NTC's AMERICAN ENGLISH LEARNER'S DICTIONARY

THE ESSENTIAL VOCABULARY OF AMERICAN LANGUAGE AND CULTURE

EDITOR-IN-CHIEF
RICHARD A. SPEARS, PH.D.

NTC Publishing Group

Library of Congress Cataloging-in-Publication Data

Spears, Richard A.
NTC's American English learner's dictionary : the essential vocabulary of American language and culture / Richard A. Spears.
p. cm.
ISBN 0-8442-5859-8 (cloth). — ISBN 0-8442-5860-1 (pbk.)
1. English language—Dictionaries. I. NTC Publishing Group.
II. Title.
PE1628.S5825 1998
423—dc21 97-42248
CIP

Editorial Staff

Editor-in-Chief
Richard A. Spears

Associate Editors
Nancy L. Dray
Steven R. Kleinedler
Carla White

Project Editor
Sharon Sofinski

Copy Editors
Marguerite S. Duffy
Judy Franklin Knudsen
Sharon T. Honaker
Deborah S. Roberts
Karen Schenkenfelder

Cover design by Nick Panos
Interior design by Terry Stone

Published by NTC Publishing Group
An imprint of NTC/Contemporary Publishing Group, Inc.
4255 West Touhy Avenue, Lincolnwood (Chicago), Illinois 60646-1975 U.S.A.

Printed in the United States of America
International Standard Book Number: 0-8442-5859-8 (cloth)
0-8442-5860-1 (paper)
18 17 16 15 14 13 12 11 10 9 8 7 6 5 4 3 2 1

Contents

Introduction

NTC's American English Learner's Dictionary is designed specifically for persons who are seeking to improve their knowledge of the English language as it is used in the United States of America. The word list is derived from a corpus of material used at the intermediate and advanced levels of English language education. It is a simplified dictionary in that it focuses on basic vocabulary presented in a clear and uncomplicated format and using a minimum of codes, abbreviations, and typographical devices.

Special attention has been paid to those elements of English with which most learners have difficulty, including pronunciation, the use of the plural, irregular forms, idioms, and phrases. Irregular forms appear as main entries, each with a pronunciation guide and a cross-reference to the full noun, verb, adjective, or adverb entry.

While the dictionary is quite suitable for learners in the early stages, it is really aimed at developing the vocabularies of learners at the intermediate and advanced levels. These learners approach dictionaries with a wide variety of needs and preexisting skills. It is not really possible for a dictionary maker to know, or even estimate, the size of the vocabulary that an individual user who is beginning to use a dictionary will have. A learner's vocabulary is always expanding and should continue to grow as the learner moves ahead in language studies. The definitions in this dictionary rely on a controlled defining vocabulary for the basic words, but do not exclude more difficult words when they are needed for more difficult concepts. In many instances, more than one definition is given, offering the learner additional help in figuring out the meaning of a word or expression. Virtually all the words used in the definitions and examples appear as entries in this dictionary, allowing the learner to unravel even the more complicated definitions.

Every full entry contains at least two full-sentence examples showing a typical use of the entry word in context. Learners will very often utilize the context-rich examples more than the definitions to figure out the exact meaning of a specific sense of a word. This dictionary provides more examples of real language use and more useful context than any other learner's dictionary. Use of this dictionary establishes or strengthens the kinds of vocabulary-acquisition skills that a learner must have to advance in language learning and to develop a vocabulary equal to that of a native speaker of English.

The dictionary was developed solely for the use of learners and was not derived from any existing dictionary. The word list, definitions, and examples were composed and edited to aid in advancing the use and understanding of the English language as it is spoken and written in the United States.

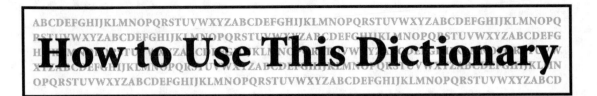

How to Use This Dictionary

If you are looking for an idiom or a phrase, look first in the Idioms and Phrases Index on page 1049.

Single words should be looked up in the body of the dictionary.

Most of the entry words in the dictionary have more than one sense. Study all the relevant senses to make sure you have found the right one.

Nouns that do not follow the regular spelling rules in the formation of the plural are marked *irreg.*, and the form of the plural is given in the entry.

Verbs that do not follow the regular rules for the formation of the past tense and past participle are marked *irreg.*, and the proper forms are given in the entry.

The comparative and superlative forms of adjectives and adverbs are listed when there are special forms—as with *red, redder, reddest*—that replace, or that exist in addition to, the comparatives and superlatives formed with *more* and *most*.

When looking up an adverb, always check for a related adjective entry as well as for a main entry for the adverb itself. Adverbs, especially those created from adjectives by adding the suffix *-ly*, are sometimes listed under related senses of the adjective. Special or important senses of such adverbs sometimes have separate entries.

After many of the definitions, you will find comments—enclosed in parentheses—containing further information about the entry word.

You will often find it informative to consult the examples before reading the definitions. In many instances, the linguistic context available in the example sentences will provide valuable clues to the understanding of the word or sense that you are consulting.

Keep in mind that the goal in using a monolingual learner's dictionary is not only to find the meanings of specific words, but also to develop the skills needed to acquire new words and senses of words from their actual use in context.

Useful Spelling Rules

The following basic spelling rules equip the learner to create and identify the most important derived and inflected forms of regular English nouns and verbs. Words that have important irregular forms that do not follow these rules are identified in the dictionary.

REGULAR VERB FORMS

Note: Many verbs that have irregular past-tense forms or irregular past participles nevertheless form the present tense and the present participle regularly.

For the third-person singular (the form used with *he*, *she*, *it*, and singular nouns) in the present tense:

♦ Add *-s* to the bare verb. (If the bare verb ends in *y* preceded by a consonant, change *y* to *ie* and then add *-s*. If the bare verb ends in *s*, *z*, *x*, *ch*, or *sh*, add *-es*.)

like	Bill likes
cry	the baby cries
walk	Anne walks
buy	the man buys
carry	a truck carries
fix	she fixes
pass	it passes
notify	he notifies
catch	she catches

For the past tense and the past participle:

♦ Add *-ed* to the bare verb. (If the bare verb ends in *y* preceded by a consonant, change *y* to *i* before adding *-ed*. If the bare verb ends in *e*, just add *-d*.)

walk	walked
like	liked
judge	judged
try	tried
carry	carried
measure	measured

For the present participle:

♦ Add *-ing* to the bare verb. (If the bare verb ends in a single *e* preceded either by a consonant or by *u*, drop the *e* before adding *-ing*. If the bare verb ends in *ie*, change *ie* to *y* before adding *-ing*.)

judge	judging
take	taking
ask	asking
carry	carrying
pay	paying
pursue	pursuing
hoe	hoeing
see	seeing
go	going
lie	lying

Doubling of consonants in participles and past-tense forms:

♦ When *-ed* or *-ing* is added to a word that ends in a consonant (other than *h*, *w*, *x*, or *y*) preceded by a single vowel, if the syllable containing these is stressed, then the consonant is normally doubled. Thus *commit* and *control*, which are accented on the last syllable, become *committed* and *controlling*, but *limit* and *cancel*, which are accented on the first syllable, become *limited* and *canceling*. Similarly, *stop* becomes *stopping*, but *look*, in which the consonant is preceded by two vowels, becomes *looking*.

♦ Within the dictionary, forms that do not follow these doubling rules are noted or illustrated in individual entries. Outside the dictionary, learners will encounter other exceptions, as well as some variation, because sometimes another option, although less familiar in American English, is also correct. The most typical exceptions to the doubling rules are words with a final *c* that becomes *ck* rather than doubling, verbs that are compounds, and verbs with closely related noun senses or more than one pronunciation.

REGULAR NOUN PLURALS

To form the plural of a regular noun:

♦ If the singular ends in *s*, *z*, *x*, *ch*, or *sh*, add *-es*.

kiss	kisses
box	boxes
match	matches
dish	dishes
bus	buses

♦ If the singular ends in *y* preceded by a consonant, change *y* to *ie* and then add *-s*.

baby	babies
library	libraries
university	universities
butterfly	butterflies

♦ For nouns ending in *o*, the regular plural may be formed by adding *-es* or by adding *-s*. For some words, both spellings are possible. In this dictionary, each entry for a noun ending in *o* specifies the correct plural form or forms for that word.

radio	radios
potato	potatoes
tornado	tornados *or* tornadoes

♦ For all other regular nouns, add *-s* to the singular to form the plural.

table	tables
boy	boys
television	televisions
valley	valleys

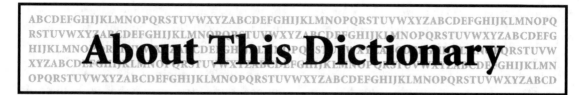

About This Dictionary

The dictionary is alphabetized letter by letter—ignoring spaces, hyphens, and punctuation. The format of the main entry is very simple. There are essentially six parts to an entry: entry word, pronunciation guide, part of speech, definition, comments, and examples. When a main entry has more than one sense, the pronunciation guide is not repeated for each numbered sense unless one or more of the senses is pronounced differently. In that case, every numbered sense is provided with a pronunciation guide. Where a word has one or more irregular forms, such as an irregular past tense or past participle for a verb, those forms are listed as a comment for the first or only sense of the word and are not repeated for each of the senses. Each sense with irregular forms is marked *irreg.*, however.

Main entries and words or expressions that are the equivalent of main entries are in **boldface sans-serif type**. Entry words that are cited or referred to in the text are in lighter sans-serif type. Putting a word in lighter sans-serif type carries with it the suggestion that the user would benefit from consulting the word that is printed in this way. Other words or phrases that are cited are placed in *italic type*. Putting a word in italic type does not carry with it the suggestion that the user consult the word. Examples are preceded by the symbol ♦ and are in *italic type*. Words, phrases, numbers, and symbols cited within the examples may appear in quotes or in roman type—not following any particular style.

The parts of speech used here are transitive verb, intransitive verb, adjectival, nominal, adverb, conjunction, preposition, article, and pronoun. Other labels are also used: idiom, phrase, interrogative, interjection, prefix, suffix, infinitive, auxiliary verb, and contraction. All grammar terms and parts of speech are defined and illustrated as regular entries in the dictionary. Phrasal verbs are labeled as transitive or intransitive verbs plus adverbs, e.g., *tv. + adv.* Verbs that take a prepositional phrase are labeled as transitive or intransitive verbs plus prepositional phrases, e.g., *tv. + prep. phr.* Patterns of this type are listed as separate senses of the verb. Phrases and idioms are placed within the main entries that offer the most semantic and formal clues to understanding them. An index at the end of the dictionary allows users to find, by looking up almost any word in a phrase or idiom, the main entry under which the phrase or idiom has been placed.

The word *something* is used in entry phrases and definitions to refer to any thing or object. The word *someone* is used to refer to any person. Sometimes *some creature* is used to emphasize that what is referred to can be a living creature other than a human. Great care has been taken to indicate which English transitive verbs take *someone* or *something* or both as an object. *One* is used in entries, definitions, and examples to refer to a hypothetical person or hypothetical persons whose sex is irrelevant. The pronouns *they*, *them*, and *their* are used only for plural antecedents.

The phrase "No plural form in this sense" is used to label noun senses that are not normally counted. This is an aid in helping learners avoid saying or writing such things as *informations* or *advices*. These are sometimes called noncount nouns, and they include a variety of subclasses of nouns. The actual explanations of semantic subclasses of nouns are too complicated for inclusion in a dictionary of this type. In many instances, there are senses of such nouns that can be made plural. The most commonly occurring senses are entries in this dictionary. Entries that are nouns in this dictionary may have additional senses that can be made plural or additional senses that must not be made plural. In some instances, suggestions are made as to how number is expressed.

Material enclosed in square brackets, [like this], is often included to clarify or limit a definition. This material is not part of the definition, but it is essential to understanding it. Some definitions are enclosed in angled brackets, <like this>. These brackets are used to enclose definitions that really describe the entry word instead of providing an equivalent for it.

A numeral enclosed in a circle, like ① or ②, is a sense number. When a number in a circle follows a word in lighter sans-serif type, as in word ③, it refers to the specific numbered sense of the word in lighter sans-serif type. That is, word ③ means the third sense of the entry **word**. A number in a circle with no word in lighter sans-serif type preceding it refers to a numbered sense within the same entry.

Many nouns can function as adjectives when they are placed before other nouns, as in *house dress*. This is a general feature of English nouns. Noun entries have been provided with separate adjectival senses only when it seems useful to do so.

Comments about a word or sense are contained in parentheses and follow the definition of the word or sense. Parentheses are also used to enclose material that is optional. In ['kæb (ə) nət], the [ə] is optional—that is, the word can be pronounced ['kæb ə nət] or ['kæb nət]. In the entry **cable (television)**, the word *television* is optional in that the entry stands for both **cable** and **cable television**, which have the same meaning in this particular sense, one of the numbered senses under the entry for **cable**. The idioms **settle** and **settle something** and **settle out of court** and **settle something out of court** are reduced to one entry through the use of parentheses: **settle (something) (out of court)**. Sometimes what is optional may be a single letter in a word; for example, **toward(s)** stands for both **toward** and **towards**.

Terms and Abbreviations

①②③, etc., are sense numbers. When they follow a word in special type that looks **like this**, they refer to an entry word outside the entry in which they are used. When there is no word in special type, they refer to senses within the entry in which they are used.

adj. adjectival.

adv. adverb.

AND follows an entry word and introduces a related or variant form of the entry word.

article a small word, such as *a, an,* or *the,* that comes before a noun.

aux. auxiliary verb.

colloquial means that the word or phrase is primarily spoken or is used more often in a spoken style than in a written style.

comp comparative.

compare with means to consider the differences in use or meaning between the entry word and the word or numbered sense that follows compare with.

conj. conjunction.

cont. contraction.

derogatory refers to words that are insulting or disparaging to someone or something.

euphemism is a word or expression that seems to be more polite or less offensive than another possible word choice.

figurative on indicates which numbered sense a figurative word or expression is based on.

formal refers to vocabulary that appears most often in writing or in polite use among educated people.

idiom is a phrase or expression that must be interpreted in a special, nonliteral way.

inf. infinitive.

informal refers to vocabulary that is casual and not used in more formal writing.

interj. interjection.

interrog. interrogative.

irreg. irregular; refers to nouns that have plural forms that do not follow the regular rules of plural formation or to verbs whose past tense and/or past participle forms do not follow the regular rules.

iv. intransitive verb.

juvenile refers to the kinds of words or expressions that are typically used by children.

n. nominal or noun.

No plural form in this sense. means that the noun in this sense is not normally counted when it has this meaning. Usually when it is possible to make such a noun plural, it has a different meaning; for example, it might mean a number of *types* of things rather than a number of things.

not prenominal refers to an adjective that does not occur before a noun.

on refers to the form from which an idiom is derived.

phr. phrase.

pl plural.

pp past participle.

prefix is a form that has meaning and is attached to the beginnings of certain words.

prenominal only refers to an adjective that can only occur before a noun.

prep. preposition.

prep. phr. prepositional phrase.

pron. pronoun.

pt past tense.

pt/pp past tense and past participle.

see means go to the entry word or numbered sense that follows the word see.

see also means to consider the meaning or form of the entry word that follows see also.

See Gazetteer. means to look up the entry word in the Gazetteer that begins on page 1081.

slang refers to very informal vocabulary that is not normally used in writing except for special effects.

suffix is a form that has meaning and is attached to the ends of certain words.

sup superlative.

term of address refers to a word or phrase that can be used as if it were someone's name.

Treated as plural. refers to a word that is treated as if it were plural even if its form is singular.

Treated as singular. refers to a word that is treated as if it were singular even if its form is plural.

Treated as singular or plural. refers to a word that can be treated as if it were singular or as if it were plural.

tv. transitive verb.

Pronunciation

The symbols of the International Phonetic Alphabet are used to show the pronunciation of the words in this dictionary. The speech represented here is that of educated people, but it is not formal or overly precise. It is more representative of the West and the middle of the country than of the East, South, or upper Midwest.

Pronunciation of American English is variable in different regions of the country, but most native speakers of American English can understand one another quite well.

The goal of the pronunciation scheme is to provide the student with one acceptable model of pronunciation for each entry. Where the numbered senses of an entry are all pronounced the same way, the phonetic representation follows the main entry word. In entries where *even one* of the numbered senses is pronounced differently from the rest, all the senses are provided with a phonetic representation.

Sounds represented here as [or] are often pronounced as [ɔr] in some parts of the East. Similarly, the sequence [ɛr] is often pronounced [ær] in parts of the East. One heavy stress is marked for each word. The dictionary user should expect to hear variation in the pronunciation of most of the words listed in this or any dictionary, but should remain confident that the model provided here is understood and accepted in all parts of the country.

The chart on the opposite page shows the symbols used here and what they correspond to in some simple English words.

Symbol	Examples	Symbol	Examples	Symbol	Examples	Symbol	Examples
[ɑ]	st**o**p, t**o**p	[ʌ]	n**u**t, sh**u**t	[n]	**n**ew, fu**nn**y	[θ]	**th**in, fai**th**
[æ]	s**a**t, tr**a**ck	[ɚ]	b**ir**d, t**ur**tle	[ŋ]	bri**ng**, thi**ng**	[u]	f**oo**d, bl**ue**
[ɑʊ]	c**ow**, n**ow**	[f]	**f**eel, i**f**	[o]	c**oa**t, wr**o**te	[ʊ]	p**u**t, l**oo**k
[ɑɪ]	b**i**te, m**y**	[g]	**g**et, fro**g**	[oɪ]	sp**oi**l, b**oy**	[v]	sa**v**e, **v**an
[b]	**b**eet, **b**u**bb**le	[h]	**h**at, **wh**o	[ɔ]	c**au**ght, y**aw**n	[w]	**w**ell, **w**ind
[d]	**d**ea**d**, bo**d**y	[i]	f**ee**t, l**ea**k	[p]	ti**p**, **p**at	[ʍ]	**wh**eel, **wh**ile
[ð]	**th**at, **th**ose	[ɪ]	b**i**t, h**i**ss	[r]	**r**at, be**rr**y	[z]	fu**zz**y, **z**oo
[dʒ]	**j**ail, **j**u**dg**e	[j]	**y**ellow, **y**ou	[s]	**s**un, fa**s**t	[ʒ]	plea**s**ure, trea**s**ure
[e]	d**a**te, s**ai**l	[k]	**c**an, **k**eep	[ʃ]	fi**sh**, **s**ure	[ˈ]	ˈwater, hoˈtel
[ɛ]	g**e**t, s**e**t	[l]	**l**awn, ye**ll**ow	[t]	**t**op, po**t**		
[ə]	**a**bove, **a**round	[m]	fa**m**ily, sla**m**	[tʃ]	**ch**eese, pi**tch**er		

A AND **a** **1.** ['e] *n.* the first letter of the alphabet. ♦ A *comes before all other letters in the Latin alphabet.* ♦ *The word* art *begins with an* a. **2. A** ['e] *n.* the first in a series; the highest grade. ♦ *John earned an A in algebra.* ♦ *I chose category A.* **3.** ['e, ə] *article* one; any. (See the note at an.) ♦ *Please give me a dollar.* ♦ *I will talk to you in a minute.* **4.** ['e, ə] *article* each; every; per. (See the note at an.) ♦ *This apartment costs nine hundred dollars a month.* ♦ *Bill drinks five cups of coffee a day.*

aardvark ['ɑrd vɑrk] *n.* an insect-eating animal of southern Africa, with claws and a long, sticky tongue. (From Afrikaans for 'earth pig.') ♦ *Our zoo has a pair of aardvarks.* ♦ *Aardvarks are active only at night.*

abandon [ə 'bæn dən] *tv.* to leave someone or something and not return; to desert someone or something. ♦ *The crew abandoned the sinking ship.* ♦ *The cat abandoned its kittens.*

abandoned [ə 'bæn dənd] *adj.* left behind; deserted. ♦ *The abandoned ship drifted aimlessly through the seas.* ♦ *The abandoned kittens were hungry and frightened.*

abbreviate [ə 'briv i et] *tv.* to make something shorter, especially a word. ♦ *I asked my teacher how to abbreviate the word* secretary. ♦ *To save space, I abbreviated as many words as I could.*

abbreviation [ə briv i 'e ʃən] *n.* a shortened word or phrase that takes the place of the full word or phrase. ♦ *The abbreviation for* North Dakota *is* N.D. ♦ *What is the abbreviation for* north?

abdicate ['æb də ket] **1.** *tv.* to leave a position of royal power; to give up one's authority or set aside one's duties. ♦ *The king abdicated the throne to marry a divorced commoner.* ♦ *The queen abdicated her royal responsibilities and fled the country.* **2.** *iv.* to step down from a position of power, especially one of royalty. ♦ *The people were surprised to hear that the king had abdicated.* ♦ *The queen abdicated after her divorce.*

abdication [æb də 'ke ʃən] *n.* giving up a position of power, especially one of royalty. (No plural form in this sense.) ♦ *After the king's abdication, his son became the new ruler.* ♦ *Upon her abdication, the queen moved to another country.*

abdomen ['æb də mən] *n.* the part of the body between the chest and the legs and the internal organs within it. ♦ *The doctors cut into my abdomen to remove my appendix.* ♦ *The ball struck John in the abdomen, and he fell to the ground.*

abdominal [æb 'dɑm ə nəl] *adj.* relating to the abdomen. (Adv: *abdominally.*) ♦ *Anne had abdominal pains, so she went to the clinic.* ♦ *The doctors cleared an abdominal obstruction.*

abduct [æb 'dʌkt] *tv.* to kidnap someone or something; to illegally take someone or something away by force. ♦ *The pirates abducted the princess and hid her in a castle.* ♦ *The criminals abducted a child and demanded a large ransom.*

abduction [æb 'dʌk ʃən] *n.* the kidnapping of someone or something. ♦ *The abduction of the baby puzzled the police for years.* ♦ *The abductions were carried out in broad daylight.*

aberration [æb ə 're ʃən] *n.* a change or difference in someone or something from what is normal or expected.

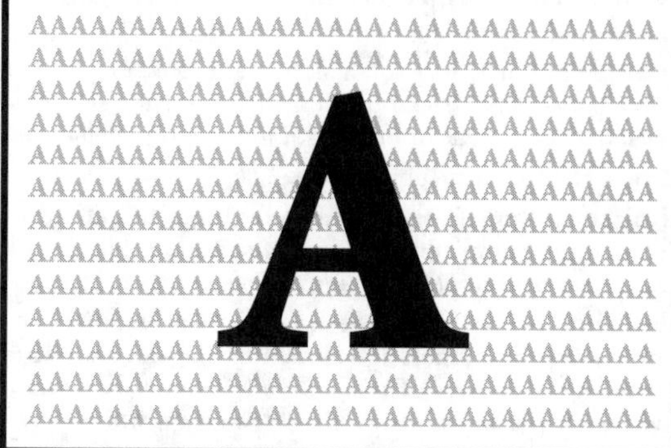

♦ *Everyone noticed the aberration in John's behavior.* ♦ *The aberrations in the data puzzled the scientists.*

abeyance [ə 'be əns] **in abeyance** *phr.* in reserve. ♦ *Until the judge determined that the evidence could be used in the trial, it was held in abeyance.* ♦ *I kept my opinion in abeyance.*

abhor [əb 'hor] *tv.* to hate someone or something very much. ♦ *Jane abhorred lima beans.* ♦ *John abhorred his neighbors, so he moved.*

abhorrence [əb 'hor əns] *n.* disgust; intense hatred. (No plural form in this sense.) ♦ *Susan could not conceal her abhorrence of the movie.* ♦ *John let his abhorrence of his nephew ruin the family gathering.*

abhorrent [əb 'hor ənt] *adj.* hateful; repellent; repulsive. (Adv: *abhorrently.*) ♦ *Bill was ashamed of his abhorrent treatment of Tom.* ♦ *Bill's abhorrent behavior shocked the community.*

abide [ə 'bɑɪd] **1.** *iv., irreg.* to remain at a place or with someone. (Older English. Pt/pp: *abided* or abode.) ♦ *The prince chose to abide in France until the war at home was over.* ♦ *Come and abide with us at our house for a while.* **2. abide by** *iv. + prep. phr.* to obey something; to follow rules; to satisfy one's obligations. ♦ *You must abide by the rules.* ♦ *I have to abide by the contract that I signed.* **3.** *tv., irreg.* to tolerate or endure someone or something. (Usually negative. Rarely in the past tenses.) ♦ *I cannot abide sweet potatoes.* ♦ *"I cannot abide your behavior," the babysitter told the twins.*

ability [ə 'bɪl ə ti] **1.** *n.* capability; the skill or power to do something. (No plural form in this sense.) ♦ *Mike has the will but lacks ability of any kind.* ♦ *Lisa is someone who has great ability.* **2.** *n.* a skill or power to do something. ♦ *I have a few abilities, but cooking is not one of them.* ♦ *John's swimming ability saved the drowning child.*

able ['e bəl] **1.** *adj.* skilled; well qualified. (Adv: *ably.*) ♦ *Your able assistant can complete the project while you are on vacation.* ♦ *In his younger days, Bill was an able gymnast.* **2. able to do something** *idiom* having the power or skill to do something. ♦ *I am able to read and write Spanish.* ♦ *Are you able to carry those bags by yourself?*

abnormal [æb 'nor məl] *adj.* not normal or usual; odd. (Adv: *abnormally.*) ♦ *The warm December weather in northern Canada was abnormal.* ♦ *There were a few abnormal oranges in the harvest.*

abnormality [æb nor 'mæl ə ti] *n.* something that is unusual or irregular. (Often refers to a physical defect.)

♦ *The puppy was born with an abnormality in its tail.* ♦ *An abnormality in the data ruined the analysis.*

aboard [ə 'bord] *prep.* on a ship, train, bus, or plane. ♦ *Jane made many friends aboard the ship when she traveled to Greece.* ♦ *Aboard the bus, I found a five-dollar bill.*

abode [ə 'bod] a pt/pp of abide.

abolish [ə 'bɑl ɪʃ] *tv.* to ban something; to get rid of something completely. ♦ *When I am king, I will abolish taxes.* ♦ *The committee abolished all entry requirements.*

abolition [æ bə 'lɪ ʃən] *n.* getting rid of something; banning something; making something illegal. (No plural form in this sense.) ♦ *The abolition of slavery was a moral victory.* ♦ *The abolition of the right to bear arms was contested bitterly.*

abolitionist [æ bə 'lɪ ʃə nəst] *n.* someone who wants to ban someone or something, especially slavery. ♦ *The abolitionists made their voices heard in the legislature.* ♦ *John's ancestors were abolitionists before the Civil War.*

abominable [ə 'bɑm (ə) nə bəl] *adj.* disgusting; horrible. (Adv: *abominably.*) ♦ *Mary nearly choked on the abominable food.* ♦ *The weather was just abominable last winter.*

abominate [ə 'bæm ə net] *tv.* to hate someone or something very much; to detest someone or something very much. ♦ *I simply abominate long lectures.* ♦ *Those who abominate sentimentalism will dislike this film.*

abomination [ə bɑm ə 'ne ʃən] *n.* someone or something that is hated, disgusting, or horrible. ♦ *The protester said that war is an abomination that cannot be justified.* ♦ *Where did you get that ugly dress? It's an abomination!*

abort [ə 'bort] **1.** *iv.* to give birth to a fetus before it can survive outside the womb. ♦ *The pregnant woman aborted in the second month.* ♦ *Mary was advised to rest to avoid aborting.* **2.** *tv.* to deliver a fetus before it can survive outside the womb. ♦ *The presence of a hereditary disease made the couple decide to abort the fetus.* ♦ *The fetus was aborted in a clinic.* **3.** *tv.* to stop something in the middle of a process; to end something prematurely. ♦ *The rocket launch was aborted at the last minute.* ♦ *The bank aborted its effort to foreclose on our mortgage.*

abortion [ə 'bor ʃən] **1.** *n.* the removal or expulsion of a fetus from the womb before it can survive outside. (No plural form in this sense.) ♦ *Abortion is sometimes used to save the mother's life.* ♦ *Abortion is controversial in the United States.* **2.** *n.* an instance of ①. ♦ *The abortion was carried out in an operating room.* ♦ *The pregnant woman considered having an abortion.*

abound [ə 'bɑʊnd] **1.** *iv.* to be abundant. ♦ *Opportunities for employment abound in the city.* ♦ *Fish abound wherever the water is clear.* **2. abound with** *iv.* + *prep. phr.* to have a lot of something; to be full of something. ♦ *The mountain streams abound with fish.* ♦ *Large cities abound with opportunities for employment.*

about [ə 'bɑʊt] **1.** *prep.* regarding someone or something; concerning someone or something. ♦ *Did you hear the news about Jane?* ♦ *In school we learned about World War II.* **2.** *prep.* back and forth and here and there in a certain place. ♦ *We walked about the house all afternoon during the storm.* ♦ *Bill drove about town, looking for Jane's house.* **3.** *adv.* approximately; nearly. ♦ *We left Jane's house about three o'clock.* ♦ *Our dog is about 12 years old.* **4.** *adv.* almost; not quite. ♦ *I was about finished with dinner when I spilled my milk.* ♦ *Are you about done?* **5. about to** *adv.* + *inf.* almost ready to do something. ♦ *Bill was about to leave when the phone rang.* ♦ *Just when I was about to give up, I finally succeeded.*

above [ə 'bʌv] **1.** *prep.* over—but not touching—someone or something. ♦ *Put this painting above the other picture.* ♦ *The jar of money was on the shelf above the refrigerator.* **2.** *prep.* greater than something. ♦ *Ice will not melt unless it is above 32 degrees.* ♦ *If the price is above $20, I don't want to buy it.* **3.** *adv.* [written about or presented] previously [in the same written work or on the same page]. ♦ *As noted above in section 2, the manager will not tolerate smoking.* ♦ *In the chart above, you can see the annual costs.* **4.** *adv.* in or at a higher place; over. ♦ *The sailor looked at the sky above.* ♦ *Above, the sun was covered with dark clouds.* **5.** *adv.* of a greater amount. ♦ *Only people five feet tall and above can ride the roller coaster.* ♦ *Only adults 21 and above may enter the bar.*

aboveboard [ə 'bʌv bord] **1.** *adj.* honest; open to scrutiny. ♦ *My lawyer is aboveboard at all times.* ♦ *Since the arrangement appeared to be aboveboard, I signed the papers.* **2.** *adv.* openly; honestly. ♦ *The lawyer practices his profession aboveboard at all times.* ♦ *The diplomat always dealt aboveboard during the negotiations.*

abrade [ə 'bred] *tv.* to scrape something; to wear down something by rubbing it. ♦ *The top of my shoe abraded my ankle.* ♦ *Many feet had abraded the threads of the worn carpet.*

abrasion [ə 'bre ʒən] *n.* a scrape on a surface of something, especially skin. ♦ *Bill received a few abrasions when he fell off his bicycle.* ♦ *The cool lotion soothed the abrasion on my elbow.*

abrasive [ə 'bre sɪv] **1.** *adj.* rough; coarse. (Adv: *abrasively.*) ♦ *The abrasive powder scratched the marble when the maid cleaned it.* ♦ *Sand is abrasive and will scratch wood floors.* **2.** *adj.* offensive; provocative. (Figurative on ①. Adv: *abrasively.*) ♦ *John's abrasive manner annoyed everyone in the room.* ♦ *Mary has an abrasive style of talking, so people avoid her.* **3.** *n.* a rough, gritty substance used for polishing or cleaning. (No plural form in this sense.) ♦ *The cook used strong abrasive to clean the stains from the sink.* ♦ *I need more abrasive to clean this dirty counter.*

abroad [ə 'brɔd] *adv.* in another country; overseas. ♦ *Jane studied abroad her junior year.* ♦ *The Browns usually travel abroad in the summer.*

abrupt [ə 'brʌpt] **1.** *adj.* sudden; unexpected. (Adv: *abruptly.*) ♦ *The passengers were jolted when the train came to an abrupt halt.* ♦ *The mystery novel came to an abrupt end without explaining the crime.* **2.** *adj.* rude; curt. (Adv: *abruptly.*) ♦ *Jane was offended by the clerk's abrupt manner.* ♦ *Because our waiter was so abrupt, we only left him a small tip.*

abscess ['æb sɛs] **1.** *n.* a swollen infection. ♦ *The doctor drained the abscess on my ankle.* ♦ *My tooth hurt because of an abscess.* **2.** *iv.* to become infected. ♦ *Jane's tooth abscessed.* ♦ *If you don't clean the wound, it will abscess.*

abscond [æb 'skɑnd] **1.** *iv.* to run away; to flee from capture or prosecution. ♦ *The robber absconded through the back door.* ♦ *One of the cashiers quickly absconded just as the theft was discovered.* **2. abscond with** *iv.* + *prep. phr.*

to flee with something, such as stolen goods; to kidnap someone. ♦ *The thief absconded with money taken in the robbery.* ♦ *The kidnapper absconded with the weeping child.*

absence ['æb səns] **1.** *n.* the quality of [someone's] not being present. (No plural form in this sense.) ♦ *Absence from the ones you love causes sadness.* ♦ *After her death, her absence was sensed even by the family dog.* **2.** *n.* a period of time when someone is not present. ♦ *How many absences does John have this month?* ♦ *An unexcused absence will result in punishment.* **3.** *n.* a lack; a deficiency. (No plural form in this sense.) ♦ *In the absence of evidence, the defendant will go free.* ♦ *Because of the absence of light, the plants died.*

absent ['æb sənt] **1.** *adj.* not present at a place; away from a place. ♦ *When Max is absent from class, the teacher calls his home.* ♦ *The president was absent, so the vice president ran the meeting.* **2.** *adj.* not in existence; not evident. ♦ *Signs of forced entry were absent, so the police believed the door was unlocked.* ♦ *A compelling motive for the crime was absent.* **3.** *adj.* [appearing] vague. (Adv: *absently.*) ♦ *Tom stood there with an absent expression, waiting for the door to open.* ♦ *Bob, tired from the trip, had an absent look in his eyes.*

absentee [æb sən 'ti] **1.** *n.* someone who is not present at a place; someone who is away from a place. ♦ *We canceled the discussion because there were so many absentees.* ♦ *The July meeting had only one absentee.* **2.** *adj.* <the adj. use of ①.> ♦ *When I vacationed in Africa, I voted in the U.S. elections by absentee ballot.* ♦ *Since our apartment is owned by an absentee landlord, nothing ever gets fixed.*

absenteeism [æb sən 'ti ɪz əm] *n.* the habit of being absent frequently. (No plural form in this sense.) ♦ *If your absenteeism doesn't stop, we're going to fire you.* ♦ *After the contract was approved, the rate of absenteeism at the factory dropped.*

absolute ['æb sə lut] *adj.* complete; total. (Adv: *absolutely.*) ♦ *When the host was insulted, an absolute silence fell across the room.* ♦ *The prime minister had absolute control of his cabinet.*

absolutely [æb sə 'lut li] **1.** *adv.* completely; without question. ♦ *Tom is absolutely broke and needs to borrow some money.* ♦ *You absolutely must clean your room today.* **2. Absolutely!** *interj.* "Certainly!"; "Of course!" ♦ *"Would you like to go to the party?" "Absolutely!"* ♦ *"Are you happy?" "Absolutely!"*

absolute zero [æb sə lut 'zi ro] *n.* [the scientific term for] the coldest temperature possible. ♦ *At absolute zero, there is no measurable heat.* ♦ *Absolute zero is –459.7 degrees Fahrenheit.*

absolution [æb sə 'lu ʃən] *n.* the official forgiveness of sins. (No plural form in this sense.) ♦ *Mary sought absolution from her sins.* ♦ *The dying man received a final absolution from the priest.*

absolve [əb 'zɑlv] **1. absolve of** *tv.* + *prep. phr.* to forgive someone of sin. ♦ *Priests can absolve penitent sinners of their sins.* ♦ *The dying man asked the priest to absolve him of his sins.* **2. absolve from** *tv.* + *prep. phr.* to free someone from guilt or blame. ♦ *The police absolved Jane from any blame in the matter.* ♦ *The teacher absolved John from guilt in the theft.* **3. absolve from** *tv.* + *prep. phr.* to release someone from duty or obligation. ♦ *Mary was absolved from further responsibility on the project.* ♦ *You are absolved from any more responsibility in this matter.*

absorb [əb 'zorb] **1.** *tv.* to soak up a liquid. ♦ *My napkin absorbed the coffee I spilled in my lap.* ♦ *I used a sponge to absorb the spilled milk.* **2.** *tv.* to learn something; to learn something easily. (Figurative on ①.) ♦ *Mary is so smart she just absorbs any book she reads.* ♦ *I had trouble absorbing algebra.*

absorbent [əb 'zor bənt] *adj.* able to soak up liquids. (Adv: *absorbently.*) ♦ *Susie's absorbent diapers kept the moisture away from her skin.* ♦ *The paper towel was so absorbent that it cleaned up all the moisture.*

absorption [əb 'zorp ʃən] *n.* the ability to soak up liquid; the capacity for soaking up a liquid. (No plural form in this sense.) ♦ *The rate of absorption for this brand of paper towel is twice that of the other brand.* ♦ *Absorption is an important quality for diapers.*

abstain [əb 'sten] **1. abstain from** *iv.* + *prep. phr.* to choose not to do something; to give up something. ♦ *Because my cholesterol is high, my doctor told me to abstain from eating fat.* ♦ *While Jane was pregnant, she abstained from smoking.* **2.** *iv.* to choose not to cast a vote; to declare that one is neither voting for nor voting against an issue. ♦ *When the issue came to a vote, four council members abstained.* ♦ *Because Jane abstained, the vote was tied 2–2.*

abstainer [əb 'sten ɚ] *n.* a person who has given up something, especially alcohol. ♦ *The abstainer politely refused the glass of wine.* ♦ *Bill would be better off as an abstainer. He always drinks too much.*

abstention [əb 'stɛn ʃən] **1.** *n.* choosing not to do something; voluntarily giving something up. (No plural form in this sense.) ♦ *Abstention from foods containing cholesterol improved Bill's health.* ♦ *Doctors recommend abstention from smoking during pregnancy.* **2.** *n.* a choice to neither vote for an issue nor vote against it; a declaration that one does not vote for an issue and does not vote against it. ♦ *Commissioner Brown's abstentions were held against him in the election.* ♦ *The final vote was five to three, with two abstentions.*

abstinence ['æb stə nəns] *n.* voluntarily avoiding or not partaking in something such as food, drink, or sex. (No plural form in this sense.) ♦ *Abstinence from fatty foods and smoking can probably lengthen your life.* ♦ *After his fifth drunken binge, Bill vowed total abstinence.*

abstinent ['æb stə nənt] *adj.* voluntarily avoiding or not partaking in something, such as food, drink, or sex. (Adv: *abstinently.*) ♦ *John remained abstinent throughout Lent.* ♦ *If teenagers would stay abstinent, there would be fewer teen pregnancies.*

abstract 1. ['æb strækt] *n.* a summary of a research paper; a summary of a document. ♦ *You can tell if a paper is worthwhile by reading its abstract.* ♦ *Anne presented the most important data in her abstract.* **2.** [æb 'strækt] *adj.* theoretical; not specific. (Adv: *abstractly.*) ♦ *I never understand Bill's abstract ideas.* ♦ *Professor Brown's books are very abstract and are hard to read.* **3.** [æb 'strækt] *tv.* to take or draw something, usually a thought, from a written document or speech. ♦ *I was only able to abstract one good quote that made sense out of context.* ♦ *Your problem in school is that you can't abstract the important points from the lectures.*

abstraction [æb 'stræk ʃən] *n.* an idea or theory drawn from actual examples. ♦ *By looking at what happened in many similar cases, we were able to create an abstraction that also covered other instances.* ♦ *After considerable thought, Mary was able to make an abstraction from the data that allowed her to predict the outcome of the experiment.*

absurd [æb 'sɚd] *adj.* foolish; ridiculous. (Adv: *absurdly.*) ♦ *Wearing a swimming suit during a snowstorm is absurd.* ♦ *John's absurd hair style made everyone laugh.*

abundance [ə 'bʌn dəns] *n.* a full supply or amount of something; more than enough of something. (No plural form in this sense.) ♦ *The abundance of wealth in the Persian Gulf is due to the oil fields.* ♦ *I am always bothered by the abundance of mosquitoes in summer.*

abundant [ə 'bʌn dənt] *adj.* full; brimming; in large amounts. (Adv: *abundantly.*) ♦ *The abundant crops would feed the village through the winter.* ♦ *Abundant rainfall made the land fertile.*

abuse 1. [ə 'bjuz] *tv.* to harm someone in some way, such as physically or emotionally; to use something in a way that damages it. ♦ *If you continue to abuse your body by smoking, you'll suffer the consequences.* ♦ *Please stop abusing your bicycle! It's all banged up!* **2.** [ə 'bjuz] *tv.* to use something badly or improperly. ♦ *If you abuse your privileges, we will take them away from you.* ♦ *Rulers who abuse their power should be removed from office.* **3.** [ə 'bjus] *n.* unfair or cruel treatment of someone; action that damages something. (No plural form in this sense.) ♦ *I could take the abuse no longer, so I ran away.* ♦ *The walls of this house show signs of abuse.* **4.** [ə 'bjus] *n.* improper use. (No plural form in this sense.) ♦ *Tom couldn't control his drug abuse, so he went for treatment.* ♦ *Alcohol abuse is a serious problem among teenagers.*

abused [ə 'bjuzd] *adj.* mistreated physically or mentally; used badly or wrongly. ♦ *The abused wife decided to leave her husband.* ♦ *The abused child was placed in a foster home.*

abusive [ə 'bju sɪv] *adj.* insulting; cruel. (Adv: *abusively.*) ♦ *The abusive teacher was fired.* ♦ *The principal punished the abusive children who made fun of Bill.*

abut [ə 'bʌt] **1.** *iv.* to touch; to share a common border. ♦ *My garage abuts with my neighbor's garage.* ♦ *Because the two buildings abutted, both were destroyed in the fire.* **2.** *tv.* to touch something; to share a common border with something. ♦ *Their garage abuts our vegetable garden.* ♦ *My office building abuts city hall.*

abysmal [ə 'bɪz məl] *adj.* very bad; as extreme as the depth of the deepest abyss is deep. (Adv: *abysmally.*) ♦ *The overcooked dinner was abysmal.* ♦ *My grades were abysmal, so I hired a tutor.*

abyss [ə 'bɪs] **1.** *n.* something—such as a hole—with a great depth. ♦ *The probe descended into the abyss of the trench.* ♦ *One step further and I would have plunged into the abyss.* **2.** *n.* something too deep to comprehend. (Figurative on ①.) ♦ *After his dad died, Bill was in an abyss of depression.* ♦ *The autistic child seemed to be lost in the abyss of her own mind.*

academic [æk ə 'dɛm ɪk] **1.** *adj.* relating to colleges and universities; scholarly. (Adv: *academically* [...ɪk li].) ♦ *Each student wore an academic gown during the graduation ceremony.* ♦ *John was invited to give an academic address at a conference.* **2.** *adj.* of abstract or theoretical interest only; moot. ♦ *Whether the event should take place was merely an academic question.* ♦ *It's too late to do anything about it now. It's all academic.* **3.** *n.* someone who is part of an academic institution; a student or professor in a college or university. ♦ *My uncle, who has been an academic all his life, teaches at a university.* ♦ *Academics are usually found in the field of education and not in business.*

academy [ə 'kæd ə mi] *n.* a school for special training in a specific area of study. ♦ *The soldier had attended a military academy.* ♦ *The singer had trained in an academy for the arts.*

accede [æk 'sid] *iv.* to go along with something; to agree to something. ♦ *Jane was unable to accede to her employer's demands.* ♦ *I was uncertain about it, but in the end, I acceded.*

accelerate [æk 'sɛl ə ret] **1.** *iv.* to go faster; to change or happen at a faster rate. ♦ *The car accelerated as it went downhill.* ♦ *Economic growth accelerated during the summer.* **2.** *tv.* to cause something to go, happen, or change faster. ♦ *Government spending accelerates the pace of inflation.* ♦ *Too much sunshine accelerates the aging process of your skin.*

acceleration [æk sɛl ə 're ʃən] *n.* going, happening, or changing faster; causing something to go, happen, or change faster; increasing something's rate of speed, growth, change, etc. (No plural form in this sense.) ♦ *The car had no brakes, so we couldn't stop its acceleration as it rolled downhill.* ♦ *The government's policies resulted in the acceleration of inflation.*

accelerator [æk 'sɛl ə ret ɚ] *n.* the part of a motor vehicle that is pressed with the foot to feed fuel to the engine. ♦ *Jane stepped on the accelerator, and the car sped off.* ♦ *When Bill pushed the accelerator to the floor, the engine roared.*

accent ['æk sɛnt] **1.** *n.* the force or stress put on a word or a part of a word during speech. ♦ *The accent in the word* hotel *is on the second syllable.* ♦ *People often put the strongest accent on a word they are contrasting with something else.* **2.** *n.* a mark written over a letter of the alphabet that gives the letter a special pronunciation or stress. ♦ *French, Italian, and Spanish use accents.* ♦ *In English, there is an accent on the word* cliché. **3.** *n.* a way of speaking a language, and especially of pronouncing a language, that is characteristic of a particular country or region where that language is spoken. ♦ *Mary used to speak with a Southern accent.* ♦ *Bill tried to speak with a British accent, but he still sounded American.* **4.** *n.* an audible indication that one is speaking something other than one's native language. ♦ *The tourist from Hungary spoke English with an accent.* ♦ *We guessed that Anne was born in Germany because she still has a slight German accent.* **5.** *tv.* to emphasize something, especially to put ① on a word or a part of a word during speech. ♦ *Not* HOtel! *You have accented the wrong syllable.* ♦ *The teacher accented the last word in each line of the poem.* **6.** *tv.* to embellish something; to make something have more visual interest. ♦ *The yellow curtains accented an otherwise dull room.* ♦ *A bit of red pepper accents the stew.*

accented ['æk sɛn tɪd] *adj.* emphasized; meant to be emphasized. ♦ *John pronounced the accented syllable too softly.* ♦ *Each accented beat is at the beginning of a musical measure.*

accentuate [æk 'sɛn tʃu et] *tv.* to stress or emphasize something; to make something more noticeable. ♦ *The drummer hit the drum harder to accentuate the first beat.* ♦ *The tall girl wore short skirts that accentuated her height, making her look even taller.*

accept [æk 'sɛpt] *tv.* to take something that is offered. ♦ *I accept your apology.* ♦ *Mary accepted a lovely gift from Jane.*

acceptable [æk 'sɛp tə bəl] *adj.* worth accepting; satisfactory; good enough. (Adv: *acceptably.*) ♦ *I hope my offer is acceptable.* ♦ *The prospective purchaser's bid on the house was acceptable.*

acceptance [æk 'sɛp təns] **1.** *n.* the taking of something that is offered; the agreement to a proposition. (No plural form in this sense.) ♦ *John's acceptance of the idea came slowly.* ♦ *We asked for the acceptance of our bid in writing.* **2. acceptance speech** *n.* a speech in which the speaker accepts something, such as an award or prize. ♦ *Anne's acceptance speech was subdued and polite.* ♦ *I had planned an acceptance speech, but I didn't win the prize.*

access 1. ['æk sɛs] *n.* the right or ability to enter, use, or obtain something. (No plural form in this sense.) ♦ *Access to education is the right of every citizen.* ♦ *Pickets blocked access to the factory.* **2.** [æk 'sɛs, 'æk sɛs] *tv.* to retrieve a file or other information from a computer. ♦ *When Jane tried to access her files, the computer crashed.* ♦ *Bill could not access any information from the computer.*

accessibility [æk sɛs ə 'bɪl ə ti] *n.* the property of something that makes it easily usable, reachable, or obtainable. (No plural form in this sense.) ♦ *The ramp increased the post office's accessibility.* ♦ *Restroom accessibility was reduced while the floors were being cleaned.*

accessible [æk 'sɛs ə bəl] *adj.* easy to reach, enter, obtain, or use. (Adv: *accessibly.*) ♦ *The post office is handicapped accessible.* ♦ *The public library is accessible to everyone.*

accessory [æk 'sɛs ə ri] **1.** *n.* a decorative item of jewelry or clothing. ♦ *Jane bought a handbag as an accessory for her suit.* ♦ *Leather accessories would look good with Bill's tweed outfit.* **2.** *n.* an extra object or detail added to something to make it more special or interesting. ♦ *What accessories are available on this automobile?* ♦ *Many useful accessories come with the food processor.* **3.** *n.* someone who helps another person commit a crime. ♦ *Max was considered an accessory to the jeweler's murder.* ♦ *Bob's alibi means that he couldn't have been an accessory.*

accident ['æk sɪ dənt] *n.* an unexpected event, usually involving harm to someone or something. ♦ *There was a car accident at our corner last night.* ♦ *I didn't mean to bump into you. It was an accident.*

accidental [æk sɪ 'dɛn təl] *adj.* unintentional; done or happening by mistake. (Adv: *accidentally.*) ♦ *The police investigated the accidental death.* ♦ *I made an accidental error on my exam.*

accident-prone ['æk sɪ dənt 'pron] *adj.* more likely to have accidents than the average person. ♦ *Bill, who is accident-prone, broke his arm again.* ♦ *The accident-prone skater fell on the ice twice last week.*

acclaim [ə 'klem] **1.** *n.* enthusiastic approval; strong praise. (No plural form in this sense.) ♦ *The art museum drew endless acclaim from visitors.* ♦ *The critic's acclaim warmed the hearts of the performers.* **2.** *tv.* to praise someone or something greatly. ♦ *The entire audience loudly acclaimed the good performances.* ♦ *The crowd acclaimed the hero as he rode through the town.*

acclamation [æk lə 'me ʃən] *n.* shouting or loud declaration of approval or praise. (No plural form in this sense.) ♦ *The audience's acclamation echoed through the theater.* ♦ *The acclamation brought tears to the singers' eyes.*

acclimate ['æk lə met] **1.** *iv.* to get used to something; to become accustomed to something. ♦ *The tourists acclimated to the new time zone slowly.* ♦ *The exotic flowers have not yet acclimated to this climate.* **2.** *tv.* to cause someone or something to get used to something; to cause someone or something to become accustomed to something. ♦ *The headmaster acclimated the new students to the joys of waking at sunrise.* ♦ *We acclimated ourselves quickly to the new time zone.*

acclimatized [ə 'klɑɪm ə tɑɪzd] *adj.* accustomed to someone or something; familiar with someone or something. ♦ *The tourists, finally acclimatized, are now sleeping normally.* ♦ *The new garden plants are now acclimatized.*

accolade ['æk ə led] *n.* strong praise; strong approval. ♦ *The audience heaped accolades on the orchestra.* ♦ *The speakers gave the mayor many accolades, praising her diplomacy.*

accommodate [ə 'kɑm ə det] **1.** *tv.* [for a place] to have enough room for someone or something. ♦ *This elevator accommodates twelve people.* ♦ *The restaurant could not accommodate the large party.* **2.** *tv.* to adjust to something; to adapt to something. ♦ *The restaurant could not accommodate my diet.* ♦ *The desk clerk said that the hotel could accommodate our special needs.*

accommodation [ə kɑm ə 'de ʃən] **1.** *n.* reconciliation or settlement of a disagreement or problem. (No plural form in this sense.) ♦ *The manager made absolutely no accommodation in response to our complaint.* ♦ *Max was unable to provide any satisfactory accommodation regarding the customer's complaint.* **2. accommodations** *n.* a place to live, stay, or sleep; lodging. ♦ *Our accommodations in the expensive hotel were luxurious.* ♦ *The visitor was able to secure accommodations at a local hotel.*

accompaniment [ə 'kʌmp (ə) nɪ mənt] **1.** *n.* something that accompanies someone or something; something that goes along with something else. ♦ *The jam was an excellent accompaniment to the freshly baked bread.* ♦ *That purple hat is not the ideal accompaniment for your red hair!* **2.** *n.* music played along with another instrument or a singer. (No plural form in this sense.) ♦ *The accompaniment was too loud, and I could not hear the violin.* ♦ *The excellent accompaniment complemented the singer's performance.*

accompanist *n.* someone who plays an instrument to provide the accompaniment for a singer or musician. ♦ *Mary made her living as an accompanist for many famous singers.* ♦ *The audience applauded the accompanist as much as the soloist.*

accompany [ə 'kʌmp ə ni] **1.** *tv.* to go with someone; to travel with someone. ♦ *If you go to the opera, I will accompany you.* ♦ *John accompanied his father on a business trip.* **2.** *tv.* to play a musical instrument along with another musician or a singer. ♦ *Mary accompanied Tom on the piano.* ♦ *I need someone to accompany me while I play the violin.*

accomplice [ə 'kɑm pləs] *n.* someone who helps someone else commit a crime or other wrongdoing. ♦ *Max and Bill were accomplices in the jewel theft.* ♦ *Bill and his accomplice Max were arrested last week.*

accomplish [ə 'kɑm plɪʃ] *tv.* to finish something; to successfully complete something. ♦ *I must accomplish a lot today.* ♦ *I was not able to accomplish all I set out to do.*

accomplished [ə 'kɑm plɪʃt] *adj.* skilled; talented. ♦ *Mary is an accomplished accompanist.* ♦ *Bill is the most accomplished musician I know.*

accomplishment [ə 'kɑm plɪʃ mənt] *n.* something that has been completed or achieved; a success. ♦ *Getting a good mortgage for our new house was quite an accomplishment.* ♦ *The president was responsible for many important accomplishments.*

accord [ə 'kord] **1.** *n.* agreement. (No plural form in this sense.) ♦ *There is no accord on what we should do now.* ♦ *We are in complete accord!* **2.** *n.* an agreement; an instance of ①. ♦ *An accord with the labor union was reached at about midnight.* ♦ *Many hours of negotiation produced an acceptable accord.*

accordance [ə 'kor dns] **in accordance with** *phr.* in agreement with; in conformity with. ♦ *In accordance with our discussion, I have prepared a contract.* ♦ *I did this in accordance with your request.*

according [ə 'kord ɪŋ] **1. according to someone or something** *idiom* as stated by someone; as indicated by something. ♦ *According to the weather report, it will rain today.* ♦ *The guests will arrive at noon, according to Mary.* **2. according to something** *idiom* in proportion to something. ♦ *You will get paid according to the number of hours that you work.* ♦ *The doctor charges patients according to their ability to pay.*

accordingly [ə 'kor dɪŋ li] *adv.* therefore; consequently. ♦ *The snow was four feet deep. Accordingly, the boss told us to go home.* ♦ *The speech was very funny. Accordingly, the audience laughed loudly.*

accordion [ə 'kor di ən] *n.* a musical instrument shaped like a rectangular box with a keyboard or buttons on the sides and bellows in the middle. (Music is made by working the bellows while pushing the keyboard or the buttons.) ♦ *Jane plays the accordion while Mary sings.* ♦ *This polka was written for an accordion and a trumpet.*

account [ə 'kaʊnt] **1.** *n.* a report; a description; one's version of what happened in an event. ♦ *John's account of the accident differed from mine.* ♦ *When you return, please give an account of your trip.* **2.** *n.* a set of accounting notations—recording income [or payments received] and expenses [or payments paid out]—assigned to a particular person, business, or class of transactions. ♦ *My checking account is almost empty.* ♦ *We have almost spent every penny budgeted in our supplies account.* **3. account for** *iv.* + *prep. phr.* to provide an explanation for something. ♦ *The treasurer could not account for the missing money.* ♦ *How do you account for what happened today?* **4. give a good account of oneself** *idiom* to do (something) well or thoroughly. ♦ *John gave a good account of himself when he gave his speech last night.* ♦ *Mary was tired, and she didn't give a good account of herself at the meeting.* **5. turn something to good account** *idiom* to use something in such a way that it is to one's advantage; to make good use of a situation, experience, etc. ♦ *Anne turned her illness to good account and did a lot of reading.* ♦ *Many people turn their retirement to good account and take up interesting hobbies.*

accountable [ə 'kaʊn tə bəl] *adj.* responsible. (Adv: *accountably.*) ♦ *My boss held me accountable for an error that someone else made.* ♦ *The insurance company says it is not accountable for the hospital's errors.*

accountant [ə 'kaʊnt nt] *n.* someone who is responsible for maintaining financial records or accounts; someone who prepares tax records. ♦ *The accountants want to know what happened to the money set aside for new construction.* ♦ *My accountant will prepare my taxes.*

accounting [ə 'kaʊn tɪŋ] *n.* the profession of examining and maintaining money, accounts, and taxes. (No plural form in this sense.) ♦ *The student studying finance went into accounting as a career.* ♦ *The person who prepared my taxes had studied accounting in school.*

accrue [ə 'kru] **1.** *iv.* [for an amount] to be added to another amount of money. ♦ *Interest accrues each month.* ♦ *How much of a penalty has accrued on this bill?* **2.** *tv.* to earn or gather a sum of monetary interest. ♦ *Will this deposit accrue any interest this month?* ♦ *My new bank account accrues interest daily.*

accumulate [ə 'kjum jə let] **1.** *iv.* to build up gradually. ♦ *My vacation days are accumulating.* ♦ *Dust accumulated under the bed.* **2.** *tv.* to build up something gradually. ♦ *I've accumulated a lot of vacation days.* ♦ *The television screen accumulates dust.*

accumulated [æ 'kjum jə let ɪd] *adj.* gradually built up. ♦ *The vase was gray with accumulated dust.* ♦ *The accumulated memories of a busy lifetime were the basis of Aunt Jane's book.*

accumulation [ə kju mjə 'le ʃən] **1.** *n.* collecting or accumulating things. (No plural form in this sense.) ♦ *Lisa is most concerned with the accumulation of wealth.* ♦ *Mike tried to prevent the accumulation of dust on the boxes in the attic by covering them with cloths.* **2.** *n.* a gradually built up mass or collection of something. ♦ *The attic contains an accumulation of old furniture and toys.* ♦ *The library represents a vast accumulation of knowledge.*

accuracy ['æk jɚ ə si] *n.* correctness; the degree of freedom from errors. (No plural form in this sense.) ♦ *She always hits the target with complete accuracy.* ♦ *There is a problem with the accuracy of your typing.*

accurate ['æk jɚ ət] *adj.* correct; exact; without error. (Adv: *accurately.*) ♦ *Your statements about the cost of the house were not accurate.* ♦ *The witness gave an accurate account of the situation.*

accusation [æk jə 'ze ʃən] *n.* a claim or charge that someone has done something, usually something wrong or illegal. ♦ *The police made an accusation that Bill was at the scene of the crime.* ♦ *Anne objected to the untrue accusations.*

accuse [ə 'kjuz] *tv.* to claim or charge that someone has done something, usually something wrong or illegal. ♦ *I accused John of hitting my dog.* ♦ *The police accused Bill of being at the scene of the crime.*

accused [ə 'kjuzd] **1.** *adj.* blamed for something; charged with a wrongdoing. ♦ *The accused man refused to speak in his own defense.* ♦ *A police officer arrested the accused murderer.* **2. the accused** *n.* someone blamed for something; a person charged with a wrongdoing. (No plural form in this sense. Treated as singular or plural.) ♦ *The accused refused to speak in his own defense.* ♦ *The judge ordered the accused to appear in court the next week.*

accuser [æ 'kjuz ɚ] *n.* someone who accuses someone else of a wrongdoing. ♦ *Mike's accuser was present at the trial.* ♦ *The accuser was lying, so the charges were dropped.*

accustom [ə 'kʌs təm] **accustom to** *tv.* + *prep. phr.* to cause someone or something to become familiar with something. ♦ *Mr. Brown accustomed himself to the noise of his new neighbors.* ♦ *We tried to accustom the children to eating late.*

accustomed [ə 'kʌs təmd] **1.** *adj.* regular; normal. ♦ *The children ate at their accustomed time.* ♦ *We met at noon in our accustomed manner.* **2. accustomed to someone or something** *idiom* used to someone or something; used to or in the habit of doing something. ♦ *The children are accustomed to eating late in the evening.* ♦ *The recent immigrants have not yet become accustomed to American food.*

ace ['es] **1.** *n.* a playing card with only one spot; a domino or the side of a die with only one spot. ♦ *Bill held four aces in his hand.* ♦ *Both of the dice showed aces.* **2.** *adj.* very skilled. (Informal. Prenominal only.) ♦ *John's father was an ace pilot in the war.* ♦ *We took the car to our ace mechanic for repairs.* **3.** *tv.* to receive an excellent score or grade on a test. (Slang.) ♦ *Susan aced her math examination.* ♦ *I hope I can ace my history test.*

acerbic [ə 'sɚ bɪk] **1.** *adj.* very sour or tart. (Adv: *acerbically* [...ɪk li].) ♦ *The lemon was so acerbic that I puckered up my lips.* ♦ *I disliked the acerbic taste of the sauce.* **2.** *adj.* [of a remark or a manner] sharp and biting. (Figurative on ①. Adv: *acerbically* [...ɪk li].) ♦ *The critic's acerbic dismissal of the play was cruel.* ♦ *Anne made an acerbic comment about Tom's efforts.*

ache ['ek] **1.** *n.* a pain; a soreness. ♦ *I have aches in both legs from running.* ♦ *There was a constant ache in Mary's ankle after her fall.* **2.** *iv.* to hurt; to be sore. ♦ *My legs ache from too much running.* ♦ *My head begins to ache when I read too much.*

achieve [ə 'tʃiv] **1.** *tv.* to accomplish what was intended; to gain or get something. ♦ *We achieved everything we intended to do.* ♦ *The team achieved victory after lots of hard work.* **2.** *iv.* to advance; to get ahead. ♦ *As hard as Bill tried, he could not achieve in school.* ♦ *Max was not the kind of child who wanted to achieve.*

achievement [ə 'tʃiv mənt] **1.** *n.* accomplishing something; accomplishment. (No plural form in this sense.) ♦ *You are capable of high achievement.* ♦ *Poor Mike shows no signs of achievement in his work.* **2.** *n.* the successful result of one's effort; an accomplishment. ♦ *Her best achievement was getting a job.* ♦ *Tom's achievements in school earned him a scholarship.*

achiever [ə' tʃiv ɚ] *n.* someone who achieves; someone who accomplishes a lot. ♦ *Tom was an achiever in high school but not in college.* ♦ *The best achievers study a lot.*

aching ['ek ɪŋ] **1.** *adj.* hurting; sore. (Adv: *achingly.*) ♦ *What can I do for an aching back?* ♦ *Sally applied heat to her aching shoulder.* **2. aching heart** *idiom* the feeling of pain or sadness because of love that is lost or has faded away, described as being in the heart, where love is said to reside. ♦ *I try to tell my aching heart that I don't love him.* ♦ *There is no medicine for an aching heart.*

acid ['æs ɪd] **1.** *n.* a corrosive substance that neutralizes alkalis. (No plural form in this sense.) ♦ *Vinegar is acid diluted with water.* ♦ *Strong acid corrodes metal.* **2.** *adj.* [of a taste] sharply sour or bitter. (Adv: *acidly.*) ♦ *The acid taste of this lemon is making my lips pucker.* ♦ *There is a slightly acid taste to the sauce.* **3.** *adj.* biting; sarcastic. (Figurative on ②. Adv: *acidly.*) ♦ *The critic's acid remarks hurt the director's feelings.* ♦ *She spoke with such an acid voice that everyone was startled.*

acidic [ə 'sɪd ɪk] **1.** *adj.* sharply sour or bitter. (Adv: *acidically* [...ɪk li].) ♦ *The sauce was too acidic, so no one could eat it.* ♦ *The acidic wine could not even be used for cooking.* **2.** *adj.* sarcastic; emotionally bitter. (Figurative on ①. Adv: *acidically* [...ɪk li].) ♦ *Her acidic remarks horrified all who heard them.* ♦ *The acidic criticism appeared in the morning paper but was forgotten by noon.*

acidity [ə 'sɪd ə ti] **1.** *n.* the acid content of something. (No plural form in this sense.) ♦ *The extreme acidity of the substance ate right through my gloves.* ♦ *High acidity is a characteristic of citrus fruits.* **2.** *n.* bitterness; sourness. (No plural form in this sense.) ♦ *The acidity of the sauce was too great.* ♦ *The cook added lemon juice to increase the recipe's acidity.* **3.** *n.* emotional bitterness. (Figurative on ②. No plural form in this sense.) ♦ *The acidity in her tone of voice frightened us all.* ♦ *There was so much acidity in his manner that I was insulted.*

acknowledge [æk 'nɑl ədʒ] **1.** *tv.* to give recognition to someone or something. ♦ *The speaker acknowledged Sue's work on the project.* ♦ *I acknowledged Tom for all of his help with the project.* **2.** *tv.* to admit something. ♦ *Bill acknowledged his failure to complete the job.* ♦ *Susan acknowledged that it was too late to help Bill.* **3.** *tv.* to report that one has received something; to report that one has received something and express that one is grateful. ♦ *I acknowledged the letter from Mary immediately.* ♦ *Susan acknowledged the gift within a week.*

acknowledgment [æk 'nɑl ɪdʒ mənt] **1.** *n.* admission; stating that something is so. (No plural form in this sense.) ♦ *Acknowledgment of Sue's part in the plot came only after much questioning.* ♦ *We knew who had taken the money although Mike offered no acknowledgment of his guilt.* **2.** *n.* the recognition given to someone for doing something well. ♦ *The speaker gave an acknowledgment of Tom's work on the project.* ♦ *We all appreciated the committee's acknowledgment of our work.* **3.** *n.* a report of having received something. ♦ *I received an acknowledgment of the gift I sent Susan.* ♦ *Tom did not get any acknowledgment of the check he sent to the bank.*

acne ['æk ni] *n.* pimples. (No plural form in this sense.) ♦ *Tom had a bad case of acne when he was a teenager.* ♦ *Eventually, you won't be bothered by acne anymore.*

acorn ['e korn] *n.* the nut that grows on an oak tree. ♦ *Squirrels gather acorns.* ♦ *Many wild animals eat acorns.*

acoustic [ə 'ku stɪk] **1.** *adj.* relating to sound. (Adv: *acoustically* [...ɪk li].) ♦ *The concert hall had excellent acoustic qualities.* ♦ *Susan is studying the acoustic nature of vowel sounds.* **2.** *adj.* relating to a musical instrument whose sound is not changed or made louder electrically. (Adv: *acoustically* [...ɪk li].) ♦ *Bill plays the acoustic guitar.* ♦ *Were they using acoustic or electric drums?* **3. acoustics** *n.* the branch of physics that deals with sound waves. (Treated as singular.) ♦ *Mary is interested in designing recital halls and is studying acoustics.* ♦ *Acoustics is not offered at all universities.* **4. acoustics** *n.* the qualities of a specific space that determine how well or how poorly sound will travel in that space. (Treated as plural.) ♦ *The acoustics of this room are not good.* ♦ *The hall's acoustics were so bad that we couldn't understand the speaker.*

acquaint [ə 'kwent] *tv.* to cause someone to get to know someone or something. ♦ *The teacher acquainted her class with the history of glass.* ♦ *I bought a book to acquaint myself with French grammar.*

acquaintance [ə 'kwent ns] *n.* someone one knows slightly. ♦ *An old acquaintance dropped by for a chat.* ♦ *I met an acquaintance of yours at the train station.*

acquiesce [æ kwi 'ɛs] *iv.* to yield [to someone] on a matter; to agree or consent. ♦ *We argued until I finally acquiesced.* ♦ *After Bill had acquiesced on the matter of payment, things went much more smoothly.*

acquiescent [æ kwi 'ɛs ənt] *adj.* tending to agree or consent. (Adv: *acquiescently.*) ♦ *If Bill were a more acquiescent person, we would not have argued.* ♦ *As a rule, Tom is quite acquiescent on the matter of salary.*

acquire [ə 'kwaɪr] *tv.* to get something; to receive something. ♦ *Susan acquired an appreciation of classical music.* ♦ *Tom acquired a famous painting from an art dealer.*

acquisition [æ kwɪ 'zɪ ʃən] **1.** *n.* receiving or obtaining something. (No plural form in this sense.) ♦ *The acquisition of the property took months.* ♦ *Tom completed the acquisition of a full set of baseball cards.* **2.** *n.* something that has been received or obtained. ♦ *Tom's newest acquisition is a luxurious sports car.* ♦ *The museum has several new acquisitions on display.*

acquisitive [ə 'kwɪz ɪ tɪv] *adj.* eager to obtain material items or knowledge; greedy. (Adv: *acquisitively.*) ♦ *Jane has an acquisitive nature and will probably want a new car just like yours.* ♦ *Bill, who is very acquisitive, has a house filled with antiques and artwork.*

acquit [ə 'kwɪt] *tv.* to declare someone innocent of wrongdoing. ♦ *The court acquitted Max of all charges.* ♦ *Susan hoped the judge would acquit her, too.*

acquittal [ə 'kwɪt əl] *n.* the official or legal declaration that someone is not guilty of a wrongdoing. (No plural form in this sense.) ♦ *Max's acquittal came just when he was giving up hope.* ♦ *The jury's verdict was an acquittal of the suspect.*

acre ['ek ɚ] *n.* a measurement of land equal to 4,840 square yards, or approximately 4,047 square meters. ♦ *The farmer planted 40 acres of wheat.* ♦ *In Mary's neighborhood, the lots are one-sixth of an acre each.*

acreage ['e kə rɪdʒ] *n.* the area of a piece of land measured in acres. (No plural form in this sense.) ♦ *The farmer put most of his acreage into wheat.* ♦ *We don't have enough acreage to raise cattle.*

acrid ['æk rɪd] *adj.* [of a taste or smell] stinging or bitter. (Adv: *acridly.*) ♦ *The acrid odor burned John's nostrils.* ♦ *An acrid wind blew in from the factory.*

acrimonious [æ kri 'mon ɪ əs] *adj.* bitter in manner, language, or temper. (Adv: *acrimoniously.*) ♦ *The court session was an acrimonious affair.* ♦ *The acrimonious debate resulted in much resentment.*

acrimony ['æ krə mon i] *n.* bitterness of manner, language, or temper. (No plural form in this sense.) ♦ *They were able to reach a decision without acrimony.* ♦ *There was a great deal of acrimony in the argument.*

acrobat ['æ krə bæt] *n.* someone who does stunts and tricks on suspended apparatus, sometimes in a circus. ♦ *The acrobats swung from trapeze to trapeze.* ♦ *The acrobat fell into the safety net.*

acrobatic [æ krə 'bæt ɪk] **1.** *adj.* of the skills or activities of an acrobat. (Adv: *acrobatically* [...ɪk li].) ♦ *Bill had no acrobatic skills and could not even jump over a stream.* ♦ *The circus presented a performer of acrobatic tricks.* **2. acrobatics** *n.* the activity of working on a trapeze or high wire as an acrobat. (Treated as singular or plural.) ♦ *Mary practiced acrobatics for years before joining the circus.* ♦ *I am sure that doing acrobatics would make me dizzy.*

acronym [æk rə nɪm] *n.* a word that is made from the initial letters of a series of words. ♦ Radar *and* scuba *are well-known acronyms.* ♦ *The* ZIP *in* ZIP code *is an acronym.*

across [ə 'krɔs] **1.** *prep.* from one side of something to the other side. ♦ *We went across the street when the light turned green.* ♦ *Bill jumped across the stream.* **2.** *prep.* on the other side of something. ♦ *We waved to our friends across the street.* ♦ *The bank is across the river, just over that bridge.* **3.** *adv.* to the other side of something. ♦ *The river was too wide for me to swim across.* ♦ *I could row across.* **4. come across someone or something; run across someone or something** *idiom* to find someone or something; to discover someone or something. ♦ *John came across a book he had been looking for.* ♦ *Where did you run across that lovely skirt?* **5. get something across (to someone)** *idiom* to succeed in explaining something to someone. ♦ *The teacher finally got the point across to the students.* ♦ *Did you ever get it across to her that you want to leave and go home?*

acrylic [ə 'krɪl ɪk] **1.** *adj.* [of paint, plastic, or fiber] made of a synthetic substance derived from resins. ♦ *The artist bought several tubes of acrylic paint.* ♦ *I have a sweater made from acrylic fibers.* **2.** *n.* acrylic paint, plastic, or fiber. (No plural form in this sense.) ♦ *Blankets made of acrylic are not as warm as blankets made of wool.* ♦ *Acrylic dries faster than most other types of paint.*

act ['ækt] **1.** *n.* a division of a play or musical. ♦ *In the first act of the play, the young lovers meet.* ♦ *The second act of this drama is shorter than the first.* **2.** *n.* one of many short performances within a longer program. ♦ *The first act consisted of four men who did acrobatics.* ♦ *The last act at the talent show was the best.* **3.** *n.* a deed; something that is done. ♦ *Susan's act of kindness was very comforting.* ♦ *Angry people sometimes commit violent acts.* **4.** *n.* a law.

♦ *The senator challenged the act that made selling alcohol illegal.* ♦ *A number of new acts were passed in this legislative session.* **5.** *iv.* to perform theatrically as a profession or hobby. ♦ *During the day, Bill is a waiter, but at night, he acts.* ♦ *Mary moved to New York so she could act for a living.* **6.** *iv.* to do [something]; to start [doing something]. ♦ *The county officials will not act on a request unless it is presented in writing.* ♦ *I have been waiting on this matter, but I expect to act soon.* **7. act as** *iv. + prep. phr.* to perform in the function or role of someone or something, especially temporarily; to serve as something. ♦ *During the mayor's illness, the vice mayor acted as mayor.* ♦ *Since I had been to Detroit before, I acted as tour guide when my family decided to go there.* **8.** *iv.* to behave [in a certain way]. ♦ *John's children act like perfect young ladies and gentlemen.* ♦ *Act as if you don't know about the party.* **9. act of God** *idiom* an occurrence (usually an accident) for which no human is responsible; an act of nature such as a storm, an earthquake, or a windstorm. (On ③.) ♦ *Will your insurance company pay for the damage caused by earthquakes and other acts of God?* ♦ *The thief tried to convince the judge that the diamonds were in his pocket due to an act of God.* **10. tough act to follow** *idiom* a stunning presentation or performance that is to be followed by one's own performance. (On ②.) ♦ *Bill's speech was excellent. It was a tough act to follow, but my speech was good also.* ♦ *Although I had a tough act to follow, I did my best.*

action ['æk ʃən] **1.** *n.* activity; movement. (No plural form in this sense.) ♦ *The continuous action of the sewing machine shook the table.* ♦ *We saw no action in the office. Everyone was at lunch.* **2.** *n.* a deed; an event; a movement. ♦ *Mary's rude actions were unacceptable.* ♦ *The protesters' actions were well planned.* **3.** *n.* the plot of a story; the events that happen in a story. (No plural form in this sense.) ♦ *The action was hard to follow toward the end of the movie.* ♦ *The real action of the story did not unfold until the last chapter.* **4.** *n.* fighting or battles during a war or conflict. (No plural form in this sense.) ♦ *There was military action on the beach during the invasion.* ♦ *My grandfather saw action in Korea.* **5. course of action** See course.

activate ['æk tə vet] *tv.* to set something in motion; to make something start or work. ♦ *The cook activated the food processor.* ♦ *The soldier activated the bomb.*

active ['æk tɪv] **1.** *adj.* moving; functioning. (Adv: *actively.*) ♦ *I am not very active at sunrise.* ♦ *I keep active, and that keeps me healthy.* **2.** *adj.* lively; moving at a rapid, steady pace. (Adv: *actively.*) ♦ *Tom's active lifestyle is expensive.* ♦ *Susan's personal life is very active.* **3.** *adj.* of or about sentences in which the subject is the doer of the action that is expressed in the verb. (The opposite of passive ②. Adv: *actively.*) ♦ *"The girl cut the flower" is an active sentence.* ♦ *"The flower was cut by the girl" is a passive sentence, not an active one.* **4. active ingredient** *n.* a chemically active ① substance, especially a substance in a medicine that makes the medicine have the desired effect. ♦ *I cannot pronounce the name of the active ingredient in this medicine.* ♦ *In addition to the active ingredient, the medicine includes some flavoring and sugar.*

activism ['æk tɪ vɪz əm] *n.* the practice of using direct actions to bring about social or political change. (No plural form in this sense.) ♦ *Bill is interested in social activism.* ♦ *Anne participated in many forms of activism in college.*

activist ['æk tɪ vəst] *n.* a person who works to bring about social or political change. ♦ *The activists favored the law that prohibited waste in government.* ♦ *Some activists blocked the entrance to the store that sold books they disagreed with.*

activity [æk 'tɪv ə ti] **1.** *n.* movement; motion. (No plural form in this sense.) ♦ *There was a lot of activity near the accident.* ♦ *Jane was confused by all the activity in the room.* **2.** *n.* something to do; an action that is being done. ♦ *When you finish this activity, please go on to the next.* ♦ *The museum offers many activities for children.*

actor ['æk tɚ] *n.* a performer, male or female, in a play, musical, or movie. (See also actress.) ♦ *The actors gathered on stage to take their bows.* ♦ *The director auditioned three actors for the leading role.*

actress ['æk trəs] *n.* a female performer in a play, musical, or movie. ♦ *The actress performed her part very well.* ♦ *Four actresses had to share one dressing room.*

actual ['æk tʃu əl] *adj.* real; existing. (Adv: *actually.*) ♦ *Is this vase an actual antique or a copy?* ♦ *I will be there at noon. When is the actual meeting?*

actuality [æk tʃu 'æl ə ti] *n.* the existence or reality of something; a true condition. (No plural form in this sense.) ♦ *Bill lived in a fantasy world and could not face the actuality of his life.* ♦ *I thought I was taller than Bill, but in actuality, he is taller.*

actually ['æk tʃu ə li] *adv.* in fact; really. ♦ *I am actually older than I look.* ♦ *Actually, Anne is the person you need to see.*

actuary ['æk tʃu ɛr i] *n.* someone who determines insurance risks, rates, and premiums. ♦ *An actuary has determined the risk of insuring cancer patients.* ♦ *The actuaries calculate the average length of life.*

actuate ['æk tʃu et] *tv.* to set something in motion; to start something. ♦ *What do I press to actuate this device?* ♦ *The supervisor actuated the assembly line by turning a switch.*

acuity [ə 'kju ə ti] *n.* exactness or preciseness, especially of sight or mental processes. (No plural form in this sense.) ♦ *Tom's visual acuity is weak, so he wears glasses.* ♦ *Despite her age, Aunt Mary has enormous mental acuity.*

acumen [ə 'kjum ən] *n.* insight; shrewdness. (No plural form in this sense.) ♦ *Bill has a lot of business acumen and earns a high salary.* ♦ *With her theatrical acumen, Mary produced a fantastic play.*

acute [ə 'kjut] **1.** *adj.* sharp; severe; intense. (Adv: *acutely.*) ♦ *Dogs have very acute hearing.* ♦ *After an acute drop in oil prices, the price of gasoline dropped.* **2.** *adj.* [in geometry] less than 90 degrees; smaller than a right angle. (Adv: *acutely.*) ♦ *The angle of the turn was so acute that I had to slow down.* ♦ *John drew a series of acute angles for geometry class.*

A.D. ['e 'di] *abbr.* "in the year of the Lord," since the birth of Christ. (From Latin *anno domini.* Properly written before a date, but often seen written after the date. It shows when something occurred in relation to the calendar that begins with the birth of Christ. Also **A.D.**) ♦ *The ancient city was founded in A.D. 800.* ♦ *Bill was born in 1954 A.D.*

ad ['æd] *n.* an advertisement. ♦ *Tom placed an ad in the paper, hoping to sell his car.* ♦ *I saw an ad for houses on sale.*

adage ['æd ɪdʒ] *n.* a wise saying. ♦ *Isn't there an old adage about a stitch in time?* ♦ *I remember the old adages I used to hear from my aunt.*

adamant ['æd ə mənt] *adj.* stubborn; [of someone's attitude] firm and immovable. (Adv: *adamantly.*) ♦ *Tom was adamant about not going to the dance.* ♦ *Mary was so adamant about it that she raised her voice.*

adapt [ə 'dæpt] **1.** *iv.* to change or modify to fit in; to adjust to new conditions. ♦ *Jane adapted quickly to the new procedures.* ♦ *Since Bill could not adapt to college life, he left school.* **2.** *tv.* to change or modify something to fit with something else; to adjust something to new conditions. ♦ *Jane adapted the room to suit her needs.* ♦ *This isn't what I need, but I can adapt it.*

adaptable [ə 'dæp tə bəl] *adj.* capable of being changed or updated easily; flexible. (Adv: *adaptably.*) ♦ *Mary is very adaptable and will do well in any situation.* ♦ *If you are not adaptable, you will feel uncomfortable in college.*

adaptation [æ dæp 'te ʃən] *n.* something that has been changed, modified, or updated. ♦ *The movie was an adaptation of a classic novel.* ♦ *This engine is an adaptation of the original one.*

adapter [ə 'dæp tɚ] *n.* a device that connects two different parts or objects. ♦ *When I went to Europe, I had to use an adapter in the electrical outlets.* ♦ *I need an adapter so I can connect these two cables.*

add ['æd] **1.** *tv.* to join something to something else; to include something with something else. ♦ *Please add some water to the vase of flowers.* ♦ *Add some milk as you cook the eggs.* **2. add (up)** *tv.* (+ *adv.*) to figure the total of two or more numbers. ♦ *Please add this column of figures.* ♦ *The waiter added up the bill, but he did not add it up correctly.*

addict 1. [ə 'dɪkt] *tv.* [for a substance or the consumption of a substance] to become habitual or irresistible to someone. ♦ *Smoking tobacco addicts many people.* ♦ *Alcohol may addict you.* **2.** ['æ dɪkt] *n.* someone who cannot stop consuming a substance or is unable to function without consuming a substance. (Usually refers to someone addicted to drugs.) ♦ *An addict stood on the street corner, begging.* ♦ *John is an addict when it comes to cigarettes.*

addicted [ə 'dɪk tɪd] *adj.* unable to stop consuming a substance; unable to function without consuming a substance. (Adv: *addictedly.*) ♦ *The addicted heroin user was put in the hospital.* ♦ *Max smokes but he is not addicted.*

addiction [ə 'dɪk ʃən] *n.* dependence on a drug or some other substance or activity. (No plural form in this sense.) ♦ *Addiction to gambling was a serious problem for Jane.* ♦ *Max suffered from addiction to a drug.*

addictive [ə 'dɪk tɪv] *adj.* habit forming; causing extreme dependence. (Adv: *addictively.*) ♦ *Cocaine and nicotine are addictive substances.* ♦ *Sweets are addictive for some people.*

addition [ə 'dɪ ʃən] **1.** *n.* the adding together of two or more numbers. (No plural form in this sense.) ♦ *There is an error in your addition.* ♦ *This calculator does addition quickly and accurately.* **2.** *n.* an instance of ①. ♦ *She did the additions in her head faster than I could do them on my calculator.* ♦ *I have a few more additions to perform before I can go home.* **3.** *n.* including something in something else. (No plural form in this sense.) ♦ *The addition of yeast made the bread dough rise.* ♦ *The play improved with the addition of a love scene.* **4.** *n.* someone or something that is added to something. ♦ *The most recent addition to our family is the new baby.* ♦ *The Browns built an addition onto their house.* **5. in addition (to something)** *phr.* additionally; further; moreover; as an additional thing or person. ♦ *In addition, I would like for you to sweep the kitchen floor.* ♦ *I put the books away, and in addition, I cleaned up my desk.*

additional [ə 'dɪʃ ə nəl] *adj.* extra; [something] further; more; added. (Adv: *additionally.*) ♦ *There is room for an additional person on this bus.* ♦ *Do you mind if I have a few additional cookies?*

additive ['æd ɪ tɪv] *n.* something that is added to something else, especially a chemical that is added to food. ♦ *This loaf of bread contains additives.* ♦ *The gasoline additives result in better gas mileage.*

address 1. ['æ drɛs, ə 'drɛs] *n.* the street name and number, city, state, and other information identifying the location of something, such as a building or residence. ♦ *Please print your address on the envelope.* ♦ *I know Bob's office address, but what is his home address?* **2.** [ə 'drɛs] *n.* a formal speech. ♦ *I am going to give an address to the English teachers.* ♦ *The address was short, thank heavens!* **3.** [ə 'drɛs] *tv.* to write the street name, number, city, state, and other information on an envelope or package. ♦ *Please address this package to the mayor.* ♦ *I have to address all these envelopes.* **4.** [ə 'drɛs] *tv.* to speak directly to a person. ♦ *I was addressing Susan, not you.* ♦ *Whom were you addressing when you asked for advice?* **5.** [ə 'drɛs] *tv.* to speak formally before a crowd of people. ♦ *John addressed the English teachers for an hour.* ♦ *Mary spoke English because she could not address the audience in Dutch.* **6.** [ə 'drɛs] *tv.* to respond to a question; to make remarks about an issue or problem. ♦ *In her speech, the manager addressed the matter of pay increases.* ♦ *Tom addressed the question that Jane asked.*

adenoid ['æd nɔɪd] *n.* an enlargement of the tissue at the back of the throat. (Usually plural.) ♦ *Bill had his adenoids removed along with his tonsils.* ♦ *I can't breathe well because of my enlarged adenoids.*

adept [ə 'dɛpt] *adj.* skilled or clever in being able to do something. (Adv: *adeptly.*) ♦ *Mary is very adept at tuning pianos.* ♦ *Max is an adept painter.*

adequacy ['æd ə kwə si] *n.* the quality or quantity of someone or something being adequate to meet some need or serve some purpose. (No plural form in this sense.) ♦ *John was unsure of the adequacy of the old stove for baking.* ♦ *We have an adequacy of paper plates for the picnic.*

adequate ['æd ə kwɪt] *adj.* just enough but not more than enough; sufficient; good enough. (Adv: *adequately.*) ♦ *I had an adequate amount of food for dinner.* ♦ *What you have given us is not adequate. You must find more.*

adhere [æd 'hɪr] **1. adhere to** *iv.* + *prep. phr.* to stick to something. ♦ *There is a piece of lettuce adhering to the side of your plate.* ♦ *The sticker adhered to the windshield.* **2. adhere to** *iv.* + *prep. phr.* to follow and obey something; to act in accordance with something, such as rules.

(Figurative on ①.) ♦ *We try to adhere to the rules.* ♦ *The monk adhered to the tenets of his religion.*

adherence [æd 'hɪr əns] **1.** *n.* the quality of sticking to something. (No plural form in this sense.) ♦ *The adherence of this glue is extraordinary.* ♦ *This tape has lost its adherence.* **2.** *n.* the loyalty of someone to someone or something. (Figurative on ①. No plural form in this sense.) ♦ *Tom's adherence to his childhood beliefs gradually faded away.* ♦ *The adherence of the dictator's followers was strained by his many acts of cruelty.*

adherent [æd 'hɪr ənt] *n.* someone who is loyal to someone or something; a follower of someone's philosophy. ♦ *The dictator's adherents object to his violence.* ♦ *The political party's loyal adherents contributed a lot of money.*

adhesion [æd 'hi ʒən] *n.* the quality of sticking to something firmly. (No plural form in this sense.) ♦ *The poor adhesion of the glue caused the stamp to fall off the letter.* ♦ *This powerful glue has great adhesion.*

adhesive [æd 'hi sɪv] **1.** *adj.* sticky; designed to adhere to things. (Adv: *adhesively.*) ♦ *I used an adhesive bandage to cover the cut on my finger.* ♦ *The adhesive power of the glue increased under pressure.* **2.** *n.* glue; paste. (No plural form in this sense.) ♦ *Put some more adhesive on the boards before you clamp them together.* ♦ *The adhesive was difficult to clean from my hands.* **3. adhesive tape** *n.* a fabric or plastic tape with a sticky side. ♦ *I need some adhesive tape to seal this package.* ♦ *Adhesive tape will keep the bandage in place.*

ad infinitum ['æd ɪn fɪ 'nɑɪt əm] *adv.* [continuing on] with no end in sight. (Latin for 'toward infinity.') ♦ *The concerto went on and on ad infinitum.* ♦ *He described the movie's flaws ad infinitum.*

adj. See adjectival.

adjacent [ə 'dʒe sənt] *adj.* neighboring; next to someone or something. (Adv: *adjacently.*) ♦ *The dog in the adjacent yard is barking.* ♦ *Tom's house is adjacent to the park.*

adjectival [æ dʒɛk 'tɑɪv əl] *adj.* serving as an adjective. (Abbreviated *adj.* Adv: *adjectivally.* Adjectival forms include true adjectives, such as *red;* adjectives made from the present participle or past participle of a verb, such as *falling* in *falling temperatures* or *fallen* in *fallen tree;* and adjectives that are simply nouns placed before other nouns, such as *city* in *city hall.*) ♦ *Many nouns have an adjectival use.* ♦ *The adjectival form of* center *is* central.

adjective ['æ dʒɛk tɪv] *n.* a word that describes or modifies a noun or nominal. ♦ *In the phrase "the red barn,"* red *is an adjective.* ♦ *Adjectives usually come before nouns in English.*

adjoin [ə 'dʒoɪn] **1.** *tv.* [for a room or building] to connect to another room or building. ♦ *Our garage adjoins the house.* ♦ *The living room adjoins the dining room.* **2.** *iv.* [for things] to touch or connect. ♦ *The living room and dining room adjoin.* ♦ *The joint where the parts adjoin is loose.*

adjoining [ə 'dʒoɪn ɪŋ] *adj.* touching; bordering; connecting. (Adv: *adjoiningly.*) ♦ *John lives in the adjoining house.* ♦ *We requested adjoining rooms at the hotel.*

adjourn [ə 'dʒɚn] **1.** *iv.* [for a meeting or session] to come to a formal end. ♦ *The meeting adjourned at four o'clock.* ♦ *The Senate hearing adjourned after the last speaker finished.* **2.** *iv.* [for a meeting or session] to stop until a later time. ♦ *Court adjourned until the end of the holiday.* ♦ *The U.S. Congress adjourns for the weekend.* **3.** *tv.* to end a meeting or session formally. ♦ *The vice president adjourned the meeting at four o'clock.* ♦ *The judge adjourned the court so she could review the evidence.* **4.** *tv.* to stop something until a later time. ♦ *The vice president asked to adjourn the meeting until the next day.* ♦ *The lawyer asked the judge to adjourn the court so he could get more witnesses.*

adjunct ['æ dʒəŋkt] *n.* an addition that is not needed; a part of something that is not needed or is not essential. ♦ *The garage was an adjunct to the house.* ♦ *As an adjunct to the lecture, the history professor showed some slides.*

adjust [ə 'dʒʌst] **1.** *tv.* to change something in a small way in order to try to make it work or fit better. ♦ *Mary adjusted the TV to get a clearer picture.* ♦ *When she lost weight, Mary had to adjust the waistline of her favorite skirt.* **2.** *iv.* to become used to someone or something; to adapt to someone or something. ♦ *It took Bill a few weeks to adjust to the colder climate.* ♦ *The adopted child adjusted to his new surroundings.*

adjustable [ə 'dʒʌst ə bəl] *adj.* changeable; able to be changed in small amounts. (Adv: *adjustably.*) ♦ *The brightness of my computer screen is adjustable.* ♦ *Adjustable mortgage rates are popular.*

adjustment [ə 'dʒʌst mənt] *n.* a slight change made to something to try to make it work or fit better. ♦ *The mechanic's adjustments fixed the car's engine.* ♦ *Mom made an adjustment to her schedule so she could see Mary's play.*

ad lib ['æd 'lɪb] **1.** *n.* a comment made up just before it is uttered. (From Latin *ad libitum,* 'at one's pleasure.') ♦ *The entertainer made one good ad lib after another.* ♦ *The funniest part of her speech was her ad lib about why she was late.* **2. ad-lib** *iv.* to think of something to say on the spot; to talk without a script. ♦ *When Tom forgot his lines, everyone began to ad-lib.* ♦ *The unprepared actor ad-libbed almost every line.*

administer [æd 'mɪn ɪs tɚ] **1.** *tv.* to manage something. ♦ *The state administers many social services.* ♦ *The personnel director administers the attendance policy.* **2.** *tv.* to give or dispense something, such as medicine, medical care, or justice, to someone. ♦ *The nurse administered medicine to the dying patient.* ♦ *The emergency-room doctor administered the treatment quickly.*

administration [æd mɪn ɪs 'tre ʃən] **1.** *n.* the work of managing and directing an organization. (No plural form in this sense.) ♦ *Lisa is involved in administration at the company she works for.* ♦ *Bob enjoyed administration but preferred more physical work.* **2.** *n.* the office and staff of an elected official. ♦ *The president's administration had little experience in foreign affairs.* ♦ *The governor's administration supported his policies.* **3.** *n.* a group of people who manage an organization. ♦ *The university's administration tried to keep tuition low.* ♦ *The company's administration often disagreed with the president.*

administrative [æd 'mɪn ə stret ɪv] *adj.* relating to the management and direction of an organization. (Adv: *administratively.*) ♦ *The administrative assistant performed clerical work.* ♦ *An administrative decision was made to limit overtime hours.*

administrator [æd 'mɪn ə stret ɚ] *n.* someone who manages and directs an organization. ♦ *The administrator of a prison is called the warden.* ♦ *The administrator of a school is the principal.*

admirable ['æd mə rə bəl] *adj.* deserving of admiration; very good. (Adv: *admirably.*) ♦ *The pianist's performance was admirable considering how cold the recital hall was.* ♦ *The child's honesty was admirable.*

admiral ['æd mə rəl] *n.* a naval officer of the highest rank. ♦ *The ship's admiral was a courageous officer.* ♦ *The little boy's dream was to be an admiral some day.*

admiration [æd mə 're ʃən] *n.* a feeling of pride, pleasure, and respect for someone or something. (No plural form in this sense.) ♦ *Bill's admiration of athletes increased when he watched the Olympics.* ♦ *Mr. Jones has a lot of admiration for his coworkers.*

admire [æd 'mɑɪr] *tv.* to regard someone or something with pride, pleasure, and respect. ♦ *I have always admired my mother's charm.* ♦ *My father admires musicians because he can't carry a tune.*

admirer [æd 'mɑɪr ɚ] **1.** *n.* someone who admires someone or something. ♦ *I've always been an admirer of people who could play the piano.* ♦ *Tom is an admirer of modern art.* **2.** *n.* someone who is fond of another person; a person who is romantically interested in another person. ♦ *A secret admirer left me a bouquet of flowers.* ♦ *Grandmother had many admirers before she married.*

admiring [æd 'mɑɪr ɪŋ] *adj.* fond; showing a favorable appraisal; with admiration. (Adv: *admiringly.*) ♦ *The bride cast an admiring glance at the groom.* ♦ *The critic had an admiring eye for the artist's work.*

admissible [æd 'mɪs ə bəl] *adj.* allowable; allowed to be included. (Adv: *admissibly.*) ♦ *The admissible evidence was not strong enough to convict the suspect.* ♦ *Are the witnesses' statements admissible in court?*

admission [æd 'mɪ ʃən] **1.** *n.* permission or the right to enter something, especially an educational program. (No plural form in this sense.) ♦ *Mary beamed when she received notice of her admission to the college.* ♦ *Admission to law school is very competitive.* **2.** *n.* an amount of money one has to pay to enter some place. (No plural form in this sense.) ♦ *How much is admission for the concert?* ♦ *The man at the gate said we had to pay admission.* **3.** *n.* a confession; some kind of evidence showing that something is true. ♦ *Tom's sheepish grin was an admission of guilt.* ♦ *The suspect's admission to being at the crime scene convinced the jury of his guilt.*

admit [æd 'mɪt] **1.** *tv.* to allow someone to enter into some place. ♦ *The usher will admit the couple to the theater.* ♦ *They would not admit us at the opera because we arrived late.* **2.** *tv.* to allow someone to become a member of a club or organization. ♦ *The sorority admitted Jane during her first year of college.* ♦ *The club was sued for refusing to admit minorities.* **3.** *tv.* to state that one has done something one is accused of; to state that something is true. ♦ *Bill was forced to admit that he had cheated on the test.* ♦ *I admit it looks like it will rain, but I wouldn't bet on it.*

admittance [æd 'mɪt ns] **1.** *n.* being allowed to enter into a place. (No plural form in this sense.) ♦ *The "No Admittance" sign scared the boys away from the empty lot.* ♦ *We presented our ticket for admittance to the concert.* **2.** *n.* being allowed to join a club or organization. (No plural form in this sense.) ♦ *Jane was quite pleased upon her admittance into the sorority.* ♦ *John finally gained admittance to the club.*

admittedly [æd 'mɪt əd li] *adv.* without denial. ♦ *The employee was admittedly late but had an excuse.* ♦ *Admittedly, you are right, but don't gloat.*

admonish [æd 'mɑn ɪʃ] *tv.* to caution someone against something. ♦ *The leader admonished his troop about wandering off in the forest.* ♦ *Mary admonished the children not to talk to strangers.*

admonition [æd mə 'nɪ ʃən] **1.** *n.* a scolding; a reprimand. ♦ *The admonition about lying made the guilty child cry.* ♦ *The public admonition embarrassed Bill.* **2.** *n.* a warning. ♦ *The children did not heed their mother's admonition and ate too much candy before dinner.* ♦ *Doctors often make admonitions about the dangers of smoking.*

adolescence [æd ə 'lɛs əns] *n.* the period of time between being a child and being an adult; the teenage years. (No plural form in this sense.) ♦ *Adolescence can be a confusing time.* ♦ *Developing friendships is an important part of adolescence.*

adolescent [æd ə 'lɛs ənt] **1.** *n.* a teenager; someone who is older than a child but not yet an adult. ♦ *The adolescent refused to sit at the children's table for the holiday dinner.* ♦ *Many of the camp counselors were adolescents.* **2.** *adj.* <the adj. use of ①.> ♦ *Eventually Max will grow out of his adolescent rebellion.* ♦ *Adolescent emotions are hard for teenagers to deal with.*

adopt [ə 'dɑpt] **1.** *iv.* to become the parent or parents of a child through legal proceedings. ♦ *Because the Johnsons couldn't have children, they adopted.* ♦ *The decision to adopt should be given much consideration.* **2.** *tv.* to acquire and become responsible for the child of someone else by a legal proceeding. ♦ *The Browns adopted the baby when she was just three months old.* ♦ *Jane adopted her niece when her sister died.* **3.** *tv.* to acquire a new practice, belief, or habit. ♦ *Susan adopted a strict diet when she learned she was sick.* ♦ *The company adopted new policies regarding maternity leave.*

adoption [ə 'dɑp ʃən] **1.** *n.* acquiring and becoming responsible for the child of someone else by a legal proceeding. (No plural form in this sense.) ♦ *They could not have children of their own, so they tried adoption.* ♦ *Adoption can provide homes for many children without parents.* **2.** *n.* an instance of ①. ♦ *No one talked about Tom's adoption until he was 13 years old.* ♦ *For years, the Johnsons pursued a legal adoption.* **3.** *n.* acquiring a new practice, belief, or habit. (No plural form in this sense.) ♦ *Mary's adoption of a strange lifestyle made her parents unhappy.* ♦ *The company's adoption of new policies caused John to look for a new job.*

adoptive [ə 'dɑp tɪv] *adj.* [of someone] related through adoption. (Adv: *adoptively.*) ♦ *The Browns love their adoptive children as much as their biological ones.* ♦ *My adoptive parents treated me like their own child.*

adorable [ə 'dor ə bəl] *adj.* very cute; worthy of being adored. (Adv: *adorably.*) ♦ *The twins were both adorable.* ♦ *The adorable puppy rolled around the lawn.*

adoration [æ do 're ʃən] *n.* worship; strong esteem. (No plural form in this sense.) ♦ *Bill's adoration of his older* *brother continued his whole life.* ♦ *Adoration was heaped upon the opera star.*

adore [ə 'dor] *tv.* to admire and be fond of someone or something. ♦ *I just adore quaint old hotels.* ♦ *Grandpa adored Grandma from the day they first met.*

adorn [ə 'dorn] *tv.* to put ornaments or decorations on someone or something. ♦ *The seamstress adorned the bridal gown with lace and pearls.* ♦ *Carvings adorned the legs of the chair.*

adornment [ə 'dorn mənt] *n.* a decoration or ornament that is put on someone or something. ♦ *A red rose was the only adornment on the table.* ♦ *The woman's adornments included earrings and a silver bracelet.*

adrenal [ə 'drin əl] **adrenal gland** *n.* a small gland that produces the hormone adrenaline. (Adv: *adrenally.*) ♦ *The adrenal glands are located above the kidneys.* ♦ *The adrenal glands secrete adrenaline and other hormones.*

adrenaline [ə 'drɛn ə lɪn] *n.* a hormone produced by the body during excitement or danger. (No plural form in this sense.) ♦ *Adrenaline provides an extra burst of energy.* ♦ *In an emergency, the body often responds by producing a burst of adrenaline.*

adroit [ə 'drɔɪt] *adj.* very clever or skillful; very good with one's hands or mind. (Adv: *adroitly.*) ♦ *The elderly man couldn't walk, but he was still adroit with his hands.* ♦ *The adroit mechanic can fix the motor very quickly.*

adulation [æ dʒə 'le ʃən] *n.* much praise; much flattery. (No plural form in this sense.) ♦ *The crowd's adulation surprised the humble performer.* ♦ *The basketball star enjoyed the adulation of his fans.*

adult [ə 'dʌlt] **1.** *adj.* mature; fully grown; fully developed. ♦ *Adult cats are not as playful as kittens.* ♦ *An adult elephant is enormous.* **2.** *adj.* exhibiting the behavior of a mature person. ♦ *I wish Jimmy would act more adult when we go out to eat.* ♦ *Max has an adult outlook on life, considering he is a teenager.* **3.** *adj.* intended for persons who are mature. (Often used referring to sex and violence in entertainment.) ♦ *Sometimes I think that adult movies are intended for the immature.* ♦ *A comedian delivered an hour of adult entertainment.* **4.** *n.* someone or something that is fully grown. ♦ *An adult has more responsibility than a child.* ♦ *The Smiths' children are adults, but they still live with their parents.*

adulterate [ə 'dʌl tə ret] *tv.* to weaken or dilute something by adding an inferior ingredient; to water something down. ♦ *Mary adulterated perfectly good iced tea with orange juice.* ♦ *Putting ice in wine adulterates the flavor.*

adultery [ə 'dʌl tri] *n.* an offense that is an act of sex between a man and a woman who are not married to each other and where either the man or the woman is married to someone else. (No plural form in this sense. Number is expressed by *act(s) of adultery.*) ♦ *The couple were caught in an act of adultery.* ♦ *Adultery was named as the reason for the divorce.*

adulthood [ə 'dʌlt hʊd] *n.* the state or condition of being an adult. (No plural form in this sense.) ♦ *The teenagers talked about the future, when they would reach adulthood.* ♦ *In adulthood, many people wish they were still teenagers.*

adv. See adverb.

advance [æd 'væns] **1.** *n.* a forward motion. ♦ *The invading army made an advance inland from the coast.* ♦ *Has the union made any advances in the negotiation?* **2. advances** *n.* an indication of romantic or sexual interest toward someone. ♦ *Bill made advances toward his sister's friend.* ♦ *Jane didn't even notice the advances of John, who adored her.* **3.** *n.* money that is given to someone ahead of schedule or before it is earned; a loan taken against money that is to be paid at a later time. ♦ *The publisher gave the author an advance against her royalties.* ♦ *Dad will never give me an advance on my allowance!* **4.** *iv.* to progress or move forward; to move to a higher or better level. ♦ *The sun advanced across the sky at a very slow speed.* ♦ *As hard as I tried, I was unable to advance in my company.* **5.** *tv.* to move someone or something forward or to a higher level. ♦ *He advanced the chess piece one space.* ♦ *The ballet teacher advanced Jane to the intermediate class.* **6.** *tv.* to give someone money ahead of schedule or before it is earned. ♦ *Mom advanced me $2. I will pay her back from my allowance.* ♦ *The contract promised to advance the author a portion of her royalties.* **7.** *adj.* prior; before the event. ♦ *The weather forecasters provided advance notice of the hurricane.* ♦ *The workers received no advance warning of the factory's closing.* **8. in advance** *phr.* [of something given, paid, or provided] before it is due; [of something prepared or obtained] before it is needed. ♦ *The bill isn't due for a month, but I paid it in advance.* ♦ *Is it cheaper if we buy our tickets in advance?*

advanced [æd 'vænst] *adj.* far ahead; very much progressed; far along. ♦ *We didn't know John had cancer until it was very advanced.* ♦ *Mary is taking an advanced German class.*

advancement [æd 'væns mənt] **1.** *n.* furthering something; moving something to a higher or better level; helping something succeed. (No plural form in this sense.) ♦ *The advancement of science is a major goal of all scientists.* ♦ *Jane took the job because it would help in the advancement of her career.* **2.** *n.* progressing; moving forward or to a higher or better level. (No plural form in this sense.) ♦ *Tom's rapid advancement at the company made his peers jealous.* ♦ *Does this job offer opportunities for advancement?* **3.** *n.* a movement forward; an advance. ♦ *In a series of small advancements, the army moved into and captured the town.* ♦ *Each advancement required careful preparation.*

advantage [æd 'væn tɪdʒ] **1.** *n.* something good or useful that will help someone with something; a benefit. ♦ *Eight years of experience as a lawyer gave Jane an advantage in the job market.* ♦ *Not everyone has the advantage of a good education.* **2. take advantage of someone** *idiom* to use someone unfairly for one's own advantage. ♦ *You took advantage of Tom by bringing a stranger to his party. He could hardly refuse to let her in!* ♦ *The government's complicated tax rules take advantage of the people who don't understand them.* **3. take advantage of something** *idiom* to make good use of something; to benefit from something; to benefit from an opportunity. ♦ *I took advantage of Max's offer of free tickets to the opera.* ♦ *Mary always takes advantage of every opportunity that comes her way.* **4. turn something to one's advantage** *idiom* to make an advantage for oneself out of something that might otherwise be a disadvantage. ♦ *Mary found a way to turn the problem to her advantage.*

♦ *The manager of the ice-cream store was able to turn the hot weather to her advantage.*

advantageous [æd væn 'te dʒɪs] *adj.* useful; beneficial; helpful. (Adv: *advantageously.*) ♦ *Speaking more than one language can be advantageous if you are traveling overseas.* ♦ *Having money saved will put you in an advantageous position.*

adventure [æd 'vɛn tʃɚ] **1.** *n.* excitement; challenge. (No plural form in this sense.) ♦ *The spy's work was filled with adventure.* ♦ *I love adventure, but I enjoy reading about it best of all.* **2.** *n.* an unusual or exciting experience. ♦ *Hiking in the mountains is an adventure.* ♦ *Lisa had quite an adventure when her car broke down on the highway.*

adventurer [æd 'vɛn tʃɚ ɚ] *n.* someone who seeks experiences that are unusual and exciting. ♦ *The adventurer told tales of his travels.* ♦ *Mary is an adventurer who will try anything once.*

adventurous [æd 'vɛn tʃɚ əs] *adj.* exciting; not ordinary; risky. (Adv: *adventurously.*) ♦ *Climbing mountains is adventurous!* ♦ *The traveler had an adventurous spirit.*

adverb ['æd vɚb] *n.* a word that modifies or describes a verb, verb phrase, adjective, or sentence or another adverb. (Abbreviated "adv:" or *adv.* here.) ♦ *Many adverbs end in* -ly. ♦ *In the sentence "The dog slowly walked away,"* slowly *is an adverb.*

adverbial [æd 'vɚb i əl] *adj.* [of a phrase, a series of words, or a clause] functioning as an adverb. (Adv: *adverbially.*) ♦ *In the sentence "When the dog starts barking, put it outside," the adverbial clause is "when the dog starts barking."* ♦ *A sentence can have more than one adverbial phrase or clause.*

adversarial [æd vɚ 'sɛr i əl] *adj.* antagonistic; argumentative. (Adv: *adversarially.*) ♦ *The former friends found themselves in an adversarial position when war broke out.* ♦ *The two employees became adversarial while working on the same project.*

adversary ['æd vɚ sɛr i] *n.* an enemy; the opposition. ♦ *The candidate's adversaries tarnished his image.* ♦ *John never thought of Mary as an adversary until she tried to blackmail him.*

adverse [æd 'vɚs] *adj.* unfavorable; contrary or in opposition to one's interests. (Adv: *adversely.*) ♦ *The adverse weather conditions made travel difficult.* ♦ *Too much stress can have an adverse effect on one's health.*

adversity [æd 'vɚs ə ti] *n.* difficulty; bad fortune. (No plural form in this sense.) ♦ *The adversity of losing one's job is difficult to bear.* ♦ *John and Mary experienced one adversity after another.*

advertise ['æd vɚ tɑɪz] **1.** *iv.* to make [something] known to the public, especially through signs, television, radio, newspapers, or magazines. ♦ *The company has advertised on television for thirty years.* ♦ *The charity advertised for weeks before the benefit.* **2.** *tv.* to make something known to the public through signs, television, radio, newspapers, magazines, or other means; to publicize something. ♦ *We advertised our sale in the local paper.* ♦ *Ms. Jones advertised her tutoring service at the local school.*

advertised ['æd vɚ tɑɪzd] *adj.* publicized; made known to the public. ♦ *The advertised radios were not available when we got to the store.* ♦ *The advertised concert was canceled due to rain.*

advertisement [æd vɚ 'tɑɪz mənt] *n.* a commercial; a notice about something, displayed to the public. ♦ *The store's advertisement about its grand opening drew customers.* ♦ *When I read the advertisement for the apartment, I knew I wanted to live there.*

advertising ['æd vɚ tɑɪz ɪŋ] **1.** *n.* publicity. (No plural form in this sense.) ♦ *The company did not spend much money on advertising, and the product didn't sell very well.* ♦ *Advertising is a good way to make sure that potential customers know about your product.* **2.** *adj.* <the adj. use of ①.> ♦ *Many creative people work in the advertising industry.* ♦ *The advertising executive approved the new marketing plan.*

advice [æd 'vɑɪs] *n.* recommendations or suggestions provided to help someone. (Compare with **advise**. No plural form in this sense. Number is expressed with *piece(s)* or *bit(s) of advice.*) ♦ *In times of trouble, people ask friends for advice.* ♦ *Bill's business failed because he followed some bad advice.*

advisability [æd vɑɪz ə 'bɪl ə ti] *n.* the degree of worthiness of a recommendation. (No plural form in this sense.) ♦ *We debated the advisability of swimming in the rain.* ♦ *The doctors considered the advisability of performing the operation.*

advisable [æd 'vɑɪz ə bəl] *adj.* sensible; recommended. (Adv: *advisably.*) ♦ *It is not advisable to swim in the rain.* ♦ *It is advisable to save part of your paycheck each month.*

advise [æd 'vɑɪz] **1.** *tv.* to give [someone] a particular kind of advice; to suggest doing something. ♦ *I advise caution in this matter.* ♦ *The weather report advised carrying an umbrella today.* **2. advise to** *tv. + inf.* to supply someone with a suggestion of something to do. ♦ *I advise you to be cautious.* ♦ *John advised Bill to get a new job before quitting the one he had.* **3. advise someone against doing something** *phr.* to supply someone with a suggestion of not doing something. ♦ *I advised Bill against quitting his job.* ♦ *Lisa advised Tom against doing it.* **4. advise against something** *phr.* to suggest that something not be done. ♦ *I advised against quitting work early.* ♦ *Lisa always advises against hasty actions.*

advisor AND **adviser** [æd 'vɑɪz ɚ] *n.* someone whose job is to give advice; someone whose job is to counsel people. ♦ *My college advisor wants me to take a literature class.* ♦ *Mary's financial advisor told her to invest her money.*

advisory [æd 'vɑɪ zə ri] **1.** *n.* a notice or warning about something. ♦ *The tornado advisory suggested seeking shelter.* ♦ *There was an advisory against international travel during the war.* **2.** *adj.* warning; giving notice or advice. ♦ *An advisory bulletin notified the people of the approaching storm.* ♦ *An advisory report warned consumers about the faulty toasters.*

advocacy ['æd və kə si] *n.* arguing or pleading for someone or something. (No plural form in this sense.) ♦ *Lisa's constant advocacy of change made the manager uneasy.* ♦ *Mike preferred quiet and persistent advocacy to blatant demands.*

advocate 1. ['æd və kət] *n.* someone who speaks for another person, especially in court. ♦ *The suspected murderer's only advocate was his attorney.* ♦ *When Anne ran* *for mayor, her husband was her best advocate.* **2.** ['æd və ket] *tv.* to recommend or urge that something be done. ♦ *The school board advocated purchasing new books.* ♦ *The social activist advocated change.*

aerial ['ɛr i əl] **1.** *adj.* seen from high in the air, as from an airplane. (Adv: *aerially.*) ♦ *The pilot took an aerial picture of our house.* ♦ *The picture showed an aerial view of the town.* **2.** *n.* an antenna; a device that receives radio and television broadcasts. ♦ *The aerial fell off our roof during the storm.* ♦ *Bob adjusted the aerial to get a better picture on the TV.*

aerobic [ɛ 'ro bɪk] **1.** *adj.* using or needing oxygen. (Adv: *aerobically* [...ɪk li].) ♦ *Bacteria that need oxygen are aerobic.* ♦ *Aerobic organisms need oxygen.* **2.** *adj.* serving to strengthen the heart and the lungs and improve blood circulation. (Adv: *aerobically* [...ɪk li].) ♦ *Aerobic exercise strengthens the heart and lungs.* ♦ *Jogging is an aerobic activity.* **3. aerobics** *n.* a program of exercise—typically done to music—that strengthens the heart and the lungs and improves blood circulation. (Treated as singular.) ♦ *Jane takes aerobics each Monday.* ♦ *Doing aerobics is a good way to stay in shape.*

aerodynamic [ɛr o daɪ 'næm ɪk] **1.** *adj.* sleek and efficient for easy passage through the air. (Adv: *aerodynamically* [...ɪk li].) ♦ *The cyclist's bike is especially aerodynamic.* ♦ *The aerodynamic properties of the plane permit very high speeds.* **2. aerodynamics** *n.* the science of the movement of gases and the effects of this movement on the objects that move through them. (Treated as singular.) ♦ *Aerodynamics is an important part of spacecraft design.* ♦ *Designers apply principles of aerodynamics more when making a sports car than when making a family sedan.* **3. aerodynamics** *n.* the qualities or design features of something that determine how smoothly and efficiently it will pass through a gas, usually air. (Usually treated as plural.) ♦ *The aerodynamics of a rocket are of major importance.* ♦ *The aerodynamics of a family car are often quite poor.*

aeronautic [ɛr ə 'nɑt ɪk] **1.** *adj.* utilizing aeronautics ②. (Adv: *aeronautically* [...ɪk li].) ♦ *Modern aeronautic design is evident in this new aircraft.* ♦ *The aeronautic principles of rocket design are complex.* **2. aeronautics** *n.* the science of the design and operation of aircraft. (Treated as singular.) ♦ *Knowledge of aeronautics is essential for pilots.* ♦ *Bob has an interest in flying and knows something of aeronautics.*

aeronautical [ɛr ə 'nɑt ɪ kəl] *adj.* utilizing aeronautics. (Adv: *aeronautically* [...ɪk li].) ♦ *The aeronautical design of the car lets it reach high speeds.* ♦ *An aeronautical engineer was consulted about the airplane's design.*

aerospace ['ɛr o spes] *adj.* associated with the industry that deals with the space around the earth and beyond. ♦ *Lisa studied to be an aerospace engineer.* ♦ *She got a job in the aerospace industry.*

aesthetic [ɛs 'θɛt ɪk] **1.** *adj.* pleasing to the eye; artistic. (Adv: *aesthetically* [...ɪk li]. Also spelled esthetic.) ♦ *I added an aesthetic touch to the living room with silk flowers.* ♦ *Your artwork has no aesthetic value.* **2. aesthetics** *n.* the study and appreciation of beauty in art and in nature. (Treated as singular.) ♦ *Aesthetics is not offered at this university.* ♦ *The designer studied aesthetics in college.* **3. aesthetics** *n.* the aesthetic ① features or details of something. (Treated as plural.) ♦ *The aesthetics of interior design are important to Jane.* ♦ *Many people question the aesthetics of modern art.*

affability [æf ə 'bɪl ə ti] *n.* good humor; friendliness. (No plural form in this sense.) ♦ *John's affability made him an excellent waiter.* ♦ *The candidate's affability made her seem like a good politician.*

affable ['æf ə bəl] *adj.* likable; friendly; easy to talk with. (Adv: *affably.*) ♦ *Slamming the door in someone's face is not an affable gesture.* ♦ *Mary is quite affable and is always invited to parties.*

affair [ə 'fer] **1.** *n.* a matter that needs attention; business. ♦ *The whole affair reeked of corruption.* ♦ *I have a few affairs to take care of this week.* **2.** *n.* an intimate relationship between two people who are not married to each other. ♦ *The politician's sordid affair soon became common knowledge.* ♦ *Mary was having an affair, so John divorced her.* **3.** *n.* a party; a social function. ♦ *There was a huge affair in the hotel's ballroom last night.* ♦ *The Joneses invited us to their annual spring affair.* **4. affairs** *n.* matters of personal or business interest. ♦ *Father's affairs were not in order at the time of his death.* ♦ *Jane's relatives often pry into her affairs.*

affect [ə 'fɛkt] **1.** *tv.* to influence someone or something; to have an effect on someone or something. (Compare with effect.) ♦ *Did the blunder affect your promotion?* ♦ *How did John's news affect Mary?* **2.** *tv.* to imitate someone or something; to make a pretense of something. ♦ *Bill affected a silly accent to entertain us.* ♦ *Jane affected a ridiculous manner to impress her friends.*

affected [ə 'fɛk tɪd] *adj.* pretentious; artificial. (Adv: *affectedly.*) ♦ *The affected accent made Professor Smith seem ridiculous.* ♦ *Jane was annoyed with her date because he had such affected table manners.*

affection [ə 'fɛk ʃən] **1.** *n.* love, caring, or fondness. (No plural form in this sense.) ♦ *The baby is full of affection for its mother.* ♦ *John has difficulty showing affection.* **2. affections** *n.* intentions and indications of love and kindness. ♦ *Susan's affections leaned toward musicians and artists.* ♦ *Bill completely ignored Lisa's affections, and that hurt her feelings.*

affectionate [ə 'fɛk ʃə nət] *adj.* showing kindness, care, or love for someone or something; loving. (Adv: *affectionately.*) ♦ *Jane gave her mother an affectionate hug.* ♦ *Dogs are very affectionate animals.*

affidavit [æf ə 'dev ɪt] *n.* a written statement, sworn to be true, used in legal proceedings. ♦ *The witness signed an affidavit stating that he saw the thief running from the crime scene.* ♦ *Did the detective get a signed affidavit from the suspect?*

affiliate 1. [ə 'fɪl i ət] *n.* a local organization or group associated with similar organizations on a national level. ♦ *The local television station is an affiliate of a national network.* ♦ *The newspaper's East Coast affiliate went bankrupt.* **2.** [ə 'fɪl i ət] *n.* someone who is associated with some group or organization. ♦ *I am not a full member, only an affiliate.* ♦ *Mike is an affiliate of our club.* **3.** [ə 'fɪl i et] *iv.* to associate with someone or something; to join with someone or something of a similar kind. ♦ *Our company affiliated with a larger firm in the same city.* ♦ *We chose not to affiliate with our competitor.*

affiliated [ə 'fɪl i e tɪd] *adj.* associated; having an affiliation. ♦ *The health-insurance company provided a list of its affiliated doctors.* ♦ *The two affiliated businesses share a single telephone system.*

affiliation [ə fɪl i 'e ʃən] *n.* a connection or relationship. ♦ *Does the university have a religious affiliation?* ♦ *The author has an affiliation with the university.*

affinity [ə 'fɪn ə ti] **1.** *n.* a relationship to something; a close likeness or similarity to something. ♦ *There is a close affinity between apes and monkeys.* ♦ *The Dutch and English languages have a fairly close affinity.* **2. affinity for something** *phr.* a strong preference for something; a strong liking for something. (No plural form in this sense.) ♦ *Cats have an affinity for seafood.* ♦ *Mary's affinity for classical music accounts for her large collection of recordings.*

affirm [ə 'fɚm] *tv.* to state, assert, or declare something to be true. ♦ *The scholar affirmed Shakespeare's authorship of the plays.* ♦ *The man's testimony affirmed the innocence of the suspect.*

affirmation [æ fɚ 'me ʃən] *n.* a statement of truth or fact; a declaration; an assertion. ♦ *The post office sent an affirmation that the letter was delivered.* ♦ *A second opinion gave us an affirmation of the doctor's diagnosis.*

affirmative [ə 'fɚm ə tɪv] **1.** *adj.* agreeing or permitting; encouraging. (Adv: *affirmatively.*) ♦ *Tom's supervisor gave an affirmative response to his plan.* ♦ *Dad gave an affirmative grunt, but he didn't look up from his paper.* **2. in the affirmative** *phr.* in the form of an answer that means 'yes.' ♦ *The soldier answered in the affirmative by nodding his head "yes."* ♦ *My manager's response was in the affirmative.*

affix 1. [ə 'fɪks] *tv.* to attach something to something else. ♦ *The king affixed his seal to the parchment.* ♦ *I affixed a label with my name on it to my coat.* **2.** ['æ fɪks] *n.* a suffix or a prefix; a part of a word added to a word to change its meaning. ♦ Non-, un-, *and* -able *are examples of affixes.* ♦ *An affix changes the meaning of a word.*

afflict [ə 'flɪkt] *tv.* to cause someone to become unhappy; to torment or distress someone. ♦ *Financial difficulties afflicted the Smiths.* ♦ *A disease broke out and severely afflicted the campers.*

afflicted [ə 'flɪk tɪd] *adj.* sick; injured; tormented; affected by some misfortune. ♦ *The severely afflicted man lay dying in bed.* ♦ *The afflicted family had the flu.*

affliction [ə 'flɪk ʃən] *n.* something that causes someone distress, suffering, pain, or grief. ♦ *Grandma's disability was an affliction for her.* ♦ *You're lucky if your worst affliction is the flu.*

affluence ['æ flu əns] *n.* wealth; a large amount of money or property. (No plural form in this sense.) ♦ *The town is known for the affluence of its citizens.* ♦ *Though she lived well, Aunt Jane did not have the affluence of her neighbors.*

affluent ['æ flu ənt] *adj.* rich; wealthy; having affluence. (Adv: *affluently.*) ♦ *The Joneses are affluent and give money to their community.* ♦ *Tom is not from an affluent family, but he has traveled a lot anyway.*

afford [ə 'ford] **1.** *tv.* to have enough money to buy something; to be able to buy something. (With *able to* or *can.*) ♦ *Can we afford a new car this year?* ♦ *Few people can afford a summer home on the lake.* **2.** *tv.* to endure the consequences of something. (With *able to* or *can.*) ♦ *Can you afford the trouble another traffic ticket will bring you?* ♦ *I don't think I can afford another of my mother's lectures.* **3. afford to** *tv.* + *inf.* to endure the consequences of doing something. (With *able to* or *can.*) ♦ *You can't afford to miss another piano lesson.* ♦ *I don't think I can afford to get another low grade.*

affordable [ə 'ford ə bəl] *adj.* low enough in price to allow a person to buy it. (Adv: *affordably.*) ♦ *The sale made the sofa Sue wanted quite affordable.* ♦ *Lobster at this time of year is not affordable for most people.*

Afghanistan [æf 'gæn ə stæn] See Gazetteer.

aficionado [ə fɪʃ i ə 'nɑ do] *n.* someone who is very much a fan of a particular sport or hobby. (From Spanish. Pl in *-s.*) ♦ *Mary is a golf aficionado and spends weekends at the driving range.* ♦ *John is not an opera aficionado and refuses to go to performances.*

afloat [ə 'flot] **1.** *adv.* floating. ♦ *The surfer drifted afloat on a broken surfboard for two days before he was rescued.* ♦ *The swimmer rested for a few minutes by lying afloat.* **2.** *adj.* floating. (Not prenominal.) ♦ *We were afloat for seven days before the ship reached the island.* ♦ *The toy boat was afloat on the pond for an hour before the rain sank it.*

afoot [ə 'fʊt] *adj.* in planning; being planned. (Not prenominal.) ♦ *"What plans are afoot for the holidays?" Bill asked his friend.* ♦ *Our parents guessed that something was afoot for their anniversary.*

aforementioned [ə 'for mɛn ʃənd] *adj.* as stated above; referred to earlier. (Used mainly in writing.) ♦ *The aforementioned matter was voted down.* ♦ *The contract stated that the aforementioned person would be referred to as "the client."*

afraid [ə 'fred] *adj.* fearful of someone or something; scared of someone or something. (Not prenominal.) ♦ *Many children are afraid of the dark.* ♦ *I am afraid to drive in the rain.*

Africa ['æf rɪ kə] See Gazetteer.

African ['æf rɪ kən] **1.** *n.* a citizen or native of one of the countries in Africa. ♦ *Bob met some Africans at the lecture.* ♦ *I know an African from Sierra Leone.* **2.** *adj.* of or about Africa. ♦ *I visited three African countries on my vacation.* ♦ *Dave studies African languages.*

African-American [æf rɪ kən ə 'mɛr ə kən] **1.** *n.* an American of African descent; a black American. ♦ *Many African-Americans supported the candidate who had worked hard for civil rights.* ♦ *An African-American wrote the poem that was read at the ceremony.* **2.** *adj.* <the adj. use of ①.> ♦ *Kwanzaa is an African-American holiday.* ♦ *Tom is majoring in African-American literature.*

African violet ['æf rɪ kən 'vɑɪ (ə) lət] *n.* a plant with heart-shaped, fuzzy leaves and white, purple, or pinkish blossoms. ♦ *African violets are popular houseplants.* ♦ *The African violets had pretty purple flowers.*

Afrikaans [ɑf rɪ 'kɑns] *n.* a language of South Africa. (No plural form in this sense.) ♦ *Afrikaans is related to Dutch.* ♦ Aardvark *is from Afrikaans.*

Afro-American [æ fro ə 'mɛr ə kən] **1.** *n.* an American of African descent; a black American. (Not heard as often as African-American.) ♦ *The new mayor is an Afro-American.* ♦ *A group of Afro-Americans greeted the ambas-*

sador from Ghana. **2.** *adj.* <the adj. use of ①.> ♦ *Two Afro-American writers teach at our school.* ♦ *Tom is fascinated with Afro-American music.*

after ['æf tɚ] **1.** *conj.* at a later time than when someone or something does something; later in time than when something happens; when something has finished happening. ♦ *You can eat the cake after you eat your dinner.* ♦ *After he came, we left.* **2.** *prep.* at a later time than something; later in time than something. ♦ *We will leave after his arrival.* ♦ *It's 20 minutes after three o'clock.* **3.** *prep.* further along in sequence than someone or something. ♦ *The letter* p *comes after the letter* o. ♦ *When you are traveling south on the West Coast, Oregon comes after Washington.* **4.** *prep.* in spite of something. ♦ *After all the plans we made for a party in his honor, Bill decided to stay home.* ♦ *After all the money we spent at the carnival, we still had enough for dinner.* **5.** *prep.* in search of someone or something; looking for someone or something. ♦ *The police are after some information on Max.* ♦ *The bank teller is in the vault, after some quarters.* **6.** *prep.* in the name of someone; in honor of someone; for someone. ♦ *The baby was named Mary after her grandmother.* ♦ *The company is named after my father, who founded it.* **7.** *adv.* behind; to the rear; following. ♦ *Jane walked in the door, and John came after.* ♦ *The mother duck arrived with five ducklings waddling after.*

aftereffect ['æf tɚ ə fɛkt] *n.* the results that follow the main action or occurrence. ♦ *One aftereffect of the layoffs was a decrease in the factory's production.* ♦ *The aftereffects of the explosion in the nuclear reactor were severe.*

afterlife ['æf tɚ lɑɪf] *n.* a period of life after death. (No plural form in this sense.) ♦ *Many religions include a belief in the afterlife.* ♦ *The hope of an afterlife comforts many mourners.*

aftermath ['æf tɚ mæθ] *n.* results or consequences occurring after an event. ♦ *In the aftermath of the hurricane, people rebuilt their homes.* ♦ *Many people were treated for injuries in the explosion's aftermath.*

afternoon [æf tɚ 'nun] **1.** *n.* the time of day from noon until the evening. (No plural form in this sense.) ♦ *I took a nap on Saturday afternoon.* ♦ *John gets more work done in the afternoon than in the morning.* **2.** *adj.* <the adj. use of ①.> ♦ *The afternoon sun shines in our western windows.* ♦ *The baby has an afternoon nap each day.* **3. afternoons** *adv.* every afternoon ①. ♦ *Dad sleeps afternoons and works through the night.* ♦ *Afternoons, we go to the zoo.*

afterthought ['æf tɚ θɔt] *n.* a thought that occurs after an event or after a first thought or action. ♦ *As an afterthought, Bill suggested that we ask Mary to come with us.* ♦ *I had an afterthought that I should have made two pies.*

afterward(s) ['æf tɚ wɚd(z)] *adv.* after; following; later. ♦ *Mary went to work, and afterward she went to dinner.* ♦ *We have to do our chores, but afterwards we'll go to the movies.*

again [ə 'gɛn] **1.** *adv.* once more; another time. ♦ *I realize you cleaned your room yesterday, but I want you to do it again.* ♦ *Please don't say that again!* **2.** *adv.* as someone or something was before. ♦ *Jane was very sick, but now she is well again.* ♦ *Bill lost his job, but now he is working again.* **3. again and again** *phr.* repeatedly; again ① and then even more. ♦ *I like going to the beach, and I will go back again and again.* ♦ *He knocked on the door again and again until I finally answered.*

against [ə 'gɛnst] **1.** *prep.* in opposition to someone or something. ♦ *Bob fought against Tom in a boxing match.* ♦ *The court case pitted two business partners against each other.* **2.** *prep.* in a direction opposite to something. ♦ *The children tried to swim against the current.* ♦ *Don't sand the wood against the grain.* **3.** *prep.* coming toward and meeting. ♦ *I tripped and fell against the railing.* ♦ *The rain splattered against the windowpanes.* **4.** *prep.* [leaning or tilting and] in contact with someone or something. ♦ *Place the rake against the side of the house.* ♦ *Stand this board up and lean it against the wall.*

age ['edʒ] **1.** *n.* the amount of time that someone or something has been alive or in existence; the progression of time while something is in existence. (No plural form in this sense.) ♦ *At ten years of age, Mary learned to swim.* ♦ *Many things become better with age.* **2.** *n.* advanced ①; evidence of advanced ①; the state of being old. (No plural form in this sense.) ♦ *Age showed on the old man's wrinkled face.* ♦ *Fifteen years after I bought it, my car finally yielded to age and stopped working.* **3.** *n.* the specific ① of a person, usually given as a number of years; the specific ① of something. ♦ *What are the ages of your children?* ♦ *The historians tried to determine the age of the old manuscript.* **4.** *n.* [for a person] the condition of having a certain ③; the time when a person has a certain ③. (The number comes after *age* and refers to years, unless some other unit, such as months, weeks, or days, is specified.) ♦ *At age three, my daughter could read very well.* ♦ *Age 2 was very difficult for Jimmy and his parents.* **5.** *n.* a period or stage of life. ♦ *Some people say that middle age begins at about 45 or 50, and that old age begins at about 65 or 70.* ♦ *Adolescence can be a difficult age.* **6.** *n.* a period of history; a generation; an era. ♦ *In this modern age, efficiency is considered very important.* ♦ *During the Ice Age, much of the earth was covered with glaciers.* **7.** *iv.* to become old; to show advancing ①. ♦ *The president seemed to age a lot during his term.* ♦ *As people age, their physical appearance changes.* **8.** *iv.* [for cheese, wine, whiskey, etc.] to mature; to reach a peak of quality, taste, and strength. ♦ *The wine aged in the oaken barrels for many years.* ♦ *The cheese aged in the cellar during the winter.* **9.** *tv.* to cause someone or something to grow old; to cause someone or something to appear to be old. ♦ *The crisis aged Mary considerably.* ♦ *An unusual amount of wear aged the door hinges prematurely.* **10. ripe old age** *idiom* a very old age. ♦ *Mr. Smith died last night, but he was at the ripe old age of ninety-nine.* ♦ *All the Smiths seem to live to a ripe old age.*

aged **1.** ['edʒd, 'edʒ ɪd] *adj.* old; elderly. ♦ *Grandma didn't look aged until she was in her nineties.* ♦ *The aged statue just fell over one day.* **2.** ['edʒd] *adj.* of a particular age; (The number comes after *aged* and refers to years, unless some other unit, such as months, weeks, or days, is specified.) ♦ *The soldier, aged twenty-three, was killed in a battle.* ♦ *Jane, aged five, announced that she didn't need afternoon naps.* **3. the aged** [ði 'edʒ ɪd] *n.* old people as a group. (No plural form in this sense. Treated as plural.) ♦ *Problems of the aged were discussed at the conference.* ♦ *We worried what would become of the aged if there were a recession.*

ageless ['edʒ ləs] *adj.* timeless; not showing age. (Adv: *agelessly.*) ♦ *The widow's ageless beauty was captured in her portrait.* ♦ *The themes of great art are ageless.*

agency ['e dʒən si] **1.** *n.* a business that arranges for certain products or services, such as houses or insurance, to be bought or sold. ♦ *My father operates an insurance agency.* ♦ *I wanted to sell my house, so I spoke with an agent at a local real-estate agency.* **2.** *n.* an office that deals with care and services for people. ♦ *The adoption agency was happy to help the Smiths adopt a baby.* ♦ *Social-service agencies provide help to needy citizens.*

agenda [ə 'dʒɛn də] **1.** *n.* a list of items to be discussed during a meeting; a schedule of events for a meeting. ♦ *Bob photocopied his agenda for the meeting but forgot to distribute it.* ♦ *"How many items are on the agenda?" growled the company's president.* **2.** *n.* someone's personal set of plans. ♦ *Bill always has a hidden agenda when he asks favors of his coworkers.* ♦ *Susan has her own agenda in her relationship with Tom.*

agent ['e dʒənt] **1.** *n.* someone who represents someone or something else; someone who has the power to act for someone or something else. ♦ *The agent from the insurance company came to our house.* ♦ *David served as an agent for the shipping company.* **2.** *n.* something that causes someone or something else to change. ♦ *Fear and dissatisfaction are often the agents of change.* ♦ *Your hard work is the agent that helped the company to succeed.* **3.** *n.* a spy. ♦ *The foreign agent stole the army's plans for a new weapon.* ♦ *The enemy arrested all of our secret agents.*

aggravate ['æg rə vet] **1.** *tv.* to make something worse; to make something more severe; to make something more serious. ♦ *Tom aggravated his financial difficulties by spending more money than he made.* ♦ *Mary aggravated her injuries by refusing treatment.* **2.** *tv.* to anger someone; to annoy someone. (Colloquial.) ♦ *Jimmy aggravated his dad by running through the house.* ♦ *It aggravates me when people are late.*

aggravated ['æg rə vet ɪd] *adj.* angered; annoyed. (Colloquial. Adv: *aggravatedly.*) ♦ *The aggravated mother heaved a sigh of relief as her toddler fell asleep.* ♦ *The aggravated judge pounded his gavel and screamed, "Silence!"*

aggravation [æ grə 've ʃən] **1.** *n.* making something worse or more serious. (No plural form in this sense.) ♦ *Carrying heavy boxes will certainly result in further aggravation of your back injury.* ♦ *Any aggravation of the tense situation could lead to war.* **2.** *n.* annoyance; bother. (Colloquial. No plural form in this sense.) ♦ *I hate the aggravation of having to drive into the city.* ♦ *Too much aggravation makes me nervous and irritable.* **3.** *n.* an annoyance; a bother. (Colloquial.) ♦ *Rock music is an aggravation to my parents.* ♦ *It's just one aggravation after another at work.*

aggregate ['æ grə gɪt] **1.** *adj.* of or about the combined total. ♦ *What is the Smith family's aggregate income?* ♦ *The company's aggregate expenses are over ten million dollars.* **2.** *n.* the sand, gravel, or pebbles that are mixed with cement to make concrete. (No plural form in this sense.) ♦ *There is not enough aggregate in this concrete.* ♦ *Make sure that the aggregate is well mixed with the cement.*

aggregation [æ grə 'ge ʃən] *n.* a combination of separate things. (No plural form in this sense.) ♦ *The stew was a delicious aggregation of vegetables and spices.* ♦ *My little shop contains an aggregation of handmade trinkets.*

aggression [ə 'grɛ ʃən] **1.** *n.* hostility; making assaults or attacks; the tendency to make assaults or attacks. (No plural form in this sense.) ♦ *Aggression frightens some people.* ♦ *War is a very serious form of aggression.* **2.** *n.* aggressive acts or manners; a feeling of ①. ♦ *Tom's bold aggression frightened many of his classmates.* ♦ *Her aggressions often got her in trouble.*

aggressive [ə 'grɛs ɪv] **1.** *adj.* hostile; belligerent. (Adv: *aggressively.*) ♦ *The country made an aggressive attack on a neighboring land.* ♦ *Tom often exhibits very aggressive behavior.* **2.** *adj.* assertive; bold; not afraid to take risks. (Adv: *aggressively.*) ♦ *The aggressive salesman gave his entire pitch to the uninterested browser.* ♦ *The aggressive journalist pushed her way to the front of the crowd.*

aggressor [ə 'grɛs ɚ] *n.* a creature that attacks someone or something; a country that attacks another country. ♦ *In the border dispute, both countries were the aggressors.* ♦ *In fistfights, Max is usually the aggressor.*

aghast [ə 'gæst] *adj.* shocked; frightened; filled with shock or fear. ♦ *Mary was aghast at the suggestion that she should dye her hair.* ♦ *The assassination of the president left the entire country aghast.*

agile ['æ dʒəl] *adj.* nimble; able to move quickly and easily. (Adv: *agilely.*) ♦ *The agile monkey swung from branch to branch.* ♦ *The coach picked the most agile athletes to compete for the prize.*

agility [ə 'dʒɪl ə ti] *n.* the ability to move quickly, easily, and nimbly. (No plural form in this sense.) ♦ *Bob's natural agility made him a great tap dancer.* ♦ *A cat's agility allows it to land on its feet when it falls.*

aging ['e dʒɪŋ] *adj.* growing older; maturing. ♦ *The aging movie star was given fewer scripts each year.* ♦ *The aging wine increased in value each year.*

agitate ['æ dʒɪ tet] **1.** *tv.* to shake, stir, or mix something. ♦ *The washing machine agitates the laundry to get it really clean.* ♦ *If you agitate a soufflé too much, it will collapse and come out flat.* **2.** *tv.* to annoy someone or some creature. ♦ *The sensational news show agitated people with its controversial topics.* ♦ *Jimmy agitated the dog by poking it with a stick.* **3.** *iv.* to stir up trouble; to attempt to gain support for one's causes. ♦ *Protesters agitated against the killing in Vietnam.* ♦ *The students agitated in favor of more dorms on campus.*

agitated ['æ dʒə tet ɪd] *adj.* troubled; annoyed. (Adv: *agitatedly.*) ♦ *The agitated victim could barely speak to the police.* ♦ *The agitated monkey pounded on the wall of its cage.*

agitation [æ dʒɪ 'te ʃən] **1.** *n.* shaking, stirring, or mixing. (No plural form in this sense.) ♦ *Agitation of some chemicals might cause them to burst into flames.* ♦ *It is the agitation of clothes in the washing machine that gets them clean.* **2.** *n.* trouble, dissent, and demands for action. ♦ *Police quelled the protesters' agitation on campus.* ♦ *After a lot of agitation from stockholders, the company president resigned.*

agitator ['æ dʒɪ tet ɚ] **1.** *n.* someone who creates public unrest; someone who causes disturbances. ♦ *The protester had gained a reputation for being an agitator.* ♦ *Three agitators were jailed after chaining themselves to a tree.* **2.**

n. a part of a washing machine that agitates the laundry inside the machine. ♦ *A washing machine with a broken agitator is useless.* ♦ *The worker installed a new agitator in the washer.*

aglow [ə 'glo] **1.** *adj.* glowing; lit up; bright. (Not prenominal.) ♦ *The stadium was aglow with newly installed lights.* ♦ *The dining room was aglow with candles.* **2.** *adj.* glowing with emotion, especially excitement or happiness. (Figurative on ①. Not prenominal.) ♦ *Mary was all aglow when John asked her for a date.* ♦ *The entire wedding party was aglow with joy.*

agnostic [æg 'nɑs tɪk] **1.** *adj.* not knowing about something, especially uncertain or undecided about the existence of God. (Adv: *agnostically* [...ɪk li].) ♦ *Bob remained agnostic on the question of a higher power.* ♦ *My agnostic friend believes that we cannot know whether or not there is a God.* **2.** *n.* someone who is uncertain or undecided about the existence of God. ♦ *Jane doesn't go to church because she is an agnostic.* ♦ *The agnostic insisted that the nature of God cannot be known.*

agnosticism [æg 'nɑs tɪ sɪz əm] *n.* the belief that the existence of God cannot be determined. (No plural form in this sense.) ♦ *Agnosticism is a form of skepticism.* ♦ *The adherent of agnosticism questioned how human beings could possibly confirm the existence of God.*

ago [ə 'go] **1.** *adv.* past; [time] already gone by. (After the noun.) ♦ *My parents moved to the United States twelve years ago.* ♦ *How many years ago did you graduate from college?* **2. long ago** *adv.* long before this time; much earlier than now. ♦ *I can't remember what happened so long ago.* ♦ *Our dog died long ago.*

agonize ['æ gə nɑɪz] *iv.* to worry very much over something; to suffer agony about something. ♦ *The host agonized over every detail of the party.* ♦ *Mr. Smith agonized over his child's violent death for many years.*

agonizing ['æg ə nɑɪz ɪŋ] *adj.* causing suffering, distress, or anxiety. (Adv: *agonizingly.*) ♦ *There was an agonizing silence while the teacher waited for the answer.* ♦ *The secretary had another agonizing day at the office.*

agony ['æ gə ni] *n.* an intense, deep pain in the mind or the body; a deep suffering. (No plural form in this sense.) ♦ *Bill was in agony as he endured his medical treatments.* ♦ *Listening to my neighbor practice the piano is agony.*

agrarian [ə 'grɛr i ən] *adj.* agricultural; relating to farms or farmland. ♦ *The professor specialized in studying agrarian reform.* ♦ *The small towns of Iowa have an agrarian economy.*

agree [ə 'gri] **1.** *iv.* [for people] to be in harmony or have the same opinion; [for people] to be in a state where there is no conflict of opinion or desire. ♦ *I am glad that we agree.* ♦ *Bill and his father used to argue a lot, but recently they have been surprised at how often they agree.* **2.** *iv.* [for facts or things] to be consistent or to harmonize. ♦ *My checkbook and my bank statement agree.* ♦ *These colors just do not agree!* **3.** *iv.* to decide together that an action should or should not be carried out; to concur that something is or is not true or that a state does or does not exist. ♦ *I agree that this is a difficult situation.* ♦ *We agreed that Lisa would represent us at the meeting.* **4. agree with** *iv.* + *prep. phr.* to concur with someone. ♦ *Mary agreed with Jane about the plan.* ♦ *Do you agree with me about this?* **5. agree with** *iv.* + *prep. phr.* to be able to be digested by someone without causing the person discomfort or sickness. ♦ *Spicy foods do not agree with Jimmy.* ♦ *My supper did not agree with me.* **6. agree to** *iv.* + *inf.* to consent to do something; to say one will do something. ♦ *I agreed to clean the house.* ♦ *The company agreed to change its policy about overtime.* **7.** *iv.* [for a form of a word] to match the form of another word grammatically. ♦ *The subject and verb of a sentence must agree.* ♦ *This verb does not agree with the pronoun that comes before it.*

agreeable [ə 'gri ə bəl] **1.** *adj.* pleasant; satisfactory. (Adv: *agreeably.*) ♦ *Our neighbor is an agreeable old man with a kind smile.* ♦ *The weather was quite agreeable for a picnic.* **2.** *adj.* acceptable. ♦ *The plan was agreeable to everyone but Mary.* ♦ *Tom's solution was not universally agreeable.*

agreement [ə 'gri mənt] **1.** *n.* consent; saying yes to someone or something. (No plural form in this sense.) ♦ *Agreement to the terms is binding.* ♦ *Jane's agreement was too late, and the deal fell through.* **2.** *n.* an understanding about when and how something is to be done. ♦ *John and Jane had an agreement to meet at the golf course.* ♦ *Our agreement was that you would pay for dinner and I would pay for the movie.* **3.** *n.* a contract. ♦ *I signed the agreement as soon as I received it.* ♦ *The agreement specifies that we share the income from this product.* **4.** *n.* the correct grammatical relationship between words. (No plural form in this sense.) ♦ *Language students must learn subject-and-verb agreement.* ♦ *Agreement between the subject and the verb is a grammatical rule.* **5. in agreement** *phr.* in harmony; agreeing. ♦ *The business partners were never in agreement about marketing strategies.* ♦ *Because the partners were not in agreement, the business failed.* **6. reach an agreement** *idiom* to achieve ③; to make ③. ♦ *We reached an agreement and signed a contract.* ♦ *We could not reach an agreement, so we stopped negotiating.*

agricultural [æ grɪ 'kʌl tʃɚ əl] *adj.* concerning or associated with farming. (Adv: *agriculturally.*) ♦ *Rural Iowa is an agricultural part of the country.* ♦ *Many agricultural areas must be irrigated each year.*

agriculture ['æ grɪ kəl tʃɚ] *n.* farming; the practice of raising crops or animals. (No plural form in this sense.) ♦ *Agriculture is the leading economic activity in many countries.* ♦ *The farmer studied agriculture at the university.*

agronomy [ə 'grɑn ə mi] *n.* the study of soil and its cultivation. (No plural form in this sense.) ♦ *Tom studied agronomy at the university.* ♦ *Knowledge of agronomy is important to successful farming.*

ahead [ə 'hɛd] **1.** *adv.* at a time before something; into the future. ♦ *By planning ahead, Jane saved money.* ♦ *John smiled, thinking ahead to his vacation.* **2.** *adv.* forward; continuing in the same direction. ♦ *Go straight ahead, and then turn left at the library.* ♦ *Move ahead, please.* **3.** *adv.* into an advanced position; into a better position. ♦ *John worked hard to move ahead at the office.* ♦ *It is not easy to get ahead these days.* **4. ahead of** *adv.* at a place in front of or in advance of someone or something. ♦ *The black car is ahead of the green car.* ♦ *Sally was ahead of Tom on the waiting list.* **5. come out ahead** *idiom* to end up with a profit; to improve one's situation. (On ③.) ♦ *I hope you come out ahead with your investments.* ♦ *It took *a lot of money to buy the house, but I think I'll come out ahead.*

aid ['ed] **1.** *n.* help; assistance; support. (No plural form in this sense.) ♦ *The relief worker provided aid for the earthquake victims.* ♦ *The politician offered aid to refugees.* **2.** *n.* something that helps someone or something else. ♦ *His eyesight is weak, so he must use thick glasses as an aid to reading.* ♦ *Canes are an aid for elderly people.* **3.** *tv.* to provide someone or something with ①. ♦ *The government aided the flood victims by providing loans to rebuild their homes.* ♦ *The politicians promised to aid the refugees.*

aide ['ed] *n.* an official assistant; someone who helps someone else with official duties. ♦ *The teacher's aide passed out paper to the children.* ♦ *The president's aides wrote most of his speeches.*

AIDS ['edz] *n.* "acquired immune deficiency syndrome." (No plural form in this sense. An acronym.) ♦ *Mary contributed money to support research on AIDS.* ♦ *AIDS is a syndrome wherein the immune system is destroyed.*

ail ['el] **1.** *iv.* to be sick; to grow weak. ♦ *Grandpa is ailing and has to stay in bed.* ♦ *My plants have been ailing, and I can't seem to help them.* **2.** *tv.* [for something] to make someone or something sick or weak. ♦ *"What ails you?" the doctor asked.* ♦ *The quack said his potion would cure whatever ailed you.*

ailment ['el mənt] *n.* an illness. ♦ *The doctor studied the patient's ailment.* ♦ *An ailment of the nervous system can be serious.*

aim ['em] **1. aim at** *tv.* + *prep. phr.* to point something toward a target or a goal. ♦ *The archer aimed the arrow at the target.* ♦ *The firefighter aimed the hose at the fire.* **2. aim to** *tv.* + *inf.* to intend to do something; to mean to do something. ♦ *Mary aimed to earn her college tuition during the summer.* ♦ *John aimed to be home for dinner but was late.* **3.** *n.* a goal; a purpose; an intention. ♦ *The aim of the committee was to publicize the charity ball.* ♦ *John's aim was to give a lively talk.* **4.** *n.* the pointing of something accurately. (No plural form in this sense.) ♦ *The archer has good aim.* ♦ *I need to improve my aim.*

aimless ['em ləs] *adj.* without purpose or goal. (Adv: *aimlessly.*) ♦ *Bob told another long and aimless tale from his childhood.* ♦ *Mary's future seemed aimless until she became interested in law.*

aimlessness ['em ləs nəs] *n.* lacking a purpose; not having a goal. (No plural form in this sense.) ♦ *Aimlessness is not a good quality in a person.* ♦ *Bill's aimlessness is a problem in the workplace.*

ain't ['ent] *cont.* "am not"; "is not"; "are not." (Regarded as uneducated or nonstandard, this contraction is also used informally and for effect by educated speakers.) ♦ *Ain't you ready yet?* ♦ *They ain't here.*

air ['er] **1.** *n.* the mixture of gases that surrounds the earth; the mixture of gases that people normally breathe. (No plural form in this sense.) ♦ *Jane took a deep breath of fresh mountain air.* ♦ *The balloon floated through the air above our heads.* **2.** *n.* a mood or atmosphere. (No plural form in this sense.) ♦ *Sally's fancy dress gave her a glamorous air.* ♦ *The balloons gave the room a festive air.* **3.** *n.* a tune. ♦ *The violinist played a little air.* ♦ *The melodious air sounded familiar to me.* **4. airs** *n.* ways of acting that make one seem more important than one really is. (Treated as plural.) ♦ *John's airs make him seem conceited and arrogant.* ♦ *Don't let her airs fool you, she is very nice.* **5. air out** *tv.* + *adv.* to ventilate something; to freshen something by exposing it to fresh air ①. ♦ *Air the sleeping bags out before putting them away.* ♦ *Mary opened all the windows to air out the room.* **6.** *tv.* to express a view or an opinion in public; to make something known. ♦ *The flustered employee aired his grievances.* ♦ *I try to air my opinions at family meetings, but no one listens.* **7. in the air** *idiom* everywhere; all about. ♦ *There is such a feeling of joy in the air.* ♦ *We felt a sense of tension in the air.* **8. on the air** *idiom* broadcasting a radio or television program. ♦ *The radio station came back on the air shortly after the storm.* ♦ *We were on the air for two hours.* **9. out of thin air** *idiom* out of nowhere; out of nothing. ♦ *Suddenly—out of thin air—the messenger appeared.* ♦ *You just made that up out of thin air.* **10. put on airs** *idiom* to act superior. (On ④.) ♦ *Stop putting on airs. You're just human like the rest of us.* ♦ *Anne is always putting on airs. You'd think she was a queen.* **11. up in the air** *idiom* undecided; uncertain. ♦ *I don't know what Sally plans to do. Things were sort of up in the air the last time we talked.* ♦ *Let's leave this question up in the air until next week.* **12. walk on air** *idiom* to be very happy; to be euphoric. ♦ *Anne was walking on air when she got the job.* ♦ *On the last day of school, all the children are walking on air.*

air bag ['er bæg] *n.* a protective device, installed in a car in front of the driver or a front-seat passenger, that explodes and provides a cushion of air when the car strikes something hard. ♦ *The old car was not equipped with air bags.* ♦ *When John crashed into the tree, the air bag saved his life.*

airborne ['er born] *adj.* aloft; in the air; flying. ♦ *The glider was only airborne for a minute before it crashed.* ♦ *The airborne dust and pollen make me sneeze.*

air-condition ['er kən di ʃən] *tv.* to provide a vehicle, room, home, or building with air conditioning. ♦ *We air-conditioned our house because it gets so hot in the summer.* ♦ *It is very expensive to air-condition a bus.*

air-conditioned ['er kən di ʃənd] *adj.* equipped with air conditioning. ♦ *We have to have an air-conditioned car because it is so hot in the summer.* ♦ *Our house is air-conditioned, too.*

air conditioner ['er kən dɪ ʃən ɚ] *n.* a machine that cools indoor air. ♦ *Mary turns on the air conditioner on hot summer days.* ♦ *Not all cars have air conditioners.*

air conditioning ['er kən dɪ ʃə nɪŋ] **1.** *n.* the mechanical system that cools indoor air. (No plural form in this sense.) ♦ *The prospective tenant wanted an apartment with air conditioning.* ♦ *John turned the air conditioning on as soon as he got home.* **2.** *n.* the cool or cold air that comes from ①. (No plural form in this sense.) ♦ *The air conditioning in the restaurant was too cold.* ♦ *In the movie theater, the air conditioning is much too cool.*

aircraft ['er kræft] *n., irreg.* a machine, such as an airplane or a helicopter, that flies in the air. (Pl: *aircraft.*) ♦ *The aircraft we flew here on was extremely fast.* ♦ *Several aircraft at the far end of the field were waiting to be serviced.*

airfield ['er fild] *n.* a place for planes to take off and land, usually less well equipped than a large airport. ♦ *John owns a small airplane which he flies from a small airfield* *near his home.* ♦ *The small airfield had grown into a large airport with a terminal building and hangars.*

airline ['er lɑɪn] *n.* a company that operates a fleet of aircraft for passengers, cargo, etc. ♦ *"Which airline do you prefer to fly on?" the travel agent asked.* ♦ *The airline provides meals on some flights.*

airmail ['er mel] **1.** *n.* a system for sending international mail by airplane; international mail that is carried by airplane. (No plural form in this sense.) ♦ *The postmaster stamped the letter to Japan "Airmail."* ♦ *A package arrived by airmail from France.* **2.** *adv.* [sending mail] by ①. ♦ *How much does it cost to send a small package to France airmail?* ♦ *Grandma sent her letter to England airmail.* **3.** *tv.* to send something by ①. ♦ *Please airmail the postcards to the children overseas.* ♦ *Did Grandma airmail her letter to Japan?*

airplane ['er plen] *n.* a heavier-than-air vehicle that flies through the air. ♦ *We went to Detroit by airplane.* ♦ *John owns an airplane, but he doesn't have a pilot's license.*

airport ['er port] *n.* a place where airplanes land and take off. ♦ *John's uncle watched the planes land at the airport.* ♦ *If there are no airports around, the pilot will land the airplane in a field.*

airsick ['er sɪk] *adj.* feeling ill from the motion of flight in an airplane or something similar. ♦ *I was afraid I would be airsick on the rough flight, but I wasn't.* ♦ *A number of the passengers became airsick because of the motion of the plane.*

airspace ['er spes] *n.* the space above a country that is considered part of it. (No plural form in this sense.) ♦ *The airplane took a special route to avoid entering the hostile country's airspace.* ♦ *Once in enemy airspace, the pilot dropped the bomb.*

airstrip ['er strɪp] *n.* a long, straight stretch of ground where planes take off and land; a runway. ♦ *The airstrip at the rural airport was not paved.* ♦ *The island didn't really have an airport—just a grassy airstrip where planes could land in emergencies.*

airtight ['er tɑɪt] **1.** *adj.* sealed so that air cannot enter or leave. ♦ *The storage container was not airtight, so the food spoiled.* ♦ *Our refrigerator is airtight when the door is closed.* **2. airtight alibi** *n.* an alibi having no weak points and able to withstand every challenge. (Figurative on ①.) ♦ *Max had an airtight alibi, and everyone believed him.* ♦ *The suspect's airtight alibi saved him from being arrested.*

aisle ['ɑɪl] *n.* a walkway between rows of seats, as in a theater, or between rows of shelves, as in a supermarket. ♦ *John stretched his legs into the aisle of the airplane.* ♦ *I walked down the aisle to the front of the church.*

ajar [ə 'dʒɑr] *adj.* partially open. (Not prenominal.) ♦ *The door was kept slightly ajar so a little light could get in.* ♦ *Dad left the door ajar, and the cat snuck out.*

akin [ə 'kɪn] *adj.* related; similar. (Not prenominal.) ♦ *Custard is akin to pudding.* ♦ *Although different, the two approaches are closely akin and equally effective.*

Alabama [æ lə 'bæm ə] See Gazetteer.

alarm [ə 'lɑrm] **1.** *n.* a warning sound or signal. ♦ *The burglar heard the alarm and fled.* ♦ *Bob's cry of alarm alerted us to the fire.* **2.** *n.* a machine that makes a warning sound or signal. ♦ *Dad set the house's burglar alarm before we went on vacation.* ♦ *The fire alarm sounded when the house began to fill with smoke.* **3.** *n.* anxiety or shock. (No plural form in this sense.) ♦ *Jane's alarm increased as the fire trucks came closer.* ♦ *The bright student's failure was cause for alarm.* **4.** *n.* a clock that has a bell or other signal that is sounded to wake someone up. ♦ *The alarm's buzzer was so soft that John slept through it.* ♦ *I set the alarm before I went to bed.* **5.** *tv.* to frighten or scare someone; to make someone afraid or fearful of danger. ♦ *The "Don't Feed the Bears" signs alarmed the campers.* ♦ *Jane's test results alarmed her doctors.*

alarming [ə 'lɑr mɪŋ] *adj.* frightening; causing fear and shock. (Adv: *alarmingly.*) ♦ *Jane's unexpected bad news was alarming.* ♦ *An alarming number of children do not get medical care.*

alarmist [ə 'lɑr məst] *n.* someone who makes other people feel scared, afraid, or anxious without a good reason. ♦ *John is such an alarmist that no one asks him for advice.* ♦ *An alarmist gets excited and nervous about almost anything.*

Alaska [ə 'læs kə] See Gazetteer.

Albania [æl 'be ni ə] See Gazetteer.

albatross ['æl bə trɔs] *n.* a type of bird with a huge wingspread that lives near or on the ocean. ♦ *The albatross can hover for hours without moving its wings.* ♦ *When it needs to rest, an albatross can float on the sea.*

albinism ['æl bə nɪz əm] *n.* an absence of pigment in the skin. (No plural form in this sense.) ♦ *Rabbits exhibiting albinism have pink eyes.* ♦ *Albinism is found among all peoples.*

albino [æl 'bɑɪ no] *n.* a human or an animal that has no pigment. (Pl in *-s.*) ♦ *The zoo's white alligator was an albino and very valuable.* ♦ *The child was so pale that the other children said she was an albino.*

album ['æl bəm] **1.** *n.* a large book with blank pages to be filled with photographs, stamps, writings, autographs, etc. ♦ *Jane had several albums of photographs of her family.* ♦ *The author kept all his rejection letters in an album.* **2.** *n.* a sound recording that is to be played on a record player or turntable. ♦ *My old albums are all scratched.* ♦ *Albums have been replaced by cassette tapes and CDs.*

alcohol ['æl kə hɔl] **1.** *n.* a solvent and disinfectant. (No plural unless referring to different kinds of ①.) ♦ *Jane cleaned her scratch with alcohol.* ♦ *Susan used a little alcohol to get the glue off the counter.* **2.** *n.* the intoxicating substance found in beer, wine, and hard liquors. (No plural form in this sense.) ♦ *There is more alcohol in hard liquor than in wine.* ♦ *Beer contains a small amount of alcohol.* **3.** *n.* beer, wine, hard liquor, spirits; drinks that contain alcohol. (No plural form in this sense.) ♦ *Mary does not serve alcohol at her parties.* ♦ *Our restaurant only sells soft drinks, but you can bring your own alcohol if you wish.*

alcoholic [æl kə 'hɔl ɪk] **1.** *adj.* containing alcohol. ♦ *Mr. Smith prefers alcoholic beverages to lemonade.* ♦ *Jane made an alcoholic punch for the adults.* **2.** *adj.* relating to alcoholism; relating to ③; typical of ③. (Adv: *alcoholically* [...ɪk li].) ♦ *Mary is still troubled by her alcoholic tendencies.* ♦ *Tom had another alcoholic binge last week.* **3.** *n.* someone who is addicted to alcohol; someone who drinks too much alcohol too often. ♦ *It was many years before we realized that John was an alcoholic.* ♦ *There are many organizations to help alcoholics.*

alcoholism ['æl kə hɔl ɪz əm] *n.* addiction to alcohol. (No plural form in this sense.) ♦ *Alcoholism is more common than people think.* ♦ *John lost his job due to his problem with alcoholism.*

alcove ['æl kov] *n.* a small room or a small space set off from a larger room. ♦ *A small alcove in the back of the church had a statue in it.* ♦ *The alcove in the hall is a telephone booth.*

alderman ['ɔl dɚ mən] *n., irreg.* a member of the city council; an elected legislator of a city. (Pl: **aldermen**.) ♦ *I wrote a letter of complaint to my alderman.* ♦ *Our alderman rode in the parade.*

aldermen ['ɔl dɚ mən] pl of **alderman**.

alderwoman ['ɔl dɚ wʊm ən] *n., irreg.* a female member of the city council; a female elected legislator of a city. (Pl: **alderwomen**.) ♦ *I wrote a letter of complaint to my alderwoman.* ♦ *Our alderwoman rode in the parade.*

alderwomen ['ɔl dɚ wɪm ən] pl of **alderwoman**.

ale ['el] *n.* a kind of strong beer. (No plural form in this sense.) ♦ *The Irish and English love to drink ale.* ♦ *John prefers drinking dark ale to light ale.*

alert [ə 'lɚt] **1.** *adj.* wary; aware; watchful. (Adv: *alertly.*) ♦ *The alert baby smiled at everyone.* ♦ *Mary was awake but not very alert when the alarm rang.* **2.** *n.* a loud warning sound, such as a bell or a siren. ♦ *An alert sounded and the sailors assembled on the deck.* ♦ *The alert sounded for five minutes before anyone realized it was not a drill.* **3.** *tv.* to warn someone about something, especially danger. ♦ *Make sure that your neighbors have been alerted about the tornado warning.* ♦ *We alerted the police to watch for the missing child.*

alfalfa [æl 'fæl fə] *n.* a plant that is grown to feed farm animals. (No plural form in this sense.) ♦ *Alfalfa is a good grazing plant for cows.* ♦ *We made hay out of our crop of alfalfa.*

algae ['æl dʒi] *n.* small plants without stems, roots, or leaves, that live in water or wet places. (*Algae* is actually a Latin plural of *alga,* but it is usually treated as singular in English.) ♦ *Algae grows on rocks in the lake.* ♦ *Bill slipped on some algae while climbing up a ladder to the dock.*

algebra ['æl dʒə brə] *n.* a branch of mathematics using letters and other symbols to represent numbers or sets of numbers in equations. (No plural form in this sense.) ♦ *High-school students must take algebra.* ♦ *Mary studied diligently for her test in algebra.*

algebraic [æl dʒə 'bre ɪk] *adj.* relating to algebra. (Adv: *algebraically* [...ɪk li].) ♦ *Bill could not solve the algebraic problem on his test.* ♦ *Anne remembered the algebraic formula after the test.*

Algeria [æl 'dʒir i ə] See Gazetteer.

alias ['e li əs] **1.** *adv.* also known as; otherwise known as. (From Latin for 'otherwise.') ♦ *Max Jones, alias Max Smith, kept trying to pass forged checks.* ♦ *Bill Brown, alias Bill the Butcher, was accused of the murder.* **2.** *n.* an assumed name; a name other than one's real name. ♦ *The spy uses an alias on secret missions.* ♦ *Max's alias was useless because the witnesses recognized him.*

alibi ['æl ə bɑɪ] **1.** *n.* a story that explains why a criminal suspect could not have committed a certain crime. (From Latin for 'in another place.') ♦ *The murder suspect had an alibi for the night of the crime.* ♦ *The judge did not think the suspect's alibi was a good one.* **2.** *n.* an excuse. (Figurative on ①.) ♦ *John's mother did not believe his alibi.* ♦ *What was Bill's alibi for standing you up Saturday night?*

alien ['e li ən] **1.** *n.* a foreign-born resident of a country, who is not a citizen of the country. ♦ *It is hard for an alien to get a job in this country.* ♦ *Some aliens are in the United States illegally.* **2.** *n.* a visitor from space. ♦ *Many movies have been made about aliens coming to earth.* ♦ *What do you think an alien would look like?* **3.** *adj.* unknown; strange; very different. ♦ *Making a cake from a mix is an alien idea to the pastry chef.* ♦ *Swimming outdoors in the winter is an alien concept for most people.* **4.** *adj.* foreign; from another place. ♦ *Rabbits are really alien creatures in Australia.* ♦ *Someone introduced an alien plant into the Florida swamp.*

alienate ['e li ə net] *tv.* to repel someone; to make someone feel like leaving or withdrawing from whatever or whoever is alienating them. ♦ *The comedian alienated his audience by making mean jokes that weren't funny.* ♦ *The club president alienated the new member by ignoring her.*

alienation [e li ə 'ne ʃən] *n.* feeling unwanted or distant from other people. (No plural form in this sense.) ♦ *Bob felt a sense of alienation when his roommates ignored him.* ♦ *Much alienation has resulted from years of racial hatred.*

alight [ə 'lɑɪt] *iv., irreg.* to step out of or down from a vehicle; to dismount from something. (Pt/pp: *alighted* and, less commonly, **alit**.) ♦ *The rider alighted from her horse after her ride.* ♦ *As soon as the passengers had alighted, the bus drove away.*

align [ə 'lɑɪn] **1.** *tv.* to place things in a line; to put something into proper adjustment. ♦ *The mechanic aligned the front end of my car.* ♦ *Align the patterns on the pieces of wallpaper to hide the seam.* **2. align with** *tv.* + *prep. phr.* to join oneself with someone whose opinions one agrees with; to take someone's side on an issue. (Takes a reflexive object.) ♦ *Jane aligned herself with Mary and John, because she agreed with them.* ♦ *The workers aligned themselves with the union officials.* **3. align with** *iv.* + *prep. phr.* to take someone's side on an issue. ♦ *Jane aligned with Mary and John on the issue.* ♦ *During family arguments, Bill always aligns with Dad.*

alignment [ə 'lɑɪn mənt] *n.* being lined up in a row; being in good order or positioning. (No plural form in this sense.) ♦ *The accident knocked the front end of the car out of alignment.* ♦ *The alignment of the striped wallpaper was wrong and made me dizzy.*

alike [ə 'lɑɪk] **1.** *adj.* similar; the same or almost the same. (Not prenominal.) ♦ *The habits of John and his father are alike.* ♦ *Your answers on these tests are too much alike. You must have cheated.* **2.** *adv.* in the same manner. ♦ *John and his dad walk very much alike.* ♦ *The twins look alike, but they don't act alike.* **3.** *adv.* equally; in the same amount or degree. ♦ *The dean is respected by professors and students alike.* ♦ *Big people, little people, black people, white people—we treat them all alike.*

alikeness [ə 'lɑɪk nəs] *n.* similarity; sameness. (No plural form in this sense.) ♦ *The alikeness of the twins was confusing.* ♦ *The degree of alikeness between the boys was amazing.*

alimentary [æl ə 'mɛn tə ri] **alimentary canal** *n.* the passageway inside the body that forms the route taken by food through the body, from the mouth to the anus. (Adv: *alimentarily* [æl ə mɛn 'tɛr ə li].) ♦ *Our food passes through the alimentary canal.* ♦ *John has some sort of disorder of the alimentary canal.*

alimony ['æl ə mon i] *n.* money paid [by a former spouse] to a former spouse after a divorce. (No plural form in this sense.) ♦ *John pays his alimony to his ex-wife on time.* ♦ *Can I count the alimony that I pay as a deduction on my taxes?*

alit [ə 'lɪt] a pt/pp of alight.

alive [ə 'lɑɪv] **1.** *adj.* living; not dead. (Not prenominal.) ♦ *Jimmy looked at the sleeping hamster and asked, "Is it alive?"* ♦ *The rescuers were not sure the victims would be alive by the time help reached them.* **2.** *adj.* active; lively; full of energy. ♦ *Fresh air makes me feel alive!* ♦ *After recovering from the flu, Jane felt really alive.*

alkali ['æl kə lɑɪ] *n.* a chemical substance that can neutralize an acid. (No plural form in this sense.) ♦ *This soil is too acidic, and it needs to have an alkali added.* ♦ *Alkalis neutralize acids.*

all ['ɔl] **1.** *adj.* each and every one [of the people or things]; the full amount [of something]; the whole extent of [something]. ♦ *All Jane's sisters are tall, but her brothers are all short.* ♦ *The restaurant serves all types of cheese.* ♦ *Why did you drink all the milk?* **2.** *adj.* the greatest amount possible [of something]. ♦ *In all sincerity, I don't like your pie.* ♦ *The compliment was paid with all the seriousness due such a gracious person.* **3.** *pron.* everything or everyone mentioned earlier in the course of conversation or writing. ♦ *Twenty people came to my party. All left by midnight.* ♦ *All were happy and full of food.* **4.** *pron.* everything. ♦ *All is lost.* ♦ *We have all we need right here on this island.* **5.** *adv.* completely. ♦ *"All done!" the toddler shouted and threw the plate on the floor.* ♦ *Tom left, and I am all alone.*

Allah ['ɑ lɑ] *n.* [the] God; the supreme being. (No plural form. Arabic. From the Islamic religion.) ♦ *In Islam, the name of the supreme being is Allah.* ♦ *Allah and God are considered to be the same being or force.*

all-American [ɔl ə 'mɛr ə kən] **1.** *n.* an exemplary American athlete or performer who is chosen to represent the best such people in the U.S. ♦ *During her college years, Anne was an all-American.* ♦ *The all-American helped his school's team win several championships.* **2.** *adj.* completely American ④; typically American ④. ♦ *Pot roast for Sunday dinner is an all-American meal.* ♦ *Having a picnic on the Fourth of July is an all-American custom.* **3.** *adj.* <the adj. use of ①.> ♦ *Bill was on the all-American football team.* ♦ *Mary played basketball in college and was chosen for the all-American team three years in a row.*

all-(a)round ['ɔl (ə) 'rɑʊnd] *adj.* in general; in all aspects. (Prenominal only.) ♦ *Mr. Smith is an all-around gentleman.* ♦ *The play was an all-round success.*

all day ['ɔl de] **1.** *adv.* for the entire day. ♦ *I worked in the office all day without stopping.* ♦ *Tom doesn't like to sit around doing nothing all day.* **2. all-day** *adj.* lasting for the whole day. (Prenominal only.) ♦ *The company picnic was an all-day affair.* ♦ *Painting the living room turned into an all-day project.*

allegation [æl ə 'ge ʃən] *n.* a claim; an accusation. ♦ *The allegations against the treasurer involved fraud.* ♦ *What allegations has Mary made against her attacker?*

allege [ə 'lɛdʒ] *tv.* to state something as fact before it has been proved. ♦ *The company alleged that the employee tampered with the computer system.* ♦ *The report alleged that the prominent lawyer was caught shoplifting.*

alleged [ə 'lɛdʒd] *adj.* suspected or claimed to be. (Adv: *allegedly* [ə 'lɛdʒ əd li].) ♦ *The alleged murderer was taken to the police station.* ♦ *The alleged suspect resisted arrest.*

allegedly [ə 'lɛdʒ əd li] *adv.* according to a claim, charge, or accusation. ♦ *Allegedly, the parents abandoned their baby.* ♦ *The man allegedly was driving a stolen car, but his lawyers say the car was given to him.*

allegiance [ə 'li dʒəns] *n.* loyalty; faithfulness. (No plural form in this sense.) ♦ *The politician has the allegiance of the voters.* ♦ *The two old friends have an undying allegiance to each other.*

allegorical [æl ə 'gor ɪ kəl] *adj.* symbolic. (Adv: *allegorically* [...ɪk li].) ♦ *The reader was unaware of the story's allegorical meaning.* ♦ *The novel's main character was an allegorical figure representing the devil.*

allergen ['æl ɚ dʒɛn] *n.* something that causes an allergy in someone. ♦ *Mold can be an allergen for many people.* ♦ *Pollen is an allergen for people with hay fever.*

allergenic [æl ɚ 'dʒɛn ɪk] *adj.* causing an allergic reaction. (Adv: *allergenically* [...ɪk li].) ♦ *The allergenic properties of household dust are well known.* ♦ *Pollen grains are allergenic particles that affect many people.*

allergic [ə 'lɚ dʒɪk] **1.** *adj.* having an allergy to something. (Adv: *allergically* [...ɪk li].) ♦ *Mary is allergic to cats.* ♦ *I am not allergic to any food.* **2.** *adj.* caused by an allergy. (Adv: *allergically* [...ɪk li].) ♦ *Sneezing is an allergic response to allergens in the air.* ♦ *The baby's hives were an allergic reaction to milk.*

allergist ['æl ɚ dʒəst] *n.* a doctor who diagnoses and treats people who have an allergy. ♦ *John sees an allergist twice a week to get shots.* ♦ *The allergist said that I am allergic to chocolate.*

allergy ['æl ɚ dʒi] *n.* a physical response to a substance—an allergen—causing sneezing, itching, a rash, or other symptoms. ♦ *John has an allergy to dogs. They make him sneeze.* ♦ *Mary recently developed allergies to dairy products.*

alleviate [ə 'liv i et] *tv.* to make a burden lighter; to make a problem less severe or bad. ♦ *Winning the lottery alleviated the couple's financial problems.* ♦ *The drug alleviated the pain of Mary's broken leg.*

alleviation [ə liv i 'e ʃən] *n.* making a problem less severe or bad; making a burden lighter. (No plural form in this sense.) ♦ *The new plan provided for the alleviation of our most serious problems.* ♦ *This medicine is used for the alleviation of pain.*

alley ['æl i] **1.** *n.* a narrow road or pathway behind buildings or between buildings. ♦ *John parked his car in the alley.* ♦ *The cat crept down the alley.* **2. (bowling) alley** *n.* the path down which one rolls a bowling ball in the game of bowling. ♦ *The bowling ball rolled halfway down the alley and then fell into the gutter.* ♦ *I try to keep the ball in the middle of the alley as much as possible.* **3. (bowling) alley** *n.* the building that houses a number of ②. ♦ *We went to the bowling alley for the evening.* ♦ *There is an alley on Maple Street where we can bowl for half price tonight.* **4. up a blind alley** *idiom* at a dead end; on a route that leads nowhere. ♦ *I have been trying to find out something about my ancestors, but I'm up a blind alley. I can't find anything.* ♦ *The police are up a blind alley in their investigation of the crime.*

alliance [ə 'laɪ əns] *n.* an association of countries or businesses whose members agree to help each other. ♦ *The chamber of commerce is an alliance of businesses.* ♦ *The two countries formed an alliance to protect themselves against enemies.*

alligator ['æl ə get ɚ] *n.* a large reptile of the crocodile family. ♦ *The alligator crawled onto the riverbank.* ♦ *There are many alligators in Florida.*

all-important ['ɔl ɪm 'port nt] *adj.* most important; most critical; key; most necessary. (Adv: *all-importantly.*) ♦ *An all-important goal for Bill was to make the football team.* ♦ *Getting good grades in school is all-important to Jane.*

all-inclusive ['ɔl ɪn 'klus ɪv] *adj.* including everything or everyone; [of a price] including everything. (Adv: *all-inclusively.*) ♦ *The invitation to the neighborhood party was all-inclusive—everyone was invited.* ♦ *The Browns took a vacation for an all-inclusive price of $2,000.*

all night ['ɔl 'nɑɪt] **1.** *adv.* for the entire night. ♦ *I'm very tired because I worked all night to finish the report.* ♦ *This store is open all night.* **2. all-night** *adj.* lasting the entire night; open or available for the entire night. (Prenominal only.) ♦ *We went to an all-night diner and bought some hamburgers at midnight.* ♦ *The dance contest was an all-night affair.*

allocate ['æl ə ket] *tv.* to give or assign a portion of something. ♦ *The government allocated funds to aid flood victims.* ♦ *The teacher allocated time during class to answer questions.*

allocation [æl ə 'ke ʃən] **1.** *n.* allocating or dividing something into portions or shares. (No plural form in this sense.) ♦ *The allocation of funds was done by the company officers.* ♦ *My department is concerned with the allocation of resources.* **2.** *n.* a share; an allotment. ♦ *My allocation of food was more than I could eat.* ♦ *Each worker's allocation of company profits was small.*

allot [ə 'lɑt] *tv.* to give a portion of something to someone or something. ♦ *Mom allotted us three cookies each.* ♦ *The refugee camp allotted each family a small living space and a weekly food ration.*

allotment [ə 'lɑt mənt] *n.* a portion of something; a share. ♦ *Jimmy was not happy with his allotment of ice cream.* ♦ *Mary's allotment from her parents' estate was large.*

all-out ['ɔl 'ɑʊt] *adj.* to the furthest degree; using all possible energy. ♦ *The team made an all-out effort to win the game.* ♦ *The soldiers fought an all-out battle for the town.*

allow [ə 'lɑʊ] **1.** *tv.* to permit someone to do something; to let someone do something. ♦ *Do you allow your children to cross the street by themselves?* ♦ *Allow me to introduce myself.* **2.** *tv.* to make sure that there is a certain amount of time for something to be done. ♦ *Allow six to eight weeks for delivery.* ♦ *Traffic is very heavy, so allow enough time.*

allowable [ə 'lɑʊ ə bəl] *adj.* permitted; permissible. (Adv: *allowably.*) ♦ *You are carrying more baggage than is allowable.* ♦ *I don't know if it is allowable to smoke in here.*

allowance [ə 'lɑʊ əns] **1.** *n.* an amount of something, such as money, given to someone. ♦ *Bill's allowance is twenty dollars a week.* ♦ *This cereal provides the recommended daily allowance of many vitamins.* **2. make allowances for something** *idiom* to keep something in mind when making a decision or policy. ♦ *I will have to make allowances for the possibility of an extra guest at dinner.* ♦ *The company made no allowances for bad weather in its attendance policy.* **3. make allowances for someone** *idiom* to make excuses for someone's behavior. ♦ *You make too many allowances for your children's bad behavior.* ♦ *I have to make allowances for John. He hasn't been well lately.*

alloy ['æ lɔɪ] **1.** *n.* a mixture of metals. ♦ *Alloys are usually stronger than pure metals.* ♦ *Copper and tin are used to make an alloy called bronze.* **2.** *tv.* to mix one metal with one or more other metals. ♦ *Copper is alloyed with tin to make bronze.* ♦ *Gold is alloyed with other metals to strengthen it.*

all-purpose ['ɔl 'pɚp əs] *adj.* serving many or all purposes or needs. ♦ *I used an all-purpose paint on the garage floor.* ♦ *Please buy the all-purpose grind of coffee at the store.*

all right ['ɔl 'rɑɪt] **1.** *adj.* OK; fine; acceptable; satisfactory. ♦ *Is it all right if we stop at the store?* ♦ *"It's all right with me," Bill said.* **2.** *adv.* in a good way; satisfactorily. ♦ *Susan dances all right and sings very well.* ♦ *Did you sleep all right last night?* **3.** *interj.* "yes." (Colloquial.) ♦ *All right, I will do it.* ♦ *All right, I'll clean the garage tomorrow.*

all-star 1. ['ɔl stɑr] *n.* one of the best athletes. ♦ *Jimmy hopes to be a basketball all-star when he grows up.* ♦ *How many in the league were voted all-stars this year?* **2.** ['ɔl 'stɑr] *adj.* composed of the very best of a particular group, especially athletes or entertainers. (Prenominal only.) ♦ *The new musical featured an all-star cast.* ♦ *The Olympic athletes formed an all-star team.*

all-time ['ɔl 'tɑɪm] **1.** *adj.* of all time. (Prenominal only.) ♦ *I just broke my own all-time record.* ♦ *The river is at an all-time high.* **2.** *adv.* up to this point in time; of all time. ♦ *Pizza is my all-time favorite food.* ♦ *Bill was the all-time best athlete at his school.*

allude [ə 'lud] **allude to** *iv.* + *prep. phr.* to refer to someone or something indirectly; to hint at something. ♦ *John alluded to leaving the party early.* ♦ *Jane alluded to her birthday, hoping I would buy her a present.*

allure [ə 'lʊr] *n.* attraction; charm; appeal. (No plural form in this sense.) ♦ *Exotic vacations have an allure for many people.* ♦ *The allure of money makes some people greedy.*

alluring [ə 'lur ɪŋ] *adj.* appealing; fascinating; inviting. (Adv: *alluringly.*) ♦ *A piece of string is very alluring to a kitten.* ♦ *I ran across the sand and dove into the warm and alluring azure sea.*

allusion [ə 'lu ʒən] *n.* a slight reference to something; a small hint; an indirect mention. (Compare with **illusion**.) ♦ *John made an allusion to the money Bill owed him.* ♦ *The movie director made several allusions to corrupt leaders.*

ally 1. ['æl ɑɪ] *n.* someone or something that cooperates with someone or something else; a member of an alliance; a friend. ♦ *The two countries were once allies but are now enemies.* ♦ *Tom found an ally in Bill, who backed him on all issues.* **2.** [ə 'lɑɪ] *iv.* to join with someone or something. ♦ *During World War II, Great Britain allied with the United States.* ♦ *The country to the north is attempting to ally against us with the country to our west.* **3.** [ə 'lɑɪ] *tv.* to join oneself with someone or something. (Takes a reflexive object.) ♦ *Russia allied itself with the United States during World War II.* ♦ *Tom and Susan allied themselves against John.*

alma mater [æl mə 'mɑt ɚ] **1.** *n.* the school, college, or university from which one has graduated. (Latin for 'fostering mother.') ♦ *John remained loyal to his alma mater his entire life.* ♦ *Mary is a member of the alumni club of her alma mater.* **2.** *n.* the official song of a school, college, or university. ♦ *The college choir sang the alma mater at the game.* ♦ *Mary hummed her alma mater as she walked across campus.*

almanac ['ɔl mə næk] *n.* a book of statistical facts, news, and information for a particular year. ♦ *Dad bought me an almanac as a resource for my school project.* ♦ *Once, farmers used an almanac to determine the best times to plant crops.*

almighty [ɔl 'mɑɪt i] **1.** *adj.* having the power to do anything. ♦ *When the almighty ruler of nations visits our kingdom, we will welcome him with feasts and festivals.* ♦ *The almighty dictator ruled with an iron fist.* **2. the Almighty** *n.* God. (No plural form in this sense. Treated as singular.) ♦ *With the help of the Almighty, I'll conquer this disease!* ♦ *The choir praised the Almighty with a fine anthem.* **3. almighty dollar** *idiom* the U.S. dollar, worshiped as a god; money, viewed as more important and powerful than anything else. ♦ *Bill was a slave to the almighty dollar.* ♦ *It's the almighty dollar that drives the whole country.*

almond ['ɑ mənd] *n.* a kind of oval-shaped nut. ♦ *Almonds can be used to make pastries.* ♦ *Mary prefers almonds to peanuts as a snack.*

almost ['ɔl most] *adv.* not quite; nearly. ♦ *I'm almost done making dinner, so go wash your hands.* ♦ *"Are we almost there yet?" the tired children whined.*

alms ['ɑmz] *n.* gifts given to poor people. (Treated as singular or a plural.) ♦ *The man regularly gave alms to the poor.* ♦ *Many charities collect alms for the needy.*

aloft [ə 'lɔft] **1.** *adj.* in a higher place; in the air. (Not prenominal.) ♦ *You cannot use a cellular telephone while the plane is aloft.* ♦ *Once we are aloft, you will be served a small snack.* **2.** *adv.* to a higher place; into the air. ♦ *The balloon broke loose from Jimmy and zoomed aloft in seconds.* ♦ *Bill went aloft to repair the TV antenna on the roof.*

alone [ə 'lon] **1.** *adj.* by oneself; having no one else nearby. (Not prenominal.) ♦ *I was lonely because I was all alone.* ♦ *Mary was alone for an hour in the small room.* **2.** *adv.* by oneself; with no help. ♦ *Susan wrote this report alone.* ♦ *I can't lift this piano alone.*

along [ə 'lɔŋ] **1.** *prep.* next to something for a distance; in a linear path parallel to something. ♦ *Tom and Jane walked along the bank of the river each morning.* ♦ *A wallpaper border ran along the molding on the wall.* **2. get along** *iv.* + *adv.* to be friends or friendly with someone. ♦ *Nothing ever gets done because the committee members don't get along with each other.* ♦ *Bill and Mary get along quite well.* **3. along with** *phr.* in addition to; together with. ♦ *Jane went to the mall along with David.* ♦ *I ate some chocolates along with some fruit.* **4. get along on a shoestring** *idiom* to live on very little money. ♦ *For the last two years, we have had to get along on a shoestring.* ♦ *With so little money, we are getting along on a shoestring.*

alongside [ə 'lɔŋ 'sɑɪd] **1.** *prep.* next to someone or something; close beside someone or something. ♦ *The dog lay in the sun alongside the house.* ♦ *Put the pepper alongside the salt on the table.* **2.** *adv.* to the side of; next to. ♦ *Jane jogged through the park with her dog alongside.* ♦ *I drove through the lovely forest with my wife alongside, following the map.*

aloof [ə 'luf] *adj.* unfriendly; reserved; unsympathetic. (Adv: *aloofly.*) ♦ *When no one applauded after his speech, Bob became quite aloof.* ♦ *Jane is aloof and businesslike at the office.*

aloofness [ə 'luf nəs] *n.* distance; indifference. (No plural form in this sense.) ♦ *Natural shyness can be mistaken for aloofness.* ♦ *Jane's aloofness has prevented her from making friends.*

aloud [ə 'lɑʊd] *adv.* audibly; [of speech] spoken so that it can be heard. ♦ *John reads aloud to his children every night.* ♦ *Bill never has the courage to say aloud what he's thinking.*

alphabet ['æl fə bɛt] *n.* the list of letters used to write a language. ♦ *Children learn the alphabet in kindergarten.* ♦ *The Russian language uses the Cyrillic alphabet.*

alphabetical [æl fə 'bɛt ɪ kəl] *adj.* arranged in the order of the letters in the alphabet. (Adv: *alphabetically* [...ɪk li].) ♦ *Dictionaries list words in alphabetical order.* ♦ *Please give me an alphabetical list of the guests.*

alphabetization [æl fə bɛ tɪ 'ze ʃən] ♦ *n.* arranging words in the order of the alphabet. (No plural form in this sense.) ♦ *Alphabetization is a skill learned in second grade.* ♦ *The alphabetization of these files was incorrect.*

alphabetize ['æl fə bə tɑɪz] *tv.* to place things in an order based on the order of the letters of the alphabet. ♦ *The very young students learned to alphabetize a list of words.* ♦ *The library does not alphabetize its record albums.*

alphabetized ['æl fə bə tɑɪzd] *adj.* in the same order as the letters of the alphabet. ♦ *It's easy to find books on Mary's alphabetized bookshelves.* ♦ *The alphabetized files fell off the cabinet and got out of order.*

already [ɔl 'rɛd i] *adv.* by now; by this point in time. (This is different from *all ready.*) ♦ *I have already washed the dishes.* ♦ *John had eaten dinner already, but he joined his friends for dessert.*

also ['ɔl so] *adv.* as well; too; in addition. ♦ *I must buy some bread also.* ♦ *Does the dry cleaner also do alterations?*

also-ran ['ɔl so ræn] *n.* someone who is not successful, especially in a competition. (Someone who wins no prize in a race could be called an also-ran.) ♦ *Most of my dates turn out to be also-rans.* ♦ *Everyone thought John was an also-ran, but he became very successful.*

altar ['ɔl tɚ] *n.* a table used in religious ceremonies. (Compare with alter.) ♦ *The altar was adorned with a bouquet of flowers.* ♦ *There are two candles on the altar, and they are lit on Sundays.*

alter ['ɔl tɚ] *tv.* to change something; to make something different. (Compare with altar.) ♦ *Dad altered his old pants because they didn't fit anymore.* ♦ *The editor altered the manuscript only slightly.*

alteration [ɔl tə 're ʃən] **1.** *n.* change caused intentionally. (No plural form in this sense.) ♦ *With proper planning, alteration would not be necessary.* ♦ *No time was left for alteration, so things had to stay the way they were.* **2.** *n.* the result of a change. ♦ *What has caused the alterations in your personality?* ♦ *I made an alteration to your design.*

altercation [ɔl tɚ 'ke ʃən] *n.* an argument; a dispute; a fight. ♦ *Altercations often break out between siblings.* ♦ *Jane and Mary would not let the altercation ruin their friendship.*

altered ['ɔl tɚd] *adj.* [of a design, garment, plans, etc.] having one or more dimensions changed. ♦ *The altered dress still doesn't fit.* ♦ *I need a copy of the altered blueprints.*

alternate 1. ['ɔl tɚ net] *iv.* to take turns back and forth; to do something in turns. ♦ *Mary and Bob alternate with each other, each watching the children a few hours a week.* ♦ *The cook alternates between meatless days and days on which meat is served.* **2.** ['ɔl tɚ nət] *n.* a substitute; an official stand-in. ♦ *Tom is an alternate in my bowling league.* ♦ *Substitute teachers are alternates for regular teachers.* **3.** ['ɔl tɚ nət] *adj.* substitute; other. (Adv: *alternately.*) ♦ *Who is the alternate telephone operator today? Mary is ill.* ♦ *There were no white towels in stock, so we picked an alternate color.* **4.** ['ɔl tɚ nət] *adj.* every second person or thing; every other person or thing. (Adv: *alternately.*) ♦ *Our committee meets on alternate Thursdays.* ♦ *The machine sampled alternate bottles of soda pop, testing for purity.*

alternately ['ɔl tɚ nət li] **1.** *adv.* first one and then another; switching back and forth between one and another. ♦ *The traffic lights flashed red and yellow alternately.* ♦ *Mary alternately stirred the gravy and sliced tomatoes.* **2.** *adv.* on the other hand; as another choice; alternatively. (Some people prefer alternatively for this sense.) ♦ *I'd like to have a picnic, but alternately we could eat inside.* ♦ *Mary planned to vacation in June or, alternately, in December.*

alternating current ['ɔl tɚ net ɪŋ 'kɚ ənt] *n.* electric current that reverses the polarity of its flow a fixed number of times per second. (No plural form in this sense. Abbreviated *A.C.*) ♦ *Does this run on alternating current or direct current?* ♦ *Alternating current travels better over long distances.*

alternative [ɔl 'tɚ nə tɪv] **1.** *n.* someone or something that takes the place of someone or something else; a choice; an option. ♦ *What are the alternatives to watching a movie tonight?* ♦ *At the restaurant, the only alternative to chicken was beef.* **2.** *adj.* other; another. (Adv: *alternatively.*) ♦ *I have an alternative plan in case it rains during the picnic.* ♦ *Does anyone have an alternative idea for raising funds?* **3.** *adj.* not typical or appreciated by most people. ♦ *The movie festival showed a lot of alternative films.* ♦ *John is an alternative dresser. He wears only motorcycle gear.*

alternatively [ɔl 'tɚ nə tɪv li] *adv.* on the other hand; as another choice; instead. ♦ *We could alternatively go to the movies instead of the zoo.* ♦ *Alternatively, Tom could take the first turn at driving.*

although [ɔl 'ðo] *conj.* despite; in spite of; even though. ♦ *We stayed at the outdoor concert although it rained.* ♦ *Although Jane and Mary like different things, they are great friends.*

altimeter [æl 'tɪm ə tɚ] *n.* a device that measures altitude. ♦ *The pilot looked at the altimeter to see how high the plane was.* ♦ *The altimeter was broken, so the pilot had to land the plane before sundown.*

altitude ['æl tɪ tud] *n.* the distance above sea level; the height above sea level. (No plural form in this sense.) ♦ *The pilot announced that our altitude was 30,000 feet.* ♦ *The altitude in the mountains is higher than in the valleys.*

alto ['æl to] **1.** *n.* a woman having the lower of the two female singing voices; a person who sings in the second-highest vocal range. (See also soprano. Pl in *-s.*) ♦ *The voice of the talented alto blended with that of the soprano.* ♦ *There are three altos in the choir.* **2. the alto** *n.* the musical part written for ①; the notes usually sung by ①. (No plural form in this sense. Treated as singular.) ♦ *I am a soprano, but I can sing the alto if necessary.* ♦ *The alto in this piece is extremely difficult.* **3.** *adj.* <the adj. use of ①.> ♦ *The alto part seldom carries the melody.* ♦ *Jane has a lovely alto voice.*

altogether ['ɔl tə gɛð ɚ] *adv.* completely. (Different from *all together.*) ♦ *Tom was altogether unprepared for college.* ♦ *We were shocked altogether when we heard the news.*

altruism ['ɔl tru ɪz əm] *n.* a philosophy of selflessness; doing good deeds for other people. (No plural form in this sense.) ♦ *Altruism means doing good things simply because the good things are worth doing.* ♦ *The scholarship was funded by the millionaire's altruism.*

altruist ['ɔl tru əst] *n.* someone who does good things unselfishly. ♦ *Anne is an altruist who donates her time to charity work.* ♦ *Altruists expect nothing in return for their good deeds.*

altruistic [ɔl tru 'ɪs tɪk] *adj.* unselfish; kind. (Adv: *altruistically* [...ɪk li].) ♦ *Altruistic people are usually not selfish.* ♦ *The charity was staffed by altruistic volunteers.*

aluminum [ə 'lum ə nəm] **1.** *n.* a metallic chemical element that is lightweight and does not rust easily. (No plural form in this sense.) ♦ *Aluminum's atomic number is 13, and its symbol is Al.* ♦ *The siding on our house was made of aluminum.* **2.** *adj.* made of ①. ♦ *We have aluminum gutters on our house.* ♦ *Most soft drinks come in aluminum cans.*

alumna [ə 'lʌm nə] *n., irreg.* a female graduate of a school, college, or university. (Latin feminine singular. The Latin feminine plural is alumnae.) ♦ *The alumna donated thousands of dollars to her alma mater.* ♦ *My mother and my sister are alumnae of the same university.*

alumnae [ə 'lʌm ni] pl of alumna.

alumni [ə 'lʌm nɑɪ] pl of alumnus.

alumnus [ə 'lʌm nəs] *n., irreg.* a male graduate of a school, college, or university. (Latin masculine singular. The Latin masculine plural is alumni.) ♦ *The alumnus gave a speech to the faculty.* ♦ *The alumnus thought fondly of his alma mater.*

always ['ɔl wez] **1.** *adv.* every time; repeatedly. ♦ *Jane always goes to her favorite restaurant on Monday.* ♦ *The phone always rings while we are eating dinner.* **2.** *adv.* forever; without end. ♦ *I will always love you.* ♦ *Jane will always remember the day she graduated.*

A.M. ['e 'ɛm] *abbr.* before noon. (Used to show that a time is between morning and noon. An abbreviation for Latin *ante meridiem,* 'before midday.' Also **A.M.** and **a.m.**) ♦ *I am at work every morning by 8:00 A.M.* ♦ *Anne has a meeting with her staff at 10:00 A.M.*

am ['æm] *iv., irreg.* <the first-person present singular form of be.> (Reduced to *'m* in the contraction I'm.) ♦ *I am eager to learn English.* ♦ *I think that I am fat, so I am going to start exercising.*

amalgamate [ə 'mæl gə met] **1.** *tv.* to mix something with something else; to combine something with something else. ♦ *Due to poor economic times, we ought to amalgamate the two companies.* ♦ *The two boards of directors were amalgamated by a vote of the stockholders of both companies.* **2.** *iv.* to join with something; to merge. ♦ *The two firms decided not to amalgamate.* ♦ *Our school amalgamated with another school in the same district.*

amaryllis [æm ə 'rɪl əs] *n.* a bulbous plant with a long stalk and large flowers, native to the tropics. ♦ *We grow an amaryllis indoors every winter.* ♦ *The amaryllis usually blooms before it grows its leaves.*

amass [ə 'mæs] **1.** *tv.* to gather people or things together; to gather or accumulate an amount of something. ♦ *While in college, John amassed a shelf full of reference books.* ♦ *Jane amassed the neighbors and organized a club.* **2.** *iv.* to collect; to gather into a group. ♦ *The guests amassed in the kitchen to see the host cut the elaborate cake.* ♦ *The shellfish amassed around the rocks in the shallow water.*

amateur ['æ mə tʃɚ] *n.* someone who does an activity for fun and does not get paid for it; someone who is not an expert. ♦ *The amateur clown was not very entertaining.* ♦ *The band was made up of amateur musicians.*

amateurish ['æ mə tʃɚ ɪʃ] *adj.* nonprofessional; without skill; shoddy. (Adv: *amateurishly.*) ♦ *The college graduate's résumé looked amateurish.* ♦ *Some inexperienced painters did an amateurish job on our house.*

amaze [ə 'mez] *tv.* to astound someone; to astonish someone. ♦ *The magician amazed the children with interesting tricks.* ♦ *My neighbor's lies never cease to amaze me.*

amazed [ə 'mezd] *adj.* surprised; astonished. (Adv: *amazedly* [ə 'mez əd li].) ♦ *An amazed audience applauded the acrobatic dancer.* ♦ *John's amazed coworkers couldn't believe he had quit his job.*

amazement [æ 'mez mənt] *n.* surprise; astonishment. (No plural form in this sense.) ♦ *To the amazement of her family, Jane announced that she had joined the Peace Corps.* ♦ *The children stared in amazement at the beautiful mosaic.*

amazing [ə 'mez ɪŋ] *adj.* astounding; astonishing. (Adv: *amazingly.*) ♦ *The amazing stunts of the trapeze artist entertained the crowd.* ♦ *It was amazing that no one was hurt in the earthquake.*

ambassador [æm 'bæs ə dɚ] **1.** *n.* a diplomat assigned to represent one country to another country, usually residing in the foreign country. ♦ *The French ambassador gave a speech at the banquet.* ♦ *The American ambassador to France lives in Paris.* **2.** *n.* someone who represents an organization in an official manner. ♦ *Bill served as the student union's ambassador to the university's administration.* ♦ *Mr. Smith acted as an ambassador for the charity organization.*

amber ['æm bɚ] **1.** *n.* an ancient, yellowish-orange resin. (No plural form in this sense.) ♦ *The queen's beads were made of amber.* ♦ *Ancient insects are often trapped inside amber.* **2.** *adj.* yellowish-orange in color. ♦ *The porch was lit by an amber glow.* ♦ *The fur of Mary's cat is amber.*

ambiance AND **ambience** ['æm bi əns] *n.* the mood or atmosphere of a place. (From French. No plural form in this sense.) ♦ *The restaurant had a pleasant ambiance.* ♦ *The candles and music gave the room a nice ambiance.*

ambidextrous [æm bə 'dɛks trəs] *adj.* able to use both hands equally well. (Adv: *ambidextrously.*) ♦ *"Are you left-handed or right-handed?" "Neither—I'm ambidextrous."* ♦ *Jimmy's parents thought he was ambidextrous, because he could draw pictures using either hand.*

ambience ['æm bi əns] See ambiance.

ambient ['æm bi ənt] *adj.* relating to the surroundings; surrounding. ♦ *The level of ambient noise made it difficult to hear the lecturer.* ♦ *The library used special cases to protect the rare books from the ambient humidity.*

ambiguity [æm bɪ 'gju ə ti] **1.** *n.* the quality of having more than one meaning or interpretation. (No plural form in this sense.) ♦ *The ambiguity of the teacher's response made us realize he did not know the answer.* ♦ *Due to an ambiguity in the law, the judge was uncertain how to proceed.* **2.** *n.* something, such as a word or expression, that has more than one meaning or interpretation. ♦ *The ambiguities in the article made it hard to understand.* ♦ *The editor pointed out the ambiguities in my manuscript.*

ambiguous [æm 'bɪg ju əs] *adj.* confusing; having more than one meaning or interpretation. (Adv: *ambiguously.*) ♦ *Poor grammar can lead to ambiguous sentences.* ♦ *The professor gave an ambiguous answer to Jane's question.*

ambition [æm 'bɪ ʃən] **1.** *n.* the desire to achieve something; the desire to make oneself better. (No plural form in this sense.) ♦ *Too much ambition caused Bill to act selfishly.* ♦ *Mary has a lot of ambition, but she often changes her goals.* **2.** *n.* the object or goal that one desires; the achievement that one wishes to accomplish. ♦ *Mary's ambition was to learn to fly.* ♦ *John had no ambitions, so he never achieved anything.*

ambitious [æm 'bɪ ʃəs] *adj.* eager; wanting to achieve something; wanting to make oneself better. (Adv: *ambitiously.*) ♦ *The ambitious lawyer worked 18 hours every day.* ♦ *We watched the ambitious beaver cut down many trees to build the dam.*

ambivalence [æm 'bɪv ə ləns] *n.* an inability to decide; mixed feelings about something. (No plural form in this sense.) ♦ *John felt some ambivalence toward moving 1,000 miles away.* ♦ *Ambivalence is natural when one makes a big decision.*

ambivalent [æm 'bɪv ə lənt] *adj.* having mixed feelings about something; not being able to decide between two or more things. (Adv: *ambivalently.*) ♦ *Mary had an ambivalent attitude about quitting her job.* ♦ *The Joneses were ambivalent concerning where to go on vacation.*

amble ['æm bəl] *iv.* to walk slowly; to walk in a leisurely manner. ♦ *The elderly couple ambled arm in arm through the park.* ♦ *Jimmy ran on ahead, while his dad ambled along with the dog.*

ambrosia [æm 'bro ʒə] **1.** *n.* the mythical food of the Greek and Roman gods that made them immortal. (No plural form in this sense.) ♦ *The ancient Greek gods were thought to eat ambrosia all day.* ♦ *Ambrosia supposedly granted immortality to the gods of Greece and Rome.* **2.** *n.* a dessert made with coconut and oranges. (No plural form in this sense.) ♦ *Mom makes ambrosia on Thanksgiving.* ♦ *David asked Sue for her recipe for ambrosia.*

ambulance ['æm bjə ləns] *n.* a vehicle for taking sick or injured people to the hospital. ♦ *The ambulance is equipped with life-saving equipment.* ♦ *Paramedics jumped out of the ambulance and ran into the house.*

ambulatory ['æm bjə lə tor i] *adj.* able to walk; walking. ♦ *After his stroke, John wasn't ambulatory for six weeks.* ♦ *Susan's baby isn't ambulatory yet.*

ambush ['æm bʊʃ] **1.** *tv.* to attack someone from a hidden place; to attack someone by surprise. ♦ *The thieves ambushed the travelers as they rode through the forest.* ♦ *My older brother ambushed me and took my candy bar.* **2.** *n.* a surprise attack by a hidden attacker. ♦ *The robbers planned an ambush from behind the rock.* ♦ *The stagecoach driver was injured in the ambush.*

ameba AND **amoeba** [ə 'mi bə] *n.* a simple organism, having only one cell, that lives in water or inside other creatures as a parasite. ♦ *The biology teacher drew an ameba on the chalkboard.* ♦ *The class looked at an amoeba under the microscope.*

ameliorate [ə 'mil i ə ret] **1.** *iv.* to become better; to improve. ♦ *The political situation did not ameliorate, and everyone expected there to be a war.* ♦ *When economic conditions ameliorate, we will be able to get a loan.* **2.** *tv.* to make something better; to improve something. ♦ *Winning the lottery ameliorated John's financial difficulties.* ♦ *I could not ameliorate my financial condition, so I had to sell my car.*

amelioration [ə mil i ə 're ʃən] *n.* improvement; betterment. (No plural form in this sense.) ♦ *The stormy weather showed no sign of amelioration.* ♦ *The labor union fought for the amelioration of conditions at the factory.*

amen ['ɑ 'mɛn] *interj.* <the formal ending of a prayer.> ♦ *When the minister finished the prayer, the congregation said, "Amen."* ♦ *John said "amen" whenever he agreed with someone.*

amenable [ə 'mɛn ə bəl] **amenable (to)** *adj.* (+ *prep. phr.*) cooperative in relation to something; agreeable to something; open to suggestions concerning something; responsive to something. (Adv: *amenably.*) ♦ *The committee was amenable to delegating some responsibilities to a subcommittee.* ♦ *If everyone is amenable, let's have the picnic on Sunday.*

amend [ə 'mɛnd] **1.** *tv.* to change something; to modify something; especially to make a change in a constitution. ♦ *The publisher amended the contract to accommodate the author's demands.* ♦ *Did Grandma amend her will before her death?* **2. make amends (for something)** *idiom* to compensate; to do something as an act of restitution or to make up for some error, injury, or loss that one has caused. ♦ *After the argument, Jane later called her friend to make amends.* ♦ *After amends had been made, Jane took her friend to dinner.*

amendment [ə 'mɛnd mənt] *n.* a change made by correcting or adding to something. ♦ *The amendment to the contract gave the author more money.* ♦ *After much debate, several amendments were added to the constitution.*

amenity [ə 'mɛn ə ti] *n.* something extra or special that makes an occasion or location more enjoyable or convenient. ♦ *The hotel's amenities included a whirlpool and a tennis court.* ♦ *The camp offered no amenities, only an outhouse.*

America [ə 'mɛr ɪ kə] **1.** *n.* the continents of the New World. ♦ *America extends from northern Alaska and Canada to the tip of Argentina.* ♦ *All kinds of climates can be found in America.* **2.** *n.* the United States of America. ♦ *America has been called the land of opportunity.* ♦ *Our flight to America landed at New York City.* **3. the Americas** *n.* North and South America. (Treated as plural.) ♦ *The wildlife of the Americas is different from that found in Europe.* ♦ *There were many civilizations in the Americas before the arrival of Columbus.*

American [ə 'mɛr ə kən] **1.** *n.* someone who is a citizen or native of one of the countries of North America or South America. ♦ *Americans from all over the continent gathered for a meeting in Panama.* ♦ *Americans speak four major languages: Spanish, French, Portuguese, and English.* **2.** *n.* a citizen or native of the United States of America. ♦ *My uncle, who lives in Kansas, is an American.* ♦ *Americans mostly speak English, but many other languages are also spoken.* **3.** *adj.* of, for, or about North America, South America, or ①. ♦ *A conference was held to discuss American trade.* ♦ *The largest American bear is the grizzly.* **4.** *adj.* of, for, or about the United States of America, or ②. ♦ *My uncle, who lives in Kansas, is an American citizen.* ♦ *Is the most famous American food really hamburgers?*

American Indian [ə 'mɛr ə kən 'ɪn di ən] **1.** *n.* a person belonging to one of the indigenous groups of people in North America when the Europeans arrived; a Native American ①. ♦ *American Indians could be found all across the entire continent when the Europeans arrived.* ♦ *My grandmother is an American Indian whose people used to live in Florida.* **2.** *n.* <the adj. use of ①.> ♦ *An American Indian village was discovered by some hikers walking along the river.* ♦ *When we were in Arizona, we visited an American Indian reservation.*

Amerindian [æ mɚ 'ɪn di ən] **1.** *n.* a person belonging to one of the indigenous groups of people in North America when the Europeans arrived; an American Indian; a Native American ①. ♦ *My uncle is an anthropologist who studies the Amerindians.* ♦ *Amerindians were in America before the Europeans.* **2.** *adj.* <the adj. use of ①.> ♦ *The anthropologist studies Amerindian culture.* ♦ *Most of the Amerindian languages are no longer spoken.*

amiability [e mi ə 'bɪl ə ti] *n.* kindness; friendliness. (No plural form in this sense.) ♦ *The boy's amiability made him a favorite of his teachers.* ♦ *Sue's amiability helped her get elected class president.*

amiable ['em i ə bəl] *adj.* pleasant; kind; friendly; good-natured. (Adv: *amiably.*) ♦ *Dave is quite amiable and is always making new friends.* ♦ *Sue is an amiable woman, but her boyfriend is aloof.*

amicability [æm ə kə 'bɪl ə ti] *n.* friendliness; a pleasant and friendly manner. (No plural form in this sense.) ♦ *The mayor's amicability was in evidence at her press conference.* ♦ *The divorced couple's amicability surprised and impressed us.*

amicable ['æm ə kə bəl] *adj.* [of something] showing friendly intentions and pleasant agreement; [of something] not hostile. (Adv: *amicably.*) ♦ *Although we had argued, our parting was amicable.* ♦ *We had a pleasant discussion and soon reached an amicable agreement.*

Amish ['ɑ mɪʃ] **1. the Amish** *n.* members of a religious group who live in their own communities in Pennsylvania, the Midwestern United States, and Canada. (No plural form in this sense. Treated as plural.) ♦ *The Amish have a strong sense of community.* ♦ *Many of the Amish seem quite old-fashioned.* **2.** *adj.* <the adj. use of ①.> ♦ *Amish crafts are simple but beautiful.* ♦ *Tractors are not used on most Amish farms.*

ammonia [ə 'mon jə] **1.** *n.* a colorless gas made of hydrogen and nitrogen, having a strong smell. (No plural form in this sense.) ♦ *Ammonia can be dangerous if inhaled.* ♦ *The ammonia in the cleaning fluid made my eyes water.* **2.** *n.* ① mixed with water, used for cleaning and disinfecting. (No plural form in this sense.) ♦ *The janitor cleaned the floor with ammonia.* ♦ *Tom sprayed ammonia on the windows and wiped them clean.*

ammunition [æm jə 'nɪ ʃən] **1.** *n.* bullets and shells for weapons. (No plural form in this sense.) ♦ *The hunter carried his ammunition in his backpack.* ♦ *The army ran out of ammunition and was soon defeated by the enemy.* **2.** *n.* words or facts that are used to attack or defend someone or something. (Figurative on ①. No plural form in this sense.) ♦ *The lawyer gathered ammunition to be used against the suspect.* ♦ *John's mistakes became ammunition for his boss when she fired him.*

amnesia [æm 'ni ʒə] *n.* a condition where someone cannot remember anything or cannot remember certain things. (No plural form in this sense.) ♦ *The accident victim had amnesia for three days.* ♦ *Amnesia is usually not a permanent condition.*

amnesiac [æm 'niz i æk] *n.* someone whose memory is lost. ♦ *The amnesiac didn't recognize her relatives.* ♦ *Bob became an amnesiac after the accident.*

amnesty ['æm nəs ti] *n.* the forgiveness or the pardoning of someone or of a group. (No plural form in this sense.) ♦ *The rebels were granted amnesty and were released from prison.* ♦ *Tom joined an organization that works for the amnesty of political prisoners.*

amoeba [ə 'mi bə] See ameba.

among [ə 'mʌŋ] **1.** *prep.* in the midst of things; surrounded by things. ♦ *There was one pink daisy among the roses.* ♦ *Jane found her gray skirt in her closet among her other clothes.* **2.** *prep.* within a group; within a set of choices or possibilities. (Use between with two items. Use among with more than two items.) ♦ *Bob, John, and Anne divided the oranges among themselves.* ♦ *Please choose among these four.*

amorous ['æm ə rəs] *adj.* romantic; showing or feeling romantic or sexual interest. (Adv: *amorously.*) ♦ *The moonlight made Mary feel amorous.* ♦ *John had amorous feelings for his date.*

amorousness ['æm ə rəs nəs] *n.* romance; romantic or sexual interest. (No plural form in this sense.) ♦ *Mary's amorousness annoyed John.* ♦ *Mary wished John's amorousness were directed toward her.*

amorphous [ə 'mor fəs] **1.** *adj.* shapeless; formless. (Adv: *amorphously.*) ♦ *I spilled my gelatin, and it fell to the floor in an amorphous mass.* ♦ *Amoebas are an amorphous form of life.* **2.** *adj.* [of writing, ideas, thoughts, etc.] without organization or structure. (Figurative on ①. Adv: *amorphously.*) ♦ *Tom's writing is so amorphous that I cannot make sense of it.* ♦ *I don't have a plan at the moment, only a few amorphous thoughts.*

amorphousness [ə 'mor fəs nəs] *n.* the lack of shape or form. (No plural form in this sense.) ♦ *The amorphousness of your plan is very disappointing.* ♦ *Some bacteria exhibit a high degree of amorphousness.*

amortization [æm ɚ tɪ 'ze ʃən] *n.* the gradual payment of the principal of a sum of money. (No plural form in this sense.) ♦ *The amortization of the mortgage was carried out over 20 years.* ♦ *The amortization of his debts must proceed at a faster pace.*

amortize ['æm ɚ tɑɪz] *tv.* to arrange to spread payments of money over a period of time. ♦ *They amortized the debt over a ten-year period.* ♦ *The expenditure was amortized over just two years.*

amount [ə 'mɑʊnt] **1.** *n.* how much there is of something; a quantity. ♦ *I doubled the amount of sugar in the recipe.* ♦ *What is the total amount of money in the account?* **2. amount to** *iv.* + *prep. phr.* to be equal to a numerical figure; to total up to something. ♦ *The damage after the fire amounted to $50,000.* ♦ *These three projects amount to a lot of work!* **3. amount to** *iv.* + *prep. phr.* to have the same effect, value, or meaning as something; to constitute something; to develop into something. ♦ *Some people think that running away from a crime amounts to an admission of guilt.* ♦ *The unruly teenager never amounted to anything.*

amphibian [æm 'fɪb i ən] *n.* any of a class of animals that live in water and on land, such as frogs. ♦ *Jimmy collected some amphibians from the pond.* ♦ *Toads, newts, and salamanders are all amphibians.*

amphibious [æm 'fɪb i əs] **1.** *adj.* able to live both in water and on land. (Adv: *amphibiously.*) ♦ *Toads and newts are amphibious creatures.* ♦ *Dogs are not amphibious, although they can swim.* **2.** *adj.* able to be used both in water and on land. (Figurative on ①. Adv: *amphibiously.*) ♦ *The military has some amphibious vehicles.* ♦ *In the forties, someone invented an amphibious car, but it sank.*

amphitheater ['æm fə θi ə tɚ] *n.* a hall or building where the seating surrounds an arena in rising tiers. ♦ *Ancient Romans watched trained warriors fight in amphitheaters.* ♦ *Remains of an amphitheater called the Coliseum can be seen in Rome.*

ample ['æm pəl] *adj.* sufficient and adequate. (Adv: *amply.* Comp: *ampler;* sup: *amplest.*) ♦ *My income is small, but it is ample for my needs.* ♦ *We have an ample supply of food for three days.*

amplification [æm plɪ fə 'ke ʃən] *n.* an amount of increased loudness. (No plural form in this sense.) ♦ *The weak sound needs more amplification.* ♦ *The amplification in the auditorium is set too high.*

amplifier ['æm plɪ fɑɪ ɚ] *n.* an electronic device that makes sounds louder. ♦ *The amplifier broke, so the speaker used a bullhorn to address the crowd.* ♦ *John spilled water on the amplifier, and it never worked again.*

amplify ['æm plɪ fɑɪ] **1.** *tv.* to make someone or something louder. ♦ *Can you amplify the sound so we can hear* *it better?* ♦ *The structure of the room amplifies the music.* **2.** *tv.* to make something larger or stronger. ♦ *Seeing the ballet amplified Jane's desire to learn to dance.* ♦ *Would you care to amplify your objections?*

amputate ['æm pjə tet] *tv.* to cut off all or part of a body part, especially an arm, a leg, a finger, or a toe. ♦ *The doctors amputated the mangled leg.* ♦ *The medical students are learning to amputate limbs.*

amputation [æm pjə 'te ʃən] **1.** *n.* the removal of an arm, a leg, a finger, or a toe, or of part of such a body part. (No plural form in this sense.) ♦ *The doctors felt amputation would save the patient.* ♦ *Amputation was the only way to keep the cancer from spreading.* **2.** *n.* an act of ①. ♦ *The amputation was successful in stopping the infection.* ♦ *During the war, the doctor performed amputations without anesthetic.*

amputee [æm pjə 'ti] *n.* someone who has had one or more limbs removed; someone who has had an amputation. ♦ *The amputee had physical therapy to help her adjust to losing a leg.* ♦ *Many soldiers became amputees during the bloody war.*

amulet ['æm jə lət] *n.* an ornament worn to protect against evil. ♦ *The princess wore an amulet around her neck.* ♦ *The chief carried a small stone as a good-luck amulet.*

amuse [ə 'mjuz] *tv.* to make someone laugh or smile; to give someone pleasure. ♦ *The playful kitten always amuses Grandma.* ♦ *This cartoon amuses me.*

amusement [ə 'mjuz mənt] **1.** *n.* happiness; pleasure; enjoyment. (No plural form in this sense.) ♦ *Jane couldn't hide her amusement as she watched the funny movie.* ♦ *To our amusement, the kittens tried to climb onto the chair.* **2.** *n.* something that makes someone happy; entertainment. ♦ *The guest entertained herself with some small amusements.* ♦ *What type of amusement do you like on the weekends?*

amusing [ə 'mjuz ɪŋ] *adj.* funny; entertaining. (Adv: *amusingly.*) ♦ *Not all comedians are amusing.* ♦ *The amusing child danced on one foot for us.*

an [æn] **1.** *article* one; any. (Note: The indefinite article a is used before words that begin with a consonant sound; the indefinite article an is used before words that begin with a vowel sound.) ♦ *I will be there in an hour.* ♦ *Mary ate an apple and a banana for lunch.* **2.** *article* each; per. (See note at ①.) ♦ *The clerk earned $12 an hour, which is $96 a day.* ♦ *At the farmers' market, corn was twenty-five cents an ear.*

analgesic [æn əl 'dʒiz ɪk] **1.** *adj.* relieving pain; making pain hurt less. (Adv: *analgesically* [...ɪk li].) ♦ *Jane took an analgesic medicine for her headache.* ♦ *The doctor recommended an analgesic ointment.* **2.** *n.* a drug that takes pain away; a drug that relieves pain. ♦ *Aspirin is an analgesic.* ♦ *John took analgesics when he sprained his ankle.*

analog ['æn ə lɔg] **1.** *adj.* the opposite of digital; transmitted mechanically or by waves and not by digital code. ♦ *Digital sound must be converted to analog sound before it can be sent to a loudspeaker.* ♦ *The hands on this analog watch glow in the dark.* **2.** AND **analogue** *n.* something that is similar to something else in function or in other characteristics; something that plays the same role as something else but in a different context. ♦ *A fish's gills can be thought of as an analogue to our lungs.* ♦ *This formula is an analogue of a formula developed by the other scientists.*

analogous [ə 'næl ə gəs] *adj.* similar; like; comparable. (Adv: *analogously.*) ♦ *A fish's gills are analogous to a person's lungs.* ♦ *In certain ways, a computer is analogous to the human brain.*

analogy [ə 'næl ə dʒi] *n.* a similarity shared by two things that are compared; a comparison of two things, focusing on their similarities. ♦ *There is no analogy between my problems and your problems. They are completely different.* ♦ *The teacher made an analogy between the lens of a camera and the lens of an eye.*

analyses [ə 'næl ə siz] pl of analysis.

analysis [ə 'næl ə sɪs] **1.** *n.* the process of analyzing or of examining something very closely. (No plural form in this sense.) ♦ *Good analysis is important in all problem solving.* ♦ *The initial analysis is more important than any subsequent examination.* **2.** *n., irreg.* an in-depth examination of an issue or topic. (Pl: analyses.) ♦ *The governor gave his analysis of the state's economic problems.* ♦ *Your analysis of the problem helps me understand it.* **3.** *n.* psychoanalysis. (No plural form in this sense.) ♦ *Analysis might help you with your depression.* ♦ *Tom goes to a psychoanalyst for analysis every week.*

analyst ['æn ə ləst] **1.** *n.* a psychoanalyst. ♦ *Dr. Smith is a good analyst who has helped many people.* ♦ *Jane went to see an analyst because her physician couldn't detect any physical problems.* **2.** *n.* someone who studies something in depth; an expert who knows very much about a particular subject. ♦ *The professor was a well-known analyst of Middle Eastern politics.* ♦ *The market analyst was fired because he didn't foresee the drop in stock prices.*

analytic [æn ə 'lɪt ɪk] *adj.* examining something very closely; analytical. (Adv: *analytically* [...ɪk li].) ♦ *The analytic investigator thought about the problem intently.* ♦ *Lisa is a very analytic person, and she makes careful scientific observations.*

analytical [æn ə 'lɪt ɪ kəl] *adj.* using analysis; examining something very closely. (Adv: *analytically* [...ɪk li].) ♦ *The analytical methods of the investigator revealed the identity of the murderer.* ♦ *Analytical skills should be taught in elementary school.*

analytically [æn ə 'lɪt ɪk li] *adv.* in a logical fashion; with careful thought and study. ♦ *The detective analytically deduced the motive for the crime.* ♦ *By approaching the problem analytically, I was able to solve it.*

analyzable ['æn ə lɑɪz ə bəl] *adj.* able to be studied; able to be examined. (Adv: *analyzably.*) ♦ *Many peculiar dreams are easily analyzable.* ♦ *This blood sample is not analyzable because it was contaminated.*

analyze ['æn ə lɑɪz] *tv.* to examine something in depth. ♦ *The lab technician analyzed the blood samples.* ♦ *The company hired a consultant to analyze its budget.*

anarchic [æn 'ɑr kɪk] *adj.* lawless; opposing order and government. (Adv: *anarchically* [...ɪk li].) ♦ *The scene in the besieged capital was anarchic.* ♦ *The new teacher tried to take control of the anarchic classroom.*

anarchist ['æn ɑr kəst] *n.* someone who seeks the abolition of government and laws. ♦ *Because John is an anarchist, he never votes in elections.* ♦ *Most anarchists oppose all forms of government.*

anarchy ['æn ɑr ki] **1.** *n.* a lack of orderly government and laws. (No plural form in this sense.) ♦ *A period of anarchy followed the rebel coup.* ♦ *We were not surprised to find anarchy in the newly independent nation.* **2.** *n.* chaos; disorder. (Figurative on ①. No plural form in this sense.) ♦ *The school principal was shocked at the total anarchy in the classroom.* ♦ *Anarchy erupted on the football field when the two teams began fighting.*

anathema [ə 'næθ ə mə] *n.* someone or something hated or despised. (No plural form in this sense.) ♦ *Smokers were treated as anathema at the health-food store.* ♦ *Taxes are anathema to the people of this district.*

anatomical [æn ə 'tɑm ɪ kəl] *adj.* relating to the structure of the bodies of plants or animals. (Adv: *anatomically* [...ɪk li].) ♦ *The medical student hung an anatomical chart on the wall.* ♦ *The veterinarian studied anatomical diagrams of different kinds of animals.*

anatomist [ə 'næt ə məst] *n.* someone who studies anatomy. ♦ *The anatomist dissected the pig for the class.* ♦ *The anatomist studied the structure of whales.*

anatomy [ə 'næt ə mi] **1.** *n.* the study of the structure of the bodies of plants and animals. (No plural form in this sense.) ♦ *Tom had to study anatomy in medical school.* ♦ *Anne studied the anatomy of the cat for a whole semester.* **2.** *n.* the structure and details of a plan; an analysis. (No plural form in this sense. Figurative on ①.) ♦ *The anatomy of a legal argument can be quite fascinating.* ♦ *The teacher discussed the anatomy of the novel's plot.*

ancestor ['æn sɛs tɚ] *n.* a person, usually no longer living, from whom a person descends. ♦ *Ancestors are revered in most East Asian cultures.* ♦ *Mr. Macdonald's ancestors came from Scotland.*

ancestral [æn 'sɛs trəl] *adj.* relating to one's ancestors. (Adv: *ancestrally.*) ♦ *My family's ancestral home is in Scotland.* ♦ *John's family continues its ancestral traditions.*

ancestry ['æn sɛs tri] *n.* all of one's ancestors; the history of a person's ancestors. (No plural form in this sense.) ♦ *Jane's ancestry can be traced back five generations.* ♦ *John's ancestry is Turkish.*

anchor ['æŋk ɚ] **1.** *n.* a heavy object, attached to a ship or boat, that catches on the sea bottom to keep the ship or boat from drifting away. ♦ *Dad threw the anchor overboard at our fishing spot.* ♦ *A heavy anchor prevented our boat from drifting from that spot.* **2.** *n.* something that holds something else in place; something that secures something else. ♦ *The centerpiece was an anchor for the balloons.* ♦ *The campers used a rock as an anchor to keep the tent flap in place.* **3.** *n.* a newscaster; a central newscaster who introduces news reports from other people. (From anchorman.) ♦ *The news anchor ran to her seat as the news began.* ♦ *The anchor on the nine o'clock news wears a toupee.* **4.** *tv.* to keep a ship in place by lowering an ① into the water. ♦ *John anchored the boat just offshore.* ♦ *The sailors anchored the vessel near the island.* **5.** *tv.* to secure something; to hold something in place. ♦ *I anchored the flowerpot to the porch step with strong glue.* ♦ *Anne anchored the bracket to the wall with a long bolt.* **6.** *iv.* [for a ship] to remain in a place by dropping its anchor. ♦ *The clipper anchored out in the bay.* ♦ *The ship could not anchor fast enough and was blown onto the rocks.*

anchorage ['æŋk ə rɪdʒ] *n.* a place, such as a harbor, where a ship can anchor safely. ♦ *Fortunately, we found a safe anchorage before nightfall.* ♦ *The anchorage was free of high waves during the storm.*

anchorman ['æŋ kɚ mæn] *n., irreg.* a central male newscaster who introduces news reports from other people. (So named because he worked from an *anchor desk* and moderated complicated news reporting from there. Pl: anchormen.) ♦ *The anchorman soberly reported the latest war news.* ♦ *The network anchormen have well-trained speaking voices.*

anchormen ['æŋ kɚ mɛn] pl of anchorman.

anchorperson ['æŋ kɚ pɚ sən] *n.* a central newscaster, male or female, who introduces news reports from other people. ♦ *The anchorperson opened the nightly news with an uplifting story.* ♦ *The anchorpersons spoke among themselves before the broadcast.*

anchorwoman ['æŋ kɚ wʊm ən] *n., irreg.* a female anchorperson. (Pl: anchorwomen.) ♦ *Jane is an anchorwoman on the five o'clock news.* ♦ *The anchorwoman read the report about the downtown fire.*

anchorwomen ['æŋ kɚ wɪm ɪn] pl of anchorwoman.

ancient ['en tʃənt] **1.** *adj.* from long ago in history. ♦ *The ancient peoples of Europe spoke many different languages.* ♦ *The archaeologists found an ancient manuscript in the cave.* **2.** *adj.* very old. (An exaggeration.) ♦ *I would never drive that ancient car anywhere!* ♦ *This dress is ancient! I can't wear it to the party.* **3.** *n.* someone who lived long ago. ♦ *The poem was written by an ancient in the Chinese Empire.* ♦ *The drawings were done by the ancients of North America.*

ancientness ['en tʃənt nəs] *n.* a state of being very old; great age. (No plural form in this sense.) ♦ *To the little children, Grandpa had an air of ancientness.* ♦ *The manuscript's ancientness made it very fragile.*

and [ænd] **1.** *conj.* in addition to; plus; also. ♦ *Be on time, and don't forget to dress nicely.* ♦ *Remember to buy both apples and oranges.* **2.** *conj.* then; as a result. ♦ *Bill got dressed and drove to work.* ♦ *The driver stopped paying attention to his driving, and he hit another car.*

anecdotal ['æn ɛk dot əl] *adj.* <the adj. form of anecdote.> (Adv: *anecdotally.*) ♦ *The speaker's anecdotal asides kept the audience awake.* ♦ *The funny sermon was more anecdotal than religious.*

anecdote ['æn ɛk dot] *n.* a short, often humorous story; a brief account of something interesting. ♦ *Mr. Smith told his friends an anecdote about his grandson.* ♦ *The professor opened her lecture with a brief anecdote.*

anemia [ə 'nim i ə] *n.* a lack of red blood cells, causing a lack of energy. (No plural form in this sense.) ♦ *Mary was tired for months before she realized she had anemia.* ♦ *Bill took iron supplements to compensate for his anemia.*

anemic [ə 'nim ɪk] **1.** *adj.* having anemia, and thus pallid and lacking energy. (Adv: *anemically* [...ɪk li].) ♦ *The anemic patient was pale and lethargic.* ♦ *The anemic child did not receive enough nourishment.* **2.** *adj.* inadequate. (Informal. Figurative on ①. Adv: *anemically* [...ɪk li].) ♦ *I cannot possibly survive on this anemic amount of money!* ♦ *Your efforts to help me have been quite anemic.*

anesthesia [æn ɛs 'θi ʒə] *n.* the loss of the feeling of pain or any sensation. (No plural form in this sense.) ♦ *Only partial anesthesia is required for this surgery to be performed.* ♦ *Under general anesthesia, the patient is asleep.*

anesthesiologist [æn ɛs θi zi 'ɑl ə dʒəst] *n.* someone who gives an anesthetic to a patient before or during surgery. ♦ *The group of medical personnel in the operating room included an anesthesiologist.* ♦ *The anesthesiologist injected an anesthetic into my arm.*

anesthetic [æn ɛs 'θɛt ɪk] **1.** *n.* a chemical agent that produces anesthesia. ♦ *The dentist used an anesthetic before he drilled into my tooth.* ♦ *After the patient received the anesthetic, her foot was numb.* **2.** *adj.* producing anesthesia. (Adv: *anesthetically* [...ɪk li].) ♦ *The drug's anesthetic effect knocked me unconscious.* ♦ *The anesthetic drug was too weak to numb the pain I felt.*

anesthetist [ə 'nɛs θə təst] *n.* someone who gives an anesthetic. ♦ *The anesthetist charged almost as much as the surgeon!* ♦ *My anesthetist chose to use a gas rather than a chemical injection.*

anesthetize [ə 'nɛs θə tɑɪz] *tv.* to render someone insensitive to pain or any sensation with an anesthetic. ♦ *The lab technicians anesthetized the animals before doing their tests.* ♦ *The patient was anesthetized quickly, and surgery began immediately.*

angel ['en dʒəl] **1.** *n.* a heavenly being; a messenger of God. ♦ *There are many mentions of angels in the Bible.* ♦ *In many stories, angels are dressed in white robes and have large wings.* **2.** *n.* a very kind, sweet person. (Figurative on ①.) ♦ *You're an angel to babysit for us on such short notice.* ♦ *You're such an angel for baking a cake for my birthday!*

angelic [æn 'dʒɛl ɪk] **1.** *adj.* heavenly; serene. (Adv: *angelically* [...ɪk li].) ♦ *The happy child had an angelic smile.* ♦ *The chimes of the bells had an angelic sound.* **2.** *adj.* pure; innocent like an angel; very kind or good. (Adv: *angelically* [...ɪk li].) ♦ *The angelic child had been taught good manners.* ♦ *Jane had such an angelic appearance that no one guessed she stole the cookies.*

anger ['æŋ gɚ] **1.** *n.* great displeasure; strong feelings of annoyance. (No plural form in this sense.) ♦ *John's anger erupted when he learned that his car had been stolen.* ♦ *Mary got an ulcer because she doesn't express her anger.* **2.** *tv.* to upset someone; to annoy someone very much. ♦ *The stain on the carpet angered Mom, and she punished us.* ♦ *Threatening phone calls angered Bob, so he called the police.*

angle ['æŋ gəl] **1.** *n.* a figure formed where two lines or surfaces intersect. (See also **right angle**.) ♦ *John used a compass to draw a right angle.* ♦ *One line intersected the other at a 45-degree angle.* **2.** *n.* a point of view; a way of looking at an issue or idea. (Informal.) ♦ *I have a good angle for a story on the high cost of housing.* ♦ *Mary presented an interesting angle on the energy crisis.* **3.** *tv.* to place two surfaces or lines so that they intersect. ♦ *Mary angled the books so they would stand up by themselves.* ♦ *The architect angled the walls so each room received a lot of sunlight.* **4.** *iv.* to turn, perhaps sharply. ♦ *The street angles to the right just past the post office.* ♦ *The snake angled sharply toward the ledge and escaped underneath it.* **5.** *iv.* to fish [for some kind of fish] using a hook and line. ♦ *Mary was angling when she fell into the stream.* ♦ *What are you angling for? Catfish?* **6. angle for** *iv.* + *prep. phr.* to seek something. (Figurative on ⑤.) ♦ *The arrogant poet seemed to be angling for a compliment.* ♦ *The lawyer seemed to be angling for some sort of a confession.*

angler ['æŋ glɚ] *n.* someone who fishes using a hook and line. ♦ *This stream is a favorite of local anglers.* ♦ *The anglers in my family go fishing every weekend in the summer.*

angry ['æŋ gri] *adj.* irate; upset; annoyed. (Adv: *angrily.* Comp: *angrier;* sup: *angriest.*) ♦ *Susan was so angry with me that she yelled quite loudly.* ♦ *The angry customer asked to see the clerk's manager.*

anguish ['æŋ gwɪʃ] **1.** *n.* mental pain or suffering; grief. (No plural form in this sense.) ♦ *John experienced anguish over his brother's death.* ♦ *Work-related stress can cause someone anguish.* **2. anguish over** *iv.* + *prep. phr.* to grieve or suffer over something; to have great mental pain or suffering concerning something. ♦ *Mary anguished over the death of her pet cat.* ♦ *Mike anguished over not getting the promotion.*

angular ['æŋ gjə lɚ] *adj.* having angles; having features that seem like angles. (Adv: *angularly.*) ♦ *The sculpture was made of metal beams and was quite angular.* ♦ *The suspect was tall and had an angular build.*

animal ['æn ə məl] **1.** *n.* a living creature that is not a plant. ♦ *Many people keep animals as pets.* ♦ *Many types of animals can be seen at the zoo.* **2.** *n.* an unruly person, usually a male; a brute. (Figurative on ①.) ♦ *John turns into an animal when he's angry.* ♦ *Those guys are animals—just look at the mess they left here!* **3.** *adj.* relating to living creatures that are not plants. ♦ *Animal fat is bad for your health.* ♦ *Leather is an animal product.* **4.** *adj.* relating to functions of the body instead of the mind. ♦ *John was not able to control his more violent animal instincts.* ♦ *When the starving man saw the apple tree, his animal nature took over and he stole some apples.*

animate 1. ['æn ə mət] *adj.* alive; living. ♦ *The scientists did not expect to find any animate creatures at the bomb site.* ♦ *Human beings are animate, but tables and chairs are not.* **2.** ['æn ə met] *tv.* to make something come alive; to make someone or something become more lively or energetic. ♦ *The wine animated Jane, and she sang for her guests.* ♦ *I heard a story about a magician who animated a child's doll.* **3.** ['æn ə met] *tv.* to make the drawings or models for a cartoon, by hand or by computer. ♦ *It took three years to animate the story.* ♦ *The class was taught how to animate cartoons on a computer.*

animated ['æn ə met ɪd] **1.** *adj.* lively; spirited; alive. (Adv: *animatedly.*) ♦ *After her nap, the baby was quite animated.* ♦ *The speaker spoke well but was not animated enough.* **2.** *adj.* referring to a cartoon instead of a film or video of actual things. ♦ *Do you like animated movies?* ♦ *We love to watch the old animated films.*

animation [æn ə 'me ʃən] **1.** *n.* movement; lively movement. (No plural form in this sense.) ♦ *The dancer's fluid animation charmed the audience.* ♦ *The puppet's animation was controlled by the puppeteer.* **2.** *n.* the art, business, and process of making cartoons on film or video. (No plural form in this sense.) ♦ *Bob works with animation in the film industry.* ♦ *What kind of training do you need to work in animation?*

animator ['æn ə met ɚ] *n.* someone who makes cartoons on film or video. ♦ *Sue is an experienced video animator.* ♦ *The animator and the producer could not agree on how long to make the cartoon.*

animosity [æn ə 'mɑs ə ti] *n.* hostility; anger. (No plural form in this sense.) ♦ *Much animosity existed between the two opponents.* ♦ *Animosity among the committee members prevented work from getting done.*

ankle ['æŋ kəl] *n.* the joint that connects the foot with the leg. ♦ *The skates were too tight around Jane's ankles.* ♦ *John stepped in a hole and twisted his ankle.*

anklebone ['æŋ kəl bon] *n.* the main bone of the ankle. ♦ *Something in Bill's boot rubbed against his anklebone.* ♦ *Mary broke her anklebone when she fell off the ladder.*

annalist ['æn ə ləst] *n.* a historian; someone who writes down and keeps track of events year by year. (Compare with analyst.) ♦ *An annalist of American politics wrote an essay about past presidents.* ♦ *The annalists of the future will be surprised by what we did here today.*

annals ['æn əlz] *n.* the written records of something recorded year by year. (Treated as plural.) ♦ *The university's annals are kept in the library's attic.* ♦ *This event will be written in the company's annals and be remembered forever.*

annex 1. ['æn ɛks] *n.* an addition to a building. ♦ *The annex was built for storage of old files and papers.* ♦ *The Joneses had so many children, they had to build an annex onto their house.* **2.** [ə 'nɛks] *tv.* to assume political control over a piece of land. ♦ *The dictator tried to annex the neighboring country.* ♦ *The powerful nation annexed the small islands near its coast.*

annexation [æn ɛk 'se ʃən] *n.* assuming political control over a piece of land. (No plural form in this sense.) ♦ *Annexation of the islands would probably start a war.* ♦ *The residents of the area fought the proposed annexation in the courts.*

annihilate [ə 'nɑɪ ə let] *tv.* to kill or destroy someone or something thoroughly. ♦ *The chemicals annihilated the bugs on our rosebushes.* ♦ *The leaders of the country tried to annihilate poverty.*

annihilation [ə nɑɪ ə 'le ʃən] *n.* complete destruction; total elimination. (No plural form in this sense.) ♦ *The bombing resulted in the annihilation of an entire town.* ♦ *The annihilation of cancer has long been a dream of doctors.*

anniversary [æn ə 'vɚ sə ri] *n.* the annual commemoration of the date of an event that occurred in the past. ♦ *My parents were in Europe on their fiftieth wedding anniversary.* ♦ *Is September fifteenth the anniversary of a famous battle?*

annotate ['æn ə tet] *tv.* to add explanatory notes to a piece of writing. ♦ *You need to annotate your narrative to help us understand it.* ♦ *The publisher annotated the new edition of Shakespeare's plays.*

annotated ['æn ə tet ɪd] *adj.* provided with explanatory notes. ♦ *I bought the annotated edition of the novel.* ♦ *The teacher's annotated textbook included suggestions for class projects.*

annotation [æn ə 'te ʃən] *n.* an explanatory note added to a piece of writing. ♦ *Annotations helped the class understand the complex poem.* ♦ *This edition of Shakespeare's plays includes annotations by a famous scholar.*

announce [ə 'nɑʊns] **1.** *tv.* to make something known to people. ♦ *The butler announced that dinner was served.* ♦ *John and Mary announced their engagement last night.* **2.** *tv.* to speak out the name of someone who is arriving. ♦ *Please don't announce me. I want to surprise the hostess.* ♦ *The butler announced the guests one by one as they arrived.*

announcement [ə 'nɑʊns mənt] *n.* a declaration; a public statement. ♦ *When it started to rain, an announcement canceling the parade was made.* ♦ *The Smiths sent out an announcement of their baby's birth.*

announcer [ə 'nɑʊn sɚ] *n.* someone who provides information on the radio or on television. ♦ *The radio announcer identified the radio station once each hour.* ♦ *The announcer read the latest news headlines.*

annoy [ə 'nɔɪ] *tv.* to bother or pester someone. ♦ *John's little brother annoyed him by changing the TV channel.* ♦ *Jimmy annoyed his sister by stealing her diary.*

annoyance [ə 'nɔɪ əns] *n.* a bother; a pest; an irritation. ♦ *Car alarms are an annoyance when they make noise at night.* ♦ *Bugs are an annoyance at picnics.*

annoyed [ə 'nɔɪd] *adj.* bothered; irritated; angered. (Adv: *annoyedly* [ə 'nɔɪ əd li].) ♦ *The annoyed customer complained to the store manager.* ♦ *John is annoyed with your unreasonable excuses.*

annoying [ə 'nɔɪ ɪŋ] *adj.* bothersome; irritating. (Adv: *annoyingly.*) ♦ *An annoying car alarm continued to sound throughout the night.* ♦ *Jane thinks little children are annoying.*

annual ['æn ju əl] *adj.* happening once a year; happening every year; happening yearly. (Adv: *annually.*) ♦ *The annual company barbecue was a success.* ♦ *Every employee is reviewed on an annual basis.*

annuity [ə 'nu ə ti] *n.* A financial instrument that pays out a sum of money month by month. (It often includes insurance that will allow payments to continue throughout the life of the recipient even after the principal has been exhausted.) ♦ *Her annuity was not enough to support her.* ♦ *Before he retired, he put his money into an annuity so that he would always have enough income to support himself.*

annul [ə 'nʌl] *tv.* to make something, such as a marriage, void. ♦ *Jane's marriage was annulled after six months.* ♦ *After his first marriage was annulled, John was free to marry again.*

annulment [ə 'nʌl mənt] *n.* a declaration that cancels a marriage or makes it invalid. ♦ *The annulment of Jane's marriage was completed in court this morning.* ♦ *The Catholic church grants annulments but not divorces.*

anoint [ə 'nɔɪnt] **1.** *tv.* to apply oil to someone as a religious rite. ♦ *A priest anointed the dying man and prayed for him.* ♦ *They anointed his head with oil as was their custom.* **2.** *tv.* to rub medication onto something. ♦ *The nurse anointed the swollen area with an ointment.* ♦ *He anointed his chest with a pungent cream in order to soothe his cough.*

anomalous [ə 'nɑm ə ləs] *adj.* different from what is usual; strange. (Adv: *anomalously.*) ♦ *An anomalous yellow rose stuck out in the bouquet of red roses.* ♦ *The results of the medical tests were anomalous.*

anomaly [ə 'nɑm ə li] *n.* someone or something that does not fit an expected pattern. ♦ *The test results contained anomalies that the scientists could not explain.* ♦ *My siblings all became musicians. I was the anomaly and became a painter.*

anonymity [æn ə 'nɪm ə ti] *n.* the state of not having one's name known. (No plural form in this sense.) ♦ *The author maintained her anonymity by using a pen name.* ♦ *The charity respected the donor's wish for anonymity.*

anonymous [ə 'nɑn ə məs] *adj.* unnamed; from an unknown source; created or done without revealing the name or identity of the creator or doer. (Adv: *anonymously.*) ♦ *An anonymous donor gave a million dollars to the charity.* ♦ *The club's votes for president were anonymous.*

anonymously [ə 'nɑn ə məs li] *adv.* without revealing the source of something or the name of its creator. ♦ *The bouquet was sent anonymously, but Jane suspected that John sent it.* ♦ *Some generous person donated $5,000 to the charity anonymously.*

another [ə 'nʌð ɚ] **1.** *pron.* an additional one; a different one. ♦ *If you don't like that dress, get another.* ♦ *If you don't like my recipe for apple pie, here is another to try.* **2.** *adj.* consisting of one more of the same kind; [an] additional [one]. ♦ *The musician needed another rehearsal before the recital.* ♦ *I asked the hostess for another helping of the casserole.* **3. one thing or person after another** *idiom* a series of things or people that seems without limit. ♦ *It's just one problem after another.* ♦ *One customer after another has been buying shoes today!*

answer ['æn sɚ] **1.** *n.* a reply; a response to a question; a solution to a problem on a test. ♦ *The answer to question 5 is "Walt Whitman."* ♦ *I asked Tom what he'd like for supper, but he gave no answer.* **2.** *n.* a response to a situation; a way of solving a problem. ♦ *Hiring more police was the mayor's answer to the crime problem.* ♦ *My answer to a stressful day at the office is to eat a big bar of chocolate as soon as I get home.* **3.** *tv.* to give a response to something, such as a test question or a letter. ♦ *Jane answered all of the problems on the exam correctly.* ♦ *The president of the company answered all his mail personally.* **4.** *tv.* to reply to someone. ♦ *Please answer me!* ♦ *Every time Lisa answers Jimmy, he asks another question.* **5.** *iv.* to give a reply. ♦ *When you wrote to Mary about the meeting, did she answer?* ♦ *I called out Bill's name, but he didn't answer.* **6. answer the door** *idiom* [after hearing the doorbell or a knock] to go to the door to see who is there. ♦ *Would you please answer the door? I am busy.* ♦ *I wish someone would answer the door. I can't wait all day.*

answerable ['æn sɚ ə bəl] *adj.* capable of being responded to with a correct answer. (Adv: *answerably.*) ♦ *The student's question was so complex that it wasn't answerable during the lecture.* ♦ *Some questions in life just aren't answerable.*

ant ['ænt] *n.* a small insect that lives in a colony. ♦ *The house is infested with ants.* ♦ *Jimmy studied the ants on the sidewalk.*

antacid [ænt 'æs ɪd] *n.* a medicine that soothes an acidic or upset stomach. (No plural form in this sense.) ♦ *After eating the spicy food, John took some antacid.* ♦ *Will antacid help Jane's upset stomach?*

antagonism [æn 'tæg ə nɪz əm] *n.* opposition; hostility. (No plural form in this sense.) ♦ *John felt antagonism toward the winner of the contest.* ♦ *Jane saw a lot of antagonism between her children.*

antagonist [æn 'tæg ə nəst] *n.* an opponent; a hostile person. ♦ *The rebels were antagonists of the ruling party.* ♦ *Her antagonist in the argument was an arrogant graduate student.*

antagonistic [æn tæg ə 'nɪs tɪk] *adj.* hostile; characterized by opposition. (Adv: *antagonistically* [...ɪk li].) ♦ *I didn't know John was so antagonistic until he began arguing with me.* ♦ *The candidate's tone was antagonistic as she described her opponent.*

antagonize [æn 'tæg ə nɑɪz] *tv.* to make someone or something hostile or angry; to torment someone or something. ♦ *Stop antagonizing your sister!* ♦ *Do not antagonize the cat!*

antarctic [ænt 'ɑrk tɪk] **1. the Antarctic** *n.* the area including the South Pole; Antarctica and the Arctic Ocean. (No plural form in this sense. Treated as singular.) ♦ *Temperatures in the Antarctic can get very, very low.* ♦ *There are some scientists and researchers living in the Antarctic.* **2.** *adj.* <the adj. use of ①.> ♦ *Antarctic temperatures can be extremely cold.* ♦ *The penguin is a well-known antarctic bird.*

Antarctica [ænt 'ɑrk tɪ kə] See Gazetteer.

ante ['æn ti] **1.** *n.* the amount of money required to receive another card in many card games; the amount of money required at the start of a game of cards. (Typical of poker.) ♦ *John increased the ante by five dollars, and everyone else quit.* ♦ *Ten cents is too little for the ante!* **2. ante up** *iv.* + *adv.* to place the proper bet before receiving cards in a game of cards. ♦ *We can't continue with the game until you ante up.* ♦ *As soon as Tom antes up, I can deal him some cards.*

anteater ['ænt it ɚ] *n.* an animal that eats ants and termites and that has claws and a long, sticky tongue. ♦ *Anteaters have long snouts.* ♦ *There are anteaters that are nearly six feet long, if you count the tail.*

antebellum [æn ti 'bɛl əm] *adj.* relating to the period of time before a war, and especially the time before the American Civil War, which began in the 1860s. (From Latin for 'before the war.') ♦ *The antebellum period was the height of Southern culture.* ♦ *We love to visit the antebellum mansions of the Old South.*

antecedent [æn tə 'sid nt] **1.** *n.* something that has occurred before an event; something that leads up to an event. ♦ *What are the antecedents of the event we are talking about?* ♦ *Which idea was the antecedent of the present notion?* **2. antecedents** *n.* ancestors; people, things, or circumstances from earlier times in one's life. ♦ *Jane's antecedents included several famous lawyers.* ♦ *The orphan knew nothing of his antecedents.* **3.** *n.* a word or a phrase to which a pronoun refers. ♦ Tom *is the antecedent of* he *in the sentence "Tom wanted to know when he should arrive."* ♦ *A pronoun's antecedent appears before the pronoun in simple sentences.*

antelope ['æn tə lop] *n., irreg.* a deer-like animal related to the sheep and the goat. (Pl: *antelope* or *antelopes.*) ♦ *Many antelopes are found in Asia and Africa.* ♦ *Can you see the herd of antelope on the plain?*

antenna [æn 'tɛn ə] **1.** *n.* a device that collects or receives electromagnetic signals that are broadcast. (Pl: *antennas.*) ♦ *There is a microwave antenna on top of the tallest building in town.* ♦ *Our television antenna needs adjustment.* **2.** *n., irreg.* a sensitive feeler found in pairs on the heads of insects and some shelled sea creatures. (Pl:

antennae or *antennas.*) ♦ *Susie asked her teacher why butterflies have antennae and people don't.* ♦ *The moth had a feathery antenna on each side of its head.*

antennae [æn 'tɛn i] a pl of antenna ②.

anterior [æn 'tɪr i ɚ] *adj.* more forward; toward the front; on the front side [of the human body]; on the underside [of the body of a four-legged animal]. (Adv: *anteriorly.*) ♦ *The anterior side of the turtle's shell is lighter in color.* ♦ *The surgeon made a short anterior incision.*

anthem ['æn θəm] **1.** *n.* a religious song of praise, usually sung by a choir. ♦ *The congregation joined in singing the final anthem.* ♦ *The choir director chose two anthems for each worship service.* **2.** *n.* the official song of a country, state, school, or organization. ♦ *All the children sang the school's anthem at the assembly.* ♦ *The country adopted a new national anthem.*

anthill ['ænt hɪl] *n.* a mound of dirt on top of an ant's nest or colony. ♦ *We saw several anthills along the edge of the sidewalk.* ♦ *The cat watched the ants scurry around the anthill.*

anthology [æn 'θɑl ə dʒi] *n.* a book that is a collection of written works on a common theme or by the same author. ♦ *John owns three anthologies of poetry.* ♦ *This literature class uses an anthology as a text.*

anthropoid ['æn θrə pɔɪd] *adj.* like a human being; similar to humans. ♦ *Large anthropoid apes can be found in Africa.* ♦ *The chimpanzee has many anthropoid facial features.*

antiaircraft [æn ti 'er kræft] *adj.* relating to an armed defense against an attack by enemy aircraft. ♦ *A great deal of antiaircraft fire was aimed at the attackers.* ♦ *Many antiaircraft guns were destroyed by the rocket attack.*

antibacterial [æn ti bæk 'tɪr i əl] *adj.* destroying bacteria; slowing the growth of bacteria. (Adv: *antibacterially.*) ♦ *The doctors washed their hands with an antibacterial soap.* ♦ *The nurse gave me an antibacterial ointment to put on my cut.*

antibiotic [æn ti baɪ 'ɑt ɪk] **1.** *adj.* relating to medicine that kills or inhibits the growth of organisms that cause disease. (Adv: *antibiotically* [...ɪk li].) ♦ *The doctor recommended antibiotic treatment to cure the infection.* ♦ *Antibiotic drugs such as penicillin have saved many lives.* **2.** *n.* a medicine that kills or inhibits the growth of disease-causing organisms. ♦ *The doctor gave me an antibiotic to cure my infection.* ♦ *This antibiotic is useful against ear infections.* **3. antibiotics** *n.* a class of medicines that fight infections. (Treated as plural.) ♦ *Antibiotics are used to fight infections.* ♦ *Some people are allergic to antibiotics.*

antibody ['æn ti bɑd i] *n.* a substance made by the body in response to a foreign protein in the body. ♦ *The vaccination caused Jimmy's body to make its own antibodies against the disease.* ♦ *When you catch the flu, your body starts making antibodies immediately.*

antic ['æn tɪk] **1.** *n.* a playful or silly act. (Often plural.) ♦ *The antics of the playful kitten made us laugh.* ♦ *Jimmy's antics in class did not amuse the teacher.* **2.** *adj.* silly; playful. (Adv: *anticly* or *antically* [...ɪk li].) ♦ *The antic expressions of the clown made the children laugh.* ♦ *The antic activity of the children entertained Grandma for hours.*

anticipate [æn 'tɪs ə pet] *tv.* to expect something to happen; to prepare for something that is expected to happen. ♦ *We anticipated the storm and brought raincoats.* ♦ *I did not anticipate the expense of buying a new car.*

anticipated [æn 'tɪs ə pe tɪd] *adj.* expected; foreseen. ♦ *John's anticipated promotion never came.* ♦ *The anticipated storm blew to the north of us.*

anticipation [æn tɪs ə 'pe ʃən] *n.* waiting for or expecting something to occur; the feeling of eagerness or anxiousness while waiting for something to occur. (No plural form in this sense.) ♦ *Jimmy was full of anticipation on his fifth birthday.* ♦ *The anticipation of waiting to hear whether I got the job was very stressful.*

anticipatory [æn 'tɪs ə pə tor i] *adj.* [of an action] done while one is waiting for or expecting something to occur. (Adv: *anticipatorily* [æn tɪs ə pə 'tor ə li].) ♦ *Before her baby was born, Mary made the anticipatory preparations of buying a crib and baby clothes.* ♦ *A slight anticipatory movement of his sword signaled his opponent that Sir John was about to strike.*

anticlimactic ['æn ti klaɪ 'mæk tɪk] *adj.* not as exciting as earlier; not as exciting as expected; climaxing weakly after a stronger and earlier climax. (Adv: *anticlimactically* [...ɪk li].) ♦ *Everyday life was anticlimactic for the gold-medal winner after the Olympics.* ♦ *Seeing the movie was anticlimactic after hearing so many reviews of it.*

anticlimax ['æn ti 'klaɪ mæks] *n.* something that is not as exciting or important as expected, or as what came before it; a weak climax after a stronger and earlier climax. ♦ *Seeing the movie was an anticlimax after hearing so many reviews of it.* ♦ *The community picnic after the fireworks display was an anticlimax.*

antidepressant [æn ti də 'prɛs ənt] *n.* a drug that relieves depression. ♦ *Mary took an antidepressant to help deal with her excessive grief.* ♦ *The psychiatrist prescribed an antidepressant for John.*

antidote ['æn ti dot] **1.** *n.* a substance that stops poison from working. ♦ *John was given an antidote to the poison just in time.* ♦ *The scientist created an antidote for the poison.* **2.** *n.* a solution to a problem. (Figurative on ①.) ♦ *One antidote to crime is creating jobs.* ♦ *What is the antidote for a broken heart?*

antifreeze ['æn ti friz] *n.* a liquid substance that will not freeze that is put into a car's radiator. (No plural form in this sense.) ♦ *Mary puts new antifreeze in her car's radiator each winter.* ♦ *The mechanic recommended using a new kind of antifreeze in the car.*

antigen ['æn ti dʒən] *n.* a foreign substance in the body that causes the creation of antibodies. ♦ *The injection contained an effective antigen.* ♦ *Mike has had a number of diseases, so his blood carries many different antigens.*

antihistamine ['æn ti 'hɪs tə min] *n.* a remedy for the symptoms of allergies and colds. ♦ *Mary takes an antihistamine for her allergies.* ♦ *An antihistamine will relieve your cold symptoms.*

antipathy [æn 'tɪp ə θi] *n.* dislike; hatred. (No plural form in this sense.) ♦ *The antipathy among the students was obvious. They were always fighting.* ♦ *Jane felt antipathy toward her job, but she hid it well.*

antiperspirant [æn ti 'pɚ spɚ ənt] *n.* a substance that prevents or reduces perspiration when applied to the skin. ♦ *The sweaty worker clearly needed to use an antiper-*

spirant. ♦ *Lisa uses an antiperspirant so she won't have perspiration stains on her clothing.*

antiquated ['æn ti kwet ɪd] *adj.* old-fashioned; very old; out-of-date. (Adv: *antiquatedly.*) ♦ *Nobody wanted the antiquated lamp.* ♦ *The company's accounting system is very antiquated.*

antique [æn 'tik] **1.** *adj.* old, especially if valuable; belonging to a time long ago. ♦ *I collect antique china.* ♦ *Grandma's house is filled with quaint, antique furniture.* **2.** *n.* an object that was made long ago. ♦ *Be careful with that bowl; it's an antique.* ♦ *Firefighters rescued the antiques from the burning museum.*

antiquity [æn 'tɪ kwə ti] *n.* ancient history; ancient times. (No plural form in this sense.) ♦ *Humans have created art since early antiquity.* ♦ *In antiquity, documents were written on parchment.*

anti-Semite [æn ti 'sɛm ɑɪt] *n.* a person who is prejudiced against Jews and Judaism; a person who practices anti-Semitism. ♦ *Some anti-Semite desecrated the Jewish cemetery.* ♦ *Bill was shocked to learn that his coworker was an anti-Semite.*

anti-Semitic [æn ti sə 'mɪt ɪk] *adj.* prejudiced against Jews and Judaism. (Adv: *anti-Semitically* [...ɪk li].) ♦ *The speaker was criticized for making anti-Semitic remarks.* ♦ *The company was sued because of its anti-Semitic policies.*

anti-Semitism [æn ti 'sɛm ɪ tɪz əm] *n.* prejudice against Jews and Judaism. (No plural form in this sense.) ♦ *There is evidence of anti-Semitism in the political campaign.* ♦ *The desecration of the Jewish cemetery was an act of anti-Semitism.*

antiseptic ['æn ti 'sɛp tɪk] **1.** *n.* a substance used to kill germs. (No plural form in this sense.) ♦ *Tom put antiseptic on his scratch.* ♦ *You'd better get some antiseptic for that cut!* **2.** *adj.* <the adj. use of ①.> (Adv: *antiseptically* [...ɪk li].) ♦ *This antiseptic salve prevents infection.* ♦ *John used an antiseptic spray to clean the bathroom.*

antisocial [æn ti 'so ʃəl] **1.** *adj.* not social; preferring to remain alone; withdrawn. (Adv: *antisocially.*) ♦ *John didn't have many friends because of his antisocial behavior.* ♦ *The antisocial manager always worked through lunch.* **2.** *adj.* against society; against social norms or expectations. (Adv: *antisocially.*) ♦ *The criminal had a history of antisocial behavior.* ♦ *The artist said that his antisocial activities were a form of expression.*

antithesis [æn 'tɪθ ə səs] *n.* the exact opposite of something. ♦ *John's reaction was the antithesis of what Mary expected.* ♦ *The tabloid article was the antithesis of the truth.*

antitoxin [æn ti 'tɑk sən] *n.* a substance or drug that reverses the effect of a poison or is manufactured by the body to fight toxins. ♦ *There was not enough of the antitoxin to treat everyone who had been poisoned.* ♦ *The child received an injection of an antitoxin that would halt the effects of the toxin.*

antitrust law [æn ti 'trʌst 'lɔ] *n.* a law that prevents monopolistic business practices. ♦ *The large conglomerate was thwarted by the new antitrust laws.* ♦ *Some lawyers specialize in cases involving antitrust laws.*

antonym ['æn tə nɪm] *n.* a word that means the opposite of another word. ♦ Fast *is the antonym of* slow. ♦ *The language test included sections where the students were asked to find the antonyms.*

antonymous [æn 'tɑn ə məs] *adj.* opposite. (Adv: *antonymously.*) ♦ *The meaning of the word* hot *is antonymous to the meaning of the word* cold. ♦ *The meanings of* fast *and* slow *are antonymous.*

anus ['e nəs] *n.* the lower or rear opening of the bowel. ♦ *The anus of the snake is concealed beneath one of its anterior scales.* ♦ *Some animals have tails that serve to protect the anus.*

anvil ['æn vəl] **1.** *n.* a large iron block on which metal is shaped, usually by a blacksmith. ♦ *The blacksmith pounded the hot horseshoe on the anvil.* ♦ *The museum exhibited old horseshoes and anvils.* **2.** *n.* a small bone in the inner ear. ♦ *The three bones in the inner ear are called the hammer, the anvil, and the stirrup.* ♦ *The anvil, a tiny bone in the inner ear, had developed incorrectly and prevented Bill from hearing well.*

anxiety [æŋ 'zɑɪ ə ti] **1.** *n.* nervousness; worry. (No plural form in this sense.) ♦ *Before the recital, the pianist felt a lot of anxiety.* ♦ *Anxiety and depression are very common and can be reduced by counseling.* **2.** *n.* a nervous fear; a worry. ♦ *Mary's anxieties prevented her from starting a new job.* ♦ *The psychologist helped Bill work through his anxieties.*

anxious ['æŋk ʃəs] **1.** *adj.* nervous; worried; troubled, especially with a feeling of dread or concern. (Adv: *anxiously.*) ♦ *Mary was anxious as she waited for her teenage daughter to come home.* ♦ *The host was anxious about how the party would go.* **2. anxious (to)** *adj.* (+ *inf.*) eager to do something; excited in anticipation. (Adv: *anxiously.*) ♦ *Jane was anxious to read the book she had just bought.* ♦ *The anxious children opened the gifts quickly.*

any ['ɛn i] **1.** *pron.* whichever one or ones. ♦ *You may take home with you any that you like.* ♦ *I need three of them. Any will do.* **2.** *pron.* even the smallest amount or number. (Always in the negative or questions. Use **some** in affirmative statements or commands.) ♦ *Would you like any of this ice cream?* ♦ *Don't give the baby any of those cookies. Give her some of these.* **3.** *adj.* whichever [one or ones]. (To point out one from a group of two, use **either**.) ♦ *"Test-drive any car you like," the salesperson said.* ♦ *Just hand me any book from that shelf. It doesn't matter which one.* **4.** *adj.* even the smallest amount or number [of something]. (Always in the negative or questions. Use **some** in affirmative statements or commands.) ♦ *"I told you not to give her any candy," Mary said to Tom.* ♦ *"Did any letters come for me in the mail?" Tom asked.* **5.** *adv.* even the smallest amount. ♦ *Have you gotten any stronger since you began lifting weights?* ♦ *"I can't run any further," the winner said after the marathon.*

anybody ['ɛn i bɑd i] **1.** *pron.* some person; any person; anyone; even one person. (Always in the negative or questions. Use **somebody** in affirmative statements or commands. No plural form in this sense.) ♦ *Isn't there anybody who can help me?* ♦ *"Is anybody home?" the visitor asked.* **2.** *n.* an important person. (Used in the negative or questions; use **somebody** in affirmative statements or commands. No plural form in this sense.) ♦ *"You won't be anybody after I finish with you," the reporter told the mayor.* ♦ *You're not anybody! Why are you acting so important?* **3.** *n.* any random person; whoever; no matter who. (No plural form in this sense.) ♦ *I don't date just anybody, you realize.* ♦ *Pick anybody handy to help with the work.*

anyhow ['ɛn i haʊ] *adv.* at any rate; in any case; anyway. ♦ *"Anyhow, let's get back to the point," said the professor.* ♦ *He knows it is impolite, but John swears anyhow.*

anymore [æn i 'mor] **1.** *adv.* at the present time in contrast to an earlier time. (This is different from *any more.* Usually in negative sentences.) ♦ *Bill doesn't live here anymore.* ♦ *The family doesn't take vacations together anymore.* **2.** *adv.* nowadays; recently. (This is different from *any more.* Colloquial. Common but not viewed as standard English.) ♦ *She is such a pest anymore.* ♦ *Anymore, my back hurts all the time.*

anyone ['ɛn i wən] **1.** *pron.* some person; any person; anybody. (Always in the negative or questions. Use someone in the affirmative. No plural form in this sense.) ♦ *Isn't there anyone who can help me?* ♦ *"Is anyone home?" the visitor asked.* **2.** *n.* any random person; whoever; no matter who. (No plural form in this sense.) ♦ *I don't date just anyone, you realize.* ♦ *Pick anyone handy to help with the work.*

anyplace ['ɛn i ples] **1.** *adv.* no matter where; in, at, or to any place; wherever. (See also anywhere.) ♦ *I'll go anyplace where I know how to speak the language.* ♦ *Set that box down anyplace. I don't care where you put it.* **2.** *adv.* [not] in, at, or to any place; [not] in, at, or to even one place. (Always in the negative or questions. Use someplace in the affirmative. See also anywhere.) ♦ *You never go anyplace with me anymore.* ♦ *I can't find John anyplace.*

anything ['ɛn i θɪŋ] **1.** *n.* any thing, object, or event whatever; no matter what thing, object, or event. (No plural form in this sense.) ♦ *The gifted singer can sing anything.* ♦ *I will be happy to eat anything, I am so hungry.* **2.** *n.* [not] a single thing; [not] even one thing, object, or event. (Always in the negative or questions. Use something in the affirmative. No plural form in this sense.) ♦ *Can't you do anything right?* ♦ *I didn't get anything done today.* **3.** *adv.* in any way. (Always in the negative or questions.) ♦ *This doesn't taste anything like buttermilk!* ♦ *Bob and John are twins, but they don't look anything alike.*

anytime ['ɛn i taɪm] *adv.* whenever; at any time; no matter when. ♦ *"Use our pool anytime," Anne told her neighbors.* ♦ *John goes on vacation anytime he wants.*

anyway ['ɛn i we] *adv.* at any rate; in any case. ♦ *"Anyway," said Bob, changing the subject, "please do it right next time."* ♦ *I know you don't like it, but I don't care. I'm buying it anyway.*

anywhere ['ɛn i ʍɛr] **1.** *adv.* anyplace; wherever; in, at, or to any place; in, at, or to whatever place. ♦ *Please just put that box anywhere.* ♦ *Anywhere is fine with me.* **2.** *adv.* [not] somewhere; [not] in, at, or to even one place. (Always in the negative or questions. Use somewhere in affirmative statements and commands.) ♦ *I never stay anywhere there is cigarette smoke.* ♦ *Why don't you want to go anywhere for dinner?*

aorta [e 'or tə] *n.* the main artery carrying blood from the heart. ♦ *A blockage in the aorta caused Tom's health problems.* ♦ *The aorta is a major blood vessel.*

apart [ə 'pɑrt] **1.** *adv.* not together; separately. ♦ *Mary and her husband currently live apart because they have jobs in different cities.* ♦ *Dave was feeling sad and stood apart from the crowd.* **2.** *adv.* in pieces; into pieces. ♦ *Bob pulled the radio apart to see how it worked.* ♦ *The puzzle fell apart when the cat knocked it on the floor.* **3. fall apart** *idiom* to break into pieces; to become disconnected; to break into parts. ♦ *My old car is about ready to fall apart.* ♦ *The old book fell apart as soon as I opened it.*

apartheid [ə 'pɑrt haɪt] *n.* the legal segregation once practiced in South Africa. (No plural form in this sense. From Afrikaans for 'apartness.') ♦ *Apartheid is no longer legal in South Africa.* ♦ *With the end of apartheid in South Africa, all citizens gained the right to vote.*

apartment [ə 'pɑrt mənt] *n.* a residence or set of rooms within a building; living quarters. ♦ *I have rented an apartment for three years.* ♦ *Some people prefer renting an apartment to owning a house.*

apartness [ə 'pɑrt nəs] *n.* the state of being separate; the state of not being together. (No plural form in this sense.) ♦ *The apartness that the couple experienced strained their marriage.* ♦ *Some of the workers in the isolated area liked the feeling of apartness.*

apathetic [æp ə 'θɛt ɪk] *adj.* not caring; without interest. (Adv: *apathetically* [...ɪk li].) ♦ *John became apathetic when he lost his job.* ♦ *Jane's boss felt she was apathetic about her work.*

apathy ['æp ə θi] *n.* a lack of desire; a lack of interest; a lack of caring. (No plural form in this sense.) ♦ *The clerk's apathy offended many customers.* ♦ *Low grades revealed the smart student's apathy to school.*

ape ['ep] **1.** *n.* a large primate without a tail. ♦ *We love to watch the apes at the zoo.* ♦ *The preacher refused to believe that humans are related to apes.* **2.** *tv.* to mimic someone or something; to imitate someone or something. ♦ *John aped his little sister until she cried.* ♦ *We love to watch Dad ape the actors on television.*

aperture ['æp ɚ tʃɚ] *n.* an opening, especially the opening that allows light into a camera. ♦ *It is dark now, so the camera's aperture should be fairly large.* ♦ *John adjusted the aperture of the camera lens.*

apex ['e pɛks] **1.** *n., irreg.* the peak; the summit. (Pl: *apexes* or apices.) ♦ *The apex of the structure was 400 feet from the ground.* ♦ *The pointed apex of the mountain was obscured by clouds.* **2.** *n., irreg.* the period of greatest fame or accomplishment. (Figurative on ①.) ♦ *Mary reached the apex of her vocal career as a teenager.* ♦ *The apex of Tom's career occurred three months before his death.*

aphasia [ə 'fe ʒə] *n.* a disability involving loss of the use or understanding of words. (No plural form in this sense.) ♦ *After the accident, the patient showed signs of aphasia.* ♦ *Aphasia caused by a stroke made it difficult for Grandma to speak.*

aphrodisiac [æ frə 'diz i æk] *n.* something that increases sexual desire. ♦ *Oysters have been thought to be an aphrodisiac.* ♦ *The loving couple believed the sound of the sea was an aphrodisiac.*

apices ['e pə siz] a pl of apex.

apiece [ə 'pis] *adv.* each; per every one. ♦ *The children were given five dollars apiece.* ♦ *These books cost ten dollars apiece.*

apologetic [ə pɑl ə 'dʒɛt ɪk] *adj.* sorry; making apologies. (Adv: *apologetically* [...ɪk li].) ♦ *Mary was apologetic* *about forgetting her appointment.* ♦ *The apologetic waiter refused to accept a tip.*

apologist [ə 'pɑl ə dʒəst] *n.* someone who defends something by speaking in support of it. ♦ *The mayor's opponent accused him of being an apologist for scoundrels.* ♦ *The senator was a weak apologist for the administration's failed policies.*

apologize [ə 'pɑl ə dʒɑɪz] *iv.* to express regret for doing something; to make an apology. ♦ *I continued to apologize for breaking the vase.* ♦ *Max apologized for hurting our feelings.*

apology [ə 'pɑl ə dʒi] *n.* a statement of regret for having done something. ♦ *"No apology is necessary," said Jane.* ♦ *Bill's apology did not seem sincere.*

apostle [ə 'pɑs əl] *n.* [in the Christian religion] one of the twelve original followers of Jesus Christ. (Sometimes capitalized. Ultimately from Greek.) ♦ *John was the name of one of the apostles.* ♦ *The Apostles James and John were brothers.*

apostrophe [ə 'pɑs trə fi] **1.** *n.* the mark of punctuation (') showing where one or more letters have been omitted. ♦ *The proofreader added an apostrophe to the contraction.* ♦ *Words that are contractions are written with apostrophes in English, as in* can't *and* I'm. **2.** *n.* the mark of punctuation (') used to show possession in nouns. (In regular, singular nouns, add the apostrophe plus an *s.* In regular, plural nouns, add the apostrophe after the plural *s.*) ♦ *The teacher taught the children to add an apostrophe and the letter* s *to a noun to indicate possession.* ♦ *The apostrophe in* Bob's *indicates possession.*

appall [ə 'pɔl] *tv.* to disgust someone; to shock someone; to horrify someone. ♦ *The squalor of the room appalled everyone who came in.* ♦ *The host's rude manners appalled the guests.*

appalling [ə 'pɔl ɪŋ] *adj.* [of morals or aesthetics] horrifying and shocking. (Adv: *appallingly.*) ♦ *The amount of crime in this country is appalling.* ♦ *An appalling number of students cheat.*

appallingly [ə 'pɔl ɪŋ li] *adv.* in an appalling manner. ♦ *The expensive house was appallingly decorated with tacky furniture.* ♦ *An appallingly large number of students cheat.*

apparatus [æp ə 'ræt əs] *n.* a device; equipment. (No plural form in this sense. Number is expressed with *piece(s) of apparatus.*) ♦ *The science lab purchased a new piece of apparatus.* ♦ *What kind of apparatus does the gymnast compete on?*

apparel [ə 'pɛr əl] *n.* clothing; garments. (No plural form in this sense.) ♦ *Where in the store can we find women's apparel?* ♦ *Bill's daily apparel was not very attractive.*

apparent [ə 'pɛr ənt] *adj.* obvious; evident; from all appearances. (Adv: *apparently.*) ♦ *The cause of the problem was apparent when we entered the room and saw the smoke.* ♦ *The apparent cause of the accident turned out not to be the real cause.*

apparently [ə 'pɛr ənt li] *adv.* evidently. ♦ *You apparently did not understand the instructions.* ♦ *Apparently, your checking account is overdrawn.*

appeal [ə 'pil] **1.** *n.* a plea for help; a request. ♦ *My appeal for justice went unnoticed.* ♦ *Max made an appeal for a new computer.* **2.** *n.* a legal request that a verdict be examined by a higher judge or court. ♦ *The convicted killer vowed to make an appeal.* ♦ *The lawyer made an appeal to the Supreme Court.* **3.** *n.* attraction; something that draws someone or something closer. (No plural form in this sense.) ♦ *Florida has great appeal for many people during the winter months.* ♦ *I never understood the appeal of living in the city.* **4.** *tv.* to request that a verdict or case be examined by a higher judge or court. ♦ *The innocent woman appealed the verdict and won.* ♦ *The lawyer appealed the case to a higher court.* **5. appeal to** *iv.* + *prep. phr.* to ask someone for something; to make a plea for something. ♦ *Bill appealed to his mother for a larger allowance, but she said no.* ♦ *The charity appealed to everyone in town for contributions.* **6. appeal to** *iv.* + *prep. phr.* to be attractive to someone. ♦ *A glamorous career appealed to the model.* ♦ *Fast cars appeal to John, but he can't afford one.*

appealing [ə 'pil ɪŋ] *adj.* attractive; pleasing; enticing. (Adv: *appealingly.*) ♦ *Dinner had an appealing aroma.* ♦ *This perfume has an appealing scent.*

appear [ə 'pɪr] **1.** *iv.* to become visible; to come into sight. ♦ *The sun appeared on the horizon at five o'clock this morning.* ♦ *On the other side of river, the outline of the city appeared.* **2.** *iv.* to seem to be a certain way; to look a certain way. ♦ *Bill appears to be very upset this morning.* ♦ *The lost dog appears lonely.* **3. appear before** *iv.* + *prep. phr.* to be in attendance in court before a judge or similar legal authority. ♦ *Susan appeared before the judge to testify against her neighbor.* ♦ *Jane appeared before the Senate committee.*

appearance [ə 'pɪr əns] **1.** *n.* the way someone or something looks. (No plural form in this sense.) ♦ *My manager's appearance is always impeccable.* ♦ *The old building's ramshackle appearance made it difficult to sell.* **2.** *n.* an act of becoming a visible presence; becoming seen. ♦ *The appearance of a cat in the road caused Susan to swerve.* ♦ *With the appearance of the president, everyone rose.*

appease [ə 'piz] *tv.* to pacify someone or something; to make someone or something less hostile or more content. ♦ *A cookie will usually appease a crying child.* ♦ *John appeased his angry boss by offering to work overtime.*

appeasement [ə 'piz mənt] *n.* pacification; giving in to someone's demands; doing something to make someone or something less hostile or more content. (No plural form in this sense.) ♦ *Your constant appeasement of your children will spoil them.* ♦ *The diplomat tried every kind of appeasement to get the other country to stop its aggression.*

append [ə 'pɛnd] *tv.* to add something to the end of something else; to add something as a supplement to something else. ♦ *We appended some more data to the report after it was finished.* ♦ *When you send the application, please append a list of references.*

appendage [ə 'pɛn dɪdʒ] **1.** *n.* a part extending away from a creature's main body. ♦ *Human arms are considered appendages.* ♦ *Fish have appendages called fins.* **2.** *n.* a smaller attachment to something larger and more important. (Figurative on ①.) ♦ *The firm's publications department is an appendage to its main business.* ♦ *A small appendage on the side of the suitcase could be used as a handle.*

appendectomy [æ pən 'dɛk tə mi] *n.* the surgical removal of the appendix from a person. ♦ *Jane had an* *emergency appendectomy.* ♦ *When Bill had severe abdominal pain, the doctor said he needed an appendectomy.*

appendices [ə 'pɛn də siz] a pl of appendix ②.

appendicitis [ə pɛn də 'sɑɪ tɪs] *n.* a painful inflammation of the appendix. (No plural form in this sense.) ♦ *Susan's stomach pains were due to appendicitis.* ♦ *Appendicitis can strike at any age.*

appendix [ə 'pɛn dɪks] **1.** *n.* a small growth at the end of the large intestine. (Pl: *appendixes.*) ♦ *The appendix has no known function in the human body.* ♦ *Bob had his appendix removed because it was infected.* **2.** *n., irreg.* a section at the end of a book or document that gives additional information. (Pl: appendices or *appendixes.*) ♦ *The almanac listed important dates in an appendix.* ♦ *The author forgot to include the appendix in the book.*

appetite ['æp ə tɑɪt] *n.* a desire for something, especially food or drink. ♦ *The stout man had a large appetite.* ♦ *The children's appetite was ruined by too much candy.*

appetizer ['æp ə tɑɪz ɚ] *n.* a small snack that is served to stimulate the appetite for the main course. ♦ *Cheese and crackers make a good appetizer before dinner.* ♦ *Mary offered to bring appetizers to the dinner party.*

applaud [ə 'plɔd] **1.** *iv.* to clap the hands together to show appreciation or approval. ♦ *At the end of the performance, the audience applauded loudly.* ♦ *The comedian was not funny, and no one applauded.* **2.** *tv.* to show appreciation for someone or something by clapping one's hands together. ♦ *The audience rose to applaud the famous singer.* ♦ *The other athletes applauded the gymnast's amazing performance.*

applause [ə 'plɔz] *n.* a show of approval by clapping one's hands together. (No plural form in this sense.) ♦ *The applause was thunderous.* ♦ *The host asked the members of the audience to hold their applause until the end.*

apple ['æp əl] *n.* a firm, round fruit that has red, green, or yellow skin and is white inside. ♦ *We pick apples in the country each fall.* ♦ *An apple a day keeps the doctor away.*

applesauce ['æp əl sɔs] *n.* a food made from apples, mashed and cooked with sugar and spices. (No plural form in this sense.) ♦ *Jane always serves applesauce with pork chops.* ♦ *I made applesauce with the leftover apples.*

appliance [ə 'plɑɪ əns] *n.* a machine, usually found in the home, with a specific function. ♦ *None of the kitchen appliances worked when the power went out.* ♦ *The newlyweds got many appliances as wedding gifts.*

applicability ['æ plə kə 'bɪl ə ti] *n.* appropriateness; relevance. (No plural form in this sense.) ♦ *These guidelines are only of limited applicability.* ♦ *That law has almost no applicability in cases like this one.*

applicable ['æ plə kə bəl] *adj.* appropriate; fitting. (Adv: *applicably.*) ♦ *Some questions on the questionnaire were not applicable to me.* ♦ *Each suggestion was applicable to at least one student.*

applicant ['æ plə kənt] *n.* someone who applies for something, usually by filling out an application form. ♦ *Hundreds of applicants applied for the position.* ♦ *Anne interviewed three applicants for the job.*

application [æ plə 'ke ʃən] **1.** *n.* applying for something. (No plural form in this sense.) ♦ *Application must be made early for a seat at the banquet.* ♦ *The counselor recommended application to several colleges.* **2.** *n.* an instance of ①. ♦ *Mary's first application for a loan was not successful.* ♦ *In future applications for jobs, you should be more honest.* **3.** *n.* a printed form used in applying for something, such as a job. ♦ *John filled out many applications for different colleges.* ♦ *I got an application for a credit card in the mail.* **4.** *n.* spreading something on something else. (No plural form in this sense.) ♦ *Proper application of the salve is important to prevent infection.* ♦ *The application of a good varnish is recommended.* **5.** *n.* an act or instance of ④. ♦ *The first application of white paint did not completely cover the dark color underneath.* ♦ *Let the paint dry between applications.* **6.** *n.* a specific use for something. ♦ *This theory has many practical applications.* ♦ *I can't think of a single application for your invention!*

applicator ['æ plə ket ɚ] *n.* a device that applies something. ♦ *The shoe polish came with a special applicator.* ♦ *Spread the glue with the applicator.*

applied [ə 'plɑɪd] *adj.* of practical use; for practical purposes; not theoretical. ♦ *Applied science concentrates on problem solving.* ♦ *Writing dictionaries is an example of applied linguistics.*

appliqué [æ plə 'ke] *n.* a decorative piece of fabric that is attached to another piece of cloth by sewing or by other means. (From French.) ♦ *The tablecloth had tiny appliqués along its edge.* ♦ *Mary ironed an appliqué onto her T-shirt.*

apply [ə 'plɑɪ] **1.** *tv.* to put something on something else. ♦ *I applied the stain remover to the spot.* ♦ *John applied the wallpaper to the wall with a special paste.* **2.** *tv.* to use something; to make use of something. ♦ *You have to apply all the strength you have to lift this crate.* ♦ *Jane applied her knowledge of geometry in determining the area of the circle.* **3.** *tv.* to cause oneself to work or study hard. (Takes a reflexive object.) ♦ *Once Jane applied herself, she did better in school.* ♦ *If you apply yourself, you'll get good grades.* **4. apply for** *iv.* + *prep. phr.* to request something that requires approval—for example, a loan, a job, or admission to a school—usually in writing or through some other formal process. ♦ *We applied for a loan to buy a house.* ♦ *How many jobs did Bob apply for?* **5. apply to** *iv.* + *prep. phr.* to be appropriate or relevant to someone or something. ♦ *"Well, these rules don't apply to me," the president told the board.* ♦ *Each of these remarks applies to everyone in the room.*

appoint [ə 'pɔɪnt] **1.** *tv.* to choose someone for a job or position; to assign someone to a position. ♦ *Tom appointed Mary manager.* ♦ *I appointed Bill to be my assistant.* **2.** *tv.* to fill a vacant office, position, or job; to determine who will serve in an office, position, or job. ♦ *Max will appoint the new manager tomorrow.* ♦ *Who will appoint the committee?* **3.** *tv.* to set a time. ♦ *The new manager will appoint a time for the final report.* ♦ *The committee appointed a time for the next meeting.*

appointed [ə 'pɔɪn tɪd] *adj.* [of a time] chosen or assigned. ♦ *The show began at the appointed time.* ♦ *The appointed time for the meeting is noon.*

appointment [ə 'pɔɪnt mənt] **1.** *n.* choosing someone to fill a position or to take a job. (No plural form in this sense.) ♦ *Appointment of a committee head took weeks.* ♦ *The appointment of a replacement is very important.* **2.** *n.* being chosen to fill a position or to take a job. (No plural form in this sense.) ♦ *Was Jane pleased about her appoint-*

ment to the committee? ♦ *The judge's appointment was challenged by people who said he was not qualified.* **3.** *n.* a job or position to which someone has been assigned or for which someone has been chosen, especially a position at a high level of responsibility. ♦ *Anne does not enjoy her new appointment, and she misses her old job.* ♦ *In each of my appointments, I have faced different challenges and learned valuable skills.* **4.** *n.* an act or instance of ①. ♦ *The company's president named the new vice president and also made several other high-level appointments.* ♦ *Several political appointments were announced today.* **5.** *n.* an arranged meeting; an agreement to meet at a specific time and place. ♦ *Bob was late for his appointment with his boss.* ♦ *I have an appointment with the dentist at four o'clock.*

apportion [ə 'por ʃən] *tv.* to allot portions of something. ♦ *The city council apportions all the tax money to the different departments.* ♦ *The church apportioned the usable clothes to needy families.*

apportionment [ə 'por ʃən mənt] *n.* dividing something up; splitting something up. (No plural form in this sense.) ♦ *The fair apportionment of toys among the children was not easy.* ♦ *Mr. Wilson's heirs argued about the apportionment of his estate.*

appraisal [ə 'prez əl] *n.* a knowledgeable estimate of the value of something. ♦ *Jane took her ring to the jeweler for an appraisal.* ♦ *Susan's appraisal of the writer's work was favorable.*

appraise [ə 'prez] *tv.* [for an expert] to estimate the value of something. ♦ *An antique dealer appraised my china and silver.* ♦ *The museum curator appraised an old painting we found in our attic.*

appraiser [ə 'prez ɚ] *n.* a qualified person who estimates the value of something. ♦ *The librarian became an appraiser of rare books.* ♦ *An appraiser valued the house at $100,000.*

appreciable [ə 'priʃ ɪ ə bəl] *adj.* considerable; perceptible. (Adv: *appreciably.*) ♦ *The improvement in your tennis game is quite appreciable.* ♦ *My pay raise was an appreciable sum.*

appreciate [ə 'priʃ i et] **1.** *tv.* to be grateful for someone or something; to value someone or something. ♦ *We appreciated the help of our friends.* ♦ *John appreciates fine art.* **2.** *iv.* to increase in value. ♦ *Our house appreciated, and we made a profit when we sold it.* ♦ *Unfortunately, new cars do not appreciate after you buy them.*

appreciation [ə pri ʃi 'e ʃən] **1.** *n.* a feeling of being grateful for someone or something. (No plural form in this sense.) ♦ *Mary showed her appreciation for the gift by writing a thank-you note.* ♦ *A box of candy is often given as a token of appreciation for hospitality.* **2.** *n.* the recognition of the value of something. (No plural form in this sense.) ♦ *The Smiths are teaching their children appreciation of the fine arts.* ♦ *John does not have an appreciation of good literature.* **3.** *n.* a rise in value; an increase in value. (No plural form in this sense.) ♦ *The appreciation of the house forces us to increase our insurance coverage.* ♦ *Do not expect any appreciation of an automobile.*

appreciative [ə 'priʃ ɪ ə tɪv] *adj.* thankful; grateful. (Adv: *appreciatively.*) ♦ *The college student was most appreciative of the scholarship.* ♦ *An appreciative guest sent the hostess some flowers.*

apprehend [æ prɪ 'hɛnd] *tv.* to locate and arrest someone. ♦ *The police officer apprehended the criminal on the street.* ♦ *Were the police able to apprehend the suspect?*

apprehension [æ prɪ 'hɛn ʃən] **1.** *n.* fear or dread in general. (No plural form in this sense.) ♦ *The biology test caused me a lot of apprehension.* ♦ *Apprehension and anxiety are very similar.* **2.** *n.* specific fear and worries. ♦ *Max had lots of apprehensions about going away to college.* ♦ *Bill was afraid of flying, but he boarded the plane despite his apprehensions.* **3.** *n.* the capture of someone who breaks the law. (No plural form in this sense.) ♦ *The apprehension of the drug dealers took three weeks.* ♦ *The apprehension of speeders is a priority for small-town police.*

apprehensive [æ prɪ 'hɛn sɪv] *adj.* afraid; dreading something; nervous or fearful about something. (Adv: *apprehensively.*) ♦ *Jane was apprehensive about moving to a new apartment.* ♦ *The apprehensive buyer decided not to put a deposit on the condominium.*

apprentice [ə 'prɛn tɪs] *n.* someone who learns a skill by working under an expert. ♦ *The carpenter's apprentice built this beautiful bookcase.* ♦ *The plumber sent his apprentice to fix our sink.*

apprenticeship [ə 'prɛn tɪs ʃɪp] *n.* the state or position of being an apprentice. (No plural form in this sense.) ♦ *Bob's apprenticeship with a plumber will prepare him to work on his own.* ♦ *After high school, Anne served an apprenticeship in carpentry.*

approach [ə 'protʃ] **1.** *tv.* to go near someone or something; to get closer to someone or something in time or space. ♦ *As we approached the park, we saw children playing catch.* ♦ *Approaching the end of our vacation, we dreaded going home.* **2.** *iv.* [for someone or something] to come closer in time or space. ♦ *We stood still as the deer approached.* ♦ *As the end of our vacation approached, we dreaded going home.* **3.** *n.* a way of solving a problem. ♦ *What approach did the school district take to the teacher shortage?* ♦ *The manager uses a direct approach to get things done quickly.* **4.** *n.* an entrance; a path to something. ♦ *The approach to the mansion is hidden by a stone wall.* ♦ *A tree-lined driveway formed the approach to the historic house.* **5.** *n.* an instance of [something] coming closer. ♦ *We could hear the approach of the trains.* ♦ *The airplane's approach to the runway was smooth.*

appropriate 1. [ə 'pro pri ɪt] *adj.* correct; suitable; proper. (Adv: *appropriately.*) ♦ *A tuxedo is appropriate dress for the opera.* ♦ *Vulgar language is not appropriate in the workplace.* **2.** [ə 'pro pri et] *tv.* to take something for one's own use; to steal something. (Euphemistic for steal.) ♦ *Max appropriated a carton of pencils from work.* ♦ *John appropriated the chair his little sister was sitting in.* **3.** [ə 'pro pri et] *tv.* to set aside money for a specific purpose; to budget funds. ♦ *The Smiths appropriated money for their daughter's education.* ♦ *The city appropriated funds to fix the roads.*

appropriateness [ə 'pro pri ət nəs] *n.* suitability for a particular situation. (No plural form in this sense.) ♦ *I doubt the appropriateness of wearing a tuxedo to play basketball!* ♦ *Your comments lacked appropriateness for the readers of our newsletter.*

appropriation [ə pro pri 'e ʃən] **1.** *n.* the process of budgeting or setting aside money for a particular purpose. (No plural form in this sense.) ♦ *The taxpayers objected* *to the appropriation of more funds to fix the roads.* ♦ *The appropriation of funds requires the approval of the company treasurer.* **2.** *n.* an amount of money budgeted for a specific use. ♦ *We need larger appropriations this year.* ♦ *The city's appropriation was not sufficient to pay for the road repairs.* **3.** *n.* taking something for one's own use; stealing. (Euphemistic. No plural form in this sense.) ♦ *John was arrested for the appropriation of company property.* ♦ *Appropriation of another country's land is likely to cause a war.*

approval [ə 'pruv əl] **1.** *n.* the acceptance of someone or something as satisfactory; confirmation of the acceptance of someone or something as satisfactory. (No plural form in this sense.) ♦ *Max needs lots of approval from his peers.* ♦ *You must have approval for your plan before you can start.* **2.** *n.* an act of giving ①; a statement, signature, or document showing that someone has given ①. ♦ *I need your approval of this plan today, please.* ♦ *Have they all given their approvals?*

approve [ə 'pruv] **1. approve (of)** *iv.* (+ *prep. phr.*) to judge someone or something to be satisfactory or agreeable. ♦ *My parents approved of my date.* ♦ *I simply do not approve.* **2.** *tv.* to grant approval of someone or something. ♦ *The author approved the editor's changes.* ♦ *The principal approved the new curriculum.*

approved [ə 'pruvd] *adj.* accepted; determined to be acceptable. ♦ *An approved copy of the manuscript was sent to the printer.* ♦ *The approved schedule was sent to the conference participants.*

approximate 1. [ə 'prɑk sə mɪt] *adj.* estimated; not exact. (Adv: *approximately.*) ♦ *What is the approximate travel time from your house to your job?* ♦ *The salesclerk told us the approximate cost of the new radio.* **2.** [ə 'prɑk sə met] *tv.* to estimate something; to guess the amount of something. ♦ *Can you approximate the distance from here to New York City?* ♦ *The editor could only approximate the number of entries in the dictionary.* **3.** [ə 'prɑk sə met] *tv.* to be similar to someone or something; to appear to be almost the same as someone or something. ♦ *The picture frame approximates the size of the picture.* ♦ *The costume approximates authentic seventeenth-century dress.*

approximately [ə 'prɑk sə mət li] *adv.* about; close to; by estimation. ♦ *I have approximately fifty dollars in my bank account.* ♦ *Approximately how long does it take to drive to the city?*

approximation [ə prɑk sə 'me ʃən] *n.* an estimation; a guess. ♦ *The approximation of the amount needed was low.* ♦ *The company offered us an approximation of the final bill.*

apricot ['e prə kɑt] **1.** *n.* a soft, fuzzy, yellowish fruit with a large pit. ♦ *Apricots are Jane's favorite fruit.* ♦ *Tom just loved to eat canned apricots for dessert.* **2.** *adj.* made with ①. ♦ *I love biscuits with apricot preserves.* ♦ *I made an apricot tart for dessert.*

April ['e prəl] *n.* the fourth month of the year. ♦ *Spring usually arrives in early April.* ♦ *You must file your taxes by April 15th.*

April Fools' Day ['e prəl 'fulz 'de] the first day of April, when practical jokes are played on people. ♦ *It's April Fools' Day, so I am going to call the zoo and ask for Mr. Wolf.* ♦ *Because it was April Fools' Day, the newspaper had silly headlines on every page.*

apron ['e prən] **1.** *n.* a protective skirt worn over one's clothing; a protective covering for the front of one's clothing. ♦ *Mary put an apron on to cook dinner.* ♦ *Bob loves to cook, so we gave him an apron for his birthday.* **2.** *n.* the part of a theater stage that is in front of where the curtain hangs. ♦ *There was a short scene on the apron while the scenery was being changed for the next act.* ♦ *When the main curtain closed, a chair remained out on the apron.*

apropos [æ prə 'po] *adj.* appropriate; suitable; fitting; relevant. (From French.) ♦ *An apropos response to "Thank you" is "You're welcome."* ♦ *Your gift of a suitcase is very apropos. I'm leaving on a trip tomorrow!*

apt ['æpt] **1. apt to** *adj.* + *inf.* likely to do something; prone to doing something. ♦ *I am apt to watch football games on television all weekend.* ♦ *Bill is apt to forget half of the groceries if he doesn't make a list.* **2.** *adj.* clever; easily taught. ♦ *John is an apt pupil and learns his lessons quickly.* ♦ *The carpenter was pleased to have such an apt apprentice.* **3.** *adj.* suitable; appropriate; fitting. (Adv: *aptly.*) ♦ *"Haste makes waste" is an apt expression to use about John, who works too quickly and makes mistakes.* ♦ *The professor made an apt analogy to explain his point.*

aptitude ['æp tɪ tud] *n.* ability; skill; the natural ability to learn new things quickly. (No plural form in this sense.) ♦ *I have no musical aptitude. I can't even sing a simple tune.* ♦ *The students in the biology class have great aptitude for science.*

aptness ['æpt nəs] **1.** *n.* appropriateness. (No plural form in this sense.) ♦ *Bill was impressed at the aptness of the speaker's remarks.* ♦ *My boss was unaware of the aptness of the occasion when he gave me a raise on my birthday.* **2.** *n.* the ability to learn. (No plural form in this sense.) ♦ *The student's aptness became apparent in a short time.* ♦ *The teacher was pleasantly surprised at the class's aptness.*

aquaria [ə 'kwɛr i ə] a pl of aquarium.

aquarium [ə 'kwɛr i əm] **1.** *n., irreg.* a container for aquatic plants and animals. (Pl: *aquariums* or aquaria.) ♦ *There is a leak in my aquarium.* ♦ *The pet store has a sale on aquaria.* **2.** *n., irreg.* a public building containing ① for public viewing. ♦ *We spent the afternoon at the aquarium, looking at the fish.* ♦ *Feeding hours at the aquarium are popular with the children.*

aquatic [ə 'kwɑt ɪk] *adj.* relating to water. (Adv: *aquatically* [...ɪk li].) ♦ *A painting of the aquatic scene represents a school of fish.* ♦ *Aquatic animals can be seen at the aquarium.*

aqueduct ['æ kwɪ dəkt] *n.* a large channel or pipe for carrying running water. ♦ *The Romans built aqueducts in ancient times.* ♦ *The rural community built an aqueduct to irrigate the land.*

aqueous ['e kwi əs] **aqueous solution** *n.* a solution made with water; a mixture of water and something else that is dissolved in it. ♦ *The medication is taken in an aqueous solution.* ♦ *The marine aquarium contains an aqueous solution of sea salts.*

Arab ['ɛr əb] **1.** *n.* someone who lives in or comes from the Middle East and speaks Arabic. ♦ *Many Arabs live in Saudi Arabia.* ♦ *Arabs are usually Muslims.* **2.** of or about

① or the nations and cultures associated with ①. ♦ *I read a book about the history of the Arab peoples.* ♦ *The international conference included representatives from all the Arab nations.*

Arabia [ə 'reb i ə] *n.* a peninsula in the Middle East where Saudi Arabia and several other countries are located. (No plural form in this sense.) ♦ *Bill has traveled to several countries in Arabia.* ♦ *In ancient Arabia, the people were mostly nomads.*

Arabian [ə 'reb i ən] *adj.* relating to the people and culture of Arabia; originating in Arabia. ♦ *We studied Arabian history in our class on the cultures of the Middle East.* ♦ *Bob found the Arabian horses to be the most beautiful.*

Arabic ['ɛr ə bɪk] **1.** *n.* the Semitic language spoken by the Arab peoples. (No plural form in this sense.) ♦ *Arabic is not written in the Latin alphabet.* ♦ *Bob is learning to read and write Arabic.* **2.** *adj.* <the adj. use of ①.> ♦ *Jane is fluent in several Arabic dialects.* ♦ *Some Arabic sounds are hard for English speakers to produce.* **3.** *adj.* relating to the people and culture of Arabia; originating in Arabia. ♦ *Arabic art and architecture seem quite exotic to Americans.* ♦ *The historian studied the Arabic influence on Spanish architecture.*

Arabic numeral ['ɛr ə bɪk 'num ə rəl] See numeral.

arbitrary ['ɑr bə trɛr i] **1.** *adj.* random; based on chance or an individual's opinion instead of on reason, principle, or discussion. (Adv: *arbitrarily.*) ♦ *Buying a home should not be an arbitrary decision.* ♦ *The supervisor made an arbitrary decision to promote an employee.* **2.** *adj.* prone to making arbitrary ① decisions; autocratic. (Adv: *arbitrarily.*) ♦ *Bill is sometimes a very arbitrary person and won't explain his decisions.* ♦ *If you would be less arbitrary when you deal with employees, they would be more loyal.*

arbitrate ['ɑr bə tret] *tv.* [for a disinterested party] to listen to both sides of an issue and help both sides resolve the issue. ♦ *The couple asked the counselor to arbitrate their argument.* ♦ *A team of lawyers arbitrated the property dispute.*

arbitration [ɑr bə 'tre ʃən] *n.* settling a dispute through the use of an arbitrator. (No plural form in this sense.) ♦ *After much arbitration, the union and the company finally settled their differences.* ♦ *The matter was sent into arbitration to avoid the costs of a court trial.*

arbitrator ['ɑr bə tret ɚ] *n.* someone who listens to both sides of an issue and helps resolve the issue. ♦ *The arbitrator proposed a satisfactory compromise.* ♦ *The disputing parties agreed to accept the decision of the arbitrator.*

arbor ['ɑr bɚ] **1.** *n.* a shady place formed by trees or other plants. ♦ *I like to sit and read in the arbor on summer afternoons.* ♦ *In the corner of the garden was an arbor where it was always cool and quiet.* **2.** *n.* a decorative structure made of wood or metal that supports vines or climbing plants. ♦ *An arbor covered with vines marked the entrance to the garden.* ♦ *A decorative grape arbor stood at the back of the house.*

arboreal [ɑr 'bor ɪ əl] *adj.* relating to trees; dwelling in trees. (Adv: *arboreally.*) ♦ *The sloth is an arboreal animal.* ♦ *There are many arboreal creatures in the rain forest.*

arc ['ɑrk] **1.** *n.* a curve; a portion of a circle. ♦ *The buildings formed an arc around the courtyard, partially enclosing it.* ♦ *The stream twisted through the forest in a series of arcs.* **2.** *iv.* to form a curve; to take the shape of a curve. ♦ *The rocket's path arced gracefully over the sea.* ♦ *The airplane gradually arced to the left as it approached the airport.*

arcade [ɑr 'ked] **1.** *n.* a public place offering several video games or other game machines. ♦ *The children spent their money at the arcade.* ♦ *The arcade has modern video games that attract young teenagers.* **2.** *n.* a walkway covered with an arched roof. (Merchants sell goods from shops or stalls on either side of the walkway.) ♦ *The vendors set up stands along the arcade.* ♦ *After dinner, the couple strolled hand-in-hand along the arcade.*

arch ['ɑrtʃ] **1.** *n.* a curved structure over an opening, usually holding the weight of the wall above it. ♦ *The front of the museum had three main arches in it.* ♦ *We huddled under the arch of the bridge during the storm.* **2.** *n.* the curved part of the bottom of the foot. ♦ *These shoes are designed to support your arches.* ♦ *The dancer had high arches.* **3.** *iv.* to bend in the shape of ①; to curve like ①. ♦ *The trees arched over the road.* ♦ *The bird's wing arched over the chicks, keeping the rain off.*

archaeological [ɑr ki ə 'lɑdʒ ɪ kəl] *adj.* relating to the study of the physical remains of older human cultures. (Adv: *archaeologically* [...ɪk li].) ♦ *The scientist started an archaeological excavation in the desert.* ♦ *Archaeological research has taught us a lot about how people lived in ancient times.*

archaeologist [ɑr ki 'ɑl ə dʒəst] *n.* someone who studies the physical remains of older human cultures. ♦ *Archaeologists helped with the reconstruction of the excavated town.* ♦ *The archaeologist speculated about how the ancient people prepared their food.*

archaeology [ɑr ki 'ɑl ə dʒi] *n.* the study of the physical remains of older human cultures. (No plural form in this sense.) ♦ *Mary took a course in archaeology and learned a lot about ancient artifacts.* ♦ *Her archaeology class took a field trip to an ancient burial ground.*

archaic [ɑr 'ke ɪk] *adj.* characteristic of an earlier time; antiquated; out-of-date; obsolete; no longer used. (Adv: *archaically* [...ɪk li].) ♦ *The archaeologist dug up an archaic lantern.* ♦ *The archaic ship was just like the ones used centuries earlier.*

archangel ['ɑrk 'en ðʒəl] *n.* a chief angel; the major angel. ♦ *Archangels are described in the Bible as messengers.* ♦ *Gabriel is perhaps the best-known archangel.*

archbishop ['ɑrtʃ 'bɪʃ əp] *n.* a church leader ranking above a bishop. ♦ *England has two archbishops.* ♦ *The archbishop is responsible for making church policy.*

arched ['ɑrtʃt] *adj.* curved; shaped like an arch. ♦ *Arched windows do not fit this style of architecture.* ♦ *The arched doorway made the room seem more elegant.*

archenemy ['ɑrtʃ 'ɛn ə mi] *n.* someone or something's primary opponent. ♦ *The candidate ran in the election against her archenemy.* ♦ *The cat chased its archenemy, the mouse.*

archer ['ɑrtʃ ɚ] *n.* someone who uses a bow and arrow; someone skilled at archery. ♦ *Bill is an archer who loves shooting at targets.* ♦ *The archer aimed at the target.*

archery ['ɑrtʃ ə ri] *n.* the sport or skill of shooting with a bow and arrow. (No plural form in this sense.) ♦ *The* *students are learning archery in gym class.* ♦ *Archery is a sport requiring good aim.*

architect ['ɑrk ə tɛkt] *n.* someone who designs buildings. ♦ *The architect has won awards for his designs.* ♦ *We hired an architect to design the addition to our home.*

architectural [ɑr kə 'tɛk tʃə rəl] *adj.* relating to the design of buildings. (Adv: *architecturally.*) ♦ *This church has several unusual architectural features.* ♦ *The architectural plans for the house showed exactly where each wall should be.*

architecture ['ɑrk ɪ tɛk tʃɚ] **1.** *n.* the designing of buildings; the study of building design. (No plural form in this sense.) ♦ *Jane is training for a career in architecture.* ♦ *The field of architecture offers many opportunities.* **2.** *n.* the particular design of a building. (No plural form in this sense.) ♦ *The modern architecture of the church is not at all traditional.* ♦ *We admired the architecture of the stately old homes.*

archival ['ɑr kɑɪv əl] **1.** *adj.* of or about archives. (Adv: *archivally.*) ♦ *Jane took a course in archival techniques.* ♦ *The librarian's archival practices were out-of-date.* **2.** *adj.* [of a copy of a document, photograph, or computer file] kept in reserve or as a backup. (Adv: *archivally.*) ♦ *All the archival disks are stored in the other building.* ♦ *One archival copy remains, but I cannot let you have that one.*

archive ['ɑr kɑɪv] **1.** *n.* a collection of documents and records on a specific topic; a collection of important documents and historical records. (Often plural.) ♦ *You might find the legal papers you want in the archive of old wills.* ♦ *Please put this document in the archives with the other contracts.* **2.** *n.* the place where ① is stored. (Often plural.) ♦ *I sometimes study in the archive because it's so quiet.* ♦ *You will find the company's archives on the first floor of this building.* **3.** *tv.* to place something in ①. ♦ *Please archive this as soon as possible.* ♦ *The computer disk was becoming full, so we had to archive some files.*

archivist ['ɑr kə vəst] *n.* someone who keeps archives; someone who maintains a collection of historical documents and records. ♦ *The archivist was not able to locate the records in the archives.* ♦ *Only the archivist is allowed in the rare-manuscript section.*

archway ['ɑrtʃ we] *n.* a doorway or passageway with a rounded top. ♦ *The couple stepped through the archway into the garden.* ♦ *The only entrance to the estate is through the archway.*

arctic ['ɑrk tɪk] **1. the Arctic** *n.* the area around the Arctic Ocean, near the North Pole. (No plural form in this sense. Treated as singular.) ♦ *I would hate to be lost in the Arctic.* ♦ *Polar bears live in the Arctic.* **2.** *adj.* relating to ①. (Sometimes capitalized.) ♦ *The Arctic explorers wore special clothing to keep warm.* ♦ *Polar bears live in the arctic region.* **3.** *adj.* very cold; freezing. (Adv: *arctically* [...ɪk li].) ♦ *I wore very warm sweaters because of the arctic weather we were having.* ♦ *The arctic temperatures in the city this winter have caused several deaths.*

Arctic Ocean ['ɑrk tɪk 'o ʃən] See Gazetteer.

ardent ['ɑrd nt] *adj.* eager; full of intense desire or passion. (Adv: *ardently.*) ♦ *Jane's ardent admirer sent her flowers every day.* ♦ *The president is an ardent supporter of civil rights.*

ardor ['ɑrd ɚ] *n.* intense desire or passion for someone or something; zeal for someone or something. (No plural form in this sense.) ♦ *The teacher was impressed by Bill's ardor for learning.* ♦ *Mary attacked the weeds in her garden with ardor.*

arduous ['ɑr dʒu əs] *adj.* strenuous; very difficult. (Adv: *arduously.*) ♦ *Cutting the grass is an arduous task for the elderly man.* ♦ *The travelers were glad that the arduous journey across the desert was almost finished.*

are [ɑr] *iv., irreg.* <a form of the verb be used in the second-person singular present and in all three persons in the present-tense plural.> (Reduced to *'re* in contractions.) ♦ *They are on vacation this week, but we are still at work.* ♦ *Jane, you are the only person who can help me.*

area ['ɛr i ə] **1.** *n.* a space; a section. ♦ *Please keep out of this restricted area.* ♦ *There is a strange smell in the area around the refrigerator.* **2.** *n.* a measure of a section of a flat surface, determined by multiplying the length of the surface by its width. ♦ *The surveyor determined the area of the yard.* ♦ *Mary measured the area of the floor before ordering the new carpet.* **3.** *n.* a subject; a field of interest or study. ♦ *What is your principal area of study?* ♦ *Physics is an area I don't know much about.* **4. gray area** *idiom* an area ③ of a subject or question that is difficult to put into a particular category because it is not clearly defined and may have connections or associations with more than one category. ♦ *The responsibility for social studies in the college is a gray area. Several departments are involved.* ♦ *Publicity is a gray area in that firm. It is shared between the marketing and design divisions.*

area code ['ɛr i ə kod] *n.* a numerical prefix, used especially when making a long-distance phone call, that identifies the general location of the person being called. ♦ *What is the area code for downtown Chicago?* ♦ *Please give me your telephone number, area code first.*

arena [ə 'rin ə] *n.* a large open space surrounded by tiers of seats, where performances and sporting events take place. ♦ *The basketball game was held at the arena.* ♦ *The arena was closed to the public while it was being renovated.*

aren't [ɑrnt] **1.** *cont.* "are not." ♦ *We aren't going to the park because it's raining.* ♦ *Aren't you going to introduce me to your friend?* **2. aren't I** *cont.* "am I not." (Used in the asking of certain questions. See also ain't.) ♦ *I'm a friendly person, aren't I?* ♦ *Aren't I the best cook in town?*

Argentina [ɑr dʒən 'ti nə] See Gazetteer.

arguable ['ɑr gju ə bəl] **1.** *adj.* subject to dispute; doubtful. ♦ *Whether we can afford a new house is arguable.* ♦ *That she is qualified for the job is an arguable point.* **2.** *adj.* capable of withstanding an opposing argument; likely; plausible. (Adv: *arguably.*) ♦ *The matter is not arguable and should be dropped.* ♦ *The case is arguable, and we should go ahead and take it into court.*

arguably ['ɑr gju ə bli] *adv.* likely; [of an assertion] worthy of being argued in favor of. ♦ *The Dragon Inn is arguably the best Chinese restaurant in town.* ♦ *Arguably, we will achieve everything we want if we follow this course.*

argue ['ɑr gju] **1.** *iv.* to disagree [with someone] verbally; to quarrel [with someone] verbally. ♦ *Susan and her brother argued over which television program to watch.* ♦ *"Don't argue!" Dad warned Bob.* **2.** *tv.* to debate a point or issue by means of an argument. ♦ *Jane argued her point* *well.* ♦ *Bob's son argued that the more expensive car was the better value, but Bob bought the cheaper one anyway.*

argument ['ɑr gjə mənt] **1.** *n.* a quarrel, especially if verbal; a dispute. ♦ *The children had an argument about who should close the door.* ♦ *What started the argument?* **2.** *n.* a debate or discussion of an issue of contention. ♦ *The argument was presented to the judge.* ♦ *Your argument contains several flaws.*

argumentation [ɑr gjə mən 'te ʃən] *n.* statements made to persuade or convince someone. (No plural form in this sense.) ♦ *The argumentation in the scientific paper was very logical.* ♦ *The professor found weaknesses in the student's argumentation.*

argumentative [ɑr gjə 'mɛn tə tɪv] *adj.* liking to argue; contentious. (Adv: *argumentatively.*) ♦ *Jane was in an argumentative mood and disagreed with everything I said.* ♦ *The salesclerk was annoyed with the argumentative customer.*

aria ['ɑr i ə] *n.* a song in an opera that is sung by only one person; an operatic solo. (From Italian.) ♦ *My favorite opera has several beautiful arias in it.* ♦ *The soloist sang arias from famous operas.*

arid ['ɛr ɪd] *adj.* very dry; without water, humidity, or rain. (Adv: *aridly.*) ♦ *The desert is an arid place.* ♦ *The Joneses were anxious to retire to an arid climate.*

arise [ə 'rɑɪz] **1.** *iv., irreg.* to get up; to rise; to stand up. (Pt: arose; pp: arisen.) ♦ *The princess saw the vampire arise from the coffin.* ♦ *When the actors appeared, the audience arose and applauded.* **2.** *iv., irreg.* to develop; to happen. ♦ *Here's the phone number where I will be. Call me if trouble arises.* ♦ *If something unexpected arises at the office, I will be home late.*

arisen [ə 'rɪz ən] pp of arise.

aristocracy [æ rɪ 'stɑ krə si] *n.* the upper class; the ruling families. (No plural form in this sense.) ♦ *The local aristocracy was very much concerned with propriety.* ♦ *Members of the aristocracy were executed during the revolution.*

aristocrat [ə 'rɪs tə kræt] *n.* a member of the upper class. ♦ *The young aristocrat was educated overseas.* ♦ *The fancy ball was attended by wealthy aristocrats.*

aristocratic [ə rɪs tə 'kræt ɪk] *adj.* relating to or characteristic of the people and manners of the upper class. (Adv: *aristocratically* [...ɪk li].) ♦ *The students at the exclusive school were from aristocratic families.* ♦ *I found my roommate's aristocratic behavior to be annoying.*

arithmetic [ə 'rɪθ mə tɪk] **1.** *n.* the part of mathematics using numbers to perform addition, subtraction, multiplication, and division. ♦ *Mary got an A on her arithmetic test.* ♦ *Arithmetic is a basic school subject.* **2.** [ɛr ɪθ 'mɛt ɪk] *adj.* <the adj. use of ①.> (Adv: *arithmetically* [...ɪk li].) ♦ *This arithmetic formula is very complex.* ♦ *Max caught on to arithmetic principles almost at once.*

arithmetical [ɛ rɪθ 'mɛt ɪ kəl] *adj.* of or about arithmetic. (Adv: *arithmetically* [...ɪk li].) ♦ *Architects use arithmetical formulas in their work.* ♦ *Bob took an arithmetical approach to solving the problem.*

arithmetically [ɛ rɪθ 'mɛt ɪk li] *adv.* using arithmetic. ♦ *The engineering problem can be solved arithmetically.* ♦ *The cook determined arithmetically how much flour was needed for three cakes.*

Arizona [ɛr ə 'zon ə] See Gazetteer.

ark ['ɑrk] *n.* a large boat of the type built by Noah in the biblical story of the flood. ♦ *Noah built the ark as a means of saving pairs of all creatures.* ♦ *The ark had to be very large to hold samples of all the land animals in the world.*

Arkansas ['ɑr kən sɔ] See Gazetteer.

arm ['ɑrm] **1.** *n.* one of the upper limbs of a human being. ♦ *Grandma hugged the child in her arms.* ♦ *My arms ached after moving the heavy boxes.* **2.** *n.* something that extends from the main part of something; a branch of something. (Figurative on ①.) ♦ *The Adriatic Sea is an arm of the Mediterranean Sea.* ♦ *The accounting arm of the company also handles customer service.* **3. arms** *n.* guns; weapons. ♦ *The traitor sold arms to the enemy during the war.* ♦ *The troops were ordered to lay down their arms.* **4.** *n.* the part of a chair that supports the arms of someone who sits in the chair. ♦ *The frail man used the arms of the chair to lift himself up.* ♦ *One of the arms of the chair broke off as I leaned on it.* **5.** *tv.* to equip someone or something with weapons. ♦ *The gun manufacturer secretly armed the rebels.* ♦ *The knight armed himself for battle, putting on armor and carrying a lance and shield.* **6. arm in arm** *idiom* [of persons] linked or hooked together by the arms. ♦ *The two lovers walked arm in arm down the street.* ♦ *Arm in arm, the line of dancers kicked high, and the audience roared its approval.* **7. give one's right arm (for someone or something)** *idiom* to be willing to give something of great value for someone or something. ♦ *I'd give my right arm for a nice cool drink.* ♦ *I'd give my right arm to be there.* **8. shot in the arm** *idiom* a boost; something that gives someone energy. ♦ *Thank you for cheering me up. It was a real shot in the arm.* ♦ *Your friendly greeting card was just what I needed—a real shot in the arm.* **9. up in arms** *idiom* rising up in anger, as if armed with weapons. ♦ *My father was really up in arms when he got his tax bill this year.* ♦ *The citizens were up in arms, pounding on the gates of the palace, demanding justice.*

armada [ɑr 'mɑd ə] *n.* a group of warships; a fleet of warships. (From Spanish.) ♦ *Spain had a powerful armada a few centuries ago.* ♦ *The armada encountered pirates off the coast of Spain.*

armament ['ɑr mə mənt] **1.** *n.* providing the military with equipment for war; arming. (No plural form in this sense.) ♦ *Armament is thought to be a protection against aggression.* ♦ *The citizens protested the government's plans for armament.* **2.** *n.* military weapons and equipment. ♦ *The tiny country had enough armaments to conquer the enemy.* ♦ *The army keeps armaments on military bases.*

armchair ['ɑrm tʃɛr] *n.* a seat, usually cushioned, with raised arms ④. ♦ *Grandpa always sits in the armchair by the window.* ♦ *My favorite armchair is in the living room.*

armed ['ɑrmd] **1.** *adj.* carrying a gun or other weapons. ♦ *The armed suspect was considered to be dangerous.* ♦ *The armed police officer stopped the robbery.* **2.** *adj.* ready for war; prepared for battle. ♦ *The armed soldiers marched toward the battlefield.* ♦ *An armed group of rebels started the revolution.* **3. armed to the teeth** *idiom* heavily armed with deadly weapons. ♦ *The bank robber was armed to the teeth when he was caught.* ♦ *There are too many guns around. The entire country is armed to the teeth.*

Armenia [ɑr 'min i ə] See Gazetteer.

armful ['ɑrm fʊl] *n.* the amount of something that can be carried in someone's arms; an armload. ♦ *I carried an armful of dirty clothes into the laundry room.* ♦ *I can only carry one armful at a time.*

armhole ['ɑrm hol] *n.* a hole in clothing for an arm. ♦ *The seamstress pinned the armhole of the dress.* ♦ *John pushed his arms through the armholes of the vest.*

armistice ['ɑr mɪs tɪs] *n.* a truce. ♦ *The battling countries agreed to an armistice after three years of fighting.* ♦ *After the armistice, there was supposed to be no gunfire.*

Armistice Day ['ɑr mɪs tɪs 'de] *n.* November 11, the anniversary of the truce that ended World War I in 1918. (Now known in the U.S. as Veterans Day.) ♦ *There was a parade through town on Armistice Day.* ♦ *Tom laid a wreath on his grandfather's grave on Armistice Day.*

armload ['ɑrm lod] *n.* the amount of something that can be carried in someone's arms; an armful. ♦ *We carried an armload of clothes to the washing machine.* ♦ *Tom placed an armload of wood on the hearth.*

armoire [ɑrm 'wɑr] *n.* a large, movable cupboard, typically used to hold clothing. (Originally, a cabinet that held guns and other arms.) ♦ *Bill used the armoire as a cabinet for his stereo components.* ♦ *I keep my sweaters in an armoire in the bedroom.*

armor ['ɑrm ɚ] **1.** *n.* a shell of metal used to protect the body when fighting. (Used by knights and warriors in the Middle Ages. No plural form in this sense. Number is expressed with *piece(s)* or *suit(s) of armor.*) ♦ *The museum had an exhibit of medieval armor last month.* ♦ *A knight's armor must have been quite uncomfortable.* **2.** *n.* something that shields or protects someone or something. (No plural form in this sense.) ♦ *A turtle has a soft body, but it also has the armor of a hard shell to protect it.* ♦ *The military vehicles were covered with bulletproof armor.*

armored ['ɑrm ɚd] *adj.* protected; shielded; covered with a hard substance. ♦ *A security officer parked the armored truck in front of the bank.* ♦ *The soldiers rode in an armored tank.*

armory ['ɑrm ə ri] *n.* a place where weapons and ammunition are kept. ♦ *The old armory is now used as a meeting hall.* ♦ *The cannon shells are stored in the armory.*

armpit ['ɑrm pɪt] *n.* the hollow underneath the place where the arm joins the shoulder. ♦ *Bob said his jacket had become too tight under the armpits.* ♦ *Mary applied deodorant to her armpits.*

armrest ['ɑrm rɛst] *n.* the part of a chair or seat that supports someone's arms. ♦ *Jane placed both arms on the armrests and relaxed completely.* ♦ *One of the armrests on this chair is loose.*

army ['ɑrm i] **1.** *n.* a large group of land-based soldiers. ♦ *The army invaded at dawn.* ♦ *Have you served in the army?* **2.** *n.* a large group of creatures, typically people or ants. (Figurative on ①.) ♦ *Jane had a small army helping her move to her new apartment.* ♦ *An army of ants quickly collected around the picnic table.*

aroma [ə 'rom ə] *n.* an odor, especially one that is pleasant or agreeable. ♦ *The roses gave the room a pleasant aroma.* ♦ *The aroma of dinner cooking on the stove made us hungry.*

aromatic [ɛr ə 'mæt ɪk] *adj.* fragrant; pleasing to smell; having a strong aroma. (Adv: *aromatically* […ɪk li].) ♦ *Anne bought an aromatic spray to freshen her car.* ♦ *The pie baking in the oven was very aromatic.*

arose [ə 'roz] pt of arise.

around [ə 'rɑʊnd] **1.** *prep.* encircling someone or something; surrounding. ♦ *The students stood around the piano and sang.* ♦ *A ring of flowers grew around the base of the tree.* **2.** *prep.* close to a certain time or location. ♦ *Bob lives somewhere around 48th Street and Main.* ♦ *The meeting will start around three o'clock.* **3.** *prep.* in avoidance of someone or something. ♦ *There is no way around it. You must do it.* ♦ *You can't get around paying your taxes!* **4.** *prep.* in various places in something; at different locations within something. (With verbs such as *run around, walk around, go around, crawl around, travel around, drive around, jog around.*) ♦ *Susan and Bill walked around the mall looking for a mailbox.* ♦ *I spent last summer driving around Europe.* **5.** *prep.* revolving, with respect to something; moving in a circular pathway. ♦ *The earth goes around the sun once a year.* ♦ *They walked around the lake.* **6.** *prep.* in a direction that changes or turns at a corner. ♦ *The water fountain is around the corner to your left.* ♦ *Reach around the bookcase and plug in the lamp.* **7.** *adv.* on every side; on all sides. ♦ *After the accident, people gathered around.* ♦ *The spectators stood around waiting for the race to start.* **8.** *adv.* along a perimeter or circumference for a distance. ♦ *The track is ⅝ of a mile around.* ♦ *The cylinder measured six inches around.* **9.** *adv.* here and there; in no particular direction or location. (Used with verbs such as *bounce around, run around, chase around.*) ♦ *We drove around for a few hours.* ♦ *Anne wandered around for a while.* **10.** *adv.* in a manner so as to face the opposite way. ♦ *Anne swung her chair around so that she was facing me.* ♦ *The model turned around so the audience could see the back of her outfit.* **11.** *adv.* in a circular manner; in circles. ♦ *The wheel went around and around.* ♦ *The hands of the clock turn around slowly.* **12.** *adv.* present; available. ♦ *The boss is around somewhere.* ♦ *"That part hasn't been around for years," the mechanic said.*

around the clock [ə 'rɑʊnd ðə 'klɑk] **1.** *adv.* always; during the day and night; all the time. ♦ *This store is open around the clock.* ♦ *The hospital patients are monitored around the clock.* **2. around-the-clock** *adj.* always available or functioning; continuing for 24 hours each day; happening or available all the time; never stopping. ♦ *This hotel provides around-the-clock food service for its guests.* ♦ *The police used around-the-clock surveillance to catch the criminal.*

arouse [ə 'rɑʊz] **1.** *tv.* to wake someone up. ♦ *I did not have to arouse the children on Saturday morning.* ♦ *The alarm clock aroused the family at 6:00 A.M.* **2.** *tv.* to awaken someone's interest, causing curiosity, anger, sexual stimulation, or general interest. ♦ *A book with a very colorful cover aroused Bill's interest.* ♦ *Rudeness like Tom's always arouses my anger.* **3.** *tv.* to interest or stimulate someone sexually. ♦ *The explicit movie was too dull to arouse anyone!* ♦ *Bob claimed that almost anything would arouse him.*

arraign [ə 'ren] *tv.* to bring someone before a court or a judge to answer an indictment. ♦ *The suspect was arraigned on charges of fraud.* ♦ *The court arraigned each of the alleged crooks.*

arraignment [ə 'ren mənt] *n.* the bringing of someone before a court or a judge to answer an indictment. (No plural form in this sense.) ♦ *After the suspect's arraignment, the case was dismissed.* ♦ *The arraignment of the senator in the real-estate scandal was televised.*

arrange [ə 'rendʒ] **1.** *tv.* to put things in a particular order; to put things in specific locations. ♦ *The artist arranged her paintings for the exhibit.* ♦ *The florist arranged the roses in the vase.* **2.** *tv.* to prepare plans for something; to plan details for something. ♦ *Can you arrange a ride to the airport?* ♦ *Bob arranged a party for Mary's birthday.* **3.** *tv.* to adapt a piece of music in a particular way. ♦ *The composer arranged the musical score for piano and violin.* ♦ *The conductor arranged the music for a duet.*

arrangement [ə 'rendʒ mənt] **1.** *n.* the order or positions in which things have been put or placed. ♦ *The students messed up the librarian's arrangement of books on the shelf.* ♦ *The caterer carefully planned the arrangement of food on the buffet table.* **2. make arrangements** *n.* a plan or plans; a scheme that is worked out in advance. ♦ *John made arrangements to meet Mary at eight o'clock.* ♦ *Bob made arrangements to arrive at the same time as I would.* **3.** *n.* a particular version or adaptation of a piece of music. ♦ *Do you recognize this arrangement of the song?* ♦ *The orchestra played two arrangements of the piece.* **4.** *n.* a group of flowers arranged in a pleasing way. ♦ *There was a lovely arrangement on the table.* ♦ *The florist created an arrangement of roses for the funeral.*

arranger [ə 'ren dʒɚ] *n.* a musician who adapts a piece of music; a person who arranges music. ♦ *The arranger changed the cello part in the piece.* ♦ *The arranger rewrote the song in a lower key so that I could sing it.*

array [ə 're] **1.** *n.* a display of things; a collection of things. ♦ *The store had a vast array of toys to choose from.* ♦ *The colorful array of candy made the children's eyes bulge.* **2.** *tv.* to arrange things in a particular way or in a particular order. ♦ *Array the flowers so that the colors are mixed together.* ♦ *The gifts were arrayed on the table so everyone could see them.* **3.** *tv.* to dress someone or something in fancy clothes; to adorn someone or something. ♦ *The king and queen were arrayed in elegant robes.* ♦ *The bride arrayed the bridesmaids in lace and ribbons.*

arrears [ə 'rɪrz] **1.** *n.* a debt or payment that is overdue. (Treated as plural.) ♦ *Please pay the arrears immediately.* ♦ *Further credit is denied until the arrears are removed from this account.* **2. in arrears** *phr.* [of debts] overdue. ♦ *Jane's student-loan payments are in arrears.* ♦ *The accounts of the bankrupt company were in arrears.*

arrest [ə 'rɛst] **1.** *n.* the seizure of someone in the name of the law. ♦ *The arrest of the drug dealers was made quickly.* ♦ *How many arrests do the police make each month?* **2.** *tv.* to seize and take someone to jail in the name of the law. ♦ *The chief ordered the officers to arrest the suspect.* ♦ *The police arrested the purse snatcher.* **3.** *tv.* to stop something from moving or working; to bring something to an end. ♦ *The doctors hoped the medicine would arrest the spread of the infection.* ♦ *The loss of funding arrested the scientists' progress.*

arrested [ə 'rɛs tɪd] *adj.* stopped or slowed; impaired. ♦ *Are your bad manners due to rudeness or arrested development?* ♦ *The long drought was responsible for the plants' arrested growth.*

arresting [ə 'rɛs tɪŋ] *adj.* interesting; eye-catching. (Adv: *arrestingly.*) ♦ *The singer's pink hair was an arresting sight.* ♦ *"What an arresting view!" said Mary as she gazed across the canyon.*

arrival [ə 'rɑɪ vəl] *n.* the reaching of a destination. ♦ *The politician's arrival was hailed with music and speeches.* ♦ *Our flight's arrival is scheduled for eight o'clock.*

arrive [ə 'rɑɪv] **1.** *iv.* to reach a destination. ♦ *Did the package arrive in good condition?* ♦ *Our guests arrived late in the evening.* **2. have arrived** *idiom* to reach a position of power, authority, or prominence. ♦ *Jane saw her picture on the cover of the magazine and felt that she had finally arrived.* ♦ *When I got an office with a window, I knew that I had arrived.*

arrogance ['ɛr ə gəns] *n.* an offensive air of superiority; excessive pride. (No plural form in this sense.) ♦ *My business partner's arrogance makes her difficult to work with.* ♦ *We didn't tip the waiter because of his arrogance toward us.*

arrogant ['ɛr ə gənt] *adj.* with an offensive air of superiority; showing arrogance. (Adv: *arrogantly.*) ♦ *The tennis player's arrogant reaction offended the fans.* ♦ *Our waiter's arrogant manner cost him his job.*

arrow ['ɛr o] **1.** *n.* a thin, sharply pointed shaft that is shot from a bow. ♦ *The hunter put an arrow in his bow.* ♦ *The campers sharpened their arrows before going hunting.* **2.** *n.* a pointed symbol, indicating direction or position. ♦ *An arrow painted on the wall showed the way to the restrooms.* ♦ *An arrow on the loan application indicated where to sign.*

arrowhead ['ɛr o hɛd] *n.* the pointed tip of an arrow. ♦ *John found an old arrowhead in the field in back of his house.* ♦ *The arrowhead was stuck tightly in the target.*

arsenal ['ɑr sə nəl] **1.** *n.* a supply of weapons and ammunition belonging to a military unit. ♦ *The whole arsenal exploded when the bomb struck it.* ♦ *The spy discovered a secret underground arsenal.* **2.** *n.* a factory that makes weapons and ammunition. ♦ *The arsenal produced thousands of missiles each year.* ♦ *The government arsenal supplied the army with guns and ammunition.*

arsenic ['ɑr sə nɪk] *n.* a poisonous chemical element. (No plural form in this sense.) ♦ *In the mystery novel, the victim was poisoned with arsenic.* ♦ *The landlady used arsenic to kill rats.*

arson ['ɑr sən] *n.* the illegal act of destroying something by fire. (No plural form in this sense.) ♦ *The mysterious fire was believed to be a case of arson.* ♦ *When the inspectors found empty gasoline cans, they suspected arson.*

arsonist ['ɑr sə nəst] *n.* someone who commits arson. ♦ *The arsonist was a disgruntled employee who set fire to his boss's house.* ♦ *The police identified the arsonist's fingerprints.*

art ['ɑrt] **1.** *n.* the skilled creation of things of beauty or significant interest. (No plural form in this sense. Typically painting, drawing, sculpture, fiction, poetry, theater, dance, music, film, and photography.) ♦ *The summer class at the museum exposed the children to art.* ♦ *John got a degree in art and made his living as a sculptor.* **2.** *n.* the product of ①, such as a painting, drawing, or sculpture. (No plural form in this sense.) ♦ *I love to see the art* *on display at the museum.* ♦ *My house is decorated with a few important pieces of art.* **3.** *n.* the skill required to do or to make something creative; a creative craft. ♦ *The gourmet chef is a master at the art of cooking.* ♦ *The art of arranging flowers is difficult to learn.* **4. the arts** *n.* areas of activity associated with ①. (These are also called the *fine arts* and are distinguished from the humanities and the sciences. See also liberal arts under liberal. Treated as plural.) ♦ *Funding for the arts has been cut at many schools.* ♦ *Many of the arts are supported by charitable donations.*

arterial [ɑr 'tɪr ɪ əl] **1.** *adj.* relating to an artery ①. (Adv: *arterially.*) ♦ *The patient was hospitalized with an arterial blockage.* ♦ *Your arterial abnormality may lead to heart trouble.* **2.** *adj.* relating to an artery ②. (Adv: *arterially.*) ♦ *The arterial congestion at rush hour reached an impossible level.* ♦ *Due to the program of arterial repairs, there were many traffic jams.*

arteriosclerosis [ɑr 'tɪr i o sklə 'ro sɪs] *n.* hardening or clogging of the arteries ①. (No plural form in this sense.) ♦ *Excess cholesterol can cause arteriosclerosis.* ♦ *Arteriosclerosis can lead to a heart attack.*

artery ['ɑrt ə ri] **1.** *n.* a vessel that carries blood from the heart to the rest of the body. ♦ *If you cut an artery, you will bleed profusely.* ♦ *The arteries leading to the brain are on both sides of the neck.* **2.** *n.* a main road. (Figurative on ①.) ♦ *When the city's main artery was closed for construction, the side roads backed up with traffic.* ♦ *Most of the busiest arteries have traffic lights.*

arthritic [ɑr 'θrɪ tɪk] *adj.* relating to arthritis; afflicted with arthritis. (Adv: *arthritically* [...ɪk li].) ♦ *The pianist's arthritic hands prevented her from performing.* ♦ *Arthritic joints can be quite painful.*

arthritis [ɑr 'θrɑɪ tɪs] *n.* an inflammation of the joints. (No plural form in this sense.) ♦ *Many older people suffer from arthritis.* ♦ *Arthritis causes pain and swelling in the joints.*

article ['ɑrt ɪ kəl] **1.** *n.* a small part or section of a written document, especially an official document such as a contract. ♦ *The third article of the U.S. Constitution describes the Supreme Court.* ♦ *The last article in the publisher's contract explained the author's rights.* **2.** *n.* a specific item; a piece of something. ♦ *Jane had several articles of clothing that needed to be washed.* ♦ *Various articles used in the preparation of food are kept on this shelf.* **3.** *n.* a part of speech that makes a noun specific or general, such as a, an, and the in English. ♦ *If a noun begins with a vowel sound, it takes the article* an *rather than* a. ♦ *Some languages, like Russian, do not have articles.* **4.** *n.* a small section of writing in a larger work, as in a newspaper or an encyclopedia. ♦ *Mary often writes short articles for the local newspaper.* ♦ *Bill looked up the article on computers in the encyclopedia.*

articulate 1. [ɑr 'tɪk jə lɪt] *adj.* [of someone] speaking clearly and distinctly. (Adv: *articulately.*) ♦ *An articulate speaker does not mumble.* ♦ *Please practice your speech until you are more articulate.* **2.** [ɑr 'tɪk jə let] *iv.* to speak clearly and distinctly. ♦ *Speech disorders can make it difficult for a speaker to articulate.* ♦ *The announcer has a cold and can't articulate properly.* **3.** [ɑr 'tɪk jə let] *tv.* to create an element of speech, using the speech organs. ♦ *The baby could not articulate specific words.* ♦ *People learning a foreign language often have difficulty articulating certain sounds.* **4.** [ɑr 'tɪk jə let] *tv.* to describe something, especially an idea, logically or distinctly. ♦ *John did not articulate his argument well, so he lost the debate.* ♦ *The six-year-old could not articulate his feelings.*

articulated [ɑr 'tɪk jə let ɪd] *adj.* segmented; connected at a movable joint. ♦ *The doctor had an articulated human skeleton hanging in his office.* ♦ *The artist sketched from an articulated model of the human body.*

articulateness [ɑr 'tɪk jə lət nəs] *n.* clarity and effectiveness in speech. (No plural form in this sense.) ♦ *The broadcasting school taught articulateness and poise.* ♦ *The lecturer's articulateness made the complex ideas simple to comprehend.*

articulation [ɑr tɪk jə 'le ʃən] **1.** *n.* the creation of speech sounds by moving the speech organs. (No plural form in this sense.) ♦ *The foreigner's articulation of the "th" sound was not correct.* ♦ *Bill had trouble with the articulation of the German "ch" sounds.* **2.** *n.* the clear and logical presentation of an idea. (No plural form in this sense.) ♦ *Articulation of complex ideas came easy for Max.* ♦ *Mary was very good at the articulation of her ideas.* **3.** *n.* the movement of the bones meeting at a joint. (No plural form in this sense.) ♦ *Because of arthritis, the articulation of my knee joints is painful.* ♦ *In anatomy class we studied the articulation of the ankle bones.*

artifact ['ɑrt ə fækt] *n.* something that is made by human hands and not by nature. ♦ *The archaeologist discovered ancient artifacts.* ♦ *The museum is filled with artifacts from various cultures.*

artificial [ɑrt ə 'fɪʃ əl] *adj.* not authentic; not occurring in nature; synthetic. (Adv: *artificially.*) ♦ *Many snack foods have artificial flavors.* ♦ *The soldier who lost a leg in battle now has an artificial limb.*

artificiality [ɑrt ə fɪʃ i 'æl ə ti] *n.* the quality of being synthetic or not authentic. (No plural form in this sense.) ♦ *Aside from the artificiality of the flowers, the room's decorations were lovely.* ♦ *The artificiality of the fake leather upholstery didn't bother the customer.*

artificialness [ɑrt ə 'fɪʃ əl nəs] *n.* the state of being an imitation. (No plural form in this sense.) ♦ *The artificialness of the plastic flowers offended Jane.* ♦ *All the bright colors in the room gave it an air of pretense and artificialness.*

artisan ['ɑr tə zən] *n.* someone skilled in a craft or trade. ♦ *Many artisans came to the craft show to sell their goods.* ♦ *Blacksmiths are artisans whose craft has almost disappeared.*

artist ['ɑr təst] *n.* someone who creates art ② or practices art ①. ♦ *The painting was a portrait of the artist's parents.* ♦ *The artist's works were exhibited at the museum.*

artistic [ɑr 'tɪs tɪk] **1.** *adj.* aesthetically pleasing; showing creativity. (Adv: *artistically* [...ɪk li].) ♦ *The hostess presented a platter containing an artistic arrangement of appetizers.* ♦ *The ugly painting had no artistic merit.* **2.** *adj.* using creativity; using artistry. (Adv: *artistically* [...ɪk li].) ♦ *Mary's artistic touch was evident in her exquisite drawings.* ♦ *Bob has no artistic talents.*

artistry ['ɑr tə stri] *n.* skill or talent in creating art. (No plural form in this sense.) ♦ *The writer had a great artistry with words.* ♦ *The spectator admired the sculptor's artistry.*

artwork ['ɑrt wɚk] **1.** *n.* one or more pieces of art, such as a painting or a sculpture. (No plural form in this sense.) ♦ *We enjoyed seeing the artwork on exhibit at the gallery.* ♦ *I own only one piece of original artwork.* **2.** *n.* the pictures or illustrations that appear with written text. (No plural form in this sense.) ♦ *The picture book featured original artwork by the author.* ♦ *Max's book has lots of color artwork in it.*

as [æz] **1. as...as** *conj.* to the same extent or degree; equally; in the same way. ♦ *Susan is as tall as Bob.* ♦ *Mary is as busy as ever.* **2.** *conj.* while; during; at the same time. ♦ *The performer sang as she juggled the oranges.* ♦ *The librarian spoke to us as he took the books from the shelves.* **3.** *conj.* in the way that. ♦ *I filled out the form as I had been instructed to do.* ♦ *Do your work as I told you to do it.* **4.** *conj.* because; since. ♦ *As I didn't know how to drive, I crashed the car into a tree.* ♦ *Mary left the movie early as she felt ill.* **5. as if** *conj.* in the same way that it would be if [something were to happen]. ♦ *Jane's voice sounded as if she had just woken up.* ♦ *The pale man looked as if he had seen a ghost.* **6. as though** *conj.* as if ⑤. ♦ *Mary looked outside and said that the sky looked as though it would rain.* ♦ *The cat, sleeping in the sunlight, lay motionless as though it were dead.* **7. as for** *phr.* in regards to; concerning; relative to. ♦ *"As for you," the teacher yelled at the rude pupil, "you can go to the principal's office."* ♦ *As for the window you broke, you'll have to pay for it out of your allowance.* **8. as to** *phr.* regarding; concerning; about. ♦ *Susan has absolutely no idea as to what to name the puppy.* ♦ *What can you tell us as to the whereabouts of Jimmy's runaway cat?* **9.** *prep.* in the role or function of something. ♦ *John worked as a carpenter.* ♦ *She used her table as a desk.*

asbestos [æs 'bɛs təs] *n.* a mineral fiber that will not burn. (No plural form in this sense. Some varieties are considered to be a health hazard.) ♦ *The school was closed while the asbestos was removed.* ♦ *Asbestos is used to make fireproof materials.*

ascend [ə 'sɛnd] **1.** *iv.* to go upwards; to rise. ♦ *The businessman steadily ascended in the ranks of his company.* ♦ *The hot-air balloon slowly ascended into the sky.* **2.** *tv.* to go up stairs; to climb something; to go up something. ♦ *The guests ascended the stairs to the second floor.* ♦ *As Jane ascended the mountain, Bill took pictures.*

ascension [ə 'sɛn ʃən] *n.* rising or going upward. (No plural form in this sense.) ♦ *The ascension of the ladder was no easy task.* ♦ *The balloon's ascension took place in the early morning.*

ascent [ə 'sɛnt] *n.* an act of climbing or going upward. ♦ *The rock climbers made their ascent slowly.* ♦ *The plane's ascent during the storm was quite rough.*

ascertain [æs ɚ 'ten] *tv.* to find out something; to determine something. ♦ *Did the doctor ascertain the cause of your pain?* ♦ *The students ascertained that the professor was not too knowledgeable.*

ascertainable [æs ɚ 'ten ə bəl] *adj.* capable of being determined or found out; verifiable. (Adv: *ascertainably.*) ♦ *The future is just not ascertainable.* ♦ *The sex of an unborn baby is ascertainable with special tests.*

ascribe [ə 'skrɑɪb] **1. ascribe to** *tv + prep. phr.* to identify something as the product of someone or something. ♦ *Dr. Smith ascribed the painting to a German monk.* ♦ *The monument was ascribed to an ancient civilization.* **2. ascribe to** *tv. + prep. phr.* to identify something as the cause of something. ♦ *To what do you ascribe your success?* ♦ *I ascribed his bad humor to his illness.*

aseptic [e 'sɛp tɪk] *adj.* free of germs; completely clean and free of germs. (Adv: *aseptically* [...ɪk li].) ♦ *A hospital operating room is almost totally aseptic.* ♦ *The man who was obsessed with germs wanted to live in an aseptic house.*

asexual [e 'sɛk ʃu əl] **1.** *adj.* able to reproduce without sexual activity. (Adv: *asexually.*) ♦ *Asexual reproduction in plants is quite common.* ♦ *Some worms use asexual reproduction.* **2.** *adj.* not involving sex; unaffected by sex. (Adv: *asexually.*) ♦ *Tom lived an essentially asexual existence.* ♦ *Many people view the elderly as asexual, but this is not always so.*

asexually [e 'sɛk ʃu ə li] *adv.* without sexual connection with another organism. ♦ *Many cells reproduce asexually by splitting into two.* ♦ *Fungus reproduces asexually by releasing spores.*

ash ['æʃ] **1.** *n.* what remains after matter has burned or exploded. (Made plural when referring to the individual particles and pieces.) ♦ *Ash from the volcano's eruption drifted down into the village.* ♦ *Your cigarette is leaving ashes all over the table.* **2.** *n.* a tree of the olive family. ♦ *I planted an ash and an oak in the backyard.* ♦ *The ash in front of our house was hit by lightning.* **3.** *n.* the wood of ②. (No plural form in this sense.) ♦ *The carpenter ordered a large shipment of oak, ash, and pine.* ♦ *Don't waste ash by burning it in the fireplace.* **4.** *adj.* made from ③. ♦ *Solid ash paneling is found throughout the house.* ♦ *Ash beams supported the ceiling of the large room.*

ashamed [ə 'ʃemd] *adj.* burdened with guilt, shame, or embarrassment. (Adv: *ashamedly* [ə 'ʃem əd li].) ♦ *The little child was ashamed when she was caught lying.* ♦ *Aren't you ashamed to wear those old clothes?*

ashen ['æʃ ən] *adj.* pale; pallid; drained of color. (Adv: *ashenly.*) ♦ *Jane turned ashen when she heard the bad news.* ♦ *I could tell John was ill by looking at his ashen face.*

ashore [ə 'ʃor] **1.** *adv.* to or onto the shore [from the water]. ♦ *After swimming for an hour, Bob went ashore.* ♦ *Some dead fish washed ashore.* **2.** *adv.* on the beach or on land next to water, as opposed to in or on the water. ♦ *During the boat trip, we stopped and had a barbecue ashore.* ♦ *When we are ashore, you will not feel seasick any longer.*

ashtray ['æʃ tre] *n.* a small bowl for receiving tobacco ashes. ♦ *I made an ashtray in ceramics class.* ♦ *Anne extinguished her cigarette in the metal ashtray.*

Asia ['e ʒə] See Gazetteer.

Asian ['e ʒən] **1.** *n.* a person originating in Asia; a person originating in the eastern part of Eurasia. ♦ *Some of the Asians of the far north are called Eskimos.* ♦ *Many Asians crossed from Siberia to Alaska thousands of years ago.* **2.** *n.* Asians ① originating in the southern and eastern parts of Asia—including China and Japan—and the islands adjacent to this area. (Used as a replacement for *Oriental.*) ♦ *Asians from Japan and China have come to the United States.* ♦ *Many Asians eat with chopsticks.* **3.** *adj.* <an adj. form of ②>; of, from, or about Asia. ♦ *A number of my Asian classmates are from Japan.* ♦ *I love to eat Asian food—especially Chinese food.*

Asiatic [e ʒi 'æt ɪk] *adj.* <an adj. form of Asia.> (Not used for people. Adv: *Asiatically* [...ɪk li].) ♦ *The Asiatic elephant is slightly smaller than the African elephant.* ♦ *There are many Asiatic species of flowers.*

aside [ə 'saɪd] **1.** *n.* an utterance not meant to be heard by all present; a remark made by an actor to the audience; an utterance apart from the main theme. ♦ *The actor's aside made the audience laugh.* ♦ *Shakespeare's plays include many asides.* **2.** *adv.* to the side; to one side; apart from someone or something. ♦ *Please stand aside. You are in the way.* ♦ *Susan moved aside so the cart could pass.* **3.** *adv.* away from oneself; to the side of oneself. ♦ *Susan pushed the textbook aside and began writing her paper.* ♦ *The baby pushed its bottle aside.* **4. aside from** *phr.* except for someone or something; not including someone or something. ♦ *Aside from Alaska and Hawaii, every American state is between Canada and Mexico.* ♦ *Aside from chocolate, Bob's favorite food is steak.* **5. as an aside** *idiom* [said] as a comment that is not supposed to be heard by everyone. (On ①.) ♦ *At the wedding, Tom said as an aside, "The bride doesn't look well."* ♦ *At the ballet, Billy said as an aside to his mother, "I hope the dancers fall off the stage!"*

asinine ['æs ə naɪn] *adj.* ridiculous; very stupid. (Adv: *asininely.*) ♦ *The television show had an asinine plot.* ♦ *The politician's impromptu comments were absolutely asinine.*

ask ['æsk] **1.** *tv.* to put a question to someone. ♦ *Did you ask Dad to buy milk?* ♦ *I asked the visitor her name.* **2.** *tv.* to request information in the form of a question. ♦ *Don't ask that question again.* ♦ *Mary asked, "What time is it?"* **3. ask of** *tv. + prep. phr.* to request something of someone. ♦ *Can I ask a favor of you?* ♦ *What did the manager ask of you?* **4. ask for** *tv. + prep. phr.* to request that someone do something or provide something. ♦ *Can I ask you for some more tea?* ♦ *Mary asked me for a ride to work.* **5. ask about** *tv. + prep. phr.* to question someone about someone or something. ♦ *The suspect was asked about his whereabouts on the night of the accident.* ♦ *I asked Mary about her vacation in Florida.* **6.** *tv.* to invite someone to do something; to suggest that someone do something. ♦ *John asked Mary to the school dance.* ♦ *We asked some friends over for a barbecue.*

askew [ə 'skju] *adj.* slanted; not aligned; twisted. (Not prenominal.) ♦ *I straightened the painting that was askew.* ♦ *The curtain didn't hang properly because the curtain rod was askew.*

asleep [ə 'slip] **1.** *adj.* sleeping; not awake. (Not prenominal.) ♦ *We peeked at the baby while he was asleep.* ♦ *Be quiet. Anne is asleep on the couch.* **2.** *adj.* [of limbs] temporarily not feeling sensation. (Not prenominal.) ♦ *I sat in the same position for too long, and my right leg is now asleep.* ♦ *When my foot is asleep, I cannot walk on it.* **3. asleep at the switch** *idiom* not attending to one's job; failing to do one's duty at the proper time. ♦ *The guard was asleep at the switch when the robber broke in.* ♦ *If I hadn't been asleep at the switch, I'd have noticed the stolen car.*

asocial ['e so ʃəl] *adj.* avoiding other people; shy. (Adv: *asocially.*) ♦ *John is asocial and feels uncomfortable in groups.* ♦ *Sue, who is usually asocial, was surprisingly friendly tonight.*

asparagus [ə 'spɛr ə gəs] *n.* a green vegetable that grows in thin, edible stalks. (No plural form in this sense. Number is expressed with *stalk(s), spear(s),* or *shoot(s) of asparagus.*) ♦ *Asparagus is Bob's favorite vegetable.* ♦ *The restaurant served asparagus with a lemon sauce.*

aspect ['æs pɛkt] **1.** *n.* a way that something can be viewed; a part of the nature of something; a feature or characteristic of something. ♦ *What aspect of your job is most difficult, and what aspect is most rewarding?* ♦ *I asked my lawyer to explain the legal aspects of the problem.* **2.** *n.* a quality of a verb that shows time relationships. ♦ *The aspect of a verb is quite different from its tense.* ♦ *Different aspects express the beginning of an action, the ending of an action, repeating an action, or continuing an action.*

aspersion [ə 'spɚ ʒən] **cast aspersions on someone** *idiom* to make a rude and insulting remark. ♦ *I resent your casting aspersions on my brother and his ability!* ♦ *It is rude to cast aspersions on people in general.*

asphalt ['æs fɔlt] **1.** *n.* a black, tar-like substance used for pavement. (No plural form in this sense.) ♦ *The cracked driveway needs a new coat of asphalt.* ♦ *The asphalt on the road has worn down to a light gray.* **2.** *tv.* to cover the surface of something with asphalt. ♦ *John asphalted his driveway.* ♦ *The workers asphalted the road.*

asphyxiate [æs 'fɪk si et] *tv.* to smother someone or something; to make someone or something unable to breathe. ♦ *I was afraid that the smoke would asphyxiate all of us.* ♦ *The victim had been asphyxiated by the killer.*

asphyxiation [æs fɪk si 'e ʃən] *n.* smothering; suffocation. (No plural form in this sense.) ♦ *I was worried about asphyxiation from all the cigarette smoke.* ♦ *Asphyxiation is a horrible way to die.*

aspirant [æ 'spaɪ rənt] *n.* someone with an ambition to be or do something. ♦ *The divinity student was an aspirant to the ministry.* ♦ *David's brother—a very eager aspirant—hopes to get a part in the play.*

aspirate ['æs pə ret] *tv.* to clear a body cavity of fluid through suction. ♦ *The doctor aspirated the newborn's throat soon after birth.* ♦ *A nurse had to aspirate the lungs of the pneumonia patient.*

aspiration [æs pə 're ʃən] **1.** *n.* an ambition; a wish or desire. ♦ *Children often have big aspirations.* ♦ *Jane worked eighty hours a week to fulfill her aspirations.* **2.** *n.* a forced puff of air after a speech sound, such as after the [p] in "puff." (No plural form in this sense.) ♦ *Three of the English consonants can have aspiration when they are pronounced.* ♦ *When you say "top," the [t] is pronounced with heavy aspiration.*

aspire [ə 'spaɪr] *iv.* to have the ambition to do or be something. ♦ *Whoever thought that Bill would aspire to be president?* ♦ *I aspire to being the president of a bank.*

aspirin ['æs prɪn] *n.* a medication for relieving pain, used especially for headaches. (Can be plural when referring to individual tablets.) ♦ *I took two aspirin when I got to work because I knew it was going to be a difficult day.* ♦ *The nurse gave me an aspirin for my headache.*

aspiring [ə 'spaɪr ɪŋ] *adj.* having the ambition to be something; having aspirations. (Adv: *aspiringly.*) ♦ *The aspiring actress worked as a waitress during the day.* ♦ *The aspiring medical students listened carefully to the lecture.*

ass ['æs] **1.** *n.* a long-eared animal that is similar to a horse; a donkey. ♦ *The folk painting showed a man riding an ass.* ♦ *Asses are strong animals that can carry a heavy load.* **2.** *n.* a stubborn and foolish person. (Derogatory.) ♦ *Bob acted like an ass at the party and embarrassed his date.* ♦ *Oh, stop being such an ass and behave like a responsible adult!* **3.** *n.* the buttocks, rump, or backside. (Vulgar.) ♦ *Bill threatened to kick Max in the ass.* ♦ *Max slipped on the ice and fell on his ass.*

assail [ə 'sel] **1.** *tv.* to attack someone or something. ♦ *The shopkeeper assailed the thief with curses and kicking.* ♦ *A police officer assailed the crook with a baton.* **2.** *tv.* to criticize someone or something strongly. ♦ *The public assailed the newspaper editor for his editorial on smoking.* ♦ *Angry voices assailed the mayor for her lack of honesty.*

assailant [ə 'sel ənt] *n.* someone who attacks someone or something. ♦ *The assailant was apprehended not far from the crime scene.* ♦ *Did the victim know his assailant?*

assassin [ə 'sæs ən] *n.* someone who murders someone, especially for political purposes. ♦ *The spy was a trained assassin.* ♦ *An assassin tried to kill the president.*

assassinate [ə 'sæs ə net] *tv.* to murder someone, usually for political reasons. ♦ *The spy overheard a plot to assassinate the president.* ♦ *A horrible war began when the terrorist assassinated a government official.*

assassination [ə sæs ə 'ne ʃən] *n.* the murder of someone famous or important, especially for political reasons. ♦ *The nation was shocked by the president's assassination.* ♦ *The revolution began with the assassination of several government leaders.*

assault [ə 'sɔlt] **1.** *tv.* to attack someone. ♦ *The mugger assaulted his victims as they waited for the bus.* ♦ *Mike very unwisely assaulted a police officer.* **2.** *tv.* to attack someone sexually. ♦ *Mary testified against the man who had assaulted her.* ♦ *The man who tried to assault the woman was beaten by people who came to her aid.* **3.** *n.* an act of attacking someone or something. ♦ *Bob was arrested for an assault on an elderly person.* ♦ *The criminal was charged with assault with a deadly weapon.* **4.** *adj.* <the adj. use of ③.> ♦ *Congress debated banning assault weapons.* ♦ *The troops underwent three weeks of assault training.*

assay 1. ['æ se] *n.* an analysis of a metallic ore to determine its purity. ♦ *The assay showed the ore to be worthless.* ♦ *When the assay was completed, the sample was determined to be mostly silver.* **2.** [ə 'se] *tv.* to test a metallic ore for purity. ♦ *The technician assayed the sample and gave the results to the prospector.* ♦ *Hurry, take this sample into town to be assayed.*

assemblage [ə 'sɛm blɪdʒ] *n.* a group of people or things gathered together. ♦ *At the special event we found an assemblage of the town's most prominent citizens.* ♦ *Can the detectives interpret this assemblage of seemingly unrelated facts?*

assemble [ə 'sɛm bəl] **1.** *tv.* to bring things or people into a collection or group. ♦ *I assembled all the ingredients for the cake.* ♦ *After assembling the things he needed, Bob baked a beautiful cake.* **2.** *tv.* to put something together; to construct something from its parts. ♦ *The clerk assembled the bicycle for a $25 charge.* ♦ *It was difficult to assemble the miniature airplane.*

assembled [ə 'sɛm bəld] **1.** *adj.* put together; fitted together out of parts. ♦ *The assembled dollhouse was hidden in the attic until Jane's birthday.* ♦ *The instructions showed how the assembled bike should look.* **2.** *adj.* collected together. ♦ *The assembled crowd demanded a speech from the president.* ♦ *The assembled club members waited for the meeting to begin.*

assembly [ə 'sɛm bli] **1.** *n.* a meeting, especially a large one. ♦ *An assembly was called so that everyone could vote on the issue.* ♦ *The students were required to attend weekly assemblies in the school's auditorium.* **2.** *n.* putting something together. (No plural form in this sense.) ♦ *Assembly of the model plane required parts not included in the kit.* ♦ *The toy company's catalog noted that assembly was required for many of the toys.* **3.** *n.* [in some U.S. states] the lower house of the legislature. ♦ *The general assembly tabled several items on the agenda.* ♦ *The state assembly has finished meeting for the year.*

assent [ə 'sɛnt] **1.** *n.* an agreement; an affirmation. (No plural form in this sense.) ♦ *Bob refused to give his assent to the proposal.* ♦ *John's assent was needed in order for the meeting to continue.* **2.** *iv.* to agree to something. ♦ *John assented, and everything went as had been planned.* ♦ *Bob refused to assent to the proposal.*

assert [ə 'sɚt] **1.** *tv.* to claim something as a fact; to state something positively. ♦ *The lawyer asserted that his client was innocent.* ♦ *Jane strongly asserted her opinion about the election.* **2.** *tv.* to make one's control or authority evident; to insist on one's rights. (Takes a reflexive object.) ♦ *Mary asserted herself and said that she would not work overtime.* ♦ *At midnight, John finally asserted himself and insisted that his guests go home.*

assertion [ə 'sɚ ʃən] *n.* a claim; something that is said or claimed. ♦ *The witness's assertion that the suspect was innocent was a turning point in the case.* ♦ *The journalist withdrew her assertions in a printed apology.*

assertive [ə 'sɚ tɪv] *adj.* forceful; direct. (Adv: *assertively.*) ♦ *Assertive people generally get what they want.* ♦ *Try to act confident and assertive during a job interview.*

assertiveness [ə 'ʃɚ tɪv nəs] *n.* forceful and direct behavior. (No plural form in this sense.) ♦ *Sometimes assertiveness can be perceived as rudeness.* ♦ *The managers took courses that trained them in assertiveness.*

assess [ə 'sɛs] **1.** *tv.* to determine the state or amount of something. ♦ *It took a while to assess the damage from the tornado.* ♦ *A consultant was hired to assess the company's problems.* **2.** *tv.* to assign a value to property for the purpose of taxing it. ♦ *The assessor assessed the property at much less than it was worth.* ♦ *The Smiths' house was assessed at $250,000.* **3.** *tv.* to charge someone a sum of money, often as a tax. ♦ *The city assessed each home owner for the cost of the new sidewalks.* ♦ *The condominium owners were assessed for the cost of the improvements.*

assessment [ə 'sɛs mənt] **1.** *n.* an amount of money that is owed annually. ♦ *The tax assessment was much higher than we had thought it would be.* ♦ *My club dues included a special assessment for new furniture for the lounge.* **2.** *n.* the analysis of a situation; an evaluation of something; a determination of something. ♦ *The mechanic's assessment was that the car couldn't be fixed.* ♦ *What is your assessment of the situation?*

assessor [ə 'sɛs ɚ] *n.* someone who determines the value of property for taxation or insurance. ♦ *The assessor underestimated the worth of the property.* ♦ *The tax assessor claims that we have a basement, but we don't.*

asset ['æ sɛt] **1.** *n.* an item of value; an item of property. ♦ *The Joneses lived so simply that no one guessed their assets were so large.* ♦ *The loan application asked about the applicant's assets.* **2.** *n.* a useful skill; a useful quality. ♦ *Her excellent reasoning skill is a great asset in her job.* ♦ *My sense of direction was an asset when I got lost.*

assiduous [ə 'sɪ dʒu əs] *adj.* persevering; diligent; attentive. (Adv: *assiduously.*) ♦ *The assiduous student worked hard to earn her degree.* ♦ *Through years of assiduous research, the scientists finally found a cure for the disease.*

assign [ə 'saɪn] **1. assign to** *tv.* + *prep. phr.* to designate someone for something. ♦ *The manager assigned Bill to the Jones project.* ♦ *Two cops are assigned to each squad car.* **2. assign to** *tv.* + *prep. phr.* to allocate something to someone. ♦ *The manager assigned the Jones contract to Bill.* ♦ *Certain household chores were assigned to each child.* **3. assign to** *tv.* + *prep. phr.* to transfer something to someone under law. ♦ *The court assigned the widow's assets to her granddaughter.* ♦ *According to the contract, the publishers cannot assign the book's copyright to anyone else.*

assignable [ə 'saɪn ə bəl] *adj.* able to be transferred. ♦ *This contract is assignable only if the company is sold.* ♦ *These insurance benefits are assignable to the hospital.*

assigned [ə 'saɪnd] *adj.* appointed; allocated. ♦ *The students sat in their assigned seats.* ♦ *The schedule listed the assigned tasks for each person.*

assignment [ə 'saɪn mənt] **1.** *n.* a job or a task that has been assigned to someone. ♦ *The editor had a new assignment for the reporter.* ♦ *I have a large assignment for history class.* **2.** *n.* the legal transfer of something from someone to someone else. (No plural form in this sense.) ♦ *The contract permitted the assignment of the property.* ♦ *The insurance contract does not permit assignment of the benefits.*

assimilate [ə 'sɪm ə let] **1.** *tv.* to absorb something; to incorporate something into one's own thinking, behavior, or body. ♦ *I have not quite assimilated the new rules, so I sometimes violate them by mistake.* ♦ *I cannot assimilate all this new information so quickly.* **2.** *tv.* to incorporate someone or something into a culture or group. ♦ *The friendly community readily assimilated the new immigrants.* ♦ *The company quickly assimilated the new employees.*

assimilation [ə sɪm ə 'le ʃən] *n.* becoming a part of something else. (No plural form in this sense.) ♦ *The assimilation of so many immigrants strained the small town's resources.* ♦ *The assimilation of so many facts was very difficult for John.*

assist [ə 'sɪst] **1.** *tv.* to help someone or something; to help someone with something. ♦ *A nurse assisted the surgeon during the operation.* ♦ *If you will assist me in writing this report, I will assist you with your next project.* **2.** *n.* an act of assistance. ♦ *The visiting accountant gave Bill a much-needed assist in his bookkeeping.* ♦ *Thanks to his teammate's assist, the athlete was able to score the winning goal.*

assistance [ə 'sɪs təns] *n.* help; aid; cooperation. (No plural form in this sense.) ♦ *The agency offered financial assistance to single mothers.* ♦ *The government asked for the assistance of the Army during the riots.*

assistant [ə 'sɪs tənt] *n.* someone who helps someone; someone whose job is to help someone. ♦ *The editor hired an assistant to work on the manuscripts.* ♦ *The bank president began her career as an assistant to a loan officer.*

associate 1. [ə 'so si ət] *n.* a colleague; someone who works with someone else. ♦ *John ran into an associate from work at the concert.* ♦ *Anne ate lunch with a business associate.* **2.** [ə 'so si ət] *adj.* [of a job or position] not at the highest level, but typically at a higher level than an assistant. ♦ *Mary is an associate editor at a publishing house.* ♦ *The associate sales manager left the meeting early.* **3.** [ə 'so si et] *iv.* to make social contact with someone. ♦ *I do not associate with people who use vulgar language.* ♦ *John and his coworkers do not associate on weekends.* **4. associate with** [ə 'so si et...] *tv.* + *prep. phr.* to connect thoughts about two things mentally; to think of something because something else has reminded one of it. ♦ *I always associate orange juice with breakfast.* ♦ *Tom associates the sound of the sea with swimming.*

association [ə so si 'e ʃən] **1.** *n.* a connection or link between two things, people, or thoughts. ♦ *What is the nature of your association with the organization?* ♦ *The dog made an association between hearing a bell and receiving food.* **2.** *n.* an organization; an alliance. ♦ *The athletic association sold candy to raise money.* ♦ *The reference book listed all the medical associations in the country.* **3.** *n.* a friendship; a relationship. ♦ *The two poets wrote letters for years and formed a close association.* ♦ *Business relationships often lead to close personal associations.*

associative [ə 'so si ə tɪv] *adj.* connecting; resulting from associating. (Adv: *associatively.*) ♦ *Jane formed an associative link between snow and Christmas.* ♦ *Bill, who lacks associative powers, could not see the connection between candy and dental pain.*

assorted [ə 'sort ɪd] *adj.* various; mixed. (Adv: *assortedly.*) ♦ *I bought a box of assorted chocolates.* ♦ *The store sold ice cream in assorted flavors.*

assortment [ə 'sort mənt] *n.* a collection of different types of things; a mix of things. ♦ *The eccentric woman has an assortment of pets.* ♦ *The orchestra played an assortment of pieces.*

assume [ə 'sum] **1.** *tv.* to take something for granted; to suppose something is true. ♦ *Mary mistakenly assumed that she would get the job.* ♦ *A pessimist usually assumes the worst.* **2.** *tv.* to take control of something; to move into a role of leadership or responsibility for something. ♦ *The prince assumed the throne after the king's death.* ♦ *The vice president assumed the presidency after the assassination.*

assumption [ə 'sʌmp ʃən] **1.** *n.* something that is taken for granted; something that is accepted as true without question. ♦ *My assumption was that you would remember the appointment, so I didn't remind you.* ♦ *People often make assumptions that turn out to be false.* **2.** *n.* the taking on of something, especially responsibility, power, or a particular role, usually of leadership. (No plural form in this sense.) ♦ *The rebels' sudden assumption of power shocked the small nation.* ♦ *The vice president's assumption of the presidency occurred as soon as the president died.*

assurance [ə 'ʃʊr əns] **1.** *n.* a promise; a guarantee; a pledge of support. ♦ *Tom gave his assurance that he would not be late.* ♦ *Despite all your assurances, I still don't believe that you will pay me back.* **2.** *n.* confidence. (No plural form in this sense.) ♦ *The experienced teacher had an air of assurance.* ♦ *"I'm positive that John's birthday is today," Jane said with assurance.*

assure [ə 'ʃʊr] *tv.* to make a guarantee to someone about something; to promise someone something. ♦ *Bob assured me that he would pay back the loan.* ♦ *The doctor assured the patient that everything would be all right.*

assuredly [ə 'ʃʊr əd li] *adv.* surely; certainly; without a doubt. ♦ *The guard told the prisoners that any attempt to escape would assuredly fail.* ♦ *This is assuredly the worst movie I have ever seen.*

aster ['æs tɚ] *n.* one of a number of flowering herbs that bloom in the fall. ♦ *Asters can have white, pink, blue, or purple flowers.* ♦ *The asters bloomed well into the early fall.*

asterisk ['æs tə rɪsk] *n.* a starlike symbol (*) that is typically used to highlight something or to direct the reader's attention to a related note. ♦ *Jane put an asterisk by the most important points in her report.* ♦ *Asterisks on the supervisor's list indicated which people were getting raises.*

asthma ['æz mə] *n.* an illness involving difficulty in breathing. (No plural form in this sense.) ♦ *The child with asthma could not take gym class.* ♦ *Bob's asthma is aggravated by cigarette smoke.*

asthmatic [æz 'mæt ɪk] *adj.* <the adjective form of asthma.> (Adv: *asthmatically* [...ɪk li].) ♦ *The asthmatic child couldn't run very far.* ♦ *His breathing sounds asthmatic, and he should see a doctor.*

astigmatic [e stɪg 'mæt ɪk] *adj.* of or about **astigmatism**. (Adv: *astigmatically* [...ɪk li].) ♦ *The optician told me that my right eye was astigmatic.* ♦ *My eyes are astigmatic, so I wear glasses.*

astigmatism [ə 'stɪg mə tɪz əm] *n.* an irregularity in the lens of the eye that causes vision to be distorted. ♦ *The optometrist told Mary she had an astigmatism in her left eye.* ♦ *Bob wears glasses to correct his astigmatism.*

astonish [ə 'stɑn ɪʃ] *tv.* to surprise someone; to amaze someone. ♦ *The magician astonished the children.* ♦ *The ending of the book will astonish you.*

astonished [ə 'stɑn ɪʃt] *adj.* amazed; surprised. (Adv: *astonishedly.*) ♦ *The astonished audience applauded the magician.* ♦ *A hush fell over the astonished crowd as the governor announced his resignation.*

astonishing [ə 'stɑn ɪʃ ɪŋ] *adj.* amazing; surprising. (Adv: *astonishingly.*) ♦ *Highly skilled and gracious, Jane is an astonishing woman.* ♦ *The crime rate in the city is simply astonishing.*

astonishment [ə 'stɑn ɪʃ mənt] *n.* surprise; extreme amazement. (No plural form in this sense.) ♦ *She was speechless in astonishment over winning the lottery.* ♦ *To his parents' astonishment, Bob announced that he was getting married.*

astound [ə 'staʊnd] *tv.* to surprise someone; to amaze someone. ♦ *The scientist astounded his colleagues with the experiment.* ♦ *The daredevil astounded the audience with a dangerous feat.*

astounding [ə 'staʊn dɪŋ] *adj.* amazing; surprising. (Adv: *astoundingly.*) ♦ *The astounding discovery won fame for the scientist.* ♦ *The athlete's astounding popularity surpassed that of any movie star.*

astride [ə 'strɑɪd] *prep.* sitting or standing on top of something with one leg on either side. ♦ *The girl's feet just reached the pedals when she sat astride the bicycle.* ♦ *The princess rode sidesaddle, rather than astride the horse.*

astrologer [ə 'strɑl ə dʒɚ] *n.* someone who practices astrology. ♦ *The astrologer described how my future might be.* ♦ *The astrologer asked for John's date of birth so she could predict his future.*

astrological [æs trə 'lɑdʒ ɪ kəl] *adj.* relating to the practice of astrology. (Adv: *astrologically* [...ɪk li].) ♦ *Jane read astrological predictions about her future.* ♦ *A little shop in the alley sold astrological maps.*

astrology [ə 'strɑl ə dʒi] *n.* using the positions of stars and planets to predict the future. (No plural form in this sense.) ♦ *Astrology is an ancient art.* ♦ *Many people do not believe the predictions of astrology.*

astronaut ['æs trə nɑt] *n.* someone who is trained to travel in space. ♦ *In 1969, astronauts walked on the moon for the first time.* ♦ *Astronauts receive years of scientific training.*

astronomer [ə 'strɑn ə mɚ] *n.* someone who studies astronomy. ♦ *The astronomer saw a new comet through a telescope.* ♦ *The astronomer at the planetarium gave a lecture about the history of the universe.*

astronomic [æs trə 'nɑm ɪk] **1.** *adj.* relating to astronomy. (Adv: *astronomically* [...ɪk li].) ♦ *The scientist offered an astronomic explanation for the strange lights we had seen in the sky.* ♦ *The team used the powerful telescope for astronomic research.* **2.** *adj.* immense; huge; incredibly large. (Figurative on ①. Adv: *astronomically* [...ɪk li].) ♦ *The car-repair bill was astronomic.* ♦ *The economist predicted an astronomic increase in unemployment.*

astronomical [æs trə 'nɑm ɪ kəl] **1.** *adj.* relating to astronomy. (Adv: *astronomically* [...ɪk li].) ♦ *The astronomical observatory was built near the top of the mountain.* ♦ *Congress appropriated funds for astronomical research.* **2.** *adj.* immense; huge; incredibly large. (Figurative on ①. Adv: *astronomically* [...ɪk li].) ♦ *An astronomical amount of money is wasted on ineffective medicine.* ♦ *The catering bill for the wedding was astronomical.*

astronomy [ə 'strɑn ə mi] *n.* the study of the universe and the objects in it, such as stars and planets. (No plural form in this sense.) ♦ *Because I was interested in stars, I bought a book about astronomy.* ♦ *I took a class in astronomy at the local planetarium.*

astrophysicist [æs tro 'fɪz ə səst] *n.* someone who studies astrophysics. ♦ *The astrophysicist speculated about the origin of the solar system.* ♦ *Astrophysicists study the physical properties of the universe.*

astrophysics [æs tro 'fɪz ɪks] *n.* the study of the physical properties of the universe and of the objects in it, such as stars and planets. (Treated as singular.) ♦ *Astrophysics deals with the entire universe.* ♦ *To earn a degree in astrophysics, Mary took many courses in advanced mathematics.*

astute [ə 'stut] *adj.* clever; wise; intelligent; observant; insightful. (Adv: *astutely.*) ♦ *The astute reader noticed that* *the author had ignored a crucial fact.* ♦ *The boss appreciated Mary's astute observations about how to improve the company's image.*

astuteness [ə 'stut nəs] *n.* shrewdness; intelligence; wisdom. (No plural form in this sense.) ♦ *The advice columnist was well known for her astuteness about human nature.* ♦ *John's astuteness enabled him to make the most lucrative business deals.*

asylum [ə 'sɑɪ ləm] **1.** *n.* a place of refuge or shelter, often a country; a state or condition of safety. (No plural form in this sense.) ♦ *The refugee requested asylum when she entered the country.* ♦ *The three brothers sought asylum in a European country.* **2.** *n.* an institution for the mentally ill; a place where the mentally ill can live. ♦ *The asylum housed hundreds of patients in simple rooms.* ♦ *The insane criminal spent most of his life in an asylum.*

at [æt] **1.** *prep.* located on a point or in a place. (Used to show location in time or space.) ♦ *We will meet you at the café at three o'clock.* ♦ *The children waited at the corner for the bus.* **2.** *prep.* in the direction of; toward. ♦ *Bill threw a rock at the window.* ♦ *I sent a warning look at John when he yawned.* **3.** *prep.* engaged in; in a state of being. ♦ *The yellow sign warned that there were men at work.* ♦ *The children at play were covered with dirt.* **4.** *prep.* toward. (Used to show the object of an emotion.) ♦ *Yesterday, my teacher was mad at me.* ♦ *Sue got annoyed at me for giving her bad directions.*

ate ['et] pt of eat.

atheism ['e θi ɪz əm] *n.* the belief that there is no God or supreme being. (No plural form in this sense.) ♦ *Despite his atheism, Bill liked studying the history of religions.* ♦ *Anne's atheism contrasted with her friend's strong religious beliefs.*

atheist ['e θi əst] *n.* someone who believes that there is no God or supreme being. ♦ *The atheist argued with the Christian about religion.* ♦ *Bill is an atheist and does not attend church.*

atheistic [e θi 'ɪs tɪk] *adj.* relating to atheism. (Adv: *atheistically* [...ɪk li].) ♦ *Tom's parents are very religious and are puzzled by his atheistic beliefs.* ♦ *The religious leaders discussed the atheistic tendencies in modern-day society.*

athlete ['æθ lit] *n.* someone who participates in sports actively, especially a team member. ♦ *An athlete must eat well and exercise often.* ♦ *The soccer team consists of a dozen well-trained athletes.*

athlete's foot ['æθ lits fʊt] *n.* a fungal infection of the skin of the feet. (No plural form in this sense.) ♦ *The members of the track team all got athlete's foot.* ♦ *Walking barefoot in the locker room gave me athlete's foot.*

athletic [æθ 'lɛt ɪk] **1.** *adj.* strong; active; in good physical condition. (Adv: *athletically* [...ɪk li].) ♦ *The athletic old man ran five miles each day.* ♦ *Until she discovered tennis, Jane never thought of herself as athletic.* **2.** *adj.* relating to athletes; in or for athletics ③. (Adv: *athletically* [...ɪk li].) ♦ *Bill is naturally a fast runner, but he hasn't had any athletic training.* ♦ *The university's athletic facilities attracted many students.* **3. athletics** *n.* active sports; exercise and training associated with sports. (Treated as singular or plural.) ♦ *The quiet scholar never cared for athletics.* ♦ *Mary spent a lot of time participating in athletics and outdoor activities.*

Atlantic Ocean [æt 'læn tɪk 'o ʃən] See Gazetteer.

atlas ['æt ləs] *n.* a book of maps. ♦ *As a child, Bob loved to look at atlases and take journeys in his mind.* ♦ *The Smiths took a road atlas on their trip in case they got lost.*

atmosphere ['æt məs fɪr] **1.** *n.* the mixture of gases that surrounds a planet, especially the air that surrounds Earth. (No plural form in this sense.) ♦ *The earth's atmosphere is many miles thick.* ♦ *The scientists determined that the atmosphere was getting more polluted.* **2.** *n.* the air in the immediate vicinity; the air that one is breathing. (No plural form in this sense.) ♦ *The atmosphere was thick with smog and dust.* ♦ *The atmosphere in the room was heavy with cigarette smoke.* **3.** *n.* the mood or feeling in a particular place. ♦ *The Smiths' favorite restaurant has a friendly, relaxed atmosphere.* ♦ *The atmosphere at the conference was so formal that I started calling everyone "Sir" or "Ma'am."*

atmospheric [æt məs 'fɛr ɪk] *adj.* relating to the atmosphere. (Adv: *atmospherically* [...ɪk li].) ♦ *Atmospheric conditions may cause many airplane flights to be delayed or canceled today.* ♦ *A change in atmospheric pressure indicated that a storm was approaching.*

atom ['æt əm] *n.* the smallest component of an element having the chemical properties of the element. ♦ *An atom is made up of protons, neutrons, and one or more electrons.* ♦ *A molecule of water has two atoms of hydrogen and one atom of oxygen.*

atomic [ə 'tɑm ɪk] **1.** *adj.* of or about atoms. (Adv: *atomically* [...ɪk li].) ♦ *This chart gives the symbol and the atomic weight for each element.* ♦ *The scientist wrote a paper about the atomic structure of uranium.* **2.** *adj.* using the energy from the atom; using nuclear energy. (Adv: *atomically* [...ɪk li].) ♦ *The scientists constructed an atomic bomb.* ♦ *The bomb can create an enormous atomic explosion.*

atomizer ['æt ə mɑɪ zɚ] *n.* a device that changes a liquid into a spray or a mist. ♦ *The perfume bottle came with an atomizer.* ♦ *The singer used an atomizer to moisten his throat with water.*

atone [ə 'ton] **atone for** *iv.* + *prep. phr.* to make amends for something; to make right something that one has done wrong. ♦ *There was no way Tom could atone for the wrong he had done.* ♦ *Jane felt the need to atone for her misdeeds.*

atonement [ə 'ton mənt] *n.* making up for something; an act performed to make up for having done something wrong. (No plural form in this sense.) ♦ *As an act of atonement, he apologized and replaced the broken vase.* ♦ *Mary's atonement was inadequate, and Bill became angry.*

atop [ə 'tɑp] *prep.* on top of something. ♦ *Atop the post was an ornament in the shape of an eagle.* ♦ *We put five blankets on the bed, one atop the other.*

atria ['e tri ə] the Latin plural of atrium.

atrium ['e tri əm] *n., irreg.* a large open space inside a building, often with a glass ceiling that allows light in. (Pl: atria or *atriums*.) ♦ *Mary bought a house with an atrium in it.* ♦ *Ancient Roman houses often had an atrium in the center.*

atrocious [ə 'tro ʃəs] *adj.* disgusting; horrifying; shockingly bad. (Adv: *atrociously*.) ♦ *The living conditions in the* *refugee camp were atrocious.* ♦ *The murderer's atrocious crimes shocked the world.*

atrociousness [ə 'tro ʃəs nəs] *n.* shocking cruelty. (No plural form in this sense.) ♦ *The atrociousness of the crime made us angry.* ♦ *We could not believe the atrociousness of the suggestion.*

atrocity [ə 'trɑs ə ti] **1.** *n.* a specific act of cruelty. ♦ *The soldiers were tried for the atrocities they committed during the war.* ♦ *The atrocities involved in the crime sickened the jury.* **2.** *n.* something done very badly. (Figurative on ①.) ♦ *The first half of the movie was an atrocity. The second half was even worse.* ♦ *That ugly building is both an atrocity and a monstrosity.*

atrophy ['æ trə fi] *iv.* to wither from lack of use; to grow limp. ♦ *The bedridden patient's muscles began to atrophy.* ♦ *Severe nerve damage caused the patient's limbs to atrophy.*

attach [ə 'tætʃ] **1.** *tv.* to fasten something to something else. ♦ *Heavy thread attached the buttons firmly to my winter coat.* ♦ *Bill attached a big bow to the birthday present.* **2.** *tv.* to assign a quality to someone or something; to attribute something to someone or something. ♦ *Tom attached all the blame to me.* ♦ *I attach no significance to this matter.*

attached [ə 'tætʃt] **1.** *adj.* connected to something. ♦ *Please study the attached report.* ♦ *This letter and the attached photographs should be filed in a safe place.* **2.** *adj.* married; in a steady romantic relationship with one person. ♦ *Is the new employee attached or single?* ♦ *Bob said he couldn't accept the offer of a date because he's already attached.* **3. attached to someone or something** *idiom* fond of something or something. ♦ *John is really attached to his old-fashioned ideas.* ♦ *I'm really attached to this old house.*

attachment [ə 'tætʃ mənt] **1.** *n.* an auxiliary piece of equipment that connects to the main piece. ♦ *The vacuum cleaner has six different attachments.* ♦ *Does this electric mixer have an attachment for grinding nuts?* **2.** *n.* affection for someone or something; a bond. ♦ *John has a strong attachment to his old-fashioned ideas.* ♦ *Mary has such an attachment to the old house that she'll never sell it.*

attack [ə 'tæk] **1.** *tv.* to try to harm someone or something, physically or verbally. ♦ *The journalist attacked the politician with questions.* ♦ *Our dog attacked the neighbor's cat.* **2.** *tv.* to begin work on a problem. (Figurative on ①.) ♦ *The children attacked their homework after dinner.* ♦ *The houseguests attacked the puzzle with enthusiasm.* **3.** *n.* an act of violence against someone or something, physical or verbal. ♦ *The attack left the victim with a broken arm.* ♦ *Did the cat survive the attack by the neighbor's dog?* **4.** *n.* a sudden period of sickness or disease. ♦ *Bob had an attack of appendicitis.* ♦ *After a severe asthma attack, Jane went to the doctor.*

attain [ə 'ten] *tv.* to reach a goal; to get something. ♦ *The museum attained its goal for the restoration by raising three million dollars.* ♦ *John finally attained the degree he sought for so many years in college.*

attainability [ə ten ə 'bɪl ə ti] *n.* the potential for something to be attained; the probability of a goal being reached. (No plural form in this sense.) ♦ *Jane doubted the attainability of a new vase just like the one she had broken.* ♦ *Many people set goals without considering their attainability.*

attainable [ə 'ten ə bəl] *adj.* able to be reached or achieved; able to be acquired. (Adv: *attainably.*) ♦ *Jane's goal of quitting smoking was attainable.* ♦ *The director of the charity felt that raising a million dollars was an attainable goal.*

attainment [ə 'ten mənt] *n.* the achievement of something. (No plural form in this sense.) ♦ *Attainment of the Olympic gold medal thrilled the athlete.* ♦ *Mary was pleased at her attainment of the promotion.*

attempt [ə 'tɛmpt] **1.** *n.* an effort to do something; a try at doing something. ♦ *The teacher suggested that the student make an attempt at writing the essay.* ♦ *My attempt to make a cake failed miserably.* **2.** *tv.* to make an effort at doing something. ♦ *The paramedics attempted the resuscitation of the boy.* ♦ *I attempted a second try, being more careful this time.* **3. attempt to** *iv.* + *inf.* to try to do something. ♦ *Max attempted to resuscitate the boy.* ♦ *We will attempt to do it better this time.*

attempted [ə 'tɛmp tɪd] *adj.* [having been] tried, especially unsuccessfully. ♦ *Tom's attempted evasion of responsibility failed.* ♦ *The police responded to a call about an attempted murder.*

attend [ə 'tɛnd] **1.** *tv.* to be present at a place or event; to be present somewhere over a period of time. ♦ *Two hundred people attended the wedding.* ♦ *Bob attended school until he was 17.* **2. attend to** *iv.* + *prep. phr.* to stay with and care for someone. ♦ *Mary has attended to her ailing grandmother for years.* ♦ *She attended to her grandmother's needs with loving care.* **3. attend to** *iv.* + *prep. phr.* to deal with someone or something; to manage something. ♦ *All the details of the party have been attended to.* ♦ *Please attend to the customers waiting in line.*

attendance [ə 'tɛn dəns] **1.** *n.* someone's presence at a location or event. (No plural form in this sense.) ♦ *Attendance at the meeting is mandatory.* ♦ *His attendance at the meeting wasn't even noticed by the other members.* **2.** *n.* the number of people present; the identity of the people attending something. (No plural form in this sense.) ♦ *Attendance was quite good at the fair—thousands came.* ♦ *Was there a large attendance at the baseball game?* **3. take attendance** *phr.* to make a record of persons attending something. ♦ *The teacher took attendance before starting the class.* ♦ *I will take attendance each day.* **4.** *adj.* <the adj. use of ①.> ♦ *The company has a strict attendance policy.* ♦ *The employee's attendance rate is getting worse.*

attendant [ə 'tɛn dənt] *n.* someone who assists or helps someone else, especially someone important. ♦ *The president was surrounded by his attendants and secretaries.* ♦ *The queen's attendants went everywhere with her.*

attention [ə 'tɛn ʃən] **1.** *n.* careful consideration; focus of awareness. (No plural form in this sense.) ♦ *After our vacation, we turned our attention to work.* ♦ *Special attention was given to the elderly at the church.* **2. attentions** *n.* ① that indicates a romantic interest. ♦ *Mary did not like the waiter's attentions.* ♦ *John turned his attentions toward his single neighbor.* **3. pay attention (to someone or something)** *idiom* to give attention (to someone or something). ♦ *Please pay attention to the teacher.* ♦ *Max always pays careful attention to what is being told to him.*

attentive [ə 'tɛn tɪv] *adj.* observant; paying attention; aware. (Adv: *attentively.*) ♦ *The psychologist was atten-*

tive to his client's words. ♦ *The teacher enjoyed teaching the attentive students.*

attentiveness [ə 'tɛn tɪv nəs] *n.* careful attention; alert awareness. (No plural form in this sense.) ♦ *John's lack of attentiveness almost got him fired.* ♦ *Jane was hired because of her attentiveness to detail.*

attic ['æt ɪk] *n.* the room at the top of a house, just under the roof. ♦ *Grandma's attic is full of old clothes.* ♦ *The attic of our house is a large room with slanted walls.*

attire [ə 'taɪr] **1.** *n.* clothes, especially formal or very good clothing. (No plural form in this sense.) ♦ *Bob inquired as to what proper attire for the party would be.* ♦ *The members of the wedding party all bought special attire to wear at the wedding.* **2.** *tv.* to dress someone in formal or elegant clothing. (Formal.) ♦ *The executive attired herself in expensive clothing.* ♦ *Jimmy's mom had attired him in a tiny suit.*

attitude ['æt ə tud] **1.** *n.* a way of thinking, behaving, or feeling. ♦ *John's attitude about his job improved when he was promoted.* ♦ *The clerk had a bad attitude and treated customers poorly.* **2.** *n.* a particular position, especially of an aircraft. ♦ *The attitude of an airplane as it lands is very important to a successful landing.* ♦ *A computer controls the attitude of the aircraft.* **3. wait-and-see attitude** *idiom* a skeptical attitude; an uncertain attitude in which someone will just wait to see what happens before reacting. ♦ *John thought that Mary couldn't do it, but he took a wait-and-see attitude.* ♦ *His wait-and-see attitude seemed to indicate that he didn't really care what happened.*

attorney [ə 'tɚ ni] *n.* a lawyer. ♦ *Bob hired an attorney to get a patent for his invention.* ♦ *Mary went to law school and became an attorney.*

attorney general [ə 'tɚ ni 'dʒɛn (ə) rəl] *n., irreg.* the chief legal officer of a governmental body. (Pl: attorneys general or sometimes *attorney generals.*) ♦ *The attorney general was accused of taking bribes.* ♦ *The president appointed a new attorney general.*

attorneys general [ə 'tɚ niz 'dʒɛn (ə) rəl] a pl of attorney general.

attract [ə 'trækt] *tv.* to draw someone or something closer; to get the attention of someone or something. ♦ *The picnic food attracted many ants.* ♦ *The sculpture attracted pedestrians, and a crowd formed around it.*

attraction [ə 'træk ʃən] **1.** *n.* the process or quality of drawing interest, attention, customers, etc. (No plural form in this sense.) ♦ *I don't understand the attraction of that new restaurant. It's not very good.* ♦ *The university spent a lot of money on the attraction of new students.* **2.** *n.* something that delights or draws interest or attention. ♦ *The attractions at the theme park caused thousands of people to come last weekend.* ♦ *People are lined up to see the latest attraction at the movie theater.* **3.** *n.* the force that draws people or things together. ♦ *Bob's attraction to Sue did not last long.* ♦ *Bob's mother noticed an attraction between Bob and Mary.*

attractive [ə 'træk tɪv] *adj.* pretty; pleasing to the eye; handsome; arousing interest. (Adv: *attractively.*) ♦ *The flowers looked attractive on the kitchen table.* ♦ *We've chosen an attractive wallpaper for the nursery.*

attractiveness [ə 'træk tɪv nəs] **1.** *n.* prettiness; handsomeness; a pleasant quality that draws attention. (No plural form in this sense.) ♦ *At his class reunion, John's former classmates were stunned by his attractiveness.* ♦ *Susan's attractiveness brought her lots of attention.* **2.** *n.* a quality that makes something draw interest or consideration, especially because it seems good or favorable. (No plural form in this sense.) ♦ *Changing careers held some attractiveness for Jane.* ♦ *Bill was lured by the attractiveness of the investment.*

attributable [ə 'trɪb jə tə bəl] *adj.* able to be blamed for something or ascribed to someone or something. ♦ *Her lateness was attributable to the heavy traffic.* ♦ *The damage to the car is attributable to Jane's reckless driving.*

attribute 1. ['æ trə bjut] *n.* a feature of someone or something; a quality present in someone or something; a property of someone or something. ♦ *What attributes of the car enticed you to buy it?* ♦ *Jane has many good attributes that make her eligible for the job.* **2. attribute to** [ə 'trɪb jut...] *tv.* + *prep. phr.* to ascribe something to someone; to give the credit for something to someone; to say that something is the result of someone's effort or was produced by someone. ♦ *The discovery of electricity is attributed to Benjamin Franklin.* ♦ *The author mistakenly attributed this quote to the wrong person.* **3. attribute to** [ə 'trɪb jut...] *tv.* + *prep. phr.* to ascribe something to something; to cite something as a cause. ♦ *Jane attributed her lateness to the heavy traffic.* ♦ *To what do you attribute your success?*

attune [ə 'tun] **attune to** *tv.* + *prep. phr.* to adjust oneself to something. (Takes a reflexive object.) ♦ *Once I attuned myself to the local culture, I fit in better.* ♦ *Mary quickly attuned herself to living in a college dormitory.*

attuned [ə 'tund] **attuned to** *adj.* + *prep. phr.* adjusted to; comfortable with. ♦ *Jane became attuned to Japanese culture after living in Japan.* ♦ *Bill, attuned to his supervisor's moods, knows when to leave him alone.*

atypical [e 'tɪp ɪ kəl] *adj.* unusual; abnormal; not typical. (Adv: *atypically* [...ɪk li].) ♦ *Hiring someone with no experience is atypical for most businesses.* ♦ *Bob was surprised by his child's atypical behavior.*

auburn ['ɔ bɚn] **1.** *n.* a reddish-brown color. (No plural form in this sense.) ♦ *Auburn is a reddish shade of brown.* ♦ *The color of the wood is more auburn than brown.* **2.** *adj.* <the adj. use of ①.> ♦ *The stylist's next customer was a woman with auburn hair.* ♦ *John's green tie clashed with his auburn hair.*

auction ['ɔk ʃən] **1.** *n.* a sale where each item is sold to the person offering to pay the highest price. ♦ *The charity held an auction to benefit medical research.* ♦ *Tom made a bid on an antique dresser at the auction.* **2. auction (off)** *tv.* (+ *adv.*) to sell something to the person who will pay the most money for it, as with ①. ♦ *The artist auctioned off his works shortly before he died.* ♦ *Only a few large firms auction valuable art to wealthy collectors.*

auctioneer [ɔk ʃə 'nɪr] *n.* someone who conducts auctions. ♦ *The auctioneer urged the audience to bid on each piece.* ♦ *The mayor was the auctioneer for the city's auction of old office furniture.*

audacious [ɔ 'de ʃəs] *adj.* very bold or daring; shockingly bold; brazen. (Adv: *audaciously.*) ♦ *It was audacious* *of you to come to the party uninvited.* ♦ *The audacious employee asked the manager for a second raise.*

audaciousness [ɔ 'de ʃəs nəs] *n.* boldness, especially daring or shocking boldness. (No plural form in this sense.) ♦ *The audience was shocked by the comedian's audaciousness.* ♦ *Through her boisterous audaciousness, the popular singer gained a lot of publicity.*

audacity [ɔ 'dæs ə ti] *n.* boldness, especially arrogant or shameless boldness. (No plural form in this sense.) ♦ *You had a lot of audacity to let your baby cry during the wedding!* ♦ *John's audacity has made him unpopular at the office.*

audibility [ɔ də 'bɪl ə ti] *n.* the quality of being loud enough to be heard. (No plural form in this sense.) ♦ *The sound of the breeze is below the level of audibility for most people.* ♦ *To improve the audibility of your lecture, please use this microphone.*

audible ['ɔ də bəl] *adj.* capable of being heard; loud enough to be heard. (Adv: *audibly.*) ♦ *The shy speaker was barely audible at the back of the theater.* ♦ *An amplifier makes a soft voice audible even in a large hall.*

audience ['ɔ di əns] **1.** *n.* a group of spectators who watch and listen to someone or something. ♦ *A large audience gathered around the street musicians.* ♦ *The audience loved the opera and gave it a standing ovation.* **2.** *n.* the group of people who are reached by a particular film, TV show, book, etc. ♦ *The marketing agency targeted a wide audience with its ads.* ♦ *The animated film was written for a young audience.* **3.** *n.* a formal interview or meeting with a very important person. (Usually with someone of very high rank.) ♦ *The ambassador sought an audience with the duke.* ♦ *The countess had an afternoon audience with Her Majesty.*

audio ['ɔ di o] **1.** *n.* broadcast or recorded sound, as opposed to video; the part of television that can be heard; the sound that comes from a computer's speakers. (No plural form in this sense.) ♦ *Even though the video was perfect, the audio was no good because the microphone was damaged.* ♦ *Who did the audio for the commercial?* **2.** *adj.* <the adj. use of ①.> ♦ *The audio control on the television set broke.* ♦ *The substitute teacher didn't know how to work the audio equipment and could not play the recording.*

audiology [ɔ di 'ɑl ə dʒi] *n.* the study of the ear and hearing and the treatment of hearing disorders. (No plural form in this sense.) ♦ *A student of audiology gave each child a hearing test.* ♦ *The hospital's department of audiology fits people with hearing aids.*

audiotape ['ɔd i o 'tep] **1.** *n.* a tape made for recording sound only. (No plural form in this sense. See also **videotape.**) ♦ *The cassette contains a length of audiotape.* ♦ *Audiotape is narrower than videotape.* **2.** *n.* a reel or cassette of ①; a copy of a sound recording on ①. ♦ *I liked the song so well that I bought both a CD and an audiotape of it.* ♦ *Tom collects audiotapes and must have hundreds of them.*

audiovisual ['ɔ di o 'vɪ ʒu əl] **1.** *adj.* relating to both sound and visual images or the equipment that produces sound and visual images. (Adv: *audiovisually.*) ♦ *The substitute teacher had difficulty working the audiovisual machines.* ♦ *Does your presentation have audiovisual effects?* **2. audiovisuals** *n.* elements of a presentation including sound and images. ♦ *The audiovisuals of the presentation kept the audience awake.* ♦ *The teacher used many audiovisuals to clarify the lecture.*

audit ['ɔ dɪt] **1.** *n.* an inspection of financial records by an accountant; an official check of financial records by an accountant. ♦ *The audit of the man's estate revealed unpaid taxes.* ♦ *I'm dreading the audit of my federal income-tax return.* **2.** *tv.* to go over the financial records of someone or something; to inspect the financial records of someone or something. ♦ *The government audits thousands of people each year.* ♦ *The company hired an accounting firm to audit the books.* **3.** *tv.* to attend a college class as a visiting student rather than as an enrolled student. ♦ *I'm auditing a class at the local university this fall.* ♦ *Some students are auditing the art class, but most are taking it for credit.*

audition [ɔ 'dɪ ʃən] **1.** *n.* a tryout; a test of one's performance skills. ♦ *The orchestra held auditions for a new cellist.* ♦ *Jane did so well at her audition that she was cast in the movie.* **2. audition for** *iv.* + *prep. phr.* to try out for a part in a performance; to perform for someone who is selecting performers for a performance. ♦ *Five violinists auditioned for the orchestra.* ♦ *Three actors auditioned for the leading role.* **3.** *tv.* to observe and evaluate the performances of people who are trying out. ♦ *The director auditioned thousands of children for the movie.* ♦ *One director auditioned dancers for the production, and another auditioned singers.*

auditor ['ɔ dɪt ɚ] **1.** *n.* someone who conducts a financial audit; someone who carefully goes over the financial records of someone or something. ♦ *The company hired an auditor to study the accounts.* ♦ *The auditor found mistakes in the accounting.* **2.** *n.* someone who audits a class. ♦ *The auditor asked more questions than the students who were taking the course for a grade.* ♦ *You can save money if you take a class as an auditor.*

auditorium [ɔ dɪ 'tor i əm] **1.** *n.* the part of a performance hall where the audience sits. ♦ *The new auditorium had velvet seats.* ♦ *The crowd filled every seat in the auditorium.* **2.** *n.* a large room or building used for public meetings, lectures, and the like. ♦ *The acoustics in the high-school auditorium are not very good.* ♦ *The students assembled in the auditorium to hear the principal speak.*

auditory ['ɔ də tor i] *adj.* relating to hearing and the ears. (Adv: *auditorily* [ɔ də 'tor ə li].) ♦ *The explosion damaged the worker's auditory nerve.* ♦ *Some ear diseases cause auditory problems.*

augment [ɔg 'mɛnt] *tv.* to add to, increase, or enhance something. ♦ *The addition to the house greatly augmented its value.* ♦ *We augmented the presentation with the addition of audiovisuals.*

august 1. [ɔ 'gʌst] *adj.* dignified; majestic; noble. (Adv: *augustly.*) ♦ *The august gentleman stepped to the microphone.* ♦ *The poet wrote poems about august heroes and heroines.* **2. August** ['ɔg əst] *n.* the eighth month of the year. ♦ *The students bought school supplies at the end of August.* ♦ *The long, hot days of August mark the end of summer.*

au jus [o 'ʒu(s)] *adv.* [of meat] with its own gravy or juice. (French for 'with the juice.') ♦ *The roast beef is served au jus.* ♦ *A steak does not usually come au jus.*

aunt ['ænt] *n.* the sister of one's mother or father; the wife of the brother of one's mother or father; the wife of one's uncle. (Also a term of address.) ♦ *Dad has five sisters, so I have at least five aunts.* ♦ *Aunt Mary sent me a birthday card last week.*

auspicious [ɔ 'spɪ ʃəs] *adj.* showing signs of good fortune or success; favorable. (Adv: *auspiciously.*) ♦ *Spring is an auspicious time to begin new activities.* ♦ *On this auspicious occasion, I am pleased to award this prize to our distinguished guest.*

auspiciousness [ɔ 'spɪ ʃəs nəs] *n.* the appearance of being favorable. (No plural form in this sense.) ♦ *The auspiciousness of the beginning of the day faded dismally by noon.* ♦ *The auspiciousness with which Tom began the school year continued until the first examination.*

austere [ɔ 'stɪr] **1.** *adj.* stern; severe in appearance. (Adv: *austerely.*) ♦ *The austere professor never smiled.* ♦ *The austere painting was done in grays, browns, and blacks.* **2.** *adj.* very simple; without luxury. (Adv: *austerely.*) ♦ *The Smiths led an austere life until they won the lottery.* ♦ *The mountain cabin had austere rooms and no indoor plumbing.*

austerity [ɔ 'stɛr ə ti] *n.* plainness; frugalness. (No plural form in this sense.) ♦ *The austerity of the room made me uncomfortable.* ♦ *Austerity is the chosen lifestyle of a monk.*

Australia [ɔ 'strel jə] See Gazetteer.

Austria ['ɔ stri ə] See Gazetteer.

authentic [ɔ 'θɛn tɪk] *adj.* real; genuine; known to be real or true. (Adv: *authentically* [...ɪk li].) ♦ *The museum had an exhibit of authentic Indian artifacts.* ♦ *Is your diamond ring authentic?*

authenticate [ɔ 'θɛn tɪ ket] *tv.* to prove that something is real; to show that a claim is true. ♦ *The expert authenticated the famous athlete's signature.* ♦ *Can you authenticate your claim that you are a descendant of the first president?*

authentication [ɔ θɛn tɪ 'ke ʃən] *n.* proving that something is real or true; certification of something as genuine. (No plural form in this sense.) ♦ *The authentication of the artifact took months.* ♦ *The dealer in antiques specializes in the authentication of autographs.*

authenticity [ɔ θɛn 'tɪs ə ti] *n.* the state of being genuine; the state of being real. (No plural form in this sense.) ♦ *We questioned the authenticity of the old manuscript.* ♦ *After we got to know the man who said he was our lost cousin, we began to wonder about his authenticity.*

author ['ɔθ ɚ] **1.** *n.* someone who writes books, poems, plays, articles, or similar compositions. ♦ *Who is the author of the play we saw last night?* ♦ *The author of the book researched the subject for many years.* **2.** *tv.* to write something; to compose something. ♦ *Mary has authored three books about plants.* ♦ *We could not find anyone to author a book on our town's history.*

authoritarian [ə θor ə 'tɛr i ən] **1.** *n.* a bossy person. ♦ *My parents are such authoritarians!* ♦ *My boss is an authoritarian who likes everything to be done his way.* **2.** *adj.* demanding obedience to authority; taking complete control over others. (Adv: *authoritarianly.*) ♦ *Jane takes an authoritarian approach to supervising her employees.* ♦ *The timid child was raised by authoritarian parents.*

authoritative [ə 'θor ɪ tet ɪv] **1.** *adj.* accepted as true or reliable; trusted. (Adv: *authoritatively.*) ♦ *This newspaper is considered the most authoritative paper in the country.* ♦ *Make sure you ask an authoritative source for directions.* **2.** *adj.* having an air of authority; commanding obedience. (Adv: *authoritatively.*) ♦ *The babysitter announced in an authoritative voice that it was time for bed.* ♦ *The authoritative manager was well respected.*

authority [ə 'θor ə ti] **1.** *n.* the power and right to do something; control and management in general. (No plural form in this sense.) ♦ *The mayor has authority over all the city departments.* ♦ *The teacher gave her assistant the authority to grade papers.* **2.** *n.* an expert. ♦ *Jane is an authority on 17th-century art.* ♦ *Tom thinks he is an authority on baseball statistics, but he isn't.* **3. authorities** *n.* members of an organization who have the authority to do something, especially to make or enforce rules; the police; the government. ♦ *The authorities arrested the suspect on drug charges.* ♦ *We reported the car accident to the local authorities.*

authorization [ɔ θə rɪ 'ze ʃən] **1.** *n.* official permission to do something. (No plural form in this sense.) ♦ *The school required parental authorization for the students to take a field trip.* ♦ *Did the couple receive authorization from the foreign government to adopt the baby?* **2.** *n.* a document showing ①. ♦ *Did you bring the authorization that will allow you to enter the building?* ♦ *Unless you can present some sort of authorization, I cannot allow you to remove the papers you are asking for.*

authorize ['ɔ θə raɪz] *tv.* to give someone the power and right to do something. ♦ *The teacher authorized her assistant to grade papers.* ♦ *A visa authorizes a person to enter and leave a country.*

authorized ['ɔ θə raɪzd] **1.** *adj.* having the authority to do something. ♦ *The authorized employee opened the safe.* ♦ *Only authorized personnel are allowed beyond this barrier.* **2.** *adj.* approved; sanctioned; legal. ♦ *The authorized biography was a bit dull.* ♦ *Do not spend more than the authorized amount of money on the new equipment.*

authorship ['ɔθ ɚ ʃɪp] *n.* the state of being the author (of something). (No plural form in this sense.) ♦ *Authorship of the book was attributed to two university scholars.* ♦ *Is anyone willing to undertake the authorship of a book about the town's history?*

auto ['ɔ to] *n.* a car; an automobile. ♦ *My auto was in the shop, so I took a bus to work.* ♦ *John bought his first auto when he was twenty.*

autobiographical [ɔ to baɪ ə 'græf ɪ kəl] *adj.* of or about an autobiography; stating the details from one's own life. (Adv: *autobiographically* [...ɪk li].) ♦ *No one realized the poet's poems were autobiographical.* ♦ *The book is an autobiographical account of a child's experience of the war.*

autobiography [ɔ to baɪ 'ɑ grə fi] *n.* a story that one writes about one's own life. ♦ *John wrote his autobiography, but no one would publish it.* ♦ *The president wrote a fascinating autobiography.*

autocracy [ɔ 'tɑ krə si] *n.* a government run by an autocrat; a dictatorship. ♦ *An autocracy is not a democratic form of government.* ♦ *The tiny island country is an autocracy.*

autocrat ['ɔt ə kræt] *n.* someone who has complete control over a government; a dictator. ♦ *The autocrat ruled the country unjustly.* ♦ *A rebellion overthrew the cruel autocrat.*

autocratic [ɔt ə 'kræt ɪk] *adj.* dictatorial; having complete control over an organization. (Adv: *autocratically* [...ɪk li].) ♦ *Bill's boss runs an autocratic office and doesn't give his employees much freedom.* ♦ *The autocratic ruler was criticized by other world leaders.*

autograph ['ɔt ə græf] **1.** *n.* someone's signature, especially the signature of a famous person. ♦ *Could I have your autograph, please?* ♦ *I have more than 100 autographs of famous people.* **2.** *adj.* <the adj. use of ①.> ♦ *I took my autograph book with me on my vacation.* ♦ *My autograph collection numbers more than 100.* **3.** *tv.* to sign one's name on something. ♦ *The child held up a program for the singer to autograph.* ♦ *Did the author autograph your copy of the book?*

automate ['ɔt o met] **1.** *tv.* to make a process automatic. ♦ *The washing machine automated the laundry process.* ♦ *The inventor wanted to automate window washing.* **2.** *tv.* to bring a system under computer control or management. ♦ *When the billing department was automated, fewer workers were needed.* ♦ *The library automated the circulation system.* **3.** *iv.* to equip an office or business with computers and other office equipment. ♦ *This company decided to automate before the competing companies did.* ♦ *The accounting office automated so that it could become more efficient.*

automated ['ɔt o met ɪd] *adj.* [of a machine or system] controlled automatically, often by a computer; not requiring help from a human. (Adv: *automatedly.*) ♦ *Jane pushed buttons on the automated banking machine to request a cash withdrawal.* ♦ *At the grocery store, the entire ordering process is automated.*

automatic [ɔt ə 'mæt ɪk] **1.** *adj.* [of a machine] acting by itself; not needing outside help to perform a process. (Adv: *automatically* [...ɪk li].) ♦ *The Smiths bought an automatic dishwasher.* ♦ *The automatic garage door opens at the press of a button.* **2.** *adj.* done without thinking; done out of habit or by instinct. (Adv: *automatically* [...ɪk li].) ♦ *Blinking is an automatic response.* ♦ *Fear is an automatic reaction to a threat.*

automation [ɔt ə 'me ʃən] **1.** *n.* making a process automatic instead of dependent on humans. (No plural form in this sense.) ♦ *The automation of the billing department took only a few weeks.* ♦ *The library's automation took years to accomplish.* **2.** *n.* the control of something by computers or other machines. (No plural form in this sense.) ♦ *Many workers are replaced by automation.* ♦ *The large company turned to automation to cut costs.*

automobile [ɔt ə mo 'bil] *n.* a car; a vehicle that can carry a small number of passengers. ♦ *Tom drove to work in a new automobile.* ♦ *Mary is learning to repair automobiles.*

automotive [ɔt ə 'mot ɪv] *adj.* relating to automobiles. (Adv: *automotively.*) ♦ *The automotive industry is a large part of the economy.* ♦ *The local high school offers a class in automotive repairs.*

autonomous [ɔ 'tɑn ə məs] *adj.* self-governing; independent. (Adv: *autonomously.*) ♦ *The colony wished to become an autonomous state.* ♦ *The smaller company was once a part of the conglomerate, but has been autonomous since last spring.*

autonomy [ɔ 'tɑn ə mi] *n.* independence; self-government. (No plural form in this sense.) ♦ *The thirteen original U.S. colonies won their autonomy after the American Revolution.* ♦ *The nation's autonomy was compromised by the treaty.*

autopsy ['ɔ tɑp si] *n.* the medical examination of a dead body, usually to determine the cause of death. ♦ *The coroner determined the cause of death by doing an autopsy.* ♦ *The autopsy revealed that the victim had drowned.*

autumn ['ɔt əm] *n.* fall; in the Northern Hemisphere, the time of year from September 22 to December 21; the season between summer and winter. ♦ *In the autumn, the leaves turn colors and fall off the trees.* ♦ *Every autumn, a new academic year begins at the university.*

autumnal [ɔ 'tʌm nəl] *adj.* relating to autumn. (Adv: *autumnally.*) ♦ *The brisk autumnal winds precede the arrival of winter.* ♦ *Halloween is an autumnal festival.*

aux. See auxiliary verb.

auxiliary [ɔg 'zɪl jə ri] **1.** *adj.* secondary; supplementary; substitute. ♦ *The auxiliary power unit turned on during the storm.* ♦ *An auxiliary supply of light bulbs is kept in the basement.* **2. auxiliary verb** AND **verbal auxiliary** *n.* a word that is used before a verb to affect its tense, aspect, or mood. (Also called a *helping verb.* Abbreviated *aux.* here. Examples: *can, could, did, do, had, has, have, may, might, must, ought, shall, should, will, would.*) ♦ *Some auxiliary verbs, such as* do *and* have, *are also regular verbs.* ♦ *In the sentence "I have done it,"* have *is an auxiliary verb.*

avail [ə 'vel] **1. avail oneself of something** *idiom* to help oneself by making use of something that is available. ♦ *We availed ourselves of Tom's goodwill and let him repair the fence.* ♦ *The campers availed themselves of the first chance in a week to take a shower.* **2. to no avail** *idiom* of no benefit or help. ♦ *We struggled to no avail and lost the battle.* ♦ *We called to tell Jane the concert was canceled, but to no avail—she had already left home.*

availability [ə vel ə 'bɪl ə ti] *n.* readiness or willingness to serve some purpose; accessibility. (No plural form in this sense.) ♦ *What is the babysitter's availability for Saturday night?* ♦ *The availability of fresh greens during the winter is limited.*

available [ə 'vel ə bəl] *adj.* ready; accessible and not assigned or committed to something else. ♦ *The hotel is available for the wedding reception next week.* ♦ *Are you available to serve on the committee?*

avalanche ['æ və læntʃ] **1.** *n.* the sudden movement of a vast amount of snow on the side of a mountain from a higher place to a lower place. ♦ *The skiers were trapped in an avalanche but were rescued quickly.* ♦ *Tons of snow rushed down the mountain in the avalanche.* **2.** *n.* the sudden appearance of a large number of people or a lot of something. (Figurative on ①.) ♦ *The emergency room received an avalanche of accident victims.* ♦ *An avalanche of work was waiting for me after my vacation.*

avant-garde ['ɑ vɑnt 'gɑrd] **1.** *adj.* experimental, innovative, and daring, especially in the arts. ♦ *The art school encourages its students to try avant-garde projects.* ♦ *I wrote a paper about avant-garde filmmaking.* **2. the avant-garde** *n.* experimental, innovative, and daring qualities in the performing arts and the artists associated with these qualities. (No plural form in this sense. Treated as singular or plural. From French.) ♦ *The art critic wrote regularly about the avant-garde in her column.* ♦ *The avant-garde is so common nowadays that it has lost some of its novelty.*

avarice ['æv ə rɪs] *n.* greed. (No plural form in this sense.) ♦ *Avarice has caused the downfall of many people.* ♦ *The minister preached against the sin of avarice.*

avaricious [æv ə 'rɪ ʃəs] *adj.* greedy. (Adv: *avariciously.*) ♦ *The avaricious nature of children can be seen when they learn the word* mine. ♦ *Bill is so avaricious that he donates nothing to charity.*

avenge [ə 'vɛndʒ] *tv.* to take revenge for something or on behalf of someone. (See also **revenge.**) ♦ *The girl avenged her father's death by poisoning his murderer.* ♦ *I was too weak to avenge myself and was satisfied with having escaped with my life.*

avenger [ə 'vɛn dʒɚ] *n.* someone who takes revenge. ♦ *The avenger had waited years to carry out her revenge.* ♦ *The avenger was stopped by the police before he had harmed anyone.*

avenue ['æv ə nu] **1.** *n.* a wide street in a city, sometimes lined with trees. ♦ *Shops are located all along the avenue.* ♦ *The city planted trees along Washington Avenue.* **2.** *n.* a pathway—often figurative—such as the way a problem is approached. ♦ *What avenues did the school board explore toward solving the teacher shortage?* ♦ *We explored all the avenues, but this is the only solution that is reasonable.* **3. avenue of escape** *idiom* the pathway or route along which someone or something escapes. ♦ *The open window was the bird's only avenue of escape from the house.* ♦ *Bill saw that his one avenue of escape was through the back door.*

average ['æv (ə) rɪdʒ] **1.** *n.* a sum obtained by adding several numbers together and then dividing that total by the number of figures that were added. ♦ *The average daily rainfall for January in Minneapolis is quite low.* ♦ *The average of 10, 22, and 34 is 22.* **2.** *n.* something that is usual, typical, or normal. (No plural form in this sense.) ♦ *As to skills, Tom is the average, being neither excellent nor poor.* ♦ *There is nothing unique about this. This is just the average.* **3. average (up)** *tv.* (+ *adv.*) to add several figures and then divide that total by the number of figures that were added. ♦ *Please average the figures and report back to me.* ♦ *I have to average up these numbers for the boss.* **4.** *adj.* usual; typical; normal; ordinary. (Adv: *averagely.*) ♦ *John is an average, hardworking businessman.* ♦ *On an average day, I receive three or four telephone calls.* **5. on the average** *idiom* generally; usually. ♦ *On the average, you can expect about a 10 percent failure rate.* ♦ *This report looks OK, on the average.* **6. above average** *idiom* higher or better than the average. ♦ *Max's grades are always above average.* ♦ *His intelligence is clearly above average.* **7. below average** *idiom* lower or worse than average. ♦ *Tom's strength is below average for a child his size.* ♦ *Dad asked why my grades are below average.*

averse [ə 'vɚs] **averse to** *adj.* + *prep. phr.* opposed to doing something. (Adv: *aversely.*) ♦ *Our dog is averse to having a bath.* ♦ *Not even stormy weather makes me averse to traveling.*

aversion [ə 'vɚ ʒən] *n.* a strong dislike of something; a dislike of doing something. ♦ *Her aversion to buses makes it necessary for her to own a car.* ♦ *Our family's cat has an aversion to water.*

avert [ə 'vɚt] **1.** *tv.* to turn something away, especially to turn one's face, eyes, or gaze away. ♦ *When she realized she was staring at the stranger, Mary averted her eyes.* ♦ *Bill averted his gaze when his enemy passed.* **2.** *tv.* to stop something bad from happening; to prevent a disaster from happening. ♦ *As hard as he tried, the driver could not avert having an accident.* ♦ *Tom was able to avert the disaster, but just barely.*

aviary ['ev i ɛr i] *n.* a large enclosure where birds are kept. ♦ *My favorite place in the zoo is the aviary.* ♦ *Twenty types of birds were kept in the aviary.*

aviation [ev i 'e ʃən] *n.* the flying of aircraft; the management of flying aircraft. (No plural form in this sense.) ♦ *We bought a book on the history of aviation.* ♦ *Tom wanted to study aviation, but his eyesight was not good enough.*

aviator ['ev i et ɚ] *n.* a pilot; someone who flies an aircraft. ♦ *The navy aviator had trained for many years.* ♦ *The aviator tried to contact the control tower before the crash.*

avid ['æv ɪd] *adj.* enthusiastic about something. (Adv: *avidly.*) ♦ *The avid reader went to the library every day.* ♦ *The avid tennis fans cheered for their favorite tennis player.*

avocado [ɑv ə 'kɑd o] **1.** *n.* a tropical fruit with rough green, black, or purple skin, soft green flesh, and a large pit. (Pl in *-s.*) ♦ *Avocados are popular in Mexican cooking.* ♦ *The dip was made from avocados and lemon juice.* **2.** *n.* the edible part of ①. (No plural form in this sense.) ♦ *I put some avocado in the salad.* ♦ *Max has a recipe for a delicious spread made with avocado.* **3.** *adj.* made from ②. ♦ *I just love this avocado spread!* ♦ *Your avocado salad is delicious.*

avocation [æv o 'ke ʃən] *n.* a hobby. (Compare with **vocation.**) ♦ *Volunteer work is an avocation for John, who is an accountant.* ♦ *For some people, watching television is an avocation.*

avoid [ə 'vɔɪd] **1.** *tv.* to elude contact with someone or something; to manage not to make contact with someone or something. ♦ *Mary avoided John at school after they stopped dating.* ♦ *To avoid the snarling dog, I turned around and ran away.* **2.** *tv.* to prevent something from occurring. ♦ *I drove carefully to avoid an accident.* ♦ *Try to avoid getting soap in your eyes.*

avoidable [ə 'vɔɪd ə bəl] *adj.* preventable; capable of being avoided. (Adv: *avoidably.*) ♦ *The accident was avoidable, but John wasn't looking where he was going.* ♦ *The argument was avoidable, but both parties were eager to argue.*

avoidance [ə 'vɔɪd ns] *n.* staying away from someone or something; ignoring someone or something; not doing something. (No plural form in this sense.) ♦ *Tom's behavior was characterized by an avoidance of the important issues.* ♦ *Mary's avoidance of her friends indicated the extent of her despair.*

avowed [ə 'vɑʊd] *adj.* admitted; declared. (Adv: *avowedly* [ə 'vɑʊ əd li].) ♦ *An avowed football fan, Tom watched every Monday-night game.* ♦ *Max is an avowed music lover and loves to go to the symphony.*

await [ə 'wet] *tv.* to expect someone or something to arrive; to wait for the arrival of someone or something. ♦ *Jane awaited the mail each day, expecting a letter.* ♦ *The farmer awaited the arrival of spring so planting could begin.*

awake [ə 'wek] **1.** *adj.* not asleep; alert. (Not prenominal.) ♦ *The alarm went off at six o'clock, but John was already awake.* ♦ *The playful kitten was wide awake and wouldn't let me fall asleep.* **2.** *iv., irreg.* to stop sleeping; to wake. (Pt: awoke; pp: awoken. See also awaken.) ♦ *Since the children would awake from their naps soon, I hurried to finish my work.* ♦ *Tom awoke early and finished studying for the exam.* **3.** *tv., irreg.* to make someone or something stop sleeping; to wake someone or something up. (See also awaken.) ♦ *Tom awoke his roommate at dawn.* ♦ *The alarm awoke the residents of the burning house.* **4.** *tv., irreg.* to bring back into consciousness thoughts or memories of someone or something. (Figurative on ③. See also awaken.) ♦ *The sight of the sea awoke old memories in the mind of the old sailor.* ♦ *The sound of the thunder awoke terrors in those who had survived the war.*

awaken [ə 'wek ən] **1.** *iv.* to stop sleeping; to wake. (See also awake.) ♦ *The children will awaken from their naps soon.* ♦ *Tom awakened and got ready for work.* **2.** *tv.* to make someone or something stop sleeping; to wake someone or something up. (See also awake.) ♦ *Tom awakened his roommate just in time for breakfast.* ♦ *The kittens awakened their mother because they were hungry.* **3.** *tv.* to bring back into consciousness thoughts or memories of someone or something; to arouse in someone a new or hidden feeling, interest, talent, awareness, or emotion. (Figurative on ②. See also awake.) ♦ *The smells of the sea awakened old memories in the mind of the sailor.* ♦ *The teacher hoped that visiting the laboratory would awaken the children's interest in science.*

award [ə 'word] **1.** *n.* something given to someone as repayment or compensation; something given to someone as a prize. ♦ *The firefighter received an award for saving people's lives.* ♦ *The committee gave Mary an award for excellence.* **2.** *tv.* to give something to someone as the result of an official legal decision; to order the payment of money as compensation in a court of law. ♦ *The judge awarded $10,000 to the plaintiff.* ♦ *The jury awarded custody to the grandparents of the child.* **3.** *tv.* to give a prize to someone; to give someone something as the result of an official decision. ♦ *The judges awarded a gold medal to the gymnast from Romania.* ♦ *The jury awarded the grandparents custody of the child.*

aware [ə 'wɛr] **1.** *adj.* alert; conscious; having control of one's senses. (Not usually prenominal.) ♦ *Tom just isn't very aware at this time of the morning.* ♦ *The cat is half asleep, but she is more aware than you might think.* **2. aware of** *adj. + prep. phr.* conscious of someone or something. ♦ *I am not aware of ever having been here before.* ♦ *Are you aware of the problems that you have caused?* **3.** *adj.* knowledgeable; in a state of knowing something. (Takes a clause.) ♦ *We were not aware that we left the car lights on.* ♦ *John was aware that he was being rude, but he didn't care.*

awareness [ə 'wɛr nəs] *n.* consciousness; the knowledge of something; alertness. (No plural form in this sense.) ♦ *A therapist needs to have an awareness of other people's feelings.* ♦ *From the newspaper article, we gained an awareness of other people's problems.*

away [ə 'we] **1.** *adj.* at some distance; apart in distance. (Not prenominal.) ♦ *Boston is too far away from Seattle for us to drive there in one day.* ♦ *The ship on the horizon was actually more than 60 miles away.* **2.** *adj.* [of a game] not played on the home team's court or field. ♦ *The school's baseball team lost every away game last year.* ♦ *The team traveled for an hour to get to the final away game.* **3.** *adv.* from one position or direction to another; from one state or position to another. ♦ *The busy lawyer pushed the beggar away.* ♦ *I turned my head away from the bloody accident.* **4.** *adv.* without stopping; continuously. ♦ *Bob banged away at the piano.* ♦ *Jane worked away at packing until all the books were in boxes.* **5. go away empty-handed** *idiom* to leave without what one came for. ♦ *I hate for you to go away empty-handed, but I cannot afford to contribute any money.* ♦ *They came hoping for some food, but they had to go away empty-handed.*

awe ['ɔ] **1.** *n.* a strong feeling of amazement and respect. (No plural form in this sense.) ♦ *The children gazed in awe at the gigantic dinosaur bones.* ♦ *I am always in awe of people who can cook well.* **2.** *tv.* to fill someone with amazement and respect. ♦ *The beauty of the symphony awed the audience.* ♦ *The campers were always awed by a beautiful sunset.*

awe-inspiring ['ɔ ɪn spaɪr ɪŋ] *adj.* causing the feeling of awe. (Adv: *awe-inspiringly.*) ♦ *The view of the mountains from our cabin was awe-inspiring.* ♦ *Several awe-inspiring paintings were on exhibit at the museum.*

awesome ['ɔ səm] **1.** *adj.* frightening and amazing; awe-inspiring. (Adv: *awesomely.*) ♦ *An awesome storm overtook the small ship.* ♦ *The painter was known for his enormous, awesome landscapes.* **2.** *adj.* excellent; very good. (Slang. Adv: *awesomely.*) ♦ *"This pizza is totally awesome!" the kids exclaimed.* ♦ *The teenagers said they had an awesome time at the party.*

awesomeness ['ɔ səm nəs] *n.* the quality of being very impressive; the quality of inspiring awe. (No plural form in this sense.) ♦ *The awesomeness of the view impressed us.* ♦ *The awesomeness of my accomplishments amazed my parents.*

awestruck ['ɔ strək] *adj.* full of amazement and wonder. ♦ *The winner of the lottery was awestruck and could hardly speak.* ♦ *The awestruck child stared at the huge birthday cake.*

awful ['ɔ fʊl] *adj.* horrible; terrible; very bad. (Adv: *awfully.*) ♦ *Monday was an awful day—everything went wrong.* ♦ *The food at the restaurant was awful, but the service was excellent.*

awfully ['ɔf (ə) li] **1.** *adv.* terribly; horribly; badly. ♦ *Bob scored awfully on his test.* ♦ *The performer at the talent show sang awfully and left in tears.* **2.** *adv.* very; really. ♦ *This soup is awfully good.* ♦ *This movie is awfully bad.*

awfulness ['ɔ fʊl nəs] *n.* a bad or horrible quality of something. (No plural form in this sense.) ♦ *The awfulness of the crime shocked the community.* ♦ *The first act was one hour of awfulness, and the second act was worse.*

awhile [ə 'ʍaɪl] *adv.* for a short length of time; for a little bit of time. ♦ *The birds sat awhile on the telephone wire.* ♦ *Let's rest awhile before finishing our hike.*

awkward ['ɔk wɚd] **1.** *adj.* clumsy; not graceful. (Adv: *awkwardly.*) ♦ *The growing teenager went through an awkward stage.* ♦ *The old arthritic man was a bit awkward and walked with a cane.* **2.** *adj.* hard to manage; hard to control; not easily used. (Adv: *awkwardly.*) ♦ *The tennis racket was too big and awkward for Jane.* ♦ *These are awkward shoes, and I know I will trip when I wear them.* **3.** *adj.* embarrassing. (Adv: *awkwardly.*) ♦ *It was an awkward moment when the preacher fell in church.* ♦ *Tom was always a bit awkward when meeting new people.*

awkwardly ['ɔk wɚd li] *adv.* with embarrassment. ♦ *Bob smiled awkwardly and said, "Thank you."* ♦ *The boy giggled awkwardly and turned away.*

awkwardness ['ɔk wɚd nəs] **1.** *n.* clumsiness. (No plural form in this sense.) ♦ *The teenager's friends were sympathetic to his awkwardness.* ♦ *With considerable awkwardness, Sue got her cane and hobbled to the door.* **2.** *n.* shy embarrassment. (No plural form in this sense.) ♦ *There is always a certain awkwardness on the first date with someone new.* ♦ *Bob greeted people at the door with a little awkwardness, but he became more confident as the evening went on.*

awning ['ɔn ɪŋ] *n.* a covering, extending over a walkway, door, or window, to deflect rain and snow. ♦ *The striped awnings gave the house a festive look.* ♦ *When the storm started, we ran under the awning.*

awoke [ə 'wok] pt of awake.

awoken [ə 'wok ən] pp of awake.

ax(e) ['æks] **1.** *n.* a tool that consists of a heavy metal wedge attached to a handle, used to chop wood. (Pl: axes.) ♦ *The campers chopped their wood with an ax.* ♦ *The axe had been left in the rain and was rusted.* **2. have an ax(e) to grind** *idiom* to have something to complain about. ♦ *Tom, I need to talk to you. I have an ax to grind.* ♦ *Bill and Bob went into the other room to argue. They had an axe to grind.*

axes 1. ['æk siz] pl of axis. **2.** ['æk sɪz] pl of axe and ax.

axiom ['æks i əm] *n.* a statement that need not be proved and is accepted as true. ♦ *John recited the old axiom about a stitch in time saving nine.* ♦ *Some basic axioms of mathematics have been accepted as true since ancient times.*

axiomatic [æks i o 'mæt ɪk] *adj.* relating to statements that cannot be proved but are accepted as true. (Adv: *axiomatically* [...ɪk li].) ♦ *The author's philosophy of life was based on axiomatic generalizations.* ♦ *The consultant's advice was little more than axiomatic clichés.*

axis ['æks ɪs] **1.** *n., irreg.* an imaginary line that goes through the center point of a sphere or a ball. (Pl: **axes.**) ♦ *The earth spins on its axis.* ♦ *A rod runs along the axis of my globe and is attached to the stand that supports the globe.* **2.** *n., irreg.* a base line used when placing points on a graph. ♦ *Start at the horizontal axis and draw a line up to 10 units.* ♦ *In Chicago, State Street is the axis between east and west addresses.*

axle ['æks əl] *n.* the rod that connects a pair of wheels. ♦ *John broke the axle on his car by driving on rough roads.* ♦ *Trucks often have more than two axles.*

azalea [ə 'zel jə] *n.* a type of shrub and the flowers found on it, similar to a rhododendron. ♦ *Azaleas require a very acidic soil.* ♦ *Many azaleas live through the winter in the north.*

azure ['æ ʒɚ] *adj.* blue, especially the color of a clear sky or deep water. ♦ *Bill gazed into the azure sky and thought of his home far away.* ♦ *From the ship we saw azure water in all directions.*

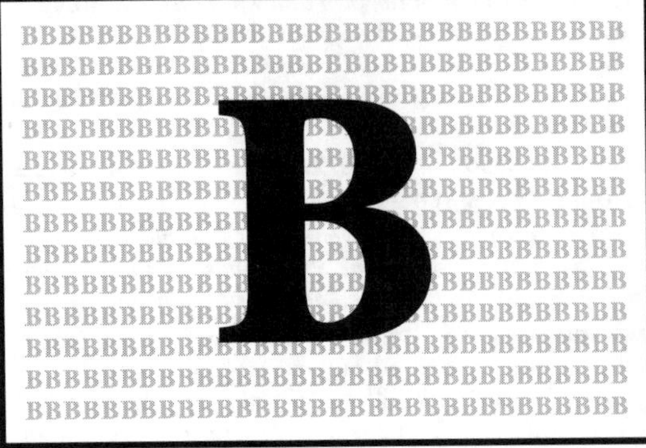

B AND **b** ['bi] **1.** *n.* the second letter of the alphabet. ♦ *The letter* b *comes after the letter* a *in the alphabet.* ♦ *The word* boy *begins with* b. **2. B** *n.* the second highest school mark. ♦ *John earned a B in algebra.* ♦ *I got a B on my paper.*

baa ['bɑ] *n.* the sound made by sheep and lambs. ♦ *The sheep said "baa" as the child touched it.* ♦ *All the little lamb said was "baa."*

babble ['bæb əl] **1.** *iv.* to talk without making much sense. ♦ *The old friends babbled for hours in the café.* ♦ *Is the baby babbling yet?* **2.** *iv.* to make a bubbling noise, as with flowing water. ♦ *The brook babbled as it made its way toward the lake.* ♦ *The water babbled as it leapt from rock to rock.* **3.** *n.* silly talk; chatter. (No plural form in this sense.) ♦ *The babble at the company picnic was boring.* ♦ *The dinner party babble turned to a discussion of politics.*

babbling ['bæb lɪŋ] *adj.* bubbling, as with the sound of flowing water. ♦ *The children jumped over the babbling brook.* ♦ *The deer drank from the babbling stream.*

babe ['beb] **1.** *n.* a baby. ♦ *The tiny babe slept peacefully in its crib.* ♦ *The mother carried her babe in a basket.* **2. babe in the woods** *idiom* a naive or innocent person; an inexperienced person. ♦ *Bill is a babe in the woods when it comes to dealing with plumbers.* ♦ *As a painter, Mary is fine, but she's a babe in the woods as a musician.*

baboon [bæ 'bun] *n.* a large Asian or African ape with a doglike face. ♦ *The baboons have a strong social structure.* ♦ *Baboons will eat almost anything.*

baby ['beb i] **1.** *n.* an infant; a newborn child. ♦ *The Smiths named their new baby Anne.* ♦ *Sue played with her baby every day.* **2.** *tv.* to treat someone or something like a baby. ♦ *Jane babies her children, and they are very attached to her.* ♦ *If you baby your children, they will become spoiled.* **3.** *adj.* <the adj. use of ①.> ♦ *Please buy a bottle of baby shampoo.* ♦ *The baby elephant must weigh 200 pounds!*

babyish ['beb i ɪʃ] *adj.* acting or looking like a baby. (Adv: *babyishly.*) ♦ *The child's babyish tantrums annoyed everybody.* ♦ *That dress looks babyish on you.*

babysat ['beb i sæt] pt/pp of **babysit.**

babysit ['beb i sɪt] **1.** *iv., irreg.* to care for someone else's children. (Pt/pp: **babysat.**) ♦ *Can Mary babysit for Jimmy Saturday night?* ♦ *Children aren't invited to the wedding, so we'll need someone to babysit.* **2.** *tv., irreg.* to take care of children whose parents are away. ♦ *Jane babysat her nephew last night.* ♦ *John babysits his younger siblings when his parents go out.*

babysitter ['beb i sɪt ɚ] *n.* someone who takes care of children whose parents are away. ♦ *The Wilsons hired a babysitter whom they can trust.* ♦ *The babysitter put the children to bed at nine o'clock.*

babysitting ['beb i sɪt ɪŋ] *n.* taking care of children whose parents are away. (No plural form in this sense.) ♦ *Mary started doing babysitting when she was thirteen.* ♦ *Babysitting is a big responsibility.*

bachelor ['bætʃ (ə) lɚ] *n.* a man who is not married. ♦ *Bill is a confirmed bachelor with no plans to marry.* ♦ *There aren't many eligible bachelors left in town.*

bachelorhood ['bæθʃ ə lɚ hʊd] *n.* the state of being an unmarried man. (No plural form in this sense.) ♦ *Bachelorhood suited the young man quite well.* ♦ *John has a lot of free time, owing to his bachelorhood.*

back ['bæk] **1.** *n.* the part of a body along the spine. ♦ *The children stood with their backs pressed to the wall.* ♦ *John hurt his back helping a friend move some furniture.* **2.** *n.* the rear part of something. ♦ *We entered at the back of the house.* ♦ *The back of your shirt has a tear in it.* **3.** *n.* the part of a chair that supports ①. ♦ *The back of the chair was broken, and I fell off.* ♦ *The airplane passengers reclined their seat backs.* **4. in back of** *prep.* behind someone or something. ♦ *Jane hid in back of the shed.* ♦ *Please put the broom in back of the door.* **5. back up; back off** *iv.* + *adv.* to move backwards, away from someone or something. ♦ *Back up! You're in my way.* ♦ *The cat backed off when it saw the dog approach.* **6. back out (of something)** *iv.* + *adv.* (+ *prep. phr.*) to move backwards out of something. ♦ *Please back out of the driveway carefully.* ♦ *There are children playing in the street. Be careful when you back out.* **7. back up** *tv.* + *adv.* to make a copy of one's computer work for safekeeping. ♦ *I forgot to back up my computer files the day the power went out.* ♦ *Does the secretary back up the computers each night?* **8. back out (of something)** *tv.* + *adv.* (+ *prep. phr.*) to make someone or something go backwards out of something; to make someone or something move back and go out of something. ♦ *Susan backed the car out of the garage.* ♦ *The kids backed their bicycles out of the way so that the pedestrian could pass.* **9.** *tv.* to support someone or something; to agree with someone or something. ♦ *Jane backed my idea of moving the meeting time to 4:30.* ♦ *I always back my boss on department policy.* **10.** *tv.* to support someone or something with money. ♦ *The wealthy banker backed the entire opera season.* ♦ *An anonymous patron backed the struggling artist.* **11.** *adj.* rear; opposite the front. ♦ *The four friends sat in the back row of the movie theater.* ♦ *There was a pool table in the bar's back room.* **12.** *adj.* past; not current. ♦ *Mary called the magazine publisher to order a back issue.* ♦ *The union negotiated back pay for its members.* **13.** *adv.* to the rear; backwards. ♦ *The museum guard made us step back from the painting.* ♦ *I moved back to let the busy clerk pass me.* **14.** *adv.* in or to the original place. ♦ *Please put the cookie jar back where it belongs.* ♦ *You never put the scissors back when you are done with them.* **15.** *adv.* earlier; in or to the past. ♦ *The time travelers went back to the year 1392.* ♦ *Sue suddenly realized that she should have gotten off the bus three stops back.* **16.** *adv.* in reply; in repayment of something. ♦ *Six months after I borrowed the money, I paid back the loan.* ♦ *Jane is trying to teach her kids not to answer back rudely.* **17. back and forth** *phr.* moving in one direction and then the other repeatedly; moving from one to the other repeatedly. ♦ *We tossed the ball back and forth between us.* ♦ *The tiger paced back and forth in its cage.*

backboard ['bæk bord] *n.* a vertically mounted board to which a basketball hoop is attached. ♦ *The basketball bounced off the backboard and missed the basket.* ♦ *The school bought new backboards for the basketball court.*

backbone ['bæk bon] **1.** *n.* the spine. ♦ *The hiker's backbone broke in the fall.* ♦ *The human backbone is a delicate structure.* **2.** *n.* willpower; courage. (Figurative on ①. No plural form in this sense.) ♦ *John has no backbone and lets people take advantage of him constantly.* ♦ *Jane got some backbone and asked for a raise.*

backbreaker ['bæk brek ɚ] *n.* a difficult task. ♦ *Spring cleaning is really a backbreaker!* ♦ *This project my boss assigned me is a real backbreaker!*

backbreaking ['bæk brek ɪŋ] *adj.* requiring much strength and endurance. (Adv: *backbreakingly.*) ♦ *Moving the piano is a backbreaking task.* ♦ *The backbreaking work made me very tired.*

backer ['bæk ɚ] *n.* someone who provides money or support, sometimes without hope of a return of the money. ♦ *The artist's backer is wealthy but demanding.* ♦ *The backers of the new play are confident about its success.*

backfield ['bæk fild] *n.* the players on a football team who are positioned behind the linemen on offense and behind the linebackers on defense. ♦ *The backfield played poorly and caused the loss of the game.* ♦ *The coach replaced the whole backfield after the play.*

backfire ['bæk fɑɪr] **1.** *iv.* to cause the opposite from what was intended or expected. ♦ *The surprise party backfired because Anne already knew about it.* ♦ *After the plan backfired, things were worse than before.* **2.** *iv.* [for gasoline in an engine] to explode too soon, causing a loud noise. ♦ *John's old car backfires every time he starts it.* ♦ *Does the mechanic know what is making the engine backfire?*

backgammon ['bæk gæm ən] *n.* a board game played with dice and movable tokens. (No plural form in this sense.) ♦ *Grandma and Grandpa love to play backgammon.* ♦ *You win backgammon by clearing your tokens from the board.*

background ['bæk grɑʊnd] **1.** *n.* [in a picture] the scene behind the main subject. ♦ *The Rocky Mountains formed the background of the photo.* ♦ *We sat in front of a blue background when our portrait was taken.* **2.** *n.* the events leading up to something. (No plural form in this sense.) ♦ *The lawyer provided the jury with the background of the case.* ♦ *We arrived late for the movie and didn't know the background of the story.* **3.** *n.* the past training, education, and experience of someone. ♦ *Jane told the foster parents about the child's background.* ♦ *During a job interview, you will be asked to talk about your background.*

backhand ['bæk hænd] *n.* a swift movement of a racket or a paddle with the back part of the hand facing forward. ♦ *The tennis player was known for his powerful backhand.* ♦ *Anne went to the tennis court to practice her backhand.*

backhanded ['bæk hæn dɪd] *adj.* [of an insult] disguised as a compliment. (Adv: *backhandedly.*) ♦ *The committee was insulted by John's backhanded compliments.* ♦ *Mary's backhanded praise offended me.*

backing ['bæk ɪŋ] **1.** *n.* financial support for a large project. (No plural form in this sense.) ♦ *The community project did not receive enough backing and was abandoned.* ♦ *A wealthy family provided backing for the festival.* **2.** *n.* moral support. (No plural form in this sense.) ♦ *Jane turns to her family for their backing in difficult situations.* ♦ *Tom happily gave his backing to his younger brother.* **3.** *n.* something placed behind something else to strengthen, protect, or support it. (No plural form in this sense.) ♦ *The backing on the poster came loose and it fell off the wall.* ♦ *After many years, the carpet's backing disintegrated.*

backlash ['bæk læʃ] *n.* an adverse social or political reaction. ♦ *A large backlash was anticipated when taxes were raised.* ♦ *There was a voter backlash when the promised budget savings did not materialize.*

backlog ['bæk lɔg] *n.* an accumulation of things that need to be done. ♦ *After his vacation, Bob had a backlog of telephone calls to return.* ♦ *A backlog developed in the understaffed company.*

backorder ['bæk or dɚ] **1.** *n.* an order for an item that is out of stock. ♦ *I placed a backorder for the book I wanted.* ♦ *Does the company do backorders for out-of-stock products?* **2.** *tv.* to record an order for an item that is not currently available. ♦ *The clerk backordered the books that were out of stock.* ♦ *That is out of stock. Do you want me to backorder it for you?*

backpack ['bæk pæk] **1.** *n.* a bag that hangs from the shoulders and rests on the back. ♦ *Each child got a new backpack for school.* ♦ *John lost his backpack on the hike.* **2.** *iv.* to hike or camp, carrying necessary belongings in ①. ♦ *Jane loves to backpack in the mountains.* ♦ *The family backpacks every summer.*

backpacker ['bæk pæk ɚ] *n.* someone who travels with a backpack. ♦ *The backpacker got lost in the woods.* ♦ *We ran into other backpackers on our trip across Europe.*

backpedal ['bæk pɛd əl] **1.** *iv.* to slow or stop a bicycle with pedal-operated brakes by moving the pedals backwards. ♦ *The kids on the bikes backpedaled to make a quick stop.* ♦ *Tom had to backpedal very hard to slow down before striking the tree.* **2.** *iv.* to retreat from an originally held position or belief. (Figurative on ①.) ♦ *When forced to explain her prejudices, Mary backpedaled quickly.* ♦ *The official backpedaled on his campaign promises after the election.*

backrest ['bæk rɛst] *n.* the vertical part of a chair that supports someone's back. ♦ *Don't sit on that chair. Its backrest is broken.* ♦ *Anne leaned against the backrest of the chair and relaxed.*

back seat ['bæk 'sit] **1.** *n.* the rear seat of a car; a seat behind the other seats. ♦ *I hate to sit in the back seat!* ♦ *If the children sit in the back seat, make sure they lock the rear doors.* **2. take a back seat (to someone or something)** *idiom* to become not as important as someone or something else. ♦ *My homework had to take a back seat to football during the playoffs.* ♦ *Jimmy always took a back seat to his older brother, Bill, until Bill went away to college.*

backside ['bæk sɑɪd] **1.** *n.* the back part of something. ♦ *The movers scratched the backside of the bookcase.* ♦ *The* *scratch isn't visible because it's on the backside.* **2.** *n.* the buttocks; the rump. ♦ *Tom fell on his backside while skating.* ♦ *You spend too much time sitting on your backside.*

backslash ['bæk slæʃ] *n.* the symbol "\." ♦ *I get the backslash mixed up with the regular slash.* ♦ *Please put the foreign words in backslashes so I can locate them easily in the computer file.*

backslid ['bæk slɪd] pt/pp of backslide.

backslide ['bæk slaɪd] *iv., irreg.* to have a moral lapse; to return to a bad habit. (Pt/pp: backslid.) ♦ *After not smoking for six months, Dave was afraid of backsliding.* ♦ *We all tend to backslide if we don't pay attention to what we do.*

backslider ['bæk slaɪd ɚ] *n.* someone who returns to a bad habit; someone who has a moral lapse. ♦ *Dave felt like a backslider when he had a cigarette.* ♦ *Bill is a backslider who must be watched at work.*

backspace ['bæk spes] **1.** *n.* the key on a keyboard that moves a cursor or a typewriter carriage back one position. ♦ *Where is the backspace on this machine?* ♦ *Press the backspace to erase a single letter.* **2.** *iv.* to press the key on a keyboard that moves a cursor or a typewriter carriage back one position. ♦ *Backspace and type over the blank space that you typed by mistake.* ♦ *You had better backspace over that extra letter.*

backstage ['bæk 'stedʒ] *adv.* toward or in the area behind or to the side of a stage. ♦ *The stage crew stored the props backstage.* ♦ *The actress waited backstage for her cue.*

backstop ['bæk stɑp] **1.** *n.* [in baseball] a large mesh fence behind home plate that protects spectators from foul balls. ♦ *The batter hit the ball into the backstop.* ♦ *The pitch was too high and hit the backstop.* **2.** *n.* [in baseball] the catcher. (See also shortstop.) ♦ *Tom usually played backstop.* ♦ *The batter barely missed the backstop when he swung.*

backstretch ['bæk strɛtʃ] *n.* [in racing] the part of a racetrack opposite the homestretch. ♦ *The horses ran nose to nose in the backstretch.* ♦ *My horse pulled ahead in the backstretch but was behind again in the homestretch.*

backstroke ['bæk strok] *n.* a swimming stroke made while on one's back. ♦ *The swimmers were tested on the backstroke.* ♦ *Jimmy likes the backstroke because he doesn't like to put his face in the water.*

backup ['bæk əp] **1.** *n.* a substitute or replacement for someone or something. ♦ *Is there a backup for John? He is sick.* ♦ *Carry these batteries as a backup in case those wear out.* **2.** *n.* [in computers] a copy of a computer file or document. ♦ *Did you make backups of your files?* ♦ *I erased the file accidentally, and there is no backup!* **3.** *adj.* spare; extra. ♦ *Susan had some backup film for the camera.* ♦ *I own a backup flashlight in case the power goes out.*

backward(s) ['bæk wɚd(z)] **1.** *adv.* toward the rear. ♦ *The kitten inched backwards when it saw the dog.* ♦ *The outfielder ran backward to catch the fly ball.* **2.** *adv.* opposite the normal direction. ♦ *Since the code was written from right to left, Jane never realized she was reading the message backward.* ♦ *The appliance didn't work because it was assembled backwards.* **3.** *adj.* directed toward the back or the starting point. ♦ *With a backward glance from the ship, I saw my mother crying on the dock.* ♦ *He jerked with a slight backward motion, falling over his own feet.* **4.** *adj.* in a worse or earlier state; not modern. (Adv: *backwardly.*) ♦ *Bob was from a backward area that didn't have electricity.* ♦ *The senator's backward views were very uneducated.* **5.** *adj.* hesitant or shy. (Adv: *backwardly.*) ♦ *Tom was a little backward around the other students.* ♦ *Mary was a backward child but became a successful businesswoman.*

backwoods ['bæk 'wʊdz] **1.** *n.* a place deep in the woods. (Treated as singular.) ♦ *We spent two weeks camping in the backwoods.* ♦ *The forest fire threatened even the deepest backwoods.* **2.** *adj.* rural; rustic. ♦ *Sue is from a small, backwoods community where everyone knows each other.* ♦ *Bill talks with a deep backwoods accent. Where is he from?*

backyard ['bæk 'jɑrd] *n.* the lawn or area behind a house. ♦ *The children were playing tag in the backyard.* ♦ *Anne planted some trees in her backyard.*

bacon ['bek ən] *n.* meat from the back and sides of a hog. (No plural form in this sense.) ♦ *I love crisp bacon, but it is not good for me.* ♦ *Bacon and eggs are Bill's favorite breakfast food.*

bacteria [bæk 'tɪr i ə] *n.* a group of tiny one-celled organisms. (Bacteria is the plural of bacterium.) ♦ *One must look through a microscope to see bacteria.* ♦ *Some bacteria cause harmful diseases.*

bacterial [bæk 'tɪr i əl] *adj.* relating to or caused by bacteria. (Adv: *bacterially.*) ♦ *The illness is caused by a bacterial infection.* ♦ *The disease presented a serious problem in bacterial identification.*

bacteriologist [bæk tɪr i 'ɑl ə dʒəst] *n.* a scientist who studies bacteria. ♦ *The bacteriologists were not able to identify the specimen.* ♦ *The lab employs bacteriologists to identify the germs that cause diseases.*

bacteriology [bæk tɪr i 'ɑl ə dʒi] *n.* the study of bacteria. (No plural form in this sense.) ♦ *The biologist began studying bacteriology in college.* ♦ *The department of bacteriology has a new laboratory.*

bacterium [bæk 'tɪr i əm] *n.* a small one-celled organism; a species of bacteria. (Pl: bacteria.) ♦ *A single bacterium is unlikely to cause a disease.* ♦ *Which bacterium do they say caused the infection?*

bad ['bæd] **1.** *adj., irreg.* wicked; evil; not good. (Adv: *badly.* Comp: worse; sup: worst.) ♦ *The children found the house of a very bad witch.* ♦ *John has done some bad things, but he is not really a bad person.* **2.** *adj., irreg.* of poor quality; inferior; worthless; defective; not good. (Adv: *badly.*) ♦ *Driving while drunk is a bad idea.* ♦ *One of my knees is bad, so I can't run well.* **3.** *adj., irreg.* serious; severe. (Adv: *badly.*) ♦ *Tom has a bad cold.* ♦ *Jane suffered from a bad case of food poisoning.* **4.** *adj., irreg.* harmful; not healthful. ♦ *Smoking is bad for your lungs.* ♦ *Fatty foods are bad for your health.* **5.** *adj., irreg.* [of a person, a creature, or a part of one's body feeling or appearing] sick, hurt, or unwell. ♦ *If you still feel bad this afternoon, you should go to the doctor.* ♦ *After Mary sprained her ankle, it felt bad for several weeks.* **6.** *adj., irreg.* unpleasant; disagreeable; not nice. (Adv: *badly.*) ♦ *I was upset because I had a bad day.* ♦ *Jimmy was punished for using bad words.* **7.** *adj.* [of food] decayed or spoiled. ♦ *Mary didn't refrigerate the eggs, and they went bad.* ♦ *The milk turned bad* *overnight.* **8.** *adv.* intensely; severely. (Colloquial.) ♦ *I have to go to the bathroom bad!* ♦ *This cut really hurts bad!*

badge ['bædʒ] **1.** *n.* a pin or medal worn to show allegiance to or membership in an organization. ♦ *The officer handed out badges to the new members.* ♦ *How many badges did the club president order?* **2.** *n.* a symbol or a sign of something. ♦ *The soldier wore his medal as a badge of honor.* ♦ *I wear my badges on my uniform.*

badger ['bæ dʒɚ] **1.** *n.* a nocturnal, burrowing animal found in North America, Asia, and Europe. ♦ *The hunter trapped a badger in the field.* ♦ *Last summer, badgers burrowed under our bushes.* **2.** *tv.* to pester someone; to bother someone. (Figurative on ①.) ♦ *Quit badgering me for a raise in your allowance!* ♦ *I don't mean to badger you, but when will you do the job?*

badly ['bæd li] **1.** *adv.* in an inferior or defective manner; poorly; not well. ♦ *The boring play was performed badly.* ♦ *I like to play chess, but I play it badly.* **2.** *adv.* unpleasantly; disagreeably; not well. ♦ *I was upset because my day went very badly.* ♦ *Jimmy behaved badly at dinner and was sent to his room.* **3.** *adv.* seriously; severely. ♦ *Was Bill badly injured in the accident?* ♦ *The storm badly damaged our house.* **4.** *adv.* very much; to a great extent. (Figurative on ③.) ♦ *I wanted a new bicycle very badly.* ♦ *The children wanted badly to stay up late.*

badminton ['bæd mɪ(n)t n] *n.* a game in which players on a court use rackets to hit a shuttlecock back and forth over a net. (No plural form in this sense.) ♦ *Badminton is a relaxing sport.* ♦ *We played badminton at the company picnic.*

bad-mouth ['bæd mɑʊθ] *tv.* to say bad things about someone; to tell lies about someone. (Informal.) ♦ *Don't bad-mouth your boss. He might be listening.* ♦ *Jane felt guilty after bad-mouthing her neighbor.*

baffle ['bæf əl] *tv.* to puzzle or confuse someone or something; to be difficult for someone or something to solve. ♦ *The detective was baffled by the case.* ♦ *The jigsaw puzzle baffled us until we realized pieces were missing.*

baffling ['bæf lɪŋ] *adj.* confusing; puzzling. (Adv: *bafflingly.*) ♦ *Bob read a baffling mystery on his vacation.* ♦ *The question of what happened to the missing money was baffling.*

bag ['bæg] **1.** *n.* a sack; a pouch-like container. ♦ *Jane packed her lunch in a bag.* ♦ *I carried the groceries in a plastic bag.* **2.** *n.* the contents of ①. ♦ *Bill and Sue used a whole bag of apples when they made pies.* ♦ *Put a whole bag of nuts in the recipe.* **3.** *n.* a pouch or fold of loose skin. ♦ *The obese man had bags of flesh on his legs.* ♦ *I did exercises to tighten up the bags under my arms.* **4.** *tv.* to put items into a bag. ♦ *The clerk broke the eggs when she bagged my groceries.* ♦ *I bagged the laundry before we went to the Laundromat.* **5.** *tv.* to kill wild game. ♦ *We didn't bag any deer while we were hunting.* ♦ *The hunter bagged a large duck.* **6.** *iv.* to hang loosely; to bulge; for extra cloth to form a pouch. ♦ *Since the pants were four sizes too large, they bagged around my waist.* ♦ *The poorly hung curtains bagged horribly.* **7. bag of tricks** *idiom* a collection of special techniques or methods. ♦ *What have you got in your bag of tricks that could help me with this problem?* ♦ *Here comes Mother with her bag of tricks. I'm sure she can help us.* **8. leave someone holding the bag** *idiom* to allow someone to take all the blame; to leave someone appearing guilty. ♦ *They all ran off and left me holding the bag. It wasn't even my fault.* ♦ *It was the mayor's fault, but he wasn't left holding the bag.* **9. a mixed bag** *idiom* a varied collection of people or things. ♦ *The new pupils are a mixed bag—some bright, some positively stupid.* ♦ *The furniture I bought is a mixed bag. Some of it is valuable, and the rest is worthless.*

bagel ['beg əl] *n.* a bread roll in the shape of a doughnut, prepared by boiling and then baking dough. (From Yiddish.) ♦ *I ate some lox and bagels for breakfast.* ♦ *The bakery sold bagels by the dozen.*

baggage ['bæg ɪdʒ] **1.** *n.* luggage or suitcases. (No plural form in this sense. Number is expressed with *piece(s) of baggage.*) ♦ *The airline lost our baggage!* ♦ *How much baggage can we take on the plane?* **2.** *n.* unpleasant memories or guilt; mental problems. (No plural form in this sense. Figurative on ①.) ♦ *Bill's past baggage prevented him from having healthy relationships.* ♦ *Once Anne left her mental baggage behind, she was much happier.*

baggy ['bæg i] *adj.* puffy; having extra material that hangs in loose folds. (Adv: *baggily.* Comp: *baggier;* sup: *baggiest.*) ♦ *I don't like how those baggy pants look on you.* ♦ *The tailor altered the baggy dress for the bridesmaid.*

bagpipes ['bæg pɑɪps] *n.* a musical instrument consisting of pipes connected to a bag serving as an air reservoir. (Treated as plural.) ♦ *Jane wanted bagpipes at her wedding.* ♦ *Dave practiced the bagpipes for many years, but did not improve.*

Bahamas [bə 'hɑm əz] See Gazetteer.

bail ['bel] **1.** *n.* the amount of money needed to release someone from jail prior to a court appearance. (No plural form in this sense.) ♦ *The killer was released on half a million dollars bail.* ♦ *The poor suspect could not raise bail.* **2. bail out** *tv.* + *adv.* to deposit money to release someone from jail prior to a court appearance. ♦ *David bailed his roommate out of jail.* ♦ *Was the suspect's family able to bail him out?* **3. bail (out)** *tv.* (+ *adv.*) to scoop water from a boat using a bucket. ♦ *We bailed out all the water that had leaked in.* ♦ *Please help me bail this water out!* **4. bail (out)** *tv.* (+ *adv.*) to free a boat of water by scooping it out. ♦ *Let's bail out this old boat and see if it will float.* ♦ *The first thing the sailor taught us was how to bail out the boat.* **5. bail out from; bail out of** *iv.* + *adv.* + *prep. phr.* to jump out of an airplane wearing a parachute. ♦ *The pilot bailed out from the downed plane.* ♦ *The soldiers bailed from the warplane when it was damaged during the battle.* **6. bail out of** *iv.* + *adv.* + *prep. phr.* to depart; to quit an enterprise. (Figurative on ⑤.) ♦ *I had to bail out of the deal before I lost all my money.* ♦ *We bailed out of the failed investment just in time.*

bailiff ['bel ɪf] *n.* an officer of the law who serves as an assistant to the sheriff, especially in a courtroom. ♦ *The bailiff removed the unruly defendant from the courtroom.* ♦ *Before the judge appeared, the bailiff called for order.*

bait ['bet] **1.** *n.* someone or something used as a lure or temptation. (No plural form in this sense.) ♦ *Cheese is good bait for catfish.* ♦ *What bait did you use to persuade the kids to clean their rooms?* **2.** *tv.* to put a worm or some kind of food on a hook in order to attract fish. ♦ *Bill used artificial lures so he wouldn't have to bait his fishing hook.* ♦ *Dad didn't catch any fish because he forgot to bait his hook.* **3.** *tv.* to put a lure into a trap. ♦ *Anne baited the* *mousetrap with peanut butter.* ♦ *The hunters baited their traps carefully.* **4.** *tv.* to bother or torment someone or something. ♦ *Please don't bait your little sister like that!* ♦ *The children were always baiting Jimmy because of his height.* **5. fish or cut bait** *idiom* either do the job you are supposed to be doing, or quit and let someone else do it. ♦ *Mary is doing much better on the job since her manager told her to fish or cut bait.* ♦ *The boss told Tom, "Quit wasting time! Fish or cut bait!"*

bake ['bek] **1.** *tv.* to cook something using dry heat, usually in an oven. ♦ *Jane baked pies and cookies for the bake sale.* ♦ *The recipe says to bake the casserole for an hour.* **2.** *tv.* to place someone or something in the sun on a hot day. (Figurative on ①.) ♦ *I love to bake myself at the beach in the summer.* ♦ *The sun baked the clay bricks for a week.* **3.** *iv.* to cook food by placing it in a hot oven. ♦ *Bill is at home baking for the coming week.* ♦ *Jane learned to bake when she lived alone.* **4.** *iv.* [for someone or something] to undergo baking. ♦ *How long should the potatoes bake?* ♦ *Let the bread bake for one hour.* **5.** *iv.* to be in the sun on a hot day; to be in a place heated by the sun. (Figurative on ④.) ♦ *Let's go to the beach and bake.* ♦ *The cat loved to sit by the window and bake all day.*

baked ['bekt] *adj.* cooked by baking. ♦ *We ate baked beans at the picnic.* ♦ *My baked chicken was too dry.*

baker ['bek ɚ] *n.* someone who bakes foods, usually breads or pastries. ♦ *Jane asked the baker to make a birthday cake.* ♦ *Tom went to cooking school to become a baker.*

bakery ['bek ri] *n.* a store where bread products and pastries are prepared and sold. ♦ *I bought a fancy cake at the local bakery.* ♦ *It is very busy at the bakery before sunrise.*

baking powder ['bek ɪŋ paʊ dɚ] *n.* a substance used in cooking in place of yeast to make dough rise. (No plural form in this sense.) ♦ *Mary accidentally used too much baking powder in her cake.* ♦ *Without baking powder, a cake would be flat.*

balance ['bæl əns] **1.** *n.* an even placement of weight; equilibrium. (No plural form in this sense.) ♦ *I lost my balance and fell.* ♦ *The mobile was in perfect balance.* **2.** *n.* a device that compares the weight of two objects. ♦ *The merchant weighed the goods on an old balance.* ♦ *An old-fashioned balance was on display at the museum.* **3.** *n.* an equality in weight, proportion, or value; harmony. (No plural form in this sense.) ♦ *The pictures achieved a good balance on the wall.* ♦ *Even though some pieces of furniture were modern and some antiques, there was a balance between them.* **4.** *n.* the amount of money remaining on a bill after part of it has been paid; the amount of money remaining in an account after a transaction. (No plural form in this sense.) ♦ *The balance in my checking account is low.* ♦ *After winning the lottery, Tom paid the balance on all his loans.* **5.** *tv.* to place something in such a way that it is stable. ♦ *I balanced the book on top of the stack.* ♦ *Jimmy tried to balance his blocks on the table.* **6.** *tv.* to apply credits and debits to an account to determine the correct amount of money in the account. ♦ *Jane balances her checking account each month.* ♦ *The company balances its books once a year.* **7.** *tv.* to make something harmonious in appearance or character. ♦ *The decorator balanced the colors perfectly.* ♦ *Mary balanced the planting in her garden carefully.* **8. catch someone off-balance** *idiom* to discover a person who is not prepared; to surprise someone. ♦ *Sorry I acted so flustered. You caught me off-balance.* ♦ *The robbers caught Anne off-balance and stole her purse.* **9. hang in the balance** *idiom* to be in an undecided state; to be between two equal possibilities. ♦ *The prisoner stood before the judge with his life hanging in the balance.* ♦ *This whole issue will have to hang in the balance until Jane gets back from her vacation.* **10. strike a balance (between two things)** *idiom* to find a satisfactory compromise between two extremes. ♦ *The political party must strike a balance between the right wing and the left wing.* ♦ *Jane is overdressed for the party and Sally is underdressed. What a pity they didn't strike a balance between them.*

balanced ['bæl ənst] *adj.* [of a diet] sensible or leading to good healthy. ♦ *Eating from all the food groups ensures a balanced diet.* ♦ *My family eats balanced meals.*

balcony ['bæl kən i] **1.** *n.* a platform that extends outward from a room that is higher than ground level. ♦ *The bedrooms on the second floor of the house had balconies.* ♦ *We ate breakfast on the balcony at the ski lodge.* **2.** *n.* [in a hall or auditorium] an upper level of seats that extends over the main floor. ♦ *Our seats at the opera were in the balcony.* ♦ *We took our opera glasses so we could see the stage from the third balcony.*

bald ['bɔld] *adj.* having no hair on the head; without hair. (Comp: *balder;* sup: *baldest.*) ♦ *The bald man wore a hat to protect his head from the sun.* ♦ *Many new babies are bald.*

bald eagle ['bɔld 'i gəl] *n.* a large, brown eagle with a white head and tail, native to the United States. ♦ *The bald eagle is the national bird of the United States of America.* ♦ *Fish is an important part of a bald eagle's diet.*

baldness ['bɔld nəs] *n.* the condition of having no hair. (No plural form in this sense.) ♦ *Bob's baldness made him look older.* ♦ *Anne thought her husband's baldness was attractive.*

bale ['bel] **1.** *n.* a rectangular bundle of something, especially hay or straw. ♦ *The children played in the bales of hay in the barn.* ♦ *The farm workers made bales until the sun set.* **2.** *tv.* to put something, especially hay or straw, into a bundle. ♦ *The farmer baled hay all day.* ♦ *The farmer hired some help to bale the straw.*

balk ['bɔk] **1.** *iv.* [in baseball] to pretend to be beginning to pitch the ball and then stop. ♦ *This pitcher balks in every game.* ♦ *Tom balked twice in the second inning.* **2. balk at** *iv.* + *prep. phr.* to stop short of doing something; to hesitate or refuse to do something. ♦ *Jane balked at the thought of lying to me.* ♦ *Many people do not balk at the idea of cheating on their taxes.*

ball ['bɔl] **1.** *n.* a round object; a sphere. ♦ *I crinkled the aluminum foil into a ball.* ♦ *The yarn was wound into a ball.* **2.** *n.* a toy that is a round object. ♦ *The baby played with a cloth ball in its crib.* ♦ *The children threw the ball back and forth.* **3.** *n.* [in baseball] a pitched ball that fails to pass through the strike zone, where it must be struck at by the batter. ♦ *The batter had two balls before hitting a home run.* ♦ *The umpire cried, "Ball!" but it was really a strike.* **4.** *n.* an elegant dance or party. ♦ *Mary danced at the ball for several hours.* ♦ *Each year the club held a ball to raise money for charity.* **5. balls of one's feet** *phr.* the bottom part of the feet just under the toes. ♦ *Mary got blisters on the balls of her feet from playing tennis.* ♦ *The* *dancer balanced on the balls of his feet.* **6. have a ball** *idiom* to have a good time; to have fun. ♦ *We had a ball on our vacation.* ♦ *The kids had a ball playing in the leaves.* **7. carry the ball** *idiom* to be in charge; to make sure that a job gets done. ♦ *We need someone who knows how to get the job done. Hey, Sally! Why don't you carry the ball for us?* ♦ *John can't carry the ball. He isn't organized enough.* **8. drop the ball** *idiom* to make a blunder; to fail in some way. ♦ *Everything was going fine in the election until my campaign manager dropped the ball.* ♦ *You can't trust John to do the job right. He's always dropping the ball.*

ballad ['bæl əd] *n.* a poem or song that tells a story, especially a love story. ♦ *The folk singer was known for her emotional ballads.* ♦ *The performer sang three ballads and a folk song at the concert.*

ballast ['bæl əst] *n.* heavy material that provides stability in ships and hot-air balloons. (No plural form in this sense.) ♦ *The sailing ships carried many tons of stone ballast.* ♦ *The ship used the heavy cargo as ballast for its journey across the ocean.*

ballerina [bæl ə 'rin ə] *n.* a female ballet dancer. ♦ *The ballerina rehearsed for hours with her partner.* ♦ *The young girl practiced every day after school to become a ballerina.*

ballet [bæ 'le] *n.* a form of graceful and precise dance that tells a story without using speech or singing. (No plural form in this sense.) ♦ *Which ballet did you see?* ♦ Swan Lake *is the name of a famous ballet.*

ballistics [bə 'lɪs tɪks] *n.* the study of the motion of objects that are hurled through space such as bullets, rockets, and missiles. (Treated as singular.) ♦ *An expert on ballistics testified about the gunshot.* ♦ *The soldiers learned about ballistics during their training.*

balloon [bə 'lun] **1.** *n.* a container of rubber, fabric, or some other membrane that can be filled with air or gas. ♦ *The party room was decorated with colorful balloons.* ♦ *A ride in the hot-air balloon gave us a wonderful view of the town.* **2.** *iv.* to swell or inflate; to grow rapidly. (Figurative on ①.) ♦ *Tom's sprained ankle ballooned during the night.* ♦ *The scandal ballooned out of control.*

ballot ['bæl ət] **1.** *n.* a method of voting involving pieces of paper or machines. ♦ *The club's president is elected by ballot.* ♦ *Should we vote by raising our hands or by ballot?* **2.** *n.* a piece of paper on which one's vote is marked. ♦ *The voters stuffed their ballots into a special box.* ♦ *Who will count the ballots?* **3.** *n.* the list of candidates to be voted for in an election. ♦ *Many fine candidates are on the ballot.* ♦ *We discussed the candidates we thought would be on the ballot.*

ballpark ['bɔl pɑrk] *n.* a baseball field or stadium; any place baseball is played. ♦ *Grandpa takes me to the ballpark each summer.* ♦ *The best hot dogs in the world are served in ballparks!*

ballplayer ['bɔl ple ɚ] *n.* someone who plays baseball, football, or basketball. ♦ *Tom just wanted to be a ballplayer—he didn't care what kind.* ♦ *The ballplayers practiced every morning.*

ballpoint pen ['bɔl pɔɪnt 'pɛn] *n.* a kind of pen having a small metal ball in the tip. ♦ *The children drew with ballpoint pens.* ♦ *I prefer using ballpoint pen to pencil.*

ballroom ['bɔl rum] *n.* a large room for formal parties and dancing. ♦ *The ballroom in the old mansion was used only one night a year.* ♦ *The decoration committee transformed the ballroom into a spring garden.*

baloney [bə 'lon i] *n.* nonsense; pointless talk and lies. (No plural form in this sense. Slang. See also **bologna.**) ♦ *I'm tired of listening to all your baloney!* ♦ *The president's speech was a lot of baloney.*

Baltic Sea [bɔl tɪk 'si] See Gazetteer.

bamboo [bæm 'bu] **1.** *n.* a type of very tall grass found in tropical places. (No plural form in this sense.) ♦ *Bamboo has a long, hollow stem, which, when dried, becomes hard and can be used as a pole to make many different kinds of objects.* ♦ *Bamboo is sometimes used to make furniture.* **2.** *adj.* made from bamboo stems or wood. ♦ *The bamboo chair blended into the living room nicely.* ♦ *Those picture frames are bamboo.*

ban ['bæn] **1.** *n.* a prohibition; a statement by an official that something is illegal. ♦ *The principal announced a ban on guns at the school.* ♦ *During the 1920s, the government put a ban on alcohol.* **2.** *tv.* to make an activity illegal; to forbid the doing of something. ♦ *The college banned alcohol from parties on campus.* ♦ *Mom banned television in our house on weeknights.*

banana [bə 'næn ə] **1.** *n.* a long, tropical fruit with a yellow skin around a soft, white edible pulp. ♦ *The cook made bread out of the ripe bananas.* ♦ *The gorillas at the zoo love bananas.* **2.** *adj.* made of or flavored with ①. ♦ *Max loves banana ice cream.* ♦ *Banana bread is especially good when it's warm.*

band ['bænd] **1.** *n.* a group of musicians, often including singers. ♦ *Dave and his friends formed a band that practiced on the weekends.* ♦ *The couple hired a band to play at their wedding reception.* **2.** *n.* a flat, thin strip of some material that is used to hold objects together; a ribbon. ♦ *Each cigar in the box had a paper band around it.* ♦ *I sealed the box with a band of tape.* **3.** *n.* a stripe. ♦ *The shirt was covered with wide bands of bright color.* ♦ *A band of red accented the design.* **4.** *n.* a tribe; a group of people. ♦ *The band of hunters took shelter in the cave.* ♦ *The anthropologist studied a band of people in the jungle.* **5. band together** *iv.* + *adv.* to come together; to assemble; to unite. ♦ *The community banded together after the flood.* ♦ *The tragedy caused the family to band together.*

bandage ['bæn dɪdʒ] **1.** *n.* a wrapping used to cover and protect a wound against dirt, germs, and infection. ♦ *Jane put a bandage on the cut on her finger.* ♦ *The bandage kept the dirt out of the soldier's wound.* **2.** *tv.* to place ① on someone or something. ♦ *The school nurse bandaged Jimmy's skinned knees.* ♦ *I had to bandage my own sprained ankle.*

bandaged ['bæn dɪdʒd] *adj.* covered or protected with a bandage. ♦ *Tom's bandaged wound became infected.* ♦ *Jane limped along on her bandaged foot.*

bandit ['bæn dɪt] *n.* a robber, especially one belonging to a band of outlaws. ♦ *The bandit tried to hide from the sheriff.* ♦ *No one in the town could catch the notorious bandit.*

bandwagon ['bænd wæg ən] *n.* a political or social movement; a popular or trendy train of thought. ♦ *Dad has jumped on the environmental bandwagon.* ♦ *The senator's presence on the conservative bandwagon angered his liberal supporters.*

bang ['bæŋ] **1.** *n.* a sudden, loud noise; the sound of an explosion. ♦ *The baby cried when the balloon popped and made a bang.* ♦ *I heard a bang and went to see what had fallen.* **2.** *n.* a thrill; a feeling of excitement. (Slang.) ♦ *Watching old black-and-white movies gives me a bang.* ♦ *Grandma and Grandpa really get a bang out of their new granddaughter.* **3. bangs** *n.* hair that hangs down over the forehead or eyes rather than being combed back. ♦ *Jane told the hairdresser to cut her bangs.* ♦ *My bangs are too long and keep getting in my eyes.* **4.** *tv.* to hit something against something else, making a loud noise. ♦ *Bang the lid of the jar on the counter, and it will open more easily.* ♦ *Bob banged the TV with his fist, and the picture cleared.* **5. bang into** *tv.* + *prep. phr.* to push or crash something into someone or something. ♦ *Who banged their car into my car?* ♦ *Tom banged his shopping cart into the stack of boxes.* **6. bang into** *iv.* + *prep. phr.* to crash into someone or something. ♦ *I accidentally banged into the wall.* ♦ *Who banged into my car?* **7.** *iv.* to make loud noises by striking [something]. ♦ *Bang on the door and see if the Joneses are home.* ♦ *Who is banging around in the kitchen?* **8. go over with a bang** *idiom* [for something] to be funny or entertaining. ♦ *The play was a success. It really went over with a bang.* ♦ *That's a great joke. It went over with a bang.*

banging ['bæŋ ɪŋ] *n.* a series of loud noises; the continuous sound of crashing things. (No plural form in this sense.) ♦ *I got a headache from the banging made by the construction workers.* ♦ *What is that banging in the basement?*

Bangladesh [bæŋ glə 'dɛʃ] See Gazetteer.

banish ['bæn ɪʃ] **1.** *tv.* to expel someone from a certain place; to forbid someone to return to a certain place. ♦ *The king banished his nephew to France for many years.* ♦ *The naughty child was banished to his room until dinner.* **2.** *tv.* to send or drive something, such as a problem, away. (Figurative on ①.) ♦ *Bill made a resolution to banish sorrow from his life.* ♦ *The president promised to banish poverty from the land.*

banishment ['bæn ɪʃ mənt] *n.* exile; being forced to leave and remain away from a certain location; forcing someone to leave a certain location. (No plural form in this sense.) ♦ *The duke endured his banishment while plotting against the king.* ♦ *The tyrant's sentence was banishment from the land.*

banjo ['bæn dʒo] *n.* a musical instrument similar to a small guitar, with a wooden body covered with a tight skin like a drum. (Pl in *-s* or *-es*.) ♦ *Susan plays the banjo in a band.* ♦ *How many strings does a banjo have?*

bank ['bæŋk] **1.** *n.* a corporation that lends, saves, and protects money. ♦ *We got a personal loan from the bank.* ♦ *I opened a savings account at a local bank.* **2.** *n.* the building where money is loaned, saved, and protected. ♦ *I walked to the bank after work to cash a check.* ♦ *The post office is across the street from the bank.* **3.** *n.* a place to store certain objects. ♦ *The community contributed to the blood bank by donating blood each spring.* ♦ *Bill made a contribution to the food bank.* **4.** *n.* the land along the side of a river, stream, or canal. ♦ *The lovers sat on the bank of the river and had a picnic.* ♦ *The little bridge enabled the children to run from one bank of the stream to the other.* **5.** *n.* a row or set of objects. ♦ *It was a perfect day until a bank of clouds covered the sun.* ♦ *We installed a bank of lights in the ceiling of our basement.* **6.** *iv.* to do business with a bank. ♦ *I bank at Citizen's Bank and Trust Company.* ♦ *John banks where there are no service charges.* **7.** *tv.* to place money in an account at a bank. ♦ *Sue banks her paycheck every Friday.* ♦ *If I could bank half my money each month, I would save more money.* **8.** *tv.* to tilt an airplane to the side in flight in order to turn right or left. ♦ *The pilot banked the plane as we made a turn.* ♦ *In flying school, we learned to bank the plane.* **9. bank on something** *idiom* to count on something; to rely on something. ♦ *The weather service said it wouldn't rain, but I wouldn't bank on it.* ♦ *My word is to be trusted. You can bank on it.* **10. break the bank** *idiom* to leave someone without any money. ♦ *It will hardly break the bank if we go out to dinner just once.* ♦ *Buying a new dress at that price won't break the bank.*

banker ['bæŋk ɚ] *n.* someone who is an owner of or an important officer in a bank. ♦ *The wealthy banker donated $10,000 to the worthy charity.* ♦ *The firm hired a retired banker to manage its money.*

bank robber ['bæŋk rɑb ɚ] *n.* someone who steals money from a bank, usually by threatening violence. ♦ *The bank robber handed the teller a note demanding money.* ♦ *The bank robber was caught counting his loot back at his hideout.*

bankrupt ['bæŋk rəpt] **1.** *adj.* having no money; destitute; not able to pay off debts. ♦ *The company was bankrupt after its first year of business.* ♦ *The bankrupt woman had to ask for financial assistance.* **2.** *adj.* lacking in something that is needed; ruined, corrupt, or worthless. (Figurative on ①.) ♦ *The parents complained that the teacher's morally bankrupt behavior was bad for their children.* ♦ *The president's bankrupt policies will end at the next election.* **3.** *tv.* to send someone or something into financial ruin. ♦ *The inept investment broker bankrupted all of his clients.* ♦ *The bad business deal bankrupted poor Tom.*

bankruptcy ['bæŋk rəp si] *n.* a state of not having enough money to pay off debts. (No plural form in this sense.) ♦ *Sue couldn't pay her debts, so she declared bankruptcy.* ♦ *The failed company went into bankruptcy.*

banner ['bæn ɚ] **1.** *n.* a large piece of fabric or paper with words or pictures on it, attached to a pole or flat surface. ♦ *Our school slogan is written on the banner that hangs in our school lobby.* ♦ *Halfway through the parade, the banner fell and was trampled.* **2.** *n.* a flag. ♦ *The country's colorful new banner waved in the wind.* ♦ *The referee waved a banner to start the auto race.* **3.** *adj.* very successful; outstanding. ♦ *It was a banner year for the Smiths—two grandchildren and two weddings.* ♦ *The citizens' group did a banner job of cleaning up the parks.*

banquet ['bæŋ kwɪt] **1.** *n.* a dinner and speeches, usually connected with a celebration or an event. ♦ *Each year the boss hosts a banquet for the company's employees.* ♦ *The banquet is held at the same hotel each year.* **2.** *n.* a large dinner with an extensive menu; a feast. ♦ *Mary served us a banquet that was fit for a king.* ♦ *We gasped at the beautiful banquet laid upon the table.*

baptism ['bæp tɪz əm] **1.** *n.* a Christian rite involving immersion in or sprinkling with water, initiating a person into the church. (No plural form in this sense.) ♦ *The Browns presented their baby for baptism last Sunday.* ♦

Baptism is usually done in the church. **2.** *n.* an experience that is an introduction to a new and important change in life. (Figurative on ①. No plural form in this sense.) ♦ *The editorial assistant's job was a baptism into the publishing industry.* ♦ *Starting work at a department store during a sale is a real baptism.*

baptismal ['bæp tɪz məl] *adj.* relating to baptism. ♦ *The baptismal font was filled with holy water.* ♦ *The baby wore a white baptismal gown.*

Baptist ['bæp təst] **1.** *n.* a member of the Baptist denomination of the Christian religion. ♦ *There's a larger percentage of Baptists in the south than in the north.* ♦ *Baptists generally believe in adult baptism.* **2.** *adj.* relating to the Baptist denomination of the Christian religion. ♦ *There is a Baptist church at the end of our block.* ♦ *The couple were wed by a Baptist minister.*

baptize [bæp 'tɑɪz, 'bæp tɑɪz] *tv.* to perform the Christian rite of baptism on someone. ♦ *Our baby daughter was baptized last Sunday.* ♦ *The preacher baptized three adults on Sunday.*

bar ['bɑr] **1.** *n.* a counter or flat surface that someone stands behind to prepare and serve people drinks or food. ♦ *John walked up to the bar and asked for another drink.* ♦ *The bartender stood behind the bar serving drinks all night.* **2.** *n.* a counter or flat surface where different kinds of food items are kept, from which people choose whatever they would like to eat. ♦ *The salad bar included spinach, carrots, and tomatoes.* ♦ *The wedding dinner included a pasta bar and dessert.* **3.** *n.* a place where people can buy alcoholic drinks. ♦ *They went to the bar and had a few drinks.* ♦ *Tom and Bill spend every Saturday night at the bar.* **4.** *n.* a rigid rod of metal, wood, or some other material. ♦ *A bar of iron fell off the truck and struck a car.* ♦ *The police used an iron bar to pry open the door.* **5.** *n.* a rectangular object made of certain kinds of material, such as soap or various metals. ♦ *The treasure chest contained a few bars of gold.* ♦ *Are there any bars of soap in the linen closet?* **6.** *n.* a hindrance; something that gets in the way of something else. ♦ *Max's poor communication skills were a bar to his promotion.* ♦ *Poor manners can be a bar to social success.* **7.** *n.* a deposit of sand or silt in a river or lake. ♦ *We swam as far as the sand bar before we got tired.* ♦ *The current created a bar of silt in the stream.* **8.** *n.* a narrow band, a stripe. ♦ *My sweatshirt has red and blue bars across it.* ♦ *The tapestry has narrow bars of gold along its borders.* **9. the bar** *n.* the legal profession. (No plural form in this sense. Treated as singular.) ♦ *Grandpa joined the bar in 1939.* ♦ *Dave consulted a member of the bar for legal advice.* **10.** *n.* a measure in a piece of music. ♦ *Dave could only remember three bars of his recital piece.* ♦ *There was a mistake in the third bar of the music.* **11. bar from** *tv. + prep. phr.* to prevent or forbid someone or some creature from doing something. ♦ *Mary barred the dog from entering into the living room.* ♦ *The gate was put up to bar the children from leaving.* **12.** *tv.* to secure a door or window by placing a bar across it. ♦ *The frightened family barred the door against the intruder.* ♦ *We barred the windows with some old pieces of wood.*

barb ['bɑrb] **1.** *n.* a small, backward-pointing metal spike on a hook that makes it difficult to pull the hook out of something. ♦ *The barb on the fish hook stabbed me.* ♦ *The head of the spear had a barb on it.* **2.** *n.* a small metal spike found on certain wire fences. ♦ *The barbs on the fence were rusty and could give you a nasty cut.* ♦ *Watch out for the barbs on that fence!* **3.** *n.* an insult; a statement that is mean or cutting. (Figurative on ①.) ♦ *The unexpected barb offended me.* ♦ *Max's feelings were hurt by his coworker's barbs.*

barbarian [bɑr 'bɛr i ən] **1.** *n.* an uncivilized person. ♦ *The warriors were considered barbarians when they invaded our land.* ♦ *Bob's manners are worse than a barbarian's.* **2.** *n.* a cruel or mean person. ♦ *Bob is just a barbarian who treats everyone poorly.* ♦ *What kind of a barbarian would behave so badly?*

barbaric [bɑr 'bɛr ɪk] *adj.* uncivilized; unsophisticated; cruel; mean. (Adv: *barbarically* [...ɪk li].) ♦ *That type of barbaric behavior will not be tolerated.* ♦ *Your table manners are simply barbaric.*

barbecue AND **barbeque** ['bɑr bə kju] **1.** *n.* an outdoor grill used to cook food. ♦ *Jane set up the barbecue in the backyard before the picnic.* ♦ *Meat is cooking on the barbecue.* **2.** *n.* a party or meal where people eat food cooked on a grill. ♦ *Let's have our friends over for a barbecue Saturday!* ♦ *It rained on our barbecue, so the guests left.* **3.** *n.* the food that is prepared on an outdoor grill, especially food cooked with a spicy tomato sauce. ♦ *John's barbecue tasted bad because it was too salty.* ♦ *We ate some of the best barbecue in Texas.* **4.** *tv.* to cook food on a grill, especially with a spicy tomato sauce. ♦ *David barbecued dinner on the grill.* ♦ *This cookbook tells how to barbecue vegetables.* **5.** *iv.* [for food] to cook on an outdoor grill, especially with a spicy, tomato-based sauce. ♦ *The hot dogs were barbecuing while we played volleyball.* ♦ *Please set the table while dinner is barbecuing.*

barbecued ['bɑr bə kjud] *adj.* cooked on a grill and often covered with a spicy tomato sauce. ♦ *I love the taste of barbecued chicken!* ♦ *My favorite restaurant serves barbecued vegetables.*

barbell ['bɑr bɛl] *n.* a weight that someone lifts to develop muscle strength or size. ♦ *The barbell weighed about 20 pounds.* ♦ *The weightlifter lifted the barbell as if it were a feather.*

barbeque ['bɑr bə kju] See barbecue.

barber ['bɑr bɚ] *n.* someone who cuts or styles hair. ♦ *The barber had a shop on Main Street for thirty years.* ♦ *Not many men go to the barber for a shave anymore.*

bar code ['bɑr kod] *n.* a code—usually containing price and identification information—represented by a series of parallel black stripes. (Found on many retail products.) ♦ *Bar codes are read by a laser, and the information is processed by a computer.* ♦ *The clerk ran the bar code over the laser.*

bard ['bɑrd] *n.* a poet, especially one of national stature. ♦ *Perhaps the greatest bard was Shakespeare.* ♦ *The bard entertained the court with a ballad.*

bare ['bɛr] **1.** *tv.* to uncover. ♦ *I bared the mattress of the bed by removing the blankets and sheets.* ♦ *The dog bared its teeth and growled.* **2.** *tv.* to cause something to be seen; to reveal something. (Figurative on ①.) ♦ *Mary bared her soul to her friend.* ♦ *Sue bared her embarrassing story to her friends.* **3.** *adj.* naked; exposed. (Adv: *barely.* Comp: *barer;* sup: *barest.*) ♦ *The edge of the bathtub is cold on my bare bottom.* ♦ *The foolish woman had bare arms in the* *middle of winter.* **4.** *adj.* empty. (Adv: *barely.* Comp: *barer;* sup: *barest.*) ♦ *The cupboard was bare, so I went to the grocery store.* ♦ *The walls look so bare without any pictures!* **5. the bare something** *idiom* the smallest amount of something possible. ♦ *Bob did the bare minimum of work to pass the class.* ♦ *Food, clothing, and shelter are the bare necessities of life.*

bareback ['bɛr bæk] *adv.* [riding] without a saddle. ♦ *Sue rode the horse bareback across the field.* ♦ *Tom rode bareback on the pony into town.*

barefaced ['bɛr fest] *adj.* [of a lie told] without shame or guilt. (Adv: *barefacedly* [bɛr 'fes əd li].) ♦ *That clerk told me a barefaced lie!* ♦ *The naughty student told a barefaced lie to the teacher.*

barefoot(ed) ['bɛr fʊt(əd)] **1.** *adv.* without shoes or socks; with nothing on the feet. ♦ *On the first day of summer, Bill walked barefooted around town.* ♦ *The children ran barefoot in the grass.* **2.** *adj.* not wearing shoes or socks; having nothing on the feet. ♦ *The barefoot child stepped on a piece of glass.* ♦ *Barefoot people are not allowed in the store.*

barehanded ['bɛr hæn dɪd] *adv.* with nothing on or over the hands; without gloves. ♦ *The young ballplayer caught the fly ball barehanded during practice.* ♦ *Max picked up the snake barehanded.*

bareheaded ['bɛr hɛd ɪd] **1.** *adv.* without anything covering the head; without a hat. ♦ *Anne walked through the blizzard bareheaded, and her ears almost froze.* ♦ *The bald man never went anywhere bareheaded.* **2.** *adj.* wearing nothing on the head; without a hat. ♦ *The bareheaded joggers needed hats to prevent sunstroke.* ♦ *The bareheaded children all had sun-bleached hair.*

barely ['bɛr li] *adv.* hardly; only just; not quite. ♦ *There was barely enough food to go around.* ♦ *The Browns had barely started their vacation when the children got sick.*

bare verb ['bɛr 'vɚb] *n.* the infinitive form of a verb without the *to.* ♦ *If the infinitive is "to take," the bare verb is "take."* ♦ *The sentence "I did nothing but sleep" uses the bare verb "sleep."*

bargain ['bɑr gən] **1.** *n.* something that was bought for less money than it would normally cost; something that is inexpensive. ♦ *The new car I bought on sale was quite a bargain.* ♦ *We shopped all day but didn't see any bargains.* **2.** *n.* an agreement. ♦ *Mother made a bargain with Jimmy about bedtime.* ♦ *The union and management finally reached a bargain that would settle the dispute.* **3. bargain with** *iv.* + *prep. phr.* to set the terms of an agreement or a sale with someone. ♦ *The antique collector bargained with the shopkeeper.* ♦ *John bargained with the salesman over the price of the used car.* **4. bargain on; bargain for** *iv.* + *prep. phr.* to expect. ♦ *I hadn't bargained on the party ending by midnight.* ♦ *The car repairs were an expense that I hadn't bargained for.* **5. drive a hard bargain** *idiom* to work hard to negotiate prices or agreements in one's own favor. ♦ *All right, sir, you drive a hard bargain. I'll sell you this car for $12,450.* ♦ *You drive a hard bargain, Jane, but I'll sign the contract.* **6. in the bargain** *idiom* in addition to what was agreed on. ♦ *I bought a car, and in the bargain, they gave me a plastic coffee mug!* ♦ *I get a new job and a place to live in the bargain.* **7. throw something into the bargain** *idiom* to include something in a deal. ♦ *To encourage me to buy a new car, the car dealer threw a free radio into the bargain.* ♦ *If you purchase three pounds of chocolates, I'll throw one pound of salted nuts into the bargain.*

bargaining ['bɑr gən ɪŋ] *adj.* relating to negotiations. ♦ *The company brought three proposals to the bargaining table.* ♦ *Mary's position as president gave her real bargaining power.*

barge ['bɑrdʒ] *n.* a flat-bottomed boat that carries bulky cargo. ♦ *The barge floated down the river pushed by the tugboat.* ♦ *The material will be transported by barge to the building site.*

baritone ['bɛr ə ton] **1.** *n.* a male singer whose range is lower than that of a tenor and higher than that of a bass. ♦ *The opera starred a magnificent baritone.* ♦ *The choir included only one baritone.* **2.** *n.* a large brass musical instrument like a large trumpet coiled in an oval shape. ♦ *Mary played the baritone in the marching band.* ♦ *The band director recruited Tom to play the baritone.* **3.** *adj.* having the musical range of ①. ♦ *The chorus's magnificent baritone section stole the show.* ♦ *The baritone part was difficult to sing.*

barium ['bɛr i əm] *n.* a soft, silver-white metallic chemical element. (No plural form in this sense.) ♦ *I had to drink something with barium in it before my stomach X-ray.* ♦ *The atomic symbol of barium is Ba, and its atomic number is 56.*

bark ['bɑrk] **1.** *n.* the outer surface of a tree. (No plural form in this sense.) ♦ *A message was etched into the bark of the tree.* ♦ *The dog had chewed the bark of the tree to which it was chained.* **2.** *n.* the sound that is made by a dog. (No plural form in this sense.) ♦ *The bark of the fierce dog frightened us.* ♦ *Sue's little poodle has an annoying bark.* **3.** *iv.* to make the noise of a dog. ♦ *Why is that dog barking all the time?* ♦ *Our neighbor's dog barks constantly.* **4. bark up the wrong tree** *idiom* to make the wrong choice; to ask the wrong person; to follow the wrong course. ♦ *If you think I'm the guilty person, you're barking up the wrong tree.* ♦ *The baseball players blamed their bad record on the pitcher, but they were barking up the wrong tree.*

barker ['bɑr kɚ] *n.* someone at a carnival or a fair who encourages people to visit a certain attraction. ♦ *The barker attracted many people to the juggling act.* ♦ *We got tired of listening to the barker, so we moved away from the stage.*

barley ['bɑr li] *n.* a cereal grain eaten by people and animals and used to make alcoholic drinks. (No plural form in this sense.) ♦ *The chef added some barley to the soup.* ♦ *The farmer harvests the barley in the autumn.*

bar mitzvah [bɑr 'mɪts və] **1.** *n.* a ceremony in the Jewish religion marking the entrance of a 13-year-old boy to adult responsibilities in his religion. (Compare with bat mitzvah.) ♦ *Dave had his bar mitzvah in Jerusalem.* ♦ *We attended three bar mitzvahs last year.* **2.** *n.* a young man celebrating his ①. ♦ *The young bar mitzvah read his scriptures confidently.* ♦ *We sent a gift to the bar mitzvah because we couldn't deliver it personally.*

barn ['bɑrn] **1.** *n.* a large farm building for keeping livestock and storing supplies and equipment. ♦ *Farm animals are kept in barns.* ♦ *The photo showed an old red barn on a farm.* **2.** *n.* a large building where trucks and buses are kept and serviced. ♦ *John fell asleep and rode the bus* *back to the barn.* ♦ *The train was sent to the barn for repairs.*

barnacle ['bɑr nɪk əl] *n.* a hard-shelled marine animal that attaches itself to underwater objects. ♦ *The bottom of the boat was covered with barnacles.* ♦ *We found barnacles on the rocks at low tide.*

barnstorm ['bɑrn storm] **1.** *tv.* [for a pilot] to do airplane stunts at rural fairs. ♦ *The performers barnstormed the town and frightened its residents.* ♦ *Uncle John barnstormed the Midwest towns in an old plane.* **2.** *tv.* [for someone, such as a politician] to conduct a fast tour of a group of small towns. (Figurative on ①.) ♦ *The president barnstormed Iowa, trying to pick up some votes.* ♦ *The candidate barnstormed the Midwest twice during the campaign.*

barnyard ['bɑrn jɑrd] *n.* the fenced area surrounding a barn; a farmyard. ♦ *Cows, pigs, sheep, chickens, and other farm animals are kept in the barnyard.* ♦ *Dozens of chickens ran around the barnyard.*

barometer [bə 'rɑm ə tɚ] **1.** *n.* a device that measures atmospheric pressure. ♦ *A barometer is useful in predicting the weather.* ♦ *The barometer indicated that the air pressure was dropping.* **2.** *n.* an indicator of possible changes. (Figurative on ①.) ♦ *The newspaper is a barometer for public sentiment.* ♦ *The stock market is a barometer for the state of the economy.*

baron ['bɛr ən] **1.** *n.* a low-ranking male member of the nobility. (Also a term of address.) ♦ *The baron had a small parcel of land north of the kingdom.* ♦ *The baron and the baroness attended the royal ball.* **2.** *n.* someone with much power and influence. (Mainly in compounds.) ♦ *The rubber barons founded a city in the middle of the Amazon jungle.* ♦ *The college's founder had been a 19th-century steel baron.*

baroness ['bɛr ə nəs] *n.* the female counterpart of a baron; the wife or widow of a baron. (Also a term of address.) ♦ *The baroness is a dignified woman of fifty.* ♦ *The baron and the baroness vacationed in the south of France.*

barrack ['bɛr ək] **1.** *n.* a building that serves as the living quarters of military or police personnel. (Usually plural.) ♦ *The barracks housed enlisted men before the military base closed.* ♦ *The prisoners were kept in barracks at the camp.* **2.** *n.* any large building where many people can be housed. (Usually plural.) ♦ *The orphans were housed in barracks.* ♦ *The boarding school built large barracks for the students.*

barracuda [bɛr ə 'kud ə] *n., irreg.* a long, slender marine fish known for its vicious feeding habits. (Pl: *barracuda* or *barracudas.*) ♦ *We saw a barracuda at the aquarium.* ♦ *The barracuda has large, sharp teeth.*

barrage [bə 'rɑʒ] *n.* a continuous flow of something, such as bullets or words. (No plural form in this sense.) ♦ *The barrage of work exhausted the crew.* ♦ *The oil company got a barrage of letters protesting its policies.*

barred ['bɑrd] **1.** *adj.* marked with **bars** ⑧. ♦ *The zebra bears a barred pattern of black and white.* ♦ *The cloth had a barred pattern across brightly colored circles.* **2.** *adj.* having iron or steel **bars** ④, as with a window or prison cell. ♦ *The barred windows gave us added security in our neighborhood.* ♦ *The jeweler's shop had a barred door.*

barrel ['bɛr əl] **1.** *n.* a large, rounded wooden container with a flat top and bottom. ♦ *The barrels were full of grain.* ♦ *The workers unloaded three barrels from the cart.* **2.** *n.* the contents of ①. (The exact amount depends on the contents of the barrel.) ♦ *The pigs were fed an entire barrel of feed each week.* ♦ *A small barrel of pickles was delivered to the deli.* **3.** *n.* the standard measurement of petroleum oil, equal to 42 U.S. gallons. ♦ *The small country consumed about 10,000 barrels of oil per day.* ♦ *We use hundreds of thousands of barrels of oil each day.* **4.** *n.* the part of a gun through which the bullets travel. ♦ *The soldier rested the barrel of his gun in the hole in the fort's wall.* ♦ *Susan has a special tool to clean the barrel of her gun.* **5. barrel through** *iv.* + *prep. phr.* to move very quickly and awkwardly through an area or a group of people. ♦ *The quarterback barreled through the other players.* ♦ *We barreled through the crowd to get a better view of the action.* **6. lock, stock, and barrel** *idiom* everything. ♦ *We had to move everything out of the house—lock, stock, and barrel.* ♦ *We lost everything—lock, stock, and barrel—in the fire.* **7. scrape the bottom of the barrel** *idiom* to select from among the worst; to choose from what is left over. ♦ *You've bought a bad-looking car. You really scraped the bottom of the barrel to get that one.* ♦ *The worker you sent over was the worst I've ever seen. Send me another—and don't scrape the bottom of the barrel.*

barren ['bɛr ən] **1.** *adj.* [of a female] not capable of producing offspring; [of a female] sterile. ♦ *The woman wanted to have children, but she was barren.* ♦ *All mules are barren.* **2.** *adj.* not capable of supporting plant life. ♦ *The farmer's soil was overworked and barren.* ♦ *The desert only seems barren. There is actually a lot of life there.*

barrette [bə 'rɛt] *n.* a clip used to hold hair in place. ♦ *Jane pulled her hair back with barrettes.* ♦ *Barrettes held the child's hair out of her face.*

barricade ['bɛr ə ked] **1.** *n.* something that blocks a passageway. ♦ *The students erected a barricade on campus as a protest.* ♦ *The police barricade kept looters away from the crime scene.* **2.** *tv.* to block off a passageway or a pathway. ♦ *The workers barricaded the driveway after they poured the cement.* ♦ *The police barricaded the crime scene to keep people out.*

barrier ['bɛr i ɚ] **1.** *n.* something that physically separates people or things. ♦ *The barrier between the desks gave both workers some privacy.* ♦ *The police officers moved the protesters behind the concrete barrier.* **2.** *n.* something that emotionally or spiritually separates people or things. (Figurative on ①.) ♦ *The two tourists had a language barrier and could not understand each other.* ♦ *Tom's and Anne's political beliefs are a barrier to their friendship.*

barroom ['bɑr rum] *n.* a tavern; a place where alcoholic drinks are served. ♦ *The barroom was packed on Friday night.* ♦ *A drunken brawl broke out in the barroom last night.*

bartender ['bɑr tɛn dɚ] *n.* someone who mixes and serves drinks at a bar. ♦ *The bartender tried to break up the brawl.* ♦ *The bartender had never heard of the drink I ordered.*

barter ['bɑr tɚ] **1.** *n.* trade conducted without money. (No plural form in this sense.) ♦ *Barter is an ancient way of doing business.* ♦ *The ancient town had an economy based on barter.* **2. barter with** *iv.* + *prep. phr.* to conduct trade with someone by exchanging products and services instead of money. ♦ *The pioneers bartered with each other at the frontier store.* ♦ *Will the shopkeeper barter with you?*

base ['bes] **1.** *n.* the bottom, supporting part of something. ♦ *The base of the lamp is made of wood.* ♦ *Three legs formed the base of the stool.* **2.** *n.* a starting point; the foundation from which other things develop. ♦ *The theory was built on a flawed base.* ♦ *This theory forms the base of the argument.* **3.** *n.* a center of operations; the main site of a business or organization. ♦ *The steel company's base was in Pittsburgh.* ♦ *The company chose a small suburb for the base of its operations.* **4.** *n.* a military headquarters. ♦ *When the base was shut down last year, the soldiers departed.* ♦ *Most of the soldiers live on the base.* **5.** *n.* a chemical that is the opposite of an acid. ♦ *All alkalis are base.* ♦ *A base will neutralize an acid.* **6.** *n.* [in baseball] one of the four points of the baseball diamond. ♦ *A batter must touch each base in order to score a run.* ♦ *The runner stood on the base and waited for the pitch.* **7.** *n.* the part of a word to which a suffix or prefix is attached. ♦ *The past participle is forming by adding* -ed *to the base of a verb.* ♦ *The present participle is formed by adding* -ing *to the base of a verb.* **8.** *adj.* morally low; inferior; unworthy. (Adv: *basely.*) ♦ *The base man bragged about his shady business deals.* ♦ *Jane ignored her coworker who made the base comment.* **9.** *adj.* forming or serving as a base; acting as a foundation. ♦ *The base price for this car is $20,000.* ♦ *For this job the base salary is $25,000.* **10. base on** *tv.* + *prep. phr.* to establish something as a cause or basis for something else; to establish something on some kind of foundation or basis. ♦ *The success of the firm was based on providing good service.* ♦ *I based my opinion about Tom on what I had heard.* **11.** *tv.* to establish a center of activity in a certain place. ♦ *The firm was based in New York.* ♦ *They chose to base the company in Atlanta.* **12. off base** *idiom* unrealistic; inexact; wrong. ♦ *I'm afraid you're off base when you state that this problem will take care of itself.* ♦ *You are quite confused. You're way off base!* **13. steal a base** *idiom* to sneak from one base to another in baseball. ♦ *The runner stole second base, but he nearly got put out on the way.* ♦ *Tom runs so slowly that he never tries to steal a base.*

baseball ['bes bɔl] **1.** *n.* a team sport played with two teams of nine members each. (No plural form in this sense.) ♦ *Baseball is a very popular sport in America.* ♦ *No professional baseball was played during the year of the strike.* **2.** *n.* the white, leather-covered ball used in ①. ♦ *The catcher caught the baseball in his glove.* ♦ *The baseball sailed over the fence—it was a home run!*

baseboard ['bes bord] *n.* a decorative board running along the lower edge of a wall. ♦ *I cleaned the baseboards in the living room.* ♦ *The painter had to scrape the baseboards before they could be painted.*

baseless ['bes ləs] *adj.* without any reason; not based in fact. (Adv: *baselessly.*) ♦ *The suspect's alibi is baseless.* ♦ *The rumor about the celebrity was baseless.*

baseline ['bes lɑɪn] **1.** *n.* a basic value or measurement against which other measurements can be compared. ♦ *What is the baseline amount used in this experiment?* ♦ *A baseline for the budget for this project is $5,000.* **2.** *n.* one of the imaginary lines that connects the bases of a baseball diamond. ♦ *The player threw down the bat and ran along the baseline.* ♦ *The ball rolled across the baseline.*

basement ['bes mənt] *n.* a space within the foundations of a building, tall enough to permit a person to stand upright. ♦ *The Smiths furnished their basement as a family room.* ♦ *We stored all our old things in the basement.*

bases ['bes iz] pl of **basis.**

bash ['bæʃ] **1.** *tv.* to strike someone or something. ♦ *Susan accidentally bashed the wall with the chair.* ♦ *Bill bashed the robber's nose with his fist.* **2.** *tv.* to belittle someone or something. (Informal. Figurative on ①.) ♦ *The newspaper bashed the candidate for being greedy.* ♦ *The conservative senator bashed the judge for being too liberal.* **3. bash into** *iv.* + *prep. phr.* to crash into someone or something; to run into someone or something violently. ♦ *The runner bashed into the wall by accident.* ♦ *The car bashed into a brick wall after being hit by the truck.* **4.** *n.* a large, wild party; a large social event. (Informal.) ♦ *My parents warned me not to have a bash while they were away.* ♦ *Each year the fraternity has a bash and invites the whole school.*

bashful ['bæʃ fʊl] *adj.* easily embarrassed; shy. (Adv: *bashfully.*) ♦ *The bashful child hid behind his mother.* ♦ *The salesclerk was a bashful man who mumbled when speaking to customers.*

bashfulness ['bæʃ fʊl nəs] *n.* shyness. (No plural form in this sense.) ♦ *John got over his bashfulness and asked Jane out.* ♦ *Mary's bashfulness kept her from speaking her mind.*

basic ['bes ɪk] **1.** *adj.* fundamental; essential. (Adv: *basically* [...ɪk li].) ♦ *Freedom of speech is a basic right in the United States.* ♦ *Vegetables contain basic nutrients.* **2.** *adj.* simple. (Adv: *basically* [...ɪk li].) ♦ *I signed up for a basic German class, but it was too easy.* ♦ *The seamstress used a very basic pattern for this dress.* **3. the basics** *n.* the fundamental principles of something. (Treated as plural.) ♦ *The florist taught me the basics of flower arranging.* ♦ *Where did you learn the basics of business?*

basically ['bes ɪk li] *adv.* fundamentally; essentially. ♦ *Basically, it's a bad idea.* ♦ *Your answer is basically right.*

basin ['bes ən] **1.** *n.* a large shallow bowl, or similar structure. ♦ *The sink basin was filled with water.* ♦ *John emptied the basin into the toilet.* **2.** *n.* the contents of ①. ♦ *Pour another basin of water onto the plants.* ♦ *The mechanic poured the basin of used oil into a steel barrel.* **3.** *n.* the area of land that is drained by a river or a system of rivers. ♦ *The soil along the river basin was very good for farming.* ♦ *The Amazon basin covers a vast amount of land.*

basis ['bes ɪs] **1.** *n., irreg.* the foundation of something; the part of something from which other things develop. (Pl: **bases.**) ♦ *The professor's new theory formed the basis for her lecture.* ♦ *Dissatisfaction with the government was the basis for the new political movement.* **2.** *n., irreg.* an agreed-upon standard or status. ♦ *The secretary was hired on a temporary basis.* ♦ *The skilled worker was hired on a permanent basis.*

basket ['bæs kɪt] **1.** *n.* a container woven of strips of wood, twigs, or similar material. ♦ *My basket is woven from dried grass.* ♦ *I filled my basket with vegetables at the market.* **2.** *n.* the contents of ①. ♦ *Mary brought a basket* *of pears to the picnic.* ♦ *We bought a basket of flowers.* **3.** *n.* a container with a specific use. ♦ *I carried the laundry basket to the washing machine.* ♦ *The wastepaper baskets were overflowing with trash.* **4.** *n.* the cylindrical net, and the hoop to which it is attached, that is part of a basketball goal. ♦ *The basketball dropped through the basket.* ♦ *Jimmy didn't get the ball through the basket, but he kept trying.* **5.** *n.* a goal or score in the game of basketball. ♦ *How many baskets were made in last night's game?* ♦ *The referee didn't see the basket.*

basketball ['bæs kɪt bɔl] **1.** *n.* a team sport where a goal is made by sending a ball through a basket ④. (No plural form in this sense.) ♦ *The movie was about the sport of basketball.* ♦ *Basketball is played at both the college and professional level.* **2.** *n.* a ball used in the game of basketball. ♦ *The basketball missed the hoop and fell to the ground.* ♦ *Jimmy bounced his new basketball against the pavement.*

bass 1. ['bes] *n.* a man having the lowest of the male singing voices. (See also tenor and baritone.) ♦ *Tom is the only bass in the church choir.* ♦ *The bass sang a magnificent solo.* **2.** ['bes] *n.* the music written for ①; the musical part written for ①. ♦ *I usually sing bass, but I will sing tenor if you wish.* ♦ *The bass is very easy in this piece.* **3.** ['bes] *n.* the largest stringed instrument in the violin family. ♦ *The orchestra has two basses.* ♦ *Mary plays the bass in a small string orchestra.* **4.** ['bæs] *n., irreg.* a type of edible freshwater or marine fish. (Pl: *bass.*) ♦ *We went fishing for bass but caught none.* ♦ *We all ate the huge bass Bob caught for dinner last night.* **5.** ['bes] *adj.* <the adj. use of ① or ②.> ♦ *The bass section of the choir is weak.* ♦ *Did you study the bass part of this anthem?* **6.** ['bes] *adj.* sounding low or deep. ♦ *The bass howl of the wind made us uneasy.* ♦ *The orchestra's bass notes made a gloomy sound.*

bassinet [bæs ə 'nɛt] *n.* a small, movable crib with a hood over one end. ♦ *The bassinet was decorated with white lace.* ♦ *Susan placed her baby in the bassinet.*

bassoon [bə 'sun] *n.* the lowest-pitched musical instrument of the woodwind family. ♦ *In this arrangement, the oboes play the melody, and the bassoons play the harmony.* ♦ *The bassoon uses a double reed and plays in the lowest tonal range.*

bastard ['bæs tɚd] **1.** *n.* a child of parents who are not married to each other; an illegitimate child. (Not in polite use except technical use.) ♦ *As a bastard, he had no claim to his parents' fortune.* ♦ *Since he was a bastard, the young man could make no claim to the land.* **2.** *n.* someone who is obnoxious, annoying, or disliked. (Vulgar. Also a provocative term of address.) ♦ *"That bastard stole my money!" yelled Mike.* ♦ *"You bastard!" Anne yelled angrily at her boyfriend.* **3.** *adj.* having parents who are not married to each other; illegitimate. (Not in polite use except technical use.) ♦ *The bastard child was raised in an orphanage.* ♦ *The couple's bastard son sued to receive an inheritance.*

baste ['best] *tv.* to keep food—usually meat—moist during cooking by pouring on fat or cooking juices. ♦ *Jane basted the turkey every half hour.* ♦ *The recipe said to baste the roast frequently.*

bastion ['bæs tʃən] **1.** *n.* something that is strong, especially a fort or building. ♦ *The fort was a bastion that protected the pioneers from attacks.* ♦ *Citizens fled to the bastion as the enemy soldiers rode into the town.* **2.** *n.* someone or something that is strong. (Figurative on ①.) ♦ *The judge was considered a bastion of justice in the town.* ♦ *Our club president is a bastion of good taste.*

bat ['bæt] **1.** *n.* a nocturnal, mouse-like mammal with large wings. ♦ *There are bats in the old house's attic.* ♦ *Bats hung upside down from the rafters.* **2.** *n.* a wood or metal club used in the game of baseball. ♦ *The player swung the bat a few times before approaching the mound.* ♦ *The baseball player threw down the bat and ran for first base.* **3.** *tv.* to hit a ball with ②. ♦ *Max batted the ball as hard as he could.* ♦ *Everyone laughed at the way Bill batted the ball.* **4.** *tv.* to hit something; to slap at something. ♦ *Tom batted the flies away from him.* ♦ *My older sister playfully batted me on the head.* **5.** *iv.* [in baseball] to take one's turn as a batter; to swing [a baseball bat]. ♦ *Mary batted first in the third inning.* ♦ *When Bob batted, he struck out.* **6. go to bat for someone** *idiom* to support or help someone. ♦ *I tried to go to bat for Bill, but he said he didn't want any help.* ♦ *I heard them gossiping about Sally, so I went to bat for her.* **7. have bats in one's belfry** *idiom* to be slightly crazy. ♦ *Poor old Tom has bats in his belfry.* ♦ *Don't act so silly, John. People will think you have bats in your belfry.* **8. right off the bat** *idiom* immediately; first thing. ♦ *When he was learning to ride a bicycle, he fell on his head right off the bat.* ♦ *The new manager demanded new office furniture right off the bat.*

batch ['bætʃ] **1.** *n.* a group of things that is processed at the same time. ♦ *I paid a batch of bills last night.* ♦ *This batch of cookies is burned.* **2.** *tv.* to group things together. ♦ *Batch last week's newspapers and tie them with string.* ♦ *We batched the photographs by year.*

bath ['bæθ] **1.** *n.* the washing of someone or something. ♦ *I'm going to take a bath tonight after supper.* ♦ *Jimmy really needs a bath.* **2.** *n.* water drawn for bathing. ♦ *Mary sprinkled some oil into her bath.* ♦ *The babysitter ran a bath for the children.* **3.** *n.* a bathtub; a tub used for bathing. ♦ *This bath really needs scrubbing.* ♦ *Bill installed a new bath and toilet in his bathroom.* **4.** *n.* a bathroom; a room with bathtub or shower. ♦ *My parent' house has five bedrooms and two baths.* ♦ *The decorator put striped wallpaper in the bath.*

bathe ['beð] **1.** *iv.* to take a bath; to wash. ♦ *I bathed for an hour before dinner to soothe my nerves.* ♦ *Max wanted to ask his coworker to bathe more frequently.* **2.** *tv.* to clean or wash someone or something; to give someone a bath. ♦ *I bathed the children and tucked them into bed.* ♦ *The nurse bathed the wound with antiseptic.* **3.** *tv.* to put water on something; to make something wet or moist. ♦ *After leaving the smoky bar, Jane wanted to bathe her eyes with warm water.* ♦ *Grandpa bathes his feet in hot water each night.* **4.** *tv.* to surround or immerse someone or something in something. (Figurative on ③.) ♦ *A soft pink light bathed the dancers on the stage.* ♦ *We were bathed in the steamy Florida air once we left the plane.*

bathmat ['bæθ mæt] *n.* a cloth mat placed outside a bathtub or shower. ♦ *The bathmat in the hotel room was quite large.* ♦ *You might slip without a bathmat on the floor.*

bathrobe ['bæθ rob] *n.* a loose, coat-like garment worn before or after bathing or over pajamas. (See also robe.) ♦ *David wore his bathrobe around the house after his* *shower.* ♦ *Jane got out of the shower and reached for her bathrobe.*

bathroom ['bæθ rum] **1.** *n.* a room having at least a toilet and sink, and often a bathtub or shower. ♦ *How many bathrooms does the new house have?* ♦ *The tub overflowed and ruined the floor in the bathroom.* **2. go to the bathroom** *idiom* to use the toilet; to urinate; to defecate. ♦ *Jimmy has to go to the bathroom right now.* ♦ *Mommy, the puppy is going to the bathroom on the carpet.*

bathtub ['bæθ təb] *n.* a large tub for bathing. ♦ *Jimmy loves to play with his boats in the bathtub.* ♦ *The rooms in the old hotel had antique bathtubs with feet.*

bathwater ['bæθ wɑt ɚ] *n.* water for bathing; the water contained in a bathtub. (No plural form in this sense.) ♦ *I relaxed while soaking in the bathwater.* ♦ *Make sure that baby's bathwater isn't too hot!*

bat mitzvah [bɑt 'mɪts və] **1.** *n.* a ceremony in the Jewish religion marking the entrance of a young woman to adult responsibilities in her religion. (Compare with bar mitzvah.) ♦ *Jane had her bat mitzvah in Israel.* ♦ *All of Susan's family attended her bat mitzvah.* **2.** *n.* the young woman celebrating her ①. ♦ *The bat mitzvah read the Torah confidently.* ♦ *We sent the bat mitzvah a gift of money.*

baton [bə 'tɑn] **1.** *n.* a stick or club carried by police officers. ♦ *The officer swung his baton at the crowd menacingly.* ♦ *The cop knocked the suspect unconscious with a blow from his baton.* **2.** *n.* a thin stick used by a conductor to show the beat of the music. ♦ *The conductor led the orchestra with a synthetic ivory baton.* ♦ *The orchestra members follow the tempo of the moving baton.* **3.** *n.* a rod or tube passed from runner to runner in a relay race. ♦ *Dave dropped the baton during the relay race.* ♦ *Susan handed the baton to the next runner.* **4.** *n.* a rod or tube that is tossed and twirled during parades and sporting events. ♦ *The cheerleaders twirled their batons in the parade.* ♦ *Jane rapidly twirled the baton.*

battalion [bə 'tæl jən] *n.* a large unit of soldiers, consisting of two or more companies. (Two or more battalions form a regiment.) ♦ *The battalion waited near the front for an order to attack.* ♦ *Five battalions were slaughtered in the battle.*

batter ['bæt ɚ] **1.** *n.* a mixture—thinner than dough—of flour, eggs, sugar, water, etc., which, when baked, becomes cake, cookies, etc. (No plural form in this sense.) ♦ *The cook tasted the batter, and then added more sugar.* ♦ *The children licked the cake batter from the mixing spoon.* **2.** *n.* a mixture of flour, water, and other ingredients into which meat, fish, or vegetables are dipped and then fried. (No plural form in this sense.) ♦ *The fish fillets were fried in batter.* ♦ *Jane picked the batter off her chicken before eating it.* **3.** *n.* [in baseball] a player with a bat who tries to hit balls thrown to him by a pitcher. ♦ *The pitcher hit the batter with the ball by mistake.* ♦ *The batter hit a home run.* **4.** *tv.* to hit someone or something many times; to physically abuse someone or something. ♦ *The man who battered his wife was sent to jail.* ♦ *The wind battered the flag against the house.*

battered ['bæt ɚd] **1.** *adj.* food that has been dipped in a mixture of flour, water, and other ingredients and then fried. ♦ *I put the battered chicken in the fryer.* ♦ *"Are the fish fillets battered?" I asked the waitress.* **2.** *adj.* physically beaten or abused repeatedly. ♦ *People from the social-service agency counseled the battered woman.* ♦ *The battered cat slunk through the back door.*

battery ['bæt ə ri] **1.** *n.* a cylindrical or square object inserted into flashlights, portable radios, cameras, etc., to provide electrical power. ♦ *The batteries in my camera were dead.* ♦ *Do we have any extra batteries for the alarm clock?* **2.** *n.* beating someone; striking and harming someone. (No plural form in this sense.) ♦ *The abusive man was arrested for battery.* ♦ *The police interrupted the battery taking place on the subway platform.* **3.** *n.* a group of many large guns or other weapons. ♦ *A battery of cannons was installed on the wall of the fortress.* ♦ *The huge guns were placed in seven batteries overlooking the bay.* **4.** *n.* a series of tests or examinations. ♦ *The doctor ordered a battery of tests.* ♦ *After undergoing a battery of blood tests, Bill was diagnosed as anemic.*

batting ['bæt ɪŋ] *n.* fibers pressed into layers, and placed between two layers of cloth to provide warmth. (No plural form in this sense.) ♦ *The batting in my winter coat is falling out.* ♦ *The seamstress lined the coat with batting.*

battle ['bæt əl] **1.** *n.* a fight between two enemy forces during a war. ♦ *The enemy troops met in an open field, and a battle ensued.* ♦ *The outcome of the battle would determine the fate of the country.* **2.** *n.* a fight or crusade against someone or something. (Figurative on ①.) ♦ *Our class president led a battle against drunk drivers.* ♦ *The battle against smoking has been won.* **3.** *tv.* to fight someone or something. ♦ *Bill had to battle his competition to get a promotion.* ♦ *The business owner battled city hall over zoning regulations.* **4. battle for; battle against** *iv.* + *prep. phr.* to fight for or against someone or something; to struggle for or against someone or something. ♦ *After Bill's accident, his parents began battling against drunk driving.* ♦ *The lawyer battled for her client's freedom.*

battlefield ['bæt l fild] **1.** *n.* an area where a battle is fought. ♦ *The old battlefield is now a graveyard.* ♦ *The wounded soldiers lay on the battlefield.* **2.** *n.* a place of conflict; an area of conflict. (Figurative on ①.) ♦ *The three brothers' bedroom became their battlefield.* ♦ *Our office became a battlefield of politics during the election.*

battleship ['bæt l ʃɪp] *n.* a warship; a ship armed with heavy weapons. ♦ *The battleship was sunk by a torpedo.* ♦ *During the war, thousands of sailors served on battleships.*

bauble ['bɔb əl] *n.* a cheap piece of jewelry; a trinket. ♦ *The tacky celebrity was covered with gaudy baubles.* ♦ *I can't afford good jewelry, so I buy cheap baubles.*

bawl ['bɔl] **1.** *iv.* to cry very loudly; to sob. ♦ *When Susie's dollhouse broke, she bawled for an hour.* ♦ *Jimmy bawled when his mother left the house.* **2. bawl out** *tv.* + *adv.* to reprimand someone. ♦ *Tommy's parents bawled him out for breaking Susie's dollhouse.* ♦ *The teacher bawled out Jimmy for talking during class.*

bay ['be] **1.** *n.* an inlet in the shoreline of an ocean, sea, or lake, capable of sheltering ships. ♦ *Our favorite fishing spot is in the bay.* ♦ *The sailboat got stranded in the bay when the wind died.* **2.** *n.* a vertical section of windows between two structural elements. ♦ *The room has a bay of huge windows on the longest wall and another smaller window opposite from it.* ♦ *One large bay was damaged by the storm.* **3.** *n.* a horse with a reddish-brown body and black mane, tail, and legs. ♦ *Sue dreamed of riding a bay* *across the prairie.* ♦ *Her favorite horse is a bay with a long, thick mane.* **4.** *iv.* to howl; to make a long, deep howl like a dog, wolf, etc. ♦ *The wolves bayed at the moon all night long.* ♦ *Your dog was baying while you were away!* **5. at bay** *phr.* at a distance. ♦ *I have to keep the bill collectors at bay until I get my check.* ♦ *The wolves will not remain at bay for very long.*

bayonet ['be ə nɛt] **1.** *n.* a sword attached to the end of a rifle. ♦ *The museum has a collection of bayonets from the Revolutionary War.* ♦ *Soldiers still use bayonets in battles.* **2.** *tv.* to stab someone or something with ①. ♦ *The soldier bayoneted the enemy.* ♦ *The troops were trained to bayonet their enemies.*

bayou ['bɑɪ u] *n.* a swamp, especially as found in Louisiana. (From French.) ♦ *We rowed a boat through the bayou.* ♦ *The murderer hid the body in the bayous.*

bazaar [bə 'zɑr] **1.** *n.* a marketplace, especially in the Middle East. (From Persian.) ♦ *All types of food are available at the bazaar.* ♦ *Many vendors sell their goods at the bazaar.* **2.** *n.* a marketplace where crafts and food are sold, often to benefit some organization. ♦ *The committee organized a bazaar to raise funds.* ♦ *We bought some used furniture at the bazaar.*

bazooka [bə 'zuk ə] *n.* a small, portable weapon that shoots powerful rockets capable of penetrating tank armor. ♦ *The illegal arms deal involved bazookas and grenades.* ♦ *The enemy fired its bazooka into our camp.*

B.C. ['bi 'si] *abbr.* before Christ. (Used after dates to indicate when something occurred in relation to the calendar that begins with the birth of Christ. Also **B.C.**) ♦ *The ancient city was founded in 328 B.C.* ♦ *In 400 B.C., this great army marched across the desert.*

be ['bi] **1.** *iv., irreg.* to exist in a certain way or as a certain thing; to exist in a certain state or condition. (The linking verb or copula. The conjugation of *be:* Present tense: *I am, you are, he is, she is, it is, we are, you are, they are.* Past tense: *I was, you were, he was, she was, it was, we were, you were, they were.* Past participle: been. Present participle: *being.*) ♦ *Jimmy is a little boy.* ♦ *The sunrise was beautiful.* ♦ *Anne is very tired.* **2.** *iv., irreg.* to occur; to happen. ♦ *Our vacation will be next week.* ♦ *There was an accident on the freeway last night.* **3.** *iv., irreg.* to have a location; to exist at a specific place. ♦ *Where is my umbrella?* ♦ *The magazine is on the coffee table.* **4.** *iv., irreg.* to exist. (Usually with there ③.) ♦ *Do you believe there is a heaven?* ♦ *As long as there is life, there is hope.* **5.** *iv., irreg.* to be ① in the process of doing something. (The progressive tenses are formed when a form of be comes before a verb ending in -ing.) ♦ *The birds are singing.* ♦ *The trees were swaying in the breeze.* **6.** *iv., irreg.* to have been ① done [by someone or something]. (The passive voice is formed when a form of be comes before the past participle of another verb.) ♦ *The task has been completed.* ♦ *The leaves were raked by Dad.* **7. be to do something** *idiom* to be obliged to do something; to be expected or directed to do something. ♦ *Am I to clean up the entire kitchen by myself?* ♦ *John is to take the money to the bank.*

beach ['bitʃ] **1.** *n.* a shoreline covered with sand, pebbles, or stones. ♦ *We sat on the beach and watched the waves.* ♦ *The children collected shells at the beach.* **2.** *tv.* to run or drive something onto the shore. ♦ *Dave beached the boat and ran ashore.* ♦ *The whales had beached themselves on the sand.*

beachcomber ['bitʃ kom ɚ] *n.* someone who lives on or near a beach and collects things found on the shore. ♦ *Beachcombers often found valuable objects in the sand.* ♦ *I have often wanted to quit my job and become a beachcomber!*

beachhead ['bitʃ hɛd] *n.* the part of a beach or a shore where invading soldiers first land during a war or battle. ♦ *The first soldier on the beachhead faced the enemy.* ♦ *The beachhead where the invasion would occur was veiled in fog.*

beacon ['bik ən] **1.** *n.* a radio signal used in navigation. ♦ *The beacon is broadcast from a small hut near the end of the runway.* ♦ *It was foggy and the pilot had to rely on the radio beacon.* **2.** *n.* a lighthouse; a tower with a signal at the top to warn someone or something of something. ♦ *The sailor saw the beacon on the coast.* ♦ *An old sailor has run the beacon for forty years.*

bead ['bid] **1.** *n.* a small piece of wood, metal, glass, plastic, stone, gemstone, or other material, usually with a hole through it for a string or a thread. ♦ *The necklace was made of beads strung together.* ♦ *The wedding gown had glass beads sewn to it.* **2.** *n.* a droplet of a liquid. ♦ *Beads of sweat clung to the gymnast's forehead.* ♦ *A bead of water slid across the newly waxed car.* **3.** *tv.* to make jewelry or decorate clothing by attaching ①. ♦ *The craftsman beaded the headpiece with great skill.* ♦ *I asked the seamstress to bead my gown.* **4. bead (up)** *iv.* (+ *adv.*) [for something wet] to form into a droplet. ♦ *Sweat began to bead on the jogger's forehead.* ♦ *Water beaded up on the newly waxed car.*

beagle ['big əl] *n.* a small hound with black, tan, and white markings, often used in hunting. ♦ *Mom and Dad always wanted a beagle for a pet.* ♦ *The cute little beagle won the dog show.*

beak ['bik] *n.* the bill of a bird; the hard mouth structure of a bird or a turtle. ♦ *The bird held a worm in its beak.* ♦ *The woodpecker jammed its beak against the tree trunk.*

beam ['bim] **1.** *n.* a long, flat piece of wood, concrete, or metal. ♦ *The worker examined the beams in the ceiling.* ♦ *How thick are the beams in the wall?* **2.** *n.* a ray of light; a stream of light; a stream of laser energy. ♦ *The surgeon used a laser beam to destroy the diseased cells.* ♦ *The cat relaxed in a beam of sunlight.* **3.** *iv.* to radiate light; to emit light. ♦ *The sun was beaming while we played on the beach.* ♦ *The front porch light beamed in the dark of the night.* **4.** *iv.* to smile brightly; to look very happy. ♦ *Susan beamed when she heard the good news.* ♦ *The children beamed from ear to ear when school was canceled.* **5.** *tv.* to send light out; to radiate light; to emit light. ♦ *The sun beamed bright light down on our picnic.* ♦ *The spotlight beamed light onto the stage.* **6.** *tv.* to aim something, especially something producing a signal or a light, in a certain direction. ♦ *A tall antenna beamed the television signal to the suburbs.* ♦ *Jimmy beamed the flashlight into the closet looking for monsters.*

bean ['bin] **1.** *n.* a seed of a certain plant, and sometimes its pod, used as food. ♦ *The coffee beans smelled wonderful.* ♦ *The farmer grew nothing but beans.* **2.** *tv.* to hit someone on the head. (Informal.) ♦ *The pitcher beaned* *the batter with a fast ball.* ♦ *Don't bean yourself on the top of the doorway.*

bean sprout ['bin sprɑʊt] *n.* a sprout of a particular type of bean, eaten as a vegetable. (Usually plural.) ♦ *This salad contains bean sprouts.* ♦ *The recipe called for a cup of bean sprouts.*

bear ['bɛr] **1.** *n.* a powerful, furry animal with a short tail and claws. ♦ *The ranger at the park warned us against feeding the bears.* ♦ *The bear pulled a fish out the stream with its paw.* **2.** *n.* a grouch; a gruff person. (Informal. Figurative on ①.) ♦ *My boss is just a bear on Monday mornings.* ♦ *"Don't be a bear!" I said to my grouchy roommate.* **3.** *n.* someone who is bearish ②. ♦ *The bears have sold all their stock and are waiting for the market to fall.* ♦ *Bob is a bear on the stock market and will not risk his money.* **4.** *tv., irreg.* to carry or transport something. (Pt: bore; pp: borne.) ♦ *The travelers bore the contraband into the U.S. unknowingly.* ♦ *The camels bore their cargo across the desert without complaint.* **5.** *tv., irreg.* to accept or endure the consequences of something; to take responsibility for something. ♦ *We bore the consequences of the young employees' mistakes.* ♦ *The company will have to bear the responsibility for the accident.* **6.** *tv., irreg.* to manage to support someone or something; to carry the weight of someone or something. ♦ *Can this old chair bear my weight?* ♦ *The bookcase could not bear the weight of all the books, and it collapsed.* **7.** *tv., irreg.* to undergo something; to suffer and endure something. ♦ *Can the patient bear the pain of further tests?* ♦ *How can the couple bear the loss of their only child?* **8.** *tv., irreg.* to produce offspring; to give birth to a child. (When this sense is used in the passive and focuses on the child, as in *Jimmy was born in 1996*, the past participle is born; otherwise, the past participle is borne.) ♦ *Jane bore a child last spring.* ♦ *Mrs. Jones has borne five children already and prefers not to have another.* ♦ *All of Mary's children have been born in this hospital.* **9.** *tv., irreg.* [for a plant] to produce or yield something, such as fruit, flowers, or leaves. ♦ *Despite daily care, the tree never bore any fruit.* ♦ *Does this plant bear blossoms every year?* **10.** *iv., irreg.* to turn; to go in a certain direction. ♦ *Bear right at the second stoplight.* ♦ *Should we bear left or right when we reach the fork in the road?* **11. bear down on** *iv., irreg.* + *adv.* + *prep. phr.* to put pressure on someone or something. ♦ *Don't bear down on your pencil so hard.* ♦ *Dad bore down on the handle and twisted with all his might.* **12. bear in mind** *idiom* to remember something; to consider something. ♦ *Bear in mind that the trip will be expensive.* ♦ *I asked the teacher to bear in mind that I am just a beginner.* **13. bear watching** *idiom* to need watching; to deserve observation or monitoring. ♦ *This problem will bear watching.* ♦ *This is a very serious disease, and it will bear watching for further developments.*

bearable ['bɛr ə bəl] *adj.* able to be dealt with; endurable. (Adv: *bearably.*) ♦ *Food at the cheap restaurant was almost bearable.* ♦ *The school band concert was bearable, but we were glad when it was over.*

beard ['bɪrd] *n.* hair that grows on the side of the face, chin, and neck, usually of the male. ♦ *Bob grew a beard during the winter.* ♦ *Bill trims his beard each day.*

bearded ['bɪrd ɪd] *adj.* having a beard. ♦ *Mary identified the bearded man as her attacker.* ♦ *Max is bearded each winter and clean-shaven each summer.*

bearing ['bɛr ɪŋ] **1. one's bearings** *n.* a direction or location; knowledge of where one is. ♦ *The campers used a compass to get their bearings.* ♦ *We lost our bearings and suddenly were lost.* **2.** *n.* posture; behavior; the way that someone stands or acts. (No plural form in this sense.) ♦ *Mary's bearing indicated that she was timid.* ♦ *The teacher's formidable bearing frightened the younger students.* **3.** *n.* a part of a structure or machine that supports moving or rotating parts. ♦ *Each bearing needs oil or it will get too hot.* ♦ *The bearings of the car wheels must be packed in grease.* **4. have bearing on something** *idiom* the effect or influence that something has on something else. ♦ *The worker's opinion has no bearing on the boss's decision.* ♦ *What bearing does John's decision have on the situation?*

bearish ['bɛr ɪʃ] **1.** *adj.* in the rough and grouchy manner of a bear. (Adv: *bearishly.*) ♦ *The manager was somewhat bearish in the grumpy way he sat in his office and gave orders.* ♦ *Your bearish behavior at the party offended almost everyone there.* **2.** *adj.* pessimistic about the prospects for a particular financial market or financial instrument. (Compare with bullish ②. Adv: *bearishly.*) ♦ *I'm very bearish in the stock market since the increase in interest rates.* ♦ *Investors were bearish on foreign stocks because of a war in Asia.*

beast ['bist] **1.** *n.* a monster; a scary creature. ♦ *The beast arose from its lair and roared at the trespassers.* ♦ *A brave knight stabbed the beast with his sword.* **2.** *n.* an animal, especially one with four feet. ♦ *The beast was so sickly, we couldn't tell if it was a wolf or a dog.* ♦ *The hunter would shoot at any beast along the path.* **3.** *n.* someone or something that is horrible or ugly. (Figurative on ①.) ♦ *Don't act like such a beast!* ♦ *That beast of a piano will take four strong people to move it.*

beastly ['bist li] *adj.* horrible; intolerable. ♦ *The beastly criminal was locked up for his deeds.* ♦ *The hot weather was simply beastly!*

beat ['bit] **1.** *n.* the rhythm of poetry or music. ♦ *Grandpa tapped his foot to the beat of the music.* ♦ *The untalented dancer couldn't find the beat of the music.* **2.** *n.* one unit of a musical measure. ♦ *How many beats are there in a measure of music in 4/4 time?* ♦ *The conductor indicated each beat with his baton.* **3.** *n.* the area or route that someone, especially a police officer, walks on a regular basis. ♦ *Officer Brown walked the same beat for thirty years.* ♦ *The new cop was given a dangerous beat.* **4.** *tv., irreg.* to hit someone or something over and over. (Pt: *beat;* pp: beaten.) ♦ *Bill beat the dust out of the rug.* ♦ *The beastly man beat his dog.* **5.** *tv., irreg.* to mix food ingredients with a kitchen tool. ♦ *Tom beat the eggs with a fork.* ♦ *The recipe says to beat the batter for five minutes.* **6.** *tv., irreg.* to win a game against someone or something; to triumph over someone or something in a competition. ♦ *Everyone cheered when Mary beat the other tennis player.* ♦ *Did the rival team beat your team again?* **7. beat up** *tv.* + *adv.* to beat someone; to hit someone repeatedly with the fists. ♦ *Two bullies tried to beat Max up.* ♦ *The muggers beat up the old lady and robbed her.* **8.** *iv., irreg.* to hit against someone or something over and over. ♦ *The shutter is beating against the side of the house.* ♦ *The rain is beating on the roof.* **9.** *iv., irreg.* to throb; to pulse over and over. ♦ *My heart is beating very fast.* ♦ *The metronome beats to keep time.* **10.** *adj.* exhausted; tired; worn out. (Informal.) ♦ *We were just beat after raking all the leaves.* ♦ *The busy teacher is always beat on Friday night.*

beaten ['bit n] pp of beat.

beating ['bit ɪŋ] **1.** *n.* the repeated hitting of someone or something; a whipping. ♦ *The poor child got a beating for misbehaving.* ♦ *A dangerous criminal was arrested and charged with the beating.* **2.** *adj.* throbbing; thumping; [of a heart] pumping. ♦ *I could feel my beating heart in my chest.* ♦ *The doctor could not detect any beating sound and declared the patient to be dead.*

beautician [bju 'tɪ ʃən] *n.* someone trained to beautify someone's skin and hair. ♦ *The beautician recommended putting highlights in Mary's hair.* ♦ *My hairdresser is a licensed beautician.*

beautification [bju tə fɪ 'ke ʃən] *n.* making someone or something more beautiful. (No plural form in this sense.) ♦ *The beautification of the hotel lobby was quite expensive.* ♦ *Beautification of the town square included installing a new fountain.*

beautiful ['bju tə fʊl] **1.** *adj.* having great beauty; very pretty. (Adv: *beautifully* ['bju tə fli].) ♦ *The flowers in the garden were beautiful.* ♦ *The ugly duckling turned out be a beautiful swan.* **2.** *adj.* excellent. (Informal. Adv: *beautifully* ['bju tə fli].) ♦ *The surgeon did a beautiful job closing the incision.* ♦ *Your performance was beautiful!*

beautify ['bju tə fɑɪ] *tv.* to make someone or something look beautiful. ♦ *The people raised funds to beautify the town square.* ♦ *A few flowers will beautify any room.*

beauty ['bjut i] **1.** *n.* the quality that makes someone or something very pleasing to look at. (No plural form in this sense.) ♦ *Mary has a natural beauty and needs no makeup.* ♦ *We were awed by the beauty of the scenery.* **2.** *n.* someone or something that is beautiful or excellent. ♦ *That horse is a beauty!* ♦ *We had a beauty of a day for the picnic.* **3.** *n.* excellence; suitability; cleverness. (No plural form in this sense.) ♦ *The beauty of the plan is its simplicity.* ♦ *"That's the beauty of it. No one will ever know," Jane said.*

beaver ['bi vɚ] **1.** *n., irreg.* a furry, plant-eating animal that dams up streams to form a pond in which it builds its house or lodge. (Pl: *beaver* or *beavers.*) ♦ *Beavers gnawed at the tree until it fell.* ♦ *The beaver's dam hindered the stream's flow.* **2. eager beaver** *idiom* someone who is very enthusiastic; someone who works very hard. (The plural is always *eager beavers.*) ♦ *New volunteers are always eager beavers.* ♦ *The young assistant gets to work very early. She's a real eager beaver.*

became [bɪ 'kem] pt of become.

because [bɪ 'kɔz] *conj.* due to; on account of; for the reason that. ♦ *Because of the rain, the hike was canceled.* ♦ *Jane was late for work because her car broke down.*

beckon ['bɛk ən] **1. beckon (to)** *iv.* (+ *prep. phr.*) to signal to someone to come nearer. ♦ *The restaurant's sign beckoned to hungry travelers.* ♦ *The lights in the house beckoned in an inviting manner.* **2.** *tv.* to make a motion indicating that someone is to come nearer. ♦ *The tour guide beckoned us over to look at the painting.* ♦ *Jimmy knew he was in trouble when his mother beckoned him.*

become [bɪ 'kʌm] **1.** *iv., irreg.* to come to be something; to grow to be something. (Pt: became; pp: *become.*) ♦ *The student became quite an accomplished musician.* ♦ *Tom plans to become a teacher.* **2.** *iv., irreg.* to turn into something. ♦ *The ugly duckling became a beautiful swan.* ♦ *The sky became cloudy suddenly.* **3.** *tv., irreg.* [for clothing or ornament] to look good on someone; to make someone look attractive. ♦ *These ugly clothes do not become you.* ♦ *That fancy style really becomes you!*

becoming [bɪ 'kʌm ɪŋ] *adj.* [of clothing or personal ornamentation] flattering and pleasant looking. (Adv: *becomingly.*) ♦ *John's new haircut is very becoming.* ♦ *My most becoming dress is very expensive.*

bed ['bɛd] **1.** *n.* a piece of furniture used to sleep on, usually raised and with a mattress, sheets, and blankets. ♦ *The large bed barely fit in the small room.* ♦ *The maid changed the sheets on the bed each day.* **2.** *n.* a flat base; a foundation; a bottom layer of support. ♦ *We loaded the lumber onto the bed of the truck.* ♦ *A bed of gravel lay under the concrete floor.* **3.** *n.* the earth on the bottom of a body of water. ♦ *The lake bed yielded fossils of sea animals.* ♦ *Divers examined the bed of the sea.* **4.** *n.* an area of soil where flowers and other plants grow. ♦ *The kids ran right through the bed of flowers.* ♦ *The rabbits hopped straight to the lettuce bed and began to eat.* **5. go to bed** *idiom* to go to where one's bed ① is, get into it, and go to sleep. ♦ *It's time for me to go to bed.* ♦ *I want to go to bed, but there is too much work to do.* **6. put someone to bed; send someone to bed** *idiom* to make someone go to bed. ♦ *Mother put Jimmy to bed and kissed him.* ♦ *Sally was naughty and was sent to bed.* **7. put something to bed** *idiom* to complete work on something and send it on to the next step in production, especially in publishing. ♦ *This edition is finished. Let's put it to bed.* ♦ *Finish the editing of this book and put it to bed.* **8. should have stood in bed** *idiom* should have stayed in one's bed ①. ♦ *What a horrible day! I should have stood in bed.* ♦ *The minute I got up and heard the news this morning, I knew I should have stood in bed.*

bedclothes ['bɛd kloz] *n.* covering for a bed; sheets and a blanket. (Treated as plural.) ♦ *The maid changed the bedclothes every morning.* ♦ *I stripped the bed of its bedclothes after I got up.*

bedding ['bɛd ɪŋ] *n.* the mattress coverings, sheets, and blankets used on a bed. (No plural form in this sense.) ♦ *Bedding is kept in the linen closet.* ♦ *The bedding at the hotel is changed every day.*

bedfellow ['bɛd fɛl o] *n.* an associate; an ally. ♦ *The newspaper said that the politician and the labor leader make strange bedfellows.* ♦ *The two bankers have been loyal and supportive bedfellows for many years.*

bedlam ['bɛd ləm] *n.* chaos; a state of noisy confusion. (No plural form in this sense.) ♦ *The playground was in bedlam during recess.* ♦ *When the director quit, play rehearsals turned into total bedlam.*

bedpan ['bɛd pæn] *n.* a pan for excrement, used by people who cannot get out of bed. ♦ *A nurse kindly helped the patient with the bedpan.* ♦ *The patient groaned upon seeing the bedpan.*

bed rest ['bɛd rɛst] *n.* rest taken lying in bed. ♦ *Mary's serious illness required bed rest.* ♦ *The recovering patient needs extensive bed rest.*

bedridden ['bɛd rɪd n] *adj.* too sick or weak to get out of bed. ♦ *The volunteer read to the bedridden patient.* ♦ *After the accident, Grandpa was bedridden for months.*

bedrock ['bɛd rɑk] *n.* the layer of solid rock beneath other layers of soil and stones. (No plural form in this sense.) ♦ *The construction workers hit bedrock with their drills.* ♦ *The building's foundation went down to the bedrock.*

bedroll ['bɛd rol] *n.* a sleeping bag or other bedding that can be rolled or folded and carried. ♦ *The hikers carried bedrolls on their backs.* ♦ *The campers placed their bedrolls near the fire.*

bedroom ['bɛd rum] *n.* a room in a dwelling place where someone sleeps. ♦ *Bill was asleep in the bedroom when the fire started.* ♦ *The decorator painted the bedroom blue.*

bed sheet ['bɛd ʃit] *n.* one of the sheets of cloth that people sleep between. ♦ *The bed sheets became all twisted during the night.* ♦ *I stripped the dirty bed sheets from the bed.*

bedside ['bɛd saɪd] **1.** *n.* the side of a bed; the area beside a bed. ♦ *The devoted husband sat by his wife's bedside until she was well.* ♦ *The doctor reached the patient's bedside just as he died.* **2.** *adj.* beside a bed. ♦ *An alarm clock sat on the bedside table.* ♦ *The bedroom had matching bedside tables.*

bedsore ['bɛd sor] *n.* a sore on the body caused by lying too long in the same position. ♦ *A special cushion prevented the patient from getting bedsores.* ♦ *The nurse turned the patient over to prevent bedsores.*

bedspread ['bɛd sprɛd] *n.* a decorative quilt or blanket that rests on top of the bedclothes. ♦ *The baby spilled milk on the new bedspread.* ♦ *The bedspread matched the paint in the bedroom.*

bedstead ['bɛd stɛd] *n.* the metal or wood pieces that fit together to form the frame of a bed. ♦ *I inherited my great-grandmother's bedstead.* ♦ *The children broke the bedstead when they jumped on the bed.*

bedtime ['bɛd taɪm] *n.* the time when someone usually goes to bed. ♦ *The toddler's bedtime is eight o'clock.* ♦ *I remained awake past my bedtime.*

bee ['bi] **1.** *n.* a small insect that can sting and that makes honey. ♦ *The bee gathered pollen from the flowers.* ♦ *Jimmy got stung by a bee in the pasture.* **2. have a bee in one's bonnet** *idiom* to have an idea or a thought remain in one's mind; to have an obsession. ♦ *I have a bee in my bonnet that you'd be a good manager.* ♦ *I had a bee in my bonnet about swimming. I couldn't stop wanting to go swimming.*

beef ['bif] **1.** *n.* the meat of a cow, steer, or bull. (No plural form in this sense.) ♦ *Hamburger is generally made from beef.* ♦ *Beef has a higher fat content than turkey.* **2.** *n.* a complaint; a gripe. (Slang.) ♦ *The teenager's beef was about her allowance.* ♦ *Some employees always have a beef.*

beefsteak ['bif stek] *n.* a slice of the flesh of a cow, steer, or bull, eaten as food. (Usually **steak**.) ♦ *The server brought our beefsteaks quickly.* ♦ *Bill craved a good beefsteak about once a week.*

beehive ['bi haɪv] *n.* a place where bees live, reproduce, and make honey. ♦ *Bees swarmed around the beehive.* ♦ *The beehive was full of honey.*

beekeeper ['bi kip ɚ] *n.* someone who raises bees and harvests their honey. ♦ *The professional beekeeper sold honey at the market.* ♦ *The beekeeper explained to the children how bees make honey.*

beeline ['bi laɪn] **make a beeline for someone or something** *idiom* to head straight toward someone or something. ♦ *Billy came into the kitchen and made a beeline for the cookies.* ♦ *After the game, we all made a beeline for John, who was serving cold drinks.*

been [bɪn] pp of be.

beep ['bip] **1.** *n.* a short, high-pitched, audible signal, usually made by a mechanical device such as a car horn or an answering machine. ♦ *The timer gave three short beeps.* ♦ *The car alarm is making an annoying beep.* **2.** *iv.* [for a machine] to make a short, high-pitched, audible signal. ♦ *The answering machine beeped and then played back our messages.* ♦ *When the timer beeps, the cake will be finished baking.* **3.** *tv.* [for someone] to cause a mechanical device to sound a short, high-pitched, audible signal. ♦ *I beeped the car horn at the slow driver.* ♦ *The hospital beeped Mary's pager.* **4.** *tv.* to signal someone by way of a pager. ♦ *I told David to beep me if there was an emergency.* ♦ *The nurse beeped the doctor when the patient took a turn for the worse.*

beeper ['bip ɚ] **1.** *n.* a small electronic device that sounds a signal or vibrates to notify someone of something, such as a waiting telephone message; a **pager**. ♦ *Mary's beeper went off in the middle of the opera.* ♦ *Dr. Smith left his beeper in the car and missed the hospital's call.* **2.** *n.* any small device that makes a beep. ♦ *My computer's beeper alerted me to a mistake.* ♦ *The beeper in the alarm clock broke.*

beer ['bɪr] **1.** *n.* a fermented alcoholic beverage made from grain and flavored with hops. (No plural form in this sense.) ♦ *I prefer German beer to domestic beer.* ♦ *Beer always goes well with pizza.* **2.** *n.* a glass or can of ①; a serving of ①. ♦ *I would like a beer, please.* ♦ *How many beers did he drink?*

beeswax ['biz wæks] *n.* wax produced by bees as they make honeycombs. (No plural form in this sense.) ♦ *Beeswax made a good lubricant for drawers and other wood parts.* ♦ *The ointment contained beeswax.*

beet ['bit] *n.* a plant with a large red root that is eaten as a vegetable. ♦ *The farmer's main crop was beets.* ♦ *The juice of the beet can stain your clothing.*

beetle ['bit əl] *n.* a small insect whose wings are hard and protect its body. ♦ *There are thousands of types of beetles.* ♦ *The cat batted the beetle around on the sidewalk.*

befall [bɪ 'fɔl] *tv., irreg.* to happen to someone or something. (Pt: **befell**; pp: **befallen**. Formal.) ♦ *Something terrible has befallen Tom.* ♦ *What has befallen the princess?*

befallen [bɪ 'fɔl ən] pp of **befall**.

befell [bɪ 'fɛl] pt of **befall**.

before [bɪ 'for] **1.** *conj.* earlier than a certain time; previous to a certain time. ♦ *I will be ready before you arrive.* ♦ *Before Sue eats, she always washes her hands.* **2.** *prep.* earlier than; previous to. ♦ *Before noon, we washed the laundry.* ♦ *Let's eat dinner before dark.* **3.** *prep.* in front of. ♦ *The students who started the fight stood before the principal.* ♦ *Bill and Mary were married before their friends and families.* **4.** *adv.* earlier; previous. ♦ *The party starts at 9:00, and not a moment before.* ♦ *The leader of the expedition had left an hour before.* **5.** *adv.* until this moment in time; in the past. ♦ *Bob had never tried caviar before,* *but he was willing to try.* ♦ *I had never sailed before, but I loved it immediately.*

beforehand [bɪ 'for hænd] *adv.* ahead of time; in advance. ♦ *The cook fried the bacon beforehand, so preparing breakfast would not take as long.* ♦ *Please make a reservation at the restaurant beforehand so we don't have to wait.*

befuddled [bɪ 'fʌd ld] *adj.* confused. (Adv: *befuddledly.*) ♦ *The befuddled deer could not move out of the path of the car.* ♦ *The police found the befuddled old man in the park.*

beg ['bɛg] **1.** *iv.* to plead for something; to ask for something very humbly. ♦ *The woman begged for spare change to feed her family.* ♦ *The children begged to stay up late.* **2. beg to** *tv.* + *inf.* to ask someone, very humbly, to do something. ♦ *Anne begged her friend to forgive her.* ♦ *The children begged their parents to let them stay up late.*

began [bɪ 'gæn] pt of begin.

beggar ['bɛg ɚ] *n.* someone who asks for charity, especially money or food; a panhandler. ♦ *The beggar made about $50 a day.* ♦ *Tom tossed the beggar some change.*

begin [bɪ 'gɪn] **1.** *iv., irreg.* to start [to do] something; to commence [doing] something. (Pt: began; pp: begun.) ♦ *Please begin on page ten.* ♦ *When does the concert begin?* **2. begin to** *iv., irreg.* + *inf.* to start to do something. ♦ *It is beginning to rain.* ♦ *Tommy is beginning to look like a movie star.* **3.** *tv., irreg.* to start something; to commence something. ♦ *Mary began her studies when she was a child.* ♦ *The professor will begin the lecture with slides.*

beginner [bɪ 'gɪn ɚ] *n.* someone just learning to do something; an amateur. ♦ *The skater is just a beginner but shows great promise.* ♦ *My German class is full of beginners.*

beginning [bɪ 'gɪn ɪŋ] **1.** *n.* the start; the origin. (No plural form in this sense.) ♦ *The beginning of the play is depressing, but it ends happily.* ♦ *In the beginning, I thought Max was a good guy.* **2. beginnings** *n.* the earliest stage of the origin of someone or something. ♦ *This problem goes back to the beginnings of the earth itself.* ♦ *My beginnings were quite humble.*

begonia [bɪ 'gon jə] *n.* any of a group of popular house or garden plants with colorful flowers and shiny, sometimes colorful, leaves. ♦ *The begonia plants were in full blossom.* ♦ *When I was in the hospital, someone sent me a begonia.*

begun [bɪ 'gʌn] pp of begin.

behalf [bɪ 'hæf] **1. in behalf of; on behalf of** *idiom* in representing someone; speaking for someone. ♦ *The actor's agent accepted the award on behalf of her client.* ♦ *The club president spoke on behalf of the committee.* **2. on someone's behalf; in someone's behalf** *idiom* as a help to something; to the benefit of someone. ♦ *A donation was made in the victim's behalf.* ♦ *The memorial was established on John's behalf.*

behave [bɪ 'hev] **1.** *iv.* to act in a specified way. (Refers to good behavior unless there are words indicating bad behavior.) ♦ *The unruly student behaved badly in class.* ♦ *When will your children learn to behave?* **2.** *tv.* to conduct oneself in a proper manner. (Takes a reflexive object.) ♦ *"Behave yourself!" the mother warned her child.* ♦ *I was pleased that Jimmy behaved himself at the party.*

behavior [bɪ 'hev jɚ] **1.** *n.* the manner in which someone acts or behaves; conduct; manners. (No plural form in this sense.) ♦ *The chairman's behavior was unbecoming to his position.* ♦ *The children's behavior improved after they were warned.* **2.** *n.* the manner in which someone or something responds or reacts in a certain situation. ♦ *The sociologist studies the behavior of crowds.* ♦ *The researcher wrote an article on animal behavior.*

behead [bɪ 'hɛd] *tv.* to cut off someone or something's head; to chop off a criminal's head as punishment. ♦ *The chef beheaded the fish before cooking it.* ♦ *The queen gave the order to behead the treasonous spy.*

beheld [bɪ 'hɛld] pt/pp of behold.

behind [bɪ 'hɑɪnd] **1.** *prep.* in or to a place farther back than something else; at the rear of someone or something. ♦ *Put the plant behind the table.* ♦ *The shed was behind the house.* **2.** *prep.* late; later than scheduled. ♦ *This project is behind schedule.* ♦ *Max is always behind with his work.* **3.** *prep.* serving as the reason for something. ♦ *The facts behind his death are not available to the public.* ♦ *What is behind these practical jokes?* **4.** *prep.* in support of someone. ♦ *"I'm behind you 100 percent," the lawyer said to the defendant.* ♦ *The fans stood behind the losing baseball team.* **5.** *adv.* toward the back; further back in place or time. ♦ *I am falling behind in my work.* ♦ *Please don't give me more work; I'm falling behind as it is.* **6.** *n.* the backside; the buttocks. ♦ *Jimmy fell on his behind while skating.* ♦ *Bob's behind got warm as he stood facing away from the fire.*

behold [bɪ 'hold] **1.** *tv., irreg.* to see someone or something; to gaze upon someone or something. (Pt/pp: beheld.) ♦ *I screamed when I beheld the mess in the kitchen.* ♦ *The crowds clamored to behold the famous rock group.* **2.** *interj.* Look!; See! ♦ *And behold, the ugly duckling had become a swan.* ♦ *"Behold, his majesty!" the knight bellowed.*

beige ['beʒ] **1.** *n.* a pale, light brown color. (No plural form in this sense.) ♦ *Beige looks terrible against your pale skin.* ♦ *Beige is a neutral tone.* **2.** *adj.* pale, light brown in color. ♦ *The apartment had beige carpeting and walls.* ♦ *Your beige shoes clash with your black belt.*

being ['bi ɪŋ] **1. into being** *phr.* into existence. ♦ *The new law brought more problems into being.* ♦ *That idea came into being centuries ago.* **2.** *n.* a living thing; a living creature. ♦ *All sorts of beings live in the desert.* ♦ *Every human being should have the same basic rights.*

belabor [bɪ 'leb ɚ] *tv.* to talk or write about a subject too much. ♦ *The newspaper belabored the kidnapping story long after the child's rescue.* ♦ *Let's not belabor the point.*

Belarus [bɛl ə 'rus] See Gazetteer.

belated [bɪ 'let ɪd] *adj.* late; not on time; done after the proper time. (Adv: *belatedly.*) ♦ *Sue forgot Jane's birthday but sent a belated card to her.* ♦ *Your belated congratulations are still appreciated.*

belch ['bɛltʃ] **1.** *n.* an audible release of stomach gas through the mouth. ♦ *The baby made a belch, and everyone laughed.* ♦ *The rude guest let out a belch at dinner.* **2.** *n.* a puff of smoke or other vapors released or pushed out. ♦ *The belch of smoke from the factory was pale green.* ♦ *A belch of smoke from the fireplace filled the room.* **3.** *iv.* to make ①. ♦ *The baby belched, and everyone laughed.* ♦ *The rude child belched during the meal.* **4.** *iv.* [for large volumes of smoke or other vapors] to escape. ♦ *Smoke belched from the windows of the burning building.* ♦

Because the flue was shut, smoke from the fireplace belched into the living room. **5.** *tv.* to release smoke or other vapors. ♦ *The fireplace belched smoke into the living room.* ♦ *The smoke stacks belched poisonous fumes into the air.*

Belgium ['bɛl dʒəm] See Gazetteer.

belief [bɪ 'lif] **1.** *n.* something that is thought to be true; an opinion; a conviction. ♦ *John held the belief that people are basically good.* ♦ *Mary didn't share that belief with us.* **2.** *n.* a trust in someone. ♦ *John's belief in Mary supported her during the crisis.* ♦ *I have no belief in you, and I can't trust you at all.* **3.** *n.* a tenet of a religion or faith. (Often plural.) ♦ *Different religions have different beliefs.* ♦ *Mary's beliefs are centered around God.*

believe [bɪ 'liv] **1.** *tv.* to accept that someone or something is true or real. ♦ *The judge did not believe our story.* ♦ *Mary believed the witness's testimony.* **2.** *tv.* to have an opinion about something; to suppose something. (Takes a clause.) ♦ *I believe that you are correct.* ♦ *The coach believes that we can win the game.* **3. believe in** *iv.* + *prep. phr.* to accept that someone or something exists or is real. ♦ *Do you believe in ghosts?* ♦ *Jimmy believes in Santa Claus.* **4. believe in** *iv.* + *prep. phr.* to have faith in someone or something; to trust someone or something. ♦ *Jane believes in the fairness of the legal system.* ♦ *Tom believes in his ability to succeed.* **5. believe it or not** *idiom* to choose to believe something or not. ♦ *Believe it or not, I just got home from work.* ♦ *I'm over fifty years old, believe it or not.*

believer [bɪ 'liv ɚ] **1.** *n.* someone who believes in someone or something. ♦ *Tom is a believer in home remedies.* ♦ *The president is a real believer in making government smaller.* **2.** *n.* someone who follows a certain religion or faith. ♦ *This religion has millions of believers.* ♦ *The faithful believers always went to church.*

belittle [bɪ 'lɪt əl] *tv.* to make fun of or insult someone; to make something seem small and unimportant. ♦ *The children were reprimanded for belittling each other at the dinner table.* ♦ *The reporter's comments belittled the candidate.*

Belize [bə 'liz] See Gazetteer.

bell ['bɛl] **1.** *n.* a cupped, metal shell that makes a ringing sound when struck. ♦ *The church bells rang each noon.* ♦ *Mother rang a bell to call the children home.* **2.** *n.* the sound made by ① to mark the start or the finish of a period of time. ♦ *All students not in their classes at the bell will be marked late.* ♦ *When we heard the bell, we all got up and left.* **3. saved by the bell** *idiom* rescued from a difficult or dangerous situation just in time by something that brings the situation to a sudden end. ♦ *James didn't know the answer to the question, but he was saved by the bell when the teacher was called away from the room.* ♦ *I couldn't think of anything to say to the woman at the bus stop, but I was saved by the bell when the bus arrived.*

bellicose ['bɛl ə kos] *adj.* warlike; ready to fight. (Adv: *bellicosely.*) ♦ *The bellicose man threatened to hit me.* ♦ *The old senator was known for his bellicose attitude.*

belligerence [bə 'lɪdʒ ə rəns] *n.* a display of a warlike attitude or aggressive behavior; aggressiveness; hostility. (No plural form in this sense.) ♦ *The teacher would not tolerate any belligerence in her classroom.* ♦ *The boy's voice had a tone of belligerence.*

belligerent [bə 'lɪdʒ ə rənt] *adj.* warlike; aggressive; hostile. (Adv: *belligerently.*) ♦ *The belligerent boy was sent to the principal's office.* ♦ *It is unwise to take a belligerent attitude.*

bellow ['bɛl o] **1.** *n.* a loud, deep roar. ♦ *Dave let out a bellow when he realized that his car had been stolen.* ♦ *We heard angry bellows coming from the locker room after the game.* **2.** *iv.* to roar; to yell. ♦ *The lion bellowed at the visitors to the zoo.* ♦ *Mary vowed she would never bellow like her parents.* **3. bellow (out)** *tv.* (+ *adv.*) to yell something. ♦ *The coach bellowed out the play numbers to the team.* ♦ *Bob bellowed his complaints to the service representative.*

belly ['bɛl i] **1.** *n.* the stomach; the abdomen. ♦ *Our bellies ached after we ate the rich dessert.* ♦ *I tickled the baby's belly, and he laughed.* **2.** *n.* the inside of certain things. ♦ *The belly of the castle was filled with weapons.* ♦ *Gold was hidden in the belly of the ship.* **3.** *n.* the underside of certain things. ♦ *The belly of the plane scraped the trees before the crash.* ♦ *A lizard's belly is usually soft and white.*

bellyache ['bɛl i ek] *n.* a sick feeling in the stomach; a stomachache. (Colloquial.) ♦ *Eating the raw cookie dough gave Mary a bellyache.* ♦ *I drink herbal tea when I have a bellyache.*

belong [bɪ 'lɔŋ] **1.** *iv.* [for someone or something] to have a proper or appropriate placement. ♦ *The fork belongs to the left of the knife.* ♦ *Clothes belong in the closet.* **2. belong to** *iv.* + *prep. phr.* to be the property of someone or something. ♦ *Does this book belong to you?* ♦ *The cat belongs to the Smiths, but it begs for food at the Browns' house.* **3. belong to** *iv.* + *prep. phr.* to be a member of something. ♦ *Lions and tigers belong to the cat family.* ♦ *John and I belong to the same club.*

belongings [bɪ 'lɔŋ ɪŋz] *n.* the things that one owns; a possession. (Treated as plural.) ♦ *Mary told Bill to gather his belongings and leave.* ♦ *We left our belongings in the locker at school.*

beloved [bɪ 'lʌvd, bɪ 'lʌvəd] **1.** *adj.* cherished; dearly loved. ♦ *Jane buried her beloved father last year.* ♦ *The rich man left each of his beloved grandchildren a large inheritance.* **2.** *n.* someone who is dearly loved; someone who is cherished. (No plural form in this sense.) ♦ *I sent my beloved a letter.* ♦ *My beloved sent me flowers.*

below [bɪ 'lo] **1.** *prep.* beneath; under; lower than. ♦ *Below each painting was a plaque showing its name.* ♦ *Pots and pans are kept below the kitchen counter.* **2.** *prep.* lower in status. ♦ *Detroit ranks below New York in terms of population.* ♦ *The students' test scores were below the national average.* **3.** *adv.* to a lower deck on a ship. ♦ *The sailor went below to talk to the ship's captain.* ♦ *All the officers are below eating supper.* **4.** *adv.* after or following. (Usually in a book or other printed material.) ♦ *See Figure 14 below.* ♦ *The complete story is told below.*

belt ['bɛlt] **1.** *n.* a strip of leather or similar material fastened around the waist. ♦ *Bill fastened his belt and put on his tie.* ♦ *After I lost thirty pounds, my belt was too big.* **2.** *n.* a region; an area with a common characteristic. (In compounds.) ♦ *During the early 1980s, many people left the Rust Belt in the industrial Midwest for southern states.* ♦ *The southern states are sometimes referred to as the Bible Belt.* **3.** *n.* a long, continuous loop of strong, flexible material used in machinery to transfer power. ♦ *One of* *the engine's belts broke, causing the car to stall.* ♦ *The parts needed in the factory are transported by a conveyor belt.* **4.** *n.* a seat belt; a strap in a car that holds people securely in the seat. ♦ *Anne asked me to latch my belt before starting the car.* ♦ *Is your belt attached?* **5. belt in; belt up** *tv. + adv.* to put a seat belt on oneself. (Takes a reflexive object.) ♦ *I belted myself up and started the car.* ♦ *"Belt yourselves in," the driver instructed.* **6.** *tv.* to hit someone hard; to beat someone. (Informal.) ♦ *Bob belted the guy who insulted his sister.* ♦ *The angry clerk really wanted to belt the rude customer.* **7. tighten one's belt** *idiom* to manage to spend less money. ♦ *Things are beginning to cost more and more. It looks like we'll all have to tighten our belts.* ♦ *Times are hard, and prices are high. I can tighten my belt for only so long.*

beltway ['bɛlt we] *n.* a road, freeway, or tollway that forms a circle around a city or area. (When capitalized, the *Beltway* refers to the expressway that circles Washington, D.C.) ♦ *The truck broke down in the middle of the beltway.* ♦ *The beltway was crowded with traffic during rush hour.*

bench ['bɛntʃ] **1.** *n.* a seat—often unpadded—for two or more people. ♦ *The city put new benches in all the parks.* ♦ *Bob sat on the bench at the bus stop.* **2.** *n.* a place where players on a sports team sit when they are not playing. ♦ *Anne never got off the bench during her softball game.* ♦ *The players waited on the bench to be put in the game.* **3.** *n.* the seat a judge sits on. ♦ *Judge Brown sat down on the bench and called the court to order.* ♦ *The judge rose from the bench and demanded order in the court.* **4.** *n.* a judge or a group of judges in a court of law. ♦ *The decision came from the bench just after noon.* ♦ *The bench ruled against the motion.* **5.** *tv.* to take an athlete out of a game to sit on the bench. ♦ *The coach benched the quarterback for most of the game.* ♦ *After too many fouls, the referee benched the basketball player.* **6. warm the bench** *idiom* [for a player] to remain out of play during a game—seated on a bench. ♦ *John spent the whole game warming the bench.* ♦ *Mary never warms the bench. She plays from the beginning to the end.*

bend ['bɛnd] **1.** *n.* a curve; a turn. ♦ *The car raced around the bend in the road.* ♦ *The hikers left the path at the bend by the lake.* **2.** *iv., irreg.* to change one's mind; to yield. (Pt/pp: bent.) ♦ *Dad bent a little on the issue of curfews.* ♦ *Do you think we can get the teacher to bend on the due date?* **3.** *iv., irreg.* to become curved or crooked; to go in a direction away from a straight line. ♦ *The road bends a lot in the mountains.* ♦ *Thin wire bends easily.* **4.** *tv., irreg.* to cause an object to curve; to change the shape of a flexible object. ♦ *We bent the pipe so that it would fit against the wall.* ♦ *If you bend the antenna wire, you'll get a better reception.*

beneath [bɪ 'niθ] **1.** *prep.* under; below; lower than someone or something. ♦ *Hide the letter beneath the newspaper.* ♦ *Hang the picture beneath the photograph.* **2.** *prep.* inferior; worse than someone or something. ♦ *Bob felt physical labor was beneath him.* ♦ *Jane wouldn't associate with anyone she felt was beneath her.*

benediction [bɛn ə 'dɪk ʃən] *n.* a blessing given at the close of a religious service. ♦ *After the last prayer, the minister gave a benediction.* ♦ *The congregation left after the benediction.*

benefactor ['bɛn ə fæk tɚ] *n.* someone who gives money to an organization, institution, or person. ♦ *The generous benefactor remained anonymous.* ♦ *The museum must find a benefactor to donate some money.*

beneficent [bə 'nɛf ə sənt] *adj.* charitable; kind. (Adv: *beneficently.*) ♦ *Max's beneficent act went unnoticed.* ♦ *The beneficent woman came to the rescue of her needy relatives.*

beneficial [bɛn ə 'fɪʃ əl] *adj.* having an advantage or benefit. (Adv: *beneficially.*) ♦ *The medication was beneficial in curing the disease.* ♦ *Mary's college classes were beneficial to her career path.*

beneficiary [bɛn ə 'fɪʃ ɪ ɛr i] **1.** *n.* someone or a group that receives money or benefits; the recipient of a gift. ♦ *The museum was the beneficiary of Mary's generosity.* ♦ *The whole office was the beneficiary of the boss's good cheer.* **2.** *n.* someone who legally receives money or property from a will, trust, or other legal document. ♦ *Anne was the beneficiary of the aunt's estate.* ♦ *Mary named her husband the beneficiary of her life insurance policy.*

benefit ['bɛn ə fɪt] **1.** *n.* an advantage; something that is helpful or has a good effect. ♦ *What are the benefits of doing it your way?* ♦ *There are many benefits to a well-rounded education.* **2.** *n.* the sum of money paid to someone under the terms of an insurance or retirement contract; the sum of money paid to someone as an entitlement. (Often plural.) ♦ *There are no benefits for smoking-related illnesses listed in your insurance policy.* ♦ *The insurance policy listed no benefits for illnesses related to smoking.* **3.** *n.* something that one receives—in addition to salary—as part of one's compensation for working, such as health insurance, life insurance, etc. ♦ *Where I work, the salaries are not too good, but the benefits are excellent.* ♦ *Health insurance is a benefit that all workers expect to receive.* **4.** *n.* a special entertainment given to raise money for a worthy cause. ♦ *The benefit raised money for medical research.* ♦ *Where will the church benefit be held this year?* **5.** *tv.* to serve to the good of someone or something. ♦ *Volunteer work benefits society.* ♦ *A healthy economy benefits everyone.* **6.** *iv.* to improve or to profit from something; to be better because of something. ♦ *If violence could be stopped, society would benefit.* ♦ *The students would benefit from better instruction.* **7. the benefit of the doubt** *idiom* a judgment in one's favor when the evidence is neither for one nor against one. ♦ *I was right between a B and an A. I got the benefit of the doubt—an A.* ♦ *I thought I should have had the benefit of the doubt, but the judge made me pay a fine.*

benevolence [bə 'nɛv ə ləns] *n.* good will; the desire to help other people. (No plural form in this sense.) ♦ *My kind grandmother was known for her benevolence.* ♦ *Susan's great benevolence was truly appreciated by everyone.*

benevolent [bə 'nɛv ə lənt] *adj.* kind; wishing to help other people; charitable. (Adv: *benevolently.*) ♦ *The benevolent doctor donated time and skills to the neighborhood clinic.* ♦ *Some benevolent soul donated clothes to the orphanage.*

benign [bɪ 'nɑɪn] **1.** *adj.* gentle; harmless. (Adv: *benignly.*) ♦ *Mary's words were quite benign, but John took offense at them.* ♦ *The burly man had a benign manner.* **2.** *adj.* [of a tumor] not malignant. (Adv: *benignly.*) ♦ *Mary was relieved to learn that her tumor was benign.* ♦ *The doctor determined that the growth was benign.*

bent ['bɛnt] **1.** pt/pp of bend. **2.** *n.* a special skill or talent; a knack; an inclination. ♦ *Mary has a bent for crafts and makes beautiful things.* ♦ *Jimmy showed a bent for music, so his parents let him take piano lessons.* **3.** *adj.* crooked or curved; not straight. ♦ *The bent antenna ruined the television's reception.* ♦ *Dave used a bent hanger to unlock the car door.* **4. bent on doing something** *idiom* resolved to do something; intent on doing something. ♦ *The kids were bent on going to the amusement park, rain or shine.* ♦ *The boss is bent on increasing production this quarter.*

bequeath [bɪ 'kwið] *tv.* to will money or property to someone or something. ♦ *The woman bequeathed her estate to the church.* ♦ *My uncles were irate that Grandpa had not bequeathed them his money.*

bequest [bɪ 'kwɛst] *n.* an asset willed to someone or something; a legacy. ♦ *The poor family welcomed the unexpected bequest of cash.* ♦ *The bequest was subject to heavy taxes.*

berate [bɪ 'ret] *tv.* to chastise someone; to reprimand someone. ♦ *Tom berated Bob for leaving him without a ride.* ♦ *The teacher berated the students for being late.*

bereave [bɪ 'riv] **bereave of** *tv., irreg.* + *prep. phr.* to deprive someone of someone or something. (Usually past tense. Pt/pp: bereft or *bereaved.*) ♦ *The children grieved that they were bereft of their favorite pet.* ♦ *John found himself bereft of his beloved wife at a young age.*

bereaved [bɪ 'rivd] **the bereaved** *n.* the family and friends of someone who has died. (No plural form in this sense. Treated as singular or plural.) ♦ *The bereaved gathered at the cemetery.* ♦ *It is not always easy to comfort the bereaved.*

bereavement [bɪ 'riv mənt] *n.* the sorrow caused by the death of someone. (No plural form in this sense.) ♦ *Mary thought she couldn't endure another bereavement.* ♦ *The family members drew closer together in their bereavement.*

bereft [bɪ 'rɛft] pt/pp of bereave.

beret [bə 're] *n.* a soft, round cap with a flat top, without a bill or visor. ♦ *The spy always wore a blue beret.* ♦ *Jane's beret flew off her head in the wind.*

berry ['bɛr i] *n.* the small, juicy fruit of a bush or shrub. ♦ *We picked berries in the garden all afternoon.* ♦ *Anne put fresh berries in her cereal.*

berserk [bɚ 'zɚk] *adj.* crazy; frenzied. (Adv: *berserkly.*) ♦ *The angry employee went berserk.* ♦ *The berserk customer started pulling items off the shelf.*

berth ['bɚθ] **1.** *n.* a bed on a ship or a train, often narrow and attached to the wall. ♦ *The cabin's berth was so small that it was uncomfortable.* ♦ *Our berth on the train was very small.* **2.** *n.* the space allotted to a ship at anchor or tied to a dock. ♦ *After the long journey, the ocean liner slipped into its berth.* ♦ *A sailboat was in the ship's berth, leaving no place to dock.* **3. give someone or something a wide berth** *idiom* to keep a reasonable distance from someone or something; to steer clear of someone or something. (Originally referred to sailing ships.) ♦ *The dog we are approaching is very mean. Better give it a wide berth.* ♦ *Give Mary a wide berth. She's in a very bad mood.*

beseech [bɪ 'sitʃ] **beseech to** *tv.* + *inf.* to implore someone to do something; to beg someone to do something. ♦ *We beseeched the teacher to let us take the exam again.* ♦ *The knight beseeched the queen to pardon him.*

beset [bɪ 'sɛt] *tv., irreg.* to attack someone or something on all sides; to surround someone or something. (Pt/pp: *beset.* Often passive.) ♦ *The small town was beset by enemy troops.* ♦ *The citizens were beset by attackers.*

beside [bɪ 'saɪd] **1.** *prep.* at, by, or to the side of something; next to someone or something. ♦ *The umbrella stand is beside the front door.* ♦ *Put the bookcase beside the piano.* **2. besides** *prep.* as well as someone or something; in addition to someone or something. ♦ *Besides hot dogs, we had chips and potato salad.* ♦ *What games should we play besides checkers?* **3. besides** *adv.* also, further; in any case; at any rate. ♦ *Besides, nothing bad is going to happen.* ♦ *You interrupted me, and you're late besides!* **4. beside oneself** *idiom* very upset; distressed. ♦ *She was beside herself over breaking the antique vase.* ♦ *The whole family was beside itself with grief.*

besiege [bɪ 'siʒ] **1.** *tv.* to attack a place, as in battle. ♦ *The troops besieged the tiny island.* ♦ *The town was besieged by enemy soldiers.* **2.** *tv.* to overwhelm someone or something. (Often passive.) ♦ *The speaker was besieged with questions.* ♦ *Piles of paperwork besieged the tiny office.* **3.** *tv.* to hem someone or something in; to crowd around someone or something; to surround someone or something. ♦ *The crowd besieged the candidate.* ♦ *The hungry cats besieged the mouse.*

besieged [bɪ 'siʒd] **1.** *adj.* surrounded by soldiers; captive. ♦ *The besieged city sent cries for help over the airwaves.* ♦ *The besieged troops surrendered.* **2.** *adj.* surrounded; harassed. ♦ *The besieged candidate quickly jumped into a cab.* ♦ *The besieged performer became very uncomfortable in the crowd.*

best ['bɛst] **1.** *adj.* the most excellent [something]. (The superlative form of good. See also better.) ♦ *Mario's serves the best pizza in town.* ♦ *The teacher explained the best way to solve the problem.* **2.** *adv.* most excellently. (The superlative form of well. See also better.) ♦ *This one best suits your purposes.* ♦ *Of all the children, Jane behaves best.* **3.** *tv.* to defeat someone; to outdo someone; to outwit someone. ♦ *Your cooking bests that of any fancy restaurant.* ♦ *Once again Jane bested Bill at chess.* **4. the best** *n.* someone or something that is better than anything else. (Stands for singular or plural nominals.) ♦ *These are all great, but this one is the best.* ♦ *They are doing the best they can.* **5. at one's best; at its best** *idiom* the utmost; to the highest degree possible. ♦ *This restaurant serves gourmet food at its best.* ♦ *The singer was at her best when she performed ballads.*

bestial ['bis ti əl] *adj.* savage; wild; brutal. (Adv: *bestially.*) ♦ *The slaves were treated in a bestial manner.* ♦ *The bestial murder was never solved.*

best-liked ['bɛst laɪkt] *adj.* most popular; favorite. ♦ *Sue was named the best-liked student in her graduating class.* ♦ *The toddler carried her best-liked doll everywhere.*

bestow [bɪ 'sto] **bestow on** *tv.* + *prep. phr.* to give praise to someone; to present an award to someone. ♦ *Praise was bestowed on the graduate.* ♦ *The committee bestowed an engraved plaque on the contest winner.*

best-seller ['bɛst 'sɛl ɚ] *n.* a book, recording, magazine, or similar item that has sold more copies than similar items in a specific period of time. ♦ *The writer's first novel* *was a best-seller.* ♦ *John read a best-seller while riding the bus.*

bet ['bɛt] **1.** *n.* an amount of money gambled on something; a wager. ♦ *John placed a three-dollar bet on his favorite horse.* ♦ *The bet was only twenty dollars.* **2.** *tv., irreg.* to make a wager. (Pt/pp: *bet.*) ♦ *What will you bet that Bill is late?* ♦ *Mary bet twenty dollars that her favorite horse would win.* **3.** *tv., irreg.* to predict something; to make a guess that something will happen. (Takes a clause.) ♦ *I bet that John and Anne will leave the party together.* ♦ *I bet it snows this weekend.* **4. bet on** *iv., irreg. + prep. phr.* to gamble on the success of a participant in a contest. ♦ *Tom bet on the black horse.* ♦ *Susan bet on the home team.*

betray [bɪ 'tre] **1.** *tv.* to be disloyal to someone or something; to be unfaithful to someone or something. ♦ *John betrayed my trust when he told my secret.* ♦ *Mary betrayed Bill by having a love affair.* **2.** *tv.* to show a sign of something; to reveal something. ♦ *Susan's facial expression betrayed her feelings.* ♦ *John's prying questions betrayed his motives.*

betrothed [bɪ 'troðd] **1.** *adj.* engaged to be married. ♦ *The princess has been betrothed to a distant cousin for years.* ♦ *Anne and John were betrothed for years before their marriage.* **2.** *n.* someone who is engaged to be married. (No plural form in this sense.) ♦ *The soldier wrote to his betrothed daily when he was at war.* ♦ *After Mary argued with her betrothed, she postponed the wedding.*

better ['bɛt ɚ] **1.** *adj.* of more goodness; of greater benefit. (The comparative form of good. See also best.) ♦ *I have a better idea than that.* ♦ *Jane chose the better plan of the two.* **2.** *adj.* improved in health. (The comparative form of good.) ♦ *I felt better after the operation.* ♦ *Did the medicine make John feel better?* **3.** *adv.* with more quality; with greater benefit. (The comparative form of well. See also best.) ♦ *John skates better than the rest of us.* ♦ *After being in France for a year, Mary speaks French better.* **4.** *tv.* to improve someone or something; to make someone or something better ②. ♦ *Mary tried to better herself by taking a class.* ♦ *A salary increase bettered Susan's financial situation.* **5.** *n.* See bettor. **6. the better** *n.* [of a choice of two things] the one that is superior or more excellent. (No plural form in this sense. Treated as singular.) ♦ *Which one of the two options is the better?* ♦ *Of the two cakes, this one is the better.* **7. had better** *aux.* is obliged to; should. (Often *-'d better.*) ♦ *He had better be here on time!* ♦ *You'd better plan your activities carefully.*

betterment ['bɛt ɚ mənt] *n.* improvement; making something better. (No plural form in this sense.) ♦ *The governor claimed his policies were for the betterment of his state.* ♦ *The money was used for the orphanage's betterment.*

bettor AND **better** ['bɛt ɚ] *n.* someone who bets. ♦ *The bettor made a silly bet and lost his money.* ♦ *Everyone was amazed at the risks the bettor took.*

between [bɪ 'twin] **1.** *prep.* in the middle of two things; with something on both sides. (See the note at among.) ♦ *The couch is between the end tables.* ♦ *John put some frosting between the layers of the cake.* **2.** *prep.* together; in combination. (Requires the objective form of the pronoun in standard English.) ♦ *Between Bill and Mary, they have 30 years of experience.* ♦ *Just between you and me, John is giving Jane a surprise party.* **3.** *prep.* in comparison. ♦ *Do you know the difference between right and left?* ♦ *We noted the similarities between Bill's story and Mary's.* **4. in between** *phr.* located in the middle of two things. ♦ *It not hot or cold. It's in between.* ♦ *A sandwich consists of two slices of bread with some other food in between.*

bevel ['bɛv əl] **1.** *n.* the edge of one surface that does not intersect a second surface at a right angle. ♦ *The woodworking class learned how to make a bevel.* ♦ *The bevel on the tabletop was crooked.* **2.** *tv.* to slant an edge or surface. ♦ *The carpenter beveled the edge of the coffee table.* ♦ *The woodworking class learned how to bevel the edge of a counter.*

beverage ['bɛv (ə) rɪdʒ] *n.* a drink other than water. ♦ *What sort of beverages should we serve at the party?* ♦ *Can I get you a beverage?*

bevy ['bɛv i] **1.** *n.* a group of certain animals. ♦ *A bevy of quail flew overhead.* ♦ *Several small deer moved in a close bevy through the open field.* **2.** *n.* a collection of someone or something. (Figurative on ①.) ♦ *A bevy of children were invited to the birthday party.* ♦ *Bill has collected a bevy of old campaign buttons.*

beware [bɪ 'wɛr] **1.** *tv.* to be cautious with something; to be alert to a problem. (Almost always a command.) ♦ *Beware the dangers of eating uncooked meat.* ♦ *Beware the stranger who acts too friendly.* **2. beware of** *iv. + prep. phr.* to use caution with someone or something. (Almost always a command. More common than ①.) ♦ *The sign said, "Beware of the dog!"* ♦ *Beware of the ice on the sidewalk.*

bewilder [bɪ 'wɪl dɚ] *tv.* to confuse someone or something; to perplex someone or something. ♦ *The end of the novel bewildered me.* ♦ *Jimmy's strange behavior bewildered his parents.*

bewildered [bɪ 'wɪl dɚd] *adj.* confused; puzzled; perplexed. (Adv: *bewilderedly.*) ♦ *The bewildered audience waited for something to happen on stage.* ♦ *The bewildered doctor could not diagnose his patient's illness.*

bewilderment [bɪ 'wɪl dɚ mənt] *n.* the state of being puzzled or perplexed. (No plural form in this sense.) ♦ *The dog searched in bewilderment for its owner.* ♦ *Our first reaction to the news was bewilderment.*

beyond [bi 'jɑnd] **1.** *prep.* farther; on the other side of someone or something. ♦ *Beyond the stream, the deer frolicked.* ♦ *Our hike took us beyond the marked trail.* **2.** *prep.* past the ability to understand or comprehend. ♦ *Why John traveled to Greenland is beyond me.* ♦ *Algebra is beyond the understanding of many students.* **3.** *adv.* past; further; on the other side of someone or something. ♦ *Bill traveled to the lake, and Tom went beyond.* ♦ *I'd like to rent the room for June and beyond.* **4.** *n.* the unknown; life after death. (No plural form in this sense.) ♦ *The medium claimed she had contact with spirits in the great beyond.* ♦ *Many philosophers have speculated about the beyond.*

biannual [bɑɪ 'æn ju əl] **1.** *adj.* happening twice every year; semiannual. (Adv: *biannually.*) ♦ *The garden show is held on a biannual basis.* ♦ *Each employee has a biannual review.* **2.** *adj.* happening every two years; biennial. ♦ *The town's biannual festival is held in even-numbered years.* ♦ *John looked forward to his family's biannual reunion.*

bias ['baɪ əs] **1.** *n.* an inclination toward one opinion or preference; a prejudice. ♦ *A political bias was evident in the newspaper article.* ♦ *The classical music reviewer had a bias against rock music.* **2. on a bias; on the bias** *phr.* on a diagonal line; on a diagonal pathway or direction. ♦ *The panels of the dress were cut on a bias.* ♦ *The seamstress sewed the fabric on the bias.* **3.** *tv.* to prejudice someone. ♦ *The journalist tried to bias the readers with his article.* ♦ *The jury was biased by the false testimony.*

biased ['baɪ əst] *adj.* prejudiced; favoring one over another. (Adv: *biasedly.*) ♦ *The biased article told only one side of the issue.* ♦ *The senator was biased against low-income groups.*

bib ['bɪb] *n.* a napkin or piece of cloth worn around the neck. ♦ *Babies wear bibs to catch stray bits of food.* ♦ *I had to wear a bib when I ate lobster in the restaurant.*

bible ['baɪb əl] **1. Bible** *n.* the holy writings of the Jewish religion; the Hebrew Scriptures. ♦ *In Judaism, the Bible is what Christians call the Old Testament.* ♦ *The rabbi read from the Bible.* **2. Bible** *n.* the holy writings of the Christian religion. ♦ *In Christianity, the Bible consists of the Old and New Testaments.* ♦ *The minister read from the Bible at the pulpit.* **3.** *n.* a manual; a guidebook; a book of authority. ♦ *A style manual is an editor's bible.* ♦ *That cookbook is the chef's bible.*

biblical ['bɪb lɪ kəl] *adj.* relating to the Bible. (Adv: *biblically* [...ɪk li].) ♦ *The Sunday school class learned about biblical characters.* ♦ *The paintings in the pastor's office had a biblical theme.*

bibliography [bɪb li 'ɔ grə fi] **1.** *n.* a section at the end of a book, article, or other document that lists all of the sources of information used to write the work. ♦ *The author included a lengthy bibliography at the end of the book.* ♦ *How many books were listed in the bibliography?* **2.** *n.* a list of books or articles about a specific subject. ♦ *The professor handed out a bibliography of outstanding books on the subject.* ♦ *A bibliography of recommended reading was given to all students.*

bicker ['bɪk ɚ] *iv.* to argue with someone about something that is unimportant. ♦ *The couple bickered over little things.* ♦ *The parents were annoyed when their children began to bicker.*

bickering ['bɪk ɚ ɪŋ] *n.* a petty argument about something that is not important. (No plural form in this sense.) ♦ *Susan and Bob's endless bickering drove their guests home early.* ♦ *Our friendship was ruined by bickering.*

bicycle ['baɪ sɪ kəl] **1.** *n.* a vehicle with a metal frame and two wheels, operated by foot pedals. ♦ *Jimmy got his first bicycle on his fifth birthday.* ♦ *Anne rode her bicycle to school.* **2.** *iv.* to travel by ①. ♦ *The kids bicycled to school every day.* ♦ *Unless it rains, David bicycles to work.*

bicycling ['baɪ sɪk lɪŋ] *n.* the activity and sport of riding a bicycle. (No plural form in this sense.) ♦ *Bill enjoys hiking and bicycling.* ♦ *Bicycling is very good exercise.*

bicyclist ['baɪ sɪk lɪst] *n.* someone who rides a bicycle. ♦ *Anne dreamed of becoming a famous bicyclist.* ♦ *The bicyclist was not badly injured when hit by the car.*

bid ['bɪd] **1.** *n.* an offer of an amount of money for something for sale, especially at an auction. ♦ *I made a small bid on the antique dresser.* ♦ *My bid on the furniture was doubled by another bidder.* **2.** *n.* the presentation of the price for one's services, especially in a competition joined by others to do the same work. ♦ *John's bid for the job indicated how long the job would take.* ♦ *Mary's firm submitted the lowest bid for the project.* **3.** *n.* an attempt to take power or control of something. ♦ *Bill's bid for the open position at his company went unnoticed.* ♦ *The judge made a bid for the court's attention by rapping his gavel loudly.* **4.** *tv., irreg.* to offer an amount of money for something, especially at an auction. (Pt/pp: *bid.*) ♦ *Mary bid two hundred dollars on a painting.* ♦ *We just couldn't bid more money at the auction.* **5.** *tv., irreg.* to state the price that one will charge for goods or services. (Pt/pp: *bid.*) ♦ *The contractor who bid $5,000 for the job was not awarded the contract.* ♦ *John bid the lowest amount possible, but another contractor bid lower.* **6. bid on** *iv., irreg.* + *prep. phr.* to make an offer of a certain amount of money for something, especially at an auction. (Pt/pp: bid.) ♦ *How much did Susan bid on the antique?* ♦ *I bid on the painting at the auction.*

bidding ['bɪd ɪŋ] **do someone's bidding** *idiom* to do what is requested. ♦ *The servant grumbled but did his employer's bidding.* ♦ *Am I expected to do your bidding whenever you ask?*

biennial [baɪ 'ɛn i əl] **1.** *adj.* occurring once every two years; occurring once every other year. (Adv: *biennially.*) ♦ *The biennial picnic was postponed due to rain.* ♦ *I always go to the biennial convention of the association I belong to.* **2.** *adj.* [of plants] living for two years and blooming in the second year. ♦ *I planted some biennial bushes near the house.* ♦ *The biennial plants in our garden will bloom next year.*

bier ['bɪr] *n.* a platform on which a coffin or corpse rests before burial. ♦ *The mourners surrounded the funeral bier.* ♦ *Hundreds of flowers were placed at the base of the bier.*

bifocal ['baɪ fok əl] **1.** *adj.* having two focal points. (Optics.) ♦ *We will have to fit you with bifocal lenses.* ♦ *Mary requires bifocal correction in both eyes.* **2. bifocals** *n.* eyeglasses having lenses with two focal lengths—one for distance and one for close up. (Treated as plural.) ♦ *Jane got bifocals so she won't have to take her glasses off and put them on repeatedly.* ♦ *As Bill became older, he needed to wear bifocals.*

big ['bɪg] **1.** *adj.* large; great in amount or size. (Comp: *bigger;* sup: *biggest.*) ♦ *A big ship entered the harbor.* ♦ *I asked for a big helping of mashed potatoes.* **2.** *adj.* important. (Comp: *bigger;* sup: *biggest.*) ♦ *Bill strutted around the office as if he were a big man.* ♦ *The big executives all ate lunch together.* **3.** *adj.* adult; grown-up. (Comp: *bigger;* sup: *biggest.*) ♦ *"When I get big, I won't eat vegetables," said Jimmy.* ♦ *The big people ate at a separate table from the children.* **4. one's eyes are bigger than one's stomach** *idiom* [for one] to take more food than one can eat. ♦ *I can't eat all this. I'm afraid that my eyes were bigger than my stomach.* ♦ *Try to take less food. Your eyes are bigger than your stomach at every meal.*

bigamy ['bɪg ə mi] *n.* being married to more than one person at the same time. (No plural form in this sense.) ♦ *Bigamy is illegal in almost every Western culture.* ♦ *The man with two wives was charged with bigamy.*

bigheaded ['bɪg hɛd ɪd] *adj.* arrogant; thinking one is more important than one really is. (Informal. Adv: *bigheadedly.*) ♦ *Her frequent successes made Jane a bit* *bigheaded.* ♦ *After getting a reprimand, Bill wasn't so bigheaded anymore.*

bighearted ['bɪg hɑrt ɪd] *adj.* kind and generous; charitable. (Adv: *bigheartedly.*) ♦ *The bighearted store owner donated money to the church.* ♦ *Jane's kind words showed her bighearted nature.*

bigmouth ['bɪg mɑʊθ] *n.* someone who talks constantly; a person who cannot keep a secret. (Informal.) ♦ *My neighbor is a bigmouth who can't keep a secret.* ♦ *Sue didn't trust the office bigmouth with her news.*

bigot ['bɪg ət] *n.* someone who is intolerant of differences in race, religion, or opinions. ♦ *The bigot was vocally opposed to desegregation.* ♦ *The bigot yelled racial slurs at some marchers in the parade.*

bigoted ['bɪg ə tɪd] *adj.* intolerant; showing intolerance. (Adv: *bigotedly.*) ♦ *The judge was removed from the bench after making bigoted comments.* ♦ *The bigoted manager refused to hire minority workers.*

bigotry ['bɪg ə tri] *n.* intolerance. (No plural form in this sense.) ♦ *The social activist strived to end bigotry.* ♦ *Bigotry caused the family to move to a more integrated neighborhood.*

bike ['bɑɪk] **1.** *n.* a bicycle. ♦ *Jimmy fell off his bike and skinned his knees.* ♦ *Susie rode her bike to school.* **2.** *n.* a motorcycle. ♦ *Dave sat on his bike at the intersection and revved the engine.* ♦ *The gang members got on their bikes and drove off.* **3.** *iv.* to ride a bicycle. ♦ *Anne bikes to work, rain or shine.* ♦ *Jimmy learned to bike last summer.* **4.** *iv.* to ride a motorcycle. ♦ *The friends biked everywhere together.* ♦ *Unless it's raining, Bill and Anne bike every weekend.*

biker ['bɑɪk ɚ] **1.** *n.* someone who rides a bicycle. ♦ *The biker wore highly reflective clothing.* ♦ *The car just barely missed hitting the biker.* **2.** *n.* someone who rides a motorcycle. ♦ *The bikers drove down the freeway in a large pack.* ♦ *The biker wore a leather jacket for protection.*

bikini [bɪ 'kin i] **1.** *n.* a brief, two-piece woman's bathing suit. ♦ *The sunbathers wore bikinis on the beach.* ♦ *Jane owns a bikini and a one-piece bathing suit.* **2.** *n.* a brief, close-fitting pair of men's swimming trunks or underpants. ♦ *Tom prefers regular trunks to bikinis.* ♦ *Dave lounged around the pool in his bikini.*

bilabial [bɑɪ 'leb i əl] **1.** *adj.* [of sounds] made by bringing both lips together. (Adv: *bilabially.*) ♦ *Both lips are used in the production of* [b] *and* [p], *which are both bilabial stops.* ♦ *The symbol* [w] *also stands for a bilabial sound.* **2.** *n.* a sound, such as [b], [p], [m], or [w], that is made by bringing both lips together. ♦ *The word* blue *starts with a bilabial.* ♦ *The sound* [m] *is a bilabial that is also nasal.*

bilateral [bɑɪ 'læt ə rəl] **1.** *adj.* symmetrical; having two equal sides. (Adv: *bilaterally.*) ♦ *The geometry teacher drew a bilateral triangle.* ♦ *The left and right sides of the bilateral painting were mirror images of each other.* **2.** *adj.* involving, serving, or referring to two sides or factions. (Adv: *bilaterally.*) ♦ *The two countries worked out a bilateral agreement.* ♦ *The bilateral talks between Russia and the U.S. produced an important agreement.*

bile ['bɑɪl] **1.** *n.* a bitter liquid produced by the liver to aid in the digestion of food. (No plural form in this sense.) ♦ *The sick patient vomited bile.* ♦ *There was nothing in the starving child's stomach but bile.* **2.** *n.* ill-tempered verbal abuse. (No plural form in this sense. Figurative on ①.) ♦ *The angry protester shouted bile at the official.* ♦ *The crabby critic's review was full of bile.*

bilingual [bɑɪ 'lɪŋ gwəl] **1.** *adj.* [of a person] able to speak two languages. (Adv: *bilingually.*) ♦ *The bilingual child spoke both English and Spanish.* ♦ *Many immigrants are bilingual.* **2.** *adj.* referring to two languages. (Adv: *bilingually.*) ♦ *The company develops bilingual dictionaries for students.* ♦ *The teachers promoted bilingual education.*

bilk ['bɪlk] **bilk (out of)** *tv.* (+ *adv.* + *prep. phr.*) to cheat or defraud someone or something out of something. ♦ *The con man bilked the old couple out of their life savings.* ♦ *Jimmy bilked his sister out of her allowance.*

bill ['bɪl] **1.** *n.* a written notice of money owed. ♦ *My mailbox was full of bills.* ♦ *The bill for the car repairs was quite high.* **2.** *n.* a legal draft of a proposed law. ♦ *The bill passed both the House and the Senate, and then the president signed it into law.* ♦ *The proposed bill would limit government officials' terms.* **3.** *n.* a piece of printed money, as opposed to a coin. ♦ *I only had bills in my wallet.* ♦ *Bob handed the cashier a five-dollar bill.* **4.** *n.* the visor of a cap; the part of a cap that extends from the head and shields the eyes from the sun. ♦ *Mary wore her cap with the bill in the back.* ♦ *The cap had the team's name on its bill.* **5.** *n.* the hard part of a bird's mouth. ♦ *The bird had a bright yellow bill.* ♦ *The bird pecked at the tree with its bill.* **6.** *tv.* to present a notice of charges to someone or something. ♦ *The doctor billed me for the medical tests.* ♦ *"Please bill me," I told the mechanic.* **7. fill the bill** *idiom* to be exactly the thing that is needed. ♦ *Ah, this steak is great. It really fills the bill.* ♦ *This new pair of shoes fills the bill nicely.* **8. foot the bill** *idiom* to pay the bill; to pay (for something). ♦ *Let's go out and eat. I'll foot the bill.* ♦ *If the bank goes broke, don't worry. The government will foot the bill.* **9. pad the bill** *idiom* to put unnecessary items on a bill to make the total cost higher. ♦ *The plumber had padded the bill with things we didn't need.* ♦ *I was falsely accused of padding the bill.* **10. sell someone a bill of goods** *idiom* to get someone to believe something that isn't true; to deceive someone. ♦ *Don't pay any attention to what John says. He's just trying to sell you a bill of goods.* ♦ *I'm not selling you a bill of goods. What I say is true.*

billboard ['bɪl bord] *n.* a large outdoor sign used for advertising. ♦ *The highway was lined with billboards.* ♦ *The business rented a billboard to advertise its product.*

billfold ['bɪl fold] *n.* a wallet; a small, folding holder for money, credit cards, and identification. ♦ *Mary held onto her billfold tightly when she rode the bus.* ♦ *I put the cash into my billfold.*

billiards ['bɪl jɚdz] *n.* a game similar to pool, but with fewer balls and on a table without pockets for the balls to go into. (Treated as singular.) ♦ *Billiards is played with sticks and hard balls on a cloth-covered table.* ♦ *We play billiards every Saturday night at the bar.*

billion ['bɪl jən] **1.** *n.* 1,000,000,000; a thousand million. (A British billion is a million million. Additional numbers formed as with *two billion, three billion, four billion,* etc.) ♦ *The country is more than two billion in debt.* ♦ *Nobody can count to a billion.* **2.** *adj.* amounting to

1,000,000,000 of something. ♦ *The government's debt was over a billion dollars.* ♦ *Over one billion people live on this continent.*

billionth ['bɪl jənθ] [a] 1,000,000,000th. See fourth for senses and examples.

billow ['bɪl o] **1.** *n.* a large moving volume of smoke or air. ♦ *A billow of smoke surged from the factory.* ♦ *Billows of fresh air made the house smell good.* **2.** *iv.* to move along with the action of wind. ♦ *The flag billowed in the breeze.* ♦ *The clothes hanging on the clothes line billowed in the strong wind.*

bimonthly [bɑɪ 'mʌnθ li] **1.** *adj.* occurring once every two months. ♦ *She attended all six bimonthly concerts last year.* ♦ *I subscribe to a popular bimonthly magazine.* **2.** *adj.* appearing twice a month; semimonthly. ♦ *The employees are paid on a bimonthly basis.* ♦ *This bimonthly newsletter is never late.* **3.** *adv.* once every two months. ♦ *Lectures at the museum are given bimonthly.* ♦ *Political discussions are held bimonthly.* **4.** *adv.* twice a month. ♦ *My favorite magazine is delivered bimonthly.* ♦ *The employees are paid bimonthly, or 24 times a year.*

bin ['bɪn] a container or enclosed space used for storage. ♦ *Onions and potatoes are stored in the basement in bins.* ♦ *The farmer's bins were full of grain after the harvest.*

binary ['bɑɪ nɛr i] *adj.* relating to a system of numbering where all amounts are expressed using only "0" and "1." (This is the basic system used for storing and transmitting computer information.) ♦ *The information is recorded in a series of binary numbers.* ♦ *The computer uses a type of binary transmission.*

bind ['bɑɪnd] **1.** *tv., irreg.* to secure something to something else with a tie or band; to tie something together with something else. (Pt/pp: bound.) ♦ *Bind the newspapers in a stack so we can carry them out.* ♦ *The paramedic bound the wounds with bandages.* **2. bind to** *tv., irreg. + prep. phr.* to hold someone or something by force; to tie someone or something to something. ♦ *Bind the vine to the fence so it will cover the fence with foliage.* ♦ *The guards bound the prisoner to his bed.* **3.** *tv., irreg.* to attach a cover to the pages of a book. ♦ *The manufacturer will bind the books with the covers we supply.* ♦ *The publisher planned to bind the book in a special plastic cover.* **4. bind to** *tv., irreg. + prep. phr.* [for a contract] to oblige someone to do obey or abide by something. ♦ *The contract bound me to a specific course of action.* ♦ *I am bound by the agreement to the terms of the agreement.* **5. bind to** *tv., irreg. + inf.* to legally obligate someone to do something. ♦ *The contract bound me to follow a specific course of action.* ♦ *I am bound by the contract to pay you on time.* **6.** *iv., irreg.* to be stuck and thus fail to move. ♦ *The window binds against the window frame.* ♦ *The door is binding and won't open easily.* **7. bound hand and foot** *idiom* with hands and feet tied up. ♦ *The robbers left us bound hand and foot.* ♦ *We remained bound hand and foot until the maid found us and untied us.* **8. in a bind** *idiom* in a difficult situation. ♦ *I was really in a bind when I lost my job.* ♦ *What kind of bind have you gotten yourself into now?* **9. bound to do something** See bound.

binder ['bɑɪnd ɚ] **1.** *n.* a person or machine that fastens book covers to stacks of pages. ♦ *The binder worked quickly to get the books out on time.* ♦ *How many books go through the binder each hour?* **2.** *n.* a folder or notebook that holds loose pieces of paper. ♦ *Each semester the student bought a new binder for class notes.* ♦ *I like to keep my lecture notes in a binder rather than a notebook.*

binding ['bɑɪnd ɪŋ] *adj.* [of a contract] firm and permanently agreed to by all parties. ♦ *The contract is binding, and you must do what it says.* ♦ *Your agreement is binding. There is no legal way to ignore it.*

binge ['bɪndʒ] **1.** *n.* a drinking spree. ♦ *The two guys went on a binge Friday and were sick all day Saturday.* ♦ *The alcoholic went on a binge every week.* **2.** *n.* a period of indulging in too much of a particular thing. (Figurative on ①.) ♦ *During final exams, I tend to go on a potato chip binge.* ♦ *I've been on a dessert binge since the holidays began.* **3. binge on** *iv. + prep. phr.* to indulge in too much of a particular thing. ♦ *Last weekend, we binged on pizza and were sick until Monday.* ♦ *During the holidays, I tend to binge on chocolate.*

bingo ['bɪŋ go] **1.** *n.* a game of chance in which players mark the numbers that appear on their cards as someone calls out a random series of numbers. (No plural form in this sense. The first person to complete a line of marked numbers wins.) ♦ *Grandma plays bingo every week at church.* ♦ *Bingo is a form of gambling.* **2. Bingo!** *interj.* <a word shouted when a player wins in ①.> ♦ *"Bingo!" the winner yelled excitedly.* ♦ *All her friends groaned as Grandma yelled, "Bingo!" for the fifth time.* **3. Bingo!** *interj.* "Exactly!"; "You guessed it!" (Informal.) ♦ *"Bingo!" Dad said when we asked if we had to clean our rooms.* ♦ *We guessed the answer, and the teacher said, "Bingo!"*

binocular [bə 'nɑk jə lɚ] **1.** *adj.* relating to both eyes; involving both eyes. ♦ *Most animals have binocular vision.* ♦ *Because he can only see with one eye, Dave's binocular vision is impaired.* **2. binoculars** *n.* a viewing device made of two small telescopes, side by side. (Treated as a plural. Number is expressed with *pair(s) of binoculars.*) ♦ *The binoculars were so strong, we could see craters on the moon!* ♦ *I took a pair of binoculars to the football game so I could see better.*

biochemistry [bɑɪ o 'kɛm ɪs tri] *n.* the study of the chemistry of living things. (No plural form in this sense.) ♦ *I majored in biochemistry and then became a researcher.* ♦ *The state university has a good program in biochemistry.*

biodegradable [bɑɪ o də 'gred ə bəl] *adj.* able to decay naturally. ♦ *Certain biodegradable materials, such as paper, are also recyclable.* ♦ *Vegetable matter is biodegradable.*

biographer [bɑɪ 'ɑ grəf ɚ] *n.* someone who writes about the lives of other people. ♦ *A biographer published a scandalous book about the celebrity.* ♦ *This biographer writes about the lives of politicians.*

biographical [bɑɪ ə 'græf ɪ kəl] *adj.* relating to the story of someone's life. (Adv: *biographically* [...ɪk li].) ♦ *The documentary was a biographical account of the military leader.* ♦ *We thought the movie was fiction, but it was really biographical.*

biography [bɑɪ 'ɑ grə fi] *n.* the story of someone's life; a book about someone's life. ♦ *Jane read the biography of her favorite singer.* ♦ *I am looking for a biography of Shakespeare.*

biological [bɑɪ ə 'lɑ dʒɪ kəl] **1.** *adj.* relating to living things. (Adv: *biologically* [...ɪk li].) ♦ *Respiration is a biological function.* ♦ *The science class performed a biological experiment.* **2.** *adj.* related by blood as opposed to adoption. (Adv: *biologically* [...ɪk li].) ♦ *The court awarded custody to the biological parents.* ♦ *The test proved that Bill was the child's biological father.*

biologist [bɑɪ 'ɑl ə dʒəst] *n.* someone who studies biology; a person who studies living things. ♦ *The biologist collected samples from the river.* ♦ *The biologist observed the organism through the microscope.*

biology [bɑɪ 'ɑl ə dʒi] *n.* the scientific study of plants and animals. (No plural form in this sense.) ♦ *Every sophomore is required to take biology.* ♦ *Biology deals with the study of animals.*

biophysics [bɑɪ o 'fɪz ɪks] *n.* the study of living things through the methods of physics. (Treated as singular.) ♦ *All science majors must take biophysics at the university.* ♦ *Professor Brown taught biophysics and chemistry.*

biopsy ['bɑɪ ɑp si] *n.* the removal and examination of living tissue. ♦ *The doctor performed a biopsy before diagnosing the illness.* ♦ *The tissue removed in the biopsy was examined under a microscope.*

bipartisan [bɑɪ 'pɑrt ɪ zən] *adj.* relating to two political parties; supported by both the Republican and Democratic parties. (Adv: *bipartisanly.*) ♦ *The bill received bipartisan support.* ♦ *The new legislation is a bipartisan issue.*

biracial [bɑɪ 're ʃəl] *adj.* relating to two races; belonging to two races. (Adv: *biracially.*) ♦ *Jimmy is the child of a biracial couple.* ♦ *The biracial student left the blank next to "race" on the form empty.*

birch ['bɚtʃ] **1.** *n.* a kind of tree whose bark is often white and peels off in thin layers. ♦ *We noticed several birches as we walked through the woods.* ♦ *I could see the white trunks of the birches from across the lake.* **2.** *n.* wood from ①. (No plural form in this sense.) ♦ *The cabinet is made of birch.* ♦ *After removing the paint from the table we discovered it was made of birch.* **3.** *adj.* made out of ②. ♦ *The birch cabinet was stained a deep brown.* ♦ *A few birch carvings stood on the mantle.*

bird ['bɚd] **1.** *n.* an animal that has feathers and wings and lays eggs. ♦ *A bird perched on the telephone wire.* ♦ *A beautiful blue bird flew right by us.* **2. bird of prey** *n.* ① that lives by killing and eating other animals. (Pl: *birds of prey.*) ♦ *The hawk is a well-known bird of prey.* ♦ *Many birds of prey eat other birds.* **3. early bird** *idiom* someone who gets up or arrives early; someone who starts something very promptly, especially someone who gains an advantage of some kind by so doing. ♦ *The Smiths are early birds. They caught the first ferry to the island.* ♦ *I was an early bird and got the best selection of flowers at the store.* **4. eat like a bird** *idiom* to eat only small amounts of food; to peck at one's food. ♦ *Jane is very slim because she eats like a bird.* ♦ *Bill is trying to lose weight by eating like a bird.* **5. kill two birds with one stone** *idiom* to solve two problems with one solution. ♦ *John learned the words to his part in the play while peeling potatoes. He was killing two birds with one stone.* ♦ *I have to cash a check and make a payment on my bank loan. I'll kill two birds with one stone by doing them both in one trip to the bank.* **6. the birds and the bees** *idiom* human reproduction. (A euphemistic way of referring to human sex and reproduction.) ♦ *My father tried to teach me about the birds and the bees.* ♦ *He's twenty years old and doesn't understand about the birds and the bees!*

bird's-eye view ['bɚdz ɑɪ 'vju] *n.* a view of the ground from the air; an image from an elevated viewpoint. ♦ *In the second row of the balcony, we had a bird's-eye view of the stage.* ♦ *The apartment roof offered a bird's-eye view of the baseball field.*

birth ['bɚθ] **1.** *n.* the process of being born. ♦ *The difficult birth took twenty hours.* ♦ *John stood by Mary at the birth of their first child.* **2.** *n.* parentage; heritage. (No plural form in this sense.) ♦ *Few citizens are of noble birth nowadays.* ♦ *John is German by birth, but he came to the United States as a baby.* **3.** *n.* the origin of something; the way something has come into being. (Figurative on ①.) ♦ *The birth of jazz took place in the 19th century.* ♦ *The discovery of nuclear energy led to the birth of the atomic age.* **4. give birth to someone or some creature** *idiom* to bring a baby or other offspring into the world through birth. ♦ *Mary gave birth to a lovely baby girl.* ♦ *The raccoon gave birth to 6 little raccoons.* **5. give birth to something** *idiom* to create, start, or yield something. ♦ *Poverty and a lack of discipline give birth to crime and more poverty.* ♦ *The discovery of gold in the West gave birth to the settlement of California.*

birth control ['bɚθ kən trol] **1.** *n.* procedures, methods, techniques, and devices that prevent the conception of humans. (No plural form in this sense.) ♦ *John and Mary practice birth control.* ♦ *Many countries need birth control to control population size.* **2. birth-control** *adj.* <the adj. use of ①.> ♦ *Birth-control devices are available at drugstores.* ♦ *Modern birth-control methods are very effective.*

birthday ['bɚθ de] *n.* the date on which someone is born; a date of birth. ♦ *Mother saved the newspaper from my birthday, May 1, 1975.* ♦ *I plan to celebrate my birthday tomorrow with my family.*

birthmark ['bɚθ mɑrk] *n.* a pigmented mark on the skin, usually red, brown, black, or purple, present from birth. ♦ *The baby had a tiny birthmark on its arm.* ♦ *Mary had the birthmark on her cheek removed.*

birthplace ['bɚθ ples] *n.* the city and country where someone is born. ♦ *Jane's family tree listed the birthplaces of her relatives.* ♦ *Dave visited his birthplace overseas last year.*

birthrate ['bɚθ ret] *n.* the number of live births for every 100 or 1,000 people in a particular place during a certain length of time. ♦ *Many developing countries have a very high birthrate.* ♦ *The birthrate dropped sharply during the second year of the war.*

birthright ['bɚt rɑɪt] *n.* a right accorded to a person because of the circumstances surrounding the person's birth. (For example, being the eldest child, being born in a particular country, being born into royalty, etc.) ♦ *The young boy was, by birthright, heir to the throne.* ♦ *Her father's business empire was Mary's birthright.*

birthstone ['bɚθ ston] *n.* a stone or jewel associated with the month of one's birth. (Each month is assigned a specific gemstone.) ♦ *Mary received a necklace with her birthstone on her birthday.* ♦ *Diamond is the birthstone for April.*

biscuit ['bɪs kɪt] *n.* a round, flat cake of bread, made with baking powder. ♦ *Biscuits with gravy are my favorite!* ♦ *This restaurant is well known for its biscuits and roast beef.*

bisect ['baɪ sɛkt] *tv.* to cut something into two equal parts; to split something down the middle. ♦ *The partition bisected the room into two smaller rooms.* ♦ *We bisected circles in geometry class today.*

bisexual [baɪ 'sɛk ʃu əl] **1.** *adj.* having both male and female reproductive characteristics. (Adv: *bisexually.*) ♦ *Earthworms are bisexual.* ♦ *Garden snails are usually bisexual.* **2.** *adj.* related to sexual attraction to both male and female; sexually attracted to both men and women. (Adv: *bisexually.*) ♦ *The romantic movie had a bisexual theme.* ♦ *The sociologist studied bisexual relationships in the city.* **3.** *n.* someone who is sexually attracted to both men and women. ♦ *Because Mary is a bisexual, she dates both men and women.* ♦ *Tom realized he was a bisexual when he was 18.*

bishop ['bɪʃ əp] **1.** *n.* a church official who supervises a number of churches. ♦ *The bishop visited each of his churches.* ♦ *A special service was held during the bishop's visit.* **2.** *n.* a chess piece that moves only in a diagonal direction. ♦ *Bill slowly moved his bishop across the chess board.* ♦ *Anne captured Bill's bishop first in the chess game.*

bison ['baɪ sən] *n., irreg.* a type of wild ox native to North America. (Pl: *bison.*) ♦ *The bison is better known as the American buffalo.* ♦ *The wall of the cave had bison painted on it.*

bit ['bɪt] **1.** pt of bite. **2.** *n.* a small amount of something. (No plural form in this sense.) ♦ *Can I have a bit of your dessert?* ♦ *I spilled a bit of the rice on the floor.* **3. a bit** *n.* a short amount of time or distance; a small amount of time or distance. (No plural form in this sense.) ♦ *We'll be home in a bit.* ♦ *The store is just up the road a bit.* **4.** *n.* the mouthpiece on a bridle, used to control a horse. ♦ *Mary put the bit into the horse's mouth.* ♦ *The horse soon became cooperative when the bit was in its mouth.* **5.** *n.* the basic unit of information in a computer; a binary digit. ♦ *There are usually 8 bits in a computer character.* ♦ *My modem only transmits 9,600 bits per second.* **6.** *n.* one eighth of a dollar. (Usually in the plural, *two bits, four bits, six bits.*) ♦ *"My allowance was two bits when I was young," Grandpa said.* ♦ *Tom found two bits on the ground.* **7.** *n.* the end of a drilling tool that bores or cuts holes. ♦ *Dave has many different bits for his drill.* ♦ *Jane used a large bit to drill the hole in the wall.* **8.** *adj.* [of an acting role] small and not important. ♦ *Dave's acting career started with a bit role in a local production.* ♦ *Jane landed a bit part in the action movie.* **9. a little bit** *phr.* a small amount; some. ♦ *Can I have a little bit of candy?* ♦ *I need a little bit of time to finish this essay.* **10. in a little bit** *idiom* in a small amount of time. ♦ *I will be there in a little bit. Please wait.* ♦ *In a little bit, we can go outside and play.*

bitch ['bɪtʃ] **1.** *n.* a female dog. ♦ *The bitch had a large litter of pups.* ♦ *The bitch suckled her pups.* **2.** *n.* a malicious woman. (Derogatory. Figurative on ①. Alluding to the bad temper of ① in heat.) ♦ *Jane's bad attitude earned her a reputation for being a bitch.* ♦ *"Only a bitch would do something like that!" exclaimed Sue.* **3. a bitch** *n.* a difficult task; something that causes a lot of problems. (Slang.) ♦ *Trying to get this old key to unlock the door is a bitch.* ♦ *The final exam was really a bitch.* **4. bitch about** *iv. + prep. phr.* to grumble or complain about something. (Slang.) ♦ *Don't bitch to me about your problems.* ♦ *Sue's friends were tired of hearing her bitch about her job.*

bitchy ['bɪtʃ i] *adj.* spiteful; complaining. (Derogatory slang. Adv: *bitchily.* Comp: *bitchier;* sup: *bitchiest.*) ♦ *Sue's bitchy attitude did not help her make friends.* ♦ *Why are you being so bitchy today?*

bite ['baɪt] **1.** *n.* a mouthful of food; the amount of food taken in at one time. ♦ *Dave swallowed a large bite of food.* ♦ *The baby shoved a huge bite of food into his mouth.* **2.** *n.* a light meal; a snack; a small amount of food. ♦ *Let's get a bite to eat before the movie.* ♦ *Sue had a quick bite for breakfast and ran to catch the train.* **3.** *n.* the mark or wound made on the skin when someone is bitten by an animal or stung by an insect. ♦ *The camper woke up with a spider bite.* ♦ *David kept scratching his mosquito bites.* **4.** *n.* the alignment of the top and bottom teeth when the mouth is closed. ♦ *The orthodontist tried to fix the child's bite.* ♦ *The dentist told Mary she has a perfect bite.* **5.** *tv., irreg.* to grip or tear something with the teeth; to close the teeth around an object. (Pt: bit; pp: bitten.) ♦ *Anne bit the top off the cupcake.* ♦ *Dave bites his fingernails.* **6.** *tv., irreg.* [for a creature] to pierce skin with its teeth; to clamp someone or something hard with the teeth. ♦ *The large dog bit Tom on the leg.* ♦ *That mouse bit me!* **7.** *iv., irreg.* [for a creature] to be able to pierce skin with its teeth. ♦ *Our dog bites, so be careful.* ♦ *Don't worry, our cat doesn't bite.* **8.** *iv., irreg.* [for a fish] to take a lure. ♦ *In the creek behind my house, the fish bite more in the evening than in the morning.* ♦ *I hope the fish are biting tonight!* **9.** *iv., irreg.* to fall for or go along with a joke; to accept a gamble. (Informal. Figurative on ⑧.) ♦ *OK, I'll bite. What's the joke?* ♦ *I bet Bill $20 that it would rain, but he wouldn't bite.* **10. bite off more than one can chew** *idiom* to take (on) more than one can deal with; to be overconfident. ♦ *Billy, stopping biting off more than you can chew. You're doing too many activities.* ♦ *Anne is exhausted again. She's always biting off more than she can chew.*

biting ['baɪt ɪŋ] **1.** *adj.* scathing; sharp; very critical. (Adv: *bitingly.*) ♦ *The biting review of the play infuriated the cast.* ♦ *I asked my friend to stop making biting remarks.* **2.** *adj.* bitter cold; very wintry. (Adv: *bitingly.*) ♦ *A biting wind swept across the plains.* ♦ *Mary put on a scarf to protect herself from the biting cold.*

bitten ['bɪt n] pp of bite.

bitter ['bɪt ɚ] **1.** *adj.* very acrid or harsh in taste. (Adv: *bitterly.* As one of the four basic tastes, not sweet, salty, or sour.) ♦ *Unsweetened chocolate is very bitter.* ♦ *This lettuce is old and bitter.* **2.** *adj.* extremely cold; biting. (Adv: *bitterly.*) ♦ *The wind is bitter today.* ♦ *I hate this bitter weather!* **3.** *adj.* emotionally painful; distressful. (Adv: *bitterly.*) ♦ *Not getting the promotion was a bitter experience for Anne.* ♦ *I had some bitter moments during the discussion, but when it was over I felt better.* **4.** *adj.* resentful; hateful. (Adv: *bitterly.*) ♦ *Tom felt very bitter toward Jane after the argument.* ♦ *The opponents flung bitter words at each other.* **5. take the bitter with the sweet** *idiom* to accept the bad things along with the good things. ♦ *We all have disappointments. You have to learn to take the bitter with the sweet.* ♦ *There are good days and bad days, but every day you take the bitter with the sweet. That's life.*

bitterness ['bɪt ɚ nəs] **1.** *n.* the quality of have a bitter taste. (No plural form in this sense.) ♦ *I didn't care for the bitterness of the fruit.* ♦ *The food's bitterness made it inedible.* **2.** *n.* hostility. (No plural form in this sense.) ♦ *The bitterness between the angry enemies was evident.* ♦ *After a few drinks, all traces of bitterness between the opponents vanished.* **3.** *n.* resentfulness. (No plural form in this sense.) ♦ *Jimmy could not hide the bitterness he felt toward the baby.* ♦ *Mary hid her bitterness with an angelic expression.* **4.** *n.* an extreme coldness of the climate. (No plural form in this sense.) ♦ *We moved south to escape the bitterness of Minneapolis winters.* ♦ *I dread the bitterness of our winter winds.*

bittersweet ['bɪt ɚ swit] **1.** *adj.* tasting both bitter and sweet at the same time. ♦ *I am very fond of bittersweet chocolate.* ♦ *The sauce had a bittersweet flavor that didn't go well with the meat.* **2.** *adj.* joyful and sorrowful at the same time. (Figurative on ①.) ♦ *The emotional ending of the movie was bittersweet.* ♦ *It was a bittersweet moment for the widow when only one of her sons returned from the war.*

biweekly [bɑɪ 'wik li] **1.** *adj.* occurring once every two weeks. ♦ *The employees are paid on a biweekly basis.* ♦ *Our biweekly newsletter comes out next week, not this week.* **2.** *adj.* occurring twice a week. ♦ *Mary has biweekly sessions with her physical therapist.* ♦ *Susan enrolled in a biweekly class in psychology.* **3.** *adv.* once every two weeks. ♦ *David visits his parents biweekly, that is, twice a month.* ♦ *Anne is paid biweekly, on every other Friday.* **4.** *adv.* twice a week. ♦ *I do the laundry biweekly, on Tuesday and Friday.* ♦ *The school newspaper is published biweekly, every Monday and Thursday.*

bizarre [bɪ 'zɑr] *adj.* very strange; eccentric; weird. (Adv: *bizarrely.*) ♦ *A bizarre series of events preceded the murder.* ♦ *The odd sailor had a reputation for bizarre behavior.*

black ['blæk] **1.** *adj.* the color of coal; the color of the darkest night; the opposite of white. (Comp: *blacker;* sup: *blackest.*) ♦ *I have black boots to match my coat.* ♦ *It was very black outside last night.* **2.** *adj.* [of coffee served] without cream or milk. ♦ *I asked for a cup of black coffee.* ♦ *The server poured some more black coffee into my cup.* **3.** *adj.* evil; wicked. (Adv: *blackly.* Comp: *blacker;* sup: *blackest.*) ♦ *The villain gloated over his black deed.* ♦ *The black plan unfolded as the evil king had planned.* **4.** *adj.* angry; sullen; gloomy. (Adv: *blackly.* Comp: *blacker;* sup: *blackest.*) ♦ *Jane was in a black mood the day she got fired.* ♦ *It was hard not to think black thoughts after getting fired.* **5.** *adj.* [of people, usually of African decent] having dark-colored skin. (Occasionally capitalized.) ♦ *A kindly black lady shook our hands as we entered.* ♦ *Tom is studying Black culture in school.* **6.** *adv.* [of coffee served] without cream or milk. ♦ *The restaurant ran out of cream, so we had to have our coffee black.* ♦ *John drinks his coffee black.* **7.** *n.* someone who is of African descent having dark-colored skin. (Sometimes capitalized.) ♦ *The crowd at the concert was a mix of blacks and whites.* ♦ *Both blacks and whites are among Tom's friends.* **8. black and blue** *idiom* bruised; [of skin] showing signs of physical injury. ♦ *The child was black and blue after having been beaten.* ♦ *She was black and blue all over after falling out of the tree.* **9. in the black** *idiom* not in debt; in a financially profitable condition. (See also in the red.) ♦ *I wish my accounts were in the black.* ♦ *Sally moved the company into the black.*

black and white ['blæk ən ʍɑɪt] **1.** *adj.* [of photography] in shades of black, gray, and white, rather than in color. (Hyphenated before nominals.) ♦ *Jane took some black-and-white photographs on her vacation.* ♦ *The newspaper printed a black-and-white picture of the suspect.* **2.** *adj.* simple and easily decided; either right or wrong and nothing in between. (Hyphenated before nominals.) ♦ *This is not a black-and-white issue. There are many different aspects to this problem.* ♦ *If the problem were black and white, it would be easy to figure out a solution.* **3.** *phr.* absolute terms; clearly definable positions. (No plural form in this sense.) ♦ *John sees everything in black and white.* ♦ *Mary discussed the problem in terms of black and white.* **4. in black and white** *idiom* printed, as in a contract. ♦ *We need to get the terms of the agreement in black and white.* ♦ *I have your very words right here in black and white.*

blackball ['blæk bɔl] *tv.* to vote against inviting someone to be a member in an organization. (In this voting, a white ball means acceptance and even one black ball means rejection.) ♦ *David was blackballed from the fraternity again this year.* ♦ *Who blackballed Anne? She would make a good member.*

blackberry ['blæk bɛr i] **1.** *n.* a small black or purple berry. ♦ *The children were sent to pick blackberries for the pie.* ♦ *Bill smeared jam made from blackberries all over his toast.* **2.** *adj.* made of ①. ♦ *I spread some blackberry jam on the bread.* ♦ *We ordered blackberry pie for dessert.*

blackbird ['blæk bɚd] *n.* any of several birds with all black feathers. ♦ *The telephone wire was covered with blackbirds.* ♦ *That ugly blackbird won't leave our yard.*

blackboard ['blæk bord] *n.* a chalkboard; a flat surface—usually black—designed to be written on with chalk, mounted at the front of a classroom. ♦ *The teacher wrote the quiz on the blackboard.* ♦ *The students solved the problems on the blackboard.*

blacken ['blæk ən] **1.** *tv.* to make something black; to cause something to become black. ♦ *Smoke from the fire blackened the wallpaper.* ♦ *The artist blackened the canvas to make a background for the painting.* **2.** *iv.* to become very dark or black; to turn black. ♦ *The sky blackened just before the storm.* ♦ *The wood blackened in the fire.*

blackened ['blæk ənd] *adj.* of cooked or grilled food that has been coated with spices and charred. ♦ *The restaurant's special tonight is blackened catfish.* ♦ *Blackened food is usually very spicy.*

blackjack ['blæk dʒæk] **1.** *n.* a card game in which the players try to score 21 points before the dealer does. ♦ *Bob won $1,000 playing blackjack in Las Vegas.* ♦ *Mary taught her friends how to play blackjack.* **2.** *n.* a very short club with a flexible handle, used as a weapon. ♦ *The assailant was armed with a blackjack.* ♦ *The victim was beaten with a blackjack.*

blacklist ['blæk lɪst] **1.** *n.* a list of people under suspicion; a list of disliked people. ♦ *The company kept a blacklist of vendors it would not use.* ♦ *The government kept a blacklist of political dissidents.* **2.** *tv.* to put someone or something on a blacklist. ♦ *The labor union blacklisted the two companies.* ♦ *The dictator blacklisted the political dissident.*

blackmail ['blæk mel] **1.** *tv.* to demand money or favors from a person in exchange for concealing damaging information about the person. ♦ *The crooks had blackmailed the senator for years.* ♦ *The gangsters who knew of Bill's past crimes tried to blackmail him.* **2.** *n.* the crime of demanding money as in ①. (No plural form in this sense.) ♦ *Blackmail is illegal in most countries.* ♦ *The gangster was convicted of blackmail.*

blackness ['blæk nəs] *n.* the state of being black. (No plural form in this sense.) ♦ *The blackness of the night startled the campers from the city.* ♦ *I was surprised by the blackness of the sky.*

blackout ['blæk ɑʊt] **1.** *n.* a complete loss of all electricity or power; a complete darkness caused by the lack of any light. ♦ *The storm caused a blackout in our neighborhood.* ♦ *Luckily, we had candles ready in case of a blackout.* **2.** *n.* the darkening of the lights of a city during World War II, so enemy bombers could not locate the city. ♦ *A blackout of the city was ordered to prevent damage from the bombing attack.* ♦ *During the blackout, we listened to the radio for war news.* **3.** *n.* the banning of a local television or radio broadcast of a local sports event. ♦ *There was a blackout on the home football game.* ♦ *The blackout of the local games was an annoyance to people who couldn't afford tickets to attend the game.* **4.** *n.* a period of time when a special airfare is not available, as during holiday periods. ♦ *The airline imposed a blackout over the holidays.* ♦ *An airline blackout was in effect during my vacation.* **5.** *n.* not allowing information about something, such as an invasion or court trial, to be covered by the press. ♦ *The court case was so controversial that the judge ordered a blackout.* ♦ *The judge ordered a blackout to prevent the jurors from being influenced by the media.* **6.** *n.* a loss of consciousness. ♦ *Jane had a short blackout after she fell and broke her foot.* ♦ *Tom had a blackout lasting a few seconds just after his stomach pains started.*

Black Sea ['blæk 'si] See Gazetteer.

blacksmith ['blæk smɪθ] *n.* someone who produces objects made of iron, especially horseshoes. ♦ *The museum exhibit showed the workshop of a blacksmith.* ♦ *The blacksmith made shoes for the farmer's horse.*

blacktop ['blæk tɑp] **1.** *n.* asphalt pavement; the asphalt used for pavement. (No plural form in this sense.) ♦ *It was too hot outside to walk barefoot on the playground blacktop.* ♦ *Anne wanted the dirt driveway to be covered with blacktop.* **2.** *tv.* to pave something with ①. ♦ *David blacktopped the driveway.* ♦ *The workers blacktopped the parking lot at the new shopping mall.*

bladder ['blæd ɚ] *n.* a sac-like organ for holding fluids or gases. (Usually used in reference to the urinary bladder.) ♦ *My bladder was full, and I searched desperately for a bathroom.* ♦ *Air escaped from the fish's swim bladder when I cut it open.*

blade ['bled] **1.** *n.* the flat, sharpened edge of a knife or tool. ♦ *The blade of the knife sliced through the roast.* ♦ *The rusty saw blade would not cut the wood.* **2.** *n.* the flat, wide part of an oar or propeller. ♦ *The blade of the oar made gentle ripples in the water.* ♦ *An unlucky fish got caught in the blades of the boat's propeller.* **3.** *n.* a long, flat leaf of grass or other plant. ♦ *A beetle crawled up the blade of grass.* ♦ *The children had blades of grass stuck to their clothing from rolling down the hill.* **4.** *n.* the metal part of an ice skate that makes contact with the ice. ♦ *The skater's blades glided across the ice.* ♦ *New blades were put on the skates before the competition.*

blame ['blem] **1.** *n.* the responsibility for causing something that is bad or wrong. (No plural form in this sense.) ♦ *Who took the blame for the unsuccessful project?* ♦ *The blame for the broken window fell on Jimmy.* **2.** *tv.* to accuse someone of doing something badly or wrongly. ♦ *Mother blamed Jimmy for the mud on the carpet.* ♦ *Jane could not blame anyone but herself when she was late.*

blameless ['blem ləs] *adj.* innocent; without blame or fault. (Adv: *blamelessly.*) ♦ *The officer was blameless and could not have prevented the accident.* ♦ *The students were found blameless in the incident.*

bland ['blænd] **1.** *adj.* having no taste; not spicy. (Adv: *blandly.* Comp: *blander;* sup: *blandest.*) ♦ *The cafeteria's food was really bland.* ♦ *Mary added spices to the bland casserole.* **2.** *adj.* having no excitement; boring; dull. (Figurative on ①. Adv: *blandly.* Comp: *blander;* sup: *blandest.*) ♦ *We spent another bland evening at home last Saturday.* ♦ *Mary stopped dating Bill because he's so bland.*

blank ['blæŋk] **1.** *n.* an empty line or a space on a form. ♦ *The applicant filled in the blanks on the form.* ♦ *I wrote my name in the wrong blank on the application.* **2.** *n.* a form that has not been filled out. ♦ *Fill out this application blank and return it to me.* ♦ *We filled out an entry blank for the contest.* **3. a blank** *n.* a void; a lack of memory about someone or something. ♦ *Jane's memory of her childhood is a blank—she's blocked it out.* ♦ *My mind is just a blank. I can't remember your name.* **4.** *n.* a fake bullet that makes a noise when it is fired. ♦ *The pistol used in the play fired blanks.* ♦ *I didn't know the gun was loaded with blanks, so I jumped when it was fired.* **5.** *adj.* without marks; having no writing. (Comp: *blanker;* sup: *blankest.*) ♦ *The writer just sat and stared at the blank sheets of paper.* ♦ *The teacher handed a blank test booklet to each student.* **6.** *adj.* [of a facial expression] not showing recognition or response. (Adv: *blankly.* Comp: *blanker;* sup: *blankest.*) ♦ *The teacher's scolding drew a blank look from the student.* ♦ *The victim was still in shock and had a blank expression on his face.* **7. blank (out) on** *iv.* (+ *adv.*) + *prep. phr.* to suddenly forget an answer or an idea; to lose one's thoughts. (Informal.) ♦ *Paul blanked on the name of his interviewer.* ♦ *I always blank out on the answers to test questions.*

blank check ['blæŋk 'tʃɛk] **1.** *n.* a signed check on which the payee fills in an amount. ♦ *I keep all my blank checks locked in a drawer.* ♦ *Never lose a blank check!* **2. give someone a blank check** *idiom* to give someone permission to spend an unlimited amount of money. ♦ *Tom gave the mechanic a blank check to make the repairs.* ♦ *The foundation gave the agency a blank check to plan a program.*

blanket ['blæŋ kɪt] **1.** *n.* a piece of thick fabric, used to keep someone warm. ♦ *We curled up in blankets while watching television.* ♦ *During the winter Jane keeps three blankets on her bed.* **2.** *n.* a covering of something. (Figurative on ①.) ♦ *The snow lay in a thick blanket over the garden.* ♦ *The cake was covered with a blanket of powdered sugar.* **3.** *tv.* to cover something (with something). ♦ *The storm blanketed the neighborhood with snow.* ♦ *Presents blanketed the table at the wedding.* **4. wet blanket** *idiom* a dull or depressing person who spoils other people's enjoyment. ♦ *Jack is fun at parties, but his brother is a wet blanket.* ♦ *I was tired of being with Anne because she was a real wet blanket.*

blare ['blɛr] **1.** *n.* a loud, harsh noise. ♦ *The sleepy campers woke to the blare of the trumpet.* ♦ *The blare of a car horn startled Mary.* **2.** *iv.* to make a loud, harsh noise. ♦ *Your radio is blaring! Turn it down!* ♦ *The trumpets blared as the bride and groom left the church.* **3.** *tv.* to bellow something loudly and harshly. ♦ *The radio blared the news about the blizzard.* ♦ *Their loud discussion blared the embarrassing story across the room.*

blaspheme [blæs 'fim] **1.** *tv.* to curse the name of God or sacred things. ♦ *John blasphemed God when he cursed.* ♦ *The religious leaders claimed the book blasphemed Islam.* **2.** *iv.* to revile God or sacred things. ♦ *The preacher said that the man had blasphemed by breaking the commandments.* ♦ *The woman blasphemed and immediately regretted it.*

blasphemous ['blæs fə məs] *adj.* contemptuous towards God or sacred things. (Adv: *blasphemously.*) ♦ *The writer was condemned for making a blasphemous statement.* ♦ *The minister warned against the blasphemous new ideas.*

blasphemy ['blæs fə mi] *n.* an expression of contempt for God or sacred things. (No plural form in this sense.) ♦ *The youths who damaged the church were accused of vandalism and blasphemy.* ♦ *The preacher said the scientist was guilty of blasphemy.*

blast ['blæst] **1.** *n.* a strong, sudden gust of air; a sudden, heavy wind. ♦ *A sudden blast of air blew the lawn furniture over.* ♦ *The leaves were lifted into the air by a sudden blast of wind.* **2.** *n.* the noise and violent gust of air created by an explosion. ♦ *The blast from the truck's tailpipe startled the other drivers.* ♦ *The dynamite made a loud blast when it exploded.* **3.** *n.* an explosion. ♦ *The building was torn apart by the blast.* ♦ *The miners braced for the dynamite blast.* **4.** *tv.* to blow something up; to explode something. ♦ *The workers blasted the mine entrance.* ♦ *The robbers blasted the bank vault open.*

blatant ['blet nt] *adj.* obvious; flagrant. (Adv: *blatantly.*) ♦ *The experiment results contained a blatant error.* ♦ *The villain's evil intentions were blatant.*

blaze ['blez] **1.** *n.* a fire; a flame. ♦ *The fire department rushed to the blaze.* ♦ *The blaze had been set by an arsonist.* **2.** *n.* a bright outburst; a passionate outburst. (Figurative on ①.) ♦ *In a blaze of passion, John and Jane decided to get married.* ♦ *The scientist solved the problem in a blaze of insight.* **3.** *iv.* to be on fire; to burn. ♦ *The apartment building blazed far into the night.* ♦ *The logs in the fireplace blazed brightly.* **4.** *tv.* to mark a trail or pathway so that others can follow. ♦ *The pioneers blazed a trail across the United States.* ♦ *The kids blazed a path through the forest preserve.*

blazer ['blez ɚ] *n.* a sportscoat; a jacket, usually with metal buttons. ♦ *The boys' school required a uniform that included a blue blazer.* ♦ *There's a sale on blazers at the department store.*

blazing ['blez ɪŋ] *adj.* on fire; fiery. (Adv: *blazingly.*) ♦ *Sue started a blazing fire in the fireplace.* ♦ *The blazing conflagration burned out of control.*

bleach ['blitʃ] **1.** *n.* a substance that removes color or stains. (No plural form in this sense.) ♦ *You can remove some stains from white shirts with a little bleach.* ♦ *The spilled bleach ruined the plaid shirt.* **2.** *iv.* to become white or lighter; to turn white or lighter. ♦ *The dark pants bleached in the wash.* ♦ *Will this stain bleach away?* **3.** *tv.* to turn something white or lighter; to cause something to become white or lighter. ♦ *I bleached the stain out of my white shirt.* ♦ *The hair stylist bleached my hair.*

bleachers ['blitʃ ɚz] *n.* the tiered rows of seats at a sporting event or in a gymnasium. (Treated as plural. Rarely singular.) ♦ *The bleachers were filled with fans during the football game.* ♦ *The athlete looked up to see her family in the bleachers.*

bleak ['blik] *adj.* dreary; colorless; dismal. (Adv: *bleakly.* Comp: *bleaker;* sup: *bleakest.*) ♦ *The bleak day made us feel rather gloomy.* ♦ *The bleak look on my manager's face means that he has bad news.*

bleary ['blɪr i] *adj.* [of eyes] blurred and watery. (Adv: *blearily.* Comp: *blearier;* sup: *bleariest.*) ♦ *I wiped the tears from my crying child's bleary eyes.* ♦ *The bleary-eyed friends said good-bye at the train station.*

bled ['blɛd] pt/pp of bleed.

bleed ['blid] **1.** *iv., irreg.* to lose blood as from a wound. (Pt/pp: bled.) ♦ *Your cut will bleed if you pick the scab.* ♦ *Did the crash survivor bleed much after the accident?* **2.** *iv., irreg.* [for color, ink, or dye] to seep or soak into other colors or dyes. ♦ *The ink from the pen bled into my pocket.* ♦ *The dyes in this shirt bled when I washed it.*

blemish ['blɛm ɪʃ] **1.** *n.* a mark; a defect. ♦ *The fabric had a tiny blemish in it.* ♦ *I found a small blemish on my new mirror, so I returned it.* **2.** *tv.* to mark, spoil, or tarnish something. ♦ *The water spot blemished the finish on the table.* ♦ *One illness will blemish your perfect attendance record.*

blend ['blɛnd] **1.** *n.* a mixture. ♦ *This blend of spices tastes delicious.* ♦ *The room's decor was a good blend of traditional and modern pieces.* **2.** *tv.* to combine something with something else. ♦ *The artist blended painting with etching.* ♦ *The decor blends traditional furniture with modern pieces.* **3.** *iv.* to harmonize; to mix with people or things. ♦ *The draperies blend well with the rest of the room.* ♦ *Tom can blend with just about any group of people.*

blender ['blɛn dɚ] *n.* a kitchen appliance that chops and mixes foods. ♦ *We use our blender to mix fruit drinks.* ♦ *The couple received three blenders as wedding gifts!*

bless ['blɛs] **1.** *tv.* to make someone or something holy through a religious ritual; to consecrate someone or something. ♦ *At the baptism, the priest blessed the baby.* ♦ *We asked the minister to bless our new house.* **2.** *tv.* to ask God to bestow favor on the food that is to be eaten. ♦ *Dad blessed the food at the dinner table.* ♦ *The preacher blessed the meal, and everyone started eating.*

blessed **1.** ['blɛs ɪd] *adj.* holy. ♦ *The worshiper prayed to the blessed saint.* ♦ *The blessed infant was laid in the manger.* **2.** ['blɛst] *adj.* fortunate; happy. (Adv: *blessedly* ['blɛs əd li].) ♦ *We are surely blessed because we escaped the hotel fire.* ♦ *Mary felt blessed that her newborn baby was healthy.* **3.** ['blɛs ɪd] *adj.* cursed. (Informal euphemism or sarcasm.) ♦ *This blessed jar just won't open!* ♦ *Don't slam that blessed door again!*

blessing ['blɛs ɪŋ] **1.** *n.* a prayer invoking God's favor or protection. ♦ *Mary gave a blessing before dinner.* ♦ *A spe-*

cial blessing was asked for the sick man. **2.** *n.* God's favor or good fortune given to someone or something. ♦ *Bill was thankful for his many blessings.* ♦ *The blessing of good health fell upon the family.* **3.** *n.* approval; sanction. ♦ *The couple sought their parents' blessings before getting married.* ♦ *The committee members gave their blessing to the budget proposal.* **4.** *n.* a fortunate event. ♦ *Losing my job was a blessing in disguise, because I quickly found a much better one.* ♦ *What a blessing that you can help out at the sale!* **5. be thankful for small blessings** *idiom* to be grateful for any small benefits or advantages one has, especially in a generally difficult situation. ♦ *We have very little money, but we must be thankful for small blessings. At least we have enough food.* ♦ *Bob was badly injured in the accident, but at least he's still alive. Let's be thankful for small blessings.*

blew ['blu] pt of blow.

blight ['blaɪt] **1.** *n.* a plant disease characterized by withering. (No plural form in this sense.) ♦ *A blight spread across the field of grain.* ♦ *The new species we planted is immune to blight.* **2.** *n.* a state of decay or deterioration. (No plural form in this sense. Figurative on ①.) ♦ *The mayoral candidate vowed to reverse urban blight.* ♦ *The blight of this neighborhood was due to the closing of many factories.*

blimp ['blɪmp] *n.* a nonrigid, balloon-like airship; a dirigible. ♦ *An advertising blimp hovered for hours over the football field.* ♦ *The blimp burst and fell to earth.*

blind ['blaɪnd] **1.** *adj.* unable to see; sightless. (Adv: *blindly.* Comp: *blinder;* sup: *blindest.*) ♦ *A blind woman tapped the sidewalk with her white cane.* ♦ *The blind man had a dog that led him around.* **2.** *adj.* [of anger] irrational. (Adv: *blindly.* Comp: *blinder;* sup: *blindest.*) ♦ *Tom flew out of the house in a blind fury.* ♦ *Anne, in a blind rage, crushed her computer mouse.* **3.** *adv.* without insight or knowledge. ♦ *Without a prepared lecture, the professor was just flying blind.* ♦ *I'm working blind on this project—I have no help from anyone!* **4.** *tv.* to take away someone or something's sight permanently or temporarily. ♦ *Dave was blinded by a childhood illness.* ♦ *The oncoming headlights blinded the driver.* **5.** *n.* a place where hunters hide while shooting at game. ♦ *The blind resounded with gunfire.* ♦ *The hunter crouched quietly in the duck blind.* **6. blinds** *n.* a kind of window shade made of horizontal, or sometimes vertical, slats that can be tilted to cut off vision. ♦ *The blinds were covered with dust.* ♦ *I adjusted the blinds so the carpet would not fade from the sunlight.* **7. blind date** *n.* a date where the two individuals concerned have not met each other before the date. ♦ *I went on a blind date with Jane, and we later got married.* ♦ *Bill arranged a blind date for the two shy people.* **8. blind date** *n.* either of the people in ⑦. ♦ *My blind date turned out to be a charming person.* ♦ *It turned out that I had known my blind date for years.*

blindfold ['blaɪnd fold] **1.** *n.* a piece of cloth covering the eyes. ♦ *The child wore a blindfold during the game.* ♦ *The blindfold prevented the hostages from seeing the kidnappers.* **2.** *tv.* to cover someone's eyes with a cloth; to attach ① to a person. ♦ *The robbers blindfolded me so that I could not see.* ♦ *The physician blindfolded the boy with bandages after the operation.*

blinding ['blaɪn dɪŋ] *adj.* causing [temporary] blindness. (Adv: *blindingly.*) ♦ *The oncoming truck's blinding headlights hurt my eyes.* ♦ *A blinding light flashed around the crowd.*

blindly ['blaɪnd li] **1.** *adv.* as if blinded; without being able to see. ♦ *John stumbled blindly through the darkened room.* ♦ *Mary groped blindly through the medicine cabinet.* **2.** *adv.* without thought, attention, or understanding. (Figurative on ①.) ♦ *The child ran blindly across the street.* ♦ *The supervisor made decisions blindly without consulting the staff.*

blindness ['blaɪnd nəs] *n.* the condition of being unable to see. (No plural form in this sense.) ♦ *Some diseases cause blindness.* ♦ *Anne's blindness was caused by a car accident.*

blink ['blɪŋk] **1.** *iv.* an action in which the eyes close and open quickly. (Compare with wink.) ♦ *The flashing lights made me blink.* ♦ *Every time we take John's picture, he blinks.* **2.** *iv.* [for a light] to flash on and off quickly. ♦ *The lights in the theater blinked at the end of intermission.* ♦ *A power surge made the lights blink a couple of times.* **3.** *tv.* to close and open one's eyes quickly. ♦ *"Blink your eyes if you can hear me," the doctor said.* ♦ *The patient slowly blinked her eyes.* **4.** *tv.* to turn a light on and off quickly; to flash a light. ♦ *At the end of intermission, Sue blinked the lights to let the audience know it was time to sit down.* ♦ *Blink the lights in the backyard to tell the children it's time to come in and go to bed.*

blinker ['blɪŋk ɚ] *n.* a turn signal on a car. ♦ *Mary turned her left blinker on before she turned.* ♦ *Both blinkers on my car are burned out.*

bliss ['blɪs] *n.* complete happiness; joy. (No plural form in this sense.) ♦ *The couple felt tremendous bliss on their honeymoon.* ♦ *Jane was in a state of bliss after getting her degree.*

blissful ['blɪs fʊl] *adj.* joyful. (Adv: *blissfully.*) ♦ *The new parents' blissful mood lasted for weeks.* ♦ *Our vacation was a very blissful time for us.*

blister ['blɪs tɚ] **1.** *n.* a bubble of fluid under the skin, formed by a burn or irritation. ♦ *I got blisters on the back of my heel from jogging.* ♦ *The rowboat's oars gave my hands blisters.* **2.** *iv.* [for a part of the skin] to raise up and fill with fluid in response to a burn or irritation. ♦ *After playing tennis for an hour, my hands began to blister.* ♦ *My skin blistered from the sunburn.* **3.** *tv.* to cause a blister to form on someone or something. ♦ *The sun blistered the swimmer's skin.* ♦ *This tennis racket blistered my palm.*

blistering ['blɪs tɚ ɪŋ] *adj.* hot enough to cause blisters. (Adv: *blisteringly.*) ♦ *The workers toiled in the blistering sun all day.* ♦ *The blistering weather made us tired.*

blithe ['blaɪð] **1.** *adj.* merry; cheerful; unworried. (Adv: *blithely.* Comp: *blither;* sup: *blithest.*) ♦ *The whole office was in blithe spirits the day before the holidays.* ♦ *With a blithe smile, the clerk helped all the customers.* **2.** *adj.* casual; nonchalant; unworried when worry is appropriate. (Adv: *blithely.* Comp: *blither;* sup: *blithest.*) ♦ *Even in a crisis, Jane remains blithe and indifferent.* ♦ *The president's blithe response angered the people.*

blizzard ['blɪz ɚd] *n.* an intense snowstorm with strong winds, heavy snow, and possible thunder and lightning.

♦ *Wow! There's a blizzard outside!* ♦ *The weather report stated that a blizzard was approaching.*

bloat ['blot] **1.** *iv.* to swell, usually with water or gas. ♦ *The very salty food made me bloat.* ♦ *The child's stomach bloated from too much food.* **2.** *n.* swelling due to retained water or gas. (No plural form in this sense.) ♦ *I suffered from bloat after eating all the potato chips.* ♦ *Bill's bloat made his ring too tight.*

bloated ['blot ɪd] **1.** *adj.* swollen; puffy; full of something. ♦ *Mary's rings would not fit on her bloated fingers.* ♦ *The lion's bloated belly indicated that it had just eaten.* **2.** *adj.* overly full. (Figurative on ①.) ♦ *The candidate borrowed money from the campaign fund's bloated coffers.* ♦ *Your essay is bloated with too many long sentences.*

blob ['blɑb] *n.* a soft, shapeless mass of something. ♦ *The cook kneaded a blob of dough.* ♦ *The wet tissues lay in a blob on the floor.*

block ['blɑk] **1.** *n.* a solid piece of something, such as wood, stone, or ice. ♦ *A heavy block of wood props the door open.* ♦ *The patio was lined with stone blocks.* **2.** *n.* a large, flat piece of stone or wood on which items are cut, chopped, or split. ♦ *The hatchet lay on the chopping block.* ♦ *The turkey glistened on the carving block.* **3.** *n.* the distance along a street from one intersection to the next. ♦ *Jane lives three blocks from my house.* ♦ *We know all the neighbors on our block.* **4.** *n.* a kind of mental obstacle. ♦ *The novelist had writer's block and hadn't written in months.* ♦ *I had a mental block and couldn't seem to remember the man's name.* **5.** *n.* a group of adjacent seats or tickets for seats, as for the theater, an airline flight, or sporting event. ♦ *The hotel reserved a block of rooms for the conference.* ♦ *We reserved the best block of seats in the theater.* **6.** *tv.* to obstruct something. ♦ *The gate blocked the entrance to the driveway.* ♦ *The lobbyists blocked the passage of the bill.* **7. stumbling block** *idiom* something that prevents or obstructs progress. ♦ *We'd like to buy that house, but the high price is the stumbling block.* ♦ *Jim's age is a stumbling block to getting another job. He's over sixty.*

blockade [blɑ 'ked] **1.** *n.* an impediment to the movement or progress of something. ♦ *The police formed a blockade on the main roads to prevent the suspect from escaping.* ♦ *The committee raised many blockades to prevent the budget cuts.* **2.** *n.* a military action that prevents people and goods from entering or leaving a place. ♦ *The government imposed a blockade to keep food out of the warring nations.* ♦ *Airlifts bypassed the blockade and delivered food to the starving people.* **3.** *tv.* to start a military action that prevents people and goods from entering or leaving a place. ♦ *The government blockaded the roads used to supply the rebels.* ♦ *They blockaded the town to starve the people into surrendering.*

blockage ['blɑk ɪdʒ] *n.* an obstruction; something that blocks something else. ♦ *The medical tests showed there was a blockage in one of my arteries.* ♦ *A plumber removed the blockage from the pipe.*

blockbuster ['blɑk bəs tɚ] **1.** *n.* something, especially an entertainment event, that is very successful. ♦ *The scandalous novel was a blockbuster.* ♦ *The blockbuster earned its producers a lot of money.* **2.** *adj.* very successful. ♦ *The blockbuster novel sold more than a million copies.* ♦ *The Smiths went to see the blockbuster Broadway musical.*

blocked ['blɑkt] *adj.* clogged; obstructed. ♦ *The road was blocked by the fire engines.* ♦ *The crowd filed past the blocked passageway.*

blond ['blɑnd] **1.** *adj.* [of hair] fair or light in color. (Comp: *blonder;* sup: *blondest.*) ♦ *Bob's hair is blond, and his sister's is brunette.* ♦ *I have always admired Tom's blond hair.* **2.** *n.* someone with light-colored hair. (**Blonde** is sometimes used for females.) ♦ *My brothers are all blonds with blue eyes.* ♦ *The models in the magazine were blonds.*

blonde ['blɑnd] *n.* a woman or a girl with light-colored hair. ♦ *Bill's sisters are all blondes.* ♦ *Do you know the name of the blonde sitting next to John?*

blood ['blʌd] **1.** *n.* a dark, red fluid circulating in the human body that carries oxygen and nutrients. (No plural form in this sense.) ♦ *The technician drew blood from the patient.* ♦ *Blood from the wound dripped onto the floor.* **2. blue blood** *idiom* the blood [heredity] of a noble family; aristocratic ancestry. ♦ *The earl refuses to allow anyone who is not of blue blood to marry his son.* ♦ *Although Mary's family is poor, she has blue blood in her veins.* **3. new blood** *idiom* a new and energetic person; new and energetic people. (No plural form in this sense.) ♦ *The company fired some employees and hired new blood.* ♦ *A little new blood on the committee wouldn't hurt.* **4. have someone's blood on one's hands** *idiom* to be responsible for someone's death; to be guilty of causing someone's death. (No plural form in this sense.) ♦ *The teenager's blood was on the policeman's hands.* ♦ *The king's blood was on the hands of the murderer who killed him.* **5. make someone's blood boil** *idiom* to make someone very angry. ♦ *It just makes my blood boil to think of the amount of food that gets wasted around here.* ♦ *Whenever I think of that dishonest mess, it makes my blood boil.*

bloodhound ['blʌd haʊnd] *n.* a dog with a very good sense of smell that is used to search for someone or something. ♦ *The police used bloodhounds to locate the suspect.* ♦ *The bloodhound led the police right to the man.*

bloodless ['blʌd ləs] *adj.* without bloodshed, death, or violence. (Adv: *bloodlessly.*) ♦ *The bloodless murder involved a rare poison.* ♦ *The civil-rights leader led a bloodless protest against government policies.*

bloodshed ['blʌd ʃɛd] *n.* injury and death caused by violence. (No plural form in this sense.) ♦ *The skirmish between troops ended in bloodshed.* ♦ *The bloodshed in the streets of the war-torn country was appalling.*

bloodshot ['blʌd ʃɑt] *adj.* [for eyes to be] inflamed and swollen. ♦ *We knew Bill had been drinking because of his bloodshot eyes.* ♦ *Your eyes are bloodshot from crying.*

bloodstain ['blʌd sten] *n.* a spot of blood. ♦ *A little bleach and cold water will remove that bloodstain.* ♦ *The detective noted the bloodstains on the carpet.*

bloodstained ['blʌd stend] *adj.* marked with spots of blood. ♦ *The lawyer submitted a bloodstained glove as evidence.* ♦ *The woman's clothes were bloodstained from the accident.*

bloodstream ['blʌd strim] *n.* the flow of blood in the body. (No plural form in this sense.) ♦ *The patient felt relief as the painkillers entered his bloodstream.* ♦ *The bloodstream carries nutrients to all parts of the body.*

bloody ['blʌd i] **1.** *adj.* covered or stained with blood. (Adv: *bloodily.* Comp: *bloodier;* sup: *bloodiest.*) ♦ *The* *police found a bloody glove at the scene of the murder.* ♦ *The murderer soaked the bloody shirt in some cold water and bleach.* **2.** *adj.* involving killing or bloodshed. (Comp: *bloodier*; sup: *bloodiest*.) ♦ *The bloody war killed thousands of people.* ♦ *The peaceful protest turned into a bloody skirmish.*

bloom ['blum] **1.** *iv.* [for a plant] to produce flowers or blossoms. ♦ *The bulbs broke through the soil but never bloomed.* ♦ *My roses bloomed early this year.* **2.** *iv.* to become healthy, beautiful, or vigorous. (Figurative on ①.) ♦ *At about age eighteen, the sickly teenager bloomed.* ♦ *After retirement, Grandma and Grandpa bloomed again as they became more active.* **3.** *iv.* [for a flower bud] to open. ♦ *The rosebuds bloomed into huge, fluffy flowers.* ♦ *The buds didn't bloom, but withered because of the frost.* **4.** *n.* a condition in which one is most healthy, beautiful, vigorous, etc. (No plural form in this sense.) ♦ *The young movie star was in the bloom of youth.* ♦ *Jane was in the bloom of her life and looked forward to a productive career.* **5. in bloom** *idiom* with many flowers; at the peak of blooming. ♦ *The garden is beautiful when it is in bloom.* ♦ *The roses are in bloom and they smell so sweet!*

blossom ['blɑs əm] **1.** *n.* a flower. ♦ *The gentleman wore a white blossom in his lapel.* ♦ *I wore a hat decorated with ribbons and blossoms.* **2.** *iv.* to produce flowers; to bloom. ♦ *The daffodils blossomed early this year.* ♦ *When does this type of plant blossom?* **3.** *iv.* [for a flower bud] to open. ♦ *The rosebuds blossomed into huge, fluffy flowers.* ♦ *We picked the flowers after they blossomed.* **4.** *iv.* to flourish; to be in a very good physical condition. (Figurative on ③.) ♦ *A little exercise will make anyone blossom.* ♦ *The pale child blossomed in the sun.* **5. in blossom** *idiom* with many flowers; at the peak of blooming. ♦ *The peonies are in blossom early this spring.* ♦ *If the daffodils are in blossom, spring is on the way.*

blot ['blɑt] **1.** *n.* a spot or smeared area of ink. ♦ *The letter had a tiny blot of ink in the corner.* ♦ *A blot of ink covered the most important word in the sentence.* **2.** *n.* a record of something bad. (Figurative on ①.) ♦ *The scandalous affair was a blot on the politician's reputation.* ♦ *Getting fired is a blot on one's employment record.* **3.** *tv.* to remove an excess amount of moisture by placing an absorbent paper over it and pressing. ♦ *Blot the ink before you put the letter in the envelope.* ♦ *I blotted my fresh lipstick with a white handkerchief.* **4.** *tv.* to dry or clean something by placing an absorbent paper over it and pressing. ♦ *Susan blotted her lips on the tissue.* ♦ *John blotted his letter before folding it.*

blotch ['blɑtʃ] **1.** *n.* a spot or stain of something, such as blood, ink, or paint. ♦ *Dave made a blotch on the page with coffee.* ♦ *Who is responsible for that ugly blotch on the wall?* **2.** *n.* a mark on the skin. ♦ *Jane was embarrassed by the red blotches on her face.* ♦ *Jimmy is allergic to chocolate—it gives him red blotches all over his body.*

blotter ['blɑt ɚ] **1.** *n.* a piece of thick, absorbent paper used to dry wet ink. ♦ *Bill bought a new blotter for his fountain pen.* ♦ *The old blotter was spotted with ink.* **2.** *n.* a book for recording events, especially arrests at a police station. (Slang.) ♦ *Lisa's arrest was recorded in the blotter.* ♦ *The court used the police blotter as evidence.*

blouse ['blɑʊs] *n.* a woman's shirt. ♦ *Mary bought a white blouse and a red skirt on sale.* ♦ *The dry cleaner got the spot out of my blouse.*

blow ['blo] **1.** *iv., irreg.* [for wind or air] to be in motion. (Pt: *blew*; pp: *blown*.) ♦ *The wind blew all night and kept us awake.* ♦ *Fresh air blew through the open windows.* **2.** *iv., irreg.* [for something] to be lifted or carried in the air or wind. ♦ *The flag blew in the breeze.* ♦ *Our kite blew up into the tree.* **3.** *iv., irreg.* [for a sound-producing device, such as a horn] to make sound. ♦ *A whistle blows at the factory at the end of the day.* ♦ *Many horns were blowing as the cars waited behind the stalled car.* **4.** *iv., irreg.* [for a fuse] to burn out. ♦ *This is the second fuse that blew today.* ♦ *The fuse blew, so I went downstairs to replace it.* **5. blow up** *iv.* + *adv.* to break suddenly and violently into pieces, with a loud noise. ♦ *A bomb blew up and injured four people.* ♦ *A whole box of firecrackers blew up and scared us all.* **6. blow up** *iv.* + *adv.* to lose one's temper. ♦ *My father got mad and blew up at me.* ♦ *There is no need to blow up. I won't do it again.* **7. blow up** *tv.* + *adv.* to cause something to explode. ♦ *Tom blew up a whole box of firecrackers.* ♦ *Using dynamite, Bob blew up the old building.* **8. blow up** *tv.* + *adv.* to inflate something; to push air into something so that it becomes full of air. ♦ *I am so tired that I can't blow up Jimmy's balloon.* ♦ *I had to use a pump to blow up the basketball.* **9.** *tv., irreg.* [for air or wind] to carry someone or something in the air. ♦ *The breeze blew the dust and dirt into the house.* ♦ *The wind blew the laundry off the clothesline.* **10.** *tv., irreg.* to exhale air or smoke. ♦ *The rude smoker blew smoke into our faces at the table.* ♦ *John blew air out of his mouth loudly in exasperation.* **11.** *tv., irreg.* to move something outward or away from a source by forcing air at it. ♦ *The children blew the balloons back and forth to each other.* ♦ *I tried to gently blow the cigarette smoke away from the baby.* **12.** *tv., irreg.* to sound a whistle or a horn, trumpet, or similar instrument. ♦ *The children merrily blew their whistles.* ♦ *All the cars were blowing their horns at once.* **13.** *tv., irreg.* to spend an amount of money foolishly. (Slang.) ♦ *Every Saturday the children blew their allowance at the record store.* ♦ *Dave won the prize money but blew it right away.* **14.** *tv., irreg.* to form or shape something with air. ♦ *The worker blew a glass ball from the molten glass.* ♦ *Jimmy loves to blow bubbles with his gum.* **15.** *n.* a hard hit or knock. ♦ *The boxer took a hard blow to his head and collapsed in the ring.* ♦ *A few blows with the hammer, and the nail was in the wall.* **16.** *n.* a misfortune; a setback. (Figurative on ⑮.) ♦ *Losing her job was a real blow for Mary, who had three children to support.* ♦ *Anne didn't let the blow stop her from achieving her goal.* **17. blow a fuse** *idiom* to burn out a fuse. ♦ *The microwave oven blew a fuse, so we had no power.* ♦ *You'll blow a fuse if you use too many appliances at once.* **18. blow one's nose** *idiom* to drive mucus and other material from the nose using air pressure. ♦ *Excuse me, I have to blow my nose.* ♦ *Bill blew his nose into his handkerchief.*

blown ['blon] pp of blow.

blubber ['blʌb ɚ] **1.** *n.* the fat of whales and other marine mammals. (No plural form in this sense.) ♦ *Whale blubber was once a valuable commodity.* ♦ *Blubber insulates marine animals against the cold.* **2.** *n.* the fat on people. (Figurative on ①. No plural form in this sense.) ♦ *The large football player was mostly blubber.* ♦ *David vowed to* *lose some of his blubber.* **3.** *iv.* to cry wetly; to sob. ♦ *We blubbered during the movie's emotional ending.* ♦ *The child blubbered quietly when he didn't get any more cake.*

bludgeon ['blʌdʒ ən] **1.** *n.* a club used for beating people or other creatures. ♦ *The museum had a bludgeon from medieval times on display.* ♦ *The hunter carried a bludgeon in case he was attacked by an animal.* **2.** *tv.* to strike someone with a heavy object, such as a club. ♦ *The victim was bludgeoned to death by the intruder.* ♦ *The trapper bludgeoned the furry animal to kill it quickly.*

blue ['blu] **1.** *n.* the color of a clear sky on a bright day; the color of a deep, clear ocean. (No plural form in this sense.) ♦ *The living room was painted a beautiful pale blue.* ♦ *Bob's favorite color is blue.* **2. blues** *n.* a type of music, similar to slow jazz. (Treated as plural.) ♦ *Bill's musical taste includes blues.* ♦ *The blues are very popular in Chicago.* **3. the blues** *n.* sadness; depression. (Treated as singular or plural.) ♦ *Many people get the blues on Sunday night.* ♦ *Mary had the blues for months after her mother's death.* **4.** *adj.* <the adj. use of ①.> (Comp: *bluer;* sup: *bluest.*) ♦ *We bought the blue car.* ♦ *The blue suit looks better on you than the brown one.* **5.** *adj.* sad. (Adv: *bluely.* Comp: *bluer;* sup: *bluest.*) ♦ *The movie's ending made us a little blue.* ♦ *The children were blue when their vacation was canceled.*

blueberry ['blu bɛr i] **1.** *n.* a small, round, dark blue or purple fruit, used in pies and jams. ♦ *Blueberries are in season during the summer.* ♦ *I made a pie with the blueberries I picked.* **2.** *adj.* made of or flavored with ①. ♦ *I love blueberry jam.* ♦ *Max baked a blueberry pie for dessert.*

bluebird ['blu bɚd] *n.* any of several species of small, bluish birds. ♦ *We saw a bluebird sitting on the fence.* ♦ *Bluebirds are very common in the Midwest.*

bluegill ['blu gɪl] *n.* a small, edible freshwater fish. ♦ *All we caught on our fishing trip were bluegills.* ♦ *The lake was full of bluegills!*

blue jay ['blu dʒe] See jay.

blue jeans ['blu dʒinz] *n.* a popular type of trousers made out of blue denim. (Treated as plural. Number is expressed with *pair(s) of blue jeans.*) ♦ *Dave bought some new blue jeans.* ♦ *No wardrobe is complete without a few pairs of blue jeans.*

blueprint ['blu prɪnt] *n.* a design; a plan that shows the basic design of something to be constructed. (In years past, blueprints appeared as white lines on blue paper.) ♦ *The architect unrolled the blueprints.* ♦ *The blueprints of the house showed the location of each room.*

bluff ['blʌf] **1.** *n.* a steep hill or cliff with a wide front. ♦ *The view of the lake from the bluff was magnificent.* ♦ *The hikers descended the bluff into the ravine.* **2.** *n.* a hollow threat; an instance of bluffing. ♦ *John's bluff was challenged by his coworkers.* ♦ *I ignored the card player's bluff.* **3.** *n.* someone or some creature who bluffs someone or something. ♦ *John is just a big bluff who tries to get us to work harder.* ♦ *The possum is nature's cleverest bluff.* **4.** *tv.* to deceive someone or some creature; to mislead someone or some creature into doing something. ♦ *The possum bluffed the bear into leaving.* ♦ *Dave bluffed us and took a shortcut to school.*

bluish ['blu ɪʃ] *adj.* having some qualities of the color blue. ♦ *The choking child's face turned a bluish color.* ♦ *The fabric had a bluish tint to it.*

blunder ['blʌn dɚ] **1.** *n.* a stupid mistake; a clumsy error. ♦ *Not turning in the report was a real blunder.* ♦ *The accountant made several serious blunders on my taxes.* **2.** *iv.* to make a stupid mistake. ♦ *I really blundered when I forgot to introduce my friends.* ♦ *The accountant blundered when adding up this column.* **3. blunder into** *iv.* + *prep. phr.* to meet with something unexpectedly and in a clumsy manner. ♦ *The scientists blundered into the discovery while trying to solve another problem.* ♦ *Columbus wanted to reach India but blundered into North America.*

blunt ['blʌnt] **1.** *adj.* without a sharp edge or point. (Adv: *bluntly.* Comp: *blunter;* sup: *bluntest.*) ♦ *The knife was too blunt to cut through the tough meat.* ♦ *The recipe said to pound the meat with a blunt instrument.* **2.** *adj.* to the point; frank; not subtle. (Adv: *bluntly.* Comp: *blunter;* sup: *bluntest.*) ♦ *The politician's blunt statements offended many people.* ♦ *The newspaper article contained a few blunt observations.* **3.** *tv.* to make something dull; to make something less sharp. ♦ *Constant use blunted the blade of the knife.* ♦ *The action of the waves blunted the sharp pieces of glass on the beach.*

blur ['blɚ] **1.** *n.* an indistinct shape or image. ♦ *I could not tell who the blur in the photograph was.* ♦ *The birds were a blur as they zoomed past my window.* **2.** *n.* a smear; a smudge. ♦ *The wet ink made a blur on the page.* ♦ *A messy blur on the newspaper page made part of an article unreadable.* **3.** *iv.* to appear vague or indistinct. ♦ *The television picture blurred every time a plane went over.* ♦ *My vision blurred as tears filled my eyes.* **4.** *tv.* to make something vague or indistinct. ♦ *Tears blurred David's vision.* ♦ *The rain on the windshield blurred our view.*

blurred ['blɚd] *adj.* having been made hazy or indistinct. ♦ *A blurred image in the photograph was unidentifiable.* ♦ *Eyeglasses corrected my blurred vision.*

blurry ['blɚ i] *adj.* hazy; indistinct. (Adv: *blurrily.* Comp: *blurrier;* sup: *blurriest.*) ♦ *The drugs made my vision blurry.* ♦ *The page appeared blurry to Bob, who wasn't wearing his glasses.*

blurt ['blɚt] **blurt out** *tv.* + *adv.* to say something loudly without thinking. ♦ *The excited children blurted out the answer to the teacher's question.* ♦ *Dave blurted out the news and gave away the surprise.*

blush ['blʌʃ] **1.** *n.* a reddening of the face, especially the cheeks, usually when one is embarrassed or excited. ♦ *A blush appeared on the embarrassed man's cheeks.* ♦ *Before the party, Sue had a blush of anticipation on her face.* **2.** *n.* makeup that is put on the cheeks to add color; rouge. (No plural form in this sense.) ♦ *The beautician suggested a rose-colored blush for Sue.* ♦ *The garish clerk had too much blush on.* **3.** *iv.* to turn red in the face from emotion. ♦ *Lisa blushes easily.* ♦ *Max blushed with embarrassment.*

blushing ['blʌʃ ɪŋ] *adj.* red-faced with emotion. (Adv: *blushingly.*) ♦ *The blushing bride walked down the aisle.* ♦ *After winning the award, the blushing man gave a short speech.*

bluster ['blʌs tɚ] **1.** *n.* bold, threatening talk or action; a threatening attitude. (No plural form in this sense.) ♦ *The president's bluster intimidated the reporter.* ♦ *The sen-*

ator's bluster gives people a bad impression. **2.** *iv.* to move or talk threateningly or boastfully; to swagger. ♦ *The cowboy blustered into the tavern and ordered a shot of whiskey.* ♦ *We just laugh at Tom when he blusters about, trying to look important.*

boa constrictor ['bo ə kən strɪk tɚ] *n.* a large snake found mainly in tropical parts of the Americas that squeezes the breath out of its prey. ♦ *The zookeeper fed the boa constrictor some live rats.* ♦ *We watched a boa constrictor squeeze its prey.*

board ['bord] **1.** *n.* a flat, thin piece of wood; a plank. ♦ *We put a wide board under the mattress to make it more firm.* ♦ *Boards were nailed over the windows of the deserted house.* **2.** *n.* a flat piece of wood or other rigid material, used for a specific purpose. ♦ *The clean laundry was heaped on the ironing board.* ♦ *The children's artwork was pinned to the bulletin board.* **3. the board** *n.* a chalkboard; a blackboard. (No plural form in this sense. Treated as singular.) ♦ *Jane went to the board and wrote the correct answer.* ♦ *The teacher erased the board and began writing math problems on it.* **4.** *n.* daily meals. (No plural form in this sense.) ♦ *The college provided room and board for the first-year students.* ♦ *Bob offered to work for his board.* **5.** *n.* a group of people who manage a company or other organization. ♦ *The board of directors voted to expand the business.* ♦ *The school board chose a new curriculum.* **6.** *n.* a flat, sturdy piece of material on which a game is played. ♦ *Jimmy lifted the board and checkers flew everywhere.* ♦ *Where is the game board?* **7. board game** *n.* a game like checkers or chess that is played on a special board having special patterns on it. ♦ *Checkers is my favorite board game.* ♦ *Board games are fun except for when you lose the board.* **8. board up** *tv.* + *adv.* to cover the windows and the doors of a building with boards. ♦ *They boarded up the house to keep prowlers out.* ♦ *The outside entrance to the basement has been boarded up for years.* **9.** *tv.* to get on a ship, bus, train, or plane. ♦ *Please watch your step as you board the train.* ♦ *The passengers stood in line to board the bus.* **10.** *iv.* to receive meals and living space in exchange for money or work. ♦ *Bill boards in town while he goes to college.* ♦ *The college student boarded with our family in exchange for doing all the yard work.* **11. back to the drawing board** *idiom* time to start over again; time to plan something over again. ♦ *It didn't work. Back to the drawing board.* ♦ *I flunked English this semester. Well, back to the old drawing board.*

boarder ['bord ɚ] *n.* a renter who is given regular meals. ♦ *The family supported itself by taking in boarders.* ♦ *The boarder helped out with chores around the house.*

boarding house ['bord ɪŋ hɑʊs] *n., irreg.* a large house where rooms are rented and daily meals are served. (Pl: [...hɑʊ zəz].) ♦ *The boarding house was large enough for the owners and five boarders.* ♦ *All meals were included in the rent at the boarding house.*

boarding school ['bord ɪŋ skul] *n.* a private school at which students live. ♦ *The wealthy family's children were sent to boarding school.* ♦ *The Smiths threatened their children with boarding school if they didn't behave properly.*

boardwalk ['bord wɔk] *n.* a path made of boards on a beach or shore along an ocean, lake, or river. ♦ *The tourists strolled down the boardwalk by the casinos.* ♦ *Restaurants and taverns lined the boardwalk.*

boast ['bost] **1.** *n.* a bragging statement. ♦ *Tom's boast was that he could beat anyone at cards.* ♦ *Anne made many boasts about her business.* **2.** *iv.* to brag or exaggerate. ♦ *Jimmy boasted about his grades often.* ♦ *It is not polite to boast.* **3.** *tv.* to offer or have a particular characteristic. ♦ *The new hotel boasted a casino, a swimming pool, and a dance hall.* ♦ *The car boasted cruise control and automatic seats.*

boastful ['bost fʊl] *adj.* bragging; exaggerating. (Adv: *boastfully.*) ♦ *Bill's boastful attitude angered his colleagues.* ♦ *When telling of her successes, Mary tried not to be boastful.*

boat ['bot] **1.** *n.* a vessel designed to float on top of water; a small ship. ♦ *We rowed across the lake in a boat.* ♦ *The boat set sail at noon.* **2. in the same boat** *idiom* in the same situation; having the same problem. ♦ *"I'm broke. Can you lend me twenty dollars?" "Sorry. I'm in the same boat."* ♦ *Jane and Mary are in the same boat. They both have been called for jury duty.* **3. rock the boat** *idiom* to cause trouble where none is welcome; to disturb a situation that is otherwise stable and satisfactory. ♦ *Look, Tom, everything is going fine here. Don't rock the boat!* ♦ *You can depend on Tom to mess things up by rocking the boat.*

bob ['bɑb] **1.** *n.* a quick up and down movement. ♦ *We noticed the bob of the cork in the water.* ♦ *I made a quick bob of the head in agreement.* **2.** *iv.* move up and down quickly, as with something floating on water. ♦ *The ball bobbed up and down in the pool.* ♦ *The log bobbed as it washed down the stream.* **3.** *tv.* to cut something, especially hair, short. ♦ *The hairdresser bobbed the woman's hair.* ♦ *Have you considered bobbing your hair?*

bobcat ['bɑb kæt] *n.* a wildcat of North America that lives in swamps and wooded or mountainous areas. ♦ *The television program was about the habitat of the bobcat.* ♦ *The campers saw bobcats in the woods.*

bobsled ['bɑb slɛd] **1.** *n.* a sled having two runners, brakes, and a steering device. ♦ *The team jumped on the bobsled as the race began.* ♦ *The bobsled raced down the track.* **2.** *iv.* to ride down a snowy hill on ①. ♦ *The kids bobsledded all afternoon.* ♦ *Has the team ever bobsledded in a competition?*

bodice ['bɑd ɪs] *n.* the upper part of a woman's dress; the part of a woman's dress above the waist. ♦ *The bodice of the gown was covered with sequins.* ♦ *The tight bodice caused the young woman to faint.*

bodies politic ['bɑd iz 'pɑl ə tɪk] pl of body politic. See politic ⑦.

bodily ['bɑd ə li] **1.** *adj.* relating to the human body. ♦ *Tom didn't sustain any bodily injuries in the accident.* ♦ *Mary promised to do Bob bodily harm if she ever saw him again.* **2.** *adv.* in a manner involving the whole body. ♦ *The teacher picked up the hysterical student bodily from the floor.* ♦ *We lifted the injured victim bodily from the street.*

body ['bɑd i] **1.** *n.* the whole physical structure of a living creature or plant. ♦ *The zebra's body is covered with stripes.* ♦ *The athlete pushed her body to its limit.* **2.** *n.* a dead human or animal; a corpse. ♦ *The funeral home received a body last night.* ♦ *The body was badly decomposed by the time it was found.* **3.** *n.* the main part of something. ♦ *The body of evidence convinced the jury of* *the suspect's guilt.* ♦ *The body of the text needed no revision.* **4.** *n.* a collection of people or things taken as a group; a group; a collection. ♦ *They arrived as a body.* ♦ *Has the entire body voted yet on the new procedures?* **5.** *n.* a large mass of something; an object. ♦ *We looked through the telescope at heavenly bodies.* ♦ *The geography class learned the major bodies of water in the world.* **6.** *n.* the basic, external structure of a motor vehicle. (This excludes engines, brakes, steering, etc.) ♦ *The accident didn't cause any damage to the body of the car.* ♦ *The body of Bill's car is red.* **7. body politic.** See politic.

bodybuilding ['bɑd i 'bɪld ɪŋ] *n.* exercise that strengthens and firms the muscles of the human body. (No plural form in this sense.) ♦ *The wiry boy began a course in bodybuilding to gain strength.* ♦ *The athletic club offers training in bodybuilding.*

bodyguard ['bɑd i gɑrd] *n.* someone who guards and protects someone else. ♦ *The queen's bodyguards accompany her wherever she goes.* ♦ *A bodyguard was hired to protect the witness.*

body shop ['bɑd i ʃɑp] *n.* a place where vehicle bodies are built or repaired. ♦ *The body shop repaired the dent on my car.* ♦ *Will the body shop charge a lot to paint your car?*

bodywork ['bɑd i wɚk] *n.* work that is done to repair damaged vehicle bodies. (No plural form in this sense.) ♦ *After the accident, the car needed some bodywork.* ♦ *The bodywork on our car included new paint.*

bog ['bɔg] **1.** *n.* a marsh; wet, soft, muddy ground. ♦ *Cranberries grow in bogs.* ♦ *The hikers walked around the bog.* **2. bog down** *tv.* to cause someone or something to get stuck or slow down. ♦ *The accusations bogged the senator down until the courts decided the issues.* ♦ *Special problems bogged down the legislative process.* **3. bog down** *iv.* + *adv.* to get stuck, as if sinking in mud; to come to a halt, as if mired. ♦ *The hikers bogged down in the mud.* ♦ *The project bogged down because of poor management.*

bogeyman ['bʊg i mæn] *n., irreg.* an imaginary scary creature, used to frighten children. (Pl: bogeymen.) ♦ *Don't get up in the night, or the bogeyman will get you.* ♦ *Jimmy made his Dad check under the bed for the bogeyman.*

bogeymen ['bʊg i mɛn] pl of bogeyman.

bogus ['bog əs] *adj.* fake; false; counterfeit. (Adv: *bogusly.*) ♦ *The bogus money was distributed throughout the city.* ♦ *The museum quickly discovered that the painting was bogus.*

boil ['bɔɪl] **1.** *n.* a painful skin inflammation surrounding an infected core of tissue. ♦ *The patient's body was covered with painful boils.* ♦ *The doctor examined the boil on my foot.* **2.** *n.* the condition of something that is boiling. (No plural form in this sense.) ♦ *When the water comes to a boil, turn down the heat.* ♦ *I let the water reach a rapid boil and then added the pasta.* **3.** *tv.* to make a liquid so hot that it bubbles and turns into vapor. ♦ *"Bill could barely boil water without burning it!" his wife exclaimed.* ♦ *Don't let the milk boil when you make pudding.* **4.** *tv.* to cook something by putting it in a boiling liquid. ♦ *Boil the eggs for three minutes.* ♦ *I boiled the pasta for our dinner.* **5.** *iv.* [for a liquid] to become so hot that it bubbles and turns into vapor. ♦ *The water will boil in about 3 minutes.* ♦ *I waited 10 minutes for the pot of soup to boil.* **6. boil off** *iv.* + *adv.* [for a liquid] to turn into a gas or vapor with the application of heat. ♦ *When you cook with wine, the alcohol boils off, leaving just the flavor.* ♦ *I forgot about the cooking pasta, and the whole pan of water boiled off.* **7.** *iv.* [for something] to cook in a boiling liquid. ♦ *The eggs boiled for fifteen minutes.* ♦ *The chicken boiled slowly.* **8.** *iv.* to be very angry; to seethe. ♦ *Tom's promotion made Bill boil, because he thought he deserved one also.* ♦ *Losing to her worst enemy made Mary boil.*

boiled ['bɔɪld] *adj.* cooked in boiling water or other liquid. ♦ *For breakfast each morning, Sue ate two boiled eggs.* ♦ *The boiled chicken was added to the soup.*

boiler ['bɔɪl ɚ] *n.* a large, heated tank that makes hot water or steam. ♦ *The boiler broke, and our house became very cold.* ♦ *My apartment is heated by a boiler.*

boiling ['bɔɪl ɪŋ] **1.** *adj.* [of a liquid] heated to the point of bubbling and turning into vapor. ♦ *Add the pasta to the boiling water.* ♦ *The clothes were washed in a vat of boiling water.* **2. boiling mad** *adj.* very mad. ♦ *Max was boiling mad when he heard the news.* ♦ *This really makes me boiling mad!* **3. have a low boiling point** *idiom* to become angry easily. ♦ *Be nice to John. He's upset and has a low boiling point.* ♦ *Mr. Jones sure has a low boiling point. I hardly said anything, and he got angry.*

boisterous ['bɔɪs trəs] *adj.* noisy and happy; rough, loud, and playful. (Adv: *boisterously.*) ♦ *The boisterous antics of the children warmed Grandma's heart.* ♦ *The friends played a boisterous game of football.*

bold ['bold] **1.** *adj.* confident; sure of oneself; courageous. (Adv: *boldly.* Comp: *bolder;* sup: *boldest.*) ♦ *The bold employee insisted on better working conditions.* ♦ *It was very bold of you to support Jane in front of the boss.* **2.** *adj.* without shame; rude; impudent. (Adv: *boldly.* Comp: *bolder;* sup: *boldest.*) ♦ *Cutting in front of the people waiting in line was a bold action.* ♦ *The employee paid for his bold remark by getting extra work.* **3.** *adj.* [of printing] darker and thicker. (Comp: *bolder;* sup: *boldest.*) ♦ *My computer printer has bold and italic fonts.* ♦ *The word "poison" appeared in bold letters on the label.*

boldfaced ['bold fest] *adj.* [of letters] darker and thicker. ♦ *The title of the book appeared in boldfaced type.* ♦ *The boldfaced words in the text caught our attention.*

boldness ['bold nəs] *n.* courage; bravery. (No plural form in this sense.) ♦ *The soldiers were decorated for their boldness.* ♦ *Uncle Bob acquired his boldness in business where timidness is never rewarded.*

Bolivia [bo 'lɪv i ə] See Gazetteer.

bologna [bə 'lo ni] **1.** *n.* a kind of seasoned sausage made of finely ground, smoked meat. (No plural form in this sense. From Italian. Number is expressed with *slice(s) of bologna.* See also baloney.) ♦ *The butcher sliced the bologna and wrapped it for me.* ♦ *I bought salami and bologna at the store.* **2.** *n.* a whole roll or length of ①. ♦ *Three large bolognas hung at the back of the butcher shop.* ♦ *For the party, we need a whole bologna and six pounds of cheese.* **3.** *adj.* made with ①. ♦ *Anne eats a bologna sandwich with cheese every day for lunch.* ♦ *They served tiny bologna snacks at the party.*

bolster ['bol stɚ] **1.** *n.* a cylindrical pillow or cushion. ♦ *We bought a new bolster for Jimmy's bed.* ♦ *Jane leaned her* *back comfortably against the bolster on the sofa.* **2.** *tv.* to (figuratively) support or uphold someone or something. ♦ *Dave bolstered his courage to ask for a raise.* ♦ *The evidence bolstered the prospector's claim to the land.*

bolt ['bolt] **1.** *n.* a metal pin or rod, completely or partially threaded, used to connect or attach things. ♦ *The bolt fell out of the steel beam.* ♦ *The carpenter connected the boards with three bolts.* **2.** *n.* a rod that fastens a door, window, or gate. ♦ *The door was secured with a bolt.* ♦ *The bolt on the gate was not engaged, so the dog escaped.* **3.** *n.* a flash or streak of lightning. ♦ *A bolt of lightning lit up the sky.* ♦ *We saw the bolt against the purple sky.* **4.** *n.* a sudden, quick movement; an unexpected, quick movement. ♦ *The cat made a bolt for the door.* ♦ *Her sudden bolt from the table was caused by the ringing of the telephone.* **5.** *n.* a roll of cloth. ♦ *The salesperson cut two yards of wool off the bolt.* ♦ *The tailor bought a whole bolt of calico.* **6.** *tv.* to fasten two or more objects together with a bolt. ♦ *The walls of the shed were bolted together.* ♦ *Anne bolted the shelves to the wall.* **7.** *tv.* to lock a door, gate, or a window by sliding the bolt closed. ♦ *Please bolt the door before you go to bed.* ♦ *As the storm approached, we raced to bolt the barn door closed.* **8.** *iv.* to run away from someone or something; to move away from someone or something quickly and suddenly. ♦ *Mary bolted down the platform when the train was about to leave.* ♦ *The cat bolted when it saw the dog coming.*

bomb ['bɑm] **1.** *n.* an explosive weapon. ♦ *The terrorist constructed several bombs.* ♦ *The army dropped bombs on the war-torn country.* **2.** *n.* a big failure; someone or something that is not successful. (Slang.) ♦ *The movie was a bomb—everyone hated it.* ♦ *Jane worried that her party would be a bomb, but everyone enjoyed it very much.* **3.** *tv.* to attack an area by dropping bombs on it from planes. ♦ *The air force bombed the country until it surrendered.* ♦ *The Germans bombed England during the war.* **4.** *tv.* to cause damage and injury by setting off explosions. ♦ *The terrorists bombed the building.* ♦ *The protesters bombed the government office.* **5.** *tv.* to fail [at doing] something. (Slang.) ♦ *I really bombed this test.* ♦ *The lazy student bombed the entire first semester in college.* **6.** *iv.* to be a failure; to do badly on a test or an exam. (Slang.) ♦ *The movie bombed in Boston.* ♦ *This time, I really bombed on the test.*

bombard [bɑm 'bɑrd] *tv.* to pelt someone or something with something continuously. ♦ *The audience bombarded the stage with rotten fruit.* ♦ *The speaker was bombarded with questions.*

bombardment [bɑm 'bɑrd mənt] *n.* attacking someone or something constantly with something. (No plural form in this sense.) ♦ *The bombardment of the senator with letters was very effective.* ♦ *Aerial bombardment of the city continued throughout the war.*

bomber ['bɑm ɚ] *n.* an airplane that drops bombs. ♦ *Three bombers were housed at the air force base.* ♦ *The bombers went on secret missions every night.*

bombshell ['bɑm ʃɛl] **1.** *n.* a bomb. ♦ *Deadly bombshells rained on the sleeping city.* ♦ *Children found an old bombshell on the beach.* **2.** *n.* a complete surprise; a very shocking surprise. (Figurative on ①.) ♦ *News of the company's bankruptcy was a bombshell for everyone.* ♦ *Dave dropped a bombshell when he announced his marriage plans.* **3.** *n.* someone who attracts people's attention through sex appeal. (Figurative on ①.) ♦ *The striking young model was a very attractive bombshell.* ♦ *The bombshell at the bar caught the attention of many patrons.*

bona fide ['bon ə fɑɪd] *adj.* genuine; authentic; true. (Latin.) ♦ *This lamp is a bona fide antique.* ♦ *Is the fossil bona fide, or is it another fake?*

bonanza [bə 'næn zə] *n.* something that brings great wealth suddenly. (No plural form in this sense.) ♦ *John's promotion was a financial bonanza for him.* ♦ *Winning the lottery was a bonanza for the Browns.*

bond ['bɑnd] **1.** *n.* a link or something in common that brings together two people or two groups of people. ♦ *The common experience forged a bond between Bill and Tom.* ♦ *Mary shared many bonds with her daughter.* **2.** *n.* something that causes two objects to stick together. (No plural form in this sense.) ♦ *The bond holding the broken cup together gave out.* ♦ *Glue acted as a strong bond between the layers of cardboard.* **3.** *n.* a financial instrument wherein someone or something promises to pay back a specified sum of money by a particular date. ♦ *Grandma bought all her grandchildren bonds when they were born.* ♦ *Let's cash in our bonds and buy the house.* **4.** *iv.* [for an adhesive or paint] to become firmly attached. ♦ *The adhesive bonded very quickly.* ♦ *This paint will bond to the wall very well.* **5.** *iv.* [for two or more people] to develop the ties that make a friendship. ♦ *The college roommates quickly bonded and were lifelong friends.* ♦ *The members of the book club bonded together.*

bondage ['bɑn dɪdʒ] *n.* slavery; involuntary servitude. (No plural form in this sense.) ♦ *The criminals kidnapped young children and forced them into bondage.* ♦ *Lincoln emancipated the slaves from their bondage.*

bone ['bon] **1.** *n.* the hard substance of which ② is made. (No plural form in this sense.) ♦ *The archaeologist uncovered an ancient rattle made of bone.* ♦ *The old flute was made of bone.* **2.** *n.* any one of the many parts of an animal's skeleton. ♦ *The human skeleton is made of more than two hundred bones.* ♦ *The skier broke several bones in the skiing accident.* **3.** *tv.* to remove the bones of meat before cooking it. ♦ *You must bone the chicken before it can be added to the soup.* ♦ *I asked the butcher to bone the roast for me.* **4. bone of contention** *idiom* the subject or point of an argument; an unsettled point of disagreement. ♦ *We've fought for so long that we've forgotten what the bone of contention is.* ♦ *The question of a fence between the houses has become quite a bone of contention.* **5. chilled to the bone** *idiom* very cold. ♦ *I was chilled to the bone in that snowstorm.* ♦ *The children were chilled to the bone in that unheated room.* **6. have a bone to pick (with someone)** *idiom* to have a matter to discuss with someone; to have something to argue about with someone. ♦ *Hey, Bill. I've got a bone to pick with you. Where is the money you owe me?* ♦ *I had a bone to pick with her, but she was so sweet that I forgot about it.*

bone-dry ['bon 'drɑɪ] *adj.* very dry; completely dry. ♦ *The well was bone-dry.* ♦ *During the drought, the riverbed was bone-dry.*

boneless ['bon ləs] **1.** *adj.* having no bones; lacking bones. ♦ *Slugs are boneless creatures.* ♦ *Insects are boneless, but some have a hard shell.* **2.** *adj.* [of a piece of meat] with the bone(s) removed. ♦ *The boneless roast looked* *delicious.* ♦ *The restaurant served boneless chicken breasts cooked in many ways.*

bonfire ['bɑn fɑɪr] *n.* a large, controlled, outdoor fire. ♦ *The teenagers had a bonfire on the beach.* ♦ *The campers sat around the bonfire.*

bong ['bɔŋ] **1.** *n.* the deep, sustained sound of a gong, chime, or bell. ♦ *The bong of the church bells could be heard all over town.* ♦ *A loud bong called us to the dinner table.* **2.** *iv.* [for a bell, chime, gong, etc.] to sound. ♦ *The church bell bonged during the night.* ♦ *I heard the bell bong, and I went to dinner.*

bonnet ['bɑn ɪt] **1.** *n.* a type of cap—worn by women and girls—that ties under the chin. ♦ *The pioneer women wore calico bonnets to protect their faces from the sun.* ♦ *The baby wore a lacy white bonnet.* **2.** *n.* any hat worn by women. ♦ *Some of the women in church wore frilly bonnets.* ♦ *The actress's costume included a brimmed bonnet and a long dress.*

bonus ['bon əs] **1.** *n.* something extra. ♦ *At the end of the year, the employees all received cash bonuses.* ♦ *This year our company gave out hams as a bonus.* **2.** *adj.* extra; offering more than expected. ♦ *I clipped a bonus coupon for laundry detergent from the newspaper.* ♦ *The huge store offered many bonus buys.*

boo ['bu] **1. Boo!** *interj.* <a word uttered to frighten people.> (Usually said quickly and loudly.) ♦ *The children put sheets over their heads and ran around shouting, "Boo!"* ♦ *Jane waited behind the door and yelled "Boo!" as John walked by.* **2. Boo!** *interj.* <a noise used to show displeasure with a speaker or performer.> (Usually loud and drawn out.) ♦ *The audience shouted "Boo! Boo!" when the show's cancellation was announced.* ♦ *"Boo!" yelled the audience at the poor performance.* **3.** *n.* a noise of displeasure or disagreement. (Pl in *-s.*) ♦ *The crowd's boos overpowered the applause.* ♦ *The politician's unpopular ideas got boos from the crowd.* **4.** *iv.* to make ③ to show displeasure or disagreement. ♦ *The audience applauded, but a few people booed.* ♦ *Shh! It's not polite to boo in the theater.* **5.** *tv.* to show someone or something displeasure or disagreement by making a booing noise. ♦ *The crowd booed the politician's unpopular ideas.* ♦ *The audience booed the singer who had done so badly.*

booby trap ['bub i træp] *n.* a concealed trap, possibly containing something harmful, like a bomb. ♦ *The eccentric man carefully concealed the booby trap.* ♦ *Enemy soldiers mined the field with booby traps.*

book ['bʊk] **1.** *n.* a stack of pages, held within a cover. ♦ *The children read books in the car.* ♦ *There are thousands of books on the library's shelves.* **2.** *n.* a subdivision of a longer literary work contained within a book. ♦ *The books of the Bible are further divided into chapters and verses.* ♦ *The first volume contained books one and two.* **3.** *n.* a set of objects that are held together under a cover. ♦ *Please stop by the post office and buy a book of stamps.* ♦ *I found a book of matches in my pocket.* **4. books** *n.* the financial records of a company or organization. (Treated as plural.) ♦ *The bookkeeper spent days balancing the books.* ♦ *The government sent someone to audit the company's books.* **5.** *tv.* to process a charge against someone who has been arrested for committing a crime. ♦ *The police officer booked the criminal.* ♦ *"Book him!" the officer said.* **6.** *tv.* to reserve space in advance for something, such as a play, an airplane flight, a room in a hotel, a table in a restaurant. etc. ♦ *The Smiths booked their flight to Europe three months before their trip.* ♦ *The tourists couldn't book a hotel room because there were no vacancies.* **7.** *tv.* to reserve the services of a performer in advance. ♦ *Bill and Mary booked a singer for their wedding.* ♦ *The party organizer wanted to book an entire orchestra for the dance.* **8. open book** *idiom* someone or something that is easy to understand. ♦ *Jane's an open book. I always know what she is going to do next.* ♦ *The council is an open book. It wants to save money.*

bookcase ['bʊk kes] *n.* a set of shelves for books. ♦ *The bookcase held all sorts of interesting books.* ♦ *There's no more room in the bookcase, so I piled books on the floor.*

bookend ['bʊk ɛnd] *n.* one of a pair of heavy supports that are placed at either end of a row of books. ♦ *Bookends kept the books on the desk upright.* ♦ *I need some bookends for the books on my mantle.*

bookish ['bʊk ɪʃ] *adj.* learned; studious; more interested in books than in people. (Adv: *bookishly.*) ♦ *The bookish professor was also a renowned lecturer.* ♦ *The bookish philosopher wrote dozens of essays.*

bookkeeper ['bʊk kip ɚ] *n.* someone who keeps track of the financial records and transactions of a company or an organization; someone who takes care of the books. ♦ *The company employed three bookkeepers to do the accounting.* ♦ *A bookkeeper at the bank helped me balance my account.*

bookkeeping ['bʊk kip ɪŋ] *n.* the job of keeping track of the financial records and transactions of a company or any organization. (No plural form in this sense.) ♦ *Bookkeeping requires a sharp mind and a knowledge of accounting.* ♦ *Mary does the bookkeeping for her family.*

booklet ['bʊk lɪt] *n.* a thin book; a pamphlet. ♦ *A stranger on the street corner handed me a religious booklet.* ♦ *The dentist gave me a booklet about dental hygiene.*

bookmark ['bʊk mɑrk] *n.* something placed between the pages of a book to keep the reader's place. ♦ *The bookmark fell out of Jane's book, and she lost her place.* ♦ *Bill gave me a book and a pretty bookmark for my birthday.*

bookmobile ['bʊk mo bil] *n.* a van or bus equipped as a library on wheels. ♦ *The library parks the bookmobile near the grocery store.* ♦ *The children love to check out books at the bookmobile.*

bookshelf ['bʊk ʃɛlf] *n., irreg.* a horizontal board for holding and displaying books. (Often one of several such shelves, positioned one over the other in a **bookcase**. Pl: **bookshelves**.) ♦ *The bookshelf only had a few books on it.* ♦ *A thin layer of dust covered the bookshelf.*

bookshelves ['bʊk ʃɛlvz] pl of **bookshelf**.

bookshop ['bʊk ʃɑp] *n.* a store where books are sold. ♦ *I went to a bookshop to buy a cookbook.* ♦ *The bookshop had sofas and chairs for browsers to relax on.*

bookstore ['bʊk stor] *n.* a store where books are sold; a store where books are sold on a college campus. ♦ *The bookstore held a children's story hour each week.* ♦ *I called the bookstore to order a book.*

bookworm ['bʊk wɚm] *n.* someone who is always reading and studying. ♦ *The high-school bookworm received a full scholarship for college.* ♦ *The library is full of bookworms after school.*

boom ['bum] **1.** *n.* a large, echoing noise made when something explodes or crashes. ♦ *We heard a boom and then saw a car go up in flames.* ♦ *The crash of the airplane made a deafening boom.* **2.** *n.* a time of strong economic growth. ♦ *During the boom, many companies hired lots of people.* ♦ *The war industry resulted in a boom for the country.* **3.** *iv.* to make a large, echoing noise like an explosion or a crash. ♦ *The announcer's voice boomed over the loudspeaker.* ♦ *The waterfall boomed down into the canyon and hit the rocks.*

boomerang ['bum ə ræŋ] **1.** *n.* a curved wooden stick, which, when thrown, returns to the person who threw it. ♦ *The children played outside with the boomerang.* ♦ *The boomerang flew out and came sailing back to the children.* **2.** *iv.* to recoil; to return unexpectedly; to backfire. (Figurative on ①.) ♦ *The plan for the military takeover boomeranged, and the rebels were arrested.* ♦ *Bob's scheme for revenge against Lisa boomeranged.*

booming ['bum ɪŋ] *adj.* prospering strongly; very successful. ♦ *The booming business was very profitable.* ♦ *The small town is booming now that more businesses have moved to the area.*

boon ['bun] *n.* something that is a great benefit. ♦ *Having a parent who was a teacher was a real boon to the kids.* ♦ *The new businesses were a real boon for the struggling town.*

boor ['bʊr] *n.* someone who is obnoxious or annoying. ♦ *Bob is just a boor who always dominates conversations.* ♦ *After dating boor after boor, Jane finally met someone nice.*

boorish ['bʊr ɪʃ] *adj.* obnoxious; ill-mannered. (Adv: *boorishly.*) ♦ *The boorish guest ruined the banquet.* ♦ *Did any of the guests behave in a boorish way?*

boost ['bust] **1.** *n.* an upward push; an upward thrust; an upward movement. ♦ *Could you give me a boost? I can't reach the top shelf.* ♦ *The cowhand gave me a boost onto the horse.* **2.** *n.* an encouraging act of cheering someone up. ♦ *The promotion gave Mary's morale a boost.* ♦ *Jimmy lost his dog and could really use a boost.* **3.** *n.* an increase; a rise. ♦ *With a small boost in my salary, I could afford to go on vacation.* ♦ *The fierce, winter weather resulted in a boost in the sales of snow shovels.* **4.** *tv.* to push someone or something upward from beneath. ♦ *The cowhand boosted Bill onto the horse.* ♦ *Boost the baby into the chair, please.* **5.** *tv.* to increase something; to raise something. ♦ *Inflation has boosted the cost of living.* ♦ *The landlord boosted our rent.*

boot ['but] **1.** *n.* a heavy shoe, often waterproof. ♦ *Jane couldn't get the tight boot off her foot.* ♦ *One of my boots has a hole in the sole.* **2.** *tv.* to kick someone or something. ♦ *The cruel man booted the cat across the room.* ♦ *The soccer player booted the ball into the goal.* **3.** *tv.* to start a computer, causing it to undergo a series of checks and set up its operating system. ♦ *Something went wrong with my computer, and I had to boot it a few times before it worked right.* ♦ *I booted my computer when I first bought it, and I have never turned it off since.*

booth ['buθ] **1.** *n.* a seating area in a restaurant or club having bench seats with backs, on either side of the table. ♦ *The secluded booth in the restaurant was very romantic.* ♦ *The hostess asked if we would prefer a table or a booth.* **2.** *n.* a small, enclosed space, such as the enclosure containing a public telephone. ♦ *The voting booth had a curtain for privacy.* ♦ *As a stunt, we tried to see how many people could fit in the phone booth.* **3.** *n.* a display table or area—possibly enclosed—at a fair or a market. ♦ *Jane sold her work in a booth at the fair.* ♦ *At the farmers' market, people gathered around the booth where flowers were sold.*

bootleg ['but lɛg] **1.** *tv.* to sell alcohol when such sales were banned in the US. ♦ *Many people made a fortune bootlegging whiskey during Prohibition.* ♦ *The police tried to catch people who bootlegged booze.* **2.** *tv.* to sell any illegal goods or contraband. ♦ *The prison inmates bootlegged all sorts of illegal items.* ♦ *The teenagers bootlegged tapes of the rock concert.* **3.** *n.* homemade liquor, especially during Prohibition. (No plural form in this sense.) ♦ *John was caught making bootleg in his basement.* ♦ *The flappers carried their bootleg in tiny flasks.* **4.** *adj.* made and sold illegally. ♦ *The bootleg tapes of the concert were sold quickly.* ♦ *The police confiscated the bootleg alcohol.*

booty ['but i] *n.* things that are stolen; stolen goods. (No plural form in this sense.) ♦ *The burglar crept out of the house with his booty.* ♦ *The pirate booty sank to the bottom of the ocean along with the ship.*

booze ['buz] **1.** *n.* alcoholic drinks; beer, wine, and hard liquor. (Informal. No plural form in this sense.) ♦ *Bill will drink almost any kind of booze.* ♦ *No booze was served at the wedding.* **2.** *iv.* to drink a lot of alcohol; to get drunk and party. (Informal.) ♦ *The friends went to the bar to booze.* ♦ *Everyone boozed at the party.*

borax ['bor æks] *n.* the crystallized form of the chemical element boron. (No plural form in this sense.) ♦ *Many laundry detergents contain borax.* ♦ *The soap was made of borax.*

border ['bor dɚ] **1.** *n.* the area around the edge of something and the edge itself. ♦ *The wall had a stenciled border at the top.* ♦ *The square cake had decorations all along its borders.* **2.** *n.* the dividing line between two countries, states, or other political units. ♦ *Skirmishes frequently occurred on the border of the two countries.* ♦ *The government securely guards its borders.* **3.** *tv.* to adjoin a particular area. ♦ *The United States borders Mexico and Canada.* ♦ *The shrubs border our yard and the Joneses'.*

borderline ['bor dɚ laɪn] **1.** *n.* the dividing line between two areas. ♦ *The borderline between Missouri and Illinois is the Mississippi River.* ♦ *This street forms a borderline between the suburbs.* **2.** *adj.* difficult to identify as being one thing or quality or another. ♦ *Mary did a borderline job on her homework assignment.* ♦ *Sometimes I think my boss is a borderline idiot.* **3. on the borderline** *idiom* in an uncertain position between two statuses; undecided. ♦ *Bill was on the borderline between an A and a B in biology.* ♦ *Jane was on the borderline of joining the navy.*

bore ['bor] **1.** pt of bear. **2.** *n.* someone or something that is boring; someone or something that is dull. ♦ *The lecture on economic theory was a real bore.* ♦ *My guest was such a bore that I began to yawn.* **3.** *n.* the hollow part of a tube, such as the barrel of a gun, and the diameter of that tube. ♦ *The bore of the rifle wasn't properly aligned.* ♦ *Bob uses a large bore shotgun when he hunts.* **4.** *tv.* to drill a hole in something. ♦ *The carpenter bored a hole in the tabletop.* ♦ *The electrician bored an opening in the wall for the wires.* **5.** *tv.* to make someone tired by being dull. ♦ *The uninteresting lecture bored me very much.* ♦ *That pro-*

fessor's voice would bore anyone. **6.** *iv.* to drill; to make a hole. ♦ *This special drill can bore through solid rock.* ♦ *Is this the right size drill bit to bore through the wall?*

bored ['bord] *adj.* having no interest in what is going on. (Adv: *boredly.*) ♦ *The bored students had to listen to a long lecture about philosophy.* ♦ *The bored audience began to talk among themselves.*

boredom ['bor dəm] *n.* the condition of not being interested in anything or not being stimulated by anything. (No plural form in this sense.) ♦ *The exciting novel chased away Jane's boredom.* ♦ *The children's boredom resulted from having nothing to do on a rainy day.*

boring ['bor ɪŋ] *adj.* dull; tedious. (Adv: *boringly.*) ♦ *Dave found the lecture on art history to be very boring.* ♦ *Since it rained, the children spent a boring afternoon cleaning the basement.*

born ['born] **1.** a pp of bear ⑧. **2.** *adj.* possessing a certain quality or character since birth; by birth; natural. ♦ *The musician announced that her child was a born pianist.* ♦ *Bill was a born loser. Nothing ever seems to go right for him.* **3.** *adj.* having a specified place of birth or national heritage. (Usually in hyphenated combinations.) ♦ *The immigrant's children were all American-born.* ♦ *My relatives are all native-born Canadians.*

borne ['born] a pp of bear.

borough ['bor o] *n.* a town, or a district within a town, that is a unit of government, especially in New York City. ♦ *Bill was a councilman in his borough.* ♦ *I grew up in the borough of Manhattan.*

borrow ['bɑr o] **1.** *tv.* to ask for, accept, and use something from someone with the intention of returning or replacing it. ♦ *Sue borrowed my dress to wear to the party.* ♦ *I borrowed a cup of sugar from the neighbor and replaced it the next day.* **2.** *tv.* to take something, such as a custom, trait, or idea, and use it as one's own. ♦ *The tribe borrowed the rituals of a neighboring tribe.* ♦ *The melody in this piece of music is borrowed from a folk song.*

borrowed ['bɑr od] *adj.* belonging to someone else; taken from some other source. ♦ *I spilled wine all over the borrowed dress.* ♦ *Tom drove a borrowed car at college.*

bosom ['bʊz əm] **1.** *n.* the chest of a human. (Formal or literary.) ♦ *The baby nestled against his father's bosom.* ♦ *The patriot's bosom swelled with pride.* **2.** *n.* the center of feeling in a human. (Literary.) ♦ *She felt anguish in her bosom.* ♦ *Pain shot through his bosom like fire.* **3.** *n.* the [pair of] breasts of a woman. (No plural form in this sense.) ♦ *The dress is too tight across my bosom.* ♦ *Her bosom was too small for the large costume.* **4.** *adj.* close; intimate; trusted. ♦ *Bosom pals don't come along every day.* ♦ *Jane and Mary are bosom buddies.*

boss ['bɔs] **1.** *n.* a supervisor; someone who is in charge of other people's work. ♦ *Bill has a meeting with his boss each week to go over his work.* ♦ *Anne's boss asked her to work over the weekend.* **2.** *tv.* to tell someone what to do; to order someone to do something. ♦ *Susan bossed us the entire time we were at her house.* ♦ *Mary doesn't let anyone boss her.* **3. boss around** *tv.* + *adv.* to order someone about. ♦ *I was bossed around all day, and now I want to do it my way.* ♦ *Dave is always bossing his friends around.*

bossy ['bɔs i] *adj.* overbearing; domineering. (Adv: *bossily.* Comp: *bossier;* sup: *bossiest.*) ♦ *Mary taught her children not to be bossy.* ♦ *The bossy old man didn't have very many friends.*

botanist ['bɑt n ɪʃt] *n.* someone who studies plants; a scientist who studies plants. ♦ *The botanist identified plants at the national park.* ♦ *Botanists have produced many hybrid plants.*

botany ['bɑt n i] **1.** *n.* the study of plants. (No plural form in this sense.) ♦ *Mary liked plants so much, she decided to study botany at the university.* ♦ *The science teacher introduced her students to botany.* **2.** *n.* the description of plant life in a certain area. (No plural form in this sense.) ♦ *The book outlined the botany of the New England area.* ♦ *We were fascinated by the botany of the national park we visited.*

both ['boθ] **1.** *adj.* one and one other; the two [things or people]. (See also each and every.) ♦ *Both trees in the front yard lost their leaves in October.* ♦ *I spoke to both Anne and David about the problem.* **2.** *pron.* one thing or person and another thing or person; the two things or people. ♦ *When offered pizza and hamburgers, I chose both.* ♦ *"Did you talk to Bill or Sue?" Anne asked. "I talked to both," I replied.*

bother ['bɑð ɚ] **1.** *n.* something that is time-consuming or annoying to do. ♦ *Picking up the dry cleaning is such a bother—there is never any place to park.* ♦ *We'll do it. It's no bother at all.* **2.** *tv.* to annoy someone or something; to upset someone or something. ♦ *What's bothering you?* ♦ *Mosquitos really bother me.* **3.** *tv.* to interrupt or disturb someone. ♦ *I'm trying to study. Please don't bother me right now.* ♦ *Don't bother your dad. He's sleeping.*

bothered ['bɑð ɚd] *adj.* upset; troubled. ♦ *Mary was quite bothered to learn that her car was stolen.* ♦ *Tom was bothered by the tragic news.*

bothersome ['bɑð ɚ səm] **1.** *adj.* time-consuming; annoying. (Adv: *bothersomely.*) ♦ *Shopping for gifts can be a bothersome task.* ♦ *Jimmy thinks practicing the piano is bothersome.* **2.** *adj.* upsetting; annoying. (Adv: *bothersomely.*) ♦ *Bothersome gossip always angers Mary.* ♦ *The bothersome news of possible layoffs at work worried Bill.* **3.** *adj.* disturbing; interruptive. (Adv: *bothersomely.*) ♦ *The bothersome dripping of the faucet drove Bill mad.* ♦ *The noisy typewriter in the next room is really bothersome.*

Botswana [bɑt 'swɑn ə] See Gazetteer.

bottle ['bɑt əl] **1.** *n.* a container, usually glass or plastic, with an opening at the end of a short or long neck. ♦ *The rack is full of bottles of wine.* ♦ *The glass bottle broke into pieces when it fell to the floor.* **2.** *n.* the contents of ①. ♦ *I drank two bottles of orange juice.* ♦ *The recipe calls for a whole bottle of soy sauce.* **3.** *tv.* to put something in a bottle, usually for future use or sale. ♦ *The company bottles all sorts of juices.* ♦ *You ought to bottle this tomato sauce! It's so good!*

bottled ['bɑt ld] *adj.* contained in a bottle; packaged and sealed in a bottle. ♦ *Bottled water is a popular drink.* ♦ *The cupboard was full of bottled juices.*

bottleneck ['bɑt l nɛk] *n.* a narrow or crowded way, like the neck of a bottle. ♦ *The bottleneck where the two freeways merged causes large traffic jams.* ♦ *Anne squeezed through the bottleneck at the doorway.*

bottom ['bɑt əm] **1.** *n.* the lowest level of something; the deepest point of something. ♦ *I retrieved some water from* *the bottom of the well.* ♦ *The mules walked along the river at the bottom of the canyon.* **2.** *n.* the underside of something; the lowest surface of something. ♦ *The bottom of the plane scraped the runway before it crashed.* ♦ *My aquarium has a glass bottom.* **3.** *n.* land underneath water; the ground under a body of water. ♦ *The crab walked along the bottom of the ocean.* ♦ *The river had a muddy bottom.* **4.** *n.* the buttocks. ♦ *Jane spanked her unruly child on his bottom.* ♦ *Our bottoms hurt from sitting on the hard wooden bench for too long.* **5.** *adj.* relating to the lowest part of something; relating to the underneath part of something. ♦ *The socks are in the bottom drawer of the dresser.* ♦ *The kitten slept on the bottom stair.* **6. get to the bottom of something** *idiom* to get an understanding of the causes of something. ♦ *We must get to the bottom of this problem immediately.* ♦ *There is clearly something wrong here, and I want to get to the bottom of it.* **7. hit bottom** *idiom* to reach the lowest or worst point. ♦ *Our profits have hit bottom. This is our worst year ever.* ♦ *When my life hit bottom, I began to feel much better. I knew that if there was going to be any change, it would be for the better.*

botulism ['batʃ ə lɪz əm] *n.* a disease of the nervous system acquired from improperly canned foods. (No plural form in this sense.) ♦ *Botulism can be fatal.* ♦ *The can of tuna was contaminated with botulism.*

bough ['baʊ] *n.* a large tree branch. ♦ *Delicious apples hang from the boughs of the tree.* ♦ *The children swung on the bough of the weeping willow tree.*

bought ['bɔt] pt/pp of buy.

bouillon ['bʊl jan] *n.* a clear broth or soup. (From French. No plural form in this sense.) ♦ *The recipe called for a cup of bouillon.* ♦ *The sick man sipped bouillon from a mug.*

boulder ['bol dɚ] *n.* a large stone, especially one rounded by erosion. ♦ *The highway was lined with boulders.* ♦ *The farmer had to plow around the boulder in the field.*

boulevard ['bʊl ə vard] *n.* a wide city street, usually lined with trees. ♦ *The artist was known for paintings of tree-lined boulevards.* ♦ *Anne lives on Maple Boulevard near the park.*

bounce ['baʊns] **1.** *n.* the rebounding of an object when it hits a surface. ♦ *I hit the tennis ball after two bounces.* ♦ *The basketball made a quick bounce off the backboard.* **2.** *n.* energy; liveliness; vigor. (No plural form in this sense.) ♦ *Grandma may be ninety, but she sure has a bounce in her step.* ♦ *Bill's good mood was obvious from the bounce in his walk.* **3.** *iv.* to rebound from hitting a surface. ♦ *The rubber ball bounced on the floor many times before it stopped moving.* ♦ *Susie bounced on her bed so much that it broke.* **4.** *iv.* [for a check] not to be honored by the bank owing to insufficient funds. ♦ *My rent check bounced, so I paid my landlord in cash.* ♦ *My checks never bounce because I always balance my checkbook.* **5.** *tv.* [for a bank] not to honor a check owing to insufficient funds. ♦ *The bank bounced my check because I had withdrawn too much money.* ♦ *Will the bank bounce your check?* **6.** *tv.* to toss someone upward gently, causing bouncing as in ③. ♦ *Grandma bounced the baby on her lap.* ♦ *Dad bounced Jimmy on his knee.* **7.** *tv.* to cause something to hit against a surface and rebound. ♦ *The youngster bounced a rubber ball on the floor all day long.* ♦ *Stop bouncing that ball!* **8.** *tv.* to write a check that is valueless owing to insufficient funds. ♦ *I forgot to deposit my paycheck, so I bounced four checks in one week.* ♦ *If you bounce a check, often your bank will charge you a fee.* **9.** *tv.* to eject someone from a place, usually a drinking establishment. ♦ *The 20-year-olds were bounced from the bar for underage drinking.* ♦ *Bill was bounced from the tavern when he wouldn't pay for the drinks.*

bounced ['baʊnst] *adj.* [of a check] returned by the bank owing to insufficient funds. ♦ *My bounced check was returned to the grocery store.* ♦ *Mike had three bounced checks this month.*

bouncer ['baʊn sɚ] *n.* someone who checks the identification of persons wishing to go into a drinking establishment to make sure they are of legal drinking age and removes those who aren't. ♦ *The bouncer at the bar was also a weightlifter.* ♦ *The bouncer kicked the drunken men out of the bar.*

bouncy ['baʊn si] **1.** *adj.* [of something] able to bounce when it hits a surface. (Comp: *bouncier;* sup: *bounciest.*) ♦ *Rubber is bouncy and good for making balls.* ♦ *The children played with soft, bouncy toys.* **2.** *adj.* springy; relating to something that bends up and down; pliant. (Adv: *bouncily.* Comp: *bouncier;* sup: *bounciest.*) ♦ *The new carpeting is a bit bouncy.* ♦ *My hair is shiny and bouncy.* **3.** *adj.* energetic; full of energy; full of life. (Adv: *bouncily.* Comp: *bouncier;* sup: *bounciest.*) ♦ *The children were bouncy from morning until bedtime.* ♦ *Mice are bouncy little animals.*

bound ['baʊnd] **1.** pt/pp of bind. **2.** *adj.* tied up; fastened; glued into covers. ♦ *The bound papers did not separate.* ♦ *John put the bound copies of the magazines onto the reading table.* **3.** *iv.* to jump; to leap forward; to bounce up. ♦ *The children bounded out of bed on Christmas morning.* ♦ *As soon as the lecture was over, the students bounded to the exit.* **4.** *n.* an upward jump; a forward jump. ♦ *The rabbit took great bounds across the road.* ♦ *In one bound, Bill jumped across the stream.* **5. bound to do something** *idiom* certain to do something; confident of something. ♦ *The Mets are bound to win the pennant eventually.* ♦ *You're bound to publish a novel some day.* **6. bound for somewhere** *idiom* headed for a specific goal destination. ♦ *Bill accidentally got on a bus bound for Miami.* ♦ *Our baseball team is bound for glory.*

boundary ['baʊn dri] *n.* a border; a line that marks the edge of a thing or a place. ♦ *Where is the boundary of your property?* ♦ *A fence marked the boundary of the woods.*

bountiful ['baʊn tə fʊl] *adj.* abundant; having plenty of something. (Adv: *bountifully* ['baʊn tə fli].) ♦ *The harvest was bountiful this year.* ♦ *The pantry is stocked with a bountiful supply of canned vegetables.*

bouquet [bo 'ke] **1.** *n.* an arrangement of cut flowers; a grouping of cut flowers that can be held in one hand. (From French.) ♦ *John sent me a bouquet of flowers for my birthday.* ♦ *The bouquet was made up of tulips, daffodils, and jonquils.* **2.** *n.* the characteristic aroma of a type of wine. ♦ *David tested the wine's bouquet by sniffing the wine in his glass.* ♦ *How would you describe the wine's bouquet?*

bourbon ['bɚ bən] *n.* a type of American whiskey made from corn and other grains. (No plural form in this sense. Named for Bourbon County, Kentucky, where it was first made. From French.) ♦ *The cake was flavored* *with bourbon.* ♦ *The liquor store had a lot of bourbon in stock.*

bout ['bɑʊt] **1.** *n.* an attack of a disease. ♦ *Mary is still weak after her bout with the flu.* ♦ *When it's rainy, Grandpa suffers from bouts of arthritis.* **2.** *n.* a period of heavy alcoholic drinking. ♦ *The cowboys went on a drinking bout after a long day on the ranch.* ♦ *The drunken bout ended when the sailors passed out.* **3.** *n.* a specific contest or event, especially a boxing match. ♦ *The boxer prepared for the major bout.* ♦ *The best fighter won the bout.*

boutique [bu 'tik] *n.* a small store, or a department within a larger store, that sells fancy clothes, accessories, or other personal items. (From French.) ♦ *I bought a birthday gift at a local boutique.* ♦ *The new boutique had a promotion on imported perfumes.*

bovine ['bo vɑɪn] *adj.* cattle-like; relating to cattle. ♦ *A large number of bovine creatures grazed on the plains.* ♦ *The rancher killed many cattle to prevent the bovine disease from spreading.*

bow 1. ['bo] *n.* a decorative knot, usually with two or more large loops. ♦ *The wreath had a huge velvet bow.* ♦ *The little girl wore bows in her hair.* **2.** ['bo] *n.* a weapon that shoots arrows. ♦ *The archer drew his bow as the deer entered the clearing.* ♦ *The arrow flew from the bow as the archer released the string.* **3.** ['bo] *n.* a stick with strings of hair stretched from end to end, used to play a stringed instrument, such as a violin. ♦ *The violinist waved her bow in the air with a flourish as she finished playing.* ♦ *The musician drew his bow across the strings of his cello.* **4.** ['bɑʊ] *n.* an act of bending the body in deference or in acknowledgment. ♦ *I made a bow to my host as I entered the room.* ♦ *When I was in Japan, I greeted my host with a deep bow.* **5.** ['bɑʊ] *n.* the front part of a ship or a boat. ♦ *The bow of the ship pointed north as we left the harbor.* ♦ *Mary sat in the bow of the rowboat.* **6.** ['bo] *iv.* to bend into a curve, like the shape of ②; to form a curve. ♦ *The old man's legs bowed slightly.* ♦ *The walls of the wooden shed bowed because they were not strong enough to support the roof.* **7.** ['bɑʊ] *iv.* to bend the body in deference; to bend the body when greeting someone. ♦ *The servant bowed before the king.* ♦ *We bowed to each other upon meeting.* **8.** ['bɑʊ] *iv.* to acknowledge applause by bending at the waist. ♦ *The singer bowed before the audience.* ♦ *The jester bowed before the king and queen.* **9. bow to** ['bɑʊ...] *iv.* + *prep. phr.* to comply with someone's wishes; to consent to someone's wishes; to defer to someone else's desires. ♦ *I bow to your greater wisdom.* ♦ *Bill bowed to his parents' wishes that he go to law school.* **10.** ['bo] *tv.* to cause something to bend into a curve, like the curve of ②; to cause something straight to form a curve. ♦ *The weight of the books bowed the shelf.* ♦ *The heavy roof bowed the walls of the wooden shack.* **11. bow and scrape** ['bɑʊ...] *idiom* to be very humble and subservient. (On ⑦.) ♦ *Please don't bow and scrape. We are all equal here.* ♦ *The salesclerk came in, bowing and scraping, and asked if he could help us.*

bowel ['bɑʊ əl] **1.** *n.* the upper or lower intestine; the upper and lower intestine. ♦ *The spicy meal wreaked havoc with Bill's bowels.* ♦ *Tom was afflicted with a severe pain in the upper bowel.* **2. bowels** *n.* the inner part of something; the deep interior of something; the inner workings of something. (Figurative on ①.) ♦ *The cave led the geologist to the bowels of the earth.* ♦ *The supplies were stored in the bowels of the building.* **3. bowel movement** *n.* an act of expelling feces. ♦ *The pain in his abdomen was relieved by a bowel movement.* ♦ *I usually have a bowel movement once a day.*

bowl ['bol] **1.** *n.* a deep, rounded dish; a deep, rounded container. ♦ *The bowl on the kitchen table had apples and oranges in it.* ♦ *We made small bowls in ceramics class.* **2.** *n.* the contents of ①. ♦ *Every morning Bill eats a bowl of cereal for breakfast.* ♦ *I offered our guests a bowl of fruit.* **3.** *n.* the part of a pipe that holds the tobacco. ♦ *David packed the tobacco into the bowl of his pipe.* ♦ *When he was finished, David tapped the bowl of his pipe into the ashtray.* **4.** *n.* a special football game; a championship football game. ♦ *Which teams are playing in the Rose Bowl this year?* ♦ *The college team hoped to play in one of the bowls.* **5.** *iv.* to go bowling; to play the game of bowling. ♦ *Jane and Sue bowl every Friday night.* ♦ *John bowls on a league every Wednesday night.* **6. bowl someone over** *idiom* to overwhelm or surprise someone. ♦ *We were bowled over by the expensive wedding gift.* ♦ *David bowled his parents over with his report card.*

bowlegged ['bo lɛg ɪd] *adj.* having legs that bow outward. (Adv: *bowleggedly.*) ♦ *The newborn calf was a bit bowlegged.* ♦ *The pediatrician examined the bowlegged child.*

bowler ['bol ɚ] *n.* someone who plays the game of bowling. ♦ *An experienced bowler does not roll balls into the gutter very often.* ♦ *The tournament I went to was for beginning bowlers.*

bowling ['bol ɪŋ] *n.* a game where a player rolls a large, hard ball along a narrow wooden floor in order to knock down as many as possible of the ten pins at the other end. (No plural form in this sense. See also alley.) ♦ *We went bowling at the alley near my house.* ♦ *I find bowling to be a very relaxing pastime.*

bow-wow ['bɑʊ 'wɑʊ] *n.* a sound made by barking dogs. ♦ *The puppy went "bow-wow" at the cat.* ♦ *The toy dog said "bow-wow" when its tail was pulled.*

box ['bɑks] **1.** *n.* a rigid, cube-shaped container, used for storage or delivery. ♦ *The books were stored in boxes in the basement.* ♦ *The present came in a fancy box.* **2.** *n.* the contents of ①. ♦ *The cookie recipe called for a box of raisins.* ♦ *I used a whole box of nails repairing the fence.* **3.** *n.* a private seating area in a sports stadium, theater, etc. ♦ *We sat in a box at the baseball field.* ♦ *The opera house had private boxes for wealthy patrons.* **4.** *n.* a square printed on a piece of paper or on a form. ♦ *Check the box when you complete the task.* ♦ *I checked the box that indicated my salary range.* **5.** *n.* [in baseball] the place where a batter stands to hit a ball. ♦ *The player approached the box, swinging the bat.* ♦ *The batter readied himself at the box for the pitch.* **6.** *n.* [in soccer and hockey] the place where penalized players sit. ♦ *The angry player was sent to the penalty box.* ♦ *The hockey players filled the box after the brawl.* **7.** *n.* any of a number of different square or rectangular containers or receptacles. ♦ *I went to the letter box to mail my letter.* ♦ *The employee dropped an angry note in the suggestion box.* **8.** *n.* a hit or a punch, especially to the ears. ♦ *The unruly boy received a sharp box on the ears.* ♦ *The kitten gave the ball a box.* **9.** *iv.* to fight in a boxing match. ♦ *The two fighters boxed in the ring.* ♦ *The heavyweight champ was injured and no longer boxes.*

10. *tv.* to strike someone on the ear. ♦ *The old man boxed the boy's ears.* ♦ *The schoolmaster was reprimanded for boxing ears.* **11. box (up)** *tv.* (+ *adv.*) to put something into a box; to wrap something up in a box. ♦ *The salesclerk boxed the gift that I had purchased.* ♦ *I boxed up the dishes for the move.* **12. stuff the ballot box** *idiom* to put fraudulent ballots into a ballot box; to cheat in counting the votes in an election. ♦ *The election judge was caught stuffing the ballot box in the election yesterday.* ♦ *Election officials are supposed to guard against stuffing the ballot box.*

boxcar ['bɑks kɑr] *n.* an enclosed railway car that carries freight. ♦ *The boxcars were filled with cargo.* ♦ *A few hobos traveled in the boxcars of freight trains.*

boxer ['bɑks ɚ] **1.** *n.* someone who boxes; someone who fights in boxing matches. ♦ *The boxer suffered brain damage in his last bout.* ♦ *The boxers climbed into the ring to begin the fight.* **2.** *n.* a breed of medium-sized dog, tan with a somewhat flat face. ♦ *Bill likes dogs—especially boxers.* ♦ *Three boxers were entered in the dog show.* **3. boxers** See boxer shorts.

boxer shorts AND **boxers** ['bɑks ɚ 'ʃorts, 'bɑks ɚz] *n.* men's underpants having loose, short legs. (Treated as plural.) ♦ *Bob prefers boxers to briefs.* ♦ *Dave wears boxers, briefs, and bikinis—he is not particular.*

boxing ['bɑks ɪŋ] *n.* the sport of fighting with fists or gloved fists. (No plural form in this sense.) ♦ *Boxing is a dangerous sport.* ♦ *My roommates like to watch boxing on TV and bet on which fighter will win.*

boy ['bɔɪ] **1.** *n.* a male human, not yet fully matured. ♦ *The boy often plays with toy trucks.* ♦ *The boys organized a football game at school.* **2.** *n.* a man of any age; one of a group of male friends; one of a group of men. ♦ *The boys are coming over for poker tonight.* ♦ *Dave went out with the boys, and Mary spent the day with the grandchildren.* **3. (Oh,) boy!** *interj.* <an exclamation of excitement, surprise, dismay, etc.> ♦ *"Boy! That was a good movie!" Jimmy exclaimed.* ♦ *Oh, boy! Cake for dessert!*

boycott ['bɔɪ kɑt] **1.** *n.* an organized effort where people refuse to have dealings with someone or something as a means of coercion. ♦ *The boycott was organized to protest human rights violations.* ♦ *A few citizens organized a boycott of the grocery store.* **2.** *tv.* to refuse to have dealing with someone or something as a means of coercion. ♦ *All the angry customers boycotted the grocery store.* ♦ *Our country boycotted the nation accused of human rights violations.*

boyfriend ['bɔɪ frɛnd] *n.* a male sweetheart; a male lover. ♦ *Jane finally brought her boyfriend home to meet her parents.* ♦ *Mary had a lot of boyfriends before she married.*

boyhood ['bɔɪ hʊd] *n.* the period of time when a male is a (young) boy; youth. (No plural form in this sense.) ♦ *Dave's boyhood was spent on a farm in Minnesota.* ♦ *A few photographs were Dad's only record of his boyhood.*

boyish ['bɔɪ ɪʃ] *adj.* like a boy. (Adv: *boyishly.*) ♦ *Mary's boyish haircut looks good on her.* ♦ *Even as an adult, Tom had a boyish face.*

bra ['brɑ] *n.* a piece of women's underclothing that gives support to the breasts; a brassiere. ♦ *The department store had a sale on bras and other undergarments.* ♦ *Mary adjusted the straps on her bra.*

brace ['bres] **1.** *n.* a support; something that holds something else in place. ♦ *The physical therapist gave Jane a brace for her injured knee.* ♦ *The rope acted as a brace to hold the tree upright.* **2.** *n.* a printed character used to set off items or to enclose a set of words; { and }. (Compare with bracket ②.) ♦ *Put the sentence in braces.* ♦ *The information was enclosed in braces.* **3.** *tv.* to prepare oneself for an impact or other dislocating force. (Takes a reflexive object.) ♦ *Brace yourself. We are going around a curve.* ♦ *Just before the accident, Sue braced herself.* **4.** *tv.* to prepare oneself for bad news. (Takes a reflexive object.) ♦ *I braced myself when the test scores were announced.* ♦ *When the telegram arrived, we braced ourselves for the worst.* **5. braces** *n.* metal wires or bands attached to teeth to straighten them. ♦ *The orthodontist put braces on Bill's teeth.* ♦ *Jane has worn braces for three years.*

bracelet ['bres lɪt] *n.* a piece of jewelry worn around the wrist. ♦ *I received a gold bracelet for my birthday.* ♦ *The gold bracelet fell off Bob's wrist, and he never found it.*

bracket ['bræk ɪt] **1.** *n.* an L-shaped object attached to a wall to support a shelf. ♦ *The shelf rested on the brackets.* ♦ *When books were put on the shelf, the bracket came loose from the wall.* **2.** *n.* a printed character used to set off items or to enclose a set of words; [and]. ♦ *The extra information is in brackets.* ♦ *The notation in brackets is important.* **3. (tax) bracket** *n.* one of a series of federal income-tax rates. ♦ *Jane's raise put her in a higher tax bracket.* ♦ *The upper bracket gets taxed more than the lower ones.* **4.** *tv.* to enclose something in brackets [such as these words]. ♦ *Bracket the words you want removed from the text.* ♦ *The editor bracketed the unimportant words.*

brackish ['bræk ɪʃ] *adj.* salty; tasting of salt. ♦ *The glass of water has a brackish taste to it.* ♦ *The freshwater fish could not live in the brackish water.*

brad ['bræd] *n.* a small nail. ♦ *I repaired the picture frame with a few brads.* ♦ *The hardware store had a sale on brads.*

brag ['bræg] **1.** *iv.* to boast; to speak too highly of oneself. ♦ *The boss bragged about himself all the time.* ♦ *Bill is always bragging!* **2.** *tv.* to claim something in a boastful manner. (Takes a clause.) ♦ *Sue bragged that she could eat an entire pie in two minutes.* ♦ *Everyone was tired of hearing John brag that he was wealthy.*

braggart ['bræg ɚt] *n.* someone who brags; someone who boasts. ♦ *Soon, everyone at the office ignored the braggart.* ♦ *Mary is a braggart who talks about her successes constantly.*

braid ['bred] **1.** *tv.* to interweave three or more strands of rope or bundles of hair, string, etc., into one rope-like band. ♦ *Jane braided her long hair every morning.* ♦ *The artisan braided the grass to make a basket.* **2.** *n.* a rope-like band made of interwoven strands. ♦ *Jane's braids swung from side to side.* ♦ *The basket was made from braids of grass.*

Braille ['brel] *n.* an alphabet for blind people, made up of raised dots that are read with the fingers. (Named for Louis Braille, who developed the system. No plural form in this sense.) ♦ *The library stocked a lot of books published in Braille.* ♦ *The blind child had only two books in Braille.*

brain ['bren] **1.** *n.* the part of the central nervous system inside the head that is the center of thinking and feeling and that controls the movement and operation of the body. ♦ *The scientists compared the brains of different types* *of animals.* ♦ *The surgeons removed a tumor from the patient's brain.* **2.** *n.* a very smart person; a genius. (Informal.) ♦ *Tom is no brain at calculus.* ♦ *I don't know anyone who is a real brain at physics.* **3.** *tv.* to smash someone's skull; to strike someone's head very hard. ♦ *In the cartoon, the mouse brained the cat with a frying pan.* ♦ *Bob really brained the quarterback during football practice.*

brainchild ['bren tʃɑɪld] *n.* an invention; a discovery; an original work. (No plural form in this sense. The figurative offspring of one's intellect.) ♦ *Mary's brainchild was organizing a recycling drive.* ♦ *The social programs were the president's brainchild.*

brainless ['bren ləs] *adj.* stupid; dumb; not smart. (Adv: *brainlessly.*) ♦ *Forgetting to turn the oven on was really a brainless thing to do.* ♦ *The brainless student spoke before thinking.*

brainstorm ['bren storm] **1.** *n.* an idea; an inspiration; a sudden thought that solves a problem. ♦ *I had a brainstorm as I was falling asleep last night.* ♦ *Dave's brainstorm saved the company a lot of money.* **2.** *iv.* [for a group of people] to work together to think up many possible solutions to a problem. ♦ *Tom and Mary brainstorm whenever there is a problem.* ♦ *The manager told us to get together and brainstorm.*

brainwash ['bren wɑʃ] *tv.* to systematically indoctrinate someone with new attitudes and thoughts. ♦ *The enemy brainwashed its prisoners of war.* ♦ *The cult leaders tried to brainwash their followers.*

brainy ['bren i] *adj.* smart; intelligent. (Informal. Adv: *brainily.* Comp: *brainier;* sup: *brainiest.*) ♦ *I asked my brainy friend to help me with my homework.* ♦ *The brainy students participated in the science fair.*

braise ['brez] *tv.* to cook food with a small amount of liquid slowly in a covered pot. ♦ *The chef braised the pot roast slowly.* ♦ *The recipe said to braise the turkey leg in a skillet for an hour.*

brake ['brek] **1.** *n.* a device that slows or stops a machine or vehicle. (Often plural. Compare with **break.**) ♦ *Mary's car needs new brakes.* ♦ *I crashed because the brakes on my bike were faulty.* **2.** *tv.* to cause something to stop or slow down. (Pt/pp: *braked.*) ♦ *Brake the car to slow down.* ♦ *The engineer braked the train to bring it to a stop.* **3.** *iv.* to stop or slow down. ♦ *The bicyclists braked at the stop sign.* ♦ *The driver didn't bother to brake for the pedestrians.* **4. break up** *iv.* + *adv.* [for something] to reach an end. ♦ *The meeting broke up about noon.* ♦ *Their marriage broke up, and both Jane and Bob left town.*

bramble ['bræm bəl] *n.* a prickly shrub; a prickly bush of the rose family. ♦ *Deer roamed through the brambles in the forest.* ♦ *The once-beautiful garden was overrun with brambles.*

bran ['bræn] *n.* the edible skin or husk of grains, ground away and separated from the flour. (No plural form in this sense.) ♦ *I love muffins made with bran.* ♦ *Bran provides a good source of fiber.*

branch ['bræntʃ] **1.** *n.* a part of a tree that grows out of the trunk; an arm-like part of a tree. ♦ *The branches had ripe apples on them.* ♦ *Bill gathered some dry branches for the fire.* **2.** *n.* a small stream or river that joins to a larger river. ♦ *The map showed all of the river's branches.* ♦ *The explorers followed a dried-up branch.* **3.** *n.* a division of a company; a subsidiary of a larger company. ♦ *The company has many branches that produce other products.* ♦ *Susan moved from one branch of her company to another.* **4. branch (out) into** *iv.* (+ *adv.*) + *prep. phr.* to diversify into something. ♦ *The painter branched into sculpting late in her career.* ♦ *The publisher branched out into electronic products.*

brand ['brænd] **1.** *n.* a trade name; the name of a product by which the product is widely recognized. ♦ *The recipe calls for a certain brand of mayonnaise.* ♦ *To save money, I buy generic brands rather than well-known brands.* **2.** *n.* a special kind or type of something. ♦ *The dictator's brand of democracy is not really democracy at all.* ♦ *The owner's brand of management is unfair to the employees.* **3.** *n.* an identification mark burned into the skin of cattle. ♦ *The cattle bore the brand of the Triple D ranch.* ♦ *Mary thinks it's cruel to give animals brands.* **4.** *tv.* to mark cattle with identification marks by burning them into their skin. ♦ *The cattle were branded with a red-hot iron.* ♦ *The ranchers branded their calves each spring.* **5.** *tv.* to accuse someone of being something; to stigmatize someone. (Figurative on ④.) ♦ *The student was branded a cheater by the teachers.* ♦ *The government branded the company as corrupt.*

brandish ['bræn dɪʃ] *tv.* to display something in a threatening way. ♦ *Mary brandished her report while she argued with her boss.* ♦ *The robber brandished a gun.*

brand-new ['brænd 'nu] *adj.* completely new; entirely new. ♦ *The showroom was filled with brand-new cars.* ♦ *Jane showed me her brand-new ring.*

brandy ['bræn di] **1.** *n.* an alcoholic drink distilled from wine or other fermented fruit juices. (No plural form in this sense.) ♦ *After the meal, expensive brandy was served.* ♦ *I use brandy in fine cooking, but I couldn't afford to drink it!* **2.** *n.* a serving of ①. ♦ *I ordered a brandy after dinner.* ♦ *Shall we have brandies after dinner?*

brash ['bræʃ] *adj.* bold; rash; recklessly showy. (Adv: *brashly.* Comp: *brasher;* sup: *brashest.*) ♦ *The brash patron demanded to be served ahead of the others.* ♦ *Bill made a brash suggestion at work and was ignored.*

brashness ['bræʃ nəs] *n.* recklessness; impudence. (No plural form in this sense.) ♦ *The teenager's brashness led to an early death.* ♦ *Bob is known for his brashness in dealing with late employees.*

brass ['bræs] **1.** *n.* a metal made from copper and zinc. (No plural form in this sense.) ♦ *The door knocker was made of brass.* ♦ *Our new candlesticks were made of solid brass.* **2.** *n.* the family of wind instruments made of brass or some other metal, including the trumpet, trombone, and tuba. (No plural form in this sense.) ♦ *Bill especially likes the sound of brass.* ♦ *The brass played powerfully, but the strings were weak.* **3. the brass** *n.* important people within the military or other organization; the bosses. (No plural form in this sense. Treated as singular or plural.) ♦ *The military base was cleaned up for the brass's visit.* ♦ *The company brass paid a visit to the factory.* **4.** *adj.* made out of ①. ♦ *The old brass candlesticks were badly tarnished.* ♦ *Mary fastened a brass knocker to the front door.* **5.** *adj.* <the adj. use of ②.> ♦ *There were three trumpets in the brass section of the orchestra.* ♦ *Jane played the trombone in a brass band.*

brassiere [brə 'zɪr] *n.* a piece of women's underclothing that gives support to the breasts. (From French.) ♦ *The department store had a sale of brassieres and other undergarments.* ♦ *Mary bought a new brassiere and a slip.*

brat ['bræt] *n.* an unruly child; an ill-behaved child. (Derogatory.) ♦ *By the day's end, the teacher was frustrated with the brats in class.* ♦ *The little brat asked the adults how much money they made.*

brava ['brɑ və] See bravo.

bravado [brə 'vɑd o] *n.* a show of unnecessary boldness. (No plural form in this sense.) ♦ *The commander's bravado did not impress the soldiers.* ♦ *The princess was shocked by the knight's bravado.*

brave ['brev] **1.** *n.* an Amerindian warrior. ♦ *The braves rode their horses to the white settlement.* ♦ *The pioneers ran into the Indian braves on the prairie.* **2.** *adj.* showing courage; willing to face danger. (Adv: *bravely.* Comp: *braver;* sup: *bravest.*) ♦ *The brave little boy stood up to the bully.* ♦ *The brave patient faced a very complex surgery.* **3.** *tv.* to withstand something; to face something without fear. ♦ *Anne braved the storm in order to make it to the wedding.* ♦ *We braved Anne's temper and told her about the broken vase.*

bravery ['brev ə ri] *n.* courage; fearlessness. (No plural form in this sense.) ♦ *The firefighter became known for bravery.* ♦ *It takes a lot of bravery to face the unknown.*

bravo AND **brava** ['brɑv o, 'brɑ vɑ] **Bravo!; Brava!** *interj.* "Well done!" (Called out at the end of a performance where a performer has done excellent work. In opera, Bravo! is used for males, and Brava! is used for females. *Bravi* is used occasionally as the plural.) ♦ *The conductor bowed to cheers of "Bravo, bravo!"* ♦ *Not a single "Bravo" was heard in the theater, but the applause was thunderous.*

brawl ['brɔl] **1.** *n.* a fight; a loud, violent argument. ♦ *The disagreement soon erupted into a brawl.* ♦ *The pool hall was the site of a bloody brawl.* **2.** *iv.* to fight; to argue loudly. ♦ *The children brawled with each other constantly.* ♦ *The two men were always brawling about some stupid thing.*

brawny ['brɔn i] *adj.* muscular; of a large and muscular appearance. (Adv: *brawnily.* Comp: *brawnier;* sup: *brawniest.*) ♦ *The construction workers were all brawny.* ♦ *The brawny weightlifter exercised every day.*

brazen ['brez ən] **1.** *adj.* made of brass. ♦ *Brazen doorknobs decorated the heavy door.* ♦ *The museum exhibited some brazen artifacts from West Africa.* **2.** *adj.* shameless; impudent. (Adv: *brazenly.*) ♦ *The brazen hussy flirted with the police officer.* ♦ *The brazen accusation was denied.*

Brazil [brə 'zɪl] See Gazetteer.

breach ['britʃ] **1.** *n.* a crack; a gap; a break. (Compare with breech.) ♦ *The flood was caused by a small breach in the dam.* ♦ *The rude comment was a real breach of etiquette.* **2.** *tv.* to break a promise; not to do what was agreed upon. ♦ *The real-estate agent breached the agreement with her clients.* ♦ *Tom breached his contract with the company.* **3.** *tv.* to split something; to break into something. ♦ *The enemy breached the wall of the fort.* ♦ *The force of the water breached the dam and caused the flood.*

bread ['brɛd] **1.** *n.* a type of food made by baking a mixture of flour, yeast, and water. (No plural form in this sense. Treated as singular. Number expressed with *piece(s)* or *slice(s)* or *loaves of bread.*) ♦ *I eat bread with every meal.* ♦ *Mike bought a fresh loaf of bread at the bakery.* **2.** *tv.* to cover food with crumbs or meal before cooking it. ♦ *The scallops were breaded before they were sautéed.* ♦ *The cook breaded the pork chops before frying them.* **3. bread and butter** *idiom* someone's livelihood or income. ♦ *Selling cars is a lot of hard work, but it's my bread and butter.* ♦ *It was hard to give up my bread and butter, but I felt it was time to retire.*

breadbox ['brɛd bɑks] *n.* a container that bread and other baked goods are kept in. ♦ *A little mouse crept into the breadbox on the counter.* ♦ *I placed the dinner rolls in the breadbox.*

breadcrumb ['brɛd krəm] *n.* a tiny crumb of bread. ♦ *The peasants were starving for even a breadcrumb.* ♦ *Breadcrumbs were sprinkled on top of the casserole.*

breadth ['brɛdθ] **1.** *n.* width; the measurement of something from side to side. ♦ *The shelf has a breadth of two feet.* ♦ *We measured the length of the couch but forgot to measure its breadth.* **2.** *n.* extent. ♦ *The breadth of the project was larger than I had thought.* ♦ *Bill has a wide breadth of experience from his travels.*

breadwinner ['brɛd wɪn ɚ] *n.* one person who supports the others in a family. ♦ *John is the breadwinner in his family.* ♦ *Mary became the sole breadwinner when her husband lost his job.*

break ['brek] **1.** *n.* a fracture. ♦ *The doctor suspected a break when the boy came in limping badly.* ♦ *A serious break in his wrist bone prevented Bob from writing.* **2.** *n.* a gap; a split. ♦ *A small break in a blood vessel caused some internal bleeding.* ♦ *We noticed a break in the windowpane.* **3.** *n.* a short period of rest from work. ♦ *I took a break from mowing the lawn because I was tired.* ♦ *The workers took a coffee break at 2:30.* **4.** *n.* the period of time between school terms. ♦ *Jane worked at a bank during her break.* ♦ *We went to Florida for spring break.* **5.** *n.* a breaking out of jail or prison. ♦ *The break was thwarted when prison guards discovered the plot.* ♦ *Only one break occurred at the prison in ten years.* **6.** *n.* the ending of a relationship with someone or something; the ending of an association with someone or something. ♦ *Jane tried to make the break easy for Bill, but he took it badly.* ♦ *Bill made a clean break with his business partner.* **7.** *n.* a stop in a continuous action; an interruption. ♦ *A power outage caused a break in our routine.* ♦ *A break in telephone service meant that I missed an important call.* **8.** *n.* a chance to do something; an opportunity to do something. ♦ *The performer got his first break when he was twenty.* ♦ *All Jane needed was a break, and her career would be a success.* **9.** *n.* the opening shot in a game of pool that scatters all of the balls from their original set-up. ♦ *Max will only play pool if he can make the break.* ♦ *The pool player made a bad break.* **10.** *tv., irreg.* to cause something to fall apart; to smash something; to make something fall apart. (Pt: broke; pp: broken.) ♦ *I broke the cookie in two and gave half to Anne.* ♦ *The queen broke a bottle of champagne to christen the ship.* **11.** *tv., irreg.* to damage something; to make something not work correctly; to make something unusable. ♦ *The children broke the remote control for the television.* ♦ *Jane accidentally broke her sister's camera.* **12.** *tv., irreg.* to crack something; to fracture something, especially a bone. ♦ *Jane broke her leg in three places.* ♦ *Bill broke his collarbone when he fell down the stairs.* **13. break of** *tv.,* *irreg.* + *prep. phr.* to cause oneself to stop doing something. ♦ *Bill finally broke the dog of its bad habits.* ♦ *I just can't seem to break myself of the smoking habit.* **14.** *tv., irreg.* to violate an agreement or promise by failing to do what was promised. ♦ *That company is known for breaking its promises.* ♦ *Jane broke her agreement with her business partner.* **15.** *tv., irreg.* to exchange a large unit of money for the same amount of money in smaller units. ♦ *Bill asked the cashier to break a hundred-dollar bill.* ♦ *The cab driver couldn't break our twenty-dollar bill.* **16.** *iv., irreg.* to shatter; to smash; to fall apart. ♦ *The glass broke when it hit the tile floor.* ♦ *How did this vase break?* **17.** *iv., irreg.* to fail to operate; not to function. ♦ *How did the camera break?* ♦ *The clock broke, so we were all late for work.* **18.** *iv., irreg.* to crack; to fracture. ♦ *The ice broke as it started to thaw.* ♦ *His leg broke when he fell.* **19.** *iv., irreg.* [for someone's voice] to crack because of the onset of puberty or from emotion. ♦ *I was so upset that my voice broke when I spoke.* ♦ *Jimmy's voice began to break when he was thirteen.* **20. break into** *iv., irreg.* + *prep. phr.* to enter a closed area by force. ♦ *The crooks broke into the office and stole some files.* ♦ *I forgot my key and had to break into my own house!* **21. break a code** *idiom* to figure out a code; to decipher a code. ♦ *The intelligence agents finally broke the enemy's code.* ♦ *When they broke the code, they were able to decipher messages.* **22. break a habit; break the habit; break one's habit** *idiom* to end a habit. ♦ *I was not able to break the habit of snoring.* ♦ *It's hard to break a habit that you have had for a long time.* **23. break a record** *idiom* to destroy a previously set high record by setting a new one. ♦ *The athlete broke all the school records in swimming.* ♦ *The record was broken after thirty years.* **24. break up (with someone)** *idiom* to end a romantic relationship with someone. ♦ *Tom broke up with Mary and started dating Lisa.* ♦ *We broke up in March, after an argument.* **25. make a break for something** *idiom* to make a sudden rush toward something. ♦ *When it started raining, we made a break for shelter.* ♦ *The cat made a break for the door when it was opened.* **26. break something to someone** *idiom* to tell bad news to someone. ♦ *I hated to break the news to Dad about his car.* ♦ *Bill broke it to his employees gently.*

breakable ['brek ə bəl] *adj.* fragile; capable of being broken. (Adv: *breakably.*) ♦ *Careful—those antiques are quite breakable!* ♦ *We packed the breakable items in newspaper.*

breakage ['brek ɪdʒ] *n.* damage—where things are broken—to goods or property. (No plural form in this sense.) ♦ *The store reported considerable breakage in the shipment of glasses.* ♦ *The insurance agent surveyed the breakage after the storm.*

breakdown ['brek daʊn] **1.** *n.* the cessation of correct operation; a mechanical failure. ♦ *My car is always having a breakdown.* ♦ *The computer breakdown was not caused by anything serious.* **2.** *n.* a study or an analysis of the various parts that make up something. ♦ *The committee presented a breakdown of the budget.* ♦ *Please give me a breakdown of all the areas of responsibility.* **3.** *n.* a nervous collapse; a crisis caused by mental fatigue. (Figurative on ①.) ♦ *After his father's death, we feared Tom was on the verge of a breakdown.* ♦ *We urged Susan to take a vacation so she wouldn't have a breakdown.*

breaker ['brek ɚ] *n.* a large wave with a white crest. ♦ *We sat on the beach and watched the breakers come in.* ♦ *Breakers pounded the shore with incredible force.*

breakfast ['brɛk fəst] **1.** *n.* the first meal of the day. ♦ *My breakfast is usually just coffee and toast.* ♦ *On Sundays, we have waffles and eggs for breakfast.* **2.** *iv.* to eat ① [somewhere]. ♦ *In the summer, we breakfast on the porch.* ♦ *We breakfasted at the local restaurant.*

breakneck ['brek nɛk] *adj.* [of speed] very fast, dangerous, or reckless. ♦ *The children did their chores at breakneck speed.* ♦ *The traffic went by at a breakneck pace.*

breakthrough ['brek θru] *n.* a sudden discovery; a major discovery of a crucial fact. ♦ *The scientists were hoping to make a breakthrough in cancer treatments.* ♦ *After years of experimenting, the inventor finally had a breakthrough.*

breast ['brɛst] **1.** *n.* the chest; the part of the body between the neck and the stomach. (Formal or literary.) ♦ *The baby nestled on its mother's breast.* ♦ *Grandpa rested the book on his breast and took a nap.* **2.** *n.* the edible upper body of a fowl. ♦ *As he cut up the chicken, Dad asked who wanted a breast and who wanted a leg.* ♦ *We cooked the chicken breasts on the barbecue.* **3.** *n.* one of the two milk-producing glands on the chest of the human female. ♦ *Each breast was examined for cancer.* ♦ *The baby fed at its mother's breast.* **4. make a clean breast of something** *idiom* to confess something. ♦ *You'll feel better if you make a clean breast of it. Now tell us what happened.* ♦ *I was forced to make a clean breast of the whole affair.*

breastbone ['brɛst bon] *n.* the thin, flat bone to which the ribs are connected over the heart. ♦ *The ribs are attached to the breastbone.* ♦ *Bill broke his breastbone in the car accident.*

breast-fed ['brɛst fɛd] *adj.* fed at the breast in infancy, rather than from a bottle. ♦ *Breast-fed infants receive many nutrients from their mothers' milk.* ♦ *The breast-fed baby was weaned at six months.*

breaststroke ['brɛst strok] *n.* a way of swimming in a prone position where the arms are worked together as oars. (No plural form in this sense.) ♦ *Jane did the breaststroke so she wouldn't get her hair wet.* ♦ *Bill won the backstroke but lost in the breaststroke.*

breath ['brɛθ] **1.** *n.* the air that moves in and out of the body during breathing. ♦ *I drew a breath of the fresh air and felt very much alive.* ♦ *When Bob took a breath of the stale air, he almost choked.* **2.** *n.* someone's exhaled air, especially if felt or smelled. ♦ *No one wanted to tell Bill that he had bad breath.* ♦ *Jane could feel the baby's breath on her neck.* **3. time to catch one's breath** *idiom* to find enough time to relax or behave normally. ♦ *When things slow down around here, I'll get time to catch my breath.* ♦ *Sally was so busy she didn't even have time to catch her breath.* **4. in the same breath** *idiom* [stated or said] almost at the same time; as part of the same thought or conversation. ♦ *He told me I was lazy, but then in the same breath he said I was doing a good job.* ♦ *The teacher said that the students were working hard and, in the same breath, that they were not working hard enough.* **5. take someone's breath away** *idiom* to overwhelm someone with beauty or grandeur. ♦ *The magnificent painting took my breath away.* ♦ *Ann looked so beautiful that she took my breath away.* **6. waste one's breath**

idiom to waste one's time talking; to talk in vain. ♦ *Don't waste your breath talking to her. She won't listen.* ♦ *You can't persuade me. You're just wasting your breath.*

breathe ['brið] **1.** *iv.* to take air into the lungs and expel air from the lungs. ♦ *I could hardly breathe when the weather became hot and humid.* ♦ *The athlete breathed heavily after the strenuous workout.* **2.** *tv.* to inhale or exhale something; to take something into the lungs or expel something from the lungs or throat. ♦ *The hikers breathed the fresh mountain air.* ♦ *The label on the can of paint warned that breathing paint fumes may be dangerous.* **3. breathe down someone's neck** *idiom* to try to hurry someone along; to make someone get something done on time. ♦ *I have to finish my taxes today. The tax collector is breathing down my neck.* ♦ *I have a deadline breathing down my neck.* **4. breathe one's last** *idiom* to die; to take one's last breath. ♦ *Mrs. Smith breathed her last this morning.* ♦ *I'll keep running every day until I breathe my last.* **5. hardly have time to breathe** *idiom* to be very busy. ♦ *This was such a busy day. I hardly had time to breathe.* ♦ *They made him work so hard that he hardly had time to breathe.*

breathless ['brɛθ ləs] *adj.* out of breath; gasping for air owing to hard work, exercise, etc. (Adv: *breathlessly.*) ♦ *Jane and Bill were breathless after their run.* ♦ *The breathless child tried to tell what he'd seen.*

breathlessly ['brɛθ ləs li] *adv.* holding one's breath in anticipation. ♦ *We waited breathlessly to hear the name of the contest winner.* ♦ *The children sat breathlessly waiting to open their presents.*

breathtaking ['brɛθ tek ɪŋ] *adj.* spectacular; awesome; overwhelming. (Adv: *breathtakingly.*) ♦ *The artist's painting was simply breathtaking.* ♦ *We watched the breathtaking sunset without speaking.*

breathy ['brɛθ i] *adj.* having a whispered voice; speaking so that breathing is also heard. (Adv: *breathily.* Comp: *breathier;* sup: *breathiest.*) ♦ *The obscene phone caller spoke in a breathy voice.* ♦ *Mary had a breathy voice because she smoked so much.*

bred ['brɛd] pt/pp of breed.

breech ['britʃ] **1.** *n.* the lower portion of a gun, cannon, barrel, etc. (Compare with breach.) ♦ *John carefully took the breech of the gun in his hands.* ♦ *Anne polished the breech of her rifle.* **2.** *adj.* [of birth] with the buttocks first; [of a baby] born with buttocks first. ♦ *Jane had a breech birth with her second child.* ♦ *The doctors delivered the breech baby as quickly as possible.*

breed ['brid] **1.** *n.* a group within a species; a subgroup of a certain species. ♦ *Anne only likes certain breeds of dogs.* ♦ *Our dog is a mixed breed.* **2.** *n.* a kind of something; a class of something. ♦ *After they became wealthy, the Browns had a new breed of problems to contend with.* ♦ *This decade has produced a new breed of politician.* **3.** *iv., irreg.* to propagate; to mate. (Pt/pp: bred.) ♦ *How does that type of insect breed?* ♦ *The two dogs bred and produced a large litter.* **4.** *tv., irreg.* to propagate a species, often for specific genetic traits. ♦ *The local veterinarian also breeds horses.* ♦ *The Smiths tried to breed their dog with the neighbor's.* **5.** *tv., irreg.* to cause something; to produce something; to generate something. (Figurative on ④.) ♦ *"Familiarity breeds contempt," an old saying says.* ♦ *Spoiling a child breeds selfish behavior.*

breeder ['brid ɚ] *n.* someone who breeds plants or animals, often for specific genetic traits. ♦ *The breeder came up with a new hybrid tulip.* ♦ *The breeder only worked with healthy animals.*

breeze ['briz] **1.** *n.* a light wind; a gentle wind. ♦ *The wind chimes tinkled in the gentle breeze.* ♦ *A gentle breeze swept over the porch and cooled us.* **2.** *n.* something that is very easy; something that is easily done. (Informal.) ♦ *The test was a breeze!* ♦ *Cooking might be a breeze for you, but it's not for me.* **3. breeze through** *iv. + prep. phr.* to progress easily and swiftly through something. ♦ *The athlete breezed through the workout.* ♦ *The children breezed through their homework.*

breezeway ['briz we] *n.* a room or covered path between a garage and a house. ♦ *Please take your shoes off in the breezeway.* ♦ *Mary locked the door between the garage and the breezeway.*

breezy ['briz i] *adj.* with a gentle wind blowing. (Adv: *breezily.* Comp: *breezier;* sup: *breeziest.*) ♦ *It was breezy along the coast today.* ♦ *Riding in the convertible was breezy.*

brevity ['brɛv ə ti] *n.* shortness; the quality of being brief. (No plural form in this sense.) ♦ *The employees appreciated the brevity of the president's speech.* ♦ *The students appreciated the brevity of the weekend homework assignment.*

brew ['bru] **1.** *n.* a liquid drink produced by heating various ingredients. ♦ *The wizard made a special brew to cure the sick man.* ♦ *The witch stirred her brew in a cauldron.* **2.** *n.* a beer; a kind of beer. (Informal.) ♦ *The tavern served many different brews.* ♦ *Which brew do you prefer?* **3.** *tv.* to make a liquid drink by mixing and heating various ingredients. ♦ *Jane brews her tea in a special way.* ♦ *The witch brewed a love potion.* **4.** *tv.* to make beer or ale. ♦ *John brews his own beer at home.* ♦ *The clerk at the brewery explained how to brew beer.* **5.** *iv.* to develop; to gather; to form. ♦ *We could tell by the clouds that a storm was brewing.* ♦ *"Trouble is brewing," Mary said.* **6.** *iv.* [for a liquid drink] to develop into its final form. ♦ *I could smell the beer that was brewing at the brewery.* ♦ *Some sort of herb tea was brewing in the kitchen.* **7.** *iv.* [for a plot] to develop. (See ⑨.) ♦ *The teacher overheard a plot brewing at recess.* ♦ *The king suspected that a plot was brewing among his knights.* **8.** *iv.* [for a storm] to develop. ♦ *A storm was brewing to the east.* ♦ *The thunderclouds alerted us that a storm was brewing.* **9. brew a plot** *idiom* to plot something; to make a plot. ♦ *The children brewed an evil plot to get revenge on their teacher.* ♦ *We brewed a plot so that we would not have to help with dinner.*

brewer ['bru ɚ] *n.* someone who makes beer; someone who brews beer. ♦ *The brewer made several types of beer.* ♦ *This beer comes from a brewer in Germany.*

brewery ['bru ɚ i] *n.* a place where beer is made. ♦ *Our guests wanted to take a tour of the brewery.* ♦ *You can smell the neighborhood brewery a mile away.*

bribe ['brɑɪb] **1.** *n.* an offer of something, especially money, in exchange for a favor from someone. ♦ *Sue offered Jimmy a bribe of cake if he ate all of his carrots.* ♦ *The politician was accused of accepting bribes.* **2.** *tv.* to offer someone something, especially money, in exchange for a favor. ♦ *Sue had to bribe Jimmy to get him to eat his vegetables.* ♦ *The prisoner bribed the guard to look the other way as he escaped.*

bribery ['brɑɪb ə ri] *n.* giving someone an exchange of money for a favor. (No plural form in this sense.) ♦ *Dave had to resort to bribery to get his son to behave.* ♦ *The politician was accused of bribery.*

brick ['brɪk] **1.** *n.* a rectangular block—used in building things—made of cement or baked clay. ♦ *The front of my house is faced with bricks.* ♦ *Bob laid bricks in the backyard to form a patio.* **2.** *adj.* built of ①. ♦ *The brick house was more than a hundred years old.* ♦ *Anne laid a brick patio in her backyard.* **3. brick up** *tv.* + *adv.* to cover an opening with bricks. ♦ *The mason bricked up the hole in the wall.* ♦ *Previous owners of our house bricked the fireplace up.* **4. hit (someone) like a ton of bricks** *idiom* to surprise, startle, or shock someone. ♦ *Suddenly, the truth hit me like a ton of bricks.* ♦ *The sudden tax increase hit like a ton of bricks. Everyone became angry.*

bricklayer ['brɪk le ɚ] *n.* someone who puts bricks into place; a mason. ♦ *It took three bricklayers to complete the fireplace on schedule.* ♦ *This wall was constructed by professional bricklayers.*

bridal ['brɑɪd l] **1.** *adj.* relating to a wedding, especially the bride. ♦ *The picture showed the entire bridal party in front of the church.* ♦ *Sue tossed her bridal bouquet to the bridesmaids.* **2. bridal registry** See registry.

bride ['brɑɪd] **1.** *n.* a woman who is about to be married or has just been married. ♦ *The bride received many beautiful gifts as wedding presents.* ♦ *Everyone congratulated the bride and groom after the ceremony.* **2. give the bride away** *idiom* [for the father of ①] to accompany ① to where the groom is standing in a wedding ceremony. ♦ *Mr. Brown is ill. Who'll give the bride away?* ♦ *In the traditional wedding ceremony, the bride's father gives the bride away.*

bridegroom ['brɑɪd grum] *n.* a groom; a man who is about to be married or has just been married. ♦ *The bridegroom waited anxiously at the altar.* ♦ *The bridegroom made a toast to his new bride.*

bridesmaid ['brɑɪdz med] *n.* a woman who attends the bride at a wedding. ♦ *Jane was a bridesmaid at her best friend's wedding.* ♦ *How many bridesmaids were in Anne's wedding?*

bridge ['brɪdʒ] **1.** *n.* an elevated way over a river, street, train tracks, etc. ♦ *A wooden bridge spanned the creek.* ♦ *San Francisco is known for its Golden Gate Bridge.* **2.** *n.* something that links people or things. (Figurative on ①.) ♦ *The deal formed a bridge between the two companies.* ♦ *The marriage created a bridge between the feuding families.* **3.** *n.* the navigation and control center of a ship. ♦ *The captain stood on the bridge of the ship.* ♦ *The entire crew reported to the bridge to take the captain's orders.* **4.** *n.* the upper part of the nose; the part of the nose between the eyes. ♦ *These glasses don't fit the bridge of my nose well.* ♦ *The ball hit Bill on the bridge of his nose.* **5.** *n.* the part of a pair of eyeglasses that rests on the nose. ♦ *The optometrist adjusted the bridge of my glasses.* ♦ *I don't like the bridge on that style of glasses.* **6.** *n.* a type of card game for four people. (No plural form in this sense.) ♦ *Bill, Tom, Jane, and Mary played bridge all day.* ♦ *Jane found a deck of cards, so we all played bridge.* **7.** *tv.* to resolve a conflict between two people, two groups of people, or different ideas. (Figurative on ②.) ♦ *A counselor helped the couple bridge their differences.* ♦ *The peace plan bridged the conflicts between the warring nations.* **8. cross a bridge before one comes to it** *idiom* to worry excessively about something before it happens. ♦ *There is no sense in crossing that bridge before you come to it.* ♦ *She's always crossing bridges before coming to them. She needs to learn to relax.* **9. water under the bridge** *idiom* [of a problem] past and forgotten. ♦ *Please don't worry about it anymore. It's all water under the bridge.* ♦ *I can't change the past. It's water under the bridge.* **10. burn one's bridges (behind one)** *idiom* to make decisions that cannot be changed in the future. ♦ *If you drop out of school now, you'll be burning your bridges behind you.* ♦ *You're too young to burn your bridges that way.*

bridle ['brɑɪd l] **1.** *n.* a set of straps that fit on a horse's head and allow a rider to control the horse. ♦ *The rider adjusted the horse's bridle.* ♦ *Mary yanked on the bridle to stop the horse.* **2.** *tv.* to put ① on a horse. ♦ *Jane bridled her horse before leaving the stable.* ♦ *Mary decided to ride bareback and didn't bridle or saddle the horse.* **3.** *tv.* to restrain something, usually anger or something similar. ♦ *Sue bridled her anger at the inconvenience.* ♦ *John had to bridle his resentment at Tom's good fortune.*

brief ['brif] **1.** *adj.* short in time; to the point. (Adv: *briefly.* Comp: *briefer;* sup: *briefest.*) ♦ *The police chief gave a brief statement on the status of the case.* ♦ *We'll have a brief meeting tomorrow morning.* **2.** *n.* [in law] a document that describes certain facts or information about a case or a client. ♦ *The law students wrote many briefs during the semester.* ♦ *The paralegal wrote a brief for the attorney.* **3. briefs** *n.* short and close-fitting underpants. (Treated as plural.) ♦ *Tom prefers white cotton briefs.* ♦ *Bill sat around the house in briefs and a T-shirt on hot days.* **4.** *tv.* to acquaint someone with certain facts or information. ♦ *Our manager briefed us on company sales for the year.* ♦ *The general briefed the troops about their mission.*

briefcase ['brif kes] *n.* a flat case with a handle, for carrying papers and documents. ♦ *The college graduate received a briefcase as a present.* ♦ *Dave left his briefcase on the train this morning.*

briefing ['brif ɪŋ] *n.* a meeting where someone provides information about something. ♦ *The troop's briefing was held at dawn.* ♦ *The police held a briefing to update the press on the case.*

briefly ['brif li] **1.** *adv.* in as few words as possible; concisely. ♦ *Please tell me briefly everything that you saw.* ♦ *The director briefly described the new policy and then asked if we had any questions.* **2.** *adv.* for a short time. ♦ *I can only meet with you briefly.* ♦ *Jane had to wait briefly at the doctor's office.*

brigand ['brɪg ənd] *n.* a bandit; a robber. ♦ *The brigands who held up the stagecoach were never caught.* ♦ *Jesse James is a famous brigand of the 1800s.*

bright ['brɑɪt] **1.** *adj.* shiny; full of light; reflecting much light. (Adv: *brightly.* Comp: *brighter;* sup: *brightest.*) ♦ *I wore dark glasses because the sun was so bright.* ♦ *The restaurant was too bright to have a romantic atmosphere.* **2.** *adj.* smart; intelligent. (Adv: *brightly.* Comp: *brighter;* sup: *brightest.*) ♦ *The bright students asked the curator many questions about the dinosaur exhibit.* ♦ *It was not very bright to leave the tools out in the rain.* **3.** *adj.* vivid; brilliant. (Adv: *brightly.* Comp: *brighter;* sup: *brightest.*)

♦ *Tom is wearing a bright green shirt.* ♦ *The reds in the colorful painting were very bright.*

brighten ['brɑɪt n] **1.** *iv.* to give off more light; to become brighter. ♦ *The room brightened when we turned on the overhead light.* ♦ *The silver tea set brightened as I polished it.* **2.** *tv.* to make something shiny; to cause something to reflect more light; to polish something. ♦ *A little furniture polish will brighten that old table.* ♦ *The lamp brightened the work space.* **3.** *tv.* to make someone or something cheerier. ♦ *Your kind words really brightened my day.* ♦ *A few paintings will brighten the room.*

brightly ['brɑɪt li] *adv.* with much light. ♦ *The street lamps shone brightly against the night.* ♦ *The moon glowed brightly in the nighttime sky.*

brightness ['brɑɪt nəs] **1.** *n.* the quality of being shiny or well lit. (No plural form in this sense.) ♦ *The photographer adjusted the brightness of the lamps.* ♦ *Our eyes quickly adjusted to the brightness when the sun came out.* **2.** *n.* intelligence. (No plural form in this sense.) ♦ *Jimmy tried to hide his brightness because the other kids teased him.* ♦ *No one doubted Jimmy's brightness, but he got terrible grades.*

brilliance ['brɪl jəns] **1.** *n.* brightness; shininess. (No plural form in this sense.) ♦ *The brilliance of the gem contrasted with the black velvet of its case.* ♦ *I was astounded by the brilliance of the sunlight on the ocean.* **2.** *n.* intelligence; a talent for a skill or an art. (No plural form in this sense.) ♦ *The violinist's musical brilliance was evident at an early age.* ♦ *The scientist's brilliance is evident from these experiments.*

brilliant ['brɪl jənt] **1.** *adj.* bright; shiny. (Adv: *brilliantly.*) ♦ *The brilliant light of noon made me squint.* ♦ *The brilliant sun scorched the desert.* **2.** *adj.* intelligent; smart; talented. (Adv: *brilliantly.*) ♦ *The brilliant student was accepted by numerous universities.* ♦ *The students at the music camp are all thought to be brilliant.* **3.** *adj.* excellent. (Adv: *brilliantly.*) ♦ *Mary gave a brilliant presentation to the committee.* ♦ *Her brilliant performance received good reviews from the critics.*

brilliantly ['brɪl jənt li] *adv.* brightly; shinily. ♦ *The ocean sparkled brilliantly in the setting sun.* ♦ *The sun shone brilliantly on the snow-covered mountains.*

brim ['brɪm] **1.** *n.* the top edge of something, such as a cup. ♦ *I filled my coffee cup to the brim.* ♦ *A bird perched on the brim of the flowerpot.* **2.** *n.* the circular, flat, projecting edge of a hat. ♦ *The brim of the hat was decorated with a clump of silk flowers.* ♦ *The wind caught the brim of my hat, and it blew off my head.* **3. brimming with something** *idiom* full to the point of overflowing. ♦ *Tom's glass was brimming with milk.* ♦ *The pool was brimming with water.* **4. brimming with something** *idiom* full of some kind of happy behavior. ♦ *The volunteer worker was brimming with goodwill.* ♦ *The giggling children were brimming with joy.*

brine ['brɑɪn] **1.** *n.* sea water. (No plural form in this sense.) ♦ *Many tiny creatures live in the brine.* ♦ *This fish cannot live in fresh water—it needs brine.* **2.** *n.* a mixture of salt and water, as used for pickling. (No plural form in this sense.) ♦ *The pickles were bottled in brine.* ♦ *Rinse the brine off the pickle before eating it.*

bring ['brɪŋ] **1.** *tv., irreg.* to carry or escort someone or something from a more distant place to a closer place. (Pt/pp: brought.) ♦ *Please bring that package to me.* ♦ *Please bring your son into the doctor's office.* **2.** *tv., irreg.* to cause something to happen; to result in something. ♦ *April showers bring May flowers.* ♦ *The pill brought me quick relief from my headache.* **3. bring with** *tv., irreg. + prep. phr.* to carry or escort someone or something along with oneself. ♦ *Don't worry. I will bring it with me.* ♦ *Bring a friend with you when you come to the picnic.* **4. bring to** *tv., irreg. + prep. phr.* to cause oneself to do something. (Takes a reflexive object.) ♦ *Anne brought herself to the point of asking for a raise.* ♦ *I couldn't bring myself to leave my hometown.* **5.** *tv., irreg.* to cause something to enter into a different state. ♦ *Jane brought her car to a stop and got out.* ♦ *Let's bring this matter to an end.* **6. bring someone or something up** *idiom* to mention a topic, question, or person's name. ♦ *Why did you have to bring Bob's name up while I am eating?* ♦ *I want to bring this matter up for a vote.*

brink ['brɪŋk] **1.** *n.* the edge of a surface or space next to a steep drop. ♦ *I stood on the brink of the chasm and peered over the edge.* ♦ *A fence was built along the brink of the cliff to prevent accidents.* **2.** *n.* the moment just before something happens. ♦ *We rose at the brink of dawn and saw the sunrise.* ♦ *The nation waited nervously on the brink of war for some good news.*

brisk ['brɪsk] **1.** *adj.* [of movement, actions, activity, or rhythm] quick, rapid, or swift; [of rhythm, music, or activity] lively. (Adv: *briskly.* Comp: *brisker;* sup: *briskest.*) ♦ *A brisk walk before breakfast is a good way to start the day.* ♦ *The band played a brisk march as the soldiers paraded down the street.* **2.** *adj.* abrupt. (Adv: *briskly.* Comp: *brisker;* sup: *briskest.*) ♦ *The doctor, after a few brisk inquiries, gave a diagnosis.* ♦ *John was known for his brisk manner around the office.* **3.** *adj.* stimulating; chilly. (Adv: *briskly.* Comp: *brisker;* sup: *briskest.*) ♦ *A brisk wind blew from the north.* ♦ *We hiked through the forest on a brisk fall day.*

bristle ['brɪs əl] **1.** *n.* short, stiff hair, as on a brush. ♦ *The hog's back was covered with coarse bristles.* ♦ *The bristles on the brush scratched Mary's scalp.* **2.** *iv.* [for an animal's hairs or bristles] to raise up, showing anger or as a threat. ♦ *The cat's fur bristled when it saw the chipmunk.* ♦ *The hair on the dog's neck bristled as we approached.* **3.** *iv.* to adopt a posture or facial expression indicating anger or a threat; to display anger or resentment. (Figurative on ②.) ♦ *Dave bristled when he heard about his demotion.* ♦ *Mary bristled when she discovered that Anne lied to her.*

Britain ['brɪt n] See Gazetteer.

British ['brɪt ɪʃ] **1.** *n.* the English people. (No plural form in this sense. Also used for the people of Great Britain: the English, Scottish, and Welsh people. This sense is not always acceptable to the Scottish and Welsh people.) ♦ *The British can trace their history back many centuries.* ♦ *The British are fond of their monarchs.* **2.** *adj.* <the adj. use of ①.> (Adv: *Britishly.*) ♦ *Tea in the afternoon is a British tradition.* ♦ *Australia, India, and Canada are former British colonies.*

brittle ['brɪt əl] *adj.* hard, but easily cracked or broken. (Comp: *brittler;* sup: *brittlest.*) ♦ *Dried flowers are very brittle.* ♦ *The brittle plastic cup broke when it hit the floor.*

broad ['brɔd] **1.** *adj.* wide; vast; extensive; far-reaching. (Adv: *broadly.* Comp: *broader;* sup: *broadest.*) ♦ *The plains* *are broad and flat.* ♦ *We crossed the broad river by ferry.* **2.** *adj.* main; general. (Adv: *broadly.* Comp: *broader;* sup: *broadest.*) ♦ *The professor explained the theory in very broad terms.* ♦ *Please give me a broad explanation.* **3. in broad daylight** *idiom* in the open; clearly visible. ♦ *The crime was committed in broad daylight.* ♦ *Bill stood there in broad daylight, but we never saw him.*

broadcast ['brɔd kæst] **1.** *n.* a television or radio program. ♦ *The broadcast of the program was interrupted for a special report.* ♦ *The radio station gave a broadcast of the baseball game.* **2.** *tv.* to transmit a radio or television signal or program. ♦ *The baseball game was broadcast on the radio.* ♦ *The station would not broadcast the comedian's foul language.* **3.** *tv.* to make news widely known; to tell something to many people. ♦ *Bill broadcast the news of Mary's promotion to the entire office.* ♦ *The company buyout was broadcast by the media.* **4.** *iv.* to transmit radio waves. ♦ *The new station will start broadcasting tomorrow.* ♦ *This station doesn't broadcast after midnight.*

broadcaster ['brɔd kæs tɚ] **1.** *n.* someone who reads news or information aloud on the radio or television. ♦ *The news broadcaster began laughing during the report.* ♦ *The broadcaster always spoke with a dignified voice.* **2.** *n.* a company in the business of operating a radio or a television station. ♦ *The broadcaster was known for its excellent news service.* ♦ *A local broadcaster was sued by an angry listener.*

broaden ['brɔd n] **1.** *tv.* to make something that is flat wider than it was. ♦ *The clothing designer wanted to broaden the lapels of the jacket, but it was too late.* ♦ *The city broadened the road at the dangerous turn.* **2.** *tv.* to increase the scope of something. ♦ *The company tried to broaden the appeal of its product.* ♦ *Bill started to broaden his interests in college.* **3.** *iv.* to become wider; to widen. ♦ *The river broadens after it goes through the canyon.* ♦ *Bill's shoulders broadened as he became a teenager.*

broad-minded ['brɔd 'mɑɪn dɪd] *adj.* tolerant; liberal; open-minded. (Adv: *broad-mindedly.*) ♦ *The broad-minded couple became strict and traditional once they started raising children.* ♦ *The broad-minded professor was popular with the young students.*

broadside ['brɔd sɑɪd] **1.** *adv.* sideways; to the side of something; on the side of something. ♦ *The tank rammed the car broadside.* ♦ *A truck ran a red light and hit a taxi broadside.* **2.** *tv.* to ram into the side of something; to run into the side of something; to crash into the side of something. ♦ *The truck broadsided the car and destroyed it.* ♦ *Our car was broadsided in the accident.* **3.** *tv.* to attack strongly. (Figurative on ②.) ♦ *The movie was broadsided by a bitter critic.* ♦ *The media broadsided the politician at every opportunity.*

Broadway ['brɔd we] **1.** *n.* the theater district in New York City, thought of as the center of theater in the U.S. (No plural form in this sense.) ♦ *Someday I hope to go to Broadway and be a star.* ♦ *Broadway is where all the best plays and musicals are performed.* **2.** *adj.* <the adj. use of ①.> ♦ *Tom is starring in a Broadway musical.* ♦ *Whenever I am in New York, I go see a Broadway show.* **3. on Broadway** *idiom* located in ①; currently performing or being performed in ①. ♦ *Our musical is the best thing on Broadway!* ♦ *I want to be a star on Broadway someday.*

brocade [bro 'ked] *n.* cloth that has a raised pattern woven into it. (No plural form in this sense.) ♦ *The wedding dress was made of a beautiful brocade.* ♦ *The delicate curtains are made of brocade.*

broccoli ['brɑk ə li] *n.* a green vegetable that grows in branched stalks ending in clumps of buds. (From Italian. No plural form in this sense.) ♦ *I had meatloaf and broccoli for dinner.* ♦ *The grocery store offered lots of fresh broccoli.*

brochure [bro 'ʃʊr] *n.* a pamphlet; a piece of paper or booklet that describes something. ♦ *The preacher stood on the street corner handing out brochures.* ♦ *The manager of the repair shop printed a brochure about his shop's services.*

brogue ['brog] **1.** *n.* a kind of Irish or Scots accent in spoken English. ♦ *We guessed that the man with the brogue was from Ireland.* ♦ *The actor spoke with a brogue for his role as an Irishman.* **2.** *n.* any heavy, regional accent. ♦ *From John's brogue, I knew he was from Scotland.* ♦ *The immigrant didn't lose her gentle brogue for years.*

broil ['broɪl] **1.** *tv.* to cook something by placing it over an open flame in a grill or under an oven's broiler. ♦ *Mary broiled salmon steaks for her dinner party.* ♦ *I will broil the pork chops.* **2.** *iv.* [for food] to cook over an open flame on a grill or under an oven's broiler. ♦ *The meat is broiling on the grill.* ♦ *The chef on TV said that fish broils well over a hot fire.*

broiled ['broɪld] *adj.* [of food] grilled over an open flame or under a broiler. ♦ *My favorite dinner is broiled pork chops.* ♦ *Broiled meat has fewer calories than fried meat.*

broiler ['broɪl ɚ] **1.** *n.* a cooking device that sears food with radiant heat. ♦ *Tom put the steaks under the oven's broiler.* ♦ *Anne has an outdoor broiler for summer cooking.* **2.** *n.* a tender, young chicken raised to be broiled. ♦ *David bought a broiler at the grocery store.* ♦ *The butcher wrapped up a broiler for Mary.*

broke ['brok] **1.** pt of break. **2.** *adj.* having no money; completely without money; penniless. ♦ *I was broke after buying a new car.* ♦ *Mary stayed home last weekend because she was broke.* **3. flat broke** *idiom* having no money at all. ♦ *I spent my last dollar, and I'm flat broke.* ♦ *The bank closed its doors to the public. It was flat broke!*

broken ['brok ən] **1.** pp of break. **2.** *adj.* not working; not functioning; not operating; busted; out of order. ♦ *The carpenter repaired the broken rung of a ladder.* ♦ *I took the broken television set to the repair shop.* **3. broken English** *n.* English as spoken by someone who does not speak English well. ♦ *The man talked to me in broken English, and I could not be certain what he said.* ♦ *Many people in the countries I visited spoke only broken English.*

broken-down ['brok ən 'dɑʊn] *adj.* not working; worn out. ♦ *We bought a broken-down house and renovated it.* ♦ *John finally sold his broken-down car.*

brokenhearted ['brok ən 'hɑrt ɪd] *adj.* grieving; unhappy; full of sadness. (Adv: *brokenheartedly.*) ♦ *The family was brokenhearted when they had to sell the house.* ♦ *The brokenhearted man said he'd never date again.*

broker ['brok ɚ] *n.* someone who manages the exchange of goods or a service for a commission. ♦ *Our stockbroker helped us choose our investments.* ♦ *A real-estate broker helped us buy our house.*

brokerage ['brok ə rɪdʒ] *n.* a company that arranges the sale of something—stock or real estate—in exchange for commission. ♦ *Our stock brokerage advised us on our investments.* ♦ *I contacted a real-estate brokerage because I wanted to buy a house.*

bronchitis [brɑŋ 'kɑɪt ɪs] *n.* an illness where the air passages leading to the lungs are inflamed or infected. (No plural form in this sense.) ♦ *The smoker developed a chronic case of bronchitis.* ♦ *Bronchitis made it difficult for Dave to breathe.*

bronco ['brɑŋ ko] *n.* a wild horse; an untamed horse. (From Mexican Spanish. Pl in *-s*.) ♦ *The cowboy was unable to tame the wild bronco.* ♦ *We saw a herd of broncos from a distance.*

bronze ['brɑnz] **1.** *n.* a brownish metal made from copper and tin. (No plural form in this sense.) ♦ *The statue was cast in bronze.* ♦ *Bronze carries electricity well.* **2.** *n.* a third-place medal; an award for coming in third place in a competition. ♦ *The skater took the bronze three years in a row.* ♦ *The winner of the bronze smiled for the photographers.* **3.** *adj.* made from ①. ♦ *The bronze statue stood in the courtyard.* ♦ *The athlete proudly wore her bronze medal.* **4.** *adj.* the color of ①; yellowish or reddish brown. ♦ *The tourist was bronze after two weeks in the Mediterranean sun.* ♦ *The couch was a bronze and black plaid.* **5.** *tv.* to cover something with ①; to coat something with ①. ♦ *Mary bronzed her children's baby shoes.* ♦ *The baseball museum bronzed the famous catcher's mitt.* **6.** *iv.* to become tan; to get a tan from the sun. ♦ *The tourists bronzed in the Mediterranean sun.* ♦ *Bill is fair and does not bronze in the sun.*

bronzed ['brɑnzd] **1.** *adj.* covered with bronze; coated with bronze. ♦ *Bill and Anne preserved the bronzed baby shoes.* ♦ *The museum curator unveiled the bronzed statue.* **2.** *adj.* tan; dark golden-brown. ♦ *The bronzed tourists went to the beach every day.* ♦ *Jane's bronzed skin was dried out from the sun.*

brooch ['brotʃ] *n.* a decorative pin used as a piece of jewelry. ♦ *Grandma always wore a brooch on her collar.* ♦ *Jane wore her mother's brooch to the party.*

brood ['brud] **1.** *n.* a group of birds that are hatched at the same time. ♦ *The duck herded her brood around the park.* ♦ *The quacking brood of ducks waddled in circles.* **2.** *n.* a group of brothers and sisters. (Informal.) ♦ *John and Mary took their brood to the museum.* ♦ *The whole Smith brood attended the same university.* **3.** *tv.* [for a bird] to sit on eggs to hatch them or to sit on its young. ♦ *The robin brooded her eggs protectively.* ♦ *We could not tell if the bird was brooding its eggs or not.* **4. brood about; brood on** *iv.* + *prep. phr.* to dwell on a thought or a problem; to worry over a problem; to ponder a problem. ♦ *The manager brooded over the problem for days.* ♦ *The jury brooded on the verdict for three days.*

brooding ['brud ɪŋ] **1.** *adj.* [of a bird] sitting on chicks or hatching eggs. ♦ *The brooding bird looked around its nest anxiously.* ♦ *Quite please. Don't disturb the brooding hen on her nest.* **2.** *adj.* dwelling on a thought; fretting; worrying. (Figurative on ①. Adv: *broodingly*.) ♦ *The brooding prisoner simply stared at the wall.* ♦ *The brooding expression on Bill's face was troubling.*

brook ['brʊk] *n.* a stream; a creek; a small river. ♦ *The brook tumbled over the round stones as it flowed down the slope.* ♦ *The kids discovered a brook in the woods.*

broom ['brum] *n.* a brush with a long handle that is used to sweep floors. ♦ *I used a broom to sweep up the sawdust from my project.* ♦ *Sue swept the patio with a broom.*

broomstick ['brum stɪk] *n.* the long handle of a broom. ♦ *Bill gripped the broomstick tightly as he swept the floor.* ♦ *I poked at the snake with the end of a broomstick.*

broth ['brɔθ] *n.* the liquid part of soup. (No plural form in this sense.) ♦ *The soup is made of chicken broth and rice.* ♦ *I ate only broth when I had the flu.*

brothel ['brɔθ əl] *n.* the place of business for one or more prostitutes. ♦ *The sheriff closed down the local brothel.* ♦ *The sleazy hotel was actually a brothel.*

brother ['brʌð ɚ] **1.** *n.* a male sibling. ♦ *Jane has three brothers and a sister.* ♦ *My brother has three children.* **2.** *n.* a male comrade; a male member of the same union, profession, or organization as another male. ♦ *John and Bill are fraternity brothers.* ♦ *The soldiers were brothers in battle.* **3.** *n.* a member of a religious order who is not a priest; a man who is studying to become a priest. (Also a term of address.) ♦ *A devotional prayer was led by the brother.* ♦ *Brother Thomas led the monks in song.* **4. (Oh,) brother!** *interj.* <an expression of mild annoyance or surprise.> (Informal.) ♦ *Brother! What a mess!* ♦ *Oh, brother! Meatloaf again.*

brotherhood ['brʌð ɚ hʊd] **1.** *n.* the bond between brothers ①. (No plural form in this sense.) ♦ *Their brotherhood was evident in their actions towards each other.* ♦ *Brotherhood meant a great deal to Bill and Tom Jones.* **2.** *n.* the bond between brothers ②. (No plural form in this sense.) ♦ *The fraternity was based on brotherhood.* ♦ *The church stressed the importance of brotherhood.* **3.** *n.* the bond of peace between peaceful people. (No plural form in this sense.) ♦ *The president's speech mentioned the brotherhood of world peace.* ♦ *The organization worked to establish brotherhood of all citizens.*

brother-in-law ['brʌð ɚ ɪn lɔ] *n., irreg.* the husband of one's sister; the husband of the sister of one's spouse. (Pl: brothers-in-law.) ♦ *My brother-in-law is a musician.* ♦ *My sister's husband is my brother-in-law.*

brotherly ['brʌð ɚ li] *adj.* kind and helpful like a good brother. ♦ *Bill was always ready to lend a brotherly hand to Jane.* ♦ *Anne appreciated the brotherly advice from her neighbor.*

brothers-in-law ['brʌð ɚs ɪn lɔ] pl of brother-in-law.

brought ['brɔt] pt/pp of bring.

brow ['brɑʊ] **1.** *n.* the forehead. (See also eyebrow.) ♦ *The police officer's brow wrinkled as he listened to our story.* ♦ *Susan wiped the sweat from her brow while she exercised.* **2.** *n.* the top of a steep place. ♦ *The deer stood at the brow of the hill.* ♦ *The hikers made it to the brow of the mountain.* **3. knit one's brow** *idiom* to make wrinkles in ①, especially by frowning. ♦ *The woman knit her brow and asked us what we wanted from her.* ♦ *While he read his book, John knit his brow occasionally. He must not have agreed with what he was reading.*

brown ['brɑʊn] **1.** *n.* a deep, reddish tan color similar to the color of dirt or wood. (No plural form in this sense.) ♦ *The dreary painting was painted in grays and browns.* ♦

The walls were painted a dark brown. **2.** *adj.* of the color of ①. (Comp: *browner;* sup: *brownest.*) ♦ *My brown shoes matched my brown belt.* ♦ *The trees had brown trunks, except for the birches.* **3.** *tv.* to cook something until it turns dark or gets crisp. ♦ *Brown the ground beef in the skillet before adding it to the sauce.* ♦ *The cook browned the potatoes in the oven.* **4.** *iv.* [for food] to cook until it becomes ②. ♦ *How long will it take the ground beef to brown in the skillet?* ♦ *The potatoes are browning in the oven.*

brownie ['braʊn i] *n.* a rich, flat, chewy piece of chocolate cake. ♦ *Dave ate brownies and ice cream for dessert.* ♦ *Each child had a homemade brownie after lunch.*

brownout ['braʊn aʊt] *n.* a reduction of electrical power when there is not enough electricity to supply everyone. ♦ *The city suffered several brownouts last summer.* ♦ *During the energy crisis, brownouts were common.*

browse ['braʊz] **1.** *iv.* to look through goods casually when shopping. ♦ *Mary browsed through the shelves at the bookstore.* ♦ *We browsed among the racks of clothes but didn't intend to buy anything.* **2.** *iv.* [for an animal] to eat by nibbling. ♦ *The deer browsed on the grass near the woods.* ♦ *A huge giraffe browsed among the top branches of the tree.* **3.** *tv.* to search (through) the various sites on the Internet. ♦ *I found this recipe while I was browsing the Internet last night.* ♦ *The student who browsed the Net six hours a day had few other interests in life.*

browser ['braʊz ɚ] *n.* a type of computer software used to browse ③ the Internet, especially the World Wide Web. ♦ *My new browser is much faster and more useful than my old one.* ♦ *Without a good browser, you will never know what's on the World Wide Web.*

bruin ['bru ən] *n.* a bear; a brown bear. ♦ *The ranger warned that the park was full of young bruins.* ♦ *The bruins came close to our camp and gave us a scare.*

bruise ['bruz] **1.** *n.* a mark on the skin caused by being struck. ♦ *Mary got a bruise where she bumped against the table.* ♦ *The tennis ball made a bruise where it struck Bill.* **2.** *tv.* to cause ① by striking the body. ♦ *The tennis ball bruised Bill's arm when it struck him.* ♦ *The injuries bruised Jane's legs.*

bruised ['bruzd] *adj.* having colored marks on one's skin from injuries. ♦ *Sue showed everyone her bruised arm.* ♦ *Bill sustained a bruised back from the car accident.*

brunch ['brʌntʃ] *n.* a late breakfast or an early lunch. (**Br**eakfast + l**unch**.) ♦ *It was too early for lunch and too late for breakfast, so we had brunch.* ♦ *The tourists ate brunch at the hotel.*

brunette [bru 'nɛt] **1.** *n.* someone with brown or dark hair. ♦ *Jane was blonde as a child, but now she's a brunette.* ♦ *Bill's children are all brunettes.* **2.** *adj.* [of hair] brown or dark. ♦ *The suspect was tall and had brunette hair.* ♦ *The actor wore a brunette wig on stage.*

brunt ['brʌnt] *n.* the heaviest impact of something; the main force of something. (No plural form in this sense.) ♦ *The brunt of the work fell on the employees.* ♦ *The coastal village was hit with the brunt of the storm.*

brush ['brʌʃ] **1.** *n.* a device used for cleaning, combing, or painting—made of hard bristles attached to a handle. ♦ *I removed the rust from the car with a steel brush.* ♦ *Sue stroked her long hair with a brush.* **2.** *n.* a brief contact; an encounter. ♦ *After a brush with death, Dave's outlook on life improved.* ♦ *Mary had a brush with the law when she was pulled over for speeding.* **3.** *tv.* to clean something, such as one's teeth, with ①. ♦ *The children forgot to brush their teeth before bed.* ♦ *Jane brushed her dog's coat.* **4. brush on** *tv.* + *adv.* to apply paint or some other substance to a surface with ①. ♦ *Bill brushed the varnish on carefully.* ♦ *The painters brushed the second coat of paint on this morning.* **5.** *tv.* to arrange or groom hair with ①. ♦ *Go back upstairs and brush your hair!* ♦ *Each night before bed, Sue brushes her hair.* **6.** *tv.* to come in contact with something; to touch something lightly but not collide. ♦ *I am not hurt. The ball just brushed my ear.* ♦ *The bullet just brushed the officer's arm.*

brusque ['brʌsk] *adj.* abrupt and impolite; curt. (Adv: *brusquely.*) ♦ *The brusque salesclerk wasn't very helpful.* ♦ *Our brusque and careless waiter was lacking in manners.*

brutal ['brut əl] *adj.* violent and cruel; vicious. (Adv: *brutally.*) ♦ *The brutal king tortured his opponents.* ♦ *The brutal beast tore the deer to pieces.*

brutality [bru 'tæl ə ti] *n.* extreme violence. (No plural form in this sense.) ♦ *The newspapers published stories about the dictator's brutality.* ♦ *The brutality of the hunters angered the citizens.*

brutalize ['brut ə laɪz] *tv.* to be vicious and cruel to someone or something. ♦ *The tyrant brutalized the peasants for many years.* ♦ *The gang brutalized the neighborhood.*

brute ['brut] **1.** *n.* any animal except humans; a beast. ♦ *The brute charged the hunter.* ♦ *Bill came face to face with the furry brute.* **2.** *n.* a bully; someone who is cruel. ♦ *The brute met his match when a bigger and meaner boy came to school.* ♦ *The children wished someone would punish the brute.* **3.** *adj.* great [strength]; powerful [force]. ♦ *With brute strength, Bill pried open the door.* ♦ *The brute force of the tide can be very dangerous.*

bubble ['bʌb əl] **1.** *n.* a thin, spherical film of liquid that encloses a pocket of gas or air. ♦ *The soap made bubbles in the water.* ♦ *The children blew bubbles all day long.* **2.** *n.* a sphere of air within a solid or a liquid. ♦ *There were lots of tiny bubbles in the soft drink.* ♦ *Make sure you get the bubbles out of the cement.* **3.** *iv.* [for moving liquid] to make a sound that includes the popping or collapsing of ① or ②. ♦ *The water bubbled in the pot on the stove.* ♦ *The brook bubbled merrily along its way.* **4.** *iv.* to show much happiness, especially in one's speech. ♦ *Sue bubbled with excitement when she received her final grade.* ♦ *Bill always bubbles and giggles when he says hello to Mary.*

buck ['bʌk] **1.** *n.* the male of certain kinds of animals, such as deer and rabbits. ♦ *A large buck stood in the clearing in the forest.* ♦ *The buck had six points on its horns.* **2.** *n.* one American dollar bill; a dollar. (Slang.) ♦ *"Give me a few bucks for the groceries," Bill said.* ♦ *Jane found a couple of bucks under the sofa.* **3.** *iv.* [for an animal that is being ridden] to jump in an attempt to throw its rider. ♦ *Mary was afraid her horse would buck if it saw any cars.* ♦ *The horse bucked when the saddle was put on.* **4. pass the buck** *idiom* to pass the blame for something to someone else; to give the responsibility for something to someone else. ♦ *Don't try to pass the buck! It's your fault, and everybody knows it.* ♦ *Some people try to pass the buck whenever they can.*

bucket ['bʌk ɪt] **1.** *n.* a pail; an open-topped container with a curved wire handle. ♦ *The janitor rinsed the mop in a bucket of water.* ♦ *The farmer poured the cow's milk into a bucket.* **2.** *n.* the contents of ①. ♦ *The farmer spilled a bucket of milk in the barn.* ♦ *I mixed a small amount of soap with a bucket of water.*

buckle ['bʌk əl] **1.** *n.* a fastener for securing a belt or strap. ♦ *The buckle on my belt broke.* ♦ *The jacket had little brass buckles instead of buttons.* **2.** *tv.* to fasten a shoe, belt, etc., by using ①. ♦ *"One, two, buckle your shoe," starts the little poem.* ♦ *Sue buckled the belt around her waist.* **3.** *tv.* to cause pavement to bend and raise up. ♦ *The earthquake buckled several stretches of highway along the California coast.* ♦ *The summer heat buckled the roads.* **4.** *iv.* to be able to be fastened by means of a ①. ♦ *None of my shoes buckle, because they've all got laces.* ♦ *The belt is so old, it won't buckle anymore.* **5.** *iv.* [for pavement] to rise, fold, or break due to a force such as an earthquake or expansion caused by excessive heat. ♦ *The highway buckled during the earthquake.* ♦ *The hot sun made the sidewalk buckle.* **6.** *iv.* [for pavement] to raise up from expansion or pressure. ♦ *The highway buckled for miles along the coast during the earthquake.* ♦ *The sidewalk buckled in front of our house.* **7.** *iv.* [for someone's knees] to fold or collapse. ♦ *Anne's knees buckled when she fainted.* ♦ *Bill's knees almost buckled under the weight of the bricks he was carrying.*

buckshot ['bʌk ʃɑt] *n.* large, coarse, lead shot used in shotgun shells for hunting animals. (No plural form in this sense.) ♦ *Bill picked the buckshot out of the duck before he cooked it.* ♦ *The bottom of the pond was covered with hunters' buckshot.*

buckskin ['bʌk skɪn] **1.** *n.* leather made from the skin of a male deer. (No plural form in this sense.) ♦ *Buckskin is strong and supple.* ♦ *Fine gloves can be made from buckskin.* **2.** *adj.* made of ①. ♦ *Jane has a new buckskin jacket.* ♦ *Where are my buckskin gloves?*

buckteeth ['bʌk 'tiθ] pl of bucktooth.

bucktooth ['bʌk 'tuθ] *n., irreg.* an upper incisor that protrudes. (Pl: buckteeth.) ♦ *The orthodontist tried to fix John's bucktooth.* ♦ *Jimmy was adorable, even with his buckteeth.*

bud ['bʌd] **1.** *n.* the part of a plant that becomes a leaf or a flower. ♦ *In the spring, tiny buds appeared on all the trees.* ♦ *The cluster of buds bloomed into a gorgeous bouquet.* **2.** *n.* a flower that has not opened all the way; a flower whose petals are still wrapped together. ♦ *The bud of the flower never opened.* ♦ *Jimmy picked the flowers when they were just buds.* **3.** *iv.* [for a plant] to develop and open the parts that become leaves of flowers. ♦ *The trees budded in early April.* ♦ *The stunted rosebush never budded.* **4. nip something in the bud** *idiom* to put an end to something at an early stage. ♦ *John is getting into bad habits, and it's best to nip them in the bud.* ♦ *There was trouble in the classroom, but the teacher nipped it in the bud.*

Buddha ['bu də] *n.* an Indian religious leader—living around 500 B.C.—and the founder of Buddhism. (No plural form in this sense.) ♦ *Statues representing Buddha can be found in many parts of Southeast Asia.* ♦ *Buddha has attained full enlightenment.*

Buddhism ['bu dɪ zəm] *n.* one of the major religions of the world, practiced primarily in India, China, Japan, Tibet, and other Southeast Asian countries. (No plural form in this sense.) ♦ *Buddhism teaches that enlightenment can end human suffering.* ♦ *Buddhism is also practiced in Western countries.*

Buddhist ['bud əst] **1.** *n.* someone who practices Buddhism. ♦ *My nephew is a practicing Buddhist.* ♦ *Buddhists seek enlightenment.* **2.** *adj.* <the adj. use of ①.> ♦ *Buddhist monks sat in a row and recited prayers.* ♦ *We were advised to behave in a respectful manner when we visited the Buddhist temple.*

budding ['bʌd ɪŋ] *adj.* developing; up-and-coming; maturing; emerging. ♦ *The budding violinist loved to perform.* ♦ *The budding executive ignored ethical concerns.*

buddy ['bʌd i] *n.* a friend; a pal. (Also a term of address for a male whose full name is not known.) ♦ *Bill and his buddy went to a movie.* ♦ *Hey, buddy, move your car!*

budge ['bʌdʒ] **1.** *iv.* to move a little; to move a small amount due to great effort. (Usually in the negative.) ♦ *The bookcase would not budge when we tried to move it.* ♦ *The lid of the jar was stuck tight and would not budge.* **2.** *tv.* to move something a little; to move something a small amount with great effort. (Usually in the negative.) ♦ *Mother could not budge the bookcase, which must have weighed a ton.* ♦ *The door was stuck, and we couldn't budge it a bit.*

budget ['bʌdʒ ət] **1.** *n.* a financial plan; an estimate of how much money will be earned and spent during a period of time. ♦ *Sue was careful about adhering to her budget.* ♦ *The department's budget did not include money for electricity.* **2.** *n.* an amount of money allocated for a particular purpose. ♦ *Is there a budget for office supplies?* ♦ *The budget for groceries is two hundred dollars a month.* **3.** *tv.* to allocate or set aside an amount of money for a particular purpose. ♦ *We've budgeted $1,000 for advertising.* ♦ *Anne had not budgeted anything for emergencies.* **4.** *adj.* cheap; economical. ♦ *I don't mind buying the budget brands at the grocery store.* ♦ *The department store always has a budget rack of clothing.*

budgetary ['bʌdʒ ə tɛr i] *adj.* relating to a budget. (Adv: *budgetarily* [bədʒ ə 'tɛr ə li].) ♦ *Jane's vacation was canceled because of budgetary matters.* ♦ *The finance committee made a list of budgetary considerations.*

buff ['bʌf] **1.** *n.* a yellowish tan color. (No plural form in this sense.) ♦ *The hospital walls were painted in buff.* ♦ *Buff is not a becoming color on pale people.* **2.** *adj.* dull yellow in color; a yellowish tan. ♦ *All the kitchen appliances are buff.* ♦ *The walls of the school are painted a buff color.* **3.** *adj.* muscularly good-looking. (Slang. Comp: *buffer;* sup: *buffest.*) ♦ *The surfer was really buff.* ♦ *The models in the advertisement were all buff young men.* **4.** *tv.* to make something shiny or smooth by rubbing. ♦ *The manicurist buffed my nails.* ♦ *The maid buffed the silver tea set.*

buffalo ['bʌf ə lo] *n., irreg.* a type of wild ox native to Asia, Africa, and the Americas. (Pl: *buffalo, buffalos,* or *buffaloes.*) ♦ *The Indians hunted buffalo for food and hides.* ♦ *Cave drawings sometimes depict buffalos and other animals.*

buffer ['bʌf ɚ] **1.** *n.* a neutral space between two things, especially enemies. ♦ *The small strip of land acted as a buffer between the warring factions.* ♦ *The buffer didn't remain neutral for long.* **2.** *n.* someone or something that absorbs shock; someone or something that decreases the shock or impact between two things. ♦ *The talk-show moderator acted as a buffer between the guests.* ♦ *Sue was a buffer between her boss and the angry customers.* **3.** *n.* a portion of electronic memory in a computer used for the temporary storage of data. ♦ *The buffer was not large enough to hold the data.* ♦ *The computer stored the information temporarily in a buffer.* **4.** *n.* a machine used for polishing floors or other surfaces. ♦ *The janitor used a buffer on the wooden school floors.* ♦ *Bob rented a buffer from the local hardware store.*

buffet 1. [bə 'fe] *n.* a large cabinet for holding silverware and table linen, with a top from which food can be served. (From French.) ♦ *The buffet stood against the wall in the dining room.* ♦ *Grandma keeps the good china in the buffet.* **2.** [bə 'fe] *n.* a table or counter laden with food that diners can serve themselves. ♦ *The buffet featured all of our favorite foods.* ♦ *The restaurant offers a large and varied buffet.* **3.** [bə 'fe] *adj.* <the adj. use of ②.> ♦ *The church had a buffet supper.* ♦ *Anne arranged a lovely buffet table for her guests.* **4.** ['bʌf ət] *tv.* to bang someone or something around; to knock someone or something around. ♦ *The wind buffeted the travelers as they struggled to walk along the shore.* ♦ *The cat buffeted the chipmunk around.*

buffoon [bə 'fun] *n.* a fool; a clown; someone who tells a lot of jokes. ♦ *Bill always turns into a buffoon at parties.* ♦ *I thought Mary would be serious, but she's really quite a buffoon.*

bug ['bʌg] **1.** *n.* any small insect; any annoying insect. ♦ *Bugs crawled all over the plant.* ♦ *Bill saw a bug and quickly stepped on it.* **2.** *n.* the flu; any minor sickness. (Informal.) ♦ *Mary felt sick and thought she might have a bug.* ♦ *This particular bug gives its victims diarrhea.* **3.** *n.* some kind of electronic device that permits someone to eavesdrop on another person. ♦ *The police planted a bug in the suspect's apartment.* ♦ *With the bug, the detective listened to the conversations in the suspect's apartment.* **4.** *n.* a problem; something that is wrong with a system, especially in a computer program. ♦ *The programmer could not get all the bugs out of the computer program.* ♦ *Every time a bug appeared, the program crashed.* **5.** *tv.* to bother someone or something; to annoy someone or something. ♦ *Sue bugged her brother until he took her to the park.* ♦ *The dripping faucet bugged me, but not enough to fix it.* **6.** *tv.* to equip a room, telephone, etc., with ③. ♦ *The detective bugged the suspect's telephone.* ♦ *The suspect knew that her room had been bugged.* **7.** *iv.* [for someone's eyes] to open up and become very apparent. ♦ *Anne's eyes bugged when she heard the news.* ♦ *Jimmy's eyes bugged at the suggestion of a bath.*

buggy ['bʌg i] **1.** *n.* a carriage pulled by horses. ♦ *The servant pulled the buggy up to the house.* ♦ *The buggy was drawn by two black horses.* **2.** *adj.* full of bugs; full of insects. (Comp: *buggier;* sup: *buggiest.*) ♦ *The carved pumpkin was pretty buggy after a few weeks outdoors.* ♦ *We had a buggy picnic. Ants were everywhere!*

bugle ['bjug əl] *n.* a trumpet-like brass horn, used to sound military signals. ♦ *Dad used to march in a drum and bugle corps.* ♦ *Mary learned to play the bugle at age ten.*

bugler ['bjug lɚ] *n.* someone who plays a bugle, usually for signaling purposes. ♦ *The bugler woke everyone up each morning.* ♦ *Bill was the bugler in his camp.*

build ['bɪld] **1.** *tv., irreg.* to make something from separate pieces; to construct something. (Pt/pp: **built**.) ♦ *The kids built an airplane from wooden sticks.* ♦ *Anne helped Dad build a fence with old boards.* **2.** *tv., irreg.* to develop something; to establish something a little bit at a time. ♦ *Anne tried to build her child's confidence.* ♦ *Max built the business slowly over many years.* **3.** *iv., irreg.* [for something] to increase. ♦ *The volume of the music kept building until it was deafening.* ♦ *The tension between the feuding neighbors was building.* **4. build up** *iv., irreg. + adv.* to accumulate; to gather things bit by bit; to increase steadily. ♦ *Dust is building up on top of the refrigerator.* ♦ *Grease keeps building up in the kitchen drain.* **5.** *n.* form of the body; shape of the body; the muscle structure of the body. ♦ *The police say the suspect has a large build.* ♦ *Tom worked at the gym to develop a muscular build.*

builder ['bɪld ɚ] *n.* someone who builds buildings for a living. ♦ *We hired a builder to complete the construction job.* ♦ *Bill tried to build the deck himself but ended up hiring a builder.*

building ['bɪld ɪŋ] **1.** *n.* a structure where people live, work, or play. ♦ *The apartment building housed fifty people.* ♦ *The school built another building for all the new students.* **2.** *n.* the business of constructing ①. (No plural form in this sense.) ♦ *After I quit my office job, I went into building.* ♦ *Our carpenter had been in building for thirty years.* **3.** *adj.* <the adj. use of ②.> ♦ *The building trade is booming these days.* ♦ *Does this structure meet all the building codes?*

built ['bɪlt] pt/pp of build.

built-in ['bɪlt 'ɪn] *adj.* not removable; part of a larger unit. ♦ *Is the dishwasher built-in or portable?* ♦ *The apartment has built-in bookcases.*

bulb ['bʌlb] **1.** *n.* any rounded or globular-shaped object. ♦ *The vase had a narrow neck and a bulb as a base.* ♦ *The pottery was shaped into a fat bulb.* **2.** *n.* a glass globe that contains a filament and is used to create light from electricity. ♦ *The lamp needs a new bulb—the old one is burned out.* ♦ *Screw the new bulb into the socket carefully.* **3.** *n.* the fleshy root of some plants. ♦ *Jane planted tulip bulbs in the garden.* ♦ *These bulbs will grow into beautiful daffodils in the spring.* **4.** *n.* a species of flower that is grown from a bulb. ♦ *My bulbs were beautiful, but my annuals were disappointing.* ♦ *I've never had good luck growing bulbs.*

bulbous ['bʌl bəs] *adj.* shaped like a bulb. (Adv: *bulbously.*) ♦ *The funny clown had a bulbous nose.* ♦ *The bulbous pears hung from the branches of the tree.*

Bulgaria [bəl 'gɛr i ə] See Gazetteer.

bulge ['bʌldʒ] **1.** *n.* a bump, a round swelling; a protrusion. ♦ *My arm had a big bulge on it before the bruise appeared.* ♦ *There was a bulge around Sue's waist where she had tucked in her sweater.* **2.** *iv.* to swell; to protrude. ♦ *Our stomachs bulged after we ate too much.* ♦ *The frog's throat bulged just before it croaked.* **3.** *tv.* to cause something to curve outward. ♦ *Max bulged his muscles to impress his friends.* ♦ *The wind bulged the glass of the large window inward.*

bulging ['bʌl dʒɪŋ] *adj.* swollen; curving outward or inward. (Adv: *bulgingly.*) ♦ *Acorns filled the squirrel's bulging cheeks.* ♦ *The pregnant woman patted her bulging abdomen lovingly.*

bulk ['bʌlk] **1.** *n.* a great amount; a large amount of something. (No plural form in this sense.) ♦ *The heavy bulk of the block of steel almost crushed the delivery truck.* ♦ *Dave placed his great bulk on the tiny chair, and it broke.* **2.** *n.* the major portion of something; the largest and most important part. (No plural form in this sense.) ♦ *The bulk of the work after the flood was cleaning the mud out of the basement.* ♦ *The caterer did the bulk of the cooking for the party.* **3.** *adj.* [containing] large [quantities or amounts]. ♦ *The warehouse was filled with huge bulk containers.* ♦ *Jane made a bulk purchase of office supplies for her company.* **4. in bulk** *idiom* in large quantities or amounts, rather than smaller, more convenient quantities or amounts. ♦ *Jane always bought office supplies in bulk to save money.* ♦ *Dave purchased cereal in bulk because his family used so much of it.*

bulky ['bʌlk i] *adj.* taking up a lot of space; hard to hold because of its great size. (Adv: *bulkily.* Comp: *bulkier;* sup: *bulkiest.*) ♦ *The bulky boxes won't fit in the trunk of the car.* ♦ *The sack of groceries was too bulky to handle.*

bull ['bʊl] **1.** *n.* a male bovine animal, if it is able to breed. (Compare with **steer** ④.) ♦ *A huge and dangerous bull stood in the pasture and looked straight at us.* ♦ *The bull grazed on the land around the farm.* **2.** *n.* someone who believes that prices on a particular financial market will rise. ♦ *Bill is a bull on the technology stock.* ♦ *The bulls expect the market to break another record this week.* **3.** *adj.* [of certain animals] male. ♦ *The zoo had two bull mooses.* ♦ *The bull elephants tramped through the tall grass.*

bulldog ['bʊl dɔg] *n.* a small, muscular dog with a protruding lower jaw. ♦ *The bulldog growled at the postal carrier.* ♦ *My bulldog snarls at everyone who comes to the door.*

bulldoze ['bʊl doz] *tv.* to knock something over with a bulldozer; to flatten something with a bulldozer. ♦ *The construction crew bulldozed the site until it was flat.* ♦ *The city bulldozed the old building.*

bulldozer ['bʊl doz ɚ] *n.* a powerful tractor equipped with a strong blade that can push dirt and rubble. ♦ *A huge bulldozer was parked at the construction site.* ♦ *The bulldozer scraped up a huge amount of rubble.*

bullet ['bʊl ɪt] *n.* a small piece of lead fired from a gun. ♦ *This pistol holds six bullets.* ♦ *The hunters brought extra bullets.*

bulletin ['bʊl ə tən] **1.** *n.* a special news report; a piece of news; official information. ♦ *The television news bulletin reported the outbreak of war.* ♦ *The bulletin announced a change in the date of the rocket launch.* **2.** *n.* a journal or newsletter published by a specific group or interest. ♦ *The medical association publishes a bulletin each month.* ♦ *The organization's latest bulletin was delayed in the mail.* **3. bulletin board** *n.* a board where notices and signs can be posted. ♦ *There is a notice about the dress code on the bulletin board.* ♦ *No advertisements can be posted on the company bulletin board.*

bulletproof ['bʊl ɪt pruf] *adj.* able to withstand bullets; resistant to bullets. ♦ *All police officers were required to wear bulletproof vests.* ♦ *The windows on the president's limousine are bulletproof.*

bullfight ['bʊl fɑɪt] *n.* a fight between a man and a bull. (A traditional Spanish and Mexican sport.) ♦ *A bullfight ends when the bull dies.* ♦ *Huge crowds packed the arena to see the bullfight.*

bullfighter ['bʊl fɑɪt ɚ] *n.* a man who fights bulls for public entertainment; a matador. ♦ *The bullfighter carried a red cape.* ♦ *The bull nearly killed the bullfighter.*

bullfrog ['bʊl frɔg] *n.* a large frog with a deep, loud croak. ♦ *The boys snuck their bullfrogs into school as a joke.* ♦ *The swamp was full of bullfrogs.*

bullheaded ['bʊl hɛd ɪd] *adj.* stubborn; obstinate; headstrong; not willing to listen to reason. (Adv: *bullheadedly.*) ♦ *Bill was quite bullheaded and would not change his plans.* ♦ *The bullheaded toddler said "No" to everything I suggested.*

bullhorn ['bʊl horn] *n.* a loud, amplified megaphone. ♦ *The sheriff addressed the crowd through the bullhorn.* ♦ *The principal spoke to the students with a bullhorn.*

bullish ['bʊl ɪʃ] **1.** *adj.* in the aggressive manner of a bull. (Adv: *bullishly.*) ♦ *The manager was somewhat bullish in the way he tried to force people to think his way.* ♦ *Your bullish behavior was inexcusable.* **2.** *adj.* optimistic about the prospects for a particular financial market or financial instrument. (Compare with **bearish.** Adv: *bullishly.*) ♦ *I'm not so bullish these days, since the increase in interest rates.* ♦ *The investor was bullish on the new computer company.*

bullpen ['bʊl pɛn] **1.** *n.* a place where bulls are kept or raised. ♦ *The bullpen was fenced in.* ♦ *The gate was open and the bullpen was empty.* **2.** *n.* the area in a baseball stadium where pitchers practice before going onto the field. ♦ *The pitcher warmed up in the bullpen.* ♦ *Balls flew back and forth in the bullpen as the players practiced.*

bullring ['bʊl rɪŋ] *n.* the stadium or arena where a bullfight takes place. ♦ *The matador entered the bullring confidently.* ♦ *The crowd jeered as the bullfighter ran from the bullring.*

bull's-eye ['bʊl zɑɪ] **1.** *n.* the exact center of a target. ♦ *The archer's arrow hit the bull's-eye.* ♦ *All my darts hit outside of the bull's-eye.* **2.** *n.* a shot or throw that hits the center of the target. ♦ *The archer hit three bull's-eyes.* ♦ *I love to play darts but have never made a bull's-eye.* **3. hit the bull's-eye** *idiom* to achieve the goal perfectly. ♦ *Your idea really hit the bull's-eye. Thank you!* ♦ *Jill has a lot of insight. She knows how to hit the bull's-eye.*

bully ['bʊl i] **1.** *n.* someone, usually a male, who is mean or threatening. ♦ *The students were threatened by a bully who took their money.* ♦ *The bully became more polite when a bigger, meaner boy came to school.* **2.** *tv.* to threaten someone; to be overly aggressive with someone. ♦ *The older students bullied the younger ones on the playground.* ♦ *"Don't bully me anymore!" the young child screamed.*

bum ['bʌm] **1.** *n.* a tramp; a good-for-nothing. (Derogatory.) ♦ *I told the bum begging for money to get a job.* ♦ *We thought Bill was a bum until he started his own business.* **2.** *tv.* to ask for something with no intention of repayment; to take advantage of other people. (Slang.) ♦ *I was out of cigarettes, so I bummed one off my best friend.* ♦ *Sue bummed some quarters to do her laundry.* **3.** *adj.* of poor quality; not good. (Informal.) ♦ *Grandpa hobbled around slowly on his bum leg.* ♦ *The advice to make that investment was really a bum idea.*

bumble ['bʌm bəl] **1.** *iv.* to trip; to stumble; to move clumsily. ♦ *The clown bumbled around on the stage.* ♦ *The drunk bumbled down the street.* **2. bumble through** *iv.* + *prep. phr.* to speak haltingly; to stammer and mumble. ♦ *Bill bumbled nervously through his speech.* ♦ *The frightened thief bumbled through his alibi.*

bumblebee ['bʌm bəl bi] *n.* a large, hairy, black and yellow bee. ♦ *The bumblebee frightened me.* ♦ *A huge bumblebee nestled in the flower.*

bumbling ['bʌmb lɪŋ] *adj.* clumsy; awkward; not doing something in a skilled way. (Adv: *bumblingly.*) ♦ *The children laughed at the bumbling magician.* ♦ *The bumbling employee was fired.*

bump ['bʌmp] **1.** *n.* a lump or swelling in an otherwise flat area. ♦ *How did that bump in the floor get there?* ♦ *Our car ran over a big bump in the road.* **2.** *n.* a knock; a blow; a hit; a forceful contact. ♦ *Suddenly, I felt a bump and knew that someone had hit my car.* ♦ *The truck behind us gave us a bump from the rear.* **3.** *tv.* to make forceful contact with someone or something. ♦ *The waitress bumped our table as she hurried by.* ♦ *I bumped the wall and got wet paint on my shirt.* **4.** *tv.* [for an airline] to cancel someone's airplane reservation without warning. ♦ *Our vacation was ruined when the airline bumped us.* ♦ *Do airlines bump passengers often?* **5. bump into** *iv.* + *prep. phr.* to make contact with something; to run into something. ♦ *I bumped into the wall by mistake.* ♦ *My car bumped into the car in front of me.* **6. bump into** *iv.* + *prep. phr.* to have a surprise meeting with someone. ♦ *Sue bumped into Bob at the supermarket.* ♦ *It was a surprise to bump into our old schoolteacher.*

bumper ['bʌm pɚ] **1.** *n.* a strong, protective metal bar in the front and back of vehicle. ♦ *The bumper minimized the damage from the accident.* ♦ *The accident caused the car's bumper to fall off.* **2.** *n.* any device designed to absorb an impact. ♦ *A rubber bumper protected the wall from damage from the doorknob.* ♦ *The baby's crib had a soft bumper around the inside.* **3.** *adj.* large; abundant; plentiful. ♦ *The farmer had a bumper crop three years in a row.* ♦ *We had a bumper harvest this year.*

bumpy ['bʌm pi] *adj.* having many bumps. (Adv: *bumpily.* Comp: *bumpier;* sup: *bumpiest.*) ♦ *Let's not drive on that bumpy road.* ♦ *The plastered wall was bumpy.*

bun ['bʌn] **1.** *n.* a bread product, such as used to hold cooked hamburger meat or a frankfurter. ♦ *Anne brought the hamburgers and hot dogs, but forgot the buns.* ♦ *The guests ate their hamburgers on bread instead of buns.* **2.** *n.* a sweetened bread roll, sometimes with fruit or other fillings. ♦ *I bought some fresh buns at the bakery.* ♦ *Cinnamon buns are our favorite.* **3.** *n.* a knot of hair that is gathered up at the back of the head. ♦ *Aunt Mary wore her hair in a bun for thirty years.* ♦ *Ballet dancers often wear their hair in buns.*

bunch ['bʌntʃ] **1.** *n.* a group of things that grow together or are placed together. ♦ *Jane arranged a bunch of flowers in the vase.* ♦ *A bunch of mushrooms grew near the pine tree.* **2.** *n.* a group of things or people; an indefinite number of things or people. ♦ *The whole bunch of politicians is crooked.* ♦ *I saved a bunch of boxes for our next move.* **3. bunch up** *iv.* + *adv.* [for people or things] to gather together closely. ♦ *The students bunched up in the hallway.* ♦ *We bunched up to make room for another person to sit down.*

bundle ['bʌn dəl] **1.** *n.* a group of things gathered together. ♦ *The mailman put a bundle of mail in our mailbox.* ♦ *Mary gave a bundle of clothes to charity.* **2.** *n.* a large amount of something; many things. (No plural form in this sense.) ♦ *Bill had a bundle of chores to finish before he could go outside to play.* ♦ *A trip overseas would cost a bundle of money.* **3. bundle up** *tv.* + *adv.* to wrap someone or something up; to wrap someone or something tightly. ♦ *Bundle the children up well—it's bitterly cold today.* ♦ *Sue bundled the package up with the others before taking them to the post office.* **4.** *tv.* to include a selection of software with the sale of computer hardware. ♦ *The company bundled software that it claimed was worth $900.* ♦ *The marketing department likes to bundle the computer products.*

bundled ['bʌn dəld] *adj.* [of computer software] included with the purchase of hardware. ♦ *Bundled products sell faster.* ♦ *The sales of computers with bundled software has risen this year.*

bungalow ['bʌŋ gə lo] **1.** *n.* a one-story cottage. ♦ *Tom rented a bungalow for his vacation.* ♦ *We stayed in a bungalow near the shore.* **2.** *n.* a specific house design of one and one-half stories with a pitched roof on all sides. ♦ *Our family bought a bungalow on the north side of town.* ♦ *The real-estate agent showed Anne a bungalow and a two-story house.*

bungle ['bʌŋ gəl] *tv.* to do something badly or awkwardly. ♦ *Jane bungled the job so badly that Mary did it herself.* ♦ *I just knew you would bungle the whole matter!*

bunion ['bʌn jən] *n.* a painful swelling of the joint of the big toe. ♦ *The surgeon corrected Mary's bunion.* ♦ *John's bunion had caused him a lot of pain.*

bunk ['bʌŋk] **1.** *n.* a narrow bed. (See also bunk bed.) ♦ *The campers slept in bunks in the lodge.* ♦ *The dormitory has two bunks to a room.* **2.** *n.* nonsense. (Informal. No plural form in this sense.) ♦ *I don't want to listen to any more of this bunk.* ♦ *I've heard enough of your bunk.* **3. bunk down** *iv.* + *adv.* to prepare for sleep. ♦ *Bill and Tom got ready to bunk down for the night.* ♦ *We bunked down in the barn.* **4. bunk with** *iv.* + *prep. phr.* to share a bedroom or sleeping area. ♦ *Tom bunked with Bill on the camping trip.* ♦ *The leaders bunked with the officers.*

bunk bed ['bʌŋk bɛd] **1.** *n.* one of a set of two beds built into a frame that positions one bed over the other to save space. ♦ *Bob and Bill slept in bunk beds until they were teenagers.* ♦ *The bunk beds made extra space in the small bedroom.* **2.** *n.* a pair of ① set one over the other. ♦ *We spent the night in a shaky bunk bed.* ♦ *The twins slept in a bunk bed, with Susie on top.*

bunker ['bʌŋk ɚ] **1.** *n.* a steel or concrete shelter or fortification. ♦ *The soldiers took refuge in the bunker.* ♦ *The cave made a natural bunker.* **2.** *n.* a stretch of sand or a mound of soil on a golf course that creates an obstacle to play. ♦ *Dave hit the ball into a sandy bunker.* ♦ *Mary had to hit balls from the bunker three times.*

bunny ['bʌn i] *n.* a rabbit; a hare. (Juvenile.) ♦ *The child pointed at the little white bunny.* ♦ *The Easter basket contained a chocolate bunny.*

bunt ['bʌnt] **1.** *n.* a way of stopping a baseball with the bat so it drops to the ground in front of the batter. ♦ *The batter fooled the pitcher with a bunt.* ♦ *Tom held the bat near each end and performed a classic bunt.* **2.** *tv.* to hit a baseball gently so that it does not go very far. ♦ *That batter always bunts the ball.* ♦ *The kids learned to bunt a ball at baseball practice.* **3.** *iv.* to swing a bat gently so that the ball it strikes does not go very far. ♦ *That batter always bunts.* ♦ *The kids learned to bunt at baseball practice.*

buoy ['bɔi, bu i] **1.** *n.* a floating aid to navigation, used to display warnings or directions. ♦ *The lifeguard swam out to the buoy and back.* ♦ *Buoys marked off the swimming area at the beach.* **2.** *n.* a floating ring that can support a person in the water. ♦ *The ship's deck held buoys in case of an emergency.* ♦ *We threw the passenger who had fallen overboard a buoy.* **3. buoy (up)** *tv.* (+ *adv.*) to prevent someone or something from sinking; to keep someone or something afloat. ♦ *A life jacket buoyed the child who fell from the boat.* ♦ *The floating board buoyed the swimmer up.* **4. buoy (up)** *tv.* (+ *adv.*) to make someone happy; to cheer someone up. (Figurative on ③.) ♦ *The good news buoyed Jane through another day.* ♦ *The smiling baby buoyed up Grandma.*

buoyant ['bɔɪ ənt] **1.** *adj.* able to float. (Adv: *buoyantly.*) ♦ *The plastic bathtub toys were very buoyant.* ♦ *Life vests made us buoyant in the water.* **2.** *adj.* happy; cheerful. (Figurative on ①. Adv: *buoyantly.*) ♦ *My neighbor has a buoyant personality.* ♦ *Anne and Bill were really friendly and buoyant today.*

burden ['bɚd n] **1.** *n.* a heavy load. ♦ *The mule struggled under the burden on its back.* ♦ *The burden of five grocery bags slowed me down.* **2.** *n.* a heavy responsibility that strains a person. (Figurative on ①.) ♦ *Buying a new car this year was a financial burden for me.* ♦ *At sixteen, Jane was not ready for the burden of college.* **3.** *tv.* to give someone or something a heavy load. ♦ *The mule was burdened with too big a load.* ♦ *We burdened each of the campers with loads of the same weight.* **4.** *tv.* to depress someone; [for a problem] to serve as ②. (Figurative on ③.) ♦ *A lack of money burdens many people.* ♦ *Mary was burdened by a death in her family.*

burdensome ['bɚd n səm] *adj.* difficult; troublesome. (Adv: *burdensomely.*) ♦ *Cleaning the garage is a burdensome task.* ♦ *We thought long and hard about the burdensome dilemma.*

bureau ['bjʊr o] **1.** *n.* a department or agency, especially one relating to government. (From French.) ♦ *A special bureau in each state handles licenses for drivers.* ♦ *What bureau handles the records of births and deaths?* **2.** *n.* a chest of drawers; a piece of furniture that clothes are kept in. ♦ *Sue inherited her grandparents' bureau.* ♦ *Put your clothes away in the bureau.*

bureaucracy [bjʊr 'ɑ krə si] **1.** *n.* government offices and agencies. ♦ *Some of the bureaucracy is housed in large buildings in the city.* ♦ *The bureaucracy is usually an inefficient form of government.* **2.** *n.* the annoyances and complications of dealing with bureaucrats. (No plural form in this sense.) ♦ *Too much bureaucracy drove people crazy with petty rules.* ♦ *A lot of complicated bureaucracy is involved in immigration.*

bureaucrat ['bjʊr ə kræt] *n.* a government worker; someone who is part of a bureaucracy and follows policies rigidly. ♦ *The bureaucrat at the tax office gave us many forms to fill out.* ♦ *By the time John got a building permit, he was very annoyed with bureaucrats.*

bureaucratic [bjʊr ə 'kræt ɪk] *adj.* relating to bureaucracy. (Adv: *bureaucratically* [...ɪk li].) ♦ *The office manager makes a lot of bureaucratic decisions.* ♦ *The governor promised to eliminate a layer of bureaucratic management.*

burglar ['bɚg lɚ] *n.* a criminal who enters someplace illegally to steal things. ♦ *Anne caught the burglar stealing her jewelry.* ♦ *Bill thought he heard a burglar downstairs, but it was only the dog.*

burglarize ['bɚg lə rɑɪz] *tv.* to enter a building to steal things. ♦ *Some crooks burglarized the equipment room at school.* ♦ *Mary knew her house had been burglarized—things had been thrown everywhere.*

burglary ['bɚg lə ri] *n.* an act of breaking into a building to rob or steal something. ♦ *Sue reported the burglary to the police immediately.* ♦ *What was taken from the home during the burglary?*

burgundy ['bɚ gən di] **1.** *n.* a type of wine made in the Burgundy region of France. (No plural form in this sense.) ♦ *The beef was served with a nice burgundy.* ♦ *The glass of burgundy was a deep, ruby red color.* **2.** *adj.* a deep, ruby red color that resembles the color of red wine. ♦ *The walls of the library were decorated with burgundy paint.* ♦ *The school uniform includes a burgundy and blue tie.*

burial ['bɛr i əl] **1.** *n.* the burying of something, especially a dead body. ♦ *The undertaker finished the burial after the mourners had left.* ♦ *The sailor had a burial at sea.* **2.** *adj.* relating to ①. ♦ *The burial site was in the man's hometown.* ♦ *The mourners gathered together for the burial service.*

burlap ['bɚ læp] **1.** *n.* a rough cloth woven from twine or hemp. (No plural form in this sense.) ♦ *The large pieces of iron were wrapped in burlap before they were shipped.* ♦ *The banner was burlap and had red letters painted on it.* **2.** *adj.* made of ①. ♦ *The potatoes are in a burlap sack in the basement.* ♦ *The roots of the new tree were covered with a burlap wrapping.*

burlesque [bɚ 'lɛsk] **1.** *n.* a satire; art that mocks something serious. (From French.) ♦ *The actors did a burlesque of an opera.* ♦ *The spontaneous burlesque of rowdy behavior was out of place.* **2.** *n.* vulgar theater consisting of sexy acts and crude comedians. (No plural form in this sense.) ♦ *Mary worked in burlesque to earn money for school.* ♦ *Burlesque was popular in the days of vaudeville.* **3.** *adj.* mocking something serious. (Adv: *burlesquely.*) ♦ *The burlesque interpretation of Shakespeare insulted the audience.* ♦ *The burlesque performance of the opera was very funny.*

burly ['bɚl i] *adj.* big, strong, and muscular. (Comp: *burlier;* sup: *burliest.*) ♦ *The burly wrestler growled at his opponent.* ♦ *A burly bear lumbered through the forest, looking for food.*

Burma ['bɚ mə] See Gazetteer.

burn ['bɚn] **1.** *n.* the mark caused by a flame or something that is very hot. ♦ *How did this burn get on the coffee table?* ♦ *The cigarette made a burn in Jane's pants.* **2.** *n.* an injury caused to someone who has been harmed by high heat. ♦ *Tom has a burn on his hand from the hot skillet.* ♦ *The firefighter suffered burns during the rescue.*

3. *tv., irreg.* to set fire to something; to destroy something by fire. (Pt/pp are usually *burned,* but sometimes burnt.) ♦ *The novelist burned his private papers before he died.* ♦ *The arsonist burned the building to the ground.* **4.** *tv., irreg.* to damage someone or something by heat; to sear someone or something. ♦ *The faulty oven burned my dinner.* ♦ *Anne burned her finger on the oven door.* **5.** *tv., irreg.* to consume a fuel or an energy source. ♦ *During the last winter we burned a barrel of oil.* ♦ *Turn off the lights, you're burning too much electricity.* **6.** *tv., irreg.* to sting something; to cause something to have a sharp sensation of heat. ♦ *The hot pepper sauce burned Mary's mouth.* ♦ *The cheap whiskey burned Max's throat.* **7. burn out** *tv., irreg. + adv.* to cause an electrical device to wear out or burn its components and fail. ♦ *You ran the toaster too much and burned it out.* ♦ *Who burned out the motor of the vacuum cleaner?* **8. burn out** *iv., irreg. + adv.* [for an electrical device] to fail as in ⑦; [for a flame] to exhaust its fuel and stop burning. ♦ *The candles burned out at about midnight.* ♦ *The toaster burned out yesterday morning.* **9.** *iv., irreg.* to provide light; to give off light. ♦ *Lights were burning in every room of the house.* ♦ *The fire burned bright.* **10.** *iv., irreg.* to sting. ♦ *The disinfectant burned when I put it on the wound.* ♦ *A spider bite burns.* **11.** *iv., irreg.* to be on fire. ♦ *The fire burned brightly.* ♦ *The candles burned on the mantle.* **12.** *iv., irreg.* [for food] to become scorched from overcooking. ♦ *Dinner is burning again!* ♦ *What is burning in the kitchen?* **13. burn someone up** *idiom* to anger someone; to make someone mad. ♦ *Seeing people throw litter on the ground just burns me up.* ♦ *It burns Jane up when people don't respond to her invitations.*

burner ['bɚn ɚ] *n.* a device that makes a controlled flame for cooking or heating. ♦ *The cook had something cooking on every burner.* ♦ *The chemist lit the gas burner and heated the chemicals.*

burnish ['bɚ nɪʃ] *tv.* to give a permanent brightness to metal by rubbing it. ♦ *The craftsman burnished the brass plates until they glowed.* ♦ *Jane used a powerful machine to burnish the bronze statue.*

burnished ['bɚ nɪʃt] *adj.* polished; shiny. ♦ *Anne's reflection shone in the burnished platter.* ♦ *The burnished copper belt buckle cost too much.*

burnt ['bɚnt] **1.** a pt/pp of burn. **2.** *adj.* [of something] damaged by fire or heat. (Also *burned.*) ♦ *The workers tore down the remains of the burnt building.* ♦ *I can't stand burnt toast!*

burp ['bɚp] **1.** *n.* a noise made when gas is released from the stomach up through the mouth; a belch. ♦ *The baby made a loud burp after finishing her bottle.* ♦ *Who let out that burp?* **2.** *iv.* to make noise when gas is released upward from the stomach; to belch. ♦ *The baby burped after finishing her bottle.* ♦ *The spicy food made Bill burp.* **3.** *tv.* to make a baby burp ② after feeding by patting it lightly on its back. ♦ *You must burp the baby after he has his bottle.* ♦ *Please burp the baby after its bottle.*

burr ['bɚ] **1.** *n.* a prickly seed case of some plants. ♦ *After my walk in the woods, some burrs were stuck to my jeans.* ♦ *Just to be mean, Bob rubbed burrs in his friend's hair.* **2.** *n.* small, rough spikes that remain on a metal surface after cutting or drilling. ♦ *Please file down these burrs before someone gets cut.* ♦ *Drilling in the metal left a lot of burrs that had to be removed.*

burro ['bɚ o] *n.* a small donkey. (Pl in *-s.*) ♦ *The farmer rode a burro to the village.* ♦ *The peasants used burros to ride to town and back.*

burrow ['bɚ o] **1.** *n.* a hole that an animal digs in the ground for shelter. ♦ *The groundhog's burrow was under the bush.* ♦ *We saw the rabbits in our yard, but we could never find their burrow.* **2.** *iv.* [for a small animal] to work its way, digging, into soil, leaves, snow, etc. ♦ *The mole burrowed in the soil, looking for worms.* ♦ *The rabbits burrowed into the leaves to try to keep warm.* **3.** *iv.* [for someone] to dig through something in search of something. ♦ *John burrowed through the objects in the kitchen drawer looking for matches.* ♦ *Jane burrowed in her desk for an eraser.*

bursitis [bɚ 'saɪ tɪs] *n.* a painful inflammation of a sac of fluid surrounding a joint. (No plural form in this sense. The fluid serves as a lubricant for the joint.) ♦ *The soreness of Tom's joints was due to bursitis.* ♦ *Anne's bursitis was bothering her, so she couldn't play tennis.*

burst ['bɚst] **1.** *tv., irreg.* to break something open; to cause something to explode. ♦ *A sharp stick burst the balloon.* ♦ *The flood of water burst the dam.* **2.** *iv., irreg.* to explode; to suddenly break open. (Pt/pp: *burst.*) ♦ *The pipes burst from the cold.* ♦ *The balloon burst and everyone jumped at the noise.* **3. burst with** *iv., irreg. + prep. phr.* to be exuberant with some happy feeling or energy. ♦ *After a good night's sleep we were bursting with energy.* ♦ *Mary's parents burst with pride at her graduation ceremony.* **4. burst into** *iv., irreg. + prep. phr.* to do something suddenly and strongly; to act suddenly. (See ⑦.) ♦ *The choir burst into song.* ♦ *David burst into laughter at my joke.* **5.** *n.* a sudden outbreak; a violent outbreak; a barrage. ♦ *The troops were surprised by a burst of enemy gunfire.* ♦ *A burst of thunder preceded the deluge of rain.* **6.** *n.* a spurt; a quick, intense event. ♦ *At midnight Jane got a burst of energy and began exercising.* ♦ *The runner had a burst of adrenaline and sprinted towards the finish line.* **7. burst into flame(s)** *idiom* [for something] to catch fire and become a large fire quickly. ♦ *As soon as a piece of the drapery touched the candle, the entire wall seemed to burst into flames.* ♦ *The two cars burst into flames soon after the collision.*

Burundi [bʊ 'rʊn di] See Gazetteer.

bury ['bɛr i] **1.** *tv.* to put something in the ground, to cover something with dirt or soil. ♦ *Bury the tulip bulbs about three inches deep.* ♦ *The dog buried its bone in the yard.* **2.** *tv.* to place a dead person or other creature in the ground. ♦ *The family buried their father in the cemetery.* ♦ *Jimmy buried his dead hamster in the backyard.* **3.** *tv.* to conceal someone or something; to hide someone or something. ♦ *The kids buried themselves under the covers to hide from their parents.* ♦ *Jane buried the birthday present in the back of the closet so Bob wouldn't find it.*

bus ['bʌs] **1.** *n.* an enclosed motor vehicle that carries many passengers. ♦ *Do buses pick up passengers at this corner?* ♦ *Mary rides the bus to work every day.* **2.** *n.* [in a computer] a circuit that allows new devices and equipment to be connected to the main computer. ♦ *The new model has a huge bus that lets me install ten circuit boards.* ♦ *This board plugs directly into the bus.* **3.** *tv.* to move children from one school to another, daily, by bus, in order to achieve racial balance. ♦ *The school district bussed the children across town to school.* ♦ *Children were bussed to a school in a different district.* **4.** *tv.* to remove dirty dishes from a table after a meal in a restaurant or cafeteria. ♦ *A sign directs customers to bus their own tables.* ♦ *The waitress bussed the table so new customers could be seated.*

busboy ['bʌs bɔɪ] *n.* a restaurant or cafeteria employee who removes dirty plates from a table, wipes the table clean, and sets the table for the next customer. ♦ *The busboy quickly set the table while the customers waited.* ♦ *Our table was cleared by the busboy.*

bush ['bʊʃ] **1.** *n.* a plant with several woody branches. ♦ *There is a row of bushes at the end of our backyard.* ♦ *The bush had beautiful yellow blossoms on it.* **2.** *n.* undeveloped land with a mixture of trees and shrubs. (No plural form in this sense.) ♦ *The hunters searched for the wild boar in the bush.* ♦ *Most animals in the bush are wild.*

bushed ['bʊʃt] *adj.* completely exhausted. ♦ *We were just bushed after a hard day's work.* ♦ *The bushed campers fell into their bunks.*

bushel ['bʊʃ əl] **1.** *n.* a unit of measurement of dry goods, especially crops, equal to 64 pints, 32 quarts, or 4 pecks. ♦ *Sue and Bill picked a bushel of apples at the orchard.* ♦ *We were given a bushel of pears as a gift.* **2.** *adj.* holding or containing ①. ♦ *The bushel basket was full of apples.* ♦ *Please buy a bushel bag of oranges when you go to the store.*

bushy ['bʊʃ i] *adj.* [of hair or fur] thick, dense, and shaggy. (Adv: *bushily.* Comp: *bushier;* sup: *bushiest.*) ♦ *The dog with long bushy fur needs a haircut and a bath.* ♦ *My history teacher has very bushy eyebrows.*

business ['bɪz nəs] **1.** *n.* a profession; an occupation. ♦ *What type of business are you in?* ♦ *Bill's business is roofing.* **2.** *n.* buying, selling, or trading. (No plural form in this sense.) ♦ *The air-conditioning firm did a lot of business during the heat wave.* ♦ *Anne's gift shop has a lot of business during the holidays.* **3.** *n.* a corporation; a company; a commercial enterprise. ♦ *Our family business was founded in 1901.* ♦ *The business owes thousands of dollars in back taxes.* **4.** *n.* affair; concern; matter of interest. (No plural form in this sense.) ♦ *"That is none of your business," Jane told her nosy friend.* ♦ *Okay, I'll mind my own business.* **5. do a land-office business** *idiom* to do a large amount of buying or selling in a short period of time. ♦ *The ice-cream shop always does a land-office business on a hot day.* ♦ *The tax collector's office did a land-office business on the day that taxes were due.* **6. drum up some business** *idiom* to stimulate or encourage people to buy what one is selling. ♦ *A little bit of advertising would drum up some business.* ♦ *I need to do something to drum some business up.* **7. funny business** *idiom* trickery or deception; illegal activity. ♦ *From the silence as she entered the room, the teacher knew there was some funny business going on.* ♦ *There's some funny business going on at the warehouse. Stock keeps disappearing.* **8. go about one's business** *idiom* to move elsewhere and tend to one's own affairs. ♦ *Leave me alone! Just go about your business!* ♦ *I have no more to say. I would be pleased if you would go about your business.* **9. mind one's own business** *idiom* to attend only to the things that concern one. ♦ *Leave me alone, Bill. Mind your own business.* ♦ *I'd be fine if John would mind his own business.* **10. place of business** *idiom* a place where ② is done; a factory or office. ♦ *Our place of business opens at 9:00 A.M. each day.* ♦ *You will have to come to our place of business to make a purchase.* **11. send one about one's business** *idiom* to send someone away, usually in an unfriendly way. ♦ *Is that annoying man on the telephone again? Please send him about his business.* ♦ *Ann, I can't clean up the house with you running around. I'm going to have to send you about your business.* **12. the business end of something** *idiom* the part or end of something that actually does the work or carries out the procedure. ♦ *Keep away from the business end of the electric drill in case you get hurt.* ♦ *Don't point the business end of that gun at anyone. It might go off.*

businesslike ['bɪz nəs lɑɪk] *adj.* professional; managed like a well-run business. ♦ *The businesslike clerk served us quickly.* ♦ *The meeting was run in a businesslike manner, and it was over quickly.*

businessman ['bɪz nəs mæn] *n., irreg.* a man whose career is in business; a professional man. (Pl: businessmen. See also businessperson, businesswoman.) ♦ *The businessman rode the train to work.* ♦ *The plane was full of businessmen on their way home.*

businessmen ['bɪz nəs mɛn] pl of businessman.

businesspeople ['bɪz nəs pi pəl] pl of businessperson.

businessperson ['bɪz nəs pɚ sən] *n.* someone whose career is in business; a professional; an executive. (Pl: businesspeople. See also businessman, businesswoman.) ♦ *This book is a good reference for businesspeople.* ♦ *The restaurant serves lunch to a lot of businesspeople.*

businesswoman ['bɪz nəs wʊm ən] *n., irreg.* a woman whose career is in business; a female professional; a female executive. (Pl: businesswomen. See also businessman, businessperson.) ♦ *The businesswoman rode the train to work every day.* ♦ *A group of businesswomen discussed the deal during lunch.*

businesswomen ['bɪz nəs wɪm ən] pl of businesswoman.

busing ['bʌs ɪŋ] *n.* the practice of sending children to a distant school rather than their neighborhood school in order to provide racial balance. (No plural form in this sense.) ♦ *The residents objected to the busing of their children across town.* ♦ *Busing the children across town was an issue in the school board elections.*

bus stop ['bʌs stɑp] *n.* a place where a bus picks up and drops off passengers. ♦ *The bus stops at every bus stop along the route.* ♦ *The students waited at the bus stop.*

bust ['bʌst] **1.** *n.* a sculpture of someone's head and shoulders. ♦ *The sculptor unveiled the bust at the museum.* ♦ *John had a bust of himself made for the study.* **2.** *n.* a woman's bosom, taken as a whole, particularly in reference to the shape of women's clothing. ♦ *The seamstress measured Mary's waist and bust for the dress.* ♦ *The actress's costume was too tight in the bust.* **3.** *n.* a complete failure; a bankruptcy; an insolvency. (Colloquial.) ♦ *The whole project was a bust.* ♦ *My first business was a bust.* **4.** *tv.* to break something. (Colloquial.) ♦ *Don't bust that antique vase!* ♦ *The baseball busted a window of our house.* **5.** *tv.* to place someone under arrest. (Slang.) ♦ *The police busted Max for drug possession.* ♦ *After years of trying, the detective finally busted the smugglers.* **6.** *iv.* not to work;

to break down; to not function. (Colloquial.) ♦ *The television busted again!* ♦ *Just when we got the radiator fixed, the fuel pump busted.*

busted ['bʌs tɪd] **1.** *adj.* broken; not working; inoperable; in need of repair. (Colloquial.) ♦ *The busted coffeepot was not repairable.* ♦ *What did you do with the busted chair?* **2.** *adj.* caught; arrested. (Slang.) ♦ *Four busted teenagers had to call their parents to pick them up.* ♦ *Max posted bail for his busted friend.*

bustle ['bʌs əl] *iv.* to rush about busily; to hurry around. ♦ *The server bustled here and there, but she never brought us our food.* ♦ *The children bustled about, getting ready for school.*

busy ['bɪz i] **1.** *adj.* working; at work; having things to do. (Adv: *busily.* Comp: *busier;* sup: *busiest.*) ♦ *The busy clerk waited on customers all day.* ♦ *All the clerks were busy, and we couldn't get any service.* **2.** *adj.* [of a telephone connection] in use. (Comp: *busier;* sup: *busiest.*) ♦ *I keep trying to call Jane, but her line is busy.* ♦ *The busy phone really annoyed me.* **3.** *adj.* occupied with something else at the time. (Comp: *busier;* sup: *busiest.*) ♦ *I can't do it tomorrow because I'm busy all day.* ♦ *We invited the Smiths to dinner, but they were busy.* **4.** *adj.* distracting to look at because of clashing patterns; having too much detail. (Adv: *busily.* Comp: *busier;* sup: *busiest.*) ♦ *The flowered wallpaper is too busy.* ♦ *Take some of the books off the mantle. It's too busy.* **5.** *tv.* to make work for oneself; to occupy oneself with something. (Takes a reflexive object.) ♦ *I choose to busy myself with community affairs.* ♦ *Anne busied herself preparing for the interview.*

busybody ['bɪz i bɑd i] *n.* someone who meddles in other people's concerns. ♦ *Don't tell that old busybody anything personal!* ♦ *The inspector got a lot of information from the neighborhood busybody.*

but [bət] **1.** *conj.* on the contrary; however. ♦ *John ordered peas, but he was served carrots.* ♦ *The weather forecaster said it would be sunny, but it rained instead.* **2.** *conj.* except. (Takes a bare verb.) ♦ *I could not do anything but sit there and cry.* ♦ *He did nothing but ask a simple question.* **3.** *prep.* except; except for; other than; besides. ♦ *No one but the best student passed the exam.* ♦ *I don't trust anyone but my accountant to do my taxes.* **4.** *adv.* only; merely; just. ♦ *That nonsense is but a figment of your imagination.* ♦ *The expense is but a fraction of the return.*

butane ['bju ten] *n.* a colorless, flammable gas derived from natural gas and crude oil. (No plural form in this sense.) ♦ *Butane is often used in cigarette lighters.* ♦ *Some curling irons are fueled by butane.*

butcher ['bʊtʃ ɚ] **1.** *n.* someone who slaughters animals for meat. ♦ *The cattle filed into the factory to face the butchers.* ♦ *The butcher plans to slaughter the hogs today.* **2.** *n.* someone who cuts up and sells the meat of animals. ♦ *The butcher cut a thick slice of beef for me.* ♦ *The butcher weighed the roast and told me how much it cost.* **3.** *tv.* to kill and cut up an animal for food. ♦ *The farmer butchered all his own food.* ♦ *Dave butchered a pig for the pig roast.* **4.** *tv.* to kill someone or something with great cruelty. ♦ *The maniac butchered his victims.* ♦ *All of the butchered victims were children.*

butler ['bʌt lɚ] *n.* a male servant in a household. ♦ *The butler answered the door and announced the guests.* ♦ *Not many people have butlers to serve them.*

butt ['bʌt] **1.** *n.* the end or base of something. ♦ *John placed the butt of his rifle against his shoulder.* ♦ *The butt of the log rammed hard against the back of the fireplace, loosening some bricks.* **2.** *n.* the leftover end of a cigar or cigarette. ♦ *The sidewalk near the doorway was littered with butts.* ♦ *Please take your stale cigar butt out of this house!* **3.** *n.* a cigarette. (Slang.) ♦ *Can I borrow a butt?* ♦ *How much is a pack of butts around here?* **4.** *n.* the buttocks. (Informal.) ♦ *Tom tripped and fell on his butt.* ♦ *Get off your butt and help me move the piano!* **5.** *n.* someone who is the victim of ridicule or the object of jokes or rudeness. ♦ *Bill was always the butt of Tom's ridicule.* ♦ *I hate being the butt of the joke.* **6.** *n.* a cut of meat from the shoulder of the pig. ♦ *At our picnic, we had a smoked butt and lots of fried chicken.* ♦ *A butt isn't big enough to feed a lot of people. I need to buy a whole ham instead.* **7.** *tv.* to strike or push hard against someone or something with the head. (Said especially of animals with horns.) ♦ *The goat butted the dog and forced it out of the barnyard.* ♦ *If the sheep butts you, you will suffer severe injuries.* **8.** **butt in (on)** *iv.* + *adv.* (+ *prep. phr.*) to interrupt someone or something. ♦ *Please stop butting in.* ♦ *Excuse me for butting in on you, but I need an answer now.*

butter ['bʌt ɚ] **1.** *n.* the semi-solid, fatty part of milk after it has been churned. (No plural form in this sense.) ♦ *Bread and butter was served with dinner.* ♦ *The recipe calls for unsalted butter.* **2.** *n.* certain foods mashed into a spreadable substance. ♦ *Dave spread apple butter on his toast.* ♦ *Peanut butter is made from crushed peanuts.* **3.** *tv.* to put butter on something, usually bread. ♦ *Mary buttered her toast.* ♦ *Please butter the bread for the sandwiches.* **4.** **butter up** *tv.* + *adv.* to flatter someone; to praise someone. ♦ *Bill buttered up the boss before he asked for a raise.* ♦ *You should butter Sue up if you're going to ask a favor.* **5.** **look as if butter wouldn't melt in one's mouth** *idiom* to appear to be cold and unfeeling (despite any information to the contrary). ♦ *Sally looks as if butter wouldn't melt in her mouth. She can be so cruel.* ♦ *What a sour face. He looks as if butter wouldn't melt in his mouth.*

buttercup ['bʌt ɚ kəp] *n.* a small, bright yellow flower. ♦ *The lawn was dotted with buttercups.* ♦ *Jimmy brought his mom a bouquet of buttercups.*

butterfat ['bʌt ɚ fæt] *n.* the fat found in milk. (No plural form in this sense.) ♦ *The baby cannot eat butterfat.* ♦ *Ice cream with lots of butterfat tastes very rich.*

butterfly ['bʌt ɚ flɑɪ] *n.* an insect with large, brightly colored wings, ♦ *A large butterfly with orange and black wings just flew by.* ♦ *A butterfly lighted on the picnic table.*

buttermilk ['bʌt ɚ mɪlk] *n.* a drink made from milk with certain bacterial cultures added. (No plural form in this sense.) ♦ *The recipe calls for buttermilk, rather than regular milk.* ♦ *Buttermilk is very sour.*

buttery ['bʌt ə ri] **1.** *adj.* tasting or appearing like butter. ♦ *Margarine has a buttery taste.* ♦ *I enjoyed the popcorn's buttery flavor.* **2.** *adj.* smooth and creamy like butter. ♦ *The caramel was buttery and delicious.* ♦ *Jimmy loved the buttery frosting on the cake.*

buttock ['bʌt ək] *n.* one of the two large muscles that people sit on. (Usually plural.) ♦ *The babysitter put powder on the baby's buttocks after his bath.* ♦ *My buttocks were sore after driving for 10 hours in the car.*

button ['bʌt n] **1.** *n.* a small hard disc, used to fasten clothes or fabric. ♦ *The buttons on my sweater are black and white.* ♦ *A button fell from my coat.* **2.** *n.* a small disc or similar device that is pressed to close an electrical circuit. ♦ *I had to push in the button in order to use my hair dryer.* ♦ *Push the button to complete the circuit.* **3.** *n.* a badge bearing a message, worn on the clothing. ♦ *The campaign button had a catchy slogan on it.* ♦ *The voter's jacket was covered with political buttons.* **4.** *tv.* to fasten or close two pieces of fabric together with ①. ♦ *Jane buttoned her jacket against the wind.* ♦ *The designer buttoned the model's gown.* **5. on the button** *idiom* exactly right; in exactly the right place; at exactly the right time. ♦ *That's it! You're right on the button.* ♦ *He got here at one o'clock on the button.*

buttonhole ['bʌt n hol] **1.** *n.* an opening in cloth that a button passes through. ♦ *John pushed the buttons through the buttonholes.* ♦ *David wore a rose in his buttonhole.* **2.** *tv.* [for someone] to detain someone for a conversation. (Figurative on ①.) ♦ *The reporter buttonholed me in the lobby and started asking personal questions.* ♦ *The boss buttonholed us and demanded the report.*

buxom ['bʌks əm] *adj.* [of a woman] having a large bosom. (Adv: *buxomly.*) ♦ *The opera singer was a large, buxom woman.* ♦ *The buxom shopper bought her clothes at a store that carried large sizes.*

buy ['bɑɪ] **1.** *tv., irreg.* to purchase something; to pay money in exchange for something. (Pt/pp: bought.) ♦ *I bought groceries today.* ♦ *Bill bought me a birthday present.* **2.** *tv., irreg.* to acquire something, such as time. (Figurative on ①.) ♦ *By coming into work early, I bought myself some time to finish the project.* ♦ *The supervisor's absence bought us another day to finish the project.* **3.** *tv., irreg.* to believe something. (Informal.) ♦ *Mary bought my story about being away on business.* ♦ *The teacher didn't buy the student's poor excuse.* **4.** *n.* something that is offered for sale at a very good price. ♦ *This outfit was a great buy.* ♦ *The department store is offering several special buys.* **5. buy something for a song** *idiom* to purchase something cheaply. ♦ *No one else wanted it, so I bought it for a song.* ♦ *I could buy this house for a song, because it's so ugly.* **6. buy something sight unseen** *idiom* to purchase something without seeing it first. ♦ *I bought this land sight unseen. I didn't know it was so rocky.* ♦ *It isn't usually safe to buy something sight unseen.*

buzz ['bʌz] **1.** *n.* the sound that bees make; a rapid humming sound; the vibrating noise that an electric buzzer makes. (No plural form in this sense.) ♦ *I heard the buzz and knew that my guests had arrived.* ♦ *The buzz of the alarm clock woke me from my sleep.* **2.** *n.* the sound of many people talking quietly at the same time. (Figurative on ①. No plural form in this sense.) ♦ *The buzz of many voices was very loud.* ♦ *Throughout the performance, the actors could hear the buzz of the audience.* **3.** *n.* the feeling of being intoxicated. (Slang.) ♦ *Bill got a buzz from one beer.* ♦ *The wine gave Anne a little buzz, and she couldn't stop talking.* **4.** *n.* a telephone call. (Informal.) ♦ *I'll give you a buzz before I pick you up.* ♦ *I gave Bill a buzz to see if he wanted to play basketball.* **5.** *iv.* to make a loud humming sound like bees. ♦ *The airplane engine buzzed overhead.* ♦ *The swarm of insects buzzed all night.* **6.** *iv.* [for many people] to talk quietly at the same time. ♦ *The audience buzzed throughout the performance.* ♦ *The children could not stop buzzing during class.* **7. buzz around** *iv. + adv.* to run around busily. ♦ *We buzzed around town trying to get our errands done.* ♦ *Bill is always buzzing around his yard.* **8.** *tv.* to call someone by telephone; to phone someone. ♦ *Bob buzzed Bill to see if he could go golfing.* ♦ *Buzz me before you come over.* **9.** *tv.* to ring someone's apartment buzzer from the lobby. ♦ *Mary's guests buzzed her apartment.* ♦ *When you get to the lobby, buzz my place.*

buzzard ['bʌz ɚd] **1.** *n.* a large scavenger bird. ♦ *A large buzzard circled above the deer carcass.* ♦ *Buzzards ate the dead rabbit.* **2. old buzzard** *n.* an old man. (Informal. Mildly derogatory.) ♦ *The old buzzard next door keeps kicking our cat.* ♦ *The old buzzard softened up a bit when we asked him to dinner.*

buzzer ['bʌz ɚ] *n.* an electric device that makes a loud vibrating noise. ♦ *The door buzzer for my apartment is broken.* ♦ *The buzzer of my alarm clock is very loud.*

buzzing ['bʌz ɪŋ] *adj.* humming; describing a steady electrically produced vibration. ♦ *The radio is making a buzzing noise.* ♦ *Bill heard a buzzing in his ears when he had the flu.*

by ['bɑɪ] **1.** *prep.* near; next to; alongside; beside. ♦ *I sat in the chair by the window.* ♦ *Put the umbrella by the door.* **2.** *prep.* [passing] nearby. ♦ *Tom and Jane walked by the fountain.* ♦ *We drove by the zoo today.* **3.** *prep.* by way of; through the use of. ♦ *Bill traveled to Dallas by the new expressway.* ♦ *Tom traveled through Europe by train.* **4.** *prep.* through the cause of. (Indicating who or what did something in a passive sentence.) ♦ *The party was hosted by Bob.* ♦ *The carpet was ruined by the leaky pen.* **5.** *prep.* [done] through the process of doing something. ♦ *Tom broke the computer by throwing a brick at the screen.* ♦ *John amused his class by telling funny stories.* **6.** *prep.* indicating a dimension of a square area. ♦ *This office measures 12 feet by 8 feet.* ♦ *Each group of 100 soldiers marched 10 by 10.* **7.** *prep.* before; not later than. ♦ *You must read the next chapter by tomorrow.* ♦ *Please be home by midnight.* **8.** *prep.* [surpassing someone or something] according to a specific amount. ♦ *Sue is older than Tom by three years.* ♦ *This path is longer than that one by a mile.* **9.** *prep.* allotted according to; in units of. ♦ *The grocer sold orange juice by the bottle or by the crate.* ♦ *Eggs are usually sold by the dozen.* **10.** *prep.* with the aid of a particular light source. ♦ *We gathered in the living room and read by firelight.* ♦ *The inspector searched the garden by moonlight.* **11.** *adv.* past; beyond. ♦ *An ambulance rushed by.* ♦ *Anne waved as she walked by.* **12. by day; by night** *phr.* during the day; during the night. ♦ *By day, Mary worked in an office; by night, she took classes.* ♦ *Dave slept by day and worked by night.* **13. by the way** *phr.* in addition to what I just said; while I think of it; incidentally. ♦ *By the way, I think your tie is stunning.* ♦ *By the way, you left the car unlocked when you used it last.*

bye ['bɑɪ] **1.** *n.* a bypass of the first round of a sports tournament by a player or team that is not paired against another player or team. ♦ *The players were given a bye for the first playoff game.* ♦ *Our team got a bye for Sunday's game.* **2.** See Bye-bye.

Bye(-bye) ['bɑɪ ('bɑɪ)] *interj.* "Good-bye"; "Farewell." ♦ *The baby waved and said, "Bye-bye."* ♦ *Bill said "Bye" and hung up the phone.*

bylaw ['baɪ lɔ] *n.* an official rule of an organization. ♦ *It is against the club's bylaws to vote without the president in attendance.* ♦ *The bylaws of our organization are listed in this pamphlet.*

byline ['baɪ laɪn] *n.* the name of the author of an article printed on a separate line of an article. ♦ *Jane was pleased when she finally had a byline in the local paper.* ♦ *The journalist's byline was right under the headline.*

bypass ['baɪ pæs] **1.** *tv.* to avoid something by taking a route that goes around it. ♦ *Let's bypass the city by taking this old road.* ♦ *We decided to bypass the major problem area.* **2.** *n.* a surgical operation where a passageway is constructed to go around a diseased or blocked part of the body, usually the heart. ♦ *Bill had a coronary bypass to improve his heart condition.* ♦ *Dr. Smith performs a bypass at least once a week.* **3.** *n.* a highway that goes around a congested area. ♦ *The sign suggested taking the bypass around the congested area.* ♦ *Bill always takes the bypass to avoid the city traffic.*

by-product ['baɪ prɑ dəkt] *n.* a secondary result; a secondary thing that is made in the process of making something else. ♦ *Molasses is a by-product of sugar.* ♦ *The by-products made when processing oranges are fed to cattle.*

bystander ['baɪ stæn dɚ] *n.* someone who witnesses something but is not part of it. ♦ *An innocent bystander was shot in the burglary.* ♦ *A bystander helped the accident victims.*

byte ['baɪt] *n.* a unit of computer data, made up of eight bits. ♦ *Each byte represents a single letter or number.* ♦ *How many bytes of memory does your computer have?*

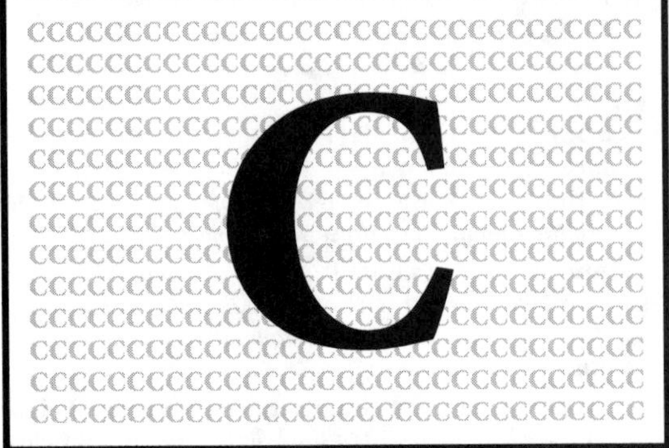

C and **c** ['si] **1.** *n.* the third letter of the alphabet. ♦ C *comes after* B *and before* D. ♦ *Please use a capital* C *when writing the word* Canada. **2. C** *n.* a letter grade of C, meaning average work. ♦ *Mary got a C on her homework.* ♦ *The teacher gave Tom a C on the test.*

cabaret [kæb ə 're] **1.** *n.* a small nightclub; an informal nightclub. (From French.) ♦ *The singer at the cabaret had a large audience.* ♦ *After dinner, we enjoyed a drink at the cabaret.* **2.** *n.* the music, singing, or other entertainment found in a small nightclub. (No plural form in this sense.) ♦ *The Smiths love opera, but they also enjoy cabaret.* ♦ *Was the cabaret at the club entertaining?*

cabbage ['kæb ɪdʒ] *n.* a large, round vegetable with green or purple leaves. (No plural form in this sense. Number is expressed with *head(s) of cabbage.*) ♦ *The salad was made with cabbage and mayonnaise.* ♦ *The grocery store had a sale on heads of cabbage.*

cabin ['kæb ən] **1.** *n.* a small house made of wood, especially in a remote area. ♦ *The cabin had one room with a small fireplace.* ♦ *Bill stayed in a cabin in the woods when he went camping.* **2.** *n.* a private room on a ship. ♦ *The ship's cabin had a sink and bunks.* ♦ *During the storm at sea, the passengers stayed in their cabins.* **3.** *n.* the part of an airplane where the passengers sit. ♦ *It was noisy in the cabin, so no one heard the pilot's announcement.* ♦ *The air pressure changed quickly in the plane's cabin.*

cabinet ['kæb (ə) nət] **1.** *n.* a piece of furniture with shelves, used for storing or displaying something. ♦ *The pots and pans are in the cabinet.* ♦ *Who left the doors of the cabinet open?* **2.** *n.* the board of advisors for a president, prime minister, etc. ♦ *The prime minister consulted his cabinet on the issue.* ♦ *Lisa was appointed to the president's cabinet.*

cabinetmaker ['kæb (ə) nət mek ɚ] *n.* someone who constructs cabinets and other furniture. ♦ *The cabinetmaker carefully sanded the wood.* ♦ *We bought a handmade chest from the cabinetmaker.*

cable ['keb əl] **1.** *n.* a thick, heavy, strong length of wire or rope. ♦ *The stereo was connected to the speakers with cables.* ♦ *A wire cable ran the length of the flagpole.* **2.** *n.* a telegram. (These were once sent over a telegraph cable.) ♦ *Mother sent a cable to let us know her arrival date.* ♦ *The cable contained bad news from my office.* **3. cable (television)** *n.* television programming received over a cable. (No plural form in this sense.) ♦ *The movie was shown only on cable.* ♦ *The company installed cable television in our house.* **4.** *tv.* to fasten something with heavy rope or wire. ♦ *The trucker cabled the cargo securely into the bed of the truck.* ♦ *John cabled the trellis to the side of the house.* **5.** *tv.* to send a message by telegraph. ♦ *Anne cabled us to let us know her arrival time.* ♦ *Cable me to let me know when your plane will be in.*

caboose [kə 'bus] *n.* the last car of a freight train. ♦ *The kids waited anxiously to see the train's caboose.* ♦ *The engineer in the caboose waved to the children.*

cache ['keʃ] **1.** *n.* a hiding place. ♦ *Jimmy's dresser drawer was a cache for his baseball cards.* ♦ *When we go on vacation, we put our jewelry in a cache under the bed.* **2.** *n.* something that is hidden; a hidden supply of something. ♦ *Bob found his brother's cache of baseball cards.* ♦ *The burglar discovered the cache of jewels.* **3.** *tv.* to hide something; to put something in a hiding place. ♦ *David cached his passport in his dresser drawer.* ♦ *Anne cached her jewels in the wall safe.*

cackle ['kæk əl] **1.** *n.* the sound of a hen. ♦ *The hen gave a cackle as it pecked at its food.* ♦ *Loud cackles came from the barnyard.* **2.** *n.* laughter like the sound of a hen. ♦ *Bill gave a cackle and grinned mischievously.* ♦ *Anne's cackle sounded throughout the house.* **3.** *iv.* to make the sound of a hen. ♦ *The hens cackled and pecked at their food.* ♦ *A hen cackled outside the window.* **4.** *iv.* to laugh with the sound of a hen. ♦ *The audience cackled at the lewd joke.* ♦ *Bill cackled and grinned mischievously.*

cacti ['kæk tɑɪ] a pl of **cactus**.

cactus ['kæk təs] *n., irreg.* a desert plant, pulpy inside, with needles on the outside. (Pl: **cacti** or *cactuses*.) ♦ *Cacti do not need much water.* ♦ *The cactus had a blossom on it.*

cad ['kæd] *n.* a rude man; a man without manners. ♦ *Mary stopped dating the cad she had been seeing.* ♦ *Only a cad would say something so rude.*

cadaver [kə 'dæv ɚ] *n.* a corpse; a dead body. ♦ *The medical students dissected the cadaver.* ♦ *The cadaver lay on the table covered with a sheet.*

cadet [kə 'dɛt] *n.* someone in a military or police academy. ♦ *The cadets stood while the national anthem was sung.* ♦ *The cadet wore a blue uniform and a white hat.*

café [kæ 'fe] *n.* a place to buy simple meals; a small restaurant. ♦ *Bill and Jane spent the afternoon reading at the café.* ♦ *There is a small café near our apartment.*

cafeteria [kæf ə 'tɪr i ə] *n.* a self-service restaurant where one can choose from many selections, generally by passing by the items and placing one's choice of food on a tray. ♦ *The cafeteria had an extensive menu.* ♦ *Bill and Bob had lunch in the school cafeteria.*

caffeine [kæ 'fin] *n.* the stimulant found in coffee, cola, cocoa, and tea. (No plural form in this sense.) ♦ *Caffeine makes some people nervous.* ♦ *Mary had too much caffeine and couldn't sleep.*

cage ['kedʒ] **1.** *n.* an enclosure with bars or wires, where living creatures are kept. ♦ *The bird sat on a perch in its cage.* ♦ *Animals live in large cages at the zoo.* **2.** *tv.* to put someone or something in a cage. ♦ *Jane cages her bird at night, but during the day it flies free.* ♦ *The zookeeper caged the dangerous animals.*

caged ['kedʒd] *adj.* enclosed; not free. ♦ *The caged animals grew weak and helpless.* ♦ *The Wilsons keep caged birds in their living room.*

cahoots [kə 'huts] **in cahoots with** *n.* in partnership with someone; in a conspiracy with someone. ♦ *John, in cahoots with his friends, had triggered the false alarm.* ♦ *The lawyer was in cahoots with the mayor in the scandal.*

cajole [kə 'dʒol] *tv.* to coax someone into doing something. ♦ *Susan cajoled the baby into eating the vegetables.* ♦ *Bill was cajoled into volunteering his time.*

Cajun ['ke dʒən] **1.** *n.* a person of French descent who immigrated to Louisiana by way of Eastern Canada. (From *Acadian.*) ♦ *We loved to go to the docks and listen to the old Cajuns talk.* ♦ *My grandfather was a Cajun and lived in Louisiana.* **2.** *adj.* <the adj. use of ①.> ♦ *Cajun cooking is very spicy.* ♦ *The band played Cajun music.*

cake ['kek] **1.** *n.* a sweet, baked, bread-like food. (No plural form in this sense. Number of expressed with *slice(s)* or *piece(s) of cake.*) ♦ *Shall I bake cake or pie for the picnic?* ♦ *Cake with lots of frosting is my favorite dessert.* **2.** *n.* a single, complete unit of ①. ♦ *I baked three cakes for the picnic.* ♦ *We cut the cake into eight equal pieces.* **3. slice of the cake** *idiom* a share of something. ♦ *There's so much work to do that everyone must get a slice of the cake.* ♦ *This company makes huge profits, and the workers want a slice of the cake.*

calamari [kæl ə 'mɑr i] *n.* squid, eaten as food. (No plural form in this sense. The Italian word for **squid**.) ♦ *Max's seafood restaurant serves excellent calamari.* ♦ *The calamari was fried in butter.*

calamity [kə 'læm ə ti] *n.* a disaster; a catastrophe. (No plural form in this sense.) ♦ *Calamity struck when the tent collapsed during the storm.* ♦ *The circus experienced a calamity when the tigers escaped from their cages.*

calcium ['kæl si əm] *n.* a chemical element and essential nutrient, important for strong teeth and bones. (No plural form in this sense.) ♦ *Milk contains calcium.* ♦ *A good diet includes foods with calcium.*

calculate ['kæl kjə let] **1.** *iv.* to estimate; to figure out values. ♦ *Please be quiet. I'm calculating.* ♦ *The computer has not stopped running. It is calculating.* **2.** *tv.* to add, subtract, multiply, or divide numbers; to estimate the value of something; to figure out the value of something. ♦ *Mary calculated her monthly expenses.* ♦ *We couldn't calculate the value of the house without going inside.*

calculated ['kælk jə let ɪd] *adj.* carefully planned; thought out; premeditated. ♦ *I only take calculated risks.* ♦ *Tom's actions appeared completely cold and calculated.*

calculating ['kælk jə let ɪŋ] *adj.* shrewd; cunning; scheming. (Adv: *calculatingly.*) ♦ *The calculating man tried to cheat his friends.* ♦ *The successful businesswoman was very calculating.*

calculation [kæl kjə 'le ʃən] **1.** *n.* adding, subtracting, dividing, or multiplying numbers and the results of these activities. ♦ *Mary's calculation of her monthly expenses was correct.* ♦ *The teacher corrected the student's calculations.* **2.** *n.* deliberate planning or thinking. (Figurative on ①. No plural form in this sense.) ♦ *Calculation and manipulation were the qualities that Mike used to get people to do things his way.* ♦ *It was deliberate calculation, not an accident that caused this!*

calculator ['kæl kjə let ɚ] *n.* a machine that adds, subtracts, multiplies, and divides figures and performs other mathematical functions. ♦ *Accountants keep calculators on their desks.* ♦ *A calculator is useful when balancing a checkbook.*

calculus ['kæl kjə ləs] **1.** *n.* a branch of higher mathematics using algebraic symbols and operations. (No plural form in this sense.) ♦ *I failed my course in calculus three times.* ♦ *You have to study calculus and trigonometry to be an engineer.* **2.** *n.* a dark, granular substance built up on the teeth from dead bacteria. (No plural form in this sense. See also **tartar**.) ♦ *The dentist removed the calculus from between Tom's teeth.* ♦ *Regular brushing will keep calculus from forming.*

calendar ['kæl ən dɚ] **1.** *n.* a system for keeping track of years and the divisions of years. ♦ *Carvings in the stone showed an ancient calendar.* ♦ *Our modern calendar is only a few centuries old.* **2.** *n.* a chart or table showing days, weeks, and months. ♦ *A calendar hangs on the kitchen wall.* ♦ *The calendar shows each month separately.* **3.** *n.* a schedule of events; a list of events. ♦ *The busy manager's calendar is full this month.* ♦ *My health club published a calendar of exercise classes.*

calf ['kæf] **1.** *n., irreg.* a young cow or bull. (Pl: **calves**.) ♦ *The new calf stood up on wobbly legs.* ♦ *In the spring, several new calves were born.* **2.** *n.* the back of the leg from the knee to the ankle. ♦ *Tom had a bruise on his calf where the horse kicked him.* ♦ *The exercises were designed to strengthen the calves.* **3. kill the fatted calf** *idiom* to prepare an elaborate celebration or banquet (in someone's honor). ♦ *When Bob got back from college, his parents killed the fatted calf and threw a great party.* ♦ *Sorry this meal isn't much, John. We didn't have time to kill the fatted calf.*

calfskin ['kæf skɪn] **1.** *n.* leather from the skin of a young cow or bull. (No plural form in this sense.) ♦ *The wallet was made of calfskin.* ♦ *David bought a belt of calfskin.* **2.** *adj.* made of ①. ♦ *John got a calfskin wallet for his birthday.* ♦ *David grew too large for his calfskin belt.*

caliber ['kæl ə bɚ] **1.** *n.* the inside diameter of a narrow cylinder; [of a gun having] a barrel of a particular diameter. ♦ *A revolver usually has a small caliber.* ♦ *The victim was shot with a gun having a large caliber.* **2.** *n.* the diameter of a bullet. ♦ *What caliber is this bullet?* ♦ *They found the shell of a bullet with a large caliber near the victim.* **3.** *n.* the degree of worthiness; rank. (No plural form in this sense.) ♦ *The new opera singer is of the highest caliber.* ♦ *Students of low caliber do not get into the best colleges.*

calibrate ['kæl ə bret] **1.** *tv.* to adjust something so it is more accurate. ♦ *The astronomer calibrated the telescope.* ♦ *Scales must be calibrated regularly.* **2.** *tv.* to put the correct measuring marks on something. ♦ *Someone had calibrated the glass cylinder incorrectly.* ♦ *The thermometer was calibrated at the factory.*

calibration [kæl ə 'bre ʃən] *n.* the proper adjustment of a measuring device. (No plural form in this sense.) ♦ *The astronomer checked the calibration of the telescope.* ♦ *The butcher's scales needed calibration frequently.*

calico ['kæl i ko] **1.** *n.* a patterned, cotton fabric. (Pl in *-s* or *-es.*) ♦ *The new summer dresses were made of bright calico.* ♦ *Calico is an inexpensive fabric.* **2.** *adj.* made of ①. ♦ *Mary's favorite dress is a bright calico frock.* ♦ *The farmer bought a few yards of calico cloth to take home to his wife.* **3.** *adj.* [of a cat] having patches of fur of many different colors. ♦ *Tom has a long-haired, calico cat.* ♦ *Our calico cat lived to be 19 years old.*

California [kæl ə 'forn jə] See Gazetteer.

calisthenics [kæl ɪs 'θɛn ɪks] *n.* exercises for physical fitness. (Treated as singular or plural.) ♦ *The army recruits did calisthenics every morning.* ♦ *In order to lose weight, Mike did calisthenics.*

call ['kɔl] **1.** *n.* a shout; a cry. ♦ *A call for help came from the burning house.* ♦ *The injured man gave a faint call to his fellow passenger.* **2. (phone) call** *n.* a message or conversation using the telephone. ♦ *There was a phone call for you earlier today.* ♦ *There were a few calls while you were out.* **3.** *n.* a decision; a choice. ♦ *It's your call—do you want Chinese or Italian food for dinner?* ♦ *I made a wrong call about Mike's character.* **4.** *n.* a need; a demand. (No plural form in this sense.) ♦ *There's no call for being rude!* ♦ *There is a real call for leaders in this country.* **5. call to** *iv.* + *prep. phr.* to speak loudly or shout toward someone, usually to attract the person's attention. ♦ *Jane called to the children downstairs.* ♦ *I called to my friend across the park, but she didn't hear me.* **6.** *tv.* to call someone on the telephone; to try to contact someone by telephone. ♦ *Call Mary and see if she wants to join us for dinner.* ♦ *David calls his mother every day.* **7.** *tv.* to summon someone. ♦ *Anne called the children, and they came immediately.* ♦ *The family was called to the dying man's bedside.* **8.** *tv.* to name someone or something; to refer to or address someone or something as something. ♦ *We call the dog Rover.* ♦ *The boy's name is Randolph, but he's called Randy.* **9.** *tv.* [for an umpire] to make a decision in a ball game. ♦ *The umpire called a strike.* ♦ *The umpire called it wrong!* **10. call off** *tv.* + *adv.* to cancel something, especially an event that has been planned for a certain date. ♦ *The picnic was called off due to rain.* ♦ *The nervous groom called the wedding off.* **11. call a meeting to order** *idiom* to announce that a meeting is about to begin. ♦ *The president called the meeting to order.* ♦ *The meeting will be called to order at noon.* **12. call for someone or something** *idiom* to need, require, or demand something or the services of someone. ♦ *The recipe calls for two cups of flour.* ♦ *This job calls for someone with good eyesight.* **13. call on someone** *idiom* to visit someone. ♦ *I have to call on my aunt this Sunday.* ♦ *Bill called on his brother in the hospital.* **14. call out (to someone)** *idiom* to shout to someone. ♦ *Mike called out to Tom that there was a telephone call for him.* ♦ *I heard someone call out, but I could see no one.* **15. issue a call for something** *idiom* to make an invitation or request for something. ♦ *The prime minister made a call for peace.* ♦ *The person who organized the writing contest issued a call for entries.* **16. pay a call on someone** *idiom* to visit someone. ♦ *Grandmother always paid us a call on Sundays.* ♦ *Let's pay a call on Mary at the hospital.*

caller ['kɔl ɚ] **1.** *n.* someone who makes a telephone call. ♦ *The caller left a message on the answering machine.* ♦ *The last caller hung up on me.* **2.** *n.* a visitor. ♦ *A caller left his business card.* ♦ *The socialite did not accept callers in the morning.*

calligrapher [kə 'lɪ grə fɚ] *n.* someone who is skilled in calligraphy; someone who can write with fine, artistic penmanship. ♦ *The calligrapher does exquisite lettering.* ♦ *Mary hired a calligrapher to address the invitations.*

calligraphy [kə 'lɪ grə fi] *n.* a style of elaborate, artistic handwriting. (No plural form in this sense.) ♦ *Jane took a class in calligraphy.* ♦ *The old manuscript was done in beautiful calligraphy.*

calling ['kɔl ɪŋ] *n.* one's vocation; one's job. (No plural form in this sense.) ♦ *What is your calling in life?* ♦ *The nun felt her calling was to help the poor.*

callous ['kæl əs] **1.** *adj.* [of skin] hardened and thickened. (See also **callus.**) ♦ *Mike has callous lumps on his hands from playing tennis.* ♦ *A painful callous protrusion rubbed against the inside of Anne's shoe.* **2.** *adj.* unsympathetic; without compassion. (Figurative on ①. Adv: *callously.*) ♦ *The callous executive laughed at the beggar.* ♦ *Only someone who is callous would refuse to help someone in need.*

callousness ['kæl əs nəs] *n.* the condition of being without feeling or compassion. (No plural form in this sense.) ♦ *The voters were tired of the politicians' callousness.* ♦ *The uncaring clerk lost a lot of sales because of his callousness.*

callus ['kæl əs] *n.* a hard, thick piece of skin. (See also **callous.**) ♦ *Mike got a callus from playing tennis.* ♦ *The blister turned into a callus.*

calm ['kɑm] **1.** *adj.* quiet; serene; at peace. (Adv: *calmly.* Comp: *calmer;* sup: *calmest.*) ♦ *Bill seemed calm, but inside he was seething.* ♦ *The canoe glided across the calm water.* **2.** *n.* a time of quiet; a time of serenity. (No plural form in this sense.) ♦ *At sunset, a calm came over the lake.* ♦ *Max sat in the chapel and enjoyed the calm.* **3. calm (down)** *tv.* (+ *adv.*) to soothe someone or something; to cause someone or something to relax. ♦ *The trainer calmed the dog after gaining its trust.* ♦ *Mary tried to calm down the hysterical child.* **4. calm (down)** *iv.* (+ *adv.*) to relax; to become tranquil. ♦ *After everyone had calmed down, the company president explained the cutbacks.* ♦ *The storm soon calmed, and the sun came out.*

calorie ['kæl ə ri] **1.** *n.* a unit equal to the amount of energy required to raise the temperature of one gram of water one degree Celsius (a small calorie). ♦ *The chemical reaction produced only 22 calories of heat.* ♦ *Our instruments detected only 18 calories.* **2.** *n.* a unit of energy equal to the amount of energy required to raise the temperature of one kilogram of water one degree Celsius (a large calorie). ♦ *The tiny furnace produced enough calories to heat the entire room.* ♦ *How many calories are required to boil a cup of water?* **3.** *n.* a unit of energy supplied by food. ♦ *I always eat meals low in calories.* ♦ *How many calories are in this candy?*

calves ['kævz] pl of calf.

camaraderie [kɑm ə 'rɑd ə ri] *n.* a spirit of togetherness; friendship among friends. (No plural form in this sense.) ♦ *The company ran smoothly because the workers had a sense of camaraderie.* ♦ *The friends had great camaraderie on the camping trip.*

Cambodia [kæm 'bod i ə] See Gazetteer.

came ['kem] pt of come.

camel ['kæm əl] *n.* a large desert animal with one or two fatty humps on its back. ♦ *The nomads traveled across the desert by camel.* ♦ *While on vacation in the Middle East, Mary rode a camel.*

cameo ['kæm i o] **1.** *n.* a small piece of jewelry showing a raised profile against a background. (Pl in *-s.*) ♦ *This* *cameo is a family heirloom.* ♦ *The museum had a display of antique cameos.* **2.** *n.* a brief appearance of someone famous in a movie or play. (Pl in *-s.*) ♦ *The singer did a cameo on the popular TV show.* ♦ *The movie included cameos by several celebrities.* **3.** *adj.* <the adj. use of ②.> ♦ *The famous celebrity played a cameo role in the movie.* ♦ *The singer made a cameo appearance on the popular TV show.*

camera ['kæm (ə) rə] **1.** *n.* a device that takes pictures; a device that makes photographs. ♦ *We forgot the camera when we went to the park.* ♦ *Mary's camera takes great pictures.* **2.** *n.* a device that records live action for television or movies. (As used for movies or video recording.) ♦ *The cameras were poised, waiting for the star to appear.* ♦ *Mike took his video camera on vacation.*

Cameroon [kæm ə 'run] See Gazetteer.

camouflage ['kæm ə flɑʒ] **1.** *n.* material that disguises or conceals someone or something. (No plural form in this sense.) ♦ *The soldiers wore camouflage in the jungle.* ♦ *A chameleon has a natural camouflage.* **2.** *tv.* to disguise or conceal someone or something, making the person or thing blend with the background. ♦ *Tan uniforms camouflaged the soldiers in the desert.* ♦ *Sue used some makeup to camouflage her rash.*

camouflaged ['kæm ə flɑʒd] *adj.* concealed or hidden; made to blend in with the surroundings. ♦ *The camouflaged soldiers were well hidden.* ♦ *I could not see the naturally camouflaged snake among the leaves.*

camp ['kæmp] **1.** *n.* a remote or rural temporary residence, such as for soldiers, pioneers, refugees, people on vacation, etc. ♦ *We made our camp on the bank of the river.* ♦ *The pioneers set up a camp while they built houses.* **2.** *n.* a remote or rural place where children are sent in the summer. ♦ *The camp provided horseback riding and archery lessons.* ♦ *Jimmy got homesick at camp last summer.* **3.** *n.* a permanent training and residence area for training and retraining members of various military organizations. ♦ *John's father trained at Camp Pendleton decades ago.* ♦ *The buildings at the camp were painted every year.* **4.** *iv.* to take a vacation in a natural setting; to stay outside in a remote or rural area, in a tent or a camper instead of a hotel. ♦ *We camped at a large national park for a week.* ♦ *It rained when we wanted to camp, so we rented a cabin instead.* **5. have a foot in both camps** *idiom* to have an interest in, or to support each of, two opposing groups of people. ♦ *The foreman has been promised a promotion and so had a foot in both camps—workers and management—during the strike.* ♦ *Mr. Smith has a foot in both camps in the parent/teacher dispute. He teaches math, but he has a son at the school.*

campaign [kæm 'pen] **1.** *n.* the period of time before an election when the candidates try to persuade people to vote for them. ♦ *The campaign was a long one, but Mike won the election.* ♦ *The presidential campaign lasted for months.* **2.** *n.* a coordinated series of events with a specific goal or purpose. ♦ *Our marketing campaign will increase sales.* ♦ *The charity started a campaign against poverty.* **3.** *iv.* to try to persuade people to agree with someone's point of view. ♦ *Our office manager campaigned for a new computer system.* ♦ *Mike campaigned for a new car, and Mary finally agreed.* **4. smear campaign (against someone)** *idiom* a campaign aimed at damaging someone's reputation by making accusations and spreading rumors. ♦ *The politician's opponents are engaging in a smear campaign against him.* ♦ *Jack started a smear campaign against Tom so that Tom wouldn't get the manager's job.*

camper ['kæm pɚ] **1.** *n.* someone who goes camping; someone who takes a vacation out in rural or remote areas. ♦ *The wealthy campers had expensive tents and equipment.* ♦ *The Smiths aren't campers—they prefer elegant hotels.* **2.** *n.* a special vehicle, designed for camping. ♦ *Some campers fit on the back of a small truck, and others are almost homes that can be driven wherever you want.* ♦ *My neighbors did not want me to park my camper in my front yard.*

campfire ['kæmp fɑɪr] *n.* a fire that campers cook on and sit around at night to keep warm while telling stories and enjoying the outdoors. ♦ *As the campfire died down, the campers sang songs and told stories.* ♦ *The campers huddled near the campfire to keep warm.*

camphor ['kæm fɚ] *n.* a fragrant substance from a resinous tree. (No plural form in this sense.) ♦ *Grandma kept a bit of camphor in her cabinet full of knickknacks.* ♦ *Camphor can be used to stop itching.*

campsite ['kæmp sɑɪt] *n.* the area where campers set up their tents. ♦ *Each park has campsites designated for overnight campers.* ♦ *The campsite had a public shower and bathroom in a nearby building.*

campus ['kæmp əs] **1.** *n.* the buildings and grounds of a school, college, or university. ♦ *A civil engineer designed the college's campus.* ♦ *The campus of the university is very old and beautiful.* **2.** *n.* the buildings and grounds of a large company. ♦ *The company's campus has benches surrounding a little fountain.* ♦ *The building was built on a large campus in the suburbs.* **3.** *adj.* <the adj. use of ①.> ♦ *The campus buildings had been built decades ago.* ♦ *Campus life is interesting, and living in a dormitory can be fun.* **4. off campus** *phr.* not located on the grounds of a college or university. ♦ *Tom has an apartment off campus.* ♦ *The dean is off campus and cannot be reached.* **5. on campus** *phr.* located or being on the grounds of a college or university. ♦ *Do you live on campus or off campus?* ♦ *I don't think that Lisa is on campus right now.*

can ['kæn] **1.** *aux.* <a form indicating ability to do something.> (The related form associated with action in the past is could.) ♦ *We can go to the movie because I have enough money.* ♦ *Mary can ski really well.* **2.** *aux.* <a form indicating permission to do something.> (In general use but considered informal. In more formal English, may is used for this function.) ♦ *Mother says we can go to the movies.* ♦ *Can I have some more salad?* **3.** *tv.* to preserve food by sealing it in an airtight container. (Pt: *canned.*) ♦ *Mary cans the vegetables that grow in her garden.* ♦ *We ate some carrots from our garden and canned the rest.* **4.** *tv.* to fire someone; to get rid of someone. (Slang.) ♦ *A lazy employee was canned last Friday.* ♦ *Will the boss can you for that mistake?* **5.** *n.* a cylindrical container, usually made of metal. ♦ *We always buy coffee in a can.* ♦ *The nails are in a can on the workbench.* **6.** *n.* the contents of ⑤. ♦ *Add one can of tomato paste to the casserole.* ♦ *I ate a can of beans for supper.*

Canada ['kæn ə də] See Gazetteer.

Canadian [kə 'ned i ən] **1.** *n.* a citizen or native of Canada. ♦ *Some Canadians speak French and other Canadians speak English.* ♦ *Canadians and U.S. citizens visit each other's countries often.* **2.** *adj.* of or about Canada or ①. ♦ *The Canadian winter can be very cold.* ♦ *We have a lovely week at a Canadian hotel in the mountains.*

canal [kə 'næl] **1.** *n.* a long, navigable waterway—usually man-made—that is not a river. ♦ *A canal linked the two bodies of water.* ♦ *The Panama Canal links the Atlantic and Pacific Oceans.* **2.** *n.* an internal passageway in plants and animals. ♦ *John's stomach pains are a disorder of the alimentary canal.* ♦ *The baby passed through the birth canal head first.*

canary [kə 'nɛr i] *n.* a small, yellow bird that sings. ♦ *In the living room was a small cage with a canary in it.* ♦ *Our canary sings sweetly.*

cancel ['kæn səl] **1.** *tv.* to end or stop something that is occurring or planned. ♦ *Please cancel your plans and come with me.* ♦ *The boss canceled the meeting.* **2. cancel out** *tv.* + *adv.* to neutralize something; to balance something. ♦ *The music coming over my headphones canceled out the sound of the plane's engines.* ♦ *The antacid cancels out the extra acid in your stomach.* **3.** *tv.* to place a mark on a postage stamp, check, ticket, and the like, so that it cannot be used again. ♦ *The post office cancels the postage on each letter.* ♦ *The train conductor canceled the expired train pass.*

canceled ['kæn səld] *adj.* rendered useless; stopped; ended. ♦ *We rescheduled the canceled picnic.* ♦ *I wrote the network asking it to restore the canceled television show.*

cancellation [kæn sə 'le ʃən] *n.* the ending or stopping of something occurring or planned. ♦ *The cancellation of the party disappointed the children.* ♦ *The restaurant often gets cancellations of reservations.*

cancer ['kæn sɚ] **1.** *n.* a disease characterized by a tumor or tumors growing and spreading throughout the body. (No plural form in this sense.) ♦ *Cancer ravaged the body of the scientist exposed to radiation.* ♦ *The doctor suspected that the patient had cancer.* **2.** *n.* a tumor caused by ①; a case of ①. ♦ *The doctor removed the cancer during an operation.* ♦ *Bill's cancer has not spread, and he will get well.* **3.** *n.* something evil or horrible that spreads out over an area. (Figurative on ②.) ♦ *Low morale was a cancer in the company.* ♦ *Crime is an evil cancer in many cities.*

cancerous ['kæn sə rəs] **1.** *adj.* malignant; diseased with cancer. (Adv: *cancerously.*) ♦ *The surgeon removed the cancerous tumor.* ♦ *The pathologist studied the cancerous organ.* **2.** *adj.* evil and destructive. (Figurative on ①. Adv: *cancerously.*) ♦ *A cancerous attitude spread throughout the company.* ♦ *Cancerous cynicism affected the relationship.*

candid ['kæn dɪd] *adj.* frank and open. (Adv: *candidly.*) ♦ *I can always count on a candid answer from my advisor.* ♦ *The candid article described the artist's strengths and weaknesses.*

candidate ['kæn dɪ det] **1.** *n.* someone who is seeking a public office or other job. ♦ *The presidential candidate gave speeches all over the country.* ♦ *The reporter asked the candidate some tough questions.* **2.** *n.* a recommended or possible choice of a thing or person. ♦ *Who is a likely candidate to make the next pot of coffee?* ♦ *My car is a good candidate for the rubbish heap!*

candied ['kæn did] *adj.* dried and coated with sugar. ♦ *I ate a lot of candied fruit over the holidays.* ♦ *Bob placed a dish of candied nuts on the coffee table.*

candle ['kæn dəl] **1.** *n.* an object made of wax molded around a string or wick. (The wick burns and gives off light.) ♦ *The dining room was lit with candles.* ♦ *Mary extinguished the candles at the end of the evening.* **2. burn the candle at both ends** *idiom* to work very hard and stay up very late at night. ♦ *No wonder Mary is ill. She has been burning the candle at both ends for a long time.* ♦ *You can't keep on burning the candle at both ends.* **3. can't hold a candle to someone** *idiom* not equal to someone; not worthy to associate with someone; unable to measure up to someone. ♦ *Mary can't hold a candle to Anne when it comes to auto racing.* ♦ *As for singing, John can't hold a candle to Jane.*

candlestick ['kæn dəl stɪk] *n.* a holder for a candle. ♦ *The gift box held a beautiful set of silver candlesticks.* ♦ *The burning candle dripped wax onto the candlestick.*

candor ['kæn dɚ] *n.* frankness; straightforwardness. (No plural form in this sense.) ♦ *Mary appreciated her friend's candor.* ♦ *Candor is an appealing quality in a politician.*

candy ['kæn di] **1.** *n.* a sweet food or confection made with sugar and additional flavors or components. (No plural form in this sense.) ♦ *Jimmy spent his allowance on candy.* ♦ *Jane took a box of candy to her friend as a gift.* **2.** *n.* a piece or serving of ①. ♦ *There was a bowl of little candies on the table.* ♦ *Can I have a candy?*

cane ['ken] **1.** *n.* a stick used as an aid in walking. ♦ *Grandfather's cane is carved from oak.* ♦ *The disabled woman leaned on her cane.* **2.** *tv.* to beat someone with a stick, as punishment. ♦ *The boy was caned as punishment for his misbehavior.* ♦ *Some countries still cane people for committing crimes.*

canine ['ke naɪn] **1.** *n.* a dog. ♦ *The police department used canines to sniff out drugs.* ♦ *The friendly canine worked as a guide dog.* **2.** *adj.* <the adj. use of ①.> ♦ *The police department has a canine patrol.* ♦ *Many blind people have canine companions that guide them.* **3.** *n.* a pointed upper tooth, used for cutting or tearing. ♦ *The canines of walruses are very long tusks.* ♦ *The dentist filled a cavity in my left canine.*

canister ['kæn ɪ stɚ] *n.* a small box for storing foods in the kitchen. ♦ *Flour and sugar are kept in canisters on the kitchen counter.* ♦ *I bought a set of canisters for my kitchen.*

canker (sore) ['kæŋ kɚ (sor)] *n.* an ulcer or sore, in or around the mouth. ♦ *A canker on my lip hurt when I ate salty food.* ♦ *The ointment was good for curing canker sores.*

canned ['kænd] *adj.* preserved; sealed into a container. ♦ *The grocery store had a sale on canned vegetables.* ♦ *I gave David some homemade canned tomatoes from my garden.*

cannery ['kæn ə ri] *n.* a factory where food is canned. ♦ *The workers at the cannery went on strike.* ♦ *The grocery store received a shipment of vegetables directly from the cannery.*

cannibal ['kæn ə bəl] **1.** *n.* someone who eats the flesh of humans. ♦ *The tribe of cannibals killed and ate their enemies.* ♦ *Cannibals sometimes ate human flesh as part of a ritual.* **2.** *n.* an animal that eats members of its own species. ♦ *Lobsters are well known as cannibals.* ♦ *Sometimes large cats turn into cannibals when food is scarce.*

cannibalism ['kæn ə bə lɪz əm] *n.* the practice of eating the flesh of one's own species. ♦ *Cannibalism is taboo among most human groups.* ♦ *Cannibalism has been eliminated from most of the world's cultures.*

cannibalize ['kæn ə bə lɑɪz] *tv.* to take parts from one machine to repair another machine. ♦ *Tom cannibalized parts from four old trucks to get his truck running again.* ♦ *The soldiers had to cannibalize the damaged tanks for parts.*

cannon ['kæn ən] *n., irreg.* a large gun. (Pl: *cannon* or *cannons.*) ♦ *The historic fort was lined with cannons once used for defense.* ♦ *An ancient cannon sat in the middle of the town square.*

cannonball ['kɑn ən bɔl] *n.* a large, metal ball that is fired from a cannon. ♦ *The kids tried to lift the cannonballs on display at the museum.* ♦ *Hundreds of cannonballs were discovered in the shipwreck.*

cannot [kə 'nɑt] *aux.* the negative form of can. (See also can't.) ♦ *As hard as I try, I cannot get the computer to work.* ♦ *I cannot remember which street Bill lives on.*

canoe [kə 'nu] **1.** *n.* a small boat that is moved by paddling. ♦ *The canoe glided silently over the still lake.* ♦ *The campers learned to paddle a canoe.* **2.** *iv.* to travel by ①. ♦ *We canoed around the lake at dawn, trying to find a place to fish.* ♦ *The children canoed to the island for a picnic.* **3. paddle one's own canoe** *idiom* to do something by oneself; to be alone. ♦ *I've been left to paddle my own canoe too many times.* ♦ *Sally isn't with us. She's off paddling her own canoe.*

canonize ['kæn ə nɑɪz] *tv.* to declare officially that someone is a saint. ♦ *The Church canonized the martyr in 1012.* ♦ *The pious woman was canonized a century after her death.*

canopy ['kæn ə pi] *n.* a fabric cover that hangs over something. ♦ *The antique bed had a canopy.* ♦ *We waited under the store's canopy for the rain to stop.*

can't [kænt] *cont.* "cannot." ♦ *You can't compare apples and oranges.* ♦ *Jimmy can't go out and play today because he's sick.*

cantaloupe ['kæn tə lop] *n.* a round melon with a hard skin and an orange inner pulp. ♦ *The restaurant served cantaloupe for breakfast.* ♦ *The grocer thumped the cantaloupe to see if it was ripe.*

cantankerous [kæn 'tæŋk ə rəs] *adj.* grouchy; disagreeable. (Adv: *cantankerously.*) ♦ *The cantankerous customer snapped at the salesclerk.* ♦ *My boss is acting a little cantankerous today.*

canteen [kæn 'tin] **1.** *n.* a container for carrying water. ♦ *The campers filled their canteens before the hike.* ♦ *By the end of the hike, my canteen was empty.* **2.** *n.* a recreation room and informal eating area for military personnel. ♦ *The enlisted soldiers met in the canteen.* ♦ *The canteen had a pool table for the soldiers.* **3.** *n.* a place to purchase food, snacks, and personal needs. ♦ *I bought some toothpaste at the canteen.* ♦ *We ate lunch at the canteen in the amusement park.*

canter ['kæn tɚ] **1.** *n.* the pace of a horse that is slower than a gallop but faster than a trot. ♦ *The horse's canter was a little jerky.* ♦ *The horse moved at a canter across the field.* **2.** *iv.* [for a horse] to move at a canter ①. ♦ *The horse cantered through the countryside.* ♦ *Jane commanded the horse to canter.*

canvas ['kæn vəs] **1.** *n.* a heavy, sturdy fabric made from cotton or hemp. (No plural form in this sense.) ♦ *The tent was made of waterproof canvas.* ♦ *The student carried library books in a bag made of canvas.* **2.** *n.* a panel fabric—usually stretched on a frame—that painters paint on. ♦ *The artist applied a light coat of white paint to the canvas.* ♦ *My art instructor likes to paint on large canvases.* **3.** *n.* a painting that has been painted on ②. ♦ *This canvas shows the artist's use of blue.* ♦ *The decorator placed many small canvases on the walls.*

canvass ['kæn vəs] *tv.* to visit many people and ask them to vote for or against someone or something or ask them their opinion about someone or something. ♦ *The campaign workers canvassed the neighborhood.* ♦ *Let's canvass the town with a petition.*

canyon ['kæn jən] *n.* a deep, narrow valley, often with a river running through it. ♦ *This photo shows a beautiful canyon in the wilderness.* ♦ *The floor of the canyon was home to all types of wildlife.*

cap ['kæp] **1.** *n.* a head covering, often with a bill or visor. ♦ *Bill took his cap off when he entered the house.* ♦ *A little cap protected the baby from the sun.* **2.** *n.* the covering or the top of a bottle or small jar; a small lid. ♦ *Remember to put the cap on the paste, or it will dry out.* ♦ *I lost the cap to the aspirin bottle.* **3.** *tv.* to close something with ②; to put ② on something. ♦ *Cap the glue tightly, or it will dry out.* ♦ *I capped the water bottle and put it back into the refrigerator.* **4.** *tv.* to limit something at a specific point. ♦ *We need to cap spending in every department.* ♦ *The law capped the amount rents could be increased in one year.* **5. put a cap on something** *idiom* to put a limit on something. (On ④.) ♦ *We need to put a cap on spending on every department.* ♦ *The city put a cap on the amount each landlord could charge.*

capability [kep ə 'bɪl ɪt i] *n.* the mental or physical ability to do something. (No plural form in this sense.) ♦ *Each of my students has the capability of being an excellent student.* ♦ *This computer has the capabilities needed to perform all sorts of functions.*

capable ['kep ə bəl] **1.** *adj.* able; having the power or ability to do something. (Adv: *capably.*) ♦ *The very capable caterer fed everyone well at the party.* ♦ *The parents hired a capable babysitter to watch their children.* **2. capable of doing something** *idiom* having the ability to do something. ♦ *Do you think Tom is capable of lifting 200 pounds?* ♦ *No one I know is capable of such a crime!*

capacity [kə 'pæs ə ti] **1.** *n.* the amount of something that a space will hold. (No plural form in this sense.) ♦ *The maximum capacity of the room is 200 people.* ♦ *The bottle's capacity is one liter.* **2.** *n.* the ability to accommodate someone or something. (No plural form in this sense.) ♦ *The hotel has the capacity to hold large banquets.* ♦ *The computer has a large memory capacity.* **3.** *n.* a job or set of responsibilities. (No plural form in this sense.) ♦ *What is your capacity at the company?* ♦ *In his capacity as company president, Bill has the final say on all policies.*

cape ['kep] **1.** *n.* a long, sleeveless garment worn over clothes; a cloak. ♦ *Anne swept into the room wearing a long cape over her riding clothes.* ♦ *The magician's cape was lined with red satin and had a hood.* **2.** *n.* a piece of land that juts out into a body of water. ♦ *The lighthouse is at the end* *of the cape.* ♦ *The explorer sailed around the Cape of Good Hope.*

caper ['kep ɚ] **1.** *n.* a prank; a wild and silly episode or event. ♦ *Bill is known for his wild capers.* ♦ *I enjoyed watching the young bears and their juvenile capers.* **2.** *n.* the flower bud of a species of shrub, pickled and used as a seasoning. ♦ *The sauce on the fish has capers in it.* ♦ *I bought a jar of capers at the grocery store.*

capillary ['kæp ə lɛr i] *n.* the smallest blood vessel. ♦ *Broken capillaries can cause red marks on the face.* ♦ *The blow broke some capillaries in my arm.*

capital ['kæp ɪ təl] **1.** *n.* a city that is the center of a government, province, territory, or country. (Compare with capitol.) ♦ *Des Moines is the capital of Iowa.* ♦ *The capital is the seat of state government.* **2.** *n.* any special or central city, with reference to a certain attribute. ♦ *Holland, Michigan, is the tulip capital of the United States.* ♦ *Nashville, Tennessee, is the country-music capital of the world.* **3.** *n.* an uppercase letter of the alphabet; a majuscule. ♦ *A sentence begins with a capital.* ♦ *The ransom note was typed in capitals.* **4.** *n.* money that is invested with the hopes it will earn more money. (No plural form in this sense.) ♦ *The investor made a fortune from a hundred dollars of capital.* ♦ *The banker lost both earnings and capital in the bad investment.* **5.** *adj.* relating to money used as an investment. ♦ *The investor suffered a capital loss when the stock market plunged.* ♦ *The university held a capital funds drive.* **6.** *adj.* [of a crime] punishable by death. ♦ *Murder is a capital crime.* ♦ *The minister argued with the politician about capital punishment.*

capitalism ['kæp ɪ təl ɪz əm] *n.* the economic system basic to the free exchange of goods and services. (No plural form in this sense.) ♦ *Capitalism encourages the ownership of companies by the general population.* ♦ *Capitalism, in some form, is spreading throughout much of the world.*

capitalist ['kæp ɪ təl əst] **1.** *n.* someone who practices or favors capitalism. ♦ *The U.S. is a country of capitalists.* ♦ *The capitalist earned a great deal of money from investments.* **2.** *n.* an investor; someone who invests money. ♦ *Everyone who has a company pension is a capitalist.* ♦ *Capitalists provide the money for development around the world.*

capitalize ['kæp ɪ təl ɑɪz] **1.** *tv.* to write a letter of the alphabet in uppercase. ♦ *In the German language, all nouns are capitalized.* ♦ *Always capitalize the first word in a sentence.* **2.** *tv.* to turn earnings into capital; to use an investment as capital. ♦ *The firm capitalized its dividend and paid it to the stockholders in more stock.* ♦ *The company tried to capitalize its debt and sell stock to pay off the bond holders.* **3. capitalize on** *iv.* + *prep. phr.* to take advantage of a situation. ♦ *The teens capitalized on the fact that their parents were away and threw a large party.* ♦ *Let's capitalize on the good weather and go to the beach.*

capitol ['kæp ɪ təl] **1.** *n.* the building where lawmakers do their work. (Compare with capital.) ♦ *The capitol is a large government building.* ♦ *Our state capitol is in the center of the city I live in.* **2. Capitol** *n.* the building in Washington, D.C., where the Senate and the House of Representatives do their work. ♦ *New federal laws are proposed in the Capitol.* ♦ *We took a tour of the Capitol in Washington, D.C.*

capitulate [kə 'pɪtʃ ə let] *iv.* to give in to someone or something; to surrender to someone or something. ♦ *Dave finally capitulated to his roommate's wishes and washed the dishes.* ♦ *Bill held his ground and refused to capitulate on his principles.*

capitulation [kə pi tʃə 'le ʃən] *n.* surrender; yielding. (No plural form in this sense.) ♦ *Dave's capitulation on the matter of washing dishes prevented a serious argument.* ♦ *The general sent word of the army's capitulation via telegram.*

caprice [kə 'pris] *n.* sudden changes of mind or behavior; whimsy. (No plural form in this sense.) ♦ *Mary's actions are unpredictable. She is known for her caprice.* ♦ *John's nature was a blend of caprice and creativity.*

capricious [kə 'pri ʃəs] *adj.* whimsical; impulsive. (Adv: *capriciously.*) ♦ *Flying to Paris on a day's notice is a capricious thing to do.* ♦ *Mary is a bit capricious, but she is delightful.*

capsize ['kæp sɑɪz] **1.** *tv.* to overturn something in the water. ♦ *The large waves capsized the boat.* ♦ *Jimmy capsized Susie's raft in the pool.* **2.** *iv.* to turn over in the water. ♦ *Our boat capsized in the middle of the lake.* ♦ *What did you do when the canoe capsized?*

capsized ['kæp sɑɪzd] *adj.* turned over; turned upside down in the water. ♦ *The Coast Guard spotted the capsized boat.* ♦ *The capsized vessel was capable of floating that way for days.*

capsule ['kæp səl] **1.** *n.* a dose of medicine in a gelatin shell that dissolves when swallowed. ♦ *The doctor gave Bill some capsules of antibiotics for his infection.* ♦ *Pain killers come in tablets and capsules.* **2.** *n.* the part of a spaceship where astronauts live and work. ♦ *The photographs showed the astronauts in the capsule of their ship.* ♦ *The space capsule held three astronauts.*

captain ['kæp tən] **1.** *n.* someone in charge of a ship, boat, or airplane. ♦ *The captain announced that the plane would take off soon.* ♦ *During our cruise, we never saw the ship's captain.* **2.** *n.* an officer in the military or the police. ♦ *The mayor hired a new police captain to help combat crime.* ♦ *My grandfather was an army captain who ran his house like a barracks.* **3.** *n.* the leader of a team. ♦ *The football captain motioned for the team to gather together.* ♦ *The captain of the chess club started the meeting.*

caption ['kæp ʃən] **1.** *n.* an explanation under a picture. ♦ *A short caption gave the names of the people in the picture.* ♦ *The editor wrote captions for the pictures.* **2.** *n.* a translation of a foreign language appearing at the bottom of a movie or television screen. ♦ *The film was in French, but it had captions in English.* ♦ *I prefer foreign films with captions to those where the actors speak one language but we hear another language.*

captivate ['kæp tə vet] *tv.* to hold someone or something spellbound; to fascinate someone or something. ♦ *A compelling drama captivated the audience.* ♦ *The entertaining game captivated the children.*

captive ['kæp tɪv] **1.** *n.* a prisoner. ♦ *The captive begged for food.* ♦ *The duke was held as a captive by his own soldiers.* **2.** *adj.* imprisoned; trapped. (Adv: *captively.*) ♦ *Many hostages were held captive by the enemy troops.* ♦ *The performer had a captive audience. Everyone was too polite to leave.*

captivity [kæp 'tɪv ɪt i] *n.* imprisonment; the condition of not being free. (No plural form in this sense.) ♦ *During her captivity, Jane wrote a book about jails.* ♦ *Zoo animals are kept in captivity.*

captor ['kæp tɚ] *n.* someone who makes someone or something a captive; someone who captures someone or something. ♦ *The prisoners of war begged their captors for food.* ♦ *The captor treated the hostages well.*

capture ['kæp tʃɚ] **1.** *tv.* to catch someone or something; to make someone or something a captive. ♦ *The capture of the bear was difficult and dangerous.* ♦ *The war was ended when we captured the enemy's major city.* **2.** *tv.* to take something by force; to take control of something. ♦ *The troops captured the enemy beach.* ♦ *The hunters captured and killed the gorilla.* **3.** *tv.* to accurately depict a feeling or atmosphere through artistic expression. ♦ *Jane's photo captured Bill's cheerful personality.* ♦ *This painting captures the joy of swimming at the lake.*

car ['kɑr] **1.** *n.* an automobile; a vehicle that can carry a small number of passengers. ♦ *I don't drive a car to work because parking is expensive downtown.* ♦ *The Smiths plan to buy a new car this year.* **2.** *n.* one unit of a train. ♦ *We counted the cars of the train while waiting for it to pass.* ♦ *The last car of a train is called a caboose.* **3.** *n.* any of a number of different conveyances for carrying goods or people. ♦ *You should move to the rear of an elevator car.* ♦ *The two mountain resorts were connected by cable car.*

carafe [kə 'ræf] **1.** *n.* a glass container from which wine is poured at the table. (It is more elegant than a bottle.) ♦ *The waiter poured the wine from its bottle into a carafe.* ♦ *I placed a lovely crystal carafe on the mantel.* **2.** *n.* the contents of ①. ♦ *The couple drank a carafe of wine at dinner.* ♦ *A large carafe of wine cost less than buying individual glasses.*

caramel ['kɛr ə məl, 'kɑr məl] **1.** *n.* a kind of candy made by heating sugar. (No plural form in this sense.) ♦ *The piece of candy was caramel with a chocolate coating.* ♦ *Caramel is my favorite candy.* **2.** *adj.* made with or flavored with ①. ♦ *Could I please have some caramel topping on my sundae?* ♦ *I love caramel candy, but it sticks to my teeth.*

carat ['kɛr ət] *n.* a unit of weight for gemstones, equal to about 200 milligrams. ♦ *The diamond weighed just under a carat.* ♦ *How many carats is that huge emerald?*

caravan ['kɛr ə væn] *n.* a group of travelers moving as a group, now especially a line of vehicles. ♦ *The long caravan of cars was a funeral party on its way to the cemetery.* ♦ *The caravan of huge trucks stretched over a mile.*

carbohydrate [kɑr bə 'hɑɪ dret] *n.* a natural class of food that provides energy to the body. ♦ *Sugars and starches are two kinds of carbohydrates.* ♦ *There are a lot of carbohydrates in pasta.*

carbon ['kɑr bən] **1.** *n.* a chemical element occurring in nature as coal, graphite, and diamonds. (No plural form in this sense.) ♦ *There is one carbon atom in a molecule of carbon dioxide.* ♦ *Carbon's atomic symbol is C, and its atomic number is 6.* **2. carbon (copy)** *n.* a copy of a typewritten document made on carbon paper. ♦ *How many carbon copies do you want of this letter?* ♦ *Send the original, and file the carbon.* **3. carbon copy** *n.* someone or something that is almost identical to someone or something else. (Figurative on ②.) ♦ *Anne is a carbon copy of her mother.* ♦ *At work, each day was just a carbon copy of every other day.*

carbonated ['kɑr bə net ɪd] *adj.* filled with carbonation; bubbly with carbon dioxide. ♦ *Carbonated beverages are very pleasant to drink in the summer.* ♦ *I like to drink fruit juices mixed with carbonated water.*

carbonation ['kɑr bə 'ne ʃən] *n.* tiny bubbles of carbon dioxide dispersed in drinks such as soda, soda water, soda pop. (No plural form in this sense.) ♦ *The carbonation in this drink tickles my tongue.* ♦ *Too much carbonation makes me belch.*

carbon dioxide ['kɑr bən dɑɪ 'ɑk sɑɪd] *n.* a colorless, odorless gas produced as waste from breathing and combustion. (No plural form in this sense.) ♦ *Carbon dioxide does not burn.* ♦ *Living plants absorb carbon dioxide.*

carbon monoxide ['kɑr bən mən 'ɑk sɑɪd] *n.* a poisonous, colorless, odorless gas produced by burning carbon compounds when not enough oxygen is present. (No plural form in this sense.) ♦ *Carbon monoxide kills many people each year.* ♦ *A faulty furnace can produce deadly carbon monoxide.*

carbon paper ['kɑr bən pe pɚ] *n.* paper or plastic in thin sheets, coated on one side with a colored substance. (No plural form in this sense. When placed—with the coated side down—between sheets of paper, whatever is typed or written on the top sheet will be transferred to the bottom sheet.) ♦ *Jane put a sheet of carbon paper under her fancy stationery, and a sheet of plain paper below that.* ♦ *Some kinds of carbon paper can be used over and over to make lots of carbon copies.*

carburetor ['kɑr bə ret ɚ] *n.* the part of an engine that mixes fuel with air. ♦ *My car's carburetor needs adjustment.* ♦ *The mechanic cleaned the carburetor, and now the engine runs smoothly.*

carcass ['kɑr kəs] **1.** *n.* the body of an animal used for food. ♦ *Vultures circled the antelope's carcass in the desert.* ♦ *The lions gnawed at the bloody carcass.* **2.** *n.* a living human body. (Informal.) ♦ *"Sit your carcass down and let's have a chat," Grandpa said.* ♦ *The kids plopped their carcasses down on the floor in front of the TV set.*

carcinogen [kɑr 'sɪn ə dʒən] *n.* something that causes cancer. (No plural form in this sense.) ♦ *Some cleaning fluids are carcinogens.* ♦ *The tests indicated that the chemical was a carcinogen in laboratory rats.*

carcinogenic [kɑr sɪn ə 'dʒɛn ɪk] *adj.* causing cancer. (Adv: *carcinogenically* [...ɪk li].) ♦ *I eat organic produce in hopes of avoiding carcinogenic pesticides.* ♦ *Many chemicals are known to be carcinogenic.*

carcinoma [kɑr sə 'nom ə] *n.* a cancerous tumor. ♦ *The surgeon removed the carcinoma.* ♦ *The X-ray showed a carcinoma on the lung.*

card ['kɑrd] **1.** *n.* a playing card; one of a deck of cards, used in playing card games. ♦ *The poker players laid their cards on the table.* ♦ *Mary dealt the cards, and the game began.* **2.** *n.* a stiff, rectangular piece of paper. ♦ *Cards indicating the seating arrangement were placed on the table.* ♦ *I wrote the recipe on a note card.* **3.** *n.* someone who is funny or amusing. (Informal.) ♦ *Bill is such a card—he is always saying the oddest things.* ♦ *Don't be a card. Try to blend in with the group.* **4.** *tv.* to check someone's age on an identification card ②. ♦ *The bouncer at* *the bar carded the students at the entrance.* ♦ *We were carded before we could enter the disco.* **5. in the cards** *idiom* in the future. ♦ *Well, what do you think is in the cards for tomorrow?* ♦ *I asked the boss if there was a raise in the cards for me.* **6. credit card** See credit. **7. card catalog** See catalog.

cardboard ['kɑrd bord] **1.** *n.* a heavy, thick, stiff paper. (No plural form in this sense.) ♦ *The gift came in a box made of cardboard.* ♦ *The sign was backed with cardboard.* **2.** *adj.* made of ①. ♦ *He put all his books into a cardboard box.* ♦ *Jimmy built a cardboard garage for his toy cars.*

cardiac ['kɑr di æk] *adj.* relating to the heart. ♦ *The patients on this floor all have cardiac conditions.* ♦ *The hospital just built a new cardiac treatment unit.*

cardiac arrest ['kɑr di æk ə 'rɛst] *n.* a stoppage of the heart; a heart attack. (No plural form in this sense.) ♦ *Paramedics saved the life of the woman in cardiac arrest.* ♦ *The patient went into cardiac arrest on the operating table.*

cardigan ['kɑr dɪ gən] *n.* a sweater that buttons in front. ♦ *Jane wore a black cardigan to keep warm.* ♦ *I bought a bright red cardigan with fancy metal buttons.*

cardinal ['kɑrd nəl] **1.** *n.* a bird—the males of which are bright red—with a crest on its head. ♦ *A cardinal perched on the bird feeder.* ♦ *With the binoculars, we could see a nest of cardinals in the tree.* **2.** *n.* a high-ranking official of the Roman Catholic Church. ♦ *The pope is chosen from among the cardinals.* ♦ *The cardinals wear red robes.*

cardinal (numeral) AND **cardinal (number)** ['kɑrd (ə) nəl...] *n.* a number used in counting, such as one, two, three. (See also ordinal numeral.) ♦ Three *is a cardinal numeral, and the corresponding ordinal numeral is (the)* third. ♦ *Cardinal numbers are used when adding figures.*

cardiogram ['kɑr di ə græm] *n.* a graph that shows the electrical properties of a human's heartbeat; an electrocardiogram. (Abbreviated *EKG* and *ECG*.) ♦ *The doctor studied the patient's cardiogram.* ♦ *The insurance company asked for a copy of the cardiogram.*

cardiology [kɑr di 'ɑl ə dʒi] *n.* the medical study of the heart and the treatment of its diseases. (No plural form in this sense.) ♦ *Dr. Smith's specialty is cardiology.* ♦ *A specialist in cardiology examined my heart.*

care ['kɛr] **1.** *n.* serious attention; focused thought; caution. (No plural form in this sense.) ♦ *The architects put a lot of care into their designs.* ♦ *Please handle those fragile vases with care.* **2.** *n.* the responsibility of providing for, protecting, or medically treating someone. (No plural form in this sense.) ♦ *The visiting nurse provided good care for her patient.* ♦ *Mary and John gave loving care to their elderly grandmother.* **3.** *n.* worry; anxiety; concern. ♦ *I am happy and I don't have a care in the world.* ♦ *Bill's cares and worries gave him an ulcer.* **4. care (about)** *iv.* (+ *prep. phr.*) to have concern for someone or something; to show serious interest in the welfare of someone or something. ♦ *My teacher really cares about each student.* ♦ *Mary's little gestures of kindness showed that she cared.* **5. care for** *iv.* + *prep. phr.* to be responsible for someone or something; to watch over someone or something. ♦ *Will you care for my cat while I'm on vacation?* ♦ *The orphans were cared for by an elderly uncle.* **6. care for** *iv.* + *prep. phr.* to like something; to want something. ♦ *David did not care for the sun-dried tomatoes in his spinach salad.* ♦ *Would you care for a second helping?* **7. take care of someone or something** *idiom* to provide ② for someone or something. ♦ *John and Mary took care of their aged grandmother.* ♦ *Please take care of my plants while I am on vacation.* **8. take care of someone or something** *idiom* to deal with someone or something; to handle or manage someone or something. ♦ *Would you please take care of this little problem?* ♦ *This is an easy thing to take care of. I will fix it immediately.*

career [kə 'rɪɚ] **1.** *n.* one's chosen work; one's line of work. ♦ *Mary's career is in computers.* ♦ *Bill trained for years for his career.* **2.** *adj.* [concerning] lifelong [employment]. ♦ *Mary is a career diplomat, serving in Russia.* ♦ *The lower levels of government are populated by career bureaucrats.*

carefree ['kɛr fri] *adj.* without fear, worry, or responsibility. ♦ *The carefree children played happily.* ♦ *Tom enjoyed having a carefree spirit while traveling in Europe.*

careful ['kɛr fʊl] **1.** *adj.* cautious; avoiding danger or damage. (Adv: *carefully.*) ♦ *Be careful. The steps are wet.* ♦ *Mary was very careful as she handled the antique vase.* **2.** *adj.* detailed; thorough. (Adv: *carefully.*) ♦ *Bill did a careful job preparing the statistics for his report.* ♦ *Take a careful look at this picture and tell me who is in it.*

careless ['kɛr ləs] *adj.* without care; clumsy; done without thought; haphazard. (Adv: *carelessly.*) ♦ *It was careless of you to forget to invite Bob to the party.* ♦ *Consider your options instead of making a careless decision.*

carelessness ['kɛr ləs nəs] *n.* a lack of concern; a lack of carefulness. (No plural form in this sense.) ♦ *The teacher became concerned about the student's carelessness.* ♦ *Carelessness with matches may cause a fire.*

caress [kə 'rɛs] **1.** *n.* a gentle, loving touch. ♦ *The child gave the kitten a caress.* ♦ *I gave the baby's face a gentle caress.* **2.** *tv.* to touch someone or something gently and lovingly. ♦ *The child caressed the kitten's fur.* ♦ *Bill caressed my back as we danced.*

caretaker ['kɛr tek ɚ] **1.** *n.* someone who watches over and protects a building or property. ♦ *The caretaker tended the flowers around the building.* ♦ *The cemetery's caretaker also worked at the adjoining church.* **2.** *n.* someone who takes care of someone else. ♦ *The sick woman's caretaker was her oldest daughter.* ♦ *Who is the children's caretaker while their parents work?*

careworn ['kɛr worn] *adj.* showing signs of anxiety or worry. ♦ *After a hard day at the office, Bill often has a careworn look.* ♦ *The careworn manager slumped in his chair, waiting for the day to end.*

cargo ['kɑr go] *n.* a load of goods on a vehicle; freight. (Pl in *-s* or *-es.*) ♦ *The truck had no cargo—it was empty.* ♦ *The train had a cargo of grain.*

Caribbean Sea [kɛr ə bi ən 'si, kə 'rɪb i ən 'si] See Gazetteer.

caricature ['kɛr ɪ kə tʃɚ] **1.** *n.* a sketched portrait that exaggerates the unique features of the subject. ♦ *I didn't like the caricature that made my ears look so big.* ♦ *Political cartoons are often caricatures of politicians.* **2.** *n.* an imitation of someone that exaggerates the faults and quirks of the subject. ♦ *The comedian's act included a caricature of the president.* ♦ *Bill's boss walked in while he was doing a caricature of her.* **3.** *tv.* to draw someone's picture in a way that exaggerates the person's features. ♦ *The* *cartoonist caricatured the politician's mouth.* ♦ *The sidewalk artist caricatured Mary, emphasizing her ears.* **4.** *tv.* to imitate someone in an exaggerated style. ♦ *Bill rudely caricatured his boss.* ♦ *The politician was caricatured by the comedian.*

caring ['kɛr ɪŋ] *adj.* showing affectionate concern. (Adv: *caringly.*) ♦ *Mary's caring ways endear her to everyone.* ♦ *A caring word will make people feel comfortable.*

carjack ['kɑr dʒɑk] *tv.* to seize an automobile from its driver by force. (Compare with **hijack.**) ♦ *Tom's new car was carjacked by a pair of thugs.* ♦ *The crooks used a gun to carjack the helpless couple's car.*

carjacker ['kɑr jæk ɚ] *n.* someone who carjacks an automobile. ♦ *The carjacker used a gun to persuade Tom to give up his car.* ♦ *The cops caught the carjacker and recovered Tom's car.*

carload ['kɑr lod] **1.** *n.* the amount of goods that can be put into a freight car. ♦ *Two carloads of lumber arrived in town today.* ♦ *Bob ordered a carload of wallboard.* **2.** *n.* a car full of people or things. ♦ *We moved a carload of furniture to our new house today.* ♦ *Bill drove a carload of children to the movie.*

carnation [kɑr 'ne ʃən] *n.* a small flower with a strong clove-like scent, usually white, pink, or red. ♦ *The bouquet had carnations and roses in it.* ♦ *David wore a carnation in his buttonhole at the party.*

carnival ['kɑr nə vəl] *n.* a circus; a traveling amusement enterprise. ♦ *Each summer the town holds a carnival.* ♦ *The carnival had clowns and acrobats.*

carnivorous [kɑr 'nɪv ə rəs] *adj.* meat-eating. (Adv: *carnivorously.*) ♦ *Vultures are carnivorous birds.* ♦ *Not all dinosaurs were carnivorous—some were vegetarians.*

carol ['kɛr əl] **1.** *n.* a song of joy, especially a Christmas song. ♦ *The choir sang well-known carols.* ♦ *We all sang the carols together.* **2.** *iv.* to sing joyfully, especially singing ①. ♦ *The choir caroled in the nursing home.* ♦ *The children caroled happily during the religious service.*

carousel ['kɛr ə sɛl] *n.* a merry-go-round; a circular ride where the riders sit on figures of animals. ♦ *The children rode the carousel five times at the carnival.* ♦ *The carnival had an antique carousel.*

carp ['kɑrp] **1.** *n., irreg.* any one of a large family of freshwater fish, especially a type of bony food fish. (Pl: *carp.*) ♦ *Bill went to the river to fish for carp.* ♦ *The rural lake was full of carp.* **2.** *iv.* to complain about something. ♦ *Quit carping and do your chores!* ♦ *The lazy employee carped constantly about his job.*

carpenter ['kɑr pən tɚ] *n.* someone who builds things with wood. ♦ *I hired a carpenter to build my bookshelves.* ♦ *A skilled carpenter built an addition to my house.*

carpentry ['kɑr pən tri] *n.* the craft of building things out of wood. (No plural form in this sense.) ♦ *When I built a bookcase, I developed an interest in carpentry.* ♦ *The carpentry of the cabinet is exquisite.*

carpet ['kɑr pɪt] **1.** *n.* a rug; a floor covering made out of fabric. (See also **carpeting.**) ♦ *David spilled grape juice on the carpet.* ♦ *Jane vacuumed the dark green carpet in her living room.* **2.** *tv.* to cover a floor with ①. ♦ *Not many people carpet their kitchen floors.* ♦ *Bill carpeted his bedroom with a cream-colored carpet.* **3. call someone on the carpet** *idiom* to reprimand a person. ♦ *One more error like that, and the boss will call you on the carpet.* ♦ *I'm sorry it went wrong. I really hope he doesn't call me on the carpet again.* **4. get the red-carpet treatment** *idiom* to receive very special treatment; to receive royal treatment. ♦ *I love to go to fancy stores where I get the red-carpet treatment.* ♦ *The queen expects to get the red-carpet treatment wherever she goes.*

carpeted ['kɑr pɪt ɪd] *adj.* covered with carpet. ♦ *Our basement floor is not carpeted.* ♦ *The Smiths prefer a carpeted bedroom.*

carpeting ['kɑr pɪ tɪŋ] *n.* carpet. (No plural form in this sense.) ♦ *The dirty carpeting in this room needs to be replaced.* ♦ *What do you think of the new carpeting?*

carport ['kɑr port] *n.* a roofed shelter for a car, lacking a door. ♦ *Our lawn mower is stored in the carport.* ♦ *Our carport is big enough for two cars.*

carriage ['kɛr ɪdʒ] **1.** *n.* a buggy; a vehicle pulled by horses. ♦ *The carriage was drawn by two white ponies.* ♦ *We arrived at the fancy ball in a horse-drawn carriage.* **2.** *n.* the part of an older model typewriter that carries the paper and moves from right to left as one types. ♦ *Jane pushed the carriage on the typewriter when she reached the end of the line.* ♦ *The electric typewriter had an automatic carriage.*

carrier ['kɛr i ɚ] **1.** *n.* a transportation or freight company. ♦ *Which carrier does the company use to ship its packages?* ♦ *The carrier will not deliver packages overseas.* **2.** *n.* something that carries someone or something. ♦ *The cat has a special carrier for traveling in the car.* ♦ *The inventor devised a baby carrier with wheels.* **3.** *n.* someone or some creature who does not outwardly suffer from a disease but who can pass it on to someone else. ♦ *Mosquitos can be carriers of malaria.* ♦ *A typhoid carrier who works in a restaurant can transmit the disease to many people.*

carrot ['kɛr ət] *n.* a vegetable with a long, thin edible orange root. ♦ *Carrots are Jane's favorite vegetables.* ♦ *A rabbit ate some carrots from our garden.*

carry ['kɛr i] **1.** *tv.* to pick up and take someone or something somewhere. ♦ *I carried the baby into the nursery.* ♦ *Mary carried one suitcase onto the plane.* **2.** *tv.* to support the weight of something. ♦ *My car will not carry all that weight.* ♦ *This beam will carry over three tons.* **3.** *tv.* to spread a disease or sickness. ♦ *The immigrant was carrying hepatitis when he immigrated.* ♦ *The dog carried rabies and had to be destroyed.* **4.** *tv.* to win the vote of a state or district. ♦ *The Democrats carried Illinois in the 1992 election.* ♦ *Polls showed that the dishonest politician carried the third ward.* **5.** *tv.* [when adding a column of numbers, if the result is greater than 9] to transfer units of ten to the next column to the left as units of one. ♦ *7 + 7 is 14. That's four, carry the one.* ♦ *Your answer is wrong because you forgot to carry the 2.* **6.** *tv.* [for a store] to have an item in stock and available for sale. ♦ *Do you carry women's clothing in large sizes?* ♦ *The clothing store carries only small sizes.* **7. carry out** *tv.* + *adv.* to complete, accomplish, achieve, or execute a task, order, or assignment. ♦ *I was not able to carry out my orders.* ♦ *John will carry out his assignment on time.* **8.** *iv.* [for a voice or sound] to travel far. ♦ *You have a peculiar laugh that carries a long way.* ♦ *The announcement over the loudspeaker carried through the office.*

carry-on ['kɛr i ɔn] *n.* a piece of luggage someone carries onto a plane, train, or bus. ♦ *Jane took two carry-ons onto the plane with her.* ♦ *Bill packed his shaving kit in his carry-on.*

carryover ['kɛr i ov ɚ] *n.* excess things that remain and are saved for future use. (No plural form in this sense.) ♦ *We had enough money to live on because there was some carryover from last year.* ♦ *Do not order any more paper this month. We still have some carryover from last month.*

carsick ['kɑr sɪk] *adj.* sick because of the motion of riding in a moving car. ♦ *The Smith children get carsick on long trips.* ♦ *The carsick passenger was pale and moaning.*

cart ['kɑrt] **1.** *n.* a vehicle pulled by a horse, mule, dog, etc. ♦ *The cart was loaded with hay to take into town.* ♦ *A small boy snuck a ride on the back of the cart.* **2.** *n.* a large basket on wheels, such as those found in grocery stores and other shops. ♦ *I filled my cart with groceries.* ♦ *A runaway shopping cart rolled across the parking lot.* **3. cart away** *tv. + adv.* to carry something away; to haul something away. ♦ *The garbage men carted away our old refrigerator.* ♦ *The scavengers carted away the old clothes from the alley.* **4. upset the apple cart** *idiom* to mess up or ruin something. ♦ *Tom really upset the apple cart by telling Mary the truth about Jane.* ♦ *I always knew he'd upset the apple cart.*

carte blanche ['kɑrt 'blɑntʃ] *adv.* without restriction; with complete authority to follow one's own judgment. (From French for *blank paper.*) ♦ *They gave me carte blanche to make my own deal.* ♦ *Tom has carte blanche to spend as much money as is required.*

cartel [kɑr 'tɛl] *n.* a group of businesses that conspire together to eliminate competition. ♦ *A well-known diamond cartel has operated in Europe for years.* ♦ *The authorities are investigating the oil cartel.*

cartilage ['kɑrt (ə) lɪdʒ] *n.* fibrous tissue attached to bones of people and animals. (No plural form in this sense.) ♦ *A piece of cartilage was left in the meat.* ♦ *The cartilage in John's nose was broken when it was hit.*

carton ['kɑrt n] **1.** *n.* a cardboard or plastic container or package. ♦ *The eggs were packaged in a carton of cardboard.* ♦ *In the refrigerator, milk was leaking from its carton.* **2.** *n.* a carton considered as a measurement of something. ♦ *I bought a carton of eggs at the market.* ♦ *Please pick up a carton of milk on the way home from work.*

cartoon [kɑr 'tun] **1.** *n.* a drawing or series of drawings that is usually intended to be funny. ♦ *The newspaper has a large section of cartoons.* ♦ *Today's editorial cartoon was very funny.* **2.** *n.* a film where the each frame is a drawing. (Also an *animated cartoon.*) ♦ *Many children's movies are cartoons.* ♦ *On Saturday mornings, the kids watch cartoons.*

cartoonist [kɑr 'tun əst] *n.* someone who draws cartoons. ♦ *The famous cartoonist's works were published in almost every newspaper.* ♦ *The political cartoonist satirized the government.*

cartridge ['kɑr trɪdʒ] **1.** *n.* a tube that holds gunpowder and a metal shot; a bullet or the casing of a bullet. ♦ *The inspector found four empty cartridges near the body.* ♦ *You can see the bottom of the cartridges loaded into a revolver.* **2.** *n.* a bullet. ♦ *Bill bought a box of cartridges before his hunting trip.* ♦ *Mary loaded the shotgun with two cartridges.* **3.** *n.* a container for holding a specific substance, such as ink, tape, or black powder, used within a larger device or machine. ♦ *Mary loaded a new toner cartridge into the copying machine.* ♦ *David placed the tape cartridge in the video recorder.*

cartwheel ['kɑrt ʌil] **1.** *n.* a rotating motion of the body, in a circle, sideways, with the arms and legs extended and only the hands and feet touching the ground in sequence. ♦ *A clever gymnast did a cartwheel on the balance beam.* ♦ *The kids turned cartwheels on the lawn.* **2.** *iv.* to move forward making ①. ♦ *The gymnast cartwheeled across the mat.* ♦ *The children cartwheeled in the backyard.*

carve ['kɑrv] **1.** *tv.* to cut or sculpt wood, ivory, soap, or some other substance into a shape. ♦ *The candlesticks on the mantle were carved by hand.* ♦ *The artisan carved a statuette from the block of jade.* **2. carve into** *tv. + prep. phr.* to cut something into a surface. ♦ *Bill carved his initials into the wet cement.* ♦ *A scene was carved into the wooden plaque.* **3.** *tv.* to slice or cut up cooked meat for serving at a meal. ♦ *Bill carved the Thanksgiving turkey.* ♦ *Please carve some slices of ham for our sandwiches.*

carving ['kɑr vɪŋ] **1.** *adj.* cutting; used for cutting. ♦ *Anne lifted the carving knife and began to cut the meat.* ♦ *The carpenter bought some new carving tools.* **2.** *n.* an object that has been shaped by cutting. ♦ *The museum displayed the valuable carvings.* ♦ *I looked at the carving of an eagle on the table.*

car wash ['kɑr wɑʃ] *n.* a business operation that cleans cars. ♦ *The car was filthy until we took it to the car wash.* ♦ *The school held a car wash to raise money.*

case ['kes] **1.** *n.* a crate; a box. ♦ *We unloaded five cases of canned vegetables from the truck.* ♦ *The watch I got for my birthday is still in its case.* **2.** *n.* a fixed number—usually 24 in the instance of units of drink—sold in a box. ♦ *After the keg ran out, Ed ran to the corner store to buy a few more cases of beer.* ♦ *In celebration, we opened the case of wine stored in the basement.* **3.** *n.* an instance; an occurrence. ♦ *This is a simple case of failure to complete an agreement.* ♦ *The school nurse saw four cases of chickenpox on Monday.* **4.** *n.* a legal action or lawsuit. ♦ *The jury ruled in favor of the defendant in the case.* ♦ *The jurors could not discuss the case with anyone.* **5.** *n.* a grammatical category of nouns, adjectives, and pronouns that shows their relationship to each other and to the verb of the sentence or clause. ♦ *The word* I *is in the nominative case.* ♦ *The word* me *is in the objective case.* **6.** *n.* the manner in which a letter of the alphabet is written, either in the *uppercase* or in the *lowercase.* (See **majuscule, minuscule, uppercase, lowercase.**) ♦ *The first letter of a person's name is written in the uppercase.* ♦ *Most of this sentence is written with letters in the lowercase.* **7. a case in point** *idiom* an example of what one is talking about. ♦ *Now, as a case in point, let's look at nineteenth-century England.* ♦ *Fireworks can be dangerous. For a case in point, look at what happened to Bob Smith last week.* **8. in case of something** *idiom* if a problem occurs; if something happens; in the event that something happens. ♦ *What do we do in case of fire?* ♦ *In case of an accident, call the police.* **9. in case** *idiom* in the event (that). ♦ *What do we do in case the building catches fire?* ♦ *We should close the windows just in case it rains.* **10. be the case** *idiom* to be true; to describe an actual situation. ♦ *I think Bill is a vegetarian, and if that is the case, we should not serve him meat.* ♦ *Susie believes animals can talk, but that is not the case.* **11. open and**

shut case *idiom* something that is simple and straightforward without complications. ♦ *The murder trial was an open and shut case. The defendant was caught with the murder weapon.* ♦ *Bob's death was an open and shut case of suicide. He left a suicide note.*

cash ['kæʃ] **1.** *n.* money; currency, as opposed to check or a credit card. (No plural form in this sense.) ♦ *We had enough cash with us to go out to dinner.* ♦ *That store accepts cash and credit cards—no checks.* **2.** *tv.* to exchange a check for currency. ♦ *Sally cashed her paycheck every Friday.* ♦ *Where can I cash this check?* **3.** *tv.* to give money in exchange for a check. ♦ *The bank will not cash out-of-state checks unless you have three forms of identification.* ♦ *The restaurant would not cash our traveler's checks.* **4. cash in (on something)** *idiom* to earn a lot of money at something; to make a profit at something. ♦ *This is a good year for farming, and you can cash in on it if you're smart.* ♦ *It's too late to cash in on that particular clothing fad.*

cashew ['kæ ʃu] **1.** *n.* a tropical American tree producing edible nuts. ♦ *Cashews have leaves like leather and yellow flowers.* ♦ *We tried to grow a cashew for its delicious nuts.* **2.** *n.* the kidney-shaped nutmeat of ①. ♦ *I made a tasty casserole that contained cashews.* ♦ *Bill loves nuts, especially cashews.*

cashier [kæ 'ʃɪr] *n.* someone who handles the paying out and taking in of money, especially at a store or bank. ♦ *The incompetent cashier gave me the incorrect change.* ♦ *The cashier took the money and put my purchase in a box.*

cashmere ['kæʒ mɪr] *n.* soft, fine wool made from the coats of goats from south Asia. (No plural form in this sense.) ♦ *My best sweater is made of cashmere.* ♦ *Cashmere is a very expensive material.*

casino [kə 'sin o] *n.* a place for gambling; a gambling house. (Pl in *-s*.) ♦ *There are many casinos in Las Vegas.* ♦ *Bill and Mary go to the casino to gamble every Saturday night.*

cask ['kæsk] *n.* a barrel, usually used to store and hold liquids, such as wine. ♦ *Casks filled with wine lined the cellar of the winery.* ♦ *The wine was aged in oak casks.*

casket ['kæs kɪt] *n.* a coffin; a case that dead people are placed in and buried in. ♦ *The soldier was buried in a simple wooden casket.* ♦ *Old friends of the deceased carried the casket to the grave.*

casserole ['kæs ə rol] **1.** *n.* a deep baking dish. ♦ *The cake should be baked in a 9- × 13-inch casserole.* ♦ *I loaned my best casserole to my neighbor.* **2.** *n.* a mixture of different kinds of food cooked in ①. ♦ *Casseroles are a type of economical, tasty meal.* ♦ *We had a vegetable casserole for dinner.*

cassette [kə 'sɛt] *n.* a plastic case containing a pair of reels of magnetic audiotape or videotape. ♦ *John put his favorite cassette into the tape player.* ♦ *Mary's car radio also plays cassettes.*

cassette player [kə 'sɛt ple ɚ] *n.* a device that plays back sound recorded on cassette. ♦ *Our neighbors played their cassette player loudly all night.* ♦ *Bill put the tape into the cassette player, and music soon filled the room.*

cassette recorder [kə 'sɛt rɪ 'kor dɚ] *n.* a device that records sound onto a cassette and plays it back. ♦ *The children recorded the sound of their voices on the cassette recorder.* ♦ *The cassette recorder played back the recorded message.*

cast ['kæst] **1.** *n.* all of the performers in a play, musical, TV show, or movie. ♦ *The cast of the sequel included the stars from the original film.* ♦ *After the play, the audience applauded the cast.* **2.** *n.* a protective support for a broken bone, often made from plaster. ♦ *John's broken arm was in a cast for two months.* ♦ *Susan's friends signed the cast on her leg.* **3.** *tv., irreg.* to throw something. (Pt/pp: *cast*.) ♦ *Don't cast your pearls before swine!* ♦ *Anne cast a stone into the water.* **4.** *tv., irreg.* to throw a fishing lure into the water; to drop a fishing net into the water. ♦ *Bill cast his line into the lake, hoping to catch a fish for dinner.* ♦ *Jane's lure sailed through the air as she cast her line.* **5.** *tv., irreg.* to create a shadow on something. ♦ *Jane's figure cast a shadow on the wall in the cabin.* ♦ *The tree cast a long shadow on the lawn.* **6.** *tv., irreg.* to move and aim one's eyes or line of sight at someone or something. ♦ *The moment Bill cast his eyes on Mary, he wanted to ask her for a date.* ♦ *The teacher cast a look at Jimmy that stopped him in his tracks.* **7.** *tv., irreg.* to select the performers for a play, film, opera, etc. ♦ *The director cast an unknown singer to play the lead in the new Broadway musical.* ♦ *Tom hoped to be cast in the play.* **8.** *tv., irreg.* to create an object by pouring a soft substance into a mold and letting it harden into the shape of the mold. ♦ *The bell was cast from molten bronze.* ♦ *The sculptor cast the statue in bronze.* **9. cast one's vote** *idiom* to vote; to place one's ballot in the ballot box. ♦ *The citizens cast their votes for president.* ♦ *The wait in line to cast one's vote was almost an hour.*

castanet [kæs tə 'nɛt] *n.* one of a pair of hollow clappers worn on the fingers and clicked together in a rhythm. (Usually plural.) ♦ *The young students learned to play the castanets in music class.* ♦ *Castanets are a Spanish percussion instrument.*

castaway ['kæst ə we] **1.** *n.* someone who has survived a shipwreck. ♦ *The castaways were impressed with the professor's inventions made from bamboo and coconuts.* ♦ *The castaway later wrote a book about his adventures.* **2.** *adj.* shipwrecked; marooned. ♦ *Three castaway sailors swam ashore.* ♦ *The castaway passengers were soon rescued by another ship.*

caste ['kæst] *n.* a social class or social rank. ♦ *Some south Asian societies are based on a system of caste.* ♦ *The blacksmiths belong to a special caste.*

castigate ['kæs tɪ get] *tv.* to punish someone; to chastise someone. ♦ *The boss castigated Bill in front of his coworkers for the blunder.* ♦ *It is not good to castigate children too harshly.*

castle ['kæs əl] **1.** *n.* a large fortress where a country's king and queen live. ♦ *The castle was surrounded by a large moat.* ♦ *The king and queen lived comfortably in their fancy castle.* **2.** *n.* a game piece in chess, usually shaped like a castle. ♦ *Mary moved her castle across the chessboard.* ♦ *Bill lost both castles early in the chess game.*

cast-off ['kæst ɔf] **1.** *n.* something that has been abandoned, thrown away, or thrown out. ♦ *The charity was happy to take cast-offs of all sorts.* ♦ *Max relied on other people's cast-offs for clothing.* **2.** *adj.* <the adj. use of ①.> ♦ *Max was happy to get a cast-off winter coat.* ♦ *Boxes filled with cast-off toys were taken to the offices of the charity.*

castrate ['kæs tret] *tv.* to remove the testicles from a male creature. ♦ *A bull is castrated to make it a steer.* ♦ *Male pets are castrated to keep them from breeding.*

casual ['kæʒ ju əl] **1.** *adj.* [of someone] easygoing; [of an event] not formal. (Adv: *casually.*) ♦ *The picnic was casual, so we all wore shorts and T-shirts.* ♦ *Tom is a happy, casual guy who always has a smile.* **2.** *adj.* done without thought or planning. (Adv: *casually.*) ♦ *Bill regretted his casual comment about quitting his job.* ♦ *The Smiths dropped in yesterday for a casual visit.*

casualness ['kæʒ ju (ə)l nəs] *n.* the quality of being casual. (No plural form in this sense.) ♦ *The casualness of the party made us feel relaxed.* ♦ *The comfortable furniture gave the room an air of casualness.*

casualty ['kæʒ ju (ə)l ti] **1.** *n.* a serious accident. ♦ *Jane saw a casualty on the highway and phoned the police.* ♦ *The police arrived quickly at the scene of the casualty.* **2.** *n.* someone who has been injured or has died in an accident or in war. ♦ *There were thousands of casualties after the powerful earthquake.* ♦ *The car accident resulted in three casualties.*

cat ['kæt] **1.** *n.* the family of mammals that includes domestic cats, lions, leopards, tigers, jaguars, and lynxes. ♦ *Our favorite animals at the zoo are the cats.* ♦ *The documentary was about the cats of Africa.* **2.** *n.* a small, feline animal often kept as a pet. ♦ *Jane got a cat for her birthday.* ♦ *The cat sat at the window and watched the birds all day.* **3. let the cat out of the bag** *idiom* to reveal a secret or a surprise by accident. ♦ *When Bill glanced at the door, he let the cat out of the bag. We knew then that he was expecting someone to arrive.* ♦ *We are planning a surprise party for Jane. Don't let the cat out of the bag.*

cataclysm ['kæt ə klɪz əm] *n.* a violent natural catastrophe; a violent upheaval or change. ♦ *The early spring typhoon became a horrendous cataclysm when it struck our island.* ♦ *The eruption of the volcano was an unexpected cataclysm.*

catalog AND **catalogue** ['kæt ə lɔg] **1.** *n.* a book or list containing descriptions of things, often of things that are for sale. ♦ *Jane flipped through the catalog, looking at the products for sale.* ♦ *The company mails out a catalog of its products.* **2. (card) catalog** *n.* the files of cards listing the books and publications in a library and their locations within the library—or the equivalent information stored in computer files. ♦ *I am sure you will find the book you want in the catalog if you look it up.* ♦ *You must consult the card catalog to find out where a book is to be found in a library.* **3.** *tv.* to arrange or categorize items on a list or in ① or ②. ♦ *The librarian cataloged the new books.* ♦ *The auction house cataloged the items it had available for purchase.*

catalyst ['kæt ə ləst] **1.** *n.* a chemical substance that speeds up a chemical action without changing itself. ♦ *The reaction would not take place until the catalyst was added.* ♦ *Common salt served as the catalyst for the reaction.* **2.** *n.* something that makes it possible for something else to happen. (Figurative on ①.) ♦ *The new taxes imposed by the government were a catalyst for revolution.* ♦ *Losing his job served as Bill's catalyst to change careers.*

catamaran ['kæt ə mə ræn] *n.* a boat with two hulls side by side. ♦ *A sailing catamaran is very stable.* ♦ *We took a cruise around the bay on a large catamaran.*

catapult ['kæt ə pʊlt] **1.** *n.* a device for throwing or launching a missile. ♦ *A slingshot is a type of catapult.* ♦ *The army used a catapult to heave large stones against the fortress walls.* **2.** *tv.* to propel someone or something somewhere using a slingshot or ①. ♦ *The stone was catapulted against the wall.* ♦ *The army catapulted a boulder into the castle door.*

cataract ['kæt ə rækt] **1.** *n.* a waterfall; an area of rough water in a fast flowing river. ♦ *The hikers watched the cataract tumble down the mountain.* ♦ *The rafters were not skilled enough to pass through the cataract.* **2.** *n.* a cloudy patch on the lens of the eye. ♦ *Many older people suffer from cataracts.* ♦ *A cataract affects the vision in my left eye.*

catastrophe [kə 'tæs trə fi] *n.* a very large and serious disaster. ♦ *Jane suffered the catastrophe of losing her job.* ♦ *The crash of the stock market was a financial catastrophe.*

catch ['kætʃ] **1.** *n.* a game or pastime where people throw and catch a ball back and forth. ♦ *Susie and Jimmy played catch all afternoon.* ♦ *When his friends went to summer camp, Bill had no one to play catch with.* **2.** *n.* something that is caught, especially a fish. ♦ *The campers cooked the catch of the day over the campfire.* ♦ *The fishermen sold their catch right off the boat.* **3.** *n.* an act of catching something. ♦ *Bob wanted to make the catch, but Bill beat him to it.* ♦ *The baseball player made a great catch.* **4.** *n.* a good choice in a marriage partner. (Informal.) ♦ *Bill is a good catch. He'll make someone a great husband.* ♦ *John got a good catch when he married Anne.* **5.** *n.* a fastener; a locking or latching device. ♦ *The catch on the door prevented us from entering.* ♦ *The cat got out because the catch wasn't hooked.* **6.** *n.* a drawback; a negative factor. (Informal.) ♦ *I knew there was a catch when my allowance was doubled.* ♦ *The catch was that I had to do my own laundry.* **7.** *tv., irreg.* to seize and hold someone or something. (Pt/pp: **caught.**) ♦ *The cat tried to catch the mouse.* ♦ *I caught the ball that Mary threw toward me.* **8.** *tv., irreg.* to find someone in the act of doing something. ♦ *Emily caught Dave in the kitchen eating her muffins.* ♦ *The teacher caught Jimmy lying.* **9.** *tv., irreg.* to get a disease caused by bacteria or viruses. ♦ *I caught a cold at the office.* ♦ *I hope I don't catch the flu this winter.* **10.** *tv., irreg.* to reach or make contact with someone or something just in time. ♦ *If you don't hurry, you won't catch your bus.* ♦ *Can you catch Mary before she leaves the office?* **11.** *tv., irreg.* to experience something through one of the senses; to understand someone or something. ♦ *I never quite catch what the professor is saying.* ♦ *Yesterday, I caught a glimpse of a deer in the forest.* **12.** *tv., irreg.* [for something] to snare or entangle someone or something. ♦ *A small nail caught some threads in my sweater and made a hole in it.* ♦ *The drawer handle caught the edge of my pants pocket.* **13. catch one's breath** *idiom* to struggle for normal breathing after strenuous activity. ♦ *The jogger stopped to catch her breath.* ♦ *It took Jimmy a minute to catch his breath after being punched in the stomach.* **14. catch someone's eye** *idiom* to appear and attract someone's interest. ♦ *I small red car passing by caught my eye.* ♦ *One of the books on the top shelf caught my eye, and I took it down to look at it.* **15. catch someone's eye** *idiom* to cause someone to notice at you; to get someone's attention. ♦ *I tried to catch Jane's eye so I could talk to her, but she didn't notice me.* ♦ *He waved, trying to catch my eye, but I didn't recognize him.*

catchall ['kætʃ ɔl] *n.* something that holds or attracts a variety of things. ♦ *That kitchen drawer is a catchall for junk.* ♦ *This is not a theory. It is just a catchall for vague ideas.*

catcher ['kætʃ ɚ] *n.* [in baseball] the player who squats behind home plate behind the batter. ♦ *The catcher tossed the ball back to the pitcher.* ♦ *The catcher wears a protective mask.*

catching ['kætʃ ɪŋ] *adj.* contagious; spreadable. ♦ *Anne stayed at home from work because her sickness was catching.* ♦ *Your cold is catching if someone else can catch it from you.*

categorical [kæt ə 'gor ɪ kəl] *adj.* unconditional and—usually—negative. (Adv: *categorically* [...ɪk li].) ♦ *The senator made a categorical denial of the charges in the indictment.* ♦ *The boss gave a categorical no for an answer.*

categorize ['kæt ə gə rɑɪz] *tv.* to put someone or something into a category. ♦ *How would you categorize this piece of art?* ♦ *This painting is categorized as abstract art.*

category ['kæt ə gor i] *n.* a division or subdivision. ♦ *Who won the award in the best-athlete category?* ♦ *Which literary category would this book go in?*

cater ['ket ɚ] **1.** *tv.* to provide food for an event as a business. ♦ *An exclusive hotel catered the wedding.* ♦ *Jane caters large parties for a living.* **2. cater to** *iv.* + *prep. phr.* to be very attentive to someone. ♦ *I cater to my boss's every whim.* ♦ *Will the restaurant cater to our special requests?*

caterer ['ket ɚ ɚ] *n.* a person or company whose business it is to provide food service for events, such as a party. ♦ *This caterer is known for delicious desserts.* ♦ *We hired a caterer to prepare and serve the food at our party.*

caterpillar ['kæt ə pɪl ɚ] *n.* the creature, something like a worm, that is the larva of a butterfly or a moth. ♦ *Susie caught a caterpillar and put it in a jar.* ♦ *The caterpillar rested on a leaf on the bush.*

catfish ['kæt fɪʃ] **1.** *n., irreg.* any of a number of species of fish having whiskers around the mouth. (Pl: *catfish.*) ♦ *From the pier, we could see catfish swimming in the water below.* ♦ *Bill caught a catfish, but he threw it back in the water.* **2.** *n.* the flesh of ①, eaten as food. (No plural form in this sense.) ♦ *The restaurant served fried catfish.* ♦ *Catfish is a strong-flavored fish that tastes very good fried.*

catgut ['kæt gət] *n.* a strong string made from sheep intestines, used for the strings of tennis rackets and some stringed musical instruments. (No plural form in this sense.) ♦ *The violin has catgut strings.* ♦ *Jane prefers a tennis racket that has catgut strings.*

catharsis [kə 'θɑr sɪs] *n.* the release of strong emotion; the purging of tension or strong feelings. (No plural form in this sense.) ♦ *An angry outburst proved to be a catharsis for Bill.* ♦ *Building things is a catharsis for Mary.*

cathartic [kə 'θɑr tɪk] **1.** *n.* a laxative. ♦ *The doctor prescribed a cathartic for Tom's bowel problem.* ♦ *Hot water and castor oil served as a cathartic for Mary.* **2.** *adj.* helping release strong feelings or emotion. (Adv: *cathartically* [...ɪk li].) ♦ *Swimming was a cathartic activity for Mary.* ♦ *Talking his problems over with a friend is cathartic for Bill.*

cathedral [kə 'θi drəl] *n.* a large, important church, especially a church that is the seat of a bishop. ♦ *The ordination was held at the cathedral.* ♦ *The tourists admired the stained glass windows of the cathedral.*

catheter ['kæθ ɪ tɚ] *n.* a tube that is inserted into the body to extract or inject fluids. ♦ *The unconscious patient required a urinary catheter.* ♦ *The catheter drained away bodily waste.*

catheterize ['kæθ ɪ tə rɑɪz] *tv.* to insert a catheter into someone. ♦ *A nurse catheterized the patient.* ♦ *The doctor found it necessary to catheterize the patient's bladder.*

catholic ['kæθ (ə) lɪk] **1.** *adj.* universal; wide ranging. (Adv: *catholically* [...ɪk li].) ♦ *Bill had very catholic interests in reading matter.* ♦ *Her musical tastes were catholic and ranged from classical to jazz.* **2. Catholic** *adj.* <the adj. use of ③.> ♦ *There is a Catholic church at the end of our block.* ♦ *As a child, Mary went to Catholic school.* **3. Catholic** *n.* a member of the Roman Catholic Church. ♦ *Although Mary is a devout Catholic, she married a Jewish man.* ♦ *Grandma became a Catholic late in life.*

Catholicism [kə 'θɑl ə sɪz əm] *n.* the religion and doctrine of the Roman Catholic Church. (No plural form in this sense.) ♦ *The religion class spent a week discussing Catholicism.* ♦ *Mike converted to Catholicism from a Protestant denomination.*

catnap ['kæt næp] **1.** *n.* a brief period of sleep. ♦ *After a short catnap, Mary had a burst of energy.* ♦ *Bob took a catnap after lunch.* **2.** *iv.* to sleep just for a little while; to rest a little by sleeping. (Pt/pp: *catnapped.*) ♦ *Grandpa catnaps after lunch every day.* ♦ *If you catnap for a few minutes, you'll feel more energetic.*

catnip ['kæt nɪp] *n.* a scented plant of the mint family that attracts cats. (No plural form in this sense.) ♦ *Tabby, our cat, loves catnip.* ♦ *The kitten nibbled the catnip growing in the garden.*

catsup ['kæt səp] See ketchup.

cattle ['kæt əl] *n.* the general name for cows and bulls. (No plural form in this sense. Treated as plural. Number is expressed with *head of cattle*, as in *10 head of cattle.*) ♦ *The cattle grazed on the mountainside.* ♦ *The farmer raised cattle as well as crops.*

catty ['kæt i] *adj.* spiteful; mean-spirited. (Adv: *cattily.* Comp: *cattier;* sup: *cattiest.*) ♦ *Mary regretted making catty comments about her friend.* ♦ *Bill made a catty comment about his teammate's abilities.*

catwalk ['kæt wɔk] *n.* a very narrow, suspended walkway under a high ceiling. ♦ *The janitor had to travel on a narrow catwalk to change the light bulbs.* ♦ *The theater had several catwalks over the stage area.*

Caucasian [kɔ 'ke ʒən] **1.** *adj.* [of a person, usually of European descent] having light-colored skin; white ③. (In common, but not technical, use.) ♦ *Bill is Chinese, but he is married to a Caucasian woman.* ♦ *The suspect was described as being tall and Caucasian.* **2.** *n.* a person having white skin. ♦ *The murder suspect is a male Caucasian about thirty years old.* ♦ *Three Caucasians and two blacks entered the rear of the building.*

caucus ['kɔk əs] *n.* a meeting, often of members of a political party, held in order to choose a candidate or set policy. ♦ *The party caucus was held at a conference room in a downtown hotel.* ♦ *Only the regular party members were invited to the caucus.*

caught ['kɔt] pt/pp of catch.

cauldron ['kɔl drən] *n.* a very large pot used for boiling large amounts of water. ♦ *The witch's cauldron was filled with a bubbling liquid.* ♦ *The whalers boiled blubber in huge cauldrons.*

cauliflower ['kɑl ə flɑʊ ɚ] *n.* a vegetable having a large solid head made of tiny white buds. (No plural form in this sense. Number is expressed with *head(s) of cauliflower.*) ♦ *The casserole had cauliflower and broccoli in it.* ♦ *Cauliflower grows poorly in our garden.*

caulk ['kɔk] **1.** *n.* a substance used to fill gaps and seams, especially to make something watertight or airtight. (No plural form in this sense.) ♦ *Tom put some caulk around the edge of the window frame.* ♦ *The old caulk cracked, causing a leak.* **2.** *tv.* to place ① into an open seam or a gap. ♦ *Anne caulked the gaps in the window frame.* ♦ *The boat builder caulked the seams of the hull.*

causal ['kɔz əl] *adj.* <the adj. form of cause.> (Adv: *causally.*) ♦ *The doctor identified a causal relationship between the drug and Mary's rash.* ♦ *Jimmy understood the causal relationship between misbehaving and being punished.*

causality [kɔ 'zæl ə ti] *n.* the relationship between cause and effect. (No plural form in this sense.) ♦ *Mary analyzed the different patterns of causality in the collapse of economic systems.* ♦ *Susie understood the causality of misbehaving and being punished.*

cause ['kɔz] **1.** *tv.* to make something happen. ♦ *The earthquake caused a mudslide.* ♦ *Jane's angry words caused a fight.* **2.** *n.* someone or something that makes something happen; someone or something that produces an effect. ♦ *What was the cause of the accident?* ♦ *Max is the cause of all this trouble.* **3.** *n.* a philosophy or a movement; a political, charitable, or social movement. ♦ *David donated money to his favorite cause.* ♦ *The editorial supported the cause of freedom of speech.* **4. good cause** *n.* a beneficial organization, such as a charity, and its goals. ♦ *Please contribute money to this charity. It's for a good cause.* ♦ *I am always willing to contribute to a good cause.*

causeway ['kɔz we] *n.* a raised roadway built over wetlands, marshy ground, or shallow water. ♦ *The kids rode their bikes along the causeway across the swamp.* ♦ *A solidly built causeway prevented vehicles from getting stuck in the mud.*

caustic ['kɔ stɪk] **1.** *adj.* corrosive; relating to chemicals that corrode or burn. (Adv: *caustically* [...ɪk li].) ♦ *The battery leaked some kind of caustic acid.* ♦ *A caustic substance burned my skin.* **2.** *adj.* sarcastic; acerbic; cutting. (Figurative on ①. Adv: *caustically* [...ɪk li].) ♦ *The caustic remark caused the candidate to lose the election.* ♦ *By the end of our vacation, we were all a little caustic with one another.*

cauterize ['kɔt ə rɑɪz] *tv.* to seal an open wound with searing heat. ♦ *If the bleeding does not stop, the doctor will have to cauterize this cut.* ♦ *The doctor cauterized the wound to stop the bleeding.*

caution ['kɔ ʃən] **1.** *n.* great care; prudence. (No plural form in this sense.) ♦ *The hunter approached the lion with caution.* ♦ *The firemen used caution when searching the burning house.* **2.** *n.* a warning; an admonition. ♦ *The teacher gave the students a caution against talking to strangers.* ♦ *The stockbroker's caution against the unwise investment prevented the loss of the client's money.* **3.** *tv.* to warn someone. ♦ *The teacher cautioned the students about talking to strangers.* ♦ *Jane cautioned her client against the investment.* **4. throw caution to the wind** *idiom* to become very careless. ♦ *Jane, who is usually cautious, threw caution to the wind and went swimming in the ocean.* ♦ *I don't mind taking a little chance now and then, but I'm not the type of person who throws caution to the wind.*

cautionary ['kɔ ʃən ɛr i] *adj.* advising; urging carefulness. ♦ *Ignoring my cautionary remarks, the children dived into the lake.* ♦ *A cautionary warning is printed on packages of cigarettes.*

cautious ['kɔ ʃəs] *adj.* careful; prudent. (Adv: *cautiously.*) ♦ *David is always cautious about his investments.* ♦ *Be cautious when you approach strangers.*

cavalcade ['kæv əl ked] *n.* a procession on horseback. ♦ *A cavalcade of mounted police officers were part of the parade.* ♦ *The cavalcade of cowboys made its way down main street to the saloon.*

cavalier [kæv ə 'lɪr] **1.** *n.* a soldier on horseback, as part of the cavalry. ♦ *A group of cavaliers rode into the courtyard.* ♦ *The cavaliers stopped at the brook to water their horses.* **2.** *adj.* haughty; (blatantly) arrogant. (Adv: *cavalierly.*) ♦ *A driver with a cavalier view of politeness drove right in front of me.* ♦ *The cavalier shopper stepped in front of the other customers.* **3.** *adj.* casual; nonchalant. (Adv: *cavalierly.*) ♦ *Mary's cavalier attitude got her into trouble at work.* ♦ *John is just too cavalier about spending money. He needs to make a budget.*

cavalry ['kæv əl ri] *n.* a group of soldiers fighting on horseback; a troupe of cavaliers. (No plural form in this sense.) ♦ *The cavalry was stationed at the fort in the desert.* ♦ *The cavalry arrived just in time to drive back the attackers.*

cave ['kev] *n.* a natural chamber or tunnel inside a mountain or under the earth. ♦ *Drawings of wild animals were found inside the cave.* ♦ *The hikers stayed in the cave until it stopped raining.*

cave-in ['kev ɪn] *n.* the collapse of something into a hollow area underneath. ♦ *The explosion in the mine caused a cave-in of the tunnels.* ♦ *Fifty people were rescued from the cave-in.*

cavern ['kæv ɚn] *n.* a large cave; a large chamber in a cave. ♦ *The tunnel led to a cavern deep within the earth.* ♦ *Inside the cavern were the remnants of an ancient fire.*

caviar ['kæv i ɑr] *n.* the eggs of certain fish, such as the sturgeon, eaten as an appetizer. (No plural form in this sense.) ♦ *Black caviar from Russia is very expensive.* ♦ *Caviar is often served as an appetizer.*

cavity ['kæv ɪt i] **1.** *n.* a hole; a hollow, enclosed space. ♦ *A rabbit nestled in a cavity of the old tree trunk.* ♦ *A brick fell out, leaving a dark cavity in the wall.* **2.** *n.* a rotten place on a tooth. ♦ *The dentist repaired the cavity in my tooth.* ♦ *The cavity caused Jane a lot of pain before she went to the dentist.*

cavort [kə 'vort] *iv.* to jump around; to frolic. ♦ *Three young colts cavorted in the pasture.* ♦ *Dave and Mary cavorted around the living room after winning the lottery.*

caw ['kɔ] *n.* the sound made by a crow and other large birds. ♦ *The caws of the birds woke us up each morning.* ♦ *I thought I heard the caw of a bird, but none was in sight.*

CD ['si 'di] See Compact Disc.

cease ['sis] **1.** *tv.* to stop doing something; to quit doing something. ♦ *The baby ceased his tantrum after half an hour.* ♦ *Jimmy ceased tormenting Susie as he became more mature.* **2.** *iv.* to stop; to finish. ♦ *When the rain ceased, the kids went out to play.* ♦ *The music ceased, and the audience broke into applause.*

cease-fire ['sis 'faɪr] *n.* an agreement to stop shooting in a war. ♦ *The warring countries agreed to a cease-fire.* ♦ *The guerrillas broke the cease-fire when they attacked the truck.*

ceaseless ['sis ləs] *adj.* unending; ongoing. (Adv: *ceaselessly.*) ♦ *The manager was annoyed by the worker's ceaseless complaining.* ♦ *The ceaseless noise of the dripping faucet drove us crazy.*

cedar ['sid ɚ] **1.** *n.* an evergreen tree with fragrant wood. ♦ *The mountainside was covered with cedars.* ♦ *The fox surprised a rabbit under the cedar.* **2.** *n.* wood from ①. (No plural form in this sense.) ♦ *The chest was made of fragrant cedar.* ♦ *What color did Bill stain the cedar he is using for his bookcase?* **3.** *adj.* made from ②. ♦ *The cedar chest was a family heirloom.* ♦ *The cedar wood was left a natural color.*

ceiling ['si lɪŋ] **1.** *n.* the underside of a roof; a surface that forms the overhead part of a room. ♦ *The ceiling in the living room was leaking water.* ♦ *The carpenter replaced the beams in the ceiling.* **2.** *n.* the upper limit of something, especially of costs. ♦ *My father put an absolute ceiling on my college expenditures.* ♦ *The president ordered a ceiling on prices to hold down inflation.*

celebrate ['sɛl ə bret] **1.** *tv.* to observe a day or an occasion with festivity. ♦ *Let's go to dinner and celebrate your promotion.* ♦ *Bill doesn't celebrate his birthday now that he's over fifty.* **2.** *tv.* to perform a rite or a ritual. ♦ *The priest celebrates Mass each day.* ♦ *Yom Kippur is a Jewish holiday celebrated by fasting and praying.* **3.** *tv.* to praise someone or something. ♦ *The critics celebrated the performer's talents.* ♦ *A museum exhibit celebrated the invention of electricity.* **4.** *iv.* to be festive for a certain reason. ♦ *It was a beautiful sunny day, so we celebrated by having a picnic.* ♦ *We celebrated with champagne.*

celebrated ['sɛl ə bret ɪd] *adj.* known and admired; famous. ♦ *A celebrated artist died last week.* ♦ *The celebrated chef published a cookbook.*

celebration [sɛl ə 'bre ʃən] *n.* a festival; festivity. ♦ *The celebration was held at the country club.* ♦ *A celebration honoring the graduates was held Friday night.*

celebrity [sə 'lɛb rɪt i] *n.* someone who is famous; someone who is well known. ♦ *The unknown actress became a celebrity when her first film was released.* ♦ *The celebrity stopped to sign autographs for his fans.*

celery ['sɛl ə ri] *n.* a light green vegetable with long, crisp stalks and leafy ends. (No plural form in this sense. Number is expressed with *stick(s)* or *stalk(s) of celery.*) ♦ *I added chopped celery to the soup.* ♦ *Celery is a healthful snack.*

celestial [sə 'lɛs tʃəl] **1.** *adj.* relating to the sky; relating to outer space, far from the earth. (Adv: *celestially.*) ♦ *The book showed a map of the celestial realms.* ♦ *The picture showed the celestial bodies in position.* **2.** *adj.* heavenly; relating to heaven and divinity. ♦ *The angel in the painting had a celestial smile.* ♦ *As I lay dying, I thought I heard celestial music.*

celibacy ['sɛl ə bə si] *n.* the state of being unmarried and not having sex. (No plural form in this sense.) ♦ *Bob didn't choose celibacy, he just never married.* ♦ *Celibacy did not agree with Anne, so she sought to get married.*

celibate ['sɛl ə bət] **1.** *n.* someone who does not marry or have sexual experiences. ♦ *Mary did not choose to remain a celibate—she just never married.* ♦ *Roman Catholic priests are celibates.* **2.** *adj.* not having sexual experiences; having taken a vow to not marry. (Adv: *celibately.*) ♦ *The celibate woman joined a convent.* ♦ *Roman Catholic priests are celibate.*

cell ['sɛl] **1.** *n.* the basic biological unit of living tissue. ♦ *The biology class studied the structure of a cell.* ♦ *The students examined the cell under a microscope.* **2.** *n.* a subdivision of certain things, such as a beehive or zones for portable, wireless telephones. ♦ *The queen lays one egg in each cell.* ♦ *When using my cellular telephone, I can drive through various cells and still carry on a telephone conversation.* **3.** *n.* a cage-like room for keeping prisoners. ♦ *The prison had hundreds of cells.* ♦ *The cell had a metal door rather than bars.* **4.** *n.* a small, simple room, typically for a monk. ♦ *The monk prayed in his modest cell.* ♦ *The university provided cells for graduate students.* **5.** *n.* a battery; one of the sections of a battery. ♦ *My flashlight uses 6 cells.* ♦ *One of the cells of the battery is dead.*

cellar ['sɛl ɚ] *n.* basement; an underground room. ♦ *We stored canned vegetables in the cellar beneath the house.* ♦ *During the tornado, we sought refuge in the storm cellar.*

cellist ['tʃɛl əst] *n.* someone who plays a cello. ♦ *The orchestra had six cellists.* ♦ *The pianist and the cellist played a duet.*

cello ['tʃɛl o] *n.* a stringed instrument, similar to a violin but larger, held upright between the player's knees. (Pl ends in *-s.*) ♦ *John carried his cello to the orchestra rehearsal.* ♦ *The cello makes beautiful, low tones.*

cellular ['sɛl jə lɚ] (Adv: *cellularly.*) **1.** *adj.* <the adj. form of cell ①.> ♦ *The scientist examined the cellular structure of the leaf under the microscope.* ♦ *In my science class, we studied cellular biology.* **2. cellular telephone; cell phone** *n.* a portable telephone using radio-wave transmission within a large area that is divided into smaller cells, allowing the same radio frequency to be used in different cells by different users. ♦ *Tom bought a new cellular telephone to use in his car.* ♦ *My new cellular telephone is small enough to fit in my pocket.*

cellulose ['sɛl jə los] *n.* the substance found in the cell walls of plants, used to make paper, plastics, textile fibers, etc. (No plural form in this sense.) ♦ *Cellulose helps support green plants.* ♦ *Cellulose from wood is used to make paper.*

Celsius ['sel si əs] **1.** *n.* the metric system of measuring temperature. (No plural form in this sense. Named for the Swedish astronomer Anders Celsius. The same as centigrade. Abbreviated *C.*) ♦ *Celsius is used in most countries except the U.S.* ♦ *The Canadian forecaster gave the temperatures in Celsius.* **2.** *adj.* <the adj. use of ①.> (② follows degrees. Abbreviated *C.*) ♦ *Water boils at 100 degrees Celsius and freezes at 0 degrees Celsius.* ♦ *At 38 degrees C., I am very warm.*

cement [sɪ 'mɛnt] **1.** *n.* something like glue, that joins things together. (No plural form in this sense.) ♦ *Wallpaper paste is a cement that attaches paper to walls.* ♦ *The kids used rubber cement to glue sheets of construction paper together.* **2.** *n.* a gray powder made of clay and limestone that hardens when mixed with water. (No plural form in this sense.) ♦ *The construction workers mixed cement for the foundation.* ♦ *Bags of cement sat out in the rain and were ruined.* **3.** *tv.* to join two things together. ♦ *The wallpaper paste cemented the paper to the wall.* ♦ *I cemented the broken cup together with glue.*

cemetery ['sɛm ə tɛr i] *n.* a graveyard; a place where dead people are buried. ♦ *My relatives are buried in the town cemetery.* ♦ *The children were frightened to walk through the cemetery at night.*

censor ['sɛn sɚ] **1.** *n.* someone who seeks to remove objectionable words and pictures from material seen by the public. ♦ *The censor sought to change the TV script.* ♦ *After the book's publication, the censor objected to its vulgar language.* **2.** *tv.* to suppress the publication or performance of objectionable material. ♦ *The obscene outburst was censored from the TV show.* ♦ *The dictator censored news of the war.*

censorship ['sɛn sɚ ʃɪp] *n.* the suppression of the publication or performance of objectionable material. (No plural form in this sense.) ♦ *The candidate opposed censorship and spoke about freedom of speech.* ♦ *The dictator controlled the censorship of the media.*

censure ['sɛn ʃɚ] **1.** *n.* the placing of official blame on someone. (No plural form in this sense.) ♦ *Bill received a censure from his boss for the failure of the project.* ♦ *The guard got a letter of censure for letting the prisoner escape.* **2.** *tv.* to reprimand someone officially. ♦ *Congress threatened to censure the senator who accepted the bribe.* ♦ *The warden censured the guard for letting the prisoner escape.*

census ['sɛn səs] **1.** *n.* the process of counting the number of people who live in an area. ♦ *The small town was preparing to take a census.* ♦ *The census recorded the age and occupation of the people in the town.* **2.** *n.* the official number of people who live in an area; a report of what was found in collecting information for ①. ♦ *According to the last census, the population of Smithville is 5,000.* ♦ *The town took a census every few years.*

cent ['sɛnt] **1.** *n.* a penny; one one-hundredth of a dollar. ♦ *I was just one cent short of what I needed to buy the groceries.* ♦ *I'm not lending you another cent until you pay me what you owe me.* **2. put in one's two cents(' worth)** *idiom* to add one's comments (to something). ♦ *Can I put in my two cents' worth?* ♦ *Sure, go ahead—put your two cents in.*

centenarian [sɛn tə 'nɛr i ən] **1.** *n.* someone who is 100 years old or older. ♦ *My grandmother is 99 and will be a centenarian next year.* ♦ *The centenarian said the world had changed a lot since he was born.* **2.** *adj.* <the adj. use of ①.> ♦ *A huge festival for the centenarian residents of the nursing home was held last week.* ♦ *A centenarian resident living in our apartment building had a birthday party.*

centennial [sɛn 'tɛn i əl] **1.** *n.* a 100-year anniversary. ♦ *The town celebrated its centennial last year.* ♦ *The centennial of the town library was a big event.* **2.** *adj.* <the adj. use of ①.> (Adv: *centennially.*) ♦ *The town held its centennial celebration.* ♦ *My grandfather will have his centennial birthday this year.*

center ['sɛn tɚ] **1.** *n.* the point in the middle of a circle or sphere which is the same distance to all points on the circle or sphere. ♦ *Please place a dot in the center of the circle.* ♦ *The teacher stood in the center of the circle of children.* **2.** *n.* the major site or focus of an activity. ♦ *This city is the leading manufacturing center in the state.* ♦ *The university is a center of learning.* **3.** *adj.* middle. ♦ *The magician turned the center card over.* ♦ *In the hallway, the center door was locked, but the ones on the ends were open.* **4.** *tv.* to place someone or something in the middle of something. ♦ *The decorator centered the picture on the wall.* ♦ *The family was centered in the photograph.* **5. centered around; centered on** *iv.* + *prep. phr.* to be directed toward or around a particular point. ♦ *The argument centered around where to go for dinner.* ♦ *The lecture centered on the art of the Renaissance.*

centerpiece ['sɛn tɚ pis] **1.** *n.* a flower arrangement or other ornament placed in the center of a table. ♦ *The basket of flowers made a lovely centerpiece for the table.* ♦ *The guests could not see each other because the centerpiece on the table was so tall.* **2.** *n.* the central idea or theme. (Figurative on ①.) ♦ *The book's centerpiece was the author's political views.* ♦ *Mary's idea was the centerpiece of the whole plan.*

centigrade ['sɛnt ə gred] **1.** *n.* the metric system of measuring temperature. (No plural form in this sense. The same as **Celsius**. Abbreviated *C.*) ♦ *Centigrade is used in most countries except the U.S.* ♦ *The Canadian forecaster gave the temperatures in centigrade.* **2.** *n.* a measure of temperature in the metric system. (The same as **Celsius**.) ♦ *The temperatures of foreign cities were given in centigrade.* ♦ *It is nearly 40 degrees centigrade, so I'm sweating.*

centimeter ['sɛnt ə mit ɚ] *n.* a measure of length, equal to one one-hundredth of a meter. (An inch is 2.54 centimeters.) ♦ *There are a hundred centimeters in one meter.* ♦ *This grasshopper is two centimeters long.*

centipede ['sɛnt ə pid] *n.* a small worm-like animal with several sets of legs. ♦ *The children were delighted to find a centipede.* ♦ *The centipede was a few inches long.*

central ['sɛn trəl] **1.** *adj.* near the center. (Adv: *centrally.*) ♦ *The friends met at a central location in the city.* ♦ *City hall is in a central area.* **2.** *adj.* primary; essential. (Adv: *centrally.*) ♦ *The evidence was central to the lawyer's argument.* ♦ *Honor was the central theme of the book.*

Central African Republic [sɛn trəl æ frɪ kən rɪ 'pʌb lɪk] See Gazetteer.

Central America ['sɛn trəl ə 'mɛr ə kə] *n.* a region consisting of the seven countries located between Mexico and Colombia. ♦ *Belize, Costa Rica, Guatemala, Honduras, El Salvador, Nicaragua, and Panama are what is called Central America.* ♦ *Spanish is the language of Central America.*

centralize ['sɛn trə lɑɪz] *tv.* to bring things or people together to a central location or under central control. ♦ *The mayor centralized the operations of city hall.* ♦ *Our company centralized all its billing in one department.*

centrifugal [sɛn 'trɪf ə gəl] *adj.* relating to a force that moves things away from the center of a rotating object. (Adv: *centrifugally.*) ♦ *Centrifugal force caused the child to* *fall off the merry-go-round.* ♦ *A centrifuge provides a means of utilizing centrifugal force.*

centrifuge ['sɛn trə fjudʒ] *n.* a machine that spins a substance very fast, separating the heavier from the lighter parts. ♦ *The lab technician put the specimens in the centrifuge.* ♦ *The centrifuge spins at very high speeds.*

centrist ['sɛn trəst] **1.** *n.* someone who is politically moderate. ♦ *Mary was regarded as a centrist in the political area.* ♦ *Tom, a political centrist, ran for Congress last year.* **2.** *adj.* politically moderate. ♦ *The voters preferred centrist politicians in the last election.* ♦ *The president managed to present a centrist image to the public.*

century ['sɛn tʃə ri] **1.** *n.* one hundred years. ♦ *The documentary explored a century of inventions.* ♦ *This antique vase is a century old.* **2.** *n.* a block of time that begins every one hundred years, starting with the birth of Jesus Christ or some other specific event. ♦ *The 21st century begins on January 1, 2001, and ends on December 31, 2100.* ♦ *Some people think the 21st century begins in the year 2000.*

ceramic [sə 'ræm ɪk] **1.** *adj.* made of hard, baked clay, able to withstand great heat. ♦ *Coffee was served in ceramic mugs.* ♦ *The ceramic pot can be used in a hot oven.* **2. ceramics** *n.* the making of pottery by shaping clay and baking it until it hardens. (Treated as singular.) ♦ *Bill took a class in ceramics and made all sorts of pottery.* ♦ *The instructor of ceramics showed us how to glaze a pot.*

cereal ['sɪr i əl] **1.** *n.* one of a number of plants that provides grain. ♦ *A number of important cereals are grown in my state.* ♦ *We eat five cereals: wheat, oats, barley, corn, and rice.* **2.** *n.* a food product made from grains, usually served at breakfast with milk. ♦ *Hurry up and eat your cereal!* ♦ *Anne's favorite cereal is oatmeal.*

cerebral ['sɛr ə brəl] **1.** *adj.* of or about the cerebrum; relating to the brain. (Adv: *cerebrally.*) ♦ *She suffered from a cerebral hemorrhage.* ♦ *A severe blow to the cerebral region damaged his brain.* **2.** *adj.* using reason; requiring reason; analytic. (Figurative on ①. Adv: *cerebrally.*) ♦ *This problem is just too cerebral for me.* ♦ *The very young students don't do very well with cerebral matters.*

cerebrum [sə 'ri brəm] *n.* the largest part of the brain. ♦ *Dave suffered a blow to the head that damaged his cerebrum.* ♦ *Most of our voluntary movements are controlled by the cerebrum.*

ceremonial [sɛr ə 'mon i əl] *adj.* done according to ceremony; involving ceremony. (Adv: *ceremonially.*) ♦ *The mayor was dressed in ceremonial clothing, including a purple cape.* ♦ *Churches observe many ceremonial occasions.*

ceremonious [sɛr ə 'mon i əs] *adj.* very formal; following or observing ceremony. (Adv: *ceremoniously.*) ♦ *The symphony conductor took a ceremonious bow.* ♦ *The awards were given in a very ceremonious manner.*

ceremony ['sɛr ə mon i] **1.** *n.* a ritual associated with a particular event. ♦ *The wedding ceremony took place in a garden.* ♦ *A committee of four people was in charge of the award ceremony.* **2.** *n.* the etiquette and protocol observed in certain religious, social, or political events. (No plural form in this sense.) ♦ *Jane thrives on ceremony and makes everything more formal than it needs to be.* ♦ *Sue is uncomfortable with too much formal ceremony.*

certain ['sɚt n] **1. certain to** *adj.* + *inf.* bound to do something; sure to do something. ♦ *Jane is certain to be late because traffic is so bad.* ♦ *If we have a picnic, it's certain to rain.* **2.** *adj.* definite or known, but not specified; particular and specific, but not identified. ♦ *Certain students are not turning in their homework on time.* ♦ *Certain aspects of this problem still confuse me.*

certainly ['sɚt n li] **1.** *adv.* definitely; surely; positively. ♦ *You are certainly welcome in our home.* ♦ *That is certainly a beautiful dress.* **2.** *adv.* yes, by all means. (An answer to a question.) ♦ *"Can I stop by tonight?" Bob asked. "Certainly!" Jane replied.* ♦ *Certainly. Help yourself.*

certainty ['sɚt n ti] **1.** *n.* the state of being sure or certain. (No plural form in this sense.) ♦ *Bill couldn't say with any certainty when he'd be home.* ♦ *I can say with certainty that we like your work.* **2.** *n.* something that is known to be true. ♦ *It is a certainty that the sun will rise each day.* ♦ *Our own death is a certainty.*

certificate [sɚ 'tɪf ə kɪt] **1.** *n.* an official document pledging that the statements written on it are true. ♦ *The death certificate stated the cause of death.* ♦ *Mary had to present her birth certificate to get a driver's license.* **2.** *n.* an official document that shows that someone has achieved a certain kind of training or education. ♦ *Lisa received her teaching certificate in the mail.* ♦ *Many certificates of achievement hung on Mary's walls.*

certification [sɚt ə fɪ 'ke ʃən] **1.** *n.* the process of certifying someone or something. (No plural form in this sense.) ♦ *Bill was working towards certification in scuba diving.* ♦ *Earning certification as a paramedic is a long process.* **2.** *n.* something, such as letters or documents, proving that one has undergone ①. (No plural form in this sense.) ♦ *My scuba diving certification arrived in the mail last week.* ♦ *The court asked the lawyer to produce her professional certification.*

certified ['sɚt ə fɑɪd] *adj.* having a certificate or certification that asserts one's fitness for a specific job or task. ♦ *Tom is a certified diver.* ♦ *Sue is studying to be a certified accountant.*

certify ['sɚt ə fɑɪ] **1.** *tv.* to guarantee something, usually in writing. ♦ *I can certify in writing that the statement is true.* ♦ *The card certified that the owner had car insurance.* **2. certify as** *tv.* + *prep. phr.* to officially state that someone has met the requirements that are necessary for certification. ♦ *The board certified Mary as qualified.* ♦ *John was certified as a professional.*

cervical ['sɚv ɪ kəl] **1.** *adj.* of or about the neck. (Adv: *cervically* [...ɪk li].) ♦ *Cervical X-rays were taken to examine the vertebrae.* ♦ *The accident victim suffered cervical injuries.* **2.** *adj.* of or about to the neck of the uterus, the cervix. (Adv: *cervically* [...ɪk li].) ♦ *Can good nutrition help prevent cervical cancer?* ♦ *The doctor performed a biopsy of tissues taken from the cervical area.*

cervix ['sɚ vɪks] **1.** *n.* the neck. ♦ *The X-rays showed the accident victim's spine, including the bones of the cervix.* ♦ *There were some small fractures on the bones of the cervix.* **2.** *n.* the neck of, or entrance to, the uterus. ♦ *During labor, the cervix dilates.* ♦ *The doctor examined the cervix for signs of disease.*

cessation [sɛ 'se ʃən] *n.* the stopping of something; a pause. (No plural form in this sense.) ♦ *The cessation of* *armed conflict was a relief to the people of the nation.* ♦ *Death came with the cessation of the patient's heart.*

cesspool ['sɛs pul] **1.** *n.* a pit that waste empties into; a sewage pit. ♦ *The city made them replace the cesspool with a septic tank.* ♦ *Many cesspools overflowed during the heavy rains.* **2.** *n.* a filthy place. (Figurative on ①.) ♦ *Bill's parents thought his apartment was a cesspool, but Bill loved it.* ♦ *The horrible neighborhood was the cesspool of the city.*

Chad ['tʃæd] See Gazetteer.

chafe ['tʃef] **1.** *tv.* to rub something; to irritate a surface by rubbing. ♦ *The tag on Jimmy's shirt chafed his neck.* ♦ *Coarse fabric will chafe your skin.* **2.** *tv.* to warm one's hands by rubbing; to rub something to warm it. ♦ *Tom chafed his hands together to warm them.* ♦ *Anne chafed her arms, trying to get them warm again.* **3.** *iv.* to rub. ♦ *Does this garment chafe?* ♦ *John squirmed because his collar was chafing.*

chaff ['tʃæf] **1.** *n.* shells or husks separated from the seeds of grains. (No plural form in this sense.) ♦ *The farmer threw the chaff into the fire.* ♦ *Most of the chaff blew away when the grain was tossed into the air.* **2.** *n.* something worthless, especially unnecessary talk. (No plural form in this sense. Figurative on ①.) ♦ *The boss yelled at Tom for having so much chaff in his presentation.* ♦ *I hear too much chaff and not enough substance!*

chafing dish ['tʃef ɪŋ dɪʃ] *n.* a metal serving dish, heated when in use. ♦ *The eggs steamed in a chafing dish on the brunch table.* ♦ *The caterer ran out of chafing dishes, so some of the food was served cold.*

chagrin [ʃə 'grɪn] **1.** *n.* disappointment; humiliation. (No plural form in this sense.) ♦ *I experienced some chagrin when admitting my mistake.* ♦ *Tom displayed his chagrin when the error was pointed out.* **2.** *tv.* to embarrass someone; to humiliate someone. (Pt/pp: *chagrined.* Usually passive.) ♦ *Bill was chagrined by his brother's actions.* ♦ *Mary was chagrined by her manager's comments.*

chain ['tʃen] **1.** *n.* links or rings that are joined together in a row. ♦ *The yard was roped off with a metal chain.* ♦ *Mary is wearing a gold chain around her neck.* **2.** *n.* events that are linked together, one following the other. (Figurative on ①.) ♦ *A strange chain of events led to the car accident.* ♦ *A chain of unfortunate incidents plagued the construction project.* **3.** *n.* one of a group of stores or businesses with the same name, owned by the same company or person. (A *chain store.*) ♦ *Is that restaurant part of a chain?* ♦ *The local bookstore was put out of business by competition from chains.* **4.** *adj.* occurring in sequence; part of a larger sequence or order. ♦ *Mary received a chain letter that instructed her to mail it to the next person on the list.* ♦ *The prisoners formed a chain gang to work outside the prison.* **5. chain to** *tv.* + *prep. phr.* to fasten someone or something to something else with ①; to secure someone or something with ①. ♦ *The bank clerk chained the pen to the counter so that no one would take it.* ♦ *The thirsty dog was chained to a tree.* **6.** *tv.* to bind someone or something with chains ①. ♦ *The performing bear had been chained to keep it from attacking people.* ♦ *The sheriff chained the criminal to keep him from escaping.*

chain-smoker ['tʃen smok ɚ] *n.* someone who smokes cigarettes constantly, one after another; someone who lights a new cigarette from the end of the cigarette just smoked. ♦ *Chain-smokers are endangering their health.* ♦ *My brother was a chain-smoker and smoked two packs of cigarettes a day.*

chair ['tʃɛr] **1.** *n.* a piece of furniture for sitting, sometimes with arms. (See also armchair.) ♦ *Five chairs stood around the dining room table.* ♦ *Mary placed the chair in front of the fire and sat in it.* **2.** *n.* the position of authority held by a chairman, chairwoman, chairperson, or presiding officer. ♦ *The chair has a lot of power.* ♦ *Please direct your questions to the chair.* **3.** *n.* the head of a department or committee. ♦ *Who is the chair of the finance committee?* ♦ *The chair of the department made a unilateral decision.* **4.** *tv.* to preside over a meeting, department, or committee. ♦ *Mary chairs the finance committee.* ♦ *Who will chair the meeting if Lisa is absent?*

chairlift ['tʃɛr lɪft] *n.* a system of seats attached to cables that carry people up the side of a mountain. ♦ *The skiers rode the chairlift up the mountain.* ♦ *My tickets to ride the chairlift cost a fortune.*

chairman ['tʃɛr mən] *n., irreg.* the head of a department or committee; the person in charge of a meeting. (Either male or female. Pl: chairmen. See also chairperson.) ♦ *The committee elects a new chairman each year.* ♦ *The chairman asked that the meeting begin.*

chairmanship ['tʃɛr mən ʃɪp] *n.* the position of authority held by a chairman. ♦ *Mary is hoping to get the chairmanship of the music department at the local university.* ♦ *The chairmanship was given to the most competent person.*

chairmen ['tʃɛr mən] pl of chairman.

chairperson ['tʃer pɚ sən] *n.* the head of a department or committee; the person in charge of a meeting. ♦ *Jane is the chairperson of the finance committee.* ♦ *The chairperson ended the meeting.*

chairwoman ['tʃer wʊm ən] *n., irreg.* a woman who is the head of a department or committee; the woman in charge of a meeting. (Pl: chairwomen.) ♦ *Anne is the chairwoman of the book club.* ♦ *The chairwoman recruited new club members.*

chairwomen ['tʃer wɪm ən] pl of chairwoman.

chalet [ʃæ 'le] *n.* a small wooden house or cottage, as found in Switzerland. ♦ *The skiers stayed in a chalet near the slopes.* ♦ *The chalet had flower boxes in the windows.*

chalk ['tʃɔk] **1.** *n.* a soft, white limestone. (No plural form in this sense.) ♦ *They discovered deposits of chalk near the coast.* ♦ *Chalk is a crumbly substance.* **2.** *n.* a stick of ① used for writing, as on a chalkboard. (No plural form in this sense. Number is expressed with *piece(s)* or *stick(s) of chalk.*) ♦ *The teacher used colored chalk on the blackboard.* ♦ *The chalk erases easily from the board at the end of the day.* **3.** *tv.* to draw or write something with ②. ♦ *The kids chalked pictures onto the sidewalk.* ♦ *The student chalked a math problem on the blackboard.* **4. chalk up** *tv.* + *prep. phr.* to score a point, as in a game or argument. ♦ *When Jane won the argument she chalked up a point for herself.* ♦ *Bill tried to chalk up a few points by bringing Anne flowers after the argument.*

chalkboard ['tʃɔk bord] *n.* a large, smooth writing surface, mounted on the wall of a classroom or lecture hall; a blackboard. ♦ *The teacher used colored chalk to write on the chalkboard.* ♦ *Jimmy erased the chalkboard.*

chalky ['tʃɔk i] *adj.* white or powdery, like powdered chalk. (Adv: *chalkily.* Comp: *chalkier;* sup: *chalkiest.*) ♦

The teacher's hands were chalky after teaching the class. ♦ *The children got their clothes chalky while drawing on the pavement.*

challenge ['tʃæl ɪndʒ] **1.** *n.* a dare; an invitation to compete. ♦ *The boss presented his employees with a challenge to increase production.* ♦ *Bill issued a challenge to Mary to solve the puzzle before he did.* **2.** *n.* a difficult task. ♦ *It was a challenge to convince Dave to take a vacation.* ♦ *Getting his kids to behave is a challenge for Bill.* **3. challenge to** *tv.* + *prep. phr.* to dare or invite someone to compete. ♦ *I challenged Jane to a tennis match.* ♦ *The gentleman was challenged to a duel by his enemy.* **4.** *tv.* [for a difficult task] to test someone or something. ♦ *The homework assignment challenged Bill.* ♦ *The crisis challenged Mary's ability to deal with stress.*

challenging ['tʃæl ɪndʒ ɪŋ] *adj.* difficult; testing one's ability; requiring deep thought or hard work. (Adv: *challengingly.*) ♦ *A challenging task is good for everyone now and then.* ♦ *The challenging competition left the athletes exhausted.*

chamber ['tʃem bɚ] **1.** *n.* a room. ♦ *The sparsely furnished chamber had only a bed and dresser.* ♦ *The rare book collection is kept in a chamber just off the dining room.* **2.** *n.* a division of government, such as the House of Representatives or the Senate of the United States Congress, separately; certain organizations such as the Chamber of Commerce. ♦ *The entire chamber voted on the proposed law.* ♦ *Each chamber consists of elected officials.* **3.** *n.* a compartment within something; an enclosed space inside the body. ♦ *The human heart consists of four chambers.* ♦ *The seashell had several chambers.*

chamber music ['tʃem bɚ mju zɪk] *n.* music intended for a small hall, played by a small group of musicians. (No plural form in this sense.) ♦ *Chamber music was played at the reception.* ♦ *The Smiths went to a concert of chamber music last night.*

chameleon [kə 'mil (i) jən] **1.** *n.* a lizard that changes the color of its skin to match its surroundings. ♦ *The students keep a chameleon in a large jar in the classroom.* ♦ *The chameleon turned green when it rested on the leaf.* **2.** *n.* someone who is very changeable. (Figurative on ①.) ♦ *Jane is such a chameleon. Her reactions are changeable and predictable.* ♦ *Bill is fickle—a real chameleon.*

champ ['tʃæmp] *n.* a champion; a winner. ♦ *The boxing champ pranced around the ring, poking at his opponent.* ♦ *Bill has been wrestling champ for the last three years.*

champagne [ʃæm 'pen] **1.** *n.* a sparkling white wine made in the Champagne area of France or similar wines made elsewhere. (No plural form in this sense.) ♦ *We opened a bottle of champagne to celebrate.* ♦ *Champagne is a sparkling white wine.* **2. champagnes** *n.* kinds or types of ①. ♦ *We tried a number of champagnes, and this is the best.* ♦ *The French champagnes are good, but so are those from California.*

champion ['tʃæmp i ən] **1.** *n.* a winner; someone who has won a contest or competition. ♦ *The champion graciously accepted her medal.* ♦ *Do you think there will be a new boxing champion after the match?* **2.** *n.* someone who supports or advocates someone or something. ♦ *The lawyer was a champion of civil rights.* ♦ *The candidate needs a wealthy champion.* **3.** *tv.* to support or advocate someone or something. ♦ *Bill championed the party's nominee for president.* ♦ *One popular candidate champions tax reform.*

championship ['tʃæmp i ən ʃɪp] **1.** *n.* the first-place position in a contest. (No plural form in this sense.) ♦ *The championship went to the defending champion.* ♦ *Jane is trying to win the horseback riding championship.* **2.** *n.* the contest or event that will determine who the champion will be. ♦ *Entries for the championship must be made by Saturday.* ♦ *Twenty people entered the archery championship.*

chance ['tʃæns] **1.** *n.* fate; fortune. (No plural form in this sense.) ♦ *Chance will determine who will win the lottery.* ♦ *We can't predict the weather. It is a matter of chance.* **2.** *n.* the probability that something might happen. (No plural form in this sense.) ♦ *There is a chance we will take a vacation this year.* ♦ *Is there a chance Mary will come to the party?* **3.** *n.* an opportunity. ♦ *Bill got a chance to go hiking in the Rocky Mountains.* ♦ *This job is the chance of a lifetime.* **4.** *tv.* to risk something. ♦ *Max chanced his whole paycheck on a horse.* ♦ *Let's leave the umbrella at home and chance it. It won't rain.* **5. by chance** *idiom* accidentally; randomly; without planning. ♦ *I found this book by chance at a book sale.* ♦ *We met by chance in a class in college.* **6. fat chance** *idiom* very little likelihood. ♦ *Fat chance he has of getting the promotion.* ♦ *You think she'll lend you the money? Fat chance!* **7. fighting chance** *idiom* a good possibility of success, especially if every effort is made. ♦ *They have at least a fighting chance of winning the race.* ♦ *The patient could die, but he has a fighting chance since the operation.* **8. let the chance slip by** *idiom* to lose the opportunity (to do something). ♦ *When I was younger, I wanted to become a doctor, but I let the chance slip by.* ♦ *Don't let the chance slip by. Do it now!* **9. on the off-chance** *idiom* because of a slight possibility that something may happen or might be the case; just in case. ♦ *I went to the theater on the off-chance that there were tickets for the show left.* ♦ *We didn't think we would get into the football game, but we went on the off-chance.* **10. sporting chance** *idiom* a reasonably good chance. ♦ *If you hurry, you have a sporting chance of catching the bus.* ♦ *The firm has only a sporting chance of getting the export order.* **11. take a chance** *idiom* to take a gamble or a risk. ♦ *Max took a chance and bet on the underdog horse.* ♦ *Don't take a chance. Look before you cross the street.*

chancellor ['tʃæns (ə) lɚ] **1.** *n.* the head of a university. ♦ *The chancellor of the university gave a very long speech.* ♦ *The chancellor attended the annual board meeting.* **2.** *n.* the prime minister of Germany or Austria. ♦ *Chancellor Schmidt gave a long speech on television.* ♦ *The American president met with the German chancellor in Berlin.*

chancy ['tʃæn si] **1.** *adj.* risky. (Comp: *chancier;* sup: *chanciest.*) ♦ *Jane made a chancy investment in the stock market.* ♦ *It was a chancy plan, but it worked.* **2.** *adj.* not very likely; undecided. (Comp: *chancier;* sup: *chanciest.*) ♦ *It is chancy that Bill will come to the party.* ♦ *It's still chancy whether Anne will be able to attend.*

chandelier [ʃæn də 'lɪr] *n.* a large, hanging light fixture having several sources of light. ♦ *I needed a ladder in order to clean the chandelier.* ♦ *A beautiful chandelier was suspended over the table.*

change ['tʃendʒ] **1.** *n.* the process of becoming something different. (No plural form in this sense.) ♦ *A change in routine upset the child.* ♦ *After a long winter, a change of weather is welcome.* **2.** *n.* something new or different; something that replaces something else. ♦ *A vacation would be a good change right now.* ♦ *Moving to a new town provided a needed change.* **3.** *n.* bills or coins of lower value given in exchange for bills or coins of a higher value; the money returned to someone who had paid with a sum higher than the price. (No plural form in this sense.) ♦ *The traveler handed the clerk a $20 bill and asked for change in five-dollar bills.* ♦ *Dave handed the clerk a $5 bill when he bought the newspaper, and his change was $4.50.* **4.** *n.* loose coins. (No plural form in this sense.) ♦ *I always have some change at the bottom of my purse.* ♦ *The loose change under the couch went into the vacuum cleaner!* **5.** *tv.* to replace something. ♦ *Please change the burned out light bulb in the kitchen.* ♦ *The hotel maid changes the sheets on the bed every day.* **6.** *tv.* to cause something to become different. ♦ *The dye changed the color of the fabric.* ♦ *Bill changed his hair style.* **7.** *tv.* to remove clothing and put on different clothing. ♦ *The store had a dressing room where you could change your clothes.* ♦ *Bill changed his clothes for the party.* **8.** *tv.* to replace a baby's dirty diaper with a clean one. ♦ *No one wanted to change the baby's diapers.* ♦ *I finally changed the baby.* **9.** *iv.* to become different. ♦ *While she was away at school, Jane changed a lot.* ♦ *One is never too old to change.* **10.** *iv.* to take off one set of clothes and put on another. ♦ *I have to change before I can go out.* ♦ *After you have changed, we have to leave immediately.*

changeable ['tʃendʒ ə bəl] *adj.* capable of being changed; flexible. (Adv: *changeably.*) ♦ *The weather is so changeable in some parts of the country.* ♦ *The plan is changeable if you don't like it.*

changed ['tʃendʒd] *adj.* made different; affected. ♦ *The soldier returned from the war a changed man.* ♦ *The worker's changed attitudes were evident by an improved performance.*

changeover ['tʃendʒ ov ɚ] *n.* a shift from one thing or state to another. ♦ *The changeover from one boss to another was difficult for the workers.* ♦ *The baby made a changeover from baby food to solid food.*

channel ['tʃæn əl] **1.** *n.* a deeper passage through a harbor, where vessels can sail safely; the deepest part of a river or stream. ♦ *The boat moved through the channel to the open sea.* ♦ *The English Channel separates Great Britain from France.* **2.** *n.* the band of frequencies assigned to a particular television station. ♦ *In Chicago, channel 5 is the NBC network station.* ♦ *What channel is the football game on?* **3. channel into** *tv.* + *prep. phr.* to concentrate one's energy on a particular matter. ♦ *Bill channeled his energy into passing the test.* ♦ *Mary's efforts were channeled into starting a business.* **4. go through channels** *idiom* to proceed by consulting the proper persons or offices. ♦ *If you want an answer to your questions, you'll have to go through channels.* ♦ *If you know the answers, why do I have to go through channels?*

chant ['tʃænt] **1.** *n.* a prayer sung with several words in a row on the same note. ♦ *The chant of the monks echoed through the cloister.* ♦ *The choir repeated the chant several times.* **2.** *n.* a phrase that is repeated over and over. ♦ *A chant of "No justice, no peace!" rose from the angry crowd.* ♦ *A chant for food rose up from the starving crowd.* **3.** *tv.* to sing several words in a row on the same note. ♦ *We chanted our prayers and then had a simple meal.* ♦ *The service was spoken, rather than chanted.* **4.** *tv.* to shout slogans or phrases over and over. ♦ *They chanted "No justice, no peace!" until the mayor came out.* ♦ *The cheerleaders chanted their support for the team.* **5.** *iv.* to sing with several words in a row on the same note. ♦ *We had to chant over and over to let people know how we hated war.* ♦ *The monks chanted for an hour before the evening meal.*

Chanukah See Hanukkah.

chaos ['ke ɑs] *n.* complete confusion; complete disorder; anarchy. ♦ *The house was in a state of chaos while my parents were away.* ♦ *Chaos broke out when the fire alarm went off.*

chaotic [ke 'ɑt ɪk] *adj.* completely confused; without law or order. (Adv: *chaotically* [...ɪk li].) ♦ *The scene of the accident was chaotic.* ♦ *The rummage sale turned into a chaotic affair because so many people came.*

chap ['tʃæp] **1.** *n.* a guy; a fellow; a man. ♦ *Bill's a nice chap after you get to know him.* ♦ *My uncle is a jolly old chap.* **2.** *tv.* [for weather conditions] to cause the skin or lips to roughen and crack. ♦ *The wind chapped my lips.* ♦ *Sun can chap one's lips, too.* **3.** *iv.* [for the skin or lips] to become cracked or rough. ♦ *After skiing for a week, my lips had chapped.* ♦ *Bill's skin chapped in the sun.*

chapel ['tʃæp əl] *n.* a place of worship that is smaller than a sanctuary. ♦ *The service was held in the chapel of the church.* ♦ *The chapel had beautiful stained glass windows.*

chaplain ['tʃæp lɪn] *n.* a member of the clergy assigned to an institution, such as a hospital, prison, university, or the military. ♦ *When Mary was in the hospital, a chaplain came to see her.* ♦ *The chaplain spoke to the troops before the battle.*

chapter ['tʃæp tɚ] **1.** *n.* a division within a book; a section of a book. ♦ *Bill finished the chapter of the book before going to bed.* ♦ *The book was divided into five chapters.* **2.** *n.* a division of an organization or society. ♦ *Bill joined the local chapter of the club.* ♦ *The northwest chapter of the society held a fair to raise money.*

char ['tʃɑr] **1.** *iv.* [for something, usually food] to become scorched; [for something] to become slightly burned. ♦ *The underside of the hamburger charred because I forgot to flip it.* ♦ *Toasted marshmallows are best when you let them char.* **2.** *tv.* to burn something; to scorch something. ♦ *Mary charred her marshmallow in the fire.* ♦ *The chef charred the meat accidentally.*

character ['kɛr ɪk tɚ] **1.** *n.* a person in a book, movie, play, television show, etc. ♦ *Readers identified with the main character of the book.* ♦ *That actress plays my favorite character on a television show.* **2.** *n.* the amount of virtuous integrity someone has. (No plural form in this sense.) ♦ *The esteemed officer had a noble character.* ♦ *Hard work builds character.* **3.** *n.* an eccentric person. ♦ *Mary is such a character. She's always making jokes.* ♦ *Bill is a character, and I don't understand him at all.* **4.** *n.* a symbol used in writing, such as a letter, number, or other symbol. ♦ *Each stroke on the keyboard produced a character on the computer screen.* ♦ *The characters on the ransom note were cut from magazines.*

characteristic [kɛr ɪk tə 'rɪs tɪk] **1.** *n.* a single feature or trait; a single aspect of someone or something. ♦ *Heavy snow is a characteristic of winter around here.* ♦ *Scary monsters are a characteristic of some horror films.* **2.** *adj.* relating to the traits or features of something. (Adv: *characteristically* [...ɪk li].) ♦ *Sunny, warm days are the characteristic weather of the summer months.* ♦ *Bill has the characteristic symptoms of the flu.*

characterization [kɛr ɪk tə rɪ 'ze ʃən] **1.** *n.* a description of someone or something. ♦ *The author's characterization of the battle was shocking.* ♦ *The witness provided an accurate characterization of the event.* **2.** *n.* providing a distinct personality for the characters in a play, movie, television show, book, etc. ♦ *The actor's characterization of the villain was unique.* ♦ *The director's characterizations were always interesting and appealing.*

characterize ['kɛr ɪk tə raɪz] **characterize as** *tv.* + *prep. phr.* to describe someone or something as something. ♦ *Bill characterized the movie as boring.* ♦ *The suspect was characterized as eccentric and dangerous.*

charade [ʃə 'red] **1.** *n.* a rough acting out of a phrase, word, or event, especially as part of a game. ♦ *Jane did her charade so well that everyone guessed the answer immediately.* ♦ *Tom performed a charade that no one could guess!* **2. charades** *n.* a game involving guessing the meanings of a series of **charades** ①. (Treated as singular.) ♦ *The children played charades at the party.* ♦ *John is shy and hates to play charades.* **3.** *n.* an event that is meaningless and deceptive. (Figurative on ①.) ♦ *This whole affair is simply a silly charade.* ♦ *These negotiations aren't sincere! They're a charade!*

charcoal ['tʃɑr kol] *n.* a carbon-based fuel made by burning wood partially. (No plural form in this sense.) ♦ *Jane loves to cook meat over burning charcoal.* ♦ *Tom bought a bag of charcoal to use in the barbecue.*

charge ['tʃɑɚdʒ] **1.** *n.* the cost of something; the amount of money needed to pay for something. (Often plural.) ♦ *The charge to repair the shoes is ten dollars.* ♦ *The bill listed the charges for the doctor's services.* **2.** *n.* control [of someone or something]. (No plural form in this sense.) ♦ *Since Jane was the oldest child, when her parents were away, she had charge of her younger brothers and sisters.* ♦ *After the sudden death of the sheriff, the deputy took charge.* **3.** *n.* someone or something that must be watched over. ♦ *The babysitter's young charges ran around the house in their diapers.* ♦ *Each tutor had three charges to help.* **4.** *n.* an accusation; a statement that someone has done something criminal. ♦ *The charge was murder in the second degree.* ♦ *The company made a charge of embezzlement against the employee.* **5.** *n.* a sudden, moving attack. ♦ *The dog made a charge at the cat.* ♦ *The infantry's charge at the enemy camp was repelled.* **6.** *n.* the amount of electrical energy stored in a battery or a particle of matter. (No plural form in this sense.) ♦ *This battery has no charge left in it.* ♦ *There is a negative charge on the particles of matter in the test chamber.* **7.** *n.* the explosive material used in one explosion. ♦ *When the charge exploded, it nearly deafened us.* ♦ *The fireworks maker packed each charge carefully.* **8.** *tv.* to present a claim of a sum of money for goods or services. ♦ *The hotel charged us for the extra bed.* ♦ *The lawyer will charge the client for time spent on the phone.* **9.** *tv.* to place the charges for something on an account instead of paying cash. ♦ *Mary charged the meal on her credit card.* ♦ *I don't have any cash, so I'll have to charge the purchase.* **10.** *tv.* to rush toward someone or something in attack. ♦ *The dog charged the intruder and bit him.* ♦ *The home owner charged the burglar with a bat.* **11. charge with** *tv.* + *prep. phr.* to accuse someone of something. ♦ *Mary charged her employee with theft.* ♦ *The absent parents were charged with neglect.* **12.** *tv.* to provide a battery with energy; to send electricity through something, such as a circuit. ♦ *The car charges its own battery while the engine is running.* ♦ *I will have to charge this battery before I can use it again.* **13. charge at** *iv.* + *prep. phr.* to rush toward someone or something in attack. ♦ *The kids charged at the presents.* ♦ *The cat charged at the open door in hopes of escaping.* **14.** *iv.* to ask for pay at a certain rate. ♦ *My electrician charges by the hour.* ♦ *The designer charges $50 an hour.*

chariot ['tʃɛr i ət] *n.* a vehicle with two wheels, pulled by horses, and used in battles in ancient times. ♦ *The king rode in a golden chariot.* ♦ *Chariot races were once a popular sporting event.*

charisma [kə 'rɪz mə] *n.* a personality quality that draws people to one and gives one control over them. (No plural form in this sense.) ♦ *Even though they were poor, the people were captivated by the dictator's charisma.* ♦ *The performer's charisma kept our attention and caused us to listen to everything she said.*

charismatic [kɛr ɪz 'mæt ɪk] **1.** *adj.* having charisma. (Adv: *charismatically* [...ɪk li].) ♦ *The charismatic leader was revered by her followers.* ♦ *I ended up buying more than I wanted from the charismatic salesman.* **2.** *adj.* [of religious practices] involving ecstasy and frenzy. (Adv: *charismatically* [...ɪk li].) ♦ *The man belongs to a charismatic Christian denomination.* ♦ *Susan believed that she had the charismatic gift of prophecy.*

charitable ['tʃɛr ɪ tə bəl] **1.** *adj.* generous; willing to assist other people, especially those who need assistance. (Adv: *charitably.*) ♦ *Offering shelter for a poor family was a charitable act.* ♦ *Mary encouraged her children to be charitable.* **2.** *adj.* of or about charities. ♦ *The Smiths make charitable donations each year.* ♦ *Charitable organizations help the needy.* **3.** *adj.* lenient. (Adv: *charitably.*) ♦ *Because it was Susan's first offense, the judge was charitable and gave her probation.* ♦ *The paper was terrible, but the professor was charitable when she gave the grade.*

charity ['tʃɛr ɪt i] **1.** *n.* love, kindness, and generosity shown toward other people. (No plural form in this sense.) ♦ *The woman tried to practice charity in her daily life.* ♦ *The quality of charity is always welcome.* **2.** *n.* an organization that helps people in need. ♦ *The charity's goal is to help people help themselves.* ♦ *Funds were raised by the charity to help people in emergencies.*

charlatan ['ʃɑr lə tən] *n.* a fraud; an impostor. (From Italian.) ♦ *The "doctor" was just a charlatan who sold worthless cures.* ♦ *That charlatan cheated us out of our money!*

charm ['tʃɑrm] **1.** *n.* a pleasing, attractive personality trait. (No plural form in this sense.) ♦ *The speaker had a lot of charm and kept the audience's attention.* ♦ *My mother had lots of personal charm.* **2. charms** *n.* specific physical and personality traits that are attractive. ♦ *I used all of my charms to impress Bill.* ♦ *Of all your charms, I love* *your smiling eyes the best.* **3.** *n.* a trinket worn on a necklace or bracelet. ♦ *The girls collected charms for their bracelets.* ♦ *I lost the charm that hung on my necklace.* **4.** *n.* something that has magical powers. ♦ *The fairy gave the princess a charm to use if she were in danger.* ♦ *The superstitious man carried a charm to ward off evil.* **5.** *tv.* to influence someone by using ①. ♦ *The speaker charmed the audience.* ♦ *Grandpa was charmed by the toddler's antics.*

charmed ['tʃɑɚmd] **1.** *adj.* delighted; pleased; feeling happy and pleasant. ♦ *The charmed audience listened intently to the speaker.* ♦ *I am really charmed to meet you.* **2.** *adj.* protected, as if by magical influence; fortunate. ♦ *David led a charmed life until he lost his job.* ♦ *Jane has led a charmed existence, suffering no serious problems until she died.*

charmer ['tʃɑrm ɚ] *n.* someone who is charming; someone who charms or fascinates someone. ♦ *The baby was a real charmer—she smiled endlessly.* ♦ *Mary's date was a suave charmer and took her to an elegant restaurant.*

charming ['tʃɑrm ɪŋ] *adj.* pleasant; attractive. (Adv: *charmingly.*) ♦ *The cottage on the lake was charming.* ♦ *The charming waiter was most helpful.*

charred ['tʃɑrd] *adj.* blackened; burned. ♦ *We ate the charred hot dogs we cooked over the campfire.* ♦ *Charred meat smells horrible to a vegetarian.*

chart ['tʃɑrt] **1.** *n.* a statistical table; a graph, table, or diagram. ♦ *The chart showed the change in property values over the years.* ♦ *The nurse recorded the patient's condition on a chart.* **2.** *n.* a map, especially a map for navigation on water. ♦ *The captain looked at his chart of the harbor.* ♦ *Our chart of the islands was not accurate.* **3.** *tv.* to plan one's route on a map. ♦ *At the beginning of our trip, we charted our course across the country.* ♦ *Let's chart the path we'll take to the park.* **4.** *tv.* to arrange a set of figures or statistics on ①. ♦ *The economist charted several predictions for the stock market.* ♦ *The business owner charted the growth of her company.*

charter ['tʃɑrt ɚ] **1.** *n.* a formal document detailing the rights and privileges of a city, town, university, corporation, or branch of an organization. ♦ *The university received a charter from the state.* ♦ *The state took back the charter of the village, and it was disbanded.* **2. charter(ed bus); charter(ed train); chart(er plane).** *n.* a vehicle or airplane hired to go to a specific place. ♦ *We took a charter from the mainland to the island.* ♦ *The charter runs twice a day to the site.* **3.** *tv.* to hire a bus or an airplane for a specified journey. ♦ *John chartered a helicopter to take him to the remote island.* ♦ *There are no buses in the rural area—we'll have to charter a plane.* **4.** *tv.* to establish a city, town, university, corporation, or branch of an organization. ♦ *The famed university was chartered in the 1600s.* ♦ *The village was chartered by the state a century ago.* **5. charter member** *n.* someone who has belonged to an organization since the beginning of the organization, when its charter ① was signed. ♦ *Mary and Bill are charter members of the club.* ♦ *Most of the charter members have died, and the whole organization is collapsing.*

chase ['tʃes] **1.** *n.* the act of running after someone or something. ♦ *The dog seems to enjoy the chase more than catching rabbits.* ♦ *After a long chase, the lion killed its prey.* **2.** *tv.* to run after someone or something. ♦ *During the hunt, the dogs chased the raccoon up a tree.* ♦ *The babysitter chased the kids around the yard.* **3. lead someone on a merry chase** *idiom* to lead someone in a purposeless pursuit. ♦ *What a waste of time. You really led me on a merry chase.* ♦ *Jane led Bill on a merry chase trying to find an antique lamp.* **4. wild-goose chase** *idiom* a worthless hunt or chase ①; a futile pursuit. ♦ *I wasted all afternoon on a wild-goose chase.* ♦ *John was angry because he was sent out on a wild-goose chase.*

chasm ['kæz əm] *n.* a deep gorge; a steep valley. ♦ *The photo showed the depth of the chasm in the earth.* ♦ *Shifting of the earth's crust created the chasm.*

chassis ['tʃæs i] *n.* the frame of a vehicle. (From French.) ♦ *The chassis of the car was bent out of shape.* ♦ *This car is just a new body on an old chassis.*

chaste ['tʃest] **1.** *adj.* refraining from having any sexual intercourse that is illegal, immoral, or against the teachings of a religion. (Adv: *chastely.*) ♦ *The students were advised to remain chaste until marriage.* ♦ *It is thought that being chaste is too demanding for the general populace.* **2.** *adj.* pure; modest; very decent and not sexual. (Adv: *chastely.*) ♦ *The chaste woman blushed at the innuendo.* ♦ *The prudish man read only chaste literature.*

chasten ['tʃes ən] *tv.* to discipline someone; to reprimand someone. ♦ *The child was chastened by his parents for lying.* ♦ *Mary chastened her friend for being rude.*

chastened ['tʃes ənd] *adj.* made meek; punished; reprimanded. ♦ *The chastened child felt ashamed.* ♦ *We were chastened by the criticism.*

chastise [tʃæs 'tɑɪz] *tv.* to punish someone; to scold someone. ♦ *Mary chastised me for tracking mud into the house.* ♦ *The editorial writer chastised the corrupt politicians.*

chastity ['tʃæs tɪ ti] *n.* the condition of being chaste; a state of sexual abstinence. (No plural form in this sense.) ♦ *The nun made a vow of chastity.* ♦ *Chastity, widely practiced, could reduce the population.*

chat ['tʃæt] **1.** *iv.* to talk; to have a friendly talk. ♦ *The two friends sat on the porch and chatted.* ♦ *Dave chatted on the telephone all evening.* **2.** *n.* a pleasant conversation; a friendly talk. ♦ *The two friends sat on the porch and had a chat.* ♦ *Our chat was about things we did long ago.*

chatter ['tʃæt ɚ] **1.** *iv.* to talk about unimportant things. ♦ *The bored audience began to chatter during the performance.* ♦ *Anne and Dave chattered while they fished.* **2.** *iv.* [for one's teeth] to click together because of fear or coldness. ♦ *The kids' teeth chattered while they swam in the cold water.* ♦ *Mary's teeth chattered with the cold.* **3.** *n.* unimportant talk. (No plural form in this sense.) ♦ *The chatter of the audience distracted the performers.* ♦ *Mary was tired of Bill's chatter by the end of the evening.*

chatterbox ['tʃæt ɚ bɑks] *n.* someone who talks a lot. ♦ *Bill is known around the office as a chatterbox.* ♦ *Grandma is a chatterbox and loves to talk on the phone.*

chatty ['tʃæt i] *adj.* talkative; full of unimportant information. (Adv: *chattily.* Comp: *chattier;* sup: *chattiest.*) ♦ *The new boss is not very chatty. He just grunts.* ♦ *My chatty neighbor likes to gossip.*

chauffeur ['ʃof ɚ] **1.** *n.* someone whose job it is to drive a limousine or car. (From French.) ♦ *The chauffeur was waiting in the limousine in front of the hotel.* ♦ *The limou-*

sine was driven by the chauffeur. **2.** *tv.* to drive someone to some place. ♦ *Mike chauffeured his kids to their swimming lessons.* ♦ *The driver chauffeured us to the opera.*

chauvinism ['ʃov ə nɪz əm] **1.** *n.* excessive pride in one's country. (No plural form in this sense. From the French name *Chauvin.*) ♦ *Mary displayed considerable chauvinism when discussing her country.* ♦ *The speaker's chauvinism was not welcomed by the international audience.* **2. (male) chauvinism** *n.* aggressive bias in favor of males and against females. (No plural form in this sense.) ♦ *Mary accused Bill of blatant chauvinism.* ♦ *Jane felt that only male chauvinism kept her from getting her promotion.*

chauvinist ['ʃo və nɪst] **1.** *n.* one who has excessive pride in one's country; someone who practices chauvinism ①. ♦ *Mary was a chauvinist when it came to discussing the good points of her country.* ♦ *The chauvinist was not welcomed by the international audience.* **2.** *n.* someone who practices chauvinism ②. ♦ *Bill, who was always a perfect gentleman, denied being a chauvinist.* ♦ *Jane claimed that the entire company was dominated by chauvinists who hated women subconsciously.*

chauvinistic [ʃo və 'nɪst ɪk] **1.** *adj.* acting or behaving like a chauvinist ①; displaying chauvinism ①. (Adv: *chauvinistically* [...ɪk li].) ♦ *The patriot was too chauvinistic for the international audience.* ♦ *The chauvinistic lecturer made the audience angry.* **2.** *adj.* acting or behaving like a chauvinist ②; displaying chauvinism ②. (Adv: *chauvinistically* [...ɪk li].) ♦ *Bill's chauvinistic attitude kept him from advancing in his company.* ♦ *"Don't be so chauvinistic!" said Mary when Bill opened the car door for her.*

cheap ['tʃip] **1.** *adj.* inexpensive; not costing a lot of money. (Adv: *cheaply.* Comp: *cheaper;* sup: *cheapest.*) ♦ *The cheap detergent is just as good as the expensive detergent.* ♦ *Mary bought some cheap curtains for her apartment.* **2.** *adj.* poorly made; of poor quality; of poor value. (Adv: *cheaply.* Comp: *cheaper;* sup: *cheapest.*) ♦ *Those cheap clothes look really terrible.* ♦ *This cheap hammer broke while I was using it.*

cheapen ['tʃip ən] *tv.* to reduce the value or quality of something. ♦ *The gaudy costume jewelry cheapens the elegant outfit.* ♦ *The man cheapened himself by associating with criminals.*

cheapskate ['tʃip sket] *n.* someone who will not spend money even when necessary. ♦ *The cheapskate walked to work instead of repairing his car.* ♦ *Mary has a reputation of being a cheapskate, but she is merely frugal.*

cheat ['tʃit] **1.** *tv.* to deceive someone in a game or in commerce, as a means of gaining money. ♦ *Anne cheated her friends while playing cards.* ♦ *The auto dealer cheated his customers.* **2.** *iv.* to succeed by not working or playing fairly. ♦ *The students cheated on the test but were soon caught.* ♦ *Many people cheat on their taxes.* **3.** *n.* someone who cheats as in ① or ②; someone does not play fairly. ♦ *No one will play cards with Mike because he is a cheat.* ♦ *The cheat was sent away from the poker game.*

check ['tʃɛk] **1.** *n.* a written order to a bank to pay an amount of money to someone or something. ♦ *Bill wrote a check to pay for the groceries.* ♦ *The store accepted personal checks.* **2.** *n.* the mark "✓." ♦ *I put a check on the list by the chores I had completed.* ♦ *Please put a check in the appropriate box on the form.* **3.** *n.* the bill for a meal in a restaurant. ♦ *The waitress put our check on the table.* ♦ *I took the check to the cashier and paid it.* **4.** *n.* something that stops or restrains someone or something. ♦ *The store's security force is a check against shoplifters.* ♦ *The balance of government powers is a check against corrupt government.* **5.** *n.* a brief look at someone or something; an inspection of someone or something. ♦ *Could you give my work a quick check?* ♦ *A check of the heating system revealed a malfunction.* **6.** See traveler's check. **7. check off** *tv.* + *adv.* to place a "✓" by an item on a list after it has been examined or accounted for. ♦ *Mary checked the completed chores off of her list.* ♦ *Bill checked off the names of the people who had paid for the trip.* **8.** *tv.* to examine something; to look at something closely but quickly. ♦ *The boss said she would check Mike's work.* ♦ *An engineer checked the system but could find no malfunction.* **9.** *tv.* to put one's belongings into the care of someone—receiving a receipt for the property. ♦ *We checked our coats at the restaurant.* ♦ *Bill checked his luggage before boarding the plane.* **10.** *tv.* to restrain someone or something; to stop someone or something. ♦ *The tug on the leash checked the dog as it wandered about.* ♦ *The policy checked politicians from abusing their power.* **11. check (up) on** *iv.* (+ *adv.*) + *prep. phr.* to investigate; to seek out the facts about something. ♦ *The waitress checked on our order.* ♦ *The babysitter checked up on the sleeping children.* **12. by check** *phr.* by using a check. ♦ *He paid for the book by check.* ♦ *You will be paid by check.* **13. blank check** *idiom* freedom or permission to act as one wishes or thinks necessary. ♦ *He's been given a blank check with regard to reorganizing the work force.* ♦ *The manager has been given no instructions about how to train the staff. He just has a blank check.* **14. honor someone's check** *idiom* to accept someone's personal check ① in payment of an obligation. ♦ *The clerk at the store wouldn't honor my check. I had to pay cash.* ♦ *The bank didn't honor your check when I tried to deposit it. Please give me cash.*

checkbook ['tʃɛk bʊk] *n.* a pad of blank checks printed for a particular bank account. ♦ *Mary put her checkbook into her purse.* ♦ *Bill tore a check out of his checkbook.*

checker ['tʃɛk ɚ] **1. checkers** *n.* a game played by two people on a checkerboard, using 12 pieces apiece. (Treated as singular.) ♦ *The kids played checkers when it rained.* ♦ *Do you want to play checkers or chess?* **2.** *n.* any of the pieces used for ①. ♦ *One of the checkers was missing, so we couldn't play the game.* ♦ *The checkers are red and black.*

checkerboard ['tʃɛk ɚ bord] **1.** *n.* an array of 64 squares, arranged in 8 rows and 8 columns, with alternating colors, on which the game of checkers is played. (The same as a chessboard.) ♦ *Bill laid the checkerboard on the table and got the checkers out.* ♦ *The checkerboard had only red checkers on it at the end of the game.* **2.** *adj.* arrayed with alternately colored squares. ♦ *The tile in the bathroom has a checkerboard pattern.* ♦ *A checkerboard tablecloth brightened the kitchen table.*

checkered ['tʃɛk ɚd] **1.** *adj.* patterned with alternately colored squares. ♦ *Checkered curtains hung in the window.* ♦ *The flooring is checkered tile.* **2. checkered past** *n.* a past life that is a mixture of good and bad. ♦ *David had a checkered past, and we did not know what he might do in the future.* ♦ *I believe Bill is trustworthy, despite his checkered past.*

checkmate ['tʃɛk met] **1.** *n.* the final move in a game of chess, resulting in a situation where the king of one of the players would be captured no matter what move that player made. ♦ *"Checkmate," Mary said as she won the chess game.* ♦ *Mary knew Tom would have a checkmate if she didn't make the right move.* **2.** *tv.* to make the final move in a game of chess that does not end in a draw. ♦ *Grandma laughed before she checkmated Billy.* ♦ *The experienced chess player checkmated his opponent in a short game.*

checkroom ['tʃɛk rum] *n.* a secure room where people can leave coats and other personal belongings with an attendant. ♦ *Bill and Sue left their coats in the checkroom.* ♦ *There was no checkroom at the theater.*

checkup ['tʃɛk əp] *n.* a physical examination done by a physician; a mechanical inspection done by a mechanic. ♦ *Each employee must have a checkup every year.* ♦ *The mechanic gave the van a thorough checkup.*

cheddar ['tʃɛd ɚ] **cheddar (cheese)** *n.* a kind of yellow-orange cheese. (No plural form in this sense.) ♦ *The recipe called for cheddar, but I only had Swiss cheese.* ♦ *The grocery store was out of cheddar.*

cheek ['tʃik] **1.** *n.* the part of the face below the eye. ♦ *The baby laid its cheek on the pillow.* ♦ *Mary slapped me across the cheek.* **2.** *n.* either side of the inside of the mouth. ♦ *Mary had a sore on her cheek.* ♦ *Bill bit his cheek and howled in pain.* **3.** *n.* either of the buttocks. ♦ *The nurse gave me a shot in the left cheek.* ♦ *Both cheeks were sore from my fall on the ice.* **4.** *n.* impudence; rudeness. (No plural form in this sense.) ♦ *The students dared not give the principal any cheek.* ♦ *It took some cheek to ask the woman her age.* **5. turn the other cheek** *idiom* to ignore abuse or an insult. ♦ *When Bob got mad at Mary and yelled at her, she just turned the other cheek.* ♦ *Usually I turn the other cheek when someone is rude to me.*

cheekbone ['tʃik bon] *n.* the bone just below the eye. ♦ *The beautician applied makeup along my cheekbone.* ♦ *Sue's haircut flattered her cheekbones.*

cheep ['tʃip] **1.** *n.* a chirp; the noise that a young chicken or baby bird makes. ♦ *The chick made a cheep.* ♦ *Did you hear the cheep of the baby birds?* **2.** *iv.* to chirp or make ①. ♦ *The baby birds cheeped in their nest.* ♦ *Chicks cheep constantly.*

cheer ['tʃɪr] **1.** *n.* an encouraging yell; a supportive burst of applause and shouting. ♦ *The crowd gave a cheer when the team scored.* ♦ *The cheer echoed throughout the stadium.* **2.** *n.* happiness; a good state of mind. (No plural form in this sense.) ♦ *Bill is always in good cheer.* ♦ *The office was in need of some cheer.* **3.** *iv.* to yell and shout in support of someone or something; to yell in encouragement. ♦ *The crowed cheered for the team.* ♦ *Come to the game and cheer for us.* **4.** *tv.* to encourage someone by shouts of support. ♦ *The crowd cheered the team.* ♦ *The parents cheered their children's efforts.* **5. cheer (up)** *tv.* (+ *adv.*) to improve someone's mood or morale; to make someone happy. ♦ *Chocolate always cheers Bob up when he is sad.* ♦ *A letter from home cheered the homesick camper.*

cheerful ['tʃɪr fʊl] **1.** *adj.* in good spirits; full of cheer; happy. (Adv: *cheerfully.*) ♦ *The friendly nurse had a cheerful manner.* ♦ *Bill felt cheerful all day because it was his birthday.* **2.** *adj.* pleasant; [of something] bright and pleasing. (Adv: *cheerfully.*) ♦ *The cheerful sitting room was sunny.* ♦ *The seaside is a cheerful place on a sunny day.*

cheerfulness ['tʃɪr fʊl nəs] *n.* happiness; visible happiness. (No plural form in this sense.) ♦ *The nurse's cheerfulness made the patients feel happier.* ♦ *We could tell by Bill's scowl that he was not full of cheerfulness today.*

cheerleader ['tʃɪr lid ɚ] *n.* someone who leads crowds in organized cheers of support, especially at sporting events. ♦ *The cheerleaders supported the football team.* ♦ *If you want to be a cheerleader, auditions are tomorrow.*

cheery ['tʃɪr i] **1.** *adj.* full of cheer; showing cheer. (Adv: *cheerily.* Comp: *cheerier;* sup: *cheeriest.*) ♦ *The nurse always has a cheery smile.* ♦ *My teacher is a cheery person—always smiling and laughing.* **2.** *adj.* bright and cheerful; causing cheer. (Adv: *cheerily.* Comp: *cheerier;* sup: *cheeriest.*) ♦ *The restaurant had a cheery atmosphere.* ♦ *This drab room is not cheery!*

cheese ['tʃiz] **1.** *n.* a food made from the solid parts of curdled milk. (No plural form in this sense.) ♦ *The hostess served cheese and crackers for an appetizer.* ♦ *The dairy farmer produced cheese as well as milk.* **2.** *adj.* <the adj. use of ①.> ♦ *Could I please have a cheese sandwich?* ♦ *I served a cheese sauce on the asparagus.*

cheeseburger ['tʃiz bɚ gɚ] *n.* a hamburger sandwich with a slice of cheese on the meat. ♦ *The kids ate cheeseburgers at the restaurant.* ♦ *The cheeseburgers had Swiss cheese on them.*

cheesecake ['tʃiz kek] **1.** *n.* a sweet, rich food made with sweetened cream cheese or cottage cheese and resembling a cake or a pie. (No plural form in this sense. Number is expressed with *piece(s)* or *slice(s) of cheesecake.*) ♦ *Dessert was chocolate cheesecake.* ♦ *Would you like another slice of cheesecake?* **2.** *n.* a single, complete unit of ①. ♦ *Please buy a cheesecake at the grocery store.* ♦ *The cheesecake was made with cream cheese and sour cream.*

cheetah ['tʃi tə] *n.* a large, fast-running animal of the cat family. ♦ *The cheetah pounced on its prey.* ♦ *Cheetahs roam the grassland, looking for food.*

chef ['ʃɛf] **1.** *n.* a professional cook; the head cook in a restaurant. ♦ *The chef had trained in France.* ♦ *Pastries are the chef's specialty.* **2.** *n.* any cook; whoever is doing the cooking. ♦ *Ask the chef to cook another hamburger for me.* ♦ *Who's the chef around your house?*

chemical ['kɛm ɪ kəl] **1.** *n.* an element or a compound of basic elements. ♦ *All the chemicals were stored in large jars in the storeroom.* ♦ *The students carefully mixed the chemicals together.* **2.** *adj.* of or about chemistry. (Adv: *chemically* [...ɪk li].) ♦ *Mary performed the chemical analysis rapidly and accurately.* ♦ *What is the chemical composition of this substance?*

chemist ['kɛm əst] *n.* a scientist whose specialty is chemistry. ♦ *The chemist produced a new type of plastic in the lab.* ♦ *A chemist can analyze the unknown substance and find out what it is.*

chemistry ['kɛm ɪs tri] **1.** *n.* the science involving the elements and their compounds, the reactions of elements when they are mixed together, and the properties of the elements under different conditions. (No plural form in this sense.) ♦ *Susan studied chemistry in high school and college.* ♦ *We do our chemistry in this laboratory.* **2.** *n.* the way that two people interact with each other. (No plural form in this sense. Figurative on ①.) ♦ *The chemistry between Bill and Mike was bad—they never got along.* ♦ *Sue and Bill seem to like each other, but there is no chemistry there.*

chemotherapy [kim o 'θɛr ə pi] *n.* a treatment for diseases that uses chemicals. (No plural form in this sense.) ♦ *The cancer patient had chemotherapy twice a week.* ♦ *Chemotherapy is a treatment for cancer.*

cherish ['tʃɛr ɪʃ] **1.** *tv.* to treat someone or something very lovingly; to have great fondness for someone or something. ♦ *The new parents cherished their baby.* ♦ *We cherished the time we could spend together.* **2.** *tv.* to cling to an idea or hope; to keep the idea of someone or something in one's mind. ♦ *Mary cherished the idea of touring the castles of Europe.* ♦ *Bill cherished the thought of owning his own boat.*

cherished ['tʃɛr ɪʃt] *adj.* cared for; loved; close to one's mind or heart. ♦ *Bill mourned his cherished wife after her death.* ♦ *Grandma has many cherished memories.*

cherry ['tʃɛr i] **1.** *n.* a tree that produces small, round, bright red fruits with one pit, and an attractive, useful wood. ♦ *We planted cherries and oaks along the fence.* ♦ *Mike sprayed the old cherry with insecticide.* **2.** *n.* wood from ①. (No plural form in this sense.) ♦ *The cabinet was made of cherry.* ♦ *Cherry has a reddish color to it.* **3.** *n.* the fruit of ①. ♦ *The tree was full of cherries ready to be picked.* ♦ *I prepared the cherries for the pie.* **4.** *n.* the bright red color of ③. ♦ *This bright red is called cherry.* ♦ *Cherry is a vibrant color.* **5.** *adj.* bright red; colored like ③. ♦ *The car was a bright cherry red.* ♦ *Jane hung cherry towels in her bathroom.* **6.** *adj.* made with or flavored with ③. ♦ *We all ate cherry pie for dessert.* ♦ *Have you ever eaten cherry ice cream?* **7.** *adj.* made from ②. ♦ *Tom placed the cherry cabinet next to the window.* ♦ *Cherry wood is very attractive but very expensive.*

chess ['tʃɛs] *n.* a game played by two people on a chessboard, with 32 pieces. (No plural form in this sense.) ♦ *I taught Bill how to play chess.* ♦ *Not everyone enjoys playing chess.*

chessboard ['tʃɛs bord] *n.* an array of 64 squares, arranged in 8 rows and 8 columns, with alternating colors, on which the game of chess is played. (The same as a checkerboard.) ♦ *A chessboard sat on the coffee table.* ♦ *The kids played chess on the chessboard.*

chest ['tʃɛst] **1.** *n.* the upper front part of the torso of the body. ♦ *The ball hit John right in the chest.* ♦ *Mary's chest ached when she had a cold.* **2.** *n.* a piece of furniture with drawers, used to store clothes, linen, and other items. ♦ *An old chest of drawers stood in the attic gathering dust.* ♦ *The chest was full of old clothes and photographs.* **3.** *n.* a large, wooden storage box. ♦ *Grandma's wedding dress was stored in a chest.* ♦ *The wooden chest held many mementos of trips I had taken.* **4. get something off one's chest** *idiom* to tell something that has been bothering oneself. ♦ *I have to get this off my chest. I broke your window with a stone.* ♦ *I knew I'd feel better when I had that off my chest.*

chestnut ['tʃɛs nət] **1.** *n.* a kind of tree that produces large reddish brown nuts. ♦ *Tom planted a chestnut in the front yard.* ♦ *There are two chestnuts and one elm in the backyard.* **2.** *n.* the nutmeat of ①; the nutmeat and shell of ①. ♦ *Roasted chestnuts are a real delicacy.* ♦ *Bill put the chestnuts near the fire.* **3.** *n.* wood from ①. (No plural form in this sense.) ♦ *The cabinet was made of chestnut.* ♦ *Oak is easier to find than aged chestnut.* **4.** *adj.* reddish-brown in color, used especially for reddish-brown horses. ♦ *Bill has chestnut hair and brown eyes.* ♦ *The horse has a chestnut coat and looks sleek and powerful.* **5.** *adj.* made of ③. ♦ *Susan's chestnut cabinet is very heavy.* ♦ *Bill polished the chestnut piano.*

chew ['tʃu] **1.** *tv.* to crush food with the teeth before swallowing it. ♦ *It was difficult to chew the tough meat.* ♦ *Chew your food carefully, so you don't choke.* **2.** *iv.* to bite down with the teeth. ♦ *The meat was tough and difficult to chew.* ♦ *Bob's teeth hurt, so he couldn't chew.*

chewable ['tʃu ə bəl] *adj.* capable of being chewed. (Used especially to describe medicine for children that can be chewed instead of swallowed whole.) ♦ *The children take chewable vitamin tablets.* ♦ *The chewable aspirin is orange flavored.*

chewy ['tʃu i] *adj.* [of a food] soft and easy to chew. (Adv: *chewily.* Comp: *chewier;* sup: *chewiest.*) ♦ *The store sold chewy caramel candy.* ♦ *Mary likes chewy cookies rather than crunchy ones.*

chic ['ʃik] *adj.* elegant; stylish; fashionable. (From French. Adv: *chicly.* Comp: *chicer;* sup: *chicest.*) ♦ *Only chic clothes are sold in this store.* ♦ *A very chic woman stepped off the train, and everybody stared.*

Chicago [sɪ 'kɔ go] See Gazetteer.

chick ['tʃɪk] *n.* a baby chicken or baby bird. ♦ *The barnyard was filled with chicks last spring.* ♦ *The chick cheeped.*

chickadee ['tʃɪk ə di] *n.* a small bird native to the woodlands of North America. ♦ *The chickadee makes a sound similar to its name.* ♦ *The yard around the bird feeder was filled with chickadees.*

chicken ['tʃɪk ən] **1.** *n.* a bird raised on a farm for meat and eggs; a hen or a rooster. ♦ *The farmer raised chickens.* ♦ *Coyotes attacked the chickens at night.* **2.** *n.* the meat of ①. (No plural form in this sense.) ♦ *We have chicken for dinner every night.* ♦ *This recipe can be made with either chicken or beef.* **3.** *n.* someone who is scared of everything; someone who is too scared to do something. (Informal.) ♦ *You're just a chicken when it comes to swimming.* ♦ *Don't be a chicken—be brave!* **4.** *adj.* made with or flavored with ②. ♦ *Susan ordered a chicken sandwich for lunch.* ♦ *A nice big bowl of chicken soup will make you feel better.* **5. no spring chicken** *idiom* no longer young. ♦ *I don't get around very well anymore. I'm no spring chicken, you know.* ♦ *Even though John is no spring chicken, he still plays tennis twice a week.*

chickenpox ['tʃɪk ən pɑks] *n.* a childhood illness that causes red blisters to appear on the skin and also causes fever and itching. (No plural form in this sense.) ♦ *The Smith children have chickenpox.* ♦ *Once you have had chickenpox, you are immune from getting it again.*

chide ['tʃaɪd] *tv.* to rebuke someone, usually mildly or in a teasing manner. ♦ *My mother chided me for eating junk food.* ♦ *The personnel director chided the employees for complaining too much.*

chief ['tʃif] **1.** *n.* the head of an organization or group; the leader. ♦ *The chief of the fire department talked about fire prevention.* ♦ *Bill is the chief of this committee.* **2.** *adj.* most important; principal; main. (Adv: *chiefly.*) ♦ *Mary* *spoke about the chief point of the lecture.* ♦ *Mike is chief chef at the exclusive hotel.*

chigger ['tʃɪg ɚ] *n.* an insect that burrows under the skin and causes severe itching. ♦ *We all got chigger bites when we went camping.* ♦ *A chigger burrows into your skin and causes itching.*

child ['tʃaɪld] **1.** *n., irreg.* a young person; a boy or a girl; someone's son or daughter. (Pl: children.) ♦ *The children took the bus to school.* ♦ *Mary's child has blue eyes and brown hair.* **2. expecting (a child)** *idiom* pregnant. ♦ *Tommy's mother is expecting a child.* ♦ *Oh, I didn't know she was expecting.* **3. child's play** *idiom* to perform something effortlessly. ♦ *The exam was child's play to her.* ♦ *Finding the right street is child's play with a map.*

childbirth ['tʃaɪld bɚθ] *n.* giving birth to a child. (No plural form in this sense.) ♦ *Sue had a difficult childbirth.* ♦ *The pregnant woman bought a book about childbirth.*

childhood ['tʃaɪld hʊd] **1.** *n.* the period of time between birth and puberty; the time when someone is a child. (No plural form in this sense.) ♦ *Bill spent his childhood on the coast of Maine.* ♦ *Some people do not remember much of their childhood.* **2. in one's second childhood** *idiom* being interested in things or people that normally interest children. ♦ *My father bought himself a toy train, and my mother said he was in his second childhood.* ♦ *Whenever I go to the river and throw stones, I feel as though I'm in my second childhood.*

childish ['tʃaɪld ɪʃ] *adj.* behaving like a child; immature. (Adv: *childishly.*) ♦ *The childish tantrum of the president shocked the committee.* ♦ *Mary told Bill it was childish to get mad about little things.*

childishness ['tʃaɪld ɪʃ nəs] *n.* a state of immaturity; a state of acting like a child. (No plural form in this sense.) ♦ *The parents tolerated the childishness of their teenager.* ♦ *Mary's childishness showed when she cried when she lost the contest.*

childless ['tʃaɪld ləs] *adj.* having no children; without children. (Adv: *childlessly.*) ♦ *The childless couple adopted a baby.* ♦ *Bill and Sue remained childless for their entire marriage.*

childlike ['tʃaɪld laɪk] *adj.* like a child; innocent; naive; simple. ♦ *The man had a childlike faith in God.* ♦ *The woman spoke in a childlike voice to her baby.*

children ['tʃɪl drɪn] pl of child.

Chile ['tʃi le, 'tʃɪl i] See Gazetteer.

chili ['tʃɪl i] **1.** *n.* hot, spicy peppers, used as a spice. (No plural form in this sense.) ♦ *The sauce needs hot chili.* ♦ *Chili is a major ingredient in my cooking.* **2.** *n.* a single unit of ①. ♦ *There are lots of chilis mixed with the meat.* ♦ *The chilis were so hot we burned our mouths.* **3.** *n.* a thick, spicy stew with ①, kidney beans, and other ingredients, especially meat. (No plural form in this sense.) ♦ *We always have chili for lunch on Sundays.* ♦ *At the party, we had chili with sour cream and cheese.*

chill ['tʃɪl] **1.** *n.* a coldness, especially a damp coldness. ♦ *Mary felt a chill in the air.* ♦ *Bill wore a coat against the chill of the November day.* **2.** *n.* a lasting cold feeling caused by being in the cold too long. ♦ *The child got a chill while playing in the snow.* ♦ *A freezing draft gave everyone in the room a chill.* **3.** *n.* a cold manner; an unpleasant attitude; an unfriendly attitude. (Figurative on ②.) ♦ *There was a chill in the complaining customer's voice.* ♦ *The argument caused a chill to fall in the room.* **4.** *n.* a sense of severe fright, possibly accompanied with the feeling of ②. ♦ *The thought of falling off the cliff gave me a chill.* ♦ *A chill raced up my spine when I heard the bad news.* **5.** *tv.* to cool something. ♦ *I chilled the champagne before serving it.* ♦ *A draft chilled the room.* **6.** *iv.* to become cool or cold. ♦ *The tea is chilling in the refrigerator.* ♦ *After the tea chilled, I drank it.* **7.** *iv.* to become quiet; to relax. (Slang.) ♦ *Chill—everything's going to be okay.* ♦ *After playing basketball, we sat on the front porch and chilled.*

chilled ['tʃɪld] *adj.* refrigerated; made cool. ♦ *The chilled drink refreshed us on the hot day.* ♦ *My favorite restaurant serves salad on chilled plates.*

chilling ['tʃɪl ɪŋ] **1.** *adj.* biting cold; causing chills. (Adv: *chillingly.*) ♦ *A chilling wind came off the lake.* ♦ *A chilling rain fell throughout the bleak day.* **2.** *adj.* frightening; scary; terrifying. (Figurative on ①. Adv: *chillingly.*) ♦ *The chilling story kept the children up all night.* ♦ *The chilling facts of the murder case appalled us.*

chilly ['tʃɪl i] *adj.* cold; cool. (Comp: *chillier;* sup: *chilliest.*) ♦ *It is a bit chilly outside today.* ♦ *The draft in the movie theater made us feel chilly.*

chime ['tʃaɪm] **1.** *n.* a tubular bell, found in church towers, church organs, clocks, and orchestras. ♦ *The chimes rang in the breeze.* ♦ *A single chime hung above the hermit's door.* **2.** *n.* the sound of a bell or ①. ♦ *At the chime of the bell, the students went to lunch.* ♦ *I heard the chime of the old clock as I fell asleep.* **3.** *iv.* to make a bell-like noise. ♦ *The bell will chime at noon.* ♦ *The long brass chimes chimed the notes of a well-known song.*

chimney ['tʃɪm ni] *n.* the structure that carries smoke to the outside and above a building. ♦ *Smoke billowed out of the chimney.* ♦ *The mansion had a slate roof and six chimneys.*

chimp ['tʃɪmp] *n.* a chimpanzee. ♦ *The chimps at the zoo were entertaining.* ♦ *The zoologist carried a baby chimp in her arms.*

chimpanzee [tʃɪm 'pæn zi] *n.* an African ape, closely related to humans. ♦ *A chimpanzee swung from branch to branch in the forest.* ♦ *The Smiths are doing research on the abilities of the chimpanzees.*

chin ['tʃɪn] **1.** *n.* the part of the face below the lower lip. ♦ *Milk dribbled down Jimmy's chin.* ♦ *David rested his chin in his hand and thought about the problem.* **2. take it on the chin** *idiom* to experience and endure a direct blow or assault. ♦ *The bad news was a real shock, and John took it on the chin.* ♦ *The worst luck comes my way, and I always end up taking it on the chin.*

china ['tʃaɪn ə] **1.** *n.* porcelain dishware; high-quality dishes, cups, and saucers. (No plural form in this sense.) ♦ *On holidays, we use the good china.* ♦ *Please place the china on the table carefully.* **2. China** See Gazetteer.

Chinese [tʃaɪ 'niz] **1.** *n., irreg.* a citizen or native of China or Taiwan. (Pl: *Chinese.*) ♦ *I met three Chinese at the lecture.* ♦ *Billions of Chinese live in China.* **2. the Chinese** *n.* the people of China and Taiwan. (Treated as plural.) ♦ *The Chinese are known for their cooking and fine arts.* ♦ *The Chinese are experiencing rapid economic development.* **3.** *n.* one of the native languages spoken by ②. (No plural form in this sense.) ♦ *I am trying to learn to speak Chinese.* ♦ *It will be many years before I can write Chinese.* **4.** *adj.* of or about China or ②. ♦ *I love Chinese cooking.* ♦ *The Chinese language is very hard to read and write.*

chintz ['tʃɪnts] **1.** *n.* a type of cotton cloth with a printed pattern. (No plural form in this sense.) ♦ *My new dress is made of chintz.* ♦ *The fabric store has dozens of bolts of chintz to choose from.* **2.** *adj.* made of ①. ♦ *Chintz curtains hung in the powder room.* ♦ *The friends wore matching chintz dresses.*

chintzy ['tʃɪnt si] **1.** *adj.* cheaply made; of low quality. (Comp: *chintzier;* sup: *chintziest.*) ♦ *The chintzy furniture soon wore out.* ♦ *The suit looked chintzy, but it was actually expensive.* **2.** *adj.* [of a person] cheap. (Comp: *chintzier;* sup: *chintziest.*) ♦ *Mary is very chintzy and doesn't tip very well.* ♦ *Bill was such a chintzy date that I had to pay for my own meal.*

chip ['tʃɪp] **1.** *n.* a small piece that has broken off a larger object. ♦ *I stepped on a chip of stone and bruised my heel.* ♦ *Mary put some ice chips into her drink.* **2.** *n.* the dent that is left where a small piece of something has broken off. ♦ *Mary noticed the chip in the plate right away.* ♦ *I made a chip in the cup when I dropped it.* **3. (potato) chip** *n.* a thin slice of potato, fried until it is very crisp. (Often plural.) ♦ *The restaurant served potato chips with the fish.* ♦ *Chips and dip are Bill's favorite snack.* **4.** *tv.* to break off a small piece of something. ♦ *I chipped some ice off the block.* ♦ *The mover chipped the plaster with the leg of the chair.* **5.** *tv.* to shape something by picking away or cutting away at it piece by piece. ♦ *The sculptor chipped the marble with the chisel.* ♦ *The artisan chipped the wood block to form a candlestick.* **6.** *iv.* [for something] to lose a small bit, through chipping. ♦ *Be careful, the mirror will chip if you're not careful when you carry it.* ♦ *The pitcher chipped when I knocked it off the counter.* **7. a chip off the old block** *idiom* a person, usually a male, who behaves in the same way as his father or resembles his father. ♦ *John looks like his father—a real chip off the old block.* ♦ *Bill Jones, Jr., is a chip off the old block. He's a banker just like his father.* **8. have a chip on one's shoulder** *idiom* to be tempting someone to an argument or a fight. ♦ *Who are you mad at? You always seem to have a chip on your shoulder.* ♦ *John has had a chip on his shoulder ever since he got his speeding ticket.*

chipmunk ['tʃɪp məŋk] *n.* a rodent similar to a small squirrel with stripes. ♦ *The cat watched the chipmunks, waiting to pounce.* ♦ *A chipmunk jumped onto the bird feeder and scared the birds away.*

chipper ['tʃɪp ɚ] *adj.* happy; upbeat; cheerful. ♦ *After a good night's sleep, Bill was chipper again.* ♦ *No one at the funeral was very chipper.*

chiropodist [ʃə 'rɑp ə dəst] *n.* a doctor who specializes in treating feet. ♦ *The chiropodist removed my bunions.* ♦ *The man with sore feet made an appointment with a chiropodist.*

chirp ['tʃɚp] **1.** *n.* the short, sharp noise that a bird makes. ♦ *Jane heard the chirps of the baby birds in the nest.* ♦ *The injured bird did not move or make a chirp.* **2.** *iv.* [for a bird] to make a short sharp squeak or whistle. ♦ *The baby birds chirped from their nest.* ♦ *The injured bird could not chirp.*

chisel ['tʃɪz əl] **1.** *n.* a sharp-edged tool for removing pieces from wood or stone. ♦ *The sculptor positioned the chisel and began to tap on it.* ♦ *Mike used a chisel to cut out huge chunks of the marble.* **2.** *tv.* to shape something with a chisel. ♦ *The artist chiseled the marble with great skill.* ♦ *The kids chiseled ice to make a statue.* **3. chisel someone or something out of something** *idiom* to cheat someone or something to get money or belongings. ♦ *The company tried to chisel the government out of taxes it owed.* ♦ *Bill chiseled his little sister out of her allowance.*

chivalrous ['ʃɪv əl rəs] *adj.* [of a man] displaying chivalry; honorable; courteous. (Adv: *chivalrously.*) ♦ *I appreciate chivalrous acts such as holding doors open.* ♦ *The chivalrous man treated his date very well.*

chivalry ['ʃɪv əl ri] **1.** *n.* the ancient system of knights and their activities. (No plural form in this sense.) ♦ *The customs of chivalry are no longer practiced.* ♦ *One student wrote about chivalry in medieval times.* **2.** *n.* polite behavior—by a man—towards other people, particularly women. (No plural form in this sense.) ♦ *Mike sought to teach his boys a few elements of chivalry.* ♦ *The kindly man extended his old-fashioned chivalry to everyone he met.*

chive ['tʃɑɪvz] *n.* a small onion-like herb with thin, tubular, edible leaves. (Usually plural.) ♦ *There are some chives growing in my garden.* ♦ *The recipe required a teaspoon of chives.*

chlorinate ['klor ə net] *tv.* to add chlorine to something; to disinfect water with chlorine. ♦ *The park district chlorinated the public pool.* ♦ *In order to kill germs, the city chlorinates the water supply.*

chlorine ['klor in] *n.* a poisonous, greenish-yellow gaseous chemical element. (No plural form in this sense.) ♦ *We could smell the chlorine dissolved in the swimming pool water.* ♦ *The symbol for chlorine is Cl, and its atomic number is 17.*

chocolate ['tʃɑk (ə) lət] **1.** *n.* a tasty, candy-like food made from roasted cacao beans, usually in the form of candy, syrup, a brewed beverage, or a condiment in cooking. (No plural form in this sense.) ♦ *Chocolate is a popular candy.* ♦ *The cake was covered with chocolate—yummy!* **2.** *adj.* made with or flavored with ①. ♦ *Would you like some chocolate cake?* ♦ *I covered the cupcake with chocolate frosting.*

choice ['tʃoɪs] **1.** *n.* the ability or right to choose. (No plural form in this sense.) ♦ *Does she have any choice about what she is to do?* ♦ *I had no choice in the matter.* **2.** *n.* a selection from which one can choose. (No plural form in this sense.) ♦ *The store had a very wide choice of hats.* ♦ *There is very little choice on this menu.* **3.** *n.* the actual selection; someone or something chosen or selected. ♦ *My choice for club president was Anne.* ♦ *Did Mary make her choice yet?* **4.** *adj.* of very high quality; excellent; best; optimal. (Adv: *choicely.*) ♦ *Bill grilled some really choice cuts of meat for dinner.* ♦ *We had a choice table at the restaurant.*

choir ['kwɑɪr] **1.** *n.* a singing group, especially one in a church. ♦ *The choir rehearsed for several days before the concert.* ♦ *The choir sang Grandma's favorite hymn at her funeral.* **2. choir loft** See loft.

choke ['tʃok] **1.** *n.* the part of an engine that controls the amount of air that goes into the engine. ♦ *Most new* *cars have an automatic choke.* ♦ *My lawn mower has a choke that I have to adjust frequently.* **2.** *tv.* to cut off someone's or some creature's air supply. ♦ *The tight collar choked the dog.* ♦ *The assailant tried to choke his victim.* **3.** *iv.* to react at having the air supply cut off. ♦ *Bill choked on the apple.* ♦ *Anne laughed so hard at the joke, she choked.*

cholesterol [kə 'lɛs tə rɑl] *n.* a waxy fat found in meats, egg yolks, and some other foods. (No plural form in this sense.) ♦ *The doctor told me not to eat too much cholesterol.* ♦ *Oatmeal has no cholesterol, but eggs have a lot of it.*

chomp ['tʃɑmp] **1. chomp on** *iv.* + *prep. phr.* to bite something hard; to take a big bite of food. ♦ *The dog chomped on its rawhide bone.* ♦ *The kids chomped on carrots while they watched television.* **2.** *iv.* to eat noisily; to eat, taking large bites. ♦ *"Stop chomping!" father ordered.* ♦ *Bill chomped and chomped, more like a pig than a boy.*

choose ['tʃuz] **1.** *tv., irreg.* to pick someone or something from a group. (Pt: chose; pp: chosen.) ♦ *You can choose the classes you want to take.* ♦ *The team captains began to choose players for their teams.* **2.** *iv., irreg.* to do the process of selection. ♦ *You choose this time. I chose the last time.* ♦ *The kids chose, and we did what they wanted.*

choosy ['tʃuz i] *adj.* hard to please; hard to make happy. (Adv: *choosily.* Comp: *choosier;* sup: *choosiest.*) ♦ *Anne is very choosy about the fruit she buys.* ♦ *Bill's not too choosy when it comes to friends.*

chop ['tʃɑp] **1.** *n.* a movement with an axe or blade that cuts into something; a blow that cuts into something. ♦ *The log split with the third chop of Bill's axe.* ♦ *The butcher gave the meat a final chop with the cleaver.* **2.** *n.* a jab; a hit. ♦ *The boxer landed a hard chop to his opponent's jaw.* ♦ *The karate expert broke the block of wood with a quick chop.* **3.** *n.* a slice of meat, including some bone, especially lamb or pork. ♦ *We ate lamb chops for dinner.* ♦ *The butcher had a special on chops.* **4.** *tv.* to cut someone or something by hitting it with something sharp. ♦ *Anne chopped the logs in two with an axe.* ♦ *The cook chopped vegetables for the Chinese dish.* **5. chop up** *tv.* + *adv.* to cut someone or something into pieces. ♦ *Bill chopped up the carrots for the stew.* ♦ *Mary worked hard to chop up the wood into smaller sticks.*

chopped ['tʃɑpt] *adj.* cut into tiny pieces; minced. ♦ *The recipe called for a cup of chopped onions.* ♦ *The chopped carrots were great in the stew.*

choppy ['tʃɑp i] **1.** *adj.* [of water at sea] rough. (Adv: *choppily.* Comp: *choppier;* sup: *choppiest.*) ♦ *The lake was a bit choppy for canoeing, so we took the motorboat instead.* ♦ *We could see waves on the choppy lake.* **2.** *adj.* [of writing] uneven in style and having abrupt transitions. (Comp: *choppier;* sup: *choppiest.*) ♦ *This chapter is too choppy and must be rewritten.* ♦ *There is a choppy transition between the episodes in the final chapter.*

chopstick ['tʃɑp stɪk] *n.* one of a pair of long thin sticks used to eat the kinds of food prepared in east and southeast Asian countries. (Usually plural.) ♦ *Chopsticks are offered in Chinese restaurants.* ♦ *I couldn't use the chopsticks, so I asked for a fork.*

chop suey [tʃɑp 'su i] *n.* a type of Chinese food for Americans, made with chopped meat and vegetables. (No plural form in this sense.) ♦ *We have chop suey for dinner every Thursday.* ♦ *The chop suey was served over rice.*

chord ['kord] **1.** *n.* two or more musical tones played at the same time. ♦ *The guitarist strummed a few chords.* ♦ *The music began with a loud chord.* **2.** *n.* a straight line that connects two points on a curve. ♦ *A chord that passes through the center of a circle is its diameter.* ♦ *I drew a chord through the circle.* **3. strike a chord (with someone)** *idiom* to cause someone to remember something; to remind someone of something; to be familiar. ♦ *The woman in the portrait struck a chord with me, and I realized that it was my grandmother.* ♦ *His name strikes a chord, but I don't know why.*

chore ['tʃor] *n.* a regular task; an assignment. ♦ *Doing laundry at the Laundromat is a real chore.* ♦ *After doing their chores, the kids went outside to play.*

choreograph ['kor i ə græf] **1.** *tv.* to plan the way dancers in a play or movie will move. ♦ *The dance instructor choreographed the ballet.* ♦ *The musical was choreographed by a famous dancer.* **2.** *tv.* to manage the details of something. (Figurative on ①.) ♦ *The surprise party was choreographed by Bill's best friend.* ♦ *The executive choreographed the merger of the two companies.*

choreographer [kor i 'ɑ grə fɚ] *n.* someone who choreographs something. ♦ *After dancing for many years, Bill became a choreographer.* ♦ *The choreographer started a new dance troupe.*

choreography [kor i 'ɑ grə fi] *n.* the planning of the movements of dancers. (No plural form in this sense.) ♦ *Mary did the choreography for the variety show.* ♦ *The audience didn't think the choreography was very good.*

chortle ['tʃort əl] **1.** *n.* a hearty laugh; a loud chuckle. ♦ *Anne gave a chortle at the comedian's joke.* ♦ *I knew the audience enjoyed the movie because I could hear their chortles.* **2.** *iv.* to chuckle loudly. ♦ *The kids chortled at the joke.* ♦ *The audience chortled throughout the funny movie.*

chorus ['kor əs] **1.** *n.* a group of people who sing together; a choir. ♦ *A chorus accompanied the orchestra.* ♦ *Jane and Bill are members of the high-school chorus.* **2.** *n.* the part of a song that is repeated after each verse. ♦ *The chorus of this song is the part that everyone knows.* ♦ *The audience sang the chorus with the performers.* **3.** *n.* words or noises that are said together or at the same time. ♦ *The mayor's proposal was met with a chorus of "no's."* ♦ *The children gave a chorus of approval at the idea of swimming.*

chose ['tʃoz] pt of choose.

chosen ['tʃoz ən] pp of choose.

chowder ['tʃaʊ dɚ] *n.* a thick soup, usually made with seafood and milk. (No plural form in this sense.) ♦ *The seafood restaurant was known for its clam chowder.* ♦ *Hot chowder tastes good on a rainy day.*

chow mein [tʃaʊ 'men] *n.* a type of Chinese food for Americans made with fried noodles, chopped meat, and vegetables. (No plural form in this sense.) ♦ *The chow mein had pork in it.* ♦ *The cook on TV taught viewers how to make chow mein.*

Christ ['kraɪst] *n.* Jesus Christ. ♦ *The Bible story tells of the birth of Jesus Christ.* ♦ *The New Testament tells the story of Christ's life.*

christen ['krɪs ən] **1.** *tv.* to admit someone—usually an infant—into a Christian church. ♦ *Five babies were chris-*

tened last Sunday. ♦ *The minister christened the children in a group.* **2.** *tv.* to give a name to someone or something; to name someone or something. ♦ *The boat was christened the* Mayflower. ♦ *The baby was christened Frances Marie, after her grandmother.*

christening ['krɪs ə nɪŋ] **1.** *n.* a baptism, usually of an infant. ♦ *The christening took place at the church.* ♦ *The baby's christening was followed by a celebration.* **2.** *n.* a ceremony of naming. ♦ *The boat was named* Francine *at its christening.* ♦ *The child will be officially named at the christening.*

Christian ['krɪs tʃən] **1. Christian religion** *n.* a religion whose roots are in the teachings of Jesus Christ. ♦ *The lecture contrasted the Christian religion with Jewish beliefs.* ♦ *The Christian religion in Europe and the Americas is divided into Protestant and Catholic, and a few other varieties.* **2.** *n.* a member of a Christian religion. ♦ *The special conference drew Christians, Jews, and Muslims.* ♦ *Mary became a Christian when she was thirty.*

Christianity [krɪs tʃi 'æn ɪt i] *n.* the religion based on the teachings of Jesus Christ. (No plural form in this sense.) ♦ *Mary took a religion class on Christianity.* ♦ *The missionary tried to convert the villagers to Christianity.*

Christmas ['krɪs məs] *n.* December 25th; the day on which the birth of Christ is celebrated by many Christians. ♦ *An early service was held at the church on Christmas.* ♦ *Every Christmas, we decorate a pine tree.*

Christmas Eve ['krɪs məs 'iv] *n.* the night before Christmas; the night of December 24. ♦ *On Christmas Eve, the Smiths went caroling.* ♦ *The pageant was held on Christmas Eve.*

Christmas tree ['krɪs məs tri] *n.* a decorated tree placed in homes during the Christmas season. ♦ *Tom and Jane decorated the Christmas tree on Christmas Eve.* ♦ *Our Christmas tree fell over and crushed some gifts.*

chromatic [kro 'mæt ɪk] **1.** *adj.* of or about color. (Adv: *chromatically* [...ɪk li].) ♦ *The painting had too much chromatic intensity.* ♦ *The basic layout of your picture is good, but there is not enough chromatic contrast between the elements of the design.* **2.** *adj.* of or about a musical scale that is made up of 12 half-steps. (Adv: *chromatically* [...ɪk li].) ♦ *Bill has to practice playing the chromatic scales very rapidly in every key.* ♦ *When practicing chromatic scales, you play 13 notes.*

chrome ['krom] **1.** *n.* chromium or metal plated with chromium. (No plural form in this sense.) ♦ *The bumpers on the old car were made of real chrome.* ♦ *Polished chrome shines in the sunlight.* **2.** *adj.* covered or plated with chromium. ♦ *The chrome bumpers on the car gleamed in the sunshine.* ♦ *The kitchen had chrome appliances.*

chromium ['krom i əm] *n.* a brittle metallic element. (No plural form in this sense.) ♦ *The symbol for chromium is Cr, and its atomic weight is 24.* ♦ *Metals are sometimes plated with chromium for protection from rust and to make them shiny.*

chromosome ['krom ə som] *n.* one of many microscopic cellular structures containing genes. ♦ *Humans have 23 pairs of chromosomes.* ♦ *Chromosomes can be seen with a powerful microscope.*

chronic ['krɑn ɪk] *adj.* persistent or ongoing, said especially of sickness or pain. (Adv: *chronically* [...ɪk li].) ♦ *A chronic disease troubled John his whole life.* ♦ *The employee's chronic complaint was that working conditions at the factory were unsafe.*

chronicle ['krɑn ɪk əl] **1.** *n.* a list of events in the order that they happened; an account of an event from beginning to end. ♦ *The book was a chronicle of the city's history.* ♦ *The newspaper gave a chronicle of the war.* **2.** *tv.* to list events and describe them in the order that they happened. ♦ *The reporter chronicled the events of the day.* ♦ *John is in the process of chronicling our family history.*

chronological [krɑn ə 'lɑdʒ ɪ kəl] *adj.* arranged in order from beginning to end or the earliest to the latest. (Adv: *chronologically* [...ɪk li].) ♦ *These photos are arranged in chronological order.* ♦ *The textbook gave a chronological history of the world.*

chronology [krə 'nɑl ə dʒi] *n.* an account of events in the order in which they happened. ♦ *Several important dates were missing from the chronology of the war.* ♦ *The professor gave a chronology of the development of modern medicine.*

chrysanthemum [krɪ 'sæn θə məm] *n.* a plant whose brightly colored flowers bloom in the fall. (Also **mum**.) ♦ *The florist watered the chrysanthemums growing in the greenhouse.* ♦ *David planted chrysanthemums in the garden.*

chubby ['tʃʌb i] *adj.* somewhat fat; plump. (Comp: *chubbier;* sup: *chubbiest.*) ♦ *The baby was quite chubby but still very cute.* ♦ *I became chubby because I ate too many pastries.*

chuck ['tʃʌk] **1.** *tv.* to throw something; to toss something. ♦ *The pen ran out of ink, so I chucked it into the trash.* ♦ *Bill decided to chuck his unfinished woodcarving project.* **2.** *n.* a piece of beef from an area between the neck and the shoulder. (No plural form in this sense.) ♦ *The recipe called for chuck rather than tenderloin.* ♦ *The butcher had a sale on beef chuck.* **3.** *n.* the part of a drill, lathe, or similar machine that holds removable cutting tools. ♦ *Bob put the drill bit into the drill and tightened the chuck.* ♦ *Anne used a special tool to tighten the chuck.*

chuckhole ['tʃʌk hol] *n.* a large hole in a street or road. ♦ *The car was damaged by hitting a chuckhole.* ♦ *The construction crew finally repaired the chuckhole.*

chuckle ['tʃʌk əl] **1.** *n.* a soft, happy laugh. ♦ *Anne gave a chuckle at my joke.* ♦ *The comedian couldn't get even a chuckle out of the audience.* **2.** *iv.* to laugh softly and happily. ♦ *The children chuckled at the clown's funny antics.* ♦ *Bill chuckled for several minutes after I told him the joke.*

chum ['tʃʌm] **1.** *n.* a good friend; a buddy. ♦ *Max played chess with his chums after school.* ♦ *The new girl at school soon became chums with her classmates.* **2. chum around** *iv.* + *adv.* to keep company with friends. ♦ *My friends chum around together on the weekends.* ♦ *We chummed around all afternoon at the mall.*

chump ['tʃʌmp] *n.* a fool; a stupid-acting person. (Informal.) ♦ *Mary thought Bill was just a chump and treated him poorly.* ♦ *The thief took advantage of poor chumps.*

chunk ['tʃʌŋk] *n.* an irregularly shaped piece of something. ♦ *A big chunk of plaster fell from the ceiling.* ♦ *Bill cut himself a chunk of chocolate cake.*

chunky ['tʃʌŋ ki] **1.** *adj.* thick; solid; stocky. (Adv: *chunkily.* Comp: *chunkier;* sup: *chunkiest.*) ♦ *The chunky* *construction worker lifted the lumber with ease.* ♦ *Chunky children often become thinner during adolescence.* **2.** *adj.* not smooth; having lumps or chunks. (Adv: *chunkily.*) ♦ *Mary likes chunky peanut butter.* ♦ *The cake batter should be smooth, not chunky.*

church ['tʃɚtʃ] **1.** *n.* a building where Christians gather to worship. ♦ *The church was filled on Easter morning.* ♦ *The church was adorned with stained glass windows.* **2.** *n.* the worship service celebrated within a church. (No plural form in this sense.) ♦ *Jane and Bill attend church once a week.* ♦ *Mary's parents took her to church when she was young.* **3.** *n.* the members of a particular church or denomination. ♦ *The church held a benefit to earn money.* ♦ *When Mary was ill, the church helped her out.* **4.** *n.* the institutional organization of a religious body, its policies, and practices, as opposed to the state. (No plural form in this sense.) ♦ *We believe in the separation of the church and state.* ♦ *Some people think the churches should stay out of politics.*

churn ['tʃɚn] **1.** *n.* a device that turns cream into butter by stirring it. ♦ *Pioneers used to make butter with a churn.* ♦ *The children each took a turn working the churn.* **2.** *tv.* to turn cream into butter by stirring it rapidly. ♦ *Aunt Mary churned the butter quickly.* ♦ *The students churned butter when they studied pioneer life.*

chute ['ʃut] **1.** *n.* a slide or tube used to send something from an upper level to a lower level. ♦ *A laundry chute connected the bathroom and the laundry room.* ♦ *The old building had a mail chute.* **2.** *n.* a parachute. ♦ *For a moment I was afraid my chute wouldn't open when I pulled the cord.* ♦ *We saw someone attached to a chute floating in the sky.*

cicada [sɪ 'ke də] *n.* a large insect with four wings, known for its loud buzzing sound. ♦ *The cicadas sang all night, making it hard for us to sleep.* ♦ *The almanac predicted there would be a lot of cicadas this year.*

cider ['sɑɪ dɚ] *n.* apple juice; juice pressed from apples. (No plural form in this sense.) ♦ *The cider was made from the apples we picked at the orchard.* ♦ *I served cider and cookies to my guests.*

cigar [sɪ 'gɑr] *n.* a carefully packed roll of dried tobacco leaves, used for smoking. ♦ *Bill puffed on a cigar as he watched the sun set.* ♦ *The room smelled like stale cigars.*

cigarette [sɪg ə 'rɛt] *n.* a small roll of cut tobacco wrapped in paper, used for smoking. ♦ *Mary smoked a cigarette while she waited for the bus.* ♦ *Bill went out to buy a package of cigarettes.*

cinch ['sɪntʃ] **1.** *n.* something easy to do. ♦ *For Mary, fixing things is a cinch.* ♦ *It will be a cinch to get Bill to agree to the plan.* **2.** *n.* something certain. ♦ *It is a cinch that Jane will get the promotion.* ♦ *That the sun will rise every morning is a cinch.* **3.** *n.* the strap or belt that holds a saddle on a horse. ♦ *Tom tightened the cinch before he got on the horse.* ♦ *The cinch broke and dumped the rider off the horse.*

cinder ['sɪn dɚ] **1.** *n.* a piece of ash from burned coal. ♦ *Bill carried out the cinders from the furnace.* ♦ *All that was left of the fire was cinders.* **2.** *n.* a small piece of mostly burned coal or wood that can cause other objects to catch fire. ♦ *The cinders blew onto the carpet and started a fire.* ♦ *A cinder burned my hand when I added wood to the fire.*

cinema ['sɪn ə mə] **1.** *n.* the business of making motion pictures; the movies. (No plural form in this sense.) ♦ *The stage actor always wanted to work in cinema.* ♦ *The politician developed a ratings system for the cinema.* **2.** *n.* a movie theater. ♦ *I went to see the latest release at the local cinema.* ♦ *The floor of the cinema had popcorn all over it.*

cinematographer [sɪn ə mə 'tɑ grə fɚ] *n.* someone who films motion pictures; someone in charge of the actual film exposure in the making of movies. ♦ *The cinematographer discussed the important shot with the director.* ♦ *Lisa won an award for her work as a cinematographer.*

cinematography [sɪn ə mə 'tɑ grə fi] *n.* the art of filming motion pictures. (No plural form in this sense.) ♦ *Bill admired the foreign film's exotic cinematography.* ♦ *The film school offers many classes in cinematography.*

cinnamon ['sɪn ə mən] **1.** *n.* a spice made from the bark of a tropical tree grown in South and Southeast Asia. (No plural form in this sense.) ♦ *The coffee had a hint of cinnamon in it.* ♦ *The pastries were flavored with cinnamon.* **2.** *adj.* flavored with ①. ♦ *Bill ordered cinnamon coffee.* ♦ *I ate cinnamon buns at brunch.*

cipher ['sɑɪ fɚ] **1.** *n.* the symbol for zero: 0; nothing. ♦ *The result of all her hard work was a cipher—zero.* ♦ *The final score was a pair of ciphers. That means 0–0.* **2.** *n.* a message that has been written in code. (See also decipher.) ♦ *Spies intercepted the cipher but could not decode it.* ♦ *The cipher described the position of the enemy army.* **3.** *n.* the secret code that explains the pattern for encoding and decoding a secret message. ♦ *Only top military officials knew the cipher to decode the message.* ♦ *The spy explained the cipher needed to decode the code.*

circle ['sɚk əl] **1.** *n.* a curved line where every point on the line is the same distance from a center point. ♦ *The geometry students drew circles with compasses.* ♦ *The teacher drew a circle around the correct answer.* **2.** *n.* anything shaped like ①; a ring. ♦ *The children sat in a circle around the storyteller.* ♦ *The dog ran in circles chasing its tail.* **3.** *n.* a group of people with related interests. ♦ *Bill's circle included many fans of baseball.* ♦ *Mary had a wide circle of friends when she was in college.* **4.** *tv.* to form a ring around someone or something. ♦ *Huge rings of rocks circle the planet Saturn.* ♦ *Flowers circle the base of the tree.* **5.** *tv.* to draw a ring around something that is written or printed. ♦ *The instructions said to circle the correct answer.* ♦ *The teacher circled the verb in the sentence on the chalkboard.* **6.** *iv.* to move in a circle around someone or something. ♦ *Hyenas circled the carcass before devouring it.* ♦ *The earth circles the sun.* **7. go round in circles** *idiom* to keep going over the same ideas or repeating the same actions, often resulting in confusion and without reaching a satisfactory decision or conclusion. ♦ *We're just going round in circles discussing the problems of the plan. We need to consult someone else to get a new point of view.* ♦ *Mike's trying to find out what's happened but he's going round in circles. No one will tell him anything useful.* **8. in a vicious circle** *idiom* in a situation in which the solution of one problem leads to a second problem, and the solution of the second problem brings back the first problem, etc. ♦ *I put lemon in my tea to make it sour, then sugar to make it sweet. I'm in a vicious circle.* ♦ *Don't let your life get into a vicious circle.* **9. talk in circles** *idiom* to talk in a confusing or roundabout manner. ♦ *I couldn't understand a thing he said. All he did was talk in circles.* ♦ *We argued for a long time and finally decided that we were talking in circles.*

circuit ['sɚk ɪt] **1.** *n.* a complete trip around something. ♦ *The bus driver makes three circuits around the city each day.* ♦ *The singer made a circuit around the stage while singing.* **2.** *n.* the path that the flow of electricity follows. ♦ *The electrician connected the last wire and completed the circuit.* ♦ *There was a problem in one of the power circuits in my computer.*

circuit breaker ['sɚk ɪt brek ɚ] *n.* a device that interrupts an electric current flowing through a circuit. ♦ *The overload caused the circuit breaker to turn off.* ♦ *Mary reset the circuit breaker, and the lights came back on again.*

circuitous [sɚ 'kju ɪ təs] *adj.* roundabout; indirect. (Adv: *circuitously.*) ♦ *Bill's weak argument was circuitous.* ♦ *We could tell Mary was evading our question when she gave a circuitous response.*

circular ['sɚ kjə lɚ] **1.** *n.* a printed sheet that is sent to many people. ♦ *The circular announced the store's upcoming sale.* ♦ *The club mailed a circular each month.* **2.** *adj.* in the shape of a circle; round; ring-like. (Adv: *circularly.*) ♦ *The carpenter used a special saw to cut a circular hole.* ♦ *The freeway followed a circular route around the city.*

circulate ['sɚ kjə let] **1.** *tv.* to send something from person to person; to send something from place to place. ♦ *Bill circulated the magazine article among his friends.* ♦ *The company circulated brochures to its clients.* **2.** *tv.* to carry something, such as medicine, by way of the circulation of blood. ♦ *The bloodstream will circulate the medicine throughout the body.* ♦ *The poison was circulated by the victim's blood.* **3.** *iv.* to go around from person to person. ♦ *The rumor circulated through the office.* ♦ *The magazine will circulate to all employees.* **4.** *iv.* [for blood] to flow from the heart through the body and back to the heart. ♦ *As long as your blood is circulating normally, you should be all right.* ♦ *This medicine circulates through the body through the bloodstream.*

circulation [sɚ kjə 'le ʃən] **1.** *n.* the movement of blood from the heart to the body and back to the heart. (No plural form in this sense.) ♦ *Exercise improved the sick patient's circulation.* ♦ *A tight ring cut off circulation to my finger.* **2.** *n.* the movement of someone or something going from place to place. (No plural form in this sense.) ♦ *The circulation of the memo through the office took about a week.* ♦ *Circulation of the party guests was hampered because the hall was so crowded.* **3.** *n.* the number of copies of a newspaper or magazine that are sold. (No plural form in this sense.) ♦ *Because of the magazine's low circulation, no one would advertise in it.* ♦ *The popular magazine quickly exceeded its goal for circulation.* **4. out of circulation** *idiom* not interacting socially with other people. ♦ *I don't know what's happening because I've been out of circulation for a while.* ♦ *My cold has kept me out of circulation for a few weeks.*

circumcise ['sɚ kəm saɪz] *tv.* to cut off the foreskin from the penis, typically for religious reasons. ♦ *A doctor circumcised the baby boy at the hospital.* ♦ *There was a short ceremony when the infant boy was circumcised.*

circumcision [sɚ kəm 'sɪ ʒən] *n.* cutting off the foreskin from the penis. (No plural form in this sense.) ♦ *Some doctors do not approve of circumcision.* ♦ *Circumcision is practiced among a number of different cultures.*

circumference [sɚ 'kʌm frəns] *n.* the distance around a circle. ♦ *The circumference of the round table is five feet.* ♦ *A geometry student calculated the circumference of the circle.*

circumlocution [sɚ kəm lo 'kju ʃən] *n.* using many words when fewer words would do just as well. (No plural form in this sense.) ♦ *The writing teacher advised against unnecessary circumlocution.* ♦ *Circumlocution is just talking around a subject instead of dealing with it directly.*

circumnavigate [sɚ kəm 'næv ə get] *tv.* to sail all the way around the world. ♦ *The sailor's dream was to circumnavigate the earth.* ♦ *The ship was prevented from circumnavigating the world when it ran out of provisions.*

circumscribe ['sɚ kəm skraɪb] *tv.* to set the boundaries for something; to limit something. ♦ *The moves you can make in a chess game are circumscribed by the rules of the game.* ♦ *Rules set down by Anne's parents circumscribed her activities.*

circumspect ['sɚ kəm spɛkt] *adj.* cautious; watching on all sides. (Adv: *circumspectly.*) ♦ *The investor was circumspect when making predictions about the economy.* ♦ *Never very circumspect in expressing his views, Bill annoyed almost everyone at the party.*

circumstance ['sɚ kəm stæns] *n.* a condition, fact, or detail related to an event or action. ♦ *What were the circumstances surrounding the crime?* ♦ *Mary's difficult financial circumstances led to her bankruptcy.*

circumvent ['sɚ kəm vɛnt] *tv.* to find a way around something that one wants to avoid; to avoid someone or something. ♦ *The detour circumvents the construction site.* ♦ *The corrupt politician found a way to circumvent paying taxes.*

circus ['sɚk əs] **1.** *n.* a traveling show featuring clowns, acrobats, animals, magicians, and other similar acts. ♦ *The circus is coming to town this summer!* ♦ *At the circus, we saw elephants and acrobats.* **2. like a three-ring circus** *idiom* chaotic; exciting and busy. ♦ *Our household is like a three-ring circus on Monday mornings.* ♦ *This meeting is like a three-ring circus. Quiet down and listen!*

cirrhosis [sɪ 'ros ɪs] *n.* a fibrous disease of the liver. (No plural form in this sense.) ♦ *The patient's cirrhosis was caused by alcoholism.* ♦ *The doctor diagnosed cirrhosis of the liver.*

cirrus ['sɪr əs] *adj.* [of a cloud] thin, wispy, and higher in the sky than most clouds. ♦ *The sky was streaked with delicate cirrus clouds.* ♦ *The afternoon was bright with only a few high cirrus clouds.*

cistern ['sɪs tɚn] *n.* a underground water tank. ♦ *Most of our drinking water comes from the cistern near our house.* ♦ *The rainwater that falls on the roof goes right into the cistern.*

citation [saɪ 'te ʃən] **1.** *n.* a reference or quote that is given to support a fact. ♦ *The student supported her thesis with citations from other works.* ♦ *The author's citations were not accurately quoted.* **2.** *n.* an award given to someone who has performed exceptionally well. ♦ *Mr. Smith received a citation for outstanding performance for two years in a row.* ♦ *A teacher from our school received a cita-*

tion for excellence. **3.** *n.* a summons to appear in court. ♦ *The police officer gave Mary a citation for speeding.* ♦ *The citation said that I had to go to traffic court.*

cite ['sɑɪt] **1.** *tv.* to use someone or something as a reference to support a fact. ♦ *The boss cited Bill's excessive absences when he fired him.* ♦ *The newspaper article cited the philanthropist's good works.* **2.** *tv.* to refer to or list a citation. ♦ *The science article cited an ancient book on astronomy.* ♦ *Mary could cite five incidents of Bill being late.* **3.** *tv.* to acknowledge someone for having done an exceptional deed. ♦ *The commanding officer cited the troops for their extreme bravery.* ♦ *The critic cited Mary's outstanding performance.* **4.** *tv.* to give someone a summons to appear in court. ♦ *A police officer cited me for speeding.* ♦ *The pedestrian was cited for jaywalking.*

citizen ['sɪt ə zən] *n.* someone who is a legal resident of a political subdivision. ♦ *The refugee wanted to become a legal citizen of this country.* ♦ *Citizens protested loudly against the tax increase.*

citizenry ['sɪt ə zən ri] *n.* the population of a village, town, city, state, country, etc. (No plural form in this sense.) ♦ *The citizenry of the colonies protested the new taxes.* ♦ *The candidate addressed the city's citizenry.*

citizenship ['sɪt ə zən ʃɪp] **1.** *n.* the state of being an official citizen. (No plural form in this sense.) ♦ *Citizenship is earned by thousands of people each year.* ♦ *The immigrant's goal was to achieve citizenship.* **2.** *n.* the behavior expected of a citizen. (No plural form in this sense.) ♦ *The teacher promoted good citizenship among the students.* ♦ *Terrorists hardly demonstrate good citizenship!*

citrus ['sɪ trəs] **1.** *n.* a family of fruit including oranges, tangerines, grapefruit, limes, lemons, etc. (No plural form in this sense.) ♦ *Jane really wanted the sharpness of citrus.* ♦ *The juice—whatever it was—had the tangy taste of citrus.* **2.** *adj.* <the adj. use of ①.> ♦ *Jane really prefers citrus fruit.* ♦ *I drink some kind of citrus juice each morning.*

city ['sɪt i] **1.** *n.* a large town; a large residential and business center. ♦ *Bill grew up in the city but moved to the country later in life.* ♦ *The city offered many business and cultural opportunities.* **2.** *adj.* <the adj. use of ①.> ♦ *Bill just prefers city life.* ♦ *The city government has the power to tax its citizens.*

city hall ['sɪt i 'hɔl] **1.** *n.* the administrative building for a city government. (Sometimes capitalized.) ♦ *City hall is located downtown, next to the library.* ♦ *A new wing was added to city hall to create more space for offices.* **2.** a city government or administration; the offices in ① and the government leaders working in ①. (Sometimes capitalized.) ♦ *I complained to city hall about the poor condition of the roads.* ♦ *City hall raised our local taxes again this year.*

civic ['sɪv ɪk] **1.** *adj.* of or about citizenship or cities and their government. (Adv: *civically* [...ɪk li].) ♦ *The civic center has a theater and a gymnasium.* ♦ *It is our civic duty to vote in local elections.* **2. civics** *n.* the study of citizenship and local government. (Treated as singular.) ♦ *The students studied government structure in civics.* ♦ *Civics is a course taught in most high schools.*

civil ['sɪv əl] **1.** *adj.* of or about citizens and their government, activities, rights, and responsibilities. ♦ *Following the court decision, there was a lot of civil unrest.* ♦ *The citizens practiced civil disobedience until the law was changed.* **2.** *adj.* polite; courteous; behaving properly. (Adv: *civilly.*) ♦ *Mary was very angry, but she remained civil.* ♦ *Bill spoke in a civil tone, but his words were insulting.* **3.** *adj.* relating to a legal action that does not deal with criminal law. ♦ *The judge dealt with about a dozen civil cases a week.* ♦ *The injured party filed a civil suit against the driver of the car that caused the accident.*

civil engineer ['sɪv əl ɛn dʒə 'nɪr] *n.* someone who designs public works, such as bridges, sewers, public buildings, roads, and subways. ♦ *The city employed civil engineers to design the new bridge.* ♦ *Civil engineers contribute to city planning.*

civilian [sɪ 'vɪl jən] *n.* a citizen who is not in the military. ♦ *After thirty years in the military, Bob retired and became a civilian.* ♦ *The civilians watched the soldiers marching in the parade.*

civility [sɪ 'vɪl ə ti] *n.* courtesy; politeness. (No plural form in this sense.) ♦ *Mary treats her employees with civility.* ♦ *The store manager acted with great civility at all times.*

civilization [sɪv ə lə 'ze ʃən] **1.** *n.* complex social organization. (No plural form in this sense.) ♦ *Civilization concerns the development of cities and government in which many people can participate.* ♦ *The colonists presumed to bring civilization to savages.* **2.** *n.* a culture with a well-developed social system. ♦ *The anthropologist studied the religion of ancient civilizations.* ♦ *Many important civilizations developed around the Mediterranean Sea.* **3.** *n.* cities, as opposed to barren, rural areas. (Often jocular. No plural form in this sense.) ♦ *After years in a rural area, the Smiths moved back to civilization.* ♦ *How much farther do we have to drive on this road before we reach civilization?*

civilize ['sɪv ə lɑɪz] *tv.* to make someone or a culture more organized and less primitive. ♦ *It may take decades to fully civilize the remote peoples.* ♦ *The missionaries set out to civilize the natives.*

civilized ['sɪv ə lɑɪzd] **1.** *adj.* having a complex social, cultural, or economic system. ♦ *What appeared to be a wild tribe was really a highly civilized culture.* ♦ *Much of the Western world has been civilized for over a thousand years.* **2.** *adj.* polite; courteous; properly behaved. ♦ *Bill and Mary were very mad at each other, but they acted civilized at the party.* ♦ *Children should behave in a civilized manner.*

civil right ['sɪv əl 'rɑɪt] *n.* a legal right held by a citizen. ♦ *The Constitution upholds the civil rights of all people.* ♦ *An embargo was placed on the nation that disregarded the civil rights of its people.*

civil servant ['sɪv əl 'sɚ vənt] *n.* the people who work for the government. ♦ *Bill went to work for the state and became a civil servant.* ♦ *Government workers are often called civil servants.*

civil war ['sɪv əl 'wor] **1.** *n.* war between people who are citizens of the same country. ♦ *The country endured a bitter five-year civil war.* ♦ *A civil war broke out when one state tried to secede from the nation.* **2. Civil War** *n.* the American Civil War. ♦ *The Civil War lasted from 1861 to 1865.* ♦ *My great-great-grandfather fought in the Civil War.*

claim ['klem] **1.** *n.* a document or statement requesting that a payment be made. ♦ *Mary made a claim for her hospital bills with the insurance company.* ♦ *The insurance company paid the claim promptly.* **2.** *n.* a statement presented as fact; an assertion that something is true. ♦ *Your claim to have royal blood is ridiculous.* ♦ *The detective investigated the suspect's claims.* **3.** *n.* mining land to be registered for the use of someone. ♦ *The prospector staked his claim at the edge of the river.* ♦ *The claim did not produce any gold, unfortunately.* **4.** *tv.* to assert one's right to own something. ♦ *Bill claimed the last brownie for himself.* ♦ *The prospector claimed the land where he found a gold nugget.* **5.** *tv.* to say a statement as fact; to assert that something is true. (Takes a clause.) ♦ *The job applicant claimed he had a college degree.* ♦ *The scientist claimed that her findings were revolutionary.* **6. claim a life** *idiom* [for something] to take the life of someone. ♦ *The killer tornado claimed the lives of six people at the trailer park.* ♦ *The athlete's life was claimed in a skiing accident.*

claimant ['klem ənt] *n.* someone who makes a claim. ♦ *The insurance company refused to pay the claimant.* ♦ *The claimant sued the insurance company for withholding payment.*

clairvoyance [klɛr 'vɔɪ əns] *n.* the ability to see or hear things not in one's view. (No plural form in this sense.) ♦ *The medium's clairvoyance impressed even the skeptics.* ♦ *Through clairvoyance, Mary claimed to know what was happening in the next room.*

clairvoyant [klɛr 'vɔɪ ənt] **1.** *n.* someone who can experience sensations beyond the normal range of sight, hearing, smell, taste, and touch. ♦ *When Bill seemed to read her mind, Mary thought he must be clairvoyant.* ♦ *Eager to find the missing ring, I consulted a clairvoyant.* **2.** *adj.* able to experience sensations beyond the normal range of sight, hearing, smell, taste, and touch. (Adv: *clairvoyantly.*) ♦ *The clairvoyant woman told me where my missing ring was.* ♦ *The man who predicted the disaster is clairvoyant.*

clam ['klæm] **1.** *n.* an edible marine animal having a pair of hinged shells. ♦ *The cook put a lot of clams in the chowder.* ♦ *The scuba diver saw many clams on the floor of the sea.* **2.** *adj.* made with or flavored with ①. ♦ *Susan bought bottles of clam juice at the store.* ♦ *Bill made a huge kettle of clam chowder for the picnic.* **3.** *adj.* <the adj. use of ①.> ♦ *Jimmy found lots of clam shells on the beach.* ♦ *We had a clam hunt just before dinner time.*

clammy ['klæm i] *adj.* sticky; humid; damp. (Comp: *clammier;* sup: *clammiest.*) ♦ *The children felt clammy after playing baseball on the hot day.* ♦ *The sick patient had clammy hands.*

clamor ['klæm ɚ] **1.** *n.* a noisy disturbance; a noisy protest. ♦ *The clamor from the backyard drew us out of the house.* ♦ *"What is all the clamor for?" John asked the noisy children.* **2.** *iv.* to protest loudly; to make an uproar. ♦ *The children clamored for their mother's attention.* ♦ *What is this endless clamoring about?*

clamp ['klæmp] **1.** *n.* a device that holds things together with pressure. ♦ *John put a clamp on the two pieces of wood when he glued them together.* ♦ *A clamp held the board firmly while Jane sawed it.* **2.** *tv.* to hold things together with pressure. ♦ *The carpenter clamped the board to the bench.* ♦ *I glued and clamped the broken plate.*

clan ['klæn] *n.* a group of related families. (Used especially in Scotland.) ♦ *Each clan had its own design of plaid fabric.* ♦ *The two clans have been enemies for hundreds of years.*

clandestine [klæn 'dɛs tən] *adj.* secret; done in secret; concealed. (Adv: *clandestinely.*) ♦ *The lovers had a clandestine meeting in the garden.* ♦ *Some angry peasants had a clandestine plan to overthrow the leader.*

clang ['klæŋ] **1.** *n.* the loud ringing noise that a bell makes; the loud ringing noise made by hitting metal. ♦ *The cook made a loud clang to let the workers know lunch was ready.* ♦ *The clang of the school bell startled the children.* **2.** *iv.* to make a loud ringing noise, like metal that has been hit. ♦ *The school bell clanged at the end of recess.* ♦ *The lid on the pot clanged, revealing that someone was checking on dinner.*

clank ['klæŋk] **1.** *n.* the loud noise metal makes when it is hit by another piece of metal. ♦ *The car gave a loud clank and sputtered to a stop.* ♦ *The clank caused by the pots falling from the shelf startled me.* **2.** *iv.* [for two pieces of metal] to make a loud noise when knocked together. ♦ *The door of the cell clanked as Max was locked in jail.* ♦ *The pipes clanked all night, so I couldn't fall asleep.*

clap ['klæp] **1.** *n.* the sound made when one brings one's palms together in applause. ♦ *The guard gave a clap to get my attention.* ♦ *A single clap broke the silence.* **2.** *n.* a loud burst of thunder. ♦ *Lightning followed the clap of thunder.* ♦ *We all jumped when we heard the clap of thunder.* **3. clap for** *iv.* + *prep. phr.* to slap one's hands together in applause for someone or something. ♦ *Everybody clapped hard for the new mayor.* ♦ *I clapped for Susie when she took her first steps.* **4.** *iv.* to make applause. ♦ *The actors bowed and the audience clapped.* ♦ *Please do not clap until the end of the entire symphony.*

clarification [klɛr ə fɪ 'ke ʃən] *n.* added information to make something easier to understand. ♦ *The newspaper printed clarifications of the incorrect statements.* ♦ *I asked my boss for clarification, and she explained the project to me again.*

clarify ['klɛr ə fɑɪ] *tv.* to make something easier to understand; to explain something in greater detail. ♦ *The student wanted to clarify her point for the rest of the class.* ♦ *The explanation clarified the details of the plan.*

clarinet [klɛr ə 'nɛt] *n.* a tubular musical instrument of the woodwind family. ♦ *The school band included five clarinets.* ♦ *A lot of music is written for the jazz clarinet.*

clarity ['klɛr ɪ ti] *n.* clearness. (No plural form in this sense.) ♦ *The teacher praised the clarity of expression in the student's essay.* ♦ *The clarity of the musician's playing was beautiful.*

clash ['klæʃ] **1.** *n.* a fight; a battle; a skirmish. ♦ *The clash grew into a bitter war.* ♦ *A pair of politicians had a clash of words on national television.* **2. clash (with)** *iv.* (+ *prep. phr.*) to quarrel or fight with someone. ♦ *The troops clashed briefly at the border.* ♦ *Mary clashed with her parents over her curfew.* **3. clash (with)** *iv.* (+ *prep. phr.*) to be in conflict with something else. ♦ *The vertical pattern of his shirt clashed with his plaid pants.* ♦ *I think bright orange and red clash terribly.*

clasp ['klæsp] **1.** *n.* a hook or fastener that holds something closed. ♦ *The clasp on your dress is undone.* ♦ *I lost my necklace when its clasp broke.* **2.** *n.* a firm grasp; the holding of something tightly. ♦ *The baby had a tight clasp on my finger as it toddled across the room.* ♦ *Mary tightened her clasp on Bob's arm when the movie became scary.* **3.** *tv.* to take hold of someone or something firmly; to hold someone or something tightly. ♦ *The baby clasped my hand as it took its first steps.* ♦ *I clasped the steering wheel and started the car.*

class ['klæs] **1.** *n.* a group of similar things. ♦ *This particular class of antique furniture is very valuable.* ♦ *Susan uses an advanced class of software on her computer.* **2.** *n.* someone's social and economic ranking. ♦ *Most people marry within their own class.* ♦ *The income of the middle class is higher than that of the lower class.* **3.** *n.* a course that is taught; a subject that is taught. ♦ *I think my history class is the most interesting one this term.* ♦ *The busy professor taught four classes last term.* **4.** *n.* a specific session of learning; a period of time spent in instruction. ♦ *Mary was late for class and the teacher glared at her.* ♦ *After an hour of the class, Bob began to fall asleep.* **5.** *n.* all the people in a certain grade or year of schooling. ♦ *The sophomore class sponsored a dance after the basketball game.* ♦ *The gift of the Class of '84 was a new tree for the courtyard.* **6.** *n.* <a term of address for a group of students in a classroom.> (No plural form in this sense.) ♦ *Now, class, let's turn to page twelve.* ♦ *Class! You are too noisy!* **7.** *n.* the ability to behave properly, politely, or elegantly. (No plural form in this sense.) ♦ *Ignoring rude people shows a lot of class.* ♦ *I'd prefer to date someone with class.* **8.** *tv.* to classify someone or something. ♦ *The appraiser classed the jewelry as junk.* ♦ *The tomato is actually classed as a fruit rather than a vegetable.* **9. cut class** *idiom* to skip going to class ④. ♦ *If Mary keeps cutting classes, she'll fail the course.* ♦ *I can't cut that class. I've missed too many already.*

classic ['klæs ɪk] **1.** *n.* something, especially art, music, or writing, that is of very high quality and will be or is remembered through history. ♦ *The students studied the classics of Western culture.* ♦ *Bill wanted to read the classics of English literature.* **2.** *adj.* of high quality; the best; of great and enduring importance; serving as a standard for others of its kind. ♦ *The scientist was best known for his classic study of human behavior.* ♦ Gone with the Wind *is a classic historical romance.* **3.** *adj.* typical; just as one would anticipate. ♦ *Running out of gas is the classic excuse for getting home late.* ♦ *Someone who works 80 hours a week is a classic example of a workaholic.*

classical ['klæs ɪ kəl] **1.** *adj.* of or about ancient Greece and Rome. (Adv: *classically* [...ɪk li].) ♦ *Jane majored in classical studies.* ♦ *The class discussed the art of classical cultures.* **2.** *adj.* [of music, such as symphonies, operas, chamber music, or dance and other art forms] serious and requiring a high degree of training and skill. ♦ *Bill likes all classical music, from symphonies to chamber music.* ♦ *Although she has studied classical ballet, Mary also enjoys tap dancing.*

classification [klæs ə fə 'ke ʃən] **1.** *n.* the process of assigning things to specific categories. (No plural form in this sense.) ♦ *Proper classification of the newly discovered plants is important.* ♦ *What scheme of classification is used in this library?* **2.** *n.* a system of classes or categories. ♦ *Our biology class learned the classification of the animal kingdom.* ♦ *The florist knew the scientific classifications of the plants in the greenhouse.*

classified ['klæs ə fɑɪd] **1.** *adj.* of or about newspaper advertisements arranged according to topic. ♦ *The company placed a classified ad to attract prospective employees.* ♦ *People place classified ads to buy and sell things.* **2.** *adj.* secret; confidential; restricted. ♦ *The astronomical engineer worked on classified projects for the government.* ♦ *The spy vowed to die rather than divulge classified information.*

classify ['klæs ə fɑɪ] **1.** *tv.* to place something in a specific class or category. ♦ *The botanist classified all the flowers on the island.* ♦ *How would you classify that piece of music?* **2.** *tv.* [for a government] to declare information to be secret. ♦ *The government classified the details of the case.* ♦ *The engineering firm classified the details of its satellite.*

classmate ['klæs met] *n.* someone in the same class at school. ♦ *Jimmy played with his classmates at recess.* ♦ *Susie invited five classmates to her birthday party.*

classroom ['klæs rum] *n.* a room in a school or building where classes are held. ♦ *The classroom held twenty desks.* ♦ *The teacher arrived in the classroom before the students.*

classy ['klæs i] *adj.* stylish; chic; elegant. (Comp: *classier;* sup: *classiest.*) ♦ *The designer made clothes that looked very classy.* ♦ *The company is known for its classy advertisements.*

clatter ['klæt ɚ] **1.** *n.* the noise of several things hitting together. ♦ *The plates made a clatter when they were dropped.* ♦ *The clatter in the kitchen disrupted our conversation.* **2.** *iv.* to hit together; to crash together. ♦ *The plates clattered when they hit the floor.* ♦ *The pots and pans clattered when Susie banged them together.*

clause ['klɔz] **1.** *n.* a phrase that has a subject and a verb. ♦ *A clause can be introduced with* that *or* which. ♦ *The sentence had too many clauses in it.* **2.** *n.* a single provision in a legal document. ♦ *The publisher added a clause to the contract.* ♦ *The author agreed to all but one clause in the contract.*

claustrophobia [klɔ strə 'fob i ə] *n.* the fear of being closed in a small space. (No plural form in this sense.) ♦ *Mary's claustrophobia bothered her when she got stuck in an elevator.* ♦ *Because of Bill's claustrophobia, he sleeps with his bedroom door open.*

clavichord ['klæv ə kord] *n.* an earlier version of the piano. ♦ *An old clavichord was on display at the museum.* ♦ *Some classical music was composed for a clavichord.*

clavicle ['klæv ɪ kəl] *n.* the collarbone; the bone that connects the shoulder bone to the breastbone. ♦ *The doctor examined the athlete's broken clavicle.* ♦ *The X-ray showed the patient's clavicle and ribs.*

claw ['klɔ] **1.** *n.* a sharp, hard, curved nail on the foot of an animal or a bird. ♦ *The cat's claw snagged my sweater.* ♦ *The hawk sank its claws into its prey and took flight.* **2.** *n.* the pinchers of a lobster, crab, or other shellfish. ♦ *The crab snapped its claw as the beachcomber picked it up.* ♦ *The restaurant served lobster claws.* **3.** *n.* the part of the hammer that is used for removing nails. ♦ *Anne used the claw of the hammer to remove the old, rusty nail.* ♦ *David raised the hammer and almost injured himself with the claw.* **4.** *tv.* to scratch or tear someone or something with claws. ♦ *The assailant clawed the police officer.* ♦ *The cat tried to claw me.* **5. claw at** *iv.* + *prep. phr.* to scratch at someone or something. ♦ *The cat clawed at the door, begging to go outside.* ♦ *My dog clawed at the dirt, trying to unearth its bone.*

clay ['kle] **1.** *n.* a kind of sticky soil, used for pottery. (No plural form in this sense.) ♦ *The children liked any craft that involved clay.* ♦ *The potter shaped the clay into a flower pot.* **2.** *adj.* made of or concerning ①. ♦ *The clay pot was filled with flowers.* ♦ *The clay sculpture hardened when I placed it in the kiln.* **3. have feet of clay** *idiom* [for a strong person] to have a defect of character. ♦ *All human beings have feet of clay. No one is perfect.* ♦ *Sally was popular and successful. She was nearly fifty before she learned that she, too, had feet of clay.*

clean ['klin] **1.** *adj.* tidy; not dirty. (Adv: *cleanly.*) ♦ *Bill washed his hands until they were clean.* ♦ *After working outside all day, Jane wanted a shower and clean clothes.* **2.** *adj.* new; fresh; unused. ♦ *The writer picked up a clean piece of paper and began to write.* ♦ *The maid put clean sheets on the bed.* **3.** *adj.* ethically or morally pure; not obscene. (Adv: *cleanly.*) ♦ *The parents allowed their children to watch only clean movies.* ♦ *The minister urged the congregation to think clean thoughts.* **4.** *adj.* smooth; even; not rough. (Adv: *cleanly.*) ♦ *The barber gave John a clean outline around his ears.* ♦ *The saw made a clean cut through the wood.* **5.** *tv.* to make something ①. ♦ *The maid was hired to clean the house once a week.* ♦ *I cleaned the kitchen after dinner.* **6.** *tv.* to prepare an animal for cooking and eating by removing the parts that cannot be eaten. ♦ *The hunters cleaned their kill.* ♦ *Anne cleaned the fish that she had caught.*

clean-cut ['klin 'kʌt] *adj.* [of a man] typically neatly shaved and groomed. ♦ *The next job applicant was a very clean-cut young man.* ♦ *Employers tend to hire clean-cut men instead of sloppy ones.*

cleaner ['klin ɚ] **1.** *n.* soap, bleach, detergent, disinfectant, or another product that cleans. (No plural form in this sense.) ♦ *The cleaner removed the stains in the kitchen sink.* ♦ *Some cleaners are dangerous if they are inhaled.* **2.** *n.* someone who cleans clothing and fabric for a living. ♦ *The cleaner got the spot out of my blouse.* ♦ *My cleaner raised the rates for cleaning delicate fabrics.* **3. cleaners** *n.* a business that launders or dry-cleans clothing and other items. ♦ *I took my dry cleaning to the cleaners.* ♦ *Don't forget to pick up your shirts at the cleaners.*

cleanliness ['klɛn li nəs] *n.* the quality of being clean. (No plural form in this sense.) ♦ *"Cleanliness is next to godliness," says an old proverb.* ♦ *I was disgusted with my roommate's lack of cleanliness.*

cleanse ['klɛnz] *tv.* to clean something well; to purify something. ♦ *Mary cleansed her face with special soap each evening.* ♦ *The nurse cleansed the wound before sewing it up.*

cleanser ['klɛn zɚ] *n.* a product that thoroughly cleans something; a soap; a detergent. (No plural form in this sense.) ♦ *The cleanser was very effective on the stains in the tub.* ♦ *This powerful cleanser removes dirt very well.*

clean-shaven ['klin 'ʃev ən] *adj.* [of a man] smooth-faced; not having a mustache or beard. ♦ *Anne described the mugger as clean-shaven.* ♦ *The school dress code requires the boys to be clean-shaven.*

cleansing ['klɛn zɪŋ] *adj.* purifying. ♦ *The laundry detergent has a special cleansing agent to remove tough stains.* ♦ *The beautician recommended a gentle cleansing cream for my skin.*

clear ['klɪr] **1.** *adj.* transparent; allowing light through. (Adv: *clearly.* Comp: *clearer;* sup: *clearest.*) ♦ *The stems of the flowers could be seen through the clear glass vase.* ♦ *The shower curtain was clear plastic.* **2.** *adj.* bright; free from clouds or haze. (Adv: *clearly.* Comp: *clearer;* sup: *clearest.*) ♦ *On a clear day you can see the mountains from here.* ♦ *This morning it was cloudy, but now it is clear.* **3.** *adj.* without blemishes; without defects. (Comp: *clearer;* sup: *clearest.*) ♦ *The teenager wished for a clear face.* ♦ *The best grade of clear lumber has no knotholes.* **4.** *adj.* easy to understand; lucid; making perfect sense. (Adv: *clearly.* Comp: *clearer;* sup: *clearest.*) ♦ *The professor gave a clear explanation of the theory.* ♦ *The instructions were clear, but we still couldn't put the toy together.* **5.** *adj.* perceptible; easy to hear or see. (Adv: *clearly.* Comp: *clearer;* sup: *clearest.*) ♦ *The careless thief left clear fingerprints all over the house.* ♦ *Because it was so quiet, the sound of Dave's voice was quite clear.* **6.** *adj.* certain; easy to understand. (Adv: *clearly.* Comp: *clearer;* sup: *clearest.*) ♦ *The reason for the accident may never be clear.* ♦ *It is not clear why the inflation rate rose last month.* **7.** *adj.* without anything in the way. (Comp: *clearer;* sup: *clearest.*) ♦ *The way was clear, so we crossed the road.* ♦ *The cat had a clear path to the open door.* **8.** *adv.* completely; all the way. ♦ *The dog jumped clear over the sleeping cats.* ♦ *Bob swam clear to the other side of the pond.* **9. clear of something** *phr.* without touching something; away from something. ♦ *Please stand clear of the doors while the train is moving.* ♦ *Make sure the dog moves clear of the driveway before backing the car up.* **10.** *tv.* to move someone or something so that the way is clear ⑦. ♦ *The police cleared the onlookers from the accident area.* ♦ *Please clear all that stuff out of here!* ♦ *The police officer asked all of the people to clear the street so the fire engine could get through.* **11.** *tv.* to make an area empty by removing things or people. ♦ *Would you please clear the table.* ♦ *Clear the area!* **12.** *tv.* to chop down trees and remove stones from the land. ♦ *The woodcutters cleared the forest.* ♦ *The land had been cleared to make a pasture.* **13.** *tv.* to remove blame or guilt from someone. ♦ *The court cleared the suspect of all the charges.* ♦ *John's name was cleared as a result of the investigation.* **14.** *tv.* to remove something so one can start fresh. ♦ *Sherbet is served to clear the palate between courses of a meal.* ♦ *I took a walk to clear my mind of my worries.* **15.** *tv.* to make a certain amount of profit; to earn an amount of money. ♦ *The company cleared a million dollars last year.* ♦ *I hope we clear enough money to live off this year.* **16.** *tv.* [for a bank] to send a check successfully through procedures necessary to have the check paid. ♦ *The bank cleared your check yesterday.* ♦ *The torn check will not be cleared until the bank examines the signature.* **17.** *tv.* to give someone permission or authority to do something. ♦ *The manager cleared the trusted employee for classified projects.* ♦ *New employees must be cleared before working on certain projects.* **18.** *iv.* [for a check] to successfully travel through the procedures necessary to assure payment. ♦ *You cannot have the cash until the check clears.* ♦ *It took three days for the check from another state to clear.* **19.** *iv.* [for the sky] to become free of clouds. ♦ *The sky cleared and the sun came out.* ♦ *The weather forecaster said the sky would clear by noon, but it didn't.*

clearance ['klɪr əns] **1.** *n.* the authority or the permission to be able to do something. (No plural form in this sense.) ♦ *The employee was given security clearance to work on classified projects.* ♦ *The pilot did not have clearance to take off.* **2.** *n.* space between things that must pass one another without touching. (No plural form in this sense.) ♦ *The clearance under the bridge is twelve feet.* ♦ *There was not enough clearance on the staircase to move the mattress upstairs.* **3.** *n.* removing everything from a specific place. (No plural form in this sense.) ♦ *Clearance of the rubble after the earthquake took months.* ♦ *The convention ended with the clearance of the exhibits.* **4. clearance (sale)** *n.* a sale where a store is emptied of all goods or certain classes of goods. ♦ *They're holding a big clearance at the department store, and the low prices are advertised in the newspaper.* ♦ *Many stores hold clearances at the end of the year.* **5.** *adj.* <the adj. use of ④.> ♦ *I bought this dress at a clearance price.* ♦ *The furniture store had a clearance sale.*

clear-cut ['klɪr 'kʌt] *adj.* obvious; doubtless. ♦ *The solution to your problem is clear-cut.* ♦ *The suspect gave the police a clear-cut alibi.*

clearing ['klɪr ɪŋ] *n.* an open space, especially one that is surrounded by trees. ♦ *Two deer stepped into the clearing.* ♦ *Remains of a recent campfire were evident in the clearing.*

cleavage ['kliv ɪdʒ] **1.** *n.* a split or a gap; a crease. ♦ *What caused the cleavage in the pavement?* ♦ *A cleavage in the beam grew into a dangerous crack.* **2.** *n.* the space between a woman's breasts, when visible. ♦ *Mary thought the dress showed too much cleavage.* ♦ *Anne covered her cleavage with a shawl.*

cleave ['kliv] **1.** *tv.* to split something apart. (Pt: *cleaved,* cleft, or clove. Pp: *cleaved,* cleft or cloven.) ♦ *Bob cleaved the logs with his axe.* ♦ *The board was cleft by a sharp blow of the athlete's hand.* **2.** *iv.* to split apart; to split open. ♦ *The earth cleaved, leaving a deep and dangerous gorge.* ♦ *The beam cleaved during the earthquake.*

cleaver ['kliv ɚ] *n.* a big, sharp-bladed knife with a short handle, used for cutting or chopping meat. ♦ *The butcher raised his cleaver and chopped the meat.* ♦ *The meat cleaver is in a drawer in the kitchen.*

cleft ['klɛft] **1.** a pt and a pp of cleave. **2.** *adj.* partially cut; partially divided. ♦ *The baby was born with a cleft palate.* ♦ *A small tree grew out of the cleft rock.* **3.** *n.* a crack; a split; a crevice. ♦ *Wildflowers grew in narrow clefts in the earth.* ♦ *The earthquake left a wide cleft in the land.*

clemency ['klɛm ən si] *n.* mercy; lenient treatment of someone. (No plural form in this sense.) ♦ *The death-row inmate asked the governor for clemency.* ♦ *The governor granted clemency to the murderer.*

clench ['klɛntʃ] **1.** *tv.* to close something tightly, such as one's teeth or fists; to hold something together forcefully. ♦ *The baby clenched his fists and began to cry.* ♦ *Bill clenched his teeth and tried to control his rage.* **2.** *tv.* to grip someone or something tightly. ♦ *Mary clenched the letter in her hand as she read it aloud.* ♦ *The baby clenched my hand in fright upon seeing the dog.*

clenched ['klɛntʃt] *adj.* [of teeth or fists] closed tightly. ♦ *The angry customer spoke through clenched teeth.* ♦ *Bill hit his assailant with his clenched fist.*

clergy ['klɚdʒ i] *n.* ministers; priests; pastors. (No plural form in this sense. Number is expressed by *member(s) of the clergy.*) ♦ *The clergy conducted the memorial service.* ♦ *Bill and his wife are both members of the clergy.*

clergyman ['klɚdʒ i mən] *n., irreg.* a member of the clergy. (Pl: clergymen.) ♦ *The wedding was performed by a clergyman.* ♦ *The clergyman went to the dying man's bedside.*

clergymen ['klɚ dʒi mən] pl of clergyman.

clergyperson ['klɚ dʒi pɚ sən] *n.* a member of the clergy. ♦ *The wedding was performed by a clergyperson.* ♦ *The clergyperson went to the dying man's bedside.*

clergywoman ['klɚ dʒi wʊ mən] *n., irreg.* a female member of the clergy. (Pl: clergywomen.) ♦ *The wedding was performed by a clergywoman.* ♦ *The clergywoman went to the dying man's bedside.*

clergywomen ['klɚ dʒi wɪ mən] pl of clergywoman.

cleric ['klɛr ɪk] *n.* a minister; a priest; a pastor; a clergyman. ♦ *The cleric officiated at the funeral.* ♦ *The elderly cleric had been in the same parish for fifty years.*

clerical ['klɛr ɪ kəl] **1.** *adj.* of or about clerks; of or about the office work done by clerks: filing, typing, copying. (Adv: *clerically* [...ɪk li].) ♦ *Anne supported herself by doing clerical work.* ♦ *The job requires excellent clerical skills.* **2.** *adj.* of or about the clergy. (Adv: *clerically* [...ɪk li].) ♦ *The priest always wears his clerical collar in public.* ♦ *Tending the sick and needy is a clerical responsibility.*

clerk ['klɚk] **1.** *n.* an office worker, especially one who keeps track of records, files, and information. ♦ *The clerk spent the afternoon filing documents.* ♦ *Bill is a clerk at a law firm.* **2.** *n.* someone who helps customers with merchandise and sales; someone who works behind a counter and helps customers. ♦ *Mary could not find a clerk at the department store to help her.* ♦ *The clerk at the post office sold me some stamps.*

clever ['klɛv ɚ] **1.** *adj.* [of someone or a creature] capable of innovative and creative activities. (Adv: *cleverly.* Comp: *cleverer;* sup: *cleverest.*) ♦ *The clever children wrote a little play to perform for their parents.* ♦ *Our dog is clever enough to open the front door.* **2.** *adj.* innovative and creative. (Adv: *cleverly.* Comp: *cleverer;* sup: *cleverest.*) ♦ *The gymnast did some clever tricks.* ♦ *What a clever idea!*

cleverness ['klɛv ɚ nəs] *n.* the quality of being clever. (No plural form in this sense.) ♦ *Susan was known for her cleverness at fixing things.* ♦ *The child's cleverness got him into mischief.*

cliché [kli 'she] *n.* an overused expression that is trite and tiresome. ♦ *Stop speaking in tiresome clichés. Try to make sense.* ♦ *"A fine time was had by one and all" is a good example of a cliché.*

click ['klɪk] **1.** *n.* a short, quick noise; a snapping sound. ♦ *The shutter of the camera made a click as the picture was taken.* ♦ *The padlock closed with a click.* **2.** *tv.* to make a noise by snapping things together. ♦ *The dancer clicked the castanets in time to the music.* ♦ *The photographer clicked the shutter on the camera.* **3.** *iv.* to snap; to make a snapping noise. ♦ *The castanets clicked in time to the music.* ♦ *The camera clicked as the button was pushed.*

client ['klɑɪ ənt] *n.* someone served by a company or a professional, such as a lawyer. ♦ *The client was pleased with the advertising company's service.* ♦ *Mary is a real-estate agent who helps clients buy and sell homes.*

clientele [klɑɪ ən 'tɛl] *n.* the people a business serves. (From French. No plural form in this sense. Treated as plural.) ♦ *The fancy restaurant has a wealthy clientele.* ♦ *The clientele who come to this boutique are sophisticated.*

cliff ['klɪf] *n.* a high, steep wall of rock or earth. ♦ *The swimmer dove off the top of the cliff into the river below.* ♦ *The dangerous road ran along the edge of the cliff.*

cliffhanger ['klɪf hæŋ ɚ] *n.* a story with suspenseful elements that are not resolved until the very last part of the story. ♦ *The soap opera ends every day with a cliffhanger.* ♦ *Mary always tells absorbing cliffhangers at parties.*

climate ['klɑɪ mət] **1.** *n.* the typical weather conditions of a certain area. ♦ *The climate in this part of the country is very mild.* ♦ *The climate of the rain forest is tropical and steamy.* **2.** *n.* the general atmosphere, mood, attitude, or feeling. (No plural form in this sense.) ♦ *The emotional climate at the company after the layoffs was tense.* ♦ *The climate at the party became joyous when the presents were opened.*

climax ['klɑɪ mæks] **1.** *n.* the most exciting point in an event; the most intense part of an event; the most dramatic point of a story. ♦ *The climax of the week is when I get paid.* ♦ *Romantic music marked the climax of the love scene.* **2.** *iv.* to reach the most exciting point in an event. ♦ *The movie climaxed with Tom revealing he was really the child's father.* ♦ *The climax of the novel was on the next to the last page.*

climb ['klɑɪm] **1.** *n.* an ascent made with the hands and feet. ♦ *Our climb up the mountain was strenuous, but the scenery was gorgeous.* ♦ *The long climb up the ladder to the roof was scary.* **2.** *tv.* to ascend using the hands and feet. ♦ *The firefighter quickly climbed the ladder.* ♦ *The hikers slowly climbed the mountain.* **3.** *iv.* to go to a higher level. ♦ *Mary climbed from the position of secretary to that of vice president.* ♦ *The temperature climbed and climbed until it was almost too hot to breathe.*

climber ['klɑɪm ɚ] **1.** *n.* someone who hikes up mountains, cliffs, slopes, etc. ♦ *The climber bought special hiking equipment.* ♦ *The rock climbers went to Yosemite National Park.* **2.** *n.* a plant that grows up something. ♦ *The gardener planted a climber along the side of the house.* ♦ *The climber clung tightly to the post.*

clinch ['klɪntʃ] **1.** *n.* a strong hold on a person or thing. ♦ *The two students were locked in a clinch until the teacher broke them up.* ♦ *The wrestler got his opponent in a clinch.* **2.** *tv.* to settle something; to complete an agreement. ♦ *Tom clinched the deal with Mary's company. They will sign the contract tomorrow.* ♦ *That clinches the deal! We have reached an agreement!*

clincher ['klɪnt ʃɚ] *n.* something that settles an issue; a decisive event or point. ♦ *The rain was the clincher in the decision to cancel the picnic.* ♦ *What was the clincher that made you decide to come here?*

cling ['klɪŋ] *iv., irreg.* to stick to someone or something; to hold on tightly to someone or something; to remain attached to someone or something. (Pt/pp: **clung**.) ♦ *The tight clothing clung to the model's body.* ♦ *The child clung to his mother, begging her not to leave.*

clinging ['klɪŋ ɪŋ] *adj.* holding on; firmly attached. (Adv: *clingingly.*) ♦ *The clinging child begged to go with her mother.* ♦ *The workers removed the clinging vine from the brick wall.*

clinic ['klɪn ɪk] **1.** *n.* a medical office where minor medical problems are treated. ♦ *Mary took her sick child to the clinic.* ♦ *The nurse worked at a clinic in the inner city.* **2.** *n.* a seminar or instructional course for a specific topic. ♦ *The reporter took a writing clinic last summer.* ♦ *The young athletes attended a baseball clinic led by a famous player.*

clinical ['klɪn ɪ kəl] *adj.* of or about patient treatment, as opposed to experiments and theory. (Adv: *clinically* [...ɪk li].) ♦ *The researchers took a clinical approach to developing new drugs.* ♦ *Bob spoke to a clinical psychologist about his problems.*

clinician [klɪ 'nɪ ʃən] *n.* a doctor who works in clinical medicine. ♦ *The clinician thought the researcher's theories were unrealistic.* ♦ *A competent clinician examined the child's broken leg.*

clink ['klɪŋk] **1.** *n.* a light metallic sound; the sound of glass hitting glass. ♦ *Our glasses made a clink when we touched them together.* ♦ *I heard a clink when my ring fell into the sink.* **2.** *tv.* to cause things to make a sound as in ①. ♦ *We clinked our glasses together as we toasted Mike's success.* ♦ *My ring clinked the glass as I tapped the glass door.* **3.** *iv.* to make a light, ringing noise, like glasses being hit lightly together. ♦ *My ring clinked as I tapped the glass door.* ♦ *Glasses clinked at the end of the toast.*

clip ['klɪp] **1.** *n.* a device that holds sheets of paper together; a small device for gripping or holding things together. ♦ *The papers were held together with a metal clip.* ♦ *This clip marks where Chapter 7 begins.* **2.** *n.* a brief part of a film, book, magazine, or newspaper. ♦ *The movie theater showed clips of upcoming movies.* ♦ *My father mailed me a clip from the local newspaper.* **3.** *tv.* to hold things together with ①. ♦ *I clipped the memo to the book and placed it on the shelf.* ♦ *The papers were clipped together so they wouldn't get separated.* **4. clip off** *tv.* + *adv.* to cut something away [from something larger]. ♦ *The barber clipped off Mike's hair.* ♦ *Mary clipped a few roses off from the bushes.* **5.** *tv.* to strike or bump someone or something. ♦ *Bob's punch clipped Mike in the chin.* ♦ *The careless driver clipped our bumper.*

clipper ['klɪp ɚ] **1.** *n.* a fast sailing ship. ♦ *The clipper sailed around the cape at a good speed.* ♦ *A clipper has many sails.* **2. clippers** *n.* a tool used for cutting or shearing. ♦ *I trimmed the overgrown bushes with a pair of clippers.* ♦ *The barber used the clippers on Bill's hair.*

clique ['klik, 'klɪk] *n.* a small group of people who associate only with themselves and exclude others. (From French.) ♦ *The snobbish clique of popular students always made fun of David.* ♦ *Mary was not part of any clique at the high school.*

cliquish ['klik ɪʃ, 'klɪk ɪʃ] *adj.* snobbish; stuck-up. (Adv: *cliquishly.*) ♦ *The cliquish students ignored the new student at school.* ♦ *Some of the football players were known for their cliquish behavior.*

cloak ['klok] **1.** *n.* a long coat without sleeves; an outer garment like a cape. ♦ *The princess wore a long velvet cloak.* ♦ *The peasant wore a heavy cloak because it was very cold.* **2.** *n.* something that conceals someone or something. ♦ *Under the cloak of darkness, the spy slipped across the border into enemy territory.* ♦ *Underneath his cloak of sincerity, Mike was a cold-hearted man.* **3. cloak in** *tv.* + *prep. phr.* to clothe someone with ①. ♦ *The elegant model was* *cloaked in velvet.* ♦ *The mayor arrived at the airport cloaked in heavy tweed.* **4.** *tv.* to cover something up; to obscure something. ♦ *Mary cloaked her true feelings and smiled bravely.* ♦ *The spies cloaked their intentions in sincere talk.*

cloakroom ['klok rum] *n.* a small room where coats and hats are kept. ♦ *After class, the children went to the cloakroom to put on their coats.* ♦ *The guests hung their coats in the cloakroom.*

clobber ['klɑb ɚ] **1.** *tv.* to hit someone or something hard again and again; to beat someone. (Informal.) ♦ *The football players clobbered the quarterback.* ♦ *Susie clobbered Jimmy for messing with her toys.* **2.** *tv.* to win a game by a very large point difference. (Informal.) ♦ *The Dragons were clobbered 72–0 at their homecoming game.* ♦ *The visiting team clobbered the home team by 50 points.*

clock ['klɑk] **1.** *n.* a machine that keeps track of the time of day; a timepiece. ♦ *The clock struck five, and then the workers went home.* ♦ *The Smiths have a clock in every room of their house.* **2.** *tv.* to measure the length of time it takes for someone or something to do something; to measure a rate of speed. ♦ *Mike clocked his run at ten minutes.* ♦ *The police clocked the speeding car at seventy miles an hour.* **3. clock in** *iv.* + *adv.* to register or record an event at a certain time. ♦ *At the end of the marathon, the winner runner clocked in at 3 hours.* ♦ *I clocked in as soon as I arrived at work.*

clockwise ['klɑk wɑɪz] **1.** *adj.* moving in the direction that the hands of a clock move. ♦ *The model train circled the track in a clockwise direction.* ♦ *The party guests danced in a clockwise circle.* **2.** *adv.* in the direction that the hands of a clock move. ♦ *The actor turned clockwise and faced the audience.* ♦ *The children walked clockwise in a circle.*

clod ['klɑd] **1.** *n.* a lump of something, especially dirt or soil. ♦ *The plough turned up clods of rich, dark soil.* ♦ *The children tracked clods of dirt from the woods into the house.* **2.** *n.* a stupid-acting person; a clumsy person. (Derogatory.) ♦ *Bill is just a clod who is always breaking things.* ♦ *Don't be a clod. Mind your manners.*

clog ['klɔg] **1.** *n.* something that prevents something else from moving through a passage; a blockage. ♦ *The clog in the drain was caused by hair.* ♦ *The plumber fixed the clog in the toilet.* **2.** *n.* a heavy wooden shoe. ♦ *Clogs are wooden shoes often associated with the Dutch.* ♦ *Jane has a special pair of clogs for working in the garden.* **3.** *tv.* to block the flow of something; to block the passage of something. ♦ *The drain in the kitchen sink was clogged with grease.* ♦ *The accident clogged the highway and caused a traffic jam.* **4. clog (up)** *iv.* (+ *adv.*) to become blocked. ♦ *The sink clogged again.* ♦ *My ears clogged up when I had a cold.*

clogged ['klɔgd] *adj.* blocked. ♦ *The plumber fixed the clogged toilet.* ♦ *Clogged sinuses can be very painful.*

cloister ['klɔɪs tɚ] **1.** *n.* a covered walkway, especially that found in a monastery or a convent. ♦ *The monks walked quietly through the cloister.* ♦ *The cloister was lined with flowering plants.* **2.** *n.* a monastery; a convent. ♦ *The orphan entered the cloister as a young child.* ♦ *The manuscripts were copied in the cloister's library.* **3.** *tv.* to take someone to a quiet, secluded place to live. ♦ *The earl cloistered his family in his large castle.* ♦ *The old witch cloistered herself in a cave in the woods.*

close 1. ['klos] *adj.* near in space or time. (Adv: *closely.* Comp: *closer;* sup: *closest.*) ♦ *The closest store was only two blocks from our house.* ♦ *It's close to bedtime, so go brush your teeth.* **2.** ['klos] *adj.* near in spirit; dear; intimate; confidential. (Adv: *closely.* Comp: *closer;* sup: *closest.*) ♦ *Bill and Mary have become very close friends.* ♦ *Tom was very close to his grandmother before she died.* **3.** ['klos] *adj.* careful; strict. (Adv: *closely.* Comp: *closer;* sup: *closest.*) ♦ *The babysitter kept a close eye on the children.* ♦ *I paid close attention to my boss's instructions.* **4.** ['klos] *adj.* almost equal; almost the same. (Adv: *closely.* Comp: *closer;* sup: *closest.*) ♦ *It was a close game, but our team ultimately won in the last ten seconds.* ♦ *There is a close resemblance between Mary and her daughter.* **5.** ['kloz] *adj.* [of air] stuffy or stagnant. (Adv: *closely.* Comp: *closer;* sup: *closest.*) ♦ *The house had a close atmosphere.* ♦ *The air in the elevator was quite close.* **6.** ['klos] *adv.* near in space or time. ♦ *Don't stand so close to me!* ♦ *My birthday is getting close.* **7.** ['kloz] *tv.* to shut something. ♦ *I closed the windows when the thunderstorm began.* ♦ *Please close the door when you leave.* **8.** ['kloz] *tv.* to bring something to an end; to conclude something. ♦ *The professor closed the lecture with a funny story.* ♦ *We closed the evening with a toast to the happy couple.* **9.** ['kloz] *tv.* to complete an electrical circuit. ♦ *Susan turned the switch and closed the circuit.* ♦ *The lights went on when the circuit was closed.* **10.** ['kloz] *iv.* to shut. ♦ *The door closed with a loud bang, scaring everyone in the room.* ♦ *The curtain closed after the last act of the play.* **11.** ['kloz] *iv.* to end; to finish; to bring to an end; to conclude. ♦ *The book closed with a happy ending.* ♦ *The service closed with a hymn.* **12.** ['kloz] **close in (on)** *iv.* + *adv.* (+ *prep. phr.*) to bring near; to surround. ♦ *The gang closed in on their target.* ♦ *The emery was closing in, and we were frightened.* **13.** ['kloz] *n.* the end; the finish; the conclusion. ♦ *At the close of the day, Jane swept the studio and took out the trash.* ♦ *At the close of his life, Grandpa had no regrets.*

closed ['klozd] *adj.* not open; shut. ♦ *The closed door signaled that a meeting was taking place.* ♦ *The closed shutters prevented light from getting into the room.*

closefisted ['klos 'fɪst ɪd] *adj.* stingy; miserly; frugal. (Adv: *closefistedly.*) ♦ *The closefisted old man hoarded his money and possessions.* ♦ *The closefisted miser watched every cent she spent.*

close-knit ['klos 'nɪt] *adj.* [of people who are] held together by common interests, beliefs, or activities. ♦ *Bill comes from a large, close-knit family.* ♦ *The close-knit family spends a lot of time together.*

closeness ['klos nəs] **1.** *n.* being near someone or something in time or space. (No plural form in this sense.) ♦ *The closeness of the elevator to our room helped us go in and out easily.* ♦ *In August, the closeness of the beginning of the school year excited the children.* **2.** *n.* intimacy; familiarity. (No plural form in this sense.) ♦ *The sister and brother have always had a special closeness.* ♦ *The closeness of the family helped them face difficult times together.*

closet ['klɔz ɪt] **1.** *n.* a small room where clothing and personal objects are kept. ♦ *Mary hung her coat in the closet.* ♦ *Bill stored some boxes on the floor in his bedroom closet.* **2.** *adj.* secret; hiding; covert. ♦ *John is a closet alcoholic and always drinks in private.* ♦ *Susan was a closet poet who never shared her work.* **3. skeleton in the closet** *idiom* a hidden and shocking secret; a secret fact about oneself. ♦ *You can ask anyone about how reliable I am. I don't mind. I don't have any skeletons in the closet.* ♦ *My uncle was in jail for a day once. That's our family's skeleton in the closet.*

closeup ['klos əp] **1.** *n.* a picture taken with a camera very near the person or thing being photographed. ♦ *The closeup showed just our faces.* ♦ *The biology book contained a closeup of some bacteria.* **2.** *n.* a detailed examination; an in-depth report. (Figurative on ①.) ♦ *The news program featured a closeup on the effects of the earthquake.* ♦ *A closeup on the accused murderer was broadcast late in the evening.*

closure ['klo ʒɚ] *n.* the process of bringing something to an end. (No plural form in this sense.) ♦ *The committee tried to reach closure on the issue.* ♦ *The angry manager could not produce a sense of closure to the affair.*

clot ['klɑt] **1.** *n.* a lump of hardened or thickened liquid. ♦ *Dave was hospitalized because of a dangerous blood clot in his left leg.* ♦ *The wound was covered with a clot of blood.* **2.** *tv.* to cause something to form ①. ♦ *The old lady used a strange herb to clot the blood coming from the wound.* ♦ *A bit of lemon juice will clot the cream.* **3.** *iv.* to form ①. ♦ *This medicine can cause your blood to clot.* ♦ *Blood had begun to clot around the gaping wound.*

cloth ['klɔθ] **1.** *n.* woven material; woven fabric. (No plural form in this sense.) ♦ *The seamstress showed me a beautiful piece of cloth.* ♦ *The dress was made from imported cotton cloth.* **2.** *n.* a piece of woven material or fabric. ♦ *John wiped up the spill with a cloth.* ♦ *Anne polished the furniture with soft cloths.*

clothe ['kloð] **1.** *tv.* to put clothes on someone or something; to dress someone or something. ♦ *Susie clothed the doll in frilly dresses.* ♦ *The manager clothed himself in an expensive suit.* **2. clothes** ['kloz] *n.* clothing; garments. (Treated as plural.) ♦ *Bill bought new clothes when he got his new job.* ♦ *After playing in the dirt, the children had to change their clothes.*

clothes hanger ['kloz hæŋ ɚ] *n.* a wire, metal or plastic frame with a hook. ♦ *The closet was full of empty clothes hangers.* ♦ *The dry cleaner hangs our clothes on clothes hangers.*

clothesline ['kloz lɑɪn] *n.* a length of rope positioned so as to hold drying clothing. ♦ *A clothesline stretched across the yard from the house to the tree.* ♦ *I hung the sheets on the clothesline to dry.*

clothespin ['kloz pɪn] *n.* a wooden or plastic clip used to attach damp clothes to a clothesline. ♦ *Wooden clothespins dotted the clothesline.* ♦ *The clothes were hung on the line with clothespins.*

clothier ['kloð i ɚ] *n.* someone who makes or sells clothes. ♦ *John bought his suit from an expensive clothier.* ♦ *The largest clothier in town was having a sale.*

clothing ['kloð ɪŋ] *n.* clothes; garments. (No plural form in this sense.) ♦ *Mary's clothing consists mainly of blue jeans and T-shirts.* ♦ *The children were instructed to keep their clothing clean.*

cloud ['klɑʊd] **1.** *n.* a large white or gray mass in the sky, made of water vapor. ♦ *The sky filled with clouds, and it began to rain.* ♦ *A fluffy white cloud floated through the sky above us.* **2.** *n.* a large billow of smoke or dust; a visible mass of gas or particles that hover or move in the air. ♦ *A cloud of dust rose from the trunk when I opened it.* ♦ *The burning building was enveloped in a cloud of smoke.* **3.** *tv.* to obscure something; to hide something. ♦ *Alcohol clouded John's judgment.* ♦ *Moisture clouded the windshield.* **4. have one's head in the clouds** *idiom* to be unaware of what is going on. ♦ *"Bob, do you have your head in the clouds?" asked the teacher.* ♦ *She walks around all day with her head in the clouds. She must be in love.* **5. under a cloud (of suspicion)** *idiom* suspected of something. ♦ *Someone stole some money at work, and now everyone is under a cloud of suspicion.* ♦ *Even the manager is under a cloud.*

cloudburst ['klɑʊd bɚst] *n.* a thunderstorm; a short, pounding rain. ♦ *The cloudburst soaked everyone on the golf course.* ♦ *The steamy day ended in a cloudburst.*

cloudy ['klɑʊd i] **1.** *adj.* [of sky] having clouds. (Adv: *cloudily.* Comp: *cloudier;* sup: *cloudiest.*) ♦ *We lay on our backs in the field and gazed at the cloudy sky.* ♦ *A cloudy sky doesn't always mean that it's going to rain.* **2.** *adj.* not able to be seen through clearly. (Figurative on ①. Adv: *cloudily.* Comp: *cloudier;* sup: *cloudiest.*) ♦ *The old glass was cloudy with dirt.* ♦ *The water was a bit cloudy, and no one would drink it.*

clout ['klɑʊt] **1.** *n.* a blow; an act of striking someone or something. ♦ *Mary gave the mugger a good clout with her backpack.* ♦ *Bob was bruised by a clout to his face during the fight.* **2.** *n.* power; influence. (No plural form in this sense. Informal.) ♦ *The scheming business owner had a lot of clout with the mayor.* ♦ *The performer used her clout to get a good table at the restaurant.* **3.** *tv.* to hit someone; to strike someone. ♦ *Anne clouted the mugger with her fist.* ♦ *The bully clouted Bill in the face.*

clove ['klov] **1.** a pt of cleave. **2.** *n.* the dried flower of a certain tropical tree, used as a spice. ♦ *I added a few cloves to the ham before I baked it.* ♦ *The kitchen smelled of cinnamon and cloves.* **3.** *n.* one segment of a bulb of garlic. ♦ *The recipe called for one clove of crushed garlic.* ♦ *A bulb of garlic has many cloves.*

cloven ['klov ən] **1.** a pp of cleave. **2.** *adj.* partially divided; partially split. (Used mainly in reference to hooves.) ♦ *Goats have cloven hooves.* ♦ *We found the print of a cloven hoof in the snow.*

clover ['klov ɚ] *n.* a kind of herb having three-part circular leaves. (No plural form in this sense.) ♦ *The lawn was covered with wild clover.* ♦ *The children picked the pink and white clover from the field.*

cloverleaf ['klov ɚ lif] **1.** *n., irreg.* the small round petals that are the leaves of clover, usually appearing in groups of three, but sometimes of four. (Pl: *cloverleafs* or cloverleaves.) ♦ *The kids looked for cloverleaves with four parts.* ♦ *The material for the curtains had a pattern of cloverleaves.* **2.** *n., irreg.* a junction between an expressway and another road. (Seen from above, this junction looks like a cluster of four cloverleaves ①.) ♦ *The map showed the cloverleaf exit from the highway.* ♦ *The cloverleaf took up many acres of what had been farmland.*

cloverleaves ['klov ɚ livz] a pl of cloverleaf.

clown ['klɑʊn] **1.** *n.* a performer in funny costume and makeup who tries to make people laugh. ♦ *The clowns at the circus hit each other with rubber bats.* ♦ *A clown entertained the kids at the birthday party.* **2.** *n.* someone who is always making jokes and trying to make other people laugh. ♦ *Bill is such a clown, even when I'm trying to be serious.* ♦ *My office is full of clowns who are always making jokes.*

clownish ['klaʊn ɪʃ] *adj.* like a clown; funny; not serious. (Adv: *clownishly.*) ♦ *The clownish behavior made the children laugh.* ♦ *Stop acting clownish and be serious!*

club ['klʌb] **1.** *n.* a large, thick, blunt wooden stick. ♦ *The police officer carried a club for protection.* ♦ *The injured hiker used a club as a cane.* **2. (golf) club** *n.* a long, metal mallet used in the game of golf. ♦ *Bill left his clubs at the golf course.* ♦ *Old golf clubs sometimes had wooden handles.* **3.** *n.* a nightclub; a place where liquor is served or where people can dance. ♦ *Let's go to the club and dance.* ♦ *The club was having a special on mixed drinks.* **4.** *n.* an organization or group of people who meet to pursue a specific activity. ♦ *The Smiths joined a bird-watching club.* ♦ *The club began its meeting at eight o'clock.* **5.** *n.* one of four different symbols found in a deck of playing cards; the symbol "♣." ♦ *The club looks something like clover.* ♦ *The rules of the card game required that the clubs be set aside.* **6.** *tv.* to beat someone or something with ①. ♦ *The police officers clubbed the thief.* ♦ *The mail carrier clubbed the attacking dog.*

clubfeet ['klʌb fit] pl of clubfoot.

clubfoot ['klʌb 'fʊt] *n.* a deformed foot. (Pl: clubfeet.) ♦ *The baby was born with a clubfoot.* ♦ *The orthopedic surgeon specialized in treating clubfeet.*

clubhouse ['klʌb haʊs] **1.** *n., irreg.* the place where people belonging to a particular club meet. (Pl: [...haʊ zəz].) ♦ *The clubhouse was packed the night of the awards banquet.* ♦ *A special pass is needed to get into the team's clubhouse.* **2.** *n., irreg.* a room or building used for social purposes and recreation. ♦ *The party was held in the clubhouse at the condominium.* ♦ *The Smiths play cards at the clubhouse each week.* **3.** *n., irreg.* a tree house; an outdoor playhouse for children. ♦ *The children made a clubhouse in the backyard.* ♦ *The tent served as a clubhouse for the boys.*

cluck ['klʌk] **1.** *n.* the short noise made by a hen. ♦ *The hen gave a loud cluck as the farmer chased it with an axe.* ♦ *We heard clucks coming from the barn and knew a fox must have gotten in.* **2.** *iv.* to make a short noise like ①; [for a hen] to make ①. ♦ *The hens in the barn clucked furiously at the sight of the fox.* ♦ *Anne clucked disapprovingly when she heard what we had done.*

clue ['klu] *n.* a hint; some information that will help to solve a problem. ♦ *Bill gave his friend a clue to the secret.* ♦ *I don't have a clue about how to solve the problem.*

clump ['klʌmp] **1.** *n.* a group of something; a mass of something. ♦ *The plow turned up huge clumps of earth.* ♦ *The bulldozer moved the huge clumps of cement.* **2.** *tv.* to group things together; to gather something into clumps ①. ♦ *I clumped all the tools together in one box.* ♦ *Susan clumped the soil around the roots of the plant.* **3. clump together** *iv.* + *adv.* to group together; to gather together. ♦ *The mice clumped together at one end of the cage.* ♦ *The buffalo clumped together to keep warm.* **4.** *iv.* to walk very heavily or loudly. ♦ *John clumped down the stairs in his work boots.* ♦ *The elephant clumped slowly along the path.*

clumsily ['klʌm zɪ li] *adv.* awkwardly. ♦ *The skinny teenager danced clumsily at the party.* ♦ *The inexperienced clerk clumsily wrapped my purchase.*

clumsiness ['klʌm zi nəs] *n.* awkwardness. (No plural form in this sense.) ♦ *Maybe ballet lessons will rid you of your clumsiness.* ♦ *The clerk at the store that sells crystal was fired because of clumsiness.*

clumsy ['klʌm zi] *adj.* awkward; uncoordinated; likely to trip or stumble on something. (Adv: *clumsily.* Comp: *clumsier;* sup: *clumsiest.*) ♦ *The clumsy waiter dropped my dinner on the floor.* ♦ *I feel so clumsy when I'm ice skating.*

clung ['klʌŋ] pt/pp of cling.

cluster ['klʌs tɚ] **1.** *n.* a group of people or things. ♦ *A cluster of strawberries grew in the field.* ♦ *A cluster of people appeared at the scene of the accident.* **2.** *n.* two or more speech consonant sounds in sequence. ♦ *The sequence* pr *is an example of a consonant cluster.* ♦ *There are three consonants in the cluster* spr. **3.** *tv.* to group people or things together somewhere. ♦ *The mourners clustered themselves around the grave.* ♦ *Jane clustered the chairs near the table.* **4.** *iv.* to group together; to come together near something. ♦ *The mourners clustered around the grave.* ♦ *Wildflowers clustered near the trunk of the tree.*

clutch ['klʌtʃ] **1.** *n.* a part of a machine that controls the coupling of two moving parts. ♦ *Some cars have a pedal that operates the clutch.* ♦ *Our car has an automatic clutch.* **2.** *n.* a [tight] grip; a [firm] hold. ♦ *Jimmy had a tight clutch on my arm during the scary parts of the movie.* ♦ *Anne held on to the banister with a firm clutch as she descended the stairs.* **3.** *tv.* to hold something tightly; to grip something tightly. ♦ *The crying child clutched her father around the neck.* ♦ *The speaker nervously clutched his notes.* **4. in(to) someone's clutches** *idiom* in the control of someone who has power or authority over someone else. ♦ *Snow White fell into the clutches of the evil witch.* ♦ *Once you're in my clutches, I'll ruin you.*

clutter ['klʌt ɚ] **1.** *n.* a mess; disorder. (No plural form in this sense.) ♦ *My office is filled with useless clutter.* ♦ *Clutter filled the room so that it was difficult to walk through.* **2.** *tv.* to mess up a place; to place things about without plan or order. ♦ *Papers and junk cluttered the office.* ♦ *Old furniture cluttered the attic.*

coach ['kotʃ] **1.** *n.* someone who is in charge of a team; someone who trains players on a team. ♦ *The coach made the team practice for three hours every day.* ♦ *The team members admired their coach.* **2.** *n.* someone who trains someone else. ♦ *Jane's voice coach advised her not to talk until her throat healed.* ♦ *Bill has a coach to help him stay on his diet.* **3.** *n.* an enclosed carriage, typically pulled by horses. ♦ *The coach stopped in front of the theater, and the passengers got out.* ♦ *The duke's coach was pulled by four horses.* **4.** *n.* a railway coach ③ where passengers ride in seats. (As opposed to cars where people can eat or lie down to sleep.) ♦ *The rail coach had uncomfortable seats.* ♦ *We took a railway coach across the country.* **5.** *n.* a cross-country bus; a touring bus. ♦ *Susan traveled by coach from Detroit to Miami.* ♦ *The tour coach took the passengers to their hotels.* **6.** *n.* the tourist section of an airplane; the cheapest class of air travel. (No plural form in this sense.) ♦ *I always fly in coach.* ♦ *The flight attendant offered coffee to the passengers sitting in coach.* **7.** *adv.* [traveling] in the coach section of an airplane. ♦ *Dave* *couldn't imagine traveling coach all the way to Europe!* ♦ *Flying coach is more affordable than going first class.* **8.** *tv.* to instruct someone in a sport, skill, or craft. ♦ *Anne coached Mary on her public speaking skills.* ♦ *Susan coached her children on appropriate table manners.*

coaching ['kotʃ ɪŋ] **1.** *n.* the profession or hobby of training people. (No plural form in this sense.) ♦ *Coaching a football team takes lots of energy.* ♦ *My history teacher makes extra money from coaching on weekends.* **2.** *n.* advice, instruction, or education. (No plural form in this sense.) ♦ *The children received coaching on good manners from their parents.* ♦ *The tennis pro gave me some coaching on how to improve my game.*

coagulate [ko 'æg jə let] **1.** *tv.* to cause something to thicken or make clots. ♦ *This chemical will coagulate only certain types of blood.* ♦ *Heat is used to coagulate the mixture.* **2.** *iv.* to thicken; to become thicker; to clot. ♦ *The blood coagulated, and the wound began to heal.* ♦ *Because of his disease, Bill's blood would not coagulate when he was wounded.*

coagulation [ko ɑg jə 'le ʃən] *n.* the thickening of something, such as blood or pudding. (No plural form in this sense.) ♦ *The coagulation of blood is a necessary part of healing a wound.* ♦ *Cooling the pudding caused its rapid coagulation.*

coal ['kol] **1.** *n.* a black mineral made of carbon, used as fuel. (No plural form in this sense.) ♦ *The furnace was fueled with coal.* ♦ *The servant hauled coal into the cellar.* **2. coals** *n.* hot, glowing chunks of burning ① or charcoal. ♦ *The old furnace was filled with hot coals.* ♦ *When the barbecue had lots of glowing coals, Lisa put the meat on it.*

coalesce [ko ə 'les] *iv.* to come together; to be brought together. ♦ *Three old political parties coalesced to form a new one.* ♦ *Our days of planning coalesced into a perfect evening.*

coalition [ko ə 'lɪ ʃən] *n.* a union or alliance of things or people. ♦ *The tenants and the landlord formed a coalition to make the property better.* ♦ *A coalition of laywers defended the workers in court.*

coarse ['kors] **1.** *adj.* having a rough texture; not smooth. (Adv: *coarsely.* Comp: *coarser;* sup: *coarsest.*) ♦ *I put some lotion on my coarse skin.* ♦ *The sandpaper was coarse enough to remove the varnish from the furniture.* **2.** *adj.* vulgar; crude. (Adv: *coarsely.* Comp: *coarser;* sup: *coarsest.*) ♦ *Bill's coarse manners were becoming quite offensive.* ♦ *Swearing is a coarse habit.*

coast ['kost] **1.** *n.* land alongside a large body of water, especially alongside the sea. ♦ *The coast along the lake was lined with houses.* ♦ *We walked along the coast and watched the sunset.* **2.** *iv.* to glide without using energy. ♦ *The kids coasted on their bicycles down the hill.* ♦ *The car ran out of gas and coasted downhill to a stop.*

coastal ['kos təl] *adj.* along the coast; on the coast. (Adv: *coastally.*) ♦ *San Francisco is a coastal city on the Pacific Ocean.* ♦ *Coastal weather is often cooler than the weather inland.*

coaster ['kost ɚ] *n.* a small dish placed under a bottle, can, or glass, to protect a wooden surface beneath from moisture. ♦ *Mary put her glass on a coaster so that the table's finish wouldn't be ruined.* ♦ *Coasters protect a surface from stains from wet glasses.*

Coast Guard ['kost gɑrd] *n.* a military service that patrols the coast. ♦ *The Coast Guard rescued the capsized boaters.* ♦ *Bill joined the Coast Guard when he was 18.*

coastline ['kost lɑɪn] *n.* the coast; the shoreline. ♦ *The coastline was lined with charming cottages.* ♦ *Volunteers picked up litter from along the coastline.*

coat ['kot] **1.** *n.* a heavy item of clothing, worn over one's other clothes during cold weather. ♦ *Each winter I buy a new wool coat.* ♦ *The crossing guard's coat is waterproof.* **2.** *n.* the fur of an animal; the pelt of an animal. ♦ *The dog's coat was matted with dirt.* ♦ *My little kitten has a fluffy coat of white fur.* **3.** *n.* a layer of something, such as paint, that covers a surface. ♦ *I scraped three coats of paint from the old table.* ♦ *Mary put a coat of paint on the fence.* **4.** *tv.* to cover the surface of something with a layer of something. ♦ *The workers coated the roof with tar.* ♦ *The beach was coated with oil from the shipwreck.*

coating ['kot ɪŋ] *n.* a coat; a layer of something that covers a surface. (No plural form in this sense.) ♦ *The candy had a chocolate coating.* ♦ *The old windows had a thick coating of grime.*

coauthor ['ko to ɚ] **1.** *n.* one of a number of authors who work together. ♦ *The coauthors split the royalties from the book.* ♦ *One coauthor had to proofread the entire book.* **2.** *tv.* to write something along with someone else. ♦ *The writers who coauthored the book no longer speak to each other.* ♦ *Tom and Susan coauthored the research report.*

coax ['koks] *tv.* to urge someone to do something by being pleasant and agreeable. ♦ *I had to coax Jimmy into eating his vegetables.* ♦ *Jane coaxed her parents to see the movie.*

cob ['kɑb] See corncob.

cobbler ['kɑb lɚ] **1.** *n.* someone who repairs shoes. (See also shoemaker.) ♦ *The cobbler said my shoes were beyond repair.* ♦ *The cobbler put new soles on the shoes.* **2.** *n.* a kind of dessert, usually having a fruit filling and a crust on top. (No plural form in this sense.) ♦ *John made cherry cobbler with ice cream for dessert.* ♦ *Anne served rhubarb cobbler after dinner.*

cobblestone ['kɑb əl ston] **1.** *n.* a round stone used for paving streets. ♦ *The historic street was lined with cobblestones.* ♦ *The horse had difficulty walking on the cobblestones.* **2.** *adj.* consisting of ①; paved with ①. ♦ *The historic neighborhood had cobblestone streets.* ♦ *A cobblestone path led to the village cemetery.*

cobra ['ko brə] *n.* a kind of poisonous snake from Africa or Asia. ♦ *The cobra's bite can kill its prey rapidly.* ♦ *A cobra sank its fangs into the dog and killed it.*

cobweb ['kɑb wɛb] *n.* a spider's web, especially when old and filled with dust. ♦ *The attic was filled with cobwebs.* ♦ *Mary wiped the cobwebs from the corners of the room.*

cocaine [ko 'ken] *n.* a highly addictive drug made from the leaves of a South American bush. (No plural form in this sense.) ♦ *It is easy to get addicted to cocaine.* ♦ *Doctors treat many people who are addicted to cocaine.*

cock ['kɑk] **1.** *n.* a rooster; a male chicken. ♦ *The oldest cock ruled the barnyard.* ♦ *A cock strutted across the barnyard.* **2.** *tv.* to pull back the hammer of a gun so that it is ready to shoot. ♦ *Tom cocked the gun in preparation for firing.* ♦ *The gun was cocked and ready.* **3.** *tv.* to turn the head to the side or at an angle. ♦ *Bill cocked his head as* *he listened attentively to the lecture.* ♦ *The puppy cocked its head and whined for food.*

cock-a-doodle-doo ['kɑk ə dud l du] *n.* the sound of a crowing rooster. (Pl in *-s.*) ♦ *I heard the rooster's cock-a-doodle-doo and knew it was time to get up.* ♦ *The cock-a-doodle-doo of the rooster woke me up at 5:00 A.M.*

cockeyed ['kɑk ɑɪd] **1.** *adj.* cross-eyed. (Informal.) ♦ *Don't give me that cockeyed look! That's rude!* ♦ *The cockeyed puppy looked adorable.* **2.** *adj.* tilted; turned to the side; askew; not straight. (Informal.) ♦ *Mary adjusted the cockeyed painting.* ♦ *Bill's cap was cockeyed.* **3.** *adj.* stupid; foolish; silly. (Informal.) ♦ *Going fishing with no bait is cockeyed.* ♦ *Bill came up with some cockeyed plan to make a million dollars.*

cockfight ['kɑk fɑɪt] *n.* a fight between two roosters that are wearing sharp spurs. ♦ *Cockfights are illegal in most parts of the United States.* ♦ *The police arrested the men who arranged the cockfight in the abandoned building.*

cockiness ['kɑk i nəs] *n.* impertinence; conceit; excessive pride. (No plural form in this sense.) ♦ *The man's cockiness fooled people into believing he was competent.* ♦ *In his cockiness, Bill insulted everyone else at the meeting.*

cockpit ['kɑk pɪt] **1.** *n.* an enclosure for a cockfight. ♦ *The cocks fought bitterly in the cockpit.* ♦ *An illegal cockpit was found in a vacant warehouse.* **2.** *n.* the place from which a sailboat is piloted. ♦ *No one was in the cockpit, and the boat drifted off course.* ♦ *The sailor steered the boat from the cockpit.* **3.** *n.* the cabin at the front of an airplane where the pilot operates the airplane. ♦ *The pilot talked from the cockpit to the passengers.* ♦ *The passengers could not see into the cockpit but listened to the pilot over the loudspeaker.*

cockroach ['kɑk rotʃ] *n.* a large, nocturnal insect that infests houses. ♦ *Jane looked for cockroaches before renting the apartment.* ♦ *Bill called the exterminator when he found a cockroach in his bedroom.*

cocksure ['kɑk 'sʊr] **1.** *adj.* very sure of something; very confident of something. (Adv: *cocksurely.*) ♦ *Mary has always been cocksure of her musical abilities.* ♦ *Bill was cocksure that he would win the scholarship.* **2.** *adj.* too confident of something. (Adv: *cocksurely.*) ♦ *The cocksure student failed to study enough for the test and failed.* ♦ *The cocksure customer swaggered to the head of the line.*

cocktail ['kɑk tel] **1.** *n.* a mixed alcoholic drink. ♦ *We had a few cocktails at the bar last night.* ♦ *The Smiths served cocktails at their dinner party.* **2.** *n.* an appetizer of specially prepared seafood or fruit. (Always in compounds.) ♦ *Shrimp cocktail makes a good appetizer to any meal.* ♦ *Most fruit cocktail comes right out of a can.*

cocky ['kɑk i] *adj.* conceited; overly proud; impertinent; arrogant. (Adv: *cockily.* Comp: *cockier;* sup: *cockiest.*) ♦ *The cocky student didn't study and was surprised to learn he failed the test.* ♦ *The cocky athlete skipped football practice.*

cocoa ['ko ko] **1.** *n.* a powder made by processing *cacao* seeds; powdered chocolate. (No plural form in this sense.) ♦ *The hot chocolate was made from cocoa, milk, and sugar.* ♦ *I can't make brownies because I have no cocoa.* **2.** *n.* a drink made by mixing powdered chocolate with milk and sugar. (No plural form in this sense.) ♦ *Cocoa tastes great after a day of skiing.* ♦ *The hot cocoa made the little child sleepy.*

coconut ['ko kə nət] **1.** *n.* a large, round nut that grows on some species of palm tree. ♦ *The workers harvested coconuts from the palm trees.* ♦ *The meat of the coconut is used for salads or baking.* **2.** *adj.* made with or flavored with ①. ♦ *Coconut cake is my favorite.* ♦ *Mary ate the coconut donut and asked for another.*

cocoon [kə 'kun] **1.** *n.* the protective shell in which a caterpillar wraps itself while it transforms into a butterfly or a moth. ♦ *A little cocoon was attached to the fallen branch.* ♦ *The butterfly emerged from its cocoon and flew away.* **2.** *n.* a protective shelter; a room or a house that someone never leaves. (Figurative on ①.) ♦ *The teenager escaped his parents in the cocoon of his bedroom.* ♦ *Anne's apartment is more of a cocoon than a place to live. She hardly ever leaves it.* **3.** *tv.* to provide protection like a cocoon ② for oneself. (Takes a reflexive object.) ♦ *The hermit had cocooned himself in the cottage in the woods.* ♦ *John never ventured into the dangerous city at night, but cocooned himself inside his safe apartment.*

cod ['kɑd] **1.** *n., irreg.* a kind of edible fish that lives in cold water. (Pl: *cod.*) ♦ *Cod used to be extremely plentiful near the eastern coast of Canada.* ♦ *The fishermen went out on their boats to fish for cod.* **2.** *n.* the flesh of ①, eaten as food. (No plural form in this sense.) ♦ *The restaurant offered a special on fried cod.* ♦ *Lisa bought some cod and took it home for dinner.*

coddle ['kɑd l] *tv.* to pamper someone; to do everything that someone wants. ♦ *You coddle your children too much. They are getting spoiled.* ♦ *The private nurse coddled the sick patient.*

code ['kod] **1.** *n.* a secret writing system; a system of symbols used for communication. ♦ *The spy sent his message in a secret code.* ♦ *The spy deciphered the code easily.* **2.** See **area code**. **3.** See **zip code**. **4.** *n.* a set of laws; a set of rules. ♦ *The boarding school had a code of conduct for its students.* ♦ *The apartment building violated the city's safety code.* **5.** *tv.* to translate a message into ①. ♦ *The army general coded the message in case the enemy intercepted it.* ♦ *The cryptographer coded the message by typing each word backwards.* **6.** *tv.* to mark an object with a special number or symbol. ♦ *The customs officer coded each piece of baggage with a mysterious symbol.* ♦ *The electrical wires were coded by color.*

coded ['kod ɪd] *adj.* written in a system of symbols; written in code. ♦ *The coded message arrived safely with the President.* ♦ *The children wrote in a coded script so their parents couldn't read their plans.*

codeine ['ko din] *n.* a powerful drug used to relieve pain and to cause sleep. (No plural form in this sense.) ♦ *The dentist gave Bill some codeine for his pain.* ♦ *The codeine put the patient to sleep.*

codfish ['kɑd fɪʃ] **1.** *n., irreg.* cod, a kind of edible fish that lives in cold water. (Pl: *codfish.*) ♦ *Codfish live in the northern part of the ocean.* ♦ *The local fishermen caught fewer codfish this year than they did last year.* **2.** the meat of ①. (No plural form in this sense.) ♦ *The restaurant served codfish in a stew.* ♦ *David bought some codfish and ate it for dinner.*

codicil ['kɑd ə səl] *n.* a clause added to a will. ♦ *A codicil added to my uncle's will made me his only heir.* ♦ *The judge ruled the codicil invalid, and the money went to charity.*

codify ['kɑd ə fɑɪ] *tv.* to write out rules; to arrange rules into an organized system. ♦ *The manager codified the procedure so others would do it the same way.* ♦ *This is the most complicated case to occur since our laws were codified.*

coed AND **co-ed** ['ko ɛd] **1.** *n.* a female student in a school for both sexes. (Some people object to this term. From coeducational *student.)* ♦ *Several co-eds joined the chemistry club.* ♦ *Mary was the only coed in the chess club.* **2.** *adj.* educating both males and females in the same school; [of a school, program, or residence] for or serving both males and females. (From coeducational.) ♦ *The private school was once a school for girls, but now it is coed.* ♦ *Many students live in co-ed dormitories.*

coeducational [ko ɛdʒ ə 'ke ʃə nəl] *adj.* of, about, or providing education for both sexes in the same school. (Adv: *coeducationally.*) ♦ *The courts forced the college to develop coeducational athletic programs.* ♦ *Dave preferred to enroll in a coeducational institution.*

coerce [ko 'ɚs] *tv.* to force someone into doing something. ♦ *The terrorists coerced the government into meeting their demands by taking hostages.* ♦ *The bully coerced Billy to give him his allowance.*

coercion [ko 'ɚ ʃən] *n.* forcing one to do something against one's will. (No plural form in this sense.) ♦ *The terrorists used coercion to get their way.* ♦ *I took piano lessons only after threats and coercion from my parents.*

coexist [ko ɛg 'zɪst] *iv.* to exist at the same time, peaceably. ♦ *Those two nations have never coexisted peacefully.* ♦ *Many political movements coexisted during the tumultuous period.*

coffee ['kɔf i] **1.** *n.* the roasted beans of the coffee tree, either whole or ground. (No plural form in this sense.) ♦ *The coffee in the canister smelled fresh.* ♦ *The farmer grew many acres of coffee.* **2.** *n.* a drink made from roasted, ground coffee beans. (No plural form in this sense.) ♦ *Bill needs a cup of coffee each morning before he can work.* ♦ *Coffee contains a stimulant called caffeine.*

coffee break ['kɔf i brek] *n.* a rest period during which coffee or some other refreshment is enjoyed. ♦ *The workers took a coffee break each morning.* ♦ *Bill and his boss went on a coffee break together.*

coffeepot ['kɔf i pɑt] *n.* a pot used to brew and serve coffee. ♦ *Lisa brewed the coffee in a new coffeepot.* ♦ *I washed the coffeepot after drinking all of the coffee.*

coffee table ['kɔf i 'te bəl] *n.* a low table that usually sits in front of a sofa, used for serving food or drink, such as coffee or tea, and to hold decorations, books, or magazines. ♦ *Please don't put your feet on the coffee table!* ♦ *I will have to take the old newspapers off the coffee table before our guests come.*

coffin ['kɔf ən] *n.* a box in which the body of a dead person is buried. ♦ *The soldier was buried in a simple pine coffin.* ♦ *The funeral ended as the coffin was lowered into the ground.*

cog ['kɔg] *n.* one of the teeth on the edge of a gear. ♦ *One of the cogs was broken and had jammed the machine.* ♦ *The mechanic had to weld a new cog to the gear.*

cogent ['ko dʒənt] *adj.* convincing; compelling. (Adv: *cogently.*) ♦ *The defense attorney's cogent argument was persuasive.* ♦ *The teenager made a cogent appeal for a higher allowance.*

cogitate ['kɑdʒ ɪ tet] *iv.* to think deeply; to think hard about something; to ponder. ♦ *The minister suggested that I take the time to cogitate about my problem.* ♦ *The elderly man watched the sunset and cogitated peacefully.*

cognac ['kɔn jæk] *n.* a brandy made from wine from area around Cognac, France. (No plural form in this sense.) ♦ *After dinner, the hostess served a delicious cognac.* ♦ *The sauce on the meat was flavored with cognac.*

cognizance ['kɑg nɪ zəns] *n.* awareness; knowledge; perception. (No plural form in this sense.) ♦ *The lost tourist had no cognizance of where he was.* ♦ *Cognizance of the problem is the first step to solving it.*

cognizant ['kɑg nɪ zənt] *adj.* knowing about someone or something; being aware of someone or something. ♦ *Bill is not cognizant of my financial problems.* ♦ *The teacher was not cognizant of the cheating going on in class.*

coherent [ko 'hɪr ənt] *adj.* clear; lucid; logical; making sense. (Adv: *coherently.*) ♦ *The debater presented a coherent argument.* ♦ *The student had a coherent explanation for being late.*

cohesion [ko 'hi ʒən] **1.** *n.* the property of stickiness. (No plural form in this sense.) ♦ *The tape has no cohesion left, so you will have to get a new piece.* ♦ *The strength of cohesion produced by this cement is quite high.* **2.** *n.* the property that holds ideas together. (Figurative on ①. No plural form in this sense.) ♦ *You argument has little cohesion and can easily be overturned.* ♦ *Since Bob's paper had no cohesion and merely listed facts, he received a failing grade.*

cohort ['ko hort] **1.** *n.* an accomplice; a companion. ♦ *The two cohorts were inseparable.* ♦ *Bill and his cohort go to a baseball game every week.* **2.** *n.* a group of people sharing some characteristic. ♦ *A cohort of algebra students met to work on the difficult assignment together.* ♦ *This year's cohort of transfer students went to a meeting with the dean.*

coil ['koɪl] **1.** *n.* a length of something, such as rope, wound into a stack of circular loops. ♦ *Coils of rope sat on the deck of the ship.* ♦ *The electrician set the coil of wire on the workbench.* **2.** *n.* a circular loop. ♦ *A coil of rope slipped around my foot and nearly tripped me.* ♦ *Place a coil over the post and tie it tight.* **3.** *tv.* to wrap something around and around into a circle. ♦ *The vines coiled the tree trunk.* ♦ *The snake coiled itself around its prey.* **4.** *iv.* to form into a circular loop. ♦ *The woman's bracelet coiled around her wrist.* ♦ *The colorful garland coiled around the post.*

coin ['koɪn] **1.** *n.* a piece of money made from metal. ♦ *Bill's pocket was full of coins.* ♦ *The vending machine only accepted coins.* **2.** *tv.* to stamp metal into money; to make money from metal. ♦ *On our vacation, we toured a mint where they coined money.* ♦ *The huge machine was designed to coin money.* **3.** *tv.* to invent a new word; to make up a new word. ♦ *The advertising company coined a new word to use to name the new product.* ♦ *Many new scientific words are coined each year.*

coincide [ko ɪn 'sɑɪd] **1.** *iv.* [for two or more things] to happen at the same time. ♦ *Our vacations coincided, so we traveled together.* ♦ *Our trips to town coincided each week, so we saw each other often.* **2. coincide with** *iv.* + *prep. phr.* [for something] to happen at the same time as something else. ♦ *My vacation coincided with Mary's, so we took* *a trip together.* ♦ *My trip to the bank coincided with John's trip to the bakery.*

coincidence [ko 'ɪn sɪ dəns] *n.* [for two or more things] to happen the same way or at the same time, by chance; [for two or more people] to share remarkable similarities, by chance. ♦ *It was a coincidence that Anne and I were at the same resort at the same time.* ♦ *It was just a coincidence that Bill and Mary had the same last name.*

coincidental [ko ɪn sɪ 'dɛn təl] *adj.* [of an event] happening purely by chance. (Adv: *coincidentally.*) ♦ *Bill and Mike had a coincidental meeting at the hardware store.* ♦ *It was purely coincidental that we both walked to work today.*

coke ['kok] **1.** *n.* the substance that is left after gas has been removed from coal, which—when burned—gives off very strong heat. (No plural form in this sense.) ♦ *The factory has an oven that produces coke from ordinary coal.* ♦ *The coke is used to produce steel.* **2. Coke** *n.* Coca-Cola™, the protected trade name of a soft drink. ♦ *There were about twenty commercials for Coke during the baseball game.* ♦ *Mary ordered a Coke with her meal.* **3.** *n.* a generic name for cola drinks. (Never capitalized. Objected to as an infringement of the Coca-Cola™ trade name.) ♦ *The waitress forget to bring our cokes with our meal.* ♦ *We stopped for a coke because we were so thirsty.* **4.** *n.* cocaine. (Slang. No plural form in this sense.) ♦ *The drug user was heavily addicted to coke.* ♦ *The police found coke in the suspect's apartment.*

colander ['kɑl ən dɚ] *n.* a bowl with holes in the bottom and sides, used for draining wet foods. ♦ *I dumped the pasta in the colander to drain after it was cooked.* ♦ *Bob used a colander to rinse the vegetables.*

cold ['kold] **1.** *n.* a physical state or property of something having relatively less heat. (No plural form in this sense.) ♦ *The cold of the stone floor was unbearable on our bare feet.* ♦ *Cold is really the absence of heat.* **2.** *n.* cold weather; a lack of warmth in the outside temperature. (No plural form in this sense.) ♦ *I can't stand the cold of winter, so I moved to Florida.* ♦ *When I came in from the cold, I sat near the fireplace.* **3.** *n.* a common illness that causes sneezing, a runny nose, a sore throat, etc. ♦ *I caught a cold from one of my coworkers.* ♦ *Mary's cold started with a sore throat.* **4.** *adj.* not hot; not having heat. (Comp: *colder;* sup: *coldest.*) ♦ *We lit a fire to warm up the cold room.* ♦ *The cold vegetables had to be heated for dinner.* **5.** *adj.* uncomfortable from not having heat. (Adv: *coldly.* Comp: *colder;* sup: *coldest.*) ♦ *I got very cold swimming in the lake.* ♦ *Mary put on another sweater because she felt cold.* **6.** *adj.* mean; unfriendly; unpleasant. (Adv: *coldly.* Comp: *colder;* sup: *coldest.*) ♦ *The cold clerk didn't help me find what I was looking for.* ♦ *Jane can be very cold to people she does not know.* **7. out cold** *idiom* unconscious. ♦ *The boxer knocked his opponent out cold.* ♦ *The robbery victim was knocked out cold.*

cold-blooded ['kold 'blʌd ɪd] **1.** *adj.* [of an animal] having a variable body temperature that is the same as the outside air. ♦ *Lizards are all cold-blooded creatures.* ♦ *The zoo kept the cold-blooded snakes in a room at a constant temperature.* **2.** *adj.* cruel; without mercy; without compassion. (Figurative on ①. Adv: *cold-bloodedly.*) ♦ *The judge punished the criminal for the cold-blooded crime.* ♦ *The child's cold-blooded behavior worried his parents.*

cold cuts ['kold kəts] *n.* slices of meat and cheese that are ready to eat. ♦ *I made a sandwich from assorted cold cuts.* ♦ *Bill buys his cold cuts at the local delicatessen.*

coldness ['kold nəs] **1.** *n.* the quality of lacking heat. (No plural form in this sense.) ♦ *We lit a fire to combat the coldness of the room.* ♦ *Bill can't stand the coldness of winter.* **2.** *n.* unfriendliness. (No plural form in this sense.) ♦ *David's coldness prevented him from making friends easily.* ♦ *Mary's shyness was misinterpreted as coldness.*

cold sore ['kold sor] *n.* a blister on the lip or in the mouth. ♦ *Mary bought some ointment for her cold sore.* ♦ *John's cold sore burned when he ate spicy foods.*

coleslaw ['kol slɔ] *n.* a salad made of chopped cabbage. (No plural form in this sense.) ♦ *Susan served coleslaw at the barbecue.* ♦ *Bill shredded the cabbage for the coleslaw, and Jane made the dressing.*

colic ['kɑl ɪk] *n.* a sharp abdominal pain; a sharp pain in the intestines. (No plural form in this sense.) ♦ *The baby is crying because it has colic.* ♦ *Our baby has colic after almost every meal.*

coliseum [kɑl ə 'si əm] *n.* a large arena or stadium where sporting events or concerts are held. ♦ *The remains of a huge coliseum can be seen in Rome.* ♦ *Athletic events were held at the coliseum in ancient times.*

collaborate [kə 'læb ə ret] *iv.* [for two or more people] to work together on something. ♦ *The composers collaborated on the musical. One wrote the lyrics, and the other wrote the music.* ♦ *The prisoners collaborated to plan the escape.*

collaboration [kə læb ə 're ʃən] *n.* working together on something. (No plural form in this sense.) ♦ *The author and editor succeeded in their collaboration on the book.* ♦ *This project is the result of the collaboration of many researchers.*

collaborator [kə 'læb ə ret ɚ] *n.* someone who collaborates [with someone]. ♦ *Anne and her collaborator meet frequently to discuss their work.* ♦ *Bill could not cooperate with his collaborator, so he finished the project alone.*

collage [kə 'lɑʒ] *n.* a piece of art made of fragments, pasted together. ♦ *The children made collages from pictures cut out of old magazines.* ♦ *Making collages was popular as an art form during the 1920s.*

collapse [kə 'læps] **1.** *n.* an instance of falling down; the total ruin of something; a deflating of something. (No plural form in this sense.) ♦ *People were penniless after the bank's collapse.* ♦ *After the collapse of his business, John declared bankruptcy.* **2.** *n.* a mental or physical breakdown of a person. ♦ *Mary was in the hospital for a month after her collapse.* ♦ *John's collapse was caused by stress.* **3.** *iv.* to fall down; to become ruined; to deflate. ♦ *The house made of blocks collapsed when Jimmy struck it.* ♦ *The building collapsed during the earthquake.* **4.** *iv.* to fail; to break down completely. ♦ *Jane's marriage collapsed after only three years.* ♦ *When negotiations collapsed, the union called a strike.* **5.** *tv.* to cause something to fall down; to deflate, crush, or fold something. ♦ *Bill collapsed the lawn chairs and put them in the garage.* ♦ *I collapsed the box that the present was packed in.*

collapsible [kə 'læps ɪ bəl] *adj.* capable of being broken down, folded up, or deflated. (Adv: *collapsibly.*) ♦ *We* *bought collapsible chairs for the patio.* ♦ *This table is collapsible and can be put in the car.*

collar ['kɑl ɚ] **1.** *n.* the part of a piece of clothing that wraps around the neck. ♦ *Jane buttoned the top button of her collar.* ♦ *The collar of Bill's shirt is too tight.* **2.** *n.* a band around the neck of an animal. ♦ *The cat wore a collar with identification.* ♦ *I attached the leash to the dog's collar and took it for a walk.* **3.** *tv.* to catch someone; to arrest someone. (Slang.) ♦ *The police collar about 30 shoplifters each week.* ♦ *Mary finally collared the child who was stealing her newspapers.*

collarbone ['kɑl ɚ bon] *n.* the bone that goes from the shoulder blade to the breastbone; the clavicle. ♦ *Jimmy broke his collarbone when he fell from the tree.* ♦ *A broken collarbone takes a long time to heal.*

collate ['ko let] **1.** *tv.* to arrange pages in the proper order. ♦ *The secretary collated and distributed the reports.* ♦ *The sophisticated copier collated the pages as it copied them.* **2.** *iv.* to arrange [things] in the proper order. ♦ *Our office copier collates but does not staple.* ♦ *Susan laid out all the papers and began to collate.*

collateral [kə 'læt ɚ əl] *n.* an asset used as security for a loan; an asset pledged as payment for a loan in case the borrower does not pay the loan as promised. (No plural form in this sense.) ♦ *The Smiths used valuable jewelry as collateral for their loan.* ♦ *I have no collateral, so the bank probably won't give me a loan.*

colleague ['kɑl ig] *n.* an associate who works with someone. ♦ *I often go to dinner with my colleagues after work.* ♦ *Bill is on good terms with all his colleagues.*

collect [kə 'lɛkt] **1.** *tv.* to ask for or to receive money that is owed. ♦ *The landlord collects the rent every month.* ♦ *The office manager also collected the delinquent accounts.* **2.** *tv.* to gather items together; to bring items together. ♦ *I collected the dirty dishes from around the house and placed them in the sink.* ♦ *The old newspapers were collected and thrown away.* **3.** *tv.* to get or keep control of oneself or one's senses after a big surprise or change of emotion. ♦ *Jane was nervous before her speech, so she took a deep breath and collected her wits.* ♦ *After the shocking news, Bill left the room to collect himself.* **4.** *tv.* to accumulate something or a class of things as a hobby. ♦ *Anne collects stamps.* ♦ *John began to collect insects in a jar when he was 10.* **5.** *iv.* to assemble somewhere; to gather together somewhere. ♦ *The mourners collected around the graveside.* ♦ *The family began to collect in the dining room when it was time to eat.* **6.** *adj.* [of a telephone call] charged to the person or number called. ♦ *Bill made a collect call to his parents.* ♦ *Mary did not accept the collect call.* **7.** *adv.* charging a telephone call to the person or telephone number called. ♦ *Bill called his parents collect.* ♦ *Mary became angry when David called her collect.*

collection [kə 'lɛk ʃən] **1.** *n.* the collecting of things. (No plural form in this sense.) ♦ *How long did the collection of all those insects take?* ♦ *Garbage collection in our town occurs once a week.* **2.** *n.* the donation of money during a church service or some other types of meetings. ♦ *The choir sang a hymn, and then came the collection.* ♦ *The collection did not bring in much money this week.* **3.** *n.* a group of similar objects gathered together. ♦ *The museum has a large collection of 19th-century sculpture.* ♦ *Bob took his insect collection to school.* **4.** *n.* a group of people. ♦ *Mary has an interesting collection of friends.* ♦ *Mike and Susan had an odd collection of guests at their wedding.* **5.** *n.* the (amount of) money donated during a church service or in a similar setting. ♦ *How much is the collection?* ♦ *This week's collection will go to help feed the poor.*

collective [kə 'lɛk tɪv] **1.** *n.* a farm operated by a group of workers, under central governmental control. ♦ *The students visited a collective when they were in Russia.* ♦ *Most of the food they ate was grown on the collective.* **2.** *adj.* joined together; total; as a group. (Adv: *collectively.*) ♦ *In its collective wisdom, the board decided to abandon the project.* ♦ *Using our collective resources, we made a bid for the property.*

collector [kə 'lɛk tɚ] **1.** *n.* someone who collects things, either as a hobby or as an investment. ♦ *Bill is a collector of Chinese art.* ♦ *The collector bought antiques from a local dealer.* **2.** *n.* someone who collects money that is owed. ♦ *Jane's job as a collector involves making people pay their bills.* ♦ *The collector left several messages about the delinquent account.*

college ['kɑl ɪdʒ] *n.* a school of higher education; an undergraduate division within a university. ♦ *Mary went to a large college after she graduated from high school.* ♦ *Bill's counselor helped him apply to colleges.*

collegiate [kə 'lidʒ ɪt] *adj.* of or about college or college life. (Adv: *collegiately.*) ♦ *Bill was not talented enough to play collegiate sports.* ♦ *Studying is a large part of collegiate life.*

collide [kə 'lɑɪd] *iv.* [for two or more things or people] to crash into each other. ♦ *Two planes collided in midair.* ♦ *Mary collided with her boss in the hallway.*

collie ['kɑl i] *n.* a kind of long-haired dog. ♦ *Lassie was a talented collie that appeared in many movies.* ♦ *I combed the collie's long hair.*

collision [kə 'lɪ ʒən] *n.* a forceful crash. ♦ *The collision was caused when the brakes on Bill's car failed.* ♦ *An explosion resulted from the collision of the oil tanker and the truck.*

colloquial [kə 'lo kwi əl] *adj.* [of words or a language style] best suited for conversation rather than writing; informal; appropriate for everyday speech and writing but not for formal speech and writing. (Adv: *colloquially.*) ♦ *Bob deletes colloquial expressions from his formal writing.* ♦ *The speech was given in a colloquial tone.*

colloquialism [kə 'lo kwi ə lɪz əm] *n.* a word or phrase that is part of informal, everyday speech. ♦ *Many of the catchy phrases we use each day are colloquialisms.* ♦ *A formal report should not include colloquialisms.*

cologne [kə 'lon] *n.* a scented liquid, used in the manner of perfume. ♦ *Mary's cologne smelled like lavender.* ♦ *I received a vial of cologne for my birthday.*

Colombia [kə 'lʌm bi ə] See Gazetteer.

colon ['ko lən] **1.** *n.* the punctuation mark ":" used to introduce a list of things. ♦ *The proofreader inserted a colon between the clauses.* ♦ *A colon often introduces a list of things.* **2.** *n.* the lower part of the large intestine. ♦ *The patient was diagnosed with cancer of the colon.* ♦ *Many people have ulcers in their colons.*

colonel ['kɚ nəl] *n.* a military rank above a lieutenant colonel and below a brigadier general, equal to captain in the U.S. Navy. ♦ *Two officers were promoted to colonel* *in the army last week.* ♦ *The colonel stood solemnly at his court martial, awaiting his fate.*

colonial [kə 'lon i əl] **1.** *adj.* of or about a colony. (Adv: *colonially.*) ♦ *Britain had colonial holdings in Africa until the 1960s.* ♦ *The colonial government worked with the local governments to keep order.* **2.** *adj.* of or about the original thirteen colonies of the United States. (Adv: *colonially.*) ♦ *In colonial days, men often wore fancy wigs.* ♦ *Colonial unrest worsened with the imposition of unfair taxes.* **3.** *n.* a person who lives in a colony. ♦ *The colonials supported the revolt against the mother country.* ♦ *Some towns in New England are named for famous colonials.*

colonialism [kə 'lon i ə lɪz əm] *n.* the practice of one country setting up settlements of its citizens in another country. (No plural form in this sense.) ♦ *Almost all of Africa was affected by colonialism in the last century.* ♦ *Some of the European languages spread around the world in the period of colonialism.*

colonist ['kɑl ə nəst] *n.* someone who settles in a colony. ♦ *Colonists established settlements near the coast.* ♦ *The colonists soon found that tobacco was a profitable crop.*

colonize ['kɑl ə nɑɪz] *tv.* [for a country] to create settlements of its own citizens in a foreign country or territory. ♦ *Several European nations sought to colonize the African continent.* ♦ *Our forebears colonized this country.*

colony ['kɑl ə ni] **1.** *n.* an area in one country settled and ruled by another country. ♦ *England had thirteen colonies in America.* ♦ *Algeria was once a colony of France.* **2.** *n.* the place where a social group of ants or termites live and breed. ♦ *A colony of ants lives under our driveway.* ♦ *There is a colony of termites that is destroying our house!*

color ['kʌl ɚ] **1.** *n.* the quality of light that causes people to see the differences among red, orange, yellow, blue, green, purple, etc.; a hue; a tint. ♦ *John was unable to see much color in the dark photograph.* ♦ *Mary decorated the room with bright colors.* **2.** *tv.* to give something ①; to paint or draw with ①. ♦ *John colored the drawing of the horse green.* ♦ *Mary colored the picture with crayons.* **3.** *tv.* to affect something; to give a nuance to something; to influence something. (Figurative on ②.) ♦ *Anne colored her remarks with clever allusions.* ♦ *The day's events were colored by the loud argument.* **4.** *iv.* to blush; to look flushed. ♦ *Jane colored when she said something embarrassing to her.* ♦ *Bill's face colored in the fresh air.* **5.** *iv.* to draw with crayons or colored markers. ♦ *The children colored all afternoon.* ♦ *Susie colored with a new box of crayons.* **6.** *adj.* [of photographic film or video recording] using all the colors, not just black and white. ♦ The Wizard of Oz *is both a color film and a black-and-white one.* ♦ *The color photographs turned out better than the black-and-white ones.* **7. show one's (true) colors** *idiom* to show what one is really like or what one is really thinking. ♦ *Whose side are you on, John? Come on. Show your colors.* ♦ *It's hard to tell what Mary is thinking. She never shows her true colors.* **8. with flying colors** *idiom* easily and excellently. ♦ *John passed his geometry test with flying colors.* ♦ *Sally qualified for the race with flying colors.*

Colorado [kɑ lə 'rɑ do] See Gazetteer.

coloration [kəl ə 're ʃən] *n.* the coloring of someone or something; the way something is colored. (No plural form in this sense.) ♦ *The horse had a unique coloration.* ♦ *The coloration of chameleons changes with their environment.*

color-blind ['kʌl ɚ blɑɪnd] **1.** *adj.* of or about people who cannot see the difference between certain colors, usually red and green. ♦ *Dave's clothes never match because he is color-blind.* ♦ *The color-blind driver could not tell the difference between green and red.* **2.** *adj.* ignoring differences of skin color or race. (A reinterpretation of ①.) ♦ *Little children are color-blind—they accept everyone impartially.* ♦ *Mike claimed he was color-blind, but his actions seemed prejudiced.*

colored ['kʌl ɚd] *adj.* having color. ♦ *The kids made collages with colored paper.* ♦ *The candlesticks were made of colored glass.*

colorful ['kʌl ɚ fʊl] **1.** *adj.* full of color; brightly colored. (Adv: *colorfully* ['kʌl ɚ fli].) ♦ *The room was decorated with colorful streamers.* ♦ *Colorful flowers dotted the landscape.* **2.** *adj.* interesting; exciting. (Adv: *colorfully* ['kʌl ɚ fli].) ♦ *Bill has many colorful friends who lead exotic lives.* ♦ *We enjoyed the lecturer's colorful narrative during the slide show.*

colorless ['kʌl ɚ ləs] **1.** *adj.* without color. (Adv: *colorlessly.*) ♦ *I applied a colorless ointment to my rash.* ♦ *Water is colorless.* **2.** *adj.* boring; dreary. (Adv: *colorlessly.*) ♦ *Bob's colorless lecture caused the audience to become sleepy.* ♦ *The boring reporter read the news in a colorless way.*

colossal [kə 'lɑs əl] *adj.* very large; huge; enormous. (Adv: *colossally.*) ♦ *Buying computers for an entire company is a colossal expense.* ♦ *Bill made a colossal mistake when he bought that used car.*

colossus [kə 'lɑs əs] **1.** *n.* something that is very large. ♦ *That skyscraper is a colossus among the neighboring buildings.* ♦ *We flew to Europe on a colossus of an airplane.* **2.** *n.* someone or something that is very important. (Figurative on ①.) ♦ *The composer was a colossus among his peers.* ♦ *Professor Jones is a colossus in the field of mathematics.*

colt ['kolt] *n.* a young male horse. (Compare with **filly**.) ♦ *The colt galloped across the moors.* ♦ *The young colt was afraid of its owner.*

Columbus Day [kə 'lʌm bəs de] *n.* a national holiday in the United States, celebrating Christopher Columbus's landing in the New World on October 12, 1492. ♦ *On Columbus Day, we remember the voyage of Christopher Columbus.* ♦ *Columbus Day is a holiday where I work.*

column ['kɑl əm] **1.** *n.* a supporting pillar. ♦ *The columns supporting the house were in decay.* ♦ *The architecture class studied the characteristics of different columns.* **2.** *n.* a series of words or symbols arranged in a line from top to bottom. ♦ *I only read the first column of the lengthy magazine article.* ♦ *The computer aligned the columns of text.* **3.** *n.* a narrow, vertical strip of writing from top to bottom on a page. ♦ *I wrote my grocery list in one column down the page.* ♦ *The accountant's ledger was a series of columns.* **4.** *n.* a newspaper article, especially one written by a columnist. (On ②.) ♦ *The editor wrote a weekly column for the newspaper.* ♦ *The column was about proper treatment of children.*

columnist ['kɑl əm nəst] *n.* someone who writes commentary for newspapers on a regular basis. ♦ *The columnist's favorite topic was politics.* ♦ *Humor was the columnist's greatest strength.*

coma ['kom ə] *n.* a deep, unconscious state; a very long period of unconsciousness. ♦ *The accident victim went into a coma and never recovered.* ♦ *Bob's diabetic coma resulted from a lack of insulin.*

comatose ['kɑm ə tos] *adj.* unconscious. (Adv: *comatosely.*) ♦ *The patient was comatose when she arrived in the emergency room.* ♦ *Eventually, the comatose patient revived.*

comb ['kom] **1.** *n.* a toothed strip of plastic or the like, used for arranging hair. ♦ *Run a comb through your hair before you leave.* ♦ *My hair was so tangled the comb would not go through it.* **2.** *n.* the red growth on top of the heads of chickens and turkeys. ♦ *The turkey's comb bobbed as it waddled through the barnyard.* ♦ *The chicken has a bright red comb.* **3.** *tv.* to arrange one's hair with a comb. ♦ *Comb your hair before dinner.* ♦ *Bill combed his hair in the car while driving to his office.* **4.** *tv.* to thoroughly look through an area for something; to search for something. ♦ *We combed the house for the missing key.* ♦ *The police combed the mall looking for the suspect.*

combat 1. ['kɑm bæt] *n.* a war; a conflict; a battle. (No plural form in this sense.) ♦ *The soldiers were trained for combat.* ♦ *The fighting children were locked in combat on the basement floor.* **2.** ['kɑm bæt] *adj.* <the adj. use of ①.> ♦ *The soldiers were unprepared for combat stress.* ♦ *Bill wore combat boots to the rock concert.* **3.** [kəm 'bæt] *tv.* to fight someone or something; to battle someone or something. (Pt/pp: *combated.*) ♦ *Bill used a club to combat the intruder.* ♦ *The doctors are combating cancer with new drugs.*

combatant [kəm 'bæt nt] *n.* one of the parties in a fight. ♦ *All the combatants shot at each other.* ♦ *The combatants stopped fighting when one fell, wounded.*

combative [kəm 'bæt ɪv] *adj.* prone to fighting; argumentative. (Adv: *combatively.*) ♦ *The combative children are always fighting.* ♦ *Bill's combative attitude got him into trouble at work.*

combination [kɑm bɪ 'ne ʃən] **1.** *n.* the process of combining. (No plural form in this sense.) ♦ *The combination of ammonia and bleach creates dangerous fumes.* ♦ *The safe combination of the two chemicals required a complicated chemical process.* **2.** *n.* something that is made by an act of combining. ♦ *John wears some pretty strange-looking combinations of clothing.* ♦ *This is a combination of two powerful ingredients.* **3.** *n.* the sequence of numbers needed to open a combination lock. ♦ *Bill couldn't remember the combination to the lock on the shed.* ♦ *The safe requires a combination to be opened.* **4. combination lock** *n.* a lock that opens by turning a dial to a secret combination of numbers or by pressing numbered buttons in the proper sequence, instead of with a key. ♦ *I have a combination lock on the door to my shed.* ♦ *I keep losing my keys, so I use combination locks wherever I can.*

combine 1. ['kɑm bɑɪn] *n.* a farm machine that harvests seeds from stalks as it is driven across a field. ♦ *The farmer drove the combine over the fields.* ♦ *The bank gave me a loan to buy a new combine for my farm.* **2.** ['kɑm bɑɪn] *tv.* to drive ① through a field to harvest grain. ♦ *Frank combined his fields last week.* ♦ *The farmer hired extra help to combine the corn.* **3.** [kəm 'bɑɪn] *tv.* to join two or more things together. ♦ *I combined the eggs with the flour mixture.* ♦ *The mechanic combined the nuts and bolts by putting them in one box.* **4.** [kəm 'bɑɪn] *iv.* to unite; to join. ♦ *The army and navy units combined to fight the war.* ♦ *Mary's and Bob's businesses combined to form a new company.*

combined [kəm 'bɑɪnd] *adj.* united; joined. ♦ *The combined forces were no match for enemy troops.* ♦ *Jane did a combined workout of aerobics and weightlifting at the gym.*

combo ['kɑm bo] *n.* a group of jazz musicians. (From *combination.* Pl in *-s.*) ♦ *The combo was great—especially the trombone player.* ♦ *A local combo played at the senior center.*

combustibility [kəm bəs tə 'bɪl ɪt i] *n.* the quality of being likely to catch fire or to burst into flames. (No plural form in this sense.) ♦ *The combustibility of dry leaves is quite high.* ♦ *Oily rags have a great deal of combustibility.*

combustible [kəm 'bʌs tə bəl] **1.** *adj.* likely to catch fire; flammable. (Adv: *combustibly.*) ♦ *Gasoline is highly combustible.* ♦ *Insulation should be made from material that is not combustible.* **2.** *n.* an object or substance that is likely to catch fire. ♦ *Combustibles should be stored separately from the other materials.* ♦ *Gasoline is a very volatile combustible.*

combustion [kəm 'bʌs tʃən] *n.* burning; catching fire. (No plural form in this sense.) ♦ *The quick combustion of the dry forest was caused by the lack of rain.* ♦ *Good combustion in damp air is difficult to achieve.*

come ['kʌm] **1.** *iv., irreg.* to move towards someone or something; to move toward the location of the speaker. (Pt: came; pp: *come.*) ♦ *Come here, please.* ♦ *Please come over to my house at three o'clock.* **2.** *iv., irreg.* to arrive; to get somewhere. ♦ *We came to the theater early to get a good seat.* ♦ *When Bill comes, we'll eat.* **3. come to** *iv., irreg. + prep. phr.* to arrive at or reach a critical or important state or point. (Figurative an ②.) ♦ *I came to the point where I couldn't stand my job anymore.* ♦ *If it comes to having to buy a new car, that's what we'll do.* **4. come in** *iv., irreg. + prep. phr.* to be available in. ♦ *This carpet comes in blue, gray, or black.* ♦ *This dress does not come in a size two.* **5.** *iv., irreg.* [for goods that have been purchased] to arrive equipped in a certain way. ♦ *This computer comes with a full-color terminal and a fax modem.* ♦ *This vacuum cleaner comes fully equipped.* **6. come to** *iv., irreg. + prep. phr.* [for something] to arrive in someone's thinking. ♦ *It suddenly came to me that Bill hates his job.* ♦ *I forgot what I was going to say. Oh well, it will come to me later.* **7. come from** *iv., irreg. + prep. phr.* to be from a certain place; to have been in a certain place before one's arrival. (When used in the past tense, it usually refers to the place where one has just been. When used in the present tense, it usually refers to the place where one lived for a long time or where one was raised.) ♦ *I came from St. Louis by bus; that is, I just arrived from St. Louis on a bus.* ♦ *I come from St. Louis; that is, I was born and raised in St. Louis.* **8. come by something** *idiom* to find or get something. ♦ *How did you come by that haircut?* ♦ *Where did you come by that new shirt?* **9. come down in the world** *idiom* to lose one's social position or financial standing. ♦ *Mr. Jones has really come down in the world since he lost his job.* ♦ *If I were unemployed, I'm sure I'd come down in the world, too.*

comedian [kə 'mid i ən] *n.* a performer who tells jokes and funny stories. ♦ *The comedian was known for his very funny jokes.* ♦ *Bill wanted to be a comedian, but he wasn't funny.*

comedienne [kə mid i 'ɛn] *n.* a female performer who tells jokes and funny stories. ♦ *The comedienne made a lot of jokes about men.* ♦ *The club hired a comedienne to attract female patrons.*

comedy ['kɑm ə di] **1.** *n.* a funny play or movie; the opposite of a tragedy. ♦ *Bill likes to see plays if they are comedies.* ♦ *The popular TV show was a comedy about elderly women.* **2.** *n.* the element of movies or plays that make people laugh; the opposite of tragedy. (No plural form in this sense.) ♦ *The comedy of the play lay in the clever dialogue.* ♦ *Timing is very important in comedy.*

comely ['kʌm li] *adj.* attractive; pretty; handsome. (Comp: *comelier;* sup: *comeliest.*) ♦ *The knight swept the comely princess onto his horse.* ♦ *Mary's child was quite gentle and comely.*

come-on ['kʌm ɔn] **1.** *n.* an attempt to get someone's attention or attract customers. ♦ *The offer of a free vacation was an insincere come-on.* ♦ *The car dealer offered free car washes for a year as a come-on.* **2.** *n.* an attempt to flirt with someone. ♦ *Asking someone's sign of the zodiac is a weak come-on.* ♦ *The flight attendant ignored the passenger's come-on.*

comet ['kɑm ət] *n.* a rapidly moving bright celestial body with a long tail. ♦ *The comet swung around the sun and headed out into space.* ♦ *A huge comet is approaching the earth and will be visible for a few months.*

comeuppance [kəm 'ʌp əns] *n.* a rebuke; a well-deserved rebuke. (No plural form in this sense.) ♦ *The nasty child got his comeuppance from the principal.* ♦ *The arrogant club president got her comeuppance when she was voted out of office.*

comfort ['kʌm fɚt] **1.** *n.* being at ease; the state of being free from pain. (No plural form in this sense.) ♦ *The nurse tended to the comfort of the patients.* ♦ *The luxurious comfort of the hotel was very relaxing.* **2.** *n.* the lessening of pain, suffering, grief, and sorrow. (No plural form in this sense.) ♦ *Jane was grateful for the comfort given by her friends in her time of need.* ♦ *We provided Bill with emotional comfort when his father died.* **3.** *n.* someone or something who provides relief from pain, suffering, grief, and sorrow. ♦ *Your understanding is a real comfort to me.* ♦ *Mary was a comfort to her widowed friend.* **4.** *tv.* to provide someone ease and contentment. ♦ *John comforted his crying child.* ♦ *The preacher tried to comfort the mourners at the funeral.* **5. cold comfort** *idiom* no comfort or consolation at all. ♦ *She knows there are others worse off than her, but that's cold comfort.* ♦ *It was cold comfort to the student that others had failed as he had done.*

comfortable ['kʌm fɚ tə bəl] **1.** *adj.* [of something] providing physical comfort. (Adv: *comfortably.*) ♦ *This is a very comfortable chair.* ♦ *Lisa moved to a more comfortable seat.* **2.** *adj.* physically and mentally at ease. (Adv: *comfortably.*) ♦ *Are you comfortable with the plan?* ♦ *I am not comfortable in this cold room. Please turn on the heat.*

comforter ['kʌm fɚ tɚ] *n.* a thick quilt used as a bed covering. ♦ *The children burrowed under the fluffy comforter.* ♦ *The bed was covered with a warm comforter.*

comfy ['kʌm fi] *adj.* comfortable. (Informal. Adv: *comfily.* Comp: *comfier;* sup: *comfiest.*) ♦ *This couch is so comfy!* ♦ *Make yourself comfy, and I'll get you something to drink.*

comic ['kɑm ɪk] **1.** *adj.* funny; humorous. (Adv: *comically* [...ɪk li].) ♦ *John's speech provided a comic interlude between the boring lectures.* ♦ *The comic movie lifted our spirits.* **2.** *n.* a pamphlet printed in color on cheap paper where stories are told in **comic strips**. (From *comic book.*) ♦ *Bill has a big stack of old comics in his attic.* ♦ *When my grandfather was a little boy, he bought a new comic every time he got ten cents.* **3.** *n.* a comedian. ♦ *The comic stood in front of the microphone but forgot his jokes.* ♦ *There was a stand-up comic at the nightclub.* **4. comics** *n.* the newspaper pages containing the cartoons. (Treated as plural.) ♦ *Billy reads the comics every Sunday morning.* ♦ *The comics weren't very funny today.* **5. comic strip** *n.* a cartoon series that appears daily or weekly, usually in newspapers. ♦ *The newspaper prints comic strips every day.* ♦ *On Sunday, the comic strips are in color.*

comical ['kɑm ɪk əl] *adj.* funny; causing laughter. (Adv: *comically* [...ɪk li].) ♦ *The comical waiter entertained the diners.* ♦ *My kitten's antics are often quite comical.*

coming ['kʌm ɪŋ] **1.** *n.* the arrival of someone or something. (No plural form in this sense.) ♦ *With the coming of spring, the flowers bloom.* ♦ *We prepared for the coming of the new employee.* **2.** *adj.* next; future. ♦ *The movie theater showed clips of coming attractions.* ♦ *We are going to the zoo this coming Saturday.*

comma ['kɑm ə] *n.* a punctuation mark "," used to show a pause in a sentence or a break in the structure of the sentence. ♦ *Commas separated the items on the list.* ♦ *Some sentences use a comma before a conjunction.*

command [kə 'mænd] **1.** *n.* an order; a statement that tells someone what to do; a direction; an instruction. ♦ *The soldiers took commands from the sergeant.* ♦ *Mike's guide dog learned many verbal commands.* **2.** *n.* the authority to order other people what to do. (No plural form in this sense.) ♦ *The captain of the ship is first in command.* ♦ *Mary turned the command of the department over to her assistant.* **3.** *tv.* to give an order to someone. ♦ *The general commanded the troops to surrender.* ♦ *Bob commanded his dog to sit.* **4.** *tv.* to control someone or something. ♦ *The ship's captain commands the crew.* ♦ *Blind people command their guide dogs.* **5.** *tv.* [for someone or someone's character] to deserve and receive respect and attention. ♦ *The distinguished scholar commanded respect.* ♦ *The charismatic speaker commanded our attention.* **6. have a good command of something; have a poor command of something** *idiom* to possess the understanding necessary to do something well. ♦ *Anne has a good command of the German language.* ♦ *Dave has a poor command of his computer's operation.*

commandeer [kɑ mən 'dɪr] **1.** *tv.* [for the military] to seize something for its use. (Originally from French.) ♦ *The soldiers commandeered a city bus.* ♦ *The buildings were commandeered by the troops for command posts.* **2.** *tv.* to seize control of something. ♦ *The hijackers commandeered the plane.* ♦ *Bill commandeered the remote control for the TV from me.*

commander [kə 'mæn dɚ] **1.** *n.* a military officer in charge of a ship, fort, armed forces unit, etc. ♦ *The commander ordered the troops into battle.* ♦ *The soldiers stood* *at attention while their commander inspected them.* **2.** *n.* an officer in the Navy above a lieutenant commander and below a captain. ♦ *The commander gave the signal to submerge the submarine.* ♦ *Commander Smith gave the signal to submerge the submarine.*

commanding [kə 'mæn dɪŋ] **1.** *adj.* superb; superior; dominant. (Adv: *commandingly.*) ♦ *The voters gave the mayor a commanding lead over his opponent.* ♦ *The opera singer's commanding rendition of the aria won great applause.* **2. commanding view** *n.* a wide view, as from a high place. ♦ *From the fiftieth floor we got a commanding view of the city.* ♦ *The performer had a commanding view of the audience from the stage.*

commando [kə 'mæn do] *n.* a soldier trained for dangerous surprise raids. (Pl in *-s* or *-es.*) ♦ *Commandos led the surprise attack.* ♦ *The town was not prepared to defend itself against the commandos.*

commemorate [kə 'mɛm ə ret] *tv.* to celebrate a special occasion; to honor the memory of someone or something. ♦ *The celebration commemorated the founding of the town.* ♦ *We will commemorate our anniversary tomorrow.*

commemoration [kə mɛm ə 're ʃən] **1.** *n.* commemorating; remembrance. (No plural form in this sense.) ♦ *They planned a meeting for the commemoration of the anniversary of the death of the president.* ♦ *A tree was planted in commemoration of the killed soldiers.* **2.** *n.* a ceremony honoring the memory of someone or something. ♦ *The commemoration began with a toast.* ♦ *We attended a commemoration of the lives of the tornado victims.*

commemorative [kə 'mɛm ə rə tɪv] *adj.* in memory and honor of someone or something. (Adv: *commemoratively.*) ♦ *A commemorative plaque was attached to the wall of the fire station.* ♦ *The government minted commemorative coins in honor of the presidents.*

commence [kə 'mɛns] **1.** *tv.* to begin something; to start something. (More formal than **begin**.) ♦ *The professor commenced the lecture ten minutes late.* ♦ *The orchestra commenced playing when the conductor raised his baton.* **2.** *iv.* to begin; to start. ♦ *Sit down. The ceremony is about to commence.* ♦ *The lecture commenced promptly at noon.*

commencement [kə 'mɛns mənt] **1.** *n.* the start of something; the beginning of something. (More formal than **start**. No plural form in this sense.) ♦ *Music announced the commencement of the church service.* ♦ *The commencement of the day was marked by a moment of silence.* **2.** *n.* the graduation ceremony where diplomas are awarded. ♦ *Jane's whole family went to her high-school commencement.* ♦ *A celebrity gave the address at commencement.*

commend [kə 'mɛnd] *tv.* to praise someone. ♦ *My teacher commended me on my essay.* ♦ *The employees were commended with a bonus.*

commendable [kə 'mɛnd ə bəl] *adj.* worthy of praise; deserving praise. (Adv: *commendably.*) ♦ *Bob always does commendable work in school.* ♦ *Your efforts are most commendable.*

commendation [kɑ mən 'de ʃən] **1.** *n.* praise and recognition. (No plural form in this sense.) ♦ *Bob craved the kind of commendation he felt he deserved.* ♦ *Lisa never received any commendation for her efforts.* **2.** *n.* an award for doing something commendable. ♦ *The mayor gave the police officer a commendation for saving the child's life.* ♦ *This bonus is a commendation for exceeding the sales goals.*

commensurate [kə 'mɛn sə rɪt] **commensurate (with)** *adj.* (+ *prep. phr.*) proportionate; in proportion to. (Adv: *commensurately.*) ♦ *Your salary is commensurate with your experience level.* ♦ *What you receive is commensurate with what you give.*

comment ['kɑm ɛnt] **1.** *n.* a remark about something; a statement about something; an observation. ♦ *Bill made a casual comment about scuba diving.* ♦ *Mary whispered her comments, but everyone heard her.* **2. comment on** *iv.* + *prep. phr.* to make a statement about something; to remark about something. ♦ *Bill commented favorably on my new haircut.* ♦ *I asked the professor to comment on my writing style.* **3.** *tv.* to state that; to remark that. (Takes a clause.) ♦ *Anne commented that she wanted to eat pizza for dinner.* ♦ *"I didn't like the movie very much," Bill commented.*

commentary ['kɑm ən tɛr i] *n.* a series of comments linked to a series of events. (No plural form in this sense.) ♦ *After the movie, we listened to Bill's commentary about it.* ♦ *The writer's commentary outlines the history of the war.*

commentator ['kɑm ən tet ɚ] *n.* a newscaster; an announcer; someone who talks about current events on television or the radio. ♦ *The commentator reported the football game.* ♦ *The sports commentator had his own radio program.*

commerce ['kɑm ɚs] *n.* the buying and selling of products and services; trade. (No plural form in this sense.) ♦ *Commerce flourished between the two friendly countries.* ♦ *During the war, commerce between the nations halted.*

commercial [kə 'mɚ ʃəl] **1.** *adj.* of or about commerce. (Adv: *commercially.*) ♦ *Susan's hobby turned into a commercial venture.* ♦ *Tom was very much interested in the commercial aspects of his invention.* **2.** *n.* an advertisement on television or radio. (From *commercial announcement.*) ♦ *I hate commercials on television!* ♦ *Bill changes the TV channel when commercials are broadcast.*

commercialize [kə 'mɚ ʃə lɑɪz] *tv.* to attempt to make something more commercial or more concerned with the making of money. ♦ *Christmas became commercialized many years ago.* ♦ *Attempts to commercialize the Internet have met with great success.*

commingle [ko 'mɪŋ gəl] **1.** *tv.* to blend monetary accounts; to mix amounts of money intended for different purposes. ♦ *These amounts should not have been commingled. This will cause tax problems.* ♦ *The lawyer advised us not to commingle our business and personal accounts.* **2.** *iv.* to blend; to mix. ♦ *As the newlyweds kissed, their spirits commingled.* ♦ *The scents of the flowers commingled in the fresh breeze.*

commiserate [kə 'mɪz ə ret] *iv.* to suffer along with someone. ♦ *After losing their jobs, Bill and Anne commiserated with each other.* ♦ *Jane had the flu, and we commiserated because I also had it.*

commissary ['kɑm ə sɛr i] **1.** *n.* a store that stocks food and equipment, especially one on a military base. ♦ *The soldiers bought their groceries at the commissary.* ♦ *The commissary was open only to military personnel.* **2.** *n.* a snack shop or cafeteria at a film or television studio. ♦ *The panelists sat in the commissary eating peanuts until show time.* ♦ *Is there a commissary where we can get coffee between rehearsals?*

commission [kə 'mɪ ʃən] **1.** *n.* a group of people who are given the authority to do a certain thing. ♦ *The medical commission urged the vaccination of children.* ♦ *The president appointed a commission to study poverty.* **2.** *n.* money earned based on a percentage of profit; payment to a seller based on the amount of sales. ♦ *The salesman lived off the commissions he made selling cars.* ♦ *The salesclerk will get a commission on everything she sells.* **3.** *tv.* to appoint someone to do something; to give someone the authority to do something. ♦ *An artist was commissioned to paint the mayor's portrait.* ♦ *The city commissioned an architect to design the new library.* **4. out of commission** *idiom* broken, unserviceable, or inoperable. ♦ *My watch is out of commission and is running slowly.* ♦ *I can't run in the marathon because my knees are out of commission.*

commissioner [kə 'mɪʃ ən ɚ] *n.* a government official in charge of a department. ♦ *The police commissioner worked on the case himself.* ♦ *Commissioner Davis voted against the controversial measure.*

commit [kə 'mɪt] **1.** *tv.* to do a crime; to do something illegal. ♦ *The criminal had committed several murders.* ♦ *The police do not know who committed the robberies.* **2. commit to** *tv.* + *prep. phr.* to place someone under the control or authority of a hospital, institution, or prison. ♦ *John committed his sick father to the hospital.* ♦ *The judge committed the criminal to prison for thirty years.* **3. commit to** *tv.* + *prep. phr.* to pledge oneself to do something. ♦ *Dave committed himself to working for the good of all people.* ♦ *I am committed to babysitting my nephew tonight.* **4.** *tv.* to place someone (in a mental institution). ♦ *The court committed the senile man to protect him from harm.* ♦ *Mike finally got so mentally disturbed that he was committed.*

commitment [kə 'mɪt mənt] **1.** *n.* a pledge; a promise; an obligation. ♦ *Jane made a commitment to help her friend move.* ♦ *Bill has a commitment to donate $3,000 to the charity.* **2.** *n.* dedication; devotion. (No plural form in this sense.) ♦ *Lisa displays a lot of commitment to her job.* ♦ *Bob was criticized for the lack of commitment he showed in his religious practices.*

committed [kə 'mɪt ɪd] *adj.* devoted; dedicated. (Adv: *committedly.*) ♦ *Lisa is a very committed geometry teacher.* ♦ *The mayor is a very committed politician.*

committee [kə 'mɪt i] *n.* a group of people who meet to perform a specific duty, usually as part of a larger organization. ♦ *The committee planned the club's budget for next year.* ♦ *How many members are on the finance committee?*

commode [kə 'mod] **1.** *n.* a low cabinet or chest of drawers. ♦ *The commode held table linens and candles.* ♦ *There was a commode full of towels next to the bed.* **2.** *n.* a toilet. (Typical in the South. From a Latin word for *convenient.*) ♦ *The commode continued to run for a long time after it was flushed.* ♦ *The plumber had to be called to repair the commode.*

commodity [kə 'mɑd tɪ i] *n.* unprocessed foods or metals. ♦ *Wheat is an important international commodity.* ♦ *John, who deals in commodities, invests in coffee and orange juice.*

commodore ['kɑm ə dor] **1.** *n.* an officer in the navy above a captain and below a rear admiral. ♦ *A commodore has a larger cabin than a captain.* ♦ *The admiral saluted the commodore as they passed each other.* **2.** *n.* the director of a yacht club. ♦ *The commodore hosted a lovely spring formal dance.* ♦ *Before dinner at the club, the commodore gave a short speech.*

common ['kɑm ən] **1.** *adj.* usual; typical; frequently encountered; widespread. (Adv: *commonly.* Comp: *commoner;* sup: *commonest.*) ♦ *Colds and flu are common in the winter months.* ♦ *Sprained ankles are not very common among trained athletes.* **2.** *adj.* shared or used by two or more people. (Adv: *commonly.*) ♦ *These two bedrooms share a common bathroom.* ♦ *Bill and Bob have a common interest in gardening.* **3.** *adj.* without distinction; ordinary. (Adv: *commonly.* Comp: *commoner;* sup: *commonest.*) ♦ *This is the common variety of daisy.* ♦ *Bill studies hard, but he's just a common student.* **4. common noun** *n.* a noun referring to the general name of a class, as opposed to specific members within a class. ♦ *For instance,* France *is a proper noun and* country *is a common noun.* ♦ *Common nouns are not capitalized in English, unless they are at the beginning of the sentence.* **5. commons** *n.* an area of land that is available for use by all the people of a city or town; a central town park. (Treated as singular or plural. Primarily in New England.) ♦ *The students lounged on the commons between classes.* ♦ *A war memorial was erected in the commons.* **6. common sense** *n.* basic reasonable and practical thinking. ♦ *If you had any common sense, you wouldn't have to ask such silly questions!* ♦ *He has a lot of common sense and doesn't panic in a bad situation.*

commonplace ['kɑm ən ples] *adj.* plain and ordinary. ♦ *Meatloaf is a commonplace American meal.* ♦ *We grow a commonplace variety of daisy in our garden.*

commonwealth ['kɑm ən wɛlθ] **1.** *n.* a group of sovereign states. ♦ *The small countries bonded together as a commonwealth.* ♦ *The island county did not join the commonwealth, thinking it could do better on its own.* **2. Commonwealth** *n.* [part of] the official name of Kentucky, Massachusetts, Pennsylvania, and Virginia, as well as Puerto Rico. ♦ *The great Commonwealth of Kentucky invites you to visit.* ♦ *We will struggle for the good of the Commonwealth.*

commotion [kə 'mo ʃən] *n.* a disturbance; a clamor; a noisy interruption. ♦ *Bill went to see what the commotion down the hall was.* ♦ *There was a noisy commotion in the kitchen when someone dropped a lot of plates.*

communal [kə 'mjun əl] *adj.* owned by the members of a community; used by the members of a community; common to all. (Adv: *communally.*) ♦ *My roommates and I share a communal bathroom.* ♦ *The editors shared a set of communal computers for their work.*

commune 1. ['kɑ mjun] *n.* the site where a group of people live and work together, have no private belongings, and share everything. ♦ *Twenty students live in a peaceful religious commune.* ♦ *There was some lack of privacy in the commune.* **2. commune with** [kə 'mjun…] *iv.* + *prep. phr.* to communicate intimately with someone or something. ♦ *Susan goes to the woods to commune with nature.* ♦ *John communes with God through prayer.*

communicable [kə 'mjun ə kə bəl] **1.** *adj.* able to be communicated. (Adv: *communicably.*) ♦ *The child's vague desires were not communicable.* ♦ *The bad news was not communicable over the telephone.* **2.** *adj.* contagious. (Adv: *communicably.*) ♦ *Flu is a communicable disease.* ♦ *Medical professionals are exposed to communicable viruses every day.*

communicate [kə 'mjun ɪ ket] **1.** *tv.* to make something known; to tell something. ♦ *Mary communicated the news as tactfully as she could.* ♦ *The bereaved mourner could not communicate the depth of his grief.* **2.** *iv.* to exchange information; to send out information. ♦ *Before her first cup of coffee in the morning, Mary communicates poorly.* ♦ *The boss communicates with her staff by memo.*

communication [kə mjun ɪ 'ke ʃən] **1.** *n.* sending and receiving information. (No plural form in this sense.) ♦ *Communication is an integral part of any relationship.* ♦ *Bill has had no communication with his brother for 10 years.* **2.** *n.* an announcement or statement in written or spoken form. ♦ *The messenger left a communication informing us that one of my cousins had died.* ♦ *A communication from the office outlined the new dress code.*

communicative [kə 'mjun ɪ kə tɪv] *adj.* likely to give information; informative. (Adv: *communicatively.*) ♦ *Mary is not too communicative about her true feelings.* ♦ *A communicative boss is the best kind.*

communion [kə 'mjun jən] **1.** *n.* the exchange of ideas and beliefs; the sharing of ideas and beliefs. (No plural form in this sense.) ♦ *Jane and Mary shared a lovely communion of thought.* ♦ *The lovers sat alone, lost in their own communion.* **2. Communion** *n.* the Christian sacrament in which bread and wine are blessed and eaten in remembrance of Christ's Last Supper. ♦ *Some churches serve Communion every Sunday.* ♦ *Bread and wine are sometimes distributed at Communion.*

communiqué [kə 'mjun ə ke] *n.* an official message; an official statement. (From French.) ♦ *The spy intercepted a government communiqué.* ♦ *The communiqué detailed the next offensive in the war.*

communism ['kɑm jə nɪz əm] *n.* a social and economic system where everything is owned and operated by the people or by the government in the name of the people. (No plural form in this sense.) ♦ *The country's political system was that of communism.* ♦ *Communism promotes the sharing of a nation's wealth among all its citizens.*

communist ['kɑm jə nəst] **1.** *n.* someone who practices communism; someone who admires the theory of communism. ♦ *The members of the ruling party were all communists.* ♦ *In the 1950s, many U.S. entertainers were thought to be communists.* **2.** *adj.* of or about communism. ♦ *The democratic government leaders feared a communist takeover.* ♦ *The hostile actions were thought to be a communist plot.*

community [kə 'mjun ə ti] **1.** *n.* an area or region where people live and interact with each other; a neighborhood or town. ♦ *We live in a suburban community.* ♦ *There are seven churches in our community.* **2.** *n.* a group of people who have a common interest, occupation, or background. ♦ *A church is sometimes called a community of believers.* ♦ *The Hispanic community in our town celebrates a holiday in May.* **3.** *adj.* <the adj. use of ①.> ♦ *The convicted criminal was forced to do community service.* ♦ *Bill is involved with the local community theater.*

commute [kə 'mjut] **1.** *iv.* to travel from home to work and back in a car, train, bus, etc. ♦ *Many people commute each day by train.* ♦ *Mary commutes to school rather than living on campus.* **2.** *tv.* to lessen the sentence of a convicted criminal. ♦ *The governor commuted Bill's sentence when new evidence proved he was innocent.* ♦ *The sentence was commuted from death to life imprisonment.* **3.** *n.* the trip from work or home or from home to work. ♦ *The commute was terrible today because of the rain!* ♦ *I like to read during my commute on the train.*

commuter [kə 'mjut ɚ] *n.* someone who commutes. ♦ *The commuters waited for the train that would take them into the city.* ♦ *When the subway company went on strike, many commuters had to ride the bus.*

comp See comparative ④.

compact 1. [kəm 'pækt] *adj.* packed together; close together; small. (Adv: *compactly.*) ♦ *Jane has a compact kitchen with room for only one person.* ♦ *The compact umbrella collapsed into a small tube.* **2.** ['kɑm pækt] *n.* a small makeup case holding face powder and a mirror. ♦ *Mary's compact fell out of her purse.* ♦ *I bought a new compact when I ran out of powder.* **3.** ['kɑm pækt] *n.* a small car; a compact ① car. ♦ *The Smiths wanted to buy a compact to replace their station wagon.* ♦ *Some people believe compacts are not as safe as larger cars.* **4.** ['kɑm pækt] *n.* an agreement between two countries or groups. ♦ *The compact between the nations ended the war.* ♦ *The nation violated the compact by arming its troops.* **5.** [kəm 'pækt] *tv.* to pack something densely. ♦ *Someone compacted all the ice cream so tightly that I could not get it out of the container.* ♦ *Dave compacted the trash so it would fit in the bin.*

Compact Disc™ ['kɑm pækt 'dɪsk] *n.* a disk encoded with digital information, either music or computer data and programs. (A protected trade name for a kind of disk encoded in this way. Abbreviated CD.) ♦ *Bill bought a few Compact Discs to play on his stereo.* ♦ *The encyclopedia is available on Compact Disc.*

companion [kəm 'pæn jən] **1.** *n.* someone with whom time is spent. ♦ *Jane and Mary, her constant companion, go to the symphony each month.* ♦ *My companions and I went to the museum.* **2.** *n.* something that matches something else; something that is part of a set. ♦ *I cannot find a companion to this black sock.* ♦ *The large glass pitcher is a companion to the set of glasses.*

companionship [kəm 'pæn jən ʃɪp] *n.* the friendship between two people who are together a lot or between a person or a pet. (No plural form in this sense.) ♦ *Mary appreciates the companionship of her friends.* ♦ *The companionship of a pet is prized by many people.*

company ['kʌm pə ni] **1.** *n.* a business entity; a business. ♦ *Mary works for a computer software company.* ♦ *My former company went out of business last year.* **2.** *n.* guests; visitors. (No plural form in this sense. Treated as singular.) ♦ *We are having company tonight, so we must clean the house.* ♦ *The company that was expected never arrived.* **3.** *n.* a division of an army that is commanded by a captain. ♦ *Company Eight was at the front line of the war.* ♦ *Our company was called up for service.* **4. keep company** *idiom* to associate with or visit someone often. ♦

Anne keeps company with many neighbors on her block. ♦ *Bill and Mary have been keeping company a lot lately.*

comparable ['kɑm pɚ ə bəl] *adj.* similar. (Adv: *comparably.*) ♦ *All the clothes in the store were of comparable quality.* ♦ *I suggested two comparable solutions to the problem.*

comparative [kəm 'pɛr ə tɪv] **1.** *adj.* of or about studies based on comparison. (Adv: *comparatively.*) ♦ *Mike is a student of comparative religions.* ♦ *Susan took a course in comparative languages.* **2.** *adj.* of or about a form of an adverb or adjective that typically has an *-er* suffix or is a combination of the adverb or adjective and the word *more.* (Some adverbs and adjectives have irregular comparatives ④, however.) ♦ Better *is the comparative form of* good. ♦ *In grammar class we learned about comparative adjectives.* **3.** *adj.* as compared with others. (Adv: *comparatively.*) ♦ *Bill is a comparative stranger in town. He just moved here.* ♦ *Bob, as strong as he is, is a comparative weakling at the gym.* **4.** *n.* the comparative ② form of an adjective or adverb. (Abbreviated "comp:" here.) ♦ Better *is the comparative of* good. ♦ *In grammar class we learned about comparatives and superlatives.*

compare [kəm 'pɛr] **1.** *tv.* to determine or show how two things are the same or different. ♦ *The teacher compared the two historical events.* ♦ *Bob compared the socks to see if one was longer than the other.* **2. compare with** *tv.* + *prep. phr.* to determine or show how things or people resemble or differ from other things or people. ♦ *If you compare this book with that one, you will find that that one is larger.* ♦ *Tom compared Bill with Bob to see who was taller.* **3. compare to** *tv.* + *prep. phr.* to point out the similarities between a person or thing and another person or thing that is otherwise quite different. ♦ *Bob compared Mary's messy hair to a bird's nest.* ♦ *The poet compared the building's beauty to a bright summer's day.*

comparison [kəm 'pɛr ɪ sən] **1.** *n.* showing how things are the same or different. (No plural form in this sense.) ♦ *Your comparison of the two ideas is very insightful.* ♦ *Mary made a comparison between the story and her own life.* **2.** *n.* an instance of comparing things or people. ♦ *Since Tom is not standing up straight, checking his height against Bob's is a poor comparison.* ♦ *A comparison between the two stories is to be found in your textbook.*

compartment [kəm 'pɑrt mənt] *n.* a separate, enclosed space, such as the inside of a cabinet or cupboard. ♦ *There are separate compartments in my desk for various kinds of bills and papers.* ♦ *The maps are in the glove compartment of the car.*

compass ['kʌm pəs] **1.** *n.* a device that points to the north and indicates direction for the purposes of travel or finding out where one is located. ♦ *The soldier used his compass to locate the direction he should go in.* ♦ *Mary used a compass when she became lost in the strange town.* **2.** *n.* a simple device used to draw circles or parts of circles. ♦ *The geometry students drew circles with their compasses.* ♦ *The architect made an arc on the blueprint with the compass.* **3.** *n.* an area with a certain boundary; a range. ♦ *The television station broadcasts over a wide compass.* ♦ *The compass of the king's rule was vast but not infinite.*

compassion [kəm 'pæ ʃən] *n.* pity or sympathy. (No plural form in this sense. Number is expressed with *act(s) of compassion.*) ♦ *The nurse had compassion for the sick patient.* ♦ *Everyone felt compassion for the mourning family.*

compassionate [kəm 'pæ ʃə nət] *adj.* showing compassion; showing pity or sympathy. (Adv: *compassionately.*) ♦ *The compassionate woman helped the poor family.* ♦ *Bill is compassionate and likes to help those less fortunate than himself.*

compatibility [kəm pæt ə 'bɪl ə ti] **1.** *n.* the ability for two or more things to work smoothly together. (No plural form in this sense.) ♦ *I had a lot of problems with the compatibility of the software in my new computer.* ♦ *This software does not have any compatibility with my hardware.* **2.** *n.* the ability for two or more people to get along well together. (No plural form in this sense.) ♦ *We misjudged the compatibility of Bill and Mary. They didn't like each other at all.* ♦ *The couple divorced when they realized there was no compatibility between them.*

compatible [kəm 'pæt ə bəl] **1.** *adj.* able to work or function well together. (Adv: *compatibly.*) ♦ *Our two styles of management are not compatible.* ♦ *Is this software compatible with my computer?* **2.** *adj.* able to get along well with someone else; able to live with someone else. (Adv: *compatibly.*) ♦ *Bill is hoping to find a compatible roommate.* ♦ *My coworker and I are not compatible at all.*

compatriot [kəm 'pe tri ət] *n.* someone who is from one's own country. ♦ *The two compatriots fought in the war together.* ♦ *In France, Bob bumped into a compatriot from Denver.*

compel [kəm 'pɛl] *tv.* to make someone do something necessary; to oblige someone to do something. ♦ *I was compelled to go to Mike's birthday party.* ♦ *The boss compelled us to work over the weekend.*

compelling [kəm 'pɛl ɪŋ] *adj.* irresistible; arousing interest. (*Adv: compellingly.*) ♦ *Mike finds classical music very compelling.* ♦ *The children listened attentively to the compelling story.*

compendium [kəm 'pɛn di əm] *n.* a collection of information in one volume. ♦ *The book was a compendium of several novels.* ♦ *This reference work is a complete compendium of travel information.*

compensate ['kɑm pən set] **1.** *tv.* to give someone something equal in value to what has been taken or used. ♦ *I compensated Mary for the cup of sugar I borrowed.* ♦ *The volunteers were not compensated for their time.* **2.** *tv.* to pay someone a salary; to pay someone wages. ♦ *The company compensated its officers quite well.* ♦ *My company compensates me quite well.* **3. compensate for** *iv.* + *prep. phr.* to make up for something else; to offset or balance something, often by payments of money. ♦ *Bill was compensated by the insurance company for his medical costs.* ♦ *The company compensated its employees for working overtime by giving them longer vacations.*

compensation [kɑm pən 'se ʃən] **1.** *n.* something given to make up for something; something given to balance or make up for something. (No plural form in this sense.) ♦ *Max received his compensation in stock rather than cash.* ♦ *The volunteers' compensation was the smiles on the faces of the people they'd helped.* **2.** *n.* pay; wages; earnings. (No plural form in this sense.) ♦ *The employees received compensation twice a month.* ♦ *Jimmy gets some compensation for cutting the grass each week.* **3.** *n.* a behavior pattern where someone makes up for one trait by overemphasizing another trait. (No plural form in this sense.) ♦ *Mike's compensation for his shyness is telling a lot of jokes.* ♦ *Acting very brave is sometimes a compensation for insecurity.*

compete [kəm 'pit] *iv.* to participate in a game or competition; to take part in a game or competition. ♦ *Expert chess players competed for the championship.* ♦ *Children sometimes compete for their parents' attention.*

competence ['kɑm pə təns] *n.* the ability to do something well. (No plural form in this sense.) ♦ *The doctor's competence came into question when the surgery was botched.* ♦ *Mary looked for a stockbroker with competence in investing.*

competent ['kɑm pə tənt] *adj.* able to do something well; skilled; able. (*Adv: competently.*) ♦ *Mike did a competent job fixing my car.* ♦ *Dr. Smith is a competent surgeon.*

competing [kəm 'pit ɪŋ] *adj.* rival; referring to a competitor. ♦ *John took a job with a competing company.* ♦ *A competing product lowered the sales of our new device.*

competition [kɑm pɪ 'tɪ ʃən] **1.** *n.* a contest. ♦ *The wrestling competition was held in the gymnasium.* ♦ *Twenty people entered the baking competition.* **2.** *n.* rivalry. (No plural form in this sense.) ♦ *The sporting goods store has a lot of competition.* ♦ *The best students were in competition with each other at school.* **3.** *n.* a rival or a group of rivals. (No plural form in this sense.) ♦ *Anne wanted to put her competition out of business.* ♦ *The gymnast checked out his competition at the championship meet.*

competitive [kəm 'pɛt ɪ tɪv] **1.** *adj.* eager to compete; aggressive in competition. (*Adv: competitively.*) ♦ *My brother and I are very competitive with each other.* ♦ *Susan is quite competitive when she plays baseball.* **2.** *adj.* low in price; [of a low price] able to compete. (*Adv: competitively.*) ♦ *The computer store's prices are competitive with those of other stores.* ♦ *The advertising firm's fees are competitive.* **3.** *adj.* involving competition. (*Adv: competitively.*) ♦ *Advertising is a very competitive business.* ♦ *Fishing is not a competitive sport.*

competitor [kəm 'pɛt ɪt ɚ] *n.* someone or something that competes; a rival. ♦ *Bill shook hands with his competitor before the tennis match began.* ♦ *Mary was confident she would beat her competitor.*

compilation [kɑm pə 'le ʃən] **1.** *n.* the process of collecting together similar things from different sources. (No plural form in this sense.) ♦ *The compilation of this dictionary took ten years.* ♦ *Bill worked hard on the compilation of data for the report.* **2.** *n.* a collection of similar items taken from different places; a book whose information is taken from several sources. ♦ *The cookbook is a compilation of recipes from all over the world.* ♦ *This reference work is a compilation of older sources.*

compile [kəm 'pɑɪl] *tv.* to assemble a collection of similar items taken from different places; to collect information for a book from different sources. ♦ *The scientists compiled a great amount of data to help develop their theory.* ♦ *I compiled the favorite recipes of all my friends.*

complacency [kəm 'ple sən si] *n.* contentment; satisfaction with the way things are; a self-satisfied state. (No plural form in this sense.) ♦ *Lisa always has a look of complacency on her face.* ♦ *Because of his complacency about his job, Bill never got promoted.*

complacent [kəm 'ples ənt] *adj.* self-satisfied; uninterested in change. (*Adv: complacently.*) ♦ *The complacent citizens reelected the mayor.* ♦ *Mary was complacent about her position at the firm.*

complain [kəm 'plen] *iv.* to express discontent or annoyance. ♦ *We complained to the manager that our food was cold.* ♦ *I taught my children not to complain too much.*

complainer [kəm 'plen ɚ] *n.* someone who expresses annoyance about almost everything. ♦ *Every office has a complainer who is unhappy with working there.* ♦ *Mike is a real complainer. Nothing is ever right for him.*

complaint [kəm 'plent] **1.** *n.* a statement expressing annoyance or discontent. ♦ *Mary made a strong complaint at the department store.* ♦ *The boss had a complaint about Bill's tardiness.* **2.** *n.* an accusation; a statement that a crime has been committed. ♦ *The mugging victim filed a complaint at the police department.* ♦ *An old complaint against Bob stayed in his personnel records permanently.* **3.** *n.* a sickness; an illness. ♦ *Mike told the doctor of his sinus complaint.* ♦ *The doctor could not diagnose Bill's complaint.*

complement ['kɑm plə mənt] **1.** *tv.* to complete or enhance something; to add something that completes what is already there. (Compare with **compliment**.) ♦ *Tall white candles complemented the formal table setting nicely.* ♦ *Bill's green sweater complemented his dark green trousers.* **2.** *n.* something added that completes what is already there. ♦ *Wine is the perfect complement to any meal.* ♦ *The small chairs on the lawn complemented the seating provided by the furniture on the deck.* **3.** *n.* the normal amount of something; the amount of something required. (No plural form in this sense.) ♦ *I arrived with an entire complement of brothers, sisters, and cousins.* ♦ *The queen had a large complement of attendants at the ball.*

complementary [kɑm plə 'mɛn tə ri] *adj.* in way that completes or enhances something; making up for something that is lacking. (Compare with **complimentary**. Adv: *complementarily* [kɑm plə məm 'tɛr ə li].) ♦ *The green sweater is complementary to Bill's trousers.* ♦ *Travel is complementary to a formal education.*

complete [kəm 'plit] **1.** *adj.* entire; whole; with all the necessary parts. (Adv: *completely.*) ♦ *When the report was complete, Bill distributed it to his coworkers.* ♦ *Bill told us the complete story over coffee.* **2.** *tv.* to finish something; to end something; to do something until it is done. ♦ *I will complete my schooling next year.* ♦ *When I complete this book, I'll start another.* **3.** *tv.* to make something whole; to fill in all the parts of something. ♦ *Please complete the application form for the job.* ♦ *The art students were instructed to complete the drawing that had been started.*

completeness [kəm 'plit nəs] *n.* a state of being finished; a state of being whole. (No plural form in this sense.) ♦ *Mike does not care for completeness. He never finishes projects.* ♦ *The teacher insisted on completeness in every assignment.*

completion [kəm 'pli ʃən] *n.* ending; termination. (No plural form in this sense.) ♦ *The completion of the construction is expected in June.* ♦ *Bill's career is near its completion. He's retiring next month.*

complex 1. ['kɑm plɛks] *n.* a set of related buildings. ♦ *Our office complex has a courtyard with a fountain.* ♦ *The* *complex will be complete when two more buildings are finished.* **2.** ['kɑm plɛks] *n.* a psychological condition. ♦ *Mary has a complex about being late.* ♦ *Bill has had an insecurity complex since he was a child.* **3.** [kəm 'plɛks, 'kɑm plɛks] *adj.* difficult; complicated; hard to understand. (Adv: *complexly.*) ♦ *The student thought the algebraic formula was complex.* ♦ *Poverty is a complex problem in many of the world's cities.* **4.** [kəm 'plɛks, kɑm plɛks] *adj.* made of several parts; multifaceted. ♦ *This food is full of complex carbohydrates.* ♦ *The scientists had difficulty producing the complex molecule.*

complexion [kəm 'plɛk ʃən] **1.** *n.* the color or appearance of someone's facial skin. ♦ *Mary has dark eyes and a fair complexion.* ♦ *The dermatologist gave Bill some cream for his complexion.* **2.** *n.* the character of something; the nature of some matter or affair. (No plural form in this sense.) ♦ *Your statement puts a very different complexion on the matter.* ♦ *The whole business takes on a sinister complexion now that I understand it.*

complexity [kəm 'plɛks ɪ ti] **1.** *n.* intricacy; complication. (No plural form in this sense.) ♦ *I was surprised by the complexity of the novel's plot.* ♦ *The architect was not fazed by the complexity of the design.* **2.** *n.* something that is complex. ♦ *Bill's statement added unnecessary complexities to the problem.* ♦ *Another complexity in the matter is Tom's absence from the meeting.*

compliance [kəm 'plɑɪ əns] *n.* obeying a law or a command. (No plural form in this sense.) ♦ *Compliance with the city ordinance involves buying a vehicle sticker each year.* ♦ *Pay your parking tickets and be in compliance with city laws.*

compliant [kəm 'plɑɪ ənt] *adj.* going along with someone else's wishes; obedient; yielding. (Adv: *compliantly.*) ♦ *The salesclerk was compliant with the customer's wishes.* ♦ *The children were usually compliant, but today they would not obey.*

complicate ['kɑm plɪ ket] **1.** *tv.* to make something more confusing; to make something more intricate. ♦ *Changing the time of the party will complicate the plan.* ♦ *The detour complicated my commute to work.* **2.** *tv.* to make something worse. ♦ *Getting angry with each other will only complicate the matter.* ♦ *Mary's recovery from surgery was complicated when she got the flu.*

complicated ['kɑm plɪ ket ɪd] *adj.* confusing; difficult; made of many different parts. (Adv: *complicatedly.*) ♦ *The architect worked on the complicated blueprints for weeks.* ♦ *We got lost because the directions to the party were too complicated.*

complication [kɑm plɪ 'ke ʃən] *n.* something that makes something more confusing or difficult; something that makes something harder to deal with. ♦ *Complications arose as John recovered from a heart attack.* ♦ *The project faced another complication when the computer broke down.*

complicity [kəm 'plɪs ɪt i] *n.* helping someone do something wrong or illegal. (No plural form in this sense.) ♦ *Two people are suspected of complicity in the robbery.* ♦ *Several students were suspended because of their complicity in the cheating scandal.*

compliment 1. ['kɑm plɪ mənt] *n.* something nice that is said about someone or something. (Compare with **complement**.) ♦ *Max paid Mary a compliment on her outfit.* ♦ *The artist received many compliments on her paintings.* **2.** ['kɑm plɪ mɛnt] *tv.* to praise someone; to say something nice about someone or something. ♦ *The conductor complimented Tom on his violin solo.* ♦ *We wanted to compliment the chef on our delicious meal.* **3. fish for a compliment** [...'kɑm plɪ mənt] *idiom* to try to get someone to pay oneself a compliment. ♦ *When she showed me her new dress, I could tell that she was fishing for a compliment.* ♦ *Tom was certainly fishing for a compliment when he modeled his fancy haircut for his friends.*

complimentary [kɑm plə 'mɛn tri] **1.** *adj.* kind; [made] as a compliment. (Compare with **complementary**. Adv: *complimentarily* [kɑm plə məm 'tɛr ə li].) ♦ *The professor rarely makes complimentary remarks to students.* ♦ *The guest made a complimentary comment about the food.* **2.** *adj.* free; without charge. (Adv: *complimentarily.*) ♦ *The restaurant served us complimentary champagne.* ♦ *The actor gave his friends complimentary tickets to the play.*

comply [kəm 'plɑɪ] **comply (with)** *iv.* (+ *prep. phr.*) to obey a rule or request. ♦ *We bought a sticker for our car to comply with the city ordinance.* ♦ *A good citizen complies with the laws of the country.*

component [kəm 'po nənt] *n.* a part of something. ♦ *An essay question is one component of the test.* ♦ *An important component of the system malfunctioned.*

comportment [kəm 'port mənt] *n.* behavior; attitude. (No plural form in this sense.) ♦ *The polite children exhibited good comportment.* ♦ *Anne's comportment made people think she was haughty.*

compose [kəm 'poz] **1.** *tv.* to write music; to create and write down music, letters, poetry, or stories. ♦ *In the music class, students learned to compose melodies.* ♦ *While sitting under a tree, I composed a poem.* **2. compose of** *tv.* + *prep. phr.* to form or structure something of a selected group of people. (Usually passive.) ♦ *Our team is composed of the best players.* ♦ *The committee was composed of students and faculty.* **3.** *tv.* to calm oneself. (Takes a reflexive object.) ♦ *Jane tried to compose herself after losing her temper.* ♦ *After forgetting his lines, the actor composed himself and continued.* **4.** *iv.* to write [music or words]. ♦ *Jane plays the guitar as well as composes.* ♦ *Symphonies are difficult to compose.*

composer [kəm 'poz ɚ] *n.* someone who writes music. ♦ *The composer became famous late in his career.* ♦ *Who is the composer of this symphony?*

composite [kəm 'pɑz ɪt] **1.** *n.* something that is made up of many things. ♦ *The frame held a composite of pictures of me when I was younger.* ♦ *The quilt is a composite of old scraps of material.* **2.** *adj.* made of many things; made of many parts. (Adv: *compositely.*) ♦ *The police drew a composite sketch of the suspect.* ♦ *This is a composite map made from a number of smaller maps.*

composition [kɑm pə 'zɪ ʃən] **1.** *n.* the process of putting things together to form one whole thing. (No plural form in this sense.) ♦ *The composition of the family tree took years.* ♦ *The composition of the quilt was a lengthy process.* **2.** *n.* the arrangement of the parts of something. (No plural form in this sense.) ♦ *The composition of the photograph was perfectly balanced.* ♦ *The teacher praised the student's artistic composition.* **3.** *n.* a piece of music, a symphony; a piece of writing, an essay, a poem. ♦ *The orchestra played compositions by classical composers.* ♦ *Jane memorized the piano composition for the* *recital.* **4.** *n.* composing a piece of properly written writing. (No plural form in this sense.) ♦ *All first-year students must take a course in composition.* ♦ *The teacher instructed the students in composition.* **5.** *n.* the things that make up something; the ingredients of something; the parts of something. (No plural form in this sense.) ♦ *What is the composition of this sticky substance?* ♦ *The lab assistant lost the formula for the compound's composition.*

compost ['kɑm post] *n.* decaying organic matter used as fertilizer. (No plural form in this sense.) ♦ *We fertilized the garden with compost.* ♦ *Jane added potato peels to the compost.*

composure [kəm 'po ʒɚ] *n.* calmness; self-control. (No plural form in this sense.) ♦ *The irate customer lost his composure and yelled at the clerk.* ♦ *Once Jane regained her composure, she was no longer angry.*

compote ['kɑm pot] **1.** *n.* a portion of fruit stewed with sugar. ♦ *Dessert was a delicious fruit compote.* ♦ *The compote was made of peaches and plums.* **2.** *n.* a footed, covered dish for serving nuts, candy, etc. ♦ *A compote on the coffee table is full of candy.* ♦ *The children opened the compote and ate all the candy.*

compound 1. ['kɑm paʊnd] *n.* a chemical substance made from two or more elements. ♦ *Water is a chemical compound of oxygen and hydrogen.* ♦ *This compound will clean glass without leaving streaks.* **2.** ['kɑm paʊnd] *n.* a group of buildings within the walls or a fence; a group of buildings forming an enclosure. ♦ *The compound protected the settlers from enemy attacks.* ♦ *My office building is in the northeast corner of the compound.* **3.** ['kɑm pæund] *n.* two or more words that are used as a single word. ♦ *An example of a noun compound is* cable television. ♦ *The word* backyard *is also a compound.* **4.** ['kɑm pæund] *adj.* made of two or more parts; having two or more segments. ♦ Backyard *is a compound noun.* ♦ *A compound sentence has at least two clauses.* **5.** [kəm 'paʊnd] *tv.* to make something worse by adding to it. ♦ *Running out of gas compounded the problem of being lost.* ♦ *Tom compounded our problems by being absent from the meeting.*

comprehend [kɑm prɪ 'hɛnd] *tv.* to understand something. ♦ *I could not comprehend the instructions for operating the computer.* ♦ *The test determined if the students comprehended the material.*

comprehension [kɑm prɪ 'hɛn ʃən] *n.* understanding; the ability to understand someone or something. (No plural form in this sense.) ♦ *The student had a good comprehension of the material and passed the test.* ♦ *The noise prevented our comprehension of the speech.*

comprehensive [kɑm prɪ 'hɛn sɪv] *adj.* inclusive; thorough; wide ranging. (Adv: *comprehensively.*) ♦ *A comprehensive survey was used to determine public opinion.* ♦ *A single, comprehensive history class covered the years 1066 to 1945.*

compress 1. ['kɑm prɛs] *n.* a cloth pad that is pressed onto a wound or injury. ♦ *The nurse applied a cold compress to the patient's bruise.* ♦ *A compress reduced the swelling of the wound.* **2.** [kəm 'prɛs] *tv.* to apply pressure to squeeze something tighter; to press something to try to make it take less space. ♦ *A powerful pump compressed the air in the scuba diving tank.* ♦ *I had to compress my clothes in order to close the suitcase.* **3.** [kəm 'prɛs] *tv.* to reduce the size of a sequence of digital code, such as a computer file. ♦ *I have a small program that compresses my computer files so they take less space on the disk.* ♦ *A transmitter compresses the digital signal as it is sent.*

compressed [kəm 'prɛst] *adj.* squeezed; condensed; made more compact. ♦ *Our diving tanks are filled with compressed air.* ♦ *The tightly compressed contents made the suitcase bulge.*

compression [kəm 'prɛ ʃən] *n.* the packing of more of something into a space. (No plural form in this sense.) ♦ *Digital compression allowed large documents to be transmitted quickly.* ♦ *The compression of air into a diver's tank takes several minutes.*

compressor [kəm 'prɛs ɚ] *n.* a machine that compresses a gas. ♦ *The compressor filled the diver's tanks with air.* ♦ *The house painter attached a compressor to the paint sprayer.*

comprise [kəm 'prɑɪz] *tv.* to be made up of something; to contain something. ♦ *The continent of Africa comprises many countries.* ♦ *The cookbook comprises hundreds of recipes.*

compromise ['kɑm prə mɑɪz] **1.** *n.* an agreement to settle an argument where both sides yield a little. ♦ *After long negotiations the warring nations reached a compromise.* ♦ *Our compromise was that we would eat before seeing the movie.* **2.** *iv.* to come to an agreement by which both sides yield a little. ♦ *After arguing for an hour, we finally compromised on the issue.* ♦ *Bill and Jane learned to compromise in their marriage.* **3.** *tv.* to endanger someone's reputation, position, or morals. ♦ *The rumor compromised the mayor's standing in the community.* ♦ *Lying would compromise my morals.* **4. reach a compromise** *idiom* to achieve ①; to make ①. ♦ *After many hours of discussion, we finally reached a compromise.* ♦ *We were unable to reach a compromise and quit trying.*

compromising ['kɑm prə mɑɪz ɪŋ] *adj.* threatening to someone's reputation. (Adv: *compromisingly.*) ♦ *Your illegal actions have put me in a compromising position.* ♦ *Bill apologized to me for his compromising comment.*

comptroller [kən 'trol ɚ] *n.* a company treasurer; someone who controls the finances of a company. ♦ *The comptroller signs the company's paychecks.* ♦ *The owner realized the comptroller had been embezzling funds.*

compulsion [kəm 'pʌl ʃən] *n.* an obsession to do something irrational. (No plural form in this sense.) ♦ *Bill won't throw anything away because of his compulsion to save everything.* ♦ *Mary had a compulsion to wash her hands several times each hour.*

compulsive [kəm 'pʌl sɪv] *adj.* obsessed; irrational. (Adv: *compulsively.*) ♦ *The psychologist observed compulsive behavior in her client.* ♦ *Bill is compulsive about saving everything. He can't throw anything away.*

compulsory [kəm 'pʌl sə ri] *adj.* mandatory; required. ♦ *A composition class is compulsory for all college students.* ♦ *Each gymnast performed a compulsory routine.*

compunction [kəm 'pʌŋk ʃən] *n.* regret; remorse, guilt, or shame. (No plural form in this sense.) ♦ *John spoke with compunction about his mistakes and regrets.* ♦ *The suspect had no compunction about lying to the police.*

computation [kɑm pju 'te ʃən] *n.* computing; calculating. ♦ *The students' computations were incorrect.* ♦ *The decorator did a few computations to determine how much wallpaper was needed.*

compute [kəm 'pjut] *tv.* to add, subtract, divide, or multiply numbers; to calculate. ♦ *The cashier computed the bill with a calculator.* ♦ *Let's compute the cost of taking a vacation.*

computer [kəm 'pjut ɚ] **1.** *n.* an electronic machine that processes data at high speeds. ♦ *All of the billing information is kept in files on that computer.* ♦ *I installed some new software on my computer.* **2.** *adj.* <the adj. use of ①.> ♦ *I just bought some new computer software.* ♦ *My computer keyboard needs cleaning.*

computerize [kəm 'pjut ə rɑɪz] **1.** *tv.* to reorganize an office so that computers are used in many places. ♦ *The office manager decided to computerize the company.* ♦ *The consultant recommended that we computerize our office.* **2.** *tv.* to begin to handle certain tasks with a computer. ♦ *The secretary computerized the mailing list.* ♦ *The office slowly computerized its records.*

computerized [kəm 'pjut ə rɑɪzd] **1.** *adj.* computer operated; computer controlled. ♦ *The computerized records were easy to access.* ♦ *The accountant got the information from a computerized database.* **2.** *adj.* equipped with computers. ♦ *A computerized office can be very efficient.* ♦ *The computerized firm was more productive than its competition.*

comrade ['kɑm ræd] *n.* a friend; a companion. ♦ *Jane went golfing with her comrades from work.* ♦ *The Russian spy drank vodka with his comrades.*

con ['kɑn] **1.** *n.* a reason for not doing something. (The opposite of pro ①.) ♦ *There are many cons and no pros, so I won't do it.* ♦ *Anne listed the pros and cons of quitting her job.* **2.** *n.* someone who is against something. (The opposite of pro ②.) ♦ *The cons outnumber the pros.* ♦ *In the final vote, the cons won.* **3.** *n.* a fraud; a trick used to deceive someone. (Slang.) ♦ *The land sale in Florida was just a con.* ♦ *Mary was not fooled by the salesman's con.* **4.** *n.* a convict. (Slang.) ♦ *The cons played basketball in the prison yard.* ♦ *The con's family visited every Sunday.* **5. con someone out of something** *idiom* to trick someone out of money or something of value. (Slang.) ♦ *Anne conned her little sister out of her allowance.* ♦ *Dave conned me out of my autographed baseball.*

concave [kɑn 'kev] *adj.* bending inward; curved inward like the inside of a cup. (Compare with convex. Adv: *concavely.*) ♦ *I filled the concave part of the spoon with soup.* ♦ *My glasses are convex on the front and concave on the back.*

conceal [kən 'sil] *tv.* to hide someone or something. ♦ *The criminal concealed the knife in his boot.* ♦ *Mary concealed her husband's present in the closet.*

concealed [kən 'sild] *adj.* hidden; blocked from view. (Adv: *concealedly.*) ♦ *It is illegal to carry a concealed weapon in some states.* ♦ *The burglar didn't find the concealed safe.*

concealment [kən 'sil mənt] **1.** *n.* hiding someone or something; being hidden. (No plural form in this sense.) ♦ *The people were arrested for the concealment of the fugitives.* ♦ *We were suspicious about Bill's concealment of his past.* **2.** *n.* a place in which to hide. (No plural form in this sense. Number is expressed with *place(s) of concealment.*) ♦ *The fugitives were preparing for their concealment in a deserted building.* ♦ *The stolen painting is in concealment in another country.*

concede [kən 'sid] **1.** *iv.* to give in; to yield. ♦ *I conceded and admitted I was wrong.* ♦ *The company president conceded, and the argument was finished.* **2.** *tv.* to yield on a point in an argument. ♦ *Mary conceded that her argument was not logical.* ♦ *Once Bill explained his opinion, I conceded the point.* **3. concede to** *tv.* + *prep. phr.* to yield something to someone or something. ♦ *The player conceded the point to her opponent.* ♦ *The large country conceded a portion of the river to its neighboring country.*

conceit [kən 'sit] *n.* exaggerated pride in oneself; vanity. (No plural form in this sense.) ♦ *The popular athlete was known for conceit and arrogance.* ♦ *More people would like you if it weren't for your conceit.*

conceited [kən 'sit ɪd] *adj.* vain; thinking too much of oneself. (Adv: *conceitedly.*) ♦ *The arrogant host made several conceited comments about himself.* ♦ *If you weren't so conceited, more people might like you.*

conceivable [kən 'siv ə bəl] *adj.* thinkable; imaginable; possible. (Adv: *conceivably.*) ♦ *It's conceivable that we could take a vacation this year.* ♦ *We looked in every conceivable place, but we could not find the key.*

conceive [kən 'siv] **1.** *tv.* to invent something. ♦ *The inventor conceived a new gadget.* ♦ *The spy conceived an unbreakable code.* **2.** *tv.* [for a woman] to become pregnant with a child. ♦ *Jane conceived her first child when she was 25.* ♦ *The pregnancy test indicated that Mary had conceived a child.* **3. conceive of** *iv.* + *prep. phr.* to think of something; to imagine something. ♦ *I cannot conceive of a reason you shouldn't go to the party.* ♦ *I conceived of the idea as I was falling asleep one night.*

concentrate ['kɑn sən tret] **1. concentrate on** *iv.* + *prep. phr.* to think hard about something; to give close attention to something. ♦ *I couldn't concentrate on my homework because of the loud music.* ♦ *Bill concentrated on overcoming the obstacles to getting a job.* **2.** *tv.* to make some liquid more potent by removing excess water. ♦ *The bottled juice was concentrated to save on shipping costs.* ♦ *I concentrated the solution of cleaner to make it stronger.* **3.** *n.* something that is not diluted. ♦ *The orange juice was made from a frozen concentrate.* ♦ *The cleaner is sold as a concentrate that must be diluted.*

concentrated ['kɑn sən tret ɪd] **1.** *adj.* less diluted; not diluted. (Adv: *concentratedly.*) ♦ *The concentrated orange juice was not as good as the freshly squeezed juice.* ♦ *Concentrated cleaner must be diluted before you use it.* **2.** *adj.* brought together to one place; focused. (Adv: *concentratedly.*) ♦ *A single concentrated company of soldiers defended the town.* ♦ *I made a concentrated effort to finish the work on time.*

concentration [kɑn sən 'tre ʃən] **1.** *n.* close attention. (No plural form in this sense.) ♦ *I need total silence to achieve full concentration.* ♦ *The committee focused its concentration on raising funds.* **2.** *n.* focusing or concentrating on something. (No plural form in this sense.) ♦ *Concentration on your studies will result in good grades.* ♦ *Your tennis game will improve with a little concentration.* **3.** *n.* things massed together; a collection. ♦ *There is a concen-*

tration of cars near the exit of the highway. ♦ *Near the footpath is a dense concentration of flowers.*

concentric [kən 'sɛn trɪk] *adj.* [of circles or ellipses of different radiuses] having the same center. (Adv: *concentrically* [...ɪk li].) ♦ *The design consisted of three concentric circles, each of a different color.* ♦ *The nine planets have concentric orbits.*

concept ['kɑn sɛpt] *n.* a thought; an idea; a notion. ♦ *The inventor patented his concept for the gadget.* ♦ *Our teacher explained the concept of gravity.*

conception [kən 'sɛp ʃən] **1.** *n.* the moment when an ovum is fertilized by sperm. (No plural form in this sense.) ♦ *Through the microscope, I witnessed the moment of conception.* ♦ *Conception took place soon after sexual intercourse.* **2.** *n.* the understanding of something; the basic idea of something; the general notion of something. (No plural form in this sense.) ♦ *You have no conception of your lack of talent as a photographer.* ♦ *Bill's conception of making dinner is microwaving food.* **3.** *n.* developing an idea or thought; the thought process. (Figurative on ①. No plural form in this sense.) ♦ *The conception of the novel took the author half an hour.* ♦ *The song was only a hazy conception in the composer's mind.*

conceptual [kən 'sɛp ʃu əl] *adj.* of or about a concept; of or about an idea; based on an idea, plan, or structure. (Adv: *conceptually.*) ♦ *The designer has a good conceptual framework of how the building should look.* ♦ *Tom starts without planning. He does not use a conceptual approach.*

conceptualization [kən sɛp tʃu ə lə 'ze ʃən] *n.* a thought; a plan; a concept; a notion. (No plural form in this sense.) ♦ *This unique design was the engineer's own conceptualization.* ♦ *The committee's conceptualization of organization was unacceptable.*

conceptualize [kən 'sɛp tʃu ə lɑɪz] **1.** *tv.* to think thoughts; to form a concept; to envision something. ♦ *I tried to conceptualize unlimited wealth, but I couldn't.* ♦ *Can you conceptualize the laws of physics?* **2.** *iv.* to be able to form concepts; to be able to think thoughts. ♦ *A monkey cannot be trained to conceptualize.* ♦ *Most humans are able to conceptualize easily.*

concern [kən 'sɚn] **1.** *tv.* to matter to someone; to be important to someone; to worry someone. ♦ *Crime concerns the mayor very much.* ♦ *Earning enough money to live on concerns each of us.* **2.** *tv.* to be about something; to have to do with something; to deal with something. ♦ *This book concerns wildflowers.* ♦ *Our conversation concerned our plans for the future.* **3.** *n.* a matter of interest; a matter of importance; something that is of interest. ♦ *This matter is not a concern of yours.* ♦ *Mr. Smith considered the accident his own personal concern.* **4.** *n.* a worry; a cause for worry; an anxiety. ♦ *The increasing number of deer is a major concern.* ♦ *My concern is that we will be late for the movie.* **5.** *n.* care; worry; anxiety. (No plural form in this sense.) ♦ *John's lack of concern for his safety disturbed his parents.* ♦ *Do you think this new policy is a cause for concern?* **6.** *n.* a business; a firm. ♦ *I worked for three years with an insurance concern downtown.* ♦ *The shipping concern is hiring more people.*

concerned [kən 'sɚnd] **1. concerned with** *adj.* + *prep. phr.* dealing with [something]; of or about [something]. ♦ *The lecture was concerned with Revolutionary War politics.* ♦ *Mary is concerned with finishing her work before 5:00.* **2.** *adj.* worried; troubled. (Adv: *concernedly.*) ♦ *I am concerned about the rash on my arm.* ♦ *When his son was late getting home, Bill became concerned.*

concerning [kən 'sɚ nɪŋ] *prep.* about; regarding; relating to. ♦ *The prisoner wrote a letter to the governor concerning clemency.* ♦ *Jane addressed the issue concerning her raise.*

concert ['kɑn sɚt] **1.** *n.* a musical performance by one or more musicians. ♦ *The string quartet gave a short concert last night.* ♦ *The pianist will give a concert at the high school.* **2.** *adj.* <the adj. use of ①.> ♦ *Mary is a concert violinist.* ♦ *There was a biography of each musician in the concert program.*

concerted [kən 'sɚt ɪd] *adj.* arranged by an agreement and accomplished as a group effort. (Adv: *concertedly.*) ♦ *We made a concerted effort to get to the movie on time.* ♦ *They made a concerted attempt to finish the work by 5:00.*

concerti [kən 'tʃɛr ti] a pl of concerto.

concerto [kən 'tʃɛr to] *n., irreg.* a piece of music written for orchestra and one or more solo instruments. (Italian plural is concerti; English plural is *concertos.*) ♦ *The composer has written five piano concertos.* ♦ *The orchestra performed a violin concerto and then a piano concerto.*

concession [kən 'sɛ ʃən] **1.** *n.* something that is conceded; something that is yielded. ♦ *The governor would make no concessions on the issue of crime.* ♦ *The mayor's concessions on all the major issues were welcomed by the city council.* **2.** *n.* a stall or booth selling snacks, drinks, or souvenirs at sporting events, fairs, etc. ♦ *Our company runs a concession at the county fair.* ♦ *The fair charged the owner of each concession for rent each day.*

conciliate [kən 'sɪl i et] **1.** *tv.* to bring two arguing parties to an agreement; to reconcile a disagreement. ♦ *Mary tried to conciliate the angry guests, but it did no good.* ♦ *The mediator conciliated the dispute between the two sides.* **2.** *iv.* to create an agreement among people who disagree about something. ♦ *Mary offered to conciliate in the matter.* ♦ *As John and Anne argued, Tom tried to conciliate as best as he could.*

conciliation [kən sɪl i 'e ʃən] *n.* winning someone over; gaining the favor of opponents. (No plural form in this sense.) ♦ *The attempt at conciliation failed, and the argument continued.* ♦ *Mary's conciliation helped bring the arguing parties together.*

conciliatory [kən 'sɪl i ə tor i] *adj.* placating; offering conciliation. (Adv: *conciliatorily* [kən sɪl i ə 'tor ə li].) ♦ *In a gesture of peace, the leader made a conciliatory speech about the war.* ♦ *One of the diplomats made a few conciliatory suggestions that helped bring about a truce.*

concise [kən 'sɑɪs] *adj.* brief; saying a lot in as few words as possible. (Adv: *concisely.*) ♦ *This book is a concise collection of short stories.* ♦ *The winner of the award gave a short and concise acceptance speech.*

conciseness [kən 'sɑɪs nəs] *n.* shortness; brevity. (No plural form in this sense.) ♦ *Bill is known for conciseness when it comes to making speeches.* ♦ *The teacher encouraged conciseness in the student's papers.*

conclave ['kɑn klev] *n.* a meeting or gathering of people. ♦ *The professors held a conclave to design a new cur-*

riculum. ♦ *The mayor called a conclave with her staff before the press conference.*

conclude [kən 'klud] **1.** *tv.* to finish something; to come to the end of something. ♦ *Let's conclude this meeting before 5:00.* ♦ *The opera concluded at midnight.* **2.** *tv.* to reach an opinion by thinking about something. ♦ *Mary concluded that Bill was going to be late.* ♦ *The scientist examined the data and concluded that the theory was invalid.* **3.** *iv.* to come to a conclusion. ♦ *Finally, the droning professor concluded, and we left the lecture hall.* ♦ *The movie concludes at ten o'clock.*

concluding [kən 'klud ɪŋ] *adj.* final; ending. ♦ *The concluding notes of the symphony faded, and the audience applauded.* ♦ *The lawyers for both parties made concluding remarks.*

conclusion [kən 'kluʒ ən] **1.** *n.* the end of something. ♦ *At the conclusion of my story, everyone laughed.* ♦ *I will talk to you again after the conclusion of the meeting.* **2.** *n.* the final decision reached by thinking about something. ♦ *Jane's parents reached the conclusion that her allowance should be raised.* ♦ *The scientist's conclusions were based on the experiment's results.*

conclusive [kən 'klus ɪv] *adj.* definitive; decisive; final and certain. (Adv: *conclusively.*) ♦ *The tests results were conclusive and indicated cancer.* ♦ *The committee didn't reach any conclusive decision.*

concoct [kən 'kɑkt] **1.** *tv.* to prepare something, especially food or chemical mixtures. ♦ *Bill concocted a dessert made of oranges and ice cream.* ♦ *The scientist tried to concoct a new medication for warts.* **2.** *tv.* to make up something, such as a story. ♦ *The suspect hastily concocted an alibi.* ♦ *The children concocted a fantastic story to explain the broken window.*

concoction [kən 'kɑk ʃən] *n.* a mixture; something that has been concocted. ♦ *Bill's concoction of oranges and ice cream was delicious.* ♦ *The story was a concoction of unrelated events and lies.*

concord ['kɑn kord] *n.* agreement; peace. (No plural form in this sense.) ♦ *The concord between the nations lasted for a century.* ♦ *The school board members were in concord over the new policies.*

concourse ['kɑn kors] *n.* a wide passageway or walkway. ♦ *A large crowd stood in the concourse, waiting for the auditorium doors to open.* ♦ *A brightly lit concourse led from the stadium to the parking lot.*

concrete 1. ['kɑn krit] *n.* a stone-like material made from cement, sand, gravel, and water, used in construction and paving. (No plural form in this sense.) ♦ *The construction workers poured the concrete for the house's foundation.* ♦ *Jimmy hit his head on the concrete when he fell off his tricycle.* **2.** ['kɑn krit] *adj.* made from ①. ♦ *The workers poured a concrete foundation for the house.* ♦ *Jimmy banged his head on the concrete sidewalk when he fell.* **3.** [kɑn 'krit] *adj.* actual; existing; real; definite; not abstract. (Adv: *concretely.*) ♦ *The scientist had no concrete data to support his theory.* ♦ *Bill prefers concrete facts to abstract ideas.*

concur [kən 'kɚ] **1. concur with** *iv.* + *prep. phr.* to agree with someone or something. ♦ *After hearing my point, Bill concurred with me.* ♦ *The lawyer made a statement, and the judge concurred with it.* **2.** *iv.* [for two or more people] to agree. ♦ *Jane and I concur on the matter of gun control.* ♦ *The lawyer and the judge both concurred.*

concurrent [kən 'kɚ ənt] *adj.* happening at the same time; simultaneous. (Adv: *concurrently.*) ♦ *The circus presented three concurrent acts.* ♦ *There were several concurrent attempts to climb the mountain.*

concurrently [kən 'kɚ ənt li] *adv.* at the same time. ♦ *I ate dinner and watched television concurrently.* ♦ *The loss of water pressure and the power outage occurred concurrently.*

concussion [kən 'kʌ ʃən] **1.** *n.* a shock caused by a collision or explosion. ♦ *The concussion of the car crash left the driver unconscious.* ♦ *The concussion from the explosion could be felt in our office building.* **2.** *n.* an injury to the brain, caused by being hit or shaken violently or falling against something hard. ♦ *The driver received a concussion when her head hit the windshield.* ♦ *A minor concussion made Bill feel dizzy for a few days.*

condemn [kən 'dɛm] **1.** *tv.* to state one's disapproval of someone or something. ♦ *The principal condemned smoking by students at school.* ♦ *The newspaper editorial condemned the court's decision.* **2.** *tv.* to declare that something is unfit for use. ♦ *The city condemned the abandoned building.* ♦ *This room is so messy, it should be condemned!* **3.** *tv.* [for a government] to declare that property is needed for public use, and thus purchase it from its owners. ♦ *The government condemned the office building and put a parking lot in its place.* ♦ *The county condemned 40 acres of land when it built a new freeway interchange.* **4. condemn to** *tv.* + *prep. phr.* to officially sentence someone for a crime. ♦ *The judge condemned the man to life in prison.* ♦ *The court condemned the peasant to the dungeon for a year.*

condemnation [kɑn dɛm 'ne ʃən] **1.** *n.* the declaration that something is unfit for use. (No plural form in this sense.) ♦ *After the condemnation of the building, it was demolished.* ♦ *The mayor endorsed the condemnation of deserted factories.* **2.** *n.* [for government] to procure property for public use by purchasing it from its owners. (No plural form in this sense.) ♦ *The old building's condemnation provided land for a new parking lot.* ♦ *The court determined the final price for the condemnation.*

condemned [kən 'dɛmd] **1.** *adj.* sentenced; pronounced guilty; declared guilty. ♦ *The condemned criminal hung his head in despair.* ♦ *Three condemned outlaws were executed.* **2.** *adj.* declared unfit; shut down by the government. ♦ *The condemned building was destroyed.* ♦ *Gangsters hid in the condemned factory.*

condensation [kɑn dɛn 'se ʃən] **1.** *n.* the process of condensing a vapor to a liquid. (No plural form in this sense.) ♦ *Condensation occurs as warm, moist air touches something cool.* ♦ *The condensation of water vapor made it difficult to see through the windshield.* **2.** *n.* moisture that has been condensed. (No plural form in this sense.) ♦ *On a hot day, condensation will form on a cold glass.* ♦ *The condensation running down the glass made a ring on the wood table.*

condense [kən 'dɛns] **1.** *tv.* to cause a gas or vapor to become a liquid by cooling it. ♦ *The chemistry teacher condensed a gas into a liquid.* ♦ *Extreme cold will condense helium gas.* **2.** *tv.* to make a document or speech shorter. ♦ *The magazine condensed the novel for its readers.* ♦ *I con-*

densed my speech because it was too long. **3.** *tv.* to make a liquid more dense. ♦ *Milk can be condensed with steam heat for use in cooking.* ♦ *The chef used heat to condense the sauce.* **4.** *iv.* to change from vapor to liquid. ♦ *The steam condensed into water drops.* ♦ *The gas condensed in the test tube.*

condensed [kən 'dɛnst] **1.** *adj.* very concentrated. ♦ *The recipe required condensed milk.* ♦ *A condensed cleaning product removed the stubborn stain.* **2.** *adj.* shortened; made briefer. ♦ *Jane gave a condensed oral report to the committee and submitted a longer, written one.* ♦ *The condensed story had fewer elements of suspense than the original, longer one did.*

condescend [kɑn dɪ 'sɛnd] *iv.* to appear to come down from a higher standing to deal with someone or something; [for an important person] to associate with people of a lower social standing. ♦ *The haughty lawyer would not condescend to take public transportation.* ♦ *The boss condescends to eat lunch in the company cafeteria.*

condescending [kɑn dɪ 'sɛnd ɪŋ] *adj.* treating other people as if they are inferior. (Adv: *condescendingly.*) ♦ *Mary made a condescending remark about Bill's failure.* ♦ *The professor had a condescending attitude toward uneducated people.*

condescension [kɑn dɪ 'sɛn ʃən] *n.* treating people as if they are not as good as oneself. (No plural form in this sense.) ♦ *Condescension is a trait that makes one seem arrogant.* ♦ *The owner treated the employees with condescension.*

condiment ['kɑn də mənt] *n.* something that gives flavor to food, such as mustard, ketchup, or salt and pepper. ♦ *I placed the condiments for the hot dogs on the table.* ♦ *The only condiments I like on my hamburger are ketchup and mustard.*

condition [kən 'dɪ ʃən] **1.** *n.* a state of being; a situation that someone or something is in. (No plural form in this sense.) ♦ *Although the building was old, it was in very good condition.* ♦ *My shoes are in bad condition and need to be replaced.* **2.** *n.* the state of someone's health. (No plural form in this sense.) ♦ *The physician said Bill was in great condition.* ♦ *The sick woman's condition improved with proper medical treatment.* **3.** *n.* something that is necessary before something else can happen. ♦ *Passing a drug test was a condition of employment at the company.* ♦ *Cleaning her room was a condition for Jane getting her allowance.* **4.** *tv.* to shape someone or something's behavior; to train someone or something. ♦ *We conditioned our dog to fetch the newspaper.* ♦ *The children were conditioned to say "You're welcome" when they were thanked.* **5.** *tv.* to cause someone to become more physically fit. ♦ *Running every day helped condition me for the race.* ♦ *The trainer designed exercises to condition the athlete.* **6. in mint condition** *idiom* in perfect condition. ♦ *This is a fine car. It runs well and is in mint condition.* ♦ *We put our house in mint condition before we sold it.*

conditional [kən 'dɪ ʃən əl] **1.** *adj.* depending on certain restrictions or conditions. (Adv: *conditionally.*) ♦ *I have given your request conditional approval that will become final after an audit of your account. Continued employment here is conditional on good performance.* ♦ *Going on vacation is conditional upon finishing the project on time.* **2.** *adj.* <referring to words, phrases, and clauses that express a conditional ① meaning.> ♦ *"If he is here on time, we can go" is a conditional sentence.* ♦ *"Whether you like it or not, we are leaving" expresses a conditional meaning.*

conditionally [kən 'dɪʃ ən (ə) li] *adv.* under certain conditions; only if a certain state exists. ♦ *Bill was given the job conditionally.* ♦ *Mary said she'd accept the assignment conditionally.*

conditioner [kən 'dɪ ʃən ɚ] *n.* a product for hair that us used with or after shampoo to make hair softer and easier to comb. ♦ *The conditioner made Bill's hair limp.* ♦ *The beautician recommended a conditioner for Mary's hair.*

conditioning [kən 'dɪ ʃən ɪŋ] *n.* training that makes someone or something respond a certain way to a certain stimulus. (No plural form in this sense.) ♦ *The children received conditioning in good manners at school.* ♦ *The coach spent a lot of time on the conditioning of his athletes.*

condolences [kən 'dol ən sɪz] *n.* expressions of sympathy. (Treated as plural. Sometimes singular.) ♦ *Mary expressed her condolences at the death of Jane's mother.* ♦ *Bill received many condolences at his father's funeral.*

condom ['kɑn dəm] *n.* a thin covering worn over the penis during copulation. (It can prevent conception and the spread of some diseases.) ♦ *Condoms can be purchased at a drugstore.* ♦ *Some disease organisms can pass through some kinds of condoms.*

condominium AND **condo** [kɑn də 'mɪn i əm, 'kɑn do] **1.** *n.* a building containing dwellings that are owned by different individuals. ♦ *The developer built three condominiums on the property.* ♦ *The condominiums on this block are very expensive.* **2.** *n.* an individually owned apartment in a building where all apartments are similarly owned. ♦ *Our condominium is on the twentieth floor and has a view of the lake.* ♦ *The Smiths sold their house and bought a condo when their children moved out.*

condone [kən 'don] *tv.* to overlook something that is wrong. ♦ *"I will not condone cheating," the teacher said.* ♦ *The physician did not condone euthanasia.*

conducive [kən 'dus ɪv] **conducive to** *adj. + prep. phr.* helpful in something; favorable to something. ♦ *Mary finds silence conducive to studying.* ♦ *Living in a foreign country is conducive to learning its language.*

conduct 1. ['kɑn dəkt] *n.* behavior; the way someone behaves. (No plural form in this sense.) ♦ *My uncle's conduct was always gentlemanly.* ♦ *The children were sent to the principal because of their bad conduct.* **2.** [kən 'dʌkt] *tv.* to lead someone or something; to guide someone or something. ♦ *The psychologist conducted a seminar on self-esteem.* ♦ *The mountaineer conducted the hikers along the trail.* **3.** [kən 'dʌkt] *tv.* to behave [oneself] in a particular manner. (Takes a reflexive object.) ♦ *Please conduct yourself properly.* ♦ *I tried to conduct myself appropriately at the funeral.* **4.** [kən 'dʌkt] *tv.* to provide a path for electricity or heat to travel. ♦ *Copper conducts electricity well.* ♦ *Metal conducts heat very well.* **5.** [kən 'dʌkt] *iv.* to direct a group of musicians. ♦ *My piano teacher also conducts the school orchestra.* ♦ *The quartet was conducted by a skilled musician.*

conductor [kən 'dʌk tɚ] **1.** *n.* someone who directs an orchestra, band, choir, or other musical group. ♦ *When the conductor approached the podium, the audience* *applauded.* ♦ *The conductor stopped the rehearsal and corrected the woodwinds.* **2.** *n.* someone who checks tickets and collects fares on a train. ♦ *A conductor announced the name of each station.* ♦ *The conductor punched every commuter's ticket.* **3.** *n.* a substance electricity or heat can travel through. ♦ *Copper is an excellent conductor of electricity.* ♦ *Wood is a poor conductor of heat.*

conduit ['kɑn du ɪt] **1.** *n.* a pipe or channel that moves a fluid from place to place. ♦ *Fluid was led through a brick conduit to the river, where it was released into the water.* ♦ *A broken water conduit caused the street to flood.* **2.** *n.* a metal tube that protects electrical wires. ♦ *The electrician installed a length of conduit and pulled the wires through it.* ♦ *The conduit protects the wires that are in the walls.* **3.** *n.* someone or something that conveys knowledge or information. ♦ *An encyclopedia is a conduit to all types of knowledge.* ♦ *The radio serves as a conduit to the outside world.*

cone ['kon] **1.** *n.* a solid geometric shape that tapers from a circle at one end to a point at the other end. ♦ *Geometry students determined the volume of the cone.* ♦ *The top of a cone comes to a sharp point.* **2.** *n.* something shaped like ①. ♦ *The megaphone was a cone with a hole at the narrow end.* ♦ *Fresh flowers were held in a kind of glass cone mounted on the wall.* **3.** *n.* a crisp, thin, cone-shaped wafer, used for holding ice cream; an ice-cream cone. ♦ *The child crunched the cone after the ice cream was gone.* ♦ *The ice cream melted around the edges of the cone.* **4.** *n.* the seed-bearing fruit of a pine tree. ♦ *The forest floor was covered with pine cones.* ♦ *The wreath was decorated with pine cones.*

confection [kən 'fɛk ʃən] *n.* a dessert; a sweet food or candy. ♦ *The gourmet candy store sold expensive confections.* ♦ *I made a sugary confection for dessert.*

confectionery [kən 'fɛk ʃə nɛr i] *n.* a candy store; a place where candies are made and sold. ♦ *I stopped at the confectionery and bought some chocolate.* ♦ *The confectionery also sold nuts and coffee.*

confederacy [kən 'fɛd ə rə si] **1.** *n.* a political union of states or people. ♦ *Some states seceded from the republic and formed a confederacy.* ♦ *Four independent nations joined together to form a confederacy.* **2. Confederacy** *n.* the eleven southern states that broke away from the United States of America during the mid-1800s and who fought against the North during the War Between the States; the Confederate States of America. ♦ *The Confederacy disagreed with the Union over issues concerning slavery.* ♦ *The heroes of the Confederacy are still remembered in the South.*

confederate [kən 'fɛd ə rɪt] **1.** *n.* an accomplice; a partner in crime; an accessory. ♦ *The gangster and his confederates were arrested.* ♦ *The criminal recruited a confederate to help rob the bank.* **2. Confederate** *n.* a citizen of the Confederate States of America. ♦ *The Confederates lost the War Between the States.* ♦ *Thousands of Confederates were killed during the war.* **3.** *adj.* of or about the Confederate States of America. ♦ *The Confederate capital was located in Virginia.* ♦ *The Confederate Army and the Union Army both suffered heavy losses.*

confederation [kən fɛd ə 're ʃən] *n.* a confederacy; a group of people or states joined together to give each other support. ♦ *A confederation of sovereign states signed a treaty with the enemy.* ♦ *The confederation collapsed because of the quarreling of its members.*

confer [kən 'fɚ] **1.** *iv.* to discuss something with someone; to talk about ideas with someone. ♦ *I conferred with my friends about what we should eat for dinner.* ♦ *The tourists conferred among themselves about what sights they should see.* **2. confer (up)on** *tv.* + *prep. phr.* to give an award or honor to someone; to bestow an honor upon someone. ♦ *A lifetime achievement award was conferred upon the distinguished actor.* ♦ *The general conferred a high honor on the brave soldier.*

conference ['kɑn fə rəns] *n.* a meeting to discuss a specific topic. ♦ *Conferences on ending poverty were held in the nation's capital.* ♦ *Anne had a conference with her son's teacher to discuss his progress.*

confess [kən 'fɛs] **1.** *tv.* to admit something; to acknowledge that one has done something wrong. ♦ *The suspect never confessed the crime.* ♦ *John confessed that he broke the window.* **2. confess to** *iv.* + *prep. phr.* to admit doing something; to acknowledge that one has done something wrong. ♦ *Jimmy confessed to breaking the window.* ♦ *The driver would not confess to being the cause of the accident.* **3.** *iv.* to tell one's sins to a priest. ♦ *Catholic school children are encouraged to confess regularly.* ♦ *Mary confessed before Mass.*

confessed [kən 'fɛst] *adj.* admitted; having made a confession. ♦ *As a confessed thief, Max was a suspect in many unsolved crimes.* ♦ *The confessed murderer went to prison for life.*

confession [kən 'fɛ ʃən] **1.** *n.* the process or activity of confessing or admitting something. (No plural form in this sense.) ♦ *Confession of one's errors is an honest thing to do.* ♦ *Only confession will relieve the guilt that you feel.* **2.** *n.* the confessing of something; a spoken or written act of ①. ♦ *The newspaper printed the crook's confession.* ♦ *Jimmy told his parents he had a confession to make.*

confetti [kən 'fɛt i] *n.* small bits of paper and similar materials that are thrown into the air during celebrations. (The Italian plural of *confetto*. Treated as singular.) ♦ *The wedding guests threw confetti at the bride and groom.* ♦ *Confetti and balloons fell from the ceiling at midnight on New Year's Eve.*

confidant ['kɑn fɪ dɑnt] *n.* someone with whom one shares one's secrets. ♦ *Mary has many confidants with whom she shares her secrets.* ♦ *Bill didn't trust even his closest confidant with the information.*

confide [kən 'fɑɪd] **1. confide in** *iv.* + *prep. phr.* to talk about private matters with someone one trusts. ♦ *Bill confided in his priest.* ♦ *Mary confided in John that she had lost her job.* **2.** *tv.* to tell a secret to someone that one trusts. ♦ *Jane always confides her secrets to me.* ♦ *The student confided her fears to her teacher.*

confidence ['kɑn fɪ dəns] **1.** *n.* a strong trust in someone or something; a strong belief in someone or something. (No plural form in this sense.) ♦ *I have confidence that you will pass the test.* ♦ *The patient had confidence in her surgeon's skills.* **2.** *n.* a feeling of assurance; a belief in oneself and one's abilities. (No plural form in this sense.) ♦ *Bill has a lot of confidence. He's almost arrogant.* ♦ *A series of failures undermined the child's confidence.* **3.** *n.* the trust that someone will not tell a secret. (No plural form in this sense.) ♦ *Jane told me in confidence that she* *accepted a new job.* ♦ *"Can I have your confidence?" Bill asked before he told Mary the news.* **4. vote of confidence** *idiom* a poll taken to discover whether or not a person, party, etc., still has the majority's support. ♦ *The government easily won the vote of confidence called for by the opposition.* ♦ *The president of the club resigned when one of the members called for a vote of confidence in his leadership.*

confident ['kɑn fɪ dənt] **1.** *adj.* certain that something will happen; sure. (Takes a clause. Adv: *confidently.*) ♦ *We were confident that eventually winter would end.* ♦ *I am confident that he will pay his bills.* **2.** *adj.* sure of or about someone's abilities. (Adv: *confidently.*) ♦ *The promotion made Anne very confident in herself.* ♦ *Tom does not seem confident when he speaks in public.*

confidential [kɑn fɪ 'dɛn ʃəl] **1.** *adj.* secret; kept as secret. (Adv: *confidentially.*) ♦ *The confidential memo was delivered to me in a sealed envelope.* ♦ *The government file was confidential.* **2.** *adj.* [of someone] trusted with secrets. ♦ *Tom's confidential secretary would not let me talk to him.* ♦ *Jane's confidential advisor handled her financial matters.*

configuration [kən fɪg jə 're ʃən] *n.* the way that something is arranged. ♦ *The awkward configuration of the kitchen is very inefficient.* ♦ *Please place the chairs in the normal configuration around the table.*

confine [kən 'fɑɪn] **1.** *tv.* to keep someone or a creature in a small space; to enclose someone or some creature in a small space. ♦ *Bill confined his dog to the house all day.* ♦ *The prisoners were confined to their cells for all but two hours each day.* **2.** *tv.* to restrict or limit conversation or statements to a particular subject. ♦ *Please confine your remarks to the subject we are discussing.* ♦ *The judge ordered the witness to confine her testimony to the case being tried.*

confined [kən 'fɑɪnd] **1.** *adj.* kept in a small spaced; enclosed; imprisoned. ♦ *The confined puppy barked for attention.* ♦ *I can't tolerate being confined for very long.* **2.** *adj.* [of a space] restrictive or limiting. ♦ *Elephants cannot be kept in a confined area.* ♦ *I feel uncomfortable in confined spaces such as elevators.*

confinement [kən 'fɑɪn mənt] **1.** *n.* imprisonment; enclosing someone or something in something limiting. (No plural form in this sense.) ♦ *Confinement of criminals protects society.* ♦ *Many wild animals cannot tolerate confinement.* **2.** *n.* an instance of imprisonment or being confined somewhere. ♦ *The prisoner spent his confinement in a 6-by-9-foot cell.* ♦ *Max had had a number of confinements since he was a teenager.*

confining [kən 'fɑɪn ɪŋ] *adj.* limiting or restricting movement. (Adv: *confiningly.*) ♦ *Confining clothes hindered the gymnast's movements.* ♦ *I don't like to sit in the confining back seat of a car.*

confirm [kən 'fɚm] **1.** *tv.* to check something to make certain it is true, accurate, complete, or still in effect. ♦ *Please confirm our reservations at the restaurant.* ♦ *Will you confirm that the amounts on your bill are correct?* **2.** *tv.* to approve and agree that someone should be officially chosen for office. ♦ *Max, a successful lawyer, was confirmed as a Supreme Court justice last week.* ♦ *The Senate confirmed the president's choice for the cabinet post.* **3.** *tv.* to admit someone as a full member of a church. ♦ *Three young people were confirmed last Sunday at my church.* ♦ *Mary was confirmed in her family's church.*

confirmation [kɑn fɚ 'me ʃən] **1.** *n.* assurance that something is true, accurate, complete, or still in effect. (No plural form in this sense.) ♦ *The appraiser provided confirmation that the diamond was authentic.* ♦ *I called the restaurant seeking confirmation of our reservation.* **2.** *n.* a statement that something is true. ♦ *The airline mailed a confirmation of the ticket purchase.* ♦ *Witnesses provided numerous confirmations that the suspect was at the crime scene.* **3.** *n.* an act of formally approving of someone to serve in an office. ♦ *The confirmation of the new judge was done by committee.* ♦ *The Senate's confirmation of the new cabinet member was reported on the news.*

confirmed [kən 'fɚmd] **1.** *adj.* shown to be true, accurate, complete, or still in effect. ♦ *Your flights are confirmed, and your tickets have been purchased. Have a nice trip.* ♦ *Two passengers held confirmed reservations for the same seat.* **2.** *adj.* determined to remain in a particular state. ♦ *Susan is a confirmed believer in eating fat-free food.* ♦ *The confirmed bachelor vowed that he would never marry.*

confiscate ['kɑn fɪ sket] *tv.* to make an authorized seizure. ♦ *The teacher confiscated the student's toy gun.* ♦ *The police confiscated drugs from the apartment.*

confiscated ['kɑn fɪ sket ɪd] *adj.* taken by an authority. ♦ *The confiscated drugs were held at the police station.* ♦ *The teacher's desk contained many confiscated items.*

conflagration [kɑn flə 'gre ʃən] *n.* a large and destructive fire. ♦ *The firefighters fought the conflagration for hours.* ♦ *The national park was partially destroyed by the conflagration.*

conflict 1. ['kɑn flɪkt] *n.* disagreement; fighting. ♦ *We try to avoid conflict when it is possible to do so.* ♦ *I don't respond well to conflict. It upsets me.* **2.** ['kɑn flɪkt] *n.* an instance of ①; a fight; a disagreement. ♦ *Many citizens were killed in an armed conflict with a neighboring country.* ♦ *The conflict lasted until the town was destroyed in battle.* **3.** [kən 'flɪkt] *iv.* [for things] to differ or disagree. ♦ *The ideas in these two statements conflict.* ♦ *Does a meeting at two o'clock conflict with your schedule?*

conflicting [kən 'flɪk tɪŋ] *adj.* differing; clashing; disagreeing. (Adv: *conflictingly.*) ♦ *The editor noticed a number of conflicting statements in the article.* ♦ *The committee had conflicting opinions about how to allocate the budget.*

confluence ['kɑn flu əns] **1.** *n.* the place where two or more rivers flow together. (No plural form in this sense.) ♦ *A great city was built at the confluence of the rivers.* ♦ *A muddy brook and a clear stream created a swirling confluence where they met.* **2.** *n.* a place where a large number of people or things flow together. (No plural form in this sense. Figurative on ①.) ♦ *The confluence of the people arriving from all directions created a huge crowd.* ♦ *The confluence of the traffic from the two busy roads created a bottleneck.*

conform [kən 'form] **1. conform (to)** *iv.* (+ *prep. phr.*) to become similar to something in form; to begin to adopt the form or shape of something. ♦ *The wax conforms perfectly to the mold.* ♦ *My feet will never conform to these tight shoes.* **2. conform (to)** *iv.* (+ *prep. phr.*) to adapt to the nature or practices of a new situation. (Figurative on ①.) ♦ *The new furniture does not conform to the design of the new room.* ♦ *The foreign student soon conformed to his new surroundings.* **3. conform (to)** *iv.* (+ *prep. phr.*) to obey the rules. ♦ *The children conformed reluctantly to their parents' requests.* ♦ *The measurements conform properly.*

conformist [kən 'for məst] *n.* someone who conforms readily or willingly to the norms of society. ♦ *Rather than trying new ideas and trying to change things, most people are just dull conformists.* ♦ *The poet ridiculed the conformists in society.*

conformity [kən 'form ə ti] **1.** *n.* being like other things or people. (No plural form in this sense.) ♦ *Tom likes to be different and cannot stand conformity.* ♦ *A high degree of conformity is expected among soldiers.* **2.** *n.* being in agreement with laws, especially laws concerning how buildings are built and situated. (No plural form in this sense.) ♦ *This house is not in conformity with the plumbing code.* ♦ *The city planners stressed conformity with the law.*

confound [kɑn 'fɑʊnd] *tv.* to confuse and puzzle someone or some creature. ♦ *The confusing plot of the mystery novel confounded John.* ♦ *My computer confounds and annoys me daily.*

confront [kən 'frʌnt] *tv.* to face someone with an issue. ♦ *The jury was confronted with conflicting testimonies.* ♦ *Many serious problems confronted the early pioneers.*

confrontation [kɑn frən 'te ʃən] **1.** *n.* an awkward situation where opponents must come face to face and deal with a problem. (No plural form in this sense.) ♦ *My lawyer does not really like confrontation. He would rather write letters.* ♦ *Sometimes, confrontation is the best way to begin to solve a problem.* **2.** *n.* coming face to face with someone or something regarding a dispute. ♦ *Bill had a few angry confrontations with his boss.* ♦ *The cat avoided a confrontation with the dog by running away.*

confuse [kən 'fjuz] **1.** *tv.* to bewilder someone; to puzzle someone. ♦ *The whole problem confuses me. Could you explain it again?* ♦ *Algebra just confused many of the students.* **2. confuse with** *tv.* + *prep. phr.* to mistake someone or something for someone or something else. ♦ *I often confused the twins with each other because they looked alike.* ♦ *Mike confused the flour with the powdered sugar because they looked similar.*

confused [kən 'fjuzd] **1.** *adj.* bewildered; puzzled. (Adv: *confusedly* [kən 'fjuz əd li].) ♦ *The confused driver wondered whether to turn left or right.* ♦ *We were confused by the signs in the foreign country.* **2.** *adj.* mixed up; in the wrong order; disorderly. (Adv: *confusedly* [kən 'fjuz əd li].) ♦ *The poorly written report contained many confused facts and sentences.* ♦ *The master of ceremonies had a confused list of events.*

confusing [kən 'fjuz ɪŋ] *adj.* puzzling; bewildering. (Adv: *confusingly.*) ♦ *The confusing signs were all in a foreign language.* ♦ *The story was so long and confusing that I stopped reading it.*

confusion [kən 'fju ʒən] **1.** *n.* a feeling of being confused; being mixed-up. (No plural form in this sense.) ♦ *I experience confusion whenever I look at a map.* ♦ *The boss's explanation eliminated all confusion about the matter.* **2.** *n.* a state of noisy disorder. (No plural form in this sense.) ♦ *Confusion broke out when the fire alarm went off.* ♦ *The teacher yelled for quiet in the confusion.*

congeal [kən 'dʒil] **1.** *iv.* to become more solid; to thicken; to stiffen. ♦ *The fat in the soup congealed in the refrigerator.* ♦ *The blood from the wound congealed, and the bleeding stopped.* **2.** *tv.* to cause something to thicken; to cause something to clot. ♦ *The coldness of the refrigerator congealed the fat in the soup.* ♦ *Pressure on the wound will help the blood congeal.*

congealed [kən 'dʒild] *adj.* thickened; made more solid. ♦ *The congealed fat was easy to skim from the soup.* ♦ *The accident victim was covered with congealed blood.*

congenial [kən 'dʒin ɪ əl] *adj.* pleasant; pleasing; agreeable. (Adv: *congenially.*) ♦ *The popular restaurant had a congenial atmosphere.* ♦ *The Smiths are very congenial and accepting of others.*

congeniality [kən dʒin i 'æl ɪ ti] *n.* friendliness; agreeableness; compatibility. (No plural form in this sense.) ♦ *I enjoy talking to Mary because of her congeniality.* ♦ *Bill was thankful for the congeniality of his coworkers.*

congenital [kən 'dʒɛn ɪ təl] *adj.* [of a physical problem] present since birth. (Adv: *congenitally.*) ♦ *Some congenital defects can be corrected without surgery.* ♦ *The surgeons operated on the baby's congenital heart defect.*

congested [kən 'dʒɛs tɪd] *adj.* clogged; blocked; overcrowded. ♦ *The congested elevator would not hold another person.* ♦ *The congested highway made many commuters late for work.*

congestion [kən 'dʒɛs tʃən] *n.* blockage; crowding. (No plural form in this sense.) ♦ *The congestion in my lungs made it difficult to breathe.* ♦ *Congestion on the highway made me late for work.*

conglomerate 1. [kən 'glɑm ə rət] *n.* something that is made from a combination of things. (No plural form in this sense.) ♦ *The sculpture was a conglomerate of old pieces of wood, metal, and fabric.* ♦ *The sandwich was a conglomerate of leftovers from the refrigerator.* **2.** [kən 'glɑm ə rət] *n.* a large corporation made up of other companies. ♦ *The publishing company is owned by a large media conglomerate.* ♦ *The conglomerate sold a few of its smaller companies.* **3.** [kən 'glɑm ə ret] *iv.* to gather together; to crowd together. ♦ *Everyone conglomerated around my desk to hear the gossip.* ♦ *At my parties, people always conglomerate in the kitchen.*

conglomeration [kən glɑm ə 're ʃən] *n.* a crowd of things massed together. ♦ *The art critic hated the conglomeration the artist called a sculpture.* ♦ *This casserole is just a conglomeration of leftovers and a can of mushroom soup.*

Congo ['kɔŋ go] See Gazetteer.

congratulate [kən 'grætʃ ə let] *tv.* to extend one's good wishes to someone. ♦ *I congratulated Jane on her engagement.* ♦ *The principal congratulated each student as she handed out diplomas.*

congratulation [kən grætʃ ə 'le ʃən] **1.** *n.* good wishes that are communicated to someone. (No plural form in this sense.) ♦ *I sent a card of congratulation to the newly married couple.* ♦ *Tom's note of congratulation arrived long after I graduated.* **2. congratulations** *n.* an expression of happiness that one is doing well or has done something good. (Treated as plural.) ♦ *I sent my congratula-*

tions along with a present. ♦ *I gave John my congratulations on his promotion.* **3. Congratulations!** *interj.* "I congratulate you!" ♦ *Congratulations! I am very happy for you!* ♦ *We all cried "Congratulations!" to the newlyweds.*

congratulatory [kən 'grætʃ ə lə tor i] *adj.* expressing congratulations. ♦ *The principal made congratulatory remarks as he talked to the students.* ♦ *A congratulatory party was given for the graduates.*

congregate ['kɑŋ grə get] *iv.* to gather together; to assemble. ♦ *The townspeople congregated in the park to hear the mayor speak.* ♦ *Each morning people at work congregate around the coffeepot.*

congregation [kɑŋ grə 'ge ʃən] *n.* a group of people, especially in a church service. ♦ *The congregation sang the closing hymn.* ♦ *Half of the congregation fell asleep during the service.*

congress ['kɑŋ grəs] **1.** *n.* the group of people elected to make laws. ♦ *Congress will vote on the measure in the next session.* ♦ *The congress passed a law to punish drug dealers.* **2.** *n.* a meeting of representatives to or members of an organization. ♦ *I attended the Fifth Congress of Hotel Administrators last year.* ♦ *I was a delegate to a congress of book sellers.* **3. Congress** *n.* the House of Representatives and the Senate of the United States. (No plural form in this sense.) ♦ *The U.S. Congress set forth the annual budget.* ♦ *The lobbyists spoke to each member of Congress.*

congressional [kən 'grɛʃ ə nəl] *adj.* of or about a congress; of or about a meeting of lawmakers. (Often capitalized when referring to the U.S. Congress. Adv: *congressionally.*) ♦ *I attended the Congressional hearing on the proposed law.* ♦ *Bob visited his representative's congressional offices.*

congressman ['kɑŋ grəs mən] *n., irreg.* someone who is a member of a congress; someone who is a member of the United States House of Representatives; a male member of a congress; a male member of the U.S. House of Representatives. (Pl: congressmen.) ♦ *If you disagree with the law, you should write to your congressman.* ♦ *Five congressmen spoke in favor of the amendment.*

congressmen ['kɑŋ grɪs mən] pl of congressman.

congresswoman ['kɑŋ grɛs wʊm ən] *n., irreg.* a woman who is a member of a congress; a female member of the United States Senate or House of Representatives. (Pl: congresswomen.) ♦ *I complained to my congresswoman about the poor mail service in my area.* ♦ *The congresswoman for the fourth district will not run for reelection.*

congresswomen ['kɑŋ grɛs wɪm ən] pl of congresswoman.

conj. See conjunction ②.

conjecture [kən 'dʒɛk tʃɚ] **1.** *n.* guesswork; a group of opinions and guesses. (No plural form in this sense.) ♦ *Conjecture is a poor substitute for facts.* ♦ *The boss was tired of conjecture. She wanted hard data.* **2.** *n.* a guess; a supposition. ♦ *I am tired of your silly conjectures. Get some facts.* ♦ *Bob was good at making one conjecture after another.* **3.** *tv.* to guess something; to form an opinion about something. (Takes a clause.) ♦ *I could only conjecture why Jane was late.* ♦ *Tom conjectured that I had been stuck in traffic.* **4. conjecture about** *iv.* + *prep. phr.* to speculate about something; to form an opinion about someone or something. ♦ *I tried not to conjecture about the future.* ♦ *The lawyer conjectured about the suspects' motives for the crime.*

conjugal ['kɑn dʒə gəl] *adj.* of or about marriage. (Adv: *conjugally.*) ♦ *The law gives each partner certain conjugal rights and obligations.* ♦ *Mary and John looked forward to decades of conjugal bliss.*

conjugate ['kɑn dʒə get] *tv.* to cite the forms of a verb in a language. ♦ *The German class conjugated verbs every afternoon.* ♦ *I don't know how to conjugate that verb because it is irregular.*

conjugation [kɑn dʒə 'ge ʃən] *n.* a list or chart of the inflected forms of a verb in a language. ♦ *The book gave the conjugation of irregular verbs.* ♦ *The present-tense conjugation of "to be" is:* I am, you are, he is, we are, you are, they are.

conjunction [kən 'dʒʌŋk ʃən] **1.** *n.* the place where two or more linear things come together. (No plural form in this sense.) ♦ *Turn right at the conjunction of Maple and Elm Streets.* ♦ *The conjunction of the diagonal lines marked the center of the square.* **2.** *n.* a part of speech that connects words, phrases, and clauses. (Abbreviated *conj.* here.) ♦ *Conjunctions—including* and, but, for, or, nor, *and* yet*—connect words, phrases, and clauses to each other.* ♦ *Use a comma before a conjunction when it joins two clauses.*

conjure ['kɑn dʒɚ] **conjure up** *tv.* + *adv.* to cause someone or something to appear or come into being as if by magic. ♦ *The committee conjured up a theme for the dance.* ♦ *I don't know how I'll conjure up the money, but I'll pay rent tomorrow.*

connect [kə 'nɛkt] **1.** *tv.* to serve as a link between two things. ♦ *A bridge connects the two sides of the river.* ♦ *A short hallway connects my bedroom to the bathroom.* **2.** *tv.* to join or attach certain electronic devices. ♦ *Please connect the keyboard to the computer.* ♦ *Connect the telephone by plugging it in!* **3.** *tv.* to link someone to someone or something through an electronic means. ♦ *Operator, please connect me to the police department.* ♦ *What commands will connect me to your Web site?* **4.** *tv.* to relate something to something else; to associate one thought with another. ♦ *I didn't connect your face with your name until long after we had met.* ♦ *I couldn't connect the points the professor was making.* **5. connect with** *iv.* + *prep. phr.* to make contact with someone, such as by telephone. ♦ *I finally connected with Mary after leaving several messages.* ♦ *Once I connect with Bill, I will find out if he's coming to the party.* **6.** *iv.* to link with something; to link to something. ♦ *The knee bone connects to the leg bone.* ♦ *This road connects with the main road to town.* **7.** *iv.* to go on foot from one airplane flight to another at an intermediate stop. ♦ *When flying from Chicago to Boston, I had to connect at Cleveland.* ♦ *After my plane landed, I had only a few minutes to connect.*

Connecticut [kə 'nɛt ɪ kət] See Gazetteer.

connecting [kə 'nɛk tɪŋ] **1.** *adj.* [of an airplane flight] serving as a link to another flight. ♦ *Mary ran through the airport to catch her connecting flight.* ♦ *I had to make a connecting flight to get to my transatlantic flight back home.* **2.** *adj.* making a connection; forming a connection. ♦ *Finally, the city built a connecting street, so we can* *now reach the expressway easily.* ♦ *The connecting wires had been cut.*

connection [kə 'nɛk ʃən] **1.** *n.* the physical link among or between things. ♦ *A thin rope was the only connection between the boat and the dock.* ♦ *Our street is busy because it serves as a connection to the expressway.* **2.** *n.* the relationship among or between thoughts. ♦ *I easily made the connection between the two ideas.* ♦ *I thought there was no connection between the two theories.* **3.** *n.* the electronic link that connects two people by telephone. ♦ *This connection is very bad. Please call back later.* ♦ *There is noise on this connection. I can hardly hear you.* **4.** *n.* an airplane flight that one boards at an intermediate stop. ♦ *Your seats are confirmed for this flight and for the connection at Boston.* ♦ *The agent announced gate numbers for passengers making connections.* **5.** *n.* someone who is a social or business contact. ♦ *I have several connections at that firm, and perhaps I could get you a job interview.* ♦ *After twenty years in the industry, David had many connections.*

connective [kə 'nɛk tɪv] *adj.* [of tissue] connecting parts within the body. ♦ *Jane tore some connective tissue in her ankle.* ♦ *The meat was tough because of all the connective tissue.*

connector [kə 'nɛk tɚ] *n.* something that connects electrical and electronic things together. ♦ *Attach the red connector to the left channel of the stereo.* ♦ *The connector is broken, so I cannot plug it in.*

connive [kə 'nɑɪv] *iv.* to scheme; to plot. ♦ *Mary was always conniving to make extra money.* ♦ *Bill spent the afternoon conniving with Tom.*

conniving [kə 'nɑɪv ɪŋ] *adj.* of or about people who connive and scheme. (Adv: *connivingly.*) ♦ *The conniving child pretended to cry in order to get his way.* ♦ *The conniving employee plotted to get promoted.*

connoisseur [kɑn ə 'sʊr] *n.* an expert or critic in a certain field, especially art or food. (From French.) ♦ *The Smiths are wine connoisseurs and purchase very expensive wines.* ♦ *The art connoisseur thought the exhibit was distasteful.*

conquer ['kɑŋ kɚ] **1.** *tv.* to defeat someone in war; to subdue a people, army, or land. ♦ *The Romans conquered many lands.* ♦ *The dictator had plans to conquer the whole world.* **2.** *tv.* to overcome a difficulty. ♦ *Bill finally conquered his habitual giggling.* ♦ *With counseling, Sue conquered her fear of elevators.*

conquered ['kɑŋ kɚd] *adj.* defeated; taken over. ♦ *The conquered people were forced to adopt the customs of their conquerors.* ♦ *After a bloody fight, the conquered army surrendered.*

conqueror ['kɑŋ kɚ ɚ] *n.* the winner of a battle or a war. ♦ *The conqueror led the soldiers into battle without regard for the loss of life.* ♦ *Tom emerged from the fight as the conqueror.*

conquest ['kɑŋ kwɛst] **1.** *n.* the attempt to subdue, defeat, or conquer a people or a country. (No plural form in this sense.) ♦ *The conquest of England in 1066 is called the Norman Conquest.* ♦ *Conquest is exciting for some, devastating for others.* **2.** *n.* the object or target of ①. ♦ *It was likely that the knights' conquest would be destroyed during the battle.* ♦ *The city of Rome was the conquest that tempted the mad adventurer.* **3.** *n.* someone who is the target of a romantic or sexual quest. ♦ *Mary was just another of Mike's conquests. He really didn't care at all for her.* ♦ *Susan didn't mind being someone's conquest, as long he was her conquest too.*

conscience ['kɑn ʃəns] *n.* one's own sense of right and wrong. (No plural form in this sense.) ♦ *My conscience made me tell the truth.* ♦ *Max has no conscience. He cheats on his taxes.*

conscientious [kɑn ʃi 'ɛn ʃəs] *adj.* careful and hardworking. (Adv: *conscientiously.*) ♦ *The conscientious employee arrived at work early each day.* ♦ *I checked my work twice in an effort to be conscientious.*

conscious ['kɑn ʃəs] **1.** *adj.* awake, alert, and aware of immediate surroundings. (Adv: *consciously.*) ♦ *I fainted briefly but was conscious again in a few seconds.* ♦ *The patient did not want to be conscious during the surgery.* **2. conscious of** *adj.* + *prep. phr.* aware or knowledgeable about something. ♦ *I'm not conscious of any inaccuracies in the report.* ♦ *Tom is conscious of a small problem with his finances.* **3.** *adj.* intentional; intended. (Adv: *consciously.*) ♦ *I made a conscious effort to get to work on time.* ♦ *The host made a conscious attempt to talk to everyone at the party.*

consciousness ['kɑn ʃəs nəs] *n.* the condition of being awake, alert, and aware. (No plural form in this sense.) ♦ *The patient regained consciousness a few hours after the surgery.* ♦ *His period of consciousness was brief and was soon replaced by the stillness of death.*

conscript 1. [kən 'skrɪpt] *tv.* to call someone into the military; to require service in the military by law; to **draft** ⑥ someone. ♦ *The soldier had been conscripted by the army against his will.* ♦ *During the war, physicians were conscripted to treat the wounded.* **2.** ['kɑn skrɪpt] *n.* someone who is called into military service; a draftee. ♦ *My grandfather was a conscript in the army during World War II.* ♦ *The conscripts went through basic training before battle.*

conscription [kən 'skrɪp ʃən] *n.* the practice of requiring people—in the U.S., young men—to serve in the military; the draft. (No plural form in this sense.) ♦ *Many people opposed conscription during the war.* ♦ *Bill dreaded the day that he would be informed of his conscription.*

consecrate ['kɑn sə kret] **1.** *tv.* to declare something to be sacred; to declare a solemn purpose for someone or something. ♦ *The priest consecrated the water in the baptismal font.* ♦ *We always consecrated the burial grounds of our people.* **2. consecrate to** *tv.* + *prep. phr.* to devote someone or something to a noble purpose. ♦ *The monk consecrated his life to the service of God.* ♦ *The doctor consecrated his work to the saving of human life.*

consecration [kɑn sə 'kre ʃən] *n.* the process of declaring something sacred. (No plural form in this sense.) ♦ *Only a member of the clergy can perform the consecration of the Communion elements.* ♦ *The Gettysburg Address was given as part of the consecration of a graveyard.*

consecutive [kən 'sɛk jə tɪv] *adj.* in a row or series; in sequence. (Adv: *consecutively.*) ♦ *We went to Florida on vacation for two consecutive years.* ♦ *The baseball team played three consecutive games at home.*

consensus [kən 'sɛn səs] *n.* the general opinion; a general agreement among people. ♦ *The Smiths were all in* *consensus about where to eat dinner.* ♦ *The school board could not reach a consensus on the curriculum.*

consent [kən 'sɛnt] **1.** *iv.* to agree; to give approval. ♦ *He did not consent.* ♦ *I would consent if you would ask me politely.* **2. consent to** *iv.* + *prep. phr.* to agree to something; to permit something. ♦ *I refuse to consent to your request!* ♦ *The boss did not consent to your proposal.* **3.** *n.* permission; approval. (No plural form in this sense.) ♦ *The parents were required to sign a form of consent for the children's field trip.* ♦ *The manager happily gave his consent to my request.*

consenting [kən 'sɛn tɪŋ] *adj.* giving consent; in agreement. (Adv: *consentingly.*) ♦ *A new drug was tested on consenting subjects.* ♦ *Only children of consenting parents were allowed to go to the museum.*

consequence ['kɑn sə kwɛns] **1.** *n.* a result; an outcome. ♦ *You must deal with the consequences of your actions.* ♦ *We got stuck in traffic, and as a consequence, we missed the movie.* **2.** *n.* importance; something having important significance. (No plural form in this sense.) ♦ *The cheap novel was of no consequence to the literary world.* ♦ *The serious mistake was of great consequence.*

consequent ['kɑn sə kwɛnt] *adj.* [of something that occurs] as a result of a previous action. (Adv: *consequently.*) ♦ *Bill's mistake and consequent dismissal depressed him.* ♦ *The rain and the consequent cancellation of the baseball game left us with nothing to do.*

conservation [kɑn sɚ 've ʃən] *n.* the practice of conserving, protecting, or preserving something, such as water, the state of the land, or other resources. (No plural form in this sense.) ♦ *Our company practices conservation by recycling its waste.* ♦ *The government encourages the conservation of natural gas.*

conservative [kən 'sɚv ə tɪv] **1.** *adj.* modest; cautious, moderate. (Adv: *conservatively.*) ♦ *A conservative estimate of the cost to repair the car is $500.* ♦ *Dr. Jones takes a conservative approach to prescribing medication.* **2.** *adj.* politically not radical ② or liberal ③. (Adv: *conservatively.*) ♦ *The conservative viewpoint is usually the opposite from the liberal agenda.* ♦ *Conservative politicians think there are problems that government does not know how to solve.* **3.** *n.* someone who is a member of or supports a conservative ② political philosophy. ♦ *Bill is a conservative who opposes expanding the welfare system.* ♦ *As a conservative, Mary always votes for conservative candidates.*

conservatory [kən 'sɚv ə tor i] **1.** *n.* a school for the arts; a theater, music, dance, or art school. ♦ *Twenty students were accepted to the music conservatory this year.* ♦ *Each year the dance conservatory gives a recital.* **2.** *n.* a greenhouse; a structure where plants are kept and grown. ♦ *The mansion has a conservatory where orange trees are grown.* ♦ *Jane, a botanist, spends much of her time in the conservatory.*

conserve [kən 'sɚv] *tv.* to preserve a supply of something by not wasting it or by using less than you might otherwise use. ♦ *The government is trying to get us to conserve water.* ♦ *Turning off the lights as you leave a room conserves energy.*

consider [kən 'sɪd ɚ] **1.** *tv.* to think carefully about something. ♦ *I considered taking a trip to the coast.* ♦ *Mary considered each option before making a decision.* **2.** *tv.* to think of someone or something in a certain way. ♦ *Mary likes her job so much she doesn't consider it to be work.* ♦ *Bill considers chocolate cake to be the best dessert.* **3.** *tv.* to take something into account. ♦ *I considered the reasons why Jane might be in a bad mood.* ♦ *Before you take a trip, consider your budget.*

considerable [kən 'sɪd ɚ ə bəl] *adj.* rather large; not small or minimal. (Adv: *considerably.*) ♦ *Mike inherited a considerable amount of money from his parents.* ♦ *Having no car is a considerable inconvenience.*

considerate [kən 'sɪd ə rɪt] *adj.* thoughtful of other people. (Adv: *considerately.*) ♦ *"Be considerate and don't wake your brother," Mary said.* ♦ *Jane is so considerate. She's always doing favors for people.*

consideration [kən sɪd ə 're ʃən] **1.** *n.* the thought given toward a decision. (No plural form in this sense.) ♦ *After much consideration, the Smiths decided to adopt a child.* ♦ *The jury gave the case a lot of consideration.* **2.** *n.* something to be kept in mind when making a decision. ♦ *One consideration in choosing a college is the cost.* ♦ *The weather was a consideration in planning the camping trip.* **3.** *n.* respect for other people's feelings and opinions. (No plural form in this sense.) ♦ *Mary exercises consideration of her friends' views before she speaks.* ♦ *David had no consideration for my position.*

consign [kən 'saɪn] *tv.* to place goods in the possession of someone who will attempt to sell the goods or return them to the owner if they are not sold. ♦ *The company consigned 400 copies of the book to one distributor.* ♦ *The artist consigned her paintings to the art dealer.*

consignment [kən 'saɪn mənt] **1.** *n.* a shipment of goods. ♦ *When the next consignment arrives, we will stock the shelves immediately.* ♦ *The consignment of new hats is stored in the warehouse.* **2. on consignment** *phr.* [of goods] having been placed in a store for sale, without transferring the title of the goods to the operator of the store. ♦ *The artist placed his work in a gallery on consignment.* ♦ *I will attempt to sell your clothing on consignment.*

consist [kən 'sɪst] **consist of** *iv.* + *prep. phr.* to be made of something. ♦ *This farm consists of forty acres.* ♦ *The United States consists of fifty states.*

consistency [kən 'sɪs tən si] **1.** *n.* the degree of thickness; the degree of firmness; the kind of texture of something. (No plural form in this sense.) ♦ *The pastry chef mixed the batter to the proper consistency.* ♦ *Bill does not like the consistency of avocados.* **2.** *n.* evenness in the way that something is done. (No plural form in this sense.) ♦ *John's tennis game suffers from a lack of consistency.* ♦ *Children need consistency in their daily activities.*

consistent [kən 'sɪs tənt] *adj.* unwavering; uniform; unchanging. (Adv: *consistently.*) ♦ *Jane and Bill are consistent role models for their children.* ♦ *The witness's testimony was consistent with the victim's observations at the time of the accident.*

consolation [kɑn sə 'le ʃən] **1.** *n.* solace; the comforting of someone in time of sadness. (No plural form in this sense.) ♦ *Tom, who just lost his job, welcomed consolation from his friends.* ♦ *The rabbi offered words of consolation at the funeral.* **2.** *n.* someone or something that is a comfort in time of sadness; a comfort. ♦ *After the fire, one consolation was having home insurance.* ♦ *Mary was a consolation to her grieving friend.*

console 1. ['kɑn sol] *n.* a panel where the controls for a machine are; a control panel. ♦ *Mary sat at the console and pressed the flashing button.* ♦ *The console has many signal lights and knobs.* **2.** ['kɑn sol] *n.* a cabinet designed to stand on the floor, holding electronic equipment, such as stereo equipment. ♦ *Tom bought a console with the stereo equipment already installed in it.* ♦ *My grandparents had both a portable radio and a radio console.* **3.** [kən 'sol] *tv.* to provide comfort to someone who is sad; to give someone sympathy. ♦ *David consoled his crying child.* ♦ *The physician consoled the parents of the accident victim.*

consolidate [kən 'sɑl ɪ det] *tv.* to bring things together into one place; to reduce something in such a way to make the original smaller, more compact, or less spread out. ♦ *I consolidated all the supplies into one box.* ♦ *The two schools were consolidated to reduce costs.*

consolidation [kən sɑl ɪ 'de ʃən] *n.* the combining of businesses, schools, churches, or offices into a single strong entity. (No plural form in this sense.) ♦ *The parents strongly opposed the consolidation of the schools.* ♦ *Two small congregations consolidated last year.*

consonant ['kɑn sə nənt] **1.** *n.* a speech sound that is made by restricting the flow of sound or air in the vocal tract; a speech sound that is not a vowel. (The word has different meanings depending on whether one is talking about sounds or spelling letters.) ♦ *The consonants among the sounds used in English are* p, t, k, b, d, g, f, h, s, m, n, ŋ, *v, z,* ʒ, ʃ, θ, ð, l, r, w, j. ♦ *There are two consonants in the word* thin. **2.** *n.* a letter of an alphabet that represents ①. ♦ *The consonants included in English spelling are* b, c, d, f, g, h, j, k, l, m, n, p, q, r, s, t, v, w, x, y, z. ♦ *There are three consonants in the word* sweet.

consortia [kən ˌsor ʃə] pl of consortium.

consortium [kən 'sor ʃəm] *n.* a group or association formed for a specific task. (Pl: consortia, occasionally *consortiums.*) ♦ *The consortium met yearly to discuss advancements in medicine.* ♦ *Six colleges combined into a consortium and hired a lobbyist to work with the state legislature.*

conspicuous [kən 'spɪk ju əs] *adj.* obvious; very noticeable. (Adv: *conspicuously.*) ♦ *Mary was conspicuous in her absence.* ♦ *The crack in the ceiling was very conspicuous.*

conspiracy [kən 'spɪr ə si] *n.* a secret plan of two or more people to do something illegal or evil. ♦ *The police officer uncovered a conspiracy to assassinate the president.* ♦ *The two friends were convicted of conspiracy to commit murder.*

conspirator [kən 'spɪr ə tɚ] *n.* someone who secretly plans to do something illegal with at least one other person. ♦ *The conspirator denied his plans to assassinate the president.* ♦ *Max and Tom were both conspirators in the plot.*

conspire [kən 'spɑɪr] **1.** *iv.* to plan secretly to do something illegal with one or more other people. ♦ *The bank tellers conspired to rob the bank.* ♦ *Mary and Lisa conspired to steal a car.* **2.** *iv.* [for events] to happen together or in harmony. (Figurative on ①.) ♦ *The unfortunate events of the day conspired to make me tired and miserable.* ♦ *A lack of education and an inability to speak the language conspired to make employment difficult for the immigrant.*

constancy ['kɑn stən si] *n.* faithfulness; loyalty. (No plural form in this sense.) ♦ *Jane knew that she could count on the constancy of her friends.* ♦ *No creature displays more constancy than my dog.*

constant ['kɑn stənt] **1.** *adj.* continuous; incessant. (Adv: *constantly.*) ♦ *The constant noise from the road crew gave Bill a headache.* ♦ *Please stop tormenting me with your constant questions.* **2.** *adj.* loyal; faithful; unchanging. (Adv: *constantly.*) ♦ *Bill's constant companion was his dog.* ♦ *John remained a constant source of humor for his friends.* **3.** *n.* a figure, quality, or measurement that stays the same. ♦ *In this equation, the constant* c *equals the speed of light.* ♦ *The temperature was always a constant in the experiment.*

constellation [kɑn stə 'le ʃən] *n.* a particular group of stars. ♦ *The astronomer described the different constellations to us.* ♦ *It was so cloudy we couldn't see any of the constellations.*

consternation [kɑn stɚ 'ne ʃən] *n.* puzzled amazement and annoyance. (No plural form in this sense.) ♦ *Dave's consternation grew when he couldn't figure out the puzzle.* ♦ *Much to our consternation, the phone kept ringing.*

constipate ['kɑn stə pet] *tv.* to hinder someone's bowel movements. ♦ *Bananas tend to constipate me.* ♦ *Too much tea will constipate you.*

constipated ['kɑn stə pet ɪd] *adj.* temporarily unable to have a regular bowel movement. ♦ *John was constipated from eating too many green bananas.* ♦ *The constipated patient sat uncomfortably in the doctor's waiting room.*

constipating ['kɑn stə pet ɪŋ] *adj.* causing constipation. ♦ *Some foods are known to be constipating.* ♦ *Ripe apples are not at all constipating.*

constipation [kɑn stə 'pe ʃən] *n.* difficulty with moving the bowels. (No plural form in this sense.) ♦ *Anne is home ill, suffering from severe constipation.* ♦ *Eating an apple a day will often prevent constipation.*

constituency [kən 'stɪ tʃu ən si] *n.* the voters who are eligible to vote for the legislative representative of a particular area or district. ♦ *The politicians listened to the ideas of their constituencies.* ♦ *The entire constituency opposed raising taxes.*

constituent [kən 'stɪtʃ u ənt] **1.** *n.* a part of something; a part of a whole; a component. ♦ *This chapter is only one small constituent of the whole book.* ♦ *Friendliness is an important constituent of a pleasant personality.* **2.** *n.* someone who lives in the district represented by a particular politician. ♦ *The mayor talked to the angry constituent for a long time.* ♦ *The constituent wrote letters to her senators.* **3.** *adj.* being a part of a whole; being a component of something. ♦ *The chapter is an important constituent element of the whole book.* ♦ *The constituent parts of the radio were scattered across the workbench.*

constitute ['kɑn stɪ tut] **1.** *tv.* to make up something; to be the parts of something. ♦ *Organic matter, sand, and clay constitute the soil I plant in.* ♦ *Three houses and fifty acres of land constitute this estate.* **2.** *tv.* to be equal to; to be the same as. ♦ *Not telling the whole truth constitutes lying.* ♦ *Her explanation of why she did it constitutes a full confession.*

constitution [kɑn stɪ 'tu ʃən] **1.** *n.* the document that tells the rules that govern a country or an organization.

(Usually capitalized when it refers to the U.S. Constitution.) ♦ *The original Constitution of the United States is kept in Washington, D.C.* ♦ *The newly independent country drafted a constitution.* **2.** *n.* the state of health of the body or the mind. ♦ *My doctor said I had a hearty constitution.* ♦ *My manager's weak constitution was caused by stress.*

constitutional [kɑn stɪ 'tu ʃə nəl] **1.** *adj.* of or about a constitution. (Adv: *constitutionally.*) ♦ *Problems in the government created a constitutional crisis.* ♦ *The senator proposed a constitutional amendment.* **2.** *adj.* prescribed by or in accordance with a constitution. ♦ *Censorship violates the constitutional right to free speech.* ♦ *I know that the law is constitutional and that the courts will agree.* **3.** *n.* a walk or other exercise taken for one's health. ♦ *I went on a constitutional each morning after I retired.* ♦ *During today's constitutional, we strolled through the park.*

constrain [kən 'stren] **1.** *tv.* to make someone do something; to oblige someone to do something. ♦ *I was constrained by etiquette to write a thank-you note for the gift.* ♦ *Hunger constrained the orphan to beg for food.* **2.** *tv.* to confine someone or something; to restrain someone or something. ♦ *I constrained my desire to tell Anne what I thought of her idea.* ♦ *Bill constrained his sense of humor at the funeral.*

constraint [kən 'strent] **1.** *n.* restraint; limitation; holding back of one's natural behavior. (No plural form in this sense.) ♦ *Bill ignored all constraint and lost his temper.* ♦ *Please exercise some constraint when you criticize the queen.* **2.** *n.* a limitation; a limit. ♦ *With two kids in college, the Smiths have constraints on their budget.* ♦ *There is one important constraint, and that is that I don't have the time to do what you ask.*

constrict [kən 'strɪkt] *tv.* to tighten something; to make something narrower; to make something contract. ♦ *The snake constricted its body around its prey and killed it.* ♦ *Bill complained that a tie would constrict his breathing.*

constrictor [kən 'strɪk tɚ] *n.* a kind of snake that kills by suffocating its prey. ♦ *A rabbit became the prey of a hungry constrictor.* ♦ *The python is a well-known constrictor.*

construct 1. [kən 'strʌkt] *tv.* to build something; to put something together. ♦ *A famous architect constructed a model of a new cathedral.* ♦ *The workers constructed a fountain in the town square.* **2.** ['kɑn strʌkt] *n.* a theory; an abstract concept. ♦ *My idea for a story is only a theoretical construct.* ♦ *The professor outlined a social construct and asked us to comment on it.*

construction [kən 'strʌk ʃən] **1.** *n.* the process of building. (No plural form in this sense.) ♦ *Construction of the building was halted during the winter months.* ♦ *Our project, the construction of a garage, was completed in three weeks.* **2.** *n.* the business of building buildings; the business of constructing buildings. (No plural form in this sense.) ♦ *Mike has been in construction for twenty years.* ♦ *During the recession, construction in the city declined.* **3.** **under construction** *idiom* in the process of being built or repaired. ♦ *We cannot travel on this road because it's under construction.* ♦ *Our new home has been under construction all summer. We hope to move in next month.*

constructive [kən 'strʌk tɪv] *adj.* helpful; able to be used in a helpful way. (Adv: *constructively.*) ♦ *The professor wrote some constructive criticisms on the student's paper.* ♦ *I welcome constructive comments on my work.*

construe [kən 'stru] *tv.* to interpret something in a particular way; to take something as having a particular meaning. ♦ *I construed Sue's remark to mean she is happy working here.* ♦ *The offended customer had construed my words to mean something I didn't mean at all!*

consul ['kɑn səl] *n.* a government official who resides in a foreign country. (Compare with **counsel** and **council**.) ♦ *The consul and his family lived in a luxurious apartment.* ♦ *The American consul occupied a lovely home in the capital city.*

consulate ['kɑn sə lɪt] *n.* the office of a consul. ♦ *The consulate was located in the center of the capital.* ♦ *The tourist went to the consulate to fill out some official paperwork.*

consult [kən 'sʌlt] **1.** *tv.* to seek advice or information from someone or something. ♦ *I consulted the weather report before planning the picnic.* ♦ *Bill consulted his boss about the deal.* **2.** *iv.* to offer and supply technical business advice as a profession. ♦ *I used to work for a company, but now I consult for a living.* ♦ *I have been consulting for more than three years.* **3.** **consult with** *iv. + prep. phr.* to discuss something with someone, seeking advice. ♦ *I consulted with a lawyer about what to do.* ♦ *Mary consulted with a doctor on this problem last month.*

consultant [kən 'sʌl tənt] *n.* someone who consults; someone who is hired by a company to give advice. ♦ *The consultant recommended changes to increase productivity.* ♦ *The company hired a consultant to develop a new computer system.*

consultation [kɑn səl 'te ʃən] *n.* a meeting where someone consults with someone else. ♦ *During the consultation, the doctor told Mary that her tumor was benign.* ♦ *Billy's parents had a consultation with his teacher.*

consulting [kən 'sʌl tɪŋ] *adj.* giving advice; [of someone or something] providing a consultation. ♦ *After working in management for ten years, Lisa started a consulting firm.* ♦ *My doctor confirmed the diagnosis with a consulting physician.*

consume [kən 'sum] **1.** *tv.* to eat or drink something. ♦ *Americans consume a huge amount of sugar each year.* ♦ *At our Thanksgiving dinner, we consumed an entire turkey.* **2.** *tv.* to use something up. ♦ *This old car consumes too much gas.* ♦ *The Smiths consume a lot of goods each year.*

consumer [kən 'sum ɚ] *n.* someone who buys a product or a service. ♦ *A marketing company surveyed consumers.* ♦ *Consumers should know the ingredients of the products they use.*

consuming [kən 'sum ɪŋ] *adj.* demanding and urgent. (Adv: *consumingly.*) ♦ *Getting enough money for rent is a consuming need for Mary.* ♦ *Bill has a consuming desire to fly to Paris.*

consummate 1. ['kɑn sə mɪt] *adj.* perfect; quintessential; total. (Adv: *consummately.*) ♦ *After years of training, Mary is a consummate violinist.* ♦ *Bill has the consummate roommate—he's never home and always pays the rent.* **2.** ['kɑn sə met] *tv.* to fulfill something; to complete something; to make something complete. ♦ *Signing the contract consummated the deal.* ♦ *The agreement will be consummated when the fee has been paid.* **3.** ['kɑn sə met] *tv.* to make a marriage complete by having sex. ♦ *The newlyweds consummated their marriage during the honeymoon.* ♦ *It is easier to annul a marriage if it has never been consummated.*

consumption [kən 'sʌm ʃən] *n.* the process or activity of consuming something. (No plural form in this sense.) ♦ *My consumption of junk food increased when I quit smoking.* ♦ *The country's consumption of potatoes fell when the crops failed.*

cont. See contraction ③.

contact ['kɑn tækt] **1.** *tv.* to communicate with someone; to get in touch with someone. ♦ *I contacted Bill to see how he was doing.* ♦ *The furniture store contacted us when the couch that we had ordered arrived.* **2.** *tv.* to touch someone or something. ♦ *When the fly contacted the flypaper, it was unable to fly away.* ♦ *The copper wire must contact the brass screw to complete the circuit.* **3.** *n.* touching; coming together. (No plural form in this sense.) ♦ *The contact between the copper wire and the brass screw completed the circuit.* ♦ *When the fly came into contact with the sticky substance, it got stuck.* **4.** *n.* a person inside an organization through whom one can get needed information or favors. ♦ *Bill has contacts at the state attorney's office.* ♦ *Mary used her university contacts to get a job.* **5.** *n.* a metal part that touches another metal part, closing an electrical circuit. ♦ *When the contacts closed, the lights went on.* ♦ *The switch contacts were dirty, and the switch did not work.* **6. have contact with someone** *idiom* a link to someone resulting in communication. ♦ *I have had no contact with Bill since he left town.* ♦ *Tom had contact with a known criminal last month.*

contagious [kən 'tedʒ əs] *adj.* [of an illness] easily passed from person to person. (Adv: *contagiously.*) ♦ *The flu is a highly contagious disease.* ♦ *Cancer is not contagious, so you shouldn't be afraid to touch someone with cancer.*

contain [kən 'ten] **1.** *tv.* to hold someone or something; to have someone or something as a constituent. ♦ *Maple syrup contains a great deal of sugar.* ♦ *The glass jar contained two thousand jelly beans.* **2.** *tv.* to hold back something; to restrain something; to keep something in control. ♦ *The firefighters contained the fire in the barn, and the house was spared.* ♦ *The oil spill was contained in a small area along the coast.* **3.** *tv.* to control oneself or one's emotions. ♦ *I was so excited I could hardly contain myself.* ♦ *Mary tried to contain her amusement, but erupted in laughter anyway.*

container [kən 'ten ɚ] *n.* something that contains something. ♦ *The peanut butter was sold in a plastic container.* ♦ *The perfume was in a beautiful glass container.*

contaminate [kən 'tæm ə net] *tv.* to taint something; to make something impure. ♦ *The stream water was contaminated with pollutants.* ♦ *Bill contaminated the food by leaving it where flies could get on it.*

contaminated [kən 'tæm ɪ net ɪd] *adj.* tainted; polluted. ♦ *The children were told not to drink from the contaminated stream.* ♦ *The contaminated milk was removed from the grocery store.*

contamination [kən tæm ə 'ne ʃən] **1.** *n.* making something impure; polluting something. (No plural form in this sense.) ♦ *The water contamination was caused by improper waste management.* ♦ *Dumping garbage in the ocean resulted in contamination.* **2.** *n.* a substance that causes ①. (No plural form in this sense.) ♦ *Laboratory tests showed a lot of contamination in the water.* ♦ *Once food has spoiled, there is no way to remove all the contamination.*

contemplate ['kɑn təm plet] *tv.* to think about something carefully. ♦ *Philosophers contemplate the existence of humankind.* ♦ *The disgruntled worker carefully contemplated changing careers.*

contemplation [kɑn təm 'ple ʃən] **1.** *n.* serious thought; consideration. (No plural form in this sense.) ♦ *Mike found relaxed contemplation almost impossible.* ♦ *Contemplation and meditation keep me calm and serene.* **2.** *n.* an instance of ①. ♦ *She was lost in her contemplations of the meaning of life.* ♦ *I hate to interrupt your contemplations, but there is a telephone call for you.*

contemporary [kən 'tɛmp ə rɛ ri] **1.** *adj.* current; present day. ♦ *The museum specializes in contemporary art.* ♦ *The sociologist studied contemporary issues of urban poverty.* **2.** *n.* someone who lived during the same time period as someone else. ♦ *John and Mary, each born in 1900, were contemporaries.* ♦ *My grandparents were contemporaries of Dwight D. Eisenhower.*

contempt [kən 'tempt] **1.** *n.* hatred; loathing. (No plural form in this sense.) ♦ *The scholar had great contempt for his lazy colleagues.* ♦ *Jane's voice was filled with contempt as she described her family.* **2. in contempt (of court)** *idiom* disrespect for a judge or courtroom procedures. ♦ *The bailiff ejected the lawyer who was held in contempt.* ♦ *The judge found the juror in contempt of court when she screamed at the attorney.*

contemptible [kən 'tɛmp tə bəl] *adj.* worthy of contempt; worthy of being hated. (Adv: *contemptibly.*) ♦ *Tom's rude behavior is contemptible.* ♦ *Mary felt her friend's politics were contemptible.*

contemptuous [kən 'tɛmp tʃu əs] *adj.* showing scorn; showing contempt; hateful. (Adv: *contemptuously.*) ♦ *The contemptuous crowd heckled the speaker at the political rally.* ♦ *Mike is contemptuous of people who smoke around him.*

contend [kən 'tɛnd] **1.** *tv.* to state that something is a fact; to assert something. ♦ *Lisa contended that her theory was correct.* ♦ *I still contend that my advice was the best you ever got.* **2. contend with** *iv.* + *prep. phr.* to struggle with someone or something; to fight against someone or something. ♦ *The supervisor contended with the malfunctioning of the machinery.* ♦ *After a hard day of work, Mary had to contend with traffic.*

contender [kən 'tɛn dɚ] *n.* someone who competes against someone else in a sporting event, especially in boxing; a competitor who is seeking to be victorious. ♦ *The two friends were contenders at the track meet.* ♦ *Bob is the leading heavyweight contender for the boxing championship.*

content 1. [kən 'tɛnt] *adj.* satisfied; pleased. (Adv: *contently.*) ♦ *After a good meal and good conversation, we were all content.* ♦ *Tom looked quite content as he lay sleeping.* **2.** ['kɑn tɛnt] *n.* something that is contained within something, such as the text of a book or the components of food. (No plural form in this sense.) ♦ *This dessert has a high fat content.* ♦ *The content of the book has to do with food preparation.* **3. contents** ['kɑn tɛnts] *n.* the ingredients that make up something; everything that is contained within something. (Treated as plural. Sometimes singular.) ♦ *Mike put all the contents of the casserole into a baking dish and put it in the oven.* ♦ *Food producers must list the product's contents on its container.* **4. (table of) contents** [...'kɑn tɛnts] *n.* a list at the beginning of a book showing what is in the book and the page number of each part. ♦ *Bill skimmed the book's contents to see if he was interested in it.* ♦ *The contents listed the chapter titles and page numbers.* **5. to one's heart's content** [...kən 'tɛnt] *idiom* as much as one wants. (On ①.) ♦ *John wanted a week's vacation so he could go to the lake and fish to his heart's content.* ♦ *I just sat there, eating chocolate to my heart's content.*

contented [kən 'tɛn tɪd] *adj.* satisfied; pleased; happy with things the way they are. (Adv: *contentedly.*) ♦ *The baby gave a contented sigh and fell asleep.* ♦ *At thirty, Mary was quite contented.*

contention [kən 'tɛn ʃən] **1.** *n.* a point of dispute; a claim. ♦ *The scientist's contention was that one day people would live on the moon.* ♦ *Where to eat dinner was a matter of contention between John and me.* **2.** *n.* struggling together; competition. (No plural form in this sense.) ♦ *The contention between the two employees was obvious to everyone.* ♦ *The high level of contention in the office hurt productivity.*

contentious [kən 'tɛn tʃəs] *adj.* eager to argue; tending to argue. (Adv: *contentiously.*) ♦ *The contentious student started arguments over silly matters.* ♦ *Billy becomes contentious when the subject of his bedtime arises.*

contentment [kən 'tɛnt mənt] *n.* satisfaction. (No plural form in this sense.) ♦ *For Mike, contentment is sitting in front of the fireplace with a book.* ♦ *Jazz puts Mary in a mood of perfect contentment.*

contest 1. ['kɑn tɛst] *n.* a competition that will determine a winner. ♦ *A pie-eating contest was held at the country fair.* ♦ *It was always a contest between Bill and Mike to see whose car was faster.* **2.** [kən 'tɛst] *tv.* to challenge something, especially in a court of law. ♦ *The lawyer contested the judge's ruling.* ♦ *Mary contested her mother's will in court.*

contestant [kən 'tɛs tənt] *n.* someone who competes in a contest; a competitor. ♦ *The game show had three contestants.* ♦ *The contestants stretched their muscles before the race.*

context ['kɑn tɛkst] **1.** *n.* the words before and after another word that help determine its meaning. ♦ *The reporter took the mayor's quote out of context and distorted the meaning.* ♦ *I guessed the meaning of the word from its context in the paragraph.* **2. in the context of something** *idiom* in the circumstances under which something has happened. ♦ *In the context of a funeral, laughing loudly is inappropriate.* ♦ *In the context of an argument, it is fine to speak firmly.*

contiguous [kən 'tɪg ju əs] *adj.* touching; adjoining; next to and touching. (Adv: *contiguously.*) ♦ *The free plane ticket was good to anywhere in the contiguous United States, so we could not choose to go to Alaska or Hawaii.* ♦ *The borders of the park and the school grounds are contiguous.*

continent ['kɑn tə nənt] *n.* one of the large landmasses of Earth: Africa, Australia, North America, South America, Antarctica, Europe, and Asia. ♦ *The continent of Europe contains many countries.* ♦ *Explorers have traveled on every continent on Earth.*

continental [kɑn tə 'nɛn təl] **1.** *adj.* of or about a continent; contained within a continent. (Adv: *continentally.*) ♦ *Tom studied continental movements in geology class.* ♦ *Hawaii is not located in the continental United States.* **2.** *adj.* of or about the continent of Europe and the cultures and people found there. (England is sometimes included.) ♦ *My father, who was born in France, had a cultured, continental view of the world.* ♦ *I really enjoy continental cooking styles, and Spanish cooking in particular.*

contingency [kən 'tɪn dʒən si] *n.* a troublesome possibility. ♦ *It is not possible to foresee every contingency.* ♦ *The manager had a plan for every contingency.*

contingent [kən 'tɪn dʒənt] **1. contingent (up)on** *adj.* + *prep. phr.* dependent on something happening. (Adv: *contingently.*) ♦ *Getting dessert is contingent on eating your vegetables.* ♦ *Mary's offer to buy the house was contingent upon her getting a mortgage.* **2.** *n.* a group of people, often representative of a larger body. ♦ *Mayor Smith tried to appease every contingent of the city's voters.* ♦ *The diplomat arrived on a chartered flight with his contingent of advisors and lawyers.*

continual [kən 'tɪn ju əl] *adj.* happening again and again; repeated; over and over. (Compare with continuous. Continual and continuous are often used interchangeably at all levels of speech and writing. Adv: *continually.*) ♦ *Bill's continual failure to do his homework resulted in his failing the class.* ♦ *I have grown tired of Jane's continual complaining about her job.*

continuation [kən tɪn ju 'e ʃən] *n.* something that is continued on from an earlier beginning. ♦ *Highway 51 is a continuation of State Road 12 at the county line.* ♦ *Dad promised a continuation of the discussion about my allowance.*

continue [kən 'tɪn ju] **1.** *tv.* to make something keep on happening. (Takes a gerund as an object.) ♦ *The singer continued performing even though the audience had left.* ♦ *Jane continued taking piano lessons until she was twenty.* **2.** *tv.* to resume something after an interruption. ♦ *The radio station continued its broadcast after the announcement.* ♦ *The speaker continued speaking after the interruption.* **3.** *tv.* to postpone a trial until a later time. ♦ *Judge Smith continued the trial until the following Wednesday.* ♦ *The trial was continued until next month.* **4. continue to** *tv.* + *inf.* to do something again and again. ♦ *The singer continued to perform even though the audience had left.* ♦ *Jane continued to take piano lessons until she was twenty.* **5.** *iv.* to go on happening; to remain the same way. ♦ *The audience left, but the pianist continued.* ♦ *The rain continued all afternoon.* **6.** *iv.* to resume after being stopped. ♦ *The speaker paused, looked at his notes, and then continued.* ♦ *The television show continued after the commercial.*

continuing [kən 'tɪn ju ɪŋ] *adj.* ongoing; not stopping. ♦ *Tom and Jane have a continuing battle over which one should wash the dishes.* ♦ *Theft of office supplies has been a continuing problem for the company.*

continuity [kɑn tə 'nu ə ti] *n.* continuing in a sequence without breaks or interruptions. (No plural form in this sense.) ♦ *The movie editor is responsible for making sure that the continuity of the script is preserved in the final film.* ♦ *Many interruptions ruined the continuity of our conversation.*

continuous [kən 'tɪn ju əs] *adj.* without stopping; without an interruption; ongoing. (See also continual. Adv: *continuously.*) ♦ *I grew tired of Bill's continuous complaining about work.* ♦ *The weather forecaster predicted continuous rain throughout the day.*

continuum [kən 'tɪn ju əm] *n.* a series that cannot be separated into parts. ♦ *Each student's performance was graded on a continuum ranging from excellent to horrible.* ♦ *The graph of sales was an unbroken continuum from good to bad.*

contort [kən 'tort] *tv.* to twist something out of shape; to bend something out of shape. ♦ *The baby contorted her face and began to cry.* ♦ *He had to contort his hand in order to reach into the hole to get the tool he dropped.*

contorted [kən 'tor tɪd] *adj.* twisted; bent; distorted. (Adv: *contortedly.*) ♦ *The clown's contorted face was comical.* ♦ *The contorted body of the victim indicated a traumatic death.*

contour ['kɑn tʊr] *n.* the rounded or flowing shape of someone or something. ♦ *The contours of the car made it very aerodynamic.* ♦ *The artist accentuated the model's contours.*

contraband ['kɑn trə bænd] **1.** *n.* goods or substances that are banned from a place, such as a prison. (No plural form in this sense.) ♦ *The guards found contraband in the prisoner's cell.* ♦ *Guards often sold contraband to the prisoners.* **2.** *n.* goods that are not to be imported into a country. (No plural form in this sense.) ♦ *The dogs were taught to sniff out contraband in luggage.* ♦ *A tourist was caught carrying contraband into the country.* **3.** *adj.* <the adj. use of ①.> ♦ *The gang members smuggled contraband drugs into prison.* ♦ *The prison guards inspected the cell for contraband items.* **4.** *adj.* <the adj. use of ②.> ♦ *A tourist was caught carrying contraband sausage into the country.* ♦ *All contraband meat or plants are destroyed when found by U.S. customs.*

contraception [kɑn trə 'sɛp ʃən] *n.* birth prevention. (No plural form in this sense.) ♦ *The nurse discussed several different forms of contraception.* ♦ *Some religions do not approve of contraception.*

contraceptive [kɑn trə 'sɛp tɪv] **1.** *adj.* of or about birth prevention. (Adv: *contraceptively.*) ♦ *A large medical company invented a new contraceptive system.* ♦ *The hospital provides contraceptive counseling.* **2. contraceptive (device)** *n.* a device for birth prevention. ♦ *Most drugstores sell contraceptives.* ♦ *No contraceptive device is 100% effective.*

contract 1. ['kɑn trækt] *n.* a legal document that describes an agreement between two or more people or companies. ♦ *The singer signed a contract with a recording company to make three albums.* ♦ *The contract outlined the author's royalty rates.* **2.** [kən 'trækt] *tv.* to hire someone under a contract for a specific project. ♦ *The Smiths contracted a designer to remodel their kitchen.* ♦ *Bill contracted an artist to paint his portrait.* **3.** [kən 'trækt] *tv.* to catch a disease. ♦ *The child contracted chickenpox from a classmate.* ♦ *Jane has a limp because she contracted polio as a child.* **4.** [kən 'trækt] *iv.* to enter into an agreement with someone; to agree to do something by contract. ♦ *Bob, a house painter, contracted to paint the outside of the house.* ♦ *The author contracted to write a book.* **5.** [kən 'trækt] *iv.* to shrink; to shorten; to come together; to become narrow. ♦ *The drug caused my muscles to contract.* ♦ *I pulled the elastic, and then it contracted when I let go.*

contraction [kən 'træk ʃən] **1.** *n.* shrinkage. (No plural form in this sense.) ♦ *The contraction of spending led to a recession.* ♦ *In cold weather, the contraction of the bricks makes the pavement seem loose.* **2.** *n.* the tensing of a muscle, especially of the uterus during childbirth. ♦ *Jane felt her contractions begin, and she knew she was in labor.* ♦ *When contractions were 3 minutes apart, the doctor was notified.* **3.** *n.* a shortened word, made by replacing a letter or letters with an apostrophe ('); the shortening of a spoken word by removing a sound or sounds. (Abbreviated *cont.* here.) ♦ *The students learned to form contractions in grammar class.* ♦ Wouldn't *is a contraction of* would not.

contractor ['kɑn træk tɚ] *n.* someone who provides general building and construction services by entering into agreements with workers and supply companies. ♦ *We hired a contractor to supervise the renovation of our house.* ♦ *The contractor, in turn, hired people to do the work.*

contractual [kən 'træk tʃu əl] *adj.* of or about a contract. (Adv: *contractually.*) ♦ *Your company has a contractual obligation to complete the building.* ♦ *Bill and Bob entered into a contractual agreement.*

contradict [kɑn trə 'dɪkt] *tv.* to say something that is contrary to what someone else has said; to correct or argue with an alleged error of fact. ♦ *Jane often contradicted her annoying roommate just to annoy her.* ♦ *I hate to contradict your statement, but there are many snakes in Australia.*

contradiction [kɑn trə 'dɪk ʃən] *n.* a statement that is the opposite of something that has been said. ♦ *The lawyer pointed out a contradiction in the witness's statement.* ♦ *The proofreader found a contradiction of a previous statement in the article.*

contradictory [kɑn trə 'dɪk tə ri] **1.** *adj.* opposite; contrary; conflicting. ♦ *The editor deleted a contradictory statement in the last paragraph.* ♦ *Max made two contradictory statements to the police.* **2.** *adj.* likely to contradict; prone to making contradictions. ♦ *The contradictory witness angered the judge.* ♦ *"Don't be contradictory," Mary told Billy.*

contraption [kən 'træp ʃən] *n.* a device; a machine. ♦ *Dave bought a new contraption that gets golf balls out of ponds.* ♦ *This contraption is used to grate cheese.*

contrary 1. ['kɑn trɛr i] *adj.* completely opposite; opposed. (Adv: *contrarily* [kɑn 'trɛr ə li].) ♦ *Bill and Jane hold contrary opinions about many things, but they disagree most about politics.* ♦ *The results were contrary to what we expected.* **2.** [kən 'trɛr i, 'kɑn trɛr i] *adj.* stubborn; refusing to do what is wanted. (Adv: *contrarily* [kɑn 'trɛr ə li].) ♦ *The contrary student angered the teacher.* ♦ *The contrary clerk refused to check the stockroom for more shoes.* **3. contrary to something** ['kɑn trɛr i . . .] *idiom* in spite of something; regardless of something. ♦ *Contrary to what you might think, I am neat and tidy.* ♦ *Contrary to public opinion, my uncle is well and healthy.* **4. on the contrary** [. . . 'kɑn trɛr i] *idiom* in opposition to what has just been said. ♦ *I'm not ill. On the contrary, I'm very healthy.* ♦ *She's not in a bad mood. On the contrary, she's as happy as a lark.*

contrast 1. ['kɑn træst] *n.* a noticeable difference; an obvious difference. ♦ *Mary's modern apartment is a real contrast to her old, shabby one.* ♦ *Today's rain is a sharp contrast to yesterday's sunshine.* **2.** ['kɑn træst] *n.* noticeable differences between the light and dark parts of an image. (No plural form in this sense.) ♦ *There is too much contrast in the picture. The blacks are too black, and the whites are blinding.* ♦ *My computer monitor has no contrast left. I will have to get a new one.* **3.** [kən 'træst] *tv.* to compare the differences found in two or more things. ♦ *The essay contrasts two characters in the book.* ♦ *This short article contrasts the views of the politicians.* **4.** [kən 'træst] *iv.* to be noticeably different. ♦ *His black jacket contrasted sharply with his white pants.* ♦ *The mansion contrasted with the small houses that surrounded it.*

contrasting [kɑn 'træs tɪŋ] *adj.* noticeably different; differing; showing a difference. (Adv: *contrastingly.*) ♦ *The contrasting colors actually looked good together.* ♦ *Bill and Mary have contrasting personalities, but they get along well.*

contribute [kən 'trɪb jut] **1.** *tv.* to give money, time, or labor, usually for a good cause. ♦ *The Smiths contribute money to the same charity each year.* ♦ *Bill contributed his old clothes to the needy.* **2.** *iv.* to give [something] to someone or something. ♦ *When they pass the basket around in church, I usually contribute.* ♦ *We need your financial support. Please contribute.*

contribution [kɑn trɪ 'bju ʃən] *n.* a gift of money, time, labor, or help; a donation. ♦ *The contributions went to help the school for the blind.* ♦ *Jane was commended for her contribution to the project.*

contributor [kən 'trɪb jət ɚ] **1.** *n.* someone who gives money, time, labor, or help; a donor. ♦ *The contributor wanted to remain anonymous.* ♦ *Mike, the contributor of the team's sports equipment, was publicly acknowledged.* **2.** *n.* someone who writes articles for a newspaper, magazine, etc. ♦ *The editor asked contributors to write editorials for the magazine.* ♦ *The history professor was a frequent contributor to the local newspaper.*

contrite [kən 'trɑɪt] *adj.* showing remorse owing to guilt. (Adv: *contritely.*) ♦ *Jimmy was very contrite about breaking the window.* ♦ *The driver who caused the car accident was very contrite over it.*

contrition [kən 'trɪ ʃən] *n.* remorse; sincere sorrow for one's wrongs. (No plural form in this sense.) ♦ *Paying for the broken window was Jimmy's act of contrition.* ♦ *The businessman felt no contrition about cheating his customers.*

contrivance [kən 'trɑɪv əns] *n.* a machine; something that has been contrived. ♦ *This small contrivance is an apple corer and slicer.* ♦ *My elderly uncle invented many useless contrivances.*

contrive [kən 'trɑɪv] **1.** *tv.* to invent something; to design an invention; to come up with an invention. ♦ *My uncle, the inventor, contrived many useless appliances.* ♦ *A group of scientists contrived a new synthetic plastic.* **2. contrive to** *iv.* + *inf.* to plan in order to make something happen. ♦ *Jane's friends contrived to give her a surprise party.* ♦ *The teenagers contrived to go to the party against their parents' wishes.*

contrived [kən 'trɑɪvd] *adj.* forced; not natural; schemed. ♦ *The tardy student's excuse seemed very contrived.* ♦ *The dialogue in the novel was contrived and stilted.*

control [kən 'trol] **1.** *n.* authority; the power to direct someone or something. ♦ *We have no control over the weather.* ♦ *Bill has complete control of the operations of the factory.* **2.** *n.* a lever, knob, or other device used to operate machinery or electronics. (Often plural.) ♦ *The cockpit of an airplane is full of controls.* ♦ *Mike spilled coffee on the controls of the machine, and the machine stopped working.* **3.** *tv.* to have power over something; to have authority over something; to direct someone or something; to rule someone or something. ♦ *The president of the company controls its spending.* ♦ *No one can control the weather.* **4.** *tv.* to exercise the power to restrain, regulate, steer, guide, or command someone or something. ♦ *I could not control the car on the icy road.* ♦ *The babysitter could not control the children.* **5. out of control** *idiom* not manageable; not restrained; disorderly. ♦ *We called the police when things got out of control.* ♦ *The children are out of control and need to be disciplined.* **6. under control** *idiom* manageable; restrained and controlled; not out of control. ♦ *We finally got things under control and functioning smoothly.* ♦ *The doctor felt she had the disease under control and that I would get well soon.*

controller [kən 'trol ɚ] *n.* a comptroller; someone who manages the financial affairs of a company. ♦ *Dave was appointed the controller of the company.* ♦ *You will have to discuss accounting questions with the controller.*

controversial [kɑn trə 'vɚ ʃəl] *adj.* causing controversy. (Adv: *controversially.*) ♦ *Mike wrote a very controversial book about the weakness of our political leaders.* ♦ *Abortion is a controversial issue.*

controversy ['kɑn trə vɚ si] **1.** *n.* contention over an issue or something that a person has done. (No plural form in this sense.) ♦ *Controversy makes good newspaper stories.* ♦ *I am really tired of public controversy concerning the morals of the president.* **2.** *n.* a particular issue of contention and opinion causing discussion and debate. ♦ *The controversy over the new policies caused an uproar at the company.* ♦ *Every single news program discussed the controversy about the new tax law.*

contusion [kən 'tu ʒən] *n.* a bruise. ♦ *Bill suffered minor contusions when he fell down the stairs.* ♦ *The paramedic treated the accident victims for contusions and shock.*

convalesce [kɑn və 'lɛs] *iv.* to get better after an illness; to regain one's health after an illness. ♦ *After the surgery, Jane convalesced at home for a week.* ♦ *The tuberculosis patient convalesced in a warm, dry climate.*

convalescence [kɑn və 'lɛs əns] **1.** *n.* the process of regaining one's health after an illness. (No plural form in this sense.) ♦ *The patient's convalescence was marked by relapses.* ♦ *After the accident, Bill had a long convalescence.* **2.** *n.* a period of time while someone gets better after an illness. (No plural form in this sense.) ♦ *Bill spent his convalescence in the country.* ♦ *Jane's convalescence took three months.*

convalescent [kɑn və 'lɛs ənt] **1.** *adj.* of or about getting better after an illness. ♦ *During his convalescent* *period, John rested at home.* ♦ *The convalescent patient remained in bed most of the day.* **2.** *n.* someone who is recovering from an illness. ♦ *Jane, a convalescent, watched movies and read all day.* ♦ *A nurse took care of the convalescent.*

convenience [kən 'vin jəns] **1.** *n.* the quality of being easy to use and making life easier or more pleasant. (No plural form in this sense.) ♦ *We go the nearest grocery store because of its convenience.* ♦ *I do not have the convenience of owning a washing machine.* **2.** *n.* something that is easy to use and makes life easier or more pleasant. ♦ *Our cabin in the woods had no modern conveniences.* ♦ *The luxurious hotel had all the conveniences of home.*

convenient [kən 'vin jənt] **1.** *adj.* suitable. (Adv: *conveniently.*) ♦ *I am sorry, but the meeting you have called is not convenient.* ♦ *Tom picked a convenient time to come for a visit.* **2.** *adj.* available; within reach. (Adv: *conveniently.*) ♦ *The paper towels are kept in a convenient place above the sink.* ♦ *The extra bedroom was convenient when guests stayed overnight.*

convent ['kɑn vɛnt] **1.** *n.* a building, often next to a Catholic church, where nuns live and work. ♦ *The convent housed twenty nuns.* ♦ *The church and the convent are next to a cemetery.* **2.** *n.* a religious order or community, especially of nuns. ♦ *Mary joined the convent when she was seventeen.* ♦ *After two years, Jane left the convent and became a teacher.*

convention [kən 'vɛn ʃən] **1.** *n.* a large meeting; a group of people gathered together for a specific purpose. ♦ *The medical association annually holds a large convention in a major city.* ♦ *The convention was held to discuss innovation in the field of medicine.* **2.** *n.* a formal agreement between countries. ♦ *The Warsaw Convention primarily concerns the luggage of airline passengers.* ♦ *The Geneva Convention addresses the treatment of prisoners of war.* **3.** *n.* the way things are typically done; the way things are expected to be done. ♦ *The rude guest paid no attention to etiquette or convention.* ♦ *Students of the 1960s rebelled against everyday conventions.*

conventional [kən 'vɛn ʃə nəl] *adj.* typical; customary. (Adv: *conventionally.*) ♦ *Mary thought marriage and a family was too conventional so she joined the army.* ♦ *"Don't count your chickens before they hatch" is a piece of conventional wisdom.*

converge [kən 'vɚdʒ] *iv.* [for things, such as lines, roads, trails] to come together. ♦ *All the trails converge here and form a single large trail.* ♦ *All the radiuses of the circle converge at the center of the circle.*

conversant [kən 'vɚs ənt] *adj.* familiar with someone or something; well acquainted with someone or something. ♦ *My literature professor is conversant with all types of literature.* ♦ *I am not conversant with that type of computer system.*

conversation [kɑn vɚ 'se ʃən] **1.** *n.* discussion; talk between people. (No plural form in this sense.) ♦ *The art of conversation is acquired through practice.* ♦ *Conversation is difficult when the room is extremely noisy.* **2.** *n.* a discussion; a dialogue. ♦ *Our conversation focused on vacations we had taken.* ♦ *Mary and Bill had a long conversation on the telephone.*

conversational [kɑn vɚ 'se ʃən əl] *adj.* of or about conversation. (Adv: *conversationally.*) ♦ *The lecturer spoke with a friendly, conversational manner.* ♦ *I took a class in conversational Spanish.*

converse 1. the converse [...'kɑn vɚs] *n.* the opposite or contrary of something that is said or done. (No plural form in this sense. Treated as singular.) ♦ *You did the converse of what I would have done in that situation.* ♦ *No matter what I say, Bill says the converse.* **2.** ['kɑn vɚs] *adj.* opposite; contrary; reversed. (Adv: *conversely.*) ♦ *If that plan doesn't work, try the converse approach.* ♦ *Mary always adopts a converse opinion whenever I state my ideas.* **3.** [kən 'vɚs] *iv.* to have a conversation with someone. ♦ *We never have time to converse these days.* ♦ *Lisa went into the conference room to converse with her boss.*

conversely [kɑn 'vɚs li] *adv.* in the opposite way; on the other hand. ♦ *Conversely, we could go to the movie first and then out to dinner.* ♦ *Do it this way or, conversely, do it the other way.*

conversion [kən 'vɚʒ ən] **1.** *n.* converting something from one state to another. (No plural form in this sense.) ♦ *The conversion of the computer system took a week.* ♦ *The Smiths planned a conversion of their basement into a study.* **2.** *n.* a statement of how a value in one scheme is expressed in another scheme. ♦ *The cookbook gave a chart of conversions for standard measures.* ♦ *What is the conversion from cups to quarts?* **3.** *n.* the changing of money from one currency to another. (No plural form in this sense.) ♦ *The bank charged a fee for the conversion of American money into foreign currencies.* ♦ *The conversion from dollars to pesos can be done at the border.* **4.** *n.* a complete change in one's beliefs; a change in religion or beliefs. (No plural form in this sense.) ♦ *The criminal underwent a conversion to Christianity in prison.* ♦ *Bill's sudden conversion startled his family.*

convert 1. ['kɑn vɚt] *n.* someone who has adopted a new set of beliefs or practices, often religious beliefs or practices. ♦ *The convert fastidiously practiced his new religion.* ♦ *Describing my new diet to the group, I was hoping to make some converts.* **2. convert into** [kən 'vɚt...] *tv.* + *prep. phr.* to change something into something else; to adapt something into a new use. ♦ *I converted the spare bedroom into a reading room.* ♦ *This couch converts into a bed.* **3.** [kən 'vɚt] *tv.* to cause someone to adopt a new set of beliefs or practices. ♦ *Mary tried to convert her friends to her new method of dieting.* ♦ *Bill resisted the minister's attempts to convert him.* **4.** [kən 'vɚt] *tv.* to change a measurement into the equivalent measurement in another measuring system. ♦ *I used a calculator to convert miles to kilometers.* ♦ *The students quickly learned how to convert quarts into liters.* **5.** [kən 'vɚt] *tv.* to change the money of one country into an equivalent amount of money of another country. ♦ *We forgot to convert our dollars before the trip.* ♦ *The bank converts foreign currency for its customers.* **6.** [kən 'vɚt] *iv.* to have a complete change in beliefs; to change one's religion. ♦ *Bill, a Protestant since birth, had no desire to convert.* ♦ *The evangelist urged people on the street to convert.*

converted [kən 'vɚt ɪd] **1.** *adj.* changed; transformed; adapted. ♦ *The converted room became a study.* ♦ *Once converted, the sofa was a comfortable bed.* **2.** *adj.* brought into a new religion. ♦ *The converted man was baptized into the Christian faith.* ♦ *Converted believers were welcomed into the church.*

convertible [kən 'vɚt ə bəl] **1.** *adj.* able to be changed back and forth from one state to another. (Adv: *convertibly.*) ♦ *The crib is convertible into a bed for a toddler.* ♦ *The convertible sofa was convenient to use when guests stayed overnight.* **2.** *n.* a car with a roof that can be removed or folded down. ♦ *Bill looked at the convertibles in the showroom.* ♦ *We were driving in the convertible when it began to rain.*

convex [kɑn 'vɛks] *adj.* of or about the outside of a curve. (Compare with concave. Adv: *convexly.*) ♦ *The outside of a ball is convex.* ♦ *A convex lens bulges outward.*

convey [kən 've] **1.** *tv.* to take someone or something from one place to another. ♦ *Trucks conveyed the goods from the distributor to the buyer.* ♦ *The moving belt conveyed the product down the assembly line.* **2.** *tv.* to express something; to communicate something. (Figurative on ①.) ♦ *This award conveys our congratulations on your achievement.* ♦ *The expression on Bill's face conveyed his thoughts.*

conveyance [kən 've əns] **1.** *n.* the process of moving someone or something from one place to another. (No plural form in this sense.) ♦ *When we moved, my company paid for the conveyance of our furniture.* ♦ *What is the cost of the conveyance of the goods?* **2.** *n.* the expression of one's thoughts; a communication. (No plural form in this sense.) ♦ *Facial expressions are a conveyance of emotion.* ♦ *The officer's conveyance of the bad news was quite abrupt.* **3.** *n.* a vehicle that moves someone or something from one place to another. ♦ *The bus is a convenient conveyance for travel in the city.* ♦ *The quickest conveyance is probably the airplane.*

convict 1. ['kɑn vɪkt] *n.* someone who has been convicted of a crime; a prisoner in a jail. ♦ *The convicts were allowed outside for one hour each day.* ♦ *The convict was serving a twenty-year sentence.* **2.** [kən 'vɪkt] *tv.* [for a judge or a jury] to declare someone guilty of a crime. ♦ *The jury convicted the man, and he was sentenced to twenty years in prison.* ♦ *The defendant was convicted of murder.*

convicted [kən 'vɪk tɪd] *adj.* found guilty; declared guilty. ♦ *The convicted woman spent ten years in prison.* ♦ *The suspect was a previously convicted felon.*

conviction [kən 'vɪk ʃən] **1.** *n.* belief; strong belief. (No plural form in this sense.) ♦ *John believes in his religion with conviction.* ♦ *The preacher spoke with great conviction.* **2.** *n.* the act of convicting someone who is guilty of a crime. ♦ *The newspapers reported the conviction of the terrorists in the bombing.* ♦ *The defendant appealed his conviction to a higher court.* **3. convictions** *n.* strong beliefs. (Treated as plural.) ♦ *My minister has strong religious convictions.* ♦ *I have no convictions about the proper way to raise children.*

convince [kən 'vɪns] **1.** *tv.* to persuade someone. ♦ *I understand your argument, but you will never convince me.* ♦ *What can I do to convince you of the truth?* **2. convince to** *tv.* + *inf.* to persuade someone to do something. ♦ *I convinced Mary to cut her hair short.* ♦ *Bill convinced his father to buy a new car.*

convincing [kən 'vɪn sɪŋ] **1.** *adj.* persuasive. (Adv: *convincingly.*) ♦ *Mary always has convincing arguments to justify her political views.* ♦ *The dean's convincing words encouraged Tom to study harder.* **2.** *adj.* realistic; like the real thing. (Adv: *convincingly.*) ♦ *The movie gave a convincing portrayal of medieval life.* ♦ *The manipulative child gave a convincing excuse for his failings.*

convivial [kən 'vɪv i əl] *adj.* sociable and friendly. (Adv: *convivially.*) ♦ *You will find my friends convivial and eager to make you feel at home.* ♦ *This restaurant is quite convivial, and I am sure you will feel welcome.*

convocation [kɑn və 'ke ʃən] *n.* an assembly, especially the assembly of students at a graduation ceremony. ♦ *Jane's parents attended her convocation.* ♦ *The dean spoke at the convocation ceremony.*

convoluted [kɑn və 'lut ɪd] **1.** *adj.* twisted and tangled. (Adv: *convolutedly.*) ♦ *The rope lay on the deck of the shop, tangled and convoluted.* ♦ *The pipes under our house look like a convoluted maze of metal.* **2.** *adj.* [of writing] seeming to be twisted and confused. (Figurative on ①. Adv: *convolutedly.*) ♦ *The message was so convoluted that Bill couldn't understand it.* ♦ *I have never read such an awkward and convoluted sentence.*

convolution [kɑn və 'lu ʃən] *n.* a coil; a twist. ♦ *The sailor tripped over the convolutions of rope on the ship's deck.* ♦ *A single convolution of the garden hose looked like a snake in the grass.*

convoy ['kɑn voɪ] *n.* a group of ships or vehicles, traveling together, often for protection. ♦ *The army sent a convoy of supply trucks to the center of the battle.* ♦ *The Pilgrims came in a convoy of ships to the New World.*

convulsion [kən 'vʌl ʃən] *n.* a spasm; an uncontrollable, violent jerking of muscles. ♦ *Epilepsy can cause serious convulsions.* ♦ *The children collapsed on the floor in convulsions of laughter.*

convulsive [kən 'vʌl sɪv] *adj.* having spasms; likely to have spasms. (Adv: *convulsively.*) ♦ *The doctor sedated the convulsive patient.* ♦ *Bill was kept in the hospital room until he was no longer convulsive.*

coo ['ku] **1.** *n.* a soft murmur, such as those made to and by babies. (Pl in *-s.*) ♦ *The baby gave a few soft coos before it fell asleep.* ♦ *The mother's coos soothed the infant into sleep.* **2.** *iv.* [for a pigeon or dove] to make ①. ♦ *We could hear the pigeons coo outside our window.* ♦ *We could not hear the birds coo over the noise of the train.* **3.** *iv.* to speak in a gentle, loving murmur. ♦ *Jimmy cooed softly to his tiny, new puppy.* ♦ *Susan cooed and cooed to soothe her crying baby.*

cook ['kʊk] **1.** *n.* someone who prepares food to be eaten. ♦ *The cook prepared a three-course dinner.* ♦ *Bill is a great cook and invents his own recipes.* **2.** *tv.* to prepare food for eating by heating it. ♦ *I cooked the chicken for an hour in the oven.* ♦ *After a long day at work, I never want to cook dinner.* **3.** *tv.* to make something hot; to heat something. (Informal. Figurative on ②.) ♦ *The sun cooked Lisa and David as they biked along the lake.* ♦ *Heat from the fire cooked Bill's backside as he stood in front of the fireplace.* **4.** *iv.* to prepare food; to work as ①. ♦ *John cooked in the army for 4 years.* ♦ *I hate to cook!* **5.** *iv.* to undergo cooking. ♦ *I sliced potatoes while the ham cooked in the oven.* ♦ *The roast cooked evenly in the new oven.*

cookbook ['kʊk bʊk] *n.* a book that gives detailed instructions on how to prepare different kinds of food; a recipe book. ♦ *Bill and Jane received several cookbooks as wedding presents.* ♦ *The cookbook contained hundreds of recipes.*

cooked ['kʊkt] *adj.* heated and ready to eat; made hot; prepared for eating by being heated. ♦ *Is the chicken cooked yet?* ♦ *I like cooked carrots better than raw carrots.*

cookie ['kʊk i] *n.* a small, hard, sweet cake made of flour, sugar, eggs, and other ingredients. ♦ *The jar was full of cookies for the children.* ♦ *There are hundreds of types of cookies to choose from at the store.*

cooking ['kʊk ɪŋ] *n.* food preparation; performing as a cook. (No plural form in this sense.) ♦ *Every night, Bob did the cooking and Lisa did the cleaning.* ♦ *I took a course in gourmet cooking in my spare time.*

cookout ['kʊk ɑʊt] *n.* a party where food is prepared outdoors on a grill or over a fire. ♦ *The cookout lasted long into the night.* ♦ *We roasted marshmallows at the cookout.*

cool ['kul] **1.** *adj.* between warm and cold. (Adv: *coolly.* Comp: *cooler;* sup: *coolest.*) ♦ *It was a cool spring day.* ♦ *If it is not too cool, we'll go swimming this afternoon.* **2.** *adj.* calm, not excited; relaxed. (Informal. Adv: *coolly.* Comp: *cooler;* sup: *coolest.*) ♦ *Bill tried to remain cool after winning the lottery.* ♦ *A police officer should always remain cool and composed.* **3.** *adj.* less than friendly; unfriendly; reserved. (Adv: *coolly.* Comp: *cooler;* sup: *coolest.*) ♦ *I was disturbed by the cool reception I got at the party.* ♦ *Lisa was cool towards Bob because she was mad at him.* **4.** *adj.* admirable; very good. (Informal. Comp: *cooler;* sup: *coolest.*) ♦ *It's so cool that Bill won the lottery.* ♦ *My neighbors are very cool. They let us swim in their pool.* **5.** *tv.* to make something less warm. ♦ *I cooled the cake on a wire rack before frosting it.* ♦ *The breeze cooled the steamy room a bit.* **6.** *iv.* to become less warm. ♦ *The air cooled as evening approached.* ♦ *As we got closer to the lake, the temperature cooled.*

coolant ['kul ənt] *n.* something that is used to cool something. (No plural form in this sense.) ♦ *The car needed more engine coolant for lubrication.* ♦ *I spilled some coolant, and it killed the grass near the driveway.*

cooler ['kul ɚ] *n.* a small insulated box that maintains a cool temperature when ice is put inside it. ♦ *I packed the cooler for our picnic.* ♦ *We put the perishable items in the cooler.*

cooling ['kul ɪŋ] *adj.* causing someone or something to become more cool. ♦ *A cooling breeze wafted in through the window.* ♦ *After a humid day, a cooling rain shower is very pleasant.*

coolly ['kul li] **1.** *adv.* calmly; not in an excited way. ♦ *Bill coolly asked how much money he had won.* ♦ *Jane coolly announced her promotion.* **2.** *adv.* not in a friendly way; unenthusiastically. ♦ *The rude salesclerk spoke to us coolly.* ♦ *Bill acted coolly towards Jane because he was mad at her.*

coolness ['kul nəs] **1.** *n.* a cool quality, feeling, or state. (No plural form in this sense.) ♦ *In the hot sun, we longed for the coolness of the shade.* ♦ *Coolness descended on us as the rainstorm approached.* **2.** *n.* calmness. (No plural form in this sense.) ♦ *Bill's coolness when he won the lottery was amazing.* ♦ *Calmly, John responded to the amazing news with coolness.* **3.** *n.* unfriendliness. (No plural form in this sense.) ♦ *Anne's coolness prevented her from making friends.* ♦ *Bill didn't realize his coolness bothered people.*

co-op ['ko ɑp] *n.* something, such as an apartment building or store that is owned by the people who benefit from the ownership; a **cooperative**. (Also spelled *coop.*) ♦ *John lives in a co-op in the center of town.* ♦ *Mary shovels snow because that is her job in the co-op she lives in.*

coop ['kup] **1.** *n.* a small cage or building for chickens. ♦ *At night the chickens were locked in the coop.* ♦ *The coop protected the chickens from the coyotes.* **2. coop up** *tv.* + *adv.* to confine someone or something; to keep someone or something in a small space. ♦ *Bill hates being cooped up in the office all day.* ♦ *It rained during our vacation, and we were cooped up in the cabin a lot.*

cooperate [ko 'ɑp ə ret] *iv.* to work together with someone do get something done; to unite in order to get something done more easily. ♦ *The art department cooperated with the editorial department to produce the book.* ♦ *The children learned to cooperate and did the project together.*

cooperation [ko ɑp ə 're ʃən] *n.* working together in order to get something done; working together willingly. (No plural form in this sense.) ♦ *I need your cooperation to get this project done on time.* ♦ *Without everyone's cooperation, we will fail.*

cooperative [ko 'ɑp ə rə tɪv] **1.** *adj.* willing to work with someone; helpful. (Adv: *cooperatively.*) ♦ *Susie became cooperative when she thought she might get a cookie.* ♦ *Please try to be more cooperative and help us when you are asked.* **2.** *adj.* [of a building or enterprise] operated by its owners for their benefit. (Also **co-op**. Adv: *cooperatively.*) ♦ *Mary lives in an inexpensive cooperative apartment.* ♦ *Each person living in the cooperative living units must help out with service and maintenance.* **3.** *n.* a building or enterprise where the profits and losses are divided among people who own the building or enterprise. ♦ *Most of the local dairy farmers belonged to the milk cooperative.* ♦ *My family lives in a cooperative and shares in the chores around the building.*

coordinate 1. [ko 'or dɪ nət] *n.* one of a number of measurements that determine the position of a point on a plane. ♦ *The pilot gave his coordinates to the tower as he approached the airport.* ♦ *The captain tried to signal the ship's coordinates to the rescuers.* **2.** [ko 'or də net] *tv.* to organize something; to direct a complicated set of events or procedures. ♦ *The literature seminars were coordinated by the head of the English department.* ♦ *The office manager coordinated the large project.*

coordinated [ko 'or dɪ net ɪd] **1.** *adj.* graceful; having good coordination. (Adv: *coordinatedly.*) ♦ *The clumsy teenager studied ballet in hopes of becoming more coordinated.* ♦ *Bill is not too coordinated. He's always tripping or dropping something.* **2.** *adj.* [of things] arranged so they match; [of things] looking good or working well together. ♦ *I have nice clothes, but they are not coordinated.* ♦ *The living-room furniture is coordinated with that in the dining room.*

coordination [ko or dɪ 'ne ʃən] **1.** *n.* the way that muscles work together to create movement; to move properly using the muscles. (No plural form in this sense.) ♦ *The toddler had good coordination.* ♦ *I can't play the piano because my manual coordination is so bad.* **2.** *n.* the organization of an event so that things run smoothly and efficiently. (No plural form in this sense.) ♦ *The fair was a failure because the coordination of the events was poor.* ♦ *The surprise birthday party took a lot of coordination.*

coordinator [ko 'or dɪ net ɚ] *n.* someone who coordinates; someone who makes sure all arrangements are made. ♦ *The coordinator thanked the employees for their cooperation.* ♦ *An English professor was the coordinator of the debate.*

cop ['kɑp] **1.** *n.* a police officer. (Informal.) ♦ *I called the cops when I saw a thief break into a car.* ♦ *The cop said I was speeding, but I wasn't.* **2.** *tv.* to snatch something; to grab something; to capture something. (Slang.) ♦ *I copped a donut on my way through the cafeteria.* ♦ *The student copped the textbook from his friend.*

cope ['kop] *iv.* to deal with something successfully; to face a problem adequately. ♦ *Counseling has helped me cope with my disappointments.* ♦ *The teacher could not cope any longer. The ill-behaved children were just too much.*

copier ['kɑp i ɚ] *n.* a photocopier; a machine that makes copies of documents. ♦ *I went to the copier to make a copy of a letter I just typed.* ♦ *There is a line of people waiting to use the copier.*

copilot ['ko pɑɪ lət] *n.* someone who helps a pilot fly an aircraft; an assistant pilot. ♦ *The copilot spoke to the passengers over the intercom.* ♦ *When the pilot passed out, the copilot landed the plane.*

copious ['kop i əs] *adj.* abundant; full; plentiful. (Adv: *copiously.*) ♦ *There's a copious supply of food in the pantry.* ♦ *The students took copious notes during the lecture.*

copout ['kɑp ɑʊt] *n.* a poor excuse for not taking responsibility. (Slang.) ♦ *Bill's reason for not finishing his work was a copout for his laziness.* ♦ *Your excuse for being late is nothing but a copout.*

copper ['kɑp ɚ] *n.* a soft, reddish-tan metal element. (No plural form in this sense.) ♦ *Pennies are made from copper.* ♦ *The building's roof was covered with a layer of copper.*

copperhead ['kɑp ɚ hɛd] *n.* a poisonous snake with brown and copper marks, native to the United States. ♦ *The hiker saw a copperhead and moved quickly away from it.* ♦ *Copperheads are very poisonous.*

copula ['kɑp jə lə] See linking verb.

copulate ['kɑp jə let] *iv.* [for two creatures] to join together sexually. ♦ *Two dogs copulated in the barnyard.* ♦ *Soon after the birds copulated, the female laid six eggs.*

copulation [kɑp jə 'le ʃən] *n.* sexual intercourse; joining together sexually. (No plural form in this sense. Number is expressed with *act(s) of copulation.*) ♦ *As a result of copulation, the female dog became pregnant.* ♦ *The copulation of frogs occurs early in the spring, near the water.*

copy ['kɑp i] **1.** *n.* a duplicate; a replica. ♦ *This work of art is a copy of a famous painting.* ♦ *Our house is a copy of a Roman villa.* **2.** *n.* a single issue of a newspaper, book, or magazine. ♦ *Can I borrow your copy of the book?* ♦ *This copy has been autographed by the author.* **3.** *n.* written material that is ready to be proofread or edited. (No plural form in this sense.) ♦ *The editor stared glumly at the stack of copy on her desk.* ♦ *The copy was so bad it had to be rewritten.* **4.** *tv.* to make a duplicate of something. ♦ *Bill copied the original article for his personal use.* ♦ *It is illegal to copy an entire book without permission.* **5.** *tv.* to imitate someone's actions. ♦ *I copied my sister's decorating scheme.* ♦ *Jimmy copied everything his older sister said.* **6.** *tv.* to reproduce written material by writing it by hand. ♦ *The teacher told the children to copy the word into their notebooks.* ♦ *The calligrapher copied the words onto parchment.* **7.** *tv.* to cheat on a test by writing the answers from someone else's paper. ♦ *Dave copied Bill's answers to the test.* ♦ *The teacher saw the student copy the answers.* **8. copy from** *iv.* + *prep. phr.* to cheat by writing down the answers that one sees on someone else's paper. ♦ *After Jimmy failed the test, Bill knew not to copy from Jimmy.* ♦ *When John copied from Anne, they both failed the test.*

copyright ['kɑp i rɑɪt] **1.** *n.* the exclusive legal right to produce, publish, or sell a book, play, song, movie, or other work of music, or literature. ♦ *The composer owns the copyright to this music.* ♦ *A copyright is indicated by the symbol "©."* **2.** *tv.* to protect one's exclusive right to publish a work of music or literature by registering one's ownership with the federal copyright office. ♦ *The publishing company copyrighted the novel.* ♦ *Older works cannot be copyrighted.*

coral ['kor əl] **1.** *n.* stationary marine animals that live in groups—with some species secreting a hard skeleton that grows over long periods of time into a rock-like substance. (No plural form in this sense. Usually refers to a mass of such creatures.) ♦ *Some coral can sting badly if you touch it.* ♦ *Coral makes many interesting shapes as it grows.* **2.** *n.* the hard substance by ①. (No plural form in this sense.) ♦ *It is illegal to gather coral in most places.* ♦ *I scraped my hand on the coral while I was diving.* **3.** *adj.* made from ②. ♦ *I gave Lisa a coral necklace for her birthday.* ♦ *I bought some coral jewelry when I visited Hawaii.*

coral snake ['kor əl snek] *n.* an extremely poisonous, brightly colored snake found in the Western Hemisphere. ♦ *The colored rings of the coral snake are black, red, and yellow.* ♦ *Most coral snakes are gentle and not aggressive.*

cord ['kord] **1.** *n.* a thick string; a thin rope. (No plural form in this sense.) ♦ *The package was tied with some strong cord.* ♦ *The swing in the tree was suspended by a heavy cord.* **2.** *n.* a wire with a protective covering, especially those that connect an electrical appliance to an electrical outlet. ♦ *The cord of the electric fan would not stretch to the outlet.* ♦ *I tripped over the cord of the television set.* **3.** *n.* a tendon, a muscle, or a part of the body that looks like ①. ♦ *As John lifted the weights, the cords stood out from his neck.* ♦ *Anne has little body fat, and the cords of her muscles can be clearly seen.* **4.** *n.* a unit of measurement of cut wood, 4 feet high, 4 feet wide, and 8 feet long. ♦ *We bought two cords and didn't need it all.* ♦ *How many cords do you burn each winter?*

cordial ['kor dʒəl] *adj.* friendly; sincerely pleasant. (Adv: *cordially.*) ♦ *Our cordial hostess offered to hang up our coats.* ♦ *The president of the company is always cordial when I have to meet with him.*

cordiality [kor dʒi 'æl ɪ ti] *n.* friendliness. (No plural form in this sense.) ♦ *I appreciated the cordiality of the staff at the hotel.* ♦ *Although Bill is known for his cordiality, he's also quite a gossip.*

cordless ['kord ləs] *adj.* not having or needing an electrical power cord; operated by battery. (Adv: *cordlessly.*) ♦ *I took my cordless phone onto the patio.* ♦ *Mike takes a cordless razor on business trips.*

corduroy ['kor də roɪ] **1.** *n.* a thick, heavy cotton fabric with raised ridges. (No plural form in this sense.) ♦ *The jacket was made of heavy, blue corduroy.* ♦ *Corduroy is a good fabric for winter clothes.* **2. corduroys.** *n.* a pair of pants made from ①. (Treated as plural.) ♦ *Dave wore some warm corduroys to the football game.* ♦ *Corduroys are often worn in the winter months.* **3.** *adj.* made of ①. ♦ *I bought a corduroy jacket from the thrift store.* ♦ *The stylish teenager refused to wear corduroy clothes.*

core ['kor] **1.** *n.* the center of something; the heart of something; the important part. ♦ *Politics or religion is at the core of most of our arguments.* ♦ *The core of the issue is money.* **2.** *n.* the hard part of the inside of fruit; the pit. ♦ *John accidentally ate the apple core.* ♦ *This utensil will remove the core of fruit.* **3.** *tv.* to cut ① from a piece of fruit. ♦ *The apples must be cored before they are sliced.* ♦ *This little machine can be used to core apples.*

cork ['kork] **1.** *n.* the light, springy bark of the cork oak tree, used in many products. (No plural form in this sense.) ♦ *The bulletin board was made of cork.* ♦ *I sealed the wine bottle with a piece of cork.* **2.** *n.* the piece of shaped cork that fits in the neck of a bottle. ♦ *The wine bottle has a cork in it.* ♦ *The cork flew out of the champagne bottle.* **3.** *adj.* made of ①. ♦ *Sue set her glass on a cork coaster to keep the moisture off the table.* ♦ *I sealed the bottle with a cork stopper.* **4.** *tv.* to seal a bottle by putting ② into the neck of the bottle. ♦ *A machine corked the wine bottles and put on the labels.* ♦ *Please cork the bottle after you have poured your drink.*

corkscrew ['kork skru] *n.* a twisted spiral of metal attached to a handle, used to pull a cork out of a bottle. ♦ *The wine connoisseur owned many corkscrews.* ♦ *I need a corkscrew so I can open the bottle of wine.*

corn ['korn] **1.** *n.* a tall cereal plant producing large grains on long ears, sometimes called maize. (No plural form in this sense. Number is expressed with *corn stalk(s).*) ♦ *Corn is an important crop of the Midwest.* ♦ *The corn was ready to be harvested at the end of the summer.* **2.** *n.* the soft and tender young grains of corn eaten by humans as a vegetable. (No plural form in this sense. Number is expressed with *kernel(s) of corn* for the individual grains. *Ear(s) of corn* refers to ② still attached to the cob it grows on.) ♦ *We had corn with our meat loaf.* ♦ *John sprinkled some salt on his corn.* **3.** *n.* hard grains from ①, eaten by livestock or processed into other foods. (No plural form in this sense. Number is expressed with *ear(s) of corn* or *kernel(s) of corn* as with ②.) ♦ *The cows were in the field, eating corn.* ♦ *A huge machine ground the kernels of corn into cornmeal.* **4.** *n.* a hard, painful patch of skin on the foot or toe. ♦ *The podiatrist removed Bill's painful corn.* ♦ *The corn was caused by shoes that didn't fit properly.* **5.** *adj.* made from ③; having ③ as an ingredient. ♦ *Corn bread is made from cornmeal.* ♦ *Corn syrup is used to sweeten many food products.*

corncob AND **cob** ['korn kɑb, 'kɑb] *n.* the cylinder of fiber that corn grows on. ♦ *Dry corncobs can be burned or chopped up and used as mulch.* ♦ *We pick corn fresh in the field and then roast it while it is still on the cob.*

cornea ['kor ni ə] *n.* the clear outside covering of the iris and pupil of the eye. ♦ *The flying debris scratched Bill's cornea and harmed his vision.* ♦ *The cornea is transparent.*

corner ['kor nɚ] **1.** *n.* the point where two lines meet; the line formed where two surfaces meet. ♦ *This room has four corners.* ♦ *I put the cup on the corner of the counter.* **2.** *n.* the space where two walls meet. ♦ *The cat lay curled in one corner of the room.* ♦ *Cobwebs collected in the corners of the ceiling.* **3.** *n.* one of the four squared areas nearest to the intersection of two streets. ♦ *The school is located at the corner of Main Street and 4th Street.* ♦ *I waited on the corner for the bus.* **4.** *tv.* to trap someone or some creature in a place or situation from which it is difficult or impossible to escape. ♦ *The boss cornered me and asked me to work extra hours.* ♦ *The mouse was cornered by the cat.* **5.** *iv.* [for a wheeled vehicle] to travel around a corner. ♦ *The van corners well for a vehicle of such great size.* ♦ *The test car did not corner safely.* **6. out of the corner of one's eye** *idiom* [seeing something] at a glance; glimpsing (something). ♦ *Out of the corner of my eye, I saw someone do it. It might have been Jane who did it.* ♦ *I only saw the accident out of the corner of my eye. I don't know who is at fault.*

cornered ['kor nɚd] *adj.* stuck in a corner; trapped with no chance of escape. ♦ *Bill sat in his seat at the banquet like a cornered animal.* ♦ *The cornered celebrity had to shake hands and sign autographs.*

cornerstone ['kor nɚ ston] **1.** *n.* a large stone at the outside corner of two exterior walls. ♦ *The cornerstone often bears the date of construction and may also be hollow, containing artifacts from the time the cornerstone was laid.* ♦ *The cornerstone of the church was dated 1803.* **2.** *n.* a foundation; a basis; something that everything else is built on. ♦ *Democracy is the cornerstone of this nation.* ♦ *Honesty is the cornerstone of a good relationship.*

cornfield ['korn fild] *n.* a field where corn is grown; a field of corn. ♦ *The farmer placed a scarecrow in the cornfield.* ♦ *The cows are in the cornfield, eating the corn.*

cornflakes ['korn fleks] *n.* a breakfast cereal of toasted flakes of corn. (Treated as singular or plural.) ♦ *The company has produced cornflakes for many years.* ♦ *I poured some milk over a bowl of cornflakes for breakfast.*

cornstarch ['korn stɑrtʃ] *n.* a white flour made from corn. (No plural form in this sense.) ♦ *Cornstarch is good for thickening gravy.* ♦ *Cornstarch is useful for cleaning up spills on the carpet.*

cornucopia [korn ə 'kop i ə] **1.** *n.* a horn-shaped container, usually holding fruit, vegetables, flowers, or decorations. ♦ *The centerpiece at our Thanksgiving dinner was a cornucopia full of apples.* ♦ *The party favors were cornucopias filled with candy.* **2.** *n.* a large supply; an abundance of things. (Figurative on ①.) ♦ *The garage sale was a cornucopia of items for sale.* ♦ *Anne's yard is just a cornucopia of flowers!*

corny ['kor ni] *adj.* silly; trite; banal; unsophisticated. (Adv: *cornily.* Comp: *cornier;* sup: *corniest.*) ♦ *The comic strips contained many corny jokes today.* ♦ *The film was just a corny comedy!*

coronary ['kor ə nɛr i] **1.** *adj.* of or about the arteries of the heart. ♦ *The patient's coronary artery was blocked.* ♦ *John was wheeled into the emergency room with a coronary emergency.* **2. coronary (occlusion)** *n.* a heart attack. ♦ *The patient had a coronary and died in the emergency room.* ♦ *Many people have coronaries and recover completely.*

coronation [kor ə 'ne ʃən] *n.* the ceremony in which someone is crowned king or queen. ♦ *The coronation of the new monarch was a festive occasion.* ♦ *Special music was written for the queen's coronation.*

coroner ['kor ə nɚ] *n.* a public official who determines the cause of someone's death. ♦ *The coroner established the time and cause of death.* ♦ *The death certificate was signed by the coroner.*

corporal ['kor prəl] **1.** *n.* the lowest rank of noncommissioned officer in the military, just below a sergeant. ♦ *I can't help you. Please talk to the corporal.* ♦ *The sergeant ordered the corporal to wake him up in the morning.* **2. corporal punishment** *n.* punishment in which the person being punished is made to suffer physical pain. (No plural form in this sense.) ♦ *The state does not allow the use of corporal punishment in schools.* ♦ *My grandfather felt that corporal punishment was usually very effective.*

corporate ['kor prɪt] *adj.* of or about a corporation. (Adv: *corporately.*) ♦ *The young intern set out to succeed in the corporate world.* ♦ *The personnel director decides the company's corporate policies.*

corporation [kor pə 're ʃən] *n.* a business, firm, or company. ♦ *Mary works for a corporation that produces computers.* ♦ *The corporation I work for was bought by a competing company.*

corps ['kor] *n.* a military group that is trained for a special duty. (Treated as singular.) ♦ *Bill left home and joined the Marine Corps.* ♦ *Susan worked for the Peace Corps for two years in Central America.*

corpse ['korps] *n.* a dead body. ♦ *A corpse was found in the park.* ♦ *The mortician dressed and made up the corpse.*

corpulent ['korp jə lənt] *adj.* fat; obese. (Adv: *corpulently.*) ♦ *The doctor advised the corpulent patient to diet and exercise.* ♦ *The famous painter was known for painting corpulent women.*

corpuscle ['kor pəs əl] *n.* a red blood cell or a white blood cell. ♦ *The biologist examined hundreds of corpuscles under a microscope.* ♦ *Red corpuscles float freely in the bloodstream.*

corral [kə 'ræl] **1.** *n.* a fenced area where horses and cattle are kept. ♦ *A corral behind the barn had three horses in it.* ♦ *The ranchers built several corrals for their livestock.* **2.** *tv.* to put livestock into ①. ♦ *The cowboys corralled the cattle to brand them.* ♦ *The rancher corralled the animals at night for their protection.* **3.** *tv.* to surround someone or something; to capture someone or something. (Figurative on ②.) ♦ *The boss corralled Dave in the hall and asked why his report wasn't finished.* ♦ *The hunt ended when the hounds corralled the fox.*

correct [kə 'rɛkt] **1.** *adj.* right; without error; true. (Adv: *correctly.*) ♦ *The correct answers are given at the back of the workbook.* ♦ *Mary's response to the teacher's question was correct.* **2.** *adj.* proper; acceptable. (Adv: *correctly.*) ♦ *Writing a thank-you note is the correct response to receiving a gift.* ♦ *I learned the correct way to wrap a gift.* **3.** *tv.* to mark answers on a test as right or wrong; to point out the mistakes. ♦ *Mary likes teaching but hates to correct papers.* ♦ *The teacher corrected the students' grammar.* **4.** *tv.* to fix a mistake; to change a wrong answer to the right answer; to make something right. ♦ *I corrected my mistake in the report and resubmitted it.* ♦ *The astronomer corrected the settings on the telescope.* **5. stand corrected** *idiom* to admit that one has been wrong. ♦ *I realize that I accused him wrongly. I stand corrected.* ♦ *We appreciate now that our conclusions were wrong. We stand corrected.*

corrected [kə 'rɛk tɪd] *adj.* repaired; made right; amended; made more accurate. ♦ *The corrected sentence read much better.* ♦ *I would like read the corrected version when you have finished.*

correction [kə 'rɛkt ʃən] **1.** *n.* a change that is made when something wrong is replaced with something right. ♦ *Corrections of the errors in the newspaper are published in later editions.* ♦ *My teacher's corrections on my paper were written in red ink.* **2.** *n.* jailing; imprisonment. (Sometimes plural.) ♦ *Each state has a department of corrections.* ♦ *The State House of Correction is really a jail.*

correctness [kə 'rɛkt nəs] *n.* the degree of rightness of something, such as an answer or statement. (No plural form in this sense.) ♦ *I was not sure of the correctness of my answer.* ♦ *Mary questioned the correctness of Tom's actions.*

correlate 1. ['kor ə let] *tv.* to establish and show a relationship between two things. ♦ *The scientist could not correlate the data with his hypothesis.* ♦ *The article correlated population growth and sociological factors.* **2.** ['kor ə let] *iv.* to be related to something else. ♦ *Fatigue often correlates to a hidden disease.* ♦ *This graph correlates with the description in the text.* **3.** ['kor ə lət] *n.* something that is related to something else; one of a pair of related things. ♦ *Fatigue and cancer are often correlates.* ♦ *Poverty is a correlate of the lack of education.*

correlated ['kor ə let ɪd] *adj.* related to each other; showing a relationship between two things. ♦ *The researcher examined the correlated effects of pollution and industry on the environment.* ♦ *Smoking and alcohol were correlated factors in John's ailment.*

correlation [kor ə 'le ʃən] *n.* a clear relationship between things that correlate. ♦ *There seems to be a correlation between cancer and excessive radiation.* ♦ *The scientist's paper showed a correlation of the data to his hypothesis.*

correspond [kor ə 'spɑnd] **1.** *iv.* to match. ♦ *The peak on this graph corresponds to an increase in sales last year.* ♦ *Unfortunately, these sets of figures don't seem to correspond.* **2.** *iv.* [for two people] to exchange letters. ♦ *The two poets corresponded for many years without ever meeting.* ♦ *Bill corresponded with us by postcard while we were out of the country.*

correspondence [kor ə 'spɑn dəns] **1. correspondence between** *n.* + *prep. phr.* the similarity between two things; the likeness of two things; the resemblance of two things. ♦ *There is close correspondence between my handwriting and yours.* ♦ *There is no correspondence between these two medicines. They are completely different.* **2.** *n.* letters; records of communication. (No plural form in this sense.) ♦ *Jane saved all of her grandmother's correspondence.* ♦ *The archives of the historical society are filled with old correspondence.*

correspondent [kor ə 'spɑn dənt] **1.** *n.* someone who exchanges letters with someone else. ♦ *Mary has never met her correspondent, but they are close friends.* ♦ *Susan is expecting a letter from her correspondent any day.* **2.** *n.* a reporter who transmits news stories or reports from a distant location to the home office. ♦ *A news correspondent in Egypt reports on politics there.* ♦ *The foreign correspondent filed a report to the news agency.*

corridor ['kor ə dɚ] **1.** *n.* a hallway; a passage between two rows of rooms. ♦ *The high school's corridors were lined* *with lockers.* ♦ *John ran down the corridor because he was late for the meeting.* **2.** *n.* a narrow strip of land allowing a city or country to be connected to the sea or to distant parts of the same city or country. ♦ *A narrow corridor of disputed land led from the capital to the sea.* ♦ *Most of the city's taxes came from a profitable industrial corridor.*

corroborate [kə 'rɑb ə ret] *tv.* to provide evidence that supports another reported fact. ♦ *The witness corroborated the suspect's story.* ♦ *These data corroborate the hypothesis of the experiment.*

corrode [kə 'rod] **1.** *tv.* to cause something to rust; [for chemicals] to slowly eat away at something. ♦ *The rain corroded the metal gutter.* ♦ *Battery acid corroded the inside of the camera.* **2.** *iv.* to rust; to become rusty; to be eaten away by chemicals. ♦ *If the tools are left in the rain, they'll corrode.* ♦ *The metal case of the old battery began to corrode.*

corroded [kə 'rod ɪd] *adj.* rusted; oxidized; eaten away by chemicals. (Adv: *corrodedly.*) ♦ *Be careful not to touch the corroded battery.* ♦ *I drove the corroded car to the junkyard.*

corrosion [kə 'ro ʒən] *n.* rust; a substance made by something corroding. (No plural form in this sense.) ♦ *Corrosion in the camera was caused by a leaky battery.* ♦ *The mechanic checked the engine parts for corrosion.*

corrosive [kə 'ro sɪv] *adj.* causing something to corrode; causing something to rust. (Adv: *corrosively.*) ♦ *The corrosive liquid ruined the tabletop.* ♦ *Strong acids are very corrosive.*

corrugated ['kor ə get ɪd] *adj.* shaped in a wavy series of ridges and grooves. ♦ *The delicate dishes were packed in corrugated cardboard.* ♦ *The roof of the shed is corrugated aluminum.*

corrupt [kə 'rʌpt] **1.** *adj.* not honest; [of politicians] easily bribed. (Adv: *corruptly.*) ♦ *The corrupt witness committed perjury during the trial.* ♦ *The reporter exposed the corrupt politician.* **2.** *tv.* to make someone become bad; to make a good person become bad; to make a moral person become immoral. ♦ *Bill corrupted his younger brother by teaching him to smoke.* ♦ *Greed corrupted the mayor.* **3.** *tv.* to ruin something in the execution of a process. ♦ *The painter corrupted the original artwork by trying to improve it.* ♦ *The computer file was corrupted during the transfer.*

corruptible [kə 'rʌp tɪ bəl] *adj.* willing to be influenced by a bribe. (Adv: *corruptibly.*) ♦ *The mayor is quite ethical and is not corruptible.* ♦ *A few corruptible athletes were enticed by greed to fix the game.*

corruption [kə 'rʌp ʃən] **1.** *n.* making someone or something evil or wicked; the process of becoming evil or wicked. (No plural form in this sense.) ♦ *Bill took a perverse pride in the corruption of his little brother.* ♦ *Mary credits her corruption to drug abuse.* **2.** *n.* dishonesty; bribery. (No plural form in this sense.) ♦ *The article exposed corruption in the mayor's office.* ♦ *The corruption of public officials makes the government look bad.* **3.** *n.* rottenness; putrification. (No plural form in this sense.) ♦ *The physician cleaned the wound of its corruption.* ♦ *The corpse leaked corruption, but the coroner was used to that.*

corsage [kor 'sɑʒ] *n.* a small bouquet of one or more flowers that is pinned to a woman's clothing or worn around a woman's wrist. ♦ *Mary pinned a small orchid corsage to her lapel.* ♦ *Bill bought a corsage for his mother to wear to church.*

corset ['kor sɪt] *n.* a garment worn under the clothing to shape and contain the figure or to stabilize an injured spine. ♦ *Aunt Mary has a corset made of bone.* ♦ *Corsets were used to make a woman's waistline smaller.*

cortex ['kor tɛks] *n.* the outer layer of an internal organ, such as that of the brain or the kidneys. ♦ *In the fall, Anne experienced an injury to the cortex of her brain.* ♦ *The surgeon cut through the cortex when removing the brain tumor.*

cortisone ['kor tɪ zon] *n.* a hormone made by the adrenal glands (or artificially), used to treat allergies, arthritis, and inflammation. (No plural form in this sense.) ♦ *The doctor gave Mary a shot of cortisone when she injured her arm.* ♦ *Cortisone eased the rash Tom got due to an allergy.*

cosign ['ko saɪn] **1.** *tv.* to add one's signature as a guarantee of someone else's signature; for two or more people to sign a document together. ♦ *Bill's mom cosigned the application for his car loan.* ♦ *The contract had to be consigned by all the parties involved.* **2.** *iv.* to sign [a document] along with someone else. ♦ *When I bought a car, I asked my father to cosign.* ♦ *For me to get a student loan, my parents had to cosign.*

cosigner ['ko saɪn ɚ] *n.* someone who signs an agreement along with someone else, thereby guaranteeing the signer's ability to satisfy the terms of the agreement. ♦ *To get the loan, Mary needed a cosigner.* ♦ *The bank required a cosigner for my car loan.*

cosmetic [kɑz 'mɛt ɪk] **1. cosmetics** *n.* a substance applied to the face or the body to improve looks. (Treated as plural.) ♦ *The drugstore sells many cosmetics.* ♦ *Lotions, makeup, and perfume are considered cosmetics.* **2.** *adj.* making someone or something look better, at least on the surface. (Adv: *cosmetically* [...ɪk li].) ♦ *The celebrity entered the hospital for cosmetic surgery.* ♦ *The run-down house looked better after some cosmetic changes—a new coat of paint and some yard work.*

cosmic ['kɑz mɪk] **1.** *adj.* of or about the whole universe and its enormous size; of or about the cosmos. (Adv: *cosmically* [...ɪk li].) ♦ *The eccentric scientist's cosmic theory was immediately disproved.* ♦ *Did the universe start with a giant cosmic explosion?* **2.** *adj.* huge; immense; vast; of extreme importance. (Figurative on ①. Adv: *cosmically* [...ɪk li].) ♦ *The mayor tackled the cosmic problem of crime in the city.* ♦ *The discovery of the cure for the flu was a cosmic breakthrough in medicine.*

cosmopolitan [kɑz mə 'pɑl ɪ tən] *adj.* not limited to one region or country; international. (Adv: *cosmopolitanly.*) ♦ *The cosmopolitan traveler had been to fifty countries.* ♦ *The farmer was unused to the cosmopolitan ways of life in a large city.*

cosmos ['kɑz mos] *n.* the universe. (No plural form in this sense.) ♦ *In the movie, the spaceship traveled through the cosmos.* ♦ *The exact origin of the cosmos is unknown.*

cost ['kɔst] **1.** *n.* the price of something; the amount of money that one must pay to buy something. (No plural form in this sense.) ♦ *The cost of seeing a movie is seven dollars.* ♦ *What is the cost of this car?* **2. costs** *n.* the sums of money needed to develop or produce something. ♦ *We* *have to control costs carefully, or we will not make a profit.* ♦ *The project was stopped because of excessive development costs.* **3.** *n.* a sacrifice; the loss of something in order to achieve something. ♦ *Catching a cold was the cost of not wearing a coat.* ♦ *Losing his job was the cost Bill paid for keeping his integrity.* **4.** *tv., irreg.* to require a specific amount of money for purchase. (Pt/pp: *cost.*) ♦ *The groceries cost two hundred dollars.* ♦ *How much did the car repairs cost?* **5.** *tv., irreg.* to cause the loss of something; to sacrifice something. ♦ *The mistake cost Jane her job.* ♦ *Tripping his opponent cost Bill his reputation.* **6.** *tv., irreg.* to require the expenditure of time, work, or energy. ♦ *This silly project is going to cost me a full day's work.* ♦ *The project was canceled because it costs too much in time.* **7. cost a pretty penny** *idiom* to cost a lot of money. ♦ *I'll bet that diamond cost a pretty penny.* ♦ *You can be sure that house cost a pretty penny. It has seven bathrooms.*

costar 1. ['ko stɑr] *n.* a famous actor who appears with another famous actor in a movie, television show, or play. ♦ *The actor appeared with the same costar in six films.* ♦ *The reporter interviewed both costars of the popular show.* **2.** ['ko 'stɑr] *iv.* [for a famous actor] to appear in a movie, television show, or play with another famous actor. ♦ *The actor and actress costarred in five films together.* ♦ *The unknown actor costarred with a famous dancer in a Broadway play.*

Costa Rica [kɔs tə 'ri kə] See Gazetteer.

cost-effective ['kɔst ə fɛk tɪv] *adj.* worth the cost. ♦ *The committee chose the most cost-effective plan.* ♦ *It is not cost-effective to have three workers doing a job intended for one person.*

costly ['kɔst li] **1.** *adj.* costing a lot of money; expensive. (Comp: *costlier;* sup: *costliest.*) ♦ *The car needed some costly repairs.* ♦ *This house is too costly for us to buy.* **2.** *adj.* serious; troublesome; unfortunate. (Comp: *costlier;* sup: *costliest.*) ♦ *Driving drunk can be a costly mistake.* ♦ *Betraying his friend was a costly error for Bill.*

costume ['kɑs tum] *n.* clothes that are worn when someone is pretending to be someone else or from another time or place; clothes that represent another culture, time period, or person, as in a theatrical production. ♦ *The actors in the play had beautiful costumes.* ♦ *Mary and Bill wore costumes to the Halloween party.*

costume jewelry ['kɑs tum 'dʒu (ə)l ri] *n.* jewelry made from glass, rhinestone, and other cheap materials; cheap jewelry. (No plural form in this sense.) ♦ *The department store had a large selection of costume jewelry.* ♦ *The ring was costume jewelry with a large glass stone in it.*

cot ['kɑt] *n.* a narrow bed made of a piece of canvas stretched over a frame, used especially for camping. ♦ *The hotel sent an extra cot to our room for our daughter.* ♦ *The farmhand slept in a cot in the barn.*

Côte d'Ivoire ['kot di 'vwɑr] See Gazetteer.

cottage ['kɑt ɪdʒ] *n.* a small house, especially a small second home in the country; a vacation house. ♦ *Sue and Bill bought a cottage on the lake.* ♦ *The little cottage had only a fireplace for heat.*

cottage cheese ['kɑt ɪdʒ tʃiz] *n.* a white, lumpy cheese made from the curds of sour milk. (No plural form in this sense.) ♦ *The restaurant always served cottage cheese as a side dish.* ♦ *I ate a lot of cottage cheese when I was on a diet.*

cotton ['kɑt n] **1.** *n.* a soft white fiber used to make yarn, thread, and fabric. (No plural form in this sense. Number is expressed with *bale(s) of cotton.*) ♦ *The huge machine spun the cotton into cloth.* ♦ *Bales of cotton were loaded onto the steamship.* **2.** *n.* cloth woven of ①. (No plural form in this sense.) ♦ *The summer dress was made of cotton.* ♦ *I bought three yards of cotton for the dress.* **3.** *n.* the plant that produces ①. (No plural form in this sense.) ♦ *Cotton is a major crop of the southern United States.* ♦ *The plantation workers harvested the cotton.* **4.** *adj.* made out of ① or ②. ♦ *Mary prefers cotton clothing to polyester.* ♦ *The cotton dress kept me cool on the hot day.*

cottontail ['kɑt n tel] *n.* a rabbit with a white, fluffy tail. ♦ *Bill saw a cottontail run across the backyard.* ♦ *The zoo had a cage with two cottontails in it.*

couch ['kɑʊtʃ] **1.** *n.* a long piece of furniture that two or more people can sit on or that someone can lie down on; a sofa. ♦ *The children sat on the couch while watching TV.* ♦ *The couch in front of the fireplace is very comfortable to sleep on.* **2. couch in** *tv. + prep. phr.* to express something in a gentle or concealed manner. ♦ *The boss couched her order in pleasant words.* ♦ *Lisa's criticism was couched in a generally positive review.*

cougar ['kug ɚ] *n.* a large, tan, wild cat; a mountain lion; a panther. ♦ *The cougar chased the antelope across the field.* ♦ *Cougars can be found in the mountains of Arizona.*

cough ['kɔf] **1.** *n.* the act or sound of forcing air from the lungs quickly and with force, making a dry, rough noise through the throat. ♦ *The doctor heard Bill's cough and prescribed some medicine.* ♦ *Anne went to the baby's room when she heard a cough.* **2.** *iv.* to force air out of the lungs as in ①. ♦ *Mary knew she was getting a cold when she started to cough.* ♦ *The smoke-filled room made us cough.*

cough drop ['kɔf drɑp] *n.* a piece of medicated material that is held in the mouth to soothe a sore throat and prevent coughing. ♦ *A cough drop helped me to stop coughing.* ♦ *John sucked a cough drop so his coughing wouldn't interrupt the performance.*

coughing ['kɔf ɪŋ] *n.* repeated or continual coughs. (No plural form in this sense.) ♦ *The coughing made Bill's voice hoarse.* ♦ *Mary's coughing kept me awake all night long.*

could ['kʊd] **1.** *aux.* <the past form of **can** ①, expressing ability.> ♦ *I thought I could do it, but I was not strong enough.* ♦ *Tom could not get his work done on time.* **2.** *aux.* <the past form of **can** ②, expressing permission.> ♦ *Yesterday, Aunt Mary said I could go to the park.* ♦ *I was told that I could not keep the dollar I found because it did not belong to me.* **3.** *aux.* <a form of **can** ①, used in making polite requests.> ♦ *Could you please pass me the salt?* ♦ *Could you speak more clearly, please.* **4.** *aux.* <a form of **can** ① expressing conjecture, possibility, or an explanation.> ♦ *Where do you think Bill could be? He's ten minutes late!* ♦ *Bill could be late because he is caught in heavy traffic.*

couldn't ['kʊd nt] **1.** *cont.* "could not." ♦ *We couldn't believe the length of the line at the movie theater.* ♦ *Mike couldn't remember where he had parked his car.* **2.** *cont.* "could not"; wouldn't you please? ♦ *Couldn't you hurry up a little bit?* ♦ *Couldn't you please be a little quieter?*

could've ['kʊd əv] *cont.* "could have," where **have** is an auxiliary. ♦ *We could've gone, but we didn't.* ♦ *Tom could've won the race if he had tried harder.*

council ['kaʊn səl] *n.* a group of people who are appointed or elected to make laws for a city, school, church, or other organization. (Compare with counsel and consul.) ♦ *The town council meets twice a month.* ♦ *Anne was elected to the student council.*

councilman ['kaʊn səl mən] *n., irreg.* someone who is on a (town) council; a male member of a council. (Pl: councilmen.) ♦ *My brother is running for election to the office of councilman.* ♦ *Seven councilmen were late, so the meeting did not start on time.*

councilmen ['kaʊn səl mən] pl of councilman.

councilwoman ['kaʊn səl wum ən] *n., irreg.* a woman who is on a council; a female representative on a council. (Pl: councilwomen.) ♦ *Mary has been a city councilwoman for three years.* ♦ *Three councilwomen objected to the proposal.*

councilwomen ['kaʊn səl wɪm ən] pl of councilwoman.

counsel ['kaʊn səl] **1.** *tv.* to advise someone; to give someone advice. (Compare with council and consul.) ♦ *Mary counseled her daughter about good study habits.* ♦ *The rabbi counseled the couple on their marriage.* **2.** *n.* advice; a piece of advice. (No plural form in this sense.) ♦ *Mary always received good counsel from her friends.* ♦ *I asked my father for his counsel.*

counselor ['kaʊn sə lɚ] **1.** *n.* someone who advises people; someone who gives advice. ♦ *A counselor talks to many troubled people each day.* ♦ *The career counselor helps people find jobs.* **2.** *n.* someone who is in charge of children at a camp. ♦ *The camp counselor taught the children to swim.* ♦ *Each counselor was in charge of six campers.* **3.** *n.* a lawyer. (Also a term of address for a lawyer.) ♦ *"Approach the bench, counselor," the judge instructed.* ♦ *John hired an expert counselor when he was sued.*

count ['kaʊnt] **1.** *n.* the number that is reached when something is being counted. ♦ *I took a count of the people at the meeting.* ♦ *The prison guard began a count of inmates.* **2.** *n.* a male European nobleman. (The female form is countess.) ♦ *The count inherited the family estate.* ♦ *Count Grimshaw had no duties except to report to the king every year.* **3. count noun** *n.* of or about a noun that can be counted. (See explanation at noncount.) ♦ Hat *is a count noun, and you can make it plural.* ♦ Advice *is not a count noun, and it cannot be made plural.* **4.** *tv.* to figure out how many; to determine how many. ♦ *The child counted the blocks.* ♦ *The theater manager counted the people in the audience.* **5. count as** *tv. + prep. phr.* to include someone or something; to think of someone or something; to consider someone or something. ♦ *We count Jimmy as one of our own children—he spends so much time at our house.* ♦ *Susie counts her dog as one of the family.* **6.** *iv.* to be able to say the numbers in order; to know how to count as in ④. ♦ *Even though Anne is only three, she can count to one hundred.* ♦ *By age five, Bob could read, write, and count.* **7.** *iv.* to be taken into consideration; to be included. ♦ *Pets do not count as family members.* ♦ *Those points don't count because you were cheating!* **8. count on someone or something** *idiom* to rely on someone or something; to depend on someone or something. ♦ *I can count on Bill to get the job done.* ♦ *Can I count on this car to start every morning of the year?* **9. stand up and be counted** *idiom* to state one's support (for someone or something). ♦ *If you believe in more government help for farmers, write your representative—stand up and be counted.* ♦ *I'm generally in favor of what you propose, but not enough to stand up and be counted.*

countable ['kaʊn tə bəl] *adj.* [of a noun] that can be counted; of or about a count noun. (See noncount.) ♦ Hat *is countable and can be made plural.* ♦ *The word* advice *is not countable and cannot be made plural.*

countdown ['kaʊnt daʊn] *n.* the act of counting the seconds backwards down to zero before an event, such as before the firing of a rocket or before midnight on New Year's Eve. ♦ *Everyone at the New Year's party called out the countdown to midnight.* ♦ *The astronauts waited for the countdown to be completed before the launch of the rocket.*

countenance ['kaʊn tə nəns] **1.** *n.* someone's face; the look on someone's face; the expression on someone's face. ♦ *Bill's countenance revealed his anxiety.* ♦ *Anne's joy shone in her countenance.* **2.** *tv.* to permit something; to tolerate something. ♦ *David would not countenance disobedience from his children.* ♦ *The insurance company will not countenance fraudulent claims.*

counter ['kaʊn tɚ] **1.** *n.* a flat surface at which customers sit or stand to be served in a fast-food store, bank, or other establishment. ♦ *The clerk put all my purchases on the counter.* ♦ *I went to the customer-service counter at the store.* **2.** *n.* [in a kitchen] a flat surface where food is prepared. ♦ *The kitchen did not have a big enough counter for food preparation.* ♦ *The cat jumped onto the kitchen counter and ate our supper.* **3.** *n.* a device that is used to count objects or people; a device that keeps track of the number of objects or people. ♦ *The bank teller used a mechanical counter to count the pennies.* ♦ *An electronic counter kept track of the number of people passing through the turnstile.* **4.** *tv.* to challenge something in a response; to go against someone or something in a response; to act against someone or something. ♦ *Mary countered all of my moves in the chess game.* ♦ *The politician countered the attacks on his character.* **5.** *tv.* to answer a question by asking another question. ♦ *Bill countered my question with another of his own.* ♦ *You only counter my questions. You never answer them!*

counteract [kaʊn tɚ 'ækt] *tv.* to reduce the effect of something by causing the opposite effect; to seek to balance the effect of something. ♦ *This antidote will counteract the poison.* ♦ *Antacid will counteract the excess acid in your stomach.*

counterattack ['kaʊn tɚ ə tæk] *n.* an attack made on an attacker. ♦ *The cornered dog made a counterattack and chased off its attacker.* ♦ *The boxer dodged his opponent and made a counterattack.*

counterclockwise ['kaʊn tɚ 'klɑk waɪz] **1.** *adj.* opposite to the movement of a clock's hands. ♦ *Traffic went around the circle in a counterclockwise direction.* ♦ *The top spun in a counterclockwise direction.* **2.** *adv.* [moving] in a direction that is opposite to the movement of a clock's hands. ♦ *The top spun counterclockwise.* ♦ *To warm up, we turned clockwise and then counterclockwise.*

counterfeit ['kaʊn tɚ fɪt] **1.** *adj.* fake; imitation; not genuine. ♦ *This counterfeit money is obviously an imitation.* ♦ *The curator identified the counterfeit painting.* **2.** *n.* a forgery; an illegal copy; a fake. ♦ *The curator determined that the painting was a counterfeit.* ♦ *The banker did not notice that the bills were counterfeits.* **3.** *tv.* to make an illegal copy of something, especially money. ♦ *The mobsters were arrested for counterfeiting bonds.* ♦ *The young artist had counterfeited the masterpieces.*

countermand ['kaʊn tɚ mænd] *tv.* to cancel an order by giving another one; to withdraw a command that has been made. ♦ *Mary knew better than to countermand her boss's orders.* ♦ *The principal countermanded the teacher's unfair demands.*

counterpart ['kaʊn tɚ pɑrt] *n.* someone or something that has the same function as someone or something else; someone or something that is similar to someone or something else. ♦ *In London, the counterpart of the New York subway is called the "tube."* ♦ *Our art director spoke with her counterpart at another company at the conference.*

countersign ['kaʊn tɚ saɪn] *tv.* to sign something that has first been signed by someone else, as an authentication of the first signature. ♦ *A bank officer had to countersign the large cashier's check that I asked for.* ♦ *The car salesman had to have his manager countersign the purchase contract to authenticate the deal.*

countertop ['kaʊn tə tɑp] *n.* the flat, upper surface of a counter. ♦ *Don't cut directly on the countertop with the knife.* ♦ *I cleaned the stains from the white countertop.*

countess ['kaʊn tɪs] *n.* a European noblewoman; the wife or widow of a count. ♦ *The peasant became a countess when she married the count.* ♦ *The countess was a powerful woman at the royal court.*

countless ['kaʊnt ləs] *adj.* not capable of being counted; too numerous to be counted. (Adv: *countlessly.*) ♦ *Countless children go hungry every day.* ♦ *A countless number of stars shone in the nighttime sky.*

country ['kʌn tri] **1.** *n.* a nation, including its land and its people; a political subdivision. ♦ *The tiny country declared its independence.* ♦ *Russia is the largest country in the world, in terms of area.* **2.** *n.* land without many people or buildings; the opposite of *city.* ♦ *Many city dwellers escape to the country on weekends.* ♦ *In the country, there is more open space.* **3.** *adj.* <the adj. use of ②.> ♦ *We stopped at a small country store to buy fresh fruit.* ♦ *I crossed the state on a beautiful country road.*

countryman ['kʌn tri mən] *n., irreg.* someone from one's own country; a fellow citizen of one's own country. (Pl: countrymen.) ♦ *The spy betrayed his fellow countrymen.* ♦ *The politician appealed to the nationalism of his countrymen.*

countrymen ['kʌn tri mən] pl of countryman.

countryside ['kʌn tri saɪd] *n.* the land outside of cities, used for farming or left in its natural wild state; a rural area. (No plural form in this sense.) ♦ *We went to the countryside for a picnic.* ♦ *Beautiful wildflowers grow in the countryside.*

county ['kaʊn ti] *n.* a political division of most U.S. states. (See also parish ②.) ♦ *I work in a county adjacent to the one I live in.* ♦ *Chicago is one of many cities in Cook County, Illinois.*

coup ['ku] **1.** *n.* an unexpected action. (Pl: ['kuz].) ♦ *Being able to take two vacations this year was a real coup for Mary.* ♦ *Finally getting a promotion was a real coup for Bill.* **2. coup (d'état)** ['ku de 'tɑ] *n.* a sudden hostile takeover of a government. (French.) ♦ *The president was thrown out of office by a coup d'état.* ♦ *After the coup, the government was run by the military.*

coupe ['kup] *n.* a car with two doors instead of four. ♦ *The Smiths bought a new coupe last week.* ♦ *To get into the back seat of a coupe, you often have to push the front seat down.*

couple ['kʌp əl] **1.** *n.* two people, usually male and female, usually sharing a romantic interest. (Treated as singular when thinking of a unit and plural when thinking of the individuals.) ♦ *The young couple got engaged before they finished college.* ♦ *Eventually, the feuding couple broke up.* **2. a couple of** *phr.* two; two or three; a few; some; not many. ♦ *Bill grabbed a couple of beers from the refrigerator.* ♦ *I hung a couple of pictures on the wall.* **3. couple together** *tv.* + *adv.* to join two things together; to connect two things together; to link two things together. ♦ *The worker coupled the railroad cars together securely.* ♦ *Couple these two parts together, and the assembly will be complete.* **4.** *iv.* to copulate; to join sexually. ♦ *When the birds are fluttering close together, they are coupling.* ♦ *Lions couple frequently during the breeding season.*

coupon ['ku pɑn, 'kju pɑn] *n.* a printed form that offers a discount for a product or service. ♦ *The manufacturer mailed out coupons for its products.* ♦ *I presented my coupon to the cashier.*

courage ['kɚ ɪdʒ] **1.** *n.* bravery; fearlessness; resolve in spite of fear. (No plural form in this sense.) ♦ *Dave mustered his courage and walked into the dark room.* ♦ *The young warriors showed a lot of courage in battle.* **2. screw up one's courage** *idiom* to build up one's courage. ♦ *I guess I have to screw up my courage and go to the dentist.* ♦ *I spent all morning screwing up my courage to take my driver's test.*

courageous [kə 're dʒəs] *adj.* fearless; facing danger in spite of fear. (Adv: *courageously.*) ♦ *The courageous soldiers were awarded for their brave acts.* ♦ *The courageous firefighter saved five people's lives.*

courier ['kɚ i ɚ] *n.* a messenger; someone who transports documents or other valuable items. ♦ *A courier delivered the package to our house.* ♦ *We sent a courier to pick up the contracts.*

course ['kors] **1.** *n.* the pathway or route of someone or something. ♦ *The helium balloon took an upward course.* ♦ *I followed the course of the bear up the mountain with my binoculars.* **2.** *n.* a prescribed sequence of actions. ♦ *The disease is best treated with a two-week course of medication.* ♦ *The university requires a certain course of study for each major.* **3.** *n.* a class offered by a school or an instructor. ♦ *Mary took a biology course at the local university.* ♦ *I've always wanted to take a course in colonial literature.* **4.** *n.* a part of a meal; one of the many parts of a meal is served separately. ♦ *The third course of the banquet was a green salad.* ♦ *Dessert was the final course of the meal.* **5.** *n.* the land where certain sporting events take place, such as golfing and racing. ♦ *The golf course was green and lush.* ♦ *The spectators lined the race course to watch the race.* **6.** *iv.* [for water] to flow in a river; [for tears] to run down one's face. ♦ *Tears of joy coursed down my face when I heard the good news.* ♦ *During the storm, water coursed along, roaring and foaming.* **7. course of action** *phr.* the procedures or sequence of actions that someone will follow to accomplish a goal; **course** ②. ♦ *I plan to follow a course of action that will produce the best results.* ♦ *The committee planned a course of action that would reduce costs and eliminate employees.*

court ['kort] **1.** *n.* the place where legal matters are decided and the people who are present there, such as a judge and other officials. (No plural form in this sense.) ♦ *I have to go to court today to give evidence in a trial.* ♦ *Court was recessed for an hour for lunch.* **2. the court** *n.* the judge, often speaking for the entire **court** ①. (No plural form in this sense. Treated as singular.) ♦ *The court declined to dismiss the case.* ♦ *The court will now hear the prosecutor's evidence.* **3. the courts** *n.* the entire legal system; the judicial system. (Treated as plural.) ♦ *This matter will have to be settled by the courts.* ♦ *Is this something to be dealt with by the legislature or by the courts?* **4.** *n.* the attendants and nobles who associate with a sovereign ruler, usually a king or queen. (No plural form in this sense.) ♦ *The queen's court accompanied her everywhere.* ♦ *The entire court was present at the coronation.* **5.** See **courtyard**. **6.** *n.* the space where certain games such as basketball and tennis are played. ♦ *The basketball players sat near the court after the game.* ♦ *The tennis match was played on a clay court.* **7.** *n.* a kind of short street that usually comes to an end and goes no further. (Abbreviated *Ct.*) ♦ *Our house is at the end of the court.* ♦ *At the end of the court, we turned the car around.* **8.** *tv.* [for a man] to try to win a woman's favor, often with marriage as a goal. ♦ *Grandpa courted Grandma for three years before their marriage.* ♦ *When Bill courted Anne, she had to be home by midnight.* **9.** *tv.* to try to win the favor of someone or something. (Figurative on ⑧.) ♦ *Bill courted his supervisor's favor with flattery and gifts.* ♦ *The reporter courted the mayor's goodwill by visiting her office frequently.* **10. laugh something out of court** *idiom* to dismiss something as ridiculous. ♦ *The committee laughed the suggestion out of court.* ♦ *Bob's request for a large salary increase was laughed out of court.*

courteous ['kɚ ti əs] *adj.* showing courtesy; polite; well mannered. (Adv: *courteously.*) ♦ *The courteous child always said "please" and "thank you."* ♦ *The courteous gentleman opened the door for the hotel guests.*

courtesy ['kɚ tɪs i] **1.** *n.* politeness; thoughtfulness. (No plural form in this sense.) ♦ *The rude man was not known for his courtesy.* ♦ *The students showed their teacher courtesy and respect.* **2.** *n.* an act of kindness; a favor; a thoughtful act. ♦ *I appreciated your many small courtesies when I visited your offices.* ♦ *Mary extends many courtesies to her houseguests.*

courthouse ['kort hɑʊs] **1.** *n., irreg.* a building containing courtrooms where court is held. (Pl: [...hɑʊ zəz].) ♦ *The case was heard in the town's courthouse.* ♦ *Many spectators went to hear the case at the courthouse.* **2.** *n., irreg.* the building that houses the government offices—including the county court—of a particular county. ♦ *County census records are stored at the county courthouse.* ♦ *Bill and Lisa got their marriage license at the courthouse.*

courtly ['kort li] *adj.* elegant; refined; dignified. (Comp: *courtlier*; sup: *courtliest.*) ♦ *A courtly gentleman introduced himself to me as the owner of the house.* ♦ *The nobleman had a courtly appearance.*

court-martial ['kort mɑr ʃəl] **1.** *n., irreg.* a military court that deals with matters of military law. (From French. Pl: **courts-martial** or *court-martials.*) ♦ *The soldier faced a court-martial for disobeying orders.* ♦ *The general testified at the major's court-martial.* **2.** *tv.* to arraign and try someone in a military court. ♦ *The soldier was court-martialed for disobeying orders.* ♦ *The navy court-martialed the captain for leaving his post.*

courtroom ['kort rum] *n.* a room where a session of court is held. ♦ *The courtroom is full of newspaper reporters wanting an exciting story.* ♦ *When the judge entered the courtroom, everyone stood up.*

courtship ['kort ʃɪp] *n.* the process of wooing someone, usually with marriage in mind. (No plural form in this sense.) ♦ *My grandparents' courtship lasted a year.* ♦ *Early in their courtship, Bill proposed to Mary.*

courts-martial ['korts mɑr ʃəl] a pl of **court-martial**.

court(yard) ['kort jɑrd] *n.* a space, usually open to the sky, enclosed by walls or buildings. ♦ *Each apartment in the building faced the court.* ♦ *There are six statues in the museum's courtyard.*

cousin ['kʌz ən] *n.* the child of one's aunt or uncle; the nephew or niece of one's parent. ♦ *When I visited my aunt, I ate dinner with my cousins.* ♦ *All of my relatives were at the reunion except for two cousins.*

cove ['kov] *n.* a small bay along a coastline; a small inlet. ♦ *Our boat drifted into the tiny cove.* ♦ *That cove is a good place to catch fish.*

covenant ['kʌv ə nənt] *n.* a pact; a formal agreement; a contract. ♦ *The old war buddies made a covenant to meet again on the battlefield when they were 60.* ♦ *In the deed, there is a covenant that prevents you from building a house on the land.*

cover ['kʌv ɚ] **1.** *n.* the protective top—like a lid—for something. ♦ *The cover for the garbage can is missing.* ♦ *Please put a cover over the leftover food.* **2.** *n.* the front and back of a book, magazine, or pamphlet. ♦ *The book had a beautifully designed cover.* ♦ *The cover of the magazine ripped when I removed it from the mailbox.* **3.** *n.* shelter; protection; something that provides protection. (No plural form in this sense.) ♦ *The animals hid under the cover of the evergreen bush.* ♦ *The slaves escaped under the cover of darkness.* **4.** *n.* a blanket. ♦ *Mary sleeps with two covers on her bed.* ♦ *Tom put another cover on his bed because it was cold.* **5.** *n.* something that is hiding a secret; a legal business that is operating as a disguise for an illegal business. ♦ *The laundry was just a cover for the smugglers.* ♦ *Taking Bill to the restaurant to meet a friend was a cover for his surprise party that was to be held there.* **6.** *adj.* appearing on the cover of a magazine. ♦ *The cover photo on the nature magazine was of a beautiful sunset.* ♦ *Mary liked the cover art on the CD she bought.* **7.** *tv.* to place something on top of something else to protect or hide it; to spread something on top of something else to protect or hide it. ♦ *I covered the leftovers and put them in the refrigerator.* ♦ *The painter covered the furniture with a tarp.* **8.** *tv.* to coat the surface of something; to spread over something. ♦ *The piece of candy was covered with chocolate.* ♦ *Oil that spilled from the wrecked ship covered some of the birds.* **9.** *tv.* to amount to enough money to pay for something. ♦ *Twenty dollars ought to cover dinner, shouldn't it?* ♦ *The insurance check did not cover all the car* *repairs.* **10.** *tv.* to include something; to discuss or reveal something; to address an issue. ♦ *The professor covered one chapter with each lecture.* ♦ *Did your discussion with the babysitter cover all the important safety issues?* **11.** *tv.* to travel a certain distance. ♦ *The travelers covered about two hundred miles a day.* ♦ *Mary can't cover very much territory in the store when I go with her.* **12.** *tv.* to occupy a certain area; to extend over a certain area. ♦ *The tablecloth covers the length and width of the table.* ♦ *Our farm covers 640 acres.* **13.** *tv.* to shelter someone or something; to provide shelter for someone or something. ♦ *The screen porch covered us during the rain.* ♦ *The roof of the birdhouse covered the bird's nest.* **14.** *tv.* to report news; for a reporter to talk about an event or incident. ♦ *Tom was the first reporter to cover the story.* ♦ *Jane covered the big fire on Maple Street.* **15. cover for** *iv + prep. phr.* to take someone's place; to substitute for someone who is absent. ♦ *Please cover for me while I am out of the office.* ♦ *I had to cover for Mary when she was on vacation.*

coverage ['kʌv ɚ ɪdʒ] **1.** *n.* protection provided by insurance. (No plural form in this sense.) ♦ *This policy provides no coverage for dental work.* ♦ *The Smiths' coverage does not include damages caused by floods.* **2.** *n.* the amount and quality of discussion in the news of a particular topic. (No plural form in this sense.) ♦ *The coverage of the football game was scanty. All we heard was the scores.* ♦ *I turned on the radio to hear the coverage of the earthquake.* **3.** *n.* the amount of a population that is reached by a television station, radio station, newspaper, or other form of media. (No plural form in this sense.) ♦ *Does this magazine have wide coverage?* ♦ *The coverage of this station is so great that you can hear it throughout the Midwest.*

covering ['kʌv ɚ ɪŋ] *n.* a top layer; something that covers something else. ♦ *The frame had a thin covering of gold on it.* ♦ *The shed had a metal covering across the top.*

covert ['ko vɚt] *adj.* secret; hidden; concealed. (Adv: *covertly.*) ♦ *No one knew of the covert government mission.* ♦ *The gangsters arranged a covert meeting.*

covet ['kʌv ɪt] *tv.* to want someone else's possession. ♦ *I coveted my grandmother's cameo shamefully.* ♦ *John's neighbors coveted his beautiful antique car.*

cow ['kaʊ] **1.** *n.* an adult female member of the bovine family, raised on farms for their milk. ♦ *The farmer milked the cows every morning.* ♦ *The milk we drink comes from cows.* **2.** *n.* the female of certain animals, including the elephant. ♦ *The cow helped up her baby with her trunk.* ♦ *The mature cow looked small next to the large bull elephant.* **3.** *tv.* to threaten someone; to cause someone to yield. ♦ *Bill cowed me into helping him move.* ♦ *Your threats will not cow me!* **4. sacred cow** *idiom* something that is regarded by some people with such respect and veneration that they don't like it being criticized by anyone in any way. ♦ *University education is a sacred cow in the Smith family. Mike is regarded as a failure because he left school at sixteen.* ♦ *Don't talk about eating meat to Sally. Vegetarianism is one of her sacred cows.*

coward ['kaʊ ɚd] *n.* someone who has no courage; someone who runs away from danger. ♦ *The coward was frightened by shadows on the wall.* ♦ *Don't be a coward. Face your fears.*

cowardice ['kaʊ ɚ dɪs] *n.* lack of courage. (No plural form in this sense.) ♦ *Cowardice prevented Bill from accepting the challenge.* ♦ *The sergeant interpreted the soldier's hesitation as cowardice.*

cowardly ['kaʊ ɚd li] *adj.* having no courage. ♦ *John felt cowardly about sleeping in the large, empty house.* ♦ *The cowardly dog ran away from the raccoon.*

cowboy ['kaʊ bɔɪ] *n.* someone, usually a male, who works on a cattle ranch. ♦ *The cowboy groomed his horse in the stable.* ♦ *The cattle were rounded up by the cowboys at the end of the day.*

cower ['kaʊ ɚ] *iv.* to cringe; to draw back from something in fear; to crouch in fear. ♦ *John cowered in fear when he saw a snake.* ♦ *The children cowered each time they heard the thunder.*

cowhide ['kaʊ haɪd] *n.* leather made from the skin of a cow. (No plural form in this sense.) ♦ *My wallet is made of cowhide.* ♦ *Cowhide is an inexpensive leather.*

coworker ['ko wɚk ɚ] *n.* a fellow worker; someone with whom one works. ♦ *Jane's coworkers bought her a small gift for her birthday.* ♦ *On his first day of work, Mike met all his coworkers.*

coy ['kɔɪ] *adj.* acting shy or reserved; pretending to be shy or reserved. (Adv: *coyly.* Comp: *coyer;* sup: *coyest.*) ♦ *Don't be so coy. Let me take your picture!* ♦ *Our coy hostess said she couldn't possibly play the piano for such a big audience, but we all knew she was actually an accomplished performer.*

coyote [kaɪ 'ot i] *n.* an animal, similar to a large, skinny dog, that lives in western North America. ♦ *We heard the coyotes howling in the desert.* ♦ *The chickens on the farm were attacked by a coyote.*

cozy ['koz i] *adj.* snug; warm and comfortable. (Adv: *cozily.* Comp: *cozier;* sup: *coziest.*) ♦ *Sitting in front of a fire on a snowy day is quite cozy.* ♦ *The Smiths own a cozy little cabin by a lake.*

crab ['kræb] **1.** *n.* an edible sea creature with a hard shell, four pairs of legs, and one pair of claws. ♦ *A tiny crab crawled on the bottom of the fish tank.* ♦ *Along the beach, we saw many crabs.* **2. crab** *n.* the meat of ① eaten as food. (No plural form in this sense.) ♦ *The appetizer is made from crab.* ♦ *Crab can be served in a soup.* **3.** *n.* a grouchy person; a grumpy person; a person who complains a lot. ♦ *Having a crab in the office can lower morale.* ♦ *After he lost the race, Mike was a real crab.*

crabby ['kræb i] *adj.* grouchy; grumpy; irritable. (Adv: *crabbily.* Comp: *crabbier;* sup: *crabbiest.*) ♦ *Anne is always crabby in the morning.* ♦ *Mike became crabby because he was hungry.*

crab grass ['kræb græs] *n.* a kind of weed that infests lawns, replacing regular grass. (No plural form in this sense.) ♦ *No matter how I try to kill it, the crab grass grows back.* ♦ *There was no trace of crab grass in the lush golf course.*

crack ['kræk] **1.** *n.* the line that is made in something when it splits or breaks; a narrow opening in something or between two things. ♦ *The old wall had many cracks in it.* ♦ *I could see into the house through a crack in the door.* **2.** *n.* a short, sharp noise like the noise of a powerful slap. ♦ *The whip made a crack as it hit the horse's back.* ♦ *The bat made a loud crack as it hit the baseball.* **3.** *n.* a snide remark; a cutting remark; a sarcastic remark. ♦ *The crack about John's pimples hurt his feelings.* ♦ *Anne made a crack about my cooking.* **4.** *n.* a very addictive form of cocaine that is smoked. (No plural form in this sense.) ♦ *The police found crack in the suspect's apartment.* ♦ *The teachers were shocked that students were smoking crack at school.* **5.** *tv.* to break something without separating it into pieces; to fracture something. ♦ *The movers cracked the pitcher when they moved it.* ♦ *Twisting the lid too tight will crack the jar.* **6.** *tv.* to strike someone; to hit someone somewhere. ♦ *I cracked the robber over the head with an empty bottle.* ♦ *The boxer cracked his opponent on the chin.* **7.** *tv.* to tell a joke. (Informal.) ♦ *Mary cracked a funny joke and made me laugh.* ♦ *The minister cracked a good one during the sermon.* **8.** *tv.* to decipher a code; to solve or figure out a mystery. ♦ *The spy cracked the enemy's code.* ♦ *The detective could not crack the mystery.* **9.** *tv.* to break into a safe. (Informal.) ♦ *The thief was unable to crack the safe.* ♦ *Max cracked his employer's safe and stole some money.* **10.** *iv.* [for something] to break without separating into pieces. ♦ *The vase fell and cracked.* ♦ *After the pitcher cracked, it would not hold water.* **11.** *iv.* [for one's voice] to break while speaking. ♦ *The teenager's voice cracked as he spoke.* ♦ *The audience laughed when the singer's voice cracked.* **12.** *iv.* to have a nervous breakdown; [for someone] to break down under pressure. (Informal.) ♦ *After the death of his parents, Bill cracked.* ♦ *Mary thought the pressure at work would make her crack.* **13. make cracks (about someone or something)** *idiom* to ridicule or make jokes about someone or something. (On ③.) ♦ *Please stop making cracks about my haircut. It's the new style.* ♦ *Some people can't help making cracks. They are just rude.*

cracked ['krækt] *adj.* fractured; broken, but not in pieces. ♦ *The cracked pitcher would not hold water.* ♦ *Superstition says a cracked mirror is bad luck.*

cracker ['kræk ɚ] *n.* a flat, thin, square, unsweetened biscuit, often salted. ♦ *I brought a box of crackers to the party.* ♦ *For a snack, we had cheese and crackers.*

crackle ['kræk əl] **1.** *n.* a soft snapping sound, like logs burning in a fire. (No plural form in this sense.) ♦ *The fire made a soft crackle.* ♦ *The logs made crackles and pops as they burned.* **2.** *iv.* to make a crackling noise. ♦ *The fire crackled softly.* ♦ *The telephone line crackled as we tried to use the telephone during the storm.*

crackpot ['kræk pɑt] **1.** *n.* someone who is very odd; someone who is eccentric. ♦ *We live next door to an old crackpot who is always calling the police.* ♦ *The wealthy crackpot kept many ugly statues in his yard.* **2.** *adj.* weird; odd; eccentric. ♦ *Bill's crackpot theory proved to be wrong, of course.* ♦ *Mary is always coming up with crackpot schemes for making money.*

cradle ['kred l] **1.** *n.* a small, rocking bed for a baby or a doll. ♦ *The baby smiled as he lay in his cradle.* ♦ *I placed the baby in her cradle and rocked her to sleep.* **2.** *n.* the place where something begins; the origin of something. ♦ *Greece is called the cradle of civilization.* ♦ *Africa may to be the cradle of humankind.* **3.** *tv.* to hold a baby in one's arms while rocking it back and forth; to hold something carefully. ♦ *The new father gently cradled the infant in his arms.* ♦ *Mary cradled the antique vase as she carried it through the house.*

craft ['kræft] **1.** *n.* a special skill; a special talent. ♦ *Bill is an expert in the craft of bookbinding.* ♦ *After she retired, Sue learned the craft of making pottery.* **2.** *n.* a small boat. ♦ *Dave rowed the craft away from the pier.* ♦ *The coast guard issued a warning for small craft to return to shore before the storm begins.* **3.** *tv.* to build or create something that requires skill or talent. ♦ *The artist crafted a delicate woodcut.* ♦ *The early explorers crafted canoes from huge trees.*

craftsman ['kræfts mən] *n., irreg.* an artisan; someone who builds something by hand. (Pl: **craftsmen**.) ♦ *We hired a craftsman to build a deck in our backyard.* ♦ *The craftsman showed his wares at the art show.*

craftsmanship ['kræfts mən ʃɪp] *n.* the skill or talent of a craftsman; the high quality of skill that goes into a piece of work. (No plural form in this sense.) ♦ *The woodcarver exhibited expert craftsmanship in his work.* ♦ *Because of her craftsmanship, Sue charged high prices for her works.*

craftsmen ['kræfts mən] pl of **craftsman**.

crafty ['kræf ti] *adj.* sneaky; sly; clever. (Adv: *craftily.* Comp: *craftier;* sup: *craftiest.*) ♦ *Some crafty little boy ate all the cookies!* ♦ *The spy thought of a crafty plan to steal the documents.*

crag ['kræg] *n.* a steep, rocky projection. ♦ *The hiker stood on a crag and surveyed the valley.* ♦ *The mountaintop was lined with jagged crags.*

cram ['kræm] **1.** *tv.* to force someone or something into a small space. ♦ *I crammed as many clothes as I could into the suitcase.* ♦ *Mary crammed herself onto the crowded bus.* **2.** *tv.* to fill a space too full; to stuff too many things or people into a space. ♦ *The students crammed the auditorium.* ♦ *The decorator crammed the room with antique furniture.*

cramp ['kræmp] **1.** *n.* a sudden, painful tightening of a muscle. ♦ *The runner experienced a painful cramp.* ♦ *It is dangerous to get cramps while swimming.* **2.** *iv.* [for a muscle or body part] to tighten suddenly and painfully. ♦ *In the middle of the night, my leg suddenly cramped.* ♦ *It can be very painful when a muscle cramps.*

cramped ['kræmpt] **1.** *adj.* tightened; contracted. ♦ *The physical therapist slowly rubbed the runner's cramped muscles.* ♦ *I woke up with a cramped leg this morning.* **2.** *adj.* confined; restricted; limited as to space. ♦ *The cramped kennel was filled with too many dogs.* ♦ *No more people could fit into the cramped elevator.*

cranberry ['kræn bɛr i] **1.** *n.* a tart red berry often served as a jelly. ♦ *We picked wild cranberries growing in the bog.* ♦ *Anne loved the cranberries served at Thanksgiving dinner.* **2.** *adj.* made of ①. ♦ *We had cranberry sauce with our Thanksgiving turkey.* ♦ *Mary thinks that cranberry juice is too tart.*

crane ['kren] **1.** *n.* a bird with long legs and a long neck—usually feeding on fish, frogs, etc. ♦ *I saw a flock of cranes near the bay.* ♦ *Suddenly, a crane darted from the bushes.* **2.** *n.* a large machine with a movable arm that moves and lifts very heavy things. ♦ *The crane lifted some steel beams to the top of the structure.* ♦ *The construction worker operated the crane skillfully.* **3.** *tv.* to stretch one's neck as far as it can go in order to see something. ♦ *I craned my neck around to see who was behind me.* ♦ *From the highest balcony, we craned our necks to see the stage.* **4.** *iv.* to stretch or seem to lengthen one's neck in order to gain height to see something. ♦ *We craned to get a glimpse of the celebrity in the crowd.* ♦ *I craned to see the movie over the tall man in front of me.*

crania ['kren i ə] a pl of cranium.

cranial ['kren i əl] *adj.* of or about the upper skull. (Adv: *cranially.*) ♦ *The cranial cavity of the reptile is quite small.* ♦ *The cranial bones are flat and curved, fitting together at the edges.*

cranium ['kren i əm] *n.* the upper skull, especially the part that covers and protects the brain. (The English plural is *craniums;* the Latin plural is crania.) ♦ *The anthropologist compared the crania of the two species.* ♦ *Apes have very thick craniums.*

crank ['kræŋk] **1.** *n.* an arm or lever that transfers rotating motion to a shaft or axle. ♦ *The first automobiles were started by turning a crank.* ♦ *I turned the hand mixer's crank to beat the eggs.* **2.** *n.* someone who annoys other people; someone who is eccentric. (Slang.) ♦ *The old crank next door collects junk.* ♦ *Some crank on the phone asked me if my refrigerator was running.* **3.** *tv.* to make something work by turning ①. ♦ *John cranked the hand mixer to beat the eggs.* ♦ *Dave cranked the antique car, and it started immediately.*

crankcase ['kræŋk kes] *n.* the metal box that is the bottom part of an engine, below the crankshaft. ♦ *The crankcase contains oil that must be changed periodically.* ♦ *The oil dripped onto the garage floor through a crack in the crankcase.*

crankshaft ['kræŋk ʃæft] *n.* the shaft in an engine to which the pistons are attached. ♦ *The rotation of the crankshaft in a car is transferred to the wheels.* ♦ *If the crankshaft is bent, the engine will not run.*

cranky ['kræŋ ki] *adj.* irritable; easily upset; cross. (Adv: *crankily.* Comp: *crankier;* sup: *crankiest.*) ♦ *The cranky toddler needed a nap.* ♦ *Waiting in line makes many customers cranky.*

crash ['kræʃ] **1.** *n.* the loud sound of something hitting something else. ♦ *When we heard a crash, we ran to see what had fallen.* ♦ *The picture made a loud crash when it hit the floor.* **2.** *n.* a sudden economic disaster; a time when the stock market falls rapidly. ♦ *My family had lost everything in the crash of 1929.* ♦ *The economist predicted that the market would crash soon.* **3.** *n.* a vehicle accident; a loud collision of vehicles. ♦ *The careful driver had never had a car crash.* ♦ *The crash involved five cars.* **4.** *tv.* to cause a loud collision of vehicles. ♦ *The drivers crashed the demolition cars.* ♦ *John lost control of the car and crashed it against a tree.* **5.** *tv.* to attend a party without an invitation; to show up somewhere uninvited. (Informal.) ♦ *The students who weren't invited to the party crashed it anyway.* ♦ *Bill rudely crashed my party, and my parents made him leave.* **6.** *iv.* to break with a loud noise; to smash. ♦ *The vase crashed when it fell off the bookcase.* ♦ *The pane of glass crashed when it hit the floor.* **7.** *iv.* to make a sudden, loud noise. ♦ *Something crashed in the middle of the night and woke me up.* ♦ *The pots and pans crashed when they fell.* **8.** *iv.* to stay the night at someone's place without previous notice. (Slang.) ♦ *Jane crashed at Anne's while her own apartment was being sprayed for bugs.* ♦ *Can I crash here tonight? I'm too tired to drive home.* **9.** *iv.* to fall asleep quickly. (Slang.) ♦ *After the long drive, Bob crashed on the couch.* ♦ *After a hard day at work, Anne crashed once she got home.* **10.** *adj.* sudden; of or about an intense effort in order to get results quickly. ♦ *Going on a crash diet can be dangerous.* ♦ *I took a crash course in skiing before going on vacation.*

crass ['kræs] *adj.* rude and unthinking; vulgar. (Adv: *crassly.* Comp: *crasser;* sup: *crassest.*) ♦ *The movie had a lot of crass language in it.* ♦ *It is crass to talk with your mouth full.*

crate ['kret] **1.** *n.* a rough wooden or plastic shipping box. ♦ *The warehouse was full of empty crates.* ♦ *The goods were shipped overseas in a crate.* **2. crate (up)** *tv.* (+ *adv.*) to pack something in ①. ♦ *The goods were crated up in the warehouse.* ♦ *The store will crate up your purchase and ship it for you.*

crater ['kret ɚ] **1.** *n.* a large depression made by a falling bomb or meteor. ♦ *The geologist examined the crater in the field.* ♦ *The moon's surface is covered with craters.* **2.** *n.* the depression at the top of a volcano. ♦ *Lava oozed from the volcano's crater.* ♦ *From the helicopter, we could see deep into the crater.*

crave ['krev] *tv.* to have a very strong desire for something; to want something very badly. ♦ *Anne craved unusual foods when she was pregnant.* ♦ *The captives craved freedom.*

craving ['krev ɪŋ] *n.* a strong desire; a desperate need, usually for a kind of food. ♦ *Pregnant women often experience cravings for certain foods.* ♦ *I felt a craving that could only be satisfied with ice cream.*

crawfish ['krɔ fɪʃ] See crayfish.

crawl ['krɔl] **1.** *iv.* to move on one's hands and knees; to move forward in a prone position. ♦ *Most babies learn to crawl before they walk.* ♦ *In case of fire, it's best to crawl to safety.* **2.** *iv.* [for something] to move very slowly. (Figurative on ①.) ♦ *Traffic was crawling on the expressway this morning.* ♦ *The freight train crawled along while we waited at the tracks.*

crayfish AND **crawfish** ['kre fɪʃ, 'krɔ fɪʃ] *n., irreg.* an edible crustacean found in the lakes and rivers of the Americas, Europe, Asia, and Australia. (Pl: *crayfish, crawfish.*) ♦ *The tails of crayfish are edible and can be cooked in a number of ways.* ♦ *A crawfish is somewhat like a lobster, but smaller.*

crayon ['kre ɑn] *n.* a colored stick of wax, used for drawing on paper or making pictures. ♦ *The child's picture was drawn with crayons.* ♦ *Sue bought a new box of crayons for her art class.*

craze ['krez] *n.* a fad; a current fashion that lasts a short time. ♦ *Bell-bottomed pants and pet rocks were crazes of the 1970s.* ♦ *Mike's parents urged him not to follow every craze that comes along.*

crazed ['krezd] *adj.* insane; crazy. (Adv: *crazedly.*) ♦ *Tom screamed like a crazed man when he won the lottery.* ♦ *The crazed passenger on the bus made the other riders nervous.*

crazily ['krez ə li] *adv.* in a crazy way; out of control. ♦ *We crazily tried to finish the project before the weekend.* ♦ *The car spun crazily on the ice.*

crazy ['krez i] **1.** *adj.* insane; mentally ill. (Adv: *crazily.* Comp: *crazier;* sup: *craziest.*) ♦ *After the death of his family, Bill went crazy.* ♦ *The crazy defendant was declared unfit to stand trial.* **2.** *adj.* stupid; foolish. (Adv: *crazily.*

Comp: *crazier;* sup: *craziest.*) ♦ *Driving while drunk is plain crazy.* ♦ *It is crazy to think you'll get ahead without an education.* **3.** *adj.* wild; bizarre. (Adv: *crazily.* Comp: *crazier;* sup: *craziest.*) ♦ *The crazy party lasted until the wee hours of the night.* ♦ *I won't listen to any more of your crazy talk.* **4. crazy about someone or something** *idiom* very fond of someone or something; very enthusiastic about someone or something. ♦ *I'm crazy about camping.* ♦ *Grandpa and Grandma are still crazy about each other.* **5. go crazy** *idiom* to become crazy ①, ②, or ③, disorientated, or frustrated. ♦ *It is so busy here that I think I will go crazy.* ♦ *Bob went crazy because his car got a flat tire.*

creak ['krik] **1.** *n.* a squeaking or grating noise made by rubbing. ♦ *The creaks in the attic were due to squirrels nesting up there.* ♦ *The house made eerie creaks at night that scared the children.* **2.** *iv.* to make ①. ♦ *The floor of the house creaks when you walk on it.* ♦ *The rocking chair creaked as I rocked in it.*

cream ['krim] **1.** *n.* the fatty part of cow's milk that rises to the top. (No plural form in this sense.) ♦ *A special machine separated the milk and the cream.* ♦ *Sue always drinks her coffee with cream in it.* **2.** *n.* a soft, thick substance used to benefit or carry medicine to the skin. (No plural form in this sense.) ♦ *This medicated cream will relieve dry skin.* ♦ *The doctor applied some cream to my rash.* **3.** *n.* an off-white color; a slightly yellowish white. (No plural form in this sense.) ♦ *The room was painted in a soft cream.* ♦ *Cream is a very difficult color to keep clean.* **4.** *adj.* <the adj. use of ①.> ♦ *I love a good cream sauce on chicken.* ♦ *Cream soups are very rich in flavor.* **5.** *adj.* having an off-white color; of the color of ①. ♦ *We painted the house a pretty cream color.* ♦ *The cream carpet was very hard to keep clean.* **6.** *tv.* to mash something to a creamy consistency. ♦ *The first step in making cake is to cream the butter and sugar together.* ♦ *The cook creamed the shortening with the other ingredients.*

cream cheese ['krim tʃiz] *n.* a soft, thick, white cheese made from cream and milk. (No plural form in this sense.) ♦ *The cheesecake recipe calls for cream cheese.* ♦ *I spread cream cheese on my bagel.*

creamer ['krim ɚ] *n.* a small pitcher for serving cream or milk for coffee or tea. ♦ *I see the sugar bowl, but where is the creamer?* ♦ *Our creamer is a tiny pitcher shaped like a cat.*

creamy ['krim i] *adj.* containing a lot of cream; as smooth as cream. (Adv: *creamily.* Comp: *creamier;* sup: *creamiest.*) ♦ *Pasta is good with a creamy sauce.* ♦ *The cake had a creamy frosting.*

crease ['kris] **1.** *n.* a deep fold; a line made in something by folding it and pressing down along the fold. ♦ *I ironed my trousers along the crease.* ♦ *I made a crease in the paper when I folded it in half.* **2.** *tv.* to make a line in something, such as paper or fabric, by folding it and pressing down. ♦ *Crease the paper, and it will be easy to tear.* ♦ *The dry cleaner creased my pleated skirt.* **3.** *iv.* to acquire ①; to become wrinkled. ♦ *Linen creases easily.* ♦ *Hang your clothes up so they don't crease.*

create [kri 'et] **1.** *tv.* to bring something new into being; to invent something. ♦ *The sculptor created a good likeness of his model.* ♦ *An inventor created a new time-saving device.* **2.** *tv.* to cause something to happen; to bring about something. ♦ *The fight created a rift in the family.* ♦ *Music creates a relaxing atmosphere.*

creation [kri 'e ʃən] **1.** *n.* bringing something new into being. (No plural form in this sense.) ♦ *The artist explained the creation of his work in detail.* ♦ *Music aids in the creation of a restful atmosphere.* **2.** *n.* the process of bringing the universe into being. (No plural form in this sense.) ♦ *The sun has shone since the beginning of creation.* ♦ *The substances that make up earth have been around since creation.* **3.** *n.* the universe; everything created by God. (No plural form in this sense.) ♦ *All the creatures of creation are part of the life on this planet.* ♦ *The naturalist thought all creation was beautiful.* **4.** *n.* something that is invented; something that is produced or made for the first time. ♦ *The chef was proud of his new creation.* ♦ *The war resulted in the creation of a new nation.*

creative [kri 'e tɪv] *adj.* able to think of new ideas or new ways to solve problems; artistic; able to develop works of art. (Adv: *creatively.*) ♦ *The engineers developed a creative solution to the problem.* ♦ *Susie's art project was very creative.*

creativity [kri e 'tɪv ɪt i] *n.* the ability to use one's imagination; the ability to think of new ideas or new ways to solve problems. (No plural form in this sense.) ♦ *Invention requires creativity.* ♦ *The art teacher encouraged creativity in her students.*

creator [kri 'et ɚ] **1.** *n.* someone who creates something; an inventor. ♦ *The interview with the creator of the play was interesting.* ♦ *The creator of the machine demonstrated it at the fair.* **2. the Creator** *n.* the deity; God. (No plural form in this sense. Treated as singular.) ♦ *The religious ceremony honored the Creator.* ♦ *Religious people praise the Creator.*

creature ['kri tʃɚ] *n.* a living animal; a living being. ♦ *The veterinarian treats all creatures, except people, of course.* ♦ *A little creature scampered across the yard.*

credential [krɪ 'dɛn ʃəl] **1.** *n.* a document certifying one's training and ability; a license that serves as ②. ♦ *Mary earned a credential in math teaching.* ♦ *The state mailed me my credential too late for me to get the job that required it.* **2. credentials** *n.* documents showing who one is; documents showing what one is qualified to do. (Treated as plural.) ♦ *The customs agent asked to see my credentials.* ♦ *The dentist's professional credentials hung on the office wall.*

credibility [krɛd ə 'bɪl ɪt i] *n.* the condition of being believable; the condition of being credible. (No plural form in this sense.) ♦ *The credibility of the witness was questioned by the prosecutor.* ♦ *The reporter trusted her source's credibility.*

credible ['krɛd ə bəl] *adj.* believable; worthy of belief; worthy of trust. (Adv: *credibly.*) ♦ *The scientist proposed a credible theory, but no one paid any attention.* ♦ *Are the reporter's sources credible?*

credit ['krɛd ɪt] **1.** *n.* confidence in the ability of people to pay a debt at a later date shown by allowing them to purchase goods or services now and pay later. (No plural form in this sense.) ♦ *I could not get a loan from the bank because my credit was bad.* ♦ *If you have good credit, you can buy things now and pay for them later.* **2. credit card** *n.* a plastic card that allows someone to use ① extended by a bank. ♦ *I bought a new refrigerator using my credit* *card.* ♦ *I never carry any cash these days. I just use my credit card.* **3.** *n.* the amount of money in an account; an account balance greater than zero. ♦ *My records show a credit of $120.00 because you paid us too much.* ♦ *The checking account has a credit of $200.00, meaning you have that much to spend.* **4.** *n.* an amount of money that is added to an account. ♦ *The bank teller recorded a credit to my account after I made a payment.* ♦ *A credit has already been made for the book you returned.* **5.** *n.* trust; faith; belief. (No plural form in this sense.) ♦ *Anne doesn't put much credit in astrology.* ♦ *Grandma puts a lot of credit in her religious beliefs.* **6.** *n.* recognition given to someone for having done something. (No plural form in this sense.) ♦ *Mike gets a lot of credit for paying his own college bills.* ♦ *The author was not given proper credit for writing the book.* **7.** *n.* a unit of schoolwork that is earned when a student passes a course. ♦ *This college course is worth three credits.* ♦ *Bill audited a class, rather than taking it for credit.* **8.** *n.* mention of someone's contributions to a book, movie, or performance appearing in a list of similar contributors. ♦ *I got a credit in the movie for saying just one word on camera.* ♦ *A list of credits for the people who helped is on the back page.* **9. credit with** *tv.* + *prep. phr.* to cite someone for doing something significant. ♦ *The newspaper credited the mayor with the drop in unemployment in the city.* ♦ *Christopher Columbus has been credited with discovering the New World.* **10. a credit to someone or something** *idiom* someone or something that makes someone proud; someone or something that is worthy of honor. ♦ *John, the chemist, is a credit to his discipline.* ♦ *Well-behaved children are a credit to their parents.* **11. extend credit (to someone)** *idiom* to grant someone ①. ♦ *The bank would not extend me any credit, because I have a poor credit record.* ♦ *The grocery store used to extend credit, but they stopped doing it a few years ago.* **12. on credit** *idiom* using ①; buying something using ①. ♦ *I tried to buy a new suit on credit, but I was refused.* ♦ *The Smiths buy everything on credit and are very much in debt.*

creditor ['krɛd ɪ tɚ] *n.* someone to whom one owes money. ♦ *Jane's creditors were trying to collect money from her.* ♦ *The bankrupt man evaded his creditors.*

creed ['krid] *n.* a statement of beliefs and principles. ♦ *The newspaper prints its creed on the front page every day.* ♦ *Whatever your creed, you can see the virtue in Jane's proposal.*

creek ['krik] *n.* a small, narrow river; a small stream. ♦ *The children threw rocks into the creek.* ♦ *The horses stopped to drink from Miller's Creek.*

creep ['krip] **1.** *iv., irreg.* to move slowly, with the body close to the ground. (Pt/pp: *creeped* or **crept**.) ♦ *Four prisoners trying to escape crept through the open field.* ♦ *The cat slowly crept along the floor.* **2.** *iv., irreg.* to grow along a surface; to grow up a wall. ♦ *Over the years, the ivy slowly crept up the side of the house.* ♦ *Grass had crept over the new grave by the end of the year.* **3.** *n.* a very slow movement. (No plural form in this sense.) ♦ *The train went from a speed of 60 miles an hour down to a creep.* ♦ *The stealthy creep of the cat brought it within a foot of the mouse.* **4. the creeps** *n.* an uncomfortable feeling; the feeling that things are crawling all over one's body. (Slang. Treated as singular or plural.) ♦ *I always get the creeps when it's dark outside.* ♦ *The scary movie gave me the creeps.* **5.** *n.* someone who is not enjoyable to be around; an undesirable person. (Slang.) ♦ *Some creep stole the other kids' lunch money.* ♦ *My boss is a creep who overworks all of the employees.*

creepy ['krip i] *adj.* causing an uncomfortable feeling; scary. (Adv: *creepily.* Comp: *creepier;* sup: *creepiest.*) ♦ *Mysterious sounds from outdoors gave us a creepy feeling.* ♦ *A creepy lunatic wandered the neighborhood at night.*

cremate ['krim et] *tv.* to burn a dead body to ashes, as a funeral rite. ♦ *The Smiths cremated their dead dog.* ♦ *David wishes to be cremated rather than buried.*

cremation [kri 'me ʃən] *n.* burning a dead body to ashes. (No plural form in this sense.) ♦ *Many people prefer cremation to burial.* ♦ *After cremation, the ashes can be returned to the family.*

Creole ['kri ol] **1.** *n.* a descendant of the original French settlers in Louisiana. ♦ *It is hard for me to understand the speech of the Creoles in Louisiana.* ♦ *The Creoles have an interesting language and culture.* **2. creole** *n.* a type of mixed language, resulting from the contact of two or more languages, learned as one's first language. ♦ *Creoles are spoken in Haiti and Sierra Leone.* ♦ *The formation of creoles usually involves at least one European language.* **3.** *n.* a French-based language variety spoken in Louisiana. ♦ *Creole is not taught in schools in Louisiana.* ♦ *My relatives in the bayous speak English, French, and Creole.* **4.** *adj.* <the adj. use of ①.> ♦ *Creole cooking is very popular and is often called Cajun.* ♦ *I really like crayfish tails with a Creole sauce.*

crepe ['krep] *n.* very thin pancakes that are usually rolled up and served with powdered sugar or jam. (From French. Usually plural.) ♦ *The crepes were stuffed with spinach and served in a cream sauce.* ♦ *We served strawberry crepes for dessert.*

crept ['krɛpt] a pt/pp of **creep**.

crescendo [krə 'ʃɛn do] *n.* an increase in volume; an increase in force. (Pl in *-s* or *-es.*) ♦ *The orchestra made a crescendo at the end of the symphony.* ♦ *A crescendo at the beginning of the second movement became almost too loud.*

crescent ['krɛs ənt] *n.* something that is shaped like a C. ♦ *The beach was covered with crescents of seaweed.* ♦ *A few days after the new moon, it appears in the sky like a crescent.*

crest ['krɛst] **1.** *n.* the top of something; the top of a mountain; the top of a wave; the high point of a flood. ♦ *The crest of the wave was white.* ♦ *We hiked to the crest of the hill and admired the view.* **2.** *n.* a tuft of feathers on the head of a bird; a tuft of fur on the head of an animal. ♦ *The crane has a fluffy crest on its head.* ♦ *The bird lowered its crest, shrieked, and appeared to threaten its owner.* **3.** *n.* a particular decoration that a family uses on stationery and other personal objects. (Often alluding to one's ancestors.) ♦ *The ancient shield was painted with the family crest.* ♦ *A large crest hung above the castle's fireplace.* **4.** *iv.* [for a flood or a wave] to reach its high point. ♦ *The river crested two days after the rains ended.* ♦ *Fortunately, the river crested an inch below flood stage.*

crestfallen ['krɛst fɔl ən] *adj.* sad; disappointed; downcast; with one's head down. (Adv: *crestfallenly.*) ♦ *Jimmy was crestfallen when he didn't win the race.* ♦ *The crestfallen child sulked for days.*

crevice ['krɛv ɪs] *n.* a split; a crack; a small, narrow opening; a fissure. ♦ *The mountain climber slipped his foot into a crevice in the cliff.* ♦ *The rain came in through a crevice in the cabin wall.*

crew ['kru] **1.** *n.* a group of people who work together, especially on a ship, a plane, backstage at a theater, etc. ♦ *The stage crew worked hard to build the set for the play.* ♦ *The flight crew made sure the passengers were comfortable.* **2.** *n.* the people on a rowing team. ♦ *The crew guided the rowboat into the water.* ♦ *The crew rowed the boat up and down the river.* **3.** *n.* the sport of rowing. (No plural form in this sense.) ♦ *John went out for crew in his second year at school.* ♦ *After a year of crew, Bill had strong arms.*

crew neck ['kru nɛk] **1.** *n.* a sweater with a round opening at the neck, as opposed to a V-shaped neck opening. ♦ *Dave looked dashing in his new crew neck.* ♦ *Mary bought a cardigan and a crew neck for herself.* **2. crew-neck** *adj.* <the adj. use of ①.> ♦ *The skiers wore crew-neck sweaters with turtleneck shirts underneath.* ♦ *The crew-neck sweatshirt was too small for Tom.*

crib ['krɪb] **1.** *n.* a baby's bed that has sides so the baby can't fall out. ♦ *The infant slept in the crib.* ♦ *The baby bottle was in the crib with the baby.* **2.** *n.* a storage shed for grain. ♦ *The farmer found a dead mouse in the crib where the corn is stored.* ♦ *One huge crib held the entire harvest of wheat.*

crick ['krɪk] *n.* a cramp; a sore or stiff place in a muscle. ♦ *The elderly patient complained of aches and cricks.* ♦ *Mary woke up with a crick in her neck.*

cricket ['krɪk ɪt] **1.** *n.* a small insect similar to the grasshopper, the male of which makes a chirping noise by rubbing his front wings together. ♦ *From the porch we could hear the crickets chirping.* ♦ *A tiny cricket hopped along the pavement.* **2.** *n.* an outdoor sport played in England with a (flat) bat and a ball. (No plural form in this sense.) ♦ *The kids watched their friends play cricket.* ♦ *When visiting London, I watched games of cricket on television.*

crime ['krɑɪm] **1.** *n.* the breaking of laws in general. (No plural form in this sense.) ♦ *Crime ran rampant in the city.* ♦ *The president announced a program to fight crime.* **2.** *n.* an illegal act; an act that is against the law. (No plural form in this sense.) ♦ *Kidnapping is a very serious crime.* ♦ *It is not a crime to tell a small lie.*

criminal ['krɪm ə nəl] *n.* someone who commits a crime; someone who breaks a law. ♦ *The criminal was sentenced to prison.* ♦ *The clever criminal was never caught by the police.*

criminologist [krɪm ɪ 'nɑl ə dʒəst] *n.* someone who studies crime and criminals. ♦ *This troublesome crime is being studied by a famous criminologist.* ♦ *The criminologist studied the killer's psychology.*

criminology [krɪm ɪ 'nɑl ə dʒi] *n.* the study of crime and criminals. (No plural form in this sense.) ♦ *The police detective took courses in criminology.* ♦ *An expert in criminology testified in the court.*

crimp ['krɪmp] **1.** *tv.* to press something into small waves or folds. ♦ *The hairdresser crimped my hair.* ♦ *The worker crimped the metal edge to make it decorative.* **2.** *n.* a fold or wave in something, especially hair or fabric. ♦ *The seamstress put crimps in the curtains.* ♦ *I accidentally ironed a crimp into the tablecloth.*

crimson ['krɪm zən] **1.** *n.* a deep red color. (No plural form in this sense.) ♦ *The artist painted the sunset in crimson.* ♦ *I prefer crimson to scarlet.* **2.** *adj.* of a deep red color. ♦ *The dress was made of crimson velvet.* ♦ *Crimson blood flowed from the wound.*

cringe ['krɪndʒ] *iv.* to recoil in fear; to bend back in fear; to shrink with fear; to shudder. ♦ *The news of the accident made me cringe.* ♦ *The child cringed at the sight of the enormous dog.*

crinkle ['krɪŋ kəl] **1. crinkle up** *tv.* + *adv.* to crush something, such as paper, causing many tiny lines to form. ♦ *Mary crinkled up the used wrapping paper and threw it away.* ♦ *The cook crinkled up the used plastic wrap.* **2. crinkle (up)** *iv.* (+ *adv.*) to make a lot of tiny lines; to make a lot of tiny folds or wrinkles. ♦ *Being in the suitcase caused the clothes to crinkle up.* ♦ *The paper crinkled badly when Tom sat on it.* **3.** *n.* a wrinkle in material or paper; a small, messy fold. ♦ *The clothing has crinkles from being folded in the suitcase.* ♦ *I ironed the crinkles out of the tablecloth.*

cripple ['krɪp əl] **1.** *n.* someone with one or more damaged limbs. (Some people object to this term.) ♦ *The war veteran was a cripple and needed a wheelchair.* ♦ *The accident victim now had to go through life as a cripple.* **2.** *tv.* to injure someone or some creature, causing lameness. ♦ *The accident crippled the driver.* ♦ *The blow to his legs crippled the football player for a few months.* **3.** *tv.* to weaken someone or something. (Figurative on ②.) ♦ *The strike crippled the company.* ♦ *We were crippled by the failure of the telephone system.*

crippled ['krɪp əld] *adj.* lame; physically handicapped. ♦ *Our family made a donation to the hospital for crippled children.* ♦ *The crippled soldier walked with crutches.*

crises ['krɑɪ siz] pl of crisis.

crisis ['krɑɪ sɪs] *n., irreg.* a serious and threatening situation, the resolution of which will determine the future; a turning point. (Pl: crises.) ♦ *The hijacking became an international crisis.* ♦ *In a crisis, we can count on our neighbors for help.*

crisp ['krɪsp] **1.** *adj.* brittle and dry; easily broken; easily snapped. (Adv: *crisply.* Comp: *crisper;* sup: *crispest.*) ♦ *The autumn leaves were dry and crisp.* ♦ *I spread butter on a crisp piece of toast.* **2.** *adj.* fresh; firm. (Adv: *crisply.* Comp: *crisper;* sup: *crispest.*) ♦ *The bank teller gave me two crisp, new ten-dollar bills.* ♦ *The lettuce in the salad was crisp and fresh.* **3.** *adj.* [of air] cool and refreshing. (Adv: *crisply.* Comp: *crisper;* sup: *crispest.*) ♦ *We walked in the park on a crisp autumn day.* ♦ *The crisp air invigorated us as we walked.*

crispy ['krɪsp i] *adj.* [of food] crisp or crunchy, snapping or breaking slightly when chewed. (Adv: *crispily.* Comp: *crispier;* sup: *crispiest.*) ♦ *I bit into the delicious crispy cookie.* ♦ *Mary served crispy vegetables and dip at the party.*

crisscross ['krɪs krɔs] **1.** *tv.* to follow a pattern that moves back and forth across something in a jagged pattern. ♦ *The trail crisscrossed the road a number of times, but we were able to follow it.* ♦ *The decorative pattern crisscrossed the top of the cake in an attractive way.* **2.** *adj.* concerning the pattern described in ①. ♦ *The cake is decorated with a crisscross pattern.* ♦ *We followed a crisscross trail through the woods.*

criteria [krɑɪ 'tɪr i ə] a pl of criterion.

criterion [krɑɪ 'tɪr i ən] *n., irreg.* a principle used in decided something. (Pl: **criteria** or *criterions.*) ♦ *What were the criteria for hiring the new employee?* ♦ *My primary criterion when I am buying a car is quality.*

critic ['krɪt ɪk] **1.** *n.* someone who writes evaluations of artistic or literary works or performances. ♦ *Art critics praised the young artist's work.* ♦ *The newspaper hired a critic to review the community theater performance.* **2.** *n.* someone who finds fault with people or things. ♦ *The columnist was a social critic and disliked most politicians.* ♦ *Most of the students were critics of the poorly run school system.*

critical ['krɪt ɪ kəl] **1.** *adj.* making criticisms; finding fault. (Adv: *critically* [...ɪk li].) ♦ *Bill grew tired of his critical friend.* ♦ *The movie review was critical of the director's casting choices.* **2.** *adj.* for evaluation; doing evaluation. (Adv: *critically* [...ɪk li].) ♦ *The manuscript was submitted for a critical review.* ♦ *The plan was given a critical appraisal by the company president.* **3.** *adj.* extremely important or serious. (Adv: *critically* [...ɪk li].) ♦ *Flour is a critical ingredient in a cake recipe.* ♦ *The victim of the car accident is in critical condition.*

criticism ['krɪt ə sɪz əm] **1.** *n.* the process of evaluating and presenting critical statements. (No plural form in this sense.) ♦ *Criticism is an important part of the study of literature.* ♦ *There are a number of academic journals devoted to criticism.* **2.** *n.* an act of criticism; a statement of criticism; a critical remark. (Usually negative unless specifically positive.) ♦ *Tom's helpful criticisms made Lisa feel good.* ♦ *Billy was upset by his parents' constant criticism.*

criticize ['krɪt ə sɑɪz] **1.** *tv.* to find fault with someone or something. ♦ *A long newspaper article criticized the mayor's actions.* ♦ *Please don't criticize my haircut.* **2.** *iv.* to judge the good and bad points of something, usually negative unless specifically positive. ♦ *The literature critic criticizes in a balanced and respectful way.* ♦ *Please don't criticize all the time!*

critique [krɪ 'tik] **1.** *n.* an evaluation of the good and bad points of something; an article written by a critic. (From French.) ♦ *The critique praised the film's originality.* ♦ *The critique of the new civic center pointed out its flaws.* **2.** *tv.* to judge the good and bad points of something. ♦ *The editor critiqued the manuscript.* ♦ *I asked my teacher to critique my work.*

critter ['krɪt ɚ] *n.* a creature; an animal. (A colloquial version of **creature**.) ♦ *The old farmhouse was crawling with critters.* ♦ *Our picnic was ruined by all sorts of insects and critters.*

croak ['krok] **1.** *n.* the noise that a frog makes. ♦ *The frog made a loud croak.* ♦ *We could tell by the croak we heard that a frog was trapped under the porch steps.* **2.** *iv.* to make the characteristic sound of a frog. ♦ *In the cabin we could hear the frogs croaking down by the swamp.* ♦ *The nature film explained why frogs croak.* **3.** *iv.* to make a noise like ①. ♦ *The laryngitis patient croaked for water.* ♦ *The choking man croaked and gasped.* **4.** *iv.* to die. (Slang.) ♦ *After twenty years, my pet cat finally croaked.* ♦ *I thought I would croak during the five-mile race!*

crochet [kro 'ʃe] **1.** *tv.* to make something out of yarn using a hooked needle. (From French.) ♦ *My cousin crocheted a blanket for my new baby.* ♦ *I passed time on the subway by crocheting scarves.* **2.** *iv.* to do the action in ①. ♦ *When did you learn to crochet?* ♦ *During the plane trip, I crocheted to pass the time.*

crock ['krɑk] *n.* a large earthenware jar, used for pickling cucumbers and storing food. ♦ *The general store sold out of crocks for homemade pickles.* ♦ *I placed a dozen cucumbers in the crock.*

crocodile ['krɑk ə dɑɪl] **1.** *n.* a large, dangerous reptile with many teeth and a powerful tail. ♦ *The hunters shot the crocodile for its skin.* ♦ *Crocodiles live in the rivers of many parts of the world.* **2.** *adj.* made from the skin of ①. ♦ *The boutique sold crocodile purses.* ♦ *Crocodile shoes are very expensive.* **3. shed crocodile tears** *idiom* to shed false tears; to pretend that one is weeping. ♦ *The child wasn't hurt, but she shed crocodile tears anyway.* ♦ *He thought he could get his way if he shed crocodile tears.*

crocus ['krok əs] *n.* a small purple, yellow, or white flower that blooms in the spring. ♦ *When I saw a crocus, I knew spring was coming.* ♦ *On a walk through the woods, we saw patches of crocuses.*

croissant [krə 'sɑnt] *n.* a light, flaky pastry shaped like a crescent. (French for **crescent**.) ♦ *The sandwich was made on a croissant rather than regular bread.* ♦ *I spread some jam on a croissant for breakfast.*

crony ['kron i] *n.* a close friend; an ally. (Occasionally derogatory.) ♦ *Dave gets together with his cronies to play poker.* ♦ *The sailor met an old crony at the tavern.*

crook ['krʊk] **1.** *n.* a criminal; a thief. ♦ *Our downstairs neighbor turned out to be a crook.* ♦ *The police caught the crook red-handed.* **2.** *n.* a bent part of something; a hooked part of something. ♦ *The crook of the hanger rests on the rod.* ♦ *Dave held my baby in the crook of his arm.* **3.** *tv.* to bend something; to make a bend or a hook in something. ♦ *The glove won't go on because you've crooked your fingers.* ♦ *I crooked my arm to hold the baby.* **4.** *iv.* to bend. ♦ *The stream crooks to the left and then to the right.* ♦ *The top of the tree crooks a bit toward the house.*

crooked ['krʊk ɪd] **1.** *adj.* bent; not straight; twisted; angled. (Adv: *crookedly.*) ♦ *The picture on the wall is crooked.* ♦ *The electrician straightened the crooked wires.* **2.** *adj.* not honest; thieving; criminal. (Adv: *crookedly.*) ♦ *The bank president turned out to be quite crooked.* ♦ *The crooked accountant was caught embezzling funds.*

croon ['krun] **1.** *tv.* to sing a song in a soft voice. ♦ *The babysitter crooned an old folk song to the child.* ♦ *Bill crooned a tune as he worked.* **2.** *iv.* to sing in a soft voice; to sing romantically or lovingly. ♦ *Mary's suitor crooned to her as they sat on the front porch swing.* ♦ *I crooned to the sleeping baby in my arms.*

crop ['krɑp] **1.** *n.* a plant or food product grown and harvested by a farmer. ♦ *After the rains, the farmers had to replant their crops.* ♦ *What types of crops are grown in the Midwest?* **2.** *n.* the amount of a particular food grown during one season. (No plural form in this sense.) ♦ *The farmer harvested his corn crop in early autumn.* ♦ *An entire crop of potatoes was damaged by insects.* **3.** *n.* a short, looped whip. ♦ *The jockey used a crop to get the horse to run faster.* ♦ *The horse felt the crop and ran faster.* **4.** *tv.* to cut or trim something. ♦ *Mary got tired of her long hair and cropped it.* ♦ *The photographer cropped the photo to fit in the frame.*

croquet [kro 'ke] *n.* an outdoor game played with wooden mallets, wooden balls, and wire wickets. (No plural form in this sense.) ♦ *Max's large estate had an excellent lawn for playing croquet.* ♦ *At the barbecue, the children played croquet on the lawn.*

cross ['krɔs] **1.** *n.* a sign or structure in a form similar to an X. ♦ *Tom drew a cross on the wall where he was to drill the hole.* ♦ *A small cross on the sidewalk indicates the property line.* **2.** *n.* a post with another post crossing it near the top that people were attached to as a punishment in ancient times. ♦ *In biblical times, criminals were often executed on a cross.* ♦ *The dead man was removed from the cross.* **3.** *n.* the shape of the Christian cross, representing ②. ♦ *The cross is the main symbol of Christianity.* ♦ *Lisa received a gold cross on a chain at her confirmation.* **4.** *n.* a combination or blend; a hybrid. ♦ *The zoo had an animal that was a cross between a tiger and a lion.* ♦ *Anne's expression was a cross between wonder and disbelief.* **5.** *tv.* to move from one side of something to the other; to go across something. ♦ *The horses easily crossed the stream.* ♦ *I watched the ant slowly cross the sidewalk.* **6.** *tv.* to intersect something; to form a cross with something else. ♦ *Main Street crosses First Avenue downtown.* ♦ *The main highway crosses Smith Road just south of here.* **7.** *tv.* to make the sign of the cross on one's body. (A ritual practiced by some Christian religions where one touches one's hand on one's head, the middle of one's chest, and both shoulders. Reflexive.) ♦ *As the priest gave the blessing, the parishioners crossed themselves.* ♦ *Mary crossed herself when she heard the bad news.* **8.** *tv.* to anger someone; to upset someone. ♦ *Don't cross Dave when he is in a bad mood.* ♦ *The employee who crossed the owner was soon fired.* **9.** *tv.* to breed species or varieties of animals in such a way as to give yet a different creature. ♦ *A mule is the result of crossing a horse and a donkey.* ♦ *The trainer tried to cross the two breeds of horses.* **10.** *iv.* to intersect; to form a cross. ♦ *State Street and Madison Street cross in downtown Chicago.* ♦ *Parallel lines never cross.*

cross-country ['krɔs 'kʌn tri] **1.** *adj.* moving across the country through fields and nature, instead of by roads; [of skiing] done in relatively flat areas, typically traveling through the countryside or woods, rather than down steep hills or mountains. ♦ *Bill prefers cross-country skiing to downhill skiing.* ♦ *The hikers took a cross-country trek through the mountains.* **2.** *adj.* across the country; from one side of the country to the other. ♦ *The cross-country train trip took nearly a week.* ♦ *The Smiths took a cross-country trip from New York to Los Angeles.* **3.** *adv.* traveling across the country. ♦ *We drove cross-country to see the sites.* ♦ *During the summer, John biked cross-country.*

cross-examine ['krɔs ɛg 'zæm ɪn] **1.** *tv.* to question someone thoroughly. ♦ *The officer cross-examined the suspect at the police station.* ♦ *My parents cross-examined me when I broke my curfew.* **2.** *tv.* to question someone again in a court trial. (One attorney questions a witness, and the opposing attorney reviews the same questions with the witness.) ♦ *The prosecutor cross-examined the witness for the defense.* ♦ *The judge said to the attorney, "You may cross-examine the witness."*

cross-eyed ['krɔs ɑɪd] *adj.* having eyes that are turned toward the nose. ♦ *Susie is just a little cross-eyed.* ♦ *The eye doctor examined the cross-eyed child.*

crossfire ['krɔs fɑɪr] **1.** *n.* the firing of bullets from both sides of a battle. (No plural form in this sense.) ♦ *The pedestrians were caught in the crossfire of the snipers.* ♦ *A small child was killed in the crossfire during the gang battle.* **2.** *n.* an attack from two or more different directions. (No plural form in this sense. Figurative on ①.) ♦ *The host was caught in the crossfire of the arguing guests.* ♦ *The employee was caught in the crossfire of the managers' argument.*

crossing ['krɔs ɪŋ] *n.* the place where one path, road, or railway crosses another pathway. ♦ *The children waited for cars to stop at the crossing.* ♦ *There was a stop sign at the railroad crossing.*

cross-reference ['krɔs 'rɛf rəns] *n.* a reference from one part of a document to another. ♦ *The encyclopedia article had several cross-references in it.* ♦ *The editor made a cross-reference to another part of the book.*

crossroad ['krɔs rod] **1.** *n.* a road that intersects with the road that one is traveling on. ♦ *The hikers came to a crossroad and made a left turn.* ♦ *At the crossroad, Mike looked for the name of the street.* **2. crossroads** *n.* the junction formed where two roads intersect. (Treated as singular or plural.) ♦ *There are some shops down near the crossroads.* ♦ *At all four corners of the crossroads, there is a stop sign.* **3.** *n.* the point at which a decision has to be made. (Figurative on ①.) ♦ *We are at the crossroads of a great decision on the occasion of this election.* ♦ *The company president must consult the board at each major crossroad in the firm's operation.*

crosswalk ['krɔs wɔk] *n.* a marked path across a street where people can cross safely. ♦ *The crosswalk is painted on the cement in white paint.* ♦ *Cross only at the crosswalk. Don't jaywalk.*

crossword puzzle ['krɔs wɚd 'pʌz əl] *n.* a word puzzle where the answers to clues are entered onto a grid. ♦ *The newspaper contains a crossword puzzle every day.* ♦ *Do you work crossword puzzles in ink?*

crotch ['krɑtʃ] **1.** *n.* the space where two tree branches come together. ♦ *The bird made its nest in a crotch of the tree.* ♦ *A crotch in a tree is a good place to build a tree house.* **2.** *n.* the part of the body where the two legs come together. ♦ *John's pants were too tight in the crotch.* ♦ *He had a terrible itch in the crotch.* **3.** *n.* the part of clothing that covers ②. ♦ *His underwear has a cotton crotch.* ♦ *The crotch of these pants is too tight.*

crotchety ['krɑtʃ ɪt i] *adj.* full of complaints; arguing; irritable. ♦ *The crotchety customer yelled at the salesclerk.* ♦ *Bill is always crotchety when he is tired.*

crouch ['kræutʃ] *iv.* to hunch the body over and stoop down. ♦ *I crouched down so the football wouldn't hit me.* ♦ *Mary crouched in order to look for her shoes under the couch.*

crouton ['kru tɑn] *n.* a small cube of crunchy bread served with soups or salads. ♦ *I make croutons from old bread.* ♦ *The salad was sprinkled with flavorful croutons.*

crow ['kro] **1.** *n.* a large, black bird; a raven. ♦ *The yard was filled with crows.* ♦ *The scarecrow frightened the crows away from the farmer's crops.* **2.** *iv.* [for a rooster] to make its loud noise. ♦ *The rooster crowed at sunrise.* ♦ *The farmyard was filled with the sound of roosters crowing.* **3.** *iv.* to boast about something; to talk about something with pride. ♦ *John crowed endlessly about his success at gambling.* ♦ *Don't crow over your victories!* **4. as the crow flies** *idiom* straight across the land, as opposed to distances measured on a road, river, etc. (On ①.) ♦ *It's twenty miles to town on the highway, but only ten miles as the crow flies.* ♦ *Our house is only a few miles from the lake as the crow flies.*

crowbar ['kro bɑr] *n.* a strong iron bar that is used as a lever. ♦ *You'll need a crowbar to get that locked chest open.* ♦ *The mechanic used the crowbar to take the hubcap off the car.*

crowd ['krɑʊd] **1.** *n.* a large group of people; a gathering of people. ♦ *A crowd waited to enter the museum for the special exhibit.* ♦ *The shy student was not comfortable in crowds.* **2.** *n.* a specific group of people; one's social group. ♦ *Bill's crowd is rowdy and drinks a lot.* ♦ *The high-school student dreamed of being in the popular crowd.* **3. crowd into** *tv.* + *prep. phr.* to fill or overfill something with someone or something. ♦ *Jimmy crowded three brownies into his mouth.* ♦ *I crowded as many clothes into the suitcase as I could.* **4.** *iv.* [for many people or creatures] to gather closely together. ♦ *The fans crowded around the famous singer.* ♦ *Seven teenagers crowded into the small car.*

crowded ['krɑʊd ɪd] *adj.* packed; full; too full. (Adv: *crowdedly.*) ♦ *The crowded room became warm and stuffy.* ♦ *Bill dreaded entering the crowded hall.*

crown ['krɑʊn] **1.** *n.* the circular head ornament worn by royal persons. ♦ *The queen's crown was decorated with jewels.* ♦ *The king adjusted his crown on his head.* **2.** *n.* something that is worn around the head. ♦ *The model had a crown of golden hair.* ♦ *The actress wore a crown of flowers in her hair for the part.* **3.** *n.* the office or authority of a monarch. (No plural form in this sense.) ♦ *In a constitutional monarchy, the crown has little authority.* ♦ *In medieval days, the crown owned all the land.* **4.** *n.* the top part of something, especially a tooth, a hat, or a mountain. ♦ *A wide ribbon circled the crown of the hat.* ♦ *The crown of my tooth is made of gold.* **5.** *tv.* to make someone king or queen. ♦ *The prince was crowned king when he reached eighteen.* ♦ *The archbishop crowned the woman queen.*

crucial ['kru ʃəl] *adj.* very important; decisive; critical. (Adv: *crucially.*) ♦ *The spy played a crucial role in the coup.* ♦ *Knowing first aid is crucial for saving lives.*

crucifixion [krus ə 'fɪk ʃən] **1.** *n.* attaching someone to a cross to be left to die. ♦ *The ancient Romans executed people by crucifixion.* ♦ *Crucifixion is a slow and painful way to die.* **2. Crucifixion** *n.* the killing of Jesus Christ on the cross. (No plural form in this sense.) ♦ *The story of Christ's Crucifixion is told in the Gospels.* ♦ *The painting portrays the Crucifixion.*

crucify ['krus ə fɑɪ] **1.** *tv.* to attach someone to a cross as a death penalty. ♦ *The Romans crucified criminals.* ♦ *Jesus was crucified among a group of criminals.* **2.** *tv.* to punish someone severely; to criticize someone or something severely. (Figurative on ①.) ♦ *My parents will just crucify me if I am late!* ♦ *The reviewer crucified the poorly made movie.*

crude ['krud] **1.** *adj.* in a natural state; not refined; raw. (Adv: *crudely.* Comp: *cruder;* sup: *crudest.*) ♦ *Crude oil has to be refined before it can be used.* ♦ *The computer will analyze the crude data and give us a report.* **2.** *adj.* vulgar; mannerless. (Adv: *crudely.* Comp: *cruder;* sup: *crudest.*) ♦ *I'd appreciate it if you didn't tell any crude jokes around me.* ♦ *Bill's crude manners embarrassed everyone at the table.* **3.** *adj.* rudimentary; not expertly done. (Adv: *crudely.* Comp: *cruder;* sup: *crudest.*) ♦ *I could only make a crude translation of the document.* ♦ *The archaeologist unearthed some crude tools.*

crudeness ['krud nəs] **1.** *n.* vulgarity; a quality lacking in manners or consideration. (No plural form in this sense.) ♦ *The audience was appalled by the crudeness of the speaker's remark.* ♦ *Everyone soon tired of Bill's crudeness.* **2.** *n.* roughness; an unrefined state. (No plural form in this sense.) ♦ *From the crudeness of the tool, the archaeologist dated it very early in the period.* ♦ *Examining the back of the cabinet revealed the crudeness of the manufacturer's techniques.*

cruel ['kru əl] **1.** *adj.* evil; wicked; fond of causing pain. (Adv: *cruelly.* Comp: *crueler;* sup: *cruelest.*) ♦ *The cruel man kicked his dog.* ♦ *The cruel ruler allowed the peasants to starve.* **2.** *adj.* causing pain; causing suffering. (Adv: *cruelly.* Comp: *crueler;* sup: *cruelest.*) ♦ *The student never forgot the teacher's cruel words.* ♦ *The corrupt mayor had a cruel heart.*

cruelty ['kru əl ti] **1.** *n.* harshness; the qualities of causing pain and distress. (No plural form in this sense.) ♦ *The dictator was known for his cruelty to dissidents.* ♦ *The organization sought to prevent cruelty to animals.* **2.** *n.* a cruel act; an act of meanness; a brutal act. ♦ *The war criminal was tried for cruelties committed during the war.* ♦ *Bill was dealt one cruelty after another, so he ran away from home.*

cruise ['kruz] **1.** *n.* a trip on a boat for pleasure; a vacation on a boat or ship. ♦ *The Smiths took a cruise to Alaska.* ♦ *A few passengers became seasick during the cruise.* **2.** *iv.* to travel at a constant speed. ♦ *The ship cruised comfortably at 14 knots.* ♦ *My car can cruise along at 70 miles per hour on the freeway.*

cruiser ['kruz ɚ] **1.** *n.* a medium-sized battleship. ♦ *The submarine sank a cruiser with a torpedo.* ♦ *John was stationed on a cruiser during World War II.* **2.** *n.* a police car. (Informal.) ♦ *Three cruisers patrolled the neighborhood where the robbery occurred.* ♦ *The policeman got out of his cruiser and went into the doughnut shop.*

cruise ship ['kruz ʃɪp] *n.* a large passenger ship designed for vacations on lakes, rivers, and seas. ♦ *The cruise ship we traveled on was like a floating hotel.* ♦ *Our cruise ship is so big that it won't fit through the Panama Canal.*

crumb ['krʌm] *n.* a particle of bread or cake. ♦ *I brushed crumbs from the cake off the kitchen counter.* ♦ *My recipe for fried chicken requires crumbs of stale bread.*

crumble ['krʌm bəl] **1.** *tv.* to cause something to fall apart into tiny pieces; to break something up into tiny pieces. ♦ *Bill crumbled crackers into his soup.* ♦ *The cook crumbled chocolate over the top of the cake.* **2.** *iv.* to fall apart into tiny pieces. ♦ *The pie crust crumbled when it was sliced.* ♦ *My cookie crumbled when I dropped it.*

crumbled ['krʌm bəld] *adj.* broken into tiny pieces; in crumbs. ♦ *The ducks quickly ate the crumbled bread.* ♦ *I sprinkled crumbled crackers over the casserole.*

crumbling ['krʌm blɪŋ] *adj.* falling apart; breaking apart. (Adv: *crumblingly.*) ♦ *The crumbling building was condemned by the city.* ♦ *Jane and Bill tried to save their crumbling marriage.*

crumple ['krʌm pəl] **1. crumple (up)** *tv.* (+ *adv.*) to make random folds in something while crushing it. ♦ *Anne crumpled the letter and threw it into the wastebasket.* ♦ *Dave crumpled his clothes while packing the suitcase.* **2.** *iv.* to collapse as if undergoing the action of ①. ♦ *The building crumpled when the dynamite exploded.* ♦ *The house of cards crumpled when Bill knocked the table.*

crumpled ['krʌm pəld] *adj.* crushed; wadded up; folded in a disorderly fashion. ♦ *The wastebasket is full of crumpled paper.* ♦ *I ironed the crumpled clothes.*

crunch ['krʌntʃ] **1.** *n.* the sound of something snapping and breaking, especially of something being chewed. ♦ *The cookies made a loud crunch as the children ate them.* ♦ *John bit into a stalk of celery with a loud crunch.* **2.** *n.* the pressure felt when many deadlines happen at the same time. ♦ *There is always a crunch at work towards the end of the year.* ♦ *The boss caused a crunch by poor scheduling.*

crunchy ['krʌn tʃi] *adj.* brittle; making a breaking noise when chewed. (Adv: *crunchily.* Comp: *crunchier;* sup: *crunchiest.*) ♦ *Bill likes his cookies crunchy rather than chewy.* ♦ *I served crunchy vegetables as an appetizer.*

crusade [kru 'sed] **1. the Crusades** *n.* the religious expeditions of the Christians against the Moslems in the twelfth and thirteenth centuries. (Treated as plural.) ♦ *Soldiers and knights fought in the Crusades.* ♦ *A very large number of people died in the Crusades.* **2.** *n.* a fight against something bad; a fight for something good. ♦ *Lisa's organization led a crusade against drunk driving.* ♦ *The people in the neighborhood succeeded in their crusade to install a stop sign.* **3.** *iv.* to fight against something bad; to fight for something good. ♦ *The researcher crusaded against cancer.* ♦ *The president of the country crusaded against poverty.*

crusader [kru 'sed ɚ] **1.** *n.* someone who fought in the Crusades. ♦ *The crusader fought on the road to Jerusalem.* ♦ *The historian lectured about the crusaders and their battles.* **2.** *n.* someone who fights for something good; someone who fights against something bad. ♦ *The activist was a crusader for civil rights.* ♦ *The mayor had a reputation of being a crusader for justice.*

crush ['krʌʃ] **1.** *tv.* to compress something with great force and collapse it. ♦ *A powerful machine at the junkyard crushed the cars.* ♦ *The box was crushed under the heavier crates.* **2.** *tv.* to break something into small pieces by pressing or pounding. ♦ *The huge machine crushed the rocks into small stones.* ♦ *Sugar can be crushed into a fine powder.* **3.** *tv.* to stop a revolt; to conquer someone. (Figurative on ②.) ♦ *The military crushed the rebels.* ♦ *Our army crushed the attackers.* **4.** *tv.* to force juice out of fruit by squeezing it. ♦ *The wine press crushed the grapes.* ♦ *I have a juicer that crushes oranges to make fresh juice.* **5.** *n.* a strong desire for someone; an infatuation with someone. ♦ *John had a crush on one of his classmates.* ♦ *Mary can still remember her first crush in school.*

crushed ['krʌʃt] *adj.* flattened; squeezed into another shape. ♦ *Crushed cars were stacked in the corner of the junkyard.* ♦ *The recipe called for crushed pineapple.*

crushing ['krʌʃ ɪŋ] **1.** *adj.* causing something to be crushed; harmful. (Adv: *crushingly.*) ♦ *Crushing pressure was applied to the bodies of the cars.* ♦ *Tom was dealt a crushing blow that put him in the hospital.* **2.** *adj.* powerful and shocking. (Figurative on ①. Adv: *crushingly.*) ♦ *The Smiths were shocked when they received the crushing news of their son's death.* ♦ *The news of the accident was totally crushing.*

crust ['krʌst] *n.* the hard outside layer of something, including the earth, a pie, a loaf of bread, etc. ♦ *The crust of the pie was delicious.* ♦ *I cut the crusts from the bread I use for my sandwiches.*

crustacean [krə 'ste ʃən] *n.* a sea animal having a hard shell, such as a lobster, a shrimp, or a crab. ♦ *Many of the crustaceans are good to eat.* ♦ *When crustaceans are eaten, the shell must be removed.*

crutch ['krʌtʃ] *n.* an under-arm support that helps a lame person walk. ♦ *The injured man hobbled along on a crutch.* ♦ *After I broke my leg, I used crutches for a long time.*

crux ['krʌks] *n.* the most important part of a problem; the issue central to something. ♦ *The crux of the problem is that we have no money.* ♦ *The professor presented the crux of her argument in a short lecture.*

cry ['kraɪ] **1.** *n.* an expression of pain or anger; a loud expression of emotion. ♦ *The baby gave a cry as her mother walked away.* ♦ *We could hear the cries of the cat outside in the rain.* **2.** *n.* a shout; a call. ♦ *I gave a cry to my friend across the park.* ♦ *Bill did not hear my cry to him from across the street.* **3.** *n.* a period of weeping. ♦ *During the sad movie, I had a good cry.* ♦ *The child's cry lasted a few seconds, and then he was happy again.* **4.** *iv.* to weep; to sob; to shed tears. ♦ *Jane cried because she was very frustrated.* ♦ *Bill started to cry when he heard the sad news.* **5. cry to** *iv.* + *prep. phr.* to call out loudly to someone. ♦ *Bill cried to Anne from across the street, but Anne did not hear him.* ♦ *I cried to him to stop, but he kept going.* **6. cry one's eyes out** *idiom* to cry very hard. ♦ *When we heard the news, we cried our eyes out with joy.* ♦ *She cried her eyes out after his death.*

crybaby ['kraɪ be bi] *n.* someone who cries and complains a lot; someone who cries and complains when there is no reason to. ♦ *Susie called her little sister a crybaby.* ♦ *The crybaby dried his tears and stuck his tongue out at his brother.*

crypt ['krɪpt] *n.* an underground burial room under a church. ♦ *Famous people are buried in the cathedral's crypt.* ♦ *The pastor locked the door leading to the crypt.*

cryptic ['krɪp tɪk] *adj.* secret; coded; intelligible. (Adv: *cryptically* [...ɪk li].) ♦ *Can you explain this cryptic message I got from my boss?* ♦ *I do not understand your cryptic remarks!*

cryptographer [krɪp 'tɑ grəf ɚ] *n.* someone who writes in a code; someone who tries to figure out codes. ♦ *During the war, the government employed cryptographers.* ♦ *The cryptographer could not break the enemy code.*

crystal ['krɪs təl] **1.** *n.* a solid chemical compound occurring in a regular, angular shape. ♦ *Salt crystals can be found in every home.* ♦ *The chemist stored various chemical crystals on the shelf.* **2.** *n.* clear, expensive glass containing a lot of lead. (No plural form in this sense.) ♦ *The crystal used at the fashionable dinner party was very deli-*

cate. ♦ *Mary received her crystal as a wedding gift.* **3.** *n.* the clear cover over the face of a watch. ♦ *I scratched the crystal of my watch against the desk.* ♦ *The jeweler put a new crystal on my watch.* **4.** *adj.* made from ②. ♦ *I poured some sherry from a crystal decanter.* ♦ *The room was lit by a crystal chandelier.* **5.** *adj.* clear; transparent. ♦ *Sue wanted to swim in the crystal water of the lake.* ♦ *I gazed into the crystal depths of the pool.*

crystal-clear ['krɪs təl 'klɪr] **1.** *adj.* clear; transparent; completely clear; very clear; sparklingly clear. ♦ *Keep polishing until your glasses are crystal-clear.* ♦ *The clean windows were crystal-clear.* **2.** *adj.* easy to understand; simple; lucid. (Figurative on ①.) ♦ *You may not leave this house. Is that crystal-clear?* ♦ *It is crystal-clear that Bill and Mary don't like each other.*

crystallize ['krɪs tə lɑɪz] **1.** *iv.* to turn into crystals; to harden into the shape of a crystal. ♦ *The cooling candy crystallized before my very eyes.* ♦ *Sugar crystallized in the mixture making it gritty.* **2.** *iv.* [for an idea or a plan] to become understandable and more clear. (Figurative on ①.) ♦ *Once our plans have crystallized, I can tell you what your task will be.* ♦ *As the idea crystallized, I realized that it was impossible.*

Ct. See court.

cub ['kʌb] *n.* one of the young of certain animals, including bears, lions, and foxes. ♦ *The lion nudged her cub along.* ♦ *The bear cubs wrestled with each other.*

Cuba ['kju bə] See Gazetteer.

cubbyhole ['kʌb i hol] *n.* a small, enclosed space. ♦ *The children put their backpacks in their cubbyholes at school.* ♦ *I kept my house key in a cubbyhole near the mailbox.*

cube ['kjub] **1.** *n.* a solid object having six square sides all the same size. ♦ *I put some ice cubes in my drink.* ♦ *Mary made some broth from bouillon cubes.* **2.** *n.* the number that is the result of multiplying some other number by itself two times. ♦ *The cube of three is 3 × 3 × 3, or 27.* ♦ *The cube of 5 is 125.* **3.** *tv.* to multiply a number by itself two times, that is, number × number × number. ♦ *When you cube three, you get 27.* ♦ *Do you get 125 when you cube 5?* **4.** *tv.* to cut up food into tiny little cubes. ♦ *Mike cubed the chicken for chicken salad.* ♦ *Anne cubed the fruit for the dessert recipe.*

cubed ['kjubd] *adj.* cut up into tiny cubes. ♦ *Jane added the cubed cheese to the salad.* ♦ *The salad was made from cubed chunks of fruit.*

cubic ['kjub ɪk] *adj.* of a measurement of the length, breadth, and width of something. (Adv: *cubically* [...ɪk li].) ♦ *Mixed concrete is sold in cubic yards.* ♦ *The volume of a box measuring 3 inches by 4 inches by 6 inches is 3 × 4 × 6, or 72 cubic inches.*

cubicle ['kjub ɪ kəl] *n.* a small work space that is contained by thin or partial walls. ♦ *Each worker had a cubicle with a phone and a computer.* ♦ *The cubicles have only three walls.*

cubism ['kjub ɪz əm] *n.* a style of art where objects are represented as cubes, pyramids, spheres, and other geometric shapes. (No plural form in this sense.) ♦ *Cubism was an artistic movement of the early twentieth century.* ♦ *The artist's style had some elements of cubism.*

cuckoo ['ku ku] **1.** *n.* a kind of bird that makes a call that sounds like "koo koo." (Pl in *-s*.) ♦ *I heard a cuckoo in the forest yesterday.* ♦ *Cuckoos steal the nests of other birds.* **2.** *adj.* crazy; insane; weird; odd. (Informal.) ♦ *I called the police when my next-door neighbor went cuckoo.* ♦ *Your idea is completely cuckoo.*

cucumber ['kju kəm bɚ] *n.* a long, green, tubular vegetable, eaten raw in salads or pickled. ♦ *I grow cucumbers and tomatoes in my garden.* ♦ *My salad was made from sliced cucumbers.*

cud ['kʌd] *n.* a lump of chewed food that a ruminant animal, such as a cow, brings back into its mouth from its stomach in order to chew on it some more. ♦ *The cow stood in the pasture and chewed its cud.* ♦ *Cows spend many hours chewing their cud.*

cuddle ['kʌd l] *tv.* to hold someone with love and affection; to hug someone for a while. ♦ *Susie cuddled the baby kitten.* ♦ *The young lovers cuddled on the couch.*

cue ['kju] **1.** *n.* a long, narrow stick used to hit balls in billiards and pool. ♦ *The pool cues were in a rack mounted on the wall.* ♦ *In pool, the ball is hit with a cue.* **2.** *n.* something that is a signal for someone to do or say something; a line that prompts an actor to say the next line or do the next action. ♦ *The actor got his cue from the director.* ♦ *The end of the overture was the actress's cue to say the first line.* **3.** *tv.* to signal something to do or say something; to give someone ②. ♦ *The stage manager cued the actors backstage to make their entrance.* ♦ *The producer cued the orchestra conductor to begin.* **4. take one's cue from someone** *idiom* to use someone else's behavior or reactions as a guide to one's own. ♦ *If you don't know which cutlery to use at the dinner, just take your cue from John.* ♦ *The other children took their cue from Tom and ignored the new boy.*

cuff ['kʌf] **1.** *n.* the turned-up edge of cloth near the ankles on trousers; the thicker material near the wrists on shirts. ♦ *The tailor added cuffs onto the straight-legged trousers.* ♦ *Lint gets stuck in the cuffs of my pants.* **2.** *n.* one of a pair of handcuffs. ♦ *The police officer put cuffs on the suspect.* ♦ *The cuffs chafed the prisoner's wrists.* **3.** *tv.* to hit someone with one's hand. ♦ *The boxer cuffed his opponent.* ♦ *Billy cuffed the bully in the face.* **4.** *tv.* to put handcuffs on someone. ♦ *The cop cuffed the suspect.* ♦ *"Cuff him," the policeman said to his partner.*

cufflink ['kʌf lɪŋk] *n.* a piece of jewelry used in place of a button on shirts that do not have buttons at the cuff. ♦ *The tuxedo shirt needed cufflinks.* ♦ *The lawyer wore expensive jade cufflinks.*

cuisine [kwɪ 'zin] **1.** *n.* a particular way—usually national or cultural—of preparing food. ♦ *The cookbook contained recipes representing many cuisines.* ♦ *Some cuisines use hot spices.* **2.** *n.* food, especially the food of a particular country or region. ♦ *I really love Mexican cuisine.* ♦ *The restaurant served cuisine from Thailand.*

culinary ['kʌl ɪ nɛr i] *adj.* of or about food and food preparation. ♦ *The young cook had attended culinary school.* ♦ *Our chef has excellent culinary skills.*

cull ['kʌl] *tv.* to select and remove something from a group. ♦ *We culled the weak animals from the herd.* ♦ *The judges of the contest culled the worst entries immediately.*

culminate ['kʌl mɪn et] **1.** *tv.* to get to the highest point of something; to bring something to an end. ♦ *A fireworks display will culminate the celebration.* ♦ *This is the painting that culminated the artist's long career.* **2. culminate**

in *iv.* + *prep. phr.* to end with something. ♦ *The evening culminated in a midnight fireworks display.* ♦ *The plot culminated in the protagonist's suicide.*

culmination [kəl mɪ 'ne ʃən] *n.* the highest point; the climax. (No plural form in this sense.) ♦ *As the culmination of her career, Mary gave a final concert.* ♦ *The culmination of the artist's efforts can be seen in this work.*

culprit ['kʌl prɪt] *n.* someone who is guilty of a crime or wrongdoing. ♦ *The pie has been eaten! Who is the culprit?* ♦ *The teacher caught the culprit who was stealing glue.*

cult ['kʌlt] **1.** *n.* members of a strange or radical system of worship or admiration. ♦ *Tom's parents were afraid that he might move to California and join a cult.* ♦ *The cult leader believed he was the son of God.* **2.** *adj.* attracting a small number of devoted fans, who seem like ①. ♦ *The rock star has a cult following.* ♦ *I cannot understand why anyone likes this cult movie.*

cultivate ['kʌl tə vet] **1.** *tv.* to grow plants or crops. ♦ *The botanist cultivated tropical flowers.* ♦ *The farmer planned to cultivate the pasture.* **2.** *tv.* to develop an interest (in someone or something); to nurture an interest (in someone or something). (Figurative on ①.) ♦ *The teacher cultivated an appreciation of music among the students.* ♦ *John tried to cultivate his son's interest in good books.*

cultivated ['kʌl tə vet ɪd] *adj.* educated; cultured; mannered. ♦ *The distinguished gentleman married a cultivated woman.* ♦ *The guest's manners indicate that she is cultivated and cosmopolitan.*

cultivation [kəl tə 've ʃən] **1.** *n.* preparing soil for the planting of crops. (No plural form in this sense.) ♦ *All garden soils need cultivation to produce good results.* ♦ *Cultivation of the field is done after the harvest.* **2.** *n.* nurturing, developing, or improving something. (No plural form in this sense.) ♦ *Max's natural skills at painting only needed cultivation.* ♦ *The child benefited from the cultivation of her talents.* **3.** *n.* a person's level of cultural sophistication. (No plural form in this sense.) ♦ *His manners show a high level of cultivation.* ♦ *Cultivation is gained by exposure to many people, places, and things.*

cultural ['kʌl tʃɚ əl] **1.** *adj.* of or about culture. (Adv: *culturally.*) ♦ *We are all products of the cultural influences of our societies.* ♦ *The anthropologist was interested in cultural matters.* **2.** *adj.* of or about the music and the arts. (Adv: *culturally.*) ♦ *The class went on a cultural field trip to the art museum.* ♦ *Going to the symphony is a cultural experience.*

culture ['kʌl tʃɚ] **1.** *n.* the social patterns of the people in a particular domain. ♦ *The anthropologist wrote about the tribe's culture.* ♦ *Weddings and funerals are a part of most cultures.* **2.** *n.* the artistic and social tastes of a society. (No plural form in this sense.) ♦ *This book is a study of early American culture.* ♦ *Folk songs are part of American culture.* **3.** *n.* a growth of bacteria in a container in a laboratory. ♦ *The scientist studied the culture under a microscope.* ♦ *The bacterial culture became infected with a mold.*

cultured ['kʌl tʃɚd] *adj.* refined; cultivated; showing a knowledge of the arts. ♦ *Our school seeks to produce cultured students.* ♦ *Cultured people usually support the arts.*

culvert ['kʌl vɚt] *n.* a ditch or drain that runs under a road or other pathway. ♦ *The ducks waddled through the culvert.* ♦ *The culvert was a perfect hiding place for the little boy.*

cumbersome ['kʌm bɚ səm] *adj.* big and bulky; not easily movable. (Adv: *cumbersomely.*) ♦ *Bill carried a cumbersome box down the hall.* ♦ *The old, ornate furniture was cumbersome to move.*

cummerbund ['kʌm ɚ bənd] *n.* a sash worn around the waist as part of a tuxedo. ♦ *Max's tuxedo had a plaid cummerbund.* ♦ *The cummerbund on Bill's tuxedo was too tight.*

cumulative ['kjum jə lə tɪv] *adj.* accumulated; an amount resulting from adding small amounts repeatedly. (Adv: *cumulatively.*) ♦ *The effects of the drug are cumulative.* ♦ *Anne's cumulative score for the game was the highest, so she won.*

cunning ['kʌn ɪŋ] **1.** *adj.* clever; sly; tricky. (Adv: *cunningly.*) ♦ *The cunning child played a trick on her friend.* ♦ *The successful owner had developed a cunning business sense.* **2.** *n.* cleverness; slyness. (No plural form in this sense.) ♦ *The crook was well known for shrewd cunning.* ♦ *With a lot of cunning, the raccoons escaped the traps we'd set.*

cup ['kʌp] **1.** *n.* a drinking container having a loop-shaped handle. ♦ *The beggar held out a cup, hoping people would put coins in it.* ♦ *I filled my cup with coffee.* **2.** *n.* the contents of ①. ♦ *I spilled a cup of coffee and stained my shirt.* ♦ *The whole cup of juice splashed onto the floor.* **3.** *n.* a standard unit of measurement equal to eight ounces. ♦ *The recipe requires one cup of flour.* ♦ *Can I borrow a cup of sugar?* **4.** *n.* an award; a trophy. (Often shaped like a cup or a larger vessel.) ♦ *The hockey team won the most treasured cup of all.* ♦ *The victorious tennis player held the cup above her head.* **5.** *tv.* to shape something like a cup; to make something be shaped like a cup. ♦ *Mary cupped her hands to catch the water.* ♦ *The potter cupped the clay to form the base of a vessel.*

cupboard ['kʌb ɚd] *n.* a cabinet lined with shelves, used to store plates, food, or kitchen supplies. ♦ *The plates are in the cupboard above the stove.* ♦ *I opened the cupboard and removed some groceries from the shelves.*

cupcake ['kʌp kek] *n.* a small cake, shaped as if it had been cooked in a cup. ♦ *The cupcakes were contained in individual wrappers.* ♦ *The children ate cupcakes at the birthday party.*

cupful ['kʌp fʊl] *n.* the contents of a cup. ♦ *I spilled a cupful of coffee on the floor.* ♦ *The recipe calls for a cupful of milk.*

cur ['kɚ] **1.** *n.* a mongrel; a dog of no particular breed. ♦ *A band of curs roamed the alleys, tearing into the garbage.* ♦ *The animal pound was filled with curs and other unwanted dogs.* **2.** *n.* an insolent, cowardly male or otherwise despicable male. (Figurative on ①.) ♦ *You cur! How could you do that!* ♦ *Max was acting like a cur, so I left the room.*

curable ['kjʊr ə bəl] *adj.* [of a disease] able to be cured or treated; not fatal. (Adv: *curably.*) ♦ *Cancer is sometimes curable.* ♦ *The doctor said the disease is curable.*

curative ['kjʊr ə tɪv] *adj.* curing; having the ability to cure. (Adv: *curatively.*) ♦ *This herb has some curative properties.* ♦ *The curative effects were soon evident—the pain was gone!*

curator ['kjʊr et ɚ] *n.* someone in charge of the collections in a museum or art gallery. ♦ *A famous curator is in charge of the museum's collections.* ♦ *The museum curator spoke about the new exhibit.*

curb ['kɚb] **1.** *n.* the raised edge or rim of a road. ♦ *Dave ran his car over the curb and onto the sidewalk.* ♦ *The grass extends all the way to the curb.* **2.** *n.* a restraint; a control. ♦ *The drug acts as a curb on hunger.* ♦ *Taking a walk can be a curb against losing your temper.* **3.** *tv.* to restrain something; to control something; to keep something back. ♦ *Mary curbed her desire to buy the expensive book.* ♦ *Bill tried to curb his anger.*

curd ['kɚd] *n.* one of the thick parts of soured milk, separated from the liquid part. ♦ *The milk was so old that curds had begun to form.* ♦ *On the farm, we ate curds as part of every meal.*

cure ['kjʊr] **1.** *n.* a medicine that will make a sick person better; a remedy. ♦ *Sleep is a cure for exhaustion.* ♦ *This antibiotic is a cure for infections.* **2.** *tv.* to make someone well again; to get rid of a disease or a bad habit. ♦ *The medicine cured Mary.* ♦ *Bill cured himself of the habit of smoking.* **3.** *tv.* to preserve meat by salting, smoking, or drying it. ♦ *The hunter cured the salmon over a smoking fire.* ♦ *Salted meat was further cured by smoking it.*

cure-all ['kjʊr ɔl] *n.* a panacea; something that makes everything better. ♦ *Money is not a cure-all for personal problems.* ♦ *My cure-all for aches and pains is a cup of tea.*

cured ['kjʊrd] *adj.* [of meat] smoked, preserved, or salted. ♦ *Lox is cured salmon.* ♦ *The cured meat will not spoil.*

curfew ['kɚ fju] *n.* the time at which children are supposed to be home. (Sometimes set by law and sometimes set by parents.) ♦ *The teenagers must observe a curfew.* ♦ *Mike's parents set a midnight curfew for him.*

curiosity [kjʊr i 'ɑs ɪt i] **1.** *n.* the eager desire to know something; inquisitiveness. (No plural form in this sense.) ♦ *My curiosity got the better of me, and I looked in the closed file.* ♦ *Just out of curiosity, I wonder how much this apartment costs.* **2.** *n.* an oddity; an unusual thing; something strange or rare. ♦ *The circus had all sorts of curiosities on display.* ♦ *Your statement is really a curiosity. You sound very old-fashioned.*

curious ['kjʊr i əs] **1.** *adj.* inquisitive; wanting to learn about something. (Adv: *curiously.*) ♦ *The curious child asked a lot of questions.* ♦ *The book was about a curious monkey.* **2.** *adj.* weird; odd; strange; eccentric; unusual. (Adv: *curiously.*) ♦ *The family had a few curious traditions.* ♦ *My eccentric friend has some curious mannerisms.*

curl ['kɚl] **1.** *n.* a group of hairs that are looped or twisted. ♦ *The baby had a head full of curls.* ♦ *Jane made a curl and patted it into place.* **2.** *n.* twist; an amount of twisting. (No plural form in this sense.) ♦ *Mary asked her hairdresser to give her hair more curl.* ♦ *Bill does not like the curl of his hair.* **3.** *n.* something that is shaped like a loop or a spiral. ♦ *Curls of wood on the floor showed that the carpenter was at work.* ♦ *The package was decorated with red ribbon, twisted into curls.* **4.** *tv.* to cause a bunch of hairs to twist into loops or coils. ♦ *It's hard to curl my straight hair.* ♦ *The beautician curled Mary's hair.* **5.** *tv.* to cause something to wind around an object; to wind something around an object. ♦ *The cat curled itself around my ankle.* ♦ *The dog's leash curled around the stake.* **6.** *iv.* to twist into loops or coils. ♦ *This hot sauce will make your hair curl.* ♦ *This type of ribbon curls when you pull it across a scissor blade.* **7. curl up and die** *idiom* to retreat and die. (Often an exaggeration.) ♦ *When I heard you say that, I could have curled up and died.* ♦ *No, it wasn't an illness. She just curled up and died.*

curlicue ['kɚ li kju] *n.* a line or a letter with a fancy loop or twist, as found in fancy handwriting. ♦ *Bill signed his name with lots of curlicues.* ♦ *The calligrapher used plenty of curlicues on the invitations.*

curly ['kɚ li] *adj.* having curls; having loops or coils. (Comp: *curlier;* sup: *curliest.*) ♦ *The package was decorated with curly ribbon.* ♦ *Mike wished his curly hair was straight.*

currency ['kɚ ən si] **1.** *n.* the kind of money that is used in a particular country. ♦ *We exchanged our currency at a bank in the airport.* ♦ *The paper currency of the United States is green and white.* **2.** *n.* the quality of being in general use. (No plural form in this sense.) ♦ *Many good words just have no currency these days and are useless in conversation.* ♦ *Your invalid theories have no currency in modern science.*

current ['kɚ ənt] **1.** *adj.* up-to-date; recent; of or about the present time. (Adv: *currently.*) ♦ *Recent reports will give the most current news about the accident.* ♦ *At the current moment, I'm running late for work. Excuse me.* **2.** *n.* a moving stream of air or water; a flow. ♦ *This river is dangerous because of its strong current.* ♦ *The pilot studied the air currents.* **3.** *n.* the flow of electricity; the rate of the flow of electricity. ♦ *Tom turned the switch and cut the current off.* ♦ *How much current does this light bulb use?*

curriculum [kə 'rɪk jə ləm] *n.* all the courses offered at a school; a particular course of study. ♦ *The grade school's curriculum includes foreign languages.* ♦ *My high school has a good mathematics curriculum.*

curry ['kɚ i] **1.** *n.* a type of spicy dish, typically South Asian. (No plural form in this sense.) ♦ *Mary is very fond of curry and likes to eat in Indian restaurants.* ♦ *The menu included several varieties of curry, including some without meat.* **2.** *n.* an example of ①. ♦ *The exchange student made us a curry like those of India.* ♦ *Bill altered the recipe for the curry so it would not be too hot.* **3. curry (powder)** *n.* a mixture of spices used to make ① or to season other foods. (No plural form in this sense.) ♦ *This chicken dish has a little bit of curry in it.* ♦ *Curry powder can be very hot or relatively mild.* **4.** *tv.* to flavor food with ③; to prepare food in the manner of ①. ♦ *The chef curried the chicken salad.* ♦ *I couldn't decide whether to curry the lamb or serve it in a stew.* **5. curry favor with someone** *idiom* to try to get special favor from someone. ♦ *They tried to curry favor with the professor by working hard.* ♦ *Bill could never curry favor with the boss, but he kept trying.*

curse ['kɚs] **1.** *n.* a word or statement asking a supernatural power to bring evil or to harm someone or something. ♦ *This radio won't work. Is there a curse on it?* ♦ *The evil wizard placed a curse on the king.* **2.** *n.* a word used when swearing; a swear word. ♦ *Where did Jimmy learn that curse?* ♦ *Jane uttered a curse when she stubbed her toe.* **3.** *tv.* to utter ② against someone or something. (Pt/pp: ['kɚst].) ♦ *Tom cursed his pen when it ran out of ink.* ♦ *Anne was angry and cursed me for breaking her window.* **4.** *iv.* to swear; to use a swear word; to use profane language. ♦ *The minister said it was a sin to curse.* ♦ *Please stop cursing!*

cursed ['kɚs ɪd] *adj.* unfortunate; wretched; damned. (Adv: *cursedly.*) ♦ *"Damn that cursed cat!" Dave said when the cat scratched him.* ♦ *This cursed radio never works when I want it to.*

cursive ['kɚ sɪv] **1.** *adj.* written with letters that are joined together, as opposed to printing; handwritten. (Adv: *cursively.*) ♦ *Please use cursive script. Do not print.* ♦ *The note was written in large, round cursive letters.* **2.** *n.* a style of handwriting where the letters are joined together. (No plural form in this sense.) ♦ *Cursive is more difficult than printing.* ♦ *Mary prefers to print rather than write in cursive.*

cursor ['kɚs ɚ] *n.* a blinking symbol on a computer screen, used to indicate where information will be placed on the screen when it is typed. ♦ *Place the cursor on the first letter of the word you want to delete.* ♦ *The cursor stopped moving. I think the computer has stopped working.*

cursory ['kɚs ə ri] *adj.* at a glance; not paying attention to small details; hasty. ♦ *The busy manager gave the report a cursory glance.* ♦ *The reviewer gave a cursory report about the uninteresting book.*

curt ['kɚt] *adj.* rudely brief; short (with someone or something) in a rude way. (Adv: *curtly.*) ♦ *The rude customer gave the salesclerk a curt response.* ♦ *Our waiter was so curt we almost walked out.*

curtail [kɚ 'tel] *tv.* to cut something short; to reduce something; to lessen something. ♦ *The discussions were curtailed when the fire alarm went off.* ♦ *Our new budget curtailed spending.*

curtain ['kɚt n] *n.* a piece of fabric hung as a barrier to sight. ♦ *Gingham curtains hung in each window.* ♦ *A curtain separated the living room of the cabin from a sleeping area.*

curtsy AND **curtsey** ['kɚt si] **1.** *n.* a bow made by women and girls to show respect. (The knees are bent and the head and shoulders are lowered.) ♦ *The ballerina gave a curtsey at the end of her performance.* ♦ *The princess made a deep curtsy to the queen.* **2.** *iv.* to make ①. ♦ *The young princess curtsied to the queen.* ♦ *The ballerina curtsied at the end of her dance.*

curvaceous [kɚ 've ʃəs] *adj.* [of a woman] having a full and shapely figure. (Adv: *curvaceously.*) ♦ *A series of curvaceous models posed for the photographer.* ♦ *The beer advertisement featured several curvaceous women.*

curvature ['kɚv ə tʃɚ] **1.** *n.* the degree or amount that something is curved. (No plural form in this sense.) ♦ *The doctor assessed the curvature of the child's spine.* ♦ *The carpenter measured the curvature of the edge of the tabletop.* **2.** *n.* the quality of being curved. (No plural form in this sense.) ♦ *Curvature of the spine is a serious problem if not treated.* ♦ *The carpet did not quite cover the sharp curvature of the bottom stair.*

curve ['kɚv] **1.** *n.* a smooth bend; a continuously bending line. ♦ *Driving on the highway, we could see the curve of the horizon.* ♦ *The mountain road is full of curves.* **2.** **curve (ball)** *n.* a type of baseball pitch where the ball moves to either side of the batter just before the ball passes over home plate. ♦ *The pitcher threw a curve.* ♦ *The batter missed the curve and struck out.* **3.** *tv.* to make something bend; to bend something into ①. ♦ *The ballerina curved her arms above her head.* ♦ *Mary curved the cable to her mouse around the top edge of the computer keyboard.* **4.** *iv.* to bend in the shape of ①. ♦ *The willow branches curved gently downward.* ♦ *The road curves gently to the right just before the lake.* **5.** **throw someone a curve** *idiom* to confuse someone by doing something unexpected. ♦ *When you said "house," you threw me a curve. The password was supposed to be "home."* ♦ *John threw me a curve when we were making our presentation, and I forgot my speech.*

curved ['kɚvd] *adj.* having no straight lines or angles; bent smoothly; rounded. ♦ *The baby's spoon has a curved handle.* ♦ *The willow tree's curved branches seemed quite graceful in the moonlight.*

curving ['kɚv ɪŋ] *adj.* bending; moving in a curve. ♦ *The curving road was difficult to navigate.* ♦ *The wall was painted with curving lines.*

cushion ['kʊʃ ən] **1.** *n.* a padded pillow for sitting. ♦ *My rocking chair has a soft cushion.* ♦ *The sofa cushions have new upholstery.* **2.** *tv.* to soften something from shock or impact. ♦ *The carpet cushioned the fall of the vase.* ♦ *A safety net cushioned the acrobat's fall.*

cushioned ['kʊʃ nd] *adj.* padded; softened. ♦ *Let Grandma sit on the cushioned bench, rather than on that hard one.* ♦ *The body was laid in a cushioned casket.*

custard ['kʌs tɚd] *n.* a pudding made from eggs, sugar, and milk. ♦ *This lovely piece of pastry has custard inside.* ♦ *The chef made custard with caramel sauce.*

custodian [kə 'stod i ən] **1.** *n.* someone who has custody over someone else; someone who is in charge of someone or something. ♦ *Mike is the custodian of his parents' estate.* ♦ *The court appointed Mary as her nephew's custodian.* **2.** *n.* a janitor; someone who keeps someplace clean and makes small repairs. ♦ *I called the custodian when the refrigerator in my apartment broke down.* ♦ *The building's custodian fixed the boiler.*

custody ['kʌs tə di] **1.** *n.* the right to, or responsibility of, taking care of someone or something. (No plural form in this sense.) ♦ *The court awarded custody of the child to her aunt and uncle.* ♦ *Our antique vase is in the custody of the auction house that is selling it.* **2.** **in custody of someone or something; in someone's or something's custody** *idiom* the condition of being kept guarded by police. ♦ *The suspect was in the sheriff's custody awaiting a trial.* ♦ *The prisoner is in the custody of the state.*

custom ['kʌs təm] **1.** *n.* a tradition; a social tradition; a socially expected practice. ♦ *Carving pumpkins into grotesque heads is a Halloween custom in the United States.* ♦ *Eating roast turkey is a Thanksgiving custom.* **2.** *n.* a habit; a regular practice; a usual event. ♦ *It is Anne's custom to take a walk after supper.* ♦ *The annual picnic is a company custom.* **3.** *adj.* made to order; specially made for a customer. ♦ *Bill wears only custom suits.* ♦ *The cake has custom decorations.*

customarily [kəs tə 'mɛr i li] *adv.* usually; habitually; regularly. ♦ *The Smiths are customarily late.* ♦ *The bride's father customarily walks with the bride down the aisle.*

customary ['kʌs tə mɛr i] *adj.* usual; established by tradition or custom; habitual. (Adv: *customarily.*) ♦ *It is cus-*

tomary to give people presents on their birthdays. ♦ *Saying "please" and "thank you" is customary.*

customer ['kʌs təm ɚ] *n.* someone who buys a product or a service from a person or a business. ♦ *The customer returned the damaged goods to the store.* ♦ *The clerk packed the customer's groceries.*

custom-made ['kʌs təm 'med] *adj.* specially made for a customer; made to order. ♦ *Bill only wears custom-made clothes.* ♦ *The cake was custom-made for the party.*

cut ['kʌt] **1.** *n.* an incision; an opening made in the skin accidentally. ♦ *After climbing through the thorn bushes, I had cuts on my arms.* ♦ *My cut became infected.* **2.** *n.* a share of the profit. ♦ *The literary agent took a cut of the author's royalties.* ♦ *The government takes a cut of your salary in income taxes.* **3.** *n.* a reduction in an amount of money; the taking away of funds for something. ♦ *The arts suffered from government cuts in funding.* ♦ *The baseball players all took a cut in pay.* **4.** *n.* a piece of something that has been cut ⑤ from something; a piece of meat. ♦ *The butcher held a sale on some cuts of meat.* ♦ *John cooked the marinated cut of beef.* **5.** *tv., irreg.* to separate something from something else with a sharp object; to sever something from something else. (Pt/pp: *cut.*) ♦ *Jane cut the cake and served her friends.* ♦ *The butcher cut the fat from the steak.* **6.** *tv., irreg.* to make an opening in something with a sharp object; to slit something with a sharp object. ♦ *Max cut a hole in the wall with a knife.* ♦ *I had to cut a slit in the cloth to make on opening for my hand.* **7.** *tv., irreg.* to shorten something with a sharp object; to trim something with a sharp object. ♦ *The hairdresser cut my hair short.* ♦ *I cut the grass with my mower.* **8.** *tv., irreg.* to reduce something; to decrease something. ♦ *Jimmy's allowance was cut as a punishment.* ♦ *Congress voted to cut the budget.* **9.** *tv., irreg.* to dissolve something; to dilute something. ♦ *It took a strong soap to cut the grease.* ♦ *This disinfectant spray will cut the smell of garbage.* **10. cut out** *tv., irreg. + adv.* to make a shape by cutting something away. ♦ *The tailor cut the pattern for the dress out of the cloth.* ♦ *The children cut dolls out of paper.* **11.** *tv., irreg.* to grow a tooth; to have a tooth push through the gums. ♦ *The baby was cranky because he was cutting a tooth.* ♦ *Our baby cut her first tooth today.* **12.** *iv., irreg.* to slice into something; to make an incision into something. ♦ *As the surgeon cut, he hit a large blood vessel.* ♦ *I sharpened my knife and was ready to cut.* **13. Cut!** *interj.* an order made by a director to a camera operator to stop filming. ♦ *Cut! That scene looks great.* ♦ *Keep the action going until you hear "Cut!"* **14. cut-and-dried** *adj.* routine; boring; not requiring much thought or effort. ♦ *Your essay seems totally cut-and-dried and will not get a very high grade.* ♦ *This is a simple question that requires only a cut-and-dried answer.* **15. cut class; cut school** *idiom* to fail to attend a school class or a day of school. ♦ *As a joke, one day all the students cut their math class and went to lunch.* ♦ *Jane was grounded after she cut her classes.*

cutback ['kʌt bæk] *n.* a reduction of money, staff, help, or support. ♦ *The company made some cutbacks in production costs.* ♦ *The staff cutbacks didn't affect our department.*

cute ['kjut] *adj.* pretty; attractive. (Adv: *cutely.* Comp: *cuter;* sup: *cutest.*) ♦ *The baby looks so cute in that outfit!* ♦ *The flowers on your hat are really cute.*

cuticle ['kjut ɪ kəl] *n.* the hard skin at the lower edge of fingernails and toenails. ♦ *The manicurist trimmed the customer's cuticles.* ♦ *The cuticle on my little finger is sore.*

cutlass ['kʌt ləs] *n.* a short, slightly curved sword used by pirates and sailors. ♦ *The pirate waved a stolen cutlass as a threat.* ♦ *A cutlass hung from the pirate's belt.*

cutlery ['kʌt lə ri] **1.** *n.* knives and sharp kitchen tools. (No plural form in this sense.) ♦ *The kitchen drawer is filled with cutlery.* ♦ *There was no cutlery in the kitchen of the cabin.* **2.** *n.* knives, spoons, and forks used for eating. ♦ *John set the table with plates, napkins, and cutlery.* ♦ *Our cutlery set includes knives, forks, teaspoons.*

cutlet ['kʌt lət] *n.* a boneless slice of meat. ♦ *The cutlets were breaded and fried.* ♦ *The chef served veal cutlets.*

cut-rate ['kʌt 'ret] *adj.* cheaply priced. ♦ *We bought cut-rate goods at the flea market.* ♦ *The cut-rate clothing soon fell apart.*

cutter ['kʌt ɚ] *n.* a small boat that travels rapidly. ♦ *The Coast Guard operates a number of cutters.* ♦ *The drug dealer's boat was pursued by two cutters.*

cutting ['kʌt ɪŋ] **1.** *adj.* sharp; able to be used to cut [something]. ♦ *The carpenter used many cutting tools to make the furniture.* ♦ *The cutting blades on the lawn mower need sharpening.* **2.** *adj.* sarcastic; biting; bitter; mean. (Adv: *cuttingly.*) ♦ *The tone of her reprimand was cutting and insulting.* ♦ *The cutting insult hurt Max's feelings.* **3.** *n.* a part of a tree or a plant that is removed and planted to grow a new tree or plant. ♦ *The botanist transplanted the cutting into richer soil.* ♦ *A few cuttings were planted in the garden.*

cyanide ['saɪ ə naɪd] *n.* a powerful poison. (No plural form in this sense.) ♦ *The wasps were poisoned with cyanide.* ♦ *Cyanide is often used to kill vermin.*

cyberspace ['saɪ bɚ spes] *n.* the world of networked computer users, considered as an abstract location. (No plural form in this sense.) ♦ *All of my e-mail was lost in cyberspace when my computer crashed.* ♦ *I met several new friends in cyberspace.*

cycle ['saɪ kəl] **1.** *n.* one instance of a process that repeats over and over. ♦ *We went through a complete cycle of system maintenance in three months.* ♦ *The rinse cycle of the washing machine takes fifteen minutes.* **2.** *iv.* to ride a bicycle. ♦ *The kids cycled along the lake.* ♦ *My legs are too tired to cycle any longer.*

cycling ['saɪk lɪŋ] *n.* the sport and activity of riding a bicycle. (No plural form in this sense.) ♦ *I needed to exercise, so I took an interest in cycling.* ♦ *Cycling is a good way to strengthen your leg muscles.*

cyclist ['saɪk ləst] *n.* someone who rides a bicycle or motorcycle, especially as a regular activity. ♦ *Cyclists sometimes wear special clothing.* ♦ *The cyclists lined up at the starting line for the race.*

cyclone ['saɪ klon] *n.* a tornado; a strong, violent wind that moves in a circle. ♦ *The cyclone destroyed all the farms in its path.* ♦ *The radio reported a cyclone in the western part of the county.*

cylinder ['sɪl ən dɚ] **1.** *n.* a tube; a solid or hollow object with a circular top and bottom and straight sides in one dimension. ♦ *The painting was rolled up and put into a cardboard cylinder.* ♦ *A vase in the shape of a simple cylinder held a single rose.* **2.** *n.* the part of a car engine in which a piston moves back and forth. ♦ *One cylinder cracked, and the engine was ruined.* ♦ *Older car engines usually had eight cylinders.* **3. firing on all cylinders** *idiom* working at full strength; making every possible effort. (On ②.) ♦ *The team is firing on all cylinders under the new coach.* ♦ *The factory is firing on all cylinders to finish the orders on time.*

cymbal ['sɪm bəl] *n.* one of a pair of brass discs that are struck together to make a loud, ringing noise in orchestras and bands. ♦ *Percussionists play the cymbals in the orchestra.* ♦ *The sound of the cymbals told us the marching band was coming.*

cynic ['sɪn ɪk] *n.* someone who believes the worst about everything and everybody. ♦ *A cynic does not find much joy in life.* ♦ *After he lost his job, Bill became a terrible cynic.*

cynical ['sɪn ɪ kəl] *adj.* believing the worst about everything and everybody. (Adv: *cynically* [...ɪk li].) ♦ *The manager's cynical attitude depressed everyone at work.* ♦ *The cynical poet wrote very bleak poetry.*

cynicism ['sɪn ə sɪz əm] *n.* a philosophy of believing the worst about everything and everyone. (No plural form in this sense.) ♦ *It's no fun to be around Jane because of her cynicism.* ♦ *The elderly teacher's editorial about youth was marked with cynicism.*

cypress ['sɑɪ prəs] **1.** *n.* one of a group of evergreen trees that make pinecones. ♦ *The drive was lined with cypresses.* ♦ *Extremely tall cypresses are found in Florida swamps.* **2.** *n.* wood from ①. (No plural form in this sense.) ♦ *Cypress is a good wood for furniture.* ♦ *The antique desk is made of cypress.* **3.** *adj.* made of ②. ♦ *My uncle has a lot of cypress furniture.* ♦ *I use a lovely cypress desk at my office.*

Cyprus ['sɑɪ prəs] See Gazetteer.

Cyrillic [sɪ 'rɪl ik] **1.** *n.* the alphabet—derived from the Greek alphabet—that is now used for Russian, Bulgarian, and other languages. (No plural form in this sense. According to tradition, this was developed by St. Cyril.) ♦ *Russian books are printed in Cyrillic.* ♦ *Dave had to learn Cyrillic when he went to school in Russia.* **2.** *adj.* <the adj. use of ①.> ♦ *I can see some similarities between the Cyrillic alphabet and the Greek alphabet.* ♦ *Some of the Cyrillic characters look like Roman characters, but they stand for different sounds.*

cyst ['sɪst] *n.* a growth in or on the body that is hard or filled with fluid matter. ♦ *The doctor removed a benign cyst from my neck.* ♦ *The cyst on John's spine was often painful.*

czar ['zɑr] **1.** *n.* the male leader of Russia; a Russian king. (Until 1917. Also spelled **tsar**.) ♦ *The museum had a photo of the czar and his family.* ♦ *The czar ruled the country mercilessly.* **2.** *n.* a leader; someone who is in charge of something. (Figurative on ①.) ♦ *The U.S. drug czar tried to lead a war on illegal drugs.* ♦ *The energy czar was a U.S. cabinet member in charge of energy policy.*

Czech Republic ['tʃɛk rɪ 'pʌb lɪk] See Gazetteer.

D AND **d** ['di] **1.** *n.* the fourth letter of the alphabet. ♦ *D comes after* C *and before* E. ♦ *Please spell* Dave *with a capital* D. **2. D** *n.* a grade meaning poorer than average. ♦ *I got a D on my test. That's almost failing.* ♦ *Tom earned a D because he turned the assignment in late.* **3. 'd** See **had, would.**

dab ['dæb] **1.** *n.* a small amount of something. ♦ *Anne placed a dab of butter on her mashed potatoes.* ♦ *Please put a dab of this salve on my rash.* **2.** *tv.* to touch or press something lightly, as with applying or absorbing something. ♦ *Don't press on it, just dab it gently.* ♦ *Here, use this tissue to dab the tears from your eyes.*

dabble ['dæb əl] **1. dabble (at)** *iv.* (+ *prep. phr.*) to work (at something) without any real effort. ♦ *The lazy student only dabbled at the assignment.* ♦ *Stop dabbling at your work and do it properly!* **2. dabble (in); dabble (with)** *iv.* (+ *prep. phr.*) to do something as a hobby, but not very intently. ♦ *John uses watercolors when he paints, but sometimes he dabbles with oils.* ♦ *Anne works as a programmer, but sometimes she dabbles in technical support.*

dachshund ['dɑks ənt] *n.* a breed of small dog with a long body and short legs. ♦ *John wanted a dachshund, but he got a terrier instead.* ♦ *The dachshund ran along at its owner's feet.*

dad ['dæd] *n.* a father. (Also a term of address.) ♦ *My dad is taller than yours.* ♦ *Dad, can I go out tonight?*

daddy ['dæd i] *n.* a father; <a form used as a familiar nickname for a father>. (Also a term of address.) ♦ *Is your daddy at home, little boy?* ♦ *Daddy, what time is it?*

daffodil ['dæf ə dɪl] *n.* a kind of flower with large, typically yellow, trumpet-shaped blossoms. ♦ *The garden is beautiful when the daffodils are in bloom.* ♦ *Bill brought his mother a bouquet of daffodils for her birthday.*

dagger ['dæg ɚ] **1.** *n.* a type of knife with a short blade, used as a weapon. ♦ *The robber drew a dagger and threatened the tourist.* ♦ *The nobleman wore an ornate dagger at his hip.* **2. cloak-and-dagger** *idiom* involving secrecy and plotting. ♦ *A great deal of cloak-and-dagger stuff goes on in political circles.* ♦ *A lot of cloak-and-dagger activity was involved in the appointment of the director.* **3. look daggers at someone** *idiom* to give someone a strong, direct stare, signaling anger. ♦ *Tom must have been mad at Anne from the way he was looking daggers at her.* ♦ *Don't you dare look daggers at me. Don't even look cross-eyed at me!*

dahlia ['dæl jə] *n.* a round, fluffy flower with long, pointy petals. ♦ *Dahlias come in many colors.* ♦ *The florist put some dahlias in a vase.*

daily ['de li] **1.** *adj.* done or occurring every day. ♦ *John always takes his daily walk at noon.* ♦ *Jimmy's grandmother enjoys his daily visits.* **2.** *adj.* suitable for a single day; measured in terms of one day. ♦ *David ate his daily ration of chocolate quickly.* ♦ *Jane kept her daily assignments on her desk.* **3.** *adv.* on every day. ♦ *Anne goes for a walk daily through the park.* ♦ *Max called his aunt daily while she was in the hospital.* **4. daily dozen** *idiom* physical exercises done every day. ♦ *My brother always feels better after his daily dozen.* ♦ *Jane would rather do a daily dozen than go on a diet.*

dainty ['den ti] *adj.* delicate and pretty; delicate and small. (Adv: *daintily.* Comp: *daintier;* sup: *daintiest.*) ♦ *The charming baby was dressed in a dainty gown.* ♦ *John looked at the dainty teacup and asked for something less fragile.*

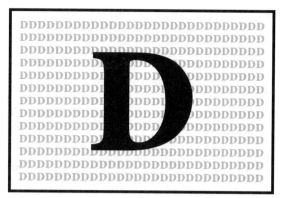

dairy ['dɛr i] **1.** *n.* a company that processes milk products. ♦ *The dairy produces safe, clean milk.* ♦ *Our local dairy produces cheese and ice cream as well as bottled milk.* **2.** *adj.* <the adj. use of ①.> ♦ *I visited my grandparents at their dairy farm.* ♦ *Bob is unable to eat or drink any dairy products.*

dais ['de əs] *n.* a raised platform from which to give a speech to an audience. (When the speech is part of a formal dinner, the **dais** may also hold the dinner table of the most important people at the event.) ♦ *Everyone on the dais rose and applauded as the speaker finished.* ♦ *The bridal party sat on the dais.*

daisy ['de zi] *n.* a long-stemmed plant bearing circular flowers, typically white with yellow centers. ♦ *We saw a whole field of daisies in the valley.* ♦ *Daisies grow wild in many places.*

dally ['dæ li] *iv.* to waste time; to move very slowly. ♦ *Please don't dally. You will make us late.* ♦ *Bob dallied lazily on his way to school.*

dam ['dæm] **1.** *n.* a solid barrier in a river or stream that holds back the flow of water. ♦ *The dam created a beautiful lake in the valley.* ♦ *Beavers built a dam in the stream.* **2. dam (up)** *tv.* (+ *prep. phr.*) to build a solid barrier in a river or a stream to hold back the flow of water. ♦ *The engineers dammed the river in order to make a lake.* ♦ *Beavers dammed up the creek.*

damage ['dæm ɪdʒ] **1.** *n.* harm; an act that causes loss or pain. (No plural form in this sense.) ♦ *The vandals inflicted much damage on the building.* ♦ *The accident caused the child a lot of emotional and physical damage.* **2. damages** *n.* charges or compensation for harm or loss. ♦ *The judge ordered the driver to pay damages to the person he struck.* ♦ *The damages as determined by the jury were very high.* **3.** *tv.* to harm something. ♦ *Someone damaged my book by spilling milk on it.* ♦ *The vandals damaged the building by breaking all the windows.*

damaged ['dæm ɪdʒd] *adj.* harmed; ruined. ♦ *Mary received damaged goods in the mail.* ♦ *The damaged furniture was sold at a discount.*

damaging ['dæm ɪdʒ ɪŋ] *adj.* harmful; incriminating. (Adv: *damagingly.*) ♦ *The witness gave twenty minutes of damaging testimony at the trial.* ♦ *The robber struck a damaging blow to his victim.*

damn ['dæm] **1.** *adj.* cursed; damned. (Used to make another word stronger or more powerful. A curse word. Use only with caution.) ♦ *That damn dog bit me!* ♦ *"I can't hit the damn ball," snarled the ballplayer.* **2. Damn!** *interj.* "I am angry!"; "I am frustrated!" (A curse word. Use only with caution.) ♦ *"Damn! I left the keys at home," said Linda when she got to her office.* ♦ *"I just missed the last train. Damn!" said the late traveler.* **3.** *tv.* to condemn something; to declare something to be bad. ♦ *Bob damned the traffic as he tried to get to the office.* ♦ *Lisa damned the rain that had ruined her new haircut.*

damnable ['dæm nə bəl] *adj.* deserving of damnation; worthy of condemnation. (Adv: *damnably.*) ♦ *The damnable key broke in the lock.* ♦ *That damnable movie was so terrible that it only played for one weekend.*

damnation [dæm 'ne ʃən] **1.** *n.* condemnation; damning someone or something. (No plural form in this sense.) ♦ *The critical damnation of the movie was too harsh.* ♦ *The cleric declared the sinner's damnation.* **2. Damnation!** *interj.* "I am angry and frustrated!" (Informal.) ♦ *Damnation! The barn is burning down.* ♦ *Anne gave the flat tire a kick and said, "Damnation!"*

damned ['dæmd] **1. the damned.** *n.* people doomed to hell. (No plural form in this sense. Treated as plural.) ♦ *Hell is the land of the damned.* ♦ *The preacher insisted that there was no mercy for the damned.* **2.** *adj.* doomed to hell. ♦ *The painting depicted damned souls descending to hell.* ♦ *The sinner, damned by the Church, begged for forgiveness.* **3.** *adj.* cursed; declared to be bad or inferior. ♦ *The damned pen leaked in my pocket!* ♦ *I tripped on that damned bucket!*

damning ['dæm ɪŋ] *adj.* causing damnation; strongly negative. (Adv: *damningly.*) ♦ *The damning evidence convicted the criminal.* ♦ *The politician was ousted after the damning criticism.*

damp ['dæmp] **1.** *adj.* moist; slightly wet. (Adv: *damply.* Comp: *damper;* sup: *dampest.*) ♦ *Tony wiped the counter with a damp rag.* ♦ *Our cat doesn't like to walk in the damp grass.* **2.** *tv.* to depress the movement of air [to a fire]. ♦ *Dave's uncle went down to the furnace to damp the fire.* ♦ *There is a control on the old iron stove to damp the fire.*

dampen ['dæmp ən] **1.** *tv.* to make something moist. ♦ *Dampen a cloth for your forehead to make your headache go away.* ♦ *Just dampen your potted plants once a week. Don't overwater them!* **2.** *tv.* to depress something, such as feelings. ♦ *The cloudy day dampened our spirits.* ♦ *I don't want to dampen your enthusiasm, but take it easy!*

damper ['dæmp ɚ] **1.** *n.* a movable plate that controls the amount of air reaching a fireplace, stove, or furnace burner. ♦ *Dave opened the damper on the furnace.* ♦ *With the damper closed, the fire was impossible to light.* **2.** *n.* a movable plate that controls air movement in an air duct. ♦ *Opening the damper will make the room warmer.* ♦ *The damper was open, providing the room with a slight breeze.* **3.** *n.* someone or something that depresses or discourages someone or something. ♦ *The rain put a damper on the swimming party.* ♦ *The teacher's criticism was a damper on the student's enthusiasm.*

damsel ['dæm zəl] *n.* a young girl; a maiden; an unmarried woman of noble rank. (Used primarily in writing, especially in fairy tales.) ♦ *The prince married a pretty damsel.* ♦ *The knight rescued the damsel in distress.*

dance ['dæns] **1.** *tv.* to perform a type of rhythmic bodily movement, usually with music. ♦ *Jane and Bill danced a slow waltz on the patio under the moonlight.* ♦ *The excited little boy danced a jig when he received some nice birthday presents.* **2.** *iv.* to move one's body rhythmically, usually to music, usually with another person. ♦ *Everyone at the nightclub danced until dawn.* ♦ *At the wedding reception, many of the guests danced.* **3.** *n.* the art and study of rhythmic movement of the body, especially to music. (No plural form in this sense.) ♦ *The choreographer had worked in dance for twenty years.* ♦ *The director was looking for actors who had studied dance.* **4.** *n.* a set series of body movements to music. ♦ *The students learned several different dances in class.* ♦ *I learned a new dance last night at the party.* **5.** *n.* an act of ②, usually performed with another person. ♦ *Excuse me. May I have this dance?* ♦ *"This dance is ours," said the groom to his bride.* **6.** *n.* a social event where music is played and people dance ②. ♦ *The high-school dance was held after the basketball game.* ♦ *The dance was enjoyed by everyone who attended.*

dandelion ['dæn də lɑɪ ən] *n.* a small weed with a bright yellow flower that turns to fluffy white seeds. ♦ *Every spring, my lawn is full of dandelions.* ♦ *Dandelions can be used to make wine.*

dander ['dæn dɚ] **1.** *n.* tiny flakes of an animal's skin. (No plural form in this sense.) ♦ *I am allergic to the dander of dogs and cats.* ♦ *The rug where the dog had slept was full of dander.* **2.** *n.* anger. (No plural form in this sense.) ♦ *The criticism got Bill's dander up.* ♦ *Government waste raises the dander of every taxpayer.*

dandruff ['dæn drəf] *n.* white, flaky dead skin cells from the scalp. (No plural form in this sense.) ♦ *Mary didn't realize there were flakes of dandruff on her sweater.* ♦ *This shampoo was supposed to eliminate dandruff.*

danger ['den dʒɚ] **1.** *n.* the possibility of harm. (No plural form in this sense.) ♦ *Danger is everywhere in a war.* ♦ *There is little danger involved in just sitting at home reading.* **2.** *n.* someone or something that could cause harm, injury, or death. ♦ *The unguarded pool was a danger to children.* ♦ *The vicious dog was a danger to trespassers.*

dangerous ['den dʒɚ əs] *adj.* risky; having the potential for harm. (Adv: *dangerously.*) ♦ *The dangerous road had several sharp turns.* ♦ *This small toy is dangerous for little babies.*

dangle ['dæŋ gəl] **1.** *iv.* to hang loosely; to swing from or above something. ♦ *A diamond pendant dangled from the gold necklace.* ♦ *The monkey loved to dangle from the branch and eat bananas.* **2.** *tv.* to cause something to hang loosely; to swing something from or above something else. ♦ *Mary dangled a string in front of the playful kitten.* ♦ *The fisherman dangled his legs off the pier.*

dank ['dæŋk] *adj.* [of an environment] unpleasantly damp and cold. (Adv: *dankly.* Comp: *dankest;* sup: *dankest.*) ♦ *Our cellar is dank and dark.* ♦ *The cloudy day was dank and dreary.*

dare ['dɛr] **1.** *n.* a challenge; a statement that challenges someone to take a risk. ♦ *Anne climbed the mountain on a dare.* ♦ *Bill was known for accepting risky dares.* **2. dare to** *tv.* + *inf.* to challenge someone to do something risky. ♦ *Bob dared Mary to pull the cat's tail.* ♦ *Anne dared me to jump into the pool.* **3.** *aux.* to have enough courage or boldness [to do something]. (Takes a bare verb. Usually used in negative sentences and questions.) ♦ *I don't dare bother David while he's writing.* ♦ *Do you dare swim in the lake without a guard?*

daredevil ['dɛr dɛv əl] *n.* someone who is reckless; someone who attempts dangerous stunts. ♦ *The daredevil jumped over ten cars on a motorcycle.* ♦ *That little daredevil ran into the street without looking!*

daring ['dɛr ɪŋ] **1.** *adj.* bold; courageous. (Adv: *daringly.*) ♦ *A daring firefighter pulled the child from the fire.* ♦ *The daring rescue caught a reporter's attention.* **2.** *n.* boldness; courage. (No plural form in this sense.) ♦ *Mike displayed great daring when he saved the drowning child.* ♦ *The driver had too much daring and not enough caution.*

dark ['dɑrk] **1.** *adj.* without light. (Adv: *darkly.* Comp: *darker*; sup: *darkest.*) ♦ *I couldn't see into the dark closet.* ♦ *Lisa took a flashlight into the dark cave.* **2.** *adj.* having little light or color. (Adv: *darkly.* Comp: *darker*; sup: *darkest.*) ♦ *Before the storm, the sky had turned a dark gray.* ♦ *I want the darker puppy, not the light one!* **3.** *n.* the absence of light; darkness; nighttime. (No plural form in this sense.) ♦ *I prefer daylight to dark.* ♦ *The children were afraid of the dark.*

darken ['dɑrk ən] **1.** *tv.* to make something darker. ♦ *The black dye darkened my hair.* ♦ *Thunderclouds darkened the sky.* **2.** *iv.* to become darker. ♦ *When the sun sets, the sky darkens.* ♦ *Bill's face darkened when he heard the bad news.*

darkening ['dɑrk ə nɪŋ] *adj.* becoming darker; becoming less light. ♦ *The old tree looks mysterious against the darkening sky.* ♦ *The audience in the darkening theater grew quiet.*

darkness ['dɑrk nəs] *n.* the quality of having no light. (No plural form in this sense.) ♦ *As the sun set, the darkness enveloped the land.* ♦ *In the darkness of the theater, Anne fell asleep.*

darkroom ['dɑrk rum] *n.* a dark, windowless room where film and photographs are processed. ♦ *The photographer was working in the darkroom when we arrived.* ♦ *Tom went into the darkroom to develop the film.*

darling ['dɑr lɪŋ] **1.** *adj.* cute; charming. (Adv: *darlingly.*) ♦ *A darling flower girl walked down the aisle.* ♦ *The darling puppy was easy to sell.* **2.** *n.* someone who is dearly loved; someone who is loved. ♦ *Susie was her father's little darling.* ♦ *The courageous child became the darling of the nurses.*

darn ['dɑrn] **1.** *adj.* <a mild form of damn ①.> (A euphemism.) ♦ *That darn dog ate the cake.* ♦ *My darn shoes are killing my feet!* **2.** *tv.* to repair a hole or tear (in clothing, especially socks) by reweaving the fabric. ♦ *I saved money by darning my old socks.* ♦ *I darned the blanket rather than buy a new one.* **3.** *iv.* to perform repairs by reweaving. ♦ *I sat in my rocking chair and darned.* ♦ *Learning to darn has saved me the expense of buying new clothes.*

darned ['dɑrnd] *adj.* <a mild form of damned ③ or damn ①.> ♦ *Why won't this darned door open?* ♦ *The darned bus is late again!*

dart ['dɑrt] **1.** *iv.* to run somewhere quickly and suddenly; to bolt. ♦ *The rabbit darted away when I opened the door.* ♦ *The child darted into the party room.* **2.** *tv.* to send a look at someone or something suddenly and quickly; to cast one line of sight at someone or something suddenly and quickly. ♦ *Bill darted his eyes around the room to make sure he was alone.* ♦ *Susan darted a look at her mischievous child.* **3.** *n.* a small object with a sharp, pointed end that is thrown either as a weapon or at a dartboard. ♦ *The dart missed the target and stuck in the wall.* ♦ *Be careful. The tips of the darts are very sharp.* **4. darts** *n.* a game in which points are scored by throwing ③ at a dartboard. ♦ *We went to the neighborhood bar to play darts.* ♦ *If you're going to play darts, please be careful.* **5. dart in and out** *idiom* [for something moving] to dart ① quickly between two things, or into a number of things, and move away again. ♦ *On the highway, a small car was darting in and out of the two right lanes of traffic.* ♦ *A small bird darted in and out of the bush, probably going into a nest inside.*

dartboard ['dɑrt bɔrd] *n.* a circular board used as a target in the game of darts. ♦ *The dart landed in the middle of the dartboard.* ♦ *The dartboard hung behind the door.*

dash ['dæʃ] **1.** *n.* a small pinch of spice or powder. ♦ *The recipe required a dash of cinnamon.* ♦ *I added a dash of sugar to my coffee.* **2.** *n.* a short, quick race; a short, quick run. ♦ *Bob made a dash for the train.* ♦ *Sue likes the 100-yard dash the best.* **3.** *n.* a straight mark (—) used in writing to indicate a pause or a break in thought. ♦ *The author added a dash to indicate a pause.* ♦ *A dash separated the two clauses.* **4.** *iv.* to run a short distance very quickly; to go somewhere quickly. (Also with over, across, around, through.) ♦ *Can you dash to the store and buy some milk?* ♦ *I dashed over to the neighbor's to borrow some sugar.* **5. dash against** *iv.* + *prep. phr.* [for something] to strike against something else. ♦ *The waves dashed against the rocks.* ♦ *The rain dashed against the windows.* **6. dash against** *tv.* + *prep. phr.* to strike something against something. ♦ *The waves dashed the boat against the rocks.* ♦ *The storm dashed the rain against the windows.*

dashboard ['dæʃ bɔrd] *n.* the front panel inside a car, just beneath the windshield. ♦ *I looked at all the controls on the dashboard.* ♦ *Mary hit her head on the dashboard in the accident.*

dashing ['dæʃ ɪŋ] *adj.* charming; full of energy; spirited. (Adv: *dashingly.*) ♦ *The dashing prince was destined to be king.* ♦ *The dashing TV star had a fan club.*

dastardly ['dæs tɚd li] *adj.* cowardly; sneaky. ♦ *The dastardly letter was unsigned.* ♦ *The dastardly villain was killed at the end of the novel.*

data ['det ə, 'dæt ə] *n.* information; pieces of information; facts; a set of facts. (The Latin plural of *datum.* Treated as singular or plural in English.) ♦ *The data were already loaded into the computer when I started working.* ♦ *The data was already loaded into the computer when I started working.*

database ['det ə bes] *n.* a collection of facts or other information organized in a way that is accessible in a number of different ways. ♦ *The library catalog is stored in a large database.* ♦ *The student tried to access the database holding the 1930 census.*

date ['det] **1.** *n.* the number of the day of a month, often including the name of the month or the name of the month and the year; the name of a month and the year; the year. (① refers to the number of the day of a month; the day of the week is called the day.) ♦ *I know the day is Thursday, but what's the date of the meeting?* ♦ *The date of* *my parents' wedding was July 10, 1965.* **2.** *n.* a brown, fleshy fruit with a long pit, grown on certain palm trees. ♦ *John ate a few dates and some toast for breakfast.* ♦ *The bread was filled with dates and nuts.* **3.** *n.* a social meeting between two people who have planned to go somewhere or do something together. (Typically male and female.) ♦ *Mary and Frank went to the movies for their first date.* ♦ *Bob was afraid to ask anyone for a date.* **4.** *tv.* to mark something with ①; to show the date ① of something. ♦ *The machine dated the ticket automatically.* ♦ *The librarian dated the slip so I would know when to return the book.* **5.** *tv.* to show or signal that someone or something is out-of-date or old-fashioned. ♦ *That old dress really dates you.* ♦ *The style of cars dated the movie.* **6.** *tv.* to have a date ③ with a particular person. ♦ *Mary dated Bill for two years before she decided to marry him.* ♦ *How long have you been dating Anne?* **7.** *iv.* to go out on dates ③ frequently or habitually. ♦ *My parents dated for two years before they got married.* ♦ *The Smiths allowed their children to date when they were 15.* **8. date (back) to** *iv. (adv.) + prep. phr.* to belong to a certain period of time. ♦ *As fashionable colors, avocado green and harvest gold date to the 1960s.* ♦ *This gun dates back to the Revolutionary War.*

dated ['det ɪd] *adj.* old-fashioned; out-of-date. (Adv: *datedly.*) ♦ *How can you wear those dated clothes in public?* ♦ *The dated movie was still quite entertaining.*

dateline ['det laɪn] *n.* the first line of a newspaper article that states where the article originated, and sometimes the date of its writing. ♦ *The dateline on the article shows it was written in New York City.* ♦ *The editor checked the dateline to make sure the story was current.*

dating ['det ɪŋ] *n.* the practice of going out on dates on a regular basis. (No plural form in this sense.) ♦ *Mary started dating when she was fifteen.* ♦ *Mike was tired of dating and wanted to get married.*

daughter ['dɔt ɚ] *n.* a female child. ♦ *John's daughter doesn't look anything like him.* ♦ *The couple had five daughters and no sons.*

daughter-in-law ['dɔt ɚ ɪn lɔ] *n., irreg.* the woman who is married to one's son. (Pl: daughters-in-law.) ♦ *The groom's parents welcomed their new daughter-in-law into the family.* ♦ *Bill and Anne's daughter-in-law was nervous about the family reunion.*

daughters-in-law ['dɔt ɚz ɪn lɔ] pl of daughter-in-law.

dauntless ['dɔnt ləs] *adj.* brave; not frightened; fearless. (Adv: *dauntlessly.*) ♦ *The dauntless pilot flew through the rough storms.* ♦ *The dauntless puppy growled at the big dog.*

davenport ['dæv ən port] *n.* a long couch with a back and arms, usually able to seat at least three people comfortably. (See also sofa, settee, couch.) ♦ *I fell asleep on the davenport after dinner.* ♦ *The children sat on the davenport and watched TV.*

dawdle ['dɔd l] *iv.* to move slowly; to waste time; to dally. ♦ *The child dawdled on the way to school.* ♦ *Don't dawdle, or we'll be late.*

dawn ['dɔn] **1.** *n.* the period of morning when light is first seen in the eastern sky; sunrise. ♦ *The light of dawn was obscured by the clouds.* ♦ *It was very peaceful by the lake just before dawn.* **2.** *n.* the beginning of something. (Figurative on ①.) ♦ *The dawn of automobile transportation brought about a more mobile society.* ♦ *The dawn of a new age began with the invention of nuclear energy.* **3.** *iv.* [for the day] to become bright or light. ♦ *The day dawned brightly and clearly.* ♦ *The search for the missing child will begin again when the day dawns.* **4. dawn on someone** *idiom* to occur to someone; to become clearly understood. ♦ *Suddenly, it dawned on me that I was late for work.* ♦ *It finally dawned on the inspector that John had stolen the money.* **5. from dawn to dusk** *idiom* during the period of the day when there is light; from the rising of the sun to the setting of the sun. ♦ *I have to work from dawn to dusk on the farm.* ♦ *The factory runs from dawn to dusk to produce hats and gloves.*

day ['de] **1.** *n.* a period of 24 hours, especially from midnight to midnight. ♦ *The paint will take a day to dry.* ♦ *The day after Wednesday is Thursday.* **2.** *n.* the period of time between sunrise and sunset; the opposite of night. ♦ *Most people work during the day and sleep at night.* ♦ *Nocturnal animals sleep during the day.* **3.** *n.* the time spent at work; the hours of work. ♦ *At work, my day begins at 7 A.M.* ♦ *"How was your day?" Bill asked when I came home.* **4.** *n.* a time; a period; an era. (No plural form in this sense.) ♦ *There was a day when women weren't allowed to vote.* ♦ *"In my day, no one had computers," the elderly man said.* **5. days** *adv.* during the daytime; during each day. ♦ *I work in the city days and have a job in the suburbs nights.* ♦ *I sleep days and work nights.* **6. call it a day** *idiom* to quit work and go home; to say that the day's work has been completed. ♦ *I'm tired. Let's call it a day.* ♦ *The boss was mad because Tom called it a day at noon and went home.* **7. have had its day** *idiom* to no longer be useful or successful. ♦ *Large cars have had their day.* ♦ *Some people think that radio has had its day, but others prefer it to television.* **8. one's days are numbered** *idiom* [for someone] to face death or dismissal. ♦ *If I don't get this contract, my days are numbered at this company.* ♦ *Uncle Bill has a terminal disease. His days are numbered.*

daybed ['de bɛd] *n.* a narrow bed that is used as a couch during the day. ♦ *When Uncle Mike comes to visit us, he sleeps on the daybed.* ♦ *The daybed was cramped, but at least I wasn't sleeping on the floor.*

daybreak ['de brek] *n.* dawn; the first light of day. (No plural form in this sense.) ♦ *The farmer awoke before daybreak.* ♦ *We need to leave at daybreak if we want to get there on time.*

day care ['de kɛr] **1.** *n.* care for children during the day when parents are working. (No plural form in this sense.) ♦ *I need day care for three children.* ♦ *Day care is very expensive, and people who need it often can't afford it.* **2. day-care center** *n.* a place where ① is available. ♦ *I have to pick up my children at the day-care center.* ♦ *There is a day-care center in the building where I work.* **3. day-care** *adj.* <the adj. use of ①.> ♦ *My day-care expenses are very high.* ♦ *I asked my legislator to vote for day-care legislation.*

daydream ['de drim] **1.** *n.* a daytime fantasy; a period of idle thoughts. ♦ *Ms. Wilson interrupted Max's daydream when she called on him.* ♦ *Anne's daydream was about winning the lottery.* **2.** *iv.* to think idle thoughts while one is awake; to have a fantasy. ♦ *John daydreamed while he lay in his hammock.* ♦ *When Mary is bored at work, she daydreams.*

day job ['de dʒɔb] *n.* a job worked at during the day, usually in addition to one worked at during the night. ♦ *I have to have a day job and a night job to make enough money to live.* ♦ *I only work 6 hours a day at my day job.*

daylight ['de lɑɪt] **1.** *n.* the light of day. (No plural form in this sense.) ♦ *The daylight streamed in through the window.* ♦ *As daylight approached, the rooster began to crow.* **2. begin to see daylight** *idiom* to begin to see the end of a long task. ♦ *I've been working on my thesis for two years, and at last I'm beginning to see daylight.* ♦ *I've been so busy. Only in the last week have I begun to see daylight.* **3. in broad daylight** *idiom* publicly visible in the daytime. ♦ *The thief stole the car in broad daylight.* ♦ *There they were, selling drugs in broad daylight.*

daytime ['de tɑɪm] **1.** *n.* the period of time during a day when it is light outside; the time of day that is not night. (No plural form in this sense.) ♦ *Most people work in the daytime and rest at night.* ♦ *Susan did all of her errands during the daytime.* **2.** *adj.* <the adj. use of ①.> ♦ *Mary gave the clerk her daytime phone number.* ♦ *Bill watched daytime television while he was on vacation.*

day-to-day ['de tə 'de] *adj.* daily; every day; happening every day. ♦ *The day-to-day chores of housekeeping are endless.* ♦ *My day-to-day expenses are small except when I go shopping.*

daze ['dez] **1.** *n.* a confused condition; a bewildered condition. ♦ *The overload of new information put the student in a daze.* ♦ *The driver recovered slowly from her daze after the accident.* **2.** *tv.* to confuse someone or some creature; to bewilder someone or some creature. ♦ *The news of his friend's death dazed Mike.* ♦ *I was dazed by your outrageous remark.*

dazzle ['dæz əl] *tv.* to impress someone with a flashy, bright performance or display. ♦ *The fireworks dazzled the crowd.* ♦ *The excellent performance dazzled the audience.*

dazzling ['dæz (ə) lɪŋ] *adj.* impressive; amazing; stunning. (Adv: *dazzlingly.*) ♦ *The dazzling dress looked stunning on the mannequin.* ♦ *The lawyer's closing statement was dazzling but not convincing.*

deactivate [di 'æk tə vet] *tv.* to adjust something so it will not work or operate. ♦ *John deactivated the cable television so his children could not watch it.* ♦ *The burglar deactivated the alarm system before entering the house.*

dead ['dɛd] **1.** *adj.* no longer living. ♦ *Susan threw the dead flowers in the trash.* ♦ *The children buried their dead goldfish in the backyard.* **2.** *adj.* not having the electrical energy to work. (Figurative on ①.) ♦ *I need new batteries for the flashlight because these are dead.* ♦ *This circuit is dead. Try another.* **3.** *adj.* not active; dull. (Figurative on ①. Comp: *deader;* sup: *deadest.*) ♦ *Things are really dead around here. Let's go.* ♦ *The library was dead, so I was able to concentrate on my studies.* **4.** *adj.* no longer used; obsolete. (Figurative on ①.) ♦ *Your old-fashioned ideas are completely dead!* ♦ *The typewriter is dead!* **5.** *adv.* completely; exactly; absolutely. ♦ *The lifeguard was dead serious about the dangers of swimming alone.* ♦ *The arrow hit the target dead center.* **6. dead ahead** *adv.* straight ahead; directly ahead. ♦ *As they drove down the road, they saw the church dead ahead.* ♦ *Be careful! There's a roadblock dead ahead.* **7. the dead** *n.* one or more dead persons. (No plural form in this sense. Treated as plural.) ♦ *We remember the dead on Memorial Day.* ♦ *A special church service was held for the dead.* **8.** *n.* the time when it is the darkest, coldest, etc. (No plural form in this sense.) ♦ *Everything is so bleak in the dead of winter.* ♦ *John works until the dead of night and then goes to sleep immediately.* **9. dead ringer** See ringer. **10. have someone dead to rights** *idiom* to have proven someone unquestionably guilty. ♦ *The police burst in on the robbers while they were at work. They had the robbers dead to rights.* ♦ *All right, Tom! I've got you dead to rights! Get your hands out of the cookie jar.*

deadbeat ['dɛd bit] *n.* someone who avoids paying for purchases or services. ♦ *That deadbeat has owed me money for two years!* ♦ *The attorney refused to take deadbeats as clients.*

deaden ['dɛd n] *tv.* to apply anesthetic to an area or a nerve in order to prevent pain. ♦ *The nurse dabbed an anesthetic on the cut to deaden the pain.* ♦ *The dentist deadened the patient's nerves before drilling.*

deadline ['dɛd lɑɪn] *n.* a due date; the time by which something must be finished. ♦ *The deadline for this article is next Tuesday.* ♦ *When is the deadline for the research report?*

deadlock ['dɛd lɑk] **1.** *n.* the point in a discussion at which neither side will agree or negotiate further. ♦ *Only war would end the deadlock between the countries over the boundary.* ♦ *The meeting reached a deadlock when both sides refused to bargain.* **2.** *tv.* to cause negotiations to come to a standstill. ♦ *A disagreement over prices deadlocked the negotiations.* ♦ *A deadly attack deadlocked the peace talks.*

deadly ['dɛd li] **1.** *adj.* causing death; fatal. (Comp: *deadlier;* sup: *deadliest.*) ♦ *A deadly poison killed the rats.* ♦ *The dog was given a deadly dose of medicine.* **2.** *adj.* suggesting death; **deathly** ②. (Comp: *deadlier;* sup: *deadliest.*) ♦ *Her face had a deadly pallor.* ♦ *Tom's skin was deadly white where the bandages were.* **3.** *adj.* dull or boring. (Comp: *deadlier;* sup: *deadliest.*) ♦ *The party was simply deadly, and most people left early.* ♦ *Her lecture was deadly, putting many students to sleep.* **4.** *adv.* in the manner of ②. ♦ *My hands are deadly cold because I forgot my gloves.* ♦ *Tom's deadly pale skin showed that he hadn't been out in the sun.* **5.** *adv.* in the manner of ③. ♦ *That was the most deadly dull speech I have ever heard.* ♦ *Mary's speech was deadly boring and almost put me to sleep.*

deadpan ['dɛd pæn] *adj.* [of a face] without a smile or not showing laughter when it is appropriate. ♦ *The comedian told the joke with a deadpan face.* ♦ *Mary's deadpan expression showed she didn't understand the joke.*

deadwood ['dɛd wʊd] *n.* useless things or people. (No plural form in this sense.) ♦ *The company president eliminated the deadwood in management.* ♦ *That old lawn mower is just deadwood and can be thrown out.*

deaf ['dɛf] **1.** *adj.* not able to hear. (Adv: *deafly.* Comp: *deafer;* sup: *deafest.*) ♦ *The partially deaf child wore a hearing aid.* ♦ *Anne communicates with her deaf sister in sign language.* **2.** *adj.* unwilling to hear; heedless. (Figurative on ①. Adv: *deafly.* Comp: *deafer;* sup: *deafest.*) ♦ *My advice fell on deaf ears.* ♦ *Max is deaf to the truth.* **3. the deaf** *n.* deaf people. (No plural form in this sense. Treated as plural.) ♦ *Mary is a teacher of the deaf.* ♦ *The deaf need special access to telephone service.*

deafen ['dɛf ən] *tv.* to make someone deaf. ♦ *The noise from the construction site almost deafened us.* ♦ *The explosion deafened several people who were near it.*

deafening ['dɛf ə nɪŋ] *adj.* incredibly loud; almost loud enough to make someone deaf. (Adv: *deafeningly.*) ♦ *The noise from the construction site was deafening.* ♦ *We complained about the deafening noise of the planes that flew over our neighborhood.*

deafness ['dɛf nəs] *n.* the condition of being deaf. (No plural form in this sense.) ♦ *Because of her deafness, Lisa often must read lips.* ♦ *Mike's deafness resulted from a childhood illness.*

deal ['dil] **1.** *tv., irreg.* to pass out cards in a card game. (Pt/pp: **dealt**.) ♦ *The casino employee dealt the cards.* ♦ *Please deal six cards to each player.* **2.** *tv., irreg.* to deliver or administer something, such as a figurative or literal blow. ♦ *The champion dealt the knockout punch in the third round.* ♦ *The scandal will deal the final blow to the candidate's campaign.* **3.** *iv., irreg.* to pass out cards in a card game. ♦ *Tom dealt and I watched him carefully.* ♦ *It is Mary's turn to deal.* **4. deal with** *iv., irreg.* + *prep. phr.* [for something, such as a book, essay, article, explanation, etc.] to tell about, discuss, or concern something. ♦ *This book deals with frogs and snakes.* ♦ *The poem deals with death.* **5. deal with** *iv., irreg.* + *prep. phr.* to cope with something; to manage to handle something; to have control of something. ♦ *I cannot deal with having roaches in the kitchen.* ♦ *You need to learn how to deal with problems like this.* **6. deal with** *iv., irreg.* + *prep. phr.* to do business with someone. ♦ *We deal with many companies in order to get the best bargains.* ♦ *I don't deal with that store because their clerks are rude.* **7.** *n.* a bargain; an agreement for the purchase of goods or services, especially if it at a cost lower than expected. ♦ *I got a really good deal on a new car!* ♦ *I made a great deal with the store owner to buy a dozen shirts for a discount.* **8. a great deal** *idiom* much; a lot. ♦ *You can learn a great deal about nature by watching television.* ♦ *This is a serious problem and it worries me a great deal.* **9. square deal** *idiom* a fair and honest transaction; fair treatment. ♦ *All the workers want is a square deal, but their boss underpays them.* ♦ *You always get a square deal with that travel firm.*

dealer ['dil ɚ] **1.** *n.* someone who passes out cards in a card game. ♦ *The dealer gave each player five cards.* ♦ *The dealer collected the discarded cards.* **2.** *n.* someone who is in the business of trade; someone who buys and sells certain products. (Usually a **retail** merchant.) ♦ *The dealer will deliver the washing machine tomorrow.* ♦ *A new car dealer is opening up in the middle of town.*

dealership ['dil ɚ ʃɪp] *n.* a business that is run by a **dealer** ②. ♦ *I went to the car dealership to look at new cars.* ♦ *The tractor dealership does business with farmers.*

dealing ['dil ɪŋ] **dealings** *n.* commerce; negotiations; transactions. (Treated as plural.) ♦ *We no longer have dealings with that company.* ♦ *After John refused to pay his bills, the store had no further dealings with him.*

dealt ['dɛlt] pt/pp of deal.

dean ['din] **1.** *n.* the head of an academic division within a university, a college, or a private school. ♦ *The dean was respected by faculty and students alike.* ♦ *Only the dean can cancel classes.* **2.** *n.* the senior member of an organization or profession. ♦ *The dean of the news broadcasters was honored at a banquet.* ♦ *The dean of the retired ballplayers gave the first toast.*

dear ['dɪr] **1.** *adj.* loved very much; precious; beloved. (Adv: *dearly.* Comp: *dearer;* sup: *dearest.*) ♦ *Come sit on my lap, dear Billy.* ♦ *My dear husband brought me roses for my birthday.* **2.** *adj.* <a form of address used at the beginning of a letter.> ♦ *"Dear Max," the letter began.* ♦ *Dear Ms. Smith: This letter is to inform you that you have won the contest.* **3.** *n.* a treasured person; a beloved person. (Also a term of address.) ♦ *Oh, Mary! You are such a dear to help!* ♦ *Dear, could you help me wash the dishes?*

dearly ['dɪr li] *adv.* at a high price; at a great cost; at great expense. ♦ *Joan paid dearly for her new car.* ♦ *The war cost both sides dearly in the loss of life.*

dearth ['dɚθ] **dearth of** *n.* + *prep. phr.* a lack of something; a shortage of something. (No plural form in this sense.) ♦ *There is a real dearth of good movies this year.* ♦ *Sometimes it seems the government has a dearth of common sense.*

death ['dɛθ] **1.** *n.* the state of being dead. (No plural form in this sense.) ♦ *In death, the troubled man finally found peace.* ♦ *The couple vowed to be faithful until death.* **2.** *n.* the act of dying; the end of life. ♦ *The patient's death came peacefully during sleep.* ♦ *The death of the beautiful swan saddened the children.* **3. death of someone or something** *idiom* the end of someone or something. (Figurative on ②. No plural form in this sense.) ♦ *This job will be the death of me!* ♦ *Rough roads are the death of tires.* **4. at death's door** *idiom* near death. ♦ *I was so ill that I was at death's door.* ♦ *The family dog was at death's door for three days, and then it finally died.*

deathbed ['dɛθ bɛd] *n.* the bed that someone dies on. ♦ *President Lincoln's deathbed was in the house across from Ford's Theater.* ♦ *I was so sick I thought I was on my deathbed.*

deathly ['dɛθ li] **1.** *adv.* [of being ill] in a way that is likely to cause death. ♦ *Bob is deathly ill with an advanced stage of cancer.* ♦ *Lisa became deathly sick after eating the chicken salad.* **2.** *adj.* death-like; similar to some aspect or part of death. (Comp: *deathlier;* sup: *deathliest.*) ♦ *After the explosion, there was only deathly silence.* ♦ *Before we saw the ghost, we felt a deathly chill in the room.*

debacle [dɪ 'bɔk əl] *n.* a complete disaster; a situation where everything possible has gone wrong. ♦ *What a debacle this party turned out to be!* ♦ *The political rally was such a debacle, even the candidate left early.*

debatable [dɪ 'bet ə bəl] *adj.* open to discussion; questionable; doubtful. (Adv: *debatably.*) ♦ *The need to increase taxes is a debatable issue.* ♦ *It is debatable as to which football team is the best.*

debate [dɪ 'bet] **1.** *n.* an event where two or more people with different points of view talk about an issue. ♦ *There's a debate in the meeting room about next year's budget.* ♦ *The city council meeting turned into a debate about the new zoning laws.* **2.** *n.* a formal, structured argumentation contest where the two sides of an issue are presented in an orderly fashion by opposing speakers. ♦ *An impartial commentator moderated the debate about taxes.* ♦ *The candidates agreed to the rules for the debate.* **3.** *n.* formal, structured argumentation practiced as an extracurricular school activity. (No plural form in this sense.) ♦ *The high-school student studied debate.* ♦ *I par-*

ticipated in debate throughout high school. **4.** *tv.* to discuss and argue something with someone. ♦ *My grandfather will debate politics with anyone.* ♦ *John debated the value of fast food with his mother.* **5.** *iv.* [for two people] to speak persuasively on the opposite sides of an issue. ♦ *We debated endlessly and finally stopped talking.* ♦ *My roommates never agree on anything and love to debate.*

debater [dɪ 'bet ɚ] **1.** *n.* someone who participates in a formal, structured debate. ♦ *After fifteen years in office, the politician was an experienced debater.* ♦ *The winning debater eventually won the election.* **2.** *n.* someone who argues with someone else in a discussion or debate. ♦ *Anne is a worthy debater who always states her case clearly.* ♦ *The Smiths are a family of debaters—they are always arguing.*

debilitating [dɪ 'bɪl ɪ tet ɪŋ] *adj.* causing weakness or feebleness. (Adv: *debilitatingly.*) ♦ *No one wanted to move in the debilitating heat.* ♦ *John must use a wheelchair because of a debilitating childhood illness.*

debit ['dɛb ɪt] **1.** *n.* a record of an amount that is owed or must be subtracted from the balance in an account. (Compare with **debt**.) ♦ *My mortgage payment is a debit in my accounts.* ♦ *Bill recorded each debit in his ledger.* **2.** *tv.* to charge a sum against someone's account. ♦ *The merchant debited $40 against Tom's account.* ♦ *My bank debited $20 for service charges last month!* **3.** *tv.* to charge someone's account with a sum. ♦ *The merchant debited Tom's account for $40.* ♦ *When the check bounced, the bank debited Sue's account.*

debonair [dɛb ə 'ner] *adj.* suave; charming; polite. (From French. Adv: *debonairly.*) ♦ *The debonair youth had perfect manners.* ♦ *The movie star was dashing and debonair at the award ceremony.*

debrief [di 'brif] *tv.* to question someone who has returned from a mission, meeting, or other task. (The opposite of **brief** ④.) ♦ *The boss debriefed the vice president after the convention.* ♦ *The president debriefed the ambassador after the peace mission.*

debriefing [di 'brif ɪŋ] *n.* a period of questioning of someone who has returned from a mission. ♦ *The FBI agent revealed helpful information during the debriefing.* ♦ *The debriefing was held immediately after the mission was complete.*

debris [də 'bri] *n.* refuse; rubbish. (No plural form in this sense.) ♦ *After the accident, debris was strewn across the road.* ♦ *The hikers picked up debris along the forest trail.*

debt ['dɛt] **1.** *n.* the condition of owing something to someone. (No plural form in this sense.) ♦ *Bill is working very hard to get out of debt.* ♦ *The Smiths don't want to increase their debt.* **2.** *n.* money that is owed. (Compare with **debit**.) ♦ *Bill's debt to Anne amounts to twenty dollars.* ♦ *John ran up a large debt when he was unemployed.* **3. in debt** *phr.* having debts; having much debt; owing money. ♦ *Mary is deeply in debt.* ♦ *I am in debt to the bank for my car loan.* **4. pay one's debt (to society)** *idiom* to serve a sentence for a crime, usually in prison. ♦ *The judge said that Mr. Simpson had to pay his debt to society.* ♦ *Mr. Brown paid his debt in state prison.*

debtor ['dɛt ɚ] *n.* someone who owes money. ♦ *When the debtor forfeited on his mortgage, the bank took his house.* ♦ *I don't borrow money because my parents told me never to be a debtor.*

debunk [dɪ 'bʌŋk] *tv.* to disprove something; to prove something to be false. ♦ *The new data debunked the theory.* ♦ *Mary debunked the rumors connecting her to the scandal.*

debut [de 'bju] **1.** *n.* the first public appearance of someone or something. (From French.) ♦ *The actor's Broadway debut was viewed favorably by critics.* ♦ *The debut of the new car model was greeted with rave reviews.* **2.** *tv.* to show someone or something for the first time; to bring someone or something before the public for the first time. ♦ *The networks will debut their new TV shows in September.* ♦ *The band debuted a new song at the concert.* **3.** *iv.* to be presented in public for the first time. ♦ *The musical production will debut in London.* ♦ *Seven new TV shows debuted in September.*

decade ['dɛk ed] **1.** *n.* a period of ten years. ♦ *I moved here a decade ago.* ♦ *The small town held a parade to celebrate its first decade.* **2.** *n.* one of the ten equal divisions of a century, such as 1950–1959. ♦ *The 1960s and 1970s were decades of social unrest.* ♦ *The Great Depression occurred in the decade of the 1930s.*

decadence ['dɛk ə dəns] **1.** *n.* moral degeneration; a decline in morals. (No plural form in this sense.) ♦ *The mayor criticized the teenagers for their decadence.* ♦ *Ancient Rome is known for its decadence.* **2.** *n.* the condition of something that is excessive. (Usually jocular or figurative. No plural form in this sense.) ♦ *This gourmet chocolate cake is the epitome of decadence!* ♦ *Buying a luxury car is pure decadence.*

decaf ['di kæf] *n.* coffee that has had its caffeine removed; decaffeinated coffee. ♦ *Mary ordered a cup of decaf after dinner.* ♦ *Decaf contains practically no caffeine.*

decaffeinated [di 'kæf ə net ɪd] *adj.* [of a drink] having had the caffeine removed. ♦ *Decaffeinated coffee will not help you stay awake.* ♦ *Bill bought a decaffeinated soft drink.*

decal [dɪ 'kæl] *n.* a plastic or paper picture that can be stuck on a flat surface. (From *decalomania.*) ♦ *The car's back bumper was covered with decals.* ♦ *Bill put a decal of the flag on each window of his house.*

decanter [dɪ 'kæn tɚ] *n.* a special, often decorative, glass bottle for serving alcoholic beverages. ♦ *The crystal decanter is only used for special occasions.* ♦ *He filled the wine glasses from the decanter.*

decapitate [dɪ 'kæp ɪ tet] *tv.* to cut off the head of someone or some creature. ♦ *The angry mob decapitated everyone in the royal family.* ♦ *The fisherman decapitated the fish.*

decathlon [dɪ 'kæθ lɑn] *n.* a sporting contest with ten separate events, usually in track and field. ♦ *The decathlon is an Olympic event.* ♦ *Twelve athletes competed in the decathlon.*

decay [dɪ 'ke] **1.** *n.* rot; the rotting of something. (No plural form in this sense.) ♦ *The wooden bridge was unsafe due to decay.* ♦ *Sugar can cause tooth decay.* **2.** *iv.* to rot. ♦ *The wooden chair decayed in the moist environment.* ♦ *The fallen tree branch will soon decay.* **3.** *iv.* to decline; to decline in power, energy, or health. (Figurative on ②.) ♦ *John's health decayed as he became older.* ♦ *The empire decayed owing to rampant corruption.* **4.** *tv.* to cause something to rot. ♦ *Moisture decayed the wood frame of the porch.* ♦ *Too much candy decayed the child's teeth.*

decayed [dɪ 'ked] *adj.* rotted; decomposed. ♦ *The decayed bench was dangerous to sit on.* ♦ *Bugs crawled all over the decayed tree trunk.*

decaying [dɪ 'ke ɪŋ] **1.** *adj.* rotting; decomposing. (Adv: *decayingly.*) ♦ *The pile of decaying leaves was home to many bugs.* ♦ *A terrible smell came from the decaying matter in the compost pile.* **2.** *adj.* declining; losing power. (Figurative on ①. Adv: *decayingly.*) ♦ *The dictator's decaying empire soon crumbled.* ♦ *The mayor's decaying influence is a result of a terrible scandal.*

decease [dɪ 'sis] *n.* death. (No plural form in this sense.) ♦ *The doctor wrote the time of decease on the death certificate.* ♦ *No one expected the sudden decease of the child.*

deceased [dɪ 'sist] **1.** *adj.* dead. ♦ *The deceased teacher was mourned by many former students.* ♦ *Hundreds of people attended the funeral of the deceased leader.* **2. the deceased** *n.* a dead person or dead people. (No plural form in this sense. Treated as singular or plural.) ♦ *The funeral for the deceased will be held tomorrow.* ♦ *The police try to notify the deceased's relatives as soon as possible.*

deceit [dɪ 'sit] **1.** *n.* dishonesty. (No plural form in this sense.) ♦ *No one trusts John because they know of his deceit.* ♦ *The government frowns on deceit on tax returns.* **2.** *n.* a dishonest act; lying, cheating, or defrauding. (No plural form in this sense.) ♦ *Once the accountant's deceit was discovered, she was fired.* ♦ *Billy thought he had gotten away with his deceit, but his teacher had found out.*

deceitful [dɪ 'sit fʊl] *adj.* dishonest; cheating. (Adv: *deceitfully.*) ♦ *The deceitful merchant's store was closed by the government.* ♦ *The teacher punished the deceitful students.*

deceive [dɪ 'siv] *tv.* to make someone believe something that is not true. ♦ *The sales representative deceived Bill about the car's mileage.* ♦ *Mary deceived the interviewer about her past experience.*

decelerate [di 'sɛl ə ret] **1.** *iv.* to slow down. ♦ *Mary decelerated as she approached the dangerous curve.* ♦ *When will the rate of inflation decelerate?* **2.** *tv.* to slow something down. ♦ *Bill decelerated the car as he neared the intersection.* ♦ *Brakes are used to decelerate a car.*

December [dɪ 'sɛm bɚ] *n.* the twelfth and last month of the year. (December comes after November and before January.) ♦ *December 31st is the last day of the year.* ♦ *Last December, our city was blanketed by heavy snow.*

decency ['di sən si] *n.* the quality of being decent; showing proper behavior. (No plural form in this sense.) ♦ *Mike expects decency and honesty in his friends and employees.* ♦ *The decency of each applicant was unquestionable.*

decent ['di sənt] **1.** *adj.* proper; well behaved; well mannered; modest. (Adv: *decently.*) ♦ *When one makes a mistake, the decent thing to do is correct it.* ♦ *Don't walk around in your underwear. Go put on some decent clothes!* **2.** *adj.* kind; nice. (Adv: *decently.*) ♦ *Holding the door open for others is a decent thing to do.* ♦ *The new librarian is every bit as decent as the previous one.* **3.** *adj.* good enough; pretty good; adequate. (Informal. Adv: *decently.*) ♦ *The restaurant serves decent portions of food, but the quality isn't great.* ♦ *The house was in decent shape when we bought it.*

decentralization [dɪ sɛn trəl ɪ 'ze ʃən] **1.** *n.* making something less centrally located or controlled; the spreading out of something. (No plural form in this sense.) ♦ *The new malls in town resulted in the decentralization of shopping.* ♦ *The decentralization of the school system gave each school more autonomy.* **2.** *n.* the result of making something less centrally located or controlled. (No plural form in this sense.) ♦ *The decentralization of the federal government means the states will have more power.* ♦ *The decentralization of power among the different departments was welcomed.*

decentralize [di 'sɛn trə lɑɪz] *tv.* to disperse something from an area of concentration. ♦ *The scattered housing projects decentralized the urban poverty.* ♦ *The company plans to decentralize its warehouse.*

deception [dɪ 'sɛp ʃən] *n.* deceiving, cheating, or defrauding. (No plural form in this sense.) ♦ *Deception and fraud were discovered in city government.* ♦ *She used deception to mislead us.*

deceptive [dɪ 'sɛp tɪv] *adj.* deceiving; misleading; dishonest. (Adv: *deceptively.*) ♦ *Many customers were angered by the deceptive ad.* ♦ *The jury did not believe the witness's deceptive answers.*

decide [dɪ 'sɑɪd] **1.** *tv.* to determine the outcome of something. ♦ *One vote decided the election.* ♦ *A single home run decided the outcome of the baseball game.* **2.** *tv.* to make a choice; to reach a decision about something. ♦ *I could not decide where to go on vacation.* ♦ *Please decide which one you want.* **3. decide on** *iv.* + *prep. phr.* to choose something; to pick something out. ♦ *I could not decide on what to order from the menu.* ♦ *The young couple could not decide on which house to buy.* **4. decide to** *iv.* + *inf.* to choose to do something. ♦ *We decided to leave the party.* ♦ *Tom decided to go on a vacation to Paris.*

decidedly [dɪ 'sɑɪd əd li] *adv.* definitely; clearly; without question. ♦ *Anne is decidedly against driving to work because parking is too expensive.* ♦ *The conservative judge decidedly opposed liberal politics.*

deciding [dɪ 'sɑɪd ɪŋ] *adj.* leading to a decision; causing a decision. ♦ *The high cost of a new car was the deciding factor in choosing to repair my old one.* ♦ *When the Senate is tied 50–50, the vice president has the deciding vote.*

deciduous [dɪ 'sɪdʒ u əs] *adj.* [of a tree or bush] bearing leaves that fall off each autumn. ♦ *Deciduous trees look barren during the winter.* ♦ *Evergreens are not deciduous trees.*

decimal ['dɛs ə məl] **1.** *adj.* based on or using the number 10. (Adv: *decimally.*) ♦ *Our currency is based on a decimal system.* ♦ *The metric system is a decimal system.* **2.** *n.* a number that contains a decimal point with figures to the right of it. ♦ *The number was written with a decimal rather than a fraction.* ♦ *One-half, written as a decimal, is .5.*

decimal point ['dɛ sə məl pɔɪnt] *n.* a period (.) that separates whole numbers from fractions. ♦ *Your numbers are right, but the decimal point is in the wrong place.* ♦ *In writing down prices, you put a decimal point between dollars and cents. For example, $2.50 is two dollars and fifty cents.*

decimate ['dɛs ə met] *tv.* to destroy a great number of things or a large proportion of something; to kill a large number of people or a large proportion of the people who are somewhere. ♦ *The tornado decimated the town.* ♦ *The ambush decimated the camp, leaving few soldiers alive.*

decimation [des ə 'me ʃən] *n.* destruction; mass killing. (No plural form in this sense.) ♦ *The cult's senseless decimation was preventable.* ♦ *The tyrant ordered the decimation of his opponents.*

decipher [dɪ 'sɑɪf ɚ] *tv.* to figure out a code; to read something that is hard or puzzling to read. (Compare with **cipher**.) ♦ *I can't decipher my doctor's handwriting.* ♦ *Can you decipher this cryptic message?*

decision [dɪ 'sɪ ʒən] *n.* a choice; a selection; a judgment; a resolution. ♦ *The judge's decision is final.* ♦ *The decision to build a new airport would raise people's taxes.*

decisive [dɪ 'sɑɪs ɪv] **1.** *adj.* leading to a definite end; causing an end result. (Adv: *decisively.*) ♦ *A winning debate was the decisive turning point in John's campaign.* ♦ *The Supreme Court made a number of decisive rulings today.* **2.** *adj.* firm; showing firmness. (Adv: *decisively.*) ♦ *Mary was quite decisive in the way she expressed herself.* ♦ *The teacher did not expect such a decisive response from the shy student.*

deck ['dɛk] **1.** *n.* a set of cards; a pack of cards. ♦ *A full deck has fifty-two cards.* ♦ *The dealer shuffled the deck and dealt the cards.* **2.** *n.* the floor of a ship. ♦ *I had a cabin on the lowest deck in the ship.* ♦ *The sailors cleaned the deck every day.* **3.** *n.* a raised, wooden patio, attached to the back door of a house. ♦ *The deck needed a coat of varnish to protect it from rain and snow.* ♦ *Tom built a deck in his backyard for parties.* **4. deck (out)** *tv.* (+ *adv.*) to make someone or something more beautiful. ♦ *The actress decked herself out in a stunning gown.* ♦ *The gardener will deck the yard with flowers this spring.* **5.** *tv.* to hit someone very hard. (Slang.) ♦ *The champion decked his opponent in the first round.* ♦ *The bully would deck the students who didn't give him money.*

declamation [dɛk lə 'me ʃən] *n.* a loud speech; a loud statement. ♦ *Anne's declamation was heard by everyone in the room.* ♦ *Tom's brief declamation concerning the mayor's error caught everyone's attention.*

declamatory [dɪ 'klæm ə tor i] *adj.* [of a statement] loud and emotional. ♦ *Excited by winning the award, Sally made a declamatory speech.* ♦ *Bob gave a declamatory eulogy for his friend.*

declaration [dɛk lə 're ʃən] *n.* a strong statement; something that is declared; an announcement. ♦ *After the disaster, a declaration was made that the flags should be flown at half-mast.* ♦ *The president issued a declaration of war.*

declare [dɪ 'klɛr] *tv.* to proclaim something; to make something known; to say something publicly. ♦ *The U.S. declared its independence from England in the 1700s.* ♦ *Five politicians declared their candidacy for mayor.*

declassified [di 'klæs ə fɑɪd] *adj.* [of secret documents] now made available to the public. ♦ *Declassified documents can be read by anyone.* ♦ *The newspaper published an article about the newly declassified government policy.*

declassify [di 'klæs ə fɑɪ] *tv.* to make a secret document available to the public. ♦ *The court's ruling declassified the secret report.* ♦ *The clerk mistakenly declassified the confidential papers.*

decline [dɪ 'klɑɪn] **1.** *iv.* to move from good to bad; to move from high to low; to go from better to worse. ♦ *As the dog grew older, its health declined.* ♦ *The quality of the restaurant's food declined over the years.* **2.** *iv.* to turn [something] down; to refuse [something]. ♦ *When asked to accept an overseas position, Mary declined.* ♦ *I offered Anne a cigarette, but she declined.* **3.** *tv.* to list the different case endings of a noun or adjective. (Compare with **conjugate**.) ♦ *Please decline the nouns on the first page.* ♦ *I learned to decline several Latin nouns today!* **4.** *tv.* to turn something down; to refuse an offer. ♦ *Susan declined my offer of help.* ♦ *Bill declined the invitation to my party.* **5.** *n.* the gradual change from high to low; the loss of power, strength, or health. ♦ *The mountain had a very steep decline.* ♦ *Jane suffered a decline in health.*

declining [dɪ 'klɑɪn ɪŋ] *adj.* having the loss of strength or health. (Adv: *decliningly.*) ♦ *The ruler—declining because of his years—decided to abdicate.* ♦ *Because of his declining health, John decided to sell his house.*

decode [di 'kod] *tv.* to decipher something; to translate a coded message. ♦ *It took the general a minute to decode the secret message.* ♦ *Can you decode this set of symbols?*

decompose [di kəm 'poz] **1.** *iv.* to decay; to rot and fall apart. ♦ *The dead tree decomposed in the damp forest.* ♦ *What caused the wooden bridge to decompose?* **2.** *tv.* to cause something to decay; to cause something to rot. ♦ *Bacteria decomposed the meat in a few days.* ♦ *Moisture will help decompose the piles of leaves quickly.*

decomposed [di kəm 'pozd] *adj.* decayed; rotten. ♦ *The compost pile was made from decomposed organic matter.* ♦ *The coroner examined the decomposed body.*

decomposition [di kɑmp ə 'zɪ ʃən] *n.* the process of decaying. (No plural form in this sense.) ♦ *Insects aided in the decomposition of the fallen tree limb.* ♦ *The complete decomposition of the carcass made it impossible to identify the animal.*

decongestant [di kən 'dʒɛs tənt] *n.* a medicine that relieves congestion in the upper respiratory tract. ♦ *The doctor prescribed Bill a decongestant for his allergies.* ♦ *When Mary had a bad cold, she took a decongestant.*

decor [de 'kor] *n.* the arrangement of decorations and furniture of a house or store. (No plural form in this sense.) ♦ *The decor in the designer's home was very stylish.* ♦ *The old department store had garish decor.*

decorate ['dɛk ə ret] **1.** *tv.* to adorn something with ornamental things; to put up decorations. ♦ *The mantle was decorated with family pictures.* ♦ *Bill decorated his office with his diplomas and awards.* **2.** *tv.* to honor a soldier with a medal. ♦ *The general will personally decorate the brave marine.* ♦ *At the ceremony, the major was decorated.* **3.** *iv.* to paint a room, put up wallpaper, hang drapes, lay carpet, or add furnishings to a room. ♦ *We have moved in, but we haven't decorated yet.* ♦ *Before we decorate, we must fix the roof.*

decoration [dɛk ə 're ʃən] **1.** *n.* an ornament; an embellishment; an object that is used to make something look pretty. ♦ *A spring wreath hung on the door as a decoration.* ♦ *There are absolutely no decorations in this room. It is totally plain.* **2.** *n.* an award or honor given to a soldier.

♦ *The soldier received the decoration at a special ceremony.* ♦ *A decoration was awarded for bravery.*

Decoration Day [dɛk ə 're ʃən de] *n.* an earlier name for Memorial Day. ♦ *Our town holds a parade on Decoration Day.* ♦ *Decoration Day is observed the last Monday in May, when we remember those who died in our country's wars.*

decorative ['dɛk ə rə tɪv] *adj.* ornamental; pretty; used for decorating. (Adv: *decoratively.*) ♦ *Lisa makes decorative pottery.* ♦ *I bought a decorative pin at the jewelry store.*

decorator ['dɛk ə ret ɚ] *n.* a designer who chooses and arranges furniture, carpeting, art, appliances, etc., for a room or a house. ♦ *My decorator chose a neutral color scheme for the room.* ♦ *The decorator carried in a box of carpet samples.*

decorum [dɪ 'kor əm] *n.* proper, formal, and dignified behavior. (No plural form in this sense.) ♦ *The gentleman always handled himself with decorum.* ♦ *Tom found the decorum at the banquet to be formal and tedious.*

decoy ['di koɪ] **1.** *n.* someone or something used as a lure. ♦ *The ducks ignored the poorly made decoy and flew away.* ♦ *Bill was used as a decoy to get Mary to the surprise party.* **2.** *tv.* to lure someone or something into a trap. ♦ *Spiders sometimes decoy insects into their webs.* ♦ *The hunter used raw meat to decoy the animal into the trap.*

decrease 1. ['di kris] *n.* a drop; a fall; a lessening; a reduction. ♦ *The church experienced a decrease in attendance.* ♦ *The store advertised a large decrease in its prices.* **2.** ['di kris] *n.* the amount that something has been reduced or lessened. ♦ *A ten-dollar decrease made the play much more affordable.* ♦ *Mary had a decrease in pay when she changed jobs.* **3.** [dɪ 'kris] *iv.* to become less; to become smaller in size or strength. ♦ *The pain decreased after I took an aspirin.* ♦ *The strong smell of the skunk decreased as we moved away from the place where we encountered it.* **4.** [dɪ 'kris] *tv.* to cause something to become less; to cause something to become smaller in size or strength. ♦ *An ice pack decreased the swelling of my sprained ankle.* ♦ *The manager decreased the size of the order.*

decreasing [dɪ 'kris ɪŋ] *adj.* growing smaller; diminishing. (Adv: *decreasingly.*) ♦ *I went shopping to replenish the decreasing food supply.* ♦ *Decreasing demand for wheat drives down the price.*

decree [dɪ 'kri] **1.** *tv.* to issue an authorized command. ♦ *The king decreed that a celebration be held for his wedding.* ♦ *A national holiday was decreed in honor of the victory.* **2.** *n.* an order from a person of authority. ♦ *The principal issued a decree to the students.* ♦ *No one dared ignore the owner's firm decree.*

decrepit [dɪ 'krɛp ɪt] *adj.* broken down; feeble due to advanced age. (Adv: *decrepitly.*) ♦ *The decrepit gate led to the secret and long-forgotten garden.* ♦ *A decrepit elderly man hobbled down the street.*

dedicate ['dɛd ə ket] **1. dedicate to** *tv.* + *prep. phr.* to declare that something be committed exclusively to a certain purpose or cause. ♦ *The committee dedicated a large sum to the renovation of the building.* ♦ *This room is dedicated to food preparation.* **2. dedicate to** *tv.* + *prep. phr.* to pledge oneself or one's effort to a cause. ♦ *I dedicated my life to eliminating cruelty to animals.* ♦ *The mayor was dedicated to fighting crime in the city.* **3. dedicate to** *tv.* + *prep. phr.* to declare that something, such as a building or a book, exists to honor a special person. ♦ *The church is dedicated to the memory of its first pastor.* ♦ *I want to dedicate this book to my mother, who encouraged me to write.*

dedicated ['dɛd ə ket ɪd] *adj.* committed; devoted. (Adv: *dedicatedly.*) ♦ *The dedicated teacher often stayed after school to help students.* ♦ *Tom is a dedicated soccer player who practices every day.*

dedicatee [dɛd ə kə 'ti] *n.* the person to whom something is dedicated. ♦ *The dedicatee of the symphony was present for its first performance.* ♦ *I have never heard of the dedicatee of this book.*

dedication [dɛd ə 'ke ʃən] **1.** *n.* the commitment of time or money to someone or something. (No plural form in this sense.) ♦ *Jane was rewarded for the dedication of her time and energy.* ♦ *The corporation made a dedication of new money to the project.* **2.** *n.* the complete commitment to a purpose or cause; the devotion to a purpose or a cause. (No plural form in this sense.) ♦ *The author's dedication to finishing the book on time meant working many late nights.* ♦ *The mayor's dedication to her town's welfare led to her reelection.* **3.** *n.* a ceremony in which something is dedicated to a special person or to a special purpose. ♦ *The building's dedication was televised on a local station.* ♦ *Many veterans attended the dedication of the war memorial.* **4.** *n.* a paragraph in a book that states that the book is dedicated to a special person. ♦ *Mary listed her parents in the dedication of her new book.* ♦ *The dedication in the children's book included the names of two dogs.*

deduce [dɪ 'dus] *tv.* to determine something by looking at the facts; to come to a conclusion by studying the facts. ♦ *Tom deduced that he would be late for work when he saw how heavy traffic was.* ♦ *The inspector deduced the murderer's identity.*

deduct [dɪ 'dʌkt] **1.** *tv.* to subtract something from a larger amount. ♦ *I deducted the amount of the check from my account balance.* ♦ *The waitress deducted the cost of the cold coffee from our bill.* **2.** *tv.* to subtract the cost of something from one's taxable income. ♦ *Bill can deduct his business costs from his income.* ♦ *The accountant deducted several items when figuring my taxes.*

deductibility [dɪ dək tə 'bɪl ɪ ti] *n.* the legality of deducting something from one's taxable income. (No plural form in this sense.) ♦ *The deductibility of an office in one's home is very questionable with the new tax laws.* ♦ *Mary asked about the deductibility of medical expenses.*

deductible [dɪ 'dʌk tɪ bəl] **1.** *adj.* able to be deducted; able to be subtracted. (Adv: *deductibly.*) ♦ *The amount of the deposit is deductible from the total bill.* ♦ *The cost of utilities is not deductible from my rent.* **2.** *n.* the amount of money that one must pay before one's insurance company makes a payment. ♦ *I pay less for a policy with a high deductible.* ♦ *The insurance company subtracted the deductible before issuing the check for the damage.*

deduction [dɪ 'dʌk ʃən] **1.** *n.* the amount that is deducted; a cost that can be deducted from one's taxable income. ♦ *Mary had a list of acceptable tax deductions.* ♦ *The tax collectors look at everyone's deductions very carefully.* **2.** *n.* a subtraction. ♦ *The bank statement showed a deduction for service charges.* ♦ *The store owner agreed to a deduction from the price of the damaged goods.* **3.** *n.* an instance of reasoning; a conclusion made by studying the facts. ♦ *The fireman made the correct deduction that the fire was just ahead when he saw clouds of smoke.* ♦ *The scientist's deduction was proved correct by the experiment.*

deed ['did] **1.** *n.* something that is performed; an act; an action. ♦ *Jimmy's good deed was carrying his neighbor's groceries.* ♦ *"Who has done this terrible deed?" shouted the king.* **2.** *n.* a legal document that officially transfers the ownership of real estate to someone. (Compare with title ④.) ♦ *When you purchase a house, you receive a deed to the property.* ♦ *The deed shows that you are legally the owner of the property.*

deem ['dim] **deem it [to be] necessary; deem that it is necessary** *idiom* to believe that something is necessary. ♦ *Mary deemed that it was necessary to leave town that night.* ♦ *Lisa deemed it necessary to go home.*

de-emphasize [di 'ɛm fə sɑɪz] *tv.* to lessen the emphasis on something. ♦ *The announcement de-emphasized the problems of the new policy.* ♦ *Makeup can de-emphasize facial blemishes.*

deep ['dip] **1.** *adj.* extending far down from the top, far in from a surface, or far back from the front; not shallow. (Adv: *deeply.* Comp: *deeper;* sup: *deepest.*) ♦ *I'm afraid to swim in deep water.* ♦ *The stage was not deep, so the actors had little room to perform in.* **2.** *adj.* reaching a specified depth; extending a certain distance downward, inward, or back; measured in extent downward, inward, or back. (Follows measure of depth. Comp: *deeper.*) ♦ *The swimming pool is five feet deep.* ♦ *These shelves are ten inches deep.* **3.** *adj.* [of a sound] low-pitched and strong. (Adv: *deeply.* Comp: *deeper;* sup: *deepest.*) ♦ *The men who sing bass in the choir have deep voices.* ♦ *The deep sound of the foghorn could be heard for miles.* **4.** *adj.* [of a color] intense. (Adv: *deeply.* Comp: *deeper;* sup: *deepest.*) ♦ *The clear mountain stream was a deep blue.* ♦ *I prefer deep colors to pastels.* **5.** *adj.* intense; strong; extreme. (Adv: *deeply.* Comp: *deeper;* sup: *deepest.*) ♦ *Mike has a deep sense of loyalty to his family.* ♦ *Jane has deep respect for her teachers.* **6.** *adj.* difficult to understand; past one's understanding. (Comp: *deeper;* sup: *deepest.*) ♦ *Many people think philosophy is a deep subject.* ♦ *The concept behind the project is too deep for me.*

deep-freeze ['dip 'friz] *n.* an appliance that freezes foods placed in it and stores them at a low temperature. ♦ *We put the perishable meat in the deep-freeze.* ♦ *When the deep-freeze broke, all of the food thawed and became spoiled.*

deep-fry ['dip frɑɪ] *tv.* to fry something in a deep pot of oil. ♦ *It is more healthful to steam vegetables than to deep-fry them.* ♦ *I deep-fried the potatoes so they are crunchy on the outside and tender inside.*

deep-rooted ['dip rut ɪd] **1.** *adj.* [of a plant] having roots that extend far into the ground. ♦ *The deep-rooted tree remained standing during the terrible storm.* ♦ *The weeds are so deep-rooted that they are almost impossible to pull out.* **2.** *adj.* ingrained; firmly established. (Figurative on ①.) ♦ *The people in this town have a deep-rooted optimism that helps them survive hardship.* ♦ *Bill's bad behavior is due to a number of deep-rooted problems.*

deep-seated [dip 'sit ɪd] *adj.* ingrained; complex and persistent. ♦ *The therapist's patient had deep-seated emotional problems.* ♦ *The feud between the families was so deep-seated that no one knew how to stop it.*

deer ['dɪr] *n., irreg.* a fast, hoofed animal, the males of which have antlers. (Pl: *deer.*) ♦ *Early one morning, I saw a deer dash across our backyard.* ♦ *Deer foraged through the forest for food.*

de-escalate [di 'ɛs kə let] *tv.* to lessen the tension of something; to make a situation less dangerous. ♦ *The president de-escalated military involvement overseas.* ♦ *The mayor sought ways to de-escalate gang violence.*

deface [dɪ 'fes] *tv.* to vandalize something by writing or drawing on it. ♦ *The gang defaced the side of the bridge with spray paint.* ♦ *The bored student defaced his textbook with doodles.*

defamation [dɛf ə 'me ʃən] *n.* an attack on someone's name or character; slander or libel. (No plural form in this sense.) ♦ *The angry politician sued the newspaper for defamation.* ♦ *The defamation of the political party was unjustified.*

defamatory [dɪ 'fæm ə tor i] *adj.* libelous; slanderous; attacking someone's name or reputation. (Adv: *defamatorily* [dɪ fæm ə 'tor ə li].) ♦ *A long, defamatory speech aroused the crowd's anger.* ♦ *The reporter was fired for writing a defamatory article without checking the facts.*

defame [dɪ 'fɛm] *tv.* to attack someone's name or reputation. ♦ *The careless historian defamed several war heroes.* ♦ *The politician defamed his opponent in his speech.*

default [dɪ 'fɔlt] **1.** *iv.* to fail to make a payment on a loan or to an account when the payment is due—thus causing the balance to become immediately due. ♦ *John defaulted on his car payment, and the bank repossessed the car.* ♦ *If they can't raise the money to pay the debt, they will have to default.* **2.** *n.* the failure to do something that a contract says one must do. (No plural form in this sense.) ♦ *The company was sued for default.* ♦ *When the loan could not be repaid, it went into default.*

defeat [dɪ 'fit] **1.** *tv.* to cause someone to lose; to beat someone in a contest or competition. ♦ *Mary defeated her opponent in the tennis match.* ♦ *The debate team defeated its rival.* **2.** *n.* loss [of a contest]; failure to win. (No plural form in this sense.) ♦ *Lisa found defeat hard to accept.* ♦ *Defeat is something that our team is quite used to.* **3.** *n.* an act of winning as in ①. ♦ *All of our team's players must play well for a successful defeat of the opponent.* ♦ *The army's defeat of the enemy was decisive.* **4.** *n.* a loss of a contest or competition. ♦ *After several frustrating defeats, our team finally won a game.* ♦ *The candidate's defeat in the last election ended his career as a politician.*

defeatist [dɪ 'fit əst] **1.** *adj.* expecting to lose; expecting the worst. ♦ *Bill's defeatist attitude was very depressing.* ♦ *You'll never win with a defeatist approach like that!* **2.** *n.* someone who expects the worst; someone who expects to lose. ♦ *Bill encouraged his children to have hope and not to be defeatists.* ♦ *Every office has a defeatist who is against new ideas.*

defecate ['dɛf ə ket] *iv.* to eject excrement (feces) from the body; to have a bowel movement. ♦ *If your dog defecates in the park, you must clean up the mess.* ♦ *The cat carefully defecated in a hole that it dug in the garden.*

defecation [dɛf ə 'ke ʃən] *n.* the elimination of excrement. (No plural form in this sense.) ♦ *Defecation is a natural act performed by most animals.* ♦ *Defecation and urination are two acts of elimination.*

defect 1. ['di fɛkt, dɪ 'fɛkt] *n.* a flaw. ♦ *The manufacturer recalled the car due to a defect in the engine.* ♦ *Because the sweater had a defect, its price was reduced.* **2.** [dɪ 'fɛkt] *iv.* to go over to the other side; to join up with one's enemies. ♦ *Normally a Republican, John defected and voted for the Democratic candidate.* ♦ *The traitor decided to defect during the night.*

defective [dɪ 'fɛk tɪv] *adj.* flawed; broken. (Adv: *defectively.*) ♦ *The defective tool would not work.* ♦ *The defective washing machine flooded the basement.*

defector [dɪ 'fɛk tɚ] *n.* someone who leaves one's group and joins the opposing group. ♦ *The Russian defector fled to the west.* ♦ *The American defector was branded as a traitor.*

defend [dɪ 'fɛnd] *tv.* to stick up for someone or something; to fight for someone or something physically or verbally. ♦ *Mary defended her actions when she was accused of cheating.* ♦ *Bill defended his little brother from the bully.*

defendant [dɪ 'fɛn dənt] *n.* someone who is the target of legal action in a court of law. ♦ *The defendant whispered to her attorney during the trial.* ♦ *The judge told the defendant to stand when the verdict was read.*

defense [dɪ 'fɛns] **1.** *n.* protection against someone or something; defending someone or something; preparation to defend against someone or something. (No plural form in this sense.) ♦ *The small boy relied on his quick thinking for defense.* ♦ *The defense provided by Bill's older brother scared the bullies away.* **2.** *n.* something that protects or shields. ♦ *A face mask is a good defense for a hockey goalie.* ♦ *A bulletproof vest is an important defense for police.* **3.** *n.* the skill of a sports team protecting its goal or in preventing the other team from scoring points. (No plural form in this sense.) ♦ *The soccer team's defense was excellent. Their opponents never scored.* ♦ *The coach hired two players to play defense on the football team.* **4.** *n.* the lawyer or lawyers who defend someone in court. ♦ *The defense presented new evidence as to the innocence of the man on trial.* ♦ *The defense was shocked by the judge's ruling.* **5.** *n.* the way that a lawyer argues a case in favor of a defendant; an argument used to defend oneself. (No plural form in this sense.) ♦ *The lawyer's defense was not adequate, and his client went to jail.* ♦ *The jury did not agree with the lawyer's defense.*

defenseless [dɪ 'fɛns ləs] *adj.* without protection; unprotected; helpless. (Adv: *defenselessly.*) ♦ *An infant is a defenseless creature.* ♦ *The defenseless town was captured by the enemy troops.*

defensive [dɪ 'fɛn sɪv] **1.** *adj.* protective; used for defense. (Adv: *defensively.*) ♦ *A defensive movement saved me from getting struck by the assailant.* ♦ *The team's defensive strategy was effective. The other team never scored.* **2. on the defensive** *idiom* overly ready to defend oneself. ♦ *John goes on the defensive when his athletic ability is questioned.* ♦ *The child was on the defensive when questioned about cheating.*

defer [dɪ 'fɚ] **1.** *tv.* [for someone] to postpone something or delay something. ♦ *I must defer the expense of a new car until next year.* ♦ *Mike deferred his judgment until he heard more explanation.* **2. defer to** *tv.* + *prep. phr.* to yield to someone else. ♦ *I'll defer to your wishes this time.* ♦ *A polite person defers to the person currently speaking.*

deference ['dɛf ə rəns] *n.* the yielding to someone who has more power. (No plural form in this sense.) ♦ *The babysitter demanded deference from the twins.* ♦ *Mary's deference to her parents' wishes was expected.*

deferential [dɛf ə 'rɛn ʃəl] *adj.* respectful; humble. (Adv: *deferentially.*) ♦ *Bill is always deferential to his parents.* ♦ *A teacher should not act too deferential to the students.*

deferment [dɪ 'fɚ mənt] **1.** *n.* postponement; delay. (No plural form in this sense.) ♦ *The deferment of the negotiations extended the strike by another day.* ♦ *This store permits deferment of payment.* **2.** *n.* a temporary delay in one's forced entry into the military service. (Part of the military draft.) ♦ *The college student was granted a deferment until after graduation.* ♦ *During the Vietnam War, many students tried to get deferments.*

defiance [dɪ 'fɑɪ əns] *n.* open resistance to authority; the failure to show respect to authority. (No plural form in this sense.) ♦ *Susie ran outside in defiance of her parents, who had sent her to bed.* ♦ *The activists were arrested for their defiance during the protest.*

defiant [dɪ 'fɑɪ ənt] *adj.* disobeying authority; not respecting authority. (Adv: *defiantly.*) ♦ *Defiant protesters blocked the busy street.* ♦ *The defiant teenager frequently skipped school.*

deficiency [dɪ 'fɪ ʃən si] *n.* a lack of something; a lack of enough of something. ♦ *An iron deficiency can make you feel tired and weak.* ♦ *The patient's illness was caused by a vitamin deficiency.*

deficient [dɪ 'fɪʃ ənt] *adj.* lacking; not having enough; incomplete. (Adv: *deficiently.*) ♦ *John's diet is deficient in fiber and vitamin E.* ♦ *You are deficient in the courses you need to graduate this year.*

deficit ['dɛf ə sɪt] *n.* the amount of money by which a sum falls short of the necessary amount. ♦ *The government tried to avoid a budget deficit.* ♦ *There's a deficit in my checking account.*

defile [dɪ 'fɑɪl] *tv.* to make someone or something impure; to pollute someone or something. ♦ *Tom defiled the pristine wilderness by building a cabin in it.* ♦ *Watching too many violent TV shows defiled the child's mind.*

define [dɪ 'fɑɪn] **1.** *tv.* to explain the meaning of a term. ♦ *The teacher defined each confusing word for the students.* ♦ *The dictionary defines thousands of words.* **2.** *tv.* to make something clear or distinct. ♦ *Can you define the problem for me?* ♦ *The president's address will define the problems the nation faces.*

definite ['dɛf ə nɪt] *adj.* certain; sure. (Adv: *definitely.*) ♦ *Dad's answer of "No" was definite.* ♦ *I got a definite response from Dr. Smith.*

definition [dɛf ə 'nɪ ʃən] **1.** *n.* an explanation of the meaning of a term. ♦ *Bill asked his teacher for the definition of the word* anemia. ♦ *Jane looked up the definition of the unfamiliar word in the dictionary.* **2.** *n.* clarity; the clearness of an image or a sound. (No plural form in this sense.) ♦ *The expensive stereo system's excellent definition caused listeners to feel like the music was in the same room.* ♦ *The definition of the skyline improved as the fog lifted.*

definitive [dɪ 'fɪn ɪ tɪv] **1.** *adj.* not able to be improved upon; quintessential. (With *the*. Adv: *definitively.*) ♦ *The prank was the definitive April Fools' Day joke.* ♦ *The skilled communicator became the definitive candidate.* **2.** *adj.*

final; conclusive. (Adv: *definitively.*) ♦ *My decision is definitive; you cannot change it.* ♦ *The Supreme Court gave a definitive ruling on the case.*

deflate [dɪ 'flet] **1.** *tv.* to let the air out of something. ♦ *A nail deflated the car tire.* ♦ *I stuck a pin in the balloon to deflate it instantly.* **2.** *tv.* to reduce the size of something that is too large. ♦ *Bill's ego is too large, so I deflated it by ridiculing him.* ♦ *The store decided to deflate its high prices.*

deflated [dɪ 'flet ɪd] **1.** *adj.* having lost air. ♦ *The hole in the deflated tire is too big to patch.* ♦ *The deflated balloon fell to the ground.* **2.** *adj.* reduced in size. ♦ *My deflated bank account meant that I couldn't go on vacation.* ♦ *The shoppers loved the deflated prices.*

deflation [dɪ 'fle ʃən] **1.** *n.* the release of air from something, such as a balloon or tire; causing air to be released from something; the state of being deflated. (No plural form in this sense.) ♦ *The gradual deflation of the tire was caused by a tiny hole.* ♦ *After each flight, the deflation of the hot-air balloon takes some time.* **2.** *n.* reduction of the money supply, causing prices to go down. (No plural form in this sense.) ♦ *During times of deflation, prices go down and the value of money increases.* ♦ *The government tried to stop the deepening deflation.*

defoliant [dɪ 'fol i ənt] *n.* a chemical that causes the leaves of trees to fall off. ♦ *The use of defoliants in the Vietnam War was strongly criticized.* ♦ *The village passed a law prohibiting the use of defoliants.*

defoliate [di 'fol i et] *tv.* to strip a tree of its leaves, especially by spraying it with chemicals. (See foliage.) ♦ *The powerful chemical defoliated the trees.* ♦ *The farmer wondered if the herbicide would defoliate trees.*

deform [dɪ 'form] *tv.* to change the shape of something, usually for the worse. ♦ *The intense heat from the fire deformed the metal chair.* ♦ *A constant wind deformed the tree.*

deformed [dɪ 'formd] *adj.* disfigured; badly shaped. (Adv: *deformedly.*) ♦ *The potter molded the deformed pot into a new vessel.* ♦ *Billy's favorite stuffed animal was a deformed teddy bear with a missing leg.*

deformity [dɪ 'form ə ti] *n.* something that is misshapen or disfigured. (No plural form in this sense.) ♦ *John's deformity was caused by the car accident.* ♦ *The deformity of his leg was corrected by surgery.*

defraud [dɪ 'frɔd] *tv.* to cheat someone of money or property; to lie to someone in order to get money or property illegally. ♦ *The tax accountant defrauded the government.* ♦ *John defrauded his employer by stealing money.*

defray [dɪ 'fre] *tv.* to pay all or part of the cost of something. ♦ *The insurance payment defrayed most of the hospital bills.* ♦ *My pay increase helped defray an increase in the cost of living.*

defrost [dɪ 'frɔst] **1.** *tv.* to remove something from a freezer in order to thaw it before cooking. ♦ *Defrost the chicken before baking it.* ♦ *The microwave oven can defrost food.* **2.** *iv.* [for something frozen] to thaw. ♦ *I set the beef on the counter to defrost.* ♦ *How long will the frozen ham take to defrost?*

deft ['dɛft] *adj.* skillful; making quick and neat movements. (Adv: *deftly.*) ♦ *The pianist's deft fingers were delightful to watch.* ♦ *With a few deft movements, the plumber fixed the leak.*

defunct [dɪ 'fʌŋkt] *adj.* no longer operating; no longer functioning. (Adv: *defunctly.*) ♦ *Those rules of etiquette have been defunct for years.* ♦ *The railroad to the city is now defunct.*

defuse [di 'fjuz] **1.** *tv.* to remove the fuse from a bomb. ♦ *Only specially trained experts should defuse a bomb.* ♦ *The soldier defused the bomb before it exploded.* **2.** *tv.* to remove the tension from a potentially dangerous situation. (Figurative on ①.) ♦ *Mary told a joke to defuse the tense atmosphere.* ♦ *The police are trained to defuse domestic disputes.*

defy [dɪ 'fɑɪ] *tv.* to resist authority; to go against a rule or a regulation. ♦ *Bill defied his superior and left work early.* ♦ *Anne defied the principal, and now she has to stay after school.*

degenerate 1. [di 'dʒɛn ə rət] *adj.* having an immoral or socially irresponsible quality. (Adv: *degenerately.*) ♦ *The critic was disgusted by the degenerate movie.* ♦ *I was shocked by the lack of morals in the degenerate book.* **2.** [di 'dʒɛn ə rət] *n.* someone with very low morals. ♦ *The degenerate went to lewd movies every day.* ♦ *The gambling ring is run by degenerates.* **3.** [di 'dʒɛn ə ret] *iv.* [for something] to worsen or break down; [for one] to lose one's morals. ♦ *As Anne grew older, her health degenerated.* ♦ *Bill's morals degenerated due to his friends' corrupt influence.*

degradation [dɛ grə 'de ʃən] **1.** *n.* breaking down to a lower state. (No plural form in this sense.) ♦ *The degradation of rocks into sand takes years.* ♦ *The hot, humid weather aided in the degradation of the carcass.* **2.** *n.* humiliation; impoverishment. (No plural form in this sense.) ♦ *In school, John suffered from one degradation after another.* ♦ *From my boss, I get only degradation, never praise.*

degrading [dɪ 'gred ɪŋ] *adj.* humiliating; taking away someone's dignity. (Adv: *degradingly.*) ♦ *The abusive parents inflicted degrading punishments on their children.* ♦ *The degrading joke met with stunned silence from the audience.*

degree [dɪ 'gri] **1.** *n.* a unit of measurement, as used for measuring temperature or angles. ♦ *There are ninety degrees in a right angle.* ♦ *The child's temperature was two degrees above normal.* **2.** *n.* the extent of something; the level of something. ♦ *The nurse treated the firefighter for first-degree burns.* ♦ *The defendant was charged with murder in the second degree.* **3.** *n.* a title awarded by a university or college to a student who has met certain requirements. ♦ *The graduate framed her degree and hung it on the wall.* ♦ *The local college offers two-year and four-year degrees.* **4.** *n.* one of the three forms in the comparison of adjectives and adverbs. ♦ *The comparative degree of* slow *is* slower. ♦ *The superlative degree of* slow *is* slowest.

dehumanize [di 'hjum ə nɑɪz] **1.** *tv.* to take away or ignore someone's human qualities. ♦ *Anne felt dehumanized by the insults she heard at her workplace.* ♦ *Conditions in the prison dehumanized the prisoners.* **2.** *tv.* to make something more mechanical and less friendly to humans. ♦ *Answering machines dehumanize telephone conversations.* ♦ *Automatic teller machines are a dehumanizing form of banking.*

dehumidifier [di hju 'mɪd ə faɪ ɚ] *n.* a device that removes moisture from the air. ♦ *The dehumidifier removed some of the moisture from the dank basement.* ♦ *The room was more comfortable with the dehumidifier operating.*

dehumidify [di hju 'mɪd ə faɪ] *tv.* to remove moisture from the air. ♦ *The doctor recommended dehumidifying the house.* ♦ *You need to dehumidify this room if you want to prevent mildew.*

dehydrate [dɪ 'haɪ dret] **1.** *iv.* to dry out; to lose moisture; to lose water. ♦ *Bob feared he would dehydrate if he didn't drink more water.* ♦ *This machine will cause fruit to dehydrate.* **2.** *tv.* to dry something out; to remove water from someone or something. ♦ *Anne dehydrated some fruit and served it as a snack.* ♦ *Working in the hot sun dehydrated the construction crew.*

dehydrated [di 'haɪ dret ɪd] *adj.* dried out; lacking water; having lost water. (Adv: *dehydratedly.*) ♦ *Give me a drink. I am completely dehydrated.* ♦ *The dehydrated worker fainted and was taken to a hospital.*

dehydration [di haɪ 'dre ʃən] *n.* the removal or loss of fluid. (No plural form in this sense.) ♦ *Lost in the desert, the hiker died of dehydration.* ♦ *Dehydration is a method of food preservation.*

de-ice [di 'ɑɪs] *tv.* to free something, such as a car window, from ice; to scrape something free of ice. ♦ *Now that I have a garage, I no longer have to de-ice my windshield.* ♦ *I was late because I had to de-ice the lock on my car door.*

deify ['di ə faɪ] *tv.* to worship someone or something as a god; to make someone or something a god. ♦ *Jimmy almost deified the famous athlete.* ♦ *A miser deifies money.*

deity ['di ə ti] **1.** *n.* a god; a goddess. ♦ *The statue was of an ancient Greek deity.* ♦ *In monotheism, only one deity is worshiped.* **2. the Deity** *n.* God; the major spiritual being in the Christian, Islamic, and Jewish religions. (No plural form in this sense. Treated as singular.) ♦ *In bad times, people often seek help from the Deity.* ♦ *The Deity is said to rule the universe.*

dejected [dɪ 'dʒɛk tɪd] *adj.* sad; discouraged. (Adv: *dejectedly.*) ♦ *Members of the dejected team walked slowly to the locker room.* ♦ *The dejected teenager wrote a lot of morose poetry.*

dejection [dɪ 'dʒɛk ʃən] *n.* sadness; discouragement. (No plural form in this sense.) ♦ *We felt a great deal of dejection after we lost the game.* ♦ *Despite the dejection he was experiencing, Mike continued to look for a job.*

Delaware ['dɛl ə wɛr] See Gazetteer.

delay [dɪ 'le] **1.** *n.* a postponement; an instance of being postponed. ♦ *The bad weather caused a lot of flight delays at the airport.* ♦ *The judge would not agree to a delay of the trial.* **2.** *tv.* to put off something until later; to cause someone or something to be late. ♦ *Bill will delay the meeting until he has all the facts.* ♦ *Cold spring weather delays the blooming of flowers.*

delayed [dɪ 'led] *adj.* postponed; put off. ♦ *The delayed meeting was held on Friday rather than Monday.* ♦ *The audience's delayed reaction made the comedian nervous.*

delectable [dɪ 'lɛk tə bəl] *adj.* delicious; tasting very good. (Adv: *delectably.*) ♦ *All the delectable food was eaten quickly.* ♦ *The chef was famous for creating delectable desserts.*

delegate 1. ['dɛl ə gɪt] *n.* someone who is chosen to represent a group of people at a meeting or convention. ♦ *The town elected two delegates to attend the conference.* ♦ *I was a delegate to the political convention.* **2.** ['dɛl ə get] *tv.* to give part of one's authority to someone else; to give the responsibility of doing something to someone else. ♦ *While on vacation, the company president delegates all his powers.* ♦ *John delegated the job of mowing the lawn to his daughter.*

delegation [dɛl ə 'ge ʃən] *n.* a group of delegates who represent the same people. ♦ *The delegation to the convention dined at one table.* ♦ *The delegation voted unanimously to adjourn the meeting.*

delete [dɪ 'lit] *tv.* to remove something from something, especially from a list or a piece of writing. ♦ *The editor deleted the untrue sentence from the manuscript.* ♦ *Mary declined the invitation, so I deleted her name from the guest list.*

deleted [dɪ 'lit ɪd] *adj.* removed. ♦ *The editor saved the deleted text for use elsewhere.* ♦ *Seven deleted names were restored to the guest list.*

deliberate 1. [dɪ 'lɪb (ə) rɪt] *adj.* on purpose; intentional; intended. (Adv: *deliberately.*) ♦ *The deliberate decision not to raise taxes was welcomed by the voters.* ♦ *Bob was thrown out of the game for making a deliberate foul.* **2.** [di 'lɪb ə ret] *iv.* to think, study, or consider carefully. ♦ *Anne deliberated for hours before replying.* ♦ *Congress in deliberating and will soon vote on the proposed law.* **3.** [di 'lɪb ə ret] *tv.* to consider something carefully. ♦ *The congress deliberated the bill for hours before voting on it.* ♦ *Anne deliberated her choices carefully.*

deliberation [dɪ lɪb ə 're ʃən] **1.** *n.* consideration; careful thought. (No plural form in this sense.) ♦ *After careful deliberation, the jury will give a verdict.* ♦ *The students were encouraged to take time for deliberation before answering the questions.* **2. deliberations** *n.* a discussion session. (Treated as plural.) ♦ *After its deliberations, the jury will reach a verdict.* ♦ *The dispute was resolved after lengthy deliberations.*

delicacy ['dɛl ə kə si] **1.** *n.* the condition of being delicate; fragility. (No plural form in this sense.) ♦ *The delicacy of the vase was obvious when it shattered.* ♦ *We were amazed at the delicacy of the hand-blown glass.* **2.** *n.* a rare or expensive food that tastes very good. ♦ *Caviar is a quite a delicacy.* ♦ *The chef is known for creating remarkable delicacies.*

delicate ['dɛl ə kɪt] **1.** *adj.* fragile; easily damaged. (Adv: *delicately.*) ♦ *The sick patient has a delicate digestive system.* ♦ *The playful dog broke the delicate lamp.* **2.** *adj.* subtly flavored. (Adv: *delicately.*) ♦ *The chicken was topped with a delicate sauce.* ♦ *Tom prefers strong spices to more delicate flavors.* **3.** *adj.* soft; tender; sensitive. (Adv: *delicately.*) ♦ *The delicate flower was silky to the touch.* ♦ *The baby's skin was delicate.*

delicately ['dɛl ə kɪt li] *adv.* gently; carefully. ♦ *Susan delicately laid her baby in the crib.* ♦ *The nurse delicately placed the bandage on my cut.*

delicatessen AND **deli** [dɛl ə kə 'tɛs ən, 'dɛl i] *n.* a store that sells food that is ready to eat, such as certain salads and the sliced meats and cheeses used for sandwiches. ♦ *The neighborhood deli is a popular place for lunch.* ♦ *When-*

ever he was hungry for a good sandwich, Bob went to the delicatessen.

delicious [dɪ 'lɪʃ əs] *adj.* tasty; pleasing to the senses, especially taste and smell. (Adv: *deliciously.*) ♦ *The food at the banquet was delicious.* ♦ *Jane made a delicious casserole from the leftovers.*

delight [dɪ 'laɪt] **1.** *n.* something that is pleasing; something that causes joy. ♦ *A roaring fire in the fireplace on a cold winter night can be quite a delight.* ♦ *Hiking in the mountains is a delight to the senses.* **2.** *tv.* to give someone pleasure; to cause someone joy; to please someone. ♦ *Lisa's story delighted the children.* ♦ *The boss delighted Anne with a promotion.* **3. delight in** *iv.* + *prep. phr.* to find pleasure in something; to be pleased by something. ♦ *Jane delights in watching birds early in the morning.* ♦ *Bill delights in watching his children play.*

delightful [dɪ 'laɪt fʊl] *adj.* causing delight; giving pleasure. (Adv: *delightfully.*) ♦ *The sunshine was delightful after four days of rain.* ♦ *The children sang a delightful song on the school bus.*

delineate [dɪ 'lɪn i et] *tv.* to mark the boundaries of something; to show the limits of something by drawing them or describing them. ♦ *The map delineated county boundaries.* ♦ *The scientist delineated the theory's capabilities.*

delinquency [dɪ 'lɪŋ kwən si] **1.** *n.* being behind on payments. (No plural form in this sense.) ♦ *Her bank repossessed Mary's car because of her delinquency.* ♦ *The credit-card company canceled Lisa's card for delinquency.* **2.** *n.* the amount of an overdue payment. ♦ *Your delinquency is due immediately.* ♦ *The bill indicated a delinquency of twenty dollars.* **3.** *n.* the behavior of people who habitually do not obey the law, especially young people. (No plural form in this sense.) ♦ *Delinquency was a problem at the high school.* ♦ *The psychologist suggested some ways to deal with delinquency.*

delinquent [dɪ 'lɪŋ kwənt] **1.** *adj.* [of someone whose payments are] overdue. (Adv: *delinquently.*) ♦ *I am usually delinquent with my monthly bills.* ♦ *The company canceled its delinquent customers' credit.* **2.** *adj.* [of a payment] that is late. ♦ *You must pay the delinquent amount now.* ♦ *Lisa's car payment is still delinquent.* **3.** *adj.* breaking laws habitually, especially minor ones; habitually getting into trouble. (Adv: *delinquently.*) ♦ *The police often call delinquent children's parents to speak about the problem.* ♦ *The principal knew the delinquent students by their first names.* **4.** *n.* a teenager who is habitually in trouble with the law. ♦ *The delinquent was sent to reform school.* ♦ *The courtroom was filled with delinquents.*

delirious [dɪ 'lɪr i əs] **1.** *adj.* out of one's mind due to illness; light-headed and not thinking well. (Adv: *deliriously.*) ♦ *The delirious patient could not answer the doctor's questions.* ♦ *John is delirious with fever.* **2.** *adj.* very excited. (Informal. Adv: *deliriously.*) ♦ *Mary and Bill were delirious with joy when they got engaged.* ♦ *The delirious ballplayers celebrated in the locker room.*

deliver [dɪ 'lɪv ɚ] **1.** *tv.* to take something [to someone or some place]. ♦ *Our mail is delivered every day at noon.* ♦ *Bill delivers pizzas for a living.* **2.** *tv.* [for a woman] to give birth to a baby. ♦ *Anne delivered a healthy set of twins.* ♦ *Mary's husband watched in awe as she delivered their first child.* **3.** *tv.* [for a doctor or midwife] to assist a baby being born. ♦ *The doctor who delivered me also delivered my sister.* ♦ *Midwives help deliver babies when women give birth at home.* **4.** *tv.* to give a speech; to read something out loud. ♦ *Bob delivered his book report in front of class.* ♦ *The attorney delivered an impassioned appeal to the jury.* **5. deliver from** *tv.* + *prep. phr.* to save someone from someone or something; to rescue someone from someone or something. (Older English.) ♦ *Mike was delivered from his troubles.* ♦ *Deliver us, Lord, from evil.*

deliverance [dɪ 'lɪv ɚ əns] **1.** *n.* rescue; being saved from danger or confinement; saving someone or something from danger or confinement. (No plural form in this sense.) ♦ *The child's deliverance from the burning building seemed like a miracle to her parents.* ♦ *Twelve firefighters were responsible for her deliverance.* **2.** *n.* religious salvation. (No plural form in this sense.) ♦ *The words of the old gospel hymn spoke of deliverance from sin.* ♦ *Bill—thinking of himself as a sinner—prayed for deliverance.*

delivery [dɪ 'lɪv ɚ i] **1.** *n.* the act of taking something to someone. ♦ *The inept worker completed the delivery of the package.* ♦ *The delivery of the ransom to the criminal assured the hostage's safety.* **2.** *n.* something that is taken to someone. ♦ *The receptionist accepted the delivery for the owner.* ♦ *The delivery arrived an hour late.* **3.** *n.* childbirth; the process of giving birth. ♦ *Anne's first delivery took ten hours.* ♦ *The hospital can handle five deliveries at the same time.* **4.** *n.* the style or manner of speaking; the style used when giving a speech. (No plural form in this sense.) ♦ *The story's humor was in its delivery.* ♦ *The speech coach aided Joan with the delivery of her speech.*

delude [dɪ 'lud] *tv.* to mislead someone; to deceive someone. ♦ *Mary was not trying to delude us, she just didn't know the facts.* ♦ *Bill deluded himself into thinking no one liked him.*

deluge ['dɛl judʒ] **1.** *n.* a great flood. ♦ *The Bible tells of Noah's deliverance from the deluge.* ♦ *The deluge took weeks to subside.* **2.** *n.* a violent rainstorm. ♦ *The plane sat on the runway waiting for the deluge to stop.* ♦ *It was hard to see through the car windshield during the deluge.* **3.** *n.* a great abundance of something. (Figurative on ②.) ♦ *I got a deluge of calls at the end of the day.* ♦ *The deluge of mail kept us busy for days.* **4.** *tv.* to overwhelm someone with a flood of something. ♦ *Calls for help deluged the police department during the riot.* ♦ *Mary's new job deluged her with heavy responsibilities.*

delusion [dɪ 'lu ʒən] *n.* a false belief. ♦ *Jane suffers from the delusion that she is unpopular.* ♦ *The daredevil had a delusion that he was immortal.*

deluxe [də 'lʌks] *adj.* of very good quality; of great luxury. (Adv: *deluxely.*) ♦ *The newlyweds spent their wedding night in a deluxe suite.* ♦ *We bought the deluxe model of the car.*

delve ['dɛlv] **1. delve into** *iv.* + *prep. phr.* to examine something; to investigate something by looking at it. ♦ *The investigator delved into the matter of Tom's sudden wealth.* ♦ *The Internal Revenue Service agent delved into our tax returns.* **2. delve through** *iv* + *prep. phr.* to search through something to find something. ♦ *I had to delve through every book in the library to find this information!* ♦ *I delved through the kitchen drawer looking for a can opener.*

demagogue AND **demagog** ['dɛm ə gɔg] *n.* someone who plays on people's emotions, fears, and prejudices. ♦ *The politician was a demagogue who stirred up trouble.* ♦ *Rational people will not be fooled by the demagogue's rhetoric.*

demagoguery [dɛm ə 'gɔg ə ri] *n.* the methods and actions used by a demagogue. (No plural form in this sense.) ♦ *The candidate's demagoguery was so obvious that many of his followers stopped supporting him.* ♦ *Mary uses demagoguery instead of rational arguments to get people to agree with her.*

demand [dɪ 'mænd] **1.** *n.* an urgent request; an insistent request; a strong order. ♦ *His demand for help could not be refused.* ♦ *The military unit made a demand for more supplies.* **2.** *n.* [the consumer's] strength of desire for a product or service. (No plural form in this sense.) ♦ *There were not enough toys to meet the demand during the holiday season.* ♦ *Consumer demand will determine the success of a product.* **3.** *tv.* to ask urgently for something; [for an authority] to request something firmly. ♦ *The angry customer demanded service.* ♦ *The injured student demanded help.* **4.** *tv.* to require something; to need something. ♦ *The injuries demanded surgery.* ♦ *This important issue demands attention.* **5.** *iv.* to make a demand ① that something be done. (Takes a clause.) ♦ *The irate customer demanded to see the manager.* ♦ *I demanded that I be allowed to enter.*

demanding [dɪ 'mæn dɪŋ] **1.** *adj.* making a lot of demands; overbearing. (Adv: *demandingly.*) ♦ *The waiter frowned at the demanding customer.* ♦ *Nurses soon learn to deal with demanding patients.* **2.** *adj.* requiring much effort, skill, and patience. (Adv: *demandingly.*) ♦ *Meditation is a demanding discipline.* ♦ *Only two runners finished the demanding course.*

demarcation [di mar 'ke ʃən] *n.* the separation of two or more things; a limitation; a boundary. (No plural form in this sense.) ♦ *This river is the demarcation between the two countries.* ♦ *The neighbors constantly fought over the demarcation of their property.*

demeanor [dɪ 'min ɚ] *n.* attitude; behavior; conduct. (No plural form in this sense.) ♦ *Bill's snobbish demeanor annoyed almost everyone.* ♦ *The speaker had a poised demeanor and spoke convincingly.*

demented [dɪ 'mɛn tɪd] *adj.* insane; crazy. (Adv: *dementedly.*) ♦ *The students eagerly agreed to the demented plan to steal the statue.* ♦ *The demented patient was restrained by a straitjacket.*

dementia [dɪ 'mɛn ʃə] *n.* confused and irrational behavior. (No plural form in this sense.) ♦ *The nursing-home patient suffered from dementia.* ♦ *Anne's dementia was caused by a horrible fever.*

demerit [di 'mɛr ɪt] *n.* a mark against someone for bad behavior. ♦ *Bill got a demerit each time he was late for work.* ♦ *The boarding school students received demerits if they misbehaved.*

demilitarize [di 'mɪl ɪ tə raɪz] *tv.* to end the military control of an area. ♦ *An order was given to demilitarize the entire territory.* ♦ *The government demilitarized the northern part of the country.*

demise [dɪ 'maɪz] **1.** *n.* death. (No plural form in this sense.) ♦ *The country mourned the president's demise.* ♦ *The demise of the elderly celebrity was no surprise.* **2.** *n.* end; the termination. (Figurative on ①. No plural form in this sense.) ♦ *The demise of the newspaper put hundreds of people out of work.* ♦ *We did not expect the demise of the local factory.*

demitasse ['dɛm i tæs] **1.** *n.* a small cup for drinking black coffee. ♦ *Steam rose from the demitasse as the coffee was poured.* ♦ *This demitasse is an antique. Don't break it.* **2.** *n.* a small amount of brewed black coffee, as is served in ①. (No plural form in this sense.) ♦ *We ordered cookies and demitasse for dessert.* ♦ *The demitasse had a wonderful aroma.*

demo ['dɛm o] **1.** *n.* a sample of something used to show how the item works; a demonstration model. (Pl in *-s.*) ♦ *The car sold for half its sticker price because it was a demo.* ♦ *The demo was broken, so no one would buy the product.* **2.** *n.* an instance of demonstrating something. (Pl in *-s.*) ♦ *We attended the new software demo, but we didn't buy anything.* ♦ *The vacuum-cleaner salesman promised a free demo in our home.*

demobilize [di 'mob ə laɪz] *tv.* to disband a military unit. ♦ *The government demobilized the military base.* ♦ *Everyone rejoiced when the commander demobilized the military hospital.*

democracy [dɪ 'ma krə si] **1.** *n.* the system of government ultimately controlled by the people who are governed. (No plural form in this sense.) ♦ *People must participate in their government if a democracy is to work.* ♦ *Democracy is spreading around the world in various forms.* **2.** *n.* a country whose government is a democracy ①. ♦ *The United States is a democracy.* ♦ *Many countries became democracies in the years following World War II.*

democrat ['dɛm ə kræt] **1.** *n.* someone who believes in democracy. ♦ *A real democrat believes that everyone should vote.* ♦ *Do democrats now outnumber communists in Russia?* **2. Democrat** *n.* a member of the Democratic Party in the United States. ♦ *A Democrat was elected mayor.* ♦ *After a series of Republican presidents, a Democrat was elected.*

democratic [dɛm ə 'kræt ɪk] **1.** *adj.* operating under the principles of democracy. (Adv: *democratically* [...ɪk li].) ♦ *The school held a democratic election for student-council officers.* ♦ *The new nation established a democratic government.* **2. Democratic** *adj.* of or about ③, its members, and policies. ♦ *The Democratic candidate met with party leaders.* ♦ *The delegates voted to accept the Democratic platform.* **3. Democratic Party** *n.* one of the two major political parties in the U.S. ♦ *The Democratic Party generally favors the active involvement of government in programs to help people.* ♦ *The Democratic Party is not particularly supportive of business and commercial interests.*

demolish [dɪ 'mal ɪʃ] *tv.* to destroy something; to tear something down. ♦ *The car was demolished in the accident.* ♦ *A hurricane demolished many coastal homes.*

demolition [dɛm ə 'lɪ ʃən] *n.* the tearing down of something; the destruction of something. (No plural form in this sense.) ♦ *The old stadium was scheduled for demolition.* ♦ *People are fascinated by the demolition of buildings.*

demon ['di mən] **1.** *n.* an evil spirit; a devil. ♦ *The deluded man thought his dog was possessed by demons.* ♦ *The ancient culture had a ritual to ward off demons.* **2.** *n.* someone who is evil; someone who is wicked. (Figurative on ①.) ♦ *The unassuming politician was a demon in disguise.* ♦ *That little demon tied my shoelaces together!*

demonstrable [dɪ 'mɑn strə bəl] *adj.* able to be demonstrated; able to be proved. (Adv: *demonstrably.*) ♦ *That the earth rotates is a demonstrable fact.* ♦ *Though intriguing, the theory's conclusions were not demonstrable.*

demonstrate ['dɛm ən stret] **1.** *tv.* to show how something is done; to show how something works. ♦ *A salesclerk demonstrated how the vacuum cleaner worked.* ♦ *The mechanic demonstrated how to change the car's oil.* **2.** *tv.* to show one's emotions; to show one's feelings. ♦ *Anne demonstrated her anger by stamping her feet.* ♦ *Mary demonstrates her love by bringing me flowers.* **3.** *iv.* to protest by marching, chanting, or rallying in public. ♦ *The citizens demonstrated against the new taxes.* ♦ *In the 1960s, students demonstrated against the Vietnam war.*

demonstrated ['dɛm ən stret ɪd] *adj.* proven; explained. ♦ *Lisa has a demonstrated talent for dealing with children.* ♦ *John had a demonstrated inability to arrive on time.*

demonstration [dɛm ən 'stre ʃən] **1.** *n.* a showing of how something works. ♦ *The demonstration was a failure because the machine leaked oil.* ♦ *To sell its new product, the company planned demonstrations at stores everywhere.* **2.** *n.* an expression of feeling; an expression of emotion. ♦ *John's demonstration of affection was touching.* ♦ *Lisa only laughed at the child's angry demonstration.* **3.** *n.* a march or rally where people express a strong feeling about something. ♦ *More than a thousand people attended the demonstration.* ♦ *To sway the vote on the bill, opponents planned a demonstration.*

demonstrative [də 'mɑn strə tɪv] **1.** *adj.* expressive; showing feelings. (Adv: *demonstratively.*) ♦ *If you were less demonstrative of your emotions, people would be more comfortable around you.* ♦ *Bill is very demonstrative of his affections.* **2.** *adj.* [of a pronoun or adjective] pointing out a reference to something. ♦ *In the sentence, "That house was bought in May," the word "that" is a demonstrative adjective.* ♦ *"This" is a demonstrative pronoun in the sentence, "This costs less than $10."*

demonstrator ['dɛm ən stret ɚ] **1.** *n.* someone who performs a demonstration. ♦ *The demonstrator was peeling apples with an apple peeler.* ♦ *The grocery store hires demonstrators to promote its products.* **2.** *n.* a protester. ♦ *The police arrested the unruly demonstrators.* ♦ *The demonstrators carried signs as they marched.*

demoralize [dɪ 'mor ə lɑɪz] *tv.* to weaken someone's spirit; to destroy someone's spirit. ♦ *A chronic illness demoralized Lisa.* ♦ *Bill's divorce demoralized him for months.*

demoralizing [dɪ 'mor ə lɑɪz ɪŋ] *adj.* destroying someone's confidence or spirit. (Adv: *demoralizingly.*) ♦ *A demoralizing review shook Dave's confidence in his acting ability.* ♦ *The demoralizing comments were very negative.*

demote [dɪ 'mot] *tv.* to reduce the rank or position of someone. ♦ *After being late to work eight times, Tom was demoted to clerk.* ♦ *The sergeant threatened to demote the corporal.*

demur [dɪ 'mɚ] *iv.* to raise an objection to something; to show that one is against something; to hesitate because one objects to something. (Compare with demure.) ♦ *Anne demurred at the suggestion that she assigned too much homework.* ♦ *John demurred when he was asked to do something that he felt was wrong.*

demure [dɪ 'mjur] *adj.* shy or modest; reserved; coy. (Adv: *demurely.* Compare with demur.) ♦ *The demure young lady hid her smile with her fan.* ♦ *Mary refuses to act demure as a way of attracting men.*

den ['dɛn] **1.** *n.* the lair or home of a wild animal. ♦ *We inadvertently uncovered a bear's den.* ♦ *The raccoons were curled up in their den.* **2.** *n.* a center of bad or illegal activities. ♦ *The local saloon was a den of vice.* ♦ *The gang hideout is a robber's den.* **3.** *n.* a room in a house used for studying or working. ♦ *The books are kept in the den.* ♦ *Mary went to the den to calculate her taxes.*

denial [dɪ 'nɑɪ əl] **1.** *n.* insisting that something does not exist or is not true; denying that something exists or is true. (No plural form in this sense.) ♦ *Denial of the problem will keep it from being solved.* ♦ *Denial is the first thing you will hear from the guilty person.* **2.** *n.* an act of ①. ♦ *The police would not believe Max's repeated denials.* ♦ *He answered each of their accusations with another denial.* **3.** **in denial** *phr.* in a state of refusing to believe something that is true. ♦ *Mary was in denial about her illness and refused treatment.* ♦ *Tom doesn't think he's an alcoholic because he's still in denial.*

denim ['dɛn əm] *n.* the material that blue jeans are made from; a strong, heavy cotton fabric. (No plural form in this sense.) ♦ *The workers wore pants made of sturdy denim.* ♦ *The denim faded after several washings.*

Denmark ['dɛn mɑrk] See Gazetteer.

denomination [dɪ nɑm ə 'ne ʃən] **1.** *n.* a religious sect; a kind of religion. ♦ *A weekly forum promotes discussion between various religious denominations.* ♦ *Each religious denomination has its own beliefs.* **2.** *n.* one of the amounts in which a particular currency is available. ♦ *The various denominations of U.S. coins are the penny, the nickel, the dime, the quarter, the half-dollar, and the dollar.* ♦ *The peso is a denomination of Mexican currency.*

denominational [dɪ nɑm ə 'ne ʃə nəl] *adj.* of or about a religious denomination. (Adv: *denominationally.*) ♦ *Max went to a denominational school run by monks.* ♦ *Presbyterians are governed by their denominational rules of order.*

denominator [dɪ 'nɑm ə net ɚ] *n.* the bottom number of a fraction. (Compare with numerator.) ♦ *To add two fractions together, make sure they have the same denominator.* ♦ *In the fraction ½, the denominator is 2.*

denounce [dɪ 'nɑʊns] *tv.* to condemn someone or something; to speak or write against someone or something; to publicly disapprove of someone or something. ♦ *An editorial denounced the Supreme Court's decision.* ♦ *Jane loudly denounces anyone who litters.*

dense ['dɛns] *adj.* thick; tightly packed together. (Adv: *densely.* Comp: *denser;* sup: *densest.*) ♦ *It was hard to see the path in the dense forest.* ♦ *The airport was closed because of the dense fog.*

density ['dɛn sə ti] *n.* the measure of the amount of people or things within a given area; the degree of how crowded something is. (No plural form in this sense.) ♦ *The population density is very high in Hong Kong.* ♦ *The city council was worried about the density of houses in the new subdivision.*

dent ['dɛnt] **1.** *n.* an indentation; a dip in a surface. ♦ *As the van backed up, it hit the car behind it, creating a large dent in the car's bumper.* ♦ *There was a dent in the kitchen counter where Mary had dropped a can of beans.* **2.** *tv.* to make a small hollow or indentation in something. ♦ *A stone falling from the back of a truck dented the hood of my car.* ♦ *The movers dented the furniture as they brought it through the narrow door.*

dental ['dɛn təl] *adj.* of or about the teeth and their care. (Adv: *dentally.*) ♦ *The dental assistant cleaned my teeth.* ♦ *My dentist follows proper dental procedures.*

dental floss ['dɛn təl flɔs] See **floss**.

dentist ['dɛn təst] *n.* a health-care professional who specializes in the care of the teeth. ♦ *The dentist recommended that I see an orthodontist.* ♦ *My dentist was as gentle as possible while cleaning my teeth.*

denture ['dɛn tʃɚ] *n.* a dental device consisting of one or more artificial teeth. (The plural often refers to a complete set of artificial teeth in two parts.) ♦ *I placed my dentures in a glass of water while I slept.* ♦ *Both of my grandparents wear dentures.*

denunciation [dɪ nən si 'e ʃən] **1.** *n.* public condemnation of someone or something. (No plural form in this sense.) ♦ *Widespread denunciation of the war forced the government to reconsider its policy.* ♦ *New taxes are usually meet with great denunciation.* **2.** *n.* an act of ①. ♦ *The editor's frequent denunciations of the war were well known.* ♦ *The protesters' loud denunciations of the dictator echoed through the streets.*

deny [dɪ 'nɑɪ] **1.** *tv.* to declare that something is not true. ♦ *The defendant denied the witness's statement.* ♦ *The students all denied cheating on the test.* **2.** *tv.* to refuse to grant someone or something permission to do something. ♦ *The sloppily dressed people were denied entrance to the restaurant.* ♦ *The state denied the elderly man a driver's license.*

deodorant [di 'od ə rənt] *n.* a substance that eliminates or disguises bad odors, typically for use in the armpits. ♦ *Using deodorant is part of good hygiene.* ♦ *Despite the advertising claims, Max's deodorant did not work.*

deodorize [di 'od ə rɑɪz] *tv.* to remove or disguise a bad odor. ♦ *Mary deodorized the kitchen after cooking the fish.* ♦ *A pine-scented spray was used to deodorize the car.*

deodorizer [di 'od ə rɑɪz ɚ] *n.* a substance that removes or disguises a bad odor. ♦ *The deodorizer had a pleasant scent of pine.* ♦ *The deodorizer eliminated the cigar smell from the living room.*

depart [dɪ 'pɑrt] **1.** *iv.* to leave; to start a journey by leaving a place. ♦ *I said good-bye and departed.* ♦ *The dog sniffed at the garbage and then departed.* **2.** *tv.* to leave from a place; to leave a state or status. ♦ *The train departs the station at 6:00 P.M. sharp.* ♦ *When we depart this life, we die.*

departed [dɪ 'pɑrt ɪd] **1.** *adj.* dead. (A euphemism.) ♦ *Jane has two sisters and a departed brother.* ♦ *Prayers were said for the departed souls.* **2. the departed** *n.* someone who has died; people who have died. (Euphemism. No plural form in this sense. Treated as singular or plural.) ♦ *Prayers were said for the departed.* ♦ *The departed was buried Monday morning.*

department [dɪ 'pɑrt mənt] **1.** *n.* a subdivision of an organization. ♦ *The new department will be responsible for marketing the company's products abroad.* ♦ *The Department of History is a part of the College of Arts.* **2.** *adj.* <the adj. use of ①.> ♦ *Do you know the department policy regarding use of the fax machine?* ♦ *The most important department records are kept in this file cabinet.*

departmental [dɪ pɑrt 'mɛn təl] *adj.* of or about a department. ♦ *We are getting ready for a departmental reorganization.* ♦ *All the departmental records are stored in this room.*

department store [dɪ 'pɑrt mənt stor] *n.* a large store where all sorts of merchandise is sold in various departments. ♦ *I bought shoes, a hat, and a new hammer at the department store.* ♦ *Some modern department stores even have a department where you can buy food.*

departure [dɪ 'pɑr tʃɚ] **1.** *n.* leaving a place. (No plural form in this sense.) ♦ *John's delayed departure from the office caused him to miss his bus.* ♦ *Mary held a press conference to announce her departure from politics.* **2. departure from** *n.* + *prep. phr.* a change or deviation from something. ♦ *Having ham rather than turkey on Thanksgiving is a departure from tradition.* ♦ *In a departure from his usual schedule, Bill worked late last night.*

depend [dɪ 'pɛnd] **1. depend (up)on** *iv.* + *prep. phr.* to place one's trust in someone or something; to rely on someone or something for help or support. ♦ *The puppies depend on their mother for food.* ♦ *I depend on my car to get to work.* **2. depend (up)on** *iv.* to be decided according to different possibilities; to be determined by something. ♦ *The outcome of the election will depend on how many people show up to vote.* ♦ *The size of the harvest depends upon the weather.*

dependability [dɪ pɛnd ə 'bɪl ə ti] *n.* reliability; trustworthiness. (No plural form in this sense.) ♦ *Everyone counts on Anne's dependability.* ♦ *Jane's dependability was questioned after she missed work twice in her first week on the job.*

dependable [dɪ 'pɛn də bəl] *adj.* trustworthy; reliable. (Adv: *dependably.*) ♦ *Our most dependable employees never call in sick.* ♦ *My manager's decisions are always dependable.*

dependence [dɪ 'pɛn dəns] **1.** *n.* reliance on something or someone else for help. (No plural form in this sense.) ♦ *Children's dependence on their parents decreases with age and maturity.* ♦ *Jane's dependence on Mike for a ride to work was a problem when Mike took a vacation.* **2.** *n.* an addiction; the need to have something habitually. (No plural form in this sense.) ♦ *The doctor warned Bill about his dependence on tobacco.* ♦ *Anne tried to hide her alcohol dependence.*

dependency [dɪ 'pɛn dən si] **1.** *n.* reliance on someone or something else for help. (No plural form in this sense.) ♦ *The agency's dependency on federal funds meant it was always in danger of closing.* ♦ *Mary's dependency on her parents lessened when she left home.* **2.** *n.* an addiction; the need to have something habitually. (No plural form in this sense.) ♦ *The celebrity's dependency on drugs was public knowledge.* ♦ *The article listed signs of possible alcohol dependency.* **3.** *n.* a political subdivision, such as a territory, that is dependent on another country. ♦ *The* *people of the dependency wanted their freedom.* ♦ *In the 1960s, many dependencies became self-governing.*

dependent [dɪ 'pɛn dənt] **1.** *adj.* relying on someone else for support; depending on someone or something. (Adv: *dependently.*) ♦ *I wish you were not so dependent! Learn to take care of yourself!* ♦ *The mare did not stray far from her dependent colt.* **2. dependent on** *adj. + prep. phr.* determined by something else; controlled by something else; resulting only if something else happens. ♦ *Holding the parade is dependent on good weather.* ♦ *The price of meat is dependent on the supply.* **3.** *n.* someone who relies on someone else for support. ♦ *Ever since his parents died, Max is a dependent of his grandparents.* ♦ *Mary is her parents' only dependent.* **4.** *n.* someone who can be listed on a wage earner's income-tax form and thereby reduce the taxes. ♦ *The Smiths claim their children as dependents on their tax returns.* ♦ *Tom has four dependents, counting his ailing mother, whom he supports.*

depict [dɪ 'pɪkt] *tv.* to show someone or something, especially by using a picture; to portray someone or something. ♦ *Mary depicted a beautiful sunset in her painting.* ♦ *This story depicts the life of whales.*

deplane [di 'plen] *iv.* to get off an airplane; to leave an airplane. ♦ *Bill deplaned after the long flight and stretched his legs.* ♦ *We deplaned briefly during the layover.*

deplete [dɪ 'plit] *tv.* to use up all or most of a supply of something. ♦ *Our long trip depleted the gas tank.* ♦ *The drought depleted the village's water supply.*

deplorable [dɪ 'plor ə bəl] *adj.* miserable; horrible. (Adv: *deplorably.*) ♦ *Lisa complained about the deplorable conditions at the orphanage.* ♦ *Max apologized for his deplorable comment.*

deplore [dɪ 'plor] **1.** *tv.* to disapprove of something. ♦ *The naturalist deplored the growth of cities.* ♦ *The pleasant teacher deplored the students' rude behavior.* **2.** *tv.* to regret something; to feel sorry about something. ♦ *I can only deplore the suffering I have caused.* ♦ *The worshipers deplored their weaknesses and sins.*

deploy [dɪ 'plɔɪ] *tv.* to position soldiers and their equipment [somewhere] before an attack. ♦ *The platoon deployed a lookout at the top of the hill.* ♦ *After the general deployed the troops and tanks, they attacked the village.*

depopulate [di 'pɑp jə let] *tv.* to reduce the number of people living somewhere. ♦ *The famine depopulated the eastern part of the country.* ♦ *Migration westward depopulated the eastern region.*

deport [dɪ 'port] **1.** *tv.* to expel someone from a country. ♦ *Customs officials deported the illegal aliens caught at the border.* ♦ *The island nation tried to deport its criminals.* **2.** *tv.* to conduct oneself in a particular manner. (Takes a reflexive object.) ♦ *Jane deported herself graciously even though she had been offended.* ♦ *Children find it almost impossible to deport themselves properly at all times.*

deportation [dɪ por 'te ʃən] **1.** *n.* sending someone out of the country. (No plural form in this sense.) ♦ *Deportation is a way of removing an unwanted foreigner from a country.* ♦ *Deportation of the refugees was halted at the last minute.* **2.** *n.* an act of ①. ♦ *The government carried out a number of deportations of known foreign criminals.* ♦ *The government demanded the dissident's immediate deportation.*

deportment [dɪ 'port mənt] *n.* behavior; conduct; the way someone acts. (No plural form in this sense.) ♦ *The deportment of the students at the private school was very refined.* ♦ *The rowdy students exhibited poor deportment on the field trip.*

deposit [dɪ 'pɑz ɪt] **1.** *n.* an amount of money paid towards a product or service. ♦ *The couple made a deposit on the new furniture.* ♦ *To purchase a car, you will probably need to make a deposit.* **2.** *n.* an amount of money paid as security on a rented dwelling. ♦ *Susan had to pay one month's rent as a deposit.* ♦ *The landlady returned our deposit after we moved from the apartment.* **3.** *n.* something that is put down; something that is laid down. ♦ *The miner found gold deposits in the riverbed.* ♦ *Thick mud deposits lay at the mouth of the river.* **4.** *n.* money that is put in a monetary account. ♦ *I made a bank deposit to cover the total amount of the checks I'd written.* ♦ *The deposit was transmitted electronically from my employer to the bank.* **5.** *tv.* to place money in a monetary account. ♦ *You need to deposit some cash before you write checks.* ♦ *The company automatically deposited the paychecks in the employees' bank accounts.* **6.** *tv.* to put something down in a specific place. ♦ *A glacier deposited a lot of rocks here during the last Ice Age.* ♦ *The tornado deposited the car in the middle of the park.*

deposition [dɛp ə 'zɪ ʃən] *n.* testimony that is given under oath; a written statement that is sworn to be true. ♦ *John contradicted his deposition and will be tried for perjury.* ♦ *The jury examined all of the depositions.*

depository [dɪ 'pɑz ɪ tor i] **1.** *n.* a place where things are kept safe; a place where things are deposited for safekeeping. ♦ *The depository was guarded by a system of alarms.* ♦ *A safety-deposit box is a type of depository.* **2.** *n.* a warehouse. ♦ *John works packing and shipping books at the book depository.* ♦ *Most of the goods are stored in a local depository.*

depot ['di po] **1.** *n.* a bus or train station. (From French.) ♦ *We waited in the bus depot for the next bus to New York.* ♦ *A new depot was built to accommodate the increase in passengers.* **2.** *n.* a place where supplies are stored, usually military supplies. ♦ *The depot burned and the army's weapons were ruined.* ♦ *The enemy tried to bomb the ammunition depot.*

depreciate [dɪ 'priʃ i et] *iv.* to lose value over time; to become worth less money over time. ♦ *People don't want their property to depreciate.* ♦ *A car depreciates rapidly.*

depreciation [dɪ priʃ i 'e ʃən] **1.** *n.* a loss in the value of something over time; a lowering in the value of something over time. (No plural form in this sense.) ♦ *The depreciation of the new car began when it was driven home.* ♦ *Because of rapid technological change, a computer has a fast depreciation.* **2.** *n.* a decrease in the value of the currency of a country. (No plural form in this sense.) ♦ *The gradual depreciation of the dollar was fueled by rising imports.* ♦ *Foreign travel is more expensive because of the dollar's depreciation.*

depress [dɪ 'prɛs] **1.** *tv.* to make someone sad; to send someone into despair. ♦ *News of Bill's departure depressed Anne.* ♦ *The cold, gray weather depressed the students on campus.* **2.** *tv.* to weaken the force or effect of something. ♦ *Some drugs depress the functions of the human body.* ♦ *The cold weather depressed the lizard's metabolism.* **3.** *tv.*

to push down on something. ♦ *I depressed the button and waited for the elevator to arrive.* ♦ *Lisa depressed the lid of the container to close it.*

depressed [dɪ 'prɛst] **1.** *adj.* sad; saddened. ♦ *Even a present could not cheer up the depressed child.* ♦ *The depressed student was unable to study.* **2.** *adj.* weakened; made less forceful; made less valuable. ♦ *The nation suffered from a depressed economy.* ♦ *Our currency is depressed, making foreign travel very expensive.*

depressing [dɪ 'prɛs ɪŋ] *adj.* saddening; causing sadness. (Adv: *depressingly.*) ♦ *I cried while watching the depressing movie.* ♦ *The patient couldn't wait to leave the depressing hospital.*

depression [dɪ 'prɛ ʃən] **1.** *n.* a part of a surface that is lower than the rest of the surface. ♦ *The children made depressions in the bed by jumping on it.* ♦ *The falling boulder caused a depression in the road.* **2.** *n.* a time of general economic weakness; a time of high unemployment and weak demand for goods and services. (When capitalized, it refers to the (U.S.) Great Depression, which lasted from October 29, 1929, until the late 1930s.) ♦ *Many people were unemployed during the Great Depression.* ♦ *Inflation often fuels fears that a depression will follow.* **3.** *n.* a state of mind where someone is hopelessly sad. ♦ *Nothing could end Mary's depression but time.* ♦ *After he attempted suicide, Dave was hospitalized for depression.*

deprivation [dɛ prə 've ʃən] *n.* depriving someone of something; the condition of being deprived of something. (No plural form in this sense.) ♦ *The lost campers suffered from food deprivation.* ♦ *Deprivation of their basic rights angered the citizens.*

deprive [dɪ 'prɑɪv] *tv.* to refuse to let someone or something use or have something; to take something away from someone or something. ♦ *The abusive parents deprived the child of proper nutrition.* ♦ *A plant will die if you deprive it of light.*

depth ['dɛpθ] **1.** *n.* deepness; the quality or extent of being deep; the distance from top to bottom; the distance from front to back. (No plural form in this sense.) ♦ *The depth of the shelf is four inches.* ♦ *The pool has a depth of twelve feet.* **2. depths** *n.* the deepest part of the ocean. ♦ *The wreckage was discovered at the ocean's depths.* ♦ *The ship sank and went to the depths of the sea.*

deputize ['dɛp jə tɑɪz] *tv.* to make someone a deputy. ♦ *The sheriff deputized five citizens to help search for the convict.* ♦ *The marshal will deputize anyone who can ride a horse.*

deputy ['dɛp jət i] *n.* someone who is authorized to act for someone else. ♦ *The sheriff has one deputy.* ♦ *The head of the company could not be there in person, so she sent her deputy.*

derail [di 'rel] **1.** *tv.* to cause a wheeled vehicle that runs on tracks to be thrown from the tracks. (The vehicle can be a train, streetcar, tram, roller-coaster wagon, etc.) ♦ *Rocks falling down the mountain derailed the train, killing several passengers.* ♦ *Extremely high winds can derail a roller coaster.* **2.** *iv.* [for a wheeled vehicle] to fall off its tracks. ♦ *The train derailed outside of town.* ♦ *The streetcar derailed during the earthquake.*

deranged [dɪ 'rendʒd] *adj.* insane; crazy. (Adv: *derangedly.*) ♦ *The doctor sedated the deranged mental patient.* ♦ *The deranged prisoner was kept in solitary confinement.*

derby ['dɚ bi] **1.** *n.* a stiff hat with a narrow brim and rounded crown. ♦ *Bill looked quite handsome wearing his grandfather's derby.* ♦ *The man wearing the black derby was easy to spot in the crowd.* **2.** *n.* an important annual horse race. ♦ *One of the most famous horse races is the Kentucky Derby.* ♦ *The racing derby will be held on Sunday.*

derelict ['dɛr ə lɪkt] **1.** *n.* someone who is abandoned by family and society; a person without a means of support. ♦ *The derelict lived in a box under the bridge.* ♦ *Our church tries to help derelicts.* **2.** *n.* an abandoned ship. ♦ *The derelict eventually sank.* ♦ *A tug towed the derelict into the harbor.* **3.** *adj.* abandoned; neglected; left to fall apart; left to fall to ruin. (Adv: *derelictly.*) ♦ *The derelict house was condemned.* ♦ *The street was lined with derelict cars and vans.*

deride [dɪ 'rɑɪd] *tv.* to insult or mock someone or something; to ridicule someone or something. ♦ *Mary derided David for his horrid taste in furniture.* ♦ *The politician derided his opponents at every opportunity.*

derision [dɪ 'rɪ ʒən] *n.* mockery; ridicule. (No plural form in this sense.) ♦ *Mike was famous for his clever derision of government officials.* ♦ *Tom's criticism was mostly derision and ridicule.*

derivation [dɛr ə 've ʃən] *n.* the history of a word and how that word was formed. ♦ *The teacher explained the derivation of the word* pathology, *showing the students how the Greek word* pathos, *meaning disease, was combined with a suffix that is often used in the names of sciences.* ♦ *Learning about Greek and Latin roots can help a student understand the derivations of many English words.*

derivative [dɪ 'rɪv ə tɪv] **1.** *n.* something that is derived from something else. ♦ *This product is a derivative of three common garden plants.* ♦ *Gasoline is a derivative of oil.* **2.** *n.* a word that is formed by adding a prefix or suffix to a base word. ♦ Preflight *is a derivative of* pre- *and* flight. ♦ *"Add a suffix to a word to form a derivative," said the teacher.*

derive [dɪ 'rɑɪv] **1. derive from** *iv. + prep. phr.* to come from a particular origin; to originally come from something. ♦ *What language does the word* pathos *derive from?* ♦ *Most of John's problems derive from his bad attitude.* **2. derive from** *tv. + prep. phr.* to get something from someone; to obtain a quality from someone or something. ♦ *Bill derives his good humor from his happy life at home.* ♦ *Jane derives great satisfaction from helping others.*

dermatitis [dɚm ə 'tɑɪt ɪs] *n.* an inflammation of the skin. (No plural form in this sense.) ♦ *Anne's dermatitis is red and itchy.* ♦ *Bob's allergy to cats causes his dermatitis.*

dermatologist [dɚm ə 'tɑl ə dʒəst] *n.* a doctor who treats diseases of the skin. ♦ *The dermatologist examined my rash.* ♦ *Jane's dermatologist gave her a prescription for her acne.*

dermatology [dɚm ə 'tɑl ə dʒi] *n.* the medical specialty of treating skin diseases. (No plural form in this sense.) ♦ *The medical doctor decided to specialize in dermatology.* ♦ *If you have a rash, you should seek a doctor who knows a lot about dermatology.*

derogate ['dɛr ə get] *tv.* to belittle someone or something; to show contempt for someone or something. ♦ *I didn't mean to derogate your new hat. It's very nice.* ♦ *Because he thinks he is superior, my unpleasant neighbor often treats people meanly and derogates them.*

derogation [dɛr ə 'ge ʃən] *n.* belittling; disparaging. (No plural form in this sense.) ♦ *The heckler's derogation disrupted the politician's speech.* ♦ *No one should be subjected to constant derogation.*

derogatory [dɪ 'rɑg ə tor i] *adj.* belittling; disparaging; showing contempt. (Adv: *derogatorily* [dɪ rɑg ə 'tor ə li].) ♦ *Anne's anger erupted when she heard the derogatory comment about her work.* ♦ *Mike's derogatory statement to the police officer almost got him arrested.*

desalinate [di 'sæl ə net] *tv.* to remove the salt from something, especially sea water. ♦ *The water-treatment plant desalinates sea water.* ♦ *All the drinking water on the island has been desalinated.*

desalination [di sæl ə 'ne ʃən] *n.* the process of removing salt from sea water. (No plural form in this sense.) ♦ *We get our drinking water through desalination.* ♦ *Desalination is expensive, but there is not natural source of fresh water on this island.*

descend [dɪ 'sɛnd] **1.** *tv.* to move from a higher part to a lower part on or along something; to climb down something. ♦ *Bill descended the stairs to the basement.* ♦ *We walked more quickly as we descended the hill.* **2.** *iv.* to go down; to go from a high place to a lower place; to move downward. ♦ *As evening came, the sun descended.* ♦ *The cattle will descend from the hill when it is feeding time.* **3.** *iv.* to come from an earlier time. ♦ *This practice descends to us from the sixteenth century.* ♦ *Your philosophy descends from the Dark Ages.* **4. descend on** *iv. + prep. phr.* to gather and attack someone or something. ♦ *Two bullies descended on Bill and beat him.* ♦ *The three large dogs descended on the smaller one.* **5. be descended from someone or some creature** *phr.* to come from an ancestor. ♦ *Anne is descended from a family of British shopkeepers.* ♦ *Mary is descended from Irish peasants.*

descendant [dɪ 'sɛn dənt] *n.* someone's child, grandchild, great-grandchild, and so on. ♦ *Jane is a descendant of George Washington.* ♦ *Mary kept the family records for the benefit of her descendants.*

descending [dɪ 'sɛn dɪŋ] *adj.* going from someplace high to a lower place. ♦ *The descending sun colored the sky with a beautiful sunset.* ♦ *Driving was becoming impossible in the descending fog.*

descent [dɪ 'sɛnt] **1.** *n.* a movement down from a higher level. ♦ *The children watched the airplane's graceful descent.* ♦ *We held our breath as the hot-air balloon made its descent through the trees.* **2.** *n.* a downward movement along a slanted surface. ♦ *Bill put the car into low gear and began his descent of the hill.* ♦ *The skier made an excellent descent down the slope.* **3.** *n.* a decline; a lowering of something. ♦ *The descent of the floodwaters was slow but steady.* ♦ *With the rapid descent in stock prices, investors became worried.*

describe [dɪ 'skrɑɪb] *tv.* to tell about someone or something in written or spoken words. ♦ *The poem describes moonlight on the lake.* ♦ *I described Jane's good qualities to Bill.*

description [dɪ 'skrɪp ʃən] *n.* a statement that describes someone or something. ♦ *Descriptions of the lost dog were posted throughout the town.* ♦ *The advertisement's description was very misleading.*

descriptive [dɪ 'skrɪp tɪv] *adj.* describing; explanatory; detailed. (Adv: *descriptively.*) ♦ *A descriptive sentence tells facts but does not ask a question.* ♦ *Susan gave a very descriptive report on forest fires to the class.*

desecrate ['dɛs ə kret] *tv.* to profane or defile something, especially something that is revered, such as something religious or sacred. ♦ *Vandals desecrated the graveyard.* ♦ *An angry mob desecrated the flag.*

desecration [dɛs ə 'kre ʃən] *n.* using sacred things or places for secular purposes; willfully defiling sacred things or places. (No plural form in this sense.) ♦ *The army's desecration of the church during the war could not be stopped.* ♦ *The vandals were arrested for the desecration of the flag.*

desegregate [di 'sɛg rə get] *tv.* to end racial separation. ♦ *The school district desegregated the students by court order.* ♦ *Some citizens resisted efforts to desegregate the city's neighborhoods.*

desegregation [di sɛ grə 'ge ʃən] *n.* the ending of the separation of the races. (No plural form in this sense.) ♦ *There were many rallies supporting and opposing desegregation.* ♦ *After desegregation, children of all races attended the same schools.*

desensitize [di 'sɛn sə tɑɪz] *tv.* to make someone less sensitive to something; to cause someone to not feel something. ♦ *Taking aspirin every day desensitizes me to the irritation of my arthritis.* ♦ *John feels that television violence has desensitized us to violence in general.*

desert 1. ['dɛz ɚt] *n.* a barren land with little rainfall and little or no human population. ♦ *We visited the desert when we went to Arizona.* ♦ *The hot, dry sand of the desert burned our feet.* **2. desert island** ['dɛz ɚt...] *n.* a remote island, usually small and uninhabited, and typically having the features of ①. ♦ *There are many stories about sailors being shipwrecked on desert islands.* ♦ *How could anyone live on a desert island with no food or water?* **3.** ['dɛz ɚt] *adj.* <the adj. use of ①.> ♦ *Many cactus plants grew in the desert sands.* ♦ *The desert climate is good for people with asthma.* **4.** [dɪ 'zɚt] *tv.* to abandon someone or something; to go away and leave someone or something behind. ♦ *The family accidentally deserted the puppy on a country road.* ♦ *Jimmy quickly deserted his friends when he was called to dinner.* **5.** [dɪ 'zɚt] *tv.* to leave a place and make it empty. ♦ *When the rains came, the people deserted the park.* ♦ *The students deserted the classroom once class was over.* **6.** [dɪ 'zɚt] *tv.* to leave military duty without permission. ♦ *The soldiers were tempted to desert their posts.* ♦ *Six soldier have deserted this unit in the past year.* **7.** [dɪ 'zɚt] *iv.* to be absent from military duty without permission. ♦ *During the Civil War, many soldiers on both sides deserted.* ♦ *The frightened soldier deserted.* **8. get one's just deserts** [...dɪ 'zɚts] *idiom* to get what one deserves. ♦ *I feel better now that Jane got her just deserts. She really insulted me.* ♦ *Bill got back exactly the treatment that he gave out. He got his just deserts.*

deserted [dɪ 'zɚt ɪd] *adj.* empty; without people; abandoned. (Adv: *desertedly.*) ♦ *The deserted town became a* *tourist attraction.* ♦ *Bob was afraid to go near the deserted barn.*

deserter [dɪ 'zɚt ɚ] *n.* someone who leaves the military without permission. ♦ *After he was caught, the deserter was court-martialed.* ♦ *After leaving his post, Bob was considered to be a deserter.*

desertion [dɪ 'zɚ ʃən] **1.** *n.* the abandonment of someone or something; the abandonment of duty. (No plural form in this sense.) ♦ *No one could understand the dog's desertion of her puppies.* ♦ *The desertion of one's children is a criminal offense.* **2.** *n.* leaving a military service without permission. (No plural form in this sense.) ♦ *The soldier was tried for desertion.* ♦ *Desertion is a very serious offense in the military services.*

deserve [dɪ 'zɚv] *tv.* to be worthy of something; to merit something. ♦ *The naughty children deserved their punishment.* ♦ *After six years in college, I think I deserve a good job.*

deserving [dɪ 'zɚ vɪŋ] *adj.* worthy of something; entitled to something. (Adv: *deservingly.*) ♦ *All deserving employees were given a promotion.* ♦ *The deserving teacher took a vacation at the end of the school year.*

design [dɪ 'zɑɪn] **1.** *n.* a plan showing how something will be made; the way something is arranged; the layout of something. ♦ *The city council approved the bridge's design.* ♦ *The design of the golf course includes a lake.* **2.** *n.* a decorative pattern. ♦ *The expensive sweater had an intricate design.* ♦ *The floor tiles were arranged in an unusual design.* **3.** *tv.* to make the plans for building or decorating something. ♦ *A professional architect will design the new stadium.* ♦ *We designed our house ourselves.* **4.** *tv.* to plan and execute a graphic work. ♦ *The artist designed the mural and painted it.* ♦ *Lisa designed the book cover for her new novel.*

designate ['dɛz ɪg net] **1.** *tv.* to assign someone to do something; to appoint someone to do something. ♦ *Four council members were designated to serve on the new committee.* ♦ *The team designated Sally as the captain.* **2.** *tv.* [for something] to mark, signify, or distinguish someone or something. ♦ *A sign designated the room used for changing clothes.* ♦ *The award designated the firefighter a hero.*

designated ['dɛz ɪg net ɪd] *adj.* assigned; appointed. ♦ *At the designated time, the president will appear on the balcony.* ♦ *Smoking is allowed only in the designated area.*

designation [dɛz ɪg 'ne ʃən] **1.** *n.* showing or indicating [something]. (No plural form in this sense.) ♦ *The designation of states on the map was clear, but some cities were hard to find.* ♦ *Special signs are erected for the designation of historical sites.* **2.** *n.* a name or a title that points someone out. ♦ *The employee's new designation is Assistant Manager.* ♦ *Our club bestowed the designation of Honorary Member on the town's mayor.*

designer [dɪ 'zɑɪn ɚ] *n.* someone who makes designs; someone who plans how buildings, clothing, rooms, or works of graphic art will look. ♦ *The designer was proud of her fall fashions.* ♦ *A graphic arts designer created the poster for the concert.*

designing [dɪ 'zɑɪn ɪŋ] **1.** *n.* the art or business of making designs. (No plural form in this sense.) ♦ *Jane got a degree in art and went into designing.* ♦ *Bill studied designing and now remodels houses.* **2.** *adj.* plotting; scheming; planning. ♦ *The designing employee intended to get a promotion somehow.* ♦ *The designing boy manipulated his parents.*

desirability [dɪ zɑɪr ə 'bɪl ə ti] *n.* being wanted; being desired; the condition or extent of being desirable. (No plural form in this sense.) ♦ *The convenient location of the house increased its desirability.* ♦ *The car's desirability was based on its comfort and cost.*

desirable [dɪ 'zɑɪr ə bəl] *adj.* worthy of desire; worth wanting; wished for. (Adv: *desirably.*) ♦ *Chocolate cakes are so desirable, the bakery can't bake enough.* ♦ *I envy Jane because her job is so desirable.*

desire [dɪ 'zɑɪr] **1.** *n.* a strong wish for something; a request for something. ♦ *Suddenly, Mary had a strong desire for chocolate.* ♦ *Bill has a desire to be a veterinarian.* **2.** *n.* someone or something that is wished for. ♦ *Chocolate is Mary's heart's desire.* ♦ *Success is Bill's desire.* **3.** *n.* lust; sexual longing. ♦ *The minister encouraged the congregation to control their desires.* ♦ *The couple kissed each other with desire.* **4.** *tv.* to want something very much. ♦ *Bill desires a good job above everything else.* ♦ *The politician desired power and would stop at nothing to get it.*

desired [dɪ 'zɑɪrd] *adj.* wished for; wanted. ♦ *All of Max's hard efforts had the desired effect, as he got the new job.* ♦ *Mary worked hard to bring about the desired end.*

desirous [dɪ 'zɑɪr əs] **desirous of** *adj.* + *prep. phr.* having a desire for something; wanting something. ♦ *I am desirous of a good job and a healthy family.* ♦ *Jane was desirous of a new car.*

desist [dɪ 'zɪst] *iv.* to stop doing something; to cease doing something. ♦ *Anne had to desist in her efforts to tame the horse.* ♦ *Mike would not stop until I ordered him to desist.*

desk ['dɛsk] *n.* a piece of furniture with a flat top and often with drawers on the lower part. ♦ *Tom does his schoolwork at his desk.* ♦ *My desk is littered with papers.*

desolate ['dɛs ə lɪt] *adj.* barren; without people. (Adv: *desolately.*) ♦ *The desolate mining town was once a booming center of activity.* ♦ *The forest looked desolate after the fire.*

desolation [dɛs ə 'le ʃən] **1.** *n.* bleakness; barrenness. (No plural form in this sense.) ♦ *We were stunned by the desolation of the deserted town.* ♦ *The desert's desolation is overwhelming.* **2.** *n.* sadness; loneliness. (No plural form in this sense.) ♦ *We could all sense Mary's desolation at the funeral.* ♦ *Bill took three months to recover from the desolation he felt from being fired.*

despair [dɪ 'spɛr] **1.** *n.* the loss of hope; hopelessness. (No plural form in this sense.) ♦ *The parents felt despair when their child was in the hospital.* ♦ *I tried to lift Mike's despair by telling him funny stories.* **2.** *iv.* to lose all hope; to believe that nothing good will happen. ♦ *After his illness, Sam despaired of ever walking again.* ♦ *The nation despaired over the senseless bombing.*

desperado [dɛs pə 'rɑd o] *n.* a criminal; an outlaw; a desperate person who will commit a crime. (Pl in *-s* or *-es.*) ♦ *The desperados all rode black horses.* ♦ *The ruthless desperado was arrested at the border.*

desperate ['dɛs pə rɪt] *adj.* willing to try anything because nothing has worked. (Adv: *desperately.*) ♦ *Mary* *was desperate for a raise because her bills were mounting.* ♦ *A desperate soldier heaved a grenade into enemy territory.*

desperately ['dɛs pə rɪt li] *adv.* acting in desperation. ♦ *The president desperately sought to avoid a war.* ♦ *The trapped passengers desperately cried for help.*

desperation [dɛs pə 're ʃən] *n.* the state of being willing to try any solution because nothing else has worked. (No plural form in this sense.) ♦ *Bill worked long hours in desperation to meet the deadline.* ♦ *I borrowed money from Jane out of sheer desperation.*

despicable [dɪ 'spɪk ə bəl] *adj.* worthy of being despised; worthy of being hated. (Adv: *despicably.*) ♦ *That despicable child trampled my flowers.* ♦ *The despicable politician was sent to prison.*

despise [dɪ 'spɑɪz] *tv.* to hate someone or something; to have a strong dislike for someone or something. ♦ *Mary despised her rude and obnoxious neighbors.* ♦ *Many people despise greasy food.*

despised [dɪ 'spɑɪzd] *adj.* scorned; hated. ♦ *The mayor's despised policies made him very unpopular.* ♦ *The police had to protect the despised defendant outside of the courtroom.*

despite [dɪ 'spɑɪt] *prep.* in spite of; even though. ♦ *Despite the rain, the game was played to the end.* ♦ *I knew I had to get on the airplane despite my fear.*

despondency [dɪ 'spɑn dən tsi] *n.* severe unhappiness; dejection; hopelessness. (No plural form in this sense.) ♦ *The unprepared student slipped into a state of despondency.* ♦ *Despondency overcame the unhappy workers.*

despondent [dɪ 'spɑn dənt] *adj.* dejected; discouraged. (Adv: *despondently.*) ♦ *The Smiths were despondent over the death of their child.* ♦ *I thought a movie might cheer up my despondent friend.*

despot ['dɛs pət] *n.* a tyrant; an oppressive ruler. ♦ *The despot taxed the people heavily.* ♦ *The manager enforced company policy like a despot.*

despotism ['dɛs pə tiz əm] *n.* complete power; oppression. (No plural form in this sense.) ♦ *The people hated the despotism of the ruler.* ♦ *Despotism was rampant in the empire.*

dessert [dɪ 'zɚt] *n.* a special, often sweet, food served at the end of a meal. ♦ *For dessert, we ate ice cream.* ♦ *Dessert is the last course of a meal.*

destination [dɛs tə 'ne ʃən] *n.* the place where someone or something is going; the place where someone or something is being sent. ♦ *We should reach our destination before nightfall.* ♦ *Our vacation destination is Phoenix.*

destine ['dɛs tən] **1. destine for** *tv.* + *prep. phr.* [for something] to intend someone or something for a particular purpose, rank, status, etc.; [for something] to determine that someone or something is appropriate for a particular purpose. (Often passive.) ♦ *Lisa is destined for the presidency.* ♦ *A tear in the sleeve destined my old coat for charity.* **2. destine to** *tv.* + *inf.* to assign or appoint someone to do something; to determine that someone is to do something. (Often passive.) ♦ *Lisa is destined to become president.* ♦ *My leg injury destined me to be a spectator rather than a player.*

destiny ['dɛs tə ni] **1.** *n.* the force that determines future events. (No plural form in this sense.) ♦ *I didn't plan for my future. Instead, I left it to destiny.* ♦ *Leave tomorrow to destiny.* **2.** *n.* the future of someone or something; the course of events that will happen. ♦ *None of us know our destinies.* ♦ *The destiny of the castaways was unknown.*

destitute ['dɛs tɪ tut] *adj.* very poor; without money for the necessities of life. (Adv: *destitutely.*) ♦ *During the Great Depression, many people became destitute.* ♦ *The fire left the family destitute.*

destroy [dɪ 'strɔɪ] *tv.* to make someone or something completely useless; to do away with someone or something. ♦ *The child destroyed the toy in a fit of anger.* ♦ *The accident destroyed the car.*

destroyer [dɪ 'strɔɪ ɚ] **1.** *n.* someone or something that destroys. ♦ *Divorce is often a destroyer of families.* ♦ *The war was a destroyer of the nation's economy.* **2.** *n.* a small warship with torpedoes. ♦ *The enemy used a torpedo to sink the destroyer.* ♦ *The fleet of destroyers sailed out of port.*

destruction [dɪ 'strʌk ʃən] **1.** *n.* ruining or destroying something. (No plural form in this sense.) ♦ *The tornado caused the destruction of the town.* ♦ *A large crowd watched the destruction of the old building.* **2.** *n.* ruins; the result of destroying. (No plural form in this sense.) ♦ *The destruction caused by the tornado lay all around.* ♦ *The photographer captured the explosions and the resulting destruction.*

destructive [dɪ 'strʌk tɪv] *adj.* causing destruction; likely to destroy something. (Adv: *destructively.*) ♦ *The destructive winds carried away the roof of the house.* ♦ *The convicted criminal had been destructive as a child.*

detach [dɪ 'tætʃ] *tv.* to separate something from something else; to disconnect something from something else. ♦ *Sally detached the spray nozzle from the hose.* ♦ *The mechanic detached the oil filter.*

detachable [dɪ 'tætʃ ə bəl] *adj.* able to be separated; able to be disconnected. (Adv: *detachably.*) ♦ *The hose has a detachable nozzle.* ♦ *My coat has a detachable hood.*

detached [dɪ 'tætʃt] **1.** *adj.* separate; not attached. ♦ *The house has a detached garage rather than an adjoining one.* ♦ *The detached nozzle of the hose lay in the grass.* **2.** *adj.* impartial; indifferent; unbiased. (Figurative on ①.) ♦ *The detached spectator didn't care who won the softball game.* ♦ *Bob's detached attitude about school often gets him in trouble.*

detachment [dɪ 'tætʃ mənt] **1.** *n.* soldiers on a special mission who are separate from a main group of soldiers. ♦ *A detachment was sent to scout the next ridge.* ♦ *Gunfire told us that the detachment had found the enemy.* **2.** *n.* aloofness; indifference; a lack of concern for someone or something. (No plural form in this sense.) ♦ *Bill feigns detachment, but he really cares about his friends.* ♦ *Lonely people feel detachment from other people.*

detail 1. ['di tel, dɪ 'tel] *n.* a small fact about something. ♦ *The newspaper story provided the details of the proposed amendment.* ♦ *Mary shortened the story by omitting a few details.* **2.** ['di tel] *n.* a drawing that shows all of the fine or small parts of something. ♦ *The picture is a detail of a larger painting.* ♦ *The architect examined the details of the stairway and the front entrance.* **3.** [dɪ 'tel] *tv.* to give all the facts of a story or issue. ♦ *The victim detailed the crime for the police officer.* ♦ *The reporter detailed the scandal in an exclusive story.* **4. in detail** [...dɪ 'tel, ...'di tel] *phr.*

with lots of details; giving all the details. ♦ *I explained the policy to the customer in detail.* ♦ *We planned the entire project in great detail.* **5. go into detail** [...dɪ 'tel, ...'di tel] *idiom* to give all the details; to present and discuss the details. ♦ *The clerk went into detail about the product with the customer.* ♦ *I just want a simple answer. Don't go into detail.*

detailed [dɪ 'teld] **1.** *adj.* having many details. ♦ *The detailed proposal was over one hundred pages long.* ♦ *The decorator chose a detailed wallpaper pattern for our kitchen.* **2.** *adj.* exact; precise; including every part. ♦ *Anne gave me detailed directions to her house.* ♦ *Following these detailed instructions, anyone could build a bookcase.*

detailing ['di tel ɪŋ] *n.* the small details that are found on a finished product. (No plural form in this sense.) ♦ *Washing the sweater ruined the embroidered detailing.* ♦ *The detailing on the Victorian house was very intricate.*

detain [dɪ 'ten] **1.** *tv.* to delay someone or something; to keep someone or something from leaving. ♦ *The officer detained Bill while writing the traffic ticket.* ♦ *Please do not detain me. I am in a hurry.* **2.** *tv.* to keep someone in police custody; to keep someone in confinement. ♦ *The police detained the suspect for questioning.* ♦ *The travelers were detained while customs officials looked through their luggage.*

detect [dɪ 'tɛkt] *tv.* to become aware of something; to discover something. ♦ *The bird detected the worm in the grass and dived down to get it.* ♦ *I detected Bob's lie because he wouldn't look at me directly.*

detectable [dɪ 'tɛk tə bəl] *adj.* able to be detected; noticeable. (Adv: *detectably.*) ♦ *The small dog in the airport was trained to sense any detectable odor of food in the passengers' luggage.* ♦ *The teenagers had a detectable odor of cigarette smoke about them.*

detection [dɪ 'tɛk ʃən] *n.* noticing someone or something; discovering someone or something. (No plural form in this sense.) ♦ *A device for smoke detection is essential for every home.* ♦ *The FBI agent took credit for the detection of the crime.*

detective [dɪ 'tɛk tɪv] *n.* a police officer or other licensed person who searches for information about crimes. ♦ *The police recruit wanted to become a detective.* ♦ *The detective specialized in missing-persons cases.*

detector [dɪ 'tɛk tɚ] *n.* something that detects something. ♦ *The family woke up when the smoke detector sounded an alarm.* ♦ *The metal detector buzzed when I walked through it.*

detention [dɪ 'tɛn ʃən] *n.* keeping someone from leaving; keeping someone in [police] custody. (No plural form in this sense.) ♦ *Jane threatened to sue the officer for her unlawful detention.* ♦ *The political dissident was starved during his detention.*

deter [dɪ 'tɚ] *tv.* to stop someone from doing something; to prevent someone from doing something. ♦ *The light rain did not deter the children from playing outside.* ♦ *Road work will deter drivers from taking that route.*

detergent [dɪ 'tɚ dʒənt] *n.* a product used for cleaning clothes and dishes. (Unlike soap, **detergent** is not fat based. No plural form in this sense.) ♦ *Bill used some strong detergent to clean the dirty work clothes.* ♦ *I forgot to put detergent in the dishwasher before starting it.*

deteriorate [dɪ 'tɪr i ə ret] *iv.* to decline; to fall apart; to worsen. ♦ *The old wooden fence is deteriorating.* ♦ *People's health often deteriorates as they grow older.*

deteriorating [dɪ 'tɪr i ə ret ɪŋ] **1.** *adj.* falling apart; losing strength or health; losing quality. (Adv: *deterioratingly.*) ♦ *I was saddened by my parents' deteriorating relationship.* ♦ *The deteriorating bridge worried the engineers.* **2.** *adj.* causing deterioration. ♦ *Wind and rain served as deteriorating forces in the erosion of the mountain.* ♦ *The deteriorating rays of the sun caused the drapes to fall apart.*

deterioration [dɪ tɪr i ə 're ʃən] **1.** *n.* falling apart; becoming worn or damaged; declining in strength, quality, or condition. (No plural form in this sense.) ♦ *After your caustic remarks, the deterioration of our friendship is inevitable.* ♦ *The deterioration of our national parks is cause for alarm.* **2.** *n.* evidence of ①; the effects of ①. (No plural form in this sense.) ♦ *See this deterioration on the corner? It is caused by rust.* ♦ *The engineer found deterioration in several areas of the bridge.*

determination [dɪ tɚ mɪ 'ne ʃən] **1.** *n.* a strong will to do something. (No plural form in this sense.) ♦ *Jane's determination to overcome her handicap was an inspiration to everyone on the team.* ♦ *A baby's determination to walk overcomes many bumps and bruises.* **2.** *n.* findings; ascertainment. ♦ *The committee's determinations will be published in the local newspaper.* ♦ *The mayor must make a determination about the possibility of building a factory here.*

determine [dɪ 'tɚ mɪn] *tv.* to figure something out; to ascertain something. ♦ *The coroner determined the cause of death.* ♦ *Anne has determined that she will win the election.*

determined [dɪ 'tɚ mɪnd] **1.** *adj.* intending to do something; driven to do something; having the will to do something. (Adv: *determinedly.*) ♦ *The determined college graduate applied for every job she could.* ♦ *The fence did not stop the determined dog from escaping.* **2. determined to** *adj.* + *inf.* intent, eager, and willful to do something. ♦ *Bob was determined to break his smoking habit.* ♦ *Anne is determined to finish the project by noon.*

determining [dɪ 'tɚ mɪn ɪŋ] *adj.* deciding; resolving. ♦ *The vice president cast the determining vote on the Senate bill.* ♦ *Mosquitos were a determining factor in canceling the picnic.*

deterrent [dɪ 'tɚ ənt] *n.* something that keeps someone or something from doing something; something that encourages someone or something not to do something. ♦ *Thoughts of his parents' anger served as a strong deterrent when Mike considered misbehaving.* ♦ *The forecast of rain was a deterrent to our attendance at the outdoor concert.*

detest [dɪ 'tɛst] *tv.* to hate someone or something very much. ♦ *The students detested the bully in their class.* ♦ *My children detest onions.*

detestable [dɪ 'tɛst ə bəl] *adj.* worthy of hatred; deserving hatred. (Adv: *detestably.*) ♦ *I find green beans to be a detestable vegetable.* ♦ *The citizens protested the police officer's detestable behavior.*

dethrone [di 'θron] *tv.* to remove someone from dominance or power, especially a king or queen. ♦ *The soldiers dethroned the king and queen by force.* ♦ *The young tennis player dethroned the reigning champion.*

detonate ['dɛt ə net] **1.** *tv.* to set off a bomb; to cause something to explode. ♦ *The engineer detonated the charge that demolished the old building.* ♦ *The terrorist detonated a bomb on the bus.* **2.** *iv.* to explode. ♦ *The bomb never detonated. It was a dud.* ♦ *A fire caused the fireworks to detonate.*

detonation [dɛt ə 'ne ʃən] *n.* causing something to explode. (No plural form in this sense.) ♦ *The soldier disconnected the bomb before detonation could take place.* ♦ *The detonation of the bomb was triggered by a timer.*

detour ['di tu ɚ] **1.** *n.* an alternate route, taken to avoid someone or something. ♦ *The detour sent Jane ten miles out of her way.* ♦ *Bill took a detour through the office to avoid his boss.* **2.** *iv.* to use ①; to travel the long way around something. ♦ *To avoid the traffic, Jane detoured around the town.* ♦ *The construction was minor and did not require anyone to detour.*

detract [dɪ 'trækt] *iv.* to lessen the importance of something. ♦ *Bad weather detracted from the wedding.* ♦ *Their argument detracted from the otherwise pleasant conversation.*

detractor [dɪ 'træk tɚ] *n.* someone who criticizes, ridicules, or heckles. ♦ *The speaker asked the detractors to leave.* ♦ *The popular author responded to her detractors and her admirers.*

detriment ['dɛ trə mənt] **1.** *n.* damage; harm. (No plural form in this sense.) ♦ *Your actions have caused great detriment to the project.* ♦ *The detriment caused by your thoughtless remark will never be forgotten.* **2.** *n.* something that causes damage or harm. ♦ *The stockbroker's trading practices were a detriment to the firm.* ♦ *The jokes were a detriment to the serious speech.*

detrimental [dɛ trə 'mɛn təl] *adj.* damaging; harmful. (Adv: *detrimentally.*) ♦ *The detrimental newspaper article may lead to a lawsuit.* ♦ *Smoking cigarettes is detrimental to your health.*

deuce ['dus] *n.* a playing card with two hearts, clubs, diamonds, or spades; the side of a die with two spots on it. ♦ *There are four deuces in a deck of cards.* ♦ *Bill rolled the dice and got a deuce and a five.*

devaluation [di væl ju 'e ʃən] *n.* a reduction in the value of something. (No plural form in this sense.) ♦ *Rumors of the devaluation of the dollar scared the investors.* ♦ *The devaluation of the company prompted me to sell all of my stocks.*

devalue [di 'væl ju] *tv.* to reduce the value of something. ♦ *Poor monetary policies eventually devalued the currency.* ♦ *The antique table was devalued by the scratches in its top.*

devastate ['dɛv ə stet] **1.** *tv.* to ruin something. ♦ *The flood devastated the house.* ♦ *A malpractice case devastated the doctor's career.* **2.** *tv.* to cause emotional distress to someone. (Figurative on ①.) ♦ *The loss of her family devastated Mary.* ♦ *The news of the fire devastated John.*

devastated ['dɛv ə stet ɪd] **1.** *adj.* destroyed; ruined. ♦ *It will take years to restore the devastated forest.* ♦ *Bill tried to reconstruct his devastated career.* **2.** *adj.* emotionally crushed; overwhelmed with misfortune. (Adv: *devastatedly.*) ♦ *The devastated owner picked through the rubble of the house.* ♦ *The devastated little boy was orphaned during the war.*

devastating ['dɛv ə stet ɪŋ] **1.** *adj.* destructive; causing great damage. (Adv: *devastatingly.*) ♦ *The devastating winds damaged the house.* ♦ *The detective made a devastating revelation about the suspect.* **2.** *adj.* overwhelming and effective. (Figurative on ①. Adv: *devastatingly.*) ♦ *The actress is known for her devastating beauty.* ♦ *A single devastating look in Tom's direction made him stop.*

develop [dɪ 'vɛl əp] **1.** *tv.* to create something and attempt to cause it to flourish. ♦ *Tom and Mary developed their relationship slowly.* ♦ *The committee developed a plan for a new product.* **2.** *tv.* to cause images to appear on exposed photographic film through chemical processes. ♦ *The photographic laboratory will develop the film today.* ♦ *Special chemicals are needed to develop film.* **3.** *tv.* [for someone or some creature] to begin to show signs of something or experience something. ♦ *I will develop a headache if it gets too hot.* ♦ *Mary developed an allergy to dogs.* **4.** *tv.* to build houses, buildings, and stores on empty land. ♦ *An investor is developing a strip mall near my house.* ♦ *The realty company developed thousands of acres of farmland.* **5.** *iv.* to grow and mature. ♦ *As the tree developed, its growing roots cracked the sidewalk.* ♦ *The polite child developed into a thoughtful teenager.* **6.** *iv.* to grow and prosper; to strengthen; to mature. ♦ *With careful planning, the business continued to develop.* ♦ *My creativity developed in art class.*

developed [dɪ 'vɛl əpt] *adj.* built up; having houses and buildings. ♦ *The developed areas along the river often flooded.* ♦ *Once an open prairie, the developed land was now full of houses and offices.*

developer [dɪ 'vɛl əp ɚ] **1.** *n.* a chemical used to process photographic film. (No plural form in this sense.) ♦ *I wore gloves while handling developer.* ♦ *Jane bought some developer for her photographic studio.* **2.** *n.* someone who builds houses, stores, or other buildings on large areas of land. ♦ *The developer paid dearly for the vacant lot in the middle of town.* ♦ *The developer transformed the farmland into a subdivision.*

development [dɪ 'vɛl əp mənt] **1.** *n.* a stage in the process of something developing. (No plural form in this sense.) ♦ *The illness arrested the child's development.* ♦ *The teacher encouraged the child's artistic development.* **2.** *n.* one or more buildings built on a large area of empty land. ♦ *The housing development was approved by the city council.* ♦ *The development was intended for people with low incomes.* **3.** *n.* a recent change in a situation, particularly a newsworthy situation. ♦ *The new development was supposed to be classified information.* ♦ *Reporters gathered at city hall to hear the latest developments in the scandal.*

deviate ['div i et] **deviate from** *iv.* + *prep. phr.* to be different from normal; to turn aside from the standard path. ♦ *I do not like to deviate from the set schedule.* ♦ *The manager deviated from the company's policy.*

deviation [div i 'e ʃən] *n.* a difference from what is expected; the degree of difference from what is expected. ♦ *No one noticed the small deviations from the pattern.* ♦ *The deviation from his schedule upset and confused Bob.*

device [dɪ 'vɑɪs] **1.** *n.* a tool or apparatus. ♦ *This device will hold the loose piece in place.* ♦ *Dave bought a special device to peel potatoes.* **2.** *n.* an element in a story or narrative. ♦ *The use of a fairy in the story to deliver the good* *news is an interesting device, but not very realistic.* ♦ *The flashback is a useful literary device.*

devil ['dɛv əl] **1.** *n.* an evil spirit; a demon. ♦ *One ancient culture had a ritual to drive away devils.* ♦ *The chant was supposed to rid the room of devils.* **2.** *n.* Satan; the supreme spirit of evil. (Sometimes capitalized.) ♦ *The sinner believed he was being tempted by the Devil.* ♦ *The cult claims to worship the devil.* **3.** *n.* someone who is mischievous. ♦ *Our youngest son is a little devil and always in trouble.* ♦ *"You're a devil, Bob!" Mary said when he tricked her.* **4. speak of the devil** *idiom* <a phrase said when someone whose name has just been mentioned appears or is heard from.> ♦ *Well, speak of the devil! Hello, Tom. We were just talking about you.* ♦ *I had just mentioned Sally, when—speak of the devil—she walked in the door.*

devilish ['dɛv ə lɪʃ] **1.** *adj.* impish; mischievous. (Adv: *devilishly.*) ♦ *A clever prank was planned by the devilish teenager.* ♦ *Bill's devilish response to the question was greeted with laughter.* **2.** *adj.* like the devil; evil; diabolical. (Adv: *devilishly.*) ♦ *The villain hatched the devilish plot.* ♦ *The committee called the censored book devilish.*

devious ['div i əs] *adj.* crafty; scheming; not straightforward. (Adv: *deviously.*) ♦ *We concocted a devious plan to trick Max.* ♦ *A devious crook swindled the old couple.*

devise [dɪ 'vaɪz] *tv.* to create or invent something. ♦ *The inventor devised a new gadget for squeezing oranges.* ♦ *The student devised a way to skip class without being caught.*

devitalize [di 'vaɪt ə laɪz] *tv.* to weaken someone or something; to take away the vitality of someone or something. ♦ *Anne's long illness devitalized her and left her disabled.* ♦ *Bob was afraid that the diet would devitalize him and leave him weak.*

devoid [dɪ 'vɔɪd] **devoid of** *adj.* + *prep. phr.* completely without something. ♦ *The mean teacher was devoid of any compassion.* ♦ *The hot air was devoid of even the slightest amount of moisture.*

devote [dɪ 'vot] **1. devote to** *tv.* + *prep. phr.* to allot something to something. ♦ *Sally devoted an extra hour to completing the project.* ♦ *Mike devotes his time to fixing up his house.* **2. devote to** *tv.* + *prep. phr.* to pledge oneself to someone or something. ♦ *The parents devoted themselves to their children.* ♦ *The farmer was devoted to conservation.*

devoted [dɪ 'vot ɪd] *adj.* pledged or loyal to someone or something. (Adv: *devotedly.*) ♦ *The devoted employee never missed a meeting.* ♦ *Mary is a devoted member of her church.*

devotee [dɛv o 'ti] *n.* a fan of someone or something. ♦ *Lisa is a devotee of rock groups and owns many albums.* ♦ *Ever since he went to his first baseball game, Bob has been a devotee of baseball.*

devotion [dɪ 'vo ʃən] **1.** *n.* loyalty; religious attention. (No plural form in this sense.) ♦ *Is it true that dogs show strong devotion to their masters?* ♦ *Anne says her prayers with great devotion.* **2.** *n.* a prayer; a meditation. ♦ *The book was a collection of daily devotions.* ♦ *A local minister led the devotions at the meeting.*

devour [dɪ 'vaʊ ɚ] **1.** *tv.* to eat something quickly and completely. ♦ *The starving animal devoured the food in the garbage can.* ♦ *Halfway up the mountain, the hungry hikers devoured their sandwiches.* **2.** *tv.* to encompass and destroy something. (Figurative on ①.) ♦ *If it's not stopped, the fire will devour the forest.* ♦ *The windswept waves devoured the pier, crashing it against the shore.* **3.** *tv.* to read or learn something voraciously. (Figurative on ①.) ♦ *The student devoured the text on astronomy.* ♦ *Anne sat on the bench with a book and devoured poem after poem.*

devout [dɪ 'vaʊt] **1.** *adj.* actively religious; prayerful; reverent. (Adv: *devoutly.*) ♦ *The devout worshiper attended church each week.* ♦ *The members of the minister's family are all very devout.* **2.** *adj.* sincere; deeply committed. (Figurative on ①. Adv: *devoutly.*) ♦ *Bill is a devout believer in exercise.* ♦ *Max, a devout reader, loves mystery novels.* **3. the devout** *n.* religious people. (No plural form in this sense. Treated as plural.) ♦ *This prayer book is written for the devout.* ♦ *The minister addressed the devout.*

dew ['du] *n.* droplets of water condensed from cooling air. (No plural form in this sense.) ♦ *In the morning, the dew covered the car.* ♦ *The only water the flowers got was the dew.*

dewdrop ['du drɑp] *n.* a droplet of dew. ♦ *The dewdrops slid down the windshield when I started the car.* ♦ *The flower's petals were weighted down with the heavy dewdrops.*

dewy ['du i] *adj.* covered with dew; wet with dew. (Comp: *dewier;* sup: *dewiest.*) ♦ *The children had fun sliding on the dewy grass.* ♦ *I picked a dewy flower and shook off the moisture.*

dexterity [dɛk 'stɛr ə ti] *n.* skill, especially the skillfulness of one's hands. (No plural form in this sense.) ♦ *The artisan's skill and dexterity amazed us.* ♦ *Mary's hands flew with great dexterity over the piano keys.*

diabetes [daɪ ə 'bit ɪs] *n.* a disease where there is too much sugar in the blood and urine. (Treated as singular.) ♦ *Lisa had to take insulin for her diabetes.* ♦ *The benefit will raise money to do research on the causes of diabetes.*

diabetic [daɪ ə 'bɛt ɪk] **1.** *adj.* having diabetes. (Adv: *diabetically* [...ɪk li].) ♦ *Diabetic people must watch their diet carefully.* ♦ *The sick child was diagnosed as being diabetic.* **2.** *adj.* of, for, or about diabetes; caused by diabetes. (Adv: *diabetically* [...ɪk li].) ♦ *Bill has a diabetic condition.* ♦ *There are many new diabetic medicines available now.* **3.** *n.* someone who has diabetes. ♦ *Every day, the diabetic had to have a shot of insulin.* ♦ *The doctor ordered the diabetic to follow a special diet.*

diabolic [daɪ ə 'bɑl ɪk] *adj.* devilish; like the devil. (Adv: *diabolically* [...ɪk li].) ♦ *The diabolic plot to kidnap the queen was discovered in time.* ♦ *When Tom found out about the diabolic attempt to spoil the fireworks show, he warned the police.*

diabolical [daɪ ə 'bɑl ɪ kəl] *adj.* devilish; like the devil. (Adv: *diabolically* [...ɪk li].) ♦ *The diabolical teenager was well known by the police.* ♦ *The burglar concocted a diabolical plan to rob the museum.*

diagnose ['daɪ əg nos] **1.** *tv.* to identify a disease in an organism; to determine the nature and cause of symptoms of illness. ♦ *A pathologist diagnosed the fatal virus.* ♦ *The tumor was diagnosed as malignant.* **2.** *tv.* to determine the cause of a problem. ♦ *The mechanic diagnosed the cause of the engine's failure.* ♦ *The manager diagnosed the cause of the low morale among the workers.*

diagnoses [dɑɪ əg 'no siz] pl of **diagnosis**.

diagnosis [dɑɪ əg 'no sɪs] **1.** *n.* finding the identity of a problem, especially a disease. (No plural form in this sense.) ♦ *The diagnosis of this illness will require more blood tests.* ♦ *Dr. Jones is very skilled at diagnosis.* **2.** *n., irreg.* a decision, reached through ①, about the nature or identity of a problem, especially a disease; a statement of what has caused a disease or condition. (Pl: **diagnoses**.) ♦ *More blood tests were needed to reach a diagnosis.* ♦ *We were very confused after the two doctors gave us two different diagnoses.*

diagnostic [dɑɪ əg 'nɑs tɪk] *adj.* of or about a diagnosis or diagnosing. (Adv: *diagnostically* [...ɪk li].) ♦ *Mike was sent to the hospital for diagnostic tests.* ♦ *The patient questioned the pathologist's diagnostic report.*

diagonal [dɑɪ 'æg ə nəl] **1.** *adj.* at an angle, but not perpendicular. (Adv: *diagonally.*) ♦ *Draw a diagonal line from one corner to another.* ♦ *The wood has a diagonal grain.* **2.** *n.* a line that goes from one corner of a four-sided figure to the opposite corner. ♦ *A rectangle can be divided into two symmetrical triangles by drawing a diagonal.* ♦ *A diagonal splits the square into two triangles.*

diagram ['dɑɪ ə græm] **1.** *n.* a drawing that helps explain something. ♦ *A good diagram helped me assemble the bike.* ♦ *The tourist looked at a diagram of the subway system.* **2.** *tv.* to make a drawing to help explain something. ♦ *The football coach diagramed the play for the offense.* ♦ *The mechanic diagramed how a piston works.* **3.** *tv.* to make a drawing that shows the relationships between the parts of a sentence. ♦ *The teacher asked the students to diagram several sentences.* ♦ *To diagram a sentence, you must understand grammar.*

dial ['dɑɪl] **1.** *n.* a rotating control knob that controls some electronic device, usually the tuning of a radio. ♦ *Mary turned the dial to get another station.* ♦ *The radio dial has lighted numbers and letters.* **2.** *n.* the rotary wheel on an older telephone that is turned in order to make a telephone call. ♦ *Telephones with dials are almost obsolete.* ♦ *Anne used the end of a pencil to turn the telephone's dial.* **3.** *n.* the part of a watch or a clock that has the numbers on it; the face of a watch or clock. ♦ *The watch is worthless because the dial is rusty.* ♦ *The dial of the watch has Roman numerals on it.* **4. dial tone** *n.* the sound heard when one picks up a telephone receiver, indicating that a telephone call can be made. ♦ *This phone must be out of order, because there is no dial tone.* ♦ *Sometimes a dial tone can be heard if the telephone receiver has not been properly replaced.* **5.** *tv.* to place a telephone call by rotating the dial of a telephone or pushing the buttons of a touch-tone telephone. ♦ *I have to dial the office to get my messages.* ♦ *The lonely college student dialed his parents.* **6.** *iv.* to operate a telephone by turning a wheel or pushing buttons. ♦ *I dialed several times, but I got a busy signal each time.* ♦ *I put money into the pay phone before I dialed.*

dialect ['dɑɪ ə lɛkt] *n.* a variety of a language. ♦ *John's Southern dialect is hard for me to understand.* ♦ *My grandfather spoke a rural Greek dialect.*

dialogue AND **dialog** ['dɑɪ ə lɔg] **1.** *n.* speech between two or more people. (No plural form in this sense.) ♦ *The students overheard the dialogue between the principal and the teacher.* ♦ *The entire play consisted of dialogue and no movement.* **2.** *n.* a discussion between two or more people who express differences of opinion. ♦ *The religious leaders of different faiths began a dialogue.* ♦ *The political dialogue between the candidates has grown heated.*

diameter [dɑɪ 'æm ɪt ɚ] *n.* the length of a straight line going through the center of a circle. ♦ *The students had to calculate the diameter of the circle.* ♦ *The diameter of the pipe is three inches.*

diamond ['dɑɪ (ə) mənd] **1.** *n.* an equilateral four-sided figure viewed standing on one of its points. ♦ *The infield in baseball is shaped like a diamond.* ♦ *The window in the front door was a diamond.* **2.** *n.* a playing card that has one or more **diamond** ① shapes on it. ♦ *A diamond is printed in red.* ♦ *In bridge, diamonds are a minor suit.* **3.** *n.* a clear gemstone formed from crystallized carbon. ♦ *My engagement ring had three small diamonds.* ♦ *A diamond can cut glass.* **4.** *n.* [in baseball] the space bounded by the three bases and home plate. ♦ *The pitcher stands in the middle of the baseball diamond.* ♦ *The players slowly walked out to the diamond to take their positions.*

diaper ['dɑɪp ɚ] **1.** *n.* a piece of cloth or other fiber that a baby wears between its legs before the baby has learned to use a toilet. ♦ *The baby's diaper needed to be changed.* ♦ *Many people now use disposable diapers instead of cloth ones.* **2.** *tv.* to put ① on a baby. ♦ *The babysitter diapered the infant.* ♦ *The new father quickly learned to diaper the baby.*

diaphragm ['dɑɪ ə fræm] **1.** *n.* a large, flat muscle separating the chest cavity from the abdomen, used to help expand the lungs and control breathing. ♦ *Your diaphragm expands and contracts every time you breathe.* ♦ *The biology students identified the diaphragm on the sketch.* **2.** *n.* a membrane or rigid disk used to transmit sound waves to or from telephones and to microphones. ♦ *When a person speaks into the telephone, the diaphragm vibrates, transmitting the voice.* ♦ *If the diaphragm breaks, the microphone will not work.* **3.** *n.* a birth-control device that is placed over the opening of the uterus. ♦ *Since the couple did not want children now, the doctor recommended a diaphragm.* ♦ *The diaphragm has a good record for accuracy in preventing pregnancy.*

diarrhea [dɑɪ ə 'ri ə] *n.* liquid **stool** ②; runny bowel movements. (No plural form in this sense.) ♦ *The baby's diarrhea leaked out of the diaper.* ♦ *Food poisoning caused Lisa's diarrhea.*

diary ['dɑɪ ri] *n.* a journal; a book in which one records the events in one's life. ♦ *A diary is a very personal book.* ♦ *Each evening, Susan wrote something in her diary.*

diatribe ['dɑɪ ə trɑɪb] *n.* an angry, lengthy criticism. ♦ *Susie ignored her mother's long diatribe.* ♦ *Our neighbor gave us a diatribe about dogs roaming the neighborhood.*

dice ['dɑɪs] **1.** pl of **die** ⑤. **2.** *tv.* to chop a food up into tiny cubes. ♦ *The cook diced the potatoes and then fried them.* ♦ *I diced the onions and added them to the salad.*

dichotomy [dɑɪ 'kɑt ə mi] *n.* a division of something into two parts. (No plural form in this sense.) ♦ *Human beings can be split into a dichotomy of females and males.* ♦ *The two characters in the play formed an interesting dichotomy. One was kind and the other was mean.*

dicker ['dɪk ɚ] *iv.* to argue over the price of something with someone. ♦ *When I go to garage sales, I love to dicker.* ♦ *Even millionaires sometimes dicker over prices.*

dictate ['dɪk tet] **1. dictates** *n.* directions; orders that must be obeyed. ♦ *People should follow the dictates of their own consciences.* ♦ *The soldier followed the dictates of the commanding officer without question.* **2.** *tv.* to determine the outcome of some process. ♦ *The weather will dictate what we do on the weekend.* ♦ *The absence of the star basketball player dictated the outcome of the game.* **3.** *tv.* to speak a message that is recorded in shorthand or electronically for later transcription. ♦ *Mary prefers to dictate her memos to her secretary.* ♦ *The manager dictated the letter into the tape recorder.* **4.** *iv.* to say something that is being recorded for later transcription. ♦ *Since my boss doesn't like to type, she dictates.* ♦ *As David dictated, the stenographer wrote furiously.*

dictation [dɪk 'te ʃən] **1.** *n.* speaking something aloud for someone to write down or type, as for students to write down as a classroom exercise or for a secretary to type on a typewriter or computer. (The speech is sometimes recorded and then transcribed later. No plural form in this sense.) ♦ *The teacher uses dictation to teach listening skills.* ♦ *My boss does not like dictation and prefers to type his own letters.* **2.** *n.* the words that are spoken, recorded, or transcribed as in ①. (No plural form in this sense.) ♦ *I must type all of this dictation before I can go home.* ♦ *The secretary was unable to transcribe the dictation before 5:00.*

dictator ['dɪk tet ɚ] *n.* a tyrant; a ruler who has absolute authority and power. ♦ *The dictator and his allies crushed the struggling democracy.* ♦ *The coup against the dictator failed, and rebels were executed.*

dictatorship [dɪk 'tet ɚ ʃɪp] *n.* a government run by a dictator; a government where one person has absolute authority and power. ♦ *The general seized power and established a dictatorship.* ♦ *No one would speak out against the cruelties of the dictatorship.*

diction ['dɪk ʃən] *n.* the clarity of someone's speech; the way that someone pronounces words. (No plural form in this sense.) ♦ *After Bob lost his two front teeth, his diction was slurred.* ♦ *The actress was proud of her precise diction.*

dictionary ['dɪk ʃə nɛr i] *n.* a book that explains the meanings of words. ♦ *A bilingual dictionary explains what a word in one language means in another language.* ♦ *The dictionary gives the pronunciation for each word.*

did [dɪd] pt of do.

didn't ['dɪd nt] *cont.* "did not." ♦ *Billy didn't want to tell his parents that he broke the window.* ♦ *You washed the dishes last night, didn't you?*

die ['dɑɪ] **1.** *iv.* to stop living; to become dead. (The present participle is spelled dying.) ♦ *Every living thing eventually dies.* ♦ *Each fall, the flowers in our garden die.* **2. die for** *iv. + prep. phr.* to want something very much. (Informal.) ♦ *At the end of the day, Jane was dying for a drink.* ♦ *The busy employee was dying for a vacation.* **3.** *iv.* [for a machine] to stop working. ♦ *The lawn mower died when it ran out of gas.* ♦ *One day, our old car just died.* **4. die out; die down** *iv. + adv.* to fade away. ♦ *As the train pulled away, the shouts of farewells died out.* ♦ *Once the lights were turned off, the children's voices began to die down.* **5.** *n., irreg.* a small cube that has a different number of spots. (Usually from 1 to 6 on each side, used in different games of chance. Pl: dice. Usually plural.) ♦ *Who throws the dice next?* ♦ *To see who goes first in the game, throw one die.* **6.** *n.* a strong metal part used to carve or shape metal or plastic. (Pl: *dies.*) ♦ *This factory makes dies for the plastic industry.* ♦ *That die is used to shape cylinders.*

diehard ['dɑɪ hɑrd] **1.** *n.* a stubborn person; someone who will not yield. ♦ *The diehards refused to leave the ballpark even though it had been raining for two hours.* ♦ *Several diehards refused to sell their houses to the developer.* **2.** *adj.* stubborn; unyielding. ♦ *The ushers had to ask the diehard fan to leave the ballpark.* ♦ *The diehard tax collector refused to believe the couple had paid all their taxes.*

diesel ['di zəl] **1.** *adj.* of or about a type of internal combustion engine where a light fuel oil is ignited in the cylinders by high pressure and heat. (Invented by Rudolf Diesel.) ♦ *The gas station at the corner sells fuel for diesel engines.* ♦ *Diesel trucks are supposed to be more powerful.* **2. diesel (fuel)** *n.* fuel for a diesel ① engine. (No plural form in this sense.) ♦ *The attendant pumped the diesel fuel into the engine.* ♦ *Around here, diesel fuel is cheaper than gasoline.*

diet ['dɑɪ ɪt] **1.** *n.* the food that a person or an animal habitually eats. ♦ *Pizza was the staple of the college student's diet.* ♦ *A rabbit's diet includes grass and leaves.* **2.** *n.* a controlled or prescribed selection of foods. ♦ *The doctor placed the overweight patient on a strict diet.* ♦ *John cheated on his diet by eating ice cream.* **3.** *iv.* to control one's choice of foods for the purpose of losing weight. ♦ *Anne's dieted to restrict her fat intake.* ♦ *Bill was dieting because his clothes no longer fit.*

dietary ['dɑɪ ə tɛr i] *adj.* of or about a diet. (Adv: *dietarily* [dɑɪ ə 'tɛr ə li].) ♦ *The doctor listed a number of dietary restrictions that Max would have to follow.* ♦ *Vitamin tablets are a dietary supplement.*

dietician [dɑɪ ə 'tɪ ʃən] *n.* someone who is trained to select proper foods, especially for hospital patients and growing children. ♦ *A dietician visits the classroom each week to talk about healthy foods.* ♦ *The dietician recommends low-fat foods for heart-attack victims.*

differ ['dɪf ɚ] **1. differ from** *iv. + prep. phr.* to be different from something else. ♦ *Although the chairs look alike, they differ from each other in their construction.* ♦ *High school differs from grade school in many ways.* **2. differ with** *iv. + prep. phr.* to disagree with someone. ♦ *Whatever you say, Mary will differ with you.* ♦ *Children constantly differ with their parents.*

difference ['dɪf (ə) rəns] **1.** *n.* a way that two things or people are not alike. (No plural form in this sense.) ♦ *The differences between a large city and a rural farm area are obvious.* ♦ *The difference between perennials and annuals is that you have to plant annuals every year.* **2.** *n.* the degree to which two things are different. (No plural form in this sense.) ♦ *The difference in the width of the paintings is just two inches.* ♦ *There is only a minor difference in the shades of the color.* **3.** *n.* the amount remaining when one amount is subtracted from another. (No plural form in this sense.) ♦ *After the charges are subtracted, the difference is $10.* ♦ *The difference between ten and eight is two.*

different ['dɪf (ə) rənt] **1.** *adj.* not the same. (Adv: *differently.*) ♦ *The school decided to put the twins in different classrooms.* ♦ *Could I please have a different book? I've read this one already.* **2. different from** *adj. + prep. phr.* not like; not the same. (Also with than. Adv: *differently.*) ♦ *The metric system is different from the measuring system used in the United States.* ♦ *Bill's account of the party was different from Bob's account.*

differential [dɪf ə 'rɛn ʃəl] **1.** *n.* a difference, or the specific amount of difference, between comparable things, especially costs, rates of speed, and other numbered values. ♦ *The price differential is very small, so let's buy the better product.* ♦ *The differential between our salaries accounts for the fact that you can afford a bigger house.* **2.** *n.* a device located where the driveshaft meets the rear axle in a wheeled vehicle. (It allows the wheels to rotate at different speeds when the car turns.) ♦ *As Jane turned the car, she could tell the car's differential wasn't working right.* ♦ *Pretending he knew what he was doing, Dave looked under the car for the differential.*

differentiate [dɪf ə 'rɛn ʃi et] **1.** *tv.* to detect the distinction between two or more things or people. ♦ *Only the parents could differentiate the identical twins.* ♦ *For the geology test, students had to differentiate rock specimens.* **2. differentiate from** *tv.* + *prep. phr.* to make something different from something else. ♦ *Mike scratched a number on his bike to differentiate it from the others.* ♦ *The weight of the material differentiates the winter suit from the summer suit.* **3. differentiate between; differentiate among** *iv.* + *prep. phr.* to show or detect a difference between two or more things or people or among more than two things or people. ♦ *Mary cannot differentiate between honest and dishonest people.* ♦ *Only an expert can differentiate between a fake and a real diamond.*

difficult ['dɪf ə kəlt] *adj.* hard to do; hard to understand. (Adv: *difficultly.*) ♦ *No one could solve the difficult math problem.* ♦ *Juggling objects is difficult for many people.*

difficulty ['dɪf ə kəl ti] **1.** *n.* the quality of being hard to do or understand. (No plural form in this sense.) ♦ *The judges recognized the difficulty of the gymnastic stunt.* ♦ *Sue walked with difficulty after the accident.* **2.** *n.* a problem. ♦ *Call the doctor if you have any difficulties after surgery.* ♦ *Some difficulties are more serious than others.*

diffuse 1. [dɪ 'fjus] *adj.* spread out; not at a single point. (Adv: *diffusely.*) ♦ *A diffuse light spread through the smoky room.* ♦ *The smoke detector detected the diffuse smoke in the air.* **2.** [dɪ 'fjuz] *tv.* to spread someone or something out in every direction. ♦ *The winds diffused the smoke throughout the neighborhood.* ♦ *The air conditioning diffused the odor into all the rooms of the house.* **3. diffuse through** [dɪ 'fjuz 'θru] *iv.* + *prep. phr.* to spread out in every direction through something. ♦ *The smell of the landfill diffused through the town.* ♦ *The sunlight diffused through the clouds.*

dig ['dɪg] *tv., irreg.* to make a hole or other depression in something by removing part of it, as with removing soil with a shovel. (Pt/pp: dug.) ♦ *The gardener dug a hole for the new tree.* ♦ *Dave will dig a hole in the backyard for the new tree.*

digest 1. ['dɑɪ dʒɛst] *n.* a short version of a long piece of writing; a summary or a collection of summaries. ♦ *The digest contained summaries of the articles.* ♦ *The movie digest told about new films.* **2.** [dɪ 'dʒɛst] *tv.* to dissolve food in the stomach so that it can be changed into a form that will give nourishment to the rest of the body. ♦ *Some people are unable to digest milk products.* ♦ *Bill felt better after his food had been digested.* **3.** [dɪ 'dʒɛst] *tv.* to absorb thoughts into the mind; to think about something very deeply and incorporate it into one's thoughts. (Figurative on ②.) ♦ *Before I form my opinion, let me digest your arguments.* ♦ *Bob digested the difficult article slowly.*

digestible [dɪ 'dʒɛs tɪ bəl] *adj.* able to be digested. (Adv: *digestibly.*) ♦ *For many people, milk is not digestible.* ♦ *Is chewing gum digestible?*

digestion [dɪ 'dʒɛs tʃən] *n.* the process of breaking down food in the stomach so that it can be changed into a form that will give nourishment to the rest of the body. (No plural form in this sense.) ♦ *We studied digestion in our biology class.* ♦ *Chewing your food well will aid your digestion.*

digestive [dɪ 'dʒɛs tɪv] *adj.* of or about digestion. (Adv: *digestively.*) ♦ *The doctor suspected a problem with the patient's digestive system.* ♦ *The students learned how digestive enzymes break food down.*

digit ['dɪdʒ ɪt] **1.** *n.* a number from 0 through 9. ♦ *The number 567 has three digits.* ♦ *The number 10 is formed from two digits, one and zero.* **2.** *n.* a finger or a toe. ♦ *Humans have five digits on each hand.* ♦ *The surgeon reattached the digit that had been cut off.*

digital ['dɪdʒ ɪ təl] **1.** *adj.* [of a clock or watch] using numbers rather than hands. (Compare with analog. Adv: *digitally.*) ♦ *A digital clock uses numbers instead of hands to tell the time.* ♦ *I prefer real hands to the symbols on a digital watch.* **2.** *adj.* of or about storing, retrieving, and working with information that is stored electronically using the digits 0 and 1. (Adv: *digitally.*) ♦ *The digital computer revolutionized the way information is processed.* ♦ *Digital memory stores all of its information in patterns of 0s and 1s.*

dignified ['dɪg nə fɑɪd] *adj.* noble; showing decorum. (Adv: *dignifiedly.*) ♦ *Bob gave a dignified response to the insult.* ♦ *The dignified woman did not lose her temper.*

dignify ['dɪg nə fɑɪ] *tv.* to give dignity to someone or something; to make something worthy. ♦ *Mary did not dignify the insult with a response.* ♦ *The president dignified the gathering by giving a short speech.*

dignitary ['dɪg nɪ tɛr i] *n.* an important person; someone who is important; someone who has a high-ranking job or position, especially in politics or religion. ♦ *The foreign dignitary was met at the plane by the vice president.* ♦ *Many dignitaries assembled at the embassy for a reception.*

dignity ['dɪg nə ti] *n.* self-respect; personal worth. (No plural form in this sense.) ♦ *Bill went through hard times, but he never lost his dignity.* ♦ *The black robes of a judge give a look of dignity.*

digress [dɑɪ 'grɛs] *iv.* to stray from the main subject being discussed. ♦ *Mary digressed and forgot what she was originally talking about.* ♦ *Forgetting the purpose of the meeting, Bob digressed, and the audience grew restless.*

digression [dɑɪ 'grɛ ʃən] *n.* an instance of straying from the main subject. ♦ *Bill's digression was more interesting than the actual subject of the lecture.* ♦ *As the attorney's digression continued, the judge warned him to return to the facts.*

dike ['dɑɪk] *n.* a wall that is built to hold back water; a wall that is built to control flooding. ♦ *The town erected* *a dike to protect against flooding.* ♦ *The dike had a small crack in it that no one noticed until water seeped through.*

dilapidated [dɪ 'læp ɪ det ɪd] *adj.* falling apart; falling to pieces. (Adv: *dilapidatedly.*) ♦ *The dilapidated barn had a big hole in the roof.* ♦ *The contractor was ordered to tear down the dilapidated building.*

dilate [dɑɪ 'let] **1.** *tv.* to make something larger; to expand something; to stretch something open further. ♦ *I dilated the opening in the turkey and pushed the stuffing in.* ♦ *The ophthalmologist dilated Mike's eyes by putting drops in them.* **2.** *iv.* to become larger; to expand; to become wider; to be stretched open further. ♦ *The pupils of Bill's eyes dilated when the medicine was applied.* ♦ *The birth canal dilates slowly during labor.*

dilation [dɑɪ 'le ʃən] *n.* expanding, widening, or stretching open further. (No plural form in this sense.) ♦ *The medical students watched with fascination the dilation of the patient's eye.* ♦ *Dilation of the birth canal occurs during labor.*

dilemma [dɪ 'lɛm ə] **1.** *n.* a difficult choice between two options. ♦ *The boss was in a dilemma over the problem.* ♦ *I have the dilemma of choosing a new car or a computer.* **2. on the horns of a dilemma** *idiom* having to decide between two things, people, etc.; balanced between one choice and another. ♦ *Mary found herself on the horns of a dilemma. She didn't know which to choose.* ♦ *I make up my mind easily. I'm not on the horns of a dilemma very often.*

diligence ['dɪl ə dʒəns] *n.* hard work; careful work; the proper attention. (No plural form in this sense.) ♦ *Anne's diligence meant her work was always of the best quality.* ♦ *It required diligence, but the project was finished by Friday.*

diligent ['dɪl ə dʒənt] *adj.* hardworking; industrious; attentive to one's job. (Adv: *diligently.*) ♦ *The diligent bird built a nest in a few hours.* ♦ *The diligent workers finished the project on time.*

dill ['dɪl] *n.* an herb used for flavoring, especially in pickling vegetables. (No plural form in this sense.) ♦ *The sauce had a lot of dill in it.* ♦ *Dill is a member of the carrot family.*

dilly-dally ['dɪl i dæl i] *iv.* to waste time; to dawdle; to loiter. ♦ *We spent the afternoon dilly-dallying in the park.* ♦ *The lazy employee dilly-dallied instead of doing work.*

dilute [dɪ 'lut] **1.** *tv.* to weaken something by the addition of a fluid. ♦ *As the ice melted, it diluted my drink.* ♦ *Water is used to dilute the concentrated detergent.* **2.** *tv.* to make something weaker; to make something less severe. (Figurative on ①.) ♦ *The way you stared at the wall while you spoke diluted the effectiveness of your comments.* ♦ *John's smile and light tone of voice diluted his criticism.*

dim ['dɪm] **1.** *adj.* barely lit; not bright. (Adv: *dimly.* Comp: *dimmer;* sup: *dimmest.*) ♦ *Mike's eyes adjusted to the dim room.* ♦ *It was difficult to find our seats in the dim theater.* **2.** *adj.* vague; unclear in the mind; hard to remember. (Adv: *dimly.* Comp: *dimmer;* sup: *dimmest.*) ♦ *After five years, John only had a dim recollection of the event.* ♦ *I have a dim memory of my grandfather who died many years ago.*

dime ['dɑɪm] *n.* a coin worth 10 U.S. cents. ♦ *The parking meter took nickels, dimes, and quarters.* ♦ *Ten dimes equal one dollar.*

dimension [dɪ 'mɛn ʃən] *n.* the measurement of something in one direction; the length, the width, or the depth of something. ♦ *What are the dimensions of the painting?* ♦ *What is the longest dimension of this room?*

diminish [dɪ 'mɪn ɪʃ] **1.** *tv.* to cause something to become smaller; to cause something to become less important; to reduce something. ♦ *Unexpected expenses diminished the size of my bank account.* ♦ *Adding a patio to the house will diminish the size of your lawn.* **2.** *iv.* to become smaller; to become less important; to decrease. ♦ *After the reorganization, Mike's staff diminished to just two people.* ♦ *The food supply diminished gradually.*

diminutive [dɪ 'mɪn jə tɪv] **1.** *adj.* small; little. (Adv: *diminutively.*) ♦ *Dressed in a suit and tie, the little boy looked like a diminutive man.* ♦ *The child placed the cute, diminutive furniture in the dollhouse.* **2.** *n.* a word or a syllable that indicates smallness or littleness. ♦ *In the word* piglet, let *is the diminutive.* ♦ *Suffixes such as* -let *and* -ette *are diminutives.*

dimple ['dɪm pəl] *n.* a small dent or pucker, especially in the skin of one's cheeks or chin. ♦ *Lisa has one dimple in her left cheek when she smiles.* ♦ *The baby has a dimple in his chin, just like his father.*

dimwit ['dɪm wɪt] *n.* someone who appears to be stupid. ♦ *I felt like a dimwit when I forgot your friend's name.* ♦ *Max was too shy to talk, so people thought he was a dimwit.*

din ['dɪn] *n.* a loud, continuous, annoying noise. (No plural form in this sense.) ♦ *The din of the bowling alley gave me a headache.* ♦ *I couldn't hear over the din of the crowd.*

dine ['dɑɪn] *iv.* to eat a meal, especially to eat dinner. ♦ *I usually dine at 7:00 P.M.* ♦ *The guests at the barbecue dined outdoors.*

diner ['dɑɪn ɚ] **1.** *n.* a restaurant; a small café that serves only food. ♦ *Max and Mike met for lunch at the diner.* ♦ *The diner serves simple food and sandwiches.* **2.** *n.* someone who dines in a restaurant. ♦ *The diner ordered a second cup of coffee.* ♦ *All the diners at the restaurant ordered fish, and the restaurant didn't have enough.*

dinette [dɑɪ 'nɛt] **1.** *n.* a small dining room, usually in or near the kitchen. ♦ *We ate breakfast in the dinette.* ♦ *A dinette is more informal than a dining room.* **2.** *n.* a table and set of chairs used in the kitchen for informal meals. ♦ *The movers placed the dinette near the kitchen window.* ♦ *Our dinette has a wooden tabletop and matching chairs.*

dingy ['dɪn dʒi] *adj.* old-looking; dirty; faded; drab; discolored. (Adv: *dingily.* Comp: *dingier;* sup: *dingiest.*) ♦ *The dog ran off with the dingy sweater that had been thrown out in the garbage.* ♦ *After many washings, the colored shirt looked dingy.*

dining room ['dɑɪn ɪŋ 'rum] *n.* the room of a house or a building, where meals are served. ♦ *Our house does not have a dining room, so we eat in the kitchen.* ♦ *A beautiful chandelier hung over the table in the dining room.*

dinner ['dɪn ɚ] **1.** *n.* the main meal of the day; either a large midday meal or a large evening meal. ♦ *Since Mike works in the evenings, he eats his dinner at noon.* ♦ *Dinner is served at 6 P.M. in my dormitory.* **2.** *n.* a formal event where an evening meal is served. ♦ *The company held a* *dinner in honor of the retiring president.* ♦ *Many rich donors attended the museum's annual dinner.*

dinosaur ['daɪn ə sor] *n.* a large, prehistoric reptile that is now extinct. ♦ *A dinosaur's skeleton was displayed in the museum's main hall.* ♦ *The young students were fascinated by dinosaurs.*

dip ['dɪp] **1.** *n.* an abrupt downward slope. ♦ *The dip in the path caught me by surprise, and I fell off my bike.* ♦ *The ball gained speed as it rolled down the dip in the driveway.* **2.** *n.* a quick plunge into water or other liquid; a quick swim in water. ♦ *The dog took a dip in the pool.* ♦ *After work, Mary likes to take a quick dip in the lake.* **3.** *n.* a creamy mixture of foods or a thick, often tomato-based sauce that is eaten with crackers, potato chips, or vegetables. (The crackers, potato chips, or vegetables are dipped into ④ it. No plural form in this sense.) ♦ *Dip is sometimes made with sour cream or mayonnaise.* ♦ *We served vegetables and dip at the party.* **4. dip in(to)** *tv.* + *prep. phr.* to put something in a liquid and pull it right back out. ♦ *As he washed the windows, Bill dipped the sponge in the water several times.* ♦ *Anne dipped her toe in the cold water.* **5.** *tv.* to lower and raise something quickly. ♦ *The plane dipped its wing as it flew over.* ♦ *The marchers dipped the flag as a salute when they passed the president.* **6.** *iv.* to move downward; to go downward. ♦ *The driveway dips toward the garage.* ♦ *The company's profits dipped last quarter.*

diphtheria ['dɪf 'θɪr i ə] *n.* a type of severe, contagious throat infection. (No plural form in this sense.) ♦ *Outbreaks of diphtheria used to kill many people.* ♦ *There is a vaccination to prevent diphtheria.*

diphthong ['dɪf θɔŋ] *n.* a vowel sound that starts with one vowel sound and ends with another. ♦ *In* house, *the diphthong is* ou. ♦ *The* o *and* y *form a diphthong in the word* toy.

diploma [dɪ 'plom ə] *n.* a certificate of graduation from a school or college. ♦ *Jane framed her college diploma and hung it on the wall in her office.* ♦ *The graduate clutched his diploma after the ceremony.*

diplomacy [dɪ 'plom ə si] **1.** *n.* tact; skill used in dealing with people. (No plural form in this sense.) ♦ *The clerk spoke with diplomacy to the angry customer.* ♦ *Bill's diplomacy keeps him on good behavior with everybody.* **2.** *n.* the business of maintaining good relationships between countries. (No plural form in this sense.) ♦ *The prime minister is a master at diplomacy.* ♦ *Diplomacy between the two countries is strained.*

diplomat ['dɪp lə mæt] **1.** *n.* an official representative of one country to the government of another country. ♦ *Many diplomats live in Washington, D.C.* ♦ *The diplomats discussed trade regulations.* **2.** *n.* someone who is notably tactful. ♦ *A diplomat was needed to resolve the argument.* ♦ *Acting as the diplomat, Mike discussed the property line with his neighbor.*

diplomatic [dɪp lə 'mæt ɪk] **1.** *adj.* tactful; skilled in dealing with people. (Adv: *diplomatically* [...ɪk li].) ♦ *The president gave a diplomatic response to the question.* ♦ *The manager praised Bill for his diplomatic treatment of customers.* **2.** *adj.* of or about the job of a diplomat. (Adv: *diplomatically* [...ɪk li].) ♦ *The courier put the message in the diplomatic pouch and headed for the consulate.* ♦ *Forgetting his diplomatic duties, the foreign representative stubbornly refused to talk about the tariffs.*

dipper ['dɪp ɚ] *n.* a ladle; a large spoon used to take liquid out of a container. ♦ *Tom drank the well water from a dipper.* ♦ *The cook used a big dipper to scoop the soup out of the kettle.*

dipstick ['dɪp stɪk] *n.* a rod that shows how much oil is in a car engine. ♦ *The mechanic pulled out the dipstick to check the oil.* ♦ *The dipstick indicated that the engine needed oil.*

dire ['daɪr] **1.** *adj.* desperate; extremely urgent; of utmost importance or seriousness. (Adv: *direly.*) ♦ *Jane was in dire need of assistance when her car broke down.* ♦ *The dire circumstances created by the flood caused a lot of anxiety.* **2.** *adj.* negative; warning of future trouble. ♦ *Mary scared Bob with her dire prediction about his future.* ♦ *After the teacher's dire warning, the students studied feverishly for the test.*

direct [dɪ 'rɛkt] **1.** *adj.* going from one place to another place without deviating from the path; going the straightest or shortest way. (Adv: *directly.*) ♦ *I would like to fly to Chicago by the most direct route.* ♦ *Instead of taking the direct route home, Sally drove along country roads.* **2.** *adj.* exact; to the point; forthright. (Adv: *directly.*) ♦ *Jane gave a direct response to a question.* ♦ *The students appreciated the professor's direct comments.* **3.** *adv.* without deviating from a route or path, especially with airplane flights. ♦ *I flew to London direct and arrived in only five hours.* ♦ *We prefer to fly direct in order to save time.* **4.** *tv.* to guide someone or something; to be in charge of someone or something. ♦ *The camp counselors direct programs for the children.* ♦ *The conductor directs the orchestra.* **5. direct to** *tv.* + *inf.* to order someone to do something; to tell someone to do something. ♦ *The manager directed Jane to handle the irate customer.* ♦ *The cop directed us to leave at once.* **6. direct to** *tv.* + *prep. phr.* to tell someone how to get somewhere; to show someone the way to some place; to give someone directions. ♦ *The police officer directed Bill to the post office.* ♦ *The receptionist's job is to direct people to the correct office.* **7. direct at** *tv.* + *prep. phr.* to aim something straight toward someone or something. ♦ *The archer directed the arrow at the target.* ♦ *Don't direct that gun at me!* **8. direct at** *tv.* + *prep. phr.* to say something straight at someone. ♦ *The teacher directed her remarks at the students who cheated on the exam.* ♦ *Trying to reach a wide audience, the minister directs his sermons at everyone.* **9.** *tv.* to establish and oversee the design and execution of a play or a film, particularly overseeing the actor's performances; to instruct actors how to perform in a particular play, opera, film, commercial, etc. ♦ *John directed the play in which Mary Smith played a major role.* ♦ *John hopes to go to Hollywood and direct a movie.*

directing [dɪ 'rɛk tɪŋ] *n.* the activity of leading or managing the performance of musicians or actors. (No plural form in this sense.) ♦ *Many actors move into directing later in their careers.* ♦ *Five people were nominated for their excellence in directing.*

direction [dɪ 'rɛk ʃən] **1.** *n.* the guidance or control of something. (No plural form in this sense.) ♦ *I work under the direction of a manager.* ♦ *The pilot follows the direction of the air-traffic controller.* **2.** *n.* the path taken by something that moves; movement. ♦ *No one knows what direction a ball will take in a pinball machine.* ♦ *The birds all flew in the same direction.* **3.** *n.* the way that someone or something faces: to the north, south, east, west. ♦ *The direction faced by the chapel is east.* ♦ *The compass will show you the right direction.* **4. directions.** *n.* instructions. ♦ *The man stopped to ask for directions to the beach.* ♦ *The directions for assembling the desk were printed on the box.*

directive [dɪ 'rɛk tɪv] *n.* an official order; an official instruction. ♦ *The sergeant received the directive to retreat.* ♦ *The manager sent a directive stating that all employees had to work overtime.*

directly [dɪ 'rɛkt li] *adv.* soon; in a few moments. ♦ *I will be there directly.* ♦ *Mike said he would be off the phone directly.*

direct object [də 'rɛkt 'ɑb dʒɛkt] *n.* a noun, pronoun, or phrase that receives the action of a transitive verb; a noun, pronoun, or phrase on which the verb operates. (In the examples, *flower* is the direct object, and *Mary* is the indirect object.) ♦ *I gave Mary a flower.* ♦ *I gave a flower to Mary.*

director [dɪ 'rɛk tɚ] **1.** *n.* someone who leads a group of musicians as they perform; a conductor; someone who directs ⑨ actors, films, plays, etc. ♦ *Who is the director of this year's student play?* ♦ *The movie director rehearsed the scene twice before filming it.* **2.** *n.* someone who is in charge of an institution, company, school, or department. ♦ *The company director ordered all of the employees to go home.* ♦ *The curriculum director gave a speech at the graduation ceremonies.*

directory [dɪ 'rɛk tə ri] **1.** *n.* a list of names arranged in alphabetical order, usually including addresses and telephone numbers. ♦ *Anne's telephone number was not in the directory.* ♦ *Bill looked up his old college roommate in the alumni directory.* **2.** *n.* any list that shows where to find someone or something. ♦ *I looked at the store directory to find where shoes were located.* ♦ *The video store has a complete directory of its movies.*

dirigible ['dɪr ɪ dʒə bəl] *n.* a type of aircraft that is lighter than air, like a balloon, but can be steered. ♦ *It was once possible to cross the Atlantic Ocean in a dirigible.* ♦ *The balloon part of the dirigible is very big, but the compartment for passengers is very small.*

dirt ['dɚt] **1.** *n.* soil; earth. (No plural form in this sense.) ♦ *The river eroded the dirt along its banks.* ♦ *My children love to dig in dirt and get filthy.* **2.** *n.* filth; debris such as dust, grime, mud. (No plural form in this sense.) ♦ *My car is so covered with dirt that you can't tell what color it is.* ♦ *The air was filled with dirt raised by the construction crew.* **3.** *n.* gossip; news about someone. (Slang. No plural form in this sense.) ♦ *Mary called Bill to get the dirt on Sue.* ♦ *You should know better than to spread dirt about your boss!*

dirty ['dɚt i] **1.** *adj.* not clean. (Adv: *dirtily.* Comp: *dirtier;* sup: *dirtiest.*) ♦ *Bill washed the dirty floor.* ♦ *Near the factory smokestacks, the dirty air smells terrible.* **2.** *adj.* obscene; of or about sex or excrement in a vulgar way. (Adv: *dirtily.* Comp: *dirtier;* sup: *dirtiest.*) ♦ *I did not laugh when I heard the dirty joke.* ♦ *The bar patrons laughed as they told dirty stories.* **3.** *tv.* to cause something to become unclean. ♦ *Driving through the puddle dirtied the car.* ♦ *The dog dirtied the carpet with its muddy paws.*

disability [dɪs ə 'bɪl ə ti] *n.* a physical or mental handicap; an impairment. ♦ *We have insurance that pays money if we develop disabilities.* ♦ *The bus was specially equipped to accommodate passengers with disabilities.*

disable [dɪs 'e bəl] *tv.* to make something not work; to make someone or something powerless. ♦ *The power failure disabled our air conditioning.* ♦ *A severe accident disabled John for a few months.*

disabled [dɪs 'e bəld] **1.** *adj.* made powerless; unable to do something; not functioning. ♦ *The electrician reconnected the disabled power lines.* ♦ *A mechanic was needed to fix the disabled vehicle.* **2. the disabled** *n.* people who have disabilities; people who are unable to do something. (No plural form in this sense. Treated as plural.) ♦ *The ramp accommodates the wheelchairs of the disabled.* ♦ *The bus for the disabled has a wheelchair lift and special seats.*

disabling [dɪs 'eb lɪŋ] *adj.* making someone or something powerless; making someone or something unable to do something. (Adv: *disablingly.*) ♦ *Because of a disabling disease, Mary must use a wheelchair.* ♦ *The disabling power failure brought the commuter trains to a halt.*

disadvantage [dɪs əd 'væn tɪdʒ] *n.* an unfavorable condition; an unfavorable circumstance. ♦ *The child suffered the disadvantage of not having a warm coat.* ♦ *The disadvantages of not having studied became apparent when I took the test.*

disagree [dɪs ə 'gri] **1.** *iv.* not to agree with someone; to have an opinion different from someone else's opinion. ♦ *Mary often disagrees with Bob on political issues.* ♦ *I gave the answer to the question, but Mark disagreed.* **2. disagree with** *iv.* + *prep. phr.* [for food] to cause someone to have an upset stomach. ♦ *Onions disagree with me.* ♦ *The broccoli disagreed with the child.*

disagreeable [dɪs ə 'gri ə bəl] *adj.* not pleasant; unpleasant. (Adv: *disagreeably.*) ♦ *I would have gone to the park if it hadn't been such a disagreeable day.* ♦ *The children avoided their disagreeable neighbor.*

disagreement [dɪs ə 'gri mənt] **1.** *n.* a difference in opinion; a failure to agree. (No plural form in this sense.) ♦ *Bill and Jane were in disagreement over who would prepare dinner.* ♦ *Disagreements can lead to arguments.* **2.** *n.* an argument; a dispute. ♦ *The disagreement ended in a fight.* ♦ *The neighbors had a long-standing disagreement over the boundary line.*

disallow [dɪs ə 'lɑʊ] *tv.* to refuse to allow something; to refuse to allow someone to do something. ♦ *The principal disallowed the students' request for a rally.* ♦ *My employer disallowed some items on my expense report.*

disappear [dɪs ə 'piɚ] **1.** *iv.* to vanish; to cease to appear; to go out of sight. ♦ *One minute the letter was on the desk, and then it just disappeared.* ♦ *I was so embarrassed, I wished I could disappear.* **2.** *iv.* to cease to exist in a place; to be no longer in a place. ♦ *When its funding was cut, the federal program simply disappeared.* ♦ *The food disappeared quickly from the hungry man's plate.*

disappearance [dɪs ə 'piɚ əns] *n.* disappearing; vanishing. ♦ *No one could explain the statue's disappearance from the town square.* ♦ *Bill's sudden disappearance surprised even his closest friends.*

disappearing [dɪs ə 'piɚ ɪŋ] **1.** *adj.* vanishing; going out of sight. ♦ *How did the magician create the illusion of a disappearing rabbit?* ♦ *The spy wrote the secret message in disappearing ink.* **2.** *adj.* becoming nonexistent at a place;

going out of existence at a place. ♦ *The ecologist worried about the disappearing shoreline.* ♦ *The squirrels are responsible for the disappearing birdseed.*

disappoint [dɪs ə 'pɔɪnt] *tv.* to fail to please someone; to make someone unhappy by not doing something that was expected or desired; to make someone unhappy by not being or happening as expected or desired. ♦ *Tom disappointed his parents repeatedly.* ♦ *Sue was disappointed by the cheap gift.*

disappointed [dɪs ə 'pɔɪnt ɪd] *adj.* made unhappy because something did not happen. (Adv: *disappointedly.*) ♦ *The disappointed candidate vowed to run again.* ♦ *A very disappointed child missed the picnic because he had chickenpox.*

disappointing [dɪs ə 'pɔɪnt ɪŋ] *adj.* causing unhappiness; causing dissatisfaction; failing to please. (Adv: *disappointingly.*) ♦ *After the disappointing loss, the team agreed to practice more.* ♦ *I was happy to end the disappointing day.*

disappointment [dɪs ə 'pɔɪnt mənt] **1.** *n.* sorrow; dismay. (No plural form in this sense.) ♦ *Disappointment hung on the children's faces because it was raining outside.* ♦ *Have you recovered from the disappointment of losing the contest?* **2.** *n.* someone or something who causes someone to be disappointed; someone or something who fails to please someone. ♦ *The bland food was a disappointment to the diners.* ♦ *The unfortunate refugees endured one disappointment after another.*

disapproval [dɪs ə 'pruv əl] *n.* rejection; the failure to give approval to someone or something; unfavorable opinion. (No plural form in this sense.) ♦ *Mary married Bob despite her parents' disapproval.* ♦ *Tom could not hide his disapproval of the new manager.*

disapprove [dɪs ə 'pruv] **disapprove (of)** *iv.* (+ *prep. phr.*) to have a bad opinion of someone or something. ♦ *The neighbors disapproved of the city's plans to build a landfill.* ♦ *It is fine with me, but Bill disapproves.*

disarm [dɪs 'ɑrm] **1.** *tv.* to take a weapon away from someone. ♦ *The security guard disarmed the robber.* ♦ *The woman who knew karate disarmed her attacker.* **2.** *tv.* to make someone feel more at ease; to make someone feel less suspicious. ♦ *The thief uses charm to disarm people before swindling them.* ♦ *Mary's pleasant manner disarmed the guests at our table.* **3.** *iv.* [for a country] to reduce or eliminate weapons. ♦ *The countries disarmed according to the treaty.* ♦ *After World War II, a number of countries were forced to disarm.*

disarmament [dɪs 'ɑrm ə mənt] *n.* the reduction or elimination of weapons. (No plural form in this sense.) ♦ *Despite the treaty, disarmament never occurred.* ♦ *Critics of disarmament say we must remain prepared for a conflict.*

disarming [dɪs 'ɑrm ɪŋ] *adj.* putting someone at ease; making someone feel less suspicious. (Adv: *disarmingly.*) ♦ *The child's disarming smile was contagious.* ♦ *The spy's disarming nature earned other people's trust.*

disarray [dɪs ə 're] *n.* disorder. (No plural form in this sense.) ♦ *The student's dormitory room was in disarray after the party.* ♦ *I couldn't find the papers in all the disarray on my desk.*

disassemble [dɪs ə 'sɛm bəl] *tv.* to take something apart piece by piece. ♦ *To fix the refrigerator, I had to disassemble it completely.* ♦ *The curious child disassembled the clock.*

disassociate [dɪs ə 'so ʃi et] **disassociate from** *tv.* + *prep. phr.* to break off relations with someone or something; to avoid someone or something. (See also **dissociate**. Takes a reflexive object.) ♦ *After her disagreement with my brother, Mary disassociated herself from our whole family.* ♦ *When members refused to obey the law, Mike disassociated himself from his gun club.*

disaster [dɪ 'zæs tɚ] *n.* a catastrophe; a terrible misfortune. ♦ *It took a disaster to bring the townspeople together.* ♦ *The month-long period of rain was a disaster for the farmer.*

disastrous [dɪ 'zæs trəs] *adj.* causing disaster; serious and devastating. (Adv: *disastrously.*) ♦ *A few disastrous investments ruined the company.* ♦ *Lisa and Mike decided to rebuild their house after the disastrous fire.*

disband [dɪs 'bænd] **1.** *iv.* [for a group] to break apart; [for a group] to separate. ♦ *The rock group disbanded after its first concert.* ♦ *After graduating, the students went their own way, and the old college gang disbanded.* **2.** *tv.* to break up a group; to separate a group. ♦ *The band leader disbanded the rock band.* ♦ *We were forced to disband the club since we had no place to meet.*

disbar [dɪs 'bɑr] *tv.* to take away the legal right for a lawyer to practice law. ♦ *The judge threatened to disbar the troublesome attorney.* ♦ *After the attorneys ignored the judge's warning, the judge disbarred them.*

disbelief [dɪs bə 'lif] *n.* not believing something; a lack of belief. (No plural form in this sense.) ♦ *Mike asserted his disbelief in the existence of God.* ♦ *Mary looked at me in disbelief when she heard the bad news.*

disburse [dɪs 'bɚs] *tv.* to pay out money. ♦ *On payday, the manager disburses our pay.* ♦ *The government disbursed the tax refunds.*

disc ['dɪsk] See **disk**, **Compact Disc**.

discard 1. ['dɪs kɑrd] *n.* something that is thrown away. ♦ *The discards were put in the trash.* ♦ *We collected old discards to give to charity.* **2.** [dɪ 'skɑrd] *tv.* to throw something away; to throw something out; to get rid of something. ♦ *Bill discarded his torn pants.* ♦ *I tried to discard the old toys, but the children found them and put them back in the toy box.* **3.** [dɪ 'skɑrd] *iv.* [during a card game] to remove from one's hand a card that is not needed. ♦ *Bob could not decide which card to discard.* ♦ *Dave could not play until Lisa had discarded.*

discarded [dɪ 'skɑrd ɪd] *adj.* thrown away; gotten rid of. ♦ *The garbage can overflowed with discarded items.* ♦ *Some money was mistakenly thrown out with the discarded papers.*

discern [dɪ 'sɚn] *tv.* to be able to perceive or distinguish something clearly. ♦ *Bob was able to discern the constellations in the clear night sky.* ♦ *I can't discern the difference between ice cream and frozen yogurt.*

discerning [dɪ 'sɚ nɪŋ] *adj.* discriminating; showing good taste. (Adv: *discerningly.*) ♦ *When it comes to cars, Bob is very discerning.* ♦ *The discerning critic liked the new play.*

discharge 1. ['dɪs tʃɑrdʒ] *n.* the sound of setting off of an explosion; the firing of a gun. ♦ *The discharge of a gun* *startled the quiet neighborhood.* ♦ *A child was wounded by the accidental discharge of the handgun.* **2.** ['dɪs tʃɑrdʒ] *n.* the release of someone or something, especially when this requires official approval. ♦ *The soldier received a discharge from the service.* ♦ *The doctor approved the patient's discharge from the hospital.* **3.** ['dɪs tʃɑrdʒ] *n.* the carrying out of one's duties; the performance of one's duties. (No plural form in this sense.) ♦ *In the military, the proper discharge of one's duties is essential.* ♦ *Our employees' primary concern should be the discharge of their responsibilities.* **4.** ['dɪs tʃɑrdʒ] *n.* giving something off; releasing something. (No plural form in this sense.) ♦ *The discharge of pollutants into the air is illegal.* ♦ *Press the bandage against the wound to stop the discharge of blood.* **5.** ['dɪs tʃɑrdʒ] *n.* something that is given off; something that is let out. ♦ *A poisonous discharge seeped into the river from the pipe.* ♦ *Tears are just a normal discharge from the eye.* **6.** [dɪs 'tʃɑrdʒ] *tv.* to fire an explosive or a gun; to cause an explosion. ♦ *Lisa discharged her gun repeatedly during target practice.* ♦ *The hunter accidentally discharged his gun while cleaning it.* **7.** [dɪs 'tʃɑrdʒ] *tv.* to dismiss someone from employment. ♦ *The company discharged 200 employees to cut costs.* ♦ *The Smiths discharged the butler who had been stealing silverware.* **8.** [dɪs 'tʃɑrdʒ] *tv.* to let something out; to pour something out. ♦ *The mechanic discharged the air from the tire.* ♦ *The engine discharged a stream of oil onto the floor.* **9.** [dɪs 'tʃɑrdʒ] *tv.* to do one's duty; to keep a promise; to repay a debt. ♦ *The mayor discharged his duty to the voters with style and energy.* ♦ *The judge ordered Mike to discharge his debts.*

disciple [dɪ 'sɑɪp əl] *n.* a follower of a teacher; someone who follows the teachings of a great leader. ♦ *The religious disciples preached on the street corner.* ♦ *Jesus had twelve disciples.*

discipline ['dɪs ə plɪn] **1.** *n.* controlled behavior achieved as the result of training; order. (No plural form in this sense.) ♦ *Practicing a musical instrument requires discipline.* ♦ *The soldier lived a life of discipline.* **2.** *n.* a field or branch of learning. ♦ *The scientist's discipline is microbiology.* ♦ *The student chose the discipline of anthropology.* **3.** *tv.* to punish someone. ♦ *The principal disciplined the unruly student.* ♦ *The child was disciplined for telling a lie.* **4.** *tv.* to train someone or something to behave; to train someone or something to be obedient. ♦ *The sergeant disciplined the recruits.* ♦ *We disciplined our children well, and they are very well behaved.*

disc jockey ['dɪsk dʒɑk i] *n.* someone who plays records for a living at a radio station, nightclub, or private parties. (Abbreviated *D.J.* or *deejay.*) ♦ *At our wedding reception, the music was played by a disc jockey.* ♦ *Who is the most popular disc jockey at the radio station?*

disclaim [dɪs 'klem] *tv.* to deny something; to say that one has no responsibility or knowledge of something. ♦ *The suspect disclaimed any knowledge of the bank robbery.* ♦ *Each employee disclaimed responsibility for the mistake.*

disclaimer [dɪs 'klem ɚ] *n.* a statement that denies someone's responsibility for something. ♦ *The manufacturer issued a disclaimer about the alleged product.* ♦ *I read the disclaimer at the bottom of the contract closely.*

disclose [dɪ 'skloz] *tv.* to make something known; to reveal something. ♦ *Mary disclosed her family's private affairs to the press.* ♦ *Some of the candidates will not disclose their income.*

disclosure [dɪ 'kloʒ ɚ] **1.** *n.* making something known; revealing a piece of information. (No plural form in this sense.) ♦ *Full disclosure of the defendant's finances was required by the court.* ♦ *The candidate would not agree to the disclosure of her personal affairs.* **2.** *n.* something that has been made known; a piece of information that has been revealed. ♦ *Mary made a surprise disclosure about her divorce last week.* ♦ *What was the nature of the politician's disclosures to the press conference?*

disco ['dɪs ko] **1.** *n.* a style of popular music in the late 1970s. (No plural form in this sense.) ♦ *I left the dance floor when the disc jockey played disco.* ♦ *When Bill is nostalgic for the 1970s, he listens to disco.* **2.** *n.* a bar where people dance to recorded music instead of live music. (A shortening of *discotheque.* Pl in *-s.*) ♦ *Loud music from the disco could be heard from the street.* ♦ *The teenagers went to the disco to dance.* **3.** *adj.* concerning ①. ♦ *Lisa buys a new disco album every week.* ♦ *My father can't stand disco music.*

discolor [dɪs 'kʌl ɚ] **1.** *tv.* to cause something to change color in a bad way; to make something fade; to stain something. ♦ *The dripping water discolored the paint on the ceiling.* ♦ *Sunlight discolored the curtains.* **2.** *iv.* to change color in a bad way; to fade; to become stained. ♦ *The smoker's teeth discolored.* ♦ *The wallpaper has discolored with age.*

discomfort [dɪs 'kʌm fɚt] **1.** *n.* an uncomfortable feeling; uneasiness. ♦ *Anne felt some discomfort in her legs during the hike.* ♦ *Bill's discomfort was evident from the look on his face.* **2.** *n.* something that causes an uncomfortable feeling. ♦ *A leak in the tent caused serious discomfort to the campers.* ♦ *A soft mattress gives Bill considerable discomfort.*

disconcert [dɪs kən 'sɚt] *tv.* to fluster someone; to cause someone to lose composure. ♦ *The shocking news disconcerted the crowd.* ♦ *The shouting and angry citizens disconcerted the mayor.*

disconcerted [dɪs kən 'sɚt ɪd] *adj.* flustered; upset; having lost composure. (Adv: *disconcertedly.*) ♦ *The frightened baby gave a disconcerted wail.* ♦ *I tried to console the disconcerted family at the funeral.*

disconcerting [dɪs kən 'sɚt ɪŋ] *adj.* flustering; upsetting. (Adv: *disconcertingly.*) ♦ *The malicious rumor was quite disconcerting.* ♦ *Her sudden laughter during the ceremony was disconcerting to those around her.*

disconnect [dɪs kə 'nɛkt] **1.** *tv.* to cause something to be no longer connected; to break a connection. ♦ *An operator accidentally disconnected our phone call.* ♦ *Bill disconnected the modem on his computer.* **2.** *iv.* to hang up a telephone. ♦ *The telephone solicitor disconnected when the answering machine started its announcement.* ♦ *Hanging up the telephone causes the line to disconnect.*

disconnected [dɪs kə 'nɛk tɪd] **1.** *adj.* no longer connected. ♦ *The electrician reattached the disconnected wires.* ♦ *This disconnected speaker is the problem with your stereo system.* **2.** *adj.* unconnected; not flowing from part to part. (Adv: *disconnectedly.*) ♦ *You have presented several disconnected ideas, but we need a coherent report.* ♦ *It was hard to understand Bill's disconnected thoughts.*

discontent [dɪs kən 'tɛnt] *n.* feeling that one is not content; dissatisfaction. (No plural form in this sense.) ♦ *Mary's discontent with her job caused her to quit.* ♦ *Bill expressed his discontent with the product to the manufacturer.*

discontented [dɪs kən 'tɛn tɪd] *adj.* not content; not satisfied; dissatisfied; expressing discontent. (Adv: *discontentedly.*) ♦ *Mary gave a discontented sigh because she was bored.* ♦ *The discontented student hated classes and wanted to quit school.*

discontinue [dɪs kən 'tɪn ju] *tv.* to stop doing or having something. ♦ *The government discontinued its funding of the agency.* ♦ *We discontinued our newspaper subscription.*

discontinued [dɪs kən 'tɪn jud] *adj.* no longer in stock; no longer made. ♦ *The discontinued drug had been found to be dangerous.* ♦ *The parts needed for our car had been discontinued and were not available.*

discord ['dɪs kord] **1.** *n.* disagreement. (No plural form in this sense.) ♦ *Discord threatened to end the harmony in the fraternity.* ♦ *The Senate hearings were marked with discord.* **2.** *n.* musical sounds that are not in harmony. (No plural form in this sense.) ♦ *The modern symphony was filled with discord and strange rhythms.* ♦ *The student band's music was full of discord.*

discordant [dɪs 'kord ənt] **1.** *adj.* [of sounds] not in harmony. (Adv: *discordantly.*) ♦ *The conductor shuddered upon hearing the discordant notes from the violins.* ♦ *The music leaped from one discordant cluster of notes to another.* **2.** *adj.* not in agreement; clashing. (Adv: *discordantly.*) ♦ *John always introduces a discordant element into any discussion. He loves to argue.* ♦ *Discordant voices could be heard from the meeting room.*

discount **1.** ['dɪs kaʊnt] *n.* an amount subtracted from the cost of a product or service; a savings in cost. ♦ *Mary gets an employee discount at the department store.* ♦ *The coupon was good for a twenty-five-cent discount.* **2.** ['dɪs kaʊnt] *tv.* to subtract an amount from the cost of a product or service. ♦ *The clerk discounted the cost of Mary's purchase by 10%.* ♦ *The plumber discounts his rate for friends.* **3.** [dɪs 'kaʊnt] *tv.* to disregard someone or something; to disregard what someone says or does; to not believe something. ♦ *The jury was told to discount the false testimony.* ♦ *I tend to discount anything that Sally says. She exaggerates so much!*

discounted ['dɪs kaʊnt ɪd] **1.** *adj.* [of a price] including a discount. ♦ *The plumber worked at a discounted rate for friends.* ♦ *Since the item was defective, the manager agreed to a discounted price.* **2.** *adj.* [of goods] sold at an amount that is less than what is normally charged. ♦ *The discounted T-shirts were a bargain and sold quickly.* ♦ *The store put a red tag on discounted items.*

discourage [dɪ 'skɚ ɪdʒ] **1.** *tv.* to cause someone to feel dejected; to take away someone's interest or excitement in something. ♦ *Poor grades discouraged the student who had studied very hard.* ♦ *The loss of the game discouraged the whole team.* **2.** *tv.* to try to talk someone out of doing something; to try to persuade someone not to do something. ♦ *The doctor discouraged David from smoking.* ♦ *Bob wanted to swim alone in the lake, but his mother discouraged him.*

discouraged [dɪ 'skɚ ɪdʒd] *tv.* dejected; not hopeful; not confident. (Adv: *discouragedly.*) ♦ *The discouraged student quit the class after failing the first test.* ♦ *Don't be so discouraged. If you work hard, you will do better next time.*

discouragement [dɪ 'skɚ ɪdʒ mənt] **1.** *n.* something that is discouraging. (No plural form in this sense.) ♦ *The discouragement of failing the test overcame the student.* ♦ *The company's poor financial results were a discouragement to potential investors.* **2.** *n.* something that discourages someone from doing something. (No plural form in this sense.) ♦ *We heeded the government's discouragement of foreign travel.* ♦ *We needed no discouragement to stay out of dangerous neighborhoods.* **3.** *n.* the feeling of being discouraged. (No plural form in this sense.) ♦ *The losing athlete's discouragement showed on her face.* ♦ *In his discouragement, the unsuccessful author vowed to give up writing.*

discouraging [dɪ 'skɚ ɪ dʒɪŋ] *adj.* dejecting; making someone feel less excited or interested. (Adv: *discouragingly.*) ♦ *Bob sold his stock after hearing some discouraging financial news.* ♦ *The teacher made a discouraging comment about the student's ability.*

discourse ['dɪs kors] **1.** *n.* conversation. (No plural form in this sense.) ♦ *Eventually the discourse at the party came around to politics.* ♦ *During the discourse, each person got to speak.* **2.** *n.* a formal speech; a lecture. ♦ *The doctor presented a discourse on patient management.* ♦ *The philosopher's discourse was published recently.*

discourteous [dɪs 'kɚ ti əs] *adj.* not courteous; impolite; rude. (Adv: *discourteously.*) ♦ *Mary received discourteous treatment from the arrogant clerk.* ♦ *David made a discourteous comment about John's clothes.*

discourtesy [dɪs 'kɚ tɪ si] **1.** *n.* rudeness; a lack of courtesy. (No plural form in this sense.) ♦ *Billy was reprimanded for his discourtesy to his grandparents.* ♦ *Discourtesy will not get you ahead in business.* **2.** *n.* a rude or impolite act. ♦ *Not replying to an invitation is a discourtesy.* ♦ *I was offended by the rude clerk's discourtesy.*

discover [dɪ 'skʌv ɚ] *tv.* to find something for the first time; to become aware of something for the first time; to find out for the first time how something functions or happens. ♦ *The puppy discovered my slippers and started chewing them.* ♦ *We discovered a new restaurant in the city.*

discovery [dɪ 'skʌv ə ri] **1.** *n.* an act of discovering something. ♦ *The scientific discovery was rewarded with the Nobel Prize.* ♦ *Researchers in this laboratory have made several important discoveries.* **2.** *n.* someone or something that has been discovered; something not known of before. ♦ *The dog hid his discovery—a bone.* ♦ *The astronomer's discovery was a new star.*

discredit [dɪs 'krɛd ɪt] **1.** *tv.* to destroy someone's reputation; to cause people to no longer trust someone; to ruin someone's name. ♦ *The scandal discredited the minister.* ♦ *The many typos in the cookbook discredited the publisher.* **2.** *tv.* to refuse to believe something; to cause people to no longer believe something. ♦ *The evidence discredited the idea that Bob was guilty of the crime.* ♦ *New experiments discredited the old theory.*

discredited [dɪs 'krɛd ɪ tɪd] *adj.* no longer believed. ♦ *The suspect's discredited story led to his arrest.* ♦ *The misinformed scientist clung to the discredited theory.*

discreet [dɪ 'skrit] *adj.* very cautious, so as not to catch anyone's attention; able to keep a secret. (Compare with discrete. Adv: *discreetly.*) ♦ *No one suspected the discreet couple of having an affair.* ♦ *You can tell Jane anything. She is very discreet.*

discrepancy [dɪ 'skrɛp ən si] *n.* a difference in things that are supposed to be the same; an inconsistency. (No plural form in this sense.) ♦ *The accountant found a discrepancy in the two columns of figures.* ♦ *There is a wide discrepancy between how much we spend and how much we earn.*

discrete [dɪ 'skrit] *adj.* separate; not connected; distinct. (Compare with discreet. Adv: *discretely.*) ♦ *Mary's plan contained seven discrete ideas.* ♦ *A computer can perform millions of discrete functions per second.*

discretion [dɪ 'skrɛ ʃən] **1.** *n.* careful judgment; discreet behavior; being discreet. (No plural form in this sense.) ♦ *The decorator showed no discretion in her purchases for our new house—everything cost too much money.* ♦ *Because of John and Mary's discretion, no one suspected they were having an affair.* **2.** *n.* the freedom to do things according to one's own judgment. (No plural form in this sense.) ♦ *The manager has complete discretion in hiring employees.* ♦ *I have granted my attorney little discretion in my affairs.*

discriminate [dɪ 'skrɪm ə net] **1. discriminate between** *iv.* + *prep. phr.* to be able to tell a difference between two things. ♦ *The color-blind person could not discriminate between green and red.* ♦ *The antique dealer can discriminate between authentic pieces and fakes.* **2. discriminate (against)** *iv.* (+ *prep. phr.*) to treat someone differently from someone else because of a prejudice or dislike. ♦ *Mike was fired for discriminating against the handicapped employee.* ♦ *Mary's firm does not discriminate.*

discriminating [dɪ 'skrɪm ə net ɪŋ] *adj.* choosy; selective; having excellent taste or judgment in choosing things. (Adv: *discriminatingly.*) ♦ *The discriminating child selected the most expensive shoes in the store.* ♦ *A discriminating shopper shops at only the best stores.*

discrimination [dɪ skrɪm ə 'ne ʃən] **1.** *n.* the ability to choose and appreciate the finest things. (No plural form in this sense.) ♦ *Your discrimination in home furnishings has proved expensive.* ♦ *Though they were wealthy, the Smiths had no discrimination in the area of art.* **2.** *n.* treating people differently because of prejudice. (No plural form in this sense.) ♦ *Certain kinds of discrimination are illegal.* ♦ *Different groups of people in many countries of the world face discrimination.*

discriminatory [dɪ 'skrɪm ə nə tor i] *adj.* treating someone differently because of illegal discrimination. (Adv: *discriminatorily* [dɪ skrɪm ə nə 'tor ə li].) ♦ *The policy was discriminatory against senior citizens.* ♦ *The court outlawed the discriminatory policy.*

discuss [dɪ 'skʌs] *tv.* to talk about something; to have a conversation about something. ♦ *The two friends discussed their summer vacations.* ♦ *The employees like to discuss their work at lunch.*

discussion [dɪ 'skʌ ʃən] *n.* a conversation, often with more than two people. ♦ *The public discussions on the library drew 200 people.* ♦ *I had a discussion with Mary about the problem.*

disdain [dɪs 'den] *n.* scorn; a lack of respect for someone or something. (No plural form in this sense.) ♦ *Jane's disdain for the movie was obvious when she turned down free tickets.* ♦ *The students treated the substitute teacher with great disdain.*

disdainful [dɪs 'den fʊl] *adj.* scornful; disrespectful. (Adv: *disdainfully.*) ♦ *The classical musician was disdainful of rock music.* ♦ *David gave the litterbug a disdainful look.*

disease [dɪ 'ziz] *n.* an illness; a sickness. ♦ *There are no cures for many diseases.* ♦ *My disease was diagnosed after several tests were done.*

diseased [dɪ 'zizd] *adj.* sick; having a disease; unhealthy. ♦ *The gardener trimmed the diseased branch from the tree.* ♦ *The doctor fought to save the soldier's diseased leg.*

disembark [dɪs ɛm 'bɑrk] *iv.* to depart from a ship or airplane at one's destination. ♦ *The train passengers disembarked as they reached their stops.* ♦ *The elderly passengers needed help to disembark.*

disfavor [dɪs 'fev ɚ] *n.* dislike. (No plural form in this sense.) ♦ *Most of my friends meet with my father's disfavor.* ♦ *The count fell into the ruler's disfavor.*

disfigure [dɪs 'fɪg jɚ] *tv.* to ruin the beauty of someone or something; to cause someone or something to look deformed. ♦ *A car accident had disfigured the driver badly.* ♦ *The forest fire disfigured the landscape.*

disgrace [dɪs 'gres] **1.** *n.* shame; dishonor. (No plural form in this sense.) ♦ *The disgrace caused by the shooting incident affected the soldier for many years.* ♦ *The wayward son was the source of the family's disgrace.* **2.** *n.* someone or something that is shameful. (No plural form in this sense.) ♦ *The children's messy clothes were a disgrace.* ♦ *The teacher warned the students not to be a disgrace to their school at the game.* **3.** *tv.* to bring shame upon someone. ♦ *The prince's silly antics disgraced the entire royal family.* ♦ *The scandal disgraced the government.*

disgraceful [dɪs 'gres fʊl] *adj.* shameful; causing scandal. (Adv: *disgracefully.*) ♦ *Your date has disgraceful manners!* ♦ *Bob heard some disgraceful news about his neighbors, but did not tell anyone else.*

disgruntled [dɪs 'grʌn təld] *adj.* upset; annoyed; disgusted. (Adv: *disgruntledly.*) ♦ *The supervisor was threatened by a disgruntled employee.* ♦ *A refund was given to the disgruntled customer.*

disguise [dɪs 'gɑɪz] **1.** *n.* something that conceals someone's or something's true identity. ♦ *The spy was an artist of disguise.* ♦ *A clever disguise concealed the burglar's identity.* **2.** *tv.* to change the appearance of a thing or a person to make identification difficult. ♦ *Mary disguised the gift so that Bob could not guess what it was.* ♦ *Bill disguised himself as a soldier for Halloween.* **3. in disguise** *idiom* hidden behind a disguise; looking like something else. ♦ *Santa Claus was really the little child's father in disguise.* ♦ *What I thought was terrible turned out to be a blessing in disguise!*

disguised [dɪs 'gɑɪzd] *adj.* with the true identity concealed by a disguise. ♦ *The disguised suspect slipped by the police.* ♦ *The detective went to the party and caught the disguised thief stealing jewelry.*

disgust [dɪs 'gʌst] **1.** *n.* a strong feeling of dislike; a loathing for someone or something. (No plural form in this sense.) ♦ *The gory horror film filled Mike with disgust.* ♦ *After her bitter divorce, Jane felt disgust for her former husband.* **2.** *tv.* to revolt someone; to offend someone. ♦ *The raw fish disgusted me, so I left the table.* ♦ *The candidate's dirty joke disgusted many voters.*

disgusted [dɪs 'kʌs tɪd] *adj.* offended; sickened. (Adv: *disgustedly.*) ♦ *Disgusted voters decided to support another candidate.* ♦ *The disgusted customer returned the merchandise to the store.*

disgusting [dɪs 'kʌs tɪŋ] *adj.* causing disgust; offensive; sickening. (Adv: *disgustingly.*) ♦ *Even the dog would not eat this disgusting food!* ♦ *A disgusting smell came from the garbage.*

dish ['dɪʃ] **1.** *n.* a plate; a flat, circular object used to serve food or to eat from. ♦ *The dishes are in the bottom cupboard.* ♦ *Mike took a dish from the buffet table and loaded it with food.* **2.** *n.* a particular food that is served at a meal. ♦ *Meatloaf is my favorite dish.* ♦ *The restaurant is famous for its chicken dishes.* **3.** *n.* a slightly concave object; something shaped like ①. ♦ *Our satellite dish receives over 200 channels.* ♦ *The potter fashioned a dish to hold paper clips.* **4. do the dishes** *idiom* to wash and dry dishes after a meal. ♦ *Bill, you cannot go out and play until you've done the dishes.* ♦ *Why am I always the one who has to do the dishes?*

dishearten [dɪs 'hɑrt n] *tv.* to make someone lose hope; to discourage someone. ♦ *The rejection notice disheartened the writer.* ♦ *A long losing streak disheartened the team's coach.*

disheartening [dɪs 'hɑrt n ɪŋ] *adj.* causing someone to lose hope; discouraging. (Adv: *dishearteningly.*) ♦ *The doctor hated giving patients disheartening news.* ♦ *After reading the disheartening letter, Tom sat and wept.*

disheveled [dɪ 'ʃɛv əld] *adj.* rumpled; messed up. (Adv: *disheveledly.*) ♦ *Mary looks disheveled after a bad day at work.* ♦ *A disheveled panhandler asked us for money.*

dishonest [dɪs 'ɑn əst] *adj.* not honest. (Adv: *dishonestly.*) ♦ *The dishonest student lied to the teacher.* ♦ *The senator was accused of engaging in dishonest activities.*

dishonesty [dɪs 'ɑn ɪs ti] *n.* deceit; untruthfulness. (No plural form in this sense.) ♦ *The child was punished for dishonesty.* ♦ *Dishonesty is not a virtue.*

dishonor [dɪs 'ɑn ɚ] **1.** *n.* shame; disgrace. (No plural form in this sense.) ♦ *The troublesome soldiers brought dishonor on their unit.* ♦ *The family felt dishonor because of their child's problems with the law.* **2.** *n.* someone or something that causes a loss of honor. (No plural form in this sense.) ♦ *Treason is a dishonor to one's country.* ♦ *Impeachment was a severe dishonor for the president.* **3.** *tv.* to cause the loss of someone's or something's honor. ♦ *Our family was dishonored by my cousin's fraudulent actions.* ♦ *The soldiers were trained to never dishonor the flag.*

dishwasher ['dɪʃ wɑʃ ɚ] **1.** *n.* someone who washes dishes. ♦ *Mary took a job as dishwasher at the new restaurant.* ♦ *One of the children's chores was to be the dishwasher.* **2.** *n.* a machine that washes dishes. ♦ *The dishwasher is a time-saving appliance.* ♦ *I placed the dirty dishes in the dishwasher.*

dishwater ['dɪʃ wɑt ɚ] *n.* the water that dishes are washed in; water that dishes have been washed in. (No plural form in this sense.) ♦ *The dishwater was warm and soapy.* ♦ *The sponge is somewhere in the dirty dishwater.*

disillusioned [dɪs ə 'lu ʒənd] *adj.* freed from illusion. ♦ *The disillusioned student was very cynical about life.* ♦ *The disillusioned child had finally realized that keeping a puppy is a lot of work.*

disillusionment [dɪs ə 'lu ʒən mənt] *n.* a state wherein one's faith, trust, or expectations have been destroyed. (No plural form in this sense.) ♦ *The worker's disillusionment resulted from tyrannical management.* ♦ *Mike blamed his disillusionment with school on poor teachers.*

disinfect [dɪs ɪn 'fɛkt] *tv.* to clean something by killing germs or bacteria. ♦ *I disinfected the bathroom tiles with bleach.* ♦ *The technician disinfected the operating room.*

disinfectant [dɪs ɪn 'fɛk tənt] *n.* something that kills germs or bacteria; something that prevents infection by killing germs or bacteria. (No plural form in this sense.) ♦ *Chlorine is a disinfectant used in swimming pools.* ♦ *Tom put a disinfectant in the toilet bowl to kill the germs and the odor.*

disintegrate [dɪ 'sɪn tə gret] **1.** *tv.* to cause something to break up into little bits and pieces; to turn something into powder. ♦ *I disintegrated the soft rock by crushing it between my fingers.* ♦ *The weight of the boulder disintegrated the stone wall.* **2.** *iv.* [for something] to break down as if through grinding or rotting. ♦ *The rotten tree branch disintegrated when I touched it.* ♦ *The ancient fabric from the tomb disintegrated when it was exposed to air.* **3.** *iv.* to break down or dissipate. (Figurative on ②.) ♦ *Opposition to the plan disintegrated when it was shown that it would cost no money.* ♦ *My anger disintegrated when I learned that nothing was wrong.*

disintegration [dɪ sɪn tə 'gre ʃən] **1.** *n.* breaking apart into bits. (No plural form in this sense.) ♦ *The disintegration of the stone wall was caused by erosion.* ♦ *Endless bombing caused the disintegration of all the buildings in the town.* **2.** *n.* declining or yielding; breaking down. (No plural form in this sense.) ♦ *The disintegration of the opposition to the plan was welcomed by the planners.* ♦ *The shock nearly caused the disintegration of his mind.*

disinterested [dɪs 'ɪn trɪs tɪd] **1.** *adj.* impartial; unbiased. (Compare with uninterested. Adv: *disinterestedly.*) ♦ *Mary is completely disinterested in the matter and can judge fairly.* ♦ *The two neighbors looked for a disinterested person to settle their dispute.* **2.** *adj.* indifferent; uninterested. (Some people object to this word used in this way. Adv: *disinterestedly.*) ♦ *As the teacher lectured, the disinterested student looked out the window.* ♦ *Mary was disinterested in food when she was sick.*

disjointed [dɪs 'dʒoɪn tɪd] **1.** *adj.* disconnected at the joints. ♦ *The disjointed chicken was placed in the pot.* ♦ *Mike ordered a disjointed duck from the butcher.* **2.** *adj.* incoherent; hard to understand; not connected; hard to follow. (Figurative on ①. Adv: *disjointedly.*) ♦ *The audience became impatient during the disjointed lecture.* ♦ *Bill's disjointed essay received a low grade.*

disk AND **disc** ['dɪsk] **1.** *n.* a thin, flat, and circular object. ♦ *Each of the table legs rested on a thin metal disk.* ♦ *A coaster is a disk that is placed under a glass or cup.* **2.** *n.* a piece of cartilage between two vertebrae. ♦ *The accident crushed a disk in Mary's back.* ♦ *Bob was suffering from a slipped disk.* **3.** See diskette, floppy disk.

disk drive ['dɪsk drɑɪv] *n.* a device inside a computer used for storing digital information on a spinning disk. ♦ *My disk drive is too full to hold any more software.* ♦ *The information was lost when the broken disk drive could not be repaired.*

diskette [dɪ 'skɛt] *n.* a device—usually held in a square of plastic—for storing digital computer information. (See also **disk**.) ♦ *Bob loaded the program onto his computer from the diskette.* ♦ *One diskette could not store all of the information on the hard drive.*

dislike [dɪs 'lɑɪk] **1.** *n.* the condition of not liking someone or something; an aversion to someone or something. ♦ *Bob's dislike for hot weather prompted him to move north.* ♦ *The puppy has an intense dislike of water and hates getting bathed.* **2.** *tv.* not to like someone or something; to have an aversion to someone or something. ♦ *Mike disliked spinach and refused to eat it.* ♦ *The children disliked their stern babysitter.*

dislocate ['dɪs lo ket] *tv.* to cause a bone to come out of its socket. ♦ *Mary dislocated her shoulder when she slipped on the ice.* ♦ *A fast ball dislocated the baseball player's middle finger.*

dislodge [dɪs 'lɑdʒ] *tv.* to remove something that is stuck or jammed. ♦ *The paramedic dislodged the food stuck in the child's throat.* ♦ *The city workers dislodged the tree trunk that was damming the river.*

disloyal [dɪs 'lɔɪ əl] *adj.* not loyal; not faithful. (Adv: *disloyally.*) ♦ *The disloyal employee gave company information to a competitor.* ♦ *The fans became disloyal when the team lost most of the games.*

dismal ['dɪz məl] *adj.* dreary; bleak; depressing. (Adv: *dismally.*) ♦ *The dismal, cold day depressed Bill.* ♦ *Mary cried during the dismal movie.*

dismantle [dɪs 'mæn təl] *tv.* to take something apart. ♦ *The child dismantled the toy and then could not reassemble it.* ♦ *The chimney was dismantled brick by brick and then rebuilt.*

dismay [dɪs 'me] **1.** *n.* disheartening fear or alarm. (No plural form in this sense.) ♦ *John showed considerable dismay at his child's bad behavior.* ♦ *The investors watched in dismay as the stock market fell.* **2.** *tv.* to trouble someone. ♦ *The news dismayed Anne, and she began to worry.* ♦ *The loss dismayed the team members, who had practiced so hard.*

dismaying [dɪs 'me ɪŋ] *adj.* disheartening; troublesome. (Adv: *dismayingly.*) ♦ *Jane shared the dismaying news about her illness with her friends.* ♦ *We heard the dismaying story of the bombing on the news.*

dismiss [dɪs 'mɪs] **1.** *tv.* to allow people to leave; to send people away. ♦ *At the end of the lecture, the professor dismissed the students.* ♦ *The mayor finished the press conference and dismissed the reporters.* **2.** *tv.* to terminate someone's employment. ♦ *Mary dismissed one of her employees today.* ♦ *As sales declined, the manager had to dismiss several workers.* **3.** *tv.* to refuse to consider something; to refuse to listen to someone or something. ♦ *The parent dismissed the child's constant requests.* ♦ *I dismissed Bill's constant complaining as childish.*

dismissal [dɪs 'mɪs əl] **1.** *n.* sending someone away; being sent away. (No plural form in this sense.) ♦ *A bell signals the school's dismissal of the students at three o'clock.* ♦ *His sudden dismissal from the meeting made Bill livid.* **2.** *n.* firing someone. (No plural form in this sense.) ♦ *The employees sued the company over their unfair dismissal.* ♦ *If John does not improve his work, he may face dismissal.* **3.** *n.* ignoring someone or something; refusing to deal with someone or something; discounting something. (No plural form in this sense.) ♦ *The manager's dismissal of the idea was shortsighted.* ♦ *Anne was angered by John's quick dismissal of her suggestion.*

dismount **1.** ['dɪs mɑʊnt] *n.* an act of getting off of something; an act of getting down from something. ♦ *The rider made a quick dismount from the horse.* ♦ *The gymnast did an impressive dismount from the balance beam.* **2.** [dɪs 'mɑʊnt] *iv.* to get down from a horse, a bicycle, or gymnastic equipment. ♦ *The gymnast dismounted and bowed.* ♦ *Riding up to the barn and stopping, the rider dismounted.*

disobedience [dɪs ə 'bid i əns] *n.* the refusal or failure to obey. (No plural form in this sense.) ♦ *The naughty children were punished for their disobedience.* ♦ *Disobedience of the speed limit can result in a traffic ticket.*

disobedient [dɪs ə 'bid i ənt] *adj.* not obedient; not following instructions. (Adv: *disobediently.*) ♦ *The disobedient puppy kept scratching the furniture.* ♦ *The stern teacher would not tolerate disobedient children.*

disobey [dɪs ə 'be] *tv.* not to do as one has been told. ♦ *Jimmy disobeyed his parents' orders to do his homework.* ♦ *The manager disobeyed a company rule and told the employees to go home early.*

disorder [dɪs 'or dɚ] **1.** *n.* confusion; the lack of order. (No plural form in this sense.) ♦ *Noise and disorder in the office made work difficult.* ♦ *The cook will not tolerate disorder in the kitchen.* **2.** *n.* a disturbance; a riot. ♦ *Police were called to control the disorder.* ♦ *The disorder caused by the hecklers interrupted the political debate.*

disorderly [dɪs 'or dɚ li] **1.** *adj.* not in order; messy. ♦ *My mom ordered me to clean my disorderly room before I went to swim.* ♦ *The teacher frowned at Bill's disorderly report.* **2.** *adj.* unruly; causing trouble. ♦ *The disorderly crowd soon turned into an angry mob.* ♦ *A protester was arrested for disorderly conduct.*

disoriented [dɪs 'or i ɛn tɪd] *adj.* mixed up; confused; dazed. (Adv: *disorientedly.*) ♦ *The car-crash victim was disoriented and could only mumble a few words.* ♦ *I was disoriented when I woke up suddenly in the middle of the night.*

disown [dɪs 'on] *tv.* to no longer claim ownership of or responsibility for someone or something. ♦ *The rich woman disowned her greedy relatives.* ♦ *No matter what I do, my family will never disown me.*

disparaging [dɪ 'spɛr ɪdʒ ɪŋ] *adj.* unkind; contemptuous; belittling. (Adv: *disparagingly.*) ♦ *Bill grumbled a disparaging comment about his boss.* ♦ *Anne give the talkative member of the audience a disparaging look.*

disparate ['dɪs pɚ ət] *adj.* distinct; different; varied. (Adv: *disparately.*) ♦ *The two scientists presented disparate theories.* ♦ *The witnesses gave disparate accounts of the incident.*

dispatch [dɪ 'spætʃ] **1.** *tv.* to send someone or something somewhere quickly; to mail something or send something away by courier. ♦ *Jane will dispatch the letter* *tomorrow.* ♦ *The teacher dispatched the student to the principal's office.* **2.** *n.* a message; a document containing up-to-date news; a shipment of goods. ♦ *A dispatch from headquarters advised the general of the attack.* ♦ *A courier carried the dispatch to the ambassador.* **3.** *n.* the sending, shipping, or mailing of something. (No plural form in this sense.) ♦ *Please ensure the prompt dispatch of this shipment.* ♦ *This office is responsible for the dispatch of updated information to the president every hour.*

dispatcher [dɪ 'spætʃ ɚ] *n.* someone who sends something out. ♦ *The dispatcher sent a taxi to our house exactly on time.* ♦ *The dispatcher sent the shipment to the customer.*

dispel [dɪ 'spɛl] **1.** *tv.* to disperse or dissipate something. ♦ *A warm sun quickly dispelled the morning fog.* ♦ *A strong wind began to dispel the rain clouds.* **2.** *tv.* to make something go away or vanish (figuratively). ♦ *I sang to Billy to dispel his fear of the dark.* ♦ *Tom dispelled all doubts about his health by running in the marathon.*

dispensable [dɪ 'spɛn sə bəl] *adj.* not necessary; not important; easily discarded. (Adv: *dispensably.*) ♦ *Even the president of this company is dispensable.* ♦ *This magazine is dispensable, so let's discontinue our subscription.*

dispensary [dɪ 'spɛn sə ri] *n.* a place where medicine and medical advice are given out. ♦ *The sick soldier was taken to the dispensary.* ♦ *Several nurses worked at the dispensary.*

dispense [dɪ 'spɛns] **1.** *tv.* to give something out; to hand something out, usually to a number of people. ♦ *The political candidate dispensed lots of leaflets.* ♦ *The nursery school teacher dispensed cookies at snack time.* **2.** *tv.* to prepare medicine and give it out. ♦ *A pharmacy dispenses medicine.* ♦ *The nurses dispensed the medicine to their patients.* **3. dispense with** *iv.* + *prep. phr.* to do away with something; to need something no longer. ♦ *Mary and Bob dispensed with formality and called each other by their first names.* ♦ *Susan dispensed with her typewriter when she bought a computer.*

disperse [dɪ 'spɝs] **1.** *tv.* to scatter something; to spread something out. ♦ *The wind dispersed the seeds around the garden.* ♦ *The gardener dispersed the fertilizer.* **2.** *iv.* to scatter; to spread out. ♦ *As the wind grew stronger, the clouds dispersed.* ♦ *After school, the children slowly dispersed.*

displace [dɪs 'ples] **1.** *tv.* to take the place of someone or something. ♦ *My computer has displaced my old typewriter.* ♦ *My new friends could never displace my old ones.* **2.** *tv.* to force people to move, especially during a war. ♦ *The bombing displaced the entire village.* ♦ *As the army advanced, they displaced the citizens to other areas.*

display [dɪ 'sple] **1.** *tv.* to show something; to exhibit something. ♦ *Five artists will display their work at the gallery.* ♦ *Antique-car owners often display their cars at county fairs.* **2.** *n.* something that is shown; something that is exhibited. ♦ *The display of antique cars drew a large crowd.* ♦ *The children running through the store knocked over the card display.*

displease [dɪs 'pliz] *tv.* to offend someone; to upset someone; to anger someone. ♦ *Mike's rude comment to the customer displeased his boss.* ♦ *Having to wait in line displeases me very much.*

displeasure [dɪs 'plɛʒ ɚ] *n.* the feeling of being displeased; anger. (No plural form in this sense.) ♦ *The child showed his displeasure by stomping his feet.* ♦ *John's rudeness sparked Mary's displeasure.*

disposable [dɪ 'spoz ə bəl] *adj.* meant to be thrown away after use. (Adv: *disposably.*) ♦ *Disposable diapers are more common than cloth ones nowadays.* ♦ *John shaved his beard with a disposable razor.*

disposal [dɪ 'spoz əl] **1.** *n.* the removal of something. (No plural form in this sense.) ♦ *The community members must pay for their trash disposal.* ♦ *The disposal of the old, heavy furniture required several strong movers.* **2. (garbage) disposal** *n.* a machine that grinds up wet garbage and sends it into the sewer system. ♦ *Mary put the onion peels in the garbage disposal.* ♦ *The disposal is full of table scraps.*

dispose [dɪ 'spoz] **1. dispose to** *tv.* + *inf.* to prepare someone for something. ♦ *Mary's nursing training disposes her to help anyone who is hurt.* ♦ *Bill's interest in the outdoors disposes him to go fishing often.* **2. dispose of** *iv.* + *prep. phr.* to get rid of something; to throw something away. ♦ *The murderer disposed of the incriminating evidence.* ♦ *I disposed of the dirty rags when I finished using them.*

disposition [dɪs pə 'zɪ ʃən] **1.** *n.* [a person's] mood, behavior, or nature. (No plural form in this sense.) ♦ *The happy clerk had a pleasant disposition.* ♦ *The teacher called Bob's parents to talk about their son's unkind disposition.* **2.** *n.* the state of a legal case or a matter under discussion. (No plural form in this sense.) ♦ *What is the disposition of the Jones case?* ♦ *The judge asked for an update on the disposition of the motion.*

dispossess [dɪs pə 'zɛs] **dispossess of** *tv.* + *prep. phr.* to take someone's property away. ♦ *The rebels dispossessed the king of his castle.* ♦ *We were dispossessed of all we owned by the tax collector.*

disproportionate [dɪs prə 'por ʃən] *adj.* out of proportion; not equal to; not the same as; too large or too small. (Adv: *disproportionately.*) ♦ *The tycoon left his children disproportionate amounts of money.* ♦ *Tom cut himself a disproportionate piece of pie, taking almost half of it.*

disprove [dɪs 'pruv] *tv.* to prove that something is false. ♦ *These facts disprove your theory.* ♦ *The research disproved information I had taken for granted.*

dispute [dɪ 'spjut] **1.** *n.* a disagreement; a debate; a fight. ♦ *Our upstairs neighbors were having a loud dispute about their children.* ♦ *The participants in the dispute were asked to leave the ballpark quietly.* **2.** *tv.* to question something; to doubt something is true; to disagree with something. ♦ *The teacher disputed Tom's claim that he had written the paper himself.* ♦ *My manager disputes every issue that arises.*

disqualification [dɪs kwɑl ɪ fə 'ke ʃən] *n.* disqualifying someone or something; being disqualified. (No plural form in this sense.) ♦ *The runner's disqualification was announced just before the race.* ♦ *Disqualification will result if any rules are violated.*

disqualify [dɪs 'kwɑl ə faɪ] *tv.* to make someone or something ineligible for something; to declare that someone is not allowed to participate in something. ♦ *The judge disqualified Mike for tripping another runner.* ♦ *The boy's age disqualified him from entering the contest.*

disquieting [dɪs 'kwɑɪ ə tɪŋ] *adj.* disturbing; unsettling. (Adv: *disquietingly.*) ♦ *Thoughts about the disquieting remark made it hard for John to fall asleep.* ♦ *Mary tried to ignore the disquieting rumor that the land she owned was worthless.*

disregard [dɪs rɪ 'gɑrd] **1.** *n.* neglect; indifference. (No plural form in this sense.) ♦ *Bill showed a total disregard for Jane's privacy when he read her mail.* ♦ *Suffering from his owner's disregard, the starving dog ran away.* **2.** *tv.* to treat someone or something indifferently; to treat someone or something as unimportant; to pay no attention to someone or something; to not take someone or something into account. ♦ *The children disregarded the No Swimming sign and jumped into the pond.* ♦ *Tom disregarded the teacher's warning that the test would be difficult.*

disreputable [dɪs 'rɛp jə tə bəl] *adj.* having a bad reputation; (Adv: *disreputably.*) ♦ *The disreputable car dealer soon went out of business.* ♦ *The newspaper reported about the senator's disreputable conduct.*

disrespect [dɪs rɪ 'spɛkt] *n.* a lack of respect; impoliteness. (No plural form in this sense.) ♦ *Billy's parents punished him for his disrespect.* ♦ *The mayor showed the citizens disrespect by not listening to their viewpoints.*

disrespectful [dɪs rɪ 'spɛkt fʊl] *adj.* lacking respect; not showing respect. (Adv: *disrespectfully.*) ♦ *Heckling is disrespectful of the person who is trying to talk.* ♦ *Forgetting to send a thank-you note is disrespectful.*

disrupt [dɪs 'rʌpt] **1.** *tv.* to stop something in progress; to interrupt something. ♦ *An emergency announcement disrupted the TV show.* ♦ *The slide lecture was disrupted by a power failure.* **2.** *tv.* to interfere with something by causing turmoil. ♦ *The devastating tornado disrupted the lives of everyone in its path.* ♦ *Ugly rumors threatened to disrupt the celebrity's career.*

disruptive [dɪs 'rʌp tɪv] *adj.* interrupting; causing disorder; causing turmoil. (Adv: *disruptively.*) ♦ *Disruptive weather made traveling difficult.* ♦ *The convention could not resume until the disruptive people left.*

dissatisfaction [dɪs sæt ɪs 'fæk ʃən] **1.** *n.* displeasure; not being at ease. (No plural form in this sense.) ♦ *Susie expressed her dissatisfaction by stomping her feet.* ♦ *The manager's dissatisfaction with the tardy employee was obvious.* **2.** *n.* a specific cause of ①. ♦ *Bill discussed his list of dissatisfactions with his supervisor.* ♦ *Anne had very few dissatisfactions in life.*

dissect [dɪ 'sɛkt] **1.** *tv.* to take a once-living thing apart piece by piece. ♦ *The students had to dissect a frog.* ♦ *Bill dissected a small shark in anatomy class.* **2.** *tv.* to examine something, such as an idea, part by part. (Figurative on ①.) ♦ *Bob asked the committee to dissect the proposal and determine its value.* ♦ *The students dissected the motivation of the characters in the novel.*

dissemble [dɪ 'sɛm bəl] *iv.* to conceal one's true intentions; to be hypocritical. ♦ *The teacher dissembled when she was explaining the problem to the principal.* ♦ *The criminal suspect was dissembling when he said he was asleep in bed at the time of the crime.*

disseminate [dɪ 'sɛm ə net] *tv.* to spread something out, especially information. ♦ *The public relations department disseminates information about the company.* ♦ *During a weather emergency, the radio station disseminated important information.*

dissension [dɪ 'sɛn ʃən] *n.* disagreement. (No plural form in this sense.) ♦ *The ruin of the company was caused by dissension between the owners.* ♦ *There was a lot of dissension among the students when the cost of tuition was raised.*

dissent [dɪ 'sɛnt] **1.** *n.* disagreement with a rule, policy, position, or general consensus. (No plural form in this sense.) ♦ *Tom's dissent was ignored by his boss.* ♦ *There is rarely any dissent among the club members.* **2.** *iv.* to disagree as in ①. ♦ *How many club members dissented?* ♦ *When asked for objections, no one in the group dissented.*

dissertation [dɪs ɚ 'te ʃən] *n.* a lengthy, formal paper submitted at the end of one's studies in order to receive a degree. ♦ *Anne's dissertation was on education in Russia.* ♦ *The graduate student spent months at the library researching his dissertation.*

disservice [dɪs 'sɚ vɪs] *n.* a harmful act; an act that is not helpful. (No plural form in this sense.) ♦ *Dr. Smith did John a disservice by ignoring his weight problem.* ♦ *Failing to teach children manners is a real disservice.*

dissimilar [dɪ 'sɪm ə lɚ] *adj.* not similar; not alike; different. (Adv: *dissimilarly.*) ♦ *The dissimilar candlesticks did not make a pretty pair.* ♦ *Your children are so dissimilar, it is hard to believe they are related.*

dissipate ['dɪs ə pet] **1.** *iv.* [for fog, smoke, clouds, etc.] to disperse. ♦ *The fog is dissipating.* ♦ *When the smoke dissipated, we could see the damage done by the explosion.* **2.** *tv.* to cause something to fade away; to cause something to disperse. ♦ *The whirlpool dissipated my muscle pain.* ♦ *Wind will dissipate the fog.* **3.** *tv.* to spend money foolishly; to squander money. ♦ *David dissipated his fortune by gambling.* ♦ *The company dissipated its funds buying unnecessary computers.*

dissipated ['dɪs ə pe tɪd] *adj.* [of someone] worn out or wasted. (Adv: *dissipatedly.*) ♦ *John looks quite dissipated from his frequent drinking bouts.* ♦ *Anne is dissipated and run down from too many parties.*

dissociate [dɪs 'so ʃi et] **dissociate from** *tv. + prep. phr.* to draw oneself away from an association with someone or something. (The same as disassociate. Takes a reflexive object.) ♦ *Max dissociated himself from the radical group.* ♦ *Mary dissociated herself from dishonest employees.*

dissolution [dɪs ə 'lu ʃən] *n.* the breaking up of an association. (No plural form in this sense.) ♦ *Many regional companies were formed after the dissolution of the conglomerate.* ♦ *The union's dissolution was caused by arguments among its members.*

dissolve [dɪ 'zɑlv] **1.** *tv.* to melt a solid, such as sugar, into a liquid; to liquefy something. ♦ *The recipe says to dissolve the sugar in the melted butter.* ♦ *Soap dissolved the globs of grease quickly.* **2.** *tv.* to break up a union or a bond; to end an association. ♦ *The president dissolved the committee when there was no longer a need for it.* ♦ *Divorce dissolves the union of marriage.* **3.** *iv.* [for a solid] to become dispersed throughout a liquid. ♦ *The sugar dissolved in the boiling water.* ♦ *As I stirred the mixture, the salt dissolved.* **4.** *iv.* to break up; to come to a formal end. ♦ *The committee dissolved after the report was read.* ♦ *You are free to do what you please once the agreement is dissolved.*

distance ['dɪs təns] **1.** *n.* the length of the space between two things. (No plural form in this sense.) ♦ *Mary walked the short distance between the drugstore and the library.* ♦ *The distance between my house and my office is 5 miles.* **2.** *n.* aloofness. (No plural form in this sense.) ♦ *Mary sensed a distance in her relationship with Bob.* ♦ *Lisa's distance from people masked her shyness.* **3. go the distance** *idiom* to do the whole amount; to play the entire game; to run the whole race. ♦ *That horse runs fast. I hope it can go the distance.* ♦ *This is going to be a long, hard project. I hope I can go the distance.*

distant ['dɪs tənt] **1.** *adj.* far away; not near in space or time. (Adv: *distantly.*) ♦ *The distant stars flickered.* ♦ *My parents live in a distant state, and I rarely see them.* **2.** *adj.* not very friendly; aloof. (Adv: *distantly.*) ♦ *John has a distant way of talking about his private life.* ♦ *Susan seems a little distant since she got a promotion at work.*

distaste [dɪs 'test] *n.* dislike; aversion to someone or something. (No plural form in this sense.) ♦ *I have considerable distaste for loud parties.* ♦ *The art collector viewed modern paintings with distaste.*

distasteful [dɪs 'test fʊl] *adj.* causing distaste; not pleasant; offensive. (Adv: *distastefully.*) ♦ *No one volunteered for the distasteful task.* ♦ *The distasteful food was left untouched on the buffet table.*

distended [dɪs 'tɛnd ɪd] *adj.* stretched out abnormally; bloated. (Adv: *distendedly.*) ♦ *The pregnant dog had a very distended abdomen.* ♦ *We discovered the distended body of a dead deer in the woods.*

distill [dɪ 'stɪl] **1.** *tv.* to vaporize liquid by heating it and then condensing the vapor. (See also **still** ⑤.) ♦ *A treatment plant on the ship distills water for drinking.* ♦ *The still was made to distill alcohol.* **2.** *tv.* to condense the presentation of an idea; to abstract the important points of something. (Figurative on ①.) ♦ *The professor distilled the lecture into four key points.* ♦ *Knowing his time was short, the salesman distilled his sales pitch.*

distillation [dɪ stə 'le ʃən] *n.* the process of vaporizing a substance in order to separate it from another substance. (No plural form in this sense.) ♦ *Alcohol is made by distillation.* ♦ *Distillation is used to produce very pure water.*

distilled [dɪ 'stɪld] *adj.* made into a gas and condensed back into a liquid. ♦ *The distilled water was suitable for drinking.* ♦ *The farmer stored the distilled alcohol in jugs.*

distinct [dɪ 'stɪŋkt] **1.** *adj.* different; separate; able to be distinguished. (Adv: *distinctly.*) ♦ *These are two distinct problems, and we must deal with them separately.* ♦ *The twins may look alike, but they have very distinct personalities.* **2.** *adj.* clearly identifiable; obvious; unmistakable. (Adv: *distinctly.*) ♦ *There was a distinct smell of gas in the room before the explosion.* ♦ *Ten years after the accident, Bill still walked with a distinct limp.*

distinction [dɪ 'stɪŋk ʃən] **1.** *n.* a noticeable difference between things. ♦ *The teacher discussed the distinctions between frogs and toads.* ♦ *The twins are so alike it is difficult to make a distinction between them.* **2.** *n.* a special difference; an honor. (No plural form in this sense.) ♦ *The military awarded its highest distinction to the brave soldier.* ♦ *The firefighter received a special distinction for saving the family.* **3.** *n.* excellence; a very good quality. (No plural form in this sense.) ♦ *David thought the foreign car gave him a mark of distinction.* ♦ *The esteemed lawyer was a woman of distinction.*

distinctive [dɪ 'stɪŋk tɪv] **1.** *adj.* noticeably different; special or unusual; worthy of notice. (Adv: *distinctively.*) ♦ *The store displayed its most distinctive products in the front window.* ♦ *The car's distinctive color made it easy to spot.* **2.** *adj.* serving as a unique characteristic that makes someone or something easily identifiable. (Adv: *distinctively.*) ♦ *I recognized the children by their distinctive voices.* ♦ *Each team has its own distinctive uniform.*

distinguish [dɪ 'stɪŋ gwɪʃ] **1.** *tv.* to set someone or something apart from someone or something else; to cause someone or something to stand out from everything else. ♦ *John's red hair distinguishes him from his relatives with black hair.* ♦ *The church's tall steeple distinguishes it from the other buildings in the village.* **2.** *tv.* to sense or know the difference between two things; to be able to see, hear, taste, feel, smell, or understand the difference between two things. ♦ *The twins giggled when the teacher could not distinguish them.* ♦ *Its delightful flavor distinguishes this wine from lesser wines.*

distinguishable [dɪ 'stɪŋ gwɪʃ ə bəl] *adj.* clearly perceivable. (Adv: *distinguishably.*) ♦ *The only distinguishable light on the whole island came from the lighthouse.* ♦ *The scientist looked for distinguishable patterns in the data.*

distinguished [dɪ 'stɪŋ gwɪʃt] **1.** *adj.* famous; well known; celebrated; important. (Adv: *distinguishedly.*) ♦ *A distinguished actor starred in the play.* ♦ *A room full of flowers greeted the distinguished hotel guest.* **2.** *adj.* having an air of distinction; looking important and dignified. (Adv: *distinguishedly.*) ♦ *Mary's gray hair makes her even more distinguished.* ♦ *My father is the tall, distinguished gentleman standing by the door.*

distort [dɪ 'stort] **1.** *tv.* to twist something out of shape; to bend something out of shape. ♦ *The old mirror distorted my reflection.* ♦ *An electrical disturbance distorted the picture on the television set.* **2.** *tv.* to misrepresent the facts of a matter. ♦ *Bill distorted the story, trying to place the blame on his brother.* ♦ *The scandalous magazine distorted the report of the star's divorce.* **3.** *iv.* [for something] to twist out of shape. ♦ *The image in the mirror will distort if the mirror is cracked.* ♦ *The patient's face distorted with pain.*

distorted [dɪ 'stort ɪd] **1.** *adj.* twisted out of shape; changed in an unusual way. (Adv: *distortedly.*) ♦ *A strangely distorted tree grew from the side of the cliff.* ♦ *Mary saw a distorted image of herself in the mirror.* **2.** *adj.* [of facts] misrepresented. (Figurative on ①. Adv: *distortedly.*) ♦ *Despite the distorted story, the truth was eventually revealed.* ♦ *The police did not believe the suspect's distorted account.*

distract [dɪ 'strækt] *tv.* to pull one's attention away from something. ♦ *The thunderstorm distracted Mike from his homework.* ♦ *The loud stereo of Mary's neighbor distracted her.*

distracting [dɪ 'stræk tɪŋ] *adj.* drawing away one's attention from something else. (Adv: *distractingly.*) ♦ *Mary couldn't read because of the distracting noise of the birds.* ♦ *We turned off the distracting TV during dinner.*

distraction [dɪ 'stræk ʃən] *n.* something that takes one's attention away from something. ♦ *The distractions of* *daily life made it hard for Susan to concentrate.* ♦ *The radio is a distraction when I am reading.*

distraught [dɪ 'strɔt] *adj.* extremely upset; extremely worried. (Adv: *distraughtly.*) ♦ *I tried to console the distraught family at the hospital.* ♦ *Bill's parents were distraught when he came home so late.*

distress [dɪ 'strɛs] **1.** *n.* grief; anxiety; discomfort; suffering. (No plural form in this sense.) ♦ *The doctor could see the parents' distress over their child's health.* ♦ *In her distress, Jane called her best friend.* **2.** *tv.* to trouble someone; to cause someone to feel anxiety, discomfort, or suffering. ♦ *The car accident distressed John so much that he wouldn't drive for several weeks.* ♦ *The unpleasant rumor distressed the celebrity.*

distressing [dɪ 'strɛs ɪŋ] *adj.* worrying; troubling; upsetting. (Adv: *distressingly.*) ♦ *Bill stopped reading the paper because of all the distressing news.* ♦ *I couldn't sleep after reading the distressing story about the tax increase.*

distribute [dɪ 'strɪb jut] *tv.* to give or sell something [to someone]; to divide something among several people. ♦ *The manager happily distributed the paychecks on Friday.* ♦ *Someone dressed in a rabbit costume distributed leaflets to passersby.*

distribution [dɪ strɪ 'bju ʃən] **1.** *n.* the giving out of something; dispersing something. (No plural form in this sense.) ♦ *The company has an efficient method of distribution of its project.* ♦ *The secretary was responsible for the distribution of the memos.* **2.** *n.* the way that something is spread out or placed. (No plural form in this sense.) ♦ *The distribution of flu cases was spread across the state.* ♦ *The chart showed the distribution of costs over the past five years.*

distributor [dɪ 'strɪb jə tɚ] **1.** *n.* someone or something that distributes something. ♦ *Mary is the distributor of assignments at our office.* ♦ *This engine part is the distributor. It distributes electricity to the spark plugs.* **2.** *n.* someone who buys products from the manufacturer and sells them to store owners. ♦ *The store called the distributor to order more products.* ♦ *Our magazine distributor is late with the most recent shipment.*

district ['dɪs trɪkt] *n.* an area; a region; a part of a country, state, county, or city. ♦ *What district does that representative represent?* ♦ *The farmer lived in the largest farming district in the state.*

District of Columbia ['dɪs trɪkt əv kə 'lʌm bi ə] See Gazetteer.

distrust [dɪs 'trʌst] **1.** *n.* a lack of trust; suspicion. (No plural form in this sense.) ♦ *Lisa's father did not hide his distrust of her husband.* ♦ *The child had a distrust of strangers.* **2.** *tv.* not to trust someone or something; not to put one's trust in someone or something. ♦ *The citizens distrusted the mayor and did not reelect him.* ♦ *The dog distrusts John and won't go near him.*

disturb [dɪ 'stɚb] **1.** *tv.* to bother or annoy someone or something; to interrupt someone or something. ♦ *Every morning the birds disturb my sleep.* ♦ *Jimmy disturbed his parents' conversation and was scolded for interrupting.* **2.** *tv.* to change, handle, or move something. ♦ *Every time Anne visits, she disturbs my furniture.* ♦ *The sudden gust of wind disturbed the pile of leaves.*

disturbance [dɪ 'stɚb əns] *n.* a bother; an annoyance. ♦ *The teacher frowned at the disturbance in the back of the class.* ♦ *Bill apologized for his disturbance of his parents' conversation.*

disturbed [dɪ 'stɚbd] *adj.* mentally unbalanced; mentally unstable. ♦ *The disturbed patient sought psychiatric help.* ♦ *The police were afraid that the disturbed criminal would harm someone else.*

disturbing [dɪ 'stɚb ɪŋ] *adj.* causing worry; upsetting. (Adv: *disturbingly.*) ♦ *The disturbing news about the economy brought down prices on the stock market.* ♦ *Just before the storm, there was a disturbing silence.*

disuse [dɪs 'jus] *n.* the lack of use. (No plural form in this sense.) ♦ *The machine rusted from disuse.* ♦ *Disuse had caused my muscles to weaken.*

ditch ['dɪtʃ] **1.** *n.* a long, narrow trench used to convey or drain water. ♦ *Bob drove the car off the road and into the ditch.* ♦ *The two fields were separated by a ditch.* **2.** *tv.* to land an airplane in the water and abandon it. ♦ *The pilot missed the runway and ditched the plane in the lake.* ♦ *When an engine caught fire over the ocean, the pilot had to ditch the plane.* **3.** *tv.* to abandon someone or something. (Slang.) ♦ *John ditched his younger brother and went to the carnival alone.* ♦ *The driver pulled over and ditched the unwanted dog.*

divan [dɪ 'væn] *n.* a sofa or couch often having no arms. ♦ *The living room had a divan and wicker chairs.* ♦ *Two people can sit comfortably on this divan.*

dive ['dɑɪv] **1.** *n.* a headfirst jump into something, especially water. ♦ *The athlete performed a somersault dive.* ♦ *The splash from the dive soaked everyone sitting by the pool.* **2.** *n.* an underwater excursion, as with snorkeling or scuba diving; time spent underwater. ♦ *John went on a dive in the Caribbean.* ♦ *Lisa was fascinated by all of the creatures she saw during the dive.* **3.** *n.* a downward plunge; a quick downward movement. ♦ *The submarine made a sudden dive when enemy planes were spotted.* ♦ *Anne caused the kite to dive by pulling on the string.* **4.** *n.* a seedy or disreputable bar or nightclub. ♦ *The bar in the run-down neighborhood was nothing but a dive.* ♦ *The police raided the dive looking for drugs.* **5.** *iv., irreg.* to jump into water headfirst. (Pt: *dived* or **dove**; pp: *dived.*) ♦ *Anne dove from the highest diving board.* ♦ *Bill is afraid to dive, so he just jumps in.* **6.** *iv., irreg.* to spend time underwater, as with scuba diving. ♦ *My friends and I dove every day when we went to the Caribbean.* ♦ *Bill dives for coral.* **7.** *iv., irreg.* to go downward quickly; to plunge downward. ♦ *The submarine dived toward the sea bottom.* ♦ *The kite dove and became tangled in the tree.* **8.** *iv., irreg.* to move out of sight quickly. ♦ *At the sound of their parents' car in the driveway, the children dove for their beds and pretended to be asleep.* ♦ *The frightened kitten dived under the couch.*

diver ['dɑɪv ɚ] **1.** *n.* someone who dives into water, especially in competition with other divers. ♦ *The diver received a perfect score from the judges.* ♦ *The diver did a complicated dive off the high diving board.* **2.** *n.* someone who goes on underwater expeditions, as with scuba diving. ♦ *The diver was continually fascinated by the beauty of the sea.* ♦ *I watched the bubbles that followed the diver's path.*

divergent [dɪ 'vɚdʒ ənt] *adj.* breaking off into two or more different paths. (Adv: *divergently.*) ♦ *A series of divergent paths wound through the woods.* ♦ *Thousands of divergent tree branches made a thick canopy overhead.*

diverse [dɪ 'vɚs] *adj.* varied; different. (Adv: *diversely.*) ♦ *Jane made a pretty bouquet of diverse flowers.* ♦ *Dave required a lot of time to study the diverse menu.*

diversion [dɪ 'vɚ ʒən] **1.** *n.* a change in one's route; a detour. ♦ *We had to make a little diversion in order to cash a check at the bank.* ♦ *A short diversion from our path lead us to a quiet stream.* **2.** *n.* an activity that is new or interesting. ♦ *When the exhausting project was completed, Tom planned a weekend diversion.* ♦ *The welcome diversion of visiting relatives relieved the boredom of summer.*

diversity [dɪ 'vɚs ə ti] **1.** *n.* variety. (No plural form in this sense.) ♦ *To appeal to a wide audience, the theater offers a diversity of plays.* ♦ *There is considerable intellectual diversity among the members of my book group.* **2.** *n.* a mix of races, sexes, cultures, and income levels. (No plural form in this sense.) ♦ *The faculty insisted that there be diversity on the college campus.* ♦ *There is considerable diversity where I work.*

divert [dɪ 'vɚt] **1.** *tv.* to cause someone or something to change direction. ♦ *The wind diverted the boat from its course.* ♦ *The air-traffic controller diverted the plane to another airport.* **2.** *tv.* to embezzle money; to intercept money that belongs to someone else. ♦ *The accountant had diverted company funds into her own account.* ♦ *A government employee was arrested for diverting tax payments into his bank account.* **3.** *tv.* to distract or gain the interest of someone or some creature. ♦ *The child diverted the kitten with a piece of string.* ♦ *One robber diverted the cashier while the other stole the money.*

diverting [dɪ 'vɚt ɪŋ] *adj.* amusing; done in order to get one's mind off something. (Adv: *divertingly.*) ♦ *Trying to ignore the storm, Mary told a diverting tale of life in a castle.* ♦ *The novel is a diverting narrative of a summer romance.*

divide [dɪ 'vɑɪd] **1. divide into** *tv.* + *prep. phr.* to determine what a number must be multiplied by to result in a given number; to determine how many times a number goes into a given number. ♦ *Divide 10 into 70 and you'll get 7.* ♦ *If you divide seven into four, the answer is a fraction.* **2. divide by** *tv.* + *prep. phr.* to split the amount represented by a number into the specified number of equal parts; to determine how many times a number can be divided into ① by another number. (The symbol "÷" means *divided by.*) ♦ *If you divide 70 by 10, you'll get 7.* ♦ *When 12 is divided by 4, the result is 3, just as when 12 people are split into 4 equal groups, each group has 3 people in it.* **3.** *tv.* to split something into smaller portions. ♦ *The charity divided the money between the medical clinic and the drug-prevention program.* ♦ *The woman's estate was divided among her children.* **4.** *iv.* to separate; to split up. ♦ *The feuding family divided into two angry groups.* ♦ *Our group divided at the crossroads and continued walking.* **5. divide by** *iv.* + *prep. phr.* to split [the amount represented by a number] into a given number of equal parts; to divide ② [a number] by another number. ♦ *The teacher told the children that to figure out what half of an amount is, they can divide by two.* ♦ *To get a monthly average, Bob added up the column of numbers and then divided by 12.*

dividend ['dɪv ə dɛnd] **1.** *n.* a number that is divided by another number. ♦ *In the equation "fourteen divided by seven equals two," fourteen is the dividend.* ♦ *The student circled the dividend of the equation.* **2.** *n.* a part of the profit of a company given to the shareholders of the company. ♦ *Mary received her dividend in the mail by check.* ♦ *When its profits increased, the company raised its dividend.* **3.** *n.* a benefit; something that is gained from doing something. ♦ *A dividend of my going to college was making new friends.* ♦ *As an extra dividend for doing the job well, Lisa was promoted.*

divine [dɪ 'vɑɪn] **1.** *adj.* of or about God; holy; sacred. (Adv: *divinely.*) ♦ *Every Sunday the minister preached about the divine word.* ♦ *The anthropologist made a distinction between sacred and divine objects.* **2.** *adj.* fabulous; excellent; wonderful. (Figurative on ①. Adv: *divinely.*) ♦ *You make such divine fudge!* ♦ *A divine dress is hanging on the mannequin in the store window.*

diving ['dɑɪv ɪŋ] **1.** *n.* the sport of jumping into water headfirst. (No plural form in this sense.) ♦ *The swimmer took some lessons in diving.* ♦ *In the Summer Olympics, diving is a popular event.* **2.** *n.* the activity of remaining underwater for periods of time, as with scuba diving. (No plural form in this sense.) ♦ *The family went diving during their Caribbean vacation.* ♦ *Bob put air in his scuba tank so that he could go diving.*

divinity [dɪ 'vɪn ə ti] **1.** *n.* a god; someone or something that is divine. ♦ *The Hindu religion includes more than one divinity.* ♦ *A shrine was built to honor the divinity.* **2.** *n.* the study of religion; the study of God; theology. (No plural form in this sense.) ♦ *The student decided to go to a school of divinity.* ♦ *Divinity proved to be the most thought-provoking course I took in college.*

divisible [dɪ 'vɪz ə bəl] **1.** *adj.* [of a number] able to be divided by another number with no remainder. (Adv: *divisibly.*) ♦ *Fourteen is divisible by 1, 2, 7, and 14.* ♦ *Twelve is not divisible by 5.* **2.** *adj.* able to be divided; able to be separated. (Adv: *divisibly.*) ♦ *This novel is not divisible into chapters. The story just flows from one event to another.* ♦ *The problem is divisible into a number of smaller difficulties that can be solved one at a time.*

division [dɪ 'vɪ ʒən] **1.** *n.* the process of dividing one number by another number. (No plural form in this sense.) ♦ *The teacher taught the third graders division.* ♦ *Division is the reverse of multiplication.* **2.** *n.* a split; a physical separation; a dividing line. ♦ *After the first hole, the division between the professional and amateur golfers was quite clear.* ♦ *The fence marked the division between the neighbors' yards.* **3.** *n.* the cause of ②. ♦ *The couple went to a marriage counselor to overcome the division that separated them.* ♦ *The division over the inheritance tore the family apart.* **4.** *n.* a major part of a very large company. ♦ *The manufacturing division was sold to another company.* ♦ *The large corporation had divisions in various states.* **5.** *n.* apportionment; dividing into portions. (No plural form in this sense.) ♦ *The division of work between my coworkers and me is unfair.* ♦ *Tom's will mandated the division of his estate between his favorite charities.*

divisive [dɪ 'vɑɪ sɪv] *adj.* causing opposition; causing arguments. (Adv: *divisively.*) ♦ *Politics can be a divisive issue even among friends.* ♦ *After many years, no one could *remember the divisive comment that started the family feud.*

divisor [dɪ 'vɑɪ zɚ] *n.* a number that is divided into another number. ♦ *In the equation "30 divided by 10 equals 3," 10 is the divisor.* ♦ *You can say that you divide the dividend by the divisor or that you divide the divisor into the dividend. These are two ways to refer to the same thing.*

divorce [dɪ 'vors] **1.** *n.* the legal termination of a marriage. (No plural form in this sense.) ♦ *The counselor suggested that divorce might be the best solution.* ♦ *Divorce is unpleasant for everyone involved.* **2.** *n.* an instance of ①. ♦ *The children were upset by their parents' divorce.* ♦ *Mary and Tom got a divorce after one year of marriage.* **3.** *tv.* to end one's marriage to someone. ♦ *Tom divorced Anne because they weren't compatible.* ♦ *Bill and Jane divorced each other.* **4.** *tv.* to grant ① to a husband and wife. ♦ *The judge divorced the couple.* ♦ *The decree officially divorced the feuding couple.* **5.** *iv.* to separate oneself from something else. (Takes a reflexive object.) ♦ *As my troubles mounted, I divorced myself from reality.* ♦ *Bill divorced himself from office politics.*

divorced [dɪ 'vorst] *adj.* having had one's marriage terminated in a court of law. ♦ *The divorced woman did not want to remarry.* ♦ *A support group has been formed for the children of divorced parents.*

divorcée [dɪ 'vor 'si] *n.* a divorced woman. (From French.) ♦ *The divorcée was happy to be rid of her husband.* ♦ *The divorcée enjoyed quiet evenings with her girlfriends.*

divulge [dɪ 'vʌldʒ] *tv.* to tell a secret; to reveal something. ♦ *Betraying a confidence, John divulged the secret to Mary.* ♦ *The president asked the managers not to divulge the news of the merger.*

dizziness ['dɪz i nəs] *n.* giddiness; lightheadedness. (No plural form in this sense.) ♦ *The medication caused terrible dizziness.* ♦ *Tom lay down until his dizziness passed.*

dizzy ['dɪz i] **1.** *adj.* feeling like everything is spinning around; not steady. (Adv: *dizzily.* Comp: *dizzier;* sup: *dizziest.*) ♦ *The toddler was dizzy after spinning around in circles.* ♦ *Watching the spinning top makes me dizzy.* **2.** *adj.* confusing; hectic. (Informal. Adv: *dizzily.* Comp: *dizzier;* sup: *dizziest.*) ♦ *After a few dizzy days, things calmed down at the office.* ♦ *We worked at a dizzy pace for three hours and then collapsed.*

dizzying ['dɪz i ɪŋ] **1.** *adj.* causing dizziness; causing someone to be unsteady. (Adv: *dizzyingly.*) ♦ *The dizzying roller coaster was the most popular ride at the carnival.* ♦ *This drug may have a dizzying effect.* **2.** *adj.* rapid and chaotic. (Figurative on ①. Adv: *dizzyingly.*) ♦ *After the dizzying pace of business, Bob looks forward to his annual vacation.* ♦ *My social schedule was dizzying when I was in high school.*

D.J. See disc jockey.

do ['du] **1.** *tv.* to perform an action; to finish an action; to end an action. (Pt: did; pp: done. See does, the third-person singular.) ♦ *I do exercises every morning.* ♦ *I did the report last night.* **2.** *tv.* to solve something; to find an answer. ♦ *Jimmy did the puzzle very quickly.* ♦ *I need a pencil and paper to do this math problem.* **3.** *tv.* to cover a distance; to go at a certain speed. ♦ *The racecar does over 100 miles per hour.* ♦ *We can do the entire trip on one tank of gas.* **4.** *iv.* to be OK; to suit one's needs. ♦ *Any salad dressing will do.* ♦ *I don't need a fancy car, my old car does fine.* **5.** *iv.* to fare; to get along. (Used to ask if someone is feeling all right, to inquire of someone's health.) ♦ *"How do you do?"* ♦ *Sally was doing fine with her new job.* **6.** *aux.* <a question word in the present and past tenses.> (In the future tense, will is used. Takes a bare verb.) ♦ *Do you want peas or carrots with dinner?* ♦ *Did you go to New York or Boston last year?* **7.** *aux.* <a form used to make negative constructions.> (Takes a bare verb.) ♦ *I don't want any peas, thank you.* ♦ *Bob didn't want to tell his teacher that he'd forgotten his homework.* **8.** *aux.* <a form used to emphasize a verb.> (Takes a bare verb.) ♦ *I do want carrots tonight!* ♦ *I did know how to get to Minneapolis, but I've forgotten.* **9.** *aux.* <a particle used to repeat a verb that has already been said or written.> ♦ *I want to go to the mall. So do I.* ♦ *Brian knocked his milk over, and after it was cleaned up, he did it again.*

docile ['dɑs əl] *adj.* tame; submissive; obedient. (Adv: *docilely.*) ♦ *The docile dog allowed the little girl to put a hat on him.* ♦ *After a good meal, Tom became very docile and friendly.*

dock ['dɑk] **1.** *n.* a pier; a platform built for moving things and people on and off boats and ships. ♦ *Several people were fishing off the dock early in the morning.* ♦ *The boat pulled up to the dock to let the passengers get on.* **2.** *n.* a platform for loading and unloading goods. ♦ *The dock for loading trucks is at the back of the factory.* ♦ *John blew his horn as he pulled the truck up to the dock.* **3.** *tv.* to bring a ship or boat up to a dock. ♦ *The captain gently docked the boat.* ♦ *The storm made it difficult to dock the huge ship.* **4.** *tv.* to deduct money from someone's paycheck or allowance as a punishment. ♦ *Bob's pay was docked because he had been late twice.* ♦ *I'm docking your allowance until the broken window is paid for.* **5.** *iv.* [for a boat or ship] to come into a dock; [for a boat or ship] to tie up to a dock. ♦ *The ship from Europe docks tonight.* ♦ *The crowd watched from the pier as the ship docked.*

doctor ['dɑk tɚ] **1.** *n.* someone who has received a doctorate from a university. ♦ *The program is run by a doctor of economics.* ♦ *The banker consulted with a doctor of finance.* **2.** *n.* someone who is licensed to practice medicine; a medical doctor. (Abbreviated *Dr.*) ♦ *The doctor agreed to perform the operation.* ♦ *Only doctors can write prescriptions.* **3.** *tv.* [for anyone] to treat someone who is sick; [for anyone] to nurse someone. ♦ *Anne doctored her sick children.* ♦ *The pioneers had to doctor each other on the long wagon trails.* **4.** *tv.* to add something to something, especially to food or drink. (Informal.) ♦ *Lisa doctored the punch.* ♦ *I doctored the strawberries with a little sugar.*

doctorate ['dɑk tɚ ɪt] *n.* the highest degree awarded by a university. ♦ *The university awarded the company president an honorary doctorate.* ♦ *Bob's doctorate hangs on a wall in his office.*

doctrinaire [dɑk trə 'ner] *adj.* dogmatic; devoted to a particular doctrine. (Adv: *doctrinairely.*) ♦ *The doctrinaire researcher would not consider the validity of another theory.* ♦ *Do not be so doctrinaire. Be more flexible.*

doctrine ['dɑk trɪn] *n.* a statement of policy; a set of beliefs. ♦ *The new manager promoted her doctrine of management.* ♦ *How are the doctrines of the two churches different?*

document ['dɑk jə mənt] **1.** *n.* a piece of paper with writing or printing on it; a text. ♦ *The computer printed my document.* ♦ *A marriage certificate is an official document.* **2.** *tv.* to prepare oneself to prove something by making a written record. ♦ *The manager documented the employee's errors and deceptions.* ♦ *The teacher documented the student's bad behavior.* **3.** *tv.* to provide references that will support what one has written. ♦ *Students must document their sources in their reports.* ♦ *I documented all the dates of birth in the family tree.* **4.** *tv.* to record something in detail over time. ♦ *The historian documented the rule of a series of dictators in the small country.* ♦ *Grandma's diary documented her entire life.*

documentary [dɑk jə 'mɛn tə ri] **1.** *n.* a film that presents factual material instead of a made-up story. ♦ *Mike made a documentary about the life of a cancer patient.* ♦ *The teacher showed the class a documentary about butterflies.* **2.** *adj.* presenting factual material instead of something made up. ♦ *The inaccuracies in the documentary account of World War II angered many veterans.* ♦ *The documentary movie was excellent, but few people went to see it.*

documentation [dɑk jə mɛn 'te ʃən] **1.** *n.* documents that support one's claim; documents that prove one's point. (No plural form in this sense.) ♦ *Mary provided the immigration clerk with documentation of her citizenship.* ♦ *The documentation about the benefits of the new drug was flawed.* **2.** *n.* instructions for operating a computer; instructions for running computer software. (No plural form in this sense.) ♦ *I hate reading documentation, and I would rather just experiment.* ♦ *When Bob had trouble with the computer, he read the documentation for help.*

dodge ['dɑdʒ] **1.** *tv.* to get out of the way of someone or something. ♦ *Mike dodged the cars as he ran through the parking lot.* ♦ *Anne dodged the snowballs that Mary threw at her.* **2.** *tv.* to avoid something; to evade something. (Figurative on ①.) ♦ *Mike tried to dodge the question because he didn't know the answer.* ♦ *The politician dodged many controversial issues in her speech.*

doe ['do] *n.* a female of certain animals, such as the deer, antelope, rabbit, etc. ♦ *Does of the deer family do not have antlers.* ♦ *A doe and her baby ate foliage in the woods.*

doer ['du ɚ] **1.** *n.* someone who does something. ♦ *Who is the doer of this deed?* ♦ *The doer of the action is called the subject of the verb.* **2.** *n.* someone who does things well or fast; someone who gets results. ♦ *A real doer was needed to take charge of the project.* ♦ *The lazy employer was not a doer.*

does ['dʌz] <the third-person present singular of **do**.>

doeskin ['do skɪn] **1.** *n.* leather made from the skin of female deer. (No plural form in this sense.) ♦ *My wallet was made from doeskin.* ♦ *Doeskin is soft and pliable.* **2.** *adj.* made from ①. ♦ *A doeskin jacket is very soft.* ♦ *Mary bought an expensive doeskin purse.*

doesn't ['dʌz ənt] *cont.* "does not." ♦ *Jimmy doesn't like to go to school.* ♦ *The judge doesn't want the trial to last for a month.*

dog ['dɔg] **1.** *n.* a domesticated canine animal usually kept as a pet. ♦ *Collies, terriers, and beagles are all types of dogs.* ♦ *The dog and its puppies ran outside to play with the children.* **2.** *tv.* to follow someone closely; to pursue someone diligently. ♦ *The toddler dogged his mother around the house, frightened of being alone.* ♦ *Reporters dogged the candidate until they caught him in a scandal.* **3.** *tv.* to afflict someone or something; to bother someone or something. (Figurative on ②.) ♦ *John's deficient memory dogged him throughout his career.* ♦ *Anne's stuttering dogged her until she saw a speech therapist.* **4. dog-eat-dog** *idiom* a situation in which one has to act ruthlessly in order to survive or succeed; ruthless competition. ♦ *It is dog-eat-dog in the world of business these days.* ♦ *Universities are not quiet, peaceful places. It's a case of dog-eat-dog for promotion.* **5. hair of the dog that bit one** *idiom* a drink of liquor taken when one has a hangover; a drink of liquor taken when one is recovering from drinking too much liquor. ♦ *Oh, I'm miserable. I need some of the hair of the dog that bit me.* ♦ *That's some hangover you've got there, Bob. Here, drink this. It's the hair of the dog that bit you.*

doghouse ['dɔg hɑʊs] **1.** *n., irreg.* a small outdoor shelter for a dog to sleep in; a kennel. (Pl: [...hɑʊ zəz].) ♦ *I wrote the name of my dog over the doghouse's door.* ♦ *Bob built a doghouse for his dog.* **2. in the doghouse** *idiom* in trouble; in (someone's) disfavor. ♦ *I'm really in the doghouse. I was late for an appointment.* ♦ *I hate being in the doghouse all the time. I don't know why I can't stay out of trouble.*

dogma ['dɔg mə] **1.** *n.* the beliefs taught by a particular religion. (No plural form in this sense.) ♦ *Tom rejected the dogma of his church and joined another.* ♦ *The religion that I am a member of has no dogma at all.* **2.** *n.* an obligatory doctrine. (No plural form in this sense.) ♦ *The older teacher retired rather than support modern educational dogma.* ♦ *No longer able to accept the company management's dogma, Bob left.*

dogmatic [dɔg 'mæt ɪk] **1.** *adj.* of or about dogma. (Adv: *dogmatically* [...ɪk li].) ♦ *The book explained the dogmatic principles of the religion.* ♦ *The pastor was quite concerned with dogmatic matters.* **2.** *adj.* overbearing; arrogant in supporting one's beliefs or opinions. (Adv: *dogmatically* [...ɪk li].) ♦ *Bob has very dogmatic religious opinions.* ♦ *Mary's dogmatic approach to managing employees sometimes backfired.*

doings ['du ɪŋz] *n.* an event; something that happens. (Treated as plural. No singular form.) ♦ *There were big doings planned for the celebration.* ♦ *The family planned the doings to celebrate the couple's anniversary.*

doldrums ['dol drəmz] **1.** *n.* an area of light winds, at sea, north of the equator. (Treated as plural.) ♦ *The yacht and crew spent two weeks drifting, unable to move from the doldrums.* ♦ *In the doldrums, the sailboat barely moved.* **2.** *n.* inactivity; gloominess; boredom. (Treated as plural.) ♦ *During the doldrums of the summer, I began to look forward to school.* ♦ *The rainy, cold weather only reinforced the doldrums I found myself in.*

dole ['dol] **1. dole out** *tv.* + *adv.* to give something out a piece at time; to give a small amount of something out. ♦ *Anne doled out the cookies to everyone at the table.* ♦ *The children waited for their mother to dole out their allowances.* **2.** *n.* money that is received from charity or the government; welfare. (No plural form in this sense.) ♦ *Mary received government dole while she was unemployed.* ♦ *The charity does not like to refer to the money it gives out as the dole.*

doll ['dɑl] **1.** *n.* a figure of a human or animal, often a baby, used as a toy. ♦ *The children were playing with action figure dolls.* ♦ *The child gently laid the doll in the crib.* **2.** *n.* an attractive or cute male or female of any age. (Informal.) ♦ *Bob's girlfriend is quite a doll.* ♦ *Jane thought her boyfriend was a real doll.* **3. get (all) dolled up** *idiom* to dress (oneself) up. ♦ *I have to get all dolled up for the dance tonight.* ♦ *I just love to get dolled up in my best clothes.*

dollar ['dɑl ɚ] *n.* the main unit of money in the United States; $1; 100 cents. (The dollar is also the name of the main unit of money in several other countries, but each is worth a different value than the U.S. dollar.) ♦ *A dollar is equal to four quarters, ten dimes, or twenty nickels.* ♦ *The prices were rounded to the nearest dollar.*

dollop ['dɑl əp] *n.* a lump or gob of something. ♦ *The sundae had a dollop of whipped cream on top.* ♦ *Bob put a large dollop of sour cream on the baked potato.*

dolly ['dɑl i] **1.** *n.* a (small) doll. ♦ *Susie slept in bed with her dolly.* ♦ *The dolly was dressed in cute little clothes.* **2.** *n.* a frame with wheels, used to move heavy things. ♦ *The mover loaded the freezer on a dolly.* ♦ *The crates were moved on the dolly.*

dolphin ['dɑl fɪn] *n.* a species of sleek, intelligent mammal that lives in the ocean; a kind of porpoise. ♦ *We watched the dolphins leaping in the ocean waves.* ♦ *Dolphins are thought of as friendly animals.*

dolt ['dolt] *n.* a stupid person; a fool; an idiot. ♦ *I felt like a dolt when I forgot the woman's name.* ♦ *Jane's date turned out to be a dolt.*

domain [do 'men] **1.** *n.* the area where someone or something is typically found. ♦ *My dog's domain is the backyard, but it's usually in my bed instead.* ♦ *The library is my domain during the school year.* **2.** *n.* the area under the control of a ruler. (No plural form in this sense.) ♦ *The ruler's domain stretches from the ocean to the river.* ♦ *The chief marked the bounds of his domain with special symbols.* **3.** *n.* an area of interest or knowledge. ♦ *History is not my domain, but I still know some basic facts.* ♦ *You will have to ask someone whose domain is mathematics.*

dome ['dom] *n.* a rounded roof; the top of a building shaped like an upside-down bowl. ♦ *The church's dome could be seen for miles.* ♦ *The Capitol in Washington, D.C., is a white building with a large dome.*

domestic [də 'mɛs tɪk] **1.** *adj.* of or about the home; of, about, or within the family. (Adv: *domestically* [...ɪk li].) ♦ *The police called the fight between the husband and wife a domestic quarrel.* ♦ *When I arrive home from work, I must attend to my domestic chores.* **2.** *adj.* not imported; not foreign. (Adv: *domestically* [...ɪk li].) ♦ *Jane bought a domestic car.* ♦ *Mary prefers domestic wines, especially ones from California.* **3.** *adj.* tame; not wild. (Adv: *domestically* [...ɪk li].) ♦ *Dogs are domestic animals.* ♦ *In the West, there are domestic and wild horses.* **4.** *n.* a servant who helps in one's home. ♦ *The Smiths are so wealthy, they can afford two domestics.* ♦ *The immigrant worked as a domestic for many years.*

domesticate [də 'mɛs tə ket] *tv.* to make something tame; to make a wild animal tame. ♦ *Lisa tried to domesticate the baby raccoon, but it ran away.* ♦ *I was unable to domesticate the wild dog.*

domicile ['dɑm ə saɪl] **1.** *n.* a house; a home; the place where someone lives. (Formal.) ♦ *The hermit never left his humble domicile.* ♦ *Bill goes to school in Iowa, but his legal domicile is in Illinois.* **2.** *tv.* to provide someone with housing, usually temporarily. ♦ *The university had to domiciles the extra students in a motel for a few weeks.* ♦ *The army will domicile the recruits on the base.*

dominant ['dɑm ə nənt] **1.** *adj.* having the most influence; foremost and strongest. (Adv: *dominantly.*) ♦ *The dominant color in the design is red.* ♦ *The dominant country threatened to invade its neighboring countries.* **2.** *adj.* [of one of a group of competing genes] more powerful than competing genes. (Adv: *dominantly.*) ♦ *The gene for dark hair is dominant.* ♦ *The gene for brown eyes is dominant; the gene for blue eyes is recessive.*

dominate ['dɑm ə net] *tv.* to overshadow someone or something; to be foremost among certain people or things. ♦ *The older brother dominated his younger siblings.* ♦ *One very tall building dominates the city's skyline.*

dominating ['dɑm ɪ net ɪŋ] *adj.* foremost; tending to dominate someone or something. (Adv: *dominatingly.*) ♦ *Billy cowered when his dominating brother gave orders.* ♦ *The enormous monument is the dominating structure in the park.*

domination [dɑm ə 'ne ʃən] *n.* practicing or executing control. (No plural form in this sense.) ♦ *People suffered the dictator's domination for years.* ♦ *Bob's constant domination of the conversation is annoying.*

domineering [dɑm ə 'nɪr ɪŋ] *adj.* having a controlling or dominating manner. (Adv: *domineeringly.*) ♦ *The domineering father made every decision in his children's lives.* ♦ *Congress battled the domineering president for power.*

dominion [də 'mɪn jən] **1.** *n.* rule; authority. (No plural form in this sense.) ♦ *The king has dominion over all the lands.* ♦ *My parents always had complete dominion over the child's welfare.* **2.** *n.* all the lands under the rule of one government. (No plural form in this sense.) ♦ *Great Britain once had a huge dominion.* ♦ *Canada was once called the Dominion of Canada.*

domino ['dɑ mɪ no] **1.** *n.* a rectangular block—about 1″ × 2″ × ¼″—used in dominoes ②. (Pl in *-es.*) ♦ *Mike likes to set up dominoes in a row and then watch them fall.* ♦ *At the beginning of the game, each domino is upside down.* **2. dominoes** *n.* a game played with ① where each player tries to match up tiles by placing together ends of tiles that have the same number of dots. (Treated as plural.) ♦ *Several people played dominoes in the park.* ♦ *I didn't know how to play dominoes, so Bob taught me.*

don ['dɑn] *tv.* to put on a piece of clothing; to put on clothing. ♦ *Billy donned his bathing suit before he went to the beach.* ♦ *I donned a coat and hat before going outside.*

donate ['do net] *tv.* to give something to a charity or other organization. ♦ *Steve donated the old couch to charity.* ♦ *Mary donates money to several charities regularly.*

donation [do 'ne ʃən] *n.* money or goods given to a charity or other organization. ♦ *The donation of food was quickly used by hungry people.* ♦ *Anne gives a donation to her church every week.*

done [dən] **1.** pp of do. **2.** *adj.* completed; finished. (Not compared.) ♦ *Tell me when you are done.* ♦ *John reread his essay when it was done.* **3.** *adj.* [of cooking] completed.

(Can be compared.) ♦ *The cake is done when the tester comes out clean.* ♦ *Your steak is more done than mine.*

donkey ['dɔŋ ki] *n.* an ass; an animal smaller than a horse, used to carry things or people. ♦ *Donkeys carried the heavy load.* ♦ *The donkey walked slowly up the path.*

donor ['don ɚ] *n.* someone who gives something; someone who makes a donation. ♦ *The hospital asked for blood donors.* ♦ *The donor of the money asked to remain anonymous.*

don't [dont] *cont.* "do not." ♦ *Don't move!* ♦ *If I don't finish mowing the lawn, I can't go to the movie.*

donut ['do nət] See doughnut.

doodle ['dud l] **1.** *n.* a design made when someone is bored or not paying attention. ♦ *Even the artist's doodles brought high prices at the auction.* ♦ *Bored, John made doodles on his pad during the meeting.* **2.** *iv.* to make drawings when one is not paying attention. ♦ *While he waited for Susan to return, Bob doodled.* ♦ *The teacher became very annoyed when he saw the student doodling.*

doom ['dum] **1.** *n.* a horrible fate; a death that cannot be avoided. (No plural form in this sense.) ♦ *I feared that doom and disaster were in my future.* ♦ *The hero saved the city from doom.* **2.** *tv.* to cause something to fail; to destine something to be ruined or destroyed. ♦ *The factory closings doomed the city's economy.* ♦ *An order from the mayor doomed the run-down building.* **3.** *tv.* [for something] to condemn someone to an unpleasant future. ♦ *The horrible disease doomed its victims to a painful death.* ♦ *The prison sentence doomed the thief to many years in jail.*

doomed ['dumd] **1.** *adj.* destined to fail. ♦ *The marriage was doomed from the beginning.* ♦ *This voyage is doomed, and nothing good can come from it.* **2.** *adj.* condemned to an unpleasant future. ♦ *The doomed sailors were marooned on a desert island.* ♦ *The doomed criminal begged for forgiveness.*

doomsday ['dumz de] **1.** *n.* the end of the world. (No plural form in this sense.) ♦ *No one knows when doomsday will come.* ♦ *The leader of the religious cult says doomsday will come July 15.* **2.** *adj.* <the adj. use of ①.> ♦ *The cult leader made a doomsday prophecy.* ♦ *The doomsday date came and went, and the world still existed.*

door ['dor] **1.** *n.* a movable panel of wood, glass, or metal that fits into an opening through which someone or something may pass. ♦ *A fireman broke down the door to rescue the child from the burning house.* ♦ *The door swung open in the wind.* **2.** *n.* a doorway; the opening into which ① fits. ♦ *When Jane walked down the stairs, she saw Bill at the door.* ♦ *Bob walked through the door carrying an armload of packages.* **3.** *n.* the (figurative) route or pathway to something, such as opportunity. (Figurative on ②.) ♦ *College is the door to greater financial success.* ♦ *The influence of Mary's friends opened the door to her finding a job.* **4.** *n.* a room or a house that has a door. (Used to describe where one location is in relation to another location.) ♦ *My friend's apartment is two doors away from mine.* ♦ *The classroom is two doors down the hall from the gymnasium.*

doorbell ['dor bɛl] **1.** *n.* a bell or similar signal—located near a door—that sounds when a visitor activates it. ♦ *My dog always barks at the sound of the doorbell.* ♦ *I ran to open the door when I heard the doorbell.* **2.** *n.* the button that activates the signal that someone is at the door. ♦ *The doorbell has a light so that it can be easily seen at night.* ♦ *An impatient visitor pushed the doorbell several times.*

doorman ['dor mən] *n., irreg.* someone, usually a male, who works in the lobby of an apartment building or hotel to guard the entrance, hold the door open for people, call taxis, etc. (Pl: doormen.) ♦ *Our doorman knows everyone who lives in our apartment building.* ♦ *The doorman opened the door for me.*

doormat ['dor mæt] **1.** *n.* a mat in front of a door on which people wipe their feet. ♦ *We wiped our muddy feet on the doormat.* ♦ *The homeowner's initials were woven into the doormat.* **2.** *n.* someone who is humiliated by other people. (Figurative on ①.) ♦ *Mary says that Bill is a doormat who lets people take advantage of him, but I think he's just a nice guy who likes to help people.* ♦ *Don't be a doormat. Insist on your rights!*

doormen ['dor mən] pl of doorman.

doorstep ['dor stɛp] **1.** *n.* a step just outside a door. ♦ *The newspaper is delivered to our doorstep every morning.* ♦ *Reaching for the doorbell, Bill tripped on the doorstep.* **2. at someone's doorstep, on my doorstep** *idiom* in someone's care; as someone's responsibility. ♦ *Why do you always have to lay your problems at my doorstep?* ♦ *I don't want it left on my doorstep.*

doorway ['dor we] *n.* the opening in a wall through which a person can walk to enter or exit a room; the opening into which a door fits. ♦ *Jane stood in the doorway but didn't enter the room.* ♦ *The basketball player had to duck when walking through the doorway.*

dope ['dop] **1.** *n.* illegal drugs. (Slang.) ♦ *A few students were smoking dope in the bathroom.* ♦ *John was punished when dope was found in his locker.* **2.** *n.* information; news; gossip. (Slang.) ♦ *Mary called David to get the dope on Bill.* ♦ *The local newspaper printed the latest dope on the mayor's scandal.* **3.** *n.* an idiot; a fool; a stupid person. (Slang.) ♦ *Billy acts like a dope when his parents aren't around.* ♦ *That dope told the teacher I was cutting class!*

dorm ['dorm] *n.* a dormitory; a building in which students live on a college campus. ♦ *Jane was assigned to a coed dorm at college.* ♦ *Living in the dorm was cheaper than living in a fraternity house.*

dormant ['dor mənt] **1.** *adj.* temporarily inactive, as if sleeping. (Adv: *dormantly.*) ♦ *Mary reactivated her dormant credit-card account.* ♦ *The dormant volcano has not erupted in two hundred years.* **2.** *adj.* [of plant tissue] alive but not growing. (Adv: *dormantly.*) ♦ *The dormant grass will grow again when the drought ends.* ♦ *Many kinds of trees are dormant during the winter.*

dormitory ['dorm ɪ tor i] **1.** *n.* a building or room containing communal sleeping facilities, especially on a college campus. (See also dorm.) ♦ *The university has five dormitories to house students.* ♦ *The prison dormitory is heavily guarded.* **2.** *n.* a room housing communal sleeping facilities. ♦ *The crew's dormitory was near the ship's engine room.* ♦ *The hostel's dormitory is on the second floor.*

dosage ['dos ɪdʒ] *n.* a recommended amount of medicine. (No plural form in this sense.) ♦ *Recommendations for the proper dosage of cold medicine are printed on the box.* ♦ *This prescription is for a low dosage of painkiller.*

dose ['dos] **1.** *n.* the amount of medicine that is to be taken at one time. ♦ *Bill forgot to take the second dose of his medication.* ♦ *Jane took a dose of medicine when her cold got worse.* **2.** *tv.* to give someone or something a specific amount of medicine. ♦ *The nurse dosed the patient as directed by the doctor.* ♦ *The sick man dosed himself with cold medicine.*

dossier ['dɔs i e] *n.* a set of papers containing information about a person and the events relating to that person. (French.) ♦ *The government agency kept a dossier on the suspected arsonist.* ♦ *When he applied for the position, Bill gave the university his dossier.*

dot ['dɑt] **1.** *n.* a small spot; a small round mark. ♦ *The leaking pen left dots of ink on the tablecloth.* ♦ *The dot at the end of this sentence is called a period.* **2.** *tv.* to provide something with a small spot. ♦ *The penmanship teacher reminded the students to dot each* i. ♦ *The light rain dotted the car's windshield with tiny drops.* **3. on the dot** *idiom* at exactly the right time. ♦ *I'll be there at noon on the dot.* ♦ *I expect to see you here at eight o'clock on the dot.*

dote ['dot] **dote on** *iv.* + *prep. phr.* to coddle someone; to pamper someone; to spoil someone. ♦ *The new parents doted on their baby.* ♦ *The newlyweds doted on each other.*

dotted ['dɑt ɪd] **dotted line** *n.* a printed line made of a row of dots, such as "...............". ♦ *Please sign your name on the dotted line.* ♦ *The form was covered with boxes for check marks and a lot of dotted lines to sign my name on.*

double ['dʌb əl] **1.** *adj.* having twice the amount as something else. (Adv: *doubly.*) ♦ *I made a double batch of cookies.* ♦ *Feeling very hungry, Mike ordered a double hamburger.* **2.** *n.* someone who looks exactly like someone else. ♦ *The twins are perfect doubles.* ♦ *When the makeup artist finished, the stuntman was the star's double.* **3.** *n.* [in baseball] an instance of hitting the ball in which the batter reaches second base safely. ♦ *After leading off the inning with a double, Lisa stole third base.* ♦ *Mary hit a double, and the crowd cheered wildly.* **4. double over** *tv.* + *adv.* to fold something in half in order to make it twice as thick. ♦ *To fit the letter in the envelope, Susan doubled it over.* ♦ *The mail carrier doubled over the magazine to get it in the mailbox.* **5.** *tv.* to cause something to become twice the amount that it previously was. ♦ *I doubled the cake recipe because I was making two cakes.* ♦ *Adding six new chapters doubled the size of the textbook.* **6.** *iv.* to become twice the amount that something was previously. ♦ *In nine years, money deposited at eight percent interest will double.* ♦ *As the bread dough rises, it will double in size.* **7. double as** *iv.* + *prep. phr.* [for someone or something] to be used as someone or something else. ♦ *When Billy was an infant, his buggy doubled as a bed.* ♦ *As a salesman, Bob's car often doubles as his office.* **8. double up** *iv.* + *adv.* to share facilities of some type. ♦ *There aren't enough beds, so some of you will have to double up.* ♦ *We doubled up because there weren't enough menus for our table.* **9. see double** *idiom* to see two of everything instead of one. ♦ *When I was driving, I saw two people on the road instead of one. I'm seeing double. There's something wrong with my eyes.* ♦ *Mike thought he was seeing double when he saw Mary with her sister. He didn't know she had a twin.*

double-barreled ['dʌb əl 'bɛr əld] **1.** *adj.* [of a gun] with two barrels. ♦ *The sheriff held a double-barreled shotgun.* ♦ *It takes longer to load a double-barreled gun.* **2.** *adj.* powerful; having twice the expected impact. (Figurative on ①.) ♦ *The double-barreled energy of Mike's speech whipped the crowd into a frenzy.* ♦ *To win the nomination, Mary knew she had to make a double-barreled presentation that would generate trust and enthusiasm.*

double-breasted ['dʌb əl 'brɛs tɪd] *adj.* [of a coat or suit coat] with a large front overlap and parallel rows of buttons. ♦ *Double-breasted coats have two rows of buttons down the front.* ♦ *A double-breasted suit coat looks best when buttoned.*

double-cross ['dʌb əl 'krɔs] **1.** *tv.* to betray someone with whom you have agreed to swindle another person, in a way that the first person is harmed. ♦ *Mike and Max robbed a bank, but then Max double-crossed Mike by running away with the money.* ♦ *After the partners took the money, one double-crossed the other by going to the police.* **2.** *tv.* to betray someone. ♦ *Sally double-crossed her friend by revealing the secret.* ♦ *The spy double-crossed the government he was spying for.*

double-crosser [dəb əl 'krɔs ɚ] *n.* someone who betrays someone. ♦ *Bob is a double-crosser who shouldn't be trusted.* ♦ *John was quite a double-crosser for revealing Mary's secret.*

double-decker ['dʌb əl 'dɛk ɚ] *adj.* [of things] having two layers or levels. ♦ *The double-decker sandwich was so big, I couldn't open my mouth wide enough to eat it.* ♦ *An old-fashioned double-decker bus took tourists around the city.*

doubleheader ['dʌb əl 'hɛd ɚ] *n.* two sporting events played on the same day, the second immediately after the first. ♦ *Our team lost both games of the doubleheader.* ♦ *The first game of the doubleheader begins at 1:00 P.M.*

double-jointed ['dʌb əl 'dʒɔɪnt ɪd] *adj.* [having joints] very limber and able to bend backwards. (Adv: *double-jointedly.*) ♦ *The double-jointed gymnast was an amazing athlete.* ♦ *A double-jointed thumb can bend backward into an awkward position.*

double-space ['dʌb əl 'spes] *tv.* to create a document so that each line of text is between two blank lines. ♦ *The students were required to double-space their reports.* ♦ *Reporters often double-space their stories so that they can use the blank space for corrections.*

doubly ['dʌb li] *adv.* twice [as much]; in a manner that has twice the amount of something. ♦ *I was doubly glad that the weather was clear because I had two outdoor activities planned.* ♦ *After rechecking the answers to the math problems, I was doubly sure they were correct.*

doubt ['dɑʊt] **1.** *n.* lack of belief; uncertainty. (No plural form in this sense.) ♦ *Widespread doubt about the candidate's ability to do a good job caused him to lose the election.* ♦ *There is little doubt that it will rain today.* **2.** *n.* a feeling of disbelief about something; a feeling of uncertainty about something. (Often plural.) ♦ *After he lost the game, Bill had doubts about his athletic ability.* ♦ *The confident boxer had no doubts about his chances of winning.* **3.** *tv.* to not believe or not trust something; to be uncertain about something; to consider something unlikely. ♦ *The police officer doubted Mike's story.* ♦ *No one doubts Mary's abilities at the office.* **4. doubting Thomas** *idiom* someone who will not easily believe something without strong proof or evidence. ♦ *Mary won't believe that I have a dog until she sees him. She's such a doubting Thomas.* ♦ *This school is full of doubting Thomases. They want to see Jimmy's new bike with their own eyes.*

doubtful ['dɑʊt fʊl] **1.** *adj.* [of someone] having doubts. (Adv: *doubtfully.*) ♦ *The doubtful police officer didn't know whether to believe the story.* ♦ *John felt doubtful about getting married.* **2.** *adj.* not likely to succeed; not promising. (Adv: *doubtfully.*) ♦ *A more doubtful proposition has never been presented to Congress!* ♦ *This old car has a doubtful future.*

doubtless ['dɑʊt ləs] **1.** *adv.* without doubt; certainly; surely. ♦ *You will doubtless pass the test.* ♦ *The lost cat will doubtless find its way home again.* **2.** *adj.* free from doubt. (Adv: *doubtlessly.*) ♦ *Anne was doubtless about her decision to accept the job offer.* ♦ *Bill remains doubtless concerning the quality of his professional skills.*

douche ['duʃ] *iv.* to use a current of water to clean a body cavity, usually the vagina. ♦ *Anne douched in the privacy of her bathroom.* ♦ *To relieve Mary's discomfort, the gynecologist recommended that she douche.*

dough ['do] **1.** *n.* a soft mixture of flour, water, and possibly other ingredients. (No plural form in this sense.) ♦ *The bread dough was put into pans and baked.* ♦ *I added chocolate chips to the cookie dough.* **2.** *n.* money. (Slang. No plural form in this sense.) ♦ *The teenager needed some dough in order to go to the movies.* ♦ *Bob spent a lot of dough on vacation.*

doughnut AND **donut** ['do nət] *n.* a small, deep-fried cake shaped in a ring. ♦ *Bob ordered a doughnut and cup of coffee for breakfast.* ♦ *Anne dunked her donut in a glass of milk.*

douse ['dɑʊs] **1.** *tv.* to get someone or something very wet; to drench someone or something. ♦ *The thunderstorm doused Tom as he ran from the car to the store.* ♦ *Max doused the cat with the hose.* **2.** *iv.* to put out a flame with water. ♦ *The campers made sure the fire was completely doused.* ♦ *After burning most of the forest, the fire was finally doused.*

dove 1. ['dov] a pt of dive. **2.** ['dʌv] *n.* a gray or white bird, a little smaller than a pigeon. (Often thought of as a symbol of peace.) ♦ *The peace organization's flag has a dove on it.* ♦ *Seeing a dove is considered a good omen.* **3.** ['dʌv] *n.* someone who is against war. (Figurative on ①.) ♦ *Bill was called a dove when he protested rather than fight in the war.* ♦ *There were more hawks than doves, so the peace initiative was defeated.*

dovetail ['dʌv tel] **1.** *n.* one of a series of projections at the end of a board, shaped to fit snugly—at a right angle—into slots in another piece. (A way of joining the ends of boards tightly at a right angle. The projection is said to be shaped like the tail of a dove.) ♦ *The carpenter sanded the dovetail until it was smooth.* ♦ *All of our drawers have dovetails joining the side to the fronts.* **2.** *tv.* to connect wooden parts at a right angle with ①. ♦ *The carpenter dovetailed the sides of the drawers to the fronts of the drawers.* ♦ *I dovetailed the joints to form the strongest possible joint.* **3.** *iv.* [for parts, ideas, plans, etc.] to fit together exactly; to come together perfectly. (Figurative on ②.) ♦ *Bill's plans dovetailed with Mike's, so they took a trip together.* ♦ *Although two people separately made the surprise-party plans, the arrangements dovetailed perfectly.*

dowager ['dɑʊ ə dʒɚ] **1.** *n.* a widow who retains the title or property of her dead husband. ♦ *When Mrs. Wilson's husband died, she became a dowager.* ♦ *The dowager retained the title of "Duchess."* **2.** *n.* an impressive or dignified older woman. ♦ *The queen was a dignified dowager and greatly admired.* ♦ *The retired actress is a gracious dowager who continues to impress her fans.*

dowdy ['dɑʊ di] *adj.* old-fashioned; not in style; shabby. (Adv: *dowdily.* Comp: *dowdier;* sup: *dowdiest.*) ♦ *The dowdy old woman always wears gray.* ♦ *Sometimes dowdy fashions later come back into style.*

down ['dɑʊn] **1.** *adj.* aimed downward. ♦ *Take the down escalator to get to the toy section.* ♦ *Please do not go up the down staircase.* **2.** *adj.* sad; depressed. ♦ *Susie felt down when she lost her doll.* ♦ *John really looks down. Let's go try to cheer him up!* **3.** *adj.* finished; completed. (Not prenominal.) ♦ *Mary's got three applications down and only two more that she still has to finish.* ♦ *One chore down, three to be completed.* **4.** *adv.* from a higher place to a lower place; in a direction from a higher place to a lower place. ♦ *Please put that book down!* ♦ *The burglar knocked the lamp down.* **5.** *adv.* from an earlier time to a later time. ♦ *The pocket watch was handed down from father to son over the years.* ♦ *The children loved to hear the family stories that have come down from generation to generation.* **6.** *adv.* to travel south; to go to a place which corresponds to "down" or south on a map. ♦ *Lisa asked her friends in Canada to come down for a visit.* ♦ *Every winter my parents leave the snow behind and go down to Florida.* **7.** *adv.* onto paper; into writing. ♦ *John put his thoughts down on paper.* ♦ *Anne writes her appointments down on her calendar.* **8.** *adv.* as an advance payment against the purchase price. ♦ *If you put 25% down, you can pay for the rest later.* ♦ *The Smiths put a deposit down on a new house.* **9.** *adv.* with less energy, strength, production, volume, or intensity. ♦ *Production at the factory went down after the layoffs.* ♦ *Please calm down.* **10.** *adv.* over to; in a specific direction. (Informal.) ♦ *I went down to the store to buy groceries.* ♦ *If you go down to the corner, you can buy a newspaper there.* **11.** *prep.* to a lower place. ♦ *Doug ran down the stairs to the basement.* ♦ *The road wound down the hill.* **12.** *prep.* to the end of something; along the length of something. ♦ *Jane looked down the pier, but she didn't see Bob anywhere.* ♦ *Lost in thought, Mary walked down the empty beach.* **13.** *tv.* to knock someone down; to knock someone over. (Informal.) ♦ *The police officer downed the burglar.* ♦ *Not looking where he was running, Billy downed the toddler.* **14.** *tv.* to eat or swallow something very quickly and without much chewing. ♦ *Mike downed a glazed doughnut in one bite.* ♦ *The coyote downed the chicken and fled.* **15.** *n.* soft feathers, used to stuff pillows, quilts, etc. (No plural form in this sense.) ♦ *I am allergic to pillows made of down.* ♦ *Comforters stuffed with down are warm and cozy on cold winter nights.* **16. come down with something; be down with something** *idiom* to become or to be sick with some illness. ♦ *Susan came down with a bad cold and had to cancel her trip.* ♦ *I didn't go to work because I was down with the flu.* **17. down by some amount** *idiom* having a score that is lower, by the specified amount, than someone else's score or the other team's score. ♦ *At halftime, the home team* *was down by 14 points.* ♦ *Down by one run, the team scored two runs in the ninth inning and won the game.* **18. down and out** *idiom* having no money or means of support. ♦ *There are many young people down and out in the city.* ♦ *John gambled away all his fortune and is now completely down and out.* **19. down in the dumps** *idiom* sad or depressed. ♦ *I've been down in the dumps for the past few days.* ♦ *Try to cheer Jane up. She's down in the dumps for some reason.* **20. down in the mouth** *idiom* sad-faced; depressed and unsmiling. ♦ *Since her dog died, Lisa has been down in the mouth.* ♦ *Bob has been down in the mouth since the car wreck.*

downcast ['daʊn kæst] **1.** *adj.* sad; feeling low; depressed. ♦ *I was downcast for weeks after my best friend moved.* ♦ *The downcast student couldn't believe that he'd failed the test.* **2.** *adj.* [of eyes] aimed downward. ♦ *Bill's downcast gaze indicated he was lying.* ♦ *His downcast eyes indicate how depressed he is.*

downfall ['daʊn fɔl] *n.* ruin; collapse; the loss of power or control of something. (No plural form in this sense.) ♦ *The downfall of the monarchy occurred over several years.* ♦ *Inefficiency and bad management caused the company's downfall.*

downgrade ['daʊn gred] *tv.* to decrease the importance or severity of something; to decrease the status of someone or something. ♦ *The doctor downgraded the patient's condition from good to serious.* ♦ *When John left the company, his position was downgraded so the next person could be hired at a lower salary.*

downhearted [daʊn 'hɑr tɪd] *adj.* sad; depressed. (Adv: *downheartedly.*) ♦ *The depressing novel is about a sick, downhearted child.* ♦ *We were all downhearted at the death of our friend.*

downhill ['daʊn 'hɪl] **1.** *adv.* down the side of a hill; downward. ♦ *The children slid downhill, laughing all the way.* ♦ *The ball rolled downhill and landed in a puddle.* **2.** *adj.* moving downward; in a downward direction. ♦ *Investors were panicked by the downhill slide of the stock market.* ♦ *Tom won the downhill race in the ski competition.* **3.** *adj.* sloping downward. ♦ *The skiers picked up speed on the downhill slope.* ♦ *Anne shifted her car into a lower gear on the steep downhill grade.* **4. go downhill** *idiom* becoming worse; worsening. ♦ *Everything went downhill for the team when the star athlete retired.* ♦ *Employee morale went downhill after the layoffs.*

downpour ['daʊn por] *n.* a very heavy rainfall. ♦ *The sudden downpour caught the picnickers by surprise.* ♦ *The streets were flooded by the downpour.*

downright ['daʊn rɑɪt] **1.** *adv.* completely; absolutely; thoroughly. ♦ *My boss was downright cruel today!* ♦ *Not responding to an invitation is downright rude.* **2.** *adj.* complete; absolute. ♦ *Jimmy told his mother a downright lie.* ♦ *It is a downright shame that Mike didn't get the promotion.*

downstairs ['daʊn 'stɛrz] **1.** *n.* a basement; a cellar. (Treated as singular.) ♦ *The ranch house does not have a downstairs.* ♦ *Our downstairs has two furnished bedrooms.* **2.** *n.* the first level of a house or building with more than one level. (Treated as singular.) ♦ *The downstairs is cooler than the upstairs.* ♦ *The downstairs was built two years before the second floor was added on.* **3.** *adv.* down a set of stairs. ♦ *I ran downstairs, tripped on some toys, and fell.* ♦ *You must walk downstairs to get to the front door.* **4.** *adv.* on a lower level of a house or building. ♦ *The Smiths live downstairs and have rented the upstairs to another family.* ♦ *The children are playing with toys downstairs.* **5.** *adj.* on a lower floor or level. ♦ *Jane says the downstairs bathroom is for the children.* ♦ *The downstairs wine cellar is always cool.*

downstream ['daʊn 'strim] **1.** *adv.* in the direction that a stream is flowing or moving. ♦ *The leaf fell off the tree and floated downstream.* ♦ *The boat drifted slowly downstream.* **2.** *adv.* at a place further down a stream in the direction that the stream is flowing. (Not prenominal.) ♦ *Anne and Bill live in a small wooden cabin downstream from us.* ♦ *The bridge is downstream and can be reached from the village near the river.* **3.** *adj.* in the direction that a stream is flowing or moving. ♦ *The downstream movement of the water was slowed by the dam.* ♦ *The strong downstream currents pulled the swimmers down the river.*

down-to-earth ['daʊn tə 'ɝθ] *adj.* realistic; straightforward; practical. ♦ *Sue is down-to-earth, so you can always count on her for advice.* ♦ *The manager liked Bill's down-to-earth attitude about work.*

downtown ['daʊn 'tɑʊn] **1.** *adv.* toward the center of a town or city; into the center of a town or city. ♦ *We went downtown after work.* ♦ *I took the subway downtown from the suburbs.* **2.** *adv.* at the center of a town or city. ♦ *We ate lunch downtown.* ♦ *I live in the suburbs, but I work downtown.* **3.** *adj.* in the center of a city; in the business district of a city. ♦ *The downtown branch of the bank is open until 5:00 P.M. on Wednesdays.* ♦ *I live 14 miles away from my downtown office.* **4.** *n.* the center of a town or city; the business district of a town or city. (No plural form in this sense.) ♦ *Driving through downtown during rush hour is not a good idea.* ♦ *There's a huge statue in the center of downtown.*

downtrodden ['daʊn trɑd n] *adj.* oppressed; (figuratively) trampled on. (Adv: *downtroddenly.*) ♦ *The downtrodden people overthrew the dictator.* ♦ *Bob felt downtrodden by his demanding boss.*

downward ['daʊn wɚd] **1. downward(s)** *adv.* toward a lower position; toward a lower level. ♦ *The plane moved downward toward the airport.* ♦ *The feather floated slowly downward.* **2.** *adj.* moving or directed toward a lower position; moving toward a lower level. (Adv: *downwardly.*) ♦ *The downward movement of the stock averages worried the investors.* ♦ *A quick downward glance confirmed that my shoes were untied.*

downy ['daʊn i] *adj.* soft; fluffy; covered with soft feathers. (Comp: *downier;* sup: *downiest.*) ♦ *The baby chick was downy and yellow.* ♦ *Sue sank down into the downy comforter.*

dowry ['dɑʊ ri] *n.* money or property that a woman, or a woman's family, brings to her husband when she marries him. (No plural form in this sense.) ♦ *In many countries, a woman brings a dowry to her marriage.* ♦ *The poor woman's family had no money for a dowry.*

doze ['doz] **1.** *n.* a nap; a small amount of sleep. ♦ *Jane felt refreshed after a short doze.* ♦ *Have a doze on the couch, and I'll wake you when it's time to leave.* **2.** *iv.* to take a nap; to sleep for a short period of time. ♦ *Mary dozed peacefully after a long day at work.* ♦ *The student dozed during the film.*

dozen ['dʌz ən] **1.** *n.* a set of 12 things. ♦ *You can't buy just one egg. You have to buy a dozen.* ♦ *The napkins were sold by the dozen.* **2.** *adj.* twelve; a set or total of twelve. ♦ *There were about two dozen people at the party.* ♦ *The baker gave me a dozen bagels plus one.*

Dr. ['dɑk tɚ] *n.* the abbreviation of doctor. ♦ *Dr. Williams is an internist.* ♦ *I finally paid Dr. Smith's bill.*

drab ['dræb] *adj.* dull; gray; boring; not exciting. (Adv: *drably.* Comp: *drabber;* sup: *drabbest.*) ♦ *The prison cells were painted a drab color.* ♦ *The inspector wore an old, drab coat.*

draft ['dræft] **1.** *n.* a current of air—usually cold—inside an enclosed space. ♦ *The draft was so strong in the office, it blew papers onto the floor.* ♦ *It is warm by the fire, but there is a draft by the door.* **2.** *n.* the depth to which a ship's hull is submerged at a given load. ♦ *As the cargo was loaded, an officer checked the draft.* ♦ *The draft of the ship was too deep for the channel.* **3.** *n.* a roughly drawn plan; an early version of a document before the final copy is written. ♦ *An engineer studied the draft of the satellite plans.* ♦ *Bill wrote the first draft of his paper.* **4. the draft** *n.* the process of selecting people to serve in the military. (No plural form in this sense. Treated as singular.) ♦ *Tom avoided the draft by going to Canada.* ♦ *The draft called the nation's young men into military service.* **5.** *tv.* to oblige someone to serve in the military; to force someone to join the military. ♦ *The government drafted its citizens for the army.* ♦ *The military used to draft young men over the age of 18.* **6.** *tv.* to choose someone to do a job or a task. (Figurative on ⑤.) ♦ *The manager will draft the strongest workers to move the heavy boxes.* ♦ *The teacher drafted Tom and Sue as the leads for the class play.* **7.** *adj.* [of beer] drawn from a keg. ♦ *The waiter recited a list of the brands of draft and bottled beer available.* ♦ *When the keg ran dry, there was no more draft beer.*

draftee ['dræf 'ti] *n.* someone who has been required to serve in the military. ♦ *Draftees all hate army food.* ♦ *The draftee headed for the barracks.*

draftsman ['dræfts mən] *n., irreg.* someone who draws plans and sketches for things that are to be made or built. (Pl: draftsmen.) ♦ *The draftsman sketched the plans for the new stadium.* ♦ *Tom had to take engineering courses in college to become a draftsman.*

draftsmen ['dræfts mən] pl of draftsman.

drag ['dræg] **1.** *tv.* to pull someone or something along on the ground. ♦ *Billy dragged the toy duck behind him.* ♦ *I dragged Mary across the snow on the sled.* **2. drag out** *tv.* + *adv.* to make an event last a long time; to make something last longer. ♦ *The preacher dragged the sermon out for three hours.* ♦ *Please don't drag this meeting out too long.* **3.** *tv.* to bring someone or something along with oneself unwillingly. ♦ *I had to drag my sister to the beach with me.* ♦ *Jimmy's mom will have to drag him into the house for a bath.* **4. drag on** *iv.* + *adv.* to lag; to move slowly through space or time. ♦ *The candidate's acceptance speech dragged on for an hour.* ♦ *Tom fell asleep as the movie dragged on.* **5.** *iv.* [for someone or something] to touch the ground as it is being moved. ♦ *The flag dragged on the ground as John carried it carelessly.* ♦ *The curtains were too long and dragged on the floor.* **6.** *n.* someone or something unexciting or boring. (Slang. No plural form in this sense.) ♦ *Mowing the grass can be a real drag when it is very hot outside.* ♦ *I can't go out tonight. What a drag!* **7. in drag** *idiom* in the clothing of the opposite sex. (Usually refers to a man wearing women's clothing.) ♦ *The actor played the woman's part in drag.* ♦ *We all went to the costume party dressed in drag.*

dragon ['dræg ən] *n.* a mythical reptile that has wings and can exhale fire. ♦ *Susie dreamed of flying through space on a friendly dragon.* ♦ *The brave soldiers slew the ferocious dragon.*

dragonfly ['dræg ən flɑɪ] *n.* a large insect, with two pairs of wings and a long, needle-shaped body, that lives near water and eats mosquitoes. ♦ *A swarm of dragonflies hovered just above the lake.* ♦ *I screamed when the large dragonfly landed on my arm.*

drain ['dren] **1.** *n.* a pipe or ditch that takes liquids away from an area. ♦ *The drain in the kitchen sink was plugged with food scraps.* ♦ *The developer planned to build a drain so that the house would not flood.* **2.** *n.* something that takes away something else a little bit at a time; something that slowly takes something else away. ♦ *John's illness was a drain on his mental health, too.* ♦ *Trying to repair the old house was a drain on our finances.* **3. drain plug** See plug. **4.** *tv.* to draw liquid away from a place. ♦ *An electric pump drained the water from the aquarium.* ♦ *The doctor drained fluid from the wound.* **5.** *tv.* to empty a container of a liquid. ♦ *John drained his swimming pool at the end of summer.* ♦ *To drain the bathtub, just pull the plug out.* **6.** *tv.* to take something away slowly, a bit at a time. (Figurative on ④ or ⑤.) ♦ *Little by little, the medical bills drained our bank account.* ♦ *The heat drained our energy.* **7.** *tv.* to drink all the contents of a glass or container. ♦ *Anne drained the juice from her glass at breakfast.* ♦ *After the walk, Bill drained the contents of a huge bottle of water.* **8.** *tv.* to empty something by drinking all the liquid from it. ♦ *The athlete drained the water bottle.* ♦ *The tired driver drained the thermos of coffee.* **9.** *tv.* to remove someone's energy, endurance, or other quality. ♦ *The marathon drained me of all my strength.* ♦ *Watching the sentimental movie drained me emotionally.* **10.** *iv.* [for something] to lose liquid slowly. ♦ *Eventually, the partially clogged sink drained.* ♦ *The wound drained into the bandage.* **11. down the drain** *idiom* lost forever; wasted. ♦ *I just hate to see all that money go down the drain.* ♦ *Well, there goes the whole project, right down the drain.*

drainage ['dren ɪdʒ] **1.** *n.* removing liquid from something or some place. (No plural form in this sense.) ♦ *Drainage of the field must be completed before any construction can begin.* ♦ *Drainage of the wound will promote healing.* **2.** *n.* the ability of an area to drain properly. (No plural form in this sense.) ♦ *A damp basement can be a sign of poor drainage.* ♦ *The drainage on the golf course is excellent.* **3.** *n.* the liquid that is drained from a place or a container. (No plural form in this sense.) ♦ *The drainage was pumped out the window.* ♦ *Inspectors checked the drainage for contamination.*

drained ['drend] *adj.* tired and exhausted. (Not prenominal.) ♦ *After the test, I felt drained.* ♦ *I am always drained after a big race.*

drainpipe ['dren pɑɪp] *n.* a tube used to remove water from a place. ♦ *When the drainpipe cracked, the area flooded.* ♦ *The plumber cleaned out the clogged drainpipe.*

drake ['drek] *n.* a male duck. ♦ *The drake was swimming on the pond.* ♦ *The mallard drake has a beautiful green head.*

drama ['drɑm ə] **1.** *n.* the academic study of plays and the theater. (No plural form in this sense.) ♦ *The Theater Department offers rigorous training in drama.* ♦ *The famous director had studied drama in college.* **2.** *n.* a serious play or movie; a play or movie that is not a comedy. ♦ *The drama was so depressing that the whole audience was crying.* ♦ Gone with the Wind *is a famous drama.* **3.** *n.* emotional, exciting, or thrilling events. (No plural form in this sense.) ♦ *I needed a vacation because there's been too much drama at work.* ♦ *Sue related the drama of getting lost in the foreign city.*

dramatic [drə 'mæt ɪk] **1.** *adj.* of or about live theater and plays. (Adv: *dramatically* [...ɪk li].) ♦ *The actors produced a dramatic version of a popular TV show.* ♦ *The novelist decided to try dramatic writing.* **2.** *adj.* exciting; full of emotion; impressive. (Adv: *dramatically* [...ɪk li].) ♦ *Mary's dramatic story left us speechless.* ♦ *The dramatic speech got a standing ovation.*

dramatist ['drɑm ə təst] *n.* someone who writes plays. ♦ *The dramatist had based this play on an old myth.* ♦ *The dramatist sent her latest script to her publisher.*

dramatize ['drɑm ə tɑɪz] *tv.* to make a play or film script out of a book or a real-life event. ♦ *The television movie dramatized the historical event.* ♦ *The play dramatizes a true story.*

drank ['dræŋk] pt of drink.

drape ['drep] **1.** *n.* a heavy curtain; one panel of material that makes up drapery. (Often plural.) ♦ *Mary opened the drapes to let the sunlight in.* ♦ *The drapes were closed against the bright sunlight.* **2.** *n.* a curving fold of fabric. ♦ *The skirt had a loose drape on both hips.* ♦ *The top of the gown was little more than a drape of satin.* **3.** *n.* the particular way that fabric hangs. (No plural form in this sense.) ♦ *The silk had an elegant drape to it.* ♦ *The drape of your dress complements your figure.* **4.** *tv.* to cover someone or something with fabric that hangs down in a decorative way. ♦ *An American flag draped the casket.* ♦ *Mary draped the table with a tablecloth.*

drapery ['drep ri] *n.* pleated fabric panels that hang in front of windows. (Sometimes plural with the same meaning.) ♦ *When the cleaners shrunk the draperies, they were too small for the windows.* ♦ *John hid behind the draperies while listening to Bill and Anne's conversation.*

drastic ['dræs tɪk] *adj.* severe; extreme. (Adv: *drastically* [...ɪk li].) ♦ *The principal felt that the cheater's punishment should be drastic.* ♦ *The emergency called for drastic measures.*

draw ['drɔ] **1. a draw** *n.* a tie; a game where both teams have the same score. ♦ *The two teams agreed to a draw when the score remained tied after fifteen innings.* ♦ *If a football game ends in a draw, it goes into overtime.* **2.** *n.* an attraction; a reason people go to a particular place. ♦ *The amusement park's new roller coaster is quite a draw with teenagers.* ♦ *Florida's climate is one of its draws.* **3.** *iv., irreg.* to make pictures using pen, pencil, crayon, etc. (Pt: drew; pp: drawn.) ♦ *Would you prefer to draw with colored pencils or crayons?* ♦ *The artist draws very well.* **4.** *iv., irreg.* to approach someone or something; to get closer to someone or something. ♦ *As the school year drew nearer, Jane prepared for classes.* ♦ *As the car drew closer, I honked my horn.* **5.** *tv., irreg.* to make a picture with a pen, pencil, crayon, marker, etc. ♦ *The artist likes to draw cats.* ♦ *Jimmy used a crayon to draw pictures.* **6.** *tv., irreg.* to attract someone or something. ♦ *The blockbuster movie will draw a big crowd on its opening night.* ♦ *The sound of music drew people to the park.* **7. draw out** *tv., irreg.* + *adv.* to pull something out; to withdraw something. ♦ *The puppy whined as I drew the thorn out from its paw.* ♦ *Draw the frankfurters out of the boiling water and set them aside.* **8. draw out** *tv., irreg.* + *adv.* to encourage someone to say or tell something. ♦ *Mary drew the truth out of her son.* ♦ *It took hours to draw out the location of the money from the robbers.* **9. draw out** *tv., irreg.* + *adv.* to make something longer in time or length. ♦ *The politician drew the speech out, and the crowd became restless.* ♦ *The meal was drawn out as seven courses were served.* **10.** *tv., irreg.* to take a breath; to take in air. ♦ *Lisa drew a large breath of fresh air.* ♦ *The injured patient had trouble drawing breath.* **11.** *tv., irreg.* to remove or collect a sample of blood. ♦ *The nurse drew some blood from Jane's arm.* ♦ *The doctor requested that blood be drawn from the infant.* **12. draw a line between something and something else** *idiom* to separate two things; to distinguish or differentiate between two things. ♦ *It's necessary to draw a line between bumping into people and striking them.* ♦ *It's very hard to draw the line between slamming a door and just closing it loudly.*

drawback ['drɔ bæk] *n.* a disadvantage; a difficulty. ♦ *The drawback to working the morning shift is having to get up early.* ♦ *Dealing with traffic is a drawback to living in the city.*

drawbridge ['drɔ brɪdʒ] **1.** *n.* a bridge that can be raised to permit water traffic to pass beneath. ♦ *City traffic backed up because the drawbridges were raised for the sailboats.* ♦ *The drawbridges were lowered as soon as the boats were through.* **2.** *n.* a movable bridge over a castle moat. ♦ *The castle's drawbridge spanned the moat.* ♦ *Many soldiers guarded the castle drawbridge.*

drawer ['drɔr] *n.* a storage box or compartment that slides in and out of a desk, cabinet, dresser, etc. ♦ *The silverware is in the top drawer of the cabinet.* ♦ *When the desk drawer stuck, Mike forced it open with a knife.*

drawing ['drɔ ɪŋ] **1.** *n.* making pictures with a pen, pencil, crayon, etc. (No plural form in this sense.) ♦ *The art students practiced their drawing.* ♦ *Children enjoy drawing during their free time.* **2.** *n.* a picture that is drawn; a sketch. ♦ *Bob's drawing won first place in the art contest.* ♦ *The painter sketched a quick drawing before beginning the painting.*

drawl ['drɔl] *n.* a variety of speech in which the vowels are spoken slowly. ♦ *My friends from Georgia have a southern drawl.* ♦ *It was hard to understand the cowboy's drawl.*

drawn ['drɔn] pp of draw.

drawstring ['drɔ strɪŋ] *n.* a string that is used to tighten or close an opening or to pull something together. ♦ *Mike tightened the drawstring on his sweatpants.* ♦ *The duffel bag has a drawstring.*

dread ['drɛd] **1.** *n.* strong apprehension. (No plural form in this sense.) ♦ *The defendant faced the judge with dread.* ♦ *The child listened to the scolding with dread.* **2.** *tv.* to approach something in the future with a great deal of apprehension. ♦ *John dreads calculating his taxes.* ♦ *Sally dreads appointments with her dentist.*

dreaded ['drɛd ɪd] *adj.* feared; causing strong apprehension. ♦ *The dreaded day came when Max was fired.* ♦ *Despite her apprehension, Sally easily passed the dreaded exam.*

dreadful ['drɛd fʊl] *adj.* horrible; terrible. (Adv: *dreadfully.*) ♦ *Children should not be allowed to see that dreadful movie!* ♦ *The mayor denied the dreadful rumor about attending a wild party.*

dream ['drim] **1.** *iv., irreg.* [for one] to have thoughts and images while one sleeps. (Pt/pp: *dreamed* or dreamt.) ♦ *John began to dream while taking a nap during class.* ♦ *Mary was dreaming when the alarm clock woke her up.* **2. dream of** *iv., irreg. + prep. phr.* to think wishfully about something. ♦ *Anne dreams of owning her own business.* ♦ *Every week, Lisa buys lottery tickets and dreams of winning.* **3.** *tv., irreg.* to envision something in one's dreams. (Takes a clause.) ♦ *Last night I dreamed that I was king of the world.* ♦ *Mary dreamed that she saw her dead parents.* **4.** *n.* the thoughts and images one has while sleeping. ♦ *When she awakes, Lisa writes down her dreams.* ♦ *Tom told his therapist about his dreams.* **5.** *n.* a desire; a wish; an ambition. ♦ *Bob's dream is to become rich.* ♦ *Owning a pony is Susie's dream.* **6. a dream** *n.* a very beautiful person or thing; something excellent; something that is of high quality. (No plural form in this sense.) ♦ *We needed a smart, efficient worker, and Mary proved to be a dream.* ♦ *In the beautiful dress, the debutante looked like a dream.* **7. pipe dream** *idiom* a wish or an idea that is impossible to achieve or carry out. ♦ *Going to Hawaii is a pipe dream. We'll never have enough money.* ♦ *Your hopes of winning a lot of money are just a silly pipe dream.*

dreamer ['drim ɚ] *n.* someone whose ambitions or wishes are unrealistic or impractical. ♦ *The dreamer thought success would come without hard work.* ♦ *The students who struggled against the government were called dreamers.*

dreamt ['drɛmt] a pt/pp of dream.

dreamy ['drim i] *adj.* soothing; restful; wonderful. (Adv: *dreamily.* Comp: *dreamier;* sup: *dreamiest.*) ♦ *I love dreamy evenings sitting on the patio and watching the stars.* ♦ *The dreamy music put Susan to sleep.*

dreary ['drɪ ri] *adj.* drab; gloomy. (Adv: *drearily.* Comp: *drearier;* sup: *dreariest.*) ♦ *The dreary day ended with a thunderstorm.* ♦ *A bright coat of paint will liven up this dreary room.*

dredge ['drɛdʒ] **1.** *tv.* to remove soil from the bottom of a river, channel, canal, or lake. ♦ *The engineers dredged the lake, trying to deepen it.* ♦ *The police dredged the channel to make it deeper.* **2. dredge up** *tv. + adv.* to bring something to the surface of the water as with ①. ♦ *The police dredged up the murder weapon from the river.* ♦ *They dredged up tons and tons of muddy sand.* **3. dredge up** *tv. + adv.* to bring up an incident from the past; to bring up old memories. (Figurative on ②.) ♦ *Bill's boss is known for dredging up old mistakes.* ♦ *You should know better than to dredge up old arguments with me.* **4.** *n.* a machine that brings up soil from the bottom of a river or lake. ♦ *The dredge deepened the lake.* ♦ *The water level was too low for the dredge to work.*

dregs ['drɛgz] **1.** *n.* particles and bits that sink to the bottom of a container of liquid. (Treated as plural.) ♦ *The last cup of coffee usually includes the dregs.* ♦ *The dregs of the tea settled to the bottom of the cup.* **2.** *n.* the lowest quality of people or things. (Figurative on ①. Treated as plural.) ♦ *Only the dregs were left after the store's clearance sale.* ♦ *Jane gave away the dregs of her wardrobe to charity.*

drench ['drɛntʃ] *tv.* to cover someone or something with liquid—water unless specified. ♦ *Jane drenched her french fries with ketchup.* ♦ *The rainstorm drenched the children who were outside playing.*

dress ['drɛs] **1.** *n.* an item of women's clothing covering an area from the shoulders to somewhere along the legs. ♦ *Mary bought a new dress to wear to the wedding.* ♦ *Anne's dress had a belt at the waist.* **2.** *n.* clothing in general. (No plural form in this sense.) ♦ *What is the proper dress for the party?* ♦ *The invitation said that formal dress was required.* **3.** *adj.* [of clothing, shoes, etc.] formal. ♦ *Tom hated wearing his dress clothes.* ♦ *I have several pairs of casual shoes but only one pair of dress shoes.* **4.** *tv.* to put clothes on someone. ♦ *Susie carefully dressed her doll.* ♦ *Jimmy's mother still dresses him.* **5.** *tv.* to bandage a wound or incision. ♦ *The nurse dressed the cut and gave the child a lollipop.* ♦ *The nurse dressed the patient's incision.* **6.** *tv.* to prepare an animal's body for cooking or for market. ♦ *The hunter dressed the deer for eating.* ♦ *The butcher dressed the chicken quickly.* **7.** *tv.* to make something straight and orderly. ♦ *Anne dressed the wires close to the edge of the circuit board.* ♦ *The sergeant ordered the squad to dress ranks, so they all lined up straight.* **8.** *iv.* to cause someone to be dressed; to put clothes on oneself. ♦ *Mary dressed early on the day of the interview.* ♦ *I will have to dress in the dark because the electricity is not working.*

dress code ['drɛs kod] *n.* a set of rules telling how people are expected to dress. ♦ *Many high schools have dress codes that govern how students look.* ♦ *The dress code for our Caribbean cruise requires tuxedos for the men on some nights.*

dresser ['drɛs ɚ] *n.* a piece of furniture with several drawers that clothes are kept in; a chest of drawers. ♦ *The movers placed the dresser in the bedroom.* ♦ *The dresser has five drawers.*

dressing ['drɛs ɪŋ] **1.** *n.* a sauce for a salad. (No plural form in this sense. From *salad dressing.*) ♦ *This dressing is made from oil and vinegar.* ♦ *The salad has a tasty dressing on it.* **2.** *n.* a stuffing of bread and spices, cooked inside a fowl. (No plural form in this sense.) ♦ *David stuffed the turkey with dressing.* ♦ *Anne puts onion and celery in her dressing.* **3.** *n.* bandages used to cover a wound. ♦ *The nurse put a dressing over the cut.* ♦ *The doctor removed the dressings from the patient's eyes.*

dressmaker ['drɛs mek ɚ] *n.* someone who makes or alters women's clothing. ♦ *The dressmaker fitted the wedding gown on Anne.* ♦ *The boutique hired a dressmaker to do alterations.*

dress rehearsal ['drɛs rɪ 'hɚs əl] **1.** *n.* a final practice of something before its actual performance. ♦ *The organizer ran a dress rehearsal to make sure the ceremony would run smoothly.* ♦ *The day before the wedding, all the participants attended a dress rehearsal.* **2.** *n.* a rehearsal in full costume before the first public performance of a play. ♦

The director and producer were pleased with the dress rehearsal. ♦ *The actors invited a few friends to watch the dress rehearsal.*

drew ['dru] pt of draw.

dribble ['drɪb əl] **1.** *tv.* to permit food or saliva to fall from the mouth. ♦ *The panting dog dribbled saliva from its mouth.* ♦ *The child dribbled cereal down his chin.* **2.** *tv.* to allow a liquid to fall from some place in drops. ♦ *Jimmy's cup was too full, and he dribbled some juice onto the rug.* ♦ *Anne dribbled the last drops of water onto the plant.* **3.** *tv.* to bounce a basketball; to move a soccer ball or hockey puck with one's foot or stick. ♦ *The guard dribbled the ball along the court.* ♦ *Trying to show off, Bill tried to dribble the basketball behind himself.* **4.** *iv.* [for a liquid] to fall in drops; [for food, drink, or saliva] to fall from the mouth. ♦ *The heavy dew dribbled off the tree leaves.* ♦ *Saliva dribbled from the dog's mouth.* **5.** *iv.* to permit [food, drink, or saliva] to fall from the mouth. ♦ *The child dribbled onto her bib.* ♦ *The dog dribbled as it lapped the water.* **6.** *iv.* to bounce [a basketball] with one's hand; to move [a soccer ball or hockey puck] with one's foot or stick. ♦ *John dribbled as he ran down the court.* ♦ *Waiting for a teammate to break free, the player just dribbled.*

dried ['drɑɪd] *adj.* having had moisture removed; without moisture. ♦ *Dried spices are used in cooking.* ♦ *This wreath is made of colorful dried flowers.*

drift ['drɪft] **1.** *n.* a mass of snow or sand that is moved by the wind. ♦ *Drifts of snow blocked the end of the driveway.* ♦ *The strong wind made the desert sand form drifts.* **2.** *n.* a gradual movement toward someone or something. (No plural form in this sense.) ♦ *The citizens hardly noticed the government's drift toward autocracy.* ♦ *I pulled on the string, trying to stop the kite's drift toward the tree.* **3.** *tv.* [for wind] to move something, such as snow or sand. ♦ *The storm drifted snow onto the highway.* ♦ *A strong wind drifted the sand into a huge pile at the end of the beach.* **4.** *iv.* to move toward something or away from something gradually; to move gradually in some direction. ♦ *Our conversation drifted away from the topic that we had intended to discuss.* ♦ *The sailboat drifted toward shore.* **5.** *iv.* [for a person] to move aimlessly from one place to another; [for someone] to move from place to place without a purpose or established plan. ♦ *Tom drifted from town to town looking for work.* ♦ *The migrant workers drift from state to state.* **6. get the drift of something** *idiom* to understand the general idea of something. ♦ *I knew enough German to get the drift of this article.* ♦ *I don't get the drift of what you're trying to tell me.*

drifting ['drɪf tɪŋ] *adj.* forming piles of snow or sand, especially as moved by the wind. ♦ *The drifting sand was very hot to the touch.* ♦ *Drifting snow piled up around our house.*

driftwood ['drɪft wʊd] *n.* wood floating on a body of water; wood that is washed ashore from a body of water. (No plural form in this sense.) ♦ *I made an interesting lamp out of a piece of driftwood.* ♦ *Anne threw a piece of driftwood back into the ocean.*

drill ['drɪl] **1.** *n.* a machine that is used to make a hole in something. ♦ *The installation of the new door required a drill.* ♦ *Dave made a small hole in the wall with a drill.* **2.** *n.* a classroom practice exercise. ♦ *Every morning the students did a math drill.* ♦ *The students had to finish their spelling drill before recess.* **3.** *n.* an event where people practice what they would do in a real emergency. ♦ *The principal ordered a fire drill to prepare the students.* ♦ *The alarm sounded on the ship, but it was just a drill.* **4.** *tv.* to make a hole in something with a drill. ♦ *Bob drilled an opening in the door for the lock.* ♦ *The carpenter drilled a hole in the wall.* **5.** *tv.* to train people by having them practice. ♦ *The police captain drilled the new recruits.* ♦ *The teacher drilled the students in math.* **6.** *iv.* to make holes with ①. ♦ *The carpenter drilled through the thick beam.* ♦ *Dentists don't like to drill, but sometimes they have to.*

drink ['drɪŋk] **1.** *tv., irreg.* to swallow a liquid. (Pt: drank; pp: drunk.) ♦ *The thirsty guests drank a lot of pop.* ♦ *The ballplayer drank the water in one gulp.* **2. drink in** *tv., irreg. + adv.* to take in something; to absorb something. (Figurative on ①.) ♦ *Susan plans to drink in the sights on her vacation in the mountains.* ♦ *Bill drank in all the stories that his grandmother told him.* **3.** *iv., irreg.* to drink ① [alcohol]. ♦ *Lisa always drinks heavily during the holidays.* ♦ *Mary doesn't drink because of health reasons.* **4.** *n.* a liquid meant to be swallowed. ♦ *I really need a drink. I am thirsty.* ♦ *I provided cold drinks for everyone sitting on the porch.* **5.** *n.* a container of a liquid meant to be swallowed. ♦ *I handed Mary a drink from the refrigerator.* ♦ *I packed a drink in my lunch box.* **6.** *n.* an alcoholic beverage. ♦ *Bill needed a drink after his stressful day.* ♦ *Joan took some whiskey from the cupboard and mixed a drink.* **7. food and drink** *n.* something to eat and something to drink. (No plural form in this sense.) ♦ *We have to have food and drink to live.* ♦ *There was plenty of food and drink at Thanksgiving dinner.*

drinker ['drɪŋk ɚ] *n.* someone who drinks alcohol. ♦ *The Smiths are drinkers—they love gin.* ♦ *Mary bought a lot of beer for the party because her friends are heavy drinkers.*

drinking ['drɪŋk ɪŋ] **1.** *n.* swallowing liquid. (No plural form in this sense.) ♦ *Drinking a lot of water is important on a hot day.* ♦ *Drinking is difficult when you have a toothache.* **2.** *n.* swallowing alcohol in general or on a specific occasion. (No plural form in this sense.) ♦ *Drinking and driving is not safe.* ♦ *Drinking is bad for athletes.* **3. drinking water** *n.* water that is used or intended for swallowing; water that is safe for swallowing. ♦ *The sailors on the lost boat only had enough drinking water for three days.* ♦ *We bought drinking water in plastic bottles at the store.* **4.** *adj.* designed to be used for ①. ♦ *On the hot day, there was a long line of children at the drinking fountain.* ♦ *The empty drinking glasses need to be washed.*

drip ['drɪp] **1.** *n.* the action of liquid falling one drop at a time. ♦ *Jane could see a steady drip of fluid under her car.* ♦ *If the faucet is not turned off completely, the water keeps coming out in a slow drip.* **2.** *n.* the sound of a liquid falling one drop at a time. ♦ *The drip of a leaky faucet can be very annoying.* ♦ *The drip isn't very loud, but it still keeps me awake.* **3.** *tv.* to cause something to fall one drop at a time. ♦ *Please don't drip coffee on the tablecloth.* ♦ *The garden hose was not turned off completely, and it dripped water all afternoon.* **4.** *iv.* to fall one drop at a time; to leak; to release one drop at a time. ♦ *The leaky faucet dripped all day long.* ♦ *The ice cream dripped as it melted.*

dripping ['drɪp ɪŋ] **1.** *adj.* soaked; causing water to fall in drops. ♦ *Tom put his dripping clothes in the dryer.* ♦ *The dripping leaves drenched the children huddled underneath* *the tree.* **2. drippings** *n.* fat and juice that falls from meat when it is being cooked. (Treated as plural.) ♦ *This gravy is made from turkey drippings.* ♦ *The cook used the meat drippings to make the sauce.*

drive ['drɑɪv] **1.** *tv., irreg.* to cause a car or other vehicle to move and to direct its movement. (Pt: **drove**; pp: **driven**.) ♦ *Lisa drove her car to work every day.* ♦ *The driver drove the bus along the route.* **2.** *tv., irreg.* to take someone in a vehicle to some place. ♦ *Jane drove her children to school.* ♦ *Bob drives his little brother to baseball practice every day.* **3.** *tv., irreg.* to ram or force something into or through something else. ♦ *I drove the nail into the board with a hammer.* ♦ *The force of the wind drove a branch through the window.* **4.** *tv., irreg. + inf.* to force someone to do something. ♦ *Ambition drove Lisa to finish graduate school in three years.* ♦ *Having a large amount of debt has driven Mike to work two jobs.* **5.** *iv., irreg.* to ride in and steer or direct [a vehicle]. ♦ *Anne drove to the airport to pick up her brother.* ♦ *The farmer drove to town on his tractor.* **6.** *n.* a trip in a car or other vehicle; the act of driving. ♦ *The drive to the grocery store is only two miles.* ♦ *Young children can make a long drive miserable.* **7.** *n.* the energy to do something; ambition. (No plural form in this sense.) ♦ *Mike has the drive to work hard and succeed.* ♦ *For an athlete, the drive to compete is strong.* **8.** *n.* a driveway; a place to drive a car between a road and a house or garage. ♦ *The drive leading to the garage is concrete.* ♦ *Five cars were parked in the drive on the night of the party.* **9. drive someone crazy; drive someone insane; drive one out of one's mind** *idiom* to force someone into a state. ♦ *The sound of the wind howling drove me crazy.* ♦ *The dog's constant barking drove me insane.*

drive-in ['drɑɪv ɪn] **1.** *n.* an outdoor movie theater where people watch the movie from their cars. ♦ *The drive-in is packed with cars on Saturday night.* ♦ *A van blocked our view of the screen at the drive-in.* **2.** *n.* a restaurant where the food is delivered to customers, who eat in their cars. ♦ *The teenagers hung out at the drive-in.* ♦ *The drive-in only serves hamburgers and hot dogs.* **3.** *adj.* designed to do business with people who remain in their cars. ♦ *John pulled up to the drive-in dry cleaner and opened his window.* ♦ *There were five cars waiting at the drive-in restaurant.*

drivel ['drɪv əl] *n.* nonsense; foolish talk. (No plural form in this sense.) ♦ *I ignored the silly drivel I heard at the meeting!* ♦ *The speech was typical political drivel.*

driven ['drɪv ən] pp of **drive**.

driver ['drɑɪv ɚ] *n.* someone who drives a car or other vehicle. ♦ *The driver slammed on the brakes to avoid hitting a deer.* ♦ *The police officer gave the driver a speeding ticket.*

driveshaft ['drɑɪv ʃæft] *n.* the part of a vehicle that transfers power from the engine in the front to the wheels in the rear. ♦ *Most modern cars do not need a driveshaft because they send power to the front wheels.* ♦ *A driveshaft is very strong and heavy and turns very fast.*

drive-through ['drɑɪv θru] *adj.* allowing for business to be conducted with customers in their cars—for example, through a window in the side of a building. ♦ *You can place your order for food through an intercom and pick up your meal at the drive-through window.* ♦ *The fast-food restaurant also has drive-through service for people who are really in a hurry.*

driveway ['drɑɪv we] *n.* a short length of road from the street to a house or garage. (See also **drive** ⑧.) ♦ *My car is parked in the driveway.* ♦ *Our driveway is on the right side of our house.*

driving ['drɑɪv ɪŋ] **1.** *n.* the operation of a vehicle, including starting, steering, stopping, etc. (No plural form in this sense.) ♦ *Mary's driving has improved as she's gotten more practice.* ♦ *John was ticketed for poor and dangerous driving.* **2.** *adj.* <the adj. use of ①.> ♦ *The racecar driver used special driving gloves.* ♦ *I took driving lessons when I was 15.* **3.** *adj.* hard; forceful; severe; moving rapidly. ♦ *Driving rain pelted the window.* ♦ *We could not see very far because of the driving snow.*

drizzle ['drɪz əl] **1.** *n.* misty rain; rain that falls in tiny drops. (No plural form in this sense.) ♦ *A light drizzle ruined the outdoor picnic.* ♦ *The children continued to play, even in the drizzle.* **2.** *iv.* to mist; to rain lightly. ♦ *Today it drizzled and was cold.* ♦ *The weak lawn sprinkler just drizzled on the grass.* **3. drizzle on** *tv. + prep. phr.* to pour a tiny, thin stream of a liquid on something. ♦ *Jane drizzled chocolate sauce on her ice cream.* ♦ *The cook drizzled icing on the cake.*

dromedary ['drɑm ə dɛr i] *n.* a one-humped camel found in India, the Middle East, and Africa. ♦ *A dromedary stores food in its hump.* ♦ *Dromedaries are used to transport goods and passengers.*

drone ['dron] **1.** *n.* a monotonous noise; a loud, low-pitched hum. (No plural form in this sense.) ♦ *The drone of the airplane engines continued as the passengers boarded.* ♦ *Mary looked up in alarm as she heard the drone of approaching bees.* **2.** *n.* a male bee. ♦ *The biologist studied the function of the drone in the bee colony.* ♦ *The queen bee was fertilized by a drone.* **3.** *n.* a mechanism or device that is operated by remote control, such as a rocket, boat, or an exploding airplane. ♦ *The island was attacked by the enemy's drones during the war.* ♦ *The drone was detonated as it flew over the ammunition factory.* **4. drone (out)** *tv. (+ adv.)* to say something monotonously. ♦ *The minister droned out the endless sermon to a bored congregation.* ♦ *The unenthusiastic student droned his answer to the question.* **5.** *iv.* to make a loud, low-pitched hum. ♦ *The airplane engine droned loudly throughout the long flight.* ♦ *Our car droned for hours and hours across Kansas.* **6. drone (on)** *iv. (+ adv.)* to talk in a monotonous voice; to talk in a boring way. ♦ *The speaker droned on for two hours.* ♦ *The lecturer seemed to drone on for a very long time, even when people started leaving.*

drool ['drul] **1.** *n.* saliva or juice that rolls out of the mouth. (No plural form in this sense.) ♦ *The dog's drool fell on the new carpet.* ♦ *Please wipe the drool off the baby's face.* **2.** *iv.* to permit saliva or food to roll out of the mouth. ♦ *The dog drooled while sitting in the hot car.* ♦ *Infants often drool when their teeth begin to grow.* **3.** *iv.* to show excitement over or pleasure about someone or something. (Informal.) ♦ *Bob was drooling about the front-row concert tickets.* ♦ *Jane drooled over the powerful computer on display.*

droop ['drup] *iv.* to sag; to wilt; to hang down. ♦ *The dry flowers drooped in the heat.* ♦ *These drapes are meant to droop over the window.*

droopy ['drup i] **1.** *adj.* sagging; wilted; hanging down. (Adv: *droopily.* Comp: *droopier;* sup: *droopiest.*) ♦ *Our dog is the kind that has droopy ears.* ♦ *The droopy flowers sprang up after they were watered.* **2.** *adj.* looking sad or depressed. (Adv: *droopily.* Comp: *droopier;* sup: *droopiest.*) ♦ *The child was droopy for days after the puppy died.* ♦ *You seem sort of droopy. Is something wrong?*

drop ['drɑp] **1.** *n.* a small ball of liquid; a small amount of liquid. ♦ *We need to buy more milk. There isn't a drop left in the carton.* ♦ *Drops of water ran down the windshield.* **2.** *n.* a small amount of anything. (Figurative on ①.) ♦ *If you had a single drop of decency, you would apologize!* ♦ *You have no courage at all. Not a drop!* **3.** *n.* a sudden fall; a sudden downward movement. ♦ *An earthquake caused a sudden drop in the road, causing several accidents.* ♦ *The drop in the price of the company's stock was bad news.* **4.** *n.* the length of a fall. ♦ *From the top of the roof to the ground is a drop of forty feet.* ♦ *There is a ten-foot drop between the cliff and the beach.* **5.** *tv.* to let someone or something fall, either by accident or on purpose. ♦ *The swimming teacher gently dropped the boy into the pool.* ♦ *The tree dropped acorns onto the patio.* **6.** *tv.* to leave something out; to omit something. ♦ *The editor dropped the quotation from the article.* ♦ *The typesetter inadvertently dropped the last sentence.* **7.** *tv.* to stop something; to end something; to stop talking about something. ♦ *The university dropped some courses due to lack of enrollment.* ♦ *Sally agreed to drop the lawsuit against her neighbor.* **8. drop off** *tv.* + *adv.* to let someone get out of a vehicle at a certain place. ♦ *Jane dropped Sue off at the library.* ♦ *The bus driver dropped the children off in front of the school.* **9. drop off** *tv.* + *adv.* to deliver something [somewhere] while one is traveling to some other place. ♦ *Could you drop this book off at the library, please?* ♦ *Tom dropped off his laundry at the cleaners on his way to work.* **10.** *iv.* to fall; to go lower; to sink. ♦ *As the weather changed, the temperature dropped seven degrees.* ♦ *Acorns dropped from the tree.* **11. drop by** *iv.* + *prep. phr.* to stop at someone's house; to make a quick stop somewhere. ♦ *The Smiths dropped by the local café after dinner.* ♦ *Please drop by our house when you have time.* **12. drop by** *iv.* + *adv.* to stop for an informal visit. ♦ *Drop by when you have time.* ♦ *We were hoping you could drop by next Friday.*

droplet ['drɑp lət] *n.* a small drop. ♦ *The infant needed only a tiny droplet of the medicine.* ♦ *A droplet of blood was placed on the microscope slide.*

droppings ['drɑp ɪŋz] *n.* animal dung. (Treated as plural.) ♦ *We tracked the deer by following their droppings.* ♦ *I get angry when I find dog droppings on my lawn.*

drought ['drɑʊt] *n.* a long period of time without any rain; a long dry period; a lack of rain. ♦ *As the drought continued, forest fires raged out of control.* ♦ *The lawns turned brown and the trees lost their leaves during the drought.*

drove ['drov] **1.** pt of drive. **2.** *n.* a large group of animals that move together. ♦ *A drove of sheep grazed in the pasture.* ♦ *I could barely see the drove of cattle in the distance.* **3. droves** *n.* a large crowd of people. (Treated as plural.) ♦ *People arrived in droves, crowding into the stadium.* ♦ *Droves of opera lovers cheered as the great singer finished singing.*

drown ['drɑʊn] **1.** *tv.* to kill someone or something by suffocation underwater. ♦ *The farmer drowned the unwanted kittens.* ♦ *The powerful tide pulled the swimmer under and drowned him.* **2.** *tv.* to flood an area with a liquid. ♦ *Heavy rains drowned the newly planted fields.* ♦ *The old village was drowned under the water of the new lake.* **3. drown out** *tv.* + *adv.* to cover up a sound by making a louder noise. ♦ *The few boos were drowned out by the cheers.* ♦ *The children's loud voices drowned out the caller on the telephone.* **4.** *iv.* to die underwater from suffocation. ♦ *After falling overboard, the dog drowned.* ♦ *The exhausted swimmer drowned.*

drowning ['drɑʊn ɪŋ] **1.** *n.* a form of death where someone suffocates underwater. (No plural form in this sense.) ♦ *Drowning is a horrible way to die.* ♦ *The boy was worried about drowning until he took swimming lessons.* **2.** *n.* an instance of ①. ♦ *News of the drowning was in the paper today.* ♦ *The shipwreck resulted in the drowning of the crew.* **3.** *adj.* [of someone or something] dying from suffocation underwater. ♦ *The guard dove into the lake to rescue the drowning swimmer.* ♦ *Lisa jumped into the pool to save the drowning cat.*

drowse ['drɑʊz] *iv.* to sleep a little; to take a nap. ♦ *I like to drowse on the porch in the afternoons.* ♦ *As the fireplace warmed the room, Anne drowsed a little.*

drowsy ['drɑʊz i] *adj.* tired; sleepy. (Adv: *drowsily.* Comp: *drowsier;* sup: *drowsiest.*) ♦ *Tom carried his drowsy son to bed.* ♦ *The heat made us all drowsy.*

drudge ['drʌdʒ] **1.** *iv.* to do hard, boring work. ♦ *All day long I drudge through my boring job.* ♦ *Our trash collector drudges along in all kinds of weather.* **2.** *n.* someone who does hard, boring work. ♦ *Bob is a dependable drudge who does what no one else wants to do.* ♦ *After being a drudge for a year, Jane was promoted to manager.*

drudgery ['drʌdʒ ə ri] *n.* work that is difficult and boring. (No plural form in this sense.) ♦ *The drudgery of her job made Susan quit.* ♦ *I don't mind drudgery if it pays well.*

drug ['drʌg] **1.** *n.* a medicine. ♦ *The doctor wrote a prescription for a drug to cure the infection.* ♦ *The drug made the patient feel better.* **2.** *n.* a substance used illegally for its pleasurable effects. ♦ *The drug was smuggled into the country.* ♦ *The government tried to stop the import of illegal drugs.* **3.** *tv.* to give someone ①. ♦ *The nurse drugged the patient to ease her pain.* ♦ *The patient was drugged before surgery.*

drugged ['drʌgd] **1.** *adj.* under the influence of a drug. ♦ *The drugged patient slept peacefully.* ♦ *The police arrested the drugged assailant.* **2.** *adj.* containing a drug. ♦ *The king drank the drugged wine and fell into a deep sleep.* ♦ *We gave the dog drugged meat so it would relax.*

druggist ['drʌg əst] *n.* someone who is licensed to package and sell medications. ♦ *Ask the druggist to fill your prescription.* ♦ *My druggist recommended some medicine for my cold.*

drugstore ['drʌg stor] *n.* a pharmacy; a place where medicine is sold, along with cosmetics and many other items. ♦ *I bought some aspirin at the drugstore on the corner.* ♦ *Today drugstores carry many things besides medicine and medical supplies.*

drum ['drʌm] **1.** *n.* a musical instrument, usually cylindrical, with a membrane stretched over one or both ends. ♦ *Jane played drums in a local rock band.* ♦ *Mike carried the big bass drum in the parade.* **2.** *n.* a container shaped like ①. ♦ *The oil is stored in metal drums.* ♦ *One of the drums had a leak, and oil flowed everywhere.* **3. drum something into someone('s head)** *idiom* to make someone learn something through persistent repetition. ♦ *Yes, I know that. They drummed it into me as a child.* ♦ *I will drum it into their heads day and night.*

drumhead ['drʌm hɛd] *n.* the membrane that is stretched over the frame of a drum. ♦ *The musician struck the drumhead with precision.* ♦ *A drumhead can be made of animal skin or plastic.*

drummer ['drʌm ɚ] *n.* someone who plays a drum. ♦ *The drummer twirled the drumsticks in the air.* ♦ *Mike wants to be a drummer, but his parents hope he'll play the violin.*

drumming ['drʌm ɪŋ] **1.** *n.* playing a drum. (No plural form in this sense.) ♦ *Every afternoon, Lisa practiced her drumming in the garage.* ♦ *I'm weary of hearing my neighbor's drumming.* **2.** *adj.* pounding; repetitive; throbbing. (Adv: *drummingly.*) ♦ *John's drumming headache was making his life miserable.* ♦ *I couldn't stand the drumming noise of the machinery.*

drumstick ['drʌm stɪk] **1.** *n.* the stick or mallet used to play a drum. ♦ *The drummer broke a pair of drumsticks during the concert.* ♦ *I always take my drumsticks home after practice.* **2.** *n.* the leg of a chicken or a turkey when served as food. (Figurative on ①.) ♦ *Bill usually asks for a drumstick at Thanksgiving dinner.* ♦ *The cook brushed the drumsticks with barbecue sauce.*

drunk ['drʌŋk] **1.** pp of drink. **2.** *n.* someone who drinks too much alcohol; an alcoholic. ♦ *The hopeless drunk begged for money on the sidewalk.* ♦ *Jane finally divorced the drunk she'd been married to for years.* **3.** *adj.* intoxicated; having had too much alcohol. (Drunk is usually used after a linking verb. Drunken is usually used before nouns.) ♦ *Bill was very drunk, so a sober friend drove him home.* ♦ *Mary doesn't drink often, and she never gets drunk.*

drunkard ['drʌŋk ɚd] *n.* an alcoholic; someone who drinks too much alcohol. ♦ *Once Tom admitted he was a drunkard, he was on his way to getting better.* ♦ *The police arrested the drunkard for driving under the influence of alcohol.*

drunken ['drʌŋk ən] *adj.* intoxicated. (Drunken is usually used before nouns. Drunk is usually used after a linking verb. Adv: *drunkenly.*) ♦ *A drunken spectator was escorted from the ballgame.* ♦ *The drunken man crashed into the wall and fell to the floor.*

dry ['drɑɪ] **1.** *adj.* not wet; not moist; without water. (Adv: *dryly.* Comp: *drier;* sup: *driest.*) ♦ *I grabbed a dry towel after I finished my shower.* ♦ *The thirsty animals gathered at the dry riverbed.* **2.** *adj.* not allowing alcohol to be sold; without alcohol. (Comp: *drier;* sup: *driest.*) ♦ *The mayor wants to have a dry town.* ♦ *That restaurant is dry, so you can't have a beer.* **3.** *adj.* boring; not interesting. (Adv: *dryly.* Comp: *drier;* sup: *driest.*) ♦ *The dry lecture put many students to sleep.* ♦ *The very dry speaker caused me to yawn.* **4.** *adj.* funny but appearing to be serious. (Adv: *dryly.* Comp: *drier;* sup: *driest.*) ♦ *The author's dry humor appealed to some readers.* ♦ *Bob's dry wit often livened up a dull meeting.* **5.** *tv.* to cause something to dry; to remove all the moisture from something. ♦ *The sun dried the towels.* ♦ *The heat of the kiln will dry the pottery.* **6.** *iv.* to become dry; to completely lose moisture. ♦ *Our sheets dried on the clothesline.* ♦ *The sweater should dry in the clothes dryer.* **7. dry someone out** *idiom* to cause someone to become sober; to cause someone to stop drinking alcohol to excess. ♦ *If the doctor at the clinic can't dry him out, no one can.* ♦ *Mary needs to be dried out. She's been drinking heavily since her divorce.* **8. dry up** *idiom* to become silent; to stop talking. ♦ *The young lecturer was so nervous that he forgot what he was going to say and dried up.* ♦ *Actors have a fear of drying up on stage.*

dry-clean ['drɑɪ klin] *tv.* to clean garments with chemicals rather than water. ♦ *I have to dry-clean this coat because water would shrink it.* ♦ *Many modern fabrics have to be dry-cleaned.*

dry cleaner(s) ['drɑɪ klin ɚr(z)] *n.* a business that dry-cleans clothing, drapes, blankets, etc. ♦ *Please take my suit to the dry cleaners today.* ♦ *Do you think the dry cleaner can remove these spots?*

dry cleaning ['drɑɪ klin ɪŋ] *n.* clothing or fabric that is ready to be or has been dry-cleaned. ♦ *I have to stop at the dry cleaners to pick up the dry cleaning.* ♦ *Please take the dry cleaning to the dry cleaners.*

dryer ['drɑɪ ɚ] *n.* a machine that dries clothes. ♦ *Bill put the clothes from the washing machine into the dryer.* ♦ *Rather than use the dryer, Jane hung her laundry on a clothesline.*

dry goods ['drɑɪ gʊdz] *n.* cloth, fabric, textiles. (Treated as plural. Sometimes singular.) ♦ *The little store specialized in dry goods and sewing supplies.* ♦ *Dry goods are usually sold by the yard.*

dryness ['drɑɪ nəs] *n.* a state of low moisture; a state of no moisture. (No plural form in this sense.) ♦ *The dryness of the forest raised concerns about forest fires.* ♦ *Arizona is known for the dryness of its climate, even though it can be very humid there.*

dual ['du əl] *adj.* having two parts; having two purposes. (Adv: *dually.*) ♦ *This stove has dual ovens, so you can bake bread and roast meat at the same time.* ♦ *The television special had a dual purpose—to entertain and to educate.*

dub ['dʌb] **1.** *tv.* to give someone a name; to name someone. ♦ *Robert was dubbed* Bob *by his friends.* ♦ *The parents dubbed their new baby David, after his grandfather.* **2.** *tv.* to make a man a knight in an official ceremony in which he is given the title "Sir." (Not a U.S. practice.) ♦ *The famous inventor was dubbed a knight.* ♦ *The queen will dub the man Sir George in honor of his bravery.* **3. dub in** *tv. + adv.* to record the words of a film in a different language; to provide the voice for someone in a movie. ♦ *The actors dubbed in their own voices.* ♦ *All of the Spanish dialogue was dubbed in.* **4.** *tv.* to duplicate something; to make a copy of an audiotape or a videotape on a blank tape. ♦ *Jane dubbed the videotape of her brother's wedding so that she could have a copy.* ♦ *You'd better not dub that tape. It would be illegal.*

dubious ['dub i əs] **1.** *adj.* uncertain; unsure; full of doubt. (Adv: *dubiously.*) ♦ *The dubious employees shook their heads as they carried out the order.* ♦ *I am dubious that a new stove will improve my cooking.* **2.** *adj.* [of character, reputation, or integrity] questionable or uncertain. (Adv: *dubiously.*) ♦ *The angry young man had a dubious reputation.* ♦ *The manager decided not to hire the dubious applicant.*

duchess ['dʌtʃ əs] *n.* the wife or widow of a duke. (Not a U.S. title.) ♦ *The duchess waved to the crowd from the balcony of the castle.* ♦ *England's royal family includes several dukes and duchesses.*

duck ['dʌk] **1.** *n.* a kind of fowl that lives near water, having a bill and webbed feet. ♦ *The ducks flew south for the winter.* ♦ *Little children enjoy feeding the ducks at the pond.* **2.** *n.* the female of ①, when compared with the drake. ♦ *The duck waddled after the drake.* ♦ *From a distance, the hunter could not tell if the bird was a duck or a drake.* **3.** *n.* the meat of ①. (No plural form in this sense.) ♦ *Duck is very tender and flavorful.* ♦ *I prefer duck to chicken, because it is juicier.* **4.** *n.* a sturdy kind of cotton cloth. (No plural form in this sense.) ♦ *Susan asked the tailor to make the summer jacket out of cotton duck.* ♦ *Duck is a very strong fabric, once used for tents and awnings.* **5.** *iv.* to stoop down so that one doesn't get hit by something; to dip one's head so one doesn't hit it into something. ♦ *The children ducked as the ball flew over their heads.* ♦ *My tall friends must duck when they enter through my low doorway.* **6.** *tv.* to dip one's head down so that it is not hit against something. ♦ *Jane had to duck her head to get through the low doorway.* ♦ *The basketball player ducked his head as he walked down the stairs.* **7.** *tv.* to avoid being seen by moving quickly somewhere. ♦ *Mike ducked around the corner to avoid Susan because he owed her money.* ♦ *Billy ducked behind the couch, trying to hide from his parents.* **8. get one's ducks in a row** *idiom* to put one's affairs in order; to get things ready. ♦ *You can't hope to go into a company and sell something until you get your ducks in a row.* ♦ *As soon as you people get your ducks in a row, we'll leave.*

duct ['dʌkt] **1.** *n.* a pipe or channel that carries air, electrical wires, phone wires, etc. ♦ *I cleaned the furnace ducts with a vacuum.* ♦ *The air could not flow through the clogged duct.* **2.** *n.* a tube inside a plant or an animal that carries water, liquids, air, etc. ♦ *The doctor examined the patient's infected tear ducts.* ♦ *A stone was lodged in Anne's bile duct.*

dud ['dʌd] **1.** *n.* an explosive device that fails to explode. ♦ *The bomb placed in the building by a madman was a dud, so no damage was done.* ♦ *At the fireworks display, there were quite a few duds that didn't explode.* **2.** *n.* someone or something that is worthless. (Figurative on ①.) ♦ *The broken-down car was a dud.* ♦ *If you weren't such a dud, you'd go out and get a job!*

dude ['dud] **1.** *n.* [from the point of view of a rancher or westerner] a visitor from the city. ♦ *The cowboys laughed as the city dude tried to get on the horse.* ♦ *After their first trail ride, the dudes were sore.* **2.** *n.* a person; a guy. (Slang. Also used as a term of address.) ♦ *Dude! What's happening?* ♦ *Some dude stole my bike today.*

due ['du] **1. dues** *n.* a sum of money owed by each member of an organization. (Treated as plural.) ♦ *The association charges dues to pay for its administration.* ♦ *Each member must pay the dues in order to attend meetings.* **2.** *adj.* owing; having to be paid. (Not prenominal.) ♦ *This bill was due two weeks ago, but I forgot to pay it.* ♦ *A payment is due now.* **3.** *adj.* expected and appropriate. (Adv: *duly.*) ♦ *The esteemed actor's fans paid him due homage.* ♦ *With all due respect, I do not understand what you are doing.* **4.** *adv.* directly; in the exact direction; straight. ♦ *We drove due north from Ohio into Michigan.* ♦ *The troops marched due south.* **5. due to** *prep.* owing to; because of. (This use is objected to by some.) ♦ *Due to the drought, the price of fruit is higher than usual.* ♦ *The play was canceled due to unavoidable circumstances.*

duel ['du əl] **1.** *n.* a formal battle between two men, once fought with guns or swords, to settle a quarrel of honor. ♦ *The man fought a duel to defend his honor.* ♦ *The men agreed to the rules before the duel was fought.* **2.** *tv.* [for two men] to fight each other in a formalistic battle to avenge an insult to one of them. ♦ *When his courage was questioned, the Southerner dueled the Northerner.* ♦ *Aaron Burr dueled Alexander Hamilton and killed him.* **3.** *iv.* [for two men] to fight a battle of honor according to a formal code. ♦ *The two men dueled to the death.* ♦ *The count and his enemy agreed to duel.*

duet [du 'ɛt] *n.* music to be performed by two people. ♦ *The composer wrote a duet for an alto and soprano.* ♦ *The conductor chose two musicians to play the duet.*

duffel bag ['dʌf əl bæg] *n.* a cloth bag used to carry clothes and other personal items. ♦ *The college student brought her laundry home in a duffel bag.* ♦ *The soldier threw his duffel bag into the back of the jeep.*

dug ['dʌg] pt/pp of dig.

dugout ['dʌg ɑʊt] *n.* the place in a baseball stadium where players sit when they are not on the baseball field. ♦ *The manager sat in the dugout watching the game.* ♦ *The players sat in the dugout waiting for the rain to stop.*

duke ['duk] *n.* a nobleman of high rank, higher than a marquis and lower than a prince. (Not a U.S. title.) ♦ *When Mary married the duke, she became a duchess.* ♦ *The prince invited the duke to the royal party.*

dull ['dʌl] **1.** *adj.* not sharp; blunt. (Adv: *dully.* Comp: *duller;* sup: *dullest.*) ♦ *The dull scissors would not even cut paper.* ♦ *The butcher sharpened the dull knife.* **2.** *adj.* not exciting; boring. (Adv: *dully.* Comp: *duller;* sup: *dullest.*) ♦ *I fell asleep during the dull movie.* ♦ *The book was so dull, Lisa didn't finish reading it.* **3.** *adj.* not shiny; tarnished. (Adv: *dully.* Comp: *duller;* sup: *dullest.*) ♦ *Dull silver should be polished.* ♦ *Whoever cleaned the mirror left streaks that made the mirror dull.* **4.** *adj.* not smart; somewhat stupid. (Adv: *dully.* Comp: *duller;* sup: *dullest.*) ♦ *Our dog is exceptionally dull and is hard to train.* ♦ *The teacher spent extra time with the dull students.* **5.** *tv.* to make an object blunt; to make an object less sharp. ♦ *Skinning the deer dulled the knife.* ♦ *Cutting the heavy paper dulled the scissors.* **6.** *tv.* to lessen physical or emotional pain. ♦ *Anesthesia dulled the pain.* ♦ *The soft music dulled Mary's sorrow.* **7.** *tv.* to make nerves less responsive. ♦ *Alcohol and drugs dull one's senses.* ♦ *A lack of sleep dulled the driver's reflexes.*

duly ['du li] *adv.* at the appropriate time; in the appropriate way; properly. ♦ *The clerk duly responded to my request.* ♦ *Bill duly held the door for the person behind him.*

dumb ['dʌm] **1.** *adj.* stupid; foolish; not smart. (Adv: *dumbly.* Comp: *dumber;* sup: *dumbest.*) ♦ *Mike regretted the dumb remark the moment he said it.* ♦ *Sometimes you seem so dumb!* **2.** *adj.* [of animals] not able to speak. (Can be offensive when applied to humans. Adv: *dumbly.* Comp: *dumber;* sup: *dumbest.*) ♦ *Animals—except for humans, of course—are dumb.* ♦ *The dolphin may be dumb, but it seems to want to communicate.*

dumbfounded [dəm 'fɑʊn dɪd] *adj.* shocked and speechless. (Adv: *dumbfoundedly.*) ♦ *The dumbfounded students were horrified by their low grades.* ♦ *Mary was dumbfounded by the personal question and refused to respond.*

dummy ['dʌm i] **1.** *n.* something that takes the place of the real thing; a substitute. ♦ *An accident was simulated with a crash dummy.* ♦ *The book is not real. It is only a dummy to show what the final book will look like.* **2.** *n.* a mannequin; a store display model having a human form. ♦ *The designer dressed the department store dummy in the window.* ♦ *There are finely dressed dummies throughout the store.* **3.** *n.* a large doll with a movable mouth used by a ventriloquist in performances. ♦ *The dummy sat on the ventriloquist's lap.* ♦ *The performer's dummy is really a large wooden puppet.* **4.** *n.* someone who acts stupid. (Derogatory.) ♦ *The quiet child seemed like a dummy but was really just shy.* ♦ *The kids made fun of the boy who they thought was a dummy.*

dump ['dʌmp] **1.** *n.* a junkyard; a landfill; a place where trash is thrown away. ♦ *The garbage is hauled to the dump each week.* ♦ *We went to the dump to look for spare auto parts.* **2.** *n.* a place that is not clean; a place that is run-down. (Figurative on ①. Slang.) ♦ *You should clean up your apartment. It's quite a dump.* ♦ *The inspectors closed the restaurant because it was a dump.* **3.** *tv.* to unload something into a pile; to empty something into a pile. ♦ *Susie dumped the contents of her purse on the table.* ♦ *A big truck dumped the sand into the backyard.* **4.** *tv.* to get rid of someone or something. (Informal.) ♦ *Jane finally dumped her boyfriend, who was cheating on her.* ♦ *My company dumped 10% of its staff last week.*

Dumpster™ ['dʌmp stɚ] *n.* the protected trade name for a large metal receptacle for refuse, designed to be easily emptied by a special truck. ♦ *I threw the garbage into the Dumpster in the backyard.* ♦ *The Dumpster was full of rotten food.*

dun ['dʌn] **1.** *tv.* to demand that someone pay a debt. ♦ *Someone called to dun Jane for payment of her credit-card bill.* ♦ *Stop dunning me! I don't owe you anything.* **2.** *n.* someone who demands the payment of a debt. ♦ *The loan company hired several duns to collect late payments.* ♦ *Bill is a dun for a local bill collector.* **3.** *n.* a demand that someone pay a debt, delivered in writing or by telephone. ♦ *Mary received another dun from the bank about her auto loan.* ♦ *There were only three pieces of mail, and all were duns.*

dunce ['dʌns] *n.* a stupid-acting person; someone who learns things slowly. ♦ *The children cruelly called the new student a dunce.* ♦ *Mike feels like a dunce when it comes to algebra.*

dune ['dun] *n.* a ridge or mound of sand, usually deposited by the action of the wind. ♦ *The desert is filled with huge sand dunes.* ♦ *Tom loves to play in the dunes near the shore of the lake.*

dune buggy ['dun bəg i] *n.* a recreational vehicle used to drive over hills of sand. ♦ *The dune buggies flew over the beach.* ♦ *Mike was hurt when his dune buggy tipped over.*

dung ['dʌŋ] *n.* feces; manure. (No plural form in this sense.) ♦ *Dried buffalo dung was used as fuel many years ago.* ♦ *The pasture was littered with cow dung.*

dungarees [dəŋ gə 'riz] *n.* blue jeans; pants made from denim. (Treated as plural.) ♦ *Mike dresses casually, and usually wears dungarees.* ♦ *The dungarees faded to a light blue after several washings.*

dungeon ['dʌn dʒən] *n.* an underground prison; a prison under a castle. ♦ *The prince was locked in the evil king's dungeon.* ♦ *The old dungeon was cold, damp, and eerie.*

dunk ['dʌŋk] **1.** *tv.* to push someone underwater for a few moments. ♦ *The children dunked each other in the swimming pool.* ♦ *Laughing, the children tried to dunk their father.* **2. dunk in(to)** *tv. + prep. phr.* to dip something, especially a piece of food, into liquid. ♦ *The policeman dunked a doughnut into his coffee.* ♦ *When he is alone, Mike often dunks his bread in his soup.*

dupe ['dup] **1.** *tv.* to trick someone; to play a trick on someone. ♦ *On April Fools' Day, my friend tried to dupe me.* ♦ *Billy duped his father into buying another ice-cream cone.* **2.** *tv.* to duplicate something. (Informal.) ♦ *The secretary will dupe the report and distribute it.* ♦ *It is illegal to dupe this videocassette.* **3.** *n.* someone who is tricked; someone who is the victim of deceit. ♦ *The crook looked around the subway platform, looking for dupes.* ♦ *Dad laughed at the joke even when he realized he had been the dupe.* **4.** *n.* a duplicate. ♦ *A dupe of the movie will be made by tomorrow.* ♦ *The dupe was so good, no one could tell which was the original.*

duplex ['du plɛks] **1.** *n.* a building that has two separate dwelling units, one over the other or side by side. ♦ *Tom bought a duplex, planning to live on one side and rent the other.* ♦ *The sisters lived in different apartments in the same duplex.* **2.** *n.* an apartment occupying parts of two different floor of a building. ♦ *Stairs connected the two floors of Bob's duplex.* ♦ *The bedrooms were on the second floor of the duplex.*

duplicate 1. ['du plə kət] *n.* a copy; a replica; something that looks or works exactly like something else. ♦ *This table is a duplicate of the table in our living room.* ♦ *The duplicate was hard to read, so Mary searched for the original document.* **2.** ['du plə ket] *tv.* to copy something exactly; to make an exact copy of something. ♦ *The bank duplicated the title to the house and sent the copy to the new owners.* ♦ *The jeweler tried to duplicate the lost ring from a picture of it.*

duplicity [du 'plɪs ə ti] *n.* deception. (No plural form in this sense.) ♦ *Tom's duplicity cost him his job as an accountant.* ♦ *Duplicity and lying are both undesirable characteristics.*

durable ['dɚ ə bəl] *adj.* strong; hard; able to withstand rough use; long-lasting. (Adv: *durably.*) ♦ *This very durable watch is both waterproof and shatterproof.* ♦ *The strong toddler was unable to break the durable toy.*

duration [dɚ 'e ʃən] **1.** *n.* the amount of time that something lasts. (No plural form in this sense.) ♦ *Fortunately the rough flight was of short duration.* ♦ *Throughout the duration of the test, John kept coughing.* **2. for the duration** *idiom* for the whole time that something continues; for the entire period of time required for something to be completed; for as long as something takes. ♦ *We are in this war for the duration.* ♦ *However long it takes, we'll wait. We are here for the duration.*

duress [dɚ 'ɛs] *n.* threats that are used to force someone to do something. (No plural form in this sense.) ♦ *Under* *duress from her lawyer, Mary reluctantly signed the papers.* ♦ *Bill signed the contract, but only because of duress.*

during ['dɚ ɪŋ] **1.** *prep.* throughout a period of time; all through a period of time. ♦ *During the winter, our swimming pool has no water in it.* ♦ *During class, the students sit at their desks.* **2.** *prep.* at some point in time; at some time within a period of time. ♦ *Susan left the theater for a moment during intermission.* ♦ *The alarm rang twice during history class.*

dusk ['dʌsk] *n.* the period of the day after the sun sets but before it is completely dark; twilight. ♦ *I enjoy taking a walk along the beach at dusk.* ♦ *The stars begin to twinkle at dusk.*

dust ['dʌst] **1.** *n.* a fine powder of dried earth. (No plural form in this sense.) ♦ *The wind blew the dust across the baseball field.* ♦ *Dust blew into my eyes and stung them.* **2.** *n.* a fine powder, especially particles that settle from the air and coat indoor surfaces. (No plural form in this sense.) ♦ *Soot and dust from the fire settled on the furniture.* ♦ *The dust on the antique table was thick.* **3.** *tv.* to clean a surface or a place by removing ②. ♦ *I quickly dusted the furniture before the guests arrived.* ♦ *The maid dusted the room until it was spotless.* **4.** *tv.* to cover something with ① or ②. ♦ *The baker dusted the cake with powdered sugar.* ♦ *The wind will dust the patio furniture with dirt.* **5.** *tv.* to spray crops with insecticide or weed-killer. (Referred originally to powdered chemicals.) ♦ *Each spring the farmer dusted the crops thoroughly.* ♦ *The plane will dust the corn from the sky.* **6.** *iv.* to remove dust from something or a place as a part of cleaning. ♦ *I haven't dusted in the family room yet.* ♦ *Mary shut the windows and then dusted.* **7. bite the dust** *idiom* to fall to defeat; to die. ♦ *A bullet hit the sheriff in the chest, and he bit the dust.* ♦ *Poor old Bill bit the dust while mowing the lawn. They buried him yesterday.*

dusting ['dʌst ɪŋ] **1.** *n.* the task of cleaning a surface of accumulated dust. (No plural form in this sense.) ♦ *The maid did the dusting quickly and efficiently.* ♦ *Dusting is my least favorite chore.* **2.** *n.* coating a surface with dust, especially coating a field with insecticide or weed-killer. ♦ *Can crop dusting be done when there are strong winds?* ♦ *Environmentalists generally object to the dusting of food crops.*

dustpan ['dʌst pæn] *n.* a flat, shovel-shaped pan with a handle into which dust is swept for disposal. ♦ *Please empty the dustpan into the trash can.* ♦ *The broom and dustpan are kept in the pantry.*

dusty ['dʌs ti] **1.** *adj.* covered with dust; full of dust. (Adv: *dustily.* Comp: *dustier;* sup: *dustiest.*) ♦ *I cleaned the dusty seat before sitting on it.* ♦ *It was hard to recognize the dusty old painting.* **2.** *adj.* like dust; dust-colored. (Comp: *dustier;* sup: *dustiest.*) ♦ *The carpet was a dusty gray.* ♦ *The decorator painted the walls a dusty rose.*

Dutch ['dʌtʃ] **1.** *n.* the language of the Netherlands. (No plural form in this sense.) ♦ *Dutch is related to English.* ♦ *It is not too difficult for a speaker of English to learn Dutch.* **2. go Dutch** *idiom* to share the cost of a meal or some other event. ♦ *"Let's go out and eat." "OK, but let's go Dutch."* ♦ *It's getting expensive to have Sally for a friend. She never wants to go Dutch.*

duty ['dut i] **1.** *n.* a task; an obligation; a responsibility. ♦ *The officer's first duty was to balance the company's budget.* ♦ *Raising children with good manners is every parent's duty.* **2.** *n.* a tax placed on products from another country. ♦ *Congress voted to raise the duty on imported cars.* ♦ *The duty will add about twenty dollars to the cost of an imported car.* **3. in the line of duty** *idiom* as part of one's expected duties. ♦ *When soldiers fight people in a war, it's in the line of duty.* ♦ *Police officers have to do things they may not like in the line of duty.* **4. on active duty** *idiom* in battle or ready to go into battle. ♦ *The soldier was on active duty for ten months.* ♦ *That was a long time to be on active duty.* **5. on duty** *idiom* at work; currently doing one's work. ♦ *I can't help you now, but I'll be on duty in about an hour.* ♦ *Who is on duty here? I need some help.*

duty-free ['dut i 'fri] *adj.* free of import tax. ♦ *Items purchased on the cruise ship are duty-free.* ♦ *The tourists bought a lot of duty-free items.*

dwarf ['dworf] **1.** *n., irreg.* someone or something that is smaller than normal or typical. (Pl: dwarves or *dwarfs.*) ♦ *We love apple trees and planted a few dwarfs in our small backyard.* ♦ *Mike is a dwarf, but he prefers to be called a little person.* **2.** *adj.* smaller than expected; smaller than normally found. ♦ *The scientist developed a number of dwarf species of apple trees.* ♦ *A dwarf evergreen is smaller than a normal evergreen.* **3.** *tv.* [for someone or something large] to make someone or something appear even smaller in a comparison. ♦ *The professional basketball player dwarfed the boys he was coaching.* ♦ *The giant oak dwarfed the seedling.*

dwarves ['dworvz] a pl of dwarf.

dwell ['dwɛl] **1.** *iv., irreg.* to live some place; to live in a place. (Pt/pp: *dwelled* or dwelt.) ♦ *Many people dwell in the mountains and love it.* ♦ *Jane was raised in the city but wanted to dwell in the country.* **2. dwell on** *iv. + prep. phr.* to linger on something; to stay on an idea. ♦ *It is best not to dwell on your misfortunes.* ♦ *The candidate dwelled on his opponent's flaws.*

dweller ['dwɛl ɚ] *n.* someone who lives in a particular place; an inhabitant. ♦ *City dwellers get used to urban noise.* ♦ *Bill loves being an apartment dweller because he doesn't like mowing the grass.*

dwelling ['dwɛl ɪŋ] *n.* a residence; a place where someone lives. ♦ *The dwelling of the sorcerer was a large cave in the side of the mountain.* ♦ *A dormitory is the typical dwelling of a college student.*

dwelt ['dwɛlt] a pt/pp of dwell.

dwindle ['dwɪnd l] *iv.* to decrease piece by piece; to get smaller gradually. ♦ *The sunlight dwindled as the sun set.* ♦ *The stream will continue to dwindle if it doesn't rain.*

dwindling ['dwɪnd lɪŋ] *adj.* getting smaller; decreasing; diminishing; shrinking. (Adv: *dwindlingly.*) ♦ *The dwindling food supply was rationed among the marooned survivors.* ♦ *My dwindling finances began to alarm me.*

dye ['daɪ] **1.** *n.* a liquid that is used to color fabric or hair. ♦ *The dye transformed the old, plain dress.* ♦ *We asked for a green dye, but they sent yellow.* **2.** *tv.* to color something by placing it in ①; to color something with ①. (The present participle is *dyeing.*) ♦ *I asked the hairdresser to dye my hair blond.* ♦ *Why is Anne dyeing her scarf to match that ugly dress?*

dying ['daɪ ɪŋ] **1.** present participle of die. **2.** *adj.* about to die; near death; in the process of approaching death;

almost dead. ♦ *The family members were summoned to say good-bye to their dying grandfather.* ♦ *The dying tree had to be cut down.* **3.** *adj.* fading. ♦ *The dying light of the sunset brought a stillness to the forest.* ♦ *We could hear the dying sounds of the train for a long time.*

dynamic [dɑɪ 'næ mɪk] **1.** *adj.* active; energetic; full of energy. (Adv: *dynamically* [...ɪk li].) ♦ *The audience applauded the dynamic dancers.* ♦ *A dynamic speaker spoke at my graduation ceremony.* **2. dynamics** *n.* the range of energy or force from the lowest to the strongest. (Treated as plural.) ♦ *The dynamics of the business cycle were evident in the economic reports from the past decade.* ♦ *It's difficult to explain the continually changing dynamics of my job.*

dynamite ['dɑɪ nə mɑɪt] **1.** *n.* an explosive chemical, usually ammonium nitrate. (No plural form in this sense.) ♦ *The dynamite exploded prematurely, hurting several people standing nearby.* ♦ *The engineers used dynamite to destroy the old warehouse.* **2.** *n.* someone or something that causes a great shock or surprise; someone or something spectacular that attracts a lot of attention or interest. (Figurative on ①. Informal.) ♦ *The economic news was simply dynamite in the office today.* ♦ *These clothes would be dynamite on you!* **3.** *tv.* to destroy something by an explosion with ①. ♦ *The construction workers dynamited the side of the mountain to build the road.* ♦ *The demolition crew dynamited the old warehouse.*

dynamo ['dɑɪ nə mo] **1.** *n.* a machine that turns energy into electricity. (An old term for a generator. Pl in *-s*.) ♦ *When the dynamo broke down, everything went dark.* ♦ *My bicycle has a small dynamo that makes electrical power for a headlight.* **2.** *n.* someone who is very energetic. (Pl in *-s*.) ♦ *Sally is quite a dynamo, so ask her if you need anything done.* ♦ *The twins ran around the house like little dynamos.*

dysentery ['dɪs ən tɛr i] **1.** *n.* a painful bowel disease with frequent stools having blood and mucus. (No plural form in this sense.) ♦ *To avoid dysentery while traveling, make sure the water you drink is absolutely pure.* ♦ *The troops couldn't march because of dysentery.* **2.** *n.* diarrhea. (No plural form in this sense.) ♦ *I was miserable on the flight home because of dysentery.* ♦ *The people who ate the badly prepared food developed dysentery.*

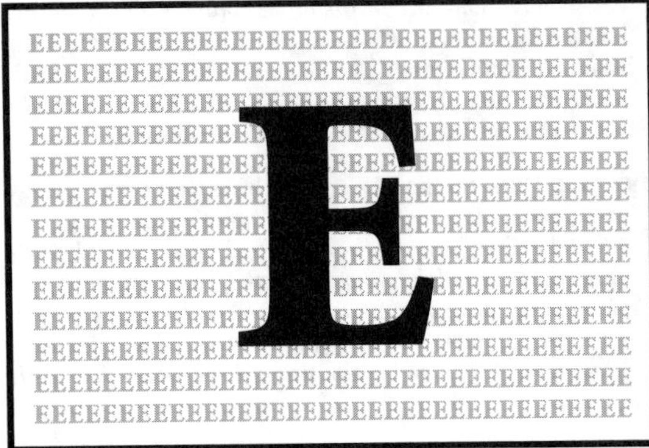

E AND **e** ['i] *n.* the fifth letter of the alphabet. ♦ E *is located between* D *and* F *in the alphabet.* ♦ *The word* elephant *starts with an* e.

each ['itʃ] **1.** *adj.* every [one]. ♦ *Each egg in the carton was broken.* ♦ *Mary washed each piece of fruit.* **2.** *pron.* every one [of those mentioned before]; every thing [of those mentioned before]. ♦ *I have two little puppies. Each is soft and cuddly.* ♦ *Mike, Bill, and Lisa work for the newspaper, each in a different department.* **3.** *adv.* apiece; for every one. ♦ *These light bulbs cost $1 each.* ♦ *The children were given one cookie each.*

eager ['ig ɚ] *adj.* full of desire and anticipation; having a strong desire to do something. (Adv: *eagerly.*) ♦ *Bill was eager to go fishing for the weekend.* ♦ *The eager puppy jumped around at our feet.*

eagerness ['ig ɚ nəs] *n.* enthusiasm. (No plural form in this sense.) ♦ *Bill took advantage of Jane's eagerness to please everyone.* ♦ *The coach loved Jimmy's eagerness to play.*

eagle ['ig əl] *n.* a strong bird of prey of the hawk family, having excellent eyesight. ♦ *The bald eagle is the national bird of the United States of America.* ♦ *An eagle soared above our heads.*

eagle-eyed ['ig əl ɑɪd] **1.** *adj.* able to see very well; having very good eyesight. ♦ *Grandpa may be ninety, but he's still eagle-eyed.* ♦ *An eagle-eyed editor spotted the error.* **2.** *adj.* observant; watchful. ♦ *The private investigator was eagle-eyed and didn't miss a clue.* ♦ *An eagle-eyed guard thwarted the escape.*

ear ['ɪr] **1.** *n.* the organ of hearing, one of which is located on either side of the head. ♦ *I have some hearing loss in my right ear.* ♦ *Bill's ears were ringing after the loud concert.* **2.** *n.* the external, visible part of the organ of hearing. ♦ *I hung gold earrings from my ears.* ♦ *The girl brushed her hair behind her ears.* **3. ear of corn** *n.* the rod-like, fibrous core on which grains of corn grow. ♦ *They served me two ears of corn at the picnic.* ♦ *I just love to eat a freshly picked ear of corn.* **4. bend someone's ear** *idiom* to talk to someone, perhaps annoyingly. ♦ *Tom is over there, bending Jane's ear about something.* ♦ *I'm sorry. I didn't mean to bend your ear for an hour.* **5. dry behind the ears** *idiom* very young and immature. ♦ *Tom is going into business by himself? Why, he's hardly dry behind the ears.* ♦ *That kid isn't dry behind the ears. He'll go broke in a month.* **6. get someone's ear** *idiom* to get someone to listen (to you); to have someone's attention. ♦ *He got my ear and talked for an hour.* ♦ *While I have your ear, I'd like to tell you about something I'm selling.* **7. go in one ear and out the other** *idiom* [for something] to be heard and then forgotten. ♦ *Everything I say to you seems to go in one ear and out the other. Why don't you pay attention?* ♦ *I can't concentrate. Things people say to me just go in one ear and out the other.* **8. have an ear for something** *idiom* to have the ability to learn music or languages. ♦ *Bill doesn't have an ear for music. He can't carry a tune.* ♦ *Mary has a good ear for languages.* **9. keep one's ear to the ground** *idiom* to listen carefully, hoping to get advance warning of something. ♦ *John kept his ear to the ground, hoping to find out about new ideas in computers.* ♦ *His boss told him to keep his ear to the ground so that he'd be the first to know of a new idea.* **10. lend an ear (to someone)** *idiom* to listen to someone. ♦ *Lend an ear to John. Hear what he has to say.* ♦ *I'd be delighted to lend an ear. I find great wisdom in everything John has to say.* **11. prick up one's ears** *idiom* to listen more closely. ♦ *At the sound of my voice, my dog pricked up her ears.* ♦ *I pricked up my ears when I heard my name mentioned.* **12. turn a deaf ear (to something)** *idiom* to ignore what someone says; to ignore a cry for help. ♦ *How can you just turn a deaf ear to their cries for food and shelter?* ♦ *The government has turned a deaf ear.*

earache ['ɪr ek] *n.* a pain in the inner part of the ear. ♦ *The baby cried because of an earache.* ♦ *The wind gave me an earache.*

eardrum ['ɪr drəm] *n.* a membrane inside the ear that vibrates when struck by sound waves. ♦ *The child's eardrum was ruptured by a blow to the head.* ♦ *Anne's right eardrum was operated on by an ear specialist.*

early ['ɚ li] **1.** *adj.* happening toward the first part of something. (Comp: *earlier;* sup: *earliest.*) ♦ *The disagreement started early in the meeting.* ♦ *Early in the marriage things began to go wrong.* **2.** *adj.* arriving before the expected time. (Comp: *earlier;* sup: *earliest.*) ♦ *The train is never early. It is always on time.* ♦ *The guests are early.* **3.** *adj.* ancient; happening long ago in time. (Comp: *earlier;* sup: *earliest.*) ♦ *Early humans hunted and gathered their food.* ♦ *The archaeologist studied early civilizations.* **4.** *adv.* happening toward the first part of something. ♦ *Each morning, classes start early and break for lunch at noon.* ♦ *The mail carrier comes early in the day.* **5.** *adv.* happening before the expected time. ♦ *The bus arrived early this morning.* ♦ *Let's leave early for the beach.*

earmark ['ɪr mɑrk] *tv.* to set something aside, especially money, for a specific reason. ♦ *Jimmy had earmarked his allowance for a bicycle.* ♦ *The committee earmarked some funds for publicity.*

earmuff ['ɪr məf] *n.* one of a pair of warm coverings for the ears. ♦ *Jane bought new earmuffs for the winter weather.* ♦ *Earmuffs protected your ears from the wind.*

earn ['ɚn] **1.** *tv.* to gain a sum of money, or something else of value. ♦ *Jane earns $40,000 a year.* ♦ *Bill earned his keep by cleaning the house.* **2.** *tv.* to merit something. (Figurative on ①.) ♦ *The student earned the professor's praise.* ♦ *Mary earned a promotion at work.*

earnest ['ɚn əst] **1.** *adj.* very serious; sincere; determined. (Adv: *earnestly.*) ♦ *The earnest student studied constantly.* ♦ *Bill appreciated his boss's earnest advice.* **2. in earnest** *idiom* with sincerity. ♦ *I spent the day writing* *the paper in earnest.* ♦ *Mary's comments were in earnest. She really meant them.*

earnestness ['ɚn ɪst nəs] *n.* seriousness; sincerity; determination. (No plural form in this sense.) ♦ *The student's earnestness impressed the professor.* ♦ *The salesclerk's polite earnestness helped her sell merchandise.*

earnings ['ɚ nɪŋz] *n.* the amount of money someone makes by working; income. (Treated as plural.) ♦ *Bill saves a third of his earnings.* ♦ *A large percentage of my earnings goes to taxes.*

earphone ['ɪr fon] *n.* a small sound-producing device that fits over or in the ear. (A pair is often used.) ♦ *Jane listened to the radio through her earphones.* ♦ *The television newscaster got up-to-date information from the producer through her hidden earphone.*

earring ['ɪr rɪŋ] *n.* a piece of jewelry worn on the ear. ♦ *Anne's earrings match her necklace.* ♦ *Jane lost an earring on the camping trip.*

earshot ['ɪr ʃɑt] **out of earshot** *idiom* too far from the source of a sound to hear the sound. ♦ *I was out of earshot and could not hear the conversation.* ♦ *Mary waited until her children were out of earshot before mentioning the party to Bill.*

earth ['ɚθ] **1.** *n.* the planet we live on; the third planet from the sun in our solar system. (Often capitalized.) ♦ *Earth and Jupiter are just two of the planets that orbit the sun.* ♦ *More than two-thirds of the earth is covered with water.* **2.** *n.* soil; land. (No plural form in this sense.) ♦ *Blades of grass emerged from the damp earth.* ♦ *The bulbs were planted in the rich earth last fall.* **3.** *n.* the surface of this planet. (No plural form in this sense.) ♦ *The plane fell to earth.* ♦ *The traveler roamed the earth looking for adventure.* **4. like nothing on earth** *idiom* not normal or expected; shocking and surprising. ♦ *Jane arrived at the office looking like nothing on earth. She was a mess.* ♦ *The cake was like nothing on earth. It was delicious!* **5. run someone or something to earth** *idiom* to find something after a search. ♦ *Lisa finally ran her long-lost cousin to earth in Paris.* ♦ *After months of searching, I ran a copy of Jim's book to earth.* **6. to the ends of the earth** *idiom* to the remotest and most inaccessible points on the earth. ♦ *I'll pursue him to the ends of the earth.* ♦ *We've traveled to the ends of the earth trying to learn about our world!*

earthen ['ɚθ ən] *adj.* made of soil; made of clay. ♦ *The corpse was lowered to its earthen resting place.* ♦ *Large earthen pots held grain for the long winter.*

earthenware ['ɚθ ɚn wɛr] **1.** *adj.* made of baked soil or clay. ♦ *The earthenware pots were very old.* ♦ *Some of the food supplies were stored in earthenware pots.* **2.** *n.* dishes or pottery made from baked soil or clay. (No plural form in this sense.) ♦ *The potter made earthenware from clay.* ♦ *The archaeologist dug up earthenware from the ruins.*

earthly ['ɚθ li] *adj.* of or on the earth; of a part of life on earth rather than in heaven. ♦ *The preacher urged us to ignore our earthly desires.* ♦ *This earthly life will soon come to an end.*

earthquake AND **quake** ['ɚθ kwek, 'kwek] *n.* a violent shaking of the ground by natural forces. ♦ *An earthquake struck the coastal city.* ♦ *The earthquake's damage was devastating.*

earthward ['ɚθ wɚd] **1.** *adv.* moving toward the earth. ♦ *The plane ran out of fuel during flight and fell earthward.* ♦ *A meteor sped earthward, leaving a trail of light.* **2.** *adj.* toward the earth. ♦ *The kite responded to an earthward tug.* ♦ *Gravity exerts an earthward pull on us.*

earthworm ['ɚθ wɚm] *n.* a worm that lives in the soil. ♦ *Earthworms burrow through the soil.* ♦ *After the storm, the sidewalk was covered with earthworms.*

earthy ['ɚθ i] **1.** *adj.* coarse; not refined; frank. (Adv: *earthily.* Comp: *earthier;* sup: *earthiest.*) ♦ *The earthy young woman said exactly what she thought.* ♦ *My earthy sense of humor offends some people.* **2.** *adj.* of earth or soil. (Comp: *earthier;* sup: *earthiest.*) ♦ *The room was decorated in earthy colors.* ♦ *The forest had an earthy fragrance that made our walk pleasant.*

ease ['iz] **1.** *tv.* to make something less hard to do; to make something easier. ♦ *A burst of energy eased Bill's task.* ♦ *Anne prayed every night for God to ease her burdens.* **2.** *tv.* to make something less severe. ♦ *The drugs eased my pain.* ♦ *The joke eased the feeling of tension in the room.* **3.** *tv.* to move something [somewhere] gently and carefully. ♦ *Jane eased the car out of the garage.* ♦ *Bill eased the gift into the box.* **4.** *iv.* to become less hard, less difficult, or less severe. ♦ *Jane's work finally eased towards the end of the year.* ♦ *The tense situation in the apartment eased once Tom's roommate moved out.* **5.** *n.* freedom from problems or annoyances; peaceful rest. (No plural form in this sense.) ♦ *If I had enough money I would live a life of ease.* ♦ *Grandfather sits in his rocking chair and enjoys the ease of his retirement.* **6. at ease** *phr.* without worry or anxiety. ♦ *The performer is at ease on the stage.* ♦ *After she had met a few people, Mary felt at ease with the group.* **7. with ease** *phr.* without effort. ♦ *The smart student passed the test with ease.* ♦ *The gymnast did a back flip with ease.*

easel ['iz əl] *n.* a stand that holds an artist's canvas. ♦ *The canvas rested on the easel.* ♦ *The artist carried the easel outdoors.*

east ['ist] **1.** *n.* the direction to the right of someone or something facing north; the direction in which the sun appears to rise. (No plural form in this sense.) ♦ *The Atlantic Ocean is to the east of the United States.* ♦ *We watched the sun rise in the east.* **2.** *adj.* in ①; from ①; toward ①; eastern. ♦ *We live on the east side of the street.* ♦ *Susan attended a college on the East Coast.* **3.** *adv.* moving toward ①. ♦ *Jerry drove east until he reached the Atlantic Ocean.* ♦ *When you get to the corner, turn east.*

Easter ['ist ɚ] **1.** *n.* the Christian holiday celebrating the resurrection of Jesus Christ. ♦ *Easter is a spring holiday.* ♦ *I went to church early in the morning on Easter.* **2.** *adj.* <the adj. use of ①.> ♦ *The children dyed Easter eggs on Saturday afternoon.* ♦ *Jane wore a new Easter dress to church.*

easterly ['ist ɚ li] **1.** *adj.* toward the east. ♦ *Lisa chose the bedroom with the easterly outlook.* ♦ *We sailed in an easterly direction across the lake.* **2.** *adj.* from the east, especially used to describe wind. ♦ *The easterly wind picked up speed and sprayed water from the ocean onto the beach.* ♦ *An easterly wind blew through the yard.*

eastern ['ist ɚn] *adj.* of or about the east. ♦ *There is a rabbit hole in the eastern part of our yard.* ♦ *Bill plowed the eastern portion of his farm today.*

Eastern Hemisphere ['ist ɚn 'hɛm əs fɪr] *n.* the half of the earth that includes Asia, Australia, Africa, and most of Europe. ♦ *The Eastern Hemisphere includes what is called the "Old World."* ♦ *All of Russia is in the Eastern Hemisphere.*

eastward ['ist wɚd] *adv.* toward the east; in the direction of the rising sun. ♦ *Dave drove the car eastward toward Cleveland from Chicago.* ♦ *The crowd faced eastward as they paused for a moment of silence.*

easy ['i zi] **1.** *adj.* simple; not hard; not difficult. (Adv: *easily.* Comp: *easier;* sup: *easiest.*) ♦ *Jane saved the easy tasks for last.* ♦ *Algebra is not easy for many people.* **2.** *adv.* without stress; without worry; relaxed. ♦ *Let's just take it easy today and go to the beach.* ♦ *Don't lift those heavy boxes. Go easy on yourself.* **3. easy come, easy go** *idiom* <said to explain the loss of something that required only a small amount of effort to get in the first place.> ♦ *Anne found twenty dollars in the morning and spent it foolishly at noon. "Easy come, easy go," she said.* ♦ *John spends his money as fast as he can earn it. With John it's easy come, easy go.* **4. free and easy** *idiom* casual. ♦ *John is so free and easy. How can anyone be so relaxed?* ♦ *Just act free and easy. No one will know you're nervous.*

easygoing [i zi 'go ɪŋ] *adj.* without worry; taking life easy; relaxed. ♦ *Bill has a calm and easygoing personality.* ♦ *An easygoing manner is helpful in stressful situations.*

eat ['it] **1.** *tv.* to put food in one's mouth, chew, and swallow it. (Pt: ate; pp: eaten.) ♦ *Let's eat hamburgers for dinner.* ♦ *We ate lunch in a restaurant.* **2.** *tv.* [for acid or alkali] to erode or corrode something. ♦ *Acid can eat metal.* ♦ *The spilled acid ate the surface of the wooden table.* **3.** *tv.* to create a hole by chewing or eroding. ♦ *The acid ate a hole in the metal.* ♦ *A mouse ate a hole in the cereal box.* **4. eat up** *tv. + adv.* to consume all of some food. ♦ *Who ate up the cheese?* ♦ *We ate up all the turkey at Thanksgiving dinner.* **5. eat up** *tv. + adv.* to use all of something. (Figurative on ④.) ♦ *Paying for the car repairs ate up all my savings.* ♦ *Leaving the lights on eats up electricity.* **6.** *iv.* to nourish the body by taking in food. ♦ *We ate at noon and again at 6:00 P.M.* ♦ *When are we going to eat? I'm hungry.* **7. eat someone out of house and home** *idiom* to eat a lot of food (in someone's home); to eat all the food in the house. ♦ *Billy has a huge appetite. He almost eats us out of house and home.* ♦ *When the kids come home from college, they always eat us out of house and home.*

eaten ['ɪt n] pp of eat.

eatery ['it ə ri] *n.* a place where people go to eat meals; a restaurant. (Informal.) ♦ *There's a small eatery in the basement of the museum.* ♦ *Bill stopped at an eatery for a snack.*

eaves ['ivz] *n.* the edge of a roof that hangs over the side of a building. (Treated as plural.) ♦ *The birds made a nest under the eaves of the house.* ♦ *Tom hung lights on the eaves of the house in December.*

eavesdrop ['ivz drɑp] **eavesdrop (on)** *iv.* (+ *prep. phr.*) to secretly listen to other people talking in private. (Pt/pp: *eavesdropped.*) ♦ *Jimmy tried to eavesdrop on his parents, but they caught him.* ♦ *It is not polite to eavesdrop!*

ebb ['ɛb] **1.** *iv.* [for the tide] to flow away from the shore. ♦ *Water washed up on the shore, then slowly ebbed away.* ♦ *As the waves ebbed, the children picked up shells on the sand.* **2.** *iv.* to weaken; to decline. (Figurative on ①.) ♦ *The politician's popularity has ebbed with the voters.* ♦ *John's fortune ebbed as he sold off his valuable collection.* **3.** *n.* the flowing away of the tide from the shore; the receding of water. (No plural form in this sense.) ♦ *The children picked up shells in the ebb of the tide.* ♦ *The bird landed on the sand during the tide's ebb.* **4.** *n.* a period of decline; the time when someone or something is weakened. (No plural form in this sense. Figurative on ③.) ♦ *The candidate's finances were at an ebb.* ♦ *The stock market was at a critical ebb.* **5.** *n.* a low point in the decline of something. (No plural form in this sense.) ♦ *Bill retired at the ebb of his career.* ♦ *We bought our house during an ebb in the real-estate market.*

ebony ['ɛb ə ni] **1.** *n.* a kind of dense, black hardwood from a variety of tropical trees. (No plural form in this sense.) ♦ *The black keys on my piano are made from ebony.* ♦ *The beads of my necklace are made of ebony.* **2.** *n.* a jet black color. (No plural form in this sense.) ♦ *The lacquered box was ebony in color.* ♦ *The sky is ebony and the moon is brilliant white.* **3.** *adj.* made of ①. ♦ *Ebony beads hung around Anne's neck.* ♦ *The documents were kept in a heavy ebony box.* **4.** *adj.* black. ♦ *The moon shone bright in the ebony sky.* ♦ *The cat had ebony feet.*

eccentric [ɛk 'sɛn trɪk] **1.** *adj.* odd; strange; peculiar. (Adv: *eccentrically* [...ɪk li].) ♦ *The poet has eccentric taste in clothing.* ♦ *My neighbor's eccentric behavior is sometimes frightening.* **2.** *n.* someone who is odd or peculiar. ♦ *There's an eccentric with 100 cats who lives in our town.* ♦ *The nurse told the old eccentric to leave the other patients alone.*

eccentricity [ɛk sɛn 'trɪs ə ti] **1.** *n.* the quality or condition of being odd, strange, or peculiar. (No plural form in this sense.) ♦ *Bill's eccentricity has made him unpopular with some people.* ♦ *Our neighbor's general eccentricity does not bother us.* **2.** *n.* an odd, strange, or peculiar habit. ♦ *Bill has several eccentricities, but is generally amiable.* ♦ *One of my eccentricities is that I won't use plastic forks.*

ecclesiastic [ɪ kliz i 'æs tɪk] **1.** *adj.* of or about the church or the clergy. (Adv: *ecclesiastically* [...ɪk li].) ♦ *The priest attended the ecclesiastic conference in Rome.* ♦ *The ecclesiastic representatives discussed changes in the church.* **2.** *n.* a priest, minister, pastor, or other person who is a member of the clergy. ♦ *The members of the commission were all ecclesiastics.* ♦ *Our religion class studied the works of several well-known ecclesiastics.*

ecclesiastical [ɪ kli zi 'æs tɪ kəl] *adj.* of or about the church or religious matters. (Adv: *ecclesiastically* [...ɪk li].) ♦ *The ecclesiastical commission set forth new church doctrine.* ♦ *The minister was concerned with all ecclesiastical matters.*

ECG See electrocardiogram.

echelon ['ɛʃ ə lɑn] *n.* a rank or level of authority or power. ♦ *Mary was promoted to the upper echelon of management at her company.* ♦ *The government's lower echelon consists of career bureaucrats.*

echo ['ɛk o] **1.** *n.* a sound that is heard twice because the sound waves have bounced off a surface and returned. (Pl in *-es.*) ♦ *An echo bounced off the bluff.* ♦ *The hikers heard an echo from the valley.* **2.** *iv.* [for a sound] to reflect back. ♦ *The hiker's voice echoed clearly.* ♦ *The thunder echoed loudly through the valley.* **3.** *tv.* to reflect sound; to repeat a sound. ♦ *The hills echoed the shepherd's voice.* ♦

The mountains echoed the thunder. **4.** *tv.* to repeat something that someone has said. ♦ *Susan echoed everything her mother said.* ♦ *David timidly echoed the opinions of his boss.* **5.** *tv.* to agree with or support someone's opinion. ♦ *The editorial echoed the viewpoints of conservative politicians.* ♦ *David echoed his parents' opinions.*

eclectic [ɛ 'klɛk tɪk] *adj.* varied; taken from many different places or systems. (Adv: *eclectically* [...ɪk li].) ♦ *Mary's taste in music is eclectic. She likes everything from classical to country.* ♦ *The man with an eclectic taste in clothes wore sneakers with a tuxedo.*

eclipse [ɪ 'klɪps] **1.** *n.* the darkening of a celestial body when another body passes between it and the star that gives it light. ♦ *We observed the eclipse with a special, protective viewer.* ♦ *An eclipse occurs when the moon passes between the sun and the earth.* **2.** *tv.* to block the light from the sun or the moon. ♦ *The moon eclipsed the sun, cutting off part of its light to the earth.* ♦ *The earth eclipsed part of the moon.* **3.** *tv.* to surpass someone; to make someone become less important than oneself. (Figurative on ②.) ♦ *The young opera star eclipsed the established singer.* ♦ *Bill's success has eclipsed his brother's ambitions.*

ecological [ɛk ə 'lɑdʒ ɪk əl] **1.** *adj.* of or about ecology. (Adv: *ecologically* [...ɪk li].) ♦ *The botanist did an ecological study of the mouse population.* ♦ *The politician addressed ecological issues.* **2.** *adj.* serving to preserve the environment. (Adv: *ecologically* [...ɪk li].) ♦ *Conservation has ecological benefits.* ♦ *The scientist proposed an ecological study before building the dam.*

ecology [ɪ 'kɑl ə dʒi] *n.* the study and science of living things and the way they interact with their environment. (No plural form in this sense.) ♦ *The scientist wrote about the ecology of the prairie.* ♦ *The sixth graders discussed ecology in their science class.*

economic [ɛk ə 'nɑm ɪk] **1.** *adj.* of or about ③. (Adv: *economically* [...ɪk li].) ♦ *The newspaper featured an article about the nation's economic future.* ♦ *Our city suffered economic turmoil when the factory closed.* **2.** *adj.* saving money; thrifty; economical. (Adv: *economically* [...ɪk li].) ♦ *Buying in bulk is an economic way to shop.* ♦ *I look for the most economic products when I shop for groceries.* **3. economics** *n.* financial matters or issues. (Usually treated as singular.) ♦ *The investor considered the economics of opening a factory in the run-down neighborhood.* ♦ *A committee was formed to study the economics of closing some military bases.* **4. economics** *n.* the study of the production and use of goods and services in a society. (Treated as singular.) ♦ *Mary is a specialist in U.S. economics.* ♦ *The stockbroker has a degree in economics.*

economical [ɛk ə 'nɑm ɪ kəl] *adj.* [of a purchase] good value; money-saving; thrifty. (Adv: *economically* [...ɪk li].) ♦ *Comparing prices is an economical way to shop for groceries.* ♦ *Purchasing clothing that will only be worn once is not very economical.*

economist [ɪ 'kɑn ə məst] *n.* someone who studies the production and use of goods and services in industry and trade. ♦ *The economist predicted the nation would experience a recession.* ♦ *The government economist advised the president on monetary policies.*

economize [ɪ 'kɑn ə mɑɪz] *iv.* to reduce the spending of money. ♦ *When they bought a house, the family had to economize to pay their mortgage.* ♦ *We could afford to go on vacation only after economizing for a year.*

economy [ɪ 'kɑn ə mi] **1.** *n.* thriftiness; spending time, energy, or money wisely. (No plural form in this sense.) ♦ *Not known for his economy, Mike often spends money on things he doesn't need.* ♦ *Economy is a major consideration when I shop for clothes.* **2. economies** *n.* acts of saving money or being thrifty. (Treated as plural.) ♦ *We are able to make small economies in our daily living.* ♦ *The company was forced to achieve economies wherever possible.* **3.** *n.* the system and management of industry and trade within a country. ♦ *The small country had a solid economy.* ♦ *The country's economy collapsed when the stock market crashed.*

ecosystem ['ɛk o sɪs təm] *n.* a specific environment in which certain plants and animals interact. ♦ *Logging has destroyed the ecosystem of the forest.* ♦ *This type of frog cannot survive outside its ecosystem.*

ecru ['ɛ kru] **1.** *n.* a pale brown color; a light brown color; a tan color. (No plural form in this sense.) ♦ *The walls were painted a pleasant shade of ecru.* ♦ *Ecru is not a color that looks good with my hair.* **2.** *adj.* <the adj. use of ①.> ♦ *The room has ecru walls and brown woodwork.* ♦ *My new sports jacket is ecru linen.*

ecstasy ['ɛk stə si] *n.* extreme joy; extreme delight; very intense happiness. (No plural form in this sense.) ♦ *Bill and Anne experienced the ecstasy of becoming parents.* ♦ *Mary was in ecstasy when she won the piano competition.*

ecstatic [ɛk 'stæt ɪk] *adj.* extremely happy; extremely joyful. (Adv: *ecstatically* [...ɪk li].) ♦ *I was ecstatic when I got the job.* ♦ *At the start of her vacation, Mary was in an ecstatic mood.*

Ecuador ['ɛ kwə dor] See Gazetteer.

ecumenical [ɛ kju 'mɛn ɪ kəl] *adj.* causing or encouraging unity among the different Christian religions. (Adv: *ecumenically* [...ɪk li].) ♦ *Several churches participated in an ecumenical service.* ♦ *There are many clerics on the ecumenical committee.*

ecumenism [ɛ kju 'mɛn ɪz əm] *n.* the idea of Christian unity; a movement concerned with Christian unity. (No plural form in this sense.) ♦ *Ecumenism seeks to overcome differences between religious denominations.* ♦ *Conflicting theologies prevented ecumenism between the churches.*

-ed *suffix* <a form that marks the past tense and some past participles of regular English verbs.> (Past participles are freely used as adjectives in English, especially when they are preceded by an adverb. Examples: *well-cleaned pot, newly poured wine, poorly printed document, much talked-about news, often-repeated story.*)

edema [ɛ 'dim ə] *n.* a medical condition where body tissues are swollen with fluid. (No plural form in this sense.) ♦ *Jane was diagnosed with edema in her ankles.* ♦ *Bill's edema was serious enough to require hospitalization.*

edge ['ɛdʒ] **1.** *n.* the rim of something; the outer border of something; the brink of something. ♦ *The edge of the plate has a gold rim around it.* ♦ *The children stood at the edge of the pond.* **2.** *n.* the edge or cutting part of a cutting tool or instrument. ♦ *The butter knife has a dull edge.* ♦ *The edge of the knife was not sharp enough to cut the meat.* **3.** *n.* an advantage. ♦ *A good education will give you an edge in the job market.* ♦ *John was a natural athlete who always had an edge in team sports.* **4.** *n.* a sharpness of

[food] flavor or [speech] intonation. (Figurative on ②.) ♦ *Jane's voice had an edge to it when she told us the bad news.* ♦ *The flavor of the chili had a spicy edge to it.* **5.** *tv.* to provide something with a border. ♦ *I edged the curtains with lace.* ♦ *The ceiling has been edged with wood.* **6.** *iv.* to move [in some direction] a little bit at a time. ♦ *The new driver edged out of the driveway carefully.* ♦ *The toddler slowly edged away from her parents.*

edgewise ['ɛdʒ wɑɪz] *adv.* leading with an edge; with the edge going first. ♦ *Bill tried to squeeze through the narrow opening edgewise.* ♦ *Put the coin into the slot edgewise.*

edging ['ɛdʒ ɪŋ] *n.* a border; something that is placed at the edge of something. (No plural form in this sense.) ♦ *The edging on the dress is handmade lace.* ♦ *Flowers formed an edging for the lawn.*

edgy ['ɛdʒ i] *adj.* easily upset; irritable; nervous. (Adv: *edgily.* Comp: *edgier;* sup: *edgiest.*) ♦ *Mary has been really edgy since she lost her job.* ♦ *Loud noises make me edgy.*

edible ['ɛd ə bəl] *adj.* able to be eaten. (Adv: *edibly.*) ♦ *The cake was garnished with edible decorations.* ♦ *Your cooking is simply not edible.*

edict ['i dɪkt] *n.* an official order or decree; an official command. ♦ *Management gave an edict that we have to cut production costs.* ♦ *According to the teacher's edict, no one can chew gum in class.*

edification [ɛd ə fɪ 'ke ʃən] *n.* an improvement, especially to one's character or mind. (No plural form in this sense.) ♦ *Jane read the article to Tom for his edification.* ♦ *I don't need any further edification in this matter.*

edifice ['ɛd ə fɪs] *n.* a large, impressive building. ♦ *This huge edifice is a tribute to modern architecture.* ♦ *The limestone edifice on the corner was built in the 1930s.*

edify ['ɛd ə fɑɪ] *tv.* to enlighten or uplift someone. ♦ *A trip to the art museum edified the tourists and helped them understand the local culture better.* ♦ *Max helped plan a religious pageant that would edify all those who watched it.*

edifying ['ɛd ə fɑɪ ɪŋ] *adj.* enlightening; instructive; uplifting. (Adv: *edifyingly.*) ♦ *Max thanked the preacher for his edifying remarks.* ♦ *We spent an edifying afternoon at the art museum.*

edit ['ɛd ɪt] *tv.* to prepare text, video, or audio for publication or production. ♦ *Jane edited Anne's writing and suggested changes.* ♦ *You must edit this video before it goes on television.*

edited ['ɛd ɪt ɪd] *adj.* corrected, amended, or revised. ♦ *The edited copy is clear and concise.* ♦ *The author is unhappy with the edited manuscript.*

edition [ɪ 'dɪ ʃən] *n.* the copies of one book made in one printing or series of printings until the text is changed or revised. ♦ *The antique dealer specializes in first editions.* ♦ *A new edition of the dictionary is coming out soon.*

editor ['ɛd ɪt ɚ] **1.** *n.* someone who prepares text for publication; someone who prepares film, video, or audio for production. ♦ *Bill is an editor for a book publishing company.* ♦ *The editor reformatted the film for television viewing.* **2.** *n.* someone who works for a newspaper, a magazine, or a book publisher, overseeing acquisition of new material, editing, and production. ♦ *The city editor removed the reporter's story from page one.* ♦ *The acquisitions editor is responsible for getting new manuscripts.*

editorial [ɛd ə 'tor i əl] **1.** *n.* a short essay written by an editor of a newspaper. ♦ *Today's editorial criticized the mayor for the city's crime problems.* ♦ *The editorial addressed the upcoming presidential election.* **2.** *adj.* of or about editing or an editor's job. (Adv: *editorially.*) ♦ *Susan interviewed for an editorial position with the publishing company.* ♦ *Books and magazines cluttered the editorial office.*

editorialize [ɛd ɪ 'tor i ə lɑɪz] *iv.* to give personal comments instead of reporting objectively. ♦ *Don't editorialize. Just give me the facts.* ♦ *The city editor did not want his reporters to editorialize.*

educable ['ɛdʒ ə kə bəl] *adj.* able to be taught; able to learn. (Adv: *educably.*) ♦ *The depressed teacher wondered if some of the students were educable.* ♦ *You're still educable even after graduation.*

educate ['ɛdʒ ə ket] *tv.* to teach someone something; to instruct someone how to do something. ♦ *Anne educated her mathematics class in subtraction.* ♦ *Please educate Bill in the rules of basic etiquette.*

education [ɛdʒ ə 'ke ʃən] **1.** *n.* the teaching of knowledge and skills; a system for teaching knowledge and skills and then certifying the student's degree of success. (No plural form in this sense.) ♦ *What could be more important than the education of our children?* ♦ *The teachers protested when the government reduced its support for education.* **2.** *n.* the learning or knowledge that is obtained by studying or being taught. (No plural form in this sense.) ♦ *I have applied my education to all aspects in my life.* ♦ *Bill's advanced education helped him obtain his current job.*

educational [ɛdʒ ə 'ke ʃə nəl] **1.** *adj.* of or about education. (Adv: *educationally.*) ♦ *The educational system in this district needs improving.* ♦ *Will this school meet the educational needs of your children?* **2.** *adj.* instructive. (Adv: *educationally.*) ♦ *The field trip to the museum was an educational experience.* ♦ *I did not feel the speech was interesting or educational.*

eel ['il] **1.** *n.* a long, finless, snake-like fish. ♦ *Eels have smooth, slimy skin.* ♦ *We caught several eels in the water of the canal.* **2.** *n.* the edible flesh of ①. (No plural form in this sense.) ♦ *The restaurant serves eel as a delicacy.* ♦ *Pickled eel is a tasty kind of food.*

eerie ['ɪr i] *adj.* strange; peculiar; weird; frightening. (Adv: *eerily* ['ɪr ɪ li]. Comp: *eerier;* sup: *eeriest.*) ♦ *I had an eerie feeling as we walked through the abandoned house.* ♦ *The stranger across the room gave me an eerie look.*

efface [ɪ 'fes] **1.** *tv.* to erase something; to eliminate writing, etc., from the surface of something. ♦ *The vandals effaced the name and date from the old tombstone.* ♦ *The plaque beside the door had been effaced and could not be read.* **2.** *tv.* to destroy a memory. (Figurative on ①.) ♦ *It is not possible to efface the memory of a loved one.* ♦ *Through all these years, his memory had not been effaced by time.*

effect [ɪ 'fɛkt] **1.** *n.* a result; something that happens because of something else. (Compare with **affect**.) ♦ *What will the effect be on the twins if they are separated?* ♦ *Noise from airplanes has an effect on people who live near the airport.* **2.** *tv.* to cause a result; to produce a result. ♦ *The once hostile countries effected a peace treaty.* ♦ *People's enthusiasm for the product effected an increase in sales.*

3. in effect *idiom* in existence; applicable. ♦ *A reduced rate at the hotel is in effect until the end of the year.* ♦ *The curfew is in effect for all minors.* **4. in effect** *idiom* producing a particular effect; effectively. ♦ *In effect, this new law will raise taxes for most people.* ♦ *This policy harms domestic manufacturers. In effect, all our clothing will be made in foreign countries.*

effective [ɪ 'fɛk tɪv] **1.** *adj.* good at producing or causing results. (Adv: *effectively.*) ♦ *Anne is an effective sales representative.* ♦ *The effective politician cut waste from the budget.* **2.** *adj.* applicable; in effect. ♦ *The curfew will be effective once the mayor signs the law authorizing it.* ♦ *The agreement is not effective until both parties sign the document.*

effectively [ɪ 'fɛk tɪv li] **1.** *adv.* in a way that causes favorable results. ♦ *Bill handled the difficult situation at work effectively.* ♦ *Anne worked effectively to find a solution to the problem.* **2.** *adv.* in effect; causing a particular effect. ♦ *When the fortress is destroyed, effectively, the war is over.* ♦ *Effectively, the new law will raise taxes for most people, rather than lower them.*

effectiveness [ɪ 'fɛk tɪv nəs] *n.* the ability to be effective. (No plural form in this sense.) ♦ *Are you sure about the effectiveness of this medicine?* ♦ *I have no doubts concerning the effectiveness of your product.*

effeminacy [ɪ 'fɛm ə nə si] *n.* feminineness [in a male]; the lack of masculine qualities [in a male]. (No plural form in this sense.) ♦ *Bill's laughter had a touch of effeminacy.* ♦ *The boy's effeminacy caused him to be mocked at school.*

effeminate [ɪ 'fɛm ə nɪt] *adj.* [of a male] having some female characteristics. (Adv: *effeminately.*) ♦ *John's effeminate gestures were ridiculed by his classmates.* ♦ *Bill spoke with an effeminate voice when he imitated his sister.*

effervesce [ɛf ɚ 'vɛs] **1.** *iv.* to bubble; to produce gas bubbles. ♦ *Don't shake the bottle, or the champagne will effervesce and explode.* ♦ *The pop effervesced as I drank it, and it tickled my nose.* **2.** *iv.* to display enthusiasm. (Figurative on ①.) ♦ *The children at the party effervesced with excitement.* ♦ *The cheerleaders effervesced before the crowd.*

effervescence [ɛf ɚ 'vɛs əns] **1.** *n.* the presence of gas bubbles, especially in a drink. (No plural form in this sense.) ♦ *The pop's effervescence was lost soon after the bottle was opened.* ♦ *The winemaker closely observed the effervescence of the champagne.* **2.** *n.* liveliness; cheeriness. (Figurative on ①. No plural form in this sense.) ♦ *Jane's effervescence made everyone else happy as well.* ♦ *It was exciting to see Bill's effervescence after he had been sick for so long.*

effervescent [ɛf ɚ 'vɛs ənt] **1.** *adj.* producing gas bubbles; giving off gas bubbles. (Adv: *effervescently.*) ♦ *I enjoyed an effervescent glass of champagne.* ♦ *The soda water was strongly effervescent.* **2.** *adj.* lively; cheery; upbeat. (Figurative on ①. Adv: *effervescently.*) ♦ *Bill's effervescent attitude made our train ride together enjoyable.* ♦ *Anne's effervescent smile made me feel less unhappy.*

efficacious [ɛf ə 'ke ʃəs] *adj.* causing a desired result; effective. (Adv: *efficaciously.*) ♦ *Your solution to our ongoing problem is quite efficacious.* ♦ *Our accountant made an efficacious suggestion concerning our tax situation.*

efficiency [ɪ 'fɪ ʃən si] **1.** *n.* the ability to produce a desired effect without wasting time, energy, or money. (No plural form in this sense.) ♦ *Jane performs her office duties with great efficiency.* ♦ *Bill's efficiency at work impressed his boss.* **2. efficiency (apartment)** *n.* a studio apartment; a one-room apartment. ♦ *I live in a cozy efficiency in the city.* ♦ *Mary's efficiency is very small and constricted.* **3.** *adj.* <the adj. use of ①.> ♦ *The boss brought in an efficiency expert to give us suggestions on being more efficient.* ♦ *This brand of refrigerator has a high efficiency rating.*

efficient [ɪ 'fɪ ʃənt] *adj.* organized; using time, energy, and money with efficiency. (Adv: *efficiently.*) ♦ *Anne is an efficient and conscientious worker.* ♦ *The financial analyst found efficient ways for the company to save money.*

effigy ['ɛf ə dʒi] **1.** *n.* a crude representation of a disliked person, usually made for ridicule or mocking. ♦ *The angry mob burned an effigy of their ruler.* ♦ *The mayor's effigy hung in the village square.* **2. hang someone in effigy** *idiom* to hang a dummy or some other figure representing a hated person. ♦ *They hanged the dictator in effigy.* ♦ *The angry mob hanged the president in effigy.*

effort ['ɛ fɚt] *n.* the use of physical or mental energy to do hard work. ♦ *Please make an effort to bring up your grades at school.* ♦ *Put some effort into cutting the lawn. If you don't, it will take all day.*

effortless ['ɛ fɚt ləs] *adj.* without effort; very easy; not requiring much physical or mental energy; not requiring strength. (Adv: *effortlessly.*) ♦ *The military takeover of the small country was effortless.* ♦ *John's effortless running of the race impressed the coach.*

effusive [ə 'fju sɪv] *adj.* emotional; showing much emotion or feeling. (Adv: *effusively.*) ♦ *My best friend is quite jolly and has an effusive personality.* ♦ *The excited children couldn't control their effusive nature.*

egalitarian [ɪ gæl ɪ 'tɛr i ən] **1.** *n.* someone who believes in equality. ♦ *The senator is a staunch egalitarian.* ♦ *My parents were egalitarians and support equality for everyone.* **2.** *adj.* believing in equality; supporting, promoting, or characterized by equality. (Adv: *egalitarianly.*) ♦ *The students supported all egalitarian causes.* ♦ *Susan's egalitarian beliefs created problems where she worked.*

egg ['ɛg] **1.** *n.* an ovum; the female reproductive cell. ♦ *The fertilized egg attached itself to the lining of the uterus.* ♦ *An egg descends from the ovaries to the uterus each month.* **2.** *n.* a round object, containing ①, covered with a shell, produced by a female bird or reptile and often used for food. ♦ *The hen sat on her egg until it hatched.* ♦ *A yellow chick came out of the egg.* **3.** *n.* the edible part of ②. ♦ *I had two eggs for breakfast.* ♦ *You should put an egg in the cake batter.* **4.** *n.* the edible part of ②. (No plural form in this sense.) ♦ *Please rewash the plate. There is still egg on it.* ♦ *Did you use egg in this cake?* **5. lay an egg** *idiom* to give a bad performance. ♦ *The cast of the play really laid an egg last night.* ♦ *I hope I don't lay an egg when it's my turn to sing.* **6. put all one's eggs in one basket** *idiom* to risk everything at once. ♦ *Don't put all your eggs in one basket. Then everything won't be lost if there is a catastrophe.* ♦ *John only applied to the one college he wanted to attend. He put all his eggs in one basket.*

eggbeater ['ɛg bit ɚ] *n.* a kitchen utensil used to whip an egg until the yellow and the white are well mixed. ♦ *Use the eggbeater to scramble the eggs for an omelet.* ♦ *The newlyweds received four eggbeaters as wedding presents!*

eggnog ['ɛg nɑg] *n.* a drink made from eggs, milk or cream, sugar, and often some kind of alcohol, served especially during winter holidays. (No plural form in this sense.) ♦ *Eggnog is rich and creamy.* ♦ *We sat in front of the fireplace and drank some cold eggnog.*

eggplant ['ɛg plænt] **1.** *n.* a large, round, purple vegetable of the nightshade family and the plant it grows on. ♦ *Please buy two eggplants at the store.* ♦ *I harvested two dozen eggplants from my garden.* **2.** *n.* the fruit of ① used as food. (No plural form in this sense.) ♦ *Anne cut up some eggplant and added it to the tomato sauce.* ♦ *Eggplant is good to eat with cheese and tomato sauce.*

eggshell ['ɛg ʃɛl] *n.* the hard, protective, outside layer of a bird's egg. ♦ *The eggshell was cracked, so I did not use the egg.* ♦ *I cracked open the eggshell, and the white and the yolk fell into the frying pan.*

ego ['i go] **1.** *n.* one's sense of self-esteem. (Pl in *-s*.) ♦ *You should be careful not to wound your child's ego.* ♦ *Bill's ego is very fragile today. Be nice to him.* **2.** *n.* conceit; an overly large sense of self-esteem. (Pl in *-s*.) ♦ *Bill's ego is enormous. Someone should bring him back to reality.* ♦ *The actor's huge ego is ruining the play.*

egocentric [i go 'sɛn trɪk] *adj.* thinking only of oneself; selfish; self-centered. (Adv: *egocentrically* [...ɪk li].) ♦ *Must you always be so selfish and egocentric?* ♦ *Your egocentric attitude will not win friends.*

egotism ['i gə tɪz əm] *n.* conceit; thinking one is better than everyone else. (No plural form in this sense.) ♦ *Because of his egotism, Bob had few friends.* ♦ *Your latest article is just another example of your egotism.*

egotist ['i gə təst] *n.* a conceited person. ♦ *Tom lost many promotions at work due to his behavior as a selfish egotist.* ♦ *I was appalled to learn that I was regarded as an egotist by my colleagues.*

egret ['i grɪt] *n.* a type of heron, a bird with a long neck, legs, and bill. ♦ *The egret was once hunted for its feathers.* ♦ *The feathers of the egret are usually white.*

Egypt ['i dʒəpt] See Gazetteer.

eight ['et] 8. See four for senses and examples.

eighteen ['et tin] 18. See four for senses and examples.

eighteenth [eit 'tinθ] 18th. See fourth for senses and examples.

eighth ['etθ] 8th. See fourth for senses and examples.

eightieth ['ɛt i əθ] 80th. See fourth for senses and examples.

eighty ['et i] 80. See forty for senses and examples.

either ['i ðɚ] **1.** *adj.* marking a choice of one or the other. (With *or*.) ♦ *You can have either milk or iced tea with your meal.* ♦ *I needed to talk to either Bob or Anne about the problem.* **2.** *adj.* both; one and the other. ♦ *There is a light switch at either end of the hall.* ♦ *The new tires should be placed on either side of the car.* **3.** *pron.* one thing or the other thing; one thing from a choice of two things. ♦ *Either will work fine, but if given a choice, I prefer the red one.* ♦ *Here are two apples. Do you want either?* **4.** *conj.* one or the other from a choice of two things. ♦ *Either eat your peas, or go to your room.* ♦ *Either finish the project by 5:00, or you will be fired.* **5.** *adv.* as well; in addition; also. (Only in negative constructions.) ♦ *I don't like the zoo, and I don't like the museum, either.* ♦ *I won't eat carrots, and I won't eat peas, either.*

ejaculate [ɪ 'dʒæk jə let] **1.** *tv.* to squirt out, typically, to release or propel semen. ♦ *When the bull ejaculates semen, the conception of a calf may follow.* ♦ *The next step in fertilization is for the male to ejaculate sperm.* **2.** *iv.* to release [semen]. ♦ *The doctor's patient was unable to ejaculate.* ♦ *When the bull ejaculates, the conception of a calf may follow.*

ejaculation [ɪ dʒæk ju 'le ʃən] **1.** *n.* a discharge of semen. ♦ *Without an ejaculation, the semen would not reach the egg.* ♦ *The ejaculation produced enough sperm to fertilize the egg.* **2.** *n.* an outburst; an exclamation; something said loudly and abruptly. ♦ *Everyone in the room heard my loud ejaculation.* ♦ *The loud ejaculation of "yes" from the crowd startled the speaker.*

eject [ɪ 'dʒɛkt] **1.** *tv.* to force something out; to expel something with force. ♦ *The baseball manager was ejected from the game for arguing with the umpire.* ♦ *The machine ejected finished parts faster than we could count them.* **2.** *iv.* to leave an airplane—as in an emergency—by being thrust out by an explosive mechanism. ♦ *Because the plane was going to crash, the pilot decided to eject.* ♦ *The pilot safely ejected from the airplane.*

EKG See electrocardiogram.

elaborate 1. [ɪ 'læb (ə) rɪt] *adj.* having many details; complex. (Adv: *elaborately*.) ♦ *Mary wore an elaborate costume to the party.* ♦ *David devised an elaborate excuse for being late.* **2.** [ɪ 'læb ə ret] *iv.* to explain [something], using many details. ♦ *Bill elaborated his ideas carefully.* ♦ *Don't elaborate! I don't want to hear every little detail.*

elapse [ɪ 'læps] *iv.* [for time] to pass. ♦ *Time elapsed slowly while I waited for the bus.* ♦ *One year has elapsed since John began college.*

elastic [ə 'læs tɪk] **1.** *adj.* [of something that is] able to return to its original shape after being stretched. (Adv: *elastically* [...ɪk li].) ♦ *The skirt has an elastic band around its waist.* ♦ *Rubber bands are very elastic.* **2.** *n.* [in clothing] a band of fabric and rubber that can stretch. (No plural form in this sense.) ♦ *I replaced the skirt's original waistband with elastic.* ♦ *The elastic tore from my underwear in the washing machine.*

elated [ɪ 'let ɪd] *adj.* very happy; joyous; excited. (Adv: *elatedly*.) ♦ *The elated young couple moved into their new home.* ♦ *Tom was elated when I told him the good news.*

elation [ɪ 'le ʃən] *n.* a state of excited joyfulness. (No plural form in this sense.) ♦ *Anne's good news filled me with elation.* ♦ *John's elation is apparent from the huge smile on his face.*

elbow ['ɛl bo] **1.** *n.* the joint where the arm bends at the middle. ♦ *I could not bend my elbow when my arm was in a cast.* ♦ *I screamed when I struck my elbow against the doorway.* **2.** *n.* a pipe that is bent, curved, or shaped like the angle of an elbow. ♦ *The plumber replaced the cracked elbow under the sink.* ♦ *The iron elbow allowed the pipes to make a 90-degree turn.* **3.** *tv.* to push a pathway through a crowd using one's elbows. ♦ *I elbowed my way to the front of the crowded lobby.* ♦ *John elbowed a path through the concert crowd.*

elder ['ɛld ɚ] **1.** *n.* someone who is considered to be among the older members of a group or society. ♦ *You should respect your elders.* ♦ *I'd like to speak to Tom Smith, the elder, not Tom Smith, junior.* **2.** *n.* the leader of certain churches, ethnic groups, or communities. ♦ *I asked the town elder for advice.* ♦ *The church elders voted to build an addition to the church.* **3.** *adj.* older. (Used especially with kinship terms.) ♦ *My elder sister is getting married next month.* ♦ *I dated John's elder brother in high school.*

elderly ['ɛld ɚ li] **1.** *adj.* [of people or pets] old. ♦ *My elderly aunt spends an hour tending her garden each day.* ♦ *Jane lives with her elderly cousin in a large mansion.* **2. the elderly** *n.* old people. (No plural form in this sense. Treated as plural.) ♦ *Many of the elderly do not have access to proper dental care.* ♦ *The elderly in that neighborhood have formed groups to combat crime.*

eldest ['ɛld əst] **1. the eldest** *n.* someone who is the oldest of a group of people. (No plural form in this sense. Treated as singular.) ♦ *As the eldest, Anne had to babysit her siblings.* ♦ *My mother is the eldest of her brothers and sisters.* **2.** *adj.* oldest. (A superlative of old.) ♦ *Their eldest sister lives in the country.* ♦ *My eldest brother died many years ago.*

elect [ɪ 'lɛkt] **1.** *tv.* [for a group of voters] to pick someone to fill an elective office; to choose someone by voting. ♦ *The students elected David as junior class president.* ♦ *Our district elected Susan Smith to represent us in the state senate.* **2. elect to** *iv.* + *inf.* to choose to do something. ♦ *I elected to take the bus home after work.* ♦ *Bill elected to take a salary cut rather than lose his job.* **3.** *adj.* chosen, as in ①, but not yet serving in office. (This follows the noun.) ♦ *John is mayor-elect of the city.* ♦ *I am president-elect of the library association.*

election [ɪ 'lɛk ʃən] *n.* the process of voting to choose between two or more options. ♦ *I voted for Mayor Smith in the local election.* ♦ *How many people voted in the last election?*

electioneering [ə lɛk ʃə 'nɪr ɪŋ] *n.* the work done during a political campaign to get someone elected. (No plural form in this sense.) ♦ *The volunteers' electioneering helped Mary win the election.* ♦ *Bill continued electioneering until the day of the election.*

elective [ə 'lɛk tɪv] **1.** *adj.* [of an office or position] filled by the election process. (Adv: *electively.*) ♦ *Judge Smith holds an elective position.* ♦ *State representatives are elective officials.* **2.** *n.* an optional course in one's schooling; a course that can be taken but is not required. ♦ *Tom took a photography class as an elective.* ♦ *The guidance counselor asked Mary which electives she wanted to take.*

electoral college [ɪ 'lɛk tə təl 'kɑl ɪdʒ] *n.* a group of people elected to elect the U.S. president. ♦ *A state's members in the electoral college generally vote for the candidate who received the most votes in that state.* ♦ *The electoral college meets once every four years to elect the president.*

electorate [ɪ 'lɛk tɚ ɪt] *n.* the people who have the right to vote in a particular election. ♦ *The politicians spoke to the electorate, urging them to vote.* ♦ *The electorate voted the corrupt politician out of office.*

electric [ɪ 'lɛk trɪk] **1.** *adj.* carrying electricity; of or about electricity. (Adv: *electrically* [...ɪk li].) ♦ *The electric wiring needs to be replaced in the old house.* ♦ *Electric cables ran underneath the office building.* **2.** *adj.* producing electricity. ♦ *The hospital can use the electric generator in an emergency.* ♦ *The electric utility company increased its rates.* **3.** *adj.* powered by electricity. (Adv: *electrically* [...ɪk li].) ♦ *I bought a new electric motor for the washing machine.* ♦ *Our apartment has electric heat.* **4.** *adj.* exciting; full of excitement; thrilling. (Adv: *electrically* [...ɪk li].) ♦ *The actor's debut on stage was absolutely electric!* ♦ *Mary's vibrantly electric speech stunned the audience.* **5. electric plug** See plug.

electrical [ɪ 'lɛk trɪ kəl] *adj.* electric; producing or carrying electricity; of or about electricity. (Adv: *electrically* [...ɪk li].) ♦ *The electrical system in the old building needs to be rewired.* ♦ *The severe thunderstorm knocked out the electrical power in our neighborhood.*

electrician [ɪ lɛk 'trɪ ʃən] *n.* someone who installs and repairs electrical wiring, equipment, or products. ♦ *If you can't fix the electric garage door opener, call an electrician.* ♦ *The electrician installed all the wiring in the new house.*

electricity [ɪ lɛk 'trɪs ə ti] **1.** *n.* a source of power obtainable from batteries, generators, and natural phenomena like friction and lightning. (No plural form in this sense.) ♦ *The dam produced electricity for the whole valley.* ♦ *I got a shock from the static electricity in the carpet.* **2.** *n.* contagious excitement, especially in a group of people. (Figurative on ①. See also electric ④. No plural form in this sense.) ♦ *You could feel the electricity in the audience as the curtain slowly rose on the stage.* ♦ *The players felt the electricity of the roaring crowd at the football game.*

electrification [ɪ lɛk trɪ fə 'ke ʃən] *n.* the installation of a wiring system to distribute electricity where there was none before. (No plural form in this sense.) ♦ *John is responsible for the complete electrification of the new school building.* ♦ *The electricians discussed the building's electrification.*

electrify [ɪ 'lɛk trə fɑɪ] **1.** *tv.* to install electricity in an area; to change a system so that it runs on electricity instead of some other form of energy. ♦ *The technician electrified the old building's heating system.* ♦ *The entire town was electrified by 1906.* **2.** *tv.* to shock someone; to excite someone; to thrill someone. (Figurative on ①.) ♦ *The skilled musician knew how to electrify the audience.* ♦ *The action movie electrified the audience.*

electrocardiogram [ɪ lɛk tro 'kɑr di ə græm] *n.* a graph that shows the changes in the electric current generated by the heart muscle. (Abbreviated EKG or ECG.) ♦ *Tom had an electrocardiogram during his stay at the hospital.* ♦ *The physician examined the patient's electrocardiogram.*

electrocute [ɪ 'lɛk trə kjut] *tv.* to kill someone or something with electricity. ♦ *The convicted killer was electrocuted at the state prison.* ♦ *Don't leave your radio plugged in near the bathtub. If it falls in, it will electrocute you.*

electrolysis [ɪ lɛk 'trɑl ə sɪs] *n.* the destruction of hair roots or other tissue through the use of an electric current. (No plural form in this sense.) ♦ *Anne had unwanted hair on her arms removed by electrolysis.* ♦ *The model underwent electrolysis before the photo shoot.*

electromagnet [ɪ lɛk tro 'mæg nət] *n.* a wire-wrapped core of iron, or other material, that will attract iron when electricity flows through the wire. ♦ *We lifted the beams with a powerful electromagnet.* ♦ *The electromagnet transported the steel rods to the truck.*

electromagnetic [ɛ lɛk tro mæg 'nɛt ɪk] *adj.* concerning electric and magnetic waves, especially as used in broadcasting. (Adv: *electromagnetically* [...ɪk li].) ♦ *The antenna on top of the tallest building in town radiates elec-*

tromagnetic waves. ♦ *Electromagnetic waves carry information to radios, television sets, and cellular telephones.*

electron [ɪ 'lɛk trɑn] *n.* a negatively charged atomic particle. ♦ *Electrons orbit around an atom's nucleus.* ♦ *Atoms are made up of electrons, neutrons, and protons.*

electronic [ɪ lɛk 'trɑn ɪk] **1.** *adj.* of or about ③. (Adv: *electronically* [...ɪk li].) ♦ *I took a course in electronic technology.* ♦ *The electronic technician repaired the television set.* **2.** *adj.* involving electrical circuits that use semiconductors. (Adv: *electronically* [...ɪk li].) ♦ *I repaired the electronic circuit board in the computer.* ♦ *The radio station experienced electronic problems.* **3. electronics** *n.* the study and design of the electrical circuits used in computers, transistors, etc. (Treated as singular.) ♦ *Susan took a basic course in electronics at the university.* ♦ *The field of modern electronics has grown rapidly.*

elegance ['ɛl ə gəns] *n.* impressive style, grace, and beauty. (No plural form in this sense.) ♦ *The model's elegance enhanced the designer's clothing.* ♦ *Bill is known for his charm and quiet elegance.*

elegant ['ɛl ə gənt] *adj.* graceful; beautiful; having good taste. (Adv: *elegantly.*) ♦ *Anne wore an elegant gown to the party.* ♦ *Bob has elegant taste in clothing.*

elegiac [ɛl ə 'dʒi ɪk] *adj.* in the manner of an elegy. ♦ *I wrote an elegiac poem in memory of my grandmother.* ♦ *Her song was a moving, almost elegiac, tribute to death.*

elegy ['ɛl ɪ dʒi] *n.* a poem or song of mourning, usually written honoring someone who has died. ♦ *The president read an elegy for the soldiers killed in combat.* ♦ *The poet wrote a beautiful elegy for her deceased grandfather.*

element ['ɛl ə mənt] **1.** *n.* one of several kinds of basic matter that cannot be broken down further into other kinds of basic matter. ♦ *The periodic table of elements lists each element by atomic number.* ♦ *Water is made of the elements oxygen and hydrogen.* **2.** *n.* a piece of a larger theme. ♦ *Many vital elements are missing in your version of the story.* ♦ *The film lacked some of the elements needed for a good thriller.* **3. the elements** *n.* the weather; air, wind, rain, and sunlight. (Treated as plural.) ♦ *The elements caused the doorknob to tarnish.* ♦ *Please don't leave your toys out in the elements.* **4. out of one's element** *idiom* not in a natural or comfortable situation. ♦ *When it comes to computers, I'm out of my element.* ♦ *Sally's out of her element in math.*

elemental [ɛl ə 'mɛn təl] **1.** *adj.* of or about the elements. (Adv: *elementally.*) ♦ *The elemental force of the hurricane completely destroyed the island.* ♦ *We were frightened by the elemental fury of the storm.* **2.** *adj.* necessary; being a basic part of the whole. (Adv: *elementally.*) ♦ *The eggs are an elemental ingredient in the recipe.* ♦ *Dim lighting is elemental to the play's success.*

elementary [ɛl ə 'mɛn tri] *adj.* basic; introductory. ♦ *I went to elementary school from first to fifth grade.* ♦ *I took a course in elementary chemistry.*

elephant ['ɛl ə fənt] **1.** *n.* a large land mammal of Africa and Asia, with tough gray skin, large ears, and a long trunk. ♦ *The elephant squirted water into its mouth with its trunk.* ♦ *The baby elephant performed tricks at the circus.* **2. white elephant** *idiom* something that is useless and is either a nuisance or expensive to keep up. ♦ *Bob's father-in-law has given him an old Rolls Royce, but it's a real white elephant. He has no place to park it and can't afford the gas for it.* ♦ *Those antique vases Aunt Mary gave me are white elephants. They're ugly and take ages to clean.*

elevate ['ɛl ə vet] **1.** *tv.* to raise or lift someone or something from a lower level to a higher level. ♦ *The marchers elevated the flag as they passed the president.* ♦ *I elevated my arms over my head.* **2.** *tv.* to raise something, such as someone's spirits or hope. ♦ *When it stopped raining, it elevated my hopes that we could go on a picnic.* ♦ *I elevated my aunt's spirits by visiting her in the hospital.*

elevated ['ɛl ə vet ɪd] *adj.* at a higher level than typical, normal, or expected. ♦ *The sick child had an elevated temperature.* ♦ *I rode an elevated train across town.*

elevation [ɛl ə 've ʃən] **1.** *n.* the distance something is above sea level. ♦ *That mountain has an elevation of more than 10,000 feet.* ♦ *There is snow on the mountain at that elevation.* **2.** *n.* a drawing of the front, side, or back view of a building, especially in architectural plans. ♦ *The architect explained the drawing of the front elevation.* ♦ *The rear elevation did not show the porch we had asked for.*

elevator ['ɛl ə vet ɚ] *n.* a moving cage or chamber that carries people and things from floor to floor in a building with more than one story. ♦ *Does this elevator go to the 32nd floor?* ♦ *I love to ride the elevators in skyscrapers.*

eleven [ɪ 'lɛv ən] 11. See **four** for senses and examples.

eleventh [ɪ 'lɛv ənθ] 11th. See **fourth** for senses and examples.

elf ['ɛlf] *n., irreg.* a small mischievous human-like creature of fairy tales and myths. (Pl: **elves.**) ♦ *Susie read a story about Santa Claus and his elves.* ♦ *Jimmy looks like a little elf in his green costume.*

elicit [ɛ 'lɪs ɪt] *tv.* to draw out information from someone; to bring out a response from someone. ♦ *Try to elicit an explanation of what's bothering John.* ♦ *The lawyer elicited a response from the defendant.*

eligibility [ɛl ə dʒə 'bɪl ə ti] **1.** *n.* being allowed or able to participate in a contest or event. (No plural form in this sense.) ♦ *Dave must meet academic eligibility before he can play on the football team.* ♦ *Did you follow the rules of eligibility when entering the contest?* **2.** *n.* meeting the proper requirements to be considered for a job, school, club, etc. (No plural form in this sense.) ♦ *Your eligibility for the position is in doubt.* ♦ *Anne's eligibility for club membership has been approved.*

eligible ['ɛl ɪ dʒə bəl] *adj.* having met the proper requirements. (Adv: *eligibly.*) ♦ *Are you eligible for the scholarship?* ♦ *Because of John's medical problem, he is not eligible to join the navy.*

eliminate [ɪ 'lɪm ə net] *tv.* to get rid of someone or something completely. ♦ *The mayor tried to eliminate gang activity in the city.* ♦ *Will the stain remover eliminate the grease spot on my shirt?*

elimination [ɪ lɪm ə 'ne ʃən] **1.** *n.* removal; eliminating. (No plural form in this sense.) ♦ *The soccer team qualified for elimination when it forfeited the game.* ♦ *The elimination of drug-related crime is one of the mayor's goals.* **2.** *n.* defecation and urination. (No plural form in this sense.) ♦ *Babies have no control over their elimination.* ♦ *At the hospital, a nurse helped the injured patient with elimination.*

elite [i 'lit] **1. the elite** *n.* the upper class; a group of people who have or expect special privileges. (No plural form in this sense. Treated as singular or plural.) ♦ *The movie star felt like one of the elite.* ♦ *This exclusive department store sells only to the elite.* **2.** *n.* a size of print where there are 12 letters per inch. (No plural form in this sense.) ♦ *Is this letter typed in pica or elite?* ♦ *The copy was difficult to read in elite.* **3.** *adj.* for the upper class; exclusive. (Adv: *elitely.*) ♦ *Anne joined an elite organization for successful lawyers.* ♦ *An elite group of students was chosen to receive scholarships.*

elk ['ɛlk] **1.** *n., irreg.* [in North America] a large deer, the males of which have large, spreading antlers. (Pl: *elk* or *elks.*) ♦ *Tom hunts elk each fall.* ♦ *The campers saw two elks at the top of the ridge.* **2.** *n., irreg.* [in Europe] the moose. ♦ *There are many elk in Sweden and Russia.* ♦ *Elk roam the European forests.*

ellipse [ɪ 'lɪps] *n.* an oval; a flattened circle. ♦ *The pancake batter formed an ellipse in the frying pan.* ♦ *Earth's orbit is not a perfect circle. It is an ellipse.*

ellipses [ɪ 'lɪp siz] pl of ellipsis.

ellipsis [ɪ 'lɪp sɪs] *n., irreg.* a place in a text where words have been taken out; a series of periods that replaces words that have been left out of a sentence. (Pl: ellipses.) ♦ *The phrase "I have nine...do you have more?" contains an ellipsis.* ♦ *The speaker paused for each ellipsis when she read the text aloud.*

elliptical [ɪ 'lɪp tɪ kəl] **1.** *adj.* oval; shaped like an ellipse. (Adv: *elliptically* [...ɪk li].) ♦ *A small, elliptical gem decorates the simple wedding ring.* ♦ *An elliptical room serves as the president's office.* **2.** *adj.* having words that are left out. (Adv: *elliptically* [...ɪk li].) ♦ *I could not understand Dave's elliptical note.* ♦ *The elliptical message was quite cryptic.*

elm ['ɛlm] **1.** *n.* a large, deciduous shade tree. ♦ *We sat under an elm in the shade.* ♦ *The fallen leaves from the elm covered the ground.* **2.** *n.* wood from ①. (No plural form in this sense.) ♦ *This picnic bench is made of elm.* ♦ *Elm is usually not used to make furniture.* **3.** *adj.* made of ②. ♦ *We sat on a handmade elm picnic bench at lunch.* ♦ *The large table in the dining room has elm veneer on top.*

elocution [ɛl ə 'kju ʃən] *n.* the art of being able to speak clearly in public. (No plural form in this sense.) ♦ *Tom takes great pride in his elocution.* ♦ *Mary's skills in elocution led her to a career in politics.*

elongate [ɪ 'lɔŋ get] **1.** *iv.* to become longer; to lengthen; to extend. ♦ *The short weekend jaunt elongated into a full week.* ♦ *The fire engine's ladder elongated, reaching to the top of the building.* **2.** *tv.* to make something longer; to lengthen something. ♦ *The elephant elongated its trunk so it could reach the peanut I was holding.* ♦ *I elongated the garden to make more room for some new roses I bought.*

elongated [ɪ 'lɔŋ get ɪd] *adj.* made longer; lengthened. (Adv: *elongatedly* [ɪ lɔŋ 'get əd li].) ♦ *The elongated bridal train proved difficult to walk in.* ♦ *An oval is an elongated circle.*

elope [ɪ 'lop] *iv.* [for two lovers] to run away in secret in order to get married. ♦ *Bill and Anne eloped last night, and they went to Florida for their honeymoon.* ♦ *The couple did not want a large wedding, so they decided to elope.*

eloquence ['ɛl ə kwəns] *n.* beauty, expressiveness, and persuasive power in speech. (No plural form in this sense.) ♦ *Because of her eloquence, Anne made an excellent lobbyist.* ♦ *The lecturer's eloquence was appreciated by his audience.*

eloquent ['ɛl ə kwənt] **1.** *adj.* capable of beautiful and expressive public speaking. (Adv: *eloquently.*) ♦ *The eloquent lecturer was interesting to listen to.* ♦ *I could listen to Mary speak all day because she's so eloquent.* **2.** *adj.* [of speech that is] beautiful and expressive. (Adv: *eloquently.*) ♦ *Susan gave an eloquent speech to her graduating class.* ♦ *The eulogy at Bill's funeral was touching and eloquent.*

El Salvador [ɛl 'sæl və dor] See Gazetteer.

else ['ɛls] **1.** *adj.* otherwise; apart from someone or something; instead. ♦ *Tom and Sue went to Los Angeles, but everyone else decided to go to San Diego.* ♦ *Bill wasn't invited to the party, but everybody else at the office was.* **2.** *adj.* in addition to someone or something; as well. ♦ *"Who else did you invite to the party?" Sally asked Anne as more and more guests arrived.* ♦ *What else do you want for your birthday?* **3. or else** *idiom* or suffer the consequences. ♦ *Do what I tell you, or else.* ♦ *Don't be late for work, or else!*

elsewhere ['ɛls ʍɛr] *adv.* in some other place. ♦ *After searching in the park for an hour for his lost kitten, Dave decided to look elsewhere.* ♦ *My house keys were not where I left them last night. I knew I would have to search elsewhere to find them.*

elucidate [ɪ 'lus ə det] **1.** *iv.* to communicate in such a way as to make something clearer. ♦ *That is an interesting idea. Would you care to elucidate?* ♦ *Could you elucidate further on this topic?* **2.** *tv.* to make something clearer through careful explanation. ♦ *John carefully elucidated his theory.* ♦ *Lisa simply cannot elucidate her ideas well enough to carry on a reasonable conversation!*

elucidation [ɪ lus ə 'de ʃən] *n.* explanation and clarification. (No plural form in this sense.) ♦ *The teacher's elucidation of the complex poem enlightened the class.* ♦ *The lawyer asked John for an elucidation of his comments.*

elude [ɪ 'lud] **1.** *tv.* to evade or avoid capture, often by cunning. ♦ *The robber's immediate goal was to elude capture.* ♦ *The gangster eluded the police.* **2.** *tv.* [for an understanding of something] to be hard to remember or grasp. ♦ *The correct answer eludes me.* ♦ *Do you know who that man is? His name eludes me right now.*

elusive [ɪ 'lus ɪv] *adj.* [of someone or something that is] hard to find or hard to catch. (Adv: *elusively.*) ♦ *We got a glimpse of the elusive movie star as he entered his limousine.* ♦ *The elusive butterfly escaped the scientist's net.*

elves ['ɛlvz] pl of elf.

em- See in ⑬.

emaciated [ɪ 'me ʃi et ɪd] *adj.* gaunt; very thin because of starvation. (Adv: *emaciatedly.*) ♦ *The emaciated man was sent to a hospital, where he was fed a good selection of nourishing foods.* ♦ *A bus transported the emaciated refugees to the camp.*

e-mail AND **email** ['i mel] **1.** *n.* electronic mail of the kind that is sent from computer to computer. (No plural form in this sense.) ♦ *I don't have e-mail, so you will have to fax me.* ♦ *I get over one hundred messages a day via e-mail.* **2.** *n.* a message sent by ①. ♦ *Mary sent me an e-mail about our dinner plans for the evening.* ♦ *When my computer crashed, it deleted the e-mail you sent me.* **3.** *adj.*

<the adj. use of ①.> ♦ *My e-mail account has expired and I cannot get any messages.* ♦ *The e-mail software I use is not very up-to-date.* **4.** *tv.* to send a message to someone by ①. ♦ *I'll e-mail you my answer tomorrow.* ♦ *Tom e-mailed his order to the manufacturer.*

emanate ['ɛm ə net] **1. emanate from** *iv.* + *prep. phr.* to come from something; to come out from something; to be emitted from something. ♦ *Your emotions emanate from within.* ♦ *Dense fumes emanated from the exhaust pipe.* **2.** *tv.* to emit something; to send something out. ♦ *David emanated kindness to everyone he met.* ♦ *The exhaust pipe emanated dense fumes.*

emanation [ɛm ə 'ne ʃən] *n.* something that is given off by something; something that is emitted by something. ♦ *The factory's toxic emanations were outlawed by the government.* ♦ *Emanations of evil billowed from the haunted house.*

emancipate [ɪ 'mæn sə pet] *tv.* to free someone from slavery; to set someone free. ♦ *Abraham Lincoln emancipated the slaves.* ♦ *The prisoners of war were emancipated after the peace treaty was signed.*

emancipated [ɪ 'mæn sə pet ɪd] *adj.* freed; made free. ♦ *The emancipated prisoners were reunited with their families.* ♦ *After her difficult marriage, the divorce made Mary feel like an emancipated woman.*

emancipation [ɪ mæn sə 'pe ʃən] *n.* setting someone free from authority or control; gaining one's freedom. (No plural form in this sense.) ♦ *The young movie star took his parents to court to obtain legal emancipation at age 16.* ♦ *Mary took delight in her emancipation from years of hardship.*

emasculate [ɪ 'mæs kjə let] **1.** *tv.* to castrate someone or some creature; to remove a male's testicles. ♦ *The veterinarian emasculated the racehorse.* ♦ *David was emasculated by the physician to prevent the spread of the cancer.* **2.** *tv.* to reduce the power and vitality of something. (Figurative on ①.) ♦ *The editor simply emasculated my novel by cutting out the best part!* ♦ *The president's rather strong speech was emasculated at the last minute by an overly cautious speech writer.*

emasculation [ɪ mæs kju 'le ʃən] **1.** *n.* castration. (No plural form in this sense.) ♦ *The dog suffered emasculation in the horrible fight.* ♦ *The emasculation of the male cats controlled the feline population dramatically.* **2.** *n.* reduction of the power and vitality of something. (No plural form in this sense. Figurative on ①.) ♦ *The author objected to the editor's emasculation of the force and vitality of the paragraph.* ♦ *Most of the president's strong speech will undergo some degree of emasculation to keep from offending anyone.*

embalm [ɛm 'bɑm] *tv.* to apply chemicals to a corpse to preserve it. ♦ *The body was embalmed a few days before the funeral.* ♦ *Ancient Egyptians used oils and natural substances to embalm their dead.*

embankment [ɛm 'bæŋk mənt] *n.* a ridge or bank built alongside a river to prevent flooding or to elevate a road that passes over low ground. ♦ *There's an embankment between the parking lot and the river.* ♦ *A concrete embankment protects the small village from flooding.*

embargo [ɛm 'bɑr go] *n.* a restriction on trade with a particular country. (Pl in *-es.*) ♦ *The trade minister placed an embargo on goods from the hostile country.* ♦ *The oil embargo was violated repeatedly by neighboring allies.*

embark [ɛm 'bɑrk] **1. embark on** *iv.* + *prep. phr.* to begin a trip; to begin a journey. ♦ *Mary embarked on a safari shortly after arriving in Africa.* ♦ *Jimmy got on the bus and embarked on a short trip to the bank.* **2.** *iv.* to board [a ship or airplane]. ♦ *Jane embarked before the other passengers on the ship.* ♦ *David embarked without his luggage.*

embarrass [ɛm 'bɛr əs] *tv.* to make someone feel ashamed, uncomfortable, or self-conscious. ♦ *Please don't embarrass me in public again!* ♦ *Anne's older brother tried to embarrass her in front of her friends.*

embarrassed [ɛm 'bɛr əst] *adj.* uncomfortably self-conscious. (Adv: *embarrassedly.*) ♦ *I was embarrassed when I saw the food stains on my shirt.* ♦ *The embarrassed student's face turned bright red.*

embarrassing [ɛm 'bɛr əs ɪŋ] *adj.* causing embarrassment. (Adv: *embarrassingly.*) ♦ *I tried to ignore the embarrassing situation.* ♦ *Bill was caught in an embarrassing lie.*

embarrassment [ɛm 'bɛr əs mənt] **1.** *n.* an uncomfortable, self-conscious feeling; public shame. (No plural form in this sense.) ♦ *John's criminal record caused embarrassment to his family.* ♦ *When my pants split, I experienced true embarrassment.* **2.** *n.* someone or something that causes someone to feel uncomfortable, self-conscious, or ashamed. ♦ *My rude date was quite an embarrassment at the restaurant.* ♦ *I can usually endure the small embarrassments of life, but not the serious ones.*

embassy ['ɛm bə si] *n.* the building where an ambassador from a foreign country lives or works. ♦ *I renewed my passport at the American embassy in London.* ♦ *I visited the new ambassador in the Polish embassy in New York.*

embellish [ɛm 'bɛl ɪʃ] **1. embellish with** *tv.* + *prep. phr.* to decorate something with some extra ornamentation. ♦ *Anne embellished the shirt collar with lace.* ♦ *The jeweler embellished the ring with a few extra stones on each side of the diamond.* **2.** *tv.* to make a story more exciting by adding small details that are not true. ♦ *Jimmy embellished the tale of his fishing trip to make it sound more exciting.* ♦ *Dave embellished his version of the child's rescue to the reporter.*

ember ['ɛm bɚ] *n.* a piece of wood or coal that is red-hot and glowing but no longer burning. ♦ *The glow of the ember slowly faded.* ♦ *Don't touch that ember! It's still hot.*

embezzle [ɛm 'bɛz əl] *tv.* to steal money or other assets from one's employer. ♦ *The clerk embezzled money from the bank.* ♦ *Two employees planned to embezzle a million dollars over a period of years.*

embezzlement [ɛm 'bɛz əl mənt] *n.* embezzling something. (No plural form in this sense.) ♦ *John's embezzlement of company funds was a shock to everyone in the office.* ♦ *The crime of embezzlement will be punished severely.*

embitter [ɛm 'bɪt ɚ] *tv.* to make someone feel bitter. ♦ *David had been embittered toward his wealthy neighbors who ignored him.* ♦ *The bad experience embittered Tom and led him to quit his job.*

emblem ['ɛm bləm] *n.* a symbol that signifies something; something that is a symbol for something. ♦ *Bill wears a* *large school emblem on his shirt.* ♦ *The emblem on Mary's coat signified her political beliefs.*

embolism ['ɛm bə lɪz əm] *n.* a foreign substance that blocks a vein or artery; the blockage of a vein or artery. ♦ *The physician tried to dissolve the embolism with drugs.* ♦ *If the embolism is not removed, the patient might die.*

emboss [ɛm 'bɔs] *tv.* to decorate something, such as paper or a thin sheet of metal, with a raised design. ♦ *The printer embossed my company's name on my business cards.* ♦ *The book's title is embossed on the cover in gold lettering.*

embossed [ɛm 'bɔst] *adj.* [of paper or a thin sheet of metal] decorated with a raised design. ♦ *An embossed business card listed the company's name, address, and phone number.* ♦ *Mary wrote the memo on the corporation's embossed letterhead.*

embrace [ɛm 'bres] **1.** *tv.* to hug someone closely; to take someone into one's arms. ♦ *I embraced my mother when I picked her up at the airport.* ♦ *The students tearfully embraced each other on their last day of school.* **2.** *tv.* to accept something, such as a belief, tenet, or policy. ♦ *Anne embraces vegetarianism because it is healthy.* ♦ *I cannot embrace the tenets of your religion.* **3.** *iv.* for two people to hug one another. ♦ *The lovers embraced passionately as they parted.* ♦ *We tearfully embraced, and I boarded my plane.*

embroider [ɛm 'broɪ dɚ] **1.** *tv.* to make a design on a piece of fabric by stitching colored thread onto it in a specific pattern. ♦ *I embroidered flowers on the baby's blanket.* ♦ *I decided to embroider a design on the edge of the pillowcase.* **2.** *tv.* to decorate a piece of fabric by stitching colored thread onto it in a specific pattern. ♦ *I embroidered the baby's blanket with a floral design.* ♦ *Susan embroidered the edges of all her pillowcases.* **3.** *tv.* to add detail to something; to make a story sound better. (Figurative on ②.) ♦ *The witness embroidered her testimony with a few opinions.* ♦ *John has a tendency to embroider a story to make it more interesting.*

embroidery [ɛm 'broɪd (ə) ri] **1.** *n.* the craft of decorating a piece of fabric by stitching colored thread onto it in a specific pattern. (No plural form in this sense.) ♦ *I teach a class in embroidery at the community arts center.* ♦ *Grandma takes great pride in her embroidery.* **2.** *n.* designs stitched onto fabric. (No plural form in this sense.) ♦ *The intricate embroidery on the tablecloth is beautiful.* ♦ *The church vestments were decorated with fine embroidery.*

embroil [ɛm 'broɪl] **embroil (in)** *tv.* (+ *prep. phr.*) to cause someone to become involved in a dispute; to involve someone in an argument. ♦ *The opposing political parties were embroiled in a fierce conflict over taxation.* ♦ *This is not my argument. Please don't embroil me.*

embryo ['ɛm bri o] **1.** *n.* the earliest stage of an unborn creature's development. (Pl in *-s.*) ♦ *The embryo is attached to the uterine wall.* ♦ *The embryo develops into a fetus.* **2.** *n.* the beginning of something; the first stage or first step of something. (Figurative on ①. Pl in *-s.*) ♦ *The idea for my invention is still just an embryo.* ♦ *The embryo of the novel's plot occurred in a dream.*

embryology [ɛm bri 'ɑl ə dʒi] *n.* the biological study of the growth and development of embryos. (No plural form in this sense.) ♦ *The university offered a course in embryology.* ♦ *To learn about embryology, the students observed the development of a chick.*

embryonic [ɛm bri 'ɑn ɪk] **1.** *adj.* of or about an embryo. (Adv: *embryonically* [...ɪk li].) ♦ *The embryonic development of living creatures can be harmed by chemicals.* ♦ *We studied the chick at its embryonic stage of development.* **2.** *adj.* not fully developed. (Figurative on ①. Adv: *embryonically* [...ɪk li].) ♦ *The plan was still in an embryonic state.* ♦ *The architect steered the designs through the embryonic stage.*

emcee ['ɛm 'si] *n.* a master of ceremonies; someone who introduces people or hosts an event. (From the initial *m* and *c* in the phrase *master of ceremonies.*) ♦ *The emcee for the fashion show announced the name of each designer.* ♦ *The talent show's emcee told the audience who the winner was.*

emerald ['ɛm ə rəld] **1.** *n.* a bright green gemstone. ♦ *The sparkling stone in this ring is an emerald.* ♦ *I gave my mother an emerald for her 50th birthday.* **2.** *n.* a bright green color. ♦ *The shamrock is emerald in color.* ♦ *Anne's red hair is accentuated when she wears emerald.* **3.** *adj.* bright green. ♦ *I wore emerald clothing on St. Patrick's Day.* ♦ *Bill wears garish emerald pants when he plays golf.*

emerge [ɪ 'mɚdʒ] **1.** *iv.* to come out from someplace; to come into view from someplace. ♦ *The inspector emerged from the shadows and cornered the suspect.* ♦ *The divers emerged from the water.* **2.** *iv.* to become apparent. ♦ *The facts of the case slowly emerged during the investigation.* ♦ *The candidate's old-fashioned views emerged during the campaign.*

emergence [ɪ 'mɚdʒ əns] *n.* the coming into view; the gradual appearance of someone or something. (No plural form in this sense.) ♦ *The royal trumpets sounded upon the queen's emergence from the castle.* ♦ *The plane's emergence from the storm clouds calmed the shaky passengers.*

emergency [ɪ 'mɚdʒ ənsi] **1.** *n.* a time when urgent action is needed; a dangerous situation that must be taken care of at once. ♦ *The devastating earthquake created an emergency.* ♦ *In case of emergency, the phone number for the police is 9–1–1.* **2. emergency room** *n.* the place in a hospital where emergency ③ cases are treated. ♦ *We took Bill to the emergency room because he had pains in his chest.* ♦ *Doctors in the emergency room tried to save Lisa's life.* **3.** *adj.* <the adj. use of ①.> ♦ *The emergency vehicles arrived soon at the scene of the accident.* ♦ *We keep an emergency food supply in the basement.*

emeritus [ə 'mɛr ɪ təs] *adj.* retired retaining title or rank. (Sometimes comes after the noun.) ♦ *An emeritus professor of biology was a guest lecturer in my class today.* ♦ *The chairman emeritus of the board of directors still attends some of the meetings.*

emigrant ['ɛm ə grənt] **1.** *n.* someone who emigrates to another country. (Compare with immigrant.) ♦ *The emigrants boarded the ship and sailed toward America.* ♦ *Many emigrants from the Middle East have settled in this neighborhood.* **2.** *adj.* <the adj. use of ①.> ♦ *The emigrant student sought asylum in the United States.* ♦ *The emigrant family hoped to find a new home abroad.*

emigrate ['ɛm ə gret] *iv.* to leave one's home country and live in another one. (Compare with immigrate.) ♦ *The family emigrated during the war to escape the dictator's* *rule.* ♦ *Mary emigrated from Germany to France during World War II.*

emigration [ɛm ə 'gre ʃən] *n.* leaving one's country to live in another. (No plural form in this sense. Compare with **immigration**.) ♦ *What are the legal restrictions on emigration?* ♦ *The persecuted family looked forward to emigration.*

eminence ['ɛm ə nəns] *n.* fame; a position or rank above all others; superiority. (No plural form in this sense.) ♦ *The bishop holds a position of eminence in the church.* ♦ *Tom's eminence in medicine was unquestioned by his colleagues.*

eminent ['ɛm ə nənt] *adj.* positioned or ranked above all others; distinguished. (Adv: *eminently.*) ♦ *The eminent poet won numerous awards.* ♦ *The politician's eminent status guarantees media coverage.*

emissary ['ɛm ə sɛr i] *n.* someone who is sent on a mission; someone who is sent to deliver a special message. ♦ *The prime minister sent an emissary to Egypt.* ♦ *Our president greeted the foreign emissary at the airport.*

emission [i 'mɪ ʃən] **1.** *n.* the sending out of something, such as a gas or fluid. ♦ *An emission of gas from the volcano fouled the atmosphere.* ♦ *An emission of smoke showed that there was a fire in the house.* **2.** *n.* something that is discharged. ♦ *The mechanic reduced the amount of emissions that the car produced.* ♦ *The emissions from the power plant were dangerous.*

emit [i 'mit] *tv.* to discharge something; to let something out; to send something out. ♦ *The bus emitted noxious fumes.* ♦ *The alarm emitted a shrill whine.*

emotion [i 'mo ʃən] **1.** *n.* feeling—other than with the physical senses—or a show of feeling. (No plural form in this sense.) ♦ *Emotion can be the enemy of rational thinking.* ♦ *Jane's poems usually have a lot of emotion.* **2.** *n.* a feeling, such as sadness, joy, anxiety, etc. ♦ *Mary sang the song with great emotion.* ♦ *Bill was overcome with emotion as he read the poem.*

emotional [i 'mo ʃə nəl] **1.** *adj.* full of feeling; full of emotion; passionate. (Adv: *emotionally.*) ♦ *The opera singer sang an emotional aria.* ♦ *Anne's emotional eulogy made everyone cry.* **2.** *adj.* easily affected by feelings or emotions. ♦ *The emotional child was upset by the scary bedtime story.* ♦ *Bill's emotional nature often gets him into trouble at work.* **3.** *adj.* irrational; ruled by emotion rather than logic. (Adv: *emotionally.*) ♦ *Calm down. Don't get emotional!* ♦ *You should not become so emotional about trivial things.* **4.** *adj.* of or related to feelings. (Adv: *emotionally.*) ♦ *John made no emotional response to the bad news.* ♦ *What was your emotional reaction to that experience?*

empathize ['ɛmp ə θɑɪz] *iv.* to identify with someone; to share someone's feelings by imagining what those feelings are like. ♦ *My own mother died recently, so I can empathize with your loss.* ♦ *Jane's friends empathized with her when she lost her job.*

empathy ['ɛmp ə θi] *n.* the sharing of someone's feelings by imagining what those feelings are like. (No plural form in this sense.) ♦ *I feel tremendous empathy for the families of the people who died in the crash.* ♦ *The counselor felt a lot of empathy with his troubled students.*

emperor ['ɛmp ɚ rɚ] *n.* someone who rules an empire. (See also **empress**.) ♦ *The emperor issued a decree on taxes.* ♦ *When the emperor died, his eldest son took his place.*

emphases ['ɛm fə siz] pl of **emphasis**.

emphasis ['ɛm fə sɪs] **1.** *n.* importance that is place on or given to something. (No plural form in this sense.) ♦ *Mary places great emphasis on reaching her job-related goals.* ♦ *I want you to give this idea extra emphasis in your letter.* **2.** *n., irreg.* something that has received or should receive ①. (Pl: **emphases**.) ♦ *Two of the emphases of her speech were patience and teamwork.* ♦ *Money is too much of an emphasis in his life.* **3.** *n.* increased loudness or (verbal) stress given to particular syllables, words, or phrases. (No plural form in this sense.) ♦ *I want you to give this word a lot of emphasis when you read it aloud.* ♦ *Place more emphasis on the first syllable.*

emphasize ['ɛm fə sɑɪz] **1.** *tv.* to place special importance on something. ♦ *I tried to emphasize the importance of good grades to Tom.* ♦ *The speaker will emphasize teamwork and patience in her speech.* **2.** *tv.* to stress something, especially a syllable, word, or phrase. ♦ *You need not emphasize the last syllable so much.* ♦ *The preacher emphasized the word* not *whenever he preached.*

emphatic [ɛm 'fæt ɪk] *adj.* stressed; spoken with stress; expressed with force. (Adv: *emphatically* [...ɪk li].) ♦ *I talked to the children about their chores in an emphatic tone.* ♦ *The supervisor's emphatic speech on worker productivity produced amazing results.*

emphysema [ɛm fə 'zi mə] *n.* a lung disease where the air spaces are enlarged and the tissue is disintegrating. (No plural form in this sense.) ♦ *Smokers often develop emphysema.* ♦ *Emphysema makes it difficult to breathe.*

empire ['ɛm pɑɪr] *n.* all the land and territory that is controlled by a country; a group of countries controlled by one ruler. ♦ *The king's empire stretched across the globe.* ♦ *India was once part of the British empire.*

empirical [ɛm 'pɪr ɪ kəl] *adj.* based on observation instead of theory; based on experience in the real world. (Adv: *empirically* [...ɪk li].) ♦ *The scientist considered the empirical evidence before writing a report.* ♦ *Lisa's argument was proven by empirical data.*

employ [ɛm 'ploɪ] **1.** *tv.* to hire someone to do work for pay. ♦ *The contractor must employ more workers to complete the job by May.* ♦ *Do you have the authority to employ these applicants?* **2.** *tv.* to use something for a particular purpose. ♦ *Susan employed all the resources available to her.* ♦ *Please employ your wisdom to the fullest in this matter.*

employable [ɛm 'ploɪ ə bəl] *adj.* suitable for employment. (Adv: *employably.*) ♦ *Jane is certainly employable in any executive position.* ♦ *I'm not sure if you are an employable candidate, but we'll keep your résumé on file.*

employee [ɛm 'ploɪ i] *n.* someone who works for a company or a person for pay. ♦ *The factory employees must arrive by 7:30 A.M.* ♦ *There are over 100 employees at this company.*

employer [ɛm 'ploɪ ɚ] *n.* a person or company that employs people. ♦ *Bill's employer is fair and honest.* ♦ *I asked my employer for a raise.*

employment [ɛm 'ploɪ mənt] **1.** *n.* the condition of holding a job. (No plural form in this sense.) ♦ *Mary* *listed her previous employment on the job application.* ♦ *I searched for employment in the classified ads of the newspaper.* **2.** *n.* the work that one does; one's job. (No plural form in this sense.) ♦ *John enjoys his employment as a photographer.* ♦ *Susan looks forward to full-time employment after she graduates.*

emporium [ɛm 'por i əm] *n.* a department store; a large store that sells many different products. (Less used than department store.) ♦ *David bought a new chair at our town's only emporium.* ♦ *The merchants sold their goods at a downtown emporium.*

empower [ɛm 'pɑʊ ɚ] *tv.* to give someone the power or authority to do something. ♦ *A congressional vote empowered the government to raise taxes.* ♦ *The owner empowered Jane to hire new employees for the store.*

empress ['ɛm prəs] **1.** *n.* a woman who rules an empire. ♦ *Catherine the Great was the empress of Russia in the late 1700s.* ♦ *The empress ordered the troops to guard the palace.* **2.** *n.* the wife of an emperor. ♦ *The emperor and empress were visited by a foreign dignitary.* ♦ *The empress bore an heir to the throne.*

emptiness ['ɛmp ti nəs] *n.* the state of being empty. (No plural form in this sense.) ♦ *John experienced a sense of emptiness on his first day of retirement.* ♦ *My voice echoed through the emptiness of the immense castle.*

empty ['ɛmp ti] **1.** *adj.* having nothing or no one within; vacant. (Comp: *emptier;* sup: *emptiest.*) ♦ *The room is empty. All the furniture has been removed.* ♦ *I lined the empty garbage can with a trash bag.* **2.** *adj.* without meaning; without purpose; senseless. (Figurative on ①. Adv: *emptily.* Comp: *emptier;* sup: *emptiest.*) ♦ *If your life is empty, you should develop a hobby.* ♦ *I have an empty feeling in my heart now that you are gone.* **3.** *tv.* to cause something to be ① by removing all the contents. ♦ *Bill emptied the fish bucket into the sink.* ♦ *I emptied the kitchen cabinets and packed the dishes into a box.* **4.** *iv.* [for something] to become empty ①. ♦ *The bathtub emptied slowly after I pulled the drain plug.* ♦ *The stadium emptied quickly after the game.*

empty-handed ['ɛmp ti 'hæn dɪd] *adj.* [leaving a place] with nothing. ♦ *Did you come away empty-handed from your last job?* ♦ *I hated to leave the amusement park empty-handed, so I bought a souvenir.*

emulate ['ɛm jə let] *tv.* to try to be like someone or something else; to try to do something as well as someone or something else. ♦ *Tom emulated his manager at work, hoping for a raise.* ♦ *I tried to emulate Mary's skill at playing the piano.*

emulsion [ɪ 'mʌl ʃən] *n.* a mixture of two or more substances that are not dissolved but are evenly mixed together. ♦ *House paint is a special kind of emulsion.* ♦ *I accidentally scratched some of the emulsion off the photographic negative.*

-en *suffix* <a form that marks the past participle of many irregular English verbs.> (Compare with -ed. Examples: *driven, spoken, written.*)

en- See in ⑬.

enable [ɛn 'e bəl] *tv.* to give someone or something the capability of doing something. ♦ *An unexpected inheritance enabled me to buy a house.* ♦ *The judge's ruling enabled the prosecutor to bring the controversial evidence before the jury.*

enact [ɛn 'ækt] **1.** *tv.* to make a bill into a law; to pass a law. ♦ *Congress enacted the new crime bill.* ♦ *The city council enacted the curfew law for minors.* **2.** *tv.* to perform a part in a play or a movie; to act something out. ♦ *Jane enacted the emotional scene from the play's first act.* ♦ *The cast enacted the entire play in a church.*

enactment [ɛn 'ækt mənt] **1.** *n.* the passage of laws. (No plural form in this sense.) ♦ *The law's enactment was very controversial.* ♦ *The senators of both political parties took credit for the bill's enactment.* **2.** *n.* a performance of something, such as a play; something that is acted out. ♦ *Bill's enactment of the dramatic scene was quite moving.* ♦ *Anne's convincing enactment of the crime held the jurors' attention.*

enamel [ɪ 'næm əl] **1.** *n.* a paint that dries to make a hard protective glaze or coat. (No plural form in this sense.) ♦ *Anne painted the bathroom walls with enamel.* ♦ *Mary brushed red enamel on her long fingernails.* **2.** *n.* a hard surface coating, usually made of porcelain. (No plural form in this sense.) ♦ *The bathtub is coated with a light-blue enamel.* ♦ *There is a chip in the enamel of the kitchen sink.* **3.** *n.* the hard outer layer of teeth. (No plural form in this sense.) ♦ *In the accident, Anne chipped the enamel on her front teeth.* ♦ *David grinds his teeth and has worn away much of his tooth enamel.* **4.** *tv.* to cover something with ①. ♦ *The kitchen walls were enameled in white.* ♦ *The worker enameled the metal with one coat.*

encapsulate [ɛn 'kæp sə let] *tv.* to put something into a capsule. ♦ *The machine encapsulated the medication, making thousands of bright yellow pills.* ♦ *The caterpillar encapsulated itself in a cocoon of silk.*

encephalitis [ɛn sɛf ə 'lɑɪ tɪs] *n.* a viral disease causing an inflammation of the brain. ♦ *The patient was diagnosed with encephalitis.* ♦ *Encephalitis is also known as sleeping sickness.*

enchant [ɛn 'tʃænt] **1.** *tv.* to cast a magic spell over someone or something. ♦ *The witch enchanted the handsome knight, turning him into a frog.* ♦ *A wizard had enchanted the gate so it would only open for good people.* **2.** *tv.* to charm someone or something; to delight someone or something. ♦ *Susan enchanted us with her singing.* ♦ *Tom thought he could enchant me with his quick wit and clever personality.*

enchantment [ɛn 'tʃænt mənt] **1.** *n.* a magic spell. ♦ *The wizard's enchantment caused the hut to appear to be a palace.* ♦ *The knight was under the enchantment of a powerful witch.* **2.** *n.* great delight. (No plural form in this sense.) ♦ *We were filled with enchantment on the opening night of the opera.* ♦ *The enchantment of a crisp, starry night is indescribable.*

enchantress [ɛn 'tʃæntrɪs] *n.* an enchanting woman; an alluring woman. ♦ *Even though her looks were simple, she was an enchantress.* ♦ *The enchantress lured David into a life of crime.*

encircle [ɛn 'sɚk əl] *tv.* to form a circle around someone or something; to surround someone or something. ♦ *The enemy troops encircled our camp.* ♦ *The children held hands and encircled their teacher.*

enclose [ɛn 'kloz] **1.** *tv.* [for a box or envelope] to contain something, especially something made of paper. ♦ *A scented envelope enclosed the romantic letter.* ♦ *The large, brown box enclosed my typed manuscript.* **2.** *tv.* to close something in on all sides; to put walls up around something. ♦ *Workers enclosed the yard with a wooden fence.* ♦ *A tall, concrete wall enclosed the prison.*

enclosed [ɛn 'klozd] **1.** *adj.* included in an envelope or a package. ♦ *Please look at the enclosed list.* ♦ *The letter said that the enclosed check is a gift.* **2.** *adj.* shut in on all sides; surrounded; having walls around on all sides. ♦ *The dog ran around in the enclosed yard.* ♦ *The inmates could not escape the enclosed prison courtyard.*

enclosure [ɛn 'klo ʒɚ] **1.** *n.* something that is put or included in an envelope or package. ♦ *Did you see the enclosure I stapled to the letter?* ♦ *There is an enclosure inside the large package.* **2.** *n.* a space that is surrounded by walls. ♦ *The dog ran loose in the enclosure.* ♦ *The prisoners exercised in the small enclosure.*

encore ['ɑŋ kor] **1.** *n.* the performance of an additional piece of music, or a repeat of a piece of music, after the end of a concert, at the demand of the audience. ♦ *The singer returned to the stage for an encore.* ♦ *The audience clapped loudly after the band's encore.* **2.** *adj.* repeated. ♦ *The television station ran an encore showing of its series on cancer.* ♦ *The comedian did an encore performance of his best routine.*

encounter [ɛn 'kaʊn tɚ] **1.** *tv.* to meet someone or something by chance. ♦ *While skipping school, Bill encountered his principal at the mall.* ♦ *I encountered a lot of difficulty when I tried to take the test.* **2.** *n.* a meeting, especially by chance. ♦ *Our encounter at the train station caught me by surprise.* ♦ *The two old high-school friends had an unexpected encounter.*

encourage [ɛn 'kɚ ɪdʒ] *tv.* to give someone the courage or confidence to do something. ♦ *The coach encouraged Jimmy to practice more often.* ♦ *Jane encouraged me to work hard in school.*

encouragement [ɛn 'kɚ ɪdʒ mənt] *n.* words or actions that encourage someone. (No plural form in this sense.) ♦ *The athlete acknowledged our cries of encouragement by waving at us.* ♦ *I gave Anne a great deal of encouragement before the talent show.*

encouraging [ɛn 'kɚ ɪdʒ ɪŋ] *adj.* giving confidence; giving courage; giving hope. (Adv: *encouragingly.*) ♦ *Mary's quick recovery from surgery was an encouraging sign.* ♦ *I gave Bill an encouraging pat on the back.*

encroach [ɛn 'krotʃ] **encroach (up)on** *iv.* + *prep. phr.* to go beyond a legal limit or boundary. ♦ *Don't encroach upon our property!* ♦ *The reporter encroached on my privacy.*

encumbrance [ɛn 'kʌm brəns] *n.* an obstacle or burden. ♦ *Our many debts are a serious encumbrance.* ♦ *John fell out of the boat and found his wet clothing to be an encumbrance when trying to get back in.*

encyclopedia [ɛn saɪ klə 'pid i ə] *n.* a collection of books that provides detailed information on many subjects. ♦ *Sue read about different kinds of rocks in her encyclopedia.* ♦ *There are many types of encyclopedias at your local library.*

end ['ɛnd] **1.** *n.* the final stopping point of a continuing process. (No plural form in this sense.) ♦ *The end of the warfare came when the treaty was signed.* ♦ *I will love you until the end of time.* **2.** *n.* the last part of something. ♦ *The end of the movie was actually quite boring.* ♦ *I turned on the television to watch the end of the football game.* **3.** *n.* death. (A euphemism.) ♦ *The old man's end came just before dawn.* ♦ *The doomed passengers realized the end was near.* **4.** *n.* a purpose; an intended outcome; a result. ♦ *Your actions are not a means to an end.* ♦ *When you plan something, you should have certain ends in mind.* **5.** *iv.* to stop; to finish; to exist no longer. ♦ *With death, his pain finally ended.* ♦ *The movie ended abruptly, leaving many questions unanswered.* **6.** *tv.* to stop something; to finish something. ♦ *Let's end this discussion right now.* ♦ *We ended our friendship over a silly argument.* **7. come to a dead end** *idiom* to come to an absolute stopping point. ♦ *The building project came to a dead end.* ♦ *The street came to a dead end.* **8. come to an untimely end** *idiom* to come to an early death. ♦ *Poor Mr. Jones came to an untimely end in a car accident.* ♦ *Cancer caused Mrs. Smith to come to an untimely end.* **9. end in itself** *idiom* for its own sake; toward its own ends; toward no purpose but its own. ♦ *For Bob, art is an end in itself. He doesn't hope to make any money from it.* ♦ *Learning is an end in itself. Knowledge does not have to have a practical application.* **10. hold up one's end (of the bargain)** *idiom* to do one's part as agreed; to attend to one's responsibilities as agreed. ♦ *Tom has to learn to cooperate. He must hold up his end of the bargain.* ♦ *If you don't hold your end up, the whole project will fail.* **11. meet one's end** *idiom* to die. ♦ *The dog met his end under the wheels of a car.* ♦ *I don't intend to meet my end until I'm 100 years old.* **12. put an end to something** *idiom* to end something; to terminate something. (The same as **put a stop to something** at **stop** ⑩.) ♦ *The teacher put an end to the fight between the boys.* ♦ *The coming of fall put an end to the blooming of the roses.*

endanger [ɛn 'den dʒɚ] *tv.* to put someone or something in a dangerous position; to put someone or something at risk of injury or death. ♦ *Driving while drunk endangers everyone on the road.* ♦ *The animals that lived in the marsh were endangered by the drought.*

endangered species [ɛn 'den dʒɚd 'spi siz] *n.* a species that has declined in number and has thus acquired governmental protection. ♦ *The government protected the endangered species.* ♦ *An endangered species of owl lives in this forest.*

endearing [ɛn 'dɪr ɪŋ] *adj.* charming; sweet; worthy of love; lovable. (Adv: *endearingly.*) ♦ *My best friend has many endearing qualities.* ♦ *Anne has made numerous friends because of her endearing nature.*

endeavor [ɛn 'dɛv ɚ] **1. endeavor to** *tv.* + *inf.* to try to do something; to try very hard to do something. ♦ *Susan endeavored to run the marathon.* ♦ *Tom endeavored to get better grades in college.* **2.** *n.* an attempt to do something; a struggle to do something. ♦ *Bill's well-planned and sincere endeavor failed.* ♦ *Would you please make an endeavor to stay out of trouble?*

ending ['ɛnd ɪŋ] *n.* the final part of something; the last part of something; the conclusion. ♦ *Did you understand the ending of that movie?* ♦ *This novel has a happy ending.*

endless ['ɛnd ləs] *adj.* without end; continuous; without stopping. (Adv: *endlessly.*) ♦ *I wish you'd stop your endless complaining.* ♦ *The long and boring drive seemed endless.*

endocrine ['ɛnd o krɪn] *adj.* [of a gland that is capable of] releasing fluid directly into the blood or lymph. ♦ *The physician found a problem with Bill's endocrine glands.* ♦ *A lack of certain endocrine secretions made Lisa tired all the time.*

endocrinology [ɛnd o krɪ 'nɑl ə dʒi] *n.* the study of the endocrine glands. (No plural form in this sense.) ♦ *The medical student took a course in endocrinology.* ♦ *Dr. Jones specializes in endocrinology.*

endorse [ɛn 'dors] **1.** *tv.* to support someone; to approve someone for something. ♦ *The labor union endorsed the democratic candidate for president.* ♦ *I do not endorse your choice of friends.* **2.** *tv.* to write one's name on the back of a check when cashing it. ♦ *Dave endorsed his paycheck.* ♦ *The bank teller reminded me to endorse the check I was cashing.*

endorsement [ɛn 'dors mənt] **1.** *n.* approval. (No plural form in this sense.) ♦ *My application for a loan requires the endorsement of a bank officer.* ♦ *Without your endorsement, I would never have gotten permission to carry out my plan.* **2.** *n.* a statement of approval. ♦ *You must write your endorsement on the back of the form.* ♦ *John wrote his endorsement in a brief note on the application.* **3.** *n.* the name of a candidate that someone recommends to the voters for election. ♦ *The newspaper listed its endorsements for city council.* ♦ *I carried a list of endorsements with me when I voted.* **4.** *n.* a name written on the back of a check, indicating who guarantees payment of the check. ♦ *Is there an endorsement on the check?* ♦ *The bank teller verified the endorsement before cashing the check.*

endow [ɛn 'dɑʊ] **1.** *tv.* to present a school, charity, hospital, church, or fund with an asset or cash. ♦ *A large manufacturing company endowed a new wing of the local hospital.* ♦ *After Mary became successful, she endowed her former university in the amount of $500,000.* **2. endow with** *tv.* + *prep. phr.* to furnish someone with a good quality or benefit at birth. ♦ *Nature endowed Jane with a pleasant smile.* ♦ *Bill was endowed with a sweet personality.*

endowment [ɛn 'dɑʊ mənt] **1.** *n.* a large sum of money given to a school, charity, hospital, church, or fund to support the institution for a period of time. ♦ *The university received a substantial endowment from the automotive company.* ♦ *The endowment helped the hospital buy new equipment.* **2.** *n.* a good quality or talent that is present at one's birth. ♦ *Mary's quick mind was an endowment that served her well in college.* ♦ *Among his natural endowments, Dave has a head of wavy hair.*

endurance [ɛn 'dɚ əns] *n.* the ability to keep going; the ability to endure. (No plural form in this sense.) ♦ *Do you have the endurance needed to run this marathon?* ♦ *I don't know if I have the endurance required for this task.*

endure [ɛn 'dɚ] **1.** *tv.* to withstand something; to put up with something; to tolerate something. ♦ *I hope our house will endure the coming hurricane.* ♦ *I can't endure your tasteless humor.* **2.** *iv.* to last; to keep going. ♦ *No matter what hardships face this family, we will endure.* ♦ *I don't know how long this old car will endure.*

enduring [ɛn 'dɚ ɪŋ] *adj.* long-lasting; continuous; ongoing; permanent. (Adv: *enduringly.*) ♦ *The couple had an enduring love for each other.* ♦ *Your tardiness at work is an enduring problem that must be resolved.*

enema ['ɛn ə mə] **1.** *n.* a treatment that causes a bowel movement by introducing water into the rectum. ♦ *The nurse administered an enema to the patient.* ♦ *The patient received an enema before surgery.* **2.** *n.* a device for administering ①. ♦ *The nurse disposed of the enema after administering it.* ♦ *John bought a disposable enema at the drugstore.*

enemy ['ɛn ə mi] **1.** *n.* an opponent of someone or something; someone who fights against someone or something. ♦ *The rival football teams regarded each other as enemies.* ♦ *The popular celebrity didn't have an enemy in the world.* **2.** *n.* a country that another country fights against during a war; an opposing army or other unit of military service. ♦ *The enemy forced the troops to retreat.* ♦ *The small group of soldiers was victorious against the enemy.*

energetic [ɛn ɚ 'dʒɛt ɪk] *adj.* having a lot of energy; full of life. (Adv: *energetically* [...ɪk li].) ♦ *The boss appreciated the energetic workers.* ♦ *The energetic athlete runs 5 miles every day.*

energize ['ɛn ɚ dʒɑɪz] **1.** *tv.* to provide the needed power to something; to start something up. ♦ *Bill energized the battery with a charger.* ♦ *I energized the motor when I turned on the electric switch.* **2.** *tv.* to stimulate or motivate someone. (Figurative on ①.) ♦ *The coach energized the team before the game with a pep talk.* ♦ *The motivational speaker energized the audience.*

energy ['ɛn ɚ dʒi] *n.* the power needed to do something; the force that powers people or machines. (No plural form in this sense.) ♦ *The energy used to power most cars comes from gasoline.* ♦ *I don't have the energy to clean house after working all day.*

enervate ['ɛn ɚ vet] *tv.* to weaken someone's spirit or vigor. ♦ *The coach's negative lecture enervated the football team.* ♦ *The dullness of the lecture as well as the heat of the day enervated the students, who were all too tired to do anything.*

enervating ['ɛn ɚ ve tɪŋ] *adj.* weakening someone's spirit or vigor. (Adv: *enervatingly.*) ♦ *This is the most enervating day I have ever had at work.* ♦ *The heat has an enervating effect on me.*

enfold [ɛn 'fold] *tv.* to embrace someone. ♦ *Mary enfolded the tearful child in her arms.* ♦ *Bill enfolded Mary lovingly when they met at the airport.*

enforce [ɛn 'fors] **1.** *tv.* to put a law or regulation into force; to make certain that a law is obeyed. ♦ *Patrol officers enforce a speed limit on the roads.* ♦ *Local police enforce the law in our town.* **2. enforce on** *tv.* + *prep. phr.* to impose something on a person. ♦ *The physician enforced a strict diet on the cardiac patient.* ♦ *The teacher did not like to enforce rigid rules on the children.*

enforceable [ɛn 'fors ə bəl] *adj.* [of something] capable of being enforced. (Adv: *enforceably.*) ♦ *The speed limit is an enforceable law.* ♦ *The contract is an agreement that is enforceable by law.*

enforcement [ɛn 'fors mənt] *n.* using the force of an existing law; using legal police powers. (No plural form in this sense.) ♦ *The courts vowed stern enforcement of all laws and regulations.* ♦ *The mayoral candidate promised vigorous law enforcement in the city.*

enfranchise [ɛn 'fræn tʃɑɪz] *tv.* to give someone the right to vote. ♦ *Women were enfranchised in the United States in 1920.* ♦ *The 26th Amendment, ratified in 1971, enfranchised 18-, 19-, and 20-year-olds.*

engage [ɛn 'gedʒ] **1.** *tv.* to take up someone's time; to keep someone busy. ♦ *The matter engaged a considerable amount of our time.* ♦ *The children were busily engaged in a baseball game during recess.* **2.** *tv.* to obtain the services of someone. ♦ *We engaged a trio of trumpeters for the ceremony.* ♦ *David engaged an expensive caterer for the party.* **3.** *tv.* to rent something or a place. ♦ *Anne engaged the largest hall in town for the party.* ♦ *The couple engaged a limousine to take them from the church to the reception.* **4.** *tv.* to occupy the attentions of an opposing army with fighting. ♦ *The troops engaged the enemy just before dawn.* ♦ *The soldiers engaged the opposing army on the battlefield.* **5.** *tv.* to cause a mechanical part to interlock with another mechanical part. ♦ *John engaged a lower gear when driving up the steep incline.* ♦ *Jane engaged the clutch, and the car started to move.* **6.** *iv.* to enter into a conflict. ♦ *The opposing armies engaged just before dawn.* ♦ *The troops engaged on the battlefield.* **7.** *iv.* [for mechanical parts] to interlock. ♦ *The car's gears engaged just in time.* ♦ *The watch was not running because the gears did not engage properly.*

engaged [ɛn 'gedʒd] *adj.* pledged to marry a particular person. ♦ *Susan will become engaged to marry Tom next spring.* ♦ *The engaged couple are high-school sweethearts.*

engagement [ɛn 'gedʒ mənt] **1.** *n.* the pledge of marriage made by a man and woman. ♦ *Anne and Bob announced their engagement in the local newspaper.* ♦ *Both families were happy with news of the engagement.* **2.** *n.* a period of time before a wedding when a man and a woman are engaged. ♦ *Our engagement lasted for two years before we finally married.* ♦ *John and Mary had a terrible argument that ended their three-month engagement.* **3.** *n.* a military battle. ♦ *The generals drew battle plans for the military engagement.* ♦ *The soldiers fought a decisive engagement.* **4.** *n.* an appointment; a scheduled time to meet with someone. ♦ *I can't meet with you for lunch today. I have a previous engagement.* ♦ *Tom called Susan to verify their business engagement.*

engaging [ɛn 'gedʒ ɪŋ] *adj.* pleasant; charming; capturing someone's interest. (Adv: *engagingly.*) ♦ *The talk-show host had an engaging personality.* ♦ *David's engaging nature puts everyone at ease.*

engender [ɛn 'dʒɛn dɚ] *tv.* to produce something; to bring about the existence of something. ♦ *I hope my actions will engender your trust.* ♦ *John's acts of kindness engendered my friendship.*

engine ['ɛn dʒən] **1.** *n.* a machine that uses power from gas, electricity, water pressure, steam, etc., to create mechanical energy. ♦ *The airplane has a jet engine.* ♦ *The locomotive was powered by a steam engine.* **2.** *n.* a powered train car that pulls or pushes the other train cars; a locomotive. ♦ *The children looked at the old steam engine in the museum.* ♦ *The engine blew its whistle as it roared through town.*

engineer [ɛn dʒə 'nɪr] **1.** *n.* someone who drives a locomotive engine. ♦ *The engineer blew the loud whistle as a warning to cars near the railroad crossing.* ♦ *The engineer drove the train through the tunnel.* **2.** *n.* someone who has training in a branch of engineering. ♦ *The car company employed dozens of automotive engineers.* ♦ *An electrical engineer accompanied the building inspector during the inspection.* **3.** *tv.* [for ②] to do the designing and planning of something, such as a building, bridge, computer, automobile, etc. ♦ *Bob helped engineer the complex new bridge.* ♦ *Lisa engineered a part of the powerful computer circuits.* **4.** *tv.* to plan something; to bring something about. (Figurative on ③.) ♦ *The contractor engineered the construction of the skyscraper.* ♦ *The board of directors engineered the library director's downfall.*

engineering [ɛn dʒə 'nɪr ɪŋ] *n.* the field of mathematical and physical sciences, especially in the design of buildings, roads, bridges, and other structures. (No plural form in this sense.) ♦ *I took a course in engineering at the university.* ♦ *Does this college offer courses in industrial engineering?*

England ['ɪŋ glənd] See Gazetteer.

English ['ɪŋ glɪʃ] **1. the English** *n.* the citizens of England, considered as a group. (No plural form in this sense. Treated as plural.) ♦ *The English are proud of their country and its traditions.* ♦ *The English import many American products.* **2.** *n.* the primary language spoken by the people of the United States of America, England and the rest of the United Kingdom, Canada, Australia, and New Zealand, as well as one of the official languages of South Africa and India. (No plural form in this sense.) ♦ *English is one of the international languages of business.* ♦ *Some sounds are pronounced differently in British English than in American English.* **3.** *adj.* of or about the English people and their culture. ♦ *Most English subjects are loyal to the queen.* ♦ *We visited an English castle last summer.*

engrave [ɛn 'grev] **1.** *tv.* to cut a pattern or letters into something; to carve a design into something. ♦ *My initials are engraved on the bracelet I wear.* ♦ *The jeweler engraved a heart-shaped symbol on the inside of the gold ring.* **2.** *tv.* to carve into something, creating a pattern or letters. ♦ *I engraved the bracelet with a special message.* ♦ *Bill engraved a heart on the oak tree.*

engraved [ɛn 'grevd] *adj.* having a carved design; decorated with an engraving. ♦ *The couple exchanged engraved rings at the wedding.* ♦ *I wore an ornately engraved bracelet to the party.*

engraving [ɛn 'grev ɪŋ] **1.** *n.* cutting or carving a design into something. (No plural form in this sense.) ♦ *Engraving requires a steady hand.* ♦ *Dave learned the techniques of fine engraving from a jeweler.* **2.** *n.* a picture that has been printed from a metal or wood plate that has been engraved. ♦ *The artist enclosed the engraving in a glass frame.* ♦ *The engraving was made from a wooden plaque near the historical landmark.*

engross [ɛn 'grɔs] *tv.* to engage one totally and take all of one's time and attention. ♦ *The football game engrossed Tom completely.* ♦ *Nothing engrosses me as much as my work.*

engrossing [ɛn 'gros ɪŋ] *adj.* intriguing; occupying one's complete attention. (Adv: *engrossingly.*) ♦ *I stayed awake until 3:00 A.M. to finish the engrossing novel.* ♦ *The magician's engrossing act kept the members of the audience on the edge of their seats.*

engulf [ɛn 'gʌlf] **1.** *tv.* to submerge something; to wash over and submerge something. ♦ *Huge waves engulfed the* *small boat.* ♦ *The flames engulfed the building.* **2.** *tv.* to overwhelm someone or something. (Figurative on ①. Not prenominal.) ♦ *I feared that the assignment would engulf me in problems I could not solve.* ♦ *Sorrow engulfed Susan at her brother's funeral.*

enhance [ɛn 'hæns] *tv.* to add to the quality of something; to cause something to appear more important, valuable, functional, or beautiful. ♦ *Small improvements enhanced the value of the house.* ♦ *You can enhance your appearance with makeup.*

enhanced [ɛn 'hænst] *adj.* improved; added to; made more valuable. ♦ *Bill's enhanced appearance—owing to a new tie—was quite fashionable.* ♦ *I purchased an enhanced version of the software package.*

enhancement [ɛn 'hæns mənt] **1.** *n.* improvement, especially in quality. (No plural form in this sense.) ♦ *We felt that enhancement of our product line this year was very important.* ♦ *The continued enhancement of the software helped it retain its value.* **2.** *n.* an addition that makes something more important or beautiful; an improvement. ♦ *An acoustic guitar is played without electronic enhancements.* ♦ *A new coat of paint is one of the enhancements our house would benefit from.*

enigma [ɪ 'nɪg mə] *n.* a puzzle; someone or something that is hard to understand. ♦ *The enigma surrounding the murder perplexed the detective.* ♦ *Bill's contradictory political beliefs are an enigma to me.*

enigmatic [ɪ nɪg 'mæt ɪk] *adj.* puzzling; hard to understand; baffling. (Adv: *enigmatically* [...ɪk li].) ♦ *The Egyptian pyramids seem quite enigmatic to the people of modern times.* ♦ *I couldn't tell where the enigmatic candidate stood on most issues.*

enjoy [ɛn 'dʒoɪ] *tv.* to have something that is good; to be fortunate to have something. ♦ *Throughout her life, Mary always enjoyed good health.* ♦ *I have enjoyed my fulfilling career in law.*

enjoyable [ɛn 'dʒoɪ ə bəl] *adj.* causing joy; pleasant. (Adv: *enjoyably.*) ♦ *The wedding was an enjoyable occasion.* ♦ *I looked forward to an enjoyable weekend away from work.*

enjoyment [ɛn 'dʒoɪ mənt] **1.** *n.* joy; pleasure; happiness. (No plural form in this sense.) ♦ *The bride and groom both felt tremendous enjoyment at the wedding.* ♦ *I take great enjoyment in climbing mountains.* **2.** *n.* something that causes joy, pleasure, or happiness. ♦ *Collecting rare postage stamps is Mary's greatest enjoyment.* ♦ *Eating is one of my few enjoyments.*

enlarge [ɛn 'lɑrdʒ] **1.** *tv.* to make something larger; to make something bigger. ♦ *The photographer enlarged the photograph.* ♦ *You should enlarge the size of the lettering so that it's easier to read.* **2.** *iv.* to become larger; to become bigger. ♦ *The doctor noted that the tumor enlarged since last month.* ♦ *The trunk of the tree will enlarge as the tree grows.*

enlargement [ɛn 'lɑrdʒ mənt] **1.** *n.* growing or enlarging. (No plural form in this sense.) ♦ *The enlargement of the injured joint is abnormal.* ♦ *The physician detected an enlargement of the liver.* **2.** *n.* a photograph that is larger than normal or larger than the original photograph. ♦ *Jane had enlargements of her favorite picture made.* ♦ *The enlargements fit into a 5" × 7" frame.*

enlighten [ɛn 'lɑɪt n] *tv.* to inform someone about something. ♦ *The speaker enlightened the students about the dangers of drinking.* ♦ *The warden wrote a newspaper editorial that enlightened the public on prison conditions.*

enlightened [ɛn 'lɑɪt nd] *adj.* informed; knowledgeable; intellectually aware. (Adv: *enlightenedly.*) ♦ *The enlightened public voted the corrupt mayor out of office.* ♦ *The author responded to questions from her enlightened readers.*

enlightenment [ɛn 'lɑɪt n mənt] *n.* explaining something to someone; giving someone information. (No plural form in this sense.) ♦ *The devastating automobile accident provided enlightenment about the dangers of driving drunk.* ♦ *Susan experienced a spiritual enlightenment of her faith.*

enlist [ɛn 'lɪst] **1.** *tv.* to ask or persuade someone to help do something. ♦ *I enlisted Mary and Bill to help decorate the party room.* ♦ *The coach enlisted Tom to put the equipment away after practice.* **2.** *iv.* to sign up for military duty; to join the military. ♦ *I enlisted in the army when I turned 18.* ♦ *You can enlist at any recruiting station.*

enlisted [ɛn 'lɪst ɪd] *adj.* signed up for military duty; in the military. ♦ *Forty enlisted soldiers boarded the bus.* ♦ *The enlisted men were trained for combat.*

enliven [ɛn 'lɑɪ vən] *tv.* to make something more exciting; to make something more active. ♦ *My funny coworker always enlivens the office atmosphere.* ♦ *Play some music. Let's enliven this dull party!*

en masse [ɛn 'mæs] *adv.* [moving] all together; [moving] as a group. (From French.) ♦ *The children entered the museum en masse.* ♦ *Our guests arrived en masse and made a horrible crowd at the doorway.*

enmity ['ɛn mə ti] *n.* hatred; the feeling one has for an enemy. (No plural form in this sense.) ♦ *I don't feel any enmity for those who have hurt me in the past.* ♦ *John felt enmity toward the people who discriminated against him.*

enormity [ɪ 'nor mɪt i] **1.** *n.* largeness, especially overwhelming largeness; magnitude; enormousness. (No plural form in this sense.) ♦ *The supervisor was overwhelmed by the enormity of the problem.* ♦ *No one was prepared for the enormity of the destruction caused by the earthquake.* **2.** *n.* extreme evil; wickedness; the degree of evilness of a crime. (No plural form in this sense.) ♦ *Even the jaded detectives were shocked by the enormity of the crime.* ♦ *The public demanded an investigation into the enormity of the political scandal.*

enormous [ɪ 'nor məs] *adj.* huge; large; very big. (Adv: *enormously.*) ♦ *We ate an enormous dinner because we were very hungry.* ♦ *The truck hauled an enormous load from the warehouse.*

enormously [ɪ 'nor məs li] *adv.* extremely; very much. ♦ *We are enormously excited about your promotion.* ♦ *I am enormously thankful for everything you have done for me.*

enormousness [ɪ 'nor məs nəs] *n.* hugeness; largeness. (No plural form in this sense.) ♦ *The enormousness of the load strained the movers.* ♦ *I could not believe the enormousness of the waves that the hurricane caused.*

enough [ɪ 'nʌf] **1.** *adj.* as much as is needed; as much as is necessary; adequate. ♦ *I don't have enough money to buy a new car, so I will have to buy a used one.* ♦ *Do you have enough change to pay the bill?* **2.** *pron.* a necessary amount; an adequate amount. ♦ *I have enough. I don't need more.* ♦ *I have had enough of your excuses!* **3.** *adv.* adequately; to an adequate degree. (Follows an adjective.) ♦ *You don't exercise long enough to do your body any good.* ♦ *I am hungry enough to eat a horse.*

enquire [ɛn 'kwɑɪ ɚ] See inquire.

enquiry [ɛn 'kwɑɪ rɪ] See inquiry.

enrage [ɛn 'redʒ] *tv.* to make someone very mad; to make someone very upset. ♦ *John's insolence enraged his supervisor.* ♦ *The arrogant criminal enraged the judge.*

enrich [ɛn 'rɪtʃ] **1.** *tv.* to make something richer by adding flavor or something fatty. ♦ *I enriched my coffee with cream and sugar.* ♦ *The cook enriched the batter with real butter.* **2.** *tv.* to add vitamins or minerals to food; to fortify food with vitamins or minerals. ♦ *The manufacturer has enriched the cereal with lots of vitamins.* ♦ *My orange juice has been enriched with extra nutrients.* **3.** *tv.* to increase someone or something's wealth. ♦ *Don't pay the extra interest. It will only enrich the bank.* ♦ *The taxes you pay will enrich the treasury.*

enriched [ɛn 'rɪtʃt] *adj.* fortified; having vitamins or minerals added. ♦ *Enriched bread is highly nutritious.* ♦ *I bought a box of enriched cereal.*

enriching [ɛn 'rɪtʃ ɪŋ] *adj.* causing moral, spiritual, or intellectual improvement. (Adv: *enrichingly.*) ♦ *Traveling across the globe was an enriching experience.* ♦ *I enjoy my enriching career as a social worker.*

enroll AND **enrol** [ɛn 'rol] **1. enroll (in)** *iv.* (+ *prep. phr.*) to become a member of a club, school, or other group. ♦ *I enrolled early, long before school actually started.* ♦ *Lisa will enroll in the club when the first meeting is held.* **2.** *tv.* to sign someone up for a club, school, or other group. ♦ *Our club enrolled seven new members at the last meeting.* ♦ *Twenty students have enrolled in the art class.*

enrollment [ɛn 'rol mənt] **1.** *n.* signing someone up for a school, club, or other group. (No plural form in this sense.) ♦ *You must pay your tuition upon enrollment.* ♦ *Enrollment for college classes went smoothly.* **2.** *n.* a name on a list of people who have enrolled for something; a list of people who have enrolled for something. ♦ *Enrollments for first grade are higher this year than last.* ♦ *There was only one late enrollment for physics.*

en route [ɛn rɑʊt, ɛn 'rut] *adv.* (From French.) on the way; on the path or road toward someplace. ♦ *We were en route to the airport when the accident occurred.* ♦ *The grocery store is en route to the party.*

ensemble [ɑn 'sɑm bəl] **1.** *n.* a group of people, working together, usually musicians or other performers. ♦ *The woodwind ensemble performed pieces by Handel and Schubert.* ♦ *The acting ensemble performed* Romeo and Juliet. **2.** *n.* a coordinated set of clothing and accessories. ♦ *Jane's ensemble consisted of a lavender dress with matching shoes.* ♦ *John's ensemble included a top hat and a cane.*

ensign ['ɛn sɪn] **1.** *n.* a flag, especially one used on a ship to indicate what country the ship is from. ♦ *The ensign identified the French ship.* ♦ *The ship's ensign flew from the mast.* **2.** *n.* the lowest rank of commissioned officer in the navy. ♦ *One of the ensigns swabbed the deck.* ♦ *The ensign saluted the admiral.*

enslave [ɛn 'slev] *tv.* to make someone a slave; to take someone's freedom away. ♦ *The ruler enslaved the captured troops.* ♦ *The addict was enslaved by drugs.*

ensue [ɛn 'su] *iv.* to follow after something else; to happen after something else. ♦ *I will have to see what ensues before I make a decision.* ♦ *A serious traffic jam ensued after the accident.*

ensuing [ɛn 'su ɪŋ] *adj.* following; happening next; coming after. ♦ *When the computer crashed, the ensuing problems gave me a headache.* ♦ *Further questions about the project will be addressed at the ensuing meeting.*

ensure [ɛn 'ʃʊr] *tv.* to make sure that something happens; to make something certain to happen. (Compare with insure.) ♦ *I will do what is necessary to ensure that things go well.* ♦ *Prompt payment will ensure good service.*

entail [ɛn 'tel] *tv.* to require something; to involve or utilize something. ♦ *The project will entail many hours of overtime at the office.* ♦ *The task entailed strict attention to procedure.*

entangle [ɛn 'tæŋ gəl] **1.** *tv.* to tangle things or people together, where one of the tangled items is string, rope, cord, wire, hair, etc. ♦ *Bill entangled the leg of his desk chair in the lamp cord.* ♦ *The fishing line became entangled in the weeds.* **2.** *tv.* to cause someone or something to become involved in something; to involve someone or something in a situation. (Figurative on ①.) ♦ *I don't like to get entangled in other people's affairs.* ♦ *John entangled us in a difficult financial situation.*

enter ['ɛn tɚ] **1.** *tv.* to go into a place; to come into a place. ♦ *Knock on the door before you enter the room.* ♦ *We entered the building through the front door.* **2.** *tv.* to join something; to begin a career or course of study. ♦ *John entered the ministry.* ♦ *Susan entered the advertising business after college.* **3.** *tv.* to write down something in a journal, log, or record book. ♦ *I entered my thoughts in a diary.* ♦ *Bill entered the amount of each check in his checkbook.* **4.** *tv.* to type data or other information into a computer. ♦ *Dave entered all the data in only a few hours.* ♦ *I entered the results of the experiment into the computer file.* **5.** *n.* the key labeled "enter" or the "(carriage) return" key on a computer keyboard. ♦ *Press "enter" to move on to the next question.* ♦ *I hit "enter" to save the information.*

enterprise ['ɛn tɚ prɑɪz] **1.** *n.* a business or company. ♦ *Bill manages a publishing enterprise.* ♦ *The new enterprise will require additional staff and equipment.* **2.** *n.* a plan; a project. ♦ *The committee hopes to complete the enterprise by January.* ♦ *Our department's new enterprise is fraught with problems.*

enterprising ['ɛn tɚ prɑɪz ɪŋ] *adj.* energetic; ready or eager to innovate. (Adv: *enterprisingly.*) ♦ *Dave is an enterprising salesman.* ♦ *This position requires an enterprising worker.*

entertain [ɛn tɚ 'ten] **1.** *tv.* to amuse someone; to provide an audience with amusement. ♦ *The clown entertained the children.* ♦ *Dave is fun to be around. He always finds ways to entertain us.* **2.** *tv.* to provide guests or associates with food, amusement, and hospitality. ♦ *Our Japanese hosts entertained us very well.* ♦ *We entertained a group of exchange students from Sweden.* **3.** *tv.* to consider something; to think about something. ♦ *How could you even entertain such an idea?* ♦ *I entertained going back to school for a degree in law.*

entertainer [ɛn tɚ 'ten ɚ] *n.* a performer; someone who entertains; a singer, an actor, a musician, etc. ♦ *John wanted to be an entertainer ever since he was young.* ♦ *Anne was an accomplished entertainer in the music industry.*

entertaining [ɛn tɚ 'ten ɪŋ] *adj.* amusing; interesting. (Adv: *entertainingly.*) ♦ *My grandmother told us an entertaining story.* ♦ *I couldn't put down the entertaining novel.*

entertainment [ɛn tɚ 'ten mənt] **1.** *n.* amusement; an entertaining performance. (No plural form in this sense.) ♦ *Who will provide the entertainment for the child's party?* ♦ *The bride's parents arranged for the entertainment at the reception.* **2.** *n.* something that is entertaining; a performance. (No plural form in this sense.) ♦ *The public park provides all sorts of entertainment for children.* ♦ *The musical entertainment this evening will be provided by a jazz quartet.*

enthrall [ɛn 'θrɑl] *tv.* to capture and hold someone's attention; to fascinate someone. ♦ *The magician enthralled us with fascinating tricks.* ♦ *The politician enthralled the crowd with a lively speech.*

enthralling [ɛn 'θrɑl ɪŋ] *adj.* captivating; fascinating. (Adv: *enthrallingly.*) ♦ *The enthralling action movie excited the audience.* ♦ *We closely watched the enthralling trapeze artists.*

enthusiasm [ɛn 'θuz ɪ æz əm] *n.* excited interest; zeal. (No plural form in this sense.) ♦ *Jane's enthusiasm for gardening is evident by all of these beautiful flowers.* ♦ *The neighborhood committee expressed enthusiasm for the new playground.*

enthusiast [ɛn 'θuz ɪ əst] *n.* someone who enjoys doing something; someone who enjoys a certain hobby; a devotee. ♦ *Susan is a tennis enthusiast.* ♦ *The hiking enthusiast climbed many mountains in New England.*

enthusiastic [ɛn θuz ɪ 'æs tɪk] *adj.* full of enthusiasm; excited; interested. (Adv: *enthusiastically* [...ɪk li].) ♦ *I am very enthusiastic about my new job.* ♦ *The enthusiastic student did very well in school.*

entice [ɛn 'tɑɪs] *tv.* to lure, attract, tempt, or lead someone or some creature into doing what one wishes. ♦ *The fisherman enticed the fish with a big, fat worm.* ♦ *I enticed Mary to dinner by offering to pay for her meal.*

enticement [ɛn 'tɑɪs mənt] *n.* a lure; something that attracts; an allurement. ♦ *I used dessert as an enticement to get the children to eat dinner.* ♦ *Mary used a promotion as an enticement for Tom to stay on the job.*

enticing [ɛn 'tɑɪs ɪŋ] *adj.* alluring; tempting. (Adv: *enticingly.*) ♦ *Tom could not resist the enticing offer of free tickets to the football game.* ♦ *I must have a piece of that enticing chocolate cake.*

entire [ɛn 'tɑɪr] *adj.* whole; complete; all. (Adv: *entirely.*) ♦ *Bill ate the entire apple pie by himself.* ♦ *The entire class passed the exam.*

entirely [ɛn 'tɑɪr li] *adv.* completely; totally. ♦ *That color looks entirely wrong on you.* ♦ *The witness wasn't entirely sure of what he had seen.*

entirety [ɛn 'tɑɪr ə ti] **in its entirety, in their entirety** *idiom* in a state of completeness. ♦ *I watched the basketball game in its entirety.* ♦ *My friends and I ate the two large pizzas in their entirety.*

entitle [ɛn 'tɑɪt əl] **1.** *tv.* to give a title to a book, essay, or other written document. ♦ *The author entitled the book My Life Story.* ♦ *My favorite poem is entitled "Summer Rain."* **2.** *tv.* to give someone the authority or right to do something. ♦ *This paper entitles my lawyer to handle all my legal affairs.* ♦ *Your job does not entitle you to bend the rules.*

entitlement [ɛn 'tɑɪt l mənt] *n.* a sum of money from the government that one is entitled to under law. ♦ *Social security is an entitlement that most workers receive when they retire.* ♦ *The cost of entitlements makes the federal budget very high.*

entity ['ɛn tə ti] *n.* a being, something like an organization or a business, that has its own rights and responsibilities. ♦ *My company and your company are separate business entities.* ♦ *My brother works for a large banking entity.*

entomologist [ɛn tə 'mɑl ə dʒəst] *n.* a scientist who studies insects. ♦ *The entomologist collected beetles in specimen jars.* ♦ *The entomologist explained the difference between ants and flies.*

entomology [ɛn tə 'mɑl ə dʒi] *n.* the study and classification of insects. (No plural form in this sense.) ♦ *The scientist gave an interesting lecture on entomology.* ♦ *The biology department offered a course in entomology.*

entourage ['ɑn tə rɑʒ] *n.* a group of people who follow someone important. (From French.) ♦ *The president's entourage protected him from assassins.* ♦ *The queen was surrounded by an entourage of advisers and bodyguards.*

entrance 1. ['ɛn trəns] *n.* the right to go into a place; the right to enter a place. (No plural form in this sense.) ♦ *The heckler was refused entrance to the comedian's performance.* ♦ *We gained entrance to the concert with special passes.* **2.** ['ɛn trəns] *n.* an act of entering. ♦ *The movie star made a dramatic entrance onto the stage.* ♦ *The singer's entrance was greeted with a standing ovation.* **3.** ['ɛn trəns] *n.* the way into a room or place; the door to a room or other place. ♦ *You must come in through the back entrance of the building.* ♦ *The school's front entrance is locked after three o'clock.* **4.** [ɛn 'træns] *tv.* to charm someone; to intrigue someone. (Usually passive.) ♦ *The cat was entranced by the bird outside the window.* ♦ *Anne was entranced by the charming stranger on the train.*

entrant ['ɛn trənt] *n.* someone who takes part in a contest or competition; someone who has entered a competition. ♦ *Bill was an entrant in the pie-eating contest.* ♦ *Five entrants were disqualified because they were professionals.*

entrap [ɛn 'træp] *tv.* to trap someone or something; to lure someone or something into a trap. ♦ *The hounds entrapped the fox.* ♦ *The police entrapped the criminal in the corner of a warehouse.*

entrapment [ɛn 'træp mənt] *n.* unfairly luring someone into illegal behavior. (No plural form in this sense.) ♦ *The police officials were accused of entrapment.* ♦ *Federal agents used entrapment to catch the senator committing a crime.*

entreat [ɛn 'trit] **entreat to** *tv.* + *inf.* to beg or implore someone to do something. ♦ *The convicted criminal entreated the judge to give him a light sentence.* ♦ *The peasants entreated the prince to leave them alone.*

entreaty [ɛn 'trit i] *n.* a plea; a humble request. ♦ *The king ignored the peasants' repeated entreaties for protection* *against the invading army.* ♦ *Mary responded to my entreaty by agreeing to marry me.*

entrée ['ɑn tre] *n.* the main course of a meal. (From French.) ♦ *The entrée consisted of shrimp and lobster.* ♦ *The waiter brought the entrées to our table.*

entrench [ɛn 'trɛntʃ] *tv.* firmly established. (Usually passive.) ♦ *The troops were entrenched on the battlefield.* ♦ *The board's new policy serves only to further entrench the existing management.*

entrenchment [ɛn 'trɛntʃ mənt] *n.* establishment of a firmly held position. (No plural form in this sense.) ♦ *When under attack from all sides, the soldiers chose entrenchment over surrender.* ♦ *The book company enjoyed its firm entrenchment in the publishing field.*

entrepreneur [ɑn trə prə 'nɚ] *n.* someone who develops a business. ♦ *The entrepreneur in the international export business made a lot of money.* ♦ *The entrepreneur considered investing in the daring financial proposal.*

entrust [ɛn 'trʌst] **1. entrust with** *tv.* + *prep. phr.* to charge someone or some entity with the care of someone or something. ♦ *I entrusted the bank with my money.* ♦ *We entrusted the babysitter with our children.* **2. entrust to** *tv.* + *prep. phr.* to place someone or something in the care of someone or something. ♦ *I entrusted my money to the bank.* ♦ *Mary and Bill entrusted their children to the babysitter.*

entry ['ɛn tri] **1.** *n.* going into a place or a room. ♦ *The actress made a dramatic entry on the stage.* ♦ *The actor's grand entry caused the audience to applaud.* **2.** *n.* an entrance; the way into a room or a place. ♦ *Is there a back entry into the house?* ♦ *The entry is blocked by moving boxes.* **3.** *n.* a piece of information or data that is put into a computer, journal, database, record book, or on a list. ♦ *Jane verified the entry she made in her checking account with her bank.* ♦ *The auditor checked the entries in my journal.* **4.** *n.* the right to go into a room or place. (No plural form in this sense.) ♦ *We could not gain entry to the private clubhouse.* ♦ *Entry to the party is permitted only if you have an invitation.*

enumerate [ɪ 'num ə ret] *tv.* to make a numbered list of things or people one by one; to name things one by one. ♦ *Sam can enumerate all the presidents of the United States.* ♦ *I enumerated the main points of my speech.*

enunciate [ɪ 'nʌn si et] **1.** *tv.* to speak words clearly and distinctly; to speak words clearly so that they can be understood. ♦ *You must enunciate your lines, or the audience will never understand you.* ♦ *Please enunciate the words carefully when you are singing the song.* **2.** *iv.* to speak clearly and distinctly. ♦ *The actors enunciated well enough so everyone could understand them.* ♦ *The speaker enunciated clearly and loudly.*

enunciation [ɪ nən si 'e ʃən] *n.* the pronouncing of words. (No plural form in this sense.) ♦ *The actor's enunciation was perfect.* ♦ *My enunciation needs some improvement. People say that I mumble.*

envelop [ɛn 'vɛl əp] *tv.* to wrap around someone or something; to completely cover someone or something. ♦ *Swirling snow enveloped the hikers.* ♦ *I was enveloped by Bill's comforting hug.*

envelope ['ɛn və lop] *n.* a paper covering that letters and documents are placed in for mailing. ♦ *I folded the letter and put it in an envelope.* ♦ *I put a stamp on the envelope and mailed it.*

enviable ['ɛn vi ə bəl] *adj.* worthy of envy; desirable. (Adv: *enviably.*) ♦ *The class president was in an enviable position to influence the administration.* ♦ *Sue's high-paying job placed her in an enviable situation.*

envious ['ɛn vi əs] *adj.* feeling envy; wanting something that someone else has. (Adv: *enviously.*) ♦ *I don't like to have envious feelings about others.* ♦ *The envious boy wanted his brother's bicycle.*

environment [ɛn 'vɑɪ rən mənt] **1.** *n.* the state and nature of the immediate surroundings. ♦ *I don't feel safe in this dangerous environment.* ♦ *The work environment at this factory is unhealthy.* **2.** *n.* a living organism's natural surroundings. ♦ *At the modern zoo, you can see each animal in its natural environment.* ♦ *The deer were free to roam within their typical environment.* **3. the environment** *n.* the natural realm including the atmosphere, oceans, lands, and all creatures. (No plural form in this sense. Treated as singular.) ♦ *Using too much water is said to harm the environment.* ♦ *We will all work to produce a clean and healthy environment.*

environmental [ɛn vɑɪ rən 'mɛn təl] *adj.* of or about the environment. (Adv: *environmentally.*) ♦ *The oil spill was an environmental disaster.* ♦ *The environmental damage caused by factories cannot be ignored.*

environmentalist [ɛn vɑɪ rən 'mɛn tə ləst] *n.* someone who advocates actions that protect the environment. ♦ *The environmentalists fought to save endangered species.* ♦ *Environmentalists helped clean up after the oil spill.*

environs [ɛn 'vɑɪ rənz] **1.** *n.* surroundings; environment. (Treated as plural.) ♦ *Our environs were unsafe, so we moved to a safer neighborhood.* ♦ *The workers cleared the environs of all debris.* **2.** *n.* suburbs; the smaller towns that surround a city. (Treated as plural.) ♦ *The subway serves the city and its adjacent environs.* ♦ *The weather forecaster predicted snow for Chicago and its environs.*

envisage [ɛn 'vɪz ɪdʒ] *tv.* to visualize or foresee something. ♦ *As I stood in front of a mirror, I envisaged myself as a movie star.* ♦ *Susan envisaged her graduation day.*

envision [ɛn 'vɪ ʒən] *tv.* to imagine something; to see in the mind what something will be like. ♦ *I tried to envision what Sue would look like in 10 years.* ♦ *The owner of the business envisioned making a fortune in the coming years.*

envoy ['ɑn vɔɪ] *n.* a messenger, especially someone sent by one government to another government. (From French.) ♦ *A special envoy to the Middle East carried an important message from the president.* ♦ *The envoy traveled regularly to foreign countries.*

envy ['ɛn vi] **1.** *n.* a negative feeling toward someone who has someone or something that one wants. (No plural form in this sense.) ♦ *I felt a great deal of envy when Mary got the job I wanted.* ♦ *Tom tried to ignore his feelings of envy when Bill bought a new car.* **2.** *tv.* to have a negative feeling toward someone who has someone or something that one wants. ♦ *Do you envy the rich?* ♦ *I envy people who drive expensive cars.* **3. green with envy** *idiom* envious; jealous. ♦ *When Sally saw me with Tom, she turned green with envy. She likes him a lot.* ♦ *I feel green with envy whenever I see you in your new car.*

enzyme ['ɛn zɑɪm] *n.* a chemical protein that helps bring about a change in plants or animals without being changed itself; a protein that is a catalyst. ♦ *Enzymes are a type of protein.* ♦ *Certain enzymes help us digest our food.*

ephemeral [ɪ 'fɛm ə rəl] *adj.* short-lived; lasting only a short time. (Adv: *ephemerally.*) ♦ *Life is so ephemeral. It goes by so quickly.* ♦ *Our relationship has been more than ephemeral.*

epic ['ɛp ɪk] **1.** *n.* a long narrative poem, especially one that describes the adventures of heroes and gods. ♦ The Iliad *is a Greek epic.* ♦ *We read a Scandinavian epic in literature class.* **2.** *adj.* of great size. ♦ *The newspaper reported a scandal of epic proportions.* ♦ *We crossed the desert on our epic journey.*

epidemic [ɛp ə 'dɛm ɪk] **1.** *n.* a disease that spreads very rapidly from person to person. ♦ *The epidemic killed thousands of people.* ♦ *The Black Plague was an epidemic in the Middle Ages.* **2.** *adj.* <the adj. use of ①.> (Adv: *epidemically* [...ɪk li].) ♦ *The disease quickly reached epidemic proportions.* ♦ *The epidemic sickness terrified everyone.* **3.** *adj.* spreading rapidly like ①. (Figurative on ②. Adv: *epidemically* [...ɪk li].) ♦ *Hysteria became epidemic and there was nearly a riot.* ♦ *Fear was epidemic, and people ran screaming in the streets.*

epilepsy ['ɛp ə lɛp si] *n.* a disorder of the nervous system having symptoms ranging from loss of attention to convulsions. (No plural form in this sense.) ♦ *Proper medication can help control epilepsy.* ♦ *John experienced convulsions in his episodes of epilepsy.*

epileptic [ɛp ə 'lɛp tɪk] **1.** *adj.* of, for, or about epilepsy; caused by epilepsy. (Adv: *epileptically* [...ɪk li].) ♦ *John's medicine helped prevent severe epileptic seizures.* ♦ *A variety of epileptic medications provide relief from the disorder.* **2.** *adj.* having epilepsy. (Adv: *epileptically* [...ɪk li].) ♦ *My cousin is epileptic and takes medicine every day to prevent seizures.* ♦ *The epileptic patient asked her doctor for more information about the disorder.* **3.** *n.* someone who suffers from epilepsy. ♦ *John has been an epileptic for many years.* ♦ *The hospital developed a special program for epileptics.*

epilogue AND **epilog** ['ɛp ə lɔg] *n.* a concluding part added to the end of a novel or a play. ♦ *The murderer's name was revealed in the mystery's epilogue.* ♦ *The epilogue was written after the author's death.*

Episcopal AND **Episcopalian** [ə 'pɪs kə pəl, ə pɪs kə 'pel jən] *adj.* of or about the Episcopalian Church in America. ♦ *Mary and Bill were married by an Episcopal priest.* ♦ *I attended an Episcopal service on Easter Sunday.*

Episcopalian [ə pɪs kə 'pel jən] **1.** *n.* someone who is a member of the Episcopalian Church in America. ♦ *Most of the people in this neighborhood are Episcopalians.* ♦ *Presidents who were Episcopalians include George Washington and George Bush.* **2.** *adj.* Episcopal.

episode ['ɛp ə sod] **1.** *n.* one thing that is part of a series; one incident; a separate event. ♦ *The witness related the entire episode to the jury.* ♦ *The long lecture I got from my boss was an episode I did not want to undergo a second time.* **2.** *n.* one radio or television program out of a series; a fully developed story in a series of stories or a novel. ♦ *Let's watch another episode of* Life Can Be Beautiful. ♦ *I missed Tuesday night's episode of the television police drama.*

epitaph ['ɛp i tæf] *n.* a statement written on someone's gravestone. ♦ *Bill's epitaph humorously read, "I told you I was sick."* ♦ *I don't want a lengthy epitaph carved on my headstone.*

epitome [ə 'pɪt ə mi] *n.* the typical example; someone or something that exhibits many characteristics of a specified class. (No plural form in this sense.) ♦ *Bob is the epitome of charm and attractiveness. He should be the emcee for the talent show.* ♦ *Lisa is the epitome of intelligence. She can help us solve our problem.*

epitomize [ə 'pɪt ə mɑɪz] *tv.* to exemplify something; to exhibit many characteristics of a specified class. ♦ *The work you've done on this report epitomizes sloppiness and ignorance!* ♦ *The court case epitomized everything I respect in the legal system.*

epoxy [ɪ 'pɑk si] *n.* a strong synthetic adhesive. (No plural form in this sense.) ♦ *Use epoxy to repair the broken cup.* ♦ *I need some epoxy to mend the cracked dish.*

equal ['i kwəl] **1.** *adj.* the same as someone or something; in the same amount or degree. (Adv: *equally.*) ♦ *Put an equal amount of sugar into both bowls.* ♦ *The union required equal pay for equal work.* **2.** *tv.* to be the same as someone or something else; to have the same amount or degree of something as someone or something else. ♦ *Two plus three equals five.* ♦ *Three plus one does not equal six. It equals four.* **3.** *n.* a person who is on the same level as someone else—in social standing, in productivity, in rank, etc.; a peer. ♦ *Bill and Mary are equals at the office, and they report to the same supervisor.* ♦ *When it comes to getting work done quickly and efficiently, my secretary has no equal.*

equality [ɪ 'kwɑl ə ti] *n.* the condition of having the same amount or degree of something as someone or something else. (No plural form in this sense.) ♦ *There was no equality in the funding of school districts across the state. Poor districts suffered terribly.* ♦ *I believe in equality for all people.*

equalize ['i kwə lɑɪz] *tv.* to cause something to equal something else. ♦ *Bob equalized the amount of soup in the bowls he was filling.* ♦ *It is difficult to equalize the work at my office.*

equalizer ['i kwə lɑɪz ɚ] *n.* a complex electronic control for adjusting the loudness of various bands of the sound spectrum. ♦ *My stereo has an equalizer that can increase the bass and decrease the mid-range frequencies.* ♦ *Mary has an equalizer on her car radio which makes it sound like a home stereo system.*

equally ['i kwə li] *adv.* in the same way; at the same level or degree; as much as; the same as. ♦ *Bob and Sally treat their children equally.* ♦ *We will share the candy equally among ourselves.*

equanimity [ɛ kwə 'nɪm ə ti] *n.* emotional stability; composure. (No plural form in this sense.) ♦ *Jane's equanimity during her brother's funeral was impressive.* ♦ *Bill showed a great deal of equanimity during the crisis.*

equate [ɪ 'kwet] **equate with** *tv.* + *prep. phr.* to consider something to be equal; to think of something as the same as something else. ♦ *Do you equate money with happiness? They are different, you know.* ♦ *Our teacher equates talking in class with being late. They both result in a scolding.*

equation [ɪ 'kwe ʒən] *n.* a statement showing that two amounts are equal. ♦ *In an equation, the "=" symbol is used to mean "is equal to."* ♦ *5 + 4 = 9 is a simple equation.*

equator [ɪ 'kwet ɚ] *n.* the imaginary line around the middle of the earth (or any planet); halfway between the north and south poles. ♦ *The weather is warmer near the equator.* ♦ *The ship sailed across the equator.*

equatorial [ɛ kwə 'tor ɪ əl] *adj.* of or about the equator. (Adv: *equatorially.*) ♦ *I found the equatorial sun much hotter than I had expected.* ♦ *Equatorial weather is usually hot and humid.*

equestrian [ɪ 'kwɛs tri ən] **1.** *n.* someone who rides horses. ♦ *Anne is an award-winning equestrian.* ♦ *The equestrian fell off his horse.* **2.** *adj.* <the adj. use of ①.> ♦ *There is a safe equestrian crossing halfway down the street.* ♦ *Jane won a prize in the equestrian competition.*

equidistant [i kwɪ 'dɪs tənt] *adj.* being the same distance from one point as from another; equally near or far. (Adv: *equidistantly.*) ♦ *The shopping center is equidistant from my office and my house.* ♦ *Look on the map and see if these locations are equidistant.*

equilibrium [i kwə 'lɪb ri əm] *n.* balance; the condition of being completely balanced. (No plural form in this sense.) ♦ *The gymnast has perfect equilibrium.* ♦ *Bill's equilibrium was impaired after he drank alcohol.*

equip [ɪ 'kwɪp] **1. equip with** *tv.* + *prep. phr.* to provide someone with the necessary supplies. ♦ *The campers were equipped with sleeping bags and tents.* ♦ *The manager equipped each worker with a cellular telephone.* **2. equip with** *tv.* + *prep. phr.* to provide something with accessories or attachments. ♦ *The television was not equipped with a remote control.* ♦ *The manufacturer had equipped our car with seat belts.*

equipment [ɪ 'kwɪp mənt] *n.* things that are furnished or supplied, especially the tools and supplies needed to do a job. (No plural form in this sense. Number is expressed with *piece(s) of equipment.*) ♦ *Bill lacked the proper equipment to fix the faucet.* ♦ *Do you have the equipment you need to repair the photocopier?*

equitable ['ɛ kwə tə bəl] *adj.* fair; just. (Adv: *equitably.*) ♦ *Twenty dollars is an equitable price for this lamp.* ♦ *The workers staged a strike for equitable pay.*

equity ['ɛ kwə ti] **1.** *n.* fairness; the quality of not being partial. (No plural form in this sense.) ♦ *The verdict was based on fairness and equity for both parties.* ♦ *Bill mediated the matter with the equity of a judge.* **2.** *n.* the amount that an asset is worth, less money that is owed for it. (No plural form in this sense.) ♦ *Do you have any equity in the house?* ♦ *Our equity in the property is not worth much.* **3. equities** *n.* stock or shares in a company as opposed to bonds. ♦ *Equities are doing better than bonds at this time.* ♦ *The prices of equities have fallen a great deal in the last year.*

equivalent [ɪ 'kwɪv ə lənt] *adj.* same; equal in level or degree. (Adv: *equivalently.*) ♦ *Both of them expressed their agreement with equivalent statements.* ♦ *My donations to both charities were equivalent.*

equivocal [ɪ 'kwɪv ə kəl] *adj.* ambiguous; vague; having more than one meaning. (Adv: *equivocally* [ɪ 'kwɪv ə kli].) ♦ *The confusing movie had an equivocal ending.* ♦ *John's comment was purposely equivocal so we would have no idea what he really thinks.*

equivocate [ɪ 'kwɪv ə ket] *iv.* to say something with a double meaning in order to hide the truth; to mislead someone by being vague or ambiguous. ♦ *Don't equivocate! Just tell me the truth.* ♦ *If you equivocate on the witness stand, you might be charged with perjury.*

-er 1. *suffix* <a form that marks the comparative of many adjectives and adverbs.> (Examples: *nearer, redder, smarter, tastier, wider.*) **2.** *suffix* <a suffix used to form nouns from verbs, resulting in a noun that means a doer of the action of the verb.> (Examples: *abstainer, babysitter, caller, dealer, farmer.*)

era ['ɛr ə] *n.* a period of time characterized in a particular way. ♦ *Charles Dickens wrote novels about the social conditions in the early part of the Industrial Era.* ♦ *In the United States, the last years of the 1960s were an era of civil unrest and turmoil.*

eradicate [ɪ 'ræd ə ket] *tv.* to completely get rid of or destroy someone or something. ♦ *I will eradicate poverty from the face of the earth!* ♦ *The mayor wanted to eradicate crime within five years.*

erase [ɪ 'res] **1.** *tv.* to remove something written or drawn in pencil, ink, or chalk by rubbing it with an eraser. ♦ *Please erase that word from the chalkboard.* ♦ *Bill erased his mistake before turning in his assignment.* **2.** *tv.* to wipe something, such as a chalkboard, clean by removing the writing on it. ♦ *Please erase the blackboard.* ♦ *I need to erase the chalkboard before class.* **3.** *tv.* to remove something completely. (Figurative on ①.) ♦ *Jane tried to erase the scary thoughts from her memory.* ♦ *Bob couldn't erase the nightmares from his dreams.*

eraser [ɪ 'res ɚ] *n.* a small rubber object that rubs out pencil markings; a rectangular block of felt that rubs out chalk markings. ♦ *Use the eraser to clean the blackboard.* ♦ *Jane borrowed my pencil eraser.*

erect [ɪ 'rɛkt] **1.** *adj.* standing straight up; upright. (Adv: *erectly.*) ♦ *Stately, erect poplars lined both sides of the road.* ♦ *The erect model had excellent posture.* **2.** *tv.* to build something. ♦ *The workers required only a year to erect the new skyscraper.* ♦ *Jimmy and his friends erected a tree house.* **3.** *tv.* to cause something to stand upright. ♦ *The citizens erected a flagpole in the town square.* ♦ *The company I work for erected a statue in memory of its founder.* **4.** *adv.* upright; straight up. ♦ *John always walks very erect.* ♦ *Please sit erect and look interested during the lecture, no matter how dull it is.*

erection [ɪ 'rɛk ʃən] **1.** *n.* something that has been constructed, especially a building. (No plural form in this sense.) ♦ *The skyscraper's erection was funded by bank loans.* ♦ *The erection of the building was completed in record time.* **2.** *n.* a stiff penis, usually due to sexual arousal. ♦ *The monkeys in the zoo were always getting erections.* ♦ *All male mammals get erections when they mate.*

erode [ɪ 'rod] **1.** *tv.* to wear something away gradually; to rub something away gradually. ♦ *A constant stream of water eroded the rock mountain.* ♦ *Strong winds eroded the shoreline.* **2.** *iv.* to become worn away; to become rubbed away. ♦ *The coastline eroded gradually.* ♦ *The epitaph on the gravestone eroded over time.*

erosion [ɪ 'ro ʒən] **1.** *n.* the gradual destruction of rock or land by the action of wind and water. (No plural form in this sense.) ♦ *The erosion of the shoreline ruined the beach.* ♦ *Erosion of the soil made the farmer's land less valuable.* **2.** *n.* the breaking down or diminishing of something gradually. (No plural form in this sense. Figurative on ①.) ♦ *Tom experienced an erosion of faith and stopped going to church.* ♦ *Jane and Tom worked hard to prevent the erosion of their marriage.*

erotic [ɛ 'rɑt ɪk] *adj.* [of something] portraying or stimulating sexual responses. (Adv: *erotically* [...ɪk li].) ♦ *One of our cable channels shows erotic movies at night.* ♦ *I borrowed an erotic novel from the library.*

err [ɛr, ɚ] *iv.* to make a mistake; to be wrong. ♦ *I erred when making the calculation.* ♦ *Bill erred when he said Detroit is the capital of Michigan.*

errand ['ɛr ənd] **1.** *n.* a small task that someone goes someplace to do or is sent someplace to do. ♦ *The manager sent David on an errand across town.* ♦ *We do all of our errands on Saturday.* **2. run an errand** *idiom* to perform ①. ♦ *I have to run an errand and I will be back soon.* ♦ *Will you run an errand for me?*

erratic [ɛ 'ræt ɪk] *adj.* not regular; irregular; uneven. (Adv: *erratically* [...ɪk li].) ♦ *Mary's behavior becomes erratic when she drinks alcohol.* ♦ *Bill's erratic moods upset everyone in our office.*

erroneous [ɛ 'ron i əs] *adj.* mistaken; having errors; wrong. (Adv: *erroneously.*) ♦ *The so-called facts you gave me were totally erroneous.* ♦ *The boss looked upset after reading the erroneous report.*

error ['ɛr ɚ] **1.** *n.* a mistake; something that is wrong. ♦ *Jane made an error on her tax return.* ♦ *The teacher corrected the errors in Bill's term paper.* **2.** *n.* a bad play by someone on a baseball team. ♦ *The shortstop made an error that cost the team the game.* ♦ *The coach replaced the outfielder who had made three errors.*

erstwhile ['ərst ʍaɪl] *adj.* former; previous; in the past. ♦ *My erstwhile friends have achieved great success in their respective fields.* ♦ *The mayor was an erstwhile companion of mine.*

erudite ['ɛr ju dɑɪt] *adj.* intelligent; learned and exclusive; educated. (Adv: *eruditely.*) ♦ *One of the more erudite students was chosen as valedictorian.* ♦ *Anne gave an erudite speech about life in Paris.*

erudition [ɛr ju 'dɪ ʃən] *n.* intelligence gained from schooling; learning. (No plural form in this sense.) ♦ *Erudition is a fine quality in a professor.* ♦ *Mike's erudition makes him seem quite haughty.*

erupt [ɪ 'rʌpt] **1.** *iv.* [for a volcano] to explode. ♦ *The volcano erupted violently.* ♦ *We feared that the volcano would erupt again.* **2.** *iv.* [for anger, violence, arguments, etc.] to be released suddenly. ♦ *A fight erupted in the park and the police were called.* ♦ *We were afraid that violence would erupt again, so we left.* **3. erupt in; erupt with** *iv.* + *prep. phr.* to break out in a rash. ♦ *My body erupts with hives if I eat chocolate.* ♦ *John's face erupted in a rash due to the heat.*

eruption [ɪ 'rʌp ʃən] **1.** *n.* an explosive outburst of a volcano. ♦ *An eruption of the volcano threw the citizens into a panic.* ♦ *This is the forth eruption this year.* **2.** *n.* a bursting forth of anger, violence, fighting, etc. ♦ *Small eruptions of fighting occurred here and there after the rebels attacked.* ♦ *Lisa's eruption of anger shocked all of us.*

-es *suffix* <a form that marks the plural in certain English nouns.> (Used with nouns ending in *ch, s, sh, x,* or *z.* Compare with -s. Examples: *boxes, bushes, classes, gases, masses, witches.*)

escalate ['ɛs kə let] **1.** *tv.* to cause a problem to get worse; to cause the intensity of a problem to increase. ♦ *An assassination attempt escalated the tension between the two countries.* ♦ *As the election drew nearer, the candidates escalated their attacks against each other.* **2.** *iv.* [for intensity or magnitude] to increase. ♦ *Tension escalated as the hostage crisis worsened.* ♦ *Fighting escalated on both fronts.*

escalator ['ɛs kə let ɚ] *n.* a moving staircase that carries people to a higher or lower floor of a building. ♦ *I rode up the escalator to the department store.* ♦ *Please do not bring baby carriages onto the escalator.*

escapade ['ɛs kə ped] *n.* a wild adventure; an exciting incident, often involving breaking rules. ♦ *The three friends skipped school and went on a silly escapade.* ♦ *The soldiers were punished for their wild escapades in town.*

escape [ɛ 'skep] **1.** *n.* getting free of someone or something; getting out of a dangerous place, an enclosed place, or a bad situation. (No plural form in this sense.) ♦ *As he sat in his prison cell, escape was always on his mind.* ♦ *Escape is the goal of every trapped animal.* **2.** *n.* something that relieves boredom. (No plural form in this sense.) ♦ *I read fantasy books as an escape from my dull life.* ♦ *This vacation was my escape from the city.* **3.** *n.* fleeing a dangerous place, an enclosed place, or a bad situation. ♦ *The prisoners of war made a daring escape from their captors.* ♦ *The hostage knew that an escape was impossible.* **4.** *iv.* to become free; to get away. ♦ *The prisoners escaped when it was very dark.* ♦ *My birds escaped when I accidentally left their cage open.* **5.** *iv.* to leak out from a container. ♦ *A trickle of milk escaped from the damaged carton.* ♦ *Deadly carbon monoxide escaped from the broken furnace.* **6.** *iv.* to elude being caught; to avoid being caught. ♦ *The robbers escaped during the chaos after the robbery.* ♦ *I escaped even though the bully was right behind me most of the way.* **7.** *tv.* to avoid or elude someone or something. ♦ *In order to escape capture, I hid in a cornfield.* ♦ *The robber escaped the police by running very fast.* **8.** *tv.* to avoid being seen, heard, remembered, etc. ♦ *I escaped the notice of the guard at the door and went in.* ♦ *Tom's address has escaped my memory.*

escaped [ɛ 'skept] *adj.* having become free; having gotten away from someone or someplace, without being noticed or caught. ♦ *The escaped prisoner hid in an abandoned barn.* ♦ *A reporter interviewed the escaped hostage.*

escapism [ɛ 'skep ɪz əm] *n.* avoiding reality or boredom by doing something or fantasizing. (No plural form in this sense.) ♦ *Television is Dave's prime means of escapism.* ♦ *Escapism eases the stresses of our everyday lives.*

eschew [ɛs 'tʃu] *tv.* to shun someone or something; to avoid associating with someone or something. ♦ *Bill eschewed the rude behavior of his older brother.* ♦ *Jane eschews both alcohol and tobacco.*

escort 1. ['ɛ skort] *n.* someone who accompanies someone else as a companion. ♦ *I didn't want to go to the party unless I had an escort.* ♦ *My escort got sick two days before the dance.* **2.** [ɛ 'skort] *tv.* to accompany someone else; to guide someone; to lead someone; to guard someone.

♦ *A bodyguard escorted the celebrity around town.* ♦ *Bill escorted Mary to the prom.*

Eskimo ['ɛ skə mo] **1.** *n.* an Amerindian of the arctic areas of northern Canada and Alaska, Greenland, and northeast Asia. (The Eskimos of the New World and Greenland refer to themselves as Inuit, which means 'the people.' Pl in *-s.*) ♦ *Many Eskimos live in igloos.* ♦ *Our guide on the Alaskan journey was an Eskimo.* **2.** *adj.* <the adj. use of ①.> ♦ *Most Eskimo people get their food and clothing from sea mammals.* ♦ *The Eskimo hunters built shelters from blocks of snow.*

esophagus [ɪ 'sɑf ə gəs] *n.* the tube that carries food from the throat to the stomach. ♦ *John choked when a chicken bone got caught in his esophagus.* ♦ *The doctor performed an emergency operation on John's esophagus.*

esoteric [ɛs ə 'tɛr ɪk] *adj.* [of a topic or issue] understandable only to people who are already familiar with the topic being discussed. (Adv: *esoterically* [...ɪk li].) ♦ *The esoteric article baffled the general readers, even though it was perfectly clear to the specialists.* ♦ *The professor tried to explain the esoteric essay to his class.*

especially [ɛ 'spɛʃ ə li] *adv.* mainly; chiefly; primarily; particularly. ♦ *John is especially proud of his children.* ♦ *I like all kinds of food, especially pizza and fried chicken.*

Esperanto [ɛs pə 'rɑn to] *n.* an artificial language based on a number of European languages. (No plural form in this sense.) ♦ *In Esperanto, all nouns end in "-o".* ♦ *A Polish physician invented Esperanto.*

espionage ['ɛs pi ə nɑʒ] *n.* the use of spies to get secret information; the work of spies. (No plural form in this sense.) ♦ *The spies received lengthy prison terms for espionage.* ♦ *Tom committed industrial espionage for his corporation.*

espouse [ɛ 'spɑʊz] *tv.* to undertake to support a belief or a cause. ♦ *I do not espouse your beliefs on the death penalty.* ♦ *The principal espoused the proposal for a dress code.*

espresso [ɛ 'sprɛs o] **1.** *n.* very strong, concentrated black coffee. (No plural form in this sense. From Italian.) ♦ *Mary served us some espresso after dinner.* ♦ *A café that serves espresso has opened up down the street.* **2.** *n.* a cup of ①. (Pl in *-s.*) ♦ *I had an espresso and a muffin for breakfast.* ♦ *Lisa put quite a lot of sugar in her espresso.*

essay ['ɛs e] *n.* a composition about a specific topic. ♦ *The student wrote an essay on nuclear weapons.* ♦ *Your essay contains far too many mistakes.*

essayist ['ɛs e əst] *n.* someone who writes essays. ♦ *The newspaper editor is also a well-known essayist.* ♦ *Ralph Waldo Emerson was a famous essayist and poet.*

essence ['ɛs əns] **1.** *n.* the most important part of something; the important features that make up someone or something. (No plural form in this sense.) ♦ *Do you understand the essence of this novel?* ♦ *The foreign movie star had an exotic essence about his speech and mannerisms.* **2.** *n.* a perfume or a cologne. ♦ *This essence reminds me of wildflowers.* ♦ *Anne placed a drop of the essence behind her ears.* **3. in essence** *idiom* basically; essentially. ♦ *I have lots of detailed advice for you, but in essence, I want you to do the best you can.* ♦ *In essence, lightning is just a giant spark of electricity.*

essential [ɪ 'sɛn ʃəl] **1.** *adj.* necessary; needed. (Adv: *essentially.*) ♦ *Do you have the essential piece needed to repair the air conditioner?* ♦ *It is essential that you phone me as soon as you arrive home.* **2.** *adj.* basic; constituting the nature or foundation of something. (Adv: *essentially.*) ♦ *Cells are an essential structure in living organisms.* ♦ *Oxygen and hydrogen are the essential elements in water.* **3. essentials** *n.* the basic and necessary elements. ♦ *I will deal only with the essentials in my discussion.* ♦ *I didn't bring every tool I own, only the essentials.*

essentially [ɪ 'sɛn ʃə li] **1.** *adv.* more this characteristic than another. ♦ *I trust Mary because she is an essentially honest person.* ♦ *Bob is essentially hardworking even if he is late occasionally.* **2.** *adv.* necessarily; basically. ♦ *Essentially, I need more sleep than most people.* ♦ *Tom is essentially lazy.*

-est *suffix* <a form that marks the superlative of many adjectives and adverbs.> (Examples: *fastest, happiest, longest, narrowest, sweetest.*)

establish [ɛ 'stæb lɪʃ] **1.** *tv.* to start an organization; to found an organization. ♦ *Three former college friends joined together to establish a computer company.* ♦ *The college established a scholarship for poor students.* **2.** *tv.* to start something, such as a policy or plan. ♦ *The hospital established new procedures regarding admission.* ♦ *The head of personnel established a rigid policy regarding absences.* **3.** *tv.* to place oneself or itself as something or in a specific role. (Takes a reflexive object.) ♦ *The company established itself as a good employer.* ♦ *Bill established himself as head of the new division.* **4.** *tv.* to prove something; to determine the truth of something. ♦ *Can you establish the truth of that statement?* ♦ *Jane established her identity for the police officer.*

establishment [ɛ 'stæb lɪʃ mənt] **1.** *n.* establishing something. (No plural form in this sense.) ♦ *I believe in the establishment of good housing for everyone.* ♦ *The establishment of the United States of America occurred in 1776.* **2.** *n.* a company or organization. ♦ *How long have you worked at this establishment?* ♦ *The establishment I work for provides medical and dental insurance.* **3. the establishment** *n.* the elite class of people who control politics, government, or society. (No plural form in this sense. Treated as singular. Sometimes capitalized.) ♦ *Members of the establishment urged the mayor to run for governor.* ♦ *The activists protested against The Establishment.*

estate [ɛ 'stet] **1.** *n.* everything that someone owns; the property of someone who has just died. ♦ *All of Bill's relatives made claims on his estate after he died.* ♦ *My accountant estimated the value of my estate.* **2.** *n.* a house and related buildings set on a large piece of property. ♦ *My grandparents' estate includes stables, a pool, and a forest.* ♦ *The rich couple live at an estate in the country.*

esteem [ɛ 'stim] **1.** *n.* opinion or regard, favorable unless indicated otherwise. (No plural form in this sense.) ♦ *My manager holds me in the highest esteem as an employee.* ♦ *I have a great deal of esteem for my parents.* **2.** *tv.* to have a very good opinion of someone; to respect someone deeply. ♦ *Jane esteems Mary above all others as her friend.* ♦ *The committee greatly esteems your work on this project.*

esteemed [ɛ 'stimd] *adj.* respected; held in high regard. ♦ *The senator said, "I give the floor to my esteemed col-*

league." ♦ Dr. Smith is an esteemed physician in our community.

esthetic [ɛs 'θɛt ɪk] See aesthetic.

estimate 1. ['est ə mət] *n.* a preliminary calculation of an amount. ♦ *I made a quick estimate of the cost of the groceries in my cart.* ♦ *Do you have an estimate of the value of your car?* **2.** ['est ə mət] *n.* a statement that shows about how much someone will charge to do a certain amount of work. ♦ *The mechanic gave Jane an estimate for the car repairs.* ♦ *The carpenter handed Dave an estimate for the kitchen renovations.* **3.** ['est ə met] *tv.* an opinion about someone or something. (Takes a clause.) ♦ *Mary estimates that she will win the contest.* ♦ *I estimate that Tom will be promoted to department manager.* **4.** ['est ə met] *tv.* to calculate how much something will cost; to determine an approximate figure. ♦ *Can you estimate what the sales tax will be on these items?* ♦ *I estimate the cost at $4,000.*

estimation [est ə 'me ʃən] *n.* one's opinion or judgment. (No plural form in this sense.) ♦ *In my estimation, the cheaters should be expelled from school.* ♦ *What is your estimation of the problem we are facing?*

Estonia [ɛs 'ton i ə] See Gazetteer.

estranged [ɛ 'strendʒd] *adj.* alienated; separated. ♦ *John reconciled with his estranged wife.* ♦ *My parents are estranged and live in different apartments.*

estrogen ['ɛ strə dʒən] *n.* a hormone that maintains female body characteristics. (No plural form in this sense.) ♦ *The physician prescribed estrogen for Jane.* ♦ *Estrogen is used in some important medications.*

etc. See et cetera.

et cetera [ɛt 'sɛt ɚ ə] *adv.* and so on; and the rest. (Abbreviated *etc.* From Latin for 'and other things.' Used at the end of a list to indicate the presence of further examples.) ♦ *Bob studied Slavic languages, including Czech, Polish, Russian, etc.* ♦ *When you go camping, don't forget to bring your equipment, such as a backpack, a sleeping bag, a flashlight, etc.*

etch ['ɛtʃ] **1.** *tv.* to cut into a surface. ♦ *Sand blown by the wind etched into the painted surface.* ♦ *Tom used a strong acid to etch the glass.* **2. etch onto** *tv.* + *prep. phr.* to carve letters or a picture into a metal plate. (Ink is put on the metal plate, and the plate is pressed onto paper or canvas.) ♦ *Jane etched a complex design onto the plate.* ♦ *The carver etched the message backwards onto the sheet of copper.*

etching ['ɛtʃ ɪŋ] *n.* a picture that is made by placing paper over a metal plate covered with ink that has an image etched into it. ♦ *Jane's etchings were displayed at the art show.* ♦ *Mike has an etching of the plaque on Shakespeare's tomb.*

eternal [ɪ 'tɚ nəl] *adj.* without ending; existing forever. (Adv: *eternally.*) ♦ *The bride and groom pledged their eternal love to each other.* ♦ *Parents share an eternal bond with their children.*

eternity [ɪ 'tɚ nə ti] **1.** *n.* time without beginning or end. (No plural form in this sense.) ♦ *The minister said that God exists throughout eternity.* ♦ *I felt this boring movie would last for eternity.* **2.** *n.* the endless time after one's death. (No plural form in this sense.) ♦ *The patient dying of cancer looked forward to a peaceful eternity.* ♦ *The evangelist preached to the congregation about the happiness they would experience in eternity.*

ethereal [ɪ 'θɪr ɪ əl] **1.** *adj.* heavenly; celestial. (Adv: *ethereally.*) ♦ *The artist captured the model's ethereal beauty on canvas.* ♦ *We entered the cathedral and found there an incredible ethereal experience.* **2.** *adj.* light and airy; fragile and imaginary. (Adv: *ethereally.*) ♦ *The troubled child lived in an ethereal world of his imagination.* ♦ *Mary saw ethereal shapes and faces in the clouds.*

ethic ['ɛθ ɪk] **1.** *n.* the body of morals governing a person or a group. (No plural form in this sense.) ♦ *I only hire employees with a strong work ethic.* ♦ *Dishonesty is not part of Mary's personal ethic.* **2. ethics** *n.* the standards of right and wrong within a society. (Treated as plural.) ♦ *The judge's ethics were unquestionable.* ♦ *Lisa has very high ethics.* **3. ethics** *n.* the study of the standards of right and wrong; the study of morals. (Treated as singular.) ♦ *The philosophy department offered a course in ethics.* ♦ *I wrote an essay on morality for my class in ethics.*

ethical ['ɛθ ɪ kəl] **1.** *adj.* of or about ethics. (Adv: *ethically* [...ɪk li].) ♦ *The Smiths taught their children many important ethical principles.* ♦ *The philosopher studied the ethical implications of war.* **2.** *adj.* right; moral; in accordance with moral principles. (Adv: *ethically* [...ɪk li].) ♦ *I questioned whether John's behavior was ethical.* ♦ *Returning the money is the only ethical course of action.* **3.** *adj.* according to the rules of one's profession. (Adv: *ethically* [...ɪk li].) ♦ *John was barred from practicing law because his conduct as a lawyer was not ethical.* ♦ *The doctor taught the medical students about the ethical treatment of patients.*

Ethiopia [i θi 'o pi ə] See Gazetteer.

ethnic ['ɛθ nɪk] *adj.* of or about a particular variety, group, or subgroup of people, such as divisions along racial, national, or linguistic lines. (Adv: *ethnically* [...ɪk li].) ♦ *The largest ethnic group represents the Italians, followed by the Mexicans.* ♦ *The chef prepared many ethnic dishes.*

ethnic group ['ɛθ nɪk 'grup] *n.* a subdivision of human types representing differences in culture, language, and religion. ♦ *Many different ethnic groups can be found in the United States.* ♦ *People from India form an important ethnic group in Trinidad.*

etiology [i ti 'ɑl ə dʒi] *n.* the origin or cause of a disease. ♦ *The scientists are baffled by the etiology of the virus.* ♦ *Dr. Smith's innovative article describes the etiology of diabetes.*

etiquette ['ɛt ə kɪt] *n.* the rules of good manners; proper or appropriate behavior. (No plural form in this sense.) ♦ *Etiquette demands that you use different forks for different parts of a formally served meal.* ♦ *I consulted a book of etiquette before I attended the formal dance.*

etymology [ɛt ə 'mɑl ə dʒi] **1.** *n.* the study of the linguistic changes in words through history. (No plural form in this sense.) ♦ *The linguist wrote a book on etymology in the English language.* ♦ *While studying etymology, I saw how many English words are related to German.* **2.** *n.* an explanation of the origin of a word; the derivation of a word. ♦ *Where can I find the etymology of the word* dictionary? ♦ *Unabridged dictionaries provide the etymologies of most entry words.*

eulogize ['jul ə dʒɑɪz] *tv.* to honor someone who has died by presenting a formal statement of praise. ♦ *Mary eulogized her former colleague at a private service.* ♦ *Bill eulogized his father at his funeral.*

eulogy ['jul ə dʒi] *n.* a statement of praise, especially for someone who has just died. ♦ *Tom read the eulogy with great emotion.* ♦ *The minister's eulogy was very sad.*

euphemism ['ju fə mɪz əm] *n.* a word or phrase that replaces a less polite or more harsh word or expression. ♦ Large *is a word often used as a euphemism for the word* fat. ♦ *Tom used the word* fragrant *as a euphemism for the word* smelly.

euphemistic [ju fə 'mɪs tɪk] *adj.* showing or exhibiting euphemism. (Adv: *euphemistically* [...ɪk li].) ♦ *To be polite, John used a euphemistic expression.* ♦ *To use the word* chubby *instead of* fat *is to speak in a euphemistic way.*

euphoria [ju 'for i ə] *n.* a feeling of total happiness. (No plural form in this sense.) ♦ *I felt complete euphoria when the real-estate agent handed me the keys to my new house.* ♦ *I cannot describe the euphoria I felt when my daughter was born.*

Eurasia [jɚ 'e ʒə] See Gazetteer.

Eureka! [jʊ 'ri kə] *interj.* "Aha!" (Used when one figures something out or when one has solved a difficult problem. From Greek for 'I have found it!') ♦ *Eureka! I have found the cure for baldness!* ♦ *Mary yelled "Eureka!" when she figured out the complex explanation.*

Europe ['jɚ əp] See Gazetteer.

European [jʊr ə 'pi ən] **1.** *n.* a citizen of one of the countries of Europe. ♦ *Europeans speak more foreign languages than Americans.* ♦ *Many Europeans visit the United States on vacations.* **2.** *adj.* of or about Europe or ①. ♦ *Big European cities are very much like U.S. cities.* ♦ *We are planning a European vacation for next spring.*

euthanasia [ju θə 'ne ʒə] *n.* painlessly killing someone or some creature who is suffering terribly from a painful disease. (No plural form in this sense.) ♦ *There are legal and medical questions concerning euthanasia.* ♦ *The doctor was accused of performing euthanasia on a suffering patient.*

evacuate [ɪ 'væk ju et] **1.** *tv.* to remove endangered people from a dangerous situation or area. ♦ *The police evacuated the citizens before the hurricane reached the coast.* ♦ *The authorities ordered the soldiers to evacuate the townspeople.* **2.** *tv.* to leave a place, often in an emergency. ♦ *We were asked to evacuate the area during the emergency.* ♦ *Everyone must evacuate the building immediately!* **3. evacuate from** *tv. + prep. phr.* to remove a fluid from a container. ♦ *The authorities evacuated the poisonous gas from the railway tank car.* ♦ *Anne evacuated all the air from the chamber.* **4.** *tv.* to empty the bowels. (Medical.) ♦ *The patient was told to evacuate his bowels before coming to the hospital for tests.* ♦ *Anne was not able to evacuate her bowels without the help of medication.* **5.** *iv.* to leave a place, often in an emergency. ♦ *Fearing the worst, we evacuated immediately.* ♦ *The neighborhood residents evacuated when they heard the news of the danger.*

evacuated [ɪ 'væk ju et ɪd] *adj.* cleared out; removed; emptied. ♦ *The citizens were warned to stay out of the evacuated area.* ♦ *Rioters looted the evacuated town.*

evacuation [ɪ væk ju 'e ʃən] **1.** *n.* removing all the people from an area that is in danger. (No plural form in this sense.) ♦ *Police assisted in the town's evacuation.* ♦ *The evacuation was done in a calm and orderly manner.* **2.** *n.* making something empty. (No plural form in this sense.) ♦ *The evacuation of the gas from the tank progressed slowly.* ♦ *Complete evacuation was the only way to remove the air from the room.*

evade [ɪ 'ved] *tv.* to avoid doing something; to get out of doing something. ♦ *Jane evaded doing her chores at home by pretending to be sick.* ♦ *Bill evaded answering the questions I asked him.*

evaluate [ɪ 'væl ju et] **1.** *tv.* to judge or establish the monetary value of something. ♦ *The assessor evaluated the plot of land before Anne sold it.* ♦ *Bill needs time to evaluate the stock before he buys it.* **2.** *tv.* to make a judgment about someone or something. ♦ *The students' skills were evaluated on the basis of test results.* ♦ *I want to evaluate my options thoroughly before making a decision.*

evaluation [ɪ væl ju 'e ʃən] **1.** *n.* studying the worth, value, or status of something. (No plural form in this sense.) ♦ *Evaluation of something complex will take a lot of time.* ♦ *Medical evaluation of such a complex problem will cost a lot of money.* **2.** *n.* a judgment about the status or quality of someone or something. ♦ *The teachers made evaluations of the work of the students.* ♦ *The manager gave the lazy employee a negative job evaluation.*

evangelism [ɪ 'væn dʒə lɪz əm] *n.* spreading the Christian gospel. (No plural form in this sense.) ♦ *The minister's evangelism spread far beyond his church.* ♦ *Evangelism is the work of the missionary.*

evangelist [ɪ 'væn dʒə ləst] *n.* someone who practices or preaches evangelism. ♦ *The evangelist gave an exciting sermon in the church.* ♦ *The television evangelists asked their viewers to send donations.*

evaporate [ɪ 'væp ə ret] **1.** *iv.* to turn into a gas or vapor; to disappear by turning into a gas or a vapor. ♦ *The steaming water evaporated quickly.* ♦ *The rubbing alcohol evaporated as soon as the nurse dabbed it on the patient's arm.* **2.** *iv.* to disappear. (Figurative on ①.) ♦ *My good intentions evaporated once I discovered that Bill was trying to cheat me.* ♦ *Our hopes evaporated when it became apparent that our team would lose.* **3.** *tv.* to cause something to turn into a gas or vapor. ♦ *The extremely hot weather evaporated the shallow stream.* ♦ *Applying heat will evaporate water.*

evaporation [ɪ væp ə 're ʃən] *n.* the process of turning into a gas or a vapor. (No plural form in this sense.) ♦ *The hot sun accelerated the water's evaporation.* ♦ *During evaporation, a lot of steam was produced.*

evasion [ɪ 've ʒən] **1.** *n.* evading someone or something. (No plural form in this sense.) ♦ *The soldiers were reprimanded for the evasion of their duties.* ♦ *John's evasion of questions about where he was last night alarmed his parents.* **2.** *n.* a statement that avoids telling the truth. ♦ *I want an answer, not an evasion!* ♦ *The witness's repeated evasions on the witness stand angered the judge.*

evasive [ɪ 've sɪv] *adj.* not giving a direct answer; not straightforward. (Adv: *evasively.*) ♦ *Anne's evasive manner caused me to doubt everything she said.* ♦ *John gave an evasive answer when asked about the broken vase.*

evasiveness [ɪ 'vе sɪv nəs] *n.* the behavior of someone who is seeking to evade or elude someone or something. (No plural form in this sense.) ♦ *Tom's evasiveness about marriage convinced Mary that their relationship was about to end.* ♦ *John's evasiveness made the police suspicious.*

eve ['iv] *n.* the night or day before an important day. ♦ *Jimmy slept restlessly on the eve of his birthday.* ♦ *On Christmas Eve, I placed some gifts under the Christmas tree.*

even ['iv ən] **1.** *adj.* smooth; not rough; level; on the same level; uniform. (Adv: *evenly.*) ♦ *The children skated on the sidewalk's even concrete surface.* ♦ *It was easy to apply wallpaper to the even walls.* **2.** *adj.* [of a number] able to be divided by 2 with nothing left over. ♦ *2, 4, 6, and 8 are examples of even numbers.* (Adv: *evenly.*) ♦ *If you add two even numbers together, the result will be an even number as well.* **3.** *adj.* equal. (Adv: *evenly.*) ♦ *Jane's salary is even with mine.* ♦ *I divided the candy among the children in even proportions.* **4.** *adj.* [of a debtor and lender who are] no longer indebted or owed. (Not prenominal.) ♦ *Lisa used to owe me $100, but she paid me last week, and now we are even.* ♦ *Here's the $5 I owe you. At last, we're even.* **5.** *adv.* still more. (Used to make a comparison stronger.) ♦ *Jane is tall, Mary is taller, and Susan is even taller.* ♦ *This horror movie is even scarier than the one we saw last week.* **6.** *adv.* more than expected; in a way that would not be expected. ♦ *Even the young children listened patiently to the guest speaker at school.* ♦ *Even a candle seems bright after one has been in total darkness.* **7.** *tv.* to smooth something out; to make something smooth; to make something level. ♦ *The bricklayer evened the cement with a trowel.* ♦ *The gardener evened the hedge by trimming it with shears.* **8. get even (with someone)** *idiom* to retaliate against someone; to repay a person for something bad the person has done. ♦ *I will get even with you for breaking my baseball bat!* ♦ *Jimmy got even with Bill by punching him in the nose.*

evenhanded ['iv ən 'hæn dɪd] *adj.* fair; just. (Adv: *evenhandedly.*) ♦ *I appreciated the fact that my boss is evenhanded.* ♦ *The reporter gave an evenhanded account of the story.*

evening ['iv (ə) nɪŋ] **1.** *n.* the last part of the day; the period of the day after the afternoon and before the night. (No plural form in this sense.) ♦ *We always eat dinner at seven o'clock in the evening.* ♦ *I have invited the neighbors to come over tomorrow evening.* **2.** *adj.* <the adj. use of ①.> ♦ *Would you like to go for an evening walk with me?* ♦ *We are going to an evening performance of the opera today.* **3. evenings** *adv.* every evening; happening every evening. ♦ *Evenings, we sit on the porch and drink lemonade.* ♦ *I work evenings, five days a week.*

event [ə 'vɛnt] **1.** *n.* something that happens; an occurrence. ♦ *Your graduation from college is an important event.* ♦ *The happy event will be celebrated by friends and family.* **2.** *n.* a particular sporting match; a competition within a series of games. ♦ *Hundreds of people attended the boxing event at the stadium.* ♦ *The sporting event drew a tremendous crowd.* **3. in the event of something** *idiom* if something happens; on the chance that something happens. ♦ *In the event of his late arrival, please call me.* ♦ *In the event of rain, the parade is canceled.*

eventful [ə 'vɛnt fʊl] **1.** *adj.* having numerous events. (Adv: *eventfully.*) ♦ *We have just had an eventful week, during which my daughter got married and my son bought a new house.* ♦ *The day was quite eventful because of the president's visit.* **2.** *adj.* important; momentous. (Adv: *eventfully.*) ♦ *The couple's 50th anniversary is an eventful occasion.* ♦ *The inauguration of the president was an eventful occasion.*

eventual [ə 'vɛn tʃu əl] *adj.* at some time in the future; ultimate. (Adv: *eventually.*) ♦ *Susan's many absences from work led to her eventual firing.* ♦ *Owning a restaurant is Bill's eventual goal, but now he is just an assistant chef.*

eventuality [ə vɛn tʃu 'æl ə ti] *n.* a possible result; a possible future occurrence. ♦ *I was not prepared for the eventuality of losing my job.* ♦ *Are you prepared for the all the eventualities related to the computerization of your accounts?*

eventually [ə 'vɛn tʃu ə li] *adv.* ultimately; at some later time. ♦ *Eventually, you will achieve your goals.* ♦ *If you keep practicing, you might eventually become a good dancer.*

ever ['ɛv ɚ] **1.** *adv.* at any time. (Used especially in negative sentences, questions, and sentences with *if*, and after comparatives with *than*, after superlatives, or after *as*.) ♦ *I can't ever seem to find my keys in the morning.* ♦ *Have you ever heard of any such thing?* ♦ *After the surgery, John felt better than ever.* **2.** *adv.* increasingly; continuously [becoming more]. (Used before a comparative. Formal.) ♦ *As the storm approached, the sky grew ever darker.* ♦ *Bill's love for his wife becomes ever stronger.* **3.** *adv.* always; forever. ♦ *I am ever indebted to your kindness.* ♦ *I will love you forever and ever.*

evergreen ['ɛv ɚ grin] **1.** *n.* a tree that does not lose its leaves in the fall and remains green the whole year, such as a pine tree. ♦ *Evergreens are common in colder climates.* ♦ *There are two evergreens planted near the foundation of our house.* **2.** *adj.* <the adj. use of ①.> ♦ *Dave planted an evergreen tree in the backyard.* ♦ *I bought three evergreen plants at the nursery.*

everlasting [ɛv ɚ 'læs tɪŋ] **1.** *adj.* without end; not stopping; unending. (Adv: *everlastingly.*) ♦ *The minister believed in everlasting life.* ♦ *I give you my everlasting love.* **2.** *adj.* lasting too long; happening too often. (Adv: *everlastingly.*) ♦ *This everlasting headache will not go away.* ♦ *Your everlasting phone calls are beginning to bother me.*

evermore [ɛv ɚ 'mor] *adv.* for all time; forever. (Formal.) ♦ *Our love will last evermore.* ♦ *I pledge my loyalty to you evermore.*

every ['ɛv ri] **1.** *adj.* all; each. (Used with more than two people or things. For two things, use **both**.) ♦ *The teacher gave every student a blank piece of paper.* ♦ *I gave every child at the party a small toy.* **2.** *adj.* per; once during each unit. ♦ *I take one vitamin every day.* ♦ *There are 10 grams of fat in every serving of this dessert.* **3.** *adj.* all possible. ♦ *I tried every option, but none would work.* ♦ *Mary used every excuse she could think of to avoid helping me with the chores.* **4. (every) Tom, Dick, and Harry** *idiom* everyone, without discrimination; ordinary people. ♦ *The golf club is very exclusive. They don't let every Tom, Dick, and Harry join.* ♦ *Mary's sending out very few invitations. She doesn't want every Tom, Dick, and Harry turning up.*

everybody ['ɛv ri bɑd i] *pron.* every person; all; every one. (Takes a singular verb.) ♦ *Everybody was talking about the new developments in the White House.* ♦ *Everybody likes to walk barefoot on the beach.*

everyday ['ɛv ri de] **1.** *adj.* happening every day. (Prenominal only.) ♦ *Rain in the tropics is an everyday occurrence.* ♦ *Taking her pills is an everyday event for Jane.* **2.** *adj.* common; ordinary; not special. (Prenominal only. Compare with *every day*, meaning 'each day.') ♦ *I usually wear my everyday clothes to the gym.* ♦ *Tom just has a typical everyday car that he drives everywhere.*

everyone ['ɛv ri wən] *pron.* every person; all; everybody. (Treated as singular.) ♦ *Everyone was talking about the new scandal in the newspaper.* ♦ *Everyone likes to walk on the beach.*

everything ['ɛv ri θɪŋ] **1.** *pron.* all things; each thing. ♦ *Tony bought everything that was on sale.* ♦ *The lawyer questioned everything that I said.* **2.** *pron.* all things that are important; all things that matter. ♦ *"Winning isn't everything," the coach told the losing team.* ♦ *I have my health, my family, and a good job. I have everything that I could possibly want.* **3. everything but the kitchen sink** *idiom* almost everything one can think of. ♦ *When Sally went off to college, she took everything but the kitchen sink.* ♦ *John orders everything but the kitchen sink when he goes out to dinner, especially if someone else is paying for it.*

everywhere ['ɛv ri ʍɛr] *adv.* in all places; in every location; at every point. ♦ *Mosquitos are everywhere this summer!* ♦ *There are rainstorms everywhere in the Midwest at this time of year.*

evict [ɪ 'vɪkt] *tv.* to force a tenant to vacate rented or leased space. ♦ *The landlord tried to evict the tenant for failing to pay the rent.* ♦ *The sheriff was asked to evict the tenants.*

eviction [ə 'vɪk ʃən] *n.* the removal of a tenant from rented or leased space. ♦ *The landlord filed the papers for three evictions in his building.* ♦ *The eviction was carried out by the local sheriff.*

evidence ['ɛv ə dəns] *n.* something that proves a claim or statement. (No plural form in this sense.) ♦ *The prosecutor displayed the evidence in front of the jury.* ♦ *This evidence does not prove the defendant's guilt.*

evident ['ɛv ə dənt] *adj.* obvious; easily seen. (Adv: *evidently.*) ♦ *It is evident that you are not telling me the truth.* ♦ *The happy couple's love for each other is very evident.*

evidently ['ɛv ə dənt li] *adv.* according to what can be observed; apparently. ♦ *Bill looks very sad. Evidently, he's quite unhappy.* ♦ *The audience evidently liked the play because they applauded for two minutes at the end.*

evil ['iv əl] **1.** *adj.* very bad; wicked; morally corrupt. (Adv: *evilly.*) ♦ *The evil witch cast a wicked spell on the knight.* ♦ *The peasants rebelled against the evil king.* **2.** *n.* wickedness; badness. (No plural form in this sense.) ♦ *You must understand the difference between good and evil.* ♦ *Good coexists with evil in this world.* **3.** *n.* something bad. ♦ *Drug abuse is one of the serious evils in the world today.* ♦ *Intolerance is an evil that harms many people.*

evoke [ɪ 'vok] *tv.* to bring to mind a certain image or feeling; to recall a certain memory. ♦ *This fragrance evokes the memory of a cool, summer evening.* ♦ *Bill's soft voice evoked a feeling of peace and calmness.*

evolution [ɛv ə 'lu ʃən] **1.** *n.* the development of something from an early stage to a more advanced stage. (No plural form in this sense.) ♦ *Mary's political beliefs have undergone a dramatic evolution since college.* ♦ *The evolution of computer technology in this century is astounding.* **2.** *n.* the scientific theory that all living creatures developed from simpler forms of life over millions of years. (No plural form in this sense.) ♦ *We studied the process of evolution in our science class.* ♦ *Some religious groups do not believe in the theory of evolution.*

evolve [ə 'vɔlv] **1.** *iv.* to develop; to become more advanced over time. ♦ *My political beliefs evolved as I got older.* ♦ *The plan to open a restaurant evolved under Anne's steady guidance.* **2. evolve from** *iv.* + *prep. phr.* to develop from a simpler form of life. ♦ *Plants have evolved from simpler kinds of plants, over millions of years.* ♦ *Modern turtles evolved from a very large, prehistoric species of turtle.*

exacerbate [ɪg 'zæs ɚ bet] *tv.* to make a problem worse; to make something worse. ♦ *My neighbor's loud stereo exacerbated my headache.* ♦ *The accident exacerbated the slow flow of traffic.*

exact [ɪg 'zækt] **1.** *adj.* without mistakes; precise; completely correct. (Adv: *exactly.*) ♦ *You need exact change for the bus.* ♦ *What is the exact amount left in your savings account?* **2. exact from** *tv.* + *prep. phr.* to demand something from someone and get it. ♦ *Tom exacted a favor from me.* ♦ *The patient exacted an honest evaluation from the doctor.*

exacting [ɪg 'zæk tɪŋ] **1.** *adj.* precise; requiring a lot of attention. (Adv: *exactingly.*) ♦ *Jane is very exacting in her work.* ♦ *The exacting task took a lot of concentration.* **2.** *adj.* demanding exactness and precision. (Adv: *exactingly.*) ♦ *My exacting piano teacher expects perfection.* ♦ *Because of my manager's exacting expectations, I often work until midnight.*

exactly [ɪg 'zækt li] **1.** *adv.* precisely; accurately; only as specified. ♦ *Exactly how would I get to Fifth Avenue from Main Street?* ♦ *Meet me at exactly 8:00* A.M. *in front of the building.* **2. Exactly!** *interj.* "That is quite right!" ♦ *Exactly! That is just the way to do it.* ♦ *"Exactly!" cried Tom when I finally threw the baseball over home plate.*

exactness [ɛg 'zækt nəs] *n.* the quality of being exact. (No plural form in this sense.) ♦ *The exactness with which Jane writes is quite admirable.* ♦ *Exactness of expression is an important quality for a writer to have.*

exaggerate [ɪg 'zædʒ ə ret] **1.** *tv.* to make something seem larger or more severe than it really is. ♦ *Mary exaggerated the size of the fish she caught.* ♦ *Bill exaggerates every story he tells his friends.* **2.** *iv.* to claim that something is more or less than it really is. ♦ *You're just exaggerating! My grandfather isn't that old!* ♦ *Just tell us the truth. Don't exaggerate.*

exaggerated [ɪg 'zædʒ ə ret ɪd] *adj.* made to seem greater than is the case; out of proportion. (Adv: *exaggeratedly.*) ♦ *The newscaster perpetuated the exaggerated reports of floods.* ♦ *The speaker's exaggerated gestures distracted from the presentation.*

exaggeration [ɪg zædʒ ə 're ʃən] **1.** *n.* claiming someone or something to be more extreme than is really true. (No plural form in this sense.) ♦ *I have heard too much exaggeration and not enough of the truth.* ♦ *Dave is known for exaggeration, but at least he is entertaining with his storytelling.* **2.** *n.* a statement that uses ①. ♦ *Jane's story about the fish that got away was an exaggeration.* ♦ *Dave's exag-*

gerations to the press damaged any credibility he might have had.

exalt [ɪg 'zɔlt] *tv.* to praise someone; to honor someone; to give glory to someone. (Compare with **exult**.) ♦ *The general exalted the heroism of the slain soldiers.* ♦ *The campaign manager's speech exalted the candidate's virtues.*

exalted [ɪg 'zɔlt ɪd] *adj.* praised; honored; praiseworthy. (Adv: *exaltedly.*) ♦ *When our exalted president spoke, everyone became silent.* ♦ *The exalted prince entered the hall and everyone stood up.*

exam [ɪg 'zæm] *n.* an **examination**. ♦ *Mary diligently studied for the upcoming medical exam.* ♦ *Do you think you passed the algebra exam?*

examination [ɪg zæm ɪ 'ne ʃən] **1.** *n.* examining, studying, or observing someone or something. (No plural form in this sense.) ♦ *Physical examination is the only way to diagnose the disease.* ♦ *Examination of your documents will take only a few minutes.* **2.** *n.* a test; a series of questions given to test someone's knowledge of a certain topic. ♦ *Bill passed his calculus examination easily.* ♦ *The law school entrance examination is often difficult.*

examine [ɪg 'zæm ɪn] **1.** *tv.* to look at someone or something very closely; to scrutinize someone or something. ♦ *I examined the old coin with a magnifying glass.* ♦ *Jane examined every clause in the contract before she signed it.* **2.** *tv.* to made a medical study of the state of someone's body. ♦ *The doctor examined the pregnant woman.* ♦ *The medical students examined patients under the supervision of a doctor.*

example [ɪg 'zæm pəl] **1.** *n.* something that clarifies what one is talking about; a sample of what is being talked about. ♦ *These two pieces of material are examples of the fabrics I want to buy.* ♦ *Can you give me an example of the type of music you like?* **2.** *n.* someone or something that should be imitated; a model. ♦ *The brave officer was a good example for the others to follow.* ♦ *Mary's years of dedicated teaching are an example to new teachers everywhere.*

exasperate [ɪg 'zæs pə ret] *tv.* to make someone very angry; to frustrate someone greatly. ♦ *The traffic jam exasperated the motorists who were caught in it.* ♦ *The heckler's constant remarks exasperated the comedian.*

exasperated [ɪg 'zæs pə ret ɪd] *adj.* angry; upset; annoyed; angered; irritated. (Adv: *exasperatedly.*) ♦ *Jane made an exasperated gesture before angrily leaving the room.* ♦ *The exasperated drivers beeped their horns in the traffic jam.*

exasperation [ɪg zæs pə 're ʃən] *n.* extreme anger; extreme annoyance; extreme frustration. (No plural form in this sense.) ♦ *In my exasperation, I slammed the door as I left the meeting.* ♦ *Bill's exasperation reached a new level when he saw the bill for the car repairs.*

excavate ['ɛk skə vet] **1.** *tv.* to create a hole in the ground by removing dirt. ♦ *The workers used shovels to excavate the dirt from the hole.* ♦ *They excavated a huge hole for the foundation of the building.* **2.** *tv.* to uncover something buried in the ground by digging. ♦ *The archaeologist and his team excavated the ruins.* ♦ *The explorers excavated the remains of an ancient temple.*

excavation [ɛk skə 've ʃən] **1.** *n.* making a hole in the ground. (No plural form in this sense.) ♦ *When the tunnel was built, most of the work involved excavation.* ♦ *Excavation is the only way to remove such a large amount of soil.* **2.** *n.* a hole in the ground that has been made by digging. ♦ *The archaeologist found ancient bones in the excavation.* ♦ *The excavation was 10 feet across and 20 feet wide.*

exceed [ɛk 'sid] **1.** *tv.* to surpass the limits of something; to surpass the upper boundary of something. ♦ *You exceeded your authority when you signed the purchase order.* ♦ *I never exceed the speed limit on the highway.* **2.** *tv.* to surpass something. ♦ *Dave's success exceeded his wildest expectations.* ♦ *Mary exceeded Susan's speed record in the track event.*

exceedingly [ɛk 'sid ɪŋ li] *adv.* extremely; very. ♦ *You have been exceedingly kind to me.* ♦ *The students were exceedingly helpful to the exchange student.*

excel [ɛk 'sɛl] *iv.* to do very well at something; to be outstanding at something. ♦ *Mary excels in school because she studies very hard.* ♦ *Anne is in good physical condition and excels at many sports.*

excellence ['ɛk sə ləns] *n.* a superior quality; the best quality possible; an extremely good quality. (No plural form in this sense.) ♦ *The senator had a record of excellence in promoting civil-rights issues.* ♦ *The valedictorian received a college scholarship for academic excellence.*

excellent ['ɛk sə lənt] *adj.* superior; extremely good; outstanding; of very high quality. (Adv: *excellently.*) ♦ *My grades this semester were excellent.* ♦ *This restaurant is known for preparing excellent dishes.*

except [ɛk 'sɛpt] **1.** *prep.* other than; besides; not including. ♦ *I like all green vegetables except spinach.* ♦ *Mary works evenings except for Friday and Saturday nights.* **2. except for** *prep.* were it not for. ♦ *I would go bowling with you, except for the fact that I have a previous engagement.* ♦ *Tom and Susan would go out to dinner after work, except for the problem of getting a babysitter at such short notice.* **3.** *tv.* to exclude someone or something; to omit someone or something. (Compare with **accept**.) ♦ *I except the people who are here when I complain about people who are always late!* ♦ *The company's rules except no one, not even the owner.*

exception [ɛk 'sɛp ʃən] **1.** *n.* someone or something that is left out; someone or something that is omitted. ♦ *Everyone passed the math test, with the exception of Tom.* ♦ *With the exception of my neighbor's house, each house on our block has a well-tended lawn.* **2.** *n.* an instance of something that does not follow a general rule; an unusual case. ♦ *Words like* child *and* mouse *are exceptions, because their plurals are* children *and* mice. ♦ *Even though your grades are not outstanding, the college will make an exception and admit you.*

exceptional [ɛk 'sɛp ʃə nəl] *adj.* standing out from what is normal; unusual; not typical; better than what is usual. (Adv: *exceptionally.*) ♦ *The exceptional tennis player won the championship.* ♦ *Mary's golf game was exceptional. She scored ten strokes under par.*

excerpt 1. ['ɛk sɚpt] *n.* a part of a larger work, such as a piece of text from a longer passage or a section of music from a longer work. ♦ *The actor auditioned by performing an excerpt from the play.* ♦ *This magazine often prints excerpts from popular new novels.* **2.** [ɛk 'sɚpt] *tv.* to extract or quote a passage from a text. ♦ *The musician excerpted a short section of the concerto for performance.*

♦ *The magazine excerpted a passage from the second chapter of the popular book.*

excess 1. ['ɛk sɛs] *n.* the amount that is over a certain limit or boundary; the part of something that is too much. (No plural form in this sense.) ♦ *The paper is too wide. Please trim off the excess.* ♦ *This meat has an excess of fat.* **2. excesses** [ɛk 'sɛs əz] *n.* acts of extravagant indulgence; waste. ♦ *The people always forgive Congress for its excesses.* ♦ *Your many excesses have caused you to go into debt.* **3.** ['ɛk sɛs] *adj.* extra; beyond the proper limit; beyond what is needed. ♦ *Please trim off the excess fat from the meat.* ♦ *Don't bring any excess baggage on this trip.* **4. do something to excess** [...ɛk 'sɛs] *idiom* to do too much of something; to consume too much of something. ♦ *Anne often drinks to excess at parties.* ♦ *John worries to excess about everything.*

excessive [ɛk 'sɛs ɪv] *adj.* extra; beyond the proper limit; beyond what is needed; too much. (Adv: *excessively.*) ♦ *I will not buy the steak if there is excessive fat on it.* ♦ *You must curb your excessive spending, or you will become penniless.*

exchange [ɛks 'tʃendʒ] **1.** *tv.* to trade something for something else; to trade someone for someone else. ♦ *I exchanged belts with Bill because mine wasn't large enough.* ♦ *The governments exchanged spies in secret on a deserted road.* **2.** *n.* giving someone something for something else; trading something for something else. ♦ *The exchange was made inside the president's office.* ♦ *The children were satisfied with the baseball card exchange.* **3.** *n.* a conversation; a short dialogue. ♦ *Our exchange was brief but informative.* ♦ *I came away from the exchange with a deeper understanding of Dave's problems.* **4.** *n.* a place where things, such as stocks, are bought and sold. ♦ *The stock exchange is often a chaotic environment.* ♦ *Every major country has a stock exchange.* **5.** *n.* a particular subset of the telephone switching system, represented by the first three digits of a local telephone number in the United States. ♦ *Our number is 555–2345. We are in the 555 exchange.* ♦ *The old exchange for our area was Lakeview. It is now known as 525.*

exchangeable [ɛks 'tʃendʒ ə bəl] *adj.* able to be exchanged; able to be traded. (Adv: *exchangeably.*) ♦ *The dress is not exchangeable. You don't have the sales receipt.* ♦ *These two parts are not exchangeable. You have to buy an exact replacement.*

exchange student [ɛks 'tʃendʒ stud nt] *n.* a student from a foreign high school or college who studies locally for a year while a local student studies in the foreign school for a year. ♦ *My parents invited the exchange students for dinner.* ♦ *All of the exchange students spoke English very well.*

excise 1. excise tax ['ɛk saɪz...] *n.* a tax on products made and used inside a county, state, country, etc. ♦ *The state legislature put an excise tax on alcohol and cigarettes.* ♦ *The excise tax on tickets for the sporting event is excessive.* **2.** [ɛk 'saɪz] *tv.* to cut something out surgically. ♦ *The surgeon excised the cancerous tumor.* ♦ *Dr. Smith excised the patient's appendix before it ruptured.* **3.** [ɛk 'saɪz] *tv.* to cut out parts of a text. ♦ *The editor excised the unconfirmed statements from the reporter's article.* ♦ *The editor excised numerous poorly written passages from the manuscript.*

excitable [ɛk 'saɪt ə bəl] *adj.* easily excited. (Adv: *excitably.*) ♦ *Our dog is very excitable and may get rough if she gets too excited.* ♦ *Tom is too excitable in the classroom. It is hard for him to pay attention to what is going on.*

excite [ɛk 'saɪt] *tv.* to arouse or interest someone or something; to stimulate someone or something. ♦ *Rumors of the musician's surprise appearance excited the crowd.* ♦ *Tom excited my interest in antique cars when he bought a 1959 convertible.*

excited [ɛk 'saɪt ɪd] *adj.* aroused; stimulated; caused to be very interested. (Adv: *excitedly.*) ♦ *The excited children were unable to fall asleep.* ♦ *The excited performers bowed before the enthusiastic crowd.*

excitement [ɛk 'saɪt mənt] *n.* the feeling of great interest, expectation, stimulation, and arousal. (No plural form in this sense.) ♦ *The children's excitement grew as they opened their presents.* ♦ *Excitement flowed through the crowd when the famous athlete entered the room.*

exciting [ɛk 'saɪt ɪŋ] *adj.* causing excitement; very interesting; stimulating. (Adv: *excitingly.*) ♦ *We had an exciting time at the amusement park.* ♦ *The critic praised the exciting book.*

exclaim [ɛk 'sklem] *tv.* to shout something; to say something with strong feeling. (Takes a clause.) ♦ *When interrupted, David exclaimed that he wanted to be left alone.* ♦ *Mary exclaimed that someone forgot to turn the water off in the bathroom.*

exclamation [ɛk sklə 'me ʃən] *n.* a loud statement; a statement made with strong feeling or emotion. ♦ *The contractor's angry exclamation could be heard all over the construction site.* ♦ *The lifeguard's exclamation about seeing a shark startled the swimmers.*

exclamation point [ɛk sklə 'me ʃən pɔɪnt] *n.* a punctuation mark "!" written at the end of a word, phrase, or sentence that is an exclamation. ♦ *Commands and warnings such as "Stop!" and "Look out!" and interjections such as "Eureka!" are often written with exclamation points.* ♦ *I wrote an exclamation point after "I love chocolate" to show how strongly I meant it.*

exclude [ɛk 'sklud] *tv.* to leave someone or something out; to omit someone or something; to fail to include someone or something. ♦ *The other students always excluded Max at lunch.* ♦ *Please don't exclude grains from your diet.*

exclusion [ɛk 'sklu ʒən] **1.** *n.* the condition of being excluded; the condition of being left out. (No plural form in this sense.) ♦ *You are my best friend, to the exclusion of all others.* ♦ *Bill's exclusion from the party made him feel sad.* **2.** *n.* someone or something that has been excluded. ♦ *There is room for another person at the party, so you can put one of the exclusions back on the list.* ♦ *The contract covers everything with no exclusions stated.*

exclusive [ɛk 'sklu sɪv] **1.** *adj.* limited or restricted to one or some and no others. (Adv: *exclusively.*) ♦ *The university president belongs to an exclusive club.* ♦ *I buy all my clothing at an exclusive men's shop.* **2.** *adj.* sole; personal; not shared with other people. (Adv: *exclusively.*) ♦ *Tom and Susan have an exclusive relationship.* ♦ *The author has an exclusive contract with the publisher.* **3.** *n.* an important story or revelation given to only one publisher or broadcaster. ♦ *The reporter got an exclusive on the* *movie star's scandalous past.* ♦ *We read the exclusive in the tabloid magazine.*

excommunicate [ɛks kə 'mju nə ket] **1.** *tv.* to expel someone from church membership, especially in the Roman Catholic Church. ♦ *The church authorities excommunicated the theologian for heresy.* ♦ *The bishop excommunicated the priest for offenses against church law.* **2.** *tv.* to remove someone from a group. (Figurative on ①.) ♦ *The senators excommunicated those who didn't agree to their platform from the party.* ♦ *The committee tried to excommunicate Jane from their group for her outspoken views.*

excommunication [ɛks kə mju nə 'ke ʃən] *n.* expelling someone from church membership. (No plural form in this sense.) ♦ *The Vatican announced the priest's excommunication in a formal statement.* ♦ *After excommunication, one cannot be buried in the same cemetery as church members.*

excrement ['ɛk skrə mənt] *n.* feces; solid waste from the bowels. (No plural form in this sense.) ♦ *The zookeeper cleaned the animal excrement from the cage.* ♦ *David found dog excrement on his lawn every morning.*

excrete [ɛk 'skrit] *tv.* to release solid waste from the body; to defecate. ♦ *The baby excreted waste into a diaper.* ♦ *The cat excreted feces in its litter box.*

excruciating [ɛk 'skru ʃi et ɪŋ] **1.** *adj.* extremely painful; causing extreme mental or physical suffering. (Adv: *excruciatingly.*) ♦ *Anne has been in excruciating pain ever since she fell and broke her hip.* ♦ *John's death caused his family excruciating suffering.* **2.** *adj.* intense or elaborate. (Adv: *excruciatingly.*) ♦ *Bill painted the doll's face with excruciating precision.* ♦ *Anne does all her work with excruciating care.*

excursion [ɛk 'skɚ ʒən] *n.* a trip; a journey. ♦ *Our family took a two-week excursion to France.* ♦ *We saw the pyramids during our excursion to Egypt.*

excuse 1. [ɛk 'skjus] *n.* a reason that attempts to explain or justify a wrongdoing. ♦ *Jimmy could not think of a good excuse for losing his homework.* ♦ *Tina had a good excuse for missing work yesterday.* **2.** [ɛk 'skjuz] *tv.* to forgive someone for bad manners; to pardon someone. ♦ *Please excuse me for interrupting you.* ♦ *I cannot excuse your unspeakable behavior.* **3.** [ɛk 'skjuz] *tv.* to grant permission for someone to leave. ♦ *Mother excused Jane who had to leave the dinner table to answer the telephone.* ♦ *Please excuse me. I must go.* **4. excuse someone from something** [ɛk 'skjuz…] *idiom* to free someone from a duty or obligation. ♦ *Dad excused me from cutting the grass on Saturday.* ♦ *The teacher excused Susan from taking the quiz because she was ill.*

execute ['ɛks ə kjut] **1.** *tv.* to do something as ordered; to carry out something; to perform an act. ♦ *The soldier executed the general's order.* ♦ *The ice skaters executed their routine with great skill.* **2.** *tv.* to kill someone as a punishment; to punish someone with death. (To **execute** ① a sentence of death on someone.) ♦ *The government was finally able to execute the serial killer.* ♦ *The mobster executed a rival gang member.* **3.** *tv.* to make a document effective as of a certain date by signing it. ♦ *The two parties executed the contract in the lawyer's office.* ♦ *Bill executed the agreement in front of two witnesses.*

execution [ɛks ə 'kju ʃən] **1.** *n.* the doing of something; the carrying out of an order. (No plural form in this sense.) ♦ *The execution of the soldier's duties was done without question.* ♦ *The execution of the gymnast's routine was flawless.* **2.** *n.* the killing of someone as a punishment. ♦ *Members of the press were allowed to view the criminal's execution.* ♦ *The convict's execution was delayed for 24 hours.* **3.** *n.* the signing of a document to make the document legal. ♦ *Two witnesses were present at the execution of the agreement.* ♦ *Upon execution, copies of the contract were sent to our lawyers.*

executioner [ɛks ə 'kju ʃən ɚ] *n.* someone who carries out the sentence of death on someone. ♦ *The executioner gave the prisoner a lethal injection.* ♦ *In earlier times, the executioner wore a black mask.*

executive [ɛg 'zɛk jə tɪv] **1.** *n.* someone who manages an organization in business or government. ♦ *The advertising executive approved the ideas for the new commercials.* ♦ *The chief executive called a meeting of the company's board of directors.* **2.** *adj.* in the manner of ①; firm and authoritative. ♦ *The business owner made an executive decision to fire 500 workers.* ♦ *The bank's executive vice president was convicted of embezzlement.* **3.** *adj.* of or about the branch of government that manages, as opposed to the branches that make laws and run the courts. ♦ *The president of the United States is the head of the executive branch of government.* ♦ *The president issued an executive order.*

executor [ɛg 'zɛk jət ɚ] *n.* someone who is named in a will to carry out the requests listed in the will. ♦ *Jane's brother was named as executor of her estate.* ♦ *My oldest sister is executor of our parents' will.*

exemplary [ɛg 'zɛm plɚ i] *adj.* setting a good example; being a perfect example; worthy of imitation. ♦ *The soldier was decorated for exemplary heroism in combat.* ♦ *The principal rewarded Susan for her exemplary performance in school.*

exemplify [ɪg 'zɛm plə fɑɪ] *tv.* to represent someone or something as a good example. ♦ *The soldier exemplified courage in the line of duty.* ♦ *Your diligence exemplifies the characteristics of a good employee.*

exempt [ɪg 'zɛmpt] **1.** *tv.* to free someone from a duty or obligation. ♦ *The teacher exempted the smartest students from taking the quiz.* ♦ *The doctor's note exempted Mary from gym class.* **2.** *adj.* free from a duty or obligation. ♦ *You are not exempt from the rules!* ♦ *The exempt workers received a paid holiday.*

exercise ['ɛk sɚ sɑɪz] **1.** *n.* active use of the muscles of the body. (No plural form in this sense.) ♦ *Vigorous exercise stimulates the body and mind.* ♦ *I find it difficult to insert an hour of exercise into my daily routine.* **2.** *n.* a specific act of ①. ♦ *I have to do exercises to strengthen my leg muscles.* ♦ *Please do this exercise fifty times without stopping.* **3.** *n.* a question or problem designed to train someone in problem solving. ♦ *We had to do a lot of exercises in French class today.* ♦ *The mathematical exercise was a challenge to the class.* **4.** *n.* an activity designed to train someone for a military task. ♦ *The soldiers had to do a training exercise in the hot sun.* ♦ *The entire Pacific fleet is involved in naval exercises this month.* **5. graduation exercises** *n.* graduation ceremonies. (Often plural.) ♦ *Bill attended his graduation exercises in a black cap and* *gown.* ♦ *The graduating students were handed their diplomas at the college's annual graduation exercises.* **6.** *tv.* to actively use one or more muscles or areas of the body. ♦ *I exercised my leg muscles by riding a bike.* ♦ *At the gym, you exercise every part of your body.* **7.** *tv.* to actively use something, such as a power, right, privilege, or option. ♦ *Citizens should exercise their right to vote.* ♦ *I exercise my right to free speech by writing letters to the editor of the local newspaper.* **8.** *iv.* to be physically active in order to strengthen the heart and muscles or to lose weight. ♦ *Bill exercised on a regular basis in order to lose weight.* ♦ *Mary exercises at the health club.*

exert [ɛg 'zɝt] **1.** *tv.* to apply strength, force, or pressure. ♦ *The piano and the bookcase both exert a lot of force on the floor that supports them.* ♦ *The nurse exerted pressure on the patient's bleeding wound.* **2.** *tv.* to use one's influence. (Figurative on ①.) ♦ *The mayor exerted his influence in order to halt the investigation.* ♦ *I wish you would exert more control on your children.*

exertion [ɛg 'zɝ ʃən] *n.* the strength or effort needed to do something. (No plural form in this sense.) ♦ *A great exertion of force was required to open the locked door.* ♦ *The exertion of my job makes my muscles sore.*

exhale [ɛks'hel] **1.** *iv.* to breathe out; to push air out from the lungs. ♦ *Mary sighed and exhaled slowly.* ♦ *Bill inhaled the cigarette smoke and then exhaled deeply.* **2.** *tv.* to breathe air or smoke out of the body. ♦ *Bill exhaled the cigar smoke.* ♦ *Jane exhaled her breath in the freezing weather and her breath turned to fog.*

exhaust [ɛg 'zɔst] **1.** *n.* steam, gas, or vapor that is the waste product of burning. (No plural form in this sense.) ♦ *Buses produce black, smelly exhaust.* ♦ *The fumes and particles of the exhaust float up into the atmosphere.* **2.** *tv.* to use up all of someone or something's resources or energy. ♦ *I give up. I've exhausted every idea I have.* ♦ *The children thoroughly exhausted their mother's patience.* **3.** *tv.* to cause someone to become very tired. ♦ *The noisy children exhausted the babysitter.* ♦ *The tedious work exhausted the employee.*

exhaustion [ɛg 'zɔs tʃən] *n.* being completely tired or without energy; fatigue. (No plural form in this sense.) ♦ *Tom suffered from extreme exhaustion after working for 32 hours.* ♦ *The busy graduate student was hospitalized for exhaustion.*

exhaustive [ɛg 'zɔs tɪv] *adj.* complete; comprehensive; thorough. (Adv: *exhaustively.*) ♦ *Please make an exhaustive inventory of everything in the supply room.* ♦ *The real-estate agent gave the prospective buyers an exhaustive tour of the new house.*

exhibit [ɛg 'zɪb ət] **1.** *tv.* to show signs of something; to indicate something. ♦ *The patient exhibited symptoms of malaria.* ♦ *Mary exhibited signs of genius in her piano playing.* **2.** *tv.* to display one's works of art in a public place. ♦ *Jane exhibited her sculptures at the art museum.* ♦ *The artist exhibited his paintings in a local gallery.* **3.** *n.* a show of one's artwork, as in an exhibition. ♦ *Bill's art exhibit is a success with the critics.* ♦ *A critic wrote a flattering article about the sculpture exhibit.* **4.** *n.* a piece of evidence used in a court trial. ♦ *The prosecutor introduced the exhibit as evidence of the defendant's guilt.* ♦ *Each jury member looked at the exhibit closely.*

exhibition [ɛk sə 'bɪʃ ən] *n.* the public display of something, usually works of art. ♦ *The museum exhibition of Egyptian mummies always draws great crowds.* ♦ *Mary attended the art exhibition with her art class.*

exhibitionism [ɛk sə 'bɪʃ ə nɪz əm] **1.** *n.* the behavior of someone who wants a lot of attention. (No plural form in this sense.) ♦ *Mary's noisy and self-centered exhibitionism in class made her fellow students angry.* ♦ *The principal punished Tom for his exhibitionism.* **2.** *n.* indecent exposure; revealing one's genitals in public. (No plural form in this sense.) ♦ *A mentally troubled old man was arrested in the park for exhibitionism.* ♦ *Put your pants on! Do you want to be accused of exhibitionism?*

exhilarating [ɛg 'zɪl ə ret ɪŋ] *adj.* very exciting; very stimulating. (Adv: *exhilaratingly.*) ♦ *The children screamed with delight on the exhilarating carnival ride.* ♦ *An exhilarating shower woke me up enough to go to work.*

exhort [ɛg 'zort] **exhort to** *tv.* + *inf.* to urge someone to do something; to advise someone strongly to do something. ♦ *I exhort you to pay off all your bills before you go into debt.* ♦ *The teacher exhorted the students to study for the quiz.*

exhume [ɛg 'zum] *tv.* to dig up the remains of a dead body. ♦ *The court ordered the authorities to exhume the murder victim.* ♦ *The coroner exhumed the body in order to perform tests regarding the cause of death.*

exile ['ɛg zaɪl] **1.** *n.* forcing one out of one's home country. (No plural form in this sense.) ♦ *Exile is the only way to remove the king without killing him.* ♦ *The king preferred exile to death.* **2.** *n.* someone who has been banished. ♦ *The exile went from country to country seeking asylum.* ♦ *The political exile went into hiding.* **3.** *tv.* to banish someone; to force one from one's homeland. ♦ *The king exiled the duke who tried to usurp his throne.* ♦ *The government exiled the corrupt politician.*

exist [ɛg 'zɪst] **1.** *iv.* to be; to be in reality. ♦ *Good and evil both exist in the real world.* ♦ *Everyone knows that ghosts do not exist.* **2.** *iv.* to last through time; to continue to be. ♦ *Our love will exist eternally.* ♦ *Memories exist forever in our hearts.* **3.** *iv.* to manage to live with only the minimum of physical needs met. ♦ *The turtle exists on very little food.* ♦ *The prisoners existed on bread and water.*

existence [ɛg 'zɪs təns] **1.** *n.* being; the condition of actually being. (No plural form in this sense.) ♦ *Do you believe in the existence of ghosts?* ♦ *Most religious faiths believe in the existence of a Supreme Being.* **2.** *n.* living; continuing to be; a way of living. (No plural form in this sense.) ♦ *I cannot continue my meager existence on this low salary.* ♦ *Susan's very existence now depends on the surgeon's skills.* **3. in existence** *phr.* now existing; currently and actually being. ♦ *The tiger may not be in existence in a few decades.* ♦ *All the oil in existence will not last the world for another century.*

existing [ɛg 'zɪs tɪŋ] *adj.* being; actually being; current. ♦ *You must obey the existing traffic laws.* ♦ *Existing circumstances at work have forced me to look for a new job.*

exit ['ɛg zɪt] **1.** *n.* the way out, especially from a place or room. ♦ *The theater's exits were marked with lighted signs.* ♦ *A police officer blocked the only exit from the room.* **2.** *n.* the roadway leading off an expressway. ♦ *I missed my exit and had to drive to the next town and turn around.* ♦ *The exit from the freeway onto Route 28 was blocked.* **3.** *n.* leaving someplace, especially a stage. ♦ *The actress made a dramatic exit after her speech.* ♦ *Bill's angry exit from the meeting shocked everyone.* **4.** *iv.* to leave [a place], such as a stage or an expressway. ♦ *The performers exited from the stage gracefully.* ♦ *The cars exited off the expressway.* **5.** *tv.* to leave a place. ♦ *The actor exited the stage gracefully.* ♦ *I have to exit the expressway at the next exit.*

exodus ['ɛk sə dəs] *n.* a departure of many people; a mass emigration. ♦ *The refugees made an exodus to a safe place.* ♦ *The exodus included refugees from all parts of the country.*

ex officio ['ɛks ə 'fɪʃ i o] *adj.* "because of one's office," having the right to do something because of one's rank or position. (From Latin 'out of [because of] the office.') ♦ *Since I am only ex officio, the rules do not allow me to vote.* ♦ *An ex officio member of the board made a motion to dismiss the company president immediately.*

exonerate [ɛg 'zɑn ə ret] *tv.* to free someone from blame; to determine that someone is innocent. ♦ *The jury exonerated the defendant.* ♦ *I exonerated John from all blame in the accident.*

exorbitant [ɛg 'zor bɪ tənt] *adj.* greater than what is reasonable; too expensive. (Adv: *exorbitantly.*) ♦ *How can this company charge such exorbitant prices for its merchandise?* ♦ *I will not pay such an exorbitant price for these shoes!*

exotic [ɛg 'zɑt ɪk] **1.** *adj.* not native to a country; foreign. ♦ *Susan and Bill love to eat spicy and exotic food dishes.* ♦ *There are a number of exotic bird species in Florida.* **2.** *adj.* having a strange beauty; having a strange allure. (Adv: *exotically* [...ɪk li].) ♦ *Jane dabbed some exotic perfume behind her ears.* ♦ *Warm, exotic evenings in the tropics are very relaxing.*

expand [ɛk 'spænd] **1.** *tv.* to enlarge something; to make something wider or longer; to cause something to grow bigger. ♦ *The highway construction workers expanded the intersection.* ♦ *The producer expanded the broadcast from thirty minutes to an hour.* **2.** *iv.* to enlarge; to make wider or longer; to swell up; to grow bigger. ♦ *The large balloon expanded slowly.* ♦ *The population expanded by 4 percent last year.* **3. expand on** *iv.* + *prep. phr.* to explain something using more details. ♦ *Please expand on your comments.* ♦ *The reporter expanded on the story, giving it more details.*

expanse [ɛk 'spæns] *n.* a large, unbroken space; a large, wide-open space. ♦ *A vast expanse of water surrounded the island.* ♦ *The skater glided across an expanse of ice.*

expansion [ɛk 'spæn ʃən] **1.** *n.* growth; enlargement. (No plural form in this sense.) ♦ *The plumber was concerned with the expansion of the water pipes.* ♦ *We cannot afford the constant expansion of our welfare system.* **2.** *n.* a part of something added on to the original part. ♦ *The new airport expansion opens next month.* ♦ *The expansion provided for 6 additional offices and a small cafeteria.*

expansive [ɛk 'spæn sɪv] **1.** *adj.* spread-out; wide; comprehensive. (Adv: *expansively.*) ♦ *From our balcony, we had an expansive view of the city.* ♦ *The book's expansive index listed hundreds of important terms.* **2.** *adj.* openly showing feelings and emotions; open; friendly. (Adv: *expansively.*) ♦ *Because of Jane's expansive nature, some people try to take advantage of her.* ♦ *People with expansive personalities make new friends easily.*

expatriate [ɛks 'pe tri ət] **1.** *n.* one living outside of one's native country. ♦ *The expatriate missed his family and friends.* ♦ *The expatriate made her new home in France.* **2.** *adj.* forced or choosing to live outside one's native country. ♦ *The expatriate family found refuge with distant relatives.* ♦ *The expatriate artist lived among other artists and writers in Paris.*

expect [ɛk 'spɛkt] **1. expect to** *iv.* + *inf.* to think that something will happen; to anticipate something happening. ♦ *Jimmy expects to receive a new video game for his birthday.* ♦ *Bill expects to be promoted to the new position.* **2.** *tv.* to count on someone to do something; to rely on someone to do something. (Takes a clause.) ♦ *While you live in this house, I expect you to follow my rules.* ♦ *I expect you to be home before midnight.* **3.** *tv.* to anticipate the arrival of something; to anticipate the birth of a baby. (See also expecting.) ♦ *The doctor told Mary to expect triplets.* ♦ *The flight is expected to arrive at 2:30.* **4.** *tv.* to anticipate something. ♦ *I expect trouble if Bob comes late again.* ♦ *Rain is expected for tonight.*

expectant [ɛk 'spɛk tənt] **1.** *adj.* waiting; hoping; expecting something to happen. (Adv: *expectantly.*) ♦ *The expectant child was very eager for her birthday party to begin.* ♦ *The members of the expectant audience stamped their feet when the concert was delayed.* **2.** *adj.* expecting a baby; pregnant. ♦ *The expectant parents thought of names for the new baby.* ♦ *The expectant mother chose wallpaper for the nursery.*

expectation [ɛk spɛk 'te ʃən] **1.** *n.* looking forward to something; anticipation. (No plural form in this sense.) ♦ *All this expectation makes me nervous. When will we know what happened?* ♦ *We waited with great expectation for the fireworks to begin.* **2.** *n.* something that is hoped for; something that is looked forward to; something that is anticipated. ♦ *It is my fondest expectation that all of my children will go to college.* ♦ *The fabulous vacation went far beyond my wildest expectations.*

expecting [ɛk 'spɛk tɪŋ] *iv.* anticipating the birth of a baby; waiting for the birth of a baby. (Not prenominal.) ♦ *Jane is expecting, so she shouldn't be lifting heavy objects.* ♦ *The happy parents are expecting in March.*

expectorant [ɛk 'spɛk tə rənt] **1.** *n.* a medicine that encourages the easy coughing up of phlegm. ♦ *John took an expectorant to break up his cough.* ♦ *The child's expectorant had a sweet, cherry flavor.* **2.** *adj.* <the adj. use of ①.> ♦ *Anne swallowed a teaspoonful of an expectorant syrup.* ♦ *The doctor prescribed an expectorant medicine for my cough.*

expedience [ɛk 'spid i əns] *n.* doing things in a profitable, efficient, or advantageous way, rather than the best possible way; expediency. (No plural form in this sense.) ♦ *In their expedience, the builders of the house neglected certain safety procedures.* ♦ *For the sake of expedience, I conducted a conference from my car phone on my way home.*

expediency [ɛk 'spid i ən si] *n.* expedience. (No plural form in this sense.) ♦ *Expediency is often the course taken in politics.* ♦ *Bob favors expediency over planning and consideration.*

expedient [ɛk 'spid i ənt] **1.** *adj.* profitable, efficient, or advantageous, rather than right. (Adv: *expediently.*) ♦ *Hiring temporary workers provided an expedient answer* *to my company's labor shortage.* ♦ *Expedient solutions rarely solve long-term problems.* **2.** *n.* something that is ①. ♦ *The company used every expedient necessary to get the job done.* ♦ *The ill-advised expedient cost more money in the long run.*

expedite ['ɛk spɪ dɑɪt] *tv.* to make something happen faster or more efficiently. ♦ *The person I talked to on the phone promised to expedite the shipment of the book I ordered.* ♦ *The travel agent used my credit card to expedite the ticket purchase.*

expedition [ɛk spɪ 'dɪ ʃən] **1.** *n.* speeding something up; expediting something. (No plural form in this sense.) ♦ *The ticket agent was of little help in the expedition of our travel arrangements.* ♦ *Jane completed the job at work with considerable expedition.* **2.** *n.* a trip; a journey; a specific course of travel to a certain place. ♦ *Our senior class took an expedition to Washington, D.C.* ♦ *The explorers started on a year-long expedition down the Nile.* **3.** *n.* a group of people traveling together to a certain place. ♦ *The expedition up the mountain would take several weeks.* ♦ *An archaeologist headed the expedition in the desert.* **4. go on a fishing expedition** *idiom* to attempt to discover information. ♦ *We are going to have to go on a fishing expedition to try to find the facts.* ♦ *One lawyer went on a fishing expedition in court, and the other lawyer objected.*

expel [ɛk 'spɛl] **1.** *tv.* to force someone or something out of a place. ♦ *The army expelled the enemy troops from the town.* ♦ *When you sneeze, you expel air from your lungs.* **2.** *tv.* to ban someone from attending a school, usually for bad behavior or bad grades; to end someone's membership in an organization. ♦ *The principal expelled the student for the rest of the school year.* ♦ *The school board voted to expel John for setting fire to the school.*

expend [ɛk 'spɛnd] *tv.* to spend something, such as time or energy; to use something up. ♦ *The student expended an extraordinary amount of time on the science project.* ♦ *Susan expended a great deal of energy while exercising.*

expendable [ɛk 'spɛn də bəl] *adj.* able to be gotten rid of in order to serve a purpose; abundant enough to be used freely. (Adv: *expendably.*) ♦ *The general stated that some troops are expendable in battle.* ♦ *The paper cups and plates for the party are expendable. We have lots of them.*

expenditure [ɛk 'spɛn dɪ tʃɚ] **1.** *n.* money spent for a product or service. ♦ *The expenditure for computer equipment is included in the new budget.* ♦ *The company made a large expenditure for office furniture.* **2.** *n.* an amount of time or energy spent for a specific purpose. ♦ *The hot weather required a great expenditure of energy for air conditioning.* ♦ *The huge expenditure of effort on the project was wasted.*

expense [ɛk 'spɛns] *n.* the amount of money that a product or service costs; an item of cost, as in a budget. ♦ *Electricity is a large expense in running a business.* ♦ *Which expenses in the budget can be eliminated or cut?*

expensive [ɛk 'spɛn sɪv] *adj.* costing a lot of money; high-priced; costly. (Adv: *expensively.*) ♦ *All of the dinners at the fancy restaurant were quite expensive.* ♦ *We cannot afford an expensive vacation this summer.*

experience [ɛk 'spɪr i əns] **1.** *n.* knowledge gained from remembering past events and the results of one's actions during those events; skills gained from living one's life. (No plural form in this sense.) ♦ *To apply for this job, you must have five years of experience in sales.* ♦ *Mary has a lot of experience with cattle because her parents were ranchers.* **2.** *n.* an event that gives someone ①. ♦ *After a few bad experiences with car accidents, I gave up driving.* ♦ *I had a frightening experience while I was in the city today.* **3.** *tv.* to learn about an event by being involved in it when it happens. ♦ *Sadly, John has experienced many tragic events in his life.* ♦ *When Mary's dog died, she experienced great sorrow.*

experienced [ɛk 'spɪr i ənst] *adj.* having knowledge gained from remembering past events and the results of one's actions during those events. ♦ *The experienced parents were not as anxious as they were at the birth of their first child.* ♦ *An experienced babysitter will not panic in an emergency situation.*

experiment [ɛk 'spɛr ə mənt] **1.** *n.* a test that is carried out to prove or disprove an idea or theory. ♦ *The scientist performed an experiment on the isolated virus.* ♦ *An experiment proved the effectiveness of the new vaccine.* **2.** *iv.* to test a theory in order to prove or disprove it; to try something in order to find out about it. ♦ *The scientist spent many hours experimenting and writing about his discoveries.* ♦ *I experimented with different recipes before I made a batch of cookies I really liked.*

experimental [ɛk spɛr ə 'mɛn təl] **1.** *adj.* of or about an experiment. (Adv: *experimentally.*) ♦ *The experimental animals were kept in cages in the laboratory.* ♦ *A blue pill was given to each person in the experimental group.* **2.** *adj.* being tried out; unproven. (Adv: *experimentally.*) ♦ *The experimental drug had a miraculous effect on the sick patient.* ♦ *The experimental cancer treatment was unsuccessful.*

experimentation [ɛk spɛr ə mɛn 'te ʃən] *n.* testing or trying out a theory or device. (No plural form in this sense.) ♦ *The laboratory was designed for scientific observation and experimentation.* ♦ *The researchers published papers on their experimentation with unidentified viruses.*

expert ['ɛk spɚt] **1.** *n.* someone who is an authority on something; someone who knows a lot about a certain topic. ♦ *An expert in sports medicine examined the athlete's knee.* ♦ *The fingerprint expert testified in court.* **2.** *adj.* authoritative; knowledgeable; skilled. (Adv: *expertly.*) ♦ *The doctor's expert testimony helped the jury understand the problem.* ♦ *The museum featured several works by expert sculptors.*

expertise [ɛk spɚ 'tiz] *n.* skill; expert knowledge; expert ability. (No plural form in this sense.) ♦ *Do you have the expertise required to tune the piano?* ♦ *Because of the captain's expertise in navigation, the ship avoided the reef.*

expiration [ɛk spə 're ʃən] **1.** *n.* becoming no longer usable, valid, or authorized. (No plural form in this sense.) ♦ *On expiration, this coupon becomes invalid.* ♦ *At the time of the reservation's expiration, it became worthless.* **2.** *n.* breathing out; exhalation. (No plural form in this sense.) ♦ *Inspiration and expiration are part of breathing.* ♦ *Even though John was near death, the nurse detected a subtle expiration from his lungs.* **3. expiration (date)** *n.* the date that something, such as food or medicine, will become no longer fresh, usable, valid, or authorized. ♦ *The expiration date on the cheese is tomorrow, so we must eat it today.* ♦ *There was no expiration on the package, so I did not buy it.*

expire [ɛk 'spɑɪr] **1.** *iv.* to end; to terminate; to be valid no longer. ♦ *The coupon expires tomorrow. You'd better use it today.* ♦ *John's driver's license expired last week.* **2.** *iv.* to die. (Euphemistic.) ♦ *Bill expired in his sleep after a long illness.* ♦ *Aunt Jane expired peacefully at the age of 80.*

explain [ɛk 'splen] **1.** *tv.* to make something easier to understand; to talk in detail about something; to make something clear. ♦ *The coach explained the new football rules to the team.* ♦ *Please explain your answer so that we can understand it.* **2.** *tv.* to give an excuse for something. ♦ *How will you explain your absence at work this time?* ♦ *Can you explain why your grades are dropping at school?*

explanation [ɛk splə 'ne ʃən] **1.** *n.* information that makes something easier to understand; description. (No plural form in this sense.) ♦ *The instructions are not clear. I need more explanation.* ♦ *I need more careful explanation in order to figure out what I am supposed to do.* **2.** *n.* an act of explaining something. ♦ *The teacher's explanations of the math problems made sense.* ♦ *The doctor provided a lengthy explanation about my illness.*

explanatory [ɛk 'splæn ə tor i] *adj.* providing an explanation; making something more clear; helping explain something. (Adv: *explanatorily* [ɛk splæn ə 'tor ə li].) ♦ *Look over the explanatory section at the top of the form before you begin the test.* ♦ *The textbook contains explanatory notes at the end of each chapter.*

expletive ['ɛk splɪ tɪv] *n.* an exclamation, often profane or obscene; a taboo word. ♦ *The radio engineer prevented the broadcast of the callers' expletives.* ♦ *The coach's angry speech was filled with expletives.*

explicit [ɛk 'splɪs ɪt] **1.** *adj.* specific; clearly stated. (Adv: *explicitly.*) ♦ *I gave Bill explicit instructions about watering my plants when I went on vacation.* ♦ *The directions Jane gave me to get to her home were very explicit.* **2.** *adj.* showing sex activity. (Euphemistic. Adv: *explicitly.*) ♦ *We don't allow our children to watch explicit movies.* ♦ *I blushed when I read parts of the explicit novel.*

explode [ɛk 'splod] **1.** *iv.* to blow up; to burst. ♦ *The fireworks exploded high in the sky.* ♦ *The red balloon exploded when I popped it with a pin.* **2.** *iv.* to get very mad; to get violently angry. (Figurative on ①.) ♦ *The coach exploded with anger at the losing team.* ♦ *I exploded when I found another parking ticket on my car.*

exploit 1. ['ɛk splɔɪt] *n.* an adventure; an act of daring; a bold action. ♦ *Dave's mountain-climbing exploit brought him fame.* ♦ *The soldiers each won a medal for their exploits in combat.* **2.** [ɛk 'splɔɪt] *tv.* to cheat someone; to take advantage of someone; to use someone or something unfairly for one's own gain. ♦ *The housing developer exploited the farmer by paying him an extremely low price for his land.* ♦ *The company exploited the workers by falsely promising them pay raises.*

exploitation [ɛk splɔɪ 'te ʃən] *n.* using someone or something for one's own advantage or gain; the unfair use of someone or something for one's own gain. (No plural form in this sense.) ♦ *The government forced the company to end exploitation of its employees.* ♦ *Child labor laws protect children from exploitation.*

exploration [ɛk splor 'e ʃən] *n.* the examination and study of some place; a journey to a place for study. (Sometimes plural with the same meaning.) ♦ *The university funded the marine biologist's underwater explorations.* ♦ *The astronaut talked about the possible exploration of Mars.*

exploratory [ɛk 'splor ə tor i] *adj.* for the purpose of exploration. (Adv: *exploratorily* [ɛk splor ə 'tor ə li].) ♦ *The patient underwent exploratory surgery.* ♦ *The oil company drilled an exploratory well.*

explore [ɛk 'splor] **1.** *tv.* to study and examine a place that has not been examined before. ♦ *The adventurer explored a dangerous underground cave.* ♦ *The survivors from the shipwreck explored the deserted island.* **2.** *tv.* to examine or consider a plan or idea carefully. (Figurative on ①.) ♦ *John explored the idea of using paper money of different colors in the U.S.* ♦ *The physician explored current theories of cancer treatment.*

explorer [ɛk 'splor ɚ] *n.* someone who travels to and through areas that are relatively unknown to the major cultural centers of the world. ♦ *The explorers were last seen entering the jungle.* ♦ *A dozen explorers traveled to the uncharted section of the Antarctic.*

explosion [ɛk 'splo ʒən] **1.** *n.* a loud, violent burst; an act of exploding; the blowing up of something. ♦ *An explosion ripped through the walls of the fort.* ♦ *An explosion in the plane's baggage compartment injured many passengers.* **2.** *n.* a noisy commotion; a noisy outburst. (Figurative on ①.) ♦ *The boss reprimanded Tom for his frequent explosions in the office.* ♦ *The crowd burst into an explosion of laughter when the clown tripped on a banana peel.*

explosive [ɛk 'splo sɪv] **1.** *adj.* likely to explode; capable of exploding. (Adv: *explosively.*) ♦ *Dynamite is highly explosive.* ♦ *Do not mix these two explosive chemicals together.* **2.** *adj.* dangerous; having the potential for leading to violence or disorder. (Figurative on ①. Adv: *explosively.*) ♦ *The teacher's explosive personality frightened the children.* ♦ *The police monitored the explosive hostage situation.* **3.** *n.* something that is used to blow something up, such as dynamite; a material that will explode. ♦ *The terrorists bought explosives to make a bomb.* ♦ *The explosives were made harmless by soaking them in oil.*

exponent [ɛk 'spo nənt] **1.** *n.* someone who explains or advocates someone or something. ♦ *The senator is a staunch exponent of civil rights.* ♦ *The prison warden is one of the death penalty's strongest exponents.* **2.** *n.* [in mathematics] a number that indicates how many times another number is to be multiplied by itself. ♦ *The number 3 is an exponent in the expression 2^3.* ♦ *The exponent is written higher and smaller than the rest of the numbers.*

exponential [ɛk spo ˌnɛn ʃəl] *adj.* of or about the number of times something is to be multiplied; having the effect of being multiplied many times. (Adv: *exponentially.*) ♦ *The exponential value of the expression was 27 digits long.* ♦ *We are experiencing exponential growth in our business.*

export 1. ['ɛk sport] *n.* a product that is shipped to another country; a product that is sold to another country. ♦ *Grain and cotton are exports from the United States.* ♦ *The government placed a tariff on all exports from hostile nations.* **2.** ['ɛk sport] *adj.* <the adj. use of ①.> ♦ *The owner of the export firm had business contacts across the globe.* ♦ *We will not meet our export quota for the coming year.* **3.** [ɛk 'sport] *tv.* to ship a product to another country for sale; to sell a product in another country. ♦ *The*

United States used to export wheat to Russia. ♦ *Japan exports automobiles to the United States.*

exportation [ɛk spor 'te ʃən] *n.* sending products to other countries for sale. (No plural form in this sense.) ♦ *The Swiss encourage the exportation of cheese to the United States.* ♦ *The exportation of Western ideas is often due to television.*

exporter [ɛk 'sport ɚ] *n.* someone or a company that sends products to other countries for sale. ♦ *Korea is a large exporter of electronic goods.* ♦ *Watches are the main product of the Swiss exporter.*

exposé [ɛk spo 'ze] *n.* a published story revealing something of importance that had been kept a secret. (From French.) ♦ *The exposé about the celebrity was quite shocking.* ♦ *The journalist verified the content of the exposé with two reliable sources.*

expose [ɛk 'spoz] **1.** *tv.* to cause something to be open to public knowledge; to remove something from hiding; to make something known. ♦ *The reporter exposed the corruption in the city government.* ♦ *Bill exposed my secret by telling Mary about it.* **2.** *tv.* to unmask someone; to cause someone's faults or wrongdoing to be revealed. ♦ *A newspaper story exposed the mayor as a crook.* ♦ *The mayor knew that her enemies wanted to expose her past errors.* **3.** *tv.* to allow photographic film to be touched by light rays. ♦ *Tom exposed the film and ruined it when he opened the camera.* ♦ *The photographer exposed the photographic film, and the image of the mountain was captured.*

exposed [ɛk 'spozd] **1.** *adj.* uncovered. ♦ *The exposed areas of the carpet had faded. Under the sofa, the carpet is still colorful.* ♦ *Bright sunlight affects exposed skin.* **2.** *adj.* [of photographic film that has been] touched by light rays. ♦ *The photographer developed the exposed film in a dark room.* ♦ *The exposed film was ruined.*

exposition [ɛk spə 'zɪ ʃən] **1.** *n.* a speech or text that explains something in detail. ♦ *Jane read an exposition of her views on space exploration.* ♦ *John's exposition on gun control was criticized by several classmates.* **2.** *n.* an exhibition; a trade show that displays products that are available for sale or retail. ♦ *Thousands of people attended the car exposition at the stadium.* ♦ *The attendance at the boat exposition set a new record.*

expostulate [ɛk 'spɑs tu let] *iv.* to argue and reason vigorously. ♦ *The lawyer expostulated endlessly about the virtues of his client.* ♦ *Dave expostulated with his children about the necessity of doing the household chores.*

exposure [ɛk 'spo ʒɚ] **1.** *n.* showing something to the public; uncovering or revealing something that was hidden. (No plural form in this sense.) ♦ *The undercover officer was responsible for the exposure of corruption in the police department.* ♦ *Because of the reporter's exposure of fraud, the bank president was sentenced to prison.* **2.** *n.* attention given to someone or something by newspapers, television, magazines, etc. (No plural form in this sense.) ♦ *The police department received a considerable amount of unwanted exposure in the press.* ♦ *Lots of advertising gave the new product a nationwide exposure.* **3.** *n.* a section of photographic film that will produce a single image. ♦ *How many exposures are there on this roll of film?* ♦ *There are 24 exposures on this roll.* **4.** *n.* an act of exposing photographic film to light. ♦ *Double exposure results from exposing the same photographic film twice.* ♦ *The photographer shot several exposures of each pose.* **5.** *n.* the settings of a camera that determine the amount of light that touches the film and the amount of time the light touches the film. ♦ *The expensive camera regulated the amount of exposure for each shot automatically.* ♦ *Without proper photographic exposure, your photos would be too light or too dark.*

expound [ɛk 'spaʊnd] **1.** *tv.* to state something in detail. ♦ *A neighborhood representative was allowed to expound the minority view.* ♦ *Mary expounded her own opinions as facts.* **2. expound on** *iv.* + *prep. phr.* to explain in detail; to talk or write about something in detail in order to make it clear or understood. ♦ *Jane expounded on the controversial views of the political candidates.* ♦ *David expounded on the budget proposal for half an hour.*

express [ɛk 'sprɛs] **1.** *tv.* to put a thought or idea into words. ♦ *It's difficult to express my ideas about the meaning of life.* ♦ *Mary expressed her complex thoughts eloquently.* **2.** *tv.* to convey a feeling or emotion through words, signs, gestures, or writing. ♦ *Tom expressed his anger by yelling at everyone.* ♦ *He expressed his love for camping through poetry.* **3.** *tv.* to indicate something; to show something. ♦ *His poetry expresses a lot of anger.* ♦ *Jimmy's sad face expressed his disappointment.* **4.** *adj.* [of transportation] traveling without stopping or with fewer stops. ♦ *The express train zoomed past the waiting commuters.* ♦ *We took the express bus downtown.* **5.** *adj.* explicit; clear; intended. (Adv: *expressly.*) ♦ *It is my express wish that my money go to a charitable foundation after my death.* ♦ *I came to the train station for the express purpose of meeting the spy.* **6.** *adj.* of or about a rapid means of shipment or delivery. ♦ *We sent the box by express delivery.* ♦ *I need the shipment right away. Does your company offer express service?*

expression [ɛk 'sprɛ ʃən] **1.** *n.* the look on one's face that indicates how one feels. ♦ *Tom wore a sorrowful expression when he walked into the room.* ♦ *The expression on Mary's face indicated that she was shocked.* **2.** *n.* the process of expressing oneself in some way. (No plural form in this sense.) ♦ *Jane needed an outlet for her artistic expression.* ♦ *David's verbal expression is improving because of his speech therapy.* **3.** *n.* a phrase or clause that is used to express an idea; an idiom. ♦ *Lisa used an idiomatic expression I hadn't heard in years.* ♦ *What does the expression "in seventh heaven" mean?*

expressive [ɛk 'sprɛs ɪv] *adj.* showing feeling and emotion; full of meaning. (Adv: *expressively.*) ♦ *I gave Jane an expressive look of gratitude.* ♦ *Dave's expressive smile comforted the child.*

expressly [ɛk 'sprɛs li] *adv.* clearly; distinctly; definitely. ♦ *John expressly stated that he didn't want to attend the party.* ♦ *The children were expressly forbidden to go near the woods.*

expressway [ɛk 'sprɛs we] *n.* a highway that does not intersect with any roads, but has ramps that allow one to get on and off at junctions. ♦ *Mary took the expressway every day to work.* ♦ *An accident on the expressway tied up traffic for miles.*

expropriate [ɛks 'pro pri et] **1.** *tv.* [for a government or a military organization] to take property away from someone or something. ♦ *The government expropriated*

Bill's house for use as military headquarters. ♦ *The army expropriated our barn and all the animals in it.* **2.** *tv.* to take away anyone's property; to steal something. ♦ *The clerk expropriated a thousand dollars from the company.* ♦ *The developers expropriated the land illegally.*

expulsion [ɛk 'spʌl ʃən] **1.** *n.* removal of someone from an office, status, or location. (No plural form in this sense.) ♦ *The board of directors voted on the expulsion of the president of the company.* ♦ *The expulsion of the dictator was accomplished by the army.* **2.** *n.* ① of someone from school or membership in an organization. (No plural form in this sense.) ♦ *The school administration ordered the child's expulsion.* ♦ *Is the student's expulsion permanent?*

expunge [ɛk 'spʌndʒ] **1.** *tv.* to clear a book or document of negative material. ♦ *The judge expunged Dave's records so that the juvenile arrest did not appear any longer.* ♦ *The editor expunged the book of its libelous content.* **2. expunge from** *tv.* + *prep. phr.* to permanently remove something; to erase something from a written record. ♦ *The court expunged the charge from the juvenile's police record.* ♦ *The judge expunged the statement from the court transcript.*

exquisite ['ɛk skwɪz ɪt] *adj.* of an excellent beauty; very fine. (Adv: *exquisitely.*) ♦ *The exquisite lace dress was very expensive.* ♦ *Tom bid on the exquisite vase at the auction.*

extemporaneous [ɛk stɛm pə 'ren i əs] *adj.* [a speech that is] made up while one is speaking; improvised. (Adv: *extemporaneously.*) ♦ *I gave an extemporaneous lecture because the invited speaker was late.* ♦ *The coach's extemporaneous speech inspired the team to victory.*

extemporize [ɛk 'stɛm pə rɑɪz] *iv.* to improvise while one is speaking. ♦ *The tennis player extemporized about her desire to win.* ♦ *The other actors extemporized extensively when John fainted just before he was to go on stage.*

extend [ɛk 'stɛnd] **1.** *tv.* to stretch something, making it longer. ♦ *I extended my arms above my head while painting the ceiling.* ♦ *Tom extended the telescope to its full length.* **2.** *tv.* to make something last longer in time. (Figurative on ①.) ♦ *The judge extended the prisoner's sentence.* ♦ *The government extended the deadline for filing federal taxes.* **3.** *tv.* to present an offer; to utter an offer or a wish. ♦ *Let me extend an offer of help to you.* ♦ *Dave extended his good wishes to the newly married couple.* **4.** *iv.* to increase in length. ♦ *The turtle's neck extended so it could reach its food.* ♦ *The rubber band extended as it was stretched.* **5.** *iv.* to spread out in all directions. ♦ *Cornfields extend over the entire landscape.* ♦ *The farmer's property extended into the next county.* **6.** *iv.* to continue in space or time. ♦ *The murderer's prison sentence extends into the distant future.* ♦ *My cousin's visit extended longer than expected.*

extended [ɛk 'stɛnd ɪd] *adj.* lengthy; long. ♦ *What I need is an extended vacation on a tropical island.* ♦ *Our lives were interrupted by our guest's extended visit.*

extension [ɛk 'stɛn ʃən] **1.** *n.* something that is added to something to make it longer or larger; an additional part. ♦ *The handle isn't long enough. I need an extension.* ♦ *The watering can has an extension on it that allows me to water hanging flower baskets.* **2. extension (telephone)** *n.* an additional telephone instrument added to an existing telephone line. ♦ *We added an extension so we could answer the telephone in the bedroom.* ♦ *Tom! Please pick up the extension. This phone call is for you.* **3. extension (cord)** *n.* a length of electrical cord with a plug in one end and a receptacle on the other. ♦ *The cord to the iron won't reach a receptacle. I need an extension.* ♦ *Where is the extension cord? It is never where it should be.* **4. extension ladder** *n.* a two-part ladder that can be extended to increase its length. ♦ *I fell off my extension ladder and broke my leg.* ♦ *The painters used an extension ladder to reach the top part of the house.* **5.** *n.* extra time given beyond a deadline. ♦ *The students were given a two-day extension to turn in their projects.* ♦ *I requested an extension from the government for filing my taxes.*

extensive [ɛk 'stɛn sɪv] *adj.* far reaching; stretched out; comprehensive; covering many areas or topics; wide ranging; large. (Adv: *extensively.*) ♦ *The editor made extensive changes in the manuscript.* ♦ *The doctor said the patient needed extensive physical therapy in order to walk again.*

extent [ɛk 'stɛnt] *n.* the distance or degree to which something extends; the degree to which something is extensive; the scope of something. ♦ *What is the extent of your interest in this matter?* ♦ *We tried to find out the extent of the problem.*

extenuating [ɛk 'stɛn ju et ɪŋ] *adj.* making [something] seem less serious by providing an excuse or explanation. ♦ *Even noting the extenuating circumstances, I must still ask for your resignation.* ♦ *The judge looked at the extenuating factors in the case before sentencing the defendant.*

exterior [ɛk 'stɪr i ɚ] **1.** *n.* the outside of something. (No plural form in this sense.) ♦ *There's a dent on the exterior of the box.* ♦ *The exterior of my house suffered some damage from the fire next door.* **2.** *adj.* <the adj. use of ①.> ♦ *The exterior walls of my house are painted green.* ♦ *There are scratches on the exterior surface of the box.*

exterminate [ɛk 'stɚ mə net] **1.** *tv.* to kill all of a group of living creatures. ♦ *The soldiers exterminated the enemy troops.* ♦ *Illegal hunters have exterminated many of the elephants in Africa.* **2.** *tv.* to kill insects, rats, and other pests in an area. ♦ *The landlord exterminated the rats in the cellar.* ♦ *I exterminated the ants with pesticide.*

exterminator [ɛk 'stɚ mə net ɚ] *n.* someone who kills insects, mice, rats, and other pests. ♦ *The exterminator got rid of the termites in the house.* ♦ *I think it's time we called an exterminator. I saw bugs in the attic.*

external [ɛk 'stɚ nəl] **1.** *adj.* outside; outer. (Adv: *externally.*) ♦ *The crab's external shell must be removed before you eat the meat inside.* ♦ *The electric wires are covered with an external plastic sheath.* **2.** *adj.* coming from the outside; being affected by someone or something on the outside. (Adv: *externally.*) ♦ *The judge would not allow external sources to influence her opinion of the case.* ♦ *The external pressures on his life made his job too much for Bill to handle.* **3. external use** *n.* application or use on the outside of the body. (No plural form in this sense.) ♦ *This medicine is for external use only.* ♦ *The contents of this bottle are for external use.*

extinct [ɛk 'stɪŋkt] **1.** *adj.* [of a plant or animal species that is] no longer in existence. ♦ *Scientists examined fossils of the extinct plant.* ♦ *It is natural for some species to become extinct every decade.* **2.** *adj.* [of a volcano] no longer capable of erupting. ♦ *We visited the extinct vol-*

cano on the island. ♦ *Some Caribbean islands are the tips of extinct volcanoes resting on the ocean floor.*

extinction [ɛk 'stɪŋk ʃən] *n.* the death of a species of plant or animal. (No plural form in this sense.) ♦ *What caused the extinction of the dinosaurs?* ♦ *There are many animals in danger of extinction.*

extinguish [ɛk 'stɪŋ gwɪʃ] **1.** *tv.* to put out a fire or a flame; to stop something from burning. ♦ *The firefighters extinguished the fire in the office building.* ♦ *John extinguished the campfire with water.* **2.** *tv.* to put an end to something. (Figurative on ①.) ♦ *Anne's knee injury extinguished any chance she had for a place on the softball team.* ♦ *Jane extinguished John's hopes of going out on a date.*

extol [ɛk 'stol] *tv.* to praise the virtues of someone or something; to praise someone or something. ♦ *Movie critics extolled the young performer's acting debut.* ♦ *The general extolled David for his bravery.*

extort [ɛk 'stort] *tv.* to demand money or something from someone by making threats. ♦ *The business owner extorted favors from the politician.* ♦ *A blackmailer extorted thousands of dollars from the millionaire.*

extortion [ɛk 'stor ʃən] *n.* using threats to force someone into giving up money or property. (No plural form in this sense.) ♦ *The criminals went to jail for extortion.* ♦ *The blackmailer was charged with extortion.*

extra ['ɛk strə] **1.** *adj.* more or greater than is expected; more or greater than usual; additional. ♦ *John asked for an extra scoop of ice cream.* ♦ *Did you eat an extra bowl of cereal this morning?* **2.** *adv.* more; additional. ♦ *An enlarged color portrait costs twenty dollars extra.* ♦ *You'll have to pay a little extra to get cheese on the hamburgers.* **3.** *n.* an actor that is hired to be part of the background or part of a crowd. ♦ *Hundreds of extras were hired for the new action movie.* ♦ *Mary was an extra in the restaurant scene on the soap opera.*

extract 1. ['ɛk strækt] *n.* something that is taken from a text; an excerpt; a quote. ♦ *The author began the first chapter with an extract from the Bible.* ♦ *The teacher read the students an extract from one of Shakespeare's plays.* **2.** ['ɛk strækt] *n.* a concentrated substance, such as a flavor. ♦ *Add a little lemon extract to the cheesecake recipe.* ♦ *I added a teaspoon of vanilla extract to the cake batter.* **3.** [ɛk 'strækt] *tv.* to remove something from some place; to pull something out from some place. ♦ *The dentist extracted the patient's abscessed tooth.* ♦ *Anne extracted her car keys from her purse.* **4.** [ɛk 'strækt] *tv.* to remove something from something by using a machine or chemicals. ♦ *The doctor extracted the snake's poison from the bite.* ♦ *A special process extracts the ink from the recycled newspapers.*

extraction [ɛk 'stræk ʃən] **1.** *n.* pulling something out; removing something. (No plural form in this sense.) ♦ *The extraction of the tooth was extremely painful.* ♦ *Miners use heavy equipment for the extraction of coal.* **2.** *n.* the act of pulling a tooth. ♦ *I am sorry but I will have to perform an extraction on this tooth.* ♦ *Sally was sent to a dentist who does nothing but extractions.* **3.** *n.* family descent; lineage; parentage. (No plural form in this sense.) ♦ *Anne's German extraction was evident in her accent.* ♦ *My roommate is of Japanese extraction.*

extracurricular [ɛk strə kə 'rɪk jə lɚ] **1.** *adj.* of or about hobbies and activities, such as sports clubs, outside of regular schoolwork. (Adv: *extracurricularly.*) ♦ *I don't want your extracurricular activities to interfere with your schoolwork.* ♦ *The shy students participated in no extracurricular activities.* **2.** *adj.* outside the limits of one's duties or responsibilities. (Figurative on ①. Adv: *extracurricularly.*) ♦ *Taking work home from the office was an extracurricular task for John.* ♦ *Mary was fired for doing extracurricular work as a freelancer for a competing company.*

extradite ['ɛk strə dɑɪt] *tv.* to order an accused criminal moved from one jurisdiction to another for trial. (Can be from one state, country, or county to another.) ♦ *The authorities extradited the fugitive from Canada to the United States.* ♦ *The accused killer was extradited from Arizona to Texas.*

extradition [ɛk srtə 'dɪ ʃən] *n.* moving an accused criminal from one jurisdiction to another. (No plural form in this sense.) ♦ *The fugitive's lawyer fought the extradition in court.* ♦ *The order of extradition was waived.*

extramarital [ɛk strə 'mɛr ə təl] *adj.* outside of a marriage. (Adv: *extramaritally.*) ♦ *The former candidate had been accused of an extramarital love affair.* ♦ *Bill and Mary divorced due to his extramarital affair.*

extraneous [ɛk 'stren i əs] *adj.* not belonging to something; not related to something; foreign or alien to something. (Adv: *extraneously.*) ♦ *The editor cut the extraneous material from the first chapter.* ♦ *The lawyer's extraneous remarks were removed from the court record on the orders of the judge.*

extraordinary [ɛk 'stror də nɛr i] *adj.* out of the ordinary; beyond what is expected or required; remarkable; unusual. (Adv: *extraordinarily* [ɛk stror də 'nɛr ə li].) ♦ *The explorer lived an extraordinary life.* ♦ *Mary wrote a book about her extraordinary adventures during the war.*

extrapolate [ɛk 'stræp ə let] *tv.* to make a guess about something, based on what is already known. ♦ *The stockbroker extrapolated the future price of the stock based on its historical growth patterns.* ♦ *You are able to extrapolate the population growth from previous census figures.*

extrasensory [ɛk strə 'sɛn sə ri] *adj.* beyond the normal range of sight, hearing, taste, touch, and smell; intuitive. ♦ *This dog seems to use some sort of extrasensory faculties for hunting.* ♦ *The psychic claimed to have extrasensory perception.*

extraterrestrial [ɛk strə tə 'rɛs tri əl] *adj.* from outer space; existing on another celestial body; alien. (Adv: *extraterrestrially.*) ♦ *I don't believe that you've had an extraterrestrial encounter.* ♦ *Do you think that extraterrestrial life exists?*

extravagance [ɛk 'stræv ə gəns] **1.** *n.* expensive and unnecessary things; expenditures that are costly and unnecessary. (No plural form in this sense.) ♦ *Few people can afford the extravagance of buying a new car every year.* ♦ *Max claims that the federal government excels in extravagance and waste.* **2.** *n.* a wasteful expense of money; an unnecessary luxury. ♦ *John's three-week vacation in Paris is certainly an extravagance.* ♦ *My new ring is an extravagance, but I wanted it so much!*

extravagant [ɛk 'stræv ə gənt] *adj.* wasteful and excessive. (Adv: *extravagantly.*) ♦ *I went on an extravagant shopping spree with my parents' credit card.* ♦ *The accountant warned the owner against extravagant purchases.*

extravaganza [ɛk stræv ə 'gæn zə] *n.* an expensive or elaborate performance or piece of entertainment. ♦ *I attended the musical extravaganza held at the auditorium.* ♦ *All tickets for the extravaganza were sold out.*

extreme [ɛk 'strim] **1.** *adj.* to the greatest degree; to the furthest point possible in any direction; furthest. (Adv: *extremely.*) ♦ *Bill was in extreme pain when he broke his foot.* ♦ *I felt extreme grief when my brother died.* **2.** *n.* one of two things that are as far apart from each other as possible. ♦ *Tom's mood has gone from one extreme to another today.* ♦ *Good and evil are two extremes that co-exist in this world.* **3.** *n.* the greatest degree of a measure of something. ♦ *The heat reached an extreme of 106 degrees this summer.* ♦ *The pregnant woman's labor pains have reached the extreme.*

extremism [ɛk 'strim ɪz əm] *n.* [in political philosophy] exhibiting extreme or radical behavior in the espousal of one's beliefs. (No plural form in this sense.) ♦ *Mary's liberal extremism conflicted with her parents' beliefs.* ♦ *I could not support Bill's antigovernment extremism.*

extremist [ɛk 'strim əst] **1.** *n.* someone who exhibits extreme or radical behavior regarding a political or other philosophy. ♦ *The conservative students heckled the liberal extremist.* ♦ *Extremists threatened to place a bomb in the subway.* **2.** *adj.* <the adj. use of ①.> ♦ *Most extremist political positions are offensive to me.* ♦ *I have heard enough of your extremist talk!*

extremity [ɛk 'strɛm ə ti] **1.** *n.* intensity; the extremist nature [of something]. (No plural form in this sense.) ♦ *I was alarmed by the extremity of your statement.* ♦ *I was pushed to the extremity of my patience.* **2. extremities** *n.* the end of one's hand or foot; the part of the body furthest from the heart. ♦ *Dave experienced numbness in his extremities due to the cold weather.* ♦ *I felt pain and weakness in my extremities.*

extricate ['ɛk strə ket] *tv.* to remove something from a delicate situation; to remove something that is stuck; to untangle someone or something. ♦ *The emergency rescue crew extricated the injured people from the wrecked vehicle.* ♦ *Jane extricated herself from an unhappy relationship with her mother.*

extrication [ɛk strə 'ke ʃən] *n.* removing someone or something from a delicate situation. (No plural form in this sense.) ♦ *The extrication of the injured passengers from the accident was successful.* ♦ *Why should the extrication of a splinter be so difficult and painful?*

extrinsic [ɛk 'strɪn sɪk] *adj.* additional; not inherent; coming from the outside of something. (Adv: *extrinsically* [...ɪk li].) ♦ *The intrinsic problems were easily settled, but the extrinsic difficulties caused by unknown outside forces were almost impossible to settle.* ♦ *Dave discussed the extrinsic difficulties associated with the project.*

extrovert ['ɛk strə vɚt] *n.* someone who enjoys being with other people instead of being alone; someone who is very outgoing and cheerful. ♦ *Even though Susan is an actress, I would not consider her an extrovert.* ♦ *John has all the social characteristics of an extrovert.*

extrude [ɛk 'strud] *tv.* to push something out with force; to force something out. ♦ *The powerful machine extruded copper tubing with ease.* ♦ *We have a machine that extrudes pasta.*

exuberance [ɛg 'zub ə rəns] *n.* joy, enthusiasm, and cheerfulness. (No plural form in this sense.) ♦ *Bill's exuberance influenced the entire soccer team.* ♦ *Jane's exuberance made it easier for all of us to work on the difficult task.*

exuberant [ɛg 'zub ə rənt] *adj.* enthusiastic; cheerful; full of life and cheer. (Adv: *exuberantly.*) ♦ *After your long illness, it is good to see you active and exuberant.* ♦ *The exuberant children jumped into the swimming pool.*

exude [ɛg 'zud] **1.** *tv.* to cause something to ooze out; to cause something to drip out. ♦ *The wound exuded a clear substance.* ♦ *The runner exuded sweat.* **2.** *tv.* to utter or display something, such as a feeling, or verbal sweetness. (Figurative on ①.) ♦ *John exudes confidence in his work.* ♦ *The applicant exuded charm during the interview.* **3.** *iv.* to ooze; to drip. ♦ *Drops of sweat exuded from every pore.* ♦ *Blood exuded from the wound.*

exult [ɛg 'zʌlt] *iv.* to rejoice; to be joyful. (Compare with exalt.) ♦ *Along the route of the parade, citizens exulted in celebration of their independence and freedom.* ♦ *The members of the soccer team exulted over their winning season.*

eye ['ɑɪ] **1.** *n.* one of the two organs of sight; an **eyeball**. ♦ *The eye doctor shined a bright light in each of my eyes.* ♦ *I covered my eyes to protect them from blowing dust.* **2.** *n.* the ring of color on someone's eye; the iris. ♦ *My eyes are dark brown.* ♦ *The color of your sweater matches your eyes.* **3. eye of the needle** *n.* a small hole for thread in one end of a needle. ♦ *I can't get the thread through the eye of the needle.* ♦ *The thread has to go through the eye of the needle.* **4.** *tv.* to glance at or look at someone or something; to watch someone or something. (The present participle is *eying* or *eyeing.*) ♦ *Jane eyed her watch and started toward the door.* ♦ *Bill eyed the door, waiting for Mary to arrive.* **5. eye of the hurricane, eye of the storm** *idiom* the area of calm in the center of a tornado, hurricane, or cyclone. ♦ *It is calm and peaceful in the eye of the storm.* ♦ *The helicopter flew into the eye of the hurricane.* **6. eye of the storm** *idiom* the center of a problem; the center of a commotion or a disturbance. ♦ *Tom, finding himself at the eye of the storm, tried to blame someone else for the problem.* ♦ *The manager's office was known as the eye of the storm since all the major problems ended up there.* **7. give someone the eye** *idiom* to look at someone in a way that communicates romantic interest. ♦ *Anne gave John the eye. It really surprised him.* ♦ *Tom kept giving Sally the eye. She finally left.* **8. have an eye for something, have a good eye for something** *idiom* to have the ability to see small details; to have the ability to see the difference between two things that are similar. ♦ *The designer had a good eye for color.* ♦ *The teacher has an eye for identifying promising students.* **9. have eyes in the back of one's head** *idiom* to seem to be able to sense what is going on outside of one's vision. ♦ *My teacher seems to have eyes in the back of her head.* ♦ *My teacher doesn't need to have eyes in the back of his head. He watches us very carefully.* **10. hit someone (right) between the eyes** *idiom* to become completely apparent; to surprise or impress someone. ♦ *Suddenly, it hit me right between the eyes. John and Mary were in love.* ♦ *Then—as he was talking—the exact nature of the evil plan hit me between the eyes.* **11. in one's mind's eye** *idiom* in one's mind. ♦ *In my mind's eye, I can see trouble ahead.* ♦ *In her mind's eye, she could see a beautiful building beside the river. She decided to design such a building.* **12. in the**

public eye *idiom* publicly; visible to all; conspicuous. ♦ *Elected officials find themselves constantly in the public eye.* ♦ *The mayor made it a practice to get into the public eye as much as possible.* **13. turn a blind eye (to someone or something)** *idiom* to ignore something and pretend one does not see it. ♦ *The usher turned a blind eye to the little boy who sneaked into the theater.* ♦ *How can you turn a blind eye to all those starving children?* **14. with the naked eye** See naked ③.

eyeball ['aɪ bɔl] **1.** *n.* the round part of the eye that sits in the socket. (The same as eye ①.) ♦ *Susan's eyeballs were red from the smoke in the bar.* ♦ *John placed the contact lens on his eyeball.* **2.** *tv.* to look at someone or something closely; to watch someone or something closely. (Informal.) ♦ *The sergeant eyeballed the new recruits.* ♦ *I eyeballed the contract before I signed it.* **3. eyeball-to-eyeball** *idiom* person-to-person; face-to-face. ♦ *The discussions will have to be eyeball-to-eyeball to be effective.* ♦ *Telephone conversations are a waste of time. We need to talk eyeball-to-eyeball.*

eyebrow ['aɪ brɑʊ] **1.** *n.* the curved ridge of hair on one's brow, just above the eye. ♦ *Bill has bushy red eyebrows and small, green eyes.* ♦ *Mary dyed her eyebrows a lighter color.* **2. cause (some) eyebrows to raise** *idiom* to shock people; to surprise and dismay people. ♦ *John caused some eyebrows to raise when he married a poor girl from Toledo.* ♦ *If you want to cause eyebrows to raise, just start singing as you walk down the street.*

eyedrops ['aɪ drɑps] *n.* a soothing medicine that is placed in the eyes to relieve irritation and redness. (Treated as plural.) ♦ *The doctor prescribed eyedrops for Bill's infection.* ♦ *The eyedrops relieved the itching in Susan's eyes.*

eyeful ['aɪ fʊl] **get an eyeful (of someone or something)** *idiom* to see everything; to see a shocking or surprising sight. ♦ *The office door opened for a minute, and I got an eyeful of the interior.* ♦ *Mary got an eyeful of the company's extravagant spending when she peeked into the conference room.*

eyeglasses ['aɪ glæs əz] *n.* two lenses held together by a frame; worn in front of the eyes to improve vision. (Treated as plural. See also **glasses, spectacles.**) ♦ *Bill couldn't read the newspaper because he couldn't find his eyeglasses.* ♦ *Mary needs to wear eyeglasses when she drives.*

eyelash ['aɪ læʃ] *n.* one of the many small, thin hairs that grow on the edge of the eyelid. ♦ *Jane applied mascara to her eyelashes to make them look darker.* ♦ *When an eyelash fell into my eye, my eye began to water.*

eyelet ['aɪ lɪt] *n.* a small hole that is shaped like an eye; a small round hole, such as found on shoes, that shoelaces are put through. ♦ *I threaded the shoelace through the eyelet.* ♦ *The soldiers' boots had metal eyelets.*

eyelid ['aɪ lɪd] *n.* the fold of skin that moves over the eye. ♦ *The accident victim's eyelids were swollen shut.* ♦ *Mary wore blue eye shadow on her eyelids.*

eye-opener ['aɪ o pən ɚ] *n.* a discovery that is surprising or shocking; news or information that changes the way someone thinks about something. ♦ *The extent of the storm's damage was quite an eye-opener.* ♦ *The doctor confronted Bill with the eye-opener that he only had a year to live.*

eyepiece ['aɪ pis] *n.* the lens of a microscope or telescope. ♦ *The eyepiece of the telescope needs cleaning.* ♦ *The scientist looked through the eyepieces of the microscope at the cells.*

eye shadow ['aɪ ʃæ do] *n.* makeup that is placed on the eyelids to give them color. (No plural form in this sense.) ♦ *The actress applied her eye shadow after putting on her costume.* ♦ *The dark eye shadow makes you look like you're depressed.*

eyesight ['aɪ sɑɪt] *n.* vision; the ability to see. (No plural form in this sense.) ♦ *Each year I have my eyesight checked.* ♦ *Dave's eyesight is poor, so he wears corrective glasses.*

eyewitness ['aɪ 'wɪt nəs] *n.* someone who sees an event happen; someone who sees an accident or crime take place. ♦ *An eyewitness to the crime testified against the suspect.* ♦ *Eyewitnesses reported the accident to the police.*

F AND **f** ['ɛf] **1.** *n.* the sixth letter of the English alphabet. ♦ *The word* leaf *ends with the letter* F. ♦ E *comes before* F. **2. F** *n.* the grade of F; a grade that indicates failure. ♦ *Bob didn't study, so he got an F on his test.* ♦ *Susan had hoped for a C but got an F.*

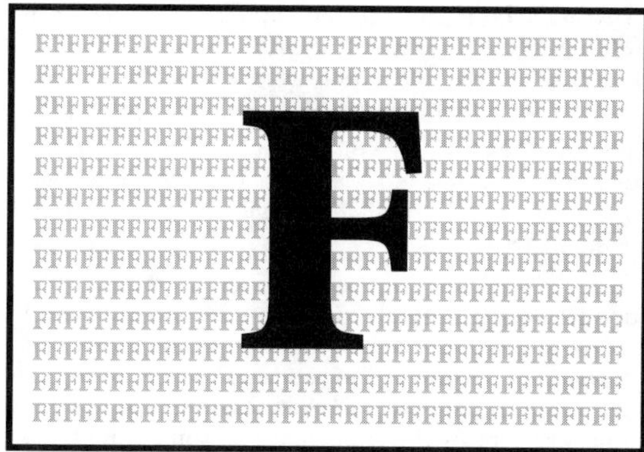

fable ['fe bəl] **1.** *n.* a story that teaches a lesson, often using animals as the characters of the story. ♦ *I read an ancient fable about the race between the tortoise and the hare.* ♦ *Many fables were first told by an old Greek storyteller named Aesop.* **2.** *n.* a lie; a description of an event that didn't really happen. ♦ *The teacher did not believe John's fable that the dog ate his homework.* ♦ *I want to know why you're late, and don't tell me any fables!*

fabric ['fæb rɪk] **1.** *n.* material or cloth made by weaving thread together. (No plural form in this sense.) ♦ *My shirt is made of cotton fabric.* ♦ *I repaired the tear in the fabric with a needle and thread.* **2. fabrics** *n.* kinds or types of ①. ♦ *I looked at colored fabrics at the department store.* ♦ *They have a wide selection of fabrics at that store.* **3.** *n.* a framework or structure. (Figurative on ①. No plural form in this sense.) ♦ *The lawyer slowly unraveled the defendant's fabric of lies.* ♦ *Crime threatens the fabric of society.*

fabricate ['fæb rɪ ket] **1.** *tv.* to build something. ♦ *The factory fabricated one hundred cars every day.* ♦ *We were able to fabricate a temporary pen in which to keep the new pony.* **2.** *tv.* to make up a story or a lie; to invent an excuse. (Figurative on ①.) ♦ *Jane fabricated the story that she was late because she was caught in traffic.* ♦ *John fabricated an excuse for missing the meeting.*

fabrication [fæb rɪ 'ke ʃən] **1.** *n.* construction; manufacture. (No plural form in this sense.) ♦ *The fabrication of the farmer's barn took only one day.* ♦ *Fabrication of the huge machine took three months.* **2.** *n.* a lie; an excuse; a story that is made up or invented. ♦ *Your story of being caught in traffic is a fabrication, isn't it?* ♦ *Although my excuse was a fabrication, my teacher believed it.*

fabulous ['fæb jə ləs] *adj.* amazing; wonderful; tremendous. (Adv: *fabulously.*) ♦ *Dave made a fabulous salad for the dinner party.* ♦ *We had a fabulous time at the beach last Saturday.*

facade AND **façade** [fə 'sɑd] **1.** *n.* the front of a building; the part of a building that faces the street. (From French.) ♦ *During the earthquake, the facade of the small shop collapsed.* ♦ *The façades of the stores had been freshly painted.* **2.** *n.* [someone's] false appearance that covers up something real. (Figurative on ①.) ♦ *Bill's smile is just a façade. Really he's very mad at you.* ♦ *In spite of Anne's cheerful facade, I knew she was very unhappy.*

face ['fes] **1.** *n.* the front part of the head from the hairline to the chin. ♦ *The baseball struck John's face, just to the left of his nose.* ♦ *The old man's face was lined with wrinkles.* **2.** *n.* a look; an expression; the way ① looks. ♦ *What a sad face! Is something bothering you?* ♦ *The clown with a silly face made the children laugh.* **3.** *n.* the front part or surface of something. ♦ *The face of the building was decorated with colorful brick.* ♦ *The out-of-control car tumbled down the face of the cliff.* **4.** *iv.* to look toward someone or something or toward a particular direction; to be directed toward a particular direction. ♦ *The same side of the moon always faces toward the earth.* ♦ *My bedroom window faces to the east.* **5.** *tv.* to look toward someone or something or in a particular direction. ♦ *Tom faced Mary directly while they ate dinner.* ♦ *Anne faced the east, looking at the sunrise.* **6.** *tv.* to stand in front of people; to confront someone or something. ♦ *The young soldier faced a line of enemy fighters.* ♦ *The mayor faced the angry citizens to explain the tax increase.* **7.** *tv.* to deal with someone or something; to have to cope with someone or something. ♦ *You have to face the facts and realize it's time to get on with your life.* ♦ *The mayor faced the accusations with dignity.* **8.** *tv.* to cover the front part of something or the edges of something with a decoration. ♦ *The designer faced the side wall with marble tile.* ♦ *The cabinet is faced with panels of oak.* **9. have egg on one's face** *idiom* to be embarrassed because of an error that is obvious to everyone. ♦ *Bob has egg on his face because he wore jeans to the party and everyone else wore formal clothing.* ♦ *John was completely wrong about the weather for the picnic. It snowed! Now he has egg on his face.* **10. keep a straight face** *idiom* to make one's face stay free from laughter. ♦ *It's hard to keep a straight face when someone tells a funny joke.* ♦ *I knew it was John who played the trick. He couldn't keep a straight face.* **11. lose face** *idiom* to lose status; to become less respectable. ♦ *John is more afraid of losing face than of losing money.* ♦ *Things will go better if you can explain to him where he was wrong without making him lose face.* **12. make a face** *idiom* to twist one's face into a strange expression in order to show one's dislike, ridicule, etc., or in order to make someone laugh. ♦ *The comedian made faces in order to amuse the children.* ♦ *Jane made a face when she was asked to work late.* **13. not show one's face** *idiom* not to appear (somewhere). ♦ *After what she said, she had better not show her face around here again.* ♦ *If I don't say I'm sorry, I'll never be able to show my face again.* **14. put on a brave face** *idiom* to try to appear happy or satisfied when faced with misfortune or danger. ♦ *We've lost all our money, but we must put a brave face on for the sake of the children.* ♦ *Jim's lost his job and is worried, but he's putting on a brave face.* **15. slap in the face** *idiom* an insult; an act that causes disappointment or discouragement. ♦ *Losing the election was a slap in the face for the club president.* ♦ *Failing to get into graduate school was a slap in the face to Max after his year of study.* **16. stare someone in the face** *idiom* [for something] to be very obvious to someone; [for something] to be very easy for someone to see or understand. ♦ *Her child's need for special teachers must have been staring Sally in the face, but she ignored it.* ♦ *It's staring Max in the face that the boss is displeased with him.* **17. tell one**

to one's face *idiom* to tell (something) to someone directly. ♦ *I'm sorry that Sally feels that way about me. I wish she had told me to my face.* ♦ *I won't tell Tom that you're mad at him. You should tell him to his face.*

faceless ['fes ləs] *adj.* without an identity; impersonal; without character. (Adv: *facelessly.*) ♦ *Not one of the faceless bureaucrats at city hall was able to help me.* ♦ *In the hospital, I was treated by a faceless staff of indifferent doctors and nurses.*

facelift ['fes lɪft] **1.** *n.* a kind of surgery where the skin of the face is pulled tighter in order to remove wrinkles. ♦ *My facelift makes me look ten years younger.* ♦ *My plastic surgeon specializes in facelifts.* **2.** *n.* a renovation; the improvement of the appearance of something that is worn down. (Figurative on ①.) ♦ *The bank loaned $100,000 to the restaurant for a badly needed facelift.* ♦ *More people than ever visited the mall after its facelift.*

facet ['fæs ɪt] **1.** *n.* a side of a polished or cut gemstone. ♦ *Each facet of the diamond reflected the sunlight.* ♦ *The jeweler carefully polished each facet of the ruby.* **2.** *n.* an aspect of something; a part of something; a feature of something. (Figurative on ①.) ♦ *The most important facet of the mayor's plan was a balanced budget.* ♦ *The teacher carefully explained each facet of the theory.*

facetious [fə 'si ʃəs] *adj.* not serious; meant as a joke; meant to be funny. (Adv: *facetiously.*) ♦ *Don't be offended; it was just a facetious remark.* ♦ *The teacher didn't appreciate Bob's facetious comment.*

facial ['fe ʃəl] **1.** *adj.* of or about the face. (Adv: *facially.*) ♦ *The company didn't allow its workers to grow facial hair.* ♦ *Jane's facial expression indicated that she was very mad.* **2.** *n.* a service provided by someone who massages, cleans, and applies makeup to someone's face. ♦ *Sue received a manicure, a haircut, and a facial for $75.* ♦ *I made an appointment for a facial for the day before my wedding.*

facile ['fæs ɛl] **1.** *adj.* easily done; easy to use; too easy; simplistic. ♦ *I'm bored at work because my boss only gives me facile assignments.* ♦ *I completed the facile task quickly.* **2.** *adj.* moving or functioning easily and with skill. (Adv: *facilely.*) ♦ *Jane's facile mind could follow the complicated explanation easily.* ♦ *With her skilled and facile fingers, the seamstress finished the dress quickly.*

facilitate [fə 'sɪl ə tet] *tv.* to make it easier for someone to do something; to enable something to happen. ♦ *Anne facilitated the process by alphabetizing everything.* ♦ *A calculator facilitates the processing of my income tax forms.*

facility [fə 'sɪl ə ti] **1.** *n.* a site used by a company for its business. ♦ *The receptionist suggested I call the company's Minneapolis facility.* ♦ *The company's president inspected the new facility each month.* **2. facilities** *n.* a bathroom; a restroom. (Euphemistic.) ♦ *"Excuse me, where are the facilities?" Bob asked the clerk at the front desk.* ♦ *I'm sorry, we have no facilities for public use in the store.* **3.** *n.* ease; the ability to do something easily and without problems. (No plural form in this sense.) ♦ *The stern teacher handled problem students with great facility.* ♦ *The facility with which the acrobat walked on the tightrope amazed the crowd.*

facing ['fes ɪŋ] **1.** *n.* a covering for decoration or protection. (No plural form in this sense.) ♦ *The front of the building has a wood facing.* ♦ *The wall was covered with brick facing.* **2. facing page** *n.* the opposite page. ♦ *Please refer to the graph on the facing page.* ♦ *The story is continued on the facing page.*

facsimile [fæk 'sɪm ə li] **1.** *n.* an exact copy; an exact duplicate. ♦ *This painting of sunflowers is a good facsimile of the original one.* ♦ *Could you send me the original document, or a reasonable facsimile?* **2.** *n.* the process of sending ① over telephone lines, using special transmitters and receivers. (See also fax ①.) ♦ *I'm sending you a copy by facsimile and the original by mail.* ♦ *The researcher sent the important report via facsimile.*

fact ['fækt] **1.** *n.* something that is true; something that really happened. ♦ *It's a fact that the capital of Wisconsin is Madison.* ♦ *Each of these travel books has a list of facts about the country that is the subject of the book.* **2. in fact** *phr.* truthfully. ♦ *I wasn't in California last week. In fact, I've never been there.* ♦ *In fact, you should never have asked the question.*

faction ['fæk ʃən] *n.* a small segment of a larger group of people. ♦ *An armed faction of rebels killed the leader and took control of the government.* ♦ *The president negotiated a cease-fire among the opposing factions.*

factor ['fæk tɚ] **1.** *n.* one of a number of elements that contribute to a result; an influence; a circumstance. ♦ *One factor in environmental pollution is toxic waste.* ♦ *Your bad behavior was a factor in my decision to punish you.* **2.** *n.* a whole number multiplied by another whole number to make a specific number. ♦ *Since 2 × 5 is 10, 2 and 5 are factors of 10.* ♦ *The greatest common factor of 24 and 36 is 12, because 12 is the largest number that evenly divides into both 24 and 36.* **3.** *tv.* to break down a number into ②. ♦ *If you factor 35, you get 7 and 5.* ♦ *If you factor a prime number, you can only get that number and 1.*

factory ['fæk tə ri] *n.* a building where products are made, usually with machines. ♦ *My dad works in a factory that produces cars.* ♦ *During the last recession, several factories were shut down.*

factual ['fæk tʃu əl] *adj.* real; actual; of or about facts. (Adv: *factually.*) ♦ *Many movies are based on factual experiences.* ♦ *I wrote a book involving factual events during the Civil War.*

faculty ['fæk əl ti] **1.** *n.* the teachers at a school, college, or university. ♦ *Jane is a member of the faculty at the local university.* ♦ *The faculty voted to approve a foreign-language requirement.* **2.** *n.* a skill; an ability, especially a mental ability. ♦ *Mary has a remarkable faculty for adding large numbers in her head.* ♦ *Dave has quite a faculty for memorizing long poems.* **3.** *adj.* <the adj. use of ①.> ♦ *Jane is a faculty member at the local university.* ♦ *The faculty offices are located in this building.*

fad ['fæd] *n.* a short-lived fashion; a very popular thing that everyone does or has for a short period of time. ♦ *Wearing pants with wide cuffs was a fad of the 1970s.* ♦ *Popular celebrities often start fads unintentionally.*

fade ['fed] **1.** *iv.* to lose color; to become pale; to become less bright. ♦ *Over the years, the bright red carpet faded to pink.* ♦ *During October, my suntan began to fade.* **2.** *iv.* to wither; to become weak; to lose energy; to diminish. (Figurative on ①.) ♦ *Our hopes of winning the game faded when two of our players were injured.* ♦ *The president's popularity faded because of the proposed tax increase.* **3.** *tv.*

to cause something to lose color or become pale as in ①. ♦ *The sunlight faded the red carpet.* ♦ *I faded my new blue jeans with bleach.*

faded ['fed ɪd] **1.** *adj.* paled; having lost color; having become less bright. ♦ *I wore a T-shirt and a pair of faded blue jeans to the party.* ♦ *We replaced the faded rug in the living room with wall-to-wall carpeting.* **2.** *adj.* diminished. (Figurative on ①.) ♦ *The faded hopes of yesterday are nothing but dim memories.* ♦ *Your sloth is the result of faded ambitions.*

fading ['fed ɪŋ] *adj.* losing color or brightness; becoming pale. ♦ *The fading paint on the walls was beginning to peel.* ♦ *The fading sun slowly dipped below the horizon.*

Fahrenheit ['fɛr ən hɑɪt] **1.** *n.* the nonmetric system of measuring temperature, as opposed to Celsius. (No plural form in this sense. From Gabriel Fahrenheit, a German physicist who invented the Fahrenheit scale.) ♦ *Is this temperature measured in Fahrenheit or Celsius?* ♦ *Canadians measure temperature in Celsius, and Americans measure it in Fahrenheit.* **2.** *adj.* <the adj. use of ①.> (② follows **degrees**. Abbreviated *F.*) ♦ *Water boils at 212 degrees Fahrenheit and freezes at 32 degrees Fahrenheit.* ♦ *The sick child's temperature is 103 degrees F.*

fail ['fel] **1.** *tv.* not to succeed at something, especially a course in school. ♦ *I never bothered to study, and so I failed my algebra test.* ♦ *I failed history, so I had to take it again in summer school.* **2.** *tv.* to give a student a grade indicating failure. ♦ *Mrs. Brown failed five students in her math class because they never did their homework.* ♦ *Mr. Smith failed the students who did not come to class.* **3.** *tv.* to not help someone; to let someone down. ♦ *Grandpa's eyes failed him at about the age of 90.* ♦ *My car failed me when I needed it most.* **4.** *iv.* [for part of a person's body] to become weak; [for something] to cease working; [for something] not to succeed. ♦ *When Grandma turned 85, her eyes began to fail.* ♦ *Because of the long drought, our corn crop failed.* **5.** *iv.* [for a business] to go bankrupt. ♦ *Bill's business failed because he didn't advertise enough.* ♦ *Many banks failed during the Depression.* **6.** *iv.* not to succeed in a task that one has undertaken; not to pass a school course. ♦ *I took the course three times, and I failed each time.* ♦ *John had been given a big job to do, but he failed and was fired.* **7.** *n.* a grade given for a course, test, paper, or school year showing that one has not passed. (In a grading system where the only other grade is **pass**.) ♦ *Bill worked hard in the difficult chemistry course but ended up with a fail.* ♦ *If you do not write an essay for this class, you will get a fail.*

failed ['feld] *adj.* unsuccessful; ruined; bankrupt. ♦ *The government shut down the failed bank.* ♦ *Tom lost $100,000 on his failed business venture.*

failing ['fel ɪŋ] **1.** *n.* a fault; a weakness of character. ♦ *Your failing is that you let other people order you around.* ♦ *Postponing important business is one of my failings.* **2.** *prep.* lacking; without. ♦ *Failing a change in attitude, Bob is not likely to participate.* ♦ *Failing an emergency bank loan, we won't be able to repair the water damage.*

fail-safe ['fel sef] *adj.* [a machine or system] able to go to a secure or unharmed state in case of a failure. ♦ *A fail-safe machine will not cause harm if something goes wrong.* ♦ *John developed a fail-safe system for transferring computer files.*

failure ['fel jɚ] **1.** *n.* failing; not succeeding. (No plural form in this sense.) ♦ *Failure is common to all humans. No one is perfect.* ♦ *Failure and the fear of it make us alert.* **2.** *n.* an act of ①. ♦ *Tom's failure at work was caused by his lack of skill.* ♦ *Bob was ashamed of his failure to pass the math course.* **3.** *n.* something that is not successful; something that has not lived up to expectations. ♦ *Dave's store was a total failure, and he lost his entire investment.* ♦ *The television network canceled the season's programming failures.* **4.** *n.* someone whose life has had almost no success. ♦ *After he was fired from his job, Bill felt like a failure.* ♦ *Because Sue felt like a failure, she went to see a psychiatrist.*

faint ['fent] **1.** *adj.* barely noticeable; dim; not clear. (Adv: *faintly.* Comp: *fainter;* sup: *faintest.*) ♦ *I stayed up until I saw faint rays of light from the rising sun.* ♦ *This spaghetti sauce has a faint taste of oregano.* **2.** *adj.* [of someone] weak; [of someone] about to pass out. (Adv: *faintly.* Comp: *fainter;* sup: *faintest.*) ♦ *After working for hours in the hot sun, we began to feel faint.* ♦ *I need to sit down. I'm a little faint.* **3.** *iv.* to pass out; to lose consciousness. ♦ *The news surprised Anne so much that she fainted.* ♦ *After witnessing the bloody accident, Tom fainted on the street.* **4.** *n.* a temporary loss of consciousness. (No plural form in this sense.) ♦ *John fell into a faint after the ordeal.* ♦ *After Mary's brief faint, I drove her to the hospital.*

fainthearted ['fent hɑrt ɪd] **1.** *adj.* timid; shy; not courageous. (Adv: *faintheartedly.*) ♦ *The fainthearted student refused to dissect the frog.* ♦ *The fainthearted skier decided not to go down the dangerous slope.* **2. the fainthearted** *n.* people who are ①. (No plural form in this sense. Treated as plural.) ♦ *This movie is not for the fainthearted.* ♦ *The fainthearted will want to leave before the shocking end of the movie.*

fair ['fɛɚ] **1.** *n.* an annual event held in a town, state, or county. ♦ *Farm animals and baked goods are judged at the county fair.* ♦ *We went to the fair to look at the farm animals.* **2.** *adj.* just; honest; not corrupt; giving good judgments; not favoring one thing or person over another. (Adv: *fairly.* Comp: *fairer;* sup: *fairest.*) ♦ *The fair judge listened carefully to the evidence at the trial.* ♦ *It's not fair! Why does Jimmy get more ice cream than I do?* **3.** *adj.* [of skin or hair] very light in color. (Adv: *fairly.* Comp: *fairer;* sup: *fairest.*) ♦ *Fair skin usually sunburns easily.* ♦ *My hair is brown now, but when I was younger it was very fair.* **4.** *adj.* [of someone] having **fair** ③ skin or hair. (Comp: *fairer;* sup: *fairest.*) ♦ *John is very fair and sunburns easily.* ♦ *Since Billy is fair, we keep him out of the sun.* **5.** *adj.* considerable; a lot; quite a bit. (Adv: *fairly.*) ♦ *When Bob invested in silver, he made a fair amount of money.* ♦ *I have a fair amount of work to do before I leave the office.* **6.** *adj.* not too bad; pretty good; adequate. (Adv: *fairly.* Comp: *fairer;* sup: *fairest.*) ♦ *You did a fair job on this report, but you could have done better.* ♦ *Is the new mayor doing a good, fair, or poor job?*

fair-haired ['fɛr 'hɛɚd] **1.** *adj.* having blond or light brown hair; having light-colored hair. ♦ *Fair-haired children often have freckles.* ♦ *The main suspect in the robbery is a tall, fair-haired man.* **2. fair-haired boy** *idiom* a favored person. (Not necessarily young or a boy.) ♦ *The teacher's fair-haired boy always does well on tests.* ♦ *The supervisor's son was the fair-haired boy on the construction site.*

fairly ['fɛɚ li] **1.** *adv.* honestly; justly; in an honest or just way; in accordance with the rules. ♦ *The judge listened to the evidence fairly.* ♦ *Our team always plays fairly, even if the other team cheats.* **2.** *adv.* considerably; quite a bit; rather. ♦ *That shade of blue is fairly dark.* ♦ *I ate a fairly large amount of potato salad at the picnic.* **3.** *adv.* moderately; adequately; pretty well; not too badly. ♦ *This report was fairly well done, but you could have been neater.* ♦ *This book is fairly interesting, although it's often hard to understand.*

fairness ['fɛɚ nəs] *n.* justice; freedom from bias and injustice. (No plural form in this sense.) ♦ *The defendant appreciated the fairness of the judge.* ♦ *The newscaster commented on the umpire's fairness at the baseball game.*

fairy ['fɛɚ i] *n.* a small, mythical being that looks human and does magic and sometimes has wings. (Compare with ferry.) ♦ *I told a story about a fairy who gave a poor farmer three wishes.* ♦ *I pulled out my loose tooth and put it under my pillow for the tooth fairy.*

fairyland ['fɛɚ i lænd] *n.* an imaginary place where fairies live. ♦ *I dreamed I was in a magical fairyland where I never had to work.* ♦ *I read my children a story about the queen of a mysterious fairyland.*

fairy tale ['fɛɚ i tel] *n.* a made-up story about fairies and magical creatures, dragons, kings, queens, princes, princesses, etc. ♦ *My parents read me a fairy tale every night before I went to bed.* ♦ *"Cinderella" and "Snow White" are two famous fairy tales.*

faith ['feθ] **1.** *n.* a very powerful belief in something that cannot be proved; a very powerful belief in someone or in a deity. (No plural form in this sense.) ♦ *The preacher believed that faith was a powerful force in his life.* ♦ *Faith is the basis of many of the large religions.* **2.** *n.* a particular religion; a denomination. ♦ *My family belongs to one of the Protestant faiths.* ♦ *I switched faiths when I married.* **3.** *n.* loyalty; trust. (No plural form in this sense.) ♦ *Even during the war, I kept faith with the government.* ♦ *I have lost faith in my landlord's repeated promises to make needed repairs to my apartment.* **4. in bad faith** *idiom* without sincerity; with bad or dishonest intent; with duplicity. ♦ *It appears that you acted in bad faith and didn't live up to the terms of our agreement.* ♦ *If you do things in bad faith, you'll get a bad reputation.* **5. take something on faith** *idiom* to accept or believe something on the basis of little or no evidence. ♦ *Please try to believe what I'm telling you. Just take it on faith.* ♦ *Surely you can't expect me to take a story like that on faith.*

faithful ['feθ fʊl] **1.** *adj.* loyal to someone or something; showing loyalty. (Adv: *faithfully.*) ♦ *My faithful dog sleeps at the foot of my bed.* ♦ *Our faithful cook has worked for my family for 50 years.* **2.** *adj.* showing exclusive sexual loyalty to one's spouse or lover. (Adv: *faithfully.*) ♦ *Jane divorced her husband because he was not faithful to her.* ♦ *John promised to be faithful to his girlfriend while on vacation.* **3.** *adj.* accurate; true to the facts. (Adv: *faithfully.*) ♦ *This movie is faithful to the book that it is based on.* ♦ *The researcher wrote a faithful account of the senator's life in politics.*

faithfulness ['feθ fəl nəs] **1.** *n.* loyalty; keeping one's promises. (No plural form in this sense.) ♦ *I would show more faithfulness to my company if it paid me more.* ♦ *Nothing can cause me to renounce my faithfulness to God.* **2.** *n.* complete monogamy practiced by partners in a marriage. (No plural form in this sense.) ♦ *I admire my parents' faithfulness to each other.* ♦ *Sue never questioned her husband's faithfulness.*

fake ['fek] **1.** *tv.* to make a counterfeit of something; to make a copy of something with the intent of deceiving. ♦ *Max faked $20 bills with a high-quality color photocopier.* ♦ *Anne faked her parents' signatures on her application.* **2.** *tv.* to pretend to do something or have something in order to deceive. ♦ *I faked illness so I could take the day off from work.* ♦ *I faked interest in the boring lecture because I didn't want to offend the speaker.* **3.** *n.* something that is made to take the place of an original in order to deceive; a fraud. ♦ *The new painting in the art museum was found to be a fake.* ♦ *Mary owns a lot of jewelry, but she wears glass fakes when traveling.* **4.** *n.* someone who is a fraud; an impostor. ♦ *The police arrested the fake who pretended to be a doctor.* ♦ *You're not a magician! You're a fake.* **5.** *adj.* false; not genuine; artificial; made in order to deceive. ♦ *I wear fake jewelry to parties and keep the real jewels in my safe.* ♦ *Bill tried to buy a hamburger with a fake $2 bill.*

falcon ['fæl kən] *n.* a bird of prey, related to the hawk, with long wings and a hooked beak. ♦ *People who raise falcons wear thick, heavy gloves to protect themselves from the claws.* ♦ *The falcon swooped down and picked up a small squirrel with its beak.*

fall ['fɔl] **1.** *iv., irreg.* to drop to a lower level from a higher level. (Pt: fell; pp: fallen.) ♦ *The book fell from the shelf onto the floor.* ♦ *I tripped and fell down a flight of stairs.* **2.** *iv., irreg.* to lose power; to be defeated. (Figurative on ①.) ♦ *During the revolution, the old government fell.* ♦ *The former champion fell from first place to third.* **3.** *iv., irreg.* to hang downward; to extend downward; [for vision] to aim downward. ♦ *Sue's long hair falls over her shoulders.* ♦ *Bill's eyes fell because he was too embarrassed to look at me.* **4.** *iv., irreg.* to go from a standing position to a lying position in one quick movement; to collapse. ♦ *The deer fell as it ran away.* ♦ *Don't run in the house. You'll fall and hurt yourself.* **5.** *iv., irreg.* to occur on a particular day of the week or in a particular month of the year. ♦ *January 1, 1998, falls on a Thursday.* ♦ *Last year, my birthday fell on a Saturday.* **6.** *iv., irreg.* [for an accent] to be placed in a specific place on a word. ♦ *In Czech, the accent falls on the first syllable of every word.* ♦ *There is no way to predict where an accent will fall within an English word.* **7.** *n.* the autumn; the season between summer and winter. ♦ *Fall is the period of time each year between September 22 and December 21.* ♦ *I began kindergarten in the fall of 1971.* **8.** *n.* going from an upright position to a lying position, suddenly. ♦ *The ice skater had a bad fall and twisted her ankle.* ♦ *The football player's fall was cushioned by soft, wet mud.* **9.** *n.* a decrease; a drop; a lowering. ♦ *Because of a fall in the price of gas, I drove to New York instead of flying.* ♦ *I lost a lot of money because of a fall in the value of silver.* **10.** *n.* the collapse of a political unit; a defeat, especially when at war. ♦ *After Napoleon's fall, he was exiled to a remote island.* ♦ *No one is sure what caused the fall of the Roman empire.* **11. falls** *n.* a waterfall. (Treated as plural.) ♦ *When you go canoeing, stay away from the falls.* ♦ *Thousands of tourists visit Niagara Falls each day.* **12. break someone's fall** *idiom* to cushion a falling person; to lessen the impact of a falling person. ♦ *When the* *little boy fell out of the window, the bushes broke his fall.* ♦ *The old lady slipped on the ice, but a snowbank broke her fall.* **13. fall apart** See apart. **14. fall asleep** *idiom* to go to sleep. ♦ *I fell asleep while reading the very dull book.* ♦ *I got in bed and fell asleep at once.* **15. fall down on the job** *idiom* to fail to do something properly; to fail to do one's job adequately. ♦ *The team kept losing because the coach was falling down on the job.* ♦ *Tom was fired because he fell down on the job.* **16. fall in love** *idiom* [for two people] to recognize and experience love for one another. ♦ *Bob and Lisa fell in love on a warm day in October.* ♦ *Anne has fallen in love with various guys a number of times.* **17. fall ill** *idiom* to become ill. ♦ *Tom fell ill just before he was to perform.* ♦ *We both fell ill after eating the baked fish.* **18. fall in(to) place** *idiom* to fit together; to become organized. ♦ *After we heard the whole story, things began to fall in place.* ♦ *When you get older, the different parts of your life begin to fall into place.* **19. fall to someone** *idiom* to become the responsibility of someone. ♦ *It always falls to me to apologize first.* ♦ *Why does it fall to me to answer the telephone every time it rings?* **20. riding for a fall** *idiom* risking failure or an accident, usually due to overconfidence. ♦ *Tom drives too fast, and he seems too sure of himself. He's riding for a fall.* ♦ *Bill needs to eat better and get more sleep. He's riding for a fall.*

fallacious [fə 'le ʃəs] *adj.* untrue; wrong. (Adv: *fallaciously.*) ♦ *The senator denied the accusation and called it fallacious.* ♦ *The newspaper spread fallacious gossip about the famous movie star.*

fallacy ['fæl ə si] *n.* a false belief; an error in one's thinking. ♦ *The fallacy in your thinking is based on ignorance.* ♦ *The badly written article about taxes contained numerous fallacies.*

fallen ['fɔl ən] **1.** pp of fall. **2.** *adj.* toppled; dropped. ♦ *A fallen tree blocked the road.* ♦ *I picked up the fallen branches after the storm.* **3.** *adj.* defeated; destroyed. ♦ *When the soldiers of the fallen army came home, they were jeered by the citizens.* ♦ *The fallen dictator fled the country at night.* **4.** *adj.* degraded; not worthy of respect or worship. ♦ *The fallen members of society can always start life over again.* ♦ *The movie star became a fallen idol after his arrest and imprisonment.*

fallible ['fæl ə bəl] *adj.* capable of making mistakes; likely to make a mistake. (Adv: *fallibly.*) ♦ *All of you are fallible, so please check each other's work.* ♦ *I know I am fallible, but sometimes I know I am absolutely right!*

falling-out ['fɔl ɪŋ 'ɑʊt] *n., irreg.* a disagreement; an argument; a quarrel. (Pl: fallings-out.) ♦ *After a brief falling-out, the young lovers kissed and made up.* ♦ *In forty years of marriage, we've only had a few fallings-out.*

fallings-out pl of falling-out.

fallout ['fɔl ɑʊt] **1.** *n.* radioactive dust that results from a nuclear explosion. (No plural form in this sense.) ♦ *If the nuclear bomb blast doesn't kill you, the fallout probably will.* ♦ *The scientists inside the lead shelter were protected from fallout.* **2.** *n.* negative or unexpected results of something. (No plural form in this sense. Figurative on ①.) ♦ *My boss was fired, and as part of the fallout, so was I.* ♦ *The fallout from budget cuts affected social-service agencies.*

fallow ['fæl o] **1.** *adj.* [of land] not farmed for a period of time, usually in order to help replenish the soil with nutrients. ♦ *Much of the land in the county was fallow during the war.* ♦ *The farmer tilled the fallow farmland in preparation for next year's crop.* **2. lie fallow** *idiom* [for land] to remain ①. ♦ *Each year we let a different section of our farmland lie fallow.* ♦ *The land that is lying fallow this year will be cultivated next year.* **3. lie fallow** *idiom* [for a skill and talent] to remain unused and neglected. (Figurative on ①.) ♦ *You should not let your talent lie fallow. Practice the piano before you forget how to play it.* ♦ *His writing had lain fallow for so long that he could hardly write a proper sentence.*

false ['fɔls] **1.** *adj.* not true; wrong; incorrect. (Adv: *falsely.* Comp: *falser;* sup: *falsest.*) ♦ *The criminal gave a false statement to the police.* ♦ *The detective's theory that Max committed the crime turned out to be false.* **2.** *adj.* not loyal; not faithful; like a traitor. (Adv: *falsely.* Comp: *falser;* sup: *falsest.*) ♦ *The traitor was executed for being false to the king.* ♦ *A false friend will repeat things that are told in confidence.* **3.** *adj.* not real; artificial; fake. (Comp: *falser;* sup: *falsest.*) ♦ *My grandfather takes out his false teeth every night.* ♦ *Even though it was a false alarm, the firefighters wouldn't let us return to the building.*

falsehood ['fɔls hʊd] *n.* a lie; a statement that is not true. ♦ *The preacher urged the members of the congregation not to utter falsehoods.* ♦ *Mary claimed the accusations against her were falsehoods.*

false teeth ['fɔls 'tiθ] *n.* dentures; a set of artificial teeth. (Plural. The singular refers to only one tooth.) ♦ *Most people take out their false teeth when they go to bed.* ♦ *After the dentist removed my bad teeth, I got false teeth.*

falsification [fɔl sə fə 'ke ʃən] *n.* fraudulently altering something. (No plural form in this sense.) ♦ *The commander approved the report's falsification so that the truth would not be known.* ♦ *The clerk was fired for the illegal falsification of official documents.*

falsify ['fɔl sə fɑɪ] *tv.* to change something to be false in order to trick someone. ♦ *Bob stole some money from his company and then falsified the bank balance.* ♦ *The commander decided to falsify the report in order to trick the enemy.*

falter ['fɔl tɚ] *iv.* to waiver; to lose courage; to move or talk unsteadily; to stumble. ♦ *During my speech, I got nervous and began to falter.* ♦ *The untrained soldiers faltered as they neared the battlefield.*

faltering ['fɔl tɚ ɪŋ] *adj.* stumbling; halting; wavering; hesitating with fear or weakness. (Adv: *falteringly.*) ♦ *It was difficult to understand John's faltering speech.* ♦ *The faltering soldiers ran for cover as the bombs began to fall.*

fame ['fem] *n.* the quality of being very well known. (No plural form in this sense.) ♦ *The movie star used her fame to further her political interests.* ♦ *Because of the reporter's fame, everyone recognized him.*

familiar [fə 'mɪl jɚ] **1.** *adj.* known; well known; common. (Adv: *familiarly.*) ♦ *The woman in the restaurant has a familiar face, but I can't remember how I know her.* ♦ *George Washington is probably the most familiar American president of all.* **2.** *adj.* friendly; overly friendly. (Adv: *familiarly.*) ♦ *I felt that the stranger's remarks were a little too familiar, so I moved to a different seat on the bus.* ♦ *Anne's familiar manner made it easy to get to know her.* **3. familiar with someone or something** *idiom* having a good knowledge of someone or something. ♦ *Are you familiar with changing a flat tire?* ♦ *I'm can't speak German fluently, but I'm somewhat familiar with the language.*

familiarity [fə mɪl i 'ɛr ə ti] **1.** *n.* knowledge of someone or something. (No plural form in this sense.) ♦ *Jane was hired because of her familiarity with computers.* ♦ *My familiarity with Spanish was helpful when I visited Mexico.* **2.** *n.* relaxed, open behavior, like between very close friends. (No plural form in this sense.) ♦ *I quickly developed a good level of familiarity with my new roommate.* ♦ *Because of our well-established familiarity, I can tell Mary anything.*

familiarize [fə 'mɪl jə rɑɪz] **familiarize with** *tv.* + *prep. phr.* to cause someone to know someone or something; to teach someone about someone or something. ♦ *The math teacher familiarized the students with fractions.* ♦ *Read the handbook to familiarize yourself with company policies.*

family ['fæm li] **1.** *n.* a group of people related by blood or marriage. ♦ *Dave brought Anne home to meet his family.* ♦ *Brown hair and green eyes are genetic traits that are found in my family.* **2.** *n.* a mother, father, and one child or more; a parent and one child or more. ♦ *Four different families live in my apartment building.* ♦ *My workplace provides special services for families.* **3.** *n.* a group of things that are related in some way or share common features, such as animals, plants, languages, etc. ♦ *The rodent family includes mice, chipmunks, and squirrels.* ♦ *The Romance language family includes Italian, French, and Spanish.* **4.** *adj.* <the adj. use of ①.> ♦ *I can trace my family line back to the 1700s.* ♦ *Every three years we pose for a new family portrait.* **5. run in the family** *idiom* [for a characteristic] to appear in many (or all) members of a family. ♦ *My grandparents lived well into their nineties, and it runs in the family.* ♦ *My brothers and I have red hair. It runs in the family.*

famine ['fæm ən] *n.* a period of time when there is little or no food available. (No plural form in this sense.) ♦ *The church sent canned food to the town struck by famine.* ♦ *A severe famine was caused by a terrible drought.*

famished ['fæm ɪʃt] *adj.* very hungry. ♦ *I am so famished I could eat a horse!* ♦ *The famished children pleaded with their parents to stop at the restaurant.*

famous ['fe məs] *adj.* very well known. ♦ *Bill asked the famous athlete for her autograph.* ♦ *Abraham Lincoln is a very famous president.*

famously ['fe məs li] *adv.* excellently; in a very good way. ♦ *Tom's job search is moving along quite famously.* ♦ *My roommate and I get along famously.*

fan ['fæn] **1.** *n.* someone who is a very strong admirer of someone or something. (A shortening of fanatic.) ♦ *The fans cheered wildly when the band stepped out onto the stage.* ♦ *The movie star gladly signed autographs for the excited fans.* **2.** *n.* a device or machine used to move air in order to cool someone or something. ♦ *It's getting hot in here. Would you turn on the fan, please?* ♦ *The fan blew all the papers off my desk.* **3.** *tv.* to move air onto something. ♦ *The church was very hot, so I fanned my face with my hymn book.* ♦ *The fire was dying, so I fanned it.* **4. fan out** *iv.* + *adv.* [for a group] to separate and move outward. ♦ *The hunters fanned out through the woods to surround the deer.* ♦ *The river fanned out over the valley when the dam broke.* **5. fan the flames (of something)** *idiom* to make something more intense; to make a situation worse. (Figurative on ③.) ♦ *The riot fanned the flames of racial hatred even more.* ♦ *The hostility in the school is bad enough without anyone fanning the flames.*

fanatic [fə 'næt ɪk] *n.* someone who is too enthusiastic about someone or something; a zealot. ♦ *Tom is a baseball fanatic. He goes to every game that he can.* ♦ *I screamed at the religious fanatic who had been following me.*

fanatically [fə 'næt ɪk li] *adv.* out of control; zealously. ♦ *Anne and I screamed fanatically when we greeted each other at the mall.* ♦ *Bob sped fanatically through rush-hour traffic.*

fancier ['fæn si ɚ] *n.* someone who fancies or admires someone or something. ♦ *The antique collector was a fancier of fine china.* ♦ *Since you're such a fish fancier, let's go to a seafood restaurant.*

fanciful ['fæn si fʊl] **1.** *adj.* full of imagination; imaginative. (Adv: *fancifully* ['fæn sə fli].) ♦ *Jane enjoys reading fanciful science fiction.* ♦ *The babysitter read a fanciful tale about a magical giant to the child.* **2.** *adj.* not real; imaginary; based on imagination rather than reality. (Adv: *fancifully* ['fæn sə fli].) ♦ *John was an only child, so he invented fanciful playmates.* ♦ *Although Dave's worries were only fanciful, he developed an ulcer.*

fancy ['fæn si] **1.** *adj.* ornate; elegant; stylish; decorated. (Adv: *fancily.* Comp: *fancier;* sup: *fanciest.*) ♦ *When guests come, we use our fancy dishes.* ♦ *This dress is too fancy. Do you have anything simpler?* **2.** *n.* the imagination; the ability to create imaginative ideas or images. ♦ *The artist portrayed his fancies on canvas.* ♦ *Lisa let her fancy take hold and wrote a marvelous story.* **3.** *n.* something that is imagined; a notion. ♦ *I wanted to go to Florida this summer, but it was just a passing fancy.* ♦ *It was my fancy that we'd go bowling tonight.* **4.** *n.* a fondness for someone or something; a liking for someone or something. ♦ *I have a fancy for antique cars.* ♦ *Please order whatever meal catches your fancy.* **5.** *tv.* to desire something. ♦ *Would you fancy a cool drink?* ♦ *After a hard day at work, I fancy a nice, hot bath.* **6. flight of fancy** *idiom* an idea or suggestion that is out of touch with reality or possibility. ♦ *What is the point of indulging in flights of fancy about exotic vacations when you cannot even afford the rent?* ♦ *We are tired of her flights of fancy about marrying a millionaire.* **7. strike someone's fancy** *idiom* to appeal to someone. ♦ *I'll have some ice cream, please. Chocolate strikes my fancy right now.* ♦ *Why don't you go to the store and buy a CD that strikes your fancy?* **8. take a fancy to someone or something** *idiom* to develop a liking for someone or something. ♦ *I think that Tom has taken a fancy to Mary.* ♦ *Bill took a fancy to skydiving and now he does it every weekend.* **9. tickle someone's fancy** *idiom* to interest someone; to make someone curious. ♦ *I have an interesting problem here that I think will tickle your fancy.* ♦ *This doesn't tickle my fancy at all. This is dull and boring.*

fancy-free ['fæn si 'fri] **1.** *n.* unrestrained; free to do as one wants. ♦ *Bill had too many responsibilities to be completely fancy-free.* ♦ *When Sue left her parents' house, she was young and fancy-free.* **2. footloose and fancy-free** See footloose.

fanfare ['fæn fɛr] *n.* a piece of music played on trumpets to announce an important event. ♦ *A majestic fanfare greeted the royal couple when they entered the castle.* ♦ *A military band played a lengthy fanfare before the president's speech.*

fang ['fæŋ] *n.* a long, sharp tooth. ♦ *The angry dog bared its fangs at me.* ♦ *A snake sunk its fangs deep into my arm.*

fantasize ['fæn tə sɑɪz] *iv.* + *prep. phr.* to have a fantasy about someone or something. ♦ *Anne fantasized about retiring at 50 and moving to Hawaii.* ♦ *Tom fantasized about moving to Hawaii with Anne.*

fantastic [fæn 'tæs tɪk] *adj.* wonderful; terrific; very good. (Adv: *fantastically* [...ɪk li].) ♦ *Could I have another piece of your fantastic lemon pie?* ♦ *Our vacation in Mexico was fantastic!*

fantasy ['fæn tə si] **1.** *n.* imagination; a sense of intrigue. (No plural form in this sense.) ♦ *Writing interesting movies requires a good sense of fantasy.* ♦ *Bill was an only child, so he developed his own world of fantasy.* **2.** *n.* an illusion or image made by one's imagination. ♦ *It's my fantasy to win the lottery and buy a mansion.* ♦ *In my wildest fantasies, I never thought I'd go skiing in Europe.*

far ['fɑr] **1.** *adj., irreg.* further; not as close as something else. (Comp: farther or further; sup: farthest or furthest.) ♦ *Here's a bakery, and there's a pizza shop on the far end of the street.* ♦ *Could you get me the paint? It's on the far side of the garage.* **2.** *adv., irreg.* distant in time or space; a long way away in time or space. ♦ *Dinosaurs lived far in the past.* ♦ *The planet Mars is far away from the planet Earth.* **3.** *adv.* much; a lot. ♦ *It's far hotter in Arizona than it is in Alaska.* ♦ *I like baseball far more than I like football.* **4. as far as it goes** *idiom* as much as something does, covers, or accomplishes. ♦ *Your plan is fine as far as it goes. It doesn't seem to take care of everything, though.* ♦ *As far as it goes, this law is a good one. It should require stiffer penalties, however.*

far away ['fɑr ə 'we] See far off.

farce ['fɑrs] **1.** *n.* an absurd play or movie written to make people laugh. ♦ *Last night I saw a farce that poked fun at the government.* ♦ *After writing light romantic comedies, I decided to write a farce.* **2.** *n.* a pretense; a sham; a mockery. ♦ *My job interview was a farce because they already hired someone else.* ♦ *The award show was a farce because the winner had bribed the judges.*

fare ['fɛr] **1.** *n.* the amount of money required to ride a bus, train, plane, subway, taxi, etc. ♦ *You must pay the bus fare with exact change.* ♦ *Mary and I took a taxi home from the party and split the fare.* **2.** *n.* the food that is served at a meal. (No plural form in this sense.) ♦ *The country restaurant served us a hearty fare.* ♦ *I could offer the unexpected guests only modest fare.*

farewell [fɛr 'wɛl] **1.** *n.* a departure including saying good-bye. ♦ *The mayor's farewell was short since she had to catch a plane.* ♦ *Anne's farewell at the bus terminal was quite sad.* **2.** *adj.* <the adj. use of ①.> ♦ *The mayor delivered her farewell address to the saddened crowd.* ♦ *The farewell speech took too long.* **3.** *interj.* good-bye. ♦ *Farewell! Don't forget to write!* ♦ *Bob said "farewell" to his coworkers as he left the office.*

far-fetched ['fɑr 'fɛtʃt] *adj.* hard to believe. ♦ *Are you lying to me? Your story seems a little far-fetched.* ♦ *John's scenario of how he would earn a million dollars is incredibly far-fetched.*

farm ['fɑrm] **1.** *n.* a parcel of land used to grow crops or to raise animals. ♦ *My grandparents grow wheat and soybeans on their farm.* ♦ *There used to be a farm where this shopping mall is today.* **2.** *tv.* to cultivate land; to plow land. ♦ *My grandparents farm 80 acres of land.* ♦ *Our food comes from thousands of Americans who farm the land.* **3. farm out** *tv.* + *adv.* to assign work among people; to distribute work among people. ♦ *The director farmed the assignments out to the committee members.* ♦ *While I was on vacation, my work was farmed out.* **4.** *iv.* to grow crops and raise animals as a living. ♦ *My family farms during the summer and sells firewood in the winter.* ♦ *My grandparents farmed for fifty years before they retired.* **5.** *adj.* <the adj. use of ①.> ♦ *Farm animals include horses, chickens, goats, and pigs.* ♦ *We sold all of our farm machinery at an auction.*

farmer ['fɑrm ɚ] *n.* someone who grows crops and raises animals on a farm. ♦ *The farmer milked the cows every morning at 6:00 A.M.* ♦ *The farmer harvested the corn crop in September.*

farmhand ['fɑrm hænd] *n.* someone, typically a male, who works on a farm. ♦ *During the summer, we employ five farmhands to help with the crops.* ♦ *The farmhand accidentally drove the tractor into the creek.*

farmhouse ['fɑrm hɑʊs] *n., irreg.* the house on a farm where a farmer lives. (Pl: [...hɑʊ zəz].) ♦ *John and Sue turned the old farmhouse into a country inn.* ♦ *A fire destroyed the barns, but it didn't harm the farmhouse.*

farmland ['fɑrm lænd] *n.* the land that makes up a farm. (No plural form in this sense.) ♦ *The crops were destroyed when several thousand acres of farmland flooded.* ♦ *This rich, dark soil is perfect farmland.*

far off AND **far away** ['fɑr 'ɔf, 'fɑr ə 'we] **1.** *adj.* distant in space or time. ♦ *The day when the project is finished is still quite far off.* ♦ *A place where we can buy gas for the car is still far away.* **2. far-away; far-off** *adj.* distant; remote in time or distance. ♦ *My cousin moved to some far-off country last year.* ♦ *I would like to travel in far-away lands.* **3. far-away look; far-off look** *phr.* an appearance on one's face of having one's mind in another place. ♦ *Dave had a far-away look in his eyes, so I touched him to get his attention.* ♦ *Lisa's face had a far-off look indicating that she was daydreaming.*

far-reaching ['fɑr 'ritʃ ɪŋ] *adj.* having much influence; influencing many things or people; having an effect over a large area. (Adv: *far-reachingly.*) ♦ *The nuclear bomb explosion had serious, far-reaching effects.* ♦ *The influence of cable television programming is far-reaching.*

farsighted ['fɑr sɑɪt ɪd] **1.** *adj.* able to see things that are farther away better than things that are close. (Adv: *farsightedly.*) ♦ *I have to wear glasses when I read because I'm farsighted.* ♦ *Anne squints when she talks to me. I think she's farsighted.* **2.** *adj.* wisely looking into the future. (Adv: *farsightedly.*) ♦ *Buying flood insurance was farsighted of you since you live near a river.* ♦ *I'm being farsighted by saving money for retirement now.*

farther ['fɑr ðɚ] **1.** *adj.* more far; more distant in space or time. (One of the comparative forms of far, along with further.) ♦ *Please hand me the farther book of the two.* ♦ *How much farther is it to the beach? I'm getting tired.*

2. *adv.* more far; more distant in space or time. (One of the comparative forms of **far**, along with **further**.) ♦ *I can throw a baseball farther than you can.* ♦ *We talked farther into the night than I had expected.*

farthest ['fɑr ðəst] **1.** *adj.* the most far; the most distant in space or time. (One of the superlative forms of **far**, along with **furthest**.) ♦ *The farthest planet from the sun is Pluto.* ♦ *Paying attention to traffic was the farthest thing from my mind when I got into the accident.* **2.** *adv.* most far; most distant in space or time. (One of the superlative forms of **far**, along with **furthest**.) ♦ *What's the farthest back you can remember?* ♦ *Of my friends, Bill has traveled the farthest. He's been to Russia.*

fascinate ['fæs ə net] *tv.* to attract someone's attention; to amaze someone; to interest someone very much. ♦ *Scary movies fascinate me.* ♦ *The puppet show fascinated the young children.*

fascinating ['fæs ə net ɪŋ] *adj.* very interesting; holding one's attention; attracting one's attention. (Adv: *fascinatingly.*) ♦ *I stayed up all night to finish reading the fascinating book.* ♦ *I had a fascinating conversation with your cousin at your party.*

fascination [fɑs ə 'ne ʃən] *n.* a strong interest in something; a strong attraction to something. (No plural form in this sense.) ♦ *Tom has a strong fascination for antique cars.* ♦ *I don't like your fascination with horror films.*

fascism ['fæʃ ɪz əm] *n.* the principles of government involving a dictatorship under which all business is strictly controlled by the government, and opposition to the government is forbidden. (No plural form in this sense.) ♦ *The protesters who accused the government of fascism were killed.* ♦ *My grandparents fled Germany during the 1930s because of fascism.*

fashion ['fæ ʃən] **1.** *n.* the preferred style of dress or behavior within a society. (No plural form in this sense.) ♦ *Fashion is very important among wealthy people, especially in large cities.* ♦ *Fashion has never interested me. I want comfort.* **2. fashions** *n.* designs and styles of clothing. ♦ *I have a good job, so I can afford to buy the latest fashions.* ♦ *I absolutely do not care about fashions!* **3.** *n.* the manner or way in which something is done; a method. (No plural form in this sense.) ♦ *The baseball coach instructed the players to swing their bats in a particular fashion.* ♦ *The criminal was executed in a merciless fashion.* **4.** *tv.* to form or shape something; to form something by hand. ♦ *In ceramics class, we fashioned ashtrays out of clay.* ♦ *I can fashion a swan by folding paper in a certain way.* **5. in fashion** *idiom* fitting in well with the clothing that has been designed for a particular season of a particular year. ♦ *I understand that long skirts are in fashion this year.* ♦ *I always want to find out what styles are in fashion so I can avoid them.*

fashionable ['fæʃ ə nə bəl] *adj.* in style; stylish; according to the current fashion. (Adv: *fashionably.*) ♦ *Each year we paint our mailbox in fashionable colors.* ♦ *Maintaining a fashionable wardrobe can be expensive.*

fast ['fæst] **1.** *adv.* quickly; rapidly. (Comp: *faster;* sup: *fastest.*) ♦ *Don't drive so fast. You'll have an accident.* ♦ *Move fast. We're already 20 minutes late.* **2.** *adv.* tight; without moving; securely. (Comp: *faster;* sup: *fastest.*) ♦ *The glue held the stamp fast to the envelope.* ♦ *The ropes held the mattress fast to the roof of the car.* **3.** *adj.* quick; rapid; speedy; not slow. (Comp: *faster;* sup: *fastest.*) ♦ *If you take the fast train, you'll be downtown in 10 minutes.* ♦ *My boss is impressed with my fast typing.* **4.** *adj.* [of a clock or watch] showing a time that is ahead of the real time. (Comp: *faster;* sup: *fastest.*) ♦ *My watch is fast, so we've got a little more time than you think.* ♦ *The clock in the kitchen is five minutes fast.* **5.** *adj.* not likely to fade; having colors that will stay bright. (Comp: *faster;* sup: *fastest.*) ♦ *Don't put these clothes in bleach. The colors aren't fast.* ♦ *Wash this as much as you want. The colors are fast.* **6.** *iv.* to go without food. ♦ *Members of my church are supposed to fast on Fridays during Lent.* ♦ *The protesters fasted until the mayor would speak with them.* **7.** *n.* a period of time when someone does not eat, for religious, health, or political reasons. (No plural form in this sense.) ♦ *The pilgrims continued their fast for three weeks.* ♦ *I broke my fast by eating a small piece of chicken.* **8. faster and faster** *idiom* at an increasing rate of speed; fast and then even faster. ♦ *The car went faster and faster, and I was afraid we would crash.* ♦ *The cost of education goes up faster and faster every year.*

fasten ['fæs ən] **1.** *tv.* to tie, lock, clasp, or hook something closed. ♦ *I fastened the window shut when it started to rain.* ♦ *Our gate is fastened with a strong lock.* **2.** *tv.* to attach something to someone or something. ♦ *I fastened the new handle to the oven door.* ♦ *We are supposed to fasten tassels on our graduation caps.*

fastener ['fæs ən ɚ] *n.* a device that secures or fastens something shut. ♦ *When the fastener fell off, the door popped open.* ♦ *I pressed the fastener until it was securely shut.*

fast food ['fæst 'fud] **1.** *n.* food that is prepared and served quickly, especially hamburgers, hot dogs, etc. (No plural form in this sense.) ♦ *Most fast food is fatty, so I don't eat too much of it.* ♦ *I don't have time to cook tonight. Let's go get some fast food.* **2. fast-food** *adj.* <the adj. form of ①.> ♦ *Let's stop at a fast-food restaurant.* ♦ *I used to live on a fast-food diet.*

fastidious [fæ 'stɪd i əs] **1.** *adj.* hard to please; picky. (Adv: *fastidiously.*) ♦ *The salesclerk helped the fastidious customer try on different clothes for an hour.* ♦ *Max is a fastidious eater and won't eat overcooked vegetables.* **2.** *adj.* preferring cleanliness and orderliness. (Adv: *fastidiously.*) ♦ *My roommate is a fastidious housekeeper, but I'm messy.* ♦ *I'm so fastidious that you could eat off my kitchen floor.*

fat ['fæt] **1.** *n.* oily flesh; oil-laden animal tissue, especially when used for cooking. (No plural form in this sense.) ♦ *I trimmed the fat from the pork chops before I baked them.* ♦ *I greased the pan with fat before I cooked the eggs.* **2.** *n.* the part of the body that makes creatures overweight or burdened with ①. (No plural form in this sense.) ♦ *I don't like it when people laugh at my fat.* ♦ *I decided to exercise because my fat jiggled when I walked.* **3.** *n.* an excess amount of something; an extra amount of something that is not necessary. (Informal. Figurative on ②. No plural form in this sense.) ♦ *The managers argued about how to trim the fat from the payroll.* ♦ *The senator promised to cut fat from the budget without cutting jobs.* **4.** *adj.* overweight; obese; having too much ②. (Adv: *fatly.* Comp: *fatter;* sup: *fattest.*) ♦ *When I stop exercising, I become fat.* ♦ *These movie seats are uncomfortable for fat people.* **5. live off the fat of the land** *idiom* to grow one's own food; to live on stored-up resources or abundant resources. ♦ *I would like to leave the city and live off the fat of the land.* ♦ *Many farmers live off the fat of the land.*

fatal ['fet əl] *adj.* causing death; resulting in death. (Adv: *fatally.*) ♦ *A fatal accident blocked traffic on the freeway for hours.* ♦ *My cousin had a fatal heart attack last summer.*

fatality [fə 'tæl ə ti] *n.* a death, especially one caused by an accident. ♦ *The traffic accident resulted in six fatalities.* ♦ *Reporters announced the war fatalities daily.*

fate ['fet] **1.** *n.* a force that is said to control what happens. (No plural form in this sense.) ♦ *Anne was convinced that fate brought her and her husband together.* ♦ *When I lost control of my car, my life was placed in the hands of fate.* **2.** *n.* the destiny of someone or something; what will happen to someone or something. (No plural form in this sense.) ♦ *Uncertain of my fate, I decided to take the new job and move to Florida.* ♦ *I don't know what the fate of my lost dog was, but I missed her a lot.* **3.** *tv.* [for fate ①] to determine what happens to someone or something. (Usually passive.) ♦ *I was fated to live my life in poverty.* ♦ *The airplane was fated to crash into the mountainside.* **4. leave one to one's fate** *idiom* to abandon someone to whatever may happen—possibly death or some other unpleasant event. ♦ *We couldn't rescue the miners, and we were forced to leave them to their fate.* ♦ *Please don't try to help. Just go away and leave me to my fate.*

fateful ['fet fʊl] *adj.* having a negative effect on future events; causing something unpleasant to happen. (Adv: *fatefully.*) ♦ *I'll never forget the fateful day when I got in a car accident.* ♦ *I always regretted my fateful decision to quit my job.*

father ['fɑ ðɚ] **1.** *n.* the male parent of a child. (Also a term of address.) ♦ *My father was 30 years old when I was born.* ♦ *I bought my father a tie for his birthday.* **2.** *n.* a male ancestor; a male forebear. ♦ *I was punished for the sins of my fathers.* ♦ *Old grandfather Brown was the father of the clan.* **3.** *n.* the inventor of something; the founder of something; the leader of something. (Figurative on ①.) ♦ *Alexander Graham Bell is the father of the telephone.* ♦ *George Washington is the father of the United States.* **4.** *tv.* [for a man] to fertilize an ovum, which will lead to the development of a child. ♦ *Bill fathered three children, all of whom are self-supporting now.* ♦ *Tom fathered his first child when he was 23.*

fatherhood ['fɑ ðɚ hʊd] *n.* the state of being a father. (No plural form in this sense.) ♦ *Mary told her husband that he had eight months to prepare for fatherhood.* ♦ *Bob enjoyed the new responsibilities of fatherhood.*

father-in-law ['fɑ ðɚ ɪn lɔ] *n., irreg.* the father of one's spouse. (Pl: fathers-in-law.) ♦ *Lisa took over her father-in-law's business when he retired.* ♦ *Jane remained close to her father-in-law after her husband died.*

fatherland ['fɑ ðɚ lænd] *n.* the country where someone comes from; one's native country. ♦ *Sixty years after he fled Russia, Tom returned to his fatherland.* ♦ *Every winter my parents visit their fatherland.*

fatherless ['fɑ ðɚ ləs] *adj.* having no father; without a father. ♦ *Jimmy was fatherless because his father died in a plane crash.* ♦ *Sue worked two jobs to support her fatherless children.*

fatherly ['fɑ ðɚ li] *adj.* like a kind and helpful father; paternal. ♦ *My high-school counselor had a strong fatherly influence on my life.* ♦ *My minister gave me a fatherly hug when I told him I was getting married.*

fathers-in-law ['fɑ ðɚz ɪn lɔ] pl of father-in-law.

fathom ['fæ ðəm] **1.** *n.* a unit of measurement for the depth of water, equal to six feet. ♦ *The submarine was stationed many fathoms beneath the surface of the water.* ♦ *The biologist dove several fathoms to examine coral.* **2.** *tv.* to understand something; to comprehend something. ♦ *I can't fathom how you can dance all night long and wake up at 8:00 A.M.* ♦ *Can you begin to fathom what I'm trying to say to you?*

fatigue [fə 'tig] **1.** *n.* exhaustion; weariness. (No plural form in this sense.) ♦ *After marching for days, fatigue slowed down the troops.* ♦ *I suffered from mental fatigue because of stress from my job.* **2.** *n.* the condition of a metal part that is worn out or overused. (No plural form in this sense.) ♦ *The engineer tested the degree of metal fatigue in the bridge.* ♦ *The lever in this machine has snapped from fatigue.* **3.** *tv.* to tire someone or something; to make someone or something tired. ♦ *The eighteen-hour drive to Boston fatigued me.* ♦ *Playing baseball fatigued all the kids.*

fatiguing [fə 'tig ɪŋ] *adj.* tiring; exhausting; wearing someone or something out. (Adv: *fatiguingly.*) ♦ *I am ready to quit my fatiguing job.* ♦ *I participated in a fatiguing 26-mile marathon.*

fatten ['fæt n] **1.** *tv.* to cause someone or something to grow larger. ♦ *The farmer fattened the chickens before butchering them.* ♦ *My host fattened me with homemade cakes and cookies.* **2.** *tv.* to increase the size or value of an offer. (Figurative on ①.) ♦ *The company fattened its offer by promising me a company car.* ♦ *The university fattened the deal by increasing my stipend.*

fatty ['fæt i] *adj.* full of or containing fat. (Comp: *fatter;* sup: *fattest.*) ♦ *I asked the waiter to return my steak to the kitchen because it was too fatty.* ♦ *My doctor warned me to avoid fatty foods.*

faucet ['fɔs ɪt] *n.* a valve that controls the flow of water or other liquid from a pipe or container; a tap. ♦ *The bathroom faucet dripped all night long, keeping me awake.* ♦ *Hot water comes from the left faucet.*

fault ['fɔlt] **1.** *n.* a personal shortcoming; a flawed trait. ♦ *One of your faults is that you always interrupt me when I'm talking.* ♦ *I'm willing to overlook your faults as long as you try to improve.* **2.** *n.* the responsibility for causing something bad to happen. (No plural form in this sense.) ♦ *I broke the vase, but it's not my fault. Jimmy pushed me.* ♦ *Whose fault is it that the door was left unlocked?* **3.** *n.* a crack or rift in the surface of the earth. ♦ *The houses near the fault collapsed during the earthquake.* ♦ *Our insurance premium is very high because we live on a fault.* **4. fault for** *tv.* + *prep. phr.* to blame someone for something. ♦ *Anne faulted Bill for crashing the car into the tree.* ♦ *Dave faulted Sue for leaving the cap off the toothpaste.* **5. find fault with someone or something** *idiom* to seek to find something wrong with someone or something. ♦ *My father is always finding fault with everything I do.* ♦ *I was unable to find fault with the car, so I bought it.*

faultless ['fɔlt ləs] *adj.* perfect; free from error. (Adv: *faultlessly.*) ♦ *The teacher gave the faultless project an A.* ♦ *The scientist's logic was faultless.*

faulty ['fɔl ti] *adj.* flawed; incorrect; having an error or mistake. (Adv: *faultily.* Comp: *faultier;* sup: *faultiest.*) ♦ *The building collapsed because of a faulty design.* ♦ *I don't understand your faulty logic.*

faux pas ['fo 'pɑ] *n.* a social blunder; an embarrassing action in a social situation. (From French. No plural form in this sense. Treated as singular or plural.) ♦ *Slurping your soup at a formal dinner is an embarrassing faux pas.* ♦ *Tom embarrassed his date by committing several faux pas throughout the evening.*

favor ['fev ɚ] **1.** *n.* a state of advantage or benefit from a preference. (No plural form in this sense.) ♦ *Tom sought Jane's favor by bringing her flowers.* ♦ *Anne was in the boss's favor and got easy assignments.* **2.** *n.* an act of kindness; something nice that is done for someone else. ♦ *I washed the dishes as a favor to my mother.* ♦ *Please do me a favor and shut the window.* **3.** *tv.* to prefer someone or something; to like someone or something at the expense of someone or something else. ♦ *The beautiful princess favored the good shepherd over the rich prince.* ♦ *I favor chocolate ice cream, but I will eat any flavor happily.* **4.** *tv.* to support someone or something; to support an issue, a plan, a theory, an option, etc. ♦ *I favor a state income tax instead of raising the sales tax.* ♦ *Bob favored going home early.* **5.** *tv.* to choose or expect someone or something to win. ♦ *I favored the black horse to cross the finish line first.* ♦ *The incumbent senator is favored to win the election.* **6. favor someone or something with something** *idiom* to provide someone or something with something beneficial or special. ♦ *Mary favored us with a song.* ♦ *Nature favored Bill with curly hair.*

favorable ['fev ə rə bəl] **1.** *adj.* approving; supporting. (Adv: *favorably.*) ♦ *My friend's response to my poetry was favorable.* ♦ *The new movie received a favorable review from most critics.* **2.** *adj.* beneficial; being to one's advantage; advantageous; helpful. (Adv: *favorably.*) ♦ *I like visiting Arizona in the winter because of its favorable climate.* ♦ *The scientist claimed that the new cancer treatment produced favorable results.*

favored ['fev ɚd] *adj.* special; treated in a special way. ♦ *The front seats were reserved for the favored few.* ♦ *I always resented my brother, who was clearly the favored child in my family.*

favorite ['fev ə rɪt] **1.** *adj.* preferred over every other choice; liked better than everything or everyone else. ♦ *Chocolate is my favorite ice-cream flavor.* ♦ *Mr. Smith's favorite pupil always got As on tests.* **2.** *n.* someone or something that is preferred over every other choice; someone or something who is liked better than everything or everyone else. ♦ *Anne bet $25 on the favorite to win the horse race.* ♦ *The students were all jealous of Dave, who was their teacher's favorite.*

favoritism ['fev ə rə tɪz əm] *n.* showing kindness to one person more than anyone else; treating one person better than everyone else. (No plural form in this sense.) ♦ *The impartial teacher didn't show any favoritism to any student in class.* ♦ *The mayor was accused of favoritism when he hired his sister as a consultant.*

fawn ['fɔn] **1.** *n.* a baby deer. ♦ *The doe protected her fawn from a curious raccoon.* ♦ *I watched fawns grazing in my backyard!* **2. fawn over** *iv.* + *prep. phr.* to cover someone with attention. ♦ *My grandparents fawned over my baby brother and totally ignored me.* ♦ *Bill fawned all over our waitress and asked her out on a date.*

fax ['fæks] **1.** *n.* a machine that sends an exact copy of a piece of paper to another machine, over telephone lines. ♦ *Please send the document to me by fax.* ♦ *My fax places the current time on the top of each page it prints.* **2.** *n.* a piece of paper that has been sent and received by way of ①. ♦ *The secretary handed an important fax to Sue.* ♦ *It was hard to read the fax because the print was too light.* **3.** *adj.* <the adj. use of ①.> of or about sending and receiving ②. ♦ *Does this model require special fax paper, or can I use regular white paper?* ♦ *The fax manual describes how to clear jammed paper.* **4.** *tv.* to send a document to someone by using ①. ♦ *Please fax this document to our Baltimore office.* ♦ *Did you get the report I faxed you last night?*

faze ['fez] *tv.* to bother someone; to worry someone; to upset someone or something. (Usually negative.) ♦ *The singer was not fazed by the negative reviews.* ♦ *The harsh criticism did not faze the director in the least.*

fear ['fɪr] **1.** *n.* the feeling of being afraid; the feeling of being in danger. (No plural form in this sense.) ♦ *I have a great fear of rats.* ♦ *Dogs can sense whether you have fear for them or not.* **2.** *n.* a specific source of ① and the feeling caused by that source. ♦ *Bullies are one of my greatest fears.* ♦ *I have a constant fear that I will have a car accident.* **3.** *tv.* to be afraid of someone or something. ♦ *I fear walking around the city at night.* ♦ *I want to ask for a raise, but I fear my supervisor's temper.* **4.** *tv.* to be sorry to say something; to feel obliged to say something. (Takes a clause.) ♦ *I fear that we might have to cancel our vacation.* ♦ *I fear that you're mistaken in this matter.* **5. fear for** *iv.* + *prep. phr.* to be afraid that someone or something is in danger. ♦ *I feared for my parents' safety when I heard that a tornado struck in their area.* ♦ *Even the family doctor feared for my grandfather's health.* **6. for fear of something** *idiom* out of fear for something; because of fear of something. ♦ *He doesn't drive for fear of an accident.* ♦ *They lock their doors for fear of being robbed.*

feared ['fɪrd] *adj.* causing fright; causing someone to be afraid. ♦ *The feared outcome never materialized.* ♦ *Two of the feared enemy planes bombed the town at noon.*

fearful ['fɪr fʊl] **1.** *adj.* full of fear; frightened. (Adv: *fearfully.*) ♦ *The fearful children ran from the monster.* ♦ *Tom was fearful when he got lost in the forest after dark.* **2.** *adj.* causing fear; scary; frightening; fearsome. (Adv: *fearfully.*) ♦ *The accident made a fearful noise.* ♦ *The terrorist taunted the hostages with a fearful laugh.*

fearless ['fɪr ləs] *adj.* without fear; brave; courageous. (Adv: *fearlessly.*) ♦ *The fearless soldier drove the tank into the enemy's camp.* ♦ *The fearless cat clawed at the sleeping dog's nose.*

fearsome ['fɪr səm] *adj.* causing fear; frightening; scary. (Adv: *fearsomely.*) ♦ *A fearsome crash of thunder made Jimmy cry.* ♦ *When we approached the scene of the car accident, we saw a fearsome sight.*

feasibility [fiz ə 'bɪl ə ti] *n.* the likelihood of being able to do something. (No plural form in this sense.) ♦ *What is the feasibility of your finishing this project by next week?*

♦ *The report examined the feasibility of building a freeway around the lake.*

feasible ['fiz ə bəl] *adj.* possible; easily done; able to be done without problems. (Adv: *feasibly.*) ♦ *Is it feasible that you could finish the report by next week?* ♦ *Your request seems quite feasible. I'll take care of it today.*

feast ['fist] **1.** *n.* a large meal, especially one for a special occasion; a banquet. ♦ *The chef prepared a feast in honor of the president's visit.* ♦ *Every Sunday, I cook a feast fit for a king.* **2.** *iv.* to eat a lot of food, often in the company of others, especially as part of a celebration. ♦ *On Easter my family feasts at my grandparents' house.* ♦ *My friends and I feasted royally after we learned that we passed our final exams.* **3. feast on** *iv. + prep. phr.* to eat a lot of a particular food. ♦ *We feasted on the turkey for many days.* ♦ *On my birthday, I feasted on pizza.* **4. feast one's eyes (on someone or something)** *idiom* to look at someone or something with pleasure, envy, or admiration. ♦ *Just feast your eyes on that beautiful juicy steak!* ♦ *Yes, feast your eyes. You won't see one like that again for a long time.*

feat ['fit] *n.* a remarkable accomplishment; an act or deed that shows skill or talent. ♦ *The magician's first feat was to change a parrot into a rabbit.* ♦ *It was quite a feat, but the bridge was repaired within two months after the earthquake.*

feather ['fɛð ɚ] **1.** *n.* one of many hard stems bearing fine tufts that cover the body of a bird. ♦ *My pillow is stuffed with feathers.* ♦ *A cardinal has red feathers.* **2. feather in one's cap** *idiom* an honor; a reward for something. ♦ *Getting a new client was really a feather in my cap.* ♦ *John earned a feather in his cap by getting an A in physics.* **3. ruffle someone's feathers** *idiom* to upset or annoy someone. ♦ *You certainly ruffled Mrs. Smith's feathers by criticizing her garden.* ♦ *Try to be tactful and not ruffle people's feathers.*

featherbedding ['fɛð ɚ bɛd ɪŋ] *n.* a situation where a labor union causes an employer to hire more people than are really needed. (No plural form in this sense.) ♦ *Management fired the extra people who had been hired because of featherbedding.* ♦ *The union's attempt at featherbedding annoyed management.*

featherweight ['fɛð ɚ wet] *adj.* lightweight. ♦ *I have a pair of featherweight glasses with plastic lenses.* ♦ *In the summer, even my featherweight blanket is too warm.*

feathery ['fɛð ə ri] *adj.* light and fluffy like a feather. ♦ *Moths have feathery antennas.* ♦ *Cotton has a feathery texture.*

feature ['fi tʃɚ] **1.** *n.* an important aspect of something; a quality of something that stands out. ♦ *Power steering is a standard feature on most new cars.* ♦ *The business plan's most important feature is that it will save $100,000.* **2.** *n.* a part of the face. ♦ *The police asked Bill to describe the features of his attacker.* ♦ *My features are blurred in this photograph.* **3.** *n.* a special article in a newspaper; an important news story. ♦ *Jane wrote a feature about the president's visit to China.* ♦ *The editor put Bill's feature on the front page.* **4.** *n.* a full-length movie. ♦ *Let's go eat and then see the new feature playing at the mall.* ♦ *Before the feature started, six previews were shown.* **5.** *tv.* to present or focus on an important element of something. ♦ *The car I'm offering for sale features air conditioning and airbags.* ♦ *The instruction manual features clear instructions on how to operate the computer.* **6.** *tv.* to present someone special as an actor in a movie, play, or television show. ♦ *This movie version of* Hamlet *features Sir Laurence Olivier.* ♦ *My favorite television show features Mary Tyler Moore.* **7.** *tv.* to imagine something; to imagine someone as something. (Informal.) ♦ *Feature Sue as the head of the department.* ♦ *Can you feature me in a large lobster costume?*

featured ['fi tʃɚd] *adj.* prominent; standing out as important. ♦ *The featured guest spoke at length at the reception.* ♦ *I bought the featured book in the newspaper's review section.*

February ['fɛb ru ɛr i] *n.* the second month of the year. ♦ *Valentine's Day is on February 14.* ♦ *Next February, I'm going to Mexico for two weeks.*

fecal ['fi kəl] *adj.* of or about feces or dung. ♦ *There appears to be some fecal material on the bottom of my shoe.* ♦ *The swimming pool was closed because of fecal contamination.*

feces ['fi siz] *n.* excrement; animal waste. (From Latin. Treated as plural.) ♦ *Anne cleaned up her dog's feces when she took him out for a walk.* ♦ *I had to clean my shoes because I stepped in some animal feces.*

fed ['fɛd] **1.** pt/pp of feed. **2. feds** *n.* an (unspecified) agency of the U.S. federal government. (Treated as plural.) ♦ *The feds have ruled that tobacco cannot be advertised.* ♦ *The feds raided the headquarters of the drug ring.* **3. Fed** *n.* the U.S. Federal Reserve Board, the U.S. national bank. (Treated as singular.) ♦ *The Fed raised the prime interest rate a quarter of a percent.* ♦ *The Fed took action to slow the growth of the inflation rate.*

federal ['fɛd ə rəl] **1.** *adj.* of or about a federation. (Adv: *federally.*) ♦ *My senator favors a strong federal government.* ♦ *The U.S. is a federal organization of states.* **2.** *adj.* of or about the U.S. government. (Adv: *federally.*) ♦ *Interstate commerce is governed by federal law.* ♦ *The FDIC is the Federal Deposit Insurance Corporation.*

federalize ['fɛd ə rə laɪz] **1.** *tv.* [for different governments] to join together to form a federation; to cause a government to become part of a federation. ♦ *An advantage of federalizing the independent states is a strong military system.* ♦ *Citizens from both nations protested when their governments decided to federalize the two countries.* **2.** *tv.* [for the federal government] to bring something under its control. ♦ *Do you think the welfare system should be federalized?* ♦ *If health care were federalized, would our taxes increase?*

federation [fɛd ə 're ʃən] **1.** *n.* the formation of a governmental body by smaller governments that join together while still governing their own internal affairs. (No plural form in this sense.) ♦ *The military guided the peaceful federation of the previously independent islands.* ♦ *During the federation of the country, the states decided to share a common currency.* **2.** *n.* a government formed by smaller governments that join together while each governs its own internal affairs. ♦ *The United Arab Emirates is a federation of seven Arab emirates.* ♦ *The federation decided to levy a tax on commerce between its provinces.* **3.** *n.* a league or union of people or nations. ♦ *In 1955, the American Federation of Labor and the Con-*

gress of Industrial Organizations merged. ♦ *My mother is a member of the American Federation of Teachers.*

fee ['fi] *n.* money that is paid in exchange for a service or privilege. ♦ *I'll fix your car for a modest fee.* ♦ *My lawyer's hourly fee is $130.*

feeble ['fi bəl] *adj.* weak; frail; lacking force; lacking strength. (Adv: *feebly.* Comp: *feebler;* sup: *feeblest.*) ♦ *My teacher ignored my feeble excuse for being late.* ♦ *The feeble old man hobbled as he crossed the street.*

feed ['fid] **1.** *tv., irreg.* to nourish someone or something with food; to give food to someone or something. (Pt/pp: fed.) ♦ *Tom fed the baby and put her to bed.* ♦ *What time should I feed the dog tonight?* **2.** *tv., irreg.* to supply something without stopping; to provide something without stopping. (Figurative on ①.) ♦ *This machine feeds paper into the computer printer.* ♦ *The sewing machine feeds thread through the eye of the needle.* **3.** *n.* food that is given to animals, especially on a farm. (No plural form in this sense.) ♦ *The farmer bought a dozen bags of feed for his horses.* ♦ *We grow corn for use in our cattle's feed.* **4. spoon-feed someone** *idiom* to treat someone with too much care or help; to teach someone with methods that are too easy and do not stimulate the learner to independent thinking. ♦ *The teacher spoon-feeds the pupils by dictating notes on the novel instead of getting the children to read the books themselves.* ♦ *You mustn't spoon-feed the new recruits by telling them what to do all the time. They must use their initiative.*

feedback ['fid bæk] **1.** *n.* a loud, high-pitched noise caused when amplified sound is amplified again as a microphone picks up the sound coming through the speakers. (No plural form in this sense.) ♦ *Bob turned on the microphone while standing too close to the speakers, and the feedback hurt our ears.* ♦ *The band's recording session was marred by feedback.* **2.** *n.* specific information that is given about something one has done; criticism. (No plural form in this sense. Figurative on ①.) ♦ *Would you read my report and give me some feedback?* ♦ *The actor asked the director for some feedback after the rehearsal.*

feeder ['fid ɚ] *n.* a device that provides something with supplies as they are needed. ♦ *The assembly line stopped because the feeder broke down.* ♦ *Our new laser printer has an envelope feeder.*

feel ['fil] **1.** *tv., irreg.* to touch someone or something. (Pt/pp: felt.) ♦ *I felt the cold the railing and decided I needed my gloves.* ♦ *Susan could feel the soft blanket with the tips of her fingers.* **2.** *tv., irreg.* to experience or sense being touched by someone or something. ♦ *I felt a cold wind on my neck.* ♦ *Do you feel a little pressure on your arm? I am touching you there.* **3.** *tv., irreg.* to receive information by touching; to detect something by touch. ♦ *The doctor was relieved to feel the victim's pulse.* ♦ *I felt the wet spot the drinking glass had left on the table.* **4.** *tv., irreg.* to experience an emotion; to experience something in one's mind. ♦ *I feel sadness every year on the anniversary of my father's death.* ♦ *Tom felt discomfort when he read the disturbing account of the fire.* **5.** *tv., irreg.* to consider something; to have an opinion. (Takes a clause.) ♦ *I feel that you should go home now.* ♦ *Jane felt I had made a mistake.* **6. feel for** *iv., irreg. + prep. phr.* to search for something with one's fingers instead of one's eyes. ♦ *Tom had to feel for the fuse box in total darkness.* ♦ *I reached into the tool box and felt for a hammer.* **7.** *iv., irreg.* to provide a certain kind of tactile stimulation; to provide an identifiable (physical) feeling. ♦ *This wood feels rough.* ♦ *This cloth feels like silk.* **8.** *iv., irreg.* to experience an emotion; to experience something in one's mind. ♦ *I felt angry after seeing the amount of paper they wasted.* ♦ *Bill feels unhappy every year on the anniversary of his father's death.* **9. feel for** *iv., irreg. + prep. phr.* to have pity for someone; to have sympathy for someone. ♦ *Sue felt for me when my father died of cancer.* ♦ *You have a lot of problems, and I really feel for you.* **10.** *n.* a characteristic shape or texture that can be felt. (No plural form in this sense.) ♦ *This material has the feel of silk.* ♦ *The wood has a rough feel that makes it a poor choice for furniture.* **11. feel like doing something** *idiom* to want to do something; to be in the mood to do something. ♦ *Do you feel like stopping work to eat something?* ♦ *I feel like going on a vacation.* **12. feel like something** *idiom* to have the feeling of being something, usually something bad. ♦ *I said something really stupid and I feel like a fool.* ♦ *Lisa says she feels like a failure.* **13. feel like something** *idiom* to want to have something, such as food or drink. ♦ *I really feel like a cold drink right now.* ♦ *Do you feel like a hamburger?* **14. get the feel of something** *idiom* to acquire the ability to do something; to develop the skill or talent for doing something. ♦ *Don't worry. You'll get the feel of it.* ♦ *I finally got the feel of dancing to fast music.*

feeler ['fil ɚ] **1.** *n.* an antenna; a part of the body of an insect or crustacean that is used for touching or sensing. ♦ *Lobsters sense the direction of water currents with their feelers.* ♦ *Some insects use their feelers to find food.* **2.** *n.* an inquiry or suggestion that is made to determine what other people are thinking or feeling. ♦ *While looking for a job, I sent out feelers to local law firms.* ♦ *Send out a feeler and see if the staff wants to go bowling.*

feeling ['fil ɪŋ] **1.** *n.* the sensation produced by touching something. (No plural form in this sense.) ♦ *I like the feeling of crushed velvet against my skin.* ♦ *I don't like this lotion because it has a sticky feeling.* **2.** *n.* a response to touch, pressure, heat, or pain. (No plural form in this sense.) ♦ *Because of the anesthetic, Anne had no feeling in her arm.* ♦ *John felt the burning feeling of alcohol on his throat.* **3. feelings** *n.* an emotion; the ability to feel emotions. ♦ *After the accident, I had no feelings because of shock.* ♦ *Your insult hurt my feelings.* **4.** *n.* a hunch; an idea based on what one feels; a perception. ♦ *What's your feeling on the issue?* ♦ *I have a feeling that it's going to rain soon.* **5. have mixed feelings (about someone or something)** *idiom* to be uncertain about someone or something. (On ③.) ♦ *I have mixed feelings about Bob. Sometimes I think he likes me; other times I don't.* ♦ *I have mixed feelings about my trip to England. I love the people, but the climate upsets me.*

feet ['fit] pl of foot.

feign ['fen] *tv.* to pretend something; to make believe something. ♦ *I feigned illness so I could stay home from work.* ♦ *Although Mary had heard the story, she feigned surprise when Bob told her the latest gossip.*

felicitation [fə ləs ə 'te ʃən] *n.* a statement of goodwill; an expression of congratulations. (Usually plural.) ♦ *The senator extended his felicitations to the new ambassador.* ♦ *I sent my felicitations to Anne when she graduated from college.*

felicitous [fə 'lɪs ə təs] *adj.* appropriate; apt; suitable. (Adv: *felicitously.*) ♦ *I appreciated your felicitous response to my question.* ♦ *The company handbook outlines felicitous forms of behavior at work.*

feline ['fi laɪn] **1.** *adj.* of or about cats or members of the cat family. (Adv: *felinely.*) ♦ *In biology class today, we studied feline body structure.* ♦ *Feline temperament can be described as fickle.* **2.** *n.* a cat; a member of the cat family. ♦ *Some of the large felines, like tigers, are nearly extinct.* ♦ *Our veterinarian specializes in felines and canines.*

fell ['fɛl] **1.** pt of **fall**. **2.** *tv.* to cut something down, especially a tree; to topple someone or something that is very powerful or important. (Pt/pp: **felled**.) ♦ *The woodcutter felled five trees in one hour.* ♦ *I felled the tree with a chain saw.* **3. in one fell swoop** *idiom* [accomplishing much] in one swift and damaging action. ♦ *In one fell swoop, management laid off 800 workers.* ♦ *The bear managed to capture two large fish in one fell swoop.*

felled ['fɛld] pt/pp of **fell** ②.

fellow ['fɛl o] **1.** *n.* a man; a male. ♦ *Do you know the name of that fellow on the corner?* ♦ *I spoke to some fellow from Boston during lunch.* **2.** *n.* an academic rank or status, usually without teaching responsibilities. (For either sex.) ♦ *Sue was appointed as a research fellow in the biology department.* ♦ *John is a fellow in the English department at Indiana University.* **3.** *adj.* similar; alike; sharing a common interest or occupation. (For either sex.) ♦ *I encouraged my fellow workers to join the union.* ♦ *I'd like to thank my fellow students for their help.* **4. hail-fellow-well-met** *idiom* friendly to everyone; falsely friendly to everyone. ♦ *Yes, he's friendly, sort of hail-fellow-well-met.* ♦ *He's not a very sincere person. Hail-fellow-well-met—you know the type.*

fellowship ['fɛl o ʃɪp] **1.** *n.* a group; a social organization; friendship. (Not restricted to males.) ♦ *Dave joined the Fellowship of Expert Chess Players.* ♦ *At church, Sue belongs to a fellowship of devout worshipers.* **2.** *n.* friendly interaction with other people. (No plural form in this sense.) ♦ *I enjoy the fellowship of my friends and relatives.* ♦ *After the meeting, we had refreshments and enjoyed the fellowship of the group.* **3.** *n.* a scholarship; money that is given to an advanced student for tuition. ♦ *The university awarded Anne a $10,000 fellowship.* ♦ *I couldn't afford to continue my studies without a fellowship.*

felon ['fɛl ən] *n.* someone who has been found guilty of a felony. ♦ *Many companies will not hire convicted felons.* ♦ *The felon spent 12 years in prison.*

felony ['fɛl ə ni] *n.* a serious crime; a crime that is more serious than a misdemeanor. ♦ *Murder and armed robberies are examples of felonies.* ♦ *The drug pusher had been convicted of numerous felonies.*

felt ['fɛlt] **1.** pt/pp of **feel**. **2.** *n.* a thick cloth made of intertwined, pressed fibers. (No plural form in this sense.) ♦ *My hat is made of felt.* ♦ *Black felt seems to attract lint.* **3.** *adj.* made of ②. ♦ *The wind blew my felt hat from my head.* ♦ *You can't sign these forms with a felt pen.*

female ['fi mel] **1.** *adj.* of or about women or girls; of or about animals that bear young or lay eggs, as opposed to males. ♦ *We had our female cat neutered.* ♦ *The female employees played baseball together after work.* **2.** *n.* a woman; a girl; an animal that bears young or lays eggs. ♦ *The census asks how many males and how many females live in each household.* ♦ *Breast cancer is more common in females than in males.*

feminine ['fɛm ə nɪn] **1.** *adj.* of or about the characteristics of women; of or about the qualities of women. (Adv: *femininely.*) ♦ *When I answered the phone, a feminine voice whispered, "Hello?"* ♦ *Jim asked Mary for a feminine viewpoint on the issue.* **2.** *adj.* of or about the one of the three grammatical genders that is neither masculine nor neuter. ♦ *In Spanish, many feminine nouns end in* a. ♦ *The word for* work *in German is in the feminine gender.*

feminism ['fɛm ə nɪz əm] *n.* a doctrine that advocates equal rights and equal roles for women in modern society. (No plural form in this sense.) ♦ *Feminism has brought many women into the work force.* ♦ *My sociology class examines the effect of feminism in the workplace.*

feminist ['fɛm ə nəst] *n.* someone, typically a woman, who advocates feminism. ♦ *The feminist explained her viewpoints on a talk show.* ♦ *Feminists believe in equal pay for equal work, regardless of the worker's sex.*

fence ['fɛns] **1.** *n.* a barrier that encloses a space to keep things or people from coming into or leaving that space. ♦ *A drunk driver smashed into our picket fence last night.* ♦ *The horses are safe behind the tall fence.* **2.** *n.* someone who buys and sells stolen things. ♦ *The robber took the stolen goods to the fence.* ♦ *The fence paid $50 for the stolen watch.* **3. fence in** *tv.* + *adv.* to enclose something in ①. ♦ *The farmer fenced the field in.* ♦ *The field was fenced in by the previous owner.* **4.** *iv.* to participate in a sport wherein there are engagements between two persons each armed with a long, thin sword. ♦ *I learned how to fence in college.* ♦ *Because Bill knew how to fence, the director put him in the sword-fighting scene.* **5. mend (one's) fences** *idiom* to restore good relations (with someone). ♦ *I think I had better get home and mend my fences. I had an argument with my daughter this morning.* ♦ *Sally called up her uncle to apologize and try to mend fences.* **6. sit on the fence** *idiom* not to take sides in a dispute; not to make a clear choice between two possibilities. ♦ *When Jane and Tom argue, it is well to sit on the fence, and then you won't offend either of them.* ♦ *No one knows which of the candidates Jane will vote for. She's sitting on the fence.*

fend ['fɛnd] **1. fend off** *tv.* + *adv.* to fight someone or something off; to protect oneself by fighting someone or something off; ♦ *The president was able to fend off questions from reporters.* ♦ *Mary fended off the dog by poking her umbrella at it.* **2. fend for oneself** *idiom* to take care of oneself. ♦ *My parents went on vacation, leaving me to fend for myself.* ♦ *Since you're 18, you're old enough to fend for yourself.*

fender ['fɛn dɚ] *n.* a part of a vehicle's body that forms a protective shield over the wheel of a car. ♦ *Bob crumpled the rear fender when he backed into a tree.* ♦ *I polish the fenders every time I clean my car.*

ferment **1.** [fɚ 'mɛnt] *tv.* to cause something to undergo fermentation; [for yeast] to cause sugar to change into alcohol. ♦ *If you ferment grapes, you will make wine.* ♦ *As soon as they had fermented the grape juice, they bottled the new wine.* **2.** [fɚ 'mɛnt] *iv.* to undergo fermentation as with ①. ♦ *Has the grape juice fermented into wine yet?* ♦ *This pineapple is so old, it is fermenting.* **3.** ['fɚ mɛnt] *n.*

political unrest; a commotion. (No plural form in this sense. Figurative on ①.) ♦ *The dictator ordered the army to deal with the ferment in the town square.* ♦ *The newspaper was banned as punishment for stirring up ferment.*

fermentation [fɚ mɛn 'te ʃən] *n.* the alteration of sugar into alcohol by the action of yeast. (No plural form in this sense.) ♦ *I sped up the fermentation of the wine by adding extra sugar to the grape juice.* ♦ *During fermentation, yeast emits a distinctive smell.*

fermented [fɚ 'mɛn tɪd] *adj.* having undergone a chemical change caused by an organic substance such as yeast. ♦ *Wine is made from fermented grapes.* ♦ *Lisa threw away the fermented pineapple.*

fern ['fɚn] *n.* a plant that has leaves but no flowers, and reproduces with spores instead of seeds. ♦ *I gave Jane a potted fern for her birthday.* ♦ *I planted a row of ferns in front of my house.*

ferocious [fə 'ro ʃəs] *adj.* fierce; savage; cruel. (Adv: *ferociously.*) ♦ *The ferocious lion tore its food apart with its teeth.* ♦ *The ferocious winter storm buried the roads in a foot of snow.*

ferocity [fə 'rɑs ə ti] *n.* the quality of being ferocious; fierceness. (No plural form in this sense.) ♦ *The ferocity of the hurricane scared those who had not evacuated.* ♦ *I was very upset by the ferocity of your criticism.*

ferret ['fɛr ɪt] **1.** *n.* a small furry animal similar to the weasel, sometimes kept as a pet. ♦ *My landlord won't let me keep my ferret in the apartment.* ♦ *The ferret crawled through the trash can, looking for food.* **2. ferret out** *tv. + adv.* to search something out; to discover something by looking through something. (Figurative on ①.) ♦ *I ferreted out some clues about Bob's past by looking through his files.* ♦ *The detective ferreted the information out by reading through the papers.*

ferry ['fɛr i] **1.** *n.* a ferryboat. (Compare with **fairy**.) ♦ *Travelers can take the ferry instead of driving around the lake.* ♦ *We rode across the river on a ferry.* **2.** *tv.* to carry cars, products, or people from one side of a river or lake to the other by ①. ♦ *This vessel can ferry up to 250 cars at once.* ♦ *The captain ferried the cargo to the opposite shore.* **3.** *iv.* to travel some place by ①. ♦ *We ferried to the opposite shore of the river.* ♦ *We had to ferry across the river because the bridge was out.* **4.** *adj.* <the adj. use of ①.> ♦ *The ferry landing was crowded with cars.* ♦ *We made a ferry crossing at high tide during a storm.*

ferryboat ['fɛr i] *n.* a boat that takes cars and people across a river or a lake. ♦ *How many cars does the ferryboat carry?* ♦ *The ferryboat is just now leaving the opposite shore.*

fertile ['fɚt əl] **1.** *adj.* able to reproduce easily. (Adv: *fertilely.*) ♦ *The very fertile couple had six children in eight years.* ♦ *The fertile seeds soon grew into a beautiful flower garden.* **2.** *adj.* rich in nutrients that help reproduction. (Adv: *fertilely.*) ♦ *The soil on our farm is so fertile that we don't use any fertilizer.* ♦ *The fertile farmland yielded a very large bounty of crops.* **3.** *adj.* creative; able to produce good ideas. (Figurative on ①. Adv: *fertilely.*) ♦ *Fertile minds on the committee solved the problem quickly.* ♦ *The meeting was quite fertile, with a number of fine ideas being discussed.*

fertility [fɚ 'tɪl ə ti] **1.** *n.* the ability to produce offspring; [of soil] the ability to grow plants or crops. (No plural form in this sense.) ♦ *The Johnsons have no problems with fertility—they have eight children!* ♦ *Because they were childless, the Smiths went to a doctor who specialized in the problems of fertility.* **2.** *n.* the ability for soil to produce good crops. (No plural form in this sense.) ♦ *The scientist measured the fertility of the farmer's soil.* ♦ *The farmer improved the soil's fertility by planting alfalfa every few years.* **3.** *adj.* <the adj. use of ①.> ♦ *Mary and Bob were having fertility problems and sought medical advice.* ♦ *The fertility specialist made some suggestions that resulted in conception.*

fertilization [fɚ tə lə 'ze ʃən] **1.** *n.* fertilizing crops; providing nutrients to the land so that crops will grow well. (No plural form in this sense.) ♦ *The farmer read about more efficient methods of fertilization.* ♦ *During spring fertilization, the farmer also tilled the soil.* **2.** *n.* a sperm cell uniting with an ovum. ♦ *After fertilization, the new structure is called a zygote, which will become an embryo, and then a fetus.* ♦ *The doctor specialized in test-tube fertilizations.*

fertilize ['fɚ tə lɑɪz] **1.** *tv.* to provide nutrients to the land so that crops will grow well. ♦ *We fertilized the soil with chemicals rich in nitrogen.* ♦ *The farmer fertilized the farmland every year.* **2.** *tv.* [for a male sperm] to join with the female's ovum. ♦ *The first sperm that reaches the ovum fertilizes it.* ♦ *Without birth control, the sperm can freely fertilize the ovum.* **3.** *tv.* to cause a male sperm to join with the female's ovum. ♦ *A scientist fertilized the frog ova in the laboratory.* ♦ *The farmer fertilized the cows with semen from healthy bulls.*

fertilizer ['fɚ tə lɑɪ zɚ] *n.* something that helps crops grow; nutrients for soil. ♦ *The farmer plowed organic fertilizer into the soil.* ♦ *Because the crops were stunted, the farmer applied more fertilizer.*

fervent ['fɚ vənt] *adj.* passionate; showing a warmth of spirit or sincerity. (Adv: *fervently.*) ♦ *The church members listened to their minister's fervent prayers.* ♦ *I am a fervent admirer of that highly ethical lawyer.*

fervor ['fɚ vɚ] *n.* passion; excitement; strong emotion. (No plural form in this sense.) ♦ *Lisa delivered her speech with great fervor.* ♦ *The media generated a huge amount of fervor for the presidential election.*

fester ['fɛs tɚ] **1.** *iv.* [for an injury] to become more and more infected and form pus. ♦ *Because I didn't clean it, my open wound began to fester.* ♦ *When cuts begin to fester, they turn red.* **2.** *iv.* [for a problem or difficulty] to increase in intensity. (Figurative on ①.) ♦ *Because the problem was ignored, it quickly festered into a bigger crisis.* ♦ *You should solve your problems before they begin to fester.*

festival ['fɛs tə vəl] *n.* a public celebration, especially in honor of a certain occasion. ♦ *My hometown sponsors a large festival every Fourth of July.* ♦ *The town's annual festival features bands from every high school.*

festive ['fɛs tɪv] *adj.* merry; exciting; like a celebration; joyous. (Adv: *festively.*) ♦ *The room was decorated with bright, festive colors.* ♦ *The winning team was in a festive mood after the game.*

festivity [fɛs 'tɪv ə ti] **1.** *n.* a spirit of happiness and celebration. (No plural form in this sense.) ♦ *The festivity at school increased when our team won the championship.* ♦ *I enjoyed the festivity of the crowd during the parade.* **2. festivities** *n.* particular activities involved in a celebration; things that are done during celebrations. ♦ *What festivities do you have planned for graduation weekend?* ♦ *I arrived at the party too late to join the festivities.*

festoon [fɛs 'tun] **festoon with** *tv.* + *prep. phr.* to decorate something with ribbons, streamers, flowers, or other objects that are strung together like a chain. ♦ *My roommates festooned the house with ribbons and banners for my birthday.* ♦ *The gymnasium was festooned with decorations for the dance.*

fetal ['fit əl] *adj.* of or about a fetus. (Adv: *fetally.*) ♦ *Dr. Jones specializes in fetal diseases.* ♦ *Fetal surgery corrected the child's deformity before it was born.*

fetch ['fɛtʃ] **1.** *tv.* to bring something to someone; to go somewhere and get something for someone. ♦ *Tom commanded his dog to fetch the stick he had thrown.* ♦ *Would you fetch me my slippers from the closet?* **2.** *tv.* [for something] to bring in a certain amount of money when sold. ♦ *Do you think this old painting will fetch much if I sell it?* ♦ *My vintage car fetched $75,000 at the auction.*

fetish ['fɛt ɪʃ] **1.** *n.* an idol; an object that is worshiped; an object that is said to have magical powers. ♦ *The tour guide warned against touching the sacred fetishes on the temple walls.* ♦ *The city museum displays hand-carved fetishes from ancient cultures.* **2.** *n.* an object or idea that inspires devotion, fascination, or reverence. (Figurative on ①.) ♦ *Jane made a fetish out of punctuality.* ♦ *Bob was burdened with a chocolate fetish.*

fetter ['fɛt ɚ] **1.** *n.* a chain, rope, or something similar used to bind the legs of a captive person or creature. (Often plural.) ♦ *The prisoners' legs were chained to the walls with fetters.* ♦ *The horse tried to break away from its fetters.* **2.** *tv.* to attach ① to the legs of someone or some creature. ♦ *The guard fettered the prisoner to the wall.* ♦ *The horse was fettered so that it could not run away.*

fetus ['fit əs] *n.* a stage of development of a female's offspring during pregnancy. ♦ *A fetus is more developed than an embryo.* ♦ *Sue could feel the fetus moving inside her uterus.*

feud ['fjud] **1.** *n.* an argument; a quarrel, especially a quarrel between two families or groups of families. ♦ *The feud between our families has lasted for generations.* ♦ *Anne and I ended our friendship with a bitter feud.* **2.** *iv.* to argue with someone, especially over a long period of time. ♦ *Our families have been feuding since the 1800s.* ♦ *I feuded with my parents throughout my teenage years.*

feudal ['fjud l] *adj.* of or about feudalism. (Adv: *feudally.*) ♦ *The feudal system flourished in Europe a thousand years ago.* ♦ *The servants obeyed their feudal lords.*

feudalism ['fjud ə liz əm] *n.* a system used in western Europe during the Middle Ages where people who farmed land served and were protected by the owners of the land. (No plural form in this sense.) ♦ *Under feudalism, landowners lived off the crops grown by the farmers and could use these farmers in their armies.* ♦ *My report discusses the impact of feudalism on European history.*

fever ['fiv ɚ] *n.* a state of sickness where the temperature of the body rises above normal. ♦ *I should stay home tonight because I have a fever.* ♦ *Your forehead feels very hot. I think you have a fever.*

feverish ['fiv ɚ ɪʃ] **1.** *adj.* having a higher body temperature than normal. (Adv: *feverishly.*) ♦ *I should stay home tonight because I'm feeling feverish.* ♦ *Your forehead feels very hot. Are you feverish?* **2.** *adj.* agitated; excited; restless. (Figurative on ①. Adv: *feverishly.*) ♦ *He worked with feverish intensity to complete the assignment.* ♦ *I walked at a feverish pace to get to my appointment on time.*

few ['fju] **1.** *adj.* not many but some; a smaller number than expected. (Used with items that can be counted. Compare with **little**. Without *a*. Comp: *fewer;* sup: *fewest.*) ♦ *Few people showed up for the party—not nearly the number we had expected.* ♦ *John is fortunate because he has very few problems.* **2.** *adj.* only a small number. (With *a*. Comp: *fewer;* sup: *fewest.*) ♦ *A few students were late for class, but most were on time.* ♦ *Dave has a few problems, but then, who doesn't?* **3.** *pron.* some [of those previously mentioned]; not many; a smaller number than expected. (Treated as plural.) ♦ *Many students started taking the course, but few finished it.* ♦ *I invited several people to the party, but few came.* **4. a few** *n.* a small number [of those items previously mentioned]. (Treated as plural. Use *a little* for quantities.) ♦ *Most of the guests arrived on time, but a few arrived late.* ♦ *I invited several people to the party, but only a few came.* **5. quite a few** *phr.* a fairly large number; more than expected. ♦ *Dave has quite a few problems with his car in cold weather.* ♦ *There are quite a few people waiting to see you.*

fiancé [fi 'ɑn se] *n.* the man that a woman is engaged to be married to. (From French.) ♦ *Mary's fiancé was an hour late to the wedding rehearsal.* ♦ *Jane's fiancé bought her a diamond ring.*

fiancée [fi 'ɑn se] *n.* the woman that a man is engaged to be married to. (From French.) ♦ *Bill's fiancée called off the wedding at the last minute.* ♦ *Dave told his fiancée that he wanted to get married in Bermuda.*

fiasco [fi 'æs ko] *n.* a debacle; an event where everything has gone wrong. (From Italian. Pl in *-es.*) ♦ *The party was a total fiasco. We ran out of food before all of the guests had arrived.* ♦ *My physics test was a complete fiasco. I only answered two questions.*

fiat ['fi ɑt] *n.* an order; a command; a decree. (Latin for 'Let it be done.') ♦ *The workers were given an executive fiat to use their vacation time in December.* ♦ *The plan was not thought out. It was just another fiat from one of the executives.*

fib ['fɪb] **1.** *n.* a small, harmless lie. ♦ *The teacher scolded Jimmy for telling fibs.* ♦ *I told Anne a fib because I didn't want to hurt her feelings.* **2.** *iv.* to tell ①. ♦ *I fibbed to Tom that I was busy because I didn't want to go to the party with him.* ♦ *Jimmy fibbed to his teacher that his dog ate his homework.*

fiber ['faɪb ɚ] **1.** *n.* one of many threads or strands that form many plant, animal, and artificial substances. ♦ *Fibers of asbestos can cause disease.* ♦ *My sock unraveled when I pulled a loose fiber hanging from it.* **2.** *n.* edible fiber ①. (No plural form in this sense.) ♦ *My doctor said my digestion would improve if I ate more fiber.* ♦ *Bran is a food that is high in fiber.* **3. (moral) fiber** *n.* moral strength; moral integrity. (Figurative on ①. No plural form in this sense.) ♦ *I respected and admired my father's moral fiber.* ♦ *The judge scolded the criminal for lacking fiber.*

fiberglass ['fɑɪb ɚ glæs] **1.** *n.* a very strong, durable, lightweight substance made from thin, flexible glass fibers. (No plural form in this sense.) ♦ *Boats made of fiberglass are very strong.* ♦ *Bob's fishing rod is made of fiberglass.* **2.** *adj.* made of ①. ♦ *Bob has a fiberglass fishing rod.* ♦ *Our boat has a fiberglass hull.*

fibrous ['fɑɪb (ə) rəs] *adj.* made of fiber; having many fibers. (Adv: *fibrously.*) ♦ *The biologist examined the fibrous growth under the microscope.* ♦ *We used the fibrous stalks of the plants to weave crude baskets.*

fickle ['fɪk əl] *adj.* changing often for no reason; liking someone or something one moment and not the next. ♦ *The weather along the lakefront is fickle. It's sunny now, but in a few minutes it could be raining.* ♦ *Bill is a fickle man. Every time I see him, he's with a new girlfriend.*

fiction ['fɪk ʃən] **1.** *n.* literature that is written about imagined events, as opposed to real events; a story that is made up. (No plural form in this sense.) ♦ *I hoped to win a prize for my fiction.* ♦ *The school library keeps fiction on the second floor.* **2.** *n.* an occurrence or situation invented by the mind; information that is not true but which is made up. (No plural form in this sense.) ♦ *The judge dismissed the addict's testimony as pure fiction.* ♦ *Dave's account of why he was late for work was fiction.*

fictional ['fɪk ʃə nəl] *adj.* of or about fiction; created by the imagination. (Adv: *fictionally.*) ♦ *Tiny Tim is a fictional character in a Charles Dickens novel.* ♦ *Jane gave her boss a fictional account of why she was late.*

fictitious [fɪk 'tɪʃ əs] **1.** *adj.* imaginary; invented. (Adv: *fictitiously.*) ♦ *Dave was charged with perjury for giving fictitious testimony.* ♦ *Although loosely based on fact, the TV program about the hostages was mostly fictitious.* **2.** *adj.* false; made up in order to trick someone. (Adv: *fictitiously.*) ♦ *The thief used a fictitious identity to rent the car.* ♦ *Sue filed a fictitious absence report when she returned from vacation.*

fiddle ['fɪd l] **1.** *n.* a violin. (Informal.) ♦ *Music for square dances is usually played on a fiddle.* ♦ *We sat around the campfire and sang while Bill played the fiddle.* **2.** *iv.* to play the violin. ♦ *Mary fiddled while we sang.* ♦ *Do you know how to fiddle well enough to play in our band?* **3. fiddle (around) with something** *idiom* to play aimlessly with something; to meddle with something. ♦ *Stop fiddling with the light switch!* ♦ *Bill fiddled around with the vase until he dropped it.* **4. fiddle while Rome burns** *idiom* to do something trivial or nothing while something disastrous happens. ♦ *Congress doesn't seem to be doing anything to stop this terrible problem. They're fiddling while Rome burns.* ♦ *The doctor should have sent for an ambulance right away instead of examining her. In fact, he was just fiddling while Rome burned.* **5. play second fiddle (to someone)** *idiom* to be in a subordinate position to someone. ♦ *I'm tired of playing second fiddle to John.* ♦ *I'm better trained than he, and I have more experience. I shouldn't always play second fiddle.*

fidelity [fɪ 'dɛl ə ti] **1.** *n.* the condition of being faithful to someone; loyalty to someone. (No plural form in this sense.) ♦ *I admire my parents' fidelity to each other.* ♦ *The king rewarded his servants for their fidelity.* **2.** *n.* the accuracy of a copy when it is copied from an original. (Figurative on ①. No plural form in this sense.) ♦ *The fidelity of these duplicates is 100%.* ♦ *The copier needs repair, so the fidelity of the copies is poor.*

fidget ['fɪdʒ ɪt] *iv.* to move restlessly; to shift one's body uncomfortably; to not be able to remain still. ♦ *Bob fidgeted in church during the long sermon.* ♦ *Anne told her children not to fidget while she was taking their picture.*

fidgety ['fɪdʒ ə ti] *adj.* restless; unable to remain still. ♦ *You're very fidgety today. Are you nervous about something?* ♦ *It isn't polite to be so fidgety when someone is talking to you.*

field ['fild] **1.** *n.* a large area of land used for a specific purpose, such as growing crops, grazing cattle, playing certain sports, fighting a battle, landing airplanes, etc. ♦ *The farmer harvested the field of corn behind the farmhouse.* ♦ *The baseball field was covered with mud after two weeks of rain.* **2.** *n.* an area of knowledge; an area of expertise; an area of study. ♦ *Jane is a scientist in the field of biology.* ♦ *John does research in the field of computer science.* **3.** *tv.* to catch a baseball. ♦ *The player fielded the ball expertly.* ♦ *I'm a good batter but I have problems fielding the ball.* **4. field questions** *idiom* to answer a series of questions, especially from reporters. ♦ *After her speech, Jane fielded questions from reporters.* ♦ *The president's press agents field questions from the newspaper.* **5. out in left field** *idiom* offbeat; unusual and eccentric. ♦ *Sally is a lot of fun, but she's sort of out in left field.* ♦ *What a strange idea. It's really out in left field.*

fieldwork ['fild wɚk] *n.* academic or scientific work that is done outside of a laboratory or classroom; academic or scientific work that is done in the real world. (No plural form in this sense.) ♦ *Sociologists often do fieldwork in their area of expertise.* ♦ *Sue is in Australia doing fieldwork with the native languages.*

fiend ['find] *n.* a monster; someone who is evil or cruel. ♦ *I filed charges against the fiend who assaulted me.* ♦ *My boss is such a fiend. I have to work on Christmas Day.*

fierce ['fɪrs] *adj.* violent; cruel; untamed; wild. (Adv: *fiercely.* Comp: *fiercer;* sup: *fiercest.*) ♦ *The fierce winds knocked over many telephone lines.* ♦ *I went on a safari to see fierce animals in the wild.*

fiery ['fɑɪɚ i] **1.** *adj.* burning; flaming. (Comp: *fierier;* sup: *fieriest.*) ♦ *The building was destroyed by the fiery explosion.* ♦ *Five people were killed in the fiery train wreck.* **2.** *adj.* very emotional; passionate; full of passion. (Figurative on ①. Comp: *fierier;* sup: *fieriest.*) ♦ *I became tired of my roommate's fiery temper.* ♦ *Don't upset Sue. She's very fiery when she's mad.*

fiesta [fi 'ɛs tə] *n.* a party; a festival. (From Spanish.) ♦ *Come over to my house around eight. We're having a little fiesta.* ♦ *While I was in Mexico, I went to a fiesta in a small village.*

fifteen ['fɪf 'tin] 15. See four for senses and examples.

fifteenth ['fɪf 'tinθ] 15th. See fourth for senses and examples.

fifth ['fɪfθ] **1.** 5th. See fourth for senses and examples. **2.** *n.* a fifth ① of a gallon of liquor. ♦ *Bill drank a fifth of whiskey and passed out.* ♦ *How much tax is there on a fifth of liquor?*

fiftieth ['fɪf 'ti əθ] 50th. See **fourth** for senses and examples.

fifty ['fɪf ti] 50. See **forty** for senses and examples.

fig ['fɪg] *n.* a soft, sweet fruit with many seeds. ♦ *I bought some figs for the fruitcake.* ♦ *This dessert is made with figs and dates.*

fight ['fɑɪt] **1.** *n.* a struggle; a battle; a dispute. ♦ *The principal stopped the fight that broke out in the cafeteria.* ♦ *I broke my nose in a fight.* **2.** *tv., irreg.* to combat against someone; to battle someone. (Pt/pp: **fought**.) ♦ *The soldiers fought the enemy bravely.* ♦ *Bob fought Bill at recess and got hit in the face.* **3.** *iv., irreg.* to do battle; to argue; to be in a dispute with someone. (Figurative on ②.) ♦ *My roommate and I fought all through the night.* ♦ *I don't enjoy fighting with my parents.*

fighter ['fɑɪt ɚ] **1.** *n.* someone who fights. ♦ *The teacher sent the fighters to the principal's office.* ♦ *The fighter was knocked out in round six.* **2.** *n.* someone who struggles to succeed or survive rather than give up. ♦ *Even though Grandpa has cancer, he's a fighter and he's expected to live.* ♦ *Mary's a real fighter, and learned to walk again after the accident.* **3.** *n.* an airplane used in war for attacking. ♦ *The fighter dropped many bombs and destroyed the town.* ♦ *Many fighters were shot down over the ocean.* **4.** *adj.* <the adj. use of ③.> ♦ *The veteran had been a fighter pilot in the Vietnam War.* ♦ *The fighter squadron was instructed to attack the enemy's camp at dawn.*

fighting ['fɑɪt ɪŋ] **1.** *n.* arguing, combating, or battling. (No plural form in this sense.) ♦ *The fighting between the countries went on for decades.* ♦ *The couple's fighting led to their divorce.* **2.** *adj.* <the adj. use of ①.> ♦ *The United Nations helped the fighting countries settle their dispute.* ♦ *The teacher told the fighting students to behave.*

figment ['fɪg mənt] *n.* something that is made up; something that is imagined. ♦ *The judge dismissed Bill's story as a mere figment.* ♦ *Is it a figment of my imagination, or did you get a haircut?*

figurative ['fɪg jə rə tɪv] *adj.* metaphorical; using words to indicate what something is like instead of using the words with their literal meanings. (Adv: *figuratively.*) ♦ *The professor used a figurative analogy to explain the difficult concept.* ♦ *This story is a figurative account of the experience of death.*

figure ['fɪg jɚ] **1.** *n.* a human body; the form of a human body. ♦ *The artist sketched the figure of the model's body on the canvas.* ♦ *Jane exercises a lot, so her figure is in good shape.* **2.** *n.* a person, usually well known or important. ♦ *Ronald Reagan was an important figure in politics.* ♦ *Tom wrote an essay about a famous American figure for history class.* **3.** *n.* a digit; one of the numbers from 0 to 9. ♦ *American telephone numbers consist of seven figures plus an area code.* ♦ *Please write each figure neatly in the space provided.* **4.** *n.* a total; a sum; an amount. ♦ *Have you seen the latest figures from today's stock report?* ♦ *Add your wages together and place the figure on line 5 of the tax form.* **5.** *n.* a shape; a form; the shape of an object. ♦ *Through the fog, I could barely see the figure of the building across the street.* ♦ *The clouds looked like the figure of a horse.* **6.** *n.* the name for a chart or diagram in a book that explains information in the text. ♦ *Figure 1 shows the percentage of Americans who are high-school graduates.* ♦ *Please refer to Figure 2.8 for a graph of the data discussed here.* **7. figure out** *tv.* + *adv.* to come to understand someone or something; to solve something such as a puzzle or riddle; to unravel a mystery. ♦ *I can't figure out the answer to this problem.* ♦ *The police could not figure Max out.* **8. figure (up)** *tv.* (+ *adv.*) to calculate an amount; to add, subtract, multiply, or divide. ♦ *Bob figured up the bill without a calculator.* ♦ *Max figured the totals in his head.* **9.** *tv.* to reckon something; to consider something; to believe something. (Takes a clause.) ♦ *I didn't figure that you would go to the movies without me.* ♦ *I figure that there were 25,000 people at the parade.* **10. figure on something** *idiom* to plan on something. ♦ *I figured on arriving at the party around eight o'clock.* ♦ *Jane figured on spending $25 on dinner.* **11. figure in something** *idiom* to be important; to play a role in something; to be a part of something. ♦ *The decisive battle figured in the ending of the war.* ♦ *Your medical expenses will figure in the settlement amount.*

figurehead ['fɪg jɚ hɛd] **1.** *n.* a statue or bust on the bow of a ship. ♦ *The figurehead of the sunken ship was covered with seaweed.* ♦ *I recognized the old boat by its figurehead.* **2.** *n.* someone who has a job that seems important but has no real power or authority. (Figurative on ①.) ♦ *Even though the mayor's deputy is just a figurehead, he still earns a high salary.* ♦ *In modern times, the royalty of England are only figureheads.*

figurine [fɪg jə 'rin] *n.* a small statue. ♦ *I broke several figurines when I knocked over the cabinet.* ♦ *For my birthday, my boyfriend gave me a figurine of an elephant.*

filament ['fɪl ə mənt] **1.** *n.* a very thin thread. ♦ *The complex tapestry was woven with thousands of filaments of silk.* ♦ *The doctor sewed the wound with a special surgical filament.* **2.** *n.* the very thin wire in a light bulb that gives off light when electricity passes through it. ♦ *Through the glass of the light bulb, I can see the glowing filament.* ♦ *When I dropped the light bulb, the glass shattered, but the filament remained attached.*

file ['fɑɪl] **1.** *n.* a metal tool that is scraped over rough surfaces to make them smooth and even. ♦ *Mary smoothed the burrs from the end of the metal pipe with a file.* ♦ *Use a file to smooth the rough places on the railing.* **2.** *n.* a folder used for holding and storing papers in an organized way. ♦ *Jane placed the files in alphabetical order on the desk.* ♦ *I accidentally dropped a stack of files, and all the papers fell out.* **3.** *n.* the papers within a file; the information contained in a file. ♦ *According to your file, your last dental appointment was ten months ago.* ♦ *The police chief read the young criminal's extensive file.* **4.** *n.* a line of things placed one after the other. ♦ *The children walked in a single file to the cafeteria.* ♦ *The file of trucks moved slowly down the icy road.* **5. computer file** *n.* a unit of data or information in digital form, stored on a floppy disk or disk drive. ♦ *All my computer files were lost when my disk drive broke.* ♦ *Could I have a copy of the computer file that has my letter on it?* **6.** *tv.* to smooth something with ①. ♦ *The carpenter filed the surface of the steel bar until it was smooth.* ♦ *I filed my fingernails after I cut them.* **7.** *tv.* to organize papers by putting them into the appropriate ②; to put a piece of paper in the appropriate file. ♦ *Please file this letter in Mr. Johnson's file.* ♦ *I filed the reports in alphabetical order.* **8.** *iv.* to move in or out of a place in a line. ♦ *The cars filed out of the parking lot* *and onto the highway.* ♦ *The students calmly filed out of the room during the fire drill.*

filet AND **fillet** [fɪ 'le] **1.** *n.* a thick slice of meat or fish with the bones removed. ♦ *I had a chicken-breast filet with a salad for lunch.* ♦ *Eat your fish fillet carefully because I might have missed some small bones.* **2.** *tv.* to slice a piece of meat or fish before cooking or eating it. (Pt/pp: *fileted, filleted* [fɪ 'led].) ♦ *I carefully checked for remaining bones after I filleted the fish.* ♦ *After you fillet the chicken, marinate it for ten minutes.*

filet mignon [fɪ 'le mɪn 'jɑn] *n.* the slice of the tender piece of beef that runs along either side of the spine of a cow. (No plural form in this sense.) ♦ *I wanted to order filet mignon, but it was too expensive.* ♦ *Would you like peas or carrots with your filet mignon?*

filibuster ['fɪl ə bəs tɚ] **1.** *n.* a very long speech made by a member of Congress in order to prevent or delay the passage of a bill. (From Spanish.) ♦ *Hours into his filibuster, the senator began reading from the phone book.* ♦ *There were not enough votes to stop the senator's lengthy filibuster.* **2.** *iv.* to speak endlessly to prevent or delay the passage of a bill in Congress by making a very long speech. ♦ *The senator filibustered for three days to prevent the bill from passing.* ♦ *If you want to delay this bill, I suggest you filibuster.*

filing cabinet ['fɑɪl ɪŋ kæb (ə) nɪt] *n.* a piece of office furniture that is used to hold and organize files. ♦ *My filing cabinet is locked because it holds confidential documents.* ♦ *Your file is in the filing cabinet in the top drawer.*

Filipino [fɪl ə 'pin o] **1.** *n.* a citizen or native of the Philippines. (Pl in -*s*.) ♦ *Most Filipinos are able to speak Tagalog.* ♦ *My roommate is an American, but his parents are Filipinos.* **2.** *adj.* of or about the people or culture of the Philippines. ♦ *Tagalog is a native Filipino language.* ♦ *July 4, 1946, is the date of Filipino independence from the United States.*

fill ['fɪl] **1. fill (up)** *tv.* (+ *adv.*) to put something into a container or a place until there is no more room to put anything else in; to take up all available space or time; to occupy all available space or time. ♦ *I filled the container with flour.* ♦ *The speech filled up two hours exactly.* **2.** *tv.* to provide what is requested; to supply a product when it is requested; to meet the demands of someone or something. ♦ *Our warehouse can fill your order within an hour.* ♦ *The pharmacist filled my prescription for sleeping pills.* **3. fill in** *tv.* + *adv.* to put words in blank spaces on a form. ♦ *You must fill in every blank space.* ♦ *Please fill in the blank with your name and address.* **4. fill out** *tv.* + *adv.* to complete a form. ♦ *When I applied for a loan, I had to fill out dozens of forms.* ♦ *Please fill out all these forms.* **5.** *iv.* to become full. ♦ *The field filled with water during the flood.* ♦ *Thick smoke filled the kitchen.* **6.** *n.* all that is needed; all that is required; all that is wanted. (No plural form in this sense.) ♦ *I've had my fill of your insults, so I'm going home.* ♦ *I've made a lot of food, so please eat your fill.* **7.** *n.* dirt, sand, or gravel used to fill in a hole or to make ground level. (No plural form in this sense.) ♦ *The contractor placed the fill in the hole next to the new house.* ♦ *When digging a new pond, we sold the dirt as fill.* **8. get one's fill of someone or something** *idiom* to get or have enough of someone or something. ♦ *You'll soon get your fill of Tom. He can be quite a pest.* ♦ *Three weeks of visiting grandchildren is enough. I've had my fill of them.*

filler ['fɪl ɚ] *n.* something that is put someplace in order to make it full; something that is used to take up space. (No plural form in this sense.) ♦ *The article was too short, so I added a few paragraphs of filler.* ♦ *When packing dishes, place filler along the sides of the box to prevent breakage.*

fillet ['fɪl ɪt] See filet.

filling ['fɪl ɪŋ] **1.** *n.* something that is put inside something in order to fill a space. ♦ *I have very few fillings in my teeth.* ♦ *These pastries have a custard filling.* **2.** *adj.* [of food or a meal] providing a feeling of fullness. ♦ *A small bowl of soup is not very filling.* ♦ *Max had a filling meal of meat and potatoes.*

filly ['fɪl i] *n.* a young, female horse. (See also colt.) ♦ *Anne brushed the hair of her filly.* ♦ *I placed a bright red bow on the filly's tail at the horse exhibition.*

film ['fɪlm] **1.** *n.* a movie; a motion picture. ♦ *What time does the first film at the theater start?* ♦ *Last night we went to dinner and then watched a film.* **2.** *n.* the material that photographs or movies are recorded on. (No plural form in this sense.) ♦ *The film broke while the movie was being shown, so we didn't get the see the end.* ♦ *I bought some new film for my camera.* **3.** *n.* a thin layer of something; a coating. ♦ *A thin film of dust on the mirror made it hard to see my reflection.* ♦ *The throat is covered with a thin film of mucous.* **4.** *tv.* to record someone or something on film in a particular place or manner. ♦ *The exotic movie was filmed in Europe.* ♦ *Most television shows are filmed in Los Angeles.* **5.** *iv.* to shoot film for a movie; to record a movie; to record something on videotape. ♦ *The cast and crew filmed until it began to rain.* ♦ *This show films in front of a live audience.*

filmmaker ['fɪlm mek ɚ] *n.* a director; someone who makes movies. ♦ *The filmmaker won an award for her documentary on cancer.* ♦ *Lisa hopes to become a Hollywood filmmaker someday.*

filmmaking ['fɪlm mek ɪŋ] *n.* the art, technology, and business of producing motion pictures. (No plural form in this sense.) ♦ *The center for filmmaking in the U.S. is Hollywood, California.* ♦ *Filmmaking is a major industry in California.*

filter ['fɪl tɚ] **1.** *n.* a device that strains fluids or gases to separate solids from them; a device that cleans a fluid or gas that passes through it. ♦ *Coffee filters keep coffee grounds from falling into the coffee pot.* ♦ *The filter of a cigarette helps prevent some of the tar and nicotine from entering the body.* **2.** *tv.* to pass a substance through ①. ♦ *I filter the water through a charcoal filter.* ♦ *The scientist filtered the liquid and studied the residue.* **3.** *iv.* [for a fluid or gas] to leak; [for a fluid or gas] to pass through in a small amount. ♦ *Water filtered through the crack in the dam.* ♦ *Smoke filtered out of the room.*

filtered ['fɪl tɚd] *adj.* passed through a filter. ♦ *I drink only filtered water.* ♦ *I have to live in a house that has filtered air because of my allergies.*

filth ['fɪlθ] **1.** *n.* grime; dirt that is difficult to clean off. (No plural form in this sense.) ♦ *The counter around the stove is covered with greasy filth.* ♦ *Wash that filth off your hands before you come to dinner.* **2.** *n.* something that is dirty, disgusting, vulgar, or obscene. (Figurative on ①.

No plural form in this sense.) ♦ *The minister asked the stores in the neighborhood to remove filth from their magazine racks.* ♦ *We don't allow our children to watch any filth on television.*

filthy ['fɪl θi] **1.** *adj.* grimy; grungy; very dirty. (Adv: *filthily.* Comp: *filthier;* sup: *filthiest.*) ♦ *Dave spent two hours cleaning his filthy kitchen.* ♦ *Your hands are filthy. Go wash them.* **2.** *adj.* disgusting; vulgar; obscene. (Figurative on ①. Adv: *filthily.* Comp: *filthier;* sup: *filthiest.*) ♦ *How could you let your children watch such filthy movies?* ♦ *Please don't tell any filthy jokes in front of my parents.*

fin ['fɪn] **1.** *n.* a flat, winglike projection on a fish that allows it to control its motion in the water. ♦ *The lifeguard watched the shark's fin approaching the swimmers.* ♦ *The biologist studied how fish use their fins in strong currents of water.* **2.** *n.* one of a pair of rubber or plastic feet with flat projections, used by divers to propel themselves through the water. ♦ *The diver put on her fins and dove down to the coral reef.* ♦ *It's hard to walk on land while wearing fins.*

final ['fɑɪ nəl] **1.** *adj.* last; at the end; ultimate. (Adv: *finally.*) ♦ *Mary's coworkers planned a retirement party for her final day of work.* ♦ *After the final contestant has competed, the judges will decide who won.* **2.** *n.* the last examination in a school course. (Often plural, referring to the last examinations in all of one's courses for the term or semester.) ♦ *I got an A on all the homework assignments, but I got a C on the final.* ♦ *I can't go to Florida that week because I've got finals then.*

finale [fɪ 'næl i] *n.* the ending; the finish, especially of a piece of music or a musical production. (From Italian.) ♦ *For the grand finale, the singer was surrounded by sixteen tap dancers.* ♦ *The finale of the 1812 Overture includes the firing of cannons.*

finalist ['fɑɪn ə ləst] *n.* a person or a team that makes it to the last round of a contest or competition. ♦ *The judges congratulated the finalists for having done so well.* ♦ *I was a finalist in the spelling bee, but then I lost in the last round.*

finalize ['fɑɪn ə lɑɪz] *tv.* to finish making plans for something. ♦ *Just last week I finalized my plans for the vacation.* ♦ *We finalized the menu for the party and told the caterer what we wanted.*

finally ['fɑɪn ə li] *adv.* at last, after much asking, waiting, or delay. ♦ *The baseball game finally finished after 12 innings.* ♦ *My parents finally let me drive to the concert after I asked them a dozen times.*

finance [fə 'næns] **1.** *n.* business matters dealing with money; the management and control of money. (No plural form in this sense.) ♦ *Questions of finance and the value of assets should be addressed to the controller.* ♦ *I studied finance in school, and I worked for a bank after graduation.* **2. finances** *n.* practices, policies, and controls concerning the earning, spending, and borrowing of money. ♦ *My finances are not in very good shape this month.* ♦ *The accounting department is in charge of all our finances.* **3.** *tv.* to provide someone with enough money to pay for something. ♦ *A substantial scholarship financed my college tuition.* ♦ *The government financed our construction loan.*

financial [fə 'næn ʃəl] *adj.* of or about business matters dealing with money; of or about finance ①. (Adv: *financially.*) ♦ *My lawyer explained the financial aspects of my father's will.* ♦ *If our business is successful, there will be a financial gain this year.*

finch ['fɪntʃ] **1.** *n.* any species of a large class of small songbirds. ♦ *This kind of birdseed is perfect for all kinds of finches.* ♦ *The cardinal is a kind of finch.* **2.** *n.* an individual finch ①. ♦ *This morning I was awakened by a purple finch outside my bedroom window.* ♦ *Could you feed my finch while I'm on vacation?*

find ['fɑɪnd] **1.** *tv., irreg.* to discover or locate someone or something that one was looking for. (Pt/pp: found.) ♦ *You'll find yogurt next to the milk in the dairy section.* ♦ *I found just what I needed at my neighbor's garage sale.* **2.** *tv., irreg.* to recover something; to discover something. ♦ *Cleaning my parents' attic, I found the watch I lost when I was a boy.* ♦ *The dog found an old tennis ball in the ditch.* **3. find out** *tv., irreg.* + *adv.* to learn something; to learn information. ♦ *I found out who took my book.* ♦ *Did you find out the name of the person we need to speak to?* **4.** *tv., irreg.* to decide that someone or something is satisfactory or unsatisfactory. ♦ *I found the cake delicious.* ♦ *Everyone found the movie entertaining.* **5. find someone guilty; find someone innocent** *idiom* to decide guilt or innocence and deliver a verdict in a court of law. ♦ *The judge found the defendant not guilty by reason of insanity.* ♦ *The jury found the defendant innocent.*

fine ['fɑɪn] **1.** *n.* an amount of money that must be paid as a punishment; a penalty. ♦ *The landlord who discriminated against the renters had to pay a $1,000 fine.* ♦ *I had to pay a large fine for speeding, but I was innocent!* **2.** *adj.* acceptable or suitable; very good; excellent. (Adv: *finely.* Comp: *finer;* sup: *finest.*) ♦ *Thank you. You did a fine job.* ♦ *The weather is fine for outdoor games.* **3.** *adj.* very delicate and of high quality. (Adv: *finely.* Comp: *finer;* sup: *finest.*) ♦ *The tablecloth was made of fine lace.* ♦ *We carefully packed the fine china in a cushioned box.* **4.** *adj.* not coarse; consisting of small particles; in the form of a powder. (Adv: *finely.* Comp: *finer;* sup: *finest.*) ♦ *Fine particles of dust filled the air after the explosion.* ♦ *We went to the beach and walked barefoot on the fine sand.* **5.** *adj.* very thin or slender; very small. (Adv: *finely.* Comp: *finer;* sup: *finest.*) ♦ *Would you like a pen with a fine or medium point?* ♦ *That thread isn't fine enough to fit through the eye of this needle.* **6.** *adv.* well; nicely; excellently. ♦ *My watch stopped yesterday, but now it runs fine.* ♦ *How are you? I'm doing fine.* **7.** *tv.* to charge someone or something an amount of money as a punishment or penalty. ♦ *The government fined the oil corporation millions of dollars as a result of the oil spill.* ♦ *The judge found the defendant guilty and fined him $100.*

finely ['fɑɪn li] **1.** *adv.* elegantly; with excellent style. ♦ *The ballroom was finely decorated for the party.* ♦ *The wedding invitations were finely engraved on expensive paper.* **2.** *adv.* [divided] into tiny parts or divisions. ♦ *The biologist used a finely marked ruler to measure the length of the insect.* ♦ *I added finely chopped nuts to the cookies.*

finery ['fɑɪn ə ri] *n.* fine, elegant clothes. (No plural form in this sense.) ♦ *The Smiths wore their finery to their daughter's wedding.* ♦ *The queen was clothed in exquisite finery for the ceremony.*

finesse [fɪ 'nɛs] **1.** *n.* delicate skill; deftness; subtle tact. (No plural form in this sense.) ♦ *Finesse is very important* *when dealing with angry customers.* ♦ *Our manager solved our argument with great finesse.* **2.** *tv.* to manipulate something in a subtle way that avoids conflicts. ♦ *He only finessed the question. He never really answered it.* ♦ *The director finessed the difficult situation between the feuding actors.*

finger ['fɪŋ gɚ] **1.** *n.* one of the five extensions or digits at the end of the hand. ♦ *John placed the wedding ring on Anne's finger.* ♦ *I accidentally hit my finger with a hammer.* **2.** *tv.* to feel or meddle with something with one's fingers. ♦ *Please don't finger the fabric of my dress.* ♦ *Max always fingers the telephone dial when he uses the phone.* **3. get one's fingers burned** *idiom* to have a bad experience. ♦ *I tried that once before and got my fingers burned. I won't try it again.* ♦ *If you go swimming and get your fingers burned, you won't want to swim again.* **4. have one's finger in the pie** *idiom* to be involved in something. ♦ *I like to have my finger in the pie so I can make sure things go my way.* ♦ *As long as John has his finger in the pie, things will happen slowly.* **5. lay a finger on someone or something** *idiom* to touch someone or something, even slightly, with a finger. ♦ *Don't you dare lay a finger on my pencil. Go get your own!* ♦ *If you lay a finger on me, I'll scream.* **6. point the finger at someone** *idiom* to blame someone; to identify someone as the guilty person. ♦ *Don't point the finger at me! I didn't take the money.* ♦ *The manager refused to point the finger at anyone in particular and said the whole staff was sometimes guilty of being late.* **7. slip through someone's fingers** *idiom* to get away from someone; for someone to lose track (of something or someone). ♦ *I had a copy of the book you want, but somehow it slipped through my fingers.* ♦ *There was a detective following me, but I managed to slip through his fingers.*

fingernail ['fɪŋ gɚ nel] *n.* the hard, flat covering at the end of each finger. ♦ *The singer's fingernails were painted a deep red.* ♦ *Bob cleaned the dirt from under his fingernails with a file.*

fingerprint ['fɪŋ gɚ prɪnt] *n.* the slight, oily mark left by the ridges on the skin of one's fingers. ♦ *No two people have the same fingerprints.* ♦ *The thief left his fingerprints on the doorknob.*

fingertip ['fɪŋ gɚ tɪp] *n.* the end of a finger. ♦ *John ran his fingertip along the frosted cake and tasted it.* ♦ *Anne cut her fingertip with a knife while slicing bread.*

finicky ['fɪn ɪ ki] *adj.* fussy; very particular; wanting or liking only certain specific things. ♦ *Mary is very finicky about what she wears and spends hours shopping for suitable clothing.* ♦ *Since Dave is a finicky eater, I let him cook his own meals.*

finish ['fɪn ɪʃ] **1.** *tv.* to bring something to an end; to complete or conclude something. ♦ *I finished my report by thanking the people who had helped me.* ♦ *Has he finished his dinner yet?* **2.** *tv.* to use all of something; to eat or drink something up. ♦ *I finished the coffee. Would you like me to make more?* ♦ *Finish your vegetables, or you won't get any dessert.* **3.** *tv.* to cover something made out of wood with a protective coat of varnish, lacquer, or stain. ♦ *Sue finished the old desk with a coat of varnish.* ♦ *The bookshelf was finished with a light stain.* **4.** *iv.* [for someone] to reach the end of doing something. ♦ *As soon as I finished, I went home.* ♦ *Bill finished last and had to run to catch the bus.* **5.** *n.* the end; the conclusion; the final part of something. ♦ *The horse I bet on came into first place at the very finish of the race.* ♦ *Have you reached the finish of the novel yet? It's really good.* **6.** *n.* a protective coating of paint, varnish, lacquer, or stain on a wooden surface; a protective coating on any surface. ♦ *Anne coated the wooden bookshelf with a protective finish.* ♦ *A strong finish protected the wood from rain damage.*

finished ['fɪn ɪʃt] *adj.* ended; concluded; completed; done. ♦ *Mary sent her finished manuscript to the publisher.* ♦ *I took a picture of the finished jigsaw puzzle.*

finite ['fɑɪ nɑɪt] *adj.* having an end; having a limit; able to be counted; able to be measured. (Adv: *finitely.*) ♦ *There are a finite number of books on my bookshelf.* ♦ *The number of possible radio stations in an area is finite.*

Finland ['fɪn lənd] See Gazetteer.

fir ['fɚ] *n.* an evergreen tree that has thin pointed leaves called needles that do not fall off in winter. ♦ *There are fir trees on either side of our front door.* ♦ *While traveling in the north, we drove through a forest of firs.*

fire ['fɑɪɚ] **1.** *n.* heat, flames, and light made by burning. (No plural form in this sense.) ♦ *Fire produces both heat and light.* ♦ *Fire destroyed the building quickly.* **2.** *n.* a discrete area of burning with ①. ♦ *Let's build a fire in the fireplace.* ♦ *There is a terrible fire on Maple Street.* **3.** *n.* passion; strong emotion; fervor. (Figurative on ①. No plural form in this sense.) ♦ *The police officer spoke with fire about the high crime rate.* ♦ *I was impressed by Jimmy's fire for learning.* **4.** *n.* the shooting of weapons; the noise made by shooting guns. (See gunfire. No plural form in this sense.) ♦ *I dropped to the ground when I heard the fire of bullets.* ♦ *The sergeant commanded the troops to hold their fire.* **5.** *tv.* to get rid of an employee; to terminate an employee from employment. ♦ *My boss fired me because I came late to work too many times.* ♦ *If your work does not improve, we will have to fire you.* **6.** *tv.* to burn something down. ♦ *The raiders fired the whole town.* ♦ *The arsonist fired the school, but fortunately no one was hurt.* **7. fire at** *iv.* + *prep. phr.* to shoot at someone or something. ♦ *The police fired at the criminal.* ♦ *The hunter fired at what he thought was a deer. It was a cow.* **8. catch fire** *idiom* to begin to burn; to ignite. ♦ *If the wood were not so wet, it would catch fire more easily.* ♦ *The curtains blew against the flame of the candle and caught fire.* **9. fire a gun** *idiom* to shoot a gun; to discharge a gun. ♦ *The police caught the robber who had fired the gun.* ♦ *Jane fired the gun and hit the target.* **10. on fire** *idiom* burning; being burned with flames. ♦ *Help! My car is on fire!* ♦ *That house on the corner is on fire!* **11. play with fire** *idiom* to take a big risk. ♦ *If you accuse her of stealing, you'll be playing with fire.* ♦ *I wouldn't try that if I were you—unless you like playing with fire.* **12. under fire** *idiom* during an attack. ♦ *There was a scandal in city hall, and the mayor was forced to resign under fire.* ♦ *John is a good lawyer because he can think under fire.*

firearm ['fɑɪɚ ɑrm] *n.* a weapon used for shooting; a gun. ♦ *Would banning firearms increase or decrease the murder rate?* ♦ *The robber held up the bank with a firearm.*

firecracker ['fɑɪɚ kræk ɚ] *n.* a small explosive that makes a lot of noise. ♦ *Bill set off hundreds of firecrackers on the Fourth of July.* ♦ *I was punished for setting off a firecracker on school property.*

fire engine ['fɑɪɚ ɛn dʒɪn] *n.* a truck that carries water and hoses to put out fires. ♦ *The drivers of fire engines have the authority to go through red lights.* ♦ *A fire engine arrived at the fire shortly after I placed the emergency call.*

fire escape ['fɑɪɚ ə skep] **1.** *n.* an alternate exit from a building in case the building catches fire. ♦ *City law requires the owners of buildings to post the location of the fire escapes.* ♦ *In case of fire, use the fire escape instead of the elevators.* **2.** *n.* a special metal staircase attached to the outside of the building, used as an escape route in case of fire ①. ♦ *The thief broke into my office from the fire escape.* ♦ *Our fire escape is inspected each year to make sure it is safe.*

firefighter ['fɑɪɚ fɑɪt ɚ] *n.* someone who is trained to put out destructive fires. ♦ *Firefighters battled the blaze for hours.* ♦ *The firefighter entered the burning building to save the children inside.*

firefly ['fɑɪɚ flɑɪ] *n.* a small insect that glows or gives off light at night. (The same as lightning bug.) ♦ *When I was small, I collected fireflies in a glass jar.* ♦ *The backyard flashed with the lights of hundreds of fireflies.*

fire hydrant AND **fireplug** *n.* a connection to a major water supply pipe that water can be drawn from in order to put out a destructive fire. ♦ *It is illegal to park in front of a fire hydrant.* ♦ *The fireplug was painted bright yellow so it could be seen easily.*

fireman ['fɑɪɚ mən] *n., irreg.* someone, usually a male, who is trained to put out destructive fires. (Pl: firemen. See also firefighter.) ♦ *The mayor honored the fireman who saved five children in the apartment fire.* ♦ *The fireman caught the boy who jumped out of the burning building.*

firemen ['fɑɪɚ mən] pl of fireman.

fireplace ['fɑɪɚ ples] *n.* a place in a house or building where a fire can be built to provide heat. ♦ *Smoke from the fireplace exits the house through the chimney.* ♦ *I warmed my feet in front of the fireplace.*

fireplug ['fɑɪɚ pləg] See fire hydrant.

fireproof ['fɑɪɚ pruf] **1.** *adj.* not combustible; not able to catch fire; hard to burn. ♦ *Children's clothing should be made from fireproof fabric.* ♦ *We keep our important documents in a fireproof metal box.* **2.** *tv.* to make something resistant to fire. ♦ *I fireproofed the curtains by spraying them with a special chemical.* ♦ *They used to fireproof buildings with asbestos.*

fireside ['fɑɪɚ sɑɪd] **1.** *n.* the area around a fireplace. ♦ *The fireside was tiled with marble.* ♦ *We placed the extra logs on the fireside.* **2.** *adj.* beside a fire or a fireplace. ♦ *In the president's fireside chat, he informed the public about his latest policies.* ♦ *I rested in the fireside rocking chair.*

firetrap ['fɑɪɚ træp] *n.* a dangerous building that is likely to catch fire; a dangerous building that would be hard to escape from if it caught fire. ♦ *My apartment is very cheap; unfortunately, it is also a firetrap.* ♦ *The victims of the fire had no chance of escaping from the firetrap they lived in.*

firewood ['fɑɪɚ wʊd] *n.* wood that is used to build or feed fires. (No plural form in this sense.) ♦ *I chopped the tree into smaller pieces of firewood.* ♦ *Tom set the firewood down next to the campfire.*

fireworks ['fɑɪɚ wɚks] *n.* explosives that make loud noises and beautiful displays of light and smoke when lit. (Treated as plural. Rarely singular.) ♦ *The city has a brilliant display of fireworks on the Fourth of July.* ♦ *We sat in the park, watching the fireworks over the lake.*

firm ['fɚm] **1.** *adj.* solid; hard; fixed. (Adv: *firmly.* Comp: *firmer;* sup: *firmest.*) ♦ *Bob lifts weights, so his muscles are very firm.* ♦ *I have a firm handshake.* **2.** *adj.* not easily moved; steady. (Adv: *firmly.* Comp: *firmer;* sup: *firmest.*) ♦ *The reporter spoke with a firm voice at the accident site.* ♦ *Sue never gets emotional; she always remains firm and calm.* **3.** *adj.* final and not yielding. (Adv: *firmly.* Comp: *firmer;* sup: *firmest.*) ♦ *Once Mike makes a firm decision, he never changes it.* ♦ *No, you cannot go to the ballgame. My answer is firm.* **4.** *n.* a company; a business partnership. ♦ *I worked for the firm for 30 years before I retired.* ♦ *After ten years of hard work, Anne became a partner in the law firm.* **5. firm up** *tv.* + *adv.* [to cause something] to become solid or hard. ♦ *Bill firmed up his muscles by exercising every day.* ♦ *The volunteers firmed up the dike with sandbags.* **6. firm (up)** *iv.* (+ *adv.*) [for something] to become hard or solid. ♦ *The ice firmed up as it became colder.* ♦ *The clay pottery firmed quickly.*

firmament ['fɚ mə mənt] *n.* the sky. (Literary. No plural form in this sense.) ♦ *At night, John gazed at the firmament, counting stars.* ♦ *Planes soared across the firmament, leaving white trails.*

firmness ['fɚm nəs] **1.** *n.* hardness; solidness. (No plural form in this sense.) ♦ *Dave felt the firmness of his muscles by squeezing them.* ♦ *I buy only the watermelons that have the proper firmness.* **2.** *n.* being certain; holding to one's opinions, attitudes, or orders. (No plural form in this sense.) ♦ *You have to admire Jane's firmness in her beliefs.* ♦ *The president's firmness in business decisions kept the company from going bankrupt.*

first ['fɚst] **1.** *adj.* being the initial object in a series of things; before everything or everyone else; at the beginning. (The ordinal number for one. Adv: *firstly.*) ♦ *The first letter of the alphabet is* A. ♦ *Here's a picture of my first haircut—when I was two years old.* **2.** *adv.* before anything else; before another event. ♦ *Before you enter the room, you must turn off the alarm system first.* ♦ *First, pour a cup of milk into a bowl, and then add the flour.* **3.** *adv.* never having happened before. ♦ *Bill first went to Europe when he was 12.* ♦ *Sue first studied piano when she was 5.* **4.** *n.* someone or something that is the first ① thing or person. (No plural form in this sense.) ♦ *Anne was the first to cross the finish line. She gets the prize.* ♦ *The first to arrive at parties is usually the last to leave.* **5. first of all** *idiom* as the very first ① thing; before anything else. ♦ *First of all, put your name on this piece of paper.* ♦ *First of all, we'll try to find a place to live.* **6. first thing (in the morning)** *idiom* before anything else in the morning. ♦ *Please call me first thing in the morning. I can't help you now.* ♦ *I'll do that first thing.* **7. first things first** *idiom* the most important things must be taken care of first ②. ♦ *It's more important to get a job than to buy new clothes. First things first!* ♦ *Do your homework now. Go out and play later. First things first.* **8. of the first water** *idiom* of the finest quality. ♦ *This is a very fine pearl—a pearl of the first water.* ♦ *Tom is of the first water—a true gentleman.*

first aid ['fɚst 'ed] *n.* medical care that is given to someone in an emergency. (No plural form in this sense.) ♦

After the accident, I administered first aid until the paramedics arrived. ♦ *We learned basic first aid in health class.*

first-aid kit ['fɚst 'ed kɪt] *n.* a box that holds medicine, bandages, and other useful things to take care of someone in an emergency. ♦ *I think we have some bandages in the first-aid kit.* ♦ *Mary keeps a first-aid kit in her car in case of emergencies.*

firstborn ['fɚst 'born] **1.** *n.* the first child born to a mother; the oldest child in a family. ♦ *Jane named her firstborn after her father.* ♦ *Sue had her firstborn when she was 23.* **2.** *adj.* <the adj. use of ①.> ♦ *The king's firstborn son is destined to be the next king.* ♦ *Anne promised to name her firstborn daughter after her mother.*

first class ['fɚst 'klæs] **1.** *n.* the best or highest-level class of service. (No plural form in this sense.) ♦ *Our airplane tickets are for first class, and we are looking forward to the comfortable seats.* ♦ *First class is the only way that we will travel.* **2.** *n.* mail that is sealed and goes by the fastest form of transportation. (No plural form in this sense.) ♦ *What is the cost of first class?* ♦ *Can this go by airmail, or should I send it by first class?* **3. first-class** *adj.* best; excellent; most expensive. ♦ *We stayed in a first-class hotel while on vacation.* ♦ *For our anniversary, we ate at a first-class restaurant.* **4. first-class** *adv.* in the best and most expensive section of a plane, train, etc. ♦ *The Jones family traveled to Paris first-class.* ♦ *The millionaire always flew first-class.* **5. first-class** *adv.* by the fastest form of mail delivery, usually by surface mail. ♦ *Mary sent a letter to England first-class.* ♦ *You'll have to pay extra if you want to send this letter first-class.*

firsthand ['fɚst 'hænd] **1.** *adj.* direct; coming from the source directly; witnessed. ♦ *The firsthand account of the war was written by a British soldier.* ♦ *I have firsthand knowledge of what it's like to live with a disability.* **2.** *adv.* directly; from the source. ♦ *I heard the story firsthand from Jane herself.* ♦ *Did someone tell you this news firsthand, or is it gossip?*

firstly ['fɚst li] *adv.* first. ♦ *Firstly, I think you should mind your own business.* ♦ *Firstly, make sure you have all the ingredients ready.*

first name ['fɚst 'nem] **1.** *n.* one's name, given at birth and—in English—placed before one's surname. ♦ *Please print your first name in the space provided.* ♦ *John Smith's first name is John.* **2. first-name** *adj.* familiar; characterized by the use of first names rather than more formal titles. ♦ *I'm on a first-name basis with all of my teachers.* ♦ *I don't like salespeople who talk to me as though we have a first-name relationship.*

first-rate ['fɚst 'ret] *adj.* best; superior; excellent. ♦ *I took my friends to a first-rate restaurant when I got the new job.* ♦ *Sue was thankful to have such first-rate people working for her.*

fiscal ['fɪs kəl] *adj.* financial; of or about money or taxes. (Adv: *fiscally.*) ♦ *Our company's fiscal year runs from October 1 to September 30.* ♦ *We have a treasurer who keeps track of our fiscal responsibilities.*

fish ['fɪʃ] **1.** *n., irreg.* any of various legless, vertebrate animals that live underwater, have gills instead of lungs, and typically have fins and scales. (Pl: *fish.*) ♦ *Fish are found all over the world in oceans, lakes, ponds, and rivers.* ♦ *Bob caught two large fish in this stream.* **2.** *n.* a kind or type of ①. ♦ *Either of these fishes is good broiled or fried.* ♦ *Even a marine biologist couldn't name all the fishes in the sea!* **3.** *n.* the meat of ① used as food. (No plural form in this sense.) ♦ *I love any kind of fish as long as it's fresh.* ♦ *My brother, a vegetarian, doesn't eat fish.* **4. fish tank** See tank. **5.** *iv.* to try to catch ①. ♦ *Do you want to fish early in the morning?* ♦ *Every Saturday I go to the lake to fish.* **6. fish through** *iv.* + *prep. phr.* to search through something. ♦ *I fished through my closet looking for my good shoes.* ♦ *The detective fished through the rubble looking for clues.* **7. fish in troubled waters** *idiom* to involve oneself in a difficult, confused, or dangerous situation, especially with a view to gaining an advantage. ♦ *Frank is fishing in troubled waters by buying more shares of that firm. They are supposed to be in financial difficulties.* ♦ *The company could make more money by selling weapons abroad, but it would be fishing in troubled waters.* **8. have bigger fish to fry; have other fish to fry** *idiom* to have other things to do; to have more important things to do. ♦ *I can't take time for your problem. I have other fish to fry.* ♦ *I won't waste time on your question. I have bigger fish to fry.*

fishbowl ['fɪs bol] *n.* a container that fish are kept in; a small aquarium. ♦ *Please sprinkle some fish food in the fishbowl before you leave.* ♦ *I placed the fish in the sink while I cleaned the fishbowl.*

fisherman ['fɪʃ ɚ mən] *n., irreg.* someone who catches fish for a living; a man who fishes. (Pl: **fishermen.**) ♦ *Strict limits were placed on how much fish the fishermen could catch.* ♦ *The fishermen left port early in the morning.*

fishermen ['fɪʃ ɚ mən] pl of fisherman.

fishhook ['fɪʃ hʊk] *n.* a sharp hook used to catch fish. ♦ *I baited the fishhook with a worm.* ♦ *I cut my finger on the fishhook.*

fishy ['fɪʃ i] **1.** *adj.* tasting or smelling like fish. (Comp: *fishier;* sup: *fishiest.*) ♦ *A fishy smell surrounded the cannery.* ♦ *Would you please remove this salad? It tastes fishy.* **2.** *adj.* suspicious; doubtful; seeming to be false. (Informal. Comp: *fishier;* sup: *fishiest.*) ♦ *Are you telling the truth? Your story sounds fishy to me.* ♦ *The police didn't believe the thief's fishy alibi.*

fission ['fɪ ʃən] *n.* a division; the splitting of something into parts. (No plural form in this sense.) ♦ *In biology, the reproduction of a one-celled organism by splitting into two is called fission.* ♦ *An angry debate about goals caused the fission of the company into three smaller organizations.*

fissure ['fɪʃ ɚ] *n.* a crack; a crevice; a narrow opening. ♦ *Steam rose from a fissure in the earth's crust.* ♦ *I covered the fissure in the wall with plaster.*

fist ['fɪst] *n.* the hand with the fingers closed tightly. ♦ *Tom angrily hit me with his fist.* ♦ *Nervously, I clutched my house keys in my fist.*

fit ['fɪt] **1.** *iv., irreg.* to be the right size for something. (Pt/pp: *fit* or *fitted.*) ♦ *This chair fits here between the fireplace and the table.* ♦ *Does this pair of shoes fit?* **2.** *tv., irreg.* to suit someone or something; to be matched to someone or something. ♦ *A light pastel color scheme fits the doctor's office perfectly.* ♦ *The antique furniture does not fit the room's decor.* **3.** *tv., irreg.* [for something] to be the right size for someone or something. ♦ *These shoes do not fit my feet.* ♦ *This belt fits my waist perfectly.* **4.** *tv.* to make something match something else in size or proportion. ♦ *The tailor fit the suit to my exact measurements.* ♦ *The judge tried to make the punishment fit the crime.* **5. fit in** *tv. + adv.* to make space for someone. ♦ *There is room on this bench. We can fit you in.* ♦ *We could not fit the box in, so we left it in the garage.* **6. fit in(to)** *tv. + prep. phr.* to squeeze someone into a sequence. ♦ *I will try to fit you into my busy schedule.* ♦ *The dentist could not fit me into the schedule even though I was in pain.* **7.** *adj.* suitable; appropriate; having the things that are needed. (Adv: *fitly.* Comp: *fitter;* sup: *fittest.*) ♦ *Your manuscript is not fit for publication.* ♦ *This violent movie is not fit for children.* **8.** *adj.* healthy; in good condition. (Comp: *fitter;* sup: *fittest.*) ♦ *Mary is very fit because she exercises daily.* ♦ *Grandpa is physically fit for a man his age.* **9.** *n.* the way that something fits ①. ♦ *I bought the suit because it was a good fit.* ♦ *I had gained weight, so the pants were a tight fit.* **10.** *n.* a sudden attack of sickness or emotion. (Informal.) ♦ *My boss had a fit because I deleted some computer files.* ♦ *My joke resulted in a fit of laughter from my friends.* **11. fit in with someone or something** *idiom* to belong; to seem to be part of. ♦ *Anne felt like she didn't fit in with the other students.* ♦ *Bob's teaching style didn't fit in with that of the other professors at the college.*

fitful ['fɪt fʊl] *adj.* restless; starting and stopping. (Adv: *fitfully.*) ♦ *Last night I only had a few hours of fitful sleep.* ♦ *Please sit. Your fitful pacing is bothering me.*

fitness ['fɪt nəs] *n.* good physical or mental health. (No plural form in this sense.) ♦ *Physical fitness is important for maintaining a healthy body.* ♦ *The murderer's mental fitness was questioned in court.*

fitted ['fɪt ɪd] *adj.* made to be a particular size or shape; made to fit closely. ♦ *Max placed the fitted sheet snugly around the mattress.* ♦ *I tucked the fitted shirt into my trousers.*

fitting ['fɪt ɪŋ] **1.** *adj.* proper; suitable. (Adv: *fittingly.*) ♦ *It is fitting and proper that we congratulate you for your heroism.* ♦ *Offering a reward to someone who returns something that you've lost is a fitting gesture.* **2.** *n.* an instance of trying on clothing to see if it fits properly. ♦ *The tailor arranged a fitting so that my suit would fit properly.* ♦ *During my fitting, the seamstress accidentally stuck me with a pin.*

five ['faɪv] **1.** 5. See four for senses and examples. **2.** *n.* a five-dollar bill. ♦ *I have a five in my pocket, but nothing larger.* ♦ *Can I borrow a five until next week?*

fix ['fɪks] **1.** *tv.* to repair something; to make something work again. ♦ *The repairman fixed our broken TV.* ♦ *Do you know how to fix a car engine?* **2.** *tv.* to make something firm; to place something firmly into something. ♦ *I fixed the steel rod in a vise so I could file it.* ♦ *The bench had been fixed in place and I could not move it.* **3.** *tv.* to illegally cause something to have a specific outcome; to rig an election, a trial, a game, etc. (Informal.) ♦ *The mobster fixed the trial by bribing the judge.* ♦ *John fixed the boxing match by paying one of the boxers to lose.* **4.** *tv.* to prepare food or drink. ♦ *I fixed supper when I got home from work.* ♦ *Can I fix you something to eat?* **5.** *tv.* to choose a date and time; to determine a date, time, or place. ♦ *Let's fix the appointment for 6:00 P.M.* ♦ *Max fixed the time of his arrival at noon.* **6. in a fix** *idiom* in an awkward situation. ♦ *I was in a real fix because I'd made two dates for the same night.* ♦ *Every time Dave was in a fix, he called his mother for help.*

fixation [fɪk 'se ʃən] *n.* an obsession; an unhealthy feeling for someone or something. ♦ *Bill's fixation on his injured dog affected his daily life.* ♦ *Sue watches TV daily because of her fixation with soap operas.*

fixed ['fɪkst] *adj.* not able to be moved or changed. ♦ *The North Star is a fixed point of light in the night sky.* ♦ *Mary is retired and lives on a fixed income.*

fixings ['fɪks ɪŋz] **with all the fixings** *idiom* with all the condiments that accompany a certain kind of food. ♦ *For $5.99 you get a turkey dinner with all the fixings.* ♦ *Max likes his hamburgers with all the fixings.*

fixture ['fɪks tʃɚ] **1.** *n.* a permanent part of a house or building, such as a ceiling light, a sink, or a toilet. ♦ *I installed a new light fixture above the kitchen sink.* ♦ *I bought the plumbing fixtures I needed at the hardware store.* **2.** *n.* someone or something that is well established. ♦ *Hollywood is a permanent fixture in the film industry.* ♦ *My ancestors are fixtures in the history of my hometown.*

fizz ['fɪz] **1.** *n.* carbonation; small bubbles in certain drinks. (No plural form in this sense.) ♦ *Who left the pop open? It's lost all of its fizz.* ♦ *I drank the pop too fast and the fizz made me sneeze.* **2.** *n.* the noise made by things that have ①. (No plural form in this sense.) ♦ *You can hear the fizz when you open up a can of pop.* ♦ *Hearing the fizz in the soft drink commercial made me thirsty.* **3.** *iv.* [for bubbles in carbonated drinks] to rise up and make a hissing noise. ♦ *The soda fizzed when I opened the bottle.* ♦ *I waited until the pop stopped fizzing before I drank it.*

fizzle ['fɪz əl] **1.** *iv.* to make a sputtering sound. ♦ *The candle fizzled, and then extinguished itself.* ♦ *I took my car to a mechanic when the engine started to fizzle.* **2.** *iv.* to fail. ♦ *The movie fizzled because the acting was very bad.* ♦ *Max's party fizzled because all of the guests were boring.* **3. fizzle out** *iv. + adv.* to decrease in activity; to dwindle away; to diminish. ♦ *The party fizzled out after all the food and drinks were gone.* ♦ *The fighting just fizzled out and both armies withdrew, leaving no clear winner.* **4.** *n.* a failure; something that goes wrong. ♦ *Unfortunately, the TV show I helped produce was a big fizzle.* ♦ *After my last fizzle, I was scared to make another presentation to my boss.*

fizzy ['fɪz i] *adj.* having lots of tiny bubbles, as in carbonated drinks. (Adv: *fizzily.* Comp: *fizzier;* sup: *fizziest.*) ♦ *I sneezed when I drank the fizzy drink too quickly.* ♦ *We celebrated my promotion by drinking fizzy champagne.*

flabbergast ['flæb ɚ gæst] *tv.* to make someone speechless; to amaze someone completely. ♦ *Your comments simply flabbergasted me!* ♦ *Bob liked to flabbergast his teachers by making rude comments.*

flabbergasted ['flæb ɚ gæs tɪd] *adj.* made speechless; completely amazed. (Adv: *flabbergastedly.*) ♦ *Mary's flabbergasted parents heard her perform the difficult piano piece.* ♦ *The flabbergasted teacher sent the disruptive student to the principal's office.*

flabby ['flæb i] *adj.* pudgy; overweight; not in shape. (Adv: *flabbily.* Comp: *flabbier;* sup: *flabbiest.*) ♦ *I'm exercising because I was starting to get flabby.* ♦ *I have flabby legs because I ride instead of walking.*

flaccid ['flæs ɪd] *adj.* limp; weak. (Adv: *flaccidly.*) ♦ *A flaccid handshake does not make a very good impression.* ♦ *A week after the party, a few flaccid balloons still hung on the walls.*

flag ['flæg] **1.** *n.* a piece of fabric of a certain color pattern that represents a country, state, city, school, or organization, or is used as a signal. ♦ *The colors of the American flag are red, white, and blue.* ♦ *The ship flew a flag meaning quarantine.* **2. flag down** *tv.* + *adv.* to signal someone to stop. ♦ *I flagged down a taxi and went immediately to the airport.* ♦ *The police officer flagged down the speeding car.* **3.** *iv.* to become tired; to weaken. ♦ *The runner began to flag in the last lap.* ♦ *After a week in the woods, the lost hiker's spirits began to flag.*

flagpole ['flæg pol] *n.* a pole on which a flag is mounted or attached. ♦ *The flagpole stuck out from the building at a 45-degree angle.* ♦ *Once a year, we hired someone to paint the tall flagpole.*

flagrant ['fle grənt] *adj.* obvious; shameless; in the open. (Adv: *flagrantly.*) ♦ *My manager was fired for a flagrant abuse of company funds.* ♦ *The couple's flagrant display of affection offended the other people in the restaurant.*

flagstone ['flæg ston] *n.* a flat stone that is used for paving. ♦ *The road had some large potholes where the flagstones crumbled.* ♦ *Main Street is paved with flagstone.*

flail ['flel] **1.** *tv.* to wave or jerk something about. ♦ *Bill flailed his arms in anger.* ♦ *The knight flailed his sword to threaten his enemy.* **2.** *iv.* to jerk around uncontrollably; [for someone] to wave one's arms or legs about in an uncontrolled way. ♦ *Don't just stand there and flail. Hit the bully on the chin!* ♦ *Those people on the dance floor are just flailing and are not moving their feet. What do you call that dance?*

flair ['flɛr] *n.* a special style; a talent. ♦ *Jane has a flair for designing clothing.* ♦ *My roommate took advantage of my flair for cooking.*

flak ['flæk] **1.** *n.* gunfire fired at aircraft. (No plural form in this sense.) ♦ *Our plane was hit by enemy flak.* ♦ *Flak from the ground threatened to damage the fighter plane.* **2.** *n.* negative criticism. (No plural form in this sense.) ♦ *I spent two weeks on this project, so don't give me any flak!* ♦ *Instead of giving me flak, why don't you help me improve what I've written?*

flake ['flek] **1.** *n.* a loose piece of something; a bit of something; a thin, light piece of something. ♦ *The children caught flakes of snow on their tongues.* ♦ *I ate some corn flakes for breakfast.* **2. flake off** *iv.* + *adv.* to fall off in thin, loose pieces. ♦ *The edges of the step flaked off when I rubbed my dirty shoes against them.* ♦ *Paint flaked off the old house.* **3.** *tv.* to remove something in flakes ①. ♦ *I flaked the paint from the wall with my knife.* ♦ *Sue used a stick to flake the loose chips off the rocks.* **4. flake off** *tv.* + *adv.* to cause something to separate from a large object in thin, loose pieces. ♦ *The mason flaked off some chips of stone with the chisel.* ♦ *You should flake the loose paint off before repainting.*

flamboyant [flæm 'boɪ ənt] *adj.* outrageous; very colorful; very showy. (Adv: *flamboyantly.*) ♦ *Bob's bright pink car is very flamboyant.* ♦ *The flamboyant waiter showed us to our table with a flourish of his hand.*

flame ['flem] **1.** *n.* a tongue of fire; a segment of yellow, white, blue, or red light that shoots out from a fire. ♦ *Tongues of flame from the fire warmed my hands.* ♦ *The burning house was engulfed in flames.* **2.** *n.* an angry and critical e-mail message. ♦ *I had ten e-mail messages, and half of them were flames.* ♦ *Someone sent me a nasty flame because I expressed my opinion.* **3.** *tv.* to criticize someone sharply in a message on the Internet or a computer bulletin board; to burn someone with criticism. (Slang.) ♦ *Anne flamed me for scheduling a meeting without checking with her.* ♦ *Dave was flamed for posting an insulting message on the Internet.* **4.** *iv.* to be on fire; [for a fire] to make ①. ♦ *The blaze flamed for hours before the firefighters put it out.* ♦ *A fire flamed brightly in the center of the circle of campers.* **5. burn with a low blue flame** *idiom* to be very angry. ♦ *By the time she showed up three hours late, I was burning with a low blue flame.* ♦ *Whenever Anne gets mad, she just presses her lips together and burns with a low blue flame.*

flaming ['flem ɪŋ] *adj.* on fire; burning. (Adv: *flamingly.*) ♦ *The flaming bonfire lit up the night sky.* ♦ *Bill pulled his flaming hot dog from the campfire.*

flamingo [flə 'mɪŋ go] *n.* a large wading bird with long legs, a long neck, and pink feathers. (Pl in *-s* or *-es.*) ♦ *Dozens of graceful flamingos waded near shore.* ♦ *Flamingos sleep standing, with their heads under one wing.*

flammable ['flæm ə bəl] *adj.* inflammable; likely to catch fire; easily set on fire. (Adv: *flammably.*) ♦ *We made sure our children's pajamas were not flammable.* ♦ *Gasoline is an extremely flammable liquid.*

flank ['flæŋk] **1.** *n.* the flesh of a human or an animal between the rib and the hip. ♦ *An arrow gashed my horse in its flank.* ♦ *The butcher cut off a steak from the flank and wrapped it for me.* **2.** *n.* the sides or outer edges of a marching army. ♦ *Our right flank was attacked by sniper fire.* ♦ *The left flank cut through the woods and ambushed the enemy.* **3.** *tv.* to be at the side of something; to be alongside something. ♦ *At the press conference, the president was flanked by secret service agents.* ♦ *A pair of bronze lions flanked the entrance to the museum.*

flannel ['flæn əl] **1.** *n.* a warm cloth made from cotton or wool. (No plural form in this sense.) ♦ *I'd like to buy some flannel with a plaid pattern.* ♦ *My winter shirts are made from flannel.* **2.** *adj.* made of ①. ♦ *Flannel clothing is very warm.* ♦ *In the winter, I sleep under a flannel blanket.*

flap ['flæp] **1.** *n.* a covering placed over an opening that is hinged or attached at one end. ♦ *The dog ran out of the house through a small flap at the bottom of the back door.* ♦ *I tied the tent flap closed to keep out the rain.* **2.** *n.* an argument; a quarrel. (Informal.) ♦ *My neighbor and I had a nasty flap about our property line.* ♦ *The gym manager told us to take our flap outside or he'd call the police.* **3.** *iv.* to move back and forth, as with the movement of birds' wings. ♦ *The shutters flapped in the breeze.* ♦ *Bill's mouth flaps a lot, but he never says anything important.* **4.** *tv.* to move something back and forth, as with the movement of birds' wings. ♦ *The bird flapped its wings and flew away.* ♦ *If you don't stop flapping your lips, I'm going to leave.*

flapjack ['flæp dʒæk] *n.* a pancake. ♦ *We had flapjacks and bacon for breakfast.* ♦ *Mary poured syrup on her flapjacks.*

flare ['flɛr] **1.** *n.* a bright flame. ♦ *The astronomer studied the flare of burning gas pulsing from the sun.* ♦ *I shielded my eyes from the bright flares of light bursting from the factory fire.* **2.** *n.* something that provides a bright light, used as a signal or as a warning of danger. ♦ *The police set up flares behind the broken car so no one would run into it.* ♦ *We lit flares on the island's shore in hopes of being rescued.* **3.** *n.* a part of a piece of clothing that spreads out or gets wider. ♦ *The flare of Bill's pants was quite out of style.* ♦ *A lot of material is required for the flares of hoop skirts.* **4.** *iv.* to spread out. ♦ *The dog's nostrils flared when it sensed danger.* ♦ *I have an old pair of pants that flare from the knee to the ankle.* **5.** *iv.* to create bursts of bright light. ♦ *Hundreds of stars flared in the night sky.* ♦ *Fireworks flared in the darkened sky.*

flare-up ['flɚ əp] **1.** *n.* a burst of flame. ♦ *A sudden flare-up of the campfire startled us.* ♦ *Put the fire out completely. You don't want to cause an unexpected flare-up.* **2.** *n.* a burst of anger or violence. (Figurative on ①.) ♦ *Soldiers were sent to stop the flare-up between the warring towns.* ♦ *Max quit his job after a flare-up with his boss.*

flash ['flæʃ] **1.** *n.* a quick, strong, burst of light. ♦ *The tree was struck by a flash of lightning.* ♦ *I was temporarily blinded by a flash of light.* **2.** *n.* a quick, strong, burst of feeling. (Figurative on ①.) ♦ *Dave hit me in a flash of anger.* ♦ *With a flash of excitement, Sue explained her idea to me.* **3.** *n.* an important news report, especially one that interrupts regular programming. ♦ *The TV show was interrupted by a news flash about nearby tornadoes.* ♦ *The latest news flash reported that the police had caught the dangerous criminal.* **4.** *iv.* to give off a burst of light for a brief moment. ♦ *The lights flashed twice, and then the power went out.* ♦ *Lightning flashed across the sky.* **5. flash by** *iv. + adv.* to move by quickly. (Figurative on ④.) ♦ *A red car flashed by, almost hitting me.* ♦ *The express train flashed by the people waiting on the platform.* **6.** *tv.* to make something give off a burst of light for a brief moment. ♦ *The guard flashed the light in my eyes.* ♦ *The driver flashed the blinker to indicate a left turn.* **7.** *tv.* to show something off; to make something be seen. ♦ *Don't flash your money like that, do you want to be robbed?* ♦ *I flashed my new ring to all of my friends.* **8.** *adj.* very quick; very sudden. ♦ *The cows in the valley were swept away by a flash flood.* ♦ *The accountant gave us the flash budget figures the minute they were proposed.* **9.** *adj.* [in photography] of or about the creation of a quick burst of light. ♦ *A flash attachment is built into the camera.* ♦ *Flash photos are easy to take with an automatic camera.* **10. in a flash** *idiom* quickly; immediately. (On ⑧.) ♦ *I'll be there in a flash.* ♦ *It happened in a flash. Suddenly my wallet was gone.*

flashback ['flæʃ bæk] *n.* something that happened in the past, reenacted in one's memory. (Also a device used in storytelling.) ♦ *While eating my cereal, I had a flashback of my grandma making oatmeal for me 25 years before.* ♦ *While driving down the road, Bill had a flashback of an accident he had suffered many years before.*

flashing ['flæʃ ɪŋ] **1.** *adj.* [of a light] turning on and off; blinking. ♦ *A police car's siren and flashing lights indicated that I was to stop.* ♦ *The flashing signal indicated that the car was about to turn.* **2.** *n.* pieces of metal that protect the roof and edges of a building from leaking. (No plural form in this sense.) ♦ *Heavy winds tore some flashing from our roof.* ♦ *Yesterday we replaced the shingles and the flashing on our roof.*

flashlight ['flæʃ lɑɪt] *n.* a small, portable, battery-operated light. ♦ *I keep a flashlight in the glove compartment of my car for emergencies.* ♦ *The only light in the narrow tunnel came from my weak flashlight.*

flashy ['flæʃ i] *adj.* showy; gaudy; ornate; very bright. (Adv: *flashily.* Comp: *flashier;* sup: *flashiest.*) ♦ *Mary's new sports car is very flashy and very expensive.* ♦ *Tom wore a flashy new tie to the party.*

flask ['flæsk] **1.** *n.* a small, flat container used for holding whiskey or other liquids. ♦ *Bob carried a flask with him when he went hunting in the fall.* ♦ *Jane took a flask of brandy to the baseball game.* **2.** *n.* a glass container, especially one used in laboratories. ♦ *After the science experiment, I washed the flasks.* ♦ *Carefully hand me that flask of acid, please.*

flat ['flæt] **1.** *adj.* [of a surface] level, even, and smooth. (Adv: *flatly.* Comp: *flatter;* sup: *flattest.*) ♦ *Place the vase on a flat surface so that it does not tip over.* ♦ *This region is very flat. There are no hills or mountains.* **2.** *adj.* deflated; having lost air; not pumped up with air. (Adv: *flatly.* Comp: *flatter;* sup: *flattest.*) ♦ *I drove very slowly to a gas station because I had a flat tire.* ♦ *I pumped air into the tire because it was flat.* **3.** *adj.* fixed; stable; not variable or negotiable. (Comp: *flatter;* sup: *flattest.*) ♦ *The bank charges a flat fee for checking accounts regardless of one's balance.* ♦ *Interest rates are flat right now, but they're expected to climb.* **4.** *adj.* dull; not exciting. (Adv: *flatly.* Comp: *flatter;* sup: *flattest.*) ♦ *The actor's performance was flat and insipid.* ♦ *Your writing is flat and uninspiring.* **5.** *adj.* off-key; lower in pitch than what something is supposed to be. (Adv: *flatly.* Comp: *flatter;* sup: *flattest.*) ♦ *The singer's high notes were all flat.* ♦ *Your piano is flat. You should tune it.* **6.** *n.* an apartment. ♦ *I rented a small flat in town for use while I was there on business.* ♦ *I live in a flat in New York City.* **7.** *n.* a piece of scenery for a stage, made of canvas mounted on a wooden frame. ♦ *During the scene change, the stage crew quickly moved the flats into place.* ♦ *I bumped into a flat and it fell over during the last act.* **8. flat (tire)** *n.* a tire that is low on air; a deflated tire. ♦ *I had to drive very slowly because I had a flat.* ♦ *I'm late because I had to change a flat tire on the way here.* **9.** *n.* a note that is one-half step lower in pitch than a natural note. ♦ *The sonata was written to be played on all flats and sharps.* ♦ *You are singing D, and it should be D-flat.* **10.** *adv.* horizontally; level with a surface or the ground. ♦ *Press your hand flat on the door and push it.* ♦ *I tried to get the wallpaper to stick flat against the wall.* **11.** *adv.* exactly so much time or money. (Follows the unit of time or money.) ♦ *The meal cost $20 flat.* ♦ *I ran a mile in six minutes flat.* **12. in nothing flat** *idiom* in exactly no time at all; in a very short time. (On ⑪.) ♦ *Of course I can get there in a hurry. I'll be there in nothing flat.* ♦ *We covered the distance between New York and Philadelphia in nothing flat.*

flatcar ['flæt kɑr] *n.* a railroad car without sides or a roof, looking like a sturdy platform on wheels. ♦ *Flatcars are used to transport large items across the country.* ♦ *Rolls of steel are transported from the factory on flatcars.*

flatly ['flæt li] *adv.* straightforwardly; absolutely. ♦ *I flatly told Anne, "No!"* ♦ *My boss flatly refused to give me a raise.*

flatten ['flæt n] **1.** *tv.* to cause something to become flat. ♦ *The car ran over my football and flattened it.* ♦ *You can flatten your stomach by exercising daily.* **2. flatten (out)** *iv.* (+ *adv.*) to become flat. ♦ *My papers flattened out as they dried.* ♦ *In time, the tablecloth will flatten out.*

flatter ['flæt ɚ] **1.** *tv.* to attempt to influence someone with praise, possibly insincere praise. ♦ *Before asking for a raise, I flattered my boss by praising her latest accomplishments.* ♦ *Stop trying to flatter me, and tell me what you want.* **2.** *tv.* to cause someone to feel pleased or honored. ♦ *Anne flattered me when she told me I had done a good job.* ♦ *Dave flattered his teacher by saying that he was responsible for his success.* **3.** *tv.* [for an article of clothing] to make a person look good. ♦ *Those earrings flatter the shape of your face.* ♦ *Vertical stripes can flatter your figure by making you look taller.*

flattery ['flæt ə ri] **1.** *n.* praise. (Often overstated or insincere. No plural form in this sense.) ♦ *No amount of flattery will make me change my opinion of you.* ♦ *I used flattery with my boss in an attempt to get a raise.* **2. Flattery will get you nowhere.** *idiom* "You can praise me, but I'm not going to give you what you want." ♦ *I am glad to hear that I am beautiful and talented, but flattery will get you nowhere.* ♦ *Flattery will get you nowhere, but that doesn't mean you should stop flattering me!*

flattop ['flæt tɑp] *n.* a kind of short haircut where the top is completely flat. ♦ *Bob surprised everyone when he cut off his ponytail and got a flattop.* ♦ *John got a flattop so he would look nice for his sister's wedding.*

flatulence ['flætʃ ə ləns] *n.* gas that collects in the intestines and is passed through the rectum. (No plural form in this sense.) ♦ *Eating beans can cause flatulence.* ♦ *Sue went to her doctor because she had severe cramps and flatulence.*

flatulent ['flætʃ ə lənt] *adj.* having flatulence; of or about flatulence. (Adv: *flatulently.*) ♦ *Because he felt a bit flatulent, David excused himself from the party.* ♦ *John was troubled with flatulent episodes.*

flatware ['flæt wɛr] *n.* eating utensils used at the table, such as knives, forks, and spoons. (No plural form in this sense. Often used in contrast to **silverware**.) ♦ *The newlywed couple received an expensive set of flatware as a wedding gift.* ♦ *Dave placed the flatware in its correct position around the plates.*

flaunt ['flɔnt] *tv.* to show something off; to display something too proudly. (Compare with **flout**.) ♦ *Bill always flaunts his law degree in front of his less successful friends.* ♦ *You shouldn't flaunt your money when you're out shopping.*

flautist ['flɑʊt əst] *n.* a flutist; someone who plays a flute. ♦ *The flautist polished her flute every day.* ♦ *Our symphony orchestra featured a well-known flautist.*

flavor ['flev ɚ] **1.** *n.* a specific taste; the way something tastes. ♦ *This yogurt has the flavor of strawberries.* ♦ *These chips have a strong barbecue flavor.* **2.** *n.* something that is added to a food to give it a specific taste. ♦ *These cookies have no artificial ingredients and contain only natural flavors.* ♦ *This ice cream has natural vanilla flavor.* **3.** *n.* a special quality or characteristic. ♦ *Mary's morbid paintings gave an eerie flavor to the room.* ♦ *Bands of colored paper gave the party a holiday flavor.* **4. flavor with** *tv.* + *prep. phr.* to add something to a food to give it a specific taste. ♦ *These chips are flavored with garlic.* ♦ *The cook flavored the soup with too many spices.*

flavorful ['flev ɚ fʊl] *adj.* full of flavor; tasty. (Adv: *flavorfully* ['flev ɚ fli].) ♦ *Your soup is very flavorful.* ♦ *I would prefer some nice, flavorful steamed vegetables, please.*

flavoring ['flev ɚ ɪŋ] *n.* something that is added to a food to make it taste a certain way. ♦ *I don't eat foods with artificial flavorings.* ♦ *I bought ice cream with natural chocolate flavoring.*

flavorless ['flev ɚ ləs] *adj.* having no flavor; having no taste; bland. (Adv: *flavorlessly.*) ♦ *I asked the waiter to return the flavorless soup to the kitchen.* ♦ *I added a dash of oregano to the flavorless sauce.*

flaw ['flɔ] *n.* a fault; a defect; an indication of damage. ♦ *The flaw in your theory is that you didn't account for gravity.* ♦ *A flaw in the design of the airplane caused its crash.*

flawed ['flɔd] *adj.* damaged; not perfect; in error. (Adv: *flawedly.*) ♦ *My manager asked me to correct my flawed report.* ♦ *The jeweler sold the flawed diamond at a very good price.*

flawless ['flɔ ləs] *adj.* perfect; without a flaw; undamaged; having no errors. (Adv: *flawlessly.*) ♦ *The flawless diamond was worth thousands of dollars.* ♦ *The audience applauded the acrobat's flawless performance.*

flax ['flæks] **1.** *n.* a thin, narrow plant grown for its fibers and seeds. (No plural form in this sense.) ♦ *The flax was harvested and sent to the mill.* ♦ *A useful kind of oil is made from the seeds of flax.* **2.** *n.* the fibers of ①. (No plural form in this sense.) ♦ *Linen is the fabric made from flax.* ♦ *Flax can be spun into a fine, strong thread.* **3.** *adj.* <the adj. use of ① or ②.> ♦ *The flax fibers were spun into a fine, strong thread.* ♦ *The flax plants were killed by a powerful herbicide.*

flea ['fli] *n.* a tiny insect that lives on an animal's skin, sucking blood and eating dead skin. ♦ *Our dog scratches himself because he has fleas.* ♦ *It's difficult to detect fleas on a furry animal because they are so small.*

fleck ['flɛk] **1.** *n.* a small particle of something. ♦ *I wiped the flecks of dust from the counter.* ♦ *There are flecks of chalk on the teacher's pants.* **2.** *tv.* to sprinkle something with something; to cause something to have small spots. ♦ *The passing truck flecked my windshield with droplets of water.* ♦ *The artist flecked the canvas with orange paint.*

fled ['flɛd] pt of flee.

fledge ['flɛdʒ] *iv.* [for a young bird] to grow the feathers needed for flight. (See **full-fledged**.) ♦ *The mother bird brought food to her babies until they fledged.* ♦ *The young birds left the nest after they fledged.*

fledgling ['flɛdʒ lɪŋ] **1.** *n.* a baby bird just growing the feathers it needs to fly. ♦ *The fledgling stayed close to the nest until it could fly well.* ♦ *The birds cared for their chicks until they were fledglings.* **2.** *n.* a beginner; someone who is new or inexperienced. (Figurative on ①.) ♦ *Anne is in charge of training the fledglings.* ♦ *The recently retired reporter gave the fledgling some good advice.* **3.** *adj.* inexperienced; beginning; new. ♦ *The fledgling author did not like the editor's comments.* ♦ *The veteran mason gave the fledgling bricklayer some good advice.*

flee ['fli] **1. flee (from)** *tv., irreg. (+ prep. phr.)* to run away from someone or something; to escape from danger. (Pt/pp: **fled**.) ♦ *The people who lived near the river had to flee the flooding waters.* ♦ *My grandmother fled the civil unrest in her homeland.* **2.** *iv., irreg.* to run quickly away from something or toward something. ♦ *When the rain began, we fled for cover.* ♦ *The thief fled from the police.*

fleece ['flis] **1.** *n.* the wool of a sheep. (No plural form in this sense.) ♦ *The fleece of Mary's lamb was as white as snow.* ♦ *We sheared the sheep's fleece quickly.* **2.** *tv.* to charge someone too much money. (Informal.) ♦ *The crooks fleeced the tourists by selling them overpriced junk.* ♦ *If you paid $50 for that watch, you were really fleeced.*

fleecy ['flis i] **1.** *adj.* looking or feeling soft and white. (Adv: *fleecily.* Comp: *fleecier;* sup: *fleecier.*) ♦ *The fleecy cotton candy tasted very sweet.* ♦ *I lay in the field, watching the fleecy clouds blow by.* **2.** *adj.* made of soft and fluffy fibers like clean wool. (Adv: *fleecily.* Comp: *fleecier;* sup: *fleeciest.*) ♦ *The quilt is lined with fleecy wool.* ♦ *In the winter, I wear gloves with a fleecy lining.*

fleet ['flit] **1.** *n.* all the ships of a country's navy. ♦ *Our huge fleet is docked in several different ports.* ♦ *The fleet set sail toward the enemy after war was declared.* **2.** *n.* a group of trucks, cars, or buses owned by one owner. ♦ *Dave's bus company has 200 buses in its fleet.* ♦ *I got to choose from a fleet of cars when I rented one at the airport.*

fleeting ['flit ɪŋ] *adj.* rapid; quick; swift; existing for just a moment. (Adv: *fleetingly.*) ♦ *The witness only caught a fleeting glimpse of the robber.* ♦ *I'm sorry. For a fleeting moment, I thought you were someone else.*

flesh ['flɛʃ] **1.** *n.* the soft part of the body covered by skin; fat, muscle, and tissues; meat. (No plural form in this sense.) ♦ *The dog bit deep into my flesh.* ♦ *The cook removed the chicken's flesh from its bones.* **2.** *n.* the soft part of a fruit or vegetable that can be eaten. (No plural form in this sense.) ♦ *I bit into the juicy flesh of the peach.* ♦ *The worms ate the flesh of the ripe tomatoes.* **3. the flesh** *n.* the physical body as opposed to the spirit or mind. (Figurative on ①. No plural form in this sense. Treated as singular.) ♦ *The preacher encouraged his flock to think more of the spirit and less of the flesh.* ♦ *The flesh is subject to many temptations.* **4. in the flesh** *idiom* bodily present; in person; totally real. (On ③.) ♦ *I've heard that the queen is coming here in the flesh.* ♦ *I've wanted a color television for years, and now I've got one right here in the flesh.*

fleshy ['flɛʃ i] *adj.* having a lot of meat; meaty; fat. (Adv: *fleshily.* Comp: *fleshier;* sup: *fleshiest.*) ♦ *The cook fried the fleshy chicken breasts.* ♦ *You should go on a diet. You're starting to look a little fleshy.*

flew ['flu] pt of fly.

flex ['flɛks] *tv.* to bend something, especially a muscle. ♦ *Sue flexed her arm to show how exercise had toned her muscles.* ♦ *The doctor removed my cast and told me to flex my leg.*

flexible ['flɛk sə bəl] **1.** *adj.* limber; able to bend easily; pliant; not rigid. (Adv: *flexibly.*) ♦ *After the accident, my ankle joint was no longer flexible.* ♦ *Jane easily bent the flexible wire into a loop.* **2.** *adj.* able to be changed; adaptable; able to serve a number of purposes. (Figurative on ①. Adv: *flexibly.*) ♦ *My stubborn brother does not have a flexible personality.* ♦ *My schedule is flexible. I can meet you anytime.*

flick ['flɪk] **1.** *tv.* to move something quickly and lightly; to hit someone or something quickly and lightly, as with a whip; to whip someone or something lightly. ♦ *I flicked the switch to turn on the lights.* ♦ *Max flicked the whip, and the horse went faster.* **2.** *n.* a short or sudden movement. ♦ *You can snap a whip with a flick of your wrist.* ♦ *The flick of the whip made the horse go faster.*

flicker ['flɪk ɚ] **1.** *n.* a light or flame that is not steady; a light or flame that wavers. ♦ *The only light in the room was the weak flicker of a candle.* ♦ *At night, the stars look like tiny flickers of light.* **2.** *n.* a short burst of energy or excitement that dies out quickly. (Figurative on ①.) ♦ *Since we were expecting the president, there was a flicker of excitement when the door opened, but it was just a reporter.* ♦ *I had a flicker of hope when the doctor entered the waiting room, but it was bad news.* **3.** *iv.* to burn unsteadily; to burn as a flame. ♦ *The lights began to flicker and then went out completely.* ♦ *The candle flickered in the wind.*

flickering ['flɪk ɚ ɪŋ] *adj.* burning unsteadily; burning unevenly; flashing on and off in an irregular fashion. (Adv: *flickeringly.*) ♦ *Flickering candles were the only source of light in the empty church.* ♦ *I could see someone carrying a flickering torch in the distance.*

flier AND **flyer** ['flɑɪ ɚ] *n.* a piece of paper handed out to people, having printed or written information on it. ♦ *Max passed out flyers advertising the town festival.* ♦ *The flier announced the opening of a new store in town.*

flight ['flɑɪt] **1.** *n.* flying; flying through the air. (No plural form in this sense.) ♦ *The scientist studied the mechanism of flight used by geese.* ♦ *Humans have been fascinated with flight for thousands of years.* **2.** *n.* a movement through the air accomplished though ①. ♦ *After a few shorts flights, the bird landed on my windowsill.* ♦ *The flight of the small plane ended in a crash.* **3.** *n.* a particular scheduled **flight** ② of an airline company from one airport to another; an airplane trip. ♦ *Flight #204 to Houston is now boarding at Gate 12.* ♦ *I'm sorry, this flight is full. I can put you on the 4:30 plane.* **4.** *n.* running away from someone or something; an escape from danger; fleeing. (No plural form in this sense.) ♦ *After the thieves robbed the bank, their flight into the crowd was quick and flawless.* ♦ *The soldier talked about his flight from the enemy's prison.* **5.** *n.* a set of stairs. ♦ *I have to climb three flights of stairs to get to my apartment.* ♦ *Tom fell down a flight of stairs and broke his arm.* **6. in flight** *phr.* while flying. ♦ *A passenger became ill in flight and the pilot had to return to the airport.* ♦ *I really don't care to eat in flight. I am too nervous.*

flight attendant ['flɑɪt ə tɛn dənt] *n.* someone who tends to the passengers' needs and safety on an airplane flight. ♦ *The flight attendant demonstrated how to buckle a seat belt.* ♦ *There were 12 flight attendants on the long flight across the Pacific Ocean.*

flighty ['flɑɪt i] *adj.* whimsical; likely to change one's mind; silly. (Adv: *flightily.* Comp: *flightier;* sup: *flightiest.*) ♦ *How can you be so flighty when I'm trying to have a serious conversation?* ♦ *Don't ask Bob to make a serious decision. He's too flighty.*

flimsy ['flɪm zi] *adj.* likely to fall apart; not very durable; poorly made. (Adv: *flimsily.* Comp: *flimsier;* sup: *flimsiest.*) ♦ *The flimsy kite was torn when it crashed into the tree.* ♦ *No one will believe your flimsy excuse.*

flinch ['flɪntʃ] *iv.* to wince; to shudder in pain or with emotion. ♦ *I flinched when the bee stung me.* ♦ *We all flinched when we saw the cars collide.*

fling ['flɪŋ] **1.** *n.* a throw; a toss, especially to get rid of something. ♦ *With a careless fling, Bill threw a paper cup out of the car window.* ♦ *If you don't want it, just give it a fling.* **2.** *n.* a romantic or sexual affair. ♦ *The couple met at a convention and had a fling that lasted a few months.* ♦ *Bill had hoped it was more than a fling, but soon, Jane tired of him.* **3.** *tv., irreg.* to throw something with force; to throw something out or down; to throw something aside. (Pt/pp: **flung.**) ♦ *The dishes broke when I flung them against the table.* ♦ *I flung my clean clothes onto my bed.* **4. final fling** *idiom* the last act or period of enjoyment before a change in one's circumstances or lifestyle. ♦ *You might as well have a final fling before the baby's born.* ♦ *Mary's going out with her girlfriends for a final fling. She's getting married next week.*

flint ['flɪnt] *n.* a kind of hard stone that makes sparks when struck. (No plural form in this sense.) ♦ *I always carry a piece of flint when I go hiking, in case of emergency.* ♦ *We lit the campfire using a piece of flint.*

flip ['flɪp] **1.** *n.* a throw that tosses something into the air; a tossing action that moves something. ♦ *With a flip of her wrist, Jane tossed her keys onto the counter.* ♦ *I turned on the lights with a flip of the switch.* **2.** *n.* a kind of acrobatic jump where one turns one's body in the air. ♦ *The gymnast did a backward flip off the high beam.* ♦ *The swimmer did a flip from the diving board.* **3.** *tv.* to cause something to turn about or spin through the air. ♦ *I flipped the keys across the room to Sue.* ♦ *Tom flipped the car upside down when he ran it off the road.* **4.** *adj.* **flippant**; rude. (Adv: *fliply.*) ♦ *The teacher would not tolerate flip responses from the students.* ♦ *Please don't be flip with me, and do what I told you.*

flippant ['flɪp ənt] *adj.* rude; casually disrespectful. (Adv: *flippantly.*) ♦ *If your flippant attitude doesn't improve, you're going to be fired.* ♦ *Instead of making flippant comments, why don't you offer some constructive criticism?*

flipper ['flɪp ɚ] **1.** *n.* the structure of a seal, and similar animals, that is similar to a human limb adapted for swimming. ♦ *The seal was trained to clap its flippers together and bark like a dog.* ♦ *Seals have two pairs of flippers.* **2.** *n.* one of a pair of plastic or rubber paddles worn on the feet while scuba diving or snorkeling; a fin. ♦ *Jimmy put on his flippers and jumped into the pool.* ♦ *With flippers, I can dive deeply and swim rapidly underwater.*

flirt ['flɚt] **1. flirt (with)** *iv.* (+ *prep. phr.*) to behave in a way that is intended to attract someone's attention—with romantic goals in mind. ♦ *Bob flirts with every woman in our office.* ♦ *After Anne had flirted with John for a few weeks, she was embarrassed to learn that he was married.* **2.** *n.* someone who tries to attract someone's attention romantically or sexually. ♦ *Don't be such a flirt with strangers.* ♦ *That little flirt asked me for my phone number.* **3. flirt with the idea of doing something** *idiom* to think about doing something; to toy with an idea; to consider something, but not too seriously. (Figurative on ①.) ♦ *I flirted with the idea of going to Europe for two weeks.* ♦ *Jane flirted with the idea of quitting her job.*

flirtation [flɚ 'te ʃən] *n.* flirting. (No plural form in this sense.) ♦ *Flirtation can lead to a date or even marriage.* ♦ *A little flirtation can be fun as long as both people know it's nothing serious.*

flirtatious [flɚ 'te ʃəs] *adj.* teasing; arousing someone's interest romantically or sexually. (Adv: *flirtatiously.*) ♦ *Stop paying me so much attention! You are the most flirtatious person I have ever met!* ♦ *Are you just being flirtatious, or do you really want to go out with me?*

flirting ['flɚt ɪŋ] *n.* the arousal of someone's attention sexually or romantically. (No plural form in this sense.) ♦ *Jane was well known for flirting with strange men at parties.* ♦ *Bob's constant flirting angered his wife.*

flit ['flɪt] *iv.* to move about quickly from place to place. ♦ *I flitted around the room impatiently, waiting for the guests to arrive.* ♦ *The manager flitted through the office but never paid much attention to what was happening.*

float ['flot] **1.** *iv.* to remain on top of water or a liquid; to stay above water. ♦ *Cork floats.* ♦ *Sue floated on an inflated mattress in the pool.* **2.** *iv.* to hover; to remain in the air. (Figurative on ①.) ♦ *The clouds floated in the sky.* ♦ *The hot-air balloon floated in the breeze.* **3.** *n.* a device that keeps someone or something above water; a device that keeps someone or something floating on water. ♦ *I knew I'd caught a fish when the float attached to the fishing line was pulled underwater.* ♦ *The float in the toilet tank is broken, so the water is constantly running.* **4.** *tv.* to set something afloat and into motion. ♦ *Bill floated the model boat on the pond.* ♦ *We floated the raft down the river.* **5.** *tv.* to arrange a loan of money. (Informal.) ♦ *Can you float me $25 until payday?* ♦ *I floated Bob a small loan after his wallet was lost.*

floating ['flot ɪŋ] **1.** *adj.* drifting; hovering on the surface of the water. ♦ *I took the floating bottle from the lake and read the message inside it.* ♦ *I removed the floating leaves from the pool.* **2.** *adj.* hovering in the air. ♦ *I lay in the field, watching the floating clouds above me.* ♦ *The floating balloon went higher and higher, until it was out of sight.*

flock ['flɑk] **1.** *n.* a group of certain animals clustered together, especially birds or sheep. ♦ *The shepherd tended a small flock of sheep.* ♦ *A flock of seagulls roosted on the telephone wire.* **2.** *iv.* to gather together in a place. ♦ *The crowd flocked around the movie star.* ♦ *The students flocked to the gym for the assembly.*

flog ['flɔg] *tv.* to beat someone or something violently, especially as punishment. ♦ *The thief was flogged with a whip.* ♦ *Tom was flogged with a stick by the bully.*

flood ['flʌd] **1.** *n.* a large amount of water lying on land that is normally dry. ♦ *A huge flood covered most of the farmland.* ♦ *The flood left behind tons of mud and dead fish.* **2.** *n.* a powerful surge of water moving over the land. ♦ *The flood swept through the valley in the night.* ♦ *The flood spilled over onto the land and into the town.* **3.** *n.* a large flow of anything; an outpouring of something. (Figurative on ②.) ♦ *I was comforted by the flood of support from my family when my best friend died.* ♦ *I can't leave the office now because I have a flood of paperwork to* *attend to on my desk.* **4.** *tv.* to cover an area with water; to cover something with water. ♦ *Rushing waters flooded the streets of the town.* ♦ *The heavy rains flooded the land around the river.* **5.** *iv.* to spill or overflow with great volumes of water. ♦ *This river floods every time it rains heavily.* ♦ *We had to evacuate when the town flooded.*

floodlight ['flʌd lɑɪt] **1.** *n.* a very powerful light used to cover a large area with bright light. ♦ *The guards kept watch over the prison yard with large floodlights.* ♦ *Giant floodlights light up the baseball stadium after dark.* **2.** *tv., irreg.* to cover a large area with a bright light. (Pt/pp: *floodlighted* or **floodlit**.) ♦ *The architect decided to floodlight the football field from size huge towers.* ♦ *Huge lights floodlighted the stage and auditorium for the finale.*

floodlit ['flʌd lɪt] **1.** pt/pp of **floodlight**. **2.** *adj.* lighted by floodlights. ♦ *The cast stood happily on the floodlit stage and bowed to the members of the audience, who applauded wildly.* ♦ *We played soccer on the college's floodlit field nearly every night.*

floor ['flor] **1.** *n.* the surface of a room that is walked on; the inside bottom surface of a room. ♦ *Our apartment has hardwood floors.* ♦ *I knocked the plate off the table and onto the floor.* **2.** *n.* one level of a building; a story. ♦ *My apartment building has 10 floors.* ♦ *My apartment is on the third floor.* **3.** *tv.* to install ① in a place; to install a new surface on ①. ♦ *The workers floored the kitchen with marble tile.* ♦ *My living room had been floored with hardwood, but it is now carpeted.* **4.** *tv.* to knock someone to the floor. (Informal.) ♦ *Bob's blow to John's jaw floored him.* ♦ *A huge wind burst through the door and floored the butler.* **5.** *tv.* to astound someone; to make someone speechless. (Figurative on ④.) ♦ *Your revelation absolutely floored me.* ♦ *I was floored by your rude behavior.* **6. walk the floor** *idiom* to pace nervously while waiting. ♦ *While Bill waited for news of the operation, he walked the floor for hours on end.* ♦ *Walking the floor won't help. You might as well sit down and relax.*

floorboard ['flor bord] **1.** *n.* a board that is part of a wooden floor. ♦ *The farmer kept money under the kitchen floorboards.* ♦ *That floorboard squeaks if you step on it.* **2.** *n.* the floor of a car or truck. ♦ *Our floorboard rusted out because of the salt put on the roads to melt the snow.* ♦ *I could hear the gravel hitting the underside of the floorboard as I drove down the road.*

flop ['flɑp] **1.** *tv.* to cause something flat to fall heavily somewhere. ♦ *Bob flopped the magazine on the counter.* ♦ *I flopped the hamburger onto the grill.* **2.** *iv.* [for someone] to fall heavily into or onto something. ♦ *I flopped into bed and fell asleep immediately.* ♦ *Bob flopped onto the couch and turned on the TV.* **3.** *iv.* to fail. (Informal.) ♦ *The movie flopped, so it was immediately available on video.* ♦ *I lost $50,000 when my restaurant flopped within a month.* **4. a flop** *n.* a failure. ♦ *The movie was a flop that cost the studio $25 million.* ♦ *I went back to school because my life was a total flop.*

floppy disk ['flɑp i 'dɪsk] *n.* a round, flat, magnetic computer storage medium that can be moved from computer to computer. ♦ *Keep floppy disks away from magnets.* ♦ *I saved my homework on a floppy disk and printed it out on the school's computer.*

floppy drive ['flɑp i 'drɑɪv] *n.* the device that allows a computer to read and write information to a floppy disk. ♦ *Place the disk into the floppy drive and copy the file onto the hard drive.* ♦ *Push that button when you want to remove your disk from the floppy drive.*

floral ['flor əl] *adj.* Concerning or associated with flowers. ♦ *We sent a floral arrangement to our colleague's funeral.* ♦ *I bought an air freshener with a floral scent.*

Florida ['flor ə də] See Gazetteer.

florist ['flor əst] *n.* someone who arranges and sells flowers for a living. ♦ *The florist received dozens of orders for the funeral home each day.* ♦ *I asked the florist to put together a $30 flower arrangement.*

floss ['flɑs] **1. (dental) floss** *n.* a special string used to clean between the teeth. (No plural form in this sense.) ♦ *You should clean between your teeth with dental floss after every meal.* ♦ *I always pack extra floss with me when I travel.* **2.** *tv.* to clean between someone's teeth using ①. ♦ *I floss my teeth after each meal.* ♦ *Be sure to floss your molars!* **3.** *iv.* to use ①. ♦ *The dentist told me to floss more often.* ♦ *Your gums look unhealthy; have you been flossing?*

flotilla [flo 'tɪl ə] *n.* a small group of ships; a small fleet. ♦ *A flotilla of enemy ships approached the harbor.* ♦ *Early each morning a small flotilla of fishing ships left the docks.*

flounder ['flɑʊn dɚ] **1.** *n., irreg.* any one of a number of common, flat-bodied, edible fish. (Pl: *flounder* or *flounders*.) ♦ *Bob caught two flounders and a turtle.* ♦ *Flounder and sole are both flat-bodied, but they are entirely different kinds of fish.* **2.** *n.* the meat of ①. (No plural form in this sense.) ♦ *I love baked flounder.* ♦ *Flounder is best when it is fresh.* **3.** *iv.* to move awkwardly in an attempt to regain one's balance; to plunge and stumble as through mud or water. (Compare with **founder**.) ♦ *The explorer floundered in the quicksand.* ♦ *The drunk floundered as he walked through the streets.* **4.** *iv.* to act confused and **stumble** ② with one's words. (Figurative on ③.) ♦ *Dave forgot his lines and floundered as he spoke.* ♦ *The mayor floundered while answering the question.*

flour ['flɑʊ ɚ] **1.** *n.* a powder made from grinding wheat, corn, or other grain, used in cooking. (Compare with **flower**. No plural form in this sense.) ♦ *This bread is made from whole-wheat flour.* ♦ *I bought five pounds of flour at the grocery store.* **2.** *tv.* to cover or coat food with ① in preparation for cooking. ♦ *Flour the chicken breast before you place it in the frying pan.* ♦ *The cook floured the vegetables and dropped them into the boiling oil.*

flourish ['flɚ ɪʃ] **1.** *iv.* to grow; to thrive; to do well; to live well; to be successful. ♦ *Corn and wheat flourished in the fields.* ♦ *Jane's restaurant flourished in the new location.* **2.** *tv.* to wave something around; to flaunt something; to draw attention to something. ♦ *The knight flourished his banner to indicate his presence.* ♦ *Mary dramatically flourished her fan as if to show everyone just how hot she was.* **3.** *n.* a fancy movement, decoration, or piece of music that catches people's attention. ♦ *The magician's flourish with his right hand kept the audience from watching what he did with his left hand.* ♦ *There was a flourish from a bugle to announce the queen's entrance.*

flout ['flɑʊt] *tv.* to ignore someone's orders or rules. (Compare with **flaunt**.) ♦ *Tom flouted his boss's orders all the time.* ♦ *The soldier was executed for flouting the king's request.*

flow ['flo] **1.** *n.* the movement of running water; the movement of a fluid. (No plural form in this sense.) ♦ *The dam slowed the flow of the river.* ♦ *Sue applied pressure to the cut to stop the flow of blood.* **2.** *n.* the even and ordered movement of things in a series. (No plural form in this sense. Figurative on ①.) ♦ *The flow of orders goes from the supervisors to the workers.* ♦ *This lever controls the flow of parts that come down the assembly line.* **3.** *iv.* to move like running water; to move smoothly along a route. ♦ *The Mississippi River flows by St. Louis.* ♦ *Hot water flowed from the open pipe.* **4.** *iv.* to move easily and in an orderly fashion. ♦ *Traffic flowed smoothly on the highway despite the rain.* ♦ *The students flowed in and out of the cafeteria during lunch.*

flower ['flaʊ ɚ] **1.** *n.* a plant that produces blossoms. (Compare with **flour**.) ♦ *I planted several different kinds of flowers in the garden.* ♦ *Mary bought many pots of flowers and brought them home to plant them.* **2.** *n.* a blossom; the brightly colored petals of a plant. ♦ *Red flowers include roses, carnations, and begonias.* ♦ *Anne pressed the pretty flower between the pages of a book.* **3.** *iv.* to bloom; [for a plant] to produce ②. ♦ *I looked outside and noticed that the roses had flowered.* ♦ *The petunias flowered early this year.*

flowering ['flaʊ ɚ ɪŋ] *adj.* producing blossoms; capable of producing blossoms. ♦ *My house is decorated with pots of flowering plants.* ♦ *A flowering vine covers the side of the building.*

flowerpot ['flaʊ ɚ pɑt] *n.* a pot designed to hold soil and a plant. ♦ *I filled the flowerpot with soil and added some fertilizer.* ♦ *The flowerpot broke when it fell off the window sill.*

flowery ['flaʊ ɚ i] **1.** *adj.* having a lot of flowers; like flowers. ♦ *Our bedroom carpet has a flowery design.* ♦ *The greenhouse has a flowery smell.* **2.** *adj.* fancy; expressive. (Figurative on ①.) ♦ *Your writing is too flowery for a business letter.* ♦ *The writer's flowery prose won a literary award.*

flowing ['flo ɪŋ] **1.** *adj.* [of a fluid] moving continuously, like water moving in a river. (Adv: *flowingly.*) ♦ *The flowing water carried our beach ball away.* ♦ *A flowing torrent of mud slid down the side of the mountain.* **2.** *adj.* [of a process] moving easily; moving smoothly. (Figurative on ①. Adv: *flowingly.*) ♦ *The graceful, flowing motion of the bird's wings guided it through the sky.* ♦ *I heard a lovely, flowing melody coming from the piano room.* **3.** *adj.* appearing to flow; appearing to fall smoothly as in ②. ♦ *Mary combed her flowing hair for ten minutes each day.* ♦ *The drapes hung in a flowing design across the large windows.*

flown ['flon] pp of **fly**.

flu ['flu] **the flu** *n.* influenza; a bad cold. (No plural form in this sense. Treated as singular.) ♦ *Bob caught the flu from someone at the office.* ♦ *My whole family has influenza. I thought I had a common cold, but I have the flu, just like the others.*

fluctuate ['flʌk tʃu et] *iv.* to change continually; [for a measurement] to vary. ♦ *The stock prices fluctuated wildly.* ♦ *The citizens' opinion of the president fluctuated from week to week.*

fluctuation [flək tʃu 'e ʃən] *n.* a movement up and down; a change; a variation. ♦ *The scientist could not explain the fluctuation in the data.* ♦ *The fluctuation in the price of oil affects the price of gasoline.*

flue ['flu] *n.* a pipe that carries smoke and hot gases away from a furnace or fireplace. (Compare with **flu**.) ♦ *I was covered with soot when I cleaned out our flue.* ♦ *Smoke billowed from the fireplace because we forgot to open the flue.*

fluency ['flu ən si] **1.** *n.* the ability to speak, read, write, or understand a language well. (No plural form in this sense.) ♦ *This exam is designed to test your fluency in English.* ♦ *Jane has native fluency in English and French.* **2.** *n.* the ability to express oneself well. (No plural form in this sense.) ♦ *I understood the difficult information because of the author's fluency with the subject.* ♦ *My professor's fluency in the subject needs improving.*

fluent ['flu ənt] *adj.* able to speak, read, write, or understand a language like a native speaker of that language. (Adv: *fluently.*) ♦ *I am a fluent speaker of English.* ♦ *This job requires you to be fluent in English and Spanish.*

fluff ['flʌf] **1.** *n.* soft, light fiber, such as wool, cotton, or hair. (No plural form in this sense.) ♦ *The cat pulled some of the fluff out of the cushions of the couch.* ♦ *I pulled the fluff from the dryer's lint trap.* **2.** *n.* a mass or tuft of ①. ♦ *There is a fluff of cotton inside the bottle of aspirin.* ♦ *The cushion is stuffed with fluffs of some sort of artificial fiber.* **3.** *n.* something that is not important and without much meaning. (Figurative on ①. No plural form in this sense.) ♦ *Bob objected when John dismissed his interests as fluff.* ♦ *I read complex books at school, but I read fluff on the bus.* **4. fluff (up)** *tv.* (+ *adv.*) to puff up a pillow; to make something fluffy. ♦ *Sue fluffed the cushions on the couch.* ♦ *John couldn't fall asleep, and he kept fluffing his pillow up.*

fluffy ['flʌf i] *adj.* soft, light, and airy. (Adv: *fluffily.* Comp: *fluffier;* sup: *fluffiest.*) ♦ *These pastries are light and fluffy.* ♦ *The baby's hair is fluffy when it has just been washed.*

fluid ['flu ɪd] **1.** *n.* a liquid or a gas; a substance that can flow. (No plural form in this sense.) ♦ *A mass of fluid acquires the shape of its container.* ♦ *The engineer measured the pressure of the fluid flowing in the pipe.* **2.** *n.* a liquid. ♦ *When you are sick, you should drink plenty of fluids.* ♦ *My head hurts because I have fluid in my ears.* **3.** *adj.* moving freely; flowing freely as with a liquid or a gas. (Adv: *fluidly.*) ♦ *The reptile's blood is not very fluid in cold weather.* ♦ *Sand in the deserts seem quite fluid when you walk through it.* **4.** *adj.* easily changed; unstable. (Figurative on ③. Adv: *fluidly.*) ♦ *The radio kept us informed of the current state of the fluid situation.* ♦ *Fluid assets can be easily converted to cash.*

fluke ['fluk] *n.* a lucky event; a fortunate event that happens by chance. ♦ *It was a total fluke that I found an inexpensive apartment in New York City.* ♦ *By some fluke, I was interviewed for the job by my father's old college roommate.*

flung ['flʌŋ] pt/pp of **fling**.

flunk ['flʌŋk] **1.** *tv.* to give a student a failing grade; [for a teacher] to make a judgment that prevents a student from going on to a higher grade. ♦ *If you miss three classes, I will flunk you.* ♦ *Ms. Smith flunked me in history, so I had to take the class again.* **2.** *tv.* [for a student] to fail to pass a test or to fail to qualify for promotion. ♦ *I flunked the test because I didn't study for it.* ♦ *I flunked second grade, so I didn't graduate from high school until I was 19.* **3.** *iv.* to fail to pass [a test]; to fail [to be promoted to the next academic level]. ♦ *Jane studied hard for the exam, but she still flunked.* ♦ *John was 19 when he graduated from high school because he had flunked when he was 8.*

fluorescent light ['flor ɛs ənt 'laɪt] **1.** *n.* a gas-filled glass tube that produces light when electricity is run through it. ♦ *My office uses hundreds of fluorescent lights.* ♦ *The classroom is lit by sixteen fluorescent lights.* **2.** *n.* light produced by ①. ♦ *The office was lit with harsh white fluorescent light.* ♦ *I prefer natural light to fluorescent light.*

fluoride ['flor aɪd] *n.* a chemical compound that has fluorine in it. (No plural form in this sense.) ♦ *Flouride is put in toothpaste and water to help prevent tooth decay.* ♦ *Too much fluoride can stain your teeth.*

fluorine ['flʊr in] *n.* a chemical element in the form of a poisonous, yellowish gas. (No plural form in this sense.) ♦ *Fluorine combines with other chemicals to make fluoride.* ♦ *Fluorine was discovered in 1771.*

flurry ['flɚ i] **1.** *n.* a rush of rain or snow. (No plural form in this sense.) ♦ *A flurry of rain drenched me as I ran to the bus stop.* ♦ *The snow flurry suddenly turned into a blizzard.* **2. flurries** *n.* flakes of snow; light snow. ♦ *The flurries that came into the area this morning will be over by noon.* ♦ *Flurries are expected in the northern part of the state.* **3.** *n.* a rush of something, such as excitement, activity, or emotion. (Figurative on ①. No plural form in this sense.) ♦ *John screamed at me in a flurry of anger.* ♦ *The children rushed around in a flurry of activity.*

flush ['flʌʃ] **1.** *n.* the reddening of skin, caused by heat, exertion, excitement, or embarrassment. (No plural form in this sense.) ♦ *A flush came to Anne's face as she jogged through the park.* ♦ *A flush on Bill's face indicated that he had found that his zipper was undone.* **2.** *n.* the act of releasing water to cleanse a toilet bowl. ♦ *Cleanser is released into the toilet bowl with each flush.* ♦ *The toilet is still running after the last flush.* **3.** *tv.* to clean something, especially a toilet bowl, with a stream of water. ♦ *Flush the toilet after you use it.* ♦ *The gardener flushed her boots with the garden hose to remove the mud.* **4. flush out** *tv.* + *adv.* to drive someone or some creature out of a certain place. ♦ *The hunters flushed the quail out from the bushes.* ♦ *The police flushed the criminals out of their den.* **5. flush with something** *idiom* even with something; sharing a surface with something. ♦ *The edge of the sink is flush with the counter.* ♦ *The wood flooring is flush with the carpet so people won't trip.* **6. flush with something** *idiom* having lots of something. ♦ *Our garden is flush with fresh vegetables.* ♦ *The committee was flush with helpful ideas.*

fluster ['flʌs tɚ] *tv.* to confuse someone or something; to agitate someone or something. ♦ *The complicated map flustered the tourist.* ♦ *My boss often flusters me with his confusing instructions.*

flustered ['flʌs tɚd] *adj.* confused; nervous; agitated. (Adv: *flusteredly.*) ♦ *The flustered tourist asked the police officer for directions.* ♦ *A long reading assignment overwhelmed the flustered student.*

flute ['flut] *n.* a musical instrument that is shaped like a long, thin pipe. ♦ *A flute is played by blowing over one hole near the end and covering and uncovering other holes along the pipe with one's fingers.* ♦ *I played the flute in my high school's marching band.*

flutist ['flut əst] *n.* someone who plays a flute; a flautist. ♦ *The flutists sit together behind the violinists.* ♦ *Mary is a flutist with the Boston Symphony.*

flutter ['flʌt ɚ] **1.** *iv.* [for birds, moths, butterflies, etc.] to fly though the air, moving their wings. ♦ *The bird fluttered through the air.* ♦ *The hummingbird bird fluttered close to my window.* **2. flutter around; flutter about** *iv.* + *adv.* to move back and forth quickly. (Figurative on ①.) ♦ *I fluttered around, trying to get things ready before the party.* ♦ *Don't flutter about. You're making me very nervous.* **3.** *iv.* to beat irregularly; to pulse irregularly. ♦ *My heart fluttered every time the handsome lifeguard walked by me.* ♦ *I told my doctor that my heart fluttered fairly often.* **4.** *n.* a quick but gentle movement, as with the movement of a bird's wings. ♦ *Jane complained about a little flutter in her heart when she drank coffee.* ♦ *The robin's wings gave a little flutter, but the bird settled back onto its perch.*

flux ['flʌks] **1.** *n.* a substance that helps hot solder flow onto metal. (No plural form in this sense.) ♦ *The plumber applied flux to the pipe joint before soldering it.* ♦ *I have to buy some more flux before I can finish attaching these wires.* **2. in flux; in a (constant) state of flux** *idiom* in constant change; changing. ♦ *I can't describe my job because it's in a constant state of flux.* ♦ *The price of gold is in flux.*

fly ['flaɪ] **1.** *tv., irreg.* to drive an airplane; to guide something that moves through the air. (Pt: **flew**; pp: **flown**.) ♦ *The pilot flew the plane to London.* ♦ *I flew the kite in the park.* **2.** *tv., irreg.* to raise or otherwise display a flag. ♦ *I fly the flag on every Independence Day.* ♦ *All the ships in the harbor are flying the flags of different nations.* **3.** *iv., irreg.* to move through the air; to move in the air. ♦ *The plane flew to London.* ♦ *The bird flew from its nest to the river.* **4.** *iv., irreg.* to travel by airplane. ♦ *I flew to London on business.* ♦ *Max prefers to fly except on short trips.* **5.** *iv., irreg.* [for time] to pass quickly. (Figurative on ③.) ♦ *Time flies when you're having fun.* ♦ *I was so busy at work that the time flew by.* **6.** *n.* a small insect; a bug; a mosquito. ♦ *The hungry flies at the picnic were unbearable.* ♦ *I swatted the fly sitting on the table.* **7.** *n.* a fishing lure that is made in imitation of ⑥. ♦ *My uncle and I used flies to fish in the stream behind his house.* ♦ *For years, my uncle has made his own flies.* **8.** *n.* the zipper in the front of someone's pants; the flap of material that covers a zipper in trousers. ♦ *Hey, Tom! Your fly is unzipped!* ♦ *Bob's shirt became caught in his fly when he zipped up his pants.* **9.** See **fly ball**.

fly ball AND **fly** ['flaɪ 'bɑl] *n.* a baseball that is struck so that it goes up into the air, rather than bouncing along the ground. ♦ *The last batter hit a fly ball that went out of the stadium.* ♦ *The pitcher caught the fly and made the final out of the inning.*

fly-by-night ['flaɪ baɪ naɪt] *adj.* not trustworthy; not responsible; likely to run away from one's duty. ♦ *I'd rather pay more money and rent from a well-known company than go to a fly-by-night car rental firm.* ♦ *This new company is not very reputable. I heard it was a fly-by-night operation.*

flyer ['flaɪ ɚ] See flier.

flying ['flaɪ ɪŋ] **1.** *n.* moving through the air in flight. (No plural form in this sense.) ♦ *Flying is a wonderful hobby if you can afford to buy or rent a plane.* ♦ *Dave loves flying and goes on several trips each month.* **2.** *adj.* <the adj. use of ①.> ♦ *I shot the flying bird with an arrow.* ♦ *Near the airport, the sky was filled with flying airplanes.*

flyleaf ['flaɪ lif] *n., irreg.* a blank page at the front or back of a book. (Pl: **flyleaves.**) ♦ *I made some notes on the flyleaf of my algebra book.* ♦ *Mary always writes her name on the flyleaves of her books.*

flyleaves ['flaɪ 'livz] pl of **flyleaf.**

flypaper ['flaɪ pe pɚ] *n.* paper that is covered with a sticky substance, which attracts and traps flies. (No plural form in this sense.) ♦ *A strip of flypaper hung from the light bulb in the kitchen.* ♦ *The flypaper was covered with dozens of bugs.*

foal ['fol] *n.* a young horse. ♦ *A male foal is called a colt and a female foal is called a filly.* ♦ *The young foal walked on wobbly legs towards the mare.*

foam ['fom] **1.** *n.* a collection of small bubbles; froth. (No plural form in this sense.) ♦ *The polluted stream was covered with chunks of foam.* ♦ *The dirty dishes sat in the sink under the soapy foam.* **2.** *iv.* [for foam] to form on the surface of a liquid or around the mouth. ♦ *The rabid dog foamed at the mouth.* ♦ *The soft drink foamed as I poured it into the glass.*

foamy ['fom i] *adj.* having froth or a mass of tiny bubbles. (Adv: *foamily.* Comp: *foamier;* sup: *foamiest.*) ♦ *I love foamy drinks made with soda pop and ice cream.* ♦ *Inside the candy was a foamy marshmallow layer.*

foci ['fo saɪ] a pl of **focus.**

focus ['fok əs] **1.** *n., irreg.* the position or setting of a lens that provides the clearest image. (No plural form in this sense.) ♦ *Please adjust the focus before I look through the telescope.* ♦ *The focus is not quite perfect.* **2.** *n., irreg.* the center of attention; the center of interest. (Figurative on ①. Pl: *focuses* or **foci.**) ♦ *Jimmy always wants to be the focus of attention.* ♦ *The focus of the investigation centered on the missing money.* **3. focus on** *iv.* + *prep. phr.* [for a lens] to cause light rays or lines of sight to converge on a particular point. ♦ *My eyes focused on the candle.* ♦ *I turned the knob to get the telescope to focus on the moon.* **4.** *tv.* to adjust a lens, or the eyes, so that the image that passes through them is sharp and clear. ♦ *The photographer focused the lens and then took the picture.* ♦ *I focused my eyes on the dark stain on the wall.* **5. focus on** *tv.* + *prep. phr.* to concentrate one's attention on something. (Figurative on ③.) ♦ *We will focus our attention on 19th-century American history in this course.* ♦ *Every night, I focus my thoughts on the problems of the day.*

fodder ['fɑd ɚ] **1.** *n.* food for farm animals. (No plural form in this sense.) ♦ *The farmer put the fodder in the pigs' trough.* ♦ *The farmer grew corn for fodder.* **2.** *n.* events or subject to be used by writers and performers. (Figurative on ①. No plural form in this sense.) ♦ *The scandal provided weeks of fodder for the tabloid newspapers.* ♦ *The president's failings were perfect fodder for comedians.*

foe ['fo] *n.* the enemy in general; individual enemies. ♦ *The soldiers fought with the foe on the battlefield.* ♦ *The guard asked if the traveler was friend or foe.*

fog ['fɔg] **1.** *n.* water vapor suspended in the air; a heavy mist. (No plural form in this sense.) ♦ *The airport was closed because of the heavy fog.* ♦ *The thick morning fog slowly dispersed.* **2. fog up** *tv.* + *adv.* to make something, especially glass, partially opaque with water vapor. ♦ *The moist air fogged up my glasses.* ♦ *The car windows were fogged up, so I turned the fan to high.*

fogged in ['fɔgd 'ɪn] *adj.* covered in or obscured with fog. (Not prenominal.) ♦ *The coastal areas were fogged in all morning.* ♦ *I had to land in Newark because LaGuardia Airport was fogged in.*

foggy ['fɔg i] **1.** *adj.* covered with fog. (Adv: *foggily.* Comp: *foggier;* sup: *foggiest.*) ♦ *I arrived in Scotland on a very foggy day.* ♦ *When I landed in Seattle, it was very foggy.* **2.** *adj.* confusing; unclear. (Figurative on ①. Adv: *foggily.* Comp: *foggier;* sup: *foggiest.*) ♦ *Your concept seems foggy to me. Could you explain it again?* ♦ *My recollection of the accident is rather foggy.*

foghorn ['fɔg horn] *n.* a noise-making device that ships use in the fog to warn other ships of their presence. ♦ *The ship sounded its foghorn as it sailed through the fog.* ♦ *Walking along the shore, I could hear a distant foghorn.*

foible ['foɪ bəl] *n.* a weakness; a small personal fault or quirk. ♦ *All humans have foibles that they would not like other people to know about.* ♦ *None of Sue's foibles are large enough to annoy me.*

foil ['foɪl] **1.** *n.* a thin sword, used in the sport of fencing, with a protective knob on the end. ♦ *The fencing team bought new foils at the start of the season.* ♦ *My opponent placed the tip of his foil against my shoulder.* **2.** *n.* a very thin, light sheet of metal, usually aluminum, used to wrap food or as a decoration. (No plural form in this sense.) ♦ *I wrapped the leftover cheese in foil and put it in the refrigerator.* ♦ *Each stick of chewing gum is wrapped in a separate piece of foil.* **3.** *tv.* to spoil someone's plans; to prevent something from happening. ♦ *My parents foiled my plans to go the party by not allowing me to use their car.* ♦ *The bank teller foiled the robbery by tricking the robber.*

foist ['foɪst] **foist something (off) on someone** *idiom* to force someone to take something that they don't want. ♦ *Bill tried to foist the task of washing dishes off on his sister.* ♦ *The city council foisted the new garbage dump on the poorest neighborhood in the city.*

fold ['fold] **1.** *tv.* to bend something so that part of it lies on top of the rest of it; to double something over onto itself. ♦ *Anne folded the map neatly and put it in her purse.* ♦ *I took the laundry from the dryer and then folded it.* **2.** *iv.* [for a business] to fail. ♦ *Many small downtown stores folded after the new mall opened.* ♦ *After 75 years of publishing, the local newspaper folded.* **3.** *n.* a place where sheep are kept; a sheep pen. ♦ *The shepherd herded the sheep back to their fold.* ♦ *A wolf crept into the fold and killed a sheep.* **4.** *n.* a congregation; the worshipers of a church. ♦ *How many worshipers do you have in your fold?* ♦ *The minister preached to his fold about sin.* **5. fold one's arms** *tv.* to cross one's arms and bring them close to one's body. ♦ *Mary lay down and folded her arms across her chest.* ♦ *Jane stood in the doorway, folded her arms, and refused to let me leave.*

folded ['fol dɪd] *adj.* bent back upon itself; creased; doubled over. ♦ *Please write your name on a folded sheet of paper.* ♦ *I put the folded shirts in my dresser.*

folder ['fol dɚ] *n.* a holder made of heavy paper used for filing, organizing, or storing papers. ♦ *At the end of class, I placed my notes in my folder.* ♦ *The personnel manager put Mary's review in her folder.*

folding ['fol dɪŋ] *adj.* able to be folded and made more compact. ♦ *The janitor set up folding chairs in the cafeteria for the meeting.* ♦ *We have a folding bed for when guests come to visit.*

foliage ['fo li ɪdʒ] *n.* leaves. (No plural form in this sense.) ♦ *In the fall, the foliage turns pretty shades of red and yellow.* ♦ *The photographer took pictures of the forest's lush foliage.*

folk ['fok] **1.** *n.* a group of people. (No plural form in this sense. Treated as plural.) ♦ *The good folk of the town are gathered in the church to hear the minister speak.* ♦ *The thief pleaded to the village folk for mercy.* **2. folks** *n.* people in general. (Treated as plural.) ♦ *Folks around this town don't like being told what to do.* ♦ *The president talked to folks on the street to get their opinions.* **3. someone's folks** *n.* relatives, especially one's own parents. (Treated as plural.) ♦ *I asked my folks if I could borrow the car.* ♦ *What do your folks do for a living?* **4.** *adj.* of or about the common people; traditional. ♦ *The campers sat around the campfire and sang folk songs.* ♦ *None of my doctors were helping me, so I visited a woman who practiced folk medicine.*

folklore ['fok lor] *n.* traditions, stories, customs, and beliefs that are passed down from generation to generation within a culture. (No plural form in this sense.) ♦ *The anthropologist studied the folklore of southwestern American Indians.* ♦ *Many of our fairy tales come from English folklore.*

folk song ['fok sɔŋ] *n.* a song that is in the traditional style of a country or group of people. ♦ *After the game, we gathered under the tree and sang folk songs.* ♦ *At the dance, the band played German folk songs.*

folksy ['fok si] *adj.* friendly; sociable. (Comp: *folksier;* sup: *folksiest.*) ♦ *Most of the people in my hometown are folksy and friendly.* ♦ *I chatted with the folksy barber as he cut my hair.*

follow ['fɑl o] **1.** *tv.* to come after someone or something in space or time. ♦ *Summer follows spring.* ♦ *The number 5 follows 4.* **2.** *tv.* to pursue someone or something; to go after someone or something. ♦ *The police secretly followed the bank robbers back to their hideout.* ♦ *The fox followed its prey through the woods.* **3.** *tv.* to obey a set of rules or instructions. ♦ *If you don't follow the rules, you'll be punished.* ♦ *This cake tastes bad because I didn't follow the recipe closely.* **4.** *tv.* to understand a person is who leading one through an explanation; to understand an explanation as someone explains it. ♦ *Sorry, but I don't follow you. Can you explain it again?* ♦ *I followed you up until the last part of the problem.* **5.** *tv.* to study or pay attention to or have a continuing interest in something, such as a sport. ♦ *John follows baseball and knows everything about all the teams.* ♦ *I don't follow the movies, but I did see a good one last night.* **6.** *iv.* [for something] to happen as a logical or typical result of something. ♦ *It follows that if you jump up, you have to come down.* ♦ *It just follows that if you study, you should do better in class.* **7. follow up (on something)** *idiom* to check (on something) and do what needs to be done. ♦ *I will follow up on this matter and make sure it is settled.* ♦ *There is a problem with the bank account. Will you please follow up?*

follower ['fɑl o ɚ] *n.* someone who follows someone or something; someone who obeys the teachings of someone. ♦ *The charismatic politician had millions of followers.* ♦ *The rock star's followers worshiped her.*

following ['fɑl o ɪŋ] **1.** *n.* a group of supporters. (No plural form in this sense.) ♦ *The popular politician amassed quite a following in six months.* ♦ *The leader spoke to his following by means of a radio broadcast.* **2.** *n.* the persons or things that are about to be listed or described. (No plural form in this sense.) ♦ *If you have been exposed to any of the following, please see the company nurse.* ♦ *If your name is among the following, please go to Room 101.* **3.** *adj.* next; coming after; coming next; subsequent. ♦ *In the following year, I plan to travel to Asia.* ♦ *I ate way too much, and I felt sort of sick on the following day.*

follow-up ['fɑl o əp] **1.** *n.* a second or other action that is done after an initial action. ♦ *Tom is good at making initial contacts, but he needs to work on his follow-up.* ♦ *This isn't a new story—it's just a follow-up to the one that appeared in last week's newspaper.* **2.** *adj.* [of something] done after an initial action. ♦ *I made a follow-up phone call the week after I faxed my proposal.* ♦ *Sue sent Bob a follow-up note after their date.*

folly ['fɑl i] **1.** *n.* stupid behavior; foolishness. (No plural form in this sense.) ♦ *Why are we standing in line in the cold? This is folly!* ♦ *Spend less time with folly and more time with serious matters.* **2.** *n.* a silly thing to do. ♦ *Because of my coworker's folly, I had to work late to fix the problem.* ♦ *The senator denounced the plan as a great folly.*

foment [fo 'mɛnt] *tv.* to cause trouble; to promote revolution; to excite a group of angry people. ♦ *The demonstrators fomented a riot against the police.* ♦ *The peasants fomented a revolution in response to the king's harsh policies.*

fond ['fɑnd] **1.** *adj.* loving; tender. (Adv: *fondly.* Comp: *fonder;* sup: *fondest.*) ♦ *I bid my parents a fond farewell as I left for the army.* ♦ *I gave my aunt a fond embrace as I entered her house.* **2. fond of** *adj.* + *prep. phr.* liking someone or something; having a desire for someone or something. (Comp: *fonder;* sup: *fondest.*) ♦ *I think Anne is very fond of chocolate. She eats it all the time.* ♦ *John is fond of Mary, so he sent her some flowers.*

fondle ['fɑn dəl] **1.** *tv.* to caress a part of an intimate friend in a loving way. ♦ *My boyfriend fondled my hair as we watched television.* ♦ *Jane fondled my arm as we stood in line.* **2.** *tv.* to handle a stranger sexually or intimately. ♦ *The senator was accused of fondling his aides.* ♦ *I slapped the stranger who tried to fondle me on the bus.*

fondness ['fɑnd nəs] *n.* a liking for someone or something; a desire for someone or something; a feeling of love for someone or something. (No plural form in this sense.) ♦ *John's fondness for Jane caused him to buy her flowers every week.* ♦ *I have a fondness for cheese pizza.*

fondue [fɑn 'du] *n.* a dish of melted cheese, caramel, chocolate, etc., that bread, crackers, or other food is dipped into. (From French. No plural form in this sense.) ♦ *I dipped a piece of fruit into the chocolate fondue.* ♦ *We ate cheese fondue for a snack.*

font ['fɑnt] *n.* a complete set of printing type in a particular size and style. ♦ *I printed my letter in a small font so that I would use less paper.* ♦ *This sentence is printed in an italic font.*

food ['fud] **1.** *n.* something that is eaten by animals and plants for nourishment. (No plural form in this sense.) ♦ *What kind of food do you want to eat tonight?* ♦ *I must give my dog some food and water each day.* **2.** *n.* a kind or type of ①. ♦ *I avoid eating fatty foods such as bacon and fried chicken.* ♦ *This grocery store sells all my favorite foods.* **3. food for thought** *idiom* something for someone to think about. (No plural form in this sense. Figurative on ①.) ♦ *Your essay has provided me with some interesting food for thought.* ♦ *My adviser gave me some food for thought about job opportunities.*

foodstuff ['fud stəf] *n.* something that can be eaten; something that is used as food. (Sometimes plural with the same meaning.) ♦ *We store emergency supplies and basic foodstuffs in our car.* ♦ *During the flood, the citizens of the town suffered from a lack of foodstuffs.*

fool ['ful] **1.** *n.* an idiot; a stupid person; someone who has no common sense. ♦ *You'd be a fool to quit your job now.* ♦ *Stop acting like a fool, or I'll send you to your room.* **2.** *tv.* to trick someone; to play a joke on someone. ♦ *We fooled Sue into thinking no one was home by parking around the block.* ♦ *I fooled Bill by putting sugar in the salt shaker.* **3. fool around** *iv.* + *adv.* to play around. ♦ *Stop fooling around and do your homework!* ♦ *Bob accidentally broke a vase when we were fooling around in the house.* **4. fools rush in (where angels fear to tread)** *idiom* people with little experience or knowledge often get involved in difficult or delicate situations that wiser people would avoid. ♦ *I wouldn't ask Lisa about her divorce, but Mary did. Fools rush in, as they say.* ♦ *Only the newest member of the committee questioned the chairman's decision. Fools rush in where angels fear to tread.* **5. nobody's fool** *idiom* a sensible and wise person who is not easily deceived. ♦ *Mary is nobody's fool. She watches out for people who might try to cheat her.* ♦ *Anne looks as though she's not very bright, but she's nobody's fool.* **6. on a fool's errand** *idiom* involved in a useless journey or task. ♦ *Bill went for an interview, but he was on a fool's errand. The job had already been filled.* ♦ *I was sent on a fool's errand to buy some flowers. I knew the shop would be closed by then.*

foolhardy ['ful hɑr di] *adj.* rash; acting without thinking about the risks. (Adv: *foolhardily.*) ♦ *The foolhardy students stayed up all night before the test.* ♦ *The foolhardy criminal jumped from the moving train.*

foolish ['ful ɪʃ] *adj.* silly; lacking common sense; stupid; ridiculous. (Adv: *foolishly.*) ♦ *Yelling at a police officer is a foolish thing to do.* ♦ *The foolish student tried to cheat while the teacher was watching.*

foolishness ['ful ɪʃ nəs] **1.** *n.* stupidity; the lack of common sense. (No plural form in this sense.) ♦ *Your foolishness is responsible for the failure of your project.* ♦ *The construction worker's foolishness resulted in the collapse of a wall.* **2.** *n.* silliness. (No plural form in this sense.) ♦ *My brother's foolishness annoys me.* ♦ *Stop this foolishness at once and behave seriously!*

foolproof ['ful pruf] *adj.* not capable of failing; so simple that a fool could use it without problems. ♦ *This computer program is so foolproof, even a six-year-old could use it.* ♦ *I had a foolproof plan to keep Mary away while we prepared for her surprise party.*

foot ['fʊt] **1.** *n., irreg.* the end of a leg; the part of a human or animal body that touches the ground and supports the body. (Pl: **feet.**) ♦ *After I walked all day, my feet hurt.* ♦ *I removed the thorn from my dog's foot.* **2.** *n.* the bottom or lower end of a bed, mountain, cliff, ladder, hill, page, goblet, etc. (No plural form in this sense.) ♦ *I placed the blankets at the foot of the bed.* ♦ *Mary stood at the foot of the mountain.* **3.** *n., irreg.* a unit of measurement equal to 12 inches or just over 30 centimeters. ♦ *A football field is 300 feet long.* ♦ *The first step is one foot high.* **4. on foot** *phr.* [running or walking] using the feet. ♦ *My car won't work so I have to travel on foot.* ♦ *We go everywhere on foot.* **5. foot the bill (for something)** *idiom* to pay for something; to pay for a bill. ♦ *My boss took me out for lunch and the company footed the bill.* ♦ *You paid for dinner last time. Let me foot the bill for lunch.* **6. drag one's feet** *idiom* to act very slowly, often deliberately. ♦ *The government is dragging its feet on this matter because there is not enough money.* ♦ *If the people in the planning department hadn't dragged their feet, the building would have been built by now.* **7. find one's feet** *idiom* to become used to a new situation or experience. ♦ *She was lonely when she first left home, but she is finding her feet now.* ♦ *It takes time to learn the office routine, but you will gradually find your feet.* **8. get cold feet, have cold feet** *idiom* to become timid or frightened; to have one's feet seem to freeze with fear. ♦ *I usually get cold feet when I have to speak in public.* ♦ *John got cold feet and wouldn't run in the race.* **9. get one's feet on the ground, have one's feet on the ground** *idiom* to get firmly established or reestablished. ♦ *He's new at the job, but soon he'll get his feet on the ground.* ♦ *Her productivity will improve after she gets her feet on the ground again.* **10. get one's feet wet** *idiom* to begin something; to have one's first experience of something. ♦ *Of course he can't do the job right. He's hardly got his feet wet yet.* ♦ *I'm looking forward to learning to drive. I can't wait to get behind the steering wheel and get my feet wet.* **11. get one's foot in the door** *idiom* to achieve a favorable position (for further action); to take the first step in a process. ♦ *I think I could get the job if I could only get my foot in the door.* ♦ *I have a better chance now that I have my foot in the door.* **12. get to one's feet** *idiom* to stand up. ♦ *On a signal from the director, the singers got to their feet.* ♦ *I was so weak, I could hardly get to my feet.* **13. have the shoe on the other foot** *idiom* to experience the opposite situation (from a previous situation). ♦ *I used to be a student, and now I'm the teacher. Now I have the shoe on the other foot.* ♦ *You were mean to me when you thought I was cheating. Now that I have caught you cheating, the shoe is on the other foot.* **14. put one's best foot forward** *idiom* to act or appear at one's best; to try to make a good impression. ♦ *When you apply for a job, you should always put your best foot forward.* ♦ *I try to put my best foot forward whenever I meet someone for the first time.* **15. put one's foot in one's mouth** *idiom* to say something that one regrets; to say something stupid, insulting, or hurtful. ♦ *When I told Anne that her hair was more beautiful than I had ever seen it, I really put my foot in my mouth. It was a wig.* ♦ *I put my foot in my mouth by telling John's secret.*

16. set foot somewhere *idiom* to go or enter somewhere. ♦ *If I were you, I wouldn't set foot in that town.* ♦ *I wouldn't set foot in her house! Not after the way she spoke to me.* **17. throw oneself at someone's feet** *idiom* to bow down humbly at someone's feet. ♦ *Do I have to throw myself at your feet to convince you that I'm sorry?* ♦ *I love you sincerely, Jane. I throw myself at your feet.*

footage ['fʊt ɪdʒ] *n.* a length of film or videotape; a film or video clip. (No plural form in this sense.) ♦ *The history teacher showed the class some interesting footage from World War II.* ♦ *I saw some footage of the riot on the news.*

football ['fʊt bɔl] **1.** *n.* a sport played between two teams of eleven players each, on a field having a goal on each end, using ②. (No plural form in this sense. Compare with soccer.) ♦ *In football, each team tries to score points by crossing the goal line with the ball.* ♦ *Dave played football in college.* **2.** *n.* the leather, oval-shaped ball used in ①. ♦ *Jane and I went to the park and threw a football back and forth.* ♦ *Bill threw the football to the quarterback.* **3.** *adj.* <the adj. use of ①.> ♦ *Mary loves to go to football games.* ♦ *Our football team never wins.*

footbridge ['fʊt brɪdʒ] *n.* a bridge that can only be walked on. ♦ *We carefully crossed the wooden footbridge high above the river.* ♦ *At the next town, you can cross the river by footbridge or ferry.*

foothills ['fʊt hɪlz] *n.* small hills at the base of a larger mountain. ♦ *After a day of driving through the plains, we approached the foothills of the Rocky Mountains.* ♦ *The attendant at the gas station in the foothills warned us of avalanches further up the road.*

foothold ['fʊt hold] **1.** *n.* a space for one's foot that helps one climb up or down something. (Pl: *footholds.*) ♦ *Near the top of the mountain, the footholds barely supported my toes.* ♦ *I started to slip from the foothold, but my climbing partner helped me.* **2. get a foothold (somewhere)** *idiom* an initial position of support; a starting point. (Figurative on ①.) ♦ *It's difficult to get a foothold in the education market when schools are laying off teachers.* ♦ *Max's father helped him get a foothold in the textile industry.*

footing ['fʊt ɪŋ] **1.** *n.* a place that will allow one's feet to be firmly placed so that one is balanced. (No plural form in this sense.) ♦ *I fell down a few steps, but regained my footing by grabbing the railing.* ♦ *The icy slope was too slippery to get a good footing.* **2.** *n.* a relationship; the relationship between two people or groups of people. (No plural form in this sense.) ♦ *Our principal is on a good footing with the students.* ♦ *The footing between the guards and the prisoners was very tense.* **3.** *n.* the concrete base of a foundation that supports the weight of the foundation wall evenly. (Sometimes plural with the same meaning.) ♦ *We'll pour the footing today if it stops raining by noon.* ♦ *These footings need to be reinforced with iron rods.*

footlight ['fʊt laɪt] *n.* one of a number of lights at the front edge of a stage in a theater. ♦ *The lighting designer aimed the footlights up toward the center of the stage.* ♦ *At the end of the scene, the actor was lit only from below by the footlights.*

footlocker ['fʊt lɑk ɚ] *n.* a small chest, especially one used by a soldier; a chest kept at the foot of the bed. ♦ *The soldier kept letters from home in his footlocker.* ♦ *I placed my diary in my footlocker and went to bed.*

footloose ['fʊt lus] **1.** *adj.* free to do as one pleases; not restrained; not tied to anyone or anything. ♦ *I don't have the chance to be footloose because I have to work 80 hours each week.* ♦ *Ever since Dave won the lottery, he's been footloose.* **2. footloose and fancy-free** *idiom* without responsibilities or commitments. ♦ *All the rest of the men have wives, but John is footloose and fancy-free.* ♦ *Mary never stays long in any job. She likes being footloose and fancy-free.*

footnote ['fʊt not] **1.** *n.* a note at the bottom of a page that clarifies or provides a source for something that appears higher on the page. ♦ *The footnote provided the source of the quote.* ♦ *Footnotes are usually printed in a smaller type than the main text.* **2.** *tv.* to provide ① for a piece of information. ♦ *The professor told me to footnote the direct quotes in my paper.* ♦ *I footnoted the foreign phrase and provided an English translation.*

footpath ['fʊt pæθ] *n.* a path that is made for walking. ♦ *I took the footpath through the forest to save time.* ♦ *Bicycles are not allowed on the footpath.*

footprint ['fʊt prɪnt] **1.** *n.* the mark made by the pressure of a foot in soft earth or snow. ♦ *Whose footprints do I see in the snow?* ♦ *The detective examined the footprint underneath the kitchen window.* **2.** *n.* the mark made by tracking dirt from a muddy area onto a clean floor. ♦ *Whose muddy footprints are on the carpet?* ♦ *I see someone's footprints on the kitchen floor.*

footrace ['fʊt res] *n.* a race done by people running. ♦ *I can beat you in a footrace anytime.* ♦ *We held quite a footrace to the bus stop, and we all ended up panting.*

footstep ['fʊt stɛp] **1.** *n.* a step made while walking. ♦ *I took two footsteps and stopped to listen.* ♦ *Don't come another footstep closer, or I'll scream.* **2.** *n.* the sound made by a person's step. ♦ *I heard my roommate's footsteps on the stairs.* ♦ *I turned around quickly when I heard footsteps behind me.*

footstool ['fʊt stul] *n.* a small stool, placed in front of a chair, on which one's feet can be rested. ♦ *I propped my feet up on the footstool and rested.* ♦ *I want to buy a footstool that will match this chair.*

footwear ['fʊt wer] *n.* shoes, socks, slippers, boots, and sandals. (No plural form in this sense.) ♦ *All footwear in the department store was on sale.* ♦ *Proper footwear is important when you are climbing mountains.*

footwork ['fʊt wɚk] *n.* the way one moves one's feet, especially in dancing, sports, etc. (No plural form in this sense.) ♦ *Despite our quarterback's impressive footwork, we still lost the game.* ♦ *The ice skater's fancy footwork impressed the judges.*

for [for] **1.** *prep.* meant to be used by someone or something; meant to belong to someone; meant to be given to someone. (Indicates who or what will benefit.) ♦ *I bought this present for you.* ♦ *I cooked dinner for Mary.* **2.** *prep.* meant to be used in doing something. ♦ *This soap is for cleaning your hands.* ♦ *Ink pens are used for writing.* **3.** *prep.* instead of someone or something; in place of someone or something. ♦ *I'm accepting this award for Bob, who can't be here today.* ♦ *I sat in for Anne when she was on vacation.* **4.** *prep.* in favor of someone or something; in support of someone or something; in defense of someone or something. ♦ *We are for a reduction in the size of* *the army.* ♦ *The president is for the new tax cut.* **5.** *prep.* in search of someone or something. (Indicates the target of the search.) ♦ *I spent an hour looking for a sharp knife.* ♦ *The doctor checked my body for cancerous growths.* **6.** *prep.* in a certain amount. ♦ *This one sells for a dollar.* ♦ *I will sell it to you for thirty dollars.* **7.** *prep.* during something; throughout a period of time. ♦ *I could not stay for the whole concert.* ♦ *I will be your substitute teacher for the next week.* **8.** *conj.* since; because; as. (Formal.) ♦ *Mary slept a long time, for she was exhausted.* ♦ *Bill tended to overeat, for he was a glutton.*

forage ['for ɪdʒ] **1.** *n.* animal food; fodder. (No plural form in this sense.) ♦ *We stored forage for the cattle in the silo.* ♦ *The farmer poured the forage into the trough.* **2.** *iv.* [for animals with hooves] to search for food. ♦ *The deer foraged in the woods for food.* ♦ *The starving dog foraged for food.* **3.** *iv.* to search for something. (Figurative on ②.) ♦ *I foraged through the refrigerator for something to eat.* ♦ *The detective foraged in the dark alley for evidence.*

forbade AND **forbad** [for 'bed, for 'bæd] pt of forbid.

forbear [for 'bɛr] **1.** *iv., irreg.* to hold back from doing something; to restrain from doing something. (Formal. Pt: forbore; pp: forborne.) ♦ *We encouraged David to forbear and try to control his temper.* ♦ *The remark was rude and I forbore responding.* **2.** See forebear.

forbid [for 'bɪd] **1.** *tv., irreg.* to prohibit something. (Pt: forbad or forbade; pp: forbidden.) ♦ *The principal forbade running in the hallways.* ♦ *Chewing gum in class was forbidden.* **2.** *tv.* to order someone not to do something. ♦ *I forbid you to leave your room until I say so.* ♦ *Company rules forbid me to smoke in the factory.*

forbidden [for 'bɪd n] *adj.* prohibited; banned; not allowed. ♦ *A snake encouraged Eve to eat the forbidden fruit.* ♦ *Military police kept the soldiers away from the forbidden area.*

forbore [for 'bor] pt of forbear.

forborne [for 'born] pp of forbear.

force ['fors] **1.** *n.* power; physical strength. (No plural form in this sense.) ♦ *The barn was knocked over by the force of the wind.* ♦ *The force of the collision destroyed both cars.* **2.** *n.* military strength. (No plural form in this sense.) ♦ *The soldiers took the castle by force.* ♦ *The army used force to overthrow the government.* **3.** *n.* an influence; someone or something that is an influence or inspiration. ♦ *The computer is a powerful force in modern business.* ♦ *My English professor was an inspiring force in my life.* **4.** *n.* a group of soldiers, police officers, etc. ♦ *The police force threatened to go on strike if their contract wasn't renewed.* ♦ *A well-armed force was called in to stop the riot.* **5.** *tv.* to push or move something through ①. ♦ *Bill tried to force the door open.* ♦ *Sue forced her way into the crowded room.* **6.** *tv.* to make someone do something by the use of ①. ♦ *No one can force me to eat food I don't like.* ♦ *The police forced us to leave the building.* **7. force someone's hand** *idiom* to force a person to reveal plans, strategies, or secrets. ♦ *We didn't know what she was doing until Tom forced her hand.* ♦ *We couldn't plan our game until we forced the other team's hand in the last play.*

forced ['forst] *adj.* strained; not natural; insincere. ♦ *Anne's compliments were polite, but seemed forced.* ♦ *My forced smile betrayed my true emotions.*

force-fed ['fors 'fɛd] pt/pp of force-feed.

force-feed ['fors 'fid] *tv., irreg.* to feed someone or something by force. (Pt/pp: force-fed.) ♦ *The zookeeper had to force-feed the giant snake.* ♦ *Dave angrily force-fed peas to his obstinate child.*

forceful ['fors fʊl] *adj.* full of force; powerful; full of energy; strong. (Adv: *forcefully.*) ♦ *A forceful wind knocked over the old tree.* ♦ *The building was destroyed by a forceful explosion.*

forceps ['for səps] *n.* a medical tool, similar to tongs, used to grasp things. (Treated as plural. Number is express with *pair(s) of forceps.*) ♦ *The doctor used forceps to remove the bullet.* ♦ *The nurse handed the sterile forceps to the doctor.*

forcible ['for sə bəl] *adj.* done by force; using force to do something. (Adv: *forcibly.*) ♦ *Forcible entry into the house was indicated by the broken door.* ♦ *The judge ruled in favor of the forcible removal of the squatters.*

forearm 1. ['for ɑrm] *n.* the lower part of the arm, between the elbow and the wrist. ♦ *The children grabbed onto my forearm, begging me not to leave.* ♦ *As I reached to pet the dog, it bit my forearm.* **2. forearm (against)** [for 'ɑrm...] *tv.* (+ *prep. phr.*) to prepare oneself for something before it happens. (Takes a reflexive object.) ♦ *We forearmed ourselves against any possible attack.* ♦ *The militia forearmed itself against an attack by the government.*

forebear AND **forbear** ['for ber] *n.* an ancestor. (Usually plural.) ♦ *My forebears moved to America in the 19th century from Ireland.* ♦ *All of my forebears were farmers.*

foreboding [for 'bod ɪŋ] **1.** *n.* a feeling that something bad is going to happen. (No plural form in this sense.) ♦ *There was a gloomy feeling of foreboding just before the war started.* ♦ *I was almost overcome with anxiety and foreboding before the test.* **2.** *n.* a warning. ♦ *I felt urgent forebodings to switch airplane flights at the last minute.* ♦ *The constant forebodings of death and destruction from my grandfather made me cancel my parachute jump.* **3.** *adj.* warning; ominous. (Adv: *forebodingly.*) ♦ *The foreboding clouds indicated that it would rain soon.* ♦ *In movies, foreboding music is often heard before disaster strikes.*

forecast ['for kæst] **1.** *n.* a statement of what will happen in the future. ♦ *My forecast of who would win was very accurate.* ♦ *The forecast for the stock market predicts a sharp drop over the next few weeks.* **2. (weather) forecast** *n.* a description of what the weather will be like during the next day or week. ♦ *The weather forecast predicted it would rain tomorrow.* ♦ *I listened to the forecast to see if I should take my umbrella to work.* **3.** *tv., irreg.* to say what something is going to be like. (Pt/pp: *forecast* or *forecasted.*) ♦ *The economic report forecast a sharp drop in unemployment for the next year.* ♦ *The company treasurer forecast a modest rise in profits for the remainder of the year.* **4.** *tv., irreg.* to predict the weather or weather events. ♦ *The weatherman forecast snow for northern Wisconsin.* ♦ *Rain is forecast for the entire weekend.*

foreclose [for 'kloz] **foreclose on** *iv.* + *prep. phr.* to take away the right of a borrower to repay a loan and to take possession of the property that secured the loan. ♦ *The bank foreclosed on our house because we couldn't make the payments.* ♦ *The bank threatened to foreclose on the office building if the asbestos wasn't removed.*

foreclosure [for 'klo ʒɚ] *n.* taking away the right of a borrower to repay a loan and taking the property that secured the loan. (No plural form in this sense.) ♦ *The company avoided foreclosure on its office by declaring bankruptcy.* ♦ *The bank threatened me with foreclosure if I didn't pay my mortgage within a month.*

forefather ['for fɑ ðɚ] *n.* a male ancestor; an ancestor. (Usually plural.) ♦ *My forefathers came from China in the 19th century.* ♦ *Bob's forefathers were all farmers.*

forefinger ['for fɪŋ gɚ] *n.* the first finger; the finger next to the thumb. ♦ *The forefinger is also called the index finger.* ♦ *I cut my forefinger while slicing potatoes.*

forefront ['for frənt] **at the forefront (of something); in the forefront (of something)** *phr.* in the most important place; in the place of greatest activity. ♦ *I interviewed Max Brown, the director who is in the forefront of the movie industry.* ♦ *The university I go to is at the forefront of computer technology.*

foregoing ['for go ɪŋ] *adj.* [of speaking or writing that has been] previously written or spoken. ♦ *The foregoing paragraph explains it all.* ♦ *The foregoing statement does not express my personal opinion.*

foregone ['for gɔn] **foregone conclusion** *idiom* a conclusion already reached; an inevitable result. ♦ *That the company was moving to California was a foregone conclusion.* ♦ *That the mayor will win reelection is a foregone conclusion.*

foreground ['for graʊnd] *n.* the part of a picture or scene closest to the person looking at it. (No plural form in this sense.) ♦ *A tractor appeared in the foreground of the painting of the farm.* ♦ *Most of the photo is clear, except for the objects in the foreground, which are blurry.*

forehand ['for hænd] *n.* a tennis stroke made with the palm of the hand facing forward. ♦ *My coach told me to practice my forehand.* ♦ *I sent the ball back over the net with a powerful forehand.*

forehead ['for hɛd] *n.* the part of the face between the eyebrows and the hairline. ♦ *I wiped the sweat from my forehead.* ♦ *Mary's thick bangs completely cover her forehead.*

foreign ['for ɪn] **1.** *adj.* not native to one's country; of or about a country other than one's own. (Adv: *foreignly.*) ♦ *I own a foreign car.* ♦ *Do you speak any foreign languages?* **2.** *adj.* out of place; coming from the outside of something. (Adv: *foreignly.*) ♦ *Do not place any foreign matter on the sink.* ♦ *Do not flush foreign articles down the toilet.*

foreigner ['for ən ɚ] *n.* someone who comes from another country; someone who was born in another country. ♦ *I couldn't understand what the foreigner was trying to tell me.* ♦ *The foreigner asked the police officer for directions.*

foreman ['for mən] **1.** *n., irreg.* a supervisor; someone who is in charge of workers. (Pl: foremen.) ♦ *The foreman told her crew that it was time for lunch.* ♦ *My foreman docked my pay because I was an hour late.* **2.** *n., irreg.* the head of a jury; someone who represents the jury to the court. ♦ *The foreman delivered a verdict of not guilty.* ♦ *The judge asked the foreman for the verdict.*

foremen ['for mən] pl of foreman.

foremost ['for most] **1.** *adj.* first; most important. ♦ *My foremost concern is your welfare.* ♦ *It is of foremost importance that you arrive on time.* **2.** *adv.* first; most importantly. ♦ *First and foremost, I'd like to thank John for his help.* ♦ *Jane stands foremost among her peers in the field of engineering.*

forenoon ['for nun] *n.* the time of day before noon; the late morning. ♦ *I arrived at work in the late forenoon because my alarm clock was broken.* ♦ *I finished my work during the forenoon so I could take the afternoon off.*

forensic [fə 'rɛn sɪk] **1.** *adj.* concerning the courts and the argumentation used in court. (Adv: *forensically* [...ɪk li].) ♦ *As a specialist in forensic medicine, the doctor was often called to testify in court.* ♦ *The lawyer, in a display of forensic skill, demolished the prosecutor's arguments.* **2. forensics** *n.* the art or skill of debate; debating; rhetoric. (Treated as singular.) ♦ *Forensics was my favorite activity in high school.* ♦ *My English teacher also coached us in forensics.*

forerunner ['for rən ɚ] *n.* a predecessor; someone or something that comes before someone or something more important or more developed. ♦ *The forerunner of the modern computer was extremely slow and large.* ♦ *The horse and buggy was the forerunner of the automobile.*

foresaw [for 'sɔ] pt of foresee.

foresee [for 'si] *tv., irreg.* to be aware of something before it happens; to envision that something will happen. (Pt: foresaw; pp: foreseen.) ♦ *The stockbrokers had foreseen the recession, so they were prepared when the economy soured.* ♦ *I foresaw that there would be trouble with my neighbors shortly after they moved in.*

foreseeable [for 'si ə bəl] *adj.* able to be predicted; able to be foreseen. (Adv: *foreseeably.*) ♦ *We don't plan to do any hiring in the foreseeable future.* ♦ *The ultimate results were not really foreseeable, but we prepared for them as best we could.*

foreseen [for 'sin] pp of foresee.

foreshadow [for 'ʃæd o] *tv.* [for a sign or omen] to indicate in advance that something is going to happen. ♦ *A sharp increase in bond prices foreshadowed a sharp drop in stock prices.* ♦ *Dark clouds foreshadow rain.*

foresight ['for sɑɪt] **1.** *n.* the ability to know or determine what will happen before it actually happens. (No plural form in this sense.) ♦ *Foresight and common sense could have prevented the accident.* ♦ *The treasurer had the foresight to sell the company stocks right before the market crashed.* **2.** *n.* the ability to think about the future carefully; the ability to plan ahead; the ability to anticipate anything that might go wrong and prepare for that beforehand. (No plural form in this sense.) ♦ *Anne's excellent foresight had made certain that the proposal contained all the necessary protective clauses.* ♦ *I can't believe you lacked the foresight to leave money in the bank for an emergency!*

foreskin ['for skɪn] *n.* a fold of skin that covers the end of the penis. ♦ *The foreskin is removed during circumcision.* ♦ *Every male child is born with a foreskin.*

forest ['for əst] *n.* a large area of land covered with trees. ♦ *A raging fire destroyed acres of forest.* ♦ *We own a cabin deep in a forest next to a lake.*

forestall [for 'stɔl] *tv.* to prevent something from happening; to delay or postpone something. ♦ *Bill forestalled a major crisis by taking care of small problems before they became serious.* ♦ *Financial problems were forestalled because the manager was alert.*

forestry ['for ɪs tri] *n.* the science of planting, protecting, and maintaining forests. (No plural form in this sense.) ♦ *The young ranger was a graduate of the Department of Forestry.* ♦ *Mary studied forestry because she loves the wilderness.*

foretaste ['for test] *n.* an experience of a small amount of something that is yet to come; a sample. ♦ *The excerpt in the magazine was a foretaste of the author's upcoming novel.* ♦ *The light shower was a foretaste of the impending heavy rains.*

foretell [for 'tɛl] *tv., irreg.* to predict something that is to happen in the future; to predict the future. (Pt/pp: foretold.) ♦ *A mysterious woman foretold that I was to marry a tall, handsome man.* ♦ *Thunder in the distance foretold the coming of a storm.*

forethought ['for θɔt] *n.* planning; planning for something before it happens; anticipation. (No plural form in this sense.) ♦ *Planning a large wedding requires careful forethought.* ♦ *Your weak presentation obviously lacked forethought.*

foretold [for 'told] pt/pp of foretell.

forever [for 'ɛv ɚ] *adv.* always; with no beginning and no end; throughout all time. ♦ *I promise to love you forever.* ♦ *The movie was so long, it seemed to go on forever.*

forewarn [for 'worn] *tv.* to warn someone about something ahead of time; to warn someone about something before it happens. ♦ *A spy forewarned the general of the imminent attack.* ♦ *The secretary forewarned me that I was going to be transferred to Texas.*

forewoman ['for wʊm ən] **1.** *n., irreg.* a female supervisor; a woman who is in charge of workers. (Pl: forewomen.) ♦ *The forewoman told her crew that it was time for lunch.* ♦ *My forewoman docked my pay because I was an hour late.* **2.** *n., irreg.* the female head of a jury; a female who represents the jury to the court. ♦ *The forewoman delivered a verdict of not guilty.* ♦ *The judge asked the forewoman for the verdict.*

forewomen ['for wɪm ən] pl of forewoman.

foreword ['for wɚd] *n.* the introduction to a book or speech; a preface. (Compare with forward.) ♦ *I asked a famous scientist to write the foreword to the textbook I had written.* ♦ *The foreword was written by an economist who knew the subject of the book well.*

forfeit ['for fɪt] **1.** *tv.* to give up something; to lose something as a punishment. ♦ *The criminal forfeited his right to freedom.* ♦ *Anne's driver's license was forfeited when she was arrested for drunk driving.* **2.** *n.* something that is given up, especially as a punishment or penalty. (No plural form in this sense.) ♦ *As a forfeit, John lost his claim on the land.* ♦ *He was instructed to deliver his forfeit to the bailiff.*

forgave [for 'gev] pt of forgive.

forge ['fordʒ] **1.** *n.* a furnace that heats metal until it is soft. ♦ *The blacksmith placed the iron in the forge.* ♦ *A forge has to be hot enough to make metal soft.* **2.** *tv.* to make something out of heated, softened metal. ♦ *The blacksmith forged horseshoes from iron.* ♦ *The iron was forged into a decorative wall bracket.* **3.** *tv.* to sign someone else's name to something illegally; to create an imitation of a legal document illegally for the purposes of deception. ♦ *Jimmy forged his father's name on a check.* ♦ *The criminal forged a passport in order to escape the country.* **4.** *iv.* to move ahead suddenly; to move ahead forcefully. ♦ *Although the road was covered with snow, we forged ahead.* ♦ *The general ordered the troops to forge onward.*

forged ['fordʒd] **1.** *adj.* shaped from heated and softened metal. ♦ *The forged horseshoes remained hot for quite a while.* ♦ *The wrench was made of forged steel.* **2.** *adj.* [of a document or a signature] imitated illegally for the purpose of deception. ♦ *The bank would not honor the forged checks.* ♦ *The teacher could spot report cards with forged signatures.*

forgery ['fordʒ ə ri] **1.** *n.* the crime of making an illegal imitation of something. (No plural form in this sense.) ♦ *John served two years in prison for forgery.* ♦ *Forgery of legal documents is a serious crime in all U.S. states.* **2.** *n.* an illegal imitation of something. ♦ *I could immediately tell that the painting was a forgery.* ♦ *Lisa was arrested for committing forgery.*

forget [for 'gɛt] **1.** *tv., irreg.* to lose a piece of information from one's memory. (Pt: forgot; pp: forgot or forgotten.) ♦ *Did you forget my telephone number?* ♦ *I forgot what her name is.* **2.** *tv., irreg.* to fail to remember to do something. ♦ *I forgot to turn off the iron this morning.* ♦ *Bob forgot to water his plants this week.* **3.** *tv., irreg.* to leave someone or something behind; to not take someone or something with oneself. ♦ *I forgot my briefcase at the office.* ♦ *Bob forgot his umbrella, and of course, it rained.*

forgetful [for 'gɛt fʊl] *adj.* likely to forget someone or something; having a faulty memory. (Adv: *forgetfully.*) ♦ *I'm always losing my glasses. I guess I'm becoming forgetful.* ♦ *The boss has a forgetful secretary and is always late for meetings.*

forgetfulness [for 'gɛt fʊl nəs] *n.* the quality of not remembering. (No plural form in this sense.) ♦ *My forgetfulness is getting worse. I don't even remember what I ate for breakfast.* ♦ *My father's forgetfulness gets worse as he gets older.*

forgettable [for 'gɛt ə bəl] *adj.* worth forgetting; not important enough to remember. (Adv: *forgettably.*) ♦ *I don't advise reading this most forgettable book.* ♦ *Even though he's a memorable actor, his performance is completely forgettable in this movie.*

forgivable [for 'gɪv ə bəl] *adj.* [of someone or something] easy to forgive. (Adv: *forgivably.*) ♦ *Minor offenses are often forgivable.* ♦ *John's silly comments were somewhat rude but forgivable.*

forgive [for 'gɪv] **1.** *tv., irreg.* to pardon someone for an error or wrongdoing. (Pt: forgave; pp: forgiven.) ♦ *I forgave Bill for hitting me.* ♦ *Can you ever forgive me for insulting you?* **2.** *tv., irreg.* to cancel payment of a debt; to relieve someone of a debt before it is paid back. ♦ *The bank forgave the payment of principal on our debt for six months.* ♦ *The United States aided the small nation by forgiving its debt.*

forgiven [for 'gɪv ən] pp of forgive.

forgiveness [for 'gɪv nəs] **1.** *n.* forgiving; pardon. (No plural form in this sense.) ♦ *If you ask for forgiveness, it may be granted to you.* ♦ *The sinner prayed to God for forgiveness.* **2.** *n.* allowing a debt to remain unpaid; canceling a debt. (No plural form in this sense.) ♦ *The bank's forgiveness of our loan was greatly appreciated.* ♦ *The bank's policy of forgiveness is very strict and only serves the bank's interests.*

forgiving [for 'gɪv ɪŋ] *adj.* likely to forgive; granting a pardon in a friendly way. (Adv: *forgivingly.*) ♦ *A forgiving look from Mary let me know that everything was fine.* ♦ *You must be a very forgiving person to overlook such an insult!*

forgo [for 'go] *tv., irreg.* to give something up; to make do without something. (Pt: forwent; pp: forgone.) ♦ *While I was unemployed, I had to forgo many luxuries.* ♦ *I forwent my annual trip to New York because I had to save money.*

forgone [for 'gɔn] pp of forgo.

forgot [for 'gɑt] pt of forget; a pp of forget.

forgotten [for 'gɑt n] **1.** a pp of forget. **2.** *adj.* not remembered. (Adv: *forgottenly.*) ♦ *Bob's forgotten tombstone was covered with weeds.* ♦ *The forgotten papers were hidden in the attic.*

fork ['fork] **1.** *n.* an eating tool with a handle and two, three, or four prongs, used to spear or scoop food when eating. ♦ *I eat with my fork in my right hand.* ♦ *At the picnic, we ate with plastic forks.* **2.** *n.* the place where something splits into two branches. ♦ *A streetlight shined brightly at the fork in the road.* ♦ *When you reach the fork, go left.* **3.** *n.* one of the two branches that something splits into. ♦ *Follow the left fork if you want to go to Springfield.* ♦ *I took the wrong fork and got completely lost.* **4. fork over** *tv.* + *adv.* to hand something over to someone; to relinquish something to someone. (Informal.) ♦ *Max told me to fork over the money.* ♦ *I forked over $30 to see the concert.* **5.** *iv.* to split into two branches. ♦ *The road forks six miles outside of town.* ♦ *Where the path forks, you should go to the left.* **6. fork money out (for something)** *idiom* to pay (perhaps unwillingly) for something. ♦ *Do you think I'm going to fork twenty dollars out for that book?* ♦ *I hate having to fork out money day after day for expensive lunches.*

forklift ['fork lɪft] *n.* a machine that is used for moving or lifting heavy crates. ♦ *John used a forklift to move the boxes into the warehouse.* ♦ *Bob lifted the crate with a forklift.*

forlorn [for 'lorn] *adj.* sad and neglected; sad and left alone. (Adv: *forlornly.*) ♦ *Tom has been forlorn ever since his wife left him.* ♦ *A sorrowful and forlorn woman sat alone in the corner of the restaurant.*

form ['form] **1.** *n.* a shape; the shape of someone or something; the way someone or something is shaped. ♦ *Racetracks are usually oval in form.* ♦ *The weightlifter sought to have a more muscular form.* **2.** *n.* a kind; a sort; a type. ♦ *Sue contracted some form of influenza.* ♦ *Torture is a cruel form of punishment.* **3.** *n.* a document that has blank spaces on it that need to be filled with information; a blank. ♦ *You have to fill out a lot of forms to apply for a loan.* ♦ *Anne mailed the contest entry form before the deadline.* **4.** *n.* an abbreviation, derivation, conjugation, or inflection of a word. ♦ Exam *is a shortened form of the word* examination. ♦ *In Spanish, the feminine form of* amigo, *which means friend, is* amiga. **5.** *iv.* to come into being; to be created. ♦ *Storm clouds formed on the horizon.* ♦ *Mildew formed on the shower tile.* **6. form into** *iv.* + *prep. phr.* to be shaped into something; to acquire a certain shape. ♦ *The attacking army formed into a wedge.* ♦ *The group of children formed into a single line.* **7. form into** *tv.* + *prep. phr.* to shape something into a specific form. ♦ *The sculptor formed the clay into an ashtray.* ♦ *I formed a block of ice into a swan statue.* **8. form from** *tv.* + *prep. phr.* to shape something from something else. ♦ *The sculptor formed an ashtray from the clay.* ♦ *I formed a swan from the block of ice.* **9.** *tv.* to develop something; to develop into something; to cause something to come into being. ♦ *The young deer is forming horns on top of its head.* ♦ *The council formed new policies at the meeting last night.* **10.** *tv.* to make up something; to be a component of something. ♦ *This forms a major part of the lesson for today.* ♦ *A triangle is formed with three lines.*

formal ['form əl] **1.** *adj.* according to custom; according to rules; established; conventional. (Adv: *formally.*) ♦ *Congress issued a formal declaration of war.* ♦ *The two candidates agreed to participate in a formal debate.* **2.** *adj.* [of behavior, language use, clothes, etc.] serious and proper; [of a person or situation] characterized by serious and proper behavior, dress, etc. (Adv: formally. See also informal.) ♦ *John is a very formal person, but his wife is more relaxed and casual.* ♦ *At home I wear a T-shirt and jeans, but at work I wear more formal clothes, such as a suit.* ♦ *Sometimes Bob uses formal words when informal words would be more appropriate.* **3.** *adj.* [of clothing] of the highest level or style prescribed by the rules of etiquette. (Adv: *formally.*) ♦ *Formal dress is required at the banquet.* ♦ *A tuxedo is part of formal attire for men.* **4.** *adj.* [of an event] where formal ③ clothing is expected or required. (Adv: *formally.*) ♦ *Men usually wear tuxedos at formal events.* ♦ *Mary wore a full-length gown to the formal dance.* **5.** *n.* a woman's (usually long) gown suitable for a formal ④ event. ♦ *Jane bought her formal three days before the prom.* ♦ *Sue wore an attractive blue formal to her brother's wedding.* **6.** *n.* a formal ④ dance or party. ♦ *The tickets to the spring formal cost $40 per couple.* ♦ *We drove to the formal in a limousine.*

formality [for 'mæl ə ti] **1.** *n.* formalness; the condition of being formal. (No plural form in this sense.) ♦ *Bob was annoyed by the formality of dress required for the wedding.* ♦ *There was a lot of formality in the ceremony.* **2.** *n.* tradition or policy, rigidly obeyed. (No plural form in this sense.) ♦ *Formality requires that you have an interview.* ♦ *We've decided to hire you, but we have to interview you, for the sake of formality.* **3. a formality** *n.* something that is done because it is part of tradition or custom. ♦ *Since Anne had been accepted into the sorority, signing the forms was only a formality.* ♦ *Signing the contract is a mere formality.*

formalize ['form ə laɪz] *tv.* to make something official; to put something into its proper form. ♦ *We formalized the agreement by signing a contract.* ♦ *The company formalized its policies by putting them in writing.*

format ['for mæt] **1.** *n.* the arrangement of a presentation; the way events are ordered; the way things are placed on a page. ♦ *The format of the page made it easy to* *read.* ♦ *The presentation's format will consist of a short speech followed by a question-and-answer period.* **2.** *tv.* to arrange something to look a certain way, as with the order and arrangement in the pages of a book or other document. ♦ *I formatted the page so that the crucial information was easy to spot.* ♦ *Format your report so that the page number appears at the top of each page.* **3.** *tv.* to make a computer disk ready to accept information. ♦ *Before you can store information on a disk, you have to format it.* ♦ *Have you formatted this disk for this computer?*

formation [for 'me ʃən] **1.** *n.* forming or creating. (No plural form in this sense.) ♦ *The astronomers viewed the formation of a new star.* ♦ *The meeting dealt with the formation of a new subcommittee.* **2.** *n.* the arrangement or shape [of something]. ♦ *I took a photo of the peculiar rock formation in the foothills.* ♦ *The soldiers moved in formation across the desert.*

formative ['for mə tɪv] **1.** *adj.* of or about the development of a child. (With *period, stage, years.* Adv: *formatively.*) ♦ *Discipline is important during a child's formative years.* ♦ *The psychologist was most interested in the formative stages of her clients' lives.* **2.** *adj.* in the stage of forming, developing, or shaping something. (With *period, stage, years.* Adv: *formatively.*) ♦ *In the formative period of our company's history, there were only four employees.* ♦ *The geologist examined the new volcano in its formative stage.*

formatted ['for mæt ɪd] *adj.* [of a computer disk that has been] prepared to accept data. ♦ *Store your data on a formatted disk.* ♦ *I just bought a new box of formatted disks.*

former ['form ɚ] **1. the former** *n.* the first of two things mentioned. (No plural form in this sense. Treated as singular or plural.) ♦ *I like New York and Los Angeles. I travel to the former each month.* ♦ *Roses and daisies are both beautiful, but I prefer the former because they smell so good.* **2.** *adj.* past; previous. (Adv: *formerly.*) ♦ *I'm still friendly with my former employer.* ♦ *John's former wife receives $650 a month in alimony payments.* **3. [the] former** *adj.* of or about the first of the two things mentioned. ♦ *Of red and blue, I prefer the former color.* ♦ *We visited London and Paris, and I prefer the former city.*

formidable ['for mɪ də bəl] *adj.* hard to deal with; causing fear or dread; hard to defeat. (Adv: *formidably.*) ♦ *Cancer is a formidable disease, killing thousands each year.* ♦ *The army surrendered to its formidable enemy.*

formless ['form ləs] *adj.* having no shape; shapeless. (Adv: *formlessly.*) ♦ *The baker began to knead the formless lump of dough.* ♦ *The formless sculpture vaguely reminded me of a jellyfish.*

formula ['form jə lə] **1.** *n., irreg.* a series of symbols that show the chemical composition of a substance; a prescription. (Pl: *formulas* or formulae.) ♦ *I had to learn a lot of formulas in chemistry.* ♦ *The chemical formula of salt is NaCl.* **2.** *n.* a mathematical rule that is expressed with numbers or symbols. ♦ *The formula for the circumference of a circle is* πr^2. ♦ *Because the formula for the volume of a cube is* s^3, *the volume of a cube 5 inches tall is 125 cubic inches.* **3.** *n.* a pattern or standard set of components. (Figurative on ①.) ♦ *After one type of movie is successful, many more are made using the same formula.* ♦ *Following the successful formula used in her first year of teaching, Anne patterned all her courses in the same way.* **4.** *n.* animal milk or another milk substitute for feeding babies. (No plural form in this sense.) ♦ *Mary heated her baby's formula on the stove.* ♦ *The baby finished all of the formula and cried for more.*

formulae [ˌform jə laɪ] a pl of formula.

formulate ['form jə let] *tv.* to make a plan; to devise a plan. ♦ *The prisoners formulated a plan to break out of jail.* ♦ *Congress formulated new tax laws.*

formulation [form jə 'le ʃən] **1.** *n.* development or creation of something. (No plural form in this sense.) ♦ *The debate teacher praised Mary's clear formulation of her ideas.* ♦ *The formulation of the policy took many weeks.* **2.** *n.* a substance that has been made according to a formula. ♦ *The company advertised a new formulation designed to soothe aching muscles.* ♦ *The newest formulation of the product is being tested at this moment.*

forsake [for 'sek] *tv., irreg.* to abandon someone or something; to give someone or something up. (Pt: forsook; pp: forsaken.) ♦ *I had to forsake my smoking habit because I was having trouble breathing.* ♦ *Dave forsook a college degree for a job on his uncle's ranch.*

forsaken [for 'sek ən] pp of forsake.

forsook [for 'sʊk] pt of forsake.

fort ['fort] **1.** *n.* a structure or building used for defense that can withstand enemy attack; a number of fortified buildings behind a barrier. ♦ *The enemy troops surrounded the fort and threatened to burn it.* ♦ *The soldiers stayed inside the fort until more troops arrived.* **2.** *n.* a permanent military base. ♦ *The ship docked at Fort Sheridan on the lake.* ♦ *Fort Dearborn was established at the mouth of the Chicago River.* **3. hold the fort** *idiom* to take care of a place, such as a store or one's home. ♦ *I'm going next door to visit Mrs. Jones. You stay here and hold the fort.* ♦ *You should open the store at eight o'clock and hold the fort until I get there at ten o'clock.*

forth ['forθ] *adv.* forward; onward; outward. ♦ *The soldiers marched forth into battle.* ♦ *Go forth among the people and tell them the good news.*

forthcoming ['forθ kʌm ɪŋ] **1.** *adj.* appearing soon; approaching. ♦ *The forthcoming days will be difficult because of the war.* ♦ *Bill and Anne eagerly awaited their forthcoming wedding.* **2.** *adj.* helpful; ready to help; accommodating. (Adv: *forthcomingly.*) ♦ *The hotel staff was quite forthcoming during our short stay.* ♦ *The pleasant and forthcoming police officer gave me excellent directions to the train station.*

forthright ['forθ raɪt] *adj.* frank; direct; straightforward; to the point. (Adv: *forthrightly.*) ♦ *Your forthright questions, though earnest, are rather rude.* ♦ *The witness gave forthright answers to the lawyer's questions.*

fortieth ['for ti ɪθ] 40th. See fourth for senses and examples.

fortification [for tə fɪ 'ke ʃən] **1.** *n.* making a structure stronger. (No plural form in this sense.) ♦ *This bridge will require fortification if we intend to drive large trucks across it.* ♦ *Fortification of the old castle required the help of all the peasants in the county.* **2.** *n.* a fort. ♦ *The soldiers remained safe inside the fortification.* ♦ *The enemy was unable to destroy our fortification.*

fortified ['for tə fɑɪd] **1.** *adj.* [of a building] strengthened, as if to withstand an attack or heavy use. ♦ *The fortified walls were difficult to knock down.* ♦ *The bridge had been fortified to withstand almost any attack.* **2.** *adj.* enriched with vitamins and minerals. ♦ *Fortified breakfast cereal is rich in iron.* ♦ *I drink fortified milk every morning.*

fortify ['for tə fɑɪ] **1.** *tv.* to strengthen a structure, especially to prepare for attack. ♦ *The army fortified its headquarters as the enemy moved closer.* ♦ *We fortified the bridge with extra supports.* **2.** *tv.* to enrich something with vitamins and minerals. ♦ *The manufacturer has fortified this cereal with vitamins and minerals.* ♦ *This bread has been fortified with vitamins and some important minerals.*

fortitude ['for tɪ tud] *n.* courage or bravery, especially when one is suffering. (No plural form in this sense.) ♦ *The soldiers were given a medal for their fortitude during the battle.* ♦ *I admired the fortitude of the citizens who were trapped in the war zone.*

fortress ['for trɪs] **1.** *n.* a fortified building. ♦ *The fortress was well stocked with food and ammunition.* ♦ *Soldiers attacked the enemy fortress.* **2.** *n.* a huge, towering building. (Figurative on ①.) ♦ *The World Trade Center in New York City is a fortress of steel and metal.* ♦ *My apartment building is an ugly fortress made of cement and steel.*

fortuitous [for 'tu ə təs] *adj.* happening by chance; accidental and lucky. (Adv: *fortuitously.*) ♦ *I had a fortuitous encounter with the company president in the elevator.* ♦ *It was fortuitous that I left the freeway just before the horrible accident.*

fortunate ['for tʃə nɪt] **1.** *adj.* lucky; bringing good results; representing good fortune. (Adv: *fortunately.*) ♦ *I am glad we made the fortunate decision to vacation in Mexico. It was simply wonderful.* ♦ *We celebrated the fortunate occasion with a bottle of champagne.* **2.** *adj.* having had good luck. (Adv: *fortunately.*) ♦ *Four fortunate passengers survived the train wreck.* ♦ *One fortunate player won the lottery last week.*

fortunately ['for tʃə nɪt li] *adv.* luckily; in a way that is fortunate. ♦ *Fortunately, it stopped raining before the picnic started.* ♦ *Fortunately, I was wearing my seat belt when the other car struck mine.*

fortune ['for tʃən] **1.** *n.* good luck; success. (No plural form in this sense.) ♦ *I wished the young couple good fortune throughout their lives.* ♦ *I had the fortune of going to a good college.* **2.** *n.* everything that will happen to someone in the future. (No plural form in this sense.) ♦ *The psychic offered to tell me my fortune for $10.* ♦ *My fortune consists of working every day until I retire.* **3.** *n.* the money and property that someone owns. ♦ *The stockbroker amassed a small fortune in ten years of work.* ♦ *The millionaire made her fortune in the computer industry.*

forty ['for ti] **1.** *n.* the cardinal number 40; the number between 39 and 41. (No plural form in this sense. Similar definitions and examples for twenty, thirty, forty, fifty, sixty, seventy, eighty, ninety.) ♦ *Four times ten is forty.* ♦ *Here are forty of them.* ♦ *Forty is far more than I need.* **2.** **forties** *n.* the decade beginning in 1940; the 1940s. (Similar definitions and examples for twenties, thirties, forties, fifties, sixties, seventies, eighties, nineties.) ♦ *There weren't many television programs in the forties.* ♦ *Tom was born in the forties and got married in the sixties.* **3.** *adj.* 40; consisting of 40 things; having 40 things. (Similar definitions and examples for twenty, thirty, forty, fifty, sixty, seventy, eighty, ninety.) ♦ *My paper is forty pages long.* ♦ *This shirt costs forty dollars.* **4.** *pron.* 40 things or people already mentioned or able to be determined by context. (Similar definitions and examples for twenty, thirty, forty, fifty, sixty, seventy, eighty, ninety.) ♦ *I invited one hundred people, but only forty showed up.* ♦ *Of every million parts produced by our factory, only 40 are damaged.*

forum ['for əm] *n.* a meeting where someone can discuss something; a place where someone can talk about something, especially items of public interest. ♦ *I complained about my taxes at the city council's forum.* ♦ *The angry citizens demanded a forum in which their criticism could be heard.*

forward ['for wɚd] **1.** *adv.* ahead; toward the front; into the future. (Also **forwards.** Compare with foreword.) ♦ *Each student in line faced forward.* ♦ *Can we move the meeting forward one week?* **2.** *adj.* [moving] toward the front; [looking] into the future. ♦ *The analyst's forward averages were too high.* ♦ *I fell down when the bus made a sudden forward movement.* **3.** *adj.* very bold; too sure of oneself. (Adv: *forwardly.*) ♦ *A rather forward person insisted that I was sitting in his seat.* ♦ *Perhaps you were being too forward when you bragged that you could do the job.* **4.** *n.* a basketball, soccer, or hockey player who plays closer to the action than other players. ♦ *I threw the ball to the forward.* ♦ *The forward kicked the soccer ball past the goalie.* **5.** *tv.* to have mail sent onward to a new address when one moves. ♦ *The post office is forwarding my mail to my new address.* ♦ *Don't forget to forward your mail when you move.*

forwards ['for wɚdz] See forward ①.

forwent [for 'wɛnt] pt of forgo.

fossil ['fɑs əl] **1.** *n.* bones or remains of prehistoric plants, animals, and objects that have turned into stone; impressions left in stone of prehistoric plants, animals, and objects. ♦ *Dinosaur fossils can be seen at science museums.* ♦ *The paleontologist carefully removed the fossil from the ground.* **2.** *adj.* <the adj. use of ①.> ♦ *The fossil bones of animals teach us about life in the past.* ♦ *I looked at the fossil leaves on my professor's desk.* **3.** **fossil fuel** *n.* fuel derived from life in the far past, such as oil and gas. ♦ *Our known supplies of fossil fuels will be used up in the next century.* ♦ *Almost the entire transportation system in the world is dependent on fossil fuel.*

foster ['fɔ stɚ] **1.** *tv.* to encourage the growth and development of someone or something; to help someone or something grow and develop. ♦ *The teacher fostered the intellectual development of her students.* ♦ *My interest in science was fostered by my parents.* **2.** *adj.* of or about temporary care for parenthood of a child whose own parents cannot provide suitable care for various reasons. ♦ *After John's parents died, he was placed in a foster home.* ♦ *Since Jane didn't have any children of her own, she decided to become a foster parent.* **3.** **foster child** *n., irreg.* a child raised by foster parents. (Pl: *foster children.*) ♦ *John is our foster child, and we intend to adopt him next year.* ♦ *Foster children are usually in the care of a state agency.*

fought ['fɔt] pt/pp of fight.

foul ['fɑʊl] **1.** *adj.* dirty; filthy; rotten. (Adv: *foully.* Comp: *fouler;* sup: *foulest.*) ♦ *The sewers have a foul smell.* ♦ *The* *meat turned foul because I didn't put it in the refrigerator.* **2.** *adj.* vulgar; obscene. (Adv: *foully.* Comp: *fouler;* sup: *foulest.*) ♦ *I'm not allowed to watch movies with foul language.* ♦ *I was punished for telling a foul joke.* **3.** *adj.* evil; wicked; really bad. (Figurative on ①. Adv: *foully.* Comp: *fouler;* sup: *foulest.*) ♦ *You're in a foul mood today.* ♦ *Everyone hated the foul ruler.* **4.** *adj.* [of a ball] outside the proper playing area. (Sports.) ♦ *The umpire declared that the ball was foul.* ♦ *The batter hit another foul ball.* **5.** *adj.* stormy; [of weather] bad. (Adv: *foully.* Comp: *fouler;* sup: *foulest.*) ♦ *I don't like being outside when the weather is foul.* ♦ *Foul weather caused several traffic accidents.* **6.** *tv.* to make something dirty. ♦ *The baby fouled its diapers.* ♦ *Bill fouled the food by touching it with his dirty hands.* **7. foul up** *tv. + prep. phr.* to make errors with someone or something; to mess someone or something up. (Informal.) ♦ *I am sorry that I fouled it up so bad.* ♦ *Who fouled up the plans for the picnic?* **8.** *iv.* to make ⑩ in a particular game. ♦ *The basketball player was replaced because he fouled five times.* ♦ *The referee said Tom fouled on purpose.* **9. foul up** *iv.* to make an error. (Informal.) ♦ *I am sorry that I fouled up.* ♦ *If you keep fouling up, you will be fired.* **10.** *n.* an action in a game that is against the rules. ♦ *The hockey player was penalized for an obvious foul.* ♦ *The referee called a foul on the basketball player.* **11.** *n.* [in baseball] a ball that is hit outside the proper playing area. ♦ *The umpire determines whether a ball that is hit is a foul.* ♦ *A foul counts as a strike unless it would be the third strike.* **12. fall foul of someone or something** *idiom* to do something that annoys or offends someone or something; to do something that is contrary to the rules. ♦ *He has fallen foul of the police more than once.* ♦ *The political activists fell foul of the authorities.*

foul-up ['fɑʊl əp] *n.* a mistake or error that messes something up; a blunder. (Informal.) ♦ *Because of your foul-up, we've lost $10,000.* ♦ *I was given the wrong test results due to a foul-up at the lab.*

found ['fɑʊnd] **1.** pt/pp of find. **2.** *tv.* to establish an organization; to provide money or support to help start an organization. (Pt/pp: *founded.*) ♦ *This firm was founded in 1909.* ♦ *Our theater company was founded with the support of a local grant.*

foundation [fɑʊn 'de ʃən] **1.** *n.* the base of a building. (Rarely plural.) ♦ *The building's foundation cracked as a result of the earthquake.* ♦ *The foundation for the new shopping center covered many acres.* **2.** *n.* the base of a custom or tradition; a basis. (Figurative on ①.) ♦ *The belief that everyone is equal is one of the foundations of the American government.* ♦ *The judge told the lawyer to lay a foundation for the question being asked.* **3.** *n.* an institution that gives out money or grants to special causes. ♦ *The science program was funded by a grant from the Ford Foundation.* ♦ *I researched the kinds of grants available from various foundations.*

founder ['fɑʊn dɚ] **1.** *iv.* [for a boat] to fill up with water and submerge. (Compare with flounder.) ♦ *All the passengers got wet when the boat foundered.* ♦ *The boat foundered and sank to the bottom of the ocean.* **2.** *n.* someone who establishes an organization. ♦ *The founder of our company is still its president.* ♦ *The founder of the religious cult was arrested for tax evasion.*

founding ['fɑʊn dɪŋ] *adj.* establishing; setting up; instituting. ♦ *Anne is a founding member of the organization.* ♦ *The last of the founding directors of this company turns 90 next week.*

foundry ['fɑʊn dri] *n.* a place where metal is softened with heat, then melted and shaped into specific products. ♦ *Steel rods are produced in foundries.* ♦ *Tons of ore were shipped to the foundry by train each year.*

fountain ['fɑʊnt n] **1.** *n.* a stream of water that sprays up into the air. ♦ *The geyser sprayed a fountain of hot water into the air.* ♦ *A small fountain of water squirted from the crack in the water pipe.* **2.** *n.* a structure—designed and built by humans—that sprays a stream of water into the air. ♦ *We enjoyed the dancing waters of the fountains in the public gardens.* ♦ *The fountain is lit with colored lights at night.*

four ['for] **1.** *n.* the cardinal number 4; the number between 3 and 5. (No plural form in this sense. The ordinal form is fourth. Similar definitions and examples for one, two, three, four, five, six, seven, eight, nine, ten, eleven, twelve, thirteen, fourteen, fifteen, sixteen, seventeen, eighteen, nineteen.) ♦ *I have four of them right here in this box.* ♦ *One plus three is four.* **2.** *adj.* 4; consisting of 4 things; having 4 things. (The ordinal form is fourth. This covers other terms as in ①.) ♦ *There are four seasons: spring, summer, fall, and winter.* ♦ *A quartet consists of four musicians.* **3.** *pron.* 4 people or things already mentioned or able to be determined by context. (The ordinal form is fourth. This covers other terms as in ①.) ♦ *Of the original members of the club, four have resigned.* ♦ *Four can easily be seated in this room.* **4. on all fours** *idiom* on one's hands and knees. ♦ *I dropped a contact lens and spent an hour on all fours looking for it.* ♦ *The baby can walk, but is on all fours most of the time anyway.*

foursome ['for səm] *n.* a group of four people; a group consisting of two pairs of people. (No plural form in this sense.) ♦ *The Beatles were a very famous foursome from England.* ♦ *John got a foursome together for golf.*

fourteen ['fort 'tin] 14. See four for senses and examples.

fourteenth ['fort 'tinθ] **1.** *n.* one of 14 equal parts. ♦ *A fourteenth of the people who were surveyed had no opinion.* ♦ *One fourteenth of a week is 12 hours.* **2.** *adj.* of the 14th item in a series of things; of the item in a series between the 13th and 15th. ♦ *Our office is on the fourteenth floor of the building.* ♦ *Vermont was the fourteenth state to join the Union.* **3.** *pron.* the 14th item in a series of things or people already mentioned or able to be determined by context. ♦ *There were thirteen people at dinner, so I quickly invited a fourteenth because I'm superstitious.* ♦ *Flag Day is on the 14th of June.*

fourth ['forθ] **1.** *n.* 4th; one of 4 equal parts; a quarter; a half of a half. (Similar definitions for third, fifth, sixth, seventh, eighth, ninth, tenth, eleventh, twelfth, thirteenth, fourteenth, fifteenth, sixteenth, seventeenth, eighteenth, nineteenth, twentieth, thirtieth, fortieth, fiftieth, sixtieth, seventieth, eightieth, ninetieth, [one] hundredth, [one] thousandth, [one] millionth, [one] billionth, and [one] trillionth. See also first, second.) ♦ *Here is a fourth of the sheets of paper that you wanted.* ♦ *Fold a sheet of paper into fourths.* **2.** *n.* the 4th item in a series of things or people already mentioned or able to be determined by context. (This covers other terms as in ①. See also first, second.)

♦ *There are hundreds of books listed here. What is the title of the fourth?* ♦ *I have a reply from everyone except the fourth on the list.* **3.** *adj.* of the 4th item in a series of things; of the item in a series between the 3rd and 5th. (This covers other terms as in ①. See also first, second.) ♦ *This is the fourth time we have visited here.* ♦ *This is the fourth book I have checked out of the library.* **4.** *adv.* in the 4th position or rank. (This covers other terms as in ①. See also first, second.) ♦ *John came in fourth in the marathon.* ♦ *We all got a chance to state our views. I spoke fourth in the long list of complainers.*

Fourth of July [forθ əv dʒə 'lɑɪ] *n.* an American holiday commemorating the declaration of independence from Great Britain on July 4, 1776. (The same as Independence Day.) ♦ *Many towns have parades to celebrate the Fourth of July.* ♦ *Our city has a fireworks display every Fourth of July.*

fowl ['fɑʊl] **1.** *n., irreg.* one of a number of species of domesticated birds of limited flight, kept for their eggs or meat, such as the chicken, duck, turkey, etc. (Pl: *fowl* or *fowls.*) ♦ *Each morning, I collected the eggs that our fowls had laid.* ♦ *Should I put the geese in the coop with the rest of the fowl?* **2.** *n.* the meat of ①. (No plural form in this sense.) ♦ *I don't eat red meat, but I do eat fish and fowl.* ♦ *My sister eats fowl, but only the flesh without the skin.*

fox ['fɑks] **1.** *n.* a wild animal related to the dog, having a bushy tail. ♦ *The fox crept into the farmyard and killed our chickens.* ♦ *I saw a fox running through the woods.* **2.** *n.* the fur or pelt of ①. (No plural form in this sense.) ♦ *Is your fur mink or fox?* ♦ *The collar of my coat is silver fox.* **3.** *adj.* made of ②. ♦ *How many foxes are killed to make a fox coat?* ♦ *Fox furs are no longer popular.*

foyer ['foɪ ɚ] *n.* an entrance room; a lobby; a room just inside the front door of a building, house, or apartment. ♦ *We placed our wet umbrellas and shoes in the foyer.* ♦ *I waited in the foyer until Jane came down in the elevator and joined me.*

fracas ['fre kəs] *n.* a loud argument; a disturbance; a fight. (No plural form in this sense.) ♦ *The police broke up the violent fracas outside the tavern.* ♦ *Several plates and dishes were broken in the fracas.*

fraction ['fræk ʃən] **1.** *n.* a part of a whole number. ♦ *Numbers like ½ and ¾ are fractions.* ♦ *If you convert .25 into a fraction, you get ¼.* **2.** *n.* a small piece or portion of something. (No plural form in this sense.) ♦ *The salesman promised my heating bills would be a fraction of what they are now if I bought the heat pump.* ♦ *Each month I can pay only a small fraction of my bills.*

fractious ['fræk ʃəs] *adj.* bad-tempered; complaining. (Adv: *fractiously.*) ♦ *The fractious group threatened to oppose everything the government proposed.* ♦ *My fractious roommate complains about everything.*

fracture ['fræk tʃɚ] **1.** *n.* a break or crack, especially a break in a bone. ♦ *The doctor told me my fracture would heal in 8 weeks.* ♦ *I turned the vase around so that its fracture faced the wall.* **2.** *tv.* to break something by creating a crack in it. ♦ *I fell down the steps and fractured my arm.* ♦ *I fractured the ice with a heavy icepack.* **3.** *iv.* to break; to crack. ♦ *One of the chair legs fractured when I knocked it over.* ♦ *The vase fractured into a hundred pieces.*

fractured ['fræk tʃɚd] *adj.* broken; cracked. ♦ *The doctor put my fractured leg in a cast.* ♦ *I threw the fractured mirror away.*

fragile ['frædʒ əl] *adj.* easily broken; delicate. (Adv: *fragilely.*) ♦ *Don't drop those eggs! They're fragile.* ♦ *You must cushion fragile objects carefully when you pack them.*

fragment ['fræg mənt] **1.** *n.* a small piece of something. ♦ *I cleaned up fragments of glass from the carpet.* ♦ *The dog is choking on a fragment of bone.* **2.** *iv.* to break into pieces or sections. ♦ *The ice fragmented when I stepped onto it.* ♦ *My mirror fragmented when I dropped it.* **3.** *tv.* to break something into pieces or sections. ♦ *A blow to my side fragmented my hip bone.* ♦ *A rock thrown by a child has fragmented my kitchen window.*

fragmentary ['fræg mən tɛr i] *adj.* incomplete; made up of numerous pieces. (Adv: *fragmentarily* [fræg mən 'tɛr ə li].) ♦ *I want to write a novel, but my ideas are still too fragmentary.* ♦ *Following the large earthquake, the news reports were fragmentary until a reporter flew to the site by helicopter.*

fragrance ['fre grəns] **1.** *n.* a smell or scent that is pleasant. ♦ *I love the fragrance of roses.* ♦ *The fragrance of chocolate lured me into the kitchen.* **2.** *n.* a perfume; a cologne. ♦ *Mary sprayed a sweet fragrance on her neck.* ♦ *What is the name of the fragrance you are wearing? I like it.*

fragrant ['fre grənt] *adj.* smelling good; having a nice smell. (Adv: *fragrantly.*) ♦ *There are twelve fragrant roses in the vase.* ♦ *John's cologne is very fragrant. Unfortunately, it makes me sneeze.*

frail ['frel] *adj.* thin and weak; not strong; easily hurt. (Adv: *frailly.*) ♦ *My grandmother is frail, but she's still very alert.* ♦ *The frail old man chased the thief down the street.*

frailty ['fre əl ti] *n.* weakness and physical vulnerability. (No plural form in this sense.) ♦ *Because of my frailty, I stay in bed most of the day.* ♦ *The frailty of the antique vase caused me to keep it in a padded box.*

frame ['frem] **1.** *n.* a structure that provides support for something. ♦ *The wind snapped the frame of the kite in two.* ♦ *The frame of the building was weakened by the earthquake.* **2.** *n.* a firm border that something is set into, such as a door, a window, or a picture. ♦ *This picture has an oak frame.* ♦ *I live in the old white house with brown window frames.* **3.** *n.* the shape or form of a human body; the structure of the body. ♦ *Even though Dave doesn't exercise much, he still has a sturdy frame.* ♦ *With my slight frame, I cannot carry anything heavy.* **4.** *tv.* to place something in ②. ♦ *I framed the picture with a metal frame.* ♦ *The carpenter framed the window skillfully.* **5.** *tv.* to express something in a certain way. (Figurative on ④.) ♦ *Please frame your question so we can understand it better.* ♦ *You will get a quicker response if you frame your comment in the form of a question.* **6.** *tv.* to cause someone to appear guilty of a crime by manipulating evidence or lying. ♦ *The murderer went free because he framed his best friend.* ♦ *Max said he was innocent and that the cops had framed him.*

framework ['frem wɚk] **1.** *n.* a structure that serves as a frame or skeleton. ♦ *The decorations were mounted on a wooden framework.* ♦ *The framework that supported the display was not visible from the front of the display.* **2.** *n.*

a basic structure of ideas, such as an outline of an essay or speech. (Figurative on ①.) ♦ *The framework of her plan was clearly presented in the meeting.* ♦ *The report lacked any sort of framework to organize the ideas.*

France ['fræns] See Gazetteer.

franchise ['fræn tʃɑɪz] **1.** *n.* the right sold by a company for someone to sell that company's trademarked products or services exclusively in a specific area. ♦ *My uncle owns a hamburger franchise.* ♦ *The company revoked its franchise because the owner criticized the product in a newspaper article.* **2.** *n.* a restaurant or store that sells goods and services not owned by the company itself, but by someone who has been given the right to do so by the company. ♦ *Is this store company-owned or is it a franchise?* ♦ *I'd rather shop at independent stores than franchises or chains.* **3.** *n.* the right to vote in an election. (No plural form in this sense.) ♦ *Franchise was not granted to women in America until 1920.* ♦ *The constitution now assures the franchise of every citizen.*

frank ['fræŋk] **1.** *adj.* straightforward; truthful; honest; [of someone] speaking the truth even if it hurts. (Adv: *frankly.* Comp: *franker;* sup: *frankest.*) ♦ *I'm going to be frank and tell you that you need to lose weight.* ♦ *If I may be frank, I don't think your book is very good.* **2.** *n.* a hot dog; a frankfurter. ♦ *I put mustard and onions on my franks.* ♦ *Would you like a grilled frank?*

frankfurter ['fræŋk fɚ tɚ] *n.* a meat-filled sausage named for Frankfurt, Germany; a hot dog. (See frank ②.) ♦ *I put some frankfurters and some hamburgers on the grill.* ♦ *Would you like some mustard with your frankfurter?*

frankly ['fræŋk li] *adv.* in a straightforward way; honestly; truthfully. ♦ *Frankly, I didn't like the movie at all.* ♦ *Frankly, I think you should break up with your boyfriend.*

frankness ['fræŋk nəs] *n.* honesty; truthfulness; candor. (No plural form in this sense.) ♦ *Although I appreciate your frankness, I don't feel like going on a diet.* ♦ *I don't mind frankness, as long as it's polite.*

frantic ['fræn tɪk] *adj.* very excited; wild with emotion. (Adv: *frantically* [...ɪk li].) ♦ *After a frantic search, I found my keys under the sofa cushion.* ♦ *I had a frantic conversation with my bank after they said I'd bounced five checks.*

fraternal [frə 'tɚn əl] **1.** *adj.* of or about brothers or brotherhood. (Adv: *fraternally.*) ♦ *I gave my brother a fraternal embrace.* ♦ *My brother gave me some fraternal advice.* **2.** *adj.* [of twins] from two different ova and not split from one. (Adv: *fraternally.*) ♦ *You don't look alike at all, so you must be fraternal twins, not identical twins.* ♦ *Fraternal twins can be of different sexes, whereas identical twins must be of the same sex.* **3.** *adj.* of or about a society or organization of males. (Adv: *fraternally.*) ♦ *Bill belongs to the Fraternal Order of Otters.* ♦ *Max decided not to join the fraternal organization.*

fraternity [frə 'tɚn ə ti] **1.** *n.* the quality of being brothers; the bond shared between two or more members of an organization of males. (No plural form in this sense.) ♦ *The organization stressed fraternity and equality among its members.* ♦ *I cherished the fraternity of the group because I didn't have any brothers of my own.* **2.** *n.* a society of male college students who live in the same house and socialize together. ♦ *Bob joined the most popular fraternity on campus.* ♦ *My fraternity is raising money for charity this weekend.*

fraternize ['fræt ɚ nɑɪz] **fraternize with** *iv.* + *prep. phr.* to associate with someone too intimately. ♦ *The soldier was punished for fraternizing with the enemy.* ♦ *Professors shouldn't fraternize with their students.*

fraud ['frɔd] **1.** *n.* deception; cheating; dishonest actions done to deceive someone. (No plural form in this sense.) ♦ *The senator was charged with fraud.* ♦ *A committee was formed to combat fraud in the workplace.* **2.** *n.* a deception; an act of cheating; a dishonest act. ♦ *This contest is a fraud! They'll just take your money and run.* ♦ *The contract the company promised me was a fraud.* **3.** *n.* someone who pretends to be someone or something else; someone who pretends to have certain qualifications. ♦ *I believed that the lawyer I first talked to was a fraud.* ♦ *The man claiming to be a doctor turned out to be a fraud.*

fraudulent ['frɔ dʒə lənt] *adj.* deceiving; false; dishonest. (Adv: *fraudulently.*) ♦ *The fraudulent doctor was taken to court.* ♦ *John learned of my unlisted phone number by fraudulent methods.*

fraught ['frɔt] **fraught with danger** *idiom* [of something] full of something dangerous or unpleasant. ♦ *The spy's trip to Russia was fraught with danger.* ♦ *My escape from the kidnappers was fraught with danger.*

fray ['fre] **1.** *tv.* to cause a rope or string to unravel; to separate the threads that make up string or rope. ♦ *I frayed the string into thin threads.* ♦ *Constant use had frayed the rope until it was almost ruined.* **2.** *iv.* to unravel; to become worn at the edges. ♦ *The rope frayed as it rubbed against the rock.* ♦ *My shoelaces frayed after months of use.* **3.** *n.* an argument; a brawl. ♦ *The police were called in to break up the violent fray.* ♦ *A noisy fray in the alley drew people from all directions.* **4. join the fray; jump into the fray** *idiom* to join the fight or argument. ♦ *After listening to the argument, Mary decided to jump into the fray.* ♦ *Tom joined the fray and immediately got knocked down.*

frayed ['fred] **1.** *adj.* worn at the edges; unraveled. ♦ *This frayed electric wire is a fire hazard.* ♦ *The frayed rope suddenly snapped.* **2. frayed nerves** *n.* upset or strained nerves. (Figurative on ①.) ♦ *Dave took a pill to calm his frayed nerves.* ♦ *I took a long shower to soothe my frayed nerves.*

freak ['frik] **1.** *n.* someone or something that is abnormally developed; someone or something that is misshapen. (Not polite for humans.) ♦ *We saw several freaks on display at the circus.* ♦ *A purple pumpkin would be a real freak.* **2.** *adj.* most unusual. ♦ *A freak storm caused all the power to go out.* ♦ *Mary was hurt in a freak accident involving a can opener.*

freckle ['frɛk əl] **1.** *n.* one of many small dark dots on the skin. ♦ *Sunshine darkens my freckles.* ♦ *I kissed the freckle on my baby sister's nose.* **2.** *iv.* to become covered with ①, usually because of exposure to the sun. ♦ *I freckle no matter how much sunblock I put on.* ♦ *Sue wore a big hat so her face wouldn't freckle.*

free ['fri] **1.** *adj.* independent; not subject to someone else's rule; not enslaved. (Adv: *freely.* Comp: *freer;* sup: *freest.*) ♦ *The American colonies declared themselves free from England in 1776.* ♦ *As a result of the Civil War, the slaves became free.* **2.** *adj.* costing no money; without cost. ♦ *This coupon is for a free toothbrush if you buy a tube of toothpaste.* ♦ *Some restaurants offer free coffee with meals.*

3. *adj.* not limited; not restricted; not bound by rules. (Adv: *freely.* Comp: *freer;* sup: *freest.*) ♦ *The Constitution guarantees the right to free speech.* ♦ *Censorship goes against the idea of a free press.* **4.** *adj.* not busy; unoccupied; available. (Comp: *freer;* sup: *freest.*) ♦ *Are you free Saturday evening? If so, let's go to dinner.* ♦ *I'd like to speak to you when you're free.* **5.** *adj.* empty; not being used. ♦ *Is this seat free?* ♦ *The next available table in the restaurant won't be free for at least 30 minutes.* **6.** *adj.* generous; lavish; giving. (Adv: *freely.* Comp: *freer;* sup: *freest.*) ♦ *My grandpa is a free spender and gives me whatever I want.* ♦ *If you continue to be so free with your money, you'll soon be in debt.* **7.** *adj.* clear of blockage; having an open path; having nothing in one's way. ♦ *Is the street free of debris?* ♦ *After the storm, we cleared our yard so that it was free of branches.* **8.** *adj.* not afflicted with something unpleasant; not troubled by something. (Comp: *freer;* sup: *freest.*) ♦ *The doctor declared that I was free from disease.* ♦ *Fortunately, our presentation was free of errors.* **9.** *adv.* without cost; without having to pay money. ♦ *I got into the movie free.* ♦ *This lamp came free with the living-room furniture.* **10.** *adv.* in a way that is not constrained or held; in such a way that constraints are removed; in a way that liberates. ♦ *I was able to shake myself free of his grip.* ♦ *After the Civil War, the slaves were set free.* **11.** *tv.* to release someone or something. ♦ *I caught a butterfly, but then I freed it.* ♦ *The liberating army freed the prisoners of war.* **12. free of** *tv. + prep. phr.* to rid someone or something of something. ♦ *Free your mind of all bad thoughts.* ♦ *Tom tried to free himself of his bad habits.* **13. -free** *n.* <a combining form meaning *without,* added to certain nouns.> (Examples: *debt-free, duty-free, fancy-free, fat-free, scot-free, traffic-free.*) **14. for free** *idiom* for no charge or cost; without any charge. ♦ *They let us into the movie for free.* ♦ *I will let you have a sample of the candy for free.* **15. free-for-all** *idiom* a disorganized fight or contest involving everyone; a brawl. ♦ *The party turned into a free-for-all after midnight.* ♦ *The race started out in an organized manner but ended up being a free-for-all.* **16. free translation** *idiom* a translation that is not completely accurate and not well thought out. ♦ *John gave a free translation of the sentence, which did not help us at all.* ♦ *Anne gave a very free translation of the poem.*

freedom ['fri dəm] **1.** *n.* liberty; a state where one is free from constraint. (No plural form in this sense.) ♦ *The Constitution guarantees the freedom of speech.* ♦ *On the Fourth of July, Americans celebrate their freedom from England.* **2.** *n.* a right. ♦ *We treasure our freedoms.* ♦ *Freedom of speech is one of our precious freedoms.*

freelance ['fri 'læns] **1.** *adj.* done on one's own and not as the employee of a company. ♦ *I've done freelance work in the publishing industry.* ♦ *As a freelance writer, Sue sold her stories to many different magazines.* **2.** *iv.* to work for oneself and not for a company. ♦ *Because I freelance, I only work when I want to.* ♦ *I freelanced for a few years before finding a permanent job.* **3.** See freelancer.

freelancer AND **freelance** ['fri læns (ɚ)] *n.* one who works for oneself and not for a company. ♦ *Since I'm a freelancer, I can meet with you whenever you want.* ♦ *Because Anne is a freelance, she doesn't have any insurance.*

freeway ['fri we] *n.* an expressway; a highway with limited access. ♦ *A freeway does not intersect with any roads, but has ramps that allow one to get on and off at junctions without stopping traffic.* ♦ *Take the freeway because it's much quicker than the other roads.*

freeze ['friz] **1.** *iv., irreg.* to solidify as the temperature gets colder. (Pt: froze; pp: frozen.) ♦ *The milk froze because I accidentally put it in the freezer.* ♦ *When water freezes, it is called ice.* **2.** *iv., irreg.* [for someone or some creature] to become very cold in cold weather. ♦ *Hurry up and open the door, or we will freeze!* ♦ *Close the window or I will freeze to death.* **3.** *iv., irreg.* to become completely motionless; to stop all movement. (Figurative on ①.) ♦ *The deer froze when it heard us approach.* ♦ *The robber ordered me to freeze.* **4.** *tv., irreg.* to turn something into ice; to cause something to harden as the temperature gets colder. ♦ *The cold weather froze the river quickly.* ♦ *A blast of frigid air froze the pond.* **5.** *tv., irreg.* to place food in a freezer so that it stays fresh; to preserve something at a freezing temperature. ♦ *Freeze the ice cream, otherwise it will melt.* ♦ *You should freeze the leftover hamburger so that it doesn't spoil.* **6.** *tv., irreg.* to cause someone or something to become completely motionless. ♦ *A power surge froze my computer screen.* ♦ *The accident froze traffic in all directions.* **7.** *tv., irreg.* to keep the price of something at a certain level; to not allow a sum to change. ♦ *The government froze the utilities' prices at 1976 levels.* ♦ *My company froze the rate of pay increases at the rate of inflation.* **8.** *n.* a time when the temperature is 32 degrees Fahrenheit, 0 degrees Celsius, or below. ♦ *Because of the deep freeze, not many people ventured outside.* ♦ *A sudden freeze trapped many boats in the harbor.*

freezer ['friz ɚ] *n.* an appliance with a compartment that remains at a temperature below freezing in order to preserve food and other things. ♦ *Put the milk in the refrigerator and the ice cream in the freezer.* ♦ *When our freezer broke, all of our ice melted.*

freezing ['friz ɪŋ] **1.** *adj.* below 32 degrees Fahrenheit or 0 degrees Celsius; cold enough to cause water to turn to ice. ♦ *The lake froze because of all the freezing weather we've had.* ♦ *The area has been hit with freezing conditions, so the roads may be icy.* **2.** *adj.* very cold. ♦ *The living room is warm, but the bedroom is freezing!* ♦ *Put on a hat and scarf! It's freezing outside!*

freight ['fret] **1.** *n.* cargo; products that are carried by truck, plane, train, etc. (No plural form in this sense.) ♦ *A train full of freight crashed in Oregon last night.* ♦ *Freight is hauled down the Mississippi River on barges.* **2.** *n.* the cost of shipping something as ①. ♦ *What is the freight on the last shipment of grain?* ♦ *Who will pay the freight on this order?* **3.** *adj.* <the adj. use of ①.> ♦ *We stopped at the railroad crossing while a long freight train went past.* ♦ *The freight yard is filled with freight cars.*

French ['frɛntʃ] **1.** *n.* the language spoken by the citizens or natives of France and some other countries of the world. (No plural form in this sense.) ♦ *I am studying French in school.* ♦ *French is easier to read than it is to pronounce.* **2. the French** *n.* the people of France. (No plural form in this sense. Treated as plural.) ♦ *The French love good food and drink.* ♦ *The French are very interested in French culture.* **3.** *adj.* of or about France, ①, or ②. ♦ *I am studying the French language in school.* ♦ *Bob does not like French cooking.*

french-fried ['frɛntʃ frɑɪd] *adj.* fried in deep fat. ♦ *Would you like some more french-fried potatoes?* ♦ *John just loves french-fried onions.*

french fry ['frɛntʃ frɑɪ] **1. french-fry** *tv.* to fry something in fat. ♦ *I try to avoid food that has been french-fried.* ♦ *We ordered cheese that was french-fried in vegetable oil.* **2.** *n.* a long, narrow piece of potato that has been fried in deep fat. (Usually plural.) ♦ *Would you like french fries with your hamburger?* ♦ *Jane sprinkled salt on her french fries.*

frenetic [frə 'nɛt ɪk] *adj.* very excited; frenzied. (Adv: *frenetically* [...ɪk li].) ♦ *Before the election, the candidates gave speeches at a frenetic pace.* ♦ *Things are so busy at the office that we are always frenetic and exhausted.*

frenzied ['frɛn zid] *adj.* very excited; frantic. (Adv: *frenziedly.*) ♦ *I was overwhelmed by the frenzied atmosphere at the party.* ♦ *Our frenzied waiter dropped a tray of food.*

frenzy ['frɛn zi] *n.* a wild fury; an excited state. (No plural form in this sense.) ♦ *In a frenzy of rage, the dog jumped over the fence and attacked the boys who were teasing it.* ♦ *The frenzy of the emergency room shocked the young intern.*

frequency ['fri kwən si] **1.** *n.* a repeated occurrence; a frequent occurrence. (No plural form in this sense.) ♦ *The frequency of serious crimes is decreasing.* ♦ *With increasing frequency, people are volunteering to help with today's social problems.* **2.** *n.* the number of times that something occurs within a given period of time. ♦ *In physics, the frequency of a sound wave is measured by the number of cycles produced by the wave each second.* ♦ *Middle A on the piano has a frequency of 446 cycles per second.*

frequent ['fri kwənt] **1.** *adj.* happening often; occurring often; common. (Adv: *frequently.*) ♦ *My neighbor's frequent parties are annoying.* ♦ *The couple's frequent arguments led to a divorce.* **2.** *tv.* to go to a certain place often. ♦ *We frequent our neighborhood bar.* ♦ *The restaurant was frequented by local residents.*

fresco ['frɛs ko] **1.** *n.* the art of painting onto damp plaster so that the color is absorbed into the plaster. (No plural form in this sense.) ♦ *Sue is an artist, and her specialty is fresco.* ♦ *In art class, I did some work in fresco.* **2.** *n.* a painting which is done on wet plaster. (Pl in *-es.*) ♦ *The lobby was decorated with brightly colored frescoes.* ♦ *Restoration of the frescoes revealed an intricate design.*

fresh ['frɛʃ] **1.** *adj.* new; newly or recently made, done, obtained, etc., especially if not yet used or altered. (Adv: *freshly.* Comp: *fresher;* sup: *freshest.*) ♦ *I need a fresh copy of the report because I lost the copy you gave me.* ♦ *Be careful! That's a fresh coat of paint on the door.* **2.** *adj.* not stale; not spoiled; [of foods] not canned, frozen, dried, or preserved in another way; [of fruits or vegetables] recently picked or harvested. (Adv: *freshly.* Comp: *fresher;* sup: *freshest.*) ♦ *I ordered fresh fruit for dessert.* ♦ *This milk doesn't smell fresh.* ♦ *I need some fresh air.* **3. get fresh (with someone)** *idiom* to become overly bold or impertinent. ♦ *When I tried to kiss Mary, she slapped me and shouted, "Don't get fresh with me!"* ♦ *I can't stand people who get fresh.*

freshen ['frɛ ʃən] *tv.* to renew something; to make something fresh. ♦ *The spring rain freshened the stale air.* ♦ *The author freshened the script by rewriting many of the scenes.*

freshman ['frɛʃ mən] *n., irreg.* a student in the first year of study at a high school or college. (Pl: **freshmen.**) ♦ *The university required all freshmen to live in a dormitory.* ♦ *Next year, I'll be a freshman at the University of Michigan.*

freshmen ['frɛʃ mən] pl of **freshman.**

freshness ['frɛʃ nəs] *n.* newness; the quality of being fresh. (No plural form in this sense.) ♦ *You can determine the freshness of a watermelon by knocking on its rind.* ♦ *There was a pleasant freshness in the air after the spring rain.*

fresh water ['frɛʃ 'wɑt ɚ] **1.** *n.* water that is not salty and can be made suitable for drinking. (No plural form in this sense.) ♦ *The lake is fresh water and it is full of fish.* ♦ *This fish lives only fresh water and will die in salt water.* **2. freshwater** *adj.* [of water] not salty; living in fresh water. ♦ *We ate freshwater fish for dinner.* ♦ *Trout and bass are freshwater fish.*

fret ['frɛt] **1.** *iv.* to worry about something; to be upset. ♦ *You'll get an ulcer if you continue to fret over small problems.* ♦ *Don't fret. Everything will be OK.* **2.** *n.* a ridge on the neck of a guitar or banjo which strings are pressed against to make different musical notes. ♦ *Move your second finger up one fret.* ♦ *I don't always squeeze the strings against the frets hard enough when I play the guitar.*

fretful ['frɛt fʊl] *adj.* worried; upset; anxious. (Adv: *fretfully.*) ♦ *The fretful parents stayed awake until their children were safely home.* ♦ *Even though Mary had studied, she was fretful before the biology test.*

friable ['frɑɪ ə bəl] *adj.* crumbly; easily crumbled. ♦ *The landlord was ordered to remove all friable asbestos from the building.* ♦ *The soil must be friable for anything to grow in it.*

friction ['frɪk ʃən] **1.** *n.* rubbing against something that resists the rubbing. (No plural form in this sense.) ♦ *Friction against the rock caused the rope to snap.* ♦ *The friction between the carpet and my arm reddened my skin.* **2.** *n.* the resistance that keeps one object from sliding over another object. (No plural form in this sense.) ♦ *Oil reduces friction in engines.* ♦ *There is very little friction between ice and the blade of an ice skate.* **3.** *n.* a disagreement because of differences in opinions. (No plural form in this sense.) ♦ *Most of the friction at my office has to do with politics.* ♦ *I left home because of the friction between my parents and me.*

Friday ['frɑɪ de] **1.** *n.* the sixth day of the week, between Thursday and Saturday. ♦ *I stay up late on Friday because I don't have to work on Saturday.* ♦ *I have a dentist appointment next Friday at three o'clock.* **2.** *adv.* on the next ①. ♦ *I have a dentist appointment Friday.* ♦ *I don't have to work Friday.* **3. (on) Fridays** *adv.* on each ①. ♦ *Fridays I can sleep late.* ♦ *My dentist doesn't work on Fridays.*

fried ['frɑɪd] *adj.* cooked in hot fat, vegetable oil, or butter. ♦ *We served fried onions with the steak.* ♦ *Do you want your chicken fried or broiled?*

friend ['frɛnd] **1.** *n.* someone whom someone else knows well and likes. ♦ *Dave has been my best friend for 30 years.* ♦ *I drove my friend to the airport.* **2.** *n.* a supporter; someone or something that supports or helps someone or something. ♦ *The Friends of the Zoo raised $1,000,000 for the new monkey house.* ♦ *The caller asked if I wanted to become a friend of the museum.* **3. fair-weather friend**

idiom someone who is your friend ① only when things are going well for you. ♦ *Bill wouldn't help me with my homework. He's just a fair-weather friend.* ♦ *A fair-weather friend isn't much help in an emergency.*

friendless ['frɛnd ləs] *adj.* having no friends; without friends. (Adv: *friendlessly.*) ♦ *The friendless old man lived alone in a tiny apartment.* ♦ *Bill is friendless because he spends all of his time at work.*

friendliness ['frɛnd li nəs] *n.* the quality of being friendly. (No plural form in this sense.) ♦ *I appreciated my host's friendliness when I visited England.* ♦ *Friendliness is important when dealing with customers.*

friendly ['frɛnd li] *adj.* like a friend; nice, kind, or pleasant. (Comp: *friendlier;* sup: *friendliest.*) ♦ *A friendly smile from my bus driver brightened my day.* ♦ *I held open the door for Tom as a friendly gesture.*

friendship ['frɛnd ʃɪp] **1.** *n.* being friends with someone. (No plural form in this sense.) ♦ *Friendship is very important in my life.* ♦ *Without friendship and the warmth of human kindness, life would be unendurable.* **2.** *n.* a relationship between friends; a friendly feeling about someone. ♦ *My friendship with Lisa has lasted since first grade.* ♦ *Many of my friendships came to an end as I outlived my friends.* **3. strike up a friendship** *idiom* to become friends (with someone). ♦ *I struck up a friendship with John while we were on a business trip together.* ♦ *If you're lonely, you should go out and try to strike up a friendship with someone you like.*

fright ['frɑɪt] *n.* fear; terror; the condition of being scared. (No plural form in this sense.) ♦ *I ran from the soldiers in fright.* ♦ *The fright of seeing the accident made Lisa terrified of driving.*

frighten ['frɑɪt n] *tv.* to scare someone or something; to make someone or something afraid. ♦ *The thunder frightened my younger brother.* ♦ *Scary movies frighten me.*

frightened ['frɑɪt nd] *adj.* scared; afraid. (Adv: *frightenedly.*) ♦ *The frightened child hid in the closet.* ♦ *All the frightened tourists gave the robber their money.*

frightening ['frɑɪt n ɪŋ] *adj.* scary; filling one with fear; causing fear. (Adv: *frighteningly.*) ♦ *Getting robbed is a frightening experience.* ♦ *I don't like watching frightening movies.*

frightful ['frɑɪt fʊl] **1.** *adj.* frightening; scary. (Adv: *frightfully.*) ♦ *The rough airplane ride was a frightful experience.* ♦ *Being robbed was a frightful experience.* **2.** *adj.* very bad; awful. (Adv: *frightfully.*) ♦ *The ugly painting in your living room is just frightful.* ♦ *The airport has been closed because of the frightful weather.*

frightfully ['frɑɪt fə li] *adv.* very [bad]. ♦ *The frightfully bad TV show was soon canceled.* ♦ *I removed the frightfully hideous painting from the living room.*

frigid ['frɪdʒ ɪd] **1.** *adj.* very cold. (Adv: *frigidly.*) ♦ *The weather is frigid today, so dress warmly.* ♦ *I could see my breath in the frigid air.* **2.** *adj.* not pleasant; unfriendly. (Adv: *frigidly.*) ♦ *My request for help was met with a frigid glare from the clerk.* ♦ *John cut our conversation short with a frigid response.* **3.** *adj.* [of a woman] not able to reach a sexual climax. (Adv: *frigidly.*) ♦ *She isn't frigid, she is just too tired.* ♦ *Counseling helped the frigid woman overcome her problem.*

frigidity [frɪ 'dʒɪd ə ti] **1.** *n.* the quality of being very cold; coldness. (No plural form in this sense.) ♦ *The lake froze solid because of the frigidity of the weather.* ♦ *After living in Florida for many years, I had difficulty adjusting to the frigidity of winters in Wisconsin.* **2.** *n.* the quality of being unpleasant. (No plural form in this sense.) ♦ *I was quite upset by the frigidity of the store clerk's attitude.* ♦ *Jane could not tolerate the frigidity of her new neighbor.* **3.** *n.* [in women] a lack of interest in sex; [in women] the inability to reach a sexual climax. (No plural form in this sense.) ♦ *The sex therapist discussed some causes of frigidity.* ♦ *Anne saw a therapist to determine the reasons for her frigidity.*

frill ['frɪl] **1.** *n.* an ornamental edge; a ruffle. ♦ *The hem of Mary's dress was decorated with frills.* ♦ *The tablecloth was bordered with colorful frills.* **2.** *n.* something that is an added bonus but is not necessary. (Usually plural.) ♦ *Because of budget cuts, the school eliminated all of the frills.* ♦ *First-class passengers receive many frills, such as free drinks.*

fringe ['frɪndʒ] **1.** *n.* a border for clothing or material, made of a row of threads or strings hanging loose. ♦ *The cat pawed at the fringe at the bottom of my dress.* ♦ *The bottom of the curtain was decorated with fringe.* **2.** *n.* the edge of something; something that is far away from the center. (Figurative on ①. Sometimes plural with the same meaning.) ♦ *The spaceship traveled to the outer fringe of the solar system.* ♦ *The police stood on guard at the fringes of the crowd.* **3.** *tv.* to enclose something and serve as its border. ♦ *Lovely green trees fringed the placid lake.* ♦ *The office building was fringed by parking lots.*

fringe benefit ['frɪndʒ 'bɛn ə fɪt] *n.* something of value that a company gives to a worker beyond a salary and what is required by law. (Usually plural.) ♦ *One of the fringe benefits where I work is a free meal each shift.* ♦ *My fringe benefits are worth almost $2,000 a year.*

frisk ['frɪsk] *tv.* to pat and press on the body in a search for weapons, drugs, evidence, or stolen property. ♦ *The guards frisked me when I crossed the border.* ♦ *The police frisked the students as they entered the school.*

frisky ['frɪs ki] *adj.* playful; lively. (Adv: *friskily.* Comp: *friskier;* sup: *friskiest.*) ♦ *The frisky cat pawed at the string that I was pulling.* ♦ *Jane tickled Bill because she was in a frisky mood.*

fritter ['frɪt ɚ] **1.** *n.* a lump of batter containing small pieces of a food, such as corn or fruit, fried in deep fat. ♦ *We ate corn fritters with our hamburgers.* ♦ *Wait for the apple fritter to cool before you eat it.* **2. fritter away** *tv.* + *adv.* to waste something bit by bit. ♦ *Mary always fritters away her time by playing games on her computer.* ♦ *Dave frittered the day away at the beach.*

frivolity [frɪ 'vɑl ə ti] **1.** *n.* doing something for pleasure instead of being serious. (No plural form in this sense.) ♦ *Frivolity is discouraged at my office.* ♦ *I wish I had the time for frivolity, but I have bills to pay.* **2.** *n.* something done for pleasure instead of being serious. ♦ *Your computer games are an expensive frivolity in terms of time.* ♦ *He seems concerned only with frivolities!*

frivolous ['frɪv ə ləs] *adj.* silly; not serious. (Adv: *frivolously.*) ♦ *The teacher was annoyed by frivolous questions.* ♦ *I relaxed by watching a frivolous television show.*

frizzy ['frɪz i] *adj.* [of hair] having small, tiny, tight curls. (Adv: *frizzily.* Comp: *frizzier;* sup: *frizziest.*) ♦ *Humidity makes my hair become very frizzy.* ♦ *I covered my frizzy hair with a hat.*

frog ['frɔg] **1.** *n.* a small amphibian that hops and has webbed feet. ♦ *Bill played in the creek, watching the frogs hop around.* ♦ *I was kept awake by the croaking frogs in our backyard.* **2. be a big frog in a small pond** *idiom* to be an important person in the midst of less important people. ♦ *I'd rather be a big frog in a small pond than the opposite.* ♦ *The trouble with Tom is that he's a big frog in a small pond. He needs more competition.*

frolic ['frɑl ɪk] **1.** *iv., irreg.* to play; to have fun; to run and jump around. (Pt/pp: **frolicked.** Present participle is *frolicking.*) ♦ *The little children frolicked in the swimming pool.* ♦ *The dogs frolicked on the beach.* **2.** *n.* fun; fun entertainment. (No plural form in this sense.) ♦ *The party was filled with fun and frolic.* ♦ *The junior class sponsored a Spring Frolic at the student center.*

frolicked ['frɑl ɪkt] pt/pp of **frolic.**

from ['frʌm] **1.** *prep.* starting at a particular time or place; originating at a particular time or place. ♦ *I moved from Kansas when I was 16.* ♦ *The office is open from 9 A.M. to 3 P.M.* **2.** *prep.* <a word indicating separation or difference.> ♦ *Move the oily rags away from the gasoline.* ♦ *Because Susan and Mary are identical twins, I can't tell one from the other.* **3.** *prep.* out of. ♦ *Did these buttons come from that box?* ♦ *The speeding car came from a side street and passed me.* **4.** *prep.* sent by; given by. ♦ *My scholarship is from the government.* ♦ *This present is from your aunt.* **5.** *prep.* because of; due to. ♦ *I was screaming from the pain.* ♦ *The baby was crying from hunger.*

front ['frʌnt] **1.** *n.* the part of something that faces forward. ♦ *The front of the building faces the street.* ♦ *The bullet struck Tom in the front of his chest.* **2.** *n.* a group of people fighting for a political goal. ♦ *The underground political front demanded an open election.* ♦ *Hostages were taken by an extremist front.* **3.** *n.* the border of one's territory closest to the enemy during a war. ♦ *The soldiers were sent to the battle on the western front.* ♦ *Because we won the battle, our front moved another 30 miles east.* **4.** *n.* a border between two masses of air of a different temperature or pressure. ♦ *Temperatures are expected to drop tonight as a cold front moves in from Canada.* ♦ *A warm front moved over the region, breaking the cold spell.* **5.** *n.* the way one appears to other people; the way one seems to be when around other people; an outward appearance. ♦ *Jane keeps up a good front at work even though she hates her job.* ♦ *Bob claims to be happy, but I know his smile is just a front.* **6.** *iv.* to face in a certain direction. ♦ *The office fronts toward the east.* ♦ *My apartment fronts directly onto the street.* **7.** *adj.* at the **front** ① of something. ♦ *Lock the front door on your way in.* ♦ *Sue sat in the front seat next to the driver.* **8. put up a (brave) front** *idiom* to appear to be brave (even if one is not). ♦ *Mary is frightened, but she's putting up a brave front.* ♦ *If she weren't putting up a front, I'd be more frightened than I am.*

frontage ['frʌn tɪdʒ] *n.* a part of a building, property, or land that lies alongside a road, river, lake, etc. (No plural form in this sense.) ♦ *I rented a cabin with frontage on the lake.* ♦ *Our farm is worth a lot because it has frontage along the interstate.*

frontier [frən 'tɪr] **1.** *n.* a border; a line separating two states or countries. ♦ *The soldier was ordered to guard the frontier.* ♦ *The frontier between Germany and Switzerland is mountainous.* **2.** *n.* the line separating settled areas from wild areas; the edge of an undeveloped area. ♦ *The pioneers moved into the vast frontier.* ♦ *As more people moved west, America's frontier became smaller.*

frost ['frɔst] **1.** *n.* frozen moisture on the surface of something, especially ground; small ice crystals on the surface of something. (No plural form in this sense.) ♦ *A late frost killed the flowers' blooms.* ♦ *We covered the tomato plants to protect them from frost.* **2.** *iv.* to be covered with small ice crystals; to be covered with frozen moisture. ♦ *The car window frosted as I breathed on it.* ♦ *Did it frost last night?* **3.** *tv.* to put frosting on a cake or dessert. ♦ *I frosted the cake with a plastic knife.* ♦ *You have to let the cake cool before you frost it.*

frostbite ['frɔst bɑɪt] *n.* an injury caused by exposing skin to extremely cold weather without protection. (No plural form in this sense.) ♦ *Where are your mittens? Do you want to get frostbite?* ♦ *The mountain climber's fingers were purple with frostbite.*

frosting ['frɔs tɪŋ] *n.* a sugary mixture that is spread on top of a cake or pastry. (No plural form in this sense.) ♦ *Do you like chocolate or vanilla frosting?* ♦ *Mary tasted the frosting with her finger.*

frosty ['frɔs ti] **1.** *adj.* cold; below freezing. (Adv: *frostily.* Comp: *frostier;* sup: *frostiest.*) ♦ *Dress warmly. It's really frosty outside.* ♦ *We removed the frosty dessert from the freezer.* **2.** *adj.* covered with frost; looking **frosty** ①. (Comp: *frostier;* sup: *frostiest.*) ♦ *I got a frosty box of frozen peas out of the freezer.* ♦ *In the morning, I looked out the window at the frosty landscape.*

froth ['frɔθ] **1.** *n.* foam; a mass of white bubbles that forms on top of liquids or around the mouth. (No plural form in this sense.) ♦ *The waves were topped with white froth.* ♦ *Tom served some sort of fruit drink with a sweet froth on top.* **2.** *n.* something not very serious. (No plural form in this sense.) ♦ *Where are the news stories? This newspaper is nothing but froth.* ♦ *If you can get through the froth and propaganda, this novel is pretty interesting.*

frothy ['frɔθ i] **1.** *adj.* covered with froth; foamy. (Adv: *frothily.* Comp: *frothier;* sup: *frothiest.*) ♦ *Frothy beer tastes good on a hot summer day.* ♦ *The violent winds pushed our ship through the frothy waves.* **2.** *adj.* [of something] silly and of no importance. (Adv: *frothily.* Comp: *frothier;* sup: *frothiest.*) ♦ *After a frothy introduction, the book finally got to some important matters.* ♦ *Television newscasts seem to be one frothy issue after another.*

frown ['frɑʊn] **1.** *n.* a grimace; the opposite of a smile; the look on one's face made by pulling the eyebrows together and squinting the eyes. ♦ *Jane's deep frown indicated she was upset with me.* ♦ *Jimmy's frown went away when the clown gave him a balloon.* **2.** *iv.* to pull one's eyebrows together and squint the eyes; to scowl; to look angry. ♦ *My boss frowned because I was playing video games instead of working.* ♦ *Sue frowned because she was stuck in traffic.*

froze ['froz] pt of **freeze.**

frozen ['froz ən] **1.** pp of **freeze. 2.** *adj.* turned into ice; made hard because of a very cold temperature. ♦ *We* *skated on the frozen lake.* ♦ *The fishermen cut a hole in the frozen pond for their lines.* **3.** *adj.* exposed to **freezing** temperatures; affected by **freezing** temperatures. ♦ *The frozen tomato plants died.* ♦ *I warmed my frozen body in front of the fireplace.*

frugal ['frug əl] *adj.* saving money carefully; not spending much money. (Adv: *frugally.*) ♦ *The frugal student bought only the most inexpensive food.* ♦ *After I lost my job, I became much more frugal.*

fruit ['frut] **1.** *n.* the part of a plant that contains seeds and can be eaten as food. (No plural form in this sense. Number is expressed with *piece(s) of fruit.*) ♦ *I took a piece of fruit from the table and ate it.* ♦ *This drink is made from fruit.* **2.** *n.* a kind or type of ①. ♦ *Apples, oranges, and pears are all fruits.* ♦ *It is important to eat a variety of fruits and vegetables.* **3. forbidden fruit** *idiom* someone or something that one finds attractive or desirable partly because the person or thing is unobtainable. ♦ *Jim is in love with his sister-in-law only because she's forbidden fruit.* ♦ *The boy watches that program only when his parents are out. It's forbidden fruit.* **4. fruit(s) of one's labor(s)** *idiom* the results of one's work. ♦ *We displayed the fruits of our labor at the convention.* ♦ *What have you accomplished? Where is the fruit of your labors?*

fruitcake ['frut kek] *n.* a cake that has dried fruit and spices in it. ♦ *Every year, my boss gives me a homemade fruitcake.* ♦ *This fruitcake is difficult to slice because it's too hard.*

fruitful ['frut fʊl] *adj.* producing good results; beneficial; useful. (Adv: *fruitfully.*) ♦ *The fruitful research yielded a new cancer treatment.* ♦ *The workers were rewarded for their fruitful labors.*

fruition [fru 'ɪ ʃən] *n.* the attainment of results for something that was planned or worked for; the realization of one's plans and efforts. (No plural form in this sense.) ♦ *After much planning and hard work, Mary's ideas reached fruition.* ♦ *Five years of hard work came to fruition on graduation day.*

fruitless ['frut ləs] *adj.* useless; having no results; pointless. (Adv: *fruitlessly.*) ♦ *No hostages were freed in the fruitless rescue attempt.* ♦ *After years of fruitless research, the scientist changed fields.*

frustrate ['frʌs tret] **1.** *tv.* to cause someone to feel disappointed; to discourage someone. ♦ *I frustrated Jane because I forgot our date.* ♦ *The difficult exam frustrated the entire class.* **2.** *tv.* to hamper something; to prevent someone or something from achieving a certain result. ♦ *The heavy rain frustrated our attempts to go fishing.* ♦ *The experiment was frustrated by careless researchers.*

frustrating ['frʌs tret ɪŋ] *adj.* upsetting and disappointing. (Adv: *frustratingly.*) ♦ *The situation was so frustrating that I began to cry.* ♦ *I vowed to overcome the frustrating circumstances.*

frustration [frəs 'tre ʃən] **1.** *n.* disappointment and discouragement. (No plural form in this sense.) ♦ *Frustration caused Tom to be depressed.* ♦ *The frustration of not being able to find the right size shoes made John more and more angry.* **2.** *n.* something that frustrates someone. ♦ *Life is filled with a lot of little frustrations.* ♦ *Failing eyesight is a frustration we all have to live with.*

fry ['fraɪ] **1.** *tv.* to cook something in hot fat. ♦ *Do you fry your chicken in corn oil?* ♦ *Mary fried the fish that she caught.* **2. fries** *n.* thin pieces of potato fried in hot fat; french fries. (Treated as plural.) ♦ *Would you like fries with your hamburger?* ♦ *The fries made my hands greasy.* **3.** *n., irreg.* a young fish; a recently hatched fish. (Pl: *fry.* Usually plural.) ♦ *We could see a large number of fry swimming in the shallow water.* ♦ *The fisherman threw the fry back into the lake because they hadn't reached the legal size.* **4. small fry** *idiom* an unimportant person or thing; unimportant people or things. ♦ *The police have only caught the small fry. The leader of the gang is still free.* ♦ *At the moment our business is small fry, but we're planning to expand.*

fryer ['fraɪ ɚ] **1.** *n.* a chicken that is raised to be eaten. ♦ *The farmer fed the fryers corn.* ♦ *I removed the skin from the fryer and baked it.* **2.** *n.* a pan that is used for frying things. ♦ *I put the sliced potatoes in a large fryer and cooked them.* ♦ *Hot oil sizzled in the fryer, ready for cooking.*

fuddy-duddy ['fʌd i dəd i] *n.* someone who is old-fashioned; someone who is conservative. ♦ *I'm not allowed to do anything because my parents are fuddy-duddies.* ♦ *Don't be such a fuddy-duddy, and come to the party!*

fudge ['fʌdʒ] **1.** *n.* a thick, rich chocolate candy. (No plural form in this sense.) ♦ *I ate a scoop of ice cream covered with hot fudge.* ♦ *I ignored my diet and ate a piece of rich fudge.* **2.** *iv.* to be deceptive in some manner. (Informal.) ♦ *The researcher fudged a little so the results looked better than they actually were.* ♦ *The politician fudged, and the poll results looked better than they really were.*

fuel ['fjul] **1.** *n.* material that is burned to make heat or energy. ♦ *What kind of fuel heats your home, oil or gas?* ♦ *The scientist predicted America would run out of fuel within 20 years.* **2.** *tv.* to supply something with ①. ♦ *I fueled the boat engine with unleaded gasoline.* ♦ *It's your turn to fuel the car.* **3.** *tv.* to provide someone or something with energy, stimulation, or encouragement. (Figurative on ②.) ♦ *Anne fueled the debate by disagreeing with everything John said.* ♦ *Quit arguing with John! You'll only fuel his anger.* **4. add fuel to the fire** *idiom* to make a problem worse; to say or do something that makes a bad situation worse; to make an angry person get even more angry. ♦ *To spank a crying child just adds fuel to the fire.* ♦ *Bill was shouting angrily, and Bob tried to get him to stop by laughing at him. Of course, that was just adding fuel to the fire.*

fugitive ['fjudʒ ɪ tɪv] **1.** *n.* someone who has run away from or is hiding from the law. ♦ *The fugitive left the country and never returned.* ♦ *The radio announcement said that the fugitive was headed to our town.* **2.** *adj.* hiding or escaping from the law; fleeing. ♦ *The fugitive criminal fled to the mountains.* ♦ *The police tracked down the fugitive terrorists.*

fulfill [fʊl 'fɪl] **1.** *tv.* to carry out an order, plan, or promise. ♦ *The soldiers fulfilled their sergeant's order and attacked the fort.* ♦ *I fulfilled a promise to my dying mother by finishing college.* **2.** *tv.* to satisfy a demand or a need. ♦ *The kidnapped child's parents fulfilled the kidnapper's demand for money.* ♦ *I fulfilled my hunger by going to a restaurant.*

fulfillment [fʊl 'fɪl mənt] **1.** *n.* personal satisfaction and contentment. (No plural form in this sense.) ♦ *Many of* *us are seeking a feeling of fulfillment.* ♦ *Fulfillment is the most we can hope for in life.* **2.** *n.* meeting a demand; satisfying an obligation; completing a set of goals. (No plural form in this sense.) ♦ *The fulfillment of your obligation to your country can be met by serving in the army.* ♦ *John F. Kennedy did not live to see the fulfillment of his dreams.*

full ['fʊl] **1.** *adj.* completely filled; having no empty space. (Adv: *fully.* Comp: *fuller;* sup: *fullest.*) ♦ *The jar is full. There is not room for any more.* ♦ *The full bucket was very heavy, and some water spilled out of it as I walked.* **2. full of** *adj.* + *prep. phr.* abundant with someone or something; containing a lot of someone or something. ♦ *After the gunfight, the room was full of bullet holes.* ♦ *My report was full of spelling mistakes.* **3.** *adj.* entire; complete; whole. (Adv: *fully.*) ♦ *We did not always receive our full food ration during the war.* ♦ *I placed the full amount of detergent into the washing machine.* **4.** *adj.* at the highest or greatest extent possible. ♦ *Anne graduated from the university with full honors.* ♦ *We traveled down the highway at full speed.* **5. full of oneself** *idiom* conceited; self-important. ♦ *Mary's very unpopular because she's so full of herself.* ♦ *She doesn't care about other people's feelings. She's too full of herself.* **6. have one's hands full (with someone or something)** *idiom* to be busy or totally occupied with someone or something. ♦ *I have my hands full with my three children.* ♦ *You have your hands full with the store.*

fullback ['fʊl bæk] *n.* a football player who is positioned behind the front line, primarily responsible for running with the ball. ♦ *The exhausted fullback lay in the mud.* ♦ *The fullback caught the football and ran toward the goal line.*

full-blooded ['fʊl 'blʌd ɪd] **1.** *adj.* belonging to one ethnic group only. ♦ *Both of Helen's parents came from Athens, so she is a full-blooded Greek.* ♦ *The university offered scholarships to full-blooded American Indians.* **2.** *adj.* strong; vigorous. ♦ *The fair included a lot of full-blooded dancing and heavy drinking.* ♦ *We enjoyed the loud and full-blooded singing.*

full-blown ['fʊl 'blon] *adj.* developed to the greatest extent or degree possible; completely developed. ♦ *Tom was diagnosed as having a full-blown case of the flu.* ♦ *The angry citizens demanded a full-blown investigation into the senator's conduct.*

full-fledged ['fʊl 'flɛdʒd] **1.** *adj.* [of a bird] having all its flight feathers. ♦ *The full-fledged birds finally flew from their nest.* ♦ *The bird took care of its young until they were full-fledged.* **2.** *adj.* completely developed; matured. (Figurative on ①.) ♦ *It seems that Mary was just born yesterday, but now she's a full-fledged woman.* ♦ *My coughing turned into a full-fledged case of influenza.*

fullness ['fʊl nəs] *n.* being full; having as much of something as possible. (No plural form in this sense.) ♦ *The fullness of the reservoir raised fears about flooding.* ♦ *The fullness of the sound coming from the tiny speakers was amazing.*

full-scale ['fʊl 'skel] *adj.* complete; total; thorough. ♦ *The army launched a full-scale attack on the enemy.* ♦ *Congress conducted a full-scale investigation into the president's financial affairs.*

full-time ['fʊl 'tɑɪm] **1.** *adj.* all the time; 24 hours a day. ♦ *The nuclear power plant is a full-time operation.* ♦ *Being a parent is a full-time responsibility.* **2.** *adj.* [of a job that] takes up the working day, usually 8 hours a day, 5 days a week. ♦ *My father is a full-time employee at the car factory.* ♦ *Where I work, full-time workers get three weeks of vacation.* **3.** *adv.* throughout the normal work week. ♦ *Susan works full-time at the hospital.* ♦ *Mary is not well enough to work full-time yet.*

fully ['fʊl i] *adv.* completely; entirely; wholly. ♦ *Bob was fully responsible for the car accident.* ♦ *My teacher was fully satisfied with my work.*

fumble ['fʌm bəl] **1.** *iv.* to reach for or handle [something] clumsily. ♦ *I fumbled for a pen inside my briefcase.* ♦ *Lisa fumbled with the snaps on her shirt.* **2.** *tv.* [in football] to fail to hold onto a ball after having touched it or carried it. ♦ *The quarterback fumbled the football on the 30-yard line.* ♦ *I fumbled the ball when I slipped in the mud.* **3.** *tv.* to say words in a garbled way. (Figurative on ②.) ♦ *I fumbled my words because I was so tired.* ♦ *The actor fumbled the line because he was distracted by a scream in the audience.* **4.** *n.* the act of dropping a ball as in ②. ♦ *The instant replay showed the fumble in slow motion.* ♦ *We lost the game because we had too many fumbles.*

fume ['fjum] **1.** *n.* a volume of any gas, smoke, or chemical vapor. (Usually plural.) ♦ *The firefighters almost choked on the deadly fumes.* ♦ *The fumes from the factory coated the nearby buildings with soot.* **2.** *tv.* to emit fumes; to give off smoke or gas. ♦ *The truck fumed black soot when its gears were shifted.* ♦ *The factory chimney fumed deadly gases into the atmosphere.* **3.** *iv.* to be upset; to be angry; to show that one is angry. (Figurative on ②.) ♦ *Mary fumed for days when she was fired from her job.* ♦ *Bill sat and fumed because I yelled at him.*

fumigate ['fjum ə get] *tv.* to rid a room of insects or other pests by spraying it with a poisonous smoke or gas. ♦ *My landlord fumigated our apartment for bugs.* ♦ *I fumigated my kitchen after I saw a mouse.*

fumigation [fjum ə 'ge ʃən] *n.* spraying poisonous smoke or gas into a room to kill insects, mice, and other pests; spraying clothing with a substance to rid it of insect pests. (No plural form in this sense.) ♦ *The fumigation of our kitchen cost $250.* ♦ *The cost of fumigation was paid by our landlady.*

fun ['fʌn] **1.** *n.* enjoyment, especially from play or amusement. (No plural form in this sense.) ♦ *After a long day at work, I like to have fun.* ♦ *Did you have any fun at the beach today?* **2.** *adj.* entertaining; amusing; playful. (Colloquial.) ♦ *Thanks for the party! I had a really fun time.* ♦ *We had a fun day at the beach.* **3. fun and games** *idiom* playing around; doing worthless things; activities that are a waste of time. ♦ *All right, Bill, the fun and games are over. It's time to get down to work.* ♦ *This isn't a serious course. It's nothing but fun and games.* **4. make fun of someone or something** *idiom* to tease and make jokes about someone or something; to ridicule someone; to mock someone or something. ♦ *Please don't make fun of my dog!* ♦ *Jimmy cries when people make fun of him.* **5. poke fun (at someone)** *idiom* to make fun of someone; to ridicule someone. ♦ *Stop poking fun at me! It's not nice.* ♦ *Bob is always poking fun.*

function ['fʌŋk ʃən] **1.** *n.* the proper use of something; the purpose of something. ♦ *I demonstrated the proper function of the hammer.* ♦ *What is the function of this lever?* **2.** *n.* a social gathering; an event where people get together and socialize. ♦ *I spoke with the mayor at the church function.* ♦ *I was asked to bring some potato salad to the annual social function.* **3.** *iv.* to work properly; to operate; to be in proper use. ♦ *What's wrong with the TV? It doesn't function right.* ♦ *Your toaster won't function unless you plug it in.* **4. function as** *iv.* + *prep. phr.* to work as something; to be used as something; ♦ *This couch also functions as a bed.* ♦ *My apartment also functions as an office.*

functional ['fʌŋk ʃə nəl] **1.** *adj.* working; operable; not broken. (Adv: *functionally.*) ♦ *The TV set was functional until you dropped it.* ♦ *Although my car is functional, it needs some minor repairs.* **2.** *adj.* useful; practical. (Adv: *functionally.*) ♦ *This knife holder is not very functional because none of my knives fit in it.* ♦ *This small tool is a highly functional device.*

functionary ['fʌŋk ʃə nɛr i] *n.* a bureaucrat; a civil servant. ♦ *Each functionary sent me to a different department.* ♦ *Some bureaucratic functionary asked me to fill out a stack of application forms.*

fund ['fʌnd] **1.** *n.* an amount of money that is reserved for a specific reason. ♦ *Extra money in the school's building fund will be used to fix the roof.* ♦ *Jane donated money to her university's scholarship fund.* **2. funds** money; an amount or supply of money. (Treated as plural.) ♦ *There are no funds available for repairing the roof.* ♦ *Max lacks the funds needed to continue his education. n.* **3. (mutual) fund** *n.* an investment in which a large number of people own shares of investments in many securities. ♦ *Most of Dave's savings are in a bond fund.* ♦ *My accountant calculated how much money I had in mutual funds.* **4.** *tv.* to provide someone or something with money. ♦ *The government funded the social-service agency.* ♦ *My parents funded my college education.*

fundamental [fən də 'mɛn təl] **1.** *adj.* basic; essential. (Adv: *fundamentally.*) ♦ *I studied the fundamental theories of physics.* ♦ *The agency's fundamental goal was to feed the poor.* **2.** *n.* a basic rule; a principle. ♦ *This math class covers the fundamentals of algebra.* ♦ *The Law of Gravity is a fundamental of science.*

fundamentalism [fən də 'mɛn tə lɪz əm] *n.* a belief that the Bible should be interpreted and followed literally. (No plural form in this sense.) ♦ *Belief in the Bible is the basis of fundamentalism.* ♦ *The minister's approach to religion was based in fundamentalism.*

fundamentalist [fən də 'mɛn təl əst] *n.* someone who believes in religious fundamentalism. ♦ *Fundamentalists don't usually believe in the theory of evolution.* ♦ *The conservative senator was voted into office by fundamentalists.*

funding ['fʌn dɪŋ] *n.* money that is given to support someone or something; support money. (No plural form in this sense.) ♦ *The museum relied on private funding to stay open.* ♦ *Lisa's research qualifies for federal funding.*

funeral ['fjun ə rəl] **1.** *n.* a ceremony performed when someone is buried or cremated. ♦ *My uncle gave a eulogy at my father's funeral.* ♦ *Hundreds of people attended the senator's funeral.* **2.** *adj.* <the adj. use of ①.> ♦ *The mourners crowded into the funeral home.* ♦ *The funeral procession included dozens of cars.*

funereal [fju 'nir i əl] *adj.* somber, like a funeral; solemn. (Adv: *funereally.*) ♦ *A funereal mood hung over the factory for weeks after the explosion.* ♦ *Our office had a funereal atmosphere because no one was sure who was going to be laid off next.*

fungal ['fʌŋ gəl] *adj.* of or about fungus. ♦ *Dave had a fungal infection on his foot.* ♦ *A fungal growth covered the old leather saddle.*

fungi ['fʌn dʒɑɪ] pl of fungus.

fungicide ['fʌŋ dʒɪ sɑɪd] *n.* a poison that kills fungus. (No plural form in this sense.) ♦ *Bill sprayed his toes with fungicide.* ♦ *Bob had to use a fungicide on his scalp to cure a skin disease.*

fungus ['fʌŋ gəs] *n., irreg.* a plant that does not have leaves and is not green, such as the mushroom or toadstool. (Pl: fungi or *funguses.*) ♦ *Don't eat that fungus. It might be poisonous.* ♦ *Humans sometimes are afflicted with a fungus that grows on the skin.*

fun-loving ['fʌn ləv ɪŋ] *adj.* loving fun; loving to play; playful. ♦ *I enjoy traveling with Anne and Bob because they're a fun-loving couple.* ♦ *Our fun-loving uncle came to visit us for the summer.*

funnel ['fʌn əl] **1.** *n.* a cone-shaped device with a wide mouth and a narrow spout on the bottom, used when pouring liquids from one container into another. ♦ *I poured the gasoline from the can into the tank using a funnel.* ♦ *None of the liquid came through because the funnel was clogged with dirt.* **2. funnel (cloud)** *n.* a tornado; a violent, spinning wind, shaped something like ①. ♦ *We ran into the basement when the funnel cloud was sighted.* ♦ *Several dark funnels tore through Iowa during the night.* **3. funnel into** *tv.* + *prep. phr.* to pass a liquid through a funnel. ♦ *I funneled gasoline into the tank.* ♦ *I funneled the water into the canteen.* **4.** *iv.* to pass through a narrow opening. (Figurative on ③.) ♦ *The class funneled through the narrow door to the basement laboratory.* ♦ *The cars funneled onto the bridge in single file.*

funny ['fʌn i] **1.** *adj.* amusing; causing laughter. (Comp: *funnier;* sup: *funniest.*) ♦ *Would you like to hear a funny joke?* ♦ *We all laughed at the funny story.* **2.** *adj.* strange; weird; unusual; odd. (Comp: *funnier;* sup: *funniest.*) ♦ *Do you notice something funny about John lately?* ♦ *The store manager called the police because a funny man was hanging around the parking lot.* **3. strike someone funny** *idiom* to seem funny to someone. ♦ *Sally has a great sense of humor. Everything she says strikes me funny.* ♦ *Why are you laughing? Did something I said strike you funny?*

fur ['fɚ] **1.** *n.* the short, soft hair that is grown on many mammals. (No plural form in this sense.) ♦ *I petted my cat's fur.* ♦ *These gloves are lined with rabbit fur.* **2.** *n.* a coat or other garment made from animal skin covered with ①. ♦ *I put my furs in storage for the summer.* ♦ *I wear a fur in the winter because it's very warm.* **3.** *adj.* made from animal skin covered with ①. ♦ *Dave's hands remained warm because he was wearing fur gloves.* ♦ *Mary took her fur coat to the cleaners.*

furious ['fjɚ i əs] *adj.* very angry; violently angry; very upset. (Adv: *furiously.*) ♦ *My parents were furious when* *they saw my report card.* ♦ *The furious customer asked to speak to my manager.*

furlough ['fɚ lo] **1.** *n.* a period of time granted to be away from military service. ♦ *The private was granted a furlough to attend his father's funeral.* ♦ *While on his furlough, the soldier got arrested for speeding.* **2.** *tv.* to permit someone to have ①. ♦ *The private was furloughed so that he could attend a funeral.* ♦ *The officer furloughed the soldier for a week.*

furnace ['fɚn əs] *n.* an oven that can be heated at very high temperatures to melt metal, heat a building, etc. ♦ *We have our furnace inspected each year for carbon monoxide leaks.* ♦ *This furnace is used to melt the iron that will be made into steel.*

furnish ['fɚ nɪʃ] **1. furnish (with)** *tv.* (+ *prep. phr.*) to provide someone with something; to supply someone with something. ♦ *The school district furnished each student with textbooks.* ♦ *The hotel furnished towels and sheets.* **2. furnish (with)** *tv.* (+ *prep. phr.*) to supply a house or an apartment with furniture. ♦ *We furnished the house with inexpensive furniture.* ♦ *They can't afford to furnish the house right now.*

furnished ['fɚ nɪʃt] *adj.* having furniture; supplied with furniture. ♦ *I rented a furnished studio apartment for $500 a month.* ♦ *Although the apartment was furnished, it did not have a desk.*

furniture ['fɚ nɪ tʃɚ] *n.* the objects in a house, apartment, or office that can be moved, such as tables, chairs, desks, televisions, etc. (No plural form in this sense. Number is expressed with *piece(s) of furniture.*) ♦ *I had to hire workers to move my piano.* ♦ *We received several pieces of furniture as wedding gifts.*

furor ['fjɚ or] *n.* a rage; an uproar; a burst of violent or angry energy. ♦ *A dog got into the hospital and caused a great furor.* ♦ *The furor of the citizens led them to overthrow the government.*

furrow ['fɚ o] **1.** *n.* a long groove in the earth made by a plow. ♦ *I followed the plow, planting corn in the furrows.* ♦ *During the rainstorm, the furrows filled with water.* **2.** *n.* any groove. ♦ *The surface of the record was ruined by a deep furrow.* ♦ *My brow became lined with deep furrows as I got older.*

furry ['fɚ i] *adj.* covered with fur; having fur. (Adv: *furrily.* Comp: *furrier;* sup: *furriest.*) ♦ *I combed the burrs from the hair of my furry dog.* ♦ *A bear rubbed its furry back against the tree.*

further ['fɚ ðɚ] **1.** *adj.* more far; more distant in space or time. (One of the comparative forms of **far**, along with **farther.**) ♦ *Please hand me the further book of the two on the counter.* ♦ *Which town is further from here, Adamsville or Millsville?* **2.** *adv.* more far; more distant in space or time. ♦ *I can throw a baseball further than you can.* ♦ *We talked further into the night than I had expected.* **3.** *adv.* to a greater degree or extent; to a more advanced level. ♦ *Please come back this afternoon so we can discuss this problem further.* ♦ *The advanced student has progressed further in his studies than the beginner has.* **4.** *tv.* to advance or promote someone or something. ♦ *Tom did a lot to further his own interests, but he never helped anyone else.* ♦ *Please do what you can to further this project.*

furthermore ['fɚ ðɚ mor] *adv.* also; moreover; in addition to what has been said or stated. ♦ *I woke up late, and furthermore, I got stuck in traffic.* ♦ *I demand that you be quiet! Furthermore, I think you should apologize for waking me up.*

furthest ['fɚ ðəst] **1.** *adj.* the most far; the most distant in space or time. (One of the superlative forms of **far**, along with **farthest.**) ♦ *I sat in the seat furthest from the noisy children.* ♦ *Paying attention to traffic was the furthest thing from my mind when I got into the accident.* **2.** *adv.* most far; most distant in space or time. (One of the superlative forms of **far**, along with **farthest.**) ♦ *What's the furthest back you can remember?* ♦ *Of all my friends, John traveled the furthest last summer. He went to Russia.*

furtive ['fɚ tɪv] *adj.* half-hidden; done as though one is trying to hide something. (Adv: *furtively.*) ♦ *From across the classroom, my friend flashed me a furtive smile.* ♦ *I took a furtive look at Bill during class.*

fury ['fjɚ i] **1.** *n.* violent anger; rage. (No plural form in this sense.) ♦ *I was afraid to face my parents' fury after I wrecked the car.* ♦ *Bill hid in the closet to protect himself from his roommate's fury.* **2.** *n.* power or force. ♦ *The storm's fury blew down a grove of trees.* ♦ *The governor advised the citizens to move inland to avoid the fury of the hurricane.*

fuse ['fjuz] **1.** *tv.* to melt something together with something else; to melt two things together. ♦ *The welder fused the wires together with a blow torch.* ♦ *The plumber fused the pipe to the drain with lead.* **2.** *iv.* [for two or more things] to melt together. ♦ *Because of the fire, the wiring fused together.* ♦ *The plastic cups fused into a solid block in the heat.* **3.** *n.* a part of an electrical circuit that melts and stops the flow of electricity when there is a dangerous amount of electricity flowing through the circuit. ♦ *Don't turn on the microwave while I'm ironing because you'll blow a fuse.* ♦ *I had to change the fuse in the dark because the flashlight didn't work.*

fuselage ['fjus ə lɑʒ] *n.* the body of an airplane. ♦ *The impact of the crash shattered the fuselage into hundreds of small pieces.* ♦ *The company's name was painted along the side of the fuselage of each plane it owned.*

fusion ['fju ʒən] **1.** *n.* the joining or blending of two or more things. ♦ *This recipe is a fusion of Cajun and French cooking.* ♦ *Our band plays a fusion of jazz and blues.* **2.** *n.* energy created by combining the centers of two atoms. (No plural form in this sense.) ♦ *The scientists worked to develop a reliable source of energy from nuclear fusion.* ♦ *In physics class, we learned the difference between atomic fission and fusion.*

fuss ['fʌs] **1.** *iv.* to whine, cry, and pout. ♦ *The baby is fussing again. Maybe he needs feeding.* ♦ *Jimmy fusses whenever he is tired.* **2.** *iv.* to complain; to whine and cause a disturbance. ♦ *Some people always fuss about something!* ♦ *Lisa will fuss and fuss until she gets her way.* **3.** *n.* controversy. (Informal.) ♦ *Lisa created quite a fuss by wearing that skimpy bikini.* ♦ *What is all the fuss about?*

fussy ['fʌs i] **1.** *adj.* hard to please; likely to complain about everything. (Adv: *fussily.* Comp: *fussier;* sup: *fussiest.*) ♦ *Tom's a fussy eater and refuses to eat vegetables.* ♦ *If you weren't so fussy, we could have finished shopping an hour ago.* **2.** *adj.* overly ornamented; [of decoration] overly complicated. (Adv: *fussily.* Comp: *fussier;* sup:

fussiest.) ♦ *I carefully placed the fussy porcelain dolls in the cabinet.* ♦ *I don't like the fussy design of my company's new letterhead.*

futile ['fjut əl] *adj.* hopeless; useless; worthless. (Adv: *futilely.*) ♦ *It would be futile for you to explain it again. I just don't understand algebra.* ♦ *The mayor's futile gestures to the angry citizens only angered them further.*

future ['fju tʃɚ] **1.** *adj.* coming; yet to come; later. ♦ *Taking account of my future earnings, I won't be able to repay my loans for over 10 years.* ♦ *My future plans include starting my own restaurant.* **2.** *n.* the time that is to come; events that will happen. (No plural form in this sense.) ♦ *Will humans live on the moon in the future?* ♦ *The psychic claimed that she could predict the future.* **3.** *n.* the things that are planned for one's life. (No plural form in this sense.) ♦ *My future includes another four years of college.* ♦ *I planned for my future by saving a lot of money for retirement.* **4.** *n.* <the tense of verbs that describe actions that are to happen or actions that will happen.> ♦ *In English, the words "will" or "going to" often indicate the future tense.* ♦ *Many languages show the future tense by adding an affix to the verb.*

futuristic ['fju tʃɚ 'ɪs tɪk] *adj.* looking like something from the future, especially something radical in design. (Adv: *futuristically* [...ɪk li].) ♦ *The older members of the law firm didn't like the architect's futuristic design for the new office building.* ♦ *The futuristic apartment building looked like a spaceship.*

fuzz ['fʌz] *n.* short, soft, light, fluffy hairs. (No plural form in this sense.) ♦ *Bob couldn't grow a full mustache, but his upper lip was covered with blond fuzz.* ♦ *Peaches are covered with fuzz.*

fuzzy ['fʌz i] *adj.* having fuzz; covered with fuzz. (Adv: *fuzzily.* Comp: *fuzzier;* sup: *fuzziest.*) ♦ *John's face was fuzzy because he hadn't shaved in a few days.* ♦ *The fuzzy skin of a peach can be eaten.*

G

G AND **g** ['dʒi] *n.* the seventh letter of the alphabet. ♦ G *comes after* F *and before* H. ♦ *There are three* Gs *in* giggle.

gab ['gæb] **1.** *iv.* to talk informally and rapidly; to gossip. (Informal.) ♦ *I gabbed with my friends about the movie.* ♦ *Susan gabbed for hours with Tom during the flight.* **2.** *n.* informal conversation; chatter. (Informal. No plural form in this sense.) ♦ *Long bus rides can be tedious, but we filled the time with gab.* ♦ *People who talk a lot are said to have the gift of gab.*

gabby ['gæb i] *adj.* talkative; full of talk or gossip. (Informal. Adv: *gabbily.* Comp: *gabbier;* sup: *gabbiest.*) ♦ *I wanted to speak seriously, but my gabby friends were being silly.* ♦ *When John is in a gabby mood, he'll talk for hours.*

gable ['ge bəl] *n.* a triangular part of an exterior wall, with sloping edges that follow the roof line. ♦ *The trim around the gables of the old house needed paint.* ♦ *Lightning struck the house, setting fire to the old wooden gables.*

gadfly ['gæd flɑɪ] **1.** *n.* a kind of fly that swarms around cattle. ♦ *The cow brushed a swarm of gadflies away with its tail.* ♦ *The air in the barn was thick with gadflies.* **2.** *n.* an annoying person. (Figurative on ①.) ♦ *Susan told the gadfly who was bothering her to go away.* ♦ *Curious gadflies swarmed around the movie star.*

gadget ['gædʒ ɪt] *n.* any machine, device, tool, or appliance. ♦ *The gadget controlling my car's air conditioner is broken.* ♦ *I bought some sort of a gadget to help open jar lids.*

gadgetry ['gædʒ ɪ tri] *n.* several gadgets, thought of as a group. (No plural form in this sense.) ♦ *Lisa was amazed by all the electronic gadgetry at the computer store.* ♦ *Gadgetry in various stages of development cluttered the inventor's laboratory.*

gag ['gæg] **1.** *n.* something used to block someone's mouth to prevent talking or shouting for help. ♦ *The robber put a gag in my mouth so I couldn't shout for help.* ♦ *The police removed the gags from the victims' mouths.* **2.** *n.* a practical joke; a hoax. ♦ *On April Fools' Day, people play harmless gags on each other.* ♦ *It turned out that the author's disappearance was just a gag for publicity.* **3.** *tv.* to block someone's mouth with ①. ♦ *The robber gagged me to keep me from shouting for help.* ♦ *The kidnapper gagged the child's mouth with tape.* **4.** *tv.* to cause someone or some creature to retch; to cause someone or some creature to choke. ♦ *The thick smoke was gagging me as I escaped the fire.* ♦ *The spoiled milk almost gagged me when I started to drink it.* **5.** *iv.* to choke on something; to retch. ♦ *I gag whenever I try to eat peas.* ♦ *Max gagged on the thick smoke coming from the fire.*

gaggle ['gæg əl] **1. gaggle of** *n.* + *prep. phr.* a flock of geese. ♦ *A gaggle of geese waddled toward the pond.* ♦ *I could hear a gaggle of geese flying overhead.* **2. gaggle of** *n.* + *prep. phr.* a large group of people. (Figurative on ①.) ♦ *The rock star was surrounded by a gaggle of screaming fans.* ♦ *The gaggle of photographers annoyed the basketball player.*

gaiety ['ge ə ti] *n.* happiness; lively cheerfulness. (No plural form in this sense.) ♦ *The party's gaiety ended abruptly when our neighbors called the police.* ♦ *Mary enjoyed reading about the gaiety of the Roaring Twenties.*

gaily ['ge li] *adv.* happily; in a lively and cheerful fashion. ♦ *The children played gaily in the park.* ♦ *Susan was gaily dressed for the party.*

gain ['gen] **1.** *tv.* to get something; to obtain something; to acquire something. ♦ *I gained 10 pounds during my first year in college.* ♦ *The author gained a lot of notoriety from her latest controversial book.* **2.** *tv.* [for a clock or watch] to reach a later time than it should have. ♦ *Our clock must have gained a few minutes—it's already chimed midnight.* ♦ *My watch gains five minutes every week.* **3.** *tv.* to earn or save time. ♦ *We gained an hour by taking the expressway instead of country roads.* ♦ *I gain thirty minutes by taking the subway to work instead of driving.* **4.** *iv.* to earn, get, or acquire something of value. ♦ *How much can we gain by switching long-distance phone companies?* ♦ *The company would gain a lot by merging with its competitor.* **5.** *n.* a profit. (Sometimes plural with the same meaning.) ♦ *Susan received a 10% gain on her investment.* ♦ *The thief spent his gains from the robbery on a new car.* **6.** *n.* an increase in weight. ♦ *His gain in weight was due to a lack of activity.* ♦ *During pregnancy, women normally experience weight gain.* **7. ill-gotten gains** *idiom* money or other possessions acquired in a dishonest or illegal fashion. ♦ *Bill cheated at cards and is now living on his ill-gotten gains.* ♦ *Mary is enjoying her ill-gotten gains. She deceived an old lady into leaving her $5,000 in her will.*

gait ['get] *n.* the way in which someone or some creature, such as a horse, runs or walks. ♦ *My horse's gait remained steady as I rode it to the lake.* ♦ *I suspected from his awkward gait that Bill was injured.*

galaxy ['gæl ək si] *n.* a large mass or cluster of stars and their solar systems in space. ♦ *The name of our galaxy is the Milky Way.* ♦ *We can only dream of sending rockets to distant galaxies.*

gale ['gel] **1.** *n.* a very strong wind. ♦ *The hurricane caused strong gales in its path.* ♦ *The violent gale blew the truck off the freeway.* **2.** *n.* an outburst, especially of laughter. (Often plural.) ♦ *My friends responded to my joke with gales of laughter.* ♦ *The school board's decision was met with a gale of hoots and jeers.*

gall ['gɔl] **1.** *n.* bile, a bitter liquid made by the liver. (Especially of animals. No plural form in this sense.) ♦ *Gall is released into the small intestine by the liver.* ♦ *Gall helps the body absorb food.* **2.** *n.* a sore spot on the hide of an animal, usually caused by rubbing or chafing. ♦ *The cowboy rubbed salve on the gall under the saddle.* ♦ *The veterinarian examined the gall on my horse's back.* **3.** *n.* rudeness; impudence. (No plural form in this sense.) ♦ *The mayor was astounded by the citizens' gall.* ♦ *What gall! You* *are incredibly impudent!* **4.** *tv.* to cause a sore to develop by rubbing or chafing. ♦ *The leather strap galled the horse's belly.* ♦ *Something was galling the horse, and I had to stop and find out what it was.* **5.** *tv.* to annoy or bother someone severely; to irritate someone. (Figurative on ④.) ♦ *Anne's insulting words galled me.* ♦ *The angry citizens galled the mayor during a press conference.* **6. have the gall to do something** *idiom* to have sufficient arrogance to do something. ♦ *I bet you don't have the gall to argue with the mayor.* ♦ *Only Jane has the gall to ask the boss for a second raise this month.*

gallant ['gæl ənt] *adj.* honorable; chivalrous; very polite. (Refers to men who are very polite toward women. Adv: *gallantly.*) ♦ *A gallant gentleman offered Anne his seat on the bus.* ♦ *Mary and Jane gave their gallant waiter a generous tip.*

gallery ['gæl ə ri] **1.** *n.* a balcony, often running along a wall or outside a window. ♦ *Our hotel room had a small gallery that faced a courtyard.* ♦ *We stood on the gallery and enjoyed the view.* **2.** *n.* the cheapest and highest seats in a theater. ♦ *The gallery isn't bad, but you may need binoculars.* ♦ *I couldn't afford main-floor tickets, so we sat in the gallery.* **3.** *n.* a room or building where art is displayed. ♦ *The east wing of the gallery featured modern oil paintings.* ♦ *My artwork is on display in a gallery in New York City.*

galley ['gæl i] **1.** *n.* a kind of ancient ship that is powered by oars and sometimes sails. ♦ *The prince's galley was rowed by forty strong men.* ♦ *A diver found a sunken galley off the coast of France.* **2.** *n.* a kitchen on a ship or airplane. ♦ *The ship's waiter took my undercooked food back to the galley.* ♦ *There was a loud crash in the galley when the plane flew through bad weather.*

gallium ['gæl i əm] *n.* a bluish-white chemical element used in lasers and transistors. (No plural form in this sense.) ♦ *The atomic symbol for gallium is Ga, and its atomic number is 31.* ♦ *The cost of transistors rose due to a gallium shortage.*

gallivant ['gæl ə vænt] *iv.* to wander around, often looking for entertainment. ♦ *John spent the summer gallivanting across the country.* ♦ *I met interesting people while gallivanting around Europe.*

gallon ['gæl ən] *n.* a unit of liquid measure, equal to 4 quarts, 8 pints, or almost 3.8 liters. ♦ *We buy a gallon of milk every week.* ♦ *A gallon in the U.S. is about .83 of a British gallon.*

gallop ['gæl əp] **1.** *n.* a fast gait of a horse in which all four feet are off the ground once during each stride. ♦ *The horse went into a gallop when it broke free from the reins.* ♦ *I couldn't bring my horse to a gallop because it was too tired.* **2.** *iv.* to move quickly; [for a horse] to run fast. ♦ *The horse galloped away from the fire.* ♦ *To escape from the bull, I had to gallop across the field.* **3. gallop through** *iv.* + *prep. phr.* to speed through something. (Figurative on ②.) ♦ *Congress galloped through the debate session.* ♦ *I galloped through the textbook in less than an hour.*

galloping ['gæl əp ɪŋ] **1.** *adj.* moving rapidly; moving with the gait of a gallop; rushing; hurrying. ♦ *It's hard to ride a galloping horse if you haven't done it before.* ♦ *The noise of a dozen galloping zebras frightened the sleeping antelope.* **2.** *adj.* [of something] moving or changing. (Figurative on ①.) ♦ *The office worker was unprepared for the galloping technological advances of the last decade.* ♦ *The economists were alarmed by the galloping rate of inflation.*

gallows ['gæl oz] *n.* a wooden frame used to execute criminals by hanging. (Treated as plural.) ♦ *The executioner met the prisoner at the gallows.* ♦ *The gallows broke, so the criminal was hanged from a tree.*

galore [gə 'lor] *adj.* in a great amount; plenty; lots. (Not prenominal.) ♦ *After David won the lottery, he suddenly had friends galore.* ♦ *The wedding guests were treated with drinks galore.*

galvanize ['gæl və nɑɪz] **1.** *tv.* to cover iron or steel with a thin coat of zinc to prevent rust. (A process that is carried out through the use of electricity. From Luigi Galvani, who discovered that electricity could be produced by chemical action.) ♦ *Steel used for cars is galvanized to prevent the cars from rusting.* ♦ *Workers at the mill galvanized the steel before shipping it to suppliers.* **2.** *tv.* to shock, stimulate, or excite someone into taking action. ♦ *Management's refusal to bargain galvanized the workers to strike.* ♦ *Rising waters galvanized the townspeople to work hard to prevent flooding.*

galvanized ['gæl və nɑɪzd] *adj.* coated with a protective layer of zinc to prevent rust. ♦ *Galvanized steel is almost rustproof.* ♦ *I bought galvanized nails so they wouldn't rust when exposed to rain.*

gambit ['gæm bɪt] **opening gambit** *idiom* an opening movement or statement made to secure a position that is to one's advantage. ♦ *The rebel army's opening gambit was to bomb the city's business district.* ♦ *The prosecution's opening gambit was to call a witness who linked the defendant to the scene of the crime.*

gamble ['gæm bəl] **1.** *iv.* to routinely bet money or property; to routinely play games of chance or bet on sporting events, etc. ♦ *I don't gamble if the stakes are too high.* ♦ *For vacation, I went to Las Vegas to gamble.* **2. gamble on** *iv.* + *prep. phr.* to bet money on something. ♦ *I gambled on the chestnut horse to win the derby.* ♦ *My parents warned me not to gamble on the lottery.* **3. gamble on** *iv.* + *prep. phr.* to take the chance that something will happen. (Figurative on ②.) ♦ *The union gambled on management signing a new contract.* ♦ *Bob might show up on time, but I wouldn't gamble on it.* **4.** *tv.* to risk or bet money or property on a game of chance, a sporting event, or the like. ♦ *I gambled my watch against Bill's TV that I'd win the poker game.* ♦ *Jane gambled $100 that the roulette ball would land on red.* **5.** *n.* a risk. ♦ *It was a gamble, but John got a raise by threatening to quit.* ♦ *Driving while drunk is a dangerous gamble indeed.*

gambling ['gæm blɪŋ] **1.** *n.* betting on games of chance or sporting events, involving the risk of winning or losing money. (No plural form in this sense.) ♦ *Gambling is illegal in many cities and states.* ♦ *Bob was in debt to everyone because of his gambling.* **2.** *adj.* <the adj. use of ①.> ♦ *Anne realized she had a gambling problem because she spent $250 each week on lottery tickets.* ♦ *John went bankrupt because his gambling debts were so high.*

game ['gem] **1.** *n.* a kind of contest, sporting event, or pastime played according to a set of rules. ♦ *What is your favorite game?* ♦ *Baseball is a very popular game.* **2.** *n.* an instance of playing ①. ♦ *Would you like to see a baseball* *game tonight?* ♦ *When the game is over, please come right home.* **3.** *n.* a scheme; a plan. (Informal.) ♦ *"What's your little game?" the detective asked the mysterious voice on the telephone.* ♦ *"Don't play any games with me," the babysitter warned the unruly children.* **4.** *n.* wild animals that are hunted for sport or food. (No plural form in this sense.) ♦ *Every November, I hunt for wild game, especially deer.* ♦ *I showed the warden the permit that allowed me to hunt game.* **5. be game** *idiom* to be ready for action; to be agreeable to participating in something. ♦ *"I'm game," David replied when I suggested we go bowling.* ♦ *We're going to the park to play football. Are you game?* **6. fair game** *idiom* someone or something that it is quite permissible to attack. ♦ *I don't like seeing articles exposing people's private lives, but politicians are fair game.* ♦ *Journalists always regard movie stars as fair game.*

gamut ['gæm ət] *n.* the entire range of something from one extreme to the other. (No plural form in this sense.) ♦ *In one day, Bob ran the whole gamut of emotions from very depressed to extremely happy.* ♦ *The movie included the gamut of comedy from slapstick to satire.*

gander ['gæn dɚ] *n.* a male goose. ♦ *The cook served the roast gander with potatoes and carrots.* ♦ *The farmer fed corn to the ganders.*

gang ['gæŋ] **1.** *n.* a group of people who work, play, or do things together. ♦ *The gang of prisoners picked up trash from the roadside.* ♦ *After work, John went bowling with a gang of friends.* **2.** *n.* a group of urban youths who practice crime and violence. ♦ *The Smiths moved from the inner city to the suburbs because they were afraid of gangs.* ♦ *Gangs make many cities unsafe.* **3. gang up on someone** *idiom* [for a group] to attack [someone]. ♦ *The thugs ganged up on the tourists and robbed them.* ♦ *The two bullies ganged up on Max and tried to beat him up.*

gangly ['gæŋ gli] *adj.* tall, thin, and awkward; uncoordinated. (Comp: *ganglier;* sup: *gangliest.*) ♦ *The gangly teenager had grown seven inches in one year.* ♦ *Ballet classes transformed her from a gangly young woman to a graceful dancer.*

gangrene ['gæŋ grin] *n.* the decay of part of the body caused by the cutting off of the flow of blood to that part. (No plural form in this sense.) ♦ *Gangrene set in after Bill's leg had been gouged by shrapnel.* ♦ *The doctors amputated the soldier's foot before gangrene set in.*

gangster ['gæŋ stɚ] *n.* a member of a gang of criminals; a thug. ♦ *During Prohibition, the alcohol trade was operated by gangsters.* ♦ *The gang leader killed the gangster who talked to the police.*

gangway ['gæŋ we] **1.** *n.* a passageway; a walkway. ♦ *The gangway between the houses was a great place for kids to play.* ♦ *Our dog sleeps during the night in the gangway.* **2.** *n.* an opening in the railing of a ship where a walkway leading off the ship can be attached or rested. ♦ *Jane turned and waved to her friends on shore from the gangway.* ♦ *The cruise director stood by the gangway, welcoming passengers aboard.*

gap ['gæp] **1.** *n.* an opening created by a crack; an opening created where two objects or structures do not meet. ♦ *I filled the gap around the window frame with caulk.* ♦ *The gap in the bookcase is where my dictionary belongs.* **2.** *n.* an interruption in time; a period of time between two events or the parts of an event. ♦ *There was a ten-minute gap between acts while the set was changed.* ♦ *The guests talked to each other during the two-hour gap between the wedding and the reception.* **3.** *n.* a ravine; a gorge; a pass between two mountains. ♦ *The pioneers traveled through the gap in a covered wagon.* ♦ *A rickety wooden bridge was the only way across the gap.* **4.** *n.* a measurable or noticeable difference between two things or groups. ♦ *The gap between the rich and the poor is widening in America.* ♦ *The gap between men's and women's wages is slowly narrowing.*

gape ['gep] **1.** *n.* an open-mouthed stare. ♦ *The famous actor entered the restaurant and was met by gapes and stares.* ♦ *Tom's face became one huge gape as he saw the truck coming toward him.* **2. gape at** *iv.* + *prep. phr.* to stare in amazement, wonder, or disbelief, usually with the mouth hanging open; to open one's mouth in amazement, wonder, or disbelief. ♦ *Traffic slowed as drivers stopped to gape at the accident.* ♦ *Everyone gaped at the scantily clad model in the grocery store.* **3.** *iv.* to be wide open. ♦ *After the explosion, a large hole gaped where the building had been.* ♦ *Bill's wound gaped when he extended his arm.*

gaping ['gep ɪŋ] *adj.* open wide; wide open. (Adv: *gapingly.*) ♦ *The explosion left a gaping hole where the building used to be.* ♦ *Blood flowed from the gaping bullet wound.*

garage [gə 'rɑʒ] *n.* a building used to store a car or other motor vehicle. ♦ *Mr. Smith parked his car in the garage.* ♦ *Parking garages downtown charge about $8 per hour.*

garb ['gɑrb] **1.** *n.* the clothing that one wears, especially the clothing worn by members of specific professions; one's attire. (No plural form in this sense.) ♦ *The surgeons donned their surgical garb and went into the operating room.* ♦ *The poet's garb consisted entirely of black denim.* **2. garb in** *tv.* + *prep. phr.* to clothe someone; to cover someone or something with material. ♦ *The dressmaker garbed the bride in fine silk.* ♦ *Some famous designer garbed the movie star in lavish costumes for the movie.*

garbage ['gɑr bɪdʒ] **1.** *n.* trash; rubbish; useless things that are thrown away. (No plural form in this sense.) ♦ *Please throw this garbage away now!* ♦ *I searched through the garbage for the bill I'd thrown away.* **2.** *n.* the container that holds ①. (No plural form in this sense.) ♦ *I threw the leftover food into the garbage.* ♦ *Please haul the garbage out to the curb so it can be collected.*

garble ['gɑr bəl] **1.** *tv.* to distort the meaning or understanding of something. ♦ *Static garbled my cellular phone conversation.* ♦ *The translator garbled the meaning of the diplomat's request.* **2.** *tv.* to mumble or mix up one's words. ♦ *The drunk garbled his words so badly that we couldn't understand him.* ♦ *Bob garbled his speech because he was nervous.* **3.** *n.* speech that is distorted. (No plural form in this sense.) ♦ *The cheap tape recorder made everyone's words sound like garble.* ♦ *The lawyer played the incriminating tape, but the jury couldn't understand the garble.*

garden ['gɑrd n] **1.** *n.* a piece of land where plants, flowers, or vegetables are grown. ♦ *These tomatoes are fresh from the garden.* ♦ *I weeded and watered the garden every day.* **2.** *n.* a place where people go for amusement or relaxation. ♦ *We sat in the beer garden under the moonlight.* ♦ *The students visited the zoological garden on their* *field trip.* **3.** *iv.* to cultivate plants in a garden; to raise and take care of plants grown in a garden. ♦ *My dad loves to garden.* ♦ *Mary gardens, and it is her favorite hobby.*

gardener ['gɑrd nɚ] *n.* someone who takes care of a garden; someone who plants and nourishes plants in a garden. ♦ *The gardener spread fertilizer around the tomato plants.* ♦ *Five gardeners were hired to take care of the palace garden.*

gardenia [gɑr 'din jə] **1.** *n.* a fragrant white flower that grows on a low shrub. ♦ *The fragrance from the gardenias was enchanting on the warm summer evening.* ♦ *I gave my date a corsage made of a single gardenia.* **2.** *n.* the shrub on which ① grows. ♦ *Our property line was marked with a row of gardenias.* ♦ *We have to fertilize the gardenias every year to make them bloom.*

gargle ['gɑr gəl] **1.** *iv.* to rinse one's mouth or throat with a liquid by breathing out while the liquid is in the mouth or throat. ♦ *When I have a sore throat, I gargle with warm salt water.* ♦ *After brushing my teeth, I gargle with mouthwash.* **2.** *n.* the liquid one uses for gargling as in ①. (No plural form in this sense.) ♦ *Max spit the gargle into the sink.* ♦ *I prefer a mint-flavored gargle.*

garish ['gɛr ɪʃ] *adj.* too bright or showy; gaudy. (Adv: *garishly.*) ♦ *The critic disliked the garish costumes in the movie.* ♦ *The bride's garish wedding gown was bright pink.*

garland ['gɑr lənd] **1.** *n.* a wreath or string of flowers or leaves worn around the neck or head. ♦ *The beauty pageant winner was crowned with a garland of flowers.* ♦ *In Hawaii, tourists are given garlands to wear around their necks.* **2.** *n.* a decoration made of flowers, leaves, ribbons, etc., that are linked together in a chain. ♦ *We decorated the room with garlands of fresh flowers.* ♦ *The basket was decorated with a garland of daisies.*

garlic ['gɑr lɪk] **1.** *n.* a strong-smelling plant whose bulb is made of small segments, used as a flavoring in cooking. (No plural form in this sense.) ♦ *I'd like ham and garlic on my pizza.* ♦ *I used several cloves of garlic in the spaghetti sauce.* **2.** *adj.* made from or with ①. ♦ *Mary put some garlic dressing on her salad.* ♦ *I had a garlic pizza for lunch.*

garment ['gɑr mənt] *n.* an article of clothing; a piece of clothing. ♦ *David's garments were torn in the accident.* ♦ *I took my dirty garments to the Laundromat.*

garner ['gɑr nɚ] *tv.* to earn or accumulate something. (Not for money or goods.) ♦ *The mayor garnered the respect of the townspeople.* ♦ *In four years, Mary garnered eight weeks of unused vacation.*

garnish ['gɑr nɪʃ] **1.** *tv.* to decorate food or drink with something edible that will make it look prettier or taste better. ♦ *The chef garnished the broiled fish with a sprig of parsley.* ♦ *The cool drink was garnished with a slice of lemon.* **2.** *n.* a decoration, especially one that makes a plate of food look more attractive. ♦ *The colorful garnish was made from radishes and orange peels.* ♦ *The chef placed a garnish of parsley on top of the steak.*

garrison ['gɛr ə sən] **1.** *n.* a fort; a building or small town surrounded by a stockade. ♦ *The bomb blew up the enemy garrison where supplies were stored.* ♦ *The soldiers retreated to the safety of their garrison.* **2.** *n.* the military troops stationed at ①. ♦ *The general ordered the garrison to attack the enemy at dawn.* ♦ *The entire garrison was destroyed by a bomb blast.* **3.** *tv.* to station military troops at ①. ♦ *The troops who were garrisoned at the fort protected the town.* ♦ *Soldiers were garrisoned at the fort in preparation for the final battle.*

garrulous ['gɛr ə ləs] *adj.* very talkative; constantly talking; very wordy. (Adv: *garrulously.*) ♦ *It is very difficult to interrupt a garrulous person.* ♦ *The garrulous man annoyed everyone else in the audience.*

garter ['gɑrt ɚ] *n.* an elastic band worn around the leg, or an elastic strap suspended from an undergarment, to hold up a stocking. ♦ *Jane prefers silk stockings and garters to pantyhose.* ♦ *The groom removed the bride's decorative garter and threw it into the crowd.*

gas ['gæs] **1.** *n.* a vapor; a substance that is not in a liquid or solid state at room temperature. (No plural form in this sense.) ♦ *Water turns into a gas at 212 degrees Fahrenheit.* ♦ *Carbon monoxide is a gas with no smell or color.* **2.** *n.* a naturally occurring, flammable vapor used for cooking and heating. (No plural form in this sense.) ♦ *I prefer cooking on stoves that use gas instead of electricity.* ♦ *Anne smelled gas, so she opened the windows and called the fire department.* **3. gases** *n.* kinds or types of ①. ♦ *In the chemistry lab, there are tanks of different gases in the storage room.* ♦ *The two main gases in the air we breathe are oxygen and nitrogen.* **4.** *n.* gasoline, the liquid made from petroleum that is used to operate motors and engines. (No plural form in this sense.) ♦ *My car's tank holds 12 gallons of gas.* ♦ *The arsonist doused the building with gas and set it on fire.* **5. gas up** *iv.* + *adv.* to put gasoline into a tank. ♦ *Dave gassed up with premium fuel.* ♦ *On our way to New Orleans, we had to gas up in Memphis.* **6. gas up** *tv.* + *adv.* to fill a vehicle's tank with gasoline. ♦ *Dave gassed up his car with premium fuel.* ♦ *There was a stop in Memphis, where the driver gassed the bus up.* **7.** *tv.* to kill someone or something with poisonous gas ①. ♦ *The exterminator gassed the cockroaches with poison.* ♦ *Millions of people were gassed in concentration camps during World War II.* **8. out of gas** *idiom* tired; exhausted; worn out. ♦ *What a day! I've been working since morning, and I'm really out of gas.* ♦ *This electric clock is out of gas. I'll have to get a new one.* **9. step on the gas** *idiom* to make a car go faster. ♦ *I'm in a hurry, driver. Step on the gas!* ♦ *I can't step on the gas, mister. There's too much traffic.* **10. to be a gas** *idiom* to be a wild or funny. (No plural form in this sense.) ♦ *You should have been at Susan's party last night. It was a gas.* ♦ *That movie was such a gas. I haven't laughed so hard in ages.*

gaseous ['gæs i əs] *adj.* in the form of a gas or vapor, such as air. (Adv: *gaseously.*) ♦ *The gaseous form of water is called steam.* ♦ *The gaseous poison spread easily throughout the building, killing all the termites and ants.*

gash ['gæʃ] **1.** *n.* a large or deep cut or wound; a slash. ♦ *The doctor stitched up the gash on Anne's arm.* ♦ *The meteor created a two-mile-long gash where it struck the earth.* **2.** *tv.* to slash or cut something. ♦ *Bill gashed his leg on a sharp rock when he fell off his bike.* ♦ *Mary gashed her forehead on the low ceiling above the stairs.*

gasket ['gæs kɪt] *n.* a piece of flexible material used to seal the joint between two pieces of metal to prevent air or liquid from getting in or out. ♦ *Intense pressure blew the gasket out and released hot steam.* ♦ *The mechanics checked all the joints and gaskets for leaks.*

gasoline [gæs ə 'lin] *n.* a liquid made from petroleum that is used to operate motors and engines. (No plural form in this sense.) ♦ *My lawn mower is powered by gasoline.* ♦ *Gasoline catches fire very easily.*

gasp ['gæsp] **1.** *n.* a quick, short inward breath; a quick intake of air. ♦ *There was a loud gasp from the audience when the actor collapsed.* ♦ *After running three miles, my breath came in short, quick gasps.* **2.** *iv.* to breathe in suddenly as in surprise, shock, fear, etc. ♦ *The passengers gasped as the elevator fell three floors.* ♦ *After being saved from drowning, the swimmer gasped for breath.*

gasping ['gæs pɪŋ] *adj.* breathing in suddenly, as in surprise, shock, fear, etc. (Adv: *gaspingly.*) ♦ *With gasping breaths, the witness told the jury about the murder.* ♦ *The gasping swimmer struggled to stay afloat after being injured.*

gastric ['gæs trɪk] *adj.* of or about the stomach. (Adv: *gastrically* [...ɪk li].) ♦ *Heartburn is a kind of gastric distress.* ♦ *When I smell good food, my gastric juices begin to flow.*

gate ['get] **1.** *n.* a hinged barrier that can be opened or closed, serving as the entrance and exit in a fence, wall, or other opening. ♦ *Bill closed the gate behind him to keep the dog inside the yard.* ♦ *The farmer led the cows through the open gate.* **2.** *n.* an ornamental structure, including ①, serving as a formal entrance to a park, cemetery, street, etc. ♦ *The attacking army was stopped at the gate to the city.* ♦ *I'll meet you at the gate in front of the park at three o'clock.* **3.** *n.* the point of entry at a stadium, arena, etc. ♦ *We entered the stadium through Gate 5.* ♦ *Mary stood at the gate, taking tickets as people entered the stadium.* **4.** *n.* the entrance to the passageway to an airplane in an airport. ♦ *Bill ran from Gate 12C to the other side of the airport.* ♦ *Susan met Bob at the gate when he flew into town.*

gate-crasher ['get kræʃ ɚ] *n.* someone who enters a party or an event without being invited or without paying. ♦ *The gate-crashers were arrested and removed from the banquet.* ♦ *One gate-crasher was kind enough to bring some food to the party.*

gateway ['get we] **1.** *n.* a space in a fence or a wall that frames a gate or where a gate can be placed; an entrance or exit. ♦ *We approached the gateway and hoped that the gate was not locked.* ♦ *People without tickets were not allowed through the gateway.* **2.** *n.* an (abstract) way of entering something. (Figurative on ①.) ♦ *The encyclopedia can be a gateway to knowledge.* ♦ *The preacher said rock music was a gateway to hell.*

gather ['gæð ɚ] **1.** *tv.* to bring something together; to collect something together. ♦ *Bob gathered apples that had fallen to the ground.* ♦ *Anne gathered her thoughts before answering the question.* **2.** *tv.* to assume something; to deduce something based on information that one knows or has learned. (Takes a clause.) ♦ *I gather that you'll want to leave tomorrow?* ♦ *Since you're a vegetarian, I gather that you don't want any of my grilled chicken.* **3. gather to** *tv. + prep. phr.* to pull someone or something in closely; to embrace someone or something closely. ♦ *Jane gathered her child to her bosom during the thunderstorm.* ♦ *David gathered the baby to his chest and comforted her.* **4.** *tv.* to increase speed or intensity. ♦ *The ball gathered speed as it rolled downhill.* ♦ *The hurricane gathered strength as it moved across the ocean.* **5.** *iv.* to come together into a big group. ♦ *My friends gathered together to help me after my accident.* ♦ *People gathered in the town square to hear the mayor speak.*

gathering ['gæð ɚ ɪŋ] *n.* a group of people; an assembly; a group of people who are grouped together for a specific purpose. ♦ *The senator spoke to the gathering about taxation.* ♦ *The popular band attracted a large gathering.*

gaudy ['gɔd i] *adj.* too showy; too colorful; lacking taste in style. (Adv: *gaudily.* Comp: *gaudier;* sup: *gaudiest.*) ♦ *Bob bought a gaudy polyester jacket at a thrift store.* ♦ *The tourists who wore gaudy clothes were very noticeable.*

gauge ['gedʒ] **1.** *n.* a device or instrument for displaying a measurement. ♦ *The gauge indicated that the tire needed more air.* ♦ *We'd better stop for gas soon because the gas gauge is on empty.* **2.** *n.* a measurement of the scope or range of something. ♦ *This quiz is a gauge of your capacity for learning geometry.* ♦ *The test will serve as a gauge of your knowledge of biology.* **3.** *n.* the diameter of the barrel of a shotgun or of a wire or the thickness of a sheet of metal. ♦ *Grandpa aimed his 20-gauge shotgun at the intruder.* ♦ *The electrician knew which gauge of wire to install.* **4.** *n.* the distance between the two rails of a track or between the two wheels on an axle. ♦ *Almost all railroad track in the United States has the same gauge.* ♦ *The monorail's gauge was narrower than the track in the subway.* **5.** *tv.* to estimate a distance. ♦ *Tom gauged the distance to the river to be about a mile.* ♦ *I could not gauge how many miles the town was from the farm.*

gaunt ['gɔnt] *adj.* pale and thin; looking hungry and emaciated. (Adv: *gauntly.* Comp: *gaunter;* sup: *gauntest.*) ♦ *The children orphaned during the war were sick and gaunt.* ♦ *From his hospital bed, Bill flashed a gaunt smile to his friends.*

gauze ['gɔz] *n.* a thin, loosely woven, and nearly transparent cloth. (No plural form in this sense.) ♦ *The nurse covered the wound with sterile gauze.* ♦ *The tent's entrance was covered with gauze to keep the flies out.*

gave ['gev] pt of give.

gavel ['gæ vəl] *n.* a small, wooden hammer used by a judge or an auctioneer to get people's attention and to mark the completion of an order or transaction. ♦ *The judge banged the gavel after the prisoner was sentenced.* ♦ *The auctioneer banged the gavel and yelled, "Sold to the man with the blue tie for $50!"*

gawk ['gɔk] *iv.* to stare at someone or something foolishly or stupidly. ♦ *The children gawked at the dead bird by the side of the road.* ♦ *Don't gawk! It is very rude.*

gawky ['gɔk i] *adj.* awkward; clumsy; uncoordinated. (Adv: *gawkily.* Comp: *gawkier;* sup: *gawkiest.*) ♦ *The gawky teenager tripped and fell down the stairs.* ♦ *I was gawky and uncoordinated the first time I went skating.*

gay ['ge] **1.** *adj.* happy; cheerful; brightly colored. (Adv: *gaily.* Comp: *gayer;* sup: *gayest.*) ♦ *The party room was decorated with gay balloons and ribbons.* ♦ *We had a gay old time at the reunion.* **2.** *adj.* homosexual; [of someone, usually a male] attracted to members of the same sex. (Comp: *gayer;* sup: *gayest.*) ♦ *I invited my gay uncle to my wedding.* ♦ *Mary suspected that her unmarried son was gay.* **3.** *adj.* concerning or associated with ④. ♦ *There were dozens of colorful floats in the gay parade.* ♦ *The newsstand carries a number of gay magazines.* **4.** *n.* a homosexual person, usually a male. ♦ *Gays and lesbians in different communities can communicate on the World Wide Web.* ♦ *A group of gays sued the company for discrimination.*

gaze ['gez] **1.** *n.* an intent stare. ♦ *I followed John's gaze toward the horizon.* ♦ *Anne was disturbed by the stranger's gaze toward her.* **2. gaze at** *iv.* + *prep. phr.* to stare at someone or something intently; to look at someone or something for a long time in admiration or wonder. ♦ *I lay on the grass and gazed at the stars all night.* ♦ *I gazed at the television for four hours without moving.*

gazelle [gə 'zɛl] *n., irreg.* a kind of small Asian or African antelope. (Pl: *gazelle* or *gazelles.*) ♦ *The gazelle swiftly fled from the lion.* ♦ *During a safari, we saw a herd of gazelle.*

gazetteer [gæ zə 'tɪr] *n.* a dictionary of place names and other geographical terms. ♦ *A pronouncing gazetteer tells you how to pronounce the names of places.* ♦ *This dictionary has a gazetteer at the end.*

gear ['gɪr] **1.** *n.* a wheel with teeth along its edge that moves similar wheels of differing diameters. ♦ *Gears serve to transfer power and change the direction of rotation.* ♦ *A piece of gum fell onto the gears, bringing the machine to a halt.* **2.** *n.* equipment; tools; the things required to do a certain activity. (No plural form in this sense.) ♦ *The firefighters grabbed their gear and headed toward the blaze.* ♦ *The hiker bought new gear for a two-week camping trip in Vermont.* **3.** *n.* one of a small number of different configurations of ① available to a driver of a motor vehicle. (The choice of ① ranges from low speed at high power to high speed at low power.) ♦ *While driving up the hill, Anne shifted to a lower gear.* ♦ *This car won't start if the transmission is in gear.* **4. gear (oneself) up for something** *idiom* to prepare for something. ♦ *The citizens on the coast geared up for the approaching hurricane.* ♦ *I geared up for the big presentation by eating a big breakfast.* **5. gear something to someone or something** *idiom* to cause something to match something else; to create or adapt something for a specific purpose. ♦ *Tim geared his speech to his audience.* ♦ *The newspaper geared its language to a fourth-grade reading level.*

gearshift ['gɪr ʃɪft] *n.* a rod or lever in a motor vehicle that controls which gear the vehicle is in. ♦ *Bill kept one hand on the gearshift while he drove through the mountains.* ♦ *John accidentally knocked the gearshift into neutral while his father was driving.*

geese ['gis] pl of goose.

gel ['dʒɛl] **1.** *n.* something sticky and bouncy like gelatin. (No plural form in this sense.) ♦ *This gel turns liquid at room temperature.* ♦ *Mix the glue until it turns to a gel.* **2.** *n.* a sticky substance that is used to keep hair in place. (No plural form in this sense.) ♦ *Anne rubbed hair gel through her bangs to keep them out of her eyes.* ♦ *John combed gel through his hair to keep it in place.* **3.** *iv.* [for a liquid] to thicken into ①. ♦ *The dessert will gel when you refrigerate it.* ♦ *The chemist studied the properties of liquid substances when they gel.* **4.** *iv.* to become fixed in one's mind; to become definite. (Figurative on ③.) ♦ *The important ideas of the article gelled in my mind.* ♦ *After we discussed it for a while, the plan began to gel.*

gelatin ['dʒɛl ə tən] **1.** *n.* a clear, jelly-like substance made from stewing animal bones and tissues, used in certain foods, film, glue, and other products. (No plural form in this sense.) ♦ *By the time gelatin is used for food, there is nothing left that can be identified as animal tissue.* ♦ *Gelatin is made from leftover parts of the cattle.* **2.** *n.* a sweet, clear, jelly-like food. (No plural form in this sense.) ♦ *For dessert, we ate strawberry-flavored gelatin.* ♦ *I like lime gelatin that's topped with whipped cream.*

gelding ['gɛl dɪŋ] *n.* a male animal, especially a horse, that has been castrated. ♦ *The gelding pulled the plow through the pasture.* ♦ *The veterinarian examined the gelding a week after its castration.*

gem ['dʒɛm] **1.** *n.* a jewel; a precious stone, especially one used in jewelry. ♦ *My favorite kinds of gems are sapphires and rubies.* ♦ *The gem fell out of its setting when my ring fell to the floor.* **2.** *n.* someone or something that is very beautiful or wonderful; a perfect example of someone or something. ♦ *My secretary is a real gem!* ♦ *We drove a gem of a sports car down to the beach.*

gemstone ['dʒɛm ston] *n.* a jewel; a precious stone, especially one used in jewelry. ♦ *The jeweler valued the gemstone in my ring at $750.* ♦ *The radiant gemstones in your necklace caught my eye.*

gender ['dʒɛn dɚ] **1.** *n.* [in grammar] a subdivision of nouns into masculine, feminine, and, sometimes, neuter categories. ♦ *In languages that have gender, all nouns have gender even if they represent things that do not have sexual distinctions.* ♦ *In German, the gender of the word* Hund, *meaning 'dog,' is masculine.* **2.** *n.* sex ③; the condition of being male or female. ♦ *I wrote my name, address, age, and gender on the application form.* ♦ *I couldn't determine the gender of the baby dressed in green.*

gene ['dʒin] *n.* a part of a chromosome within every living cell that determines the traits of the plant or animal. ♦ *The scientists searched for the human gene that causes senility.* ♦ *The biologist manipulated the tomato's genes to make it juicier.*

genealogy [dʒi ni 'ɑl ə dʒi] **1.** *n.* the study of the ancestors of a specific person through many generations. (No plural form in this sense.) ♦ *By studying genealogy, you can also learn a lot about history.* ♦ *The book on genealogy explained how to find family records in foreign countries.* **2.** *n.* a record or account of the ancestors of a person or family. ♦ *Anne traced her genealogy back to 12th-century Scotland.* ♦ *By tracing his genealogy, Bill learned he was related to George Washington.*

genera ['ʒɑn ə rə] the Latin plural of genus.

general ['dʒɛn ə rəl] **1.** *adj.* commonly known or understood; widespread. (Adv: *generally.*) ♦ *That two plus two equals four is general knowledge.* ♦ *Contrary to the general belief, the tomato is actually a fruit.* **2.** *adj.* not specific; not specialized. (Adv: *generally.*) ♦ *The doctor gave the patient a general anesthetic before operating.* ♦ *Bill took general courses until he chose history as a major.* **3.** *adj.* usual; regular; appropriate to most situations. (Adv: *generally.*) ♦ *The general approach to this problem is to telephone the child's parents.* ♦ *As a general rule, you should floss your teeth after eating.* **4.** *n.* a high-ranking army or air force officer. ♦ *The general led the troops into battle.* ♦ *The president honored the general for his bravery during the war.* **5. in general** *phr.* referring to the entire class being discussed; speaking of the entire range of possibilities; in most situations or circumstances. ♦ *I like vegetables in general, but not beets.* ♦ *In general, I prefer a hotel* *room on a lower floor but will take a higher room if it's special.*

generality [dʒɛn ə 'ræl ə ti] *n.* a statement or idea that is not specific or not detailed. ♦ *The mayor spoke in generalities even though we demanded specific information about the budget.* ♦ *You need to make the generalities in your paper more specific.*

generalization [dʒɛn ə rə lɪ 'ze ʃən] **1.** *n.* generalizing; obscuring detail with a general statement. (No plural form in this sense.) ♦ *Generalization simply covers up the facts.* ♦ *Your report has too much generalization and no presentation of facts.* **2.** *n.* a significant point or principle developed by studying numerous examples. ♦ *Bob made an important generalization by studying the data.* ♦ *There are no important generalizations that can be made about the growth of this plant.* **3.** *n.* a general statement or idea; a statement or idea that is not specific or not detailed; a statement or idea that is very broad. ♦ *I refuted Bill's faulty generalizations with hard facts.* ♦ *Often, prejudice is the result of unfair generalizations.*

generalize ['dʒɛn (ə) rə lɑɪz] *iv.* to make a statement or form an idea that is not specific or not detailed. ♦ *The company spokesman generalized while the audience demanded specifics.* ♦ *At the accident site, the reporter could only generalize because no specific information was yet available.*

generally ['dʒɛn (ə) rə li] **1.** *adv.* usually; commonly. ♦ *Generally, I buy groceries on Thursday.* ♦ *Rain is generally accompanied by cloudy skies.* **2.** *adv.* by almost everyone. ♦ *It is generally thought that too much sun can be bad for your skin.* ♦ *It is generally known that George Washington was the first president of the United States.* **3.** *adv.* in a way that does not consider details or specifics. ♦ *The summary described generally the things that had to be done, while the details were outlined in the actual report.* ♦ *The spokeswoman addressed the impact of the lawsuit generally, omitting the important details.*

generate ['dʒɛn ə ret] *tv.* to cause something to come into being. ♦ *The power of moving water can be used to generate electricity.* ♦ *My coworkers generate a lot of confusion.*

generation [dʒɛn ə 're ʃən] **1.** *n.* producing or creating something. (No plural form in this sense.) ♦ *The designer supervised the generation of the new clothing line.* ♦ *The generation of energy from solar power creates little pollution.* **2.** *n.* one stage in the history of a family. ♦ *The Browns' 60th anniversary brought together four generations of their family: themselves, their three children, their twelve grandchildren, and three great-grandchildren.* ♦ *My cousins belong to the same generation as I do.* **3.** *n.* all the people of the same culture who were born around the same time, taken as a group. ♦ *Jane, like many other members of her generation, grew up with TV.* ♦ *The reporter padded his article with stereotypes about the generation of Americans born in the 1960s.*

generator ['dʒɛn ə ret ɚ] *n.* a machine that changes one kind of energy into another kind of energy, especially one that changes mechanical energy into electricity. ♦ *Air conditioners place a heavy demand on electrical generators.* ♦ *During the blackout, the hospital relied on its emergency generators.*

generic [dʒə 'nɛr ɪk] **1.** *adj.* common to a whole group; referring to a whole group; general. (Adv: *generically* [...ɪk li].) ♦ *The lazy reporter wrote a few generic comments about the event instead of researching the matter.* ♦ *The politician made only generic statements to the press.* **2.** *adj.* [of a product] sold without a brand name. (Adv: *generically* [...ɪk li].) ♦ *I don't eat generic foods, but I use generic paper products a lot.* ♦ *Generic medicines are as effective as expensive name brands.* **3.** *n.* a generic ② product. ♦ *We always buy generics to save money.* ♦ *Generics are usually shelved together in grocery stores.*

generosity [dʒɛn ə 'rɑs ə ti] *n.* the quality of not being selfish; the quality of being willing to give one's time and money to others. (No plural form in this sense.) ♦ *The alumni's generosity made scholarships available to needy students.* ♦ *Susan was thankful for her friends' generosity while she was in the hospital.*

generous ['dʒɛn ə rəs] **1.** *adj.* not selfish; giving freely. (Adv: *generously.*) ♦ *The generous millionaire donated 10% of his assets to charity.* ♦ *I thanked my aunt for her generous offer to help me go to college.* **2.** *adj.* [of an amount] more than adequate. (Adv: *generously.*) ♦ *I have a generous supply of paper clips in my desk drawer.* ♦ *My mashed potatoes were covered with generous helpings of gravy.*

genesis ['dʒɛn ə sɪs] **1.** *n.* the beginning of something; the origin or something. (No plural form in this sense.) ♦ *The biologist studied life at its genesis.* ♦ *The inventive developers met to foster the genesis of new products.* **2. Genesis** *n.* the first book of the Bible. ♦ *Bill started to read the Bible, but he didn't get past Genesis.* ♦ *The Book of Genesis provides an account of creation.*

genetic [dʒə 'nɛt ɪk] **1.** *adj.* of or about genes; of or about the parts of the cell that determine traits. (Adv: *genetically* [...ɪk li].) ♦ *The genetic makeup of an organism is encoded in its DNA.* ♦ *Bill doesn't want to have children because he has an inherited genetic disorder.* **2. genetics** *n.* the study of genes; the study of heredity; the study of the inborn traits of plants and animals. (Treated as singular.) ♦ *Genetics has been a science since the 19th century.* ♦ *Genetics can explain why brown-eyed parents can have blue-eyed children.*

genial ['dʒi ni əl] *adj.* pleasant; kind; cheerful. (Adv: *genially.*) ♦ *I was greeted at the store entrance by a genial employee.* ♦ *Lisa exchanged genial greetings with the bus driver.*

genie ['dʒɪ ni] *n.* [in Arabian fairy tales] a magical spirit who has the power to grant people their wishes. ♦ *When Aladdin rubbed the magic lamp, a genie appeared.* ♦ *The genie offered to grant the young man three wishes.*

genital ['dʒɛn ə təl] **1.** *adj.* of or about the sexual organs. (Adv: *genitally.*) ♦ *Anne's gynecologist prescribed a medicated lotion for her genital rash.* ♦ *The baseball hit the pitcher in the genital area.* **2. genitals** *n.* the sex organs; genitalia. ♦ *Male athletes protect their genitals by wearing protective clothing.* ♦ *Swimming suits, no matter how skimpy, are designed to conceal the genitals.*

genitalia [dʒɛn ɪ 'tel jə] *n.* the sex organs; the genitals. (A Latin plural.) ♦ *In the painting, the nude's genitalia were covered with a fig leaf.* ♦ *Children are taught to clean their genitalia regularly.*

genius ['dʒin jəs] **1.** *n.* someone who is very smart, especially someone who is much smarter than most of the population. ♦ *Because Jane was a genius, she went to a school for gifted children.* ♦ *Because Max was a genius, he was incredibly bored in school.* **2.** *n.* someone who has a very impressive talent or skill in a specific area. (Figurative on ①.) ♦ *Ludwig van Beethoven was a musical genius.* ♦ *Emily Dickinson was a literary genius.* **3.** *n.* the talent or skill of ②. (No plural form in this sense.) ♦ *Because of Anne's creative genius, her gallery is very successful.* ♦ *Engineering genius was required to build the Golden Gate Bridge.*

genocide ['dʒɛn ə saɪd] *n.* the deliberate killing of an ethnic group. (No plural form in this sense.) ♦ *The dictator tried to make his nation ethnically pure through genocide.* ♦ *Millions of people were victims of genocide during World War II.*

genre ['ʒɑn rə] *n.* a specific style, especially of writing or art. (From French.) ♦ *Genres of writing include romance, science fiction, and westerns.* ♦ *Jazz is my favorite genre of music.*

genteel [dʒɛn 'til] *adj.* polite; refined. (Adv: *genteelly.*) ♦ *The book of etiquette emphasized genteel, middle-class manners.* ♦ *The talk-show host had a genteel way of greeting guests.*

gentle ['dʒɛn təl] *adj.* pleasantly mild; not rough; tame; kind. (Adv: *gently* ['dzɛnt li]. Comp: *gentler;* sup: *gentlest.*) ♦ *A gentle wind blew through the valley.* ♦ *I gave my favorite teacher a gentle hug on the last day of school.*

gentleman ['dʒɛnt əl mən] **1.** *n., irreg.* a man who is refined, polite, and well mannered. (Pl: gentlemen.) ♦ *A true gentleman holds the door open for the person behind him.* ♦ *Anne sighed, "For once, I'd like to date a gentleman."* **2.** *n., irreg.* a polite term for man. ♦ *Please ask the gentleman to come in.* ♦ *Ladies and gentlemen, please be seated.*

gentlemen ['dʒɛnt əl mən] pl of gentleman.

gentleness ['dʒɛnt əl nəs] *n.* the quality of being gentle; calmness; tenderness. (No plural form in this sense.) ♦ *I appreciate my dentist's gentleness while filling cavities.* ♦ *The gentleness of the massage was very soothing.*

gently ['dʒɛnt li] **1.** *adv.* kindly. ♦ *The doctor told Jane the bad news very gently.* ♦ *My teacher gently advised me to do the assignment over.* **2.** *adv.* smoothly; not roughly. ♦ *Please handle this fragile crystal very gently.* ♦ *The wind blew gently across the plains.*

genuine ['dʒɛn ju ɪn] **1.** *adj.* real; actual; not fake; not artificial. (Adv: *genuinely.*) ♦ *My necklace is made with genuine pearls.* ♦ *Genuine leather costs more than imitation leather.* **2.** *adj.* sincere; not pretending to act a certain way. (Adv: *genuinely.*) ♦ *My friends expressed genuine sorrow at my loss.* ♦ *I was touched by David's genuine display of sympathy.*

genus ['dʒin əs] *n.* [in the system of describing all living plants and animals] a group of related species. (The Latin plural is genera; the English plural is *genuses.*) ♦ Homo sapiens *is the genus and species of human beings.* ♦ *The biologist studied flies of one genus.*

geographer [dʒi 'ɑ grə fɚ] *n.* someone who works in the field of geography. ♦ *Geographers redrew political boundaries after the Soviet Union collapsed.* ♦ *The geographer explained the effects of the flood on the riverbank.*

geographically [dʒi ə 'græf ɪk li] *adv.* in a way that has to do with geography; from the standpoint of geography. ♦ *Geographically speaking, Russia is a part of both Asia and Europe.* ♦ *This map is geographically accurate, showing exactly where everything is.*

geography [dʒi 'ɑ grə fi] **1.** *n.* the study of the features of the surface of Earth, including the land and climate, countries, and the people and culture of the countries. (No plural form in this sense.) ♦ *We learned about the countries of western Africa in geography class.* ♦ *When Mrs. Miller taught geography, she was astounded how many students couldn't find the United States on a world map.* **2.** *n.* the features of the land of a certain area. (No plural form in this sense.) ♦ *The geography of Utah is mountainous.* ♦ *The geography of Illinois is mostly flat.*

geologist [dʒi 'ɑl ə dʒəst] *n.* someone who works in the field of geology. ♦ *The geologist determined that the hardened lava was 1,000 years old.* ♦ *Geologists were hired to determine likely sites for new oil wells.*

geology [dʒi 'ɑl ə dʒi] *n.* the study of the origin and the structure of Earth. (No plural form in this sense.) ♦ *The study of the composition of the earth's crust is a part of geology.* ♦ *The dinosaur fossil was excavated by scientists who studied archaeology and geology.*

geometric [dʒi ə 'mɛ trɪk] **1.** *adj.* of or about geometry. (Adv: *geometrically* [...ɪk li].) ♦ *The mathematician wrote an article about geometric solids.* ♦ *The computer program involved several geometric algorithms.* **2.** *adj.* formed by lines, curves, circles, squares, triangles, etc. (Adv: *geometrically* [...ɪk li].) ♦ *Bill's artwork is actually an intricate geometric design.* ♦ *The swimming pool was tiled in a simple geometric pattern.*

geometry [dʒi 'ɑm ɪ tri] **1.** *n.* the part of mathematics that deals with the relationships and properties of points, lines, curves, angles, surfaces, and solids. (No plural form in this sense.) ♦ *Geometry demands lots of reasoning.* ♦ *A student of geometry can easily bisect a line using a compass and a protractor.* **2.** *adj.* <the adj. use of ①.> ♦ *The geometry student figured out the radius of the circle.* ♦ *I am late for geometry class.*

geophysics [dʒi o 'fɪz ɪks] *n.* a part of geology that uses physics to study the properties of the features of Earth. (Treated as singular.) ♦ *The scientist used geophysics to explain the earthquake's effects.* ♦ *With a degree in geophysics, Anne worked for an oil company developing new ways of extracting oil from the earth.*

Georgia ['dʒor dʒə] See Gazetteer.

geranium [dʒə 'ren i əm] *n.* a common house or garden plant with red, pink, or white flowers. ♦ *The fragrance of geraniums makes me sneeze.* ♦ *I planted geraniums around the oak tree in my front yard.*

gerbil ['dʒɚ bəl] *n.* a small desert rodent, sometimes kept as a pet. ♦ *The gerbil ran for hours on its exercise wheel.* ♦ *I feed gerbils and mice to my pet snake.*

geriatric [dʒɛr i 'æ trɪk] **1.** *adj.* of or about old people; of or about human aging. (Adv: *geriatrically* [...ɪk li].) ♦ *My grandfather was admitted to the hospital's geriatric ward.* ♦ *The nursing home's staff specialized in geriatric medicine.* **2. geriatrics** *n.* the medical study and treatment of old people and diseases that affect old people. (Treated as singular.) ♦ *The staff members at the nursing home were all trained in geriatrics.* ♦ *Jane specialized in geriatrics because she wanted to help the elderly.*

germ ['dʒɚm] *n.* a very small organism that causes disease. ♦ *Germs collect on surfaces that other people have touched.* ♦ *Disinfectants are used to kill germs.*

German ['dʒɚ mən] **1.** *n.* a citizen or native of Germany. ♦ *My grandparents were both Germans.* ♦ *My teacher is a German from Berlin.* **2.** *n.* the language spoken in Germany by ①. (No plural form in this sense.) ♦ *I have studied German for three years.* ♦ *German is easy for me because my parents speak it.* **3.** *adj.* of or about Germany, ①, and ②. ♦ *I have some old German books about castles and churches.* ♦ *I have studied the German language for three years.*

germane [dʒɚ 'men] *adj.* relevant; appropriate; pertaining to what is being discussed. (Adv: *germanely.*) ♦ *At the end of her speech, Susan answered only the questions that were germane to her topic.* ♦ *David read books that were germane to his research topic.*

Germanic [dʒɚ 'mæn ɪk] **1.** *n.* a language group that includes German, English, Dutch, and the Scandinavian languages. ♦ *Germanic includes Swedish, Norwegian, Danish, and Dutch.* ♦ *Germanic is a large group of languages, some of which are widely spoken.* **2.** *adj.* <the adj. use of ①.> ♦ *English is a Germanic language, but it is also heavily influenced by Latin and French.* ♦ *Romance and Germanic languages are spoken in Switzerland.* **3.** *adj.* of or about Germany or Germans. (Adv: *Germanically* [...ɪk li].) ♦ *Blond hair and blue eyes are common Germanic traits.* ♦ *The car was built with typical Germanic precision.*

germanium [dʒɚ 'men i əm] *n.* a brittle, grayish-white chemical element used in semiconductors and transistors. (No plural form in this sense.) ♦ *The atomic symbol for germanium is Ge.* ♦ *The atomic number for germanium is 32.*

Germany ['dʒɚ mə ni] See Gazetteer.

germicide ['dʒɚm ɪ sɑɪd] *n.* something that kills germs, especially something that kills the germs that cause disease. (No plural form in this sense.) ♦ *The janitor sprayed the bathroom with a strong germicide.* ♦ *I swabbed the cut on my arm with a germicide.*

germinate ['dʒɚm ə net] **1.** *iv.* [for a seed] to sprout; to begin to develop. ♦ *The acorn germinated and began to develop into an oak tree.* ♦ *After the seeds germinated, I transplanted them to a larger pot.* **2.** *tv.* to cause something to sprout and develop. ♦ *Sun and moisture germinated the seeds we had planted.* ♦ *The warm weather germinated the flowers, but an early frost could kill them.*

gerontology [dʒɛr ən 'tɑl ə dʒi] *n.* the study of old people and the problems of aging. (No plural form in this sense.) ♦ *The mayor hired a specialist in gerontology to address the issues of the city's elderly.* ♦ *The head of the nursing home had worked in the field of gerontology all of her adult life.*

gerund ['dʒɛɚ ənd] *n.* the present participle of a verb used as a noun. ♦ *In the sentence "Writing requires concentration,"* writing *is a gerund.* ♦ *Gerunds can take adjectives, as in "Good writing requires concentration."*

gestate ['dʒɛs tet] **1.** *iv.* [for an embryo or fetus] to be carried in the womb. ♦ *Humans gestate in the womb for nine months.* ♦ *While her fetus gestated, Mary visited her doctor regularly.* **2.** *iv.* [for something, such as an idea] to develop slowly. (Figurative on ①.) ♦ *The author's novel gestated in her mind for years before she wrote it.* ♦ *Jane's latest invention gestated in her mind until she was confident that it could be built.*

gestation [dʒɛ 'ste ʃən] *n.* the time of pregnancy from conception to birth. (No plural form in this sense.) ♦ *The gestation of elephants lasts almost two years.* ♦ *Human gestation lasts 40 weeks.*

gesticulate [dʒɛ 'stɪk jə let] *iv.* to make active or animated gestures as a way of expressing oneself. ♦ *John gesticulated wildly as his speech became more emotional.* ♦ *The choking man gesticulated by waving his arms, hoping to attract attention.*

gesture ['dʒɛs tʃɚ] **1.** *n.* a movement made with a part of the body to communicate or to emphasize a statement, emotion, or feeling. ♦ *With a tiny facial gesture, Anne signaled that she wanted to leave.* ♦ *With a gesture of his hand, the waiter indicated where I should sit.* **2.** *n.* an act of kindness or courtesy; an act that demonstrates friendship. ♦ *Please accept this gift as a gesture of my appreciation.* ♦ *As a gesture of friendship, I cooked dinner for my roommates.* **3.** *tv.* to communicate something by moving a part of one's body, especially the hands. ♦ *Because her mouth was full of food, Anne could only gesture her agreement.* ♦ *My father gestured his disappointment by shaking his head.* **4.** *iv.* to use hand motions and facial movements when communicating; to make ①. ♦ *In some cultures, it is impolite or strange to gesture too broadly.* ♦ *The waiter gestured toward the table where he wanted us to sit.*

get ['gɛt] **1.** *tv., irreg.* to obtain something; to receive something. (Pt: got; pp: got or gotten.) ♦ *Jane got her first car when she was 18.* ♦ *I got a sprained ankle when I fell.* **2.** *tv., irreg.* to capture something; to bag ⑤ something. ♦ *I got a white-tailed deer with my first shot.* ♦ *John got 12 fish at the lake, and I cleaned them for dinner.* **3.** *tv., irreg.* to bring something; to fetch something. ♦ *Get your jacket from the closet because we're ready to leave.* ♦ *Could you go to the store and get a gallon of milk?* **4.** *tv., irreg.* to understand something; to comprehend something. ♦ *I don't get what you're trying to say.* ♦ *I didn't get algebra until I went to my teacher for help.* **5.** *tv., irreg.* to persuade someone to do something; to convince someone to do something. ♦ *After writing ten letters to the mayor's office, Jane finally got the city to fix the potholes on her street.* ♦ *Could I get you to do me a small favor?* **6.** *tv., irreg.* to cause something to happen to someone or something; to cause someone or something to be a certain way. ♦ *When the Browns had saved enough money, they got their house painted.* ♦ *I need a strong cup of coffee in the morning to get me going.* **7.** *iv., irreg.* to become. ♦ *This book gets more boring page after page.* ♦ *By the middle of spring, the flower garden had gotten very pretty.* **8.** *iv., irreg.* to arrive somewhere; to reach a certain point or place. (Followed by an adverb such as home, there, or somewhere or by a prepositional phrase.) ♦ *As soon as I get home, I will prepare dinner.* ♦ *When did you get to the party?* **9. get to** *iv., irreg. + inf.* to be allowed to do something; to be permitted to do something. ♦ *If you pay a $3 entrance fee, you get to go into the bar.* ♦ *Mary got to sing the national anthem before the ballgame.* **10. have got to [do something]** *phr.* to be obliged to [do something]; must [do something]. (Used only with the present tense of have that is, as *have got to* or *has got to,* and often reduced in contractions to *'ve got to* and *'s got to.* It means the same as **have to**—at **have** ⑤—which is never reduced.) ♦ *We have got to leave now.* ♦ *I've got to finish this book by tomorrow.* **11. have got [something]** *phr.* to have [something]; to possess [something]. (Used only with the present tense of **have** ⑥, that is, as *have got* or *has got,* and usually reduced in contractions to *'ve got* and *'s got.* It means the same as **have** ①, which is never reduced.) ♦ *I've got a brand-new coat.* ♦ *Have you got a pen that I could borrow?* **12. get to someone** *idiom* to affect someone emotionally in a bad way; to bother someone. ♦ *Working with abandoned children eventually got to David, and he had to transfer to another department.* ♦ *Nothing gets to me like seeing people litter.*

getaway ['gɛt ə we] *n.* an escape. ♦ *The criminal's easy getaway was an embarrassment to the police.* ♦ *The robber's getaway was blocked by a traffic jam.*

geyser ['gɑɪ zɚ] *n.* a hot spring that shoots streams of steam and hot water up from the earth. ♦ *The tourists took pictures of the steam shooting from the geyser.* ♦ *The geyser was the most popular attraction at the national park.*

Ghana ['gɑn ə] See Gazetteer.

ghastly ['gæst li] **1.** *adj.* causing fear; causing terror. (Comp: *ghastlier;* sup: *ghastliest.*) ♦ *I screamed when I heard the ghastly noise from the forest.* ♦ *The ghastly movie gave me nightmares for a week.* **2.** *adj.* very bad; very unpleasant. (Comp: *ghastlier;* sup: *ghastliest.*) ♦ *I refused to pay for the soup because it tasted ghastly.* ♦ *Jane looks ghastly because she was up all night studying.*

ghetto ['gɛt o] *n.* a contained neighborhood of a city where many very poor people live; a slum. (Pl in *-s* or *-es.*) ♦ *The candidate campaigned to bring jobs to the ghetto.* ♦ *Susan became a social worker to help the people in the ghetto where she had grown up.*

ghost ['gost] **1.** *n.* an apparent image of a dead person, moving among the living. ♦ *After my father died, I thought I saw his ghost in the garden.* ♦ *The old mansion was rumored to be haunted with ghosts.* **2.** *n.* a shadowy image; a faint image; a glimmer. (Figurative on ①.) ♦ *After Jane's long illness, she's only a ghost of her former self.* ♦ *The team doesn't have a ghost of a chance to win the World Series.*

ghostly ['gost li] *adj.* looking like a ghost; eerie. (Comp: *ghostlier;* sup: *ghostliest.*) ♦ *The teenagers screamed as the ghostly figure approached them.* ♦ *I saw a ghostly image in the background of the video I'd made.*

ghostwrite ['gost rɑɪt] *tv., irreg.* to write a book or article for someone who takes credit as the author. (Pt: **ghostwrote;** pp: **ghostwritten.**) ♦ *I was paid to ghostwrite a book for the mayor.* ♦ *Most political speeches are ghostwritten.*

ghostwriter ['gost rɑɪt ɚ] *n.* a professional writer who writes a book or article for someone who takes credit as the author. ♦ *Many famous autobiographies are actually written by ghostwriters.* ♦ *Politicians use ghostwriters to write their speeches.*

ghostwritten ['gost rɪt n] pp of **ghostwrite.**

ghostwrote ['gost rot] pt of **ghostwrite.**

giant ['dʒɑɪ ənt] **1.** *n.* a fictional or mythical human-like creature who is of enormous size. ♦ *The giant grabbed Jack and locked him up.* ♦ *In the story, the hero fought against a powerful giant.* **2.** *n.* an oversized person or animal. ♦ *The boy grew into a giant and had to have his shoes custom made.* ♦ *The huge puppy—the giant of the litter—kept knocking over his siblings.* **3.** *n.* a person who is very important or exemplary. ♦ *Bette Davis was a giant in the film industry.* ♦ *Somehow, I became a giant in banking—just like my father did.* **4.** *adj.* very large; enormous. ♦ *A giant mountain rose on the horizon.* ♦ *Four giant oak trees stood near the courthouse.*

gibberish ['dʒɪb (ə) rɪʃ] *n.* nonsense; spoken sounds that cannot be understood. (No plural form in this sense.) ♦ *The crazy man next to me on the subway shouted gibberish.* ♦ *Still in shock from the accident, Jane babbled nothing but gibberish.*

gibbon ['gɪb ən] *n.* the smallest member of the ape family, found in the forests of southeast Asia. ♦ *We visited the monkey house at the zoo to watch the gibbons play.* ♦ *The gibbon scampered up the tree away from danger.*

giblet ['dʒɪb lɪt] *n.* the heart, gizzard, or liver of a chicken or other bird. (Usually plural.) ♦ *The giblets were wrapped in paper and placed inside the frozen chicken I'd bought.* ♦ *Grandma chopped the giblets and put them in the gravy.*

giddy ['gɪd i] *adj.* light-headed; dizzy. (Adv: *giddily.* Comp: *giddier;* sup: *giddiest.*) ♦ *The fast carousel made me giddy.* ♦ *At the football game, I yelled until I was giddy.*

gift ['gɪft] **1.** *n.* a present; something that is given to someone without expecting anything in return. ♦ *My bicycle was a birthday gift from my parents.* ♦ *We give our mail carrier a small gift at the end of the year.* **2.** *n.* a special skill or talent. ♦ *Jane has a gift for the piano.* ♦ *Talented writers have a gift for words.*

gifted ['gɪf tɪd] *adj.* having a special skill or talent. (Adv: *giftedly.*) ♦ *A gifted young pianist played a very difficult piece at the recital.* ♦ *The gifted students were allowed to work at their own rate.*

gigabyte ['gɪg ə bɑɪt] *n.* 1 billion bytes [of computer memory]. ♦ *I need a magnetic tape that can store at least a gigabyte of data.* ♦ *I have over a gigabyte of disk space on my hard drive.*

gigantic [dʒɑɪ 'gæn tɪk] *adj.* very large; huge; enormous. (Adv: *gigantically* [...ɪk li].) ♦ *The ship sank when it struck a gigantic iceberg.* ♦ *John ate a gigantic pizza by himself for dinner.*

giggle ['gɪg əl] **1.** *n.* a silly laugh. ♦ *With a giggle, Susan explained why everyone was laughing at me.* ♦ *Your high-pitched giggle is very annoying.* **2.** *iv.* to laugh in a silly way. ♦ *Once John starts to giggle, he can't stop.* ♦ *I giggled when the clown's pants fell down.*

Gila monster ['hi lə mɑn stɚ] *n.* a poisonous lizard native to the southwestern United States and northern Mexico. (Named for the Gila River.) ♦ *When hiking in Arizona, watch out for Gila monsters and snakes.* ♦ *My dog was killed by a Gila monster.*

gild ['gɪld] *tv.* to coat something with a thin layer of gold or gold paint. ♦ *The picture frame was gilded with gold.* ♦ *The jeweler gilded the watch.*

gill ['gɪl] *n.* one of a pair of organs in a fish's head that allow it to take oxygen from and put carbon dioxide into water. ♦ *We watched the fish's gills flutter as it swam in the tank.* ♦ *The fish died because its gills were infected.*

gilt ['gɪlt] **1.** a pp of **gild. 2.** *adj.* covered with a thin layer of gold or gold paint. ♦ *The gilt picture frame was worth* *several hundred dollars.* ♦ *The book cover was decorated with gilt lettering.*

gimmick ['gɪm ɪk] **1.** *n.* a gadget. ♦ *This little gimmick is used to pull nails.* ♦ *I bought a gimmick that purifies water straight from the tap.* **2.** *n.* something that is used to attract attention or publicity. ♦ *The politician's gimmick to attract crowds was to offer free pizza.* ♦ *Comedians often have a unique gimmick that makes them stand out.*

gin ['dʒɪn] **1.** *n.* a kind of clear, beverage alcohol distilled from grain. (No plural form in this sense.) ♦ *After dinner, I had a gin and tonic.* ♦ *My special punch includes a fifth of gin.* **2. gin (rummy)** *n.* a kind of card game. (No plural form in this sense.) ♦ *Do you want to play gin or poker tonight?* ♦ *Gin rummy is easy to play and is a fast-moving card game.* **3.** *n.* a machine that separates cotton from cotton seeds. ♦ *The cotton gin was invented in 1793 by Eli Whitney.* ♦ *Before the cotton gin was invented, cotton seeds were separated from cotton by hand.*

ginger ['dʒɪn dʒɚ] *n.* a kind of tropical plant whose root is used as a spice. (No plural form in this sense.) ♦ *In addition to flowers, I grew ginger in my greenhouse.* ♦ *As the roots of ginger were harvested, their pungent scent filled the air.*

ginger ale ['dʒɪn dʒɚ 'el] *n.* a nonalcoholic pop or soda that is flavored with ginger. (No plural form in this sense.) ♦ *I ordered a hamburger and a cold ginger ale.* ♦ *The carbonation from the ginger ale made me sneeze.*

gingerbread ['dʒɪn dʒɚ brɛd] **1.** *n.* a sweet, soft, brown cake flavored with ginger. (No plural form in this sense.) ♦ *For dessert, Grandma served gingerbread.* ♦ *Cookies made of gingerbread are often frosted with lines of icing.* **2.** *n.* wooden decorations cut in lacy patterns, used on the outside of some kinds of Victorian houses. (No plural form in this sense. Like the lacy decorations used on cookies made of **gingerbread**.) ♦ *We painted the gingerbread light blue.* ♦ *The old house's shutters were falling down and the gingerbread was rotting.*

gingerly ['dʒɪn dʒɚ li] *adv.* cautiously; timidly; carefully. ♦ *I walked gingerly down the icy sidewalk.* ♦ *Gingerly, I strained to hear the conversation in the next room.*

gingersnap ['dʒɪn dʒɚ snæp] *n.* a hard cookie that is flavored with ginger. ♦ *After school, I ate gingersnaps and drank a cold glass of milk.* ♦ *Gingersnaps are my favorite kind of cookie.*

gingham ['gɪŋ əm] *n.* a light cotton fabric that is woven with two different colors of thread in a striped or checked pattern. (No plural form in this sense.) ♦ *Susan made a gingham dress that she could wear to church.* ♦ *In the summer, Anne wore light gingham dresses to work.*

giraffe [dʒə 'ræf] *n.* an African animal that has long legs and a very long neck. ♦ *Giraffes can eat the leaves that are high up in trees.* ♦ *The documentary explained the evolution of the giraffe's neck.*

girder ['gɚd ɚ] *n.* a large metal support beam used in building bridges and buildings. ♦ *The welder carefully walked across the girder high up in the air.* ♦ *The girders were designed to withstand earthquakes.*

girdle ['gɚd l] *n.* a binding garment worn under the clothing in order to make the wearer appear thinner or more shapely. ♦ *To fit into the costume, the somewhat plump actress playing Juliet wore a girdle.* ♦ *After wearing the tight girdle for 6 hours, Mary happily took it off.*

girl ['gɚl] **1.** *n.* a female child. ♦ *The Browns have three boys and two girls.* ♦ *My sister gave birth to a baby girl last night.* **2.** *n.* a woman. (Informal. Considered derogatory by some.) ♦ *I am going to play cards with some of the girls tonight.* ♦ *The secretaries referred to each other as girls.* **3.** *n.* a man's girlfriend. (Informal.) ♦ *Bill gave Susan a ring inscribed with the words "To my best girl."* ♦ *John took his girl out dancing every Friday.*

girlfriend ['gɚl frɛnd] **1.** *n.* a woman with whom someone is romantically involved. ♦ *Michael introduced his girlfriend to his parents.* ♦ *The senator's girlfriend threatened to tell the press about their affair.* **2.** *n.* a female friend. ♦ *Mary went to the mall with her girlfriends for lunch.* ♦ *Anne helped her girlfriend pick out a wedding dress.*

gist ['dʒɪst] *n.* the basic meaning of something; the important points of a story, argument, etc. (No plural form in this sense.) ♦ *The gist of the editorial was that people must be responsible for their actions.* ♦ *I don't have time for details; just tell me the gist of the story.*

give ['gɪv] **1.** *tv., irreg.* to cause someone or something to have or receive something; to cause something to become possessed by someone. (Pt: **gave**; pp: **given**.) ♦ *Susan gave the news to David.* ♦ *Susan gave David the news.* **2.** *tv., irreg.* to supply something; to provide something. ♦ *The sun gives heat and light.* ♦ *This book gave me the information I needed.* **3.** *tv.* to utter something; to make some sort of vocal sound. ♦ *The dog gave a loud whine when I stepped on its tail.* ♦ *Bill give a sigh of relief when the test was over.* **4.** *tv., irreg.* to present someone; to introduce someone. ♦ *The emcee of the talent show said, "I give you Bill Brown!"* ♦ *Without further delay, I give you the lovely bride and groom.* **5. give off** *tv.* + *prep. phr.* to release or send out something; to emit or exude something. ♦ *The flower gave off a wonderful scent.* ♦ *The stove gives off a lot of heat.* **6. give up** *tv.* + *adv.* to yield something or someone; to renounce ownership of something. ♦ *I will never give up my car as long as I can drive.* ♦ *Lisa refuses to give her bad habits up.* **7.** *iv., irreg.* to be flexible; to be elastic; to not break when pushed or pulled. ♦ *The thin wall gave when I pressed on it, and bounced back when I stopped.* ♦ *The branch gave a little when I sat on it, and then suddenly, it broke.* **8. give up; give in** *iv.* + *adv.* to yield; to quit. ♦ *The weak team finally gave up and quit playing.* ♦ *I will never give up! I will fight and fight to the end.* **9.** *n.* resilience; flexibility. (No plural form in this sense.) ♦ *Pull the rope a little tighter; it's still got some give.* ♦ *The couch has less give than it used to because its springs are broken.* **10. give as good as one gets** *idiom* to give as much as one receives; to pay someone back in kind. (Usually in the present tense.) ♦ *John can take care of himself in a fight. He can give as good as he gets.* ♦ *Sally usually wins a formal debate. She gives as good as she gets.* **11. give-and-take** *idiom* the cooperation between two sides who are bargaining for something; the essence of negotiation. ♦ *The union asked for a little give-and-take from management.* ♦ *The mediator praised the give-and-take shown by both sides.*

given ['gɪv ən] **1.** pp of give. **2.** *adj.* already said, stated, or provided. ♦ *Jane did not believe the given measurements were accurate.* ♦ *The given parameters left only a small* *margin for error.* **3. a given** *idiom* a fact that is taken for granted; a fact that is assumed. ♦ *That Mary will go to college is a given. The question is what she is going to study.* ♦ *It is a given that the earth revolves around the sun.* **4. given to doing something** *idiom* likely to do something; inclined to do something habitually. ♦ *Mary is given to singing in the shower.* ♦ *Bob is given to shouting when things don't go his way.*

glacial ['gle ʃəl] **1.** *adj.* of or about glaciers. (Adv: *glacially.*) ♦ *These giant stones are part of an ancient glacial deposit.* ♦ *Glacial movement is very, very slow.* **2.** *adj.* [of someone's attitude] extremely cold and distant. (Adv: *glacially.*) ♦ *The glacial stare from the librarian caused me to become quiet.* ♦ *I tried to be nice to Bill, but his disposition is too glacial.* **3.** *adj.* [of movement] as slow as a glacier. (Adv: *glacially.*) ♦ *Traffic was moving at a glacial speed, and I thought I would never get home.* ♦ *The project is moving at a glacial pace. We will never finish.*

glacier ['gle ʃɚ] *n.* a vast body of ice that moves very slowly. ♦ *This huge lake was carved out by glaciers during the last Ice Age.* ♦ *We took a cruise ship to see Alaska's majestic glaciers.*

glad ['glæd] **1.** *adj.* happy; content; pleased; joyful. (Adv: *gladly.* Comp: *gladder;* sup: *gladdest.*) ♦ *I'm glad for your good fortune.* ♦ *The workers were glad that the contract dispute was settled.* **2.** *adj.* causing happiness, contentment, pleasure, or joy. (Adv: *gladly.* Comp: *gladder;* sup: *gladdest.*) ♦ *The gladdest moment of John's life was when he got married.* ♦ *The team celebrated the glad event of winning first place.* **3. glad to** *adj.* + *inf.* willing to do something; pleased to do something. ♦ *Anne was glad to help her grandmother in the garden.* ♦ *I'd be glad to show you a dress in your size.*

gladden ['glæd n] **1.** *tv.* to cause someone to be glad. ♦ *The news that school was canceled gladdened the children.* ♦ *I am gladdened by the fact that tomorrow is Saturday.* **2.** *iv.* [for one's mood or outlook] to become glad. ♦ *Susan's spirits gladdened at the good news.* ♦ *The workers' mood gladdened when their contract was renewed.*

glade ['gled] *n.* a clearing within a forest; an open space in a forest. ♦ *We set the blanket down in the glade and ate our picnic lunch.* ♦ *I built a small cottage in the glade.*

gladly ['glæd li] *adv.* willingly; happily. ♦ *I would gladly buy a car if I had the money.* ♦ *Anne and Bill gladly took their children to the amusement park.*

gladness ['glæd nəs] *n.* joy; happiness. (No plural form in this sense.) ♦ *Gladness filled our hearts when the young couple was married.* ♦ *The gladness of the moment made everyone more friendly and outgoing.*

glamorize ['glæm ə rɑɪz] *tv.* to make someone or something seem more glamorous; to beautify someone or something. ♦ *Anne felt that the tobacco industry was glamorizing smoking.* ♦ *The hair stylist glamorized the young model by dyeing her hair.*

glamorous ['glæm ə rəs] *adj.* charming, alluring, and beautiful. (Adv: *glamorously.*) ♦ *The glamorous model was paid $5,000 an hour for a photo shoot.* ♦ *Being an actor isn't as glamorous as it sounds.*

glamour ['glæm ɚ] *n.* charm, allure, and beauty. (No plural form in this sense.) ♦ *The model seemed to radiate glamour and style.* ♦ *Mary was fascinated by the glamour of Hollywood.*

glance ['glæns] **1.** *n.* a brief look toward someone or something. ♦ *With a quick glance in each direction, Bill checked for traffic.* ♦ *The witness cast a glance at the jury during her testimony.* **2. glance at; glance through; glance over** *iv.* + *prep. phr.* to quickly look at or over someone or something; to read something through or over quickly. ♦ *I glanced at the headlines at the newspaper rack.* ♦ *The unprepared student had only glanced over the assignment.* **3. glance off** *iv.* + *prep. phr.* to strike something and bounce off at an angle. ♦ *The arrow I shot glanced off a tree and fell to the ground.* ♦ *The ball glanced off the house and bounced into the pool.*

gland ['glænd] *n.* a group of cells or an organ in the body that produces fluids (or secretions) of various types. ♦ *My throat glands were sore and tender, so I went to bed early.* ♦ *Sweat is produced by sweat glands.*

glandular ['glænd jə lɚ] *adj.* of or about glands. (Adv: *glandularly.*) ♦ *David's growth was stunted because of a glandular disorder.* ♦ *My doctor has experience treating various glandular problems.*

glare ['glɛɚ] **1.** *n.* a harsh, angry stare. ♦ *Jane's icy glare indicated that she was very mad.* ♦ *I could tell by David's glare that he knew I'd told his secret.* **2.** *n.* strong, almost blinding light. (No plural form in this sense.) ♦ *The glare on the windshield made it difficult to drive.* ♦ *I shielded my eyes from the glare of the spotlight.* **3.** *iv.* to stare angrily. ♦ *Jane glared at Dave after he spilled his wine.* ♦ *Bill glared out his car window at the driver next to him.* **4. glare down on** *iv.* + *adv.* + *prep. phr.* to give off a very bright, blinding light. ♦ *Sunlight glared down on the farmers in the field.* ♦ *The stage lights glared down on the actors.*

glaring ['glɛɚ ɪŋ] **1.** *adj.* very bright; blinding; dazzling. (Adv: *glaringly.*) ♦ *The glaring searchlight lit up the escaped prisoner.* ♦ *I wore sunglasses so I could drive in the glaring sunlight.* **2.** *adj.* very obvious; conspicuous. (Figurative on ①. Adv: *glaringly.*) ♦ *My professor commented on the glaring mistakes in my paper.* ♦ *The effects of smoking seem glaring to me, but I can't convince David of that.*

glass ['glæs] **1.** *n.* a hard, stiff, easily broken, usually clear substance, used to make windows, drinking glasses, eyeglasses, etc. (No plural form in this sense.) ♦ *Is this cup made of glass or plastic?* ♦ *Glass shatters easily.* **2.** *n.* a container that is used to drink from, usually made of ①. (The glass for drinking does not have a handle. When a vessel for drinking is not made of ①, it is often referred to as a cup.) ♦ *Susan filled her glass with milk.* ♦ *After dinner, Susan washed and dried the glasses.* **3.** *n.* the contents of ②. ♦ *Susan drank an entire glass of milk.* ♦ *I threw a glass of water on the small fire.* **4. glasses** *n.* eyeglasses; spectacles. (Treated as plural.) ♦ *Tom lost his glasses and can't see a thing!* ♦ *I can't see very well without my glasses.*

glassware ['glæs wɛr] *n.* objects made from glass. (No plural form in this sense.) ♦ *Laboratory glassware includes test tubes and flasks.* ♦ *I store the glassware to the right of the coffee cups.*

glassy ['glæs i] **1.** *adj.* smooth, like glass; transparent, like glass. (Adv: *glassily.* Comp: *glassier;* sup: *glassiest.*) ♦ *The lake was so calm that its surface was glassy.* ♦ *The glassy surface reflected the sun brightly.* **2.** *adj.* [of a facial expression] vacant, empty, and lifeless. (Adv: *glassily.* Comp: *glassier;* sup: *glassiest.*) ♦ *Anne had a glassy expression on her face while she was hypnotized.* ♦ *The drug addict* *looked toward me with a glassy stare.* **3.** *adj.* [of eyes] dull and lifeless. (Adv: *glassily.* Comp: *glassier;* sup: *glassiest.*) ♦ *The doctor peered into the glassy eyes of the unconscious patient.* ♦ *Dave's glassy eyes showed just how very tired he was.*

glaucoma [glaʊ 'ko mə] *n.* an eye disease in which there is an increase of pressure inside the eyeball. (No plural form in this sense.) ♦ *My optometrist checked for glaucoma as part of my eye exam.* ♦ *My grandmother's blindness was caused by glaucoma.*

glaze ['glez] **1.** *n.* a shiny coating applied in liquid form. (No plural form in this sense.) ♦ *The chocolate cake was coated with a delicious strawberry-flavored glaze.* ♦ *The artist applied a glaze to the pottery and waited for it to dry.* **2.** *tv.* to coat something with a liquid that makes a shiny outer layer. ♦ *John glazed the chocolate cake with a strawberry-flavored topping.* ♦ *Sue glazed the pottery and waited for it to dry.* **3.** *tv.* to cover something with glass; to install a glass pane in a window frame. ♦ *John glazed the small window in the door with opaque glass.* ♦ *This window is glazed with bulletproof glass.*

gleam ['glim] **1.** *n.* a flash of light; a ray of light. (No plural form in this sense.) ♦ *A gleam of sunlight shone through the dark clouds.* ♦ *The gleam of his flashlight showed John the trail as he walked outside after dark.* **2.** *n.* a tiny bit of something abstract. (No plural form in this sense.) ♦ *A gleam of hope that the war had ended was dashed by more gunfire.* ♦ *The senator's gleam of civility disappeared after his reelection.* **3.** *iv.* to give off light; to glow. ♦ *The porch light gleamed in the night.* ♦ *Bright lights gleamed from tall towers in the football stadium.*

gleaming ['glim ɪŋ] *adj.* reflecting light(s) brightly. (Adv: *gleamingly.*) ♦ *The gleaming jewelry was kept in a safety-deposit box.* ♦ *The cook placed the gleaming pots and pans in the cupboard.*

glean ['glin] *tv.* to pick up information slowly, carefully, and piece by piece. ♦ *The journalist gleaned her information from many sources.* ♦ *The detective gleaned some important details from nosy neighbors.*

glee ['gli] *n.* great happiness. (No plural form in this sense.) ♦ *The schoolchildren jumped with glee on the last day of school.* ♦ *The glee we felt after we won the game made us want to jump and yell.*

gleeful ['gli fʊl] *adj.* very happy; joyful. (Adv: *gleefully.*) ♦ *The gleeful members of the winning team placed their trophy in the case.* ♦ *The citizens were gleeful that the war was over.*

glib ['glɪb] *adj.* speaking fluently, quickly, and impressively, but in a way such that it is impossible for the listener to tell if the speaker is being sincere and truthful. (Adv: *glibly.* Comp: *glibber;* sup: *glibbest.*) ♦ *No one knew if Mary's glib retort to Jane was serious.* ♦ *I can't tell if John's glib response was sarcastic.*

glide ['glaɪd] **1.** *iv.* to move smoothly. ♦ *The car glided quietly into the garage.* ♦ *The tip of the pen glided across the sheet of paper.* **2.** *iv.* to move through the air without engine power. ♦ *The plane glided to a safe landing after its engines failed.* ♦ *The kite glided through the air, carried by the wind.* **3.** *tv.* to cause something to move smoothly. ♦ *The artist glided the paintbrush across the canvas.* ♦ *Jane glided her car to a smooth stop.* **4.** *n.* a smooth movement without stops or jerks. ♦ *The skater's glide across the ice makes skating seem so easy.* ♦ *A good pen gives a smooth glide over the surface of the paper.* **5.** *n.* a movement through air. ♦ *The plane entered a long glide from 2,000 feet to the end of the runway.* ♦ *The satellite tracked the long glide of the missile over the ocean.* **6.** *n.* a phonetic term for a sound like [j] in *yellow* ['jɛ lo], or [w] in *willow* ['wɪl o], which are sounds made by moving from one point of articulation to another. ♦ *In English, the glide* [j] *is usually spelled with a* y. ♦ *We studied glides in my phonetics class today.*

glider ['glaɪd ɚ] **1.** *n.* a kind of aircraft that moves through the air without power from an engine. ♦ *I soared from the cliff, strapped to a glider.* ♦ *It's too windy to use the glider today.* **2.** *n.* a porch swing that is suspended from and contained within a low framework that rests on the floor. ♦ *We swung back and forth on the glider while sipping lemonade.* ♦ *Uncle Bill sat on the glider, waiting for his wife to come home.*

glimmer ['glɪm ɚ] **1.** *n.* a brief flicker of light; a faint light that glows and then fades. (Also glimmering.) ♦ *The single candle gave off a glimmer of light in the dark room.* ♦ *Far down the road, I saw the glimmer of a pair of headlights.* **2.** *n.* a tiny bit of certain abstract things. (Figurative on ①. Also glimmering.) ♦ *I had a glimmer of hope that I might get the job.* ♦ *If you had a glimmer of intelligence, we wouldn't be lost!* **3.** *iv.* to briefly flicker; to give off a faint light that glows and subsides. ♦ *The candle glimmered in the darkness before the wind blew it out.* ♦ *The satellite glimmered in the nighttime sky.* **4.** *iv.* [for an abstract quality] to appear only for a very short time. ♦ *Hope glimmered briefly for our team, but we lost 4 to 3.* ♦ *John's understanding of algebra glimmered briefly, but he decided to drop the class.*

glimmering ['glɪm ɚ ɪŋ] **1.** *n.* a brief flicker of light; a faint light that glows and subsides. (Also glimmer.) ♦ *When I left for work at 5:00 in the morning, I saw a soft glimmering in the east.* ♦ *The glimmering of the warning light means you should replace the battery.* **2.** *n.* a slight condition or quality that appears only for a very short time. (Also glimmer.) ♦ *There was just a glimmering of hope that the war would end soon.* ♦ *Anne thought the movie lacked even a glimmering of creativity.*

glimpse ['glɪmps] **1.** *n.* a brief look at someone or something; a glance. ♦ *John caught only a glimpse of the man who mugged him.* ♦ *I got a glimpse of the accident out of the corner of my eye.* **2.** *tv.* to have only a quick look at something. ♦ *Mary only glimpsed the newspaper before leaving for work.* ♦ *I glimpsed the accident out of the corner of my eye.*

glint ['glɪnt] *n.* a quick, bright flash of light, especially one reflected from a shiny surface. ♦ *A glint of sunlight bounced off the windshield and hurt my eyes.* ♦ *A glint of bright light reflected off the face of Susan's watch.*

glisten ['glɪs ən] *iv.* to shine with reflected light; to sparkle with reflected light. ♦ *The icy streets glistened in the moonlight.* ♦ *The cat's eyes glistened in the light from the fireplace.*

glitter ['glɪt ɚ] **1.** *n.* sparkle; glistening light. (No plural form in this sense.) ♦ *The dazzling glitter from the jeweler's showcase attracted my attention.* ♦ *The glitter of the fireworks lit up the nighttime sky.* **2.** *n.* tiny pieces of shiny plastic that are sprinkled on surfaces as a decoration to reflect light. (No plural form in this sense.) ♦ *David sprinkled glitter on the card to make it sparkle.* ♦ *Mary's makeup has green and red glitter in it, making her look sort of strange.* **3.** *n.* the glamour associated with celebrities and fame. (No plural form in this sense.) ♦ *The glitter of the movie industry lures thousands of hopeful actors.* ♦ *Mary preferred the hard work of Broadway to the glitter of Hollywood.* **4.** *iv.* to give off a flashing, reflective light; to sparkle. ♦ *The jewelry on display in the lighted showcase glittered brightly.* ♦ *Mary's ring glittered as she gestured with her hands.*

gloat ['glot] *iv.* to talk about something selfishly with a look and tone of smug satisfaction. ♦ *If Bob wins, he'll gloat all night.* ♦ *I left the room when Anne began to gloat over her accomplishments.*

glob ['glɑb] *n.* a shapeless mass of something wet or moist; a blob. ♦ *Anne wiped a glob of jelly from the counter.* ♦ *I stepped in a glob of mud.*

global ['glob əl] **1.** *adj.* of or about the whole world; worldwide. (Adv: *globally.*) ♦ *One country's pollution can have global effects.* ♦ *The war started small but soon became a global crisis.* **2.** *adj.* affecting parts of a computer file, as with a complete search-and-replace command in a computer program. (Figurative on ①. Adv: *globally.*) ♦ *Mary did a global search for the words "business contract."* ♦ *One global command replaced all instances of "Rome" with "Paris."*

globe ['glob] **1.** *n.* a ball; a sphere. ♦ *Bill accidentally shattered a vase shaped like a glass globe.* ♦ *Oranges have the shape of a globe.* **2.** *n.* a ball or sphere with a map of the world on it. ♦ *Susan pointed to Italy on the globe at the front of the classroom.* ♦ *I bought a new globe after the Soviet Union was dissolved.* **3.** *n.* the earth; the world. ♦ *Anne flew across the globe to visit her sick mother in Tokyo.* ♦ *I had traveled around the globe before I was 21.*

globe-trotter ['glob trɑt ɚ] *n.* someone who regularly travels or does business all over the world. ♦ *Max, a very busy globe-trotter, was seldom home to see his family.* ♦ *Lisa works in international sales and has become quite a globe-trotter.*

globule ['glɑb jul] *n.* a small, round drop. ♦ *A small globule of blood dripped from the cut on my finger.* ♦ *John's face was coated with globules of sweat.*

gloom ['glum] **1.** *n.* a sad, depressed feeling. (No plural form in this sense.) ♦ *An air of gloom was very apparent at my brother's funeral.* ♦ *I was unable to ignore the gloom caused by the bad news.* **2.** *n.* dimness; darkness. (No plural form in this sense.) ♦ *I left the gloom of my dark apartment and went to the park.* ♦ *In the gloom of the basement, I saw a rat.*

gloomy ['glum i] *adj.* dark; dim; sad; depressing. (Adv: *gloomily.* Comp: *gloomier;* sup: *gloomiest.*) ♦ *I decided to give the gloomy apartment a fresh coat of paint.* ♦ *It's looking gloomy outside. You'd better take an umbrella.*

glorification [glor ə fə 'ke ʃən] *n.* glorifying or praising someone or something. (No plural form in this sense.) ♦ *The church promotes the glorification of God.* ♦ *The minister condemned the glorification of sex and violence on television.*

glorified ['glor ə fɑɪd] *adj.* made to seem far more important than is really so; [for someone or something of lesser quality to be] made to appear of superior quality. (Sarcastic.) ♦ *This "chopped steak" is nothing but glorified hamburger.* ♦ *It was supposed to be a scenic cave but was only a glorified hole in the ground.*

glorify ['glor ə fɑɪ] **1.** *tv.* to honor or worship someone. to praise someone or something; to extol someone or something. ♦ *The church congregation glorified God in the worship service.* ♦ *They sang a lovely hymn that glorified the wonders of nature.* **2.** *tv.* to exaggerate the importance of someone or something. ♦ *The senator glorified his uneventful days in the army.* ♦ *The director tried to glorify her mediocre movies.*

glorious ['glor i əs] *adj.* beautiful; splendid; wonderful. (Adv: *gloriously.*) ♦ *Since it's such a glorious day, let's go to the beach.* ♦ *I had a glorious time at your party. Thanks for inviting me!*

glory ['glor i] **1.** *n.* praise and honor. (No plural form in this sense.) ♦ *The worshipers gave glory to God.* ♦ *The new castle was dedicated to the glory of the king.* **2.** *n.* something of great beauty or wonder. ♦ *I opened my eyes to the glory of a new day.* ♦ *The sunset was a glory to behold.*

gloss ['glɔs] **1.** *n.* something written in the margin of a page explaining or commenting on something in the text. ♦ *I wrote a few glosses in the margin while reading the text.* ♦ *An old gloss in the margin of the book indicated that a date in the text was wrong.* **2.** *n.* a literal translation of something written in a different language. ♦ *The English gloss of the German word for submarine,* Unterseeboot, *is 'under-sea-boat.'* ♦ *A translator provided the English gloss after every foreign word.* **3.** *n.* the shine on a surface; luster. (No plural form in this sense.) ♦ *I polished the silver until its former gloss was restored.* ♦ *The gloss of the new tile wore off within a week.* **4.** *tv.* to provide a literal translation of something that is written in a different language. ♦ *I glossed the Latin sentences in English.* ♦ *The editor glossed the foreign phrases in the manuscript.* **5. gloss over** *iv.* + *prep. phr.* to deal with something important only hastily. ♦ *The local newscast glossed over the international news.* ♦ *John glossed over my contribution and spoke only of himself.*

glossary ['glɔs ə ri] *n.* a list of words and their definitions, as used within a particular text. ♦ *My editor suggested I place the technical terms in a glossary.* ♦ *Glossaries of basic computer manuals should include terms like* hardware *and* software.

glossy ['glɔs i] **1.** *adj.* shiny; lustrous. (Adv: *glossily.* Comp: *glossier;* sup: *glossiest.*) ♦ *I polished the silver until it was glossy again.* ♦ *The glossy bathroom tile reflected the light above the sink.* **2.** *adj.* produced on shiny paper, especially of photographs. (Comp: *glossier;* sup: *glossiest.*) ♦ *Do you want your photos to be printed on glossy paper?* ♦ *The actor gave his agent 100 glossy photographs and résumés.*

glottal ['glɑt əl] *adj.* of or about the glottis, and sounds made at the glottis. (Adv: *glottally.*) ♦ *Some speakers pronounce the* [t] *in* bottle *with a glottal stop.* ♦ *The human voice is a series of rapid glottal pulses.*

glottis ['glɑt ɪs] *n.* the space between the two vocal cords at the top of the windpipe. ♦ *The glottis is not an organ, but only the opening between the vocal cords.* ♦ *A glottal stop is produced by the sudden closing of the glottis.*

glove ['glʌv] **1.** *n.* one of a pair of fitted, fabric coverings for the hand with individual compartments for each finger and thumb. ♦ *The thief who wore gloves left no trace of fingerprints.* ♦ *The flower vendor cut the fingertips off her gloves so she could handle money easily.* **2.** *n.* a hand covering, similar to ① but not necessarily with individual compartments. (Generic.) ♦ *Those gloves are actually mittens.* ♦ *Put some gloves on and let's go play in the snow.* **3.** *n.* a special hand covering, similar to ① but designed for a special purpose. ♦ *Boxing gloves are heavily padded.* ♦ *The angry pitcher threw his glove at the umpire.* **4. fit like a glove** *idiom* to fit very well; to fit tightly or snugly. ♦ *My new shoes fit like a glove.* ♦ *My new coat is a little tight. It fits like a glove.* **5. hand in glove (with someone)** *idiom* very close to someone. ♦ *John is really hand in glove with Sally.* ♦ *The teacher and the principal work hand in glove.* **6. handle someone with kid gloves** *idiom* to be very careful with a touchy person; to deal with someone who is very difficult. ♦ *Bill has become so sensitive. You really have to handle him with kid gloves.* ♦ *You don't have to handle me with kid gloves. I can take it.*

glow ['glo] **1.** *iv.* to shine; to give off a weak light. ♦ *The night-light glowed in the hallway outside the bedrooms.* ♦ *The bike rider wore clothing that glowed in the dark so she could be seen more easily.* **2.** *iv.* to be very hot; to be red-hot; to be so hot as to be red, yellow, or white with heat. ♦ *The molten iron glowed red.* ♦ *The embers glowed in the fireplace for hours.* **3.** *iv.* to be very excited with emotion or energy. ♦ *Susan's face glowed with excitement during the party.* ♦ *Mr. and Mrs. Johnson glowed as their daughter received her diploma.* **4.** *iv.* to show a healthy appearance; to have bright red cheeks. ♦ *Mary's skin glowed as she jogged through the park.* ♦ *Remarkably, a week after leaving the hospital, John glowed with good health.* **5.** *n.* a weak light. (No plural form in this sense.) ♦ *Through the window, I could see the glow of Bill's television.* ♦ *In the distance, I saw the glow of headlights.* **6.** *n.* a healthy appearance; a reddened complexion. (No plural form in this sense.) ♦ *After exercising, my skin had a healthy glow.* ♦ *Anne's face shines with the glow of a healthy complexion.* **7. feel a glow of something** *idiom* to have a feeling of contentment, happiness, satisfaction, peace, etc. ♦ *Anne felt a glow of happiness as she held her new baby.* ♦ *Sitting by the lake, the lovers felt a warm glow of contentment.*

glower ['glɑʊ ɚ] **1.** *iv.* to stare angrily. ♦ *The teacher glowered at the students who came to class late.* ♦ *My mother glowered for a moment when I dropped the dishes.* **2.** *n.* an angry stare. ♦ *Because of my supervisor's stern glower, I postponed asking for a raise.* ♦ *Anne's glower slowly faded as Bill explained why he was late.*

glowing ['glo ɪŋ] **1.** *adj.* giving off light. (Adv: *glowingly.*) ♦ *The glowing light suddenly went out.* ♦ *A glowing warning light indicated I should get gas very soon.* **2.** *adj.* [of something] so hot that light and heat are given off. (Adv: *glowingly.*) ♦ *The blacksmith removed the glowing irons from the fire.* ♦ *The glowing ember crackled in the fireplace.* **3.** *adj.* with much praise. (Adv: *glowingly.*) ♦ *Susan gave a glowing report on the progress of the project.* ♦ *Bill's glowing comments reflected his pride in the matter.*

glucose ['glu kos] *n.* a form of sugar. (No plural form in this sense.) ♦ *Glucose is a sugar found naturally in food.* ♦ *Glucose is digested by the body as a carbohydrate.*

glue ['glu] **1.** *n.* a thick, sticky liquid that is used to make something stick to something else; an adhesive. (No plural form in this sense.) ♦ *Before screwing the boards together, I secured them with wood glue.* ♦ *Jimmy peeled off the dried glue that was stuck to his fingers.* **2.** *tv.* to stick something to something else using ①. ♦ *I glued pictures of movie stars to the front of my notebook.* ♦ *Anne glued the pieces of the broken vase back together.*

glum ['glʌm] *adj.* sad; disappointed. (Adv: *glumly.* Comp: *glummer;* sup: *glummest.*) ♦ *Susan was glum because she was too sick to go to the party.* ♦ *I tried to cheer up my glum friend.*

glut ['glʌt] **1.** *n.* an overabundance of something; too much of something. ♦ *I dislike the glut of violence in the movies.* ♦ *A glut of oil on the market caused its price to fall.* **2.** *tv.* to supply someone or something with too much of something. ♦ *Our office is glutted with paper supplies.* ♦ *The software company glutted the market with low-priced software.*

glutton ['glʌt n] **1.** *n.* someone who eats or drinks too much. ♦ *The glutton consumed three pizzas for dinner.* ♦ *The doctor ordered the glutton to go on a diet.* **2. glutton for punishment** *idiom* someone who is eager for a burden or some sort of difficulty; someone willing to accept a difficult task. ♦ *Tom works too hard. He is a glutton for punishment.* ♦ *I enjoy managing difficult projects, but I am a glutton for punishment.*

gluttony ['glʌt n i] *n.* eating or drinking too much. (No plural form in this sense.) ♦ *Your gluttony is disgraceful because so many people are starving.* ♦ *Gluttony is not a problem in the poorer countries.*

gnarl ['nɑrl] *tv.* to twist or knot something; to cause something to become misshapen. ♦ *The cat gnarled the ball of yarn into a knotted lump.* ♦ *Arthritis has gnarled my grandfather's hands.*

gnarled ['nɑrld] *adj.* twisted; knotted; misshapen. ♦ *The old man's gnarled fingers couldn't open the bottle of aspirin.* ♦ *I tried to untangle the gnarled volleyball net.*

gnash ['næʃ] **gnash one's teeth** *idiom* to slash about with the teeth. ♦ *Bill clenched his fists and gnashed his teeth in anger.* ♦ *The wolf gnashed its teeth and chased after the deer.*

gnat ['næt] *n.* a small fly that bites. ♦ *I swatted at the gnats with a folded newspaper.* ♦ *We were all bitten by gnats at the picnic.*

gnaw ['nɔ] **1.** *tv.* to bite or chew away at something piece by piece. ♦ *A beaver gnawed the bark of the small tree.* ♦ *The hungry dog gnawed the meat off the bone.* **2. gnaw at; gnaw on** *iv.* + *prep. phr.* to bite or chew away at something piece by piece. ♦ *I gnawed on the tough meat.* ♦ *The rat gnawed at the piece of cheese.* **3. gnaw at; gnaw on** *iv.* + *prep. phr.* (Figurative on ②.) to cause constant pain or worry. ♦ *My horrible deeds gnawed on my conscience.* ♦ *Bill's insults gnawed at my self-esteem.*

gnawing ['nɔ ɪŋ] *adj.* throbbing; hurting. (Adv: *gnawingly.*) ♦ *Mary felt a gnawing pain in her stomach.* ♦ *The starving children suffered from a gnawing hunger.*

gnu ['nu] *n., irreg.* a large African antelope with a long, ox-like head. (Pl: *gnu* or *gnus.*) ♦ *I saw a small herd of gnu at the zoo.* ♦ *On the safari, I saw gnus roaming across the land.*

go ['go] **1.** *iv., irreg.* to move from one place to another; [for time] to progress. (Pt: went; pp: gone. The third-person singular present tense is goes.) ♦ *I went downtown after school.* ♦ *Time went by very rapidly while I was on vacation.* **2.** *iv., irreg.* to travel to a place in order to do a certain action. ♦ *On Monday, I go shopping.* ♦ *Tom went skiing last week.* **3.** *iv., irreg.* to leave. ♦ *Bill looked at his watch and said it was time to go.* ♦ *When you go, please turn out the lights.* **4.** *iv., irreg.* to reach a certain time or place; to extend to a certain time or place. ♦ *This train goes to New York.* ♦ *This movie goes until 11:00.* **5.** *iv., irreg.* to work; to function. ♦ *Is the washing machine going yet, or do you need to put in more money?* ♦ *Mary assures me that her computer is still going even though it is six years old.* **6.** *iv., irreg.* to become. ♦ *Uncle John went insane after the war.* ♦ *Some diseases can make you go blind.* **7. go for** *iv., irreg. + prep. phr.* to sell for a certain price. ♦ *This watch normally goes for $500, but it's on sale for $300.* ♦ *What does this radio go for? The price tag is missing.* **8.** *iv.* to become worn out; to weaken. ♦ *The actor's voice started going during the second act.* ♦ *The radio station started to go when we were 60 miles out of town.* **9.** *iv., irreg.* to be destined for something or some place. ♦ *Last year, 25% of my income went to taxes.* ♦ *My foot doesn't go into this shoe.* **10.** *iv., irreg.* to belong in a certain place. ♦ *These letters go in the top drawer of the desk.* ♦ *The number 12 goes after the number 11.* **11.** *iv., irreg.* [for the activities in a period of time] to unfold in some way, good or bad. ♦ *How did your trip to Florida go?* ♦ *I don't think my interview went very well.* **12.** *iv., irreg.* to make a certain sound. ♦ *A cow goes "moo," and a pig goes "oink."* ♦ *The engine went "clunk, clunk, clunk," and then it stopped.* **13.** *iv., irreg.* to progress though a series of words or musical notes. ♦ *Do you know how the national anthem goes?* ♦ *How does the melody of "Moon River" go?* **14.** *iv., irreg.* to be willed to someone. ♦ *The books in my office go to my son.* ♦ *All of the millionaire's money went to charity.* **15. go with** *iv., irreg. + prep. phr.* to match; to look good together. ♦ *Your shoes don't go with your purse.* ♦ *Do these light blue pants go with this striped tie?* **16.** *iv., irreg.* to be tolerated. ♦ *In New York City, anything goes.* ♦ *Your insolent attitude doesn't go around here.* **17. go into** *iv., irreg. + prep. phr.* [for a number] to divide into another number. ♦ *Three goes into twelve four times.* ♦ *How many times does 5 go into 20?* **18. go under** *iv., irreg. + adv.* [for a business or other enterprise] to fail. ♦ *When the business went under, many people lost their jobs.* ♦ *Many small newspapers went under when the price of paper went up.* **19. from the word "go"** *idiom* from the beginning; from the very start of things. ♦ *I knew about the problem from the word "go."* ♦ *She was failing the class from the word "go."* **20. go on** *idiom* to happen; to occur. ♦ *What is going on here?* ♦ *Something is going on in the center of town. Can you hear the sirens?* **21. go out with someone** *idiom* to have a date with someone; to spend an evening with someone doing something such as seeing a movie or eating a meal. ♦ *John would like to go out with Mary but is too shy to ask her.* ♦ *Would you go out with me sometime?* **22. have a go at something** *idiom* make an attempt something. ♦ *At the carnival, my friend urged me to have a go at one of the games.* ♦ *If you can't open the pickle jar, let me have a go at it.* **23. make a go of it** *idiom* to make something work out all right. ♦ *It's a tough situation, but Anne is trying to make a go of it.* ♦ *We don't like living here, but we have to make a go of it.* **24. on the go** *idiom* busy; moving about busily. ♦ *I'm usually on the go all day long.* ♦ *I hate being on the go all the time.*

goad ['god] **1.** *n.* something that prods someone or something to do something. ♦ *The need to make his mortgage payment was a constant goad that prompted Bill to work overtime.* ♦ *The boss promised us a bonus as a goad to finish the project.* **2. goad into** *tv. + prep. phr.* to force someone or something into doing something. ♦ *My children goaded me into buying a swimming pool.* ♦ *My parents goaded me into doing my homework.*

goal ['gol] **1.** *n.* an aim; an objective; an intended purpose; a result that one would like to achieve from doing something. ♦ *The goal of this company is to make a lot of money.* ♦ *Anne's goal was to become a lawyer.* **2.** *n.* [in sports] a place where players try to send a ball or puck in order to score points. ♦ *The goalie kicked the soccer ball away from the goal.* ♦ *The football player caught the ball and ran towards the goal.* **3.** *n.* [in sports] the points earned by sending a ball or puck through or past ②. ♦ *A goal in hockey is worth one point.* ♦ *Our team scored its first goal two minutes after the game started.* **4.** *n.* the finish line; the end point of a race. ♦ *The winner broke through the tape that stretched across the goal.* ♦ *The winner of the marathon reached the goal two minutes ahead of anyone else.*

goalie ['go li] *n.* a goalkeeper. (A shortening of goalkeeper.) ♦ *The goalie bounced the soccer ball off his head.* ♦ *The puck hit the goalie in the chest.*

goalkeeper ['gol kip ɚ] *n.* [in sports] the player whose position is in front of the team's goal and who tries to prevent players on the other team from scoring. ♦ *In soccer, only goalkeepers can touch the ball with their hands.* ♦ *The goalkeeper blocked the hockey puck with his hockey stick.*

goaltender ['gol tɛn dɚ] *n.* a goalkeeper. ♦ *The goaltender kicked the soccer ball away from the goal.* ♦ *I shot the puck past the goaltender and scored a point.*

goat ['got] *n.* an animal with horns, similar to a sheep. ♦ *Goats are found in the wild and also on farms.* ♦ *Uncle John raised a goat for its milk.*

goatee [go 'ti] *n.* a short, pointed beard, often worn with the facial hair between the ear and the edge of the chin shaved off. ♦ *Bill's new job required him to shave his goatee off.* ♦ *John shaved the beard off his cheeks, so now he's got a goatee.*

gob ['gɑb] **1.** *n.* a lump of something. ♦ *I scraped a gob of gum from my shoe.* ♦ *I left a gob of rice on my plate.* **2.** *n.* a lot; a large amount. (Informal. Often plural.) ♦ *There were gobs of people at the mall today.* ♦ *I have gobs of work to do before I go home.*

gobble ['gɑb əl] **1. gobble (down); gobble (up)** *tv. (+ adv.)* to eat all of one's food very quickly. ♦ *It's not polite to gobble your food.* ♦ *I gobbled the pizza down in five minutes.* **2.** *iv.* [for a turkey] to make a noise; to make a noise like a turkey. ♦ *The turkeys gobbled as they ran around the farmyard.* ♦ *I asked Jimmy if he could gobble like a turkey.* **3.** *n.* the noise that a turkey makes. ♦ *I heard the gobble of the turkeys inside the barn.* ♦ *I was awakened at sunrise by the turkeys' gobbles.*

goblet ['gɑb lɪt] *n.* a drinking vessel with a stem and a base or foot. ♦ *The waiter filled our goblets with wine.* ♦ *The museum displayed a golden goblet from the 15th century.*

goblin ['gɑb lɪn] *n.* a small, mythical creature that frightens people or makes trouble. ♦ *The farmer was convinced that his pig was killed by goblins.* ♦ *Susan dressed up like a goblin for Halloween.*

god ['gɑd] **1.** *n.* a male spiritual being who is worshiped. (See also **God**. Compare with **goddess**.) ♦ *The ancient Greeks worshiped several gods.* ♦ *The planet Mars is named for the Roman god of war.* **2.** *n.* a human who is admired as ①. ♦ *Modern rock stars are often treated as gods.* ♦ *Babe Ruth was one of the gods of baseball.* **3. God** *n.* [in religions such as Christianity, Islam, and Judaism] the one spiritual being that is worshiped as the creator and ruler of the universe. (No plural form in this sense.) ♦ *Churches and temples are houses of God.* ♦ *I prayed to God that my mother's operation would be successful.*

goddess ['gɑd əs] *n.* a female spiritual being who is worshiped. ♦ *Athena was the Greek goddess of wisdom.* ♦ *The farmer offered a prayer to the goddess of the harvest.*

godfather ['gɑd fɑ ðɚ] *n.* a male godparent. ♦ *My godfather helped me afford to go to college.* ♦ *Bob's godfather always sends him a card on his birthday.*

godforsaken ['gɑd for 'sek ən] **1.** *adj.* forsaken by God; abandoned by God. (Adv: *godforsakenly.*) ♦ *The godforsaken sinners begged for forgiveness.* ♦ *The minister prayed for the godforsaken people of the world.* **2.** *adj.* desolate; empty; barren. (Adv: *godforsakenly.*) ♦ *My car ran out of gas on some godforsaken road in western Nebraska.* ♦ *I left Los Angeles and moved to a godforsaken beach in Mexico.*

godmother ['gɑd mə ðɚ] *n.* a female godparent. ♦ *My godmother gave me a Bible for Christmas.* ♦ *I asked my best friend to be my new baby's godmother.*

godparent ['gɑd pɛr ənt] **1.** *n.* someone who vows at a child's baptism to support in the religious upbringing of the child, especially if the parents die. ♦ *I went to live with my godparents after my parents died.* ♦ *I asked my godparents for advice when I argued with my parents.* **2.** *n.* someone formally or informally designated as a child's guardian in case the true parents die. ♦ *Bill named Bob and Anne as the godparents of his children.* ♦ *My lawyer suggested I name godparents for my children in my will.*

godsend ['gɑd sɛnd] *n.* someone or something that arrives unexpectedly but is needed very much. ♦ *The bonus of $100 I got at work was a godsend.* ♦ *The rainstorm was a godsend to the area affected by the drought.*

goes ['goz] the third-person singular, present tense of go.

goggles ['gɔg əlz] *n.* a pair of protective lenses that are worn during swimming, skiing, biking, and other activities. (Treated as plural.) ♦ *I won't open my eyes underwater unless I'm wearing goggles.* ♦ *I wear goggles while biking to keep insects and dust from flying into my eyes.*

going ['go ɪŋ] **1.** *n.* a departure; a good-bye; leaving. (No plural form in this sense.) ♦ *The traveler's going was fraught with delays.* ♦ *John's going saddened us all.* **2. slow going** *idiom* a slow and steady rate of speed when one is making progress. ♦ *It was slow going at first, but I was able to finish the project by the weekend.* ♦ *Getting the heavy rocks out of the field is slow going.* **3. the going** *idiom* the condition of a path of travel or progress. ♦ *The going was rough through the mountains.* ♦ *I decided to sell my stock while the going was still good.* **4. the going rate** *idiom* the current rate. ♦ *The going interest rate for your account is 10%.* ♦ *Our babysitter charges us the going rate.*

gold ['gold] **1.** *n.* a chemical element that is a soft, yellow metal, is very valuable, and is the standard for money in many countries. (No plural form in this sense.) ♦ *The miner struck it rich when he found a vein of gold.* ♦ *The pages of many valuable old books are edged with gold.* **2.** *n.* coins or jewelry made of gold. (No plural form in this sense.) ♦ *Anne keeps her gold in a safety-deposit box.* ♦ *Should I wear silver or gold with this outfit?* **3.** *n.* a deep yellow color. (No plural form in this sense.) ♦ *My high school's colors are black and gold.* ♦ *Our kitchen is decorated in green and harvest gold.* **4.** *adj.* made of ①. ♦ *The thief stole my gold watch.* ♦ *Should I wear a silver or gold earring with this outfit?* **5.** *adj.* deep yellow in color. (Comp: *golder*; sup: *goldest.*) ♦ *We replaced the ugly gold refrigerator with a white one.* ♦ *The field was full of gold sunflowers.* **6. worth its weight in gold, worth one's weight in gold** *idiom* very valuable. ♦ *This book is worth its weight in gold.* ♦ *Oh, Bill. You're wonderful. You're worth your weight in gold.*

golden ['gol dən] **1.** *adj.* made from gold; yellowish as if made from gold. ♦ *A large golden goblet sat at the center of the museum display.* ♦ *Anne often wears a large golden bracelet.* **2.** *adj.* prosperous; successful; fortunate. ♦ *My grandparents spent their golden years of retirement in Arizona.* ♦ *The company's golden days ended when the stock market crashed.* **3.** *adj.* [of anniversaries] the fiftieth. ♦ *My parents went to Las Vegas for their golden anniversary.* ♦ *The department store celebrated its golden anniversary by having a big sale.*

goldenrod ['gol dən rɑd] *n.* a plant that has small clusters of yellow flowers. (No plural form in this sense.) ♦ *The meadow was dotted with wild goldenrod.* ♦ *The pollen from goldenrod makes me sneeze.*

golden rule ['gol dən 'rul] *n.* a rule from the Bible that means that one should treat people the way one wants to be treated. ♦ *Most of the world's religions have a belief similar to the golden rule.* ♦ *There would be less violence if everyone followed the golden rule.*

goldfish ['gold fɪʃ] *n., irreg.* a kind of small fish, typically orange or golden, commonly kept as a pet. (Pl: *goldfish.*) ♦ *I fed the goldfish tiny flakes of fish food.* ♦ *A dead goldfish floated upside down in the tank.*

gold-plated ['gold 'plet ɪd] *adj.* coated with a layer of gold. ♦ *Is your ring solid gold or just gold-plated?* ♦ *I revealed the nickel interior when I scratched the gold-plated coin.*

golf ['gɔlf] **1.** *n.* a game played on a large area of land, where players try to hit a small ball into a hole, using as few strokes as possible. (No plural form in this sense.) ♦ *My boss discussed work with me while we played golf.* ♦ *After work, I played nine holes of golf.* **2.** *iv.* to play ①. ♦ *My family golfs every Sunday after church.* ♦ *The board members discussed business while they golfed.*

golfer ['gɔlf ɚ] *n.* someone who golfs. ♦ *The golfer hit the ball into a pond by accident.* ♦ *After playing golf, the golfers went to the clubhouse for a drink.*

gondola ['gɑn də lə] **1.** *n.* a flat-bottom boat that is used in Venice, Italy—where there are numerous canals—to transport people and goods from place to place. ♦ *In Venice, people travel by gondola instead of by car.* ♦ *David got wet when he fell out of the gondola.* **2.** *n.* the basket underneath a hot-air balloon that holds the passengers. ♦ *The gondola we used on our balloon flight was made of wicker.* ♦ *I looked over the side of the gondola to the ground far below.*

gone ['gɔn] pp of go.

goner ['gɔn ɚ] *n.* someone who is dead or who is about to die; something that is broken and cannot be fixed. ♦ *The paramedics ignored the goners and searched for survivors.* ♦ *Can the television be fixed or is it a goner?*

goo ['gu] *n.* a wet, sticky mess; an amount of any wet, sticky substance. (No plural form in this sense.) ♦ *The young child mashed her peas into a pile of green goo.* ♦ *The floor of the theater was coated with goo.*

good ['gʊd] **1.** *adj., irreg.* having positive qualities; satisfactory; suitable; not negative. (Adv: *well.* Comp: better; sup: best.) ♦ *Have you heard the good news? I won the lottery!* ♦ *My dog has a good sense of smell.* **2.** *adj., irreg.* having proper morals; virtuous; moral; not evil. ♦ *The minister was known for being a good man.* ♦ *My landlord is forgetful, but he's really a good person.* **3.** *adj., irreg.* enjoyable; pleasant; beneficial; satisfying. (Adv: *well.*) ♦ *We had a good time at the beach.* ♦ *I had a really good steak for dinner.* **4.** *adj., irreg.* complete; thorough; full. (Adv: *well.*) ♦ *Give your room a good cleaning before you leave tonight.* ♦ *You're going to get a good spanking if you don't clean your room.* **5.** *adj.* [of a total of] at least. (See also goodly.) ♦ *We drove a good 500 miles today.* ♦ *Our microwave oven cost a good three hundred dollars.* **6.** *adj., irreg.* (Adv: *well.*) skillful; talented; able to do something right. ♦ *Mary's a good golfer.* ♦ *The street musician was very good, so we gave him $5.* **7.** *adj., irreg.* properly behaved; obedient. ♦ *Dave was a good child and never gave his parents any problems.* ♦ *"Good dog," Mary said as she patted it on the head.* **8.** *adj.* ripe; edible; not spoiled; not rotten. ♦ *The grocer separated the good fruit from the bad.* ♦ *Is the milk in the refrigerator still good?* **9.** *adj.* of high quality; best available. (See also best.) ♦ *I put the good silverware on the table for the fancy party.* ♦ *Bob wore his good clothes to the interview.* **10.** *adj.* financially sound. ♦ *Is this check good, or should I wait a few days before cashing it?* ♦ *You can borrow some money from Bob. He's good for $10.* **11.** *n.* excellence; virtue; goodness. (No plural form in this sense.) ♦ *The newspaper reported very little of the good in the world.* ♦ *In the end, the forces of good will win over the forces of evil.* **12. goods** *n.* items for sale; commodities. (Treated as plural.) ♦ *What aisle are the paper goods located in?* ♦ *All goods are 25% off this week.* **13. goods** *n.* the property and things that someone owns. (Treated as plural.) ♦ *The refugees carried all of their goods on their backs.* ♦ *All of my worldly goods fit into a small van.* **14. for the good of someone or something** *idiom* for the benefit, profit, or advantage of someone or something. (No plural form in this sense.) ♦ *The president said the strict drug laws were for the good of the country.* ♦ *David took a second job for the good of his family.*

good-bye [gʊd 'bɑɪ] **1.** *interj.* "farewell," as said when someone leaves. ♦ *"Good-bye," Dave said as he dropped me off at school.* ♦ *"Good-bye," I said to my guests as they left.* **2.** *n.* a departure, including saying good-bye ①. ♦ *The lovers' good-byes were sad.* ♦ *After our angry good-bye, I knew I'd never see my boss again.* **3.** *adj.* of or about leaving; of or about a departure; of or about a parting. ♦ *John gave his mother a good-bye kiss.* ♦ *We threw our boss a good-bye party when he retired.* **4.** *adv.* as a way of expressing farewell. ♦ *Bill kissed Susan good-bye and left for the airport.* ♦ *I hugged my mother good-bye before going to school.*

good-for-nothing ['gʊd for nəθ ɪŋ] **1.** *n.* someone who is worthless or lazy. ♦ *Get off the couch, you lazy good-for-nothing, and help me clean!* ♦ *I regretted having hired such a good-for-nothing as my assistant.* **2.** *adj.* worthless; lazy; irresponsible. ♦ *My good-for-nothing roommate left his dirty dishes in the sink.* ♦ *I ended up doing the work of my good-for-nothing coworker.*

Good Friday ['gʊd 'frɑɪ de] *n.* [in the Christian religion] the Friday before Easter, honored in remembrance of the crucifixion of Jesus Christ. ♦ *Some Christians are not supposed to eat meat on Good Friday.* ♦ *Many Christians go to church services on Good Friday.*

good-hearted ['gʊd 'hɑrt ɪd] *adj.* very kind; very generous. (Adv: *good-heartedly.*) ♦ *My good-hearted landlord let me pay my rent a week late.* ♦ *My good-hearted neighbor watched my kids while I was in the hospital.*

good-looking ['gʊd 'lʊk ɪŋ] *adj.* attractive; beautiful; handsome; pretty. ♦ *The good-looking woman would not pay any attention to Dave.* ♦ *Don't you think Anne's date for the prom is very good-looking?*

good-luck [gʊd 'lʌk] *adj.* causing or thought to cause good luck. ♦ *Jane's good-luck charm lay on her dresser.* ♦ *I gave my girlfriend a good-luck kiss before her interview.*

goodly ['gʊd li] *adj.* [a] considerable [amount]; [a] large [number]. (Comp: *goodlier;* sup: *goodliest.*) ♦ *A goodly amount of money is wasted each year by the government.* ♦ *We saw a goodly number of people at the beach today.*

good-natured ['gʊd 'ne tʃɚd] *adj.* pleasant; easy going; tolerant; forgiving. (Adv: *good-naturedly.*) ♦ *My good-natured roommate helped me do my homework.* ♦ *Dave's good-natured neighbor lent him their lawn mower when Dave's broke.*

goodness ['gʊd nəs] *n.* being good, ethical, and right. (No plural form in this sense.) ♦ *I always look for the goodness in other people.* ♦ *I respected John's goodness in the face of temptation.*

good night [gʊd 'nɑɪt] **1.** *n.* <an expression used in the evening when someone leaves or goes to bed.> ♦ *"Good night," I said to my roommates as I went to my bedroom.* ♦ *"Good night," said the bus driver as I got off the bus.* **2. good-night** *adj.* <the adj. use of ①.> ♦ *John gave Mary a good-night kiss.* ♦ *Jimmy always gets a good-night hug from his daddy.*

good-sized ['gʊd 'sɑɪzd] *adj.* large; rather large. ♦ *I had a good-sized hamburger for dinner.* ♦ *Our house has a good-sized backyard.*

good-tempered ['gʊd 'tɛm pɚd] *adj.* not easily angered; cheerful; kind. (Adv: *good-temperedly.*) ♦ *My good-tempered boss laughed at the practical joke I played.* ♦ *Even though Anne was sick, she tried to remain good-tempered.*

goodwill ['gʊd wɪl] *n.* kindness and friendliness. ♦ *Bob was friendly and had goodwill for everyone.* ♦ *The volunteer worker was filled with goodwill.*

goody ['gʊd i] **1.** *interj.* <a diminutive form of *good,* especially used by children to show approval.> ♦ *Oh, goody, you ate all of your carrots!* ♦ *"Oh, goody!" Jimmy said. "We're going to the zoo!"* **2.** *n.* a small candy or other treat. ♦ *Jimmy's grandmother gave him some chocolate goodies.* ♦ *Don't eat too many goodies, or you'll spoil your dinner.*

gooey ['gu i] **1.** *adj.* sticky and messy. (Comp: *gooier;* sup: *gooiest.*) ♦ *After Jimmy ate the jelly sandwich, his face was a gooey mess.* ♦ *I washed my hands because they were all gooey.* **2.** *adj.* sentimental and sweet. (Figurative on ①. Comp: *gooier;* sup: *gooiest.*) ♦ *The movie's gooey dialogue embarrassed John on his first date with Susan.* ♦ *"Don't get all gooey!" Mary told her weeping mother as she left for the airport.*

goof ['guf] **1.** *n.* a silly person. (Informal.) ♦ *The teacher asked John to be less of a goof in the classroom.* ♦ *Did you see that guy drop his books? What a goof!* **2.** *n.* a mistake; an error. (Informal.) ♦ *Anne checked her homework for goofs.* ♦ *Bill's typographical goof cost his company $10,000.* **3. goof (up)** *iv.* (+ *adv.*) to make a mistake. (Informal.) ♦ *Sorry, I goofed.* ♦ *The waiter goofed up by bringing me the wrong food.* **4. goof off; goof around** *iv.* + *adv.* to fool around; to waste time. ♦ *Stop goofing off and get ready to leave.* ♦ *John spent the afternoon goofing off instead of working.* **5. goof up** *tv.* + *adv.* to do something wrong; to make a mess of something. (Informal.) ♦ *The waiter goofed my order up.* ♦ *I goofed my homework up, so my teacher explained how to do it.*

goofy ['guf i] *adj.* silly; stupid. (Informal. Adv: *goofily.* Comp: *goofier;* sup: *goofiest.*) ♦ *Anne gave her teacher a goofy excuse for not doing her homework.* ♦ *Bill's shirt was turned inside out, and it made him look goofy.*

goon ['gun] *n.* a stupid person. (Slang.) ♦ *The goon at the fast-food counter got my order wrong.* ♦ *Some goon driving in front of me turned without signaling.*

goop ['gup] *n.* a formless mixture of a sticky, messy substance. (No plural form in this sense. Informal.) ♦ *I poked at the goop in the bowl with my fork.* ♦ *Anne put some goop in her hair to make it stay in place.*

goopy ['gup i] *adj.* messy, sticky, and without form. (Informal. Comp: *goopier;* sup: *goopiest.*) ♦ *This soup looks goopy, but it tastes very good.* ♦ *I wiped up the goopy mess with a rag.*

goose ['gus] **1.** *n., irreg.* a long-necked bird similar to a large duck. (Pl: geese.) ♦ *I watched the large geese swim across the river.* ♦ *The baby goose tumbled as it walked behind its mother.* **2. cook someone's goose** *idiom* to damage or ruin someone. ♦ *I cooked my own goose by not showing up on time.* ♦ *Sally cooked Bob's goose for treating her the way he did.*

goose bumps ['gus bəmps] See goose pimples.

goose flesh ['gus flɛʃ] See goose pimples.

goose pimples AND **goose bumps; goose flesh** ['gus pɪm pəlz, 'gus bəmps, 'gus flɛʃ] *n.* small bumps on the skin that form when one is frightened or cold. (Treated as plural. Rarely singular.) ♦ *The movie scared me so badly that I got goose pimples.* ♦ *I put on a sweater because the cold air gave me goose pimples.*

gopher ['gof ɚ] **1.** *n.* a rat-like rodent with large front teeth and puffy cheeks. ♦ *The gopher burrows through underground tunnels.* ♦ *Gophers were destroying my manicured lawn.* **2.** *n.* a type of computer program that searches a host computer for information requested over the Internet. ♦ *You can use the gopher to access the library's computer system.* ♦ *My system's gopher was down, so I couldn't read the news on-line.*

gore ['gor] **1.** *n.* thickened or clotted blood from a wound. (No plural form in this sense.) ♦ *The nurse cleaned the gore from my wound.* ♦ *The dead soldiers were covered with gore.* **2.** *tv.* [for an animal] to stab someone or something with a horn or a tusk. ♦ *A large rhinoceros gored the hunter.* ♦ *The bullfighter died when he was gored by the bull.*

gorge ['gordʒ] **1.** *n.* a narrow valley bordered by high cliffs. ♦ *I stood on the edge of the cliff and threw a rock into the gorge.* ♦ *Drive carefully up the mountain, or you'll end up in the gorge.* **2. gorge on** *iv.* + *prep. phr.* to eat too much food. ♦ *I broke my diet when I gorged on sweets.* ♦ *I didn't have time to eat lunch, so I gorged on potato chips.* **3. gorge on** *tv.* + *prep. phr.* to stuff oneself with food. (Takes a reflexive object.) ♦ *Bill became sick because he gorged himself on pizza.* ♦ *I gorged myself on ham sandwiches.* **4. feel one's gorge rise** *idiom* to sense that one is getting very angry. ♦ *I felt my gorge rise and I knew I was going to loose my temper.* ♦ *Bob could feel his gorge rise as he read his tax bill.* **5. make someone's gorge rise** *idiom* to cause someone to become very angry. ♦ *The unnecessary accident made my gorge rise.* ♦ *Getting his tax bill made Bob's gorge rise.*

gorgeous ['gor dʒəs] *adj.* very beautiful; very pretty; very pleasant. (Adv: *gorgeously.*) ♦ *Since it was a gorgeous day, I went to the beach.* ♦ *A gorgeous model won the beauty contest.*

gorilla [gə 'rɪl ə] *n.* the largest kind of ape. (Compare with guerrilla.) ♦ *The scientist tried to teach some gorillas sign language.* ♦ *The gorilla at the zoo was kept in a cage that was too small.*

gory ['gor i] *adj.* showing gore; covered with blood and gore. (Adv: *gorily.* Comp: *gorier;* sup: *goriest.*) ♦ *The police inspected the gory remains of the victim.* ♦ *My parents wouldn't let me watch the gory movie.*

gosh ['gɑʃ] *interj.* <an exclamation used in place of God to indicate amazement or surprise.> ♦ *Gosh, do you think it will rain today?* ♦ *Gosh, it's cold in here!*

gospel ['gɑs pəl] **1. Gospel** *n.* one of the first four books of the New Testament. ♦ *The four Gospels were written by Matthew, Mark, Luke, and John, who are saints in the Catholic Church.* ♦ *The minister read from the Gospel during the service.* **2.** *n.* the absolute truth; something that is absolutely true. (Figurative on the assumed truth of the four Gospels ①.) ♦ *The police took the witness's word as gospel.* ♦ *The defendant swore her testimony was gospel.* **3. gospel (music)** *n.* a style of religious and, later, popular music, originating among blacks in the South. ♦ *The singer had begun her career by singing gospel in her church choir.* ♦ *Susan listens to gospel music while she drives.* **4. the gospel truth** *idiom* a truth that is undeniable. ♦ *The witness swore he was telling the gospel truth.* ♦ *I told my parents the gospel truth about how the vase broke.*

gossip ['gɑs əp] **1.** *n.* talk about other people, which may or may not be true; rumors about other people. (No plural form in this sense.) ♦ *According to the latest gossip, my boss is going to quit.* ♦ *I demanded to know who had spread vicious gossip about me.* **2.** *n.* someone who often talks about other people and other people's private lives. ♦ *The neighborhood gossip told me about Susan's arrest.* ♦ *I told the annoying gossip to mind his own business.* **3.** *iv.* to talk about other people and their private lives; to spread rumors about other people. ♦ *All of the neighbors gossiped about Bill's problem with alcohol.* ♦ *You shouldn't gossip, because you could hurt someone's reputation.*

got ['gɑt] **1.** pt and a pp of get. **2. have got to [do something]** See get.

Gothic ['gɔθ ɪk] **1.** *adj.* relating to the styles of art and architecture of Western Europe from the 12th century to the 16th century. (Adv: *Gothically* [...ɪk li].) ♦ *The tourists took pictures of the lovely Gothic church.* ♦ *The art museum had an entire wing containing Gothic art.* **2.** *adj.* relating to a style of literature, originating in the late 1700s, involving the supernatural, horror, gloom, and romance. (Often gothic. Adv: *Gothically* [...ɪk li].) ♦ *We read tales of Gothic horror in my literature class.* ♦ *The horror film showed a heavy Gothic influence.*

gotten ['gɑt n] a pp of get.

gouge ['gɑʊdʒ] **1.** *n.* a deep gash; a deep cut. ♦ *Dave made a gouge in the kitchen door when he slammed the edge of his tool kit into it.* ♦ *The sharp rock made a deep gouge in my leg.* **2.** *n.* a kind of chisel with a scooped blade that is used to make grooves. ♦ *I used a gouge to make a groove in the wood.* ♦ *The police determined that the murderer had used a gouge.* **3.** *tv.* to gash or cut deeply into something; to gash something by force; to scoop something out by force. ♦ *Bill gouged the wall by accident.* ♦ *I gouged the surface of the table with my penknife.* **4.** *tv.* to charge someone too much for something, especially if the person has no other options but to pay the price. ♦ *The store gouged the refugees by charging double for basic supplies.* ♦ *The tourists were gouged by the high prices.*

goulash ['gu lɑʃ] *n.* a spicy Hungarian stew with meat, vegetables, and paprika. (No plural form in this sense.) ♦ *The goulash was too spicy for me.* ♦ *Tom learned to make goulash from his grandmother, who was Hungarian.*

gourd ['gord] **1.** *n.* a hard fruit that grows on a vine along the ground, similar to a pumpkin. ♦ *Bob made a drinking cup from a dried gourd.* ♦ *The colorful Thanksgiving centerpiece was made with gourds.* **2.** *n.* a plant that produces ①. ♦ *I planted a row of gourds between the pumpkins and the squash.* ♦ *The soil around the gourds was dry, so I watered it.*

gourmet [gor 'me] **1.** *n.* someone who enjoys fine foods and wine. ♦ *The gourmet, finding nothing that suited him on the menu, left the restaurant.* ♦ *The waiter asked the gourmet if the wine was suitable.* **2.** *adj.* [of food and drink] produced according to the highest cooking standards. ♦ *We drank a bottle of gourmet wine with our steak.* ♦ *The gourmet meal cost $50 per person.* **3.** *adj.* [of cooking utensils, recipes, etc.] suitable for ①. ♦ *The gourmet frying pan was coated with a nonstick surface.* ♦ *The cook told me his secret gourmet recipe for chicken salad.*

gout ['gɑʊt] *n.* a disease that causes the toes, knees, and fingers to swell painfully. (No plural form in this sense.) ♦ *My grandfather could polka quite well until he got gout.* ♦ *My neighbor walks with a cane because she's got gout.*

govern ['gʌv ɚn] **1.** *iv.* to rule; to be the leader of a group of people. ♦ *The noble king governed until his death.* ♦ *The evil dictator governed unfairly.* **2.** *tv.* to rule or lead a group of people. ♦ *The president governed the nation for 8 years.* ♦ *The mayor governed the inhabitants of the city.* **3.** *tv.* to guide, control, or regulate something. ♦ *This lever governs the speed of the truck.* ♦ *The board of directors governed the firm's day-to-day operations.*

governess ['gʌv ɚ nəs] *n.* a woman employed to raise and teach the children of someone else's family. ♦ *Only wealthy families can afford a governess.* ♦ *The Smiths hired a governess who knew Latin.*

governing ['gʌv ɚ nɪŋ] *adj.* ruling; controlling; in charge. ♦ *The company's governing body demanded that its treasurer resign.* ♦ *The meeting was attended by 20 governing heads of state.*

government ['gʌv ɚn mənt] **1.** *n.* the system of rule over a country and its people. (No plural form in this sense.) ♦ *Government is expensive but necessary.* ♦ *There are many systems of government, but democracy is becoming more widespread.* **2.** *n.* the political organization ruling in a particular area. ♦ *The government of the United Kingdom is a constitutional monarchy.* ♦ *The professor was jailed for criticizing the authoritarian government.* **3.** *n.* the people who rule others; those who run ①. ♦ *The government received thousands of complaints about slow mail service.* ♦ *I object to the government's immigration policy.* **4.** *adj.* <the adj. use of ①.> ♦ *Everyone hates government bureaucracy.* ♦ *You can get a passport at the government office building downtown.*

governmental [gəv ɚn 'mɛn təl] *adj.* of or about the government. (Adv: *governmentally.*) ♦ *Dozens of governmental agencies were eliminated because of budget cuts.* ♦ *The bureaucrat strictly followed governmental policies.*

governor ['gʌv ɚ nɚ] **1.** *n.* the title of the executive officer of each of the United States. ♦ *The governor granted the condemned prisoner a stay of execution.* ♦ *Detroit's mayor met with the governor of Michigan to discuss crime.* **2.** *n.* someone who governs or rules certain organizations. ♦ *The governor of the board of elections ordered the polls to stay open an extra hour.* ♦ *The commission's governor vowed to cut its budget in half.* **3.** *n.* a device that controls the speed of a car or other vehicle, either keeping it at a constant speed or not allowing it to go over a certain speed. ♦ *The rental van's governor prevented speeds over 55 miles per hour.* ♦ *The delivery truck driver was fired for tampering with the truck's governor.*

gown ['gɑʊn] **1.** *n.* a formal dress for a woman. ♦ *Susan's wedding gown was made of white satin.* ♦ *The actress bought a stylish gown for the award ceremony.* **2.** *n.* a nightgown. ♦ *Anne slept in a flannel gown on cold winter nights.* ♦ *She wore a sleeveless gown to bed in the summer.* **3.** *n.* a sterile outer layer of clothing worn by doctors and nurses. ♦ *By the end of the operation, the doctor's gown was spattered with blood.* ♦ *Sterile gowns must be worn in the operating room.* **4.** *n.* a type of loose ceremonial covering or robe such as is worn at graduation ceremonies. ♦ *The graduating students lined up in their caps and gowns to receive their diplomas.* ♦ *Jane's graduation gown completely covered her dress.*

grab ['græb] **1.** *tv.* to seize and hold someone or something; to snatch someone or something; to take something rudely. ♦ *Bob grabbed the book I was reading out of my hands.* ♦ *Mary kicked the assailant who had grabbed her from behind.* **2.** *tv.* to get and bring something; to fetch something. ♦ *Please grab a cup of coffee for me while you're in the kitchen.* ♦ *Could you grab my slippers when you go upstairs?* **3.** *n.* an act of seizing as in ①. ♦ *The baseball player's grab for the ball was too late, and it went past him.* ♦ *I thwarted the thief's quick grab for my purse.* **4. grab a bite (to eat)** *idiom* to get something to eat; to get food that can be eaten quickly. ♦ *I need a few minutes to grab a bite to eat.* ♦ *Bob often tries to grab a bite between meetings.*

grace ['gres] **1.** *n.* elegance, smoothness, or attractiveness of form or motion. (No plural form in this sense.) ♦ *You have the grace and poise of a fashion model.* ♦ *We all admired the athletes' grace as they ran.* **2.** *n.* poised and tolerant elegance. (No plural form in this sense.) ♦ *After I accidentally broke a teacup, the hostess exhibited such superb grace in pardoning me that I was in awe of her good manners.* ♦ *The king was well known for the grace he showed in settling disputes between his subjects.* **3.** *n.* favor; mercy; favorable regard. (No plural form in this sense.) ♦ *The merchant's life was spared by the king's grace.* ♦ *Only through the grace of God did I survive the accident.* **4.** *n.* a prayer said before eating. (No plural form in this sense.) ♦ *Our family says grace together before every meal.* ♦ *I said grace quickly because I was rather hungry.* **5.** *n.* <a title used to address or refer to dukes, duchesses, and archbishops.> (Follows **his**, **her**, **their**, **your**.) ♦ *"Dinner is served, Your Grace," the servant said to the duke.* ♦ *His Grace, the archbishop, will see you now.* **6. grace period** *n.* a period of time between when a payment is due and when interest charges or other penalties will be added on. ♦ *The loan payment is due on the 15th, but there's a three-day grace period.* ♦ *The bank charged a late fee because my payment arrived after the grace period.* **7.** *tv.* to make something more beautiful or elegant; to add beauty or elegance to something. ♦ *Blue velvet drapes graced the doorway to the outer hall.* ♦ *Flowers graced the marble altar of the church.* **8. grace someone or something with one's presence** *idiom* to honor someone or something with one's presence. ♦ *"How nice of you to grace us with your presence," Mr. Wilson told Mary sarcastically as she entered the classroom late.* ♦ *The banquet was graced with the presence of the governor.* **9. graced with something** *idiom* made elegant by means of some ornament or decoration. ♦ *The altar was graced with lovely white flowers.* ♦ *The end of the beautiful day was graced with a beautiful sunset.* **10. fall from grace** *idiom* to cease to be held in favor, especially because of some wrong or foolish action. ♦ *He was the teacher's best pupil until he fell from grace by failing the history exam.* ♦ *Mary was the favorite grandchild until she fell from grace by running away from home.*

graceful ['gres fʊl] *adj.* moving with smoothness and grace; elegant in appearance. (Adv: *gracefully.*) ♦ *The dancers were all graceful, except for my date, who kept stumbling.* ♦ *I responded to the compliment with a graceful smile.*

graceless ['gres ləs] **1.** *adj.* awkward; clumsy; without style or elegance; not graceful. (Adv: *gracelessly.*) ♦ *The graceless student tripped walking up the stairs.* ♦ *The instructor said I was too graceless to be a ballet dancer.* **2.** *adj.* lacking good manners; lacking poise, tact, or elegance; not gracious. (Adv: *gracelessly.*) ♦ *Your graceless refusal of my generous offer offends me.* ♦ *The graceless boy stuck his tongue out at me.*

gracious ['gre ʃəs] **1.** *adj.* kind; courteous; pleasant. (Adv: *graciously.*) ♦ *I thanked Jane for her gracious hospitality.* ♦ *That rude clerk needs some lessons in gracious manners.* **2.** *adj.* of or about great comfort and good taste. (Adv: *graciously.*) ♦ *The stylish magazine featured pictures of several gracious homes.* ♦ *The president of my company lives in gracious surroundings.* **3.** *adj.* merciful; showing love and mercy. (Adv: *graciously.*) ♦ *The prisoner's life was spared by the queen's gracious act.* ♦ *The minister spoke of a gracious and loving God.* **4.** *interj.* <a mild expression of wonder or surprise.> ♦ *Gracious! It certainly is windy today, isn't it?* ♦ *Good gracious! Is this birthday cake for me?*

grackle ['græk əl] *n.* any of several species of black birds found in North and South America. ♦ *I was awakened at dawn by the harsh sound of a grackle outside my window.* ♦ *Mary threw breadcrumbs to the grackles in her backyard.*

gradation [gre 'de ʃən] *n.* one degree in the series of degrees of difference on a scale of measure. ♦ *The gradations on the ruler weren't fine enough to measure the insect's head.* ♦ *The gradations between the lightest and darkest settings are very noticeable on this copier.*

grade ['gred] **1.** *n.* a level in school corresponding to a year of study. ♦ *In American public schools, there are usually 12 grades plus kindergarten.* ♦ *Students in the 10th grade are called sophomores.* **2.** *n.* a mark given to a student for a class, test, paper, or assignment that shows how well or how poorly the student did. ♦ *Beneath my grade, the teacher wrote some comments about my paper.* ♦ *All of my grades this term were As, except for a B in History.* **3.** *n.* a degree of quality. ♦ *The grocery store stocks only grade A milk.* ♦ *Hundreds of grade B movies were filmed in the 1950s.* **4.** *n.* the slope of a road, roof, terrace, etc. ♦ *The sign warned drivers about the steep grade of the upcoming hill.* ♦ *The roof's slight grade caused rain to collect in puddles.* **5.** *tv.* to give ② for the work of a student. ♦ *Mrs. Fairbanks graded homework for an hour every evening.* ♦ *Mr. Davis graded the students' essays for grammar and creativity.* **6.** *iv.* to grade ⑤ the work of students in a particular manner. ♦ *I worked diligently because my teacher grades harshly.* ♦ *Mr. Smith grades easy, so I didn't try very hard.* **7. make the grade** *idiom* to be satisfactory; to be what is expected. ♦ *I'm sorry, but your work doesn't exactly make the grade.* ♦ *This meal doesn't just make the grade. It is excellent.*

grade school ['gred skul] *n.* a school for younger children. ♦ *Usually grade schools have kindergartens and first through fifth grades, first through sixth grades, or first through eighth grades.* ♦ *I learned how to read in grade school.*

gradual ['græ dʒu əl] *adj.* moving, happening, or changing a little bit at a time; slow. (Adv: *gradually.*) ♦ *There was a gradual change in climate as we drove north.* ♦ *The employees have received a gradual increase in pay.*

gradually ['græ dʒu ə li] *adv.* a little bit at a time; little by little; slowly. ♦ *Gradually, the flu spread across the coun-*

try. ♦ *The town's population has grown gradually since World War II.*

graduate 1. ['græ dʒu ət] *n.* someone who has received a diploma from a high school, college, or university. ♦ *The graduate looked forward to going to college in the fall.* ♦ *It's harder to get a good job if you're not a graduate.* **2. graduate (from)** ['græ dʒu et...] *iv.* (+ *prep. phr.*) to depart from a school, college, or university with a degree. ♦ *Anne graduated from the University of Michigan in 1988.* ♦ *When did you graduate from high school?* **3.** ['græ dʒu et] *tv.* to depart from a school, college, or university with a degree. (Informal.) ♦ *Bill graduated high school at 17 and went right into college.* ♦ *I graduated college when I was 21.*

graduated ['græ dʒu et ɪd] *adj.* marked to show units of measurement; calibrated. ♦ *I poured half a liter of acid into the graduated cylinder.* ♦ *The manufacturer guarantees the accuracy of its graduated instruments.*

graduation [græ dʒu 'e ʃən] **1.** *n.* the ceremony where students receive diplomas or degrees when they graduate. (No plural form in this sense.) ♦ *The students were each allowed to invite one guest to their graduation.* ♦ *I began working at a new job a week after graduation.* **2.** *n.* one or all of the marks on something that show the units of measurement. ♦ *The graduations on the flask had faded over time.* ♦ *Are the graduations on this ruler in inches or centimeters?*

graffiti [grə 'fi ti] *n.* words, symbols, or pictures that are written, scratched, or painted onto surfaces. (The Italian plural of *graffito.* Treated as singular.) ♦ *The walls of the subway station were covered with graffiti.* ♦ *I covered the graffiti on my garage door with paint.*

graft ['græft] **1.** *n.* political corruption involving bribery or the abuse of power and influence. (No plural form in this sense.) ♦ *The reporter vowed to expose graft in Washington.* ♦ *The ethical representative refused to become involved with graft.* **2.** *n.* the joint where a small twig or branch is attached to another plant. ♦ *After a few years, the graft at the base of the tree was no longer noticeable.* ♦ *The gardener tied string around the graft until the branch was secure enough to support itself.* **3.** *n.* a piece of skin or other tissue transplanted from one part of the body to another, or from one person (or creature) to another. ♦ *The nurse cleaned the patient's skin graft and covered it with sterile gauze.* ♦ *The doctors replaced the patient's burned flesh with a graft from his leg.* **4. graft onto** *tv.* + *prep. phr.* to attach something to something else so that it becomes one thing; to incorporate something into something else. ♦ *The botanist grafted a small twig onto a crook of a larger shrub.* ♦ *The doctors grafted skin from the patient's leg onto her injured arm.*

graham cracker ['græm kræk ɚ] *n.* a cracker made from unsifted whole-wheat flour. ♦ *Graham crackers are made from whole-wheat flour.* ♦ *I coated the chicken with crushed graham crackers before frying it.*

grain ['gren] **1.** *n.* grass or cereal plants grown for their edible seeds. (No plural form in this sense.) ♦ *We planted grain and turnips on the farm this year.* ♦ *This is a good year for growing grain.* **2.** *n.* the seed of ①. (No plural form in this sense.) ♦ *How much grain is stored in the silo?* ♦ *We bought enough grain to feed the cattle for a month.* **3.** *n.* an individual seed of ①. ♦ *The gardener planted one grain every four inches.* ♦ *The farmer planted two grains in each hole.* **4. grains** *n.* kinds or types of ①. ♦ *This bread is made with seven different grains.* ♦ *We planted four grains in the fields—wheat, rye, oats, and barley.* **5.** *n.* a tiny particle of something, such as sand or salt. ♦ *I removed a grain of sand from my eye.* ♦ *I sprinkled a few grains of salt on my potato.* **6.** *n.* a very small unit of measure, equal to about 64.8 milligrams. ♦ *The jeweler measured the weight of the diamond in grains.* ♦ *One ounce is equal to 480 grains.* **7.** *n.* the pattern or direction of the fibers of wood. (No plural form in this sense.) ♦ *The grain of the wood formed an interesting pattern after it was varnished.* ♦ *It was hard to saw the board because I was cutting with the grain.* **8. go against the grain** *idiom* to go against the natural direction or inclination. (On ⑦.) ♦ *Don't expect me to help you cheat. That goes against the grain.* ♦ *Would it go against the grain for you to call in sick for me?* **9. grain of truth** *idiom* even the smallest amount of truth. (On ⑥.) ♦ *The attorney was unable to find a grain of truth in the defendant's testimony.* ♦ *If there were a grain of truth to your statement, I would trust you.*

grainy ['gren i] *adj.* [of a photograph] having an image with a speckled look. (Adv: *grainily.* Comp: *grainier;* sup: *grainiest.*) ♦ *The only picture of the wanted criminal was a grainy photograph.* ♦ *The photograph of my grandparents' wedding is faded and grainy.*

gram ['græm] *n.* the basic unit for measuring weight in the metric system, equal to 1/1,000 of a kilogram or about 1/28 of an ounce. ♦ *This tablet has half a gram of aspirin.* ♦ *This coin weighs about 5 grams.*

grammar ['græm ɚ] **1.** *n.* a system of abstract rules in a language that determine how sentences are formed; the study of sentence structure and the relationships between words within sentences. (No plural form in this sense.) ♦ *I hope to be able to master English grammar and pronunciation.* ♦ *A description of the grammar of English shows how questions, commands, and statements are made.* **2.** *n.* a statement of the rules of a language that account for how sentences are formed, especially the description of what the standard form of the language is like. ♦ *There is a short Spanish grammar printed inside my Spanish dictionary.* ♦ *The linguist wrote a new grammar for English, but it was difficult to understand.* **3.** *n.* the observance of the rules of ② in the use of written and spoken language. ♦ *Jane received an A for good grammar and punctuation in her essay.* ♦ *Bill's grammar is regarded as poor by the teacher, but everybody understands him just fine.* **4. grammar school** *n.* a school at the elementary level. ♦ *I learned how to read and write in grammar school.* ♦ *I rode the bus to grammar school every morning.*

grammatical [grə 'mæt ɪ kəl] **1.** *adj.* of or about grammar. (Adv: *grammatically* [...ɪk li].) ♦ *Mary studied the grammatical structure of French.* ♦ *'Noun' is a kind of grammatical category.* **2.** *adj.* [of sentence structure] considered to be proper or correct. (Adv: *grammatically* [...ɪk li].) ♦ *It is wise to use grammatical sentences in formal situations, such as when interviewing for a job.* ♦ *"I seen it" is not grammatical in proper English.*

granary ['græn ə ri] *n.* a barn or silo where grain is stored after the harvest. ♦ *Our granaries are filled with corn.* ♦ *We stored the cattle feed in the granary.*

grand ['grænd] **1.** *adj.* impressive; magnificent. (Adv: *grandly.* Comp: *grander;* sup: *grandest.*) ♦ *The view from the hotel window was grand, and we could see all the way to the harbor.* ♦ *The cathedral in our town is a very grand building.* **2. grand total** *n.* the complete total; the final total. ♦ *A grand total of $20,000 was donated to the scholarship fund last month.* ♦ *The computer added the columns and displayed the grand total.* **3. grand (piano)** *n.* a long piano with its strings on a horizontal plane. ♦ *The grand piano fit nicely in the large living room.* ♦ *At the party, Mary sat down at the grand and began to play.* **4.** *n.* a thousand dollars. (Slang. No plural form in this sense.) ♦ *Mary won five grand in last week's lottery!* ♦ *John bought a used car for a grand.*

Grand Canyon ['grænd 'kæn jən] *n.* an enormous, beautiful canyon in Northern Arizona. ♦ *In some places, the Grand Canyon is over one mile deep.* ♦ *Bob and Mary took a trip to the Grand Canyon last year.*

grandchild ['græn(d) tʃaɪld] *n., irreg.* an offspring of one's offspring. (Pl: **grandchildren.**) ♦ *Mary watched her grandchildren while their parents were on vacation.* ♦ *John helped pay for his grandchild's education.*

grandchildren ['græn(d) tʃɪl drən] pl of **grandchild.**

granddad ['græn dæd] *n.* grandfather; the father of one's mother or father. ♦ *Jimmy often went fishing with his granddad.* ♦ *Granddad, what was my mother like when she was a little girl?*

granddaughter ['græn dɔt ɚ] *n.* the daughter of one's offspring. ♦ *Anne willed her wedding ring to her granddaughter.* ♦ *John moved in with his granddaughter when he couldn't live alone anymore.*

grandeur ['græn dʒɚ] *n.* magnificence; splendor; the quality of being impressive. (No plural form in this sense.) ♦ *The tourists were astounded by the grandeur of the Grand Canyon.* ♦ *It's hard to capture the grandeur of a beautiful sunset on film.*

grandfather ['græn(d) fɑ ðɚ] *n.* the father of one's mother or father. (Also a term of address.) ♦ *My grandfather immigrated from Italy when he was twelve.* ♦ *"Do you need any help with those bags, Grandfather?" Jimmy asked.*

grandiose ['græn di os] *adj.* pretentious; excessive; pompous; planned on a very large scale. (Adv: *grandiosely.*) ♦ *I quickly became tired of the poet's grandiose language.* ♦ *Grandiose ideas are often unrealistic.*

grandma ['græm mɑ] *n.* grandmother; the mother of one's mother or father. (Also a term of address.) ♦ *My grandma makes the best apple pie in the world.* ♦ *"Could I have some more of your cookies, Grandma?" asked Jimmy.*

grandmother ['græn(d) məð ɚ] *n.* the mother of one's mother or father. (Also a term of address.) ♦ *My grandmother went back to school when she was 65.* ♦ *Grandmother, would you like to come over for dinner tomorrow?*

grandpa ['græm pɑ] *n.* grandfather; the father of one's mother or father. (Also a term of address.) ♦ *My grandpa parked his tractor in the barn.* ♦ *Grandpa, what did you do before you met Grandma?*

grandparent ['græn(d) per ənt] *n.* a grandmother or a grandfather; the parent of one's parent. (The plural usually refers to one or more pairs consisting of a **grandmother** and a **grandfather.**) ♦ *All of my grandparents were still alive when I was 21.* ♦ *I lived with my grandparents during the summer.*

grandson ['græn(d) sən] *n.* the son of one's offspring. ♦ *John and Mary's only grandson went to college to become a lawyer.* ♦ *Bill and his grandson went hunting for deer.*

grandstand ['græn(d) stænd] *n.* the area where people sit at a racetrack, ball field, and the like. ♦ *The batter hit the ball into the grandstand.* ♦ *From my seat in the grandstand, I had a clear view of the finish line.*

granite ['græn ɪt] **1.** *n.* a hard, gray rock, used especially in constructing buildings and roads. (No plural form in this sense.) ♦ *The floor is tiled with huge slabs of granite.* ♦ *The designer suggested using marble or granite for the kitchen counter.* **2.** *adj.* made of ①. ♦ *The floor was covered with granite blocks.* ♦ *The bank's granite walls were six inches thick.*

grant ['grænt] **1.** *n.* money that is given by a government or a private agency for a worthy purpose. ♦ *Many groups and organizations receive financial support from government grants.* ♦ *Mary's research is funded by a grant from a foundation.* **2.** *tv.* to give something formally to someone. ♦ *The magician granted the prince three wishes.* ♦ *The foundation granted $10,000 to the art project.* **3.** *tv.* to give permission for something to someone. ♦ *The famous celebrity refused to grant the media an interview.* ♦ *The general granted the tourists safe passage to the American embassy during the war.* **4.** *tv.* to concede that something is true; to admit to someone that something is true. (Takes a clause.) ♦ *I grant that crime is a problem, but what can I do about it?* ♦ *I'll grant that your point is correct, but I think it's irrelevant.*

granted ['græn tɪd] **1.** *adv.* admittedly. ♦ *Granted, I was late, but I tried to call and tell you.* ♦ *Granted, I should have left the party earlier, but I was having fun.* **2. take someone or something for granted** *idiom* to accept someone or something—without gratitude—as a matter of course. ♦ *We tend to take a lot of things for granted.* ♦ *Mrs. Franklin complained that Mr. Franklin takes her for granted.*

granular ['græn jə lɚ] *adj.* looking or feeling like grains; consisting of grains. (Adv: *granularly.*) ♦ *In the ancient dwelling we found grains that had been crushed into a crude granular powder with a stone.* ♦ *I didn't like the granular texture of the cereal.*

granulated ['græn jə let ɪd] *adj.* crushed into tiny bits. ♦ *I put a spoonful of granulated sugar in my coffee.* ♦ *I put some finely granulated salt on my potato.*

granule ['græn jul] *n.* a small grain; a speck. ♦ *My shoes were filled with granules of sand.* ♦ *I extracted a granule of dirt from my eye.*

grape ['grep] **1.** *n.* a red, green, or purple fruit that grows in bunches on vines. ♦ *I picked a bunch of grapes straight off the vine.* ♦ *Lisa made homemade wine by pressing and fermenting grapes.* **2.** *adj.* made of or flavored with ①. ♦ *I drank a glass of grape juice for breakfast.* ♦ *I spread some grape jam on a slice of bread.*

grapefruit ['grep frut] **1.** *n., irreg.* a round fruit with yellow skin, similar to an orange, but larger and more tart. (This has nothing to do with grapes. Pl: *grapefruit* or *grapefruits.*) ♦ *I cut a grapefruit in half and scooped the sections out with a spoon.* ♦ *Grapefruits can be white, pink, or red inside.* **2.** *adj.* <the adj. use of ①.> ♦ *I prefer grape-*

fruit juice to orange juice. ♦ *It was so cold that our grapefruit tree nearly froze.*

grapevine ['grep vɑɪn] **1.** *n.* the plant that grapes grow on. ♦ *Our grapevine grows along wires between two posts.* ♦ *I picked bunches of grapes from the grapevines in my backyard.* **2.** *n.* the way gossip travels; a network of communication. (No plural form in this sense. Informal.) ♦ *I heard through the grapevine that you're quitting your job.* ♦ *There are no secrets in my office because of the grapevine.*

graph ['græf] **1.** *n.* a drawing that shows the difference between two or more quantities with reference to a certain measurement. ♦ *The researcher represented the data in the form of a graph.* ♦ *The graph showed the annual homicide rate in New York since 1980.* **2.** *tv.* to place information on a graph; to make a graph. ♦ *The researcher graphed the results of the experiment.* ♦ *I graphed the increase in the homicide rate over the past 20 years.*

graphic ['græf ɪk] **1.** *adj.* producing and designing drawings and charts. (Adv: *graphically* [...ɪk li].) ♦ *The firm hired a graphic artist to make the charts for the sales presentation.* ♦ *Our advertising is done by a graphic designer.* **2.** *adj.* detailed; vivid. (Adv: *graphically* [...ɪk li].) ♦ *The witness gave the police a graphic description of the accident.* ♦ *My parents won't let me see movies with graphic violence.* **3.** *n.* a chart, diagram, or similar display that presents information visually. ♦ *The graphics helped me understand the written descriptions.* ♦ *The designer created a graphic to appear on all of the company's business cards.*

graphic arts ['græf ɪk 'ɑrts] *n.* the arts that involve painting, drawing, and images displayed by various means. (Treated as singular or plural.) ♦ *The advertising agency hired a designer with a background in graphic arts.* ♦ *The gallery of graphic arts had an exhibit of etchings and engravings.*

graphite ['græ fɑɪt] *n.* a soft, black carbon used in pencils. (No plural form in this sense.) ♦ *The pencil's graphite broke because I wrote using too much pressure.* ♦ *The graphite from my pencil left marks on my shirt pocket.*

graphology [græf 'ɑl ə dʒi] *n.* the study of handwriting analysis. (No plural form in this sense.) ♦ *The police sent the ransom note to a detective skilled in graphology.* ♦ *An expert in graphology looked at my signature and said I was a creative person.*

grapple ['græ pəl] **grapple with** *iv.* + *prep. phr.* to deal with something that is very difficult; to struggle with problems relating to someone or something. ♦ *I grappled with money problems for years before I organized my finances.* ♦ *Mary had to grapple with her father's illness and her brother's death at the same time.*

grasp ['græsp] **1.** *tv.* to hold someone or something tightly with one's hands. ♦ *I grasped my keys so I wouldn't drop them.* ♦ *Anne grasped Bill and gave him a big hug.* **2.** *tv.* to understand something; to comprehend something. (Figurative on ①.) ♦ *I am unable to grasp advanced calculus.* ♦ *Mary finally grasped the material after reading the textbook very carefully.* **3.** *n.* a tight hold on someone or something; an act of holding someone or something tightly with one's hands. ♦ *My grasp on the handle was weak because it was slippery.* ♦ *The rescuer had a firm grasp on my arm and pulled me to safety.* **4.** *n.* understanding; comprehension; knowing what something is about. (Figurative on ③.) ♦ *My grasp of this article is poor because it was badly written.* ♦ *I have a good grasp of German because I grew up in Berlin.*

grasping ['græs pɪŋ] *adj.* jealously greedy and selfish. (Adv: *graspingly.*) ♦ *He was a grasping kind of man, always eager to control more people and make more money.* ♦ *Bill's wife was a grasping woman who treated him as if he were her own personal property.*

grass ['græs] *n.* a plant with thin blades instead of leaves. (No plural form in this sense.) ♦ *The grass in most lawns is cut before it grows flowers or seeds.* ♦ *I love the scent of freshly cut grass.*

grasshopper ['græs hɑp ɚ] *n.* a winged, jumping insect that produces a singing sound by rubbing its back legs together. ♦ *I love the sound of grasshoppers on a hot summer day.* ♦ *A grasshopper jumped onto my arm and frightened me.*

grassland ['græs lænd] *n.* a large stretch of land that is covered with grass. (Sometimes plural with the same meaning.) ♦ *My grandfather created his farm by plowing 180 acres of grassland.* ♦ *As the suburbs were built, the grasslands got smaller.*

grassy ['græs i] *adj.* covered with grass. (Comp: *grassier;* sup: *grassiest.*) ♦ *Many acres of grassy meadow were converted to farmland.* ♦ *We sat down to eat our picnic in a grassy area under a tree.*

grate ['gret] **1.** *n.* the metal frame that holds wood or coal in a fireplace, stove, or furnace. ♦ *Bill stacked wood on the grate of the stove and lighted it.* ♦ *I removed the ashes from under the fireplace grate.* **2.** *n.* a slotted cover placed over a vent or hole, letting air, water, or light pass through; a **grating.** ♦ *The brass grate over the air vent was clogged with dust.* ♦ *My keys fell between the slots of the sewer grate.* **3.** *tv.* to shred food into small pieces by rubbing it against a rough surface. ♦ *Please grate the cheese before you put it on the pizza.* ♦ *I grated the carrots and mixed them into the cake batter.* **4.** *tv.* to scratch or scrape something against something. ♦ *I grated my fingernails across the chalkboard to get everyone's attention.* ♦ *The bottom of the gate is grating on the pavement.* **5.** *iv.* to rub on something, making a scratching or scraping sound. ♦ *The gate grated across the sidewalk as it swung open.* ♦ *I cringed when I heard fingernails grate on the chalkboard.* **6. grate on someone('s nerves)** *idiom* to annoy someone; to bother someone. ♦ *My obnoxious brother is grating on my nerves.* ♦ *Your whining really grates on me.*

grateful ['gret fʊl] *adj.* feeling or showing gratitude toward someone or something; feeling or showing appreciation; thankful. (Adv: *gratefully.*) ♦ *I was grateful to the stranger for returning my lost wallet.* ♦ *The family was grateful that no one died in the fire.*

gratification [græt ə fɪ 'ke ʃən] *n.* satisfaction; the quality of having been gratified. (No plural form in this sense.) ♦ *I receive personal gratification from donating money to charities.* ♦ *Bob's only gratification was in the exercise of power over other people.*

gratify ['græt ə fɑɪ] *tv.* to please someone; to give someone satisfaction. ♦ *It gratifies me to see people being polite to other people.* ♦ *Anne was gratified by the manager's efforts to help her.*

grating ['gret ɪŋ] **1.** *adj.* annoying; irritating. (Adv: *gratingly.*) ♦ *Please stop chewing gum so loudly. It's very grating.* ♦ *I tried to ignore my roommate's grating habits.* **2.** *n.*

a slotted cover placed over a vent or a hole, which lets light, water, or air pass through. ♦ *I dropped my keys, and they fell through the grating on the sidewalk.* ♦ *The flow of air into the room was reduced because the grating was clogged with dust.*

gratis ['græt ɪs] **1.** *adj.* free; at no cost. (From Latin.) ♦ *Is the soup gratis or is there a charge?* ♦ *Bread is usually gratis at restaurants.* **2.** *adv.* without cost; free. (From Latin.) ♦ *The waiter gave us our salads gratis because we waited so long for our food to arrive.* ♦ *The auto shop offers the fourth tire gratis when you buy three.*

gratitude ['græt ə tud] *n.* thankfulness; the quality of being grateful; a feeling or expression of appreciation. (No plural form in this sense.) ♦ *Expressing our gratitude for what we are given is a sign of good manners.* ♦ *I gave my grandparents my undying gratitude for supporting me while I was in college.*

gratuitous [grə 'tu ɪ təs] **1.** *adj.* without justification or need. (Adv: *gratuitously.*) ♦ *John's gratuitous insult angered me.* ♦ *The movie was filled with gratuitous violence.* **2.** *adj.* done or given without payment; done or given for free. (Adv: *gratuitously.*) ♦ *The doctor offered his friend some gratuitous advice about how to stay healthy.* ♦ *I wanted to compensate my aunt somehow for her gratuitous help.*

gratuity [grə 'tu ə ti] *n.* a tip; extra money that is given to someone who has provided a service. ♦ *You should leave a 15% to 20% gratuity at a restaurant.* ♦ *Service was incredibly poor, so we left only a 10% gratuity.*

grave ['grev] **1.** *n.* the place where someone is buried; a burial site. ♦ *I visit my mother's grave on each anniversary of her death.* ♦ *The cemetery is filled with row after row of graves.* **2.** *n.* the actual hole that someone is buried in. ♦ *After the funeral service, I threw a handful of dirt into the grave.* ♦ *The pallbearers placed the casket on a framework over the grave.* **3. the grave** *n.* death. (No plural form in this sense. Treated as singular.) ♦ *After living 90 years, Susan didn't fear the grave.* ♦ *Thoughts of a long illness and then the grave disturb me often.* **4.** *adj.* very serious; dire. (Adv: *gravely.*) ♦ *Smoking has grave effects on your health.* ♦ *The grave situation demanded my immediate attention.* **5. carry a secret to the grave; carry a secret to one's grave** *idiom* to avoid telling a secret, even to the day of one's death. ♦ *John carried our secret to his grave.* ♦ *Trust me, I will carry your secret to the grave!* **6. dig one's own grave** *idiom* to be responsible for one's own downfall or ruin. ♦ *If you try to cheat the bank, you will be digging your own grave.* ♦ *Those politicians have dug their own grave with their new tax bill. They won't be reelected.* **7. turn over in one's grave** *idiom* [for a dead person] to be shocked or horrified. ♦ *If Beethoven heard Mary play one of his sonatas, he'd turn over in his grave.* ♦ *If Aunt Jane knew that you sold her good china, she would turn over in her grave.*

gravel ['græv əl] *n.* crushed rock; pebbles about the size of peas. (No plural form in this sense.) ♦ *The country road was paved with gravel.* ♦ *The workers extracted gravel from the quarry.*

gravestone ['grev ston] *n.* a tombstone; a stone placed at a burial site. ♦ *The gravestone usually lists the dead person's name and dates of birth and death.* ♦ *The vandals were caught knocking over gravestones.*

graveyard ['grev jɑrd] *n.* a cemetery; a place where dead people are buried. ♦ *I visited the graveyard where my parents were buried.* ♦ *The funeral procession moved from the church to the graveyard.*

gravitate ['græv ə tet] **1. gravitate to(ward)** *iv.* + *prep. phr.* to move lower owing to the pull of gravity. ♦ *The kite gravitated toward the ground.* ♦ *The rocket gravitated to the surface of the planet.* **2. gravitate to(ward)** *iv.* + *prep. phr.* to move toward someone or something because of an attraction. (Figurative on ①.) ♦ *The screaming fans gravitated toward the rock star.* ♦ *Why is it that people who come to my parties always gravitate to the kitchen?*

gravity ['græv ə ti] **1.** *n.* the force that pulls things toward the center of planets, suns, moons, etc.; the force that pulls things toward the center of Earth. (No plural form in this sense.) ♦ *The moon has very little gravity as compared with Earth.* ♦ *Things fall to the ground because of the effects of gravity.* **2.** *n.* seriousness; importance. (No plural form in this sense.) ♦ *The committee analyzed the gravity of the proposals.* ♦ *I don't think you understand the gravity of the situation.* **3. law of gravity** *n.* the fact that ① pulls things toward the center of the earth. (No plural form in this sense. Also *law of gravitation.*) ♦ *My watch is as dependable as the law of gravity.* ♦ *When I let go of this book, it will fall because of the law of gravity.*

gravy ['grev i] **1.** *n.* the juice that drips from meat when it cooks. (No plural form in this sense.) ♦ *Don't throw out the gravy when you take the roast from the oven.* ♦ *There was a lot of gravy in the pan from cooking the turkey.* **2.** *n.* a sauce made from the juice that drips from meat when it cooks, often thickened with flour or cornstarch. (No plural form in this sense.) ♦ *I covered the mashed potatoes with gravy.* ♦ *The cook thickened the gravy with cornstarch.*

gray ['gre] **1.** *n.* the color made when white is mixed with black. (No plural form in this sense.) ♦ *The picture on a black-and-white television actually contains several shades of gray.* ♦ *Our kitchen is decorated in blue and gray.* **2.** *n.* gray ① of the hair. (No plural form in this sense.) ♦ *Anne used a special shampoo to color her gray.* ♦ *John is only 25, but he already has some gray.* **3.** *adj.* gray ① in color. (Adv: *grayly.*) ♦ *I saw a gray cat sitting on the mat outside my door.* ♦ *The gray rain clouds blocked the sun.* **4.** *iv.* [for hair] to become ③; [for someone] to develop ②. ♦ *My hair grayed at 25.* ♦ *I'm going to dye my hair when it starts to gray.*

grayish ['gre ɪʃ] *adj.* sort of gray; somewhat gray. (Adv: *grayishly.*) ♦ *My shirt is a grayish blue.* ♦ *I watched the grayish clouds cross the sky.*

graze ['grez] **1.** *iv.* [for animals] to search for and eat grass, as in a pasture. ♦ *The cattle grazed contentedly in the field.* ♦ *Sheep graze in the pasture.* **2.** *tv.* to allow or to cause animals to graze ①. ♦ *The rancher grazes 500 head of cattle in this pasture.* ♦ *The shepherd grazed the herd of sheep in the meadow.* **3.** *tv.* to touch or scratch someone or something in passing. ♦ *A bullet grazed the side of the tank the soldiers were riding in.* ♦ *The barber's clippers just grazed my left ear.*

grease 1. ['gris] *n.* melted animal fat, or any similar oily substance. (No plural form in this sense.) ♦ *I coated the pan with grease.* ♦ *Bob tried to remove some of the grease with a paper towel.* **2.** ['griz] *tv.* to coat or lubricate something with ①. ♦ *I greased the pan before baking the cookies in it.* ♦ *The mechanic greased the hinges on my car doors.*

greasepaint ['gris pent] *n.* an oily kind of makeup used by actors, clowns, and other entertainers. (No plural form in this sense.) ♦ *The clown outlined his mouth with red greasepaint.* ♦ *My date's makeup was so heavy and thick that I thought it was greasepaint.*

greasy ['gris i] *adj.* oily; like grease; coated with grease. (Adv: *greasily.* Comp: *greasier;* sup: *greasiest.*) ♦ *I wiped the greasy table with a soapy rag.* ♦ *I have to wash my hair because it's really greasy.*

great ['gret] **1.** *adj.* large in size or importance. (Adv: *greatly.* Comp: *greater;* sup: *greatest.*) ♦ *Great storm clouds appeared on the horizon.* ♦ *The shadow of the great building darkened the entire street.* **2.** *adj.* remarkable; exceptional; notable. (Adv: *greatly.* Comp: *greater;* sup: *greatest.*) ♦ *Babe Ruth was a great baseball player.* ♦ *I thanked Bob for the great dinner that he had cooked.* **3. great deal** See deal ⑧. **4. Great!** *interj.* "Super!"; "Wonderful!" (Sometimes used sarcastically.) ♦ *"Great! The television I want is on sale!"* ♦ *"Great! It's stopped raining!"*

great-aunt ['gret 'ænt] *n.* the sister of one's grandfather or grandmother; the aunt of one's father or mother. ♦ *My great-aunt immigrated from Ireland in 1910.* ♦ *Bob's great-aunt lived to be 103.*

Great Britain [gret 'brɪt n] See Gazetteer.

great-grandchild ['gret 'græn(d) tʃaɪld] *n., irreg.* the child of one's grandchild; the grandchild of one's child. (Pl: great-grandchildren.) ♦ *Susan was 80 when her first great-grandchild was born.* ♦ *At the time of John's death, he had three children, six grandchildren, and three great-grandchildren.*

great-grandchildren ['gret 'græn(d) tʃil drən] pl of great-grandchild.

great-grandfather ['gret 'græn(d) fɑ ðɚ] *n.* the grandfather of one's mother or father; the father of one's grandfather or grandmother. ♦ *One of my great-grandfathers immigrated from France during World War I.* ♦ *My great-grandfather was still alive when I was born.*

great-grandmother ['gret 'græn(d) mə ðɚ] *n.* the grandmother of one's mother or father; the mother of one's grandfather or grandmother. ♦ *My great-grandmother came from New York on a boat.* ♦ *Tom's great-grandmother lived longer than his great-grandfather.*

great-grandparent ['gret 'græn(d) pɛr ənt] *n.* a grandparent of one's mother or father; the parent of one's grandparent. ♦ *All eight of my great-grandparents came from China.* ♦ *Five of my great-grandparents were still alive when I was born.*

greatly ['gret li] *adv.* very much so; extremely; much. ♦ *I greatly appreciate your help.* ♦ *Mary admired her aunt greatly.*

greatness ['gret nəs] **1.** *n.* importance, significance, and power. (No plural form in this sense.) ♦ *The knight stood in awe of the queen's greatness.* ♦ *The president stressed the greatness of the country's army.* **2.** *n.* vastness [of space]; enormousness [in physical size]. (No plural form in this sense.) ♦ *The tourist stood in awe of the greatness of the Grand Canyon.* ♦ *Humans have always been overwhelmed with the greatness of the skies and the stars beyond.*

great-uncle ['gret 'ʌŋ kəl] *n.* the brother of one's grandmother or grandfather; the uncle of one's father or mother. ♦ *My great-uncle owns a candy store downtown.* ♦ *I mow my great-uncle's lawn every weekend.*

Greece ['gris] See Gazetteer.

greed ['grid] *n.* an excessive desire, especially for money, possessions, or power. (No plural form in this sense.) ♦ *Bill was corrupted by his greed for power.* ♦ *Our minister urged us to remove greed from our lives.*

greedy ['gri di] *adj.* showing greed; desiring money, possessions, or power too strongly. (Adv: *greedily.* Comp: *greedier;* sup: *greediest.*) ♦ *The greedy boy refused to share his candy with his sister.* ♦ *The greedy millionaire would not donate any money to charity.*

Greek ['grik] **1.** *n.* a citizen or native of Greece. ♦ *We met a Greek at the lecture.* ♦ *There are three Greeks in my German class.* **2.** *n.* the language spoken in Greece by ①. (No plural form in this sense.) ♦ *I study Greek because my grandmother is from Greece.* ♦ *Greek is not hard, but it does not use the Latin alphabet.* **3.** *adj.* of or about Greece, ①, or ②. ♦ *We like to go to Greek restaurants.* ♦ *The Greek alphabet is easy to learn.*

green ['grin] **1.** *n.* the color of grass or the leaves of trees in the summer; the color made when blue and yellow are mixed together. (No plural form in this sense.) ♦ *After the rain, the grass was a very pretty shade of green.* ♦ *I added some green to the painting by including more trees.* **2.** *n.* a grassy area. ♦ *The jazz band played on the village green.* ♦ *The golfer carefully lined up his shot on the putting green.* **3. greens** *n.* the leaves of certain plants eaten as food. (Treated as plural.) ♦ *You're not getting dessert until you eat your greens.* ♦ *I cooked the turnip greens with ham for extra flavor.* **4.** *adj.* of a green ① color. (Comp: *greener;* sup: *greenest.*) ♦ *The green soda was lime-flavored.* ♦ *I swatted at the green insect crawling on my window.* **5.** *adj.* unripe; not yet ripe or mature. (Comp: *greener;* sup: *greenest.*) ♦ *Green bananas ripen after they're picked.* ♦ *In a few weeks, the green grapes will be dark purple.* **6.** *adj.* without experience; young; naive. (Figurative on ⑤. Comp: *greener;* sup: *greenest.*) ♦ *You did a very good job for someone who's still green.* ♦ *This job might be hard, but that's just because you're still green.* **7.** *adj.* safe for the environment and nature. (Comp: *greener;* sup: *greenest.*) ♦ *The company's green marketing campaign promoted its new recycled products.* ♦ *The protesters believed that Congress should pass more green laws.* **8.** *adj.* pale; sickly; unhealthy. (Adv: *greenly.* Comp: *greener;* sup: *greenest.*) ♦ *Bill turned green after eating the spoiled food.* ♦ *You're looking green. You should see a doctor.* **9. green with envy** *idiom* appearing jealous; appearing envious. ♦ *My new car made my neighbor green with envy.* ♦ *Bill was green with envy that I won first place.*

greenery ['grin ə ri] *n.* green plants, especially those used as decorations. (No plural form in this sense.) ♦ *Our house has so much greenery, it's like living in a forest.* ♦ *The centerpiece on the table was surrounded by greenery.*

greenhouse ['grin hɑʊs] *n., irreg.* a building with a glass roof and glass walls where the temperature is controlled so that plants can grow inside all year round. (Pl: [...hɑʊ zəz]. See also hothouse.) ♦ *Since I have a greenhouse, I can have fresh tomatoes all year.* ♦ *It was so cold outside that*

I was happy to be taking care of the plants in the greenhouse.

greenish ['grin ɪʃ] *adj.* sort of green; somewhat green. (Adv: *greenishly.*) ♦ *The pond has a greenish look, probably due to algae.* ♦ *Greenish smoke billowed from the chemical plant.*

greet ['grit] **1.** *tv.* to welcome someone; to address or acknowledge someone, especially upon meeting or arrival. ♦ *I greeted my best friend with a big hug.* ♦ *The mayor greeted the governor and invited him to sit down.* **2. greet with** *tv.* + *prep. phr.* to meet someone or something with a particular reaction. ♦ *The popular singer was greeted with cheers from the audience.* ♦ *John's offensive joke was greeted with dead silence.*

greeting ['grit ɪŋ] *n.* a word, phrase, or action—such as *Hello*—said or done when meeting someone or when answering the telephone. ♦ *The greeting on your answering machine is too long.* ♦ *"Hi!" is a common American greeting.*

greeting card ['grit ɪŋ kɑrd] *n.* a folded sheet of heavy paper having a decorative picture on the front and sentimental or clever thoughts printed on the inside. ♦ *I sent a greeting card to my mother on her birthday.* ♦ *Jane sends greeting cards to all her friends at Thanksgiving.*

gregarious [grə 'gɛr i əs] **1.** *adj.* social; eager to be around other people. (Adv: *gregariously.*) ♦ *The gregarious host mingled with all of the guests.* ♦ *My gregarious sister makes friends wherever she goes.* **2.** *adj.* living together in groups. (Adv: *gregariously.*) ♦ *Ants and bees are gregarious insects.* ♦ *The biologist studied gregarious insect colonies.*

grenade [grə 'ned] *n.* a small bomb that is thrown by hand or shot from a rifle. ♦ *The grenade exploded ten seconds after the soldier threw it.* ♦ *The soldiers launched grenades at the attacking army.*

grew ['gru] pt of grow.

greyhound ['gre hɑʊnd] *n.* a large, thin dog that runs very fast. ♦ *Bill often goes to the racetrack to bet on greyhounds.* ♦ *Greyhounds chased the mechanical rabbit around the racetrack.*

grid ['grɪd] **1.** *n.* a series of lines arranged vertically and horizontally forming squares, especially as found on maps or graphs. ♦ *It is difficult to draw a chart on a grid.* ♦ *Because the streets of Chicago form a grid, it's very easy to find addresses there.* **2.** *n.* a series of rods, bars, or wires arranged as in ①. ♦ *A wooden grid is perfect for growing flowering vines.* ♦ *A grid of iron bars covered each ground-floor window.* **3.** *n.* a network of electrical lines spread over a large area; a network of roads. ♦ *The workers shut down the power grid while they replaced a transformer.* ♦ *When lightning disabled the electrical grid near Adamsville, long-distance phone calls were routed through other regional centers.*

griddle ['grɪd l] *n.* a broad, flat, or shallow metal pan that is used for cooking; a flat surface on a stove that can be heated for cooking. ♦ *The cook poured the pancake batter onto the griddle.* ♦ *Before making pancakes, I greased the griddle with butter.*

gridiron ['grɪd ɑɪrn] *n.* a football field. ♦ *The crowd rushed onto the gridiron when the home team won the championship.* ♦ *The gridiron was littered with cans that the irate fans threw at the referee.*

grief ['grif] **1.** *n.* sorrow; distress. (No plural form in this sense.) ♦ *I comforted Bob in his grief following his mother's death.* ♦ *The unruly children caused the babysitter a lot of grief.* **2.** *n.* something that causes sorrow or distress. (Not usually plural.) ♦ *The letter carrier brought a new grief into my life. The tax bill came!* ♦ *You shouldn't let every little grief upset you so much.* **3. come to grief** *idiom* to fail; to have trouble or grief. ♦ *The artist wept when her canvas got wet and came to grief.* ♦ *The wedding party came to grief when the bride passed out.*

grief-stricken ['grif strɪk ən] *adj.* suffering with grief or sorrow, especially because of a loss; distressed; suffering. ♦ *The parents of the injured boy were too grief-stricken to talk to reporters.* ♦ *The grief-stricken widow told the reporters to leave her alone.*

grievance ['griv əns] **1.** *n.* a complaint; the problems that cause a complaint. ♦ *Overwork was the employee's main grievance.* ♦ *Management did its best to address the workers' grievances.* **2.** *n.* a statement of a complaint. ♦ *The distraught workers filed their grievance with the management.* ♦ *After management studied the stack of grievances, it finally acted.*

grieve ['griv] **1.** *tv.* to cause someone to feel grief, sorrow, or unhappiness. ♦ *The unending war grieved the citizens of the seized town.* ♦ *Anne was grieved by her son's criminal behavior.* **2.** *iv.* to feel and suffer grief ①. ♦ *The young parents grieved at the death of their infant daughter.* ♦ *The students grieved at their friend's funeral.*

grieving ['griv ɪŋ] *adj.* feeling sadness or sorrow, especially because of a loss. ♦ *The grieving widow was comforted by her family.* ♦ *The grieving family asked the reporters to leave them alone.*

grievous ['gri vəs] **1.** *adj.* causing grief. (Formal. Adv: *grievously.*) ♦ *His grievous behavior at the dance embarrassed us all.* ♦ *The grievous situation caused my ulcer to flare.* **2.** *adj.* severe; painful; hurtful. (Formal. Adv: *grievously.*) ♦ *The soldier received a grievous head wound.* ♦ *The driver suffered grievous injuries in the accident.*

grill ['grɪl] **1.** *n.* a grid of metal rods set over a fire, on which food is placed to cook. ♦ *The grill was covered with grease by the end of the day.* ♦ *Don't touch the grill! It's still hot!* **2.** *n.* an outdoor stove that cooks food placed on a framework of rows of metal bars. ♦ *Dave placed six hamburgers on the grill.* ♦ *I brought my grill to the picnic, but I didn't remember to bring charcoal.* **3.** *tv.* to cook food on ① or ②. ♦ *I was chosen to grill the hamburgers at the picnic.* ♦ *We grilled pieces of chicken for dinner.* **4.** *tv.* to question someone forcefully and without mercy. ♦ *The police grilled the suspect until he confessed.* ♦ *A lawyer grilled the witness during cross-examination.* **5.** *iv.* [for food] to be cooked on ① or ②. ♦ *The hamburgers grilled for five minutes.* ♦ *The hot dogs became plump as they grilled.*

grille ['grɪl] **1.** *n.* a grate above the front bumper of a car in front of the radiator. (Compare with **grill**.) ♦ *The grille was covered with hundreds of dead insects.* ♦ *My grille was crushed when I drove into the back of a truck.* **2.** *n.* a grid of metal bars placed in a door or window. ♦ *After my neighbor's house was robbed, I covered my first-floor windows with grilles.* ♦ *Five people died in the fire because their exit was blocked by a grille over the window.*

grilled ['grɪld] *adj.* cooked on a grill. ♦ *We ate grilled hamburgers at the picnic.* ♦ *My lunch included grilled vegetables.*

grim ['grɪm] **1.** *adj.* bleak; not likely to turn out well; not promising. (Adv: *grimly.* Comp: *grimmer;* sup: *grimmest.*) ♦ *Your job prospects will be grim if you don't finish school.* ♦ *Each day, the chance for peace became more grim.* **2.** *adj.* [looking] stern and harsh. (Adv: *grimly.* Comp: *grimmer;* sup: *grimmest.*) ♦ *The artist accentuated the old man's grim features.* ♦ *The students disliked their teacher's grim attitude.*

grimace ['grɪm əs] **1.** *n.* an ugly frown; a facial expression of pain or anger. ♦ *I knew Bob was in pain from the grimace on his face.* ♦ *John had an angry grimace on his face after he spoke to his boss.* **2.** *iv.* to frown in an ugly way; to make an exaggerated facial expression of pain or anger. ♦ *I grimaced when I bit my tongue.* ♦ *My father grimaced as he scolded me.*

grimacing ['grɪm əs ɪŋ] *adj.* frowning; making a facial expression of pain or anger. (Adv: *grimacingly.*) ♦ *The grimacing child looked at his cut hand.* ♦ *A grimacing clown approached the young children and frightened them.*

grime ['graɪm] *n.* thick, greasy dirt. (No plural form in this sense.) ♦ *The cupboard above the stove was covered with grime.* ♦ *While fixing the engine, I got grime all over my hands.*

grimy ['graɪm i] *adj.* covered with grime; dirty and greasy. (Adv: *grimily.* Comp: *grimier;* sup: *grimiest.*) ♦ *I washed my grimy hands after fixing the car engine.* ♦ *Sally threw the grimy rag in the laundry.*

grin ['grɪn] **1.** *n.* a wide smile. ♦ *Mary has a pretty grin because she takes good care of her teeth.* ♦ *David's sly grin indicated that he knew about the surprise.* **2.** *iv.* to smile widely so that one's teeth show. ♦ *Everyone grinned when Bob told the funny joke.* ♦ *Anne only grinned when I asked her how she knew the secret.* **3. grin and bear it** *idiom* to endure something unpleasant in good humor. ♦ *There is nothing you can do but grin and bear it.* ♦ *I hate having to work for rude people. I guess I have to grin and bear it.*

grind ['graɪnd] **1.** *tv., irreg.* to make something into a powder, tiny chunks, or granules by crushing or pounding it. (Pt/pp: **ground.**) ♦ *I'll grind the coffee for breakfast tomorrow morning.* ♦ *The waiter ground some pepper onto my salad.* **2.** *tv., irreg.* to grate things together; to rub things together forcefully. ♦ *Anne grinds her teeth in her sleep.* ♦ *The baseball player ground dirt into his pants when he slid into home plate.* **3. grind (down)** *tv., irreg.* (+ *adv.*) to wear something down through friction or grinding; to smooth a rough object by using friction. ♦ *I ground down the rim of the glass to make it smooth.* ♦ *Mary ground down the pencil in the electric sharpener.* **4.** *n.* a degree of the fineness of something that has been ground as in ①. ♦ *What grind of coffee do you prefer?* ♦ *I would like an all-purpose grind.*

grindstone ['graɪnd ston] **1.** *n.* a thick, round wheel of stone that is used to sharpen knives. ♦ *I have a grindstone that attaches to my electric drill, allowing me to sharpen almost anything.* ♦ *I sharpened the knives against the spinning grindstone.* **2. keep one's nose to the grindstone** *idiom* to work hard at one's job or task. ♦ *Keep your nose to the grindstone and you will succeed.* ♦ *If Tom had kept his nose to the grindstone, he would be a vice president by now.*

grinning ['grɪn ɪŋ] *adj.* smiling widely. (Adv: *grinningly.*) ♦ *The grinning audience applauded the funny comedian.* ♦ *Thirty grinning students sang "Happy Birthday" to their teacher.*

grip ['grɪp] **1.** *tv.* to hold someone or something tightly with one's hands; to grasp. ♦ *I gripped the handlebars as I biked over the bumpy road.* ♦ *My little brother and I gripped hands as we crossed the street.* **2.** *n.* a tight hold on someone or something. ♦ *My brother broke from my grip and ran into the street.* ♦ *My hands were sore from the firm grip I had on the steering wheel.* **3. come to grips with something** *idiom* to face something; to comprehend something. ♦ *He found it difficult to come to grips with his grandmother's death.* ♦ *Many students have a hard time coming to grips with algebra.* **4. grip someone's attention** *idiom* to attract and hold someone's attention. ♦ *The scary movie gripped my attention.* ♦ *The professor's interesting lecture gripped the attention of all the students.* **5. lose one's grip** *idiom* to lose control over something. ♦ *I can't seem to run things the way I used to. I'm losing my grip.* ♦ *They replaced the directors because they were losing their grip.*

gripe ['graɪp] **1.** *n.* a complaint. ♦ *The manager patiently listened to the customer's gripes.* ♦ *What do you expect me to do about your gripes?* **2. gripe (about)** *iv.* (+ *prep. phr.*) to complain about something; to whine about something. ♦ *The diners griped about the slow service.* ♦ *Bob griped endlessly through the whole trip.*

grisly ['grɪz li] *adj.* horrible; gruesome; causing horror. ♦ *The newspapers reported the grisly details of the murder over and over.* ♦ *We were shocked by the grisly scene that awaited us.*

gristle ['grɪs əl] *n.* cartilage, especially in meat served as food. (No plural form in this sense.) ♦ *Cheap meat is likely to have a lot of gristle.* ♦ *I cut the gristle from my steak with my knife.*

grit ['grɪt] **1.** *n.* grains of sand and dirt. (No plural form in this sense.) ♦ *My hair was full of grit after a day at the beach.* ♦ *The picnic food had some grit in it, blown in by the wind.* **2.** *n.* courage; determination. (No plural form in this sense.) ♦ *Being a firefighter requires a lot of hard work and grit.* ♦ *Our team won first place because of skill and grit.* **3.** *tv.* to clench one's teeth together in determination. ♦ *The soldier gritted his teeth and went into battle.* ♦ *The runner gritted her teeth as she ran toward the finish line.*

gritty ['grɪt i] **1.** *adj.* sandy and dirty with grit. (Adv: *grittily.* Comp: *grittier;* sup: *grittiest.*) ♦ *Take off your gritty shoes before you come into the house!* ♦ *I threw my gritty beach towel into the washing machine.* **2.** *adj.* (Adv: *grittily.*) full of determination and courage. (Comp: *grittier;* sup: *grittiest.*) ♦ *The gritty little kid hit the bully's nose.* ♦ *The gritty reporter got an interview with the ambassador.*

grizzly ['grɪz li] **1.** *adj.* gray-haired. (Comp: *grizzlier;* sup: *grizzliest.*) ♦ *A grizzly and ragged old man stopped us and asked for help.* ♦ *The university forced the grizzly old professor to retire at 70.* **2. grizzly (bear)** *n.* a large brown bear of North America. ♦ *The ranger warned the campers to beware of grizzlies.* ♦ *I watched a grizzly bear catch a fish with its paws.*

groan ['gron] **1.** *n.* a loud, deep noise of pain, disappointment, or disapproval. ♦ *My friends responded to my* *bad pun with a loud groan.* ♦ *After the building collapsed, groans could be heard from people trapped in the rubble.* **2.** *iv.* to make a loud, deep noise of pain, disappointment, or disapproval. ♦ *I groaned when the doctor pressed on my stomach.* ♦ *The audience groaned when the comedian told a bad joke.* **3.** *iv.* [for an enormous bulk] to make a deep noise or creak. ♦ *We heard the ship's timbers groan as the ship was tossed by the storm.* ♦ *Our new house groaned as it settled after the heavy rainstorm.* **4. groan under the weight of something.** *idiom* to suffer under the burden or domination of someone or something. (Figurative on ②.) ♦ *John groaned under the weight of his new responsibilities.* ♦ *The servant groaned under the burdens imposed by a cruel master.*

grocer ['gro sɚ] *n.* someone who owns or runs a grocery store; someone who sells food and basic supplies. ♦ *I asked the grocer if there were any bananas in stock.* ♦ *The grocer placed my purchases in a plastic bag.*

grocery ['gros (ə) ri] **1. grocery (store)** *n.* a store where food can be bought. ♦ *Could you stop at the grocery and pick up some milk?* ♦ *I'm going to the grocery now. Do you need anything?* **2. groceries** *n.* items bought at ①. (Treated as plural.) ♦ *I just spent $50 on groceries, so how can you complain that there's no food in the house?* ♦ *I paid for my groceries with a credit card.*

groggy ['grɔg i] *adj.* not fully aware because one is tired or drunk; dazed; not steady. (Adv: *groggily.* Comp: *groggier;* sup: *groggiest.*) ♦ *Mary is groggy in the morning until her first cup of coffee.* ♦ *I wouldn't let John drive his car because he was still groggy from being out all night.*

groin ['grɔɪn] **1.** *n.* the part of the body where the tops of the thighs join the trunk. (No plural form in this sense.) ♦ *The dog was trained to attack the groin and neck.* ♦ *A stray bullet hit the police officer in the groin.* **2.** *n.* the genital area of the male. (No plural form in this sense. Euphemistic.) ♦ *John collapsed on the ground when the baseball struck him in the groin.* ♦ *The doctor felt Bill's groin to see if he had a hernia.*

groom ['grum] **1.** *n.* a man who is getting married; a bridegroom. ♦ *The groom wore a tuxedo with a red bow tie.* ♦ *The bride and groom went to Hawaii for their honeymoon.* **2.** *tv.* to clean and comb a horse. ♦ *Anne groomed her family's horses every day after school.* ♦ *John has to groom his horse before the parade.* **3.** *tv.* to make someone's hair neat. ♦ *Sally spends a lot of time grooming her long hair.* ♦ *I groomed my hair and polished my shoes before I went out to the party.* **4.** *tv.* to prepare someone for a specific duty. ♦ *The reporter had been carefully groomed for the assignment in Washington.* ♦ *The Browns groomed their children to take over the store after they retired.*

grooming ['grum ɪŋ] *n.* the process of producing a clean appearance. (No plural form in this sense.) ♦ *Good grooming is important when you go on job interviews.* ♦ *My parents instilled me with a good sense of grooming.*

groove ['gruv] **1.** *n.* a long, narrow channel cut into a surface. ♦ *This piece of the clock slides back and forth in this groove.* ♦ *The woodworker cut a groove into the board with a chisel.* **2.** *n.* the continuous, circular channel on a phonograph record in which the needle rests. ♦ *I wiped the dust from the record's grooves with a piece of felt.* ♦ *Anne played the record so much that she wore down the grooves.* **3.** *tv.* to cut ① into something. ♦ *The woodworker grooved the board with a special chisel.* ♦ *Water grooved the soil as it flowed toward the river.*

grope ['grop] **1.** *iv.* to search with one's hands. ♦ *Tom groped around in the dark until he found the light switch.* ♦ *I will have to grope though the gloom to find the doorknob.* **2. grope for** *iv.* + *prep. phr.* to search for something with one's hands. ♦ *Tom groped in the darkness for the light switch.* ♦ *In the gloom, I had to grope for the doorknob.*

gross ['gros] **1.** *n., irreg.* 144; a dozen dozen (12 × 12). (Pl: *gross.*) ♦ *My boss orders reams of paper a gross at a time.* ♦ *We were shipped 20 gross of the wrong part by mistake.* **2. gross (income)** *n.* [for income-tax purposes] the amount of money one has earned, less certain exclusions. ♦ *I wrote my gross income on the tenth line of the tax form.* ♦ *My gross income last year was under $20,000.* **3.** *tv.* to receive money as payment for something. ♦ *The movie grossed $5 million in its opening weekend.* ♦ *This book will gross a profit after 10,000 copies are sold.* **4.** *adj.* large; bulky. (Comp: *grosser;* sup: *grossest.*) ♦ *The package is too gross to fit through the door.* ♦ *This shipment is not gross enough to require an entire truck.* **5.** *adj.* disgusting; sickening; vulgar. (Informal. Adv: *grossly.* Comp: *grosser;* sup: *grossest.*) ♦ *Stop playing with your food. That's really gross.* ♦ *I can't believe you told that gross joke to my parents.* **6.** *adj.* complete; obviously wrong; flagrant. (Adv: *grossly.* Comp: *grosser;* sup: *grossest.*) ♦ *The company was sued for its gross error in judgment.* ♦ *"The court has committed another gross injustice," shouted the convicted criminal.* **7.** *adj.* total [weight]. ♦ *The gross weight of a product includes the weight of its package.* ♦ *This bridge supports gross weights of up to 24 tons.*

grotesque [gro 'tɛsk] **1.** *adj.* very ugly or absurd; unnaturally ugly. (Adv: *grotesquely.*) ♦ *I covered the grotesque painting with a sheet.* ♦ *The grotesque monster was played by an actor wearing makeup.* **2.** *adj.* unpleasant. (Figurative on ①. Adv: *grotesquely.*) ♦ *Unfortunately, we had a grotesque time at John's party.* ♦ *The poor pianist played a grotesque rendition of Beethoven's "Moonlight Sonata."*

grotto ['grɑt o] *n.* a small cave, either natural or constructed. (Pl in *-s* or *-es.*) ♦ *While hiking, we took shelter in a grotto during a rainstorm.* ♦ *The waves had carved a huge grotto in the cliff, making a wonderful place for a picnic.*

grouch ['grɑʊtʃ] **1.** *iv.* to complain. ♦ *Some people just grouch all the time!* ♦ *The passengers grouched about the uncomfortable seats.* **2.** *n.* someone who complains a lot. ♦ *Don't listen to John, he's just a grouch this morning.* ♦ *I don't talk to my brother because he's such a grouch.*

grouchy ['grɑʊtʃ i] *adj.* complaining; irritable. (Adv: *grouchily.* Comp: *grouchier;* sup: *grouchiest.*) ♦ *The grouchy customer yelled at the salesclerk.* ♦ *My grouchy neighbor yelled at me for mowing the lawn early in the morning.*

ground ['grɑʊnd] **1.** pt/pp of grind. **2.** *adj.* broken or chopped into tiny chunks by grinding. ♦ *Would you like some freshly ground pepper on your salad?* ♦ *Please buy 3 pounds of ground beef at the store.* **3.** *n.* the surface of the earth. (No plural form in this sense.) ♦ *The plane landed on the ground safely.* ♦ *I tripped and fell to the ground.* **4. grounds** *n.* powdered coffee beans after coffee has been made. (Treated as plural.) ♦ *I dumped the coffee grounds* into the garbage. ♦ *I removed the grounds from my coffee with a spoon.* **5.** *tv.* to cause a pilot, airplane, or bird to stay on ③. (Pt/pp: *grounded.*) ♦ *Thick fog grounded all flights out of the city.* ♦ *The geese were grounded by the ice storm.* **6.** *tv.* to make someone stay in a certain place as punishment. (Figurative on ⑤.) ♦ *The Smiths grounded their son in his bedroom for swearing at them.* ♦ *I can't go to the party because my parents have grounded me for a week.* **7.** *tv.* to make an electrical device safer by extending a wire into ③. ♦ *The electrician grounded the wiring around our patio.* ♦ *If the wire hadn't been grounded, I would have been electrocuted.* **8. break new ground** *idiom* to begin to do something that no one else has done; to pioneer (in an enterprise). ♦ *Dr. Anderson was breaking new ground in cancer research.* ♦ *They were breaking new ground in consumer electronics.* **9. from the ground up** *idiom* from the beginning; from start to finish. ♦ *We must plan our sales campaign carefully from the ground up.* ♦ *Sorry, but you'll have to start all over again from the ground up.* **10. gain ground** *idiom* to make progress; to advance; to become more important or popular. ♦ *Our new product is gaining ground against that of our competitor.* ♦ *Since the government announced its new policies, the opposition has been gaining ground.* **11. grounded in fact** *idiom* based on facts. (Usually passive.) ♦ *This movie is grounded in fact.* ♦ *The stories in this book are all grounded in actual fact.* **12. grounds for something** *idiom* a basis or cause for legal action such as a lawsuit. ♦ *Your negligence is grounds for a lawsuit.* ♦ *Is infidelity grounds for divorce in this state?*

ground beef ['graʊnd bif] *n.* beef that has been chopped or ground fine; hamburger. (No plural form in this sense.) ♦ *I made a meatloaf out of ground beef.* ♦ *Ground beef can be baked or barbecued.*

grounder ['graʊnd ɚ] *n.* a baseball, struck by a bat, that travels along the ground instead of through the air. ♦ *The shortstop scooped up the grounder and threw it to first base.* ♦ *The grounder rolled between the ballplayer's legs.*

groundhog ['graʊnd hɔg] *n.* a heavy, furry, burrowing rodent; a woodchuck. ♦ *The groundhog popped out of its hole and looked at its shadow.* ♦ *My dog chased a groundhog back to its hole.*

grounding ['graʊnd ɪŋ] *n.* basic education in a certain subject; thorough knowledge of the basics of a certain subject. (No plural form in this sense.) ♦ *The students received a thorough grounding in biology.* ♦ *The school failed to provide students with the proper grounding needed for college.*

groundless ['graʊnd ləs] *adj.* without reason; without cause; having no basis. (Adv: *groundlessly.*) ♦ *The mayor denied the newspaper's groundless accusations.* ♦ *The police officer was reprimanded for making groundless arrests.*

groundswell ['graʊnd swɛl] **1.** *n.* deep, slow-moving waves made by a storm or earthquake. ♦ *The fishing boat was caught in the groundswell caused by the storm.* ♦ *The groundswell from the earthquake destroyed my house.* **2.** *n.* an intense and growing public interest or expression. (Figurative on ①.) ♦ *The sensational trial created a groundswell of sympathy for the victim.* ♦ *A groundswell of criticism swept the ruling party out of office.*

groundwork ['graʊnd wɚk] *n.* work that is done ahead of time before a project begins; preliminary study and preparation. (No plural form in this sense.) ♦ *If the groundwork isn't done properly, the project is doomed.* ♦ *Bob failed to do the groundwork required for his essay, and many of his facts were wrong.*

group ['grup] **1.** *n.* a number of things or people considered as a unit; a category. ♦ *I went with a group of friends to the zoo.* ♦ *Could you bring me that group of files on your desk?* **2.** *tv.* to arrange things or people into categories; to place things or people together in ①. ♦ *The teacher grouped the children according to height.* ♦ *The librarian grouped the dictionaries on one shelf.* **3.** *tv.* to place things or people with other things or people. ♦ *The teacher grouped the tall children with the older children.* ♦ *The librarian grouped the dictionaries with the encyclopedias.* **4. group together** *iv.* + *adv.* to huddle together; to gather together. ♦ *The people grouped together under the tent.* ♦ *A few sheep grouped together to keep warm.*

grove ['grov] *n.* a small forest; woods; a group of trees. ♦ *I buried the family dog in the grove behind our house.* ♦ *The children often played in the grove of trees far in the backyard.*

grovel ['grɑv əl] *iv.* to lie with one's face pointing down to the ground in fear or to humble oneself. ♦ *The prisoner groveled before the king, pleading for his life.* ♦ *I had to grovel to my boss for a raise.*

grow ['gro] **1.** *tv., irreg.* to cultivate and nourish plants. (Pt: grew; pp: grown.) ♦ *The florist grew flowers in a greenhouse.* ♦ *The farmer grows wheat and soybeans.* **2.** *tv., irreg.* to cause something to become bigger, larger, or more powerful; to cause something to increase. (Used in financial matters.) ♦ *The banker grew his profits by investing wisely.* ♦ *I sought to grow my income by taking a second job.* **3.** *iv., irreg.* to become bigger, larger, or more powerful; to increase. ♦ *Jimmy grew three inches over the summer.* ♦ *The tall oak tree had grown from a tiny acorn.* **4.** *iv., irreg.* to develop into something. ♦ *Our small problem soon grew to enormous proportions.* ♦ *The local singer grew into an international celebrity.* **5.** *iv., irreg.* to become a certain way. ♦ *I grew tired and went to bed.* ♦ *His face grew redder and redder, and he lost his temper.* **6. grow to do something** *idiom* to gradually begin to do a certain thing. (Takes a verb such as *feel, know, like, need, respect, sense, suspect, think, want, wonder,* etc.) ♦ *I grew to hate Bob over a period of years.* ♦ *As I grew to know Bob, I began to like him.*

growing ['gro ɪŋ] **1.** *adj.* developing. ♦ *The farmer watered the growing crops.* ♦ *Growing children need milk.* **2.** *adj.* increasing; becoming bigger, larger, or more powerful. (Adv: *growingly.*) ♦ *Crime is a growing problem in urban America.* ♦ *Congress tried to slow the growing national debt.*

growl ['graʊl] **1.** *n.* a deep, threatening sound, especially that made in anger. ♦ *I heard a deep growl before the dog bit me.* ♦ *The dog's growl scared the burglar away.* **2.** *iv.* to make a deep, threatening sound; to say something in a deep, threatening way, especially when angry or irritated. ♦ *The dog growls whenever anyone comes to the front door.* ♦ *My father growled at me to be quieter.*

grown ['gron] **1.** pp of grow. **2.** *adj.* fully developed; adult; mature; ripe. ♦ *You don't often see grown men cry in public.* ♦ *Why don't you act like a grown adult instead of a child?*

grown-up ['gron əp] **1.** *n.* an adult. ♦ *Jimmy wished he could eat at the grown-ups' table.* ♦ *Susie was lost, so she asked a grown-up for help.* **2.** *adj.* appropriate for an adult; of or about an adult or adult behavior. ♦ *Discussing your problems calmly would be the grown-up thing to do.* ♦ *Jimmy's parents wouldn't let him watch grown-up movies.*

growth ['groθ] **1.** *n.* development; the amount someone or something develops in a certain period of time. (No plural form in this sense.) ♦ *The biologist studied the growth of embryos.* ♦ *I am amazed at the growth of your son since I last saw him.* **2.** *n.* an increase; the process of becoming bigger, larger, or more powerful. (No plural form in this sense.) ♦ *The rapid growth of the federal government caused my taxes to increase.* ♦ *What has caused the growth in the number of words in the English language?* **3.** *n.* an unnatural or unhealthy lump of tissue; a tumor. ♦ *My doctor removed two cancerous growths from my spine.* ♦ *Someone in the laboratory examined the growth under a microscope.*

grubby ['grʌb i] *adj.* dirty; grimy. (Informal. Adv: *grubbily.* Comp: *grubbier;* sup: *grubbiest.*) ♦ *Go wash your grubby hands before you eat dinner.* ♦ *Take off your grubby shoes before you walk on the carpet!*

grudge ['grʌdʒ] **1.** *n.* a resentment held toward someone. ♦ *Anger owing to old grudges is making Dave very unhappy.* ♦ *Your grouchy statement indicates that you have a grudge.* **2. hold a grudge (against someone)** *idiom* to have a resentment against someone. ♦ *John won't talk to me because he's holding a grudge against me.* ♦ *I held a grudge against my sister for 25 years.*

grudging ['grʌdʒ ɪŋ] *adj.* unwilling. (Adv: *grudgingly.*) ♦ *I have a grudging agreement with my parents to empty the garbage.* ♦ *I dragged my grudging dance partner over to the dance floor.*

grueling ['grul ɪŋ] *adj.* very demanding; rigorous; very difficult and tiring. (Adv: *gruelingly.*) ♦ *Construction work can be very grueling at times.* ♦ *After a grueling day at work, Mary fell asleep at early in the evening.*

gruesome ['gru səm] *adj.* causing horror and disgust; sickening; revolting. (Adv: *gruesomely.*) ♦ *I left the gruesome movie before it ended.* ♦ *Bill showed me the gruesome photographs he'd taken during the war.*

gruff ['grʌf] **1.** *adj.* rough in behavior; surly. (Adv: *gruffly.* Comp: *gruffer;* sup: *gruffest.*) ♦ *The clerk's gruff response surprised me.* ♦ *Don't be so gruff with me. I'm just trying to help you.* **2.** *adj.* [of a voice or sound] deep and hoarse. (Adv: *gruffly.* Comp: *gruffer;* sup: *gruffest.*) ♦ *John's voice sounded gruff because he'd been smoking a lot.* ♦ *I couldn't understand the train conductor's gruff announcement.*

grumble ['grʌm bəl] **1.** *iv.* to speak with a low, indistinct, and possibly complaining voice. ♦ *When Bill has to wait in line, he often grumbles impatiently to himself.* ♦ *Stop grumbling, Jimmy. If you have a problem, speak so that I can understand you.* **2.** *iv.* [for something] to make a low rumbling noise, indicating stress or heaviness. (Figurative on ①.) ♦ *The wheels of the plane grumbled as they touched the ground.* ♦ *The old window grumbled as I slid it on its worn track.* **3. grumble about** *iv.* + *prep. phr.* to complain about something. ♦ *The customer grumbled about poor service.* ♦ *Anne grumbled about the lousy weather.* **4.** *n.* a low, indistinct voice. ♦ *Tom spoke with a grumble, and we could not understand him.* ♦ *He's not awake yet. He will make a grumble when he is awake.*

grumpy ['grʌm pi] *adj.* grouchy; irritable; cranky; bad-tempered. (Adv: *grumpily.* Comp: *grumpier;* sup: *grumpiest.*) ♦ *My grumpy roommate asked me to turn down my stereo.* ♦ *I hate to ask Jane anything because she's been so grumpy lately.*

grunt ['grʌnt] **1.** *iv.* to make a deep, rough sound like a pig. ♦ *The pigs grunted as they wallowed in the mud.* ♦ *The starving hikers grunted as they ate.* **2.** *n.* a deep, rough sound, like that of a pig. ♦ *My father cleared his throat with a grunt and looked like he was going to say something.* ♦ *I heard the grunt of the escaped pig from behind the barn.* **3. grunt work** *idiom* work that is hard and thankless. ♦ *During the summer, I earned money doing grunt work.* ♦ *I did all of the grunt work on the project, but my boss got all of the credit.*

guarantee [gɛr ən 'ti] **1.** *n.* a written document that promises that a certain product will operate properly for a certain amount of time. ♦ *I bought a computer with a one-year guarantee.* ♦ *The car's guarantee lasts for 12 months or 12,000 miles, whichever comes first.* **2.** *n.* a written or verbal promise that one will be responsible for someone else's debts or actions. ♦ *You have my guarantee that I will be home by midnight.* ♦ *The contractor's guarantee stated that the work would be completed in six months.* **3.** *tv.* to promise something; to pledge something. (Takes a clause.) ♦ *The manufacturer guaranteed that its knives would never break.* ♦ *Max guaranteed to fix the computer if it ever broke.* **4.** *tv.* to promise to be responsible for one's own or someone else's debts or actions. ♦ *My father guaranteed the repayment of my loan.* ♦ *The contractor guaranteed completion of the job in six months.* **5.** *tv.* to provide ① promising that a product will work properly for a period of time. ♦ *The manufacturer guaranteed its products for 12 months.* ♦ *The new car was guaranteed for two years.*

guarantor ['gɛr ən tor] *n.* someone who promises to be responsible for someone else's debts or actions. ♦ *Because John wasn't 21, the bank required one of his parents to be a guarantor of his student loan.* ♦ *If you can't repay a debt, the bank will demand payment from any guarantors.*

guard ['gɑrd] **1.** *n.* someone or some creature that watches over or protects someone or something; someone who prevents someone or some creature from escaping. ♦ *Guards protected priceless paintings at the museum.* ♦ *The guard locked the prisoner in the cell.* **2.** *n.* a defensive position in basketball. ♦ *One of the guards blocked the forward's shot.* ♦ *The guard knocked the basketball out of bounds.* **3.** *adj.* <the adj. use of ①.> ♦ *Our guard dog is trained to attack burglars.* ♦ *Don't lean against the guard rail too much. It looks weak.* **4.** *tv.* to protect someone or something: to keep someone or something from escaping. ♦ *The wardens guarded the prisoners night and day.* ♦ *Security officers guarded the bank vault.*

guarded ['gɑr dɪd] *adj.* controlled; restrained. (Adv: *guardedly.*) ♦ *The politician used guarded speech around the reporters.* ♦ *My optimism is guarded because I don't want to be disappointed if something goes wrong.*

guardian ['gɑr di ən] *n.* someone who watches over or protects someone or something, sometimes appointed to do so by a court of law. ♦ *This paper has to be signed* *by the child's parents or legal guardian.* ♦ *The children were sent to live with their guardian when their parents died.*

Guatemala [gwɑt ə 'mɑl ə] See Gazetteer.

guerrilla [gɛ 'rɪl ə] **1.** *n.* a soldier in an unofficial political army that is fighting against the government in power. (Compare with **gorilla**.) ♦ *The guerrillas blew up a bomb at the airport.* ♦ *The government was overthrown by rebel guerrillas.* **2.** *adj.* of or about the warfare or tactics of ①. ♦ *Dozens of innocent citizens were killed by guerrilla warfare.* ♦ *Guerrilla rockets bombarded the capital city.*

guess ['gɛs] **1.** *n.* an opinion or statement that is made without really knowing what is true. ♦ *It's my guess that it's about 50 degrees outside.* ♦ *What's your guess as to why the problem failed?* **2. guess at** *iv.* + *prep. phr.* to make a try at getting the right answer to a question. ♦ *I guessed at the answers on the test and got a few of them right.* ♦ *Max could only guess at the number of pages in the book.* **3.** *tv.* to make a successful try at getting the right answer to a question. ♦ *I guessed most of the answers on the surprise quiz.* ♦ *Max correctly guessed the number of pages in the book.* **4.** *tv.* to think that something will probably happen; to suppose that something will happen. (Takes a clause.) ♦ *I guess that it could rain tonight.* ♦ *I guessed that my boss would respond angrily to my request.*

guesswork ['gɛs wɚk] *n.* the process of making conclusions or estimates. (No plural form in this sense.) ♦ *My conclusions are based on guesswork. The actual data won't be known for another six months.* ♦ *The detective relied on guesswork until the police found actual clues.*

guest ['gɛst] **1.** *n.* someone who visits another person's home by invitation. ♦ *I invited Bill to be my guest whenever he came to town.* ♦ *I stayed in London as the guest of my best friend's father.* **2.** *n.* someone who is taken to dinner or to a place of entertainment by someone else, who is paying for it. ♦ *Please be my guest for dinner.* ♦ *Since you're my guest, I insist that I pay for dinner.* **3.** *n.* someone who is invited by an organization or government to visit. ♦ *The British prime minister was an honored guest at the White House.* ♦ *The invited guest spoke to the government panel about global warming.* **4.** *n.* a performer who makes a special appearance on a program. ♦ *The famous comedian appeared at the award ceremony as a special guest.* ♦ *The talk-show host's first guest was Elizabeth Taylor.* **5.** *n.* a customer of a hotel, resort, motel, etc. ♦ *We hope that all our guests will be comfortable in our hotel.* ♦ *As a guest of this resort, you can use any of our swimming pools.* **6. guest of honor** *idiom* a guest who gets special attention from everyone; the person for whom a party, celebration, or ceremony is given. ♦ *Bob is the guest of honor, and many people will make speeches about him.* ♦ *The guest of honor sits at the front of the room on the dais.*

guesthouse ['gɛst hɑʊs] *n., irreg.* a boarding house; a private house where travelers can stay for a price. (Pl: [...hɑʊ zəz].) ♦ *We stayed at a charming guesthouse in the mountains of Italy.* ♦ *My parents run a guesthouse on the coast of Florida.*

guffaw [gə 'fɔ] **1.** *n.* a loud, crude laugh. ♦ *John responded to the joke with a guffaw.* ♦ *My date's inappropriate guffaw embarrassed me.* **2.** *iv.* to make a loud, crude laugh. ♦ *The audience guffawed at the comedian's risqué joke.* ♦ *I guffawed when my brother slipped on a banana peel.*

guidance ['gɑɪd əns] **1.** *n.* advice; direction; help. (No plural form in this sense.) ♦ *Anne asked her mother for some guidance about college.* ♦ *John asked his counselor for some guidance about his career.* **2.** *adj.* <the adj. use of ①.> ♦ *My guidance counselor suggested a few colleges that she thought would be good for me.* ♦ *The guidance department at my school doesn't have enough counselors.*

guide ['gɑɪd] **1.** *n.* someone who shows someone else the way. ♦ *I looked for a guide who could show me the way to the subway.* ♦ *A guide led the inspectors around the factory.* **2.** *n.* someone who leads tours. ♦ *A guide led the tourists around the castle.* ♦ *I asked the guide some questions about the city's history.* **3.** *n.* a book or chart of information about a place; a guidebook. ♦ *I stayed in hotels that the travel guide recommended.* ♦ *According to the guide, the subway should be in the next street.* **4.** *tv.* to lead the way for someone; to show someone where to go. ♦ *The manager guided the inspectors through the factory.* ♦ *I guided the lost tourist towards the subway.* **5.** *tv.* to lead a tour. ♦ *Max guides tours for a living.* ♦ *I meet many interesting people because I guide tour groups.* **6.** *tv.* to direct the business of something; to control something. ♦ *The board of directors guides the future of the company.* ♦ *The manager will guide the growth of the new department.* **7.** *tv.* to advise someone. ♦ *I hope I can guide you to make the right decision.* ♦ *I asked my counselor to guide me as I applied for colleges.*

guidebook ['gɑɪd bʊk] *n.* a book of information, especially for tourists, about a certain area, country, or city. ♦ *I stayed only at hotels recommended by the guidebook.* ♦ *The guidebook of London includes a map of the subway system.*

guide dog ['gɑɪd dɔg] *n.* a dog that is trained to help someone who is blind. ♦ *The guide dog stopped five inches from the curb.* ♦ *The restaurant does not allow any animals inside except for guide dogs.*

guideline ['gɑɪd lɑɪn] *n.* a suggested idea for doing something; a principle. (Usually plural.) ♦ *The manual's helpful guidelines were clearly written.* ♦ *I learned how to read faster by following a few simple guidelines.*

guile ['gɑɪl] *n.* clever trickery; cunning. (No plural form in this sense.) ♦ *The politician relied on guile to win the election.* ♦ *The sly student used wit and guile to avoid attending class.*

guileless ['gɑɪl ləs] *adj.* sincere; straightforward. (Adv: *guilelessly*.) ♦ *The young man seemed guileless and eager to help, so I hired him to shovel the snow from my driveway.* ♦ *The people who live along the river are guileless and easily misled.*

guillotine ['gɪl ə tin] **1.** *n.* a device that chops off the heads of criminals. (From French.) ♦ *People gathered at the guillotine to watch an execution.* ♦ *The guillotine's sharp blade sliced the prisoner's neck.* **2.** *tv.* to cut off someone's head using ①. ♦ *The executioner guillotined the murderer.* ♦ *The spy was guillotined for treason.*

guilt ['gɪlt] **1.** *n.* the feeling that one has done something wrong or bad. (No plural form in this sense.) ♦ *A wave of guilt came over me after I lied to my parents.* ♦ *I felt a twinge of guilt for taking home pencils from work.* **2.** *n.* the burden or responsibility of having done something wrong or bad. (No plural form in this sense.) ♦ *The pros-*

ecutor was not able to prove the guilt of the accused woman. ♦ *I am free from guilt in this crime!*

guiltless ['gɪlt ləs] *adj.* innocent; without guilt ②. (Adv: *guiltlessly.*) ♦ *The person being tried for the crime was proved guiltless.* ♦ *The convict proclaimed that he was guiltless.*

guilty ['gɪl ti] **1.** *adj.* having broken a rule or done something wrong; judged in a court to have done a crime; not innocent. (Adv: *guiltily.* Comp: *guiltier;* sup: *guiltiest.*) ♦ *The jury declared the defendant to be guilty of all charges.* ♦ *The guilty murderer was led from the courtroom in handcuffs.* ♦ *I am guilty of sleeping late.* **2. feel guilty (about something)** *idiom* to feel that one is to blame for something; to feel intense regret for something that one has done. (Adv: *guiltily.*) ♦ *I feel guilty for forgetting about your birthday.* ♦ *You shouldn't feel guilty about the accident. It's not your fault.*

Guinea ['gɪn i] See Gazetteer.

guinea pig ['gɪn i pɪg] **1.** *n.* a small rodent, often kept as a pet or used in medical and scientific experiments. ♦ *The students took turns feeding the classroom's guinea pig.* ♦ *The scientist injected the guinea pig with a new vaccine.* **2.** *n.* someone who is being used in an experiment. (Figurative on ①.) ♦ *The psychologist paid 20 undergraduates to be guinea pigs.* ♦ *I volunteered to be a guinea pig in a study about sleep.*

guise ['gɑɪz] *n.* an appearance, especially one that hides the truth; a disguise. ♦ *The thief robbed houses in the guise of a mailman.* ♦ *A few students attended our high school illegally, under the guise of residents of the school district.*

guitar [gɪ 'tɑr] *n.* a musical instrument with strings that are plucked or strummed. ♦ *My brother plays a guitar in a rock band.* ♦ *Susan played the guitar while we sang songs around the campfire.*

gulch ['gʌltʃ] *n.* a narrow valley with steep sides, often having a fast-moving stream running through it. ♦ *The miner drowned when a flash flood raced through the gulch.* ♦ *A sturdy bridge was built over the dry gulch.*

gulf ['gʌlf] **1.** *n.* an area of sea, larger than a bay, surrounded by land on two or three sides. ♦ *John and Bill went fishing in the gulf.* ♦ *Last summer, Jane and I traveled to the Gulf of Mexico.* **2.** *n.* a large or wide separation. (Figurative on ①.) ♦ *An enormous gulf separated the striking workers and management.* ♦ *A mediator helped bridge the gulf between the warring armies.*

Gulf of Mexico ['gʌlf əv 'mɛk sɪ ko] See Gazetteer.

gull ['gʌl] *n.* a seagull. ♦ *As we approached the beach, we saw hundreds of gulls in the sky.* ♦ *The gull swooped down and grabbed my sandwich with its beak.*

gullible ['gʌl ə bəl] *adj.* likely to believe anything; easy to be tricked; naive. (Adv: *gullibly.*) ♦ *My gullible friend believed me when I said school was canceled.* ♦ *The gullible tourist was tricked out of $100.*

gully ['gʌl i] *n.* a deep ditch made by running water. ♦ *The heavy rain washed the farm's precious topsoil away, leaving only gullies.* ♦ *The water flowed through the gully and into the stream.*

gulp ['gʌlp] **1.** *n.* the swallowing of a large amount of food, drink, or air. ♦ *You should chew your food instead of swallowing it in gulps.* ♦ *Susan swallowed her lemonade in one gulp.* **2.** *n.* a large mouthful; a large breath of air; a large bite of food or drink. ♦ *The runner inhaled huge gulps of air after the race.* ♦ *The drowning swimmer swallowed large gulps of water.* **3. gulp (down)** *tv.* (+ *adv.*) to swallow food, drink, or air quickly. ♦ *Don't gulp your food! You'll get a stomach ache.* ♦ *I gulped the slice of pizza down in two bites.* **4. gulp for air** *idiom* to eagerly or desperately try to get air or a breath. ♦ *Tom gulped for air after trying to hold his breath for three minutes.* ♦ *Mary came up out of the water, gulping for air.*

gum ['gʌm] **1.** *n.* a sticky substance produced by certain trees and other plants. (No plural form in this sense.) ♦ *The gum of this tree has many uses in industry.* ♦ *The plants produced a large amount of gum.* **2.** *n.* a soft, sticky, flavored substance that people chew. (No plural form in this sense. Number expressed with *stick(s) of gum.*) ♦ *I freshened my breath with a stick of mint-flavored gum.* ♦ *I stepped on some gum that someone had spit out.* **3.** *n.* the upper or lower ridge of flesh that covers the jaw bones and surrounds the bases of the teeth. ♦ *I have problems with my gums if I don't have regular dental care.* ♦ *The dentist says my gums are pink and healthy.* **4.** *tv.* to chew or suck on something with toothless gums ③. ♦ *The baby gummed her pacifier contentedly.* ♦ *The toothless man had to gum all his food.*

gumdrop ['gʌm drɑp] *n.* a small jelly-like candy. ♦ *The waiter gave us each a gumdrop after dinner.* ♦ *Orange gumdrops usually taste like oranges.*

gumption ['gʌmp ʃən] *n.* initiative, energy, and resourcefulness. (No plural form in this sense.) ♦ *Bill had the gumption to work on three projects at once.* ♦ *I just don't have the gumption to build a new fence, even though the old one is falling down.*

gun ['gʌn] **1.** *n.* a weapon that shoots bullets. ♦ *The robber aimed a gun at my head and threatened to kill me.* ♦ *I took the gun in my hand and pulled the trigger.* **2.** *n.* a device or tool that has a handle and trigger like ①, used for applying or installing something. ♦ *The spray gun applied paint to the wall quickly and evenly.* ♦ *Bill used a staple gun to staple the shingles onto the roof.* **3. gun down** *tv.* + *adv.* to shoot someone who then drops down, dead or wounded. ♦ *The army gunned the rebels down.* ♦ *The store owner gunned down the robber.* **4. beat the gun** *idiom* to manage to do something before the ending signal. ♦ *The ball beat the gun and dropped through the hoop just in time.* ♦ *Tom tried to beat the gun, but he was one second too slow.* **5. gun for someone** *idiom* to be looking for someone, presumably to harm the person. ♦ *The coach is gunning for you. I think he's going to bawl you out.* ♦ *I've heard that the sheriff is gunning for me, so I'm getting out of town.* **6. jump the gun** *idiom* to start before the starting signal. ♦ *We all had to start the race again because Jane jumped the gun.* ♦ *When we took the test, Tom jumped the gun and started early.* **7. stick to one's guns** *idiom* to remain firm in one's convictions; to stand up for one's rights. ♦ *I'll stick to my guns on this matter. I'm sure I'm right.* ♦ *Bob can be persuaded to do it our way. He probably won't stick to his guns on this point.*

gunboat ['gʌn bot] *n.* a ship or a boat that is armed with guns. ♦ *The gunboat was sunk by a torpedo.* ♦ *The gunboat fired on the port city.*

gunfight ['gʌn fɑɪt] *n.* a fight between two or more people using guns. ♦ *The cowboy challenged the villain to a gunfight.* ♦ *The young gang member was killed in a violent gunfight.*

gunfire ['gʌn fɑɪr] *n.* the firing of guns; the sound made by the firing of guns. (No plural form in this sense.) ♦ *John called the police when he heard gunfire up the street.* ♦ *I fled for shelter as the gunfire rained down from the hills.*

gunman ['gʌn mən] *n., irreg.* a man who uses or carries a gun, especially to commit crimes. (Pl: gunmen.) ♦ *The police shot and killed the gunman.* ♦ *The gunman fled the bank with $50,000.*

gunmen ['gʌn mən] pl of gunman.

gunpowder ['gʌn pɑʊ dɚ] *n.* a powder that explodes when lit, used in certain guns, explosives, and fireworks. (No plural form in this sense.) ♦ *The gunpowder on the victim's shirt means he was shot at close range.* ♦ *A gun uses gunpowder to propel a chunk of lead through the barrel of the gun.*

gunshot ['gʌn ʃɑt] **1.** *n.* a shot from a gun; a bullet fired from a gun; the noise of shooting a gun. ♦ *A gunshot silenced the loud argument.* ♦ *The store owner killed the robber with a single gunshot.* **2.** *adj.* <the adj. use of ①.> ♦ *The police officer received a gunshot wound to his leg.* ♦ *The emergency-room doctor saw dozens of gunshot wounds every month.*

gunslinger ['gʌn slɪŋ ɚ] *n.* someone who carries a gun, especially referring to someone in the Old West. ♦ *The gunslinger shot the cheating poker player.* ♦ *The gunslinger challenged the sheriff to a duel.*

guppy ['gʌp i] *n.* a very small, tropical, freshwater fish. ♦ *My cat knocked over the fishbowl and ate the guppies.* ♦ *Guppies are used to eat the eggs and larvae of mosquitoes.*

gurgle ['gɚg əl] **1.** *n.* a bubbling noise, especially one made in or by water. ♦ *I heard a gurgle of water just before it streamed from the pipe.* ♦ *The baby made a happy gurgle when I smiled at him.* **2.** *iv.* to make a bubbling noise. ♦ *The water gurgled in the whirlpool.* ♦ *The baby gurgled and spit up some milk.*

guru ['gu ru] **1.** *n.* a spiritual or personal religious advisor in the Hindu religion. ♦ *I asked the guru about his philosophy of life.* ♦ *My guru helped me acquire a better approach to life.* **2.** *n.* an advisor. (Figurative on ①.) ♦ *Susan became some sort of diet guru, helping people lose weight through her books and recipes.* ♦ *The president had gurus for almost every subject or problem.*

gush ['gʌʃ] **1.** *n.* a large, noticeable flow of a fluid. ♦ *A gush of water streamed through the hole in the pipe.* ♦ *When I unclogged the hose, the water came out in a gush.* **2.** *n.* a flow of emotion or feeling. (Figurative on ①.) ♦ *I felt a sudden gush of sorrow for the victims of the fire.* ♦ *In a gush of anger, my boss threatened to fire everyone.* **3.** *iv.* to flow out rapidly and in large amounts. ♦ *Gallons of water gushed from the broken pipe.* ♦ *Oil gushed out of the well.* **4.** *iv.* to show one's emotions or enthusiasm in an affected or overbearing way, generally in speaking or writing. ♦ *The senator gushed with apologies after making offensive comments.* ♦ *The pretentious artist gushed about the new gallery.* **5.** *tv.* to discharge or emit fluid. ♦ *The broken pipe gushed gallons of water.* ♦ *The cut on my wrist gushed blood.*

gusher ['gʌʃ ɚ] *n.* an oil well of such size that oil shoots up out of the ground under pressure. ♦ *The workers dug a new well, hoping for a gusher.* ♦ *The gusher shot oil toward the sky.*

gust ['gʌst] **1.** *n.* a strong rush of wind or smoke. ♦ *A gust of wind knocked down the dead tree.* ♦ *The truck belched a gust of smoke from its exhaust pipe.* **2.** *iv.* [for the wind] to move in short, strong bursts. ♦ *The wind gusted and howled all through the night.* ♦ *Suddenly, the wind gusted mightily and blew the door open.*

gusto ['gʌs to] *n.* great enjoyment in doing something; zest; vigor. (No plural form in this sense.) ♦ *We played volleyball on the beach with great gusto.* ♦ *Anne's friends sang "Happy Birthday" to her with gusto.*

gut ['gʌt] **1.** *n.* the area of the intestine or stomach. (No plural form in this sense.) ♦ *The horse has some sort of disorder in the gut.* ♦ *There was something lodged in the gut of the fish, causing it to die.* **2. guts** *n.* the intestines. (Treated as plural. Colloquial.) ♦ *My guts were on fire after eating spicy food.* ♦ *The bully slugged Bob in the guts.* **3. guts** *n.* courage. (Treated as plural. Colloquial.) ♦ *The young child didn't have the guts to swim in the deep end.* ♦ *I wish I had the guts to challenge the corrupt mayor.* **4. guts** *n.* the inner or central core of something; the working parts of something. (Treated as plural. Informal.) ♦ *I had to have the guts of my microwave oven replaced.* ♦ *The jeweler replaced the guts of my watch.* **5.** *tv.* to take the intestines and organs out of an animal. ♦ *I cleaned and gutted the fish before I fried it.* ♦ *They gutted the swine as they slaughtered them.* **6.** *tv.* to destroy the inside of a building completely. (Figurative on ⑤.) ♦ *The city demolished the warehouse that had been gutted by fire.* ♦ *The new owner gutted the building before remodeling it.* **7.** *tv.* to steal everything inside a building; to strip a place bare. (Figurative on ⑥.) ♦ *Thieves gutted my apartment while I was on vacation.* ♦ *The disgruntled employee gutted his office before quitting.* **8. gut feeling, gut reaction, gut response** *idiom* a personal, intuitive feeling or response. ♦ *I have a gut feeling that something bad is going to happen.* ♦ *My gut reaction is that we should hire Susan for the job.* **9. hate someone's guts** *idiom* to hate someone very much. ♦ *Oh, Bob is terrible. I hate his guts!* ♦ *You may hate my guts for saying so, but I think you're getting gray hair.*

gutter ['gʌt ɚ] **1.** *n.* a metal channel hanging on the edge of a roof to carry away rainwater. ♦ *The violent storm ripped the gutters away from the roof.* ♦ *Water leaked through the roof because the gutter was clogged with leaves.* **2.** *n.* the wide, wooden channel on both sides of a bowling lane. ♦ *The bowler slipped and the ball rolled into the gutter.* ♦ *The bowling ball slowly rolled down the gutter.* **3.** *n.* a lower, formed area at the side of a paved street that leads water and other waste to the entrance of a sewer. ♦ *The street flooded because the gutter was clogged with debris.* ♦ *My wallet is wet because I dropped it in the gutter.* **4.** *n.* a low place in life; a despicable state of life. (No plural form in this sense. Figurative on ③.) ♦ *I finally finished school because I didn't want to end up in the gutter.* ♦ *His bad habits put him into the gutter.*

guy ['gɑɪ] **1.** *n.* a man; a boy. (Informal.) ♦ *A guy at the bus stop asked me for a quarter.* ♦ *Bill went drinking with the guys after work.* **2.** *n.* a person, male or female, usually in a group. (Informal.) ♦ *Have any of you guys seen my keys?* ♦ *What do you guys want to do for dinner tonight?*

guzzle ['gʌz əl] **1.** *tv.* to drink something quickly and in large amounts. ♦ *It was so hot that I guzzled a quart of lemonade.* ♦ *We guzzled some soda pop and then continued playing baseball.* **2.** *tv.* [for an engine or machine] to use a lot of something, especially fuel, energy, or oil. (Figurative on ①.) ♦ *My old car guzzles five gallons of gas per mile.* ♦ *The leaky engine guzzled a quart of oil a day.*

gym ['dʒɪm] **1.** *n.* a gymnasium. ♦ *I ran a mile at the gym today.* ♦ *I shower at the gym after I lift weights.* **2.** *adj.* <the adj. use of ①.> ♦ *I couldn't go into the fancy store wearing gym shoes.* ♦ *I carried my gym clothes in my gym bag.*

gymnasium [dʒɪm 'nez i əm] *n.* a large room or building for physical education, physical training, or certain sports events such as basketball and wrestling. (See gym.) ♦ *The janitor mopped the gymnasium before the basketball game.* ♦ *The school dance was held in the gymnasium.*

gymnast ['dʒɪm nəst] *n.* someone who is skilled in gymnastics. ♦ *The gymnast did three back flips in a row.* ♦ *If you want to be a gymnast, you have to train for it.*

gymnastic [dʒɪm 'næs tɪk] **1.** *adj.* <the adj. use of ②.> (Adv: *gymnastically* [...ɪk li].) ♦ *We practiced gymnastic exercises in gym class.* ♦ *The acrobat performed gymnastic feats on the high wire.* **2. gymnastics** *n.* the training of the body through exercise, and the skill and sport of performing these exercises. (Treated as singular.) ♦ *Sally trained in gymnastics until she injured her leg.* ♦ *The acrobat was very skilled in gymnastics.*

gynecologist [gɑɪ nə 'kɑl ə dʒəst] *n.* a doctor who works in gynecology. ♦ *I told my gynecologist that I thought I might be pregnant.* ♦ *My gynecologist specializes in diseases of the female reproductive system.*

gynecology [gɑɪ nə 'kɑl ə dʒi] *n.* the medical care and treatment of women, especially relating to the female reproductive system. (No plural form in this sense.) ♦ *The medical student specialized in gynecology.* ♦ *There have been many advances in gynecology in the past decade.*

gyp ['dʒɪp] **1.** *tv.* to cheat someone. (Pt/pp: *gypped*. From Gypsy and objected to as derogatory.) ♦ *The taxi driver gypped the tourist.* ♦ *The cashier gypped me by giving me the incorrect change.* **2.** *n.* an instance of being cheated. ♦ *What a gyp! This box of cereal is half empty.* ♦ *This gyp of a watch broke the day after I bought it.* **3. gyp someone out of something** *idiom* to deceive someone in order to get something of value. ♦ *The salesclerk gypped me out of a dollar.* ♦ *The taxi driver tried to gyp me out of a fortune by driving all over town.*

gypsum ['dʒɪp səm] *n.* a chalky mineral used to make plaster and wallboard. (No plural form in this sense.) ♦ *Gypsum is spread between two layers of heavy paper and then rolled into a flat panel.* ♦ *Workers installed the heavy panels made from gypsum.*

Gypsy ['dʒɪp si] **1.** *n.* someone who descends from people who migrated from northwest India to eastern Europe; people of the Romani ethnic group. (The less-familiar terms Roma and Romani are also used.) ♦ *A small band of Gypsies lived outside of the Hungarian village.* ♦ *The Gypsies moved from town to town, living in colorful wagons.* **2.** *adj.* <the adj. use of ①.> ♦ *I remember seeing Gypsy wagons along the highway when I was a child.* ♦ *I can play a Gypsy melody on the violin.*

gyrate ['dʒɑɪ ret] *iv.* to move in a circle or spiral; to rotate. ♦ *The wheel gyrated wildly from side to side as it started to come loose from the wagon.* ♦ *The spinning top gyrated on the tile floor.*

gyration [dʒɑɪ 're ʃən] *n.* a rotation; a circular movement. ♦ *The gyration of the spinning top made me dizzy.* ♦ *The astronomer studied the gyration of Jupiter's moons.*

H AND **h** ['etʃ] *n.* the eighth letter of the alphabet. ♦ H *comes after* G *and before* I. ♦ *The name "Henry" begins with a capital* H.

habit ['hæb ɪt] **1.** *n.* an action that is done over and over, usually without thought. ♦ *Anne made a habit of locking her door, even when she was at home.* ♦ *Bill kept practicing the scales on the piano until they became a habit.* **2.** *n.* an addiction. ♦ *Because of her smoking habit, Jane is often short of breath.* ♦ *The heroin addict went to a hospital in order to end his dangerous habit.* **3.** *n.* the uniform worn by a monk or a nun. ♦ *Only a silver cross adorned the nun's black and white habit.* ♦ *The man's habit indicated that he was a monk.*

habitable ['hæb ɪt ə bəl] *adj.* able to be lived in; suitable for a dwelling. (Adv: *habitably.*) ♦ *The hikers stayed in a small but habitable cabin during the storm.* ♦ *The pirates used a habitable cave as their hideout.*

habitat ['hæb ɪ tæt] *n.* a place where a plant or an animal lives or thrives; the home required by a plant or an animal. ♦ *The scientist spent two years researching the habitats of bats.* ♦ *The polar bear lives in a cold habitat.*

habitation [hæb ɪ 'te ʃən] **1.** *n.* a home; a dwelling; a place where someone lives. ♦ *The habitation of many college students is a college dormitory.* ♦ *A foster home is the typical habitation for orphans until they are adopted.* **2.** *n.* the use of a place as a home. (No plural form in this sense.) ♦ *A sign warned that habitation of the burned out building was illegal.* ♦ *The city officials will not allow habitation of new buildings until they are inspected.*

habitual [hə 'bɪtʃ u əl] *adj.* done regularly; done repeatedly; done as a habit. (Adv: *habitually.*) ♦ *You should try to stop your habitual complaining.* ♦ *The principal warned the student against habitual tardiness.*

hack ['hæk] **1.** *tv.* to chop something; to hit something with an axe. ♦ *The camper hacked the wood into pieces for the fire.* ♦ *The forester hacked the tree with an axe.* **2. hack at** *iv.* + *prep. phr.* to chop at something. ♦ *The burglar hacked at the wood around the door lock.* ♦ *Annoyed that he had lost the key, Tom hacked at the padlock with an axe.* **3.** *iv.* to cough; to have short, dry coughs. ♦ *Mary hacked all night when she was ill.* ♦ *I began to hack, so I put a cough drop in my mouth.* **4.** *n.* a chop; a sharp blow. ♦ *Bill was knocked unconscious by a sharp hack to his head.* ♦ *The knight's well-aimed hack knocked his opponent from his horse.* **5.** *n.* a short, dry cough. ♦ *I sucked on a cough drop to soothe my dry hack.* ♦ *Another big hack like that and you will hurt your throat.* **6.** *n.* a writer who writes poorly. ♦ *What hack wrote this nonsense?* ♦ *The hacks who worked for the small newspaper were poorly paid.*

hackneyed ['hæk nid] *adj.* trite; overused. ♦ *My teacher crossed out the hackneyed phrases in my term paper.* ♦ *No one laughed at the comic's hackneyed joke.*

hacksaw ['hæk sɔ] *n.* a saw used to cut metal. ♦ *I used a hacksaw to cut through the chain-link fence.* ♦ *The paramedic needed a hacksaw to extract the driver from the wrecked car.*

had ['hæd] **1.** pt/pp of have. (See ②.) **2.** *aux.* <the past-tense form of have ⑥, used in forming the past perfect tense.> (Used before the past participle of a verb. Reduced to *'d* in contractions. See also has.) ♦ *Bill had put the toys away.* ♦ *Where had Mary gone before she came here?* **3. been had** *idiom* been duped; been cheated. (Slang.) ♦ *I may have been had, but I'll get even.* ♦ *Tom knew he'd been had when the cheap watch stopped running the day after he bought it.*

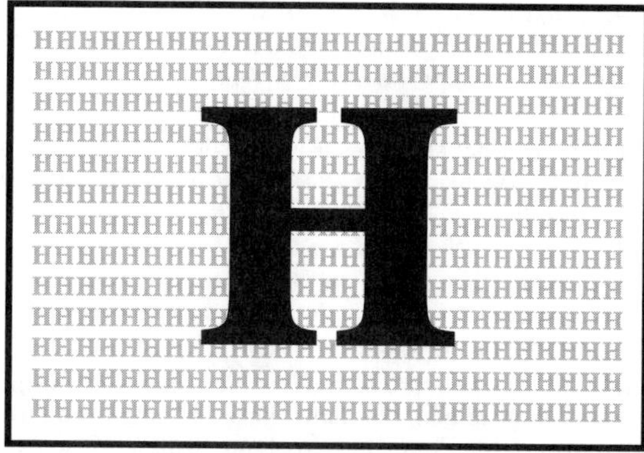

hadn't ['hæd nt] *cont.* "had not." ♦ *Anne hadn't studied, so she did poorly on the test.* ♦ *Since John hadn't eaten breakfast, he was hungry.*

hag ['hæg] *n.* an ugly old woman; a witch. ♦ *Mary dressed up as a hag for Halloween.* ♦ *It's not polite to call your teacher a hag.*

haggard ['hæg ɚd] *adj.* looking tired, as from sickness or exhaustion. (Adv: *haggardly.*) ♦ *The haggard parents chased their twins around the toy store.* ♦ *The last haggard runner finally stumbled across the finish line.*

haggle ['hæg əl] **1.** *tv.* to achieve a lower price through arguing. ♦ *Bob thought he could haggle a better price on the furniture.* ♦ *Mary tried to haggle the price down on the new car.* **2. haggle with** *iv.* + *prep. phr.* to argue with someone about the price of something; to negotiate with someone for a lower price. ♦ *I haggled with the butcher over the price of the steaks.* ♦ *Mary haggled with the salesman over the price of the new car.*

haggling ['hæg (ə) lɪŋ] *n.* negotiation about a price; dickering; wrangling. (No plural form in this sense.) ♦ *Haggling was a sport to Tom, who rarely paid full price for anything.* ♦ *The haggling went on for an hour, but we couldn't come to an agreement on a price for the used car.*

hail ['hel] **1.** *n.* round pellets of ice that fall from the sky like rain. (No plural form in this sense. Number is expressed with hailstone(s).) ♦ *Hail dented the roof of Lisa's car.* ♦ *Some of the pieces of hail were as big as stones.* **2.** *n.* a group of things that come in small, sharp units. ♦ *The troops were met by a hail of bullets as they approached the enemy town.* ♦ *The car was dented by a hail of pebbles falling from the truck ahead.* **3.** *n.* a continual barrage of demands, objections, etc. ♦ *The senator received a hail of criticism for supporting the tax increase.* ♦ *The mayor refused to answer the hail of questions about the scandal.* **4.** *tv.* to greet and honor someone. ♦ *The mayor hailed Tom as a hero for saving a family from a burning building.* ♦ *The city hailed the victorious team with a parade.* **5.** *tv.* to approve something eagerly and enthusiastically. ♦ *The president of the company hailed the contract with the union as nearly perfect.* ♦ *The president hailed the work of the legislature and signed the legislation.* **6. hail from** *iv.* + *prep. phr.* to come from a particular area or region. ♦ *Our new company president hails from*

Denver. ♦ *Judging by her accent, I think Sue hails from the South.* **7.** *iv.* [for ①] to fall from the sky. ♦ *The sidewalks were slippery after it hailed.* ♦ *Because it was hailing, the airport closed.*

hailstone ['hel ston] *n.* a round pellet of ice that falls from the sky like rain. ♦ *The largest hailstone was almost an inch in diameter.* ♦ *After the storm, the patio was littered with hailstones.*

hailstorm ['hel storm] *n.* a storm that produces or includes hail. ♦ *A brief hailstorm preceded the tornado.* ♦ *The hailstorm delayed the ballgame.*

hair ['he ɚ] **1.** *n.* the fibrous strands that grow on the body of an animal, especially the ones that grow on top of the heads of humans. (No plural form in this sense.) ♦ *Mary dyed her hair black.* ♦ *David brushed his hair after he dried it.* **2.** *n.* one of the fibrous strands that grows on the body of an animal. ♦ *The detective carefully picked up the hair with a pair of tweezers.* ♦ *Mary became angry when she found a hair in her soup.* **3. curl someone's hair** *idiom* to frighten or alarm someone severely; to shock someone with sight, sound, or taste. ♦ *Don't ever sneak up on me like that again. You really curled my hair.* ♦ *The horror film curled my hair.* **4. get in someone's hair** *idiom* to bother or irritate someone. ♦ *Billy is always getting in his mother's hair.* ♦ *I wish you'd stop getting in my hair.* **5. let one's hair down** *idiom* to become more intimate and begin to speak frankly. ♦ *Come on, Jane, let your hair down and tell me all about it.* ♦ *I have a problem. Do you mind if I let down my hair?* **6. make someone's hair stand on end** *idiom* to cause someone to be very frightened. ♦ *A horrible scream made my hair stand on end.* ♦ *The ghost story made our hair stand on end.* **7. tear one's hair** *idiom* to be anxious, frustrated, or angry. ♦ *I was so nervous, I was about to tear my hair.* ♦ *I had better get home. My parents will be tearing their hair.*

hairbrush ['he ɚ brəʃ] *n.* a brush used for aligning or smoothing hair. ♦ *Mary ran a hairbrush through her tangled hair.* ♦ *The barber combed my hair with a plastic hairbrush.*

haircut ['he ɚ kət] **1.** *n.* the act of cutting hair; especially the hair on top of someone's head. ♦ *Dave had his first haircut when he was two years old.* ♦ *I needed a haircut before going on my job interview.* **2.** *n.* the particular way that one's hair has been cut; a hair style; a hairdo. ♦ *Bob's short haircut makes him look like he's in the army.* ♦ *Ever since he began losing his hair, Bill is very particular about his haircut.*

hairdo ['he ɚ du] *n.* the style of one's hair; the way one's hair has been cut or shaped. (Pl in *-s.*) ♦ *Mary's new hairdo is a very popular style nowadays.* ♦ *Jane asked her hairdresser for a new hairdo.*

hairdresser ['he ɚ drɛs ɚ] *n.* someone who cuts and styles hair; a **hair stylist**. ♦ *Mary called her hairdresser to set up an appointment.* ♦ *I liked my hairdresser's work, so I gave him a $10 tip.*

hairdryer ['he ɚ drɑɪ ɚ] *n.* a device that blows hot air in order to dry wet hair. ♦ *My hair is so long it takes 15 minutes to dry it even with a hairdryer.* ♦ *This hairdryer has two different heat settings.*

hairline ['he ɚ lɑɪn] **1.** *n.* the place above the forehead where hair starts growing. ♦ *The older Bob gets, the more his hairline recedes.* ♦ *The newborn baby had just a little fuzz at the hairline.* **2.** *adj.* very thin; as thin as a hair. ♦ *The hairline fracture will take a couple of weeks to heal.* ♦ *The carpenter made a hairline mark with her pencil so she knew where to cut the wood.*

hairpiece ['he ɚ pis] *n.* a wig; a toupee; a piece of artificial hair. ♦ *The strong wind blew Bob's hairpiece away.* ♦ *Anne bought a hairpiece when her hair began to thin.*

hair-raising ['he ɚ rez ɪŋ] *adj.* scary; frightening; [figuratively] making one's hair stand on end. (Adv: *hair-raisingly.*) ♦ *The children couldn't sleep after hearing the hair-raising story.* ♦ *For one hair-raising hour, the bank robber held four tellers hostage.*

hair style ['hɛɚ stɑɪl] *n.* the particular way that one's hair has been cut or styled; a hairdo. ♦ *I prefer short hair styles in the summer because they feel cooler.* ♦ *My barber asked me what kind of hair style I'd like.*

hair stylist ['hɛɚ stɑɪl əst] See stylist.

hairy ['he ɚ ri] *adj.* covered with hair; having a lot of hair. (Comp: *hairier;* sup: *hairiest.*) ♦ *Bob bared his hairy chest at the beach.* ♦ *The hairy dog shed its hair all over the house.*

Haiti ['het i] See Gazetteer.

hale ['hel] **hale and hearty** *idiom* healthy. ♦ *The young infant was hale and hearty.* ♦ *The calf—hale and hearty—ran around the barnyard.*

half ['hæf] **1.** *n., irreg.* either of two equal parts that make up a whole; either of two parts that make up a whole. (Pl: **halves.**) ♦ *Mary tried to glue the halves of the broken plate together.* ♦ *Which half of the sandwich do you want?* **2.** *adj.* half in amount; of two equal parts; being one of two parts. ♦ *Jane earned a half million dollars from the sale of the house.* ♦ *We walked a half mile to the pond.* **3.** *pron.* half the amount of things or people already mentioned or able to be determined by context. (Treated as singular or plural, depending on the number of the noun that ③ stands for.) ♦ *I bought a dozen eggs, but half were spoiled and had to be thrown away.* ♦ *Of everyone in the audience, half really seemed to enjoy it.* **4.** *adv.* part of the way; not completely; halfway. ♦ *The potatoes were only half cooked.* ♦ *John was only half finished with his manuscript when he died.* **5. one's better half** *idiom* one's spouse. ♦ *I think we'd like to come for dinner, but I'll have to ask my better half.* ♦ *I have to go home now to my better half. We are going out tonight.*

half-and-half ['hæf ən 'hæf] *n.* a dairy product that is half cream and half milk, used to flavor coffee and other foods. ♦ *Bob added some half-and-half to his coffee.* ♦ *Anne asked the waiter for half-and-half.*

halfback ['hæf bæk] *n.* a position in football, rugby, or soccer. ♦ *Bill played halfback on his college football team.* ♦ *The halfback caught the pass and scored a touchdown.*

halfhearted ['hæf 'hɑrt ɪd] *adj.* not too enthusiastic; without excitement. (Adv: *halfheartedly.*) ♦ *I made a halfhearted attempt to wash the dishes, but I left most of them in the sink.* ♦ *I knew from Bob's halfhearted response that he didn't really want to see the movie.*

half-hour ['hæf 'ɑʊ ɚ] **1.** *n.* thirty minutes; half an hour. ♦ *The class will last a half-hour.* ♦ *I will meet you in a half-hour.* **2.** *adj.* lasting thirty minutes. ♦ *The half-hour program was just long enough for the small children.* ♦ *The two friends talked during the half-hour train ride.*

half-mast ['hæf 'mæst] **at half-mast** *phr.* [of a flag] hung below the top of a flagpole, nearer the midpoint of the pole. ♦ *The company flag flew at half-mast in honor of the owner's death.* ♦ *The flag was flown at half-mast for a week following the president's death.*

half-price ['hæf 'prɑɪs] **1.** *adj.* costing half as much as normal; on sale for half the normal price. ♦ *I bought some half-price books at the bookstore.* ♦ *The half-price dress was quite a bargain.* **2. half-price sale** *n.* a sale where goods are sold at half their normal prices. ♦ *The store was crowded during the half-price sale.* ♦ *The half-price sale lasted only one day.*

halftime ['hæf tɑɪm] *n.* the break between two halves of a sporting event, such as in basketball or football. (No plural form in this sense.) ♦ *The marching band performed during halftime.* ♦ *During halftime, the teams went to their locker rooms.*

half-truth ['hæf 'truθ] *n.* a statement that is only partly true. ♦ *The lawyer accused the witness of telling half-truths.* ♦ *I told John I didn't eat all of the pie. That was a half-truth, because I'd given the dog a small amount and eaten the rest.*

halfway ['hæf 'we] **1.** *adj.* at the middle; in the middle. ♦ *There's a small marker at the halfway point on the bike trail.* ♦ *On our climb up the mountain, we spent the night at a small halfway house.* **2.** *adv.* to the halfway ① point. ♦ *I can only paint halfway to the end of the hallway with this small can of paint.* ♦ *My homework is halfway finished. Can I call you in an hour?* **3. meet someone halfway** *idiom* to compromise with someone. ♦ *No, I won't give in, but I'll meet you halfway.* ♦ *They settled the argument by agreeing to meet each other halfway.*

half-wit ['hæf wɪt] *n.* an idiot; a fool. ♦ *What half-wit left a bicycle in the middle of the sidewalk?* ♦ *The children teased John about being a half-wit until he scored better than they did on the test.*

half-witted ['hæf wɪt ɪd] *adj.* stupid; foolish; idiotic. (Adv: *half-wittedly.*) ♦ *Buying this old car was the most half-witted thing I've ever done.* ♦ *The student was punished for making half-witted remarks about the teacher.*

halibut ['hæl ə bət] **1.** *n., irreg.* a large, edible fish found in cold water. (Pl: *halibut.*) ♦ *Halibut swim in the northern parts of the Atlantic and Pacific oceans.* ♦ *The fishermen caught mostly halibut and cod.* **2.** *n.* the meat of ①. (No plural form in this sense.) ♦ *John ordered halibut for dinner.* ♦ *The chef rolled pieces of halibut in batter and then fried them.*

halitosis [hæl ə 'to sɪs] *n.* bad breath; breath that smells bad. (No plural form in this sense.) ♦ *Most dogs have halitosis.* ♦ *I have halitosis in the morning, so the first thing I do is brush my teeth.*

hall ['hɔl] **1.** *n.* a corridor; a passage inside a house or building that rooms open into. ♦ *The bathroom is at the end of the hall and on the right.* ♦ *The tardy students hurried down the hall to get to their classrooms.* **2.** *n.* a large room for meetings, public gatherings, dances, etc. ♦ *The city council meets in the meeting hall every month.* ♦ *This large hall will accommodate most wedding receptions.* **3.** *n.* a building where college students live, sleep, study, or have class. ♦ *What hall are you living in?* ♦ *Jane's hall is on the other side of the campus.* **4.** *n.* a foyer; the space inside a house just inside the front door. ♦ *Please leave your coat in the hall.* ♦ *When the front door opened, Bob could see into the hall.*

hallmark ['hɔl mɑrk] **1.** *n.* an official stamp of a goldsmith or silversmith, indicating quality or purity. ♦ *The silver bowl had a famous silversmith's hallmark stamped on the bottom.* ♦ *When Mary couldn't find the hallmark on the gold goblet, she refused to buy it.* **2.** *n.* a sign of excellence; a sign of quality. (Figurative on ①.) ♦ *The name "Surrey" on china is the hallmark of fine quality.* ♦ *The employees worked hard to make the company's name the hallmark of fine clothing.* **3.** *n.* a feature or quality by which something is recognized. (Figurative on ①.) ♦ *Meticulousness and care are the hallmarks of a good proofreader.* ♦ *With his speed and size, Tom has all the hallmarks of being an excellent football player.*

hallowed ['hæl od] *adj.* sacred; regarded as sacred. (Adv: *hallowedly.*) ♦ *The hallowed grave was left undisturbed for years.* ♦ *Religious groups from around the world came to worship at the hallowed shrine.*

Halloween [hæl ə 'win] *n.* October 31; All Hallows Eve, the day before All Saint's Day. ♦ *Children love to dress up in costumes on Halloween.* ♦ *I took my children to a scary movie on Halloween.*

hallucinate [hə 'lu sə net] **1.** *tv.* to see or hear something that is really not there. (Takes a clause.) ♦ *Bob must be on drugs. He's hallucinating that there are animals in his house.* ♦ *In the hospital, Anne hallucinated that she heard voices.* **2.** *iv.* to have hallucinations. ♦ *Because John was hallucinating, he couldn't hear the doorbell.* ♦ *Some drugs can cause you to hallucinate.*

hallucination [hə lu sə 'ne ʃən] *n.* hearing or seeing something that is not there. ♦ *As he became more addicted to the drug, Tom's hallucinations could occur anywhere.* ♦ *During his hallucination, the patient saw giant blue monsters.*

hallway ['hɔl we] *n.* a hall; a corridor; a passage inside a house or building that rooms open up into. ♦ *A hallway led through the house and out to the patio.* ♦ *The teacher led the students down the hallway to the library.*

halo ['he lo] **1.** *n.* [in paintings and graphic representations] the ring of light around the head of an angel, God, or a holy person. (Pl in *-s* or *-es.*) ♦ *The painting of Christ's mother showed a halo above her head.* ♦ *The artist had drawn a halo above the angel's head.* **2.** *n.* a ring of light that can be sometimes seen around the sun, stars, the moon, or other sources of light. (Pl in *-s* or *-es.*) ♦ *The city lights were too bright for us to see the moon's halo.* ♦ *I could see a dim halo of light around the streetlight.*

halt ['hɔlt] **1.** *iv.* to stop. ♦ *The police ordered the thief to halt.* ♦ *Just before running into the fence, the dog halted.* **2.** *tv.* to cause someone or something to stop. ♦ *The fence halted the galloping horse.* ♦ *The police roadblock halted the thief.* **3. grind to a halt** *idiom* to slow to a stop; to run down. ♦ *By the end of the day, work at the factory had ground to a halt.* ♦ *The car ground to a halt, and we got out to stretch our legs.*

halter ['hɔl tɚ] *n.* a strap used to lead an animal or to tie an animal to a post. ♦ *The horse was wearing a halter, so it was easy to catch.* ♦ *I led the horse with the leather halter.*

halting ['hɔl tɪŋ] *adj.* wavering; hesitating. (Adv: *haltingly.*) ♦ *The frightened child spoke in a halting voice.* ♦ *The nervous politician delivered a halting speech.*

halve ['hæv] **1.** *tv.* to cut something into two halves; to split something into two equal halves. ♦ *Tom halved the apples with a knife.* ♦ *I halved the sandwich and placed each half in a plastic sandwich bag.* **2.** *tv.* to reduce something by half. ♦ *The finance committee halved the budget at the last minute.* ♦ *The new machine will halve the amount of time needed to do the job.*

halves ['hævz] pl of half.

ham ['hæm] **1.** *n.* the upper part of a hog's rear hip and thigh, preserved by salt and smoking. ♦ *There's a ham baking in the oven.* ♦ *I bought half a ham for the party.* **2.** *n.* meat of ①, eaten as food. (No plural form in this sense.) ♦ *Anne ate ham and eggs for breakfast.* ♦ *I don't care for ham. It's too salty.* **3.** *n.* an actor who overacts; someone who shows off. ♦ *The ham was disappointed when the crowd did not clap enthusiastically.* ♦ *The other actors were annoyed by the ham who fooled around onstage.* **4.** *n.* someone who operates an amateur radio station. ♦ *A ham in Florida heard the distress call from the boat and called for help.* ♦ *With my shortwave radio, I've made friends with hams around the world.*

hamburger ['hæm bɚg ɚ] **1.** *n.* beef that has been ground into tiny pieces. (No plural form in this sense.) ♦ *I browned the hamburger in a skillet.* ♦ *Hamburger is a cheap meat that can feed a lot of people.* **2.** *n.* a sandwich made of a patty of ground meat and a specially shaped bun. ♦ *The fast-food restaurant sold thousands of hamburgers each day.* ♦ *I put pickles, onion, and mustard on my hamburger.*

hammer ['hæm ɚ] **1.** *n.* a tool with a heavy metal head that is used to pound nails or to break things. ♦ *The carpenter drove the nail into the beam with a hammer.* ♦ *I used the claw on one end of the hammer to remove a nail.* **2.** *n.* a tiny bone in the middle ear, shaped like ①. ♦ *The hammer connects directly to the eardrum.* ♦ *The hammer, stirrup, and anvil are three bones in the middle ear that transmit vibrations.* **3.** *tv.* to hit something with a hammer; to break something with a hammer. ♦ *The thief hammered the window until it broke.* ♦ *Bob hammered the locked door, trying to open it.* **4. hammer into** *tv.* + *prep. phr.* to shape something by hitting it; to shape something with a hammer. ♦ *A blacksmith hammered the iron into a horseshoe.* ♦ *Bob hammered the metal into a rim for the barrel.* **5. hammer at** *iv.* + *prep. phr.* to pound repeatedly and forcefully on someone or something. ♦ *Tom woke up his neighbors by hammering at their door.* ♦ *The boxer hammered at his opponent until the referee stopped the fight.* **6. hammer something home** *idiom* to try extremely hard to make someone understand or realize something. ♦ *The boss hopes to hammer the firm's poor financial position home to the staff.* ♦ *I tried to hammer home to Anne the fact that she would have to get a job.*

hammock ['hæm ək] *n.* a rope net or canvas stretched between supports, on which a person can rest. ♦ *I'd love to spend a day relaxing in a hammock.* ♦ *I strung my hammock between two strong trees.*

hamper ['hæm pɚ] **1.** *n.* a covered basket for carrying or containing things. ♦ *Bob carried the picnic hamper to the table.* ♦ *Put your dirty shirt in the clothes hamper.* **2.** *tv.* to hinder or interfere with someone or something. ♦ *The fierce storm hampered our efforts to get to town by sunset.* ♦ *Bill's low grades hampered his plans to go to a private college.*

hamster ['hæm stɚ] *n.* a small, furry rodent, often kept as a pet. ♦ *After his parents said he couldn't have a dog, Bill asked for a hamster.* ♦ *The hamster escaped from its cage and scurried across the room.*

hand ['hænd] **1.** *n.* the structure at the end of the arm suitable for grasping; the most distant part of the arm, below the wrist. ♦ *Bob suffered three broken fingers when the car door slammed on his hand.* ♦ *Jane writes with her left hand.* **2.** *n.* the cards dealt to someone in a card game; one round in a game of cards. ♦ *Mary slowly picked up her hand of cards.* ♦ *I lost $2 on the last hand.* **3.** *n.* side; direction. (No plural form in this sense.) ♦ *Soldiers were fighting on either hand.* ♦ *At Bob's right hand stood his dog.* **4.** *n.* one of the pointers on a clock or watch. ♦ *The second hand no longer works on my watch.* ♦ *When the big hand is on the 3, it's 15 minutes past the hour.* **5.** *tv.* to give something to someone using one's hands ①. ♦ *The store clerk handed the package to the customer.* ♦ *Please hand that dish to me.* **6.** *adj.* <the adj. use of ①.> ♦ *There were several hand towels in the guest bathroom.* ♦ *Anne keeps a hand mirror in her purse.* **7. by hand** *phr.* made or done by one's hands; made by human hands as opposed to a machine. ♦ *This fine wooden cabinet was made by hand.* ♦ *I carved this figurine by hand.* **8. an old hand at doing something** *idiom* someone who is experienced at doing something. ♦ *The maid was an old hand at polishing silver.* ♦ *Bob is an old hand at training dogs.* **9. bite the hand that feeds one** *idiom* to do harm to someone who does good things for you. ♦ *I'm your mother! How can you bite the hand that feeds you?* ♦ *She can hardly expect much when she bites the hand that feeds her.* **10. by a show of hands** *idiom* a vote expressed by people raising their hands. ♦ *We were asked to vote for the candidates for captain by a show of hands.* ♦ *Bob wanted us to vote on paper, not by a show of hands, so that we could have a secret ballot.* **11. do something hands down** *idiom* to do something easily and without opposition. ♦ *The mayor won the election hands down.* ♦ *She was the choice of the people hands down.* **12. eat out of someone's hands** *idiom* to do what someone else wants; to obey someone eagerly. ♦ *Just wait! I'll have everyone eating out of my hands. They'll do whatever I ask.* ♦ *A lot of people are eating out of his hands.* **13. from hand to hand** *idiom* from one person to a series of other persons; passed from one hand to another. ♦ *The book traveled from hand to hand until it got back to its owner.* ♦ *By the time the baby had been passed from hand to hand, it was crying.* **14. get the upper hand (on someone)** *idiom* to get into a position superior to someone; to get the advantage over someone. ♦ *John is always trying to get the upper hand on me.* ♦ *He never ends up having the upper hand, though.* **15. give someone a hand, lend someone a hand** *idiom* to help someone. ♦ *Can you give me a hand carrying this box, please?* ♦ *After the hurricane, everyone lent a hand to help clean up the town.* **16. give someone a hand** *idiom* applause. ♦ *The audience gave the singer a big hand.* ♦ *The crowd rose and gave the politician a hand.* **17. have a hand in something** *idiom* to have an influence on something. ♦ *Tom's grandparents have always had* *a hand in helping him.* ♦ *Who had the biggest hand in your education?* **18. have clean hands** *idiom* to be guiltless. ♦ *Don't look at me. I have clean hands.* ♦ *The police took him in, but let him go again because he had clean hands.* **19. hand over fist** *idiom* [for money and merchandise to be exchanged] very rapidly. ♦ *What a busy day. We took in money hand over fist.* ♦ *They were buying things hand over fist.* **20. hand over hand** *idiom* [moving] one hand after the other (again and again). ♦ *Sally pulled in the rope hand over hand.* ♦ *The man climbed the rope hand over hand.* **21. in hand** *idiom* controlled; under control. ♦ *I thought I had my destiny in hand, but then fate played a trick on me.* ♦ *Don't worry about me. I have everything in hand.* **22. in someone's hands** *idiom* in someone's control; under someone's responsibility. ♦ *You have the whole project in your hands.* ♦ *I'm leaving the baby in your hands while I go shopping.* **23. show one's hand** *idiom* to reveal one's intentions to someone. ♦ *I don't know whether Jim's intending to marry Jane or not. He's not one to show his hand.* ♦ *If you want to get a raise, don't show the boss your hand too soon.* **24. sit on one's hands** *idiom* to do nothing; to fail to help. ♦ *When we needed help from Mary, she just sat on her hands.* ♦ *We need the cooperation of everyone. You can't sit on your hands!* **25. tie someone's hands** *idiom* to prevent someone from doing something. ♦ *I'd like to help you, but my boss has tied my hands.* ♦ *Please don't tie my hands with unnecessary restrictions. I'd like the freedom to do whatever is necessary.*

handbag ['hænd bæg] *n.* a purse; a container that serves as a purse. ♦ *The thief grabbed Mary's handbag and ran.* ♦ *I looked in my handbag for my car keys.*

handball ['hænd bɔl] **1.** *n.* a sport where two or four people hit a small ball against a wall with their hands. (No plural form in this sense.) ♦ *I went to the health club to play handball after work.* ♦ *You should wear protective goggles when playing handball.* **2.** *n.* the small, hard, rubber ball used in ①. ♦ *The handball rocketed off the wall and hit John's neck.* ♦ *I kept a canister of handballs in my locker at the health club.*

handbook ['hænd bʊk] *n.* a reference book; a guidebook; an instruction manual. ♦ *The computer came with a handbook, but Dave still couldn't figure out how to turn it on.* ♦ *That toy is so complicated to put together that it comes with a six-page handbook.*

handcuff ['hænd kəf] **1.** *n.* one of a pair of lockable metal bracelets placed on the wrists of someone who has been arrested. (Usually plural.) ♦ *The police officer put the handcuffs on the thief.* ♦ *The only way to remove the handcuffs is to use a key.* **2.** *tv.* to put ① on someone. ♦ *The police officer handcuffed the shoplifter.* ♦ *The officer arrested the suspect and handcuffed him.*

handful ['hænd fʊl] *n.* the amount of something that can be held in the hand. ♦ *Tom grabbed a handful of nuts from the bowl on the table.* ♦ *The recipe called for a handful of raisins.*

handgun ['hænd gən] *n.* a gun that can be carried in the hand; a pistol. ♦ *Even though the police officer was not working, he still carried a handgun.* ♦ *Some cities have laws prohibiting citizens from carrying handguns.*

handicap ['hæn di kæp] **1.** *n.* a disability; a disadvantage; something that hinders someone from doing something in the usual way. ♦ *A minor handicap causes Sally to use a cane when she walks.* ♦ *Because of John's handicap, he needs a wheelchair.* **2.** *n.* [in sports or games] placing restrictions on a better player in order to make the event more competitive. ♦ *The marathon runner was given a five-yard handicap, which meant he had to run five yards more than his competitors.* ♦ *When they competed against the younger children, the older children were given a handicap to make the contest more equal.* **3.** *tv.* to prevent someone from doing something in the usual way; to hinder someone. ♦ *A sore throat handicapped the singer.* ♦ *The stiff ankle handicapped the baseball player.*

handicapped ['hæn di kæpt] **1.** *adj.* disabled; impaired. ♦ *The handicapped person rode to work in a special bus.* ♦ *Susan became handicapped as a result of a car accident.* **2.** *adj.* in a weak position; not able to function satisfactorily. (Figurative on ①.) ♦ *Do you think you have been handicapped by your lack of computer skills?* ♦ *During the contract negotiations, Bob was handicapped because he didn't know what the union members wanted.* **3.** *adj.* designed or designated for handicapped people. ♦ *Dave received a ticket for parking in a handicapped parking space.* ♦ *The college built handicapped ramps so that all buildings were accessible to all students.* **4. the handicapped** *n.* people who are ①. (No plural form in this sense. Treated as plural.) ♦ *These doors are designed to accommodate the handicapped.* ♦ *The handicapped can get into all the buildings on campus.*

handicraft ['hæn di kræft] **1.** *n.* a craft or skill that is done with the hands. (No plural form in this sense.) ♦ *Quilting is a popular handicraft.* ♦ *John taught the handicraft of woodcarving to his children.* **2.** *n.* an item made by hand. ♦ *John sells his wooden handicrafts at local fairs.* ♦ *The most popular handicrafts in this store are the quilts.*

handiwork ['hæn di wɚk] **1.** *n.* something that is made by using the hands instead of machines. (No plural form in this sense.) ♦ *Although each item takes hours to complete, Jane is proud of her handiwork.* ♦ *This crocheted skirt is an example of my handiwork.* **2.** *n.* the product of someone's skills and efforts whether machines are involved or not. (Figurative on ①. No plural form in this sense.) ♦ *The new company organization is the handiwork of the president.* ♦ *The oak bookcases are the handiwork of a local carpenter.*

handkerchief ['hæŋk ɚ tʃɪf] *n.* a square of soft fabric used to wipe one's nose or face. ♦ *Throughout the sad movie, I dabbed my eyes with a handkerchief.* ♦ *Bob blew his nose into his handkerchief.*

handle ['hæn dəl] **1.** *n.* the part of an object that is held onto so that the object can be used, moved, picked up, pushed, pulled, opened, or closed. ♦ *I grabbed the handle of the pan and moved it from the burner.* ♦ *I gripped the comb's handle tightly and brushed my hair.* **2.** *tv.* to feel someone or something with one's hands; to use one's hands on someone or something. ♦ *Please be careful when you handle the fragile vases.* ♦ *The book was damaged by readers who had handled it with dirty hands.* **3.** *tv.* to deal with or be able to deal with a situation; to have control over a situation. ♦ *Susan handled the contract negotiations.* ♦ *I'm under so much pressure that I can't handle it anymore.* **4.** *iv.* [for something] to work in a certain way as the result of being used; [for a vehicle or boat] to be controllable. ♦ *The large truck handles well on the freeway.* ♦ *My little car does not handle well in the snow.* **5. fly off the handle** *idiom* to lose one's temper. ♦ *Every time anyone mentions taxes, Mrs. Brown flies off the handle.* ♦ *If she keeps flying off the handle like that, she'll have a heart attack.* **6. have a handle on something, get a handle on something** *idiom* to have or get control of something; to have or get an understanding of something ♦ *Get a handle on your temper and calm down.* ♦ *The police chief had a handle on the potential riot situation.*

handlebar ['hæn dəl bɑr] *n.* the curved metal tube by which one steers a bicycle or motorcycle. (Usually plural.) ♦ *Bob usually rode his bike with only one hand on the handlebars.* ♦ *Anne attached an air horn to her left handlebar.*

handmade ['hænd 'med] *adj.* made by hand, one at a time; not made by a machine. ♦ *I prefer handmade gifts to things bought from a store.* ♦ *Hundreds of handmade objects were sold at the county fair.*

hand-me-down ['hænd mi dɑʊn] *n.* a worn or used piece of clothing or other item that is passed down from person to person. ♦ *As the youngest child in the family, Tom wore a lot of hand-me-downs.* ♦ *Mary hated to wear hand-me-downs because they were always out of style.*

handout ['hænd ɑʊt] **1.** *n.* something that is given to someone for free, especially money, food, or clothing, as an act of charity. ♦ *Dave felt that too many people who could work were getting free handouts.* ♦ *I don't want any handouts; I can buy what I need.* **2.** *n.* a flier, leaflet, or other information that is passed out to people. ♦ *Just before an election, politicians are always passing out handouts.* ♦ *The new store advertised by passing out handouts on the sidewalk.*

handpick ['hænd 'pɪk] *tv.* to carefully choose someone or something for a specific purpose. ♦ *I've personally handpicked Anne as my successor.* ♦ *Powerful business owners tried to handpick the next mayor.*

handpicked ['hænd 'pɪkt] **1.** *adj.* [of fruit, etc.] picked carefully by hand. ♦ *The handpicked strawberries were red and tasty.* ♦ *There were very few bruises on the handpicked apples.* **2.** *adj.* chosen carefully; selected personally with great care. (Figurative on ①.) ♦ *I enjoyed receiving my friend's handpicked gift.* ♦ *John is the boss's handpicked successor.*

handrail ['hænd rel] *n.* a railing mounted to a wall or alongside a staircase that can be held for support. ♦ *Mary held on to the handrail so she wouldn't fall down the stairs.* ♦ *Without the handrail, the steep staircase would be dangerous.*

handshake ['hænd ʃek] **1.** *n.* holding and shaking someone's hand, used as a polite way of greeting someone. ♦ *Tom angrily refused his enemy's handshake.* ♦ *The photographer took a picture of the handshake between the two presidents.* **2.** *n.* ① signifying an agreement. ♦ *A handshake was as good as a contract between the old business associates.* ♦ *We sealed our deal with a handshake.*

handsome ['hænd səm] **1.** *adj.* very attractive; [of a male] very good-looking. (Adv: *handsomely.* Comp: *handsomer;* sup: *handsomest.*) ♦ *The handsome young man went out on dates every weekend.* ♦ *The handsome model was used in several advertising campaigns.* **2.** *adj.* ample; generous; more than enough. (Adv: *handsomely.* Comp: *handsomer;* sup: *handsomest.*) ♦ *Bob's aunt left him a handsome amount of money in her will.* ♦ *The antique chair brought a handsome price at the auction.*

handspring ['hænd sprɪŋ] *n.* an acrobatic movement where someone stands, flips forward or backward into a handstand, and then flips back to a standing position. ♦ *Whenever I try to do a handspring, I land flat on my back.* ♦ *The crowd applauded when the gymnast completed five handsprings in a row.*

handstand ['hænd stænd] *n.* an acrobatic movement where one is upside down, using one's hands alone for support. ♦ *Handstands give me headaches.* ♦ *Bob's feet waved in the air as he tried to hold the handstand for three minutes.*

handwork ['hænd wɚk] *n.* something that is made by using the hands instead of machines. (No plural form in this sense.) ♦ *The stitching on that tablecloth is intricate handwork requiring many hours of patience.* ♦ *The quilt's detailed handwork was done by three of my friends.*

handwriting ['hænd rɑɪt ɪŋ] **1.** *n.* writing done by hand with a pen or pencil instead of with a typewriter or computer. (No plural form in this sense.) ♦ *The handwriting on the note had faded over time.* ♦ *The old contract was written in handwriting.* **2.** *n.* one's own style of writing; a sample of one's own handwriting. (No plural form in this sense.) ♦ *Tom's handwriting isn't legible.* ♦ *I can recognize Sue's handwriting because she makes her capital T's in a distinctive way.*

handwritten ['hænd 'rɪt n] *adj.* written by hand; not written with a typewriter or computer. ♦ *The handwritten note was difficult to read.* ♦ *I prefer handwritten letters to typed ones.*

handy ['hæn di] **1.** *adj.* [of something] easy to use or convenient. (Adv: *handily.* Comp: *handier;* sup: *handiest.*) ♦ *Scissors are a handy tool to have in the kitchen.* ♦ *Our neighbors used the handy shortcut across our backyard to the park.* **2.** *adj.* [of someone] skilled or good with one's hands. (Adv: *handily.* Comp: *handier;* sup: *handiest.*) ♦ *The handy carpenter was always in demand.* ♦ *Mary is very handy with a screwdriver.*

handyman ['hæn di mæn] *n., irreg.* someone who is good at repairing things around the house; someone who is hired to do odd jobs. (Pl: handymen.) ♦ *The rental agency hired a handyman to maintain its apartments.* ♦ *The handyman fixed the electrical outlet.*

handymen ['hæn di mɛn] pl of handyman.

hang ['hæŋ] **1.** *tv., irreg.* to suspend something from a higher place, using a rope, chain, etc. (Pt/pp: hung.) ♦ *We will hang the swing from the tree branch.* ♦ *Mary decided to hang the flowers on the lamppost.* **2.** *tv., irreg.* to attach something to a wall. ♦ *Tom hung a mirror over the mantel.* ♦ *I hung the pictures after the new coat of paint had dried.* **3.** *tv., irreg.* to put a door or window on hinges so that it can swing back and forth. ♦ *The carpenter will hang the new back door.* ♦ *Bill hung the door and then tested it by swinging it open and shut.* **4.** *tv.* to execute someone by strangulation caused by hanging as in ①. (Pt/pp: *hanged* for this sense.) ♦ *A scaffold was built to hang the thief.* ♦ *The prisoner was hanged at midnight.* **5.** *iv., irreg.* to be suspended over something; to hover; to remain above someplace. ♦ *A light bulb hangs over my desk.* ♦ *The flag hung over our front window.* **6. hang (around); hang (out)** *iv., irreg. (+ adv.)* to waste time somewhere; to loiter. ♦ *The kids hung around and did nothing during the summer.* ♦ *During lunch, I hung out around the office and talked with colleagues.* **7. get the hang of something** *idiom* to learn how to do something; to learn how something works. ♦ *As soon as I get the hang of this computer, I'll be able to work faster.* ♦ *Now that I have the hang of starting the car in cold weather, I won't have to get up so early.* **8. hang fire** *idiom* to delay or wait; to be delayed. ♦ *I think we should hang fire and wait for other information.* ♦ *Our plans have to hang fire until we get planning permission.* **9. have something hanging over one's head** *idiom* to have something bothering or worrying one; to have a deadline worrying one. ♦ *I keep worrying about getting drafted. I hate to have something like that hanging over my head.* ♦ *I have a history paper that is hanging over my head.* **10. leave someone or something hanging in midair** *idiom* to suspend dealing with someone or something; to leave someone or something waiting to be finished or continued. (Also used literally.) ♦ *She left her sentence hanging in midair.* ♦ *Tell me the rest of the story. Don't leave me hanging in midair.*

hangar ['hæŋ ɚ] *n.* a large building where airplanes are stored and serviced. ♦ *The plane taxied toward the hangar.* ♦ *The damaged plane was taken to the nearest hangar for repairs.*

hanger ['hæŋ ɚ] *n.* a wooden, metal, or plastic frame for suspending clothing inside a closet. ♦ *I put the heavy fur coat on a sturdy metal hanger.* ♦ *Bob put his suit on the hanger and hung it in the closet.*

hanging ['hæŋ ɪŋ] **1.** *adj.* suspended from above; not supported from below. ♦ *The dining room was lit by a hanging chandelier.* ♦ *The hanging birdhouse rocked in the gentle breeze.* **2.** *n.* the act of killing or executing by suspending someone's body with a rope tied around the neck. ♦ *The executioner prepared the noose prior to the hanging.* ♦ *The judge set the hanging for the following week.* **3.** *n.* something that is hung on a wall, such as a tapestry or drapery. ♦ *To decorate the room, Dave used a wall hanging made of blue velvet.* ♦ *There were several expensive hangings in the conference room.*

hangnail ['hæŋ nel] *n.* a piece of skin that is ripped back from the side of a fingernail. ♦ *Don't bite your hangnails. They'll get worse.* ♦ *The manicurist put a small bandage on my hangnail.*

hangover ['hæŋ ov ɚ] *n.* the headache and sick feeling that is felt the morning after one has drunk too much alcohol. (The adjective form is **hungover**.) ♦ *After the all-night party, Tom had a terrible hangover.* ♦ *You can avoid a hangover if you don't drink to excess.*

hang-up ['hæŋ əp] **1.** *n.* a mental problem or obsession. (Informal.) ♦ *Mary has a hang-up about dirt and is always cleaning her apartment.* ♦ *Bob has a hang-up about planes and refuses to fly anywhere.* **2.** *n.* an incomplete phone call where the caller hangs up as soon as the person being called answers or as soon as an answering machine answers. (Informal.) ♦ *After receiving numerous hang-ups, Mary changed her phone number.* ♦ *There were two messages on my answering machine, but they were both hang-ups, so I don't know who called.*

hankie ['hæŋ ki] *n.* a handkerchief. ♦ *The queen waved her hankie at the crowd.* ♦ *I blew my nose into my hankie.*

Hanukkah AND **Chanukah** ['hɑn ə kə, 'tʃɑn ə kə] *n.* an eight-day Jewish festival celebrated in December, commemorating the rededication of the Temple at Jerusalem in 165 B.C. ♦ *David received a small present every night of Hanukkah.* ♦ *The whole family gathered to celebrate the first night of Hanukkah.*

haphazard ['hæp 'hæz ɚd] *adj.* random; without being planned. (Adv: *haphazardly.*) ♦ *The last-minute, haphazard vacation turned out to be a disaster because all the hotels were booked.* ♦ *Haphazard preparation leads to unpredictable results.*

hapless ['hæp ləs] *adj.* unlucky; unfortunate. (Adv: *haplessly.*) ♦ *The hapless child dropped the ice-cream cone onto the ground.* ♦ *The hapless traveler discovered that his flight had been canceled.*

happen ['hæp ən] **1.** *iv.* to occur; to take place. ♦ *We know what happens when you drop an egg. Yes, a mess.* ♦ *Accidents happen, but you should do your best to avoid them.* **2. happen to** *iv. + inf.* to have the good fortune to do something. ♦ *Bob happened to find the antique at the fair and bought it immediately.* ♦ *Did you happen to see the shooting star?* **3. happen to** *iv. + prep. phr.* to be done to someone or something; to be experienced by someone or something. ♦ *Nothing exciting ever happens to people who live around here.* ♦ *You won't believe what happened to me at the parade!*

happening ['hæp ə nɪŋ] *n.* an event; something that happens. ♦ *The canceling of the concert was an unfortunate happening.* ♦ *The students said the party was the biggest happening of the semester.*

happenstance ['hæp ən stæns] *n.* something that happens by chance. (No plural form in this sense.) ♦ *Sitting next to the senator on the plane was an interesting happenstance.* ♦ *Being stuck in an elevator was an unfortunate happenstance.*

happily ['hæp ə li] *adv.* fortunately; beneficially. ♦ *Happily, everyone was rescued from the fire.* ♦ *Happily, Mary found her keys after she had lost them.*

happiness ['hæp i nəs] *n.* being happy; gladness. (No plural form in this sense.) ♦ *The happiness of my family is very important to me.* ♦ *The wedding filled the guests with happiness.*

happy ['hæp i] **1.** *adj.* [of someone or a creature] feeling or showing joy or in a good mood; [of someone] glad, pleased, or willing. (Adv: *happily.* Comp: *happier;* sup: *happiest.*) ♦ *The happy children laughed as they played with the toys.* ♦ *I am happy to accept your kind invitation.* **2.** *adj.* causing joy; joyful. (Adv: *happily.* Comp: *happier;* sup: *happiest.*) ♦ *An anniversary is a happy occasion.* ♦ *By a happy coincidence, Bob and I were passengers on the same flight.*

happy-go-lucky ['hæp i go 'lʌk i] *adj.* without any troubles; carefree. ♦ *The happy-go-lucky child skipped to the park.* ♦ *Paul appears to be happy-go-lucky, but he really worries a lot.*

harass [hə 'ræs, 'hɛr əs] *tv.* to annoy someone again and again; to continue to bother someone. ♦ *Someone was harassing me with telephone calls, so I changed my phone number.* ♦ *I harassed my boss until I got a raise.*

harassment [hə 'ræs mənt] *n.* harassing, taunting, teasing, or bothering someone. (No plural form in this sense.) ♦ *The children's harassment of the new student was mean.* ♦ *The company issued guidelines to prevent any kind of harassment in the workplace.*

harbor ['hɑr bɚ] **1.** *n.* a sheltered port where ships and boats can anchor safely. ♦ *The tugboat guided the ship into the harbor.* ♦ *The harbor was full, so the ship anchored farther out into the lake.* **2.** *tv.* to keep something in one's mind, especially resentment or a grudge. ♦ *Bob has harbored a grudge against George ever since George sold him a worthless car.* ♦ *The bully harbored a plan for revenge against the teacher who punished him.*

hard ['hɑrd] **1.** *adj.* firm; solid; not soft. (Comp: *harder;* sup: *hardest.*) ♦ *The plants wouldn't grow in the hard ground.* ♦ *I couldn't open the pecan's hard shell with my fingers.* **2.** *adj.* difficult; not easy to do. (Comp: *harder;* sup: *hardest.*) ♦ *Few students were able to solve the hard math problem.* ♦ *It's hard to swim against the current.* **3.** *adj.* severe; harsh; not lenient; demanding. (Comp: *harder;* sup: *hardest.*) ♦ *Losing both parents was a hard experience for Jimmy.* ♦ *Why are you such a hard judge of other people?* **4.** *adj.* forceful; violent; not light. (Comp: *harder;* sup: *hardest.*) ♦ *We could hear the hard rain pounding on the roof.* ♦ *The guard was knocked unconscious by a hard blow to the head.* **5.** *adj.* [of water] having a high mineral content. (Comp: *harder;* sup: *hardest.*) ♦ *The hard water had a bitter taste.* ♦ *This filter removes many of the minerals from our hard water.* **6.** *adj.* [of drinks, except for beer and wine] having high alcohol content. (Comp: *harder;* sup: *hardest.*) ♦ *Whiskey is a type of hard liquor.* ♦ *The drinks at the reception included beer and hard liquor.* **7.** *adj.* [of drugs] very addictive. (Comp: *harder;* sup: *hardest.*) ♦ *Bob has sold almost everything he owns to buy hard drugs.* ♦ *Heroin is a hard drug.* **8.** *adj.* [of a letter] pronounced as a stop. ♦ *A hard* c *is pronounced like the* c *in* call. *A soft* c *has the sound of an* s. ♦ *The first* g *in* garage *is hard, and the second* g *is not.* **9.** *adv.* with strong energy; with great force. (Comp: *harder;* sup: *hardest.*) ♦ *The wind blows hard during a blizzard.* ♦ *The laborers worked hard to complete the project before winter.* **10.** *adv.* slowly; unwillingly. (Comp: *harder;* sup: *hardest.*) ♦ *Old habits die hard.* ♦ *The team took the defeat very hard.* **11. hard of hearing** *idiom* [of someone] unable to hear well or partially deaf. ♦ *Please speak loudly. I am hard of hearing.* ♦ *Tom is hard of hearing, but is not totally deaf.*

hard-boiled ['hɑrd 'bɔɪld] **1.** *adj.* [of an egg] boiled until the yolk and the white have become solid. ♦ *The customer ordered a hard-boiled egg and toast.* ♦ *I peeled the shell from the hard-boiled egg.* **2.** *adj.* tough; not affected by emotion or feeling. (Informal.) ♦ *The hard-boiled teacher had heard every excuse imaginable.* ♦ *John's excuse did not impress the hard-boiled police officer, who issued him a speeding ticket anyway.*

hard disk (drive) ['hɑrd 'dɪsk ('drɑɪv)] *n.* a storage device inside a computer that spins very fast and contains a lot of information in digital form. ♦ *My hard disk drive won't hold all my computer files.* ♦ *A new hard disk only costs a few hundred dollars.*

harden ['hɑrd n] **1.** *tv.* to cause something to become hard, rigid, solid, or firm. ♦ *Heat hardened the iron and made it strong.* ♦ *Baking clay in a special oven will harden it.* **2.** *iv.* to become hard, rigid, solid, or firm. ♦ *As the candy cools, it will harden.* ♦ *The plaster will harden in a few minutes.* **3.** *iv.* to become unemotional or uncaring about someone or something; to become hostile to someone or something. (Figurative on ②.) ♦ *Listening to the student's excuse, the teacher's face hardened.* ♦ *After dozens of letters begging for money, Lisa hardened to the charity's pleas.*

hardened ['hɑrd nd] **1.** *adj.* made hard, rigid, solid, or firm. ♦ *The hardened glue could not be removed from the top of the table.* ♦ *The hardened bread had sat out all night and gotten stale.* **2.** *adj.* unemotional; not easily influenced. (Figurative on ①.) ♦ *The hardened criminal's way of life could not be changed.* ♦ *From the hardened look on John's face, I'd guess that something is wrong.*

hardheaded ['hɑrd 'hɛd ɪd] *adj.* stubborn; not likely to give in. (Adv: *hardheadedly.*) ♦ *The hardheaded toddler kept trying to climb out of the crib.* ♦ *It's very difficult to try to reason with hardheaded people.*

hard-hearted ['hɑrd 'hɑrt ɪd] *adj.* cruel; unfeeling; unkind. (Adv: *hard-heartedly.*) ♦ *The hard-hearted driver did not stop to help the people in the accident.* ♦ *The hard-hearted crowd booed the politician.*

hardly ['hɑrd li] *adv.* barely; almost not at all. ♦ *With her sore throat, Mary could hardly talk.* ♦ *There was hardly enough food for everyone at the party, so I ordered some pizza.*

hardness ['hɑrd nəs] *n.* firmness; solidness. (No plural form in this sense.) ♦ *The students tested the hardness of the minerals.* ♦ *The more I exercised, the more the hardness of my muscles increased.*

hard-nosed ['hɑrd nozd] *adj.* shrewd; stubborn. ♦ *The hard-nosed reporter asked the mayor questions about the scandal.* ♦ *Bob was promoted for negotiating the hard-nosed business deal.*

hardship ['hɑrd ʃɪp] *n.* a great difficulty; something that makes life difficult; something that causes suffering. ♦ *I experienced many hardships when I was lost in the forest.* ♦ *Losing my job was a horrible hardship on me and my family.*

hard-up ['hɑrd əp] *adj.* poor; needy; destitute. (Informal.) ♦ *I didn't get paid this week so I am a little hard-up for money.* ♦ *A free clinic was opened to help hard-up people.*

hardware ['hɑrd wɛr] **1.** *n.* tools, nails, screws, door handles, electrical supplies, brackets, buckets, utensils, and similar things used in building and maintenance. (No plural form in this sense.) ♦ *I need some new hardware for this door. The old knobs and hinges are getting rusty.* ♦ *Locks, screws, and nails are examples of hardware.* **2.** *n.* heavy military equipment and weapons, as opposed to human soldiers. (No plural form in this sense.) ♦ *The navy purchased some new hardware, including forty battleships.* ♦ *Guns, tanks, and aircraft are types of military hardware.* **3.** *n.* computer equipment; the machinery of a computer, as opposed to software programs. (No plural form in this sense.) ♦ *Computer hardware includes the monitor and the printer.* ♦ *Three years after Mary bought it, her hardware was outdated.*

hardwood ['hɑrd wʊd] **1.** *n.* dense and compact wood from various trees, such as maple, oak, or walnut. (No plural form in this sense.) ♦ *Hardwood is excellent for flooring.* ♦ *The expensive dining-room furniture is made of hardwood.* **2. hardwoods** *n.* kinds of ①. ♦ *Oak and walnut are hardwoods.* ♦ *Our furniture is made from various hardwoods.* **3.** *adj.* made of ①. ♦ *The walls in the den were covered with hardwood paneling.* ♦ *Bill pulled up the ugly carpet and found beautiful hardwood floors underneath.*

hardworking ['hɑrd 'wɚk ɪŋ] *adj.* diligent; working hard. (Adv: *hardworkingly.*) ♦ *The hardworking employee was quickly promoted.* ♦ *The teacher praised the hardworking student.*

hardy ['hɑrd i] **1.** *adj.* robust; able to live under difficult conditions. (Adv: *hardily.* Comp: *hardier;* sup: *hardiest.*) ♦ *The hardy cattle survived the long journey on the trail.* ♦ *Our country was settled by hardy pioneers.* **2.** *adj.* [of a plant] able to survive a severe winter freeze. (Adv: *hardily.* Comp: *hardier;* sup: *hardiest.*) ♦ *These hardy plants will live through the winter.* ♦ *An evergreen is a hardy tree.*

hare ['he ɚ] *n.* an animal, such as the jackrabbit, that is very similar to a rabbit, but larger. ♦ *Some hares crept into my garden and ate the carrots.* ♦ *Hares have longer ears and hind legs than rabbits.*

harebrained ['he ɚ brend] *adj.* stupid; idiotic; foolish. ♦ *The company lost thousands of dollars on the harebrained scheme.* ♦ *Do you have any idea how dangerous your harebrained plan is?*

harem ['he ɚ əm] *n.* the part of a Muslim palace or household where the women live. ♦ *A large part of the palace was a guarded harem.* ♦ *The ruler's wives and children lived in a luxurious harem.*

harm ['hɑrm] **1.** *n.* mental or physical damage to someone or something. (No plural form in this sense.) ♦ *The storm caused great harm to the house.* ♦ *Losing my job caused a lot of harm to my sense of worth.* **2.** *tv.* to damage someone or something. ♦ *Five people were harmed in the accident.* ♦ *The hurricane harmed nearly every house in the coastal town.*

harmful ['hɑrm fʊl] *adj.* causing damage or harm to someone or something. (Adv: *harmfully.*) ♦ *The harmful product was withdrawn from all stores.* ♦ *The harmful rodents were trapped and destroyed.*

harmless ['hɑrm ləs] *adj.* not causing damage or harm. (Adv: *harmlessly.*) ♦ *That harmless dog won't bite anyone.* ♦ *The harmless storm passed by quickly.*

harmonica [hɑr 'mɑn ɪ kə] *n.* a small musical reed instrument, played by blowing air into or sucking air from the small chambers that contain the sound-producing reeds. ♦ *Harmonicas are popular because they are easy to carry.* ♦ *The child pulled out the harmonica and began to play a song.*

harmonious [hɑr 'mon i əs] **1.** *adj.* [of sounds] having pitches that sound good together. (Adv: *harmoniously.*) ♦ *The music was harmonious and pleasant to listen to.* ♦ *The harmonious music of the choir entertained us for an hour.* **2.** *adj.* peaceable; agreeable. (Adv: *harmoniously.*) ♦ *Management and employees tried to settle their differences during a harmonious meeting.* ♦ *The harmonious evening was interrupted by the quarrel.*

harmonize ['hɑr mə nɑɪz] **1. harmonize (with)** *iv.* (+ *prep. phr.*) to sing in harmony with other singers; [for a sound] to be in harmony with other sounds. ♦ *Our singing group harmonizes quite nicely.* ♦ *The flute and the oboe did not harmonize well.* **2. harmonize (with)** *iv.* (+ *prep. phr.*) [for colors or other qualities] to blend. (Figurative on ①.) ♦ *The colors do not harmonize with each other.* ♦ *This deep yellow does not harmonize with that shade of blue.*

harmony ['hɑr mən i] **1.** *n.* the effect of different musical notes that are played or sung together in tune. (No plural form in this sense.) ♦ *One of the singers couldn't stay in the right pitch and that ruined the harmony.* ♦ *The barbershop quartet blended their voices into perfect harmony.* **2.** *n.* agreement; accord; peace. (No plural form in this sense. Figurative on ①.) ♦ *The harmony between the countries was shattered by the terrorist's bomb.* ♦ *I lived in harmony with six friends in a large house.*

harness ['hɑr nəs] **1.** *n.* a set of straps that is placed on a horse so that it can pull a cart or a carriage. ♦ *Bill put the harness on the horse and led it out to the carriage.* ♦ *The farmer stored the horses' harnesses in the barn.* **2.** *n.* a set of straps used to attach something, such as a parachute, to someone's body. ♦ *Jane carefully checked the parachute's harness before jumping from the plane.* ♦ *Bill used a harness to pull the sled through the snow.* **3.** *tv.* to put ① on a horse. ♦ *Tell the servants to harness the horses! We must leave now.* ♦ *The child wasn't tall enough to harness the horse.* **4.** *tv.* to use a natural source of energy to produce power. (Figurative on ③.) ♦ *A windmill harnesses the energy of the wind.* ♦ *The engineers wanted to find a way to harness the river's power.*

harp ['hɑrp] **1.** *n.* a musical instrument having strings attached to a frame of wood. ♦ *Mary plucked the harp and made a beautiful tinkling sound.* ♦ *The musician's hands glided over the harp's strings.* **2. harp on** *iv.* + *prep. phr.* to keep talking about something until everyone is tired of hearing about it. (Informal.) ♦ *Please stop harping on this subject!* ♦ *All you do is harp on how dirty my room is.*

harpoon [hɑr 'pun] **1.** *n.* a large spear, attached to a rope, that is thrown or shot into a water-dwelling creature, such as a whale or large fish. ♦ *The harpoon just missed the whale.* ♦ *John thrust his harpoon into the side of the boat by accident.* **2.** *tv.* to spear and capture a water-dwelling creature with ①. ♦ *The fisherman harpooned the shark.* ♦ *Ten sailors tried to harpoon the whale.*

harpsichord ['hɑrp sɪ kord] *n.* a keyboard instrument whose strings are plucked rather than struck by hammers as in a piano. ♦ *A harpsichord must be tuned frequently.* ♦ *Many pieces of classical music were written for the harpsichord.*

harrowing ['hɛr o ɪŋ] *adj.* distressing; very upsetting. (Adv: *harrowingly.*) ♦ *After the harrowing accident, Mary refused to drive for months.* ♦ *After hearing the harrowing story about the escaped criminal, I locked all the doors and windows of my house.*

harsh ['hɑrʃ] **1.** *adj.* rough; unpleasant to look at, listen to, touch, taste, or smell. (Adv: *harshly.* Comp: *harsher;* sup: *harshest.*) ♦ *The harsh towel irritated my skin.* ♦ *The harsh colors of the wallpaper hurt my eyes.* **2.** *adj.* mean; cruel; severe. (Adv: *harshly.* Comp: *harsher;* sup: *harsh-*

est.) ♦ *The student protested the harsh punishment.* ♦ *The judge gave the criminal a harsh sentence.*

harvest ['hɑr vəst] **1.** *n.* the gathering of a crop of grain, fiber, fruit, vegetables, or the like. ♦ *The farmer's children stayed home from school to help with the harvest.* ♦ *The harvest was bountiful because we had good weather during the summer.* **2.** *n.* the total amount of grain, fiber, fruit, or vegetables produced by a given crop for a specific area. ♦ *The entire corn harvest was lost because of the rains.* ♦ *The farmers were pleased with the record wheat harvest.* **3.** *tv.* to collect a crop of grain, fiber, fruit, or vegetables when it is ready. ♦ *The workers harvested the apples.* ♦ *The cotton crop was so large that dozens of people were needed to harvest it.*

has ['hæz] **1.** *tv.* <the present-tense form of have used for the third-person singular, that is, with *he, she, it,* and singular nouns.> ♦ *Bill has a new car.* ♦ *The house has a red roof.* **2.** *aux.* <the present-tense form of have ⑥ used for the third-person singular, that is, with *he, she, it,* and singular nouns, in forming the present perfect tense.> (Used before the past participle of a verb. Reduced to *'s* in contractions.) ♦ *Bill has put the toys away.* ♦ *Where has Mary gone?*

has-been ['hæz bɪn] **1.** *n.* someone who used to be popular or successful. ♦ *The cast of the play was a few unknowns and an aging has-been.* ♦ *Bill was a popular singer in the 1960s, but now he is just a has-been.* **2.** *adj.* <the adj. use of ①.> ♦ *No one recognized the has-been rock star.* ♦ *The has-been actor had been famous twenty years ago.*

hash ['hæʃ] **1.** *n.* a dish of leftover meat, cut up into pieces and cooked again with something else, such as potatoes, vegetables, etc. (No plural form in this sense.) ♦ *The hash contained last night's chicken and fresh vegetables from the garden.* ♦ *I saved money by making hash for dinner.* **2.** *n.* a mixture of things. (Figurative on ①. No plural form in this sense.) ♦ *We don't have a particular style of furniture in our house, just a hash of many styles.* ♦ *Mary likes variety; her art collection is a hash of paintings, sculptures, and textiles.*

hasn't ['hæz ənt] *cont.* "has not." ♦ *Bob hasn't come home from work yet.* ♦ *Mary hasn't done her homework yet because she's been at softball practice.*

hassle ['hæs əl] **1.** *n.* trouble; a bother; an annoyance. ♦ *The student thought school was a hassle.* ♦ *Bob didn't want the hassle of commuting to work, so he took a job close to his home.* **2.** *n.* an argument; a fight; a dispute. ♦ *A hassle broke out when the children could not agree on which game to play.* ♦ *During the sale, there was a hassle between two customers who wanted the same item.* **3.** *tv.* to cause someone or something trouble. (Informal.) ♦ *The little boy hassled his parents until they bought the new bike.* ♦ *The obnoxious customer hassled the clerk for ten minutes.*

hassock ['hæs ək] *n.* a cushioned footstool. ♦ *Anne put her sore foot on a hassock while she watched TV.* ♦ *There were not enough chairs in the room, so Bob sat on the hassock.*

haste ['hest] *n.* speed; hurry. (No plural form in this sense.) ♦ *With great haste, I marched through the station toward my train.* ♦ *In her haste, Mary forgot to lock the door.*

hasten ['hes ən] **1.** *tv.* to cause someone or something to hurry; to cause something to happen sooner. ♦ *The researchers are working furiously to hasten the day when a cure for cancer will be found.* ♦ *Watching the dark clouds form, the teacher hastened the children inside.* **2. hasten to** *tv.* + *inf.* to hurry to do something. ♦ *Susan hastened to explain why she was late.* ♦ *I must hasten to apologize for my messy office.*

hasty ['he sti] **1.** *adj.* quick; speedy. (Adv: *hastily.* Comp: *hastier;* sup: *hastiest.*) ♦ *The doctor made a hasty diagnosis and immediately sent the patient to the hospital.* ♦ *I made a hasty trip to the store to buy some food before the party.* **2.** *adj.* carelessly fast; without proper thought. (Adv: *hastily.* Comp: *hastier;* sup: *hastiest.*) ♦ *I am afraid that I acted in a hasty manner, and I am sorry.* ♦ *The hasty decision ended up costing the company extra money.*

hat ['hæt] **1.** *n.* an article of clothing shaped so as to cover the head. ♦ *To keep his head warm, John wore a hat.* ♦ *Please take your hat off when you're indoors.* **2. at the drop of a hat** *idiom* immediately and without urging. ♦ *John was always ready to go fishing at the drop of a hat.* ♦ *If you need help, just call on me. I can come at the drop of a hat.* **3. be old hat** *idiom* to be old-fashioned; to be outmoded. ♦ *That's a silly idea. It's old hat.* ♦ *Nobody does that anymore. That's just old hat.* **4. eat one's hat** *idiom* a phrase telling the kind of thing that one would do if a very unlikely event really happens. ♦ *If we get there on time, I'll eat my hat.* ♦ *He said he'd eat his hat if she got elected.* **5. hang one's hat (up) somewhere** *idiom* to take up residence somewhere. ♦ *George loves Dallas. He's decided to buy a house and hang his hat up there.* ♦ *Bill moves from place to place and never hangs his hat anywhere.* **6. keep something under one's hat** *idiom* to keep something a secret; to keep something in one's mind (only). ♦ *Keep this under your hat, but I'm looking for a new job.* ♦ *I'm getting married, but keep it under your hat.* **7. pass the hat** *idiom* to attempt to collect money for some charitable project. ♦ *Bob is passing the hat to collect money to buy flowers for Anne.* ♦ *He's always passing the hat for something.* **8. pull something out of a hat** *idiom* to produce something as if by magic. ♦ *This is a serious problem, and we just can't pull a solution out of a hat.* ♦ *I'm sorry, but I don't have a pen. What do you want me to do, pull one out of a hat?* **9. talk through one's hat** *idiom* to talk nonsense; to brag and boast. ♦ *John isn't really as good as he says. He's just talking through his hat.* ♦ *Stop talking through your hat and start being sincere!* **10. toss one's hat into the ring** *idiom* to state that one is running for an elective office. ♦ *Jane wanted to run for treasurer, so she tossed her hat into the ring.* ♦ *The mayor never tossed his hat into the ring. Instead he announced his retirement.* **11. wear more than one hat** *idiom* to have more than one set of responsibilities; to hold more than one office. ♦ *The mayor is also the police chief. She wears more than one hat.* ♦ *I have too much to do to wear more than one hat.*

hatch ['hætʃ] **1.** *n.* an opening in a wall, ceiling, or floor. ♦ *Access to the attic is made through a hatch in the ceiling of my bedroom.* ♦ *The flight attendant closed and locked the airplane hatch.* **2.** *iv.* [for a baby bird or reptile] to break an eggshell from the inside and come out. ♦ *Four baby chicks hatched this morning.* ♦ *The children watched in awe as the baby robin hatched.* **3.** *tv.* to help or cause a baby animal to break out of an eggshell. ♦ *The heat of the incubator helped hatch the chick.* ♦ *The mother robin hatched her babies by sitting on the eggs.*

hatchback ['hætʃ bæk] **1.** *n.* a car with a sloping back door hinged to the roof. ♦ *John bought a hatchback because he often carries large items.* ♦ *I transported my new chair from the store to my home in my hatchback.* **2.** *n.* the sloping back door of ①. ♦ *Mary unlocked the hatchback, opened it, and placed her packages in the car.* ♦ *Bob left the hatchback open so that the long pieces of wood would fit in the car.*

hatchery ['hætʃ ə ri] *n.* a place of business where eggs are hatched, especially the eggs of fish and fowl. ♦ *Bob worked at a hatchery, making sure that the eggs were kept warm.* ♦ *Anne bought fish for her pond at the hatchery.*

hatchet ['hætʃ ɪt] **1.** *n.* a short axe. ♦ *The hiker carried a hatchet to cut firewood.* ♦ *Bill used a hatchet to cut off the dead tree limb.* **2. bury the hatchet** *idiom* to stop fighting or arguing; to end old resentments. ♦ *All right, you two. Calm down and bury the hatchet.* ♦ *I wish Mr. and Mrs. Franklin would bury the hatchet. They argue all the time.*

hate ['het] **1.** *n.* hatred; intense dislike. (No plural form in this sense.) ♦ *Hate can make people do terrible things.* ♦ *Driven by hate, the mob attacked the foreigner.* **2.** *tv.* to dislike someone or something intensely. ♦ *Bob hates noisy neighbors.* ♦ *Sue hates washing the car.* **3. hate to** *tv.* + *inf.* to strongly dislike doing something; to be averse to doing something. ♦ *David hates to wash the car.* ♦ *I hate to drive in heavy traffic.* **4. pet hate** *idiom* something that is disliked intensely and is a constant or repeated annoyance. ♦ *My pet hate is being put on hold on the telephone.* ♦ *Another pet hate of mine is having to stand in line.*

hateful ['het fʊl] *adj.* worthy of hate; deserving hate; detestable. (Adv: *hatefully.*) ♦ *Spreading cruel rumors about Jane was a hateful thing to do.* ♦ *Greed is a hateful human trait.*

hatred ['he trɪd] *n.* intense dislike; hate. (No plural form in this sense.) ♦ *Mistrust and hatred tore the family apart.* ♦ *I felt intense hatred toward the thief who robbed my house.*

haughty ['hɔt i] *adj.* arrogant; looking down on other people. (Adv: *haughtily.* Comp: *haughtier;* sup: *haughtiest.*) ♦ *Bill's peers despised him because he had a haughty attitude.* ♦ *The haughty woman did not respond when greeted by her servant.*

haul ['hɔl] **1.** *tv.* to carry something using force; to drag something heavy. ♦ *The sled dogs hauled the load into town.* ♦ *We hauled the boxes to the basement.* **2.** *tv.* to carry or bring someone or something by truck or other vehicle. ♦ *The train hauled the mail across the country.* ♦ *The moving truck hauled our furniture to the new house.* **3.** *n.* the time spent traveling from one place to another, especially considering the amount of effort or distance involved. ♦ *The business trip was a long haul of more than 400 miles.* ♦ *Covering the entire distance in one day will be quite a haul.* **4.** *n.* the amount of something gained as the result of negotiation, commerce, or theft. (Informal.) ♦ *The sales department got quite a haul of new orders.* ♦ *The thieves got a huge haul of jewelry from the store.* **5. over the long haul** *idiom* for a relatively long period of time. ♦ *Over the long haul, it might be better to invest in stocks.* ♦ *Over the long haul, everything will turn out all right.* **6. over the short haul** *idiom* for the immediate future. ♦ *Over the short haul, you'd be better off to put your money in the bank.* ♦ *Over the short haul, you may wish you had done something different. But things will work out all right.*

haunt ['hɔnt] **1.** *tv.* [for a ghost or spirit] to remain in a certain place and appear occasionally. ♦ *Do ghosts really haunt that old house?* ♦ *Legends tell us that spirits haunt the graveyard.* **2.** *tv.* [for someone or something annoying or disquieting] to remain in one's thoughts. (Figurative on ①.) ♦ *The car accident haunted Sue for many months.* ♦ *The idea that Bob had forgotten to do something haunted him all day.* **3.** *tv.* to visit a place often; to be in a place for long periods. (Figurative on ①.) ♦ *The café was haunted by students after school.* ♦ *My roommate and I haunted the movie theater for hours every weekend.* **4.** *n.* a place that is visited by a certain person often; a place where someone goes frequently. ♦ *My favorite haunt is the mountains.* ♦ *Trying to find Sue, Bill checked all her frequent haunts.*

haunted ['hɔnt ɪd] *adj.* bothered by a ghost or an evil spirit; frequented by a ghost. ♦ *The children ran past the haunted house on Halloween.* ♦ *I told a scary story about the haunted castle.*

haunting ['hɔnt ɪŋ] *adj.* strange and eerie and always in one's thoughts. (Adv: *hauntingly.*) ♦ *The promotion dispelled the haunting doubts Bob had about his capabilities.* ♦ *Mary hummed the haunting melody over and over.*

have ['hæv] **1.** *tv., irreg.* to own something; to possess something; to possess a quality. (Pt/pp: had; in the present tense, the third-person singular form is has.) ♦ *I have a good car.* ♦ *Bob has a wonderful sense of humor.* **2.** *tv., irreg.* to undergo something; [for something] to happen to oneself; to experience something. ♦ *John had a bad accident.* ♦ *Bill and Jane had an argument.* **3.** *tv., irreg.* to take something; to consume something. ♦ *Have another piece of pie.* ♦ *Make sure you have a glass of milk before you go to bed.* **4.** *tv., irreg.* to cause something to be done. ♦ *Please have these letters mailed before noon.* ♦ *Mary will have the laundry cleaned today.* **5. have to** *iv., irreg.* + *inf.* to be obligated to do something; must do something. ♦ *You have to finish your dinner before you go outside and play.* ♦ *Bill has to do homework tonight.* **6.** *aux.* <an auxiliary verb that is used to form the perfect tenses, which show that an action is completed.> (Used before the past participle of a verb. The form have, which is used with *I, we, you, they,* and plural nouns to form the present perfect and is also the bare verb form, is reduced to *'ve* in contractions. See also had, has.) ♦ *Mary has written to the mayor already.* ♦ *We have visited the zoo twice since June.* **7. have-nots** *n.* people who do not have enough money to live comfortably. ♦ *The have-nots are looking for ways to get ahead.* ♦ *Bob says that there are too few haves and too many have-nots in the world.* **8. haves** *n.* people who have enough assets to live comfortably; people who are rich and privileged. ♦ *There are fewer haves than have-nots in the world.* ♦ *As you can tell by his luxury car, Dave is one of the haves.* **9. have someone over** *idiom* to invite someone as a guest to one's house. ♦ *When can we have Aunt Jane over for dinner?* ♦ *I would love to have you over some time.* **10. have nothing to do with someone or something; [not] have anything to do with someone or something** *idiom* to prefer not to associate or be associated with someone or something. ♦ *I don't like Mike, so I won't have anything to do with the books he writes.* ♦ *Bob has had nothing to do with Mary since she quit her job.* **11. have something to do with something; [not] have anything to do with something; have nothing to do with something.** *idiom* to be associated with or related to something. (The first *something* does not vary.) ♦ *Does your dislike for Sally have something to do with the way she insulted you?* ♦ *My illness has something to do with my lungs.* **12. have to do with something** *idiom* to be associated with or related to something. (Similar to ⑪.) ♦ *Sally's unhappiness has to do with the way you insulted her.* ♦ *My illness has to do with my stomach.*

haven ['hev n] *n.* a safe place; a shelter; a refuge. ♦ *The little cabin was a safe haven from the furious storm.* ♦ *The soldiers sought a haven in the middle of enemy country.*

haven't ['hæv ənt] *cont.* "have not." ♦ *I haven't had time to bake the cake yet.* ♦ *Bob and Jane haven't finished their homework, so they are working on it now.*

havoc ['hæv ək] **1.** *n.* confusion; chaos; disorder. (No plural form in this sense.) ♦ *The unruly children raised havoc at the mall.* ♦ *The blizzard played havoc with the flight schedules at the airport.* **2.** *n.* destruction; ruin. (No plural form in this sense.) ♦ *A tornado created havoc in the small village.* ♦ *The angry mob caused havoc in front of city hall.*

Hawaii [hə 'wɑɪ i, hə 'vɑɪ i] See Gazetteer.

hawk ['hɔk] **1.** *n.* a bird of prey, similar to a falcon, with strong beak and claws, a long tail, and good eyesight. ♦ *The hawk soared over the mountaintop.* ♦ *The hawk caught the mouse in its claws.* **2.** *n.* someone, often a politician, who favors war or a strong military posture. ♦ *The hawks called for military intervention to settle the overseas conflict.* ♦ *Tom must be a hawk because he thinks the military should settle all international disputes.* **3.** *tv.* to sell something, especially in the street; to carry something for sale. ♦ *A vendor stood on the street corner, hawking the daily paper.* ♦ *The children hawked lemonade from a table on the sidewalk.* **4. watch someone or something like a hawk** *idiom* to watch someone or something very carefully. ♦ *The teacher watched the pupils like a hawk to make sure they did not cheat on the exam.* ♦ *We had to watch our dog like a hawk in case he ran away.*

hawker ['hɔk ɚ] *n.* someone who carries around things for sale; a vendor who sells things on the street. ♦ *Hawkers who sell things inside the stadium are required to have a permit.* ♦ *The hawker sold newspapers and magazines from a cart at the street corner.*

hay ['he] *n.* clover or alfalfa that is cut, dried, and used as food for cattle. (No plural form in this sense.) ♦ *Horses and cows eat hay.* ♦ *The farmer stored hay in a barn during the winter.*

hay fever ['he fiv ɚ] *n.* a seasonal allergy to pollen or dust, which causes a runny nose, watery eyes, and sneezing. (No plural form in this sense.) ♦ *Bob's hay fever made him miserable.* ♦ *When there's a lot of pollen in the air, Jane's hay fever worsens.*

hayloft ['he lɔft] *n.* a place in the upper part of a barn where hay is stored. ♦ *Hay is thrown from the hayloft into the animals' stalls.* ♦ *We had to lift the hay into the hayloft.*

haystack ['he stæk] *n.* a large amount of hay that is piled together to dry. ♦ *After the harvest, there were dozens of haystacks in the field.* ♦ *A huge machine turns the haystacks into bales of hay.*

haywire ['he wɑɪr] **1.** *adj.* out of control; not working correctly. (Informal.) ♦ *During the storm, my telephone was haywire.* ♦ *My radio is haywire. I can't hear anything but static.* **2. go haywire** *idiom* to begin to function incorrectly. ♦ *The telephone went haywire during the storm.* ♦ *My radio goes haywire whenever a plane flies overhead.*

hazard ['hæz ɚd] **1.** *n.* the risk of something bad happening. ♦ *A new hazard greeted the hikers at every turn in the path.* ♦ *There are many hazards in mountain climbing.* **2.** *tv.* to risk something; to put something in danger. ♦ *Tom was willing to hazard his life for his child.* ♦ *I will not hazard thousands of dollars on your silly idea.* **3. at hazard** *phr.* risked; in danger; at risk. ♦ *He is not willing to have much of his money at hazard in the stock market.* ♦ *Your entire life is at hazard unless you wear a helmet when you ride your bicycle.* **4. hazard a guess** *idiom* to make a guess. ♦ *Even if you don't know, please hazard a guess.* ♦ *If you don't know the answer, hazard a guess.* **5. hazard an opinion** *idiom* to give an opinion. ♦ *Anne asked the attorney to hazard an opinion about the strength of her lawsuit.* ♦ *Don't feel like you have to hazard an opinion on something you know nothing about.*

hazardous ['hæz ɚ dəs] *adj.* dangerous; risky. (Adv: *hazardously.*) ♦ *There were three car accidents on the hazardous road.* ♦ *The hazardous ride at the carnival was shut down.*

haze ['hez] **1.** *n.* mist; fog; smoke; smog. (No plural form in this sense.) ♦ *The haze was so thick that you couldn't see the top of the mountain.* ♦ *Airplane flights were delayed because of the dense, smoky haze.* **2.** *tv.* to harass and abuse a person as part of the induction to a club or fraternal organization. ♦ *Members of the fraternity hazed their newest members.* ♦ *If you haze anyone in this club, you will be disciplined.* **3. in a haze** *idiom* in a state of confusion. ♦ *After being hit in the head by the bat, Bill was in a haze.* ♦ *After surgery, I was in a haze until the anesthetic wore off.*

hazy ['hez i] **1.** *adj.* not clear; difficult to see through. (Adv: *hazily.* Comp: *hazier;* sup: *haziest.*) ♦ *The hazy view of the mountain became clearer as the fog lifted.* ♦ *The antique mirror reflected hazy images.* **2.** *adj.* vague; unsure. (Figurative on ①. Informal. Adv: *hazily.* Comp: *hazier;* sup: *haziest.*) ♦ *Tom was hazy about the park's location and had to ask for directions.* ♦ *The unprepared treasurer gave a hazy financial report.*

he ['hi] **1.** *pron.* <a third-person singular masculine pronoun.> (Refers to male creatures. Used as a subject of a sentence or a clause.) ♦ *John is tired. He wants to go to bed.* ♦ *My puppy is hungry. He wants to eat.* **2.** *pron.* <a third-person singular pronoun.> (Used when the sex of a grammatical subject is indeterminate, undetermined, or irrelevant. Objected to by some as actually referring only to males in this sense. Compare with ⑤. See also **they** ②.) ♦ *If someone comes in late, he should take his seat quietly.* ♦ *Each runner should get to the finish line as fast as he can.* **3.** *n.* a male. ♦ *Is your new baby a she or a he?* ♦ *The hes outnumber the shes five to one in my office.* **4. he or she** *phr.* [where there is known to be a choice between male and female] either he ① or she ①. ♦ *John and Mary arrived at noon, and either he or she left the door open.* ♦ *Both John and Mary are expecting a telephone call, so when the telephone rings, only he or she should bother to answer it.* **5. he or she** *phr.* <a third-person singular pronoun.> (Used when the sex of a grammatical subject is indeterminate, undetermined, or irrelevant. Also used to assert that both sexes are involved.) ♦ *Each runner should get to the finish line as fast as he or she can.* ♦ *If someone comes in late, he or she should take his or her seat quietly.*

head ['hɛd] **1.** *n.* the part of the body of humans and animals above the neck, including the face, eyes, nose, mouth, ears, brain, and skull. ♦ *The boxer was stunned by a blow to the head.* ♦ *Sue laid her head on her pillow and fell asleep.* **2.** *n.* the brain; the mind. ♦ *My head can't contain all the information from the three-hour lecture.* ♦ *Is it true that two heads are better than one?* **3.** *n.* an individual animal, used especially in counting cows, horses, and sheep. (No plural form in this sense. Always a singular form preceded by words that tell how many.) ♦ *Many head of cattle entered the pasture at once.* ♦ *Fourteen head were led into the corral.* **4.** *n.* the leader of a company, country, organization, group, etc.; a chief; someone who is in charge. ♦ *The head of our company eats in the cafeteria with the employees.* ♦ *Only the head of the organization can make the important decisions.* **5.** *n.* the top, front, or upper parts of things, such as a table, a page, a sheet of paper, a line, or a [school] class. ♦ *Bob arrived first and stood at the head of the line.* ♦ *The host sat at the head of the table.* **6.** *adj.* <the adj. use of ⑤.> primary; chief; foremost. ♦ *The head chef personally tasted all the food served.* ♦ *The ship's captain depended heavily on the head crew member.* **7.** *tv.* to lead a group of people or a meeting; to conduct a meeting; to be in charge of a group of people or part of a company. ♦ *Who will head the meeting?* ♦ *Jane was chosen to head the committee after Bill retired.* **8.** *iv.* to move in a certain direction. ♦ *After the movie, we headed toward the exit.* ♦ *At closing time, the shoppers headed out of the store.* **9. a head; per head** *phr.* a person; an individual. ♦ *How much do you charge per head for dinner?* ♦ *It costs four dollars a head.* **10. bring something to a head** *idiom* to cause something to come to the point when a decision has to be made or action taken. ♦ *The latest disagreement between management and the union has brought matters to a head. There will be an all-out strike now.* ♦ *It's a relief that things have been brought to a head. The disputes have been going on for months.* **11. come to a head** *idiom* to come to a crucial point; to come to a point when a problem must be solved. ♦ *Remember my problem with my neighbors? Well, last night the whole thing came to a head.* ♦ *The battle between the two factions of the city council came to a head yesterday.* **12. count heads** *idiom* to count people. ♦ *I'll tell you how many people are here after I count heads.* ♦ *Everyone is here. Let's count heads so we can order hamburgers.* **13. get one's head above water** *idiom* to get ahead of one's problems; to catch up with one's work or responsibilities. ♦ *I can't seem to get my head above water. Work just keeps piling up.* ♦ *I'll be glad when I get my head above water again.* **14. go over someone's head, pass over someone's head** *idiom* [for the intellectual content of something] to be too difficult for someone to understand. ♦ *All that talk about computers went over my head.* ♦ *I hope my lecture didn't go over the students' heads.* **15. go over someone's head** *idiom* to carry a request to someone's boss, supervisor, or superior. ♦ *I am angry because you went over my head rather than discussing the problem with me.* ♦ *If you don't agree with my proposal, I will go over your head and get your boss to agree!* **16. go to someone's head** *idiom* to make someone conceited; to make someone overly proud. ♦ *You did a fine job, but don't let it go to your head.* ♦ *He let his success go to his head, and soon he became a complete failure.* **17. have a good head on one's shoulders** *idiom* to have common sense; to be sensible and intelligent. ♦ *Mary doesn't do well in school, but she's got a good head on her shoulders.* ♦ *John has a good head on his shoulders and can be depended on to give good advice.* **18. have a head for something** *idiom* have the mental capacity for something. ♦ *Jane has a good head for directions and never gets lost.* ♦ *Bill doesn't have a head for figures and should never become an accountant.* **19. head and shoulders above someone or something** *idiom* to be clearly superior to someone or something. ♦ *This wine is head and shoulders above that one.* ♦ *John stands head and shoulders above Bob.* **20. hold one's head up** *idiom* to have one's self-respect; to retain or display one's dignity. ♦ *I've done nothing wrong. I can hold my head up in public.* ♦ *I'm so embarrassed and ashamed. I'll never be able to hold up my head again.* **21. in over one's head** *idiom* having more difficulties than one can manage. ♦ *Calculus is very hard for me. I'm in over my head.* ♦ *Anne is too busy. She's really in over her head.* **22. on someone's head** *idiom* [for something negative] to belong only to one person or group. ♦ *All the blame fell on their heads.* ♦ *I don't think that all the criticism should be on my head.* **23. over someone's head** *idiom* too difficult or clever for someone to understand. ♦ *The children have no idea what the new teacher is talking about. Her ideas are way over their heads.* ♦ *She started a physics course, but it turned out to be miles over her head.* **24. turn someone's head** *idiom* to make someone conceited. ♦ *John's compliments really turned Sally's head.* ♦ *Victory in the competition is bound to turn Tom's head. He'll think he's too good for us.*

headache ['hɛd ek] **1.** *n.* a pain in the head. ♦ *Mary took aspirin to get rid of her headache.* ♦ *The severe headache made it hard for Mike to concentrate.* **2.** *n.* a problem; a bother; a worry. (Figurative on ①.) ♦ *Work is just one headache after another.* ♦ *I don't mean to be a headache, but I need help with this problem.*

headboard ['hɛd bord] *n.* a panel that stands upright against the wall at the end of a bed. ♦ *As Bob rolled over, the headboard banged against the wall.* ♦ *The maple headboard matched the other bedroom furniture.*

headfirst ['hɛd 'fɚst] *adv.* with the head in front; with the head aimed forward. ♦ *Jane dove headfirst into the pool.* ♦ *The baseball player slid headfirst into second base.*

heading ['hɛd ɪŋ] *n.* a title that is written at the top of a chapter, section, page, or paragraph. ♦ *Each section of your term paper should have a heading.* ♦ *The author wrote the chapters first and then their headings.*

headless ['hɛd ləs] *adj.* without a head; having no head. (Adv: *headlessly.*) ♦ *Legend has it that a headless ghost haunts the graveyard.* ♦ *The story of the headless horseman is an American classic.*

headlight ['hɛd lɑɪt] **1.** *n.* a strong, bright lamp on the front of a vehicle. ♦ *You should always turn your headlights on when driving at night.* ♦ *One of the truck's headlights was broken.* **2.** *n.* the beam of light from ①. ♦ *I saw a deer in my headlights.* ♦ *The fog was so thick I could hardly see the headlights of the other cars.*

headline ['hɛd lɑɪn] **1.** *n.* the title of a newspaper article, especially at the top of the front page. ♦ *The headline caught Jane's attention, so she bought the newspaper.* ♦ *The headline announced the winner of the presidential election.* **2.** *tv.* to have a major part in a play or movie, and thus have one's name written in large print, like a headline, in the advertising for a play or movie. ♦ *A famous movie star will headline the charity benefit.* ♦ *Who will headline the new movie?*

headlong ['hɛd lɔŋ] **1.** *adv.* with the front, top, or head in front; headfirst. ♦ *The sailboat ran headlong into the wind and almost stalled.* ♦ *The swimmer dove headlong into the waves.* **2.** *adv.* quickly; hastily. ♦ *Bob's parents warned him not to rush headlong into marriage.* ♦ *Despite the warning, Anne dashed headlong into a complicated legal tangle.* **3.** *adj.* done with the front, top, or head in front. ♦ *The headlong dive into the cool water was refreshing.* ♦ *The skier was lucky to survive the headlong tumble down the hill.* **4.** *adj.* quick; hasty. ♦ *Tom lost most of his money when the stock market took a headlong plunge.* ♦ *The attorney warned Anne not to make a headlong dash into the lawsuit.*

headmaster ['hɛd mæ stɚ] *n.* the head of a school; the principal of a school. ♦ *The headmaster disciplined the truant student.* ♦ *The teacher sent the rowdy students to the headmaster.*

head-on ['hɛd 'ɔn] **1.** *adj.* with the front of something in front; especially used to describe motor vehicle accidents where the front of one vehicle hits the front of another vehicle. ♦ *The head-on car crash killed two people.* ♦ *John swerved to avoid a head-on collision.* **2.** *adv.* directly in front. ♦ *The stray puppy in the middle of the road was hit head-on and instantly killed.* ♦ *While learning to ride a bike, Jimmy ran head-on into the fence.*

headphone ['hɛd fon] *n.* an earphone; a small sound-producing device that fits over the ear. (Usually plural.) ♦ *The airplane pilot wore headphones to listen to the plane's radio.* ♦ *I listen to my stereo with headphones so I don't bother my roommates.*

headquarters ['hɛd kwort ɚz] *n.* the controlling office or location of an organization. (Treated as singular or plural.) ♦ *The company headquarters are on the East Coast.* ♦ *The hiring of new employees must be approved by headquarters.*

headrest ['hɛd rɛst] *n.* a support for the head, such as on the back of a chair or the seat of a car, airplane, bus, etc. ♦ *Dave leaned back, put his head on the headrest, and fell asleep.* ♦ *Mary raised the headrest on the back of her car seat.*

headroom ['hɛd rum] *n.* the amount of open space between the top of someone's head and the ceiling or bottom of a door frame. (No plural form in this sense.) ♦ *The short doorway provided little headroom for tall people.* ♦ *The architect designed large doorways so there would be plenty of headroom for tall people.*

head start ['hɛd 'stɑrt] *n.* an advantage, such as being able to start doing something before other people. ♦ *I got a head start on holiday shopping and finished by November 1st.* ♦ *Jimmy's brother gave him a head start in the race.*

headstrong ['hɛd strɔŋ] *adj.* determined; stubborn. (Adv: *headstrongly.*) ♦ *No one could ride the headstrong horse.* ♦ *The headstrong child kept trying to tie her shoes until she did it right.*

headway ['hɛd we] *n.* forward motion; progress. (No plural form in this sense.) ♦ *Since there was no breeze, the sailboat made little headway.* ♦ *By working together, the committee made good headway on solving the problem.*

headwind ['hɛd wɪnd] *n.* wind that is blowing in a direction that is opposite to the way that someone or something is traveling; wind that is blowing against someone or something. ♦ *A strong headwind delayed the plane's arrival.* ♦ *The captain had a hard time controlling the ship in the headwind.*

heal ['hil] **1.** *iv.* [for a wound] to return to health and become whole again. ♦ *The medicated lotion caused my cut to heal.* ♦ *The wound soon healed.* **2.** *tv.* to cause a wound to become healthy and whole. ♦ *In a few days, this medicine should help heal the wound.* ♦ *The salve will help heal your cut.* **3.** *tv.* to bring an end to conflicts between people; to close gaps between people's feelings and understanding. (Figurative on ②.) ♦ *I wanted to heal the division between Tom and his wife, but I didn't know how.* ♦ *I hope that all of you can heal your differences without fighting.*

health ['hɛlθ] **1.** *n.* freedom from diseases of the mind or the body. (No plural form in this sense.) ♦ *My grandfather's health began to fail when he was 85.* ♦ *Sue is in good health because she exercises and eats properly.* **2.** *n.* vigor; general condition. (No plural form in this sense. Figurative on ①.) ♦ *After posting record profits, the company's health was excellent.* ♦ *The general health of the nation's economy was not good.* **3.** *adj.* <the adj. use of ①>; promoting ①. ♦ *The company offered its employees health insurance.* ♦ *Many kinds of drugs were advertised at the health festival.* **4. get a clean bill of health** *idiom* [for someone] to be pronounced healthy by a physician. ♦ *Sally got a clean bill of health from the doctor.* ♦ *Now that Lisa has a clean bill of health, she can go back to work.*

healthful ['hɛlθ fʊl] *adj.* good for one's health. (Adv: *healthfully.*) ♦ *Because his father had cancer, Bob maintains a healthful diet.* ♦ *Mary takes good care of herself by leading a healthful lifestyle.*

healthy ['hɛlθ i] **1.** *adj.* in good health; free from disease. (Adv: *healthily.* Comp: *healthier;* sup: *healthiest.*) ♦ *The doctor placed the healthy newborn in the mother's arms.* ♦ *Although it was a stray, the dog seemed healthy.* **2.** *adj.* good for one's health; good for the body; healthful. (Adv: *healthily.* Comp: *healthier;* sup: *healthiest.*) ♦ *A healthy diet includes the proper amounts of nutritious food.* ♦ *Healthy foods do not include french fries and rich ice cream.* **3.** *adj.* adequate or abundant. (Figurative on ①. Comp: *healthier;* sup: *healthiest.*) ♦ *Bob was hungry and put a healthy amount of food on his plate.* ♦ *The performers were pleased to see a healthy number of people in the audience.*

heap ['hip] **1.** *n.* a large pile of things; a stack of things piled together. ♦ *After we raked the yard, there was a heap* *of leaves in the front lawn.* ♦ *Don't leave your dirty laundry in a heap in the middle of the floor!* **2. heap in(to)** *tv. + prep. phr.* to place things into ①. ♦ *The children heaped the leaves into a large pile and jumped in.* ♦ *Just heap the toys into the toy box.*

hear ['hɪr] **1.** *iv., irreg.* to be able to perceive sounds by means of the ears. (Pt/pp: heard.) ♦ *The noise of the airplane engines made it impossible to hear.* ♦ *I could hear you better if you turned the radio down.* **2.** *tv., irreg.* to perceive a certain sound or a certain utterance. ♦ *Did you hear what I said?* ♦ *The driver did not hear the siren.* **3.** *tv., irreg.* to learn that something has happened. (Takes a clause.) ♦ *The parents were surprised to hear that their child had cut classes.* ♦ *We heard that Sam had an accident.* **4.** *tv., irreg.* [for a court of law] to listen to the two sides of a court case. ♦ *The court heard the entire case in one day.* ♦ *The judge agreed to hear the case next week.* **5.** *tv., irreg.* to pay attention to someone or something; to listen to someone or something. ♦ *You didn't hear a word I said, did you?* ♦ *Because Mary was daydreaming, she didn't hear the teacher's instructions.*

heard ['hɝd] pt/pp of hear.

hearing ['hɪr ɪŋ] **1.** *n.* the sense that allows one to recognize sound; the ability to hear. (No plural form in this sense.) ♦ *Bill's hearing was poor, so he asked me to talk louder.* ♦ *An ear doctor tested the children's hearing.* **2.** *n.* an examination of basic evidence in a court of law. ♦ *The judge set the hearing for Saturday.* ♦ *There was not enough evidence presented at the hearing, so the suspect was released.* **3.** *adj.* <the adj. use of ①.> ♦ *Bill wears a hearing aid that allows him to understand better what people are saying.* ♦ *He has had a hearing disability since he was a small child.* **4.** *adj.* able to hear; not deaf. ♦ *Hearing people usually do not understand sign language.* ♦ *Tom is a hearing person, but he is not sighted.*

hearsay ['hɪr se] *n.* gossip; a rumor; rumors. (No plural form in this sense.) ♦ *It's just hearsay, but it's rumored that John is going to quit.* ♦ *I accused my colleagues of spreading hearsay about our boss.*

hearse ['hɝs] *n.* a vehicle that carries coffins to the cemetery during funerals. ♦ *The hearse led the funeral procession.* ♦ *The pallbearers removed the coffin from the hearse.*

heart ['hɑrt] **1.** *n.* a large, four-chambered muscle that pumps blood throughout the body. ♦ *The heart of the old dog finally failed and it died.* ♦ *Bill felt his heart beat by placing his hand over his chest.* **2.** *n.* ① considered as a symbol of the center of a person's emotions, thoughts, and love. (Figurative on ①.) ♦ *John gave his heart to Lisa.* ♦ *My heart belongs to Dave, and I don't want to date anyone else.* **3.** *n.* the shape ♥. ♦ *Jane's skirt had a pattern of tiny hearts all over it.* ♦ *For Valentine's Day, Bill baked a cake that looked like a heart.* **4.** *n.* a card in a suit in a deck of playing cards that is indicated by a red ♥. (See ⑥.) ♦ *Spades and hearts are the major suits in the game of bridge.* ♦ *Susan had the ace of hearts in her hand.* **5. the heart** *n.* the most central, essential, or vital part of something; the core of something. (No plural form in this sense. Treated as singular.) ♦ *Mary enjoys living in the heart of the city, near many restaurants and theaters.* ♦ *At the heart of the problem is the need for education.* **6. hearts** *n.* the suit of playing cards having the symbol ♥. (Sometimes plural with the same meaning.) ♦ *Hearts and spades are major suits in the game of bridge.* ♦ *The king of hearts captured the ten of diamonds.* **7. break someone's heart** *idiom* to cause someone emotional pain. ♦ *It just broke my heart when Tom ran away from home.* ♦ *Sally broke John's heart when she refused to marry him.* **8. die of a broken heart** *idiom* to suffer from emotional distress, especially from a failed romance. ♦ *Tom and Mary broke off their romance and both died of broken hearts.* ♦ *Please don't leave me. I know I'll die of a broken heart.* **9. do someone's heart good** *idiom* to make someone feel good emotionally. ♦ *It does my heart good to hear you talk that way.* ♦ *When she sent me a get-well card, it really did my heart good.* **10. eat one's heart out** *idiom* to be envious (of someone or something). ♦ *Do you like my new watch? Well, eat your heart out. It was the last one in the store.* ♦ *Don't eat your heart out about my new car. Go get one of your own.* **11. find it in one's heart (to do something)** *idiom* to have the courage or compassion to do something. ♦ *She couldn't find it in her heart to refuse to come home to him.* ♦ *I can't do it! I can't find it in my heart.* **12. follow one's heart** *idiom* to act according to one's feelings; to obey one's sympathetic or compassionate inclinations. ♦ *I couldn't decide what to do, so I just followed my heart.* ♦ *I trust that you will follow your heart in this matter.* **13. from the bottom of one's heart** *idiom* sincerely. ♦ *When I returned the lost kitten to Mrs. Brown, she thanked me from the bottom of her heart.* ♦ *Oh, thank you! I'm grateful from the bottom of my heart.* **14. get to the heart of the matter** *idiom* to get to the essentials of a matter. ♦ *We have to stop wasting time and get to the heart of the matter.* ♦ *You've been very helpful. You really seem to be able to get to the heart of the matter.* **15. have a heart of gold** *idiom* to be generous, sincere, and friendly. ♦ *Mary is such a lovely person. She has a heart of gold.* ♦ *You think Tom stole your watch? Impossible! He has a heart of gold.* **16. have a heart** *idiom* to be compassionate; to be generous and forgiving; to have an especially compassionate heart. ♦ *Oh, have a heart! Give me some help!* ♦ *If Anne had a heart, she'd have made us feel more welcome.* **17. have a heart of stone** *idiom* to be cold, unfeeling, and unfriendly. ♦ *Sally has a heart of stone. She never even smiles.* ♦ *The villain in the play had a heart of stone. He was an ideal villain.* **18. have a soft spot in one's heart for someone or something** *idiom* to be fond of someone or something. ♦ *John has a soft spot in his heart for Mary.* ♦ *I have a soft spot in my heart for chocolate cake.* **19. have one's heart set on something** *idiom* to be desiring and expecting something. ♦ *Jane has her heart set on going to London.* ♦ *Bob will be disappointed. He had his heart set on going to college this year.* **20. lose heart** *idiom* to lose one's courage or confidence. ♦ *Now, don't lose heart. Keep trying.* ♦ *What a disappointment! It's enough to make one lose heart.* **21. one's heart goes out to someone** *idiom* to feel great sympathy for someone. ♦ *My heart goes out to the grieving family.* ♦ *Let your heart go out to those who are suffering, and pray for their improvement.* **22. open one's heart (to someone)** *idiom* to reveal one's inmost thoughts to someone. ♦ *I always open my heart to my spouse when I have a problem.* ♦ *It's a good idea to open your heart every now and then.*

heartache ['hɑrt ek] *n.* anguish; sorrow; mental suffering. (No plural form in this sense.) ♦ *After the divorce,*

Dave refused to talk about his heartache. ♦ *Mary suffered from heartache for years after her son died.*

heartbeat ['hɑrt bit] **1.** *n.* one full pulse of the heart. ♦ *The healthy patient's heartbeat was strong.* ♦ *The doctor listened carefully to my heartbeat.* **2.** *n.* a moment; a second or two. ♦ *I'll be finished in just a heartbeat.* ♦ *It only took a heartbeat for the new parents to fall in love with their baby.* **3. be a heartbeat away from something** *idiom* to be the next ruler upon the final heartbeat of the current ruler. (Especially in reference to U.S. presidential succession.) ♦ *The vice president is just a heartbeat away from being president.* ♦ *The prince was only a heartbeat away from being king.* **4. do something in a heartbeat** *idiom* to do something almost immediately. (Typically used referring to a hypothetical situation in which the conditions are right.) ♦ *If I had the money, I would go back to college in a heartbeat.* ♦ *Just tell me that you need me and I'll come there in a heartbeat.*

heartbreak ['hɑrt brek] *n.* anguish; great emotional discomfort. (No plural form in this sense.) ♦ *David suffered terrible heartbreak when his wife died.* ♦ *The child's heartbreak after losing the contest was painful to witness.*

heartbroken ['hɑrt 'brok ən] *adj.* anguished; full of sorrow. (Adv: *heartbrokenly.*) ♦ *Sally was heartbroken as she searched for her lost dog.* ♦ *The heartbroken parents cried at their son's funeral.*

heartburn ['hɑrt bɚn] *n.* a burning feeling in the lower part of the chest. (No plural form in this sense.) ♦ *The spicy meal gave Bill heartburn.* ♦ *Bill took some medicine to relieve his heartburn.*

hearten ['hɑrt n] *tv.* to cause someone to feel happy or cheerful. ♦ *The good news heartened Mary, and she smiled.* ♦ *Passing algebra really heartened the student.*

heartfelt ['hɑrt fɛlt] *adj.* sincere; earnest. ♦ *I accepted Bob's heartfelt apology.* ♦ *I want to give you my heartfelt congratulations on winning the contest.*

hearth ['hɑrθ] *n.* the floor of a fireplace; the area in front of a fireplace. ♦ *The dog lay near the hearth, warming itself.* ♦ *Lisa put some logs on the hearth and began to build a fire.*

heartless ['hɑrt ləs] *adj.* cruel; mean; without pity. (Adv: *heartlessly.*) ♦ *Only a heartless driver would leave an injured dog in the middle of the road.* ♦ *The heartless coach wouldn't let Jimmy play because he was late for practice.*

heartrending ['hɑrt rɛn dɪŋ] *adj.* sad; causing heartbreak. (Adv: *heartrendingly.*) ♦ *Mary cried during the heartrending ending of the movie.* ♦ *I could read a good, old-fashioned, heartrending love story every day.*

heart-to-heart ['hɑrt tə 'hɑrt] *adj.* frank and sincere; candid; personal. ♦ *Dave had a heart-to-heart talk with his son about his new girlfriend.* ♦ *Mary peacefully settled her differences with her boss in a heart-to-heart conversation.*

hearty ['hɑr ti] **1.** *adj.* energetic; vigorous; strong and lively. (Adv: *heartily.* Comp: *heartier;* sup: *heartiest.*) ♦ *The hearty puppy raced around the yard.* ♦ *The comedian liked to hear hearty laughter from the audience.* **2.** *adj.* [of a meal] large and satisfying. (Adv: *heartily.* Comp: *heartier;* sup: *heartiest.*) ♦ *The hearty dinner was enough to feed an army.* ♦ *After the long hike, Tom was ready for a hearty meal.*

heat ['hit] **1.** *n.* hotness; the quality that is perceived as a relatively higher temperature. (No plural form in this sense.) ♦ *I could feel the heat of the pavement under the hot sun.* ♦ *The heat of the fire warmed the room.* **2.** *n.* hot weather. (No plural form in this sense.) ♦ *The summer heat was unbearable.* ♦ *The heat wore Susan down, and she felt physically exhausted.* **3.** *n.* passion; intense emotion; the most intense part of something. (No plural form in this sense.) ♦ *The movie captured the heat between the two lovers.* ♦ *At the heat of the argument, everyone in the room could hear Tom and Bob yelling.* **4.** *n.* a preliminary grouping of contestants in a sporting event. (The winners of different heats compete in later heats or the final event.) ♦ *Anne and Mary won their respective heats and will run against each other in the final race.* ♦ *The winners of the five heats advanced to the championship.* **5.** *tv.* to cause something to become hotter. ♦ *The sun heated the water in the lake.* ♦ *This fireplace can heat the cabin when it's cold.* **6.** *iv.* to become hotter or warmer. ♦ *Dinner is heating in the oven.* ♦ *As the sun shone, the water in the pool heated up.* **7. in a dead heat** *idiom* finishing a race at exactly the same time; tied. ♦ *The two horses finished the race in a dead heat.* ♦ *They ended the contest in a dead heat.* **8. in heat** *idiom* in a period of sexual excitement; in estrus. ♦ *Our dog is in heat.* ♦ *When my dog is in heat, I have to keep her locked in the house.*

heated ['hit ɪd] **1.** *adj.* warmed; made warm; made hot. ♦ *The heated pool water felt almost like bathwater.* ♦ *The hotel we stayed at has heated bathroom floors.* **2.** *adj.* angry. (Adv: *heatedly.*) ♦ *The couple had a heated discussion about money.* ♦ *There was a heated exchange between the police officer and the speeding driver.*

heater ['hit ɚ] *n.* a device that provides heat for heating a room, usually electric or powered by a liquid fuel. ♦ *We installed a heater to warm the bathroom.* ♦ *The heater tipped over and started a fire.*

heathen ['hið ən] **1.** *n.* someone who does not believe in the Christian, Jewish, or Muslim God. (Often derogatory.) ♦ *When I refused to go to church, my aunt called me a heathen.* ♦ *Tom preferred to leave the heathen alone, rather than covert them.* **2.** *adj.* uncivilized. (Figurative on ①.) ♦ *My mother said I couldn't play with those heathen children who were always misbehaving.* ♦ *Bob is a snob. He thinks anyone who doesn't go to college is a heathen.*

heatstroke ['hit strok] *n.* a medical condition where one passes out or collapses from too much heat. (See also sunstroke. No plural form in this sense.) ♦ *Two of the golfers in our group suffered heatstroke.* ♦ *Wearing a hat can help prevent heatstroke.*

heat wave ['hit wev] *n.* a period of very hot weather. ♦ *The heat wave lasted seven days and made everyone miserable.* ♦ *Dozens of people died during the intense heat wave.*

heave ['hiv] **1.** *tv.* to lift or throw something that requires hard work; to lift or throw something that is very heavy. ♦ *Heave that box over here.* ♦ *The volcano heaved lava from beneath the earth's surface.* **2.** *iv.* to rise and fall with effort. ♦ *After chasing the squirrel, the dog's sides heaved.* ♦ *The hospital patient's chest heaved with each gasp.* **3.** *n.* a pull; a throw; the act of heaving something as in ①. ♦

With three good heaves, the firefighter broke the door down. ♦ *It took a strong heave to get the heavy table into the truck.*

heaven ['hɛv ən] **1.** *n.* [in certain religions] the place where God resides and where the souls of good people go after death. (Usually associated with the sky. No plural form in this sense.) ♦ *Mary told her children that their grandfather was up in heaven with the angels.* ♦ *The minister asked me if I felt that I would go to heaven.* **2. the heavens** *n.* the sky; space. (Treated as plural.) ♦ *With the approaching storm, the heavens were almost black.* ♦ *The heavens opened up, and the rain came pouring down.* **3. in heaven** *idiom* in a state of absolute bliss or happiness. (Figurative on ①.) ♦ *Lisa was in heaven after winning the lottery.* ♦ *Resting in his hammock, John was simply in heaven.* **4. in seventh heaven** *idiom* in a very happy state. ♦ *Anne was really in seventh heaven when she got a car of her own.* ♦ *I'd be in seventh heaven if I had a million dollars.*

heavenly ['hɛv ən li] **1.** *adj.* perfect; wonderful. ♦ *This expensive chocolate is simply heavenly.* ♦ *In that heavenly dress, you look like a queen.* **2.** *adj.* holy; divine. (Often capitalized.) ♦ *After the service, I felt filled with a heavenly spirit.* ♦ *Jimmy was taught to start his prayers with "Heavenly Father."* **3. heavenly body** *n.* a star, moon, planet, or comet. ♦ *Astronomers study the heavenly bodies.* ♦ *The moon is the closest heavenly body to earth.*

heavenward ['hɛv ən wɚd] **1.** *adj.* directed upward; directed toward heaven. ♦ *The last Bill saw of the balloon, it was on a heavenward journey.* ♦ *The crowd watched the rocket rush along its heavenward path.* **2.** *adv.* upward; toward heaven. ♦ *The balloon soared heavenward.* ♦ *I felt a drop of rain, and I glanced heavenward.*

heavily ['hɛv ə li] **1.** *adv.* as though carrying something heavy. ♦ *On his way to school, John trudged heavily through the snow.* ♦ *Don't walk so heavily! You'll disturb the neighbors downstairs.* **2.** *adv.* in a large amount; intensely. ♦ *After losing his money gambling, Bob began drinking heavily.* ♦ *The singer never ate heavily before a concert.*

heaviness ['hɛv i nəs] *n.* weighing a lot; being heavy. (No plural form in this sense.) ♦ *Dave considered the piano's awkward heaviness, and wondered how he was going to move it.* ♦ *The heaviness of the gift box surprised Bob.*

heavy ['hɛv i] **1.** *adj.* weighing a lot; of great weight. (Adv: *heavily.* Comp: *heavier;* sup: *heaviest.*) ♦ *It took two strong workers to lift the heavy couch.* ♦ *The heavy sled had to be pulled by six dogs.* **2.** *adj.* [of sound] strong, deep, and ponderous. (Adv: *heavily.* Comp: *heavier;* sup: *heaviest.*) ♦ *The music was too heavy in the bass notes.* ♦ *The flutes could barely be heard above the heavy sounds of the trombones.* **3.** *adj.* great in amount; dense; intense; thick. (Adv: *heavily.* Comp: *heavier;* sup: *heaviest.*) ♦ *A heavy snowfall blanketed the town.* ♦ *In the traffic, it was hard to get anywhere.* **4.** *adj.* serious; requiring a lot of thought to understand. (Adv: *heavily.* Comp: *heavier;* sup: *heaviest.*) ♦ *The scientific textbook was very heavy reading.* ♦ *The heavy lecture put many students to sleep.* **5.** *n.* a villain, especially in a play or movie. ♦ *That hulking actor has played the heavy in a number of movies.* ♦ *The director wanted a group of heavies for the fight in the street.* **6. heavy drinker** *n.* someone who drinks a lot of alcohol. ♦ *John is a very heavy drinker.* ♦ *After the death of her daughter, Jane became a heavy drinker.* **7. heavy smoker** *n.* someone who smokes a lot of tobacco. ♦ *Bill is a heavy smoker and has a terrible cough.* ♦ *Heavy smokers have a hard time finding a place where it is legal to smoke.*

heavy-duty ['hɛv i 'dut i] *adj.* durable; made to be strong; made to last. ♦ *The heavy-duty truck lasted for more than fifteen years.* ♦ *I cleaned the large spill with a heavy-duty paper towel.*

heavy-handed ['hɛv i 'hæn dɪd] **1.** *adj.* harsh; severe; unnecessarily strong. (Adv: *heavy-handedly.*) ♦ *The teacher's heavy-handed criticism made the student bitter.* ♦ *After the heavy-handed movie review, no one went to see the film.* **2.** *adj.* clumsy, as if done with large, unskilled hands. (Figurative. Adv: *heavy-handedly.*) ♦ *John's heavy-handed attempt to help was too poorly planned to be of any benefit.* ♦ *The writer's exaggeration of the character flaws of the hero was heavy-handed and amateurish.*

heavyset ['hɛv i 'sɛt] *adj.* [of someone] stocky and muscular; [of someone] heavy and large, although not necessarily overweight. ♦ *The heavyset man had trouble buying clothes that fit properly.* ♦ *Two heavyset men came into the store to deliver a large box.*

heavyweight ['hɛv i wet] **1.** *n.* a boxer who weighs more than 175 pounds. ♦ *The two heavyweights entered the boxing ring.* ♦ *The heavyweights were both weighed before the bout to make sure they qualified for the match.* **2.** *n.* someone who is important. (Figurative on ①.) ♦ *Having served five terms, the senator was a heavyweight in Congress.* ♦ *Because John was a heavyweight in the company, people listened to him closely.* **3.** *adj.* <the adj. use of ①.> ♦ *The champion won the heavyweight fight in six rounds.* ♦ *The heavyweight boxer weighed almost 190 pounds.*

Hebraic [hɪ 'bre ɪk] *adj.* of or about Hebrew. (Adv: *Hebraically* [...ɪk li].) ♦ *The archaeologist found a Hebraic document in the cave.* ♦ *The song was based on an old Hebraic melody.*

Hebrew ['hi bru] **1.** *n.* the people who were the ancestors of the Jewish people. ♦ *The history of the Hebrews is contained in the Old Testament of the Bible.* ♦ *The ancient Hebrews built a temple in Jerusalem.* **2.** *n.* the language of the ancient Hebrews and of modern Israel. (No plural form in this sense.) ♦ *Hebrew is a Semitic language.* ♦ *The bat mitzvah learned to read Hebrew.* **3.** *adj.* <the adj. use of ① or ②.> ♦ *The Hebrew language is taught to children in Israel.* ♦ *The dates of Jewish holidays are determined according to the Hebrew calendar.*

heckle ['hɛk əl] *tv.* to taunt or interrupt a speaker or a performer. ♦ *The speaker left the stage because the crowd had heckled him.* ♦ *The comic insulted the people in the audience who heckled her.*

heckler ['hɛk lɚ] *n.* someone who taunts or interrupts a speaker or a performer. ♦ *A security guard removed the heckler from the crowd.* ♦ *Most of the audience jeered the heckler.*

hectic ['hɛk tɪk] *adj.* very active; very excited; very busy. (Adv: *hectically* [...ɪk li].) ♦ *After a hectic day, Jane was exhausted.* ♦ *The beginning of the school year is very hectic for teachers.*

hector ['hɛk tɚ] *tv.* to intimidate someone; to bully someone; to tease someone. ♦ *The bully began hectoring the younger students.* ♦ *The high-school student hectored the 7th grader on the bus.*

he'd ['hid] **1.** *cont.* "he would." ♦ *Dave said he'd like to go to the movies.* ♦ *The customer said he'd love another piece of pie.* **2.** *cont.* "he had," where **had** is an auxiliary. ♦ *Bill didn't want to go to the movie because he'd already seen it.* ♦ *Bob told Sue that he'd eaten dinner earlier.*

hedge ['hɛdʒ] **1.** *n.* a row of bushes planted closely together, separating two parcels of land. ♦ *The gardener trimmed the hedges.* ♦ *My neighbor's yard and mine are separated by a large hedge.* **2.** *n.* a statement that protects against a risk or danger; a statement that equivocates. ♦ *The contract contained a hedge so that it actually gave me no protection at all.* ♦ *The insurance policy looked good—until I saw the hedge that allowed the company to avoid paying benefits in most cases.* **3.** *tv.* to make a statement in an evasive way to avoid committing oneself to a certain belief or decision. ♦ *Many politicians hedge their statements about important issues when they are campaigning.* ♦ *David hedged his answer by saying "maybe" and "perhaps" a lot.* **4. hedge (in)** *tv.* (+ *adv.*) to enclose or surround something with a hedge. ♦ *My new neighbor decided to hedge in his backyard.* ♦ *Many people hedge their yards for privacy.* **5. hedge in** *tv.* + *adv.* to restrict or contain someone; to limit someone. (Figurative on ④.) ♦ *My instructions hedged me in, and I could not act as freely as I wanted to.* ♦ *Tom felt hedged in by the stress of his job, so he quit.* **6.** *iv.* to speak in an evasive way, avoiding the risks of being more specific. ♦ *When asked to comment on taxes, the mayor simply hedged.* ♦ *Did the teacher answer the question, or did she hedge?*

hedgehog ['hɛdʒ 'hɔg] *n.* one of a number of species of small nocturnal mammals with spiny coats, found in Europe, Australia, and Asia. ♦ *In the moonlight, I saw a hedgehog scurry across the yard.* ♦ *The hedgehog eats mainly insects.*

heed ['hid] **1.** *n.* close attention; regard. (No plural form in this sense.) ♦ *Bill paid no heed to the instructions, and so he flunked the test.* ♦ *If you pay careful heed to the recipe, your cake will be perfect.* **2.** *tv.* to pay close attention to something, such as advice. ♦ *The apprentice heeded the master's advice.* ♦ *Children should heed their parents' instructions.*

heedless ['hid ləs] *adj.* careless; paying no attention; not taking notice. (Adv: *heedlessly.*) ♦ *The heedless children did not realize they were ruining my garden.* ♦ *Your heedless remarks hurt Lisa's feelings.*

hee-haw ['hi hɔ] *n.* the sound made by a mule, ass, or donkey. ♦ *A loud hee-haw came from the pasture.* ♦ *The children laughed when they heard the donkey's hee-haw.*

heel ['hil] **1.** *n.* the back part of the foot; the part of the foot that bears the weight of the body. ♦ *After walking for miles, the hiker's heels were blistered.* ♦ *Bob stopped running when he injured his heel.* **2.** *n.* the part of a shoe or sock that covers ①. ♦ *The heel of Dave's sock had a hole in it.* ♦ *The heels of my shoes are worn down and need to be replaced.* **3.** *n.* the part of a shoe that supports ①. ♦ *Mary asked the clerk for a shoe with a high heel.* ♦ *I like shoes with rubber heels.* **4.** *n.* someone, usually a male, who is not very nice. ♦ *Bob is a heel because he mistreats his friends.* ♦ *To get to the door first, the heel pushed Mary aside.* **5. (high) heels** *n.* a type of women's shoe having a long or tall ③. (Treated as plural.) ♦ *Jane wore a dress and high heels to the party.* ♦ *Heels will make you look much taller.* **6. cool one's heels** *idiom* to wait (for someone). ♦ *I spent all afternoon cooling my heels in the waiting room while the doctor talked on the telephone.* ♦ *All right, if you can't behave properly, just sit down here and cool your heels until I call you.* **7. hard on someone's heels** *idiom* following someone very closely; following very closely to someone's heels. ♦ *I ran as fast as I could, but the vicious dog was still hard on my heels.* ♦ *Here comes Sally, and John is hard on her heels.* **8. on the heels of something** *idiom* soon after something. ♦ *There was a rainstorm on the heels of the windstorm.* ♦ *The team held a victory celebration on the heels of their winning season.* **9. set one back on one's heels** *idiom* to surprise, shock, or overwhelm someone. ♦ *Her sudden announcement set us all back on our heels.* ♦ *The manager scolded me, and that really set me back on my heels.* **10. take to one's heels** *idiom* to run away. ♦ *The little boy said hello and then took to his heels.* ♦ *The man took to his heels to try to get to the bus stop before the bus left.*

hefty ['hɛf ti] **1.** *adj.* [of someone] large, strong, and capable of moving great weight. (Adv: *heftily.* Comp: *heftier;* sup: *heftiest.*) ♦ *The hefty woman moved the sofa easily.* ♦ *A couple of hefty guys offered to rake my yard for ten dollars.* **2.** *adj.* large; bulky; sizable. (Comp: *heftier;* sup: *heftiest.*) ♦ *John's promotion came with a hefty raise.* ♦ *The hungry boy took a hefty helping of mashed potatoes.*

heifer ['hɛf ɚ] *n.* a young (female) cow; a cow that has not given birth to a calf. ♦ *The heifers were left in the pasture all year.* ♦ *The farmer's daughter raised a heifer as a pet.*

height ['hɑɪt] **1.** *n.* the tallness of someone or something; the length of a person or a vertical object. (No plural form in this sense.) ♦ *Abraham Lincoln was a man of great height.* ♦ *The men in our family are of average height.* **2.** *n.* the length of something from bottom to top; the distance to a higher point from a lower level. ♦ *The height of the truck was too great to allow it to pass under the low bridge.* ♦ *The height of this flagpole is 15 feet.* **3.** *n.* the most extreme example of something. ♦ *The student's poor excuse was the height of absurdity.* ♦ *Drinking and driving is the height of stupidity.* **4. at the height of something** *idiom* at the most intense or forceful aspect of something. ♦ *At the height of his career, Tom was known around the world.* ♦ *At the height of the party, there were 50 people present.*

heighten ['hɑɪt n] **1.** *tv.* to cause something to become more intense or exciting. ♦ *This juicy gossip should heighten your interest in the matter.* ♦ *The music heightened the suspense of the movie.* **2.** *iv.* to become higher or taller. ♦ *As more leaves were added, the pile heightened.* ♦ *The mountain seemed to heighten as we approached it.* **3.** *iv.* to become more intense or exciting. ♦ *The suspense of the movie heightened as the background music became louder.* ♦ *The hope for peace heightened when the leaders had a private meeting.*

heinous ['he nəs] *adj.* evil; wicked. (Adv: *heinously.*) ♦ *The heinous act of vandalism shocked everyone in town.* ♦ *Even the police were shocked by the heinous crime.*

heir ['ɛr] *n.* someone, male or female, who inherits something from its owner; someone who receives something when the owner dies. ♦ *As his mother's heir, Bill will* *inherit the house when she dies.* ♦ *When David dies, his property will be split among his heirs.*

heiress ['ɛr ɪs] *n.* the feminine form of heir; a female who has inherited a fortune. ♦ *Jane is the only heiress to the family fortune.* ♦ *Anne, a wealthy heiress, endowed a new hospital for the community.*

heirloom ['ɛr lum] *n.* something belonging to a family that has been handed down from generation to generation. ♦ *This ring is an heirloom that my grandmother gave to me.* ♦ *That desk has been a family heirloom for centuries.*

held ['hɛld] pt/pp of hold.

helicopter ['hɛl ə kɑp tɚ] *n.* an aircraft with large, rotating blades. ♦ *A helicopter can move straight up and down or hover in the air.* ♦ *The presidential helicopter landed on the White House lawn.*

helium ['hil i əm] *n.* a gaseous chemical element that is lighter than air. (No plural form in this sense.) ♦ *The balloons were filled with helium.* ♦ *Helium's atomic number is 2, and its symbol is He.*

he'll ['hil] *cont.* "he will." ♦ *Bob can't come here today. He'll come over tomorrow, though.* ♦ *Bill said he'll paint the room next week.*

hell ['hɛl] **1.** *n.* [in certain religions] the place where the devil resides and where the souls of wicked people go after death. (No plural form in this sense. Sometimes capitalized.) ♦ *Most paintings of hell show it to be fiery and hot.* ♦ *Hell sounds dull and painful, whereas heaven just sounds dull.* **2.** *n.* suffering, misery, and despair. (Figurative on ①. No plural form in this sense.) ♦ *After I broke my foot, it was just hell.* ♦ *Painful arthritis caused my aunt to live a life of hell.* **3.** *interj.* <a word used to indicate anger or surprise.> (Colloquial.) ♦ *Hell, what do you want me to do anyway?* ♦ *Hell, I didn't know you were here.* **4. give someone hell** *idiom* to scold someone severely. ♦ *David gave his son hell for telling lies.* ♦ *Don't give me hell about it! I didn't do it!*

hellish ['hɛl ɪʃ] **1.** *adj.* like hell; infernal; as hot as hell. (Adv: *hellishly.*) ♦ *Hellish flames licked the sides of the building.* ♦ *The traveler couldn't stand the hellish temperature of the desert.* **2.** *adj.* unpleasant; awful; terrible; horrible. (Figurative on ①. Adv: *hellishly.*) ♦ *Jane had a headache from her hellish day at work.* ♦ *A hellish odor made the students run out of the room.*

hello [hɛ 'lo] **1.** *n.* a greeting; an act of saying ②. (Pl in *-s.*) ♦ *I called out a friendly hello as I entered the house.* ♦ *The arriving passengers waved their hellos to those on the dock.* **2.** *interj.* <a word used in greeting someone or in answering the telephone.> ♦ *Hello, John. How are you?* ♦ *Hello, my name is Lisa.*

helm ['hɛlm] **1.** *n.* the wheel or lever used to control the direction of a ship. (No plural form in this sense.) ♦ *The captain turned the helm to steer the ship into port.* ♦ *The helm was made of polished hardwood.* **2. at the helm (of something)** *idiom* in the position of being in control of something. ♦ *The president is at the helm of the company.* ♦ *Things will go well with Anne at the helm.*

helmet ['hɛl mət] *n.* a protective covering for the head; a covering for the head that is worn for protection. ♦ *The bicyclist wore a helmet to protect her head.* ♦ *The motorcyclist wears a helmet, as required by law.*

helmsman ['hɛlmz mən] *n., irreg.* someone who controls the helm of a ship; the person who steers a boat or ship. (Pl: helmsmen.) ♦ *The helmsman stood relaxed with one hand on the helm.* ♦ *Lisa, our helmsman, steered the ship around the reef.*

helmsmen ['hɛlmz mən] pl of helmsman.

help ['hɛlp] **1.** *n.* aid; assistance. (No plural form in this sense.) ♦ *The student asked the teacher for help with some homework.* ♦ *The stranded motorist asked the police officer for help.* **2.** *n.* someone who is hired to do a job, usually a menial job. (No plural form in this sense.) ♦ *Mary asked the hired help to prune the bushes.* ♦ *After the party, the help cleaned up.* **3.** *iv.* to give assistance. ♦ *That box looks like it's heavy to move. Can I help?* ♦ *I need some assistance. Please help if you can.* **4.** *tv.* to give assistance to someone or something; to aid someone or something. (See ⑦.) ♦ *The secretary of the organization helped me.* ♦ *The pay raise helped me with my bills.* **5.** *tv.* to relieve an illness or condition; to ease the discomfort caused by something; to make a sickness or discomfort less severe. ♦ *This medicine will help your child's cough.* ♦ *This herbal tea will help your headache.* **6.** *interj.* <a cry used when one needs aid or assistance.> ♦ *Help! My coat is caught in the car door!* ♦ *Help! I've been robbed!* **7. help (someone) do something** *phr.* to assist someone [to] do something. (Takes a bare verb.) ♦ *Bill can help load the truck.* ♦ *I am too tired to help mow the grass.* ♦ *Bill can help us load the truck.* ♦ *I am too tired to help you mow the grass.* **8. cannot help doing something** *idiom* not able to refrain from doing something; not able not to do something. ♦ *Anne is such a good cook, I can't help eating everything she makes.* ♦ *Since John loves to shop, he can't help spending money.* **9. help oneself (to something)** *idiom* to take something oneself without asking permission. ♦ *The thief helped himself to the money in the safe.* ♦ *Help yourself to more dessert.*

helper ['hɛlp ɚ] *n.* an aide; someone who helps; an assistant. ♦ *The kindergarten teacher has two adult helpers.* ♦ *Volunteer helpers are a very important resource for a hospital.*

helpful ['hɛlp fʊl] *adj.* offering or providing help; useful. (Adv: *helpfully.*) ♦ *The information the librarian gave me was very helpful.* ♦ *With your helpful directions, we were able to find the bank.*

helping ['hɛlp ɪŋ] **1.** *n.* a portion of food put on a plate. ♦ *Jimmy asked for a second helping of potatoes.* ♦ *This restaurant serves large helpings of food.* **2.** *n.* an amount; a batch or allotment. (Figurative on ①.) ♦ *The thief grabbed a large helping of money from the cash drawer.* ♦ *Bob's got more than his helping of trouble this year.* **3. lend (someone) a helping hand** *idiom* to assist someone with a task. ♦ *Mary lent a helping hand at the garage sale.* ♦ *I need someone to lend me a helping hand with this job.*

helpless ['hɛlp ləs] *adj.* not able to do something by oneself; weak; dependent. (Adv: *helplessly.*) ♦ *The helpless foal could not stand up alone.* ♦ *The mother robin fed her helpless babies.*

helpmate ['hɛlp met] **1.** *n.* an aide; an assistant; a helper; someone who helps. ♦ *The manager's helpmate went to get lunch.* ♦ *The nursing home patient had several helpmates.* **2.** *n.* a married person's spouse. (Literary.) ♦ *Dave and* *his helpmate arrived at the party early.* ♦ *Mary was looking for certain qualities in a helpmate.*

hem ['hɛm] **1.** *n.* the folded and sewn edge of a piece of cloth. ♦ *The hem of Sue's dress had become unstitched.* ♦ *The seamstress measured and sewed the hem.* **2.** *tv.* to make a nice even edge on a piece of cloth by folding and sewing. ♦ *The seamstress hemmed the dress.* ♦ *I will hem your skirt tomorrow.* **3. hem in** *tv. + adv.* to surround someone or something; to enclose someone or something. ♦ *The fence hemmed in the flock of sheep.* ♦ *The children were hemmed in by two rows of bushes.*

he-man ['hi mæn] *n., irreg.* a man who is very strong or very muscular. (Pl: he-men.) ♦ *Bob thinks he's such a he-man. He's always lifting weights.* ♦ *You can see a lot of he-men showing off at the beach.*

hematologist [him ə 'tɑl ə dʒəst] *n.* someone who studies blood and blood diseases. ♦ *Blood from the patient was analyzed by a hematologist.* ♦ *The hematologist works in a hospital laboratory.*

hematology [him ə 'tɑl ə dʒi] *n.* the medical science dealing with blood and blood diseases. (No plural form in this sense.) ♦ *There are several hematology courses at the medical school.* ♦ *Hematology is one of the branches of medicine that deals with leukemia.*

he-men ['hi mɛn] pl of he-man.

hemisphere ['hɛm əs fɪr] **1.** *n.* half of a sphere; half of a ball. ♦ *The hemisphere was placed on the table with the rounded side up.* ♦ *A plane that passes through a sphere's center forms two hemispheres.* **2.** *n.* one of two halves of the earth. ♦ *The Western Hemisphere consists of the continents of North America and South America.* ♦ *The Northern Hemisphere is north of the equator.*

hemophilia [hi mə 'fil i ə] *n.* a blood disease where the blood does not clot properly. (No plural form in this sense.) ♦ *Hemophilia causes symptoms in males.* ♦ *A person with hemophilia may have trouble stopping the bleeding of even a small cut.*

hemorrhage ['hɛm (ə) rɪdʒ] **1.** *n.* a flow of blood from a damaged artery or vein. ♦ *The patient died of an internal hemorrhage.* ♦ *A nosebleed is a minor hemorrhage.* **2.** *iv.* [for blood] to flow from a damaged artery or vein. ♦ *The patient was hemorrhaging, so the surgeons had to work quickly to repair the problem.* ♦ *The crash victim hemorrhaged in the ambulance.* **3.** *iv.* [for money or other assets] to be spent very fast and be wasted. (Figurative on ②.) ♦ *The new law allowed the tax money to hemorrhage from the treasury.* ♦ *My bank account hemorrhaged again this month and I am broke again.*

hemorrhoid ['hɛm (ə) rɔɪd] *n.* a painfully swollen blood vessel in the anus and lower rectum. ♦ *If you have hemorrhoids, sitting can be uncomfortable.* ♦ *Dave needed surgery to correct his hemorrhoids.*

hen ['hɛn] *n.* a female bird, especially a female chicken. ♦ *Every morning, the farmer went to the barn to collect all the eggs that the hens had laid.* ♦ *A hen and her chicks wandered across the barnyard.*

hence ['hɛns] **1.** *adv.* from this time; from now. ♦ *Bob will leave for New York one month hence.* ♦ *Many years hence, we will laugh about this silly mistake.* **2.** *adv.* therefore; because of this. ♦ *Jane was early, and hence she was first in line.* ♦ *I'm older than you; hence, I get to stay up later.*

henceforth ['hɛns fɔrθ] *adv.* from now on; from this time forward. ♦ *The governor declared that, henceforth, the first of June would be a holiday.* ♦ *The memo said, "Henceforth, all salary raises must be approved by the president."*

henchman ['hɛntʃ mən] *n., irreg.* an unscrupulous and obedient supporter of an important person or a politician. (Pl: henchmen. Usually a male.) ♦ *The senator had many henchmen to do his bidding.* ♦ *One of the mobster's henchmen was injured in the raid.*

henchmen ['hɛntʃ mən] pl of henchman.

he or she ['hi ɔr 'ʃi] See he ④ and ⑤. See also him ③ and ④, himself ⑥, and his ⑤ and ⑥.

hepatitis [hɛp ə 'tɑɪt ɪs] *n.* an inflammatory disease of the liver. (No plural form in this sense.) ♦ *Jaundice is a symptom of hepatitis.* ♦ *Hepatitis is usually accompanied by a fever.*

her ['hɚ] **1.** *pron.* <an objective form of she, referring to females.> (Used after prepositions and as the object of verbs.) ♦ *Mary wanted to borrow my book, so I lent it to her.* ♦ *Anne asked me to help her paint the kitchen.* **2.** *pron.* <an objective form of she, referring to ships and certain countries.> (Also other informal uses.) ♦ *Pointing at his new boat, the captain said, "What do you think of her?"* ♦ *England is a great country, and we welcome her friendship.* **3.** *pron.* <the possessive form of she, referring to a female who has already been mentioned.> (Used to modify a noun. Compare with hers.) ♦ *That coat isn't Mary's. This one is her coat.* ♦ *Why did Anne leave before eating her dinner?*

herald ['hɛr əld] **1.** *n.* someone who brings news or messages from a ruler to the people. (Older English.) ♦ *The herald brought the good news of the birth of the prince.* ♦ *The new laws were read by the herald before being posted.* **2.** *n.* a sign; an indication; a forerunner. ♦ *A robin is a herald of spring.* ♦ *Sunset is the herald of night.* **3.** *tv.* to announce or indicate that something will happen. ♦ *The flyers and posters heralded the opening of the new store.* ♦ *The newspaper heralded the return of the popular comic strip.* **4. herald in** *tv. + adv.* to greet; to welcome something. ♦ *The birds heralded in the spring.* ♦ *We will herald the new year in at a community party.*

herb ['ɚb] *n.* a plant whose seeds or leaves are used as spices or medicines. ♦ *The cooks seasoned the meat with herbs.* ♦ *Sage and mint are types of herbs.*

herbicide ['hɚb ə sɑɪd] *n.* a chemical that kills plants; a weedkiller. (No plural form in this sense.) ♦ *Bill sprayed some herbicide on the lawn to kill the dandelions.* ♦ *Jane prefers organic food and refuses to use herbicide in her garden.*

herd ['hɚd] **1.** *n.* a large group of cattle or other similar large animals such as elk, buffalo, zebra, elephants, etc. ♦ *The cowboys maintained the rancher's herds.* ♦ *A single cow strayed from the herd.* **2.** *tv.* to cause a large amount of people or animals to move together as a group. ♦ *The farmhands will herd the pigs into a small pen.* ♦ *The cowboys herded the cows to the corrals.* **3.** *tv.* to take care of cattle, sheep, or other groups of animals; to tend to cattle, sheep, or other groups of animals. ♦ *Cowboys still herd cattle for a living in some states.* ♦ *The farmer's daughter herded the sheep in the meadow.* **4.** *iv.* to form into a group; to move as a group. ♦ *Cows seem to herd naturally.* ♦ *As the people left the movie, they herded into the street.*

herdsman ['hɚdz mən] *n., irreg.* someone, usually a male, who takes care of cattle, sheep, or other groups of animals; a herder. (Pl: herdsmen.) ♦ *The herdsman talked to the cattle as if they were children.* ♦ *Ten herdsmen were hired to tend the herd of sheep.*

herdsmen ['hɚdz mən] pl of herdsman.

here ['hɪr] **1.** *adv.* in, at, to, or from the location of the speaker or writer who uses this word. ♦ *Come here.* ♦ *It's raining here. How's the weather in your town?* **2.** *adv.* now; at this point in time or in a process. ♦ *The director said "Pause here!" in the middle of the actor's speech.* ♦ *I don't know what to do here. Please help me.* **3.** *adv.* <a form that begins a sentence and is followed by a verb, which then is followed by the subject of the sentence.> (Often used to point out or offer something. Takes *be, go, stand, rest,* or a similar verb.) ♦ *Here are the tickets I promised you.* ♦ *Here rest the remains of my beloved dog, Mike.* **4.** *adj.* present; in this instance. (Colloquial. Not prenominal.) ♦ *This painting here is of a bowl of fruit.* ♦ *John here took the first prize at the swimming competition.* **5.** *n.* this place. ♦ *How far is the town from here?* ♦ *Why did you bring that dog in here?*

hereafter [hɪr 'æft ɚ] **1.** *adv.* from this point on; in the future. (Formal.) ♦ *"Williams Incorporated (hereafter known as the 'Company') is located at 100 Main Street," the contract began.* ♦ *Hereafter, Mary Jones will be known as Mary Franklin.* **2.** *n.* the afterlife; life after death. (No plural form in this sense.) ♦ *The preacher said there will be no pain in the hereafter.* ♦ *The children learned about the hereafter in Sunday school.*

hereby [hɪr 'bɑɪ] *adv.* by saying this; by this utterance. (Formal. Used with the first person, present tense.) ♦ *I hereby pronounce you husband and wife.* ♦ *I hereby christen this ship the* Friendly Dolphin.

hereditary [hə 'rɛd ɪ tɛr i] **1.** *adj.* [of genetic traits] passed from generation to generation. (Adv: *hereditarily* [hə rɛd ə 'tɛr ə li].) ♦ *This hereditary illness passes from mother to son.* ♦ *Poor eyesight and color blindness are hereditary traits.* **2.** *adj.* established through inheritance; passed from generation to generation through inheritance. (Adv: *hereditarily* [hə rɛd ə 'tɛr ə li].) ♦ *The hereditary wealth of Tom's family will belong to him someday.* ♦ *Jane's hereditary title permitted her to attend certain social functions.*

heredity [hə 'rɛd ə ti] **1.** *n.* the process of transmitting genetic characteristics from a parent to an offspring, and the results of that transfer. (No plural form in this sense.) ♦ *Is heredity or environment more important in determining how a child will develop?* ♦ *Heredity plays a major role in determining how we look.* **2.** *n.* the genetic traits inherited from one's ancestors. (No plural form in this sense.) ♦ *Mary blames all her problems on her heredity.* ♦ *As an adopted child, Tom knew little about his heredity.*

heresy ['hɛr ə si] *n.* an opinion that is different from accepted beliefs, especially in religion. (No plural form in this sense.) ♦ *Taxation without representation is heresy in the United States.* ♦ *Religious heresy is considered a serious religious offense.*

heretic ['hɛr ə tɪk] *n.* someone who practices heresy. ♦ *The heretic was burned at the stake.* ♦ *I am quite a heretic when it comes to taxation policy.*

heretical [hə 'rɛt ɪk əl] *adj.* different from accepted beliefs, especially in religion. (Adv: *heretically* [...ɪk li].) ♦ *The theories of the astronomer Copernicus were heretical in his day.* ♦ *My church is not tolerant of heretical views.*

herewith [hɪr 'wɪθ] *adv.* together with this. (Formal.) ♦ *Enclosed herewith please find a check in the amount of $1,000.* ♦ *Attached herewith is a copy of the speech.*

heritage ['hɛr ɪ tɪdʒ] **1.** *n.* the cultural background of a group of people. (No plural form in this sense.) ♦ *My heritage is primarily Korean.* ♦ *Italians have a heritage rich in music.* **2.** *n.* something that is or can be inherited; something that is passed down from generation to generation. (No plural form in this sense.) ♦ *Freedom is our nation's heritage.* ♦ *The title of king is the prince's heritage.*

hermit ['hɚ mɪt] *n.* someone who moves away from society and who lives alone in isolation. ♦ *The townspeople only saw the hermit twice a year when he came to town to buy supplies.* ♦ *The hermit lived in a tiny cottage in the woods.*

hernia ['hɚn i ə] *n.* a medical condition where tissue has pushed through a containing wall into another part of the body. ♦ *Usually a hernia involves a part of the intestine.* ♦ *John doubled over from the pain of the hernia.*

hero ['hɪr o] **1.** *n.* someone who is honored and respected for bravery or courage. (Compare with heroine. Pl in *-es.*) ♦ *The war hero returned home to a parade.* ♦ *After rescuing the child, the firefighter was hailed as a hero.* **2.** *n.* the main male character in a story, movie, or play. (See also heroine. Pl in *-es.*) ♦ *In most Westerns, the hero is the good guy.* ♦ *The hero in the movie solved the mystery.*

heroic [hɪ 'ro ɪk] *adj.* courageous; brave; valiant. (Adv: *heroically* [...ɪk li].) ♦ *The firefighters' heroic actions were reported in the local newspaper.* ♦ *David was awarded a medal for his heroic rescue of the child.*

heroin ['hɛr o ɪn] *n.* a powerful, very addictive narcotic drug. ♦ *The doctors treated the teenager who was addicted to heroin.* ♦ *The sale of heroin is illegal in the U.S.*

heroine ['hɛr o ɪn] **1.** *n.* a brave and courageous woman; a woman who does heroic actions. (Compare with hero.) ♦ *The biography was about a heroine in the time of the Civil War.* ♦ *The heroine saved the children from the fire.* **2.** *n.* the main female character in a story, movie, or play. (See also hero.) ♦ *At the end of the story, the hero and heroine fall in love.* ♦ *The heroine in this musical sings five songs.*

heroism ['hɛr o ɪz əm] **1.** *n.* a heroic act; a brave or courageous act. (No plural form in this sense.) ♦ *Bob was impressed by his friend's act of heroism.* ♦ *The mayor rewarded the police officer's heroism with a plaque.* **2.** *n.* the quality of being a hero or a heroine. (No plural form in this sense.) ♦ *Anne's heroism is outstanding and an inspiration to all.* ♦ *Risking your life for another requires heroism.*

heron ['hɛr ən] *n.* any of numerous species of wading birds with long necks, beaks, and legs. ♦ *We saw a heron in the marsh.* ♦ *Herons feed on fish and frogs.*

herpes ['hɚ piz] *n.* a viral disease that causes blisters to form on the skin and the mucous membranes. (No plural form in this sense.) ♦ *Some forms of herpes are sexually transmitted.* ♦ *A cold sore is a form of herpes.*

herring ['hɛr ɪŋ] **1.** *n., irreg.* an edible fish with silver scales that swims in large groups. (Pl: *herring.*) ♦ *A herring is a very tiny fish.* ♦ *Herring are found in huge numbers in the Atlantic Ocean.* **2.** *n.* the meat of ①. (No plural form in this sense.) ♦ *Herring tastes very good with sour cream.* ♦ *Bob served pickled herring on crackers as an appetizer.*

hers ['hɚz] *pron.* <the possessive form of she, referring to a female who has already been mentioned.> (Used in place of a noun. Compare with her.) ♦ *You gave Mary my coat. The coat in the corner is hers.* ♦ *I asked my friends for a pencil, and Anne gave me one of hers.*

herself [hɚ 'sɛlf] **1.** *pron.* <the reflexive form of she.> (Used after a verb or a preposition when the subject of the sentence is the same female to which the pronoun refers.) ♦ *Anne considered herself to be quite successful.* ♦ *Did Sue hurt herself when she fell down?* **2.** *pron.* <an emphatic form of she.> (Follows the nominal that is being emphasized.) ♦ *The mayor herself will visit the injured workers.* ♦ *Susan herself greeted us at the door.* **3. by herself** *phr.* with the help of no one else. ♦ *She can do it by herself.* ♦ *Susan is unable to get there by herself.* **4. by herself** *phr.* with no one else present; alone. ♦ *She hates to go to strange places by herself.* ♦ *She sat by herself at a table big enough for six people.*

he's ['hiz] **1.** *cont.* "he is." ♦ *I don't know where John is. I know that he's not here.* ♦ *Bill said that he's going on vacation next week.* **2.** *cont.* "he has," where has is an auxiliary. ♦ *Bob said he's got a bad headache.* ♦ *I spoke to John. He's already purchased the tickets.*

hesitant ['hɛz ə tənt] *adj.* hesitating; wavering; not sure. (Adv: *hesitantly.*) ♦ *Tony was hesitant when asked about his religious beliefs.* ♦ *The inspector was intrigued by the suspect's hesitant reply.*

hesitate ['hɛz ə tet] **1.** *iv.* to waiver; to pause for a moment before doing something, especially because one is unsure of something. ♦ *Thinking his answer was wrong, John hesitated before saying anything.* ♦ *The driver hesitated while she debated which way to turn.* **2.** *iv.* to be unwilling to do something; to be reluctant to do something. ♦ *I hesitated to accept the new responsibility because I was already busy.* ♦ *John hesitated when I asked him to help me move some furniture.*

hesitation [hɛz ə 'te ʃən] *n.* a pause; a delay; a moment of doubt or uncertainty. ♦ *Dave's brief hesitation allowed someone to jump in line ahead of him.* ♦ *The hesitations in Anne's speech were added for emphasis.*

heterosexual [hɛt ə ro 'sɛk sju əl] **1.** *n.* someone who is attracted exclusively to persons of the opposite sex. (Compare with homosexual and bisexual.) ♦ *Most married people are heterosexuals.* ♦ *The researcher interviewed heterosexuals about their sex lives.* **2.** *adj.* <the adj. use of ①.> (Adv: *heterosexually.*) ♦ *There were only a few heterosexual couples at the gay bar.* ♦ *John doubted the statistics in an article concerning heterosexual sexual activity.*

heterosexuality [hɛt ə ro sɛk sju 'æl ə tɪ] *n.* attraction toward people of the opposite sex. (No plural form in this sense.) ♦ *Heterosexuality is the predominant orientation in most cultures.* ♦ *The pamphlet discussed sexually transmitted diseases with respect to heterosexuality.*

hew ['hju] *tv., irreg.* to cut something with an axe; to shape something with an axe. (Pt: *hewed;* pp: *hewed* or hewn.) ♦ *The farmer hewed the sapling into firewood.* ♦ *The timbers had been hewn from the trunks of great oak trees.*

hewn ['hjun] pp of hew.

hexagon ['hɛks ə gɑn] *n.* a shape that has six sides; a polygon that has six sides. ♦ *A stop sign has the shape of a hexagon.* ♦ *Bob cut the paper into an irregular hexagon.*

hexagonal [hɛks 'æg ə nəl] *adj.* having six sides. (Adv: *hexagonally.*) ♦ *A hexagonal figure has six sides and six angles.* ♦ *The sign was covered with graffiti, but because of its hexagonal shape, I knew it was a stop sign.*

Hey! ['he] **1.** *interj.* <a word that is used to get someone's attention.> (Colloquial.) ♦ *Hey! Come see my new bike!* ♦ *Hey, watch where you are going!* **2.** *interj.* "Hello!" (Colloquial.) ♦ *Hey! How's it going?* ♦ *Hey, Bill.*

heyday ['he de] *n.* the best time; the time of someone's or something's greatest success. ♦ *Grandpa says his heyday was when he was 21.* ♦ *The aging athlete's heyday is over.*

Hi! ['hɑɪ] *interj.* "Hello!"; <a word used in greeting someone informally.> ♦ *Hi, Sue.* ♦ *Hi! What's happening?*

hiatus [hɑɪ 'e təs] *n.* a pause in a series of things; an interruption; a gap. ♦ *In the brief hiatus between meetings, I managed to have a quick meal.* ♦ *During the hiatus between two television seasons, the actor worked on a movie.*

hibernate ['hɑɪb ɚ net] *iv.* to sleep through the winter; to spend the winter in a deep sleep-like condition. ♦ *Bears hibernate.* ♦ *During the cold winter, I wish I could hibernate.*

hibernation [hɑɪb ɚ 'ne ʃən] *n.* spending the winter in a deep sleep-like state. (No plural form in this sense.) ♦ *Hibernation is practiced by bears and a few other mammals.* ♦ *Successful hibernation can take place if the animal has stored enough fat.*

hic-cough ['hɪk əp] See hiccup.

hiccup AND **hic-cough** ['hɪk əp] **1.** *n.* a sharp, sudden gulp of air. (Usually plural.) ♦ *Bob had the hiccups so long, his stomach began to hurt.* ♦ *It was difficult for Mary to talk because of her hiccups.* **2.** *iv.* to make ①. ♦ *Jane covered her mouth as she hiccuped.* ♦ *The teacher had to stop the lecture when he began to hiccup.*

hick ['hɪk] *n.* someone who lives in the country; a rural person. (Derogatory.) ♦ *The rancher resented being referred to as a hick.* ♦ *Some city people think that most farmers are hicks.*

hickory ['hɪk (ə) ri] **1.** *n.* a North American hardwood tree that has nuts similar to the walnut. ♦ *Nuts from a hickory are sweet and can be eaten.* ♦ *Hickories are usually very tall trees.* **2.** *n.* wood from ①. (No plural form in this sense.) ♦ *Hickory is a hard wood.* ♦ *The carpenter used hickory to make the furniture.* **3.** *adj.* made from ②. ♦ *The hickory logs took a long time to burn in the fireplace.* ♦ *Bob bought a hickory table.*

hid ['hɪd] pt of hide.

hidden ['hɪd n] **1.** pp of hide. **2.** *adj.* (Adv: *hiddenly.*) not in view; concealed. ♦ *We searched for the hidden treasure but never found it.* ♦ *The children found all but one of the hidden presents.*

hide ['hɑɪd] **1.** *tv., irreg.* to place something out of view; to place something so that it cannot be seen; to conceal something. (Pt: hide; pp: hidden.) ♦ *Mary hid my birthday present in her bedroom.* ♦ *The dog hides his bones in the garden.* **2.** *iv., irreg.* to place oneself so that one cannot be seen; to conceal oneself. ♦ *I can't find Mary. Where is she hiding?* ♦ *You can't see John in this picture. He's hiding behind that tree.* **3.** *n.* the skin of an animal, especially when used to make leather. ♦ *The hunter tanned the deer's hide.* ♦ *The hide was large enough to make a few pairs of shoes.* **4. hide-and-(go-)seek** *idiom* a children's game where all the players except one hide themselves, and the remaining person tries to find them. ♦ *We played hide-and-seek and we still haven't found Jimmy.* ♦ *The children are outside playing hide-and-go-seek.* **5. hide one's light under a bushel** *idiom* to conceal one's good ideas or talents. ♦ *Jane has some good ideas, but she doesn't speak very often. She hides her light under a bushel.* ♦ *Don't hide your light under a bushel. Share your gifts with other people.*

hideaway ['hɑɪd ə we] *n.* a secret place; a secluded place. ♦ *The children had a hideaway in the bushes.* ♦ *The lovers met in their hideaway.*

hideous ['hɪd i əs] **1.** *adj.* incredibly ugly. (Adv: *hideously.*) ♦ *Despite its low price, no one would buy the hideous tie.* ♦ *Bob wore a hideous outfit to work on Halloween.* **2.** *adj.* horrible; terrible. (Adv: *hideously.*) ♦ *The hideous tale scared the children and the adults.* ♦ *Who is spreading that hideous rumor?*

hideout ['hɑɪd ɑʊt] *n.* a place where someone hides; a place where outlaws hide. ♦ *The thieves had several hideouts in the mountains.* ♦ *Jimmy wouldn't allow adults into his hideout.*

hiding ['hɑɪd ɪŋ] **go into hiding** *idiom* to conceal oneself in a hidden place for a period of time. (No plural form in this sense.) ♦ *The political dissident went into hiding.* ♦ *After robbing the bank, the bandits went into hiding for months.*

hierarchy ['hɑɪr ɑr ki] *n.* a system with levels or ranks. ♦ *The military has a rigid hierarchy with numerous ranks.* ♦ *The company president is at the top of the company hierarchy.*

high ['hɑɪ] **1.** *adj.* far above the ground; further above than the average; not low. (Comp: *higher;* sup: *highest.*) ♦ *Put the candy on the high shelf where the children can't reach it.* ♦ *I like to look at the city from a high place, such as the top floor of a tall building.* **2.** *adj.* extending a specified distance upward; at or reaching a specified distance above the ground or above sea level. (Follows the measure of height. Comp: *higher.*) ♦ *That tall building is 50 stories high.* ♦ *Right now the little tree is only two feet high, but it will grow.* **3.** *adj.* great in power, rank, or importance. (Adv: *highly.* Comp: *higher;* sup: *highest.*) ♦ *A high official in the federal government will be in our parade on Independence Day.* ♦ *An admiral is a naval officer with a very high rank.* **4.** *adj.* [of heat, number, pitch, price, velocity, intelligence, standards, etc.] great or strong, or greater or stronger than what is normal or average. (Adv: *highly.* Comp: *higher;* sup: *highest.*) ♦ *High temperatures caused us to turn on the air conditioner.* ♦ *The high winds blew down the tree.* **5.** *n.* the top point; a peak; the uppermost level. ♦ *The stock market reached a new high today.* ♦ *Our sales are at a high for the year.* **6.** *adv.* to or at a lofty place; to or at a place that is far up. (Comp: *higher;* sup: *highest.*) ♦ *The eagle was flying high.* ♦ *The painter climbed high on the ladder.* **7. act high-and-mighty** *idiom* to act proud and powerful; to act haughty. ♦ *Why does the doctor always have to act so high-and-mighty?* ♦ *If Sally wouldn't act so high-and-mighty, she'd have more friends.* **8. leave someone high and dry** *idiom* to leave someone helpless. ♦ *All my workers quit and left me high and dry.* ♦ *All the children ran away and left Billy high and dry to take the blame for the broken window.* **9. running high** *idiom* [for feelings] to be in a state of excitement or anger. ♦ *Feelings were running high as the general election approached.* ♦ *The mood of the crowd was running high when they saw the mother slap her child.*

highbrow ['hɑɪ brɑʊ] **1.** *adj.* very educated, intellectual, or cultured. ♦ *The highbrow crowd did not laugh at the vulgar comedian's jokes.* ♦ *The teenagers did not appreciate the highbrow music.* **2.** *n.* someone who is very educated, intellectual, and cultured. (Often intended as derogatory.) ♦ *The highbrow spent all day in the library reading books.* ♦ *John may be a highbrow, but he's lacking in common sense.*

highchair ['hɑɪ tʃer] *n.* a tall chair, sometimes having a tray attached, that small children sit on to eat meals. ♦ *Bill asked the waiter to bring a highchair for his child.* ♦ *The baby banged on the tray of the highchair.*

higher-up ['hɑɪ ɚ 'əp] *n.* someone who has authority or power; a superior. ♦ *The disgruntled employee had little respect for the higher-ups.* ♦ *The higher-ups all get bonuses at the end of the year.*

high fidelity [hɑɪ fɪ 'dɛl ə ti] **1.** *n.* a type of sound reproduction with a high level of faithfulness to the original. (No plural form in this sense.) ♦ *High fidelity sounds as close to the real thing as possible.* ♦ *My little radio produces sound, but it is certainly not high fidelity.* **2. high-fidelity** *adj.* [of sound reproduction] having a high level of faithfulness to the original. ♦ *The high-fidelity sound system for the stadium was very expensive.* ♦ *My new computer has high-fidelity speakers to play sounds from the Internet.*

high-handed ['hɑɪ 'hæn dɪd] *adj.* overbearing; arrogant; rude. (Adv: *high-handedly.*) ♦ *The government was being sort of high-handed when it doubled the tax on gasoline.* ♦ *The employees did not appreciate their manager's high-handed attitude.*

high heels ['hɑɪ 'hilz] See heel.

highjack ['hɑɪ dʒæk] See hijack.

highjacker ['hɑɪ dʒæk ɚ] See hijacker.

highlight ['hɑɪ lɑɪt] **1.** *n.* the most exciting part of an event. ♦ *The highlight of my year was when I got a new job.* ♦ *The students were asked to write about the highlights of their summer vacations.* **2.** *tv.* to make something visually distinctive or prominent so it gets more attention. ♦ *The editor highlighted the mistakes in the manuscript in red ink.* ♦ *Please highlight each important point in the book in yellow.* **3.** *tv.* to emphasize something; to indicate, in some way, that an idea or concept is important; to focus attention on an idea or concept. (Figurative on ②.) ♦ *The teacher highlighted the key concepts in the essay for the students.* ♦ *In his speech, the candidate highlighted the financial mess the country was in.*

highly ['haɪ li] **1.** *adv.* very; extremely; more than normal or expected. (Usually before an adjective derived from a verb.) ♦ *The movie was highly entertaining.* ♦ *Waiting for the surgery, I was highly agitated.* **2. speak highly of someone or something** *idiom* to express a very good opinion about someone or something. ♦ *Tom speaks highly of the carpenter who built his deck.* ♦ *Bill doesn't speak very highly of the new car he just bought.* **3. think highly of someone or something** *idiom* to have a very good opinion of someone or something. ♦ *Mary thinks highly of her efficient secretary.* ♦ *I think highly of this very useful encyclopedia.*

high-pitched ['haɪ 'pɪtʃt] **1.** *adj.* of a high pitch. ♦ *The phone caller had a loud, high-pitched voice.* ♦ *It was unpleasant to listen to the speaker's high-pitched voice.* **2.** *adj.* [of a roof or a slanted area] with a steep slope. ♦ *The climber slid down the high-pitched mountain slope.* ♦ *This high-pitched roof is difficult to repair.*

high-pressure ['haɪ 'prɛʃ ɚ] **1.** *adj.* made to withstand pressures above normal; operating at pressures greater than normal. ♦ *It would be dangerous if the high-pressure pipes exploded.* ♦ *The high-pressure stream of hot water easily cleaned the car.* **2.** *adj.* demanding; requiring a lot of intense effort. ♦ *When she developed an ulcer, Lisa quit her high-pressure job.* ♦ *The high-pressure performance required all of the musician's skills.* **3.** *adj.* [of sales methods] insistent and aggressive. ♦ *Used-car dealers are often accused of high-pressure sales tactics.* ♦ *The door-to-door salesman used a high-pressure approach.*

high-ranking ['haɪ 'ræŋk ɪŋ] **1.** *adj.* having a high rank. ♦ *The high-ranking officers sat at their own table.* ♦ *The private saluted all the high-ranking officers.* **2.** *adj.* important; having a lot of authority or political power. ♦ *The high-ranking government official had access to the president.* ♦ *Anne is a high-ranking manager at her company.*

high-rise ['haɪ raɪz] **1.** *n.* an apartment or office building with several stories; a skyscraper. ♦ *My first home was an apartment on the top floor of a high-rise.* ♦ *There were twelve stories in the high-rise.* **2.** *adj.* designed as ①. ♦ *The Smiths moved into a high-rise apartment when their kids had grown.* ♦ *This high-rise building has twelve floors.*

high school ['haɪ skul] **1.** *n.* a school for students who have finished elementary school or junior high school. ♦ *John will go to high school after he finishes junior high school.* ♦ *After high school, you can go to college or a trade school.* **2. high-school** *adj.* <the adj. use of ①.> ♦ *Two old high-school friends met by accident on the beach.* ♦ *I remember my high-school days very well.*

high-strung ['haɪ 'strʌŋ] *adj.* nervous; excitable. ♦ *The high-strung dog yapped all day.* ♦ *The high-strung child couldn't sit still.*

high-tech ['haɪ 'tɛk] *adj.* using advanced or high technology; complicated; using complex electronic equipment. ♦ *A music lover, Anne has the latest high-tech stereo equipment.* ♦ *We purchased the latest high-tech computer with a CD-ROM.*

highway ['haɪ we] *n.* a main road—especially one designed for high speed—used to get from one city to another. ♦ *The easiest way to get to Chicago from here is to take the main highway.* ♦ *Several major highways go right through the city.*

hijack AND **highjack** ['haɪ dʒæk] *tv.* to take over a car, bus, truck, airplane, etc., by force in order to hold the passengers hostage, demand that they drive or fly somewhere else, or to steal the things being carried on board. (See also **carjack**, **skyjack**.) ♦ *The terrorists hijacked the airplane and held the passengers hostage.* ♦ *The authorities did not know who hijacked the bus.*

hijacker AND **highjacker** ['haɪ dʒæk ɚ] *n.* someone who takes control of a bus, truck, plane, etc., by force. ♦ *The hijackers carried concealed handguns.* ♦ *The hijackers burst through the door and demanded that the pilot fly the plane to an island.*

hike ['haɪk] **1.** *n.* a long walk, especially in the woods, mountains, etc. ♦ *A hike is good exercise.* ♦ *We like to take hikes in the mountains.* **2.** *iv.* to go on ①; to take ①. ♦ *The couple hiked together through the forest.* ♦ *For exercise, I hike.* **3. hike (up)** *tv.* (+ *adv.*) to pull something up, especially to pull or lift clothing up so that it does not sag or so that the bottom does not hang as low. ♦ *Sally hiked up her pants as she crossed the stream.* ♦ *Anne had to hike up her long skirt to avoid tripping on the stairs.* **4. take a hike** *idiom* to go on a hike; to do hiking. ♦ *It's a beautiful day. Let's take a hike in the woods.* ♦ *We took a hike through the forest to visit John's cabin.* **5. Take a hike!** *idiom* "Go away!" ♦ *You are being annoying! Take a hike!* ♦ *She was bothering me, so I told her to take a hike.*

hiker ['haɪk ɚ] *n.* someone who hikes. ♦ *The hiker reached the waterfall by noon.* ♦ *As they passed on the trail, the hikers greeted each other.*

hilarious [hɪ 'lɛr i əs] *adj.* very funny. (Adv: *hilariously.*) ♦ *The audience roared at the hilarious comedy.* ♦ *I thought my jokes were hilarious but no one laughed.*

hill ['hɪl] **1.** *n.* a raised part of the earth's surface smaller than a mountain. ♦ *The hills were at the bottom of the mountain range.* ♦ *We climbed to the top of the smallest hill.* **2.** *n.* a heap or mound of earth, especially one made by an animal. ♦ *Dozens of ants were building the ant hill on the sidewalk.* ♦ *The dog made a little hill where he buried his bone.* **3. over the hill** *idiom* old; too old to do something. ♦ *Now that Mary's forty, she thinks she's over the hill.* ♦ *My grandfather was over eighty before he felt as if he was over the hill.*

hillbilly ['hɪl bɪl i] *n.* a rural person who lives in the hills or mountains of the Southeast U.S. (Usually derogatory.) ♦ *I'm just an old hillbilly from the mountains of Virginia.* ♦ *There were three families of hillbillies living back in the woods north of the town.*

hillside ['hɪl saɪd] **1.** *n.* the side of a hill. ♦ *We watched the sunset from the hillside.* ♦ *The hiker climbed up the hillside and rested at the top.* **2.** *adj.* on the side of a hill. ♦ *Bob built a hillside retreat in the woods.* ♦ *Only the ranger knew about the hillside cave.*

hilltop ['hɪl tɑp] **1.** *n.* the top of a hill. ♦ *The exhausted hiker was happy to reach the hilltop.* ♦ *The view from the hilltop was breathtaking.* **2.** *adj.* on the top of a hill. ♦ *The people in the valley could see the lights of the hilltop house.* ♦ *The hilltop vista provided a wonderful view of the river below.*

hilly ['hɪl i] *adj.* not flat; having hills. (Comp: *hillier;* sup: *hilliest.*) ♦ *The hilly countryside was beautiful in the fall.* ♦ *The hilly land was not suitable for farming.*

him ['hɪm] **1.** *pron.* <an objective form of he ①.> (The pronoun used to refer to males. Used after prepositions and as the object of verbs.) ♦ *It's Bill's birthday, so I gave him a present.* ♦ *David was sick, so I went to the store for him.* **2.** *pron.* <an objective form of he ②.> (Used when the sex of a grammatical object of a verb or preposition is indeterminate, undetermined, or irrelevant. Objected to by some as actually referring only to males in this sense. Compare with ④. See also them ②.) ♦ *Every single person will get what is coming to him.* ♦ *The agency will see that each person receives the food allotted to him.* **3. him or her** *phr.* [where there is known to be a choice between male and female] either him ① or her ①. ♦ *Both John and Mary want the book, and you have to decide whether to give it to him or her.* ♦ *Both John and Mary are expecting phone calls, so when the telephone rings it will probably be for him or her.* **4. him or her** *phr.* <a third-person plural objective pronoun.> (Used when the sex of a grammatical object of a verb or preposition is indeterminate, undetermined, or irrelevant. Also used to assert that both sexes are involved.) ♦ *When someone returns my lost wallet, I will give him or her a reward.* ♦ *If someone calls, please tell him or her to call back later.*

himself [hɪm 'sɛlf] **1.** *pron.* <the reflexive form of he ①.> (Used after a verb or a preposition when the subject of the sentence is the same male to which the pronoun refers.) ♦ *Bill talked to himself as he walked to work.* ♦ *John took himself for a quiet walk on the beach.* **2.** *pron.* <the reflexive form of he ②.> (Used after a verb or a preposition when the sex of the subject of the sentence is indeterminate, undetermined, or irrelevant. This sense is objected to by some as actually referring only to males. Compare with ⑥.) ♦ *Each citizen was asked to introduce himself to the mayor.* ♦ *Each dissenting member was told to remove himself from the room.* **3.** *pron.* <an emphatic form of him.> (Follows the nominal being emphasized.) ♦ *He himself will read his poems for us.* ♦ *The mayor himself will come to the reception.* **4. by himself** *phr.* with the help of no one else. (Refers only to a male.) ♦ *Can he do it by himself?* ♦ *The two-year-old boy can get dressed by himself.* **5. by himself** *phr.* alone; with no one else present. (Refers only to a male.) ♦ *He is home by himself tonight.* ♦ *He hates to eat by himself. It makes him feel lonely.* **6. himself or herself** *phr.* <the reflexive form of him or her.> (Used after a verb or a preposition when the sex of the subject of the sentence is indeterminate, undetermined, or irrelevant.) ♦ *Each citizen was invited to introduce himself or herself to the mayor.* ♦ *Whoever comes in late will have to find a seat for himself or herself.*

hind ['haɪnd] *adj.* positioned at the rear or back of something. ♦ *The dog's hind leg was broken.* ♦ *Tom was at the hind end of the line and did not see me.*

hinder ['hɪn dɚ] **1.** *tv.* to attempt to prevent someone or something from doing something; to block someone or something from doing something. ♦ *Jane's boss hindered her from moving to a new job.* ♦ *The tall fence hindered the children from going to the lake.* **2.** *tv.* to attempt to prevent something from happening, progressing, or succeeding; to make it difficult for something to happen, progress, or succeed. ♦ *Congress is hindering all efforts to reform taxes.* ♦ *Tree roots hinder soil erosion.*

hindrance ['hɪn drəns] *n.* someone or something that interferes with something; an obstacle. ♦ *We faced many hindrances to our plan.* ♦ *Lack of money is one hindrance to our buying a larger house.*

hindsight ['haɪnd saɪt] *n.* understanding an event only after it has happened. (No plural form in this sense.) ♦ *With the benefit of hindsight, the professor said England should have handled the Revolutionary War differently.* ♦ *In hindsight, if I'd finished college, maybe I'd have a better job now.*

Hindu ['hɪn du] *n.* a person from India, especially one who practices Hinduism. ♦ *Hindus practice the religion and culture associated with Hinduism.* ♦ *Some Hindus in this country speak English with a British accent.*

Hinduism ['hɪn du ɪz əm] *n.* a major religion of India and south central Asia. (No plural form in this sense.) ♦ *Followers of Hinduism recognize several deities and believe in reincarnation.* ♦ *Hinduism is represented by many schools of philosophy and many manners of the expression of belief.*

hinge ['hɪndʒ] **1.** *n.* a jointed device that fits two things together so that one of the things can move, such as a door or gate. ♦ *The antique chest had ornate brass hinges.* ♦ *The garden gate swung open on its hinges.* **2. hinge on something** *idiom* to depend on something. ♦ *Everything hinges on Anne's timely arrival at the party.* ♦ *My acceptance of the promotion hinges on whether or not I also get a raise in pay.*

hint ['hɪnt] **1.** *n.* a clue; a suggestion that helps solve a puzzle or answer a question. ♦ *Mary gave Bill a hint about his birthday present.* ♦ *I don't know the answer. Please give me a hint.* **2.** *n.* a small trace; a little bit of something; a small amount. ♦ *There was a hint of oregano in the tomato sauce.* ♦ *I start to cough at even the slightest hint of cigarette smoke.* **3.** *tv.* to suggest ①; to provide ①. (Takes a clause.) ♦ *The teacher hinted that the answer started with the letter B.* ♦ *John hinted that he wanted a new shirt for his birthday.* **4. hint (at)** *iv.* (+ *prep. phr.*) to give hints. ♦ *Mary is always hinting at what she wants.* ♦ *I never have to ask the children what they want for their birthdays, since they are always hinting.*

hinterland ['hɪn tɚ lænd] *n.* the undeveloped area of a region; the interior of a country away from the shore or away from a river. (From German.) ♦ *The pioneers moved westward into the hinterland.* ♦ *Wild game is abundant in the hinterland.*

hip ['hɪp] **1.** *n.* one of the two parts of the body above the thigh and below the waist; one of the two parts of the body where the leg joins the waist. ♦ *Anne slipped on the ice and broke her hip.* ♦ *The teacher stood with his hand on his hip.* **2.** *adj.* in style; fashionable. (Older slang. Comp: *hipper;* sup: *hippest.*) ♦ *What are the latest hip clothes?* ♦ *Teenagers can tell you all the hip new words.*

hippie ['hɪp i] *n.* someone, especially during the late 1960s and 1970s, who rebelled against society by growing long hair, using drugs, listening to certain kinds of rock music, and dressing in jeans, T-shirts, etc. ♦ *Many hippies protested against the Vietnam War.* ♦ *Hippies were distrustful of anyone over the age of 30.*

hippo ['hɪp o] *n.* a hippopotamus. (Pl ends in -*s.*) ♦ *Hundreds of hippos cooled off in the river.* ♦ *The hippo is a massive mammal with short legs.*

hippopotami [hɪp ə 'pɑt ə maɪ] a pl of hippopotamus.

hippopotamus [hɪp ə 'pɑt ə məs] *n.* a large, roundish African animal that lives in and near rivers, having thick skin and no hair. (From the Greek meaning 'river horse.' The English plural is *hippopotamuses* or hippopotami.) ♦ *The zoo had two hippopotamuses.* ♦ *The hippopotamus has a large head and mouth.*

hire ['hɑɪr] **1.** *tv.* to employ someone at a job; to pay someone to do work. ♦ *David hired some of his relatives to work at the factory.* ♦ *I want to hire Bill, but he wants too much money.* **2. not for hire** *idiom* [of a taxi] not available to take new passengers. ♦ *The taxi was going to pick someone up at a nearby hotel and was not for hire.* ♦ *The taxi had a lighted sign that said it was not for hire.* **3. new hire** *idiom* a person who has recently been hired; a newly employed person. ♦ *Anne is our new hire who will begin work Tuesday.* ♦ *The accounting department is full of new hires.*

hireling ['hɑɪr lɪŋ] *n.* someone who is paid to follow orders. (Usually mildly derogatory.) ♦ *I'm just a hireling, don't ask me to make decisions.* ♦ *Mary started in the company as a hireling, and now she owns it.*

his ['hɪz] **1.** *pron.* <the possessive form of he, referring to a male who has already been mentioned.> (Used to modify a noun.) ♦ *This is his coat.* ♦ *Mike said that was his idea.* **2.** *pron.* <the possessive form of he, referring to a male who has already been mentioned.> (Used in place of a noun.) ♦ *Where's Bill? This coat is his, and I want to give it to him.* ♦ *Mike said that the idea was his.* **3.** *pron.* <the possessive form of he, referring to a person who has already been mentioned.> (Used when the sex of the person referred to is indeterminate, undetermined, or irrelevant. Objected to by some as actually referring only to males in this sense. Compare with ⑥. See also their ②.) ♦ *Each student took off his jacket.* ♦ *Everyone was told to take his seat.* **4.** *pron.* <the possessive form of he, referring to a person who has already been mentioned.> (Used in place of a noun. Used when the sex of the person referred to is indeterminate, undetermined, or irrelevant. Objected to by some as actually referring only to males in this sense.) ♦ *None were left. Each student had taken his.* ♦ *Because he needed to see all the reports, the manager asked each employee to submit his immediately.* **5. his or her** *phr.* [where there is known to be a choice between male and female] either his ① or her ③. ♦ *Only John and Mary put their coats in the closet, so it must be his or her coat that has fallen to the floor.* ♦ *Both John and Mary are expecting phone calls, so when the telephone rings it will probably be his or her call.* **6. his or her** *phr.* <a third-person singular possessive pronoun.> (Used when the sex of the person referred to is indeterminate, undetermined, or irrelevant. Also used to assert that both sexes are involved.) ♦ *Each student should hang his or her coat in the closet.* ♦ *The usher will take each person to his or her seat.*

Hispanic [hɪ 'spæn ɪk] **1.** *n.* someone who is from, or whose family is from, a Latin American country where Spanish is spoken. ♦ *The Hispanics who live next door to me are from Mexico.* ♦ *David speaks Spanish with the Hispanics in his neighborhood.* **2.** *adj.* <the adj. use of ①.> ♦ *The Hispanic family spoke Spanish at home.* ♦ *We studied Hispanic culture in school.*

hiss ['hɪs] **1.** *n.* the sound that a snake makes, a long [s] sound. ♦ *The camper jumped with fright when he heard the snake's hiss.* ♦ *We heard the hiss before we saw the cat.* **2.** *iv.* to make ①. ♦ *The snake hissed at its prey.* ♦ *The escaping steam of the locomotive hissed.*

histamine ['hɪs tə mɪn] *n.* a chemical found in body tissues that is released during allergic reactions, causing irritation. (No plural form in this sense.) ♦ *The release of histamine dilates blood vessels.* ♦ *To combat histamine, allergy sufferers take an antihistamine.*

historian [hɪ 'stor i ən] *n.* someone who studies history; someone who writes about history. ♦ *The historian had authored several books on the Civil War.* ♦ *My advisor is a Revolutionary War historian.*

historic [hɪ 'stor ɪk] **1.** *adj.* famous; important in history. (Adv: *historically* [...ɪk li].) ♦ *Many historic events of the 20th century were captured on film.* ♦ *The students studied the historic treaty that ended the war.* **2.** *adj.* old and representative of something historic ①; preserved as part of an event or place in history. ♦ *The historic building is being preserved.* ♦ *The historic battlefield is now a national park.*

historical [hɪ 'stor ɪ kəl] **1.** *adj.* using or applying history. (Adv: *historically* [...ɪk li].) ♦ *The story is based on historical fact, not legend.* ♦ *The professor loved historical research about the Pilgrims.* **2.** *adj.* [of people and events] occurring in history. (Adv: *historically* [...ɪk li].) ♦ *George and Martha Washington are historical figures.* ♦ *The chronology lists the historical events in order.*

history ['hɪs tə ri] **1.** *n.* the study of events that have happened. (No plural form in this sense.) ♦ *History fascinates Jane, especially life during the Middle Ages.* ♦ *Bill developed an interest in Civil War history after visiting Gettysburg.* **2.** *n.* a record of events that have happened. ♦ *The United States has a short history compared to other nations of the world.* ♦ *We have kept a diary detailing the history of our family.* **3.** *n.* background; facts about the past of someone or something. ♦ *The history of this ship is interesting.* ♦ *Everyone knew the history of the rivalry between the colleges.*

histrionics [hɪ stri 'ɑn ɪks] *n.* overly dramatic behavior. (Treated as plural.) ♦ *No one was amused by the child's histrionics.* ♦ *The drama teacher chided the actor for his histrionics.*

hit ['hɪt] **1.** pt/pp of hit. **2.** *tv., irreg.* to strike someone or something; to contact something violently or with force. (Pt/pp: hit.) ♦ *The batter hit the ball.* ♦ *Sliding on the ice, the car hit a pedestrian.* **3.** *tv., irreg.* to reach something. ♦ *The stock market hit an all-time high today.* ♦ *Our sales hit a record low for the year.* **4.** *n.* a blow ⑮; a jab. ♦ *The boxer threw hits at the punching bag.* ♦ *He delivered a nasty hit on the chin.* **5.** *n.* someone or something that is very successful. ♦ *Everyone loved the play. It's a hit!* ♦ *The song quickly became a hit.* **6.** *n.* [in baseball] a play where the batter hits the ball and is able to get to a base safely. ♦ *The player hasn't gotten a hit yet this season.* ♦ *The batter only had two hits in the game.* **7.** *adj.* [of music or performances] popular. (Only prenominal.) ♦ *The hit musical was sold out every night.* ♦ *Everyone was humming the hit song.* **8. hit someone hard** *idiom* to affect someone's emotions strongly. ♦ *The death of his friend hit John hard.* ♦ *The investor was hit hard by the falling stock prices.*

9. make a hit (with someone or something) *idiom* to please someone. ♦ *The singer made a hit with the audience.* ♦ *John made a hit with my parents last evening.*

hit-and-run ['hɪt n 'rʌn] **1.** *n.* an accident where a driver hits someone or something with a car and drives away without stopping to help or to claim responsibility. ♦ *The police chased the driver who had caused the hit-and-run.* ♦ *Seeing the dent in her car, Mary knew she had been the victim of a hit-and-run.* **2.** *adj.* <the adj. use of ①.> ♦ *The hit-and-run accident seriously injured the pedestrian.* ♦ *The crowd cheered as the police sped after the hit-and-run driver.*

hitch ['hɪtʃ] **1.** *n.* a connection onto which something is attached, such as a trailer to a car or tractor. ♦ *There was a hitch on the back of the car to pull a trailer.* ♦ *The horse van was attached to the pickup truck by a hitch.* **2.** *n.* a problem that causes a delay; a temporary obstacle. ♦ *There was a slight hitch in our plan, so we devised a better one.* ♦ *The flat tire was an insignificant hitch in our trip.* **3.** *tv.* to fasten something to something else, especially using a rope. ♦ *The cowboy hitched his horse to the fence.* ♦ *We hitched the swing to a strong, horizontal branch of a tree.* **4. hitch up** *tv.* + *adv.* to pull clothing up. ♦ *Anne hitched up her skirt to step over the puddle.* ♦ *When John stood up, he had to hitch up his pants.* **5. hitch a ride** *idiom* to get a ride by acting as a **hitchhiker**. ♦ *The runaway teenager hitched a ride with a trucker.* ♦ *When his car ran out of gas, Bob hitched a ride with the police officer.*

hitchhike ['hɪtʃ hɑɪk] *iv.* to try to get a free ride from cars and trucks that pass on the highway. ♦ *Mary's parents warned her never to hitchhike.* ♦ *The students hitchhiked across Europe.*

hitchhiker ['hɪtʃ hɑɪk ɚ] *n.* someone who tries to get a free ride from passing cars and trucks. ♦ *The hitchhiker was picked up by a trucker.* ♦ *Bob refuses to pick up hitchhikers.*

hive ['hɑɪv] **1.** *n.* a place where many bees live. ♦ *It was fascinating to watch the bees fly in and out of their hive.* ♦ *The bees' hive was full of honey.* **2. hives** *n.* any one of various skin diseases characterized by eruptions, typical of an allergic reaction. (Treated as singular or plural.) ♦ *Eating strawberries gives me hives.* ♦ *Bob's hives hurt and required constant care.* **3. hive of activity** *idiom* the location where things are very busy. (On ①.) ♦ *The hotel lobby was a hive of activity each morning.* ♦ *During the holidays, the shopping center is a hive of activity.*

hoard ['hord] **1.** *tv.* to store a large amount of something secretly for future use. ♦ *The squirrels are hoarding acorns for the winter.* ♦ *During hurricane season, I hoard a supply of emergency rations.* **2.** *n.* a large amount of something that has been secretly stored for future use. ♦ *We kept a large hoard of canned goods in the pantry for an emergency.* ♦ *I think my coworker has a hoard of paper clips in her desk drawer.*

hoarse ['hors] **1.** *adj.* [of a voice] rough and raspy sounding from illness or misuse. (Adv: *hoarsely.* Comp: *hoarser;* sup: *hoarsest.*) ♦ *The singer had to cancel the concert due to her hoarse voice.* ♦ *Bob's hoarse voice sounded as if his throat really hurt.* **2.** *adj.* [of a person] having a voice that is rough and raspy sounding from illness or misuse. (Adv: *hoarsely.* Comp: *hoarser;* sup: *hoarsest.*) ♦ *The singer canceled his concert because he was hoarse.* ♦ *The hoarse senator had to postpone her speech.*

hoax ['hoks] *n.* a fraud; a deception; a practical joke. ♦ *April Fools' Day is a popular time to play hoaxes.* ♦ *The discovery of the historical documents turned out to be a hoax.*

hobble ['hɑb əl] **1.** *n.* a limp; a slow, stumbling movement. (No plural form in this sense.) ♦ *The wounded soldier moved with a hobble.* ♦ *My horse moved along with a slow hobble after it lost its shoe.* **2.** *iv.* to limp; to move in a slow, stumbling way. ♦ *The injured football player hobbled off the field.* ♦ *It was sad to watch the sick old dog hobble.*

hobby ['hɑb i] *n.* an activity that is done in one's spare time; an activity that one likes to do. ♦ *My hobby is reading books.* ♦ *After Anne retired, she devoted her days to her hobby of gardening.*

hobby-horse ['hɑb i hors] **1.** *n.* a toy rocking horse; a children's toy that is a stick with a figure of a horse's head on one end. ♦ *The antique hobby-horse sold for a great deal of money.* ♦ *The children ran around the yard on their hobby-horses.* **2.** *n.* a special idea or plan to which someone devotes a lot of attention. ♦ *Every time we discussed designing a new product, Bill would mention his old hobby-horse, which was to make a plastic pencil that could be resharpened.* ♦ *You are always talking about the same hobby-horse! Get some new ideas.*

hobo ['ho bo] *n.* a tramp; someone who travels from city to city looking for food or work. (Usually male. Pl in *-s* or *-es.*) ♦ *The hobo jumped on a freight train to get to the next town.* ♦ *The hobo asked the farmer if he could work in exchange for a meal.*

hock ['hɑk] **1.** *n.* the joint of an animal just above the foot; the meat just above an animal's foot. ♦ *The horse had a swollen hock and walked with a limp.* ♦ *Smoked ham hocks are country food.* **2.** *tv.* to pawn something; to give something to a pawnbroker in exchange for money. (Informal.) ♦ *The student hocked his watch for money to buy books.* ♦ *When her divorce is final, Mary will hock her wedding ring.* **3. go into hock** *idiom* go into debt. ♦ *We will have to go into hock to buy a house.* ♦ *I go further into hock every time I use my credit card.* **4. in hock** *idiom* in debt. ♦ *After buying the luxury car, Bob was in hock for years.* ♦ *I am deeply in hock and have to pay off my debts.*

hockey ['hɑk i] *n.* a game played on ice where skaters try to hit a rubber disk into a goal area. (No plural form in this sense.) ♦ *Hockey is a fast-moving sport.* ♦ *During the winter, my friends and I play hockey at the ice rink.*

hodgepodge ['hɑdʒ pɑdʒ] *n.* a mixture; a mess; things that are mixed up in no order. (No plural form in this sense.) ♦ *Dinner is a little of this and a little of that. In other words, it is a hodgepodge.* ♦ *Your room is a hodgepodge; please clean it.*

hoe ['ho] **1.** *n.* a garden tool consisting of a small blade attached to a long handle, used to remove weeds or to break up soil. ♦ *The gardener removed the weeds with the hoe.* ♦ *My hoe has a wooden handle and a metal blade.* **2.** *tv.* to use ① on something; to remove weeds or break up soil with ①. ♦ *Anne's chore was to hoe the vegetable garden.* ♦ *David hated hoeing the flowers in the hot sun.* **3. tough row to hoe** *idiom* a difficult task to undertake. ♦ *It was a tough row to hoe, but I finally got a college degree.*

♦ *Getting the contract signed is going to be a tough row to hoe, but I'm sure I can do it.*

hog ['hɔg] **1.** *n.* a full-grown pig, especially one raised for food. ♦ *The farmer planned to slaughter the hog and freeze the meat.* ♦ *Most hogs weigh more than a hundred pounds.* **2.** *n.* someone who is very greedy or messy. (Figurative on ①.) ♦ *The kids called Bob a hog because he ate so much.* ♦ *Our house is so messy, people will think we are hogs.* **3.** *tv.* to take more than one's fair share of something. (Informal.) ♦ *Starved, Bob hogged the pizza and ate more than half of it.* ♦ *My roommate hogs the TV on Sunday afternoons to watch sports.* **4. road-hog** *idiom* someone who drives carelessly and selfishly. ♦ *Look at that road-hog driving in the middle of the road and stopping other drivers from passing him.* ♦ *That road-hog nearly knocked the children over. He was driving too fast.*

hoist ['hɔɪst] **1.** *n.* a device for lifting heavy things. ♦ *The workers used a hoist to get the trailer onto the railroad car.* ♦ *We will need a hoist to get the car out of the ditch.* **2.** *tv.* to raise something using ropes and pulleys; to lift something using ropes and pulleys. ♦ *We hoisted the car out of the ditch.* ♦ *The farmhands hoisted the hay up to the barn loft.*

hold ['hold] **1.** *tv., irreg.* to keep someone or something in one's arms or hands. (Pt/pp: **held**.) ♦ *Mary held her baby in her arms.* ♦ *You should hold the railing as you walk up the stairs.* **2.** *tv., irreg.* to support the weight of someone or something; to bear the weight of someone or something. ♦ *Don't sit in that old chair, it won't hold much weight.* ♦ *The frayed rope won't hold the boat anchor for long.* **3.** *tv., irreg.* to grasp something so it remains in a certain position. ♦ *Hold the dog while I answer the door.* ♦ *Hold the mirror in the light so I can see.* **4.** *tv., irreg.* to reserve something; to set something aside, waiting for further action. ♦ *Please hold a table for two for dinner.* ♦ *I asked the clerk to hold the coat for two days until I got enough money to pay for it.* **5.** *tv., irreg.* to contain something; to have enough room for something. ♦ *The barrel is full of water and can't hold more.* ♦ *I've eaten enough; I can't hold another morsel.* **6.** *tv., irreg.* to cause an event to take place. ♦ *Let's hold the party next week.* ♦ *The church will hold a sale of baked goods at the end of the month.* **7.** *tv., irreg.* to retain a certain position or condition. ♦ *The photographer told the model to hold the pose.* ♦ *Hold that position until I get my camera.* **8.** *tv., irreg.* to restrain someone or something; to keep someone or something in control. ♦ *The police told the store owner to hold the injured thief until they arrived.* ♦ *The leash couldn't hold the strong and active dog.* **9.** *tv., irreg.* to claim something; to believe something. (Takes a clause.) ♦ *Mary holds that everyone is just too busy these days.* ♦ *The old-timer holds that a gold mine still exists in the hills.* **10.** *iv., irreg.* to withstand a strain; not to break under pressure. ♦ *Despite the heavy tug, the knot held.* ♦ *During the rain, the dike did not hold and the valley flooded.* **11.** *iv., irreg.* to remain connected to a telephone line while one's call has been temporarily suspended—so the caller or person called can talk on another telephone line. ♦ *Please hold. I've got another call coming in.* ♦ *John's on another line. Would you like to hold for a minute?* **12. hold out** *iv., irreg.* + *adv.* to endure; to last. ♦ *I cannot hold out much longer. Please help me.* ♦ *How long will the sugar supply hold out?* **13.** *n.* a grasp; a grip. ♦ *When the puppy stopped squirming, the vet relaxed her hold.* ♦ *At the bottom rung, David loosened his hold on the ladder.* **14.** *n.* a secure grasp of something. ♦ *I did not have a good hold on the dog and it ran away.* ♦ *The climber took a good hold on the rock.* **15.** *n.* the place in a ship or plane where cargo is stored. ♦ *The sailors loaded barrels into the hold.* ♦ *The hold was full when the ship left port.* **16. have a hold on someone** *idiom* to have a strong and secure influence on someone. ♦ *The strange religion seemed to have a strong hold on its followers.* ♦ *The drug has a hold on the minds of those who use it.* **17. hold someone in high regard** *idiom* to have very great respect for someone or something; to admire someone or something greatly. ♦ *We hold our employees in very high regard.* ♦ *I do not hold Bob's abilities in high regard.* **18. hold someone's attention** *idiom* to keep someone's attention; to keep someone interested. ♦ *The boring teacher could not hold the students' attention.* ♦ *The mystery novel held my attention and I couldn't put it down.* **19. on hold** *idiom* the state a person or a telephone call is in when one remains connected to a telephone line while one's call has been temporarily suspended. ♦ *John is away from his desk. Let me put you on hold and find him.* ♦ *I waited on hold for three minutes, and then I hung up.* **20. put a hold on something** *idiom* place restriction on something showing it is reserved, delayed, or inactivated. ♦ *The bank put a hold on my credit card until I paid my bill.* ♦ *The committee agreed to put a hold on the troublesome piece of business.* **21. hold out for something** *idiom* to insist on getting something; to refuse to accept less than something. ♦ *The workers are holding out for a reasonable raise.* ♦ *The teachers are holding out for a reduction in class size.*

holder ['hold ɚ] *n.* something that retains something; something that keeps something in a certain position. ♦ *Clean napkins were placed in the napkin holder.* ♦ *A candle holder is called a candlestick.*

holding ['hold ɪŋ] **holdings** *n.* something that someone legally owns, such as land, investments, and stocks. (Treated as plural.) ♦ *The baron had extensive holdings of land.* ♦ *The investor has stock holdings in several companies.*

holdup ['hold əp] **1.** *n.* a robbery, especially one at gunpoint; a stick-up. ♦ *During the bank holdup, the thieves ordered everyone to get down on the floor.* ♦ *My neighbor was the victim of a holdup at the train station.* **2.** *n.* a delay; the reason that something is not moving properly. ♦ *The rain has caused a holdup in the delivery of the package.* ♦ *The traffic holdup made Jane miss her plane.*

hole ['hol] **1.** *n.* an opening made in or through a solid object; an opening in the surface of something. ♦ *Bill angrily punched a hole in the wall.* ♦ *The carpenter cut a hole in the door for a window.* **2. in the hole** *idiom* in debt. ♦ *I'm $200 in the hole.* ♦ *I end up in the hole every month.* **3. out of the hole** *idiom* out of debt. ♦ *I get paid next week, and then I can get out of the hole.* ♦ *I can't seem to get out of the hole. I keep spending more money than I earn.*

holiday ['hɑl ə de] **1.** *n.* a period of time when most businesses and schools are closed in honor of someone or something. ♦ *Thanksgiving is a national holiday, and most businesses are closed.* ♦ *The birthdays of Abraham Lincoln and George Washington are school holidays in some states.* **2.** *n.* a holy day; a religious celebration. ♦ *Good Friday is* *a holiday for Christians.* ♦ *Important Jewish holidays are Yom Kippur and Rosh Hashanah.*

holiness ['hol i nəs] *n.* the condition or quality of being holy. (No plural form in this sense.) ♦ *The angel in the painting had an expression of holiness on its face.* ♦ *I admired the nuns for their holiness and devotion to God.*

Holland ['hɑl ənd] See Gazetteer.

holler ['hɑl ɚ] **1.** *iv.* to scream; to shout; to yell. ♦ *Your brother sure can holler loud.* ♦ *If you want me, just holler.* **2.** *tv.* to yell something. ♦ *The rescuers searched the woods, hollering the lost child's name.* ♦ *As we drove past, our neighbor waved and hollered a greeting.* **3.** *n.* a shout; a yell; a scream. ♦ *I could hear my mother's holler at least a half mile away.* ♦ *The camper's holler echoed in the canyon.*

hollow ['hɑl o] **1.** *n.* an open space inside an object; a cavity. ♦ *The fox lived in a hollow in the rocks.* ♦ *There was a hollow in the tree trunk where the birds nested.* **2.** *n.* a small valley; a sunken area of land. ♦ *The hikers walked down the hill and through the hollow.* ♦ *There was a stream at the bottom of the hollow.* **3.** *adj.* having an open space inside; not solid. (Adv: *hollowly.* Comp: *hollower;* sup: *hollowest.*) ♦ *A basketball is hollow, but a baseball is not.* ♦ *When the tree was cut down, we found that it had a hollow trunk.* **4.** *adj.* sunken. (Adv: *hollowly.* Comp: *hollower;* sup: *hollowest.*) ♦ *After the rains, the trail had several hollow stretches.* ♦ *The sick child had sad eyes and hollow cheeks.* **5.** *adj.* empty; without meaning or substance. (Adv: *hollowly.* Comp: *hollower;* sup: *hollowest.*) ♦ *Mary was tired of her employer's hollow promises to give her a raise.* ♦ *After his mother died, the holidays brought David only hollow joy.* **6. hollow out** *tv.* + *adv.* to scoop something out; to form an open space inside an object. ♦ *The carver hollowed out the wooden stick to make a flute.* ♦ *The raccoon hollowed out a log to live in.*

holly ['hɑl i] *n.* a small tree or shrub with red berries and shiny green leaves. (No plural form in this sense.) ♦ *Branches of holly are sometimes made into wreaths.* ♦ *We planted holly by the front door.*

hollyhock ['hɑli hɑk] *n.* a plant with long stalks and large, colorful flowers. (Usually plural.) ♦ *Our hollyhocks grew to more than six feet in height.* ♦ *The gardener was proud of her showy hollyhocks.*

Hollywood ['hɑ li wʊd] **1.** *n.* a section of Los Angeles, California, considered to be the center of the motion-picture industry. (No plural form in this sense.) ♦ *Lots of famous people live in or near Hollywood.* ♦ *Most of the major filmmaking studios are found in Hollywood.* **2.** *adj.* <the adj. use of ①.> ♦ *My son wants to be a Hollywood movie star.* ♦ *John is a successful Hollywood filmmaker who has made many well-known films.*

holocaust ['hɑl ə kɔst] **1.** *n.* an enormous loss of life or widespread destruction, especially by fire. ♦ *All countries must work together to avoid a nuclear holocaust.* ♦ *A small house fire became a terrible holocaust when the wind started spreading the fire.* **2. the Holocaust** *n.* the mass murder of European Jews by Germans in concentration camps during World War II. (No plural form in this sense. Treated as singular.) ♦ *Evidence of the Holocaust can be found in the countries of Europe.* ♦ *Approximately six million Jews were killed in the Holocaust.*

holster ['hol stɚ] *n.* a leather case for a gun, worn on the body or attached to a saddle. ♦ *The cowboy buckled the holster around his waist.* ♦ *The sheriff's leather holster could carry two revolvers.*

holy ['hol i] **1.** *adj.* sacred; blessed; divine. (Comp: *holier;* sup: *holiest.*) ♦ *Many people come to visit the holy shrine in our city.* ♦ *The altar is a holy place in the church.* **2.** *adj.* devoted to God; pure; virtuous. (Comp: *holier;* sup: *holiest.*) ♦ *A church building is a holy place.* ♦ *The nun vowed to lead a holy life.*

homage ['ɑm ɪdʒ] **pay homage to someone** *idiom* to praise, respect, and honor someone. ♦ *My parents taught me to pay homage to my elders.* ♦ *The widower paid homage to his dead wife by placing flowers on her grave.*

home ['hom] **1.** *n.* the place where one lives; one's house or apartment. ♦ *Dave used to live in a house in Ohio, but now his home is in Iowa.* ♦ *Mary invited me to dinner at her home.* **2.** *n.* the place where someone was born; the place where someone comes from; the place where someone grew up. ♦ *Even though she lived in the north for many years, Jane still considered Alabama her home.* ♦ *Tom's home is Los Angeles, and his parents still live there in the same house where he was born.* **3.** *n.* an institution or building where people who need special care live. ♦ *When he became too weak to care for himself, my grandfather moved to a home for the aged.* ♦ *A new home for retired nuns is being built in town.* **4.** *n.* a place where something is found, based, or located; a place where something originated or was invented. ♦ *Chicago is the home of the Chicago Cubs baseball team.* ♦ *Detroit, Michigan, is the home of the U.S. auto industry.* **5.** *adj.* <the adj. use of ①.> ♦ *The United States is Bob's home country.* ♦ *Anne's home city is Boston.* **6.** *adj.* <the adj. use of ④.> ♦ *The baseball team is playing at its home stadium.* ♦ *The basketball team won most of its games on its home court.* **7.** *adv.* at ①; to ①. ♦ *Mary phoned home once a week.* ♦ *Bill told his obnoxious neighbor to go home.* ♦ *I went to the party, but my husband stayed home.* **8. hit home; strike home** *idiom* to really make sense; [for a comment] to make a very good point. ♦ *Mary's criticism of my clothes hit home, so I changed.* ♦ *The teacher's comment struck home and the student vowed to work harder.* **9. home in on someone or something** *idiom* to cause something to go toward a specific place; to direct something in a certain direction. ♦ *The pilot homed the plane in on the beacon.* ♦ *In order to complete the race, the tired athlete homed in on the finish line.* **10. make oneself at home** *idiom* to make oneself comfortable as if one were in one's own home. ♦ *Please come in and make yourself at home.* ♦ *I'm glad you're here. During your visit, just make yourself at home.*

home cooking ['hom 'kʊk ɪŋ] *n.* the type of food and cooking that is prepared in a home rather than a restaurant. (No plural form in this sense.) ♦ *Lisa likes meatloaf and mashed potatoes and other kinds of home cooking.* ♦ *I want to eat out tonight. I am tired of home cooking.*

homeland ['hom lænd] *n.* the country that someone was born in. ♦ *Maria's homeland is Mexico.* ♦ *Germany is David's homeland.*

homeless ['hom ləs] **1.** *adj.* having no home; without a place to live. (Adv: *homelessly.*) ♦ *The homeless man slept in a box on the street corner.* ♦ *I fed a homeless cat who* *stopped in our yard.* **2. (the) homeless** *n.* people who have no place to live. (No plural form in this sense.) ♦ *The number of homeless seems to be increasing.* ♦ *There are many charities that aid the homeless.*

homelessness ['hom ləs nəs] *n.* not having a place to live; not living in an available living space by choice. (No plural form in this sense.) ♦ *Bill preferred homelessness to living in a foster home.* ♦ *Homelessness is more prevalent in the city but also occurs in the country.*

homely ['hom li] *adj.* plain; not very pretty; not attractive. (Comp: *homelier;* sup: *homeliest.*) ♦ *Bill's face is sort of homely, but he's a great guy.* ♦ *I was ashamed of my homely clothing.*

homemade ['hom 'med] *adj.* made at home; not bought in a store. ♦ *I bought some homemade pies at the country store.* ♦ *The homemade quilt was admired by the guests.*

homemaker ['hom mek ɚ] *n.* a person who manages a home, especially a married woman who manages her home and, possibly, children. ♦ *With a large house and four children, being a homemaker is a full-time job.* ♦ *The homemaker picked up her children after school at three o'clock.*

home office ['hom 'ɔfɪs] **1.** *n.* the headquarters of a company. ♦ *The business has one home office and seven branch offices.* ♦ *The company's home office is in New York.* **2.** *n.* an office in one's home. ♦ *Jane works in her home office where she has her own computer.* ♦ *Tom is a salesman and does his paperwork in his home office.*

homeowner ['hom 'on ɚ] *n.* someone who owns a home. ♦ *Older homeowners often sell their houses and move into apartments.* ♦ *Homeowners spend a lot of money on repairs.*

home plate ['hom 'plet] *n.* [in baseball] the marker that a batter stands at when hitting the ball, and that a runner must touch in order to score a run. ♦ *The next batter walked up to home plate.* ♦ *The crowd cheered as the runner crossed home plate, scoring the winning run.*

home run ['hom 'rʌn] *n.* [in baseball] a play in which a batter hits the ball and manages to touch first base, second base, third base, and then home plate safely, scoring a point. ♦ *During the game, the star player hit two home runs and a triple.* ♦ *The crowd cheered as the runner crossed home plate after hitting a home run.*

homesick ['hom sɪk] *adj.* sad and depressed because one is away from one's home. (Adv: *homesickly.*) ♦ *The homesick college student left school to return home.* ♦ *Jane was less homesick after she received a cheery letter from her parents.*

homestretch ['hom 'strɛtʃ] **1.** *n.* the straight part of a racetrack that leads up to the finish line. ♦ *The horses raced neck and neck down the homestretch.* ♦ *The winning horse led throughout the homestretch.* **2.** *n.* the last part of anything; the part of something just before the end. (Figurative on ①.) ♦ *Don't drop out of school now. You're in the homestretch.* ♦ *With only four games left in the season, the team was in the homestretch.*

hometown ['hom 'taʊn] **1.** *n.* the town where someone was born or where someone grew up. ♦ *Chicago is Jane's hometown.* ♦ *Although he had lived around the world, Dave longed to return to his family and hometown.* **2.** *n.* the town where someone is from. ♦ *At the convention in Paris, Mike was often asked where his hometown was.* ♦ *Bob's hometown is somewhere in New York.*

homeward ['hom wɚd] **1.** *adv.* toward one's home. ♦ *The homesick child was happy to be traveling homeward.* ♦ *The soldiers marched homeward after the war.* **2.** *adj.* moving toward one's home. ♦ *It was delightful to see the house at the end of the long homeward journey.* ♦ *The homeward trip was short and pleasant.*

homework ['hom wɚk] **1.** *n.* an assignment that is given at school to be completed at home; school lessons that are to be completed at home. (See also schoolwork. No plural form in this sense.) ♦ *Bill's teacher gave him a lot of homework.* ♦ *Anne does her homework at the library.* **2.** *n.* preparation that should be done before a meeting or discussion. (Figurative on ①. No plural form in this sense.) ♦ *Mary had done her homework and was able to answer all of the committee's questions.* ♦ *Before a job interview, it is good to do your homework and learn about the company.*

homicide ['hɑm ə saɪd] *n.* a murder; the act of killing a person. ♦ *The police investigated the homicide.* ♦ *There were no suspects in the violent homicide in the park.*

homogeneous [hom ə 'dʒin i əs] *adj.* similar; alike; of the same kind; made from the same kinds of things. (Adv: *homogeneously.*) ♦ *The population of the small town was homogeneous—mostly merchants and laborers.* ♦ *John had a homogeneous collection of books, all on the Civil War.*

homogenize [hə 'mɑdʒ ə naɪz] *tv.* to mix cream into milk so thoroughly that it will not separate again. ♦ *The dairy had to homogenize the milk before selling it.* ♦ *We need special equipment to homogenize milk.*

homograph ['ho mə græf] *n.* a word that is spelled the same way as another word but has a different meaning. ♦ *Many homographs are not pronounced the same way, such as* wind *(moving air) and* wind *(to form into a coil).* ♦ *Other homographs, such as* file *(a folder for documents) and* file *(a tool for making metal smooth), sound alike.*

homonym ['hɑm ə nɪm] *n.* a word that is pronounced, and sometimes also spelled, the same way as another word but has a different meaning. ♦ *Three words that are homonyms of each other are* two, too, *and* to. ♦ *Two homonyms that are also homographs are* bank *(meaning a place that stores money) and* bank *(meaning the land near the side of a river).*

homophone ['hɑm ə fon] *n.* a word that is pronounced the same way as another word but has a different meaning. ♦ *Words that sound alike but have different meanings are homophones.* ♦ *Homophones are often spelled differently, such as* ate *and* eight.

homosexual [ho mo 'sɛk ʃu əl] **1.** *n.* someone who is attracted to people of the same sex. (See gay, lesbian.) ♦ *Male homosexuals are referred to as gays, and female homosexuals are called lesbians.* ♦ *My unmarried uncle is a homosexual.* **2.** *adj.* of or about homosexuality; attracted to people of the same sex; gay; lesbian. ♦ *Several homosexual couples live in my apartment building.* ♦ *My friend told me that he is homosexual.* **3.** *adj.* of or about homosexuality; of or for homosexuals. ♦ *The newsstand carries a number of homosexual magazines.* ♦ *This sociology course deals with a few homosexual issues.*

homosexuality [ho mo sɛk ʃu 'æl ə ti] *n.* attraction toward people of the same sex; a sexual interest in persons of one's own sex. (No plural form in this sense.) ♦ *Mary discussed her homosexuality with her parents.* ♦ *The teacher answered questions about homosexuality in our sociology class.*

Honduras [hɑn 'dur əs] See Gazetteer.

honest ['ɑn əst] **1.** *adj.* truthful; not lying; able to be trusted; fair and honorable. (Adv: *honestly.*) ♦ *The honest candidate was easily elected mayor.* ♦ *The honest person returned the lost wallet to its owner.* **2.** *adj.* obtained fairly and honorably; not stolen. (Adv: *honestly.*) ♦ *Every dollar that Tom earned was an honest dollar.* ♦ *I would rather have a small but honest savings account than a fortune gained illegally.* **3.** *adj.* sincere; frank; showing sincerity. (Adv: *honestly.*) ♦ *The politician's honest reply was applauded by the crowd.* ♦ *With her honest face, Mary is trusted by everyone.*

honestly ['ɑn ɪst li] **Honestly!** *interj.* "I really can't believe it!" ♦ *Honestly! Do you expect me to believe that tale?* ♦ *Honestly, where did the time go?*

honesty ['ɑn ɪs ti] *n.* the quality of being honest; truthfulness. (No plural form in this sense.) ♦ *Honesty must be instilled in children when they are young.* ♦ *You can trust Bob, because he is well known for his honesty.*

honey ['hʌn i] *n.* a sweet, sticky food made by bees and stored in honeycombs. (No plural form in this sense.) ♦ *Mary put honey on her biscuits.* ♦ *The bees' hive was full of honey.*

honeycomb ['hʌn i kom] *n.* a waxy structure made by bees, made of a large group of six-sided cells where honey and bee eggs are placed. ♦ *The honeycomb has many cavities.* ♦ *Honey dripped from the honeycomb.*

honeymoon ['hʌn i mun] **1.** *n.* the vacation that two newly married people take after the wedding. ♦ *The couple left for their honeymoon immediately after the wedding ceremony.* ♦ *Hawaii and San Francisco are popular places for honeymoons.* **2.** *n.* a calm period of good business or political relations, especially right after someone new has come to power. (Figurative on ①.) ♦ *The new company president enjoyed a six-month honeymoon before the stockowners began to complain about profits.* ♦ *The honeymoon ended soon after Bill took the job.*

honeysuckle ['hʌn i sək əl] **1.** *n.* a shrub with pleasant-smelling white, pink, or yellow flowers. ♦ *We planted two honeysuckles by our back door.* ♦ *The smell of the honeysuckles in the backyard is delightful.* **2.** *n.* the scent of ①. (No plural form in this sense.) ♦ *Her favorite scent is honeysuckle.* ♦ *The smell of honeysuckle from the backyard was delightful.*

honk ['hɔŋk] **1.** *n.* the sound made by a horn or a goose. ♦ *We could hear the honks of the geese flying overhead.* ♦ *I heard the honk of the cab behind me.* **2.** *iv.* to make a noise like a horn or a goose. ♦ *As it pulled up in the driveway, the taxi honked.* ♦ *We were startled when we heard the geese honk overhead.* **3.** *tv.* to sound a horn; to cause a horn to make a noise. ♦ *The angry driver honked her horn at the biker.* ♦ *A speeding truck driver honked his horn when he wanted to pass.*

honor ['ɑn ɚ] **1.** *n.* the respect or regard shown to someone or something. (No plural form in this sense.) ♦ *Honor is due to those who died in battle.* ♦ *Bill's courageous actions earned him great honor.* **2.** *n.* a high degree of character, especially one that commands respect; integrity. (No plural form in this sense.) ♦ *Bob's honor is above question.* ♦ *Anne is a woman of honor.* **3.** *n.* a pleasure; a privilege. ♦ *David felt that it was a great honor to meet the famous playwright.* ♦ *It was an honor for the artist to have one of his paintings hanging in the museum.* **4. Your Honor** *n.* the polite form of address for a judge. ♦ *Your Honor, I am ready to begin.* ♦ *The attorney always addressed the judge with the words "Your Honor."* **5.** *tv.* to hold someone in high regard; to respect someone. ♦ *On Memorial Day, we honor those soldiers who died in wars.* ♦ *Jimmy honored his grandmother's memory by placing flowers on her grave.* **6.** *tv.* to make a payment as agreed; for a bank to accept a check and pay out the money that the check was written for. ♦ *When the bank honors a check, one of the tellers stamps the back of it.* ♦ *The bank will not honor a check until it makes sure there's enough money in your account.* **7. do the honors** *idiom* to act as host or hostess and serve one's guests by pouring drinks, slicing meat, making [drinking] toasts, etc. ♦ *Jane turned to her husband and said, "Bob, someone has to carve the turkey. Will you do the honors?"* ♦ *The mayor stood up and said, "I'm delighted to do the honors this evening and propose a toast to your friend and mine, Bill Jones. Bill, good luck and best wishes in your new job in Washington."*

honorable ['ɑn ɚ ə bəl] *adj.* worthy of honor; deserving honor. (Adv: *honorably.*) ♦ *The honorable judge was well respected throughout the city.* ♦ *The attorneys agreed to an honorable settlement of the lawsuit.*

honorarium [ɑn ə 'rɛr i əm] *n.* a gift of money given to someone to show appreciation for doing something. ♦ *The guest speaker was given an honorarium of $400.* ♦ *The musician accepted an honorarium for playing at the church.*

honorary ['ɑn ə rɛr i] **1.** *adj.* [of an office or title] held as an honor. (Adv: *honorarily* [ɑn ə 'rɛr ə li].) ♦ *Bill is an honorary member of our club.* ♦ *The office of president is only honorary.* **2. honorary degree** *n.* [of an award or college degree] given as an honor rather than for completion of the regular requirements. ♦ *The renowned author never attended college, but she has received several honorary degrees.* ♦ *The college gave the dignitary an honorary degree.*

hood ['hʊd] **1.** *n.* a covering for the head or face, sometimes attached to a coat. ♦ *As the cold wind blew, Jane pulled her hood over her head.* ♦ *The child hung up his coat by its hood.* **2.** *n.* the metal panel that covers the top of the front of a car. ♦ *The mechanic lifted the hood to look at the engine.* ♦ *Sitting in the driver's seat, I can see the hood of the car.* **3.** *n.* a device over a range that contains a fan that removes cooking vapors. ♦ *Most range hoods have a fan to pull the vapors and smoke out of the kitchen.* ♦ *When the meat burned, the smoke was sucked into the hood.*

hoodlum ['hʊd ləm] *n.* a minor criminal; a thug. ♦ *The hoodlum had been arrested several times before.* ♦ *That hoodlum bullied the neighborhood children.*

hoodwink ['hʊd wɪŋk] *tv.* to trick someone; to deceive someone. ♦ *The child tried to hoodwink his parents into buying a new bike.* ♦ *The magician easily hoodwinked his audience.*

hoof ['hʊf, huf] *n., irreg.* the hard, horny covering on the bottom of the foot of a horse, deer, and certain other animals. (Pl: **hooves**.) ♦ *A deer's hooves left tracks on the trail.* ♦ *I need to have a new shoe put on my horse's left hoof.*

hook ['hʊk] **1.** *n.* a bent or curved piece of plastic, wood, wire, or metal, used to catch, pull, or hold something. ♦ *I baited the fishing hook with a worm.* ♦ *I hung my coat up on a hook in the closet.* **2.** *n.* [in boxing] a short blow given while one's elbow is bent. ♦ *The fighter's hook hit his opponent in the eye.* ♦ *The boxer was known for repeated right-hand hooks.* **3.** *tv.* to catch and pull something with ①. ♦ *The angler hooked a large bass.* ♦ *The unlucky fisherman hooked a sunken log.* **4. get off the hook** *idiom* to free oneself from an obligation. ♦ *They have asked you to lead the parade, and I don't think you can get off the hook.* ♦ *I couldn't get off the hook no matter how much I pleaded.* **5. get someone off the hook** *idiom* to free someone from an obligation; to help someone out of an awkward situation. ♦ *Thanks for getting me off the hook. I didn't want to attend that meeting.* ♦ *I couldn't get myself off the hook no matter how much I pleaded.*

hoop ['hup] **1.** *n.* a circular band, usually made of metal or wood. ♦ *The wooden barrel is held together with iron hoops.* ♦ *The old-fashioned skirt had hoops in it.* **2.** *n.* [in basketball] the ① and net that the ball is thrown into. ♦ *I shot the ball through the hoop and scored two points.* ♦ *A standard basketball hoop is ten feet high.* **3. hoops** *n.* the game of basketball. (Slang. Treated as singular.) ♦ *My friends are outside playing hoops.* ♦ *Get the ball and we'll play some hoops.*

hooray [hə 're] **1.** *n.* <a shout of victory or approval.> (More informal than **hurrah**.) ♦ *The crowd cheered the winning team with hoorays.* ♦ *The hoorays from the people in the stadium were so loud we could not hear the announcements.* **2.** *interj.* "Bravo!" ♦ *Hooray! Our team won!* ♦ *When the quarterback scored the touchdown, the crowd shouted "Hooray!"*

hoot ['hut] **1.** *n.* the noise that an owl makes. ♦ *The hoot of an owl startled the hikers.* ♦ *The owl's hoot echoed through the canyon.* **2.** *n.* a jeer; a loud noise of disapproval. ♦ *The audience interrupted the speaker with hoots until he left the stage.* ♦ *The heckler's hoots were overpowered by the applause of the rest of the audience.* **3. a hoot** *n.* someone or something that is very funny or entertaining. (Slang.) ♦ *Bob is a hoot at parties.* ♦ *The joke Mary told was a real hoot.* **4.** *iv.* to make a noise like an owl. ♦ *When the owl hooted, it scared me to death!* ♦ *An owl hooted in the woods behind my house all night long.* **5.** *iv.* [for someone] to jeer by loudly making a sound like an owl. ♦ *Stop hooting and give him a chance to speak.* ♦ *The passengers hooted at the announcement that the plane was late.* **6.** *tv.* to express a feeling by hooting as in ②. ♦ *The fans hooted their disapproval of the umpire.* ♦ *The audience hooted its disgust with the inept actor.*

hooves ['huvz] pl of **hoof**.

hop ['hap] **1.** *n.* the movement made by jumping up using only one leg. ♦ *Mary did a little hop when she stepped on the hot sand.* ♦ *With a few hops, the children crossed the sidewalk and rolled on the lawn.* **2.** *n.* an airplane flight, especially a short one. ♦ *My flight is just a hop so I'll be there in about an hour.* ♦ *The hop was so short, the flight attendants never left their seats.* **3.** *iv.* to jump up and down; to jump forward a small distance. ♦ *The excited child hopped up and down in glee.* ♦ *The gymnast kept her balance by hopping once or twice at the end of her routine.* **4.** *iv.* [for frogs, rabbits, kangaroos, etc.] to move by jumping. ♦ *The frog hopped away as we approached.* ♦ *The children giggled as they watched the kangaroo hop.* **5. hop in** *iv. + prep. phr.* to get into a car, truck, van, or taxi quickly, to make a quick or short trip. ♦ *Mike hopped in a taxi and crossed town to his office.* ♦ *Anne hopped in her car and drove to the store.* **6. hop on** *iv. + prep. phr.* to board a plane, train, bus, or bicycle to make a quick trip. ♦ *Mike hopped on his bicycle and sped up the street.* ♦ *Anne hopped on a plane to go to New York.* **7.** *tv.* to board a plane, train, bus, etc. ♦ *Jane hopped a flight to Boston.* ♦ *I'll hop the next train and be home in an hour.* **8. a hop, skip, and a jump** *idiom* a short distance. ♦ *Bill lives just a hop, skip, and a jump from here. We can be there in two minutes.* ♦ *My car is parked just a hop, skip, and a jump away.*

hope ['hop] **1.** *n.* the happy feeling that something that one wants to happen will actually happen; the expectation that something good will happen. (No plural form in this sense.) ♦ *The good news about the labor contract filled the factory workers with hope.* ♦ *The negotiations provided the hostages' families with hope.* **2.** *n.* something that is desired; something that one wants to happen; an expectation. ♦ *It is our hope that Bill will go to college.* ♦ *Jane said her hope is to buy a new car next month.* **3. hope for** *iv. + prep. phr.* to wish for something to happen. ♦ *An optimist, John always hopes for the best.* ♦ *We hope for good news about your health.* **4. hope against all hope** *idiom* to have hope even when the situation appears to be hopeless. ♦ *We hope against all hope that she'll see the right thing to do and do it.* ♦ *There is little point in hoping against all hope, except that it makes you feel better.*

hopeful ['hop fʊl] **1.** *adj.* full of hope; showing hope; optimistic. (Adv: *hopefully*.) ♦ *The hopeful student expects to do well on the test.* ♦ *Susie is hopeful that she will find her lost puppy.* **2.** *adj.* causing hope; seeming like what is hoped for will happen. ♦ *Mary smiled when she heard the hopeful news that her illness could be cured.* ♦ *The meeting between the diplomats is a hopeful sign that the war might soon end.*

hopefully ['hop fə li] **1.** *adv.* in a way that is full of hope. ♦ *Jane stood hopefully by the door, waiting for the rain to stop.* ♦ *The little child wished hopefully for a puppy.* **2.** *adv.* [I am speaking] with hope; it is to be hoped that...; if what is hoped for comes true. (Some people object to this usage.) ♦ *Hopefully, I will be finished with your book by Sunday.* ♦ *Hopefully, the weather will be better for the football game.*

hopeless ['hop ləs] **1.** *adj.* without hope; showing no hope; bleak. (Adv: *hopelessly*.) ♦ *The Smiths faced a hopeless situation after the hurricane destroyed their house.* ♦ *The hopeless situation depressed the exhausted rescuers.* **2.** *adj.* in a bad state that cannot be corrected. (Adv: *hopelessly*.) ♦ *The children's toys lay in hopeless disarray.* ♦ *This house is in a hopeless condition. You can't possibly sell it.*

hopelessness ['hop ləs nəs] *n.* the condition of having no hope; the feeling that there is no hope. (No plural form in this sense.) ♦ *The burned building was a scene of hopelessness.* ♦ *No one could raise Bob from his state of hopelessness after he learned he had cancer.*

horde ['hord] *n.* a very large group of people or animals; a large crowd. ♦ *A horde of teenagers swarmed into the concert hall.* ♦ *We joined the horde watching the firefighters fight the blaze.*

horizon [hə 'rɑɪ zən] **1.** *n.* the line in the distance where the sky seems to meet the earth. ♦ *As the sun set on the horizon, the sky turned a beautiful shade of red.* ♦ *At daybreak, the sun rose up over the horizon.* **2. on the horizon** *idiom* soon to happen. ♦ *Do you know what's on the horizon?* ♦ *There is some excitement on the horizon, but I can't tell you about it.*

horizontal [hor ə 'zɑn təl] *adj.* flat; parallel to flat ground; not up and down. (Adv: *horizontally.*) ♦ *The floor is horizontal and the walls are vertical.* ♦ *We built the tree house on a large horizontal branch.*

hormone ['hor mon] *n.* one of the chemicals produced by glands in the body and carried through the body by the bloodstream. ♦ *Hormones can control certain organs within the body.* ♦ *The doctor checked the level of hormones in the patient's blood.*

horn ['horn] **1.** *n.* a hard, usually pointed growth on the heads of cattle, goats, antelope, sheep, etc.; an antler. ♦ *Rhinoceroses have either one or two horns.* ♦ *The bull lowered its horns and charged.* **2.** *n.* the hard substance that an animal's horn ① or hoof is made of. (No plural form in this sense.) ♦ *The decorative buttons were made of horn.* ♦ *A letter opener, made of horn, lay on Anne's desk.* **3.** *n.* a device that makes noise, as in a car or other vehicle. ♦ *The irritated driver blew her horn at the slow truck.* ♦ *Jimmy has a horn on his bike.* **4.** *n.* one of the brass musical instruments, played by blowing air through a shaped tube, such as the trumpet, the coronet, the tuba, the French horn, and the trombone. (Especially in compounds.) ♦ *The horns overpowered the rest of the orchestra.* ♦ *The French horn is a difficult instrument to learn to play.* **5. lock horns (with someone)** *idiom* to get into an argument with someone. ♦ *Let's settle this peacefully. I don't want to lock horns with the boss.* ♦ *Bill and Bob seem always to lock horns over the slightest problem.*

hornet ['horn ɪt] **1.** *n.* a large kind of stinging wasp. ♦ *The children were chased inside by the angry hornet.* ♦ *Hornets built a nest at the corner of our house.* **2. stir up a hornet's nest** *idiom* to create trouble or difficulties; to aggravate a bad situation. ♦ *What a mess you have made of things. You've really stirred up a hornet's nest.* ♦ *Bill stirred up a hornet's nest when he discovered the theft.*

horoscope ['hor ə skop] *n.* the prediction of a person's future based on the positions of the planets and the stars when the person was born. ♦ *Before she makes important decisions, Jane checks her horoscope.* ♦ *I read my horoscope in the newspaper every day.*

horrendous [hɔ 'rɛn dəs] *adj.* terrible; awful; horrible. (Adv: *horrendously.*) ♦ *The family was killed in a horrendous car accident.* ♦ *The horrendous fire destroyed much of the town.*

horrible ['hor ə bəl] **1.** *adj.* causing horror or terror. (Adv: *horribly.*) ♦ *Jane fainted when she saw the horrible sight.* ♦ *I ran to my window when I heard the horrible scream.* **2.** *adj.* awful; bad. (Adv: *horribly.*) ♦ *No one would eat the horrible cake.* ♦ *The play was so horrible, it closed after just one performance.*

horrid ['hor ɪd] *adj.* terrible; awful; very bad. (Adv: *horridly.*) ♦ *After the bad review, no one went to see the horrid movie.* ♦ *The newspaper showed a picture of the horrid accident.*

horrified ['hor ə fɑɪd] *adj.* frightened; scared; terrified; shocked. (Adv: *horrifiedly.*) ♦ *The horrified child screamed for help.* ♦ *A horrified soldier ran from the bloody battlefield.*

horrify ['hor ə fɑɪ] *tv.* to frighten someone very badly; to terrify someone. ♦ *The ghost story horrified the children.* ♦ *The president's assassination horrified the nation.*

horrifying ['hor ə fɑɪ ɪŋ] *adj.* frightening; scary; terrifying; shocking. (Adv: *horrifyingly.*) ♦ *The horrifying sight gave me nightmares.* ♦ *For months after the horrifying accident, Bob refused to drive at night.*

horror ['hor ɚ] **1.** *n.* intense dread or fear; fright. (No plural form in this sense.) ♦ *Ever since her friend was killed in a plane crash, the idea of flying fills Lisa with horror.* ♦ *I never felt such horror as when my house caught fire.* **2.** *n.* someone or something that causes fear or fright; an experience of ①. ♦ *I never thought I would experience such horrors.* ♦ *Nuclear war is a horror that people hope to avoid.* **3. in horror** *idiom* with intense shock or disgust. ♦ *Mike stepped back from the rattlesnake in horror.* ♦ *The jogger recoiled in horror when she came upon a body in the park.*

hors d'oeuvre [or 'dɚv] **1.** *n.* a special and appetizing food served before or at the beginning of a meal. (No plural form in this sense. From French. Formal.) ♦ *The waiter served the hors d'oeuvre first, before the rest of the meal.* ♦ *I liked the hors d'oeuvre better than the main course.* **2.** *n.* an individual portion of tasty, savory foods, often combined in a decorative way, that may be picked up with one's fingers and eaten before or instead of a larger meal—for example, a fancy cracker with a flavorful topping. (From French. Less formal than ①.) ♦ *Anne served hors d'oeuvres and cocktails before dinner.* ♦ *I ate so many shrimp hors d'oeuvres that I wasn't hungry for dinner.*

horse ['hors] **1.** *n.* an animal, larger than a donkey, that is used for carrying people and pulling heavy things, especially on farms. (See also donkey and mule.) ♦ *The horses are hitched to the wagon, so we can leave now.* ♦ *Anne rode a horse across the meadow.* **2. horse sense** See sense. **3. beat a dead horse** *idiom* to continue fighting a battle that has been won; to continue to argue a point that is settled. ♦ *Stop arguing! You have won your point. You are just beating a dead horse.* ♦ *Oh, be quiet. Stop beating a dead horse.* **4. change horses in midstream** *idiom* to make major changes in an activity that has already begun; to choose someone or something else after it is too late. ♦ *I'm already baking a cherry pie. I can't bake an apple pie. It's too late to change horses in midstream.* ♦ *The house is half-built. It's too late to hire a different architect. You can't change horses in midstream.* **5. dark horse** *idiom* someone whose abilities, plans, or feelings are little known to others. ♦ *It's difficult to predict who will win the prize, because there are two or three dark horses in the tournament.* **6. eat like a horse** *idiom* to eat large amounts of food. ♦ *No wonder he's so fat. He eats like a horse.* ♦ *John eats like a horse, but he also works like a horse, so he never gets fat.* **7. horse of another color** *idiom* another matter altogether. ♦ *I was talking* *about the tree, not the bush. That's a horse of another color.* ♦ *Gambling is not the same as investing in the stock market. It's a horse of another color.* **8. put the cart before the horse** *idiom* to have things in the wrong order; to have things confused and mixed up. ♦ *You're eating your dessert! You've put the cart before the horse.* ♦ *Slow down and get organized. Don't put the cart before the horse!* **9. straight from the horse's mouth** *idiom* from an authoritative or dependable source. ♦ *I know it's true! I heard it straight from the horse's mouth!* ♦ *This comes straight from the horse's mouth, so it has to be believed.*

horseback ['hors bæk] **1.** *adv.* on the back of a horse. ♦ *John rode horseback all the way to the river.* ♦ *The ranger rode horseback up the mountain.* **2. horseback riding** *n.* riding on the back of a horse. (No plural form in this sense.) ♦ *David hates horseback riding because he is afraid of horses.* ♦ *Anne took lessons to learn horseback riding.* **3. on horseback** *phr.* on the back of a horse. ♦ *Anne rode on horseback across the field.* ♦ *Because they loved horses, the couple decided to marry on horseback.*

horsepower ['hors paʊ ɚ] *n.* a unit of measure of the power of an engine, equal to 746 watts. (No plural form in this sense.) ♦ *How much horsepower does this car engine have?* ♦ *John's sports car has much more horsepower than mine does.*

horseradish ['hors ræd ɪʃ] **1.** *n.* a plant that has a very hot, pungent white root. (No plural form in this sense.) ♦ *You can make a very spicy sauce by grinding up the root of the horseradish.* ♦ *Our neighbors grow horseradish in their garden.* **2.** *n.* a very strong condiment made from the root of ①. (No plural form in this sense.) ♦ *Please bring me some horseradish to go with the roast beef.* ♦ *Susan likes horseradish on her steak.*

horseshoe ['hor(s) ʃu] **1.** *n.* a piece of iron, shaped like a U, that is nailed to the bottom of a horse's hoof for protection and traction. ♦ *Horseshoes are thought to bring good luck.* ♦ *The lame horse had lost a horseshoe.* **2. horseshoes** *n.* a game where players throw horseshoes ① at a stake in the ground, attempting to make them land so close to the stake that the inner curve touches it. (Treated as singular.) ♦ *The retirees played horseshoes every day.* ♦ *In horseshoes, players score points depending on where the horseshoe lands.*

horticulture ['hort ə kəl tʃɚ] *n.* the science of growing plants, fruits, and vegetables, especially in gardens. (No plural form in this sense.) ♦ *The botanist studied horticulture in college.* ♦ *Before I planted my garden, I bought a book on horticulture.*

hose ['hoz] **1.** *n.* a flexible tube used to direct water or some other liquid. (Treated as singular.) ♦ *Bob attached the sprinkler to the hose and turned on the water.* ♦ *The children sprayed each other with the garden hose.* **2.** *n.* men's socks, especially to go with formal clothing. (No plural form in this sense. Treated as plural. Number is expressed with *pair(s) of hose.*) ♦ *The only time Bill wears hose is when he has to get dressed up.* ♦ *John's nylon hose make his feet sweat.* **3.** *n.* women's long, sheer stockings, made of silk or nylon. (No plural form in this sense. Treated as plural. Number is expressed with *pair(s) of hose.*) ♦ *Mary wore black hose with the evening gown.* ♦ *During the war, nylon hose were next to impossible to get.* **4.** *n.* pantyhose. (No plural form in this sense. Treated as plural. Number is expressed with *pair(s) of hose.*) ♦ *I threw out that pair of hose because there was a hole in one of the legs.* ♦ *Most women wear hose with skirts and dresses.*

hosiery ['ho ʒə ri] *n.* nylon hose, stockings, pantyhose, etc. (No plural form in this sense.) ♦ *Hosiery can be found in most department stores.* ♦ *Jane keeps her hosiery in the top drawer of her dresser.*

hospice ['hɑs pɪs] *n.* a home or shelter for travelers or pilgrims. ♦ *The travelers stayed in a hospice overnight.* ♦ *A religious organization supported the hospice for visitors to the shrine.*

hospitable [hɑs 'pɪt ə bəl] *adj.* welcoming; kind and generous to guests and strangers; friendly. (Adv: *hospitably.*) ♦ *The hospitable family graciously invited the stranded strangers to stay.* ♦ *The hospitable host encouraged the party guests to make themselves at home.*

hospital ['hɑs pɪt əl] *n.* an institution where medical care for serious diseases or disorders is provided. ♦ *Dave went to the hospital when he broke his arm.* ♦ *After the surgery, Jane stayed in the hospital for two weeks.*

hospitality [hɑs pɪ 'tæl ə ti] *n.* kindness or generosity shown towards guests and strangers. (No plural form in this sense.) ♦ *The Smiths' hospitality makes everyone feel welcome.* ♦ *We always return to this inn because of the owners' hospitality.*

hospitalize ['hɑs pɪt ə lɑɪz] *tv.* to put someone into a hospital. ♦ *The pediatrician hospitalized the sick child.* ♦ *Bob's doctor hospitalized him for tests when he suspected he had cancer.*

host ['host] **1.** *n.* someone who receives and welcomes guests. (Male or female. See also hostess.) ♦ *The host welcomed his guests at the front door.* ♦ *There was no host at the door, so we just walked in.* **2.** *n.* the person arranging a party or gathering, especially where food is served. (Male or female. See also hostess.) ♦ *I enjoy going to Mary's parties because she is an excellent host.* ♦ *The host asked his guests to come to the table for dinner.* **3.** *n.* someone who introduces people on a television show; someone who has a talk show on television. ♦ *The talk-show host introduced each guest.* ♦ *Many hosts start their shows with a monologue.* **4.** *n.* a large number of people or things. ♦ *Our picnic drew a host of insects.* ♦ *A host of applicants replied to the help-wanted ad.* **5.** *tv.* to be ③ on a television show. ♦ *Mike hosts a local cable talk show about sports.* ♦ *A well-known actress is hosting the TV program.* **6.** *tv.* to be ① or ② at a party. ♦ *Lisa hosts our company's summer picnic every year.* ♦ *Frank hosted the poker party last Saturday.*

hostage ['hɑs tɪdʒ] **1.** *n.* someone or something held by force, to be released only when stated demands are met. ♦ *The terrorist took hostages and threatened to kill them.* ♦ *The hostage was tied up and blindfolded.* **2.** *adj.* <the adj. use of ①.> ♦ *The police tried to end the hostage crisis without bloodshed.* ♦ *The reporter covered the hostage situation at the local bank.* **3. hold someone hostage** *idiom* to keep someone as ①. ♦ *The terrorists planned to hold everyone hostage in the airplane.* ♦ *My neighbor was held hostage in his own home by a robber.* **4. take someone hostage** *idiom* to kidnap or seize someone to be ①. ♦ *The terrorists planned to take the ambassador hostage.* ♦ *The entire family was taken hostage by the robber.*

hostel ['hɑs təl] *n.* an inexpensive place for travelers to stay overnight while traveling. ♦ *The hostel wasn't fancy, but it was clean and hospitable.* ♦ *While traveling in Europe, the students stayed in hostels.*

hostess ['hos təs] **1.** *n.* a woman who receives and welcomes guests. ♦ *A hostess at the nightclub showed us to our seats.* ♦ *The hostess in the restaurant told us that our table was ready.* **2.** *n.* a woman who arranges and supervises a party or gathering, especially in her own home. ♦ *I enjoy going to Mary's parties because she is an excellent hostess.* ♦ *The hostess asked her guests to come to the table for dinner.*

hostile ['hɑs təl] **1.** *adj.* easily angered; unfriendly; antagonistic. (Adv: *hostilely.*) ♦ *The hostile teenager argued with his parents.* ♦ *The hostile cat hissed whenever I came near.* **2.** *adj.* acting like an enemy; aggressive and threatening. (Adv: *hostilely.*) ♦ *The president refused to negotiate with the leaders of the hostile country.* ♦ *The soldiers searched for the hostile army's camp.*

hostility [hɑ 'stɪl ə ti] **1.** *n.* the condition of being hostile or unfriendly. (No plural form in this sense.) ♦ *John's hostility made us all uncomfortable.* ♦ *Mary was greeted with hostility when she tried to apologize to Dave.* **2. hostilities** *n.* acts of war; fighting. (Treated as plural.) ♦ *Hostilities ceased after the treaty was signed.* ♦ *The hostilities are expected to end once the treaty is signed.*

hot ['hɑt] **1.** *adj.* having a high temperature; not cold or warm. (Adv: *hotly.* Comp: *hotter;* sup: *hottest.*) ♦ *The hot stove burned the child's finger.* ♦ *The cat sat in the hot sunlight.* **2.** *adj.* [of food] very spicy, causing a burning feeling in the mouth. (Adv: *hotly.* Comp: *hotter;* sup: *hottest.*) ♦ *That Mexican restaurant serves very hot dishes.* ♦ *Bob gulped water after eating the hot pepper.* **3.** *adj.* very intense; excited or vehement. (Figurative on ①. Adv: *hotly.* Comp: *hotter;* sup: *hottest.*) ♦ *Hot pink is a very noticeable color.* ♦ *John has a hot temper and gets angry a lot.* **4.** *adj.* currently popular; trendy. (Informal. Comp: *hotter;* sup: *hottest.*) ♦ *What kind of music is hot right now?* ♦ *The lecture is on a hot topic, so we expect a large audience.* **5.** *adj.* stolen. (Slang. Comp: *hotter;* sup: *hottest.*) ♦ *The thief tried to sell the hot car.* ♦ *The crook had four hot watches in his pocket.* **6.** *adj.* radioactive. (Informal. Comp: *hotter;* sup: *hottest.*) ♦ *The atomic explosion left the land hot for decades.* ♦ *The hot debris was buried deep in a mine.* **7. hot on something** *idiom* enthusiastic about something; very much interested in something. (Informal.) ♦ *Jane is hot on animal rights.* ♦ *Lisa is hot on modern ballet just now.*

hotbed ['hɑt bɛd] *n.* a place where the conditions for something to happen are ideal. ♦ *Crowded cities with high unemployment are often hotbeds of crime.* ♦ *The mayor's tax proposal caused a hotbed of controversy.*

hot dog ['hɑt dɔg] **1.** *n.* a relatively small sausage made of pork, beef, or pork and beef; a type of frankfurter. ♦ *I bought a dozen hot dogs for the picnic.* ♦ *Are we having hot dogs and beans again tonight?* **2.** *n.* a sandwich consisting of ① served on a specially shaped bun, usually with many condiments. ♦ *I want chili, cheese, and ketchup on my hot dog.* ♦ *Bob ate four hot dogs with nothing but ketchup and onions on them.*

hotel [ho 'tɛl] *n.* a building where people can rent a place to stay while on business or vacation. ♦ *We stayed at two hotels on our vacation.* ♦ *The large hotel had a pool and two restaurants.*

hotheaded ['hɑt hɛd ɪd] *adj.* having a bad temper; likely to become angry about something without thinking about the situation. (Adv: *hotheadedly.*) ♦ *The hotheaded teenager never thought before he spoke.* ♦ *Mike is a little hotheaded and tends to get into arguments.*

hothouse ['hɑt haʊs] *n., irreg.* a heated greenhouse; a building where the temperature is kept high for plants that would die if they were outside. (Pl: [...haʊ zəz].) ♦ *During the winter, tomatoes are grown in a hothouse.* ♦ *Although it was snowing outside, inside the hothouse it was warm and flowers were blooming.*

hot plate ['hɑt plet] *n.* a small, portable electric appliance used to cook or warm food in a pan. ♦ *I cooked soup in my room on a hot plate.* ♦ *Sue's studio had no oven, but only a hot plate.*

hound ['haʊnd] **1.** *n.* a dog, especially one used for hunting. ♦ *Bill trained his hound to hunt.* ♦ *The hound retrieved the dead quail.* **2.** *n.* a fan; someone who is very excited about a hobby or activity. (Informal.) ♦ *Mike is a sports hound and watches every game he can.* ♦ *The autograph hounds waited outside the star's dressing room.* **3.** *tv.* to chase someone; to worry someone; to harass someone. ♦ *The child hounded his parents for a new bike.* ♦ *The thought of losing her job hounded Anne constantly.*

hour ['ɑɚ] **1.** *n.* a unit of time measurement equal to 60 minutes or 1/24 of a day. ♦ *There aren't enough hours in the day to get things done.* ♦ *How many hours until we arrive?* **2.** *n.* [in school] a classroom period, usually lasting 45 to 60 minutes. ♦ *I have English first hour and Spanish second hour.* ♦ *Mike disliked having gym first hour because he was sweaty the rest of the day.* **3.** *n.* a period of time set aside for some activity. ♦ *We do not like to be disturbed during our dinner hour.* ♦ *Hospital visiting hours are in the morning and early evening.* **4.** *n.* the distance that can be traveled in ①. ♦ *My parents live an hour south of the city by car.* ♦ *Detroit is only an hour from Chicago if you are flying.* **5. at the eleventh hour** *idiom* at the last possible moment. ♦ *She always turned her term papers in at the eleventh hour.* ♦ *We don't worry about death until the eleventh hour.* **6. on the hour** *idiom* at exactly 1:00, 2:00, 3:00, 4:00, etc. ♦ *I have to take this medicine every hour on the hour.* ♦ *I expect to see you there on the hour, not one minute before and not one minute after.*

hourglass ['ɑɚ glæs] **1.** *n.* a device for measuring one hour of time, consisting of two sand-filled, conical glass sections joined at their apexes. ♦ *An hourglass is designed so that it takes one hour for the sand to flow from one section to the other.* ♦ *There is little use for the classic hourglass these days.* **2. hourglass figure** *n.* a body or form having a very thin waist and wide hips and chest. ♦ *Women once strove to have an hourglass figure.* ♦ *Having an hourglass figure is now recognized as unrealistic.*

hourly ['ɑɚ li] **1.** *adv.* every hour; once an hour. ♦ *The clock chimes hourly.* ♦ *Planes arrive hourly from New York City.* **2.** *adj.* happening every hour; happening once an hour. ♦ *The grandfather clock plays an hourly melody.* ♦ *The radio station has hourly newscasts and traffic reports.* **3.** *adj.* employed by the hour. ♦ *The hourly employee gets paid based on the number of hours worked.* ♦ *I was an hourly worker in a toy factory when I was in high school.*

4. *adj.* computed by the hour; measured by the number of hours. ♦ *The company's hourly pay is seven dollars per hour.* ♦ *I get paid hourly wages, so I can't afford to be late for work.*

house 1. ['haʊs] *n., irreg.* a building where a person or a family lives; a home. (Pl: ['haʊ zəz] or ['haʊ səz].) ♦ *We just bought a new house with four bedrooms.* ♦ *Our house is part of a condominium.* **2.** ['haʊs] *n.* a household; all the people who live in ①. (No plural form in this sense.) ♦ *The whole house was sneezing with the cold I brought home.* ♦ *The crying baby woke the entire house.* **3.** ['haʊs] *n., irreg.* a legislature; a legislative body. ♦ *Most legislative systems have two houses.* ♦ *The U.S. Senate is sometimes called a house.* **4. House** ['haʊs] *n.* the House of Representatives; an assembly of people who make laws. ♦ *The House voted on the tax law.* ♦ *The House meets at the Capitol in Washington, D.C.* **5.** ['haʊs] *n., irreg.* the part of a theater where the audience sits. ♦ *We have a full house tonight, so we will do our best.* ♦ *There are no performances on Monday, so we give the house a thorough cleaning.* **6.** ['haʊs] *n., irreg.* the people seated in ⑤; the audience in a theater. ♦ *The house is really laughing tonight.* ♦ *Max sang his best, and the house loved it!* **7.** ['haʊs] *n., irreg.* one of the 12 sections of the zodiac. ♦ *I was born in the house of Capricorn.* ♦ *The astrologer studied the twelve houses of the zodiac.* **8.** ['haʊz] *tv.* to provide shelter to someone or something. ♦ *The barn housed the farm animals.* ♦ *The abandoned cabin housed the stranded hikers during the storm.* **9. bring down the house** [...'haʊs] *idiom* to excite a theatrical audience to laughter or applause or both. ♦ *Her performance didn't bring down the house—it emptied it.* ♦ *This is a great joke. The last time I told it, it brought the house down.* **10. on the house** [...'haʊs] *idiom* [of something] given away free by a merchant. ♦ *"Here," said the waiter, "have a cup of coffee on the house."* ♦ *I went to a restaurant last night. I was the ten thousandth customer, so my dinner was on the house.*

houseboat ['haʊs bot] *n.* a boat designed to be used as someone's home. ♦ *The family rented a houseboat for a vacation.* ♦ *While he was in college, Bill lived on a houseboat during the summer.*

housebreak ['haʊs brek] *tv.* to train a pet not to defecate or urinate in the house, or in the case of a cat, outside its litter box. ♦ *We could not housebreak the puppy because he never really understood what was demanded.* ♦ *I managed to housebreak the cat in just a few days.*

housebreaker ['haʊs brek ɚ] *n.* a criminal who breaks into someone's house to commit a crime. ♦ *The housebreaker carefully watched the neighborhood and knew when someone wasn't at home.* ♦ *Some housebreaker took all our jewelry.*

housebreaking ['haʊs brek ɪŋ] *n.* breaking into someone's house against the law to commit a crime. (No plural form in this sense.) ♦ *The juvenile delinquents were charged with housebreaking.* ♦ *Dave supported his addiction by housebreaking.*

housebroken ['haʊs brok ən] *adj.* [of a dog] trained not to defecate or urinate in the house; [of a cat] trained to defecate or urinate in a litter box. ♦ *The dog was not housebroken and quickly ruined the carpet.* ♦ *Tom only wanted a housebroken cat.*

housecleaning ['haʊs klin ɪŋ] *n.* cleaning the house. (No plural form in this sense.) ♦ *In my family, everyone helps with the housecleaning.* ♦ *Before the party, our house needs a good housecleaning.*

housecoat ['haʊs kot] *n.* a woman's robe that is worn around the house. ♦ *When she's on vacation, Anne wears her housecoat until noon.* ♦ *When the doorbell rang, Lisa jumped out of bed and grabbed her housecoat.*

houseguest ['haʊs gɛst] *n.* a visitor; a guest in one's house. ♦ *We always have houseguests for the holidays.* ♦ *When his family has houseguests, Tom sleeps in the basement.*

household ['haʊs hold] **1.** *n.* the people who live in a house or apartment. (No plural form in this sense.) ♦ *There are five people in the Smith household.* ♦ *Someone in our household is always sick.* **2.** *adj.* <the adj. use of ①.> ♦ *Spot, a collie, is our household pet.* ♦ *Mike hired an accountant to manage the household expenses.*

housekeeper ['haʊs kip ɚ] **1.** *n.* someone who manages the domestic chores in a wealthy household. ♦ *The housekeeper is responsible for seeing that food is purchased and the cleaning is done properly.* ♦ *Our housekeeper has the weekend off and the cook is sick. We'll starve!* **2.** *n.* someone who manages the cleaning in a hotel, resort, hospital, or large building. ♦ *If you have any problems with your room, please call the housekeeper.* ♦ *The housekeeper inspects each hotel room and approves it before a guest is assigned to it.* **3.** *n.* a person who is paid to clean someone's house. (Euphemistic.) ♦ *Our housekeeper comes twice a month.* ♦ *Lisa told her housekeeper to vacuum and dust every room.*

house pet ['haʊs pɛt] *n.* a dog, cat, bird, fish, or other animal kept in a house as a pet. ♦ *Dave keeps a hamster as a house pet.* ♦ *The landlord does not allow house pets.*

houseplant ['haʊs plænt] *n.* an ornamental plant usually grown indoors. ♦ *Jane's house is filled with houseplants.* ♦ *The houseplant added a touch of color to the room.*

housetop ['haʊs tɑp] *n.* the roof of a house; the top part of a house. ♦ *We could see the fireworks in the park over the housetops.* ♦ *The housetops were lightly dusted with snow.*

housewarming ['haʊs wor mɪŋ] **1.** *adj.* celebrating moving into a new house or apartment. ♦ *When Lisa came to see the new house, she brought a housewarming gift.* ♦ *Everyone on the block came to the housewarming party for the new neighbors.* **2. housewarming (party)** *n.* a party celebrating moving into a new house or apartment. ♦ *Everyone enjoyed the housewarming.* ♦ *A housewarming is a wonderful way to welcome new neighbors.*

housewife ['haʊs waɪf] *n.* a married woman who manages her home and, possibly, children; a homemaker. (Objected to by some.) ♦ *To take care of her children, Lisa gave up her career and became a housewife.* ♦ *The housewife picked up her children after school.*

housework ['haʊs wɚk] *n.* cooking, cleaning, washing, and other household tasks. (No plural form in this sense.) ♦ *We have a housekeeper who makes sure the housework is done.* ♦ *The only part of housework I don't like is vacuuming.*

housing ['haʊ zɪŋ] **1.** *n.* accommodations; places to live. (No plural form in this sense.) ♦ *The college offers stu-*

dents housing in the dorms. ♦ *When Tom was in the army, his housing was in the barracks.* **2.** *adj.* <the adj. use of ①.> ♦ *During the housing boom, construction workers were in great demand.* ♦ *The housing market was tight, so there were only a few places for sale.*

hovel ['hʌv əl] *n.* a dirty, messy place to live. ♦ *Your room is a hovel, clean it immediately!* ♦ *The hermit lived in a hovel in the woods.*

hover ['hʌv ɚ] **1.** *iv.* to stay in one place in the air; to float in place over someone or something. ♦ *A helicopter hovered near the highway, watching for speeders.* ♦ *The kite hovered over our heads.* **2.** *iv.* to linger somewhere; to stay near someone or something. ♦ *Photographers hovered around the president.* ♦ *Just before dinner, the hungry children hovered by the kitchen.*

how [hɑʊ] **1.** *interrog.* in what way?; by what means? ♦ *How should I make the cake?* ♦ *How does he manage to do it?* **2.** *interrog.* to what extent?; to what degree? ♦ *How high are the clouds?* ♦ *How tall are you?* ♦ *How hot is it outside?* **3.** *interrog.* in what condition? ♦ *How are you?* ♦ *How is your new house? Do you like it?* **4. how come** *interrog.* why? (Colloquial.) ♦ *How come you didn't come to the party?* ♦ *Jimmy asked how come he had to go to school.* **5. how many** *interrog.* in what number(s)? ♦ *Tom asked how many cookies he could have.* ♦ *How many puppies did your dog have?* **6. how much** *interrog.* in what amount? ♦ *How much milk should I give Jimmy?* ♦ *I don't know how much food to bring.* **7.** *conj.* the way in which; the manner in which. ♦ *I know how to tie my shoes.* ♦ *The applicant for the job said he knew how to wash dishes.*

however [hɑʊ 'ɛv ɚ] **1.** *adv.* but; nevertheless; in spite of something. ♦ *This car costs a lot of money; however, it comes with a lot of extra options.* ♦ *It is raining; however, I think the game will be played.* **2.** *adv.* no matter how. (Followed by an adjective or adverb.) ♦ *However far away you go, I will always find you.* ♦ *Sue said she will come to the party, however busy she is.* **3.** *conj.* in whatever way; by whatever means. ♦ *You can do it however you want.* ♦ *However did you get your room so messy?*

howl ['hɑʊl] **1.** *n.* a long wail, as the cry of a wolf or the sound of a high wind. ♦ *At night the campers heard the wolf's howl.* ♦ *The howl of the storm kept me awake last night.* **2.** *iv.* to make ①. ♦ *The wolf howled.* ♦ *Lonely for his master, the dog howled.* **3.** *tv.* to cry something out. ♦ *The baby howled his displeasure at being woken up by the noise.* ♦ *Members of the audience howled their approval at the joke.*

hub ['hʌb] **1.** *n.* the center of a wheel that an axle goes through or that spokes connect to. ♦ *During the accident, the front-wheel hub on Bob's bike was damaged.* ♦ *The axle is in the middle of the hub.* **2.** *n.* a center of activity; a busy place. (Figurative on ①.) ♦ *Washington, D.C., is the hub of our government.* ♦ *In our small town, the theater and ice-cream parlor are hubs of activity.* **3.** *n.* one or more of the central airports of a large airline. (Figurative on ①.) ♦ *The airline's hub is the Chicago airport.* ♦ *We flew to Frankfurt, which is the European hub of the airline we flew on.*

hubbub ['hʌ bəb] *n.* an uproar; many loud, confused voices or noises mixed together. (No plural form in this sense.) ♦ *There was an angry hubbub from the crowd when the candidate said she supported the new airport.* ♦ *It was hard to hear over the hubbub of the party.*

hubcap ['hʌb kæp] *n.* a metal covering that fits over the hub of a wheel. ♦ *Dave paid extra for special hubcaps for his new car.* ♦ *When the car hit the bump, a hubcap flew off and rolled away.*

huckster ['hʌk stɚ] *n.* an aggressive or insistent salesperson or peddler. ♦ *Anne told the huckster to go away and slammed the door.* ♦ *The huckster was annoying but he made a lot of sales.*

huddle ['hʌd l] **1.** *n.* a group of people crowded together. ♦ *A huddle of teenagers tried to keep out of the cold wind while waiting for the bus.* ♦ *There was a huddle of cold campers around the campfire.* **2.** *n.* [in football] a group of players close together, planning the next play. ♦ *The quarterback calls the plays in the huddle.* ♦ *The team was late getting into the huddle and received a penalty for delaying the game.* **3.** *iv.* [for a number of people] to stand closely together in a small space, especially to keep warm. ♦ *The commuters huddled in the small bus station.* ♦ *The cold campers huddled around the campfire.* **4.** *iv.* [for a creature] to curl up somewhere; to bring one's arms and legs close to the body, as if to keep warm. ♦ *The kitten huddled next to the fire.* ♦ *I huddled by the wood stove to keep warm.*

hue ['hju] *n.* color; a variety, shade, or intensity of a color. ♦ *Jane's sports car is an intensely deep hue of red.* ♦ *The room was decorated in different hues of blue.*

huff ['hʌf] **1.** *iv.* to puff; to breathe heavily. ♦ *Because John smokes, he huffs whenever he walks up stairs.* ♦ *Anne began to huff toward the end of her aerobics workout.* **2. in a huff** *idiom* in an angry or offended manner. (See **huffy**.) ♦ *He heard what we had to say, then left in a huff.* ♦ *She came in a huff and ordered us to bring her something to eat.* **3. huff and puff** *idiom* to breathe very hard; to pant as one exerts effort. ♦ *John came up the stairs huffing and puffing.* ♦ *He huffed and puffed and finally got up the steep hill.*

huffy ['hʌf i] *adj.* haughty and rudely arrogant. (Adv: *huffily.* Comp: *huffier;* sup: *huffiest.*) ♦ *The huffy customer asked to speak to the store manager.* ♦ *Do as you're told and don't get huffy with me!*

hug ['hʌg] **1.** *n.* an embrace; the act of holding someone or something in one's arms in a friendly or tender way. ♦ *John gave his child a hug every morning before school.* ♦ *Sue got a hug when Bob came home from work.* **2.** *tv.* to embrace someone with ①. ♦ *Anne hugged her child every morning.* ♦ *The couple hugged each other at the airport.* **3.** *tv.* to stay close to a curb, railing, wall, or some other object as one moves along. ♦ *The car hugged the right lane as the big truck roared past.* ♦ *The bicyclist hugged the curb to stay out of the way of cars.*

huge ['hjudʒ] **1.** *adj.* [of size] very large or enormous. (Adv: *hugely.* Comp: *huger;* sup: *hugest.*) ♦ *As the huge truck roared past, the little car shook.* ♦ *The huge bear frightened the campers.* **2.** *adj.* notably large; of a notable extent. (Adv: *hugely.* Comp: *huger;* sup: *hugest.*) ♦ *The party was a huge success.* ♦ *Tom was assigned a huge responsibility and given a large raise.*

hulk ['hʌlk] **1.** *n.* the shell of a dismantled ship. ♦ *The old hulk was rusting in the harbor.* ♦ *The divers located the hulk at the bottom of the bay.* **2.** *n.* a large, clumsy person. (Figurative on ①.) ♦ *Bob was a hulk of a man, but had little* *strength and endurance.* ♦ *Almost seven feet tall and forever bumping into things, Dave was a lovable hulk.*

hulking ['hʌl kɪŋ] *adj.* large and clumsy. (Adv: *hulkingly.*) ♦ *The hulking boy turned into a graceful athlete.* ♦ *Dark silhouettes of the hulking buildings of the great city broke up the gray skies of dusk.*

hull ['hʌl] **1.** *n.* the main body of a ship. ♦ *A torpedo ripped a hole in the hull of the ship.* ♦ *The hull of the ship needs to be sanded and painted.* **2.** *n.* the outside covering of a seed. ♦ *Max used his fingers to break the hulls off the peanuts.* ♦ *There were pieces of hull left on the ground from the squirrel's feast.* **3.** *tv.* to remove the outside covering of a seed. ♦ *The animal hulled the seed with its teeth.* ♦ *Max hulled the peanuts and then ate them all.*

hullabaloo ['hʌl ə bə lu] *n.* a commotion; an uproar; a disturbance consisting of loud noises. (Pl in *-s.*) ♦ *The teacher heard the hullabaloo before he entered the classroom.* ♦ *The fight created quite a hullabaloo.*

hum ['hʌm] **1.** *n.* a long, vibrating sound, like a long "mmmmmmm"; a low murmur; a quiet buzzing sound. (No plural form in this sense.) ♦ *Before beginning the performance, the conductor paused to wait for the hum of the crowd to stop.* ♦ *We could hear the hum of the busy bees.* **2.** *iv.* to make a long, vibrating sound, like a long "mmmmmmmm"; to sing with one's mouth closed. ♦ *Jane could not remember the words to the song, so she hummed.* ♦ *I hummed with the orchestra and hoped no one could hear me.* **3.** *tv.* to sing musical notes with one's mouth closed, as in ②. ♦ *If you don't know the words, just hum the tune while the rest of us sing.* ♦ *I hummed the melody that I heard on the radio.*

human ['hju mən] **1.** *n.* a person; the most intelligent primate; a human being. ♦ *Humans are supposed to be the most intelligent beings.* ♦ *Scientists believe that humans and apes descend from an ancient, common ancestor.* **2.** *adj.* <the adj. use of ①.> (Adv: *humanly.*) ♦ *This house is not fit for human habitation.* ♦ *Human love is a very powerful emotion.* **3.** *adj.* showing feelings that people normally show. (Adv: *humanly.*) ♦ *It is only human to feel scared sometimes.* ♦ *Being angry at something that is unfair is very human.*

human being ['hju mən 'bi ɪŋ] *n.* a person; a human creature, especially considering special human characteristics, such as intelligence, kindness, sympathy, etc. ♦ *Where do you suppose that the first human being lived?* ♦ *Bob should try to act more like a human being than just a beast!*

humane [hju 'men] **1.** *adj.* kind; sympathetic; acting like a civilized human. (Adv: *humanely.*) ♦ *Mary's humane gesture brought tears to my eyes.* ♦ *Sending flowers to the funeral was humane and thoughtful.* **2.** *adj.* causing as little pain as possible. (Adv: *humanely.*) ♦ *We believe that animals used in medical testing should receive humane treatment.* ♦ *Bob asked the vet for a humane death for his suffering old dog.*

humanitarian [hju mæn ɪ 'tɛr i ən] **1.** *n.* someone who makes a living helping people; someone who tries to make other people's lives better. ♦ *Bob is a great humanitarian who has received many awards for his work.* ♦ *The missionary was a humanitarian who taught poor people how to read.* **2.** *adj.* <the adj. use of ①.> (Adv: *humanitarianly.*) ♦ *The volunteer's humanitarian efforts following the tragedy were much appreciated.* ♦ *The humanitarian award was given to the scientist who had developed a vaccine.*

humanity [hju 'mæn ə ti] **1.** *n.* the human race; all human beings; all people. (No plural form in this sense.) ♦ *Humanity will be helped by the recent advances in medicine.* ♦ *It will be a wonderful day when all humanity is properly fed.* **2.** *n.* kindness; humanness; being compassionate and caring. (No plural form in this sense.) ♦ *I will always remember your kindness and humanity while my family and I were suffering with our loss.* ♦ *The minister tried to be a good example of humanity in action in the real world.* **3. the humanities** *n.* [in college] the areas of study that are concerned with human ideas and experience, especially languages, literature, philosophy, and history. (Compare with the arts and sciences. Treated as plural.) ♦ *I decided to major in the humanities since I wasn't very good in science.* ♦ *My courses in the humanities all require a lot of reading.*

humanize ['hju mə nɑɪz] *tv.* to attempt to make someone or something more human or more suitable for humans. ♦ *The scientist humanized the robot by giving it a voice.* ♦ *We need some new colors and fabrics to humanize this drab room.*

humankind ['hju mən 'kɑɪnd] *n.* the human race; all human beings; all people. (No plural form in this sense.) ♦ *Humankind is growing at an alarming rate.* ♦ *The congregation prayed for peace for all humankind.*

humanly ['hju mən li] **everything humanly possible** *idiom* everything that is in the range of human powers. ♦ *The rescuers did everything humanly possible to find the lost campers.* ♦ *The doctor tried everything humanly possible to save the patient.*

human resources (department) ['hju mən 'ri sor səz (də 'pɑrt mənt)] *n.* a department within a company that is concerned with hiring employees, training, and employee benefits. (Often capitalized. See also personnel.) ♦ *Someone in Human Resources will be able to help you fill out the form.* ♦ *I went to the human resources department to fill out a form for insurance.*

humble ['hʌm bəl] **1.** *adj.* aware of one's faults; modest. (Adv: *humbly.* Comp: *humbler;* sup: *humblest.*) ♦ *The humble man was reluctant to accept the award.* ♦ *Jane is too humble to boast about her successes.* **2.** *adj.* simple; lowly; not elegant; not pretentious. (Adv: *humbly.* Comp: *humbler;* sup: *humblest.*) ♦ *Tom and Jane live in a humble one-room apartment.* ♦ *The poor family lived in a humble dwelling.* **3.** *tv.* to humiliate someone; to lower the position of someone; to cause someone to become ①. ♦ *The arrogant athlete was humbled by the defeat.* ♦ *The failure of the new product humbled the engineer who had designed it.* **4. eat humble pie** *idiom* to act very humble when one is shown to be wrong. ♦ *I think I'm right, but if I'm wrong, I'll eat humble pie.* ♦ *You think you're so smart. I hope you have to eat humble pie.*

humbug ['hʌm bəg] *n.* someone who is a fraud. ♦ *The wizard was proven to be a humbug.* ♦ *John exposed the expensive consultant as a humbug.*

humdrum ['hʌm 'drʌm] *adj.* [of a period of time or one's entire existence] boring and ordinary. ♦ *Max never wearied of his humdrum existence. Sameness to Max was com-*

forting. ♦ *Another humdrum day! I really need a change in my life.*

humid ['hju mɪd] *adj.* [of weather] damp; [of air] containing much moisture. (Adv: *humidly.*) ♦ *The humid weather made everyone sticky and uncomfortable.* ♦ *My laundry took a long time to dry in the humid weather.*

humidifier [hju 'mɪd ə faɪ ɚ] *n.* a machine that adds moisture to the air of a room, house, or building. ♦ *A new humidifier improved the air at our house.* ♦ *The humidifier puts gallons of moisture into the air every day.*

humidity [hju 'mɪd ə ti] *n.* moisture in air; water vapor carried in the air. (No plural form in this sense.) ♦ *After the storm, the humidity was very high.* ♦ *Humidity is higher during the summer than during the winter.*

humiliate [hju 'mɪl i et] *tv.* to embarrass someone completely; to make a fool of someone; to hurt someone's pride. ♦ *Dave's cruel jokes humiliated me.* ♦ *Being fired humiliated the employees and made them angry.*

humiliated [hju 'mɪl i et ɪd] *adj.* embarrassed; shamed; humbled. (Adv: *humiliatedly.*) ♦ *I was so humiliated by the untrue gossip!* ♦ *The humiliated student never tried to answer another question.*

humiliating [hju 'mɪl i et ɪŋ] *adj.* embarrassing; shaming; humbling; hurting one's pride or dignity. (Adv: *humiliatingly.*) ♦ *The actor's most humiliating experience was when he fell onstage.* ♦ *Mary warned me never to tell the humiliating story to anyone.*

humiliation [hju mɪl i 'e ʃən] **1.** *n.* harming someone's pride or dignity and damaging someone's sense of worth. (No plural form in this sense.) ♦ *Humiliation is not an appropriate way to teach children.* ♦ *The manager was fired for his humiliation of the employees.* **2.** *n.* something that causes ①; an instance of ①. ♦ *I suffered many humiliations at the place I used to work. I finally had to quit.* ♦ *It was a humiliation to Jane to declare bankruptcy.*

humility [hju 'mɪl ə ti] *n.* being humble; modesty. (No plural form in this sense.) ♦ *A look of humility and humanity made the old woman's harsh features seem warm and friendly.* ♦ *A hard life filled Bob with humility.*

hummingbird ['hʌm ɪŋ bɚd] *n.* a very small bird whose wings beat so fast that they make the sound of humming. ♦ *The hummingbird fluttered around the bright flowers.* ♦ *The tiny hummingbird could hover in the same place for a long time.*

humor ['hju mɚ] **1.** *n.* the quality of being funny. (No plural form in this sense.) ♦ *This author's novels have a kind of dry humor.* ♦ *There wasn't much humor in Jane's story about the accident.* **2. sense of humor** *n.* the ability to laugh at things that are funny; the ability to see the funny aspects of a situation. (No plural form in this sense.) ♦ *Mike loved his wife's sense of humor.* ♦ *I have a good sense of humor and I like to use it to make people laugh.* **3.** *tv.* to tolerate someone's seemingly odd behavior; to accept someone who has strange whims or desires. ♦ *Anne humored her son's desire to dress up like his father.* ♦ *It's best to humor Aunt Jane. She gets upset when people are disagreeable.*

humorous ['hju mə rəs] *adj.* funny; amusing; having humor. (Adv: *humorously.*) ♦ *The humorous story drew a roar of laughter from the crowd.* ♦ *Bill is a humorous guy and tells jokes well.*

hump ['hʌmp] **1.** *n.* a large, rounded bump or bulge. ♦ *The hump on the bed is the cat sleeping under the covers.* ♦ *The crippled man had a hump on his back.* **2. over the hump** *idiom* past the difficult part. ♦ *This is a difficult project, but we're over the hump now.* ♦ *I'm halfway through—over the hump—and it looks as if I may get finished after all.*

hunch ['hʌntʃ] **1.** *n.* an intuition; a guess based on how one feels. ♦ *The detective had a hunch about the case.* ♦ *The investor had a hunch that the stock would do well and bought a lot of it.* **2. hunch over** *iv.* + *prep. phr.* to bend over someone or something; to hang the upper part of one's body over someone or something. ♦ *The quarterback hunched over the players and called out the play.* ♦ *Anne hunched over her desk, solving math problems.* **3. hunch down** *iv.* + *adv.* to stoop down; to bend one's body as to take less space. ♦ *We hunched down hoping the bear would not see us.* ♦ *Tom hunched down behind the bushes to hide from his kids.*

hunchback ['hʌntʃ bæk] *n.* someone whose spine is curved, causing a rounded back. ♦ *The hunchback walked with a limping gait.* ♦ *This famous book is about a hunchback who lived in France.*

hundred ['hʌn drəd] **1.** *n.* the number 100; the number between 99 and 101. (Additional forms as with *two hundred, three hundred, four hundred,* etc.) ♦ *Fifty plus fifty is one hundred.* ♦ *Ten times twenty is two hundred.* **2.** *n.* 100 things or people. ♦ *My class is selling pens, and it's my goal to sell a hundred.* ♦ *I ordered a hundred of the colorful calendars for gifts.* **3. hundreds** *n.* the numbers found between 100 and 999, considered in groups of 100, as in a cataloging system. (Treated as plural.) ♦ *Are these items likely to be in the three hundreds or the four hundreds?* ♦ *The librarian said those shelves hold the books in the six hundreds.* **4.** *adj.* 100; consisting of 100 things; having 100 things. ♦ *The bag held a hundred beads.* ♦ *Mary agreed to bake a hundred cookies for the bake sale.*

hundredth ['hʌn drədθ] 100th. See fourth for senses and examples.

hung ['hʌŋ] **1.** a pt/pp of hang. **2.** *adj.* [of a jury] unable to reach a decision; [of a jury] not having a majority. ♦ *Because of a hung jury, the case had to be tried again.* ♦ *The hung jury could not reach a verdict and was excused.*

Hungarian [həŋ 'gɛr i ən] **1.** *n.* a citizen or native of Hungary. ♦ *There are three Hungarians in our neighborhood.* ♦ *A Hungarian gave a lecture about Eastern Europe.* **2.** *n.* the language spoken in Hungary by ①. (No plural form in this sense.) ♦ *Hungarian is not related to any of the languages spoken in nearby countries.* ♦ *Hungarian is not taught very much in the U.S.* **3.** *adj.* of or about Hungary, ①, or ②. ♦ *We like Hungarian food, especially goulash.* ♦ *We visited the Hungarian capital last winter.*

Hungary ['hʌŋ gə ri] See Gazetteer.

hunger ['hʌŋ gɚ] **1.** *n.* the feeling of a need for food; the condition of being hungry. (No plural form in this sense.) ♦ *John's hunger forced him to eat an early lunch.* ♦ *Anne's growling stomach was a sure sign of hunger.* **2.** *n.* a general lack of food. (No plural form in this sense.) ♦ *How can hunger exist when so much food is wasted every day?* ♦ *Hunger is a problem in most of the world's countries.* **3. hunger for something** *idiom* to have a strong desire for something. (Figurative on ①.) ♦ *All her life, Mary has* *had a hunger for affection.* ♦ *The prisoner was consumed with a hunger for freedom.*

hungover [həŋ 'o vɚ] *adj.* suffering from drinking too much alcohol. ♦ *John was hungover and could not remember what had happened the night before.* ♦ *The hungover employee could not do her job and was fired.*

hungry ['hʌŋ gri] **1.** *adj.* wanting food; lacking food; having an empty stomach. (Adv: *hungrily.* Comp: *hungrier;* sup: *hungriest.*) ♦ *The hungry boy gobbled his lunch.* ♦ *The hungry dog sat by its bowl and whined.* **2. hungry for something** *idiom* desiring someone or something. ♦ *The orphan was hungry for the warmth of a family.* ♦ *Bill is hungry for knowledge and always studying.*

hunk ['hʌŋk] **1.** *n.* a large, solid amount of something. ♦ *The hunk of chocolate cake on Bob's plate disappeared quickly.* ♦ *I wish I had a hunk of gold to spend as I wanted.* **2.** *n.* an attractive, sexy man. (Slang.) ♦ *Did you see that hunk on the corner?* ♦ *Who is the new hunk in class?*

hunt ['hʌnt] **1.** *tv.* to search for and kill animals for food or for sport. ♦ *Every year my cousins and I hunt deer.* ♦ *The cat hunts mice.* **2. hunt for** *iv.* + *prep. phr.* to search for someone or something. ♦ *The police hunted for the thief.* ♦ *Everyone in town hunted for the lost child.* **3.** *iv.* to search for and kill animals as in ①. ♦ *John and his friends are hunting in the woods.* ♦ *I couldn't hunt unless I absolutely needed food.*

hunter ['hʌn tɚ] *n.* someone who hunts; someone who searches for and kills animals for food or sport. ♦ *Early in the morning, the hunter went to the forest.* ♦ *As a hunter, I kill only what I can eat.*

hunting ['hʌn tɪŋ] **1.** *n.* searching for and killing animals for food or for sport. (No plural form in this sense.) ♦ *Hunting is a favorite hobby of mine.* ♦ *To Max, hunting seems cruel and barbaric.* **2.** *adj.* <the adj. use of ①.> ♦ *To avoid accidents, hunting caps and coats are bright orange.* ♦ *Bob pulled on his hunting boots and grabbed his rifle.*

hurdle ['hɚd l] **1.** *n.* a barrier that must be jumped over in certain races. ♦ *The runner knocked down a hurdle.* ♦ *The horse had more than ten hurdles to jump over.* **2.** *n.* a barrier; an obstacle. (Figurative on ①.) ♦ *Shyness is a hurdle you must overcome to succeed in business.* ♦ *A lack of money is often a hurdle to getting a college degree.* **3.** *tv.* to jump over something. ♦ *The horse hurdled the bar easily and gracefully.* ♦ *Bill hurdled the puddle as he ran to the train.* **4.** *tv.* to overcome an obstacle; to overcome a barrier. (Figurative on ③.) ♦ *The newlyweds vowed to hurdle all obstacles together.* ♦ *Mary hurdled one difficulty only to face another.*

hurl ['hɚl] **1.** *tv.* to throw someone or something with force. ♦ *Furious, Lisa hurled the plates across the kitchen.* ♦ *The sheriff hurled the rowdy cowboy out of the saloon.* **2.** *tv.* to shout something negative, such as an insult or obscene words. ♦ *As John was being arrested, he hurled obscenities at the police officer.* ♦ *A heckler hurled insults at the stand-up comedian.*

hurrah [hə 'rɑ] **1.** *n.* <a shout of victory or approval.> (See also hooray.) ♦ *Hurrahs welcomed the returning soldiers.* ♦ *The announcement of the extra holiday was greeted with hurrahs from the employees.* **2. Hurrah!** *interj.* <a shout used to indicate approval or congratulations.> ♦ *"Hurrah! Hurrah!" shouted the members of the audience.* ♦ *Hurrah! School is over for the summer!*

hurricane ['hɚ ə ken] *n.* a violent, often destructive, tropical storm. ♦ *The hurricane destroyed much of the small coastal town.* ♦ *Violent thunderstorms accompanied the hurricane.*

hurried ['hɚ id] *adj.* rushed; done in a rush. (Adv: *hurriedly.*) ♦ *After a hurried meal of a can of chili, Bob went to the library to study.* ♦ *The hurried report was sloppy and received a low grade.*

hurry ['hɚ i] **1.** *n.* haste; quick movement. (No plural form in this sense.) ♦ *In her hurry, Anne dropped her keys.* ♦ *Hurry is the enemy of careful people.* **2.** *iv.* to move quickly or hastily. ♦ *As the clouds gathered, the hikers hurried toward shelter.* ♦ *The store was closing so the shopper hurried.* **3.** *tv.* to cause someone or something to move quickly or hastily. ♦ *The rider hurried the horse back to the barn before the storm broke.* ♦ *The teacher hurried the students through their lessons.*

hurt ['hɚt] **1.** *n.* pain of the body or emotions; an ache. (No plural form in this sense.) ♦ *The hurt of losing his job made Tom depressed.* ♦ *The patient asked the doctor for medicine to ease the hurt of the wound.* **2.** *tv., irreg.* to injure a part of the body; to harm one's mental processes or emotional well-being. (Pt/pp: *hurt.*) ♦ *Picking up the box, Mary hurt her back.* ♦ *Tom's jealousy hurt his ability to reason.* **3.** *tv., irreg.* to have a bad effect on someone or something; to be bad for someone or something. ♦ *The politician's offensive comments hurt his reelection hopes.* ♦ *Losing today hurt our chances for winning the championship.* **4.** *tv., irreg.* to cause pain. ♦ *Falling off the curb hurt Jane's foot.* ♦ *Dave hurt his hand when he accidentally slammed the door on it.* **5.** *iv., irreg.* to feel pain. ♦ *After the accident, the driver hurt all over.* ♦ *Since I've been taking the medication, I don't hurt anymore.*

hurtful ['hɚt fʊl] *adj.* causing hurt; causing pain. (Adv: *hurtfully.*) ♦ *Bob's face flushed at the hurtful comments of his boss.* ♦ *Anne's eyes filled with tears when she heard the hurtful words.*

hurtle ['hɚt əl] *iv.* to move very quickly; to move at a very high speed. ♦ *The shuttle hurtled through space.* ♦ *The car recklessly hurtled down the highway.*

husband ['hʌz bənd] *n.* a married man; the man a woman is married to. ♦ *Sue introduced Dave as her husband.* ♦ *Mary and her husband are on vacation celebrating their anniversary.*

hush ['hʌʃ] **1.** *n.* silence; quiet; calm. (No plural form in this sense.) ♦ *There was an eerie hush before the tornado struck.* ♦ *Deep in the woods, where the hush is broken only by the song of birds, I like to sit and think.* **2.** *tv.* to cause someone or something to be calm and quiet. ♦ *Mary hushed her frightened child with her soft voice.* ♦ *The teacher's angry look hushed the noisy students.* **3.** *iv.* to become calm and quiet. ♦ *The students hushed and looked toward the teacher as he entered.* ♦ *As the conductor walked onstage, the audience hushed.* **4. a hush fell over someone or something** *idiom* [for silence] to envelop someone or something. ♦ *As the conductor raised his arms, a hush fell over the audience.* ♦ *The coach shouted and a hush fell over the locker room.*

hushed ['hʌʃt] *adj.* calmed and quieted. (Adv: *hushedly.*) ♦ *As the sun set, a hushed calm spread over the countryside.* ♦ *The hushed audience waited in anticipation.*

hush-hush ['hʌʃ 'hʌʃ] *adj.* secret; hidden. ♦ *The hush-hush document was leaked to the press.* ♦ *Only a few people knew the hush-hush location of the president's vacation.*

husk ['hʌsk] **1.** *n.* the outside covering of a seed; the fibrous wrapper of an ear of corn. ♦ *The poor little squirrel could not get the husk off the tough old nut.* ♦ *Before buying the corn, Jane pulled the husk down to make sure it was fresh.* **2.** *tv.* to remove the outside covering of an ear of corn. ♦ *One of my jobs was to husk the corn.* ♦ *Tom husked the corn on the porch.*

husky ['hʌs ki] **1.** *adj.* [of a voice] deep and breathy. (Adv: *huskily.* Comp: *huskier;* sup: *huskiest.*) ♦ *The announcer's husky voice was easily recognizable.* ♦ *Anne's cold made her voice husky.* **2.** *adj.* big and strong; muscular. (Adv: *huskily.* Comp: *huskier;* sup: *huskiest.*) ♦ *The husky boy worked as hard as an adult.* ♦ *It was difficult to tackle the husky football player.* **3.** *n.* a breed of dog that pulls sleds in the far north. (No plural form in this sense.) ♦ *The sled was pulled by teams of huskies.* ♦ *Huskies have long coats to keep them warm in the bitter cold.*

hussy ['hʌs i] *n.* a promiscuous woman; a flirtatious woman. (Derogatory.) ♦ *Anne never did like Mary and always referred to her as a hussy.* ♦ *Every woman at the party ignored the hussy.*

hustle ['hʌs əl] **1.** *tv.* to move someone or something to someplace quickly. ♦ *To make more money, the restaurant owner hustled customers in and out quickly.* ♦ *In the rain, Jane hustled her groceries from the house to the car.* **2.** *tv.* to sell something in an aggressive manner. ♦ *David hustled encyclopedias to pay for his college tuition.* ♦ *The telephone solicitor was hustling magazine subscriptions.* **3.** *iv.* to move quickly. (Informal.) ♦ *As dusk approached, the hikers hustled.* ♦ *The coach told us to hustle more out on the playing field.* **4. hustle and bustle** *idiom* confusion and business. ♦ *I can't stand the hustle and bustle of big cities.* ♦ *There is a lot of hustle and bustle in this office at the end of the fiscal year.*

hut ['hʌt] *n.* a small shelter; a humble dwelling. ♦ *The hermit lived in a little hut not far from the shore.* ♦ *You can warm yourself in the huts along the ski trail.*

hutch ['hʌtʃ] **1.** *n.* a cage for rabbits or other small animals. ♦ *The rabbit happily hopped into the hutch and ate a carrot.* ♦ *We kept the rabbit hutch outside.* **2.** *n.* a cupboard or cabinet with shelves. ♦ *After you wash them, put the dishes in the hutch.* ♦ *The hutch had four shelves for plates and cups and a glass door.*

hybrid ['haɪ brɪd] **1.** *n.* an animal or a plant that is a cross between two different species or varieties. ♦ *That tomato plant is a hybrid that produces heartier and larger tomatoes.* ♦ *The mule is a hybrid, having a horse and a donkey for parents.* **2.** *n.* something that has a mixed origin; something that is made by mixing two different things together. ♦ *John designed a vehicle that is a hybrid of a truck and a passenger car.* ♦ *To save space, we bought a table that is a hybrid: part desk and part computer stand.* **3.** *adj.* having a mixed origin. ♦ *The committee developed a hybrid approach to problem solving.* ♦ *The mule is a hybrid animal, being the offspring of a female horse and a male donkey.*

hydrant ['haɪ drənt] **1.** *n.* an upright water pipe alongside a street that hoses can be attached to when water is needed to fight fires. ♦ *The firefighter attached a hose to the hydrant.* ♦ *In summer, kids turn open the hydrant and play in the water.* **2.** *n.* a faucet, especially an outdoor faucet. ♦ *Tom attached the garden hose to the hydrant and watered his roses.* ♦ *Please turn off the hydrant when you finish washing the car.*

hydraulic [haɪ 'drɑl ɪk] *adj.* operated by using pressure from water, oil, or other liquids. (Adv: *hydraulically* [...ɪk li].) ♦ *The hydraulic press molds plastics or metals into various shapes.* ♦ *Hydraulic systems perform mechanical work by using oil under high pressure.*

hydrocarbon ['haɪ dro kɑr bən] *n.* one of a group of chemical compounds of hydrogen and carbon. ♦ *Some hydrocarbons burn quite easily.* ♦ *Hydrocarbons are one source of air pollution.*

hydroelectric [haɪ dro ɪ 'lɛk trɪk] **1.** *adj.* [of electricity] produced by using the energy of falling water. (Adv: *hydroelectrically* [...ɪk li].) ♦ *Hydroelectric power is an important source of energy.* ♦ *Hydroelectric energy is used by countries around the world.* **2.** *adj.* [of the production of electricity] produced by using the energy of falling water. (Adv: *hydroelectrically* [...ɪk li].) ♦ *Dams are an essential element of a hydroelectric plant.* ♦ *The valley received its electricity from the hydroelectric generators.*

hydrofoil ['haɪ drə foɪl] **1.** *n.* a wing-like fin that serves to lift a motorboat off the surface of the water at high speeds, making it more efficient. ♦ *The hydrofoil is just below a boat's water line.* ♦ *The boat's metal hydrofoil was damaged by a floating stick of wood.* **2.** *n.* a motorboat that uses ①. ♦ *At high speeds, a hydrofoil's hull is lifted above the water.* ♦ *Hydrofoils raced across the lake, leaving the sailboats behind.*

hydrogen ['haɪ drə dʒən] *n.* the simplest, lightest, and most common chemical element in the universe, which combines with oxygen to form water. (No plural form in this sense.) ♦ *Hydrogen's atomic number is 1, and its symbol is H.* ♦ *Each water molecule consists of two atoms of hydrogen and one atom of oxygen.*

hydrogen peroxide [haɪ drə dʒən pɚ 'ɑk saɪd] *n.* a chemical compound of hydrogen and oxygen that occurs as a clear liquid. (No plural form in this sense.) ♦ *Hydrogen peroxide is a kind of bleach.* ♦ *Some antiseptics contain hydrogen peroxide.*

hydrophobia [haɪ drə 'fob i ə] *n.* rabies. (A deadly disease that destroys the brain. Literally 'fear of water.' No plural form in this sense.) ♦ *After the dog bit Max, it was tested for hydrophobia.* ♦ *Max was given a series of shots to prevent hydrophobia.*

hyena [haɪ 'i nə] *n.* a wild dog-like animal that eats meat and has a loud cry that sounds like laughter. ♦ *The hyena is a nocturnal animal.* ♦ *The hyena lives in Africa and parts of Asia.*

hygiene ['haɪ dʒin] *n.* personal cleanliness; cleanliness related to the care of the body. (No plural form in this sense.) ♦ *Mary is meticulous about her hygiene.* ♦ *The dentist instructed his patients on dental hygiene.*

hymn ['hɪm] *n.* a religious song of praise meant to be sung by worshipers. ♦ *The congregation sang the familiar hymn* *at the end of the service.* ♦ *The church service included two hymns praising God's works.*

hymnal ['hɪm nəl] *n.* a book that has the words and music of hymns. ♦ *There are hymnals in each pew.* ♦ *The hymnal contains more than 400 hymns.*

hype ['hɑɪp] **1.** *n.* an extreme amount of publicity. (No plural form in this sense.) ♦ *There is always lots of hype around major sports events.* ♦ *An advertising firm was hired to generate hype about the candidate's decision to run for office.* **2.** *tv.* to provide extremely exaggerated praise for someone or something. ♦ *The record company hyped the release of the new album for months before it was available in stores.* ♦ *The White House hyped the president's upcoming speech on taxes.*

hyperactive [hɑɪp ɚ 'æk tɪv] **1.** *adj.* (Adv: *hyperactively.*) more active than normal. ♦ *His novel plans grew out of his hyperactive imagination.* ♦ *The stock price of the new company has been hyperactive all week, jumping between high and low over and over.* **2.** *adj.* [of a child] who is very active, especially in situations where calm, quiet, or concentration is called for. (Adv: *hyperactively.*) ♦ *Jimmy is hyperactive and has to take medicine to calm him down.* ♦ *Two hyperactive children in a classroom can create quite a disturbance.*

hypercritical [hɑɪp ɚ 'krɪt ɪ kəl] *adj.* very critical. (Adv: *hypercritically* [...ɪk li].) ♦ *The hypercritical teacher took the joy out of learning.* ♦ *The critic's hypercritical review of the new play angered the playwright.*

hypersensitive [hɑɪp ɚ 'sɛn sɪ tɪv] **1.** *adj.* very sensitive to other people's behavior. (Adv: *hypersensitively.*) ♦ *Susan is hypersensitive to her parents' comments.* ♦ *The hypersensitive child knew his parents had been fighting.* **2.** *adj.* reacting strongly to certain substances. (Adv: *hypersensitively.*) ♦ *The infant's skin was hypersensitive to detergents and a rash would develop if too much soap was left on his clothes.* ♦ *Jane is hypersensitive to tree pollen.*

hypertension [hɑɪp ɚ 'tɛn ʃən] *n.* high blood pressure. (No plural form in this sense.) ♦ *Dave's problem was diagnosed as hypertension.* ♦ *Jane takes medicine every day to control her hypertension.*

hyphen ['hɑɪ fən] *n.* the mark of punctuation "-". (It is placed between the parts of some compound words, between the words in certain phrases, or between syllables where a word has been split between two lines of print.) ♦ *There is a hyphen in the word "twenty-two."* ♦ *The students were taught where to place hyphens in words.*

hyphenate ['hɑɪ fə net] *tv.* to place a hyphen between two words or syllables. ♦ *The homework assignment was to hyphenate the spelling words.* ♦ *Tom correctly hyphenated "Xray" as "X-ray."*

hypnosis [hɪp 'no sɪs] *n.* a sleep-like condition of semiconsciousness, during which time the subject can be easily controlled or remember things that have happened. (No plural form in this sense.) ♦ *Under hypnosis, Bill tried to recall his childhood.* ♦ *Lisa tried hypnosis to stop smoking.*

hypnotic [hɪp 'nɑt ɪk] **1.** *adj.* under the effect of hypnosis. (Adv: *hypnotically* [...ɪk li].) ♦ *The relaxed patient was in a hypnotic state.* ♦ *People in the hypnotic state are responsive to suggestions.* **2.** *adj.* causing hypnosis. (Adv: *hypnotically* [...ɪk li].) ♦ *Hypnotic techniques include using an object the patient can concentrate on.* ♦ *The hypnotic suggestions relaxed the patient.*

hypnotism ['hɪp nə tɪz əm] **1.** *n.* the study of hypnosis as a method of exploring and influencing the mind. (No plural form in this sense.) ♦ *The psychologist found hypnotism fascinating and read everything she could find out about it.* ♦ *The medical community is not in agreement on the benefits of hypnotism.* **2.** *n.* the process of creating a state of hypnosis. (No plural form in this sense.) ♦ *When everything else failed, Bob tried hypnotism to help him stop smoking.* ♦ *Hypnotism cannot be done against a person's will.*

hypnotist ['hɪp nə təst] *n.* someone who is able to hypnotize other people. ♦ *The hypnotist agreed to help Bill stop smoking.* ♦ *The hypnotist asked Bill to close his eyes and go to sleep.*

hypnotize ['hɪp nə tɑɪz] *tv.* to place someone in a sleep-like condition of semiconsciousness. ♦ *The hypnotist hypnotized the patient and began asking questions.* ♦ *It is difficult to hypnotize some people.*

hypochondria [hɑɪ po 'kɑn dri ə] *n.* an obsessive concern for one's health, even when one is completely healthy. (No plural form in this sense.) ♦ *Hypochondria is an abnormal concern for one's health.* ♦ *With hypochondria, someone can imagine an illness and actually feel the pain.*

hypochondriac [hɑɪ po 'kɑn dri æk] *n.* someone obsessively concerned with health and well-being, finding symptoms and illnesses where none exist. ♦ *Jane's a hypochondriac and goes to the doctor several times a month.* ♦ *David is such a hypochondriac that I think he makes himself sick.*

hypocrisy [hɪ 'pɑ krə si] *n.* an instance of behavior that is contrary to what one claims to believe. (No plural form in this sense.) ♦ *Discovering his father had lied, Bill confronted him about his hypocrisy.* ♦ *John's hypocrisy is maddening. He urges me to be honest, yet he lies about everything!*

hypocrite ['hɪp ə krɪt] *n.* someone who claims to believe one thing but does the opposite thing. ♦ *Dave is a hypocrite; he says he believes in honesty but he cheats on his tax return.* ♦ *The politician proved to be a hypocrite when she said she supported the proposed law but then voted against it.*

hypocritical [hɪp ə 'krɪt ɪ kəl] *adj.* like a hypocrite; showing hypocrisy. (Adv: *hypocritically* [...ɪk li].) ♦ *The hypocritical politician was booed by the crowd.* ♦ *Because he was always preaching honesty, the hypocritical minister had a hard time explaining his lies.*

hypodermic [hɑɪ pə 'dɚ mɪk] *adj.* penetrating beneath the skin, for the injection of medication or the removal of blood. (Adv: *hypodermically* [...ɪk li].) ♦ *The nurse used a hypodermic syringe to inject the medicine beneath the patient's skin.* ♦ *The doctor ordered a hypodermic injection of the medicine.*

hypotheses [hɑɪ 'pɑθ ə siz] pl of **hypothesis**.

hypothesis [hɑɪ 'pɑθ ə sɪs] *n., irreg.* a conjecture; a possible explanation; an idea that has not been proved but that explains the facts about something. (Pl: **hypotheses**.) ♦ *The scientists agreed to have their hypothesis tested* *by other scientists.* ♦ *The detective had a hypothesis about who committed the murder but no evidence to support it.*

hysterectomy [hɪs tə 'rɛk tə mi] *n.* the surgical removal of the uterus. ♦ *Jane checked into the hospital for a hysterectomy.* ♦ *A hysterectomy was performed to stop the progress of uterine cancer.*

hysteria [hɪ 'stɛr i ə] **1.** *n.* a nervous condition where someone laughs and cries uncontrollably; an outburst of wild emotion. (No plural form in this sense.) ♦ *The teacher did not know how to handle the student's hysteria.* ♦ *The psychiatrist prescribed medicine to control David's hysteria.* **2.** *n.* a frenzy; uncontrolled excitement. (No plural form in this sense.) ♦ *The hysteria of the teenagers waiting for the rock group was frightening.* ♦ *Hysteria gripped the nation when the president was assassinated.*

hysterical [hɪ 'stɛr i kəl] **1.** *adj.* crying uncontrollably; emotionally out of control. (Adv: *hysterically* [...ɪk li].) ♦ *The hysterical child was sobbing so hard he couldn't talk.* ♦ *I was so upset that I was afraid that I would become hysterical.* **2.** *adj.* very funny; causing uncontrollable laughter. (Adv: *hysterically* [...ɪk li].) ♦ *Bill laughed so hard at the hysterical clown that his sides hurt.* ♦ *The audience roared throughout the absolutely hysterical movie.*

hysterics [hɪ 'stɛr ɪks] *n.* wild emotional outbursts. (Treated as plural.) ♦ *The judge warned everyone in the courtroom that she would not tolerate any hysterics.* ♦ *Tom was emotionally unstable and subject to hysterics.*

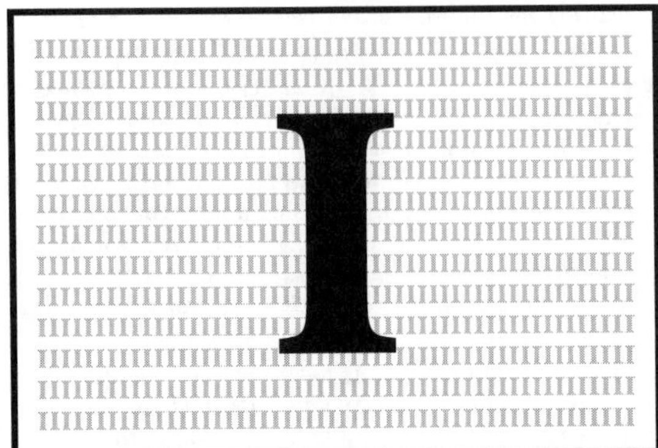

I AND **i** ['ɑɪ] **1.** *n.* the ninth letter of the alphabet. ♦ I *comes after* H *and before* J. ♦ *The word* ice *starts with* I. **2. I** *pron.* <the first-person singular pronoun—in writing, it refers to the writer, and in speaking, it refers to the speaker.> ♦ *I asked my teacher for a clean sheet of paper.* ♦ *I went to the store to buy some eggs this morning.*

ice ['ɑɪs] **1.** *n.* frozen water. (No plural form in this sense. Number is expressed with *piece(s)* or *cube(s) of ice.*) ♦ *Susan put a piece of ice in her soup to cool it.* ♦ *When the temperature is below 32 degrees, water turns into ice.* **2.** *tv.* to cover a cake with frosting. ♦ *Jane iced the cake with chocolate frosting.* ♦ *After Dave iced the cake, he ate the icing that was left over.* **3. ice up; ice over** *iv.* + *adv.* to turn into ①; to freeze into ①. ♦ *The roads iced over after the rain.* ♦ *During the snowstorm, the bridges on the freeway iced up.* **4. break the ice** *idiom* to initiate social interchanges and conversation; to get something started. ♦ *It's hard to break the ice at formal events.* ♦ *Sally broke the ice by bidding $20,000 for the painting.* **5. on thin ice** *idiom* in a risky situation. ♦ *If you try that, you'll really be on thin ice. That's too risky.* ♦ *If you don't want to find yourself on thin ice, you must be sure of your facts.*

iceberg ['ɑɪs bɚg] *n.* an enormous piece of ice that breaks off from a glacier. ♦ *From the deck of the ship, I saw seals playing on the iceberg.* ♦ *The huge ship sank after colliding with an iceberg.*

icebreaker ['ɑɪs brek ɚ] **1.** *n.* a ship with a special bow that breaks up ice when the water starts to freeze. ♦ *The captain steered the icebreaker down the narrow river.* ♦ *In November, the ice became too thick for the icebreaker to work properly.* **2.** *n.* something that helps people who don't know each other to start talking, especially at a party or a meeting. ♦ *The party served as an icebreaker on the first night of the conference.* ♦ *The party was too quiet, so, as an icebreaker, Mary suggested that everyone play a game.*

ice cream ['ɑɪs 'krim] **1.** *n.* a frozen dessert or snack food made from cream or milk. (No plural form in this sense.) ♦ *After dinner, John ate a bowl of strawberry ice cream for dessert.* ♦ *Bill put the carton of ice cream into the freezer so that it wouldn't melt.* **2. ice-cream** *adj.* <the adj. use of ①.> ♦ *I got a set of ice-cream dishes for my birthday.* ♦ *Where is the ice-cream scoop?*

ice-cream cone ['ɑɪs krim kon] **1.** *n.* a crisp, thin, cone-shaped wafer, used for holding ice cream. ♦ *Please put two scoops of chocolate ice cream in the ice-cream cone.* ♦ *I broke three ice-cream cones before I could get the ice cream placed in one.* **2.** *n.* ① and the ice cream contained in it; ① containing ice cream. ♦ *Jane licked her ice-cream cone until it started to melt.* ♦ *What flavor ice-cream cone do you want?*

ice-cream soda ['ɑɪs 'krim 'so də] See soda.

ice cube ['ɑɪs kjub] *n.* a small cube of ice, used to make drinks and liquids cold. ♦ *The ice cubes crackled when Jane added them to the lemonade.* ♦ *Susan put an ice cube in her soup to cool it.*

iced ['ɑɪst] **1.** *adj.* [of a cake or pastry] covered with frosting. ♦ *The cake was iced with a rich, sugary icing.* ♦ *The teacher gave each child an iced cupcake and a cup of milk.* **2.** *adj.* [of a drink] chilled with ice. ♦ *Dave ordered a hamburger, french fries, and an iced coffee.* ♦ *Would you like pop, juice, or iced tea?*

ice hockey ['ɑɪs hɑk i] *n.* a sport played on ice where one team tries to hit a puck into the opposite team's goal. (No plural form in this sense.) ♦ *I can't play ice hockey because I don't know how to skate.* ♦ *In ice hockey, each goal is worth one point.*

Iceland ['ɑɪs lənd] See Gazetteer.

ice skate ['ɑɪ(s) sket] **1.** *n.* a boot with a thin blade on the bottom that allows one to glide on top of ice. ♦ *If your ice skates have sharp blades, you can skate very fast.* ♦ *Bill put on his ice skates and walked carefully toward the ice rink.* **2. ice-skate** *iv.* to glide across ice while wearing ice skates. ♦ *Jane wanted to ice-skate with Bob around the rink.* ♦ *John ice-skates every day as part of his hockey training.*

icicle ['ɑɪs sɪ kəl] *n.* a pointed spike of ice that hangs from something such as a tree branch. ♦ *Icicles form when dripping water freezes.* ♦ *Max broke the icicles that hung from the edge of the roof.*

icing ['ɑɪs ɪŋ] *n.* cake frosting; a sugary coating for cakes, cookies, and other desserts. (No plural form in this sense.) ♦ *Anne's birthday cake has lemon icing.* ♦ *Max ate some icing from the cake when no one was looking.*

icon ['ɑɪ kɑn] **1.** *n.* a picture; an image; a representation of someone. ♦ *An icon of the saint was placed at the front of the church.* ♦ *The artist painted an icon of the king.* **2.** *n.* a small symbol that is part of a computer menu. (Figurative on ①.) ♦ *Bill clicked on the icon showing a pencil. Then his word processor opened.* ♦ *Sue clicked on the trash-can icon to erase the file.*

icy ['ɑɪs i] **1.** *adj.* covered with or made of ice. (Adv: *icily.* Comp: *icier;* sup: *iciest.*) ♦ *The roads are icy tonight, so drive carefully.* ♦ *Bob slipped and fell on the icy sidewalk.* **2.** *adj.* very cold; freezing cold. (Adv: *icily.* Comp: *icier;* sup: *iciest.*) ♦ *Dave decided to stay indoors because the weather was so icy.* ♦ *Susan was glad to be home after walking against the icy wind.*

I'd ['ɑɪd] **1.** *cont.* "I would." ♦ *I'd rather go to Florida than California for vacation.* ♦ *I'd like to go to the store now.* **2.** *cont.* "I had," where **had** is an auxiliary. ♦ *I returned home because I'd forgotten my schoolbooks.* ♦ *I'd wanted a dog since I was six, and I finally bought one last week.*

Idaho ['ɑɪ də ho] See Gazetteer.

idea [ɑɪ 'di ə] **1.** *n.* a thought produced by the mind; an opinion. ♦ *You have no idea how tired I am!* ♦ *Bill's ideas about raising a family were unusual.* **2.** *n.* a picture of something produced by the mind; a mental picture. ♦ *The idea of my stern principal on a motorcycle is hilari-*

ous. ♦ *My idea of the perfect house is one with gables and a picket fence.* **3.** *n.* a suggestion; a plan. ♦ *I have an idea! Let's go to the beach!* ♦ *Your idea was a good one.*

ideal [aɪ 'dil] **1. the ideal** *n.* the best example of something; the perfect type. (No plural form in this sense. Treated as singular.) ♦ *A world in which everyone lives in harmony is the ideal.* ♦ *A job that both pays well and is enjoyable is the ideal.* **2. ideals** *n.* a high moral or ethical standard; a strong moral belief. ♦ *Susan refused to act against her strong ideals.* ♦ *Max didn't understand his parents' ideals.* **3.** *adj.* perfect; perfectly suitable. (Adv: *ideally.*) ♦ *The weather was ideal, so we went to the beach to play volleyball.* ♦ *My ideal car would be one that uses very little gasoline.*

idealism [aɪ 'dil ɪz əm] *n.* the belief in or pursuit of high ideals. (No plural form in this sense.) ♦ *Bill's lofty idealism is sometimes unrealistic.* ♦ *Jane's friends thought her idealism was very noble.*

idealize [aɪ 'di ə laɪz] *tv.* to visualize someone or something as perfect. ♦ *Dave idealized his situation and didn't face his problems.* ♦ *I had idealized my parents as a perfect couple, even though they were not.*

identical [aɪ 'dɛn tɪ kəl] **1.** *adj.* equal; exactly alike. (Adv: *identically* [...ɪk li].) ♦ *The first and second printings of this book are identical.* ♦ *Bill and John have identical briefcases, and sometimes Bill picks up John's briefcase by mistake.* **2. identical to** *adj.* + *prep. phr.* exactly the same as someone or something. ♦ *The second printing of this book is identical to the first.* ♦ *The amount of milk in your glass is identical to the amount in mine.* **3.** *adj.* the same; being the same thing. ♦ *John has lived in that identical house his entire life.* ♦ *A famous actor once sat in this identical seat and used this desk.*

identification [aɪ dɛn tə fə 'ke ʃən] **1.** *n.* identifying someone or something; the condition of being identified. (No plural form in this sense.) ♦ *The police did not make an identification of the victim immediately.* ♦ *Identification of the poison will require chemical analysis.* **2.** *n.* some kind of document that identifies someone; something that proves who someone is. (No plural form in this sense.) ♦ *You should always carry your identification with you.* ♦ *The guard will ask for identification before you enter.*

identify [aɪ 'dɛn tə faɪ] **1.** *tv.* to state or declare who or what someone or something is; to assert someone's or something's identity. ♦ *The doctor identified the disease that made me sick.* ♦ *I identified Max as the thief who stole my bicycle.* **2.** *tv.* to reveal someone's identity. ♦ *His passport identified him as John Smith.* ♦ *Her graceful smile identified her as the woman I had seen yesterday in the park.* **3. identify with** *iv.* + *prep. phr.* to think of oneself as being like someone else; to feel the same way someone else does. ♦ *Susan studied law because she identified with her aunt who is a prominent lawyer.* ♦ *Mary identified with John because their fathers had both died of cancer when they were young.*

identity [aɪ 'dɛn tə ti] *n.* who or what a certain person or thing is. (No plural form in this sense.) ♦ *Only the detective knew the identity of the killer.* ♦ *I will not reveal the identity of the secret ingredient in my delicious cookies.*

ideological [ɪd i o 'lɑdʒ ɪ kəl] *adj.* of or about ideology. (Adv: *ideologically* [...ɪk li].) ♦ *The strong ideological differences between the two factions resulted in civil war.* ♦ *Dave and Mary have many ideological differences that relate to politics.*

ideology [ɪ di 'ɑl ə dʒi] *n.* the set of ideas of a political or cultural group. ♦ *The citizens of a country often do not share the same ideology.* ♦ *We're discussing the ideologies of the world's major religions in my humanities class.*

idiocy ['ɪd i ə si] *n.* stupidity; foolishness. (No plural form in this sense.) ♦ *Walking barefoot in a snowstorm is complete idiocy.* ♦ *We could not believe the idiocy of Bob's rude comments to his boss.*

idiom ['ɪd i əm] **1.** *n.* a phrase whose meaning is different from the combined literal meanings of the separate words that make up the phrase. ♦ *"To hit the hay" is an idiom which means "to go to bed" and has nothing to do with striking vegetation.* ♦ *Idioms occur in every language and make languages hard to learn.* **2.** *n.* a mode of expression or design. ♦ *Susan's clothing designs reflect a modern idiom.* ♦ *Anne and Dave had difficulty working together because they didn't share a common idiom.*

idiomatic [ɪd i o 'mæt ɪk] *adj.* acting like idioms. (Adv: *idiomatically* [...ɪk li].) ♦ *All languages have idiomatic phrases.* ♦ *The meaning of the expression "ring a bell" is idiomatic in some contexts.*

idiosyncrasy [ɪd i o 'sɪŋ krə si] *n.* a behavior of someone that is different from everyone else's behavior; a quirk; a peculiar form of behavior. ♦ *One of Dave's idiosyncrasies is putting ketchup on his cereal.* ♦ *Jane requested a new roommate because she couldn't stand Mary's annoying idiosyncrasies.*

idiosyncratic [ɪd i o sɪn 'kræt ɪk] *adj.* peculiar to one person; quirky. (Adv: *idiosyncraticly.*) ♦ *I moved to a new apartment because I didn't like my roommate's idiosyncratic behavior.* ♦ *Professor Jones's lectures are so idiosyncratic that I never know how to take notes.*

idiot ['ɪd i ət] **1.** *n.* a foolish person; a stupid person. ♦ *Anyone who crosses the street without checking for traffic is an idiot.* ♦ *What idiot put a skirt on the statue of the president of the university?* **2.** *n.* someone who is severely mentally retarded. ♦ *The man was classified as an idiot because his mental age was about 2.* ♦ *The doctor explained to the parents what it meant for their retarded child to be classified as an idiot.*

idiotic [ɪd i 'ɑt ɪk] *adj.* stupid; foolish. (Adv: *idiotically* [...ɪk li].) ♦ *Playing with matches is not only idiotic, it is also dangerous.* ♦ *Firing our staff would be an idiotic way to reduce costs.*

idle ['aɪd l] **1.** *adj.* not working; unemployed; not kept busy; [of machinery] not operating or not being used. (Adv: *idly.* Comp: *idler;* sup: *idlest.*) ♦ *The workers were idle during the strike, and so was the expensive machinery at the factory.* ♦ *I was idle for three months until I found work in another city.* **2.** *adj.* habitually lazy; not liking work. (Adv: *idly.* Comp: *idler;* sup: *idlest.*) ♦ *Max was an idle boy who never did his homework.* ♦ *A few idle troublemakers were annoying children in the park.* **3.** *adj.* not having a purpose or result; of little significance; useless; pointless. (Adv: *idly.*) ♦ *Jane accused me of adding nothing to the project except idle thoughts.* ♦ *Your idle comments aren't helping me solve this problem.* **4. idle away** *tv.* + *adv.* to waste time; to spend time doing nothing. ♦ *Max idled away the last hour of work talking on the phone.* ♦ *I* *idled my summer vacation away playing cards with my grandfather.* **5.** *tv.* to run an engine at low speed in neutral. ♦ *Max idled the engine because he liked the noise it made.* ♦ *The mechanic idled the engine to determine what was wrong with it.*

idleness ['ɑɪd l nəs] **1.** *n.* the condition of being idle; a state of doing nothing. (No plural form in this sense.) ♦ *Idleness at the company affected the owner's profits.* ♦ *I have enjoyed the idleness of the summer months, but now I must return to school.* **2.** *n.* laziness. (No plural form in this sense.) ♦ *Jane's idleness disturbed her mother, who had a lot of work to do.* ♦ *Idleness will not be tolerated in this office.*

idly ['ɑɪd li] **1.** *adv.* without purpose or direction. ♦ *Grandpa sat idly while the grandchildren unwrapped their presents.* ♦ *Bored, Jane idly stared out the window during class.* **2. sit idly by; stand idly by** *idiom* to remain close, doing nothing to help. ♦ *I do not intend to stand idly by while my children need my help.* ♦ *The wealthy man sat idly by while the poor people starved.*

idol ['ɑɪd l] **1.** *n.* something that is worshiped as sacred in an organized religion. ♦ *The villagers bowed in front of the golden idol every day at noon.* ♦ *The religion forbids the worship of idols.* **2.** *n.* someone who is extremely popular; someone whom people honor or praise. (Figurative on ①.) ♦ *Sue's older sister is her idol.* ♦ *The actor was an idol for a generation of young men.*

idolatry [ɑɪ 'dɑl ə tri] **1.** *n.* the worship of idols. (No plural form in this sense.) ♦ *Worshiping a statue of a cow is a form of idolatry.* ♦ *The anthropologist studied the practice of idolatry in other cultures.* **2.** *n.* blind devotion to someone or something. (No plural form in this sense. Figurative on ①.) ♦ *Tom dressed like a cowboy because of his idolatry of such heroes.* ♦ *The worship of money and cars is a modern form of idolatry.*

idolize ['ɑɪd ə lɑɪz] **1.** *tv.* to worship someone or something as a god. ♦ *The tribe idolized the visiting explorer.* ♦ *Thousands of fans idolized the famous movie star.* **2.** *tv.* to admire someone very much. (Figurative on ①.) ♦ *I idolize my sister because she's so successful.* ♦ *Bill idolized his professor and carefully studied all of his books.*

if ['ɪf] **1.** *conj.* in the event that; in case that; on the condition that. ♦ *I want you to come home if it begins to rain.* ♦ *If you lend me $10, I'll pay you back on Friday.* **2.** *conj.* whether. (Introduces an indirect question.) ♦ *Mary wants to know if you're going to go to the store with her.* ♦ *Have you heard if it is supposed to rain tonight?* **3.** *conj.* although; even though. ♦ *The beautiful, if poisonous, plant that grew in the backyard bloomed in the summer.* ♦ *The helpful, if scared, witness talked to the police willingly.* **4. if not** *phr.* if that is not [the case]; if that is not so; otherwise; if that does not happen. ♦ *I must leave here by 5:15. If not, I will miss my bus.* ♦ *He should be here at noon. If not, we will eat without him.* **5. if so** *phr.* if that is [the case]; if that is so. ♦ *She might be late. If so, we will eat without her.* ♦ *She is supposed to be all right. If so, we have nothing to worry about.*

igloo ['ɪg lu] *n.* a house made out of blocks of packed snow. (Pl in *-s.*) ♦ *We often think of Eskimos as living in igloos.* ♦ *When I visited the Arctic, I saw an igloo for the first time.*

ignite [ɪg 'nɑɪt] **1.** *tv.* to set fire to something; to cause something to start to burn. ♦ *A smoldering cigarette ignited the newspapers.* ♦ *An electrical spark ignited the oily rags.* **2.** *iv.* to start to burn. ♦ *My hair ignited when I leaned too close to the flame.* ♦ *The wooden building ignited easily when lightning hit it.*

ignition [ɪg 'nɪʃ ən] **1.** *n.* catching fire; bursting into flame. (No plural form in this sense.) ♦ *The process of ignition can be seen each time a match is lit.* ♦ *Ignition of the dry wood was accomplished with only one match.* **2. ignition (system)** *n.* the electric system that produces a spark that ignites the fuel in an engine. (No plural form in this sense.) ♦ *The ignition system was wet and would not function.* ♦ *The car wouldn't start, so I checked the ignition for bad wiring.* **3.** *n.* the key-operated switch that controls ②. ♦ *I put the key in the ignition and started the truck's engine.* ♦ *I turned the ignition on and tried to start the car, but the battery was dead.*

ignoramus [ɪg nə 're məs] *n.* someone who is ignorant; someone who does not know things. (Latin for 'we ignore.') ♦ *Bill didn't tell me that he couldn't read, because he thought I would call him an ignoramus.* ♦ *When it comes to geography, I am a complete ignoramus.*

ignorance ['ɪg nə rəns] *n.* a lack of knowledge; a lack of information. (No plural form in this sense.) ♦ *Ignorance of the law does not lessen one's guilt.* ♦ *I am embarrassed by my friend's ignorance of social manners.*

ignorant ['ɪg nə rənt] **1.** *adj.* without knowledge; without information; uninformed. (Adv: *ignorantly.*) ♦ *I am completely ignorant of recent changes in tax law.* ♦ *Susan was ignorant of the important issues in the upcoming election.* **2.** *adj.* caused by a lack of knowledge; resulting from a lack of knowledge. (Adv: *ignorantly.*) ♦ *Bill's ignorant responses in class showed that he didn't complete the reading assignment.* ♦ *We lost $100,000 because of your ignorant investments!*

ignore [ɪg 'nor] *tv.* to pay no attention to someone or something. ♦ *Max threw rocks at me, but I continued to ignore him.* ♦ *Mary ignored the loud noises from the street while she read.*

ignored [ɪg 'nord] *adj.* not receiving attention. ♦ *I hate to feel ignored and alone.* ♦ *Sitting in the corner, Max appeared ignored and lonely.*

iguana [ɪ 'gwɑn ə] *n.* a lizard found in tropical areas of the Western Hemisphere. ♦ *I kept my pet iguana in a large glass tank.* ♦ *On her trip to Mexico, Mary saw an iguana in the bushes and running between the rocks.*

il- *prefix* See in ⑫ and ⑬.

I'll ['ɑɪl] *cont.* "I will." ♦ *I'll clean up my room after dinner.* ♦ *I'll be back in a few minutes.*

ill ['ɪl] **1.** *adj., irreg.* sick; not well; not healthy. (Comp: worse; sup: worst. Not prenominal.) ♦ *Because Bill felt ill, he stayed home from work.* ♦ *The bad food made Mary ill.* **2. ill-** *adv.* badly. (Before a participle.) ♦ *John's entrance was ill-timed because we were planning a surprise party for him.* ♦ *You would be ill-advised to turn in your homework without checking it for spelling mistakes.* **3. ills** *n.* troubles. ♦ *I have suffered many ills in my long, hard life.* ♦ *John's list of ills was long and included several allergies.* **4.** *n.* harm. ♦ *Dave's lack of input did considerable ill to our project.* ♦ *Although I don't like you, I never wished you any ill.* **5. ill will** *phr.* hostile feelings or intentions. ♦ *I hope you* *do not have any ill will toward me because of our argument.* ♦ *Dave felt such ill will toward his family that he left his fortune to his best friend.* **6. speak ill of someone** *idiom* to say something bad about someone. ♦ *I refuse to speak ill of any of my friends.* ♦ *Max speaks ill of no one and refuses to repeat gossip.* **7. ill-disposed to doing something** *idiom* not friendly; not favorable; not well-disposed. ♦ *I am ill-disposed to doing hard labor.* ♦ *The police chief was ill-disposed to discussing the details of the case to the news reporters.*

illegal [ɪ 'lig əl] *adj.* not legal; against the law. (Adv: *illegally.*) ♦ *In some states, it is illegal to carry a concealed weapon.* ♦ *The police officer gave Sally a ticket for making an illegal left turn.*

illegible [ɪ 'lɛdʒ ə bəl] *adj.* unreadable; not clearly written or printed. (Adv: *illegibly.*) ♦ *Your handwriting is illegible. Please write more neatly.* ♦ *John's signature was an illegible scrawl.*

illegitimate [ɪl lə 'dʒɪt ə mɪt] **1.** *adj.* not legitimate; not according to the law; not authorized. (Adv: *illegitimately.*) ♦ *Since your lunch expenses are illegitimate, they will not be refunded.* ♦ *The senator used illegitimate techniques to raise campaign money.* **2.** *adj.* having parents who were not married at the time of one's birth; born out of wedlock. (Adv: *illegitimately.*) ♦ *A special commission tried to reduce the number of illegitimate births in the county.* ♦ *Susan put her illegitimate child up for adoption.*

ill-fated ['ɪl 'fet ɪd] *adj.* unlucky; cursed; doomed. ♦ *The ill-fated lovers broke up six months after they began dating.* ♦ *An ill-fated airplane crashed into a cornfield.*

Illinois [ɪl ə 'noɪ] See Gazetteer.

illiteracy [ɪ 'lɪt ə rə si] *n.* the condition of not knowing how to read or write. (No plural form in this sense.) ♦ *The president's first goal was to reduce illiteracy.* ♦ *Illiteracy is a severe problem in many poor neighborhoods.*

illiterate [ɪ 'lɪt ə rət] **1.** *adj.* unable to read or write. (Adv: *illiterately.*) ♦ *The minister established a school to teach illiterate people to read.* ♦ *John was illiterate and was unable to fill out his income-tax forms.* **2.** *adj.* ignorant of a certain subject; not knowing about a certain subject. (Adv: *illiterately.*) ♦ *I am so illiterate about computers that I can't even turn one on.* ♦ *Most people are illiterate about the law and the court system.*

illness ['ɪl nəs] **1.** *n.* a sickness; a disease. ♦ *Bill contracted a serious illness and died a few weeks later.* ♦ *Has your aunt recovered from the illness from which she has been suffering?* **2.** *n.* a period of being sick. ♦ *After an illness that lasted three months, Jane was stiff, weak, and tired.* ♦ *During Mary's long illness, she slept almost all day.*

illogical [ɪ 'lɑdʒ ɪ kəl] *adj.* not logical; not making sense. (Adv: *illogically* [...ɪk li].) ♦ *Mary's explanation was so illogical that I knew she was lying.* ♦ *For some illogical reason, Dave left his luggage at the airport.*

illuminate [ɪ 'lum ə net] **1.** *tv.* to cover someone or something with light; to spread light on someone or something; to spread light throughout a place. ♦ *The full moon illuminated the night sky.* ♦ *A single candle illuminated the small, empty room.* **2.** *tv.* to make something clearer or easier to understand. (Figurative on ①.) ♦ *A few examples illuminated the professor's ideas for the students.* ♦ *Could you please illuminate your theory with a little more explanation?*

illuminating [ɪ 'lum ə ne tɪŋ] *adj.* explanatory; insightful; informative. (Adv: *illuminatingly.*) ♦ *My doctor's answers to my questions were very illuminating.* ♦ *The professor's illuminating lecture helped me understand his theories.*

illumination [ɪ lum ə 'ne ʃən] **1.** *n.* light; a source of light. (No plural form in this sense.) ♦ *The only illumination in the room was a small lamp.* ♦ *We used candles for illumination during the blackout.* **2.** *n.* lighting; the light showing on something. (No plural form in this sense.) ♦ *A room at the back of the auditorium contains the switches that control the illumination of the stage.* ♦ *The illumination of the art exhibit is poor.* **3.** *n.* an understanding; an explanation; a clarification. (Figurative on ①. No plural form in this sense.) ♦ *The professor's insightful illumination of his theory was helpful.* ♦ *The note provided a bit of illumination on Bill's whereabouts.*

illusion [ɪ 'lu ʒən] **1.** *n.* a vision of something that is not really there; a false image. ♦ *People who are lost in deserts sometimes see illusions of water.* ♦ *The magician created the illusion that his assistant had been cut in half.* **2.** *n.* a delusion; a false belief. (Compare with allusion.) ♦ *The end of the recession was just an illusion.* ♦ *You are suffering from an illusion if you think you can sing.*

illusionary [ɪ 'lu ʒə nɛr i] *adj.* like an illusion; false. ♦ *The signals that the recession was ending were illusionary.* ♦ *The magician's illusionary tricks fascinated the audience.*

illusionist [ɪ 'lu ʒə nəst] *n.* a magician who creates illusions. ♦ *The illusionist appeared to cut his assistant in half with a saw.* ♦ *The children clapped when the illusionist seemed to change a rabbit into a bird.*

illustrate ['ɪl ə stret] **1.** *tv.* to decorate a book with pictures. ♦ *Jane illustrates children's books with colorful pictures.* ♦ *Bill has the talent and knowledge to illustrate scientific textbooks.* **2.** *tv.* to use an example to explain something. ♦ *I illustrated my point about politics with examples from a book.* ♦ *Bill illustrated the effects of gravity by dropping a heavy rock.*

illustrated ['ɪl ə stret əd] *adj.* [of a book or other printed matter] having pictures or drawings. ♦ *I gave Jimmy an illustrated book about the moon for his birthday.* ♦ *The designer created an illustrated brochure for our company.*

illustration [ɪl ə 'stre ʃən] **1.** *n.* a picture or drawing in a book, magazine, newspaper, etc. ♦ *Jane wrote a children's book, and she also drew the illustrations.* ♦ *When I was 10, I read my first book without illustrations.* **2.** *n.* an example that explains something; a demonstration of something. ♦ *A practical illustration of the theory is found on page 30.* ♦ *The teacher dropped a book as an illustration of the effects of gravity.*

illustrative [ɪ 'lʌ strə tɪv] *adj.* helping to explain; used to explain. (Adv: *illustratively.*) ♦ *The speaker used illustrative stories to explain his ideas.* ♦ *Illustrative examples are helpful when teaching a difficult subject.*

illustrator ['ɪl ə stre tɚ] *n.* someone who draws pictures for books, magazines, newspapers, etc. ♦ *Susan is an illustrator for a company that publishes children's books.* ♦ *I was hired to be the illustrator for a new comic book.*

illustrious [ɪ 'lʌ stri əs] **1.** *adj.* famous; renowned; well-known; distinguished. (Adv: *illustriously.*) ♦ *The interviewer talked to many illustrious actors each year.* ♦ *An illustrious general spoke to my history class about the war.*

2. *adj.* glorious. (Adv: *illustriously.*) ♦ *The book details the illustrious past of the Greek empire.* ♦ *The aging actress had appeared in dozens of movies during her illustrious career.*

I'm ['aɪm] *cont.* "I am." ♦ *I'm going to turn 25 next Wednesday.* ♦ *I'm flying to Hawaii this summer.*

im- *prefix* See in ⑫ and ⑬.

image ['ɪm ɪdʒ] **1.** *n.* that which is seen in a mirror or similar surface. ♦ *Jane stared at her image in the mirror.* ♦ *Looking into the curved mirror, I saw a distorted image of myself.* **2.** *n.* a sculpture, painting, or other form of art that represents someone or something. ♦ *Several of my paintings are images of the Revolutionary War.* ♦ *This sculpture is an accurate image of the mayor.* **3.** *n.* a picture of something in one's mind; a mental picture. ♦ *The detective had a clear image of the crime.* ♦ *Bill could not escape the image of the terrible accident he witnessed.* **4.** *n.* reputation; the opinion that people have about a certain person or thing. (No plural form in this sense.) ♦ *My landlord has a very negative image. She is so rude.* ♦ *The senator damaged his image by accepting the bribe.* **5.** *n.* someone or something that looks very much like someone or something else; a copy. ♦ *Bill is a perfect image of his Uncle Dave.* ♦ *Mary is the image of her mother.* **6. spit and image (of someone); spitting image (of someone)** *idiom* the exact image ① of someone. ♦ *Tom is the spit and image of his grandfather.* ♦ *My son is the spitting image of his daddy.*

imagery ['ɪm ɪdʒ ri] *n.* words, music, or pictures that represent or create images, often also evoking situations or feelings; mental pictures that are created in a person's mind, especially in response to poetry, music, art, etc. (No plural form in this sense.) ♦ *The poet used vivid imagery to evoke the excitement and hopefulness of spring after a long, cold winter.* ♦ *The imagery of death and decay in the artist's paintings made them very depressing to look at.*

imaginable [ɪ 'mædʒ ə nə bəl] *adj.* able to be pictured in one's mind; able to be thought of. (Adv: *imaginably.*) ♦ *Living on the moon is imaginable, but not very likely to happen soon.* ♦ *A thousand dollars is the highest amount imaginable that I would pay for that old car.*

imaginary [ɪ 'mædʒ ə nɛr i] *adj.* existing only in the mind; not real. (Adv: *imaginarily* [ɪ mædʒ ə 'nɛr ə li].) ♦ *Anne was an only child, so she created imaginary friends.* ♦ *The doctor believed that all of Bill's problems were imaginary.*

imagination [ɪ mædʒ ə 'ne ʃən] **1.** *n.* the part of the mind that produces thoughts and images that are not real or not experienced; the part of the mind that imagines things. (No plural form in this sense.) ♦ *Most of Bill's health problems were in his imagination.* ♦ *John's vivid stories were a product of his active imagination.* **2.** *n.* the ability to think of new and interesting ideas; the ability to imagine something. (No plural form in this sense.) ♦ *Susan shows imagination in her writing style.* ♦ *The designer's plans showed a lot of creativity and imagination.*

imaginative [ɪ 'mædʒ ə nə tɪv] *adj.* creative; using imagination in a clever and interesting way. (Adv: *imaginatively.*) ♦ *Susan writes very imaginative science-fiction stories.* ♦ *The imaginative speaker entertained the audience.*

imagine [ɪ 'mædʒ ɪn] **1.** *tv.* to think of someone or something; to form an image of someone or something in one's mind. ♦ *While sweating in the fields, the farmer imagined drinking cold lemonade.* ♦ *The soldier imagined what it would be like to be a general.* **2.** *tv.* to think something; to believe something; to suppose something; to guess something. (Takes a clause.) ♦ *Bill loves football, so I imagine that he will be watching the game today.* ♦ *I imagine your parents are quite concerned about your low grades.*

imbalance [ɪm 'bæl əns] *n.* a lack of balance. (No plural form in this sense.) ♦ *A chemical imbalance in Bob's brain caused his seizures.* ♦ *The painting had an imbalance of colors.*

imbalanced [ɪm 'bæl ənst] *adj.* lacking balance; not having balance. ♦ *Dave's diet was very imbalanced as he ate only hamburgers.* ♦ *One of my senators has an imbalanced view of world trade problems.*

imbecile ['ɪm bɪ səl] **1.** *n.* a person who has very little intelligence; someone who is mentally retarded and above the level of an **idiot.** ♦ *Most true imbeciles are institutionalized.* ♦ *Some true imbeciles are able to work, doing simple, repetitive tasks.* **2.** *n.* someone who acts stupid; someone who seems stupid. (Rude or derogatory.) ♦ *Some imbecile stepped on his brakes suddenly, and I crashed my car into his.* ♦ *Stop acting like an imbecile!*

imbecilic [ɪm bə 'sɪl ɪk] **1.** *adj.* like an imbecile; having very little intelligence. (Adv: *imbecilically* [...ɪk li].) ♦ *The new county hospital houses imbecilic patients.* ♦ *The factory received government aid for employing imbecilic workers.* **2.** *adj.* foolish; stupid. (Adv: *imbecilically* [...ɪk li].) ♦ *Bob's imbecilic behavior annoyed Mary a great deal.* ♦ *The imbecilic movie was a waste of my money.*

imbibe [ɪm 'baɪb] *tv.* to drink something, especially alcohol. ♦ *Grandpa imbibed a bit of wine each night.* ♦ *Within an hour, the poker players had imbibed a fifth of gin.*

imbue [ɪm 'bju] **imbue with** *tv.* + *prep. phr.* to inspire someone with something; to fill someone with a certain feeling. ♦ *Soft music imbues me with a feeling of romance.* ♦ *Dave's parents imbued him with a sense of personal responsibility.*

imitate ['ɪm ɪ tet] **1.** *tv.* to attempt to copy the style, behavior, or success of someone who one admires or wants to be like. ♦ *I imitated my older sister by applying to the same schools as she did.* ♦ *Anne imitated the famous artist's style in her own paintings.* **2.** *tv.* to mimic the behavior, speech, and movement of someone for amusement; to impersonate someone. ♦ *Bob can imitate the president and other politicians.* ♦ *The students laughed when I imitated our teacher.*

imitation [ɪm ɪ 'te ʃən] **1.** *n.* copying someone's actions or deeds; copying something. (No plural form in this sense.) ♦ *Imitation is a compliment to the person who is being imitated.* ♦ *Imitation may indicate a lack of originality.* **2.** *n.* a copy; a duplicate. ♦ *This poster is an imitation of a famous painting.* ♦ *After examining the diamond, I concluded it was just an imitation.* **3.** *n.* the act of imitating someone or something. ♦ *The audience laughed at Bob's imitation of the president.* ♦ *I was punished for my unflattering imitation of my teacher.* **4.** *adj.* fake; artificial; resembling something. ♦ *These gloves are made of imitation leather.* ♦ *Since I'm allergic to milk products, I eat imitation cheese.*

immaculate [ɪ 'mæk jə lɪt] *adj.* not impure; absolutely clean; spotless. (Adv: *immaculately.*) ♦ *The living room* *was immaculate when the maid finished cleaning it.* ♦ *The inspector found no mice in the restaurant's immaculate kitchen.*

immaterial [ɪm ə 'tɪr i əl] *adj.* not relevant; having nothing to do with something. (Adv: *immaterially.*) ♦ *The point I made in my court testimony was immaterial to the trial.* ♦ *The judge ordered that the lawyer's immaterial comments be removed from the record.*

immature [ɪm ə 'tʃʊr] **1.** *adj.* not mature; not completely grown; not completely developed. (Adv: *immaturely.*) ♦ *An immature apple tree is unable to bear fruit.* ♦ *Since my muscles are still immature, I am not as strong as I will be when I am grown.* **2.** *adj.* like a child; acting like a child; not acting like an adult. (Adv: *immaturely.*) ♦ *Bob's immature behavior at the dinner table upset his date.* ♦ *If you weren't so immature, I'd treat you like an adult!*

immeasurable [ɪ 'mɛʒ ə rə bəl] *adj.* not able to be measured; not able to be counted. (Adv: *immeasurably.*) ♦ *The true value of the painting was immeasurable.* ♦ *An explosion of immeasurable power destroyed the center of the city.*

immediate [ɪ 'mid i ɪt] **1.** *adj.* happening now; happening at once. (Adv: *immediately.*) ♦ *John was surprised by Anne's immediate reply to his proposal.* ♦ *The drowning swimmer required the lifeguard's immediate attention.* **2.** *adj.* closest to someone or something in space or time; next to someone or something. (Adv: *immediately.*) ♦ *The woman to my immediate right is a good friend of the governor.* ♦ *We took shelter because there was a tornado in the immediate vicinity.*

immemorial [ɪm mə 'mor i əl] **since time immemorial** *phr.* since a very long time ago. ♦ *My hometown has had a big parade on the Fourth of July since time immemorial.* ♦ *Since time immemorial, the trees have blossomed each spring.*

immense [ɪ 'mɛns] *adj.* very large; huge; enormous. (Adv: *immensely.*) ♦ *There is an immense difference between a kitten and a lion.* ♦ *The amount of money stolen from the treasury was immense.*

immerse [ɪ 'mɚs] **1. immerse in** *tv.* + *prep. phr.* to put someone or something into a liquid; to put someone or something underwater. ♦ *I immersed myself in the hot bath and relaxed.* ♦ *Sally immersed the potatoes in boiling water.* **2. immerse in** *tv.* + *prep. phr.* to become deeply involved with something; to become absorbed in something. (Figurative on ①.) ♦ *Anne immerses herself in her job, often working late into the evening.* ♦ *Dave immersed himself in the movie so deeply that he didn't hear the telephone ring.*

immersion [ɪ 'mɚ ʃən] **1.** *n.* placing something under water or in a liquid. (No plural form in this sense.) ♦ *Immersion of the whole body into a tub of hot water is an excellent way to relax.* ♦ *Immersion of a burn in cold water will ease the pain.* **2.** *n.* an act of ①. ♦ *A few brief immersions in the pool is all I need to keep me cool on a hot day.* ♦ *Repeated immersions in clear water will clean fresh vegetables of most of their sand and soil.* **3.** *n.* being completely absorbed or involved in something. (Figurative on ①. No plural form in this sense.) ♦ *Mary's immersion in school has a negative effect on her social life.* ♦ *Bill's immersion in his work caused him to neglect his family.*

immigrant ['ɪm ə grənt] **1.** *n.* someone who has come to a new country to live. (Compare with **emigrant**.) ♦ *My grandparents were immigrants who fled Russia during the revolution.* ♦ *Thousands of immigrants come to the United States each year.* **2.** *adj.* <the adj. use of ①.> ♦ *Tom was sometimes a little ashamed of his immigrant origins.* ♦ *Mary is interested in immigrant welfare and volunteers her time to assist new immigrants.*

immigrate ['ɪm ə gret] *iv.* to come into a new country to live. (Compare with **emigrate**.) ♦ *My parents immigrated to the United States from Hungary in 1956.* ♦ *Thousands fled the terrible dictator and immigrated to America.*

immigration [ɪm ə 'gre ʃən] **1.** *n.* the process of coming into a new country to live. (No plural form in this sense. Compare with **emigration**.) ♦ *The immigration of the Irish to America swelled during the Great Potato Famine.* ♦ *Congress tried to slow the rate of immigration.* **2.** *n.* an act of ①. ♦ *Repeated immigrations by Asian peoples thousands of years ago populated what is now called America.* ♦ *My uncle's immigration from England took two months on a ship.*

imminent ['ɪm ə nənt] *adj.* about to happen; happening very soon; definitely going to happen. (Adv: *imminently.*) ♦ *Black clouds usually mean rain is imminent.* ♦ *The guard warned of the imminent approach of the enemy's army.*

immobile [ɪ 'mob əl] *adj.* not able to move. (Prenominal only.) ♦ *I am completely immobile because of my broken legs.* ♦ *The damaged car is temporarily immobile.*

immobilize [ɪ 'mob ɪ lɑɪz] *tv.* to cause someone or something to be unable to move; to cause someone or something to remain in place without movement. ♦ *The doctor immobilized John's broken arm with a cast.* ♦ *The police immobilized the protesters by surrounding them.*

immoderate [ɪm 'mɑd ə rət] *adj.* excessive; more than average. (Adv: *immoderately.*) ♦ *Mary never drinks an immoderate amount of beer.* ♦ *There was an immoderate level of interest in the sensational trial.*

immodest [ɪ 'mɑd əst] **1.** *adj.* not modest; indecent; shameless. (Adv: *immodestly.*) ♦ *The immodest couple kissed passionately on the crowded subway train.* ♦ *Mary wore a very immodest outfit to the party.* **2.** *adj.* not modest about oneself; stuck-up; very bold. (Adv: *immodestly.*) ♦ *Although it may be immodest of me to boast, I have done a lot to be proud of.* ♦ *Dave is very immodest and constantly talks about himself.*

immodesty [ɪ 'mɑd əs ti] **1.** *n.* an indecent or improper way of behaving. (No plural form in this sense.) ♦ *The immodesty of Jane's comment shocked the group.* ♦ *My parents were appalled by my immodesty at the beach.* **2.** *n.* boldness; shamelessness. (No plural form in this sense.) ♦ *Dave's immodesty about his achievements bothered everyone.* ♦ *All of Anne's friends were annoyed by her immodesty.*

immoral [ɪ 'mor əl] *adj.* without morals; not moral; breaking moral rules. (Adv: *immorally.*) ♦ *The minister preached against immoral values.* ♦ *Killing is immoral.*

immortal [ɪ 'mor təl] **1.** *adj.* everlasting; never dying; lasting forever. (Adv: *immortally.*) ♦ *Throughout history, people have sought immortal life.* ♦ *The Greek gods were considered immortal.* **2.** *adj.* always remembered; never forgotten. (Adv: *immortally.*) ♦ *The students read the immortal words of William Shakespeare.* ♦ *Emily Dickinson will always be remembered for her immortal poems.*

immortality [ɪ mor 'tæl ə ti] *n.* the condition of lasting forever; the condition of living forever. (No plural form in this sense.) ♦ *The theologian discussed the immortality of the soul.* ♦ *Humans have always sought immortality, but none have found it.*

immortalize [ɪ 'mort ə laɪz] *tv.* to preserve the memories of someone or something in a book, painting, film, etc. ♦ *Dave immortalized the family picnic on videotape.* ♦ *This photo album immortalizes the boy's short life.*

immovable [ɪ 'muv ə bəl] **1.** *adj.* not able to be moved; stationary. (Adv: *immovably.*) ♦ *The piano is so heavy that it is almost immovable.* ♦ *As the cement hardened around it, the flagpole became immovable.* **2.** *adj.* not changing one's emotion; steadfast; stubborn. (Figurative on ①. Adv: *immovably.*) ♦ *Mary's position on saving money is immovable.* ♦ *Our school principal has an immovable will.*

immune [ɪ 'mjun] **1. immune (to)** *adj.* (+ *prep. phr.*) protected against a certain disease, either naturally or through medication. (Adv: *immunely.*) ♦ *You will be immune to measles if you are properly vaccinated.* ♦ *I had the mumps when I was six, so now I am immune.* **2. immune (to)** *adj.* (+ *prep. phr.*) not in danger of being affected by something; secure from the danger of something. (Figurative on ①. Adv: *immunely.*) ♦ *Susan thinks her paper is so good that it will be immune to criticism.* ♦ *No one is immune to new ideas.* **3. immune from** *adj.* + *prep. phr.* not affected by something, such as prosecution or punishment. (Figurative on ①. Adv: *immunely.*) ♦ *Jimmy thought he was immune from punishment when he did something wrong at Billy's house.* ♦ *Max cooperated on the condition that he would be immune from prosecution.*

immunity [ɪ 'mjun ə ti] **1.** *n.* the condition where one's body is protected against a certain disease, either naturally or through medication. (No plural form in this sense.) ♦ *The vaccination provides immunity to the disease.* ♦ *Immunity can occur naturally in some people.* **2.** *n.* immunity ① to a specific disease. ♦ *The nurse's body had developed an immunity to colds and flu over the years.* ♦ *Exposure to many diseases gave the doctor a number of specific immunities.* **3.** *n.* protection from arrest and prosecution. (No plural form in this sense. Figurative on ①.) ♦ *Max was given immunity from prosecution for informing on his cohorts.* ♦ *The ambassador did not have to pay parking tickets because he had diplomatic immunity.*

immunize ['ɪm jə naɪz] *tv.* to protect someone from disease through medication or by exposure to persons having the disease. ♦ *The doctor immunized the baby.* ♦ *I was immunized against most childhood diseases when I was two.*

immunology [ɪm jə 'nɑl ə dʒi] *n.* the study of the body's immunity to diseases. (No plural form in this sense.) ♦ *Mary's work with AIDS prevention led her to study immunology.* ♦ *The doctor delivered a report on recent progress in immunology.*

imp ['ɪmp] *n.* a mischievous child. ♦ *"Give me my keys, you little imp!" Mary yelled, chasing Jimmy around the house.* ♦ *Susan can be an imp at times, but usually she's well behaved.*

impact 1. ['ɪm pækt] *n.* the forceful collision of objects striking one another. ♦ *The impact of the baseball knocked me to the ground.* ♦ *The car crumpled when it made a hard impact against the solid brick wall.* **2.** ['ɪm pækt] *n.* the influence or effect of someone or something. (Figurative on ①.) ♦ *Your lectures have had a powerful impact on my thinking.* ♦ *The impact of the tax cut will not be felt for five years.* **3.** [ɪm 'pækt] *tv.* to collide with something; to hit into something. ♦ *The gasoline truck impacted the concrete wall and exploded.* ♦ *The meteor impacted the surface of the moon and left a large crater.* **4.** [ɪm 'pækt] *tv.* to affect, influence, or alter something. ♦ *The loss of federal funds has impacted our budget severely.* ♦ *The lengthy strike negatively impacted the morale of the workers.* **5. impact on** ['ɪm pækt...] *iv.* + *prep. phr.* to have an effect on something. ♦ *The loss of federal funds will impact on our budget negatively.* ♦ *The strike impacted on the morale of the workers and slowed production.* **6. upon impact** [...'ɪm pækt] *idiom* at the place or time of an impact ①. ♦ *The car crumpled upon impact with the brick wall.* ♦ *The man who fell from the top of the building died on impact.*

impair [ɪm 'per] *tv.* to damage, injure, or harm something; to cause something to be unable to work correctly; to weaken the quality or strength of something. ♦ *Listening to extremely loud music impaired my hearing permanently.* ♦ *Alcohol impairs your ability to drive a car.*

impairment [ɪm 'per mənt] *n.* a weakness or disability. ♦ *Because I have a hearing impairment, I wear a hearing aid.* ♦ *John was not drafted into the army due to a physical impairment that prevents him from walking very far.*

impart [ɪm 'pɑrt] *tv.* to give information or advice [to someone]. ♦ *My advisor imparted wisdom even when I didn't ask for it.* ♦ *The witness imparted what she knew to the police.*

impartial [ɪm 'pɑr ʃəl] *adj.* not taking any side of an argument; neutral; not biased. (Adv: *impartially.*) ♦ *It was impossible for the parents to remain impartial about their child.* ♦ *An umpire must remain impartial throughout the game.*

impassable [ɪm 'pæs ə bəl] *adj.* not passable; not permitting movement across, along, over, through, or under. (Adv: *impassably.*) ♦ *The road ahead is impassable because the bridge is washed out.* ♦ *I tried to travel along the flooded road, but it was impassable.*

impasse ['ɪm pæs] **1.** *n.* a place where movement or progress is blocked by something; a deadlock. (No plural form in this sense.) ♦ *The union went on strike because of an impasse in negotiations with management.* ♦ *The impasse was overcome through a compromise.* **2. reach an impasse** *idiom* to progress to the point that a barrier stops further progress. ♦ *When negotiations with management reached an impasse, the union went on strike.* ♦ *The discussion reached an impasse and no one was able to propose a compromise.*

impassive [ɪm 'pæs ɪv] *adj.* unemotional; showing no emotion; having no emotion. (Adv: *impassively.*) ♦ *Throughout his mother's funeral, Bob remained impassive.* ♦ *In shock, Mary spoke of the accident in an impassive voice.*

impatience [ɪm 'pe ʃəns] *n.* the lack of patience; the inability to wait for someone or something. (No plural form in this sense.) ♦ *You must wait your turn in line. I will not tolerate any impatience.* ♦ *Bill's impatience caused him to frown when he had to wait.*

impatiens [ɪm 'pe ʃəns] *n.* a flowering herb grown in temperate and northern areas. (No plural form in this sense. Treated as singular or plural.) ♦ *Clumps of impatiens grew around our summer cabin.* ♦ *Pink and white impatiens lined both sides of the sidewalk.*

impatient [ɪm 'pe ʃənt] *adj.* not patient; not able to wait for someone or something. (Adv: *impatiently.*) ♦ *Susan is impatient and refuses to wait in line for anything.* ♦ *My impatient brother paced back and forth, waiting for his date to arrive.*

impeach [ɪm 'pitʃ] *tv.* to charge a public official with misconduct. ♦ *In 1868, the House of Representatives voted to impeach President Johnson.* ♦ *The city council impeached the mayor because he had stolen money from the treasury.*

impeccable [ɪm 'pɛk ə bəl] *adj.* without fault; without flaws; completely perfect. (Adv: *impeccably.*) ♦ *Susan's impeccable taste is evident in the decor of her home.* ♦ *Bill's work is impeccable, but he never arrives at work on time.*

impede [ɪm 'pid] *tv.* to obstruct someone or something; to hinder someone or something. ♦ *Mary impeded my efforts to become the president of the council.* ♦ *Our journey was impeded by a violent snowstorm.*

impediment [ɪm 'pɛd ə mənt] **1.** *n.* something that gets in the way of someone or something; an obstacle. ♦ *Mary's accusations were an impediment to my winning the election.* ♦ *The bad weather was an impediment to getting home on time.* **2.** *n.* a physical problem that hinders speaking; a physical impairment that hinders speaking. ♦ *Therapy can sometimes correct people's speech impediments.* ♦ *A lisp is a minor speech impediment, and can usually be corrected.*

impending [ɪm 'pɛnd ɪŋ] *adj.* happening very soon; definitely going to happen. ♦ *We felt a sense of impending doom as the hurricane approached.* ♦ *John ran outside as fast as he could to escape the impending collapse of the building.*

impenetrable [ɪm 'pɛn ɪ trə bəl] **1.** *adj.* not able to be entered, even with force. (Adv: *impenetrably.*) ♦ *Fort Knox, where the nation stores its gold, is impenetrable.* ♦ *The enemy's defenses were impenetrable.* **2.** *adj.* not able to be understood; impossible to understand. (Figurative on ①. Adv: *impenetrably.*) ♦ *The mystery was impenetrable.* ♦ *My algebra textbook is so impenetrable that I need a tutor to explain it to me.*

imperative [ɪm 'per ə tɪv] **1.** *adj.* necessary; having to be done; urgent. (Adv: *imperatively.*) ♦ *Wearing a helmet is imperative when riding a motorcycle.* ♦ *It is imperative that you do it now!* **2.** *adj.* [of a verb used in] making a command. (Adv: *imperatively.*) ♦ *The imperative verb consists of the infinitive of the verb, without the word* to. ♦ *"Leave!" is an example of an imperative verb.* **3. imperative (verb)** *n.* <the form of the verb used in making commands.> ♦ *In English, the imperative consists of the infinitive of a verb without* to. ♦ *"Leave!" is an example of an imperative.* **4.** *n.* something that must be done; something that is necessary. ♦ *First on a long list of imperatives is the purchase of a new computer.* ♦ *It is an imperative that you take one year of algebra.*

imperceptible [ɪm pɚ 'sɛp tə bəl] *adj.* too small or too gradual to be noticed; not noticeable. (Adv: *imperceptibly.*) ♦ *The difference between the two shades of green was imperceptible.* ♦ *A microscope magnifies things that are imperceptible to the naked eye.*

imperfect [ɪm 'pɚ fɪkt] **1.** *adj.* not perfect; having mistakes; having flaws. (Adv: *imperfectly.*) ♦ *This imperfect diamond is less valuable than the others.* ♦ *Dave's grammar was imperfect, but he reasoned well.* **2.** *n.* <a verb form that shows an action in the past that was not completed.> ♦ *In the sentence "Mary was sleeping while Dave ate," the verb phrase "was sleeping" is in the past imperfect.* ♦ *Today in my Spanish class, we had to write 25 sentences in the imperfect.*

imperfection [ɪm pɚ 'fɛk ʃən] **1.** *n.* the condition of being imperfect. (No plural form in this sense.) ♦ *Imperfection in diamonds reduces their value.* ♦ *Bob can't stand imperfection!* **2.** *n.* something that is not perfect; a fault; a flaw. ♦ *A small imperfection on the surface of the diamond lowered its value.* ♦ *Running his hand over the woodwork, Bill felt several imperfections.*

imperial [ɪm 'pɪr i əl] *adj.* of or about an empire. (Adv: *imperially.*) ♦ *An imperial order assigned the slaves to the summer palace.* ♦ *The foreigners took pictures of the imperial palace.*

imperialism [ɪm 'pɪr i əl ɪz əm] **1.** *n.* the policy of building an empire and extending its rule by establishing dependencies and colonies. (No plural form in this sense.) ♦ *Imperialism has faded in this century, and few colonies remain in the world.* ♦ *German imperialism ended after World War I when its colonies were given to other countries.* **2.** *n.* the extension of one country's influence into territories and colonies. (No plural form in this sense.) ♦ *One effect of British imperialism is that English is spoken worldwide.* ♦ *Spanish and Portuguese imperialism brought Roman Catholicism to South America.*

impersonal [ɪm 'pɚ sə nəl] *adj.* not showing emotion; not showing feeling; cold; distant. (Adv: *impersonally.*) ♦ *The company president issued a brief, impersonal memo about the merger.* ♦ *Anne seems cold and impersonal until she gets to know you better.*

impersonate [ɪm 'pɚ sə net] **1.** *tv.* to mimic someone; to act and talk like someone as a form of entertainment. ♦ *I am able to impersonate my teacher quite well.* ♦ *The performer realistically impersonated many famous people.* **2.** *tv.* to pretend to be someone else; to pretend to be someone that one is not. ♦ *It is against the law to impersonate a police officer.* ♦ *John impersonated a minister and performed three marriages before he was caught.*

impersonator [ɪm 'pɚ sə net ɚ] *n.* someone who mimics someone; an entertainer who can act and talk exactly like certain other people. ♦ *The impersonator looked and sounded like the president.* ♦ *The very popular variety show featured four different impersonators.*

impertinent [ɪm 'pɚ tə nənt] **1.** *adj.* not pertinent; not relevant; not related. (Adv: *impertinently.*) ♦ *Your ideas about the war are impertinent to our discussion of the election.* ♦ *Don't interrupt the teacher with impertinent questions!* **2.** *adj.* rude; disrespectful. (Adv: *impertinently.*) ♦ *You should apologize for your impertinent behavior!* ♦ *The protester yelled a few impertinent comments at the mayor.*

impervious [ɪm 'pɚ vi əs] **1.** *adj.* [of something solid] not able to be penetrated by light, water, sound, etc. (Adv: *imperviously.*) ♦ *Since my watch is impervious to water, I wear it while I swim.* ♦ *This safe is impervious to fire.* **2.** *adj.* [of someone's thinking] not open to suggestions or new ideas; [of someone] resistant to begging, pleading, reasoning, suggestions, etc. (Figurative on ①. Adv: *imperviously.*) ♦ *The old professor's mind was impervious to any new theories or ideas.* ♦ *She was firm in her decision and impervious to my pleading.*

impetuous [ɪm 'pɛt tʃu əs] *adj.* rash; acting without thinking; impulsive. (Adv: *impetuously.*) ♦ *I made an impetuous decision to quit my job and move to Chicago.* ♦ *It was impetuous of John to buy four pairs of shoes.*

impetus ['ɪm pə təs] **1.** *n.* movement toward something; the force of a movement toward something; momentum. (No plural form in this sense.) ♦ *The impetus of the car as it struck the wall crushed many of the stones of the wall.* ♦ *I bumped into Bob with enough impetus to knock him over.* **2.** *n.* the reason for doing something; the stimulus for doing something. (No plural form in this sense.) ♦ *The early impetus for space travel was the need to get to the moon before the Russians.* ♦ *A severe earthquake was the impetus for Dave's move from Los Angeles to Boston.*

impinge [ɪm 'pɪndʒ] **impinge (up)on** *iv.* + *prep. phr.* to encroach on someone or something; to infringe on someone or something. ♦ *Obscenity laws impinge on the right to free speech.* ♦ *Gun control laws impinge on the right to bear arms.*

impish ['ɪm pɪʃ] *adj.* like an imp; mischievous. (Adv: *impishly.*) ♦ *With an impish grin, Jane took everyone's coats and hid them in the kitchen.* ♦ *The child's impish behavior became annoying after a while.*

implant 1. ['ɪm plænt] *n.* something that is put into the body, usually by surgery, such as tissue or a medical device. ♦ *The surgeon put an implant known as a pacemaker into Susan's body.* ♦ *Dave's heart is not his own. It is an implant from a dead person.* **2.** [ɪm 'plænt] *tv.* to put something into the body, such as tissue or a medical device. ♦ *The doctors implanted a pacemaker to regulate my heartbeat.* ♦ *The researcher developed ways of implanting healthy tissues to replace diseased ones.* **3.** [ɪm 'plænt] *tv.* to establish something in someone's mind. (Figurative on ②.) ♦ *Anne implanted all the Latin verb endings in her mind through repetition.* ♦ *Listening to the songs over and over implanted their lyrics in my brain.* **4.** [ɪm 'plænt] *tv.* to insert something inside of something. ♦ *The hero implanted a wooden stake into the vampire's heart.* ♦ *The force of the tornado had implanted a shovel into the wall of the house.*

implausible [ɪm 'plɔz ə bəl] *adj.* not likely; not plausible; seeming not to be true. (Adv: *implausibly.*) ♦ *It is implausible that the butler killed the cook, because he was in London then.* ♦ *Many cults preach implausible notions to their followers.*

implement 1. ['ɪm plə mənt] *n.* a tool; a utensil; a piece of equipment; an instrument. ♦ *A spatula is a kitchen implement.* ♦ *We needed a sharp implement to open the cardboard box.* **2.** ['ɪm plə mɛnt] *tv.* to put something in action; to carry out something, such as a plan. ♦ *Bill implemented his investment plan and quickly doubled his money.* ♦ *If you would implement my advice, you would be more successful.*

implicate ['ɪm plə ket] **implicate someone (in something)** *idiom* to suggest that someone is involved in something. ♦ *The mayor was implicated in the murder.* ♦ *Jane's essay implicated her teacher in the cheating scandal.*

implication [ɪm plə 'ke ʃən] *n.* a hint; something that is implied. ♦ *Mary's implication was that she planned to quit her job.* ♦ *Your implication that I stole the money enrages me.*

implicit [ɪm 'plɪs ɪt] **1.** *adj.* hinted; indirect; implied. (Adv: *implicitly.*) ♦ *My advisor gave me an implicit warning to study harder.* ♦ *Anne's implicit message was that Dave was not welcome any longer.* **2.** *adj.* having no doubt; absolute. (Adv: *implicitly.*) ♦ *Because of John's implicit faith in the hospital, he did not question the diagnosis that the doctor gave him.* ♦ *I have total and implicit confidence that Bob can do this job well.*

implore [ɪm 'plor] **implore to** *tv.* + *inf.* to beg someone to do something. ♦ *I implore you to listen to me!* ♦ *The convict implored me to help him escape from jail.*

imply [ɪm 'plɑɪ] *tv.* to suggest something; to indicate something without actually saying it. (Compare with infer.) ♦ *A speaker implies something, and a hearer infers it.* ♦ *The look of guilt on John's face implied that he committed the crime.*

impolite [ɪm pə 'lɑɪt] *adj.* rude; not polite; not courteous. (Adv: *impolitely.*) ♦ *Eating with one's hands at the dinner table is very impolite.* ♦ *I must apologize for my impolite behavior earlier today.*

imponderable [ɪm 'pɑn də rə bəl] **1.** *adj.* not able to be precisely evaluated or determined. (Adv: *imponderably.*) ♦ *An imponderable amount of gold is hidden in sunken ships.* ♦ *The meteor traveled an imponderable distance before it crashed into the moon.* **2.** *n.* something that cannot be precisely evaluated or determined. ♦ *The monk spent many years contemplating imponderables.* ♦ *The number of hairs on the heads of all the people who have ever lived is definitely an imponderable.*

import 1. [ɪm 'port] *tv.* to bring in a product from a foreign country. ♦ *The dealership imports cars from Japan and Germany.* ♦ *This cheese was imported from Switzerland.* **2.** ['ɪm port] *n.* a product that is brought into one country from another country. ♦ *Many imports enter the United States by ship from Europe.* ♦ *Dave decided to buy an American car instead of a Japanese import.* **3.** ['ɪm port] *n.* the meaning of something; the significance of something; the importance of something. (No plural form in this sense.) ♦ *Bill didn't understand the import of my warnings until he was robbed.* ♦ *Anne paid close attention to the import of her parents' advice.*

importance [ɪm 'port ns] **1.** *n.* the condition of being important. (No plural form in this sense.) ♦ *Bill doesn't understand the importance of being punctual.* ♦ *I have always taught my children the importance of cleanliness.* **2.** *n.* the relative standing or rank of someone or something. (No plural form in this sense.) ♦ *Behind the famous celebrities sat people of only minor importance.* ♦ *Prince John's importance was matched by that of his brother.*

important [ɪm 'port nt] *adj.* having a great effect, value, or influence. (Adv: *importantly.*) ♦ *It is important to dress warmly when it is snowing.* ♦ *I missed the most important part of the lecture.*

imported [ɪm 'por tɪd] *adj.* brought into a country from a foreign country. ♦ *Imported wine costs more than domestic wine.* ♦ *I used to buy imported cars until the quality of American cars improved.*

importer [ɪm 'pɔr tɚ] *n.* someone who brings products into a country from foreign countries. ♦ *The importer dealt in crystal from eastern Europe.* ♦ *The local grocer is an importer of Eastern foods.*

importunate [ɪm 'pɔr tʃu nət] *adj.* persistently demanding; asking again and again. (Adv: *importunately.*) ♦ *The lecturer finally responded to Bob's importunate questioning.* ♦ *If you weren't so rudely importunate, I might give you what you want!*

impose [ɪm 'poz] **1. impose on** *tv.* + *prep. phr.* to force oneself or something on someone else; to force the acceptance of something. ♦ *Mary imposed herself on her neighbor until she was finally invited for a visit.* ♦ *The United Nations imposed a permanent truce on the countries at war.* **2.** *tv.* to establish a tax on something; to fine someone; to assess a fine. ♦ *Congress imposed a luxury tax on boats and airplanes.* ♦ *The city council imposed a $100 fine for parking illegally.* **3. impose (on)** *iv.* (+ *prep. phr.*) to take advantage of someone. ♦ *Sue imposed on her neighbor for a ride after her own car broke down.* ♦ *My roommate imposes on me by borrowing my computer all the time.*

imposing [ɪm 'poz ɪŋ] *adj.* impressive; grand; stately. (Adv: *imposingly.*) ♦ *The pyramids of Egypt are imposing structures.* ♦ *An imposing figure blocked the doorway and refused to let us leave.*

imposition [ɪm pə 'zɪ ʃən] *n.* a burden. ♦ *I hope that my request is not an imposition.* ♦ *Having to take you all the way downtown is quite an imposition.*

impossibility [ɪm pɑs ə 'bɪl ə ti] *n.* something that is not possible; something that is impossible. ♦ *What you ask is simply an impossibility at this time.* ♦ *There is perhaps no greater impossibility than to travel faster than the speed of light.*

impossible [ɪm 'pɑs ə bəl] **1.** *adj.* not possible; not able to happen. (Adv: *impossibly.*) ♦ *It is impossible to be in two places at one time.* ♦ *Bill thought it was impossible to pass algebra.* **2.** *adj.* unpleasant; unendurable. (Adv: *impossibly.*) ♦ *You are simply impossible!* ♦ *Your attitude has made this an impossible situation.*

impostor [ɪm 'pɑs tɚ] *n.* someone who pretends to be someone else. ♦ *The impostor was arrested once her true identity was discovered.* ♦ *Sue was shocked to learn that the man she thought was her uncle was actually an impostor.*

impotence ['ɪm pə təns] **1.** *n.* the lack of power; the lack of strength. (No plural form in this sense.) ♦ *The impotence of the king's authority annoyed his subjects.* ♦ *The entire congress was plagued by indecision and impotence in matters of state.* **2.** *n.* [a male's] inability to perform the sex act. (Figurative on ①. No plural form in this sense.) ♦ *Bill and Mary never had children because of his impotence.* ♦ *Bob went to a doctor seeking treatment for his impotence.*

impotent ['ɪm pə tənt] **1.** *adj.* without power; without strength; weak. (Adv: *impotently.*) ♦ *The impotent president was in exile thousands of miles from his country.* ♦ *The budget committee was impotent because no one knew how to raise money.* **2.** *adj.* [of a male] unable to perform the sex act. (Figurative on ①. Adv: *impotently.*) ♦ *Bill was impotent, so he and Mary never had children.* ♦ *When Bob became impotent, he consulted his doctor.*

impound [ɪm 'pɑʊnd] *tv.* to take something legally; to seize something legally. ♦ *The police impounded the car parked in front of the fire hydrant.* ♦ *The court impounded the drug dealer's house and possessions.*

impoundment [ɪm 'pɑʊnd mənt] *n.* the seizure of something by legal means. (No plural form in this sense.) ♦ *The impoundment of John's car would have been prevented if he'd paid his tickets.* ♦ *The finance company threatened impoundment if Mary didn't make payments on her boat.*

impoverish [ɪm 'pɑv rɪʃ] *tv.* to exhaust the value or productivity of something; to reduce or destroy someone's wealth. ♦ *The high taxes on our house almost impoverished us.* ♦ *All the land in the entire region had been impoverished by the drought.*

impoverished [ɪm 'pɑv rɪʃt] **1.** *adj.* poor and suffering from poverty. (Adv: *impoverishedly.*) ♦ *Aid was given to the impoverished nation.* ♦ *The impoverished child ate only what she could steal from the other children.* **2.** *adj.* [of something] robbed of its value or productivity. (Adv: *impoverishedly.*) ♦ *Nothing would grow in the impoverished soil.* ♦ *The impoverished country struggled to regain its former glory.*

impractical [ɪm 'præk tə kəl] *adj.* not practical; not easy to do or use. (Adv: *impractically* [...ɪk li].) ♦ *Making three trips to the grocery store today was impractical.* ♦ *Buying a dress you'll wear only once is impractical.*

impregnable [ɪm 'prɛg nə bəl] **1.** *adj.* not able to be taken by force; not able to be entered; safe from attack. (Adv: *impregnably.*) ♦ *The enemy was unable to destroy the impregnable fort.* ♦ *The bank's safe was impregnable.* **2.** *adj.* [of an egg] susceptible to being impregnated. (Adv: *impregnably.*) ♦ *The fertility drugs made the ova impregnable.* ♦ *The egg was impregnable for only a short time.*

impregnate [ɪm 'prɛg net] **1.** *tv.* to cause something to be full of something; to soak something; to permeate something. ♦ *The carpet has been completely impregnated with the coffee I spilled.* ♦ *Spilled oil impregnated the rag with black oil.* **2.** *tv.* to cause a female to become pregnant. ♦ *The neighbor's dog impregnated our dog.* ♦ *Jane had been impregnated in January and had her baby in September.*

impress [ɪm 'prɛs] **1.** *tv.* to make a good impression on someone; to have a strong effect on someone; to cause someone to feel admiration. ♦ *I impressed my teacher with my essay.* ♦ *Susan impressed her boss by completing the project within a week.* **2. impress (up)on** *tv.* + *prep. phr.* to stress the importance of something to someone. ♦ *My teacher impressed the need for promptness on all the students.* ♦ *The coach impressed on the team the need to practice more.* **3. impress into** *tv.* + *prep. phr.* to press something, such as a design, into something. ♦ *I impressed my initials into the soft leather of the book's cover.* ♦ *Mike impressed his fingerprints into the soft wax.*

impression [ɪm 'prɛ ʃən] **1.** *n.* the image that someone or something causes in someone else's mind. ♦ *We got the impression that Mary was divorced.* ♦ *My impression of the speaker was that he didn't know what he was talking about.* **2.** *n.* a mark that is caused by pressing; an imprint. ♦ *I saw the impression of tiny footsteps in the mud.* ♦ *My fingers made impressions in the surface of the clay.* **3.** *n.* an impersonation; an imitation of someone or something. ♦ *The comedian is known for his impressions of famous* *politicians.* ♦ *Mary got caught doing an impression of the boss.*

impressionable [ɪm 'prɛʃ ə nə bəl] *adj.* easily influenced. (Adv: *impressionably.*) ♦ *Bob is very impressionable and agrees with everyone he talks to.* ♦ *The leader of the cult recruited impressionable young people into its membership.*

impressionism [ɪm 'prɛʃ ə nɪz əm] *n.* a style of painting or music where the artist's impressions of the subject are more important than detailed representation of the subject. (No plural form in this sense.) ♦ *The professor compared and contrasted impressionism and realism.* ♦ *An art exhibition on the theme of impressionism featured fifty paintings.*

impressionistic [ɪm prɛʃ ə 'nɪs tɪk] **1.** *adj.* of or about impressionism. (Adv: *impressionistically* [...ɪk li].) ♦ *The artist excelled at realism, but was unable to paint impressionistic works.* ♦ *I wasn't sure what feelings the impressionistic music was trying to invoke.* **2.** *adj.* of or about general impressions instead of details; subjective. (Adv: *impressionistically* [...ɪk li].) ♦ *Your poem has too much realistic detail to be labeled impressionistic.* ♦ *Jane provided impressionistic comments about her trip, leaving the details to our imagination.*

impressive [ɪm 'prɛs ɪv] *adj.* [of someone or something notably] large, strong, excellent, or important; [of someone or something] arousing admiration. (Adv: *impressively.*) ♦ *Bill has an impressive résumé and should find work easily.* ♦ *The general was an impressive war hero and had been awarded many medals.*

imprint 1. ['ɪm prɪnt] *n.* a mark made by pressing or stamping a surface. ♦ *My shoe left an imprint in the wet cement.* ♦ *My finger left an imprint in the icing of the cake where I touched it by accident.* **2. imprint on(to)** [ɪm 'prɪnt...] *tv. + prep. phr.* to make a mark or design on something by pressing something into it. ♦ *I imprinted my initials on the cover of all my books.* ♦ *Tom imprinted his name onto the outside of his computer bag.* **3. imprint with** [ɪm 'prɪnt...] *tv. + prep. phr.* to mark something with something. ♦ *The passport's pages were imprinted with stamps from many countries.* ♦ *Tom imprinted his computer bag with his name.* **4. imprint in** [ɪm 'prɪnt...] *tv. + prep. phr.* to establish something in someone's mind. (Figurative on ②.) ♦ *The events prior to the accident were firmly imprinted in my mind.* ♦ *I studied my notes until I imprinted the information in my mind.*

imprison [ɪm 'prɪz ən] **1.** *tv.* to put someone in prison. ♦ *The government agents imprisoned the foreign spy.* ♦ *Max was imprisoned for robbing a bank.* **2.** *tv.* to confine someone in a place. (Figurative on ①.) ♦ *The soldier was imprisoned in a trench until the fighting ended.* ♦ *Old age imprisoned my grandmother in her own home for a few years.*

imprisoned [ɪm 'prɪz ənd] **1.** *adj.* in prison; in jail. ♦ *The imprisoned criminal plotted an escape.* ♦ *The secret agent managed to pass information to the imprisoned spy.* **2.** *adj.* confined; unable to escape. (Figurative on ①.) ♦ *The imprisoned puppy barked inside the cage.* ♦ *I opened the window so that the imprisoned bird could escape from the room.*

imprisonment [ɪm 'prɪz ən mənt] *n.* being in prison or in a place from which one cannot escape. (No plural form in this sense.) ♦ *Bill's imprisonment lasted for twenty years.* ♦ *The criminal was found guilty and the judge ordered imprisonment.*

improbable [ɪm 'prɑb ə bəl] *adj.* not probable; not likely; doubtful. (Adv: *improbably.*) ♦ *It is improbable that we'll go on vacation this year.* ♦ *The detective thought the suspect's story was improbable.*

impromptu [ɪm 'prɑmp tu] *adj.* spontaneous; done without planning; improvised. ♦ *I was bored, so I took an impromptu trip to Minneapolis.* ♦ *The pianist gave an impromptu performance at the party.*

improper [ɪm 'prɑp ɚ] *adj.* not proper; not suitable; not appropriate. (Adv: *improperly.*) ♦ *Bob's improper behavior embarrassed his date.* ♦ *It is improper to ask someone to return a gift you've given them.*

improve [ɪm 'pruv] **1.** *tv.* to cause someone or something to become better. ♦ *Bill improved his grades by studying an extra hour each night.* ♦ *Jane improved her golf swing by playing more often.* **2.** *iv.* to become better. ♦ *After weeks of practice, my golf swing improved.* ♦ *The weather improved as summer approached.*

improved [ɪm 'pruvd] *adj.* made to be better [than before]. ♦ *A new, improved word-processing program made the secretary's work easier.* ♦ *The new surgery technique resulted in an improved survival rate.*

improvement [ɪm 'pruv mənt] **1.** *n.* getting better; improving. (No plural form in this sense.) ♦ *The quality of your work needs some improvement.* ♦ *The doctor told me that she could see improvement in my breathing.* **2.** *n.* something that makes someone or something better. ♦ *The programmer suggested some improvements to the computer system.* ♦ *Making home improvements increases the value of the house.*

improvise ['ɪm prə vɑɪz] **1.** *tv.* to make or devise something from whatever is available. ♦ *I improvised a ladder from scraps of lumber I found in the garage.* ♦ *Mary improvised a delicious meal from leftover chicken and some rice.* **2.** *tv.* to perform something without preparing for it; to make up what one is doing as one does it. ♦ *The actors improvised a scene based on an audience suggestion.* ♦ *The organist improvised a piece of music based on a simple folk tune.* **3.** *iv.* to do as well as one can with what is available. ♦ *I didn't have time to prepare a speech, so I improvised from my notes.* ♦ *There was no ladder so I improvised one.* **4.** *iv.* to perform without preparation. ♦ *In his concerts, the organist always improvises on a theme provided by a member of the audience.* ♦ *The clarinet player improvised until the drummer took over to perform a drum solo.*

improvised ['ɪm prə vɑɪzd] *adj.* made up on the spot; done without preparation. ♦ *The president's improvised speech was brief but informative.* ♦ *The audience loved the actors' improvised scene.*

imprudent [ɪm 'prud nt] *adj.* not prudent; not wise; rash. (Adv: *imprudently.*) ♦ *It is imprudent to spread rumors.* ♦ *Bill later regretted his imprudent decision to quit school.*

impudent ['ɪm pjə dənt] *adj.* rude; insolent; not showing respect. (Adv: *impudently.*) ♦ *The impudent passenger swore at the bus driver.* ♦ *John was fired because of his impudent behavior.*

impulse ['ɪm pəls] **1.** *n.* a short burst of electrical energy. ♦ *An electrical impulse shocked Mary when she touched the* *electric fence.* ♦ *The impulse generated by a pacemaker is very weak.* **2.** *n.* the sudden desire to do something; a whim. (Figurative on ①.) ♦ *Bob had an impulse to buy some roses for his wife. He did and she loved them.* ♦ *Susan had a sudden impulse to smoke a cigarette.* **3. on impulse** *phr.* after having had ②. ♦ *On impulse, Bob decided to buy a car.* ♦ *I didn't need a cellular telephone. I just bought it on impulse.*

impulsive [ɪm 'pʌl sɪv] *adj.* [of a person] tending to act without thinking, often suddenly; [of an act] done without thinking, often suddenly. (Adv: *impulsively.*) ♦ *Children are often impulsive and do dangerous things like run into the street chasing a ball.* ♦ *I made an impulsive attempt to call Mike at the last moment, just before my plane took off.*

impunity [ɪm 'pjun ə ti] **with impunity** *phr.* without risk of punishment; with immunity from the negative consequences of an act; while being exempt from punishment. (No plural form in this sense.) ♦ *The diplomat parked in illegal parking spaces with impunity.* ♦ *Bob used his brother's property with impunity.*

impure [ɪm 'pjʊr] **1.** *adj.* not pure; tainted; mixed with other things. (Adv: *impurely.*) ♦ *The impure soil contained salt and chemicals.* ♦ *Anne coughed when she breathed the impure air.* **2.** *adj.* not morally pure. (Adv: *impurely.*) ♦ *Sally felt that Bob had impure motives for dating her, and she refused to talk to him any longer.* ♦ *Almost everyone has thoughts that could be regarded as impure.*

impurity [ɪm 'pjʊr ə ti] **1.** *n.* foulness; nastiness; obscenity. (No plural form in this sense.) ♦ *Impurity of the mind leads to moral errors.* ♦ *My aunt would tolerate no impurity of thought or deed.* **2.** *n.* the condition of being impure. (No plural form in this sense.) ♦ *Impurity of the milk supply can cause widespread disease.* ♦ *The impurity of the Roman Empire's water supply is partly responsible for its fall.* **3.** *n.* a substance that makes something impure. ♦ *Lead is a dangerous impurity often found in the water supply.* ♦ *The scientist filtered the impurities from the chemical solution.*

in [ɪn] **1.** *prep.* inside; within; surrounded by something else. ♦ *Martha is in the bookstore.* ♦ *Detroit is in Michigan.* **2.** *prep.* into; entering into a space; going through a boundary and to a position that is surrounded by something else. ♦ *Patrick ran in the barn.* ♦ *The bullet hit me in the arm.* **3.** *prep.* during a certain time period. ♦ *I will go to Texas in February.* ♦ *I started college in 1984.* **4.** *prep.* after a certain period of time. ♦ *I will go to the store in two minutes.* ♦ *She will graduate from school in three years.* **5.** *prep.* during or within a certain period of time. ♦ *Mary ran a mile in seven minutes.* ♦ *I never saw anything so funny in my whole life.* **6.** *prep.* with; using; as a way of expressing something. (Concerning language or writing.) ♦ *Jane read a book written in Italian.* ♦ *John communicated in French.* **7.** *prep.* showing someone's job or affiliation. ♦ *Anne is in sales.* ♦ *Bob is in plumbing.* **8.** *prep.* showing a particular state. ♦ *Jane screamed in anger.* ♦ *We sat in silence.* **9.** *adv.* inward; indoors; into; in a way that something will be in a position where it is surrounded by something else. ♦ *"Don't get rained on, come in," Tom said.* ♦ *I went up to the door, opened it, and ran in.* **10.** *adv.* at home; at one's office; available. ♦ *Mr. Smith isn't in right now. Can I take a message?* ♦ *Dr. Fields won't be in until this afternoon.* **11.** *adj.* popular; fashionable. ♦ *Anne was part of her high school's in crowd.* ♦ *During the early 1980s, narrow ties were in.* **12. in-** *prefix* <a form freely added to adjectives and some nouns to indicate negation.> (Also il-, im-, ir-. Examples: *inactive, indecision, illiterate, illiquid, impartial, imbalance, irreligious, irregular.*) **13. in-** *prefix* <a form occurring on some verbs, usually showing emphasis of some type, or, on other word types, sometimes indicating in ①. (Also il-, im-, ir-, en-, em-. Examples: *inflame, inflate, illuminate, immense, irradiate, enable, empower.*) **14. have an in (with someone)** *idiom* to have a way to request a special favor from someone; to have influence with someone. ♦ *Do you have an in with the mayor? I have to ask him a favor.* ♦ *Sorry, I don't have an in, but I know someone who does.* **15. ins and outs of something** *idiom* the details of something. (Informal.) ♦ *Jane knows about the plan generally, but not the ins and outs of it.* ♦ *I don't know the ins and outs of their quarrel.*

inability [ɪn ə 'bɪl ə ti] *n.* a lack of ability; the condition of not being able to do something. (No plural form in this sense.) ♦ *Your inability to walk without tripping makes me laugh.* ♦ *I don't swim because of inability, not because I choose not to.*

in absentia [ɪn æb 'sɛn ʃə] *adv.* while someone is absent; while someone is not present. (Latin for 'in absence.') ♦ *The trial took place with the defendant in absentia.* ♦ *The committee elected Bob in absentia as chairman.*

inaccessible [ɪn æk 'sɛs ɪ bəl] *adj.* not accessible; not able to be reached. (Adv: *inaccessibly.*) ♦ *The second-floor bathroom was inaccessible to people in wheelchairs.* ♦ *The center of the earth is inaccessible.*

inaccurate [ɪn 'æk jɚ ɪt] *adj.* not accurate; incorrect. (Adv: *inaccurately.*) ♦ *The inaccurate news report was corrected the next day.* ♦ *The textbook contained many inaccurate statements.*

inactive [ɪn 'æk tɪv] **1.** *adj.* not active; not moving. (Adv: *inactively.*) ♦ *Bears become inactive when they hibernate.* ♦ *John works nights, so he's usually inactive during the day.* **2.** *adj.* [of someone] not or no longer working actively or actively involved. (Adv: *inactively.*) ♦ *Many of the inactive members of this organization should be removed from membership.* ♦ *Sally has become inactive and no longer participates in discussions.* **3.** *adj.* inert; having no effect. (Adv: *inactively.*) ♦ *The medicine contained a number of inactive ingredients.* ♦ *This substance is inactive until it is heated.*

inadequate [ɪn 'æd ə kwɪt] *adj.* not adequate; not having enough of something; not good enough. (Adv: *inadequately.*) ♦ *The plant died because it received an inadequate amount of water.* ♦ *Anne said that if the school can't teach children to read, spell, and do math, then it is completely inadequate.*

inadvertent [ɪn əd 'vɚt nt] *adj.* accidental; not intentional. (Adv: *inadvertently.*) ♦ *John's inadvertent comments reflect what he really thinks.* ♦ *I was charged an extra $100 due to an inadvertent computer error.*

inane [ɪ 'nen] *adj.* foolish; senseless. (Adv: *inanely.*) ♦ *No theater would produce your inane play.* ♦ *Leaving your car unlocked in New York City is inane.*

inanimate [ɪn 'æn ə mɪt] *adj.* not animate; not living. (Adv: *inanimately.*) ♦ *Rocks are inanimate objects.* ♦ *The inanimate body was taken to the morgue.*

inappropriate [ɪn ə 'pro pri ɪt] *adj.* not appropriate; not suitable; not proper. (Adv: *inappropriately.*) ♦ *A bathing suit is inappropriate attire for a business meeting.* ♦ *My boss yelled at me for asking an inappropriate question.*

inarticulate [ɪn ɑr 'tɪk jə lɪt] **1.** *adj.* not pronouncing one's words carefully. (Adv: *inarticulately.*) ♦ *It was hard to understand the inarticulate speaker.* ♦ *I am inarticulate in the morning, until I have had my coffee.* **2.** *adj.* unclearly expressed; [of a presentation] confused and badly structured. (Figurative on ①. Adv: *inarticulately.*) ♦ *No one understood Anne's inarticulate statement.* ♦ *The scientist's inarticulate explanation of the theory was confusing.*

inaugural [ɪ 'nɔg jə rəl] **1.** *adj.* initial; marking the beginning. (Adv: *inaugurally.*) ♦ *The inaugural flight of the newly designed aircraft was flawless.* ♦ *I have a photograph of the inaugural cruise of a huge, new ship.* **2.** *adj.* of or about an inauguration. (Adv: *inaugurally.*) ♦ *Every television network broadcast the president's inaugural ceremony.* ♦ *The mayor's inaugural speech was short and inspiring.*

inaugurate [ɪ 'nɔg jə ret] **1.** *tv.* to mark the beginning of something in some way. ♦ *The construction workers inaugurated the opening of the new bridge with a party.* ♦ *The team inaugurated the start of the new season by winning the game.* **2.** *tv.* to bring someone into power or office with an important ceremony. ♦ *United States presidents are usually inaugurated in January.* ♦ *Johnson was inaugurated soon after Kennedy was shot.*

inauguration [ɪ nɔg jə 're ʃən] **1.** *n.* the start of something. (No plural form in this sense.) ♦ *The inauguration of the new computer system is scheduled for this Wednesday.* ♦ *Inauguration of a new tax system is promised by our state senator.* **2.** *n.* the celebration of someone's coming into power or office. ♦ *Dave attended the president's inauguration.* ♦ *The mayor's inauguration was conducted in front of city hall.*

inborn ['ɪn born] *adj.* existing since birth; innate. ♦ *Humans have an inborn ability to learn language.* ♦ *I have an inborn desire to learn as much as possible.*

inbred ['ɪn 'brɛd] **1.** *adj.* referring to the mating of closely related organisms. ♦ *Inbred animals often have genetic disorders.* ♦ *Some species of dogs have been inbred to enhance certain characteristics.* **2.** *adj.* existing from birth or as the result of training when one was young. ♦ *Racehorses often have an inbred ability to run swiftly.* ♦ *Susan has an inbred talent for playing the piano.*

Inc. See incorporated.

incapable [ɪn 'kep ə bəl] **incapable of** *adj.* + *prep. phr.* not capable of doing something; not able to do something. ♦ *Max is incapable of ignoring a plea for money from a worthy charity.* ♦ *Mary is incapable of driving on the highway without speeding.*

incapacitate [ɪn kə 'pæs ə tet] *tv.* to disable someone or something; to take away the power to function from someone or something. ♦ *The strengthening of federal regulations would incapacitate some state laws.* ♦ *The accident incapacitated John for a few months.*

incense 1. ['ɪn sɛns] *n.* something that gives off a pleasant smell when burned. (No plural form in this sense.) ♦ *Jane burned incense to cover the smell of cigarette smoke.* ♦ *A stick of incense burned inside the temple.* **2.** [ɪn 'sɛns] *tv.* to cause someone to become very angry. ♦ *John's rude outburst incensed his classmates.* ♦ *The new tax increase incensed property owners.*

incentive [ɪn 'sɛn tɪv] *n.* something that encourages someone to do something; the promise of a reward for doing something. ♦ *As an incentive, the workers were promised a bonus if they finished the project ahead of schedule.* ♦ *As an incentive to read more, the teacher offered extra credit for each book report a student completed.*

incessant [ɪn 'sɛs ənt] *adj.* continual; without stopping. (Adv: *incessantly.*) ♦ *The incessant dripping of the leaky faucet kept me awake.* ♦ *Jane bores me with her incessant talking.*

inch ['ɪntʃ] **1.** *n.* a unit of measurement of distance, equal to 1/12 of a foot or 2.54 centimeters. ♦ *There are 12 inches in one foot.* ♦ *Jimmy grew three inches taller during the summer.* **2.** *iv.* to move very slowly; to move an inch at a time. ♦ *The snail inched along the branch of the tree.* ♦ *The hours inched along while I waited for the plane to arrive.* **3. inch by inch** *phr.* one inch at a time; little by little. ♦ *Traffic moved along inch by inch.* ♦ *Inch by inch, the snail moved across the stone.* **4. within an inch of one's life** *idiom* very close to taking one's life; almost to death. ♦ *The accident frightened me within an inch of my life.* ♦ *When Mary was seriously ill in the hospital, she came within an inch of her life.*

incidence ['ɪn sɪ dəns] *n.* the degree or amount of something. (No plural form in this sense.) ♦ *Smokers have a higher incidence of lung cancer than nonsmokers.* ♦ *There was a large incidence of loan foreclosures during the depression.*

incident ['ɪn sɪ dənt] **1.** *n.* an event; something that happens. ♦ *I told Jane about a humorous incident that happened at the zoo.* ♦ *There was a strange incident at work today.* **2.** *n.* a disturbance; an accident. ♦ *Four people were hurt in the incident at the bank.* ♦ *The investigator refused to tell the reporter about the incident in which three people were murdered.*

incidental [ɪn sɪ 'dɛn təl] **1.** *adj.* secondary to something more important. (Adv: *incidentally.*) ♦ *The film had a lot of incidental music in it.* ♦ *There are only two incidental side effects to taking this drug.* **2. incidental to** *adj.* + *prep. phr.* naturally linked. ♦ *I suffered a number of injuries incidental to the accident.* ♦ *Anne described the problems incidental to starting a small business.* **3. incidentals** *n.* small, minor expenses. ♦ *I always have a few incidentals on my expense account.* ♦ *The incidentals add up quickly, so you must budget carefully.*

incidentally [ɪn sə 'dɛnt li] *adv.* "Oh, I just happened to remember"; by the way. ♦ *Incidentally, did you remember to lock the house before we left?* ♦ *Incidentally, I forgot to mention that I saw your brother yesterday.*

incipient [ɪn 'sɪp i ənt] *adj.* beginning to be evident; starting to be recognized for what it is. (Adv: *incipiently.*) ♦ *The project we are working on is an incipient disaster.* ♦ *A runny nose is one sign of an incipient cold.*

incise [ɪn 'sɑɪz] *tv.* to cut into the surface of something; to engrave something onto something. ♦ *Bill incised his initials into the tree trunk with a knife.* ♦ *The symbols were incised onto the tabletop with a razor blade.*

incision [ɪn 'sɪ ʒən] *n.* a cut in the skin made by a surgeon. ♦ *The doctor began the operation by making an inci-*

sion in the patient's chest. ♦ *The doctor sewed up the incision with seven stitches.*

incite [ɪn 'sɑɪt] *tv.* to provoke someone or something; to encourage someone to act strongly or violently. ♦ *The police incited the protesters to violence by taunting them.* ♦ *The villain incited the villagers to attack the palace.*

inclement [ɪn 'klɛm ənt] **inclement weather** *adj.* stormy, wet, or rainy weather. ♦ *The baseball game was canceled because of inclement weather.* ♦ *We stayed home because of the inclement weather.*

inclination [ɪn klə 'ne ʃən] **1.** *n.* the amount of slant, often expressed in degrees, of an incline. (No plural form in this sense.) ♦ *The side of the hill has a 45-degree inclination.* ♦ *The roof's inclination is so small that rain collects there and leaks into the house.* **2.** *n.* an incline; a slanted surface. ♦ *This hill has a gradual inclination and is easy to climb.* ♦ *The inclination of the floor is caused by warped wood.* **3.** *n.* a tendency toward preferring to do something [rather than something else]; to lean toward doing something. ♦ *Our inclination is to rent a movie for the evening.* ♦ *Jane has an inclination to buy a house instead of renting an apartment.*

incline 1. ['ɪn klɑɪn] *n.* a slope; a slant; a surface that is on an angle to flat ground. ♦ *The sharp incline of the side of the mountain makes it difficult to climb.* ♦ *The farmer placed the board at an incline against the barn.* **2.** [ɪn 'klɑɪn] *iv.* to slope; to slant; to angle upward or downward. ♦ *The cliff inclined almost straight upward from the beach.* ♦ *The wheelchair ramp inclines at about 25 degrees.* **3. incline toward** [ɪn 'klɑɪn...] *iv. + prep. phr.* to tend to do something; to lean toward doing something. ♦ *Bill is inclining toward agreeing with his father on most subjects.* ♦ *We incline toward letting Anne go with us, but we cannot decide.*

inclined [ɪn 'klɑɪnd] **inclined to do something** *idiom* to tend to do something; to lean toward doing something. ♦ *Tom is inclined to tell jokes when he is with a group of people.* ♦ *I'm inclined to go to the beach tomorrow if it doesn't rain.*

inclose [ɪn 'kloz] See enclose.

include [ɪn 'klud] **1.** *tv.* [for something] to contain something; to comprise [a number of] things. ♦ *Does the price include tax?* ♦ *The dinner special includes an entrée, soup, and a salad.* **2.** *tv.* [for someone] to cause someone or something to be a part of something; to add something to something else. ♦ *Our server included the tip when she totaled the bill.* ♦ *Mary included a bibliography at the end of her paper.*

inclusive [ɪn 'klu sɪv] **1.** *adj.* including everything; including the numbers or times mentioned. (*Monday through Wednesday, inclusive* means *'Monday, Tuesday, and Wednesday.'* Adv: *inclusively.*) ♦ *I will be in Boston from June 22 through July 3, inclusive.* ♦ *The school year runs from September to June inclusive.* **2. inclusive of** *adj. + prep. phr.* together with; including. ♦ *The total bill, inclusive of tax, amounts to $35.00.* ♦ *Inclusive of public spaces, the office building contains 300,000 square feet.*

income ['ɪn kəm] *n.* the amount of money received as wages or return on investments. ♦ *When Mary was promoted, her yearly income increased.* ♦ *Most of Bill's income comes from stocks and bonds.*

income tax ['ɪn kəm tæks] *n.* a federal, state, or local tax on income that has been earned. ♦ *Bob was surprised that he owed so much federal income tax.* ♦ *I always pay my income tax on April 14th.*

incoming ['ɪn kəm ɪŋ] *adj.* about to enter; coming this way. ♦ *We watched in horror as the incoming airplane crashed.* ♦ *Mary was waiting for the incoming mail to be delivered.*

incomparable [ɪn 'kɑm pə rə bəl] *adj.* superior to all others; so good as to have no equal. (Adv: *incomparably.*) ♦ *This diamond is a gem of incomparable beauty.* ♦ *The millionaire served the guests an incomparable feast.*

incompetent [ɪn 'kɑm pə tənt] **1.** *adj.* not competent; not having the skill or knowledge needed to do something properly. (Adv: *incompetently.*) ♦ *The incompetent clerk could only type ten words per minute.* ♦ *The incompetent doctor was sued for malpractice.* **2.** *n.* someone who does not have the skill or knowledge needed to do something properly. ♦ *Bill is quitting his job because his boss is such an incompetent.* ♦ *Anne yelled at the incompetent who mailed her check to the wrong address.*

incomplete [ɪn kəm 'plit] *adj.* not complete; not finished. (Adv: *incompletely.*) ♦ *The composer died suddenly, leaving behind many incomplete works.* ♦ *My novel is incomplete because I don't know how to end it.*

incomprehensible [ɪn kɑm pri 'hɛn sə bəl] *adj.* not comprehensible; impossible to understand. (Adv: *incomprehensibly.*) ♦ *The legal document was incomprehensible to Bill.* ♦ *The immigrant's incomprehensible English slowly improved.*

inconceivable [ɪn kən 'siv ə bəl] *adj.* unthinkable; [almost] not able to be imagined. (Adv: *inconceivably.*) ♦ *It is inconceivable that we would miss our daughter's wedding.* ♦ *Traveling faster than the speed of light is inconceivable.*

incongruous [ɪn 'kɑŋ gru əs] *adj.* out of place; not fitting in. (Adv: *incongruously.*) ♦ *Hot dogs would be incongruous at a formal dinner.* ♦ *It would be incongruous to see a herd of buffalo in Central Park.*

inconsequential [ɪn kɑn sə 'kwɛn tʃəl] *adj.* not important; trivial. (Adv: *inconsequentially.*) ♦ *Anne deleted the inconsequential details from her proposal.* ♦ *Unfortunately, the results of the experiment were inconsequential.*

inconsiderate [ɪn kən 'sɪd ə rət] *adj.* not considerate; not thoughtful; not thinking of other people. (Adv: *inconsiderately.*) ♦ *It was inconsiderate of you to slam the door in my face.* ♦ *I asked the inconsiderate salesman not to call during dinner.*

inconsistency [ɪn kən 'sɪs tən si] **1.** *n.* a lack of consistency; the condition of not matching or agreeing. (No plural form in this sense.) ♦ *Your inconsistency in style is most noticeable in Chapter 3.* ♦ *There is inconsistency in your performance from night to night.* **2.** *n.* something that is not consistent; a discrepancy. ♦ *John found an inconsistency in my research data.* ♦ *Jane noted many inconsistencies in the two news reports.*

inconsistent [ɪn kən 'sɪs tənt] **1.** *adj.* not agreeing or matching; contradictory. (Adv: *inconsistently.*) ♦ *The witnesses' remarks were inconsistent with each other.* ♦ *The two accounts of the event were inconsistent.* **2.** *adj.* easily changing; likely to change; irregular. (Adv: *inconsis-*

tently.) ♦ *The experiment yielded inconsistent results.* ♦ *Max was fired because of his inconsistent work habits.*

inconspicuous [ɪn kən 'spɪk ju əs] *adj.* not conspicuous; not easily noticed; not attracting attention. (Adv: *inconspicuously.*) ♦ *Anne remained inconspicuous by dressing like everyone else.* ♦ *The inconspicuous restaurant was at the end of a dark alley.*

inconstant [ɪn 'kɑn stənt] *adj.* [of someone] not constant or dependable; changeable; fickle. (Adv: *inconstantly.*) ♦ *Jane was almost ready to marry John when she decided that he was too inconstant to make a good husband.* ♦ *Bill had been an inconstant friend to Bob, who never knew when he could depend on him.*

incontrovertible [ɪn kɑn tro 'vɚ tə bəl] *adj.* not able to be argued; not able to be denied. (Adv: *incontrovertibly.*) ♦ *That the president was assassinated is incontrovertible.* ♦ *The lawyer reminded the jury of the incontrovertible evidence against the accused man.*

inconvenience [ɪn kən 'vin jəns] **1.** *n.* the condition of being inconvenient. (No plural form in this sense.) ♦ *There was much inconvenience to the villagers during the water shortage.* ♦ *Inconvenience during a winter ice storm is to be expected.* **2.** *n.* something that is inconvenient; something that is troublesome. ♦ *It's a major inconvenience that the bakery went out of business.* ♦ *Pardon me for the inconveniences I caused by not being on time and failing to bring my briefcase.* **3.** *tv.* to make something difficult for someone; to cause annoyance for someone. ♦ *I hate to inconvenience you, but I need a ride to the store.* ♦ *Bob inconvenienced me by being late for our appointment.*

inconvenient [ɪn kən 'vin jənt] *adj.* not convenient; not easy to deal with; not fitting into one's schedule. (Adv: *inconveniently.*) ♦ *Your visit will be inconvenient because I will be busy that week.* ♦ *The store's hours were inconvenient. It was only open when I was at work.*

incorporate [ɪn 'kor pə ret] **1.** *tv.* to include someone or something; to make someone or something part of a whole or a group. ♦ *The school's curriculum incorporates the study of art and music.* ♦ *My theory incorporates many previously proven principles.* **2.** *tv.* to make a business into a legal corporation; to cause an organization to become a legal entity. ♦ *The owners had incorporated the company in 1925.* ♦ *After years of running a small business in his basement, John incorporated his company.* **3.** *iv.* to form a legal corporation; to become a legal organization. ♦ *Our company incorporated in 1925.* ♦ *When our partnership incorporated, we had to fill out a lot of government forms.*

incorporated [ɪn 'kor pə ret ɪd] *adj.* made into a legal organization. (Abbreviated *Inc.*) ♦ *Smith & Jones, Incorporated, sells stationery supplies.* ♦ *The secretary called every incorporated business in the city.*

incorrect [ɪn kə 'rɛkt] *adj.* not correct; wrong; false. (Adv: *incorrectly.*) ♦ *Your answer is incorrect. Would you like to try again?* ♦ *Your assumption is right, but your conclusion is incorrect.*

increase 1. ['ɪn kris] *n.* growth; becoming larger. (No plural form in this sense.) ♦ *The puppy's increase in size was noticeable.* ♦ *The army could not stop the ruler's increase in power.* **2.** ['ɪn kris] *n.* a rise in the number or amount of something; a growth in an amount. ♦ *There was an increase in accidents after the stop sign at the corner was removed.* ♦ *As part of her promotion, Susan also received an increase in pay.* **3.** [ɪn 'kris] *iv.* to become larger, faster, or more powerful; to become larger in number or amount. ♦ *The number of accidents increased after the stop sign was removed.* ♦ *As you leave town, the speed limit increases to 45 miles per hour.* **4.** [ɪn 'kris] *tv.* to cause something to become larger, faster, or more powerful; to cause something to become larger in number or amount. ♦ *Susan increased her employees' salaries.* ♦ *Congress increased the speed limit to 65 miles per hour.*

increasing [ɪn 'kris ɪŋ] *adj.* growing. (Adv: *increasingly.*) ♦ *The increasing number of robberies worried the citizens.* ♦ *After a week of exercise, Mary's increasing strength became evident.*

increasingly [ɪn 'kris ɪŋ li] *adv.* more and more. ♦ *It has become increasingly difficult to turn left at that busy intersection.* ♦ *Increasingly, people are choosing to work in the suburbs.*

incredible [ɪn 'krɛd ə bəl] **1.** *adj.* hard to believe; unbelievable. (Adv: *incredibly.*) ♦ *Bill's story was so incredible I didn't believe him.* ♦ *It's incredible, but I don't know how to drive a car.* **2.** *adj.* amazing; wonderful; really good. (Informal. Adv: *incredibly.*) ♦ *Wow! That was the most incredible movie I've ever seen!* ♦ *I love eating at Jane's because she's an incredible cook.*

incredibly [ɪn 'krɛd ə bli] **1.** *adv.* remarkably; in a way that is hard to believe. ♦ *Incredibly, no one was killed in the flood.* ♦ *Incredibly, we have enough money to pay all the bills this month!* **2.** *adv.* amazingly; wonderfully. (Informal.) ♦ *This apple pie tastes incredibly delicious.* ♦ *This is an incredibly beautiful painting.* **3.** *adv.* very. (Informal.) ♦ *I was late for work, so I ate breakfast incredibly fast.* ♦ *Your hands are incredibly dirty. Go wash them.*

increment ['ɪn krə mənt] *n.* an increase; the amount that something increases; a step in a series of increases. ♦ *Each unit on this chart corresponds to a $1,000 increment.* ♦ *The athlete added weights to the barbells in five-pound increments.*

incremental [ɪn krə 'mɛn təl] *adj.* increasing in steps. (Adv: *incrementally.*) ♦ *The citizens protested the incremental tax increase.* ♦ *Each drought caused an incremental rise in the price of coffee.*

incubator ['ɪŋ kjə bet ɚ] **1.** *n.* a container that keeps eggs warm until they hatch. ♦ *The farmer placed the eggs in an incubator.* ♦ *The baby chicken hatched in an incubator.* **2.** *n.* an apparatus in which babies that are born too early are kept for warmth and care. ♦ *The tiny baby remained in an incubator until it weighed six pounds.* ♦ *The nurse fed the baby and then returned it to the incubator.*

incumbent [ɪn 'kʌm bənt] **1.** *adj.* holding an office, especially an elected office. ♦ *The incumbent mayor was defeated in yesterday's election.* ♦ *The incumbent senator decided to retire at the end of her term.* **2.** *n.* the person currently holding an elected office. ♦ *The young politician beat the incumbent in a very close election.* ♦ *Angry voters did not reelect the incumbents.* **3. incumbent (up)on someone to do something** *idiom* obligatory for someone to do something. ♦ *It is incumbent upon me to inform you that you are up for review.* ♦ *It was incumbent on Mary to mail her application before June 1st.*

incur [ɪn 'kɚ] **1.** *tv.* to earn something; to obligate oneself to pay additional charges. ♦ *Please pay this bill today or you will incur additional expenses.* ♦ *Jane incurred a* *penalty for filing her income-tax return late.* **2.** *tv.* to earn someone's anger, wrath, hatred, displeasure, insults, etc. ♦ *John incurred his roommate's wrath for waking him up.* ♦ *Anne incurred her brother's anger for taking his radio without asking.*

incurable [ɪn ˈkjɚ ə bəl] **1.** *adj.* not able to be cured. (Adv: *incurably.*) ♦ *Bob contracted an incurable illness and died.* ♦ *Mary has an incurable form of arthritis.* **2.** *adj.* permanent; unchangeable. (Figurative on ①. Adv: *incurably.*) ♦ *Bill is an incurable optimist.* ♦ *Susan is afflicted with incurable happiness.*

incurably [ɪn ˈkjɚ ə bli] **1.** *adv.* [ill] to a degree that cannot be cured. ♦ *Susan became incurably sick and died soon after.* ♦ *Anne visited her incurably ill brother in the hospital.* **2.** *adv.* unchangeably; permanently. (Ironic and jocular. Figurative on ①.) ♦ *John is incurably optimistic, and his wife is incurably pessimistic.* ♦ *Susan is incurably happy!*

indecent [ɪn ˈdi sənt] *adj.* not decent; not proper; offensive; lewd. (Adv: *indecently.*) ♦ *The student was punished for using indecent language in class.* ♦ *The radio program was cut off because of the constant indecent remarks of the broadcasters.*

indecision [ɪn dɪ ˈsɪ ʒən] *n.* the inability to make a decision. (No plural form in this sense.) ♦ *Dave was in the video store for an hour because of his indecision in choosing a movie.* ♦ *Your indecision over the simplest choices annoys me.*

indecisive [ɪn dɪ ˈsɑɪ sɪv] *adj.* not able to make a decision; unable to make up one's mind. (Adv: *indecisively.*) ♦ *Since you're so indecisive, let me order dinner for you.* ♦ *The indecisive manager was unable to choose a new computer system.*

indeed [ɪn ˈdid] **1.** *adv.* very much so; quite. ♦ *It is indeed cold today.* ♦ *We are indeed delighted to have you as our guest.* **2.** *adv.* in fact; actually. ♦ *I am here indeed, and on time!* ♦ *"You don't need this pencil, do you?" "I do indeed!"* **3.** *interj.* "Amazing!" ♦ *"It snowed 8 inches last night." "Indeed!"* ♦ *At about 4:00 A.M., John said, "I must go now." His date sarcastically replied, "Indeed! So soon?"*

indefatigable [ɪn də ˈfæt ɪ gə bəl] *adj.* always active or moving; untiring. (Adv: *indefatigably.*) ♦ *Mary is quite indefatigable and works 16 hours a day.* ♦ *The indefatigable workers toiled through the night.*

indefensible [ɪn dɪ ˈfɛn sə bəl] **1.** *adj.* not able to be defended; not able to be protected from attack. (Adv: *indefensibly.*) ♦ *The indefensible fort was easily destroyed by the enemy.* ♦ *Your essay will get a bad grade because your research methods are indefensible.* **2.** *adj.* not able to be excused; not able to be justified. (Adv: *indefensibly.*) ♦ *Your comments are indefensible, and I cannot forgive you.* ♦ *John tried to apologize for his roommate's indefensible behavior.*

indefinite [ɪn ˈdɛf ə nɪt] **1.** *adj.* not defined; not clear; vague. (Adv: *indefinitely.*) ♦ *The police officer gave the reporters only a few indefinite answers.* ♦ *An indefinite number of robbers entered the building sometime during the night.* **2.** *adj.* not having limits or boundaries. (Adv: *indefinitely.*) ♦ *The investment has the potential to earn an indefinite amount of money.* ♦ *I'll be out of town for an indefinite period of time.*

indent [ɪn ˈdɛnt] *tv.* [in writing or typing] to begin a line a few spaces farther from the edge than the other lines, at the beginning of a paragraph. ♦ *Mary indented the first line of each paragraph.* ♦ *When I write a book, I don't indent the first paragraph of each chapter.*

indentation [ɪn dɛn ˈte ʃən] **1.** *n.* a notch; a dent; a cut. ♦ *The hail made deep indentations in the hood of the car.* ♦ *The path through the woods was indicated by small indentations carved into tree trunks.* **2.** *n.* indenting lines of type or writing. (No plural form in this sense.) ♦ *Indentation helps readers find their way on the page.* ♦ *Proper indentation is half an inch from the edge of the margin.* **3.** *n.* an instance of ②. ♦ *Your paper looks sloppy because your indentations are uneven.* ♦ *You need an indentation at the beginning of this paragraph.*

independence [ɪn dɪ ˈpɛn dəns] *n.* freedom; liberty. (No plural form in this sense.) ♦ *The United States declared independence from England in 1776.* ♦ *John proved his independence by moving out of his parents' house.*

Independence Day [ɪn dɪ ˈpɛn dəns de] *n.* Fourth of July, a United States holiday that celebrates the birth of the United States and the end of British colonial rule. ♦ *Independence Day is a federal holiday.* ♦ *The town sponsors a parade every Independence Day.*

independent [ɪn dɪ ˈpɛn dənt] **1.** *adj.* not dependent on someone or something; not controlled by others; not ruled by other people or countries. (Adv: *independently.*) ♦ *In 1776, the United States of America became an independent country.* ♦ *Many African countries became independent in the 1960s.* **2.** *adj.* not needing the support of others; self-supporting. (Adv: *independently.*) ♦ *The art exhibit is self-supporting and is independent of government funding.* ♦ *Independent television stations are not affiliated with any network.* **3.** *adj.* separate; distinct from other things. (Adv: *independently.*) ♦ *Our farmland and our apple orchard are taxed as independent parcels of land.* ♦ *Lisa runs two independent businesses.* **4.** *n.* a politician or a voter who does not belong to a political party. ♦ *The governor of that state is an independent.* ♦ *There were three candidates for president: a republican, a democrat, and an independent.*

in-depth [ˈɪn ˈdɛpθ] *adj.* in detail; thorough. ♦ *The witness provided an in-depth description of the accident.* ♦ *The reporter wrote an in-depth article about the stock market.*

indescribable [ɪn dɪ ˈskrɑɪb ə bəl] *adj.* [of something] so beautiful, impressive, or horrible that it cannot be described in words. (Adv: *indescribably.*) ♦ *The explosion created an indescribable scene of horror.*

indestructible [ɪn dɪ ˈstrʌk tə bəl] *adj.* not able to be destroyed; able to withstand attack; completely durable. (Adv: *indestructibly.*) ♦ *The soldiers were well protected inside the indestructible tank.* ♦ *John thought his house was indestructible, but it collapsed during an earthquake.*

indeterminate [ɪn dɪ ˈtɚ mə nət] *adj.* not able to be determined or decided. (Adv: *indeterminately.*) ♦ *An indeterminate number of people attended the concert without buying tickets.* ♦ *Sitting between the young man and the old man was a man of indeterminate age.*

index [ˈɪn dɛks] **1.** *n., irreg.* an alphabetical list of topics showing where the topics can be found in the main part of a book, report, magazine, journal, etc. (Pl: *indexes* or indices.) ♦ *Most book indexes are placed at the end of the book.* ♦ *Mary checked the index to see if the book had any information on Russia.* **2.** *n., irreg.* a scale where prices or amounts of certain things are compared with the prices or amounts of those same things at an earlier date. ♦ *The historical price index compares current costs to past ones.* ♦ *According to the consumer price index, the price of food doubled between 1960 and 1975.* **3.** *tv.* to locate important topics and list them and their locations, as in ①. ♦ *The editor indexed the important topics discussed in the book.* ♦ *My computer program indexes topics automatically.*

India ['ɪn di ə] See Gazetteer.

Indian ['ɪn di ən] **1.** *n.* a citizen or native of India. ♦ *My sister married an Indian from Bombay.* ♦ *Many Indians are vegetarians.* **2.** *n.* a descendant of one of the indigenous peoples of the Americas. (Also **Amerindian, American Indian, Native American.**) ♦ *The Indians and the United States Army fought many battles.* ♦ *Anthropologists have studied the languages of Indians for years.* **3.** *adj.* <the adj. use of ①>; of, about, from, or originating in India. ♦ *Many Indian dishes are flavored with curry.* ♦ *Several of my coworkers are Indian immigrants.* **4.** *adj.* <the adj. use of ②.> ♦ *The social worker observed the living conditions in Indian reservations.* ♦ *Hundreds of different Indian languages were spoken in North America before the Europeans arrived.*

Indiana [ɪn di 'æn ə] See Gazetteer.

Indian Ocean [ɪn di ən 'o ʃən] See Gazetteer.

indicate ['ɪn də ket] **1.** *tv.* to point something out verbally; to state a fact. (Takes a clause.) ♦ *The banker indicated that Monday was a federal holiday.* ♦ *John indicated that all was well with him and his family.* **2.** *tv.* to suggest that something might happen; to warn of something. ♦ *Redness around the wound indicated an infection.* ♦ *Dark clouds indicate that it may rain.* **3.** *tv.* to make something known; to draw someone's attention to something. ♦ *The teacher indicated my mistakes by circling them with red ink.* ♦ *I indicated which door I wanted the child to enter.* **4.** *tv.* [for a meter, chart, signal] to show specific information. ♦ *The meter indicated that we were nearly out of gas.* ♦ *The green signal light indicated that the machine was turned on.*

indication [ɪn də 'ke ʃən] *n.* a sign of something; something that is indicated. ♦ *Heavy, dark clouds are an indication of rain.* ♦ *Jane's silence was an indication of her anger.*

indicative [ɪn 'dɪk ə tɪv] **1.** *adj.* being a sign of something; suggestive of something. (Adv: *indicatively.*) ♦ *Redness is often indicative of an infection.* ♦ *Blond hair is often indicative of European ancestry.* **2.** *adj.* [of a form of a verb] used in making simple statements, as opposed to making commands or wishes. ♦ *You cannot ask a question or give a command with an indicative verb form.* ♦ *We learned indicative verb forms before we learned any subjunctive ones.*

indicator ['ɪn də ket ɚ] **1.** *n.* something that indicates something; something that signifies something. ♦ *Rising prices are an indicator of inflation.* ♦ *Dark clouds are an indicator of rain.* **2.** *n.* a warning light, such as on the dashboard of a car. ♦ *A red indicator blinked, showing that I needed gas, so I began looking for a gas station.* ♦ *The oil indicator lights up when the car needs more oil.*

indices ['ɪn dɪ siz] a pl of index.

indict [ɪn 'dɑɪt] *tv.* to formally accuse someone of a crime; to charge someone with a crime. ♦ *Mary was indicted on two counts of attempted murder.* ♦ *Bob has been indicted twice, but he's never been convicted.*

indictment [ɪn 'dɑɪt mənt] *n.* the formal accusation that charges someone with a crime. ♦ *The judge issued an indictment against John for armed robbery.* ♦ *The senator's indictment came shortly after his crime was discovered.*

indifference [ɪn 'dɪf rəns] *n.* the condition of being indifferent; a lack of interest, care, or concern. (No plural form in this sense.) ♦ *The students' indifference to politics frustrated the mayor.* ♦ *Bob's indifference towards Mary prompted her to date Bill.*

indifferent [ɪn 'dɪf rənt] **1.** *adj.* not interested in someone or something; not concerned about someone or something; without a preference. (Adv: *indifferently.*) ♦ *Dave is indifferent to politics.* ♦ *Jane may seem indifferent, but she really does care.* **2.** *adj.* neither good nor bad; not differentiated. (Adv: *indifferently.*) ♦ *The restaurant served food of an indifferent quality.* ♦ *We were served an indifferent wine, but we did not complain.*

indigenous [ɪn 'dɪdʒ ə nəs] **1.** *adj.* original; originally found in an area. (Adv: *indigenously.*) ♦ *The indigenous people of the area know which plants are safe to eat and which are poisonous.* ♦ *The indigenous plants of the area had been replaced by weeds and foreign plants.* **2. indigenous to** *adj.* + *prep. phr.* belonging to, found on, or native to a particular area, continent, country, region, city, etc. ♦ *People indigenous to the area know which plants are safe to eat.* ♦ *The plants indigenous to the fields were destroyed by the farmer's plow.*

indigent ['ɪn də dʒənt] **1.** *adj.* very poor; very needy; destitute. (Adv: *indigently.*) ♦ *The indigent child ate only once a day.* ♦ *The indigent family lived under a bridge.* **2.** *n.* a very poor person; a destitute person. ♦ *The indigent slept in the alley because he had no home.* ♦ *The mayor instituted a program to help the elderly indigents in the city.*

indigestion [ɪn də 'dʒɛs tʃən] *n.* an upset stomach; the digestion of food that causes pain. (No plural form in this sense.) ♦ *John ate his food too quickly, and now he's got indigestion.* ♦ *I get indigestion from spicy food.*

indignant [ɪn 'dɪg nənt] *adj.* feeling anger or resentment at something. (Adv: *indignantly.*) ♦ *People were indignant when the courts released the dangerous criminal.* ♦ *Susan was indignant that Mary was promoted instead of her.*

indignation [ɪn dɪg 'ne ʃən] *n.* anger or resentment. (No plural form in this sense.) ♦ *Your indignation over my comments is not appropriate.* ♦ *The mayor ignored the citizens' indignation over the tax increase.*

indignity [ɪn 'dɪg nə ti] *n.* something that makes one feel undignified; a blow to one's pride. ♦ *Being fired is a terrible indignity.* ♦ *John suffered the indignity of being expelled for cheating.*

indirect [ɪn də 'rɛkt] **1.** *adj.* not direct; roundabout; not in a straight line; not in the shortest way possible. (Adv: *indirectly.*) ♦ *I took an indirect route home due to the roadblock.* ♦ *The path along the river is an indirect but scenic way to get to school.* **2.** *adj.* not to the point; not answering directly. (Figurative on ①. Adv: *indirectly.*) ♦ *Jane gave an indirect response to avoid telling the truth.* ♦ *I interrupted Bill's indirect reply and asked him to get to the point.* **3.** *adj.* secondary; not resulting from something directly.

(Adv: *indirectly.*) ♦ *Gaining weight can be an indirect effect of stopping smoking.* ♦ *Anne told us about the indirect benefits of being a vegetarian.*

indirect object ['ɪn də rɛkt 'ɑb dʒɛkt] *n.* <a noun, pronoun, or phrase that is associated with the action of the verb, but is not the receiver of the action.> (In the examples, *Mary* is the indirect object and *flower* is the direct object.) ♦ *I gave Mary a flower.* ♦ *I gave a flower to Mary.*

indiscriminate [ɪn dɪ 'skrɪm ə nɪt] *adj.* not choosing carefully; not chosen carefully; random. (Adv: *indiscriminately.*) ♦ *Mary made an indiscriminate choice about which car to buy.* ♦ *Bill is quite indiscriminate in his choice of clothing.*

indispensable [ɪn dɪ 'spɛn sə bəl] *adj.* absolutely necessary; essential. (Adv: *indispensably.*) ♦ *A telephone is indispensable in most households.* ♦ *Mary is an indispensable employee.*

indistinct [ɪn dɪ 'stɪŋkt] **1.** *adj.* not distinct; not able to be clearly heard, seen, tasted, touched, or smelled. (Adv: *indistinctly.*) ♦ *I heard an indistinct whisper in the other room.* ♦ *The room had an indistinct odor that I couldn't identify.* **2.** *adj.* [of a difference] not easy to notice; [of a distinction] not pronounced. (Adv: *indistinctly.*) ♦ *The difference between dark blue and indigo is so indistinct that they look the same to me.* ♦ *In the huge parking lot filled with small gray cars, my car was indistinct from all the others.*

indistinguishable [ɪn dɪ 'stɪŋ gwɪʃ ə bəl] *adj.* not able to be distinguished from someone or something. (Adv: *indistinguishably.*) ♦ *The twins were indistinguishable from each other.* ♦ *These two red coats are indistinguishable.*

individual [ɪn də 'vɪ dʒu əl] **1.** *n.* a person; one person. ♦ *An individual was seen leaving the library late in the afternoon.* ♦ *Mary is a very funny individual.* **2.** *adj.* <the adj. use of ①.> (Adv: *individually.*) ♦ *Of course, Bill had his own individual opinion.* ♦ *We all have our individual thoughts.* **3.** *adj.* separate; single. (Adv: *individually.*) ♦ *Each individual slice of cheese was wrapped in plastic.* ♦ *There is a separate answer for each individual problem.*

individuality [ɪn də vɪ dʒu 'æl ə ti] *n.* the quality that makes a person different from everyone else. (No plural form in this sense.) ♦ *Mary expressed her individuality by dying her hair blue.* ♦ *Susan encouraged each of the twins to develop his own individuality.*

indoctrinate [ɪn 'dɑk trə net] **indoctrinate (with)** *tv.* (+ *prep. phr.*) to teach someone the doctrines or principles of something; to fill someone with a doctrine. ♦ *The professor indoctrinated her students with all the current theories.* ♦ *The children were indoctrinated with the religion of their parents.*

indoctrination [ɪn dɑk trə 'ne ʃən] *n.* indoctrinating; filling someone with a doctrine. (No plural form in this sense.) ♦ *Mary was not allowed to eat during her indoctrination to the cult.* ♦ *The process of indoctrination involved peer pressure and drugs.*

indolent ['ɪn də lənt] *adj.* lazy; not liking to work. (Adv: *indolently.*) ♦ *There are three indolent students in my class, and they will all fail.* ♦ *The boss fired the indolent employee.*

Indonesia [ɪn do 'ni ʒə] See Gazetteer.

indoor ['ɪn dor] *adj.* inside a building; kept within walls and under a roof. ♦ *Since Fluffy is an indoor cat, we had her claws removed.* ♦ *This is indoor carpeting and should not be placed outdoors.*

indoors [ɪn 'dorz] **1.** *adv.* [going] into a building. ♦ *Because it was raining, the children went indoors.* ♦ *I brought the cat indoors with me.* **2.** *adj.* [located] within a building. ♦ *The cat is indoors.* ♦ *The temperature is cooler indoors because we have air conditioning.*

induce [ɪn 'dus] **1.** *tv.* to cause something to happen; to produce some kind of a response. ♦ *The doctor induced Mary's labor so her baby would be born sooner.* ♦ *Bill induced vomiting because he ate something poisonous.* **2.** **induce to** *tv.* + *inf.* to persuade someone to do something; to influence someone to do something. ♦ *The saleswoman induced me to buy a new car.* ♦ *Can I induce you to try one of these cakes?*

inducement [ɪn 'dus mənt] *n.* something that is used to persuade or encourage someone to do something. ♦ *As an inducement for me to buy the car, the salesman lowered the price.* ♦ *John is trying to lose weight and promised himself a trip to New York as an inducement to succeed.*

induct [ɪn 'dʌkt] **1.** *tv.* to install someone in office; to bring someone on as a member. ♦ *The committee inducted the batting champion into the hall of fame.* ♦ *Susan was inducted as council president after Bill resigned.* **2.** *tv.* to bring someone into military service; to draft someone into military service. (Often passive.) ♦ *The young men were inducted into the army.* ♦ *I was inducted into the navy when I was 21.*

induction [ɪn 'dʌk ʃən] **1.** *n.* the drafting of someone into military service. (No plural form in this sense.) ♦ *Some countries require the induction of all male citizens into their armed forces.* ♦ *Bill went to England to escape induction during the Vietnam War.* **2.** *n.* bringing someone into membership in an organization. (No plural form in this sense.) ♦ *Bill's induction into the club was followed by a large banquet.* ♦ *Susan's induction as council president followed Bill's resignation.* **3.** *n.* a process of thought where one makes a conclusion loosely based on evidence. (No plural form in this sense.) ♦ *The detective solved the murder by a simple process of induction.* ♦ *Your induction must be poor, because your conclusions are wrong.* **4.** *n.* the process where electricity or magnetic force passes between two objects that are not touching each other. (No plural form in this sense.) ♦ *The experimental train is powered by electrical induction.* ♦ *The physicist studied the properties of magnetic induction.*

indulge [ɪn 'dʌldʒ] **1.** **indulge in** *iv.* + *prep. phr.* to gratify a desire; to give in to a craving; to yield to a passion. ♦ *Jane indulged in her passion for chocolate by buying some fudge.* ♦ *Bill indulged in a long, relaxing shower after a hard day.* **2.** *tv.* to gratify oneself by yielding to a craving. (Takes a reflexive object.) ♦ *Jane indulged herself by eating chocolate for dessert.* ♦ *Bill loved chocolate and indulged himself often.* **3.** *tv.* to be permissive with someone. ♦ *If you indulge your children, they might become spoiled.* ♦ *Mary indulges her grandchildren with cookies and milk.*

indulgence [ɪn 'dʌl dʒəns] **1.** *n.* gratification through something; satisfaction gained by something. (No plural form in this sense.) ♦ *Your selfish indulgence in long showers is affecting the water bill.* ♦ *Because of your indulgence, there is no milk left in the refrigerator.* **2.** *n.* permissiveness. (No plural form in this sense.) ♦ *You show too much* *indulgence toward your undisciplined children.* ♦ *Because of the teacher's indulgence, we were allowed to leave class early.* **3.** *n.* a privilege; something that is given as a favor or a privilege. ♦ *Please grant me the indulgence of listening to what I have to say.* ♦ *I ask only one small indulgence. Please permit me to turn in my paper late.*

industrial [ɪn 'dʌs tri əl] **1.** *adj.* of or about industry; of or about people who work in industry. (Adv: *industrially.*) ♦ *The factory retained a lawyer who practiced industrial law.* ♦ *Detroit's economy is primarily industrial.* **2.** *adj.* strong enough to be used by industries; powerful. ♦ *Bob used an industrial cleaner to remove the oily stain.* ♦ *Tom often uses industrial tools to do tough jobs around his house.*

industrialist [ɪn 'dʌs tri ə ləst] *n.* someone who owns, controls, or manages an industrial business. ♦ *The industrialist sold the factory at a large profit.* ♦ *The workers cursed the industrialist who fired them.*

industrious [ɪn 'dʌs tri əs] *adj.* diligent; working very hard. (Adv: *industriously.*) ♦ *My boss gave me a bonus because I'm such an industrious worker.* ♦ *The industrious ants moved objects many times their own weight.*

industry ['ɪn də stri] **1.** *n.* the production of goods; the manufacture of products. (No plural form in this sense.) ♦ *The industry of a nation suffers during a depression.* ♦ *During the early 1940s, most industry centered on the war.* **2.** *n.* the business activity concerning a specific class of product or service. ♦ *Michigan's economy hinges on the success of the car industry.* ♦ *The fast-food industry has grown rapidly.* **3.** *n.* hard work or labor; diligence. ♦ *This project required weeks of commitment and industry.* ♦ *I appreciate your industry in finishing the work so promptly.*

inebriated [ɪn 'i bri et ɪd] *adj.* drunk; under the influence of alcohol. (Adv: *inebriatedly.*) ♦ *John becomes slightly inebriated after he drinks two beers.* ♦ *The inebriated driver crashed into the stop sign.*

inedible [ɪn 'ɛd ə bəl] *adj.* not able to be eaten; not good for eating. (Adv: *inedibly.*) ♦ *Waiter, take this food back to the kitchen. It's inedible.* ♦ *The child choked on an inedible piece of fat.*

ineffective [ɪn ə 'fɛk tɪv] *adj.* not effective; not working; not producing any good results. (Adv: *ineffectively.*) ♦ *Your methods are ineffective, so let's try my idea.* ♦ *The extra police proved ineffective against the violent rioters.*

inefficiency [ɪn ɪ 'fɪʃ ən si] *n.* the condition of being inefficient. (No plural form in this sense.) ♦ *It took us twice as long to finish the report because of your inefficiency in collecting the information.* ♦ *We slowly eradicated the inefficiency that plagued our department.*

inefficient [ɪn ɪ 'fɪʃ ənt] *adj.* not efficient; not using time or materials well. (Adv: *inefficiently.*) ♦ *Carrying bricks one at a time is an inefficient way to move them.* ♦ *The inefficient design of the kitchen was a big problem for the cook.*

inept [ɪn 'ɛpt] *adj.* awkward; clumsy; unable to do something. (Adv: *ineptly.*) ♦ *The inept dancer tripped and fell over his partner's feet.* ♦ *The inept lawyer never won any cases.*

inequality [ɪn ɪ 'kwɑl ə ti] **1.** *n.* unequalness; the state of not being equal. (No plural form in this sense.) ♦ *The inequality of the weights of the two chickens means that you must start roasting the heavier one first.* ♦ *Inequality under the law is intolerable.* **2.** *n.* a specific instance of ①. ♦ *The inequalities in the hiring practices caused a lawsuit.* ♦ *I couldn't get my wheelchair through the revolving door and I had to suffer the inequality of having to enter through a side door.*

inert [ɪn 'ɚt] **1.** *adj.* not having the power to move; not having the ability to move. (Adv: *inertly.*) ♦ *Anne lay inert while the doctor examined her back.* ♦ *The rabbit was inert, hoping not to be noticed by the fox.* **2.** *adj.* not able to react with other chemical substances. (Adv: *inertly.*) ♦ *Neon is an inert gas.* ♦ *An inert solid, like gold, will not dissolve in water.*

inescapable [ɪn ɛ 'skep ə bəl] *adj.* not able to be avoided; unavoidable. (Adv: *inescapably.*) ♦ *The inescapable fact remains: you could have prevented the fire.* ♦ *The police came to the inescapable conclusion that Bob had stolen the money.*

inevitable [ɪn 'ɛv ə tə bəl] *adj.* [of something] certain to happen. (Adv: *inevitably.*) ♦ *Death is the inevitable ending of life.* ♦ *It is inevitable that Jimmy will outgrow his new shoes in three months.*

inexpensive [ɪn ɛk 'spɛn sɪv] *adj.* not expensive; cheap. (Adv: *inexpensively.*) ♦ *Let's have an inexpensive dinner since we don't have much money.* ♦ *The inexpensive watch broke three days after I bought it.*

inexperience [ɪn ɛk 'spɪr i əns] *n.* the lack of experience; the lack of knowledge that comes with experience. (No plural form in this sense.) ♦ *Despite Mary's inexperience with computers, she quickly learned to use one.* ♦ *Because of Anne's inexperience with children, she didn't get the job at the day-care center.*

inexperienced [ɪn ɛk 'spɪr i ənst] *adj.* lacking experience; lacking the knowledge that comes from experience. (Adv: *inexperiencedly.*) ♦ *The manager refused to interview inexperienced people.* ♦ *Although Mary was inexperienced with computers, she quickly learned to use one.*

inexplicable [ɪn ɛk 'splɪk ə bəl] *adj.* not able to be explained; unexplainable. (Adv: *inexplicably.*) ♦ *An inexplicable increase in water pressure burst our pipes.* ♦ *John's death was sudden and inexplicable.*

inf. See infinitive.

infallible [ɪn 'fæl ə bəl] *adj.* not fallible; always right. (Adv: *infallibly.*) ♦ *I have an infallible method for investing in the stock market!* ♦ *John believes he is infallible, but I know he makes mistakes.*

infamous ['ɪn fə məs] *adj.* having a bad reputation; notorious. (Adv: *infamously.*) ♦ *Al Capone was an infamous Chicago gangster.* ♦ *My teacher is infamous for giving difficult homework assignments.*

infancy ['ɪn fən si] **1.** *n.* the first few years of life; the early part of childhood. (No plural form in this sense.) ♦ *Infancy is a time of life we never remember.* ♦ *A baby can recognize its mother's face even in infancy.* **2.** *n.* the beginning part of development; the early part of something. (Figurative on ①. No plural form in this sense.) ♦ *In its infancy, the plan worked. Later, it became useless.* ♦ *The Constitution was written in the infancy of the United States.*

infant ['ɪn fənt] **1.** *n.* a baby; a young child. ♦ *Bill changed the infant's diaper.* ♦ *Susan laid the infant down for a nap.* **2.** *adj.* <the adj. use of ①.> ♦ *We bought an infant seat* *for the car, as required by law.* ♦ *Infant clothing is sold on the third floor.*

infantry ['ɪn fən tri] *n.* a group of soldiers who have been trained to fight on foot. (No plural form in this sense.) ♦ *The general led the infantry into battle.* ♦ *The villagers cheered when the infantry liberated their town.*

infatuate [ɪn 'fætʃ u et] *tv.* to create a senseless love for someone or something. ♦ *I am too logical and rational to allow myself to be infatuated by his pleasant manner.* ♦ *I suppose that I have somehow infatuated John, because he just gave me flowers.*

infatuated [ɪn 'fætʃ u et əd] *adj.* full of foolish love for someone or something; having a crush on someone or something. (Adv: *infatuatedly.*) ♦ *Anne is completely infatuated with her new neighbor.* ♦ *John must be infatuated with me, because he just gave me flowers.*

infatuation [ɪn fætʃ u 'e ʃən] **1.** *n.* temporary or foolish love for someone or something. (No plural form in this sense.) ♦ *Is it love or is it just infatuation that you feel for John?* ♦ *Infatuation can lead us into making foolish mistakes with our lives.* **2.** *n.* an instance of ①. ♦ *Infatuations are common during the teenage years.* ♦ *Are you really in love with Mary, or is it just an infatuation?*

infect [ɪn 'fɛkt] *tv.* to contaminate someone or something with an organism that causes disease. ♦ *Mosquitos can infect humans with malaria.* ♦ *Bill infected Susan with his cold when he kissed her.*

infected [ɪn 'fɛk təd] *adj.* contaminated. ♦ *Jane's infected finger throbbed.* ♦ *Your throat looks infected. I think you should see a doctor.*

infection [ɪn 'fɛk ʃən] **1.** *n.* the entrance and growth of disease organisms in the body. (No plural form in this sense.) ♦ *Infection takes place when germs enter the bloodstream.* ♦ *Keep the wound clean to avoid infection.* **2.** *n.* a disease caused by ①. ♦ *The infection spread quickly throughout Bill's body.* ♦ *If your throat infection is contagious, don't sneeze on me!*

infectious [ɪn 'fɛk ʃəs] **1.** *adj.* [of disease organisms] able to spread from organism to organism. (Adv: *infectiously.*) ♦ *Some infectious bacteria are resistant to drugs and vaccines.* ♦ *The flu is highly infectious and is easily spread.* **2.** *adj.* [of certain activities] spreading from one person to another. (Figurative on ①. Adv: *infectiously.*) ♦ *The audience was overcome with infectious laughter.* ♦ *The infectious gossip quickly spread through the office.*

infer [ɪn 'fɚ] **infer from** *tv.* + *prep. phr.* to reach an opinion from a study of the evidence. (Compare with imply.) ♦ *I inferred your reply from your long statement.* ♦ *Susan inferred from the text that the author disagreed with the theory.*

inference ['ɪn fə rəns] *n.* a conclusion; an opinion that is reached after studying the facts. ♦ *I made the inference that the author was a spy.* ♦ *Your inference that I was involved in the robbery is based on flawed information.*

inferior [ɪn 'fɪr i ɚ] **1.** *adj.* lower in amount, rank, power, quality, or strength than someone or something else. (Adv: *inferiorly.*) ♦ *My strength is inferior to that of a younger man.* ♦ *My old television is a cheap, inferior brand.* **2.** *n.* someone who has a lower-ranking job than someone else. ♦ *The foreman was very condescending to all of his inferiors.* ♦ *Susan was well-liked because she treated her inferiors with respect.*

inferiority [ɪn fɪr i 'or ə ti] *adj.* the condition of being inferior. (No plural form in this sense.) ♦ *Owing to the inferiority of the cloth, the new sheets ripped apart the first night they were used.* ♦ *Because of the concrete's inferiority, the floor was badly cracked.*

inferno [ɪn 'fɚ no] **1.** *n.* a large, raging fire. (Pl in *-s.*) ♦ *The firefighters were unable to keep the inferno from spreading.* ♦ *Thousands of acres of land were scorched in the deadly inferno.* **2.** *n.* someplace that is very hot. (Figurative on ①. Pl in *-s.*) ♦ *The western desert is a dry, desolate inferno.* ♦ *The pizza kitchen was an inferno because the ovens were so hot.*

infertile [ɪn 'fɚ təl] *adj.* not fertile; barren. (Adv: *infertilely.*) ♦ *The infertile soil yielded no crops.* ♦ *No trees or plants can grow on this infertile land.*

infertility [ɪn fɚ 'tɪl ə ti] *n.* the inability to produce offspring; the condition of being infertile. (No plural form in this sense.) ♦ *Mary's infertility was caused by cancer.* ♦ *The infertility of the land meant that food had to be imported.*

infest [ɪn 'fɛst] *tv.* to invade something in large numbers. ♦ *Small red ants infested our picnic site.* ♦ *Cockroaches have infested our kitchen and the basement.*

infested [ɪn 'fɛs təd] *adj.* full of pests; covered with pests. ♦ *The social worker walked through the infested apartment.* ♦ *John had lice, so he threw out all of his infested clothing.*

infighting ['ɪn fɑɪt ɪŋ] *n.* competition or arguments between two or more people within in a group. (No plural form in this sense.) ♦ *Our singing group broke up because of all of the infighting between members.* ♦ *We lost the election because of infighting in our party.*

infinite ['ɪn fə nət] *adj.* not finite; endless; immeasurably great. (Adv: *infinitely.*) ♦ *The number of grains of sand in the universe seems infinite.* ♦ *Time and space are infinite.*

infinitive [ɪn 'fɪn ə tɪv] **infinitive (form)** *n.* <a form of a verb—preceded by *to*—that does not show tense, number, or person.> (Abbreviated *inf.* here. See also bare verb.) ♦ *The infinitive form of "am" and "are" is "to be."* ♦ *Infinitives can be used after some verbs, such as "want," as in "I want to go." Bare verbs, which are infinitives without "to," are used after auxiliary verbs such as "will," as in "I will go."*

infinity [ɪn 'fɪn ə ti] **1.** *n.* infiniteness; boundlessness; limitlessness. (No plural form in this sense.) ♦ *The astronomer was awed by the infinity of space.* ♦ *There are no boundaries to infinity.* **2.** *n.* an endless amount of time or space. (No plural form in this sense.) ♦ *The boring lecture dragged on for what seemed like infinity.* ♦ *The rocket sped on into infinity.*

infirmary [ɪn 'fɚ mə ri] *n.* a hospital, clinic, or room where sick people go for treatment. ♦ *Jane's teacher helped her walk to the infirmary.* ♦ *The waiting room of the infirmary was crowded with sick people.*

infirmity [ɪn 'fɚ mə ti] *n.* a weakness of the mind or body. ♦ *Grandpa's infirmity prevented him from walking up the stairs.* ♦ *This institution is for people with mental infirmities.*

inflame [ɪn 'flem] **1.** *tv.* to excite someone's emotions; to cause someone to feel a strong emotion. ♦ *Anger inflamed Bill to the point where he had to leave the room.* ♦ *John's insults inflamed Mary's desire to hit him.* **2.** *tv.* to cause body tissue or an organ of the body to become red and swollen. ♦ *Arthritis inflamed every joint in my body.* ♦ *An allergic reaction inflamed my throat.* **3.** *iv.* to become red and swollen. ♦ *My knee inflamed painfully when I hit it against the door.* ♦ *My skin inflamed where the bees had stung me.*

inflamed [ɪn 'flemd] **1.** *adj.* angered; aroused; angry. ♦ *John becomes easily inflamed when he's challenged.* ♦ *The inflamed customer screamed at the bumbling clerk.* **2.** *adj.* red and swollen; irritated; aggravated. ♦ *John scratched his inflamed skin.* ♦ *Mary's inflamed eyes were red and swollen.*

inflammable [ɪn 'flæm ə bəl] *adj.* able to catch fire; flammable; not fireproof. (The opposite is nonflammable. Adv: *inflammably.* This *in* shows emphasis, not negativeness.) ♦ *Inflammable material should not be used in children's clothing.* ♦ *Bill's cigarette set the inflammable curtains on fire.*

inflammation [ɪn flə 'me ʃən] *n.* a red, swollen, and sore part of the body. ♦ *The spider bite caused an itchy inflammation.* ♦ *The inflammation on Anne's ankle healed slowly.*

inflatable [ɪn 'flet ə bəl] *adj.* able to be inflated; able to be blown up. (Adv: *inflatably.*) ♦ *Inflatable life jackets were stored on the boat for emergency use.* ♦ *John brought an inflatable mattress on the camping trip.*

inflate [ɪn 'flet] **1.** *tv.* to blow something up; to put air or a gas into something. ♦ *Mary inflated the balloon with helium.* ♦ *Bill inflated the bicycle tire with an air pump.* **2.** *tv.* to raise prices. (Figurative on ①.) ♦ *The flood inflated the price of lettuce.* ♦ *The grocer inflated the price of bottled water during the drought.* **3.** *tv.* to increase the supply of money in a nation's economy. (Figurative on ①.) ♦ *The treasury inflated the money supply by two percent.* ♦ *Six months after the money supply was inflated, the unemployment rate fell.*

inflated [ɪn 'flet əd] **1.** *adj.* blown up; full of air or a gas. ♦ *The wind blew the inflated balloon through the air.* ♦ *The inflated tire burst when I pierced it with a spike.* **2.** *adj.* [of prices] raised; costing more; costing too much. (Figurative on ①. Adv: *inflatedly.*) ♦ *Mary refused to pay inflated prices for vegetables she could grow herself.* ♦ *The inflated cost of cigarettes caused Anne to stop smoking.*

inflation [ɪn 'fle ʃən] **1.** *n.* the process of inflating; blowing something up. (No plural form in this sense.) ♦ *The inflation of the balloons was done with an air pump.* ♦ *After inflation, press on the ball to make sure it is not too full.* **2.** *n.* an economic condition in which too much money is available for purchasing too few goods. (No plural form in this sense.) ♦ *My salary increases are not keeping up with the rate of inflation.* ♦ *When inflation is out of control, manufacturing costs rise constantly.*

inflict [ɪn 'flɪkt] **inflict (on)** *tv.* (+ *prep. phr.*) to impose something on someone. ♦ *The guard inflicted pain on the prisoners.* ♦ *The government inflicted a very high penalty on people who paid their taxes late.*

influence ['ɪn flu əns] **1.** *n.* the power or ability to get results. (No plural form in this sense.) ♦ *The bill was passed because of the senator's influence.* ♦ *The alderman was elected because of the mayor's influence.* **2.** *n.* the effect that someone or something has on someone or something else. (No plural form in this sense.) ♦ *Bill was a good influence on his brother.* ♦ *Mary studied harder because of her teacher's influence.* **3.** *n.* a cause of some behavior. ♦ *The tides of the earth's oceans rise and fall owing to the influence of the moon.* ♦ *John drove into a tree when he was under the influence of alcohol.* **4.** *tv.* to affect someone or something. ♦ *Bill influenced the senator's vote through bribery.* ♦ *My decision was influenced by my parents' advice.* **5. under the influence** *idiom* affected by alcohol; drunk. ♦ *John was under the influence when he was driving and could have caused an accident.* ♦ *Never operate machinery if you are under the influence.* **6. under the influence of something** *idiom* experiencing the effects of something such as alcohol, drugs, or any controlling power or person. ♦ *I think that guy is under the influence of drugs.* ♦ *Bill has lived under the influence of his mother for too long.*

influential [ɪn flu 'ɛn tʃʊl] *adj.* having the power to affect someone or something; having strong influence. (Adv: *influentially.*) ♦ *The influential president helped the warring countries make peace.* ♦ *My parents have been the most influential people in my life.*

influenza [ɪn flu 'ɛn zə] *n.* the flu; an easily spread viral sickness. (No plural form in this sense. Does not take *the.* Compare with flu and cold ③.) ♦ *Between 1918 and 1920, influenza killed 20 million people.* ♦ *My whole family has influenza. I thought I had a common cold, but I have the flu, just like the others.*

influx ['ɪn fləks] *n.* the sudden arrival of many things or people. ♦ *The recent influx of immigrants caused a housing shortage in the small town.* ♦ *The morning influx of cars jammed the streets in the city.*

inform [ɪn 'form] *tv.* to tell someone about something; to let someone know about something. ♦ *My neighbor informed me of the neighborhood picnic.* ♦ *My boss informed me that he was going on vacation next week.*

informal [ɪn 'form əl] **1.** *adj.* not formal, official, or final. (Adv: *informally.*) ♦ *So far the rescue workers can only provide an informal count of the number of people killed in yesterday's earthquake.* ♦ *Anne received an informal job offer, but she wouldn't accept it until she was shown a contract.* **2.** *adj.* [of words, language, or speech] used every day but a little more relaxed than more formal speech. (Adv: *informally.*) ♦ *"Hi!" is often used as an informal greeting.* ♦ *People often end sentences with prepositions in informal speech.* **3.** *adj.* [of dress] not formal; casual. (Adv: *informally.*) ♦ *I usually wear informal clothes to work on Fridays.* ♦ *Dress at our party is informal, so please don't wear a suit.*

informality [ɪn for 'mæl ə ti] *n.* the condition of being informal. (No plural form in this sense.) ♦ *Being called by her first name was an informality of which Mrs. Smith did not approve.* ♦ *The company treated its clients with a warm informality.*

informant [ɪn 'for mənt] *n.* an informer; someone who gives information, especially to the police. ♦ *The police informant was found murdered in a dark alley.* ♦ *The informant told the police who the killer was.*

information [ɪn for 'me ʃən] *n.* news; knowledge about something; facts. (No plural form in this sense. Number is expressed by *piece(s)* or *bit(s) of information.*) ♦ *The newspaper printed information about the upcoming election.* ♦ *I asked the librarian for information on photography.*

informative [ɪn 'for mə tɪv] *adj.* giving information; giving facts; instructive. (Adv: *informatively.*) ♦ *The doctor gave an informative lecture about health care.* ♦ *My American history class is very informative.*

informed [ɪn 'formd] *adj.* aware; having the facts; having the information. ♦ *Informed citizens are essential to a democracy.* ♦ *I am not as informed about the election as I want to be.*

informer [ɪn 'for mɚ] *n.* someone who gives information, especially to the police. ♦ *The informer told the police who the drug dealers were.* ♦ *When the gang realized John was an informer, they killed him.*

infraction [ɪn 'fræk ʃən] *n.* the breaking of a law; a violation of a rule. ♦ *Speeding is a minor infraction of the law.* ♦ *Mary claimed she was not guilty of any infractions of the law.*

infrequent [ɪn 'fri kwənt] *adj.* not frequent; not often; seldom. (Adv: *infrequently.*) ♦ *I made infrequent visits to my sister in Los Angeles.* ♦ *John's use of his golf clubs was so infrequent that he sold them.*

infringe [ɪn 'frɪndʒ] **1. infringe (up)on** *iv.* + *prep. phr.* to encroach on something; to interfere with something. ♦ *The salesman infringed on our privacy by calling late at night.* ♦ *Your loud stereo infringes upon my right to peace and quiet.* **2.** *tv.* to violate or transgress something, such as a copyright, an agreement, or a set of rules. ♦ *Dave infringed the book's copyright by making illegal copies.* ♦ *We will sue your company if it infringes our agreement.*

infringement [ɪn 'frɪndʒ mənt] **1.** *n.* a violation of a copyright. ♦ *Illegally copying pages from a book is an infringement of its copyright.* ♦ *Infringement of the movie's copyright was the basis of a lawsuit.* **2.** *n.* a violation of a right, such as the right to privacy. ♦ *Calls from annoying salespersons are a constant infringement on my time at home.* ♦ *Your nosy questions are an infringement to which I object.*

infuriate [ɪn 'fjɚ i et] *tv.* to upset someone very much; to anger someone very much. ♦ *The reporter's rude questions infuriated the celebrity.* ♦ *Mary infuriated Bob by insulting him in public.*

infuriating [ɪn 'fjɚ i et ɪŋ] *adj.* causing anger. (Adv: *infuriatingly.*) ♦ *Being stuck in traffic is infuriating when you're already late.* ♦ *Do you know how infuriating your rude behavior is?*

-ing [ɪŋ] *suffix* <a form added to a verb to make a present participle.> (The resulting forms can always be used as verbs and sometimes as adjectives and nouns. See present participle.) ♦ *This ice is melting because it is getting warmer.* ♦ *Jogging in the shining sun can make you thirsty.*

ingenious [ɪn 'dʒin jəs] *adj.* inventive; showing ingenuity. (Adv: *ingeniously.*) ♦ *The prisoner developed an ingenious plan to break out of jail.* ♦ *Your ingenious ideas have saved the company millions of dollars.*

ingenuity [ɪn dʒə 'nu ə ti] *n.* the cleverness used in planning or inventing something. (No plural form in this sense.) ♦ *Anne's boss praised her for her ingenuity in designing the unusual new product.* ♦ *We have electricity because of Thomas Edison's ingenuity.*

ingest [ɪn 'jɛst] *tv.* to eat or drink something; to swallow something. ♦ *Jane called the doctor when her baby ingested a button.* ♦ *Do not ingest this medicine! It is to be rubbed on the skin.*

ingestion [ɪn 'jɛs tʃən] *n.* taking food or drink into the body; eating and drinking. (No plural form in this sense.) ♦ *The ingestion of certain mushrooms can cause death.* ♦ *Avoid the ingestion of salty foods.*

ingrain [ɪn 'gren] **ingrain in(to)** *tv.* + *prep. phr.* to teach something to someone very well. ♦ *Anne's parents ingrained responsibility in her from an early age.* ♦ *You must ingrain absolute obedience into your dog.*

ingratiate [ɪn 'gre ʃi et] **ingratiate with** *tv.* + *prep. phr.* to try to put oneself in someone else's favor. (Takes a reflexive object.) ♦ *John ingratiated himself with his boss by complimenting him frequently.* ♦ *Stop ingratiating yourself with me. It's very annoying.*

ingratiating [ɪn 'gre ʃi et ɪŋ] *adj.* meant to gain someone's favor; seeking favor or approval. (Adv: *ingratiatingly.*) ♦ *Mary's ingratiating comments flattered her boss.* ♦ *I was sure that Bill's ingratiating attitude was fake.*

ingratitude [ɪn 'græt ɪ tud] *n.* a lack of gratitude; ungratefulness. (No plural form in this sense.) ♦ *Your ingratitude is insulting after all I've done for you.* ♦ *Jane didn't thank me for the present. What ingratitude!*

ingredient [ɪn 'grid i ənt] *n.* something that is part of a mixture; an element of something; a part of something. ♦ *The ingredients in the cake included sugar, flour, eggs, and milk.* ♦ *Good communication is an ingredient of a happy marriage.*

inhabit [ɪn 'hæb ɪt] *tv.* to live in a house; to dwell in an area. ♦ *Census forms ask how many people inhabit each dwelling.* ♦ *This forest is inhabited by wild bears.*

inhabitant [ɪn 'hæb ə tənt] *n.* someone who lives in a certain place. ♦ *The woman who won the lottery is an inhabitant of Springfield.* ♦ *The soldiers protected the inhabitants of the castle.*

inhabited [ɪn 'hæb ə tɪd] *adj.* [of a dwelling] occupied; lived-in; populated. ♦ *The dilapidated house didn't look inhabited.* ♦ *The little town in the desert is inhabited by people who don't want to live in the city.*

inhale [ɪn 'hel] **1.** *iv.* to breathe in. ♦ *Mary inhaled deeply, enjoying the fresh air.* ♦ *The doctor told me to inhale, and the next thing I knew, the operation was over.* **2.** *tv.* to breathe something in. ♦ *John inhaled the smoke and began coughing immediately.* ♦ *Mary inhaled the fresh morning air.*

inherent [ɪn 'hɛr ənt] *adj.* being a natural part of something; intrinsic. (Adv: *inherently.*) ♦ *An inherent danger from smoking tobacco is the development of lung cancer.* ♦ *Jane's personality has an inherent charm.*

inherit [ɪn 'hɛr ɪt] **1.** *tv.* to receive the assets of a person when the person dies. ♦ *Mary inherited her parents' house.* ♦ *I inherited 64 acres of farmland from my grandfather.* **2.** *tv.* to receive a trait or feature from the genes of one's parents or ancestors. ♦ *Mary inherited her blue eyes from her mother.* ♦ *John inherited his curly hair from his father's side of his family.*

inheritance [ɪn 'hɛr ɪ təns] *n.* assets that are inherited from someone. ♦ *I received a $10,000 inheritance when my aunt died.* ♦ *Mary used her inheritance to pay for college.*

inherited [ɪn 'hɛr ɪ tɪd] *adj.* [of things] received from a person after the person's death. ♦ *John lived on an inherited income until he was thirty-five.* ♦ *Anne's inherited stocks are valued at $25,000.*

inhibit [ɪn 'hɪb ɪt] *tv.* to hinder someone or something; to hold someone or something back; to repress someone or something. ♦ *The new drug inhibits the growth of cancer cells.* ♦ *Dave's shyness inhibited him from meeting new people.*

inhibited [ɪn 'hɪb ɪ tɪd] *adj.* restrained; held back; repressed. (Adv: *inhibitedly.*) ♦ *An introvert is a person with an inhibited personality.* ♦ *The psychiatrist analyzed John's inhibited desires.*

inhibition [ɪn hɪ 'bɪ ʃən] **1.** *n.* inhibiting something; hindering something. (No plural form in this sense.) ♦ *Our goal is the inhibition of violence and aggression in prisons.* ♦ *The teacher suggested that Tom develop an inhibition to yawning in class.* **2. inhibitions** *n.* repressions of feelings or urges. ♦ *Mary's inhibitions prevented her from meeting new people.* ♦ *I would like to get rid of my inhibitions about the opposite sex.*

iniquity [ɪ 'nɪ kwə ti] **1.** *n.* sin; wickedness. (No plural form in this sense.) ♦ *The preacher claimed that the local bar was filled with iniquity.* ♦ *The sinner prayed to be freed from iniquity.* **2. den of iniquity** *idiom* a place filled with wickedness. ♦ *The town was a den of iniquity and vice was everywhere.* ♦ *Police raided the gambling house, calling it a den of iniquity.*

initial [ɪ 'nɪʃ əl] **1.** *n.* the first letter of a word or name when standing alone, representing the whole word or name. (Used also for a series of first letters taken from a series of words.) ♦ *The initial on my door is the first letter of my last name.* ♦ *The clerk wrote his initials on the sales receipt.* **2.** *adj.* first; occurring or appearing at the beginning of something. (Adv: *initially.*) ♦ *The initial letter of the word* Spain *is* S. ♦ *In the initial stage of the meeting, we discussed old business.* **3.** *tv.* to sign something with the initials of each word in one's name rather than with one's full name. ♦ *The clerk initialed the sales receipt.* ♦ *The boss initialed his memorandum and gave everyone a copy.*

initiate [ɪ 'nɪʃ i et] **1.** *tv.* to begin something; to start something. ♦ *Mary initiated a conversation with the man sitting next to her.* ♦ *Management initiated the negotiations, but soon withdrew from them.* **2.** *tv.* to admit someone into a club, especially during a secret ceremony. ♦ *Susan was initiated by the sorority.* ♦ *The local tennis club initiated David last night.*

initiative [ɪ 'nɪʃ ɪ tɪv] **1.** *n.* the ability to start things, especially without being told to do so. (No plural form in this sense.) ♦ *Working for oneself requires a lot of initiative.* ♦ *Susan didn't hire Bob because he didn't show any initiative.* **2. take the initiative** *idiom* to take the first action; to make the first move on an issue. ♦ *Anne took the initiative to discuss problems among the staff.* ♦ *When the ceiling started to leak, John took the initiative and fixed the roof immediately.*

inject [ɪn 'dʒɛkt] **1.** *tv.* to put a liquid into a living body through a hollow needle. ♦ *Medicine was injected into a vein by a nurse.* ♦ *A nurse injected a painkiller.* **2. inject with** *tv. + prep. phr.* to supply someone with medicine or another substance by way of an injection. ♦ *The diabetic injected himself with insulin.* ♦ *The nurse injected Tom with the medicine.* **3.** *tv.* to introduce a fluid into something under pressure. ♦ *The fuel injector was not injecting enough gasoline.* ♦ *A small hose injected the insecticide into the soil.* **4.** *tv.* to introduce a comment into a conversation. (Figurative on ①.) ♦ *John rudely injected his comments into my conversation with Anne.* ♦ *While I tried to make my point, Susan injected several helpful remarks.*

injection [ɪn 'dʒɛk ʃən] **1.** *n.* injecting something. (No plural form in this sense.) ♦ *Injection is the best way to administer some medicines.* ♦ *Electronic fuel injection is the most efficient way to get gasoline vapors into a car's engine.* **2.** *n.* a medicine, vitamins, or other liquids injected into the body. ♦ *The nurse gave the patient an injection of penicillin.* ♦ *The dentist gave me a number of injections to numb my whole upper jaw.*

injunction [ɪn 'dʒʌŋk ʃən] *n.* an order from a court that one must do or not do something. ♦ *The court issued an injunction that prevents our company from selling our products without the proper labels.* ♦ *We are seeking an injunction that will prevent the city from widening the street on which we live.*

injure ['ɪn dʒɚ] *tv.* to harm someone or something; to damage someone or something. ♦ *Anne injured her leg in the car accident.* ♦ *John injured Bob's feelings in the argument.*

injured ['ɪn dʒɚd] *adj.* harmed; damaged; hurt. ♦ *Bob's injured arm remained in a cast for six weeks.* ♦ *Everyone suffered from injured feelings after the argument.*

injury ['ɪn dʒə ri] **1.** *n.* physical or mental damage or harm; a specific act of damage or harm. ♦ *Anne suffered serious head injuries in the car crash.* ♦ *The injury to Bill's leg will heal in a few months.* **2.** *n.* something that is illegally wrong or unfair. (Figurative on ①.) ♦ *The human rights violation was an injury that Jane settled in a court of law.* ♦ *Bill discussed his claims of injury with a lawyer to determine whether he should sue.*

injustice [ɪn 'dʒʌs tɪs] **1.** *n.* the condition of not being fair or just. (No plural form in this sense.) ♦ *Injustice was rampant in the small town's court system.* ♦ *Injustice and intolerance are two serious problems in modern life.* **2.** *n.* something that is not fair; something that is not just. ♦ *The imprisonment of an innocent person is a great injustice.* ♦ *It is an outrageous injustice that Mary was not given a promotion.*

ink ['ɪŋk] **1.** *n.* a colored liquid used for writing or printing. (No plural form in this sense.) ♦ *The pen ran out of ink.* ♦ *Please sign your name in black ink.* **2.** *n.* a liquid that is injected into the water by an octopus or squid to confuse its pursuers. (No plural form in this sense.) ♦ *The octopus released a cloud of ink and fled.* ♦ *The biologist analyzed the content of the squid's ink.* **3. in ink** *phr.* written or signed with a pen that uses ink. ♦ *You should write your report in ink.* ♦ *You must sign your checks in ink.*

inkling ['ɪŋk lɪŋ] **1.** *n.* a slight suggestion or hint of something communicated to someone. ♦ *I detected an inkling of sarcasm in his remarks.* ♦ *There was an inkling of anger in Mary's voice.* **2.** *n.* a tiny suspicion. ♦ *I have an inkling* *that you ate the pizza I was saving.* ♦ *Let me see your hands. I have an inkling you didn't wash them.*

inlaid [ˈɪn led] *adj.* set in the surface; embedded in the surface. ♦ *The expensive table has an inlaid design on the top.* ♦ *Our kitchen floor has inlaid strips of gray around the border.*

inland 1. the inland [...ˈɪn lænd] *n.* the interior of a country or region; the part of a country or region that is away from a shore or a border. (No plural form in this sense. Treated as singular.) ♦ *The pioneers settled the inland much later than the coastal regions.* ♦ *Mary traveled to the inland to study agriculture.* **2.** [ˈɪn lənd] *adj.* located away from the shore or coast. ♦ *Denver, Colorado, is an inland city.* ♦ *The inland population is smaller than the coastal population.* **3.** [ˈɪn lənd] *adv.* in or toward ①. ♦ *The hurricane became less forceful as it moved inland.* ♦ *The original settlers did not travel very far inland.*

in-law [ˈɪn lɔ] *n.* one's relative by marriage; the relative of one's husband or wife. (Often plural.) ♦ *John remained friendly with his in-laws after his wife died.* ♦ *Mary met all of her in-laws for the first time at her wedding.*

inlet [ˈɪn lɛt] **1.** *n.* a small branch of a sea, ocean, or lake that stretches into the land. ♦ *The raft floated from the tip of the inlet out toward the sea.* ♦ *We camped on the shore of a narrow inlet of the Atlantic Ocean.* **2.** *n.* a narrow body of water between two islands. ♦ *Jane swam across the inlet to the neighboring island.* ♦ *This inlet is too shallow for ships to pass through.* **3.** *n.* an entrance; the way something enters. ♦ *The inlet to the hot-water heater is at the top.* ♦ *The narrow ditch is the inlet that carries water from the irrigation canal to the field.*

inmate [ˈɪn met] *n.* someone who lives in a jail or prison. ♦ *The guards punished the inmates who started the riot.* ♦ *The other inmates told me how they stole cars.*

inn [ˈɪn] *n.* a small hotel; a place that offers rooms to rent for travelers. ♦ *The guests at the inn were served breakfast each morning.* ♦ *While skiing in Switzerland, we stayed in a cozy mountain inn.*

innate [ɪ ˈnet] *adj.* present in someone since birth; inborn; instinctive. (Adv: *innately.*) ♦ *The ability to learn language is an innate human ability.* ♦ *The singer had an innate talent for music.*

inner [ˈɪn ɚ] **1.** *adj.* on the inside; nearer to the center; further inside. ♦ *I moved to the inner lane so I could make a left turn.* ♦ *John walked from the lobby into the inner room and shut the door.* **2.** *adj.* [of thoughts or emotions] private. ♦ *This book reveals the author's inner thoughts.* ♦ *Mary kept her inner emotions to herself.*

inner city [ˈɪn ɚ ˈsɪt i] **1.** *n.* an older, usually deteriorating, part of a city with many people and considerable poverty. ♦ *Many buildings in the inner city are boarded shut.* ♦ *I walked nervously through the inner city after dark.* **2. inner-city** *adj.* <the adj. use of ①.> ♦ *Susan taught music to inner-city children.* ♦ *The people in the suburbs were unaware of inner-city problems.*

inning [ˈɪn ɪŋ] *n.* [in baseball] a period of playing time that is terminated after the two teams have received three outs each during their turns batting. ♦ *Each of the two teams takes turns batting in each inning.* ♦ *The two halves of an inning are called the "top" and the "bottom."*

innocence [ˈɪn ə səns] **1.** *n.* freedom from guilt, blame, or sin. (No plural form in this sense.) ♦ *My innocence will be proved in court.* ♦ *The innocence or guilt of a defendant is determined by a judge or a jury.* **2.** *n.* harmlessness. (No plural form in this sense.) ♦ *John was insulted because he did not recognize the innocence of my humor.* ♦ *Mary explained the innocence of her actions.* **3.** *n.* the inability to recognize things that are harmful or evil. (No plural form in this sense.) ♦ *The author wrote about the innocence of childhood.* ♦ *Bill's youthful innocence was soon lost when he joined the army.*

innocent [ˈɪn ə sənt] **1.** *adj.* free from guilt or sin; not guilty. (Adv: *innocently.*) ♦ *Anne was found innocent of the crime.* ♦ *The minister said that no one is innocent of sin.* **2.** *adj.* harmless; not meant to cause harm. (Adv: *innocently.*) ♦ *It was just an innocent joke. I didn't mean to insult you.* ♦ *John gave Bill's arm an innocent, playful punch.* **3.** *adj.* too trusting; not recognizing things that are evil; inexperienced; naive. (Adv: *innocently.*) ♦ *John accompanied his innocent sister to New York City.* ♦ *The crooks took advantage of the innocent tourists.*

innocuous [ɪ ˈnɑk ju əs] *adj.* harmless; having very little effect; causing no harm. (Adv: *innocuously.*) ♦ *Your comments were so innocuous that I don't even remember them.* ♦ *I faced only a few innocuous problems at the office today.*

innovation [ɪn ə ˈve ʃən] **1.** *n.* creating new and often clever things and techniques. (No plural form in this sense.) ♦ *Innovation has given us much of our modern technology.* ♦ *Anne is often praised for her innovation.* **2.** *n.* a new, better way of doing something; a new, improved method. ♦ *For people who hate washing dishes, the dishwasher was a welcome innovation.* ♦ *Susan's design innovations saved the company a great deal of money.*

innovative [ˈɪn ə vet ɪv] *adj.* new; clever and better. (Adv: *innovatively.*) ♦ *Susan's innovative designs helped reduce production costs.* ♦ *Bill's second movie is more innovative than his first one.*

innumerable [ɪ ˈnum ə rə bəl] *adj.* not able to be counted; too many to be counted; many. (Adv: *innumerably.*) ♦ *The stars in space are innumerable.* ♦ *Innumerable deaths were caused by the earthquake.*

inoculate [ɪ ˈnɑk jə let] *tv.* to inject someone or something with a weakened or dead disease-causing agent in order to stimulate antibodies against the disease. ♦ *The doctor inoculated the children with a live polio vaccine.* ♦ *Have you been inoculated for measles yet?*

inoculation [ɪn ɑk jə ˈle ʃən] *n.* an injection of a weakened or dead disease-causing agent given to stimulate antibodies against the disease. ♦ *The doctor gave the children the inoculations they needed.* ♦ *Have you had a measles inoculation yet?*

inoffensive [ɪn ə ˈfɛn sɪv] *adj.* not offensive; harmless; not causing objection. (Adv: *inoffensively.*) ♦ *The simple painting was completely inoffensive.* ♦ *The inoffensive television show was also very boring.*

inpatient [ˈɪn pe ʃənt] **1.** *n.* a hospital patient who stays one or more nights in the hospital while getting treatment. ♦ *Inpatients stay in beds and have their meals brought to them.* ♦ *I checked into the hospital as an inpatient for my surgery.* **2.** *adj.* <the adj. use of ①.> ♦ *Anne* *went to the hospital for inpatient surgery.* ♦ *All inpatient services in the hospital are expensive.*

input ['ɪn pʊt] **1.** *n.* putting something into something. (No plural form in this sense.) ♦ *Your data input is much too slow. You'll have to type faster.* ♦ *The input of opinions at the meeting was very limited.* **2.** *n.* advice; opinions; ideas or suggestions. (Informal. No plural form in this sense.) ♦ *Your input into this matter is appreciated.* ♦ *Jane felt that John was ignoring her input.* **3.** *n.* information; data; information that is put into a computer. (No plural form in this sense.) ♦ *The disk holding all of the input was accidentally erased.* ♦ *Your input is in the wrong format.* **4.** *n.* an electronic signal that is fed into a circuit. ♦ *The input was cut off when the wire snapped.* ♦ *This switch controls the various inputs into the circuit.* **5.** *tv., irreg.* to put data into a computer. (Pt/pp: *inputted* or *input.*) ♦ *Mary input the figures into the computer program.* ♦ *The data were inputted without any mistakes.*

inquest ['ɪn kwɛst] *n.* an official court into the cause of someone's death. ♦ *At the inquest, the coroner stated that John had been poisoned.* ♦ *The inquest was held a week after John's murder.*

inquire [ɪn 'kwɑɪr] *iv.* to ask someone about something. (Also spelled enquire.) ♦ *I inquired whether any rooms at the hotel were vacant.* ♦ *Susan inquired about Bob's success.*

inquiring [ɪn 'kwɑɪr ɪŋ] *adj.* asking for information; seeking information. ♦ *My inquiring mind wanted to know who left the party with Bill.* ♦ *The convicted criminal swore at the inquiring reporters.*

inquiry [ɪn 'kwɑɪr i] **1.** *n.* a question. (Also spelled enquiry.) ♦ *Before I continue, are there any inquiries about what I've said?* ♦ *Please direct your inquiry to the information desk.* **2.** *n.* an investigation; a search for truth; a search for an answer. ♦ *The police organized an inquiry into the executive's death.* ♦ *The inquiry into the child's disappearance was never resolved.*

inquisitive [ɪn 'kwɪz ɪ tɪv] *adj.* asking a lot of questions; curious; eager to learn. (Adv: *inquisitively.*) ♦ *The teacher enjoyed teaching the inquisitive class.* ♦ *The inquisitive student reads several books each week.*

insane [ɪn 'sen] **1.** *adj.* crazy; not sane; deranged. (Adv: *insanely.*) ♦ *The murderer was judged to be insane.* ♦ *The insane soldier was sent to a mental hospital.* **2.** *adj.* owing to insanity; done because of insanity. (Adv: *insanely.*) ♦ *The serial killer was punished for his insane acts.* ♦ *The criminal's insane comments were hard to understand.* **3.** *adj.* very stupid; very foolish; very idiotic. (Informal. Adv: *insanely.*) ♦ *You'd be insane to wear a bathing suit to the wedding.* ♦ *If you think I'd quit school now, you're insane!*

insanity [ɪn 'sæn ə ti] *n.* mental derangement; the condition of being insane. (No plural form in this sense.) ♦ *The defendant was found not guilty because of insanity.* ♦ *The criminal's insanity was not in question.*

insatiable [ɪn 'se ʃə bəl] **1.** *adj.* [of a hunger for food] not able to be satisfied [easily]. (Adv: *insatiably.*) ♦ *The hungry child had an insatiable appetite.* ♦ *When she was pregnant, Anne had an insatiable desire for ice cream.* **2.** *adj.* [of a need or want] not able to be satisfied [easily]. (Figurative on ①. Adv: *insatiably.*) ♦ *Bill has an insatiable desire to fly an airplane.* ♦ *Susan has an insatiable lust for money.*

inscribe [ɪn 'skrɑɪb] **1. inscribe in(to); inscribe on(to)** *tv. + prep. phr.* to cut words or a design on the surface of something. ♦ *John inscribed the design onto the steel plate with a chisel.* ♦ *Mary inscribed her initials into the tree.* **2. inscribe with** *tv. + prep. phr.* to mark a surface with a message. ♦ *Mary inscribed the first page of the book with a personal note.* ♦ *John inscribed the greeting card with his signature.*

inscribed [ɪn 'skrɑɪbd] *adj.* written on; marked with words or a design; having an inscription. ♦ *John bought Mary an inscribed bracelet for her birthday.* ♦ *The inscribed invitations looked very pretty.*

inscription [ɪn 'skrɪp ʃən] *n.* words that are inscribed on a surface; words that are carved or cut into a surface. ♦ *The inscription on the archway read: "Peace to all who enter."* ♦ *John paid extra for a personal inscription on the bracelet.*

insect ['ɪn sɛkt] **1.** *n.* a small animal with wings and six legs. ♦ *The body of an insect consists of a head, thorax, and abdomen.* ♦ *The tiny insect carried a deadly virus.* **2.** *n.* a bug. ♦ *Some people call spiders, ticks, and centipedes insects even though they are not.* ♦ *Our picnic lunch was covered with insects.*

insecticide [ɪn 'sɛk tɪ sɑɪd] *n.* a poison that kills insects. (No plural form in this sense.) ♦ *The farmer sprayed the crops with insecticide.* ♦ *Certain mosquitoes become resistant to insecticide.*

insecure [ɪn sɪ 'kjɚ] **1.** *adj.* unsure of oneself; not self-confident. (Adv: *insecurely.*) ♦ *Bill felt insecure at the party because he didn't know anyone.* ♦ *The motivational speaker taught insecure people to be more confident.* **2.** *adj.* not firm; likely to fall, break, or collapse. (Adv: *insecurely.*) ♦ *Anne refused to cross the insecure wooden bridge.* ♦ *The insecure railing finally collapsed.*

insensible [ɪn 'sɛn sə bəl] **insensible (to)** *adj.* (+ *prep. phr.*) not conscious of something; not aware of something. (Adv: *insensibly.*) ♦ *Bill was insensible to the fact that his wife was leaving him.* ♦ *Anne passed out at the party, insensible to everything that happened.*

insensitive [ɪn 'sɛn sɪ tɪv] **1. insensitive to** *adj. + prep. phr.* not feeling pain; not able to have certain feelings. ♦ *My paralyzed leg is insensitive to pain or heat.* ♦ *Smoking cigarettes will make you insensitive to delicate flavors.* **2.** *adj.* not sensitive to other people's needs; unfeeling; tactless. (Adv: *insensitively.*) ♦ *Dave was so insensitive to Anne's feelings that he didn't know she was mad at him.* ♦ *The insensitive host offended his guests.*

inseparable [ɪn 'sɛp ə rə bəl] *adj.* not able to be separated; always together. (Adv: *inseparably.*) ♦ *John and Bill were inseparable friends.* ♦ *The parts of the case of the clock are inseparable, so I can't get inside to repair it.*

insert 1. ['ɪn sɚt] *n.* something that is placed inside of something else, especially an advertisement that is placed inside a magazine or newspaper. ♦ *Bill cut out all the coupons in the newspaper inserts.* ♦ *I removed the scented insert from the fashion magazine.* **2. insert in** [ɪn 'sɚt...] *tv. + prep. phr.* to put something inside something else. ♦ *Please insert your credit card into the slot.* ♦ *Bill inserted a bookmark into the book.*

insertion [ɪn 'sɚ ʃən] **1.** *n.* inserting something. ♦ *An insertion of a needle into Bill's arm caused him to faint.* ♦ *The insertion of the pin into the balloon caused it to pop.*

2. *n.* written material that is placed into other written material. ♦ *The editor marked in the text exactly where the insertion should be added.* ♦ *There are three insertions that must be put in my essay when it is typed again.*

in-service ['ɪn sɚ vɪs] *adj.* [attended while] on the job; [done] while at work. ♦ *The new computer system was explained at the in-service workshop.* ♦ *The students were released at noon because the teachers had an afternoon in-service conference.*

inside 1. ['ɪn 'sɑɪd] *n.* the interior of a building or an object; the part of an object that is within something. ♦ *I wonder what the inside of that house is like.* ♦ *The inside of the banana was rotten.* **2.** [ɪn 'sɑɪd, 'ɪn sɑɪd] *adj.* on the inside; interior; of or about the inside or interior. ♦ *The painter painted the inside walls light brown.* ♦ *The inside stairs of the house were steeper than the outside stairs.* **3.** [ɪn 'sɑɪd] *adv.* into a room or building; into an object. ♦ *I came inside because it started to rain.* ♦ *The dog stopped in the doorway and then ran inside.* **4.** [ɪn 'sɑɪd, 'ɪn sɑɪd] *prep.* within a room or building; within an object; within the interior; in an interior position. ♦ *It was cool inside the house because the air conditioning was on.* ♦ *Inside a pumpkin there are hundreds of seeds.*

inside out [ɪn sɑɪd 'ɑʊt] **1.** *adv.* with the inside part on the outside. (Used after the noun.) ♦ *I turned my socks inside out before I washed them.* ♦ *All my pants were inside out when I took them from the dryer.* **2. know something inside out** *idiom* to know something thoroughly; to know about something thoroughly. ♦ *I know my geometry inside out.* ♦ *I studied and studied for my driver's test until I knew the rules inside out.*

insight ['ɪn sɑɪt] **1.** *n.* the ability to make pertinent observations. (No plural form in this sense.) ♦ *My wise grandparents have a great amount of insight.* ♦ *I never questioned my teacher's insight.* **2.** *n.* a pertinent observation about someone or something. ♦ *I would like to hear more of your insights into this painting.* ♦ *I agreed with Anne's insight about the author's ideas.*

insightful ['ɪn sɑɪt fəl] *adj.* filled with insight; able to make pertinent observations. (Adv: *insightfully.*) ♦ *Anne made a few insightful remarks that helped us understand what was going on.* ♦ *Thank you for your insightful explanation of the tax system.*

insignificant [ɪn sɪg 'nɪf ə kənt] *adj.* not significant; not important; trivial. (Adv: *insignificantly.*) ♦ *The amount of money Anne spends on coffee each month is insignificant.* ♦ *John bored me with insignificant details about his vacation.*

insincere [ɪn sɪn 'sɪr] *adj.* not sincere; hypocritical. (Adv: *insincerely.*) ♦ *Bob's insincere comments insulted me.* ♦ *Jane's attitude is insincere and phony.*

insincerity [ɪn sɪn 'sɛr ə ti] *n.* a lack of sincerity. (No plural form in this sense.) ♦ *Because of the insincerity of Bill's apology, I didn't think he was really sorry.* ♦ *The insincerity of Jane's promise to visit me was obvious because she never did.*

insinuate [ɪn 'sɪn ju et] *tv.* to hint at something, especially something negative; to suggest something; to imply something negative. (Takes a clause.) ♦ *Susan insinuated that I had stolen the money, even though she didn't say so directly.* ♦ *Are you insinuating that I am responsible for the accident?*

insinuation [ɪn sin ju 'e ʃən] **1.** *n.* hinting; indirect and unpleasant suggestion. (No plural form in this sense.) ♦ *Bill tried insulting his opponent through insinuation.* ♦ *Tom used insinuation to spread rumors about his former girlfriend.* **2.** *n.* an unpleasant hint, suggestion, or implication. ♦ *I regret my insinuations that you were responsible for the accident.* ♦ *Susan's insinuation that I stole the money is unfounded.*

insipid [ɪn 'sɪp ɪd] *adj.* boring; dull; bland; uninteresting. (Adv: *insipidly.*) ♦ *Bob has an insipid personality that makes people avoid him.* ♦ *The writing was so insipid that I couldn't finish the book.*

insist [ɪn 'sɪst] **1.** *tv.* to demand something. (Takes a clause.) ♦ *Anne insisted that I stay for dinner.* ♦ *I insist that you put out that cigarette right now!* **2.** *tv.* to assert something; to state a belief about something. (Takes a clause.) ♦ *Bill insists that he was at the party, but I know he didn't go.* ♦ *The witness insisted that she saw Mary hide the gun.* **3.** *iv.* to continue to demand or assert [something] emphatically. ♦ *You must come for dinner. I insist.* ♦ *Anne insisted, so I did it.* **4. insist on** *iv.* + *prep. phr.* to remain firm or emphatic about doing something; to demand something. ♦ *My grandmother insists on cleanliness in her kitchen.* ♦ *Susan insisted on telling me how the movie ended.*

insistence [ɪn 'sɪs təns] *n.* insisting; demanding. (No plural form in this sense.) ♦ *Bill's insistence that he was being followed was laughed at by everyone.* ♦ *At Anne's insistence, we took her with us to the party.*

insistent [ɪn 'sɪs tənt] *adj.* demanding; making repeated demands. (Adv: *insistently.*) ♦ *Your insistent whining is wearing on my nerves.* ♦ *With an insistent voice, John stated his problem.*

insolence ['ɪn sə ləns] *n.* the condition of being insolent. (No plural form in this sense.) ♦ *Your insolence to your teacher is unforgivable.* ♦ *I will not put up with this insolence any longer.*

insolent ['ɪn sə lənt] *adj.* not showing respect; rude. (Adv: *insolently.*) ♦ *The insolent student yelled at his teacher.* ♦ *Anne's insolent behavior upset her parents.*

insomnia [ɪn 'sɑm ni ə] *n.* the inability to fall asleep or remain asleep. (No plural form in this sense.) ♦ *Drinking a lot of coffee at night can cause insomnia.* ♦ *My insomnia kept me awake almost all night.*

inspect [ɪn 'spɛkt] *tv.* to examine someone or something carefully. ♦ *The detective inspected the bloody knife that was used to kill the victim.* ♦ *The general inspected the troops.*

inspection [ɪn 'spɛk ʃən] **1.** *n.* study; inspecting and reviewing. (No plural form in this sense.) ♦ *Inspection of the kitchen is required every six months.* ♦ *Without frequent inspection, airplane engines would not be dependable.* **2.** *n.* a complete examination; an official examination; the act of inspecting. ♦ *An inspection of the suitcase revealed a crudely made bomb.* ♦ *The restaurant passed its last health inspection.*

inspector [ɪn 'spɛk tɚ] **1.** *n.* someone who closely examines things for mistakes or for official reasons. ♦ *The inspector carefully searched my luggage at the airport.* ♦ *The clothing inspector made sure the buttons were tightly sewn.* **2.** *n.* a police officer ranking below a police superintendent. ♦ *The inspector questioned the witnesses.* ♦ *The inspector found an important piece of evidence.*

inspiration [ɪn spɪ 'reʃən] **1.** *n.* a positive influence that causes one to want to do something good. (No plural form in this sense.) ♦ *I need some kinds of inspiration for my writing.* ♦ *The student read the works of famous philosophers for inspiration.* **2.** *n.* a good idea; an idea that has been inspired. ♦ *I just got a tremendous inspiration to write a poem.* ♦ *Attending council meetings provided me with a few inspirations about improving city government.* **3.** *n.* breathing in; inhalation. (No plural form in this sense.) ♦ *John's weak inspiration is caused by asthma.* ♦ *Inspiration was painful because of the soreness in my chest.*

inspire [ɪn 'spaɪr] **1.** *tv.* to influence someone to do something. ♦ *My mother inspired me to go to college.* ♦ *Beethoven's music inspired me to be a composer.* **2.** *tv.* to fill someone with a certain spiritual emotion or feeling; to arouse a certain emotion in someone. ♦ *The good news inspired joy in my heart.* ♦ *The hungry children inspired sorrow in me.*

inspired [ɪn 'spaɪrd] **1.** *adj.* [of something] so well done as to have been caused by a powerfully good influence. ♦ *Mary's inspired writing was published in a literary journal.* ♦ *My teacher gave a truly inspired lecture today.* **2.** *adj.* [of someone] uplifted and influenced to do something, especially by a spiritual influence. ♦ *The inspired minister preached a superb sermon.* ♦ *After a kind teacher helped him, the inspired teen decided to try to help others.*

inspiring [ɪn 'spaɪr ɪŋ] *adj.* making people feel like doing something good or helpful; encouraging; spiritually influential. (Adv: *inspiringly.*) ♦ *I cried when I read Anne's inspiring story.* ♦ *Dave relied on his parents' inspiring words for guidance.*

install [ɪn 'stɔl] **1.** *tv.* to set up a piece of equipment for use; to make something ready for use. ♦ *The worker installed cable television in the building.* ♦ *We installed a new dishwasher last week.* **2.** *tv.* to put someone in a certain job or position. ♦ *The president installed John as the new treasurer.* ♦ *The club president was installed in a joyful ceremony.*

installation [ɪn stə 'le ʃən] **1.** *n.* setting up equipment; putting equipment in place so that it will work. (No plural form in this sense.) ♦ *The installation of the dishwasher took the plumber only a few hours.* ♦ *If you want installation, it will be a separate charge.* **2.** *n.* something that has been installed; equipment that is in place and operating. ♦ *As we looked at the many transformers and wires, the engineer told us that this was a new installation.* ♦ *The whole installation had to be removed and replaced with new equipment.* **3.** *n.* putting someone in a position or office. (No plural form in this sense.) ♦ *The installation of the new president was a simple ceremony.* ♦ *The installation of the new officers takes place on May 1.*

installment [ɪn 'stɔl mənt] **1.** *n.* an episode; one part of a series of stories or reports. ♦ *The first installment of the series dealt with the Revolutionary War.* ♦ *The installment that dealt with the health-care system won an award for excellence in reporting.* **2.** *n.* one of a series of payments on a debt. ♦ *After paying the last mortgage installment, the house was ours.* ♦ *My car loan will be repaid in 36 monthly installments.*

instance ['ɪn stəns] **1.** *n.* an example; a case; an incident; an occurrence. ♦ *Each instance of food poisoning was reported to the health department.* ♦ *How many instances of tornadoes were there in 1958?* **2. for instance** *phr.* for example. ♦ *I've lived in many cities, for instance, Boston, Chicago, and Detroit.* ♦ *Jane is very generous. For instance, she volunteers her time and gives money to charities.*

instant ['ɪn stənt] **1.** *n.* one moment in time; a very short amount of time. (No plural form in this sense.) ♦ *Please wait just an instant.* ♦ *The computer calculated the figures in an instant.* **2.** *adj.* immediate; without delay. (Adv: *instantly.*) ♦ *My boss demanded an instant response to her question.* ♦ *My instant reaction to the gunfire was to hide behind a wall.* **3.** *adj.*,[of food or drink] easily and quickly prepared. ♦ *I drank instant coffee for breakfast.* ♦ *It takes 30 seconds to heat instant soup in a microwave.*

instantaneous [ɪn stən 'ten ɪ əs] **1.** *adj.* immediate; without delay; at once. (Adv: *instantaneously.*) ♦ *My instantaneous reply to John's nosy question was "No!"* ♦ *When the clown tripped and fell, my instantaneous reaction was laughter.* **2.** *adj.* happening in an instant. (Adv: *instantaneously.*) ♦ *The coroner determined that the driver's death was instantaneous.* ♦ *The explosion caused instantaneous destruction.*

instead [ɪn 'stɛd] **1.** *adv.* in place of something; as an alternative to something. ♦ *I don't want to go home. Let's go to a movie instead.* ♦ *John canceled his date with Mary so he could go out with me instead.* **2. instead of** *prep.* in place of; as a substitute for. ♦ *Instead of Florida, let's go to Mexico this winter.* ♦ *John wanted grape juice instead of orange juice.*

instill [ɪn 'stɪl] **1. instill in** *tv.* + *prep. phr.* to teach something, such as patience or manners, to someone gradually; to ingrain something in someone. ♦ *John's parents instilled good manners in him.* ♦ *Years of working as a waitress instilled a lot of patience in Anne.* **2. instill with** *tv.* + *prep. phr.* to fill someone with something, such as patience. ♦ *John's parents instilled him with good manners.* ♦ *Working as a waitress instilled Anne with patience.*

instinct ['ɪn stɪŋkt] **1.** *n.* the inborn ability to respond in a particular way. (No plural form in this sense.) ♦ *Birds migrate because of instinct.* ♦ *It is instinct that makes salmon swim upstream to lay eggs.* **2.** *n.* a natural sense or ability in a human. (Figurative on ①.) ♦ *You seem to have an instinct for getting into trouble.* ♦ *Dave's instinct for learning languages has helped him learn 7 different languages.* **3.** *n.* intuition; [someone's] perception of people and things. (Often plural.) ♦ *Anne's instincts told her that John was not to be trusted.* ♦ *John trusted his instinct to avoid the dark alley.*

instinctive [ɪn 'stɪŋk tɪv] *adj.* done by instinct; done as an automatic reaction to something. (Adv: *instinctively.*) ♦ *The cat's avoidance of fire is an instinctive response.* ♦ *The biologist studied the instinctive behavior of apes.*

institute ['ɪn stɪ tut] **1.** *n.* an organization that serves a special purpose, especially concerning science, medicine, or education. ♦ *The Institute for Mental Health raised funds for a new hospital.* ♦ *Jane got her engineering degree at the Illinois Institute of Technology.* **2.** *n.* the building where ① is located. ♦ *Mary works at the mental health institute on Elm Street.* ♦ *Inside the institute were many offices and laboratories.* **3.** *tv.* to start something new; to begin a new policy. ♦ *The foundation was instituted in 1912.* ♦ *The officers of the club instituted a stricter smoking policy.*

institution [ɪn stɪ 'tu ʃən] **1.** *n.* an institute ①; an organization that serves a special purpose. ♦ *A university is an institution of higher education.* ♦ *A seminary is an institution of religious education.* **2.** *n.* an institute ②. ♦ *The insane are treated in mental institutions.* ♦ *This institution employs 250 workers.* **3.** *n.* an established tradition; a habit; a custom. ♦ *The institution of marriage has existed for centuries.* ♦ *Ancient Greece is the birthplace of the institution of democracy.*

instruct [ɪn 'strʌkt] **1.** *tv.* to teach someone something; to educate someone about something. ♦ *Ms. Smith instructed the children in history.* ♦ *The firefighter instructed the class about how to survive a fire.* **2. instruct to** *tv.* + *inf.* to order or request someone to do something. ♦ *The teacher instructed Tom to open the window.* ♦ *Bill was instructed to leave the room.*

instruction [ɪn 'strʌk ʃən] **1.** *n.* education; teaching. (No plural form in this sense.) ♦ *The principal doubted the new teacher's methods of instruction.* ♦ *The instruction I received at the private school was very thorough.* **2. instructions** *n.* an order or set of orders, a direction or set of directions, etc. ♦ *The class followed the teacher's instructions.* ♦ *The instructions in the computer manual weren't very helpful.*

instructor [ɪn 'strʌk tɚ] *n.* a teacher; someone who instructs people about something. ♦ *The instructor is ill today, so class is canceled.* ♦ *My Spanish instructor was born in Mexico.*

instrument ['ɪn strə mənt] **1.** *n.* a thing that is used to help someone do something; a tool; a device. ♦ *The nurse handed the surgical instruments to the doctor.* ♦ *A scale is an instrument of measurement.* **2.** *n.* something that shows a measurement; a gauge. ♦ *A thermometer is an instrument used to measure temperature.* ♦ *The pilots watched the instruments on the panel in front of them.* **3.** *n.* an object that produces musical notes when played. ♦ *The trumpet, trombone, and tuba are brass instruments.* ♦ *An orchestra includes many different musical instruments.*

instrumental [ɪn strə 'mɛn təl] **1. instrumental in** *adj.* + *prep. phr.* helpful in doing something; useful in doing something. ♦ *Scholarship money was instrumental in helping me pay for college.* ♦ *Tom's good manners were instrumental in getting him the job.* **2.** *adj.* consisting of music from instruments instead of voices; [of music] without singing. (Adv: *instrumentally.*) ♦ *I listen to instrumental music when I work because singing distracts me.* ♦ *The radio played the instrumental version of the popular song.*

instrumentalist [ɪn strə 'mɛn tə ləst] *n.* a musician who plays a musical instrument. ♦ *The concert featured an instrumentalist playing original works on the guitar.* ♦ *Jane is a wonderful instrumentalist, but a bad singer.*

insufficient [ɪn sə 'fɪʃ ənt] *adj.* not sufficient; inadequate; not having enough of something. (Adv: *insufficiently.*) ♦ *There was insufficient evidence to convict John of the crime.* ♦ *There was an insufficient amount of money in my checking account to cover the check I had written.*

insulate ['ɪn sə let] **1.** *tv.* to cover something with a material that prevents the passage of electricity, heat, or sound. ♦ *We halved our heating bill when we insulated our house.* ♦ *John insulated the recording studio with material that made it soundproof.* **2. insulate from** *tv.* + *prep. phr.* to separate someone or something from other things or people by distance or a barrier. (Figurative on ①.) ♦ *The remote island was insulated from the problems of the world.* ♦ *The winter snowstorms insulated the arctic village from the outside world until April.*

insulation [ɪn sə 'le ʃən] *n.* material that prevents the passage of electricity, heat, or sound. (No plural form in this sense.) ♦ *The contractor sprayed the inside of the walls with foam insulation.* ♦ *The electrical insulation was smoldering, so I knew something was wrong with the electrical power supply.*

insulin ['ɪn sə lɪn] *n.* a hormone made by the pancreas, which regulates glucose in the body. (No plural form in this sense.) ♦ *People with diabetes must inject insulin on a regular basis.* ♦ *The medical tests showed that John was not producing enough insulin.*

insult [ɪn 'sʌlt] **1.** *n.* an offensive remark; a statement that insults. ♦ *What Anne said to Bob was a terrible insult.* ♦ *The newspaper printed the senator's insult and then his apology.* **2.** *tv.* to offend someone; to say something rude or offensive to someone. ♦ *I walked out of the room when John insulted me.* ♦ *We were all insulted by the rudeness of the taxi driver.* **3. hurl an insult (at someone)** *idiom* to direct an insult at someone; to say something insulting directly to someone. ♦ *Anne hurled an insult at Bob that made him very angry.* ♦ *If you two would stop hurling insults, we could have a serious discussion.*

insulting [ɪn 'sʌl tɪŋ] *adj.* offensive; rude. (Adv: *insultingly.*) ♦ *I could not believe how insulting you were to the waiter!* ♦ *You should apologize for your insulting behavior.*

insurance [ɪn 'ʃɚ əns] **1.** *n.* a contract that pays a sum of money in the case of a loss or injury. (No plural form in this sense. Number is expressed with insurance policy or policies.) ♦ *John had to have flood insurance when he bought a house on the coast.* ♦ *Car insurance is required by law in most states.* **2.** *n.* something that protects against a loss or an injury. (No plural form in this sense.) ♦ *Locking the doors is not insurance that your car won't be stolen.* ♦ *The bulletproof windows provided insurance that the bank tellers wouldn't be shot.* **3.** *n.* the business of writing and selling ①. (No plural form in this sense.) ♦ *The powerful banking firm decided to branch into insurance as well.* ♦ *My cousin has worked in insurance for a number of years.* **4.** *adj.* <the adj. use of ③.> ♦ *My cousin works in the insurance industry.* ♦ *Our insurance agent was very helpful after the accident.*

insurance policy [ɪn 'ʃɚ əns 'pɑl ə si] *n.* the document or contract that states the protections offered by insurance. ♦ *I keep all my insurance policies in a safe place.* ♦ *I have an insurance policy on my house and on my car.*

insure [ɪn 'ʃɚ] **1.** *tv.* to purchase insurance for someone or something. (Compare with ensure.) ♦ *John insured the package that he sent by mail.* ♦ *Susan insured her car against losses caused by accident and theft.* **2.** *tv.* [for an insurance company] to sell insurance on someone or something. ♦ *The insurance company insured city drivers at a higher cost than rural ones.* ♦ *The airline insured its passengers' luggage against loss.*

insured [ɪn 'ʃɚd] *n.* someone who owns an insurance policy on property; someone whose life or health is the subject of an insurance policy. ♦ *After the fire, the agency issued the insured a check immediately.* ♦ *The agent questioned the insured about his claim.*

intact [ɪn 'tækt] *adj.* not damaged; whole. ♦ *The tornado destroyed our garage but left our house intact.* ♦ *All the parts of the old radio were still intact.*

intake ['ɪn tek] **1.** *n.* the process of taking something in. (No plural form in this sense.) ♦ *The intake of air was blocked by a rubber stopper.* ♦ *My food intake is hindered by my severe sore throat.* **2.** *n.* an opening that allows air or liquid to enter something. ♦ *The car stalled because the fuel intake was clogged.* ♦ *John removed the blockage from the vacuum cleaner's intake.*

intangible [ɪn 'tæn dʒə bəl] **1.** *adj.* not tangible; not able to be felt by touching. (Adv: *intangibly.*) ♦ *Love and trust are intangible values.* ♦ *Thoughts and ideas are intangible things on which it is impossible to place a value.* **2. intangible asset** *n.* a business asset having a value only when considered as part of the function of the business. ♦ *The auditor questioned the figure for the company's intangible assets.* ♦ *The company had greatly overestimated the value of its intangible assets.* **3. intangibles** *n.* intangible assets in general. ♦ *Never underestimate the value of intangibles such as goodwill.* ♦ *After bankruptcy, the company's intangibles became almost worthless.*

integral ['ɪn tə grəl] **1.** *adj.* necessary; essential. (Adv: *integrally.*) ♦ *The motor is integral to the operation of a car.* ♦ *Food is an integral part of human life.* **2.** *adj.* built-in; contained within. (Adv: *integrally.*) ♦ *John's theory consists of several integral principles.* ♦ *My computer has integral fax circuitry that allows me to send faxes directly from the computer.*

integrate ['ɪn tə gret] **1.** *tv.* to incorporate something into something else. ♦ *Anne integrated the new information into her report.* ♦ *The new workers were quickly integrated into the routine.* **2.** *tv.* to incorporate persons of a minority race into a school, neighborhood, institution, or public place in a way that provides free and open access to everyone equally. ♦ *After a long court battle, the city schools were finally integrated.* ♦ *The district integrated the schools by busing the children in from different neighborhoods.* **3.** *iv.* [for people of different cultures and races] to join together; to undergo integration as in ②. ♦ *The neighborhood integrated during the 1970s.* ♦ *Our high school integrated against the wishes of the school board.*

integrated ['ɪn tə gre təd] **1.** *adj.* made whole; brought together; having parts brought together. (Adv: *integratedly.*) ♦ *The new, integrated theory combined features of earlier ones.* ♦ *Susan is in charge of an integrated network of computers.* **2.** *adj.* [of a location or institution] having people of different cultures and races joined together. (Adv: *integratedly.*) ♦ *I lived in an integrated neighborhood when I was growing up.* ♦ *The principal discussed issues of race relations with students at the newly integrated high school.*

integrity [ɪn 'tɛ grə ti] **1.** *n.* honesty; strong moral character. (No plural form in this sense.) ♦ *The president honored the heroes for their bravery and integrity.* ♦ *When he was accused of cheating, John's integrity was questioned.* **2.** *n.* completeness; the condition of being whole or unbroken. (No plural form in this sense.) ♦ *Poor construction threatened the integrity of the dam.* ♦ *The earthquake affected the structural integrity of the building.*

intellect ['ɪn tə lɛkt] *n.* understanding, thinking, and reasoning. (No plural form in this sense.) ♦ *The professor had a very sharp intellect.* ♦ *Use your well-developed intellect and help me solve this problem!*

intellectual [ɪn tə 'lɛk tʃu əl] **1.** *adj.* of or about the intellect as opposed to the emotions. (Adv: *intellectually.*) ♦ *I agree with your comments on an intellectual level.* ♦ *For intellectual stimulation, Anne reads books on philosophy.* **2.** *n.* someone who clearly has a great ability to understand, think, and reason. ♦ *The campus intellectuals discussed politics in the little café.* ♦ *John might be a brilliant intellectual, but he's not very romantic.*

intelligence [ɪn 'tɛl ɪ dʒəns] **1.** *n.* the level of someone's ability to learn and understand. (No plural form in this sense.) ♦ *Computer programming requires a high level of intelligence.* ♦ *Sometimes Bob acts like he has the intelligence of a two-year-old.* **2.** *n.* information about the enemy and the enemy's plans. (No plural form in this sense.) ♦ *The army used the intelligence provided by the spy to protect the city from attack.* ♦ *The agent tricked the government by providing false intelligence.* **3.** *n.* a department within a military service that gathers ②. (No plural form in this sense.) ♦ *The enemy soldiers were taken to the Department of Intelligence for questioning.* ♦ *Intelligence trained the best soldiers to spy on the enemy.*

intelligent [ɪn 'tɛl ɪ dʒənt] *adj.* smart; able to learn and understand things well. (Adv: *intelligently.*) ♦ *The students in my history class are all quite intelligent.* ♦ *You're intelligent enough to solve your own problems.*

intend [ɪn 'tɛnd] **1. intend to** *tv.* + *inf.* to have the purpose of doing something; to plan to do something; to mean to do something. ♦ *I intend to go to the store this afternoon.* ♦ *John intends to buy Anne a necklace for her birthday.* **2. intend for** *tv.* + *prep. phr.* to declare or designate something for someone or a purpose. ♦ *This violent movie is not intended for children.* ♦ *I intended this last piece of cake for Sally, but Susan ate it instead.*

intended [ɪn 'tɛn dɪd] *adj.* meant; having a specific purpose. ♦ *The intended effect of my suggestions was to improve your story.* ♦ *The intended message of the film was lost because of poor acting.*

intense [ɪn 'tɛns] **1.** *adj.* very powerful; very great; extreme. (Adv: *intensely.*) ♦ *An intense pain ran through the bones of my arm.* ♦ *The intense heat of the day caused most people to stay inside.* **2.** *adj.* serious; strongly emotional; showing great personal strength. (Adv: *intensely.*) ♦ *His intense glare made me stare at the floor.* ♦ *The movie was very intense, and I cried at the end.*

intensification [ɪŋ tɛn sɪ fə 'ke ʃən] *n.* The process of becoming intense or more intense. (No plural form in this sense.) ♦ *The intensification of the war upset those who prayed for peace.* ♦ *The workers decided to strike because of the intensification of problems with management.*

intensify [ɪŋ 'tɛn sə faɪ] **1.** *tv.* to make something stronger, more powerful, or more intense. ♦ *Sharing an apartment has intensified our friendship.* ♦ *The lens intensified the sun's rays and made them hot enough to start a fire.* **2.** *iv.* to become stronger, more powerful, or more intense. ♦ *As the war intensified, we had to conserve gasoline.* ♦ *As the argument continued, our anger intensified.*

intensity [ɪn 'tɛn sə ti] **1.** *n.* the degree or amount of power or strength. (No plural form in this sense.) ♦ *The electrician measured the intensity of the voltage.* ♦ *The sick actor performed with a low emotional intensity.* **2.** *n.* great strength; extreme force; great excitement. (No plural form in this sense.) ♦ *The lawyer's overwhelming intensity held the jury's attention.* ♦ *The intensity of the explosion destroyed the steel bridge.*

intensive [ɪn 'tɛn sɪv] *adj.* thorough and concentrated; paying a lot of attention to something in a small amount of time. (Adv: *intensively.*) ♦ *I learned French in an intensive six-month course.* ♦ *My first job as a naturalist required intensive research into the life of bears.*

intensive care [ɪn 'tɛn sɪv 'kɛr] **1.** *n.* the treatment of people in a hospital who need constant medical attention. (No plural form in this sense.) ♦ *The nurse was trained in intensive care.* ♦ *Our local hospital provides modern and up-to-date intensive care.* **2.** *n.* a hospital department that provides constant and intense care to its patients. (No plural form in this sense.) ♦ *After surgery, the patient was taken to intensive care.* ♦ *The hospital allows family members to visit patients in intensive care.*

intent [ɪn 'tɛnt] **1.** *n.* meaning; purpose. (No plural form in this sense.) ♦ *The intent of my experiment is to examine how mice run through mazes.* ♦ *It was not my intent to insult you.* **2. intent gaze** *n.* a direct and determined stare. ♦ *The speaker looked out to the intent gazes of the crowd.* ♦ *John's intent gaze indicated that he was angry.* **3. intent on doing something** *idiom* determined to do something. ♦ *The children were intent on making a snowman.* ♦ *The prisoner was intent on escaping.*

intention [ɪn 'tɛn ʃən] *n.* a purpose; a plan. ♦ *My intention is to examine the role of the farmer in American history.* ♦ *The intention behind my screaming was to warn you of the oncoming truck.*

intentional [ɪn 'tɛn ʃə nəl] *adj.* done on purpose; deliberate. (Adv: *intentionally.*) ♦ *Although my comments were intentional, they were not meant to be insulting.* ♦ *The lawyer proved that Bob's killing was intentional and was not at all accidental.*

intently [ɪn 'tɛnt li] *adv.* in a fixed way; with strong concentration; in an intent way. ♦ *The art student stared intently at the famous painting.* ♦ *I studied the textbook intently.*

interact [ɪn tɚ 'ækt] **1.** *iv.* to act upon one another. ♦ *Management and staff need to interact more.* ♦ *The party guests are interacting even though most have never met.* **2. interact with** *iv. + prep. phr.* to affect each other; to act upon each other. ♦ *Sales clerks must interact with their customers.* ♦ *The acid interacted with the marble tile before I could clean it up.*

intercede [ɪn tɚ 'sid] **1.** *iv.* to interrupt a disagreement to try to help settle it. ♦ *Whenever I argued with my brother, my parents would intercede.* ♦ *The students fought until their teacher interceded.* **2.** *iv.* to intervene or interrupt on someone's behalf. ♦ *The lawyer interceded on her client's behalf.* ♦ *The translator interceded on the behalf of the foreigner.*

intercept [ɪn tɚ 'sɛpt] *tv.* to stop something as it is moved from one place to another; to seize something as it is moved from one place to another. ♦ *John threw the football to Susan, but Bob intercepted it.* ♦ *I tried to hand a note to Mary, but the teacher intercepted it.*

interchange 1. ['ɪn tɚ tʃendʒ] *n.* an exchange; the switching of someone or something for someone or something else. ♦ *I made a quick interchange of the tire on my bicycle.* ♦ *The coach called for an interchange of two of the players.* **2.** ['ɪn tɚ tʃendʒ] *n.* the junction of two roads, highways, or expressways. ♦ *The highway interchange was blocked by a car accident.* ♦ *At the interchange, take I-55 toward St. Louis.* **3.** [ɪn tɚ 'tʃendʒ] *tv.* to switch two things. ♦ *Bob interchanged the tires on his bicycle.* ♦ *I interchanged my contact lenses by mistake, and as a result, I couldn't see very well.*

interchangeable [ɪn tɚ 'tʃen dʒə bəl] *adj.* able to be interchanged easily; able to be used in place of something else. (Adv: *interchangeably.*) ♦ *The vacuum-cleaner attachments are completely interchangeable.* ♦ *Fortunately, the parts were interchangeable, because I broke one.*

intercom ['ɪn tɚ kam] *n.* an electronic communication system where someone in one place can be heard speaking in another place. ♦ *I sat in my car and placed my fast-food order over an intercom.* ♦ *The principal announced over the intercom that the school bus would be late.*

intercourse ['ɪn tɚ kors] **1.** *n.* communication; interaction. (No plural form in this sense.) ♦ *Because Dave was shy, social intercourse was difficult for him.* ♦ *The sociologist studied the spoken intercourse between people of different cultures.* **2. sexual intercourse.** See sexual ③.

interest ['ɪn trəst] **1.** *n.* the attention or concern shown toward someone or something. (No plural form in this sense.) ♦ *The baby shows interest in bright lights and loud sounds.* ♦ *Jane studied biology with interest.* **2.** *n.* something that causes ①; something that attracts one's curiosity or interests someone. ♦ *Literature is a great interest of mine.* ♦ *The teacher encouraged the students' interest in science.* **3.** *n.* the money—usually a percentage of the amount borrowed—that a lender charges to someone who borrows money. (See interest rate.) ♦ *The bank charged 8% interest on my loan.* ♦ *Last year I paid over $250 in interest on my credit cards.* **4.** *n.* the money—usually a percentage of the amount held—that a bank or other financial institution pays for holding someone's money for a period of time. ♦ *My bank pays only 2% on my savings-account balance.* ♦ *My checking account earns 3%.* **5.** *tv.* to capture the attention of someone or something. ♦ *Does your line of work interest you?* ♦ *Biology interests Jane greatly.* **6. interest in** *tv. + prep. phr.* to tempt someone or something with something. ♦ *Could I interest you in a cup of coffee?* ♦ *The salesman tried to interest me in a new car.* **7. have a vested interest in something** *idiom* to have a personal or biased interest, often financial, in something. ♦ *Margaret has a vested interest in wanting her father to sell the family firm. She has shares in it and would make a large profit.* ♦ *Bob has a vested interest in keeping the village traffic-free. He has a summer home there.* **8. in the interest(s) of someone or something** *idiom* as an advantage or benefit to someone or something; in order to advance or improve someone or something. ♦ *In the interest of health, people are asked not to smoke.* ♦ *The police imprisoned the suspects in the interests of public safety.* **9. in one's (own) (best) interest(s)** *idiom* to one's advantage; as a benefit to oneself. ♦ *It is not in your own interests to share your ideas with Bob. He will say that they are his.* ♦ *Jane thought it was in the best interests of her friend to tell her mother about her illness.* **10. of interest (to someone)** *idiom* interesting to someone. ♦ *This is no longer of any interest.* ♦ *This is of little interest to me.*

interested ['ɪn trəs tɪd] **1. interested (in)** *adj.* (+ *prep. phr.*) curious about something; willing to hear or learn more information; willing to participate; willing to purchase. ♦ *Thank you for the offer, but I'm not interested.* ♦ *I'm interested in seeing a movie tonight.* **2.** *adj.* involved; [of someone] dependent on the outcome or decision. ♦ *All interested parties were eager to hear the judge's decision.* ♦ *Our company is transferring 10 people and will notify the interested individuals tomorrow.*

interesting ['ɪn trəs tɪŋ] *adj.* causing interest or curiosity; worthy of interest; keeping someone's interest. (Adv: *interestingly.*) ♦ *I listened to Anne's interesting story very closely.* ♦ *My grandmother has had a very interesting life.*

interestingly ['ɪn tə rɛs tɪŋ li] **1.** *adv.* in a way that causes or keeps someone's interest. ♦ *The lecture was interestingly presented, using slides, sound, and movies.* ♦ *The mosaic was an interestingly complex design.* **2.** *adv.* strangely; remarkably. ♦ *Interestingly, bears do not really sleep soundly all winter long.* ♦ *Interestingly enough, I, too, have a grandfather named William.*

interest rate ['ɪn trəst ret] **1.** *n.* the fee a lender charges a borrower, expressed as a percentage of the loaned amount. ♦ *The bank charges an 8% interest rate on student loans.* ♦ *Our mortgage is locked in at 9% interest rate.* **2.** *n.* the fee a borrower pays a lender, expressed as a percentage of the borrowed amount. ♦ *The interest rate on my checking account is 2.5%.* ♦ *The floating interest rate on my checking account is determined by the annual inflation rate.*

interfere [ɪn tɚ 'fɪr] **1.** *iv.* to meddle; to get involved [with something that is private or restricted]. ♦ *I am sorry I made that suggestion. I didn't mean to interfere.* ♦ *Please stop interfering. This is none of your business.* **2. interfere with** *iv.* to meddle with someone or something; to create a disturbance for someone or something; to hinder the operation of something. ♦ *My brother always interferes with my private matters.* ♦ *Our neighbor's microwave oven interferes with our television reception.*

interference [ɪn tɚ 'fɪr əns] **1.** *n.* interfering; serving as a barrier or distraction. (No plural form in this sense.) ♦ *This is a private matter and your interference is not welcome.* ♦ *Dave's interference in our problem only made the matter worse.* **2.** *n.* an electronic disturbance that prevents the clear reception of a radio or television signal. (No plural form in this sense.) ♦ *During thunderstorms, we get bad interference on channel 2.* ♦ *I couldn't hear the radio announcer because there was too much interference.*

interfering [ɪn tɚ 'fɪr ɪŋ] *adj.* [of someone] meddling or getting involved [in someone's affairs]. ♦ *Don't pay attention to my grandfather, he's just an interfering old man.* ♦ *I am sure you think I am an interfering mother-in-law, but I have a suggestion.*

interim ['ɪn tɚ ɪm] **1. in the interim (between things)** *phr.* the meantime; the time between the ending of something and the beginning of something else. ♦ *In the interim between her morning and afternoon classes, Susan rushed home to get a book she had forgotten.* ♦ *My favorite show starts in five minutes, but I'll talk to you in the interim.* **2.** *adj.* temporary; for the time being. ♦ *I was chosen as interim president until the next election.* ♦ *A few interim policies were in effect until formal ones were written.*

interior [ɪn 'tɪr i ɚ] **1.** *n.* a part or surface that is inside of something. ♦ *I heard an argument coming from the interior of the house.* ♦ *The building's interior needed to be repaired.* **2.** *n.* the space that is inside something. ♦ *I removed the pulp from the pumpkin's interior.* ♦ *The bear ran deep into the interior of the cave.* **3.** *adj.* <the adj. use of ①.> ♦ *You used interior paint on the kitchen walls, didn't you?* ♦ *The interior dimensions of the frame are 18 inches by 24 inches.*

interj. See interjection.

interjection [ɪn tɚ 'dʒɛk ʃən] *n.* <a word, expression, or phrase that is used to express an emotion.> (Abbreviated *interj.* here.) ♦ *Bob tried to make his boring story more exciting by including a lot of interjections.* ♦ Help! *is an interjection.*

interlude ['ɪn tɚ lud] **1.** *n.* an interval; the period of time between two things. ♦ *My grandmother moved to America during the interlude between the two world wars.* ♦ *I took a short nap in the interlude between the conference and dinner.* **2.** *n.* music played to fill the time between two parts of a play, opera, or radio broadcast. ♦ *The interlude between the second and third scenes of the play put me to sleep.* ♦ *The orchestra played a short interlude between the acts while the scenery was being changed.*

intermediate [ɪn tɚ 'mid i ɪt] *adj.* between two stages, levels, sizes, weights, etc. (Adv: *intermediately.*) ♦ *The express train that runs from Adamsville to Millville skips all the intermediate stops.* ♦ *We only have very small and very large sizes in stock. We've sold all the intermediate sizes.*

intermission [ɪn tɚ 'mɪ ʃən] *n.* a pause between the parts of a play, movie, opera, or other performance. ♦ *During intermission, I read the director's notes in the program.* ♦ *Do I have time to get to the restroom before the intermission ends?*

intermittent [ɪn tɚ 'mɪt nt] *adj.* off and on; stopping and starting; not continuous. (Adv: *intermittently.*) ♦ *I went to a doctor because there was an intermittent buzzing in my ears.* ♦ *We had intermittent rain all day long.*

intern ['ɪn tɚn] **1.** *n.* a doctor who has just finished medical training and is serving as a supervised member of the medical staff of a hospital. ♦ *The intern works 20 hours at a time.* ♦ *The intern assisted the doctor in surgery.* **2.** *n.* a student who is receiving on-the-job experience in addition to classes. ♦ *The newspaper intern worked harder than some of the reporters.* ♦ *I have applied to several law firms to be an intern during the summer.* **3.** *iv.* to have an internship; to serve as an intern. ♦ *John interned at the steel plant during the summer.* ♦ *Mary will intern at the city hospital after she receives her degree in pediatrics.*

internal [ɪn 'tɚ nəl] **1.** *adj.* inside; inner. (Adv: *internally.*) ♦ *Something is wrong with the internal workings of the car's engine.* ♦ *The accident injured some of the driver's internal organs.* **2.** *adj.* coming from within. (Adv: *internally.*) ♦ *In our company, internal memos are posted on the bulletin board.* ♦ *Internal pressures for expansion led the president to purchase another company.* **3.** *adj.* domestic; not foreign. (Adv: *internally.*) ♦ *The president said that our taxation system is an internal matter and is not the* *business of foreign countries.* ♦ *John felt that nations should not meddle with other nations' internal affairs.*

international [ɪn tɚ 'næʃ ə nəl] **1.** *adj.* of or about two or more countries; between two countries; among three or more countries. (Adv: *internationally.*) ♦ *Often, an important river serves as the international border between two countries.* ♦ *Mexico, Canada, and the United States signed an international trade agreement.* **2.** *adj.* global; in all nations. (Adv: *internationally.*) ♦ *After World War I, influenza was an international epidemic.* ♦ *Pollution is an international problem.*

Internet ['ɪn tɚ nɛt] *n.* a digital system of high-speed global communication and data transfer. (No plural form in this sense. Not a proper noun, but usually capitalized. Abbreviated Net.) ♦ *I just received an e-mail message over the Internet!* ♦ *Lisa's computer is hooked up to the Internet and uses a browser to visit different sites around the world.*

interpose [ɪn tɚ 'poz] *tv.* to add comments to an ongoing stream of speech. ♦ *Bill interposed jokes and clever remarks into his lecture.* ♦ *Anne continued to interpose her comments, and John continued to ignore her.*

interpret [ɪn 'tɚ prət] **1.** *tv.* to explain the meaning of something. ♦ *I did read the chapter, but I can't interpret it.* ♦ *A psychoanalyst can help you interpret your dreams.* **2.** *tv.* to translate what someone is saying in one language into another language. ♦ *I interpreted the French tourist's question so the police officer could understand it.* ♦ *Mary interpreted the German speaker's remarks for the English-speaking audience.* **3. interpret for** *iv.* + *prep. phr.* to translate for someone as in ②. ♦ *I would be happy to go to the doctor with you and interpret for you.* ♦ *My mother doesn't speak English, so I interpreted for her when we went shopping.*

interpretation [ɪn tɚ prɪ 'te ʃən] **1.** *n.* an explanation of the meaning of something. ♦ *My teacher's interpretation of the theory helped me understand it.* ♦ *Each student's interpretation of the poem was slightly different.* **2.** *n.* a subjective view or description of an event, experience, or something visual. ♦ *I like your interpretation of my painting.* ♦ *I laughed at my analyst's interpretation of my dreams.*

interpreter [ɪn 'tɚ prɪ tɚ] *n.* someone who translates what someone is saying in one language into another language. ♦ *The United Nations employs dozens of interpreters.* ♦ *There is a Spanish interpreter at the courthouse to help people who speak Spanish.*

interrelated [ɪn tə rɪ 'let əd] *adj.* related; connected; of or about each other. (Adv: *interrelatedly.*) ♦ *Many urban problems, such as drugs, poverty, and crime, are interrelated.* ♦ *Jane's comments and mine are interrelated and we should discuss them together.*

interrog. See interrogative.

interrogate [ɪn 'tɛr ə get] *tv.* to question someone; to ask questions of someone about something, especially a crime. ♦ *The police interrogated Sally about the robbery.* ♦ *The investigator interrogated everyone present during the incident.*

interrogation [ɪn tɛr ə 'ge ʃən] *n.* the process of asking someone a series of questions. ♦ *Was a lawyer present during your interrogation?* ♦ *The prisoner was tortured during his interrogation.*

interrogative [ɪn tə 'rɑg ə tɪv] **1.** *n.* <a word or expression used to ask a question.> (Who, what, when, where, how are the most common interrogatives. Abbreviated *interrog.* here.) ♦ Who *is an interrogative that asks "what person?"* ♦ *Many of the interrogatives in English are also pronouns.* **2.** *adj.* <the adj. use of ①.> ♦ Who *is an interrogative pronoun.* ♦ *The interrogative forms are usually found at the beginning of a sentence.*

interrupt [ɪn tə 'rʌpt] **1.** *iv.* to break into a conversation; to start talking while someone else is talking. ♦ *Would you stop interrupting and let me finish my sentence?* ♦ *Mary was talking about her dog until Dave interrupted with an unrelated comment.* **2.** *tv.* to stop the flow or movement of something; to stop something temporarily. (Figurative on ①.) ♦ *The doctor interrupted the flow of blood with a tourniquet.* ♦ *A three-car accident interrupted the flow of traffic.*

interruption [ɪn tə 'rʌp ʃən] **1.** *n.* interrupting; stopping and interfering in a conversation or an activity. ♦ *Your frequent interruptions during the speech were very rude.* ♦ *Please excuse my interruption, but we have to leave in five minutes.* **2.** *n.* a break in the flow of something. ♦ *We forgot to pay our phone bill so there was an interruption in our service.* ♦ *The sudden interruption in the movement of traffic was caused by an accident a mile away.*

intersect [ɪn tɚ 'sɛkt] **1.** *iv.* [for two things, such as roads, paths, or lines] to touch or cross each other. ♦ *Clark Street and North Avenue intersect near the park.* ♦ *There is smoke coming from where the wires intersect.* **2.** *tv.* [for one thing, such as a road, path, or line] to touch or cross another. ♦ *Elm Terrace intersects Main Street but does not continue on the other side.* ♦ *A path of a black cat intersected my own path.*

intersecting [ɪn tɚ 'sɛk tɪŋ] *adj.* [of things, such as roads, paths, or lines] crossing. ♦ *I was lost in a maze of intersecting streets.* ♦ *The intersecting wires are a fire hazard.*

intersection [ɪn tɚ 'sɛk ʃən] **1.** *n.* the junction of two or more roads, streets, highways, etc.; the place where roads or streets intersect. ♦ *Turn left at the next intersection.* ♦ *My bank is at the intersection of Elm Street and Maple Street.* **2.** *n.* the point at which two or more things join. ♦ *The intersection of the two air ducts is held together with tape.* ♦ *The leak is at the intersection of the two pipes.*

intersperse [ɪn tɚ 'spɚs] *tv.* to place things among other things. ♦ *I interspersed roses among the daisies when I planted the flower garden.* ♦ *The author interspersed useful charts throughout the book.*

interstate ['ɪn tɚ stet] **1.** *adj.* between two states; among three or more states. ♦ *A system of interstate highways connects most major American cities.* ♦ *Interstate commerce is federally regulated.* **2. interstate (highway)** *n.* a highway that is part of the U.S. Interstate Highway System. ♦ *Stay on the interstate until you get to Springfield, and then exit onto 12th Street.* ♦ *The interstate was crowded with people going to the concert.*

interval ['ɪn tɚ vəl] **1.** *n.* a period of time between two events. ♦ *Anne coughed during the short interval between scenes.* ♦ *There's a four-year interval between presidential elections.* **2.** *n.* the distance between two points in a series of points. ♦ *The interval between the lines on the sheets of paper is three-eighths of an inch.* ♦ *The interval between* *the fence posts of our fence is 12 feet.* **3.** *n.* a span of musical tones; the name of the distance between two musical tones. ♦ *An octave is an interval that includes eight full tones.* ♦ *The interval that is called a fifth is one-half an octave.* **4. at regular intervals** *idiom* at points that are equal in distance apart. ♦ *You will find service stations at regular intervals along the highway.* ♦ *There are street lights at regular intervals on the main street of town.*

intervene [ɪn tɚ 'vin] **1.** *iv.* to come between opposing people or groups. ♦ *In the middle of the fight, the police intervened.* ♦ *The brothers wouldn't stop arguing until their mother intervened.* **2.** *iv.* to happen or take place between two other events. ♦ *An unsteady peace intervened between the two world wars.* ♦ *A pause intervened in the middle of the debate as the opponents stopped for a drink of water.* **3.** *iv.* to get involved or interfere with something. ♦ *While I was fixing the computer, my boss intervened and made the problem worse.* ♦ *While I was telling Bob how to get to my house, my roommate intervened and completely confused him.*

intervening [ɪn tɚ 'vin ɪŋ] *adj.* coming between two things. ♦ *John studied the intervening years between the two world wars.* ♦ *In the intervening pause between the two movies, I bought popcorn.*

intervention [ɪn tɚ 'vɛn ʃən] **1.** *n.* an interruption that stops something before something bad happens or before things get worse. ♦ *If it weren't for my intervention, you could have been killed!* ♦ *The army's intervention prevented our enemies from attacking.* **2.** *n.* a confrontation between concerned people and an alcoholic or drug user, with the goal of forcing the alcoholic or drug user into treatment. ♦ *Bob's relatives participated in the intervention and told Bob just how they felt about his alcoholism.* ♦ *Bob was the subject of three different interventions before he finally decided to do something about his problem.*

interview ['ɪn tɚ vju] **1.** *n.* a meeting between an employer and a job seeker, where the employer asks questions of the job seeker. ♦ *During the interview, John truthfully answered every question.* ♦ *I bought a new suit to wear to job interviews.* **2.** *n.* a meeting where a reporter asks questions of someone. ♦ *Did you watch the president's interview last night?* ♦ *The candidate thought her interview with the reporter went very well.* **3.** *tv.* to ask questions of someone, possibly about employment; to make direct inquiries of someone. ♦ *The hotel interviewed 5,000 people for 1,000 jobs.* ♦ *The researcher interviewed people about their drinking habits.* **4.** *tv.* to ask questions of someone for a television or radio show, a newspaper or magazine article, etc. ♦ *The journalist interviewed a former president about life in the White House.* ♦ *The newspaper interviewed the mayor in depth.*

interviewer ['ɪn tɚ vju ɚ] *n.* someone who conducts an interview. ♦ *The interviewer asked me about my previous work experience.* ♦ *The interviewer asked Mary to speak into the microphone.*

intestine [ɪn 'tɛs tɪn] *n.* the digestive tract between the stomach and the anus. ♦ *Susan needed surgery because her intestines were blocked.* ♦ *The long, narrow part of the intestine is called the small intestine.*

intimacy ['ɪn tə mə si] *n.* a close relationship; the condition of being intimate. (No plural form in this sense.) ♦ *Anne's fear of intimacy interfered with her relationships.* ♦ *The couple shared a romantic intimacy that they decided was love.*

intimate 1. ['ɪn tə mɪt] *adj.* close; very personal; private. (Adv: *intimately.*) ♦ *Susan revealed her most intimate thoughts to her close friend.* ♦ *Dave and Mary shared an intimate kiss.* **2.** ['ɪn tə mɪt] *adj.* [of a place] quite, private, friendly, and inviting. (Adv: *intimately.*) ♦ *The intimate surroundings were very romantic.* ♦ *We rented a room at an intimate hotel by a lake.* **3.** ['ɪn tə met] *tv.* to hint something; to suggest something. (Takes a clause.) ♦ *Are you intimating that Jane is quitting school?* ♦ *I don't mean to intimate that you are guilty, but I did see you at the bank just before the robbery.*

intimidate [ɪn 'tɪm ə det] *tv.* to threaten someone; to frighten someone. ♦ *I don't want to intimidate you, but very few people pass this exam.* ♦ *The huge police officer intimidated the young thief.*

intimidating [ɪn 'tɪm ə det ɪŋ] *adj.* threatening; causing fear. (Adv: *intimidatingly.*) ♦ *An intimidating police officer threatened to arrest us for loitering.* ♦ *Intimidating storm clouds blew in from the west.*

into ['ɪn tu] **1.** *prep.* to the inner part of something; to the interior of something. ♦ *I reached into my pocket and pulled out a quarter.* ♦ *I went into the living room to watch TV.* **2.** *prep.* to the middle of something; to a position surrounded by something. ♦ *Jane walked into the group of people and wished them a happy New Year.* ♦ *John threw his hat into the center of the room.* **3.** *prep.* up against. ♦ *John drove the car into a tree.* ♦ *Mary ran into the wall.* **4.** *prep.* interested in something. (Informal.) ♦ *David was into watching hockey every weekend, but he could never get Jane to watch it with him.* ♦ *Mary was into mysteries, especially ones with British detectives.*

intolerable [ɪn 'tɑl ə rə bəl] *adj.* not tolerable; too hard to bear; too difficult to endure. (Adv: *intolerably.*) ♦ *The humid weather last summer was intolerable.* ♦ *I spent an intolerable vacation with three screaming children.*

intolerance [ɪn 'tɑl ə rəns] **1.** *n.* lack of respect toward people or things that are different from what one is used to. (No plural form in this sense.) ♦ *Bob's intolerance of foreigners is appalling.* ♦ *Intolerance and prejudice are often practiced by the same people.* **2.** *n.* the inability to endure something; the refusal to endure something. (No plural form in this sense.) ♦ *The teacher's intolerance of tardiness is justifiable.* ♦ *I have a severe intolerance for waiting in lines.* **3.** *n.* the inability to digest certain foods. (No plural form in this sense.) ♦ *John has an intolerance for dairy products.* ♦ *After years of being a vegetarian, Mary's body developed an intolerance to meat.*

intolerant [ɪn 'tɑl ə rənt] **1.** *adj.* lacking respect toward people or things that are different from what one is used to. (Adv: *intolerantly.*) ♦ *My neighbors are intolerant and do not like the color of my skin.* ♦ *My intolerant uncle is very prejudiced.* **2.** *adj.* unable to digest certain foods. (Often preceded by the name of the food that is not tolerated.) ♦ *Lactose-intolerant people are not able to digest milk.* ♦ *David couldn't eat most bakery goods because he was yeast intolerant.*

intoxicate [ɪn 'tɑk sə ket] *tv.* [for something] to cause someone to become drunk. ♦ *Alcohol intoxicates me rather quickly.* ♦ *The alcoholic punch intoxicated all the guests as the evening progressed.*

intoxicated [ɪn 'tɑk sə ket ɪd] *adj.* drunk; having had too much alcohol. (Adv: *intoxicatedly.*) ♦ *I took the car keys away from all the intoxicated guests.* ♦ *The intoxicated college student fell down.*

intoxicating [ɪn 'tɑk sə ket ɪŋ] *adj.* causing drunkenness. (Adv: *intoxicatingly.*) ♦ *The intoxicating punch contained vodka and gin.* ♦ *German beer is usually more intoxicating than American beer.*

intoxication [ɪn tɑk sə 'ke ʃən] *n.* drunkenness. (No plural form in this sense.) ♦ *Because of Mary's intoxication, her friends wouldn't let her drive.* ♦ *No one noticed Bill's intoxication until he spoke haltingly.*

intransitive verb [ɪn 'træn sə tɪv 'vɚb] *n.* a verb not taking a direct object. (Abbreviated *iv.* here.) ♦ *"Sleep" is an intransitive verb.* ♦ *"John eats" is a sentence containing an intransitive verb.*

intravenous [ɪn trə 'vin əs] *adj.* intended for a vein. (Adv: *intravenously.*) ♦ *The intravenous solution dripped into the patient's bloodstream.* ♦ *The nurse gave me an intravenous injection.*

intrepid [in 'trɛp ɪd] *adj.* daring; bold; without fear. (Adv: *intrepidly.*) ♦ *The soldier fascinated people with stories of his intrepid adventures.* ♦ *The intrepid explorers reached the South Pole.*

intricate ['ɪn trə kɪt] **1.** *adj.* complex; involving many parts. (Adv: *intricately.*) ♦ *The explorers were lost in an intricate maze of tunnels.* ♦ *The human eye is a very intricate part of the body.* **2.** *adj.* detailed. (Adv: *intricately.*) ♦ *Jane's intricate drawings fascinated her friends.* ♦ *On the wall, tiny pieces of tile form an intricate design.*

intrigue [ɪn 'trig] **1.** *n.* planning and plotting in a deceitful way. (No plural form in this sense.) ♦ *Spies and smugglers are involved in the kind of intrigue that makes good novels.* ♦ *There is too much intrigue and gossip in my job, so I am going to quit.* **2.** *tv.* to interest someone; to make someone curious. ♦ *John's mysterious past intrigued Mary.* ♦ *Anne's career in banking intrigued Bill.*

intrigued [ɪn 'trigd] *adj.* interested; curious. ♦ *The former president spoke to the intrigued audience.* ♦ *The intrigued reporter researched the facts surrounding the bank robbery.*

intriguing [ɪn 'trig ɪŋ] *adj.* interesting; causing curiosity or interest. (Adv: *intriguingly.*) ♦ *The reporter wrote an intriguing story about the moon.* ♦ *My grandfather has many intriguing stories about his childhood.*

intrinsic [ɪn 'trɪn sɪk] *adj.* [of something abstract] essential and inherent. (Adv: *intrinsically* [...ɪk li].) ♦ *Timing is an intrinsic part of comedy.* ♦ *Paying careful attention and responding quickly are intrinsic parts of good driving.*

introduce [ɪn trə 'dus] **1. introduce (to)** *tv.* (+ *prep. phr.*) to present someone to someone else when they meet for the first time. ♦ *John introduced Bill and Sue to each other.* ♦ *We have not been introduced.* **2. introduce to** *tv.* + *prep. phr.* to show someone something for the first time. ♦ *Last week, I introduced Tom to the pleasure of cross-country skiing.* ♦ *We introduced the baby to ice cream.* **3.** *tv.* to establish something; to bring something into use. ♦ *The company first introduced the new product in the Chicago area.* ♦ *A new model of the car was introduced in Los Angeles last week.*

introduction [ɪn trə 'dʌk ʃən] **1.** *n.* the presentation of one person to another person. ♦ *I bungled the introduction because I had forgotten the man's name.* ♦ *The meeting began with the introductions of the new staff members.* **2.** *n.* making the availability of something known to people. ♦ *The company planned an introduction of its new products for the fall.* ♦ *The introduction of the new book was delayed.* **3.** *n.* the first part of a book, chapter, or lecture that explains its purpose. ♦ *The introduction to the book is only a few pages long.* ♦ *The introduction of the biology textbook began with a quote from Darwin.* **4.** *n.* a basic presentation of essential information about a subject. ♦ *This book provides a good introduction to algebra.* ♦ *This class is meant to be an introduction to logic.*

introductory [ɪn trə 'dʌk tə ri] *adj.* preliminary; introducing a subject. (Adv: *introductorily.*) ♦ *The introductory chapters can be skipped if you are familiar with the subject.* ♦ *The introductory Spanish class was too easy for Susan.*

intrude [ɪn 'trud] **intrude ((up)on)** *iv.* (+ *prep. phr.*) to enter uninvited. ♦ *I don't mean to intrude, but you have a telephone call.* ♦ *Bill intruded upon our meeting, but we ignored him.*

intruder [ɪn 'trud ɚ] **1.** *n.* someone who enters without an invitation; someone who intrudes. ♦ *The meeting continued after the intruder left.* ♦ *When intruders were discovered in the office building, the police were called.* **2.** *n.* a robber; a criminal; someone who breaks into a house or building. ♦ *An intruder stole our television set.* ♦ *The security guard apprehended the intruder.*

intrusion [ɪn 'tru ʒən] **1.** *n.* intruding; entering into a situation where one is not wanted; a visit that is not welcome. ♦ *Bill's intrusion into the conversation was unwelcome.* ♦ *Your questions are an intrusion on my privacy.* **2.** *n.* breaking into a house or other building. ♦ *The intrusions took place after midnight.* ♦ *Three men were charged in the intrusion of the office building.*

intuition [ɪn tu 'ɪʃ ən] **1.** *n.* insight or perception not based on facts. (No plural form in this sense.) ♦ *My intuition tells me that you're right.* ♦ *I have good intuition when it comes to judging people.* **2.** *n.* a feeling about something; a hunch. ♦ *I have an intuition that it will rain today.* ♦ *Mary always followed her intuitions about people.*

intuitive [ɪn 'tu ə tɪv] *adj.* resulting from intuition. (Adv: *intuitively.*) ♦ *Anne had an intuitive distrust for her landlord.* ♦ *I had an intuitive sense of what the movie was about.*

intuitively [ɪn 'tu ɪ tɪv li] *adv.* in an intuitive way. ♦ *Bill intuitively knew that he and Bob would become friends.* ♦ *Intuitively, Susan knew her children were in danger.*

Inuit ['ɪn u ɪt] **1.** *n.* the native people of northern Canada, Alaska, and Greenland; the Eskimo people of northern Canada, Alaska, and Greenland. (No plural form in this sense. **Inuit** is a plural form. Some people use this term for all Eskimos.) ♦ *Many Inuit live north of the Arctic Circle.* ♦ *How many Inuit live in the capital of Greenland, and do they speak Danish?* **2.** *n.* a language used by ①. ♦ *The word for people in Inuit is* Inuit. ♦ *Some varieties of Inuit are written in a special alphabet.* **3.** *adj.* <the adj. use of ①.> ♦ *The Inuit artists carved beautiful stone sculptures of animals.* ♦ *There are numerous Inuit villages in northern Canada.*

inundate ['ɪn ən det] **1.** *tv.* to flood something; to cover something with water; to swamp something. ♦ *The rainstorm inundated the baseball field, so the game was canceled.* ♦ *A huge flood inundated the valley.* **2.** *tv.* to overwhelm someone or something with something; to cover something with large amounts of something. (Figurative on ①.) ♦ *My desk is inundated with paperwork.* ♦ *The angry customers inundated the clerk with complaints.*

invade [ɪn 'ved] **1.** *tv.* to enter and attack a country or place. ♦ *The Japanese invaded Pearl Harbor on December 7, 1941.* ♦ *World War II began when Germany invaded Poland in 1939.* **2.** *tv.* [for pests, bacteria, etc.] to enter a place and spread throughout. (Figurative on ①.) ♦ *The red ants invaded our picnic.* ♦ *Harmful bacteria had invaded my bloodstream causing a disease.* **3.** *tv.* to enter a place and cause a disturbance. (Figurative on ①.) ♦ *A few strangers invaded the party, but left when we threatened to call the police.* ♦ *Protesters invaded city hall demanding more jobs.*

invader [ɪn 'ved ɚ] *n.* an attacker; someone or something that invades. ♦ *The invaders surrounded and attacked the city at dawn.* ♦ *The invaders were sent out by the police.*

invading [ɪn 'ved ɪŋ] *adj.* attacking; entering by force. ♦ *The invading forces conquered the territory within a week.* ♦ *We dropped bombs on the invading army.*

invalid 1. ['ɪn və lɪd] *n.* someone who is weak because of sickness. ♦ *The invalid was ordered to remain in bed.* ♦ *My mother has been an invalid since her stroke.* **2.** ['ɪn və lɪd] *adj.* <the adj. use of ①.> ♦ *My invalid uncle is confined to bed.* ♦ *Tom visits his invalid mother once a week.* **3.** [ɪn 'væl ɪd] *adj.* not valid; useless; worthless. (Adv: *invalidly.*) ♦ *The thief was caught trying to use an invalid credit card.* ♦ *This coupon is invalid after the end of the month.*

invaluable [ɪn 'væl ju ə bəl] *adj.* priceless; very valuable; impossible to determine the value of. (The *in* is emphatic here. Adv: *invaluably.*) ♦ *The princess kept her invaluable jewels in a secure vault.* ♦ *Your friendship is invaluable to me.*

invariable [ɪn 'vɛr i ə bəl] *adj.* unchanging; constant. (Adv: *invariably.*) ♦ *The invariable interest rate on my savings account is 5%.* ♦ *The train's schedule is invariable. Every day it comes at 10:00, 1:00, and 5:00.*

invariably [ɪn 'vɛr i ə bli] *adv.* in every instance. ♦ *David invariably makes stupid jokes during dinner.* ♦ *Whenever I go camping, it invariably rains.*

invasion [ɪn 've ʒən] **1.** *n.* a military attack. ♦ *World War II began with the German invasion of Poland.* ♦ *The invasion of Pearl Harbor occurred on December 7, 1941.* **2.** *n.* the attack and spread of something bad or dangerous. (Figurative on ①.) ♦ *An invasion of locusts ate our crops.* ♦ *The child's body could not fight another invasion of disease organisms.* **3. invasion of privacy** *phr.* an intrusion that results in the loss of someone's privacy. ♦ *Your invasion of my privacy is not welcome!* ♦ *The athlete complained about the invasion of his privacy by the press.*

invent [ɪn 'vɛnt] **1.** *tv.* to create something that has never been made before. ♦ *Thomas Edison invented the light bulb.* ♦ *Alexander Graham Bell invented the telephone.* **2.** *tv.* to make up an excuse or a lie. (Figurative on ①.) ♦ *John invented an alibi to avoid punishment.* ♦ *Anne invented an excuse for why she didn't go to the party.*

invention [ɪn 'vɛn ʃən] *n.* a new device; the production of a new machine or a new process. ♦ *Before the invention of the printing press, books were copied by hand.* ♦ *The invention of the airplane eventually made travel faster and easier.*

inventive [ɪn 'vɛn tɪv] *adj.* able to invent things; creative; able to make things from the resources one has. (Adv: *inventively.*) ♦ *Thomas Edison was very inventive.* ♦ *The corporation took credit for its inventive employee's idea.*

inventor [ɪn 'vɛn tɚ] *n.* someone who invents something; someone who has invented something. ♦ *Thomas Jefferson was a president and an inventor.* ♦ *The inventor of the telephone was Alexander Graham Bell.*

inventory ['ɪn vən tor i] **1.** *n.* goods and supplies in hand or stored in a warehouse; stock waiting to be sold. (No plural form in this sense.) ♦ *How much inventory of this item do we have left?* ♦ *The roof leaked and ruined a lot of the current inventory.* **2.** *n.* a list showing the number of each item that has been packed, received, shipped, etc. ♦ *The clerk checked the inventory to see if large paper clips were available.* ♦ *Please send a copy of the inventory to the main office.* **3. take inventory** *idiom* to make ②. ♦ *They are taking inventory in the warehouse, counting each item and writing the number on a list.* ♦ *The hardware store closed once a year in order to take inventory.*

invert [ɪn 'vɚt] *tv.* to turn something upside down. ♦ *I inverted the glasses so the water would drain out of them.* ♦ *Jane inverted the bucket and dumped out the sand.*

invertebrate [ɪn 'vɚ tə bret] **1.** *n.* a type of animal that does not have a spine; a type of animal without a backbone. ♦ *Worms and flies are examples of invertebrates.* ♦ *We're studying invertebrates in biology class.* **2.** *adj.* lacking a backbone. ♦ *Shellfish are invertebrate animals.* ♦ *There are no invertebrate mammals.*

invest [ɪn 'vɛst] **1.** *tv.* to put one's money in a bank to earn interest. ♦ *I invest half of every paycheck.* ♦ *Jimmy invested his allowance in a savings account.* **2.** *tv.* to buy stocks or shares in a company to earn a part of the profits. ♦ *I invested heavily in a software company.* ♦ *Bill invested $1,500 in his company's stock.* **3. invest something in someone or something** *idiom* to place power under control of someone or something. ♦ *The constitution has invested certain powers in the federal government and left the rest to the states.* ♦ *The law invests the power to arrest criminals in the sheriff's department.* **4. invest someone with something** *idiom* to endow someone with something, such as power or privilege. ♦ *The constitution invests the vice president with the authority to act on the president's behalf in certain conditions.* ♦ *The state has invested me with the authority to unite this couple in marriage.* **5. invest someone's time in something** *idiom* to put one's time, effort, or energy into a project. ♦ *Mary invests her time in charity work.* ♦ *I invested five weeks of my time building this model ship.*

investigate [ɪn 'vɛs tə get] *tv.* to conduct an investigation; to try to find the facts of something. ♦ *The police will investigate the violent murder.* ♦ *A reporter investigated the banking scandal.*

investigation [ɪn vɛs tə 'ge ʃən] *n.* a search for information; an attempt to find out as much information about something as possible. ♦ *The investigation into the murder involved questioning many witnesses.* ♦ *The results* *of the investigation indicated that no crime had been committed.*

investigator [ɪn 'vɛs tə get ɚ] *n.* someone who conducts an investigation; a detective; someone who investigates an insurance claim. ♦ *The investigator asked the witness dozens of questions.* ♦ *Investigators searched the crime scene for clues.*

investment [ɪn 'vɛst mənt] *n.* money that is invested in a project, stocks, a bank account, etc. ♦ *John's $2,500 investment yielded a profit when he sold the stock two years later.* ♦ *You must pay taxes on the interest from investments.*

investor [ɪn 'vɛs tɚ] *n.* someone who puts money into an investment. ♦ *The investor lost all of his money in the stock-market crash.* ♦ *The movie studios rejected Anne's script, so she found private investors to finance it.*

invigorate [ɪn 'vɪg ə ret] *tv.* to give new strength and vigor to someone or something. ♦ *The massage invigorated my tired body.* ♦ *A quick breath of fresh air invigorated me and I went back to work with more energy.*

invigorating [ɪn 'vɪg ə re tɪŋ] *adj.* refreshing; causing one to feel refreshed; full of vigor. (Adv: *invigoratingly.*) ♦ *I need an invigorating shower in the morning to wake me up.* ♦ *An invigorating breath of fresh air gave me new energy.*

invisible [ɪn 'vɪz ə bəl] *adj.* not visible; unable to be seen; not seen and imaginary. (Adv: *invisibly.*) ♦ *The joint in our kitchen counter top is almost invisible.* ♦ *Oxygen is an invisible gas.*

invitation [ɪn vɪ 'te ʃən] **1.** *n.* a request for someone to attend an event; a request for someone to come for a visit. ♦ *Thank you for the invitation, but I really can't come to the wedding.* ♦ *You have an invitation to visit us whenever you want.* **2.** *n.* a written, printed, or verbal form of ①. ♦ *Susan mailed the invitations six weeks before the wedding.* ♦ *I called her yesterday with our invitation.* **3.** *n.* something that tempts or lures trouble or a problem. (Figurative on ①.) ♦ *Your skimpy bikini is just an invitation for trouble.* ♦ *Failing to lock your doors at night is an invitation to disaster.*

invite [ɪn 'vɑɪt] **1.** *tv.* to request someone to attend an event; to ask someone to come for a visit; to ask someone to join in doing something. ♦ *John and Mary invited 200 people to their wedding.* ♦ *Anne invited me to her house for the holidays.* **2.** *tv.* to tempt something to happen; to provoke something to happen, especially disaster or trouble. (Figurative on ①.) ♦ *You invite trouble when you go out dressed like that.* ♦ *John invited disaster by forgetting to shut the gas off.*

inviting [ɪn 'vɑɪt ɪŋ] *adj.* tempting; intriguing; attractive. (Adv: *invitingly.*) ♦ *Mary's warm and inviting charm made me feel welcome.* ♦ *The restaurant appeared to be cozy and inviting, so we ate there.*

invoice ['ɪn vɔɪs] **1.** *n.* a bill; a document showing how much money is owed for goods or services. ♦ *Before we can pay you, you must send us an invoice.* ♦ *John mailed his invoice directly to the accounting department.* **2.** *tv.* to present someone or a business firm with ①. ♦ *The lawyer invoiced the company for 30 hours of work.* ♦ *The contractor invoiced the Smiths before remodeling their kitchen.*

involuntarily [ɪn vɑl ən 'tɛr ɪ li] *adv.* automatically; without thought or intention. ♦ *Your leg jerks involuntarily if you hit your kneecap a certain way.* ♦ *We breathe involuntarily. Otherwise, we would never get any sleep!*

involuntary [ɪn 'vɑl ən tɛr i] **1.** *adj.* automatic; without thought or intention. (Adv: *involuntarily* [ɪn vɑl ən 'tɛr ə li].) ♦ *Breathing is an involuntary body function.* ♦ *I thanked the cashier, and his involuntary response was "Have a nice day!"* **2.** *adj.* [chosen or commanded] without volunteering; unwillingly. (Adv: *involuntarily* [ɪn vɑl ən 'tɛr ə li].) ♦ *I was sent involuntarily to the company's offices in Brazil.* ♦ *Jimmy went involuntarily to the wedding.*

involve [ɪn 'vɔlv] *tv.* to include someone or something; to make someone or something a part of something. ♦ *This project involves a lot of hard work.* ♦ *The accident involved many cars.*

involved [ɪn 'vɔlvd] **1.** *adj.* complicated. ♦ *The directions to the cabin were very involved.* ♦ *It was difficult to follow the movie's involved plot.* **2. involved (with)** *adj.* (+ *prep. phr.*) associated with or connected to someone or something. ♦ *I don't want to be involved with you anymore!* ♦ *Mary tried not to get involved with the troublesome issue.* **3. involved (in)** *adj.* (+ *prep. phr.*) included in something; being part of something. ♦ *Are you involved in this discussion? If not, be quiet.* ♦ *I'd prefer not to be involved in your illegal plan.*

involvement [ɪn 'vɔlv mənt] *n.* the state of being involved. (No plural form in this sense.) ♦ *I appreciate your involvement in organizing the conference.* ♦ *Bob was arrested for his involvement in the war protest.*

invulnerable [ɪn 'vʌl nə rə bəl] *adj.* not vulnerable; not able to be hurt; not able to be damaged. (Adv: *invulnerably.*) ♦ *My watch is invulnerable to water damage.* ♦ *The invulnerable fortress withstood the attack.*

inward ['ɪn wɚd] **1.** *adv.* toward the middle of something; toward the inside of something. ♦ *I moved inward because I was blocking the doorway.* ♦ *The bullet struck the wall and plunged inward.* **2.** *adv.* [turning] toward one's inner thoughts. ♦ *When I am alone, my thoughts turn inward.* ♦ *Once alone, Anne's mind turned inward.*

inwardly ['ɪn wɚd li] **1.** *adv.* in one's own, private thoughts. ♦ *I inwardly examined my conscience.* ♦ *Inwardly, I felt confused.* **2.** *adv.* inward; toward the middle of something. ♦ *The mouse ran inwardly to the center of the maze.* ♦ *The boxers stood in opposite corners and moved inwardly when the bell rang.*

iodine ['ɑɪ ə dɑɪn] *n.* a dark-colored, nonmetallic chemical element. (No plural form in this sense.) ♦ *The atomic symbol for iodine is I, and its atomic number is 53.* ♦ *Iodine is made into a common disinfectant.*

iota [ɑɪ 'ot ə] *n.* a very small amount. (Usually in the negative.) ♦ *Clean your room! I don't want one iota of dust here when I get back!* ♦ *John would not compromise at all. Not one iota.*

Iowa ['ɑɪ ə wə] See Gazetteer.

I.Q. ['ɑɪ 'kju] *n.* "intelligence quotient," a measure of a person's intelligence. ♦ *A genius is someone who has an I.Q. over 140.* ♦ *Everyone at this university seems to have a high I.Q.*

ir- *prefix* See in ⑫ and ⑬.

Iran [ɪ 'ræn] See Gazetteer.

Iraq [ɪ 'ræk] See Gazetteer.

irate ['ɑɪ ret] *adj.* very angry; very mad; very upset. (Adv: *irately.*) ♦ *The irate teacher demanded to know who broke the window.* ♦ *Jane was very irate because her roommate didn't clean the kitchen.*

Ireland ['ɑɪr lənd] See Gazetteer.

irides ['ɪr ə diz] a pl of iris.

iridium [ɪ 'rɪd i əm] *n.* a metallic chemical element used in surgical tools, in bearings, and in high-heat applications. (No plural form in this sense.) ♦ *The atomic symbol of iridium is Ir, and its atomic weight is 77.* ♦ *The researcher found a new technological use for iridium.*

iris ['ɑɪ rɪs] **1.** *n., irreg.* a kind of tall garden flower. (Pl: *irises* or irides.) ♦ *I put some irises in the vase on the table.* ♦ *Bill accidentally mowed down the irises with the lawn mower.* **2.** *n., irreg.* the colored part of the eyeball, around the pupil. ♦ *The iris controls the size of the pupil.* ♦ *Bill's dark brown shirt matched his irises.*

Irish ['ɑɪ rɪʃ] **1. the Irish** *n.* the people of Ireland. (No plural form in this sense. Treated as plural.) ♦ *The Irish live on a beautiful island that seems very, very green.* ♦ *We have visited the Irish and hope to return to Ireland.* **2.** *adj.* of or about Ireland or ①. ♦ *The Irish landscape is scenic and peaceful.* ♦ *My aunt collects Irish crystal.*

irk ['ɝk] *tv.* to annoy, upset, or irritate someone. ♦ *It really irks me when you bite your nails.* ♦ *We can't chew gum in class because it irks our teacher.*

iron ['ɑɪɚn] **1.** *n.* an element that is a common metal, used to make steel. (No plural form in this sense.) ♦ *The iron was cast into huge blocks.* ♦ *Anne ate a healthy meal rich in iron, zinc, and vitamin C.* **2.** *n.* a small device with a flat metal bottom, used heated to press the wrinkles out of cloth. ♦ *The old iron made a burn mark on my shirt.* ♦ *Don't forget to unplug the iron before you leave.* **3.** *adj.* made from ①. ♦ *I threw the iron horseshoe toward the stake.* ♦ *The rusted iron gate needed repair.* **4.** *tv.* to smooth the wrinkles out of clothes with ②. ♦ *John ironed a shirt every night for work the next day.* ♦ *I ironed the heavily wrinkled tablecloth.*

ironclad ['ɑɪɚn 'klæd] **1.** *adj.* covered with iron. ♦ *The rusty old ironclad ship had sunk years ago.* ♦ *The ironclad statue was too heavy for me to move.* **2.** *adj.* solid; rigid. (Figurative on ①.) ♦ *I had an ironclad excuse for missing class.* ♦ *Anne is not a suspect in the crime because her alibi is ironclad.*

ironic [ɑɪ 'rɑn ɪk] *adj.* using irony; showing irony. (Adv: *ironically* [...ɪk li].) ♦ *It was ironic that we didn't have snow until the first day of spring.* ♦ *I find it ironic that my check came in the mail just after I returned from the bank.*

ironing ['ɑɪɚ nɪŋ] *n.* a batch of clothes that need to be ironed. (No plural form in this sense.) ♦ *Leave the ironing for me to do when I get home.* ♦ *Here's a pile of ironing that needs to be done.*

irony ['ɑɪ rə ni] **1.** *n.* using words to have a meaning opposite from their literal meaning in a funny or sarcastic way. (No plural form in this sense.) ♦ *Did you mean to say that you liked the rainy weather, or were you attempting irony?* ♦ *Did you mean what you wrote, or were you using irony?* **2.** *n.* an event that has the opposite result of what was planned or expected. ♦ *The unexpected irony of finding my wallet on my dresser after I reported it stolen made me laugh.* ♦ *The irony was that it rained the entire time we were on vacation.*

irradiate [ɪ 'red i et] *tv.* to treat something with radiation; to treat food with radiation to keep it from spoiling. ♦ *The lettuce was irradiated before it was shipped.* ♦ *Very few food processors irradiate their produce.*

irrational [ɪr 'ræʃ ə nəl] **1.** *adj.* not rational; not using logic or reason. (Adv: *irrationally.*) ♦ *Your arguments are irrational and silly.* ♦ *Your argument against the project is irrational and cannot influence the decision.* **2.** *adj.* acting in a crazy or insane manner. (Adv: *irrationally.*) ♦ *The medicine caused Aunt Mary to become a little irrational and do things like take the coffee pot to bed with her.* ♦ *An irrational passenger shouted at the other subway riders.* **3. irrational number** *phr.* a number not expressible as a fraction. ♦ *The square root of 2 is an irrational number.* ♦ *Did you get an irrational number for the answer to question 3?*

irreconcilable [ɪr rɛk ən 'sɑɪl ə bəl] *adj.* not reconcilable; [of a problem] not able to be settled or solved; not able to be brought into harmony with something else. (Adv: *irreconcilably.*) ♦ *The couple divorced because of irreconcilable differences.* ♦ *My opinions were irreconcilable with those of everyone else, so I left the meeting.*

irredeemable [ɪr rɪ 'dim ə bəl] **1.** *adj.* not able to be exchanged; not able to be paid off. ♦ *These coupons are irredeemable in this state.* ♦ *These tickets are irredeemable once you purchase them.* **2.** *adj.* hopeless; beyond redemption; not able to be repaired or restored. (Adv: *irredeemably.*) ♦ *Your manners are irredeemable.* ♦ *The mayor's death is an irredeemable loss to this city.*

irrefutable [ɪr rɪ 'fjut ə bəl] *adj.* not able to be refuted; not able to be denied. (Adv: *irrefutably.*) ♦ *That the earth revolves around the sun is irrefutable.* ♦ *Why do you continue to ignore irrefutable facts?*

irreg. See irregular ④.

irregular [ɪr 'rɛg jə lɚ] **1.** *adj.* not regular; oddly shaped; uneven. (Adv: *irregularly.*) ♦ *Your haircut looks quite irregular. Did you cut it yourself?* ♦ *The fluffy cloud has an irregular shape.* **2.** *adj.* happening at differing intervals of time; not happening regularly. (Adv: *irregularly.*) ♦ *I made irregular business trips to New York throughout the year.* ♦ *My access to a computer is irregular, so don't expect a prompt reply to your e-mail message.* **3.** *adj.* different from what is normal, and therefore unacceptable. (Euphemistic.) ♦ *Your request to leave early is highly irregular.* ♦ *The teacher told Tom's father that Tom's behavior was quite irregular and that the school would not tolerate it.* **4.** *adj.* [of the form of a noun, verb, adjective, or adverb] not regular in the way it takes suffixes, such as the plural, past tense, comparative, or superlative. (Abbreviated *irreg.* here. Adv: *irregularly.*) ♦ *The verb* take *has an irregular past-tense form:* took. ♦ Geese *is the irregular plural form of* goose.

irrelevant [ɪr 'rɛl ə vənt] *adj.* not relevant; having nothing to do with what is being discussed. (Adv: *irrelevantly.*) ♦ *It is rude to interrupt with irrelevant comments.* ♦ *Bob's comments about religion were irrelevant to our discussion about politics.*

irreligious [ɪr rɪ 'lɪdʒ əs] **1.** *adj.* not religious; not caring about religion. (Adv: *irreligiously.*) ♦ *I don't go to church because I'm irreligious.* ♦ *I am indeed irreligious,* *but that doesn't mean I lack a spiritual component to my life.* **2.** *adj.* hostile to religion. (Adv: *irreligiously.*) ♦ *The mayor was heavily criticized for his irreligious remarks.* ♦ *A newspaper editorial made an irreligious attack on the problems of a local church.*

irremediable [ɪr rɪ 'mid i ə bəl] *adj.* not remediable; not repairable; not able to be fixed. (Adv: *irremediably.*) ♦ *The rift between the couple was irremediable and they split up.* ♦ *The labor union and management were locked in an irremediable dispute.*

irreparable [ɪr 'rɛp ə rə bəl] **1.** *adj.* not able to be repaired; not able to be fixed. (Adv: *irreparably.*) ♦ *The toaster was irreparable, so we bought a new one.* ♦ *A wall of the old church collapsed, leaving the building irreparable.* **2.** *adj.* [of harm or damage] permanent. (Adv: *irreparably.*) ♦ *Your heartless comments have caused irreparable harm to my reputation.* ♦ *The newspaper editorial did irreparable damage to our efforts to defeat the corrupt city officials.*

irreplaceable [ɪr rɪ 'ples ə bəl] *adj.* not replaceable; not able to be replaced. (Adv: *irreplaceably.*) ♦ *Don't drop that vase. It's irreplaceable.* ♦ *Our dog was irreplaceable. So when he died, we got a cat.*

irrepressible [ɪr rɪ 'prɛs ə bəl] *adj.* not repressible; not able to be repressed; not able to be controlled, restrained, or limited. (Adv: *irrepressibly.*) ♦ *The surging flood was irrepressible.* ♦ *John vented his irrepressible anger on his employees.*

irreproachable [ɪr rɪ 'pro tʃə bəl] *adj.* without blame; without fault. (Adv: *irreproachably.*) ♦ *The minister led a quiet, irreproachable life.* ♦ *Your intentions were irreproachable, but the result was very bad, indeed.*

irresistible [ɪ rɪ 'zɪs tə bəl] *adj.* not able to be resisted; overpowering; fascinating. (Adv: *irresistibly.*) ♦ *This cake is so irresistible that I can't stop eating it!* ♦ *I had an irresistible urge to hug the man who saved my life.*

irrespective [ɪr rɪ 'spɛk tɪv] **irrespective of** *adj. + prep. phr.* regardless of; without taking something into account. ♦ *I want you to be at the wedding, on time, irrespective of your feelings about having to dress up!* ♦ *Irrespective of Anne's wishes, I quit my job.*

irresponsible [ɪr rɪ 'spɑn sə bəl] *adj.* not responsible; reckless; not showing care or responsibility for someone or something. (Adv: *irresponsibly.*) ♦ *The irresponsible parents let their children run loose in the store.* ♦ *You're too irresponsible to work in a hospital!*

irretrievable [ɪr rɪ 'triv ə bəl] *adj.* not able to be retrieved; not able to be recovered. (Adv: *irretrievably.*) ♦ *The data file is irretrievable because you deleted it.* ♦ *The bodies buried under tons of rubble are irretrievable.*

irreverent [ɪr 'rɛv (ə) rənt] **1.** *adj.* not showing reverence; showing a lack of respect, sometimes with humor. (Adv: *irreverently.*) ♦ *Mary's aunt told her that it is irreverent to chew gum in church.* ♦ *It is irreverent to address the priest as "Dad."* **2.** *adj.* cleverly critical of someone or something. (Adv: *irreverently.*) ♦ *John was known for his irreverent remarks about the company president.* ♦ *Jane uttered an irreverent aside to Mary and made her giggle during the lecture.*

irreversible [ɪr rɪ 'vɚ sə bəl] *adj.* not reversible; not able to be reversed. (Adv: *irreversibly.*) ♦ *Once this operation is done, it is irreversible.* ♦ *My decision to work in California is irreversible because I've already signed a contract.*

irrevocable [ɪr 'rɛv ə kə bəl] *adj.* not able to be revoked; not able to be changed. (Adv: *irrevocably.*) ♦ *John signed an irrevocable one-year contract.* ♦ *I made an irrevocable gift of $10,000 to the city.*

irrigate ['ɪr ə get] *tv.* to supply land or crops with water; to bring water to land or crops. ♦ *The farmer irrigated the crops with water from the reservoir.* ♦ *Anne irrigated her lawn with a hose during the drought.*

irrigated ['ɪr ə get ɪd] *adj.* watered; supplied with water. ♦ *The irrigated fields yielded a large harvest.* ♦ *All of the land in this valley is irrigated.*

irrigation [ɪr ə 'ge ʃən] *n.* bringing water to crops or land by using pipes or artificial canals. (No plural form in this sense.) ♦ *Irrigation can bring water to crops from distant sources.* ♦ *The water used for irrigation was piped in from the mountains.*

irritable ['ɪr ɪt ə bəl] *adj.* easily upset; easily angered; grouchy. (Adv: *irritably.*) ♦ *Dave didn't sleep much last night, so he's very irritable today.* ♦ *John was irritable because he was stuck in traffic for over an hour.*

irritant ['ɪr ɪ tənt] **1.** *n.* someone or something that irritates; someone or something that causes irritation. ♦ *Smoke is an irritant that causes my eyes to water.* ♦ *Bleach is an irritant that can damage your skin.* **2.** *n.* an annoyance. ♦ *The repeated false fire alarms were quite an irritant.* ♦ *If you weren't such an unpleasant irritant, I might be nicer to you.*

irritate ['ɪr ɪ tet] **1.** *tv.* to rub on or abrade the skin; to cause a part of the body to become reddened or swollen. ♦ *The liquid detergent irritated my skin.* ♦ *The smoke irritates my eyes.* **2.** *tv.* to bother someone or something; to annoy someone or something; to pester someone or something. ♦ *My little sister irritates me when I try to study.* ♦ *I was irritated by my roommate's loud music.*

irritated ['ɪr ɪ tet əd] *adj.* inflamed; reddened; swollen. (Adv: *irritatedly.*) ♦ *I soothed my irritated skin with lotion.* ♦ *My irritated eyes began to water.*

irritating ['ɪr ɪ tet ɪŋ] **1.** *adj.* causing inflammation. (Adv: *irritatingly.*) ♦ *The irritating smoke made me cough.* ♦ *I removed an irritating sliver of glass from my finger.* **2.** *adj.* bothersome; annoying. (Adv: *irritatingly.*) ♦ *My irritating little brother followed me around the house.* ♦ *Would you please turn down that irritating music?*

irritation [ɪr ɪ 'te ʃən] **1.** *n.* an annoyance; a bother; something that irritates. ♦ *Smoking is an irritation that I cannot endure.* ♦ *My little brother is an irritation at times, but I still love him.* **2.** *n.* the condition of being sore or itchy; the condition of being irritated; soreness or tenderness of skin or other body tissues. (No plural form in this sense.) ♦ *Fumes from that chemical can cause eye irritation.* ♦ *Applying the lotion has helped, but there is still some irritation on my left arm.*

is [ɪz] *iv.* <a form of **be**, used in the present tense of the third-person singular, that is, with *he, she, it,* and singular nouns.> (Reduced to *'s* in contractions.) ♦ *It is raining.* ♦ *The cat is on the mat.*

Islam ['ɪz 'lɑm] *n.* the religion of Muslims. (No plural form in this sense.) ♦ *The holy book of Islam is called the Koran.* ♦ *Islam is the main religion of the Arab nations.*

Islamic [ɪz ˈlɑm ɪk] *adj.* of or about Islam. ♦ *A major Islamic holiday involves fasting.* ♦ *The Koran is the holy book of the Islamic religion.*

island [ˈɑɪ lənd] **1.** *n.* a piece of land that is surrounded by water and that is smaller than a continent. ♦ *We rented a cabin on a small island off the coast of Maine.* ♦ *Staten Island is part of New York City.* **2.** *n.* something that resembles ①; something that is completely surrounded by something else. (Figurative on ①.) ♦ *The island of single family homes was surrounded by large housing projects.* ♦ *An island of ice cream arose from a pool of hot fudge.*

islander [ˈɑɪ lən dɚ] *n.* someone who lives on an island. ♦ *The islanders had to go to the mainland for medical treatment.* ♦ *Hawaiian Islanders are friendly and kind to tourists.*

isle [ˈɑɪl] *n.* an island. ♦ *Ireland is sometimes called the "Emerald Isle."* ♦ *The Isle of Man is surrounded by the Irish Sea.*

isn't [ˈɪz ənt] *cont.* "is not." ♦ *John isn't here yet.* ♦ *It isn't my birthday today, but it will be tomorrow.*

isolate [ˈɑɪ sə let] *tv.* to keep someone or something separate from other things or people; to separate someone or something from other things or people. ♦ *My job isolated me from my family and friends.* ♦ *John isolated himself and spoke to no one.*

isolated [ˈɑɪ sə let ɪd] **1.** *adj.* separated by a great distance; far away from anything; kept away from other things or people. (Adv: *isolatedly.*) ♦ *My aunt and uncle live in an isolated town in northern Canada.* ♦ *The expedition reached the isolated mountaintop at sunrise.* **2.** *adj.* being the only example; not related to anything else. (Figurative on ①. Adv: *isolatedly.*) ♦ *The police believed the murder to be an isolated act of violence.* ♦ *At first, we thought John's dismissal was an isolated incident, but then six other people were fired.*

isolation [ɑɪ sə ˈle ʃən] *n.* isolating someone or something; keeping someone or something away from other things or people. (No plural form in this sense.) ♦ *The prisoner was kept in isolation.* ♦ *Isolation is practically torture for me since I am such a social person.*

isolationist [ɑɪ sə ˈle ʃə nəst] *n.* someone who believes that one's country should not be involved in international affairs. ♦ *Isolationists urged Congress to discourage involvement in foreign wars.* ♦ *The isolationists voted against the international treaty.*

Israel [ˈɪz ri əl] See Gazetteer.

issue [ˈɪ ʃu] **1.** *n.* one of a set of publications that are available regularly. ♦ *Have you read the latest issue of the magazine?* ♦ *The next issue will be available on Thursday.* **2.** *n.* the number of stamps or magazines printed at one time. ♦ *In July, we printed an issue of 40,000 copies.* ♦ *The magazine's November issue is always its largest.* **3.** *n.* a topic; the topic being discussed; a concern. ♦ *What issue are Jane and Dave arguing about now?* ♦ *Crime will be an important issue in the next election.* **4.** *n.* a discharge. (No plural form in this sense.) ♦ *The bloody issue seeped out of the wound.* ♦ *The doctor analyzed the moist issue from the side of the corpse.* **5.** *tv.* to assign something to someone; to supply something to someone. ♦ *We will issue you only one uniform. Take care of it!* ♦ *They issued one textbook to each student.* **6.** *tv.* to speak or utter a command; to deliver or publish a written command or order. ♦ *When the sergeant issues a command, everyone obeys it.* ♦ *The president issued an important memo that was delivered to all employees immediately.* **7.** *tv.* to publish a magazine, bulletin, newsletter, or newspaper. ♦ *The publisher issues four different magazines each month.* ♦ *The next edition of the newsletter will be issued in the fall.* **8. issue from** *iv. + prep. phr.* to flow out of something; to discharge; to come out from some place. ♦ *The water issuing from the pipe flooded our basement.* ♦ *Blood issued from the victim's wounds.*

it [ɪt] **1.** *pron.* <a form referring to something that is not human; a plant, an animal, or something that is not living.> (However, it is sometimes used to refer to a baby or a small child. The plural is **they**.) ♦ *The dog is sleeping on the floor. When it wakes up, I will feed it.* ♦ *The plant does not need water now, but it will later.* **2.** *pron.* <a form used as the subject of a sentence where there is no real actor or doer.> (Usually with the verb **be**, but with others also.) ♦ *It is two o'clock.* ♦ *It rains every weekend.* ♦ *It seems that the mail is late again.* ♦ *It looks like rain.* ♦ *It keeps happening again and again.* ♦ *It's five miles to town.* ♦ *How's it going?* **3.** *n.* the player who must find everyone else in a game of hide-and-seek or tag. (No plural form in this sense.) ♦ *You're it. Close your eyes and count to 25 while we hide.* ♦ *I touched Jane, and now she's it.*

Italian [ɪ ˈtæl jən] **1.** *n.* a citizen or native of Italy. ♦ *Italians live in a small country with many historical buildings and Roman ruins.* ♦ *There are two Italians in my French class.* **2.** *n.* the language spoken in Italy by ①. (No plural form in this sense.) ♦ *I am studying Italian so I can spend a year there.* ♦ *Italian is a Romance language, like French and Spanish.* **3.** *adj.* of or about Italy, ①, or ②. ♦ *I could eat Italian food all day long!* ♦ *I studied the Italian language before I went to Italy for my vacation.*

italic [ɪ ˈtæl ɪk] **1.** *adj.* [of letters] slanted; printed with slanted letters. ♦ *The underlined words in the manuscript should be printed in italic type.* ♦ *Does this word processor have italic fonts?* **2. italics** *n.* slanted printing. (Treated as singular or plural.) ♦ *All the examples in this dictionary are in italics.* ♦ *Should I underline the titles of books, or should I use italics?*

italicize [ɪ ˈtæl ə sɑɪz] *tv.* to emphasize something by printing it in italics. ♦ *The researcher italicized the important data in her article.* ♦ *In his newspaper article, the reporter italicized the words that Mary emphasized.*

Italy [ˈɪt ə li] See Gazetteer.

itch [ˈɪtʃ] **1.** *n.* a feeling on the skin that makes one want to scratch. ♦ *Mary scratched the itch on her arm.* ♦ *I felt an itch and knew I'd gotten a rash.* **2.** *iv.* [for the skin] to have ①. ♦ *This spider bite itches.* ♦ *When I began to itch, I knew a mosquito had bitten me.* **3. have an itch for something** *idiom* to have a desire for something. ♦ *I have an itch for a nice cool glass of lemonade.* ♦ *Who besides me has an itch for pizza?* **4. have an itch to do something** *idiom* to have a desire to do something. ♦ *I have an itch to see a movie tonight.* ♦ *Tom has an itch to go swimming.*

itching [ˈɪtʃ ɪŋ] *n.* the feeling of an itch. (No plural form in this sense.) ♦ *There is a continuous itching on my elbow.* ♦ *The itching became unbearable and I had to scratch.*

itchy ['ɪtʃ i] *adj.* with the feeling of itching; constantly itching. (Comp: *itchier;* sup: *itchiest.*) ♦ *My elbow is itchy.* ♦ *Bill has an itchy rash.*

it'd ['ɪt ɪd] **1.** *cont.* "it would." ♦ *It'd be a shame if we had to leave early.* ♦ *If I had a dog, it'd be named Fido.* **2.** *cont.* "it had," where **had** is an auxiliary. ♦ *Tell me your excuse, and it'd better be good!* ♦ *By midnight, it'd stopped snowing.*

item ['ɑɪ təm] *n.* one thing that is part of a list or a series; a unit; a piece of information; a piece of news. ♦ *The first item on the shopping list is bread.* ♦ *The latest news item stated that the killer had been caught.*

itemize ['ɑɪ tə mɑɪz] *tv.* to arrange items in a list, identifying each item. ♦ *The accountant itemized my expenses.* ♦ *I itemized the things I had to do in order of importance.*

itemized ['ɑɪ tə mɑɪzd] *adj.* listed and identified in an orderly fashion. ♦ *The itemized expenses total $23,000.* ♦ *I gave the insurance company an itemized list of my losses.*

itinerant [ɑɪ 'tɪn ɚ ənt] *adj.* traveling from place to place to do one's work. (Adv: *itinerantly.*) ♦ *The itinerant salesman sold vacuum cleaners.* ♦ *John worked as an itinerant carpenter for a few months.*

itinerary [ɑɪ 'tɪn ə rɛr i] **1.** *n.* a route; a plan of travel. ♦ *My itinerary takes me to Boston by way of Philadelphia.* ♦ *I bought a road map so I could plan my itinerary.* **2.** *n.* a guidebook for travelers. ♦ *The local chamber of commerce published a helpful itinerary for visitors to the region.* ♦ *The itinerary listed five reasonably priced hotels.*

it'll ['ɪt əl] *cont.* "it will." ♦ *The forecast says it'll rain tomorrow.* ♦ *I can't find my book, but I'm sure it'll appear somewhere.*

it's ['ɪts] **1.** *cont.* "it is." (Compare with **its.**) ♦ *It's raining.* ♦ *It's 2:00 A.M.* **2.** *cont.* "it has," where **has** is an auxiliary. (Compare with **its.**) ♦ *It's been a long time since I've seen you.* ♦ *Please polish the table. It's lost its shine.*

its ['ɪts] *pron.* <the possessive form of it; belonging to it.> (Compare with **it's.**) ♦ *I would buy this book, but its cover is torn.* ♦ *I own a car, but its engine needs repair.*

itself [ɪt 'sɛlf] **1.** *pron.* <the reflexive form of it.> ♦ *The baby cried itself to sleep.* ♦ *The streetlight shuts itself off automatically.* **2.** *pron.* <an emphatic form of it.> (Follows the nominal that is being emphasized.) ♦ *Please place the report itself on the table, but give the copy to me.* ♦ *Bread is very nourishing, but bread itself is not a sufficient meal.* **3. by itself** *phr.* with the help of nothing else; without the addition of anything else. ♦ *Will this be enough by itself?* ♦ *Can the dog get out of the house by itself?*

iv. See **intransitive verb.**

I've ['ɑɪv] *cont.* "I have," where **have** is an auxiliary. ♦ *I've seen that movie already.* ♦ *I've got to be leaving soon.*

ivory ['ɑɪ vri] **1.** *n.* the hard, yellow-white substance of which an elephant's tusk is made. (No plural form in this sense.) ♦ *The poachers obtained and sold the ivory illegally.* ♦ *White piano keys used to be made of ivory.* **2.** *n.* the color of ①. ♦ *We painted all the walls in our house ivory.* ♦ *Ivory is a light color, but not as light as white.* **3.** *adj.* made of ①. ♦ *The hunter killed the elephants for their ivory tusks.* ♦ *The valuable ivory necklace was stolen.* **4.** *adj.* <the adj. use of ②>; off-white. ♦ *The ivory carpet dirtied easily.* ♦ *I wore my ivory shirt to the party.*

ivy ['ɑɪv i] *n.* a plant that clings to walls, trees, etc., and climbs as it grows. (No plural form in this sense.) ♦ *The old university buildings were covered with ivy.* ♦ *I removed the ivy that covered the windows.*

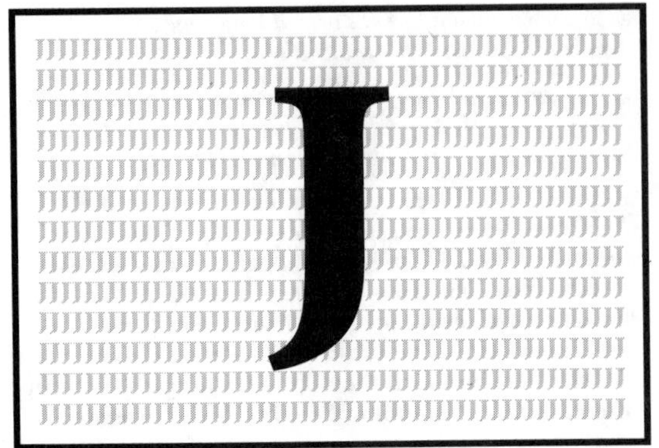

J AND **j** ['dʒe] *n.* the tenth letter of the English alphabet. ♦ J *comes after* I *and before* K. ♦ *The word* job *begins with the letter* j.

jab ['dʒæb] **1.** *tv.* to poke someone or something; to shove someone with a pointed object; to thrust something into someone or something. ♦ *Stop jabbing your finger in my chest!* ♦ *The nurse jabbed my arm with a needle.* **2.** *n.* a poke; a shove with a pointed object; a thrust. ♦ *I received a jab in the back from the person behind me.* ♦ *The bully gave Jimmy a hard jab to the ribs.*

jabber ['dʒæb ɚ] *iv.* to talk very fast but not clearly; to chatter; to talk all the time. ♦ *The parrot jabbers all day long.* ♦ *Stop jabbering! I don't understand a word you're saying.*

jack ['dʒæk] **1.** *n.* a device used to push up heavy things off the ground, especially to push up a car axle in order to change a tire. ♦ *Anne used a jack to help fix her flat tire.* ♦ *Let me borrow your jack. Mine's not in the trunk.* **2.** *n.* [in a deck of playing cards] one of four cards that has a picture of a young man on it and is signified by the letter *J.* ♦ *A pair of jacks beats a pair of tens in poker.* ♦ *The jack comes after the ten and before the queen in a deck of cards.* **3. jack up** *tv.* + *adv.* to push something up with ①. ♦ *Jack up the van so I can change the tire.* ♦ *Please help me jack up the car.* **4. jack up** *tv.* + *adv.* to raise the price of something. (Informal. Figurative on ③.) ♦ *I don't shop at those stores. They jack up their prices constantly.* ♦ *The dealer jacked up the price on the car when he found out Bob was wealthy.*

jackal ['dʒæk əl] *n.* a wild animal related to the dog family that feeds on dead animals, found in Africa and southern Asia. ♦ *Jackals swarmed around the dying animal.* ♦ *The prey escaped from the pack of jackals.*

jackass ['dʒæk æs] **1.** *n.* a male donkey. ♦ *Bill rode the jackass up the mountain trail.* ♦ *The jackass stubbornly refused to move.* **2.** *n.* someone who is annoying; a stupid fool. (Derogatory. Figurative on ①.) ♦ *Stop acting like a jackass! Everyone is laughing at us.* ♦ *Max makes a jackass of himself at every office party.*

jacket ['dʒæk ɪt] **1.** *n.* a light coat; the light coat that is part of a suit. ♦ *Put on a jacket, it's cool outside.* ♦ *Jane's new suit has a short jacket and a fitted skirt.* **2.** *n.* a covering for a book or a [vinyl] record album. ♦ *I put the album back in its jacket when I finished listening to it.* ♦ *The novel's plot is summarized on the inside of the book jacket.*

jackknife ['dʒæk nɑɪf] **1.** *n., irreg.* a knife whose blade folds into the handle. (Pl: **jackknives.** See also **penknife.**) ♦ *The store carries many kinds of jackknives.* ♦ *Dave brought a jackknife on the camping trip.* **2.** *iv.* [for a truck hauling a trailer] to go out of control and spin so that the trailer whips around at an angle to the truck. (Figurative on ①.) ♦ *The truck jackknifed on the busy highway.* ♦ *A truck can easily jackknife on icy roads in the winter.*

jackknives ['dʒæk nɑɪvz] pl of **jackknife.**

jackpot ['dʒæk pɑt] *n.* the sum of money built up in a lottery or a gambling game that will be won by the next winner. ♦ *I bought lottery tickets for Saturday's jackpot.* ♦ *The jackpot is now worth 5 million dollars.*

jackrabbit ['dʒæk ræb ət] *n.* a North American **hare,** a mammal with long ears and long back legs that moves by jumping. ♦ *The jackrabbit hopped into the woods.* ♦ *Jimmy tried to catch the jackrabbit.*

jade ['dʒed] **1.** *n.* a valuable green stone used to make jewelry or carvings. (No plural form in this sense.) ♦ *The craftsman bought the jade to fashion his own jewelry.* ♦ *Pure jade is shipped from China.* **2.** *adj.* made of ①. ♦ *Jane wore a jade necklace to the party.* ♦ *Do you have jade earrings to match the necklace?*

jaded ['dʒed ɪd] *adj.* tired or bored with something that used to be interesting; no longer impressed or excited by something. (Adv: *jadedly.*) ♦ *The jaded woman was not impressed with her date's wealth.* ♦ *The excessive violence did not affect the jaded detective.*

jagged ['dʒæg ɪd] *adj.* having a sharp or uneven edge; ragged; not smooth; sharp and pointed. (Adv: *jaggedly.*) ♦ *The jagged edge of the fence needs to be filed down.* ♦ *I trimmed the jagged edges of the paper.*

jaguar ['dʒæg wɑr] *n.* a tropical American animal like a leopard but having larger spots. ♦ *The jaguar hunted its prey.* ♦ *The jaguar is an endangered species.*

jail ['dʒel] **1.** *n.* a building where criminals are locked up or where people are locked up while waiting for a trial. ♦ *The thief was sent to jail.* ♦ *The thief sat in jail until his friend bailed him out.* **2.** *tv.* to put someone in ①; to sentence someone to spend time in ①. ♦ *The sheriff jailed the drunk driver.* ♦ *The judge decided to jail the thief for a full year.*

jailer ['dʒel ɚ] *n.* someone who is in charge of criminals in a jail. ♦ *The sheriff is the jailer in our town.* ♦ *The jailer brought the prisoners their meals.*

jailhouse ['dʒel hɑʊs] *n., irreg.* a building where prisoners are locked up as a punishment for a crime; a jail. (Pl: [...hɑʊ zəz].) ♦ *The defendants remained in the jailhouse until their court date.* ♦ *The county jailhouse is very overcrowded.*

jam ['dʒæm] **1.** *n.* a sweet food made by boiling fruit and sugar until it is thick. (No plural form in this sense.) ♦ *I like strawberry jam on my toast.* ♦ *Mike bought two jars of jam at the store.* **2.** *n.* a lot of cars that cannot move because traffic is stopped for some reason; a situation where things or people are stuck and cannot move or work properly. ♦ *There is a big traffic jam in the center of the city.* ♦ *We got stuck in a jam because an accident blocked the road.* **3.** *tv.* to cause something to become stuck; to force something to fit someplace. ♦ *I jammed the book *into the bookcase.* ♦ *Jane jammed the piece of wood under the door to hold the door open.* **4.** *tv.* to make a radio signal difficult to receive by sending out other radio signals that interfere with it. ♦ *The radio station jammed the propaganda broadcast.* ♦ *The dictator tried to jam all the foreign radio broadcasts.* **5.** *iv.* to become stuck; to be unable to work properly because something is stuck; to be unable to move because something is stuck. ♦ *When the tape recorder jammed, Anne had to pick out pieces of the tape.* ♦ *The traffic jammed in front of the drawbridge whenever it went up to let boats travel up the river.* **6. in(to) a jam** *idiom* in(to) a difficult situation. (Informal.) ♦ *Mary cannot keep track of the many times Dave got himself into a jam.* ♦ *I found myself in a jam when my car overheated on the highway.*

Jamaica [dʒə 'me kə] See Gazetteer.

janitor ['dʒæn ɪ tɚ] *n.* a custodian; someone who cleans and takes care of a building. ♦ *The janitor sweeps the hospital hallways.* ♦ *You can find the janitor's office near the basement stairs.*

janitorial [dʒæn ɪ 'tor ɪ əl] *adj.* of or about cleaning and taking care of a building. (Adv: *janitorially.*) ♦ *We hired a local janitorial service to clean our office.* ♦ *Tom took his janitorial responsibilities seriously and kept the building very clean.*

January ['dʒæn ju ɛr i] *n.* the first month of the year. ♦ *It is usually cold in January.* ♦ *The month of January has 31 days.*

Japan [dʒə 'pæn] See Gazetteer.

Japanese [dʒæp ə 'niz] **1.** *n., irreg.* a citizen or native of Japan. (Pl: *Japanese.*) ♦ *A Japanese presented a talk about life in Japan.* ♦ *Two Japanese greeted us at the door.* **2. the Japanese** *n.* the people of Japan. (Treated as plural.) ♦ *The Japanese are friendly and tolerant of foreigners.* ♦ *We learned about the Japanese and their culture on our trip to Japan.* **3.** *n.* the language spoken by ①. ♦ *Japanese is easy to learn but hard to write correctly.* ♦ *Japanese uses Chinese characters in its writing system.* **4.** *adj.* of or about Japan, ①, ②, or ③. ♦ *Japanese food is remarkably good.* ♦ *I am studying the Japanese language in school.*

jar ['dʒɑr] **1.** *n.* a container with a wide, circular top, usually made of glass or clay, and usually without handles. ♦ *I need three canning jars for the tomatoes.* ♦ *Do the jars have lids that fit?* **2.** *n.* the contents of ①. ♦ *We finished half a jar of jam.* ♦ *Tom loves pickles so much, he could eat an entire jar of them.* **3.** *tv.* to shake someone or something; to rattle someone or something. ♦ *Don't jar the aquarium. You will frighten the fish.* ♦ *Don't jar the table or you will spill my coffee.* **4.** *tv.* to shock someone or something. (Figurative on ③.) ♦ *Dave liked to jar his parents with his wild hair styles.* ♦ *Her announcement really jarred me. I was shocked!*

jargon ['dʒɑr gən] *n.* the special words that are used by people who have the same job or belong to the same group and are not normally used or understood by other people. ♦ *The word "niner" is used in pilot's jargon instead of "nine" so that it is not confused with "five."* ♦ *Police officers have their own special jargon. For them, the 25th precinct is known as the "two five."*

jaundice ['dʒɔn dɪs] **1.** *n.* the medical condition where the skin and the whites of the eyes turn yellow because there is too much bile in the blood, resulting from an illness such as hepatitis. (No plural form in this sense.) ♦ *The patient's jaundice was caused by too much bile in the blood.* ♦ *Jaundice helped diagnose Mary's hepatitis.* **2.** *tv.* to cause someone to become bitter ④ and hateful. (Figurative on ①.) ♦ *Many years of sarcasm have jaundiced her view of the world.* ♦ *Too much television will jaundice anyone's outlook on life.*

jaunt ['dʒɔnt] *n.* a short trip; a short journey. ♦ *Bob took a jaunt across town in his sports car.* ♦ *We took the children on a jaunt to the zoo.*

jaunty ['dʒɔn ti] **1.** *adj.* happy; lively; cheerful. (Adv: *jauntily.* Comp: *jauntier;* sup: *jauntiest.*) ♦ *Jim has a fun-loving and jaunty personality.* ♦ *The patients appreciated the nurse's jaunty disposition.* **2.** *adj.* [of clothing] clever and smart. (Figurative on ①. Adv: *jauntily.* Comp: *jauntier;* sup: *jauntiest.*) ♦ *Anne wore a jaunty hat.* ♦ *Tom is a jaunty dresser.*

javelin ['dʒæv ə lɪn] *n.* a long spear that is used either as a weapon or in a sporting event to see who can throw it the farthest. ♦ *The athlete threw the javelin very far.* ♦ *The hunter used a javelin to spear the wild boar.*

jaw ['dʒɔ] **1.** *n.* the upper or lower bone that forms the mouth and supports the teeth. ♦ *Anne's jaw is sore from laughing so hard.* ♦ *John broke his jaw in the car accident.* **2.** *n.* one of the two parts of a device that holds something tight, such as a vise or pliers. ♦ *The jaws of the machine held the part while it was being smoothed.* ♦ *Tom placed the piece of wood in the jaws of the vise.*

jawbone ['dʒɔ bon] *n.* the upper or lower bone that forms the mouth and supports the teeth. ♦ *Bill's jawbone was shattered in the car crash.* ♦ *Mary's face has a prominent lower jawbone.*

jay ['dʒe] **(blue) jay** *n.* a noisy bird with blue feathers that is part of the crow family. ♦ *The blue jay flew up into the tree.* ♦ *The colorful jay built a nest near our house.*

jaywalk ['dʒe wɔk] *iv.* to cross a street at a place where it is not allowed. ♦ *Don't jaywalk on this street!* ♦ *Dave jaywalked to save time, but a cop saw him and wrote him a ticket.*

jaywalker ['dʒe wɔk ɚ] *n.* someone who jaywalks. ♦ *The jaywalker was given a warning by the police officer.* ♦ *The jaywalker was almost hit by a car.*

jazz ['dʒæz] **1.** *n.* a style of music characterized by its rhythms, harmony, and improvisation. (No plural form in this sense.) ♦ *I love to listen to New Orleans jazz.* ♦ *Do you like the unusual rhythms in jazz?* **2.** *adj.* playing ①; featuring ①. ♦ *I listen to a jazz music station on the radio.* ♦ *Tom's band played in the best jazz clubs.*

jazzy ['dʒæz i] **1.** *adj.* like jazz; sounding like jazz. (Adv: *jazzily.* Comp: *jazzier;* sup: *jazziest.*) ♦ *This music has a jazzy sound.* ♦ *Bill played a jazzy piece on the clarinet.* **2.** *adj.* flashy; showy; fancy. (Informal. Figurative on ①. Adv: *jazzily.* Comp: *jazzier;* sup: *jazziest.*) ♦ *Anne is wearing a jazzy dress.* ♦ *John does not have a jazzy personality.*

jealous ['dʒɛl əs] *adj.* possessive; resentful of anyone who might try to take away one's things or the people one loves; resentful of anyone who spends time with someone one loves; resentful of one's rivals. (Adv: *jeal-*

ously.) ♦ *Tom is jealous of anyone who talks to his girlfriend.* ♦ *Anne is jealous of people who have more money than her.*

jealousy ['dʒɛl ə si] *n.* the condition of being jealous; resentment towards someone who has something one wants. (No plural form in this sense.) ♦ *I try to hide my feelings of jealousy.* ♦ *Jealousy is a negative trait.*

jeans ['dʒinz] *n.* a pair of denim pants. (Treated as plural. Number is expressed by *pair(s) of jeans.*) ♦ *Jane bought a new pair of jeans at the store.* ♦ *I put on my jeans as soon as I get home from the office.*

Jeep™ ['dʒip] *n.* the trademarked name of a powerful vehicle that can be driven over very rough land. ♦ *We drove through the mountainous terrain in our Jeep.* ♦ *Jeeps were widely used during World War II.*

jeer ['dʒɪr] **1.** *n.* a taunt; an insult; an unkind remark; a sarcastic remark. ♦ *The actor heard a loud jeer from the audience.* ♦ *The crowd's jeers were cruel and nasty.* **2.** *tv.* to insult someone; to taunt someone; to mock someone. ♦ *The unruly crowd jeered the losing hockey team.* ♦ *We jeered the boring comic every time he said anything.* **3. jeer at** *iv.* + *prep. phr.* to direct a taunt at someone or something. ♦ *The crowd jeered at the singer because she was so bad.* ♦ *The students jeered at every mistake John made.*

jeering ['dʒɪr ɪŋ] *adj.* mocking; taunting; insulting. (Adv: *jeeringly.*) ♦ *The jeering crowd booed the baseball player.* ♦ *The performers were annoyed by the jeering audience.*

jell ['dʒɛl] **1.** *iv.* to form into a gel or jelly; for a liquid to harden into a gel. ♦ *The dessert jelled quickly in the refrigerator.* ♦ *The juices of the ham jelled on the plate.* **2.** *iv.* [for an idea, plan, or intention] to become fixed, firm, or definite. (Figurative on ①.) ♦ *The more Jane studied, the more the important ideas of the text jelled in her mind.* ♦ *As John's plan jelled, he became more confident that it would work.*

jelly ['dʒɛl i] **1.** *n.* a soft food made from boiling fruit juice and sugar together, often spread on bread. (No plural form in this sense.) ♦ *I love blueberry jelly on my toast.* ♦ *When you go to the store, please buy some strawberry jelly.* **2.** *adj.* made of ①. ♦ *Jim loves to eat jelly sandwiches.* ♦ *Do you like jelly cookies?*

jellybean ['dʒɛl i bin] *n.* a small bean-sized piece of candy, with a sugar covering around a firm jelly filling. ♦ *We put different colored jellybeans in Jimmy's Easter basket.* ♦ *The pink jellybeans taste like watermelon.*

jellyfish ['dʒɛl i fɪʃ] *n., irreg.* a kind of sea creature that has a clear, dome-shaped body with long tentacles. (Pl: *jellyfish.*) ♦ *The jellyfish can sting with its tentacles.* ♦ *The children stayed close to the shore to avoid getting stung by a jellyfish.*

jenny ['dʒɛn i] *n.* a female donkey. ♦ *Dave rode the jenny on the trail.* ♦ *We bought a jenny and a jackass to help with farm chores.*

jeopardize ['dʒɛp ɚ daɪz] *tv.* to cause danger to someone or something; to put someone or something in danger. ♦ *Wear a life jacket. Don't jeopardize your safety.* ♦ *Smoking cigarettes can jeopardize your health.*

jeopardy ['dʒɛp ɚ di] **in jeopardy** *phr.* in danger; at risk; at hazard. ♦ *John puts himself in jeopardy every time he goes skydiving.* ♦ *I was in jeopardy when my car broke down on the deserted road.*

jerk ['dʒɚk] **1.** *n.* a sudden push or pull; a spasm; a movement made when something starts or stops quickly. ♦ *I felt a jerk when Bill hit the car brakes.* ♦ *A sudden jerk threw me out of my seat.* **2.** *n.* a very annoying or rude person. (Derogatory.) ♦ *John acts like a jerk when he's tired and overworked.* ♦ *Stop acting like a jerk. You're embarrassing us.* **3.** *tv.* to push or pull someone or something suddenly as the result of a sudden movement. ♦ *The police officer jerked Sue's arm to get her attention.* ♦ *My leg muscles jerked as I woke up from a frightening dream.* **4.** *iv.* to move with ①; to have a spasm; to twitch. ♦ *Bill's arm jerked involuntarily.* ♦ *The left side of Anne's face jerked before her surgery.*

jersey ['dʒɚ zi] *n.* a sweater or shirt, knitted or made of a thick, soft fabric; the upper part of a uniform worn by a sports team. ♦ *My blue jersey needs to be washed.* ♦ *Everyone in school wore a football jersey on the day of the big game.*

jest ['dʒɛst] **1.** *n.* a joke; a statement or action said or done in fun. ♦ *Don't get upset. I meant that as a jest.* ♦ *Although John's jest wasn't meant to be mean, I was upset.* **2. jest with** *iv.* + *prep. phr.* to joke with someone. ♦ *Anne liked to jest with her friends.* ♦ *The students enjoyed jesting with their teacher.*

Jesus Christ ['dʒi zəs 'kraɪst] *n.* the major figure in Christianity, who is believed by Christians to be the Son of God. (Often *Jesus.*) ♦ *Jesus was born in a stable in Bethlehem.* ♦ *Christians believe that Jesus Christ rose from the dead.*

jet ['dʒɛt] **1.** *n.* a stream of air, water, steam, or another fluid that is shot out from a small opening at high pressure. ♦ *A jet of blood sprayed from the injured soldier's neck.* ♦ *Jets of hot gases rushed out of the plane's engine.* **2. jet propulsion** *n.* a means of pushing or propelling something forward by forcing ① out of the back. ♦ *The engines of modern aircraft are powered by jet propulsion.* ♦ *Jet propulsion is noisy, but very efficient.* **3. jet engine** *n.* an engine powered by ②. ♦ *The plane has four jet engines and is fast and powerful.* ♦ *We flew on a smaller plane with two jet engines attached to the tail.* **4. jet (plane)** *n.* a high-speed plane; a plane that has one or more ③. ♦ *The pilot flew the jet plane to Jamaica.* ♦ *We flew by jet to Europe.* **5.** *iv.* [for water, steam, or another fluid] to form a stream by being forced out of a small opening under pressure. ♦ *Steam jetted out of the geyser at the park.* ♦ *Blood jetted from the open wound.* **6.** *iv.* to travel by ④. ♦ *We jetted to the Bahamas on the company plane.* ♦ *The wealthy couple jetted to Paris for the weekend.* **7.** *tv.* to cause water, steam, or another fluid to form a stream by forcing it out of a small opening under pressure. ♦ *Jimmy playfully jetted a powerful stream of water from the garden hose.* ♦ *The artist jetted the paint onto the canvas to create an abstract.* **8. jet-black** *adj.* deep, shiny black in color. ♦ *Mary has jet-black hair.* ♦ *His jet-black sports car is jazzy.*

jettison ['dʒɛt ə sən] *tv.* to throw something overboard, especially to make an aircraft or a ship lighter. ♦ *Don't jettison the anchor! We may need it.* ♦ *The pilot jettisoned the heavy cargo from the plane.*

jetty ['dʒɛt i] *n.* a structure built out into the water to protect a harbor from waves. ♦ *The boat sailed past the* *large stone jetty.* ♦ *People were standing on the jetty and fishing.*

Jew ['dʒu] *n.* a Jewish person; someone whose religion is Judaism. ♦ *Many Jews were persecuted during World War II.* ♦ *Many Jews in Israel speak Hebrew.*

jewel ['dʒu əl] **1.** *n.* a gem; a valuable stone; a piece of jewelry. ♦ *A ruby jewel fell out of my ring.* ♦ *I bought a necklace having several precious jewels.* **2.** *n.* a person who is highly valued; a person who is treasured. (Figurative on ①.) ♦ *You can't fire Jane. She is a jewel in this company.* ♦ *My secretary is an irreplaceable jewel.*

jeweler ['dʒu (ə) lɚ] *n.* someone who deals in watches, valuable gems, and precious metals. ♦ *The jeweler sold us an emerald necklace.* ♦ *I had my watch repaired by the local jeweler.*

jewelry ['dʒu əl ri] *n.* objects usually made of valuable metals or stones, such as rings, earrings, necklaces, bracelets, brooches, and pins. (No plural form in this sense. Number is expressed with *piece(s) of jewelry.*) ♦ *I only wear 24-carat gold jewelry.* ♦ *Sue keeps her expensive jewelry in a safe when she is not wearing it.*

Jewish ['dʒu ɪʃ] *adj.* of, for, or about Jews or Judaism; having Judaism as one's religion. ♦ *The Jewish family next door came from Tel Aviv.* ♦ *Yom Kippur is a Jewish holiday.*

jiffy ['dʒɪf i] **in a jiffy** *idiom* a brief moment; a short period of time. ♦ *I'll be there in a jiffy. Just wait for me.* ♦ *I'll be finished with this small job in a jiffy.*

jig ['dʒɪg] **1.** *n.* a kind of fast dance, usually involving footwork. ♦ *The dance group performed an Irish jig.* ♦ *I danced a jig when I heard about my new promotion.* **2.** *n.* the music played for ①. ♦ *The band readied their instruments for a jig.* ♦ *Do you know how to play a jig?*

jigger ['dʒɪg ɚ] **1.** *n.* a small glass used to measure an amount of alcohol when mixing drinks. ♦ *A jigger is equal to about 1.5 ounces.* ♦ *The set of glasses Jane bought came with 2 jiggers.* **2.** *n.* the contents of ①. ♦ *Bill drank a jigger of whiskey.* ♦ *They drank a toast with jiggers of vodka.*

jiggle ['dʒɪg əl] **1.** *tv.* to move someone or something up and down or from side to side. ♦ *Tom jiggled the lock with the key when the door wouldn't open.* ♦ *I jiggled the knob on the television set to try to make the picture better.* **2.** *iv.* to move up and down or from side to side. ♦ *Stop jiggling!* ♦ *John couldn't keep still. He always jiggled.* **3.** *n.* a bouncing movement. ♦ *If you give the door a jiggle it might open.* ♦ *One more jiggle, and the key should turn the lock.*

jigsaw puzzle ['dʒɪg sɔ 'pʌz əl] *n.* a puzzle that is made from a picture mounted on cardboard and then cut up into pieces of irregular shapes. ("Working" the puzzle means putting the pieces back together to form the original picture.) ♦ *It took me three days to work the jigsaw puzzle.* ♦ *I got a jigsaw puzzle as a gift for my birthday.*

jilt ['dʒɪlt] *tv.* to abandon one's sweetheart; to reject one's lover permanently. ♦ *Bill jilted Mary for another woman.* ♦ *Anne jilted Tom on their wedding day.*

jingle ['dʒɪŋ gəl] **1.** *n.* the ringing noise of metal objects gently hitting together; the noise of a small bell. ♦ *My keys made a jingle when they hit the floor.* ♦ *When the children heard the jingle of bells, they thought Santa Claus was coming.* **2.** *n.* a tune or song used in advertising. ♦ *The shampoo ad has a catchy jingle.* ♦ *Bob wrote jingles for radio commercials.* **3.** *tv.* to make ringing noises by hitting metal objects together. ♦ *Tom jingled his car keys impatiently in the living room while waiting for Mary.* ♦ *Anne jingled her bracelets as she put them on her arm.* **4.** *iv.* [for metal objects] to make noises when struck together; [for a small bell] to make a noise when shaken. ♦ *The bells on its harness jingled as the horse trotted along.* ♦ *The bumpy road made my car keys jingle.*

jinx ['dʒɪŋks] **1.** *n.* someone or something that brings bad luck. ♦ *Most hotels do not have a 13th floor because the number 13 is considered a jinx.* ♦ *Tom refers to himself as a jinx when he talks about his past bad luck.* **2.** *tv.* to bring bad luck to someone or something. ♦ *Bill jinxed the business deal by celebrating too soon.* ♦ *The football player jinxed the game with his outrageous prediction of victory.*

jittery ['dʒɪt ə ri] *adj.* nervous; anxious. ♦ *I felt a bit jittery after the thunderstorm.* ♦ *Sue reacts to most crises in a jittery manner.*

job ['dʒɑb] **1.** *n.* a career; an occupation; regular employment. ♦ *What type of job would you like when you grow up?* ♦ *Bill got a job as a botanist.* **2.** *n.* a task; a duty; a responsibility; a piece of work. ♦ *It's Mary's job to make sure the lights are off when we leave.* ♦ *It is your job to feed the cats daily.* **3.** *n.* the result of one's work. ♦ *Mary did a good job of painting the kitchen.* ♦ *Tom did a bad job of mowing the grass, because he didn't cut around the trees.*

jobber ['dʒɑb ɚ] *n.* someone who buys large amounts of products from a manufacturer and sells smaller amounts to shopkeepers. ♦ *The librarian orders books through a jobber.* ♦ *The magazine jobber sells to all of the small stores in town.*

jobless ['dʒɑb ləs] *adj.* having no job; being unemployed. (Adv: *joblessly.*) ♦ *It is difficult to pay your bills when you are jobless.* ♦ *Our temporary work agency helps many jobless clients.*

joblessness ['dʒɑb ləs nəs] *n.* unemployment; the condition of being out of work. (No plural form in this sense.) ♦ *Since many industries have moved away, our town has a high rate of joblessness.* ♦ *Joblessness affected all aspects of the local economy.*

jockey ['dʒɑk i] **1.** *n.* someone who rides a horse in horse races. ♦ *The jockey weighs only 80 pounds.* ♦ *The horse fell in the race and injured the jockey.* **2. jockey for position** *idiom* to try to push or work one's way into an advantageous position at the expense of others. (On ①.) ♦ *All the staff in that firm are jockeying for position. They all want the manager's job.* ♦ *It is unpleasant working for a firm where people are always jockeying for position.*

jog ['dʒɑg] **1.** *n.* a slow, gentle run usually done for exercise; a [human] trot. ♦ *Bill's morning jog took him through the park and by the river.* ♦ *I felt really great after a jog around the neighborhood.* **2.** *n.* a bend to the right or the left; something that causes a line not to be straight. ♦ *At the stop light, turn left, and then it's just past a jog in the road by the train station.* ♦ *Mary failed to see the jog in the road where she was supposed to turn.* **3.** *iv.* to exercise by running slowly. ♦ *Sue likes to jog in cool weather.* ♦ *Jane jogs alongside Tom every morning.* **4. jog someone's memory** *idiom* to stimulate someone's memory to recall something. ♦ *Hearing the first part of the song I'd forgot-*

ten really jogged my memory. ♦ *I tried to jog Bill's memory about our childhood antics.*

jogger ['dʒɑg ɚ] *n.* someone who exercises by jogging. ♦ *The jogger ran each morning no matter how bad the weather was.* ♦ *What brand of shoes does the jogger wear?*

join ['dʒɔɪn] **1.** *iv.* to come together; to connect; to unite. ♦ *The edges of the wall paneling join neatly at the corners of the room.* ♦ *The place where the sections of a countertop join can hardly be seen.* **2.** *tv.* to connect someone or something to someone or something else; to unite people or things into a single unit. ♦ *A local judge joined the couple in marriage.* ♦ *I joined the sections of the countertop with glue.* **3.** *tv.* to enroll in a club, class, the military, or some organization; to become a member of an organization. ♦ *Tom joined the army when he graduated from high school.* ♦ *Do you want to join the chess club?* **4. join forces** *idiom* to join together into a single large group. ♦ *Both parties joined forces to protest the tax increase.* ♦ *Our band joined forces with another band and gave a very exciting concert.* **5. join hands** *idiom* [for people] to hold hands so that each person is holding the hands of two other people; [for two people] to hold each other's hands. ♦ *Let us join hands and pray together.* ♦ *The dancers joined hands and formed a circle that moved to the left.*

joiner ['dʒɔɪn ɚ] **1.** *n.* a carpenter who makes cabinets and fine woodwork. ♦ *Tom hired a joiner to make new woodwork for his home.* ♦ *A joiner worked on all of our kitchen cabinets.* **2.** *n.* someone who joins many clubs and organizations. ♦ *Bill is a compulsive joiner who goes to various self-help groups.* ♦ *Anne is an avid joiner of charitable organizations.*

joint ['dʒɔɪnt] **1.** *n.* a place where two things join, especially bones. ♦ *The wrist and the knee are examples of joints.* ♦ *The boards fit together in a tight joint.* **2.** *n.* a bar; a nightclub; a restaurant; a café. (Informal. Often derogatory.) ♦ *John told Bill to meet him at a local joint for a bite to eat.* ♦ *The shabby street was lined with beer joints.* **3.** *adj.* (Adv: *jointly.*) done or owned together; joined; united; linked. ♦ *Mary and Jane shared joint ownership of the house.* ♦ *The divorced parents had joint custody of their children.* **4. put someone's nose out of joint** *idiom* to offend someone; to cause someone to feel slighted or insulted. ♦ *I'm afraid I put his nose out of joint by not inviting him to the picnic.* ♦ *There is no reason to put your nose out of joint. I meant no harm.*

jointly ['dʒɔɪnt li] *adv.* in a united way; together. ♦ *Bill and Anne owned the new house jointly.* ♦ *Let's do this project jointly.*

joke ['dʒok] **1.** *n.* a short story told to make people laugh. ♦ *Jimmy told his sister a silly joke.* ♦ *I told Tom a joke that was so funny he fell off his chair laughing.* **2.** *n.* someone or something that is laughed at. (Informal.) ♦ *Tom drives a run-down joke of a car.* ♦ *This movie is such a joke. I can't believe I paid good money to see it.* **3.** *tv.* to say something in a joking manner. (Takes a clause.) ♦ *Bob joked that I had more shoes than I could ever wear.* ♦ *Sue joked that she could eat three more cheeseburgers.* **4.** *iv.* to tell jokes; to play jokes; to kid or tease [someone]. ♦ *Dave jokes with everyone.* ♦ *I wasn't serious; I was just joking.* **5. all joking aside; all kidding aside** *idiom* being serious for a moment; in all seriousness. ♦ *I know I laugh at him, but all joking aside, he's a very clever scientist.* ♦ *I know I threatened to leave and go around the world, but all kidding aside, I do need a vacation.* **6. crack a joke** *idiom* to tell a joke. ♦ *She's never serious. She's always cracking jokes.* ♦ *As long as she's cracking jokes, she's okay.* **7. no joke** *idiom* not a joke; a serious matter. (Informal.) ♦ *It's no joke when you miss the last train.* ♦ *It's certainly no joke when you have to walk home.* **8. play a joke on someone** *idiom* to make a joke that tricks someone. ♦ *The children played a joke on their teacher.* ♦ *I don't like it when you play jokes on me.* **9. standing joke** *idiom* a subject that regularly and over a period of time causes amusement whenever it is mentioned. ♦ *Uncle Jim's driving was a standing joke. He used to drive incredibly slowly.* ♦ *Their mother's inability to make a decision was a standing joke in the Smith family all their lives.*

joker ['dʒok ɚ] **1.** *n.* someone who tells jokes; someone who plays jokes. ♦ *Bill is a joker; he always makes us laugh.* ♦ *Everyone likes Mary because she is the biggest joker in the classroom.* **2.** *n.* one of two extra cards in a deck of cards, which can stand for any card in some card games. ♦ *Please get rid of the jokers before you shuffle the deck.* ♦ *There are two jokers in this deck of cards.*

joking ['dʒok ɪŋ] *adj.* kidding; not serious; funny. (Adv: *jokingly.*) ♦ *Tom and Bill always talk to each other in a joking way.* ♦ *The hairdresser made a joking remark about Anne's hair.*

jokingly ['dʒok ɪŋ li] *adv.* in a joking way; in a kidding way; not seriously. ♦ *I jokingly referred to John's baldness, and he stormed out of the room.* ♦ *Anne wasn't amused when her hairdresser jokingly made a comment about the color of her hair.*

jolly ['dʒɑl i] *adj.* very happy; very cheerful. (Comp: *jollier;* sup: *jolliest.*) ♦ *Jane has a jolly disposition.* ♦ *The jolly clown performed for the children.*

jolt ['dʒolt] **1.** *n.* a sudden burst of electricity; an electrical shock. ♦ *A jolt of electricity shocked Mary when she used her hairdryer in the bathroom.* ♦ *Tom touched the electric wire and got a nasty jolt.* **2.** *n.* a sudden surprise or shock. (Figurative on ①.) ♦ *It was a real jolt to hear of your brother's death.* ♦ *Mary got a jolt when she saw her son's bad grade in science.* **3.** *n.* a sudden bump; a sudden movement. ♦ *I felt a strong jolt when the car lurched forward.* ♦ *Sue braced herself for some jolts when she turned onto the bumpy road.* **4.** *tv.* [for electricity] to shock someone or some creature. ♦ *The shock jolted the dog when it stepped on the exposed wire.* ♦ *Bob was jolted by a serious shock when his screwdriver touched the electric contact accidentally.* **5.** *tv.* to surprise someone or something; to shock someone or something. (Figurative on ④.) ♦ *Jane jolted John with the news that she was pregnant.* ♦ *Dave jolted his parents when he walked into the house with a wild hair style.* **6.** *tv.* to bump someone or something; to cause someone or something to suddenly move. ♦ *Jane jolted Mary accidentally at the crowded concert.* ♦ *When the line started to move, I jolted Tom so that he'd move too.* **7. jolt to a start; jolt to a stop** *idiom* to start or stop suddenly, causing a jolt ③. ♦ *The truck jolted to a stop at the stop sign.* ♦ *The little car jolted to a quick start and threw the passenger back in his seat.*

jonquil ['dʒɑn kwɪl] *n.* a spring plant with yellow or white flowers, related to the narcissus. ♦ *Mary placed a* *bouquet of jonquils in a vase.* ♦ *The jonquils are in full bloom.*

Jordan ['dʒor dn] See Gazetteer.

josh ['dʒɑʃ] **1.** *tv.* to make fun of someone; to tease someone; to joke around with someone; to kid someone. ♦ *Tom likes to josh his kid brother about his big ears.* ♦ *You're just joshing me!* **2.** *iv.* to tease or joke. ♦ *Don't you know I'm just joshing? I'm not serious.* ♦ *After class, Sue was joshing with Bill about his grades.*

jostle ['dʒɑs əl] **1.** *tv.* to bump into someone, especially in a crowd. ♦ *Tom jostled Dave as they stood in line to buy tickets to the game.* ♦ *I don't like it when someone jostles me.* **2.** *iv.* to move somewhere quickly, especially through a crowded area, while bumping into people or pushing people out of the way. ♦ *We had to jostle through the crowd to get to our seats.* ♦ *Some members of the audience jostled to the front rows for a better view.*

jot ['dʒɑt] **1.** *n.* a very small amount. ♦ *Just pour a jot of cream into my coffee.* ♦ *The boss gave Mary only a jot of recognition for her good work.* **2. jot (down)** *tv.* (+ *adv.*) to write something down quickly; to make a brief note. ♦ *I jotted down the items I needed from the grocery store.* ♦ *Tom quickly jotted a note to Jane.*

jounce ['dʒɑʊns] **1.** *iv.* to move up and down forcefully; to bounce forcefully. ♦ *The grocery bags jounced around in the trunk of the car.* ♦ *We were really jounced on the bumpy ride.* **2.** *tv.* to cause someone or something to move up and down with force; to bounce someone or something with force. ♦ *The truck jounced us as we drove on the gravel road.* ♦ *The rough plane ride jounced the passengers about in their seats.*

journal ['dʒɚn əl] **1.** *n.* a diary; a book where one writes down one's feelings, thoughts, or activities. ♦ *Mary writes in her journal every night.* ♦ *I keep my journal hidden. I don't want anyone to read it.* **2.** *n.* a newspaper, magazine, periodical, or academic publication. ♦ *Bill delivers the* Daily Journal *in his neighborhood every day.* ♦ *I subscribed to all the local journals after I moved into town.*

journalism ['dʒɚn ə lɪz əm] *n.* the field of gathering, writing about, and editing news for newspapers and magazines. (No plural form in this sense.) ♦ *Jane majored in journalism at the university.* ♦ *Bill pursued a career in broadcast journalism.*

journalist ['dʒɚn ə ləst] *n.* someone who gathers, writes, or edits news for newspapers and magazines. ♦ *Tom is a journalist for our local newspaper.* ♦ *The journalist interviewed many famous celebrities.*

journey ['dʒɚn i] **1.** *n.* a trip; a voyage. ♦ *We visited many exotic cities on our journey.* ♦ *Let's take a journey around the world.* **2.** *iv.* to travel. ♦ *The weary travelers journeyed on until they found a hotel.* ♦ *We journeyed to another state over the weekend.*

jovial ['dʒov i əl] *adj.* jolly; full of good humor; cheerful. (Adv: *jovially.*) ♦ *Our letter carrier always has a jovial attitude.* ♦ *Santa Claus is a jovial character.*

jowl ['dʒɑʊl] *n.* the lower jaw; extra skin that hangs from the lower jaw. ♦ *Even though it had a gentle nature, the bulldog's jowls caused it to look ferocious.* ♦ *Bill's fleshy jowls made him look years older.*

joy ['dʒoɪ] **1.** *n.* extreme pleasure or happiness. (No plural form in this sense.) ♦ *My heart is filled with joy.* ♦ *The citizens felt great joy when the war came to an end.* **2.** *n.* someone or something that causes extreme pleasure or happiness. ♦ *My child's birth was a joy.* ♦ *Seeing my daughter graduate from college was one of the joys I'll never forget.* **3. burst with joy** *idiom* [for someone] to be full to the bursting point with happiness. ♦ *When I got my grades, I could have burst with joy.* ♦ *Bill was not exactly bursting with joy when he got the news.*

joyful ['dʒoɪ fəl] **1.** *adj.* full of joy; extremely happy; very glad. (Adv: *joyfully.*) ♦ *Jane's first birthday was a joyful occasion.* ♦ *The couple's wedding was a joyful event.* **2.** *adj.* causing joy; causing extreme happiness. ♦ *The joyful news of the prince's birth was celebrated throughout the kingdom.* ♦ *We had a joyful reunion with all our relatives.*

joyous ['dʒoɪ əs] *adj.* full of joy; extremely happy; very glad. (Adv: *joyously.*) ♦ *Anne's graduation from college was a joyous occasion.* ♦ *Our wedding day will be a joyous experience.*

jubilant ['dʒub ə lənt] *adj.* showing great joy, typically because of a victory. (Adv: *jubilantly.*) ♦ *Bill was jubilant when he finally beat his older brother at chess.* ♦ *The jubilant winner happily accepted the prize.*

Judaism ['dʒud i ɪz əm] *n.* a religion based on the teachings of the Old Testament and the Talmud; the religion and the culture of Jewish people. (No plural form in this sense.) ♦ *Jane converted to Judaism before she married David.* ♦ *The rabbi instructed us in the laws of Judaism.*

judge ['dʒʌdʒ] **1.** *n.* an official who hears and settles cases in a court of law and who presides over trials. ♦ *The crowd became silent when the judge walked into the court.* ♦ *The lawyer regarded Judge Smith as fair and ethical.* **2.** *n.* someone who helps decide the winner of a contest or competition. ♦ *Dave is a judge in the pie-eating contest.* ♦ *I am a judge for the high-school science fair.* **3.** *tv.* to hear and settle a case in a court of law; to preside over a trial in a court of law. ♦ *The judge listened to the arguments and judged the case according to the law.* ♦ *Bob disagreed with the way the case was judged.* **4.** *tv.* to help decide the winner of a contest or competition. ♦ *Tom will judge the annual piano competition.* ♦ *Mary was asked to judge the competing ice skaters.* **5.** *tv.* to state an opinion about someone or something; to evaluate someone or something. ♦ *I will not judge Sue's behavior.* ♦ *Must you judge everything I do?* **6.** *tv.* to estimate something; to make a guess about something. ♦ *Bob judged that the car trip would take about five hours.* ♦ *I couldn't judge the length of string I would need to tie the package, and the piece I cut was too short.*

judgment ['dʒʌdʒ mənt] **1.** *n.* the ability to make the proper decisions; the ability to judge. (No plural form in this sense.) ♦ *You made the error because your judgment is faulty.* ♦ *You certainly exercised poor judgment in this matter.* **2.** *n.* the result of judging; the decision made by a judge or a jury. ♦ *It is the judgment of this court that you are guilty of murder.* ♦ *The court's judgment was challenged in a higher court.* **3.** *n.* an opinion. (No plural form in this sense.) ♦ *In Bob's judgment, we are all wrong.* ♦ *Sue disagreed with Tom's judgment of the situation.* **4. pass judgment (on someone or something)** *idiom* to make a judgment about someone or something. ♦ *I should* *not pass judgment on you, but I certainly could give you some good advice about how to be more pleasant.* ♦ *The judge passed judgment on the defendant who was taken away to prison.*

judicial [dʒu 'dɪʃ əl] *adj.* of or about judges and courts of law, and the system of justice. (Adv: *judicially.*) ♦ *I have great faith in our judicial system.* ♦ *The senator called for a judicial hearing into the matter.*

judiciary [dʒu 'dɪʃ i ɛr i] **the judiciary** *n.* the judges and legal professionals of a certain area, district, state, or country; the part of a government that deals with justice and the courts. (No plural form in this sense. Treated as singular.) ♦ *My cousin is a judge in the municipal judiciary.* ♦ *The federal judiciary can overrule some decisions made by individual state courts.*

jug ['dʒʌg] *n.* a container for liquids, which usually has a narrow top and a small handle. ♦ *The farmer carried cider in a brown jug.* ♦ *The water jug is empty.*

juggle ['dʒʌg əl] **1.** *iv.* to toss objects in the air as in ② for a living or as a hobby. ♦ *The clown knew how to juggle well.* ♦ *Anne juggled onstage at the state fair to entertain the children.* **2.** *tv.* to keep three or more objects moving through the air by catching and throwing them in a circle. ♦ *Tom juggled the oranges in the air.* ♦ *Can you juggle four balls at once?* **3.** *tv.* to deal with several things at the same time. (Figurative on ②.) ♦ *It can be difficult to juggle a career, marriage, and children on a daily basis.* ♦ *John had a problem juggling his numerous responsibilities at work.* **4.** *tv.* to change a financial record in order to cheat or trick someone. (Figurative on ②.) ♦ *The accountant juggled the accounts before the tax audit.* ♦ *The dishonest teller tried to juggle the figures so the bank wouldn't miss the money.*

juggler ['dʒʌg lɚ] *n.* someone who juggles; a performer who is able to juggle. ♦ *We saw a juggler perform at the circus.* ♦ *The juggler tossed five balls into the air.*

juice ['dʒus] **1.** *n.* the liquid part of fruit, vegetables, or meat. ♦ *Would you like a glass of orange juice?* ♦ *That tomato juice is spicy!* **2.** *n.* electricity. (Informal. No plural form in this sense.) ♦ *Give the motor some juice so it will run faster.* ♦ *Turn on the juice so we can test the circuits.* **3. digestive juices** *n.* liquid that is produced by the stomach to help break down food. ♦ *Your digestive juices are eating at your own stomach.* ♦ *A fly puts digestive juices into its food.* **4. stew in one's own juice** *idiom* to be left alone to suffer one's anger or disappointment. ♦ *John has such a terrible temper. When he got mad at us, we just let him go away and stew in his own juice.* ♦ *After John stewed in his own juice for a while, he decided to come back and apologize to us.*

juicy ['dʒus i] **1.** *adj.* full of juice; having much juice. (Adv: *juicily.* Comp: *juicier;* sup: *juiciest.*) ♦ *The children ate the juicy watermelon.* ♦ *Doesn't that juicy peach look good?* **2.** *adj.* interesting; provocative, especially of gossip or scandal. (Figurative on ①. Adv: *juicily.* Comp: *juicier;* sup: *juiciest.*) ♦ *Jane told me a juicy bit of gossip.* ♦ *Bill whispered the juicy story in my ear.*

jukebox ['dʒuk bɑks] *n.* a machine that holds several records or Compact Discs and will play a song that someone selects for a certain amount of money. ♦ *The jukebox contains many records from the 1950s.* ♦ *I put a quarter into the jukebox and selected a song.*

July [dʒə 'lɑɪ] *n.* the seventh month of the year. ♦ *The weather is usually warm in July.* ♦ *July comes after June and before August.*

jumble ['dʒʌm bəl] **1.** *tv.* to mix things up; to cause things to be out of order. ♦ *Jimmy jumbled the socks and underwear in his drawer.* ♦ *Mary accidentally jumbled the papers for the sales presentation.* **2.** *n.* a group of things that are mixed up; a group of things that are out of order. ♦ *The children played with the jumble of toys.* ♦ *The papers are all in a jumble. It will take me a few minutes to get them back in order.*

jumbo ['dʒʌm bo] *adj.* extra large; larger than regular. ♦ *We boarded the jumbo jet.* ♦ *I ordered jumbo shrimp at the seafood restaurant.*

jump ['dʒʌmp] **1.** *iv.* to leap up; to spring up; to push off the ground with one's legs. ♦ *The softball player jumped in the air to catch the ball.* ♦ *My cat jumped into my lap.* **2.** *iv.* to move suddenly, as if surprised or scared. ♦ *Sue jumped when I touched her shoulder.* ♦ *The cat jumped when our dog came into the room.* **3.** *iv.* to go up sharply; to increase sharply; to rise sharply. (Figurative on ①.) ♦ *The price of coffee jumped after an early frost killed most of the coffee crop.* ♦ *Have you noticed how much the price of produce has jumped in the past year?* **4. jump over** *iv. + prep. phr.* to leap over something; to push off the ground with one's legs and go over something. ♦ *The dog jumped over the tall fence.* ♦ *The runner jumped over the hurdles.* **5.** *iv.* to skip over something; to omit something. (Figurative on ①.) ♦ *In our history class, we jumped from the Civil War to World War I because we didn't have enough time to study everything.* ♦ *Using our television's remote control, we jumped past the gruesome parts of the video.* **6.** *tv.* to ambush someone; to attack someone from a hiding place. (Informal.) ♦ *The thief jumped the tourists walking through the alley.* ♦ *We were jumped and robbed in a dark parking lot.* **7.** *tv.* to start a car by connecting its battery to another car's battery. ♦ *Susan jumped Mary's car when her battery wouldn't start.* ♦ *You need cables to jump your car with mine.* **8.** *n.* a leap off the ground; a leap off the ground and over, through, or across something. ♦ *The horse and rider performed a smooth jump over the fence.* ♦ *The horse did not want to make the jump.* **9.** *n.* a sudden rise; an increase. (Figurative on ⑧.) ♦ *The jump in gas prices took us by surprise.* ♦ *The patient's temperature took a sudden jump in the evening.* **10.** *n.* the use of someone else's battery to start one's car. ♦ *I got a jump from the local service station.* ♦ *John asked his brother if he could help him get a jump for his dead battery.* **11. get the jump on someone** *idiom* to do something before someone; to get ahead of someone. ♦ *I got the jump on Tom and got a place in line ahead of him.* ♦ *We'll have to work hard to get the contract because they have the jump on us.* **12. jumping-off point** *idiom* a point or place from which to begin a venture. ♦ *The local library is a good jumping-off point for your research.* ♦ *The position in that firm would be a good jumping-off point for a job in advertising.*

jumper ['dʒʌmp ɚ] **1.** *n.* a sleeveless, one-piece article of women's clothing, like a dress but worn over a shirt or blouse. ♦ *Jane wore a white blouse with her blue jumper.* ♦

My wool jumper is lined with silk. **2. jumper** *n.* either of a pair of cables used to connect the batteries of two different cars so that the stronger battery can start the car with the weaker battery. ♦ *Connect one of the jumpers to this terminal.* ♦ *Do you have any jumpers in your trunk?*

jumpy ['dʒʌmp i] *adj.* nervous; anxious; easily scared. (Adv: *jumpily.* Comp: *jumpier;* sup: *jumpiest.*) ♦ *Mary acted jumpy every time the phone rang.* ♦ *Bill's jumpy attitude made everyone in the room nervous.*

junction ['dʒʌŋk ʃən] *n.* a place where two or more things come together, especially an intersection where roads or train tracks come together or cross. ♦ *I'll meet you at the junction of Main and Lincoln streets.* ♦ *Bill knew there was a gas station at the next junction.*

juncture ['dʒʌŋk tʃɚ] *n.* a critical point in time; a state of affairs. ♦ *I cannot make a decision at this juncture.* ♦ *We are at an important juncture in our negotiations.*

June ['dʒun] *n.* the sixth month of the year. ♦ *The first day of summer is around June 21st.* ♦ *The children get out of school in June.*

jungle ['dʒʌŋ gəl] **1.** *n.* a tropical forest of thick, lush plant growth, usually near the equator. ♦ *The explorers were lost in the jungle for days.* ♦ *The monkeys jumped from tree to tree in the jungle.* **2.** *n.* a complex and jumbled mass or collection of things. (Figurative on ①.) ♦ *I can't understand this jungle of confusing regulations.* ♦ *Sue had trouble following the jungle of rules at the university.*

junior ['dʒun jɚ] **1.** *adj.* of or about the third year of high school or college. ♦ *My parents said I could drive my car to school in my junior year.* ♦ *Tom and Anne went to the junior prom.* **2. junior to** *adj.* + *prep. phr.* lower in rank or position. ♦ *Anne is junior to Jane at the accounting firm.* ♦ *The job you applied for is junior to your current position.* **3. [someone's] junior** *n.* someone who is younger or who has a lower rank or position. ♦ *Jane is my junior at the company; she just started last week.* ♦ *Mary's younger sister is her junior by two years.* **4.** *n.* a student in the third year of high school (11th grade) or the third year of college. ♦ *I am a junior this year at college.* ♦ *The juniors in my high school are taking their college entrance examinations.*

junk ['dʒʌŋk] **1.** *n.* things that are worthless; things that should be thrown away. (No plural form in this sense.) ♦ *The cleaner left some junk near the back door.* ♦ *Throw that junk out! It's been sitting in the attic for years.* ♦ *Don't junk your bicycle. Let me see if I can fix it.* **2.** *n.* a Chinese ship that has a flat bottom and square sails. ♦ *Many junks sailed down the river in China.* ♦ *The family lived and worked on the junk.* **3.** *tv.* to throw something away. ♦ *I'm going to junk that old car. It hasn't worked right since I bought it.*

junkyard ['dʒʌŋk jɑrd] *n.* a dump; a place where junk and metal are bought and sold. ♦ *We took the old junk from the garage to a junkyard.* ♦ *The junkyard down the street sells car parts.*

jurisdiction [dʒɚ ɪs 'dɪk ʃən] **1.** *n.* the legal authority of a judge or government official. ♦ *The city cop had no jurisdiction in the matter that happened outside the city limits.* (No plural form in this sense.) ♦ *It is not within this court's jurisdiction to rule on this particular legal matter.* **2.** *n.* the area or territory where someone or something has legal authority. (No plural form in this sense.) ♦ *Is this regulation enforced in your jurisdiction?* ♦ *The lawyer wanted the case to be tried in a different jurisdiction.*

juror ['dʒɚ or] **1.** *n.* someone who is a member of a jury. ♦ *The juror was shocked by the photos of the crime scene.* ♦ *The lawyer questioned the juror about his past experience with the law.* **2.** *n.* one member of a group of people selected to judge a competition. ♦ *Mr. Brown was selected as a juror for the piano competition.* ♦ *The jurors for the science fair examined all of the projects.*

jury ['dʒɚ i] **1.** *n.* a group of people who listen to evidence at a trial in a court of law and make a decision about the truth of the facts of the case. ♦ *The jury could not reach a unanimous verdict.* ♦ *The members of the jury were interviewed individually before the trial.* **2.** *adj.* <the adj. use of ①.> ♦ *The lawyer requested a jury trial.* ♦ *Mary was called for jury duty.*

just ['dʒʌst] **1.** *adj.* fair; not biased; honest; right; in accordance with the law. (Adv: *justly.*) ♦ *The judge handed down a just ruling in the case.* ♦ *I feel I made a just decision on the matter.* **2.** *adj.* deserved; appropriate. (Adv: *justly.*) ♦ *The criminal received a just punishment.* ♦ *Jimmy collected a just sum of money when he returned the lost wallet.* **3.** *adv.* only. ♦ *There is just one cookie left in the package.* ♦ *I took just a little slice of pizza.* **4.** *adv.* hardly; barely; by just a small amount. ♦ *Bob ran quickly, but he still just missed the train.* ♦ *The sheets are too small and they just cover the top of the bed.* **5.** *adv.* exactly [the right amount and no more]. ♦ *I had just enough paint to cover the whole wall.* ♦ *I have just the right amount of change for the toll.* **6. get one's just reward(s)** *idiom* something as bad as one deserves. ♦ *The criminal who was sent to prison got his just rewards.* ♦ *I am sure that when he died, he got his just reward.*

justice ['dʒʌs tɪs] **1.** *n.* the quality or condition of being just; fairness, especially in a court of law. (No plural form in this sense.) ♦ *Justice prevailed in the court when the defendant was convicted for the crime.* ♦ *I felt that there was justice in the sentence that the criminal received.* **2.** *n.* the administration of law; the practice of law within the court system. (No plural form in this sense.) ♦ *The lawyer took a job with the Department of Justice.* ♦ *Our system of justice protects the rights of the accused person.* **3.** *n.* a judge. (Also a title and term of address.) ♦ *Justice Smith presided over the municipal court.* ♦ *Do you know who is the chief justice of the Supreme Court?* **4. poetic justice** *idiom* appropriate, ideal, or ironic punishment. ♦ *It was poetic justice that Jane won the race after Mary tried to get her banned from the race.* ♦ *The car thieves tried to steal a car with no gas. That's poetic justice.*

justification [dʒəs tə fə 'ke ʃən] **1.** *n.* the reason for doing something; justifying something that is done. (No plural form in this sense.) ♦ *I find no justification for your absence.* ♦ *Anne has a justification for every problem she creates at work.* **2.** *n.* the placement of text in relation to a margin. (No plural form in this sense.) ♦ *Check the justification of the copy before you print it out.* ♦ *The paragraph's justification was not even on the right side.*

justify ['dʒʌs tɪ fɑɪ] **1.** *tv.* to explain why one did something; to give a good reason for something. ♦ *How can you justify what you did yesterday?* ♦ *I demand that you justify your actions!* **2.** *tv.* to place text so that it lines up along the left, right, or both margins. ♦ *Justify the newsletter copy to my specifications.* ♦ *Can you justify the type along the left margin only?*

jut ['dʒʌt] **jut (out)** *iv.* (+ *adv.*) to stick out from something. ♦ *The sharp nail jutted out from the fence.* ♦ *The bill of John's hat jutted to the left.*

juvenile ['dʒu və naɪl] **1.** *n.* a child [from a legal point of view]. ♦ *Many juveniles are arrested annually for shoplifting.* ♦ *The juvenile was tried in court as an adult for the crime.* **2.** *adj.* young [animals]. ♦ *You can tell the juveniles from the adults by the color of their fur.* ♦ *The juveniles will be able to fly as soon as their feathers grow.* **3.** *adj.* youthful; for young people. ♦ *The 12-year-old actor auditioned for several juvenile roles.* ♦ *The clerk directed Jane and her mother to the juvenile clothing section of the store.* **4.** *adj.* childish; of immature behavior. (Figurative on ③.) ♦ *Must you always act so juvenile?* ♦ *Dave's juvenile behavior upsets everyone at the company.*

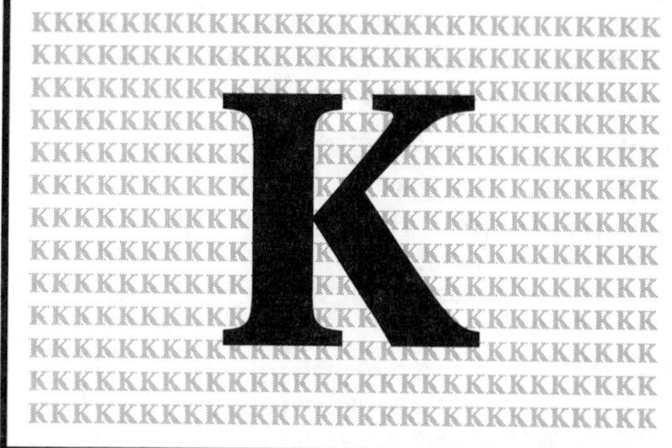

K AND **k** ['ke] *n.* the eleventh letter of the English alphabet. ♦ K *comes before* L. ♦ *The word* kidney *begins with the letter* K.

kangaroo [kæŋ gə 'ru] *n.* a large animal of Australia that hops on its hind legs. (Pl in *-s.*) ♦ *The female kangaroo has a pouch in which she carries her young.* ♦ *The kangaroo hopped across the meadow.*

Kansas ['kæn zəz] See Gazetteer.

karate [kə 'rɑt i] *n.* an east Asian method of fighting using blows from the hands and feet instead of weapons. (No plural form in this sense.) ♦ *I enrolled in a class to learn the art of karate.* ♦ *Tom used karate to ward off the attack.*

keel ['kil] **1.** *n.* the main beam along the bottom of a boat or ship from which the frame is built. ♦ *The boat's keel scraped the rocky bottom of the harbor.* ♦ *Bob laid a keel for his new boat.* **2. keep on an even keel** *idiom* to remain cool and calm. (Originally nautical.) ♦ *If Jane can keep on an even keel and not panic, she will be all right.* ♦ *Try to keep on an even keel and not get upset so easily.* **3. keep something on an even keel** *idiom* to keep something in a steady and untroubled state. ♦ *The manager cannot keep the firm on an even keel any longer.* ♦ *When the workers are unhappy, it is difficult to keep the factory on an even keel.*

keen ['kin] **1.** *adj.* [of a cutting edge] sharp. (Adv: *keenly.* Comp: *keener;* sup: *keenest.*) ♦ *I accidentally cut my finger on the knife's keen edge.* ♦ *The keen edge of the razor blade was made of special steel.* **2.** *adj.* [of a sense of taste, vision, hearing, touch, or smell] sharp. (Figurative on ①. Adv: *keenly.* Comp: *keener;* sup: *keenest.*) ♦ *John had a keen sense of hearing.* ♦ *The dog had a keen sense of smell.* **3. have a keen interest in something** *idiom* to have a strong interest in something; to be very interested in something. ♦ *Tom had always had a keen interest in music, so he started a band.* ♦ *The children have a keen interest in having a pet, so I bought them a cat.* **4. keen on doing something** *idiom* willing or eager to do something. ♦ *Dave isn't very keen on going to the opera.* ♦ *The children are keen on swimming this afternoon. Shall I take them?*

keep ['kip] **1.** *tv., irreg.* to continue doing something. (Pt/pp: kept.) ♦ *Someone kept ringing my doorbell for a long time.* ♦ *Bill keeps going on trips every month.* **2.** *tv., irreg.* to cause someone or something to remain somewhere. ♦ *Keep Mary here while I'm on the phone.* ♦ *Please keep the children in the backyard.* **3.** *tv., irreg.* to have something for a period of time; to continue to have something. ♦ *I kept my car for four years and then I sold it.* ♦ *I will keep this book in my office because I use it so often.* **4. keep up** *tv., irreg. +adv.* to maintain something; to manage something; to run, tend, or take care of something. ♦ *Sue did not keep up her grades this semester.* ♦ *You must keep up your appearance.* **5.** *iv., irreg.* to stay [quiet]. ♦ *Keep quiet about the surprise party.* ♦ *Tell the children to keep silent while I'm sleeping.* **6. earn one's keep** *idiom* to help out with chores in return for food and a place to live; to earn one's pay by doing what is expected. ♦ *I earn my keep at college by shoveling snow in the winter.* ♦ *Tom hardly earns his keep around here. He should be fired.* **7. keep a secret** *idiom* to know a secret and not tell anyone. ♦ *Please keep our little secret private.* ♦ *Do you know how to keep a secret?* **8. keep from doing something** *idiom* to avoid doing something; to refrain from doing something. ♦ *How could I keep from crying? It was so sad!* ♦ *Try to keep from falling off the ladder.* **9. keep someone from doing something** *idiom* to prevent someone from doing something. ♦ *I kept the child from falling in the lake by grabbing his collar.* ♦ *I try to keep myself from overeating, but I seem to fail frequently.* **10. keep one's eye on someone or something** *idiom* to watch someone or something carefully; to monitor someone or something. ♦ *Please keep your eye on the children while I go to the store.* ♦ *Bill kept an eye on his expenses because he was spending too much money.* **11. keep something to oneself** *idiom* to keep something a secret. ♦ *I'm quitting my job, but please keep that to yourself.* ♦ *John is always gossiping. He can't keep anything to himself.* **12. keep up (with the Joneses)** *idiom* to stay financially even with one's peers; to work hard to get the same amount of material goods that one's friends and neighbors have. ♦ *Mr. and Mrs. Brown bought a new car simply to keep up with the Joneses.* ♦ *Keeping up with the Joneses can take all your money.* **13. keep up (with the times)** *idiom* to stay in fashion; to keep up with the news; to be contemporary or modern. ♦ *I try to keep up with the times. I want to know what's going on.* ♦ *Sally learns all the new dances. She likes to keep up.*

keeper ['kip ɚ] *n.* someone who keeps something; a guardian; a protector; a guard. ♦ *The polar bear's keeper dumped a bucket of fish into the bear's enclosure.* ♦ *I don't know where Tom is; I am not his keeper.*

keepsake ['kip sek] *n.* something that is kept to remind the owner of someone or something; a memento. ♦ *My grandmother gave me a cameo for a keepsake.* ♦ *Uncle John left a small keepsake to Anne in his will.*

keg ['kɛg] **1.** *n.* a small wooden barrel, especially one that holds 100 pounds of nails. ♦ *The worker loaded the nail keg onto the truck.* ♦ *I turned the keg upside down and used it as a seat.* **2.** *n.* a small metal barrel, especially one that holds beer. ♦ *The students bought a keg for the party.* ♦ *We returned the empty kegs to the store after the party.* **3. sitting on a powder keg** *idiom* in a risky or explosive situation; in a situation where something serious or dangerous may happen at any time. ♦ *Things are very tense at work. The whole office is sitting on a powder keg.* ♦ *The fire at the oil field seems to be under control for now, but all the workers there are sitting on a powder keg.*

kennel ['kɛn əl] *n.* a place where dogs are kept. ♦ *We placed our two dogs in the local kennel when we went on vacation.* ♦ *The puppies stayed in the warm kennel.*

Kentucky [kən 'tʌk i] See Gazetteer.

Kenya ['kɛn jə] See Gazetteer.

kept ['kɛpt] pp of keep.

kerchief ['kɚ tʃɪf] *n.* a handkerchief; a square cloth worn over the head or around the neck. ♦ *I wore a kerchief while I cleaned the house.* ♦ *The cowboy wore a red kerchief around his neck.*

kernel ['kɚn əl] **1.** *n.* the edible part of a nut; a nutmeat. ♦ *The squirrel got the kernel from its shell.* ♦ *My hamster enjoys eating corn kernels.* **2.** *n.* one seed; one individual seed of corn; one piece of popcorn. ♦ *I scraped the kernels off the cob.* ♦ *Please give me more than five kernels of popcorn!* **3.** *n.* the central, most important part of something; the gist. (Figurative on ①.) ♦ *This article contains a kernel of truth, but it's hidden beneath a lot of irrelevant details and trivial errors.* ♦ *That's the kernel of the idea. I can give you a complete explanation if you're interested.*

kerosene ['kɛr ə sin] *n.* a kind of oil that is burned to make heat or light. (No plural form in this sense.) ♦ *We put kerosene in the empty lantern.* ♦ *The kerosene heater can make a lot of heat.*

ketchup ['kɛtʃ əp] *n.* a thick liquid, made from tomatoes, that is put on food for flavoring. (The same as catsup. No plural form in this sense.) ♦ *John loves ketchup on his fries.* ♦ *I added ketchup to the meatloaf.*

kettle ['kɛt əl] **1.** *n.* a large cooking pot; a pot for heating liquids. ♦ *Put the kettle of water on the stove.* ♦ *Mary stirred the soup in the kettle slowly.* **2. fine kettle of fish** *idiom* a real mess; an unsatisfactory situation. ♦ *The dog has eaten the roast we were going to have for dinner. This is a fine kettle of fish!* ♦ *This is a fine kettle of fish. It's below freezing outside, and the furnace won't work.*

key ['ki] **1.** *n.* a device that unlocks or locks a lock; something that unlocks something that is locked. (Keys are typically flat, metal, and notched along one edge.) ♦ *I used my key to unlock the car door.* ♦ *The police officer has a key that will open the handcuffs.* **2.** *n.* the solution or answer to something. (Figurative on ①.) ♦ *Use the key to solve the problem.* ♦ *The answer key is in the back of the book.* **3.** *n.* a part of a machine or instrument that is pressed down to make something happen, like on a typewriter or a piano. ♦ *John could not play the piano because one of the keys was broken.* ♦ *I pressed the "Enter" key on the computer keyboard.* **4.** *n.* a musical scale that begins on a particular note; a set of related musical notes. ♦ *You must sing the song in a higher key.* ♦ *Anne wanted the band to play her song in a particular key.* **5.** *adj.* important; essential; basic. ♦ *The recipe is lacking a key ingredient.* ♦ *The key point is missing from your speech.*

keyboard ['ki bord] **1.** *n.* a row of keys that make a certain note when pressed. ♦ *Keyboards are found on accordions, organs, pianos, harpsichords, and other similar instruments.* ♦ *Most keyboards have black and white keys.* **2.** *n.* an electronic device that creates music. ♦ *Bob played keyboard in the band.* ♦ *The electric keyboard can make all sorts of sounds.* **3.** *n.* the rows of keys standing for letters, symbols, and numbers as found on typewriters, computers, etc. ♦ *John's fingers sped across the keyboard as he typed the novel.* ♦ *Don't pound on the keyboard so hard. You'll damage it.*

keyhole ['ki hol] *n.* the small hole in a lock into which a key is placed to lock or unlock the lock. ♦ *Look through the keyhole to see if anyone is in the other room.* ♦ *This key won't fit in the keyhole.*

keynote ['ki not] *adj.* primary; main. ♦ *The senator gave the keynote speech at the convention.* ♦ *The keynote speaker was given a standing ovation.*

keypad ['ki pæd] **1.** *n.* [on a computer] a special, separate set of number keys arranged like a calculator. ♦ *Dave typed in the account number on the keypad.* ♦ *The keypad is located on the right-hand side of the keyboard.* **2.** *n.* any small control panel having an arrangement of push buttons, as found on a telephone or a calculator. ♦ *The calculator has an oversized keypad.* ♦ *The keypad numbers were very large, so they were easy to see.*

keystone ['ki ston] **1.** *n.* the center stone at the top of an arch that holds the arch in place. ♦ *The year 1991 was engraved on the keystone.* ♦ *The builder placed the keystone in the arch.* **2.** *n.* the essential part of a plan or theory. (Figurative on ①.) ♦ *The theory is the keystone in our success.* ♦ *Responsibility is the keystone of our company's philosophy.*

khaki ['kæk i] **1.** *n.* a tannish-brown, cotton fabric used to make uniforms for soldiers or regular clothing. (No plural form in this sense.) ♦ *The soldiers were outfitted in khaki.* ♦ *The tourists wore khaki as they traveled in the forest.* **2.** *n.* a tannish-brown color. (No plural form in this sense.) ♦ *Khaki goes well with white and clashes with yellow.* ♦ *Khaki is a popular color for pants.* **3. khakis** *n.* clothing made of ①; trousers made of ①. ♦ *Bob wears khakis to school almost every day.* ♦ *He looks good in khakis and a blue jacket.* **4.** *adj.* a tannish-brown; a light brown. ♦ *The soldier wore a khaki uniform.* ♦ *The prison issued khaki clothes for the inmates.*

kibitzer ['kɪb ɪt sɚ] *n.* someone who gives advice that is not wanted; someone who meddles in someone else's business. (From Yiddish.) ♦ *John is a meddlesome kibitzer when we play bridge.* ♦ *Sue is such a kibitzer that we all try to avoid her.*

kick ['kɪk] **1.** *tv.* to strike someone or something with the foot, usually the toe of a shoe or boot. ♦ *Please don't kick the cat!* ♦ *The children like to kick the ball around the yard.* **2.** *tv.* to give up a bad habit; to quit something. (Slang. Figurative on ①.) ♦ *I tried to kick cigarettes but I couldn't.* ♦ *Bill knew he would kick his drug problem.* **3. kick off** *tv. +adv.* to begin an event; to start something. ♦ *To kick off the celebration, the best athlete on the team gave a speech.* ♦ *We decided to kick the party off by having the band play a song.* **4.** *iv.* to move one's legs back and forth as if kicking something. ♦ *Kick slowly in the water or you will get tired.* ♦ *The baby lay on its back in the crib and kicked.* **5.** *n.* an act of striking someone or something with the foot, as in ①. ♦ *The kick from the mule was painful.* ♦ *I did not expect a kick in the leg from the unruly child.* **6. get a kick out of something** *idiom* something that is exciting; a thrill. ♦ *Mary got a kick out of the funny story.* ♦ *Didn't you get a kick out of the joke?* **7. kick up one's heels** *idiom* to celebrate; to act free or liberated. ♦ *After the test was over, I just wanted to go out and* *kick up my heels.* ♦ *Some of the boys like to kick up their heels on the weekend.*

kickoff ['kɪk ɔf] **1.** *n.* the start of a football game. ♦ *Let's get to the game before the kickoff.* ♦ *Everyone cheered at the moment of the kickoff.* **2.** *n.* the beginning of an event. (Figurative on ①.) ♦ *The opening speech is the kickoff of the convention.* ♦ *We gave away free books as a kickoff to the book sale.*

kid ['kɪd] **1.** *n.* a child; a youngster. ♦ *My kid loves to play with toys.* ♦ *I asked the new kid on the block what his name was.* **2.** *n.* a baby goat. ♦ *The kid nuzzled up against its mother for warmth.* ♦ *The hungry kid cried for food.* **3.** *n.* the skin of ②. (No plural form in this sense.) ♦ *I wore brown kid gloves.* ♦ *Grandma gave Mary a pair of kid gloves for her birthday.* **4.** *tv.* to tease someone; to joke with someone; to trick someone. ♦ *I don't like it when you kid me.* ♦ *We kidded Tom about his new short haircut.* **5.** *adj.* [of a brother or sister] younger. (Informal.) ♦ *My kid sister wanted to go to the mall, and I had to drive her.* ♦ *Dave's kid brother is a real pest.* **6. kid's stuff** *idiom* a very easy task. (Informal.) ♦ *Climbing that hill is kid's stuff.* ♦ *Driving an automatic car is kid's stuff.* **7. all kidding aside** See joke.

kidnap ['kɪd næp] *tv.* to take someone away by force, especially in order to make a demand for something; to abduct someone. (Pt/pp: *kidnapped.*) ♦ *A criminal tried to kidnap the rich family's children.* ♦ *Terrorists kidnapped the ambassador's brother and held him hostage.*

kidnapper ['kɪd næp ɚ] *n.* someone who kidnaps people. ♦ *The kidnapper left a ransom note.* ♦ *Pictures of the kidnapper's face were placed everywhere.*

kidnapping ['kɪd næp ɪŋ] *n.* stealing someone by force; taking someone away by force. (No plural form in this sense.) ♦ *Kidnapping is a federal offense.* ♦ *The criminal went to jail for kidnapping.*

kidney ['kɪd ni] **1.** *n.* one of the two organs that separate waste and water from the bloodstream. ♦ *After the operation, John had only one kidney left.* ♦ *The kidney filters waste from the bloodstream.* **2.** *adj.* <the adj. use of ①.> ♦ *Bill had a chronic kidney disease.* ♦ *The kidney operation was a success.*

kill ['kɪl] **1.** *tv.* to cause the death of someone or something directly. ♦ *Dave used a bow and arrow to kill the deer.* ♦ *The cat killed a mouse and brought it in the house.* **2.** *tv.* to end something; to cause something to end. (Figurative on ①.) ♦ *Kill the project. We've run out of money.* ♦ *The finance committee decided to kill the expensive proposal.* **3.** *iv.* to cause death. ♦ *Smoking kills.* ♦ *The police are worried that the crazy murderer will kill again.* **4.** *n.* an act of killing as in ①. ♦ *The hunters got ready for the next kill.* ♦ *The young lion brought down its first kill and began to eat it.* **5.** *n.* an animal that is hunted and killed ①. (No plural form in this sense.) ♦ *The hunters took their kill to their truck.* ♦ *You must clean the kill before we take it home.* **6. kill time** *idiom* to use something up, especially time. ♦ *I killed time reading a novel.* ♦ *The employees were not encouraged to kill time.*

killer ['kɪl ɚ] *n.* someone or something who kills; someone or something that causes death. ♦ *The criminal became a dangerous killer when he was provoked.* ♦ *Electricity can be a killer, so never touch loose electrical wires.*

killer whale ['kɪl ɚ 'ʍel] *n.* the orca, a large black and white marine mammal. ♦ *A killer whale swam near our ship.* ♦ *I saw a killer whale leap out of the water.*

killing ['kɪl ɪŋ] *n.* a specific death that was caused by someone or something. ♦ *The hunter participated in the killing.* ♦ *Three criminals were arrested for the killing.*

killjoy ['kɪl dʒoɪ] *n.* someone who takes all the fun out of something; someone who spoils other people's fun. ♦ *Bill is always a killjoy at parties!* ♦ *Don't be a killjoy by making us go home early!*

kilogram ['kɪl ə græm] *n.* a metric unit of measuring weight equal to 1,000 grams or about 2.2 pounds. ♦ *The infant weighed 5 kilograms.* ♦ *The flour was measured in kilograms.*

kilometer [kɪ 'lɑm ə tɚ] *n.* a metric unit of measuring distance equal to 1,000 meters or about ⅝ of a mile. ♦ *Jane ran 10 kilometers in a race.* ♦ *The town was located 30 kilometers from our home.*

kilowatt ['kɪl ə wɑt] *n.* a metric unit of electrical power equal to 1,000 watts per hour. (Abbreviated *kW* or *kw.*) ♦ *Our toaster uses 2 kilowatts.* ♦ *I have a generator that produces about 10 kW.*

kimono [kə 'mon o] *n.* a Japanese robe that is held in place by a wide sash. (Pl ends in *-s.*) ♦ *Anne wore a kimono to the party.* ♦ *The Japanese actor performed in a traditional kimono.*

kin ['kɪn] *n.* family; relatives. (No plural form in this sense. Treated as plural.) ♦ *We are kin to the Smith family in San Diego.* ♦ *My kin have always lived in the mountains of West Virginia.*

kind ['kɑɪnd] **1.** *n.* a sort; a type; a variety. (Compare with ③.) ♦ *I would like the kind of bike that Jimmy has.* ♦ *I don't want that kind. I think it's ugly.* **2.** *adj.* thoughtful; helpful. (Adv: *kindly.* Comp: *kinder;* sup: *kindest.*) ♦ *Dave is a kind and cheerful person.* ♦ *Would you be kind enough to lend me your handkerchief?* **3. a kind of something** *idiom* a variety of something that is fairly close to the real thing, even though it is not exactly the real thing. (Contrast with ①.) ♦ *I used a folded newspaper as a kind of hat to keep the rain off.* ♦ *Bill is serving as a kind of helper or assistant on this project.* **4. kind of something** *idiom* somewhat; rather; having a small or noticeable amount of a characteristic; sort of. ♦ *I am kind of tired. Let's go home.* ♦ *An orange can be kind of sweet and kind of sour at the same time.*

kindergarten ['kɪn dɚ gɑrd n] *n.* the grade before first grade, usually for children between the ages of 4 and 6. ♦ *The children took naps every day when they went to kindergarten.* ♦ *Anne learned to count to 25 when she was in kindergarten.*

kindhearted ['kɑɪnd 'hɑrt ɪd] *adj.* kind; thoughtful. (Adv: *kindheartedly.*) ♦ *My kindhearted neighbor baked me a cake for my birthday.* ♦ *The kindhearted passenger stood up so that the elderly man could sit down.*

kindle ['kɪnd əl] **1.** *tv.* to set fire to something; to set something on fire. ♦ *John kindled a fire in the stove.* ♦ *You can't kindle a fire in the rain.* **2.** *tv.* to cause something to happen; to bring something into action. (Figurative on ①.) ♦ *Bill knows how to kindle good feelings among his employees.* ♦ *I wanted to kindle a pleasant atmosphere for* *them.* **3.** *iv.* to catch fire. ♦ *The dry branches kindled easily.* ♦ *The wood kindled quickly in the fire.*

kindling ['kɪnd lɪŋ] *n.* wood that is used to start a fire. (No plural form in this sense. Number is expressed with *piece(s)* or *stick(s) of kindling.*) ♦ *Use kindling to start the campfire.* ♦ *The kindling felt damp, so I chose not to use it.*

kindly ['kɑɪnd li] **1.** *adj.* [of someone] kind; [of someone] having a kind or pleasant manner. (Comp: *kindlier;* sup: *kindliest.*) ♦ *A kindly old man held the door open for me.* ♦ *Some kindly person has volunteered to clean up the lunchroom.* **2.** *adv.* in a kind way; thoughtfully. ♦ *We were treated very kindly at the hotel.* ♦ *Bill acted kindly toward his coworkers.* **3.** *adv.* please [in questions or requests]; in an obliging manner. (Used just before the verb.) ♦ *Would you kindly lend me your pen?* ♦ *Will you kindly close the window?*

kindness ['kɑɪnd nəs] **1.** *n.* the quality of being kind. (No plural form in this sense.) ♦ *My heart overflowed with kindness.* ♦ *Mary's fears were put to rest by Tom's kindness.* **2.** *n.* a kind action. (No plural form in this sense. Number expressed with *act(s) of kindness.*) ♦ *My neighbor did a special kindness for me when he cut my grass.* ♦ *Your kindness is much appreciated.* **3. do someone a kindness** *idiom* to do a kind deed for a person. ♦ *My neighbor did me a kindness when he cut my grass.* ♦ *I am always happy to have the opportunity of doing someone a kindness.* **4. milk of human kindness** *idiom* natural kindness and sympathy shown to others. ♦ *Mary is completely hard and selfish—she has no milk of human kindness in her.* ♦ *Bob is too full of the milk of human kindness, and people take advantage of him.*

kinfolk ['kɪn fok] *n., irreg.* kin; relatives; family. (No plural form in this sense.) ♦ *My kinfolk come from Ireland.* ♦ *Do your kinfolk live around here?*

king ['kɪŋ] **1.** *n.* the male ruler of a nation governed by a monarchy. ♦ *The prince will someday become king of England.* ♦ *A king rules over his subjects.* **2.** *n.* a playing card with a picture of ① on it. ♦ *John had all four kings in his hand and won the poker game.* ♦ *Mary laid down the king of spades.* **3.** *n.* a playing piece in chess that can move one space in any direction. ♦ *It's your turn to move your king.* ♦ *If you cannot move your king to a safe square, I will win.*

kingdom ['kɪŋ dəm] **1.** *n.* a country ruled by a king or queen. ♦ *King Edward ruled over a vast kingdom.* ♦ *The queen knew the kingdom would be hers when the king died.* **2.** *n.* one of three divisions of nature—animal, vegetable, and mineral. ♦ *Humans are members of the animal kingdom.* ♦ *Roses are part of the vegetable kingdom.*

king-size(d) ['kɪŋ sɑɪz(d)] *adj.* large; larger than regular. ♦ *John bought a king-sized bed.* ♦ *This detergent comes in a king-size box.*

kink ['kɪŋk] **1.** *n.* a twist in a rope, coil, thread, etc. ♦ *I had a difficult time getting the kinks out of this rope.* ♦ *There is a kink in the gold chain.* **2.** *n.* a stiff muscle. (Figurative on ①.) ♦ *I have a kink in my shoulder.* ♦ *Please rub the kink out of my neck.* **3.** *tv.* to twist or curl a rope, coil, thread, etc. ♦ *Don't kink the rope.* ♦ *John kinked the gold chain.*

kinship ['kɪn ʃɪp] **1.** *n.* the fact of being related to someone. (No plural form in this sense.) ♦ *I can prove my kinship with George Washington.* ♦ *We cannot establish any kinship between your cousin and my uncle because they have always lived in different countries.* **2.** *n.* a relationship or affinity. (Figurative on ①. No plural form in this sense.) ♦ *I feel a strong kinship with John.* ♦ *There is a real kinship of believers in the group.*

kiss ['kɪs] **1.** *n.* a touching of one's lips to someone or something, especially someone else's lips. ♦ *My aunt's kiss left some lipstick on my cheek.* ♦ *Jane gave her boyfriend a goodnight kiss.* **2.** *n.* a gentle touch. (Figurative on ①.) ♦ *The kiss of dew made the flowers glisten.* ♦ *The kiss of the wind caressed my face.* **3.** *tv.* to touch one's lips to someone or something, especially someone else's lips. ♦ *Bob kissed Jane before he went to work.* ♦ *I kissed my boyfriend while we sat on my front porch.* **4.** *iv.* [for two people] to kiss as in ①. ♦ *Mary and Dave kissed.* ♦ *Lovers were kissing in the park.* **5. kiss and make up** *idiom* to forgive (someone) and be friends again. ♦ *They were very angry, but in the end they kissed and made up.* ♦ *I'm sorry. Let's kiss and make up.* **6. kiss of death** *idiom* an act that puts an end to someone or something. ♦ *The mayor's veto was the kiss of death for the new law.* ♦ *Fainting onstage was the kiss of death for my acting career.* **7. kiss something good-bye** *idiom* to anticipate or experience the loss of something. ♦ *If you leave your camera on a park bench, you can kiss it good-bye.* ♦ *You kissed your wallet good-bye when you left it in the store.*

kit ['kɪt] **1.** *n.* a compartment or carrying device that holds tools, equipment, or supplies for a specific purpose. ♦ *The plumber reached into his tool kit for a wrench.* ♦ *The kit in the trunk holds many tools.* **2.** *n.* the parts and instructions needed to build a particular thing, such as a model airplane. ♦ *Anne put the airplane kit together quickly.* ♦ *I bought Tom a model-car kit for his birthday.*

kitchen ['kɪtʃ ən] **1.** *n.* a room where food is stored and cooked. ♦ *Sue loves to cook, so she spends a lot of time in the kitchen.* ♦ *My kitchen has brand-new cabinets.* **2.** *adj.* <the adj. use of ①.> ♦ *The kitchen cabinet is made of maple wood.* ♦ *Push the kitchen chair into the table.*

kite ['kɑɪt] *n.* a small wooden frame covered with cloth, paper, or plastic and attached to a long string. ♦ *It is fun to fly a kite on a windy day.* ♦ *Jane flew her paper kite in the park.*

kitten ['kɪt n] *n.* a baby cat; a young cat. ♦ *The kitten slept next to its mother.* ♦ *My kitten is only two months old.*

kitty ['kɪt i] **1.** *n.* the diminutive form of kitten. ♦ *"Here kitty, kitty!" called the child.* ♦ *Our kitty is 6 weeks old.* **2.** *n.* a container that holds a fund of accumulated money and the money itself. ♦ *The extra money is in the kitty.* ♦ *Every time you have some coffee, put a quarter in the kitty.* **3. feed the kitty** *idiom* to contribute money; to put money into ②. ♦ *Please feed the kitty. Make a contribution to help sick children.* ♦ *Come on, Bill. Feed the kitty. You can afford a dollar for a good cause.*

kiwi ['ki wi] **1.** *n.* a small bird of New Zealand that has very short wings and cannot fly. ♦ *The kiwi has a long bill.* ♦ *The ostrich and kiwi are birds that cannot fly.* **2.** *n.* a soft, bright green fruit covered with a fuzzy, brown skin. ♦ *I sliced the kiwi for a snack.* ♦ *Sue lined the dessert bowl with fresh kiwi.*

knack ['næk] *n.* an ability to do something easily; a skill. ♦ *Jane had a knack for solving problems.* ♦ *Getting this box open requires a special knack.*

knapsack ['næp sæk] *n.* a backpack; a bag used to carry things that is slung over one's back. ♦ *Bill carried a knapsack on his camping trip.* ♦ *We filled the knapsack with food and clothes.*

knead ['nid] **1.** *tv.* to mix something together by squeezing it with one's hands. ♦ *I knead the dough when I make bread.* ♦ *Dave kneaded the clay before he began to shape it.* **2.** *tv.* to massage a muscle. (Figurative on ①.) ♦ *It felt good when she kneaded my sore back.* ♦ *Please knead my stiff shoulder.*

knee ['ni] **1.** *n.* the front part of the joint in the middle of the leg. ♦ *I bruised my knee when I ran into the table.* ♦ *The athlete's right knee was operated on in the hospital.* **2.** *n.* the part of a pants leg that covers ①. ♦ *Bill tore the left knee of his uniform.* ♦ *Sue ripped a hole in the knee of her pants.*

kneecap ['ni kæp] *n.* the flat bone at the front of the knee. ♦ *The football player injured his kneecap.* ♦ *Mike kicked John in the kneecap.*

knee-deep ['ni 'dip] *adj.* as deep as the height of one's knees. ♦ *Mary stood in the knee-deep mud.* ♦ *The water is knee-deep in that part of the lake.*

knee-jerk ['ni dʒɚk] **knee-jerk reaction** *adj.* automatic; involuntary; done without thinking. ♦ *Dave has a knee-jerk reaction to all books by that author.* ♦ *Must you always have a knee-jerk reaction to everything I tell you?*

kneel ['nil] *iv., irreg.* to put the weight of one's body on one or both knees. (Pt/pp: *kneeled* or knelt.) ♦ *I don't like to kneel on my right knee. It hurts.* ♦ *The worshipers knelt in church during the service.*

knell ['nɛl] **1.** *n.* the sound of bells ringing to announce a death or funeral. ♦ *The mournful knell of the bells echoed through the dismal streets.* ♦ *The church bell rang a sorrowful knell.* **2. death-knell** *n.* the sound of bells ringing to signify someone's death. ♦ *A death-knell echoed through the streets, announcing the end of another life.* ♦ *The death-knell rang from the church tower as the mourners left for the cemetery.* **3. death-knell** *n.* something that announces the end or failure of something. (Figurative on ②.) ♦ *The budget cuts for our program were the death-knell of our department.* ♦ *A rattling noise in the engine sounded the death-knell for my old car.*

knelt ['nɛlt] a pt/pp of kneel.

knew ['nu] pt of know.

knick-knack ['nɪk næk] *n.* a small trinket; a small, pretty object kept on a shelf or table. ♦ *John collected ceramic knick-knacks.* ♦ *Don't knock that knick-knack off the bookcase!*

knife ['nɑɪf] **1.** *n., irreg.* a long, flat utensil that has a handle and a sharp edge used for cutting. (Pl: knives.) ♦ *Use this knife to slice the onion.* ♦ *Anne cuts her steak with a sharp knife.* **2.** *tv.* to stab someone or something. ♦ *Battling soldiers knifed and battered each other in combat.* ♦ *The criminals were arrested for knifing their victim.*

knight ['nɑɪt] **1.** *n.* a mounted soldier in medieval times who, through honorable deeds, has risen to a high level of military rank. (Usually pictured as wearing metal armor.) ♦ *The brave knight saved the princess.* ♦ *The knight in the fairy tale slew the dragon.* **2.** *n.* a man who has been specially honored by a king or queen. ♦ *Sir John became a knight in a special ceremony in the palace.* ♦ *The queen made John a knight through a special proclamation.* **3.** *n.* a playing piece in chess that can be moved one space up or down and two spaces over or two spaces up or down and one space over. ♦ *My knight captured your pawn.* ♦ *The knight is a chess piece that has a horse's head.* **4.** *tv.* [for a king or queen] to declare someone ① or ②. ♦ *The queen knighted the politician for service to his country.* ♦ *Sir Edward had been knighted by King John.*

knit ['nɪt] **1.** *tv.* to make a fabric or clothing by using long needles to loop yarn or thread together. ♦ *I knitted a pair of mittens for myself.* ♦ *Mary likes to knit scarves in the winter.* **2. knit one's brow** *idiom* to cause one's brow to wrinkle. ♦ *Bob knitted his brow when he was confused.* ♦ *Jane knitted her brow because she was angry.*

knitted ['nɪt ɪd] *adj.* made by looping yarn or thread together with long needles. ♦ *I gave John a knitted sweater for his birthday.* ♦ *Knitted slippers are very warm.*

knitting ['nɪt ɪŋ] **1.** *n.* the hobby or pastime of people who knit. (No plural form in this sense.) ♦ *Do you enjoy knitting?* ♦ *Knitting is a very relaxing hobby for me.* **2.** *n.* something that is being knitted. (No plural form in this sense.) ♦ *My knitting is in that basket.* ♦ *I worked on some knitting during my lunch break.*

knives ['nɑɪvz] pl of knife.

knob ['nɑb] *n.* a round handle or control button. ♦ *The knob on the dresser drawer is loose.* ♦ *If you turn the knob to the right it will turn the radio off.*

knock ['nɑk] **1.** *n.* the noise made by knocking as with ⑥. ♦ *I heard a knock in the engine.* ♦ *Did you hear that knock? I think someone is at the door.* **2.** *n.* a sharp hit; a rap; a thump. ♦ *Bill received a knock on the head.* ♦ *Anne accidentally gave John a knock in the chest with her elbow.* **3.** *tv.* to hit or bump something and make it move or fall; to hit something against someone or something. ♦ *The police officer knocked the thief against the wall.* ♦ *I knocked the vase off the coffee table.* **4.** *tv.* to criticize someone or something. (Colloquial.) ♦ *Don't knock the idea until you've heard it!* ♦ *Must you always knock everything I say?* **5. knock out** *tv.* +*adv.* to make someone or some creature unconscious, typically by striking one or more blows; ♦ *A tree limb fell on my head and knocked me out.* ♦ *I hit John with my fist and knocked him out.* **6.** *iv.* to hit one's knuckles against something. ♦ *I knocked at the door.* ♦ *Sue knocked so hard that her knuckles hurt.*

knoll ['nɔl] *n.* a small hill. ♦ *A single tree grew on the grassy knoll.* ♦ *The children played on a knoll in the park where I could watch them.*

knot ['nɑt] **1.** *n.* a tight lump made where pieces of rope, cord, hair, string, etc., are tied together. ♦ *Untie the knot in the rope.* ♦ *Anne tied a knot in her scarf.* **2.** *n.* a hard circle of wood in a board, where a small branch was joined. ♦ *I pounded the knot out of the board with a hammer.* ♦ *The knot was dark brown.* **3.** *n.* a unit of distance equal to 1.15 miles, used to measure distance at sea and the speed of ships and wind at sea. ♦ *The ship was traveling at 10 knots per hour.* ♦ *Knots per hour are measured by the number of nautical miles (about 6,080 feet) covered per hour.* **4.** *tv.* to tie something in ①; to fasten something with ①. ♦ *Please knot the rope quickly.* ♦ *Can you knot the ends of the cord together?* **5.** *iv.* to become tied or twisted into ①. ♦ *As the rope twisted, it knotted.* ♦ *The cord became knotted.* **6. tie someone in knots** *idiom* to become anxious or upset. ♦ *John tied himself in knots worrying about his wife during her operation.* ♦ *This waiting and worrying really ties me in knots.*

knothole ['nɑt hol] *n.* a hole in a board where a **knot** ② used to be. ♦ *I peered through a knothole in the door.* ♦ *John's finger got stuck in the knothole.*

knotty ['nɑt i] **1.** *adj.* full of knots. (Comp: *knottier;* sup: *knottiest.*) ♦ *I was out in the wind and now my hair is all knotty.* ♦ *Mary's yarn is all knotty and she has to get the knots out before she can knit.* **2.** *adj.* difficult; hard to solve or overcome. (Figurative on ①. Comp: *knottier;* sup: *knottiest.*) ♦ *I found myself in a knotty situation.* ♦ *Bill had a knotty problem to solve.* **3. knotty pine** *n.* pine wood that is full of **knots** ②. (No plural form in this sense.) ♦ *The furniture is made of knotty pine.* ♦ *My room is paneled with knotty pine.*

know ['no] **1.** *tv., irreg.* to have met and become familiar with someone. (Pt: **knew**; pp: **known**.) ♦ *I know your family well.* ♦ *Do you know my sister from Texas?* **2.** *tv., irreg.* to understand something; to have had experience with something. ♦ *I know what you mean.* ♦ *We know calculus.* **3.** *tv., irreg.* to recognize someone or something. ♦ *Tom knew Bill the minute that he saw him walking up the street.* ♦ *I know trouble when I see it.* **4.** *iv., irreg.* to have knowledge about someone or something; to have information about someone or something. ♦ *Do you know how to change a flat tire?* ♦ *You don't have to tell me about the party. I already know about it.* **5. in the know** *idiom* knowledgeable. ♦ *Let's ask Bob. He's in the know.* ♦ *I have no knowledge of how to work this machine. I think I can get myself in the know very quickly though.* **6. know one's ABCs** *idiom* to know the most basic things, such as the letters of the alphabet, about something. ♦ *Bill can't do it. He doesn't even know his ABCs.* ♦ *You can't expect to write novels when you don't even know your ABCs.*

know-how ['no hɑʊ] *n.* the ability to do something; skill. (No plural form in this sense.) ♦ *John has the know-how to complete the task.* ♦ *I wish I had the know-how to fix this sink.*

knowing ['no ɪŋ] **1.** *adj.* aware [of what is happening]; informed. (Adv: *knowingly.*) ♦ *Mary was a knowing participant in the conspiracy.* ♦ *John was a knowing accomplice to the crime.* **2.** *adj.* shrewd; cunning. (Figurative on ①. Adv: *knowingly.*) ♦ *Bill had a knowing look on his face.* ♦ *Jane tried to hide her knowing smile.*

knowledge ['nɑl ɪdʒ] **1.** *n.* the information that is known about someone or something. (No plural form in this sense.) ♦ *I got the knowledge I needed to operate the machine by reading the manual.* ♦ *It takes special knowledge to program a computer.* **2.** *n.* familiarity with facts about something that are not generally known. (No plural form in this sense.) ♦ *I have knowledge of John's disappearance.* ♦ *Do you have any knowledge of Jane's situation?*

knowledgeable ['nɑl ɪdʒ ə bəl] *adj.* having knowledge of someone or something; knowing about someone or something; well-informed. (Adv: *knowledgeably.*) ♦ *I am knowledgeable on the use of this computer.* ♦ *Are you knowledgeable about algebra?*

known ['non] **1.** pp of know. **2.** *adj.* recognized as something [bad]. ♦ *That man is a known thief in our town.* ♦ *Bob is a known pickpocket. Watch out for him.* **3.** *n.* something that is generally recognized and understood as opposed to something that is not. ♦ *The weight of the stone is a known in this equation. Its velocity is an unknown.* ♦ *To start with, let's make a list of the knowns and the unknowns.* **4. known fact** *idiom* something that is generally recognized as a fact. ♦ *That grass is green is a known fact.* ♦ *It is a known fact that John was in Chicago on the night of the murder.* **5. known quantity** *idiom* someone whose character, personality, and behavior are recognized and understood. ♦ *We need not worry about how John will behave. He is a known quantity.* ♦ *Lisa is a known quantity and I am sure she will not surprise us by voting with the opposition.*

knuckle ['nʌk əl] *n.* the joint between the bones of a finger or the joint between the finger and the hand. ♦ *The teacher hit Jimmy on the knuckles with a ruler.* ♦ *I scraped my knuckles on the concrete wall.*

koala [ko 'ɑl ə] *n.* an animal of Australia that looks like a small bear and lives in trees. ♦ *The koala climbed the tree.* ♦ *A baby koala has thick, gray fur.*

Koran [ko 'ræn] *n.* the holy book of the Islamic religion. ♦ *Muslims read the sacred Koran.* ♦ *The Koran has 114 chapters.*

Korea [ko 'rɪ ə] See **North Korea** and **South Korea** in the Gazetteer.

Korean [kə 'ri ən] **1.** *n.* a citizen or native of North Korea or South Korea. ♦ *A family of Koreans lives on our block.* ♦ *Several Koreans attended the international business meeting.* **2.** *n.* the language spoken in North Korea or South Korea by ①. (No plural form in this sense.) ♦ *Korean is not taught in many American schools.* ♦ *My cousin studies Korean at the university.* **3.** *adj.* of or about Korea, ①, or ②. ♦ *My cousin, Mary, is studying Korean art.* ♦ *We ate at a Korean restaurant last night.*

kosher ['koʃ ɚ] **1.** *adj.* meeting the requirements of Jewish dietary laws; of or about food that is prepared in a way for Jewish people to eat in accordance with their religion. ♦ *The Jewish family ate in a kosher restaurant.* ♦ *I prepared a kosher meal for my family.* **2.** *adj.* legitimate; OK. (Informal. Figurative on ①.) ♦ *Your idea is just not kosher! It's unethical!* ♦ *Is this plan kosher with you?*

krypton ['krɪp tɑn] *n.* a colorless, gaseous chemical element used in light bulbs and electronic devices. (No plural form in this sense.) ♦ *The atomic symbol of krypton is Kr, and its atomic number is 36.* ♦ *The researcher developed new uses in electronics for krypton.*

Kuwait [ku 'wet] See Gazetteer.

Kwanzaa ['kwɑn zɑ] *n.* a harvest festival holiday, beginning on December 26 and patterned on African themes, that is celebrated by Americans of African descent in the United States. ♦ *The children celebrated Kwanzaa at their school.* ♦ *The Joneses shared Kwanzaa with their friends and loved ones.*

L AND **l** ['ɛl] *n.* the 12th letter of the English alphabet. ♦ *There are two* Ls *in the word* lily. ♦ *The letter* L *comes between* K *and* M *in the alphabet.*

lab ['læb] **1.** *n.* laboratory. ♦ *When do your blood-test results come back from the lab?* ♦ *The biologist took the specimen back to her lab.* **2. Lab** *n.* a Labrador retriever, which is a large hunting dog. ♦ *I went hunting for rabbits with my trusty Lab.* ♦ *Our Lab eats a lot of dog food every day.*

label ['leb əl] **1.** *n.* a small notice bearing important information. ♦ *The label on the bottle tells what's in it and how to use it.* ♦ *I tore the label loose from the inside of my shirt collar.* **2.** *n.* a phrase that is used to describe people or things. ♦ *When you put labels on people, you're just stereotyping them.* ♦ *John always jokes around in class, so the label of "class clown" suits him.* **3.** *tv.* to attach ① to something. ♦ *I labeled the bags of vegetables before freezing them.* ♦ *Bill labeled the children's presents with their names.* **4. label (as)** *tv.* (+ *prep. phr.*) to classify someone or something; to put someone or something into a category. ♦ *The principal labeled the unruly student as a troublemaker.* ♦ *I don't want to be labeled as a complainer, but this hotel has many faults.*

labial ['leb i əl] **1.** *adj.* of or about the lips and their role in speech. (Adv: *labially.*) ♦ *The sound* [t] *is a dental sound, not a labial one.* ♦ *Labial consonants are found in most languages.* **2.** *n.* a sound that is made using the lips, such as [p], [b], or [m]. ♦ *The sound* [m] *is an example of a labial.* ♦ *Labials are difficult for ventriloquists to produce because people can see their lips move.*

labor ['leb ɚ] **1.** *n.* a kind of work, especially hard, physical work. (No plural form in this sense.) ♦ *The prisoners were forced to do heavy labor.* ♦ *Building a house requires a lot of labor.* **2. labors** *n.* work or the product of work; effort, but usually not ①. (Treated as plural.) ♦ *After he wrote his book, John sat back and relaxed from his labors.* ♦ *Her labors were rewarded by a good salary increase.* **3.** *n.* a work force; the workers of an area, especially in contrast to people in management. (No plural form in this sense.) ♦ *The labor at the factory decided to strike.* ♦ *Management tried to convince labor that the contract was fair.* **4.** *n.* the work a woman's body does to bring about birth; the contractions of the uterus in the process of giving birth. (No plural form in this sense.) ♦ *Labor started 12 hours before the baby was born.* ♦ *The ambulance rushed the woman to the hospital when her labor began.* **5. labor pains** *n.* the pains that accompany childbirth. ♦ *Anne went to the hospital as soon as she felt labor pains.* ♦ *Susan asked for an anesthetic because she hated labor pains.* **6.** *adj.* <the adj. use of ③.> ♦ *The factory hired a consultant to examine labor problems.* ♦ *The economics professor specialized in labor issues.* **7.** *iv.* to work hard. ♦ *The construction workers labored in the hot sun.* ♦ *The crew labored for days on the difficult project.* **8. in labor** *idiom* [of a woman] experiencing the pains and exertion of ④. ♦ *Susan was in labor for nearly eight hours.* ♦ *As soon as she had been in labor for an hour, she went to the hospital.* **9. labor of love** *idiom* a task that is either unpaid or badly paid and that one does simply for one's own satisfaction or pleasure or to please someone whom one likes or loves. ♦ *Jane made no money out of the biography she wrote. She was writing about the life of a friend, and the book was a labor of love.* ♦ *Mary hates knitting, but she made a sweater for her boyfriend. What a labor of love!*

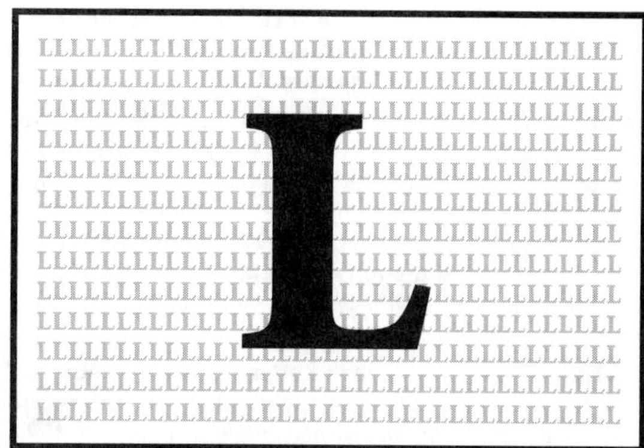

laboratory ['læb rə tor i] **1.** *n.* a room or building that contains scientific equipment for experiments, tests, manufacture, or instruction. (Abbreviated lab.) ♦ *My laboratory has a lot of sophisticated equipment.* ♦ *The intern took the blood samples to the laboratory.* **2.** *n.* a setting where experimentation can take place. (Figurative on ①.) ♦ *The forest is a laboratory for studying plant growth.* ♦ *The biologist's laboratory was the entire Atlantic Ocean.* **3.** *adj.* <the adj. use of ①.> ♦ *The laboratory animals were tested for their reactions to caffeine.* ♦ *I spilled some acid on my laboratory coat.*

Labor Day ['leb ɚ de] *n.* the first Monday in September, set aside in the United States and Canada as a holiday to honor working people. ♦ *Our company is closed on Labor Day.* ♦ *The striking union workers held a press conference on Labor Day.*

labored ['leb ɚd] *adj.* forced; done with difficulty; difficult; showing effort. ♦ *I heard labored breathing coming from inside the hospital room.* ♦ *Your breathing would be less labored if you didn't smoke so much.*

laborer ['leb ɚ ɚ] *n.* a worker, especially an unskilled worker who does hard, physical work. ♦ *The laborer worked six days a week from dawn to dusk.* ♦ *At noon, the laborers put down their tools and ate lunch.*

laborious [lə 'bor i əs] **1.** *adj.* requiring hard work. (Adv: *laboriously.*) ♦ *Rebuilding the town after the earthquake was a laborious task.* ♦ *Constructing houses is a laborious job.* **2.** *adj.* hardworking; diligent; industrious. (Adv: *laboriously.*) ♦ *The laborious worker received a bonus at the end of the year.* ♦ *Anne received a raise for her laborious efforts.*

Labrador retriever ['læb rə dor rɪ 'tri vɚ] *n.* a large hunting dog that retrieves the animals that are shot. ♦ *The Labrador retriever is from Canada.* ♦ *A Labrador retriever dived into the pond to retrieve the ducks we had shot.*

lace ['les] **1.** *n.* a delicate web of cotton or other thread woven into a design or pattern. (No plural form in this sense.) ♦ *The bride's veil was trimmed with lace.* ♦ *Her delicate shawl was made of fine lace.* **2.** *n.* a string used for tying one's shoes closed; a shoelace. ♦ *Pull the laces tight before you tie them.* ♦ *Your laces are untied.* **3. lace (up)** *tv.* (+ *adv.*) to tie one's shoes. ♦ *I taught my daughter how to lace her shoes.* ♦ *I laced up my shoes tightly.* **4.** *adj.* made of ①. ♦ *Anne's lace shawl keeps her shoulders warm.* ♦ *I washed the delicate lace tablecloth carefully.*

laceration [læs ə 're ʃən] *n.* a cut or tear in the skin. ♦ *The nurse cleaned and bandaged my lacerations.* ♦ *John's car was destroyed, but he only suffered minor lacerations.*

lack ['læk] **1.** *n.* a shortage of something; the condition of not having any of something. (No plural form in this sense.) ♦ *The city rationed water because of a lack of rain.* ♦ *The frightened soldier suffered from a lack of courage.* **2.** *tv.* to need something; to not have enough of something; to be without something. ♦ *Because the soldier lacked courage, he ran from the battle.* ♦ *I lack the money needed to go on a nice vacation.*

lackadaisical [læk ə 'dez ɪ kəl] *adj.* without a purpose; without determination or vigor. (Adv: *lackadaisically* [...ɪk li].) ♦ *The lackadaisical teenager slept all day.* ♦ *Our lackadaisical football team finished in last place.*

lackey ['læk i] *n.* someone who does what is demanded without question. ♦ *The boss asked his lackey to bring him some lunch.* ♦ *You should take your letters to the post office to be mailed. I'm not your lackey!*

lackluster ['læk ləs tɚ] *adj.* dull; not shining; not bright; without energy. ♦ *The lackluster stone was obviously not a diamond.* ♦ *I fell asleep during the lackluster movie.*

lacquer ['læk ɚ] **1.** *n.* a hard, shiny varnish that is put on objects made of wood. (No plural form in this sense.) ♦ *I coated the bookshelf with lacquer.* ♦ *The spilled acid damaged the protective layer of lacquer.* **2.** *tv.* to cover something with ①. ♦ *I lacquered my bookshelves with shiny black lacquer.* ♦ *Bob lacquered the wooden porch to protect it from rain and snow.*

lacrosse [lə 'krɔs] *n.* a sport where players use baskets with long handles to pass the ball to each other. (No plural form in this sense.) ♦ *In lacrosse, points are scored when the ball is sent through the other team's goal.* ♦ *I wanted to play lacrosse, but my high school didn't have a team.*

lactose ['læk tos] *n.* the natural sugar found in milk. (No plural form in this sense.) ♦ *I can't drink milk because my body can't digest lactose.* ♦ *The researcher measured the amount of lactose in dairy products.*

lacy ['les i] **1.** *adj.* made of lace. (Adv: *lacily.* Comp: *lacier;* sup: *laciest.*) ♦ *The lacy shawl tore easily when I caught it on a twig.* ♦ *The groom lifted the lacy veil from the bride's face and kissed her.* **2.** *adj.* delicate and intricate like lace ①; having a delicate pattern. (Figurative on ①. Adv: *lacily.* Comp: *lacier;* sup: *laciest.*) ♦ *The fly was trapped in the lacy spider web.* ♦ *Our kitchen wallpaper has a bright, lacy design.*

lad ['læd] *n.* a young man; a boy. (The opposite of lass.) ♦ *When I was a lad, I delivered newspapers.* ♦ *The coach made the lads on the football team run three miles.*

ladder ['læd ɚ] **1.** *n.* a set of steps attached to two parallel side pieces, used for climbing up to reach something or climbing down from something. ♦ *We need a ladder to reach the roof of our house.* ♦ *Be careful. The bottom rung of that ladder is broken.* **2.** *n.* something that has levels or stages that can be climbed up or down; a hierarchy. (Figurative on ①.) ♦ *Determined to be rich, Anne climbed the ladder of success.* ♦ *The rich banker was on the top rung of the city's social ladder.* **3. at the bottom of the ladder** *idiom* at the lowest level of pay and status. ♦ *Most people start work at the bottom of the ladder.* ♦ *When Anne got fired, she had to start all over again at the bottom of the ladder.*

ladle ['led l] **1.** *n.* a large, deep spoon with a long handle, used for serving liquids from a bowl. ♦ *David poured the soup into bowls with a silver ladle.* ♦ *I added more juice to the punch and stirred it with the ladle.* **2.** *n.* a cup with a long handle, used for drinking water. ♦ *The farmer drank the water from a ladle.* ♦ *It was so hot, I poured a ladle of cold water over my head.* **3.** *tv.* to serve a liquid using ① or ②. ♦ *Anne ladled the soup into my bowl.* ♦ *I ladled the punch into my glass.*

lady ['led i] **1.** *n.* a refined woman. (The female counterpart of gentleman.) ♦ *The porter opened the door for the lady as she entered the hotel.* ♦ *The gracious lady politely greeted her guests at the door.* **2.** *n.* a woman. (Also a term of address.) ♦ *Ladies and gentlemen, I'm pleased to introduce the next speaker.* ♦ *A short lady asked me to get a book from the top shelf.* **3. young lady** *n.* a young girl of any age; a female who is young relative to the speaker. (Also a term of address.) ♦ *How are you, young lady?* ♦ *These young ladies have done very well on their assignments.* **4.** *n.* <a title for certain women of nobility.> ♦ *Lord and Lady Smythe went to Italy for a vacation.* ♦ *Lady Bucknell sued the newspaper for slander.*

ladybug ['led i bəg] *n.* a small bug that has a red shell with black spots. ♦ *The ladybug eats many bothersome insects.* ♦ *I watched the ladybug walk up a blade of grass.*

ladylike ['led i laɪk] *adj.* like a lady; refined; polite. ♦ *Anne told her daughter to cross her legs in a ladylike fashion.* ♦ *Susan hoped her daughter would stop being a tomboy and behave in a ladylike manner.*

lag ['læg] **1.** *n.* a delay; the period of time between the end of one event and the start of another. ♦ *There was a short lag while the astronaut's voice was transmitted from the spaceship back to earth.* ♦ *There was a brief lag when we switched from one telephone system to another.* **2. lag behind** *iv.* + *prep. phr.* to travel behind someone or something. ♦ *The second-place runner lagged far behind the winner.* ♦ *The horse I bet on lagged behind all the others.* **3.** *tv.* to trail behind someone or something. ♦ *The second-place winner lagged the winner by 10 yards.* ♦ *The horse I bet on lagged all the others.*

laid ['led] pt/pp of lay.

lain ['len] a pp of lie.

lair ['ler] *n.* an animal's den; the place where an animal sleeps. ♦ *The skunk sleeps much of the winter in its lair.* ♦ *The hunter followed the lion back to its lair.*

laity ['le ə ti] *n.* laypeople; people who are not clergy. (No plural form in this sense.) ♦ *The pope addressed the role of the laity within the church.* ♦ *The business affairs of the parish were managed by the laity.*

lake ['lek] *n.* a large body of water surrounded by land. ♦ *I went swimming in the lake.* ♦ *Most lakes have fresh water.*

lamb ['læm] **1.** *n.* a young sheep. ♦ *The shepherd guided the young lambs to their pen.* ♦ *The farmer sheared the wool from the lambs.* **2.** *n.* the meat of ① used as food. (No plural form in this sense.) ♦ *We ate lamb and potatoes for dinner.* ♦ *The butcher sold me a pound of lamb.* **3. like a lamb to the slaughter** *idiom* quietly and without seeming to realize or complain about the likely difficulties or dangers of a situation. ♦ *Young men fighting in World War I were led like lambs to the slaughter.* ♦ *Our team went on the football field like lambs to the slaughter to meet the league leaders.*

lame ['lem] **1.** *adj.* not able to walk properly; limping; crippled. (Adv: *lamely.* Comp: *lamer;* sup: *lamest.*) ♦ *The lame man used a cane when he walked.* ♦ *I helped the lame woman cross the street.* **2.** *adj.* weak; not convincing. (Informal. Figurative on ①. Adv: *lamely.* Comp: *lamer;* sup: *lamest.*) ♦ *My teacher didn't believe my lame excuse for being late.* ♦ *John, who was very sleepy, made a lame attempt to pay attention during class.*

lame duck ['lem 'dʌk] *n.* a politician who has been voted out of office but is still serving the remainder of the term. ♦ *The lame ducks voted to give themselves a $10,000 bonus.* ♦ *The senator was a lame duck, so he didn't care if his vote angered his constituents.*

lament [lə 'mɛnt] **1.** *n.* an expression of grief; a sorrowful story or explanation. ♦ *The widow's lament at the funeral was sorrowful indeed.* ♦ *My landlord ignored my lament about the lack of hot water.* **2.** *tv.* to express grief about something. ♦ *The widow lamented the death of her husband.* ♦ *The students lamented the lack of parking spaces at school.*

laminated ['læm ə net ɪd] *adj.* [of panels of wood or other thin sheets of material] glued together under pressure. ♦ *The flooring of the house is thin, laminated wood.* ♦ *The builder used laminated beams in the house because of their superior strength.*

lamp ['læmp] **1.** *n.* a device that makes light. ♦ *There were holes in the wall where gas lamps used to be attached.* ♦ *I shielded my eyes from the glare of the electric lamp.* **2.** *n.* an ornamental stand that holds an electric light bulb. ♦ *I have matching lamps on tables at both ends of the sofa.* ♦ *I turned off the lamp and went to bed.*

lamppost ['læmp post] *n.* a post that supports a street light. ♦ *I leaned against the lamppost while waiting for the bus.* ♦ *The workers replaced the light at the top of the lamppost.*

lampshade ['læmp ʃed] *n.* a decorative cover that fits over an electric light bulb to soften the glare of the light. ♦ *The lampshade protected the light bulb when I knocked the lamp off the table.* ♦ *The light was too harsh without the lampshade.*

lance ['læns] **1.** *n.* a spear; a weapon with a long handle and a pointed metal end. ♦ *The knight carried his lance into battle.* ♦ *The hunters threw their lances at the bear.* **2.** *tv.* to open the flesh with a surgical knife. ♦ *The doctor lanced the infection on my foot.* ♦ *The surgeon lanced my skin to take out a sliver of glass.*

land ['lænd] **1.** *n.* the dry, solid part of the earth's surface; the part of the earth's surface that is not covered with water. (No plural form in this sense.) ♦ *After weeks at sea, the sailor was glad to see land.* ♦ *Amphibians live both in water and on land.* **2.** *n.* ground; dirt; soil. (No plural form in this sense.) ♦ *The plow tilled the land.* ♦ *The farmer removed large rocks from the land.* **3.** *n.* a country, region, or area. (No plural form in this sense.) ♦ *The land north of the United States is called Canada.* ♦ *The pioneers settled on the land beyond the mountains.* **4.** *n.* real estate; property. (No plural form in this sense.) ♦ *The farmer sold 40 acres of land to a developer.* ♦ *A fence surrounded the rancher's land.* **5.** *n.* a country. ♦ *I enjoy visiting foreign lands.* ♦ *My uncle was from a land across the sea.* **6. on land** *phr.* on the soil; on the land and not at sea. ♦ *The flight was rough and I feel better now that I am back on land.* ♦ *When I am at sea, I feel more relaxed than when I am on land.* **7.** *tv.* [for a pilot] to return a plane to the ground safely, as part of an airplane flight. ♦ *The pilot landed the plane during a violent storm.* ♦ *Bob landed the jet in the thick fog.* **8.** *tv.* to cause someone to end up in a place or state. ♦ *The thief's crimes landed him in jail.* ♦ *Susan's speed landed her on the track team.* **9.** *tv.* to receive something; to catch something. (Informal.) ♦ *While fishing, I landed a twelve-pound trout.* ♦ *Mary landed a job with the best law firm in town.*

landfill ['lænd fɪl] *n.* a place where trash and other waste is dumped. ♦ *I took the old refrigerator to the landfill.* ♦ *The local landfill will not accept the grass I cut with my lawn mower.*

landing ['læn dɪŋ] **1.** *n.* a place where people and cargo are loaded and unloaded from a boat or ship. ♦ *The steamboat came up to the landing where hundreds were waiting to board.* ♦ *The landing was crowded with people and goods.* **2.** *n.* [an airplane's] coming to earth; [a pilot's] act of bringing a plane to earth. ♦ *The plane's landing was smooth and safe.* ♦ *The pilot made a very skilled landing.*

landlady ['lænd led i] *n.* a woman who owns and rents out residential space; a woman who manages residential rental property. ♦ *My landlady decreased my rent because I mow the lawn.* ♦ *I asked my landlady if I could pay rent a few days late.*

landlord ['lænd lord] *n.* a person or a company that manages and collects rent for houses, apartments, and offices. ♦ *The landlord evicted the tenants for failure to pay rent.* ♦ *I asked my landlord to fix the broken refrigerator.*

landmark ['lænd mɑrk] **1.** *n.* a feature that stands out or that is easily recognized, especially used in giving directions. ♦ *I used the bridge as a landmark when giving directions to my house.* ♦ *The Statue of Liberty is a famous New York landmark.* **2.** *adj.* important; historic; noteworthy. (Figurative on ①.) ♦ *The landmark Supreme Court decision set a precedent for all related cases that followed.* ♦ *The moon landing was a landmark event in space travel.*

landowner ['lænd on ɚ] *n.* someone who owns land. ♦ *The realtor persuaded the landowner to sell her house.* ♦ *Landowners are responsible for paying property taxes.*

landscape ['lænd skep] **1.** *n.* the land and the things visible on it, such as trees, bodies of water, rocks, hills, etc. (No plural form in this sense.) ♦ *From her train window, the passenger watched the landscape go by.* ♦ *Anne sat on a hill and gazed at the landscape around her.* **2.** *n.* a painting of land or outdoor scenes. ♦ *The art show featured dozens of pastoral landscapes.* ♦ *The landscape above my sofa was done in watercolors.* **3.** *tv.* to arrange flowers, trees, bushes, hills, rocks, and other objects to make a yard look beautiful. ♦ *A designer landscaped my yard with exotic plants.* ♦ *The park was landscaped with a wide variety of bushes.*

landslide ['lænd slɑɪd] **1.** *n.* a large amount of land or rock that slides down the side of a hill or mountain. ♦ *The mountain road was blocked by a large landslide.* ♦ *The* *hikers took shelter in a cave during the landslide.* **2.** *adj.* of an election in which a large percentage of votes are for one person. (Figurative on ①.) ♦ *The incumbent senator won in a landslide vote.* ♦ *The governor's landslide victory was the largest in history.*

lane ['len] **1.** *n.* a road, path, or route. ♦ *I walked down the country lane to the pond.* ♦ *I live on Cherry Lane.* **2.** *n.* a section of a road wide enough for one line of traffic; a section of track wide enough for one runner; a division of a swimming pool wide enough for one swimmer. ♦ *The driver changed lanes in order to pass a slow car.* ♦ *The swimmer in the fifth lane won the race.*

language ['læŋ gwɪdʒ] **1.** *n.* the system of spoken and written symbols used by people to express thoughts, meaning, and emotions. (No plural form in this sense.) ♦ *The study of language is called linguistics.* ♦ *Sociologists are interested in the ways people use language.* **2.** *n.* the system of spoken and written symbols used by a specific group of people in a country or an area. ♦ *It's harder to learn a new language after the age of 12.* ♦ *German is the language spoken by most people in Germany.* **3.** *n.* any system of symbols used in a computer program. (Figurative on ②.) ♦ *John used an old programming language that few modern computers could run.* ♦ *Trying to learn two different languages at the same time was very difficult for the computer programmer.* **4.** *n.* a specific style of expression. (No plural form in this sense.) ♦ *Please do not use dirty language.* ♦ *The popular mayor spoke in a language that everyone could understand.*

languid ['læŋ gwɪd] *adj.* without energy or excitement; weak; weary; dull. (Adv: *languidly.*) ♦ *The doctor looked into the patient's languid eyes.* ♦ *Susie sat in front of the television set with a languid expression on her face.*

languish ['læŋ gwɪʃ] **1.** *iv.* to become weak; to tire; to lose energy. ♦ *The weary workers languished in the hot sun.* ♦ *The children languished as nighttime approached.* **2.** *iv.* to go through a long period of suffering; to be neglected. ♦ *Anne languished for years at her boring job in the café.* ♦ *The dog languished without food while its owner went to Florida.*

lanky ['læŋ ki] *adj.* [of someone] thin, tall, and awkward. (Adv: *lankily.* Comp: *lankier;* sup: *lankiest.*) ♦ *A lanky young man at the grocery store was kind enough to get me a can of peas from the top shelf.* ♦ *The lanky student tripped while walking up the stairs.*

lanolin ['læn ə lɪn] *n.* oil taken from wool, used in lotions and ointments. (No plural form in this sense.) ♦ *I rubbed my sunburn with lotion that contained lanolin.* ♦ *I use makeup containing lanolin because it is gentle on my skin.*

lantern ['læn tɚn] *n.* a protective case with clear sides, containing a light source. ♦ *The guard carried an electric lantern with him on his rounds.* ♦ *A dim candle flame flickered inside the lantern.*

Laos ['lɑ os] See Gazetteer.

lap ['læp] **1.** *n.* the flat surface formed by the tops of the upper legs when someone is sitting. ♦ *My young nephew sat on my lap as I read to him.* ♦ *I put the dinner plate on my lap since there was no table.* **2.** *n.* one trip around a track; one length of a swimming pool. ♦ *Each lap around this track is one-quarter of a mile.* ♦ *The swimming team members swim 20 laps each day.* **3. lap (up)** *tv.* (+ *adv.*) to drink a liquid by taking it in with the tongue, as a cat or dog does. ♦ *The dog lapped the water from its water dish.* ♦ *The cat lapped up some milk after it ate.* **4.** *iv.* [for water] to make a gently splashing noise. ♦ *Waves lapped at the rocks along the beach.* ♦ *The water lapped against the side of the pool.*

lapel [lə 'pɛl] *n.* one of the flaps at the front of a coat or jacket that is folded back toward the shoulders, just below the collar. ♦ *One of the buttons from your lapel has fallen off.* ♦ *I brushed some lint from my lapel.*

lapse ['læps] **1.** *n.* a brief failure; a small mistake. ♦ *In a lapse of good judgment, the mayor accepted the bribe.* ♦ *Bob belched loudly during dinner, showing an extreme lapse of good manners.* **2.** *n.* the period of time it takes for something to happen; the passing of time. ♦ *There's a 3-second lapse after you dial and before the phone starts ringing at the other end of the line.* ♦ *There was a brief lapse before the president responded.* **3.** *n.* the return to one's bad habits or actions after a period of not doing them. ♦ *Bill suffered a lapse into overeating after dieting for a month.* ♦ *Mary's friends were shocked by her lapse back into alcoholism.* **4.** *iv.* [for something to expire] because it was not used or renewed by a certain time. ♦ *Your privileges lapsed because you forgot to renew your license.* ♦ *I let my health club membership lapse because I never had the time to exercise there.* **5.** *iv.* to fail at an attempt to reform and return to one's old bad habits or actions. ♦ *Bill, dieting as always, lapsed and ate a whole chocolate cake.* ♦ *While on vacation, Susan lapsed and began drinking again.* **6.** *iv.* [for faith or trust] to fail. ♦ *Mary's belief in the government lapsed after the last election.* ♦ *Bill's faith in God lapsed when his wife died.* **7. lapse into** *iv.* + *prep. phr.* to change to another [bad] state. ♦ *When Bill drinks, he lapses into outrageous behavior.* ♦ *Not knowing what to say, we all lapsed into silence.* **8. lapse into a coma** *idiom* to go into a coma. ♦ *The survivor of the crash lapsed into a coma.* ♦ *Aunt Mary lapsed into a coma and died.*

larceny ['lɑr sən i] *n.* theft; stealing. ♦ *The criminal was found guilty of larceny.* ♦ *The thief had a long record of larceny and assault.*

lard ['lɑrd] *n.* pig fat, especially that used in cooking. (No plural form in this sense.) ♦ *The cook greased the pan with lard.* ♦ *The chicken was fried in lard.*

large ['lɑrdʒ] **1.** *adj.* greater in size than average; more than average; big. (Comp: *larger;* sup: *largest.*) ♦ *The large dog scared the mail carrier.* ♦ *The large building towered over the other ones.* **2.** *n.* an object, especially one for sale, that is large ① in size. ♦ *"I want a large with extra cheese," Bob said as he ordered a pizza.* ♦ *I think I need to buy a large, because the medium doesn't fit.*

largely ['lɑrdʒ li] *adv.* for the most part; primarily; essentially. ♦ *The success of this project was largely due to Mary's efforts.* ♦ *The students at the high school were largely from poor families.*

large-scale ['lɑrdʒ 'skel] *adj.* extensive; having a wide range; involved. ♦ *The country was torn apart by the large-scale war.* ♦ *The economy faltered during the large-scale recession.*

lark ['lɑrk] **1.** *n.* a kind of small, brown songbird. ♦ *There's a nest of larks on the end of that branch.* ♦ *A flock of larks flew across the sky.* **2.** *n.* something that is light, fun, and easy. ♦ *The race was not difficult. It was a lark.* ♦ *The trip to the beach was a lark for all of us.* **3. for a lark; on a**

lark *idiom* for a joke; as something done for fun. ♦ *For a lark, I wore a clown's wig to school.* ♦ *On a lark, I skipped school and drove to the beach.*

larkspur ['lɑrk spɚ] *n.* any of several popular but poisonous plants that usually have blue, pink, or white flowers. ♦ *The clump of larkspur grew on the left of the hedge.* ♦ *At the center of the bouquet was a beautiful pink larkspur.*

larva ['lɑr və] *n., irreg.* the first stage of the life of an insect after it leaves the egg. (Pl: **larvae**.) ♦ *The larva of a fly is called a maggot.* ♦ *Most larvae look somewhat like worms.*

larvae ['lɑr vi] pl of **larva**.

larynges [lə 'rɪn dʒiz] pl of **larynx**.

laryngitis [lɛr ən 'dʒɑɪ tɪs] *n.* a condition where the larynx is sore and inflamed. (No plural form in this sense.) ♦ *Laryngitis makes speech difficult or painful.* ♦ *The concert was canceled because the singer had laryngitis.*

larynx ['lɛr ɪŋks] *n., irreg.* the front part of the throat that surrounds the parts that make speech sounds. (Pl: **larynges** or *larynxes*.) ♦ *The vocal cords are found within the larynx.* ♦ *The heavy smoker developed cancer in his larynx.*

laser ['lez ɚ] **1.** *n.* a device that makes a very thin, powerful beam of light and the beam itself. (An acronym of *light amplification by simulated emission of radiation.*) ♦ *The doctor treated the patient's skin cancer with a laser.* ♦ *The aliens in the movie battled each other with lasers.* **2.** *adj.* <the adj. use of ①.> ♦ *My eyesight was corrected with laser surgery.* ♦ *I printed my résumé on a laser printer.*

lash ['læʃ] **1.** *n.* the flexible end of a whip. ♦ *I oiled the lash of the whip to keep it soft.* ♦ *The lash hit the horse's hind leg and made it move faster.* **2.** *n.* a blow from a whip. ♦ *The mules felt the lashes from the driver's whip.* ♦ *The thief received forty lashes before being thrown in jail.* **3.** *n.* an **eyelash**. ♦ *I removed a lash that fell into my eye.* ♦ *The pretty model had long, black lashes.* **4.** *tv.* to hit someone or something with a whip. ♦ *The criminal was lashed forty times.* ♦ *The rider lashed the horse to make it go faster.* **5.** *tv.* to tie someone or something up; to bind someone or something. ♦ *The robber lashed me to a chair.* ♦ *Bob accidentally lashed his shoes together.*

lashing ['læʃ ɪŋ] **1.** *n.* a rope used to tie someone or something up securely. ♦ *The trunk was strapped shut with a secure lashing.* ♦ *I couldn't break the tight lashing that bound me to the chair.* **2.** *n.* a severe whipping. ♦ *The prisoner received a lashing.* ♦ *Bill gave his son a lashing for disobeying him.* **3.** *n.* a strong attack [of wind and rain]. (No plural form in this sense. Figurative on ②.) ♦ *The lashing of the wind blew the barn down.* ♦ *The windows broke from the lashing of the storm.*

lass ['læs] *n.* a young woman; a girl. (The opposite of **lad**.) ♦ *My granddaughter is a pretty young lass.* ♦ *I helped a poor lass in the park find her lost dog.*

lasso ['læs o] **1.** *n.* a rope with a loop on one end, used to catch cattle or horses. (Pl in *-s* or *-es.*) ♦ *The cowboy threw his lasso around the horse's neck.* ♦ *The sheriff stopped the thief with his lasso.* **2.** *tv.* to catch someone or something with ①. ♦ *The cowboy lassoed the cattle that had escaped.* ♦ *I played with the cat by lassoing it with yarn.*

last ['læst] **1.** *adj.* final; at the end; after all other things or people. (Adv: *lastly.*) ♦ *The last month of the year is December.* ♦ *I was the last person in line to get tickets for the concert.* **2.** *adj.* the most recent; nearest in the past; latest. ♦ *I went to Mexico last year.* ♦ *Who was the last president?* **3.** *adj.* least likely; least appropriate. ♦ *After working all day, the last thing I want to do is go bowling.* ♦ *My selfish brother is the last person I'd ask for help.* **4.** *iv.* to continue for a length of time; to remain; to endure. ♦ *This year's theater festival begins in May and lasts through July.* ♦ *I hope my lucks lasts a little longer.* **5. the last (one)** *phr.* someone or something that is the final one in a sequence. ♦ *Anne was the last one to get concert tickets.* ♦ *The state of Hawaii was the last to enter the Union.* **6. at last** *idiom* finally; after a long wait. ♦ *The train has come at last.* ♦ *At last, we have gotten something to eat.* **7. the very last** *idiom* the end; an absolute end of something. ♦ *At the very last of the movie, the hero gets killed.* ♦ *Bill stayed at the party until the very last.* **8. last but not least** *idiom* last in sequence, but not last in importance. ♦ *The speaker said, "And now, last but not least, I'd like to present Bill Smith, who will give us some final words."* ♦ *And last but not least, here is the loser of the race.* **9. see the last of someone or something** *idiom* to have the final sight of or contact with someone or something. ♦ *I will be back to bother you again. You haven't seen the last of me!* ♦ *I'll be glad when I've seen the last of these mosquitoes.*

last-ditch ['læst 'dɪtʃ] *adj.* final and desperate; used as one's final hope; used as a last resort. ♦ *As a last-ditch effort to save the town from the flood, the residents piled sandbags along the river.* ♦ *The company's last-ditch attempt to prevent the strike failed.*

lasting ['læs tɪŋ] *adj.* enduring; continual; permanent. (Adv: *lastingly.*) ♦ *They all hoped for an end to the war and a lasting peace.* ♦ *The lasting radiation poisoned the land where the bomb fell.*

lastly ['læst li] *adv.* finally; in the last place; at the end. ♦ *Lastly, the winner thanked her coach for her guidance.* ♦ *Lastly, the speaker reminded us to be careful.*

last minute ['læst 'mɪn ɪt] **1.** *n.* the last chance; just before the end or the deadline. ♦ *Please don't wait for the last minute to do everything.* ♦ *Tom did his homework at the last minute.* **2. last-minute** *adj.* done at the last possible moment. ♦ *Tom made some last-minute changes to the book he was writing.* ♦ *The condemned prisoner received a last-minute stay of execution.*

latch ['lætʃ] **1.** *n.* a mechanism for holding a door or window closed; a lock for a door or window that can be locked and unlocked with a key. ♦ *The door won't stay shut because the latch is broken.* ♦ *I shut the window and slid the latch into place.* **2.** *tv.* to close a door or window so that ① catches and holds the door or window closed firmly. ♦ *Lisa latched the window shut.* ♦ *I latched the front door before I went to bed.* **3.** *iv.* [for ①] to catch and hold. ♦ *Did the door latch when you closed it?* ♦ *The cabinet door won't latch!*

late ['let] **1.** *adj.* not on time; past the time that something is supposed to happen; past the time that someone or something is to be in a place. (Comp: *later;* sup: *latest.*) ♦ *My brother's flight was late.* ♦ *The teacher scolded the late student.* **2.** *adj.* far into a certain period of time; toward the end of a certain period of time. (Comp: *later;* sup: *latest.*) ♦ *The test results will be back late in the week.* ♦ *The Spanish-American War was late in the 19th century.*

3. *adj.* dead. (Prenominal only.) ♦ *My late grandfather used to be a mechanic.* ♦ *The late Mr. Brown founded the company in 1902.* **4.** *adv.* after the time that something is supposed to happen. ♦ *We arrived at the movie late.* ♦ *I came to class five minutes late.* **5. late in(to)** *adv.* (+ *prep. phr.*) far into a certain period of time. ♦ *We arrived at the theater late in the performance.* ♦ *The party lasted late into the night.* **6. keep late hours** *idiom* to stay up or stay out until very late; to work late. ♦ *I'm always tired because I keep late hours.* ♦ *If I didn't keep late hours, I wouldn't sleep so late in the morning.* **7. late in the day** *idiom* far on in a project or activity; too late in a project or activity for action, decisions, etc., to be taken. ♦ *It was a bit late in the day for him to apologize.* ♦ *It's late in the day to change the plans.*

lately ['let li] *adv.* recently. ♦ *Have you seen any movies lately?* ♦ *Lately, I've been working more hours than usual.*

lateness ['let nəs] *n.* tardiness; the state of being late. (No plural form in this sense.) ♦ *The student was punished for his lateness.* ♦ *Because of my lateness, I missed my flight.*

latent ['let nt] *adj.* existing, but not noticeable; repressed; hidden. (Adv: *latently.*) ♦ *My therapist helped me discover my latent desires.* ♦ *The coach helped bring out my latent talent for swimming.*

later ['let ɚ] *adv.* at a time after the present time; at a future time. ♦ *We're going to the beach later this afternoon.* ♦ *Bob will be here later.*

lateral ['læt ə rəl] *adj.* of or about the side of something; at the side; on the side; in the side; toward the side. (Adv: *laterally.*) ♦ *I crossed each* T *with a short, lateral stroke.* ♦ *My lateral movement was restricted by the narrow walls of the passageway.*

latest ['let əst] *adj.* most recent; most up-to-date. ♦ *Mike follows all the latest fads.* ♦ *The latest styles in clothing are interesting, but too expensive.*

latex ['le tɛks] **1.** *n.* a white liquid that seeps from cuts in certain plants, especially the rubber plant, used in the production of rubber. (No plural form in this sense.) ♦ *The rubber factory processed tons of latex each day.* ♦ *Latex is harvested from trees in the tropics.* **2.** *adj.* made of ①. ♦ *The doctor wore latex gloves during surgery.* ♦ *Latex tubes are often used to connect pieces of glass laboratory equipment.*

lathe ['leð] *n.* a machine that holds and turns wood or metal against a sharp tool, giving a certain shape to the wood or metal. ♦ *The spindles in the railing were made on a lathe.* ♦ *I shaped the wooden table leg on a lathe.*

lather ['læð ɚ] **1.** *n.* white foam that is made by mixing soap with water. (No plural form in this sense.) ♦ *I covered my face with lather before shaving.* ♦ *I rinsed the lather from my body in the shower.* **2.** *iv.* to make ①. ♦ *The soap lathered easily when I mixed it with water.* ♦ *The detergent lathered in the sink.* **3.** *tv.* to cover something with ①. ♦ *I lathered my legs before I shaved them.* ♦ *I have to lather the dog with a special soap that kills fleas.*

Latin ['læt n] **1.** *n.* the language of ancient Rome. (No plural form in this sense.) ♦ *Latin can be studied in high school and college.* ♦ *French, Spanish, Portuguese, Romanian, and Italian have descended from Latin.* **2.** *adj.* of or about the people and cultures of countries whose languages developed from ①, especially the countries of Latin America where Spanish and Portuguese are spoken. ♦ *Mary danced to the Latin rhythms into the night.* ♦ *I just love music with a Latin beat.*

Latina [læ 'tin ɑ] *n.* a girl or woman of Latin American descent; a Spanish-speaking girl or woman in the U.S. ♦ *The young Latina attended a local university.* ♦ *A group of Latinas were gathered near the entrance to the theater.*

Latin America ['læt n ə 'mɛr ɪ kə] *n.* the parts of North and South America where Spanish or Portuguese is an official language; Mexico, Central America, and South America. (No plural form in this sense.) ♦ *While traveling in Latin America, I visited Guatemala.* ♦ *The climate of much of Latin America is quite warm, but it is colder in the mountains and in the south.*

Latino [læ 'tin o] **1.** *n.* someone of Latin American descent; a Spanish-speaking person in the U.S. (See also Latina. Pl in -*s*.) ♦ *The enterprising Latino opened a gourmet Mexican restaurant.* ♦ *Miami has a large population of Latinos.* **2.** *adj.* <the adj. use of ①.> ♦ *The Latino population in that city is growing.* ♦ *The elected representative was interested in Latino issues.*

latitude ['læt ə tud] **1.** *n.* the distance north or south of the equator measured in degrees. ♦ *The Tropic of Cancer is at the latitude of 23.5 degrees north of the equator.* ♦ *The South Pole is at latitude 90 degrees south.* **2.** *n.* the freedom to think or act freely. (No plural form in this sense. Figurative on ①.) ♦ *I have the latitude at work to set my own hours.* ♦ *I think children who are given wide latitude in their behavior need discipline.*

latter ['læt ɚ] **1. the latter** *n.* the second of two things that have been mentioned. (No plural form in this sense. Treated as singular or plural.) ♦ *I offered Bill peas or carrots, and he chose the latter.* ♦ *I attended both Harvard and Yale, and graduated from the latter.* **2. [the] latter** *adj.* of or about the second of two things that have been mentioned. ♦ *Of red and blue, I prefer the latter color.* ♦ *Mary has been to both Rome and Paris, but I haven't been to the latter city.*

lattice ['læt ɪs] *n.* a frame of crossed strips of wood or iron, especially used as a gate, screen, or framework for plants to grow on. ♦ *The lattice was covered with ivy.* ♦ *I removed the plants from the lattice so I could repaint it.*

Latvia ['læt vi ə] See Gazetteer.

laud ['lɔd] *tv.* to praise someone or something; to honor someone or something; to glorify someone or something. ♦ *The citizens of the town lauded their popular mayor.* ♦ *John was lauded for saving the family trapped in the fire.*

laudable ['lɔd ə bəl] *adj.* worthy of praise; deserving praise or honor. (Adv: *laudably.*) ♦ *The company rewarded its workers' laudable efforts with bonuses.* ♦ *Your desire to help the poor is laudable.*

laugh ['læf] **1.** *iv.* to express pleasure or amusement by making short, happy vocal sounds. ♦ *Mary laughed when I told her a joke.* ♦ *The children laughed when the clown fell down.* **2. laugh at** *iv.* + *prep. phr.* to make fun of someone or something with ③. ♦ *The other children laughed at me because I wore glasses.* ♦ *We laughed at the mistakes in the report.* **3.** *n.* the noise that someone makes when amused, as in ①. ♦ *My roommate's high-pitched laugh* *really annoys me.* ♦ *The comedian got a lot of laughs from people in the audience.* **4.** *n.* a funny event, usually causing laughter. (No plural form in this sense.) ♦ *The performer's comedy routine was quite a laugh.* ♦ *The comedy was one laugh after another.* **5. a laugh** *n.* someone or something that is a failure or disappointment. (No plural form in this sense. Sarcastic.) ♦ *The president's address was a laugh and no one took it seriously.* ♦ *The course was a laugh; I didn't learn anything in it.* **6. get the last laugh** *idiom* to laugh at or ridicule someone who has laughed at or ridiculed you; to put someone in the same bad position that you were once in. ♦ *John laughed when I got a D on the final exam. I got the last laugh, though. He failed the course.* ♦ *Mr. Smith said I was foolish when I bought an old building. I had the last laugh when I sold it a month later for twice what I paid for it.*

laughable ['læf ə bəl] *adj.* causing someone to laugh; worthy of being laughed at. (Adv: *laughably.*) ♦ *Bill got a bad grade on his laughable term paper.* ♦ *Your proposal is so bad that it's laughable.*

laughing ['læf ɪŋ] *adj.* making laughter because something is funny. (Adv: *laughingly.*) ♦ *The talking and laughing guests made a lot of noise.* ♦ *The laughing audience applauded the entertainer.*

laughter ['læf tɚ] *n.* the sound made when people laugh; laughing. (No plural form in this sense.) ♦ *I heard my friends' laughter, so I asked them what was so funny.* ♦ *The movie theater echoed with the audience's laughter.*

launch ['lɔntʃ] **1.** *tv.* to set a new boat or ship into the water for the first time. ♦ *The ship was launched after the Queen christened it.* ♦ *The captain launched the new boat.* **2.** *tv.* to send a rocket or its cargo into the air. ♦ *The satellite was launched into orbit.* ♦ *The astronauts launched the spaceship.* **3.** *tv.* to begin doing something, especially carrying out a plan. (Figurative on ①.) ♦ *My company launched a new insurance plan.* ♦ *After three false starts, the new plan was finally launched.* **4.** *n.* an act of sending something as in ① and ②. ♦ *We watched the rocket's launch from the control tower.* ♦ *The ship's launch was postponed because of the hurricane.* **5. launching pad** See pad ⑤.

launder ['lɔn dɚ] **1.** *tv.* to wash clothes or fabric; to wash and iron clothes or fabric. ♦ *I launder my clothes every Saturday.* ♦ *The housekeeper launders my dirty clothes and linen.* **2.** *tv.* to make money that was received illegally seem to be legal. (Informal. Figurative on ①.) ♦ *The drug dealer laundered the money before he spent it.* ♦ *The mayor laundered the bribe money by putting it in a foreign bank account.*

launderer ['lɔn dɚ ɚ] *n.* someone who washes and irons clothes or fabric. ♦ *I sent my dirty clothes and linen to the launderer.* ♦ *I showed the launderer the stain on my white shirt.*

Laundromat™ ['lɔn drə mæt] *n.* a store with washing and drying machines for rent where people can go to wash their clothes. ♦ *I carried my dirty clothes to the Laundromat.* ♦ *You need coins to operate the washers at the Laundromat.*

laundry ['lɔn dri] **1.** *n.* clothes that need to be washed; clothes that have just been washed and dried. (No plural form in this sense.) ♦ *I took my laundry to the launderer.* ♦ *I placed the laundry on the table and started folding it.* **2.** *n.* a business where clothes can be taken to be washed. ♦ *Can you drop off the clothes at the laundry on your way to work?* ♦ *The laundry charges its customers by the pound.* **3.** *n.* a location in a house where clothes are washed. ♦ *Our laundry is in the basement.* ♦ *The laundry in this house is right next to the kitchen.* **4. in the laundry** *idiom* with the clothes that are waiting to be washed. ♦ *Is my blue shirt clean or is it in the laundry?* ♦ *All my socks are in the laundry. What shall I do?*

laurel ['lor əl] **1.** *n.* a shrub with leaves that are a shiny green all year round. (No plural form in this sense.) ♦ *A leaf of laurel is called a bay leaf and is used to flavor food.* ♦ *I made a wreath out of laurel.* **2. look to one's laurels** *idiom* to take care not to lower or diminish one's reputation or position, especially in relation to that of someone else who is potentially better. ♦ *With the arrival of the new member of the football team, James will have to look to his laurels to remain the highest scorer.* ♦ *The older members of the team will have to look to their laurels when young people join.*

lava ['lɑv ə] **1.** *n.* molten rock that flows from a volcano. (No plural form in this sense.) ♦ *The lava streamed down the side of the volcano.* ♦ *The hot lava destroyed the village at the base of the volcano.* **2.** *n.* hardened ①. (No plural form in this sense.) ♦ *The geologist examined the lava at the base of the volcano.* ♦ *I brought a piece of lava home with me from Hawaii.*

lavatory ['læv ə tor i] **1.** *n.* a sink used for washing one's hands; a wash basin with running water available. ♦ *I went to the lavatory to wash my hands before dinner.* ♦ *The doctors scrubbed their hands at the lavatory before surgery.* **2.** *n.* a bathroom; a room with a toilet. (Euphemistic.) ♦ *Make sure to wash your hands after you use the lavatory.* ♦ *Can you tell me where the lavatory is?* **3. go to the lavatory** *idiom* to go somewhere and use a toilet. (See also bathroom ②.) ♦ *Bob requested to leave the room to go to the lavatory.* ♦ *Please stop the car. I have to go to the lavatory.*

lavender ['læv ən dɚ] **1.** *n.* a shrub that has a light purple flower valued for its scent. (No plural form in this sense.) ♦ *I placed a bit of lavender in the vase on the table.* ♦ *Your perfume smells like lavender.* **2.** *adj.* light purple in color; purple mixed with white. ♦ *I wore a lavender dress to the party.* ♦ *Lilacs are usually lavender or white.*

lavish ['læv ɪʃ] *adj.* in large amounts; extravagant. (Adv: *lavishly.*) ♦ *My neighbors spoiled their children with lavish gifts.* ♦ *Lisa's wealthy parents throw lavish parties.*

law ['lɔ] **1.** *n.* a rule; a statement of obligation within a legal system. ♦ *It's a federal law that you must file an income-tax return.* ♦ *When the president signed the bill, it became a law.* **2. the law** *n.* the police force; a police officer. (No plural form in this sense. Treated as singular.) ♦ *The law caught the bank robbers as they tried to escape.* ♦ *The criminal was eventually caught by the law.* **3.** *n.* a principle that describes a mathematical or scientific phenomenon. ♦ *Everything in the universe obeys natural laws.* ♦ *Grimm's Law describes sound changes in the development of Germanic languages.* **4.** *n.* the study of the system of laws ①. (No plural form in this sense.) ♦ *My lawyer studied law at Columbia University.* ♦ *After studying law, you must pass an examination before you become a lawyer.* **5. break a law; break the law** *idiom* to fail to obey a law; to act contrary to a law. ♦ *Lisa broke the law when she drove the wrong way on a one-way street.* ♦ *If you never break the law, you will never get arrested.* **6. law unto oneself** *idiom* one who makes one's own laws or rules; one who sets one's own standards of behavior. ♦ *You can't get Bill to follow the rules. He's a law unto himself.* ♦ *Jane is a law unto herself. She's totally unwilling to cooperate.* **7. take the law into one's own hands** *idiom* to attempt to administer the law; to act as a judge and jury for someone who has done something wrong. ♦ *Citizens don't have the right to take the law into their own hands.* ♦ *The shopkeeper took the law into his own hands when he tried to arrest the thief.*

law-abiding ['lɔ ə bɑɪ dɪŋ] *adj.* obeying the law. ♦ *The witness falsely accused a law-abiding citizen of theft.* ♦ *My law-abiding aunt always drives at the speed limit.*

lawful ['lɔ fʊl] *adj.* legal; permitted by law; sanctioned by law. (Adv: *lawfully.*) ♦ *The police conducted a lawful search of the suspect's car.* ♦ *John used to be a criminal, but now he runs a lawful business.*

lawless ['lɔ ləs] **1.** *adj.* having no laws; having none of the laws enforced. (Adv: *lawlessly.*) ♦ *The anarchist wanted to live in a lawless society.* ♦ *The cowboy and the bandit fought in the lawless western town.* **2.** *adj.* breaking the law; ignoring the law. (Adv: *lawlessly.*) ♦ *The government fined the lawless company for polluting.* ♦ *The lawless killer escaped from the police.*

lawmaker ['lɔ mek ɚ] *n.* someone who makes laws in a legislature; a legislator; a member of Congress. ♦ *The lawmakers voted to raise the legal speed limit.* ♦ *The lobbyist persuaded the lawmaker to change her vote.*

lawn ['lɔn] *n.* an area of ground with cut grass; a yard. ♦ *The kids tore up our lawn with their bicycles.* ♦ *The front lawn needs to be mowed.*

lawn mower ['lɔn mo ɚ] *n.* a machine with blades that cut grass. ♦ *John pushed the lawn mower into a row of flowers accidentally.* ♦ *The lawn mower ran out of gas, so I pushed it back to the garage.*

lawsuit ['lɔ sut] *n.* a claim or complaint brought into a court of law. ♦ *I filed a lawsuit against my neighbor for disturbing the peace.* ♦ *The judge dismissed the man's groundless lawsuit.*

lawyer ['lɔ jɚ] *n.* someone who is trained in law and is a member of the bar. ♦ *My lawyer argued that I was in Paris when the crime was committed.* ♦ *Lisa had to have a tax lawyer because her taxes are so complicated.*

lax ['læks] *adj.* loose; not strict; not demanding. (Adv: *laxly.* Comp: *laxer;* sup: *laxest.*) ♦ *The dress code at my office is very lax.* ♦ *I encouraged the lax parents to discipline their children more.*

laxative ['læk sə tɪv] **1.** *n.* a medicine or substance that eases bowel movements. ♦ *I took a laxative because I was constipated.* ♦ *As a joke, Jimmy replaced his friend's chocolates with a laxative.* **2.** *adj.* making it easier for the bowels to move. ♦ *Drinking prune juice has a laxative effect.* ♦ *The laxative properties of fruit help ease constipation.*

laxity ['læks ə ti] *n.* looseness; casualness; carelessness. (No plural form in this sense.) ♦ *The students took advantage of the teacher's laxity in grading.* ♦ *Due to the cashier's laxity and lack of attention, she gave me too much change.*

lay ['le] **1.** pt of lie. **2.** *adj.* not trained in a profession, such as law or medicine; not ordained as a religious leader. (See layperson.) ♦ *This book explains cancer in language that a lay reader can understand.* ♦ *The lawyers' technical terminology confused the lay observer at the trial.* **3.** *tv., irreg.* to place something on a surface or in a flat position; to put something in its place. (Compare with ④ and lie. Pt/pp: laid.) ♦ *I laid the car keys on the kitchen counter.* ♦ *Mary was sure she had laid the blanket on the shelf, but later it was not there.* **4.** *tv., irreg.* [for a hen] to produce and deposit an egg. ♦ *Our chickens laid 12 eggs this morning.* ♦ *The bird laid her eggs in the nest.* **5. lay of the land** *phr.* the arrangement of features on an area of land. ♦ *The surveyor mapped the lay of the land.* ♦ *The geologist studied the lay of the land, trying to determine if there was oil below.* **6. lay of the land** *phr.* the arrangement or organization of something other than land. (Figurative on ⑤.) ♦ *As soon as I get the lay of the land in my new job, things will go better.* ♦ *The company's corporate structure was complex, so understanding the lay of the land took time.* **7. lay someone off** *idiom* to inactivate a worker; to fire someone from a job. ♦ *The company laid off a thousand workers because there wasn't enough demand for their products.* ♦ *I hope they don't lay me off.*

layer ['le ɚ] **1.** *n.* a level; one level of thickness that is placed on a surface. ♦ *The middle layer of the cake is strawberry.* ♦ *A layer of dust covered the old desk.* **2. layer cake** *n.* a cake made of sections of cake separated by icing. ♦ *I made a delicious layer cake for Anne's birthday.* ♦ *I always prefer a white layer cake with white icing.*

layette [le 'ɛt] *n.* a complete set of clothes and bedding for a new baby. ♦ *Mary received three layettes at the baby shower.* ♦ *I bought my granddaughter a layette when she was born.*

layman ['le mən] **1.** *n., irreg.* someone who is not a member of the clergy. (See layperson. See lay ②. Pl: laymen.) ♦ *The minister's assistant was a layman.* ♦ *Due to a shortage of priests, many duties in the Catholic church are done by laymen.* **2.** *n., irreg.* someone who is not a member of a profession; someone who is not familiar with certain technical activities. ♦ *This book explains law in terms a layman can understand.* ♦ *The layman asked the doctor to explain the diagnosis clearly.*

laymen ['le mən] pl of layman.

layout ['le ɑʊt] *n.* the design of something, especially artwork for an advertisement; a drawing showing how something is arranged. ♦ *The graphic artist designed advertising layouts on her computer.* ♦ *These blueprints show the layout of the office building.*

layover ['le ov ɚ] *n.* a period of time spent in an airport or a train or bus station waiting for a connecting flight, train, or bus. (See also stopover.) ♦ *I read a book during my layover at the bus station.* ♦ *Mike visited Anne at the airport during her five-hour layover.*

laypeople ['le pi pəl] a pl of layperson.

layperson ['le pɚ sən] *n., irreg.* someone who is not a member of the clergy or the legal profession; a layman. (Pl: laypeople or *laypersons.*) ♦ *Every day, many laypeople asked the nun for her advice.* ♦ *Sometimes a layperson gives the sermon at our church.*

laziness ['lez ɪ nəs] *n.* idleness; the condition of not liking to work. (No plural form in this sense.) ♦ *John was fired from his job because of his laziness.* ♦ *When I showed signs of laziness, my boss gave me even more work.*

lazy ['lez i] **1.** *adj.* doing almost no work; avoiding work. (Adv: *lazily.* Comp: *lazier;* sup: *laziest.*) ♦ *The lazy student rarely did his homework.* ♦ *I asked our lazy waitress three times for a cup of coffee.* **2.** *adj.* moving slowly. (Figurative on ①. Adv: *lazily.* Comp: *lazier;* sup: *laziest.*) ♦ *Traffic crawled through town at a lazy pace.* ♦ *The raft moved slowly down the lazy river.* **3.** *adj.* conducive to rest and inactivity. (Figurative on ①. Adv: *lazily.* Comp: *lazier;* sup: *laziest.*) ♦ *It was a hot, lazy day, so I stayed inside and watched TV.* ♦ *I spent a lazy summer on the beaches of Florida.*

lead 1. ['lɛd] *n.* a soft grayish metallic element. (No plural form in this sense.) ♦ *The city council has banned the sale of paint that has lead in it.* ♦ *The landlord replaced the lead pipes with plastic ones.* **2.** ['lid] *n.* a clue; a hint; information that can be used to help solve a crime. ♦ *The detective followed every lead until he solved the crime.* ♦ *Following a lead, the detective questioned the victim's brother.* **3.** ['lid] *n.* the front position; the first place. ♦ *At the bottom of the fifth inning, the home team was in the lead.* ♦ *The runner from Mexico held the lead throughout the entire race.* **4.** ['lid] *n.* the distance that someone or something is ahead of someone or something else, especially in a competition. ♦ *In the last inning, the home team had a small lead over the visitors.* ♦ *The team had a big lead during the whole game.* **5.** ['lid] *n.* the main role in a movie or play. ♦ *That actor plays the lead in the new movie.* ♦ *She has played the female lead in many musicals.* **6.** ['lid] *tv., irreg.* to guide someone or something; to show someone or something the way. (Pt/pp: **led.**) ♦ *The guide led the tourists through the castle.* ♦ *I'll lead the way to Anne's house because I've been there before.* **7.** ['lid] *tv., irreg.* to cause someone or something to think some way; to cause someone or something to do something. (Takes a clause.) ♦ *Why did you lead me to believe that we were going shopping?* ♦ *I was led to think that I was invited to the party.* **8.** ['lid] *tv., irreg.* to be the leader of someone or something; to be in charge of someone or something. ♦ *General Lee led the Confederate Army.* ♦ *The researchers were led by the project director.* **9.** ['lid] *tv., irreg.* to be ahead of another team or other players in a competition. ♦ *Our team led Bill's team by five points.* ♦ *The visiting team has led our team since the game began.* **10.** ['lid] *iv., irreg.* to guide; to show the way. ♦ *You lead, and I'll follow.* ♦ *Because no one else knew the way, John led.* **11. lead to** ['lid...] *iv., irreg. + prep. phr.* to extend to somewhere; to be the way to get somewhere. ♦ *This road leads to Washington.* ♦ *This hall leads to the meeting room.* **12. lead to** ['lid...] *iv., irreg. + prep. phr.* to result in something; to have something as a result. ♦ *Smoking leads to coughing.* ♦ *Shoplifting usually leads to more dangerous crimes.* **13. follow someone's lead** [...'lid] *idiom* leadership; guidance; direction. ♦ *Just follow my lead and you will not get lost.* ♦ *John followed his father's lead and became a lawyer.* **14. lead up to something** ['lid...] *idiom* to prepare the way for something; to have something as a consequence. ♦ *His compliments were his way of leading up to asking for money.* ♦ *What were his actions leading up to?*

leader ['lid ɚ] **1.** *n.* a ruler; a director; someone who is in charge of a group of people. ♦ *The leader vowed to win the war.* ♦ *The project leader gave me a new work assignment.* **2.** *n.* an extension of something, like recording tape, that is used for placement or alignment. ♦ *I threaded the leader into the film projector.* ♦ *There was a brief silence as the leader went through the machine.*

leadership ['lid ɚ ʃɪp] **1.** *n.* the position of power or authority held by someone who rules or leads. (No plural form in this sense.) ♦ *The leadership refused to negotiate a settlement with the enemy.* ♦ *The people petitioned the leadership for a change in the law.* **2.** *n.* direction; guidance; the ability to lead. (No plural form in this sense.) ♦ *Under the president's wise leadership, the nation prospered.* ♦ *The company went bankrupt because of the owner's poor leadership.*

leading ['lid ɪŋ] **1.** *adj.* in front; ahead of other things or people; in the first position. ♦ *When the leading horse stumbled, the race was lost.* ♦ *The leading car in the race suddenly blew a tire.* **2.** *adj.* first; foremost; most popular; most important. ♦ *Nine out of ten leading doctors recommended the new cancer treatment.* ♦ *I hope to play the leading role in the opera.* **3. leading question** *idiom* a question that suggests the kind of answer that the person who asks it wants to hear. ♦ *The mayor was angered by the reporter's leading questions.* ♦ *"Don't you think that the police are failing to stop crime?" is an example of a leading question.*

leaf ['lif] **1.** *n., irreg.* the flat, usually green, part of a tree or plant that is attached to a branch or stem. (Pl: **leaves.**) ♦ *Leaves turn energy from the sun into food for the plant.* ♦ *In the fall, tree leaves turn red, orange, yellow, or brown.* **2.** *n., irreg.* a sheet of paper in a book. ♦ *Turn the leaf over to continue reading.* ♦ *I placed a bookmark between two leaves of the book.* **3.** *n., irreg.* an extra section that can be placed in a table to make it larger. ♦ *We add two leaves to the dining table when we entertain guests.* ♦ *I removed the table's extra leaves so that it would fit in the small room.* **4. take a leaf out of someone's book** *idiom* to behave or to do something in the way that someone else would. ♦ *When you act like that, you're taking a leaf out of your sister's book, and I don't like it!* ♦ *You had better do it your way. Don't take a leaf out of my book. I don't do it well.* **5. turn over a new leaf** *idiom* to start again with the intention of doing better; to begin again, ignoring past errors. ♦ *Tom promised to turn over a new leaf and do better from now on.* ♦ *After a minor accident, Sally decided to turn over a new leaf and drive more carefully.*

leaflet ['lif lət] *n.* a piece of paper with information on it, given out to people. ♦ *The demonstrators handed out leaflets explaining their concerns.* ♦ *Admission is only $5 if you bring this leaflet!*

leafy ['lif i] *adj.* having a lot of leaves; covered with leaves. (Adv: *leafily.* Comp: *leafier;* sup: *leafiest.*) ♦ *The strong wind blew many leafy branches to the ground.* ♦ *We had a picnic in the shade of a leafy tree.*

league ['lig] **1.** *n.* a group of people, organizations, or countries that work together because they have a common interest or goal. ♦ *Egypt was readmitted to the League of Arab States in 1989.* ♦ *The sculptor belonged to the local league of artists.* **2.** *n.* a group of sports teams that play against each other. ♦ *The National Football League is* *divided into two sections called conferences.* ♦ *John wants to be a ballplayer in the major leagues.* **3. in league (with someone)** *idiom* [of people] secretly cooperating, often to do something bad or illegal. ♦ *The county sheriff is in league with criminals.* ♦ *The car thieves and the police are in league to make money from stolen cars.*

leak ['lik] **1.** *n.* an opening in a channel, pipe, duct, tire, container, etc., that allows something to escape. ♦ *I patched the leak in the tire.* ♦ *I called a plumber to repair the leak in the water pipe.* **2.** *n.* something that escapes from an opening as in ①. ♦ *A leak of gasoline from my car almost caused a fire.* ♦ *The leak of hot water from the pipe burned my hands.* **3.** *n.* secret information that is revealed secretly. (Figurative on ②.) ♦ *The senator tried to stop the damaging leaks from her office.* ♦ *Who is responsible for the leak of secret information?* **4. leak from** *iv.* + *prep. phr.* [for something such as water, liquid, or air] to pass through an opening as in ①. ♦ *Water leaked from the cracked glass.* ♦ *Air leaked from the old tire.* **5.** *iv.* [for a container with an opening as in ①] to have an opening that allows water, air, or something to escape. ♦ *The beach ball leaked, so we had to blow it up every few minutes.* ♦ *If your tires leak, you should have them replaced.* **6.** *tv.* [for a container with an opening as in ①] to allow water, air, or something else to escape as in ①. ♦ *The bag leaked sand all over the floor.* ♦ *The broken cup leaked water on the kitchen counter.* **7.** *tv.* to make secret information become known secretly. ♦ *The agent leaked state secrets to the enemy.* ♦ *The secretary leaked gossip about her boss to the newspapers.*

leakage ['lik ɪdʒ] **1.** *n.* the process of leaking. (No plural form in this sense.) ♦ *The oil company was ordered to stop the leakage in its underwater pipeline.* ♦ *The leakage was increasing by the hour and threatened to flood the entire street.* **2.** *n.* something that is leaked. (No plural form in this sense.) ♦ *I wiped up the leakage from the water pipe with a mop.* ♦ *Leakage from the broken pipe made the floor slippery.*

leaking ['lik ɪŋ] *adj.* [of a pipe, channel, duct, tire, etc.] having a leak. ♦ *Water dripped from the leaking pipe.* ♦ *I temporarily repaired the leaking tire with a patch.*

leaky ['lik i] *adj.* tending to leak; likely to leak. (Adv: *leakily.* Comp: *leakier;* sup: *leakiest.*) ♦ *I used caulk to seal the leaky window frame.* ♦ *The leaky water faucet dripped all night long.*

lean ['lin] **1.** *iv.* to be slanting; to be sloped. ♦ *After the tornado, the barn leaned at a dangerous angle.* ♦ *The old tree leaned to one side.* **2. lean on; lean against** *iv.* + *prep. phr.* to rest against someone or something; to have someone's or something's weight against someone or something. ♦ *The shovel leaned against the wall of the barn.* ♦ *The tired police officer leaned against the lamppost.* **3. lean over** *iv.* + *adv.* to bend at the waist; to bend at the middle. ♦ *I leaned over to pick up some trash.* ♦ *The detective leaned over to get a better look at the body.* **4. lean on; lean against** *tv.* + *prep. phr.* to cause someone or something to rest against someone or something; to put someone's or something's weight against someone or something. ♦ *The farmer leaned the shovel against the barn wall.* ♦ *I leaned the rusty pipe against the side of the tank.* **5.** *adj.* [of someone or something] very thin or skinny. (Adv: *leanly.* Comp: *leaner;* sup: *leanest.*) ♦ *The lean model wore the latest fashions.* ♦ *Only the lean police officer could fit through the narrow opening.* **6.** *adj.* [of meat] having almost no fat. (Adv: *leanly.* Comp: *leaner;* sup: *leanest.*) ♦ *I asked the butcher for a lean cut of pork.* ♦ *I grilled some lean chicken for dinner.* **7.** *adj.* scant; not abundant; not satisfying. (Adv: *leanly.* Comp: *leaner;* sup: *leanest.*) ♦ *In lean times, we ate bread and soup.* ♦ *I barely survived on my lean salary.* **8. lean toward doing something** *idiom* to tend toward doing something; to favor doing something. ♦ *The union is leaning toward accepting the proposal.* ♦ *My friends leaned toward swimming instead of shopping.*

leap ['lip] **1.** *iv., irreg.* to jump from one place to another. (Pt/pp: *leaped* or *leapt.*) ♦ *I leaped from the car and ran upstairs.* ♦ *The frog leapt from stone to stone.* **2. leap over** *iv., irreg.* + *prep. phr.* to jump over someone or something. ♦ *I leapt over the puddle.* ♦ *The dog leaped over the fence.* **3.** *tv., irreg.* to jump over something. (② is more common.) ♦ *He leapt the ditch without getting his feet wet.* ♦ *The runner leapt every hurdle.* **4.** *n.* a jump; an instance of leaping. ♦ *John's leap from the burning building was captured on film.* ♦ *The daredevil's leap across the canyon was very dangerous.*

leapfrog ['lip frɔg] **1.** *n.* a game where someone jumps over someone else who is bending over. (No plural form in this sense.) ♦ *My mother told us not to play leapfrog in the house.* ♦ *We went outside to play a game of leapfrog.* **2. leapfrog over** *iv.* + *prep. phr.* to jump over someone or something; to play ①, jumping over someone. ♦ *The young children leapfrogged over each other.* ♦ *The children leapfrogged over their large dog.* **3.** *iv.* to move forward in stages, as though playing leapfrog; to advance in jumps or leaps. (Figurative on ①.) ♦ *John leapfrogged up the corporate ladder until he was chairman.* ♦ *The genius leapfrogged through high school.*

leaping ['lip ɪŋ] *adj.* jumping. ♦ *It was hard for me to catch the leaping rabbit.* ♦ *While in Australia, I took pictures of leaping kangaroos.*

leapt ['lɛpt] pt/pp of leap.

leap year ['lip jɪr] *n.* every fourth year, when an extra day is added to February. (This occurs only in years where the last two digits are evenly divisible by four, except for the years ending in two zeros that are not divisible by 400.) ♦ *There are 366 days in a leap year.* ♦ *February 29 only exists in leap years.*

learn ['lɚn] **1.** *tv.* to receive knowledge; to gain a particular piece of knowledge. ♦ *The detective learned the identity of the murderer.* ♦ *Today I learned that the capital of Poland is Warsaw.* **2. learn about; learn of** *iv.* + *prep. phr.* to be told about something; to receive news or information about someone or something. ♦ *Today in class we learned about fractions.* ♦ *I learned of the bank robbery from the radio newscast.* **3. learn something from the bottom up** *idiom* to learn something thoroughly, from the very beginning; to learn all aspects of something, even the least important ones. ♦ *I learned my business from the bottom up.* ♦ *I started out sweeping the floors and learned everything from the bottom up.*

learned ['lɚn ɪd] *adj.* educated; knowledgeable. (Adv: *learnedly.*) ♦ *The learned professor patiently explained the theory to me.* ♦ *The learned judge ruled in favor of the defendant.*

learner ['lɚn ɚ] *n.* someone who is learning. ♦ *At first, the learners have to drive the car in a straight line, then they learn to turn.* ♦ *The teacher spent extra time with the slow learners.*

lease ['lis] **1.** *n.* a rental contract. ♦ *The lease on my apartment lasts for one year.* ♦ *I signed a lease to rent a truck for a week.* **2. lease (from)** *tv.* (+ *prep. phr.*) to rent a property from someone. ♦ *Bob leases an apartment from Bill.* ♦ *I leased a car from the dealership instead of buying one.* **3. lease (to)** *tv.* (+ *prep. phr.*) to rent a property to someone. ♦ *My landlord leases apartment units to renters around the city.* ♦ *Bob leased a car to Mary for a year.*

leased ['list] *adj.* rented. ♦ *This skyscraper has 300,000 square feet of leased office space.* ♦ *I wasn't allowed to drive the leased car into Canada.*

leash ['liʃ] **1.** *n.* a strap that is attached to a collar of an animal in order to control the animal. ♦ *I held tightly to my dog's leash so it wouldn't run into the street.* ♦ *My dog's leash snapped, and it ran through the park.* **2.** *n.* control or a set of controls. (Figurative on ①.) ♦ *The manager held a tight leash on spending.* ♦ *Putting a leash on Mary's driving cut down on the cost of gasoline for her car.* **3.** *tv.* to attach ① onto an animal. ♦ *City law requires you to leash your dogs while in the park.* ♦ *I tried to leash my cat, but she hated it.*

least ['list] **1.** *adj.* <a superlative form of little>; the smallest [amount]. ♦ *That is still too much gravy. I want the least amount possible.* ♦ *The least amount of pepper in my food makes me sneeze.* **2.** *adv.* in the smallest amount; to the smallest degree; the opposite of most. ♦ *My history teacher is the least interesting of all my teachers.* ♦ *I watched the least offensive of the three movies available.* **3.** *pron.* the smallest amount. ♦ *Give me the least.* ♦ *The oldest child got the most, and the youngest child got the least.*

leather ['lɛð ɚ] **1.** *n.* a material made from the skin of an animal, used to make shoes, coats, belts, gloves, etc. (No plural form in this sense.) ♦ *You can keep leather in good condition by oiling it.* ♦ *The biker wore leather to the bar.* **2.** *adj.* made of ①. ♦ *I wore a leather jacket to the rock concert.* ♦ *The police officer wore leather gloves in the winter.*

leathery ['lɛð ə ri] *adj.* feeling like leather; as tough as leather. ♦ *The leathery steak was very hard to cut.* ♦ *The old man's skin was wrinkled and leathery.*

leave ['liv] **1.** *iv., irreg.* to go away; to exit from a place. (Pt/pp: left.) ♦ *I left at 5:00 and went home.* ♦ *The police ordered the loud teenagers to leave.* **2.** *tv., irreg.* to depart from a place. ♦ *The mayor left the room just after the meeting.* ♦ *I left the hospital last Friday.* **3.** *tv., irreg.* to depart [from a place], letting someone remain in the place. ♦ *I left Susan at the bank where she had to cash a check.* ♦ *Mary left her books in the library.* **4.** *tv., irreg.* to depart from and abandon someone, such as a spouse. ♦ *Jane told John that she'd leave him unless he stopped drinking.* ♦ *Bill left Mary for another woman.* **5.** *tv., irreg.* to cause someone or something to be in a certain condition. ♦ *The sad movie left me crying.* ♦ *The accident left me scratched and bruised.* **6.** *tv., irreg.* to will something to someone or something; to give something to someone or something after one dies. ♦ *The millionaire left her fortune to charity.* ♦ *My grandfather left me his gold watch.* **7.** *tv., irreg.* to entrust someone or something to someone. ♦ *Please, leave the dishes for me to wash later.* ♦ *The Browns left their kids with the babysitter for the evening.* **8.** *n.* permission. (No plural form in this sense. Formal.) ♦ *I sought the headmaster's leave to join the hockey team.* ♦ *You have my leave to go into town this evening.* **9.** *n.* an extended period of time away from one's duties. ♦ *The sailor spent his shore leave at his sister's house.* ♦ *The professor requested one semester's leave from teaching.*

leaven ['lɛv ən] *tv.* to cause dough to rise; to add something to dough to cause it to rise. ♦ *The baker leavened the dough with yeast.* ♦ *Our biscuits are leavened with baking powder.*

leavening ['lɛv ə nɪŋ] *n.* a substance, such as yeast, that causes dough to rise. (No plural form in this sense.) ♦ *The leavening caused the pastry to rise.* ♦ *The cook used baking powder for leavening.*

leaves ['livz] pl of leaf.

Lebanon ['lɛb ə nən] See Gazetteer.

lectern ['lɛk tɚn] *n.* a tall desk that someone stands behind while reading or lecturing, especially as found in a church or lecture hall. ♦ *I gave my sermon from behind the lectern.* ♦ *The professor pounded her fist on the lectern to emphasize a point.*

lecture ['lɛk tʃɚ] **1.** *n.* a lengthy talk about a certain subject; a speech. ♦ *Today's history lecture was about the War of 1812.* ♦ *I went to the auditorium to hear the lecture about modern farming techniques.* **2.** *n.* a scolding speech; a speech that warns or scolds. ♦ *The students in the back row ignored the lecture and slept.* ♦ *The police officer gave me a lecture about obeying the speed limit.* **3.** *iv.* to give a lecture; to talk about a certain subject. ♦ *The physics teacher lectured about the law of gravity.* ♦ *The professor lectured for hours, it seemed.* **4.** *tv.* to talk to people about a certain subject. ♦ *The professor lectured the class about Asian history.* ♦ *Our speaker will lecture us on politics in Mexico.* **5.** *tv.* to scold someone or something about something. ♦ *The traffic cop lectured me sternly about obeying the parking laws.* ♦ *The Smiths lectured their son about wearing a bicycle helmet.*

lecturer ['lɛk tʃɚ ɚ] **1.** *n.* someone who gives a lecture. ♦ *The lecturer talked about Russian literature.* ♦ *We are pleased to have such an entertaining lecturer to speak to us this evening.* **2.** *n.* someone who gives lectures; especially someone below the rank of professor or instructor who teaches at a university or college. ♦ *Introductory classes are often taught by lecturers.* ♦ *Bob got promoted from lecturer to instructor.*

led ['lɛd] pt/pp of lead.

ledge ['lɛdʒ] *n.* a narrow surface that sticks out along a wall or under a window; a shelf. ♦ *A bird built a nest on the ledge outside my bedroom window.* ♦ *I jumped from a third-story ledge to escape the burning building.*

ledger ['lɛdʒ ɚ] *n.* a book holding records of business transactions. ♦ *The auditor asked to examine the company's ledgers.* ♦ *Most companies use computers rather than old-fashioned ledgers.*

leech ['litʃ] **1.** *n.* a worm that sucks blood from humans or animals it is attached to. ♦ *After wading in the pond, my legs were covered with leeches.* ♦ *Many years ago, doctors used leeches to drain "bad" blood from sick people.* **2.**

n. a person who always takes things from people without ever giving anything in return. (Figurative on ①.) ♦ *My roommate is such a leech. He's always eating my food.* ♦ *Mary realized that John was just a lazy leech, so she broke up with him.*

leer ['lɪr] **1.** *n.* a look of lust; a sly look. ♦ *Mary ignored the old man's leer.* ♦ *Susan returned Bill's leer with a cold stare.* **2. leer at** *iv.* + *prep. phr.* to stare at someone lustfully. ♦ *The dirty old man leered at the waitress.* ♦ *Mary fled from the strange man who leered at her.*

leeway ['li we] **1.** *n.* extra space that someone or something is free to move in. (No plural form in this sense.) ♦ *There isn't enough leeway to turn the piano so it will go through the door to your living room.* ♦ *Interstate highway lanes have more leeway than most city streets.* **2.** *n.* the amount of freedom that one is allowed. (No plural form in this sense. Figurative on ①.) ♦ *The school paper was given a lot of leeway as to the stories it could print.* ♦ *Teenagers should be given enough leeway to let them enjoy life, but not enough to let them get into trouble.*

left ['lɛft] **1.** pt/pp of leave. **2.** *n.* one of the two directions to either side of the direction that is straight ahead. (No plural form in this sense.) ♦ *If you face north, west is to your left.* ♦ *Left is the opposite of right.* **3. the Left** *n.* politicians or citizens who are liberal ③. (No plural form in this sense. Treated as singular.) ♦ *The Left attacked the conservative senator's views.* ♦ *My senator tends to vote with the Left on social issues.* **4.** *adj.* on the left ②. ♦ *The heart is on the left side of the human body.* ♦ *About 10% of all people write with the left hand.* **5.** *adv.* toward ②. ♦ *The car in front of me veered left.* ♦ *Turn left at the next light.*

left-hand ['lɛft hænd] *adj.* left; on or at one's left side. ♦ *The salt is on the left-hand side of the napkins.* ♦ *Make a left-hand turn at the next intersection.*

left-handed ['lɛft hæn dɪd] **1.** *adj.* favoring the use of the left hand. (Adv: *left-handedly.*) ♦ *Left-handed people used to be forced to write with their right hands.* ♦ *The left-handed batter hit the ball into right field.* **2.** *adj.* designed for people who are ①. ♦ *The teacher bought some left-handed scissors for her class.* ♦ *I bought a set of left-handed golf clubs.* **3.** *adv.* [of writing] done with the left hand. ♦ *Bill writes left-handed and has done so since he was a child.* ♦ *The teacher can write both left-handed and right-handed.*

leftover ['lɛft ov ɚ] **1.** *adj.* remaining; unused and therefore extra. ♦ *We're having leftover soup tonight.* ♦ *I put the leftover dinner in the refrigerator.* **2. leftovers** *n.* portions of food left over from a meal. (Treated as plural.) ♦ *We are eating leftovers tonight.* ♦ *I put the leftovers in the refrigerator.*

left wing ['lɛft 'wɪŋ] **1.** *n.* people holding a political philosophy that is very liberal, progressive, or radical. (No plural form in this sense.) ♦ *The left wing wants to pay for everyone's health care from tax money.* ♦ *Both the left wing and the right wing agree that taxes are too high.* **2. left-wing** *adj.* <the adj. use of ①.> ♦ *There are a few left-wing politicians in Congress.* ♦ *Tom had a lot of left-wing ideas when he was young.*

leg ['lɛg] **1.** *n.* one of the two body parts that support a human; one of the four body parts that support most other mammals. ♦ *I stretched the muscles in my legs before exercising.* ♦ *The fox's leg was caught in a trap.* **2.** *n.* the part of a piece of clothing that wraps around ①. ♦ *I cut the legs off my jeans to make shorts.* ♦ *You've got mud on the left leg of your pants.* **3.** *n.* [in furniture or other structures] a vertical piece that supports weight. ♦ *I bumped my shin against the leg of the piano.* ♦ *One of the chair legs broke when I tipped the chair over.* **4.** *n.* a part of a trip; a part of a distance to be covered. ♦ *I drove 800 miles on the last leg of the trip.* ♦ *We stopped in the Bahamas on the first leg of the cruise.* **5. on someone's or something's last legs** *idiom* [for someone or something] to be almost finished. ♦ *This building is on its last legs. It should be torn down.* ♦ *I feel as if I'm on my last legs. I'm really tired.* **6. pull someone's leg** *idiom* to kid, fool, or trick someone. ♦ *You don't mean that. You're just pulling my leg.* ♦ *Don't believe him. He's just pulling your leg.* **7. stretch one's legs** *idiom* to walk around after sitting down or lying down for a time. ♦ *We wanted to stretch our legs during intermission.* ♦ *After sitting in the car all day, the travelers decided to stretch their legs.*

legacy ['lɛg ə si] **1.** *n.* assets willed to someone; money or property that someone gives away upon death. ♦ *I was able to live for years on a legacy from my late uncle.* ♦ *My farm is a legacy from my grandfather.* **2.** *n.* something that has been left behind by someone or something. (Figurative on ①.) ♦ *The long drought left a bitter legacy of famine.* ♦ *The war left a legacy of hatred between the two sides.*

legal ['lig əl] **1.** *adj.* lawful; according to the law. (Adv: *legally.*) ♦ *The inspector conducted a legal search of my property.* ♦ *It's legal to turn right at a red light in most states.* **2.** *adj.* of or about law. (Adv: *legally.*) ♦ *The legal secretary handles all of the company's contracts.* ♦ *I consulted the company's legal counsel before firing my assistant.*

legalize ['lig ə lɑɪz] *tv.* to cause something to be legal; to pass a law to make something legal. ♦ *The town council voted to legalize the sale of alcohol on Sundays.* ♦ *The students petitioned Congress to legalize some kinds of drugs.*

legal tender ['lig əl 'tɛn dɚ] See tender ④.

legation [lɪ 'ge ʃən] **1.** *n.* government officials who represent their government in a foreign country; a diplomat and the people who work with a diplomat. ♦ *Many legations fled the capital city when civil war erupted.* ♦ *The legation worked with the foreign prime minister on immigration matters.* **2.** *n.* the headquarters of ①. ♦ *The rebels set the American legation on fire.* ♦ *The prime minister met with the diplomat at the foreign legation.*

legend ['lɛdʒ ənd] **1.** *n.* an old and often repeated story; a fable; a myth. ♦ *I told the children the legend of the hare and the tortoise.* ♦ *I read a legend that was written over 300 years ago.* **2.** *n.* a very famous person; a person who might well be the subject of ①. ♦ *It is hard to predict which current celebrities will someday become legends.* ♦ *Many famous people become legends after they die.* **3.** *n.* an explanation of symbols used on a map, plan, chart, etc. ♦ *According to the legend, each inch represents 25 miles.* ♦ *I referred to the map's legend to see how toll roads were drawn.*

legendary ['lɛdʒ ɛn dɛr i] **1.** *adj.* of or about a legend; as described in a legend. ♦ *Many legendary tales have an important moral.* ♦ *Camelot is the legendary site of King Arthur's court.* **2.** *adj.* very famous; very important in one's line of work. ♦ *The legendary singer received a stand-*

ing ovation. ♦ *The legendary baseball player wrote an autobiography.*

legible ['lɛdʒ ə bəl] *adj.* able to be read; neatly printed or written. (Adv: *legibly.*) ♦ *My English teacher has very legible handwriting.* ♦ *The small print at the bottom of the contract was barely legible.*

legion ['li dʒən] **1.** *n.* a large group of soldiers; a division of an army. ♦ *The legion surrounded the rebel town.* ♦ *Bill joined the Foreign Legion during the war.* **2.** *n.* a very large group of things or people. (Figurative on ①.) ♦ *The new mayor inherited a legion of urban problems.* ♦ *There was a legion of relatives at my grandfather's funeral.*

legislate ['lɛdʒ ɪ slet] **1.** *tv.* to make laws. ♦ *Congress legislates federal laws.* ♦ *In England, laws are legislated by parliament.* **2.** *tv.* to pass a law about something. ♦ *Congress legislated new income-tax rates.* ♦ *The new drunk-driving penalties were legislated by Congress.*

legislation [lɛdʒ ɪ 'sle ʃən] **1.** *n.* writing and making laws. (No plural form in this sense.) ♦ *Careful and just legislation is the product of hard work and compromise.* ♦ *Legislation is the job of the legislative branch of government.* **2.** *n.* laws that have been made; a set of laws. (No plural form in this sense. Number is expressed with *piece(s) of legislation.*) ♦ *Congress updated the obsolete commerce legislation.* ♦ *The lawyer studied the legislation concerning fraud.*

legislative ['lɛdʒ ɪ sle tɪv] *adj.* of or about making laws or the people who make laws. (Adv: *legislatively.*) ♦ *We learned about the legislative process in government class.* ♦ *The busy senator drafted many legislative proposals.*

legislator ['lɛdʒ ɪ sle tɚ] *n.* someone who makes laws; a member of a legislature. ♦ *Many state governors started out as state legislators.* ♦ *I questioned my state legislator about his voting record.*

legislature ['lɛdʒ ɪ sle tʃɚ] *n.* the body of people who are elected or appointed to make laws. ♦ *The state legislature lowered the speed limit.* ♦ *The legislature's attempt to impose a curfew for the entire state was declared unconstitutional.*

legitimate [lɪ 'dʒɪt ə mət] **1.** *adj.* lawful; according to the law. (Adv: *legitimately.*) ♦ *It was impossible for the illegal alien to find a legitimate job.* ♦ *The banker claimed his business practices were legitimate.* **2.** *adj.* correct; valid; reasonable. (Adv: *legitimately.*) ♦ *You have a legitimate reason to be worried about pollution.* ♦ *Illness is the only legitimate excuse for missing football practice.* **3.** *adj.* [of a person] born to legally married parents; [of the birth of a person] legal. (Adv: *legitimately.*) ♦ *The city's rate of legitimate births fell 2% last year.* ♦ *The minister urged Anne to marry Bob so that their child would be legitimate.*

legitimize [lɪ 'dʒɪt ə mɑɪz] *tv.* to cause something to become legitimate; to make something legal; to legalize something. ♦ *The legislature legitimized the higher speed limit on freeways.* ♦ *Citizens accused the mayor of trying to legitimize crime by reducing the size of the police force.*

leisure ['li ʒɚ] **1.** *n.* free time; time that is not spent at work or at sleep; time when one can do what one wants. (No plural form in this sense.) ♦ *In my leisure, I like to read romance novels.* ♦ *Bill had little time for leisure because he worked two jobs.* **2.** *adj.* <the adj. use of ①.> ♦ *In my leisure time, I like to read romance novels.* ♦ *I have few leisure moments, but I like to listen to music as much as I can.*

leisurely ['li ʒɚ li] **1.** *adj.* not in a hurry; taking one's time; relaxed. ♦ *I walked to work at a leisurely pace.* ♦ *Anne was scolded for her leisurely approach to her work.* **2.** *adv.* not in a hurry; in a relaxed way. ♦ *I strolled leisurely along the bank of the river.* ♦ *We talked leisurely for several hours.*

lemon ['lɛm ən] **1.** *n.* a sour, yellow citrus fruit. ♦ *I squeezed a slice of lemon onto my seafood dinner.* ♦ *I like a piece of lemon in my iced tea.* **2.** *n.* a product, such as a car, that does not work properly and cannot be repaired. ♦ *The salesman who sold me the lemon tried to tell me it was a good car.* ♦ *This new TV doesn't work at all. It must be a lemon.* **3.** *adj.* made or flavored with ①. ♦ *I had a slice of lemon pie after dinner.* ♦ *I put some lemon juice in my tea.*

lemonade [lɛm ən 'ed] *n.* a drink made from the juice of lemons, sugar, and water. (No plural form in this sense.) ♦ *I drank a cold glass of lemonade for lunch.* ♦ *The kids sold lemonade for a quarter a cup.*

lend ['lɛnd] **1.** *tv., irreg.* to grant someone permission to use or borrow something for a period of time. (Pt/pp: lent.) ♦ *Dave lent his car to me.* ♦ *I lent Anne my book.* **2.** *tv., irreg.* to contribute an effect to something; to add a quality to something. (Figurative on ①.) ♦ *The tablecloth lent an air of style to dinner.* ♦ *The impressive speaker lent dignity to the award ceremony.* **3. lend oneself or itself to something** *idiom* [for someone or something] to be adaptable to something; [for someone or something] to be useful for something. ♦ *This room doesn't lend itself to bright colors.* ♦ *John doesn't lend himself to casual conversation.*

length ['lɛŋkθ] **1.** *n.* the measurement of something from end to end in the longest dimension; the amount of elapsed time. (No plural form in this sense.) ♦ *The length of the movie is 2 hours and 10 minutes.* ♦ *Most yardsticks are 36 inches in length.* **2.** *n.* a piece of something of a certain or known ①. ♦ *Mary sewed two lengths of cloth together to make a piece large enough to cover the table.* ♦ *The plumber bought a length of pipe four inches long.*

lengthen ['lɛŋk θən] **1.** *tv.* to make something longer. ♦ *The commercials lengthened the TV program by half an hour.* ♦ *The author lengthened her novel by adding more chapters.* **2.** *iv.* to become longer. ♦ *The days lengthened as summer approached.* ♦ *The voting lines lengthened after work.*

lengthwise AND **lengthways** ['lɛŋkθ wɑɪz, 'lɛŋkθ wez]] *adv.* along the length of something. ♦ *This broken tile measures eight inches lengthwise.* ♦ *I walked lengthwise along the pool.*

lengthy ['lɛŋk θi] **1.** *adj.* very long; covering a great distance. (Adv: *lengthily.*) ♦ *The lengthy line for concert tickets was a block long.* ♦ *I stopped for gas twice during the lengthy car trip.* **2.** *adj.* taking a long time. (Adv: *lengthily.*) ♦ *My professor's lengthy lecture was really boring.* ♦ *John's embarrassing statement was followed by a lengthy pause.*

lenient ['lin i ənt] *adj.* not strict. (Adv: *leniently.*) ♦ *A lenient judge shortened the criminal's sentence.* ♦ *The lenient parents let their kids eat whatever they wanted.*

lens ['lɛnz] **1.** *n.* a piece of curved glass that bends rays of light. ♦ *The scientist looked through the lens of the microscope.* ♦ *I wear contact lenses to correct my bad vision.* **2.** *n.* the clear, curved part of the eye—in front of the pupil—that focuses light rays on the retina. ♦ *Squinting distorts the curve of the lenses.* ♦ *The lenses of nearsighted people focus light rays in front of the retina.*

lent ['lɛnt] **1.** pt/pp of lend. **2. Lent** *n.* [in the Christian religion] a period of fasting and repentance before Easter. ♦ *Lent begins on Ash Wednesday.* ♦ *Catholics aren't supposed to eat meat on Fridays during Lent.*

leopard ['lɛp ɚd] **1.** *n.* a large animal in the cat family usually having yellowish fur with black spots. ♦ *The zookeeper fed the leopards fresh meat.* ♦ *The leopard runs very swiftly.* **2.** *n.* the fur and skin of ①. (No plural form in this sense.) ♦ *My coat is made of leopard.* ♦ *The dancer wore a cloak made from leopard.* **3.** *adj.* made of or from ②. ♦ *The model wore an expensive leopard coat.* ♦ *The leopard collar on my coat is quite stunning.*

leotard ['li ə tɑrd] *n.* a snug, one-piece article of clothing typically worn by ballet dancers and gymnasts. ♦ *I wore a leotard to aerobics class.* ♦ *The ballerina's leotard is white.*

leper ['lɛp ɚ] *n.* someone who has leprosy. ♦ *The lepers were not permitted to enter the city.* ♦ *The unpopular students were treated like lepers.*

leprosy ['lɛp rə si] *n.* a bacterial disease that causes the muscles and skin to waste away. (No plural form in this sense.) ♦ *An elderly nun cared for people dying from leprosy.* ♦ *The health agency tried to slow the spread of leprosy.*

lesbian ['lɛz bi ən] **1.** *n.* a female homosexual; a woman who is attracted to other women. ♦ *The court upheld the lesbian's claim of discrimination.* ♦ *The clinic organized a support group for lesbians with breast cancer.* **2.** *adj.* <the adj. use of ①.> ♦ *The women's bookstore had a section for lesbian fiction.* ♦ *A lesbian bar is now open for business in the city.*

lesion ['li ʒən] *n.* a wound; an injury, especially one where the structure of an organ or tissue is damaged. ♦ *The doctor bandaged my lesions carefully.* ♦ *There is a lesion on the patient's brain from the car accident.*

less ['lɛs] **1.** *adj.* <the comparative form of little, meaning a smaller amount.> (Used with things that are measured in quantities. Compare with fewer, which is used with things that can be counted. See also lesser.) ♦ *I do less walking since I bought a car.* ♦ *You gave me less rice than you gave to Jimmy.* **2.** *adv.* to a smaller extent or degree; not as much. (The opposite of more.) ♦ *I exercise less often than I used to.* ♦ *I weigh myself less frequently than you do.* **3.** *n.* a smaller amount. (No plural form in this sense.) ♦ *The actor would not settle for less than 5% of the ticket sales.* ♦ *The less that is said about the incident, the better.* **4. -less** *suffix* <a form meaning *without* that can be added to nouns and to adjectives that have come from verbs.> (The resulting adjectives can be made into nouns with the -ness suffix and into adverbs with the suffix -*ly*. The following are used in the dictionary: *ageless, aimless, aimlessness, baseless, blameless, bloodless, boneless, boundlessness, brainless, branchless, breathless, careless, carelessness, carless, ceaseless, childless, colorless, cordless, countless, dauntless, defenseless, doubtless, effortless, endless, faceless, fatherless, faultless, fearless, fearlessness, finless, flavorless, flawless, flightless, formless, friendless, fruitless, graceless, groundless, guileless, guiltless, hapless, harmless, harmlessness, headless, heartless, heedless, helpless, helplessness, homeless, homelessness, hopeless, hopelessness, jobless, joblessness, lawless, legless, lifeless, limitless, listless, mannerless, matchless, meaningless, meatless, merciless, mindless, motherless, motionless, nameless, needless, nevertheless, noiseless, nonetheless, numberless, painless, peerless, penniless, pitiless, pointless, powerless, powerlessness, priceless, purposeless, reckless, recklessness, regardless, relentless, remorseless, restless, restlessness, roofless, ruthless, seedless, selflessness, senseless, sexless, shameless, shamelessness, shapeless, shiftless, sightless, sleepless, sleeveless, speechless, spineless, spotless, tactless, tasteless, thankless, thoughtless, thoughtlessness, timeless, tireless, toothless, topless, useless, valueless, voiceless, weightless, weightlessness, windowless, wireless, worthless, worthlessness.*)

lessen ['lɛs ən] **1.** *iv.* to become less; to decrease in size, amount, or power. ♦ *The king's power lessened as he became older.* ♦ *The amount of sunlight lessens as night approaches.* **2.** *tv.* to cause someone or something to become less. ♦ *My boss lessened the amount of work I had to do.* ♦ *Seat belts lessen the impact of injury.*

lesser ['lɛs ɚ] **1.** *adj.* smaller in amount or degree. ♦ *Tom was angry and, to a lesser degree, embarrassed about his mistake.* ♦ *This brand of aspirin gives me a lesser amount of relief than the brand I used to use.* **2. the lesser (of the two)** *idiom* the smaller one (of two); the one having the least amount. ♦ *The last two pieces of pie were not quite the same size, and I chose the lesser of the two.* ♦ *Faced with a basket containing too much and one with too little, Tom chose the lesser.* **3. the lesser of two evils** *idiom* the less bad thing, of a pair of bad things. ♦ *I didn't like either politician, so I voted for the lesser of two evils.* ♦ *Given the options of going out with someone I don't like and staying home and watching a boring television program, I chose the lesser of the two evils and watched television.*

lesson ['lɛs ən] **1.** *n.* a session of instruction with a teacher; the material to be covered in one session of instruction; something, such as a school assignment, that is to be learned, studied, or prepared. ♦ *I have a piano lesson every Wednesday afternoon.* ♦ *The first lesson gives the students some very basic information.* **2.** *n.* something that one learns from an experience; an experience that one learns something from. ♦ *I learned my lesson. I'll never lie again.* ♦ *John learned a valuable lesson from the argument.*

let ['lɛt] **1.** *tv., irreg.* to allow someone or something to do something; to allow something to happen. (Pt/pp: let.) ♦ *Mr. Smith lets his son drive to school.* ♦ *Mary let the reporters ask her questions.* **2.** *tv., irreg.* [for a landlord] to rent an apartment or room (to someone). ♦ *My parents let the extra bedroom to a college student.* ♦ *The landlord finally let the studio apartment on the first floor.* **3. let go of someone or something** *idiom* to release someone or something. ♦ *Please let go of me!* ♦ *Don't let go of the steering wheel.* **4. let out a sound** *idiom* to make [some kind of a] sound. (Can be any sound an animal can make.) ♦ *Be quiet. Don't let out a sound!* ♦ *Suddenly, Jane let out a shriek.* **5. let someone know (about something)** *idiom* to tell someone something; to inform someone of something. ♦ *Please let me know* *about it soon.* ♦ *Will you be coming to the picnic? Please let me know.* **6. let us do something** *idiom* we will do something [together]. (More of an invitation or request than a command.) ♦ *Let us go in peace.* ♦ *Let us bow our heads in prayer.* **7. let someone off (the hook)** *idiom* to release someone from a responsibility. ♦ *Please let me off the hook for our appointment on Saturday. I have other plans.* ♦ *Okay, I'll let you off.*

letdown ['lɛt dɑʊn] *n.* a disappointment; something that did not happen the way one had hoped. ♦ *Our trip to the beach was a big letdown because it rained.* ♦ *My friends really liked the movie, but I thought it was a letdown.*

lethal ['liθ əl] *adj.* causing death; fatal. (Adv: *lethally.*) ♦ *Mary died when she swallowed some lethal poison.* ♦ *The lethal bullet struck John's heart.*

lethargic [lɛ 'θɑr dʒɪk] *adj.* lacking energy; slow; tired. (Adv: *lethargically* [...ɪk li].) ♦ *My brother, feeling lethargic, took a nap in the afternoon.* ♦ *The lethargic old cat walked slowly to its bowl of water.*

lethargy ['lɛθ ɚ dʒi] *n.* the lack of energy; a state of being slow and tired. (No plural form in this sense.) ♦ *John is still in bed due to lethargy.* ♦ *The hiker combated lethargy by eating a candy bar.*

let's ['lɛts] *cont.* "let us"; we will [do something]. (A gentle command or request. A response is usually expected. Compare with let us at let ⑥.) ♦ *Let's go to the movies tonight.* ♦ *Let's order pizza for dinner.*

letter ['lɛt ɚ] **1.** *n.* a written or printed symbol in an alphabet. ♦ A *is the first letter of the English alphabet.* ♦ *There are six letters in the word* picnic. **2.** *n.* a written message sent to a person or a company. ♦ *Business letters have a special structure and format.* ♦ *I just received a long letter from Aunt Jane.*

letter carrier ['lɛt ɚ kɛr i ɚ] See mail carrier.

lettering ['lɛt ɚ ɪŋ] *n.* a series of letters ①. (No plural form in this sense.) ♦ *I could barely read the lettering on the medicine bottle.* ♦ *The lettering on the envelope was written in green ink.*

lettuce ['lɛt ɪs] *n.* a leafy, green vegetable, often used in salads. (No plural form in this sense. Number is expressed with *leaf* or *leaves of lettuce* and *head(s) of lettuce.*) ♦ *What kind of dressing do you want with your lettuce?* ♦ *I placed a leaf of lettuce on my sandwich.*

letup ['lɛt əp] *n.* a pause; a reduction in or stopping of an activity. ♦ *We can only hope for a letup in Jane's insistent requests.* ♦ *There was no letup in the heavy rainfall all day.*

leukemia [lu 'ki mi ə] *n.* a blood disease where too many white blood cells are made, often causing death. (No plural form in this sense.) ♦ *The Smiths' young child died of leukemia.* ♦ *The doctor worked to find a cure for leukemia.*

levee ['lɛv i] *n.* a tall, wide ridge that is built along a riverbank to stop flooding. ♦ *The flooding river broke through the earthen levee.* ♦ *The townsfolk reinforced the levee with sandbags during the flood.*

level ['lɛv əl] **1.** *n.* a flat surface; a horizontal plane. ♦ *When we get to the level, it will be easier to walk.* ♦ *It is easier to build a house on the level than on the side of a hill.* **2.** *n.* one of the floors of a building or other structure. ♦ *My office is on the next level.* ♦ *I parked on the sixth level of the parking garage.* **3.** *n.* a layer; a step or a stage. ♦ *There are many levels of administrative power in the federal government.* ♦ *The oil well cut through several levels of rock and sand.* **4.** *n.* the amount of a measurement; a position on a scale of measurement. ♦ *Near the power plant, the level of radiation was much too high.* ♦ *The level of security at the airport is more than adequate.* **5.** *n.* a tool or device that shows when a surface is horizontal or vertical. ♦ *The level indicated the board was slightly angled.* ♦ *The carpenter placed the level on the shelf.* **6.** *n.* a fixed or known height. (No plural form in this sense.) ♦ *Our town is 600 feet above sea level.* ♦ *Water seeks its own level.* **7.** *adj.* [of a surface] exactly horizontal where every point is the same height. ♦ *You should put your computer on level surfaces only.* ♦ *The carpenter fixed the shelf so that it was level.* **8.** *adj.* steady; not changing. (Figurative on ⑦.) ♦ *Support for the president remained level throughout his term.* ♦ *The inflation rate remained level for several months.* **9.** *tv.* to knock down trees, buildings, or other objects until the land is flat. ♦ *The tornado leveled dozens of houses.* ♦ *An earthquake leveled most of the town.* **10. level off** *iv.* + *adv.* [for a surface] to become flat and ⑦; [for lines on a graph] to become flat. ♦ *Support for the president leveled off at 45%.* ♦ *The hill leveled off at 500 feet.* **11. find one's own level** *idiom* to find the position or rank to which one is best suited. ♦ *You cannot force junior staff to be ambitious. They will all find their own level.* ♦ *The new pupil is happier in the lower class. It was just a question of letting her find her own level.* **12. level something at someone** *idiom* to aim a remark at someone; to direct something at someone. ♦ *John leveled a sarcastic comment at his teacher.* ♦ *The editorial leveled its remarks at the mayor.* **13. level with someone (about someone or something)** *idiom* to be straightforward with someone about something; to be sincere about someone or something. ♦ *The police encouraged the criminal to level with them about the crime.* ♦ *Level with me, and tell me what you thought of my cake.* **14. (strictly) on the level** *idiom* honest; dependably open and fair. ♦ *How can I be sure you're on the level?* ♦ *You can trust Sally. She's strictly on the level.*

levelheaded ['lɛv əl 'hɛd ɪd] *adj.* sensible; having good judgment; calm. (Adv: *levelheadedly.*) ♦ *Jane responded to the accusation with a levelheaded remark.* ♦ *My doctor is a sensible and levelheaded person.*

lever ['lɛv ɚ] **1.** *n.* a bar of metal or wood, resting on a pivot, used to increase one's power in lifting or moving heavy objects. ♦ *I pushed down on the lever to lift the rock on the other end.* ♦ *I snapped the lever in half while trying to lift the heavy box.* **2.** *n.* a bar or handle that serves as a control device. ♦ *Push down on that red lever to start the machine.* ♦ *The emergency brake is operated with that lever next to your foot.*

leverage ['lɛv (ə) rɪdʒ] **1.** *n.* the power that is gained by using a lever. (No plural form in this sense.) ♦ *I moved the pivot so that I would have more leverage.* ♦ *I need enough leverage to lift a 100-pound box.* **2.** *n.* an advantage or influence that one has in trying to get a certain result. (Figurative on ①. No plural form in this sense.) ♦ *The senator had enough leverage to get the crime bill passed.* ♦ *Can you use your leverage to get me a job at the company you work for?*

levitate ['lɛv ɪ tet] **1.** *iv.* to rise and float in the air; to remain in the air without any support. ♦ *The glass ball magically levitated above the table.* ♦ *The blimp levitated above the sports arena.* **2.** *tv.* to cause someone or something to rise and float in the air; to cause someone or something to remain in the air without any support, presumably by magic. ♦ *The magician levitated the glass ball above the table.* ♦ *A sleeping lady was levitated over the magician's audience.*

levy ['lɛv i] **1.** *n.* a tax; a tax rate. ♦ *Which states charge a levy on medicine?* ♦ *A strict levy was imposed on all imported goods.* **2.** *tv.* to demand and collect something, especially a tax. ♦ *The state legislature levied a tax on alcohol.* ♦ *A 5% tax was levied on all imported goods.*

lewd ['lud] *adj.* crude in a sexual way; vulgar; obscene. (Adv: *lewdly.*) ♦ *They are showing another lewd movie on television tonight.* ♦ *Please stop telling those lewd jokes.*

lexicon ['lɛks ɪ kɑn] **1.** *n.* a dictionary listing the words and meanings of one language. ♦ *There are many lexicons in the public library.* ♦ *I checked the lexicon for the meaning of the word I didn't know.* **2.** *n.* a list of words; a vocabulary; someone's own vocabulary. ♦ *Most medical terms are not in the average person's lexicon.* ♦ *Some of the words in the English lexicon are derived from French.*

liability [lɑɪ ə 'bɪl ə ti] **1.** *n.* a kind of danger to people that could cause a lawsuit against whoever is responsible for creating the danger. (No plural form in this sense.) ♦ *The open pit was a liability for the construction company.* ♦ *Icy sidewalks are a liability for store owners.* **2.** *n.* a cost or [monetary] charge; a potential cost; a negative consideration. (No plural form in this sense.) ♦ *The house we want to buy needs a new roof, and that's a liability.* ♦ *The lawyers found a number of outstanding liabilities in the financial reports.* **3. assume liability** *idiom* to accept the responsibility for paying a cost. ♦ *Mr. Smith assumed liability for his son's student loans.* ♦ *The store assumed liability for the injured customer's hospital bill.*

liable ['lɑɪ ə bəl] **1.** *adj.* legally at risk for something; legally responsible for something. ♦ *The rental contract stated that I was liable for all damages.* ♦ *Yes, you are liable. You must pay all the charges.* **2. liable to** *adj.* + *inf.* apt to; likely to; prone to; tending to. ♦ *You're liable to miss your plane if you don't leave now.* ♦ *John's liable to quit his job if he doesn't get a raise.*

liaison ['li e zɑn] **1.** *n.* open communication between two or more groups of people. (No plural form in this sense.) ♦ *The allied armies required constant liaison with each other.* ♦ *Although miles apart, the research teams maintained liaison by telephone.* **2.** *n.* someone who keeps communication open between two or more groups of people. ♦ *A liaison mediated the dispute between the two sides.* ♦ *The press secretary was the liaison between the mayor and the media.* **3.** *n.* a secret romantic relationship. ♦ *The newspaper reported the mayor's liaison with an aide.* ♦ *Mrs. Jones never learned of her husband's secret liaisons.*

liar ['lɑɪ ɚ] *n.* someone who tells lies; someone who does not tell the truth. ♦ *Are you calling me a liar?* ♦ *You can never believe what Bob tells you. He's such a liar.*

libel ['lɑɪ bəl] **1.** *n.* a false and damaging statement published about someone or something. (No plural form in this sense. Compare with slander.) ♦ *The actor denounced the unflattering article as libel.* ♦ *Some tabloid magazines routinely print libel.* **2.** *n.* publishing a false and damaging statement about someone or something. (No plural form in this sense.) ♦ *The actor sued the tabloid for libel.* ♦ *The judge found the newspaper guilty of libel.* **3.** *tv.* to publish ① about someone or something. ♦ *The tabloid libeled the famous musician.* ♦ *The newspaper editors are careful not to libel anyone.*

libelous ['lɑɪ bəl əs] *adj.* serving to libel someone. (Adv: *libelously.*) ♦ *Max sued the newspaper for printing libelous statements about him.* ♦ *The book was libelous, and the person who was offended demanded that all the copies be destroyed.*

liberal ['lɪb (ə) rəl] **1.** *adj.* tolerant; broad-minded; progressive. (Adv: *liberally.*) ♦ *Most liberal people are opposed to the death penalty.* ♦ *Mary's son came home from college with many liberal ideas.* **2.** *adj.* generous; abundant; plenty; ample. (Adv: *liberally.*) ♦ *Grandma gave me liberal helpings of mashed potatoes and gravy.* ♦ *I put a liberal amount of sunblock on my skin.* **3.** *adj.* of or about political views that favor social and economic progress, very often through government control and management. (Adv: *liberally.*) ♦ *I share my senator's liberal social views.* ♦ *The conservative newspaper denounced the liberal agenda.* **4.** *n.* someone who has liberal ③ viewpoints. ♦ *The liberal voted to restore budget cuts in welfare.* ♦ *In the election, the conservative candidate was defeated by a liberal.* **5. liberal arts** *n.* subjects for study that are cultural or philosophical instead of technical or practical. (Treated as plural.) ♦ *The biology student had little interest in the liberal arts.* ♦ *Mary wanted to study philosophy and related liberal arts.*

liberate ['lɪb ə ret] *tv.* to set someone or something free; to release someone or something from control. ♦ *The army liberated the enslaved people from their masters.* ♦ *I liberated the rabbit from its cage.*

Liberia [lɑɪ 'bɪr ɪ ə] See Gazetteer.

liberty ['lɪb ɚ ti] **1.** *n.* the freedom from control or repression; the freedom to think or act for oneself. (No plural form in this sense.) ♦ *Liberty is the basis of democracy.* ♦ *The enslaved people prayed for liberty from their captors.* **2.** *n.* the permission to do something; a right or a privilege that one has been given. ♦ *Americans often take their civil liberties for granted.* ♦ *The students were given the liberty to leave campus on weekends.* **3. at liberty to do something** *idiom* not free to do something; not permitted to do something. ♦ *The general was not at liberty to divulge the military's plans.* ♦ *You are at liberty to leave anytime you wish.*

libido [lɪ 'bi do] *n.* the sexual drive; sexual desire. (No plural form in this sense. From Latin. Pl in *-s.*) ♦ *He believes that alcohol affects his libido.* ♦ *She seems to be suffering from an overactive libido.*

librarian [lɑɪ 'brɛr i ən] *n.* someone who manages or helps operate a library. ♦ *I asked the librarian where the reference section was.* ♦ *The librarian charged me a fine for the overdue book.*

library ['lɑɪ brɛr i] **1.** *n.* a building or room that has a supply of books or similar materials available for use by a number of people. ♦ *The city's public library is open to every city resident.* ♦ *I went to the library to check out books about astronomy.* **2.** *n.* a collection of books, records, videotapes, etc. ♦ *Mary has every play by Shakespeare in* *her personal library.* ♦ *John has an impressive video library of early American films.*

Libya ['lɪb i ə] See Gazetteer.

lice ['lɑɪs] pl of louse.

license ['lɑɪ səns] **1.** *n.* a document that proves that someone has permission to do or own something. ♦ *I went downtown to renew my driver's license.* ♦ *The city requires dog owners to buy a dog license each year.* **2.** *n.* the freedom of literary or other artistic expression. (No plural form in this sense.) ♦ *The differences between the movie and the original book are due to the director's artistic license.* ♦ *The critic attributed the quotes in the biography to the author's poetic license.* **3. license plate** See plate ⑦. **4.** *tv.* to give someone a license for something; to authorize someone or something; to permit someone or something. ♦ *The city licensed me to open a restaurant.* ♦ *The commander licensed the police to kill the dangerous criminal.* **5. license to do something** *idiom* permission, right, or justification to do something. ♦ *You have no license to behave in that manner!* ♦ *Who granted you license to enter my house without knocking?*

lick ['lɪk] **1.** *tv.* to move the tongue along someone or something; to taste something by moving one's tongue along someone or something; to make something wet by moving one's tongue along someone or something. ♦ *The young girl licked the ice-cream cone.* ♦ *I licked the envelope's seal.* **2.** *tv.* to beat someone in a game; to overcome someone or something. (Informal.) ♦ *The home team licked the visiting team in overtime.* ♦ *Bill licked his alcohol problem.* **3. lick at** *iv.* + *prep. phr.* [for flames] to touch something that is burning or is being ignited. ♦ *Flames licked at the garage next to the burning house.* ♦ *Yellow flames licked at the logs just piled on the fire.* **4.** *n.* the act of licking as in ①; the movement of the tongue along the surface of something. ♦ *I gave the stamp a quick lick and stuck it on the envelope.* ♦ *The dog's lick was wet and smelly.* **5.** *n.* a small amount of something that one gets by licking. ♦ *Can I have a lick of your ice-cream cone?* ♦ *You took more than one lick!* **6. a lick of work** *idiom* [not even] a bit of work. ♦ *I couldn't get her to do a lick of work all day long!* ♦ *The boys didn't do a lick of work while you were away.*

licorice ['lɪk ɚ ɪs, 'lɪk rɪʃ] **1.** *n.* a sweet, black or red, gummy candy. (No plural form in this sense.) ♦ *My grandfather gave me a dozen sticks of licorice.* ♦ *The soft licorice got stuck in my teeth.* **2.** *n.* the flavor of ①. (No plural form in this sense.) ♦ *This gum tastes like licorice.* ♦ *I flavored the cookies with licorice.* **3.** *adj.* <the adj. use of ①.> ♦ *I really do not care for licorice candy.* ♦ *This grocery store sells licorice ice cream.*

lid ['lɪd] **1.** *n.* a cover for a container, surface, hole, or other object. ♦ *The lid of the pickle jar was screwed on tightly.* ♦ *Who didn't put the lid back on the pop bottle?* **2.** *n.* the fold of skin over the eye; an eyelid. ♦ *Mary closed her lids and fell asleep.* ♦ *Anne put some makeup on her lids.*

lie ['lɑɪ] **1.** *n.* a statement that is not true that the speaker knows is not true; a false statement. ♦ *It is illegal to lie while testifying in court.* ♦ *Don't lie to me!* **2.** *n.* an action that is meant to deceive. ♦ *John's marriage is a big lie. He doesn't really love Mary.* ♦ *The agent's promise of finding me work was a lie.* **3.** *iv.* to say something that is not true; to tell ①. (Pt/pp: lied. The present participle is spelled lying.) ♦ *The judge charged John with perjury for lying under oath.* ♦ *I lied when I said Bill sings well because I didn't want to hurt his feelings.* **4.** *iv., irreg.* to be in a flat position; to place oneself in a flat position. (Pt: lay; pp: lain. See also lay. The present participle is spelled lying.) ♦ *Yesterday, I lay in bed all day.* ♦ *The baby was lying in her crib.* **5.** *iv., irreg.* to be located; to be in a certain place. ♦ *Nevada lies west of Utah.* ♦ *The newspaper is lying next to the couch.* **6.** *iv., irreg.* to remain in a place or condition; to stay in a certain condition or position. ♦ *Bears lie dormant in their caves while hibernating.* ♦ *Please lie still and don't make any noise.* **7. lie in wait (for someone or something)** *idiom* to stay still and hidden, waiting for someone or something. ♦ *Bob was lying in wait for Anne so he could scold her about something.* ♦ *The assassin lay in wait for his target to approach.* **8. take something lying down** *idiom* to endure something unpleasant without fighting back. ♦ *He insulted me publicly. You don't expect me to take that lying down, do you?* ♦ *I'm not the kind of person who'll take something like that lying down.*

lieutenant [lu 'tɛn ənt] **1.** *n.* an officer in the navy, ranking below a lieutenant commander. ♦ *The lieutenant ordered me to fire a torpedo at the enemy ship.* ♦ *I ate with Lieutenant Smith at evening mess.* **2.** *n.* a police officer, ranking below a captain. ♦ *The lieutenant filed all the reports on the crime.* ♦ *Mary spoke with Lieutenant Jones about her stolen car.* **3.** *n.* an official whose rank is one level below certain other elective offices. ♦ *The lieutenant governor was in charge while the governor was in the hospital.* ♦ *The rank of lieutenant colonel is above the rank of major.*

life ['lɑɪf] **1.** *n.* the power that causes plants and animals to exist, in general. (No plural form in this sense.) ♦ *We must have food and water in order to have life.* ♦ *As long as there is life in me, I will be a loyal party member.* **2.** *n., irreg.* an individual instance of ① that can be lived, lost, saved, spent, wasted, etc.; the period of time between birth and death or between birth and the present. (Pl: lives.) ♦ *The lifeguard saved my life!* ♦ *Our dog spent its entire life being well cared for.* **3.** *n., irreg.* a person; a living person. ♦ *Many lives were lost in the terrible accident.* ♦ *How many lives have been saved by lowering the speed limit?* **4.** *n.* a punishment where one is put in prison until death. (No plural form in this sense. From "life in prison.") ♦ *The murderer got life for his heinous crime.* ♦ *The judge sentenced the dangerous criminal to life in prison.* **5.** *n., irreg.* the activities, experiences, and habits of a person. ♦ *My life was very dull, so I decided to move to New York City.* ♦ *The traveler led an exciting, adventurous life.* **6.** *n.* excitement; vigor; vitality. (No plural form in this sense.) ♦ *I advised the playwright to put some life into the second act.* ♦ *My sweet old grandmother is still full of life.* **7.** *n.* a kind of living; a quality of living. (No plural form in this sense.) ♦ *Country life is the best for me.* ♦ *I work too hard and this is not the kind of life I want to lead.* **8.** *adj.* of or about ⑤; for an entire ②. ♦ *My father is a life member of that organization.* ♦ *The dangerous criminal received a life sentence.* **9. all walks of life** *idiom* all social, economic, and ethnic groups. ♦ *We saw people there from all walks of life.* ♦ *The people who came to the art exhibit represented all walks of life.* **10. for life** *idiom* for the remainder of one's life. ♦ *The accident caused me to become blind for life.* ♦ *She will stay in prison for life.* **11. lead the life of Riley** *idiom* to live in luxury. ♦ *If I had* *a million dollars, I could lead the life of Riley.* ♦ *The treasurer took our money to Mexico, where he led the life of Riley until the police caught him.* **12. seamy side of life** *idiom* the most unpleasant or roughest aspect of life. ♦ *Doctors in that neighborhood really see the seamy side of life.* ♦ *Mary saw the seamy side of life when she worked as a charity volunteer.*

lifeblood ['lɑɪf 'blʌd] **1.** *n.* blood; the blood that one needs to live. (No plural form in this sense.) ♦ *The soldier spilled his lifeblood on the battlefield.* ♦ *They knew they might have to give their lifeblood for their country.* **2.** *n.* a source of strength and energy. (Figurative on ①.) ♦ *Our inspiring coach is the lifeblood of our baseball team.* ♦ *The inventive genius was the lifeblood of the research department.*

lifeboat ['lɑɪf bot] *n.* a boat used to save people from a sinking ship; a boat used to save people in danger of drowning. ♦ *The passengers on the sinking ship ran toward the lifeboats.* ♦ *The survivors crowded onto the only lifeboat.*

lifeguard ['lɑɪf gɑrd] *n.* someone who works at a beach or swimming pool to encourage water safety and rescue people from drowning. ♦ *The lifeguard saved the drowning swimmer.* ♦ *One of the lifeguards warned us that a shark had been sighted.*

life jacket AND **life preserver; life vest** ['lɑɪf 'dʒæk ət, ... prə 'zɝv ɚ, ... 'vɛst] *n.* a thick jacket without sleeves that floats and will keep the person who wears it from sinking in the water. (See also lifesaver.) ♦ *You must wear a life jacket if you take a boat ride.* ♦ *My life vest even has a whistle attached to it in case I am lost at sea.*

lifeless ['lɑɪf ləs] **1.** *adj.* without life; dead. (Adv: *lifelessly.*) ♦ *The distraught mother held the lifeless body of her dead child.* ♦ *The cat carried a lifeless rat in its mouth.* **2.** *adj.* boring; inactive; without energy or interest. (Figurative on ①. Adv: *lifelessly.*) ♦ *I dropped the lifeless class after the first week.* ♦ *Most of the audience left the lifeless movie after 20 minutes.*

lifelike ['lɑɪf lɑɪk] *adj.* looking or seeming like the real person or thing. ♦ *These wax statues seem very lifelike.* ♦ *I bought a lifelike painting of the Grand Canyon.*

lifeline ['lɑɪf lɑɪn] **1.** *n.* a rope used to save people in the water; a rope or line available for sailors to grab onto for safety. ♦ *The coast guard threw a lifeline to the drowning man.* ♦ *The drowning woman grabbed the lifeline and was pulled to safety.* **2.** *n.* something that serves to help something. (Figurative on ①.) ♦ *Financial aid is the lifeline that keeps many students in school.* ♦ *My best friend acts as my lifeline when I'm depressed.*

lifelong ['lɑɪf lɔŋ] *adj.* for all of one's life; throughout one's whole life. ♦ *I've had a lifelong interest in collecting stamps.* ♦ *It's been my lifelong dream to own a restaurant.*

life preserver ['lɑɪ prə ʒɚ vɚ] See life jacket.

lifesaver ['lɑɪf sev ɚ] **1.** *n.* someone or something that saves someone's life. ♦ *The doctor on the airplane was a lifesaver when one of the passengers began choking.* ♦ *My dog's a real lifesaver. He woke me up when my house was on fire.* **2.** *n.* something that serves well in an emergency. (Figurative on ①.) ♦ *A cold drink of water is a real lifesaver on a hot day like this.* ♦ *Thanks for lending me the money. You're a lifesaver!* **3.** *n.* a flotation device used to keep someone afloat. ♦ *I clung to the lifesaver until the Coast Guard rescued me.* ♦ *The captain threw a lifesaver to the passenger who fell overboard.*

life-size(d) ['lɑɪf sɑɪz(d)] *adj.* as large as someone or something is in reality; [of a picture, sculpture, or other representation] having the same size as the object something represents. ♦ *The artist made a life-sized sculpture of John Wayne.* ♦ *The magazine printed a life-size picture of a baby kitten.*

lifestyle ['lɑɪf stɑɪl] *n.* the way a person lives; the behavior and attitudes of a person. ♦ *My parents lead a very conservative lifestyle.* ♦ *Living on a ranch is very different from my old urban lifestyle.*

lifetime ['lɑɪf tɑɪm] **1.** *n.* the time that a person or animal is living. ♦ *The computer revolution has occurred within my lifetime.* ♦ *My dog has only been lost once in its entire lifetime.* **2.** *n.* the period of time that something works or can be used. (Figurative on ①.) ♦ *This product is under warranty for its entire lifetime.* ♦ *Most batteries have a lifetime of only a few years.*

life vest ['lɑɪf vɛst] See life jacket.

lift ['lɪft] **1.** *tv.* to pick someone or something up from the ground; to raise someone or something to a higher level. ♦ *Please lift the box and put it on the table.* ♦ *I lifted the baby from his crib.* **2.** *tv.* to remove a restriction; to revoke a law. ♦ *The court lifted the ban on smoking in the hallways.* ♦ *The 21st Amendment to the U.S. Constitution lifted the ban on alcohol.* **3.** *tv.* to steal something; to shoplift something. (Slang.) ♦ *The starving man lifted a few candy bars at the drugstore.* ♦ *The thief was caught trying to lift a car stereo.* **4.** *iv.* [for clouds, fog, smoke, smog] to dissipate or evaporate. ♦ *The plane took off after the fog lifted.* ♦ *I stayed indoors until the smog lifted.* **5.** *n.* a free ride in a car or truck. (Informal.) ♦ *Can you give me a lift, please?* ♦ *The hitchhiker needed a lift to St. Louis.* **6.** *n.* something that makes someone feel happier, stronger, or more awake. ♦ *The cup of coffee gave me the lift I needed to stay awake.* ♦ *The song gave my emotions a lift.* **7.** *n.* a seat attached to a cable to take something up the side of a mountain. ♦ *Skiers use lifts to get to the top of a mountain.* ♦ *I left my ski poles on the lift.*

liftoff ['lɪft ɔf] *n.* the moment when a rocket is lifted off the launching pad. (Similar to takeoff.) ♦ *The liftoff of the rocket was witnessed by hundreds of amazed people.* ♦ *The rocket exploded moments after liftoff.*

light ['lɑɪt] **1.** *n.* illumination; a form of radiant energy that makes things visible. (No plural form in this sense.) ♦ *Stars appear as tiny dots of light in the night sky.* ♦ *It is easier to see objects in the light than in the dark.* **2.** *n.* something that produces ①; a lamp; a flame. ♦ *It's too dark in here. How do I turn on the light?* ♦ *The refrigerator light comes on when you open the door.* **3.** *n.* something, such as a match, that produces fire. (No plural form in this sense.) ♦ *I gave the guy standing next to me a light.* ♦ *Do you have a light? I forgot my matches.* **4.** *n.* the period of time when the sun is in the sky; daytime. (No plural form in this sense.) ♦ *I only walk through the park during the light of day.* ♦ *I stayed at the party until the light of dawn.* **5.** See traffic light. **6.** *n.* a view; the way that something is seen or thought of. (No plural form in this sense.) ♦ *In this light, your actions seem reasonable.* ♦ *The interview showed the actor in a favorable light.* **7.** *adj.* pale in color; not dark or deep; mixed with white. (Adv:

lightly.) ♦ *Lavender is a light purple.* ♦ *The sky was a beautiful light blue.* **8.** *adj.* not heavy; not weighing much; easy to carry. (Adv: *lightly.*) ♦ *I carried the light box with one hand.* ♦ *I took the light suitcase onto the airplane.* **9.** *adj.* not serious; not intense; not deep. (Figurative on ⑧. Adv: *lightly.*) ♦ *I watched a light comedy on television.* ♦ *The editor said my treatment of the serious subject was too light.* **10.** *adj.* not having much force; gentle. (Figurative on ⑧. Adv: *lightly.*) ♦ *A light breeze blew from the west.* ♦ *I felt a light tap on my shoulder.* **11.** *adj.* not difficult; easy. (Figurative on ⑧. Adv: *lightly.*) ♦ *I had some light reading to do before I went to bed.* ♦ *I finished the light homework assignment quickly.* **12.** *adv.* without much luggage. ♦ *I always travel light because I don't like carrying luggage.* ♦ *The hitchhiker traveled light.* **13.** *iv., irreg.* [for a creature] to land on a surface after flight. (Pt/pp: *lighted* or lit.) ♦ *The bird lit on the tree branch.* ♦ *The insect lighted on the wall.* **14. light up** *iv., irreg.* + *adv.* to become happy; to shine with happiness. ♦ *Jane's face lit up when I told her the good news.* ♦ *The children's eyes lit up with excitement.* **15.** *tv., irreg.* to set something on fire; to cause something to begin to burn. ♦ *I lit John's cigarette.* ♦ *I will light the candles.* **16.** *tv., irreg.* to cause some place to become bright; to bring light to a place. ♦ *The small room was lit with candles.* ♦ *The full moon lit the nighttime sky.* **17. light up** *tv., irreg.* + *adv.* to cause someone to become happy; to cause someone's eyes or face to shine with happiness. ♦ *The good news lit Jane's face up.* ♦ *The funny clown lit up the children's eyes.* **18. light up** *tv., irreg.* + *adv.* to light ⑮ one's cigarette, cigar, or pipe. ♦ *The moment I lit up, the train appeared around the bend.* ♦ *After Mary lit up, Susan asked her to extinguish her cigarette.* **19. begin to see the light** *idiom* to begin to understand (something). ♦ *My algebra class is hard for me, but I'm beginning to see the light.* ♦ *I was totally confused, but I began to see the light after your explanation.* **20. bring something to light** *idiom* to make something known. ♦ *The scientists brought their findings to light.* ♦ *We must bring this new evidence to light.* **21. come to light** *idiom* to become known. ♦ *Some interesting facts about your past have just come to light.* ♦ *If too many bad things come to light, you may lose your job.* **22. make light of something** *idiom* to treat something as if it were unimportant or humorous. ♦ *I wish you wouldn't make light of his problems. They're quite serious.* ♦ *I make light of my problems, and that makes me feel better.* **23. see the light (at the end of the tunnel)** *idiom* to foresee an end to one's problems after a long period of time. ♦ *I had been horribly ill for two months before I began to see the light at the end of the tunnel.* ♦ *I began to see the light one day in early spring. At that moment, I knew I'd get well.* **24. see the light (of day)** *idiom* to come to the end of a very busy time. ♦ *Finally, when the holiday season was over, we could see the light of day. We had been so busy!* ♦ *When business lets up for a while, we'll be able to see the light.* **25. shed some light on something** *idiom* to provide some knowledge or insight about something. ♦ *Can anyone shed some light on this problem?* ♦ *Max told us that he could shed some light on the mystery.*

light bulb ['lɑɪt bəlb] *n.* a glass bulb with a wire inside that gives off light when electricity is passed through it. ♦ *The light bulb shattered when I dropped it.* ♦ *I placed a light bulb in the lamp.*

lighten ['lɑɪt n] **1.** *tv.* to cause someone or something to become brighter or lighter in color. ♦ *I lightened the dark room by painting it white.* ♦ *The artist lightened the dark blue paint by mixing it with white.* **2.** *tv.* to cause something to become less of a burden. ♦ *I lightened my load because it was too heavy to carry.* ♦ *Jane lightened my burden by carrying half of my luggage.* **3.** *iv.* to become brighter. ♦ *The sky lightened at dawn.* ♦ *The room lightened when I turned on the lamp.* **4.** *iv.* [for a color] to fade. ♦ *I hope my hair color doesn't lighten in the sun.* ♦ *The deep red shirt lightened when I washed it.* **5.** *iv.* to become less heavy. ♦ *My class load lightened when I dropped biology.* ♦ *My work load lightened when my boss hired more help.* **6. lighten up** *iv.* + *adv.* to become less serious. ♦ *I asked Bill to lighten up because he was depressing me.* ♦ *My doctor told me to lighten up before I gave myself an ulcer.*

lighter ['lɑɪt ɚ] *n.* a device that makes a flame to light cigarettes or cigars. ♦ *Do you have any matches? I've lost my lighter.* ♦ *I lit Anne's cigarette with my lighter.*

lightheaded ['lɑɪt 'hɛd ɪd] *adj.* dizzy; feeling faint. (Adv: *lightheadedly.*) ♦ *After drinking some vodka, I began to get lightheaded.* ♦ *Mary stopped dancing because she was feeling lightheaded.*

lighthearted ['lɑɪt 'hɑrt ɪd] *adj.* not serious; happy; cheerful. (Adv: *lightheartedly.*) ♦ *My date and I watched a lighthearted movie.* ♦ *The teacher read a lighthearted story to the students.*

lighthouse ['lɑɪt hɑʊs] *n., irreg.* a tall structure near the sea with a bright light (or beacon) near the top that warns ships away from danger. (Pl: [...hɑʊ zəz].) ♦ *The Coast Guard operated the lighthouse out on the island.* ♦ *On a clear night, sailors could see the light in the lighthouse from miles away.*

lighting ['lɑɪt ɪŋ] **1.** *n.* light that makes things and people visible; illumination; the type or quality of light in a room or other place. (No plural form in this sense.) ♦ *The lighting at the art gallery was focused on the artwork.* ♦ *I bumped into the walls because the lighting was very dim.* **2.** *n.* the equipment that directs light, especially for effect in a television or movie studio or on a stage. (No plural form in this sense.) ♦ *The actors stood by as the technicians focused the lighting.* ♦ *A technician controlled the lighting with the help of a computer.*

lightning ['lɑɪt nɪŋ] *n.* a flash or streak of light in the sky, especially during a thunderstorm. (No plural form in this sense. Number is expressed with *bolt(s)* or *flash(es) of lightning.*) ♦ *Lightning is caused by an electrical charge moving from cloud to cloud or from a cloud to the earth.* ♦ *Loud thunder followed the bolt of lightning.*

lightning bug ['lɑɪt nɪŋ bəg] *n.* a type of beetle that is able to fly and to illuminate its abdomen in the dark. (The same as firefly.) ♦ *I caught some lightning bugs and kept them in a clear jar.* ♦ *The lightning bugs flashed in the night sky.*

lightweight ['lɑɪt wet] **1.** *n.* someone who weighs less than average. ♦ *Sally, a lightweight, was nearly blown over by the strong wind.* ♦ *The class bully picked on the lightweights.* **2.** *n.* someone who is not important in one's field; someone who does not have much power or influence. (Figurative on ①.) ♦ *The expert scoffed at the lightweight's suggestion.* ♦ *Tom will always be a lightweight in the field of painting.* **3.** *n.* a boxer who weighs between

125 and 136 pounds. ♦ *The two lightweights fought each other for the championship.* ♦ *The small boxer fought as a lightweight.* **4.** *adj.* of less weight than might be expected. ♦ *I carried the lightweight luggage onto the plane.* ♦ *I sped across town on my lightweight bicycle.*

likable ['laɪk ə bəl] *adj.* easy to like; pleasant. (Adv: *likably.*) ♦ *I like my job because my coworkers are very likable.* ♦ *Mary is a likable young woman.*

like ['laɪk] **1.** *n.* a preference; a desire; something that one likes to have or do. ♦ *The personal ad listed John's likes and dislikes.* ♦ *My likes include walking in the park and dancing.* **2.** *tv.* to enjoy someone or something; to find someone or something pleasant. ♦ *I like this house.* ♦ *John likes Mary.* **3.** *adj.* similar. (Prenominal only. See also **alike**.) ♦ *Mary and Susan have like minds because they have the same opinions about everything.* ♦ *I gave John $20 and he wrote me a check for the like amount.* **4.** *prep.* similar to someone or something; in the same way as someone or something. ♦ *Our teacher looks like my grandfather.* ♦ *This song sounds like the one you wrote.* **5.** *prep.* for instance; such as. ♦ *Many elements, like oxygen and carbon, are needed to sustain life.* ♦ *There are many problems in the world, like war, famine, and pollution.* **6.** *conj.* in the same way as someone or something does; similar to the way someone or something is. ♦ *Can you throw the ball like Daddy did?* ♦ *I solved the math problem like my teacher showed us.* **7.** *conj.* as though; as if. (Viewed as incorrect by some people.) ♦ *It is thundering like it's going to rain.* ♦ *This dog is barking like it wants to bite me.* **8. and the like** *phr.* and similar things or people. ♦ *I eat hamburgers, hot dogs, and the like.* ♦ *I bought shirts, pants, socks, and the like.* **9. the likes of someone or something** *phr.* someone or something and anyone or anything similar to that person or thing; the equal or equals of someone or something. ♦ *I never want to see the likes of you again!* ♦ *We admired the splendid old ships, the likes of which will never be built again.* **10. would like** *phr.* to want someone or something; to prefer someone or something. ♦ *I would like to have three cookies.* ♦ *I would like a piece of cake.* **11. -like** similar to ____; being much like ____; being like a ____. (Can be added to nouns to create new adjectives. Well-established pairs, such as **ladylike** and **lifelike**, are not hyphenated. For example: *arm-like, balloon-like, bear-like, bell-like, bread-like, cage-like, candy-like, clove-like, club-like, coat-like, death-like, deer-like, dog-like, finger-like, ghost-like, grass-like, hammer-like, human-like, jaw-like, jelly-like, ladylike, lifelike, onion-like, ox-like, paste-like, pouch-like, rat-like, ring-like, rock-like, rod-like, rope-like, sac-like, sand-like, shovel-like, sleep-like, snake-like, spider-like, stone-like, tangerine-like, tar-like, trumpet-like, vine-like, whip-like,* and *wing-like.*)

likelihood ['laɪk li hʊd] *n.* the chance of being likely; probability. (No plural form in this sense.) ♦ *What's the likelihood of rain tomorrow?* ♦ *In all likelihood, I'll probably go on vacation in June.*

likely ['laɪk li] **1.** *adj.* probable. ♦ *It's likely that it will rain tomorrow.* ♦ *No, it's not likely at all.* **2.** *adj.* suitable; fitting; appropriate. ♦ *John is a likely candidate for the job.* ♦ *A number of likely prospects showed up for interviews.* **3. likely to** *adj.* + *inf.* apt to do something; tending to do something. ♦ *John's likely to go to the beach tomorrow.* ♦ *It's likely to rain tomorrow.*

likeness ['laɪk nəs] **1.** *n.* a similarity; a resemblance; the condition of seeming or looking the same. (No plural form in this sense.) ♦ *There's quite a likeness between Mary and her mother.* ♦ *This painting bears a strong likeness to the one I painted.* **2.** *n.* an image of someone or something. ♦ *The artist painted a remarkable likeness of the queen.* ♦ *This picture is a poor likeness of John, but you can see he is handsome.* ♦ *The bust is a likeness of the king.*

likewise ['laɪk waɪz] *adv.* in the same way; as well; by the same token; also; similarly. ♦ *I'll help you if you need it. Likewise, I hope you'll help me.* ♦ *"It's nice to meet you," John said. "Likewise," I responded.*

liking ['laɪk ɪŋ] **1.** *n.* a fondness. (No plural form in this sense.) ♦ *John has a special liking for Mary.* ♦ *His liking for chocolate causes him to eat too much candy.* **2. to someone's liking** *idiom* fitting someone's personal preferences. ♦ *I had my house painted, but the job was not to my liking.* ♦ *Large meals with lots of fat are not to Bob's liking.*

lilac ['laɪ lək] **1.** *n.* a flowering tree or shrub with cone-shaped bunches of heavily scented lavender or white blossoms. ♦ *Lilacs bloom in the early spring.* ♦ *There is a row of lilacs beside our fence.* **2.** *n.* the blossoms from ①. ♦ *The florist put fragrant lilacs at the center of the bouquet.* ♦ *Mike picked some lilacs and gave them to Lisa.*

lilting ['lɪl tɪŋ] *adj.* [of music or a melody] light and rhythmic. (Adv: *liltingly.*) ♦ *Susan sang a lilting song about flowers in the springtime.* ♦ *Tom couldn't stop humming the lilting melody.*

lily ['lɪl i] **1.** *n.* a flower with large petals that grows from a bulb. ♦ *I sent my mother a lily for Easter.* ♦ *The surface of the river was covered with water lilies.* **2. gild the lily** *idiom* to add ornament or decoration to something that is pleasing in its original state; to attempt to improve something that is already fine the way it is. ♦ *Your house has lovely brickwork. Don't paint it. That would be gilding the lily.* ♦ *Oh, Sally. You're beautiful the way you are. You don't need makeup. You would be gilding the lily.*

lima bean [laɪ mə 'bin] *n.* a flat, edible seed that grows in pods. ♦ *Lima beans are eaten green or fully matured.* ♦ *I added some lima beans to the soup.*

limb ['lɪm] **1.** *n.* a large tree branch. ♦ *The strong wind knocked down several tree limbs.* ♦ *The bird built its nest on a strong limb.* **2.** *n.* an arm, leg, or wing. ♦ *The driver lost a limb in the car accident.* ♦ *My lower limbs were partially paralyzed after I had a stroke.* **3. out on a limb** *idiom* in a dangerous position; taking a chance. ♦ *I don't want to go out on a limb, but I think I'd agree to your request.* ♦ *She really went out on a limb when she agreed.*

limber ['lɪm bɚ] *adj.* able to bend; flexible; agile. (Adv: *limberly.* Comp: *limberer;* sup: *limberest.*) ♦ *The limber gymnast did a high, twisting jump.* ♦ *When I was more limber, I could put my leg behind my neck.*

limbo ['lɪm bo] **1. Limbo** *n.* [in Roman Catholicism] a state between heaven and hell. (No plural form in this sense.) ♦ *Limbo is a place for the souls of those who have not had a chance to avoid sin.* ♦ *The soul of the baby remains in Limbo.* **2.** *n.* a dance where people must bend backward and walk under a horizontal pole that is held lower and lower until there is only one person left who can do it. (Pl in *-s.*) ♦ *Everyone danced the limbo at the party.* ♦ *I hurt my back trying to do the limbo.* **3.** *iv.* to dance ②. ♦ *I limboed under the pole that Bob and Susan* *were holding.* ♦ *I grabbed a pole and yelled, "Everyone, let's limbo!"* **4. in limbo** *idiom* in a state of uncertainty. (Figurative on ①.) ♦ *My scholarship is in limbo until Congress finalizes the budget.* ♦ *After our huge argument, our wedding date was in limbo.*

lime ['lɑɪm] **1.** *n.* an acidic, green citrus fruit. ♦ *Please place a slice of lime in my soda water.* ♦ *I cut the lime into small wedges.* **2.** *n.* a white substance made by burning limestone, which is used to make plaster, cement, and mortar. (No plural form in this sense.) ♦ *The bricklayer added more lime to the mortar.* ♦ *They added lime to the plaster to make it white.* **3.** *adj.* made or flavored with ①. ♦ *I drank a lime soda with dinner.* ♦ *Would you care for some lime sherbet?*

limelight ['lɑɪm lɑɪt] **the limelight** *n.* the focus or target of the attention of the press; the object of public attention. (No plural form in this sense. Treated as singular.) ♦ *The famous politician enjoyed the limelight of temporary fame.* ♦ *The shy actor traveled anonymously to avoid the limelight.*

limerick ['lɪm (ə) rɪk] *n.* a poem that has five lines and a particular syllable structure, where the first, second, and fifth lines rhyme and the second and third lines rhyme. ♦ *Limericks are often humorous.* ♦ *Jimmy was punished for repeating a vulgar limerick to his class.*

limestone ['lɑɪm ston] **1.** *n.* rock made of calcium compounds used as a building material. (No plural form in this sense.) ♦ *The lobby floor was done in limestone.* ♦ *The designer imported some limestone from Italy.* **2.** *adj.* made of ①. ♦ *The building had a rough limestone surface.* ♦ *The walls are made of limestone blocks.*

limit ['lɪm ɪt] **1.** *n.* a boundary; the edge; the farthest point of something; the greatest amount allowed or possible. ♦ *The solar system's farthest limits extend beyond Pluto's orbit.* ♦ *My teacher encouraged me to follow my dreams to the limit.* **2.** *tv.* to prevent someone or something from passing a certain point or amount; to restrict something to a certain amount of space or time. ♦ *This medicine will limit the spread of your infection.* ♦ *Acceptance speeches are limited to one minute.* **3. go the limit** *idiom* to do or have as much as possible. ♦ *What do I want on my hamburger? Go the limit!* ♦ *Don't hold anything back. Go the limit.*

limitation [lɪm ɪ 'te ʃən] *n.* something that limits; a restriction. ♦ *You must overcome your limitations if you're going to succeed.* ♦ *The legislature placed a limitation on the sale of liquor on Sundays.*

limited ['lɪm ɪ tɪd] **1.** *adj.* restricted; prevented from passing a certain point or exceeding a certain amount. (Adv: *limitedly.*) ♦ *The new employee had only limited access to the computer files.* ♦ *After being released from prison, John only had a few, limited options.* **2.** *adj.* [of a selection or set of choices] small. ♦ *The store has a very limited selection of goods.* ♦ *The restaurant only had a limited number of desserts, so our choice was easy.*

limitless ['lɪm ɪt ləs] *adj.* without bounds; without limits; infinite. (Adv: *limitlessly.*) ♦ *The dictator's power was limitless.* ♦ *The dictator's limitless power was a cause for alarm.*

limousine ['lɪm ə zin] *n.* a large and usually luxurious car, usually driven by a hired chauffeur. ♦ *Bill and Mary went to the prom in a rented limousine.* ♦ *Six people rode in the back of the executive's limousine.*

limp ['lɪmp] **1.** *n.* an uneven walk; a walk where one foot drags or moves like it is injured. ♦ *I knew the dog was injured because of its limp.* ♦ *My limp gets worse when it's about to rain.* **2.** *iv.* to walk to somewhere showing ①. ♦ *I limped to the clinic after I cut my foot.* ♦ *The bruised football player limped toward the locker room.* **3.** *adj.* drooping; not stiff; having no resistance. (Adv: *limply.* Comp: *limper;* sup: *limpest.*) ♦ *I tried unsuccessfully to curl my limp hair.* ♦ *The limp leaves of the plant showed it needed to be watered.* **4.** *adj.* sagging; low and going lower; feeble and weak. (Figurative on ③. Adv: *limply.* Comp: *limper;* sup: *limpest.*) ♦ *Sales were limp, so we doubled the advertising budget.* ♦ *The tardy student gave a limp excuse for being late.*

Lincoln's Birthday [lɪŋ kənz 'bɚθ de] *n.* a U.S. holiday observing the birthday, on February 12th, of Abraham Lincoln, the 16th president of the United States. (See also Presidents' Day.) ♦ *Lincoln's Birthday is often celebrated in conjunction with Washington's Birthday on the third Monday of February.* ♦ *In some states, government offices and banks are closed on Lincoln's Birthday.*

line ['lɑɪn] **1.** *n.* a mark, straight or curved, made on the surface of something. ♦ *The child drew a line in the sand with a stick.* ♦ *The artist used a ruler to draw a straight line.* **2.** *n.* a border; a mark that shows the limit, border, or end of something. ♦ *The bus driver told me to stand behind the white line.* ♦ *The referee placed the football on the fifty-yard line.* **3.** *n.* a wide band; a stripe. ♦ *A bright white line was painted along the edge of the road.* ♦ *A sign with a diagonal red line over the letter* P *means "No Parking."* **4.** *n.* a string, rope, or cord. (On boats and ships, ropes are called lines.) ♦ *The skipper tied a line from the boat to the dock.* ♦ *My fishing line broke and the fish got away.* **5.** *n.* a wire, pipe, or cable that carries the products of a public utility company, such as electricity, water, gas, telephone, etc. ♦ *The electrical power lines were knocked down by the violent winds.* ♦ *The city installed a new sewer line under the street.* **6.** *n.* a telephone connection. ♦ *You've got a caller waiting on your line.* ♦ *I can't hear you. There's too much noise on the line.* **7.** *n.* a row or series of people, standing and waiting for a turn to do something. ♦ *I got in line to buy my ticket.* ♦ *The line at the bank was too long, so I decided to come back later.* **8.** *n.* a crease; a wrinkle; a mark with depth. ♦ *My grandmother has a lot of lines around her eyes and mouth.* ♦ *The lines on your palms are thought to reveal something about your future.* **9.** *n.* a row of words in printing or writing. ♦ *How many lines are there on each page?* ♦ *The last line is too long to fit on the page.* **10.** *n.* something that is said by an actor onstage or in film. ♦ *The actor forgot the last line of the scene.* ♦ *The director told me to say the line with more emotion.* **11.** *n.* a kind of business or job. ♦ *What line are you in?* ♦ *I went into the same line of work as my father.* **12.** *tv.* to put a lining in something; to cover the inside of something with something else. ♦ *Susan lined her coat with wool.* ♦ *These mittens are lined with fur.* **13. line up** *iv.* + *adv.* to get into ⑦; to join or form ⑦. ♦ *Please line up in a straight line.* ♦ *The visitor did not line up with the others, but went straight to the front.* **14. in line** *phr.* in a line or row of people waiting for something. ♦ *How long have you been standing in line?* ♦ *We waited in line for an hour to buy tick-*

ets. **15. drop someone a line** *idiom* to send someone a message, note, or letter. ♦ *Please drop me a line when you reach London.* ♦ *I try to drop my aunt a line every month.* **16. sign on the dotted line** *idiom* to place one's signature on a contract or other important paper. ♦ *This agreement isn't properly concluded until we both sign on the dotted line.* ♦ *Here are the papers for the purchase of your car. As soon as you sign on the dotted line, that beautiful, shiny automobile will be all yours!* **17. step out of line** *idiom* to misbehave; to do something offensive. ♦ *I'm terribly sorry. I hope I didn't step out of line.* ♦ *John is a lot of fun to go out with, but he has a tendency to step out of line.*

lineage ['lɪn i ədʒ] *n.* the direct descent from one ancestor; the line of ancestors and descendants linking two or more related people. ♦ *I traced my lineage back to the 17th century.* ♦ *The lineage of the king includes many other monarchs.*

linear ['lɪn i ɚ] *adj.* of or about lines or length. (Adv: *linearly.*) ♦ *Ants move in linear progression, following each other very closely.* ♦ *What's the linear measurement of this board?*

linebacker ['lɑɪn bæk ɚ] *n.* a football player positioned right behind the main line of players. ♦ *The linebacker tackled the quarterback.* ♦ *A powerful linebacker broke his collarbone during practice.*

lineman ['lɑɪn mən] **1.** *n., irreg.* someone who repairs and maintains telephone or other wires. (Pl: **linemen.**) ♦ *The lineman replaced the damaged electrical wires.* ♦ *Linemen are working on the wires in the backyard.* **2.** *n., irreg.* a football player whose position is in the offensive or defensive line. ♦ *The linemen knocked over the other team's quarterback.* ♦ *The team's star lineman weighed 250 pounds.*

linemen ['lɑɪn mən] pl of **lineman.**

linen ['lɪn ən] **1.** *n.* a fabric made from flax. (No plural form in this sense.) ♦ *I bought some sheets made from linen.* ♦ *John only wears shirts made from linen.* **2.** *n.* tablecloths and sheets made of ① or some other fabric. (Sometimes plural with the same meaning.) ♦ *The maid put fresh linens on the bed.* ♦ *The hospital had laundry facilities for cleaning bed linen.* **3.** *adj.* made from ①. ♦ *I placed the linen sheets on the bed.* ♦ *I took the linen suit to the dry cleaners.* **4. air someone's dirty linen in public** *idiom* to discuss private or embarrassing matters in public, especially when quarreling. ♦ *John's mother had asked him repeatedly not to air the family's dirty linen in public.* ♦ *Mr. and Mrs. Johnson are arguing again. Why must they always air their dirty linen in public?*

liner ['lɑɪn ɚ] *n.* something that lines another object; a fabric or other material put on the inside surface of something for protection. ♦ *The liners in my gloves are made from rabbit fur.* ♦ *The box was lined with a thick plastic liner.*

linger ['lɪŋ gɚ] *iv.* to remain someplace; to loiter; to be slow in moving or leaving. ♦ *Smoke lingered long after the fire was extinguished.* ♦ *The unwanted guest lingered at my house for five hours.*

lingerie [lɑn ʒə 're] *n.* women's underwear and clothing for sleeping. (From French. No plural form in this sense.) ♦ *Anne bought some fancy lingerie for her honeymoon.* ♦ *Susan wore silk lingerie to bed.*

linguist ['lɪŋ gwəst] **1.** *n.* someone who knows or speaks many languages. ♦ *My sister is a linguist who speaks six languages.* ♦ *I don't know what language this is. Is there a linguist around?* **2.** *n.* someone who studies the structure and nature of language in general. ♦ *My sister is a linguist who studies the meanings of words.* ♦ *The linguist wrote a book about modern grammar theory.*

linguistics [lɪŋ 'gwɪs tɪks] *n.* the study of language. (Treated as singular.) ♦ *I took two classes in linguistics in college.* ♦ *The teacher of the English class for foreign students has a degree in linguistics.*

liniment ['lɪn ə mənt] *n.* an oily liquid that is rubbed on the skin to relieve the pain and stiffness of sore muscles. (No plural form in this sense.) ♦ *The coach rubbed liniment on the boxer's shoulders.* ♦ *The therapist rubbed my sore muscles with liniment.*

lining ['lɑɪn ɪŋ] *n.* a fabric or other material put on the inside surface of something for protection. (No plural form in this sense.) ♦ *My gloves have a furry lining.* ♦ *I bought a jacket with a removable down lining.*

link ['lɪŋk] **1.** *n.* one of the loops or circles that make up a chain. ♦ *My bracelet consists of several gold links.* ♦ *The chain snapped when one of the links broke.* **2.** *n.* someone or something that connects someone or something to someone or something else. (Figurative on ①.) ♦ *I read a report documenting the link between smoking and cancer.* ♦ *Dinosaur fossils are a link to the past.* **3.** *tv.* to physically connect someone or something to someone or something else. ♦ *I linked the two ends of the chain together.* ♦ *The children linked arms before crossing the street.* **4. link to; link with** *tv. + prep. phr.* to associate someone or something to someone or something else. (Figurative on ③.) ♦ *Many people link the number 13 with bad luck.* ♦ *Cancer has been linked to smoking.* **5. link to; link with** *iv. + prep. phr.* to be connected to something [physically]. ♦ *This road links with the main highway.* ♦ *This wire links to the main power supply.*

linkage ['lɪŋk ɪdʒ] **1.** *n.* connecting; joining. (No plural form in this sense.) ♦ *The new software enabled the linkage of all the computers in the office.* ♦ *The linkage of the two companies created a monopoly.* **2.** *n.* a connection; a relationship [of things or ideas]. (No plural form in this sense.) ♦ *The linkage between smoking and cancer is often debated.* ♦ *The newspaper disclosed the linkage between the mayor and the mob.*

linking verb ['lɪŋ kɪŋ vɚb] *n.* a verb, such as *be, seem,* or *look,* that links two nouns or a noun and an adjective. (Also called a **copula.**) ♦ *"Be"—in the third-person singular, present-tense form "is"—is a linking verb in the sentence "The barn is red."* ♦ *A linking verb never takes an object.*

linoleum [lɪ 'nol i əm] *n.* a floor covering made by putting a mixture of powdered cork, rosin, and oil on a strong fabric backing. (No plural form in this sense.) ♦ *Peeling back the linoleum, we found a beautiful hardwood floor.* ♦ *I covered the old floor with colorful linoleum.*

lint ['lɪnt] *n.* a tiny piece of thread; a small cluster of thread, dirt, hair, etc. (No plural form in this sense.) ♦ *I removed a piece of red lint from my yellow shirt.* ♦ *The clothes in the dryer were covered with towel lint.*

lion ['lɑɪ ən] **1.** *n.* a large, wild animal in the cat family, in Africa. ♦ *The head of the male lion is surrounded by a mane of hair.* ♦ *The lion in the zoo ate all the meat in one bite.* **2. mountain lion** *n.* a large, American wildcat, also called the panther and the cougar. ♦ *A mountain lion killed one of our cows.* ♦ *The mountain lion in the U.S. is not as big as the African lion.*

lioness ['lɑɪ ən əs] *n.* a female **lion**. ♦ *The lioness protected her cubs from attack.* ♦ *Lionesses devoured the gnu very rapidly.*

lip ['lɪp] **1.** *n.* one of the two ridges of flesh on the outside of the mouth. (The adjective is **labial**.) ♦ *My lip swelled after John hit me in the mouth.* ♦ *I bit my lip accidentally while eating.* **2.** *n.* a rim; an edge, especially a part of an edge of a container. ♦ *The lip of the glass jar was chipped.* ♦ *The lip of the paint can was covered with paint.* **3.** *n.* rude statements; impudence. (No plural form in this sense. Slang.) ♦ *Don't give me any of your lip!* ♦ *My lip often got me into trouble when I was young.* **4. button one's lip** *idiom* to get quiet and stay quiet. ♦ *All right now, let's button our lips and listen to the story.* ♦ *Button your lip, Tom! I'll tell you when you can talk!* **5. keep a stiff upper lip** *idiom* to be cool and unmoved by unsettling events. ♦ *Now, Billy, don't cry. Keep a stiff upper lip.* ♦ *Bill can take it. He has a stiff upper lip.* **6. lick one's lips** *idiom* to show eagerness or pleasure about a future event. ♦ *The children licked their lips at the sight of the cake.* ♦ *The journalist was licking his lips when he went off to interview the disgraced politician.*

lipstick ['lɪp stɪk] *n.* makeup that is put on the lips to give them a different color. (No plural form in this sense.) ♦ *Susan wore bright red lipstick to the party.* ♦ *John had lipstick on his cheek where Anne kissed him.*

liquefy ['lɪ kwɪ fɑɪ] **1.** *iv.* to turn into a liquid. ♦ *The crayons liquefied when I left them out in the sun.* ♦ *Ice liquefies above 32 degrees Fahrenheit.* **2.** *tv.* to cause something to turn into a liquid. ♦ *The chemist liquefied the compound by heating it.* ♦ *The hot furnace liquefied the steel bars.*

liquid ['lɪk wɪd] **1.** *n.* a flowing substance, such as water, that is not a gas or a solid. (No plural form in this sense.) ♦ *I poured the hot liquid into a glass container.* ♦ *Mercury is a metal that is a liquid at room temperature.* **2.** *n.* the sounds [l] and [r]. ♦ *The liquids in English are sometimes made softly at the ends of words.* ♦ *Some people have trouble pronouncing the liquids* [l] *and* [r]. **3.** *adj.* in the form of ①. ♦ *I poured some liquid detergent into the washing machine.* ♦ *I washed my hands with liquid soap.* **4.** *adj.* [of an asset that can be] easily converted to cash. ♦ *Getting ready to retire, Mike converted his liquid assets into cash.* ♦ *He owns a house and two cars, but none of his assets are liquid.*

liquidate ['lɪ kwə det] **1.** *tv.* to sell assets; to convert securities into cash. ♦ *I liquidated my stocks in order to get the money to buy a house.* ♦ *The judge ordered the plaintiff to liquidate his assets so he could pay the fine.* **2.** *iv.* to sell off assets. ♦ *Things got so bad, we had to liquidate.* ♦ *When the company liquidated, everything it owned was sold.*

liquidation [lɪ kwə 'de ʃən] *n.* the sale of assets; selling goods, stocks, bonds, real estate, etc. (No plural form in this sense.) ♦ *The court ordered the liquidation of the bankrupt firm.* ♦ *Some of the company's creditors were paid as a result of its liquidation.*

liquor ['lɪk ɚ] **1.** *n.* broth or juices from cooking. (No plural form in this sense.) ♦ *I used the liquor from the roasting pan to make gravy.* ♦ *I made rice with part of the liquor from the stewing chicken.* **2.** *n.* alcohol for drinking. (No plural form in this sense.) ♦ *Would you like any liquor before dinner?* ♦ *I can smell liquor on your breath.*

lisp ['lɪsp] **1.** *n.* a speech problem where [s] and [z] are pronounced like [θ] and [ð]; a speech problem where [s] and [z] are not pronounced correctly. ♦ *The speech therapist helped correct my lisp.* ♦ *Because of his lisp, Jimmy says "kith" rather than "kiss."* **2.** *iv.* to speak with ①. ♦ *The bully made fun of Jane because she lisped.* ♦ *Jimmy lisped because his front teeth had just fallen out.* **3.** *tv.* to say something using ①. ♦ *Jimmy lisped, "Yeth, thir!"* ♦ *The speaker lisped that her speech would be short.*

list ['lɪst] **1.** *n.* a printed or written series of words, names, or items. ♦ *Can you add toothpaste to the shopping list?* ♦ *The teacher checked off every name on the class list.* **2.** *n.* a slant or tilt to one side, such as with a ship. ♦ *The list of the ship was making the passengers sick.* ♦ *The ship's list was caused by shifting cargo.* **3.** *tv.* to write things on ①. ♦ *List five states that border the Atlantic Ocean.* ♦ *I listed the advantages of buying a new computer.* **4.** *iv.* to lean to one side. ♦ *Shifting cargo caused the ship to list.* ♦ *The sinking ship listed to its left.* **5. on a waiting list** *idiom* [for someone's name to be] on a list of people waiting for an opportunity to do something. ♦ *I couldn't get a seat on the plane, but I got on a waiting list.* ♦ *There is no room for you, but we can put your name on the waiting list.*

listen ['lɪs ən] *iv.* to pay attention to a source of sound. ♦ *I listened to the radio for the weather report.* ♦ *Listen closely to the car engine. It is making a funny sound.*

listener ['lɪs ə nɚ] **1.** *n.* someone who listens to someone or something. ♦ *John does well in school because he is a good listener.* ♦ *In our experiment, listeners pushed a button when they understood the sentence on the screen.* **2.** *n.* someone who listens to a particular radio program or radio station. ♦ *The talk-show host thanked all of the listeners for tuning in.* ♦ *That classical-music station has many loyal listeners.*

listing ['lɪs tɪŋ] **1.** *n.* a list; a written series of words, names, or items. ♦ *Hand me the TV listing. I want to know what's on channel 6.* ♦ *I read the listing of people who'd donated to the charity.* **2.** *adj.* tilting to one side. ♦ *The Coast Guard saved the passengers from the listing ship.* ♦ *The listing sailboat was flooded with water.*

listless ['lɪst ləs] *adj.* having no energy; without vigor. (Adv: *listlessly*.) ♦ *The listless dog slept under the tree.* ♦ *I feel so listless. I think I need a nap.*

lit ['lɪt] a pt/pp of **light**.

liter ['lit ɚ] *n.* a liquid metric unit of measurement equal to 1.06 quarts. ♦ *A liter is the amount of liquid that can be held in a cube that is 10 centimeters long, high, and wide.* ♦ *I brought two liters of pop to the party.*

literacy ['lɪt ə rə si] *n.* the ability to read and write. (No plural form in this sense.) ♦ *The increase in the country's rate of literacy was encouraging.* ♦ *The factory offered classes to improve the literacy of its workers.*

literal ['lɪt ə rəl] **1.** *adj.* [of the meaning of a word or phrase] basic instead of secondary or figurative. (Adv: *literally.*) ♦ *The literal meaning of* hot air *is 'air that is hot.' The figurative sense means 'nonsense.'* ♦ *We seldom use the literal interpretation of* kick the bucket, *which we understand as meaning 'die.'* **2.** *adj.* exact, especially pertaining to translations; translating or interpreting one word at a time. (Adv: *literally.*) ♦ *The literal interpretation of idioms is often funny.* ♦ *The literal translation of the German word* Unterseeboot *is 'under-sea-boat.'*

literally ['lɪt ə rə li] **1.** *adv.* truly; in the literal sense of the word. ♦ *Literally everyone in our company was sick. The building was empty.* ♦ *John literally kicked the bucket, and he hurt his toe doing it.* **2.** *adv.* in an extreme state almost equal to; essentially. (Figurative on ① and *not* literal. Informal and widespread.) ♦ *After the game I was so tired I was literally dead.* ♦ *Anne was so mad she literally exploded.*

literary ['lɪt ə rɛr i] *adj.* of or about literature. (Adv: *literarily* [lɪt ə 'rɛr ə li].) ♦ *Greece has a long literary history.* ♦ *The paper's literary critic reviews a new novel each week.*

literate ['lɪt ə rət] **1.** *adj.* able to read and write. ♦ *Slowly, the immigrant became literate in English.* ♦ *I'm literate in English and French.* **2.** *adj.* educated. ♦ *John is quite literate in sociology and psychology.* ♦ *Japan is considered to have a very literate population.*

literature ['lɪt ə rə tʃɚ] **1.** *n.* writing considered as art, such as fiction, plays, and poetry. (No plural form in this sense.) ♦ *The bookstore had a special section for great works of literature.* ♦ *What kind of literature do you like to read?* **2.** *n.* all the written material of a specific subject or region. (No plural form in this sense.) ♦ *This library has a vast collection of German literature.* ♦ *I have a shelf full of literature about botany.* **3.** *n.* information; a brochure or pamphlet that has information about something. (No plural form in this sense.) ♦ *Do you have any literature about this product?* ♦ *According to the literature, this city was founded in 1840.*

lithium ['lɪθ i əm] *n.* a silver-white, metallic chemical element used to produce ceramics, enamels, and glass, as well as in medicine. (No plural form in this sense.) ♦ *The atomic symbol of lithium is Li, and its atomic number is 3.* ♦ *My psychiatrist gave me a prescription for lithium.*

lithograph ['lɪθ ə græf] *n.* a picture that is printed from a stone or metal surface treated with ink. ♦ *I hung a lithograph of a laughing clown in my living room.* ♦ *The artist only made 250 copies of her latest lithograph.*

Lithuania [lɪθ u 'wen i ə] See Gazetteer.

litigation [lɪt ɪ 'ge ʃən] *n.* legal proceedings; activity concerning a lawsuit. (No plural form in this sense.) ♦ *I avoided litigation by settling the lawsuit before the trial.* ♦ *The case was in litigation for years before it was settled.*

litmus ['lɪt məs] **1.** *n.* a substance that turns red in the presence of acid and blue in the presence of alkalis. (No plural form in this sense.) ♦ *Litmus is used in a test that determines whether something is acid or alkali.* ♦ *I dipped the strip of litmus in the colorless liquid.* **2. litmus paper** *n.* paper treated with ①, used to determine the degree of acidity. ♦ *We put a bit of litmus paper into lemon juice to see what would happen.* ♦ *Litmus paper turns red in an acid like lemon juice.* **3. litmus test** *idiom* a question or experiment that seeks to determine the state of one important factor. (Figurative on ②.) ♦ *His performance on the long exam served as a litmus test to determine whether he would go to college.* ♦ *The amount of white cells in my blood became the litmus test for diagnosing my disease.*

litter ['lɪt ɚ] **1.** *n.* bits of trash; rubbish; things that are thrown away. (No plural form in this sense.) ♦ *The boys picked up the litter along the highway.* ♦ *The driver of the car in front of me threw litter out the car window.* **2.** *n.* all the babies that an animal has from one pregnancy. ♦ *There were seven puppies in the litter.* ♦ *When my cat became pregnant, I promised my brother the best kitten from her litter.* **3.** *n.* a sand-like substance that is placed in a box for domestic cats to excrete wastes into. (No plural form in this sense.) ♦ *Could you please buy some kitty litter at the store?* ♦ *I replaced the litter in the cat box.* **4. litter box** *n.* a box filled with tiny pellets of absorbent clay, kept indoors and used by a cat for elimination. ♦ *I think that someone must clean out the litter box because it really stinks.* ♦ *I trained my cat to use a litter box.* **5.** *tv.* to throw bits of trash on the floor or ground. ♦ *The park was littered with beer cans.* ♦ *The audience littered the floor with popcorn and candy wrappers.* **6.** *iv.* to throw bits of trash on the ground as a habit. ♦ *Don't litter! Use the trash can.* ♦ *I get angry at people who litter.*

litterbug ['lɪt ɚ bəg] *n.* someone who throws bits of trash on the floor or ground habitually. ♦ *The police fined the litterbug who threw his trash in the alley.* ♦ *I yelled at the litterbug for not using the trash can.*

little ['lɪt əl] **1.** *adj.* small in size. (Comp: *littler;* sup: *littlest.*) ♦ *Jimmy is little for his age.* ♦ *The little girl asked her mother for an ice-cream cone.* **2.** *adj.* some but not much; small in amount. (With *a.* Comp: *less;* sup: *least.* For items that cannot be counted. Compare with **few**.) ♦ *Could I have a little butter with my potato?* ♦ *I can speak a little French.* **3.** *adv.* somewhat; not much. (Takes *a* before an adjective. Comp: *less;* sup: *least.*) ♦ *I was a little sad when that dog died.* ♦ *I care very little for your problems, and you care less for mine.* **4. a little** *n.* a small amount [of something mentioned before or known from the context.] (No plural form in this sense. Use **a few** for items that are counted.) ♦ *Don't drink all of the juice. I would like a little.* ♦ *I bought a pizza and gave my brother a little.* **5. little bit** See bit ⑨. **6. little by little** *idiom* gradually, a little bit at a time. ♦ *I earned enough money, little by little, to buy a car.* ♦ *Jimmy crawled, little by little, until he reached the door.*

livable ['lɪv ə bəl] *adj.* suitable to be lived in or with. (Adv: *livably.*) ♦ *The mayor promised livable housing for everyone in the city.* ♦ *Although my city neighborhood was livable, I wanted to move to the suburbs.*

live 1. ['lɑɪv] *adj.* not dead; having life. ♦ *The live fish squirmed out of my hands.* ♦ *Live lobsters crawled around in the tank at the grocery store.* **2.** ['lɑɪv] *adj.* carrying electricity; electrically charged. (Figurative on ①.) ♦ *The live wire gave me a shock.* ♦ *Don't touch that circuit! It's live.* **3.** ['lɑɪv] *adj.* on the air; not taped; broadcast at the same time something is happening. ♦ *The performer promised to be polite on the live broadcast.* ♦ *The TV show was interrupted for live news coverage of a plane crash.* **4.** ['lɑɪv] *adj.* still burning; not extinguished. (Figurative on ①.)

♦ *I doused the live embers with water.* ♦ *I dumped sand over the live fire.* **5. live audience** ['laɪv…] *n.* an audience of real people who watch a performance, especially as the whole performance is broadcast on television or as it is recorded for later broadcast on television. ♦ *Tonight's program was filmed before a live audience.* ♦ *A live audience laughs and applauds in all the right places.* **6.** ['laɪv] *adv.* while something is really happening; broadcast at the moment that something is happening. ♦ *The concert was broadcast live.* ♦ *The reporter spoke to us live from the scene of the fire.* **7.** ['lɪv] *iv.* to be; to exist; to be alive; to survive. ♦ *My grandfather lived until he was 80.* ♦ *Only two people in the plane crash lived long enough to tell us what happened.* **8.** ['lɪv] *iv.* to reside at a certain address; to reside in or at a certain place. ♦ *My best friend lives in Ohio.* ♦ *I live at 123 Main Street.* **9.** ['lɪv] *iv.* to exist in a certain way. ♦ *The allied nations lived in peace.* ♦ *When I stayed at my parents' house, I lived by very strict rules.* **10. live on** ['lɪv…] *iv. + prep. phr.* to subsist on something; to remain alive because of a certain kind of food. ♦ *The prisoner lived on bread and water.* ♦ *The lost hiker lived on nuts and berries for a week.* **11. live within one's means** ['lɪv…] *idiom* to spend no more money than one has. ♦ *We have to struggle to live within our means, but we manage.* ♦ *John is unable to live within his means.* **12. live beyond one's means** ['lɪv…] *idiom* to spend more money than one has. ♦ *We have always lived beyond our means.* ♦ *John has been living beyond his means for several years, and now he has large debts.* **13. live a life of something** ['lɪv…] *idiom* to have a life of a certain quality or style. ♦ *The movie star lived a life of luxury.* ♦ *After Anne won the lottery, she lived the life of a queen.*

livelihood ['laɪv li hʊd] *n.* the way of earning a living; employment; the source of money needed for living. (No plural form in this sense.) ♦ *What do you do for your livelihood?* ♦ *Painting houses was my livelihood when I was in college.*

liveliness ['laɪv li nəs] *n.* the quality of being lively; activity; the energy of living. (No plural form in this sense.) ♦ *The puppy's liveliness made it difficult to hold.* ♦ *Since he hadn't slept in a day, John's liveliness surprised me.*

lively ['laɪv li] *adj.* showing energy or excitement; cheerful; active. (Comp: *livelier;* sup: *liveliest.*) ♦ *Everyone had fun at the lively party.* ♦ *The lively teenagers danced until dawn.*

liver ['lɪv ɚ] **1.** *n.* an organ in the body of animals that makes bile and performs other important functions. ♦ *John's liver was damaged by alcoholism.* ♦ *The patient received a new liver in the transplant surgery.* **2.** *n.* a whole liver ① eaten as food. ♦ *I added the chicken livers to the soup.* ♦ *The recipe called for a calf's liver.* **3.** *n.* ① eaten as food. (No plural form in this sense.) ♦ *I ate liver and fried onions for dinner.* ♦ *The children just hate liver.*

lives 1. ['laɪvz] pl of life. **2.** ['lɪvz] the third-person singular of live.

livestock ['laɪv stɑk] *n.* animals that are kept on a farm or ranch, usually for the production of food. (No plural form in this sense. Treated as singular or plural.) ♦ *The farmer lost all of his livestock in the flood.* ♦ *Most of the livestock live in the barn in the winter.*

livid ['lɪv ɪd] **1.** *adj.* [of bruised skin] blue-gray in color. (Adv: *lividly.*) ♦ *The doctor noticed the livid marks around my injured ankle.* ♦ *My skin turned livid where it struck the shelf I bumped into.* **2.** *adj.* red-faced from anger. (Adv: *lividly.*) ♦ *The unhappy customer was livid with anger.* ♦ *Mary became livid when confronted with her deception.*

living ['lɪv ɪŋ] **1.** *n.* the state of being alive. (No plural form in this sense.) ♦ *Living is easy in the summertime.* ♦ *Grandma's living is comfortable in the fancy retirement home.* **2.** *n.* the money one earns to live on. (No plural form in this sense.) ♦ *After college, I set out to earn a living.* ♦ *I get a good living from construction work.* **3.** *adj.* having life; not dead. ♦ *Biologists study many living organisms.* ♦ *The paramedics rescued the barely living crash victim.* **4. do something for a living** *idiom* to do some kind of work to earn enough money to live. ♦ *John paints houses for a living.* ♦ *What do you do for a living?* **5. make a living from something; make a living by doing something** *idiom* to earn a living from something or by doing something. ♦ *John makes a living from painting houses.* ♦ *Can you really make a living by selling jewelry?*

living room ['lɪv ɪŋ rum] *n.* the main room of a house or apartment, large enough to hold a number of people. ♦ *My friends and I played cards in the living room.* ♦ *Our living room has two sofas and a chair.*

lizard ['lɪz ɚd] *n.* a reptile with legs, scaly skin, and a tail. ♦ *Unlike snakes, lizards have eyelids that move.* ♦ *The green lizard blended in with the tall grass.*

load ['lod] **1.** *n.* something that is carried; a burden; a weight. ♦ *I set down my heavy load when I reached the bus station.* ♦ *I have a load of problems to worry about.* **2.** *n.* the amount of something that can be carried. ♦ *I carried a load of bricks over to the wall.* ♦ *I dragged a load of laundry to the washing machine.* **3.** *n.* the amount of electricity used by an electrical device. ♦ *This small outlet can't carry the electrical load needed by the microwave oven.* ♦ *The refrigerator's heavy load blew a fuse.* **4. loads** *n.* a lot; a great amount. (Treated as plural.) ♦ *John has loads of problems and needs to get some help.* ♦ *Anne has loads of money, so she gives a lot to charity.* **5.** *tv.* to put film or videotape into a camera; to install computer software into a computer. ♦ *The photographer loaded the film into the camera.* ♦ *Can you help me load the software into the computer?* **6.** *tv.* to fill something with something. ♦ *We loaded the trunk with bags of groceries.* ♦ *I helped Sue load the boxes with newspapers.*

loaded ['lod ɪd] **1.** *adj.* [of a gun] full of ammunition. ♦ *Take the bullets out of the loaded gun.* ♦ *I aimed the loaded rifle at the target.* **2. loaded with** *adj. + prep. phr.* full of something. ♦ *The soup Jane made is just loaded with salt!* ♦ *That cake is loaded with calories.*

loaf ['lof] **1.** *n., irreg.* a mass of bread dough baked in one piece. (Pl: loaves.) ♦ *I bought a loaf of rye bread.* ♦ *I cut a slice of bread from the loaf.* **2.** *n., irreg.* a mass of food cooked in a shape like ①. ♦ *Mike's family is having turkey loaf for dinner.* ♦ *We love meatloaf and mashed potatoes.* **3.** *iv.* to waste time. ♦ *I loafed all day Saturday.* ♦ *Tom loafed while his boss was on vacation.*

loafer ['lof ɚ] **1.** *n.* a kind of shoe without laces that the foot is slipped into. ♦ *Bill slipped on his loafers and walked to the store.* ♦ *I kicked off my loafers and dipped my toes in the pool.* **2.** *n.* someone who wastes time; someone who loafs. ♦ *The manager fired all of the loafers at the factory.*

♦ *I was such a loafer last weekend that I didn't get anything done.*

loan ['lon] **1.** *n.* something, especially money, that is lent to someone. ♦ *I paid back my student loans after I finished college.* ♦ *Mary got a loan from the bank so she could buy a car.* **2.** *tv.* to lend something to someone; to let someone borrow something. (Some people object to the use of loan in this sense rather than lend, reserving loan for the lending of money.) ♦ *The bank loaned me money so I could buy a house.* ♦ *Can you loan me a pencil? I've forgotten mine.* **3. float a loan** *idiom* to get a loan of money; to arrange for a loan of money. ♦ *I couldn't afford to pay cash for the car, so I floated a loan.* ♦ *They needed money, so they had to float a loan.* **4. take out a loan** *idiom* to get a loan of money, especially from a bank. ♦ *Mary took out a loan to buy a car.* ♦ *We will have to take out a loan to pay the bills this month.*

loath ['loθ] **loath to** *adj.* + *inf.* not willing to do something; reluctant to do something. (See loathe.) ♦ *I am loath to drive at night.* ♦ *John is loath to ask for directions when he's lost.*

loathe ['loð] *tv.* to hate someone or something very much; to abhor someone or something. ♦ *I just loathe my neighbor's dog because it barks all the time.* ♦ *I quit my job because I loathed it.*

loathing ['loð ɪŋ] *n.* very strong hatred; disgust. (No plural form in this sense.) ♦ *My loathing for my job was so strong that I quit.* ♦ *The critic didn't hide his loathing for the new movie.*

loathsome ['loð səm] *adj.* deserving hate; worthy of hate. (Adv: *loathsomely.*) ♦ *The loathsome treatment of the refugees was shocking.* ♦ *The bigot's comments were loathsome.*

loaves ['lovz] pl of loaf.

lob ['lɑb] *tv.* to throw or hit something so that it moves in a slow, high curve. ♦ *The pitcher lobbed the baseball to the batter.* ♦ *The tennis player lobbed the ball across the court.*

lobby ['lɑb i] **1.** *n.* the entrance room of a building. ♦ *I waited in the theater's lobby for my friends to arrive.* ♦ *There's an information desk in the lobby of the museum.* **2.** *tv.* to try to influence a lawmaker to vote a certain way. ♦ *The parents lobbied the city council members for school reform.* ♦ *The tobacco company lobbied the senate for support.* **3.** *iv.* to try to influence [a lawmaker]. ♦ *The citizens lobbied for tax reform.* ♦ *The company lobbied against government regulation.*

lobbyist ['lɑb i əst] *n.* someone who is paid to try to influence the vote of a lawmaker. ♦ *The lobbyist took the influential senator to lunch.* ♦ *The representative refused all gifts from lobbyists.*

lobster ['lɑb stɚ] **1.** *n.* an edible sea animal with six legs and two claws. ♦ *Lobsters are usually caught in traps in the sea.* ♦ *There is a tank containing lobsters at the grocery store.* **2.** *n.* the meat of ① used as food. (No plural form in this sense.) ♦ *I had lobster and potatoes for dinner.* ♦ *While visiting Boston, I ate a lot of lobster.* **3.** *adj.* made or flavored with ②. ♦ *I ordered pasta with lobster sauce.* ♦ *We had a lobster casserole for the main course.*

local ['lok əl] **1.** *adj.* of or about the nearby area. (Adv: *locally.*) ♦ *The local newspaper focuses on neighborhood news.* ♦ *The doctor gave me a local anesthetic before stitching my wound.* **2.** *n.* a bus or train that stops at every station. ♦ *You have to take the local to get to my neighborhood.* ♦ *The locals run more often than the express trains.* **3.** *n.* a person who lives in the area that something is in. (Often plural.) ♦ *While vacationing, I asked a local where I should eat.* ♦ *The exchange student got along well with the locals.*

locale [lo 'kæl] *n.* a location, especially where a certain event happens. ♦ *The Ford Theater is the locale where Lincoln was shot.* ♦ *I visited the general locale where my father had been born.*

locality [lo 'kæl ə ti] *n.* a location; a place. ♦ *The house I am looking for is somewhere in this locality.* ♦ *The fast-food chain had franchises in many localities in the city.*

localize ['lok ə lɑɪz] *tv.* to restrict something to a certain area or location. ♦ *The epidemic was localized around the St. Louis area.* ♦ *The pain was localized around my kneecap.*

locate ['lo ket] **1.** *tv.* to find someone or something; to learn where someone or something is. ♦ *The student located Brazil on the map.* ♦ *I finally located my car keys that I had lost last week.* **2.** *tv.* to place someone or something in a particular place. ♦ *The company located its offices near its customers.* ♦ *The city located the tennis courts next to the park.*

location [lo 'ke ʃən] **1.** *n.* the place where someone or something is; the place where someone or something is found. ♦ *Washington, D.C., is the location of the White House, the Capitol, and other important government buildings.* ♦ *I found my wallet in the exact location that I had left it.* **2. on location** *phr.* a place, located in a place distant from the movie studio, where a movie is filmed. ♦ *This movie was shot on location in Ontario.* ♦ *The actress went on location in Spain for her latest film.*

lock ['lɑk] **1.** *n.* a device on a door opening that prevents the door from being opened without a key. ♦ *Our landlord installed a secure lock on the front door.* ♦ *The thief broke the lock with a sledgehammer.* **2.** *n.* a device similar to a ① that controls access to something. ♦ *My computer has a lock on it so no one else can use it.* ♦ *All our windows have levers that serve as locks.* **3.** *n.* a part of a canal or river between two heavy, watertight gates where the level of the water can be raised or lowered, allowing boats to move from one level of water to another. ♦ *The tourists on the boat watched the lock fill with water and lift their boat.* ♦ *The ship entered the lock, and a heavy gate closed behind it.* **4.** *n.* a small bundle of [head] hair; a strand or curl of hair. ♦ *The actress dyed her long brown locks blond.* ♦ *Mary kept a lock of John's hair in her locket.* **5. lock (up)** *tv.* (+ *adv.*) to secure something by using ①, so it cannot be opened or started without a key. ♦ *Make sure you lock the front door when you leave.* ♦ *I always lock up my car when I go shopping.* **6. lock up** *tv.* + *adv.* to put someone or something into a place that can be secured with ①; to put someone in jail. ♦ *The banker locked the money up in the vault.* ♦ *The sheriff locked up the criminal.* **7.** *iv.* to not be able to move. ♦ *The wheels locked in place as I skidded down the icy slope.* ♦ *The steering wheel locked when I tried to turn it.*

locker ['lɑk ɚ] **1.** *n.* a compartment that can be locked, where clothes and valuables are kept. ♦ *I put my biology book in my locker at school.* ♦ *My tennis shoes are in my locker at the gymnasium.* **2. go to Davy Jones's locker**

idiom to go to the bottom of the sea. ♦ *My camera fell overboard and went to Davy Jones's locker.* ♦ *My uncle was a sailor. He went to Davy Jones's locker during a terrible storm.*

locket ['lɑk ɪt] *n.* a tiny case attached to a necklace or bracelet that holds a picture or some other object. ♦ *Mary wore a heart-shaped locket around her neck.* ♦ *Susan kept a small photo of her children in her locket.*

lockjaw ['lɑk dʒɔ] *n.* a condition caused by tetanus where the jaws are locked closed by muscles. (No plural form in this sense.) ♦ *Lockjaw is rare when people are vaccinated against tetanus.* ♦ *A case of lockjaw can be fatal.*

locksmith ['lɑk smɪθ] *n.* someone who makes and repairs locks and is able to open a lock when the key is lost. ♦ *The locksmith made a duplicate of my key for me.* ♦ *I asked the locksmith to fix the lock on my front door.*

locomotion [lok ə 'mo ʃən] *n.* moving from one place to another; the ability to move from one place to another. (No plural form in this sense.) ♦ *Alcohol can impair your locomotion.* ♦ *The biologist studied the locomotion of snakes.*

locomotive [lok ə 'mot ɪv] **1.** *n.* a train engine. ♦ *The locomotive pulled twenty boxcars and a caboose.* ♦ *A speeding locomotive crashed into a stalled car.* **2.** *adj.* <the adj. use of ①.> ♦ *My uncle is a locomotive engineer.* ♦ *I could hear the locomotive whistle in the distance.*

locust ['lok əst] *n.* a kind of grasshopper that travels in large swarms and destroys crops. ♦ *A swarm of locusts destroyed the farmer's corn crop.* ♦ *Locusts descended on the valley and ate every plant.*

lodge ['lɑdʒ] **1.** *n.* a small, privately owned cabin for campers, hunters, skiers, and the like to stay in the country. ♦ *After a day of skiing, we returned to the lodge for dinner.* ♦ *We stayed in the lodge because there was a blizzard outside.* **2.** *n.* the place where a fraternal organization meets. ♦ *Only members were allowed to watch initiations at the lodge.* ♦ *On Thursdays, my dad bowls with friends from his lodge.* **3.** *n.* a place where beavers live. ♦ *The beavers built a dam to raise the water around their lodge.* ♦ *Beavers spend the winter in their lodge.* **4.** *iv.* to become stuck somewhere; to become wedged in something. ♦ *A piece of popcorn lodged in my throat.* ♦ *The bullet lodged into the wall behind me.* **5. lodge in** *tv.* + *prep. phr.* to cause something to become stuck in something; to wedge something somewhere. ♦ *I lodged the head of the axe in the stump.* ♦ *Tom lodged the packet of old letter plans in a space behind the desk.*

lodger ['lɑdʒ ɚ] *n.* someone who pays to live in someone's house; someone who rents a room in a house. ♦ *The lodger paid his rent on the first of the month.* ♦ *I rent out the spare bedroom to a lodger.*

lodging ['lɑdʒ ɪŋ] *n.* a place to stay for a short time. (Sometimes plural with the same meaning.) ♦ *The tired traveler looked for lodging for the night.* ♦ *My company pays for my lodgings when I'm on business trips.*

loft ['lɔft] **1.** *n.* an upper level in a barn or stable, where hay is kept. ♦ *The farmer pitched some hay down from the loft for the horses.* ♦ *We played in the loft, jumping into soft piles of hay.* **2.** *n.* a large apartment with high ceilings and few walls, usually renovated from an old warehouse. ♦ *The developer renovated the old factory into expensive lofts.* ♦ *The painter lived and worked in a large, almost empty loft.* **3. (choir) loft** *n.* a raised area in a church, often at the back, where the choir sits. ♦ *The new organ was placed in the center of the choir loft.* ♦ *The choir members walked up the stairs to the loft.*

lofty ['lɔf ti] **1.** *adj.* high; very tall. (Adv: *loftily.* Comp: *loftier;* sup: *loftiest.*) ♦ *The plane flew among the lofty clouds.* ♦ *The lofty mountains towered over the village that was in the valley.* **2.** *adj.* noble; dignified. (Figurative on ①. Adv: *loftily.* Comp: *loftier;* sup: *loftiest.*) ♦ *John had lofty goals but could not achieve them.* ♦ *Anne's lofty ideals became an inspiration to the others in her group.* **3.** *adj.* haughty; arrogant; as though better than other people. (Figurative on ①. Adv: *loftily.* Comp: *loftier;* sup: *loftiest.*) ♦ *I gave the waiter with the lofty attitude a small tip.* ♦ *Your lofty manner is insulting.*

log ['lɔg] **1.** *n.* a length of the trunk or main branch of a tree with all of the branches removed. ♦ *My mountain cabin is made entirely of logs.* ♦ *I put some logs in the fireplace so I could build a fire.* **2.** *n.* a detailed record of a trip written by the captain of a ship, plane, train, etc. ♦ *The captain recorded the ship's position in the log.* ♦ *A record of every change of direction is made in the log.* **3.** *tv.* to note something in ②. ♦ *The captain logged the fact that a sailor had become ill.* ♦ *The last entry was logged an hour before the ship sank.*

logic ['lɑdʒ ɪk] **1.** *n.* the science of reasoning; the part of philosophy that deals with reason. (No plural form in this sense.) ♦ *The members of the debate team studied logic.* ♦ *Logic is the key to sound reasoning.* **2.** *n.* a method of argument or reasoning. (No plural form in this sense.) ♦ *I'm having a hard time following your logic.* ♦ *According to John's logic, no one should pay taxes.* **3.** *n.* sense; rational thought; the ability to reason. (No plural form in this sense.) ♦ *The detective used logic to solve the crime.* ♦ *The mediator's logic helped settle the dispute.*

logical ['lɑdʒ ɪ kəl] **1.** *adj.* making sense; according to the rules of logic. (Adv: *logically* [...ɪk li].) ♦ *I demand a logical explanation for your behavior.* ♦ *Wouldn't it be more logical to fly to Europe instead of going by boat?* **2.** *adj.* reasoning effectively and sensibly. (Adv: *logically* [...ɪk li].) ♦ *The logical detective solved the crime.* ♦ *If you were more logical, you'd see the error of your ways.*

logistic [lo 'dʒɪs tɪk] **1. logistics** *n.* the details of the organization of a complex operation or system. (Treated as singular or plural.) ♦ *The logistics of the plan left nothing to chance.* ♦ *The manager took care of the logistics of the wedding reception.* **2.** *adj.* <the adj. use of ①.> (Adv: *logistically* [...ɪk li].) ♦ *Organizing the inefficient office was a logistic nightmare.* ♦ *I handled the logistic details of the conference.*

loin ['lɔɪn] *n.* a cut of meat from the side and lower back of an animal, between the ribs and the hips. ♦ *I ordered pork loin for dinner.* ♦ *Mary roasted a loin of beef in the oven.*

loiter ['lɔɪt ɚ] *iv.* to stand around doing nothing; to stand around idly. ♦ *The students loitered around the parking lot after school.* ♦ *The vagrants loitered in the park.*

lollipop ['lɑl i pɑp] *n.* a piece of hard candy on the end of a stick. ♦ *The little boy licked his lollipop.* ♦ *This lollipop is cherry-flavored.*

lone ['lon] *adj.* only; alone; without others. (Only prenominal. See also **alone**. Comp: none; sup: none.) ♦ *The lone survivor of the accident was a small child.* ♦ *A lone robin chirped in the tree.*

loneliness ['lon li nəs] *n.* the condition of being lonely; sadness caused by being alone. (No plural form in this sense.) ♦ *After moving to a new city, Bill suffered from loneliness.* ♦ *Mary fought loneliness by joining a club.*

lonely ['lon li] **1.** *adj.* sad because one is alone; lonesome. (Comp: *lonelier;* sup: *loneliest.*) ♦ *The lonely student ate lunch by himself.* ♦ *Mary was lonely after she graduated from school.* **2.** *adj.* isolated; desolate; without people around. (Comp: *lonelier;* sup: *loneliest.*) ♦ *The lonely farmhouse was the only building in sight.* ♦ *You couldn't reach the lonely town during the winter.*

loner ['lon ɚ] *n.* someone who prefers to be alone; someone who does not socialize with other people. ♦ *John didn't go to any parties because he was a loner.* ♦ *The loner always ate lunch by herself.*

lonesome ['lon səm] **1.** *adj.* lonely; sad because one is alone. (Adv: *lonesomely.*) ♦ *The lonesome soldier wrote to his family often.* ♦ *Susan was lonesome without her friends.* **2.** *adj.* [of something] solitary; [of something] being the only one. (Only prenominal. Adv: *lonesomely.*) ♦ *After the tornado, only one lonesome tree remained standing.* ♦ *At midnight, the lonesome car was towed from the parking lot.* **3.** *adj.* isolated; desolate; without people around. (Adv: *lonesomely.*) ♦ *The lonesome island was hundreds of miles from civilization.* ♦ *The wind rushed through the lonesome forest.*

long ['lɔŋ] **1.** *adj.* great in length or in amount of time. (Comp: *longer;* sup: *longest.*) ♦ *The long line for tickets stretched around the block.* ♦ *I fell asleep during the long lecture.* **2.** *adj.* having a certain length; lasting a certain amount of time. (Follows the measure of length or time. Comp: *longer.*) ♦ *The snake was five feet long.* ♦ *My vacation was eight days long.* **3.** *adj.* seeming to take more time than normal; seeming to be farther than normal. (Comp: *longer;* sup: *longest.*) ♦ *I spent one long week in jail.* ♦ *I walked ten long miles to the nearest gas station.* **4. all day long; all night long; all month long; all year long; all summer long; etc.** *adv.* throughout an entire period of time. ♦ *We waited all month long for our paychecks, and they were late!* ♦ *The concert lasted all night long.* **5.** *adv.* [for] such a long time. ♦ *Hurry up. I can't wait long.* ♦ *Don't worry. This won't take long.* **6.** *adv.* at a great extent of time before or after the time indicated. ♦ *Bill traveled to Europe long before his sister did.* ♦ *John stayed up long past his bedtime.* **7. as long as** *phr.* [in comparisons] of equal length. (See ①.) ♦ *Is this one as long as that one?* ♦ *This snake is as long as a car!* **8. as long as; so long as** *idiom* provided that...; on the condition that.... ♦ *I will pay you extra money so long as you promise to finish the job tomorrow.* ♦ *As long as you do what you are told, everything will be fine.* **9. as long as; so long as** *idiom* since; given the fact that.... ♦ *As long as you are going to the kitchen, please bring me some popcorn.* ♦ *As long as I have to take this check to the bank, I can also take the laundry to the Laundromat.* **10. as long as** *idiom* during or throughout the period of time that.... ♦ *As long as I have worked here, we have always had half-hour lunch breaks.* ♦ *As long as we have lived here, the basement has never flooded.*

long distance ['lɔŋ 'dɪs təns] **1.** *n.* telephone service between points that are far apart. (No plural form in this sense.) ♦ *We don't use long distance very much.* ♦ *How much do you pay for long distance?* **2. long-distance** *adj.* covering a great distance; linking people or things that are far apart. ♦ *What company provides your long-distance telephone service?* ♦ *John and Mary's long-distance relationship lasted only a year.* **3. long-distance** *adv.* in a way that covers a great distance; not locally. ♦ *I called my parents long-distance from New York.* ♦ *The salesman conducted his business long-distance over the phone.*

longevity [lɔn 'dʒɛv ə ti] *n.* the quality of [someone's] living a long time or [something's] lasting a long time. (No plural form in this sense.) ♦ *Longevity is a characteristic of my family. All my ancestors lived longer than 80 years.* ♦ *Will better gasoline increase a car's longevity?*

longhand ['lɔŋ hænd] **1.** *n.* handwriting; printing or writing made by hand instead of by machine; handwriting instead of **shorthand**. (No plural form in this sense.) ♦ *The author wrote the first draft in longhand.* ♦ *Please type, because I can't read your longhand.* **2.** *adv.* by hand instead of machine. ♦ *My computer broke, so I wrote my paper longhand.* ♦ *Please don't write longhand, because it's hard to read.*

longing ['lɔŋ ɪŋ] **1.** *n.* desire; a deep yearning. (No plural form in this sense.) ♦ *Longing is a feeling that is very close to depression.* ♦ *After David left, I was overcome with a sense of longing.* **2.** *n.* a desire; a wish for someone or something. ♦ *While on my diet, I had a longing for ice cream.* ♦ *John's longing for adventure takes him to many exciting places.* **3.** *adj.* showing desire; having a desire; yearning. (Adv: *longingly.*) ♦ *As I ate the steak, I avoided the longing look in my dog's eyes.* ♦ *My longing desire for chocolate destroyed my diet.*

longingly ['lɔŋ ɪŋ li] *adv.* in a way that shows a heartfelt want or need. ♦ *The child stared longingly at the toy train.* ♦ *The lovers looked longingly at each other.*

longitude ['lɔn dʒɪ tud] *n.* the distance, measured in degrees, to the east or west on the earth from an imaginary line that runs from the North Pole to the South Pole through Greenwich, England. ♦ *The pilot recorded the plane's latitude and longitude.* ♦ *Bremen, Germany, is located at a longitude of 10 degrees east.*

longitudinal [lɔn dʒə 'tud ɪ nəl] *adj.* of or about longitude; lengthwise; in length. (Adv: *longitudinally.*) ♦ *This graph's longitudinal axis shows the rate of change.* ♦ *The pilot recorded the plane's longitudinal coordinate.*

long-range ['lɔŋ 'rendʒ] **1.** *adj.* future; looking into the future. ♦ *My long-range goal is to have a permanent job.* ♦ *The company's long-range plans included building two new factories.* **2.** *adj.* covering a great distance. ♦ *The long-range aircraft soared across the ocean.* ♦ *The enemy fired long-range missiles at the factory.*

longshoreman ['lɔŋ 'ʃor mən] *n., irreg.* someone, usually a male, who loads and unloads ships for a living. (Pl: **longshoremen**.) ♦ *The longshoremen unloaded cargo from the ship.* ♦ *The longshoreman lived near the docks.*

longshoremen ['lɔŋ 'ʃor mən] pl of **longshoreman**.

long-term ['lɔŋ 'tɚm] *adj.* involving a long period of time. ♦ *My long-term goal has always been to become a doctor.* ♦ *The long-term effects of pollution aren't fully known yet.*

long-winded ['lɔŋ 'wɪn dɪd] **1.** *adj.* talking too much; talking for too long. (Adv: *long-windedly.*) ♦ *The long-winded speaker put me to sleep.* ♦ *My long-winded friends talked all night long.* **2.** *adj.* [of a speech] too long. ♦ *I fell asleep during the minister's long-winded sermon.* ♦ *I stopped listening to the president's long-winded speech.*

look ['lʊk] **1.** *n.* an act of looking as in ④; the deliberate act of trying to see someone or something; a glance. ♦ *Do you want to have a look at my photos?* ♦ *I need another look before I can be sure that your name is on the list.* **2.** *n.* an appearance. (Sometimes plural with the same meaning.) ♦ *I like the sleek, new look of your sports car.* ♦ *The models wore the latest looks in fashion.* **3.** *n.* an expression on the face. ♦ *John had a surprised look on his face because we'd remembered his birthday.* ♦ *Wipe that angry look off your face and eat your peas.* **4. look at** *iv.* + *prep. phr.* to move the eyes to see or examine someone or something. ♦ *The drivers slowed down to look at the accident.* ♦ *I looked at the stars in the sky.* **5.** *iv.* to seem; to appear. ♦ *Take an umbrella. It looks like it's going to rain.* ♦ *Tonight's homework assignment looks difficult.* **6.** *iv.* to face a certain direction; to be positioned in a certain direction. ♦ *The front of the store looks south.* ♦ *The bedroom window looked toward the sea.* **7. look for** *iv.* + *prep. phr.* to watch for something; to be alert for some kind of danger. ♦ *Look for glass on the floor. I just broke a glass.* ♦ *The bicyclist looked for potholes in the road.* **8. look to** *iv.* + *prep. phr.* to seek advice or help from someone or something. ♦ *Max looked to his mother for help when he failed algebra.* ♦ *I looked to the dictionary for the meaning of the word.* **9. look down on someone or something** *idiom* to look upon someone or something with dislike or scorn. ♦ *Bob looks down on me for not having my own car.* ♦ *They look down on us because we are poor.* **10. look the other way** *idiom* to ignore (something) on purpose. ♦ *John could have prevented the problem, but he looked the other way.* ♦ *By looking the other way, he actually made the problem worse.* **11. take a look at someone or something; have a look at someone or something** *idiom* to observe or examine someone or something. ♦ *I asked the doctor to take a look at my cut.* ♦ *Would you please have another look at your work? It is not complete.* **12. take a look for someone or something; have a look for someone or something** *idiom* to make a visual search for someone or something; to look for someone or something. ♦ *Please go to the library and have a look for a book about snakes.* ♦ *Take a look for a man in a black suit. He is your guide.*

lookout ['lʊk ɑʊt] **1.** *n.* a place where someone can watch for danger. ♦ *From the lookout, the scout could see the enemy approaching.* ♦ *Several soldiers were at the lookout, scanning the horizon.* **2.** *n.* someone who watches for danger. ♦ *The lookout saw the army in the distance.* ♦ *I'll act as lookout for pickpockets.* **3. on the lookout for someone or something** *idiom* to watch carefully for someone or something that might be dangerous. ♦ *The campers were on the lookout for brown bears.* ♦ *The police were on the lookout for the escaped criminal.*

loom ['lum] **1.** *n.* a machine used for weaving cloth, blankets, or rugs. ♦ *I wove this blanket on a loom.* ♦ *Mary threaded the loom with brightly colored yarn.* **2.** *iv.* to appear somewhere in a threatening or unfriendly way. ♦ *Dark clouds loomed on the horizon.* ♦ *Signs of a recession loomed in the distance.* **3. loom large** *idiom* to be of great importance, especially when referring to a possible problem, danger, or threat. ♦ *The exams were looming large.* ♦ *Eviction was looming large when the students could not pay their rent.*

loon ['lun] *n.* an aquatic bird that resembles a duck and is known for its haunting cry and ability to dive for food. ♦ *The loon caught a fish in its beak.* ♦ *At sunrise, the loons filled the air with their cries.*

loop ['lup] **1.** *n.* a circular figure formed by a line that curves and crosses itself. ♦ *The cake was decorated with loops of colored frosting.* ♦ *Our cat pawed at a loop of yarn.* **2. loop around** *iv.* + *prep. phr.* to form ① around someone or something. ♦ *The belt looped around Mary's waist.* ♦ *Elevated train tracks loop around the city's business district.* **3. loop around** *tv.* + *prep. phr.* to use something to enclose someone or something in ①. ♦ *The snake looped itself around the mouse.* ♦ *Mary looped the scarf around her neck.*

loophole ['lup hol] *n.* the inexact wording of a law that allows one to avoid complying with the law. ♦ *By exploiting loopholes in the law, the company owed no income tax.* ♦ *The factory looked for loopholes in the new environmental laws.*

loose ['lus] **1.** *adj.* not tight; having room to move. (Adv: *loosely.* Comp: *looser;* sup: *loosest.*) ♦ *I had to wear a belt because my pants were so loose.* ♦ *I wiggled my loose tooth.* **2.** *adj.* free; escaped and not confined. (Not prenominal.) ♦ *The police searched for the criminal who was loose again.* ♦ *The dog is loose. You'd better go find him.* **3.** *adj.* not exact. (Figurative on ①. Adv: *loosely.* Comp: *looser;* sup: *loosest.*) ♦ *I read a loose translation of the French president's speech.* ♦ *This movie is a very loose version of the book.* **4.** *adj.* [of morals] lax or unrestrained. (Adv: *loosely.* Comp: *looser;* sup: *loosest.*) ♦ *Bob earned a reputation for loose morals.* ♦ *The sailor flirted with the loose woman at the bar.* **5.** *tv.* to set someone or something free. ♦ *The farmer loosed the dogs on the salesman.* ♦ *The demonstrators loosed the animals from their cages.* **6.** *adv.* freely. ♦ *Dogs roam loose in the streets.* ♦ *The children ran loose through the park.* **7.** *adv.* in a way that frees or separates. ♦ *My fishing line got caught on something underwater, and I had to cut it loose.* ♦ *The dog was trapped in its leash, so its owner cut it loose.* **8. at loose ends** *idiom* restless and unsettled; unemployed. ♦ *Just before school starts, all the children are at loose ends.* ♦ *Jane has been at loose ends ever since she lost her job.*

loosen ['lus ən] **1.** *tv.* to cause something to be less tight or restraining; to untie someone or something. ♦ *I loosened the tie around my neck.* ♦ *The college loosened its entrance requirements.* **2.** *iv.* to become less tight or restraining; to unfasten. ♦ *The screws loosened slowly over time.* ♦ *The communist grip on Eastern Europe loosened in the late 1980s.*

loot ['lut] **1.** *n.* stolen money and objects. (No plural form in this sense.) ♦ *The robbers put their loot in a large bag.* ♦ *The pirates buried the loot on a remote island.* **2.** *tv.* to rob things or places, especially during a war or a riot. ♦ *The army looted the village after taking it over.* ♦ *The rioters looted the department store.* **3.** *iv.* to steal [something], especially during a war or riot. ♦ *Many were looting and causing vandalism during the riots.* ♦ *Typically, armies looted in order to survive as they crossed the country.*

lop ['lɑp] **lop off** *tv.* + *adv.* to cut something off from something else. ♦ *The barber lopped off the hair around my ears.* ♦ *I lopped the ends of the carrot off.*

lopsided ['lɑp sɑɪ dɪd] *adj.* tilted; leaning to one side; heavy on one side. (Adv: *lopsidedly.*) ♦ *I straightened the lopsided painting.* ♦ *The lopsided score at the end of the game was 84–7.*

loquacious [lo 'kwe ʃəs] *adj.* talkative; talking a lot. (Adv: *loquaciously.*) ♦ *John's very loquacious. He'll talk about any subject for hours.* ♦ *I spoke on the phone for five hours with my loquacious aunt.*

lord ['lord] **1.** *n.* a master or ruler in control. ♦ *The citizens pledged allegiance to their lord.* ♦ *The police raided the drug lord's home.* **2.** *n.* a nobleman. ♦ *The upper chamber of England's parliament is the House of Lords.* ♦ *Lord Jones has extensive business holdings in India.* **3. Lord** *n.* <a title used to address deities, such as God or Jesus Christ.> ♦ *The sinner prayed to the Lord for forgiveness.* ♦ *We ask the Lord to hear our prayers.*

lose ['luz] **1.** *tv., irreg.* to be deprived of someone or something; to fail to keep someone or something in one's possession. (Pt/pp: **lost**.) ♦ *The Browns lost everything they owned in the fire.* ♦ *Mary lost her child in the department store.* **2.** *tv., irreg.* to have less of something after doing something before. ♦ *If you want to lose weight, you should start exercising.* ♦ *I lost a lot of money playing poker last night.* **3.** *tv., irreg.* not to win or receive someone or something. ♦ *The visiting team lost the game.* ♦ *Our team lost the championship.* **4.** *tv., irreg.* to **lose** ② a period of reckoned time. ♦ *My cheap watch loses an hour every week.* ♦ *You lose an hour when you go from New York to Chicago.* **5.** *tv., irreg.* to cause someone not to understand something; to cause someone to be confused. ♦ *Could you explain that again? You've lost me.* ♦ *The professor's explanation completely lost half the class.* **6.** *iv., irreg.* not to win; to be defeated. ♦ *Our team almost lost, but ended up tying the game.* ♦ *I made a bet that the team would lose.* **7. lose oneself in something** *idiom* to have all one's attention taken up by something. ♦ *I can lose myself in a book any time.* ♦ *The children lose themselves in their favorite TV program on Saturdays.* **8. lose one's temper (at someone or something)** *idiom* to become angry at someone or something. ♦ *Lisa lost her temper and began shouting at Bob.* ♦ *I hate to lose my temper at someone. I always end up feeling guilty.*

loser ['luz ɚ] **1.** *n.* someone who did not win something; someone who is defeated or fails to win. ♦ *The loser lost the election by 250,000 votes.* ♦ *I spend a lot of money on lottery tickets, and I'm always a loser.* **2.** *n.* an unpopular person who seems to fail at everything. (Slang.) ♦ *Don't be a loser, Anne. Change your hair style and meet some new friends.* ♦ *Because John was a loser, he couldn't get any dates.*

losing ['luz ɪŋ] *adj.* not winning; having been defeated. ♦ *I voted for the losing candidate.* ♦ *The losing team left the field angrily.*

loss ['lɔs] **1.** *n.* losing someone or something; deprivation. (No plural form in this sense.) ♦ *Loss, especially through death, is very sad.* ♦ *After the tornado ruined the town, most people suffered from a sense of loss.* **2.** *n.* an instance of losing something. ♦ *I reported the loss of my car to my insurance company.* ♦ *The loss of my wallet was a major catastrophe.* **3.** *n.* the value of something that was lost; how much something lost costs; money that is lost or never earned. ♦ *The company operated at a loss of over $100,000 last month.* ♦ *The gambler wasn't fazed by his loss at the races.* **4.** *n.* the death of someone; the death of a loved one. (No plural form in this sense.) ♦ *The minister comforted the widow over her loss.* ♦ *At John's funeral, I spoke with his family about their loss.* **5.** *n.* a defeat; the failure to win. ♦ *Our team suffered a loss at the hands of the visiting team.* ♦ *Our coach said our loss was due to not practicing enough.*

lost ['lɔst] **1.** pt/pp of **lose**. **2.** *adj.* unable to be found. ♦ *I offered a reward to anyone who could find my lost wallet.* ♦ *The library charged me a fine for the lost book.* **3.** *adj.* no longer owned; no longer in one's possession. ♦ *The army vowed to take back the lost territory.* ♦ *The lost computer data had never been copied onto other disks.* **4.** *adj.* not knowing where one is; not knowing how to get to where one wants to be. ♦ *If we're lost, why don't you stop and ask for directions?* ♦ *A lost tourist asked me for directions.* **5. lost on someone** *idiom* having no effect on someone; wasted on someone. ♦ *The joke was lost on Lisa. She didn't understand it.* ♦ *The humor of the situation was lost on Mary. She was too upset to see it.*

lot ['lɑt] **1.** *n.* a portion of the available goods; an allotment or share. ♦ *I ordered a lot of 300 skirts in various styles and sizes from the manufacturer.* ♦ *We received a huge shipment of goods yesterday, but two lots had to be sent back because they were damaged.* **2.** *n.* fate; destiny; the life that fate has allotted. ♦ *It was the comedian's lot in life to make others laugh.* ♦ *I accepted my lot as a lonely taxi driver.* **3.** *n.* an area of land; a share of land; a piece of property. ♦ *Our lot is on a corner and has many trees on it.* ♦ *The Browns built their new house on a wide lot.* **4. parking lot** *n.* a portion of paved land, used to park cars on. ♦ *This used to be a vacant lot, but now it is a parking lot.* ♦ *I left my car somewhere in this huge parking lot!* **5. a lot of; lots of** *idiom* a large number of people or things; much of something. ♦ *I got a lot of presents for my birthday.* ♦ *I ate lots of cookies after dinner.* **6. draw lots** *idiom* to choose from a group of things to determine who will do something. (Typically, to choose a straw from a bundle of straws. The person with the shortest straw is selected.) ♦ *We drew lots to decide who would wash the dishes.* ♦ *The players drew lots to determine who would go first.* **7. have a lot going (for one)** *idiom* to have many things working to one's benefit. ♦ *Jane is so lucky. She has a lot going for her.* ♦ *She has a good job and a nice family. She has a lot going.*

lotion ['lo ʃən] **1.** *n.* a creamy liquid that is rubbed on the body to soothe, add moisture, or clean the skin. (No plural form in this sense.) ♦ *I put some lotion on my sunburned skin.* ♦ *The lotion put moisture into my dry skin.* **2. lotions** *n.* kinds or types of ①. ♦ *I tried all sorts of lotions, but none would help my skin.* ♦ *This store sells many different lotions.*

lottery ['lɑt ə ri] **1.** *n.* a game of chance, where chances are sold by the state and the winners get shares of the money the state has received. ♦ *The jackpot in today's lottery is $10 million.* ♦ *Anne quit her job after she won the lottery.* **2.** *n.* any system of choosing or deciding based on the drawing of tickets, numbers, tokens, etc. ♦ *I entered a lottery where the prize was a new car.* ♦ *The winner of the raffle was chosen by lottery.*

loud ['lɑʊd] **1.** *adj.* [of sound] having much volume or intensity; not quiet. (Adv: *loudly.* Comp: *louder;* sup: *loudest.*) ♦ *Please turn down your radio. It's too loud.* ♦ *My neighbors' loud argument woke me up.* **2.** *adj.* too bright; flashy; showy. (Figurative on ①. Adv: *loudly.* Comp: *louder;* sup: *loudest.*) ♦ *Mary wore a loud dress to the party.* ♦ *The painting's loud colors contrasted with the ivory walls.* **3.** *adv.* in a loud ① manner. (Comp: *louder;* sup: *loudest.*) ♦ *Please don't talk so loud.* ♦ *Speak louder so we all can hear you.*

loudmouth ['lɑʊd mɑʊθ] *n.* a person who talks too loud; a person who talks too much; a person who cannot keep a secret. ♦ *Tell that loudmouth to be quiet.* ♦ *Don't tell Bob your secret; he's a loudmouth.*

loudness ['lɑʊd nəs] **1.** *n.* the quality of being loud. (No plural form in this sense.) ♦ *The loudness of the rock concert temporarily deafened me.* ♦ *The factory worker wore earplugs due to the loudness of the machines.* **2.** *n.* the level of the strength of a sound. (No plural form in this sense.) ♦ *The engineers reduced the loudness of the aircraft.* ♦ *The sound engineer adjusted the loudness of the violins.*

loudspeaker ['lɑʊd spik ɚ] *n.* a device that changes electrical signals into sound that can be heard; a speaker. ♦ *The principal made an announcement over the loudspeaker.* ♦ *The police spoke to the crowd through a loudspeaker.*

Louisiana [lu iz i 'æn ə] See Gazetteer.

lounge ['lɑʊndʒ] **1.** *n.* a room where people can sit and relax. ♦ *During my break, I went to the lounge to smoke.* ♦ *There is a refrigerator in the lounge, along with some tables and chairs.* **2. lounge around** *iv.* + *adv.* to be idle; to pass time lazily, usually sitting or lying down. ♦ *I lounge around at the cabin on weekends.* ♦ *After class, I lounged around in the hallway.*

louse ['lɑʊs] **1.** *n., irreg.* a small insect that lives in the hair and on the body of humans and animals. (Pl: lice.) ♦ *Jimmy was sent home from school because he had lice.* ♦ *Medicated shampoo kills lice and their eggs.* **2.** *n.* someone, usually a male, who is worthless or unkind. (Derogatory. Pl: *louses.*) ♦ *I was disappointed that my daughter married such a louse.* ♦ *You louse! I can't believe you forgot our anniversary!*

lousy ['lɑʊz i] *adj.* bad; awful; terrible. (Slang.) ♦ *This was really a lousy day.* ♦ *I stopped watching the lousy movie.*

louver ['luv ɚ] *n.* [in a window or door] one of a series of overlapping wooden or metal strips that let in air but not rain. ♦ *Max adjusted the louvers to let more sunlight into the room.* ♦ *I peered outside through the louvers.*

lovable ['lʌv ə bəl] *adj.* able to be loved; deserving of being loved. (Adv: *lovably.*) ♦ *The teacher believed that every child was lovable.* ♦ *Our puppy is so lovable! He just loves to be held.*

love ['lʌv] **1.** *n.* a strong emotion of attraction, care, romance, or desire towards someone. (No plural form in this sense.) ♦ *My parents' love for each other is very strong.* ♦ *John promised his love to Mary for as long as he lived.* **2.** *n.* a strong interest in something. (No plural form in this sense.) ♦ *My love of chocolate makes it hard to stay on my diet.* ♦ *Anne donated money to the museum because of her love of art.* **3.** *n.* [in tennis] a score of zero. ♦ *Anne was ahead, 30–love.* ♦ *After the first serve, the score was 15–love.* **4.** *tv.* to care deeply for someone romantically. ♦ *After twenty years of marriage, John still loved Mary very much.* ♦ *The young couple loved each other deeply.* **5.** *tv.* to care deeply for someone; to care very much about someone. ♦ *Sally loved her children more than anything in the world.* ♦ *John loved his closest friends.* **6.** *tv.* to enjoy something; to enjoy doing something; to have an interest in doing something. ♦ *I love playing cards with my friends.* ♦ *I love to swim.* **7. love at first sight** *idiom* love established when two people first see one another. ♦ *Bill was standing at the door when Anne opened it. It was love at first sight.* ♦ *It was love at first sight when they met, but it didn't last long.*

loveliness ['lʌv li nəs] *n.* grace and beauty. (No plural form in this sense.) ♦ *John was struck by Jane's loveliness and good manners.* ♦ *The artist's painting captured the loveliness of the young girl.*

lovely ['lʌv li] *adj.* beautiful; pretty; attractive. (Comp: *lovelier;* sup: *loveliest.*) ♦ *Have you met John's lovely wife, Jane?* ♦ *Anne wore a lovely dress to the party.*

lover ['lʌv ɚ] **1.** *n.* one of two people who love each other in a romantic way. ♦ *Bill and Jane are still lovers after 30 years of marriage.* ♦ *Tom's lover lived in another town.* **2.** *n.* someone with whom one has an affair ②. ♦ *Jane learned of her husband's lover when she found lipstick on his shirt.* ♦ *The newspaper printed a picture of the senator's lover.* **3.** *n.* someone who enjoys something; someone who enjoys doing something. ♦ *John, a lover of fine books, has an extensive library.* ♦ *The chef prepared a special meal for the lover of fine food.*

loving ['lʌv ɪŋ] *adj.* caring; gentle; affectionate; showing love. (Adv: *lovingly.*) ♦ *I feel fortunate to be part of a loving family.* ♦ *The loving mother cradled her baby in her arms.*

low ['lo] **1.** *adj.* only a little way above the ground or sea level; not high. (Comp: *lower;* sup: *lowest.*) ♦ *I placed the heavy book on a low shelf.* ♦ *The low area near the river floods often.* **2.** *adj.* near the bottom of something. (Comp: *lower;* sup: *lowest.*) ♦ *Put the book on the low shelf.* ♦ *New employees usually begin at the low end of the pay scale.* **3.** *adj.* less than average in amount, power, volume, height, intensity, cost, etc. (Comp: *lower;* sup: *lowest.*) ♦ *I buy generic food because it's low in cost.* ♦ *I have a low opinion of the mayor.* **4.** *adj.* [feeling] weak or unhappy. (Comp: *lower;* sup: *lowest.*) ♦ *Mary tries to make me happy when I'm low.* ♦ *I eat ice cream when I'm feeling low.* **5.** *adj.* mean; unkind; cruel. (Comp: *lower;* sup: *lowest.*) ♦ *I didn't respond to Bob's low insult.* ♦ *The villain was a low and mean character.* **6.** *adj.* [of a supply or of strength] inadequate or not enough. (Comp: *lower;* sup: *lowest.*) ♦ *The charge in the battery is low.* ♦ *Our supplies are low, so we have to go to the store.* **7.** *adv.* to or at a position below or near the bottom of something. ♦ *I will have to stoop* *quite low to pick the pin up off the floor.* ♦ *We crouched low behind the bush to keep from being seen.* **8.** *n.* a low ③ level or amount; a low ③ setting. (No plural form in this sense.) ♦ *I microwaved the cookie on low.* ♦ *Can you put the air conditioning on low?*

lowbrow ['lo brɑʊ] **1.** *n.* someone who is not an intellectual; someone who is not interested in the arts. ♦ *The lowbrow didn't enjoy going to the art gallery.* ♦ *The haughty artist referred to television viewers as lowbrows.* **2.** *adj.* not intellectual; not interested in the arts. ♦ *The arrogant art professor scoffed at lowbrow people.* ♦ *My lowbrow roommate refused to go to the art gallery with me.*

low-cut ['lo 'kʌt] *adj.* [of or about a dress, blouse, or shirt] having a low neckline, especially where much flesh is exposed. ♦ *The model wore a low-cut blouse when she had her picture taken.* ♦ *My mom wouldn't let me out of the house in a low-cut dress.*

low-down ['lo dɑʊn] **1.** *adj.* mean; unkind; cruel. (Informal.) ♦ *That was a low-down, rotten thing to do to a friend.* ♦ *I apologized for making such a low-down insult.* **2.** *n.* the facts about a situation; information. (No plural form in this sense. Slang.) ♦ *The inspector asked for the low-down on the case.* ♦ *The spy gave us the low-down on the enemy's tactics.*

lower ['lo ɚ] **1.** *iv.* [for something] to go from a high level to a low level. ♦ *As the sun lowered in the west, it became darker.* ♦ *The curtain lowered slowly at the end of the play.* **2.** *tv.* to cause something to go from a high level to a low level; to move something down. ♦ *The stagehand lowered the curtain at the end of the play.* ♦ *I lowered the shade over the window.* **3. lower one's sights** *idiom* to set one's goals lower. ♦ *Even though you get frustrated, don't lower your sights.* ♦ *I shouldn't lower my sights. If I work hard, I can do what I want.* **4. lower oneself to some level** *idiom* to bring oneself down to some lower level or behavior. ♦ *I refuse to lower myself to your level.* ♦ *Has TV news lowered itself to the level of the tabloids?*

lowercase ['lo ɚ 'kes] *adj.* [of a letter or letters] minuscule, not capitalized. (Compare with **uppercase**.) ♦ *The e at the end of this sentence is lowercase.* ♦ *Do not use a lowercase letter at the beginning of a sentence.*

low-fat ['lo 'fæt] *adj.* having a small percentage of fat; having less fat than regular. ♦ *I had a cup of low-fat yogurt for dessert.* ♦ *My doctor put me on a low-fat diet.*

low-grade ['lo 'gred] *adj.* not of the best quality; poor quality; bad. ♦ *I filled the rental car with low-grade gasoline.* ♦ *We both fell asleep during the low-grade film.*

low-key ['lo 'ki] *adj.* quiet; having low energy; not excited; controlled. ♦ *After a hard day, I looked forward to a low-key evening at home.* ♦ *My party was low-key until the band started playing.*

lowland ['lo lænd] *n.* land that is close to sea level; land that is lower or flatter than the area around it. (Sometimes plural with the same meaning.) ♦ *The lowland flooded when the river rose above its banks.* ♦ *The army shelled the lowlands from their forts in the mountains.*

lowly ['lo li] *adj.* humble; low in rank; simple; meek. Comp: *lowlier;* sup: *lowliest.*) ♦ *The lowly peasant worked hard and was proud of his simple life.* ♦ *The manager bossed the lowly clerk unmercifully.*

low-priced ['lo praɪst] *adj.* inexpensive; costing less money than other items of the same kind. ♦ *The department store is stocked with low-priced items of clothing.* ♦ *I bought some low-priced meat for dinner. It was really tough.*

lox ['lɑks] *n.* a kind of smoked salmon. (No plural form in this sense.) ♦ *I ate some lox with cream cheese.* ♦ *I bought a pound of lox at the delicatessen.*

loyal ['lɔɪ əl] *adj.* faithful; true to one's friends, country, or promises; supportive. (Adv: *loyally.*) ♦ *My parents have always been loyal to each other.* ♦ *The soldier remained loyal to his country even when the enemy tortured him.*

loyalty ['lɔɪ əl ti] *n.* the quality of being loyal; faithfulness. (No plural form in this sense.) ♦ *The soldier was honored for his loyalty to his country.* ♦ *Anne never questioned her husband's loyalty.*

lozenge ['lɑz ɪndʒ] *n.* a small, sweet tablet of medicine that is sucked until it has dissolved. ♦ *If your throat is sore, try one of these lozenges.* ♦ *The mint lozenge soothed my throat.*

lubricant ['lu brə kənt] **1.** *n.* a substance, such as oil, that makes it easy for two things to rub against each other. ♦ *Your car doors need some lubricant badly.* ♦ *Animal fat can be an effective lubricant at low temperatures.* **2.** *n.* kinds or types of ①. ♦ *A modern automobile uses a number of different lubricants.* ♦ *This is an excellent lubricant for delicate parts, such as the parts of a clock.*

lubricate ['lu brə ket] *tv.* to put oil or another lubricant on something so that it can move against something else smoothly. ♦ *The mechanic lubricated the car's engine with motor oil.* ♦ *I lubricated the squeaky hinge with oil.*

lubrication [lu brə 'ke ʃən] **1.** *n.* lubricating; applying lubrication. (No plural form in this sense.) ♦ *Lubrication of all moving parts will make the machine run well for years.* ♦ *Proper lubrication will keep your engine running longer.* **2.** *n.* a lubricant; something that lubricates. (No plural form in this sense.) ♦ *Your dry skin needs a different kind of lubrication.* ♦ *Petroleum jelly can be used for lubrication.*

lucid ['lus ɪd] **1.** *adj.* very easy to understand; very clear. (Adv: *lucidly.*) ♦ *The witness provided a lucid description of the accident.* ♦ *John's response was surprisingly lucid, considering how frightened he was.* **2.** *adj.* able to be understood. (Adv: *lucidly.*) ♦ *The students all understood the professor's lucid lecture.* ♦ *The lucid witness clearly described the accident to the jury.*

luck ['lʌk] **1.** *n.* random chance; fortune; chance. (No plural form in this sense.) ♦ *I won the lottery by pure luck.* ♦ *With any luck, it'll stop raining before the picnic.* **2.** *n.* good or bad fortune; success or failure. (No plural form in this sense.) ♦ *Bill was thankful for his good luck in the business world.* ♦ *The number 13 is thought to be a sign of bad luck.* **3. as luck would have it** *idiom* by good or bad luck; as it turned out; by chance. ♦ *As luck would have it, we had a flat tire.* ♦ *As luck would have it, the check came in the mail today.* **4. out of luck** *idiom* without good luck; having bad fortune. ♦ *If you wanted some ice cream, you're out of luck.* ♦ *I was out of luck. I got there too late to get a seat.*

luckily ['lʌk ə li] *adv.* in a lucky way; fortunately. ♦ *Luckily, it stopped raining before the game started.* ♦ *The driver luckily was able to avoid the accident by swerving.*

lucky ['lʌk i] **1.** *adj.* [of someone] having good luck; fortunate. (Comp: *luckier;* sup: *luckiest.*) ♦ *John's such a lucky guy. He just got a new job.* ♦ *Bob must be really lucky, because he won the lottery.* **2.** *adj.* causing good luck; bringing good fortune. (Comp: *luckier;* sup: *luckiest.*) ♦ *Anne brought her lucky charm to the casino.* ♦ *Bill is superstitious and won't travel without his lucky hat.* **3.** *adj.* showing good luck; characterized by good fortune. (Adv: *luckily.* Comp: *luckier;* sup: *luckiest.*) ♦ *What a lucky coincidence that we both arrived early!* ♦ *I won the lottery! I guess it's my lucky day.*

lucrative ['lu krə tɪv] *adj.* profitable; making money. (Adv: *lucratively.*) ♦ *Real estate is a lucrative business if you buy and sell property in expensive neighborhoods.* ♦ *I made thousands of dollars in the lucrative restaurant business.*

ludicrous ['lud ə krəs] *adj.* ridiculous; very silly; absurd. (Adv: *ludicrously.*) ♦ *The teacher didn't believe Jimmy's ludicrous excuse.* ♦ *The movie's ludicrous plot made no sense.*

lug ['lʌg] **1.** *n.* a small piece that sticks out of something. ♦ *I scraped my leg against a lug on the side of the machine.* ♦ *This nut attaches to a lug on the side of the axle.* **2.** *tv.* to carry or move someone or something heavy. ♦ *Jane lugged her baby brother while her mom carried the groceries.* ♦ *I lugged the bowling ball upstairs to the attic.*

luggage ['lʌg ɪdʒ] *n.* baggage; suitcases. (No plural form in this sense. Number is expressed with *piece(s) of luggage.*) ♦ *You can only carry two pieces of luggage onto the airplane.* ♦ *My luggage was stolen at the bus station.*

lukewarm ['luk 'worm] **1.** *adj.* slightly warm; tepid. ♦ *Make sure the baby's bathwater is just lukewarm.* ♦ *The lukewarm pop did not quench my thirst.* **2.** *adj.* without excitement; without enthusiasm. (Figurative on ①. Adv: *lukewarmly.*) ♦ *The inexperienced singer got only lukewarm applause from the audience.* ♦ *The critic gave the bad movie a lukewarm review.*

lull ['lʌl] **1.** *n.* a quiet moment between long periods of noise or activity; a temporary calm. ♦ *During a lull in the storm, we quickly got back to the shore.* ♦ *Just after lunch, there is a lull in business that allows us to take a short break.* **2. lull someone to sleep** *idiom* to cause someone to fall asleep. ♦ *The mother lulled her baby to sleep.* ♦ *The boring professor lulled the students to sleep.* **3. lull before the storm** *idiom* a quiet period just before a period of great activity or excitement. ♦ *It was very quiet in the cafeteria just before the students came in for lunch. It was the lull before the storm.* ♦ *In the brief lull before the storm, the clerks prepared themselves for the doors to open and bring in thousands of shoppers.*

lullaby ['lʌl ə baɪ] *n.* a quiet song that is sung to help someone fall asleep. ♦ *The baby fell asleep after I sang a lullaby.* ♦ *The mother sang a lullaby to quiet her crying baby.*

lumber ['lʌm bɚ] **1.** *n.* timber, logs, and boards used for building. (No plural form in this sense.) ♦ *The builders needed more lumber to finish the patio.* ♦ *Every building in the town was made of lumber.* **2.** *adj.* <the adj. use of ①.> ♦ *We bought the plywood at the lumber yard.* ♦ *New environmental regulations affected the lumber industry.* **3.** *iv.* to move in a heavy or clumsy way. ♦ *I lumbered through the hall wearing boots that were too large for me.* ♦ *The tired man lumbered toward his nice warm home.*

lumberjack ['lʌm bɚ dʒæk] *n.* someone, usually a male, whose job is to cut down trees. ♦ *The lumberjack cut down the tree with an ax.* ♦ *The paper company employed 100 lumberjacks.*

luminary ['lum ə nɛr i] **1.** *adj.* of or about light. ♦ *The physicist studied the luminary properties of incandescent light.* ♦ *The sun has a considerable luminary output.* **2.** *n.* someone who is famous. ♦ *The sports luminary signed autographs after the game.* ♦ *Talk-show hosts interview dozens of luminaries each week.*

luminous ['lum ə nəs] *adj.* giving off light; glowing in the dark. (Adv: *luminously.*) ♦ *The astronomer gazed at the luminous stars.* ♦ *The center of the road is marked with luminous white stripes.*

lump ['lʌmp] **1.** *n.* a hard mass of some substance having no specific shape. ♦ *Would you like me to put a few lumps of sugar in your coffee?* ♦ *There was a lump of gum stuck to the bottom of my desk.* **2.** *n.* a tumor; a hard swelling in the body. ♦ *The doctor removed a cancerous lump from my spine.* ♦ *Anne could feel a small lump in her breast and consulted her doctor immediately.* **3. lump together** *tv.* + *prep. phr.* to think of or treat several things as a single group; to think of several things or people as being the same or as being in the same category. ♦ *Please don't lump all teenagers together. Some of us are very polite and respectful.* ♦ *The economic report lumped the former Soviet republics together into a single unit.* **4.** *adj.* [of money paid] in a single, general payment. (Figurative on ①.) ♦ *I make a monthly lump payment for the daily paper delivery.* ♦ *You must repay this loan in one lump sum.*

lumpy ['lʌm pi] *adj.* having lumps; not smooth. (Adv: *lumpily.* Comp: *lumpier;* sup: *lumpiest.*) ♦ *My oatmeal is too lumpy.* ♦ *I sat on the uncomfortably lumpy couch.*

lunacy ['lun ə si] **1.** *n.* insanity; the condition of being insane. (No plural form in this sense. No longer commonly used for a mental illness.) ♦ *Dr. Jones prescribed drugs to treat Jane's lunacy.* ♦ *Suffering from a kind of compulsive lunacy, John was sent away to an institution.* **2.** *n.* a foolish action; a crazy ② action. (No plural form in this sense. Figurative on ①.) ♦ *Swimming during a hurricane is complete lunacy.* ♦ *It's lunacy to drive at night without headlights.*

lunar ['lun ɚ] *adj.* of or about the moon. ♦ *The astronauts brought back some lunar rocks to the earth.* ♦ *I watched the lunar landing on television.*

lunatic ['lun ə tɪk] **1.** *n.* someone who is insane; someone who is crazy ①. (No longer commonly used for a mental patient.) ♦ *The horrible murder was committed by a lunatic.* ♦ *A lunatic escaped from the mental hospital.* **2.** *n.* someone who acts wild and crazy ②. (Figurative on ①.) ♦ *Mary went to Europe on a whim. She's such a lunatic!* ♦ *A couple of lunatics in my gym class threw our gym teacher into the pool.* **3. lunatic fringe** *idiom* the more extreme members of a group; ♦ *Most of the members of that religious sect are quite reasonable, but Lisa belongs to the lunatic fringe.* ♦ *Many people try to avoid eating a lot of fat, but Mary is part of the lunatic fringe and will hardly eat anything.*

lunch ['lʌntʃ] **1.** *n.* a meal eaten around noon; a meal eaten in the middle of the day. ♦ *What would you like to eat for lunch?* ♦ *I brought my lunch to work in a paper bag.* **2.** *iv.* to eat a meal around noon; to eat ①. ♦ *I lunched at the new Italian restaurant today.* ♦ *Anne lunched with her friends from work.*

luncheon ['lʌn tʃən] *n.* a formal meal in the middle of the day. (Fancier than a lunch, and usually involving a number of people.) ♦ *The senator's campaign luncheon raised $250,000.* ♦ *I accepted an invitation for luncheon at the private club.*

lunchroom ['lʌntʃ rum] *n.* a room where people in a school, office, or factory eat lunch. ♦ *Please clean up after yourself in the lunchroom.* ♦ *I will meet you in the lunchroom for lunch.*

lung ['lʌŋ] *n.* one of a pair of organs in the body that are used when breathing. ♦ *I choked as my lungs filled with smoke from the fire.* ♦ *The lungs expel carbon dioxide when we exhale.*

lunge ['lʌndʒ] **1.** *iv.* to move forward suddenly with force. ♦ *The cat lunged at the bird.* ♦ *The car suddenly lunged forward and struck the curb.* **2.** *n.* a sudden forward movement with force. ♦ *The sudden lunge of the subway car knocked me out of my seat.* ♦ *The lion made a lunge and grabbed the zebra in its claws.*

lurch ['lɚtʃ] **1.** *n.* a sudden movement that is out of control. ♦ *The airplane's sudden lurch was caused by heavy winds.* ♦ *The subway's lurch caused me to fall.* **2.** *iv.* to move in a way that is out of control; to move without control. ♦ *The elevator lurched and fell three floors.* ♦ *The heavy winds caused the airplane to lurch.* **3. leave someone in the lurch** *idiom* to leave someone waiting for or anticipating your actions. ♦ *Where were you, John? You really left me in the lurch.* ♦ *I didn't mean to leave you in the lurch. I thought we had canceled our meeting.*

lure ['lʊr] **1.** *tv.* to try to attract or catch a person or an animal by offering something the person or animal wants; to tempt someone or something. ♦ *I lured the rabbit into the trap with a carrot.* ♦ *The prospect of fame lures actors to Hollywood.* **2.** *n.* someone or something that attracts; something that is used to attract a person or animal. ♦ *The company offered me $100,000 as a lure to sign its contract.* ♦ *The trout bit the brightly colored fishing lure.*

lurid ['lʊr ɪd] *adj.* shocking; sensational; vivid. (Adv: *luridly.*) ♦ *Bill told me about his lurid affair with Mary.* ♦ *The news report described the accident in lurid detail.*

lurk ['lɚk] **1.** *iv.* to move around without being seen, especially in an evil way. ♦ *The thief lurked in the shadows, waiting for a victim.* ♦ *The shoplifter lurked by the clothes rack.* **2.** *iv.* to hang out someplace without being noticed; to be someplace without being noticed. (Figurative on ①.) ♦ *The shy student lurked in a dark corner of the café.* ♦ *Someone is lurking near my back door, and I am frightened.* **3.** *iv.* to connect to an Internet discussion and just read messages without ever sending any. ♦ *I like to get into discussion groups on the Internet, but I only lurk. I never say anything.* ♦ *There must be thousands who lurk and only a few who ever really communicate.*

luscious ['lʌʃ əs] *adj.* very delicious; having a sweet taste or smell. (Adv: *lusciously.*) ♦ *This cherry pie is luscious.* ♦ *I bought a bottle of this luscious cologne that Bob really loves!*

lush ['lʌʃ] **1.** *adj.* luxurious; comfortable. (Adv: *lushly.* Comp: *lusher;* sup: *lushest.*) ♦ *My rich relatives live in lush surroundings.* ♦ *I couldn't afford to stay at the lush hotel a second night.* **2.** *adj.* covered with plants and thick vegetation. (Adv: *lushly.* Comp: *lusher;* sup: *lushest.*) ♦ *The explorers walked through the lush jungle.* ♦ *I grew many kinds of vegetables in my lush garden.*

lust ['lʌst] **1.** *n.* a strong desire, especially for sex. (No plural form in this sense.) ♦ *The lovers looked at each other with lust.* ♦ *The cleric revealed that he had felt lust in his heart, but never acted upon it.* **2. lust after; lust for** *iv. + prep. phr.* to desire someone or something strongly; to feel ①. ♦ *John secretly lusted after his neighbor.* ♦ *The greedy politician lusted for money and power.*

luster ['lʌs tɚ] *n.* the shine of something that is polished; gloss; bright reflected light. (No plural form in this sense.) ♦ *After I polished the tarnished silver, it regained its luster.* ♦ *The luster of a gold watch caught the thief's eye.*

lustrous ['lʌs trəs] *adj.* shiny; polished; bright. (Adv: *lustrously.*) ♦ *Anne wore a strand of lustrous pearls around her neck.* ♦ *The lustrous diamond sparkled in the sunlight.*

lusty ['lʌs ti] **1.** *adj.* full of lust; showing lust. (Adv: *lustily.* Comp: *lustier;* sup: *lustiest.*) ♦ *The lusty old man flirted with his waitress.* ♦ *I decided that my lusty thoughts were no worse than anyone else's.* **2.** *adj.* full of strength; robust; full of energy. (Adv: *lustily.* Comp: *lustier;* sup: *lustiest.*) ♦ *Anne gave birth to a lusty baby boy.* ♦ *The child's lusty yell woke up everyone in the house.*

Luxembourg ['lʌk səm bɚg] See Gazetteer.

luxurious [ləg 'ʒʊr i əs] *adj.* very comfortable; elegant; lush. (Adv: *luxuriously.*) ♦ *The movie star was used to living in luxurious houses.* ♦ *We stayed in a luxurious hotel during our honeymoon.*

luxury ['lʌg ʒə ri] **1.** *n.* expensive comfort; elegance; the very best of things. (No plural form in this sense.) ♦ *Luxury is something I will never have to get used to.* ♦ *The king and queen were accustomed to luxury and the best of care.* **2.** *n.* a comfort, especially one that is expensive; an indulgence. ♦ *Good steak is a luxury I usually can't afford.* ♦ *I occasionally enjoy the luxury of a meal in a restaurant.* **3.** *n.* something that is not necessary but which is desired. ♦ *A dishwasher is a luxury many families cannot afford.* ♦ *A telephone was considered a luxury in the 1920s.* **4. in the lap of luxury** *idiom* in luxurious surroundings. ♦ *John lives in the lap of luxury because his family is very wealthy.* ♦ *When I retire, I'd like to live in the lap of luxury.*

lying ['laɪ ɪŋ] **1.** present participle of lie. **2.** *adj.* not telling the truth; telling lies. ♦ *Shut your lying mouth!* ♦ *The lying witness was charged with perjury.*

lymph ['lɪmf] **1.** *n.* a fluid made by tissues and organs of the body that has many white blood cells. (No plural form in this sense.) ♦ *Lymph, as well as blood, flows out of a wound.* ♦ *Lymph comes from glands located throughout the body.* **2. lymph node** *n.* a gland or small organ associated with ①. ♦ *The doctor felt the lymph nodes under my armpits.* ♦ *When I was sick, all of my lymph nodes were swollen.*

lynch ['lɪntʃ] *tv.* to capture and hang someone who is thought to have committed a crime. ♦ *The townsfolk lynched the man accused of killing the shopkeeper.* ♦ *The* *prisoner was taken from the sheriff and lynched by an angry mob.*

lynx ['lɪŋks] *n.* a type of wildcat with tufted ears, a short tail, and long legs. ♦ *A lynx darted across the road in front of our jeep.* ♦ *I mistook the lynx for a baby cougar.*

lyric ['lɪr ɪk] **1.** *adj.* of or about poetry that expresses the feelings of the poet. (Adv: *lyrically* [...ɪk li].) ♦ *The poems were praised for having a special lyric quality.* ♦ *Susan expressed her anger by writing lyric poetry.* **2.** *n.* a short poem. ♦ *The poet wrote a lyric in honor of his friend's death.* ♦ *My first lyric was published by a literary journal.* **3. lyrics** *n.* the words of a song. (Treated as plural.) ♦ *I don't know the lyrics of that song. I only know the melody.* ♦ *Our band needs someone to write lyrics for our music.*

lyricist ['lɪr ə sɪst] *n.* someone who writes the words for songs or operas. ♦ *The lyricist wrote the words after I'd written the music.* ♦ *I wrote a melody to go along with the lyricist's words.*

M AND **m** ['ɛm] **1.** *n.* the 13th letter of the English alphabet. ♦ *There are two* Ms *in* medium. ♦ M *is used as an abbreviation for* medium. **2.** *n.* 1,000. (A roman numeral.) ♦ *2,000 is represented in Roman numerals as MM.* ♦ *MDCCLXXVI = 1776.* **3. 'm** See am.

ma ['mɑ] *n.* mother. (Also a term of address.) ♦ *Go ask your ma if you can come to the movies with me.* ♦ *What are we having for dinner, Ma?*

ma'am ['mæm] *cont.* "madam" ①. (A polite form of address.) ♦ *Can I help you with anything, ma'am?* ♦ *Excuse me, ma'am. Do you know what time it is?*

macaroni [mæk ə 'ron i] *n.* pasta in the shape of curved tubes. (No plural form in this sense.) ♦ *Macaroni softens when it is boiled.* ♦ *Today's special is macaroni and cheese.*

macaroon [mæk ə 'run] *n.* a cookie made from sugar, egg white, and coconut or almonds. ♦ *I ate some chocolate-covered macaroons for dessert.* ♦ *I can't eat these macaroons because I'm allergic to coconut.*

macaw [mə 'kɔ] *n.* one of several species of large, long-tailed parrots found in Mexico and South and Central America. ♦ *Jane bought a macaw at an exotic pet shop.* ♦ *There's a group of colorful macaws at the zoo.*

machete [mə 'ʃɛt i] *n.* a large, heavy knife used as a tool and a weapon. (From Spanish.) ♦ *I cut through the thick vines with my machete.* ♦ *The gardener uses a machete to cut vines and weeds.*

machine [mə 'ʃin] **1.** *n.* a device created to do some kind of work. ♦ *John threw his clothes into the washing machine.* ♦ *The machine moved the components to the assembly line.* **2.** *n.* a complex political organization that controls things or people. (Figurative on ①.) ♦ *The citizens fought to destroy the machine that was controlling politics.* ♦ *The machine guaranteed the mayor a million votes in the election.*

machinery [mə 'ʃin ə ri] **1.** *n.* machines and parts of machines, in general. (No plural form in this sense.) ♦ *Factory workers usually work with heavy machinery.* ♦ *Be careful, or your sleeve will get caught in the machinery.* **2.** *n.* the system for operating an organization; a bureaucracy. (Figurative on ①. No plural form in this sense.) ♦ *New ideas slowly moved through the company's machinery.* ♦ *The reporter exposed the corrupt machinery controlling the city.*

machinist [mə 'ʃin əst] *n.* someone who operates or fixes machines. ♦ *The assembly line was stopped while the machinist worked on it.* ♦ *The machinists at the factory bargained for more money.*

mackerel ['mɑk rəl] *n., irreg.* a blue-green, edible fish related to the tuna. (Pl: *mackerel* or *mackerels.*) ♦ *I ate a grilled mackerel for lunch.* ♦ *I cooked and cleaned the mackerel that John had caught.*

mad ['mæd] **1.** *adj.* crazy; insane; mentally ill. (Adv: *madly.* Comp: *madder;* sup: *maddest.*) ♦ *After the terrible accident, John went mad.* ♦ *The mad scientist wanted to rule the world.* **2.** *adj.* angry; upset. (Comp: *madder;* sup: *maddest.*) ♦ *I get very mad when my friends are late.* ♦ *The mad teacher yelled at the unruly students.* **3. mad about someone or something; mad for someone or something** *idiom* having a strong interest in someone or something; very enthusiastic about someone or something. ♦ *I'm absolutely mad for strawberry cheesecake.* ♦ *Anne and Bill are mad about ballroom dancing.* **4. like mad** *idiom* very intensely; very much. (Informal.) ♦ *Since I was very late, I drove down the highway like mad.* ♦ *I wrote like mad, trying to meet my deadline.*

Madagascar [mæd ə 'gæs kɚ] See Gazetteer.

madam ['mæd əm] **1.** *n.* <a polite way to address a woman.> (Formal.) ♦ *Excuse me, madam, may I help you find something?* ♦ *Madam Chairman, I move that we adjourn.* **2.** *n.* a woman who manages a brothel. ♦ *The woman arrested for being a madam was shown to be innocent.* ♦ *The police brought the madam into the station for questioning.*

made ['med] pt/pp of make.

made-to-order [med tu 'or dɚ] *adj.* custom-made; made exactly as the buyer wants. ♦ *The successful lawyer wore only made-to-order suits.* ♦ *The made-to-order kitchen was beautiful, but expensive.*

made-up ['med 'əp] **1.** *adj.* invented; thought up. ♦ *No one believed the child's made-up story.* ♦ *My boss questioned my made-up excuse for being late.* **2.** *adj.* wearing makeup. ♦ *The little girls, with their made-up faces, looked like tiny ladies.* ♦ *The made-up corpse looked very lifelike in the coffin.*

madhouse ['mæd hɑʊs] **1.** *n., irreg.* an insane asylum; a mental hospital. (Pl: [...hɑʊ zəz]. Informal.) ♦ *The mentally disturbed child was sent to a madhouse.* ♦ *The judge sentenced the insane criminal to a madhouse.* **2.** *n., irreg.* a place of confusion and chaos. (Figurative on ①.) ♦ *Our office is always a madhouse on Friday.* ♦ *The mall was a madhouse with last-minute Christmas shoppers.*

madman ['mæd mæn] **1.** *n., irreg.* a man who is insane. (Pl: madmen.) ♦ *A madman threatened to blow up the stadium.* ♦ *The police arrested the madman who attacked the mayor.* **2.** *n., irreg.* a fool; an idiot. (Figurative on ①.) ♦ *Only a madman would drive in this blizzard.* ♦ *What kind of madman would punch a police officer?*

madmen ['mæd mɛn] pl of madman.

madness ['mæd nəs] **1.** *n.* insanity; mental illness. (No plural form in this sense.) ♦ *Many forms of madness can now be treated by doctors.* ♦ *John's madness was caused by his addiction to drugs.* **2.** *n.* anger; rage. (No plural form in this sense.) ♦ *Anne's madness subsided after I explained the situation.* ♦ *Bob's madness caused him to act irrationally.*

maestro ['mɑɪ stro] *n.* an eminent conductor of an orchestra; a master conductor. (Also a term of address. From Italian. Pl in -*s.*) ♦ *The maestro spent his extra time teaching children how to play the violin.* ♦ *Thank you, Maestro, for that excellent performance.*

magazine [mæg ə 'zin] *n.* a booklet that is published at regular intervals of time. ♦ *How many magazines do you subscribe to?* ♦ *I read several current magazines on my flight to New York.*

magenta [mə 'dʒɛn tə] **1.** *n.* a bright red-purple color. (No plural form in this sense.) ♦ *The designer's kitchen was done in magenta and teal.* ♦ *I think the magenta in this painting is too bright.* **2.** *adj.* <the adj. use of ①.> ♦ *The vase was filled with magenta tulips.* ♦ *John's magenta tie looks very gaudy.*

maggot ['mæg ət] *n.* the larva of a fly; a fly before it develops into an adult fly. ♦ *A maggot looks like a short white worm.* ♦ *The rotting meat was covered with maggots.*

magic ['mædʒ ɪk] **1.** *n.* sorcery, witchcraft, and the use of supernatural powers. (No plural form in this sense.) ♦ *The witch used magic to punish her enemies.* ♦ *The villagers were afraid of the wizard's magic.* **2.** *n.* the art of performing tricks that use illusion to fool an audience. (No plural form in this sense.) ♦ *The performer's act included amazing feats of magic.* ♦ *I learned some magic when I worked at the circus.* **3.** *n.* a mysterious quality or power. (Figurative on ①. No plural form in this sense.) ♦ *The unhappy couple felt that the magic had left their marriage.* ♦ *The tourist was entranced by the magic of Niagara Falls.* **4.** *adj.* <the adj. use of ①.> (Adv: *magically* [...ɪk li].) ♦ *The witch prepared a magic potion in her cauldron.* ♦ *The children were delighted by the magic tricks at the party.*

magical ['mɑdʒ i kəl] *adj.* exciting; intriguing; romantic. (Adv: *magically* [...ɪk li].) ♦ *Bill and Mary spent a few magical moments staring into each other's eyes before one of them spoke.* ♦ *Sunrise is a magical time in the tropics.*

magician [mə 'dʒɪ ʃən] **1.** *n.* someone who practices magic. ♦ *The magician cast a spell on the evil king.* ♦ *The princess asked the magician to turn her brother into a frog.* **2.** *n.* a performer who entertains by doing tricks of illusion. ♦ *The magician pulled a rabbit out of his hat.* ♦ *I went to the circus to see the magician.*

magistrate ['mædʒ ɪ stret] *n.* a minor judge; a justice of the peace. ♦ *The defendant appeared before the magistrate.* ♦ *The magistrate performed the wedding ceremony.*

magnanimous [mæg 'næn ə məs] *adj.* noble; very kind; generous. (Adv: *magnanimously.*) ♦ *The charity thanked the millionaire for his magnanimous donation.* ♦ *I thanked my host for his magnanimous hospitality.*

magnate ['mæg net] *n.* someone who is very powerful or rich in business. ♦ *The shipping magnate bought many small shipping lines.* ♦ *The board of directors accused the oil magnate of fraud.*

magnesium [mæg 'niz i əm] *n.* a very light, metallic, chemical element often used to produce aircraft parts and photographic equipment. (No plural form in this sense.) ♦ *The atomic symbol for magnesium is Mg.* ♦ *The atomic number of magnesium is 12.*

magnet ['mæg nət] **1.** *n.* an iron or steel object that draws other iron or steel toward it. ♦ *I picked up the paper clips with a magnet.* ♦ *I stuck a recipe to the refrigerator door with a magnet.* **2.** *n.* someone or something that things or people are attracted toward. (Informal. Figurative on ①.) ♦ *Jane is a magnet for depressed, lonely men.* ♦ *An unlocked car is a crime magnet.*

magnetic [mæg 'nɛt ɪk] **1.** *adj.* able to draw or attract iron or steel in the way that a magnet does. (Adv: *magnetically* [...ɪk li].) ♦ *The magnetic attraction of the north pole is evident in the movement of the needle of a compass.* ♦ *The pieces of iron were stuck together by magnetic force.* **2.** *adj.* able to be magnetized; able to be harmed or affected by magnetism. (Adv: *magnetically* [...ɪk li].) ♦ *Don't let your magnetic computer disk get too close to electrical equipment.* ♦ *I stored the data on magnetic tape.* **3.** *adj.* attracting people; captivating; alluring. (Figurative on ①. Adv: *magnetically* [...ɪk li].) ♦ *Susan's magnetic personality made everyone like her.* ♦ *I couldn't escape John's magnetic charm.*

magnetism ['mæg nɪ tɪz əm] **1.** *n.* the physical laws that explain magnets and how they attract metal. (No plural form in this sense.) ♦ *One of the properties of magnetism is that opposite poles attract.* ♦ *The physics exam will cover principles of magnetism.* **2.** *n.* a charm or attraction that attracts people toward someone; charisma. (Figurative on ①. No plural form in this sense.) ♦ *The senator's magnetism propelled him to the White House.* ♦ *The successful lawyer had a personal magnetism that no one could explain.*

magnetize ['mæg nɪ tɑɪz] **1.** *tv.* to cause an object to become magnetic. ♦ *I magnetized the paper clip by stroking it with a magnet.* ♦ *My screwdriver is magnetized, so it will pick up screws.* **2.** *tv.* to affect things or people in a way that attracts them. (Figurative on ①.) ♦ *The glamour of Hollywood magnetized the actors seeking fame.* ♦ *The cult leader magnetized all of his followers to do his bidding.*

magnification [mæg nə fə 'ke ʃən] **1.** *n.* making something appear larger, usually involving the use of a lens. (No plural form in this sense.) ♦ *Magnification makes images appear larger.* ♦ *How much magnification does this photo require to make the subject look big enough?* **2.** *n.* making someone or something seem larger or more important than it really is. (No plural form in this sense. Figurative on ①.) ♦ *The media's magnification of the mayor's faults hurt his career.* ♦ *The magnification of the problem caused a lot of undue worry.*

magnificence [mæg 'nɪf ɪ səns] *n.* impressiveness; the quality of being magnificent. (No plural form in this sense.) ♦ *I was impressed by the magnificence of the church.* ♦ *The magnificence of the sunset moved me to tears.*

magnificent [mæg 'nɪf ɪ sənt] **1.** *adj.* impressive; grand; splendid; stately. (Adv: *magnificently.*) ♦ *The prince's magnificent wedding cost millions of dollars.* ♦ *The magnificent mansion had dozens of bedrooms.* **2.** *adj.* excellent; superb; brilliant. (Adv: *magnificently.*) ♦ *Dinner was magnificent! Thank you!* ♦ *The singer's magnificent performance deserved lots of applause.*

magnify ['mæg nə fɑɪ] **1.** *tv.* to cause someone or something to seem or look larger, especially by looking through a lens. ♦ *The botanist used a microscope to magnify the plant cell 250 times.* ♦ *The scientist magnified the image so she could study it better.* **2.** *tv.* to exaggerate something; to make something seem better or worse than it is. (Figurative on ①.) ♦ *The newspaper magnified the candidate's past errors.* ♦ *Singing loudly only magnified the flaws in Lisa's voice.*

magnitude ['mæg nı tud] **1.** *n.* size; the greatness of size. (No plural form in this sense.) ♦ *An earthquake of enormous magnitude struck the small town.* ♦ *The magnitude of the epidemic amazed the doctors.* **2.** *n.* [of something] importance; a level of importance. (No plural form in this sense. Figurative on ①.) ♦ *The president deals with problems of great magnitude.* ♦ *Don't bother me with problems of such a small magnitude.* **3.** *n.* a degree of measurement of the brightness of a star. ♦ *That star has a magnitude of .5.* ♦ *Some stars have a variable magnitude and appear much brighter now and then.*

magnolia [mæg 'nol jə] **1.** *n.* a kind of tree that has large, sweet-smelling, white or pink flowers. ♦ *I never smelled a magnolia until I moved to the South.* ♦ *The garden was filled with the scent of magnolias.* **2.** *n.* the blossom of ①. ♦ *I picked a pink magnolia for my friend.* ♦ *Put this magnolia in a vase.*

mahogany [mə 'hɔg ə ni] **1.** *n.* a tree that has very hard, reddish-brown wood. ♦ *Behind the farm grew a grove of mahoganies.* ♦ *Mahoganies grows well in South and Central America.* **2.** *n.* wood from ①. (No plural form in this sense.) ♦ *Our dinner table is made of solid mahogany.* ♦ *The carpenter bought some mahogany at the lumberyard.* **3.** *adj.* made from ②. ♦ *I bought four antique mahogany chairs.* ♦ *My grandmother willed me her mahogany rocking chair.*

maid ['med] *n.* a woman who is paid to cook, clean, and do other work around the house; a female servant. ♦ *The maid brought our dinner to the table.* ♦ *The maid does laundry every Wednesday.*

maiden ['med n] **1.** *n.* an unmarried woman. (Used mostly in literature.) ♦ *The brave knight saved the maiden who was locked in the tower.* ♦ *The dragon carried the young maiden back to its cave.* **2. maiden name** *n.* the last name of an unmarried woman. ♦ *John's middle name is his mother's maiden name.* ♦ *What's your sister's maiden name?* **3. maiden voyage** *n.* first voyage; initial voyage. ♦ *The* Titanic *sank on her maiden voyage.* ♦ *We were on the maiden voyage of the new cruise ship.* **4.** *adj.* unmarried and female. ♦ *My maiden aunt has never married.* ♦ *The young duke courted the maiden princess.*

mail ['mel] **1.** *n.* letters and packages that are delivered by the post office. (No plural form in this sense. Number is expressed with *piece(s) of mail.*) ♦ *I checked my mailbox for today's mail.* ♦ *There's nothing but bills in today's mail.* **2. the mail** *n.* the postal system. (Treated as singular.) ♦ *Will this vase break if I send it through the mail?* ♦ *My check is in the mail.* **3.** *tv.* to send a letter or package by ②. ♦ *I mailed you a check last week.* ♦ *How much postage do I need to mail this package?*

mailbox ['mel bɑks] **1.** *n.* a place where mail is put so it can be picked up and taken to the post office and then delivered. ♦ *I dropped my letters in the mailbox on the corner.* ♦ *This mailbox is emptied every day at 4:00* P.M. **2.** *n.* a container into which a mail carrier delivers mail. ♦ *I checked my mailbox when I got home from work.* ♦ *My mailbox is full of bills!* **3.** *n.* the electronic version of ②, where e-mail is received. ♦ *My mailbox is filled with advertising messages.* ♦ *I erased all the e-mail in my mailbox.*

mail carrier AND **letter carrier** ['mel kɛr ı ɚ, 'lɛt ɚ kɛr ı ɚ] *n.* someone who works for the postal system and picks up and delivers mail. ♦ *The mail carrier usually gets to my house around noon.* ♦ *My dog always barks at letter carriers.*

mailman ['mel 'mæn] *n., irreg.* someone who works for the postal system and picks up and delivers mail; a mail carrier. (Pl: mailmen.) ♦ *My mailman left a large package for me at my neighbor's house.* ♦ *The mailman picks up the mail from that mailbox at noon.*

mailmen ['mel 'mɛn] pl of mailman.

maim ['mem] *tv.* to injure a part of the body so that it can no longer be used. ♦ *John's hand was maimed by a piece of heavy machinery.* ♦ *The vicious dog maimed Bill's leg.*

main ['men] **1.** *adj.* most important; primary; chief. (Adv: *mainly.*) ♦ *The main artery is known as the aorta.* ♦ *Roast beef is the main course tonight.* **2.** *n.* an important pipe that carries water, sewage, gas, etc. ♦ *When the water main burst, our street flooded.* ♦ *Our gas was shut off while the work was being done on the main.*

Maine ['men] See Gazetteer.

mainframe ['men frem] *n.* a very powerful computer system that allows many people to access, enter, or retrieve information from it at the same time. (Compare with microcomputer, minicomputer.) ♦ *The computer system manager had to boot the mainframe every morning to get it started.* ♦ *I couldn't do any work because of problems with the mainframe.*

mainland ['men lænd] *n.* the part of a country that is part of a continent; the parts of a country that are not islands. (No plural form in this sense.) ♦ *The islanders' children went to school on the mainland.* ♦ *After moving through the islands, the hurricane struck the mainland.*

mainstay ['men ste] *n.* someone or something serving as the main means of support. ♦ *My brother John is the mainstay of our family since the death of our father.* ♦ *Having good products that people will buy is the mainstay of our business.*

mainstream ['men strim] **1.** *adj.* ordinary; regular; having to do with social practices considered normal by the majority of people in a society. ♦ *Bob does not like the mainstream ideas of the middle class.* ♦ *John was bored with the mainstream education he was getting at college.* **2.** *tv.* to integrate students with disabilities into classrooms containing students who are not disabled. ♦ *The disabled students were mainstreamed by court order.* ♦ *The blind student was mainstreamed at her parents' request.* **3. in the mainstream (of something)** *idiom* following the current trends or styles that are popular or are considered normal. ♦ *Bob is too old-fashioned to be in the mainstream of modern living.* ♦ *Max likes to make fun of people in the mainstream.*

maintain [men 'ten] **1.** *tv.* to continue to do something as before; to keep doing something. ♦ *At the intersection, maintain a straight course.* ♦ *The senator maintained her dignity during the trial.* **2.** *tv.* to take care of something; to make sure that something works properly. ♦ *If you maintain an automobile properly, it will last longer.* ♦ *Mary* *maintained her computer by cleaning it regularly.* **3.** *tv.* to support someone or something, especially with money. ♦ *The very rich family maintained a large household staff.* ♦ *The art museum was maintained by a large government grant.* **4.** *tv.* to assert an opinion; to defend one's opinion when it has been contradicted. (Takes a clause.) ♦ *I continue to maintain that your ideas are old-fashioned!* ♦ *The professor maintained that the theory was flawed.*

maintenance ['men tə nəns] *n.* keeping equipment and supplies in good condition. (No plural form in this sense.) ♦ *Proper car maintenance includes checking its oil regularly.* ♦ *Without proper maintenance, mechanical equipment will break down.*

majestic [mə 'dʒɛs tɪk] *adj.* showing majesty; dignified; impressive. (Adv: *majestically* [...ɪk li].) ♦ *We went into a majestic dining room and were seated at a table that was longer than our house!* ♦ *The tourists were led around the majestic castle.*

majesty ['mædʒ ə sti] **1.** *n.* dignity; greatness. (No plural form in this sense.) ♦ *I bowed before the majesty of the king and queen.* ♦ *The tourists were impressed by the majesty of the palace.* **2. Majesty** *n.* <a title or form of address used to address a king or queen.> (Follows *Your, His, Her,* or *Their.*) ♦ *There's a likeness of Her Majesty on British currency.* ♦ *May I trouble Your Majesty with a small request?*

major ['me dʒɚ] **1.** *adj.* large in size or amount; great; important; serious. ♦ *A major fire threatened hundreds of homes.* ♦ *The president was greatly troubled by the major political crisis.* **2.** *adj.* primary; more important. ♦ *My major field of study is European history.* ♦ *Conservation has become the major effort in our community.* **3.** *n.* an officer in the army, air force, or marines above a captain and below a lieutenant colonel. (Sometimes a term of address.) ♦ *The captain received his orders from the major.* ♦ *I saluted Major Williams when I passed him on the street.* **4.** *n.* a student's primary area of study. ♦ *We want to hire someone who has a major in computer programming.* ♦ *Sue knows a lot about history because that's her major.* **5.** *n.* someone whose major ④ is in a certain subject. ♦ *There were mostly history majors at the party.* ♦ *My roommate is dating a chemistry major.* **6. major in** *iv.* + *prep. phr.* to concentrate one's studies in a certain subject. ♦ *Anne is majoring in chemistry.* ♦ *Do you know what subject you're going to major in yet?*

majority [mə 'dʒor ə ti] **1.** *n.* those people who are part of the largest group or division of people, considered as a single group. (No plural form in this sense. Treated as singular.) ♦ *The majority is always right.* ♦ *In voting, the majority rules.* **2.** *n.* [in a group] a number of people or things or people equal to more than half of the whole group, considered as individuals. (No plural form in this sense. Treated as plural. See also plurality.) ♦ *The majority of people in my neighborhood are Italian.* ♦ *The majority of the people who came to my party weren't invited.* **3.** *n.* the largest number of votes; a number of votes equal to a specific proportion of all the votes. ♦ *No one had a majority. It was a tie.* ♦ *Passage of this bill requires a two-thirds majority.* **4. age of majority** *n.* the legal age of adulthood. (No plural form in this sense.) ♦ *The age of majority in America is 18, but the drinking age is 21.* ♦ *Men must register for the draft when they reach the age of majority.*

majuscule ['mædʒ ə skjul] **1.** *adj.* [of letters that are] capitalized. (Compare with minuscule.) ♦ *The banner was printed with majuscule letters.* ♦ *The majuscule form of a is A.* **2.** *n.* a capital letter. ♦ *The poster was printed with majuscules only.* ♦ *The first letter of every chapter was an ornate majuscule.*

make ['mek] **1.** *tv., irreg.* to bring something into being; to put something together from other parts; to form something; to build something; to produce something. (Pt/pp: made.) ♦ *John made a table out of mahogany.* ♦ *I will make a peanut butter sandwich for Jane.* **2.** *tv., irreg.* to cause someone or something to be in a certain condition. ♦ *Fishing makes Grandpa happy.* ♦ *Bob's insult made me mad.* **3.** *tv., irreg.* to cause someone or something to do something; to force someone or something to do something. (Takes a bare verb.) ♦ *Jane made Bob drive her to the store.* ♦ *Anne made me tell her the truth.* **4.** *tv., irreg.* to prepare a legal document. ♦ *The union made an agreement with management.* ♦ *Grandpa made a will two weeks before he died.* **5.** *tv., irreg.* to assign someone to a job; to appoint someone to a position. ♦ *My boss made me secretary when the old one quit.* ♦ *The company made Sue manager of finance.* **6.** *tv., irreg.* to earn something; to acquire something. ♦ *My boss made $100,000 last year.* ♦ *How much money do you think I make?* **7.** *tv., irreg.* to arrive at a place; to reach something. ♦ *I didn't make the 9:00 train, so I took a taxi instead.* ♦ *If we don't stop for dinner, we can make Minneapolis in an hour.* **8. make up** *tv., irreg.* + *adv.* to put makeup on someone. ♦ *I have to make myself up before the party.* ♦ *The actors made each other up before each performance.* **9.** *iv., irreg.* to become something; to assume a certain status or job. ♦ *Susan will make a good banker when she graduates.* ♦ *Tom makes a good chef.* **10. make up** *iv., irreg.* + *adv.* to put on makeup. ♦ *Do I have enough time to make up?* ♦ *Bill made up quickly for the play, because he arrived late.* **11.** *n.* a brand; a certain style or kind. ♦ *I bought the most expensive make of television set.* ♦ *The car dealer had many foreign makes.* **12. make a bed; make someone's bed** *idiom* to fix the sheets of a bed that has been slept in. ♦ *The hotel maid made our bed.* ♦ *Billy had to make his bed before he went to school.* **13. make a friend; make friends** *idiom* to establish a link of friendship with someone. ♦ *I have never found it difficult to make friends.* ♦ *Mary had to make new friends when she changed schools.* **14. make it** *idiom* to succeed; to realize a goal. ♦ *If you don't study, you'll never make it.* ♦ *Bill was proud that he made it on his own without anyone's help.* **15. make something up** *idiom* to create a story or a lie. ♦ *That's not true! You just made it up!* ♦ *Bob made up a story about a tiny mouse and its friends.* **16. make up for something** *idiom* to give recompense for something; to provide enough of something to balance a lack of it. ♦ *Here is a cup of sugar to make up for the one that I borrowed.* ♦ *I hope this money makes up for the damage I did to your car.* **17. make up (with someone)** *idiom* to reconcile with someone; to end a disagreement (with someone). ♦ *Bill and Max decided to make up.* ♦ *They made up with each other and are still very good friends.*

makeshift ['mek ʃɪft] *adj.* working for the moment; temporarily being used in place of something. ♦ *The doctor used a scarf as a makeshift tourniquet.* ♦ *The children used Billy's book bag as a makeshift base in their game.*

makeup ['mek əp] **1.** *n.* cosmetics; something applied to the face to improve its appearance. (No plural form in this sense.) ♦ *Lipstick is a kind of makeup.* ♦ *Mary put on her makeup before she went to the party.* **2.** *n.* the contents or constituents of something. (No plural form in this sense.) ♦ *The makeup of the guest list includes family and coworkers.* ♦ *The makeup of the faculty by sex is 40% female and 60% male.* **3.** *adj.* <the adj. use of ①.> ♦ *I keep a small makeup mirror in my purse.* ♦ *My sister works at the makeup counter of a department store.*

making ['mek ɪŋ] **1.** *n.* the process of being made. (No plural form in this sense.) ♦ *The producer financed the making of the movie.* ♦ *The documentary showed the making of a nuclear bomb.* **2. have the makings of something** *idiom* to possess the qualities that are needed for something. ♦ *The young boy had the makings of a fine baseball player.* ♦ *My boss has all the makings of a prison warden.*

maladjusted [mæl ə 'dʒʌs tɪd] **1.** *adj.* [of something mechanical] not adjusted correctly. ♦ *The maladjusted printer leaked ink onto the floor.* ♦ *The maladjusted watch never gave the correct time.* **2.** *adj.* not well adjusted; having mental problems that cause unhappiness. (Figurative on ①.) ♦ *The maladjusted child set his bedroom on fire.* ♦ *The school counselor tried to help the maladjusted teenager.*

maladjustment [mæl ə 'dʒʌst mənt] **1.** *n.* the state of a mechanism that is not properly adjusted. ♦ *The mechanic corrected a small maladjustment in the engine.* ♦ *The plane crashed because of a mechanical maladjustment.* **2.** *n.* the condition of having mental problems that make one unhappy. (Figurative on ①. No plural form in this sense.) ♦ *Because of his maladjustment, Jimmy caused trouble at school.* ♦ *The tabloid commented on the famous celebrity's maladjustment.*

maladroit ['mæl ə droɪt] *adj.* [of movement] not adroit; clumsy; awkward. (From French. Adv: *maladroitly.*) ♦ *Bob's maladroit driving finally led to a serious accident.* ♦ *The mayor's maladroit handling of the press conference affected his public image.*

malady ['mæl ə di] *n.* a sickness; an illness. ♦ *My frail neighbor suffers from an incurable malady.* ♦ *The doctor treated my malady with antibiotics.*

malaise [mæ 'lez] *n.* feelings of sickness of the mind, body, or spirit; depression. (No plural form in this sense.) ♦ *After his divorce, an intense malaise confined Bill to his bed.* ♦ *The general tried to counteract the malaise that affected the troops.*

malaria [mə 'lɛr i ə] *n.* a parasitic disease carried by infected mosquitoes in tropical areas, causing chills and fever. (No plural form in this sense.) ♦ *The tourists took medication to protect themselves from malaria.* ♦ *An outbreak of malaria struck the small tropical village.*

Malaysia [mə 'le ʒə] See Gazetteer.

malcontent ['mæl kən tɛnt] **1.** *n.* someone who is not happy with the way things are; someone who is not content. ♦ *There are a few malcontents who are never happy with anything or anybody.* ♦ *The mayor suggested that the malcontents leave the country.* **2.** *adj.* not content; not satisfied; not happy with the way things are. (Adv: *malcontentedly* [mæl kən 'tɛn təd li].) ♦ *I became malcontent with the way the problem had been handled.* ♦ *The citizens were generally malcontent with government in general.*

male ['mel] **1.** *adj.* of or about men or boys; of or about animals of the sex that is, at maturity, capable of producing sperm cells. ♦ *A male sheep is called a ram.* ♦ *The Smiths named their first male child John.* **2.** *adj.* [of an electrical or electronic connector] having prongs, poles, or rods to be inserted into or between electrical contacts. ♦ *You can't connect two male plugs!* ♦ *The male connector plugs into the wall receptacle.* **3.** *n.* a male ① human or animal. ♦ *So far, all American presidents have been males.* ♦ *The males at the party challenged the females to a game of basketball.*

malefactor ['mæl ə fæk tɚ] *n.* someone who does wrong or evil; a criminal. ♦ *The malefactor plotted to overthrow the government.* ♦ *The judge sentenced the malefactor to life in prison.*

malevolent [mə 'lɛv ə lənt] *adj.* evil; seeking to do evil. (Adv: *malevolently.*) ♦ *The dictator pursued his malevolent plan.* ♦ *A malevolent wizard changed the innocent frog into a handsome prince faced with enormous responsibilities.*

malfeasance [mæl 'fi zəns] *n.* error committed by a government official who does something that is not legal or not appropriate. (No plural form in this sense. Number is expressed with *act(s) of malfeasance.*) ♦ *The senator's malfeasance led to his expulsion from the Senate.* ♦ *The governor's latest act of malfeasance was reported by the local news.*

malfunction [mæl 'fʌŋk ʃən] **1.** *n.* a failure to work properly; the inability to work properly. ♦ *I used the stairs because of a malfunction with the elevator.* ♦ *A computer malfunction destroyed the company's records.* **2.** *iv.* to fail to work properly; to be unable to work properly; to stop working properly. ♦ *When my computer malfunctioned, my term paper was deleted.* ♦ *Since the elevator had malfunctioned, we had to take the stairs.*

malice ['mæl ɪs] *n.* the desire to harm someone or something; the desire to do something evil. (No plural form in this sense.) ♦ *Bob felt a lot of malice toward his sloppy roommate.* ♦ *The thief was filled with malice for the police.*

malicious [mə 'lɪ ʃəs] *adj.* [of someone] wanting to harm someone or something. (Adv: *maliciously.*) ♦ *Some malicious person slashed my car tires.* ♦ *The bully's motives were malicious.*

malign [mə 'laɪn] *tv.* to say false, evil things about someone or something. ♦ *The reporter who maligned the actor was sued for slander.* ♦ *The mayor was unfairly maligned by an aide who'd been fired.*

malignant [mə 'lɪg nənt] **1.** *adj.* evil; causing harm; wanting to cause harm. (Adv: *malignantly.*) ♦ *The malignant appearance of the old house frightened us.* ♦ *Pretending to be a ghost, Sally scowled and made the most malignant smile I have ever seen!* **2.** *adj.* [of a tumor] cancerous. (Figurative on ①. Adv: *malignantly.*) ♦ *The doctor removed a malignant tumor from the patient's lung.* ♦ *My doctor diagnosed the growth on my skin as malignant.*

malinger [mə 'lɪŋ gɚ] *iv.* to pretend to be sick so one does not have to work. ♦ *John spent so much time malingering that he was finally fired.* ♦ *The second time the soldier malingered, he was forced to clean all the toilets.*

mall ['mɔl] **1.** *n.* a large building with many stores inside; a shopping center. ♦ *John bought a birthday present for Anne at the mall.* ♦ *After school, I met my friends at the mall.* **2.** *n.* a spacious, formal walkway, usually lined with trees. ♦ *The mall led to the front entrance of the courthouse.* ♦ *The hot dog vendor wheeled his cart down the mall in the park.*

mallard ['mæl ɚd] *n.* a common duck found throughout the Northern Hemisphere. ♦ *The pond was covered with noisy mallards.* ♦ *The hunter cooked and ate the mallard he'd shot earlier in the day.*

malleable ['mæl i ə bəl] **1.** *adj.* able to be shaped without breaking; able to be hammered into a new shape. (Adv: *malleably.*) ♦ *Pure gold is very malleable.* ♦ *The sculptor shaped the malleable clay into a bust of the mayor.* **2.** *adj.* [of someone] easily changed or influenced. (Figurative on ①. Adv: *malleably.*) ♦ *Tom is very malleable, and I can get him to do anything I want.* ♦ *I am not at all malleable, so you will have to put up with me the way I am.*

mallet ['mæl ət] *n.* a tool shaped like a hammer with a large head. ♦ *Croquet is played with a mallet that has a long handle.* ♦ *I drove the peg into the board with a mallet.*

malnourished [mæl 'nɚ ɪʃt] *adj.* not nourished enough; not getting enough nutrients; not eating enough good food. (Adv: *malnourishedly.*) ♦ *The malnourished child was sent to the hospital.* ♦ *I contributed money to help feed malnourished families.*

malnutrition [mæl nu 'trɪ ʃən] *n.* the medical condition caused by not eating enough healthy food. (No plural form in this sense.) ♦ *Malnutrition is a serious global problem.* ♦ *The neglected orphan suffered from malnutrition.*

malpractice [mæl 'præk tɪs] *n.* a harmful action by a doctor or lawyer that is not professional, ethical, or legal. (No plural form in this sense.) ♦ *The doctor who performed the wrong operation was sued for malpractice.* ♦ *The lawyer who was found guilty of malpractice was disbarred.*

malt ['mɔlt] **1.** *n.* sprouted and dried barley, or a similar grain, used especially to make beer or whisky. (No plural form in this sense.) ♦ *The brewery stored thousands of bushels of malt.* ♦ *The malt was mixed with water and fermented.* **2.** *n.* a drink made with milk or ice cream flavored with powdered ①. ♦ *I'd like a malt made with vanilla ice cream, please.* ♦ *I drank a chocolate malt with dinner.*

mama ['mɑ mə] See mommy.

mammal ['mæm əl] *n.* one of a large class of warm-blooded animals whose females are able to produce milk to feed their young. ♦ *Kinds of mammals are humans, apes, dogs, cats, rodents, cattle, sheep, horses, and bats.* ♦ *Whales and dolphins are marine mammals.*

mammoth ['mæm əθ] **1.** *n.* a large, extinct, hairy elephant with large curved tusks. ♦ *A large mammoth was on display at the museum.* ♦ *Many mammoths were trapped in large pits of tar.* **2.** *adj.* very large; huge. (Figurative on ①.) ♦ *I ate a mammoth hamburger for dinner!* ♦ *A mammoth pile of work lay on my desk.*

man ['mæn] **1.** *n., irreg.* an adult male person. (Pl: men.) ♦ *I asked the man standing next to me to tell me the time.* ♦ *My history professor is a 60-year-old man.* **2.** *n., irreg.* a human being; ① or a woman. ♦ *Sometimes the best man for a job is a woman.* ♦ *Now is the time for all good men to come to the aid of their country.* **3.** *n., irreg.* the human race; all people. (No plural form in this sense.) ♦ *Darwin wrote about the origins of man.* ♦ *Man is a warm-blooded animal.* **4.** *n., irreg.* a brave, virile, or responsible ①. ♦ *"Be a man and stand up for yourself," Mr. Smith told Billy.* ♦ *Are you a man, or do you let everyone boss you around?* **5.** *n.* <a term of address, used especially to get someone's attention.> (No plural form in this sense. Informal. Not limited to males.) ♦ *Hey, man, where have you been?* ♦ *Man, did you just hear what happened on 47th Street?* **6. young man** *n.* a boy of any age; a male who is young, relative to the speaker. (Also a term of address.) ♦ *A nice young man helped me across the street.* ♦ *Thank you, young man, for opening the door for me.* **7.** *tv.* to provide a business or organization with one's services or labor. ♦ *Volunteers manned the phones during the telethon.* ♦ *The café was manned by college students.* **8. man about town** *idiom* a fashionable man who leads a sophisticated life. ♦ *He prefers a nightclub to a quiet night at home—quite a man about town.* ♦ *Bob's too much of a man about town to go to a football game.* **9. man in the street** *idiom* the ordinary person. ♦ *Politicians rarely care what the man in the street thinks.* ♦ *The man in the street has little interest in literature.*

manage ['mæn ɪdʒ] **1.** *tv.* to be in charge of someone or something; to guide someone or something. ♦ *Mary managed the workers on the second shift.* ♦ *The football team was managed by a former player.* **2. manage to** *iv.* + *inf.* to be able to do something, even though there are problems. ♦ *I managed to finish the project on time.* ♦ *We managed to solve the problem without your help.*

manageability [mæn ɪdʒ ə 'bɪl ə ti] *n.* the ability to be managed or controlled easily. (No plural form in this sense.) ♦ *This shampoo improves the manageability of my hair.* ♦ *To improve your workers' manageability, pay them more.*

manageable ['mæn ɪdʒ ə bəl] *adj.* able to be managed or controlled easily. (Adv: *manageably.*) ♦ *This shampoo makes my hair more manageable.* ♦ *The puppy is still young and not very manageable.*

management ['mæn ɪdʒ mənt] **1.** *n.* the people in charge of a company; the people who manage an organization. (No plural form in this sense.) ♦ *The management offered the union a fair contract.* ♦ *Management laid off a portion of the work force to improve profits.* **2.** *n.* the practice of managing someone or something, such as business, time, money, or workers. (No plural form in this sense.) ♦ *The owner entrusted the management of the company to his daughter.* ♦ *The company went bankrupt because the owner wasn't skilled in management.*

manager ['mæn ə dʒɚ] *n.* someone who manages or controls someone or something. ♦ *I asked the box office manager to refund my ticket.* ♦ *The store manager took the money that was in the cash register to the bank.*

managerial [mæn ə 'dʒɪr i əl] *adj.* of or about the duties of a manager or of management. (Adv: *managerially.*) ♦ *Firing half the workers was a managerial decision.* ♦ *Hiring and firing were part of my managerial duties.*

manatee ['mæn ə ti] *n.* a large, aquatic mammal that is found in warm waters and that feeds on water plants. ♦ *The city aquarium keeps a huge manatee in a tank.* ♦ *Manatees move very slowly and can be struck by boats.*

mandarin ['mæn də rɪn] **1. Mandarin** *n.* the official language of China. (No plural form in this sense.) ♦ *I spoke Mandarin to the waiter at the Chinese restaurant.* ♦ *The grammar of Mandarin is very different from that of English.* **2. Mandarin** *n.* one of the regional cuisines of China. (No plural form in this sense.) ♦ *Do you prefer Mandarin or something more spicy?* ♦ *Mandarin would be just fine.* **3.** *n.* a small orange, much like a tangerine. ♦ *I ate some frozen yogurt that was flavored with mandarins.* ♦ *I am carrying a sandwich and two mandarins for lunch.* **4. Mandarin** *adj.* <the adj. use of ②.> ♦ *I bought a special cooking pan so I could make Mandarin dishes more easily.* ♦ *The Chinese restaurant specialized in Mandarin cuisine.* **5.** *adj.* made from or with ③. ♦ *The hostess served mandarin sherbet for dessert.* ♦ *The bakery has mandarin tarts and strawberry tarts today.*

mandate ['mæn det] **1.** *n.* an official command; an official order from a higher authority to a lower authority. ♦ *Do federal mandates interfere with the rights of the states?* ♦ *The national drug policy was set by a government mandate.* **2.** *n.* the will of the people, as spelled out by their election of a particular candidate. ♦ *The people have given me a mandate to end inflation.* ♦ *The election results are a mandate against government waste.* **3.** *tv.* to demand something; to order something. ♦ *The government mandates that the states are to comply with federal legislation.* ♦ *The government has mandated a balanced budget.*

mandatory ['mæn də tor i] *adj.* obligatory; not optional; required. (Adv: *mandatorily.*) ♦ *Many colleges have mandatory foreign-language requirements.* ♦ *The mandatory sentence for many crimes is life imprisonment.*

mandible ['mæn də bəl] **1.** *n.* the lower jaw. ♦ *The driver's mandible was broken in the car accident.* ♦ *I couldn't move my mandible until a week after surgery.* **2.** *n.* either of the two jaw-like parts of an insect's mouth that bite and crush food. ♦ *The ant held a breadcrumb between its mandibles.* ♦ *The scientist examined the beetle's mandibles underneath a microscope.*

mane ['men] *n.* the stiff, upright hairs that run down the back of a horse's neck; the long hairs that grow around a male lion's face and neck. ♦ *I held on to the horse's mane as the horse galloped across the field.* ♦ *The lion's mane makes it look fierce.*

maneuver [mə 'nu vɚ] **1.** *n.* a planned or skillful movement. ♦ *The chauffeur's skillful maneuver saved the president's life.* ♦ *At the last moment, the basketball player made a clever maneuver that allowed a goal to be made.* **2.** *iv.* to move somewhere as with ①. ♦ *The pilot maneuvered through the dark storm cloud.* ♦ *City drivers must maneuver carefully through narrow streets.* **3.** *tv.* to move something in a way that requires skill or planning. ♦ *The movers maneuvered the piano up the staircase.* ♦ *The driver maneuvered the truck through the narrow alley.*

manganese ['mæŋ gə niz] *n.* a metallic chemical element that is necessary for human and animal life. (No plural form in this sense.) ♦ *The atomic symbol for manganese is Mn, and the atomic number of manganese is 25.* ♦ *I bought vitamins that provide me with the daily requirement for manganese.*

manger ['men dʒɚ] **1.** *n.* a long box on a farm that holds food for horses, cattle, pigs, or other animals while they eat; a trough. (Not in frequent use.) ♦ *The farmer filled the manger with cattle feed.* ♦ *The hungry pigs crowded around the manger.* **2. dog in the manger** *idiom* one who prevents other people from doing or having what one does not wish them to do or have. ♦ *Jane is a real dog in the manger. She cannot drive, but she will not lend anyone her car.* ♦ *If Bob were not such a dog in the manger, he would let his brother have that tuxedo he never wears.*

mangle ['mæŋ gəl] *tv.* to crush something; to mutilate something; to cut or tear something. ♦ *My kite was mangled when it blew into the tree.* ♦ *The worker's hand was mangled when it got caught in the machine.*

manhandle ['mæn hæn dəl] *tv.* to grab or hold someone or something roughly; to move or push someone or something forcefully. ♦ *The police manhandled the criminal who had shot at them.* ♦ *My dog will bite you if you try to manhandle him.*

manhole ['mæn hol] *n.* a covered hole, usually in the pavement, that gives access to underground sewers and utility tunnels. ♦ *The manhole is covered with an iron lid.* ♦ *The city workers climbed into the tunnel through the manhole.*

manhood ['mæn hʊd] *n.* the condition of being a man; features and qualities that are associated with men. (No plural form in this sense.) ♦ *The cowboy gets into fights whenever he feels his manhood is questioned.* ♦ *The teenaged boy entered manhood by going hunting with his dad.*

manhunt ['mæn hənt] *n.* a large, organized search for a criminal or fugitive, usually a male. ♦ *The FBI conducted a nationwide manhunt for the dangerous terrorist.* ♦ *The police thoroughly searched the airport during the manhunt.*

mania ['men i ə] **1.** *n.* a disorder of the mind characterized by wild, sometimes violent, activity and excessive excitement. ♦ *The psychiatrist treated his patient's mania with drugs.* ♦ *The psychopath's mania made him very dangerous.* **2.** *n.* an obsession for someone or something; a very strong interest in someone or something. (Figurative on ①.) ♦ *I have a mania for foreign films.* ♦ *John's hobby of collecting antiques blossomed into a mania.*

maniac ['men i æk] **1.** *n.* someone who has a dangerous, sometimes violent, disorder of the mind. ♦ *The psychiatrist committed the maniac to an institution.* ♦ *The dangerous maniac was jailed in a hospital for the criminally insane.* **2.** *n.* someone who is wild and eager. (Figurative on ①.) ♦ *Did you see that maniac ignore the stop sign?* ♦ *Some maniac at the party decided to dive in the pool with his business suit on.*

manic ['mæn ɪk] *adj.* suffering from a dangerous, sometimes violent mania; overly excited or energetic. ♦ *The doctor gave a sedative to a manic patient.* ♦ *When I'm manic, I become very violent.*

manicure ['mæn ə kjɚ] **1.** *n.* a beauty treatment of the hands and fingernails. ♦ *After Jane got her hair cut, she decided to get a manicure, too.* ♦ *My favorite part of a manicure is the hand massage.* **2.** *tv.* to give someone ①. ♦ *Anne's stylist manicured her every Friday.* ♦ *My hairdresser also manicures his clients.* **3.** *tv.* to trim something, especially trees, shrubs, grass, or hedges. (Figurative on ②.) ♦ *The gardener manicured the hedges every weekend.* ♦ *I manicured the shrubs with large, sharp clippers.*

manicurist ['mæn ə kjɚ əst] *n.* a beautician who does manicures; someone who gives manicures. ♦ *I gave my manicurist a tip after she finished my nails.* ♦ *The manicurist massaged my tired hands.*

manifest ['mæn ə fɛst] *tv.* [for something] to reveal itself. ♦ *Jaundice manifests itself by turning the skin yellow.* ♦ *The audience screamed when the ghost manifested itself behind the actor.*

manifestation [mæn ə fɛ 'ste ʃən] *n.* an appearance; a display; a show. ♦ *The psychic described the ghost's manifestation.* ♦ *The doctor explained the manifestation of the new disease.*

manifold ['mæn ə fold] **1.** *adj.* multiple; having many different kinds or forms. ♦ *The medical report outlined the manifold symptoms of AIDS.* ♦ *The newlywed couple received the manifold blessings of their friends and relatives.* **2.** *n.* a pipe or channel with numerous inlets or outlets that allow substances to enter or exit at a number of points. ♦ *The mechanic replaced the cracked manifold.* ♦ *The exhaust manifold carries away hot gases.*

manipulate [mə 'nɪp jə let] **1.** *tv.* to control or handle something with skill. ♦ *The artist manipulated her paintbrush deftly.* ♦ *Because of my injured finger, I could not manipulate the television's controls.* **2.** *tv.* to control or handle someone or something for one's own benefit. (Figurative on ①.) ♦ *Anne manipulated the meeting to further her own agenda.* ♦ *Bob manipulates his friends to get what he wants.*

manipulative [mə 'nɪp jə lət tɪv] *adj.* controlling or handling people or things in a way designed to increase one's own benefit. (Adv: *manipulatively.*) ♦ *My brother is so manipulative, he always gets our mother to give him money.* ♦ *The manipulative developer persuaded me to sell my house.*

mankind [mæn 'kaɪnd] *n.* the human race; humankind. (No plural form in this sense.) ♦ *My biology teacher traced the development of mankind.* ♦ *The scientist looked for cures that would benefit mankind.*

manly ['mæn li] *adj.* masculine; having qualities or features that are usually associated with adult human males. (Comp: *manlier;* sup: *manliest.*) ♦ *My boyfriend has a deep, manly laugh.* ♦ *I mistook Anne for a man because she has a manly walk.*

man-made ['mæn 'med] *adj.* artificial; synthetic; made by humans or machines instead of being found in nature. ♦ *Many golf courses have man-made ponds.* ♦ *There's a zoo on the man-made island in the harbor.*

mannequin ['mæn ə kɪn] **1.** *n.* an object in the shape of a male or female body, used to display clothes or products in stores; a dummy. ♦ *I arranged the mannequins in the store's display window.* ♦ *This outfit looked good on the mannequin but not on me.* **2.** *n.* someone, typically a woman, who models clothing in a store for customers. ♦ *The mannequin modeled the wedding gown for Anne.* ♦ *I asked to see the dress modeled by a mannequin in my size.*

manner ['mæn ɚ] **1.** *n.* a method; a style; a way of doing something; a way of being. ♦ *My father disapproves of my manner of living.* ♦ *Anne finished her work in a diligent manner.* **2. manners** *n.* the elements of proper and polite behavior. ♦ *Mind your manners when we're at Grandma's house.* ♦ *My parents taught me very good manners.*

mannerism ['mæn ə rɪz əm] *n.* a gesture or movement of a certain person; a habit or trait of a certain person. ♦ *One of John's mannerisms is raising his eyebrows.* ♦ *The stranger's quick, jerky mannerisms frightened me.*

mannish ['mæn ɪʃ] **1.** *adj.* [of a woman] having characteristics usually associated with men. (Adv: *mannishly.*) ♦ *My cousin is a tall, mannish woman with a deep, hearty laugh.* ♦ *Jane enjoyed smoking a good cigar but didn't want to look mannish.* **2.** *adj.* styled for men; made for men. (Adv: *mannishly.*) ♦ *Anne's business suit has a very mannish cut.* ♦ *Mary got a mannish haircut when she went to college.*

manpower ['mæn paʊ ɚ] *n.* human work or energy; the work or effort of someone. (No plural form in this sense.) ♦ *It will take 2,000 hours of manpower to repair the bridge.* ♦ *Do we have enough manpower to finish the job?*

mansion ['mæn ʃən] *n.* a very large house; a large, elegant house. ♦ *Our mansion has eight guest bedrooms.* ♦ *The mansion was set back half a mile from the road.*

man-sized ['mæn saɪzd] *adj.* large enough for a man. ♦ *The growing boy wore man-sized clothing.* ♦ *Jane ate a man-sized portion of steak for dinner.*

manslaughter ['mæn slɔt ɚ] *n.* the act or crime of killing a human illegally without meaning to or by accident. (No plural form in this sense.) ♦ *The hit-and-run driver was charged with manslaughter.* ♦ *The lawyer reduced the first-degree murder charge to manslaughter.*

mantel ['mæn təl] **1.** *n.* the shelf above a fireplace. ♦ *I keep my porcelain vase on the mantel.* ♦ *Billy left milk and cookies on the mantel for Santa Claus.* **2.** *n.* the frame around the front of a fireplace. ♦ *Our fireplace mantel is made out of a slab of marble.* ♦ *Don't touch the mantel. It's hot.*

mantelpiece ['mæn təl pis] *n.* the decorative shelf above a fireplace. ♦ *The fire was so hot that it scorched the mantelpiece.* ♦ *I set the vase of flowers on the mantelpiece.*

mantle ['mæn təl] *n.* something that completely covers or weighs down on someone or something. ♦ *A mantle of snow covered the countryside.* ♦ *The mantle of responsibility fell to me after my father died.*

manual ['mæn ju əl] **1.** *n.* a book that explains how to do or use something; an instruction book; a book of information about something. ♦ *The car manual is in the glove compartment.* ♦ *I installed the computer without reading the manual.* **2.** *adj.* of or about the hand or hands. (Adv: *manually.*) ♦ *Arthritis limits manual dexterity.* ♦ *After Anne's stroke, her therapist helped her do simple manual exercises.* **3.** *adj.* done by one's hands instead of by machine or through the use of one's mind. (Adv: *manually.*) ♦ *I'm in shape because my job requires heavy manual labor.* ♦ *I am good at manual tasks, but I don't do math well.*

manufacture [mæn jə 'fæk tʃɚ] **1.** *n.* the science and business of making of products in factories or industry. (No plural form in this sense.) ♦ *Michigan's economy is linked with the manufacture of cars.* ♦ *The U.S. is no longer involved in the manufacture of television sets.* **2.** *tv.* to make something in large amounts in a factory or by using machines. ♦ *These shoes were manufactured in China.* ♦ *The U.S. manufactures many kinds of automobiles.*

manufacturer [mæn jə 'fæk tʃɚ ɚ] *n.* the person, business, or company that manufactures products. ♦ *General Motors is a major manufacturer of American cars.* ♦ *Anne sued the manufacturer when her microwave oven exploded.*

manure [mə 'nu ɚ] *n.* animal feces, especially when used as fertilizer. (No plural form in this sense.) ♦ *The gardener fertilized the tomato plants with manure.* ♦ *I smelled cow manure as I drove through the country.*

manuscript ['mæn jə skrɪpt] **1.** *n.* a book or text that is written by hand. ♦ *The author's manuscript was destroyed in a fire.* ♦ *One of the poet's original manuscripts was auctioned for a high price.* **2.** *n.* the original copy of a book or article that is sent to a publisher, either typed, printed by a computer, or as a computer file. ♦ *Manuscripts should be double-spaced.* ♦ *The author sent her manuscript to her publisher on time.*

many ['mɛn i] **1.** *adj.* numerous; of large number. (See also more and most for the comparative and superlative.) ♦ *The financial report had many flaws.* ♦ *There are many reasons why I moved to New York.* **2.** *pron.* a large number of people or things. ♦ *Many were called into service during the war.* ♦ *During the famine, many died.*

map ['mæp] **1.** *n.* a drawing that shows certain features of the earth's surface; a sketch or drawing that shows locations or relations between things or places. ♦ *The astronomer consulted a map of the stars.* ♦ *Interesting places were marked on the city map.* **2.** *tv.* to draw ①. ♦ *I mapped the quickest route to my house.* ♦ *The surveyor mapped the river's path.* **3. map out** *tv.* + *adv.* to plan something in detail. ♦ *Susan mapped out the details of her plan.* ♦ *I mapped out our itinerary for the trip.*

maple ['mep əl] **1.** *n.* a kind of tree that has sap that tastes sugary. ♦ *I made syrup from the sap of the maples in our yard.* ♦ *The maple's leaves turned bright red in the fall.* **2. maple syrup** *n.* a thick sweet syrup made by boiling the sap of ①. (No plural form in this sense.) ♦ *I ate pancakes with maple syrup.* ♦ *Real maple syrup is very expensive.* **3.** *n.* wood from ①. (No plural form in this sense.) ♦ *My bookshelf is made of maple.* ♦ *These antique chairs are made of maple.* **4.** *adj.* made out of ③. ♦ *The maple logs crackled in the fireplace.* ♦ *I sold the antique maple table.*

mar ['mɑr] **1.** *tv.* to damage something; to dent something. ♦ *The wall was marred with graffiti.* ♦ *The surface of the workbench was marred by hammer blows.* **2.** *tv.* to spoil something. (Figurative on ①.) ♦ *Your report was marred by your spelling errors.* ♦ *Our team's perfect record was marred when it lost a game.*

marathon ['mɛr ə θɑn] **1.** *n.* a 26-mile footrace. ♦ *I trained for months so I could compete in a marathon.* ♦ *I completed the marathon in just over four hours.* **2.** *n.* any contest requiring endurance. (Figurative on ①.) ♦ *The 24-hour dance marathon raised a lot of money for charity.* ♦ *The local bowling alley sponsored the sorority's bowling marathon.* **3.** *adj.* grueling and endless. (Figurative on ①.) ♦ *The marathon sales meeting dragged on for hours.* ♦ *Mike is recovering from one of his marathon drinking bouts.*

marble ['mɑr bəl] **1.** *n.* a stone that can be cut, shaped, and polished. (No plural form in this sense.) ♦ *Marble is used in construction for floors, walls, and counters.* ♦ *John carved a small statue out of marble.* **2.** *n.* a small, solid ball of colored glass, used in ③. ♦ *Bob won all of my marbles at the playground.* ♦ *I flicked my red marble toward Mary's.* **3. marbles** *n.* a game involving directing one ② into a group of ②. ♦ *The students played marbles during recess.* ♦ *I play marbles better than any of my friends.* **4.** *adj.* made of ①. ♦ *Acid in the vinegar stained the marble countertop.* ♦ *Marble tiles can be cut with a wet saw.*

march ['mɑrtʃ] **1.** *iv.* to walk in rigid steps, in the manner of a soldier. ♦ *The soldiers had to march in the hot sun.* ♦ *The children marched in a single line.* **2.** *iv.* to walk someplace with a certain goal in mind; to walk someplace for a certain reason. ♦ *The little boy marched into the kitchen and demanded to be fed.* ♦ *I marched to the manager's office with a complaint.* **3. march against; march for; march on** *iv.* to demonstrate or protest by walking around with signs and chanting. ♦ *The protesters marched against the war.* ♦ *The demonstrators marched on the White House.* **4.** *tv.* to force someone to move or walk. ♦ *The teacher marched the unruly student to the principal's office.* ♦ *The army marched the villagers into the center of town.* **5.** *n.* the act of walking in a line, like soldiers. ♦ *During the march, several soldiers fainted under the hot sun.* ♦ *The refugees' grueling march to the border took six hours.* **6.** *n.* the distance traveled by marching as in ①. ♦ *I became nervous on the short march to the principal's office.* ♦ *It's a long march to the battle front.* **7.** *n.* a demonstration or protest where people are walking with signs or chanting. ♦ *There's a march against police brutality tomorrow.* ♦ *Dozens of protesters were arrested at the march.* **8.** *n.* music that has a strong beat and is used in parades or while soldiers march ①. ♦ *Many marches are patriotic.* ♦ *The military band played lively marches at the parade.* **9. March** *n.* the third month of the year. ♦ *Spring begins during the third week of March.* ♦ *St. Patrick's Day falls on March 17th.* **10. steal a march (on someone)** *idiom* to get some sort of an advantage over someone without being noticed. ♦ *I got the contract because I was able to steal a march on my competitor.* ♦ *You have to be clever and fast—not dishonest—to steal a march.*

mare ['mɛr] *n.* an adult, female horse. ♦ *The mare whinnied in her stall.* ♦ *The mare protected her newborn foal.*

margarine ['mɑr dʒə rɪn] *n.* a food made from animal or vegetable fats, used in place of butter; a spread for bread. (No plural form in this sense.) ♦ *I spread margarine onto my toast.* ♦ *Max greased the pan with margarine before frying the fish.*

margin ['mɑr dʒɪn] **1.** *n.* the space between the edge of a text and the edge of the page. ♦ *Bill made his essay seem longer by widening the margins.* ♦ *My professor wrote comments in the margins of my term paper.* **2.** *n.* the space next to a border or an edge. ♦ *The margin of the table was decorated with ribbons.* ♦ *I planted flowers on the margin of my yard.* **3.** *n.* an extra amount; the amount that is more than what is needed. ♦ *When it comes to safety, there can be no margin for error.* ♦ *This poll has a 4% margin of error.* **4. profit margin** *n.* the percentage of total sales that is profit. ♦ *We are projecting very small profit margins for next quarter.* ♦ *Our company had very large profit margins this year.*

marginal ['mɑr dʒə nəl] **1.** *adj.* at an edge; in the margin. ♦ *My professor's marginal notes were very helpful.* ♦ *Marginal annotations made it easy to read the text.* **2.** *adj.* slight; not very much; not very important. (Adv: *marginally.*) ♦ *I only have a marginal interest in classical music.* ♦ *I deleted items of marginal importance from my essay.*

marigold ['mɛr ə gold] *n.* a small plant with bright orange or yellow flowers. ♦ *The sidewalk was lined with a row of marigolds.* ♦ *I watered the marigolds on my window sill.*

marijuana [mɛr ə 'wɑn ə] *n.* dried hemp leaves and stems used as an illegal drug that is usually smoked. (No plural form in this sense.) ♦ *The police arrested the student for selling marijuana.* ♦ *The police impounded the crop of marijuana.*

marina [mə 'rin ə] *n.* a harbor for yachts and boats used for pleasure. ♦ *We filled the boat with gas at the marina.* ♦ *We moored our boat at the marina.*

marinade ['mɛr ɪ ned] *n.* a mixture of oil, wine, and spices that food is soaked in before it is cooked. (No plural form in this sense.) ♦ *I soaked the chicken in a garlic marinade.* ♦ *I poured the marinade over the meat.*

marinate ['mɛr ɪ net] *tv.* to soak meat, fish, or some other food in a marinade before cooking it. ♦ *I marinated the chicken for an hour before grilling it.* ♦ *This steak tastes like it's been marinated in vinegar.*

marine [mə 'rin] **1.** *adj.* of or about salt water and the creatures that live in salt water. ♦ *Lobsters and dolphins are kinds of marine animals.* ♦ *Some fish are born in fresh water but spend most of their lives in a marine environment.* **2.** *adj.* of, about, from, or concerning the sea. ♦ *The marine biologist studied lobsters and crabs.* ♦ *A marine assault led to the capture of the port city.* **3.** *adj.* of or about ships and shipping on salt water. ♦ *The government regulates marine navigation.* ♦ *A cruise ship is a form of marine travel.* **4.** *n.* someone who is a member of the U.S. Marine Corps. ♦ *The marines were sent into battle.* ♦ *The young marine was homesick.* **5. marines.** See Marine Corps.

Marine Corps AND **marines** [mə 'rin kor, mə 'rinz] *n.* a branch of the United States military services that serves on land and sea and in the air. ♦ *The Marine Corps was sent first into battle.* ♦ *The prisoners of war were liberated by the Marine Corps.*

mariner ['mɛr ə nɚ] *n.* a sailor. ♦ *The dying mariner wanted to be buried at sea.* ♦ *A few weary mariners relaxed on the deck of the ship.*

marital ['mɛr ɪ təl] *adj.* of or about marriage. (Adv: *maritally.*) ♦ *The happy couple lived in marital bliss.* ♦ *The counselor specialized in marital problems.*

maritime ['mɛr ə tɑɪm] **1.** *adj.* on or near the sea. ♦ *Canada's Maritime Provinces are those east of Quebec.* ♦ *The fishermen lived in a maritime village.* **2.** *adj.* of or about the sea or shipping. ♦ *This map shows maritime shipping lanes.* ♦ *Fishing is a maritime occupation.*

mark ['mɑrk] **1.** *n.* a spot; a stain; a dent; something that spoils a clear or clean surface. ♦ *I cleaned the scuff marks from the floor.* ♦ *There are marks on the wall where someone hit it.* **2.** *n.* a line or figure made by a pencil, crayon, pen, or other writing device. ♦ *Please make a mark by the name of each person on the list who pays for a ticket.* ♦ *Bob rubbed hard to erase the mark left by the pen.* **3.** *n.* something that is a sign of something; something that stands for something else. ♦ *A gold star is often used as a mark of excellence.* ♦ *Bill wears an earring as a mark of rebellion.* **4.** *n.* a grade; a letter or a number used to grade a student's work. (Often plural.) ♦ *The lazy student never got good marks in school.* ♦ *Are my marks good enough to get into college?* **5.** *iv.* to be able to make ②. ♦ *My fountain pen marks well.* ♦ *This felt pen marks with permanent ink.* **6.** *tv.* to spot something; to stain something; to spoil an otherwise clear or clean surface with ①. ♦ *The building was marked with graffiti.* ♦ *The young child marked the wall with crayons.* **7.** *tv.* to indicate something; to symbolize something; to represent something; to stand for something. ♦ *This monument marks the place where the first atom was split.* ♦ *The trail marks the path we took to go home.* **8.** *tv.* to grade a student's work; to correct a student's work. ♦ *Mrs. Brown marked her students' papers each evening.* ♦ *My teacher marks mistakes with red ink.* **9. mark someone as** *tv.* + *prep. phr.* to label someone as something. ♦ *The spy's sale of state secrets marked him as a traitor.* ♦ *Mary's accent marks her as a Southerner.* **10. leave one's mark on someone** *idiom* [for someone like a teacher] to affect the behavior and performance of another person. ♦ *The wise professor left her mark on her students.* ♦ *My father left his mark on me, and I will always remember all his good advice.*

marked ['mɑrkt] *adj.* noticeable. (Adv: *markedly* ['mɑrk əd li].) ♦ *John has a marked tendency to criticize others.* ♦ *Anne had marked success with the project and has become its manager.*

marker ['mɑrk ɚ] *n.* a fat pen with a felt tip that makes marks that cannot be erased. ♦ *The student defaced the wall with a marker.* ♦ *She used a yellow marker to highlight the things she had to learn in her book.*

market ['mɑr kɪt] **1.** *n.* a place or building where people gather to buy and sell things. ♦ *I went to the market to buy some fresh vegetables.* ♦ *Can you pick up some milk at the market?* **2.** *n.* the stock market in general; any market for stocks or bonds. ♦ *My parents made their fortune in the market.* ♦ *I lost money when the market crashed.* **3.** *n.* an area or a country where a product is needed or used; a certain group of people for which a product is needed or used. ♦ *Suburban teenagers are a lucrative market.* ♦ *Our profits doubled when we expanded into overseas markets.* **4.** *n.* the demand for a certain product. ♦ *After the recession, the housing market improved.* ♦ *Is there a market for a painless mouse trap?* **5.** *tv.* to advertise a product; to promote a product; to make a plan for selling a product. ♦ *The new product failed because it was poorly marketed.* ♦ *Most companies use TV commercials to market their products.* **6. on the market** *idiom* available for sale; offered for sale. ♦ *I had to put my car on the market.* ♦ *This is the finest home computer on the market.* **7. in the market for something** *idiom* ready and eager to buy something. ♦ *I am in the market for a new car. Are there any good deals right now?* ♦ *Bill is in the market for a new suit.*

marketplace ['mɑr kɪt ples] **1.** *n.* a place or building containing a market. ♦ *I bought fresh corn at the country marketplace.* ♦ *Can you pick up some milk at the marketplace?* **2.** *n.* commerce; trade; buying and selling. (No plural form in this sense.) ♦ *Hundreds of new products are* *introduced to the marketplace yearly.* ♦ *The business student studied the global marketplace.*

marking ['mɑr kɪŋ] *n.* a mark; a pattern; an arrangement of marks. (Often plural.) ♦ *The police analyzed the bloody marking on the ransom note.* ♦ *The markings on the bottom of the letter were a coded message.*

marksman ['mɑrks mən] *n., irreg.* a sharpshooter; someone who can shoot a gun very well. (Pl: **marksmen**.) ♦ *The marksman shot the terrorist in the head.* ♦ *The deer was shot by the marksman.*

marksmanship ['mɑrks mən ʃɪp] *n.* the skill of being able to shoot a gun very accurately. (No plural form in this sense.) ♦ *My friends were impressed with my marksmanship.* ♦ *I proved my marksmanship at the shooting gallery.*

marksmen ['mɑrks mən] pl of marksman.

markup ['mɑrk əp] *n.* a price increase; the amount a price is raised. ♦ *The unseasonable frost led to a markup on orange juice.* ♦ *The markup in prices was caused by the embargo.*

marmalade ['mɑr mə led] *n.* a food, similar to jam, made by boiling sugar, fruit juice, fruit pulp, and the peel of the fruit together. (No plural form in this sense.) ♦ *I put orange marmalade on my toast.* ♦ *Mary opened a new jar of marmalade.*

maroon [mə 'run] **1.** *n.* a deep, dark shade of red. (No plural form in this sense.) ♦ *Our school colors are maroon and white.* ♦ *The bathroom is decorated in maroon.* **2.** *adj.* deep, dark red. ♦ *The maroon car drove off the road.* ♦ *The dried blood left a maroon stain on the ground.* **3.** *tv.* to strand someone somewhere, especially on an island. ♦ *The survivors of the shipwreck were marooned on a desert island.* ♦ *We were marooned in Brooklyn because my car broke down.*

marquee [mɑr 'ki] *n.* a large sign over the entrance to a theater that tells what shows are playing. ♦ *The theater marquee was lit with hundreds of light bulbs.* ♦ *The actor's name was misspelled on the marquee.*

marriage ['mɛr ɪdʒ] **1.** *n.* the religious or legal union of a husband and a wife. ♦ *Bill and Mary's marriage ended in divorce.* ♦ *John and Susan's taxes increased because of their marriage.* **2.** *n.* the ceremony that joins a man and a woman in ①; a wedding. ♦ *Bob and Anne had a simple marriage at the county courthouse.* ♦ *Our marriage was marred by rain.*

married ['mɛr id] **1.** *adj.* [of someone] having a husband or a wife; united in marriage. ♦ *The married couple bought a new sofa.* ♦ *My date neglected to tell me that he was a married man.* **2.** *adj.* [of a last name] acquired through marriage. ♦ *The new bride wasn't used to using her married name.* ♦ *The application asked for my married and maiden names.* **3. get married** *idiom* to become united as husband and wife. ♦ *Bill and Sally got married when they were in college.* ♦ *We got married in Texas just after we graduated from college.*

marrow ['mɛr o] *n.* soft, fatty tissue inside bones. (No plural form in this sense.) ♦ *The dog ate the marrow from the bone it was chewing on.* ♦ *The cancer had spread to my grandfather's bone marrow.*

marry ['mɛr i] **1.** *iv.* to unite with someone in a marriage. ♦ *The young couple married after graduating from college.* ♦ *I don't plan to marry until I'm 30.* **2.** *tv.* to unite two people in a marriage; to perform a wedding ceremony. ♦ *The preacher married the young couple.* ♦ *The young couple was married by a judge.* **3.** *tv.* to take someone as a husband or a wife. ♦ *John married Anne after they graduated from college.* ♦ *Bill married a famous actress.*

Mars ['mɑrz] **1.** *n.* [in Roman mythology] the god of war. ♦ *Mars is the winged messenger.* ♦ *The parents of Mars were Jupiter and Juno.* **2.** *n.* the fourth planet of the solar system, between Earth and Jupiter. ♦ *The astronaut dreamed of traveling to Mars.* ♦ *Mars has two moons.*

marsh ['mɑrʃ] *n.* a low area of land sometimes covered with water. ♦ *After the marsh was paved over, the nearby river flooded often.* ♦ *I paddled my canoe through the marsh.*

marshal ['mɑr ʃəl] **1.** *n.* an officer who is in charge of a police or fire department. (In certain U.S. cities.) ♦ *The fire marshal said the fire was started by an arsonist.* ♦ *The marshal put the thief in jail.* **2.** *n.* an officer who assists a judge and has duties like those of a sheriff. (In the U.S., not the state, court system.) ♦ *The marshal ordered the people in the courtroom to be quiet.* ♦ *The judge asked the marshal to clear the courtroom.* **3.** *n.* someone who organizes or leads a parade. ♦ *The grand marshal marched at the front of the parade.* ♦ *Parade marshals are often famous celebrities.* **4.** *tv.* to arrange things or people in the correct order; to organize things or people. ♦ *The troops were marshaled on the eve of the battle.* ♦ *The aide marshaled the graduates into line for the procession.*

marshmallow ['mɑrʃ mɛl o] **1.** *n.* a soft, spongy confection made from sugar. (Originally made from the roots of a flower called the *marsh mallow*.) ♦ *We toasted marshmallows over the campfire.* ♦ *I put some marshmallows in my hot cocoa.* **2.** *adj.* made of ①. ♦ *Do you like marshmallow sauce on your ice cream?* ♦ *We have a jar of marshmallow topping in the cupboard.*

mart ['mɑrt] *n.* a market; a store. ♦ *I bought a printer at the computer mart.* ♦ *Can you pick up a loaf of bread from the food mart?*

martial law ['mɑr ʃəl 'lɔ] *n.* the military rule of a country or area. (No plural form in this sense.) ♦ *The army imposed martial law after overthrowing the government.* ♦ *Most freedoms are restricted under martial law.*

Martian ['mɑr ʃən] **1.** *n.* of or about the planet Mars. ♦ *The rocket probe analyzed the Martian atmosphere.* ♦ *The astronomer looked at the Martian canals.* **2.** *n.* a [fictitious] creature that lives on Mars. ♦ *I saw a movie about Earth being attacked by Martians.* ♦ *The lecturer claimed to have been abducted by Martians.*

martin ['mɑrt n] *n.* one of several types of small gray or purple birds belonging to the swallow family. ♦ *The purple martin warbled in its nest.* ♦ *The bird watchers spotted a flock of martins.*

Martin Luther King Day ['mɑrt n luθ ə 'kɪŋ de] *n.* a U.S. holiday celebrated on the third Monday in January to honor the American civil-rights leader Martin Luther King, Jr. ♦ *John recited King's famous speech on Martin Luther King Day.* ♦ *Banks and government offices are closed on Martin Luther King Day.*

martyr ['mɑr tɚ] **1.** *n.* someone who dies for a cause; someone who is killed rather than abandon a belief. ♦

The pope declared the martyr to be a saint. ♦ *The martyr had set himself on fire to protest the government.* **2.** *n.* someone who suffers very much because of someone or something. (Figurative on ①.) ♦ *Instead of being such a martyr, why don't you see a doctor?* ♦ *Bill's not a martyr, he just wants you to feel sorry for him.* **3.** *tv.* to turn a person into ① by killing or seriously harming the person. ♦ *The crowd martyred the political prisoner by killing him.* ♦ *The nun was martyred for refusing to renounce her faith.*

marvel ['mɑr vəl] **1.** *n.* an amazement; someone or something that is amazing or surprising. ♦ *John is a marvel when it comes to playing the piano.* ♦ *Anne's expensive new car is a real marvel!* **2. marvel at** *iv.* + *prep. phr.* to be amazed by something; to be surprised at something. ♦ *I marveled at the paintings in the art museum.* ♦ *Jane marveled at how much money the house cost.* **3. a marvel to behold** *idiom* someone or something quite exciting or wonderful to see. ♦ *Our new house is a marvel to behold.* ♦ *Mary's lovely new baby is a marvel to behold.*

marvelous ['mɑr və ləs] *adj.* wonderful; super; great; fantastic; excellent. (Adv: *marvelously.*) ♦ *This cake tastes marvelous!* ♦ *I had a marvelous time at the party.*

Maryland ['mɛr ə lənd] See Gazetteer.

mascara [mæ 'skɛr ə] *n.* a kind of makeup that is put on the eyelashes to make them look thicker, longer, and darker. (No plural form in this sense.) ♦ *Anne went to the ladies' room to put on some mascara.* ♦ *My mascara ran down my face when I started crying.*

mascot ['mæs kɑt] *n.* a person, animal, or thing that represents a school or sports team. ♦ *My high-school mascot was a red dragon.* ♦ *Our mascot ran around the football field during the rally.*

masculine ['mæs kjə lɪn] **1.** *adj.* having features usually associated with a male; manly. (Adv: *masculinely.*) ♦ *Anne has a very masculine handshake.* ♦ *Do you think aggression is a masculine trait?* **2.** *adj.* <a grammar term describing a certain class of nouns, some of which refer to males.> (See **gender**.) ♦ *In German, the singular masculine definite article is* der. ♦ Gato, *the Spanish word for 'cat,' is masculine.*

masculinity [mɑs kjə 'lɪn ə ti] *n.* the condition of being masculine; maleness. (No plural form in this sense.) ♦ *Bob gets uptight when his masculinity is questioned.* ♦ *The actor's subtle masculinity made him a popular star.*

mash ['mæʃ] **1.** *n.* a mixture of grain and water, used as animal food or to make beer or whiskey. (No plural form in this sense.) ♦ *I fed corn mash to the chickens.* ♦ *Uncle Tom heated up the mash to make some whiskey.* **2.** *tv.* to crush something into a pulp; to beat something into a pulp. ♦ *We mashed grapes so we could make wine.* ♦ *I mashed the boiled potatoes with my fork.*

mask ['mæsk] **1.** *n.* a covering that disguises the face. ♦ *Everyone at the Halloween party wore masks.* ♦ *The bank robbers' faces were covered with masks.* **2.** *n.* something that disguises or conceals something else. (Figurative on ①.) ♦ *Anne's forced smile is a mask that covers her true feelings.* ♦ *A mask of secrecy veiled the president's travel route.* **3.** *n.* a covering that protects the face, eyes, nose, or mouth. ♦ *The smog was so bad that I wore a gas mask.* ♦ *The hockey puck bounced off the goalie's protective mask.* **4.** *tv.* to conceal something; to hide something; to put ② on someone or something. ♦ *Your medicine has masked the symptoms of a serious disease.* ♦ *The spy masked the message in a secret code.*

masochism ['mæs ə kɪz əm] **1.** *n.* the pleasure (often sexual) received from pain or humiliation; a condition where someone enjoys pain or humiliation. (No plural form in this sense. Named for von Sacher-Masoch, who first described it. Compare with **sadism**.) ♦ *Anne studied masochism in her psychology class.* ♦ *People have been injured or even killed by experimentation with masochism.* **2.** *n.* eagerness for or easy acceptance of failure, disappointment, and humiliation. (No plural form in this sense. Figurative on ①.) ♦ *Dave's masochism makes him give up easily.* ♦ *Your masochism really annoys me. Don't let people take advantage of you!*

masochist ['mæs ə kəst] **1.** *n.* someone who practices or enjoys masochism. ♦ *The masochist begged to be spanked.* ♦ *The masochist trusted his partner completely.* **2.** *n.* someone who easily accepts failure, disappointment, or humiliation. ♦ *Don't be a masochist. You don't have to accept rejection!* ♦ *Bob is such a masochist that he lets everyone take advantage of him.*

mason ['me sən] *n.* someone who makes walls of stones or bricks for a living. ♦ *The masons completed the brick wall in only two days.* ♦ *Tom mixed the mortar for the mason who was setting the stones for the walkway.*

masquerade [mæs kə 'red] **1.** *n.* a party where everyone wears a mask and a costume. ♦ *I went to the masquerade dressed as a large bee.* ♦ *I danced with several ghosts and goblins at the masquerade.* **2.** *n.* a false appearance; something pretended; a pretense. ♦ *This is not a committee meeting, it is just a foolish masquerade!* ♦ *The mayor's promises were just part of his masquerade to get reelected.* **3. masquerade as** *iv.* + *prep. phr.* to disguise oneself to look like someone or something else. ♦ *I masqueraded as my father so I could get a car loan.* ♦ *John was arrested for masquerading as a doctor.*

mass ['mæs] **1.** *n.* an amount of something with no specific shape; a lump; a heap. ♦ *The dirty clothes lay in a dark, shapeless mass on top of the washer.* ♦ *The chemist analyzed the sticky mass taken from the murder site.* **2.** *n.* the scientific term for the amount of matter in an object. (No plural form in this sense.) ♦ *The students measured the mass of the object in kilograms.* ♦ *The astronomers examined a dense mass deep in the universe.* **3. Mass** *n.* a Roman Catholic church service with Communion. ♦ *I sing in the choir at Mass.* ♦ *Catholics usually go to Mass on Sunday.* **4.** *adj.* suitable for many people or things; involving many people or things. ♦ *A mass panic seized the crowd during the earthquake.* ♦ *The government funded mass education.* **5.** *iv.* to group together somewhere in large numbers; to come together in large numbers or amounts. ♦ *The crowd massed together at the arena's entrance.* ♦ *Vultures massed around the dead coyote.* **6.** *tv.* to cause a large number of things or people to group together; to cause a large number or amount of things or people to come together. ♦ *The general massed the troops together at the river's edge.* ♦ *I massed the leaves into a large pile with a rake.*

Massachusetts [mæs ə 'tʃu sɪts] See Gazetteer.

massacre ['mæs ə kɚ] **1.** *n.* the brutal killing of many people in one battle or instance. ♦ *The horrendous mas-*

sacre was condemned by the United Nations. ♦ *Thousands of innocent villagers were slaughtered in the massacre.* **2.** *tv.* to brutally kill many people in one battle or instance. ♦ *The military massacred hundreds of members of the ruling party.* ♦ *Thousands of innocent citizens were massacred during the war.*

massage [mə 'sɑʒ] **1.** *n.* rubbing the muscles of the body in order to relax them. (No plural form in this sense.) ♦ *Massage is a good way to relax.* ♦ *My physical therapist uses massage to help heal my sprained ankle.* **2.** *n.* an act of ①. ♦ *My neck is stiff. Would you give me a massage?* ♦ *A good massage helps me fall asleep.* **3.** *tv.* to perform ① on someone or a part of someone. ♦ *My mother asked me to massage her sore back.* ♦ *A physical therapist massaged the athlete's muscles.*

masseur [mə 'sʊr] *n.* a man who is trained and paid to give massages. (From French.) ♦ *The football player saw a masseur after every game.* ♦ *The expensive health club employed a dozen masseurs.*

masseuse [mə 'sus] *n.* a woman who is trained and paid to give massages. (From French.) ♦ *After Anne's workout, she spent 15 minutes with a masseuse.* ♦ *The masseuse worked the kinks out of my neck muscles.*

massive ['mæs ɪv] *adj.* very large; enormous; imposing; powerful. (Adv: *massively.*) ♦ *John was killed by a massive heart attack.* ♦ *Congress tried to reduce the massive national debt.*

(mass) media [(mæs) 'mi di ə] *n.* all the forms of communication that reach many people in a short amount of time. (Pl of *mass medium,* which is rarely used. See medium.) ♦ *TV, radio, newspapers, magazines, and on-line computer services are mass media.* ♦ *The media became obsessed with the celebrity's murder trial.*

mass-produce ['mæs prə 'dus] *tv.* to make something in large numbers or amounts. ♦ *Our factory mass-produces household items.* ♦ *Large factories mass-produce automobiles.*

mast ['mæst] **1.** *n.* an upright beam or pole on a ship to which sails are attached. ♦ *The heavy winds cracked the ship's mast.* ♦ *I saw the mast of an enemy ship on the horizon.* **2. at half-mast** *idiom* halfway up or down. (Usually in reference to a flag.) ♦ *The flag was flying at half-mast because the general had died.* ♦ *The little boy ran out of the house with his pants at half-mast.*

mastectomy [mæ 'stɛk tə mi] *n.* a surgical operation where a diseased breast is removed. ♦ *Anne's physician suggested she have a double mastectomy.* ♦ *Mary stopped the spread of the cancer by having a mastectomy.*

master ['mæst ɚ] **1.** *n.* a man who has authority over people, animals, or things. (Compare with mistress.) ♦ *The dog returned the stick to its master.* ♦ *John was the master of the house and gave orders to the servants.* **2.** *n.* someone who is very skilled at something. ♦ *The magician is a master at creating illusions.* ♦ *Bob is a master at teaching algebra.* **3.** *n.* an original page or document that copies are made from. ♦ *The clerk placed the master on top of the 100 copies.* ♦ *Be sure to copy the master and not one of the copies.* **4. Master** *n.* <a title used to address a young boy.> (Formal. Used in formal postal addresses with first and last name and by servants with first name only.) ♦ *This letter is addressed to Master James Jones. I guess that's you, Jimmy.* ♦ *The chauffeur took Master David to school.* **5.** *adj.* <the adj. use of ③.> ♦ *Bill clumsily spilled coffee on the master copy.* ♦ *The master document was protected by a plastic pouch.* **6.** *adj.* primary; main; chief; overall; controlling everything else. ♦ *This master switch controls power to the entire factory.* ♦ *The mayor described his master plan for the city's revival.* **7.** *adj.* of professional standing or quality. ♦ *The builder hired a master carpenter to do the woodwork.* ♦ *A master plumber was needed for the complicated job.* **8.** *tv.* to become very skilled in something; to learn how to do something very well. ♦ *Susan quickly mastered the operation of her computer.* ♦ *David mastered German after living in Germany for three years.*

masterful ['mæst ɚ fʊl] *adj.* showing great skill; showing mastery. (Adv: *masterfully.*) ♦ *The pianist's masterful hands made the sonata seem easy to play.* ♦ *The driver's masterful handling of the car prevented an accident.*

mastermind ['mæst ɚ mɑɪnd] **1.** *n.* a very smart or talented person who plans and directs a complicated project. ♦ *Anne was the mastermind behind the company's growth.* ♦ *The resistance was crushed by the military mastermind.* **2.** *tv.* to plan and direct a complicated project. ♦ *The manager masterminded the sales campaign.* ♦ *The wicked king masterminded the evil plan.*

masterpiece ['mæst ɚ pis] **1.** *n.* a great work of art; a great example of a certain craft. ♦ *Many masterpieces are displayed at major art museums.* ♦ *Dante's* Inferno *is a brilliant literary masterpiece.* **2.** *n.* the best work of art done by a certain person; the best example of a craft done by a certain person. ♦ War and Peace *is Tolstoy's masterpiece.* ♦ *My masterpiece was stolen from my art studio.*

mastery ['mæst ə ri] **1.** *n.* complete skill; complete knowledge. (No plural form in this sense.) ♦ *The young student's mastery of calculus is amazing.* ♦ *I attained mastery of German while living in Berlin.* **2.** *n.* complete control. (No plural form in this sense.) ♦ *The general's mastery of the situation helped win the battle.* ♦ *The warden's mastery over the prisoners was rarely challenged.*

masticate ['mæst ɪ ket] **1.** *iv.* to chew, usually for the purposes of swallowing. ♦ *You should masticate well before you swallow.* ♦ *My teeth hurt when I masticate.* **2.** *tv.* to chew something, usually for the purposes of swallowing. ♦ *You should masticate your food thoroughly.* ♦ *I masticated the tough steak for a long time.*

masturbate ['mæst ɚ bet] **1.** *iv.* to stimulate one's own sexual organ for pleasure, especially by touching or rubbing. ♦ *The businessman told his wife that he sometimes masturbated in hotel rooms when he traveled and was away from home.* ♦ *The monkey masturbated in its cage at the zoo.* **2.** *tv.* to perform masturbation on some creature or something. ♦ *Your dog is masturbating himself against my leg.* ♦ *We were told that masturbating oneself is normal and natural.*

masturbation [mæst ɚ 'be ʃən] *n.* the stimulation of a sexual organ for pleasure, especially by touching or rubbing. (No plural form in this sense.) ♦ *The monkeys at the zoo frequently engage in masturbation.* ♦ *Our health teacher talked about masturbation.*

mat ['mæt] **1.** *n.* a piece of material for covering part of a floor, especially in front of a door. ♦ *John wiped his feet on the mat.* ♦ *My cat is sleeping on the mat.* **2.** *n.* a piece of thick, padded material used to cushion falls in certain sports. ♦ *The gymnast fell from the apparatus and landed on the mat.* ♦ *The wrestler was knocked down to the mat.* **3.** *n.* a tangled mass of hair, weeds, strings, or other things. ♦ *I had to cut the mats from my dog's fur because I couldn't comb through them.* ♦ *Mats of weeds ruined the vegetable garden.* **4.** *tv.* to tangle hair, weeds, strings, and other similar things. ♦ *The waves matted my hair on one side of my head.* ♦ *You should comb your hair because the wind matted it.*

matador ['mæt ə dor] *n.* someone, almost always a male, who fights and kills bulls for sport in a large arena; a bullfighter. (From Spanish.) ♦ *The matador waved a red cape at the bull.* ♦ *The bull tossed the matador into the air.*

match ['mætʃ] **1.** *n.* a sporting event. ♦ *Spectators at tennis matches must remain quiet.* ♦ *Do you want to go to a boxing match tonight?* **2.** *n.* someone or something that is the equal of or just like someone or something else. ♦ *I made a match by pairing the three of clubs with the three of spades.* ♦ *These two guys are a perfect match in a basketball game.* **3.** *n.* a thin stick with a chemical substance on one end, which, when struck against a hard surface, creates fire. ♦ *Do you have any matches? I lost my lighter.* ♦ *I lit the candle with a match.* **4.** *tv.* [for something] to be exactly like something else; to fit something exactly; to go with something well. ♦ *That shirt matches your pants perfectly.* ♦ *Your opinions match mine very closely.* **5. match with** *tv.* + *prep. phr.* to make a match ② of one thing with something else. ♦ *I can't seem to match these shoes with any belts.* ♦ *The designer matched the color of the curtains with the carpet.* **6.** *iv.* to be exactly alike; to go together well; to fit together well; to harmonize. ♦ *I can't find any socks that match.* ♦ *These marble tiles don't match. One is bigger than the other.* **7. a match for someone or something** *idiom* someone or some creature that is the equal of someone or some other creature, especially in a contest. ♦ *My older brother is no match for me; he's much weaker.* ♦ *Your horse is no match for mine in a race. Mine will always win.* **8. meet one's match** *idiom* to meet one's equal; to encounter one's equal. ♦ *John played tennis with Bill yesterday, and it looks as if John has finally met his match.* ♦ *Listen to Jane and Mary argue. I always thought that Jane was loud, but she has finally met her match.* **9. strike a match** *idiom* to light ③ by rubbing it on a rough surface. ♦ *Mary struck a match and lit a candle.* ♦ *When Sally struck a match to light a cigarette, Jane said quickly, "No smoking, please."* **10. whole shooting match** *idiom* the entire affair or organization. ♦ *John's not a good manager. Instead of delegating jobs to others, he runs the whole shooting match himself.* ♦ *There's not a hard worker in that whole shooting match.*

matchbox ['mætʃ bɑks] *n.* a small container that holds matches. ♦ *I threw out the matchbox because it got wet.* ♦ *I lit a match by striking it along the side of the matchbox.*

matched ['mætʃt] *adj.* meant to go together; part of a set. ♦ *I bought a matched pair of salt and pepper shakers.* ♦ *I won a set of matched luggage on the game show.*

matching ['mætʃ ɪŋ] *adj.* going along with well; looking good together; harmonizing with. ♦ *The twins wore matching clothes.* ♦ *I was careful to wear matching socks to the interview.*

matchless ['mætʃ ləs] *adj.* the best; without a match. (Adv: *matchlessly.*) ♦ *Our country's military system is matchless.* ♦ *For years, the champion boxer was matchless.*

matchmaker ['mætʃ mek ɚ] *n.* someone who arranges or tries to arrange marriages or dates. ♦ *The matchmaker slyly persuaded John and Susan to go on a date.* ♦ *I hate it when my mother tries to be a matchmaker.*

mate ['met] **1.** *n.* the sexual partner of a living creature. ♦ *The male peacock attracts mates by spreading his long tail feathers.* ♦ *A female black widow spider kills her mate after copulation.* **2.** *n.* a spouse; a husband or a wife. ♦ *The company picnic is open to workers and their mates.* ♦ *I taught my mate how to bowl.* **3.** *n.* one of a pair. (Figurative on ②.) ♦ *Can you help me find this red sock's mate?* ♦ *Here's the left glove, but I don't know where its mate is.* **4.** *n.* a friend or colleague. (In compounds.) ♦ *I drove my roommate to the airport.* ♦ *I celebrated with my teammates after we won the game.* **5.** *n.* a rank of sailor just below the captain. ♦ *The captain ordered the mate to clean the ship's deck.* ♦ *John attained the rank of first mate.* **6.** *iv.* to have sex; to breed. (Used primarily with animals.) ♦ *My dog mated with the neighbor's spaniel.* ♦ *The scientist observed the rabbits as they mated.* **7.** *tv.* to bring a male and female animal together so that breeding will result. ♦ *I mated two of my favorite rabbits.* ♦ *The breeder mated pedigreed dogs.*

material [mə 'tɪr i əl] **1.** *n.* the substance that an object is made of; a substance that can be used to make things. ♦ *The materials used to build my house included wood and brick.* ♦ *The exterior of my car is made of rustproof materials.* **2.** *n.* cloth; fabric. (No plural form in this sense.) ♦ *I made a dress from five yards of material.* ♦ *Silk and other fine material can be damaged easily.* **3.** *n.* information, knowledge, experience, or imagination used to develop a story, movie, book, program, etc. (No plural form in this sense.) ♦ *The reporter's material came from an anonymous source.* ♦ *Many comedians get their material from real-life experiences.* **4.** *adj.* of or about the physical world. (Adv: *materially.*) ♦ *We live in a material world from birth until death.* ♦ *The rich celebrity surrounded himself with material comforts.* **5.** *adj.* of importance or relevance. (Adv: *materially.*) ♦ *The material witness's testimony damaged the defendant's case.* ♦ *There's a material difference between first-degree and second-degree burns.*

materialism [mə 'tɪr i ə lɪz əm] **1.** *n.* the belief that only physical things have value and that there are no spiritual or intellectual values. (No plural form in this sense.) ♦ *The minister urged the congregation to avoid materialism.* ♦ *Spiritual values would disappear if people only cared about materialism.* **2.** *n.* a strong interest in money and the things it will buy, instead of spiritual, ethical, or intellectual values. (No plural form in this sense.) ♦ *Advertising often encourages materialism.* ♦ *The new pastor's flagrant materialism shocked the congregation.*

materialistic [mə tɪr i ə 'lɪs tɪk] *adj.* devoted to materialism and the accumulation of money. (Adv: *materialistically* [...ɪk li].) ♦ *Bill only thinks of money. He is so materialistic.* ♦ *The materialistic woman flaunted her expensive jewelry.*

materialize [mə 'tɪr i ə lɑɪz] **1.** *iv.* to happen; to become real. ♦ *As my plans materialized, I knew I would succeed.* ♦ *A tropical storm materialized off the coast of Africa.* **2.** *iv.* to appear in the form of a body; to become visible. ♦

An eerie ghost materialized at the bottom of the stairs. ♦ *A shadowy figure materialized on the videotape.*

maternal [mə 'tɚ nəl] **1.** *adj.* of or about mothers or motherhood. (Adv: *maternally.*) ♦ *Jane's maternal instinct led her to check on her baby.* ♦ *Lisa chooses to be childless because she has no maternal feelings.* **2.** *adj.* related through the mother's side of the family. (Adv: *maternally.*) ♦ *That man is not my father's brother; he's my maternal uncle.* ♦ *My maternal grandfather immigrated from Sweden.*

maternity [mə 'tɚn ə ti] **1.** *n.* motherhood; the condition of being a mother. (No plural form in this sense.) ♦ *The new bride looked forward to maternity.* ♦ *The child development class helped Mary prepare for maternity.* **2.** *adj.* <the adj. use of ①.> ♦ *Mary was given a lot of maternity clothes at the baby shower.* ♦ *The pregnant woman was rushed to the hospital's maternity ward.*

math ['mæθ] **1.** *n.* mathematics. (No plural form in this sense. Treated as singular.) ♦ *My school district requires every student to take four years of high-school math.* ♦ *I learned about fractions in math today.* **2.** *adj.* <the adj. use of ①.> ♦ *I left my math book at school.* ♦ *My math teacher says I need more practice with fractions.*

mathematic [mæθ ə 'mæt ɪk] **1.** *adj.* of or about great exactness and precision. ♦ *Mary figured the correct answer with mathematic precision.* ♦ *Anne's mathematic mind quickly figured out the consequences of the chess move.* **2.** See also mathematics.

mathematical [mæθ ə 'mæt ɪ kəl] *adj.* of or about mathematics. (Adv: *mathematically* [...ɪk li].) ♦ *I memorized mathematical formulas for the physics exam.* ♦ *The professor taught the logic class with a mathematical bent.*

mathematician [mæθ ə mə 'tɪ ʃən] *n.* someone who studies or who is skilled in mathematics. ♦ *My calculus class is taught by an expert mathematician.* ♦ *The successful computer programmer was originally a mathematician.*

mathematics [mæθ ə 'mæt ɪks] **1.** *n.* the sciences that study the properties and relationships of numbers and shapes. (Treated as singular.) ♦ *The field of mathematics includes arithmetic, algebra, geometry, trigonometry, and calculus.* ♦ *Engineering requires an understanding of mathematics.* **2.** See also mathematic.

matinée [mæt n 'ne] *n.* a movie, play, or concert shown in the afternoon. ♦ *The matinée is cheaper than the evening show.* ♦ *I took my family to the Saturday matinée.*

mating ['met ɪŋ] *adj.* of or about breeding or copulation. ♦ *The biologist studied the peacocks' mating habits.* ♦ *The state forbade deer hunting during the mating season.*

matriarch ['me tri ɑrk] *n.* a woman who controls a family or tribe. ♦ *Grandma is the matriarch of our family.* ♦ *The explorers brought gifts of exotic spices to the tribal matriarch.*

matrimonial [mæ tri 'mon i əl] *adj.* of or about matrimony or marriage. (Adv: *matrimonially.*) ♦ *The ship's captain presided over the matrimonial ceremony.* ♦ *The bride and groom exchanged matrimonial vows.*

matrimony ['mæ trə mon i] *n.* marriage. (No plural form in this sense.) ♦ *John and Mary were wed in holy matrimony.* ♦ *Bill and Susan considered matrimony after they both graduated from college.*

matron ['me trən] **1.** *n.* an older woman, usually one who is married and who has children. (Formal.) ♦ *The dignified matron held a seat on the library's board of directors.* ♦ *The matron's children had all grown up and moved away.* **2.** *n.* a female prison warden; a woman who is in charge of a group of prisoners. ♦ *The matron lit the prisoner's cigarette.* ♦ *The prison matron locked Lisa in her cell.*

matter ['mæt ɚ] **1.** *n.* anything that takes up space. (No plural form in this sense.) ♦ *The astronomer estimated the amount of matter in the solar system.* ♦ *Water, gas, gold, lead, tar, and bananas are all different kinds of matter.* **2.** *n.* a certain kind of substance. (No plural form in this sense.) ♦ *The kitchen table is coated with sticky matter.* ♦ *The inspector examined the bloody matter on the knife.* **3.** *n.* a concern; an issue; an affair; a subject of attention. ♦ *Crime is a matter of great concern.* ♦ *The candidates discussed important matters at the debate.* **4. subject matter** *n.* content; the subject that a piece of writing or speech deals with. ♦ *The subject matter of this movie is too violent for children.* ♦ *The censors found the book's subject matter offensive.* **5.** *iv.* to be important; to have meaning. ♦ *Your opinion really matters to me.* ♦ *It doesn't matter if it's raining. Let's go.* **6. a matter of life and death** *idiom* an issue of great urgency; an issue that will decide between living and dying. ♦ *We must find a doctor. It's a matter of life and death.* ♦ *A matter of life and death demands that I return home at once.* **7. gray matter** *idiom* intelligence; brains; power of thought. (Informal.) ♦ *Use your gray matter and think what will happen if the committee resigns.* ♦ *Surely they'll come up with an acceptable solution if they use a bit of gray matter.* **8. no laughing matter** *idiom* a serious issue or problem. ♦ *Be serious. This is no laughing matter.* ♦ *This disease is no laughing matter. It's quite deadly.*

mattress ['mæ trɪs] *n.* a large rectangular pad that is used to sleep on. ♦ *I prefer a large mattress since I am so tall.* ♦ *I have back problems, so I sleep on a very firm mattress.*

mature [mə 'tʃur] **1.** *adj.* [of someone] adult or grown up; [of fruit or vegetables] ripe or ready to eat. (Adv: *maturely.*) ♦ *The young child is not yet mature.* ♦ *I picked the mature grapes from the vine.* **2.** *adj.* characteristic of an adult; sensible; responsible. (Adv: *maturely.*) ♦ *My children act very mature for their age.* ♦ *The mature thing to do would be to admit your mistakes.* **3.** *tv.* to cause someone or something to become ① or ②. ♦ *I matured the peaches by placing them in a covered bowl.* ♦ *John's new job helped mature him a little more.* **4.** *iv.* to become ①. ♦ *Bananas mature after they're picked.* ♦ *The girl matured into a young woman.* **5.** *iv.* [for a bond] to reach full value; [for a payment] to be due. ♦ *My bond will be worth $10,000 when it matures.* ♦ *These bonds will mature in 10 years.*

maturity [mə 'tʃʊr ə ti] **1.** *n.* the state of being mature or developed; the degree to which someone or something is mature. (No plural form in this sense.) ♦ *The maturity of the fruit can be judged by the color of its skin.* ♦ *Mike has the maturity of a 10-year-old.* **2.** *n.* human wisdom; adult thinking. (No plural form in this sense.) ♦ *Maturity is attained through life experience.* ♦ *I relied on the maturity of my advisor.* **3.** *n.* the date when an amount of money becomes due and payable. (No plural form in this sense.) ♦ *The full value of the bond will be paid to you* *at maturity.* ♦ *Some banks charge a penalty if you repay a loan before maturity.*

maul ['mɔl] *tv.* to injure or harm someone or some creature. ♦ *The dog mauled the little kitten.* ♦ *The little boys mauled each other in a game of football.*

mausoleum [mɔ sə 'li əm] *n.* a tomb; a building in which one or more corpses are buried. ♦ *The mausoleum was located at the rear of the cemetery.* ♦ *The coffin was carried into the mausoleum.*

maverick ['mæv rɪk] **1.** *n.* a stray cow that is not branded; a cow whose ownership is not established. ♦ *The farmer found a maverick wandering through his field.* ♦ *The sheriff tried to determine the maverick's owner.* **2.** *n.* someone who thinks and acts differently from the majority. (Figurative on ①.) ♦ *The local maverick's views were unpopular but tolerated.* ♦ *The maverick was admired by some for holding to his own beliefs.* **3.** *adj.* independent; dissenting. ♦ *The maverick member of the jury could not be swayed.* ♦ *The maverick politician voted against her party's platform.*

maxim ['mæk sɪm] *n.* a wise saying; a rule of behavior; a sensible statement of truth. ♦ *"A penny saved is a penny earned" is an old maxim.* ♦ *Grandpa always gave advice in the form of maxims.*

maximal ['mæks ə məl] *adj.* to the maximum; greatest; highest; most. (Adv: *maximally.*) ♦ *The maximal rate of speed is the speed of light.* ♦ *The profitable factory operated with maximal efficiency.*

maximum ['mæk sɪ məm] **1.** *n.* the highest amount or degree possible; the upper limit or boundary. ♦ *The criminal was sentenced to a maximum of 25 years in jail.* ♦ *John turned the volume on his stereo up to the maximum.* **2.** *adj.* maximal; greatest; highest; most. ♦ *The maximum speed limit on most rural highways is 65 miles per hour.* ♦ *John turned the oven to the maximum temperature.*

may ['me] **1.** *aux.* be allowed to do something; have permission to do something. (Often can is used in place of may, even though, in standard English, can refers to ability, and may refers to permission. See also might. Takes a bare verb.) ♦ *You may go to the store after dinner.* ♦ *May I leave early today?* **2.** *aux.* be possible. (Takes a bare verb.) ♦ *It may rain today.* ♦ *I may go bowling tomorrow.* **3.** *aux.* <a form used to extend a wish or hope>; let it be that.... ♦ *May you always be healthy and happy!* ♦ *May all your wishes come true.* **4.** *aux.* will be able to. (Often can or might is used instead. Very formal. Takes a bare verb.) ♦ *I'm helping you now that you may do better next time.* ♦ *I'm completing my labors now, that I may retire early.* **5.** **May** *n.* the fifth month of the year. ♦ *Memorial Day is the last Monday in May.* ♦ *I was born on May 12.*

Maya ['mɑɪ jə] **1.** *n.* an American Indian group in southern Mexico, Belize, Guatemala, and east Honduras. ♦ *The Maya were very powerful until they were conquered by the Europeans in the early 1500s.* ♦ *The Maya developed an elaborate calendar system.* **2.** *n.* someone who is a member of ①. ♦ *Few Mayas live in Europe.* ♦ *A Maya led our tour group through the ancient ruins.* **3.** *n.* the language spoken by ①. ♦ *Nowadays, most speakers of Maya also know Spanish.* ♦ *The linguist learned Maya while living in a Mayan village.*

Mayan ['mɑɪ ən] **1.** *n.* a Maya. ♦ *The Mayans built huge structures that look like pyramids.* ♦ *No one knows what happened to the many Mayans who once lived in Central America.* **2.** *n.* the language of the Mayas. ♦ *In some places, Mayan has been influenced heavily by Spanish.* ♦ *The village children were taught in Spanish and Mayan.* **3.** *adj.* <the adj. use of ① or ②.> ♦ *Mayan families lived in small, sturdy houses.* ♦ *The Mayan people built huge structures that look like pyramids.*

maybe ['me bi] *adv.* perhaps; possibly yes, possibly no. ♦ *Maybe I'll go to the store this afternoon. I'm not sure.* ♦ *"Do you want to see a movie?" "Maybe. I'll think about it."*

mayhem ['me hɛm] **1.** *n.* the crime of harming or mutilating a person. (No plural form in this sense.) ♦ *The violent criminal was charged with mayhem.* ♦ *The pirates were known for committing murder and mayhem.* **2.** *n.* a violent action that causes injury; violent confusion or disorder. (No plural form in this sense. Figurative on ①.) ♦ *After the bomb exploded, there was general mayhem.* ♦ *Mayhem broke out when the verdict was delivered.*

mayonnaise [me ə 'nez] *n.* a creamy sauce for salads and sandwiches; a sauce made from eggs, oil, and vinegar. (No plural form in this sense.) ♦ *I spread some mayonnaise on my sandwich.* ♦ *Keep mayonnaise in the refrigerator, or it will spoil.*

mayor ['me ɚ] *n.* the elected leader of a city, town, or village. ♦ *The mayor imposed a curfew on the residents of the town.* ♦ *The city council voted against the mayor's proposed budget.*

maze ['mez] **1.** *n.* a network of connected corridors, arranged so that it is hard to get from one place to another because most of the paths are blocked. ♦ *The garden was a maze of tall shrubbery.* ♦ *The researcher watched the mouse run through the maze.* **2.** *n.* something that is as confusing as ①. (Figurative on ①.) ♦ *It's easy to get lost in Boston's maze of streets.* ♦ *Each year, the maze of tax forms gets more confusing.*

me ['mi] **1.** *pron.* <the objective form of I, the first-person singular pronoun.> (Used after prepositions and transitive verbs and as an indefinite object. When me is joined with pronouns or the names of other persons, it is usually placed last in the series.) ♦ *Would you please give me the ball?* ♦ *This package is for David and me.* **2.** *pron.* <a first-person singular form.> (Used after a contracted form of be to refer to the speaker or writer. Usually, either "It's me" or the more formal "It is I." Rarely, if ever, "It's I" or "It is me.") ♦ *It's me.* ♦ *It's nobody but little old me.*

meadow ['mɛd o] *n.* an area of grassland; an area of grassland where cows, sheep, or goats graze. ♦ *The grazing sheep stayed in the meadow.* ♦ *After it snowed, I went cross-country skiing across the meadow.*

meager ['mig ɚ] *adj.* not having enough of something; lacking; scanty. (Adv: *meagerly.*) ♦ *The workers complained about their meager wages.* ♦ *We were served a meager meal of bread and water.*

meal ['mil] **1.** *n.* a regular occasion where food is eaten, especially breakfast, lunch, or dinner. (Compare with snack.) ♦ *The three meals of the day are breakfast, lunch, and dinner.* ♦ *I'm on a diet, so I don't snack between meals.* **2.** *n.* the food that is eaten at ①. ♦ *I made a meal of the* *leftover turkey.* ♦ *The condemned prisoner chose steak as his final meal.* **3.** *n.* crushed grain; flour. (No plural form in this sense.) ♦ *The cook bought a large bag of corn meal.* ♦ *I breaded the fish in meal before frying it.* **4. square meal** *idiom* a nourishing, filling meal ②. ♦ *All you've eaten today is junk food. You should sit down to a square meal.* ♦ *The tramp hadn't had a square meal in weeks.*

mean ['min] **1.** *adj.* cruel; not kind; selfish. (Adv: *meanly.* Comp: *meaner;* sup: *meanest.*) ♦ *You should apologize for those mean things that you said.* ♦ *The mean old man refused the apple I tried to give him.* **2.** *adj.* average. (Compare with median.) ♦ *The mean wage in this state is below the national average.* ♦ *The mean age of the people I work with is 28.* **3.** *n.* an average; the average of a group of numbers. ♦ *The mean of 2, 5, and 11 is 6.* ♦ *This computer program automatically computes means.* **4.** *tv., irreg.* [for language] to represent, indicate, or express something. (Pt/pp: meant.) ♦ *Did you mean that I should stay home?* ♦ *What did you mean by that rude remark?* **5.** *tv., irreg.* to indicate or signal something. ♦ *These heavy rains mean the roads will be flooded.* ♦ *Bob's yawning. I guess that means we should go now.* **6. mean (for someone) to do something** *idiom* to intend (for someone) to do something. (The subject of the clause—the *for someone*—may be omitted if that subject is the same as the subject of the sentence.) ♦ *John meant to go with us to the zoo.* ♦ *John meant for Jane to do the dishes.* **7. meant to be** *idiom* destined to exist. ♦ *Our love was meant to be!* ♦ *It was not meant to be.* **8. meant to be something** *idiom* destined or fated to be something. ♦ *Jane was meant to be a chemist.* ♦ *I was meant to be rich, but something didn't work right!*

meander [mi 'æn dɚ] *iv.* to wander through something; to move around something with no obvious goal. ♦ *The river meandered through the countryside.* ♦ *The teenager meandered around Europe with a backpack.*

meaning ['min ɪŋ] *n.* the sense of a word, statement, or symbol; significance; an interpretation. ♦ *What's the meaning of the word* symbol? ♦ *The artist explained the meaning of her abstract painting.*

meaningful ['min ɪŋ fʊl] *adj.* full of meaning; significant. (Adv: *meaningfully.*) ♦ *John and Mary have a meaningful relationship.* ♦ *That book was meaningful to me because it mirrored my life.*

meaningless ['min ɪŋ ləs] *adj.* without meaning; without purpose; having no significance; senseless. (Adv: *meaninglessly.*) ♦ *I think your poetry is meaningless and pretentious.* ♦ *John's meaningless arguments are frustrating me.*

meant ['mɛnt] pt/pp of mean.

meantime ['min tɑɪm] **in the meantime** *phr.* the period of time between two things; the period of time between now and when something is supposed to happen. ♦ *The movie starts at 6:00. In the meantime, let's eat dinner.* ♦ *My flight was at 8:00. In the meantime, I played solitaire.*

meanwhile ['min ʌɑɪl] *adv.* at the same time; during the same time. ♦ *I need time to think about that. Meanwhile, I'll wash the dishes.* ♦ *John was in town buying supplies. Meanwhile, back at the ranch, Mary waited for him.*

measles ['mi zəlz] *n.* an easily spread disease common in children. (Treated as singular or plural, often preceded by *the.*) ♦ *Mary couldn't go to school because she had the measles.* ♦ *The measles cause a high fever and a skin rash of small red dots.*

measly ['miz li] *adj.* small in amount; skimpy; meager. ♦ *Mrs. Wilson gave me a measly $1 for mowing her lawn.* ♦ *I'm still hungry because I was served a measly portion of steak at the restaurant.*

measurable ['mɛ ʒɚ ɑ bəl] *adj.* in an amount large enough to be measured; to a degree that can be measured. (Adv: *measurably.*) ♦ *A measurable amount of salt was found in the soil.* ♦ *There's a measurable amount of pollen in the air today.*

measure ['mɛ ʒɚ] **1.** *n.* a system for determining the amount of something. (No plural form in this sense.) ♦ *A bushel is a unit of measure.* ♦ *The metric system is an international system of measure.* **2.** *n.* a unit in a system that determines the amount of something. ♦ *The inch is a measure of length.* ♦ *The hour is a measure of time.* **3.** *n.* one of the series of groups of musical notes that makes up a musical composition. ♦ *Usually, each measure has the same number of beats.* ♦ *The last measure in a piece of music contains the final note.* **4.** *n.* the extent, amount, or quantity of something. ♦ *The measure of pollution in the river was alarmingly high.* ♦ *I won the race by a considerable measure.* **5.** *n.* a course of action; a plan. ♦ *The factory took many measures to assure the workers' safety.* ♦ *I wore a life jacket as a safety measure.* **6.** *n.* a law; a proposed law; a resolution. ♦ *Congress passed a measure to punish drug dealers.* ♦ *The president vetoed the taxation measure.* **7.** *tv.* to determine the size, extent, amount, degree, etc., of something. ♦ *I measured the length and the width of the room.* ♦ *The nurse measured the child's height.* **8.** *tv.* to accomplish or provide the measurement of something. ♦ *A ruler measures length.* ♦ *A thermometer measures temperature.* **9.** *iv.* to be a certain size, extent, amount, degree, etc. ♦ *This room measures 12 feet by 15 feet.* ♦ *Billy measures precisely 4 feet tall.*

measured ['mɛ ʒɚd] *adj.* slow and careful; deliberate. (Adv: *measuredly.*) ♦ *I gave a measured response to the confusing question.* ♦ *The mayor's measured reply offended no one.*

measurement ['mɛ ʒɚ mənt] **1.** *n.* a system of measuring. (No plural form in this sense.) ♦ *Metric measurement is based on multiples of 10.* ♦ *Canada has switched to metric measurement.* **2.** *n.* the process of measuring. (No plural form in this sense.) ♦ *The measurement of the size of a bacterium requires the use of a microscope.* ♦ *A protractor is used for the measurement of angles.* **3.** *n.* the size, length, weight, or amount of something that is found by measuring. ♦ *I used trigonometry to determine the angle's measurement.* ♦ *I made a list of the measurements of everyone I wanted to buy gifts for.*

meat ['mit] **1.** *n.* the flesh of animals used as food. (No plural form in this sense. See also fish, fowl, poultry.) ♦ *Does Mary eat meat, or is she a vegetarian?* ♦ *Would you like dark meat or white meat?* **2. meats** *n.* kinds or types of ①. ♦ *Chicken and lamb are my favorite meats.* ♦ *They served three meats at the banquet.* **3.** *n.* the part of something that can be eaten. ♦ *I spread some crab meat on a cracker.* ♦ *The meat of coconuts is very tasty.* **4.** *n.* the main idea or content of something; the gist. (Figurative on ①.) ♦ *The witness responded to the meat of the lawyer's question.* ♦ *The meat of the report begins on page 6.*

meatball ['mit bɔl] *n.* a round ball of chopped meat, eaten as food. ♦ *I ate spaghetti with meatballs.* ♦ *The meatballs were made from ground beef.*

meatloaf ['mit lof] **1.** *n.* a dish of chopped meat shaped like a loaf of bread. (No plural form in this sense.) ♦ *Meatloaf is my favorite dish.* ♦ *Mike ate two slices of meatloaf for dinner.* **2.** *n.* a unit or loaf of ①. ♦ *I glazed the meatloaf with barbecue sauce.* ♦ *Please get a meatloaf out of the freezer for dinner.*

mechanic [mə 'kæn ɪk] **1.** *n.* someone who fixes cars, engines, or other machines. ♦ *The mechanic replaced the broken engine part.* ♦ *I asked the mechanic if my car could be repaired by Friday.* **2.** See also mechanics.

mechanical [mə 'kæn ɪ kəl] **1.** *adj.* concerned or associated with machines. (Adv: *mechanically* [...ɪk li].) ♦ *The fancy car was designed by a mechanical engineer.* ♦ *Fixing engines requires mechanical knowledge.* **2.** *adj.* controlled or operated by machinery; made of machinery. (Adv: *mechanically* [...ɪk li].) ♦ *A small mechanical mouse ran about on the floor.* ♦ *The mechanical arm moved the block of steel.* **3.** *adj.* like a machine; not like someone or something that is living; automatic. (Adv: *mechanically* [...ɪk li].) ♦ *The mechanical motions of the pendulum are controlled by the laws of physics.* ♦ *The engine's soft mechanical hum means it's running smoothly.* **4.** *adj.* listless; uninspired. (Figurative on ③. Adv: *mechanically* [...ɪk li].) ♦ *The mechanical delivery of the speech made me drowsy.* ♦ *The critic criticized the actor's mechanical performance.*

mechanically [mə 'kæn ɪk li] *adv.* doing something in a routine and uninspired way. ♦ *The tired worker went about his chores mechanically.* ♦ *The untalented actress delivered her lines mechanically.*

mechanics [me 'kæn ɪks] **1.** *n.* the science and study of motion and force. (Treated as singular.) ♦ *The physics exam covered the laws of mechanics.* ♦ *The force of a spring is determined by laws of mechanics.* **2.** *n.* the science, study, and design of making machines. (Treated as singular.) ♦ *The mechanic studied mechanics in a physics course.* ♦ *I learned mechanics by working in my father's garage.* **3.** See also mechanic.

mechanism ['mɛk ə nɪz əm] **1.** *n.* a machine; a moving part of a machine. ♦ *An automobile engine is a complicated mechanism.* ♦ *The jeweler repaired my watch by replacing a small mechanism.* **2.** *n.* a system whose components work together like the parts of a machine. (Figurative on ①.) ♦ *The television program detailed the mechanism of birth.* ♦ *The mechanism of chewing is more complicated than it might seem.*

mechanize ['mɛk ə naɪz] *tv.* to change from human skill and muscle power to mechanical power. ♦ *Many tasks were mechanized during the Industrial Revolution.* ♦ *The cotton gin mechanized the job of separating seeds from cotton.*

medal ['mɛd l] *n.* a small piece of metal that is given to someone as an honor. ♦ *Medals are worn about the neck on a ribbon or pinned to clothing.* ♦ *The brave soldier was awarded several medals after the war.*

medallion [mə 'dæl jən] **1.** *n.* a large medal. ♦ *The winner of the race showed her medallion to the cheering crowd.* ♦ *The brave soldier was awarded a bronze medallion.* **2.** *n.* a large design or ornament. ♦ *A gold medallion hung from Jane's necklace.* ♦ *The model's earrings were silver medallions.*

meddle ['mɛd l] **1. meddle in** *iv.* + *prep. phr.* to interfere in someone's business; to involve oneself in someone's business when one is not wanted. ♦ *Don't meddle in other people's business.* ♦ *My neighbor is always meddling in my affairs.* **2. meddle with** *iv.* + *prep. phr.* to play with and interfere with something. ♦ *Please don't meddle with my computer.* ♦ *Jimmy is meddling with the television set.*

meddling ['mɛd lɪŋ] *adj.* interfering; interrupting. (Adv: *meddlingly.*) ♦ *I told my meddling neighbor to mind his own business.* ♦ *The meddling woman told the couple how to discipline their children.*

media ['mid i ə] **1.** *n.* <the Latin plural of medium ①.> (Although it is a Latin plural, media is sometimes treated as plural in English and sometimes treated as singular.) ♦ *I think the media is unfairly criticizing the president.* ♦ *The media are interested in focusing on controversial matters.* **2.** *n.* <the Latin plural of medium ②.> (Often treated as singular.) ♦ *The scientist grew the bacteria in many different media.* ♦ *Which media is best for growing bacteria?* **3.** See mass media.

median ['mid i ən] **1.** *n.* the middle number in a series of numbers; the number in a series of numbers that has just as many numbers below it as above it. (This is not the same as mean or average.) ♦ *The median of 1, 2, 3, 500, and 1,004 is 3.* ♦ *The median of 0, 1, and 8 is 1. The average is 3.* **2.** *n.* the line or the strip of land between two lanes of a road. ♦ *The drunken driver crashed into a tree growing in the median.* ♦ *I stood in the median waiting for the traffic to clear.* **3.** *adj.* <the adj. use of ①.> ♦ *What's the median value of homes in this suburb?* ♦ *The report listed the median age of each state's population.*

mediate ['mid i et] *tv.* to settle a disagreement by helping two opposing sides agree. ♦ *The arbitrator mediated the contract dispute.* ♦ *I mediated John and Anne's rather serious disagreement.*

mediator ['mid i et ɚ] *n.* someone who helps mediate a disagreement. ♦ *The mediator urged both sides to accept the contract without changes.* ♦ *The heads of the warring armies agreed to meet with a mediator.*

medic ['mɛd ɪk] *n.* a doctor or medical student. (A front clipping of *medical personnel.*) ♦ *The medic saved the choking diner's life.* ♦ *As a medic, I have to work many hours without sleep.*

Medicaid ['mɛd ə ked] *n.* a government program that helps pay medical costs for people with a low income or no income. (No plural form in this sense.) ♦ *The presidential candidate vowed to cut Medicaid's budget.* ♦ *The destitute woman's surgery was paid for by Medicaid.*

medical ['mɛd ɪ kəl] **1.** *adj.* of or about medicine and the study and practice of medicine. (Adv: *medically* [...ɪk li].) ♦ *You need medical treatment* now! *This is an emergency.* ♦ *I need to see a medical doctor. Not a doctor of philosophy!* **2.** *n.* an examination by a physician; a physical;

a checkup. ♦ *You're due for your medical next month.* ♦ *I drove to the clinic for my annual medical.*

Medicare ['mɛd ɪ kɛr] *n.* a government program that provides health insurance for people who are at least 65 years old. (No plural form in this sense.) ♦ *My grandparents are both eligible for Medicare.* ♦ *Medicare paid for my grandmother's hip surgery.*

medicate ['mɛd ə ket] *tv.* to put medicine on or in someone or something; to treat someone or something with medicine or drugs. ♦ *I medicated the scrape on my arm with iodine.* ♦ *The sick patient was heavily medicated.*

medicated ['mɛd ɪ ket ɪd] *adj.* including medicine; containing medicine. ♦ *After brushing my teeth, I rinse with a medicated mouthwash.* ♦ *This medicated lozenge will help soothe your sore throat.*

medication [mɛd ə 'ke ʃən] **1.** *n.* the use or application of medicine. (No plural form in this sense.) ♦ *This ailment needs medication immediately.* ♦ *Medication and rest are the best way to treat your disease.* **2.** *n.* a kind of medicine; a dose of medicine. ♦ *The doctor is trying a series of new medications on my illness.* ♦ *What kind of medications are you taking for your infection?*

medicinal [mə 'dɪs ə nəl] *adj.* used as medicine; having some of the properties or characteristics of medicine. (Adv: *medicinally.*) ♦ *I soothed my sore throat with tea made from medicinal herbs.* ♦ *Bob drinks prune juice every morning for medicinal purposes.*

medicine ['mɛd ɪ sən] **1.** *n.* the science and study of preventing, diagnosing, and curing diseases in the body. (No plural form in this sense.) ♦ *You must study medicine for many years before becoming a doctor.* ♦ *Each year many important advances are made in medicine.* **2.** *n.* something that is used to treat a disease, especially something that is taken by the mouth or injected into the body. (No plural form in this sense.) ♦ *I give my dog her medicine every evening.* ♦ *The doctor gave me some medicine and sent me home.* **3.** *n.* a specific kind of ②. ♦ *I take three different medicines for my cough.* ♦ *Which of these medicines is the most effective?* **4. dose of one's own medicine; taste of one's own medicine** *idiom* the same kind of treatment that one gives to other people. ♦ *Sally never is very friendly. Someone is going to give her a dose of her own medicine someday.* ♦ *He didn't like getting a taste of his own medicine.* **5. take one's medicine** *idiom* to accept the punishment or the bad fortune that one deserves. ♦ *I know I did wrong, and I know I have to take my medicine.* ♦ *Billy knew he was going to get spanked, and he didn't want to take his medicine.*

medieval [mid i 'i vəl] *adj.* of or about the Middle Ages in Europe, from about A.D. 500 to about 1450. (Adv: *medievally.*) ♦ *Countless people died of the plague in medieval times.* ♦ *We studied the Crusades in my medieval-history class.*

mediocre [mi di 'o kɚ] *adj.* only average; halfway between good and bad; just acceptable. ♦ *The meal on the airplane was just mediocre.* ♦ *I got mediocre grades last semester.*

meditate ['mɛd ɪ tet] *iv.* to clear one's mind of ordinary thoughts and focus on one thing, often something spiritual or religious. ♦ *The monk meditated for many hours each day.* ♦ *I meditate every evening to relieve stress.*

meditation [mɛd ɪ 'te ʃən] *n.* the process of meditating; concentration on something spiritual or religious. (Noncount, but sometimes plural with the same meaning.) ♦ *The monk spent many hours each day in private meditation.* ♦ *While deep in her meditation, the nun received a message from God.*

Mediterranean Sea ['mɛd ə tə ren i ən 'si] See Gazetteer.

medium ['mid i əm] **1.** *n., irreg.* a channel or pathway for sending information. (The Latin plural is **media**, and the English plural is *mediums.* See **mass media**.) ♦ *Radio is an important medium for advertising.* ♦ *The largest media are newspapers and television.* **2.** *n., irreg.* a substance in which an organism such as a bacterium can be grown and kept alive. (Pl: **media**.) ♦ *This medium is best for growing this organism.* ♦ *Some bacteria can be grown in many different media.* **3.** *n., irreg.* the materials used by an artist. (The Latin plural is **media**, and the English plural is *mediums.*) ♦ *As a sculptor, my preferred medium is clay.* ♦ *The painter used several media, including both acrylic and oil paints.* **4.** *n.* a middle stage, level, or condition. (Pl: *mediums.*) ♦ *I think this compromise is a happy medium for all parties.* ♦ *I set the heat control on medium.* **5.** *n.* the middle size of an object for sale that comes in different sizes. (Pl: *mediums.*) ♦ *The small doesn't fit. Do you have any mediums?* ♦ *Do you want a medium or a large?* **6.** *n.* someone who claims to be able to communicate with spirits of dead people. (Pl: *mediums.*) ♦ *I asked the medium to contact the spirit of my dead mother.* ♦ *The medium looked into her crystal ball.* **7.** *adj.* being the middle size; larger than a small size and smaller than a large size. ♦ *I'd like a large order of french fries and a medium soft drink.* ♦ *Please give me a medium pizza.*

medley ['mɛd li] **1.** *n.* a song or piece of music that is made up of parts of other songs or pieces of music. ♦ *The choir sang a medley of songs from Broadway musicals.* ♦ *The band played a medley of marches.* **2.** *n.* a mixture of different things. (Figurative on ①.) ♦ *The vegetable medley consisted of peas, carrots, and corn.* ♦ *The proposed budget was met with a medley of critical remarks.*

meek ['mik] *adj.* letting others do as they want; not protesting; yielding; submissive. (Adv: *meekly.* Comp: *meeker;* sup: *meekest.*) ♦ *You're too meek. You need to stand up for yourself.* ♦ *The meek old man waited quietly in line.*

meet ['mit] **1.** *tv., irreg.* to come together with someone either by chance or on purpose; to encounter someone. (Pt/pp: **met**.) ♦ *I met an old friend for lunch today.* ♦ *Tom hoped to meet Mary at the library.* **2.** *tv., irreg.* to touch someone or something; to come into contact with someone or something. ♦ *The carpet meets the wall on all sides.* ♦ *The Ohio River meets the Mississippi River in southern Illinois.* **3.** *tv., irreg.* to be introduced to someone; to make someone's acquaintance. ♦ *I met you at the party last night, remember?* ♦ *I'd like you to meet an old friend of mine.* **4.** *tv., irreg.* to respond to something. ♦ *They will meet your announcement with cheers.* ♦ *The plan was met with a lot of resistance.* **5.** *iv., irreg.* to come together; to join; to connect; to make contact; to touch. ♦ *If you wrap each side around like this, the ends will meet.* ♦ *The two electrical wires met, giving off dangerous sparks.* **6.** *n.* a sporting event where contests of swimming, diving, running, jumping, etc., are held. ♦ *Sixty athletes competed at* *the swimming meet.* ♦ *The track meet consisted of eight different events.* **7. make (both) ends meet** *idiom* to earn and spend equal amounts of money. ♦ *I have to work at two jobs to make ends meet.* ♦ *Through better budgeting, I am learning to make both ends meet.* **8. meet one's death; meet one's end** *idiom* to experience something, especially death or problems. ♦ *After 20 years, my dog finally met his death when he got hit by a bus.* ♦ *The sky diver met his end when his parachute didn't open.*

meeting ['mit ɪŋ] **1.** *n.* an assembly; a group of people who have come together for a specific reason. ♦ *We're discussing budget cuts at today's meeting.* ♦ *Every Monday morning we have a sales meeting.* **2.** *n.* an instance of people coming together, perhaps by accident. ♦ *Our meeting yesterday in the park was a complete accident.* ♦ *After a couple of accidental meetings, the two opponents grew to be friends.* **3.** *n.* the place where two things meet or connect. ♦ *The large river was formed by the meeting of the two streams.* ♦ *The meeting of the two wires was wrapped with electrical tape.* **4. meeting of minds** *idiom* the establishment of agreement; complete agreement. ♦ *After a lot of discussion we finally reached a meeting of minds.* ♦ *We struggled to bring about a meeting of minds on the issues.*

meg ['mɛg] See megabyte.

megabyte ['mɛg ə bɑɪt] *n.* a unit consisting of about one million bytes. (The abbreviation is *Mb,* and the word is often shortened to *meg.*) ♦ *Most disks can store 1.44 megabytes of data.* ♦ *I used all the available memory on my 24-megabyte hard drive.*

megaphone ['mɛg ə fon] *n.* a kind of funnel or cone used to make one's voice louder so that it can be heard more easily and farther away. (Some are electronically amplified. See also bullhorn.) ♦ *The police officer addressed the large crowd with a megaphone.* ♦ *Speak into the small end of the megaphone, and your voice comes out quite loud at the other end.*

melancholy ['mɛl ən kɑl i] **1.** *adj.* sad; unhappy. ♦ *The melancholy song made me cry.* ♦ *I tried to cheer up my melancholy friend.* **2.** *n.* sadness; depression. (No plural form in this sense.) ♦ *When I'm suffering from melancholy, I watch a lot of television.* ♦ *I helped John combat melancholy by taking him to a funny movie.*

melee ['me le] *n.* a fight; a brawl. ♦ *Twenty people were hurt in a melee at the stadium.* ♦ *The orderly demonstration soon turned into a violent melee.*

mellow ['mɛl o] **1.** *adj.* [of colors, sounds, textures, or tastes that are] soft, deep, relaxing, or muted. (Adv: *mellowly.* Comp: *mellower;* sup: *mellowest.*) ♦ *I heard some mellow saxophone music playing in the background.* ♦ *The herbal tea had a soothing, mellow flavor.* **2.** *adj.* easygoing; relaxed; quiet. (Informal. Figurative on ①. Adv: *mellowly.* Comp: *mellower;* sup: *mellowest.*) ♦ *Good dance music puts me in a mellow mood.* ♦ *Taking a long, warm bath puts me in a mellow mood.* **3.** *tv.* to cause someone or a group to become ②. ♦ *The soft music mellowed the audience.* ♦ *The wine mellowed all of the party guests.* **4.** *iv.* to become ②. ♦ *My sister's resentment mellowed over the years.* ♦ *My temperamental father mellowed as he got older.*

melodious [mə 'lod i əs] **1.** *adj.* [of music] pleasant and having a notable melody. (Adv: *melodiously.*) ♦ *The organist played a melodious hymn.* ♦ *I sang a melodious lullaby to my baby.* **2.** *adj.* capable of making good melodies; pleasant to listen to. (Adv: *melodiously.*) ♦ *I loved listening to the soprano's melodious voice.* ♦ *The melodious birds chirped in the trees.*

melodrama ['mɛl ə drɑm ə] **1.** *n.* exaggerated emotion. (No plural form in this sense.) ♦ *Dinner at Aunt Mary's was filled with melodrama and ill feelings among the guests.* ♦ *I find the melodrama of soap operas to be unbelievable.* **2.** *n.* a play, movie, or story that is full of strong emotion and exaggerated writing or acting styles. ♦ *I don't mind a tearful melodrama occasionally.* ♦ *The melodrama was so overacted that it was fun to watch.*

melodramatic [mɛl o drə 'mæt ɪk] **1.** *adj.* showing melodrama. (Adv: *melodramatically* [...ɪk li].) ♦ *Bad acting turned the drama into a melodramatic farce.* ♦ *The actress had mastered a few melodramatic facial expressions but had no other talent.* **2.** *adj.* behaving in an exaggerated way that is meant to cause strong emotions. (Figurative on ①. Adv: *melodramatically* [...ɪk li].) ♦ *The speaker's melodramatic gestures soon became annoying.* ♦ *The poet's melodramatic reading of her poem made me cry.*

melody ['mɛl ə di] *n.* the series of notes that make up the tune of a song; a song; a tune. ♦ *My favorite radio station plays melodies from the 1950s.* ♦ *I whistled a happy melody as I walked down the street.*

melon ['mɛl ən] **1.** *n.* one of a family of large, round or oval fruit with thick rinds and pulpy insides. ♦ *The farmer picked a fine melon and cut it open.* ♦ *I knocked on the melon to see if it was ripe.* **2.** *n.* the edible part of ①. (No plural form in this sense. Number is expressed with *piece(s)* or *slice(s)* of ①.) ♦ *Could I have some melon please?* ♦ *Give Jimmy a slice of melon.*

melt ['mɛlt] **1.** *iv.* [for a solid] to become liquid; to turn into a liquid. ♦ *Ice turns into water when it melts.* ♦ *Steel melts at very high temperatures.* **2.** *tv.* to cause something solid to become liquid; to cause something solid to turn into a liquid. ♦ *The hot water melted the ice.* ♦ *The worker melted the tar in a special furnace.* **3.** *tv.* to cause something to disappear or fade. (Figurative on ②.) ♦ *This facial cream is supposed to melt your wrinkles.* ♦ *Kind words melted my fears away.* **4.** *n.* an instance of melting as in ①. ♦ *The rapid snow melt caused flash flooding.* ♦ *The sudden ice melt endangered the people who were ice fishing.*

meltdown ['mɛlt dɑʊn] *n.* a dangerous nuclear accident where the core of a nuclear reactor melts, usually releasing radiation into the air. ♦ *The aging nuclear plant was closed to prevent a nuclear meltdown.* ♦ *The radiation from the meltdown poisoned the environment.*

melting point ['mɛlt ɪŋ 'pɔɪnt] *n.* the temperature at which a solid becomes a liquid. ♦ *The melting point of water is 32 degrees Fahrenheit.* ♦ *The melting point of iron is very high.*

melting pot ['mɛlt ɪŋ pɑt] *n.* a city or country where people from different places and cultures live together, as if they were chunks of metal being melted together. ♦ *New York City is a thriving melting pot.* ♦ *The border town became a melting pot of refugees during the war.*

member ['mɛm bɚ] *n.* someone who belongs to a group or an organization. ♦ *Both senators in my state are members of the Democratic Party.* ♦ *Most health clubs are only open to members and their guests.*

membership ['mɛm bɚ ʃɪp] **1.** *n.* the connection between one person and an organization to which the person belongs. (No plural form in this sense.) ♦ *I signed up for membership at a local health club.* ♦ *I renewed my membership at the health club for another year.* **2.** *n.* all of the members of a group or organization. (No plural form in this sense.) ♦ *The president of the group spoke to the entire membership.* ♦ *The membership received an important memo from the club's leader.*

membrane ['mɛm bren] **1.** *n.* a very thin wall of cellular tissue found in plants and animals. ♦ *The biologist examined the membrane under a microscope.* ♦ *My cold inflamed the mucous membranes in my nose.* **2.** *n.* a light, thin piece of material. (Figurative on ①.) ♦ *The tent was made of a thin but strong nylon membrane.* ♦ *The silk membrane tore easily.*

memento AND **momento** [mə 'mɛn to] *n.* a souvenir; something that reminds one of someone else or of a place that one has been. ♦ *My host gave me a small gift as a memento of my trip to France.* ♦ *I keep this small lock of hair as a momento of a dear friend.*

memo ['mɛm o] *n.* a note or announcement; a memorandum. (Pl in *-s.*) ♦ *I sent a memo to all employees about the company picnic.* ♦ *Tom read the brief memo and threw it in the trash.*

memoir ['mɛm wɑr] *n.* a written story about something that happened in one's life; a written recollection; a written remembrance. (Often plural, to refer to a collection of stories about one's life.) ♦ *The former president wrote his memoirs shortly before he died.* ♦ *The actress's agent urged her to write her memoirs.*

memorable ['mɛm ɚ ə bəl] *adj.* worth remembering; notable. (Adv: *memorably.*) ♦ Hamlet *is one of Shakespeare's most memorable plays.* ♦ *I spent a memorable weekend in Palm Beach.*

memoranda [mɛm ə 'ræn də] pl of memorandum.

memorandum [mɛm ə 'ræn dəm] *n.* an official note or letter, especially from someone or some people to one or more persons in a company. (Pl: memoranda.) ♦ *The employees read many memoranda about the company's reorganization.* ♦ *The president's memorandum wished everyone a happy holiday season.*

memorial [mə 'mor i əl] **1.** *adj.* [of something] used to remind someone of a person, thing, place, or event. ♦ *The memorial service for the missing soldiers was well attended.* ♦ *The memorial ceremony marked the anniversary of the end of the war.* **2.** *n.* something that is a reminder of an event or of a person no longer living. ♦ *The music was composed as a memorial to those who died in war.* ♦ *Millions of tourists have visited the Lincoln Memorial in Washington, D.C.*

Memorial Day [mə 'mor i əl de] *n.* a U.S. holiday, celebrated on the last Monday in May, that honors all who died in war. (Memorial Day was originally instituted to remember the Civil War dead and was once known as Decoration Day.) ♦ *Banks and government offices are closed on Memorial Day.* ♦ *The amusement park was open from Memorial Day to Labor Day.*

memorize ['mɛm ə rɑɪz] *tv.* to learn and remember something; to commit something to memory. ♦ *John memorized a poem to recite in class.* ♦ *I had to memorize my speech for the meeting.*

memory ['mɛm ə ri] **1.** *n.* the brain thought of as a place where ideas, words, images, and past events reside. (No plural form in this sense.) ♦ *I committed the song to memory.* ♦ *Tom recited the story from memory.* **2.** *n.* the functioning or quality of ①; the ability of ① to function. (No plural form in this sense.) ♦ *As John got older, his memory started to fade.* ♦ *Mary has a very good memory for people's names.* **3.** *n.* an instance of remembering a past event, experience, person, or sensation; someone or something that is remembered; a recollection. ♦ *The witness's memory of the accident was faultless.* ♦ *I have no memories of my life before I was three years old.* **4.** *n.* the part of a computer where information is kept until it is needed or stored. (No plural form in this sense.) ♦ *I deleted some files because my computer's memory was full.* ♦ *My new computer has more memory than my old one.* **5. in memory of someone** *idiom* to continue the good memories ③ of someone; for the honor of a deceased person. ♦ *Many streets were renamed in memory of John F. Kennedy.* ♦ *We planted roses in memory of my deceased father.* **6. in recent memory** *idiom* the period of time in which things happened that can be remembered. ♦ *Never in recent memory has there been this much snow!* ♦ *I haven't been this happy in recent memory!* **7. know something from memory** *idiom* to have memorized something so that one does not have to consult a written version; to know something well from seeing it very often. ♦ *Mary didn't need the script because she knew the play from memory.* ♦ *The conductor went through the entire concert without music. He knew it from memory.*

men ['mɛn] pl of man.

menace ['mɛn ɪs] **1.** *n.* a threat; someone or something that threatens harm, violence, or danger. ♦ *The judge said the criminal was a menace to society.* ♦ *The enemy's huge army is a menace to peace.* **2.** *tv.* to threaten someone or something with harm, violence, or danger. ♦ *The tranquil village was menaced by dark storm clouds.* ♦ *The terrorist menaced the hostages.*

menagerie [mə 'næ ʒə ri] *n.* a collection of wild animals, usually kept in cages for the public to see; a small zoo. ♦ *Of all the animals in the menagerie, I like the monkeys the best.* ♦ *The menagerie in my town includes several lions.*

mend ['mɛnd] **1.** *tv.* to fix something; to repair something. ♦ *I mended the hole in my sock.* ♦ *Tom promised to mend the broken chair leg.* **2.** *iv.* to become healthy; to become well. ♦ *My broken bone mended within three months of the accident.* ♦ *Grandma mended slowly after a serious illness.* **3. on the mend** *idiom* getting better; becoming well again. ♦ *I cared for my father while he was on the mend.* ♦ *I took a leave of absence from work while I was on the mend.* **4. mend one's ways** *idiom* to improve one's behavior. ♦ *John used to be very wild, but he's mended his ways.* ♦ *You'll have to mend your ways if you go out with Mary. She hates people to be late.*

menial ['min i əl] **1.** *adj.* not requiring skill or knowledge; lowly. (Adv: *menially.*) ♦ *Menial jobs usually do not pay well.* ♦ *As an assistant, I performed a lot of menial tasks.* **2.** *n.* a [lowly] servant. ♦ *One of the menials cleaned up the damage from the storm.* ♦ *A few extra menials were hired to help over the holidays.*

meningitis [mɛn ɪn 'dʒɑɪ tɪs] *n.* a serious infection that causes the inflammation of the membranes surrounding the brain and spinal cord. (No plural form in this sense.) ♦ *The young child was diagnosed with spinal meningitis.* ♦ *My best friend died from meningitis.*

menopause ['mɛn ə pɔz] *n.* a period of time during which menstruation gradually ceases. (No plural form in this sense.) ♦ *After menopause, contraception is no longer necessary.* ♦ *Jane wanted to have another child before she reached menopause.*

menses ['mɛn siz] *n.* a woman's menstrual period; menstruation. (From the plural of the Latin word for 'month.' Treated as a singular or plural.) ♦ *The doctor asked Susan if her menses were unusually heavy.* ♦ *The menses cease temporarily during pregnancy.*

menstrual ['mɛn stru əl] **1.** *adj.* associated with menstruation. (Adv: *menstrually.*) ♦ *Sometimes I have painful menstrual cramps.* ♦ *Anne told her doctor about her menstrual pains.* **2. menstrual period** *n.* a time during the month when a woman menstruates. (More common as period.) ♦ *Anne felt very bad just before her menstrual period started.* ♦ *Mary thought she was pregnant because she had missed a menstrual period.*

menstruate ['mɛn str(u) et] *iv.* to experience menstruation; to have a menstrual period. ♦ *Anne realized she wasn't pregnant when she started to menstruate.* ♦ *My daughter first menstruated when she was 11 years old.*

menstruation [mɛn 'stru e ʃən] *n.* the monthly process in sexually mature women who are not pregnant in which the lining of the uterus is shed. (No plural form in this sense.) ♦ *The teacher explained menstruation to the health class.* ♦ *It's best to see a gynecologist if menstruation is very painful.*

mental ['mɛn təl] **1.** *adj.* of or about the mind; done by the mind. (Adv: *mentally.*) ♦ *My crazy neighbor has a few mental problems.* ♦ *As a mental exercise, I memorized a famous speech.* **2.** *adj.* of or about mental illness. ♦ *Tom visited a friend in a mental hospital.* ♦ *He had been a mental patient for about a month.*

mental illness ['mɛn təl 'ɪl nəs] *n.* illness of the mind, affecting one's behavior, feelings, moods, and interactions with other people. (No plural form in this sense.) ♦ *John has suffered from mental illness for some years and was sent to a mental hospital.* ♦ *Mental illness can be treated and cured.*

mentality [mɛn 'tæl ə ti] **1.** *n.* one's mind; the power to learn, remember, and reason. (No plural form in this sense.) ♦ *Drugs can adversely affect your mentality.* ♦ *His mentality began to fade as he grew older.* **2.** *n.* a way of thinking; the way that someone thinks; character. (Figurative on ①.) ♦ *I can't deal with people with prejudiced mentalities.* ♦ *If everyone had a peaceful mentality, there'd be no war.*

mention ['mɛn ʃən] **1.** *tv.* to say or write something; to tell about something briefly. (Takes a clause.) ♦ *Did I mention that I'm going to Italy next week?* ♦ *Mary mentioned that she wanted to leave soon.* **2.** *tv.* to refer to someone or something. ♦ *Just mention money, and Bill gets excited.* ♦ *When the budget was mentioned, the president changed the subject.* **3.** *n.* an act of mentioning as in ②; a brief statement; a reference. ♦ *The mayor made only a brief mention of the crime problem.* ♦ *Anne's mention of shoes reminded me that I had to buy some socks.* **4.** *n.* acknowledgment; recognition of something good. (No plural form in this sense.) ♦ *I wanted first place, but I was happy with an honorable mention.* ♦ *Although my role was small, the critic gave me a favorable mention.* **5. mention something in passing** *idiom* to say or write something casually; to mention ① something while talking about something else. ♦ *He just happened to mention in passing that the mayor had resigned.* ♦ *John mentioned in passing that he was nearly eighty years old.*

mentor ['mɛn tor] *n.* an advisor; someone who advises, helps, or guides someone else. ♦ *The young writer's editor was also his mentor.* ♦ *Jane looked to her volleyball coach as her mentor.*

menu ['mɛn ju] **1.** *n.* a list of food and drink available at a restaurant. ♦ *Waiter, could I see a menu please?* ♦ *The salads were on the first page of the menu.* **2.** *n.* a list of options or functions available in a computer program. (Figurative on ①.) ♦ *To see what options are available, click on "Menu."* ♦ *The file menu lets you edit, create, save, or delete documents.*

meow [mi 'ɑʊ] **1.** *n.* the sound a cat makes. ♦ *The cat's loud meow frightened the mouse.* ♦ *I fed my cat when I heard her meows.* **2.** *iv.* [for a cat] to make its characteristic sound. ♦ *My cat meows when I pet it.* ♦ *The cat stood on its mat and meowed.*

mercenary ['mɚ sə nɛr i] **1.** *adj.* doing something for the money only; motivated by money. (Adv: *mercinarily* [mɚ sə 'nɛr ə li].) ♦ *The corrupt lawyer had mercenary objectives.* ♦ *John's mercenary business practices made him very rich but disliked.* **2.** *n.* someone who is paid by a political group to fight or kill. ♦ *The political coup was carried out by mercenaries.* ♦ *A mercenary assassinated the foreign leader.*

merchandise 1. ['mɚtʃ ən dɑɪs] *n.* products for sale or trade; things that are for sale. (No plural form in this sense.) ♦ *That store has a lot of merchandise on sale.* ♦ *Please don't touch the merchandise. If you break it, you will pay for it.* **2.** ['mɚtʃ ən dɑɪz] *tv.* to buy and sell products; to promote products for sale; to market products for sale. ♦ *Hardware stores merchandise many kinds of tools.* ♦ *The jeweler merchandised her services in the local paper.*

merchant ['mɚtʃ ənt] *n.* someone who buys and sells products in order to make money; a retailer. ♦ *My great-grandfather was a grain merchant in Kansas.* ♦ *The merchant helped me choose a good camera.*

merciful ['mɚ sɪ fʊl] *adj.* full of mercy; compassionate; forgiving. (Adv: *mercifully.*) ♦ *Please be merciful and feed the birds in the winter months.* ♦ *The merciful judge halved the young offender's sentence.*

merciless ['mɚ sɪ ləs] *adj.* without mercy; without compassion; cruel; ruthless. (Adv: *mercilessly.*) ♦ *The merciless terrorist bombed the airport.* ♦ *The hostages were given merciless beatings.*

mercury ['mɚk jə ri] **1.** *n.* a silver-gray metallic element that is liquid at room temperature. (No plural form in this sense.) ♦ *Mercury is used in thermometers to indicate temperature.* ♦ *Mercury is an element, and its symbol is Hg.* **2. Mercury** *n.* [in Roman mythology] the messenger of the gods. ♦ *The Greek counterpart of Mercury is Hermes.* ♦ *Mercury is the son of Jupiter and Maia.* **3. Mercury** *n.* the closest planet to the sun in our solar system. ♦ *Mercury revolves around the sun once every 88 days.* ♦ *The probe sent pictures of Mercury's surface back to Earth.*

mercy ['mɚ si] *n.* kindness; pity; compassion. (No plural form in this sense.) ♦ *The judge showed mercy on the first-time offender.* ♦ *The sinner prayed to God for mercy.*

mere ['mɪr] *adj.* only; nothing more than. (Adv: *merely.* Comp: none; sup: *merest.*) ♦ *It was a mere ten degrees above zero last night.* ♦ *By mere chance, I was on the same airplane as my cousin.*

merely ['mɪr li] *adv.* this only; only this and nothing else; just. ♦ *I'm merely brushing my teeth. I'll be done in a minute.* ♦ *John and Mary are merely friends, not lovers.*

merest ['mɪr əst] *adj.* only the slightest. (The superlative form of mere.) ♦ *By the merest chance, would you have some money I could borrow?* ♦ *You always cry at the merest provocation.*

merge ['mɚdʒ] **1.** *iv.* to join with something else. ♦ *I was fired when my firm merged with another one.* ♦ *The two small companies merged into one large one.* **2.** *iv.* to enter the flow of traffic. ♦ *Merge carefully when you get on the freeway.* ♦ *The right lane ends up ahead, so merge left.* **3.** *tv.* to cause two or more things to come together and become one. ♦ *The larger company merged two smaller ones into itself.* ♦ *The corporation merged two of its divisions together.*

merger ['mɚdʒ ɚ] *n.* the act or process of joining two organizations into one. ♦ *The business merger resulted in the loss of many jobs.* ♦ *The airline merger improved service and lowered prices.*

meringue [mə 'ræŋ] **1.** *n.* a baked mixture of sugar and egg whites, used as a topping on pies or other pastry. (No plural form in this sense.) ♦ *The chef put the lemon meringue in the pie shell.* ♦ *These tarts are topped with meringue.* **2.** *n.* a pastry made from a mixture of sugar and egg whites. ♦ *I bought a dozen meringues from the bakery.* ♦ *I had a cup of coffee and a meringue for breakfast.*

merit ['mɛr ɪt] **1.** *n.* worth; excellence; value; the quality of something that deserves praise. (No plural form in this sense.) ♦ *This university offers many scholarships based on merit.* ♦ *The soldiers were honored for their merit.* **2.** *n.* a good point; a virtue. (Usually plural.) ♦ *The judge reviewed the merits of the case.* ♦ *The editors discussed the merits of the manuscript.* **3.** *tv.* to deserve something; to be worthy of something. ♦ *This movie merits a better review than the bad one I read.* ♦ *Your brave action merits a reward.*

meritorious [mɛr ɪ 'tor i əs] *adj.* worthy; deserving praise. (Adv: *meritoriously.*) ♦ *The soldier was given a medal for meritorious service.* ♦ *My boss thanked me for my meritorious efforts.*

mermaid ['mɚ med] *n.* a mythical creature that is a woman from the waist up and a fish from the waist down. ♦ *The mermaid lured the sailor into the water.* ♦ *The mermaids lived at the bottom of the ocean.*

merry ['mɛr i] **1.** *adj.* happy; cheerful; joyful. (Adv: *merrily.* Comp: *merrier;* sup: *merriest.*) ♦ *The merry children opened their presents.* ♦ *Bob was in a merry mood when he greeted us at the door.* **2. make merry** *idiom* to have fun; to have an enjoyable time. ♦ *The guests certainly made merry at the wedding.* ♦ *The children were making merry in the garden while we chatted.*

merry-go-round ['mɛr i go raʊnd] *n.* a carousel; a circular platform on which people sit on benches or wooden animals while it goes around in circles. ♦ *That merry-go-round has beautiful wooden horses to sit on.* ♦ *The line to the merry-go-round at the carnival was rather long.*

mesh ['mɛʃ] **1.** *n.* material that is woven in a way so that there are holes between the threads. ♦ *The front of the tent was covered with mesh to keep the bugs out.* ♦ *The metal mesh in the window screen was starting to rust.* **2.** *n.* the space between the threads of ①. ♦ *The wide mesh allows small particles to fall through the screen.* ♦ *The fine mesh prevented bugs from entering the tent.* **3. mesh with** *tv.* + *prep. phr.* to connect something to something else by interspersing parts of the things. (Typically refers to gears.) ♦ *This lever meshes this gear with that gear.* ♦ *The large gear cannot mesh with the smaller gear because some dirt is in the way.* **4. mesh with** *tv.* + *prep. phr.* to connect an idea with another idea. (Figurative on ③.) ♦ *Try to mesh the notion of greed with the idea of selfishness in your paper.* ♦ *My theory meshes my ideas with my professor's ideas.* **5.** *iv.* to fit in with someone or something; to join well with something else. ♦ *These pieces of the puzzle mesh to form a picture.* ♦ *The gears don't seem to mesh.* **6. mesh with** *iv.* + *prep. phr.* [for an idea] to fit in with another idea. (Figurative on ⑤.) ♦ *Your notions of freedom mesh well with the Constitution.* ♦ *Your thoughts mesh with mine.*

mesmerize ['mɛz mə raɪz] **1.** *tv.* to hypnotize someone or something. ♦ *The magician mesmerized a volunteer from the audience.* ♦ *My therapist mesmerized me at the start of the session.* **2.** *tv.* [for someone or something very fascinating] to hold an audience's attention. (Figurative on ①.) ♦ *The juggler mesmerized the children who watched him.* ♦ *The exciting movie mesmerized everyone in the theater.*

mess ['mɛs] **1.** *n.* a group of things that are not in order; a situation that is not organized; confusion; disorganization. ♦ *I can't do anything until I take care of the mess on my desk.* ♦ *School was a horrible mess while the teachers were on strike.* **2.** *n.* someone who is in mental or physical disorder. (Informal. Figurative on ①.) ♦ *You're a mess! Go take a bath.* ♦ *I've been a mess ever since the accident.* **3.** *n.* the meals that are served in the military services. ♦ *No one is ever late for mess.* ♦ *I'm hungry. What time is mess?* **4. mess up** *tv.* + *adv.* to make something dirty or unorganized. ♦ *The young child messed up the living room.* ♦ *How could you mess things up so badly in one day?*

message ['mɛs ɪdʒ] **1.** *n.* a communication between two or more people; a piece of written or spoken information for someone. ♦ *My mother left me a message to call her at 6:00.* ♦ *I listened to my answering machine for messages.* **2.** *n.* the moral of a story; a lesson that is to be learned from a story. ♦ *The teacher talked to the students about the story's message.* ♦ *I couldn't figure out the message of the confusing movie.*

messenger ['mɛs ən dʒɚ] *n.* someone who delivers messages, documents, parcels, or flowers. ♦ *The messenger* *gave me the wrong package by mistake.* ♦ *Have the messenger deliver these documents to our lawyers.*

Messiah [mə 'sɑɪ ə] **1.** *n.* the expected deliverer of the Jewish people, as promised in the Bible. ♦ *The coming of the Messiah was foretold by the prophets.* ♦ *The rabbi looked forward to the coming of the Messiah.* **2.** *n.* Jesus Christ, regarded by Christians as ①. ♦ *Christians regard Jesus Christ as the Messiah.* ♦ *The pastor tried to think how the Messiah would deal with sin today.*

messianic [mɛs ɪ 'ɑ nɪk] *adj.* of or about the Messiah. (Adv: *messianically* [...ɪk li].) ♦ *The Old Testament contains many messianic prophecies.* ♦ *The minister preached about messianic works and promises.*

messy ['mɛs i] *adj.* dirty or unorganized; not clean and tidy. (Adv: *messily.* Comp: *messier;* sup: *messiest.*) ♦ *I think it's time to clean your messy room.* ♦ *My desk is so messy that I can't see its surface.*

met ['mɛt] pt/pp of meet.

metabolism [mə 'tæb ə lɪz əm] *n.* the process by which chemical reactions in plants and animals create the energy needed to live. (No plural form in this sense.) ♦ *When I dieted, I took pills to increase my metabolism.* ♦ *Lazy people with slow metabolism tend to gain weight.*

metal ['mɛt əl] **1.** *n.* a solid mineral substance that can be worked into different shapes. (No plural form in this sense.) ♦ *Metal can be beaten or molded into different shapes.* ♦ *Is this railing made of wood or metal?* **2. metals** *n.* kinds or types of ①. ♦ *Some metals can conduct electricity.* ♦ *Most metals are mined from the earth.* **3.** *adj.* made from ①. ♦ *This roof is supported by metal beams.* ♦ *I collect old metal coins.*

metallic [mə 'tæl ɪk] *adj.* associated with metal. (Adv: *metallically* [...ɪk li].) ♦ *Armor is a protective metallic covering.* ♦ *The bell gave off a metallic ring when struck.*

metamorphosis [mɛt ə 'mor fə sɪs] *n.* the change from one stage in life to another. (No plural form in this sense.) ♦ *The process of a caterpillar changing into a butterfly is metamorphosis.* ♦ *Metamorphosis from one major stage of life to another applies mainly to the insects.*

metaphor ['mɛt ə for] *n.* an expression that is not literal; an expression in which something is linked to someone or something else in a nonliteral comparison. ♦ *The metaphor "A mighty fortress is our God" is a way of stating that "God is as mighty as a fortress" or "God is mighty just as a fortress is mighty."* ♦ *The candidate's speech contained many metaphors and little substance.*

metaphorical [mɛt ə 'for ɪ kəl] *adj.* using metaphor or comparison; not literal; figurative. (Adv: *metaphorically* [...ɪk li].) ♦ *You're obscuring your point with too many metaphorical expressions.* ♦ *Close friends are brothers, in a metaphorical sense.*

metastasis [mə 'tæs tə sɪs] *n.* the spread of cancer from one part of the body to another. (No plural form in this sense.) ♦ *Chemotherapy is used to prevent further metastasis.* ♦ *The researcher developed drugs that slowed the rate of metastasis.*

meteor ['mit i ɚ] *n.* a large rock from space that enters the earth's atmosphere. ♦ *Most meteors burn up when they enter the atmosphere.* ♦ *Dinosaurs may have become extinct when a meteor struck Earth.*

meteorite ['mit i or ɑɪt] *n.* a rock from space that did not completely burn up when it entered the atmosphere. ♦ *The meteorite was examined to see if it was radioactive.* ♦ *The fiery meteorite lit the sky as it fell to Earth.*

meteorology [mit i ə 'rɑl ə dʒi] *n.* the science and study of the atmosphere and weather conditions. (No plural form in this sense.) ♦ *Most weather reporters have degrees in meteorology.* ♦ *I studied meteorology to learn more about tornadoes.*

meter ['mit ɚ] **1.** *n.* the basic unit of the measurement of length in the metric system, equal to 39.37 inches. ♦ *The freeway exit is 100 meters ahead.* ♦ *My sister is 1.5 meters tall.* **2.** *n.* a device that measures and displays the amount of something that is used. ♦ *Someone from the gas company stopped by to read my gas meter.* ♦ *I put a dime in the parking meter for 30 minutes of parking time.* **3.** *n.* the rhythms caused by accents in poetry and music. ♦ *Free verse lacks rhyme and meter.* ♦ *Sonnets have strict meter.* **4.** *tv.* to measure the flow of something with ②. ♦ *Your electric meter meters the amount of electricity you use.* ♦ *The air flow was metered in order to maintain a steady rate.*

method ['mɛθ əd] *n.* a way of doing something; a system; a procedure. ♦ *The math teacher showed the students a new method of division.* ♦ *The principal disagreed with the teacher's methods.*

methodical [mə 'θɑd ɪ kəl] *adj.* orderly; systematic. (Adv: *methodically* [...ɪk li].) ♦ *The inspector's methodical approach ensured that nothing was overlooked.* ♦ *The accountant examined the figures in a methodical fashion.*

methodology [mɛθ ə 'dɑl ə dʒi] *n.* the system of methods used in an area of study or work; the system of procedures. (No plural form in this sense.) ♦ *Your results are wrong because your methodology was faulty.* ♦ *The researcher explained her methodology at the conference.*

meticulous [mə 'tɪk jə ləs] *adj.* very careful; very cautious; paying attention to detail. (Adv: *meticulously.*) ♦ *The inspector's meticulous questioning made me nervous.* ♦ *The meticulous doctor discovered why I was sick.*

metric ['mɛ trɪk] *adj.* of or about the system of measurement based on the meter. (Adv: *metrically* [...ɪk li].) ♦ *The meter is a metric unit of measure.* ♦ *The U.S. is one of the few countries not using the metric system.*

metronome ['mɛ trə nom] *n.* a device that provides the exact tempo that is wanted when playing music by making a signal at a specified number of times each minute. ♦ *The pianist set the metronome at 80 beats per minute.* ♦ *I heard the metronome ticking during Anne's piano lesson.*

metropolis [mə 'trɑp ə ləs] *n.* a large or important city. ♦ *New York City is the largest metropolis in the United States.* ♦ *After years of living on a farm, Mary moved to a metropolis.*

metropolitan [mɛ trə 'pɑl ɪ tən] **1.** *adj.* urban; of, about, or characteristic of a metropolis. ♦ *The company was headquartered in a metropolitan business center.* ♦ *The country is quieter in comparison to metropolitan life.* **2.** *adj.* of or about a city and its suburbs. ♦ *The Chicago metropolitan area extends into Wisconsin and Indiana.* ♦ *Our metropolitan sewer system is starting to deteriorate.*

Mexican ['mɛk sə kən] **1.** *n.* a citizen or native of Mexico. ♦ *Many Mexicans have immigrated to the United*

States. ♦ *We know the Mexicans who live in our neighborhood.* **2.** *adj.* of or about Mexico or ①. ♦ *We like Mexican food and often go to Mexican restaurants.* ♦ *They planned a vacation to a Mexican resort.*

Mexico ['mɛk sɪ ko] See Gazetteer.

mice ['mɑɪs] pl of mouse.

Michigan ['mɪʃ ə gən] See Gazetteer.

microchip ['mɑɪ kro tʃɪp] *n.* a very small piece of silicon holding a powerful electrical circuit, used in computers and electronic equipment. ♦ *My computer's microchips were destroyed by a power surge.* ♦ *The development of microchips reduced the size of computers.*

microcomputer ['mɑɪ kro kəm 'pjut ɚ] *n.* a small computer. (The typical personal computer.) ♦ *A microcomputer is smaller than a minicomputer.* ♦ *Today's microcomputers are more powerful than the mainframes of years ago.*

microphone ['mɑɪ krə fon] *n.* a device that changes sound waves into electrical waves so that the sound can be broadcast, recorded, or made louder. (Abbreviated mike.) ♦ *The singer stepped up to the microphone and began to sing.* ♦ *Speak into the microphone! We can't hear you!*

microscope ['mɑɪ krə skop] *n.* a device that magnifies very small objects so that they can be seen. ♦ *The analyst examined the blood under a microscope.* ♦ *Our lab is equipped with dozens of microscopes.*

microscopic ['mɑɪ krə 'skɑp ɪk] **1.** *adj.* of or about a microscope. (Adv: *microscopically* [...ɪk li].) ♦ *A microscopic examination of the organism reveals its cellular structure.* ♦ *The scientist placed some of the mold on a microscopic slide.* **2.** *adj.* very small; tiny; visible only with a microscope. (Figurative on ①. Adv: *microscopically* [...ɪk li].) ♦ *My bloodstream was infected with microscopic bacteria.* ♦ *Your problems are microscopic compared to mine.*

microwave ['mɑɪ kro wev] **1.** *n.* a very short radio wave, used in sending radio messages, radar, and cooking. ♦ *The microwaves cooked the potato in five minutes.* ♦ *The message was broadcast by microwaves.* **2.** *n.* an oven that uses ① to cook or heat food quickly. ♦ *I haven't used my stove ever since I bought the microwave.* ♦ *Don't put metal objects in microwaves!* **3.** *adj.* <the adj. use of ①.> ♦ *I cooked the potato in a microwave oven.* ♦ *I listened to the news report over a microwave radio.* **4.** *tv.* to cook or heat something in ②. ♦ *I microwaved the instant dinner.* ♦ *Tom microwaved the water until it began to boil.*

midair ['mɪd 'er] **1.** *adj.* in the air; not touching the ground. ♦ *The midair collision killed 40 of the plane's passengers.* ♦ *The navy pilot was skilled at midair refueling.* **2.** **in midair** *phr.* at a point high in the air. (No plural form in this sense.) ♦ *The planes crashed in midair.* ♦ *Extra fuel was released from the plane in midair.*

midday **1.** ['mɪd de] *n.* noon; the middle of the day. (No plural form in this sense.) ♦ *It started to rain at midday.* ♦ *Around midday, I began to get sleepy.* **2.** ['mɪd de] *adj.* happening in the middle of the day; happening at noon. ♦ *The midday meal is usually called lunch.* ♦ *We ordered food to eat during the midday meeting.*

middle ['mɪd l] **1.** *n.* a place or time halfway between two ends; the center. ♦ *I placed the vase in the middle of the table.* ♦ *A radius is the distance from a point on a circle to its middle.* **2.** *n.* the area of the waist; halfway along a human or other creature. ♦ *He's starting to get fat around the middle.* ♦ *These pants are too tight around my middle.* **3.** *adj.* central; at the same distance from either end; halfway between the beginning and the end. ♦ *There are three seats. Please sit in the middle one.* ♦ *John Joseph Smith's middle name is Joseph.* **4.** **middle-of-the-road** *idiom* halfway between two extremes, especially political extremes. ♦ *Jane is very liberal, but her husband is politically middle-of-the-road.* ♦ *I don't want to vote for candidates at either extreme. I prefer someone with more middle-of-the-road views.*

middle age [mɪd l 'edʒ] *n.* the time of a person's life between youth and old age, usually between 40 and 65. (No plural form in this sense.) ♦ *John hoped to have a steady job by the time he reached middle age.* ♦ *I started saving for retirement when I reached middle age.*

middle-aged ['mɪd l edʒd] *adj.* in the middle of one's life, usually between 40 and 65. ♦ *The 80-year-old woman's children were middle-aged.* ♦ *The middle-aged man started to plan for his retirement.*

Middle Ages ['mɪd l 'e dʒəz] *n.* a period in European history from about A.D. 500 until about 1450. ♦ *Many of the great cathedrals were built in the latter part of the Middle Ages.* ♦ *The Middle Ages, sometimes called the Dark Ages, ended with the beginning of the Renaissance.*

middle class ['mɪd l 'klæs] **1.** *n.* an economic class of people in a society between the upper and lower classes. ♦ *The emergence of a middle class is a relatively recent phenomenon.* ♦ *The middle class was affected most by the tax increase.* **2.** **middle-class** *adj.* <the adj. use of ①.> ♦ *The movie satirized middle-class attitudes.* ♦ *My middle-class roommate would rather watch baseball than ballet.*

Middle East ['mɪd əl 'ist] *n.* the area that includes Sudan, Syria, Egypt, Israel, Jordan, Lebanon, Saudi Arabia, Turkey, Iran, and Iraq, among other countries. (No plural form in this sense.) ♦ *John spent two years in the Middle East, teaching English.* ♦ *Arabic is the major language spoken in the Middle East.*

middleman ['mɪd l mæn] *n., irreg.* someone or a company who makes money by buying goods from a manufacturer and selling them to a store owner or consumer. (Not necessarily a male. Pl: middlemen.) ♦ *The middleman made a 10% profit in resale.* ♦ *I buy clothes from the manufacturer, eliminating the middleman.*

middlemen ['mɪd l mɛn] pl of middleman.

midget ['mɪdʒ ɪt] **1.** *adj.* small; smaller than other things of the same kind. ♦ *The jeweler worked on the watch with a midget screwdriver.* ♦ *Our furry puppy looks like a midget lion.* **2.** *n.* a small person of normal proportions. ♦ *The midget stood on a stool to reach the faucet.* ♦ *The door was so low that only a midget could get through.*

midnight ['mɪd nɑɪt] **1.** *n.* 12:00 at night; 12:00 A.M. ♦ *I went to bed at midnight.* ♦ *The stores close at midnight.* **2.** *adj.* happening at ①. ♦ *I went out to the pool for a midnight swim.* ♦ *I fell asleep during the midnight movie.*

midpoint ['mɪd pɔɪnt] *n.* the middle; the point in time or space that is halfway between the beginning and the end. ♦ *At the midpoint of the conference, we took a break.* ♦ *We stopped for dinner at the midpoint of the trip.*

midriff ['mɪd rif] **1.** *n.* the part of the body between the waist and the chest. ♦ *The school dress code does not allow bare midriffs.* ♦ *My midriff got sunburned when I went to the beach.* **2.** *n.* the section of a (women's) garment that covers ①. ♦ *Anne ironed her dress's midriff.* ♦ *My zipper is stuck at the midriff.*

midst ['mɪdst] **1.** *n.* the middle part of a group of things or people. (No plural form in this sense.) ♦ *There is a traitor in our midst.* ♦ *In the midst of the clouds, I saw a rainbow.* **2.** *n.* in the middle of something that exists over a period of time. (No plural form in this sense.) ♦ *In the midst of the storm, the roof blew off.* ♦ *I visited Alaska in the midst of summer.*

midsummer ['mɪd 'sʌm ɚ] *adj.* happening in the middle of summer. ♦ *I took a midsummer class because I was behind in my classes.* ♦ *I went canoeing on a clear midsummer night.*

midterm ['mɪd tɚm] **1.** *adj.* in the middle of a fixed period of time, such as a term of office, a pregnancy, or a school term. ♦ *Sue's midterm physical showed that both she and the baby were healthy.* ♦ *My midterm grades indicated I needed to study more.* **2.** *n.* a test that is given during a school term that covers information studied up to that point. ♦ *I failed my midterms because I didn't study.* ♦ *I can't go out tonight. I have a midterm in biology tomorrow morning.*

midway 1. ['mɪd 'we] *adj.* halfway between two points in time or space. ♦ *The speaker paused at the midway point of her speech.* ♦ *Detroit is midway between Chicago and Toronto.* **2.** ['mɪd 'we] *adv.* halfway between; halfway to the end. ♦ *The runner stumbled midway through the race.* ♦ *The plane flew midway between the two mountaintops.* **3.** ['mɪd we] *n.* the place at a carnival or fair lined with small shows and exhibits on both sides. ♦ *I walked down the midway, playing various games.* ♦ *I bought some popcorn and candy on the midway.*

midweek 1. ['mɪd wik] *adj.* in the middle of the week; on Wednesday. ♦ *On Tuesday, I began preparing for the midweek business meeting.* ♦ *I went to the health club for my midweek exercises.* **2.** ['mɪd 'wik] *adv.* done as a midweek ① activity. ♦ *I'd like to talk to you again midweek.* ♦ *I plan to drive to Houston midweek.*

Midwest [mɪd 'wɛst] **1.** *n.* the part of the United States between the states on the east coast and the states west of the Rocky Mountains and north of Texas, Arkansas, and Kentucky. (No plural form in this sense.) ♦ *Most of the nation's wheat crop is grown in the Midwest.* ♦ *The Midwest is primarily very flat.* **2.** *adj.* <the adj. use of ①.> ♦ *I grew up in a Midwest farm town.* ♦ *The news reporter had a Midwest accent.*

midwife ['mɪd waɪf] *n.* a woman who is trained to help women give birth, especially outside of a hospital. (Pl: midwives.) ♦ *The midwife came to our house when Anne went into labor.* ♦ *Mary gave birth at home with the help of a midwife.*

midwives ['mɪd waɪvz] pl of midwife.

might ['maɪt] **1.** *n.* power; strength. (No plural form in this sense.) ♦ *With lots of might, Tom lifted the end of the piano.* ♦ *Dave pushed the car with all of his might.* **2.** *aux.* <a form that expresses possibility.> (See also may. Takes a bare verb.) ♦ *I might go to Toledo next month, if I have enough money.* ♦ *It might rain tonight.* **3.** *aux.* <a form expressing permission.> (See also may and could. Takes a bare verb.) ♦ *Bob asked if he might smoke in the house.* ♦ *Anne asked if she might be excused from the dinner table.*

mighty ['maɪt i] *adj.* powerful; strong; very great. (Adv: *mightily.* Comp: *mightier;* sup: *mightiest.*) ♦ *A mighty wind blew off the barn's roof.* ♦ *A mighty torrent of water rushed through the ravine.*

migraine (headache) ['maɪ gren ('hɛd ek)] *n.* a strong, throbbing headache that often affects vision. ♦ *I couldn't fall asleep because I had a serious migraine.* ♦ *Not even Aspirin helps when I get migraines.*

migrant ['maɪ grənt] **1.** *n.* a person or an animal that moves from place to place. ♦ *The migrants traveled from city to city.* ♦ *The geese flying overhead are migrants. They fly south every winter.* **2.** *adj.* moving from place to place. ♦ *The migrant birds fly to a new location every spring.* ♦ *The migrant Gypsies traveled from city to city.*

migrate ['maɪ gret] **1.** *iv.* to move from place to place. ♦ *The refugees migrated across the continent.* ♦ *The workers migrated from farm to farm.* **2.** *iv.* to travel back and forth between two places, depending on the time of the year. ♦ *Many birds migrate south for the winter.* ♦ *Most of our friends migrate to Florida each winter.*

migrating ['maɪ gret ɪŋ] *adj.* moving from place to place. ♦ *Migrating swallows return to the same place each spring.* ♦ *The migrating refugees carried their possessions with them.*

migration [maɪ 'gre ʃən] *n.* the movement of numbers of people or creatures from place to place. ♦ *The biologist studied the route of the birds' migration.* ♦ *The researcher examined the effects of migration on refugees.*

mike ['maɪk] See microphone.

mild ['maɪld] **1.** *adj.* gentle or calm; not extreme, powerful, or severe. (Adv: *mildly.* Comp: *milder;* sup: *mildest.*) ♦ *A mild breeze blew inland from the lake.* ♦ *The temperatures became milder in September.* **2.** *adj.* bland; not spicy. (Adv: *mildly.* Comp: *milder;* sup: *mildest.*) ♦ *The chili was too mild, so I added some pepper.* ♦ *I have to eat mild food because I have an ulcer.* **3.** *adj.* lenient; light; not severe or harsh. (Adv: *mildly.* Comp: *milder;* sup: *mildest.*) ♦ *The defendant's lawyer argued for a mild sentence.* ♦ *I responded to the mild insult by walking away.*

mildew ['mɪl du] **1.** *n.* a fungus that grows on things that are warm and damp. (No plural form in this sense.) ♦ *I cleaned the mildew from the shower door.* ♦ *The damp sponge was covered with mildew.* **2.** *iv.* [for something] to acquire a growth of ①. ♦ *The shower wall is mildewing again.* ♦ *Please wash the towels. They've begun to mildew.*

mile ['maɪl] **1.** *n.* a unit of measurement of length, equal to 5,280 feet or about 1.6 kilometers. ♦ *Chicago and Los Angeles are over 2,000 miles apart.* ♦ *I live five miles from the interstate.* **2. for miles** *phr.* to or in a distance extending 2 or more miles. ♦ *The huge field of wheat extends for miles.* ♦ *We traveled for miles without stopping.*

mileage ['maɪl ɪdʒ] **1.** *n.* a distance expressed in miles. (No plural form in this sense.) ♦ *The road sign showed the mileage to the next town.* ♦ *The road atlas listed the mileage between major cities.* **2.** *n.* the total number of miles that can be traveled using one gallon of gasoline. (No plural form in this sense.) ♦ *What kind of mileage does this car* get? ♦ *This brand of gasoline will improve your mileage.* **3. get a lot of mileage out of something** *idiom* to get a lot of use from something, as if it were a car. (On ②.) ♦ *Bob always got a lot of mileage out of one joke.* ♦ *I got a lot of mileage out of my TV before it broke down.*

milestone ['maɪl ston] **1.** *n.* a stone or other marker by the side of a road showing the number of miles to the next town or village. (Now largely replaced by signs.) ♦ *The county replaced the old milestone with a large road sign.* ♦ *According to the milestone, we've got another 3 miles to go.* **2. milestone in someone's life** *idiom* a very important event or point in one's life. ♦ *Jane's wedding was a milestone in her mother's life.* ♦ *The birth of a child is a milestone in every parent's life.*

militant ['mɪl ə tənt] **1.** *adj.* aggressive and demanding. (Adv: *militantly.*) ♦ *The militant parents demanded that the principal be fired.* ♦ *Management ignored the militant workers' demands.* **2.** *n.* someone who is prepared to protest or demonstrate for a cause. ♦ *The young militants protested against the war.* ♦ *The police charged the militants in the park with disturbing the peace.*

military ['mɪl ə tɛr i] **1. the military** *n.* the armed forces; the army. (Treated as singular.) ♦ *The military was sent into the city to stop the riot.* ♦ *A large percentage of the nation's budget goes to the military.* **2.** *adj.* <the adj. use of ①.> (Adv: *militarily* [mɪl ə 'tɛr ə li].) ♦ *The popular military leader ran for president.* ♦ *Military service for young men was required during the war.*

militia [mə 'lɪʃ ə] *n.* a group of citizens that are not part of the professional army but who are trained as soldiers. ♦ *The militia trained together every Saturday afternoon.* ♦ *A local militia was blamed for the terrorist attack.*

milk ['mɪlk] **1.** *n.* the white liquid made by female mammals to feed their young. (No plural form in this sense.) ♦ *The milk of some animals is used by humans as food and to make cheese, butter, and other dairy products.* ♦ *I ordered a glass of milk and a slice of cherry pie.* **2.** *n.* a white liquid from certain plants, such as coconuts. (No plural form in this sense.) ♦ *I poured the coconut milk into a glass.* ♦ *A sticky milk seeped from the weeds' cut stems.* **3. milkshake** See shake ⑦. **4.** *tv.* to take milk from an animal. ♦ *The farmer milked the cows every morning.* ♦ *How often do cows have to be milked?* **5. cry over spilled milk** *idiom* to be unhappy about something that cannot be undone. ♦ *I'm sorry that you broke your bicycle, Tom. But there is nothing that can be done now. Don't cry over spilled milk.* ♦ *Anne is always crying over spilled milk.* **6. milk someone for something** *idiom* to pressure someone into giving information or money. ♦ *The reporter milked the mayor's aide for information.* ♦ *The thief milked me for $20.*

milky ['mɪl ki] *adj.* like milk; cloudy or whitish like milk. (Comp: *milkier;* sup: *milkiest.*) ♦ *I couldn't see the fish in the milky water.* ♦ *A milky liquid seeped from the leak.*

mill ['mɪl] **1.** *n.* a building containing the machinery needed to turn grain into meal. ♦ *Many mills were once powered by the moving water of rivers.* ♦ *The restaurant bought its flour directly from the mill.* **2.** *n.* a machine or device that crushes or pulverizes things. ♦ *The gravel mill crushes large rocks into gravel.* ♦ *This coffee mill grinds beans very finely.* **3.** *n.* a place where things are produced in great quantities, perhaps carelessly. (Figurative on ①.) ♦ *The college was accused of being nothing but a diploma mill.* ♦ *The Nevada courts are a huge divorce mill.* **4.** *tv.* to produce flour; to crush grain in ②; to process raw materials with ②. ♦ *Our job is to mill the wheat into the finest flour.* ♦ *The factory milled wood pulp into paper.* **5. been through the mill** *idiom* been badly treated; exhausted. ♦ *This has been a rough day. I've really been through the mill.* ♦ *This old car is banged up, and it hardly runs. It's been through the mill.*

millennia [mɪ 'lɛn i ə] a pl of millennium.

millennium [mɪ 'lɛn i əm] **1.** *n., irreg.* a period of 1,000 years. (Pl: *millenniums* or millennia.) ♦ *The powerful kingdom lasted for over a millennium.* ♦ *Toxic waste remains dangerous for several millennia.* **2.** *n., irreg.* the thousandth anniversary of something. ♦ *I can only hope that our country lasts long enough to celebrate its millennium.* ♦ *The ancient city celebrated its second millennium with a large parade.*

milligram ['mɪl ə græm] *n.* a unit of measurement of weight; one one-thousandth (1/1,000) of a gram. ♦ *There are 200 milligrams of sodium in one serving of these potato chips.* ♦ *Each tablet contains 500 milligrams of aspirin.*

millimeter ['mɪl ə mit ɚ] *n.* a unit of measurement of length; one one-thousandth (1/1,000) of a meter. ♦ *One inch is about 25.4 millimeters.* ♦ *The tiny insect was only a few millimeters in length.*

million ['mɪl jən] **1.** *n.* the number 1,000,000. (Additional numbers formed as with *two million, three million, four million,* etc.) ♦ *One thousand times one thousand equals one million.* ♦ *Pick a number between one and a million.* **2.** *adj.* consisting of 1,000,000 things; having 1,000,000 things. ♦ *The winner of the lottery won a million dollars.* ♦ *This TV show is being watched by ten million people.* **3. feel like a million (dollars)** *idiom* to feel well and healthy, both physically and mentally. ♦ *A quick swim in the morning makes me feel like a million dollars.* ♦ *What a beautiful day! It makes you feel like a million.*

millionaire [mɪl jə 'ner] *n.* someone who has $1,000,000 in assets after debt is subtracted. ♦ *I'm a millionaire because I have $1,100,000 in assets and only $90,000 in debts.* ♦ *Bob can afford a new car; he's a millionaire.*

millionth ['mɪl jənθ] [one] 1,000,000th. See fourth for senses and examples.

mime ['maɪm] **1.** *n.* the use of gestures instead of words to show meaning. (No plural form in this sense.) ♦ *I used mime to communicate with the woman outside the window.* ♦ *The actor expressed his request in mime.* **2.** *n.* a performer who does not use words. (See also pantomime.) ♦ *The mime performed for people in the park.* ♦ *The mime pretended to walk against a heavy wind.* **3.** *tv.* to act out a meaning using gestures instead of words. ♦ *I mimed my response because my mouth was full of food.* ♦ *Mary mimed her angry reply with a rude gesture.* **4.** *iv.* to use gestures instead of words. ♦ *I had to mime when I had a sore throat.* ♦ *The director told the actors in the background to mime.*

mimic ['mɪm ɪk] **1.** *tv., irreg.* to copy the way other people act or speak. (Pt/pp: mimicked; present participle is *mimicking.*) ♦ *The comedian mimicked the president's voice.* ♦ *I can mimic the way John walks, but it makes him mad.* **2.** *n.* someone who can copy the way other people act or speak. ♦ *The audience applauded the mimic who* *imitated the actor.* ♦ *The principal suspended the young mimic who imitated his teacher.*

mimicked ['mɪm ɪkt] pt/pp of mimic.

mince ['mɪns] **1.** *tv.* to chop or shred something into very small pieces. ♦ *The cook minced the garlic.* ♦ *Mince the onion before you add it to the sauce.* **2.** *iv.* to walk or move in affected, dainty movements. ♦ *The actor minced across the stage.* ♦ *The pretentious poet minced up to the microphone.* **3. mince (one's) words** *idiom* to soften the effect of one's words. ♦ *Tell me what you think, and don't mince your words.* ♦ *A frank person never minces words.*

minced ['mɪnst] *adj.* chopped or shredded into very small pieces. ♦ *Add a teaspoon of minced garlic to the sauce.* ♦ *The cook sprinkled minced onion over the pizza.*

mincemeat ['mɪns mit] **1.** *n.* a mixture of fruit, spices, and sometimes chopped meat, as a filling for pies. (No plural form in this sense.) ♦ *The cook filled the pie shell with mincemeat.* ♦ *The mincemeat contains raisins and dates.* **2.** *adj.* made of ①. ♦ *There is rarely any meat in mincemeat pie.* ♦ *The mincemeat filling is flavored with cinnamon.* **3. make mincemeat of someone** *idiom* to defeat someone completely. ♦ *Our football team made mincemeat of theirs.* ♦ *Bob made mincemeat of John in the tennis finals.*

mind ['mɑɪnd] **1.** *n.* the part of humans that thinks and has feelings. ♦ *Don't bother Anne. She's got a lot on her mind.* ♦ *The drugs affected Bill's mind.* **2.** *n.* memory; the ability to remember. ♦ *Deep in John's mind, he recalled his first bicycle.* ♦ *These simple mental exercises can help improve your mind.* **3.** *n.* the imagination; the creative part of humans. ♦ *Artists and musicians tend to have very creative minds.* ♦ *The young student had the mind of a genius.* **4.** *tv.* to pay attention to someone or something; to obey someone or something. ♦ *Children, mind what the babysitter tells you.* ♦ *Mind your head or you will hit it on the beam.* **5.** *tv.* to care for someone or something; to tend to someone or something. ♦ *Can you mind my cat when I'm on vacation?* ♦ *My neighbor minded my plants while I was in the hospital.* **6.** *tv.* to be opposed to something; to care if someone does something. ♦ *"Would you mind if I smoked in here?" "Yes, I do."* ♦ *Do you mind pizza for dinner?* **7.** *iv.* to be opposed; to care. ♦ *I need to smoke. Do you mind?* ♦ *"Can I borrow your car?" "Go ahead. I don't mind."* **8. enter one's mind** *idiom* [for an idea or memory] to come into one's consciousness; to be thought of. ♦ *Leave you behind? The thought never even entered my mind.* ♦ *A very interesting idea just entered my mind. What if I ran for Congress?* **9. get a load off one's mind** *idiom* to say what one is thinking. ♦ *He sure talked a long time. I guess he had to get a load off his mind.* ♦ *You aren't going to like what I'm going to say, but I have to get a load off my mind.* **10. give someone a piece of one's mind** *idiom* to bawl someone out; to tell someone off. (Actually to give someone a helping of what one is thinking about.) ♦ *I've had enough from John. I'm going to give him a piece of my mind.* ♦ *Sally, stop it, or I'll give you a piece of my mind.* **11. have a one-track mind** *idiom* to think entirely or almost entirely about one subject. ♦ *Adolescent boys often have one-track minds. All they're interested in is the opposite sex.* ♦ *Bob has a one-track mind. He can only talk about football.* **12. in one's right mind** *idiom* sane; rational and sensible. ♦ *That was a stupid thing to do. You're not in your right mind.* ♦ *You can't be in your right mind! That sounds crazy!* **13. lose one's mind** *idiom* to become crazy or insane; to become irrational. ♦ *If I don't get some sleep, I'm going to lose my mind.* ♦ *All this extra work is going to make me lose my mind!* **14. mind one's p's and q's** *idiom* to pay attention to small details of behavior. ♦ *When we go to the mayor's reception, please mind your p's and q's.* ♦ *I always mind my p's and q's when I eat at a restaurant with white tablecloths.* **15. mind you** *idiom* <a phrase indicating that something should be taken into consideration.> ♦ *He's very well dressed, but mind you, he's got plenty of money to buy clothes.* ♦ *Lisa is unfriendly to me, but mind you, she's never very nice to anyone.* **16. mind your manners** *idiom* to be careful to use good manners. ♦ *Mind your manners while we are visiting Aunt Mary's house.* ♦ *Jimmy! Mind your manners!* **17. out of one's mind** *idiom* not sane; insane; crazy; irrational. ♦ *John must have been out of his mind when he bought that ugly shirt.* ♦ *You did what? Are you out of your mind?* **18. put one's mind to something** *idiom* to give one's complete attention to something. ♦ *I could finish this job tonight if I put my mind to it.* ♦ *Please put your mind to it and concentrate on getting it finished.* **19. slip one's mind** *idiom* [for something that was to be remembered] to be forgotten. ♦ *I meant to go to the grocery store on the way home, but it slipped my mind.* ♦ *My birthday slipped my mind. I guess I wanted to forget it.* **20. on one's mind** *idiom* occupying one's thoughts; currently being thought about. ♦ *You've been on my mind all day.* ♦ *Do you have something on your mind? You look so serious.*

mindful ['mɑɪnd fʊl] *adj.* keeping something in one's mind; using concentration. (Adv: *mindfully.*) ♦ *I'm mindful of your request, but I can't approve it yet.* ♦ *The acrobat was mindful to watch where he walked.*

mindless ['mɑɪnd ləs] *adj.* not using or needing one's mind; stupid. (Adv: *mindlessly.*) ♦ *I ignored Anne's mindless suggestions.* ♦ *The mindless driver smashed his car into a tree.*

mind reader ['mɑɪnd rid ɚ] *n.* someone who claims to be able to know what other people are thinking; a psychic. ♦ *The mind reader somehow knew my name and social security number.* ♦ *I don't know what you're thinking; I'm not a mind reader.*

mine ['mɑɪn] **1.** *n.* an opening into the earth from which precious metals, minerals, or gemstones are recovered. ♦ *The lure of gold mines brought many settlers to California.* ♦ *Working in a coal mine is a dangerous profession.* **2.** *n.* a great supply. (Figurative on ①.) ♦ *The mayor's aide provided the reporter with a mine of information.* ♦ *The school library has a gold mine of source material.* **3.** *n.* a bomb that is placed under the surface of the soil or water and explodes when it is touched or activated. ♦ *Thousands of mines were planted around the country during the war.* ♦ *Many children were killed when a mine exploded near the school.* **4.** *tv.* to fetch precious metals, minerals, or gemstones from the earth. ♦ *The old prospector mined gold.* ♦ *Tons of coal are mined in West Virginia each year.* **5.** *tv.* to place bombs under the surface of the soil or water of a particular location. ♦ *The enemy soldiers mined the harbor.* ♦ *The airfield was mined with thousands of mines.* **6.** *pron.* <the first-person singular possessive pronoun.> (Used in place of a noun.) ♦ *This shoe is Bob's, and that* *one is mine.* ♦ *Your shirt is brown, and mine is black.* **7. back to the salt mines** *idiom* time to return to work, school, or something else that might be unpleasant. ♦ *It's eight o'clock. Time to go to work! Back to the salt mines.* ♦ *School starts again in the fall, and then it's back to the salt mines again.* **8. mine of information** *idiom* someone or something that is full of information. ♦ *Grandfather is a mine of information about World War I.* ♦ *The new encyclopedia is a positive mine of useful information.*

miner ['maɪn ɚ] *n.* someone who digs underground for precious metals, minerals, or gemstones; someone who works in a mine. ♦ *The miners were trapped deep in the coal mine.* ♦ *By the end of the day, the miner was almost black.*

mineral ['mɪn (ə) rəl] **1.** *n.* one of many kinds of crystalline substances and useful substances dug from the earth; a substance that is gotten by mining. ♦ *The earth's crust contains many kinds of minerals.* ♦ *Coal is a widely used mineral.* **2.** *n.* an element plants and animals need in order to function properly. ♦ *This cereal contains essential vitamins and minerals.* ♦ *Zinc is a mineral that humans need in their diets.* **3.** *adj.* <the adj. use of ①.> ♦ *The mountainous country had great mineral wealth.* ♦ *The geologist discovered a vast mineral deposit.*

mingle ['mɪŋ gəl] **1. mingle (with)** *iv.* (+ *prep. phr.*) to talk to different people; to associate with different people. ♦ *Everyone at the party mingled with each other.* ♦ *The students mingled in the hall before class.* **2.** *iv.* to blend or mix. ♦ *The dense smoke and dangerous fumes mingled in the air.* ♦ *You must chill the sauce overnight so the flavors can mingle.* **3.** *tv.* to blend or mix things together. ♦ *The cook mingled the oil with the vinegar.* ♦ *Freshmen and sophomores were mingled together in the class.*

miniature ['mɪn i ə tʃɚ] **1.** *adj.* small; on a small scale; smaller than other things of the same kind. ♦ *My aunt collects miniature teapots.* ♦ *I put miniature marshmallows in my hot cocoa.* **2.** *n.* something that is small; something that is smaller than other things of the same kind. ♦ *This model car is a miniature of a real one.* ♦ *The full-sized cherries are gone, but some miniatures are still left.*

minicomputer ['mɪn i kəm pjut ɚ] *n.* a very powerful computer that is larger than a microcomputer and smaller than a mainframe. ♦ *Should we replace the mainframe with a few minicomputers?* ♦ *The new microcomputer has made my minicomputer obsolete.*

minimal ['mɪn ə məl] *adj.* smallest possible [amount]. (Adv: *minimally.*) ♦ *The lazy student did only a minimal amount of studying.* ♦ *Sue hasn't been promoted because she only does the minimal amount of work required for the job.*

minimize ['mɪn ə maɪz] *tv.* to make something as small as possible. ♦ *I minimized my losses by selling my unprofitable stock.* ♦ *The teacher minimized the importance of the final examination.*

minimum ['mɪn ə məm] **1.** *n.* the least amount or degree possible; the smallest amount or degree possible. ♦ *At a minimum, you will be working 40 hours a week.* ♦ *You have to buy a minimum of two chickens to get the sale price.* **2.** *adj.* minimal; smallest; lowest; least. ♦ *The president vetoed any attempt to raise the minimum wage.* ♦ *The minimum speed on that highway is 45 miles per hour.*

mining ['maɪn ɪŋ] *n.* the business of removing precious metals, minerals, or gemstones from the earth. (No plural form in this sense.) ♦ *The valley was scarred from mining.* ♦ *Mining is an important industry in many countries.*

miniskirt ['mɪn i skɚt] *n.* a very short skirt. ♦ *The school principal banned miniskirts during school hours.* ♦ *The cheerleader's miniskirt matched her sweater and pompons.*

minister ['mɪn ɪ stɚ] **1.** *n.* a pastor; a preacher; the leader of a Christian church. ♦ *The minister preached the Gospel.* ♦ *Anne and Bill were married by a minister.* **2.** *n.* [in many countries] someone who is head of a government department. ♦ *The minister of education spoke at the convention.* ♦ *The defense minister urged the prime minister to declare war.*

ministerial [mɪn ɪ 'stɪr i əl] **1.** *adj.* of or about a minister ① or a ministry. ♦ *The elderly pastor was relieved of his ministerial duties.* ♦ *The ministerial school received no state or federal money.* **2.** *adj.* of or about a minister ②. ♦ *There were discussions at the ministerial level, but no policy was formulated.* ♦ *Sue was hoping for a ministerial appointment.*

ministry ['mɪn ɪs tri] **1. the ministry** *n.* the profession and religious responsibilities of a minister ①. ♦ *John joined the ministry when he was 18.* ♦ *My pastor encouraged me to enter the ministry.* **2.** *n.* a department of government headed by a minister ②. ♦ *The Education Ministry regulated the national universities.* ♦ *The Ministry of Truth dispensed government propaganda.*

mink ['mɪŋk] **1.** *n., irreg.* a small, furry animal similar to the weasel. (Pl: *mink* or *minks.*) ♦ *The fur of minks is often used to make coats.* ♦ *The trapper caught several minks in one day.* **2.** *n.* the fur of ①. (No plural form in this sense.) ♦ *My gloves are lined with mink.* ♦ *Mink is soft, warm, and expensive.* **3.** *n.* a coat made from ②. ♦ *My mink was stolen along with my favorite jewels.* ♦ *The actress wore a mink to the award ceremony.* **4.** *adj.* made from ②. ♦ *I put my mink coat in storage during the summer.* ♦ *The model wore a mink stole around her neck.*

Minnesota [mɪn ə 'sot ə] See Gazetteer.

minnow ['mɪn o] *n.* a kind of very small, thin fish that lives in fresh water. ♦ *Minnows are often used as bait for bigger fish.* ♦ *The minnows could swim through my fishing net.*

minor ['maɪn ɚ] **1.** *adj.* small in size or amount, not serious, not very important. ♦ *I survived the accident with only minor scrapes and bruises.* ♦ *My editor made a few minor changes to my article.* **2.** *adj.* <the adj. use of ③.> ♦ *Mathematics is my minor area of study.* ♦ *My minor field is closely related to my major field of study.* **3.** *n.* a student's secondary area of study. ♦ *My major is philosophy and my minor is history.* ♦ *I haven't decided on a minor yet, but my major is biology.* **4.** *n.* someone who is younger than the legal age of responsibility. ♦ *Minors aren't allowed to buy cigarettes.* ♦ *The store was fined for selling liquor to minors.* **5. minor in** *iv.* + *prep. phr.* to work in a particular secondary area of study. ♦ *The chemistry major decided to minor in physics.* ♦ *My counselor advised me to minor in biology.*

minority [maɪ 'nor ə ti] **1.** *n.* a smaller part of a group of people or things; a subgroup of things or people that are less than half of the whole amount. (No plural form in this sense.) ♦ *Only a small minority of voters voted for the convicted politician.* ♦ *The people in favor of a tax increase were in the minority.* **2.** *n.* someone who is a member of a different race, religion, or ethnic group from the majority of a population. ♦ *Minorities accounted for just 10% of the city's police force.* ♦ *The store owner was sued for discriminating against minorities.* **3.** *n.* the state of being younger than the legal age of responsibility. (No plural form in this sense.) ♦ *Because of the criminal's minority, he was spared the death penalty.* ♦ *The age of minority is determined by the courts.* **4.** *adj.* <the adj. use of ②.> ♦ *The mayor established a Department of Minority Affairs.* ♦ *I joined a minority student organization when I was in college.*

mint ['mɪnt] **1.** *n.* a small plant with leaves that have a fresh, strong flavor, and the leaves themselves. (No plural form in this sense.) ♦ *We planted mint in our garden.* ♦ *The cook added some mint to the recipe.* **2.** *n.* a candy that is flavored with ①. ♦ *I ate a mint to freshen my breath.* ♦ *The restaurant gives each customer a mint after dinner.* **3.** *n.* a building where the government makes paper money and coins. ♦ *Security is extremely tight at government mints.* ♦ *The mint where paper money is printed is named on each bill.* **4.** *n.* a very large amount of money. (Figurative on ③.) ♦ *My new sports car cost me a mint.* ♦ *I spent a mint on renovations.* **5.** *adj.* tasting like ①. ♦ *I gargled with mint mouthwash.* ♦ *I'd like a scoop of mint ice cream.* **6.** *adj.* perfect; untouched; flawless; in excellent condition. ♦ *My vintage car is in mint condition.* ♦ *I paid $1,000 for the mint first edition of the book.* **7.** *tv.* to make something, especially coins, by stamping metal. ♦ *The government mints coins from silver, nickel, copper, and zinc.* ♦ *Only 200,000 copies of the special coin were minted.*

minus ['maɪn əs] **1.** *prep.* less; reduced by; decreased by. ♦ *My weekly wages minus taxes are $500.* ♦ *Five minus three is two.* **2.** *adj.* below zero; less than zero; [of a number] negative. ♦ *It's minus five degrees outside. Dress warmly!* ♦ *Ten subtracted from three is minus seven.* **3.** *adj.* [of a school letter grade] less than the full grade. (Follows the letter. Symbolized by "–".) ♦ *I need an average of at least B– to keep my scholarship.* ♦ *I barely passed the test. I got a D minus.* **4.** *n.* a negative factor; a disadvantage; a lack. ♦ *There were more minuses to the new proposal than pluses.* ♦ *Your lack of experience is a serious minus.*

minuscule ['mɪn ə skjul] **1.** *adj.* [of letters that are] lowercase. (Compare with majuscule.) ♦ *The minuscule form of* I *is* i. ♦ *Type the warning in capital letters, not minuscule letters.* **2.** *adj.* very small. ♦ *I could hardly read the minuscule writing at the bottom of the contract.* ♦ *There's a minuscule speck of dust in my eye.*

minus sign ['maɪn əs saɪn] *n.* the "–" mark, used to show that a second number is being subtracted from a previous number, or that a number is less than zero. ♦ *That's a negative number. Don't you see the minus sign?* ♦ *Negative poles of batteries are marked with minus signs.*

minute 1. ['mɪn ɪt] *n.* a unit of the measurement of time, equal to 60 seconds or 1/60 of an hour. ♦ *The movie is 90 minutes long.* ♦ *The victim was unconscious for two minutes.* **2.** ['mɪn ɪt] *n.* a unit of the measurement of an angle, equal to 1/60 of a degree. ♦ *The latitude of Fairbanks, Alaska, is 64 degrees and 58 minutes north.* ♦ *A minute of latitude is a little longer at the poles than at the equator because Earth is not a perfect sphere.* **3. minutes** ['mɪn ɪts] *n.* a written account of what happened at a meeting. ♦ *The secretary read the minutes of the previous meeting.* ♦ *Lisa gave a copy of the minutes to the board members.* **4.** [maɪ 'nut] *adj.* very small. (Adv: *minutely.*) ♦ *There's a minute bug on the table.* ♦ *There was a minute hair floating in my soup.* **5. just a minute** [...'mɪn ɪt] *idiom* only a short time; [wait] a short period of time. ♦ *I'll be there in just a minute!* ♦ *Could I have just a minute of your time?* **6. the minute something happens** ['mɪn ɪt] *idiom* the point in time at which an event happens. ♦ *I'll be inside the minute it rains.* ♦ *Call me the minute you get to town.*

minutia [mɪ 'nu ʃə] *n., irreg.* the smallest of details. (Pl: minutiae.) ♦ *I can't be bothered with irrelevant minutiae.* ♦ *The report was perfect to the smallest minutia.*

minutiae [mɪ 'nu ʃi ə] pl of minutia.

miracle ['mɪr ə kəl] **1.** *n.* a remarkable event that cannot be explained by the laws of nature and is assumed to be supernatural. ♦ *The cancer patient's recovery was a miracle.* ♦ *The magician claims to work miracles, but he could only do tricks.* **2.** *n.* an unexpected, lucky event. (Figurative on ①.) ♦ *Tom showed up on time! It's a miracle!* ♦ *It will be a miracle if our unlucky team wins the game.*

miraculous [mɪ 'ræk jə ləs] **1.** *adj.* not explainable by the laws of nature; explained as an act of God or the supernatural. (Adv: *miraculously.*) ♦ *The patient attributed her miraculous recovery to God.* ♦ *God spoke to me in a miraculous vision.* **2.** *adj.* unexpectedly excellent. (Figurative on ①. Adv: *miraculously.*) ♦ *You ought to see how my miraculous computer does my taxes!* ♦ *I get miraculous results from my new detergent.*

mirage [mɪ 'rɑʒ] *n.* an image of something that does not really exist, especially an image of water in the desert; something that fools one's vision. ♦ *The image of an oasis was just a mirage.* ♦ *The way pavement seems to shimmer when it's hot is a mirage.*

mire ['maɪr] **1.** *n.* an area of deep mud; a bog. (No plural form in this sense.) ♦ *My car got stuck in the mire after the heavy rains.* ♦ *My shoes were ruined after my feet sank into the mire.* **2.** *n.* something that traps or stymies people. (No plural form in this sense. Figurative on ①.) ♦ *The civil war was a mire that neither side could escape.* ♦ *My job is a mire of paperwork and rules.* **3. mire in** *tv.* + *prep. phr.* to trap someone or something in mud or a bog. (Usually passive.) ♦ *My car was mired in mud.* ♦ *Don't step off the path, or you'll mire yourself in the bog.* **4. mire in** *tv.* + *prep. phr.* to trap or ensnare someone or something in something. (Figurative on ③. Usually passive.) ♦ *The fighting armies were mired in a stalemate.* ♦ *The baseball players were mired in contract negotiations.*

mirror ['mɪr ɚ] **1.** *n.* a piece of polished glass, treated in a way that makes it reflect images perfectly. ♦ *I looked in the mirror and fixed my hair.* ♦ *I saw a police car in my car's rearview mirror.* **2.** *n.* someone or something that shows what someone or something thinks, looks like, acts like, or is. (Figurative on ①.) ♦ *The eyes are said to be a mirror to the soul.* ♦ *Bob's opinions are a mirror of his mother's.* **3.** *tv.* to show something as though it were seen in a mirror; to represent something. ♦ *The senator's opinions mirror my own.* ♦ *My thoughts don't mirror the opinions of my company.*

mirth [ˈmɚθ] *n.* fun and laughter. (No plural form in this sense.) ♦ *The party was filled with mirth.* ♦ *There's no place for mirth here. I'm trying to be serious.*

misadventure [mɪs əd ˈvɛn tʃɚ] **1.** *n.* bad luck; a lack of good fortune. (No plural form in this sense.) ♦ *After a night of misadventure, John ended up in jail.* ♦ *The misadventure of getting lost in the city left me very frightened.* **2.** *n.* an accident; an unlucky adventure. ♦ *Lisa experienced a serious misadventure when she got lost.* ♦ *I told my friends about my misadventures while gambling.*

misapplication [mɪs æp lɪ ˈke ʃən] *n.* the wrong application of something; the act of applying something in the wrong way. ♦ *The misapplication of hair dye can be dangerous.* ♦ *The misapplication of the data made the report useless.*

misapply [mɪs ə ˈplɑɪ] *tv.* to apply something the wrong way; to use something in the wrong way. ♦ *The banker misapplied the funds to the wrong account.* ♦ *The wood warped because the varnish was misapplied.*

misapprehension [mɪs æp rɪ ˈhɛn ʃən] *n.* misunderstanding. ♦ *I was given an explanation that was supposed to ease my misapprehension.* ♦ *Bob stayed home because he had only misapprehension about the party.*

misappropriate [mɪs ə ˈpro pri et] *tv.* to spend money in a way other than the way it was supposed to be spent. ♦ *The bank president was arrested for misappropriating funds.* ♦ *The contractor misappropriated millions of dollars before he was caught.*

misbehave [mɪs bɪ ˈhev] *iv.* to behave badly; to behave improperly. ♦ *The children were punished because they had misbehaved.* ♦ *The students misbehaved when their teacher left the room.*

misbehavior [mɪs bɪ ˈhev jɚ] *n.* bad behavior. (No plural form in this sense.) ♦ *Billy was punished for his misbehavior at school.* ♦ *The teacher didn't tolerate any misbehavior in class.*

miscalculate [mɪs ˈkæl kjə let] **1.** *tv.* to calculate something incorrectly; to add, subtract, multiply, or divide something the wrong way. ♦ *I had miscalculated my taxes, so I still owed more money.* ♦ *The treasurer miscalculated the monthly balance.* **2.** *tv.* to guess something incorrectly; to make a bad guess or estimation. (Figurative on ①.) ♦ *I assumed Jane would stay, but I miscalculated her intentions.* ♦ *I'm late because I miscalculated the time it takes to get here.* **3.** *iv.* to calculate incorrectly; to add, subtract, multiply, or divide the wrong way. ♦ *When computers miscalculate, it's often due to human error.* ♦ *The adding machine miscalculated because it's broken.*

miscarriage [mɪs ˈkɛr ɪdʒ] **1.** *n.* giving birth to a fetus that died before it developed fully. (Compare with stillborn.) ♦ *My sister's first pregnancy ended in miscarriage.* ♦ *Some drugs increase the chance of miscarriage.* **2. miscarriage of justice** *idiom* a wrong or mistaken decision, especially one made in a court of law. ♦ *Sentencing the old man on a charge of murder proved to be a miscarriage of justice.* ♦ *The lawyer claimed that the jury had caused a miscarriage of justice.*

miscellaneous [mɪs ə ˈle ni əs] *adj.* having many different things, kinds, or types; mixed; varied. (Adv: *miscellaneously.*) ♦ *My desk drawers were full of miscellaneous junk.* ♦ *There are miscellaneous tools and cans of paint in the garage.*

mischief [ˈmɪs tʃɪf] **1.** *n.* playful trouble; bothersome deeds. (No plural form in this sense.) ♦ *My little brother causes so much mischief!* ♦ *Don't get into any mischief while I'm gone!* **2.** *n.* a source of trouble or problems. ♦ *Whenever something goes wrong in our office, we all blame Bob because he's a mischief.* ♦ *The annoying mischief was sent to the principal's office.*

mischievous [ˈmɪs tʃə vəs] *adj.* full of mischief; causing trouble, but not serious trouble. (Adv: *mischievously.*) ♦ *The mischievous kids played a practical joke on their teacher.* ♦ *My mischievous coworkers glued my desk drawer shut.*

misconception [mɪs kən ˈsɛp ʃən] *n.* an incorrect understanding of someone or something; a mistaken idea or opinion. ♦ *The doctor cleared up my misconceptions about birth control.* ♦ *The misconception that the earth is flat was dismissed long ago.*

misconduct [mɪs ˈkɑn dəkt] *n.* bad behavior; behavior that is not ethical or moral. (No plural form in this sense.) ♦ *The teacher didn't tolerate misconduct from her students.* ♦ *The officers were punished for their misconduct during the investigation.*

misconstrue [mɪs kən ˈstru] *tv.* to understand something the wrong way, by accident or on purpose. ♦ *The article was misconstrued because it was badly worded.* ♦ *The reporter misconstrued my statement, making me look stupid.*

misdeal [mɪs ˈdil] **1.** *n.* the result of a bad dealing of cards. ♦ *After the misdeal, I shuffled the cards and dealt them again.* ♦ *The dealer declared a misdeal because he dropped the cards.* **2.** *tv., irreg.* to deal cards incorrectly. (Pt/pp: misdealt.) ♦ *I think you misdealt the cards, because I've got too many.* ♦ *The careless poker player misdealt the cards.* **3.** *iv., irreg.* to deal [cards] incorrectly. ♦ *Since Tom misdealt in the last hand, we watched him carefully this time.* ♦ *You misdealt. I've got six cards instead of five.*

misdealt [mɪs ˈdɛlt] pt/pp of misdeal.

misdeed [mɪs ˈdid] *n.* a bad deed; an action that is evil or bad; a crime. ♦ *The criminal was punished for his misdeeds.* ♦ *The mayor lost the election when her misdeeds were publicized.*

misdemeanor [mɪs dɪ ˈmin ɚ] *n.* a crime that is not as serious as a felony. ♦ *The judge reduced my felony charge to a misdemeanor.* ♦ *Driving over the speed limit is a common misdemeanor.*

miser [ˈmɑɪz ɚ] *n.* someone who is very stingy. ♦ *The miser ate only simple, sparse meals.* ♦ *The charity couldn't convince the miser to donate any money.*

miserable [ˈmɪz ə rə bəl] **1.** *adj.* unhappy; very sad; depressed. (Adv: *miserably.*) ♦ *I didn't go to the party because I was feeling miserable.* ♦ *The miserable student sat in a corner and cried.* **2.** *adj.* unpleasant; depressing. (Adv: *miserably.*) ♦ *It was a miserable day outside, so I stayed in bed.* ♦ *It rained every day during my miserable vacation.* **3.** *adj.* poor; squalid; wretched. (Adv: *miserably.*) ♦ *The poor immigrants lived in a miserable dwelling.* ♦ *My miserable wages barely support my family.* **4. make life miserable for someone** *idiom* to make someone unhappy over a long period of time. ♦ *My shoes are tight, and they* *are making life miserable for me.* ♦ *Jane's boss is making life miserable for her.*

miserly ['mɑɪz ɚ li] *adj.* stingy; never spending money on anything unless it is absolutely necessary. ♦ *The miserly millionaire ate nothing but rice and spinach.* ♦ *My landlord is being miserly with the heat again.*

misery ['mɪz ə ri] **1.** *n.* a state of unhappiness, depression, and suffering. (No plural form in this sense.) ♦ *David has been in misery ever since he was fired.* ♦ *Anne's misery was made even worse by her illness.* **2.** *n.* something that causes unhappiness, depression, and suffering. (No plural form in this sense.) ♦ *My mother's death brought me misery I could not overcome.* ♦ *Bill never knew the cause of the emotional misery that tormented him.*

misfire [mɪs 'fɑɪr] **1.** *iv.* [for a gun] to fail to fire a bullet when shooting. ♦ *The president lived because the assassin's gun misfired.* ♦ *The robber pulled the trigger, but thankfully the gun misfired.* **2.** *iv.* [for a plan or joke] to fail to happen in the way intended. (Figurative on ①.) ♦ *Anne was injured when Susan's practical joke misfired.* ♦ *The company declared bankruptcy when its recovery plan misfired.*

misfit 1. ['mɪs 'fɪt] *tv.* to fit into something badly; to fit something onto something badly. ♦ *The shoddy carpenter misfit the door in the jam.* ♦ *The child's shoes were badly misfit.* **2.** ['mɪs fɪt] *n.* someone who does not fit in with other people or a situation. ♦ *The popular students laughed at the misfits.* ♦ *I never go to parties because I feel like such a misfit.*

misfortune [mɪs 'for tʃən] **1.** *n.* bad luck; bad fortune. (No plural form in this sense.) ♦ *Misfortune followed the unlucky man wherever he went.* ♦ *Misfortune and grief affected everyone in the unlucky town.* **2.** *n.* an unlucky accident. ♦ *I had the misfortune of crashing my car into a tree.* ♦ *Bill suffered two different misfortunes this week.*

misgiving [mɪs 'gɪv ɪŋ] *n.* a doubt; a feeling of distrust; a feeling of anxiety. (Often plural.) ♦ *I have a misgiving about letting Jimmy go swimming in this cold weather.* ♦ *Mary had misgivings about her mysterious new neighbor.*

misguided [mɪs 'gɑɪd əd] *adj.* behaving as if one had been given the wrong advice or instructions. (Adv: *misguidedly.*) ♦ *You are not totally wrong, you are only misguided.* ♦ *The misguided child, in a few years, became a criminal.*

mishandle [mɪs 'hænd l] **1.** *tv.* to handle something badly or roughly. ♦ *The young child mishandled the kittens.* ♦ *Don't mishandle the crystal goblet. It's very fragile.* **2.** *tv.* to deal with a situation in the wrong way. (Figurative on ①.) ♦ *I complained to the manager when the clerk mishandled my request.* ♦ *The police chief was criticized for mishandling the riot.*

mishap ['mɪs hæp] *n.* an unlucky event or accident; bad luck; an unfortunate accident. ♦ *The fisherman drowned in a boating mishap.* ♦ *The blizzard caused a lot of mishaps on the roadways.*

misinterpret [mɪs ɪn 'tɚ prɪt] *tv.* to misunderstand what someone means or says. ♦ *Don't be offended. You've misinterpreted what I said.* ♦ *I misinterpreted Jane's reply because I didn't listen carefully.*

misjudge [mɪs 'dʒʌdʒ] *tv.* to make the wrong judgment about someone or something. ♦ *Bill didn't hire the skilled applicant because he'd misjudged her.* ♦ *The capabilities of the handicapped are often misjudged.*

mislaid [mɪs 'led] **1.** pt/pp of mislay. **2.** *adj.* lost; put in a place that is no longer recalled. ♦ *I couldn't find the mislaid keys anywhere.* ♦ *I found the mislaid present six months after Max's birthday party.*

mislay [mɪs 'le] *tv., irreg.* to put something in a location that is now forgotten. (Pt/pp: mislaid.) ♦ *I'm locked out of my house because I've mislaid my keys.* ♦ *David was late because he'd mislaid his wallet.*

mislead [mɪs 'lid] **1.** *tv., irreg.* to cause someone to go the wrong direction. (Pt/pp: misled.) ♦ *The tourists were misled by the confusing directions.* ♦ *The sign misled me because it was wrong.* **2.** *tv., irreg.* to cause someone to have the wrong idea; to deceive someone. (Figurative on ①.) ♦ *The candidate's speech intentionally misled the voters.* ♦ *Bill misled us badly.*

misleading [mɪs 'lid ɪŋ] *adj.* causing one to have the wrong idea; deceiving. (Adv: *misleadingly.*) ♦ *They fixed the misleading sign so that it was more clear.* ♦ *The candidate questioned her opponent's misleading comments.*

misled [mɪs 'lɛd] pt/pp of mislead.

mismanage [mɪs 'mæn ɪdʒ] *tv.* to manage someone or something badly; to deal with someone or something badly. ♦ *My broker mismanaged my portfolio.* ♦ *The coach mismanaged the baseball team.*

mismatch [mɪs 'mætʃ] **1.** *n.* two things that do not look good together; two people who are not suited for each other. ♦ *Your plaid shirt is a mismatch with your striped pants.* ♦ *John and Mary divorced because they were such a mismatch.* **2.** *tv.* to match two things or people badly; to bring two people together who are not suited for each other. ♦ *I accidentally mismatched a black sock with a brown one.* ♦ *Somehow the contents of the book and its cover have been mismatched.*

misnomer [mɪs 'no mɚ] *n.* an incorrect or inappropriate name for something. ♦ *It is a misnomer to call a gorilla a monkey.* ♦ *Tree is a misnomer for that plant. It's a bush.*

misplace [mɪs 'ples] **1.** *tv.* to put something someplace and then forget where it is. ♦ *I was late because I'd misplaced my car keys again.* ♦ *My roommate misplaced the rent check.* **2. misplace one's trust (in someone)** *idiom* to put trust in the wrong person; to put trust in someone who does not deserve it. ♦ *The writer misplaced his trust in his editor.* ♦ *The voters misplaced their trust in the corrupt politician.*

misplaced [mɪs 'plest] **1.** *adj.* lost because one cannot remember where one put it; mislaid. ♦ *I found my misplaced wallet in a pile of dirty clothes.* ♦ *That misplaced book is due at the library today.* **2.** *adj.* undeserved. ♦ *My misplaced trust was rewarded by treachery.* ♦ *My sympathy for the criminal was probably misplaced.*

misprint ['mɪs prɪnt] **1.** *n.* a mistake in printing; something that is printed incorrectly. ♦ *The newspaper acknowledged its misprint in the next edition.* ♦ *The misprint in the manual made it impossible to assemble the bookshelf correctly.* **2.** *tv.* to print something incorrectly; to make a mistake in printing. ♦ *Somehow these pages were misprinted upside down.* ♦ *The newspaper misprinted the foreign diplomat's name.*

misquote [mɪs 'kwot] **1.** *tv.* to quote someone incorrectly. ♦ *The newspaper misquoted the mayor's speech.* ♦ *The student misquoted the words of the dean.* **2.** *n.* an incorrectly quoted part of something spoken or written. ♦ *That is a misquote! I never said it!* ♦ *The misquote made the senator look foolish.*

miss ['mɪs] **1.** *tv.* to fail to hit, catch, meet, do, or reach someone or something. ♦ *The batter missed the ball.* ♦ *I missed my appointment because traffic was so bad.* **2.** *tv.* to fail to locate or observe people or things who are where they are meant to be. ♦ *I missed my friends at the crowded beach, but I know they were there.* ♦ *I missed the fine print at the bottom of the contract.* **3.** *tv.* to notice the absence of someone or something. ♦ *I missed you at my party.* ♦ *I missed my friends at school when they were sick.* **4.** *tv.* to feel sad about the loss, departure, or absence of someone or something. ♦ *I missed my sister after she went away to school.* ♦ *I missed my favorite teacher after she retired.* **5.** *tv.* to avoid someone or something. ♦ *The driver missed hitting the tree by five feet.* ♦ *I was hoping to miss Mary's phone call because I didn't want to speak to her.* **6.** *tv.* to lack something; to fail to acquire something that is available. ♦ *We missed the first five minutes of the movie.* ♦ *I missed the circus when it was in town.* **7.** *n.* a failure to hit, reach, catch, or do something. ♦ *The catcher's miss was categorized as an error.* ♦ *The miss shook the pilot's nerves.* **8.** *n.* a girl; a young woman. ♦ *A friendly miss passed out flowers at the rest home.* ♦ *I asked the young miss behind the counter where the restroom was.* **9. Miss** *n.* <a polite form of address for girls and young women.> ♦ *May I come in, Miss?* ♦ *Excuse me, Miss, you dropped your ticket.* **10. Miss** *n.* <a title for a girl or unmarried woman.> (Compare with **Ms.**) ♦ *My history class is taught by Miss Benedict.* ♦ *Miss Johnson lives in that apartment.* **11. miss the point** See **point** ⑰.

misshapen [mɪs 'ʃep ən] *adj.* badly shaped; badly formed; deformed. (Adv: *misshapenly.*) ♦ *The bakery sold misshapen pastries for half price.* ♦ *Surgery corrected the baby's misshapen hand.*

missile ['mɪs əl] **1.** *n.* something that is thrown, shot, or fired at a target. ♦ *The missile hit the center of the target.* ♦ *The principal banned all missiles at school.* **2.** *n.* a rocket carrying bombs or weapons that can be shot at a target very far away. ♦ *Missiles rained down on the enemy's fort.* ♦ *Long-range missiles were aimed at the enemy's capital.*

missing ['mɪs ɪŋ] *adj.* not able to be found. ♦ *Dozens of volunteers helped look for the missing child.* ♦ *I searched the park for my missing dog.*

mission ['mɪ ʃən] **1.** *n.* a group of people that are sent someplace to do a specific task. ♦ *Our church set up a religious mission overseas.* ♦ *The delegates of the trade mission met with the foreign leader.* **2.** *n.* a journey to a place to do an important task. ♦ *The delegates' mission was to establish a trade agreement.* ♦ *The astronauts were sent on a mission to fix a broken satellite.* **3.** *n.* the building where people on a religious **mission** ② work and worship. ♦ *Orphaned children were raised at the mission.* ♦ *The hostile government forced the mission to close.* **4.** *n.* a specific task or duty. ♦ *The senator sent her aide on a mission to find information.* ♦ *The mayor's mission to reduce crime was successful.* **5. mission in life** *idiom* one's purpose for living; the reason for which one lives on the earth. ♦ *Bob's mission in life is to make money.* ♦ *My mission in life is to help people live in peace.*

missionary ['mɪʃ ə nɛr i] *n.* one who spreads and teaches one's religion, especially in a foreign country. ♦ *The missionary translated the Bible into the local language.* ♦ *The villagers resented the missionaries.*

Mississippi [mɪs ɪ 'sɪp i] See Gazetteer.

Missouri [mɪ 'zɝ i] See Gazetteer.

misspeak ['mɪs 'spik] *iv., irreg.* to say something other than what one meant to say; to say something incorrectly. (Pt: **misspoke**; pp: **misspoken**.) ♦ *I misspoke when I said I wanted pizza. I really want chicken.* ♦ *Politicians must be careful not to misspeak when being interviewed.*

misspell [mɪs 'spɛl] *tv.* to spell something wrongly. ♦ *The printer misspelled my name on my business cards.* ♦ *The word* misspell *is often misspelled with only one* s.

misspelled [mɪs 'spɛld] *adj.* spelled wrongly; not spelled the right way. ♦ *The first misspelled word at the spelling bee was* mischievous. ♦ *The misspelled sign cost the taxpayers a lot of money to fix.*

misspend [mɪs 'spɛnd] *tv.* to spend money wrongly or wastefully. (Pt/pp: **misspent**.) ♦ *The mayor was caught in a scheme to misspend the taxpayer's money.* ♦ *Congress misspent millions of dollars last year.*

misspent [mɪs 'spɛnt] pt/pp of **misspend**.

misspoke [mɪs 'spok] pt of **misspeak**.

misspoken [mɪs 'spok ən] pp of **misspeak**.

mist ['mɪst] **1.** *n.* a light spray of water or other liquid; a small cloud formed by spraying water or other liquid. ♦ *The ship sailed through the waterfall's mist.* ♦ *The gardener sprayed the plants with mist.* **2.** *tv.* to spray someone or something with water or other liquid; to cover something with ① or water vapor. ♦ *The gardener misted the plants with water.* ♦ *I misted my hair into place with hair spray.* **3. mist up; mist over** *iv.* + *adv.* [for something] to acquire a coating of ① or water vapor. ♦ *The car windows misted up during the rainstorm.* ♦ *The mirror in the bathroom misted over.*

mistake [mɪ 'stek] **1.** *n.* an error; something that is wrong; something that is not correct. ♦ *The teacher circled my mistakes with red ink.* ♦ *Fix the mistakes in your report before you submit it.* **2.** *tv., irreg.* to have the wrong idea about something. (Pt: **mistook**; pp: **mistaken**.) ♦ *John mistook what I said because I didn't speak loudly enough.* ♦ *You've mistaken what I said. My birthday isn't until tomorrow.* **3. mistake for** *tv., irreg.* + *prep. phr.* to think that one thing or person is another; to confuse one thing or person with another. ♦ *My grandfather mistook me for my cousin.* ♦ *I mistook Anne for her twin sister.*

mistaken [mɪ 'stek ən] **1.** pp of mistake. **2. a case of mistaken identity** *idiom* the incorrect identification of someone. ♦ *It is simply a case of mistaken identity.* ♦ *I am not the criminal you want to arrest. This is a case of mistaken identity.*

mister ['mɪs tɚ] *n.* <a title for an adult male; a form of address for men.> (The abbreviation, **Mr.**, is used in writing.) ♦ *Hey, mister! You left your car lights on.* ♦ *After he turned 18, John wanted to be called "Mr. Johnson."*

mistletoe ['mɪs əl to] *n.* a green plant with white berries, often used as a Christmas decoration. (No plural form in this sense.) ♦ *Mistletoe hung above every doorway at the Christmas party.* ♦ *It's a custom to kiss people who stand under mistletoe.*

mistook [mɪs 'tʊk] pt of mistake.

mistreat [mɪs 'trit] *tv.* to treat someone or something badly; to abuse someone or something. ♦ *Mary ran away from home because her parents mistreated her.* ♦ *No animals were mistreated in the making of this movie.*

mistress ['mɪs trɪs] **1.** *n.* a woman who is having a sexual relationship with a married man. ♦ *The newspaper revealed the identity of the mayor's mistress.* ♦ *Anne was shocked to learn that her husband had a mistress.* **2.** *n.* a woman who is in a specific position of responsibility. (Compare with master.) ♦ *The mistress of ceremonies announced the next guest.* ♦ *The actress took her ripped gown to the costume mistress.* **3.** *n.* the woman in charge of a household; a woman whom servants serve. (See also Mrs.) ♦ *The maid brought breakfast to her mistress.* ♦ *Could I speak to the mistress of the house?*

mistrial ['mɪs trɑɪl] *n.* a trial that is invalid because of an error of procedure during the trial. ♦ *The lawyer's incompetence resulted in a mistrial.* ♦ *The defendant was released when a mistrial was declared.*

mistrust [mɪs 'trʌst] **1.** *tv.* not to trust someone or something; to doubt someone or something. ♦ *John inherently mistrusted all politicians.* ♦ *I mistrusted the car salesman's claims.* **2.** *n.* distrust; doubts about someone or something. (No plural form in this sense.) ♦ *The corrupt senator reinforced my mistrust of politicians.* ♦ *My mistrust of salespeople is based on many bad experiences.*

misty ['mɪs ti] *adj.* [of a surface] covered with mist; [of air] filled with mist. (Adv: *mistily.* Comp: *mistier;* sup: *mistiest.*) ♦ *I wiped the misty windows with a rag.* ♦ *I bet our flight is late because it's so misty outside.*

misunderstand [mɪs ən dɚ 'stænd] *tv., irreg.* to understand someone or something incorrectly. (Pt/pp: misunderstood.) ♦ *Bill misunderstood his boss's garbled orders.* ♦ *I misunderstood you because you didn't speak loudly enough.*

misunderstanding [mɪs ən dɚ 'stænd ɪŋ] **1.** *n.* the failure to understand something. (No plural form in this sense.) ♦ *The instances of misunderstanding were caused by a poor telephone connection.* ♦ *There must be some misunderstanding. I know I have a reservation.* **2.** *n.* an argument; a disagreement. ♦ *We settled our misunderstanding in court.* ♦ *The loud misunderstanding led to a fight.*

misunderstood [mɪs ən dɚ 'stʊd] **1.** pt/pp of misunderstand. **2.** *adj.* not understood correctly. ♦ *The misunderstood teenager ran away from home.* ♦ *My misunderstood motives were misrepresented by the press.*

misuse 1. [mɪs 'jus] *n.* incorrect use; improper use; the act of using something wrongly. (No plural form in this sense.) ♦ *My editor chided me for my misuse of the words* sit *and* set. ♦ *The misuse of this equipment could cause an electrical shock.* **2.** [mɪs 'juz] *tv.* to use something the wrong way; to use something for a purpose for which it was not meant to be used. ♦ *I damaged the wall when I misused the drill.* ♦ *Bill started a fire when he misused the lighter.*

mitten ['mɪt n] *n.* a piece of clothing for one's hand that does not have separate parts for each finger but does have a separate area for the thumb. ♦ *I can't tie my shoelaces with my mittens on.* ♦ *Wool mittens really keep your hands warm.*

mix ['mɪks] **1.** *n.* a mixture; a combination of different things or people. ♦ *This radio station plays a mix of different kinds of music.* ♦ *My neighborhood is a mix of many ethnic groups.* **2.** *n.* a combination of different foods that is ready to be cooked or used in cooking. ♦ *I added an egg and some milk to the cake mix.* ♦ *Lisa makes pancakes from a mix.* **3.** *tv.* to combine or blend different things so that they form one thing. ♦ *The cook mixed the eggs with the flour in a blender.* ♦ *If you mix red and blue, you get purple.* **4.** *tv.* to do two things at the same time. ♦ *It's dangerous to mix drinking and driving.* ♦ *At the convention, I mixed business with pleasure.* **5.** *iv.* to socialize; to be with other people. ♦ *The popular student mixed well at the party.* ♦ *My shy guests didn't mix, so we all watched TV in silence.*

mixed ['mɪkst] **1.** *adj.* combined; blended. ♦ *Place the mixed batter in a shallow pan.* ♦ *The vinegar and oil in the mixed dressing began to separate.* **2.** *adj.* having different thoughts or feelings about something. ♦ *I have mixed emotions about that movie.* ♦ *My feelings about the candidate were mixed.* **3.** *adj.* having both males and females; for both sexes. ♦ *The school's mixed chorus sang at commencement.* ♦ *The local school offers mixed swimming classes.* **4.** *adj.* involving more than one race. ♦ *We have lived in a mixed neighborhood for years.* ♦ *Mary's parents expressed themselves about her proposed mixed marriage.*

mixed-up ['mɪkst 'əp] *adj.* confused; unsure. ♦ *Uncle Tom seems pretty mixed-up when he first gets up in the morning.* ♦ *I helped the mixed-up tourist find the freeway.*

mixer ['mɪks ɚ] **1.** *n.* a machine that mixes different things together. ♦ *The cook mixed the batter in the mixer.* ♦ *The laborer poured fresh cement from the mixer.* **2.** *n.* a party for people who are in a new place or situation to meet each other. ♦ *I attended a mixer during the first week of school.* ♦ *There's a mixer on the first evening of the convention.* **3.** *n.* water, soda, pop, juice, or some other drink that is mixed with alcohol. (No plural form in this sense.) ♦ *What kind of mixer would you like with your vodka?* ♦ *I used orange juice as a mixer.*

mixture ['mɪks tʃɚ] *n.* a combination or blend of different things or people. ♦ *The chemist tried to determine the components of the mysterious mixture.* ♦ *This city has an interesting mixture of many cultures.*

moan ['mon] **1.** *n.* a deep, long cry of despair, suffering, pain, or grief. ♦ *The hospital patient let out a loud moan.* ♦ *The firefighters could hear the moans of the victims trapped in the rubble.* **2.** *iv.* to make a deep, long cry of despair, suffering, pain, or grief. ♦ *The dog moaned in pain.* ♦ *The mourners moaned in despair at the funeral.* **3.** *iv.* to complain. (Figurative on ②.) ♦ *The customer moaned about the poor service.* ♦ *Stop moaning about your problems and do something about them.*

moaning ['mon ɪŋ] **1.** *adj.* making deep, long cries of despair, suffering, pain, or grief. ♦ *The minister consoled the moaning mourners.* ♦ *The moaning dog kept me awake all night.* **2.** *n.* low sounds of despair, pain, or grief. ♦ *The injured dog's moaning kept me awake all night.* ♦ *The patient's moaning disturbed others in the hospital.*

moat ['mot] *n.* a wide, deep ditch dug around a castle and filled with water in order to protect the castle. ♦ *The castle moat was filled with crocodiles.* ♦ *The drawbridge was lowered over the moat.*

mob ['mɑb] **1.** *n.* a large, uncontrolled group of people; a large group of people crowded around someone or something. ♦ *The police couldn't control the angry mob.* ♦ *The opera singer was surrounded by a mob of fans.* **2. the mob** *n.* a gang of criminals, especially ones involved in organized crime. (No plural form in this sense. Treated as singular.) ♦ *The mob extorted "protection" money from local businesses.* ♦ *The lone witness was killed by the mob.* **3.** *tv.* [for a large group of people] to crowd around someone or something. ♦ *Hundreds of fans mobbed the movie star.* ♦ *The reporters mobbed the mayor after the press conference.*

mobile 1. ['mob əl] *adj.* able to move easily; able to be moved easily; movable. ♦ *A laptop computer is quite mobile.* ♦ *A piano on wheels is more mobile than one without them.* **2.** ['mo bil] *n.* a hanging arrangement of balanced objects that move with air currents. (Refers to decorations, works of art, or devices to entertain infants.) ♦ *The mobile on my porch clanged in the wind.* ♦ *The baby watched the mobile hanging above her crib.*

mobile home ['mob əl 'hom] *n.* a small house on wheels that usually rests permanently in a trailer park. ♦ *The tornado destroyed a row of mobile homes.* ♦ *My aunt and uncle live in a mobile home on a tiny piece of land.*

mobility [mo 'bɪl ə ti] *n.* the ability to move; the ability to be moved. (No plural form in this sense.) ♦ *Arthritis impairs a person's mobility.* ♦ *An electrically powered wheelchair gave Bob increased mobility.*

mobilization [mob əl ɪ 'ze ʃən] *n.* the process of mobilizing something; the placement of soldiers into a position where they are ready to fight. (No plural form in this sense.) ♦ *The mobilization of our troops caused the enemy to withdraw.* ♦ *The president ordered the mobilization of the army regiment.*

mobilize ['mo bə lɑɪz] *tv.* to gather things or people together for a specific reason, especially war. ♦ *The general mobilized the troops along the border.* ♦ *The governor mobilized the citizens to pile sandbags to prevent further flooding.*

moccasin ['mɑk ə sən] *n.* a soft leather shoe without a built-up heel. ♦ *I put on my moccasins and went outside.* ♦ *I bought some moccasins at the Indian reservation.*

mock ['mɔk] **1.** *tv.* to make fun of someone; to laugh at someone, especially by copying how that person speaks or acts. ♦ *The comedian mocked the president's plans.* ♦ *Don't mock me just because I am different!* **2.** *tv.* to mimic or imitate someone or something. ♦ *Tom mocked my every word, seconds after I spoke them.* ♦ *The children loved to mock their teacher, until they got in trouble for it.* **3.** *adj.* not real. ♦ *I used chicken in the mock-turtle soup.* ♦ *The students voted in a mock presidential election.*

mockery ['mɔk ə ri] **1.** *n.* an instance of mocking or ridiculing someone or something. ♦ *This book is a mockery of my religion!* ♦ *The impersonator's act was a mockery of the president's manner.* **2.** *n.* something that is a poor substitute for the real thing or person. ♦ *This book offers only a mockery of an analysis of the problem.* ♦ *That noise is a cheap mockery of music!*

mocking ['mɔk ɪŋ] *adj.* making fun of; teasing; mimicking; ridiculing. (Adv: *mockingly.*) ♦ *The bully taunted me with a mocking laugh.* ♦ *I was hurt by David's mocking comments.*

mockingbird ['mɔk ɪŋ bɚd] *n.* a bird native to the Americas, so called because it mimics the calls or songs of other birds. ♦ *I thought I heard a robin, but it was a mockingbird.* ♦ *The mockingbird flew from tree to tree.*

mock-up ['mɔk əp] *n.* a draft or model of how something will look when it is completed. ♦ *The architect showed us a mock-up of the new skyscraper.* ♦ *The designer constructed a mock-up of the set.*

mode ['mod] **1.** *n.* a way of doing something; a method; a manner. ♦ *During the blackout, the hospital operated in an emergency mode.* ♦ *Our mode of doing business is to treat the customer royally.* **2.** *n.* style; fashion. ♦ *On Friday, we're allowed to dress in a casual mode.* ♦ *The mourners at the funeral behaved in a somber mode.* **3.** *n.* a feature of a verb that shows whether it is a statement, command, or wish; mood ②. ♦ *A word that asks a question indicates the interrogative mode.* ♦ *The imperative mode is used to form commands.*

model ['mɑd l] **1.** *n.* a copy of an object, usually made smaller than the original; a replica. ♦ *The architect showed us a model of the house she had designed for us.* ♦ *I made a model of a volcano out of clay.* **2.** *n.* someone or something that is the perfect example of something; someone or something that is to be copied or imitated; a standard. ♦ *The teacher said that I was the model of good behavior.* ♦ *The new factory soon became a model of efficiency.* **3.** *n.* someone who is paid to wear and show off clothing that is available for sale. ♦ *The fashion model walked across the stage.* ♦ *I want to buy the red dress that this model is wearing.* **4.** *n.* someone who poses for artists and photographers. ♦ *Each art student drew a picture of the model.* ♦ *The famous model appeared on the cover of many magazines.* **5.** *n.* one style of a certain product in a series of styles. ♦ *Anne's car is an American model.* ♦ *The newer model of this television set has more features than the old one.* **6.** *adj.* perfect; worthy of imitation; regarded as the perfect example. ♦ *The bully teased the model student every day.* ♦ *The model politician refused to ridicule his opponents.* **7.** *adj.* built to a smaller scale than normal. ♦ *Dad had his old model train set up in the basement.* ♦ *Bob has a collection of model cars in his room.* **8.** *iv.* to work as ④. ♦ *Anne models to make extra money for school.* ♦ *Dave has to stay fit because he models.* **9.** *tv.* to work as ③. ♦ *Mary modeled the new line of swimwear.* ♦ *John modeled the tuxedo.* **10. model on** *tv.* + *prep. phr.* to base something on something else; to create something based on something else. ♦ *Our production scheme is modeled on a Japanese system.* ♦ *Mr. Smith modeled his house on a European design.* **11. model into** *tv.* + *prep. phr.* to mold something in a certain shape; to form something into a certain shape. ♦ *The sculptor modeled the clay into an ashtray.* ♦ *Billy modeled his mashed potatoes into a giant volcano.*

modem ['mod əm] *n.* a device that connects a computer with a telephone line so that information can be sent or received over telephone lines. ♦ *My computer has a built-in modem.* ♦ *My modem transmits data at 28,800 bits per second.*

moderate 1. ['mɑd ə rɪt] *adj.* not extreme; in the center; average or medium. (Adv: *moderately.*) ♦ *The popular president pursued a moderate agenda.* ♦ *I wore a light jacket because the temperature was moderate.* **2.** ['mɑd ə rɪt] *n.* someone who is not a conservative or a liberal; someone whose views are not extreme. ♦ *The politician was elected by moderates from both parties.* ♦ *The moderate helped the extreme sides reach a compromise.* **3.** ['mɑd ə ret] *tv.* to reduce something; to cause something to be less strong. ♦ *I moderated the strength of the punch by adding some water.* ♦ *The mayor moderated the power of the city council.* **4.** ['mɑd ə ret] *tv.* to lead a discussion; to lead a meeting. ♦ *The contract negotiations were moderated by a neutral party.* ♦ *Sue moderates the sales meeting because she's the sales manager.*

moderation [mɑd ə 're ʃən] *n.* being moderate; [doing things] within reasonable limits. (No plural form in this sense.) ♦ *Moderation in all things is the secret to a good life.* ♦ *This diet allows you to eat most foods in moderation.*

moderator ['mɑd ə ret ɚ] *n.* someone who leads a discussion or a meeting. ♦ *The moderator will recognize you when it's your turn to speak.* ♦ *The moderator introduced the members of the guest panel.*

modern ['mɑd ɚn] *adj.* up-to-date; new; of or about the present or very recent time. (Adv: *modernly.*) ♦ *The professor taught modern American literature.* ♦ *The designer gave the old building a more modern look.*

modernization [mɑd ɚ nɪ 'ze ʃən] *n.* the act or process of bringing something up-to-date. (No plural form in this sense.) ♦ *The city paid for the modernization of the 100-year-old school.* ♦ *The modernization of the transit system cost millions of dollars.*

modernize ['mɑd ɚ naɪz] *tv.* to make something up-to-date; to adapt something to the current style or technology. ♦ *The factory was modernized to make it more efficient.* ♦ *The store owner hired a designer to modernize the sales area.*

modest ['mɑd əst] **1.** *adj.* shy; humble; not bragging about oneself. (Adv: *modestly.*) ♦ *The winner's modest acceptance speech was very gracious.* ♦ *The modest painter avoided the press at the gallery opening.* **2.** *adj.* not excessive; moderate; not large. (Adv: *modestly.*) ♦ *I live in a modest home in a middle-class neighborhood.* ♦ *My family survives on a modest income.* **3.** *adj.* decent; not revealing too much of one's body. (Adv: *modestly.*) ♦ *We're not leaving until you wear something more modest.* ♦ *The prudish man wore extremely modest clothing at the beach.*

modification [mɑd ə fə 'ke ʃən] *n.* a slight change; an alteration; the act of changing something. ♦ *My boss informed me of the modifications in our travel plans.* ♦ *Slight modifications to the engine caused the car to run much better.*

modified ['mɑd ə faɪd] *adj.* slightly changed. ♦ *The modified engine improved the car's gas mileage.* ♦ *My secretary faxed me a copy of the modified meeting schedule.*

modify ['mɑd ə faɪ] **1.** *tv.* to change someone or something slightly. ♦ *I modified my travel plans by staying an extra night in Rome.* ♦ *The bus route was modified to provide service to the mall.* **2.** *tv.* to change the meaning of a word or word phrase by adding an adjective or adverb to it. ♦ *Adverbs modify verbs, adjectives, or other adverbs.* ♦ *In the phrase "very fast," "very" modifies "fast."*

modulate ['mɑdʒ ə let] **1.** *tv.* [for a singer] to change the volume or tone of sound. ♦ *The opera singer modulated her voice skillfully.* ♦ *Lisa modulated her vocal quality with great skill.* **2.** *iv.* to change to a different musical key ④. ♦ *The song modulates to A minor after the second verse.* ♦ *The next theme modulates to a minor key quite suddenly.*

Mohammed AND **Muhammad** [mo 'hɑm əd] *n.* the prophet who founded the Islamic religion. ♦ *Muslims believe that Mohammed is the prophet of Allah.* ♦ *Muhammad, the prophet, was born in the year 570.*

moist ['mɔɪst] *adj.* damp; a little bit wet. (Adv: *moistly.* Comp: *moister;* sup: *moistest.*) ♦ *I wiped the sticky table with a moist sponge.* ♦ *The center of the delicious cake was moist.*

moisten ['mɔɪ sən] *tv.* to make something moist; to make something damp. ♦ *The grass was moistened with dew.* ♦ *I moistened the stamp and placed it on the envelope.*

moisture ['mɔɪs tʃɚ] *n.* dampness; wetness; condensation; water in the air; vapor. (No plural form in this sense.) ♦ *Keep this medicine away from moisture.* ♦ *I could feel the moisture in the air on the muggy day.*

moisturizer ['mɔɪs tʃə raɪz ɚ] *n.* a lotion or cream that adds moisture to something, especially the skin. ♦ *I rubbed my face with moisturizer before going to bed.* ♦ *I put moisturizer on my skin when it's dry.*

molar ['mol ɚ] *n.* one of the teeth in the back of the mouth, used for grinding food. ♦ *The dentist removed a diseased molar from my mouth.* ♦ *I have a cavity in one of my molars.*

molasses [mə 'læs ɪz] *n.* a sweet, dark, sticky liquid made in the process of making sugar. (No plural form in this sense.) ♦ *The molasses poured slowly from its container.* ♦ *I spread some molasses on my pancakes.*

mold ['mold] **1.** *n.* a fuzzy or slimy growth that forms on animal or plant matter. (No plural form in this sense.) ♦ *Don't eat that bread. There's mold on it.* ♦ *A smelly mold coated the plants' leaves.* **2.** *n.* a hollow object that has a certain shape. (Certain liquids—such as clay, resin, cement, rubber, etc.—are poured into it, and when the liquid hardens, it will have the same shape.) ♦ *Gelatin takes the shape of its mold when it sets.* ♦ *These plaster statues were made from the same mold.* **3.** *n.* something that was shaped by or made in ②. ♦ *The mold of butter was shaped like an ear of corn.* ♦ *The mold of gelatin was shaped like a dome.* **4.** *tv.* to shape something; to form something into a certain shape; to shape something using ②. ♦ *The sculptor molded the clay into a flowerpot.* ♦ *The gelatin was molded in the shape of a dome.* **5.** *iv.* to become moldy; to be covered with ①. ♦ *The bread will mold in this humidity.* ♦ *The cheese molded when I left it on the counter overnight.*

molding ['mol dɪŋ] *n.* a strip of wood where a wall meets the floor or ceiling, or around a window or a door. ♦ *The molding covered up the gap between the tile and the wall.* ♦ *The carpenter nailed the molding to the wall.*

moldy ['mol di] *adj.* covered with mold. (Comp: *moldier;* sup: *moldiest.*) ♦ *I threw the moldy bread into the garbage.* ♦ *The biologist studied the moldy growth on the tree.*

mole ['mol] *n.* a small, furry mammal that lives underground, eats worms and bugs, and cannot see well. ♦ *My lawn was torn up by holes made by moles.* ♦ *The mole burrowed deep into the soil.*

molecular [mə 'lɛk jə lɚ] *adj.* of or about molecules. (Adv: *molecularly.*) ♦ *The molecular chemist worked at the plastics factory.* ♦ *What's the molecular weight of carbon dioxide?*

molecule ['mɑl ə kjul] *n.* the smallest part into which something can be divided without changing its chemical makeup. ♦ *A salt molecule contains one sodium atom and one chlorine atom.* ♦ *A water molecule contains two hydrogen atoms and one oxygen atom.*

molest [mə 'lɛst] **1.** *tv.* to bother or disturb someone greatly. ♦ *The loud music molested me as I tried to study.* ♦ *I tried to read, but my roommate kept molesting me.* **2.** *tv.* to attack or abuse someone sexually. ♦ *The teacher was accused of molesting a student.* ♦ *The criminal was imprisoned for molesting children.*

mollify ['mɑl ə fɑɪ] *tv.* to calm someone or some creature; to soothe the temper of someone or some creature. ♦ *The waiter mollified the angry diners with a free bottle of wine.* ♦ *I mollified the nervous dog by letting it sniff my hand.*

mollusk ['mɑl əsk] *n.* a kind of animal without a backbone but with a soft body and usually a shell. ♦ *Snails, clams, mussels, oysters, squid, octopus, and slugs are mollusks.* ♦ *The cook could deal with oysters but not with any other mollusk.*

molt ['molt] **1.** *tv.* [for an animal] to shed feathers, skin, fur, or antlers. ♦ *The bird molted its feathers all over its cage.* ♦ *A snake molts its skin at least once a year.* **2.** *iv.* [for animals] to shed [something], as with ①. ♦ *As the snake molts, it leaves its skin behind.* ♦ *When the parrot molted, I kept its feathers.*

molten ['molt n] *adj.* melted; made into liquid. (Adv: *moltenly.*) ♦ *The center of the earth is molten rock.* ♦ *Molten lava flowed down the mountain from the volcano.*

mom ['mɑm] *n.* mother. (Informal. Also a term of address.) ♦ *I asked my mom if I could go to the mall.* ♦ *Dad, do you know where Mom is?*

moment ['mo mənt] **1.** *n.* an instant in time; a brief period of time. ♦ *I can't speak with you at the moment.* ♦ *If you can wait, I'll be with you in just a moment.* **2.** *n.* a certain point in time. (No plural form in this sense.) ♦ *At that moment, the inspector knew who the murderer was.* ♦ *Call me the moment you get home.* **3. on the spur of the moment** *idiom* suddenly; spontaneously. ♦ *We decided to go on the spur of the moment.* ♦ *I had to leave town on the spur of the moment.*

momentarily [mo mən 'tɛr ɪ li] **1.** *adv.* for a moment; for a brief period of time. ♦ *The fly landed momentarily on the apple.* ♦ *We'll be at this airport only momentarily, so remain in your seats.* **2.** *adv.* in a moment; soon. (Informal.) ♦ *We'll be landing momentarily, so buckle your seat belts.* ♦ *I'll be back in my office momentarily. Wait for me there.*

momentary ['mo mən tɛr i] *adj.* brief; lasting for only a moment. (Adv: *momentarily* [mom ən 'tɛr ə li].) ♦ *There will be a momentary pause in the broadcast for a commercial.* ♦ *Bill made a momentary frown when he heard the news.*

momento [mə 'mɛn to] See memento.

momentous [mo 'mɛn təs] *adj.* very important; very serious; very significant. (Adv: *momentously.*) ♦ *I celebrated the momentous occasion by giving a short speech.* ♦ *The Supreme Court issues many momentous decisions each year.*

momentum [mo 'mɛn təm] *n.* the force and speed of movement or progress. (No plural form in this sense.) ♦ *Jane's campaign gained momentum after she won the primary.* ♦ *The momentum of the car increased as it slid down the icy hill.*

mommy AND **mama** ['mɑm i, 'mɑ mə] *n.* mother. (Used especially by children. Also a term of address.) ♦ *Go ask your mama if you can come over and play.* ♦ *Where are my shoes, Mommy?*

monarch ['mɑn ɑrk] *n.* a king or a queen; the ruler of a monarchy. ♦ *The evil prince killed the reigning monarch.* ♦ *A likeness of the country's monarch appeared on its currency.*

monarchy ['mɑn ɑrk i] *n.* a system of government where a king or a queen is the absolute ruler. ♦ *The people demanded that the monarchy be abolished.* ♦ *The United States declared independence from the British monarchy in 1776.*

monastery ['mɑn ə stɛr i] *n.* a building where monks live and work secluded from society. ♦ *The monastery's library housed several rare manuscripts.* ♦ *The orphan was taken to the local monastery.*

Monday ['mʌn de] **1.** *n.* the second day of the week, between Sunday and Tuesday. ♦ *Work starts again this Monday.* ♦ *Many government holidays fall on Monday.* **2.** *adv.* on the next ①. ♦ *We can't sleep late Monday.* ♦ *I will be there Monday.* **3. (on) Mondays** *adv.* on each ①. ♦ *We always sleep late on Mondays.* ♦ *Mondays we eat dinner at a restaurant.*

monetary ['mɑn ə tɛr i] *adj.* of or about money. (Adv: *monetarily* [mɑn ə 'tɛr ə li].) ♦ *The rare necklace had a great monetary value.* ♦ *The economist criticized the nation's monetary policy.*

money ['mʌn i] **1.** *n.* currency; coins and bills issued by a government. (No plural form in this sense.) ♦ *Money is printed at federal mints.* ♦ *In Paris, I exchanged American money for French money.* **2.** *n.* wealth; riches. (No plural form in this sense.) ♦ *I have enough money to buy a mansion.* ♦ *Even though he had a lot of money, John lived frugally.* **3. have money to burn** *idiom* to have lots of ②; to have more ② than one needs; to have enough ② that some can be wasted. ♦ *Look at the way Tom buys things. You'd think he had money to burn.* ♦ *If I had money to burn, I'd just put it in the bank.* **4. hush money** *idiom* ② paid as a bribe to persuade someone to remain silent and not reveal certain information. ♦ *Bob gave his younger sister hush money so that she wouldn't tell Jane that he had gone on a date with Sue.* ♦ *The crooks paid Mike hush money to keep their whereabouts secret.* **5. make good money** *idiom* to earn a large amount of ②. ♦ *Anne makes good money at her job.* ♦ *I don't know what she does, but she makes good money.* **6. money is no object** *idiom* it does not matter how much something costs. ♦ *Please* *show me your finest automobile. Money is no object.* ♦ *I want the finest earrings you have. Don't worry about how much they cost because money is no object.* **7. money talks** *idiom* ② gives one power and influence to help get things done or get one's own way. ♦ *Don't worry. I have a way of getting things done. Money talks.* ♦ *I can't compete against rich old Mrs. Jones. She'll get her way because money talks.* **8. pour money down the drain** *idiom* to waste ②. ♦ *What a waste! You're just pouring money down the drain.* ♦ *Don't buy any more of that low-quality merchandise. That's just pouring money down the drain.* **9. throw good money after bad** *idiom* to waste additional ② after wasting ② once. ♦ *I bought a used car and then had to spend $300 on repairs. That was throwing good money after bad.* ♦ *The Browns are always throwing good money after bad. They bought an acre of land that turned out to be swamp, and then had to pay to have it filled in.*

Mongolia [maŋ 'go li ə] See Gazetteer.

mongrel ['maŋ grəl] *n.* a dog whose parents were of two different breeds. ♦ *The growling mongrel ran toward me.* ♦ *I got my mongrel from the pound.*

monitor ['man ə tɚ] **1.** *n.* a device something like a television set used to display computer information. ♦ *I bought a computer with a 17-inch monitor.* ♦ *My eyes get tired from looking at the monitor all day.* **2.** *n.* someone who watches, listens to, or keeps a record of something. ♦ *The lunchroom monitor warned me not to run.* ♦ *The hall monitor took the names of the tardy students.* **3.** *n.* a mechanism or measuring device that keeps a record of something. ♦ *The smoke monitor sounded when I burned dinner.* ♦ *The heart monitor displayed my heart rate on the screen.* **4.** *tv.* to watch, listen to, or keep a record of something. ♦ *The police monitored the criminal's every move.* ♦ *My supervisor monitors my phone conversations.*

monk ['mʌŋk] *n.* a man who lives in a monastery, devoting his life to religion as part of an all-male religious order. ♦ *The monk lived in a secluded monastery for most of his life.* ♦ *The monks said grace before eating dinner.*

monkey ['mʌŋ ki] **1.** *n.* a small, hairy primate with a long tail. (The monkeys in the Americas can use their tails as a fifth limb.) ♦ *The monkey hung from the branch by its tail.* ♦ *It is fun to watch the monkeys at the zoo.* **2. monkey around** *idiom* to fool around; to misbehave. ♦ *If you don't stop monkeying around, I'm going to leave.* ♦ *John monkeyed around while he was supposed to be working.* **3. monkey (around) with something** *idiom* to tamper or tinker with something. ♦ *I monkeyed with the antenna because the TV reception was bad.* ♦ *Don't monkey around with my stereo while I'm on vacation.* **4. monkey business** *idiom* activities that are peculiar or out of the ordinary, especially mischievous or illegal ones. ♦ *There's been some monkey business in connection with the firm's accounts.* ♦ *Bob left the firm quite suddenly. I think there was some monkey business between him and the boss's wife.*

monogamous [mə 'nag ə məs] *adj.* having only one spouse; having only one sexual partner. (Adv: *monogamously.*) ♦ *Some animals are monogamous throughout their lives.* ♦ *Most Western cultures allow only monogamous marriages.*

monogamy [mə 'nag ə mi] *n.* the practice of being married to only one spouse at a time; the practice of having only one sexual partner. (No plural form in this sense.) ♦ *Monogamy is the law in most Western cultures.* ♦ *The counselor stressed the importance of monogamy within marriage.*

monogram ['man ə græm] **1.** *n.* a design made of one or more letters, usually someone's initials, that is printed on paper, embroidered on clothing, and stamped on books and other personal belongings. ♦ *Jane's monogram appears on all of her stationery.* ♦ *I stamped my monogram on all of my books.* **2.** *tv.* to put ① on an item. ♦ *My tailor monogrammed my initials on my shirt pocket.* ♦ *My suitcases are monogrammed with my initials.*

monograph ['man ə græf] *n.* an article or book written about a single subject. ♦ *I read a monograph about World War I.* ♦ *My monograph about viral infections has just been published.*

monologue AND **monolog** ['man ə lɔg] *n.* a long, uninterrupted speech made by one person, especially in a play or movie. ♦ *The comedian was heckled during his monologue.* ♦ *The play included one of the longest and dullest monologues I have ever heard.*

monopolistic [mə nap ə 'lɪs tɪk] *adj.* seeking to establish and maintain a monopoly. (Adv: *monopolistically* [...ɪk li].) ♦ *The court ordered the monopolistic utility to relinquish its control.* ♦ *A monopolistic government prohibits competition with the state.*

monopolize [mə 'nap ə laɪz] *tv.* to establish complete control over someone or something. ♦ *My depressed friend monopolized all of my time.* ♦ *The entertainment industry is monopolized by Hollywood.*

monopoly [mə 'nap ə li] **1.** *n.* the condition existing when someone or something has complete control over something. ♦ *The electric utility has a monopoly on supplying electricity.* ♦ *The government tries to make sure that no company develops a monopoly without its permission.* **2.** *n.* a business that is the only provider of a service or product. ♦ *The local electrical utility is a monopoly.* ♦ *The breakup of the monopoly resulted in lower prices.* **3.** *n.* the right to be the only provider of a service or product, as authorized by a government. ♦ *The government granted a monopoly to the gas company.* ♦ *The court ended the telephone company's monopoly.*

monorail ['man o rel] *n.* a train system using a single rail. ♦ *A monorail connects the airport and the parking lot.* ♦ *We rode the monorail to the convention center.*

monosyllable ['man o sɪl ə bəl] *n.* a word that has only one syllable. ♦ Yes *and* no *are both monosyllables.* ♦ *John rudely answered my questions with monosyllables.*

monotheism [man ə 'θi ɪz əm] *n.* the belief or teaching that there is only one God. (No plural form in this sense.) ♦ *Christianity, Judaism, and Islam are examples of religions that practice monotheism.* ♦ *The missionaries imposed monotheism on the pagans.*

monotone ['man ə ton] *n.* a way of speaking or singing so that the voice stays on the same pitch or musical note. ♦ *The professor talked for an hour in a monotone.* ♦ *The senator was known for his dull monotone.*

monotonous [mə 'nat n nəs] **1.** *adj.* unchanging in tone; staying on the same note. (Adv: *monotonously.*) ♦ *The choir's monotonous droning grated on my nerves.* ♦ *My professor's monotonous voice puts me to sleep.* **2.** *adj.* boring; tedious; not changing; always the same. (Adv: *monoto-*

nously.) ♦ *I walked out of the monotonous lecture after 20 minutes.* ♦ *I quit my monotonous job after one year.*

monotony [mə 'nɑt n ni] *n.* boredom; tediousness; a lack of change; a lack of variety. (No plural form in this sense.) ♦ *The monotony of Bob's job caused him to quit.* ♦ *I can't stand monotony in my daily life.*

monsoon [mɑn 'sun] **1.** *n.* the wind that comes off the Indian Ocean and causes heavy rains to fall in South Asia. (From Arabic.) ♦ *The monsoon caused floods in many Indian villages.* ♦ *I sought shelter during the monsoon.* **2.** *n.* the rainy season in South Asia; the time when heavy rains fall, usually April to October. ♦ *We left India before the monsoon began.* ♦ *India received the bulk of its rainfall during the monsoon.* **3.** *adj.* <the adj. use of ②.> ♦ *When does the monsoon season start here?* ♦ *Many people get sick during the monsoon rains.*

monster ['mɑn stɚ] **1.** *n.* a large creature that scares people. ♦ *I dressed up like a monster for Halloween.* ♦ *We screamed when the monster walked down the stairs.* **2.** *n.* a wicked, cruel person. (Figurative on ①.) ♦ *Only a monster would bomb innocent citizens.* ♦ *The lawyer described the defendant as an evil monster.*

monstrosity [mɑn 'strɑs ə ti] *n.* someone or something that is huge and very ugly. ♦ *That sculpture is a monstrosity!* ♦ *The run-down building is a terrible monstrosity.*

monstrous ['mɑn strəs] **1.** *adj.* looking or acting like a monster. (Adv: *monstrously.*) ♦ *The monstrous beast frightened the children.* ♦ *The monstrous dog bit the mail carrier.* **2.** *adj.* unusually large; enormous; huge; colossal. (Adv: *monstrously.*) ♦ *We could not finish the monstrous pizza.* ♦ *The monstrous road project took five years to complete.* **3.** *adj.* shocking; horrible; terrible; atrocious. (Figurative on ①. Adv: *monstrously.*) ♦ *The criminal was punished for his monstrous deeds.* ♦ *The inspector vowed to solve the monstrous murder.*

Montana [mɑn 'tæn ə] See Gazetteer.

month ['mʌnθ] **1.** *n.* one of the 12 divisions of a year. ♦ *What month were you born in?* ♦ *January is the first month of the year.* **2.** *n.* a period of about 30 or 31 days; a period of four weeks. ♦ *Mary was so busy that she didn't watch TV for three months.* ♦ *Our baby is just six months old.*

monthly ['mʌnθ li] **1.** *adj.* happening every month; happening once a month. ♦ *I subscribe to a couple of monthly magazines.* ♦ *The workers aired their problems at the monthly meeting.* **2.** *adv.* every month; once a month. ♦ *This journal is published monthly.* ♦ *I visit my parents monthly.*

monument ['mɑn jə mənt] **1.** *n.* a structure that is built in memory of a person or event. ♦ *The Washington Monument is a well-known American landmark.* ♦ *The city built a monument for the assassinated mayor.* **2.** *n.* something that preserves the memory of a person, culture, or event. (Figurative on ①.) ♦ *This competition is a monument to a famous athlete.* ♦ *We started a scholarship fund as a monument to the founder of the college.*

monumental [mɑn jə 'men təl] **1.** *adj.* of or about a monument. ♦ *The monumental structure was a national landmark.* ♦ *The architect's monumental design used a lot of granite.* **2.** *adj.* significant, huge, and notable. (Adv: *monumentally.*) ♦ *The concert was a monumental tribute to the orchestra's first conductor.* ♦ *The new subway system was a monumental undertaking.*

moo ['mu] **1.** *n.* the noise made by a cow. (Pl in -*s*.) ♦ *I hear moos coming from inside the barn.* ♦ *Susie made a loud moo when I asked her what sound a cow makes.* **2.** *iv.* [for a cow] to make its characteristic noise. ♦ *The cow mooed softly as she was milked.* ♦ *The old cow mooed at Billy.*

mood ['mud] **1.** *n.* a state of mind; the way one is feeling. ♦ *Jane's in a good mood because she just won the lottery.* ♦ *John's in a bad mood, so I wouldn't talk to him now.* **2.** *n.* a feature of a verb that shows whether it is a statement, command, or wish; mode ③. ♦ *A word that asks a question indicates the interrogative mood.* ♦ *In Greek class, I learned the conjugation for the various moods.* **3. in no mood to do something** *idiom* not feeling like doing something; wishing not to do something. ♦ *I'm in no mood to cook dinner tonight.* ♦ *Mother is in no mood to put up with our arguing.* **4. in the mood for something; in the mood to do something** *idiom* having the proper state of mind for a particular situation or for doing something. ♦ *I'm not in the mood to see a movie tonight.* ♦ *Are you in the mood for pizza?*

moody ['mu di] **1.** *adj.* having a state of mind that changes quickly and often. (Adv: *moodily.* Comp: *moodier;* sup: *moodiest.*) ♦ *Ever since her accident, Mary's been really moody.* ♦ *The medicine's side effects make me moody.* **2.** *adj.* sad; gloomy. (Adv: *moodily.* Comp: *moodier;* sup: *moodiest.*) ♦ *I tried to console my moody friend.* ♦ *The moody movie depressed me.*

moon ['mun] **1.** *n.* a large, natural satellite that orbits around a planet. ♦ *Mars has two moons, but neither can be seen without a telescope.* ♦ *The space probe discovered a new moon that circles Jupiter.* **2.** *n.* a phase of Earth's moon ①. (One of the categories of the moon based on how much of it is lighted by the sun, such as *full moon, half-moon, new moon.*) ♦ *The night sky is was pitch black during the new moon.* ♦ *The night was lit by the light of the full moon.* **3. ask for the moon** *idiom* to ask for too much; to make great demands; to ask for something that is difficult or impossible to obtain. ♦ *When you're trying to get a job, it's unwise to ask for the moon.* ♦ *Please lend me the money. I'm not asking for the moon!* **4. once in a blue moon** *idiom* very, very rarely; once in a great, long while. ♦ *You will only get a chance like this once in a blue moon.* ♦ *Once in a blue moon, somebody asks me to go out to eat.*

moonlight ['mun lɑɪt] **1.** *n.* the light from a moon. (No plural form in this sense.) ♦ *Moonlight is light from the sun that is reflected off the moon's surface.* ♦ *In the moonlight, I saw a raccoon running across my backyard.* **2.** *adj.* while the moon is shining; clandestinely. ♦ *The moonlight theft baffled the police.* ♦ *The young boy took a moonlight swim in the neighbors' pool.* **3.** *iv.* to have a second job in the evening or at night in addition to the job one has during the day. (Pt/pp: *moonlighted.*) ♦ *The poorly paid professor moonlighted as a taxi driver.* ♦ *The underpaid office manager had to moonlight to earn enough to live.*

moonlit ['mun lɪt] *adj.* lighted with light from the moon. ♦ *I saw raccoons running through the moonlit field.* ♦ *The cat's moonlit eyes glowed brightly.*

moonshine ['mun ʃɑɪn] *n.* homemade liquor; illegally made liquor; smuggled liquor. (No plural form in this sense.) ♦ *My friends brought some moonshine to the party.*

♦ *During Prohibition, many people made their own moonshine.*

moor ['mʊr] **1.** *n.* open land with coarse grass, which is not used for farming because the soil is not good for crops. ♦ *The tourists were lost in the foggy moors of Scotland.* ♦ *The nearest village is on the other side of the moor.* **2.** *tv.* to secure a ship or boat with ropes and chains to a dock or a fixed object. ♦ *The sailor moored the ship to the dock.* ♦ *We moored our boat to the pier during the storm.*

mooring ['mʊr ɪŋ] **1.** *n.* the ropes, chains, anchors, and cables that secure a boat or ship to a dock or a fixed object. ♦ *Once the mooring was secure, the ship's cargo was unloaded.* ♦ *The thief cut the boat's mooring and sailed away.* **2.** *n.* the place where a boat or ship is moored. ♦ *The boat was cut loose from its mooring.* ♦ *The moorings were destroyed by the hurricane.*

moose ['mus] *n., irreg.* a northern animal similar to a large deer, the males of which have wide, flat antlers. (Pl: *moose.* See also elk ②.) ♦ *Bill saw several moose while he was hiking in Canada.* ♦ *A large moose stood in the middle of the road, blocking my path.*

moot ['mut] **1.** *adj.* doubtful; not decided; of little practical value. ♦ *We argued over many moot issues.* ♦ *Your opinions are moot, since the decision has already been made.* **2. moot point** *n.* an issue that is no longer relevant or is only theoretical. ♦ *We are wasting time discussing a moot point.* ♦ *Whether he should have gone there is a moot point, since he did not ever go there.*

mop ['mɑp] **1.** *n.* a group of thick, heavy strings or a sponge, attached to a pole, used wet or dry for cleaning floors. ♦ *I cleaned up the spill with a mop.* ♦ *I wrung the mop out in the bucket.* **2. mop up** *tv.* + *adv.* to clean something with ①, a towel, a sponge, etc. ♦ *I will mop the spill up before anyone falls.* ♦ *I mopped up the puddle with a sponge.* **3. mop up** *iv.* + *adv.* to clean up [liquid or debris] with ①, a towel, a sponge, etc. ♦ *I mopped up after the party.* ♦ *The city mopped up after the flood.*

mope ['mop] **1.** *iv.* to be quiet and depressed. ♦ *John moped around his apartment after he quit his job.* ♦ *Jane was moping because she didn't know anyone at her new school.* **2.** *n.* someone who is quiet and depressed. (Informal.) ♦ *Don't be such a mope, and go to the party with me.* ♦ *If you didn't act like a mope, maybe people would talk to you.*

moral ['mor əl] **1.** *adj.* of or about good and bad, according to society's standards of right and wrong. (Adv: *morally.*) ♦ *The politician was faced with a moral dilemma.* ♦ *One needs moral strength to avoid temptation.* **2.** *adj.* exhibiting or representing good behavior and values. (Adv: *morally.*) ♦ *The senator was regarded as a completely moral man.* ♦ *Jimmy was taught wholesome, moral behavior.* **3.** *n.* the lesson that can be learned from a story. ♦ *Every fable has an important moral.* ♦ *The moral of the story is that you should be yourself.* **4. morals** *n.* a person's moral principles of behavior, especially concerning sex. (Treated as plural.) ♦ *Jimmy was taught to have good morals.* ♦ *The senator's morals were unquestionable.* **5. moral support** *n.* help that is mental or psychological rather than physical or monetary. ♦ *I gave my friends moral support during exam week.* ♦ *My friends gave me moral support during my period of grief.*

morale [mə 'ræl] *n.* confidence; the amount of confidence felt by a person or group of people. (No plural form in this sense.) ♦ *The losing team's morale was low.* ♦ *The soldiers sang songs to boost their morale.*

morality [mə 'ræl ə ti] *n.* the goodness or rightness of someone's behavior; good behavior measured by society's standards of right and wrong. (No plural form in this sense.) ♦ *The minister believed America's morality was in decline.* ♦ *Max felt that the best way to improve society's morality was to improve his own.*

moratorium [mor ə 'tor i əm] *n.* an official period of delay; the length of time that a certain activity is officially stopped. ♦ *The senator proposed a moratorium on the sale of automatic weapons.* ♦ *The rulers agreed to a moratorium on nuclear testing.*

morbid ['mor bɪd] *adj.* having an unusually strong interest in death or unpleasant things. (Adv: *morbidly.*) ♦ *Jane has a morbid interest in horror films.* ♦ *I don't want to deal with any morbid matters right now. I am already sad.*

more ['mor] **1.** *adj.* <the comparative form of much or many>; a greater amount or number. ♦ *I have many books, but Susan has more books than I do.* ♦ *I don't have much money. John has more money than I do.* **2.** *pron.* <the comparative form of much or many>; a greater amount or number. ♦ *I have many ideas for the project, but Bob has more.* ♦ *I don't have much money. Anne has more than I do.* **3.** *n.* an additional amount or number. (No plural form in this sense.) ♦ *Could I have more?* ♦ *Don't take more. You have too much.* **4.** *adv.* <a word used to form the comparative form of some adjectives and adverbs.> ♦ *This apple is rotten. That apple is more rotten. Those apples are the most rotten.* ♦ *This car moves quickly, but that car moves more quickly.* **5.** *adv.* an additional time; once again. ♦ *Sing that song once more!* ♦ *Let's play cards some more.* **6. more and more** *phr.* an increasing amount; additional amounts. ♦ *As I learn more and more, I see how little I know.* ♦ *Dad seems to be smoking more and more lately.*

moreover ['mor 'ov ɚ] *adv.* in addition; further; furthermore; also. ♦ *The criminal is dangerous; moreover, he has a gun.* ♦ *Yes, we have that item in stock; moreover, it's on sale!*

morgue ['morg] *n.* a place where dead bodies are stored temporarily. ♦ *The corpse was taken to the county morgue.* ♦ *During the disaster, the school gym was used as a morgue.*

Mormon ['mor mən] **1.** *n.* a member of the Church of Jesus Christ of Latter-Day Saints, a religion established in 1830 by Joseph Smith. ♦ *Anne doesn't consume caffeine because she's a Mormon.* ♦ *Mormons are very interested in genealogy.* **2.** *adj.* <the adj. use of ①.> ♦ *The population of Utah is largely Mormon.* ♦ *We are good friends with the Mormon family living next door to us.*

morning ['mor nɪŋ] **1.** *n.* the period of the day from midnight to noon. (No plural form in this sense.) ♦ *I have to be at work at 9:00 in the morning.* ♦ *I spent the morning writing letters.* **2.** *n.* dawn; sunrise. ♦ *The birds began chirping when morning broke.* ♦ *When I left the party, I saw the light of morning.* **3.** *adj.* happening during ①. ♦ *Max has a morning meeting at 10:00.* ♦ *I missed my morning class because I overslept.* **4. mornings** *adv.* happening every ①. ♦ *I can't make a 10:00 A.M. appointment because I work mornings.* ♦ *Mornings, I work downtown.* **5. morning after (the night before)** *idiom* the morning after a night spent drinking, when one has a hangover. ♦ *Oh, I've got a headache. Talk about the morning after the night before!* ♦ *It looked like a case of the morning after the night before, and Frank asked for some aspirin.*

morning glory ['mor nɪŋ glor i] *n.* any of a group of climbing, flowering plants whose blossoms open only in the morning. ♦ *I picked some morning glories on my way to work.* ♦ *The trellis was covered with morning glories.*

Morocco [mə 'rɑk o] See Gazetteer.

moron ['mor ɑn] **1.** *n.* a person of extremely low intelligence. (Not often used in this technical sense.) ♦ *The child was classified as a moron and lived out her life in an institution.* ♦ *It is very impolite to call a mentally retarded person a moron.* **2.** *n.* someone who is very stupid or foolish. (Derogatory.) ♦ *What moron forgot to put the milk back in the refrigerator?* ♦ *You stupid moron! Watch where you're going!*

morose [mə 'ros] *adj.* generally unhappy; sullen. (Adv: *morosely.*) ♦ *The runner who lost the race was morose for the rest of the day.* ♦ *My morose friend spent hours telling me her problems.*

morphine ['mor fin] *n.* a drug made from opium, used to eliminate pain. (No plural form in this sense.) ♦ *After surgery, I was given morphine for a week.* ♦ *The nurse gave the soldier morphine while she waited for a doctor.*

morsel ['mor səl] *n.* a small piece of something, especially food. ♦ *I'm not that hungry, so just give me a morsel of cake.* ♦ *The dog ate some morsels that had fallen to the floor.*

mortal ['mor təl] **1.** *n.* a human being; someone or something that must die; someone or something that will not live forever. ♦ *Every mortal will die someday.* ♦ *I know I am only a mortal, but I want to live forever.* **2.** *adj.* unable to live forever; having to die at some time. (Adv: *mortally.*) ♦ *As mortal men, we know we may die in the service of our country.* ♦ *Because humans are mortal, we all must die.* **3.** *adj.* fatal; causing death. (Adv: *mortally.*) ♦ *The victim died from a mortal blow to the head.* ♦ *The poor man received a mortal wound in the explosion.* **4.** *adj.* dire; intense; extreme. (Adv: *mortally.*) ♦ *I live in mortal fear of snakes.* ♦ *The bombed city has a mortal need for basic supplies.*

mortality [mor 'tæl ə ti] **1.** *n.* the limitation of not being able to live forever. (No plural form in this sense.) ♦ *Humans are limited by their mortality.* ♦ *The eternal soul is free of mortality.* **2.** *n.* the number or percentage of people who die in a certain period of time or because of a certain cause. (No plural form in this sense.) ♦ *The scientists tried to slow the rate of mortality from cancer.* ♦ *The mortality of persons with heart disease is decreasing.*

mortar ['mort ɚ] **1.** *n.* a kind of cement that binds bricks or stones to each other, especially when building a wall. (No plural form in this sense.) ♦ *The mason layered the mortar on top of the brick with a trowel.* ♦ *Don't touch that wall until the mortar has dried.* **2.** *n.* a short, wide cannon that shoots shells in a high arc. ♦ *The enemy's mortars were aimed at the village.* ♦ *The shell from the mortar damaged an apartment building.* **3.** *n.* a hard bowl used to hold substances being ground into powder. ♦ *The chemist crushed the substance in the mortar with a pestle.* ♦ *The cook ground the grain in a mortar.*

mortgage ['mor gɪdʒ] **1.** *n.* an agreement by which a borrower grants a lender the ownership of an asset in exchange for a loan of money, thus protecting the loan with the asset. (When the loan is repaid, the ownership of the property is returned to the borrower. If the borrower is unable to pay the loan, then the asset then belongs to the lender.) ♦ *My mortgage has a 10% interest rate.* ♦ *We had a party when we made the last payment on our home mortgage.* **2.** *tv.* to use an asset to secure a loan. ♦ *I mortgaged the house so my children could go to college.* ♦ *The mall was mortgaged by its owner so she could buy more property.*

mortician [mor 'tɪ ʃən] *n.* someone who prepares dead bodies for burial and who arranges funerals; an undertaker. ♦ *The mortician moved the coffin into the chapel for a funeral service.* ♦ *The family was consoled by the mortician during the funeral.*

mortified ['mort ə fɑɪd] *adj.* very ashamed; embarrassed; humiliated. (Adv: *mortifiedly.*) ♦ *The student, caught cheating, became mortified and turned red with embarrassment.* ♦ *The mortified politician apologized for his son's crime.*

mortify ['mort ə fɑɪ] *tv.* to humiliate someone; to embarrass someone; to cause someone to feel ashamed. ♦ *My mother mortified me by showing my date old pictures of me.* ♦ *Susan's brother was mortified when Susan read his diary.*

mortifying ['mort ə fɑɪ ɪŋ] *adj.* humiliating; embarrassing; causing shame. (Adv: *mortifyingly.*) ♦ *Belching during my speech was the most mortifying experience of my life.* ♦ *My most mortifying event was when my bathing suit fell off while I was swimming.*

mortuary ['mor tʃu ɛr i] *n.* a place where dead bodies are kept before funerals or burials. ♦ *A mortician works in a mortuary.* ♦ *The local mortuary was full of corpses from the tornado.*

mosaic [mo 'ze ɪk] *n.* a design made from many pieces of colored substances, especially glass or stone. ♦ *The church window was a mosaic made of colored glass.* ♦ *The artist made a stone mosaic showing the president's face.*

Moslem ['mɑz ləm] See **Muslim**.

mosque ['mɑsk] *n.* an Islamic building of worship; a building where Moslems worship. ♦ *On Fridays, Moslems go to mosques to worship.* ♦ *There was a mosque at the center of the small Arab village.*

mosquito [mə 'skit o] *n., irreg.* a small insect, the female of which sucks blood from warm-blooded creatures. (Pl in *-s* or *-es.*) ♦ *I left the picnic early because there were too many mosquitoes.* ♦ *I became sick when I was bitten by an infected mosquito.*

moss ['mɔs] *n.* a small, soft green plant without flowers that grows in masses on rocks and other surfaces. (No plural form in this sense.) ♦ *I slipped on the wet moss that covered the rock.* ♦ *I sat on the moss that surrounded the base of the tree.*

most ['most] **1.** *adj.* <the superlative form of **much** or **many**>; the greatest amount or number. ♦ *Mary has the most books of all my friends.* ♦ *I know a lot of songs. Susan knows more songs than I do. Anne knows the most songs of all.* **2.** *adj.* over half; almost all. (Adv: *mostly.*) ♦ *Most fire engines are red.* ♦ *Most mornings, I'd rather stay in bed.*

3. *pron.* over half or almost all of a specified group of things or people. ♦ *Some of my friends don't smoke, but most do.* ♦ *The bananas are cheap, but most aren't ripe yet.* **4.** *adv.* <a word used to form the superlative form of some adjectives and adverbs>; to the greatest extent. ♦ *This apple is the most red of all.* ♦ *Mary's car starts the most quickly.* **5.** *adv.* very. (Used for emphasis.) ♦ *This is a most unusual book.* ♦ *I had a most difficult day at work today.* **6. at (the) most** *idiom* no more than. ♦ *"How far away is the beach?" "Ten miles at most."* ♦ *At the most, there were only 15 people in the audience.*

mostly ['most li] **1.** *adv.* more than half; chiefly; for the most part. ♦ *The wine glasses were still mostly full after the meal.* ♦ *These bananas are mostly ripe.* **2.** *adv.* most of the time; usually; ♦ *At the party, I mostly played cards.* ♦ *Mostly, I read and take naps on the weekend.*

motel [mo 'tɛl] *n.* a hotel for people traveling by car; a hotel alongside a highway. (From *MOtor* + *hoTEL.*) ♦ *I stopped at a motel because I was too tired to drive further.* ♦ *There aren't any vacancies at the motels near the beach.*

moth ['mɔθ] *n.* a small insect with large, broad wings and antennae, similar to a butterfly, but usually not as colorful. ♦ *Moths had eaten a hole in my sweater.* ♦ *I swatted the moth that was flying around my head.*

mothball ['mɔθ bɔl] *n.* a small ball of a substance that keeps moths away from clothes. ♦ *I put mothballs in my closet to keep the moths away.* ♦ *Mothballs have an unpleasant odor that keeps moths away.*

mother ['mʌð ɚ] **1.** *n.* a female who has given birth to a child or offspring. ♦ *The mother instinctively protected her cubs.* ♦ *Billy brought his mother a note from school.* **2.** *n.* <a form of address used with one's own ①.> ♦ *May I have another cookie, Mother?* ♦ *Mother, can I borrow the car tonight?* **3.** *adj.* [of one's language or country] native. ♦ *Mary's mother tongue is German.* ♦ *The immigrant returned to her mother country when she was 80.* **4.** *tv.* to nurture someone; to take care of someone in the manner of ①. ♦ *Stop mothering me! I'm old enough to take care of myself.* ♦ *My older sister mothered me after our mother died.*

motherhood ['mʌð ɚ hʊd] *n.* the state of being a mother. (No plural form in this sense.) ♦ *The pregnant woman prepared for motherhood.* ♦ *Anne had an abortion because she wasn't ready for motherhood.*

mother-in-law ['mʌð ɚ ɪn lɔ] *n., irreg.* the mother of one's husband or wife. (Pl: mothers-in-law.) ♦ *David drove his mother-in-law to the hospital.* ♦ *Anne asked her mother-in-law for her meatloaf recipe.*

motherless ['mʌð ɚ ləs] *adj.* having no mother; without a mother; having a mother who is dead. (Adv: *motherlessly.*) ♦ *I took the motherless puppies to the dog pound.* ♦ *The motherless girl asked her grandmother for advice.*

motherly ['mʌð ɚ li] *adj.* like a mother; nurturing; caring; loving; maternal. ♦ *Anne gave her daughter a motherly hug.* ♦ *Susan gave her son some motherly advice.*

mothers-in-law ['mʌð ɚz ɪn lɔ] pl of mother-in-law.

motif [mo 'tif] *n.* an idea or pattern that is used in a work of music, art, or literature; an idea or pattern that is the basis for a design. ♦ *Snow was a recurrent motif throughout the author's story.* ♦ *The composer's symphony had an obvious waltz motif.*

motion ['mo ʃən] **1.** *n.* movement; moving. (No plural form in this sense.) ♦ *I turned the ignition and set the car in motion.* ♦ *The apparent motion of the sun across the sky is from east to west.* **2.** *n.* one particular movement; a gesture. ♦ *I made a motion toward the door, but my father stopped me.* ♦ *Bob made a few subtle hand motions to get the speaker's attention.* **3.** *n.* a formal proposal that something be done, made during a meeting. ♦ *I make a motion that we adjourn the meeting.* ♦ *The council voted on the motion to cut taxes.* **4.** *tv.* to direct someone by moving a part of one's body, usually the hands. ♦ *The traffic cop motioned me to turn left.* ♦ *The clerk motioned me to come to her counter.* **5.** *iv.* to point or indicate by moving a part of one's body, usually the hands. ♦ *The mechanic motioned toward the broken engine.* ♦ *I motioned to Anne indicating that I wanted to leave the party.* **6. go through the motions** *idiom* to make a poor effort to do something; to do something insincerely. ♦ *Jane isn't doing her best. She's just going through the motions.* ♦ *Bill was supposed to be raking the yard, but he was just going through the motions.*

motionless ['mo ʃən ləs] *adj.* without moving; completely still. (Adv: *motionlessly.*) ♦ *The ventriloquist's lips were motionless while the dummy spoke.* ♦ *Our sailboat didn't move because the air was motionless.*

motion picture ['mo ʃən 'pɪk tʃɚ] *n.* a movie; a film; a story on film. ♦ *We go to the theater to see a motion picture at least once a month.* ♦ *The studio released four motion pictures during the summer.*

motivate ['mo tə vet] *tv.* to give someone an incentive to do something; to give someone a reason for doing something. ♦ *The energetic teacher motivated her students by praising them for good work.* ♦ *The supervisor motivated the workers by offering them bonuses.*

motivation [mo tɪ 've ʃən] *n.* incentive; encouragement to do something. (No plural form in this sense.) ♦ *Jimmy needs more motivation to learn in school.* ♦ *My salary is my only motivation for working.*

motive ['mot ɪv] *n.* a reason or incentive for doing something. ♦ *The inspector couldn't determine a motive for the murder.* ♦ *The motive of the robbery was greed.*

motley ['mɑt li] *adj.* consisting of different kinds of things or people. (Usually slightly derogatory.) ♦ *My coworkers are a motley crew of computer operators.* ♦ *The small diner had a motley selection of food.*

motor ['mot ɚ] *n.* an engine; a machine that changes a form of energy into a usable form of mechanical energy. ♦ *Your motor will run better if it's properly oiled.* ♦ *I had to replace my washing machine's motor when it burned out.*

motorbike ['mot ɚ bɑɪk] **1.** *n.* a motorized bicycle. ♦ *The boy liked his motorbike better than his bicycle.* ♦ *I drove my motorbike to school.* **2.** *n.* a motorcycle. ♦ *In most states, people riding motorbikes must wear helmets.* ♦ *I revved the motorbike's engine while stopped at the intersection.*

motorboat ['mot ɚ bot] *n.* a boat that is powered with a motor or engine. ♦ *I drove around the lake in my motorboat.* ♦ *The motorboat pulled the water skier behind it.*

motorcade ['mot ɚ ked] *n.* a line of cars or other motor vehicles, especially in a parade. ♦ *The presidential motorcade was 25 cars long.* ♦ *Thousands of people lined the route of the pope's motorcade.*

motorcycle ['mot ɚ saɪ kəl] *n.* a vehicle that has two wheels and a larger, heavier frame than a bicycle, and that is powered by a motor. ♦ *In most states, people riding motorcycles must wear helmets.* ♦ *A motorcycle goes much faster than a bicycle.*

motorist ['mot ə rəst] *n.* someone who drives a car. ♦ *The cop ticketed the motorist for speeding.* ♦ *Two motorists were hurt in the accident.*

motorized ['mot ə raɪzd] *adj.* equipped with a motor; receiving power from a motor. ♦ *I replaced my old mower with a motorized one.* ♦ *My handicapped uncle loves his motorized wheelchair.*

motto ['mɑt o] *n.* a short statement that expresses a belief or a rule of behavior. (Pl in *-s* or *-es.*) ♦ *The motto of New Hampshire is "Live free or die."* ♦ *The motto "In God We Trust" appears on American currency.*

mound ['mɑʊnd] *n.* a small hill or pile. ♦ *The dog made a mound of dirt when it dug up a bone.* ♦ *I put a mound of mashed potatoes on my plate.*

mount ['mɑʊnt] **1.** *n.* a support; an object that something is attached to or hung from. ♦ *The heavy shelf crashed to the floor when its mount broke.* ♦ *The mirror was fixed to the wall with a sturdy mount.* **2.** *n.* a (particular) mountain. (Abbreviated *Mt.*) ♦ *The mountain climber vowed to reach the summit of Mt. Everest.* ♦ *The eruption of Mount St. Helens covered thousands of square miles with ash.* **3.** *tv.* to get on an animal or vehicle that one must straddle in order to ride. ♦ *The jockeys mounted their horses before the start of the race.* ♦ *The children mounted their bikes and pedaled to the river.* **4.** *tv.* to climb something; to go up something; to ascend something. ♦ *The hikers mounted the hill.* ♦ *I mounted the stairs too quickly and had to rest at the top.* **5.** *tv.* to hang something to a fixed support; to attach something to a fixed support. ♦ *I mounted a mirror on the bathroom wall.* ♦ *The picture was securely mounted to the wall.* **6.** *tv.* to prepare something for production or exhibition. ♦ *The art museum mounted an exhibition of the artist's works.* ♦ *The drama class mounted a performance of the play.* **7.** *tv.* [for a taxidermist] to prepare and preserve the body of an animal by tanning its skin and stuffing it to restore the original shape. ♦ *The taxidermist mounted the large moose.* ♦ *I had my dog mounted after it died.* **8.** *iv.* to increase; to build up. ♦ *Tension mounted during contract negotiations.* ♦ *The national debt continued to mount throughout the decade.*

mountain ['mɑʊnt n] **1.** *n.* a very tall mass of land that pushes up from the surface of the earth; a very tall hill. ♦ *The Rocky Mountains are located in the western part of the U.S.* ♦ *The climber reached the top of the mountain.* **2.** *n.* a very tall pile of something; a very large amount of something. (Figurative on ①.) ♦ *There's a mountain of paperwork on my desk.* ♦ *I have a mountain of dirty laundry that I have to wash.* **3. make a mountain out of a molehill** *idiom* to make a major issue out of a minor one; to exaggerate the importance of something. ♦ *Come on, don't make a mountain out of a molehill. It's not that important.* ♦ *Mary is always making mountains out of molehills.*

mountaineer [mɑʊnt n 'nɪr] **1.** *n.* someone who climbs mountains. ♦ *The professional mountaineer saved the injured climber.* ♦ *The mountaineer reached the top of the mountain.* **2.** *n.* someone who lives in a mountainous area. ♦ *Many old mountaineers had been miners.* ♦ *The mountaineers stored a lot of food in preparation for winter.*

mountain lion ['mɑʊn tn 'laɪ ən] See lion.

mountainous ['mɑʊnt n nəs] **1.** *adj.* having many mountains. (Adv: *mountainously.*) ♦ *Utah is a very mountainous state.* ♦ *I drove slowly through the mountainous terrain.* **2.** *adj.* like a mountain; extremely tall. (Figurative on ①. Adv: *mountainously.*) ♦ *There's a mountainous heap of dirty clothes in the laundry room.* ♦ *We shoveled the snow into a mountainous pile.*

mountainside ['mɑʊnt n saɪd] **1.** *n.* the side of a mountain. ♦ *The troops on the mountainside shelled the village in the valley.* ♦ *An avalanche crashed down the mountainside.* **2.** *adj.* located on the slope of a mountain. ♦ *The skiers stayed at a mountainside inn.* ♦ *The mountainside road was blocked by falling rocks.*

mountaintop ['mɑʊnt n tɑp] *n.* the top of a mountain; the highest point of a mountain. ♦ *From the mountaintop, I could see for miles around me.* ♦ *The mountaintop was covered by clouds.*

mounting ['mɑʊn tɪŋ] **1.** *n.* a support; something that fixes an object into place. ♦ *The picture was firmly attached to its mounting.* ♦ *The sign crashed to the ground when its mounting came loose.* **2.** *adj.* growing; increasing. (Adv: *mountingly.*) ♦ *I was unable to pay my mounting debt all at once.* ♦ *The mounting hostilities led to a civil war.*

mourn ['morn] **1.** *tv.* to feel sorrow or sadness about the death or loss of someone or something. ♦ *The widow mourned the death of her husband.* ♦ *The workers mourned the death of the company president.* **2.** *iv.* to grieve; to feel sorrow or sadness. ♦ *The widower mourned at his wife's funeral.* ♦ *The nation mourned when the president was assassinated.*

mourner ['morn ɚ] *n.* someone who mourns; someone who is at a funeral. ♦ *The mourners were dressed in black.* ♦ *The minister comforted the mourners at the funeral.*

mournful ['morn fʊl] **1.** *adj.* full of sadness and sorrow; grieving. (Adv: *mournfully.*) ♦ *The mournful congregation cried during the funeral.* ♦ *The mournful family stood before the coffin.* **2.** *adj.* causing sadness and sorrow. (Adv: *mournfully.*) ♦ *I cried when I heard the mournful news.* ♦ *The minister helped me confront my mournful loss.*

mourning ['mor nɪŋ] **1.** *adj.* grieving; showing sadness and sorrow. ♦ *The mourning widow wore a black veil to the funeral.* ♦ *The soldiers' bodies were buried by their mourning families.* **2.** *n.* the period of time during which someone mourns; a state of grieving. (No plural form in this sense. Number is expressed with *period(s) of mourning.*) ♦ *The widow wore black while she was in mourning.* ♦ *Mourning occupied the land for months after the death of the queen.*

mouse ['mɑʊs] **1.** *n., irreg.* a small, furry rodent with tiny eyes and a long tail, like a rat but smaller. (Pl: mice.) ♦ *I told my landlord that I saw a mouse in my kitchen.* ♦ *The scientist tested the new drug on mice.* **2.** *n., irreg.* a computer device that can be scooted around by one hand to control the movements of the cursor on the screen. (Pl: mice or *mouses.*) ♦ *I moved the mouse until the arrow was over the right box, then I pressed a button on the mouse.* ♦ *It is hard to find a place to use my mouse on my messy desk.*

mousetrap ['maʊs træp] *n.* a simple device that is used to trap mice that are indoor pests. ♦ *The mouse was killed when the mousetrap snapped.* ♦ *I baited the mousetrap with a piece of cheese.*

mousse ['mus] **1.** *n.* a rich, creamy frozen dessert made from cream, eggs, and fruit or chocolate. (No plural form in this sense.) ♦ *For dessert, I've made some chocolate mousse.* ♦ *I served the mousse with some whipped cream.* **2.** *n.* a light, fluffy cream that is used to style hair. (No plural form in this sense. Figurative on ①.) ♦ *I sprayed some mousse onto my hand and rubbed it into my hair.* ♦ *David uses mousse to keep his hair in place.*

mouth 1. ['maʊθ] *n., irreg.* the opening on the faces of animals where food and air enters the body. (Pl: ['maʊðz].) ♦ *The teeth, gums, and tongue are inside the mouth.* ♦ *Please cover your mouth when you cough.* **2.** ['maʊθ] *n., irreg.* the opening or entrance to something. (Figurative on ①.) ♦ *The mouth of the cave was blocked by fallen rocks.* ♦ *An ice cube blocked the mouth of the pitcher.* **3.** ['maʊθ] *n., irreg.* the place where a river joins a lake, sea, or ocean. ♦ *Quebec City is at the mouth of the St. Lawrence River.* ♦ *The mouth of the river was clogged with garbage.* **4.** ['maʊð] *tv.* to move the mouth as if one were speaking but without producing actual speech. ♦ *The singer mouthed the words to the song when filming the video.* ♦ *On the other side of the window, Anne mouthed, "Come out here."* **5. foam at the mouth** [...'maʊθ] *idiom* to be very angry. ♦ *Bob was raving—foaming at the mouth. I've never seen anyone so angry.* ♦ *Bill foamed at the mouth in anger.* **6. have a big mouth** [...'maʊθ] *idiom* to be a gossiper; to be a person who tells secrets. ♦ *Mary has a big mouth. She told Bob what I was getting him for his birthday.* ♦ *You shouldn't say things like that about people all the time. Everyone will say you have a big mouth.* **7. have one's heart in one's mouth** [...'maʊθ] *idiom* to feel strongly emotional about someone or something. ♦ *"Gosh, Mary," said John, "I have my heart in my mouth whenever I see you."* ♦ *My heart is in my mouth whenever I hear the national anthem.* **8. live from hand to mouth** [...'maʊθ] *idiom* to live in poor circumstances. ♦ *When both of my parents were out of work, we lived from hand to mouth.* ♦ *We lived from hand to mouth during the war. Things were very difficult.* **9. make someone's mouth water** [...'maʊθ...] *idiom* to make someone hungry (for something); to cause someone to salivate. ♦ *That beautiful salad makes my mouth water.* ♦ *Talking about food makes my mouth water.* **10. melt in one's mouth** [...'maʊθ] *idiom* to taste very good; [for food] to be very rich and satisfying. ♦ *This cake is so good it'll melt in your mouth.* ♦ *John said that the food didn't exactly melt in his mouth.*

mouthful ['maʊθ fʊl] **1.** *n.* the contents of the mouth. ♦ *The baby spit a mouthful of peas onto the floor.* ♦ *The drowning swimmer swallowed mouthfuls of water.* **2.** *n.* something that is difficult to pronounce. (Informal.) ♦ *That foreign phrase is a real mouthful!* ♦ *That extraordinarily long name is quite a mouthful.*

mouthpiece ['maʊθ pis] **1.** *n.* the part of a musical instrument that is blown into; the part of a musical instrument that is put on or between one's lips. ♦ *The trombonist polished the mouthpiece and placed it in the case.* ♦ *Flutists blow air over the opening in the mouthpiece.* **2.** *n.* the part of a machine or device that is placed on or next to someone or something's mouth. ♦ *I covered the phone's mouthpiece with a rag to disguise my voice.* ♦ *I spoke into the mouthpiece at the drive-through restaurant.*

mouthwash ['maʊθ wɑʃ] *n.* a liquid that is used to rinse one's mouth in order to make the breath smell better or to kill germs in the mouth. ♦ *I gargled with mouthwash after eating the pizza.* ♦ *My mint-flavored mouthwash freshens my breath and kills germs.*

movable ['muv ə bəl] **1.** *adj.* able to be moved. (Adv: *movably.*) ♦ *The piano was movable because it was on wheels.* ♦ *Our mobile home is movable.* **2. movable feast** *n.* a religious holiday that changes from one date to another in different years. ♦ *Easter is a movable feast.* ♦ *The almanac listed the year's movable feasts.*

move ['muv] **1.** *iv.* to go to a different time or space; to change position in time or space. ♦ *The cat moved from my lap to the floor.* ♦ *I moved to the front row of the theater for a better view.* **2.** *iv.* to be in motion. ♦ *The car was moving when the truck crashed into it.* ♦ *A carousel moves in a circular motion.* **3.** *iv.* to change where one lives or works. ♦ *We moved from Denver to Miami.* ♦ *The accounting department moved to another location.* **4. move to** *iv.* + *inf.* to make a motion ③ to do something. ♦ *I moved to call for a vote.* ♦ *John moved to table the motion.* **5.** *tv.* to transport to a different time or space; to cause someone or something to change position. ♦ *Please move this chair into the other room.* ♦ *The network moved the popular show from Sunday to Thursday.* **6.** *tv.* to cause someone or something to remain in motion. ♦ *The motor moved the merry-go-round around and around.* ♦ *The wind moved the dust across the land.* **7.** *tv.* to affect someone's emotions or feelings. ♦ *The composer's romantic music moved me.* ♦ *The sad story moved the audience.* **8.** *tv.* to formally make a suggestion at a meeting; to formally propose something. (Takes a clause.) ♦ *I move that we adjourn the meeting.* ♦ *John moved that we pass the motion.* **9.** *n.* an act of moving as in ①; a movement. ♦ *Don't make another move, or I'll call the police.* ♦ *The robber made his move toward the cash register.* **10.** *n.* the act of going to a new house to live. ♦ *Did your recent move to the suburbs go smoothly?* ♦ *The move away from her friends was hard for Anne.* **11.** *n.* one step in a plan; an action that has a specific result. ♦ *After the evacuation, the next move was to disarm the bomb.* ♦ *The first move is to explain the situation to everyone.* **12. someone's move** *n.* a player's turn in a game. ♦ *It's your move. Roll the dice.* ♦ *I just played, so now it's John's move.* **13. move heaven and earth to do something** *idiom* to make a major effort to do something. ♦ *"I'll move heaven and earth to be with you, Mary," said Bill.* ♦ *I had to move heaven and earth to get there on time.* **14. move up (in the world)** *idiom* to advance (oneself) and become successful. ♦ *The harder I work, the more I move up in the world.* ♦ *Keep your eye on John. He's really moving up.* **15. on the move** *idiom* busy; happening busily. ♦ *What a busy day. Things are really on the move at the store.* ♦ *When all the buffalo were on the move across the plains, it must have been very exciting.*

movement ['muv mənt] **1.** *n.* moving; changing position in time or space. (No plural form in this sense.) ♦ *Your weak leg needs movement to help it heal.* ♦ *This electronic device is designed to detect movement of any kind.* **2.** *n.* an act of ①. ♦ *The mouse went past the sleeping cat* *in a series of short movements.* ♦ *The chef chopped the onions with a few quick movements of his wrist.* **3.** *n.* a division of a symphony or other classical music work. ♦ *The first movement of this symphony is better than the other two.* ♦ *The symphony's second movement is written in a minor key.* **4.** *n.* a common social or political goal and the people who work together to promote it. ♦ *Members of the environmental movement opposed the nuclear tests.* ♦ *The grass-roots movement demanded the mayor's resignation.*

mover ['muv ɚ] **1.** *n.* a highly motivated person who gets many things done. (Informal.) ♦ *It's the movers in this company who get promoted.* ♦ *The manager rewarded the movers with a bonus.* **2.** *n.* someone who moves things for other people, especially when people move to a new house or apartment. ♦ *The movers dropped my mirror and broke it.* ♦ *The movers carried my couch down the narrow stairs.*

movie ['muv i] **1.** *n.* a film; a motion picture; a story on film. ♦ *Do you want to see a movie tonight?* ♦ *I don't like watching scary movies.* **2.** *adj.* <the adj. use of ①.> ♦ *Susan wants to be a famous movie actress.* ♦ *The newspaper publishes movie reviews each Friday.*

moving ['muv ɪŋ] **1.** *adj.* affecting one's emotions or feelings. (Adv: *movingly.*) ♦ *The moving story made me cry.* ♦ *The hero's moving plight was an inspiration to us all.* **2.** *adj.* changing position in time or space; causing someone or something to change position in time or space; having or causing motion. ♦ *The radar indicated there was a moving object behind the plane.* ♦ *The moving train crashed into the stalled truck.*

mow ['mo] *tv., irreg.* to cut grass. (Pp: *mowed* or mown.) ♦ *I mow the lawn each weekend.* ♦ *The tall grass hadn't been mowed in weeks.*

mower ['mo ɚ] *n.* a machine that cuts grass. ♦ *We store our lawn mower in the garage.* ♦ *I guided the mower around the flowers.*

mown ['mon] a pp of mow.

Mozambique [mo zæm 'bik] See Gazetteer.

Mr. ['mɪst ɚ] *n.* <a title for an adult male.> (The abbreviation of mister.) ♦ *I gave my homework to Mr. Brown after class.* ♦ *Mr. President, what do you plan to do about crime?*

Mrs. ['mɪs əz] *n.* <a title for a married woman.> (An abbreviation of mistress ③, but with a different meaning.) ♦ *Mrs. Truman's first name was Bess.* ♦ *John, this is my mother, Mrs. Smith.*

Ms. ['mɪz] *n.* <a title for an adult female.> ♦ *Is Ms. Smith married?* ♦ *The students asked Ms. Jones for help with their homework.*

Mt. See mount.

much ['mʌtʃ] **1.** *adv., irreg.* to a great extent; to a great degree; a lot. (Comp: more; sup: most.) ♦ *My neighbor talks much, and I talk even more.* ♦ *I work too much and don't get enough sleep.* **2.** *adj., irreg.* a lot; quite an extent or degree. (Comp: more; sup: most.) ♦ *Anne's news brought much joy.* ♦ *The butcher gave me too much meat.* **3.** *n.* a large extent; a large degree; a large amount. (No plural form in this sense.) ♦ *Much of what he said was not clear.* ♦ *Much of my work is still unfinished.*

muck ['mʌk] *n.* dirt; filth. (No plural form in this sense.) ♦ *The gardener washed the muck from her shoes.* ♦ *The drain was clogged with muck.*

mucous ['mju kəs] *adj.* of or about mucus. ♦ *The nostrils are lined with mucous membranes.* ♦ *A mucous plug blocked Jimmy's tear duct.*

mucus ['mju kəs] *n.* the slimy substance that coats and keeps moist certain membranes. (No plural form in this sense.) ♦ *The sick patient coughed up some mucus.* ♦ *The snail left a trail of mucus as it crawled along the rock.*

mud ['mʌd] *n.* a mixture of dirt and water; very wet soil. (No plural form in this sense.) ♦ *The young children threw mud at each other.* ♦ *My car got stuck in the mud.*

muddle ['mʌd l] **1.** *n.* a confused mess; a condition of confusion. ♦ *The accountant sorted through a muddle of bills.* ♦ *My department was a muddle when my boss retired.* **2.** *tv.* to confuse something; to get things out of order. ♦ *My coworker muddled the papers on my desk.* ♦ *The confusing textbook muddled the students' minds.* **3.** *iv.* to progress or move along in a confused or disorganized fashion. ♦ *The refugees muddled toward the border.* ♦ *Half asleep, I muddled through my presentation.*

muddy ['mʌd i] **1.** *adj.* covered with mud. (Adv: *muddily.* Comp: *muddier;* sup: *muddiest.*) ♦ *Take off your muddy shoes before you come inside.* ♦ *Billy wiped his muddy hands on the clean towels.* **2.** *adj.* not clear; cloudy. (Said especially of colors or liquids. Figurative on ①. Adv: *muddily.* Comp: *muddier;* sup: *muddiest.*) ♦ *The chemist stirred the muddy liquid.* ♦ *The art teacher said my colors were too muddy.*

mudslinging ['mʌd slɪŋ ɪŋ] *n.* saying bad things to damage someone's reputation. (No plural form in this sense.) ♦ *I'm tired of the mudslinging in politician's campaigns.* ♦ *The tabloid's mudslinging damaged the actor's career.*

muff ['mʌf] *tv.* to handle something in a clumsy way, especially so that it falls. (Informal.) ♦ *The runner scored when the catcher muffed the catch.* ♦ *My company lost the account when I muffed the presentation.*

muffin ['mʌf ən] *n.* a small, thick cake or roll with a flat bottom and a rounded top. ♦ *I ate a blueberry muffin for breakfast.* ♦ *The cook took the muffins out of the oven.*

muffle ['mʌf əl] *tv.* to apply a sound-absorbent material to a sound source to make it quieter. ♦ *The silencer muffled the noise from the gunshot.* ♦ *I muffled my alarm clock with my pillow.*

muffled ['mʌf əld] **1.** *adj.* [of a sound source] wrapped or padded. ♦ *The muffled drums still produced some noise.* ♦ *Only the murderer heard the muffled gunshot.* **2.** *adj.* hard to hear; having some material in front of a source of sound that makes it hard to hear. ♦ *I heard muffled voices coming from the kitchen.* ♦ *I can hear muffled music from the next apartment.*

muffler ['mʌf lɚ] **1.** *n.* part of the exhaust system of a car that softens the noises of the engine. ♦ *The broken muffler scraped against the road as I drove.* ♦ *The noise from the car without a muffler woke up the whole neighborhood.* **2.** *n.* a scarf wrapped around the neck for warmth. ♦ *I wore a woolen muffler to the football game.* ♦ *Wear your gloves and muffler. It's cold outside!*

mug ['mʌg] **1.** *n.* a drinking cup with a handle. ♦ *My boss gave me a mug for my birthday.* ♦ *I put the dirty mugs into* *the dishwasher.* **2.** *n.* the contents of ①. ♦ *I drank a mug of coffee.* ♦ *Could I have a mug of cocoa, please?* **3.** *tv.* to attack and rob someone. ♦ *I was mugged when I walked through the park at night.* ♦ *The police caught the guy who mugged me.*

mugger ['mʌg ɚ] *n.* someone who attacks and robs people on the street. ♦ *The mugger took $50 from me.* ♦ *Muggers roam the park during the night.*

muggy ['mʌg i] *adj.* hot and humid. (Adv: *muggily.* Comp: *muggier;* sup: *muggiest.*) ♦ *After a muggy day, the cool rain was refreshing.* ♦ *I turn on my air conditioner when it's muggy outside.*

Muhammad See **Mohammed**.

mulch ['mʌltʃ] **1.** *n.* plant matter or other covering spread on plants to protect them and to retain the moisture in the soil. (No plural form in this sense.) ♦ *Instead of throwing away the wood chips, we used them for mulch.* ♦ *The gardener covered the seedlings with mulch.* **2.** *tv.* to spread ① around plants in a garden. ♦ *The gardener mulched the flowers in the spring.* ♦ *I mulched the seedling to protect it from frost.*

mule ['mjul] *n.* the offspring of one horse and one donkey. ♦ *Mules are unable to produce offspring.* ♦ *The mules pulled the plow behind them.*

mull ['mʌl] **1.** *tv.* to heat cider or wine and add sugar or spices to it. ♦ *I mulled the wine before the party.* ♦ *The host mulled a lot of cider for his guests.* **2. mull over** *tv.* + *adv.* to think about something seriously; to consider something carefully. ♦ *I mulled the job offer over before I made my decision.* ♦ *The jury mulled over the evidence before coming to a verdict.*

multilevel ['mʌl ti lɛv əl] *adj.* having more than one level. ♦ *The multilevel parking garage was attached to the mall.* ♦ *I live in a multilevel apartment building.*

multimillionaire [məl ti 'mɪl jə ner] *n.* someone who is very rich; someone who has millions of dollars in assets. ♦ *The multimillionaire made a large donation to the school.* ♦ *Many multimillionaires have made their fortunes in business.*

multiple ['mʌl tə pəl] **1.** *adj.* involving many parts; consisting of many parts. (Adv: *multiply* ['mʌl tə pli].) ♦ *The crash victim suffered from multiple fractures.* ♦ *Each question on the test seemed to have multiple answers.* **2.** *n.* a number that can be divided by another number without a remainder; a number that can be divided evenly by another number. ♦ *Twelve is a multiple of six.* ♦ *The least common multiple of 4, 5, and 6 is 60.*

multiplication [məl tə plɪ 'ke ʃən] **1.** *n.* the calculation of two numbers so that one number is added to itself the number of times shown by the other number. ("×" or "∗" indicates ①. As an example, 3 × 4 = 12, because 3 + 3 + 3 + 3 = 12. No plural form in this sense.) ♦ *On the buttons of a calculator, multiplication is sometimes indicated by "∗".* ♦ *The multiplication of any number by zero results in zero.* **2.** *n.* breeding; the process of reproduction in humans, animals, and plants. (No plural form in this sense.) ♦ *The crops were choked by the multiplication of the weeds.* ♦ *Human multiplication will eventually strain the resources of the planet.*

multiplicity [məl tə 'plɪs ə ti] *n.* a large variety; a large amount of different kinds of things. (No plural form in this sense.) ♦ *A multiplicity of products is available at the mall.* ♦ *The college graduate was faced with a multiplicity of options.*

multiply ['mʌl tə plɑɪ] **1. multiply by** *tv.* + *prep. phr.* to perform multiplication; to add an amount to itself the number of times shown by another number. ♦ *Mary multiplied 5 by 3.* ♦ *You have to multiply the length by the width to get the right answer.* **2.** *tv.* to increase something. ♦ *Health problems simply multiplied the burden that Bill had to bear.* ♦ *The new law has multiplied the number of forms we have to fill out.* **3.** *iv.* to reproduce; to have offspring; to breed. ♦ *The two rabbits will soon multiply.* ♦ *Mosquitoes seem to multiply quickly.* **4.** *iv.* to increase. ♦ *The number of bankruptcies multiplied during the recession.* ♦ *Voter disgust multiplied during the election campaign period.*

multitude ['mʌl tə tud] **1.** *n.* a large amount. ♦ *John has a multitude of problems.* ♦ *Mary used to have a multitude of friends.* **2.** *n.* a large of amount of people. (Sometimes plural.) ♦ *The president spoke to the multitudes.* ♦ *The concert was attended by multitudes of music lovers.*

mum ['mʌm] See **chrysanthemum**.

mumble ['mʌm bəl] **1.** *iv.* to speak in an unclear manner; to speak softly with poor pronunciation. ♦ *I can't hear you if you mumble.* ♦ *I didn't hear the waitress because she mumbled.* **2.** *tv.* to say something that cannot be heard clearly. ♦ *I can't hear you. You're mumbling your words.* ♦ *The guilty man mumbled his reply.* **3.** *n.* speech that cannot be heard clearly. ♦ *My teacher speaks in a soft mumble.* ♦ *A mumble of static came from the loudspeaker.*

mummy ['mʌm i] *n.* a dead body that is preserved by drying and the addition of chemicals and ointments. ♦ *Many mummies are buried in Egyptian pyramids.* ♦ *The scientist unwrapped the mummy in order to examine it.*

mumps ['mʌmps] *n.* an infection that causes glands in the throat and neck to swell, making it difficult to swallow. (Treated as singular or plural.) ♦ *Bill missed a week of school when he got the mumps.* ♦ *I've been immunized against mumps.*

munch ['mʌntʃ] **1.** *tv.* to crunch something; to eat something noisily. ♦ *The people behind me in the theater munched their popcorn loudly.* ♦ *I munched a piece of cheese for lunch.* **2. munch on** *iv.* + *prep. phr.* to eat something; to chew on something. ♦ *The dog munched on its food loudly.* ♦ *We munched on pizza while watching TV.*

mundane [mən 'den] *adj.* boring; ordinary; dull; not exciting. (Adv: *mundanely.*) ♦ *I didn't finish reading the mundane book.* ♦ *John was bored with his mundane job.*

municipal [mju 'nɪs ə pəl] *adj.* of, for, or serving a city or a municipality. (Adv: *municipally.*) ♦ *The municipal workers went on strike today.* ♦ *All municipal offices are closed on state holidays.*

municipality [mju nɪs ə 'pæl ə ti] *n.* a city, town, village, borough, or other district that governs itself. (Smaller than a **state**.) ♦ *You can't buy alcohol on Sunday in this municipality.* ♦ *The mayor of the small farming municipality was a volunteer.*

munificent [mju 'nɪf ə sənt] *adj.* very generous; very giving. (Adv: *munificently.*) ♦ *The munificent patron gave the museum a large donation.* ♦ *My munificent roommate let me borrow his leather jacket.*

munitions [mju 'nɪ ʃənz] *n.* ammunition, guns, bombs, and other military equipment and weapons used for war or defense. (Treated as plural.) ♦ *The warring country's budget went mostly to munitions.* ♦ *The missile destroyed a factory where munitions were made.*

mural ['mjʊr əl] *n.* a picture or scene that is painted on the surface of a wall. ♦ *The students painted a mural on the side of the school.* ♦ *This mural depicts the first moon landing.*

murder ['mɝ dɚ] **1.** *n.* the killing of a human, done on purpose and against the law. ♦ *The brilliant detective solved the horrible murder.* ♦ *The police charged the teenager with the murder of his parents.* **2.** *tv.* to kill someone on purpose and against the law. ♦ *The cashier was murdered during the robbery.* ♦ *The gangster murdered the police informant.* **3.** *tv.* to ruin or spoil something completely. (Informal. Figurative on ②.) ♦ *The dry weather murdered the farmer's crops.* ♦ *The untalented actor murdered the play.* **4. murder on something** *idiom* very destructive or harmful to something. ♦ *Running a marathon is murder on your knees.* ♦ *This dry weather is murder on my crops.*

murderer ['mɝ dɚ ɚ] *n.* someone who kills someone else; someone who is found guilty of murder. ♦ *The jury sentenced the murderer to death.* ♦ *The detective slowly learned the murderer's identity.*

murderous ['mɝ dɚ əs] **1.** *adj.* able to murder. (Adv: *murderously.*) ♦ *I killed the murderous assailant in self-defense.* ♦ *The robber shot at the cashier with murderous intent.* **2.** *adj.* killing; causing someone's death by murder; showing a desire to murder. (Adv: *murderously.*) ♦ *The murderous blow to John's head killed him.* ♦ *The robber had a murderous look on his face, and the clerk just gave him the money.*

murky ['mɝ ki] **1.** *adj.* dark and gloomy; dark and cloudy. (Adv: *murkily.* Comp: *murkier;* sup: *murkiest.*) ♦ *It was hard to see through the murky fog.* ♦ *The murky air in the castle was damp and cold.* **2.** *adj.* vague; obscure; hard to understand. (Figurative on ①. Adv: *murkily.* Comp: *murkier;* sup: *murkiest.*) ♦ *I didn't understand my professor's murky explanation.* ♦ *I have only a murky recollection of what happened at the party.*

murmur ['mɝ mɚ] **1.** *n.* a low, quiet sound. ♦ *The murmur of the flowing river soothed me as I slept.* ♦ *The crowd's ugly murmur soon grew into angry cries.* **2.** *n.* an irregular sound made by the heart, caused by defective heart valves. ♦ *The doctor listened to my heart murmur.* ♦ *John had surgery to correct his heart murmur.* **3.** *iv.* to make low, quiet sounds; to speak very quietly. ♦ *I have a hard time understanding people who murmur.* ♦ *The people behind me murmured while I tried to watch the movie.* **4.** *tv.* to say something very quietly. (Takes a clause.) ♦ *Embarrassed, I murmured my excuse for being late.* ♦ *The babysitter murmured a lullaby to quiet the crying baby.*

murmuring ['mɝ mɚ ɪŋ] *adj.* making low, quiet sounds. (Adv: *murmuringly.*) ♦ *A murmuring brook runs behind my house.* ♦ *The murmuring people in the movie theater annoyed me.*

muscle ['mʌs əl] **1.** *n.* a group of long tissues in the body that can be shortened to make parts of the body move. ♦ *I strained my back muscles trying to lift a heavy box.* ♦ *The weightlifter developed enormous muscles.* **2.** *n.* strength; power. (No plural form in this sense. Figurative on ①.) ♦ *My boss told me to put some muscle behind my work.* ♦ *The army used its muscle to overthrow the government.*

muscle-bound ['mʌs əl baʊnd] *adj.* having muscles that are stiff and hard to move because they have been used or exercised too much. ♦ *The muscle-bound surfer tried to impress the sunbathers.* ♦ *Max was so muscle-bound he could hardly walk.*

muscular ['mʌs kjə lɚ] **1.** *adj.* in or of the muscles. ♦ *The former athlete suffered from muscular weakness.* ♦ *I felt muscular soreness after running five miles.* **2.** *adj.* having muscles that are strong and well developed. (Adv: *muscularly.*) ♦ *Weightlifters tend to be very muscular.* ♦ *The muscular man lifted the heavy barbell over his head.*

musculature ['mʌs kjə lə tʃɚ] *n.* the system of muscles in a body. (No plural form in this sense.) ♦ *The weightlifter's musculature was sharply defined.* ♦ *My physiology book outlined the musculature of the human body.*

muse ['mjuz] **muse over** *iv.* + *prep. phr.* to think deeply about something; to ponder on something. ♦ *I mused over what I should do after I graduated.* ♦ *The cook mused over what to serve for dinner.*

museum [mju 'zi əm] *n.* a building where art or things of or about science, history, or some other subject are placed on display for the public to see and learn about. ♦ *The art museum had many famous paintings on display.* ♦ *The natural-science museum had a dinosaur-fossil exhibit.*

mush ['mʌʃ] **1.** *n.* a soft, pulpy mixture of something liquid and solid. (No plural form in this sense.) ♦ *I flattened the tomatoes into mush.* ♦ *The dust and sand turned to mush in the rain.* **2.** *tv.* to crush something and make it seem like ①. (Informal.) ♦ *Don't mush your peas, Jimmy!* ♦ *I mushed the tomato with my hand.*

mushroom ['mʌʃ rum] **1.** *n.* a kind of fungus that is often used as food. ♦ *Many mushrooms can be eaten, but some are very poisonous.* ♦ *Thousands of mushrooms covered the dark forest ground.* **2.** *iv.* to grow very quickly or suddenly. ♦ *Urban problems mushroomed under the incompetent mayor's rule.* ♦ *The number of people who needed medical care mushroomed when the free clinic was opened.*

mushy ['mʌʃ i] *adj.* soft and pulpy. (Adv: *mushily.* Comp: *mushier;* sup: *mushiest.*) ♦ *I threw out the apple because it was mushy.* ♦ *I ate only mushy food after my wisdom teeth were removed.*

music ['mju zɪk] **1.** *n.* the sounds of the voice or of instruments making pleasant tones in a series or a series of groups. (No plural form in this sense. Number is expressed with *piece(s) of music.*) ♦ *Listening to music calms my nerves.* ♦ *I listen to music all day, even at work.* **2.** *n.* a piece of paper that shows the notes of a particular song or melody. (No plural form in this sense.) ♦ *I placed the music on the stand.* ♦ *Do you know how to read music?* **3. face the music** *idiom* to receive punishment; to accept the unpleasant results of one's actions. ♦ *Mary broke a dining-room window and had to face the music when her father got home.* ♦ *After failing a math test, Tom had to go home and face the music.*

musical ['mju zɪ kəl] **1.** *adj.* causing music to be made; producing notes or tones. (Adv: *musically* [...ɪk li].) ♦ *I can play several musical instruments.* ♦ *The musical clock plays a short tune every hour.* **2.** *adj.* of or about music. (Adv: *musically* [...ɪk li].) ♦ *I have absolutely no musical ability.* ♦ *Playing in an orchestra requires musical skill.* **3.** *n.* a play or movie in which the actors sing songs, usually as a way of moving the story forward. ♦ *I got the lead in the school musical.* ♦ *In that musical, all of the dialogue is sung instead of spoken.*

musician [mju 'zɪ ʃən] *n.* someone who plays a musical instrument; someone who writes music; someone who is in a band or an orchestra. ♦ *There are 40 musicians in the school band.* ♦ *I'm a musician in a local rock band.*

musicology [mju zɪ 'kɑl ə dʒi] *n.* the science and study of music, including its history and different styles. (No plural form in this sense.) ♦ *Western classical music is only one facet of musicology.* ♦ *The university offers a degree in musicology.*

muskrat ['musk ræt] **1.** *n.* a type of aquatic rodent native to North America. ♦ *The trapper caught muskrats in the creek.* ♦ *My coat is made from the fur of muskrats.* **2.** *n.* the skin and fur of ①. (No plural form in this sense.) ♦ *My coat has a collar of muskrat.* ♦ *Bob's hat is covered with muskrat.* **3.** *adj.* made of ②. ♦ *My uncle had a muskrat hat.* ♦ *Her muskrat coat was stolen when our house was robbed.*

Muslim AND **Moslem** ['mʌz ləm, 'mɑz ləm] **1.** *n.* someone who is a member of the religion of Islam; someone who is a follower of the prophet Mohammed. ♦ *Thousands of Muslims were displaced in the war.* ♦ *The Koran is the holy book of the Moslems.* **2.** *adj.* of or about the Islamic religion. ♦ *The population of Arab countries is mostly Muslim.* ♦ *Some Muslim women wear veils.*

muss ['mʌs] **muss (up)** *tv.* (+ *adv.*) to make something messy, especially one's hair; to move someone's hair out of place. ♦ *Don't touch my hair. You'll muss it up.* ♦ *The wind mussed my hairdo.*

mussel ['mʌs əl] *n.* a kind of shellfish, usually having very dark shells, that can be eaten as food. ♦ *I ate steamed mussels for dinner.* ♦ *The cook put clams and mussels in the seafood chowder.*

must ['mʌst] **1.** *aux.* <a form showing obligation or required action>; [to] have to [do something]. (Uses *had to* for a past tense. Takes a bare verb.) ♦ *You must arrive on time, or you won't be seated.* ♦ *Must I eat my peas?* **2.** *aux.* <a form indicating probability or likelihood.> (Uses the form *has to have* plus the past participle or *must have* plus the past participle for a past tense. Takes a bare verb.) ♦ *Your book must be where you put it down when you finished reading it.* ♦ *You said it had to have been there, so I know it must be there.* ♦ *I don't see Bill here. He must not be coming to the party.* **3. must not** *phr.* <a form that indicates what one is not allowed to do.> (Takes a bare verb.) ♦ *You must not smoke inside the hospital.* ♦ *We must not be late.* **4.** *n.* something that is necessary or essential. ♦ *Wearing your seat belt is a must if you ride in my car.* ♦ *Seeing the Statue of Liberty is a must when you visit New York.*

mustache ['mʌs tæʃ] *n.* hair that grows on the upper lip. ♦ *David trimmed his mustache with a razor.* ♦ *Bob's hair is brown, but his mustache is red.*

mustang ['mʌs tæŋ] *n.* a small breed of a horse. ♦ *Most mustangs are wild.* ♦ *The cowboy rode a mustang in the rodeo.*

mustard ['mʌs tɚd] **1.** *n.* a plant with a bright yellow flower. (No plural form in this sense.) ♦ *Wild mustard grew along the banks of the creek.* ♦ *Mustard is harvested for its seed.* **2.** *n.* a condiment made from the powdered seeds of ①, water, and spices. ♦ *Mustard is spread on sandwiches and eaten with many kinds of food.* ♦ *I'd like my hot dog with mustard, please.*

muster ['mʌs tɚ] **1.** *tv.* to gather someone or something; to summon someone or something to come together. ♦ *The order came to muster the crew for battle.* ♦ *The general mustered the troops to fight against the enemy.* **2.** *iv.* to gather; to come together. ♦ *The soldiers mustered in the town square.* ♦ *The troops mustered around the flagpole.* **3. muster (up) one's courage** *idiom* to build up one's courage; to call or bring forth one's courage. ♦ *I mustered my courage and dove from the high diving board.* ♦ *He had to muster up all his courage in order to attend the dance.*

mustn't ['mʌs ənt] *cont.* "must not." (Indicates what one is not allowed to do or what one may not do.) ♦ *You mustn't smoke in hospitals.* ♦ *We mustn't be late.*

musty ['mʌs ti] *adj.* smelling old and stale; smelling like mold. (Adv: *mustily.* Comp: *mustier;* sup: *mustiest.*) ♦ *The old furniture had been stored in a musty basement.* ♦ *I pulled the musty suit out of the trunk.*

mutant ['mjut nt] *n.* a plant, animal, or human whose genetic structure is significantly different from that of its parents. ♦ *A new, mutant tomato was resistant to worms.* ♦ *The mutant fetus spontaneously aborted.*

mutate ['mju tet] **1.** *iv.* [for a plant's, animal's, or human's genetic structure] to change randomly or unpredictably. ♦ *This virus can mutate very rapidly.* ♦ *Radioactivity caused the plants to mutate.* **2.** *tv.* to cause someone or something to change, especially to cause the genetic structure of a plant, animal, or human to change. ♦ *X-rays mutated the mouse's genes.* ♦ *The scientist mutated the genetic structure of corn with radioactivity.*

mutation [mju 'te ʃən] **1.** *n.* the process of mutating; random and unpredictable genetic change. (No plural form in this sense.) ♦ *The tomato's perfect shape was brought about by mutation.* ♦ *Mutation can be caused by radiation.* **2.** *n.* a creature whose structure is the result of ①. ♦ *The mutation escaped from the mad scientist's lab.* ♦ *The scientist studied the mutation's genetic structure.*

mute ['mjut] **1.** *adj.* quiet; silent. (Adv: *mutely.*) ♦ *My roommate was mute as usual at the dinner table.* ♦ *The mute students walked through the library, thinking about their exams.* **2.** *adj.* unable to speak, as from fright. (Adv: *mutely.*) ♦ *The attacker's prey was mute from fear.* ♦ *The student stood mute before the principal, fearful and ashamed.* **3.** *adj.* physically unable to speak or make vocal sounds. ♦ *The child was born mute and never was able to talk.* ♦ *The mute children learned to communicate through sign language.* **4.** *tv.* to cause someone or something to become quieter or less intense. ♦ *I muted the loud music because I didn't want to wake my roommate.* ♦ *The artist muted the bright red paint by adding gray to it.*

mutilate ['mjut ə let] *tv.* to destroy something or some creature by stabbing, tearing, or cutting. ♦ *The wolves* *mutilated the family's dog.* ♦ *Someone mutilated all the bushes along the street.*

mutilation [mjut ə 'le ʃən] *n.* cutting, tearing, or stabbing. (No plural form in this sense.) ♦ *Mutilation of the land by loggers angered many people.* ♦ *The mutilation of the students' desks was blamed on David.*

mutinous ['mjut n nəs] *adj.* plotting or performing a mutiny. (Adv: *mutinously.*) ♦ *The leader of the mutinous sailors knocked on the captain's door.* ♦ *The captain was killed by the mutinous crew.*

mutiny ['mjut n ni] **1.** *n.* rebellion against someone in power, especially by sailors or soldiers. (No plural form in this sense.) ♦ *Mutiny is a poor way to show disagreement with the captain.* ♦ *The barbaric sergeant drove the soldiers to mutiny.* **2.** *iv.* to be part of ①. ♦ *The crew mutinied against the barbaric captain.* ♦ *The unprepared soldiers mutinied rather than die in battle.*

mutter ['mʌt ɚ] **1.** *iv.* to speak in a low, grumbling way that is hard to understand. ♦ *I can't understand you when you mutter.* ♦ *Bill muttered angrily under his breath.* **2.** *tv.* to say something as in ①. ♦ *The witness muttered his reply.* ♦ *John muttered that he was tired.*

mutton ['mʌt n] *n.* the meat of sheep used as food. (No plural form in this sense.) ♦ *This soup is flavored with mutton.* ♦ *I ordered mutton and potatoes.*

mutual ['mju tʃu əl] **1.** *adj.* shared by two or more people; equally felt or done by each person toward the other. (Adv: *mutually.*) ♦ *Bill and I have mutual respect for each other.* ♦ *My enemy and I felt a mutual hatred toward each other.* **2.** *adj.* common to two or more people; known to two or more people. (Adv: *mutually.*) ♦ *Mary is a mutual friend of Anne's and mine.* ♦ *Bill and I share a lot of mutual interests, so we are together often.*

mutual fund ['mju tʃu əl 'fʌnd] See fund.

muzzle ['mʌz əl] **1.** *n.* [in certain animals] the part of the face that sticks out. ♦ *The friendly dog stuck its muzzle into my hand and licked my fingers.* ♦ *The wolf rubbed its muzzle against its mate.* **2.** *n.* a restraint put over the mouth of an animal so that it will not bite someone or something. ♦ *The security guard covered the dogs' mouths with muzzles.* ♦ *The angry dog drooled through its muzzle.* **3.** *n.* the front end of a gun; the barrel of a gun. ♦ *Smoke trailed from the muzzle after I fired.* ♦ *The thief placed the muzzle of his gun against my neck.* **4.** *tv.* to put ② on an animal. ♦ *The security guard muzzled the guard dogs.* ♦ *I muzzle my dog when I take him for a walk.* **5.** *tv.* to silence someone, especially someone who is critical. (Figurative on ④.) ♦ *The army muzzled the opposition.* ♦ *The president muzzled his critics.*

my ['mɑɪ] **1.** *pron.* <the first-person singular possessive pronoun.> (Describes people or things belonging to the speaker or writer. Used as a modifier before a noun. Compare with mine ⑥) ♦ *My hat is on my head.* ♦ *John is my best friend.* **2.** *interj.* <a word used to show surprise.> ♦ *Oh, my! What have you done?* ♦ *My, what a beautiful baby!*

Myanmar [mɪ 'jɑn mɑr] See Gazetteer.

myopia [mɑɪ 'op i ə] **1.** *n.* the inability to see far away; the ability to see only things that are close; nearsightedness. (No plural form in this sense.) ♦ *I wear glasses because I've got myopia.* ♦ *The optometrist diagnosed me as having myopia.* **2.** *n.* the inability to foresee situations. (No plural form in this sense. Figurative on ①.) ♦ *I am frustrated by my supervisor's myopia.* ♦ *John's myopia causes him to blame others for his problems.*

myopic [mɑɪ 'ɑp ɪk] **1.** *adj.* having myopia; unable to see far away; able only to see things that are close; nearsighted. (Adv: *myopically* [...ɪk li].) ♦ *I wear glasses because I'm myopic.* ♦ *The myopic driver squinted at the road sign.* **2.** *adj.* narrow-minded; not able to foresee situations. (Figurative on ①. Adv: *myopically* [...ɪk li].) ♦ *My myopic supervisor is not suited for management.* ♦ *I'm tired of listening to your myopic concerns.*

myriad ['mɪr i əd] *adj.* unable to be counted; very many. ♦ *The band's myriad fans screamed when the band members walked on stage.* ♦ *I gazed at the myriad stars in the sky.*

myself [mɑɪ 'sɛlf] **1.** *pron.* <the first-person singular reflexive pronoun.> ♦ *I looked at myself in the mirror.* ♦ *I cut myself while shaving.* **2.** *pron.* <① used to emphasize the speaker or the writer as subject of the sentence.> ♦ *I myself do not care.* ♦ *As for myself, I'm going to bed now.* **3. by myself** *phr.* without the help of anyone else. ♦ *I did it all by myself.* ♦ *I can eat that whole pie by myself.* **4. by myself** *phr.* with no one else present; alone. ♦ *I sat at the table by myself.* ♦ *I will not be at the party. I will be at home by myself tonight.*

mysterious [mɪ 'stɪr i əs] *adj.* full of mystery; not understood or explainable; puzzling. (Adv: *mysteriously.*) ♦ *Bob found a mysterious note on the door.* ♦ *I received a mysterious package in the mail.*

mystery ['mɪs tə ri] **1.** *n.* something that is not explained or understood. (No plural form in this sense.) ♦ *Mystery is intriguing to most people.* ♦ *The identity of the murderer is veiled in mystery.* **2.** *n.* something that is unknown, secret, or hidden; an instance of ①. ♦ *The contents of my grandfather's files were a mystery until his death.* ♦ *The identity of the dead body remained a mystery.* **3.** *n.* a book that involves a crime or murder that is solved. ♦ *John hoped to write dozens of murder mysteries.* ♦ *I read a mystery almost every week.* **4.** *adj.* <the adj. use of ③.> ♦ *That is my favorite mystery novel.* ♦ *I always look in the mystery section of the bookstore.*

mystic ['mɪs tɪk] **1.** *adj.* obscure and mysterious; unclear or confusing. (Adv: *mystically* [...ɪk li].) ♦ *A strangely dressed man was performing some sort of mystic ceremony in the dimly lit cavern.* ♦ *The mystic writing on the wall could not be understood by anyone.* **2.** *n.* someone who has spiritual experiences; someone who communicates with the spiritual world. ♦ *The mystic told me she had a message from my dead father.* ♦ *I asked the mystic what the future held for me.*

mystical ['mɪs tɪ kəl] *adj.* of or about mysticism. (Adv: *mystically* [...ɪk li].) ♦ *I studied books on witchcraft, hoping to gain some strange, mystical powers.* ♦ *The inside of the huge cathedral had sort of a mystical atmosphere.*

mysticism ['mɪs tə sɪz əm] *n.* thoughts and notions that are obscure and mystical. (No plural form in this sense.) ♦ *The ancient peoples practiced some sort of strange mysticism.* ♦ *The nature of the secret society was shrouded in mysticism.*

mystified ['mɪs tə fɑɪd] *adj.* confused; puzzled; bewildered. (Adv: *mystifiedly.*) ♦ *The mystified townspeople demanded an explanation.* ♦ *The professor helped the mystified students to understand algebra.*

mystify ['mɪs tə fɑɪ] *tv.* to confuse someone; to bewilder someone; to cause someone to be puzzled. ♦ *I was mystified by Jane's strange actions.* ♦ *Algebra completely mystifies me.*

mystique [mɪ 'stik] *n.* a feeling of mystery that is associated with someone or something; a mysterious or mystical quality. (No plural form in this sense.) ♦ *John wrote about the mystique surrounding the actor's life.* ♦ *Anne's mystique makes her attractive to some people.*

myth ['mɪθ] **1.** *n.* a fable; a story that explains a mystery of nature or tells how something came into existence. ♦ *Ancient civilizations developed myths to explain natural phenomena.* ♦ *The anthropologist studied the myths found in Asian cultures.* **2.** *n.* someone or something that is imaginary or made-up; something that is not based in fact. (Figurative on ①.) ♦ *The senator dismissed the charges as pure myth.* ♦ *The monster that is supposed to be at the bottom of the lake is just a myth.*

mythical ['mɪθ ɪ kəl] *adj.* imaginary; made-up; not factual. (Adv: *mythically* [...ɪk li].) ♦ *The lonely child invented mythical friends.* ♦ *The witness provided the police with a mythical tale that included visitors from outer space.*

mythology [mɪθ 'ɑl ə dʒi] **1.** *n.* the study of myths. (No plural form in this sense.) ♦ *The literature professor taught a course in mythology.* ♦ *The classical scholar specialized in Greek mythology.* **2.** *n.* a collection of myths about someone, something, or some culture. ♦ *I like to read about the gods and heroes of ancient mythology.* ♦ *Mars was the god of war in Roman mythology.*

N

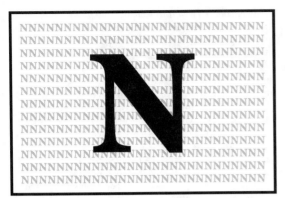

N AND **n** ['ɛn] **1.** *n.* the fourteenth letter of the alphabet. ♦ *The letter* N *represents "north" on a compass.* ♦ *Answer these questions, using a* Y *for "yes" and an* N *for "no."* **2.** *n.* See nominal.

nab ['næb] **1.** *tv.* to grab or catch something quickly or suddenly. (Slang.) ♦ *The catcher nabbed the ball before it flew into the stands.* ♦ *I nabbed the vase before it struck the ground.* **2.** *tv.* to steal something; to kidnap someone. (Slang.) ♦ *The kidnapper nabbed the ambassador's son.* ♦ *A thief nabbed a sweater while no one was watching.* **3.** *tv.* to arrest someone. (Slang.) ♦ *The police nabbed the bank robber.* ♦ *The criminal tried to escape, but the cops nabbed him.*

nag ['næg] **1.** *tv.* to continue to bother someone; to pester someone to do something by complaining all the time. ♦ *My boss kept nagging me to clean my desk.* ♦ *I nagged my roommate until she paid her share of the rent.* **2.** *iv.* to continue to be a bother and a pest. ♦ *If you didn't nag so much, more people might like you.* ♦ *Stop nagging! I'll clean my room later.* **3.** *n.* someone who pesters people habitually. ♦ *I quit my job because my boss was such a nag.* ♦ *The clerk ignored the old nag's annoying comments.* **4.** *n.* a horse, especially an old one. (Informal.) ♦ *The farmer sold the old nag to the glue factory.* ♦ *The nag walked slowly toward the stable.*

nagging ['næg ɪŋ] *adj.* persistent; annoying; bothersome. (Adv: *naggingly.*) ♦ *I had a nagging cough for a week, so I went to see a doctor.* ♦ *This nagging problem just won't go away.*

nail ['nel] **1.** *n.* a thin rod of metal, pointed on one end. ♦ *The carpenter hammered the nail into the wood.* ♦ *Be careful. There are nails sticking out of that board.* **2.** *n.* one of the hard, flat tips at the ends of fingers and toes. ♦ *I hate the sound made when nails scrape against a chalkboard.* ♦ *Jane painted her nails red.* **3.** *tv.* to attach or secure something with ①. ♦ *I nailed the message board to the wall.* ♦ *The carpenter nailed the frame into place.* **4.** **nail in someone's or something's coffin** *idiom* something that will harm or destroy someone or something. ♦ *Every word of criticism that Bob said about the firm was a nail in his coffin.* ♦ *Losing the large order was the final nail in the company's coffin.*

naive AND **naïve** [nɑɪ 'iv] *adj.* not sophisticated; childlike in thought or action; not knowing what to do because of youth or inexperience. (Adv: *naively.*) ♦ *The naive tourist was robbed in the train station.* ♦ *Con artists try to gain the trust of naive people.*

naked ['nek ɪd] **1.** *adj.* nude; wearing no clothes. ♦ *After his bath, Jimmy ran around naked until his mother caught him.* ♦ *The police arrested the naked man who ran through the park.* **2.** *adj.* not covered with anything; bare; plain and simple. (Figurative on ①. Adv: *nakedly.*) ♦ *We need a picture for that naked wall.* ♦ *The witness spoke the naked truth.* **3.** **with the naked eye** *idiom* with eyes that are not aided with the lenses of telescopes, microscopes, or binoculars. ♦ *The moon is quite visible with the naked eye.* ♦ *Bacteria are too small to be seen with the naked eye.*

nakedness ['nek ɪd nəs] **1.** *n.* a state of having no clothes on one's body; nudity. (No plural form in this sense.) ♦ *Bill concealed his nakedness with a towel.* ♦ *Max had a hard time explaining his nakedness to the police.* **2.** *n.* bareness. (Figurative on ①.) ♦ *The nakedness of the hillside after the fire was stark.* ♦ *The nakedness of the hospital room was depressing.*

name ['nem] **1.** *n.* the word that indicates someone, something, or some place. ♦ *What's the name of the main actor in that movie?* ♦ *The name of Germany's capital city is Berlin.* **2.** *n.* [someone's] fame or reputation. ♦ *My father made his name in the real-estate business.* ♦ *The actress made a name for herself in the movies.* **3.** *n.* someone who is famous or important. ♦ *Are there any big names in that movie?* ♦ *Many important names in commerce attended the charity concert.* **4.** *tv.* to give ① to someone, something, or some place. ♦ *The artist named her painting* Summertime Dance. ♦ *The new parents named their baby David.* **5.** *tv.* to state or recite the ① of someone or something. ♦ *Can you name the days of the week?* ♦ *The witness named all the people involved in the crime.* **6.** *tv.* to appoint someone; to choose someone or something. ♦ *The board of directors named Anne the new director.* ♦ *Bill was named as the chairman's successor.* **7.** **call someone names** *idiom* to give someone an abusive or insulting ①. ♦ *Billy cried when the other kids called him names.* ♦ *John was punished for calling his teacher names.* **8.** **drop names** *idiom* to mention the names ① of important or famous people as if they were personal friends. ♦ *Mary always tries to impress people by dropping the names of well-known film stars.* ♦ *Bill's such a snob. Leave it to him to drop the names of all the local gentry.* **9.** **in name only** *idiom* nominally; not actually, but only by terminology. ♦ *The president is head of the country in name only. Congress makes the laws.* ♦ *Mr. Smith is the boss of the Smith Company in name only. Mrs. Smith handles all the business affairs.*

name-calling ['nem kɔl ɪŋ] *n.* calling someone a bad or insulting name. (No plural form in this sense.) ♦ *The candidates were criticized for name-calling.* ♦ *Billy's name-calling got him in trouble.*

nameless ['nem ləs] **1.** *adj.* having no name; unable to be named or specified. (Adv: *namelessly.*) ♦ *I tried to describe my nameless fears to my friend.* ♦ *An old cabin sat at the end of the empty, nameless street.* **2.** *adj.* not named; anonymous; providing no name. (Adv: *namelessly.*) ♦ *The insulting letter was written by a nameless coward.* ♦ *This poem was written by a nameless author.*

namely ['nem li] *adv.* that is to say; that is; specifically. ♦ *For a vacation I went out west; namely, to California and Oregon.* ♦ *My diet is restricted; namely, I can't eat salt.*

namesake ['nem sek] *n.* someone whose name is taken from the name of another person. ♦ *"My nephew, Max, is also my namesake," said Max Brown.* ♦ *William Smith Sr. is very proud of his namesake—his son, William Smith Jr.*

nanny ['næn i] *n.* a woman whose job is to take care of someone else's children. ♦ *Mr. and Mrs. Smith hired a nanny to take care of their children.* ♦ *The nanny took the child to his soccer game.*

nanosecond ['næn o sɛk ənd] *n.* one-billionth of a second. ♦ *The computer solved the calculation in a few nanoseconds.* ♦ *The worker was exposed to the deadly radiation for only five nanoseconds.*

nap ['næp] **1.** *iv.* to sleep for a short period of time, especially during the day. ♦ *I was so tired that I napped at my desk at work.* ♦ *I napped before going out to see the long movie.* **2.** *n.* a short amount of sleep, especially during the day. ♦ *I need a nap. I am very tired.* ♦ *Jane put her child in bed for an afternoon nap.* **3.** *n.* the upright threads of a carpet or piece of material, such as velvet. (No plural form in this sense.) ♦ *This vacuum cleaner is designed for carpets with a high nap.* ♦ *The nap of the old velvet dress was crushed.* **4. take a nap** *idiom* to sleep as in ①. ♦ *I took a short nap just after lunch.* ♦ *The baby takes a long nap each afternoon.*

nape ['nep] *n.* the back [of the neck]. ♦ *I carried the kitten by the nape of its neck.* ♦ *The mugger knocked me out by striking the nape of my neck.*

napkin ['næp kɪn] *n.* a square of fabric or paper used for protecting one's clothes and keeping tidy at meals. ♦ *I placed the napkin in my lap before I began to eat.* ♦ *I wiped the food from the corner of my mouth with my napkin.*

narcissi [nɑr 'sɪs ɑɪ] a pl of narcissus.

narcissus [nɑr 'sɪs əs] *n., irreg.* any of a group of spring flowers, usually white or yellow, including the daffodil and jonquil. (Pl: *narcissus, narcissuses,* or narcissi.) ♦ *The florist placed a beautiful narcissus in the bouquet.* ♦ *The bride's corsage was made of narcissi.*

narcotic [nɑr 'kɑt ɪk] **1.** *n.* a drug that causes sleep or lessens pain by dulling the senses. ♦ *Most narcotics are available only with a prescription.* ♦ *It is illegal to buy or possess certain kinds of narcotics.* **2.** *adj.* <the adj. use of ①.> (Adv: *narcotically* [...ɪk li].) ♦ *The security guards found a suitcase full of narcotic drugs in the car.* ♦ *The narcotic effects of the medicine eased my pain.*

narrate ['nɛr et] **1.** *tv.* to tell a story. ♦ *At the party, John narrated the details of his accident.* ♦ *The story was narrated by the high-school speech teacher.* **2.** *iv.* to tell about events that are being shown in a film, a slide show, on television, or in some other performance setting. ♦ *Some actors mimed a scene while another actor narrated.* ♦ *John showed me pictures of his vacation while Anne narrated.*

narration [nɛr 'e ʃən] *n.* telling a story or giving an account of something that happened; narration. (No plural form in this sense.) ♦ *The movie's soundtrack was damaged, so the narration was garbled.* ♦ *The jury paid close attention to the witness's narration.*

narrative ['nɛr ə tɪv] **1.** *n.* telling a story or giving an account of something that happened; narration. (No plural form in this sense.) ♦ *Narrative is an interesting way to present history.* ♦ *Bob's use of narrative in his essay was not effective.* **2.** *n.* an instance of ①. ♦ *The narrative of the only survivor from the wreck was highly emotional.* ♦ *Jane's narrative of her trip to the circus was very funny.*

narrow ['nɛr o] **1.** *adj.* not wide; short from side to side in comparison with the length from one end to the other. (Adv: *narrowly.* Comp: *narrower;* sup: *narrowest.*) ♦ *No parking was allowed on the narrow street.* ♦ *It was difficult moving the piano through the narrow hallway.* **2.** *adj.* limited; not broad. (Figurative on ①. Adv: *narrowly.* Comp: *narrower;* sup: *narrowest.*) ♦ *I have only a narrow understanding of chemistry.* ♦ *This brochure shows a narrow sampling of this company's product.* **3.** *tv.* to cause something to become ①. ♦ *We had to narrow our garden paths so we could plant more flowers.* ♦ *Construction crews narrowed the four-lane road to two lanes.* **4.** *iv.* to become ①. ♦ *This road narrows a few hundred feet before the tunnel.* ♦ *This river narrows just before the waterfall.* **5.** *iv.* to become ②. ♦ *The competition for the job narrowed after the last round of interviews.* ♦ *Our travel options narrowed because of the hurricane.*

narrow-minded ['nɛr o 'mɑɪn dɪd] *adj.* intolerant; prejudiced; not willing to tolerate or respect other people's opinions. (Adv: *narrow-mindedly.*) ♦ *My uncle's narrow-minded viewpoints are quite irritating.* ♦ *Don't be so narrow-minded, and listen to what I'm trying to say!*

narwhal ['nɑr wəl] *n.* a type of Arctic whale, the male of which has a long tusk. ♦ *From the ship, I spotted a narwhal swimming near an iceberg.* ♦ *The fishermen harpooned a narwhal.*

nasal ['nez əl] **1.** *adj.* of or about the nose. (Adv: *nasally.*) ♦ *I took some medicine because my nasal passages were clogged.* ♦ *I can't smell anything because of nasal congestion.* **2.** *adj.* of the quality of sound heard when making the speech sounds [m], [n], or [ŋ]. (Adv: *nasally.*) ♦ *French has nasal vowels.* ♦ *The salesclerk has a very nasal voice.* **3.** *n.* a nasal ② sound, such as [m] or [n], made by opening the passage to the nose at the back of the throat. ♦ *In English, the nasals are represented by* m, n, *and* ng. ♦ *The word* nun *begins and ends with a nasal.*

nasturtium [nə 'stɚ ʃəm] *n.* a garden plant with orange, yellow, or red flowers and rounded leaves. ♦ *Orange and red nasturtiums grew by the garage.* ♦ *A large pot of nasturtiums sits beside the doorway.*

nasty ['næs ti] **1.** *adj.* mean; angry; unpleasant; bad-tempered. (Adv: *nastily.* Comp: *nastier;* sup: *nastiest.*) ♦ *The librarian gave me a nasty look when I talked too loudly.* ♦ *My boss is in a nasty mood today.* **2.** *adj.* obscene; vulgar; dirty-minded; offensive to one's morals. (Adv: *nastily.* Comp: *nastier;* sup: *nastiest.*) ♦ *Billy was punished for telling a nasty joke.* ♦ *The bookstore kept the nasty magazines on the top shelf.* **3.** *adj.* very serious; bad; dangerous. (Adv: *nastily.* Comp: *nastier;* sup: *nastiest.*) ♦ *I stayed indoors because the weather was extremely nasty.* ♦ *David had a nasty fall and broke his hip.* **4.** *adj.* not pleasant to see, hear, smell, taste, or touch. (Adv: *nastily.* Comp: *nastier;* sup: *nastiest.*) ♦ *The scene of the accident was a nasty sight.* ♦ *There's a nasty smell coming from the garbage.*

nation ['ne ʃən] **1.** *n.* a country; a country that governs itself. ♦ *How many nations fought in World War II?* ♦ *An ambassador is a representative to other nations.* **2.** *n.* the people of a country; a group of people who are ruled by the same government. ♦ *The nation was divided by the* *outcome of the sensational trial.* ♦ *The nation voted to reelect the incumbent president.*

national ['næʃ ə nəl] **1.** *adj.* of or about a nation; belonging to a nation; throughout a nation. (Adv: *nationally.*) ♦ *Every nation has a national anthem.* ♦ *Baseball is one of America's national pastimes.* **2.** *n.* a citizen of a specific nation or a particular group of nations. ♦ *My history professor is a French national.* ♦ *The bombing suspect was a foreign national.*

nationalistic [næʃ ə nə 'lɪs tɪk] *adj.* patriotic; having very strong pride in one's country. (Adv: *nationalistically* [...ɪk li].) ♦ *The strongly nationalistic president was extremely popular.* ♦ *The candidate's speeches inspired nationalistic fervor.*

nationality [næʃ ə 'næl ə ti] *n.* the state that arises from having citizenship in a particular country or being born in a particular country. ♦ *My mother's nationality is Irish, but she lives in the United States.* ♦ *The application asked for my nationality and place of birth.*

nationalize ['næʃ ə nə lɑɪz] *tv.* to bring a business under the control of the national government. ♦ *The government nationalized the telephone system years ago.* ♦ *The president threatened to nationalize the railroads.*

nationwide ['ne ʃən 'wɑɪd] **1.** *adj.* across a nation; throughout a nation. ♦ *The candidate's nationwide campaign was very expensive.* ♦ *A nationwide poll indicates dissatisfaction with Congress.* **2.** *adv.* across a nation; throughout a nation. ♦ *The presidential candidates campaigned nationwide.* ♦ *Reporters interviewed citizens nationwide for the news story.*

native ['ne tɪv] **1.** *n.* something that comes from a certain country or region. ♦ *This plant is a native of North America.* ♦ *The kangaroo is a native of Australia.* **2.** *n.* someone born in a particular place. ♦ *My parents are natives of South Carolina.* ♦ *My teacher is a Texas native.* **3.** *adj.* born or raised in a certain country or region; belonging to a certain country or region. (Adv: *natively.*) ♦ *The country called her native sons to war.* ♦ *My teacher is a native Texan.* **4. native to** *adj.* + *prep. phr.* originating in or existing naturally in a certain country or region. ♦ *The botanist studied plants that were native to the area.* ♦ *The kangaroo is native to Australia.* **5.** *adj.* innate; existing in someone since birth. (Adv: *natively.*) ♦ *The pianist's native talents were evident from an early age.* ♦ *Mary has a native ability for painting.*

Native American ['ne tɪv ə 'mɛr ə kən] **1.** *n.* a person belonging to one of the indigenous groups of people in North America when the Europeans arrived; an American Indian. (Often capitalized, but sometimes seen as *native American.*) ♦ *Native Americans immigrated from Asia thousands of years ago.* ♦ *Many Native Americans live on reservations.* **2.** *adj.* <the adj. use of ①.> ♦ *We visited a Native American reservation in Arizona.* ♦ *The museum contains weapons and items of Native American clothing.*

Nativity [nə 'tɪv ə ti] *n.* the birth of Jesus Christ. ♦ *The Nativity took place in a stable.* ♦ *The city was not allowed to display a replica of the Nativity on public grounds.*

natural ['nætʃ ə rəl] **1.** *adj.* made by nature; existing in nature; not artificial; not made by people; not affected by people. (Adv: *naturally.*) ♦ *This cake is made entirely from natural ingredients.* ♦ *Earthquakes and tornadoes are natural disasters.* **2.** *adj.* inborn; innate; existing since birth; not learned. (Adv: *naturally.*) ♦ *Anne has a natural talent for playing the piano.* ♦ *John exhibits a natural skill for playing tennis.* **3.** *n.* someone who is thought of as perfect for a certain job; someone who does something very well, especially through inborn ability. ♦ *Anne is a natural at playing the piano.* ♦ *The talented actor was a natural for the role of the villain.* **4.** *n.* a musical note that is not a sharp or a flat; one of the white keys on the piano. ♦ *You are playing a sharp where you should play a natural.* ♦ *C and E are naturals, while F sharp is not.*

naturalist ['nætʃ ə rə ləst] *n.* someone who studies plants and animals in their environment. ♦ *The naturalist watched the birds through her binoculars.* ♦ *The naturalist classified the various plants growing in the field.*

naturalized ['nætʃ ə rə lɑɪzd] *adj.* admitted as a citizen; made into a citizen. ♦ *I was born in Ireland, but now I'm a naturalized American citizen.* ♦ *Each newly naturalized citizen was issued a social security number.*

naturally ['nætʃ ə rə li] *adv.* obviously; of course. ♦ *Naturally, I'll come to your party!* ♦ *After I was robbed, naturally I called the police.*

nature ['ne tʃɚ] **1.** *n.* everything in the world except the material products of human work and thought: people, animals, plants, rocks, land, water, the weather, etc. (No plural form in this sense.) ♦ *You can learn a great deal about nature by watching television programs about plants and animals.* ♦ *Both beauty and suffering are part of nature.* **2.** *n.* the countryside; land that has not been affected by humans. (No plural form in this sense.) ♦ *I moved far away from the city in order to get back to nature.* ♦ *Developers have turned vast areas of nature into suburbs.* **3.** *n.* character; the essential qualities of someone or something; what someone or something really is. (No plural form in this sense.) ♦ *My new boss explained to me the nature of my job.* ♦ *It is Bill's nature to be shy and cautious.* **4. call of nature** *idiom* the need to go to the lavatory. ♦ *Stop the car here! I have to answer the call of nature.* ♦ *There was no interval in the meeting to take account of the call of nature.* **5. second nature to someone** *idiom* easy and natural for someone. ♦ *Swimming is second nature to Jane.* ♦ *Driving is no problem for Bob. It's second nature to him.*

naught ['nɔt] *n.* nothing. (No plural form in this sense.) ♦ *The manager's attempts at reform were all for naught.* ♦ *The score of the game was six–naught.*

naughty ['nɔ ti] **1.** *adj.* bad; behaving badly; not obeying rules. (Usually used to describe the behavior of children. Adv: *naughtily.* Comp: *naughtier;* sup: *naughtiest.*) ♦ *The parents sent the naughty child to bed early.* ♦ *The naughty students talked loudly during class.* **2.** *adj.* vulgar; indecent. (Adv: *naughtily.* Comp: *naughtier;* sup: *naughtiest.*) ♦ *A naughty limerick was written on the bathroom wall.* ♦ *Billy was punished for using naughty words.*

nausea ['nɔ zi ə] *n.* a feeling of sickness or repulsion; the feeling that one has to vomit. (No plural form in this sense.) ♦ *The rough boat ride gave me an attack of nausea.* ♦ *I was overcome with nausea at the grisly accident site.*

nauseate ['nɔ zi et] *tv.* to cause someone to feel sick or repulsed; to make someone feel like vomiting. ♦ *The horrible smell nauseated me.* ♦ *I was nauseated by the gory, violent movie.*

nauseating ['nɔ zi et ɪŋ] *adj.* sickening; causing the feeling of nausea. (Adv: *nauseatingly.*) ♦ *The nauseating food made me sick.* ♦ *The film critic deplored the nauseating movie.*

nauseous ['nɔ ʃəs, 'nɔ zi əs] **1.** *adj.* causing nausea; sickening; repulsing; causing someone to feel sick or repulsed. (Adv: *nauseously.*) ♦ *The nauseous smoke made me cough.* ♦ *I left the movie because of the nauseous violence.* **2.** *adj.* nauseated; sickened; repulsed. (Adv: *nauseously.*) ♦ *The smoke is making me nauseous.* ♦ *The violence in the movie is making me nauseous.*

nautical ['nɔt ɪ kəl] **1.** *adj.* of or about ships, shipping, or sailors. (Adv: *nautically* [...ɪk li].) ♦ *My uncle sells nautical instruments used for navigation on a ship.* ♦ *Sailors use a lot of special nautical terms.* **2. nautical mile** *n.* a measurement of distance at sea equal to about 1.15 miles on land. ♦ *Knots are measured by the number of nautical miles (about 6,080 feet) covered per hour.* ♦ *The island we are visiting is about 350 nautical miles from here.*

naval ['ne vəl] *adj.* of or about a navy. ♦ *The ensign worked at the naval base.* ♦ *The port city was under enemy naval attack.*

navel ['ne vəl] *n.* the depression in the center of the belly where the umbilical cord was removed shortly after birth. ♦ *I removed a piece of lint from my navel.* ♦ *Navels seem to serve no useful purpose in adults.*

navigability [næv ə gə 'bɪl ə ti] **1.** *n.* the capability of being sailed through safely. (No plural form in this sense.) ♦ *This channel's navigability is excellent except in the winter.* ♦ *Bad weather reduces the navigability of the river.* **2.** *n.* the ability to be steered or controlled. (No plural form in this sense.) ♦ *The violent winds affected the navigability of the small boat.* ♦ *The boat lost its navigability when I broke the rudder.*

navigable ['næv ə gə bəl] *adj.* [of a waterway] able to be sailed through safely. ♦ *Most Arctic rivers are not navigable in the winter.* ♦ *In the bay, navigable shipping lanes are marked with buoys.*

navigate ['næv ə get] **1.** *tv.* to steer a ship, plane, or other vehicle in some direction. ♦ *The captain navigated the ship around the reef.* ♦ *I navigated the car through heavy traffic.* **2.** *tv.* to travel or follow a route on the water, over land, or in the air. ♦ *The river pilot had to navigate the river in the dark.* ♦ *The pilot navigated the skies in one of the world's largest airplanes.* **3.** *iv.* to determine the proper direction or route. ♦ *I navigated while Anne drove.* ♦ *The detailed map helped me navigate through Boston.*

navigation [næv ə 'ge ʃən] **1.** *n.* the rules, skills, and science of navigating. (No plural form in this sense.) ♦ *Mary's talent for navigation comes in handy whenever I get lost.* ♦ *The rules of navigation must be learned before you launch your boat.* **2.** *n.* navigating; the practice of ①. (No plural form in this sense.) ♦ *The accident at sea was blamed on the captain's poor navigation.* ♦ *Tom's navigation got us lost.*

navigator ['næv ə ge tɚ] *n.* someone who is in charge of the navigation of a boat or other conveyance. ♦ *The navigator steered the ship through the rough waters.* ♦ *Bill drove, but since I held the map, I was the navigator.*

navy ['nev i] *n.* the branch of the military that deals with protecting the sea or fighting at sea. ♦ *Bill fought in the navy during the Vietnam War.* ♦ *The enemy navy attacked the port city.*

nay ['ne] *adv.* no. (Used especially in voting.) ♦ *Do you vote "aye" or "nay" on this issue?* ♦ *All those voting against the motion, say "nay."*

Nazi ['nɑt si] **1.** *n.* a member or supporter of the National Socialist party, organized by Adolf Hitler in Germany in 1933. ♦ *After World War II, many Nazis fled to South America.* ♦ *The Allies fought against the Nazis in World War II.* **2.** *adj.* of or about the National Socialist party, its principles, or its followers. ♦ *The British soldier shot at the Nazi troops.* ♦ *A Nazi organization claimed responsibility for the explosion.*

near ['nɪr] **1.** *prep.* at a place that is not far away; at a time that is not far away. ♦ *My house is near a lake.* ♦ *I sat near Jane on the bus.* **2.** *adj.* close in distance, time, relationship, resemblance, or effect. (Comp: *nearer;* sup: *nearest.*) ♦ *The nearest bank is five miles away.* ♦ *I expect an apology in the near future.* **3.** *adv.* at or to a place that is not far away; at or to a time that is not too distant. (Comp: *nearer;* sup: *nearest.*) ♦ *The number 6 bus travels nearer to downtown than the number 8 bus.* ♦ *I swam near to the shore.* **4.** *tv.* to come closer to someone or something; to approach someone or something. ♦ *As the shoplifter neared the exit, an alarm sounded.* ♦ *As the train neared the station, it slowed down.* **5.** *iv.* to come closer in time or space; to approach. ♦ *The time is nearing for us to leave the party.* ♦ *As the station neared, the train slowed down.*

nearby ['nɪr 'bɑɪ] **1.** *adv.* near; close; not far away. ♦ *My parents live nearby.* ♦ *Nearby, a bullet shot through the air.* **2.** *adj.* near; close; not far away. ♦ *I go shopping at a nearby supermarket.* ♦ *We went swimming at a nearby lake.*

nearly ['nɪr li] *adv.* almost; not quite. ♦ *It's nearly midnight, so I should go home.* ♦ *John walked so close to the river that he nearly fell in.*

nearsighted ['nɪr sɑɪt ɪd] *adj.* unable to see things in the distance clearly; myopic. (Adv: *nearsightedly.*) ♦ *The nearsighted driver was unable to read the road signs.* ♦ *I have to wear glasses at movies because I'm nearsighted.*

neat ['nit] **1.** *adj.* clean; tidy; orderly. (Adv: *neatly.* Comp: *neater;* sup: *neatest.*) ♦ *I keep my apartment very neat because I don't like clutter.* ♦ *My room is neat because I clean it every day.* **2.** *adj.* fine; excellent; wonderful. (Informal. Comp: *neater;* sup: *neatest.*) ♦ *I saw a really neat movie last night.* ♦ *Dave's new apartment is really neat!*

neatness ['nit nəs] *n.* cleanliness; order; the condition of being clean or orderly. (No plural form in this sense.) ♦ *The teacher stressed the importance of neatness.* ♦ *The neatness of John's apartment is amazing, considering how messy his office is at work.*

Nebraska [nə 'bræs kə] See Gazetteer.

necessarily [nɛs ə 'sɛr ə li] *adv.* because of necessity; as a necessary result; inevitably; unavoidably. (Usually with the negative.) ♦ *We don't necessarily have to go to Florida this winter.* ♦ *You're a good worker, but that doesn't necessarily mean you'll get a raise.*

necessary ['nɛs ə sɛr i] *adj.* required; needed; essential. (Adv: *necessarily* [nɛs ə 'sɛr ə li].) ♦ *A bachelor's degree is necessary for this job.* ♦ *The nurse gave the child all the necessary shots.*

necessitate [nə 'sɛs ə tet] *tv.* to make something necessary; to require something. ♦ *Your bad behavior necessitates that you be punished.* ♦ *The increase in food prices necessitated a change in our budget.*

necessity [nə 'sɛs ə ti] **1.** *n.* the quality of being necessary or needed. (No plural form in this sense.) ♦ *The college faculty questioned the necessity of certain required classes.* ♦ *The council discussed the necessity of the new anti-smoking laws.* **2.** *n.* something that is essential; something that is required; something that is necessary. ♦ *A bachelor's degree is a necessity for this job.* ♦ *Literacy is a necessity for many kinds of employment.*

neck ['nɛk] **1.** *n.* the narrow part of the body that connects the head to the rest of the body; the outside of the throat. ♦ *You should cover your neck with a scarf when it's cold.* ♦ *The mugger held a knife to my neck.* **2.** *n.* the part of clothing that goes around ①. ♦ *You stretched the neck of my sweater when you put it on the hanger.* ♦ *Why is there lipstick on the neck of your shirt?* **3.** *n.* the narrow part of something; something narrow that connects two things. (Figurative on ①.) ♦ *The strings stretch across the guitar's neck.* ♦ *Bob held his bottle of pop by the neck.* **4.** *iv.* [for two people] to kiss passionately. ♦ *The lovers necked on the beach at night.* ♦ *Jane and Bob liked to stay home on Saturday nights and neck.* **5. neck and neck** *idiom* exactly even, especially in a race or a contest. ♦ *John and Tom finished the race neck and neck.* ♦ *Mary and Anne were neck and neck in the spelling contest. Their scores were tied.* **6. stick one's neck out** *idiom* to take a risk. ♦ *Why should I stick my neck out to do something for her? What has she ever done for me?* ♦ *He made a risky investment. He stuck his neck out because he thought he could make some money.*

necklace ['nɛk ləs] *n.* a decorative band, chain, or similar object that is worn around the neck. ♦ *Anne wore a diamond necklace to the party.* ♦ *I helped Susan fasten the necklace around her neck.*

neckline ['nɛk lɑɪn] *n.* a line corresponding to the top edge of a blouse or the equivalent. ♦ *The model's revealing dress had a very low neckline.* ♦ *Susan wore a blouse with a modest neckline to work.*

necktie ['nɛk tɑɪ] *n.* a tailored strip of decorative cloth typically worn under the collar of a man's shirt. (Originally served the purpose of keeping the collar closed.) ♦ *The men were required to wear a necktie to work.* ♦ *John wore a red necktie to the party.*

nectar ['nɛk tɚ] **1.** *n.* a sweet liquid that is found in flowers and that attracts birds and insects. (No plural form in this sense.) ♦ *Some kinds of bats seek the nectar of flowers.* ♦ *The bees swarmed toward the flowers' nectar.* **2.** *n.* a kind of thick fruit juice from certain fruits. (Figurative on ①. No plural form in this sense.) ♦ *The children liked apricot nectar better than orange juice.* ♦ *The waiter served me a cold glass of mango nectar.*

nectarine [nɛk tə 'rin] **1.** *n.* a kind of peach that has no fuzz on its skin. ♦ *I washed the nectarine before eating it.* ♦ *I bought a bushel of nectarines at the orchard.* **2.** *adj.* <the adj. use of ①.> ♦ *Your nectarine pie is delicious!* ♦ *Who left nectarine peelings in the sink?*

need ['nid] **1.** *n.* something that is required or necessary; something that must be done or had; a requirement. ♦ *I have a need of some money to pay my medical bills.* ♦ *There's no need for shouting during class!* **2.** *tv.* to require something; to have to have something; to want something for a certain reason. ♦ *I need a new car because my old one doesn't work.* ♦ *These walls need a new coat of paint.* **3. need to** *iv.* + *inf.* to have to do something; to be obligated to do something. ♦ *I need to go to the store and buy some milk.* ♦ *I need to leave work fifteen minutes early.* **4. in need** *idiom* [of someone] requiring basic things like food, clothing, and housing. ♦ *Please contribute some money for those who are in need.* ♦ *The charity works with old people who are in need.* **5. in need of something** *idiom* [of someone or some creature] requiring something. ♦ *We are in need of a new car.* ♦ *The company is in need of a larger building to hold all its employees.*

needle ['nid l] **1.** *n.* a thin, pointed spike of metal having a narrow slit that thread fits through, used for sewing. ♦ *A needle's narrow opening is called an eye.* ♦ *I accidentally pricked my thumb with a needle.* **2.** *n.* a thin, hollow, pointed spike of metal used for injecting and removing body fluids. ♦ *The nurse stuck a needle in a vein in my arm and took a pint of blood.* ♦ *The doctor inoculated each child with a sterile needle.* **3.** *n.* a thin, pointed spike used to show a position on a scale or gauge. ♦ *I stopped at a gas station because the needle was on "empty."* ♦ *If the needle goes into the red zone, you're running low on oil.* **4.** *n.* the stylus of a phonograph that rides in the groove of the phonograph record. ♦ *The needle of my great-grandmother's record player was the needle of a cactus.* ♦ *The needle skipped when I bumped the phonograph.* **5.** *n.* a long, thin, sharply pointed leaf of a pine tree. ♦ *The sharp pine needles poked at my bare arms.* ♦ *Thousands of pine needles fell into our gutters.* **6.** *n.* a long, thin, sharp thorn as found on a cactus. ♦ *I bumped into a cactus and got my arm full of needles.* ♦ *Can you believe that a cactus needle was really used on early record players?* **7.** *tv.* to annoy someone. ♦ *Mary needled me with insulting comments.* ♦ *Bill needled me until I agreed to go to the store with him.*

needless ['nid ləs] *adj.* not needed; not required; not necessary. (Adv: *needlessly.*) ♦ *Many television programs contain a lot of needless violence.* ♦ *Although your concern is appreciated, it's really needless.*

needlework ['nid l wɚk] *n.* crafts that are done with a needle, such as sewing and embroidery. (No plural form in this sense.) ♦ *My grandma sold her needlework at the county fair.* ♦ *Needlework is a quiet, relaxing hobby.*

needn't ['nid nt] *cont.* "need not." ♦ *You needn't leave on my account.* ♦ *Anne needn't go to the store, because I've already gone.*

needy ['nid i] **1.** *adj.* [of someone] very poor; [of someone] needing the basic things in life. (Adv: *needily.* Comp: *needier;* sup: *neediest.*) ♦ *My church distributes food and clothing to needy people.* ♦ *The needy child begged for a dollar.* **2.** *n.* people who are ①. (No plural form in this sense. Treated as plural.) ♦ *The needy are really suffering in this cold weather.* ♦ *The charity distributes food and clothing to the needy.*

nefarious [nə 'fɛr i əs] *adj.* evil; wicked. (Adv: *nefariously.*) ♦ *Two nefarious generals assassinated the country's leader.* ♦ *The evil prince laid a nefarious plot for overthrowing the king.*

negate [nə 'get] *tv.* to make something null; to make something void; to make something ineffective. ♦ *Real-*

izing her mistake, the mayor negated her previous statements. ♦ *The new law negated the possibility of a reduction in taxes.*

negative ['nɛg ə tɪv] **1.** *adj.* meaning 'not' or 'no'; expressing 'not' or 'no'; showing refusal or denial. (Adv: *negatively.*) ♦ *When I asked Billy if he broke the window, he gave me a negative answer.* ♦ *Anne's negative response to my question surprised me.* **2.** *adj.* not positive; the opposite of positive; lacking something that makes a thing positive. (Adv: *negatively.*) ♦ *I don't like being around John because of his negative attitude.* ♦ *The critic's negative review of the movie caused people to avoid seeing it.* **3.** *adj.* fewer than zero; minus; below the number zero. ♦ *I could not write you a check because my account balance was negative.* ♦ *The temperature outdoors is a negative number!* **4.** *adj.* cynical; not optimistic; having a sad or gloomy outlook. (Adv: *negatively.*) ♦ *My depressing roommate has a very negative view of the world.* ♦ *Your negative approach to your problems is self-defeating.* **5.** *adj.* showing that the things that cause a certain disease or condition are not present. (Adv: *negatively.*) ♦ *John was happy about the negative results of his medical tests.* ♦ *The results of Jane's diabetes test were negative.* **6.** *adj.* [of some part of an electrical circuit] lower in electrical charge than other points in the same circuit, allowing electrical energy to flow from other parts of the circuit. (Adv: *negatively.*) ♦ *I connected the wire to the negative terminal.* ♦ *There is a negative charge right here at this point in the circuit.* **7.** *n.* a word or statement that means 'not' or 'no.' ♦ *The defendant responded with short negatives.* ♦ *The answer to my question was a negative—no matter whom I asked.* **8.** *n.* a piece of photographic film having dark and light reversed or colors reversed. ♦ *I made copies of the photo from its negative.* ♦ *Please handle the negatives by their edges.* **9.** *n.* a disadvantage; a negative quality. ♦ *I examined the positives and negatives before making decisions.* ♦ *I have a nice apartment, but the lack of parking is a big negative.*

neglect [nə 'glɛkt] **1.** *tv.* not to take care of someone or something; not to pay attention to someone or something; to ignore someone or something. ♦ *My flowers died because I neglected them.* ♦ *The irresponsible parents neglected their children.* **2. neglect to** *iv.* + *inf.* to forget to do something; to fail to do something. ♦ *I neglected to go to the bank today, so I'll go tomorrow.* ♦ *My plants died because I neglected to water them.* **3.** *n.* negligence; the lack of taking care of someone or something; a lack of paying attention to someone or something. (No plural form in this sense.) ♦ *The crumbling old house showed many signs of neglect.* ♦ *The state charged the irresponsible parents with neglect.*

neglected [nə 'glɛk tɪd] *adj.* not paid attention to; not taken care of; ignored; forgotten. (Adv: *neglectedly.*) ♦ *The foster family took care of neglected children.* ♦ *My neglected lawn turned yellow from a lack of water.*

negligence ['nɛg lɪ dʒəns] *n.* the lack of taking care of someone or something; a lack of attention to someone or something. (No plural form in this sense.) ♦ *The parents of the starving child were charged with negligence.* ♦ *Because of the store's negligence, Mary slipped on the wet floor and broke her hip.*

negligent ['nɛg lɪ dʒənt] *adj.* not taking care of someone or something; not paying attention to someone or something; forgetting to do something. (Adv: *negligently.*) ♦ *The negligent parents' child was placed in a foster home.* ♦ *Mary sued the negligent store owner after she was injured by the falling ceiling tile.*

negligible ['nɛg lɪ dʒə bəl] *adj.* hardly noticeable; very small; insignificant. (Adv: *negligibly.*) ♦ *I only owed the government a negligible amount of tax money.* ♦ *The difference between the two products is negligible.*

negotiable [nə 'go ʃə bəl] **1.** *adj.* able to be negotiated; able to be changed. (Adv: *negotiably.*) ♦ *I'm selling my TV for $100, but the price is negotiable.* ♦ *The contractor said that his bid was negotiable.* **2.** *adj.* able to be exchanged for cash or transferred to another owner. (Adv: *negotiably.*) ♦ *This check is negotiable at any bank in the country!* ♦ *These bonds are negotiable at any bank.*

negotiate [nə 'go ʃi et] **1.** *iv.* to discuss the matters that need to be settled before reaching an agreement. ♦ *Bob negotiated with his boss for a higher salary.* ♦ *The striking union agreed to negotiate with management.* **2.** *tv.* to make an agreement through negotiation. ♦ *The union and management negotiated a new contract.* ♦ *The actress negotiated a large raise.* **3.** *tv.* to move around or through a route successfully. ♦ *The running student was not able to negotiate the turn and slipped and fell.* ♦ *The huge ship negotiated the curve around the dock and headed out to sea.*

negotiation [nə go ʃi 'e ʃən] **1.** *n.* the process of negotiating an agreement. (No plural form in this sense.) ♦ *The successful negotiation of a contract prevented a strike.* ♦ *Once I perfected the art of negotiation, I began to make more money.* **2. negotiations** *n.* one or more meetings arranged to discuss an agreement. ♦ *The labor negotiations lasted late into the night.* ♦ *The contract negotiations concluded without a strike.*

Negro ['ni gro] **1.** *n.* a member of the dark-skinned race originating in Africa. (Spanish and Portuguese meaning 'black.' A racial term seldom used for Americans of African descent. See black and African-American. Pl in -es.) ♦ *Most African Negroes have very dark skin.* ♦ *I prefer being called black to being called a Negro.* **2.** *adj.* <the adj. use of ①.> ♦ *We are looking for a neighborhood that includes both Negro families and Caucasian families.* ♦ *My grandfather was a graduate of a Negro college in the South.*

neigh ['ne] **1.** *n.* the noise that a horse makes; a whinny. ♦ *With a loud neigh, the horse began to gallop across the field.* ♦ *I heard the horses' frightened neighs from the burning barn.* **2.** *iv.* to make a sound characteristic of a horse. ♦ *The horse neighed when I pulled on its reins.* ♦ *During the thunderstorm, the horses neighed in the barn.*

neighbor ['ne bɚ] **1.** *n.* someone who lives very close by. ♦ *There's a fence between my yard and my neighbor's yard.* ♦ *I borrowed a cup of sugar from my neighbor.* **2.** *n.* someone who is sitting or standing next to oneself. ♦ *While waiting in line, I spoke to my neighbor about the weather.* ♦ *The airplane passenger talked with her neighbor during the flight.* **3. neighbor on** *iv.* + *prep. phr.* to border on a place; to be near some place. ♦ *Several countries neighbor on Switzerland.* ♦ *My backyard neighbors on a beautiful golf course.*

neighborhood ['ne bɚ hʊd] **1.** *n.* a residential area within a larger city or town. ♦ *Most large cities have many different kinds of neighborhoods offering places to live at all price levels.* ♦ *I live in a quiet, safe neighborhood.* **2.** *n.*

the people who live in a certain area of the city. (No plural form in this sense.) ♦ *The whole neighborhood was upset when the local park was closed.* ♦ *The entire neighborhood complained about the lack of parking.* **3. (somewhere) in the neighborhood of something** *idiom* approximately a particular measurement. (No plural form in this sense.) ♦ *I take somewhere in the neighborhood of ten pills a day for my various ailments.* ♦ *My rent is in the neighborhood of $700 per month.*

neighboring ['ne bɚ ɪŋ] *adj.* adjacent; bordering. ♦ *The city's trains extend into neighboring suburbs.* ♦ *I moved from my parents' farm to a neighboring village.*

neighborly ['ne bɚ li] *adj.* friendly; nice; kind. ♦ *I appreciated my friend's neighborly advice.* ♦ *As a neighborly gesture, I shoveled the snow from the sidewalk of the house next door.*

neither ['ni ðɚ] **1.** *adj.* not either; not one person or thing nor the other; not either of two things or people. ♦ *Mary and Susan both own dogs. Neither woman owns a cat.* ♦ *Fido and Rex played in the park. Neither dog wanted to go home.* **2.** *pron.* not either; not either of two. (Treated as singular.) ♦ *Mary and Susan both own dogs. Neither owns a cat.* ♦ *John and Bill saw a new movie. Neither of them liked it.* **3.** *conj.* not. (Used before a sequence of two nouns connected by nor.) ♦ *Neither Susan nor Mary owns a cat.* ♦ *Neither snow nor rain will prevent me from coming to visit you.* **4. neither does someone** *idiom* [does] not either. (*Mary does not either* is the same as *Neither does Mary*. Note the order of words in the phrase.) ♦ *Susan does not own a cat, and neither does Mary.* ♦ *Bill doesn't want to see a movie tonight, and neither do I.* **5. neither fish nor fowl** *idiom* not any recognizable thing; not one identifiable thing or any other identifiable thing. ♦ *The vehicle that they drove up in was neither fish nor fowl. It looked like a boat with wheels.* ♦ *This television program does not entertain or inform. It is neither fish nor fowl.* **6. neither hide nor hair** *idiom* no sign or indication (of someone or something). ♦ *We could find neither hide nor hair of him. I don't know where he is.* ♦ *John came and went, leaving neither hide nor hair.*

nemesis ['nɛm ə sɪs] *n.* [someone's] serious problem or barrier; someone who is one's enemy, rival, or opponent. ♦ *Advanced algebra was my nemesis in high school.* ♦ *The general fought his nemesis on the battlefield.*

neon ['ni ɑn] **1.** *n.* a colorless gas that glows when electricity is passed through it. (No plural form in this sense.) ♦ *Glass tubes, bent into any imaginable shape, can be filled with neon to make brightly lighted signs.* ♦ *The neon escaped from the cracked glass tube.* **2.** *n.* decorative lighting using glass tubes filled with ①. (No plural form in this sense.) ♦ *At night in Las Vegas, the neon is blinding.* ♦ *Install some neon so the customers can find your store at night.* **3.** *adj.* [of light or lighting] using ②. ♦ *The neon lights glowed in the misty night.* ♦ *A neon sign saying* OPEN *hung in the window.* **4.** *adj.* [of a color] very bright to the point of glowing. ♦ *Neon yellow is a good color to wear if you want to be visible in a crowd.* ♦ *Sue's fingernails were painted a lovely neon pink.*

neophyte ['ni ə faɪt] *n.* someone who is new at doing something; a novice. ♦ *The clerk was a neophyte and accidentally locked the cash register.* ♦ *The experienced workers made the neophytes do the hard work.*

Nepal [nə 'pɔl] See Gazetteer.

nephew ['nɛf ju] *n.* the son of one's brother or sister; the son of one's spouse's brother or sister. ♦ *I became an uncle when my nephew was born.* ♦ *I raised my nephew when my brother and sister-in-law died.*

nepotism ['nɛp ə tɪz əm] *n.* the practice of employing one's relatives. (No plural form in this sense.) ♦ *The mayor's son got a city job through nepotism.* ♦ *The newspaper accused the mayor's office of nepotism.*

Neptune ['nɛp tun] **1.** *n.* the eighth planet in our solar system, between Uranus and Pluto. ♦ *Because of Pluto's odd orbit, Neptune is sometimes farther from the sun than Pluto.* ♦ *The largest moon of Neptune is called Triton.* **2.** *n.* the Roman god of the sea. ♦ *The Greek god that is the equivalent of Neptune is called Poseidon.* ♦ *Neptune is often shown carrying a three-pronged spear, or trident.*

nerve ['nɚv] **1.** *n.* a fiber in the body that carries messages to and from the brain. ♦ *The nerves in one's fingertips are very sensitive.* ♦ *The optic nerve transmits images from the eye to the brain.* **2.** *n.* courage; bravery. (No plural form in this sense.) ♦ *The fireman steeled his nerve and saved the young child.* ♦ *The soldiers were congratulated for their nerve in battle.* **3. nerves** *n.* one's temperament; one's ability to cope with one's surroundings. ♦ *After a hard day at work, my nerves are really frayed.* ♦ *John sometimes takes medication to calm his nerves.* **4. get on someone's nerves** *idiom* to irritate someone. ♦ *Please stop whistling. It's getting on my nerves.* ♦ *All this arguing is getting on their nerves.* **5. get up enough nerve (to do something)** *idiom* to get brave enough to do something. ♦ *I could never get up enough nerve to sing in public.* ♦ *I'd do it if I could get up enough nerve, but I'm shy.* **6. have got a lot of nerve; have got some nerve** *idiom* to have a lot of gall and impudence. ♦ *You've got a lot of nerve to phone me so late at night!* ♦ *You've got some nerve to treat me so rudely!* **7. of all the nerve** *idiom* how shocking; how dare [someone]. ♦ *How dare you talk to me that way! Of all the nerve!* ♦ *Imagine anyone coming to a formal dance in jeans. Of all the nerve!*

nervous ['nɚv əs] **1.** *adj.* apprehensive; worried; jumpy; edgy. (Adv: *nervously.*) ♦ *I become nervous when I drink too much coffee.* ♦ *I told the nervous job applicant to relax.* **2.** *adj.* of or about the nerves. ♦ *The drug affected my central nervous system.* ♦ *In her biology class, Jane studied the nervous responses of rats.*

nervousness ['nɛrv əs nəs] *n.* worry; apprehension. (No plural form in this sense.) ♦ *Mary's nervousness about her job interview gave her a headache.* ♦ *My hands began to shake from nervousness.*

-ness [nəs] *suffix* <a form that can be added freely to adjectives to create a noun with a parallel meaning.> (Examples: *aggressiveness, aimlessness, alertness, alikeness, aloneness, aloofness, amorousness, amorphousness, ancientness, apartness, attractiveness, audaciousness, auspiciousness, awareness, awesomeness, bitterness, blackness, bleakness, blindness, boldness, brashness, evasiveness, evenness, exactness, expressiveness, fairness, gentleness, giddiness, gladness, gloominess, goodness, greatness, nakedness, nearness, nearsightedness, neatness, negativeness, resentfulness, resourcefulness, responsiveness, restlessness, thickness, thinness, thoughtfulness, thoughtlessness, thriftiness,* *wickedness, willingness, worthiness, worthlessness, wretchedness.*)

nest ['nɛst] **1.** *n.* a structure made of twigs that is built by a bird as a shelter for its eggs and that is typically rounded and bowl-shaped. ♦ *The bird brought a worm to the baby birds in the nest.* ♦ *I saw three blue eggs in the robin's small nest.* **2.** *n.* a place where certain animals live with their young. ♦ *As I approached the alligator's nest, the mother tried to attack me.* ♦ *I sprayed the hornets' nest with insecticide.* **3.** *iv.* to build or live in ① or ②. ♦ *A robin nested in a tree in my backyard.* ♦ *A swarm of wasps nested on the roof of my house.* **4. foul one's own nest** *idiom* to harm one's own interests; to bring disadvantage upon oneself. ♦ *He tried to discredit a fellow worker but just succeeded in fouling his own nest.* ♦ *The boss really dislikes Mary. She certainly fouled her own nest when she spread those rumors about him.*

nest egg ['nɛst ɛg] *n.* money that is saved for a certain reason; savings. ♦ *I spent my nest egg on a new car.* ♦ *Jane puts some money from each paycheck into a nest egg.*

nestle ['nɛs əl] **1. nestle (down)** *iv.* (+ *adv.*) to snuggle; to rest somewhere while holding someone or something closely. ♦ *Mary nestled down with her husband in front of the fireplace.* ♦ *I nestled in my chair and got ready to watch television.* **2. nestle against** *tv.* + *prep. phr.* to cause someone or something to press against something. ♦ *The mother mouse nestled her warm body against her tiny offspring.* ♦ *Anne nestled her nursing baby against her breast.*

net ['nɛt] **1.** *n.* a mesh fabric made of string, wire, or cord. ♦ *A butterfly net is a scoop-shaped net attached to a long handle, used for catching butterflies.* ♦ *The net on a tennis court separates the two players.* **2.** *n.* the Internet. (Not a proper noun, but usually capitalized.) ♦ *I found the recipe for this pie on the Net.* ♦ *I spend three hours a day surfing the Net.* **3.** *adj.* remaining after all factors have been considered, deducted, or added, as with weight, income, cost, effect, results, outcome, etc. ♦ *Income tax is based on net income.* ♦ *A product's net weight doesn't include its packaging.* **4.** *tv.* to catch something with ①. ♦ *I netted three lovely butterflies for my collection.* ♦ *I scooped my net in my fishbowl and netted the sick goldfish.* **5.** *tv.* to catch or capture something, as with ①. (Figurative on ①.) ♦ *The cops netted four dangerous criminals over the weekend.* ♦ *Bob netted a part in the play he tried out for.* **6.** *tv.* to earn an amount of money, after taxes have been taken away; to earn as profit. ♦ *The book netted the author about $2,000 each year.* ♦ *My lawyer netted over $500,000 last year.*

Netherlands, the [ðə 'nɛ ðɚ ləndz] See Gazetteer.

network ['nɛt wɚk] **1.** *n.* a pattern of crossing lines, paths, or similar structures; a system of lines, paths, or similar structures that are interconnected. ♦ *The subway map showed the network of rail lines in detail.* ♦ *The electrician fixed the network of wires in the control panel.* **2.** *n.* a series of computers connected to each other and the systems that connect them. ♦ *I couldn't do any work because the network was down.* ♦ *Anne sent a piece of e-mail to everyone on the network.* **3.** *n.* a group of radio or television stations that broadcast the same programs. ♦ *Which network is that show on?* ♦ *Bob and Bill tried to raise enough money to establish a new network.* **4.** *n.* a collection of friends or business contacts. ♦ *I have a large network of friends, and we help each other when there are problems.* ♦ *Jane's network of business contacts helped her find a new job.* **5.** *iv.* to make social and business contacts; to talk with people in one's area of business or interest. ♦ *At the party, the actor networked with producers and directors.* ♦ *At the conference, I networked with important people in my field.*

neural ['nʊr əl] *adj.* of or about nerves. (Adv: *neurally.*) ♦ *This drug damages neural connections in rats.* ♦ *I suffered a lot of neural damage in a car accident.*

neuritis [nʊ 'raɪ tɪs] *n.* a painful inflammation of a nerve. (No plural form in this sense.) ♦ *My reflexes were weakened because of neuritis.* ♦ *John took some medicine to numb the pain of his neuritis.*

neurological [nʊ rə 'lɑdʒ ɪ kəl] *adj.* of or about neurology; of or about the science and study of nerves. (Adv: *neurologically* [...ɪk li].) ♦ *The biologist conducted a neurological study on rats.* ♦ *The doctors discovered a neurological basis for John's violent tremors.*

neurologist [nʊ 'rɑl ə dʒəst] *n.* a scientist or doctor who is trained in neurology. ♦ *I went to see a neurologist because I couldn't stop shaking.* ♦ *The neurologist treated my nervous twitch.*

neurology [nʊ 'rɑl ə dʒi] *n.* the science and study of the nerves and the nervous system. (No plural form in this sense.) ♦ *I studied neurology to learn about the structure of nerves.* ♦ *My psychiatrist specialized in neurology in medical school.*

neuroses [nʊ 'ro siz] pl of neurosis.

neurosis [nʊ 'ro sɪs] *n., irreg.* one of a number of mild mental disorders, such as obsessions and irrational fears. (Pl: neuroses.) ♦ *My psychiatrist helped me overcome my neuroses.* ♦ *Mary's always washing her hands because of a compulsive neurosis.*

neurotic [nʊ 'rɑt ɪk] **1.** *adj.* of or about a neurosis; affected by a neurosis. (Adv: *neurotically* [...ɪk li].) ♦ *Bill is neurotic about keeping his house extremely clean.* ♦ *Anne is hard to live with because of her neurotic tendencies.* **2.** *n.* someone who has a neurosis. ♦ *I had to move because my old roommate was a neurotic.* ♦ *The neurotic washed her hands compulsively.*

neuter ['nut ɚ] **1.** *adj.* neither masculine nor feminine; sexless. ♦ *Our dog was a male before his operation. Now he is neuter.* ♦ *We couldn't decide if the baby bird was male or female. We knew it wasn't neuter!* **2.** *adj.* [of a class of words] not masculine or feminine. (See gender ①.) ♦ *The German word for 'room' is neuter:* das Zimmer. ♦ *German has three genders, masculine, feminine, and neuter.* **3.** *tv.* to make someone or some creature unable to reproduce. ♦ *The veterinarian neutered our dog.* ♦ *We had our cat neutered when it turned one year old.*

neutral ['nu trəl] **1.** *adj.* not aligned with either side in a war, conflict, or argument. (Adv: *neutrally.*) ♦ *Switzerland remained neutral during World War II.* ♦ *The conflict was resolved with the help of a neutral mediator.* **2.** *adj.* at neither extreme; in the middle of a scale. (Adv: *neutrally.*) ♦ *A neutral electrical charge is neither positive nor negative.* ♦ *A neutral political viewpoint is neither conservative nor liberal.* **3. in neutral** *idiom* with the shift lever of a vehicle in the position where the motor is running but is not powering the wheels or other moving parts. ♦ *The car rolled down the hill because I'd left it in neutral.* ♦ *If you are moving and in neutral, you do not have control of your vehicle.*

neutrality [nu 'træl ə ti] **1.** *n.* the quality of being neutral. (No plural form in this sense.) ♦ *Switzerland is known for its neutrality during wars.* ♦ *Because of the mediator's neutrality, she was able to help resolve the conflict.* **2.** *n.* the quality of not being at either extreme. ♦ *The senator's neutrality appealed to a wide range of voters.* ♦ *The newspaper's neutrality annoyed both groups of extremists.*

neutralize ['nu trə lɑɪz] *tv.* to cause someone or something to become neutral; to make someone or something ineffective or harmless. ♦ *I neutralized the acid in my stomach by taking an antacid.* ♦ *The leaders neutralized the conflict by signing a treaty.*

neutron ['nu trɑn] *n.* a particle in the nucleus of an atom that has no electrical charge. ♦ *Neutrons are neutral in the sense that they have neither a positive nor a negative charge.* ♦ *Carbon-14 has 6 protons and 8 neutrons.*

Nevada [nə 'væd ə] See Gazetteer.

never ['nɛv ɚ] *adv.* not ever; at no time. ♦ *Bill has never been to California.* ♦ *I will never tell anyone your secret.*

nevertheless [nɛv ɚ ðə 'lɛs] *adv.* however; in spite of that; even so. ♦ *I don't like my job; nevertheless, I go to work every day.* ♦ *Even if you miss class for a good reason, you are nevertheless responsible for the material that is discussed.*

new ['nu] **1.** *adj.* recently done, made, bought, acquired, discovered, or built; not existing or known of before. (Adv: *newly.* Comp: *newer;* sup: *newest.*) ♦ *I ate at the new restaurant that just opened on Main Street.* ♦ *The astronomer discovered a new solar system.* **2.** *adj.* the more recent of two or more things. (Comp: *newer;* sup: *newest.*) ♦ *I looked at all the magazines on the table and picked the new one.* ♦ *Make sure you're using the new manual, not the old one.* **3.** *adj.* not familiar; strange; unknown. (Adv: *newly.* Comp: *newer;* sup: *newest.*) ♦ *My assignment was difficult because the material was new to me.* ♦ *The rocket traveled to new worlds.* **4.** *adj.* different; changed. (Adv: *newly.* Comp: *newer;* sup: *newest.*) ♦ *This year, our football team has new uniforms.* ♦ *The company developed a new strategy.* **5.** *adj.* beginning again; starting over. (Adv: *newly.* Comp: *newer;* sup: *newest.*) ♦ *January 1st is the beginning of the new year.* ♦ *The new semester begins next Monday.* **6. news** See the main entry for news below. **7. new one on someone** *idiom* something that one has not heard before and that one is not ready to believe. ♦ *Bob's poverty is a new one on me. He always seems to have plenty of money.* ♦ *The firm's difficulties are a new one on me. I thought that it was doing very well.*

newborn ['nu born] **1.** *n.* an infant; a baby that has just been born. ♦ *The nurse took the newborn to the nursery.* ♦ *Susan held her newborn in her arms.* **2.** *adj.* having just been born. ♦ *The happy parents took their newborn child home.* ♦ *Billy looked at his newborn brother sleeping in the crib.*

newcomer ['nu kəm ɚ] *n.* someone who recently arrived at a certain place. ♦ *I welcomed the newcomers to the neighborhood.* ♦ *The natives resented the arrival of the foreign newcomers.*

New England ['nu 'ɪŋ glənd] *n.* the northeastern United States, specifically Maine, Vermont, New Hampshire, Massachusetts, Rhode Island, and Connecticut. ♦ *While visiting New England, I ate some excellent clam chowder.* ♦ *Boston is the largest city in New England.*

newfound ['nu fɑʊnd] *adj.* newly found; just found. ♦ *Bill took care of the newfound kittens.* ♦ *Jane's newfound happiness has made her much more pleasant.*

New Hampshire [nu 'hæmp ʃɚ] See Gazetteer.

New Jersey [nu 'dʒɚ zi] See Gazetteer.

newly ['nu li] *adv.* recently; as of late; just. ♦ *Susan fed her newly born child.* ♦ *Our newly built house was destroyed by a tornado.*

newlywed ['nu li wɛd] *n.* someone who has recently married. ♦ *The newlyweds went to Rome for their honeymoon.* ♦ *The newlyweds danced together at the reception.*

New Mexico [nu 'mɛk sɪ ko] See Gazetteer.

news ['nuz] **1.** *n.* information, particularly current information about a person or relating to a recent event. (Treated as singular. No other singular form in this sense.) ♦ *The doctor had good news to report about my test results.* ♦ *What's the latest news about the striking workers?* **2.** *n.* a television or radio program where information about recent events is broadcast. (Treated as singular.) ♦ *I usually watch the local news while eating dinner.* ♦ *They said on the news that it's supposed to rain tomorrow.* **3. break the news (to someone)** *idiom* to tell someone some important, and usually bad, ①. ♦ *The doctor had to break the news to Jane about her husband's cancer.* ♦ *I hope that the doctor broke the news gently.*

newscaster ['nuz kæst ɚ] *n.* someone who reports the news on radio or television. ♦ *The newscaster read the latest traffic report.* ♦ *The newscaster announced that the war was over.*

newsletter ['nuz lɛt ɚ] *n.* a letter or bulletin from an organization to its members or employees. ♦ *There's an article about my boss in the company newsletter.* ♦ *The chess club prints a newsletter every month.*

newspaper ['nuz pe pɚ] *n.* a daily or weekly publication consisting of news, articles, and advertisements printed on large sheets of paper. ♦ *I read the newspaper every morning while eating breakfast.* ♦ *Did you see that article in yesterday's newspaper?*

newsprint ['nuz prɪnt] **1.** *n.* the paper on which a newspaper is printed. (No plural form in this sense.) ♦ *Newsprint is thinner and cheaper than standard paper.* ♦ *Most newsprint turns yellow when it gets old.* **2.** *n.* the ink that rubs off of a newspaper onto the reader's hands. (No plural form in this sense. Informal and inexact.) ♦ *After reading the paper, my fingers were covered with newsprint.* ♦ *The new printing technique resulted in less newsprint rubbing off.*

newsstand ['nuz stænd] *n.* a place where newspapers and magazines are sold, usually a small store or a small, sheltered structure on a sidewalk. ♦ *I buy a paper at the newsstand at the train station every day.* ♦ *The city demolished the newsstand in order to widen the street.*

newsworthy ['nuz wɚ ði] *adj.* interesting or important enough to be mentioned as news. ♦ *The TV program was interrupted for a newsworthy announcement.* ♦ *The most* *newsworthy articles used to be placed on the front page of the newspaper.*

newt ['nut] *n.* an amphibious salamander with four legs and a tail. ♦ *Newts spend some of their time in the water and some on land.* ♦ *The children bought a newt to put in their aquarium.*

New Testament ['nu 'tɛs tə mənt] *n.* the second of the two parts of the Christian Bible, including the story of the life and teachings of Jesus Christ. ♦ *The New Testament includes the gospels of Matthew, Mark, Luke, and John.* ♦ *The minister quoted from the scriptures of the New Testament.*

New World ['nu 'wɚld] *n.* the Western Hemisphere; North and South America. ♦ *Europeans exploited the resources of the New World.* ♦ *When Columbus encountered the New World, millions of people were already living there.*

New Year's Day [nu jɪrz 'de] *n.* the first day of a calendar year; January 1. ♦ *New Year's Day is a federal holiday in the United States.* ♦ *Most people do not work on New Year's Day.*

New Year's Eve ['nu jɪrz 'iv] *n.* December 31, the evening before the new year begins. ♦ *At 11:59 P.M. on New Year's Eve, everyone at the party got ready to welcome the new year.* ♦ *Billy's parents let him stay up until midnight on New Year's Eve.*

New York ['nu 'jork] See Gazetteer.

New Zealand [nu 'zi lənd] See Gazetteer.

next ['nɛkst] **1.** *adj.* following; nearest in sequence after; soonest after. ♦ *The conductor announced the next stop.* ♦ *The next day after Monday is Tuesday.* **2.** *adj.* adjacent. ♦ *Your friend is waiting for you in the next room.* ♦ *The people who live in the next house are very friendly.* **3. next to someone or something** *phr.* near to someone or something; adjacent to someone or something. ♦ *I live next to a bank.* ♦ *Please sit next to me.* **4.** *adv.* at the soonest time after now; in the nearest place or position after this one. ♦ *What shall we do next?* ♦ *The math books are here. Put the books on physics next.* **5. next door** *phr.* in or at the house or apartment next to one's own. (Hyphenated before a nominal.) ♦ *I will be next door if you need me.* ♦ *I went next door to borrow a shovel.* **6. next-door neighbor** *idiom* the person living in the house or apartment closest to one's own. ♦ *My next-door neighbor came over to borrow a shovel.* ♦ *I will be visiting our next-door neighbor if you need me.* **7. next of kin** *idiom* someone's closest living relative or relatives. ♦ *The police notified the dead man's next of kin.* ♦ *My next of kin lives 800 miles away.*

nibble ['nɪb əl] **1.** *n.* a small bite of something; a little taste of something. ♦ *I tried a nibble of the cherry pie.* ♦ *A mouse has taken a nibble out of the piece of cheese.* **2.** *iv.* to eat only a tiny bit. ♦ *Stop nibbling and eat your dinner.* ♦ *Bob stood in front of the refrigerator and nibbled.* **3. nibble at** *iv.* + *prep. phr.* to take tiny bites of something; to bite at something gently. ♦ *The bird nibbled at the breadcrumbs.* ♦ *John nibbled at his vegetables.* **4.** *tv.* to eat a tiny bite of something; to eat something in tiny bites; to bite something gently with tiny bites. ♦ *The puppy nibbled its food.* ♦ *I nibbled a snack before dinner.*

Nicaragua [nɪk ə 'rɑg wə] See Gazetteer.

nice ['nɑɪs] **1.** *adj.* pleasant; agreeable; enjoyable. (Adv: *nicely.* Comp: *nicer;* sup: *nicest.*) ♦ *The weather was nice, so I went to the beach.* ♦ *My friends and I had a nice time at the park.* **2.** *adj.* kind; friendly; considerate. (Adv: *nicely.* Comp: *nicer;* sup: *nicest.*) ♦ *My neighbors are very nice people.* ♦ *It was nice of you to care for my dog when I was on vacation.* **3.** *adj.* good; clever; well done. (Informal. Adv: *nicely.* Comp: *nicer;* sup: *nicest.*) ♦ *Bill earned a nice sum at his last job.* ♦ *That was a nice dive!* **4. nice and some quality** *idiom* enough of some quality; adequately; sufficiently. ♦ *It is nice and cool this evening.* ♦ *I think your steak is nice and done now and probably overcooked.*

nicely ['nɑɪs li] **1.** *adv.* done in a pleasing manner; pleasantly done. (Before an adjective derived from the past participle of a verb.) ♦ *Your apartment is nicely decorated.* ♦ *I am glad to say that my steak is nicely cooked.* **2.** *adv.* in a nice way; in a friendly way. (After a verb of action.) ♦ *My neighbors smiled nicely when I waved to them.* ♦ *The class applauded nicely after each student's speech.*

nicety ['nɑɪs ə ti] *n.* a fine detail; a delicate distinction. (Often plural.) ♦ *The deluxe hotel suite features many luxurious niceties.* ♦ *The decorator emphasized the niceties of his design for the living room.*

niche ['nɪtʃ] **1.** *n.* a shallow hollow in a wall with a flat surface where a statue or object of art can be placed. (From French.) ♦ *I placed a small vase of flowers in the niche in the hallway.* ♦ *A tiny fountain splashed merrily in a marble niche by the stairway.* **2.** *n.* a job or situation that suits someone well. (Figurative on ①.) ♦ *John found his niche in radio broadcasting.* ♦ *Jane created her own niche at the marketing firm.*

nick ['nɪk] **1.** *n.* a small dent or chip on the surface of something. ♦ *John noticed a small nick in his car door.* ♦ *I painted over the nicks in the wall.* **2.** *tv.* to put a small dent or chip on the surface of something. ♦ *I accidentally nicked someone's car door in the parking lot.* ♦ *I nicked the edge of the marble table when I dropped a plate.*

nickel ['nɪk əl] **1.** *n.* a metallic element that does not rust easily. (No plural form in this sense.) ♦ *Nickel is often mixed with other metals to make them stronger.* ♦ *The coin called a nickel is made of nickel and copper.* **2.** *n.* a U.S. coin worth five cents. ♦ *Two nickels make a dime. Five nickels make a quarter.* ♦ *I bought candy from the vending machine with nickels.*

nickname ['nɪk nem] **1.** *n.* an alternate, familiar, or intimate name for someone or something. ♦ *Susan's nickname is Susie.* ♦ *There are five Johns in my class, so each of them uses a nickname.* **2.** *tv.* to give someone, something, or some place ①. ♦ *Anne was nicknamed "Doodles" by her older brother.* ♦ *The students nicknamed the smoking lounge "Nicotine Alley."*

nicotine ['nɪk ə tin] *n.* a toxic substance found in tobacco. (No plural form in this sense.) ♦ *Nicotine is used to make poisons for killing insects.* ♦ *It's hard to stop smoking because nicotine is addictive.*

niece ['nis] *n.* the daughter of one's brother or sister; the daughter of one's spouse's brother or sister. ♦ *I raised my niece when my sister and her husband died.* ♦ *Since I have many brothers and sisters, I also have many nieces and nephews.*

Nigeria [nɑɪ 'dʒɪr i ə] See Gazetteer.

night ['nɑɪt] **1.** *n.* the [dark] time between sunset and sunrise. (No plural form in this sense.) ♦ *I went to see a movie last night.* ♦ *Night is very dark in the forest.* **2.** *n.* the time between sunset and midnight. ♦ *Mary studied late into the night and on into the morning hours.* ♦ *This night is over at midnight, the time that morning starts.* **3.** *n.* a specific ① or ② when something happens or is planned. ♦ *The Broadway musical's opening night was postponed for a week.* ♦ *This is my night to work late.* **4.** *n.* a unit of measure based on two or more nights ① and the period of time between them. ♦ *Five nights later, we went to Rome.* ♦ *The newlyweds honeymooned in Paris for six nights.* **5. nights** *adv.* every night; during every night; only at night. ♦ *John works nights and sleeps days.* ♦ *This subway line operates both days and nights.* **6.** *adj.* happening during ① or ②. ♦ *I have to work the night shift this week.* ♦ *I took a night flight to London and arrived in time for breakfast.* **7. at night** *phr.* during ①. ♦ *Most people sleep at night.* ♦ *Mary studies at night.*

nightcap ['nɑɪt kæp] *n.* an alcoholic drink taken as the last one of the night. ♦ *My host offered me a nightcap before I left the party.* ♦ *I drank a nightcap as I watched the late show on TV.*

nightclub ['nɑɪt kləb] *n.* a bar open at night where there is entertainment, dancing, performance, etc. ♦ *I went dancing with my friends at a nightclub downtown.* ♦ *You have to be 21 to get into this nightclub.*

nightfall ['nɑɪt fɔl] *n.* the time after sunset; dusk; the start of night. (No plural form in this sense.) ♦ *At nightfall, there was a beautiful meteor shower.* ♦ *Susan's parents told her to be home by nightfall.*

nightgown ['nɑɪt gɑʊn] *n.* an item of clothing like a dress, usually for women, that is worn in bed. ♦ *Anne bought a new nightgown for her honeymoon.* ♦ *Susan put on a nightgown after her evening bath.*

nightingale ['nɑɪt n gel] *n.* a kind of European bird, the male of which sings beautifully during the night. ♦ *I was awakened by a nightingale that sang outside my bedroom window.* ♦ *I listened to the nightingale's beautiful song.*

night job ['nɑɪt dʒɑb] *n.* a job that requires work at night rather than in the daytime. ♦ *Bill has both a night job and a day job.* ♦ *I work at a night job part-time to make enough money to live.*

nightlife ['nɑɪt lɑɪf] *n.* entertainment and social activities that take place during the night. (No plural form in this sense.) ♦ *There's not much nightlife in that small town.* ♦ *New York City has a very vibrant, diverse nightlife.*

nightly ['nɑɪt li] **1.** *adv.* every night; each night; during every night. ♦ *This bar is open nightly until 2 A.M.* ♦ *The musician performed nightly at the club.* **2.** *adj.* happening every night. ♦ *Billy's nightly bouts of coughing worried his parents.* ♦ *I watch the nightly news on television to find out what has happened during the day.*

nightmare ['nɑɪt mɛr] **1.** *n.* a frightening dream. ♦ *I awoke screaming from a horrible nightmare.* ♦ *I didn't sleep well last night because I kept having bad nightmares.* **2.** *n.* a real event that is frightening or awful. (Figurative on ①.) ♦ *The terrible hurricane was a nightmare for the coastal towns.* ♦ *Getting information from the federal government can be a nightmare.*

nighttime ['nɑɪt tɑɪm] **1.** *n.* the time during the night; the time from after sunset until sunrise. (No plural form in this sense.) ♦ *John works as a security guard during the nighttime.* ♦ *Bats are most active in the nighttime.* **2.** *adj.* happening during the night. ♦ *The young boys went to the pond for a nighttime swim.* ♦ *Nighttime strolls through city parks can be dangerous.*

nimble ['nɪm bəl] *adj.* able to move quickly and easily; agile. (Adv: *nimbly.* Comp: *nimbler;* sup: *nimblest.*) ♦ *The nimble gymnast did a triple flip.* ♦ *The nimble runner vaulted over the hurdles.*

nine ['nɑɪn] **1.** 9. See four for senses and examples. **2. on cloud nine** *idiom* very happy. ♦ *When I got my promotion, I was on cloud nine.* ♦ *When the check came, I was on cloud nine for days.*

nineteen ['nɑɪn 'tin] 19. See four for senses and examples.

nineteenth ['nɑɪn 'tinθ] 19th. See fourth for senses and examples.

ninetieth ['nɑɪn ti əθ] 90th. See fourth for senses and examples.

ninety ['nɑɪn ti] 90. See forty for senses and examples.

ninth ['nɑɪnθ] 9th. See fourth for senses and examples.

nip ['nɪp] **1.** *n.* a small drink of something, especially something alcoholic. ♦ *Could I have a nip of your brandy?* ♦ *I'd like a nip of scotch, please.* **2.** *n.* to pinch or bite someone or something. ♦ *The small dog nipped my ankle.* ♦ *The pliers nipped me because my fingers were too close to the jaws.* **3.** *tv.* to remove something by pinching or biting. ♦ *The gardener nipped the dead leaves from the flowers.* ♦ *The dog nipped the cover off the baseball.* **4. nip and tuck** *idiom* almost even; almost tied. ♦ *The horses ran nip and tuck for the first half of the race. Then my horse pulled ahead.* ♦ *In the football game last Saturday, the two teams were nip and tuck throughout the game.* **5. nip in the air** *idiom* a cold feeling; coldness. ♦ *I felt a nip in the air when I opened the window.* ♦ *There's more of a nip in the air as winter approaches.*

nipple ['nɪp əl] **1.** *n.* the tip of the breast, which, in females, gives milk. ♦ *Susan placed her nipple in her baby's mouth.* ♦ *The kittens lined up along their mother's row of nipples.* **2.** *n.* a rubber cap on a baby's milk bottle that controls the release of a liquid through a hole. (Figurative on ①.) ♦ *I washed the nipple after I dropped it on the floor.* ♦ *The baby cried when the nipple fell from its mouth.*

nitpick ['nɪt pɪk] *iv.* to find fault [with someone or something] by focusing on very small and unimportant details. ♦ *Sue is always nitpicking and making herself an annoyance.* ♦ *I don't mean to nitpick, but your collar looks worn.*

nitpicking ['nɪt pɪk ɪŋ] *n.* finding fault [with someone or something] by focusing on very small and unimportant details. (No plural form in this sense.) ♦ *My boss's nitpicking upsets all of my coworkers.* ♦ *I moved out because I couldn't stand my roommate's nitpicking.*

nitrogen ['nɑɪ trə dʒən] *n.* a gaseous element that is the main component of air. (No plural form in this sense.) ♦ *Most fertilizers are very rich in nitrogen.* ♦ *All living tissues contain nitrogen.*

nitwit ['nɪt wɪt] *n.* an idiot; someone who is foolish or stupid. ♦ *What nitwit put the ice cream in the refrigerator instead of the freezer?* ♦ *Stop being such a nitwit and start being serious!*

nix ['nɪks] *tv.* to put a stop to something; to end something; to reject something. ♦ *The president nixed the proposal.* ♦ *The producer nixed the screenwriter's script.*

no ['no] **1.** *adj.* not any; not a; not one; not any amount of. ♦ *There's no milk in the refrigerator.* ♦ *There's no reason that would compel me to support your cause.* **2.** *adv.* <a word that is used as an answer to show that one does not agree.> ♦ *"Does this dress look good on me?" "No, it doesn't."* ♦ *"It's Friday today, right?" "No, it's not. It's Thursday."* **3.** *adv.* <a word that is used to stress a negative statement.> ♦ *No, you may not go swimming today. It's too cold.* ♦ *No, Detroit is not the capital of Michigan. It's Lansing.* **4.** *n.* a negative answer. (Pl in *-s* or *-es.*) ♦ *Did I hear a no?* ♦ *The final vote was 60 nos and 40 yeses.*

nobility [no 'bɪl ə ti] **1.** *n.* privileged upper-class people, usually bearing titles given by royalty. (No plural form in this sense.) ♦ *The people who attended the event were mostly nobility.* ♦ *The king was greeted by all the nobility at the banquet.* **2.** *n.* dignity; the quality of being noble. (No plural form in this sense.) ♦ *The pastor spoke of the nobility of the deceased man.* ♦ *Because of his nobility, the diplomat was very much respected.*

noble ['nob əl] **1.** *adj.* dignified; refined; moral. (Adv: *nobly.* Comp: *nobler;* sup: *noblest.*) ♦ *The noble gentleman held the door open for me.* ♦ *Jane's offer to pay for everything was a very noble gesture.* **2.** *adj.* <the adj. use of ④.> (Adv: *nobly.* Comp: *nobler;* sup: *noblest.*) ♦ *The noble prince smiled at the dancers at the royal ball.* ♦ *Noble ladies and gentlemen entered the great hall for the banquet.* **3.** *adj.* [of a chemical element] not able to mix with other elements; [of a chemical element] not able to react with other elements. ♦ *Noble gases do not combine with other gases.* ♦ *Gold is a noble metal.* **4.** *n.* a member of the nobility. ♦ *Nowadays it is not unusual for a noble to marry a common person.* ♦ *The event at the palace was attended mostly by nobles.*

nobleman ['nob əl mən] *n., irreg.* a person who is a member of nobility. (Pl: noblemen.) ♦ *The king and queen invited the noblemen to the palace.* ♦ *The nobleman and his family lived on a large estate.*

noblemen ['nob əl mən] pl of nobleman.

nobody ['no bɑd i] **1.** *pron.* no person; no one. (No plural form in this sense.) ♦ *Nobody lives on the moon.* ♦ *Nobody likes cheese more than I do!* **2.** *n.* someone who is not important; someone who has no power. ♦ *After losing the election, the politician became a nobody.* ♦ *The reporter left the party because only nobodies were there.*

nocturnal [nɑk 'tɚ nəl] *adj.* used at night; normally awake during the night. (Adv: *nocturnally.*) ♦ *The bat is a nocturnal creature.* ♦ *John has to be nocturnal because he works nights.*

nod ['nɑd] **1.** *n.* a quick downward or up-and-down movement of the head, usually to show agreement. ♦ *Jane agreed with my suggestion with a quick nod of her head.* ♦ *My mouth was full, so I replied "yes" with a nod.* **2.** *tv.* to express something by nodding as in ③. ♦ *Jane nodded her agreement to my suggestion.* ♦ *Bill nodded yes.* **3.** *tv.* to move one's head in agreement. ♦ *Don't nod your head unless you are sure.* ♦ *Jane nodded her head in agreement.* **4.** *iv.* to move one's head down, or up and down, quickly, especially to show agreement or approval, or as a greeting. ♦ *Jane nodded when I asked her if she wanted more coffee.* ♦ *Bill nodded to indicate that he wanted to go along.* **5.** *iv.* to let one's head jerk down as one begins to fall asleep. ♦ *Everyone in the audience was beginning to nod, so the speaker finished the lecture.* ♦ *During the boring movie, I began to nod.* **6.** *iv.* [for one's head] to jerk down as one begins to fall asleep while sitting or standing. ♦ *John's head nodded as he tried to stay awake.* ♦ *My head kept nodding as I sat waiting in the doctor's office.* **7. get the nod** *idiom* to be chosen. ♦ *The boss is going to pick the new sales manager. I think Anne will get the nod.* ♦ *I got the nod for captain of the team, but I decided not to do it.*

node ['nod] **1.** *n.* a bump; a swelling; a knob. ♦ *The surface of the diseased leaf was covered with small nodes.* ♦ *The overworked singer developed nodes on his vocal cords.* **2.** See lymph.

nodule ['nɑ dʒul] *n.* a small growth; a lump; a small node. ♦ *The doctor examined the nodules on the singer's vocal cords.* ♦ *I could feel the nodules along the plant's surface.*

no-good ['no gʊd] *adj.* not good for anything; worthless. ♦ *Mr. Smith sent his no-good son out of his house.* ♦ *I threw the no-good television set in the trash.*

noise ['nɔɪz] **1.** *n.* unmusical, annoying, or unwanted sound. (No plural form in this sense.) ♦ *I study at the library because there's too much noise at home.* ♦ *Tom finds that the noise at the office keeps him from working fast enough.* **2.** *n.* instances of particular kinds of ①. ♦ *I hear noises in the attic!* ♦ *What are those noises coming from your car's engine?*

noiseless ['nɔɪz ləs] *adj.* without noise. (Adv: *noiselessly.*) ♦ *The noiseless fan circulated the air in the nursery.* ♦ *I studied in the noiseless atmosphere of the library.*

noisy ['nɔɪz i] *adj.* loud; making loud, unwanted sound. (Adv: *noisily.* Comp: *noisier;* sup: *noisiest.*) ♦ *I study in the library because my dormitory is too noisy.* ♦ *The police told everyone at the noisy party to go home.*

nomad ['no mæd] **1.** *n.* someone who does not live in one place but instead travels from place to place. ♦ *The nomads stopped at an oasis in the desert.* ♦ *Nomads can be found in some deserts.* **2.** *n.* someone who moves from town to town or from job to job. (Figurative on ①.) ♦ *Max is a nomad. He never stays in the same job for more than a year.* ♦ *The farm worker was a nomad who traveled around the country looking for work.*

nominal ['nɑm ə nəl] **1.** *n.* a noun or expression that can serve as the subject of a sentence, the direct or indirect object of a verb, or the object of a preposition. (Abbreviated *n.* here.) ♦ *The subject of a sentence is ordinarily a nominal.* ♦ *Objects of prepositions are nominals.* **2.** *adj.* functioning as ①. (Adv: *nominally.*) ♦ *Nominal constructions are found in all languages.* ♦ *"Mary's big, blue hat" is a nominal phrase.* **3.** *adj.* in name only; in theory, but not in reality. (Adv: *nominally.*) ♦ *John is a nominal member of this committee and isn't expected to do any work.* ♦ *Max is the nominal head of the company. His father, the owner, tells him what to do.* **4.** *adj.* [of a fee or charge] very small, especially as compared with what something is worth. (Adv: *nominally.*) ♦ *There's a nominal charge for parking at the beach on weekends.* ♦ *I paid a nominal fee for extra insurance when renting the car.*

nominate ['nɑm ə net] **1.** *tv.* to formally propose someone for a job or an office. ♦ *I nominate Mary for the office* *of treasurer.* ♦ *Mr. Smith nominated Ms. Jones for the job.* **2.** *tv.* to propose that someone or something receive an award. ♦ *What movies were nominated for that award in 1980?* ♦ *The board nominated Mary for the sales award for the third year in a row.*

nomination [nɑm ə 'ne ʃən] *n.* the act of nominating someone. ♦ *John's nomination of Anne was approved by the committee.* ♦ *There were three nominations for the office of president.*

nominative ['nɑm ə nə tɪv] **1.** *n.* a word in the nominative case; a word serving as the subject of a sentence or an object. (Abbreviated *n.* here.) ♦ *The pronoun* he *is a nominative.* ♦ Whom *is always an object and cannot be called a nominative.* **2.** *adj.* <the adj. use of ①.> (Adv: *nominatively.*) ♦ *The English word* he *is a nominative pronoun.* ♦ *The nominative form cannot be the object of a verb.*

nominative (case) ['nɑm ə nə tɪv 'kes] *n.* <the grammatical state of the subjects of sentences.> ♦ *A few English pronouns have a special form in the nominative case.* ♦ *Two examples of pronouns in the nominative are* he *and* I.

nominee [nɑm ə 'ni] *n.* someone who is nominated; someone who is proposed for a job, award, or office. ♦ *The manager interviewed the nominees for the job.* ♦ *The emcee announced the nominees for the award.*

non- [nɑn] *prefix* <a form meaning not that can be added freely to adjectives, giving them negative meaning.> (Not usually hyphenated. For example: *nonalcoholic, nonaligned, noncombatant, noncommissioned, noncommittal, nonconformist, noncount, nonderogatory, nondescript, nonfiction, nonflammable, nonliteral, nonlocal, nonmetallic, nonmetric, nonpartisan, nonpayment, nonplussed, nonprofessional, nonprofit, nonrestrictive, nonrigid, nonscheduled, nonsectarian, nonsmokers, nonsmoking, nonstandard, nonstick, nonstop, nontraditional, nonunion, nonviolent.*)

nonalcoholic [nɑn æl kə 'hɔl ɪk] *adj.* without alcohol; not containing alcohol. (Adv: *nonalcoholically* [...ɪk li].) ♦ *Only nonalcoholic drinks were served at the high-school dance.* ♦ *I ordered a nonalcoholic beer with my meal.*

nonaligned [nɑn ə 'lɑɪnd] *adj.* not taking sides in an argument, dispute, or war; neutral. ♦ *The nonaligned countries offered aid to the victims of the war.* ♦ *The dispute was settled by a nonaligned mediator.*

nonchalant [nɑn ʃə 'lɑnt] *adj.* indifferent; without concern. (From French. Adv: *nonchalantly.*) ♦ *The jury did not take the nonchalant witness seriously.* ♦ *The nonchalant jogger took no notice of the rain.*

noncombatant [nɑn kəm 'bæt nt] **1.** *n.* someone in the military who does not fight during wartime, such as a doctor or a chaplain. ♦ *The enemy took several noncombatants hostage.* ♦ *John served as a medical noncombatant during the war.* **2.** *n.* a civilian who does not fight during wartime. ♦ *The government rationed food and supplies to noncombatants.* ♦ *Many noncombatants worked in arms factories during the war.* **3.** *adj.* <the adj. use of ① and ②.> ♦ *Noncombatant civilians hid in their cellars during the attack.* ♦ *The noncombatant citizens prayed for their loved ones in the war.*

noncommittal [nɑn kə 'mɪt əl] *adj.* not committing oneself to an answer; not expressing an opinion; [of someone] vague. (Adv: *noncommittally.*) ♦ *My teacher was noncommittal as to the length of the final exam.* ♦ *The noncommittal candidate refused to debate the issues.*

nonconformist [nɑn kən 'for məst] **1.** *adj.* not conforming to standards of society; not following the usual way of living or thinking. ♦ *The nonconformist poet satirized American culture.* ♦ *My nonconformist friend refuses to watch television.* **2.** *n.* someone who does not conform to standards of society; someone who does not follow the usual way of living or thinking. ♦ *Ironically, many nonconformists are very similar to each other.* ♦ *The nonconformist derided popular aspects of American culture.*

noncount ['nɑn 'kɑʊnt] *adj.* [of a noun sense] not usually counted and therefore not made plural; [of a noun sense] having no plural form. (It is sometimes possible to concoct situations where nouns that are noncount can be made plural. Usually when an alleged noncount noun can be made plural, the resulting word is a different sense meaning 'different kinds, types, or instances' of what the noun refers to. Many nouns have both countable and noncount senses. In some instances, this dictionary lists only the most commonly used of the senses. In this dictionary, the notation "No plural form in this sense" marks the noun senses that are noncount. Countable nouns are not marked.) ♦ Water *is an example of a noncount noun.* ♦ *Nouns ending in* -ness *are usually noncount nouns.*

nondescript [nɑn dɪ 'skrɪpt] *adj.* plain; average; having no unusual features. (Adv: *nondescriptly.*) ♦ *Many forgettable, nondescript actors auditioned for the part.* ♦ *No one noticed the nondescript thief who stole the merchandise.*

none ['nʌn] **1.** *pron.* not one; not any; no person; no thing. ♦ *I brought ten apples to the party, but none was eaten.* ♦ *I bought some potatoes because there were none in the pantry.* **2.** *pron.* not one part; no part. ♦ *None of your bad behavior will be tolerated here!* ♦ *None of the stew was eaten.*

nonentity [nɑn 'ɛn tə ti] *n.* someone or something that is not important; someone or something that does not have power or influence. ♦ *The diplomat was insulted at being treated as a nonentity.* ♦ *The popular mayor viewed her opponents as nonentities.*

nonessential [nɑn ə 'sɛn ʃəl] *adj.* not essential; not necessary; extra. ♦ *The mountain guide told us to leave nonessential items behind.* ♦ *Please be very quiet. No nonessential talking, please.*

nonetheless [nən ðə 'lɛs] *adv.* however; nevertheless; in spite of that; still; even so. ♦ *I don't like my job; nonetheless, I go to work every day.* ♦ *Even if you miss class for a good reason, you are nonetheless responsible for the material that is discussed.*

nonexistence [nɑn ɛg 'zɪs təns] *n.* the condition of not existing. (No plural form in this sense.) ♦ *The nonexistence of a motive for the murder baffled the inspector.* ♦ *Can you prove the nonexistence of unicorns?*

nonexistent [nɑn ɛg 'zɪs tənt] *adj.* not existing; having no existence. (Adv: *nonexistently.*) ♦ *Atheists believe that God is nonexistent.* ♦ *The unicorn is a nonexistent creature.*

nonfiction [nɑn 'fɪk ʃən] *n.* writing that is not fiction; writing that concerns facts and opinions as opposed to made-up stories. (No plural form in this sense.) ♦ *The history books and biographies are in the section of the book-*

store that contains nonfiction. ♦ *Do you prefer to read fiction or nonfiction?*

nonflammable [nɑn 'flæm ə bəl] *adj.* difficult to burn; impossible to burn; not flammable. (Adv: *nonflammably.*) ♦ *Children's clothing should be made from nonflammable material.* ♦ *This tank is for hauling nonflammable liquids, such as milk.*

nonpartisan [nɑn 'pɑrt ɪ zən] **1.** *adj.* not representing a particular political party. (Adv: *nonpartisanly.*) ♦ *The political debate was sponsored by a nonpartisan organization.* ♦ *In many jurisdictions, judicial positions are nonpartisan.* **2.** *adj.* of or about a joint effort of two or more political parties. (Adv: *nonpartisanly.*) ♦ *Congress passed the nonpartisan budget proposal.* ♦ *The president signed the nonpartisan tax cut into law.*

nonplussed ['nɑn 'plʌst] *tv.* completely confused; puzzled. ♦ *The substitute teacher was nonplussed because of the students' rudeness.* ♦ *The actress was nonplussed by the reporters' intrusive questions.*

nonprofit [nɑn 'prɑf ɪt] *adj.* not making a profit; not organized or established for the purpose of making money. ♦ *Most charities are nonprofit organizations.* ♦ *Susan directed a play for a nonprofit theater company.*

nonrestrictive ['nɑn rɪ 'strɪk tɪv] *adj.* of or about a clause that serves to introduce incidental or descriptive information about a word, clause, or phrase. (The clause begins with *which* and is set off by commas, and is called a *nonrestrictive clause.* Adv: *nonrestrictively.*) ♦ *The sentence "The car, which is sitting in the driveway, belongs to my father" contains a nonrestrictive clause.* ♦ *A clause is nonrestrictive if it serves to add information and does not serve to distinguish one thing or person from another.*

nonscheduled [nɑn 'skɛ dʒld] *adj.* not scheduled; not according to a schedule or plan. ♦ *The hijacker forced the pilot to make a nonscheduled stop in Germany.* ♦ *The reporters were surprised when the president held a nonscheduled press conference.*

nonsectarian [nɑn sɛk 'tɛr i ən] *adj.* not affiliated with a certain religion. (Adv: *nonsectarianly.*) ♦ *The airport chaplain presided over a nonsectarian service.* ♦ *The president began his speech with a nonsectarian prayer.*

nonsense ['nɑn sɛns] **1.** *n.* something that does not make sense; something that is foolish. (No plural form in this sense.) ♦ *I dismissed the philosopher's rambling as nonsense.* ♦ *The crazy man stood on the subway screaming nonsense.* **2. stuff and nonsense** *idiom* foolishness; foolish talk. ♦ *Come on! Don't give me all that stuff and nonsense!* ♦ *I don't understand this book. It's all stuff and nonsense as far as I am concerned.*

nonsmoking [nɑn 'smok ɪŋ] **1.** *adj.* of or about a place where smoking is not allowed. ♦ *The law requires restaurants to provide nonsmoking sections.* ♦ *My flight to New York was nonsmoking.* **2.** *n.* the section of a public place or conveyance where smoking is not allowed. (No plural form in this sense.) ♦ *We asked to sit in nonsmoking.* ♦ *Do you want smoking or nonsmoking?*

nonstop ['nɑn 'stɑp] **1.** *adj.* without stopping; continuous; ongoing. ♦ *What airlines offer nonstop service to Berlin?* ♦ *My neighbor's nonstop chatter became annoying.* **2.** *adv.* without stopping; continuously. ♦ *This airplane flew nonstop from New York to Paris.* ♦ *At the disco, I danced nonstop until 3 A.M.*

nontraditional [nɑn trə 'dɪʃ ə nəl] *adj.* not representing a tradition. (Adv: *nontraditionally.*) ♦ *The teacher was fired for using nontraditional methods of teaching.* ♦ *My father battled cancer with nontraditional forms of treatment.*

nonunion [nɑn 'jun jən] **1.** *adj.* [of a worker] not belonging to a labor union. ♦ *Because John was a nonunion worker, he had no recourse when he was fired.* ♦ *The nonunion employees were fired when they tried to organize.* **2.** *adj.* [of an employer] not recognizing or allowing labor unions. ♦ *The nonunion factory paid its workers the minimum wage.* ♦ *Union workers picketed at the nonunion workplace.* **3.** *adj.* made by workers who are not in a labor union. ♦ *I will not buy nonunion products.* ♦ *Nonunion goods usually cost less than goods made by union workers.*

nonviolent [nɑn 'vɑɪ ə lənt] *adj.* without violence. (Adv: *nonviolently.*) ♦ *The minister led the nonviolent marchers to city hall.* ♦ *The Smiths took their children to a nonviolent family movie.*

noodle ['nud l] *n.* a strip or piece of pasta. ♦ *Boil the noodles until they're soft.* ♦ *I covered the noodles with spicy tomato sauce.*

nook ['nʊk] *n.* a corner of a room; a small room set off from a larger room. ♦ *I ate a bowl of cereal in the breakfast nook.* ♦ *I stored empty boxes in a little nook behind my office.*

noon ['nun] *n.* the time in the middle of the day between morning and afternoon; 12:00 in the daytime; midday. (No plural form in this sense.) ♦ *At noon, the church bells rang twelve times.* ♦ *People usually eat lunch around noon.*

noonday ['nun de] *adj.* happening at noon; happening in the middle of the day. ♦ *I was invited to a noonday luncheon.* ♦ *I listened to the noonday news broadcast.*

noontime ['nun tɑɪm] **1.** *n.* noon; the middle of the day. (No plural form in this sense.) ♦ *I usually eat lunch around noontime.* ♦ *Our office closes at noontime for an hour.* **2.** *adj.* happening at noon; happening in the middle of the day. ♦ *I scheduled a noontime appointment at my dentist's office.* ♦ *I ate my noontime meal in an inexpensive restaurant.*

noose ['nus] *n.* a loop tied at the end of a rope, used to trap or hang someone or something. ♦ *The executioner placed a noose around the criminal's neck.* ♦ *The cowboy threw the noose around the bull's neck.*

nor ['nor] **1.** *conj.* <a word used to connect a series of persons or things that are not options or possibilities.> ♦ *Neither Jane nor Bill was in class today.* ♦ *Neither Paraguay nor Bolivia borders an ocean.* **2. nor does someone** *idiom* not either; neither. (*Jane does not either* means the same as *nor does Jane.*) ♦ *I don't know Anne's phone number, nor does Jane.* ♦ *I don't want any sympathy, nor do I want any pity.*

norm ['norm] **1.** *n.* the normal or expected amount or quality. (No plural form in this sense.) ♦ *Eating three meals a day is considered the norm.* ♦ *The norm for a starting salary at my company is about $10 per hour.* **2.** *n.* a standard of behavior according to a society or other group. ♦ *The nonconformist ignored social norms.* ♦ *The political candidate adhered closely to all of the norms of the community.*

normal ['nor məl] **1.** *adj.* regular; typical; usual; expected. (Adv: *normally.*) ♦ *I took a detour because my normal route to work was flooded.* ♦ *Bob's weight is normal for his height.* **2.** *adj.* sane; not sick in the mind. (Adv: *normally.*) ♦ *The psychiatrist testified that the defendant was normal.* ♦ *Whoever committed this grisly crime is not normal!*

normalize ['nor mə lɑɪz] **1.** *tv.* to cause something to become normal. ♦ *These pills normalize my blood pressure.* ♦ *The diplomats attempted to normalize relations between their countries.* **2.** *iv.* to return to normal. ♦ *Living conditions normalized after the war.* ♦ *My sinus condition normalized after medical treatment.*

north ['norθ] **1.** *n.* the direction to the left of someone or something facing the rising sun. (No plural form in this sense.) ♦ *The compass indicated that we were facing north, not south.* ♦ *On most maps, north is toward the top.* **2.** *n.* the northern part of a region, country, or planet. (No plural form in this sense.) ♦ *It's cold during the winter in the north.* ♦ *The refugees fled to the mountains in the north.* **3.** *adj.* at the north; on the north side; facing the north. ♦ *If this door is locked, please use the north entrance.* ♦ *John lives on the north side of town.* **4.** *adj.* from ①. (Used especially to describe wind.) ♦ *The north wind blew cold Arctic air.* ♦ *The snowstorm was accompanied by a cold north wind.* **5.** *adv.* towards ①; into the northern part of something. ♦ *Turn north at the next stoplight.* ♦ *The front of the library faces north.*

North America [norθ ə 'mɛr ɪ kə] See Gazetteer.

North Carolina ['norθ kɛr ə 'lɑɪ nə] See Gazetteer.

North Dakota ['norθ də 'ko tə] See Gazetteer.

northeast [norθ 'ist] **1.** *n.* a direction halfway between north and east. (No plural form in this sense.) ♦ *Colorado is northeast of Arizona.* ♦ *Berlin is northeast of Paris.* **2.** *n.* an area in the northeastern part of a city, region, or country. (No plural form in this sense.) ♦ *In the U.S., the northeast is also known as New England.* ♦ *The general sent more troops to the northeast.* **3.** *adj.* in ②; toward ①; facing ①. ♦ *Chicago is in the northeast part of Illinois.* ♦ *I moved to the northeast side of town.* **4.** *adj.* [of wind] blowing from ①. ♦ *In Boston, you can smell the ocean when there's a northeast wind.* ♦ *Currently, there's a strong northeast wind at the lakefront.* **5.** *adv.* toward ①. ♦ *The road bends northeast on the other side of the river.* ♦ *The plane flew northeast from Denver to Chicago.*

northeastern [norθ 'ist ɚn] *adj.* in the northeast; toward the northeast; facing the northeast. ♦ *Vermont is one of the northeastern states.* ♦ *From the northeastern window in the kitchen, you can see the lake.*

northerly ['nor ðɚ li] **1.** *adj.* toward the north; facing the north. ♦ *I drove in a northerly direction toward Minneapolis.* ♦ *The hurricane moved on a northerly path.* **2.** *adj.* [of wind] blowing from the north. ♦ *The northerly wind blew cold Arctic air.* ♦ *A cold northerly wind is forecast for tomorrow.* **3.** *adv.* toward the north. ♦ *The plane flew northerly toward Seattle from Los Angeles.* ♦ *The tornado traveled northerly across the farmland.*

northern ['nor ðɚn] **1.** *adj.* in the north; toward the north; facing the north. ♦ *Montana shares its northern border with Canada.* ♦ *A room with northern exposure has windows on its north side.* **2.** *adj.* [of wind] blowing from the north. ♦ *The northern wind blew cold Arctic air.* ♦ *The snowstorm was accompanied by a cold northern wind.*

northerner ['nor ðɚ nɚ] *n.* someone who lives in the north part of a country, especially someone from the northern United States. ♦ *The southerner thought that northerners talked too fast.* ♦ *Northerners go to Florida in January to escape the snow.*

Northern Hemisphere ['nor ðɚn 'hɛm əs fɪr] *n.* the half of the earth that is north of the equator. ♦ *When it's spring in the Northern Hemisphere, it's fall in the Southern Hemisphere.* ♦ *Most of the world's people live in the Northern Hemisphere.*

north pole ['norθ 'pol] **1.** *n.* the point in the Arctic that is as far north as it is possible to go; the northern point on earth where the needle of a compass points straight down. ♦ *The north pole is at the northern end of earth's magnetic field.* ♦ *The north pole is exactly opposite the south pole.* **2. North Pole** *n.* the actual location of ①. ♦ *When you stand at the North Pole, all directions are south.* ♦ *There is a tradition that Santa Claus lives at the North Pole.*

North Sea ['norθ 'si] See Gazetteer.

northwest [norθ 'wɛst] **1.** *n.* a direction halfway between north and west. (No plural form in this sense.) ♦ *Utah is northwest of New Mexico.* ♦ *San Francisco is northwest of Los Angeles.* **2.** *n.* an area in the northwestern part of a region or country. (No plural form in this sense.) ♦ *The northwest includes the states of Washington, Oregon, and Idaho.* ♦ *In the U.S., fewer people live in the northwest than the northeast.* **3.** *adj.* in ②; toward ①; facing ①. ♦ *I grew up in the northwest suburbs of Detroit.* ♦ *Morocco is in the northwest part of Africa.* **4.** *adj.* [of wind] blowing from ①. ♦ *The northwest wind blew cold Arctic air.* ♦ *I biked southeast with the northwest wind at my back.* **5.** *adv.* toward ①. ♦ *The plane flew northwest from Miami to Tampa.* ♦ *Turn northwest when you get to the six-way intersection.*

northwestern [norθ 'wɛs tɚn] *adj.* in the northwest; toward the northwest; facing the northwest. ♦ *Washington is one of the northwestern states.* ♦ *Portland is in the northwestern part of Oregon.*

Norway ['nor we] See Gazetteer.

Norwegian [nor 'wi dʒ ən] **1.** *n.* a citizen or native of Norway. ♦ *My uncle is a Norwegian and likes to tell stories about his youth in Norway.* ♦ *The Norwegians eat lots of fresh fish.* **2.** *n.* the language spoken by ①. ♦ *I am studying Norwegian in school.* ♦ *Norwegian is related to English and Dutch.* **3.** *adj.* of or about Norway, ① or ②. ♦ *The Norwegian language is not hard to learn.* ♦ *I like the Norwegian people. They are friendly and speak English very well.*

nose ['noz] **1.** *n.* the structure between the mouth and the eyes in humans, being the organ used for smelling and breathing, and a similar structure in animals. ♦ *Bill's glasses slid down his nose.* ♦ *I asked for a tissue so I could blow my nose.* **2.** *n.* the sense of smell; ① used for smelling something. ♦ *This scent really appeals to my nose.* ♦ *The dog's nose led her to her puppies who had crawled away.* **3.** *n.* the front end of an airplane, a rocket, a ship, and other things. (Figurative on ①.) ♦ *There was a propeller on the nose of the small airplane.* ♦ *The captain aimed the nose of the ship between the buoys.* **4. nose through** *iv.* + *prep. phr.* to push ahead slowly with one's nose or with the front end of something. ♦ *Our boat nosed through the waves.* ♦ *The jeep nosed forward through the thick fog.* **5. nose through; nose around** *iv. + prep. phr.* to search for something that one has no business searching for; to snoop. (Figurative on ④.) ♦ *I caught my brother nosing around in my room.* ♦ *Mrs. Smith fired the maid for nosing through her closets.* **6. have a nose for something** *idiom* to have the talent for finding something. (No plural form in this sense.) ♦ *Police dogs have a good nose for drugs.* ♦ *The reporter has a nose for news.* **7. follow one's nose** *idiom* to seek the source of a smell; to go to the source of a smell. ♦ *Just follow your nose to the kitchen, and maybe Grandma will cut you a piece of pie.* ♦ *Do you want to see where the pigs are kept? Just follow your nose!* **8. follow one's nose** *idiom* to head straight in the direction that your face is pointing. ♦ *The Smith's farm is straight ahead. Just follow your nose.* ♦ *Follow your nose down the path. You can't miss seeing it.* **9. have one's nose in a book** *idiom* to be reading a book; to read books all the time. ♦ *Bob has his nose in a book every time I see him.* ♦ *His nose is always in a book. He never gets any exercise.* **10. rub someone's nose in something** *idiom* to remind someone of something one has done wrong; to remind someone of something bad or unfortunate that has happened. ♦ *When Bob failed his exam, his brother rubbed his nose in it.* ♦ *Mary knows she shouldn't have broken off her engagement. Don't rub her nose in it.* **11. thumb one's nose at someone or something** *idiom* to (figuratively or literally) make a rude gesture of disgust with one's thumb and ① at someone or something. ♦ *The tramp thumbed his nose at the lady and walked away.* ♦ *You can't just thumb your nose at people who give you trouble. You've got to learn to get along.* **12. turn one's nose up at someone or something** *idiom* to sneer at someone or something; to reject someone or something. ♦ *John turned his nose up at Anne, and that hurt her feelings.* ♦ *I never turn up my nose at dessert, no matter what it is.* **13. win by a nose** *idiom* to win by the slightest amount of difference. ♦ *I ran the fastest race I could, but I only won by a nose.* ♦ *Sally won the race, but she only won by a nose.*

nosebleed ['noz blid] *n.* a flow of blood from the nose. ♦ *The pitcher got a nosebleed when the baseball hit him in the face.* ♦ *I drove so high up into the mountains that I got a nosebleed.*

nosedive ['noz dɑɪv] **1.** *n.* a sudden drop or decline, especially the sudden fall of an airplane with the nose pointing downward. ♦ *The airplane took a nosedive after its engines failed.* ♦ *The company's stock began its nosedive when its president quit.* **2.** *iv.* to plunge with the nose pointing downward. ♦ *The airplane nosedived after its engines failed.* ♦ *The puppy nosedived off the edge of the couch.* **3.** *iv.* [for a measurement] to decline or drop suddenly. (Figurative on ②.) ♦ *The company's stock nosedived when its president was indicted.* ♦ *The employment rate nosedived during the recession.*

nostalgia [nɑ 'stæl dʒə] *n.* a desire for a time in the past; fond memories of past times. (No plural form in this sense.) ♦ *The old man remembered his college days with nostalgia.* ♦ *The popular ad campaign was based on people's nostalgia for the 1970s.*

nostril ['nɑs trəl] *n.* one of the two outside holes of the nose. ♦ *I held my nostrils closed as I dove underwater.* ♦ *We can breathe in and out through our nostrils or through our mouths.*

nosy ['noz i] *adj.* snooping; prying; rudely inquisitive. (Adv: *nosily.* Comp: *nosier;* sup: *nosiest.*) ♦ *My nosy neighbor wanted to know how much rent I paid each month.* ♦ *My brother is very nosy and always wants to know what I'm doing.*

not ['nɑt] **1.** *adv.* <a negative particle used with verbs, adverbs, participles, prepositions, nominals, and adjectives.> (Contracted to *n't.*) ♦ *We are not taking the bus to school today. We are going to walk.* ♦ *My dress is not blue. It is red.* **2.** *adv.* <a negative particle that stands for a part of a sentence that is being refused, denied, or negated.> ♦ *Are you going to the store? No, I am not [going to the store].* ♦ *Do you agree with me? No, I do not [agree with you].*

notable ['not ə bəl] **1.** *adj.* deserving to be noted; noteworthy; remarkable. (Adv: *notably.*) ♦ *One of our most notable poets won a Nobel prize.* ♦ *Frank Lloyd Wright's notable architectural achievements are known all over the world.* **2.** *n.* someone who is worth noting; someone who is remarkable. ♦ *Many notables were present for the award ceremony.* ♦ *The columnist wrote gossip about Hollywood notables.*

notaries public ['not ə riz 'pʌb lɪk] pl of notary public.

notarize ['not ə rɑɪz] *tv.* [for a notary] to certify that a signature is genuine. ♦ *You must have your signature on this document notarized for it to be official.* ♦ *The notary public notarized my will for a small fee.*

notary (public) ['not ə ri 'pʌb lɪk] *n., irreg.* someone who has the authority to certify or witness the signing of a document. (Pl: notaries public.) ♦ *The notary charged me a dollar to witness my signature.* ♦ *The banker was also licensed by the state as a notary public.*

notation [no 'te ʃən] **1.** *n.* a set of signs or symbols that is used to represent something. (No plural form in this sense.) ♦ *The mathematician explained the problem using algebraic notation.* ♦ *Can you read musical notation?* **2.** *n.* a note. ♦ *My professor made notations in the margins of my homework.* ♦ *The author wrote a personal notation in my copy of her book.*

notch ['nɑtʃ] **1.** *n.* a V-shaped cut in a surface, made for a specific reason. ♦ *The carpenter fit the wooden slats into the notch on the beam.* ♦ *The cowboy cut a notch in his gun for every wolf he killed.* **2.** *n.* a degree of quality or quantity. (Figurative on ①.) ♦ *Mary's science project was one notch above everyone else's.* ♦ *The service here is a notch below that of the restaurant across the street.* **3.** *tv.* to make a V-shaped cut for a specific reason. ♦ *The carpenter notched the wood with a chisel.* ♦ *The cowboy shot another wolf and notched his gun barrel one more time.*

note ['not] **1.** *n.* a short written message. ♦ *I left a note for my roommate on the refrigerator.* ♦ *I wrote my aunt a thank-you note for her gift.* **2.** *n.* a comment on the bottom of a page or at the end of a book that explains, clarifies, or provides the source of something in the text. (See also footnote.) ♦ *The author's notes were listed at the end of each chapter.* ♦ *A note at the bottom of the page listed the source of the quote that the author used.* **3.** *n.* a piece of paper money; a bill. ♦ *The cashier checked to make sure the $10 note wasn't counterfeit.* ♦ *I have no change, only notes and traveler's checks.* **4.** *n.* the written symbol for a specific musical tone. ♦ *The composer wrote the notes of his melody on a piece of paper.* ♦ *John wrote down the notes while I sang the tune I had made up.* **5.** *n.* a specific musical tone; one sound made by singing or playing a musical instrument. ♦ *People with perfect pitch can sing whatever note you tell them to.* ♦ *The highest note sung by the soprano was off-key.* **6.** *n.* an indication of something; a sign of something; a hint of something. ♦ *The enemy attacked at the first note of our army's weakness.* ♦ *There was a note of anger in the manager's voice.* **7. notes** *n.* information that is written down by someone while listening to a lecture or reading a book. ♦ *I studied for the exam from the notes I'd taken during class.* ♦ *Can I borrow your notes? I missed class yesterday.* **8.** *tv.* to write something as a short message. ♦ *I noted my teacher's comments in the margins of the textbook.* ♦ *The doctor noted her diagnosis on my medical records.* **9.** *tv.* to make an observation; to state something; to remark about something. ♦ *My boss noted my reluctance to work on Saturdays.* ♦ *My teacher noted that I left class early.* **10.** *tv.* to pay attention to something; to remember something. ♦ *"Note this well," my professor said, defining an important term.* ♦ *Note the way in which I thread the needle.* **11. someone of note** *idiom* a person who is famous. ♦ *We invited a speaker of note to lecture at the next meeting.* ♦ *The baseball player of note was inducted into the Hall of Fame.* **12. hit a sour note** *idiom* to signify something unpleasant. (On ⑤.) ♦ *Jane's sad announcement hit a sour note at the annual banquet.* ♦ *News of the crime hit a sour note during our holiday celebration.*

notebook ['not bʊk] *n.* a book in which notes are written. ♦ *David tore out a blank sheet of paper from his notebook.* ♦ *My notebook is full of notes from the lecture.*

noted ['not ɪd] *adj.* famous; known; renowned. ♦ *A noted scholar came to speak at our school.* ♦ *The newspaper hired a noted columnist.*

notepaper ['not pe pɚ] *n.* paper that notes, such as thank-you notes, are written on. (No plural form in this sense.) ♦ *I bought some fancy notepaper at the stationery store.* ♦ *I found matching envelopes to go with my notepaper.*

noteworthy ['not wɚ ði] *adj.* famous; worth noting; deserving to be noticed; remarkable. ♦ *A noteworthy scientist gave a lecture at our school.* ♦ *The noteworthy player won the game by hitting a home run.*

nothing ['nʌθ ɪŋ] **1.** *pron.* not one thing; not a thing. (Treated as singular.) ♦ *Nothing came for me in the mail today.* ♦ *I knew nothing about chemistry until 11th grade.* **2.** *n.* something that is without meaning; something that is not important; something that is insignificant. (No plural form in this sense.) ♦ *The labor discussions amounted to nothing, so the union went on strike.* ♦ *There's nothing worth watching on TV tonight.* **3.** *n.* zero; no amount. (No plural form in this sense.) ♦ *This watch cost me nothing. It was a gift.* ♦ *Our team lost the game ten to nothing.* **4. next to nothing** *idiom* hardly anything; almost ①. ♦ *This car's worth next to nothing. It's very rusty.* ♦ *I bought this antique chair for next to nothing.* **5. nothing but** *idiom* only; just. ♦ *Jane drinks nothing but milk.* ♦ *Dave buys nothing but expensive clothes.* **6. sweet nothings** *idiom* affectionate but unimportant or meaningless words spoken to a loved one. ♦ *Bob was whispering sweet nothings in Jane's ear when they were dancing.* ♦ *The two lovers sat in the cinema exchanging sweet nothings.* **7. want for nothing** *idiom* not to lack anything. to have everything one needs or desires. ♦ *The Smiths don't have much money, but their children seem to want for nothing.* ♦ *Lisa's husband spoils her. She wants for nothing.*

notice ['not ɪs] **1.** *tv.* to see, hear, taste, or smell someone or something; to be aware of someone or something. ♦ *Bill noticed that it was about to rain.* ♦ *The witness noticed many details about the accident.* **2.** *n.* an announcement; a sign that warns or informs; a warning. ♦ *The notice stated, in big letters, "No Trespassing."* ♦ *The store owner put up a notice about the sale.* **3.** *n.* attention; observation. (No plural form in this sense.) ♦ *The tired police officer paid no notice to the speeding car.* ♦ *Your letter escaped my notice.* **4. give (one's) notice** *idiom* to make a formal announcement that one is leaving one's job. (No plural form in this sense.) ♦ *My boss gave notice after he won the lottery.* ♦ *Jane gave her notice after she was offered a better job.* **5. sit up and take notice** *idiom* to become alert and pay attention. ♦ *A loud noise from the front of the room caused everyone to sit up and take notice.* ♦ *The company wouldn't pay any attention to my complaints. When I had my lawyer write them a letter, they sat up and took notice.*

noticeable ['not ɪs ə bəl] *adj.* able to be seen; easily seen; easily noticed. (Adv: *noticeably.*) ♦ *The surgery left a noticeable scar on my leg.* ♦ *There's been a noticeable increase in crime around here.*

notification [not ə fɪ 'ke ʃən] **1.** *n.* notifying officially; information that notifies or instructs [someone about something]. (No plural form in this sense.) ♦ *Bill received notification that his application was rejected.* ♦ *The state sent me notification that my license had expired.* **2.** *n.* an official announcement, warning, or notice. ♦ *Bill received a notification that his application was accepted.* ♦ *The state had sent me many notifications stating that my license had expired.*

notify ['not ə faɪ] *tv.* to inform someone about something; to tell someone officially about something. ♦ *The police notified Bill's parents that he'd been in an accident.* ♦ *Anne notified her landlord that her kitchen sink was broken.*

notion ['no ʃən] **1.** *n.* an opinion; a belief. ♦ *Bill's naive notions about politics surprised his friends.* ♦ *Where did you get the notion that the earth was flat?* **2.** *n.* a whim; an intention. ♦ *I have a notion to go see a movie.* ♦ *Whose silly notion was it to paint the porch floor?*

notoriety [not ə 'raɪ ə ti] *n.* the condition of being well known, sometimes for something bad. (No plural form in this sense.) ♦ *Bill gets invited to many parties because of his notoriety as a person who tells funny jokes.* ♦ *The convicted criminal's sudden notoriety surprised us all.*

notorious [no 'tor i əs] **1.** *adj.* well known for being something bad. (Adv: *notoriously.*) ♦ *Tom is one of the most notorious liars in town!* ♦ *Bill is a notorious loudmouth.* **2. notorious for** *adj.* + *prep. phr.* well known for a particular characteristic; well known for doing something. ♦ *The talk-show host was notorious for asking personal questions.* ♦ *Bill is notorious for being the first person to arrive at parties.*

noun ['naʊn] *n.* a word that refers to a person, place, thing, or idea. (See also nominal.) ♦ *The word* child *is a noun that has an irregular plural form:* children. ♦ *In the* *sentence "The cat is on the mat," the words* cat *and* mat *are nouns.*

nourish ['nɚ ɪʃ] **1.** *tv.* to feed someone or something; to give someone or something nutrients. ♦ *The children were nourished with home-cooked meals.* ♦ *The rain nourished the crops.* **2.** *tv.* to encourage something; to foster something; to support something. (Figurative on ①. Used especially with feelings and emotions.) ♦ *My mentor nourished my desire to learn.* ♦ *My grandparents nourished my respect for nature.*

nourishment ['nɚ ɪʃ mənt] *n.* food; something that nourishes (No plural form in this sense.) ♦ *The dietician made sure the orphans received proper nourishment.* ♦ *The runner ate carbohydrates after the race for nourishment.*

novel ['nɑv əl] **1.** *n.* a written story; a book of fiction. ♦ *Susan has read all of the novels written by that author.* ♦ *I read a complete novel during the airplane flight.* **2.** *adj.* new; original; not known before. ♦ *Mary had a novel idea that she wanted to patent.* ♦ *The architect won an award for his novel designs.*

novelist ['nɑv əl əst] *n.* someone who writes novels. ♦ *That novelist has won many awards for his writing.* ♦ *The famous novelist autographed my copy of her book.*

novelty ['nɑv əl ti] **1.** *n.* the quality of being novel; newness; originality. (No plural form in this sense.) ♦ *When Jane first started working here, she enjoyed the novelty of the job.* ♦ *The novelty of your poetry is very refreshing!* **2.** *n.* something that is new; something that is original. ♦ *Seeing how other people lived was a novelty that the children enjoyed.* ♦ *Bill likes popular music as a novelty, but he doesn't want to listen to it every day.* **3.** *n.* a small item, often inexpensive and usually intriguing or amusing. ♦ *The store sold novelties and decorative objects.* ♦ *Anne kept a variety of novelties in a box to amuse the children.* **4.** *adj.* cute and whimsical; intriguing and innovative. ♦ *The singer sang a few novelty songs before the serious ones.* ♦ *The shop carried some unusual novelty items.*

November [no 'vɛm bɚ] *n.* the eleventh month of the year, between October and December. ♦ *The fourth Thursday of November is the American holiday of Thanksgiving.* ♦ *Presidential elections are held in November.*

novice ['nɑv ɪs] **1.** *n.* someone who is new at a job or responsibility. ♦ *I helped my boss train the novices.* ♦ *Although I've played golf for years, I still play like a novice.* **2.** *n.* someone who has just joined a religious order and will become a monk or a nun. ♦ *The novice was instructed to remain silent when he joined the religious order.* ♦ *The head of the convent welcomed the novices.* **3.** *adj.* [of someone] new to a task. ♦ *As a novice reporter, I made many mistakes at first.* ♦ *Surprisingly, the novice chess player beat the expert.*

now ['nɑʊ] **1.** *adv.* at this moment; at this point in time; immediately. ♦ *Isn't the movie supposed to begin now?* ♦ *The pizza should be ready now.* **2.** *adv.* in these days; in modern times; nowadays. ♦ *Most American families have at least one television now.* ♦ *It's easier to operate a computer now than it was in the 1970s.* **3.** *adv.* <a word used for emphasis, to get someone's attention, with commands, and to move on to the next topic.> ♦ *Now, how did that happen?* ♦ *Now, where did I put my keys?* **4.** *conj.* because; since. (With *that* and a clause.) ♦ *Now that it's dark out, I'd better go home.* ♦ *Now that you've broken it, you'd better fix it.* **5.** *n.* the present; this time. (No plural form in this sense.) ♦ *Until now, I never understood calculus.* ♦ *For now, I'd just like a cup of coffee.* **6. now and then** *idiom* sometimes; occasionally. ♦ *I like to go to a movie now and then.* ♦ *We visit my parents now and then, but we never have a real vacation.*

nowadays ['nɑʊ ə dez] *adv.* in these times; in the present time; in modern times. ♦ *Nowadays, you can call people overseas without an operator's help.* ♦ *More people have computers nowadays than in 1980.*

nowhere ['no ʍɛr] *adv.* at no place; toward no place; not any place. ♦ *My keys are nowhere to be found.* ♦ *I gave up because all of my hard work was getting me nowhere.*

noxious ['nɑk ʃəs] *adj.* harmful; poisonous. (Adv: *noxiously.*) ♦ *The rats were poisoned by noxious fumes.* ♦ *A shed behind the factory is filled with noxious chemicals.*

nozzle ['nɑz əl] *n.* a tube located at the end of a pipe or hose, that controls and directs the fluid coming out of the pipe or hose. ♦ *Some nozzles have a valve so you can stop whatever's flowing.* ♦ *The gardener directed the nozzle of the hose at the flowers.*

n't an abbreviation of not, used in contractions, such as can't, don't, etc.

nuance ['nu ɑns] *n.* a subtle difference, usually in meaning. ♦ *This writer doesn't understand the nuance distinguishing* childish *from* childlike. ♦ *The two versions of the symphony were very similar, but the nuances made the critics prefer the second version.*

nuclear ['nu kli ɚ] *adj.* of or about the nucleus of an atom or the energy created by splitting or fusing the nuclei of atoms. ♦ *Protons and neutrons are the nuclear components of atoms.* ♦ *Nuclear energy creates radioactive waste.*

nuclei ['nu kli ɑɪ] pl of nucleus.

nucleus ['nu kli əs] **1.** *n., irreg.* the center of something; the core of something. (Pl: nuclei.) ♦ *The mayor was at the nucleus of the press conference.* ♦ *The management problems stemmed from the nucleus of the company.* **2.** *n., irreg.* the core of an atom, consisting of protons and neutrons. ♦ *The nucleus of an atom has a positive electrical charge.* ♦ *Energy is created by splitting an atom's nucleus.*

nude ['nud] **1.** *adj.* naked; not wearing any clothes. ♦ *The nude model posed in front of the art class.* ♦ *Bathing suits are required here, so you won't see any nude swimmers.* **2.** *n.* someone who is not wearing any clothes; a statue or a painting of someone who is not wearing any clothes. ♦ *The nude posed in front of the art class.* ♦ *This wing of the museum features nudes from the 17th century.* **3. in the nude** *idiom* in a state of nudity. ♦ *Bill says he sleeps in the nude.* ♦ *All the little boys swam in the nude in the creek.*

nudge ['nʌdʒ] **1.** *tv.* to bump someone or something lightly. ♦ *I accidentally nudged someone with my shopping cart.* ♦ *My dog nudged my leg with his wet nose.* **2.** *n.* a gentle bump or push. ♦ *The dog opened the door with a nudge of its nose.* ♦ *Jane's nudge on my arm reminded me that it was time to go.*

nudist ['nud əst] **1.** *n.* someone who lives without clothes as much as possible. ♦ *A group of nudists were swimming on the other side of the island.* ♦ *Bill goes each summer to a private camp for nudists.* **2.** *adj.* <the adj. use of ①.> ♦ *A reporter interviewed people at the nudist camp.* ♦ *I didn't take much luggage when I went to the nudist resort.*

nugget [ˈnʌg ɪt] **1.** *n.* a lump of metal or mineral, often gold. ♦ *The miner found a large nugget of gold in the creek.* ♦ *The bandits stole the prospector's valuable nuggets.* **2.** *n.* a bite-size piece of something, such as fried chicken or fish. ♦ *I had some chicken nuggets for lunch.* ♦ *I fried some fish nuggets for dinner.* **3.** *n.* a small measure of something, such as wisdom. (Figurative on ①.) ♦ *My boss gave me a few nuggets of wisdom before she retired.* ♦ *The columnist printed some nuggets of gossip.*

nuisance [ˈnu səns] **1.** *n.* a bother; an annoyance. ♦ *The flies were a nuisance at the picnic.* ♦ *My nosy neighbor is quite a nuisance.* **2. make a nuisance of oneself** *idiom* to be a constant bother. ♦ *I'm sorry to make a nuisance of myself, but I do need an answer to my question.* ♦ *Stop making a nuisance of yourself and wait your turn.*

null [ˈnʌl] **1.** *n.* nothing; zero. (No plural form in this sense.) ♦ *At the end of the first inning, our team's score was null.* ♦ *The correct answer is null.* **2.** *adj.* [in mathematics] empty; [numerically] without value. ♦ *Category A is a null set.* ♦ *I got null because I multiplied by a null variable.* **3. null and void** *idiom* without legal force; having no legal effect. ♦ *The judge declared the law to be null and void.* ♦ *The millionaire's will was null and void because it was unsigned.*

nullify [ˈnʌl ə fɑɪ] *tv.* to cause something to have no legal force. ♦ *Congress nullified Prohibition in 1933.* ♦ *The Supreme Court nullified the law that it determined was unconstitutional.*

numb [ˈnʌm] **1.** *adj.* unable to feel anything; unable to sense anything. (Adv: *numbly* [ˈnʌm li]. Comp: *number* [ˈnʌm ɚ]; sup: *numbest* [ˈnʌm əst].) ♦ *My hands were numb from the frigid weather.* ♦ *An injection made my mouth numb so the dentist could work on my tooth.* **2.** *tv.* to cause someone or something to be unable to feel anything; to deaden something. ♦ *The dentist numbed the area around my tooth before drilling into it.* ♦ *The cold weather numbed my fingers and toes.*

number [ˈnʌm bɚ] **1.** *n.* a symbol or a word that expresses an amount; a symbol or a word that shows how many; a digit or series of digits that has an assigned significance. ♦ *To access your account, you must enter your identification number.* ♦ *I'm thinking of a number greater than 10 and less than 100.* **2.** *n.* a specific number that identifies someone or something in a series. (Also appears as the symbol "#".) ♦ *What is your room number?* ♦ *I was number three in line to buy tickets for the concert.* **3.** *n.* a song; a piece of music. ♦ *The soloist sang a romantic number.* ♦ *The chorus ended the concert with a very lovely number.* **4.** *n.* a grammatical category evident in the inflection of words, depending on whether one or more than one person or thing is being referred to. (No plural form in this sense.) ♦ *Verbs should agree with the number of their subjects.* ♦ *In many languages, number consists of singular and plural forms.* **5. the number of things or people** *phr.* the total amount of things or people; a sum; a total. (Number is treated as singular.) ♦ *What's the number of paper clips in this box?* ♦ *The number of people at the meeting was seven.* **6. a number of things or people** *phr.* some things or people, in an indefinite amount. (Number is treated as plural.) ♦ *I subscribe to a number of different magazines.* ♦ *A number of people are here now.* **7.** See cardinal numeral. **8.** See ordinal numeral. **9.** *tv.* to assign something a ①. (Refers especially to things in a series.) ♦ *My computer automatically numbers the pages of my documents.* ♦ *The worker numbered the parts as they came down the assembly line.* **10.** *tv.* to reach a total of a certain amount; to be a certain amount. ♦ *The acres destroyed by the fire number 1,000.* ♦ *The charges against the defendant numbered five.* **11.** *iv.* [for an amount] to equal a certain figure; to total something. ♦ *My autograph collection numbers over 100 autographs.* ♦ *His typing errors number about 10 per page.* **12. in round numbers** *idiom* as an estimate; as a figure that has been rounded off to the closest whole number ②. ♦ *Please tell me in round numbers what it'll cost.* ♦ *I don't need the exact amount. Just give it to me in round numbers.*

numberless [ˈnʌm bɚ ləs] *adj.* innumerable; too many to be counted. (Adv: *numberlessly.*) ♦ *I looked with wonder at the numberless stars in the sky.* ♦ *This beach consists of numberless grains of sand.*

numeral [ˈnum ə rəl] **1.** *n.* the symbol or figure that represents a number. ♦ *In Arabic numerals, "six" is represented as 6.* ♦ *The numerals at the bottom of page were written in red ink.* **2. Arabic numeral** *n.* the most usual form of number, such as 1, 2, 3, 4, 5. (These forms are derived from Arabic script.) ♦ *Our writing system uses Roman letters and Arabic numerals.* ♦ *Arabic numerals have been used in the European languages for centuries.* **3. Roman numeral** *n.* the form of numbers made from letters, such as I, II, II, IV, V. ♦ *Many clock faces uses Roman numerals.* ♦ *Large Roman numerals, such as MCM, are hard to read.* **4.** See cardinal numeral. **5.** See ordinal numeral.

numerator [ˈnum ə ret ɚ] *n.* the number above the line in a fraction. (Compare with denominator.) ♦ *In the fraction ½, the numerator is 1.* ♦ *If a fraction's numerator is 0, then the fraction is equal to 0.*

numerical [nu ˈmɛr ɪ kəl] **1.** *adj.* of or about numbers and the normal order of numbers. (Adv: *numerically* [...ɪk li].) ♦ *The pages of a book are usually in numerical order.* ♦ *My calculator does simple numerical calculations.* **2.** *adj.* shown by using numbers; expressed with numbers. (Adv: *numerically* [...ɪk li].) ♦ *The numerical representation of "twelve" is 12.* ♦ *I entered numerical data into the computer.*

numerous [ˈnum ə rəs] *adj.* many; several; a lot. (Adv: *numerously.*) ♦ *I went to the beach numerous times last summer.* ♦ *I have numerous friends from New York City.*

numismatic [nu mɪz ˈmæt ɪk] **1.** *adj.* of or about coins or coin collecting. (Adv: *numismatically* [...ɪk li].) ♦ *The misprinted stamp had a high numismatic value.* ♦ *I bought some rare coins at a numismatic shop.* **2. numismatics** *n.* the hobby or practice of collecting coins. (Treated as singular.) ♦ *I gave the foreign money to my friend who's interested in numismatics.* ♦ *I became interested in numismatics during my first trip abroad.*

nun [ˈnʌn] *n.* a woman who is a member of a religious order. ♦ *The classes at my high school were taught by nuns.* ♦ *Every morning, the nuns at the convent go to Mass.*

nuptial [ˈnʌp ʃəl] **1.** *adj.* of or about marriage. (Adv: *nuptially.*) ♦ *The couple exchanged nuptial vows.* ♦ *A judge presided over the nuptial ceremony.* **2. nuptials** *n.* a wedding ceremony. ♦ *The nuptials were held at a small chapel* *on the university campus.* ♦ *The ministers officiated at the nuptials of Dave and Anne.*

nurse ['nɝs] **1.** *n.* someone, usually a woman, trained to provide medical care, often under the supervision of a physician. ♦ *The nurse handed the scalpel to the doctor.* ♦ *The nurse took my temperature.* **2.** *n.* a woman who raises other people's children; a woman who helps a family raise its children. ♦ *The Smiths hired a nurse to help them take care of their triplets.* ♦ *The children became very attached to their nurse.* **3.** *tv.* to feed a baby milk from one's breast. ♦ *The cat nursed her newborn kittens.* ♦ *My mother nursed all of her children.* **4.** *tv.* [for anyone] to treat a disease. ♦ *I think I can nurse this cold without seeing a doctor.* ♦ *We had to nurse our kids measles because we live so far from a doctor.* **5.** *iv.* [for a female] to feed a baby mammal as in ③. ♦ *The mother cat is nursing now. Do not disturb her.* ♦ *She nurses while sitting in a rocking chair.* **6.** *iv.* [for a baby mammal] to suckle or take milk from a female. ♦ *The baby wants to nurse every three hours.* ♦ *When Max was a baby, he nursed very noisily.* **7. nurse someone back to health** *idiom* [for anyone] to provide medical care that will restore someone to good health. ♦ *After my operation, my mother nursed me back to health.* ♦ *Lots of good food and loving care will help nurse you back to health.*

nursery ['nɝs (ə) ri] **1.** *n.* a room for babies in a hospital or residence. ♦ *We put the baby's crib in the nursery.* ♦ *There were 12 newborns in the hospital's nursery.* **2.** *n.* a place where children are watched while their parents are busy at something else. ♦ *Jane took Billy to the nursery before she went to work.* ♦ *David picked up his children at the nursery after work.* **3.** *n.* a place where plants are grown and sold. ♦ *I bought some potting soil at the nursery.* ♦ *The nursery was kept at a constant temperature all year long.*

nursing ['nɝ sɪŋ] **1.** *adj.* suckling; taking milk from the breast. ♦ *The nursing child fell asleep in her mother's arms.* ♦ *The nursing kittens meowed quietly.* **2.** *n.* the career of being a nurse. (No plural form in this sense.) ♦ *Anne studied nursing at college.* ♦ *I decided to go into nursing when I was young.*

nursing home ['nɝ sɪŋ hom] *n.* a hospital or building where old people who are ill or disabled are taken care of. ♦ *Every Sunday, I visited my mother at the nursing home.* ♦ *My grandmother recovered from her broken hip at a nursing home.*

nurture ['nɝ tʃɝ] *tv.* to care for someone or something; to raise someone. ♦ *The Smiths nurtured their children in a loving environment.* ♦ *I nurtured the sick kitten until it was well again.*

nut ['nʌt] **1.** *n.* a hard, woody shell containing a nutmeat. ♦ *I cracked the nut open with a nutcracker.* ♦ *The worker harvested the nuts from the trees.* **2.** *n.* the kernel of ①, used as food; a nutmeat. ♦ *The cook sprinkled some chopped nuts on the cake.* ♦ *The waiter put a dish of salted nuts on our table.* **3.** *n.* someone who is crazy, insane, or foolish. (Slang.) ♦ *You'd have to be a nut to go swimming in this cold weather!* ♦ *Some nut with a gun killed four people at the mall today.* **4. nuts** *adj.* crazy; insane. (Slang.) ♦ *You'd have to be nuts to spend all your money so foolishly!* ♦ *The postal worker went nuts and killed his supervisor.* **5. nuts and bolts (of something)** *idiom* the basic facts about something; the practical details of something. ♦ *Tom knows all about the nuts and bolts of the chemical process.* ♦ *Anne is familiar with the nuts and bolts of public relations.*

nutcracker ['nʌt kræk ɝ] *n.* a tool used to crack open the shells of nuts. ♦ *I used a nutcracker to crack the walnut shell.* ♦ *I needed a nutcracker to open some of the nuts.*

nutmeat ['nʌt mit] *n.* the edible part of a nut; the kernel of a nut. ♦ *I carefully removed the nutmeats from the nuts I had cracked open.* ♦ *We love to sit by the fire and eat various fruits and nutmeats.*

nutrient ['nu tri ənt] *n.* something that nourishes; a vitamin or mineral. ♦ *I prepared a dinner that is rich in several nutrients.* ♦ *Vitamin C is an important nutrient for good health.*

nutrition [nu 'trɪ ʃən] *n.* the science of providing people with information about healthy food. (No plural form in this sense.) ♦ *This book on nutrition contains several healthful recipes.* ♦ *Sue studied nutrition before becoming a dietician.*

nutritious [nu 'trɪ ʃəs] *adj.* healthy to eat; very nourishing. (Adv: *nutritiously.*) ♦ *I ate a nutritious meal after exercising at the gym.* ♦ *Bob eats a juicy, nutritious apple every day.*

nutshell ['nʌt ʃɛl] **1.** *n.* the hard, woody shell around a nutmeat. ♦ *Max cracked open the nutshell with a hammer.* ♦ *I used a nutcracker to open the thick nutshell.* **2. in a nutshell** *idiom* [of news or information] in a (figurative) capsule. ♦ *This cable channel provides the latest news in a nutshell.* ♦ *In a nutshell, what happened at work today?*

nutty ['nʌt i] **1.** *adj.* tasting like a nut; made from nuts. (Adv: *nuttily.* Comp: *nuttier;* sup: *nuttiest.*) ♦ *This frosting has a nutty flavor.* ♦ *The fresh coffee had a nutty aroma.* **2.** *adj.* crazy; insane. (Adv: *nuttily.* Comp: *nuttier;* sup: *nuttiest.*) ♦ *You'd be nutty to go outside during this blizzard.* ♦ *My neighbor went nutty and burned down his house.*

nuzzle ['nʌz əl] **1.** *tv.* to push someone or something with the nose; to push against someone or something with the nose. ♦ *My dog nuzzled the back of my knee.* ♦ *The kitten nuzzled the ball of yarn on the floor.* **2.** *iv.* to cuddle, especially if leading with the nose or face. ♦ *The lovers nuzzled on the couch while watching television.* ♦ *The puppy nuzzled against its pillow.* **3. nuzzle up to someone or something** *idiom* to nestle against someone or something, especially if leading with the nose or face. ♦ *The puppy nuzzled up to its mother.* ♦ *Tom nuzzled up to Jane and asked her for a kiss.*

nylon ['nɑɪ lɑn] **1.** *n.* a very strong, stretchy, lightweight, synthetic fiber, used especially to make clothes and material. (No plural form in this sense.) ♦ *My water-resistant tent is made from nylon.* ♦ *Do you prefer stockings made from nylon or silk?* **2. nylons** *n.* a pair of pantyhose; stockings made of ①. ♦ *Anne accidentally snagged her nylons with her fingernails.* ♦ *Susan wore black nylons with her business suit.* **3.** *adj.* made from ①. ♦ *I wore my nylon jacket because it's a little windy outside.* ♦ *The fisherman used a strong nylon thread for a fishing line.*

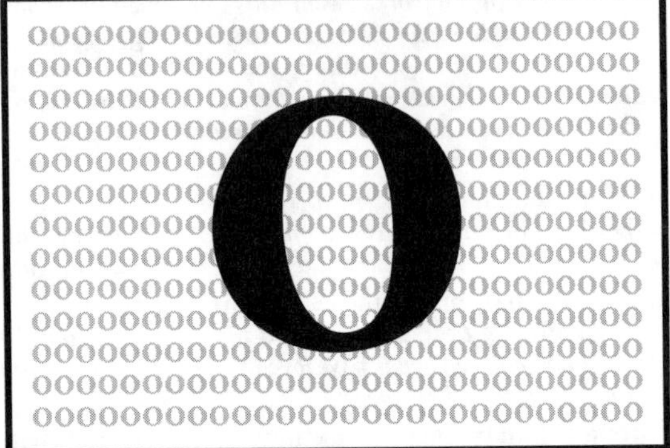

O AND **o** ['o] *n.* the fifteenth letter of the alphabet. ♦ O *comes after* N *and before* P. ♦ *The sound of the letter* o *rhymes with* crow.

oak ['ok] **1.** *n.* a kind of tree that produces acorns. ♦ *My property line is marked by a row of oaks.* ♦ *The robin built its nest in a big old oak.* **2.** *n.* wood from ①. (No plural form in this sense.) ♦ *This sturdy table is made of oak.* ♦ *The carpenter used oak when making the rocking chair.* **3.** *adj.* made from ②. ♦ *I bought a solid oak desk for my office.* ♦ *The artist placed her painting in an oak frame.*

oaken ['ok ən] *adj.* made from oak. ♦ *I removed the crystal glasses from the oaken cabinet.* ♦ *The artist placed her painting in an oaken frame.*

oar ['or] **1.** *n.* a long pole with one wide, flat end—similar to a paddle—used to steer and row boats. ♦ *The members of the rowing crew moved their oars in unison.* ♦ *The oar floated away from my boat when I accidentally dropped it.* **2. put in one's oar** *idiom* to interfere by giving advice; to add one's assistance to the general effort. ♦ *I'm sorry. I shouldn't have put in my oar.* ♦ *You don't need to put your oar in. I don't need your advice.*

oases [o 'e siz] pl of oasis.

oasis [o 'e sɪs] **1.** *n., irreg.* a place in a desert that has water and trees. (Pl: oases.) ♦ *The nomads stopped at the desert oasis to rest.* ♦ *The camels drank a lot of water at the oasis.* **2.** *n., irreg.* a refuge from problems or difficulties. (Figurative on ①.) ♦ *The teachers' lounge is an oasis, far removed from screaming children.* ♦ *The park near my house is an oasis from bustling city life.*

oat ['ot] **1. oats** *n.* a cereal grain used as food for humans and cattle. ♦ *The farmer harvested 320 acres of oats.* ♦ *My breakfast cereal is made from oats.* **2. oats** *n.* grains of ①. ♦ *The farmer spilled a few oats on the ground.* ♦ *Three oats made a meal for the tiny mouse.* **3.** *adj.* made of ①. ♦ *Mary loved the toasted oat cereal.* ♦ *We took oat muffins on our hike.* **4. sow one's wild oats** *idiom* to do wild and foolish things in one's youth. ♦ *Bill was out sowing his wild oats last night, and he's in jail this morning.* ♦ *Mrs. Smith told Mr. Smith that he was too old to be sowing his wild oats.*

oath ['oθ] **1.** *n., irreg.* a promise that one will speak only the truth; a solemn promise that one will do something; a vow. (Pl: *oaths* ['oðz].) ♦ *The politician broke his oath not to raise taxes.* ♦ *They broke their oaths when they lied.* **2. take an oath** *idiom* to make ①; to swear to something as in ①. ♦ *You must take an oath that you will never tell anyone about this.* ♦ *When I was a witness in court, I had to take an oath that I would tell the truth.* **3. under oath** *idiom* bound by ①; having taken ①. ♦ *You must tell the truth because you are under oath.* ♦ *I was placed under oath before I could testify in the trial.*

oatmeal ['ot mil] **1.** *n.* crushed oats, usually eaten with milk and sugar. (No plural form in this sense.) ♦ *I eat oatmeal every morning for breakfast.* ♦ *John puts cinnamon on his oatmeal.* **2.** *adj.* made of oats. ♦ *We have oatmeal muffins about once a week.* ♦ *Oatmeal cookies with raisins are my favorite.*

obedience [o 'bid i əns] *n.* the condition of being obedient. (No plural form in this sense.) ♦ *I was pleased by my dog's obedience to my commands.* ♦ *The unruly children showed no obedience to their parents.*

obedient [o 'bid i ənt] *adj.* obeying; following orders. (Adv: *obediently.*) ♦ *Very few children are always obedient.* ♦ *The obedient dog listened to its owner.*

obese [o 'bis] *adj.* very fat. (Adv: *obesely.*) ♦ *A bench at the mall broke when an obese customer sat on it.* ♦ *The doctor put her obese patients on a strict diet.*

obey [o 'be] **1.** *tv.* to yield to someone and do as you have been instructed; to follow instructions, commands, or rules. ♦ *The children obeyed their teacher's orders.* ♦ *You must obey the laws of the country that you're in.* **2.** *iv.* to do as one is told. ♦ *My boss told me to work until 7:00, and I obeyed.* ♦ *The members of the church congregation obeyed when the minister told them to stand.*

obituary [o 'bɪtʃ u ɛr i] **1.** *n.* a brief account of the life of someone who has recently died, usually including information about the funeral and surviving relatives. ♦ *Uncle Bill's obituary listed all of his nieces and nephews.* ♦ *The newspaper printed the bishop's obituary the day after he died.* **2. the obituaries** *n.* the section of the newspaper where ① can be found. (Treated as a plural.) ♦ *I didn't know my cousin had died until I read the obituaries.* ♦ *I found a picture of my grandfather in the obituaries from 40 years ago.*

object 1. ['ɑb dʒɛkt] *n.* a thing; something that can be seen or touched. ♦ *I studied the mysterious object that fell from the sky.* ♦ *What is that dark object lying in the street?* **2.** ['ɑb dʒɛkt] *n.* a goal; an aim; a target or objective. ♦ *The object of most diets is to lose weight.* ♦ *Jane disliked being the object of Bill's attention.* **3.** ['ɑb dʒɛkt] *n.* a noun or nominal that is affected by the action or condition of a verb, and that, if replaced with he, she, or they, would be him, her, or them; a noun or nominal within a prepositional phrase. ♦ *In the prepositional phrase "in the garden," "garden" is the object of "in."* ♦ *In "I ate the cake," "the cake" is the object.* **4. object to** [əb 'dʒɛkt…] *iv.* + *prep. phr.* to oppose something; to argue against something; to make an objection about something. ♦ *My supervisor objected to my costly proposal.* ♦ *The lawyer objected to the question asked by the defense.*

objection [əb 'dʒɛk ʃən] *n.* a stated reason for not wanting to do something. ♦ *My objection to going to the zoo is that it's too hot today.* ♦ *I see no problem. What are your objections?*

objectionable [əb 'dʒɛk ʃə nə bəl] *adj.* offensive; causing dislike or disapproval; causing objections. (Adv: *objectionably.*) ♦ *The video store removed objectionable* *movies from its shelves.* ♦ *The student was punished for using objectionable language.*

objective [əb 'dʒɛk tɪv] **1.** *adj.* not influenced by one's feelings; relying on facts rather than one's feelings. (Adv: *objectively.*) ♦ *The objective judge listened carefully to my testimony.* ♦ *John and I sought an objective solution to our disagreement.* **2.** *n.* a goal; an aim; a target; a purpose. ♦ *The teacher's objective was to teach calculus to the class.* ♦ *It's my objective to retire before I'm 60.*

objective case [ɑb 'dʒɛk tɪv ('kes)] *n.* <the grammatical state of the objects of transitive verbs and prepositions.> (There are six words in English that have a special form in the objective case: me, him, her, us, them, and whom. The remaining pronouns and the nouns have no special forms in English and will be in the objective case when they are the direct objects or indirect objects of verbs or prepositions. Direct objects are said to "receive the action" of a transitive verb, as in "John told a *good story.*" An indirect object "receives" but not directly, as in "John told *me* a good story.") ♦ Me *is always in the objective case.* ♦ *The object of a preposition is always in the objective case.*

objectivity [ɑb dʒɛk 'tɪv ə ti] *n.* the ability to deal only with facts, ignoring one's feelings and intuitions. (No plural form in this sense.) ♦ *The reporter doubted the objectivity of the corrupt judge.* ♦ *The skilled mediator was praised for her objectivity.*

obligate ['ɑ blə get] **obligate (to)** *tv.* (+ *inf.*) [for a contract or obligation] to require someone to do something. (Often passive.) ♦ *The lease obligated the tenant to pay rent each month.* ♦ *I am obligated to work at least 40 hours a week.*

obligation [ɑ blə 'ge ʃən] *n.* a responsibility or duty to do something as required by law, a contract, or a promise to someone. ♦ *Tenants have an obligation to pay rent.* ♦ *The senator promised to uphold the obligations of his office.*

obligatory [ə 'blɪg ə tor i] *adj.* required by law, contract, or promise; not optional. (Adv: *obligatorily* [ə blɪg ə 'tor ə li].) ♦ *Wearing seat belts while driving is obligatory in most states.* ♦ *The sophomores all took an obligatory writing course.*

oblige [ə 'blɑɪdʒ] **1. oblige to** *tv.* + *inf.* to require someone to do something. ♦ *A court order obliged John to get psychiatric counseling.* ♦ *The law obliges us to pay taxes.* **2.** *iv.* to do something nice for someone; to do someone a favor. ♦ *My neighbor asked me for some help, and I obliged.* ♦ *I could not oblige because I was going to be out of town.*

obliging [ə 'blɑɪdʒ ɪŋ] *adj.* helpful; willing to do things for someone. (Adv: *obligingly.*) ♦ *My obliging neighbor helped me trim my hedges.* ♦ *Our happy and obliging children did what I asked them to do.*

obliterate [ə 'blɪt ə ret] *tv.* to destroy, erase, or wipe out something completely; to remove every trace of something. ♦ *A powerful bomb obliterated the small village.* ♦ *My work was obliterated when my computer malfunctioned.*

oblivion [ə 'blɪv i ən] **1.** *n.* the state wherein someone or something is forgotten completely. (No plural form in this sense.) ♦ *The once popular writer's works were consigned to oblivion after he died.* ♦ *The fame of many modern celebrities will one day be lost in oblivion.* **2.** *n.* the state of being unaware of one's surroundings. (No plural form in this sense.) ♦ *The drunk walked around town in complete oblivion.* ♦ *In total oblivion, the hypnotized woman walked around the stage.*

oblivious [ə 'blɪv i əs] **1. oblivious to** *adj.* + *prep. phr.* not aware of someone or something. ♦ *The man reading on the bus was oblivious to the noise around him.* ♦ *Very tired, Jane slept oblivious to the loud party next door.* **2.** *adj.* unaware [of anything]. (Adv: *obliviously.*) ♦ *Before I drink coffee in the morning, I am generally oblivious.* ♦ *After the accident, John sat there, completely oblivious.*

oblong ['ɑb lɔŋ] *adj.* elongated; [especially of a circle or a rectangle] long and narrow. (Adv: *oblongly.*) ♦ *The planet Pluto has an oblong orbit.* ♦ *An oval is an oblong circle.*

obnoxious [əb 'nɑk ʃəs] *adj.* very annoying; very irritating; very offensive. (Adv: *obnoxiously.*) ♦ *I ignored my obnoxious brother and went to my room.* ♦ *The student was punished for being obnoxious in class.*

oboe ['o bo] *n.* a musical instrument that has a long, thin wooden body and a mouthpiece holding a double reed. ♦ *The oboe makes a tone that sounds somewhat nasal.* ♦ *Jane played the oboe in the city's orchestra.*

obscene [əb 'sin] *adj.* very offensive; very indecent; against a society's standard of decency. (Adv: *obscenely.*) ♦ *Bill was arrested for making obscene phone calls.* ♦ *The principal banned the obscene book from school.*

obscenity [əb 'sɛn ə ti] **1.** *n.* something that is offensive or indecent; obscene behavior. (No plural form in this sense.) ♦ *Bill isn't allowed to watch movies with a lot of obscenity.* ♦ *The obscenity of the lurid painting shocked the minister.* **2.** *n.* a curse word; a swear word; obscene language. ♦ *The newspaper would not print certain obscenities.* ♦ *Bob shouted obscenities at the driver of the car that passed him.*

obscure [əb 'skjʊr] **1.** *adj.* [of reasoning or explanation] not clearly stated or hard to understand. (Adv: *obscurely.*) ♦ *My friend mumbled some obscure reason for being late.* ♦ *The teacher's obscure explanation of the homework confused me.* **2.** *adj.* not well known; not famous. (Adv: *obscurely.*) ♦ *Nobody was familiar with the writings of the obscure author.* ♦ *The singer sang an obscure song from the 1920s at her audition.* **3.** *adj.* hard to see; hidden, especially by darkness. (Adv: *obscurely.*) ♦ *I strained to see the obscure figure in the dark alley.* ♦ *The obscure shoreline was shrouded in fog.* **4.** *tv.* to make something hard to see; to keep something from view; to dim or darken something. ♦ *The road sign was obscured by darkness.* ♦ *Fog obscured all of the downtown buildings.* **5.** *tv.* to make something difficult to understand; to cloud one's meaning. (Figurative on ④.) ♦ *John obscured his point by using big words incorrectly.* ♦ *My thinking was obscured by alcohol.*

obscurity [əb 'skjʊr ə ti] *n.* the state of being hard to see or understand. (No plural form in this sense.) ♦ *I stopped reading the textbook because of its obscurity.* ♦ *Lisa's short story was notable for its obscurity. Nothing at all made sense.*

observance [əb 'zɝ vəns] **1.** *n.* following a law or tradition. (No plural form in this sense.) ♦ *In observance of Jewish law, the rabbi ate no pork.* ♦ *As an observance of custom, no one's head was allowed to be higher than the king's head.* **2.** *n.* an event celebrating a holiday or special, serious event. ♦ *The observance of Memorial Day is a federal holiday.* ♦ *The observance of the holiday was marked with fireworks.*

observant [əb 'zɚ vənt] *adj.* observing what is happening; noticing things. (Adv: *observantly.*) ♦ *The observant driver avoided a collision.* ♦ *The observant detective found an important clue.*

observation [ɑb zɚ 've ʃən] **1.** *n.* watching or monitoring; constant watching. (No plural form in this sense.) ♦ *The sick patient was placed under continuous observation.* ♦ *The observation of the swimmers is the lifeguard's job.* **2.** *n.* an act of ①. ♦ *My observations of the situation lead me to believe that Dave made repeated errors.* ♦ *A quick observation of the room revealed a broken window and a rock on the floor.* **3.** *n.* a remark; a comment. ♦ *The reporter's observations were based on rumors.* ♦ *My friend made the observation that my shoes weren't tied.*

observatory [əb 'zɚv ə tor i] *n.* a building where people can study celestial bodies or the weather. ♦ *There are powerful telescopes at the observatory.* ♦ *The astronomer went to the observatory to examine the comet.*

observe [əb 'zɚv] **1.** *tv.* to watch something. ♦ *The scientist observed how the rat behaved in the maze.* ♦ *I observed the soccer game from a distance.* **2.** *tv.* to obey a law or custom; to pay attention to a law or custom. ♦ *Sometimes, the police don't seem to observe traffic laws.* ♦ *Mary always observes the rules of etiquette.* **3.** *tv.* to celebrate a holiday. ♦ *My company does not observe some of the state holidays.* ♦ *Our neighbors observe Ramadan.* **4.** *tv.* to make a comment. (Takes a clause.) ♦ *My teacher observed that many students had arrived late today.* ♦ *Tom observed that I was unhappy with our boss's decision.*

obsessed [əb 'sɛst] **1.** *adj.* completely preoccupied; irrationally thinking about something too much. ♦ *The psychiatrist gave the obsessed patient a sedative.* ♦ *The obsessed student couldn't stop talking about his grades.* **2.** **obsessed with** *adj.* + *prep. phr.* preoccupied with a thought or an activity. ♦ *Bill is obsessed with keeping his house clean.* ♦ *Anne was always obsessed with pleasing her parents.*

obsession [əb 'sɛ ʃən] **1.** *n.* feeling or thought that completely fills one's mind. (No plural form in this sense.) ♦ *Obsession and compulsion both cause us to do irrational things.* ♦ *Obsession for wealth has driven people to crime.* **2.** *n.* an instance or case of ①. ♦ *Bill's obsessions make him nervous and irritable.* ♦ *Anne is burdened by two serious obsessions.*

obsessive [əb 'sɛs ɪv] *adj.* having an obsession; causing an obsession. (Adv: *obsessively.*) ♦ *Mary was treated for an obsessive eating disorder.* ♦ *The obsessive fan began following the actor.*

obsolescence [ɑb sə 'lɛs əns] *n.* a state of becoming out-of-date or out of style. (No plural form in this sense.) ♦ *The obsolescence of my ten-year-old computer makes it worthless.* ♦ *Technology has caused the obsolescence of many mechanical devices.*

obsolescent [ɑb sə 'lɛs ənt] *adj.* becoming obsolete; becoming out-of-date; becoming outdated. (Adv: *obsolescently.*) ♦ *The computer I bought ten years ago is now obsolescent.* ♦ *I replaced my obsolescent adding machine with a calculator.*

obsolete ['ɑb sə lit] *adj.* no longer used; outdated; no longer as useful as something new. (Adv: *obsoletely.*) ♦ Fain *is an obsolete word that meant 'willing' or 'happy.'* ♦ *This new computer rendered my old one obsolete.*

obstacle ['ɑb stə kəl] *n.* something that is in the way of someone, something, or some action; a hindrance; a block. ♦ *Illiteracy is an obstacle to success.* ♦ *There is some sort of obstacle in the road that has caused the traffic to stop moving.*

obstetric [əb 'stɛ trɪk] **1.** *adj.* of or about the medical care of women during pregnancy, while giving birth, and after giving birth. (Adv: *obstetrically* [...ɪk li].) ♦ *The new mother left the obstetric floor of the hospital with a lovely baby.* ♦ *The midwife was knowledgeable about obstetric care.* **2. obstetrics** *n.* the branch of medicine that has to do with the care of women during pregnancy and childbirth. (Treated as singular.) ♦ *Jane studied obstetrics because she wanted to help other women.* ♦ *Nutrition is an important part of obstetrics.*

obstinacy ['ɑb stə nə si] *n.* the condition or quality of being obstinate; stubbornness. (No plural form in this sense.) ♦ *Bill's obstinacy made our vacation very unpleasant.* ♦ *Susie was punished for her obstinacy.*

obstinate ['ɑb stə nɪt] *adj.* stubborn; not willing to change one's mind; not willing to listen to other people's ideas. (Adv: *obstinately.*) ♦ *The obstinate child refused to go to bed when told to.* ♦ *The obstinate juror refused to consider the evidence.*

obstinately ['ɑb stə nət li] *adv.* stubbornly. ♦ *The child obstinately refused to eat his dinner.* ♦ *Anne obstinately ignored my suggestions.*

obstruct [əb 'strʌkt] *tv.* to get in the way of someone or something; to block someone or something; to hinder someone or something. ♦ *A stalled car obstructed traffic.* ♦ *Some paper got in the sink and obstructed the drain.*

obstruction [əb 'strʌk ʃən] *n.* something that is in the way; something that is blocking the way. ♦ *Tom was operated on to remove an obstruction in his bowels.* ♦ *The plumber removed a large obstruction from the pipes.*

obstructionist [əb 'strʌk ʃə nəst] *n.* someone who makes things difficult for other people; someone who stands in the way of progress; someone who hinders something. ♦ *Several obstructionists blocked the bill's passage in Congress.* ♦ *A petty obstructionist delayed my proposal for a week.*

obtain [əb 'ten] *tv.* to get something; to acquire something; to come to own something. ♦ *The police obtained a search warrant to enter Max's apartment.* ♦ *Jane had obtained the large oil painting from her sister.*

obtainable [əb 'ten ə bəl] *adj.* able to be gotten; able to be acquired. (Adv: *obtainably.*) ♦ *Most food items are obtainable at grocery stores.* ♦ *Tickets are obtainable at the box office.*

obtrusive [əb 'tru sɪv] *adj.* obvious and noticeable, especially in an unpleasant way; interfering. (Adv: *obtrusively.*) ♦ *Bill's obtrusive behavior is annoying.* ♦ *His visit was poorly timed and quite obtrusive.*

obvious ['ɑb vi əs] *adj.* apparent; easily seen or understood; plain; clear. (Adv: *obviously.*) ♦ *It's obvious that 2 + 2 = 4.* ♦ *Since you're late, it's obvious that you should have left earlier.*

obviously ['ɑb vi əs li] *adv.* apparently; plainly; clearly. ♦ *Obviously, you should apologize for being rude.* ♦ *The driver of the wrecked car was obviously drunk.*

occasion [ə 'ke ʒən] **1.** *n.* the time when something happens; the time when something occurs. ♦ *John met several friends on one occasion, but usually he was all alone.* ♦ *On several occasions, I've forgotten my keys.* **2.** *n.* a special event. ♦ *We celebrated the occasion with a toast of champagne.* ♦ *A wedding is a very happy occasion.* **3.** *n.* a reason for something; a cause for something. ♦ *What's the occasion for your dressing so nicely?* ♦ *The bright sunny day was the perfect occasion for a picnic.* **4. on occasion** *phr.* occasionally. ♦ *I like to go to the movies on occasion.* ♦ *On occasion, Mary would walk her dog through the park.*

occasional [ə 'ke ʒə nəl] *adj.* happening from time to time; happening once in a while; not happening all the time or regularly. (Usually with an article. Adv: *occasionally.*) ♦ *I get the occasional cold each winter.* ♦ *The silence was broken by an occasional scream.*

occlude [ə 'klud] *tv.* to block something; to stop something from passing through. ♦ *The clot occluded the flow of blood through the artery.* ♦ *The pipe was occluded by a clump of hair.*

occlusion [ə 'klu ʒən] *n.* something that blocks something. ♦ *John's stroke was caused by an occlusion in a major artery.* ♦ *The doctors ran tests to find the occlusion in the patient's intestine.*

occult [ə 'kʌlt] **1.** *n.* the supernatural, especially concerning evil; things that are hidden from regular knowledge or experience. (No plural form in this sense.) ♦ *The minister warned the children against dabbling in the occult.* ♦ *Voodoo is one of the mysteries of the occult.* **2.** *adj.* of or about the supernatural; hidden from regular knowledge; mysterious; magical. (Adv: *occultly.*) ♦ *Casting spells is an occult practice.* ♦ *The witch was questioned about her occult knowledge.*

occupancy ['ɑk jə pən si] **1.** *n.* occupying a house, building, or other piece of property. (No plural form in this sense.) ♦ *The occupancy of the abandoned building is illegal.* ♦ *My uncle maintained occupancy of his apartment for 70 years.* **2.** *n.* the number of people that a room or building is allowed to hold. (No plural form in this sense.) ♦ *The legal occupancy of this bus is 61 people.* ♦ *The sign in the lobby stated the legal occupancy of the theater.*

occupant ['ɑk jə pənt] *n.* someone who lives in a certain place; a business that occupies a certain building or space. ♦ *The building manager sent a letter to each occupant.* ♦ *The occupants of this office building are mostly lawyers.*

occupation [ɑk jə 'pe ʃən] **1.** *n.* a job; a career; what one does for a living. ♦ *I listed my occupation and salary on the credit-card application.* ♦ *Mary's occupation takes her to every state in the union.* **2.** *n.* taking or keeping possession of a geographical area. (No plural form in this sense.) ♦ *The United Nations condemned the rebels' occupation of the city.* ♦ *The occupation of the country by foreign troops frightened the residents.*

occupied ['ɑk jə pɑɪd] **1.** *adj.* not empty; being used. ♦ *The occupied bathroom was locked shut.* ♦ *Is this seat occupied, or may I sit here?* **2.** *adj.* under the control of another government; having been invaded by another government. ♦ *When the troops entered the occupied city, the citizens cheered and wept.* ♦ *Soldiers were camped in the occupied lands.*

occupy ['ɑk jə pɑɪ] **1.** *tv.* to use or consume time by doing something. (Often passive.) ♦ *I occupy my spare time with reading.* ♦ *She occupies her evenings by teaching dancing.* **2.** *tv.* to keep someone busy by doing something. ♦ *Find something to occupy the children while we go to the store.* ♦ *My boss occupied herself with preparing the monthly budget.* **3.** *tv.* to be in a certain place; to take up the space in a certain place; to live in a certain place; to have one's business in a certain place. ♦ *We occupy a small five-room house.* ♦ *Generally, dormitories are occupied by students.* **4.** *tv.* to invade and take control of another country. ♦ *Soon after World War II, Poland was occupied by the communists.* ♦ *The war began when Iraq tried to occupy Kuwait.*

occur [ə 'kɚ] **1.** *iv.* to happen; to take place. ♦ *The end of World War II occurred in 1945.* ♦ *The accident occurred when my car's brakes failed.* **2.** *iv.* to be; to exist; to be found. ♦ *Water occurs plentifully in nature.* ♦ *Snow occurs when the temperature is below freezing.* **3. occur to** *iv.* + *prep. phr.* to come to someone's mind; [for a thought] to enter into someone's mind. ♦ *It occurred to me that I should leave before midnight.* ♦ *I just remembered something that occurred to me in the middle of the night.*

occurrence [ə 'kɚ əns] **1. the occurrence of** *n.* the existence of something; the appearance or happening of something in a particular place. (No plural form in this sense.) ♦ *The occurrence of water in nature is very common.* ♦ *We have no evidence of the occurrence of water on Mars.* **2.** *n.* an event; something that happens; an incident. ♦ *A full moon is a monthly occurrence.* ♦ *English words beginning with* X *are infrequent occurrences.*

ocean ['o ʃən] **1.** *n.* a large body of salt water that covers ¾ of the earth's surface, or one of that body's four divisions: the Arctic Ocean; the Atlantic Ocean, the Indian Ocean, and the Pacific Ocean. ♦ *I washed the salt from my body after swimming in the ocean.* ♦ *The Indian Ocean lies between Africa, south Asia, and Australia.* **2. oceans of someone or something; an ocean of someone or something** *idiom* a very large amount of something. ♦ *The naughty student was in oceans of trouble.* ♦ *After a week of vacation, there was an ocean of work to do.*

o'clock [ə 'klɑk] *adv.* <a word used to indicate the time of day.> (It follows a number from 1 to 12 and means that it is that time exactly, or zero minutes past the hour. Literally, *of the clock.*) ♦ *Two o'clock is two hours after noon or midnight.* ♦ *Two o'clock is also written as 2:00.*

octagon ['ɑk tə gən] *n.* a flat figure or shape with eight sides. ♦ *Stop signs are made in the shape of an octagon.* ♦ *The geometry teacher drew a large octagon on the chalkboard.*

octave ['ɑk tɪv] *n.* a musical interval of two notes where the higher note is twelve half tones above the lower note; [on a piano] the first and eighth key in a row of eight white keys. ♦ *Each of my hands can stretch one octave on the piano.* ♦ *The soprano sang one octave higher than the alto.*

October [ɑk 'to bɚ] *n.* the tenth month of the year. ♦ *Halloween occurs on October 31st.* ♦ *October comes after September and before November.*

octogenarian [ɑk tə dʒə 'nɛr i ən] *n.* someone who is between 80 and 89 years old. ♦ *All of my grandparents lived to be octogenarians.* ♦ *Most of the people at grandmother's party are octogenarians.*

octopi ['ɑk tə pɑɪ] a pl of **octopus**.

octopus ['ɑk tə pəs] *n., irreg.* a boneless sea creature with eight legs or tentacles. (Greek for 'eight-footed.' The English plural is *octopuses* or **octopi**.) ♦ *I ate fried octopus at the seafood restaurant.* ♦ *The deep-sea diver photographed the octopus's tentacles.*

ocular ['ɑk jə lɚ] *adj.* of or about the eye. (Adv: *ocularly.*) ♦ *The eye doctor watched my ocular movements.* ♦ *I don't focus well because my ocular muscles are weak.*

odd ['ɑd] **1.** *adj.* strange; different; unusual; out of place. (Adv: *oddly.* Comp: *odder;* sup: *oddest.*) ♦ *I avoided the odd person who was talking to himself.* ♦ *Jane told me an odd but funny story.* **2.** *adj.* not even; of or about numbers that cannot be evenly divided by two. ♦ *Three and five are odd numbers.* ♦ *If you add two odd numbers together, the sum is even.* **3.** *adj.* not regular; random [occasions]; occasional. (Comp: *odder;* sup: *oddest.*) ♦ *My neighbor sometimes calls me at odd hours.* ♦ *My car brakes stop working at odd moments.* **4. the odd something** *idiom* an extra or spare something. ♦ *The tailor repaired the odd loose button on my shirt.* ♦ *When I travel, I might buy the odd trinket or two, but I never spend much money.* **5. odd man out** *idiom* an unusual or atypical person or thing. ♦ *I'm odd man out because I'm not wearing a tie.* ♦ *You had better learn to work a computer unless you want to be odd man out.* **6. for the odds to be against one** *idiom* for things to be against one generally; for one's chances to be slim. ♦ *You can give it a try, but the odds are against you.* ♦ *I know the odds are against me, but I wish to run in the race anyway.*

oddity ['ɑd ə ti] **1.** *n.* something that is odd; something that is unusual or strange. ♦ *The researcher dismissed the few oddities as exceptions.* ♦ *David looked for interesting oddities in his stamp collection.* **2.** *n.* the state of being unusual or strange. (No plural form in this sense.) ♦ *The oddity of the strange message intrigued me.* ♦ *Bill's medication is causing the oddity of his behavior.*

ode ['od] *n.* a long poem, especially a poem of praise, written about a specific person or thing. ♦ *The poet wrote an ode in memory of the assassinated president.* ♦ *The columnist's final editorial was an ode to capitalism.*

odious ['od i əs] *adj.* hateful; worthy of hate. (Adv: *odiously.*) ♦ *The judge sentenced the odious criminal to life in prison.* ♦ *The odious terrorist threatened to blow up the bank.*

odometer [o 'dɑm ɪ tɚ] *n.* a device that shows how far a car has traveled. ♦ *I couldn't determine how far I'd driven because my car's odometer is broken.* ♦ *According to the odometer, we've traveled 300 miles today.*

odor ['od ɚ] *n.* a smell; a scent; an aroma. ♦ *The odor of freshly baked apple pie came from the kitchen.* ♦ *There was an odor of sweat and socks in the locker room.*

odyssey ['ɑd ə si] *n.* a long journey with many adventures. ♦ *After graduating, Susan went on an odyssey across Asia.* ♦ *The escaped soldier went on a dangerous odyssey to freedom.*

of ['ʌv] **1.** *prep.* belonging to. ♦ *My neighbor mistakenly received a letter of mine.* ♦ *I borrowed a shirt of my roommate's.* **2.** *prep.* made from. ♦ *Anne wore a necklace of silver.* ♦ *The Spanish explorers searched for cities of gold.* **3.** *prep.* containing; including. ♦ *I ate a breakfast of eggs and bacon.* ♦ *America is the land of the free.* **4.** *prep.* <a preposition expressing an amount.> ♦ *I put eight gallons of gas into the car.* ♦ *I'd like five yards of cloth.* **5.** *prep.* referring to something; about something; concerning; about. ♦ *This matter is not of your concern.* ♦ *This movie is a story of action and adventure.* **6.** *prep.* <a preposition showing that a location is associated with another location.> ♦ *I live in the state of New York.* ♦ *I visited the city of Atlanta.* ♦ *Tom visited a friend in the Village of Glenview in Cook County.* **7.** *prep.* having a certain quality or aspect. ♦ *John wore a coat of many colors.* ♦ *I am reading a story of great importance.* **8.** *prep.* between [two]; among [more than two]. ♦ *Of the two, I prefer apples to oranges.* ♦ *Of all the jobs I've had, this one is the best.* **9.** *prep.* before a certain hour. ♦ *"Ten of six" means that it is ten minutes before 6:00.* ♦ *I have a doctor's appointment at a quarter of three.* **10.** *prep.* <a word showing the relationship between the present participle of a verb (used as a nominal) and a noun phrase, where the noun phrase would be an object of the verb, if the verb were in a simple tense.> ♦ *The ringing of the bells hurts my ears.* ♦ *The killing of the fish was an accident.*

off ['ɔf] **1.** *prep.* away from; not on. (① through ④ are often *off of,* a construction objected to by some.) ♦ *Take your books off the table.* ♦ *The calendar fell off the wall.* **2.** *prep.* less; deducted from. ♦ *The clerk took 10% off the retail price.* ♦ *The cashier took $1 off the regular price.* **3.** *prep.* leading to or from a place; turning toward or from a place. ♦ *The theater is just off Clark Street on North Avenue.* ♦ *The bathroom is off the main hallway.* **4.** *prep.* in the water near land. ♦ *Catalina Island is off the coast of California.* ♦ *The hurricane was just off the Florida coast.* **5. far off; way off** *adv.* away; in the distance or future. ♦ *The sun is far off in space.* ♦ *The meeting will be held way off in the future.* **6.** *adv.* to a separate position; away from the normal position. ♦ *Stand off a little, please. You're crowding me.* ♦ *I moved the centerpiece off to the side of the table.* **7.** *adv.* to completion; to the end; to the finish; wholly; in full. (A component of a phrasal verb.) ♦ *I finished off the pizza by eating the last slice.* ♦ *That extinct bird was killed off several centuries ago.* **8.** *adj.* stopped; not being used; causing something not to function or operate, especially by stopping the flow of electricity. ♦ *I turned off the television and went to bed.* ♦ *I switched the light off when I left the room.* **9.** *adj.* wrong. ♦ *Unless my guess is way off, it's going to rain very soon.* ♦ *My scale is off by 10 pounds.* **10.** *adj.* canceled. ♦ *The whole party is off. The host is sick.* ♦ *The meeting is off for tonight.* ♦ *After all the heavy rain in the last week, the picnic is off.* **11.** *adj.* [of a time period] free of work. ♦ *During his off hours, Bob watches television.* ♦ *During the off season, the baseball player went on vacation.* **12. off chance** *idiom* slight possibility. ♦ *I need your phone number on the off chance I need more help.* ♦ *There's an off chance that we might be hiring next month.* **13. get something off (the ground)** *idiom* to get something started. ♦ *I can relax after I get this project off the ground.* ♦ *Once I get the campaign off the ground, someone else can manage it.*

offbeat ['ɔf bit] *adj.* unusual; different; strange; not ordinary. ♦ *An offbeat poet read weird poetry at the coffee house.* ♦ *The critics liked the offbeat movie because it was different.*

off-color ['ɔf 'kʌl ɚ] **1.** *adj.* not being the proper shade of a color. ♦ *I returned the off-color invitations to the printer to be redone in pure white.* ♦ *The photos are off-color because the film was overexposed.* **2.** *adj.* indecent; improper; vulgar. (Figurative on ①.) ♦ *The entertainer's off-color jokes were censored on television.* ♦ *Jimmy was punished for telling an off-color joke.*

offend [ə 'fɛnd] *tv.* to make someone feel uncomfortable or resentful; to shock someone, especially because of one's actions, attitude, or behavior. ♦ *John's obscene language offended his mother.* ♦ *I was offended by Bob's lack of sympathy.*

offended [ə 'fɛn dɪd] *adj.* disgusted; made to feel uncomfortable or resentful; shocked. (Adv: *offendedly.*) ♦ *The offended parents tried to ban the obscene records.* ♦ *The offended customer complained to the manager.*

offender [ə 'fɛn dɚ] *n.* someone who does something wrong or illegal; someone who breaks the law. ♦ *The police officer took the offender to jail.* ♦ *The traffic offender was given a ticket.*

offending [ə 'fɛn dɪŋ] **1.** *adj.* accused of being in violation of the law. (Prenominal only.) ♦ *The offending driver was taken to the police station.* ♦ *The owner of the offending dog was ordered to go to court.* **2.** *adj.* bothersome; offensive. (Prenominal only.) ♦ *The offending song was banned from the radio.* ♦ *The offending book was removed from the shelf.*

offense 1. [ə 'fɛns] *n.* the breaking of a law; a crime; an illegal act. ♦ *The driver was ticketed for the offense of speeding.* ♦ *Certain offenses are misdemeanors, others are felonies.* **2.** [ə 'fɛns] *n.* something that is shocking or disgusting. ♦ *The book was declared to be an offense to the community.* ♦ *His rudeness was considered a serious offense.* **3.** ['ɔ fɛns] *n.* patterns or strategy of attacking. (No plural form in this sense.) ♦ *The fort fell to the enemy's forceful offense.* ♦ *The team's offense brought the football closer to the goal.* **4. take offense at someone or something** [...ə 'fɛns...] *idiom* to interpret someone or something as being offensive. ♦ *Mary took offense at Bill's ignorant statements.* ♦ *I hope you don't take offense at what I just said.*

offensive 1. [ə 'fɛn sɪv] *adj.* disgusting; shocking; annoying; causing offense. (Adv: *offensively.*) ♦ *The offensive book was banned from the school.* ♦ *The offensive joke made me blush.* **2.** ['ɔ fɛn sɪv] *adj.* of or about attacking. (Adv: *offensively.*) ♦ *The boxer assumed an offensive posture.* ♦ *The offensive team carried the ball closer to the goal.* **3.** [ə 'fɛn sɪv] *n.* an attack. ♦ *The enemy's offensive destroyed the fort.* ♦ *The team's surprise offensive won the game.*

offer ['ɔf ɚ] **1.** *tv.* to present something that can be taken or refused. ♦ *I offered some candy to the child.* ♦ *The designer offered his proposal for the remodeling job.* **2.** *tv.* to propose a price for something that is being sold. ♦ *I offered the salesman $3,500 for the used car.* ♦ *John offered $3 for the plastic bucket.* **3. offer to** *iv.* + *inf.* to indicate that one is willing to do something. ♦ *Did Tom offer to drive you home?* ♦ *My neighbor offered to help me when I was sick.* **4.** *n.* a price or amount that is **offered** as in ①. ♦ *The clerk refused my offer of $10 for the shirt.* ♦ *The saleswoman accepted my offer of $4,000 for the car.* **5.** *n.* something that is **offered** as in ①. ♦ *I refused the offer because I didn't need any help.* ♦ *I accepted my neighbor's offer to help me when I was sick.*

offering ['ɔf ɚ ɪŋ] *n.* a contribution; a donation; something that is offered, especially to a church, to a charity, or as part of a religious ritual. ♦ *Each Sunday, my family gives a $25 offering to the church.* ♦ *The worshipers sacrificed a pig as an offering to the gods.*

offhand ['ɔf 'hænd] **1.** *adj.* not thought about ahead of time; at the moment. ♦ *My offhand guess is that it's about three o'clock.* ♦ *John's offhand comment had nothing to do with the conversation.* **2.** *adv.* without thinking of something ahead of time; at the moment. ♦ *Offhand, I'd say that car is about five years old.* ♦ *I'd guess offhand that it's about three o'clock.*

office ['ɔf ɪs] **1.** *n.* a room—usually assigned to one person—where business is done. ♦ *I asked Ms. Smith if I could talk to her in her office.* ♦ *We went to my office to discuss the business proposal.* **2.** *n.* the combined work places of a number of people. ♦ *The company's employees have to be at the office by 9:00.* ♦ *Our office is closed on federal holidays.* **3.** *n.* a position of power and responsibility, especially in a government or an organization. ♦ *Three major candidates were running for the office of president.* ♦ *If elected to office, I promise to put more people to work.*

office hours ['ɔf ɪs ɑʊ ɚz] **1.** *n.* the time when an office is open. (Treated as plural. Rarely singular.) ♦ *Our office hours are from 9 A.M. to 5 P.M.* ♦ *The company's office hours were painted on the front door.* **2.** *n.* the time when a someone is available to be met with in an office. ♦ *The dentist told his neighbor to call him during office hours.* ♦ *The lawyer gave advice only during office hours.*

officer ['ɔ fə sɚ] *n.* someone in a position of authority, especially in the military, the government, or an organization. ♦ *The officers of the council met to discuss the annual budget.* ♦ *The police officer motioned for me to stop at the intersection.*

official [ə 'fɪ ʃəl] **1.** *n.* an officer; someone in a position of authority. ♦ *Dozens of foreign officials attended the prime minister's funeral.* ♦ *I spoke to an official about getting permission to enter the building.* **2.** *adj.* of or about the power, authority, and responsibility of an office or an officer. (Adv: *officially.*) ♦ *The secretary's official duties included taking minutes.* ♦ *The president issued an official statement about the crisis.*

officiate [ə 'fɪ ʃi et] **officiate (at)** *iv.* (+ *prep. phr.*) to perform the duties of an official; to act as an official; to preside. ♦ *The vice president officiates at the Senate.* ♦ *I officiated at the meeting because the president was sick.*

officiating [ə 'fɪ ʃi et ɪŋ] *adj.* presiding; performing the duties of an official. ♦ *The officiating council member called the meeting to order.* ♦ *The officiating judge entered the courtroom and we all stood.*

officious [ə 'fɪ ʃəs] *adj.* meddling; too eager to give advice where it is not wanted. (Adv: *officiously.*) ♦ *The officious clerk followed me around the store.* ♦ *My officious neighbor kept asking me personal questions.*

off-key ['ɔf 'ki] **1.** *adj.* out of tune; sung or played with notes that are a little too high (**sharp** ⑦) or low (**flat** ⑤). ♦ *I requested that the off-key piano be tuned.* ♦ *The soloist was off-key throughout the entire song!* **2.** *adv.* out of tune. ♦ *The old piano played off-key.* ♦ *The soprano sang the high notes off-key.*

offshoot ['ɔf ʃut] *n.* something that is a result or an effect of something else; something that develops from something else. ♦ *John's work was an offshoot of an earlier project.* ♦ *The café was an offshoot from the successful bakery.*

offshore ['ɔf 'ʃor] **1.** *adj.* in the water away from the shore. ♦ *A lot of oil comes from offshore drilling sites.* ♦ *The offshore hurricane quickly moved toward the coast.* **2.** *adv.* away from the shore; toward or from the water away from the shore. ♦ *The storm moved offshore.* ♦ *A lot of oil is pumped offshore.*

offspring ['ɔf sprɪŋ] *n.* [a person's] child or children; [an animal's] young. (No plural form in this sense. Treated as singular or plural.) ♦ *We took our cat's offspring to live with Mary.* ♦ *All of Mary's offspring are in Florida.*

offstage ['ɔf 'stedʒ] **1.** *adj.* adjacent to the visible part of the stage of a theater. ♦ *The scenery for the next act was offstage.* ♦ *An offstage chorus sang during the first act.* **2.** *adv.* toward or from the area adjacent to the visible part of the stage. ♦ *Mary ran offstage and changed her costume.* ♦ *The actors waited offstage for their cues to come onstage.*

off-white ['ɔf 'ʍaɪt] *adj.* not quite white in color; creamy white; a very light shade that is almost white. ♦ *The walls of the empty apartment were off-white.* ♦ *My business cards are printed on off-white paper.*

often ['ɔf ən] *adv.* frequently; happening many times. ♦ *We often go to the park during the summer.* ♦ *Anne often takes her dog for a walk after dinner.*

ogle ['ɔg əl] **1.** *tv.* to stare at someone; to look at someone with sexual desire or curiosity. ♦ *The old man ogled the young woman on the bus.* ♦ *Anne glared at the stranger who ogled her.* **2. ogle (at)** *iv.* (+ *prep. phr.*) to stare at someone or something; to look at someone with sexual desire or curiosity. ♦ *Don't ogle at me that way!* ♦ *All the boys were ogling at the bright red car.*

oh ['o] **Oh!** *interj.* <a form expressing surprise or other feelings.> (See also **boy**, **brother**.) ♦ *Oh! Is it 3:00 already?* ♦ *"Today is my birthday." "Oh, really? Happy Birthday!"*

Ohio [o 'haɪ o] See Gazetteer.

oil ['oɪl] **1.** *n.* a slick, greasy liquid that does not dissolve in water. (No plural form in this sense.) ♦ *Oil obtained from under the ground is used as a fuel.* ♦ *Oil obtained from plants and animals is used in cooking and in medicine.* **2.** *tv.* to lubricate something with oil; to make something slippery by putting oil on it; to put oil on something. ♦ *The mechanic oiled the car engine.* ♦ *The cook oiled the bottom of the frying pan.* **3. burn the midnight oil** *idiom* to stay up working, especially studying, late at night. ♦ *I have to go home and burn the midnight oil tonight.* ♦ *If you burn the midnight oil night after night, you'll probably become ill.*

oilcan ['oɪl kæn] *n.* a can that is used to apply oil as a lubricant. ♦ *The mechanic cleaned the oil that dripped from the oilcan's spout.* ♦ *I keep a full oilcan in the trunk of my car for emergencies.*

oily ['oɪl i] *adj.* made of oil; containing oil; soaked with oil. (Comp: *oilier;* sup: *oiliest.*) ♦ *The leaky engine made an oily mess on the floor.* ♦ *The fire started from a pile of oily rags.*

oink ['oɪŋk] **1.** *n.* the sound made by a pig. ♦ *The oink of the wild pig startled me.* ♦ *The pigs' oinks got louder as they got hungrier.* **2.** *iv.* to make the sound of a pig. ♦ *The pigs oinked when the farmer fed them.* ♦ *Jimmy oinked like a pig as he played in the mud.*

ointment ['oɪnt mənt] **1.** *n.* a substance that is put on the skin to heal it, soothe it, or soften it. (No plural form in this sense.) ♦ *Jane rubbed ointment on her dry skin.* ♦ *The soothing ointment felt good on my sunburned skin.* **2. fly in the ointment** *idiom* a small, unpleasant matter that spoils something; a drawback. ♦ *We enjoyed the play, but the fly in the ointment was not being able to find our car afterward.* ♦ *It sounds like a good idea, but there must be a fly in the ointment somewhere.*

OK [o 'ke] See **okay**.

okay AND **OK** [o 'ke] **1.** *adv.* all right; adequately. ♦ *If you follow directions closely, you should do OK.* ♦ *This television works okay, considering it's so old.* **2.** *adv.* a degree of intensity below "very good" but above "poor." ♦ *I like apple pie OK, but I really like blueberry pie.* ♦ *This television works okay, but it needs some repairs.* **3.** *adj.* sufficient; just good, but not excellent. ♦ *You did an OK job on your assignment.* ♦ *Bill gets okay grades, but his parents know he can do better.* **4.** *interj.* <a word used to confirm that one understands something.> ♦ *OK, I understand what you're telling me.* ♦ *"This organ here is the kidney." "Okay. What's that one?"* **5.** *interrog.* <a word used as a request for approval or permission.> ♦ *I'm going to the movies with Bob tonight, OK?* ♦ *Don't leave without me, okay?* **6.** *n.* approval. ♦ *I need your OK on this.* ♦ *The manager gave her OK to the budget proposal.* **7.** *tv.* to approve something. ♦ *My boss okayed my vacation request.* ♦ *The home owners okayed the designer's remodeling plans.*

Oklahoma [ok lə 'hom ə] See Gazetteer.

okra ['o krə] **1.** *n.* a tall plant with pods that are eaten as a vegetable. (No plural form in this sense.) ♦ *Okra grows well in hot climates.* ♦ *Okra produces pods that can be fried or put in soups and stews.* **2.** *n.* the edible pod of ①. (No plural form in this sense. Number is expressed with *piece(s) of okra.*) ♦ *Bob ordered chicken with potatoes and fried okra.* ♦ *The northerner had never eaten food like okra, and he didn't like it.*

old ['old] **1.** *adj.* having been alive for a long time; not recently born; not young. (Comp: *older;* sup: *oldest.*) ♦ *Although my grandfather is old, he is in good health.* ♦ *The old lady walked with a cane.* **2.** *adj.* having existed for a long time; not recently made; not new. (Comp: *older;* sup: *oldest.*) ♦ *My family has lived in this old house for 200 years.* ♦ *A row of oak trees lined the dusty old road.* **3.** *adj.* of a certain age. (Follows the age. Comp: *older.*) ♦ *How old are you?* ♦ *My brother turns 17 years old today.* **4.** *adj.* previous; former. (Comp: *older;* sup: *oldest.*) ♦ *We moved because our old house was too small.* ♦ *I sold my old car and bought a new one.*

old age ['old 'edʒ] **1.** *n.* the period when one is old. (No plural form in this sense.) ♦ *Old age is better than the alternative.* ♦ *In my old age, I hope to travel.* **2. old-age** *adj.* <the adj. use of ①.> ♦ *I will get a small old-age pen-*

sion from the government. ♦ *I have a few old-age aches and pains.*

old-fashioned ['old 'fæʃ ənd] *adj.* belonging to the style, actions, behavior, or rules of the past. (Adv: *old-fashionedly.*) ♦ *My old-fashioned parents insisted that I be home early.* ♦ *Anne wore an old-fashioned dress to the costume party.*

Old Testament ['old 'tɛs tə mənt] *n.* the first section of the Christian Bible. ♦ *Genesis is the first book of the Old Testament.* ♦ *The biblical account of creation is found in the Old Testament.*

old-time ['old 'tɑɪm] *adj.* of or about a past time. ♦ *Bill is an old-time friend of mine from elementary school.* ♦ *We sat around the piano singing old-time songs from the 1920s.*

olfactory [ol 'fæk tə ri] *adj.* of or about the sense of smell. ♦ *The poisonous gas damaged my olfactory nerves.* ♦ *The nose is an olfactory organ.*

olive ['ɑ lɪv] **1.** *n.* a tree grown in warm climates for its fruit. ♦ *Rows of olive trees filled the fields in southern Spain.* ♦ *We planted a few olives along with the poplar trees.* **2.** *n.* the fruit of ①, used for food. ♦ *Olives are eaten green or in their ripened black stage.* ♦ *Green olives are usually very salty.* **3. olive oil** *n.* an edible oil pressed from the seeds of ①. ♦ *Max added some olive oil to the sauce he made for his pasta.* ♦ *I rubbed olive oil on the chicken and browned it quickly.* **4.** *n.* a dark, yellowish green. (No plural form in this sense.) ♦ *Olive is not an exciting color to paint my walls.* ♦ *I prefer olive to gray.* **5.** *adj.* of a dark, yellowish green. ♦ *The soldier wore olive and brown camouflage pants.* ♦ *I repainted the ugly olive walls a brighter color.* **6. hold out the olive branch** *idiom* to offer to end a dispute and be friendly; to offer reconciliation. ♦ *Jane was the first to hold out the olive branch after our argument.* ♦ *I always try to hold out the olive branch to someone I have hurt. Life is too short for a person to bear grudges for very long.*

Olympic [ə 'lɪm pɪk] **1. Olympics** *n.* an international competition held every fourth winter and every fourth summer where athletes from several nations compete in different sporting events. (Treated as singular or plural.) ♦ *Where will the next Winter Olympics be held?* ♦ *The world's best athletes compete in the Olympics.* **2.** *adj.* <the adj. use of ①.> ♦ *The Olympic athletes participated in the opening ceremonies.* ♦ *That skater won two Olympic gold medals in skating.*

ombudsman ['ɑm bədz mən] *n., irreg.* an official who protects the rights of citizens and investigates complaints they have against bureaucratic officials. (From Swedish. Pl: ombudsmen.) ♦ *The ombudsman investigated the complaint against the mayor.* ♦ *Mary spoke with the ombudsman about her alderman's threats.*

ombudsmen ['ɑm bədz mən] pl of ombudsman.

omelet AND **omelette** ['ɑm lɪt] *n.* a dish made of beaten eggs, cooked flat and folded over, sometimes stuffed with other foods. ♦ *I ate a ham and cheese omelet for breakfast.* ♦ *I bought some eggs so I could make an omelet.*

omen ['o mən] *n.* a sign of something that will happen; a sign of things to come. ♦ *Some people think black cats are an omen of bad luck.* ♦ *Black rain clouds are an omen of heavy rainstorms.*

ominous ['ɑm ə nəs] *adj.* of or about an omen, especially a bad omen. (Adv: *ominously.*) ♦ *Ominous black clouds blew in from the west.* ♦ *I was frightened by the ominous howling of the dogs.*

omission [o 'mɪʃ ən] **1.** *n.* forgetting to list or include someone or something; omitting someone or something. (No plural form in this sense.) ♦ *The omission of the actor's name in the program angered him.* ♦ *The omission of your article from the journal was accidental.* **2.** *n.* something that has been left out; something that has been omitted. ♦ *The newspaper corrected the glaring omission in its next edition.* ♦ *Due to an omission, the author wasn't credited for her work.*

omit [o 'mɪt] *tv.* to leave someone or something out; to forget to list or include something. ♦ *I was mad that my article had been omitted from the journal.* ♦ *The publisher omitted the third chapter of the book by mistake.*

omnipotent [ɑm 'nɪp ə tənt] *adj.* more powerful than anyone else; having the power to do everything. (Adv: *omnipotently.*) ♦ *The omnipotent king killed his political enemies.* ♦ *Our minister preaches that God is omnipotent.*

omnipresent [ɑm ni 'prɛz ənt] *adj.* being everywhere at the same time. ♦ *The security force was omnipresent at the presidential rally.* ♦ *Nowadays, advertising seems to be omnipresent.*

omniscient [ɑm 'nɪʃ ənt] *adj.* all-knowing; knowing everything. (Adv: *omnisciently.*) ♦ *Parents seem to be omniscient to a three-year-old child.* ♦ *God is said to be omniscient and omnipotent.*

omnivore ['ɑm nɪ vor] *n.* an omnivorous creature. ♦ *I'm an omnivore. I'll eat whatever I am served.* ♦ *Since they eat plants, fish, and other animals, bears are omnivores.*

omnivorous [ɑm 'nɪv ɚ əs] *adj.* eating both plants and animals. (Adv: *omnivorously.*) ♦ *Most human beings are omnivorous.* ♦ *Omnivorous dinosaurs ate both plants and other dinosaurs.*

on ['ɔn] **1.** *prep.* above and supported by; covering or partially covering; touching the surface of something. ♦ *The book is on the table.* ♦ *The calendar is on the wall.* **2.** *prep.* traveling by [plane, train, boat, motorcycle, bicycle, or skateboard]. (But one travels *in* an automobile.) ♦ *Jane is on a plane to Boston.* ♦ *I hate riding on the train.* **3.** *prep.* near; at the edge of [a body of water]. ♦ *Last summer, I lived in a cottage on a stream.* ♦ *My parents have some land on the lake.* **4.** *prep.* about [a subject]. ♦ *The gardener bought a book on flowers.* ♦ *I saw a movie on the life of Queen Victoria.* **5.** *prep.* at a destination or goal. (In various idiomatic expressions.) ♦ *Our department finished the fiscal year on budget.* ♦ *Nothing is on schedule!* **6.** *prep.* happening at a specific time, date, or day. ♦ *I have a doctor's appointment on each Friday in October.* ♦ *I left for Florida on the 29th of October.* **7.** *prep.* being a member of a group. ♦ *Bill is on the publicity committee.* ♦ *I spoke to each member serving on the school board.* **8.** *prep.* taking [a drug]. ♦ *The doctor put Bill on medication to fight his infection.* ♦ *John becomes very obnoxious when he's on drugs.* **9.** *adj.* operating; turned on ⑪. ♦ *The TV set stayed on while the family ate dinner.* ♦ *Are the lights still on in the basement?* **10.** *adv.* onward; further in time or space. ♦ *The refugees walked on toward the border.* ♦ *From now on, I want you to do what you're told.* **11.** *adv.* so that something operates; so that something has the power to operate. ♦ *I turned the television on.* ♦ *Mary switched the lights on when she entered the dark room.* **12.** *adv.* still happening; not canceled; continuing as scheduled. ♦ *Is the baseball game still on for tonight?* ♦ *We're still on for dinner tomorrow, aren't we?*

once ['wʌns] **1.** *adv.* one time. ♦ *I smoked a cigarette once, and I never did it again.* ♦ *I've been to Mexico once, and I'd like to go back.* **2.** *adv.* at a time in the past; formerly. ♦ *I used to sing, once, when I was younger.* ♦ *Once, Bill had been very sociable; now he prefers to be alone.* **3. at once** *phr.* immediately; right now. ♦ *We must leave at once!* ♦ *You must come here at once.*

once-over ['wʌns ov ɚ] *n.* a quick look at something. ♦ *I gave my paper a once-over before I turned it in.* ♦ *My boss gave my proposal a once-over and approved it.*

oncoming ['ɔn kəm ɪŋ] *adj.* coming toward [oneself]; approaching. ♦ *I got off the train tracks when I saw the oncoming train.* ♦ *The driver drove over the median and crashed into an oncoming car.*

one ['wʌn] **1.** 1. See four for senses and examples. **2.** *n.* a one-dollar bill. ♦ *I have a one, but no change.* ♦ *Can I borrow a one until next week?* **3.** *adj.* on or at a particular time. ♦ *Late one evening, there was a knock at my door.* ♦ *One morning, I locked myself out of the house.* **4.** *adj.* united; together; joined. ♦ *In marriage, two people become one in spirit.* ♦ *East and West Germany became one again in 1990.* **5.** *pron.* a person or thing that is referred to. ♦ *I don't own a house now, but I plan to buy one soon.* ♦ *Those cookies look good. May I have one?* **6.** *pron.* you; anybody; a person. ♦ *What does one have to do to get service around here?* ♦ *No one saw the accident that killed the driver.* **7. as one** *idiom* as if a group were a single person. ♦ *All the dancers moved as one.* ♦ *The chorus spoke as one.*

oneself [wən 'sɛlf] **1.** *pron.* <the reflexive form of the pronoun **one** ⑥.> (Used when *one* is the subject of the sentence.) ♦ *One must behave oneself at all times.* ♦ *One should not shave oneself with a dull razor.* **2. by oneself** *phr.* with the help of no one else. ♦ *One is expected to do it by oneself.* ♦ *Can one do this by oneself?* **3. by oneself** *phr.* with no one else present; alone. ♦ *Must one sit by oneself or may one join another group?* ♦ *One just hates eating by oneself, doesn't one?*

one-sided ['wʌn 'sɑɪd ɪd] *adj.* not fair; not partial; seeing only one side of an argument. (Adv: *one-sidedly.*) ♦ *The one-sided judge ignored my lawyer.* ♦ *The one-sided editorial angered me.*

one-time ['wʌn tɑɪm] *adj.* former. ♦ *The one-time mayor returned to law after her term was over.* ♦ *The talk-show host interviewed the one-time movie star.*

ongoing ['ɔn go ɪŋ] *adj.* continuing; not stopping; in progress. ♦ *There were ongoing negotiations until the contract was settled.* ♦ *At work, there's an ongoing debate about the dress code.*

onion ['ʌn jən] **1.** *n.* a plant with a large, round edible bulb and thin green stalks. ♦ *Jane grew a row of onions in her garden.* ♦ *Bill pulled an onion from the ground by its stalk.* **2.** *n.* the edible bulb of ①, sometimes sliced or chopped. ♦ *Jane chopped up the onion with a knife.* ♦ *The chef put grilled onions on my hamburger.* **3.** *adj.* made with or flavored with ②. ♦ *I ate a ham and onion omelet for breakfast.* ♦ *I was served some onion soup.*

on-line ['ɔn 'lɑɪn] **1.** *adj.* on a computer network or the Internet. ♦ *There is lots of information about cancer on-line.* ♦ *I checked the library's on-line directory for the book I wanted.* **2.** *adv.* connecting to ①. ♦ *I went on-line to find some information on cancer.* ♦ *Max works on-line most of the day.*

onlooker ['ɔn lʊk ɚ] *n.* someone who sees but is not involved in something that is happening. ♦ *The police interviewed the onlookers who saw the accident.* ♦ *A few curious onlookers got in the way of the police.*

only ['on li] **1.** *adj.* sole; single. ♦ *My only allergy is to cats.* ♦ *This is the only house I've ever lived in.* ♦ *Only the cat sat on the mat. No other creature was on the mat.* **2.** *adv.* nothing or nobody else; merely; nothing more than. (Note the position of **only** in the examples.) ♦ *The cat only sat on the mat and did nothing else.* ♦ *The cat sat only on the mat and nowhere else.* **3.** *conj.* except that. ♦ *I want to go, only I am too frightened to do it.* ♦ *I would buy a car, only I don't have any money.*

onset ['ɔn sɛt] *n.* the beginning of something; the start of something. ♦ *From the onset, I knew this class would be difficult.* ♦ *I knew my sneezing was the onset of a major cold.*

onslaught ['ɔn slɔt] *n.* an attack; an assault. ♦ *The onslaught of missiles destroyed the town.* ♦ *The mayor faced an onslaught of angry questions.*

onstage [ɔn 'stedʒ] **1.** *adj.* on the part of a stage that an audience can see. ♦ *At the beginning of the act, all of the actors were onstage.* ♦ *Members of the onstage chorus were dressed in blue robes.* **2.** *adv.* toward or from a part of the stage that an audience can see. ♦ *John dragged the couch onstage between acts.* ♦ *The actor said his line as he ran onstage.*

onto ['ɔn tu] **1.** *prep.* to a position that is on something. ♦ *I put the vase onto the ledge.* ♦ *The pie fell onto the floor.* **2.** *prep.* knowledgeable about someone or something. (Informal.) ♦ *The teacher was onto us and caught us sneaking out of the building.* ♦ *The police are onto your plan.*

onward ['ɔn wɚd] *adv.* further in space or time; forward in space or time. ♦ *The police officer waved me onward past the accident.* ♦ *I walked onward toward the next town.*

onyx ['ɑn ɪks] **1.** *n.* a variety of quartz stone having different bands of color. (No plural form in this sense.) ♦ *The jeweler polished the onyx and set it into the ring.* ♦ *I chipped a piece of onyx out of the large rock.* **2.** *adj.* made from ①. ♦ *Jane wore an onyx ring.* ♦ *I got an onyx chess set for my birthday.*

ooze ['uz] **1.** *n.* muck; mud; slime; a thick liquid. (No plural form in this sense.) ♦ *My bike got stuck in ooze near the swamp.* ♦ *I cleaned the smelly ooze from the bottom of my refrigerator.* **2.** *iv.* to flow slowly, like mud or a very thick liquid; to seep out of a hole slowly. ♦ *Honey oozed through the hole in the container.* ♦ *The mud oozed up through the crack in the earth.*

oozy ['u zi] *adj.* slimy; having the consistency of slime. (Adv: *oozily.* Comp: *oozier;* sup: *ooziest.*) ♦ *My bike got stuck in the oozy ground.* ♦ *There's an oozy blob in the refrigerator that smells very bad.*

opal ['o pəl] **1.** *n.* a kind of stone that usually has a milky, cloudy color and is used to make jewelry. (No plural form in this sense.) ♦ *Opal is fragile and hard to work with.* ♦ *The birthstone for October is opal.* **2.** *n.* a gemstone formed of ①. ♦ *The jeweler put an opal in my ring.* ♦ *Jane has opals in her earrings.* **3.** *adj.* made from ①; made with ②. ♦ *Anne wore opal earrings to the party.* ♦ *I gave John an opal ring for his birthday.*

opaque [o 'pek] **1.** *adj.* not able to be seen through; not allowing light to pass through; not clear. (Adv: *opaquely.*) ♦ *The room was dark because all of the windows were opaque.* ♦ *The opaque wall blocked all sunlight from entering the room.* **2.** *adj.* hard to understand. (Figurative on ①. Adv: *opaquely.*) ♦ *I couldn't understand my professor's opaque lecture.* ♦ *It's very hard to read this textbook because it's so opaque.*

open ['o pən] **1.** *adj.* not shut; not closed; not sealed. ♦ *Light came through the open door.* ♦ *The food in the open container started to spoil.* **2.** *adj.* allowing customers to enter; ready for business. ♦ *The shoe store is open from 9 to 5.* ♦ *The new café will be open for business next week.* **3.** *adj.* not decided. ♦ *The council postponed a few open questions until the next meeting.* ♦ *The open issue was debated for hours by the committee.* **4.** *adj.* available; free and not restricted. (Adv: *openly.*) ♦ *There's open admission to the pageant.* ♦ *The citizens demanded open access to the city parks at all times.* **5.** *adj.* exposed; able to be seen; not hidden. (Adv: *openly.*) ♦ *Jane's open hostility to my suggestion surprised me.* ♦ *John's open disregard for the rules angered all of us.* **6.** *adj.* sincere; frank; candid; honest about one's feelings. (Adv: *openly.*) ♦ *My teacher's open attitude about drugs surprised me.* ♦ *John is very open about his feelings for Susan.* **7.** *tv.* to cause something to become ①; to allow a place to be entered into or exited from. ♦ *I opened the door and invited John inside.* ♦ *John opened the window so the bird could fly out of the room.* **8.** *tv.* to spread something out; to cause something to expand. ♦ *Mary opened the book and fanned her face with it.* ♦ *Stretching my arm opened my wound.* **9.** *tv.* to establish the beginning of something; to cause something to start. ♦ *The president opened the meeting by pounding the gavel.* ♦ *The lawyer opened the trial by describing the crime.* **10.** *iv.* to be accessible; to become more accessible. ♦ *The road opened shortly after the accident was cleared.* ♦ *The new airport finally opened to the public after several delays.* **11.** *iv.* to begin; to start doing business. ♦ *The new café opens next week.* ♦ *The store opens at 9:00.* **12. in the open** *idiom* in the outdoors; in an area that is not closed in. (No plural form in this sense.) ♦ *John's bike was stolen because he left it out in the open.* ♦ *Mary loves gardening because she loves to be in the open.* **13. open for business** *idiom* [of a shop, store, restaurant, etc.] operating and ready to do business. ♦ *The store is now open for business and invites you to come in.* ♦ *The construction will be finished in March, and we will be open for business in April.* **14. open to something** *idiom* agreeable to hear or learn about new ideas and suggestions. ♦ *The store owner was open to suggestions from her employees.* ♦ *We are always open to new ideas.*

open-ended ['o pən 'ɛnd ɪd] *adj.* not limited. (Adv: *open-endedly.*) ♦ *For our exam, we were asked three open-ended essay questions.* ♦ *Our vacation plans are open-ended, so we can do whatever we want.*

opener ['o pən ɚ] *n.* someone or something that opens something. ♦ *I opened the can of tuna with a can opener.* ♦ *I removed the cap from the soda with a bottle opener.*

opening ['o pən ɪŋ] **1.** *n.* a way into a container, compartment, or room; a way through a wall or barrier. ♦ *Milk poured from the opening of the pitcher.* ♦ *The couch barely fit through the narrow opening to the room.* **2.** *n.* the start of something; the beginning; the introduction. ♦ *Right from the opening, I knew this movie would fail.* ♦ *The opening of the book took place 20 years before the rest of it.* **3.** *n.* something that is available; a job that is available. ♦ *Our company has an opening in the accounting department.* ♦ *There's an opening for a waiter at that restaurant.* **4.** *n.* an opportunity to do something or say something. (Figurative on ①.) ♦ *When he stopped talking, it gave me an opening to present my ideas.* ♦ *If I could only get an opening, I could state my side of the matter.* **5.** *adj.* at the beginning; the first; the earliest. ♦ *On opening night of the play, several critics were in the audience.* ♦ *The lawyer presented her opening statements to the jury.*

openly ['o pən li] *adj.* clearly and obviously. ♦ *My boss was openly hostile to my suggestions.* ♦ *My friends were openly concerned about my plan to leave school.*

open-minded ['o pən 'maɪn dɪd] *adj.* willing to change one's mind; not stubborn; not prejudiced. (Adv: *open-mindedly.*) ♦ *The open-minded judge listened to both sides carefully.* ♦ *My parents are very open-minded about social issues.*

opera ['ɑ prə] **1.** *n.* the branch of theater or music where lengthy performances include solo and choral singing, orchestra music, and sometimes dance. (No plural form in this sense.) ♦ *The composer specialized in opera.* ♦ *The professor contrasted opera with musicals.* **2.** *n.* a presentation or performance of a musical production as in ①. ♦ *My favorite opera is* Madame Butterfly. ♦ *All the operas I like are sung in a foreign language.*

operable ['ɑp ɚ ə bəl] **1.** *adj.* able to be used. (Adv: *operably.*) ♦ *There was only one operable elevator in the entire building.* ♦ *The mechanic worked on the engine until it was operable.* **2.** *adj.* able to be operated on or removed by surgery. (Adv: *operably.*) ♦ *Luckily, the tumor was operable.* ♦ *The patient had a brain tumor that was not operable and also could not be treated by radiation.*

operate ['ɑp ə ret] **1.** *iv.* [for a machine or device] to work or function. ♦ *My computer operates on batteries or electricity.* ♦ *Why isn't this elevator operating?* **2.** *iv.* to perform surgery; to perform an operation. ♦ *The doctor operated with the consent of the patient.* ♦ *That surgeon talks very little while he operates.* **3. operate on** *iv.* + *prep. phr.* to perform surgery on a certain part of the body or on someone. ♦ *The surgeon operated on my kidneys.* ♦ *The surgeons operated on the patient with appendicitis.* **4.** *tv.* to cause something to work or function; to direct or manage something. ♦ *The automatic door is operated by a small motor.* ♦ *The projectionist operated the movie projector.*

operatic [ɑp ə 'ræt ɪk] *adj.* of or about opera. (Adv: *operatically* [...ɪk li].) ♦ *Mary sang an operatic aria for her audition.* ♦ *The star of the operatic movie is a famous tenor.*

operating ['ɑp ə ret ɪŋ] *adj.* working; functioning; able to be used. ♦ *The only operating elevator in this building is very slow.* ♦ *I tried three broken telephones before I found an operating one.*

operation [ɑ pə 're ʃən] **1.** *n.* surgery; a medical procedure where something is done to the body, usually involving cutting. ♦ *John had an operation to remove a cancerous tumor.* ♦ *During the operation, the patient's heartbeat remained steady.* **2.** *n.* a procedure; an activity; the way something proceeds. ♦ *The hostage situation required a bold military operation.* ♦ *My boss trained me in the operation of the equipment.*

operational [ɑp ə 're ʃə nəl] *adj.* functional; working; able to be used. ♦ *The mechanic made my car fully operational again.* ♦ *The only operational elevator in the building is running slowly.*

operator ['ɑp ə ret ɚ] **1.** *n.* someone who operates a machine. ♦ *The operator turned the machine off before repairing it.* ♦ *The operator must wear safety goggles at all times.* **2.** *n.* someone who handles telephone calls; the person one talks to when one dials "0" on a telephone. ♦ *I asked the operator what the area code for Atlanta was.* ♦ *The operator placed a collect call for me.*

ophthalmologist [ɑf θæl 'mɑl ə dʒəst] *n.* a doctor who specializes in eye diseases and disorders. ♦ *The ophthalmologist performed a corneal implant.* ♦ *Ophthalmologists can prescribe drugs and perform surgery.*

ophthalmology [ɑf θæl 'mɑl ə dʒi] *n.* the science and study of the eye and its diseases and disorders. (No plural form in this sense.) ♦ *My eye doctor has a degree in ophthalmology.* ♦ *The surgeon specialized in ophthalmology.*

opiate ['o pi ət] *n.* a drug that is made from opium and dulls pain; a drug derived from or working like opium. ♦ *The patient was given an opiate to dull his pain.* ♦ *The criminals smuggled opiates into the country.*

opinion [ə 'pɪn jən] **1.** *n.* thought, ideas, or attitudes concerning someone or something. (No plural form in this sense.) ♦ *Opinion and actual facts are not always the same.* ♦ *Are you expressing fact or only opinion?* **2.** *n.* the way that someone thinks about a certain subject; one's belief. ♦ *In my opinion, I think you could lose some weight.* ♦ *My opinion about taxation is very different from John's.* **3.** *n.* advice from a professional or an expert. ♦ *My doctor's professional opinion was that I needed surgery.* ♦ *That lawyer charges too much for simple legal opinions.* **4. form an opinion** *idiom* to think up or decide on ① or ②. ♦ *I don't know enough about the issue to form an opinion.* ♦ *Don't tell me how to think! I can form my own opinion.*

opinionated [ə 'pɪn jə ne tɪd] *adj.* stubborn; having opinions that one is not willing to change. (Adv: *opinionatedly.*) ♦ *My opinionated father refused to listen to what I had to say.* ♦ *Jane won't listen to my advice because she's too opinionated.*

opium ['o pi əm] *n.* a drug made from the seeds of the poppy plant, which is used to make people sleep and to dull pain. (No plural form in this sense.) ♦ *Opium comes from the poppy plant.* ♦ *Opium is an addictive drug.*

opossum [ə 'pɑs əm] *n.* a small furry animal with a prehensile tail. (Also possum.) ♦ *The female opossum carries her young in a pouch or on her back.* ♦ *I swerved to avoid hitting the opossum crossing the road.*

opponent [ə 'pon ənt] *n.* someone who is on the opposite side in a contest, fight, or argument. ♦ *Our football team's opponents won the game.* ♦ *The senator tried to win votes to support the proposed law.*

opportune [ɑp ɚ 'tun] *adj.* happening at a good time; happening at the right time; favorable. (Adv: *opportunely.*) ♦ *A warm, sunny day is an opportune time for a picnic.* ♦ *When the opportune moment arises, I'll ask my boss for a raise.*

opportunity [ɑp ɚ 'tun ə ti] *n.* a good chance for doing something; a favorable time for doing something. ♦ *A good education can widen your opportunities for a good job.* ♦ *Winning the lottery gave me the opportunity to quit my job.*

oppose [ə 'poz] *tv.* to be against someone or something; to fight against someone or something; to argue against someone or something. (Often passive.) ♦ *The citizens opposed the city's plan to build a new landfill.* ♦ *The incumbent was opposed by two other candidates.*

opposing [ə 'poz ɪŋ] *adj.* against; contrary. (Adv: *opposingly.*) ♦ *We lost to the opposing team by a score of 10–7.* ♦ *The opposing sides declared war on each other.*

opposite ['ɑp ə zɪt] **1.** *adj.* completely different in at least one major respect. (Adv: *oppositely.*) ♦ *My parents have the opposite viewpoint of mine on many issues.* ♦ *Taking the opposite side is easy for Bob. He loves to argue.* **2.** *adj.* of or about a location that is the farthest point away within a defined area. (Adv: *oppositely.*) ♦ *The nearest post office is on the opposite side of town.* ♦ *The plane I need to board is at the opposite end of the airport.* **3.** *prep.* across from someone or something; facing someone or something. ♦ *I sat opposite Mary at the table.* ♦ *The bakery is opposite the church.* **4.** *n.* someone or something that is opposite ① someone or something else. ♦ *The opposite of "night" is "day."* ♦ *Anne is my opposite when it comes to most political issues.* **5. opposite sex** *n.* [from the point of view of a female] a male; [from the point of view of a male] a female. ♦ *Mike has become quite interested in the opposite sex, now that he is 14.* ♦ *Mary says that she just hates the opposite sex and will never get married.*

opposition [ɑ pə 'zɪ ʃən] **1.** *n.* a state of being against someone or something; resistance; hostility. (No plural form in this sense.) ♦ *The citizens were in solid opposition to the new airport.* ♦ *The tax plan was met with strong opposition.* **2.** *n.* the people who are against something. (No plural form in this sense.) ♦ *The opposition demanded an end to the war.* ♦ *The mayor met with members of the opposition to discuss their concerns.* **3.** *n.* the political party that is not in control. (No plural form in this sense.) ♦ *The president vetoed the opposition's legislation.* ♦ *The opposition demanded a larger voice in the government.*

oppress [ə 'prɛs] *tv.* to rule someone or a group of people harshly or cruelly; to keep someone from succeeding. ♦ *The slave was oppressed by his cruel owner.* ♦ *The poor nation was oppressed by an evil tyrant.*

oppression [ə 'prɛ ʃən] *n.* the unfair or burdensome exercise of authority to the disadvantage of someone or a group. (No plural form in this sense.) ♦ *Oppression through slavery is an abuse of human rights.* ♦ *We suffered through years of oppression before laws were passed to protect us.*

oppressive [ə 'prɛs ɪv] *adj.* harsh; unfair; burdensome; cruel. (Adv: *oppressively.*) ♦ *The oppressive government enforced a strict curfew.* ♦ *Innocent people were imprisoned through the use of the oppressive laws.*

optic ['ɑp tɪk] *adj.* of or about the eye or vision. (Adv: *optically* [...ɪk li].) ♦ *The optic nerve connects the eye with the brain.* ♦ *My head injury caused severe optic distortions.*

optical ['ɑp tɪ kəl] *adj.* of or about the eye or vision. (Adv: *optically* [...ɪk li].) ♦ *Mirages and hallucinations are optical illusions.* ♦ *I was given an optical exam to determine my range of vision.*

optician [ɑp 'tɪ ʃən] *n.* someone who makes or sells eyeglasses and contact lenses. (Compare with **optometrist**.) ♦ *My optician ground the lenses according to the prescription.* ♦ *The optician fitted me with a new pair of glasses.*

optimal ['ɑp tɪ məl] *adj.* the best; the most favorable; optimum. (Adv: *optimally.*) ♦ *In my opinion, 75-degree weather is optimal.* ♦ *This is the optimal time for harvesting apples.*

optimism ['ɑp tɪ mɪz əm] *n.* a happy, positive outlook; the belief that everything will be fine; the opposite of pessimism. (No plural form in this sense.) ♦ *Bill's optimism was clouded after a series of bad accidents.* ♦ *Because of my optimism, I knew things would get better.*

optimist ['ɑp tɪ məst] *n.* someone who believes that everything will be fine; someone who looks on the positive side of everything. ♦ *The optimist felt that the war would be over soon.* ♦ *Nothing discourages Susan because she is an optimist.*

optimistic [ɑp tɪ 'mɪs tɪk] *adj.* hoping for the best; believing that everything will be fine. (Adv: *optimistically* [...ɪk li].) ♦ *The general was optimistic that the war would soon end.* ♦ *The optimistic budget report indicated there would be a surplus.*

optimum ['ɑp tə məm] **1.** *adj.* most favorable; most suitable. ♦ *The optimum temperature for baking depends on the individual oven.* ♦ *I raised my exotic plants under optimum conditions.* **2.** *n.* the best thing that suits a given purpose. (No plural form in this sense.) ♦ *The architect demanded the optimum for his working conditions.* ♦ *My pies bake best at 400 degrees, but the optimum is different at higher altitudes.*

option ['ɑp ʃən] *n.* a choice; an alternative. ♦ *The waitress offered the option of apple or blueberry pie.* ♦ *I examined all my options before making a decision.*

optional ['ɑp ʃə nəl] *adj.* having a choice; not required; not mandatory. (Adv: *optionally.*) ♦ *The history major took an optional class in psychology.* ♦ *Participating in school clubs and sports is optional.*

optometrist [ɑp 'tɑm ɪ trəst] *n.* someone who is trained to examine eyes and determine what kind of glasses or contact lenses are needed. ♦ *My optometrist gave me a prescription for contact lenses.* ♦ *The optometrist asked me which of two images was clearer.*

optometry [ɑp 'tɑm ɪ tri] *n.* the science of examining eyes to determine what kind of glasses or contact lenses are needed. (No plural form in this sense.) ♦ *I studied optometry instead of ophthalmology because surgery makes me queasy.* ♦ *David practices optometry in an office on 12th Street.*

opulent ['ɑp jə lənt] *adj.* rich; luxurious. (Adv: *opulently.*) ♦ *Bill wore a tuxedo to the opulent dinner party.* ♦ *The owner of the company owned two opulent houses.*

or ['or] **1.** *conj.* <a word used in a list of items to show a choice or difference.> ♦ *This dress is available in red, green, or blue.* ♦ *Would you like coffee, tea, or juice?* **2.** *conj.* otherwise; if not. ♦ *Listen to me, or you will suffer the consequences.* ♦ *Take your vitamins, or you will become sick.* **3.** *conj.* that is to say. ♦ *My friend, or my former friend, spread gossip about me.* ♦ *10 is one-half, or 50%, of 20.*

oral ['or əl] **1.** *adj.* of or about the mouth. (Adv: *orally.*) ♦ *The mouth contains the oral cavity.* ♦ *My cracked molar was removed by an oral surgeon.* **2.** *adj.* spoken. (Adv: *orally.*) ♦ *I presented an oral book report to the class.* ♦ *The witness gave both a written and an oral statement to the police.*

orange ['or ɪndʒ] **1.** *n.* a color of the rainbow between red and yellow, and the color of ②. (No plural form in this sense.) ♦ *Orange is the color of most pumpkins.* ♦ *I decorated the room in orange and black for Halloween.* **2.** *n.* a round, juicy, citrus fruit—of the color ①—that grows on a tree. ♦ *Oranges contain a lot of vitamin C.* ♦ *You must peel an orange before eating it.* **3.** *adj.* the color of ①. ♦ *I put some orange flowers in the vase.* ♦ *The invitations for the Halloween party were printed on orange paper.* **4.** *adj.* made with ②; flavored with ②. ♦ *I ate some orange gelatin for dessert.* ♦ *I had a glass of orange juice for breakfast.*

orangutan [ə 'ræŋ ʊ tæn, ə 'ræŋ ə tæŋ] *n.* a large, reddish ape found in the forests of Borneo and Sumatra. (From Malay.) ♦ *The orangutan has the largest arm span of all of the apes.* ♦ *Orangutans primarily eat plants, not meat.*

oration [ɔ 're ʃən] **1.** *n.* formal, public speech. (No plural form in this sense.) ♦ *Lengthy oration can be boring.* ♦ *Thousands of people listened to the minister's skilled oration.* **2.** *n.* a formal, public speech. ♦ *The preacher's oration covered a whole series of sins.* ♦ *The speaker's oration was interrupted by applause.*

orator ['or ə tɚ] *n.* someone who excels at giving a public or formal speech. ♦ *Tom is not just a speaker. He is a skilled orator.* ♦ *The university invited a famous orator to speak at commencement.*

oratorio [or ə 'tor i o] *n.* a musical composition for singers and musical instruments, usually about something religious. (Pl in *-s.*) ♦ *I listened to an oratorio about the joy of living.* ♦ *The orchestra and the chorus performed an oratorio for the festival.*

oratory ['or ə tor i] *n.* the ability to speak well in public. (No plural form in this sense.) ♦ *The popular politician was a master at public oratory.* ♦ *Mary improved her skills at oratory by taking speech classes.*

orbit ['or bɪt] **1.** *n.* a pathway around a celestial body, such as that taken by a planet, a moon, or a rocket. ♦ *The orbit of comets is elliptical.* ♦ *Our planet is in orbit around the sun.* **2.** *tv.* to move in a circle around a star or planet. ♦ *The spaceship orbited the moon.* ♦ *Earth orbits the sun every 365 days.* **3.** *iv.* to move in a circle around a star or planet. ♦ *Nine planets orbit around our sun.* ♦ *Is the satellite orbiting yet?*

orca ['or kə] *n.* the scientific name of the killer whale. ♦ *The lifeguard spotted an orca near the shore.* ♦ *A seal was killed and eaten by an orca.*

orchard ['or tʃɚd] *n.* a farm of fruit or nut trees. ♦ *I just picked these apples from the orchard.* ♦ *The cherry orchard contains hundreds of trees.*

orchestra ['or kə strə] **1.** *n.* a group of musicians and the instruments they play. ♦ *My aunt plays the violin in the city's orchestra.* ♦ *The orchestra practiced Beethoven's Fifth Symphony dozens of times.* **2. orchestra pit** See pit ③. **3. symphony orchestra** See symphony ②.

orchestral [or 'kɛs trəl] *adj.* of or about an orchestra; written for an orchestra. (Adv: *orchestrally.*) ♦ *I listened to an orchestral medley of patriotic songs.* ♦ *The composer wrote an orchestral arrangement for the popular song.*

orchestrate ['or kə stret] **1.** *tv.* to adapt a piece of music for a full orchestra. ♦ *The composer orchestrated a new symphony for the king.* ♦ *The young conductor orchestrated some popular rock-and-roll songs.* **2.** *tv.* to cause, organize, or arrange something to work smoothly. (Figurative on ①.) ♦ *Anne orchestrated the conference according to a tight schedule.* ♦ *The annual meeting was orchestrated by the chairman.*

orchid ['or kɪd] *n.* a flower with unusually shaped and brightly colored petals. ♦ *The bride's mother wore a corsage of orchids.* ♦ *The gardener planted a row of orchids next to the porch.*

ordain [or 'den] **1.** *tv.* to confer the status of being a priest or a minister on someone. ♦ *The bishop ordained five new priests last week.* ♦ *Our minister was ordained after he graduated from divinity school.* **2.** *tv.* to order something; to make something a law. (Takes a clause.) ♦ *The company president ordained that all employees work this Saturday.* ♦ *The legislature ordained that smoking in public places be illegal.*

ordeal [or 'dil] *n.* a very difficult experience. ♦ *Correcting a faulty credit record can be a horrible ordeal.* ♦ *The soldier faced many ordeals during the war.*

order ['or dɚ] **1.** *n.* the sequence in which a series of things is arranged. (No plural form in this sense.) ♦ *The secretary placed the files in alphabetical order.* ♦ *The records were filed in the order in which they were received.* **2.** *n.* a state of everything being in its proper place. (No plural form in this sense.) ♦ *My boss told me to set my messy desk in order.* ♦ *The new office manager brought order to the messy filing system.* **3.** *n.* a state of being able to be used; condition. (No plural form in this sense.) ♦ *The mechanic restored my car to working order.* ♦ *I expect my lawn mower to be returned to me in good order.* **4.** *n.* a state wherein people are following rules and behaving properly. (No plural form in this sense.) ♦ *The new sheriff promised to bring law and order to the town.* ♦ *The police restored order after the riot.* **5.** *n.* a command. ♦ *The general gave the order to attack.* ♦ *The children ignored my order to be quiet.* **6.** *n.* a request for certain goods or services. ♦ *I mailed the publisher an order for a book.* ♦ *The customer placed an order for an item that wasn't in stock.* **7.** *n.* one serving of a kind of food. ♦ *We can split an order of pancakes if you're not too hungry.* ♦ *I'd like a large order of french fries, please.* **8. (religious) order** *n.* a religious society; a group of priests, monks, or nuns. ♦ *The hospital is operated by a religious order.* ♦ *John joined a religious order immediately after high school.* **9.** *n.* a kind; a type; a division of classifying plants and animals. ♦ *In biology, "order" ranks below "class" and above "family."* ♦ *Humans and apes both belong to the order of primates.* **10. order to** *tv.* + *inf.* to tell someone what to do; to give someone a command to do something. ♦ *The private was ordered to report to the general.* ♦ *John ordered me to get him some coffee.* **11.** *tv.* to request goods or services. ♦ *John ordered a new sweater over the telephone.* ♦ *Mary ordered some skis from a catalog.* **12.** *tv.* to request a serving of food or a full meal. ♦ *I ordered a bowl of soup along with my meal.* ♦ *Anne ordered a large pizza.* **13.** *tv.* to arrange someone or something into a certain sequence. ♦ *Bill ordered the students by height.* ♦ *John ordered the cards numerically.* **14. in short order** *idiom* very quickly. ♦ *I can straighten out this mess in short order.* ♦ *The people came in and cleaned the place up in short order.* **15. order of the day** *idiom* something necessary or usual at a certain time. ♦ *Warm clothes are the order of the day when camping in the winter.* ♦ *Going to bed early was the order of the day when we were young.* **16. out of order** *idiom* not following correct parliamentary procedure. ♦ *I was declared out of order by the president.* ♦ *Anne inquired, "Isn't a motion to table the question out of order at this time?"* **17. out of order** *idiom* [of something] not in good working condition; not functioning. ♦ *This elevator is out of order!* ♦ *Her computer is out of order, and she cannot get her work done.*

orderly ['or dɚ li] **1.** *adj.* neat; in order. ♦ *John lives in a clean, orderly apartment.* ♦ *Mary was praised for her orderly penmanship.* **2.** *n.* a hospital attendant. ♦ *The orderlies changed the bed linens.* ♦ *The doctor asked the orderly for some assistance.*

ordinal (numeral) AND **ordinal (number)** ['or dɪ nəl 'nu mə rəl, 'or dɪ nəl 'nʌm bɚ] *n.* the number used to show rank or position in a series, such as first, second, third, etc. (See also cardinal numeral.) ♦ *The ordinal numerals are used when stating the order of people or things.* ♦ *When the cardinal number is* ten, *the ordinal is* tenth.

ordinance ['or də nəns] *n.* a local or state rule; a local or state regulation. ♦ *Many cities have ordinances against smoking in public places.* ♦ *By state ordinance, school buses must stop at railroad tracks.*

ordinarily [or də 'nɛr ə li] *adv.* usually; commonly. ♦ *I ordinarily do the laundry on Thursdays.* ♦ *It's ordinarily warmer in the summer than in the winter.*

ordinary ['or də nɛr i] *adj.* usual; common; typical; regular. (Adv: *ordinarily* [or də 'nɛr ə li].) ♦ *My ordinary route to work was blocked by construction.* ♦ *The magician held up an ordinary deck of playing cards.*

ore ['or] *n.* rock or dirt that contains metal. (No plural form in this sense.) ♦ *The prospector studied the ore, looking for gold.* ♦ *Tons of iron ore were taken from the mine.*

oregano [ə 'rɛg ə no] *n.* a kind of herb used as a spice in cooking. (No plural form in this sense.) ♦ *I added a pinch of oregano to the spaghetti sauce.* ♦ *The chef sprinkled some oregano on top of the salad.*

Oregon ['or ə gən] See Gazetteer.

organ ['or gən] **1.** *n.* a part of an animal that performs a specific function. ♦ *The heart is the organ that pumps blood throughout the body.* ♦ *The eye is the organ of sight.* **2.** *n.* a musical instrument with keyboards that control the air flow into many pipes of different lengths, each sounding a different note. ♦ *The choir was accompanied by an organ.* ♦ *Mr. Smith plays the organ at our church.*

organic [or 'gæn ɪk] **1.** *adj.* of or about plants or animals; of or about living or previously living things. (Adv: *organically* [...ɪk li].) ♦ *All organic substances contain carbon compounds.* ♦ *The compost pile is made from decayed organic material.* **2.** *adj.* grown without chemicals or pesticides. (Adv: *organically* [...ɪk li].) ♦ *These potato chips were made from organic potatoes.* ♦ *This grocery store stocks organic vegetables.* **3.** *adj.* underlying; basic. (Adv: *organically* [...ɪk li].) ♦ *There seemed to be no organic cause for the epidemic.* ♦ *The unruly student has organic psychological problems.*

organism ['or gə nɪz əm] *n.* a plant or an animal; a living thing. ♦ *The scientist examined the organism under the microscope.* ♦ *Thousands of microscopic organisms live in and on the human body.*

organist ['or gə nəst] *n.* a musician who plays an organ. ♦ *My church employs an organist and a choir director.* ♦ *The couple hired an organist to play at their wedding.*

organization [or gə nɪ 'ze ʃən] **1.** *n.* a group of people united for a specific purpose; a group of people who manage a business. ♦ *Every member of the organization received the company newsletter.* ♦ *Most charitable organizations are exempt from federal income tax.* **2.** *n.* the arrangement of parts to form a whole. (No plural form in this sense.) ♦ *Botanists study the structural organization of plants.* ♦ *The mechanical organization of a watch is very complex.* **3.** *n.* the way that the different parts of a whole work together; the way that different people in a group work together. (No plural form in this sense.) ♦ *Anne's methods of organization made the office more efficient.* ♦ *The consultant stated that better organization would yield higher profits.*

organize ['or gə naɪz] **1.** *tv.* to arrange different parts in a way so that they function properly; to arrange different parts into a system. ♦ *Susan organized her boss's business calendar.* ♦ *The assembly line was organized for maximum efficiency.* **2.** *tv.* to form an organization. ♦ *The students helped organize a party for the principal.* ♦ *Tom organized a stamp collecting club.* **3.** *iv.* to form a labor union; to unionize. ♦ *Against management's wishes, the factory workers organized.* ♦ *The unfairly treated workers voted to organize.*

organizer ['or gə naɪz ɚ] **1.** *n.* someone who organizes things into a system that functions well. ♦ *Since Anne is an organizer, she always knows where she's put things.* ♦ *If you were an organizer, you'd be more efficient.* **2.** *n.* someone who helps form a labor union. ♦ *The factory threatened to fire the union organizers.* ♦ *The organizer was elected as the union's first president.*

orgasm ['or gæz əm] *n.* the peak of sexual excitement. ♦ *When the male has an orgasm, he usually ejaculates semen.* ♦ *The sex therapist helped people who were unable to have orgasms.*

orgy ['or dʒi] **1.** *n.* a wild party with drinking, drugs, and sex. ♦ *A Roman orgy was depicted on the side of the ancient urn.* ♦ *Many people left the party as it turned into an orgy.* **2.** *n.* a wild or outrageous event. (Figurative on ①.) ♦ *When we won the championship, there was an orgy of celebration.* ♦ *The fraternity's annual bash is quite an orgy!*

orient ['or i ənt] **1.** *tv.* to make someone become familiar with something; to acquaint someone with something; to help someone become used to something. ♦ *The dean held a meeting to orient the new students during their first week at college.* ♦ *The manual was designed to orient the new users to the equipment.* **2.** *tv.* to face a certain direction. ♦ *Mary oriented herself toward the west.* ♦ *My bedroom windows are oriented to the north.* **3.** *tv.* to find one's bearings; to determine what direction one is facing. (Figurative on ②.) ♦ *When I arrived in Boston, it took a long time to orient myself.* ♦ *Because Chicago is laid out on a grid, it's easy to orient yourself.* **4. Orient** *n.* the countries of eastern Asia. (From the point of view of Europe. No plural form in this sense.) ♦ *The airline connected Europe with the Orient.* ♦ *Mary studied literature in the Orient for two years.*

oriental [or i 'ɛn təl] *adj.* of or about the peoples and cultures of eastern Asia and the islands to the south and east. (Adv: *orientally.* Objected to by some. **Asian** is often substituted for this term.) ♦ *Mary took a course in oriental literature.* ♦ *I'd like to have oriental food for dinner.*

orientation [or i ən 'te ʃən] **1.** *n.* becoming familiar with something; making someone familiar with something. (No plural form in this sense.) ♦ *There's a week of orientation for new students before each term.* ♦ *My orientation to the new country took some time.* **2.** *n.* the position or direction that someone or something is in; the way that someone or something is positioned. ♦ *That street has a north-south orientation.* ♦ *The astrologer studied the orientation of the constellations.*

orifice ['or ə fɪs] *n.* an opening; a hole. ♦ *A pin made a tiny orifice in the paper cup, causing it to leak.* ♦ *Your mouth is an orifice that leads to your lungs and to your stomach.*

origin ['or ə dʒən] *n.* the starting point; something that other things develop from. ♦ *The reporter tracked down the origin of the rumor.* ♦ *The origin of the river was a spring up in the mountains.*

original [ə 'rɪdʒ ə nəl] **1.** *adj.* not copied or based on something else. ♦ *This museum displays dozens of original works of art.* ♦ *The students had to write an original short story for class.* **2.** *adj.* first; earliest. (Adv: *originally.*) ♦ *I still have the original tires on my car.* ♦ *The antique doll was still in its original package.* **3.** *n.* something that copies are made from; the first example of something that other examples are based on. ♦ *The library locks up rare originals, but copies of those texts are available.* ♦ *This statue is a poor copy of the original.*

originality [ə rɪdʒ ə 'næl ə ti] *n.* the ability to think of something new; creativity. (No plural form in this sense.) ♦ *Mary's originality as an architect made her very successful.* ♦ *The author seemed to lack both imagination and originality.*

originate [ə 'rɪdʒ ə net] **1.** *tv.* to cause something to exist; to found something; to establish something, such as an organization. ♦ *The local chess club was originated by my math teacher.* ♦ *Many clothing fads are originated by fashion designers.* **2.** *iv.* to start; to begin. ♦ *Route 66 originates in Chicago.* ♦ *Flight 720, which originated in St. Louis, will arrive in 5 minutes.*

originator [ə 'rɪdʒ ə net ɚ] *n.* someone who creates or originates something. ♦ *Who was the originator of that unique style of painting?* ♦ *The theory's originator lectured my class about its applications.*

oriole ['or ɪ əl] *n.* a small songbird, the male of which has black and orange markings. ♦ *A brightly colored oriole* *nests in a tree in my yard.* ♦ *The oriole flew away when the cat jumped at it.*

ornament ['or nə mənt] **1.** *n.* decorations, in general. (No plural form in this sense.) ♦ *The entire house was devoid of any ornament.* ♦ *A lack of ornament made the room appear quite drab.* **2.** *n.* a decoration; something that makes someone or something look prettier. ♦ *The ornaments on the Christmas tree shined and sparkled.* ♦ *A few small ornaments decorated the table in the hall.* **3.** *tv.* to add ① to something; to put ② on something; to adorn something. ♦ *The children ornamented the Christmas tree with tinsel.* ♦ *The room was ornamented with paintings and expensive trinkets.*

ornamental [or nə 'mɛn təl] *adj.* used as an ornament; decorative. (Adv: *ornamentally.*) ♦ *The ornamental carvings on the wall came from Greece.* ♦ *The restaurant was decorated with ornamental lights.*

ornate [or 'net] *adj.* fancy; not simple or plain. (Adv: *ornately.*) ♦ *The Smiths spent thousands of dollars on the ornate party.* ♦ *The ornate design took Susan two months to draw.*

ornery ['or nə ri] *adj.* stubborn; perverse; cranky. (Comp: *ornerier;* sup: *orneriest.*) ♦ *The ornery old man refused to take his medicine.* ♦ *The ornery child wouldn't go to bed.*

ornithology [or nə 'θɑl ə dʒi] *n.* the study and science of birds. (No plural form in this sense.) ♦ *Ornithology is a division of zoology that concerns birds.* ♦ *I went bird watching with a friend who had studied ornithology.*

orphan ['or fən] **1.** *n.* a young child whose parents are dead or missing. ♦ *The nuns in the convent raised the orphan left on their doorstep.* ♦ *The young orphan was adopted by her foster family.* **2.** *tv.* to cause someone to be ①. (Typically passive.) ♦ *Hundreds of children were orphaned in the war.* ♦ *Jimmy was orphaned when his parents were killed in an accident.*

orphanage ['or fə nɪdʒ] *n.* an institution where orphans live. ♦ *The young couple chose to adopt a child from an orphanage.* ♦ *Jimmy moved to an orphanage after his parents died.*

orthodontic [or θə 'dɑn tɪk] **1.** *adj.* of or about the straightening of the teeth. (Adv: *orthodontically* [...ɪk li].) ♦ *I wore orthodontic braces when I was a teenager.* ♦ *Jimmy needs orthodontic treatment for his crooked teeth.* **2. orthodontics** [or θə 'dɑn tɪks] *n.* the part of dentistry concerned with straightening the teeth. (Treated as singular.) ♦ *My dentist specializes in orthodontics.* ♦ *Because of orthodontics, I now have straight teeth.*

orthodontist [or θə 'dɑn təst] *n.* a dentist who does orthodontics. ♦ *Bill had to visit the orthodontist every week for one year.* ♦ *The orthodontist gave Sue a set of braces.*

orthodox ['or θə dɑks] *adj.* having the usual, customary, or accepted beliefs and attitudes; traditional and usual. (Adv: *orthodoxly.*) ♦ *Mary is very modern and liberal, but John is more orthodox in his behavior.* ♦ *The room has an orthodox arrangement of furniture with a sofa, chair, and coffee table.*

orthopedic [or θə 'pid ɪk] **1.** *adj.* of or about the treatment of deformities and diseases of the bones. (Adv: *orthopedically* [...ɪk li].) ♦ *The child with the bone disease was referred to an orthopedic surgeon.* ♦ *An expert in orthopedic medicine advised me to include more calcium in my diet.* **2. orthopedics** *n.* the branch of medicine dealing with the treatment of deformities and diseases of the bones. (Treated as singular.) ♦ *A specialist in orthopedics examined the frail and elderly woman.* ♦ *Researchers in orthopedics look for ways to strengthen bones.*

orthopedist [or θə 'pid əst] *n.* a doctor who specializes in the treatment of deformities and diseases of the bones. ♦ *The orthopedist fitted Mary with a back brace.* ♦ *The old man's brittle bones were examined by the orthopedist.*

oscillate ['ɑs ə let] **1.** *iv.* to move back and forth regularly; to move from side to side, like a pendulum. ♦ *The seismograph needle oscillated during the earthquake.* ♦ *The car's defective fuel gauge oscillated for a moment and moved to the "empty" mark.* **2. oscillate between** *iv.* + *prep. phr.* to keep changing one's mind about two choices; to keep changing one's opinion between two options. (Figurative on ①. See also **vacillate.**) ♦ *I oscillated between vacationing in Florida or in California.* ♦ *John oscillated between ordering meat and ordering fish.*

oscillation [ɑs ə 'le ʃən] *n.* the regular movement of something back and forth or from side to side. ♦ *The seismologists measured the violent oscillations during the earthquake.* ♦ *The oscillation of the pendulum made me drowsy.*

osmosis [ɑs 'mo sɪs] *n.* the passing—through a membrane—of particles from an area of greater concentration to an area of lesser concentration. (No plural form in this sense.) ♦ *Helium in balloons escapes due to osmosis.* ♦ *Osmosis occurs until equilibrium on both sides of the membrane is reached.*

ostensible [ɑ 'stɛns ə bəl] *adj.* pretended; given as a reason without giving the real reason for doing something. (Adv: *ostensibly.*) ♦ *Bob's ostensible reason for quitting smoking is his health, but the real reason is he can't afford it.* ♦ *The ostensible motive for the crime was jealousy, but it was actually greed.*

ostentatious [ɑ stɛn 'te ʃəs] *adj.* very showy; pretentious; done to impress other people or attract attention. (Adv: *ostentatiously.*) ♦ *The actor's glittering clothing was ostentatious.* ♦ *The wealthy woman arrived at the charity event in an ostentatious limousine.*

ostracize ['ɑs trə saɪz] *tv.* to exclude someone from society or from a group. ♦ *Jimmy was ostracized because he couldn't play baseball well.* ♦ *The director was ostracized in Hollywood because he was so outspoken.*

ostrich ['ɑs trɪtʃ] *n.* a large bird that runs very quickly but cannot fly. ♦ *The poacher killed the ostrich for its feathers.* ♦ *Ostriches are naturally found in Africa.*

other ['ʌð ɚ] **1.** *pron.* the second of two; the remaining thing or person. ♦ *You take one cookie, and I'll take the other.* ♦ *John helped one of the twins, and I helped the other.* **2. others** *n.* more of the same kind of thing or people. ♦ *Anne and Mary were at the party, along with some others.* ♦ *Put this book on the shelf next to the others.* **3.** *adj.* <the adj. use of ①.> ♦ *You eat one of the cookies and I'll eat the other one.* ♦ *I'll take one of the twins in my car, and you take the other one.* **4.** *adj.* more of the same kind of thing or people. ♦ *Anne and Mary were at the party, along with some other people.* ♦ *Put this book on the shelf next to the other ones.* **5.** *adj.* not the same; belonging to someone or something else. ♦ *I don't want this book; I want the other one.* ♦ *Would you like chocolate, or would you pre-*

fer the other flavor? **6.** *adj.* additional; further; remaining. ♦ *Do you have any other thoughts on this matter?* ♦ *My boss promised to give me other work later in the week.* **7. every other** *phr.* every second person or thing; alternating. ♦ *The magician turned every other card over.* ♦ *Every other table had an ashtray on it.* **8. none other than** *idiom* the very [person]. ♦ *The new building was opened by none other than the president.* ♦ *Bob's wife turned out to be none other than my cousin.*

otherwise ['ʌð ɚ waɪz] **1.** *conj.* or else; or it is that. ♦ *The procedure is safe, otherwise we would not do it.* ♦ *You'd better quit smoking, otherwise you might get cancer.* **2.** *adv.* in another way; in a different way; differently. ♦ *This is the way to do it. We would not do it otherwise.* ♦ *Bill passed time by watching TV. John passed time otherwise.* **3.** *adv.* in every regard except [this one]; in every way except [this one]. ♦ *John is quite poor. Otherwise, he is quite happy.* ♦ *Today the cat died. Otherwise, it's been a great day.*

otter ['ɑt ɚ] **1.** *n.* a long, furry animal that lives in and near water, has webbed feet, and eats fish. ♦ *The otter swam through the water and caught a fish.* ♦ *The hunter trapped the otter for its fur.* **2.** *n.* the skin and fur of ①. (No plural form in this sense.) ♦ *Otter is an expensive fur.* ♦ *Nothing looks better in otter than an otter.* **3.** *adj.* made from ②. ♦ *I wore the warm otter coat during the snowstorm.* ♦ *The otter gloves kept my hands very warm.*

ought ['ɔt] **1. ought to** *aux.* + *inf.* have to do something; obliged to do something. ♦ *You ought to do your homework before you go out and play.* ♦ *You ought to go home after school.* **2. ought to** *aux.* + *inf.* likely to happen; should happen. ♦ *It rained in Chicago yesterday, so it ought to rain in Detroit today.* ♦ *That pumpkin ought to weigh ten pounds.*

ounce ['ɑʊns] **1.** *n.* a unit of measurement of weight equal to 1/16 of a pound or about 28 grams. ♦ *The newborn baby weighed eight pounds and four ounces.* ♦ *I needed additional postage because the letter weighed two ounces.* **2.** *n.* a unit of measurement of liquid equal to 1/16 of a pint or 1/8 of a cup. ♦ *I drank 16 ounces of diet soda.* ♦ *This container holds 32 fluid ounces.*

our ['ɑɚ] **1.** *pron.* <the first-person plural possessive pronoun including the speaker or writer.> ♦ *This is a picture of our dog.* ♦ *Our house is seventy years old.* **2. ours** *pron.* <the first-person plural possessive pronoun.> (Used in place of a noun.) ♦ *That car by the road is ours.* ♦ *John's house is white, but ours is blue.*

ourselves ['ɑɚ 'sɛlvz] **1.** *pron.* <the first-person plural reflexive pronoun.> ♦ *We completed the project by ourselves.* ♦ *Let's keep this secret to ourselves.* **2.** *pron.* <a form used to emphasize we.> ♦ *It's amazing that we ourselves managed to arrive on time.* ♦ *We ourselves are to thank for the changes that have been made.* **3. by ourselves** *phr.* with the help of no one else. ♦ *We can do it by ourselves.* ♦ *Can we lift this by ourselves, or do we need some help?* **4. by ourselves** *phr.* with no one else present; alone. ♦ *Do we have to sit here by ourselves? Can't we sit with Mary and Max?* ♦ *We like to eat by ourselves, so we can talk about private matters.*

oust ['ɑʊst] *tv.* to get rid of someone or something; to remove someone or something by force. ♦ *The city council ousted the crooked mayor.* ♦ *The landlord ousted the tenant who never paid rent.*

ouster ['ɑʊ stɚ] *n.* the forcing of someone or something from some place; the process of getting rid of someone or something. (No plural form in this sense.) ♦ *The citizens rejoiced when the mayor's ouster was announced.* ♦ *The ouster of the tenant required the help of the police.*

out ['ɑʊt] **1.** *adv.* away from a place; not in a place; not in the usual condition; not at the usual position; to a point beyond a limit. ♦ *John moved out of his parents' house last year.* ♦ *We had to stay out of the pool until the storm passed.* **2.** *adv.* in the open air; into the open air; outside; not inside. ♦ *I went out at about ten o'clock.* ♦ *Let's go out before it gets dark.* **3.** *adv.* to or toward the end; to completion. (Part of a phrasal verb.) ♦ *The losing team played out the game gracefully.* ♦ *The popular movie sold out.* **4.** *adv.* in a way that can be easily seen or understood. (Part of a phrasal verb.) ♦ *If you can't understand the instructions, let me spell them out.* ♦ *Mary stuck her tongue out.* **5.** *adv.* in a way that can no longer be seen. (Part of a phrasal verb.) ♦ *The worker painted the graffiti out.* ♦ *The writer rubbed the mistake out.* **6.** *adv.* into existence; so as to increase the intensity of an activity. (Part of a phrasal verb.) ♦ *The teenager's acne broke out before the big dance.* ♦ *The injured soldier cried out in pain.* **7.** *adv.* to others. (Part of a phrasal verb.) ♦ *The teacher handed the assignment out.* ♦ *The protester passed the fliers out.* **8.** *adv.* [in baseball] made to be out ⑭. ♦ *The player tagged the runner out.* ♦ *The catcher put the batter out by catching the foul ball.* **9.** *adj.* not at the usual position; to a point beyond a limit; not at home; not at work. (Not prenominal.) ♦ *The receptionist is out for a few moments.* ♦ *Mr. Jones is not here; he is out.* **10.** *adj.* no longer in style; old-fashioned. ♦ *Most fashions of the 1960s are now out of style.* ♦ *The magazine listed which fashions were in and which were out.* **11.** *adj.* not a consideration; not a choice. (Informal.) ♦ *Smoking is out when you're inside a public building.* ♦ *Pizza is out. Anne doesn't like it.* **12.** *adj.* no longer burning; no longer giving off light. ♦ *The campfire is out; you don't have to douse it.* ♦ *The bathroom light is out. Do you have any more bulbs?* **13.** *adj.* not working; not functioning properly. ♦ *The refrigerator is out, and my food is starting to spoil.* ♦ *John lay in bed because his back was out.* **14.** *adj.* [in baseball, of someone] no longer permitted to play in a particular turn. ♦ *The batter was out because the player caught his fly ball.* ♦ *If you get three strikes, then you're out.* **15.** *adj.* used up; no longer having more of a substance. ♦ *We're out of iced tea. Can you make more?* ♦ *Sorry, there is no more. We're out.* **16.** *adj.* unconscious; not aware; not awake. ♦ *Because John was out, he did not know what was happening.* ♦ *After getting hit in the head, Bill was out for a few seconds.* **17.** *n.* [in baseball] an instance of putting someone out ⑧; an instance of a batter's accumulating three strikes ⑬. ♦ *If there are two outs, a runner should run whenever the ball is hit.* ♦ *The catcher caught the ball, and that was the last out of the inning!* **18.** *n.* a solution; a means of escape. ♦ *Your actions leave me no out but to expel you.* ♦ *John knew that winning a scholarship was his only out.* **19. out and about** *idiom* outside the house; well enough to leave one's home. ♦ *Beth has been ill, but now she's out and about.* ♦ *As soon as I feel better, I'll be able to get out and about.*

outage ['ɑʊt ɪdʒ] *n.* a period of time when electrical power, gas, heat, telephone service, or some other service is stopped or interrupted. ♦ *The power outage was caused by an electrical storm.* ♦ *During the outage, many stores were looted.*

outboard ['aʊt bord] *adj.* on or at the outside of a boat; attached to the outside of a boat. ♦ *The anchor dented the outboard side of the hull.* ♦ *The boat was propelled by an outboard motor.*

outbound ['aʊt baʊnd] *adj.* away from a place. ♦ *The outbound train is boarding on track ten.* ♦ *Outbound traffic from the city is slow around 5:00.*

outbreak ['aʊt brek] **1.** *n.* a burst of strong emotion. ♦ *There was an outbreak of sobs from the grieving mourner.* ♦ *It was difficult to understand John's sudden outbreak of anger.* **2.** *n.* an epidemic; a sudden spread of disease. ♦ *The school nurse noticed an outbreak of measles.* ♦ *The people affected by the outbreak were quarantined.*

outburst ['aʊt bɚst] *n.* a burst of strong emotion. ♦ *Tom's outburst after hearing the bad news was heard by everyone.* ♦ *The judge threatened to empty the courtroom if there were any outbursts.*

outcast ['aʊt kæst] *n.* someone who has been rejected, abandoned, or deserted. ♦ *The outcasts from society live on the streets.* ♦ *The blacklisted director was an outcast in Hollywood.*

outcome ['aʊt kəm] *n.* the final result; the effect of something. ♦ *The outcome of the game was that our team won.* ♦ *The newspaper reported the outcome of the meeting.*

outcry ['aʊt kraɪ] **1.** *n.* a strong protest; an uproar. ♦ *The unjust verdict created a terrible outcry.* ♦ *There was an outcry when the respected leader was arrested.* **2.** *n.* a loud cry. ♦ *The outcries of the injured people were deafening.* ♦ *I heard the outcry of the woman trapped in the rubble.*

outdated [aʊt 'det ɪd] *adj.* out-of-date; no longer in style or fashion; old-fashioned. (Adv: *outdatedly.*) ♦ *The children made fun of John's outdated clothing.* ♦ *Mary's outdated computer worked very slowly.*

outdid [aʊt 'dɪd] pt of outdo.

outdistance [aʊt 'dɪs təns] *tv.* to go farther than someone or something else; to leave someone or something else behind. ♦ *The lead racecar outdistanced all the others by several laps.* ♦ *Bill outdistanced me because he left an hour before I did.*

outdo [aʊt 'du] *tv., irreg.* to do better than someone or something else; to do more than someone or something else. (Pt: outdid; pp: outdone.) ♦ *You've outdone yourself! This is your best party ever!* ♦ *John was unable to outdo his older sister at tennis.*

outdone [aʊt 'dʌn] pp of outdo.

outdoor [aʊt 'dor] **1.** *adj.* not inside; not in a building; used or done outdoors ③. ♦ *At camp, I participated in many outdoor sports.* ♦ *I bought some outdoor furniture for my back porch.* **2. outdoors** *n.* the area outside of buildings; the open air. (Treated as singular.) ♦ *I went camping in the great outdoors.* ♦ *I saw three deer in the wild outdoors.* **3. outdoors** *adv.* in the open air; not inside a building. ♦ *I let the dog outdoors so he could run around.* ♦ *According to company policy, employees must go outdoors to smoke.*

outer ['aʊt ɚ] **1.** *adj.* farther away from the center. ♦ *Pluto and Neptune are two of the outer planets of the solar system.* ♦ *The outer particles of an atom are called electrons.* **2.** *adj.* exterior; on the outside. ♦ *There's a mail slot in the outer door of my house.* ♦ *My house's outer walls need to be painted.*

outermost ['aʊt ɚ most] *adj.* the farthest away from the center of something. ♦ *John's outermost layer of clothing was a warm coat.* ♦ *Pluto and Neptune are the sun's two outermost planets.*

outer space ['aʊt ɚ 'spes] *n.* the universe beyond the atmosphere of Earth. (No plural form in this sense.) ♦ *A huge rocket was launched into outer space.* ♦ *The meteorite came from outer space.*

outfit ['aʊt fɪt] **1.** *n.* different items of clothing that are worn together. ♦ *Mary wore a stylish outfit to the dance.* ♦ *John's outfit was made by a tailor.* **2.** *n.* equipment needed for a certain job or activity. ♦ *The firefighter's outfit included extra oxygen.* ♦ *A skier's outfit includes skis and poles.* **3.** *n.* a group of people; a company or organization. (Informal.) ♦ *The entire outfit received a holiday bonus.* ♦ *So, what kind of outfit do you work for?* **4.** *tv.* to provide someone with ②. ♦ *The salesclerk outfitted the hikers with the proper shoes.* ♦ *The model was outfitted in a dark blue dress.*

outgoing ['aʊt go ɪŋ] **1.** *adj.* friendly; warm; social. ♦ *My outgoing neighbors are easy to get along with.* ♦ *The outgoing couple went to several parties each month.* **2.** *adj.* finishing a term in an office or position. ♦ *The outgoing senator returned to his law practice.* ♦ *The outgoing leader said good-bye to her supporters.*

outgrew [aʊt 'gru] pt of outgrow.

outgrow [aʊt 'gro] **1.** *tv., irreg.* to no longer fit into one's clothes because one has grown. (Pt: outgrew; pp: outgrown.) ♦ *The teenager outgrew his shoes in four months.* ♦ *Susie has outgrown last year's coat.* **2.** *tv., irreg.* to become too mature to do certain things meant for younger children. (Figurative on ①.) ♦ *At 17, Bill outgrew his interest in comic books.* ♦ *I outgrew my fascination with dolls by the time I entered high school.* **3.** *tv., irreg.* to grow to be taller or faster than someone else. ♦ *By age 16, John had outgrown his older brother.* ♦ *Mary outgrew her mother by four inches.*

outgrown [aʊt 'gron] pp of outgrow.

outhouse ['aʊt haʊs] *n., irreg.* an outdoor toilet that is in a small shed separate from the house. (Pl: [...haʊ zəz].) ♦ *Instead of a bathroom, the cabin had a small outhouse in back.* ♦ *After installing indoor plumbing, we tore down the outhouse.*

outing ['aʊt ɪŋ] *n.* a short trip; an excursion. ♦ *My family went on an outing to the park.* ♦ *Our outing at the lake was a lot of fun.*

outlandish [aʊt 'læn dɪʃ] *adj.* very unusual; strange looking; ridiculous. (Adv: *outlandishly.*) ♦ *There were a lot of outlandish costumes at the Halloween party.* ♦ *The police didn't believe the criminal's outlandish excuse.*

outlaw ['aʊt lɔ] **1.** *n.* a criminal. ♦ *The dangerous outlaw was wanted in three states.* ♦ *The sheriff put the outlaw in jail.* **2.** *tv.* to make something illegal; to declare that something is against the law. ♦ *My company outlawed smoking at the office.* ♦ *Some people would like to outlaw the sale of liquor.*

outlay ['aʊt le] *n.* money spent for a certain reason; time or energy spent for a certain reason. ♦ *The state expended a huge outlay of money on the new stadium.* ♦ *During the war, the outlay of energy and resources was rationed.*

outlet ['aʊt lɛt] **1.** *n.* the socket in a wall where something can be plugged in for electrical power. ♦ *I put my new desk near an electrical outlet.* ♦ *I needed an extension cord to plug the lamp into the outlet.* **2.** *n.* a way out for something. ♦ *This drainpipe is an outlet for water when it is raining.* ♦ *A chimney is an outlet for smoke from a fireplace.* **3.** *n.* a way to let one's feelings out; a way to use one's creativity. (Figurative on ②.) ♦ *Anne uses writing as a creative outlet.* ♦ *Boxing is an outlet for Bill's aggression.*

outline ['aʊt laɪn] **1.** *n.* the shape of someone or something; the border of someone or something. ♦ *We could see the outline of the trees against the night sky.* ♦ *This map shows the outline of the Florida coast.* **2.** *n.* a list of the main topics of a speech or text; a plan. ♦ *Mary improvised her speech from a short outline.* ♦ *John wrote a detailed outline before writing his paper.* **3.** *tv.* to draw the shape of someone; to draw the border of someone or something. ♦ *I outlined my hand by tracing it with a pen.* ♦ *The police outlined shape of the murder victim on the street with chalk.* **4.** *tv.* to list the main topics of a speech or text. ♦ *Anne outlined the primary points of her speech.* ♦ *David outlined the major topics in his report.* **5.** *tv.* to describe a plan. ♦ *Mary outlined her ideas for the party.* ♦ *The dictator outlined his plan to take over the world.*

outlive [aʊt 'lɪv] *tv.* to live longer than someone else; to work longer than something else. ♦ *My grandmother outlived her husband by five years.* ♦ *My car outlived Bill's car by 30,000 miles.*

outlook ['aʊt lʊk] **1.** *n.* an imagined view of the future course that something may take. (No plural form in this sense.) ♦ *The experts discussed the economic outlook for the coming year.* ♦ *Mary analyzed her company's outlook over the next 10 years.* **2.** *n.* the way of looking at things that happen. ♦ *Even though John was dying, he still had positive outlook on life.* ♦ *Talking to Sue is depressing because she has a very negative outlook.* **3.** *n.* the view that one sees when looking out from some place. ♦ *There's a pleasant outlook on the river from the top of the cliff.* ♦ *The outlook from my kitchen window is of the Atlantic Ocean.*

outlying ['aʊt laɪ ɪŋ] *adj.* far from the center; past a certain limit or boundary; distant. ♦ *The explosion in the city was so strong it was felt even in the outlying areas.* ♦ *The pioneers traveled to outlying lands.*

outmoded [aʊt 'mod ɪd] *adj.* no longer in style or fashion. (Adv: *outmodedly.*) ♦ *The poor children dressed in outmoded clothing.* ♦ *I wish we could get rid of that old, outmoded sofa and buy a new, stylish one.*

outnumber [aʊt 'nʌm bɚ] *tv.* to be greater in number than someone or something else. ♦ *Our army outnumbered the enemy's meager troops.* ♦ *The winning votes outnumbered the losing ones by a 2–1 margin.*

out-of-date ['aʊt əv 'det] *adj.* out of style; no longer current; old-fashioned. ♦ *Jimmy felt his parents' beliefs were very out-of-date.* ♦ *The eccentric old man wore out-of-date clothing.*

out of order ['aʊt əv 'or dɚ] *adj.* not working; not functioning; broken. ♦ *This vending machine is out of order. Don't put any money in it.* ♦ *I read a book last night because my television was out of order.*

out-of-the-way [aʊt əv ðə 'we] *adj.* not easy to be reached; hard to get to; remote; isolated. ♦ *I rested for a week at my uncle's out-of-the-way cabin.* ♦ *The postal system delivers mail even to out-of-the-way addresses.*

outpatient ['aʊt pe ʃənt] *n.* a hospital patient who does not stay in the hospital overnight. ♦ *The woman with a minor infection was treated as an outpatient.* ♦ *Each outpatient must wear a tag when inside the hospital.*

outpost ['aʊt post] *n.* the location of a group of people who are located far away from other people. ♦ *The scientist received bad news from the remote outpost.* ♦ *The soldier traveled to the outpost on horseback.*

output ['aʊt pʊt] **1.** *n.* the amount of something that is made; production. (No plural form in this sense.) ♦ *The car factory had a large output last quarter.* ♦ *The supervisor recorded the shift's output in the computer.* **2.** *n.* something that is produced. (No plural form in this sense.) ♦ *The day's entire output was put into a single packing crate.* ♦ *The oil well's output was sent to the refinery through a huge pipe.* **3.** *n.* the energy that is produced by a machine. (No plural form in this sense.) ♦ *Dams produce a large output of hydroelectric energy.* ♦ *The generator's output provided energy to the towns along the river.* **4.** *n.* information that is produced by a computer. (No plural form in this sense.) ♦ *The computer output was printed on striped paper.* ♦ *The researcher analyzed the output generated by the computer.*

outrage 1. ['aʊt redʒ] *n.* a very cruel or horrible deed. ♦ *The mayor's cruel remarks were an outrage.* ♦ *The terrorist attack was a horrible outrage.* **2.** ['aʊt redʒ] *n.* anger caused by a very cruel or horrible action. (No plural form in this sense.) ♦ *The mayor's cruel remarks caused a huge outrage.* ♦ *There was a lot of outrage over the terrorist attack.* **3.** [aʊt 'redʒ] *tv.* to anger someone greatly by doing a very cruel or horrible deed. ♦ *The mayor's cruel remarks outraged the citizens.* ♦ *The terrorist attack outraged the government and the people.*

outrageous [aʊt 'redʒ əs] **1.** *adj.* shocking; insulting; causing great anger. (Adv: *outrageously.*) ♦ *The mayor apologized for his outrageous remarks.* ♦ *The newspaper's outrageous editorial offended me.* **2.** *adj.* wild; exciting; not restrained; extravagant. (Adv: *outrageously.*) ♦ *The parents ignored their spoiled child's outrageous behavior.* ♦ *The outrageous party lasted until five in the morning.*

outran [aʊt 'ræn] pt of outrun.

outright ['aʊt raɪt] **1.** *adj.* complete; direct. ♦ *The witness accused the defendant of being an outright liar.* ♦ *It's an outright shame that you were mugged.* **2.** *adj.* [of money given] without limitations. ♦ *Tom made an outright gift of the money to the university.* ♦ *The foundation provided an outright grant of $5,000.* **3.** *adv.* without limitations. ♦ *The donor gave $100,000 to the university outright.* ♦ *Jane's grandfather willed her his total estate outright.* **4. killed outright** *idiom* killed immediately. ♦ *The driver was killed outright in the accident.* ♦ *Twenty people were killed outright in the explosion.*

outrun [aʊt 'rʌn] **1.** *tv., irreg.* to run faster than someone or something else; to run better than someone or something else. (Pt: outran; pp: outrun.) ♦ *The hunter wasn't able to outrun the hungry bear.* ♦ *The winner out-*

ran the runner in second place by four seconds. **2.** *tv., irreg.* to exceed something; to go beyond the limits of something. (Figurative on ①.) ♦ *Jimmy outran his weekly allowance in three days.* ♦ *My department outran its annual budget in October.*

outset ['aʊt sɛt] **1. at the outset** *idiom* at the very beginning. ♦ *At the outset, we were told everything we had to do.* ♦ *I learned at the outset of the project that I was to lead it.* **2. from the outset** *idiom* throughout, from the very beginning. ♦ *I felt from the outset that Lisa was the wrong one for the job.* ♦ *From the outset, I felt unwelcome in the group.*

outside ['aʊt 'saɪd] **1.** *n.* the part of something that faces away from the center of something; the surface of something that is out. (Sometimes plural with the same meaning.) ♦ *John painted the outside of his house.* ♦ *I washed the outside of my car.* **2.** *adj.* on the outside; external; not inside a building. ♦ *The paint on the outside walls is starting to peel.* ♦ *Mary turned on the outside lights so we could play in the yard after dark.* **3.** *adj.* farther from the center than something else. ♦ *The slowest runner ran in the outside lane.* ♦ *John's outside layers of clothing were totally wet.* **4.** *adj.* the greatest probable [amount]. ♦ *The mechanic's outside estimate for the job was $500.* ♦ *My outside guess is that it would take a month to fix.* **5.** *adj.* unlikely; not probable. ♦ *On the outside chance that Mary might visit, I left her a key.* ♦ *There's an outside possibility of rain, so take your umbrella.* **6.** *adj.* not associated with the inner group. ♦ *The tyrannical government banned all outside influences.* ♦ *The banker's outside partner laundered the embezzled money.* **7.** *adv.* to or toward ①. ♦ *Why don't you go outside and play?* ♦ *Jimmy didn't color outside of the lines.* **8.** *prep.* past the limit of something; beyond. ♦ *Place the bird's water dish outside the cage, please.* ♦ *The package was left outside my front door.* **9. outside of** *prep.* except for; not including. ♦ *Outside of swimming, David has no hobbies.* ♦ *Outside of strawberries, I have no allergies.*

outsider [aʊt 'saɪd ɚ] *n.* someone who is not part of a group of people; someone who is excluded from a group of people. ♦ *John felt like an outsider because he had no friends.* ♦ *The students treated the tattletale as an outsider.*

outskirts ['aʊt skɚts] *n.* the suburbs of a city; the outer edges of a city. (Treated as plural. Sometimes singular.) ♦ *I was raised in a house on the outskirts of New York City.* ♦ *The city's outskirts were assigned a new area code.*

outsmart [aʊt 'smɑrt] *tv.* to be more clever than someone and therefore win at something; to outwit someone. ♦ *I outsmart my brother every time we play chess.* ♦ *The police were outsmarted by cunning thieves.*

outspoken ['aʊt 'spok ən] *adj.* bold; frank; not holding back when one speaks; saying what one feels. (Adv: *outspokenly.*) ♦ *The outspoken activist could not be silenced by the media.* ♦ *The president's outspoken critics appeared on many talk shows.*

outstanding [aʊt 'stæn dɪŋ] **1.** *adj.* excellent; very good. (Adv: *outstandingly.*) ♦ *The talented soloist gave an outstanding performance.* ♦ *Susan's parents rewarded her for her outstanding grades.* **2.** *adj.* not paid; unpaid. ♦ *These outstanding bills are due immediately.* ♦ *I have an outstanding debt at my doctor's office.*

outstretched [aʊt 'strɛtʃt] *adj.* stretched out; wide open; open wide. ♦ *The drowning man grabbed my outstretched hand.* ♦ *At the airport, my mother ran toward me with outstretched arms.*

outstrip [aʊt 'strɪpt] *tv.* to do better than someone or something else. ♦ *Our team has outstripped all its competition.* ♦ *The most athletic student outstripped 20 other students in the race.*

outward ['aʊt wɚd] **1.** *adv.* away; away from some place; toward the outside. ♦ *The rocket traveled outward into space.* ♦ *The hurricane moved outward, leaving the coastal city behind.* **2.** *adj.* of or about one's appearance instead of one's feelings. (Adv: *outwardly.*) ♦ *Although Bob was sad, his outward appearance seemed happy.* ♦ *Mary's outward expression was one of joy.*

outweigh [aʊt 'we] **1.** *tv.* to weigh more than someone or something else. ♦ *The large truck far outweighed the small car.* ♦ *The older boxer outweighs the younger one by five pounds.* **2.** *tv.* to be more important than someone or something else. (Figurative on ①.) ♦ *John's valid reasons outweigh Bob's silly objections.* ♦ *My supervisor's decisions outweigh mine.*

outwit [aʊt 'wɪt] *tv.* to be more clever than someone and therefore win at something. ♦ *The fox outwitted the farmer and stole a chicken.* ♦ *My brother outwitted me at a game of chess.*

ova ['o və] pl of ovum.

oval ['ov əl] **1.** *adj.* shaped like an egg; almost shaped like a circle, but flatter. (Adv: *ovally.*) ♦ *That planet's moon follows an oval orbit.* ♦ *Mary served the turkey on an oval platter.* **2.** *n.* a shape like that of an egg; the shape of a flattened circle. ♦ *Earth's orbit is more like an oval than a circle.* ♦ *The lenses of my glasses are shaped like ovals.*

ovary ['o və ri] *n.* one of two glands in females that produce eggs and sex hormones. ♦ *When a female reaches puberty, her ovaries release eggs.* ♦ *The doctor removed a small cyst from Anne's left ovary.*

ovation [o 've ʃən] *n.* applause; a large expression of approval from an audience. ♦ *The brilliant performer received a standing ovation.* ♦ *The actors bowed a dozen times during the lengthy ovation.*

oven ['ʌv ən] **1.** *n.* an appliance or compartment in an appliance that can be heated to cook food. ♦ *I put the turkey in the oven.* ♦ *I heated the oven to 350 degrees before baking the cake.* **2.** *n.* a compartment that is heated to dry and harden pottery or other objects. ♦ *The sculptor set the wet clay in the oven to dry.* ♦ *The wet pottery dried in the oven.*

over ['ov ɚ] **1.** *prep.* above; higher than. ♦ *There were dark storm clouds over the house.* ♦ *I mounted the clock on the wall over the bookshelf.* **2.** *prep.* on; covering. ♦ *John placed a sheet over the mattress.* ♦ *Anne placed a cloth over the bird cage at night.* **3.** *prep.* across; from side to side; above and to the other side. ♦ *The villagers crossed the wooden bridge over the river.* ♦ *John set the grill over the burning coals.* **4.** *prep.* off and down from. ♦ *The hiker fell over the cliff.* ♦ *The mouse fell over the edge of the shelf.* **5.** *prep.* during; throughout. ♦ *Over the next three weeks, the doctors will watch my health.* ♦ *I lived in Seattle over the summer.* **6.** *prep.* more than a certain measurement; greater than. (Some people prefer *more than* to **over** in this sense.) ♦

You must be over five feet tall to ride the roller coaster. ♦ *You must be a resident for over 30 days in order to vote here.* **7.** *prep.* about; in reference to. (Part of a phrasal verb.) ♦ *My friends fought over who was going to pay for dinner.* ♦ *I talked over my problems with my psychiatrist.* **8.** *prep.* while consuming food or drink; while concerned with something. ♦ *Susan and Bob will discuss their vacation plans over dinner.* ♦ *Anne and John discussed business over a drink.* **9.** *prep.* with something noisy in the background. ♦ *I can't hear people on the phone over the television.* ♦ *It's hard to hear over all the noise from the airport.* **10.** *prep.* from [the radio, Internet, or telephone]. ♦ *I heard the news report over the radio.* ♦ *I get my news over the Internet.* **11.** *adv.* [spreading or coating] in a way that covers a surface; in a way that covers something; from side to side; from beginning to end. ♦ *I spread jelly over the muffin.* ♦ *I sprayed paint over the wall.* **12.** *adv.* on top of something else. ♦ *I wrote the correct number over the wrong one.* ♦ *I taped over the old recording.* **13.** *adv.* at some other place; on the other side of something. ♦ *The pigs are over near the barn.* ♦ *The crayons are over there by the cabinet.* **14.** *adv.* down; so that a surface faces downward. (Part of a phrasal verb.) ♦ *The baby turned over onto her back.* ♦ *The upright book fell over onto its front.* **15.** *adv.* again. ♦ *My teacher made me do my sloppy homework over.* ♦ *After I was interrupted, I started over.* **16.** *prefix* too; too much. (Usually in a compound.) ♦ *The tough steak was overcooked.* ♦ *The reporter's comments on the problem were oversimplified.* **17.** *adj.* done; finished; at the end. ♦ *When the show is over, please turn off the television.* ♦ *When the game was over, the players went to the locker room.* **18. over and over** *idiom* repeatedly; again and again. ♦ *He repeated the sentence over and over until he had it memorized.* ♦ *She will practice it over and over until she can do it perfectly.*

overall ['ov ɚ ɔl] **1.** *adj.* including everything; total. ♦ *The overall cost of the project exceeded the budget.* ♦ *I calculated the overall expense of my vacation.* **2.** *adj.* from one end to the other. ♦ *The overall length of the hallway is 40 feet.* ♦ *The overall length of the movie is 92 minutes.*

overate [ov ɚ 'et] pt of overeat.

overbearing [ov ɚ 'ber ɪŋ] *adj.* domineering; making other people do what one wants; dominating. (Adv: *overbearingly.*) ♦ *The overbearing mother ordered her children around.* ♦ *Everyone dislikes my overbearing boss.*

overboard ['ov ɚ bord] **1.** *adv.* [falling, dropping, or being thrown] from a boat or ship into the water. ♦ *The drunk passenger fell overboard.* ♦ *The sailor illegally threw garbage overboard.* **2. go overboard** *idiom* to do too much; to be extravagant. ♦ *Look, Sally, let's have a nice party, but don't go overboard. It doesn't need to be fancy.* ♦ *Okay, you can buy a big comfortable car, but don't go overboard.*

overbook [ov ɚ 'bʊk] *tv.* to book too many reservations; to accept too many reservations. ♦ *The airline overbooked my flight, so I had to take a later one.* ♦ *The restaurant had been overbooked, so we had to wait to be seated,*

overcame [ov ɚ 'kem] pt of overcome.

overcast ['ov ɚ kæst] *adj.* covered with clouds; dark and cloudy. ♦ *Unfortunately, the sky was overcast on the day of the picnic.* ♦ *My flight was delayed because the sky was so overcast.*

overcharge [ov ɚ 'tʃɑrdʒ] *tv.* to charge someone more money for something than it really costs. ♦ *The cashier overcharged me $25 for the coat.* ♦ *The store manager was fired for overcharging customers.*

overcoat ['ov ɚ kot] *n.* a heavy coat that is worn over other clothes. ♦ *Wear your overcoat. It's snowing outside.* ♦ *In the spring, I took my overcoat to the cleaners.*

overcome [ov ɚ 'kʌm] **1.** *tv., irreg.* to defeat someone or something; to fight and win against someone or something. (Pt: overcame; pp: overcome.) ♦ *The soldiers overcame their enemies and won the battle.* ♦ *I overcame my fear of flying by taking several short flights last month.* **2.** *tv., irreg.* to cause someone to become helpless, especially because of emotion. ♦ *When I was attacked, fear overcame me and I could not defend myself.* ♦ *Shame overcame the accused criminal.*

overcooked ['o vɚ 'kʊkt] *adj.* cooked too long. ♦ *The overcooked steak was too tough to eat.* ♦ *The overcooked vegetables were very soft.*

overcrowded [ov ɚ 'kraʊd ɪd] *adj.* very crowded; too crowded; packed. ♦ *The rock concert was very overcrowded.* ♦ *Passengers started to faint on the hot, overcrowded bus.*

overdid ['ov ɚ dɪd] pt of overdo.

overdo [ov ɚ 'du] **1.** *tv., irreg.* to do something too much; to do something too intensely. (Pt: overdid; pp: overdone.) ♦ *The designer overdid the colors in your living room. There is too much red.* ♦ *The doctor told me not to overdo exercise after surgery.* **2.** *iv., irreg.* to exert too much effort. ♦ *Since you are still recovering, please don't overdo.* ♦ *The doctor warned me not to overdo after surgery.*

overdone [ov ɚ 'dʌn] **1.** pp of overdo. **2.** *adj.* cooked too much. ♦ *I told the waiter to return the overdone steak to the kitchen.* ♦ *The overdone vegetables tasted very bland.*

overdose ['ov ɚ dos] **1.** *n.* a large dose of a drug that causes someone to pass out or die. ♦ *The young actor died as a result of a drug overdose.* ♦ *John committed suicide by taking an overdose of medicine.* **2.** *iv.* to become unconscious or die because one has taken too many drugs or too much medicine. ♦ *The musician overdosed on heroin.* ♦ *Mary accidentally overdosed and nearly died.*

overdraft ['ov ɚ dræft] *n.* the condition of a checking account where one has written checks for a sum greater than the amount of money in the account. ♦ *My bank charges me for each overdraft.* ♦ *I deposited some cash to cover the overdraft in my account.*

overdrawn ['ov ɚ drɔn] *adj.* [of a bank account] running a deficit owing to having one or more overdrafts. ♦ *The bank closed the overdrawn account after three weeks.* ♦ *My checking account is overdrawn because I write checks for more money than I deposit.*

overdue ['ov ɚ du] *adj.* past due; past a required time. ♦ *I was fined when I returned my overdue library books.* ♦ *Lisa finally returned the overdue video to the store.*

overeat [ov ɚ 'it] *iv., irreg.* to eat too much. (Pt: overate; pp: overeaten.) ♦ *At his birthday party, John overate until he got sick.* ♦ *I always overeat on Thanksgiving because there is so much food.*

overeaten [ov ɚ 'it n] pp of overeat.

overestimate [ov ɚ 'ɛs tɪ met] **1.** *tv.* to have too high of an opinion of something. ♦ *I think you overestimate the importance of your job.* ♦ *The manager overestimated his* *influence on his workers.* **2.** *tv.* to estimate the amount of something with a figure that is too great. ♦ *The council overestimated the budget by 10%.* ♦ *The contractor overestimated the costs by $500.* **3.** *iv.* to estimate too high of an amount. ♦ *The project came under budget because the contractor had overestimated.* ♦ *Because the mechanic overestimated, the repairs cost me less than I'd expected.*

overflow 1. ['ov ɚ flo] *n.* fluid that flows over the edge of a container or over the banks of a river. (No plural form in this sense.) ♦ *The overflow from the river flooded the nearby town.* ♦ *I cleaned up the overflow from the sink with a sponge.* **2.** ['ov ɚ flo] *n.* too many people or things; extra people or things that do not fit in a certain area. (No plural form in this sense. Figurative on ①.) ♦ *The overflow at the lecture was asked to stand at the back of the hall.* ♦ *The overflow of merchandise filled the warehouse.* **3.** [ov ɚ 'flo] *tv., irreg.* to flood something; to flow past the edge of something. (Pp: **overflown**.) ♦ *The river overflowed its banks during the flood.* ♦ *Water in the canal overflowed the sides and flooded the fields.* **4.** [ov ɚ 'flo] *iv., irreg.* [for fluid] to flow past the edge of a container. ♦ *The sink overflowed when the drain became clogged.* ♦ *The river overflowed when there was too much rain.*

overflown [ov ɚ 'flown] pp of **overflow**.

overgrew [ov ɚ 'gru] pt of **overgrow**.

overgrow [ov ɚ 'gro] *tv., irreg.* [for plants] to grow to excess in a certain area. (Pt: **overgrew**; pp: **overgrown**.) ♦ *Without proper care, these bushes will overgrow the entire yard.* ♦ *Their yard has been overgrown by weeds.*

overgrown [ov ɚ 'gron] pp of **overgrow**.

overhang ['ov ɚ hæŋ] **1.** *tv.* to hang over something; to extend over something. ♦ *An awning overhangs the store's window.* ♦ *A lovely wooden deck overhangs part of our lawn.* **2.** *n.* something that hangs over something else; something that sticks out. ♦ *I stood under the building's overhang during the rainstorm.* ♦ *There's a 4-foot overhang at the back of the truck.*

overhaul [ov ɚ 'hɔl] **1.** *tv.* to examine and repair something thoroughly; to organize something thoroughly in a different way. ♦ *The new dean overhauled the school's curriculum.* ♦ *The mechanic completely overhauled my car's engine.* **2.** *n.* a thorough examination and repair. ♦ *The citizens demanded an overhaul of the corrupt government.* ♦ *I took my car to the repair shop for a complete overhaul.*

overhead 1. ['ov ɚ hɛd] *n.* the costs of running a business; business expenses. (No plural form in this sense.) ♦ *Even after paying monthly overhead, my store made a profit last month.* ♦ *The company reduced overhead by moving to a smaller office.* **2.** ['ov ɚ hɛd] *adj.* <the adj. use of ①.> ♦ *The company cut back overhead expenses by firing three people.* ♦ *The accountant included overhead costs in the budget.* **3.** ['ov ɚ hɛd] *adj.* above one's head. ♦ *The overhead door led to a stairway to the roof.* ♦ *Fluorescent overhead lighting is too harsh for an art gallery.* **4.** ['ov ɚ hɛd] *adv.* above one's head; in the air; passing through the air. ♦ *I looked up at the plane that flew overhead.* ♦ *As the clouds passed overhead, it started to rain.*

overhear [ov ɚ 'hɪr] *tv., irreg.* to hear something by mistake; to hear something that one is not supposed to hear. (Pt/pp: **overheard**.) ♦ *I overheard that the boss is planning to fire you.* ♦ *Bill overheard me when I told Jane about the plans.*

overheard [ov ə 'hɚd] pt/pp of **overhear**.

overheat [ov ɚ 'hit] **1.** *iv.* to become too hot; to break or stop working because of being worked too hard. ♦ *My car overheated when I drove through the desert.* ♦ *The hair dryer overheated because I had it on too long.* **2.** *tv.* to cause something to become too hot. ♦ *The rough drive up the mountain overheated the engine.* ♦ *I overheated the engine when I drove through the desert.*

overjoyed [ov ɚ 'dʒɔɪd] *adj.* very happy; full of joy. (Adv: *overjoyedly*.) ♦ *The parents were overjoyed at the birth of their daughter.* ♦ *My overjoyed friends were amazed that I survived the accident.*

overkill ['ov ɚ kɪl] **1.** *n.* having more weapons than are needed to destroy the enemy or the world. (No plural form in this sense.) ♦ *Building even more nuclear weapons is overkill.* ♦ *To save money, Congress cut the overkill from the defense budget.* **2.** *n.* the condition of having more than is necessary. (Figurative on ①. No plural form in this sense.) ♦ *Buying 20 gallons of ice cream for the small party was just overkill.* ♦ *Having three different bands at the wedding reception was overkill.*

overlap [ov ɚ 'læp] **1.** *iv.* [for two or more things] to happen at the same time. ♦ *The term of Mary's contract overlapped with my term.* ♦ *The end of the first scene overlapped the beginning of the second.* **2.** *iv.* [for two or more things] to cover the same space. ♦ *The edges of the wallpaper do not overlap enough.* ♦ *The bedroom carpeting overlaps with the carpeting in the hallway.* **3.** *tv.* to partially cover something. ♦ *One sheet of wallpaper overlaps the adjacent sheet too much.* ♦ *The bedroom carpeting overlaps the carpeting in the hallway.* **4.** *tv.* to begin something before something else finishes; to place the beginning of something over the end of something else. ♦ *Mary's term of office overlaps Susan's term by two months.* ♦ *My math class overlaps my English class from noon to 12:20.* **5.** *n.* the extra part of something that extends over something else. (No plural form in this sense.) ♦ *The overlap of the carpet onto the tile floor protected the tile's fragile edge.* ♦ *I had to trim off the overlap.* **6.** *n.* the amount by which things **overlap** ① or ②. (No plural form in this sense.) ♦ *There was a half-inch overlap of the carpet onto the tile floor.* ♦ *There was a two-day overlap between the start of Mary's term and the end of mine.*

overload [ov ɚ 'lod] **1.** *n.* too great a load; too much of a burden. (No plural form in this sense.) ♦ *My counselor advised me against taking an overload of classes.* ♦ *The trucker was fined for driving with a dangerous overload.* **2.** *tv.* to load someone or something with too many things; to load someone or something with things that are too heavy. ♦ *The truck was overloaded with heavy crates.* ♦ *I overloaded my schedule with too many classes.*

overloaded [ov ɚ 'lod ɪd] *adj.* loaded with too many things; loaded too heavily. (Adv: *overloadedly*.) ♦ *The overloaded truck caused a serious accident on the hill.* ♦ *An overloaded crate broke open and spilled.*

overlook 1. ['ov ɚ lʊk] *n.* a place that looks out over another place; a place that provides a good view of another place. ♦ *The scenic overlook provides a beautiful view of the valley.* ♦ *The hikers walked up to the overlook to look at the river.* **2.** [ov ɚ 'lʊk] *tv.* to forget or neglect something. ♦ *You overlooked a few mistakes when you proofread this paper.* ♦ *When Tom was watering the plants, he overlooked the small one by the window.* **3.** [ov ɚ 'lʊk] *tv.* to disregard something. ♦ *My teacher said she'd overlook my bad behavior this time.* ♦ *My boss overlooked my good work and focused on my mistakes.*

overly ['ov ɚ li] *adv.* too; excessively; very. ♦ *Bob is overly influenced by what he sees on television.* ♦ *Don't you think this weather is overly warm for January?*

overnight 1. ['ov ɚ nɑɪt] *adj.* done during the night; lasting through the night. ♦ *I sent the important package by overnight delivery.* ♦ *The overnight bus trip is half the cost of a daytime trip.* **2.** [ov ɚ 'nɑɪt] *adv.* through the night; during the night. ♦ *The lawyer had the package delivered overnight to the client.* ♦ *If you travel overnight, the bus fare is cheaper.* **3.** [ov ɚ 'nɑɪt] *adv.* suddenly; all at once. ♦ *You don't expect me to do all this work overnight, do you?* ♦ *The new shopping mall seemed to appear overnight.*

overpower [ov ɚ 'pɑʊ ɚ] *tv.* to gain control over someone or something; to overcome someone or something; to cause someone or something to be powerless. ♦ *The store manager overpowered the thief and called the police.* ♦ *Our army overpowered the enemy.*

overproduction [ov ɚ prə 'dʌk ʃən] *n.* the production of more than is needed or can be sold. (No plural form in this sense.) ♦ *The company lost money last quarter because of overproduction.* ♦ *The firm had to rent storage space because of overproduction.*

overran ['ov ɚ 'ræn] pt of overrun.

overrate [ov ɚ 'ret] *tv.* to rate someone or something too highly; to think too much of someone or something. ♦ *I think most critics tend to overrate television programs.* ♦ *Anne loves Paris and overrates the food while ignoring the traffic.*

overrated [ov ɚ 'ret ɪd] *adj.* rated too highly; thought too much of; not as good as most people think. (Adv: *overratedly.*) ♦ *I left the overrated movie before it ended.* ♦ *We sent the overrated gourmet food back to the kitchen.*

overridden [ov ɚ 'rɪd ən] pp of override.

override [ov ɚ 'rɑɪd] **1.** *tv., irreg.* to intervene and take control of something that is automatically controlled. (Pt: overrode; pp: overriden.) ♦ *The pilot overrode the automatic controls.* ♦ *The automatic processes were overridden by the engineer.* **2.** *tv., irreg.* to prevail over someone or something; to reverse a decision. ♦ *The council will override the president's decision.* ♦ *The principal overrode the teachers' wishes.*

overrode [ov ɚ 'rod] pt of override.

overrule [ov ɚ 'rul] *tv.* to rule against the decision of someone with less authority. ♦ *The Supreme Court overruled the lower court's decision.* ♦ *The judge overruled the lawyer's objection.*

overrun [ov ɚ 'rʌn] **1.** *tv., irreg.* to spread throughout an area in a harmful way; to swarm. (Pt: overran; pp: *overrun.*) ♦ *Weeds overran my garden while I was on vacation.* ♦ *The old house was overrun with mice.* **2.** *tv., irreg.* to go past a certain limit. ♦ *These demands will overrun the federal guidelines.* ♦ *The budget was overrun with unexpected costs.*

oversaw [ov ɚ 'sɔ] pt of oversee.

overseas [ov ɚ 'siz] **1.** *adv.* across the sea; on the other side of the ocean. ♦ *Nowadays, news can be broadcast overseas instantly.* ♦ *Anne traveled overseas from New York to London.* **2.** *adj.* done, used, or about a place on the other side of the ocean. ♦ *The American company had overseas offices in Rome and Tokyo.* ♦ *I placed an overseas phone call to my friend in Paris.* **3. from overseas** *phr.* from a location on the other side of the Atlantic or Pacific Ocean, according to the point of view of someone located in the U.S. ♦ *The latest word from overseas is that the treaty has been signed.* ♦ *Is there any news from overseas about the war?*

oversee [ov ɚ 'si] *tv., irreg.* to supervise someone or something; to watch over someone or something so that something is done properly. (Pt: oversaw; pp: overseen.) ♦ *My boss oversaw the project I was working on.* ♦ *The prison workers were overseen by guards.*

overseen [ov ɚ 'sin] pp of oversee.

overseer ['ov ɚ si ɚ] *n.* a supervisor; someone who watches over someone or something. ♦ *The overseer was hired by the owner to run the plantation.* ♦ *My overseer noticed that I was ten minutes late to work.*

overshadow [ov ɚ 'ʃæd o] **1.** *tv.* to make something seem gloomy, as if putting a large shadow over it. ♦ *Our picnic was overshadowed by dark clouds.* ♦ *The party was overshadowed by the bad news.* **2.** *tv.* to be more important than someone or something else. (Figurative on ①.) ♦ *My older brother always overshadows my efforts.* ♦ *The chairman overshadowed everyone else on the committee.*

overshoot [ov ɚ 'ʃut] *tv., irreg.* to go past a target or limit. (Pt/pp: overshot.) ♦ *The archer overshot the target by twenty feet.* ♦ *The golfer overshot the putting green.*

overshot [ov ɚ 'ʃɑt] pt/pp of overshoot.

oversight ['ov ɚ sɑɪt] *n.* something that is not noticed or thought of. ♦ *Due to a major oversight, the project cost more than was expected.* ♦ *Due to an oversight in planning, I missed two appointments.*

oversleep [ov ɚ 'slip] *iv., irreg.* to sleep longer than one wanted to; to sleep too long. (Pt/pp: overslept.) ♦ *I missed my flight because I overslept.* ♦ *John was late for work because he had overslept.*

overslept [ov ɚ 'slɛpt] pt/pp of oversleep.

overstep [ov ɚ 'stɛp] *tv.* to go further past something (figuratively) than one should. ♦ *Bill's rude joke overstepped the limits of good taste.* ♦ *The police officer was reprimanded for overstepping his authority.*

overt [o 'vɚt] *adj.* obvious; noticeable; evident; not hidden. (Adv: *overtly.*) ♦ *Some overt displays of affection are inappropriate in public.* ♦ *The general made an overt grab for political power.*

overtake [ov ɚ 'tek] *tv., irreg.* to catch up to and pass someone or something else. (Pt: overtook; pp: overtaken.) ♦ *The police overtook the robbers on the highway.* ♦ *The visiting team overtook our team in the last inning.*

overtaken [ov ɚ 'tek ən] pp of overtake.

overthrew [ov ɚ 'θru] pt of overthrow.

overthrow [ov ɚ 'θro] *tv., irreg.* to remove someone or something from power. (Pt: overthrew; pp: overthrown.) ♦ *The president was overthrown by the army.* ♦ *The protesters sought to overthrow the government.*

overthrown [ov ɚ 'θron] pp of overthrow.

overtime ['ov ɚ tɑɪm] **1.** *n.* time at work past the time when one normally finishes. (No plural form in this sense.) ♦ *I am paid double my hourly wage during overtime.* ♦ *My boss asked me if I could work some overtime on Saturday.* **2.** *n.* money earned by working past the time when one normally finishes. (No plural form in this sense.) ♦ *Jane used her overtime to buy a new car.* ♦ *Overtime is taxed at the same rate as other earnings.* **3.** *n.* [in a sporting event] an extra amount of playing time allowed in order to break a tie score. (No plural form in this sense.) ♦ *Our team won the game in overtime.* ♦ *Because the teams were tied, they went into overtime.* **4.** *adv.* past the hours when one normally finishes. ♦ *I worked overtime until the project was finished.* ♦ *I'm paid double when I work overtime.* **5.** *adj.* of or about working extra as in ①. ♦ *I'm paid double for overtime hours.* ♦ *The government does not tax overtime wages at a higher rate.*

overtly [o 'vɚt li] *adv.* noticeably and easily seen; not secretly. ♦ *The general plotted against the president covertly because he would get caught if he tried to seize to power overtly.* ♦ *Overtly, Max looked like any other schoolchild. No one suspected that he was a spy.*

overtook [ov ɚ 'tʊk] pt of overtake.

overture ['ov ɚ tʃɚ] **1.** *n.* the introductory piece of music of an opera, symphony, ballet, etc. ♦ *The audience became quiet when the overture began.* ♦ *The overture of a musical usually includes parts of songs from the musical.* **2.** *n.* an initial proposal; the communication of an intention to make an offer of something. ♦ *The warring countries sent out an overture of peace.* ♦ *An overture of reconciliation was sent by messenger to the president.* **3. make overtures** *idiom* to give hints about something; to present or suggest ②. ♦ *The company made overtures about hiring me.* ♦ *Tom is making overtures about inviting us to his country home next month.*

overturn [ov ɚ 'tɚn] **1.** *iv.* to turn over. ♦ *The car overturned when it slid into the ditch.* ♦ *The trailer overturned during the earthquake.* **2.** *tv.* to cause something to turn over. ♦ *Bill overturned his car when he drove it into a ditch.* ♦ *The tornado overturned the trailer.* **3.** *tv.* to strike down a decision made by a less powerful judge or court; to rule against a decision made by a less powerful judge or court. ♦ *The Supreme Court overturned the lower court's ruling.* ♦ *My case was overturned during the appeal.*

overturned [ov ɚ 'tɚnd] *adj.* turned over; upside-down. ♦ *The driver was trapped in the overturned car.* ♦ *The magician knew what was written on the overturned card.*

overuse [ov ɚ 'jus] *n.* the state of being used too much or too often. (No plural form in this sense.) ♦ *Overuse of certain medications can be dangerous to your health.* ♦ *The old machinery in the factory suffered from overuse.*

overused [ov ɚ 'juzd] *adj.* used too much; used too often. ♦ *An overused expression is called a cliché.* ♦ *The edges of the overused book were worn.*

overweight [ov ɚ 'wet] *adj.* weighing too much. ♦ *The doctor put the overweight patient on a diet.* ♦ *The overweight puppy waddled towards its dinner dish.*

overwhelm [ov ɚ 'ʍɛlm] **1.** *tv.* to overpower someone's senses or emotions; to affect one's senses or emotions much too strongly. ♦ *Emotion overwhelmed the actor when he won an award.* ♦ *The survivor of the wreck was overwhelmed by dozens of reporters.* **2.** *tv.* to thoroughly defeat someone; to win by a very wide margin. ♦ *The visiting team was overwhelmed by our team.* ♦ *Our army overwhelmed the enemy.*

overwhelming [ov ɚ 'ʍɛlm ɪŋ] *adj.* very large; very strong; very hard to resist or oppose. (Adv: *overwhelmingly.*) ♦ *I am so angry, I have an overwhelming urge to scream!* ♦ *There was overwhelming opposition to the tax increase.*

overwork [ov ɚ 'wɚk] *tv.* to make someone or something work too hard or too long. ♦ *The factory worker overworked the machine until it broke.* ♦ *The busy lawyers overworked their only typist.*

overworked [ov ɚ 'wɚkt] *adj.* made to work too hard; made to carry too big of a burden. ♦ *The overworked employees demanded a higher salary.* ♦ *All the overworked teachers rested during the summer.*

overwrought [ov ɚ 'rɔt] *adj.* too excited; too anxious; having too much tension. ♦ *The overwrought mourners cried loudly at the funeral.* ♦ *An angry and overwrought actor broke the reporter's camera.*

ovulate ['ɑv jə let] *iv.* [for the ovary of a female] to release an egg. ♦ *Women do not ovulate before puberty or after menopause.* ♦ *Most women ovulate approximately every 28 days.*

ovulation [ɑv jə 'le ʃən] *n.* the process of releasing an egg from an ovary. ♦ *Ovulation does not occur during pregnancy.* ♦ *Chances for conception are best after ovulation.*

ovum ['ov əm] *n., irreg.* an egg. (Latin. Pl: ova.) ♦ *The ovum travels from the ovary to the uterus.* ♦ *The scientist fertilized the ova in a test tube.*

owe ['o] **1.** *tv.* to be in debt for a sum of money; to have to pay someone for something. ♦ *I owe the federal government $100 in taxes.* ♦ *John owes his sister a lot of money.* **2.** *tv.* to be obliged to give someone something. ♦ *Thanks for helping me. I owe you a favor.* ♦ *I owe Bill a dinner, because he paid for my dinner last night.* **3. owing to** *phr.* because of something; due to the fact of something. ♦ *Owing to the lateness of the evening, I must go home.* ♦ *We were late owing to the heavy traffic.*

owl ['ɑʊl] **1.** *n.* a bird that has large eyes that face the front, a short, curved beak, and is active at night. ♦ *The owls' habitat was threatened by the logging industry.* ♦ *The hoots of the owls scared the young children.* **2. night owl** *idiom* someone who stays up at night; someone who works at night. (On ①.) ♦ *My roommate is a night owl and usually reads until 5:00 A.M.* ♦ *A few night owls stayed at the café all night long.*

own ['on] **1.** *tv.* to possess something; to have something as a belonging. ♦ *I own a warm, furry hat.* ♦ *My parents own a cabin on the lake.* **2.** *adj.* belonging to oneself. ♦ *This coat is Bill's. My own coat is at the cleaners.* ♦ *I can't help Jane with her work. That's her own problem.* **3.** *pron.* <a form indicating something already mentioned as belonging to oneself.> ♦ *This hat is my own. I paid for it myself.* ♦ *That house is my brother's, but this one is my own.* **4. on one's own** *idiom* independently. ♦ *Our baby can now walk on his own.* ♦ *I have lived on my own since I was 18.* **5. hold one's own** *idiom* to do as well as anyone else. ♦ *I can hold my own in a footrace any day.* ♦ *She was unable to hold her own, and she had to quit.*

owner ['on ɚ] *n.* someone who owns something. ♦ *The owner closed the store for the weekend.* ♦ *The police officer asked to speak to the owner of the house.*

ownership ['on ɚ ʃɪp] *n.* the state of being an owner; the right one has to own something. (No plural form in this sense.) ♦ *Some cultures do not believe in the ownership of land.* ♦ *The ownership of the farm was disputed in court.*

ox ['ɑks] *n., irreg.* an adult, castrated male of a kind of cattle. (Pl: **oxen**.) ♦ *The ox pulled the plow through the field.* ♦ *The farmer put a yoke on the oxen.*

oxen ['ɑk sən] pl of **ox**.

oxygen ['ɑks ə dʒən] *n.* a gas that makes up about 20% of the air we breathe. (No plural form in this sense.) ♦ *Humans and animals cannot live without breathing oxygen.* ♦ *The atomic number for oxygen is 8, and its symbol is O.*

oyster ['oɪs tɚ] **1.** *n.* a small sea creature that lives between two hinged shells and sometimes produces pearls. ♦ *The fisherman removed the pearl from the oyster.* ♦ *Thousands of oysters are harvested from this bay.* **2.** *n.* ① used as food. ♦ *John swallowed a raw oyster.* ♦ *We ordered oysters as an appetizer before our meal.*

ozone ['o zon] *n.* a kind of oxygen produced when an electrical spark, such as lightning, passes through the air. (No plural form in this sense.) ♦ *Ozone in the upper atmosphere absorbs ultraviolet rays.* ♦ *Sometimes you can smell ozone after lightning has struck.*

P

P AND **p** ['pi] *n.* the sixteenth letter of the alphabet. ♦ *P comes after* O *and before* Q. ♦ *There are three* Ps *in* pepper.

pa ['pɑ] *n.* father. (Informal. Also a term of address.) ♦ *Is your pa at home?* ♦ *Hey, Pa, can I borrow the keys to the car?*

pace ['pes] **1.** *n.* the speed at which someone or something moves. (No plural form in this sense.) ♦ *The horse galloped across the field at a fast pace.* ♦ *The last hour of the workday crept by at a slow pace.* **2.** *n.* one step when running or walking. ♦ *The treasure is buried two paces north of the oak tree.* ♦ *The spy walked twenty paces behind the politician.* **3.** *iv.* to walk back and forth slowly and regularly. ♦ *Anne paced in the waiting room while Bill was in surgery.* ♦ *The prisoner paced back and forth in his jail cell.* **4. at a snail's pace** *idiom* very slowly. ♦ *When you watch a clock, time seems to move at a snail's pace.* ♦ *You always eat at a snail's pace. I'm tired of waiting for you.* **5. put one through one's paces** *idiom* to make one demonstrate what one can do; to make one do one's job thoroughly. ♦ *The boss really put me through my paces today. I'm tired.* ♦ *I tried out for a part in the play, and the director really put me through my paces.* **6. put something through its paces** *idiom* to demonstrate how well something operates; to demonstrate all the things something can do. ♦ *I was down by the barn, watching Sally put her horse through its paces.* ♦ *This is an excellent sewing machine. Watch me put it through its paces.*

pacemaker ['pes mek ɚ] *n.* a device that is put into the body to keep heartbeat regular. ♦ *My grandmother's pacemaker corrected her irregular heartbeat.* ♦ *John's pacemaker appears in his chest X-rays.*

pacesetter ['pes sɛt ɚ] *n.* someone or something that sets a standard or starts a trend. ♦ *The influential artist was a pacesetter in modern art styles.* ♦ *Lisa is an important pacesetter in modern banking.*

pachyderm ['pæk ə dɝm] *n.* one of a group of large mammals with thick skin, including the elephant, rhinoceros, and hippopotamus. (Usually refers to an elephant.) ♦ *The hunter killed a large pachyderm during the safari.* ♦ *Among the animals at the zoo were several pachyderms.*

Pacific Ocean [pə 'sɪf ɪk 'o ʃən] See Gazetteer.

pacifier ['pæs ə fɑɪ ɚ] *n.* a small rubber nipple with a handle that is placed in a baby's mouth so that the baby has something to suck on to keep it from crying. ♦ *The contented baby sucked on his pacifier.* ♦ *I placed a pacifier in the crying baby's mouth.*

pacifism ['pæs ə fɪz əm] *n.* the position that war or violence is not the way to solve problems. (No plural form in this sense.) ♦ *The leader's pacifism was respected.* ♦ *The senator argued against pacifism and voted to declare war.*

pacifist ['pæs ə fəst] *n.* someone who believes in pacifism and will not participate in the violence of war. ♦ *The pacifist refused to join the army.* ♦ *Thousands of pacifists protested against the war.*

pacify ['pæs ə fɑɪ] *tv.* to make someone calm or quiet; to calm someone's anger. ♦ *Jane pacified the crying baby.* ♦ *The mayor pacified the angry townspeople.*

pack ['pæk] **1.** *n.* a group of things that have been placed together—in a case, for example—so they can be carried. ♦ *That store sells packs of cigarettes.* ♦ *Anne took a pack of gum from her purse.* **2.** *n.* the standard amount of something contained in a particular kind of ①. ♦ *Anne smokes a pack of cigarettes a day.* ♦ *John chewed an entire pack of gum at once.* **3.** *n.* a backpack; a fabric container that is worn on the back and used to carry items. ♦ *Anne slung her pack over her shoulder and walked to class.* ♦ *The strap on Bill's pack broke.* **4.** *n.* a group of animals that live, hunt, and travel together. ♦ *I heard a pack of wolves howling at the moon.* ♦ *A pack of wild dogs roamed through the park.* **5.** *tv.* to fill a container completely. ♦ *I packed my small suitcase for the trip.* ♦ *Bill carefully packed the box until it was full.* **6.** *tv.* to gather, assemble, and arrange things and place them in a space or container. ♦ *Have you packed the papers yet?* ♦ *I packed them into the box.* **7. pack together** *iv.* + *prep. phr.* to crowd together. ♦ *The shoppers packed together in the elevator.* ♦ *The crowd of people packed together to stare at the accident.* **8. pack of lies** *idiom* a series of lies. ♦ *The thief told a pack of lies to cover up the crime.* ♦ *John listened to Bill's pack of lies about the fight and became very angry.*

package ['pæk ɪdʒ] **1.** *n.* a group of things that are wrapped together or boxed; a container in which goods are sold or shipped. ♦ *I removed one stick from my package of gum.* ♦ *These cupcakes are sold in a package of four.* **2.** *n.* a parcel, especially one that is wrapped in paper or something similar. ♦ *I received a large package in the mail today.* ♦ *There is a package for you on your desk.* **3.** *n.* a group of different but related products or services sold together as a unit. ♦ *The travel package included the flight, the hotel room, and a rental car.* ♦ *The two chairs, the couch, and the end table were sold as a package.* **4.** *tv.* to place something in a container, especially to make it available for sale. ♦ *Mary packaged the gift in an attractive box.* ♦ *Most kinds of breakfast cereal are packaged in cardboard boxes.*

packaging ['pæk ɪdʒ ɪŋ] *n.* the material used to contain items for sale. (No plural form in this sense.) ♦ *The product was protected by sturdy packaging.* ♦ *The shopper noticed the product's colorful packaging.*

packet ['pæk ɪt] *n.* a small package or pack. ♦ *The store sold expensive spices in small packets.* ♦ *Bill carried a packet of tobacco with him.*

pact ['pækt] *n.* an agreement; a treaty. ♦ *The warring countries signed a pact to end the war.* ♦ *Bill and John made a pact to help each other as much as possible.*

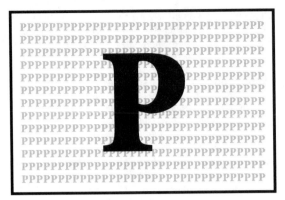

pad ['pæd] **1.** *n.* a cushion of soft material used to protect something, make something comfortable, absorb fluid, or give something a certain shape. ♦ *I put a pad on the wooden chair's hard seat.* ♦ *I removed the makeup from my face with a cotton pad.* **2.** *n.* the soft fleshy part on the bottom of the feet of animals, such as dogs, cats, rabbits, etc. ♦ *A dog's foot is made of a number of soft pads.* ♦ *The soft pads of the rabbit's feet showed clearly in its footprints in the snow.* **3.** *n.* a tablet of paper; a stack of pieces of paper that are glued together along one edge. ♦ *I wrote down the message on the pad next to the phone.* ♦ *The investigator wrote some information on her note pad.* **4. stamp pad; (ink) pad** *n.* a sponge soaked with ink for use with stamps. ♦ *The clerk pressed the rubber stamp into the stamp pad.* ♦ *I covered the ink pad so it wouldn't dry out.* **5. (launching) pad** *n.* the platform from which rockets are launched. ♦ *The rocket was moved to the launching pad.* ♦ *The reporters were gathered around the pad after the liftoff.* **6.** *iv.* to walk softly and very quietly. ♦ *No one heard the little girl padding down the hall to her room.* ♦ *The cat padded across the carpet to its favorite chair and went to sleep.* **7.** *tv.* to make a movie, book, program, etc., longer by adding extra words, longer pauses, extra performance material, etc. ♦ *John padded his term paper by writing* very *before every adjective.* ♦ *The movie was padded with three long dance numbers.*

padded ['pæd ɪd] **1.** *adj.* having a pad; protected, made comfortable, or given a shape by means of a pad. ♦ *The patrons appreciated the padded seating at the theater.* ♦ *The jacket's padded shoulders made the model look taller.* **2.** *adj.* filled with extra words, pauses, or performance material to make something longer. ♦ *The teacher gave the padded report a low grade.* ♦ *The critic said the padded movie was boring.*

padding ['pæd ɪŋ] **1.** *n.* soft material used as a pad. (No plural form in this sense.) ♦ *Anne removed the padding from the shoulders of her dress.* ♦ *The seats at the theater are covered with soft padding.* **2.** *n.* extra words, pauses, or performance material to make something longer. (No plural form in this sense.) ♦ *My teacher asked me to remove the padding from my report.* ♦ *The director added 10 minutes of padding to the short movie.*

paddle ['pæd l] **1.** *n.* a kind of oar used to steer and move a canoe or other small boat. ♦ *John accidentally dropped his paddle in the lake.* ♦ *Mary splashed water on me with her paddle.* **2.** *n.* a round or long flat object used to spank someone. ♦ *Long ago a teacher could spank a naughty child with a wooden paddle.* ♦ *Jimmy started to behave himself when his father brought out the paddle.* **3.** *n.* a round, flat object with a short handle used to hit the ball in a game of Ping-Pong. ♦ *The paddle slipped out of my sweaty hand.* ♦ *I struck the Ping-Pong ball with the paddle.* **4.** *tv.* to move a canoe with ①. ♦ *Anne paddled the canoe across the lake.* ♦ *Bill paddled the boat against the current.* **5.** *tv.* to spank someone with ② or with the hand. ♦ *Mr. Jones paddled his children when they misbehaved.* ♦ *The principal threatened to paddle the problem student.* **6.** *iv.* to propel [something] with a paddle. ♦ *Both Anne and Tom paddled furiously.* ♦ *John paddled against the current.*

padlock ['pæd lɑk] **1.** *n.* a removable lock used to secure doors, gates, cabinets, lids, etc. ♦ *I lost the key to the padlock on my school locker.* ♦ *I forgot the combination to the padlock on the gate.* **2.** *tv.* to lock a door, gate, cabinet, lid, etc. with ①. ♦ *John padlocked the heavy cabinet where he keeps his guns.* ♦ *Anne padlocked the front door behind her.*

pagan ['pe gən] **1.** *n.* someone whose religion is not Christianity, Islam, or Judaism; someone who has no religion. ♦ *The congregation prayed for pagans all around the world.* ♦ *Some groups of pagans worshiped nature in special ceremonies.* **2.** *adj.* of, by, for, or about ①. ♦ *The scholar was interested in all pagan religions.* ♦ *Tom criticized the ceremony as a pagan ritual.*

page ['pedʒ] **1.** *n.* one sheet of paper in a book. ♦ *A page has been torn from this book.* ♦ *Mary placed the bookmark between two pages.* **2.** *n.* one side of one sheet of paper in a book. ♦ *The editor found an error on the first page of the manuscript.* ♦ *I wrote some notes in the margin of the page.* **3.** *n.* a sheet of paper suitable for writing or printing or having writing or printing. ♦ *The front page of a newspaper usually has an important headline.* ♦ *A page of music fell from my music stand.* **4.** *n.* someone who runs errands and delivers messages, especially in a hotel, library, or in the legislature. ♦ *A page went through the lobby, calling out the name of someone who had a telephone call waiting.* ♦ *The page brought the photocopies to the senator.* **5.** *n.* a signal or message that someone has a message or a waiting telephone call, especially a beep from a pager. ♦ *The lawyer ignored the annoying page during dinner.* ♦ *John responded to the page by calling back on his cellular phone.* **6.** *tv.* to alert someone that a message or telephone call is waiting. ♦ *Mr. Williams is not at his desk. Let me page him for you.* ♦ *The receptionist paged Dr. Jones for a phone call.*

pageant ['pædʒ ənt] *n.* a presentation, display, or spectacle. ♦ *There was one contestant from each state at the beauty pageant.* ♦ *The schoolchildren put on a pageant for their parents.*

pageantry ['pædʒ ən tri] *n.* fancy display; pomp. (No plural form in this sense.) ♦ *The city's pageantry impressed the visiting foreign officials.* ♦ *The city taxpayers paid the bill for pageantry at the mayor's inauguration.*

pager ['pe dʒɚ] *n.* an electronic device that makes a signal to alert someone to a waiting message or telephone call. ♦ *John gave his pager to the usher before entering the theater.* ♦ *My pager started beeping during the meeting.*

paid ['ped] **1.** pt/pp of pay. **2.** *adj.* hired; employed; receiving money. ♦ *Paid workers must file income-tax returns.* ♦ *There aren't any paid employees here. We're all volunteers.*

pail ['pel] **1.** *n.* a bucket; a container without a lid and with a curved handle that connects to opposite sides of the rim. ♦ *The gardener filled the pail with water.* ♦ *Jimmy took a plastic pail and a small shovel to the beach.* **2.** *n.* the contents of ①. ♦ *The gardener poured two pails of water on the flowers.* ♦ *Jimmy emptied a pail of sand onto the beach.*

pain ['pen] **1.** *n.* hurt or ache caused by injury, sickness, or mental distress. (No plural form in this sense.) ♦ *Severe pain can result from broken bones and other injuries.* ♦ *How much pain should I expect after the operation, Doctor?* **2.** *n.* an instance of having ①; a specific case of pain. (See also shooting pain at shooting.) ♦ *John had chest pains and was rushed to the hospital.* ♦ *Too much food gives me a severe pain in the stomach.* **3.** *n.* someone who is a nuisance or a bother. (Informal. Figurative on ②.) ♦ *Stop being such a pain, and go do your work.* ♦ *My roommate is a real pain when he comes in late and makes a lot of noise.*

pained ['pend] *adj.* showing that one is upset or not pleased; showing that one's feelings are hurt. ♦ *Mary had a pained expression on her face after she was insulted.* ♦ *John gave me a pained look on his face when I asked him to leave.*

painful ['pen fʊl] *adj.* causing pain; hurting. (Adv: *painfully.*) ♦ *I covered the painful cut on my finger with a bandage.* ♦ *The death of my parents was a painful experience for me.*

painkiller ['pen kɪl ɚ] *n.* a kind of medicine or drug that ends or relieves pain. ♦ *The patient was given a lot of painkillers after surgery.* ♦ *Do you have any painkillers? I've got a really bad headache.*

painless ['pen ləs] **1.** *adj.* without pain; causing no pain. (Adv: *painlessly.*) ♦ *My dental checkup was painless because I had no cavities.* ♦ *The doctor performed some painless tests on me.* **2.** *adj.* requiring no effort and causing no distress. (Figurative on ①. Adv: *painlessly.*) ♦ *My final exam was so painless that I finished it in 20 minutes.* ♦ *I dreaded the interview, but it was painless and seemed to go well.*

painstaking ['penz tek ɪŋ] *adj.* very detailed; very careful; very thorough. (Adv: *painstakingly.*) ♦ *The artist copied the painting with painstaking accuracy.* ♦ *The diners gave the waitress a large tip for her painstaking service.*

paint ['pent] **1.** *n.* a colored liquid that is spread on a surface to give the surface color and protection and that gets hard when it dries. (No plural form in this sense.) ♦ *The old paint on the wall is starting to chip.* ♦ *Don't lean against this door. The paint is still wet.* **2.** *tv.* to cover something with ①, using a brush or something similar. ♦ *Bob painted his house last year.* ♦ *Jane painted the walls in her bedroom beige.* **3. paint with** *tv.* + *prep. phr.* to cover something with a liquid as though the liquid were ①, using a brush or something similar. ♦ *The nurse painted my wound with antiseptic.* ♦ *The cook painted the turkey with a honey glaze.* **4.** *tv.* to make a picture of someone or something using ①. ♦ *The artist painted a portrait of the mayor.* ♦ *Mary painted flowers on the canvas.* **5.** *iv.* to cover walls or other objects with ①. ♦ *My father paints for a living.* ♦ *The student painted during the summer to earn money.* **6.** *iv.* to make pictures with ①. ♦ *I'm a lawyer, but I also paint as a hobby.* ♦ *The successful artist painted for a living.* **7. paint the town red** *idiom* to have a wild celebration involving visits to bars, nightclubs, cabarets, etc. ♦ *Let's all go out and paint the town red!* ♦ *Oh, do I feel awful. I was out all last night, painting the town red.*

paintbrush ['pent 'brʌʃ] *n.* a brush used to apply paint to a surface. ♦ *Please clean the paintbrushes after you finish using them.* ♦ *The artist used a tiny paintbrush to paint the details.*

painter ['pen tɚ] **1.** *n.* someone who puts paint on houses, walls, and other objects as a job. ♦ *It took the painter five days to paint our large house.* ♦ *The painter found a color that matched my living-room carpet.* **2.** *n.* someone who paints pictures of things or people; an artist who paints pictures. ♦ *A famous painter was hired to paint the president's portrait.* ♦ *The painter supported himself by working at a movie theater.*

painting ['pen tɪŋ] **1.** *n.* the art and study of making pictures with paint. (No plural form in this sense.) ♦ *The artist had studied painting for many years.* ♦ *The art school offered night courses in painting and sculpture.* **2.** *n.* a picture that is made with paint. ♦ *There are hundreds of paintings on display at the art museum.* ♦ *A painting of my family hangs in the living room.*

pair ['pɛr] **1.** *n.* a set of two similar or matching things. ♦ *I bought a dark pair of socks.* ♦ *I had a pair of decorative bookends, but one of them broke.* **2.** *n.* an object made from two parts, neither of which can be used by itself. ♦ *John bought a new pair of pants.* ♦ *I cut the paper with a small pair of scissors.* **3.** *n.* a couple; two people who are doing something together. ♦ *Don't you think John and Mary make a lovely pair?* ♦ *My two brothers are a pair of real happy guys.* **4.** *n.* [in card games] two cards with the same number or value. ♦ *The winning poker player had two pairs: two kings and two tens.* ♦ *The card player quit because he had only one pair and the cards had a low value.* **5.** *tv.* to sort or order things or people into pairs ①. ♦ *John paired the socks together.* ♦ *The dance instructor paired the two remaining students.*

pajamas [pə 'dʒɑ məz] **1.** *n.* clothes worn in bed or worn at night before one goes to bed. (Treated as plural. Number is expressed by *pair(s) of pajamas.*) ♦ *Jimmy, go put on your pajamas and go to bed.* ♦ *We rushed out of the burning house in our pajamas.* **2. pajama** *adj.* of, by, for, or about ①. ♦ *I have lost my pajama top.* ♦ *Jimmy always leaves his pajama pants on the floor.*

Pakistan ['pæk ə stæn] See Gazetteer.

pal ['pæl] **1.** *n.* a friend; a chum; a buddy. (Informal.) ♦ *My pals and I went bowling last night.* ♦ *Would you be a pal and lend me some money until Friday?* **2. pal around with someone** *idiom* to spend much time with someone; to do things with someone who is a friend. ♦ *Anne's husband still pals around with his college friends.* ♦ *Mary palled around with her girlfriend at the mall.*

palace ['pæl ɪs] *n.* a very large, luxurious house, especially one where a king, queen, or important political leader lives or once lived. ♦ *The English queen lives in a palace.* ♦ *The ruler's palace has over one hundred rooms.*

palatable ['pæl ə tə bəl] **1.** *adj.* tasty; having an acceptable taste. (Adv: *palatably.*) ♦ *This soup isn't excellent, but it's palatable.* ♦ *Is this milk still palatable? It's two weeks old.* **2.** *adj.* agreeable; acceptable. (Figurative on ①. Adv: *palatably.*) ♦ *The proposed settlement was not palatable to either side.* ♦ *We sought to reach an agreement that was palatable to everyone concerned.*

palatal ['pæl ə təl] *adj.* of, by, for, or about the palate of the mouth. (Adv: *palatally.*) ♦ *I got a burn on the palatal area from eating hot pizza.* ♦ *The oral surgeon examined my palatal ulcer.*

palate ['pæl ɪt] **1.** *n.* the top of the inside of the mouth; the roof of the mouth; the partition of flesh and bone at the top of the mouth. ♦ *Anne clicked her tongue against her palate.* ♦ *The doctors operated on the child born with a cleft palate.* **2.** *n.* the sense of taste. ♦ *The wine expert had a very discriminating palate.* ♦ *The meal was enormously pleasing to Max's palate.*

palatial [pə 'le ʃəl] *adj.* like a palace; big and luxurious. (Adv: *palatially.*) ♦ *The banker lived on a palatial estate.* ♦ *The actor's palatial mansion was destroyed in the landslide.*

pale ['pel] **1.** *adj.* having a lighter color than usual; faded. (Adv: *palely.* Comp: *paler;* sup: *palest.*) ♦ *You look pale. Are you sick?* ♦ *Our kitchen is painted pale yellow.* **2.** *iv.* to become lighter in color; to whiten or weaken in color; to fade. ♦ *The carpet has paled where it has been exposed to sunlight.* ♦ *The flower was red in the center, but it paled to pink around the edges.* **3.** *iv.* [for someone] to become ① and appear faint. ♦ *John paled at the bad news.* ♦ *After eating the poisonous mushroom, Anne paled and fainted.* **4.** *iv.* [for something] to appear to be weak or inadequate. ♦ *Your offer paled compared to Mary's generous offering.* ♦ *Bob's sloppy work pales in comparison with David's effort.*

paleontologist [pe li ən 'tɑl ə dʒəst] *n.* someone who studies or practices paleontology. ♦ *The paleontologist carefully excavated the dinosaur fossil.* ♦ *Paleontologists cataloged the fossils at the museum.*

paleontology [pe li ən 'tɑl ə dʒi] *n.* the science and study of examining fossils to determine what prehistoric life was like. (No plural form in this sense.) ♦ *Anne enjoyed both biology and geology, so she took a course in paleontology.* ♦ *The television program on dinosaurs included interviews with many experts in paleontology.*

palladium [pə 'lɛd i əm] *n.* a silvery-white, metallic chemical element used as a catalyst and as a component of alloys. (No plural form in this sense.) ♦ *The atomic symbol for palladium is Pd.* ♦ *The atomic number for palladium is 46.*

pallbearer ['pɔl ber ɚ] *n.* one of the people who carry the coffin at a funeral. ♦ *Mr. Smith's six sons were all pallbearers at his funeral.* ♦ *The pallbearers carried the coffin from the hearse to the site of the grave.*

pallid ['pæl ɪd] *adj.* lacking in color, as though one were sick or scared; pale. (Adv: *pallidly.*) ♦ *The sick woman covered her pallid skin with makeup.* ♦ *People who work by night and sleep by day often look pallid.*

pallor ['pæl ɚ] *n.* paleness of the skin, as though one were sick, scared, or dead. (No plural form in this sense.) ♦ *The sick man's ghostly pallor frightened his wife.* ♦ *The corpse's pallor was made eerie by the dim candlelight.*

palm ['pɑm] **1.** *n.* the front of the hand between the wrist and the bottom of the fingers. ♦ *I placed my ticket in the palm of the usher's hand.* ♦ *I applauded so hard that my palms hurt.* **2.** *n.* a tropical tree with a long, branchless trunk and long, pointed leaves attached to the entire length of a long stem. ♦ *Coconuts grow on palms.* ♦ *Many streets in Los Angeles are shaded by palms.* **3.** *tv.* to hide something in one's palm ①. ♦ *The magician palmed the coin when no one was looking.* ♦ *The shoplifter palmed an expensive watch at the jewelry store.* **4. palm something off (on someone)** *idiom* to try to get something accepted as good. ♦ *The crook palmed a fake $50 bill off on me.* ♦ *Bob palmed his research off as original work, but we all knew he plagiarized it.*

palpable ['pæl pə bəl] *adj.* easily experienced or recognized; obvious; evident. (Adv: *palpably.*) ♦ *Bill's outrageous and palpable lie didn't fool anyone.* ♦ *The tension in the air during the strike was palpable.*

palpitation [pæl pɪ 'te ʃən] *n.* an irregular heartbeat; a heartbeat that is too fast. ♦ *My grandmother takes medication for her palpitations.* ♦ *The scary movie gave me palpitations.*

paltry ['pɔl tri] *adj.* meager; worthless; not significant; inadequate. ♦ *The rich old man willed his family only a paltry sum of money.* ♦ *The diner's paltry tip was an insult to the waiter.*

pamper ['pæmp ɚ] *tv.* to coddle someone or something; to be nicer than necessary to someone or something. ♦ *Max pampered his old car to try to make it last as long as possible.* ♦ *If you pamper children too much, they might become spoiled.*

pamphlet ['pæm flɪt] *n.* a booklet; a small publication that has information about a certain subject. ♦ *A stranger handed me a pamphlet about the end of the world.* ♦ *The charity's goals are described in this pamphlet.*

pan ['pæn] **1.** *n.* a wide, shallow vessel used for cooking. ♦ *I melted some butter in the pan before frying the eggs.* ♦ *When I overcooked the meat, it stuck to the bottom of the pan.* **2.** *tv.* to give a bad review about a movie, book, or play; to criticize something harshly. ♦ *The hostile critic panned the mediocre play.* ♦ *The newspapers panned the mayor's plans to raise taxes.* **3.** *iv.* [for a camera] to move while filming, traveling over a scene as one's eyes might. ♦ *The camera panned from the sky to the lone figure on the beach.* ♦ *The camera panned down the street and stopped on the old church.* **4. flash in the pan** *idiom* someone or something that draws a lot of attention for a very brief time. ♦ *I'm afraid that my success as a painter was just a flash in the pan.* ♦ *Tom had hoped to be a famous singer, but his career was only a flash in the pan.*

panacea [pæn ə 'si ə] *n.* something that will cure everything; something that will solve every problem. ♦ *Casinos are rarely the panacea needed to revive an aging city.* ♦ *The medicine was promoted as a panacea for all aches and pains.*

Panama ['pæn ə mɑ] See Gazetteer.

Panama Canal ['pæn ə mɑ kə 'næl] *n.* a canal that links the western Caribbean Sea to the Pacific Ocean. ♦ *The Panama Canal is forty miles long.* ♦ *The Panama Canal is a water link between the Atlantic and Pacific Oceans.*

pancake ['pæn kek] *n.* a thin, round cake made of flour, eggs, and milk that is cooked on both sides. ♦ *I ate a stack of pancakes for breakfast.* ♦ *Today's breakfast special is blueberry pancakes.*

pancreas ['pæn kri əs] *n.* the organ in the body near the stomach that makes insulin and puts it into the bloodstream and that makes a digestive juice and puts it into the intestines. ♦ *The malfunctioning of the pancreas can cause diabetes.* ♦ *Some medicinal insulin is obtained from the pancreases of pigs.*

panda ['pæn də] *n.* a black and white bear-like animal, found in China. ♦ *It is difficult to breed pandas in captivity.* ♦ *The panda eats bamboo shoots and leaves.*

pandemonium [pæn də 'mon i əm] *n.* chaos; wild disorder; wild confusion. (No plural form in this sense.) ♦ *The stock market crash caused pandemonium at the stock exchange.* ♦ *Dozens of people were hurt in the pandemonium caused by the fire.*

pane ['pen] *n.* a section of glass in a window or door. ♦ *The maid cleaned the panes of glass with soap and water.* ♦ *The thief broke the pane in order to unlock the door.*

panel ['pæn əl] **1.** *n.* a flat square or rectangular section of something. ♦ *The treasure was hidden behind a mov-*

able panel in the wall. ♦ *The carpenter nailed panels of wood to the beams.* **2.** *n.* a group of people who are selected to talk about something or judge someone or something. ♦ *The emcee introduced the panel of judges for the beauty contest.* ♦ *A panel of experts discussed the epidemic on the news program.* **3.** *n.* a surface that has controls, gauges, or instruments on it, used to control and monitor something. ♦ *The pilot flipped a few switches on the control panel.* ♦ *The electrician fixed the faulty wires inside the panel.* **4.** *tv.* to cover the walls of a room with ①. ♦ *We paneled our den with pine boards.* ♦ *My bedroom had been paneled with solid oak years ago.*

paneling ['pæn ə lɪŋ] *n.* a wall covering that is made of panels of wood or a similar durable material. (No plural form in this sense.) ♦ *We decided to put paneling over the ugly wallpaper.* ♦ *The carpenter glued and nailed the paneling to the wall.*

panelist ['pæn ə ləst] *n.* a member of a panel. ♦ *The panelists on the news program were experts in their fields.* ♦ *The celebrity panelists asked each contestant a question.*

pang ['pæŋ] *n.* a sudden, short, sharp feeling of hunger, pain, or emotion. ♦ *After working all morning without eating, I felt pangs of hunger.* ♦ *Pangs of guilt caused to me to confess what I had done.*

panhandler ['pæn hænd lɚ] *n.* a beggar; someone who begs for money. ♦ *The police removed the panhandler from the shopping mall.* ♦ *I gave the panhandler some food instead of money.*

panic ['pæn ɪk] **1.** *n.* uncontrollable fear; a sense of terror. (No plural form in this sense.) ♦ *After the explosion, there was panic throughout the city.* ♦ *Panic seized the entire population after the earthquake.* **2.** *iv., irreg.* to feel ①; to experience uncontrollable fear. (Pt/pp: panicked. The present participle is *panicking.*) ♦ *I panicked during the exam and left most of the questions blank.* ♦ *When the airplane lost power, many passengers panicked and began screaming.* **3.** *tv., irreg.* to cause someone or some creature to experience uncontrollable fear. ♦ *The deer were panicked by the shotgun blast.* ♦ *The earthquake panicked the people inside the tall building.*

panicked ['pæn ɪkt] pt/pp of panic.

panic-stricken ['pæn ɪk strɪk ən] *adj.* filled with uncontrollable fear or panic. ♦ *The panic-stricken deer froze in the middle of the road.* ♦ *The security guards were trampled by the panic-stricken crowd.*

panorama [pæn ə 'ræ mə] **1.** *n.* a wide display or image as viewed from a particular place. ♦ *The panorama from the edge of the Grand Canyon is breathtaking.* ♦ *From the airplane, I could see a panorama of the city beneath me.* **2.** *n.* a varied and wide set of selections or choices. ♦ *The travel brochure promised a panorama of exciting events.* ♦ *The new-home buyers were faced with a panorama of options.*

panoramic [pæn ə 'ræm ɪk] *adj.* wide like a panorama. (Adv: *panoramically* [...ɪk li].) ♦ *There's a spectacular, panoramic view from this mountaintop.* ♦ *The picture on the large movie screen was panoramic.*

pansy ['pæn zi] *n.* a plant that has colorful, rounded petals forming circular blossoms. ♦ *Mary picked some pansies and put them in a small vase.* ♦ *The gardener watered the row of pansies.*

pant ['pænt] **1.** *iv.* to make quick, shallow breaths, as with an overheated dog. ♦ *When a dog pants, its tongue sticks out of its mouth.* ♦ *Bill panted for several minutes after running up the stairs.* **2.** *n.* a gasp; a quick, shallow breath. ♦ *After Bill ran up the stairs, he breathed with short pants for several minutes.* ♦ *He was so exhausted that his breathing was only a series of quick pants.* **3. pants** *n.* trousers; clothing worn below the waist, having a separate hole or compartment for each leg. (Treated as plural. Number is expressed with *pair(s) of pants.*) ♦ *John put on his pants and went to work.* ♦ *Bill tried on three pairs of pants at the clothing store.*

panther ['pæn θɚ] *n.* a cougar; a puma; a large animal in the cat family. ♦ *The fierce panther chased the deer across the field.* ♦ *We saw a large, black panther at the zoo.*

pantomime ['pæn tə maɪm] **1.** *n.* expressing oneself, usually in a performance, by using gestures and posture instead of words. (No plural form in this sense. See also mime.) ♦ *Pantomime is an art form that requires skill and coordination.* ♦ *Separated by a thick window, Bob and Jane communicated in pantomime.* **2.** *n.* a performance done using gestures and postures instead of words. ♦ *Tom's pantomime of a man seeing his child for the first time was excellent.* ♦ *There were three pantomimes and four violin solos in the variety show!* **3.** *tv.* to express something by using gestures instead of words. ♦ *Bill pantomimed his question because his mouth was full of food.* ♦ *From across the crowded room, Anne pantomimed that I had a phone call.*

pantry ['pæn tri] *n.* a small room near a kitchen, where pots, pans, dishes, silverware, tablecloths, food, and other kitchen items are kept. ♦ *I store canned fruit and vegetables in the pantry.* ♦ *The cook went to the pantry to get a bag of flour.*

panty ['pæn ti] **1. panties** *n.* a pair of women's underpants. (Treated as plural. Number is expressed with *pair(s) of panties.*) ♦ *Lisa packed enough panties for a week when she went on vacation.* ♦ *Jane likes lacy panties made of silk.* **2.** *adj.* <the adj. use of ①.> ♦ *I keep all my panties in my panty drawer.* ♦ *There was a panty sale at the department store last week, so I bought a dozen.*

pantyhose ['pæn ti hoz] *n.* a garment that is a combination of long, sheer stockings extending from a pair of panties. (No plural form in this sense. Treated as plural. Number is expressed with *pair(s) of pantyhose.*) ♦ *Women often wear pantyhose underneath skirts.* ♦ *Mary snagged her pantyhose on the edge of the car door.*

papa ['pɑ pə] *n.* father. (Informal. Also a term of address.) ♦ *What does your papa do for a living?* ♦ *Do you know what time Papa will be home?*

papal ['pep əl] *adj.* of or about the Pope. (Adv: *papally.*) ♦ *The priest read the papal decree.* ♦ *When I was in Rome, I attended a papal Mass.*

paper ['pe pɚ] **1.** *n.* processed fiber and other substances, pressed into sheets, used for writing, printing, and drawing on. (No plural form in this sense. Number is expressed with *piece(s) of paper, sheet(s) of paper.* See also ②.) ♦ *Jane wrote her name at the top of the sheet of paper.* ♦ *Wood fiber is used in the making of paper.* **2. papers** *n.* documents; sheets of ① in groups or stacks, bearing information. (Treated as plural.) ♦ *Please stack the papers on my desk.* ♦ *The papers concerning the project are sup-*

posed to be in the filing cabinet. **3. one's papers** *n.* documents that prove who one is; one's passport or visa, carried while visiting a foreign country. (Treated as plural.) ♦ *During the war, the citizens carried their papers at all times.* ♦ *The police officer asked to look at the tourists' papers.* **4.** *n.* wallpaper; decorated paper that is glued to walls. (No plural form in this sense.) ♦ *Mary removed the old paper and painted the walls instead.* ♦ *Bob put the new paper up in strips, carefully matching the pattern at each edge.* **5.** *n.* a newspaper. ♦ *Did you read the story on the front page of today's paper?* ♦ *Anne read the morning paper during breakfast.* **6.** *n.* an article; an essay; a thesis. ♦ *The art professor published a paper on French paintings.* ♦ *Mary went to the library to work on her paper for history class.* **7.** *adj.* made from ①. ♦ *My paper hat fell apart when it got wet.* ♦ *At the picnic, we put our food on paper plates.* **8.** *tv.* to cover something with wallpaper. ♦ *The bathroom walls were papered with a pretty floral design.* ♦ *Anne papered the kitchen walls instead of painting them.* **9. put something on paper** *idiom* to write something down; to write or type an agreement on ①. ♦ *You have a great idea for a novel. Now put it on paper.* ♦ *I'm sorry, I can't discuss your offer until I see something in writing. Put it on paper, and then we'll talk.*

paperboy ['pe pɚ bɔɪ] *n.* a boy who delivers newspapers to people. ♦ *The paperboy threw our paper onto our porch.* ♦ *The paperboy finished his deliveries by 7:00 A.M.*

paper clip ['pep ɚ 'klɪp] *n.* a device made of bent wire that can hold a few sheets of paper together. ♦ *I put a paper clip on the papers and took them to Mike.* ♦ *I have a little bowl of paper clips on my desk.*

paperweight ['pe pɚ wet] *n.* a heavy object that is used to keep papers from blowing away. ♦ *The professor used a stone as a paperweight.* ♦ *When I opened the window, I had to set a paperweight on my papers.*

paperwork ['pe pɚ wɚk] *n.* the clerical tasks, such as writing letters, filling out forms, and filing documents, that are part of one's job. (No plural form in this sense.) ♦ *Jane thinks her job is boring because all she does is paperwork.* ♦ *The company I work for generates an enormous amount of paperwork.*

paprika [pæp 'ri kə] *n.* a spice made from dried red peppers. (From Hungarian. No plural form in this sense.) ♦ *The cook sprinkled paprika on top of the deviled eggs.* ♦ *I sprinkled paprika on the garlic bread before baking it.*

par ['pɑr] **1.** *n.* [in golf] the normal number of strokes that it takes to get the golf ball from the tee into the hole. (No plural form in this sense. A number may follow par.) ♦ *Because my ball landed in a sand trap, I finished the hole one over par.* ♦ *The fourteenth hole is par five, but I shot it in four.* **2. above par** *idiom* better than average or normal. ♦ *His work is above par, so he should get paid better.* ♦ *Your chances of winning the game are a little above par.* **3. below par** *idiom* not as good as average or normal. ♦ *I feel a little below par today. I think I am getting a cold.* ♦ *His work is below par, and he is paid too much money.* **4. up to par** *idiom* as good as the standard or average; up to the standard. ♦ *I'm just not feeling up to par today. I must be coming down with a cold.* ♦ *The manager said that the report was not up to par and gave it back to Mary to do over again.*

parable ['pɛr ə bəl] *n.* a story in the form of an analogy that presents a moral lesson. ♦ *Ministers sometimes preach using parables.* ♦ *Bill explained various parables from the Bible.*

parachute ['pɛr ə ʃut] **1.** *n.* a large fabric canopy attached to and supporting someone who jumps from an airplane or some other very high place. ♦ *The pilot put on a parachute and jumped from the burning plane.* ♦ *The soldier's parachute got tangled in some tree branches as he landed.* **2.** *iv.* to drift downward, wearing a parachute. ♦ *The pilot parachuted to safety from the burning plane.* ♦ *When Tom parachuted from the top of the tower, he was arrested.*

parade [pə 'red] **1.** *n.* a public event where people march or ride down a street with people watching from both sides. ♦ *On the Fourth of July, there will be a parade down Main Street.* ♦ *The parade was canceled because it rained.* **2.** *iv.* to march somewhere in a parade. ♦ *The retired soldiers paraded up the street on Veterans Day.* ♦ *A few local politicians paraded down the avenue as part of a holiday parade.* **3.** *tv.* to make someone march in front of people. ♦ *The emcee paraded the pageant winner in front of the crowd.* ♦ *The terrorist paraded the hostages in front of news cameras.*

paradise ['pɛr ə dɑɪs] **1.** *n.* heaven; the realm of God. (No plural form in this sense.) ♦ *Jane believed that when she died she would go to paradise.* ♦ *The minister talked to his congregation about paradise.* **2.** *n.* somewhere on earth that seems as lovely as ①. (No plural form in this sense.) ♦ *The expensive retirement home was paradise for the elderly.* ♦ *The beautiful Caribbean island seemed like paradise.* **3. a paradise (on earth)** *idiom* a place on earth that is as lovely as ①. ♦ *The retirement home was simply a paradise on earth.* ♦ *The beach where we went for our vacation was a paradise.* **4. fool's paradise** *idiom* a condition of apparent happiness that is based on false assumptions and will not last. ♦ *They think they can live on love alone, but they are living in a fool's paradise.* ♦ *The inhabitants of the island feel politically secure, but they are living in a fool's paradise. They could be invaded at any time.*

paradox ['pɛr ə dɑks] *n.* something that is self-contradictory. ♦ *A union of anarchists is a paradox.* ♦ *Traveling backward in time could create many paradoxes.*

paradoxically [pɛr ə 'dɑk sɪk li] *adv.* in a contradictory way. ♦ *Paradoxically, the murder victim was found in an empty room that had been locked from the inside.* ♦ *Paradoxically, the politician promised to cut taxes and provide more services.*

paraffin ['pɛr ə fən] *n.* a solid oil substance similar to wax, used in making candles and seals. (No plural form in this sense.) ♦ *The candle maker dipped the wicks into the paraffin.* ♦ *Paraffin is distilled from oil.*

paragon ['pɛr ə gɑn] *n.* the best example of something; a perfect example that should be copied. ♦ *The conscientious student was presented as a paragon of dedication.* ♦ *The judge was a paragon of honesty and fairness.*

paragraph ['pɛr ə græf] *n.* a sentence or group of sentences usually related some way in meaning. ♦ *Paragraphs break up documents into related groups of sentences.* ♦ *The first line of a paragraph is often indented.*

Paraguay ['pɛr ə gwe] See Gazetteer.

parakeet ['pɛr ə kit] *n.* a small parrot, commonly kept as a pet. ♦ *My neighbor keeps his parakeet in a cage.* ♦ *Mary fed some birdseed to her parakeet.*

paralegal [pɛr ə 'lig əl] **1.** *n.* someone who performs tasks that aid or support a lawyer. ♦ *The paralegal helped prepare documents for the trial.* ♦ *The lawyer asked the paralegal to research related cases.* **2.** *adj.* <the adj. use of ①.> ♦ *Anne received paralegal training at the law firm.* ♦ *The consultant charged $70 per hour for paralegal services.*

parallel ['pɛr ə lɛl] **1.** *adj.* [lines or plane surfaces] at the same distance apart; at an equal distance apart everywhere. ♦ *A pair of parallel lines will never meet.* ♦ *The rails of a train track are parallel to each other.* **2.** *adj.* comparable; analogous. ♦ *When I was in a parallel situation, I called the police.* ♦ *John and Mary have parallel political viewpoints.* **3.** *n.* a similarity. ♦ *The history class studied parallels between two postwar periods in the United States.* ♦ *My paper discusses parallels between the lives of two famous authors.* **4.** *n.* a line of latitude ①. (Parallel ① to the equator. ♦ *Parallels are imaginary circles that are parallel to the equator.* ♦ *The 49th parallel is the border between the western U.S. and Canada.* **5.** *tv.* to go or be in route or direction parallel to something else. ♦ *A good road parallels the river all the way to the bridge.* ♦ *The sidewalk parallels the street in most of the downtown district.*

parallelogram [pɛr ə 'lɛl ə græm] *n.* a flat figure with four sides in which the opposite sides are parallel and the same length. ♦ *A parallelogram with right angles is a rectangle.* ♦ *A square is a parallelogram whose four sides are the same length and whose angles are right angles.*

paralysis [pə 'ræl ɪ sɪs] **1.** *n.* a state of muscles that can no longer work. (No plural form in this sense.) ♦ *The accident caused paralysis in Mary's body below her waist.* ♦ *The stroke caused paralysis on the left side of Bob's body.* **2.** *n.* the stopping of movement; the inability to move or function. (No plural form in this sense. Figurative on ①.) ♦ *During rush hour, traffic is often in a state of paralysis.* ♦ *A blizzard caused a paralysis of the transportation system.*

paralyze ['pɛr ə lɑɪz] **1.** *tv.* to cause muscles to be unable to move. ♦ *A serious fall paralyzed Mary and put her in the hospital for a month.* ♦ *A car accident paralyzed Bill for the rest of his life.* **2.** *tv.* to stop something from moving. (Figurative on ①.) ♦ *An accident on Maple Street paralyzed all traffic for an hour.* ♦ *The strike by the workers paralyzed production at the factory.*

paramedic [pɛr ə 'mɛd ɪk] *n.* someone trained to assist a doctor or to give immediate aid in an emergency. ♦ *The paramedic aided the man who'd had a heart attack.* ♦ *Paramedics rushed the accident victims to the hospital.*

paramount ['pɛr ə mɑʊnt] *adj.* most important; above all other things or people; chief. (Adv: *paramountly.*) ♦ *Cutting waste was a paramount goal in the senator's tax plan.* ♦ *For the mayor, crime is an issue of paramount importance.*

paranoia [pɛr ə 'noɪ ə] *n.* an irrational state in which a person feels threatened or persecuted. (No plural form in this sense.) ♦ *Because of his paranoia, Bob always thought people were watching him.* ♦ *Anne's psychiatrist believed she was suffering from paranoia.*

paranoid ['pɛr ə noɪd] **1.** *adj.* associated with paranoia; suffering from paranoia. ♦ *The psychiatrist observed the patient's paranoid behavior.* ♦ *My paranoid neighbor accuses me of spying on her.* **2.** *n.* someone who suffers from paranoia. ♦ *Anne can't relax because she's a paranoid.* ♦ *The paranoid kept looking around to see if he was being watched.*

paraphernalia [pɛr ə fɚ 'nel jə] *n.* equipment associated with a certain activity or job. (No plural form in this sense. Treated as singular. From a Latin plural form.) ♦ *The scientist had a lot of expensive paraphernalia in the laboratory.* ♦ *Anne was shocked to find drug paraphernalia in her son's bedroom.*

paraphrase ['pɛr ə frez] **1.** *n.* a restatement of something that someone has said or has written. ♦ *The newspaper's paraphrase of the senator's speech was misleading.* ♦ *I understood Anne's paraphrase better than her original statement.* **2.** *tv.* to restate something as in ①. ♦ *Could you paraphrase your question? I don't understand you.* ♦ *The reporter paraphrased the president's comments.*

paraplegia [pɛr ə 'pli dʒi ə] *n.* paralysis from the waist down; the inability to move or feel one's legs. (No plural form in this sense.) ♦ *John's paraplegia was caused by an injury to his spine.* ♦ *Mary uses a wheelchair because of her paraplegia.*

paraplegic [pɛr ə 'pli dʒɪk] *n.* someone who is paralyzed from the waist down. ♦ *This ramp gives paraplegics easier access to the building.* ♦ *The paraplegic explained to the audience why he couldn't walk.*

parasite ['pɛr ə sɑɪt] **1.** *n.* a plant or animal completely dependent on another species of plant or animal for nourishment. (Parasites on humans and animals cause diseases or health disorders.) ♦ *The veterinarian checked my dog for parasites.* ♦ *The sick cow was infested with parasites.* **2.** *n.* someone who depends on other people for food and shelter; a useless person who is supported by other people. (Figurative on ①.) ♦ *Your roommate is a parasite and will never leave if you continue to support him.* ♦ *Susan's brother had become a real parasite and did nothing to share the cost of food or rent.*

paratrooper ['pɛr ə trup ɚ] *n.* a soldier who reaches the battleground by parachuting out of a plane. ♦ *The paratroopers landed on the beach and attacked the enemy.* ♦ *The army was reinforced by several dozen paratroopers.*

parcel ['pɑr səl] **1.** *n.* a package, especially one that is mailed or delivered; something that is wrapped up. ♦ *The mail carrier left a parcel for me on my front porch.* ♦ *The parcel was delivered to my office by a courier.* **2.** *n.* an amount of land that is sold as a unit. ♦ *I built my house on a 40-acre parcel of land.* ♦ *The developer divided the former farm into half-acre parcels.*

parcel post ['pɑr səl 'post] **1.** *n.* a class of mail in the postal system limited to small parcels. (No plural form in this sense.) ♦ *I sent my sister a book by parcel post.* ♦ *The cost of sending something by parcel post depends on its weight.* **2.** *adv.* by way of ①. ♦ *The important papers came parcel post and arrived late!* ♦ *I sent the package parcel post.*

parch ['pɑrtʃ] **1.** *iv.* to become dry because of high heat. ♦ *The land parched under the burning sun.* ♦ *During the drought, the grass parched and turned brown.* **2.** *tv.* to dry something through heating or the loss of water. ♦ *The drought parched the farmer's land.* ♦ *The dry wind parched my throat and made me thirsty.*

parchment ['partʃ mənt] **1.** *n.* the skin of a sheep or a goat, dried and used as a sheet that can be written on. (No plural form in this sense. Number is expressed with *sheet(s) of parchment.*) ♦ *My grandfather's college diploma is written on real parchment.* ♦ *Most really old parchment will crumble into dust if it is touched.* **2.** *n.* heavy paper that looks like ①. (No plural form in this sense. Number is expressed with *sheet(s) of parchment.*) ♦ *Anne printed her résumé on parchment.* ♦ *The wedding invitations were embossed on fancy parchment.*

pardon ['par dn] **1.** *n.* forgiveness. (No plural form in this sense.) ♦ *Pardon for my errors would ease my conscience.* ♦ *Your pardon in this matter is highly appreciated.* **2.** *n.* an act that keeps someone from being punished under the law. ♦ *The governor gave the young offender a pardon.* ♦ *The criminal sought a pardon from the king.* **3.** *tv.* to forgive someone; to excuse someone. ♦ *Please pardon me for interrupting you.* ♦ *Anne pardoned Bill for bumping into her.* **4.** *tv.* to release someone from jail; to order that someone not be executed; to keep someone from being punished. ♦ *The governor pardoned the young offender.* ♦ *The queen pardoned the woman who had been sentenced to die.*

pare ['pɛr] **1.** *tv.* to cut off the outer layer of something, especially to peel fruit or potatoes. ♦ *John pared the apple with a knife.* ♦ *The cook pared the pears before cutting them up for the fruit salad.* **2. pare (down)** *tv.* (+ *adv.*) to reduce something. ♦ *The school board pared down the budget by 5%.* ♦ *My work load was pared when my boss hired another worker.*

parent ['pɛr ənt] **1.** *n.* the father or the mother of a living creature. ♦ *My parents have been married for 40 years.* ♦ *I am the parent of a healthy baby boy.* **2.** *n.* a business that owns another business; the main office of one or more businesses or other organizations; the business or organization from which another business or organization has been derived. ♦ *The Jones Company is the parent of our new company.* ♦ *The headquarters of the organization—the parent of the various chapters—is located in New York.* **3.** *adj.* serving as a ②. ♦ *The parent company is located in Chicago.* ♦ *Our group has separated itself from the parent organization.*

parental [pə 'rɛn təl] *adj.* of or about the rights and responsibilities of parents. (Adv: *parentally.*) ♦ *Parental guidance is suggested for children who watch this movie.* ♦ *Drug use by teenagers is an important parental concern.*

parentheses [pə 'rɛn θə siz] pl of parenthesis.

parenthesis [pə 'rɛn θə sɪs] *n., irreg.* either of the pair of symbols "(" and ")", used to enclose information of secondary importance in writing or printing. (Pl: parentheses.) ♦ *Bill forgot to close his parenthetical statement with a right parenthesis.* ♦ *I put parentheses around the translation of the foreign phrase.*

parenthetical [pɛr ən 'θɛt ɪ kəl] *adj.* [of a word, clause, or sentence] giving an explanation or additional information. (Parenthetical information is set off by parentheses, commas, or dashes in writing and by lowering the voice in speech. Adv: *parenthetically* [...ɪk li].) ♦ *Bob, who is usually an excellent public speaker, made so many parenthetical remarks that I could hardly follow his thoughts.* ♦ *Lisa made so many detours into parenthetical comments and explanations that she forgot what she was talking about.*

parish ['pɛr ɪʃ] **1.** *n.* the residential area or district served by a church. ♦ *The new priest introduced himself to each family in the parish.* ♦ *Which parish is that minister from?* **2.** *n.* a district in the state of Louisiana similar to counties in the other states. ♦ *The city of New Orleans is in the parish of Orleans.* ♦ *There are 64 parishes in Louisiana.*

parity ['pɛr ə ti] *n.* equality; the condition of being equal. (No plural form in this sense.) ♦ *Our company ensures the parity of men's and women's salaries for the same job.* ♦ *There is no parity between the amount paid young workers and those with more seniority even if they do the same job.*

park ['park] **1.** *n.* a piece of land set aside by a city, state, county, or nation for use by the public, usually having trees, grass, and other natural features. ♦ *My friends and I had a picnic in the park.* ♦ *Anne jogs through Central Park every morning.* **2.** *tv.* to stop a car or other vehicle and leave it in a certain place for a period of time. ♦ *Bill parked his car illegally in front of the fire hydrant.* ♦ *The driver parked the bus next to the stadium during the game.* **3.** *tv.* to put or place someone or something in a certain place. (Informal. Figurative on ②.) ♦ *Park yourself in that chair. I'll be with you in a minute.* ♦ *Jane parked her bags in the corner and sat down.* **4.** *iv.* to leave a car or other vehicle in a certain place for a period of time. ♦ *I parked two blocks away from the store.* ♦ *You cannot park in an area that has a "No Parking" sign.* **5. in park** *idiom* [of an automobile transmission] having the gears locked so the automobile cannot move. ♦ *The driver stopped the car and placed it in park.* ♦ *You have to be in park in order to start this car.*

parked ['parkt] *adj.* [of a vehicle] put, placed, or left in a certain place. ♦ *The thief broke into the parked car.* ♦ *A parked truck blocked the road.*

parking ['par kɪŋ] **1.** *n.* stopping and storing a vehicle in a certain place. (No plural form in this sense.) ♦ *Parking is difficult in congested traffic.* ♦ *Bill pays $40 a month for parking in that garage.* **2.** *adj.* <the adj. use of ①.> ♦ *I left my car in a parking lot on Maple Street.* ♦ *Sally found a parking place on the street.*

parkway ['park we] *n.* a wide road or street, usually one that has trees on each side and, perhaps, trees in the middle. ♦ *Tom walked along the parkway from the lake to his house.* ♦ *When you get to Douglas Parkway, turn left.*

parliament ['par lə mənt] *n.* a government body that makes the laws for a country. ♦ *The parliament passed all of the pending legislation.* ♦ *The British Parliament consists of the House of Commons and the House of Lords.*

parlor ['par lɚ] **1.** *n.* a living room; a place in a home where guests can sit and talk. (Old-fashioned.) ♦ *Mary waited in the parlor until her date arrived.* ♦ *Aunt Susan likes to drink tea in the front parlor.* **2.** *n.* a store that sells a certain product or service, such as hair care, ice cream, or funerals. ♦ *Jane went to the beauty parlor to get her hair styled.* ♦ *I bought a chocolate sundae at the ice-cream parlor.*

parochial [pə 'rok i əl] **1. parochial school** *n.* a private school, funded by a church. ♦ *That parochial school doesn't hold classes on religious holidays.* ♦ *Jane's parents had to pay for her to attend a parochial school.* **2.** *adj.* narrow in interests or concerns. (Adv: *parochially.*) ♦ *The* *people of the small town were very parochial in their interests.* ♦ *The mayor concerned himself only with parochial matters and never thought of problems on the national level.*

parody ['pɛr ə di] **1.** *n.* a kind of art, music, literature, or film where someone mimics something in a funny way. ♦ *The audience laughed at the parody of the famous opera.* ♦ *The group of actors did a hilarious parody of mystery movies.* **2.** *n.* a mockery; something that is imitated very badly; a poor imitation of the original. (Figurative on ①.) ♦ *This horrible movie is just a parody of the book it's based on.* ♦ *Bill's article is a feeble parody of serious work in the field.* **3.** *tv.* to mimic a work of art, music, literature, or film in a funny way. ♦ *A group of students parodied classical music.* ♦ *Bob wrote a short rhyme that parodies a well-known poem.*

parole [pə 'rol] **1.** *n.* a conditional release from prison before one's sentence is finished. (No plural form in this sense. If the conditions of ① are violated, the convict must return to prison.) ♦ *Bill's parole does not permit him to leave the state, carry a weapon, use drugs, or commit a crime.* ♦ *Susan was eligible for parole after serving only half of her sentence.* **2.** *tv.* to release one from prison conditionally, before one's sentence is finished. ♦ *The judge who paroled the dangerous criminal was severely criticized.* ♦ *Susan was paroled after half of her sentence was served.* **3. (out) on parole** *idiom* out of prison, conditionally, before one's total sentence is served. ♦ *Bob was caught using drugs while out on parole and was sent back to prison.* ♦ *He has to be careful and obey the law because he is out on parole.*

parrot ['pɛr ət] **1.** *n.* a kind of tropical bird, often brightly colored, that can copy human speech. ♦ *Parrots are often kept as pets.* ♦ *My parrot repeats whatever I say.* **2.** *tv.* to repeat someone else's words or ideas without thinking. (Figurative on ①.) ♦ *The candidate only parroted the platform of his political party.* ♦ *On the test, Mary parroted her professor's comments.*

parsley ['pɑrs li] *n.* an herb used in cooking to add flavor to food or as a garnish. (No plural form in this sense. Number is expressed with *sprig(s) of parsley.*) ♦ *The chef placed a sprig of parsley on top of the fish before serving it.* ♦ *I added fresh parsley to the chicken soup.*

parson ['pɑr sən] *n.* a minister or a pastor. ♦ *My family invited our parson over for dinner.* ♦ *The parson gave an interesting sermon last Sunday.*

part ['pɑrt] **1.** *n.* a section of a whole; a piece of a whole; one of the pieces that a whole is divided into. ♦ *This stone was once part of the sidewalk.* ♦ *Part of your responsibility is to clean up after yourself.* **2.** *n.* one of a set of equal divisions. ♦ *This recipe calls for two parts sugar to three parts milk.* ♦ *Add ten parts water to one part concentrated detergent, and mix.* **3.** *n.* an actor's role in a play or movie. ♦ *Whom did the director cast in the part of the hero?* ♦ *I have an audition for a good part in a Hollywood movie.* **4.** *n.* the line between two sections of hair of the head, established when combing. ♦ *The barber asked me if I'd like my part down the middle.* ♦ *John wears his part to the side.* **5. part of speech** *n.* one of the classes or divisions of words that reflect grammatical usage, such as noun, verb, adjective, etc. ♦ *What part of speech is* house *in the sentence "He lives in the house on the corner"?* ♦ *"Adverb" and "adjective" are parts of speech.* **6.** *adv.* not completely. ♦ *Jane's plaid shirt is part red and part green.* ♦ *Come back in an hour. I'm only part finished.* **7.** *tv.* to make a pathway through a group of people or things. ♦ *The police parted the crowd of spectators so the ambulance could get through.* ♦ *The hunters parted the bushes and plants so they could walk through the woods.* **8.** *tv.* to separate one's hair along a line, especially when combing it into two sides. ♦ *Part your hair on the other side. It looks better that way.* ♦ *John parted his hair down the middle.* **9.** *iv.* to divide or separate, making an opening. ♦ *The curtains parted and the opera began.* ♦ *The crowd parted to allow the celebrity to pass through.* **10. part with** *iv.* + *prep. phr.* to give something up. ♦ *I hate to part with this old car, but it doesn't work anymore.* ♦ *Mary parted with her old computer when she bought a new one.* **11. part (with); part (from)** *iv.* (+ *prep. phr.*) to say good-bye to someone and leave. ♦ *Anne parted with her husband in a friendly way.* ♦ *After two years as roommates, John and Bob parted on friendly terms.* **12. take part (in something)** *idiom* to participate in something. ♦ *Bill refused to take part in the game.* ♦ *Everyone is asked to take part in the celebration.* **13. take someone's part** *idiom* to take a side in an argument; to support someone in an argument. ♦ *My sister took my mother's part in the family argument.* ♦ *You are always taking the part of the underdog!*

partake [pɑr 'tek] **1. partake of** *iv., irreg.* + *prep. phr.* to accept the offer of something, such as food, drink, hospitality, etc.; to join in the consumption of something. (Pt: partook; pp: partaken.) ♦ *Mary does not partake of drugs or alcohol.* ♦ *John partook of my homemade punch.* **2. partake in** *iv., irreg.* + *prep. phr.* to participate in some activity that is offered. ♦ *Won't you partake in the holiday festivities at my house?* ♦ *Anne did not partake in the celebration.*

partaken [pɑr 'tek ən] pp of partake.

partial ['pɑr ʃəl] **1.** *adj.* not complete; only part of the entire thing. (Adv: *partially.*) ♦ *John received partial credit for his late homework assignment.* ♦ *I gave only a partial answer to the question.* **2.** *adj.* favoring someone or something; biased. (Not prenominal. Adv: *partially.*) ♦ *The lawyers claimed that the judge was too partial.* ♦ *I am not partial! I am completely unbiased!* **3. partial to someone or something** *idiom* favoring or preferring something. ♦ *The boys think their teacher is partial to female students.* ♦ *I am partial to vanilla ice cream.*

participant [pɑr 'tɪs ə pənt] *n.* someone who participates in some activity. ♦ *There were ten participants in the contest.* ♦ *All of the participants in the race received a prize.*

participate [pɑr 'tɪs ə pet] **participate (in)** *iv.* (+ *prep. phr.*) to take part in something; to be one of a group of things or people doing or involved in something. ♦ *Mary participated in several school sports.* ♦ *We didn't have enough money for the raffle, so we did not participate.*

participating [pɑr 'tɪs ə pet ɪŋ] *adj.* [of a store or business] taking part in a special offer or special sale. ♦ *This coupon is valid at all participating restaurants.* ♦ *The mayor praised the participating businesses.*

participation [pɑr tɪs ə 'pe ʃən] *n.* taking part in something. (No plural form in this sense.) ♦ *Parents' participation in school activities is appreciated.* ♦ *Bob's participation in the group project was minimal.*

participial [part ə 'sɪp i əl] *adj.* of or about a participle. (Adv: *participially.*) ♦ *"Hanging by a thread" is a participial phrase.* ♦ *I think your writing uses too many participial constructions.*

participle ['part ə sɪp əl] *n.* <either the **present participle** or the **past participle**.> ♦ *The present participle of* smile *is* smiling, *and it functions as an adjective in* the smiling man. ♦ *The past participle of* freeze *is* frozen, *and it functions as an adjective in* a box of frozen vegetables.

particle ['part ɪ kəl] **1.** *n.* a small piece of something. ♦ *A particle of food was caught between my teeth.* ♦ *The cat swatted at particles of dust floating in the sunlight.* **2.** *n.* a kind of word or a part of a word that is not inflected but that affects the meaning of another word, such as conjunctions, articles, and prepositions. ♦ *Articles are particles.* ♦ *Nouns, verbs, adjectives, and adverbs are never considered particles.* **3.** *n.* a basic unit of matter, such as a proton, neutron, or electron. ♦ *Electrons are negatively charged particles.* ♦ *The proton is a particle with a positive charge.*

particular [pɑr 'tɪk jə lɚ] **1.** *adj.* specific; distinct [from others]. (Adv: *particularly.*) ♦ *I don't have any particular plans for this evening.* ♦ *"Was there a particular item you wanted?" the clerk asked me.* **2.** *adj.* unusual; noticeable; worth noticing. (Adv: *particularly.*) ♦ *The driver drove with particular care after the accident.* ♦ *Lisa wrote the letter with particular attention to her choice of words.* **3.** *adj.* very picky; demanding; hard to please. (Adv: *particularly.*) ♦ *Working for a boss who is very particular can be difficult.* ♦ *The particular diner sent the entree back to the kitchen twice.* **4. particular about** *adj. + prep. phr.* giving special attention to choice; fastidious about selecting things or people. ♦ *Tom is very particular about what he eats.* ♦ *Bob is not very particular about the clothes he wears.* **5. the particulars of something** *idiom* specific details about something. ♦ *My boss stressed the important particulars of the project.* ♦ *What are the particulars of your request?*

particularly [pɑr 'tɪk jə lɚ li] *adv.* especially; in a way that is worth mentioning. ♦ *I think this movie is particularly exciting.* ♦ *Bob smiled in a particularly friendly way.*

parting ['part ɪŋ] **1.** *n.* separating; leaving someone or something. (No plural form in this sense.) ♦ *Parting was almost more than the lovers could bear.* ♦ *The unhappy couple's parting was beneficial in the long run.* **2.** *adj.* happening as one departs or separates. ♦ *The defeated mayor's parting words were very emotional.* ♦ *As my train left the station, my wife's parting glance made me cry.*

partisan ['part ə zən] **1.** *adj.* strongly supporting a person, a political party, or a cause. (Adv: *partisanly.*) ♦ *Her partisan speech angered the opposing party.* ♦ *The senator took a partisan position, following the philosophy of his political party.* **2.** *n.* someone who supports a person, a political party, or a cause. ♦ *Since he is a partisan, you know exactly what his opinion will be.* ♦ *During the senator's speech, the room was filled with partisans who cheered everything he said.*

partition [pɑr 'tɪ ʃən] **1.** *n.* a divider; something that separates two spaces; a wall. ♦ *At my office, the work areas of individual employees are separated by partitions.* ♦ *Mary hung a calendar on her partition at work.* **2.** *tv.* to split something into two or more parts. ♦ *I partitioned the large closet into four sections.* ♦ *My supervisor partitioned the work load among four workers.*

partly ['part li] *adv.* in part; to a degree; not completely. ♦ *The other driver was partly responsible for the accident.* ♦ *The sun was partly obscured by a cloud.*

partner ['part nɚ] **1.** *n.* someone with whom one shares a business; one of the owners of a business. ♦ *I will have to discuss this contract with my partners.* ♦ *My business partner and I discussed business during lunch.* **2.** *n.* someone who shares an activity with someone else. ♦ *The thief would not reveal the names of his partner in crime.* ♦ *My partner in the relay race dropped the baton.* **3.** *n.* a person with whom one has a long-term relationship. ♦ *Bob gave his partner a dozen roses on their anniversary.* ♦ *Mary brought her partner to her parents' dinner party.*

partnership ['part nɚ ʃɪp] *n.* an association; the relationship between partners. ♦ *John and Mary's business partnership has lasted for twenty years.* ♦ *Bill set up a partnership with two other lawyers.*

partook [pɑr 'tʊk] pt of **partake**.

part-time ['part taɪm] **1.** *adj.* for only part of the time and not full-time. ♦ *Susan had a part-time job while she was in college.* ♦ *Most part-time employees aren't eligible for benefits.* **2.** *adv.* not as full-time; [working] only part of the working week. ♦ *Anne worked part-time at the library while she was in school.* ♦ *John paints houses part-time during the summer.*

party ['pɑr ti] **1.** *n.* a social gathering of people; a gathering of people who are having fun. ♦ *We played games at Anne's party.* ♦ *Bill received many gifts at his birthday party.* **2.** *n.* a group of people who are together for a specific reason. ♦ *The search party looked for the missing child for a week.* ♦ *"How many people are in your party?" asked the waiter.* **3.** *n.* a group of people united with a common goal or with common ideas, especially in politics. ♦ *Everyone in the party held a similar opinion on that issue.* ♦ *The politician's party raised money for his campaign.* **4.** *n.* a person or business entity. ♦ *Both parties came to an agreement outside of the courtroom.* ♦ *What is the name of the party you are looking for?* **5.** *adj.* <the adj. use of ③.> ♦ *The representative followed party principles.* ♦ *The party leaders boasted about their candidate.* **6.** *iv.* to celebrate; to have fun at a party. (Informal.) ♦ *The students in my dorm party every weekend.* ♦ *My friends and I partied after I got a job promotion.* **7. life of the party** *idiom* a person who is lively and helps make ① fun and exciting. ♦ *Bill is always the life of the party. Be sure to invite him.* ♦ *Bob isn't exactly the life of the party, but he's polite.* **8. party line** *idiom* the official ideas and attitudes that are adopted by the leaders of a particular group and that the other members are expected to accept. ♦ *Tom has left the club. He refused to follow the party line.* ♦ *Many politicians support the party line without thinking.*

partygoer ['pɑr ti go ɚ] *n.* someone who is at a party; someone who goes to parties. ♦ *All the partygoers wore fancy costumes.* ♦ *Each partygoer brought the host a gift.*

pass ['pæs] **1.** *tv.* to reach someone or something and go beyond. ♦ *I passed the slow car that was in front of me.* ♦ *The winner passed the finish line before the other runners.* **2.** *tv.* to succeed in a [school] course or examination; to have a medical examination where no problems are discovered. ♦ *After studying all night, I managed to pass the* *test.* ♦ *I easily passed the history exam.* **3.** *tv.* to use up a period of time [doing something]; to occupy a period of time [doing something]. ♦ *John passed the night worrying.* ♦ *Lisa passed time by reading the newspaper.* **4.** *tv.* to approve or agree to something, such as a motion, law, or resolution, by means of a vote. ♦ *The Senate passed the bill by a vote of 70–30.* ♦ *The president vetoed the law that Congress had passed.* **5.** *tv.* to hand something over to someone; to give something to someone. ♦ *I passed the bread to Anne.* ♦ *Please pass me the salt.* **6.** *tv.* to throw a ball to someone in a game. ♦ *The other player passed me the basketball.* ♦ *I passed the football to my teammate.* **7.** *iv.* to reach and go beyond. ♦ *I almost hit the car that passed on my left.* ♦ *Spectators shouted encouragement to the runners as they passed.* **8.** *iv.* to meet the requirements for successfully completing a [school] course; to undergo a medical exam where no problems are discovered. ♦ *Anne failed the test, and Jane just barely passed.* ♦ *If you attend every lecture, you should pass.* **9.** *iv.* [for a motion, law, resolution] to be approved by means of a vote. ♦ *The new law passed by a narrow margin.* ♦ *The law passed despite the public opposition to it.* **10.** *iv.* [for time] to progress or proceed. ♦ *Time passes slowly when you're bored.* ♦ *As the years passed, Bill began to regret his actions.* **11. pass across; pass over; pass through** *iv.* + *prep. phr.* to travel across, over, or through. ♦ *The cars passed through the tunnel, one by one.* ♦ *The airplane passed over the canyon.* **12. pass out** *iv.* + *adv.* to faint; to become unconscious. ♦ *It was so hot in the room that I thought I would pass out.* ♦ *When I broke my foot, I passed out from the pain.* **13.** *n.* a grade given for a course, test, paper, or school year showing that one was successful or met all the requirements. (In a grading system where the only other grade is fail.) ♦ *Bill worked hard to receive a pass in the difficult chemistry course.* ♦ *To get a pass in this class, you have to write a 20-page paper.* **14.** *n.* a ticket or document showing that one is allowed to go somewhere. ♦ *I used my free pass to see the new movie.* ♦ *My bus pass is good for 20 rides, and then I have to buy a new one.* **15.** *n.* the transfer of a ball or something similar in various sports. ♦ *The football player intercepted the pass.* ♦ *I caught my teammate's pass and threw the ball toward the basket.* **16.** *n.* a narrow path, especially through mountains. ♦ *The travelers had to get through the pass before winter.* ♦ *The avalanche blocked the only pass leading out of the mountain village.* **17. pass away** *idiom* to die. (Euphemistic.) ♦ *Mary's father passed away last week.* ♦ *When John passes away, he wants to be cremated.* **18. pass judgment (on someone or something)** *idiom* to judge someone or something. ♦ *Who are you to pass judgment on me?* ♦ *The media passed judgment on the defendant before the jury could.* **19. let something pass** *idiom* to let something go unnoticed or unchallenged. ♦ *Bob let Bill's insult pass because he didn't want to argue.* ♦ *Don't worry, I'll let this little incident pass.* **20. make a pass at someone** *idiom* to attempt to flirt with someone; to make unwanted sexual invitations to someone. ♦ *John made a pass at the woman sitting next to him at the bar.* ♦ *Mary did not want to dance with the man who had made a pass at her.* **21. pass the time** *idiom* to spend time doing something; to consume or use spare time by doing something. ♦ *I read to pass the time while waiting in the doctor's office.* ♦ *I passed the time of day by talking to Dave.*

passable ['pæs ə bəl] **1.** *adj.* able to be crossed or passed through; able to be traveled over. ♦ *This road often is not passable after a heavy rainstorm.* ♦ *We shoveled the snow to make our sidewalk passable.* **2.** *adj.* [a motion or proposition] likely to get enough votes to pass. ♦ *The senator considered the bill to be passable.* ♦ *The bill was too controversial to be passable.* **3.** *adj.* only adequate; fair; sufficient. (Adv: *passably.*) ♦ *I gave your paper a D because it was barely passable.* ♦ *Although John's work is passable, it's certainly not noteworthy.*

passage ['pæs ɪdʒ] **1.** *n.* a path, corridor, or hallway. ♦ *The passage leading to the storage room was cluttered with boxes.* ♦ *The movers maneuvered the piano through the narrow passage.* **2.** *n.* moving across, through, or over something; moving from one state or condition to another. (No plural form in this sense.) ♦ *His passage into adulthood was difficult for him.* ♦ *The passage from being an employed executive to a retired gentleman was easy.* **3.** *n.* the progress or movement of time. (No plural form in this sense.) ♦ *The passage of time is slow when you're bored.* ♦ *After the passage of three months of peace and quiet, the teacher returned to work.* **4.** *n.* the approval of a law, motion, or resolution, usually by a vote. (No plural form in this sense.) ♦ *The lobbyist supported the passage of the bill.* ♦ *The passage of the new tax law caused a public protest.* **5.** *n.* a short section of a piece of music, a speech, or a written work. ♦ *I liked the passage in your poem that dealt with darkness.* ♦ *The violinist practiced the difficult passage.*

passageway ['pæs ɪdʒ we] *n.* a hallway; a path; a passage for getting from one place to another. ♦ *The bathroom is down that passageway and to your right.* ♦ *The passageway leading to the old workshop was dark and narrow.*

passbook ['pæs bʊk] *n.* a book for keeping track of one's deposits to and withdrawals from a bank account. ♦ *The teller stamped my passbook every time I made a deposit.* ♦ *I use electronic banking and therefore do not have a passbook.*

passenger ['pæs ən dʒɚ] *n.* someone who is riding in a vehicle or conveyance but not driving it. ♦ *The driver instructed the passengers to fasten their seat belts.* ♦ *The pilot greeted the passengers as they boarded the plane.*

passerby ['pæs ɚ baɪ] *n., irreg.* someone who happens to walk by a place; someone who passes by. (Pl: passersby.) ♦ *The beggar asked each passerby for money.* ♦ *Many passersby came into the restaurant after looking at the menu posted by the door.*

passersby ['pæs ɚz 'baɪ] pl of passerby.

passing ['pæs ɪŋ] **1.** *n.* [someone's or some creature's] death. (No plural form in this sense.) ♦ *I called my brother to tell him of the passing of our father.* ♦ *My grandmother's passing brought sorrow to the whole family.* **2.** *adj.* not lasting for a long time; transient; lasting only for a short time. ♦ *Mary returned John's passing glance with a glare.* ♦ *For a few passing moments, I thought I was going to faint.* **3.** *adj.* moving; progressing. ♦ *The passing train slowed at the train crossing.* ♦ *Each passing car slowed down to look at our beautiful garden.*

passion ['pæʃ ən] **1.** *n.* strong romantic and sexual feeling. (No plural form in this sense.) ♦ *Lost in the depths of passion, the lovers did not hear the door open.* ♦ *The movie had so much passion in it that I was embarrassed.* **2. have**

a passion for someone or something *idiom* to have a strong feeling of need or desire for someone, something, or some activity. ♦ *Mary has a great passion for chocolate.* ♦ *John has a passion for fishing, so he fishes as often as he can.*

passionate ['pæʃ ə nət] **1.** *adj.* having or expressing a strong feeling of emotion for someone, something, or some activity. (Adv: *passionately.*) ♦ *John and Mary tend to get passionate about their political beliefs.* ♦ *Mary is very passionate about gardening.* **2.** *adj.* sexually interested or aroused. (Adv: *passionately.*) ♦ *When Bill started getting passionate, Mary decided to go home.* ♦ *Passionate lovers kissed in the moonlight.*

passive ['pæs ɪv] **1.** *adj.* not resisting; not active; letting others take charge or control a situation; submissive. (The opposite of active. Adv: *passively.*) ♦ *The passive guest listened to the host talk all night.* ♦ *I urged my passive friend to be more assertive.* **2.** *adj.* <concerning a grammatical state where the verb acts on the subject of the sentence.> (Adv: *passively.*) ♦ *"John is loved by Mary" is a passive construction.* ♦ *I rewrote my demand in the passive voice.* **3.** *n.* a passive ② construction. (*The house was painted by Mr. Smith* is a passive.) ♦ *There are too many passives in your writing.* ♦ *You can use the passive once or twice in your article, but not in every sentence!*

Passover ['pæs ov ɚ] *n.* an eight-day-long Jewish holiday in memory of the escape of the Hebrews from Egypt. (No plural form in this sense.) ♦ *My roommate visited his family during Passover.* ♦ *Passover is celebrated in the spring.*

passport ['pæs port] **1.** *n.* an identity document showing one's citizenship that is needed to enter certain countries. ♦ *The tourist showed his passport to the border guard.* ♦ *Mary applied for a passport four months before her trip to Asia.* **2. passport to something** *idiom* something that allows something good to happen. (On ①.) ♦ *John's new girlfriend is his passport to happiness.* ♦ *Anne's new job is a passport to financial security.*

password ['pæs wɚd] *n.* a secret word, phrase, or set of symbols that allows someone access to something. ♦ *The spy whispered the password to the guard at the door.* ♦ *John entered his password to access the computer file.*

past ['pæst] **1.** *n.* a time that has gone by; things that have happened; history. (No plural form in this sense.) ♦ *In the past, people used to travel on horseback.* ♦ *My grandfather entertained me with stories from the past.* **2. past (tense)** *n.* the tense of a verb or auxiliary verb that indicates an event or a state that has existed at a previous time. (Abbreviated "pt" here.) ♦ *In English, a verb ending in* -ed *is in the past.* ♦ *Since this happened before now, you must use the past tense to describe it.* **3.** *adj.* most recent; occurring in the time just before this time. ♦ *I'm sorry, I didn't hear the past few questions.* ♦ *I spent the past hour wondering where you were.* **4.** *adj.* previous; occurring or completed at some previous time. ♦ *The doctor read about the patient's past medical treatments.* ♦ *The student's past performance in class had been excellent.* **5.** *adj.* <the adj. use of ②.> ♦ *The past form of many English words ends in* -ed. ♦ *You need to use a past construction here because the time of the verb is in the past.* **6.** *adv.* by; toward or alongside someone or something and then beyond. ♦ *John walked past the barking dog quickly.* ♦ *The car honked when it drove past.* **7.** *prep.* farther [in space, time, ability, or quality]; beyond [in space, time, ability, or quality]. ♦ *The bank is just past the bookstore.* ♦ *The time is 15 minutes past noon.* **8. in times past** *idiom* long ago; in previous times. ♦ *In times past, you would not have been able to wear casual clothing to work.* ♦ *In times past, the air always seemed fresher and cleaner.*

pasta ['pɑs tə] *n.* a food prepared by mixing flour, water, and sometimes egg to make a dough or paste, and then shaping it into different forms; noodles. (No plural form in this sense.) ♦ *Spaghetti is a long, thin type of pasta.* ♦ *John put tomato sauce on top of his pasta.*

paste ['pest] **1.** *n.* a soft mixture that is easily spread. (No plural form in this sense.) ♦ *Max spread the tomato paste over the pizza.* ♦ *I made a paste of flour and water to use as glue.* **2.** *n.* a soft mixture that causes objects to stick together. (No plural form in this sense.) ♦ *Jimmy used paste to stick the drawing to the poster.* ♦ *I smeared the wallpaper paste on the wallpaper, and then placed it on the wall.* **3.** *tv.* to cause something to stick to something else with ②. ♦ *Jimmy pasted the picture to the top of the table.* ♦ *It took me several hours to paste all the wallpaper onto the wall.*

pastel [pæs 'tɛl] **1.** *n.* a light or pale shade of color. ♦ *Mary's bedroom was decorated in pastels.* ♦ *The designer preferred pastels to bright colors.* **2.** *n.* a piece of colored chalk. (Usually in a collection of many similarly colored pieces of chalk.) ♦ *The artist drew a picture of the flowers using pastels.* ♦ *I had to buy a set of pastels for my art class.* **3.** *adj.* soft and pale in color. ♦ *I prefer a room colored in pastel shades to one with bright colors.* ♦ *John wore a pastel shirt to the party.*

pasteurization [pæs tʃə rɪ 'ze ʃən] *n.* heating a liquid, such as milk, quickly in order to kill dangerous bacteria. (No plural form in this sense. From the name of Louis Pasteur, who invented the process.) ♦ *Pasteurization should be done under sterile conditions.* ♦ *The pasteurization of milk makes it safer to drink.*

pasteurize ['pæs tʃə rɑɪz] *tv.* to heat a liquid, especially milk, quickly in order to kill dangerous bacteria. ♦ *The dairy pasteurized the milk before putting it into bottles.* ♦ *Mary won't drink milk that hasn't been pasteurized.*

pasteurized ['pæs tʃə rɑɪzd] *adj.* sterilized; heated and then chilled so that dangerous bacteria are killed. ♦ *The dairy sold only pasteurized milk.* ♦ *All the yogurt that you buy in a store has been pasteurized.*

pastime ['pæs tɑɪm] *n.* an activity that one enjoys; an enjoyable activity that is done to pass the time. ♦ *Jane's pastimes include skiing and reading.* ♦ *My favorite pastime is reading.*

pastor ['pæs tɚ] *n.* a minister in a Christian church. ♦ *The pastor baptized our baby.* ♦ *At church, the pastor spoke about right and wrong.*

pastoral ['pæs tɚ əl] **1.** *adj.* of or about life in the country; simple; peaceful; relaxed. (Adv: *pastorally* [pæs 'tor ə li].) ♦ *The remote cabin's pastoral setting was calming.* ♦ *I prefer pastoral surroundings to the noise of large cities.* **2.** *adj.* of or about being a pastor or minister. (Adv: *pastorally* [pæs 'tor ə li].) ♦ *Pastoral duties include performing weddings, baptisms, and funerals.* ♦ *John received pastoral training at a Bible college.*

past participle ['pæst 'pɑr tə sɪp əl] *n.* <a verb form sometimes made by adding *-ed* or *-en* to a verb, and sometimes being an irregular form of the verb that must be learned.> (This form can function as a verb or as an adjective. Abbreviated "pp" here.) ♦ *"The broken vase was my father's favorite" shows a past participle as an adjective.* ♦ *"The birds have eaten the seeds" shows a past participle as a verb.*

pastry ['pe stri] **1.** *n.* baked food, typically sweet, made from a flour dough, especially the thin, flat dough used in making pies. (No plural form in this sense.) ♦ *Prepare the pastry for the pie crust before you start making the filling.* ♦ *I love to eat pieces of baked pastry left over from making pie crusts.* **2.** *n.* sweet rolls, small cakes, and other sweetened, baked food, often with fruit or sweet coatings or fillings. ♦ *The pastries at my neighborhood bakery are made fresh every day.* ♦ *Jane served a selection of pastries for dessert.*

pasture ['pæs tʃɚ] **1.** *n.* a field of grass, especially one where animals graze. ♦ *The farmer's pasture was enclosed by a wooden fence.* ♦ *The cow munched on grass in the pasture.* **2. put someone or something out to pasture** *idiom* to retire someone or something. ♦ *Please don't put me out to pasture. I have lots of good years left.* ♦ *This car has reached the end of the line. It's time to put it out to pasture.*

pat ['pæt] **1.** *n.* a gentle tap, especially with the palm of one's hand. ♦ *Uncle Bob gave Jimmy a pat on the head.* ♦ *With a few pats of his hand, the baker shaped the dough for baking.* **2.** *n.* a small amount of butter. ♦ *I put a pat of butter on my baked potato.* ♦ *The waitress brought several pats of butter to our table.* **3.** *tv.* to touch or tap someone or something gently a few times, especially with the palm of the hand. ♦ *Bill patted the puppy's head.* ♦ *Dad patted me on the back because I'd done a good job.* **4.** *adj.* perfectly, as if memorized or rehearsed. (Adv: *patly.*) ♦ *The detective was suspicious of the suspect's pat responses.* ♦ *The witness had pat answers prepared for every question.* **5. give someone a pat on the back** *idiom* to praise someone with words. ♦ *My boss gave me a pat on the back over the telephone.* ♦ *When I see Tom, I will give him a pat on the back for his patience.* **6. have something down pat** *idiom* to have learned or memorized something perfectly. ♦ *I have practiced my speech until I have it down pat.* ♦ *Tom has his part in the play down pat. He won't make any mistakes.*

patch ['pætʃ] **1.** *n.* a piece of cloth or other material used to repair a hole or a tear or to cover something. ♦ *The patch covering the tear in the couch was barely noticeable.* ♦ *I sewed a patch over the hole in my pants.* **2.** *n.* a small area of land. ♦ *John owns a patch of land by the lake.* ♦ *Anne picked some daisies from the flower patch.* **3.** *n.* a small area on a surface that is different from the area around it. ♦ *That red patch of skin on my back is a birthmark.* ♦ *The dark patch on the carpet is a permanent stain.* **4. patch (up)** *tv.* (+ *adv.*) to mend something with ①. ♦ *The tailor patched my shirt with a matching piece of cloth.* ♦ *Can you please patch up the knees of my trousers?* **5. patch something up** *idiom* [for people] to settle a quarrel and become friends again. ♦ *Bill and I patched up our little quarrel and had a cup of coffee together.* ♦ *The friends quickly patched up their disagreement.*

patchwork ['pætʃ wɚk] **1.** *adj.* made of different patches of cloth or leather, stitched together. ♦ *There is a patchwork quilt on my bed.* ♦ *Anne has a patchwork jacket made from pieces of fabric from her old clothing.* **2.** *n.* garments or coverings made of patches of cloth or leather stitched together. (No plural form in this sense.) ♦ *Lisa runs a shop that sells leather belts and patchwork.* ♦ *My hobby is making quilts and other patchwork.* **3.** *n.* held together like ②; being a mixture of or assortment of different things or styles. ♦ *The mosaic is a patchwork of brightly colored stones.* ♦ *The president's term has been a patchwork of failed ideas.*

patchy ['pætʃ i] *adj.* only in some places; not everywhere. (Adv: *patchily.* Comp: *patchier;* sup: *patchiest.*) ♦ *My flight was delayed because of patchy fog.* ♦ *The sun shone brightly through the patchy clouds.*

patent ['pæt nt] **1.** *n.* the exclusive right, registered with the government, to exploit the ownership of a process or invention. ♦ *The inventor held the patents on dozens of devices.* ♦ *Sally applied for a patent for a process she invented that makes old paint usable.* **2.** *tv.* to seek and gain ① on something. ♦ *I made sure to patent my invention as soon as it was perfected.* ♦ *The inventor patented his idea before he actually mentioned it in public.*

paternal [pə 'tɚ nəl] **1.** *adj.* of or about a father; related to one's father. (Adv: *paternally.*) ♦ *My paternal ancestors are Italian.* ♦ *I wrote my paternal grandfather a letter.* **2.** *adj.* fatherly; suitable for or typical of a helpful father. (Adv: *paternally.*) ♦ *My counselor spoke to me in a paternal way.* ♦ *Bob discovered his paternal instincts soon after his first child was born.*

paternity [pə 'tɚ nə ti] **1.** *n.* the state of being a father. (No plural form in this sense.) ♦ *Paternity was exciting for Dave, until he had to feed the baby three times a night.* ♦ *Paternity gave Bill a new sense of responsibility.* **2.** *n.* male parentage; paternal origin or source. (No plural form in this sense.) ♦ *Genetic tests proved John's paternity of Anne's child.* ♦ *The paternity of the child could not be determined.* **3.** *adj.* <the adj. use of ②.> (Especially regarding legal questions of the identity of a father.) ♦ *Anne filed a paternity suit against John.* ♦ *The judge handles about three paternity cases a month.*

path ['pæθ] **1.** *n.* a track or walkway along the earth. ♦ *Anne walked down the stone path toward the lake.* ♦ *The bicycle path was blocked by a fallen tree.* **2.** *n.* the route someone or something takes to achieve a result. (Figurative on ①.) ♦ *Gambling is the path to ruin.* ♦ *Anne has designed her own path to success.* **3. beat a path to someone's door** *idiom* [for people] to come to someone in great numbers. ♦ *I have a product so good that everyone is beating a path to my door.* ♦ *If you really become famous, people will beat a path to your door.*

pathetic [pə 'θɛt ɪk] **1.** *adj.* causing or evoking pity or sorrow. (Adv: *pathetically* [...ɪk li].) ♦ *I donated money to the pathetic victims of the earthquake.* ♦ *The refugee's pathetic story made me cry.* **2.** *adj.* hopeless; inadequate; embarrassingly bad. (Informal. Adv: *pathetically* [...ɪk li].) ♦ *Bill left the pathetic movie before it finished.* ♦ *John's pathetic apology only insulted David further.*

pathogen ['pæθ ə dʒən] *n.* a disease-causing organism. ♦ *Wash your hands to destroy the pathogens that might be on them.* ♦ *Many pathogens can be found in the soil.*

pathogenic [pæθ ə 'dʒɛn ɪk] *adj.* able to cause disease. (Adv: *pathogenically* [...ɪk li].) ♦ *A scientist found two new pathogenic bacteria.* ♦ *The researcher found a vaccine for the pathogenic virus.*

pathological [pæθ ə 'lɑdʒ ɪk əl] *adj.* of or about or caused by disease. (Adv: *pathologically* [...ɪk li].) ♦ *The doctor read the pathological symptoms on my medical chart.* ♦ *The medical textbook listed the pathological effects of the disease.*

pathway ['pæθ we] *n.* a path. ♦ *I shoveled snow off the pathway to my front door.* ♦ *Mary walked down the pathway toward the lake.*

patience ['pe ʃəns] **1.** *n.* the quality of being patient and not becoming anxious or annoyed. (No plural form in this sense.) ♦ *After waiting an hour, I started to lose patience.* ♦ *Patience is needed when you deal with very young children.* **2. try someone's patience** *idiom* to do something annoying that may cause someone to lose ①; to cause someone to be annoyed. ♦ *Stop whistling. You're trying my patience. Very soon I'm going to lose my temper.* ♦ *Some students think it's fun to try the teacher's patience.* **3. run out of patience** *idiom* to become annoyed after being patient for a while. ♦ *I finally ran out of patience and lost my temper.* ♦ *The boss ran out of patience with me and sent me back to my desk.*

patient ['pe ʃənt] **1.** *adj.* able to wait for something to happen without complaining or becoming anxious or annoyed. (Adv: *patiently.*) ♦ *The patient customers stood in line for an hour.* ♦ *Be patient! I'll help you in a moment.* **2.** *n.* someone who is getting medical help from a doctor, nurse, or hospital. ♦ *The doctor read the patient's medical history.* ♦ *The nurse prepared the patient for surgery.*

patio ['pæt i o] *n.* a paved surface connected to one's house where one can relax, socialize, barbecue food, etc. (From Spanish. Pl in *-s.*) ♦ *When it's warm, I like to eat outside on the patio.* ♦ *I set the grill on the patio in preparation for dinner.*

patriarch ['pe tri ɑrk] *n.* the male head of a large and powerful family; the male founder of a company. ♦ *When the patriarch died, he left all of his money to his wife.* ♦ *John, although aged and feeble, was still the patriarch of the family and had to be consulted in all family matters.*

patriot ['pe tri ət] *n.* one who loves and supports one's country. ♦ *Thousands of patriots fought to protect their country.* ♦ *The proud patriot voted in every election.*

patriotic [pe tri 'ɑt ɪk] **1.** *adj.* loyal to and supportive of one's country. (Adv: *patriotically* [...ɪk li].) ♦ *The patriotic citizens celebrated the anniversary of their country's founding.* ♦ *My patriotic cousin served in the Army for two years.* **2.** *adj.* expressing loyalty to and support of one's country. (Adv: *patriotically* [...ɪk li].) ♦ *Around the campfire, we sang patriotic songs and some hymns.* ♦ *The senator gave a patriotic speech at the political convention.*

patriotism ['pe tri ə tɪz əm] *n.* the feeling of love, loyalty, and support for one's country. (No plural form in this sense.) ♦ *The politician invoked patriotism in his campaign speech.* ♦ *The long, unpopular war weakened the citizens' feelings of patriotism.*

patrol [pə 'trol] **1.** *tv.* to watch over an area by walking or driving around. ♦ *The guards patrolled the museum at night.* ♦ *The police patrolled the dangerous city streets.* **2.** *iv.* to watch over [an area] by walking or driving around. ♦ *In the museum, the guards patrol on foot.* ♦ *The police patrol here often because of recent robberies.* **3.** *n.* someone who watches over an area as in ①. ♦ *The patrol responded to an alarm in their area.* ♦ *Members of the patrol remained in contact with their commander.* **4. (out) on patrol** *idiom* away from a central location, watching over an area as in ①. ♦ *Officer Smith is out on patrol and cannot see you now.* ♦ *The soldiers who are on patrol on this snowy night must be very cold.*

patron ['pe trən] **1.** *n.* a benefactor; someone who gives money to an institution or an organization. ♦ *A patron of the arts donated money to the museum each year.* ♦ *The conductor thanked the symphony's patrons for their support.* **2.** *n.* a customer; someone who supports an enterprise. ♦ *The cashier thanked the patrons for their business.* ♦ *The store informed all of its regular patrons of the upcoming sale.*

patronage ['pe trə nɪdʒ] **1.** *n.* the business provided [to a store] by a customer. (No plural form in this sense.) ♦ *The antique shop wanted to encourage patronage by wealthy customers.* ♦ *The store manager thanked the loyal customers for their patronage.* **2. political patronage** *n.* the power to give people governmental jobs and grant favors to politicians, friends, and relatives. (No plural form in this sense.) ♦ *Anne, the mayor's cousin, got a job at city hall because of political patronage.* ♦ *The reporter exposed the political patronage practiced in state government.*

patronize ['pe trə nɑɪz] **1.** *tv.* to be a regular customer of a store, restaurant, hotel, or other business. ♦ *Customers prefer to patronize stores that provide good service.* ♦ *Anne has patronized that restaurant for years.* **2.** *tv.* to act as if one is superior to someone else; to insult someone by condescending when dealing with someone. ♦ *There is no need to patronize me by simplifying your explanation. I understand everything you are telling me.* ♦ *John keeps patronizing his coworkers, even though many of them have more knowledge and experience than he does.*

patronizing ['pe trə nɑɪz ɪŋ] *adj.* condescending; seeming to be superior. (Adv: *patronizingly.*) ♦ *Rudely, the waiter spoke to me in a patronizing tone.* ♦ *The patronizing clerk annoyed the knowledgeable customer.*

patter ['pæt ɚ] **1.** *n.* a series of quick tapping sounds. (No plural form in this sense.) ♦ *I listened to the patter of rain on the roof.* ♦ *I heard the patter of footsteps running down the stairs.* **2.** *n.* quick, smooth speech; rapidly spoken, rehearsed or memorized talk that carries little information. (No plural form in this sense.) ♦ *The auctioneer interrupted his patter to yell, "Sold!"* ♦ *The politician's promises were nothing more than meaningless patter.* **3.** *iv.* [for falling rain] to make quick tapping sounds as it strikes something. ♦ *The rain pattered against the window.* ♦ *When the rain began to patter on the roof, I fell asleep.*

pattern ['pæt ɚn] **1.** *n.* a design; an arrangement of shapes and colors, especially one that is repeated. ♦ *Mary bought a dress with a flowered pattern.* ♦ *The draperies in the living room have a subtle pattern.* **2.** *n.* a repeated element in a series of events. ♦ *The detective noticed a pattern in the series of murders.* ♦ *There is no pattern to this illness. On some days there is a fever, and some days there is not.* **3.** *n.* a printed or drawn outline of the parts of a garment or something that is to be built. ♦ *The tailor* *pinned the material to the paper pattern.* ♦ *Jane bought a new pattern for a shirt for Jimmy.* **4. pattern on** *tv.* + *prep. phr.* to design something to be similar or identical to something else. ♦ *Mary patterned her sculpture on the Eiffel Tower.* ♦ *John patterned his life on that of his successful father.*

patty ['pæt i] *n.* a thin, flat disk of ground or mashed food, especially one formed of ground meat. ♦ *The cook flipped the beef patty on the grill.* ♦ *Mix the ground meat with onions, and then use your hands to shape the mixture into patties.*

paucity ['pɔs ə ti] *n.* a scarcity; a lack. (No plural form in this sense.) ♦ *We were shocked by the paucity of affordable housing in the suburbs.* ♦ *My grandmother commented on the paucity of good television programs.*

paunch ['pɔntʃ] *n.* a fat stomach or abdomen. ♦ *Santa Claus is usually depicted as having a paunch.* ♦ *After John developed a paunch, he decided to exercise.*

pauper ['pɔp ɚ] *n.* a very poor person. ♦ *The pauper begged for money in the streets.* ♦ *If I have to pay any more taxes, I will be a pauper!*

pause ['pɔz] **1.** *n.* a brief delay; a moment where someone or something stops talking, moving, or working. ♦ *There was a noticeable pause when the actor forgot his lines.* ♦ *There was an uncomfortable pause in the conversation after Bill insulted Anne.* **2.** *iv.* to stop for a moment; to stop moving or talking for a moment. ♦ *I paused at the top of the stairs to rest for a moment.* ♦ *Anne paused before she responded to Bill's insult.*

pave ['pev] *tv.* to build or cover a road, street, driveway, highway, etc., with cement, concrete, or asphalt. ♦ *The crew paved the country road with asphalt.* ♦ *The field was paved to make a new parking lot.*

pavement ['pev mənt] *n.* a flat surface of concrete, cement, or asphalt covering an area, especially covering a street or sidewalk. (No plural form in this sense.) ♦ *Jimmy fell off the swing and hit his head on the pavement.* ♦ *The car drove off the pavement and into the ditch.*

pavilion [pə 'vɪl jən] *n.* a shelter in a park or other public place, especially one where concerts or dances are held. ♦ *The town orchestra played in the pavilion in the town square.* ♦ *We ran to the pavilion when it started raining during our picnic.*

paw ['pɔ] **1.** *n.* the foot of a clawed animal. ♦ *My dog had a thorn stuck in its paw.* ♦ *Anne's cat is black with white paws.* **2. paw at** *iv.* + *prep. phr.* [for an animal] to handle someone or something with ①. ♦ *The kitten pawed at the ball of yarn.* ♦ *The dog pawed at the small kitten.* **3.** *tv.* to handle someone or something with hands or ①. ♦ *The kitten pawed the ball of yarn.* ♦ *The huge bear pawed her cubs tenderly.*

pawn ['pɔn] **1.** *n.* the chess piece having the lowest rank or least importance. ♦ *Every chess game begins with the movement of a pawn.* ♦ *Mary captured my knight with one of her pawns.* **2.** *n.* someone who is not important; someone used by a second person to the advantage of the second person. (Figurative on ①.) ♦ *The large corporation treated its employees as if they were pawns.* ♦ *The bureaucrat was merely a pawn of the government.* **3.** *tv.* to exchange something, such as personal property, for a loan, leaving the property in the shop of the lender as collateral. ♦ *John was broke, so he pawned his wedding ring.* ♦ *Mary pawned her gold necklace so she could pay her rent.*

pawnshop ['pɔn ʃɑp] *n.* a place where items are pawned. (Items left in a pawnshop will be returned—if not sold—when the money is repaid, with interest.) ♦ *David got $50 for his gold watch at the pawnshop.* ♦ *Anne went to redeem her ring at the pawnshop, but it had been sold.*

pay ['pe] **1.** *tv., irreg.* to give money (to someone) in exchange for a product or a service or to settle a debt. (Pt/pp: **paid**.) ♦ *John paid ten dollars for the book he wanted.* ♦ *I will have to pay a lot of money for that car!* **2.** *tv., irreg.* to give someone an amount of money in exchange for a product or service or to settle a debt. ♦ *John paid me the ten dollars that he owed me.* ♦ *I will have to pay John immediately.* **3.** *tv., irreg.* to settle a bill or a debt. ♦ *You must pay your debts immediately.* ♦ *I went to the cashier and paid the bill.* **4.** *tv., irreg.* [for something] to yield a certain amount of money or a certain benefit. ♦ *Mary was looking for a job that paid $15 an hour.* ♦ *My bank account pays 5% interest annually.* **5. pay (for)** *iv., irreg.* (+ *prep. phr.*) to transfer money in exchange for a product or service. ♦ *I went to the cashier to pay for the book I wanted.* ♦ *How much would I have to pay for this car?* **6.** *n.* wages; salary; the amount of money that one earns from a job. (No plural form in this sense.) ♦ *The pay for this job is $12.50 per hour.* ♦ *On Fridays, Anne deposits her pay at the bank.* **7.** *adj.* requiring money in order to be used. ♦ *Mary put a quarter in the pay phone and made a call.* ♦ *The irate shopper complained about having to use a pay toilet.* **8. pay an arm and a leg (for something)** *idiom* to pay too much money (for something). ♦ *I hate to have to pay an arm and a leg for a tank of gas.* ♦ *If you shop around, you won't have to pay an arm and a leg.* **9. pay to do something** *idiom* to be beneficial to do something; to be profitable. ♦ *It doesn't pay to drive downtown when you can take the train.* ♦ *It pays to take an umbrella with you if it's supposed to rain.* **10. pay for something** *idiom* to be punished for something. ♦ *John paid for his crime by going to jail for five years.* ♦ *The judge said that the thief would have to pay for her crimes.* **11. pay (someone or something) a visit, pay a visit to someone or something** *idiom* to visit someone or something. ♦ *Bill paid a visit to his aunt in Seattle.* ♦ *Please pay a visit to our house whenever you are in town.* **12. pay someone a compliment** *idiom* to give someone a compliment. ♦ *Tom paid Bill a compliment when he told him he was intelligent.* ♦ *Mary was very gracious when Anne paid her a compliment.* **13. pay one's last respects** *idiom* to attend the wake or funeral of someone; to approach the coffin containing someone in a final act of respect. ♦ *I went to Bill's wake to pay my last respects.* ♦ *Everyone in town came to the mayor's funeral to pay their last respects.* **14. pay attention (to someone or something)** See attention ③. **15. pay someone respect** See respect ⑥.

payable ['pe ə bəl] *adj.* due; having to be paid. ♦ *Our electricity bill is payable now.* ♦ *This bill is payable as soon as it is received.*

paycheck ['pe tʃɛk] *n.* a check given to someone in exchange for work. ♦ *Taxes are automatically deducted from my paycheck.* ♦ *Anne deposited her paycheck at her bank.*

payday ['pe de] *n.* the day on which a company pays its workers. ♦ *On payday, John paid his bills and then went shopping.* ♦ *Payday at my office is the last day of each month.*

payload ['pe lod] **1.** *n.* the cargo carried by a truck, airplane, or train. ♦ *The airplane's payload was worth over $100,000.* ♦ *The payload of the huge truck was over 2,000 pounds.* **2.** *n.* cargo, passengers, or weapons carried by an aircraft or spacecraft. ♦ *The plane's payload is 300 passengers.* ♦ *The fighter pilot emptied his payload behind enemy lines.*

payment ['pe mənt] **1.** *n.* transferring money [to someone]. (No plural form in this sense.) ♦ *Payment may be made by cash or check.* ♦ *Payment must be made on time, or interest will be charged.* **2.** *n.* an amount of money paid or to be paid; something that is paid [to someone or something]. ♦ *I paid for my new stereo in four equal payments.* ♦ *I can barely afford my monthly mortgage payments.*

payoff ['pe ɔf] **1.** *n.* an instance of making a final payment in a series. ♦ *I have had this loan for 20 years, and tomorrow is the date of the payoff.* ♦ *After the payoff of your car loan, the car will be yours.* **2.** *n.* a result; a consequence; an outcome. ♦ *After years of hard work, the payoff came when I found I could retire comfortably.* ♦ *The extra workers were costly, but the payoff was improved service.* **3.** *n.* a bribe. ♦ *The reporter secretly taped the corrupt police officer receiving a payoff.* ♦ *The company bought the senator's vote with an expensive payoff.*

payroll ['pe rol] **1.** *n.* the list of a company's employees and their salaries. ♦ *John retired after 50 years on the company's payroll.* ♦ *Many of the mayor's friends were on the city payroll.* **2.** *n.* the amount of money paid to employees during a particular period of time. ♦ *The bankrupt company was unable to find enough money for its monthly payroll.* ♦ *The treasurer deposited a check to cover the weekly payroll.*

pea ['pi] **1.** *n.* a small, round, green vegetable that grows in a pod on a vine-like plant. ♦ *The farmer shucked the peas from their pods.* ♦ *My meatloaf was served with potatoes and peas.* **2.** *n.* the plant that peas grow on. ♦ *Mary planted peas in her vegetable garden.* ♦ *John sprayed the peas with insecticide.*

peace ['pis] **1.** *n.* a condition where there is no war or fighting; a time when there is order and harmony. (No plural form in this sense.) ♦ *After the treaty was signed, there was peace at last.* ♦ *The fragile peace was broken by another outbreak of war.* **2.** *n.* silence; serenity; freedom from anxiety. (No plural form in this sense.) ♦ *Be quiet! I need peace around here!* ♦ *The student found peace and quiet in the library.* **3. hold one's peace** *idiom* to remain silent. ♦ *Bill was unable to hold his peace any longer. "Don't do it!" he cried.* ♦ *Quiet, John. Hold your peace for a little while longer.* **4. leave someone in peace** *idiom* to stop bothering someone; to go away and leave someone alone. ♦ *Please go—leave me in peace.* ♦ *Can't you see that you're upsetting her? Leave her in peace.*

peaceful ['pis fʊl] **1.** *adj.* without war, fighting, or disorder; not at war; orderly; harmonious. (Adv: *peacefully.*) ♦ *The peaceful nations sent help to the countries torn by war.* ♦ *The mediator found a peaceful solution to the disagreement.* **2.** *adj.* silent; calm; serene; free from anxiety. (Adv: *peacefully.*) ♦ *Jane took a peaceful walk along the lake.* ♦ *The baby looked peaceful as he slept in his crib.*

peacemaker ['pis mek ɚ] *n.* someone who brings about peace. ♦ *The peacemaker persuaded the warring leaders to stop fighting.* ♦ *When I argue with my father, my mother is usually the peacemaker.*

peacetime ['pis tɑɪm] **1.** *n.* a period of time when there is peace and no war. (No plural form in this sense.) ♦ *Even in peacetime, young men must register for the draft.* ♦ *During peacetime, the horrors of war are often forgotten.* **2.** *adj.* <the adj. use of ①.> ♦ *Congress decided there didn't need to be a peacetime draft.* ♦ *The peacetime army remained prepared in case of war.*

peach ['pitʃ] **1.** *n.* a soft, sweet, juicy, round fruit with a fuzzy skin, yellowish-orange pulp, and a large pit in the middle. ♦ *I washed the peach before I ate it.* ♦ *The farmer sold me a bushel of peaches.* **2.** *adj.* made with ①; tasting like ①. ♦ *I ordered some peach ice cream for dessert.* ♦ *I had a cup of peach yogurt for breakfast.*

peacock ['pi kɑk] **1.** *n.* a large male peafowl having a large, beautifully colored tail that fans out. ♦ *The peacock flirts by showing off his tail feathers.* ♦ *The brightly colored peacock strutted around the zoo.* **2.** *n.* any peafowl. ♦ *I saw a dozen peacocks at the zoo.* ♦ *The zookeeper fed some seed to the peacocks.*

peafowl ['pi fɑʊl] *n., irreg.* a large bird from Southeast Asia, the males of which have large, showy tails. (See peacock, peahen. Pl: *peafowl* or *peafowls.*) ♦ *I saw several peafowls—both peacocks and peahens—while visiting Indonesia.* ♦ *Peafowl are not native to North America.*

peahen ['pi hɛn] *n.* a female peafowl. (Compare with peacock.) ♦ *The peahen's feathers aren't as colorful as the peacock's.* ♦ *The two peacocks fought for the peahen's attention.*

peak ['pik] **1.** *n.* the top of something, especially a mountain; the highest point of something. ♦ *The explorer climbed to the peak of the mountain.* ♦ *The peak of Mt. Everest is the highest elevation on Earth.* **2.** *n.* the maximum amount of effort, accomplishment, or achievement. ♦ *The company's owner is at the peak of her career.* ♦ *As the sound reached its peak, a window broke.* **3.** *iv.* to form or rise to ①. ♦ *The mountain peaked at 15,000 feet.* ♦ *The witch's hat peaked about a foot over her head.* **4.** *iv.* to reach ②. ♦ *The runner peaked before he was halfway through the race.* ♦ *The tennis player peaked when she was 21.*

peal ['pil] **1.** *n.* the [loud], ringing sound that bells make. ♦ *A loud peal of the church bells woke me up every morning.* ♦ *When I heard the peal of the old-fashioned fire bell, I knew something was wrong.* **2.** *n.* a long, loud echoing sound. ♦ *The peal of thunder frightened the children.* ♦ *The audience responded to the comedy with peals of laughter.* **3.** *iv.* to ring loudly; to resound loudly. ♦ *The church bells pealed at the end of the church service.* ♦ *Laughter pealed from the auditorium as the comedian told his best jokes.*

peanut ['pi nət] **1.** *n.* a plant with seed pods that grow underground. ♦ *Peanuts are usually roasted, but are sometimes eaten green.* ♦ *They grow a lot of peanuts in the South.* **2.** *n.* the nutmeat of ①; the nutmeat and shell of ①. ♦ *John removed the peanuts from the shell and ate them.* ♦ *I love salted, roasted peanuts.*

peanut butter ['pi nət bət ɚ] **1.** *n.* an edible paste made from crushed peanuts. (No plural form in this sense.) ♦ *John spread the peanut butter on the bread with a knife.* ♦ *Chunky peanut butter has pieces of peanuts in it.* **2. peanut-butter** *adj.* made with ①. ♦ *Would you like a peanut-butter sandwich?* ♦ *Jane makes the best peanut-butter cookies!*

pear ['per] **1.** *n.* a yellow, brown, or green fruit that is rounded at the bottom and narrower toward the top. ♦ *David sliced some pears into wedges and served them with cheese.* ♦ *Anne went to the orchard and picked a bushel of pears.* **2.** *adj.* made with ①; tasting like ①. ♦ *I smothered the ham with a tasty pear sauce.* ♦ *We ordered pear tarts for dessert.*

pearl ['pɚl] *n.* a hard, white, round substance formed inside an oyster, usually used in jewelry. ♦ *Anne wore a string of pearls around her neck.* ♦ *When we opened the oyster, we found a beautiful pearl inside.*

peasant ['pɛz ənt] *n.* a working-class farmer, especially in Europe. ♦ *The peasants celebrated after they harvested their crops.* ♦ *The peasants work in the field all day.*

peat ['pit] *n.* a mass of partially decayed vegetable matter, used as a fertilizer and as a fuel. (No plural form in this sense.) ♦ *The gardener spread peat around the flowers.* ♦ *When it got cold, I put some more peat in the stove.*

pebble ['pɛb əl] *n.* a small stone. ♦ *I bruised my feet on the pebbles in the bed of the stream.* ♦ *Pebbles are rounded and smooth, unlike rocks or sharp stones.*

pecan [pɪ 'kɑn] **1.** *n.* a tall hickory tree native to the southern U.S. and Mexico. ♦ *A row of pecans lined the road to the house.* ♦ *They cut down the pecan for its wood.* **2.** *n.* the nutmeat of ①; the nutmeat and shell of ①. ♦ *At the party, there were bowls of salted pecans in every room.* ♦ *I sprinkled some crushed pecans on top of my ice-cream sundae.* **3.** *n.* the wood of ①. (No plural form in this sense.) ♦ *Fine furniture is made from pecan.* ♦ *Pecan is not as popular as walnut for furniture and paneling.* **4.** *adj.* made with ②. ♦ *I had a slice of pecan pie for dessert.* ♦ *I ate some pecan brownies.* **5.** *adj.* made from ③. ♦ *I love the soft tan color of pecan furniture.* ♦ *We have a pecan bookcase in the living room.*

peck ['pɛk] **1.** *n.* a sharp poke made with a bird's beak. ♦ *With each peck, the bird dug further into the tree.* ♦ *The bird cracked open the nut with a quick peck of its beak.* **2.** *n.* a quick kiss with closed lips. (Figurative on ①.) ♦ *My mother gave me a peck on the cheek before I went to bed.* ♦ *Jane gave her husband a quick peck and drove off to work.* **3.** *n.* a unit of measure of dry volume, equal to ¼ of a bushel or 8 dry quarts. ♦ *I bought a peck of apples at the market.* ♦ *The gardener sold corn by the peck.* **4. peck at** *iv.* + *prep. phr.* [for a bird] to poke something with its beak. ♦ *A woodpecker has been pecking at this tree.* ♦ *The chickens pecked at the grains of wheat on the ground.* **5. peck at** *iv.* + *prep. phr.* to eat just a little bit of something. (Figurative on ④.) ♦ *Stop pecking at your food and eat it all.* ♦ *I didn't like my dinner, so I just pecked at it.*

peculiar [pɪ 'kjul jɚ] *adj.* odd; strange; unusual. (Adv: *peculiarly.*) ♦ *A peculiar noise heard in the forest scared the campers.* ♦ *Mary was baffled by her son's peculiar eating habits.*

peculiarity [pɪ kju li 'ɛr ə ti] *n.* an oddness; a strangeness; something unusual about someone or something. ♦ *John's habit of talking to himself is a harmless peculiarity.* ♦ *The ostrich's peculiarity is that it's a bird that can't fly.*

pedagogy ['pɛd ə go dʒi] *n.* the science, study, or profession of teaching. (No plural form in this sense.) ♦ *Our principal was trained in the current theories of pedagogy.* ♦ *The old-fashioned teacher dismissed modern methods of pedagogy.*

pedal ['pɛd l] **1.** *n.* a device that controls something and is operated with the feet. ♦ *Bob pushed on the gas pedal to make the car go faster.* ♦ *Bicycles have two pedals, one for each foot.* **2.** *tv.* to ride a bicycle. ♦ *Anne pedaled her bike to school.* ♦ *Jimmy can't pedal his bike very far because he is so small.* **3.** *iv.* to ride [a bicycle] somewhere. ♦ *Anne pedaled to school.* ♦ *John pedaled down the bike trail.*

peddle ['pɛd l] *tv.* to sell things that one carries from place to place. (Informal unless used for a peddler.) ♦ *Someone on the street corner was peddling neckties and watches.* ♦ *Mary peddled cosmetics throughout her neighborhood.*

peddler ['pɛd lɚ] *n.* someone who travels around selling things. ♦ *The peddler tried to sell me a new vacuum cleaner.* ♦ *I didn't open the door when the peddler came to my house.*

pedestal ['pɛd ə stəl] *n.* a base that supports a statue, vase, pillar, column, etc. ♦ *Jimmy knocked the vase from its pedestal.* ♦ *The granite pedestal cracked under the statue's weight.*

pedestrian [pə 'dɛs tri ən] **1.** *n.* someone who walks as a means of travel; someone who is walking. ♦ *Drivers must stop for pedestrians who are in the street.* ♦ *The pedestrian waited at the street corner for the "walk" signal.* **2.** *adj.* designed for ①; serving ①. ♦ *The pedestrian crossing was clearly marked by painted lines.* ♦ *The pedestrian signal indicated that we could cross the street.* **3.** *adj.* boring; unimaginative. (Adv: *pedestrianly.*) ♦ *Your essay is a pedestrian attempt at satire and has failed, unfortunately.* ♦ *This novel has a rather pedestrian plot, involving love, marriage, and life in a small village.*

pediatric [pi di 'æ trɪk] **1.** *adj.* <the adj. use of ②.> (Adv: *pediatrically* [...ɪk li].) ♦ *The nurse took the sick child to the pediatric ward.* ♦ *Dr. Smith worked in pediatric medicine because she liked kids.* **2. pediatrics** *n.* a branch of medicine that deals with the treatment of children. (Treated as singular.) ♦ *Anne took her sick child to a doctor trained in pediatrics.* ♦ *The university hospital had a separate department for pediatrics.*

pediatrician [pi di ə 'trɪ ʃən] *n.* a doctor who specializes in treating children. ♦ *The pediatrician gave the child another vaccination.* ♦ *Mary told the pediatrician about her child's symptoms.*

pedigree ['pɛd ə gri] *n.* a chart or table showing the ancestry of a person or an animal, such as a dog or a horse. ♦ *This dog's pedigree goes back seven generations.* ♦ *Susan worked for years doing research on her family's pedigree.*

pedigreed ['pɛd ə grid] *adj.* [of an animal] having ancestors all of the same breed. ♦ *Anne entered her pedigreed poodle in the dog show.* ♦ *The director auditioned pedigreed collies for the movie.*

peek ['pik] **1.** *n.* a quick, sly look; a quick look at something that one is not supposed to look at. ♦ *David took a* *quick peek at Mary's diary.* ♦ *The nosy employee took a quick peek at the company files.* **2.** *iv.* to look quickly at something that one is not supposed to look at. ♦ *I peeked into John's refrigerator to see what he had to eat.* ♦ *John peeked at his presents a week before Christmas.* **3. peek out (from)** *iv.* + *adv.* (+ *prep. phr.*) to peer or appear to peer out from something. ♦ *The sun peeked out from behind the clouds.* ♦ *A little mouse peeked out at me when I opened the cabinet.*

peel ['pil] **1.** *n.* the outer skin of certain fruits and vegetables. (No plural form in this sense. See also **peeling**.) ♦ *You shouldn't eat the peel of an orange.* ♦ *The peel of the apple was bright red.* **2.** *tv.* to remove ①. ♦ *Mary peeled the apple with a knife.* ♦ *John peeled the orange with his fingers.* **3.** *tv.* to remove an outer layer from something. (Figurative on ②.) ♦ *The paramedics peeled the jacket off the drowning man.* ♦ *Bill peeled the plastic from the slice of cheese.* **4.** *iv.* [for an outer layer] to come off. ♦ *The plastic layer on the cover of the book began to peel.* ♦ *The old paint started to peel from the wall.*

peeling ['pil ɪŋ] *n.* a part of something, especially fruits and vegetables, that has been peeled off. (Often plural.) ♦ *Anne threw the apple peelings in the garbage.* ♦ *Please dispose of the potato peelings.*

peep ['pip] **1.** *n.* a small chirping noise, such as that made by a baby chicken. ♦ *The bird's peep was very quiet.* ♦ *The farmer listened to the peeps of the newborn chicks.* **2.** *n.* a small noise or remark. (Figurative on ①.) ♦ *Be quiet! I don't want to hear a peep out of you!* ♦ *The teacher said she would punish any student who made a peep.* **3.** *iv.* to have a quick look at something, especially in secret; a peek. ♦ *Bill peeped at his neighbors through the fence.* ♦ *I see a shadow at the window. I think someone is peeping.* **4. peep through** *iv.* + *prep. phr.* to take a quick look through something, especially in secret. ♦ *Mary peeped through the keyhole to spy on her boss.* ♦ *John peeped through the partly open doorway to check on the sleeping baby.* **5.** *iv.* to make a small chirping noise, like the noise a baby chicken makes. ♦ *The chicks peeped as they hopped about in the chicken coop.* ♦ *My smoke alarm peeps when its batteries run low.* **6. have a peep, take a peep** *idiom* to look quickly, sometimes through a small hole. ♦ *Have a peep into the refrigerator and see if we need any milk.* ♦ *I took a peep at the comet through the telescope.*

peephole ['pip hol] *n.* a small hole that someone can peep through. ♦ *Through a peephole in the fence, I could see the vicious dog on the other side.* ♦ *Anne looked through the peephole to see who was at her door.*

peer ['pɪr] **1.** *iv.* to look intently [at something]; to look closely [at something]. ♦ *The guard peered into the darkness toward the unusual sound.* ♦ *The doctor peered at the patient's X-rays for over a minute.* **2.** *n.* an equal; someone who is the same age, has the same job, or has the same social status as someone else. ♦ *My peers and I complained about our boss.* ♦ *Bill calls most of his peers by their first names.*

peerless ['pɪr ləs] *adj.* having no peers; unequaled. (Adv: *peerlessly*.) ♦ *I have purchased an automobile that is peerless in design and power.* ♦ *We are seeking employees with experience and peerless recommendations.*

peeve ['piv] **1.** *n.* something that irritates or annoys someone. ♦ *I have a real peeve with the editorial in today's newspaper.* ♦ *My only peeve with my boss is that he won't listen to what I tell him.* **2. pet peeve** *idiom* a frequent annoyance; one's "favorite" or most often encountered annoyance. ♦ *My pet peeve is someone who always comes into the theater after the show has started.* ♦ *Drivers who don't signal are John's pet peeve.*

peg ['pɛg] **1.** *n.* a thick wooden or plastic pin used to hold objects together. ♦ *The carpenter pounded a peg into the beam with a mallet.* ♦ *Three pegs held the leg onto the table.* **2.** *n.* a level; a degree. ♦ *Anne's work experience is a peg higher than mine.* ♦ *The critic considered the movie to be a few pegs below average.* **3.** *tv.* to attach something to something with ①. ♦ *The carpenter pegged the two beams together.* ♦ *Bill pegged the board to the floor.* **4. peg someone as something; have someone pegged as something** *idiom* to think of someone in a certain way. ♦ *Susan pegged the new employee as a lazy worker.* ♦ *I had you pegged as an angry rebel before I got to know you.* **5. square peg in a round hole** *idiom* a misfit. ♦ *John can't seem to get along with the people he works with. He's just a square peg in a round hole.* ♦ *I'm not a square peg in a round hole. It's just that no one understands me.*

pelican ['pɛl ɪ kən] *n.* a bird that lives on or near the water and that has a bill with a large scoop on the lower part. ♦ *Pelicans live near the sea.* ♦ *The pelican scooped up a fish with its bill.*

pellet ['pɛl ɪt] *n.* a hard, small ball of something, such as ice, wax, dirt, or metal. ♦ *Pellets of wax from the candle collected on the tablecloth.* ♦ *Tiny pellets of ice beat against my window.*

pell-mell ['pɛl 'mɛl] **1.** *adv.* rapidly in a confused, disorderly, or unorganized way. ♦ *The rowdy students ran pell-mell down the hallway.* ♦ *Frightened horses galloped pell-mell away from the fire.* **2.** *adj.* confused; unorganized; disorderly. ♦ *The rowdy students made a pell-mell rush for the beach.* ♦ *Frightened horses made a pell-mell escape from the barn.*

pelt ['pɛlt] **1.** *n.* the complete fur-covered skin of an animal. ♦ *The trapper sold the beaver pelts to a fur trader.* ♦ *My coat was made from the pelts of minks.* **2. pelt with** *tv.* + *prep. phr.* to target someone or something with something. ♦ *Angry students pelted the building with rocks.* ♦ *The crowd pelted the criminal with stones.* **3.** *tv.* to hit against someone or something repeatedly with force. ♦ *The heavy rain pelted us.* ♦ *Large hailstones pelted the homes along the coast.*

pelvis ['pɛl vəs] *n.* the hip bones and the bottom of the backbone. ♦ *Men's and women's pelvises are shaped differently.* ♦ *John fractured his pelvis in the car accident.*

pen ['pɛn] **1.** *n.* a thin writing instrument that uses ink. ♦ *I signed the forms with a pen.* ♦ *The pen in my pocket leaked ink.* **2.** *n.* a confined area where certain animals are kept. ♦ *The pigs wallowed in the mud in their pen.* ♦ *The zookeeper threw raw meat into the lizards' pen.* **3.** *tv.* to write something, usually with ①. ♦ *I penned my name on the contract.* ♦ *The author penned a new story in four months.* **4. pen in; pen up** *tv.* + *adv.* to keep someone or something in a tight space; to confine someone or something. ♦ *The police penned the robber in so he could not get away.* ♦ *During the terrible storm, I was penned up in the house for hours.*

penal ['pi nəl] *adj.* of or about punishment in a prison. (See penalty. Adv: *penally.*) ♦ *The senator promised to reform the state's penal system.* ♦ *John's crimes were a penal offense.*

penalize ['pi nə lɑɪz] *tv.* to punish someone for breaking a rule or law. ♦ *The basketball player was penalized for making a foul.* ♦ *The law penalizes drivers for parking next to fire hydrants.*

penalty ['pɛn əl ti] *n.* a punishment for breaking a rule or law. ♦ *In this city, the penalty for speeding is a $50 fine.* ♦ *John's penalty for breaking the law was a one-year jail term.*

penchant ['pɛn tʃənt] **have a penchant for something** *idiom* to have a liking for something; to have an inclination toward doing something. ♦ *My roommate has a penchant for cooking elaborate dinners.* ♦ *My nosy neighbor has a penchant for gossip.*

pencil ['pɛn səl] **1.** *n.* a thin writing instrument with a pointed core made of graphite. ♦ *I sharpened my pencil because the point was too dull.* ♦ *You cannot sign this contract with a pencil; it must be signed in ink.* **2.** *tv.* to write something with ①. ♦ *I penciled the date on the back of each photograph.* ♦ *Anne penciled her thoughts in the margins of the book.* **3. pencil in** *tv.* + *prep. phr.* to write something, such as a person's name, on a list or schedule with ① so that it can be erased if it needs to be changed. ♦ *I penciled in a meeting with my boss for next Tuesday at noon.* ♦ *I've penciled you in for a game of golf next Friday.* **4. in pencil** *phr.* written or signed with ①. ♦ *Why did you write your report in pencil?* ♦ *You can't sign a check in pencil!*

pendant ['pɛn dənt] *n.* an ornament that hangs from a piece of jewelry, especially from a necklace or bracelet. ♦ *The thief snapped Jane's necklace by pulling on the pendant.* ♦ *A beautiful jade pendant hung from the necklace.*

pending ['pɛn dɪŋ] **1.** *adj.* not decided; not settled. ♦ *The date of our next meeting is still pending.* ♦ *We will have to take care of pending business first.* **2.** *prep.* while awaiting; until. ♦ *Pending approval of the budget, our office couldn't spend any money.* ♦ *Pending the results from my blood tests, I remained in quarantine.*

pendulum ['pɛn djə ləm] *n.* an object that swings back and forth from a fixed point that it is hung from, especially the device that controls a clock. ♦ *The clock's pendulum swung back and forth once each second.* ♦ *I made a crude pendulum out of a stone tied to a string.*

penetrate ['pɛn ə tret] **1.** *tv.* to pierce through something; to enter something by force; to go through something solid. ♦ *The bullets penetrated the wall.* ♦ *The arrow penetrated the bear's skin.* **2.** *tv.* [for a fluid] to soak through something or permeate something. ♦ *Water penetrated the rugs and ruined the floor.* ♦ *The fumes penetrated the walls of the room.*

penetrating ['pɛn ə tret ɪŋ] **1.** *adj.* [of a sound] sharp and loud. (Adv: *penetratingly.*) ♦ *You have a very penetrating voice. We can hear you in the next room!* ♦ *The penetrating noise of the siren hurt my ears.* **2.** *adj.* showing critical understanding. (Adv: *penetratingly.*) ♦ *The article took a penetrating look at crime.* ♦ *I watched a penetrating documentary about drug abuse.*

penetration [pen ə 'tre ʃən] **1.** *n.* penetrating, piercing, or going through something. (No plural form in this sense.) ♦ *The bullet's penetration of the steel door surprised me.* ♦ *The penetration of the loud music into my room annoyed me.* **2.** *n.* coverage of something such as a market or a population. (No plural form in this sense.) ♦ *The unsuccessful product had no penetration into key markets.* ♦ *The penetration of the network's television coverage in the U.S. was 40%.*

penguin ['pɛŋ gwɪn] *n.* a fish-eating, black and white flightless bird found especially in Antarctica. ♦ *Most penguins can swim very fast underwater.* ♦ *The penguin waddled across the ice to the water.*

penicillin [pɛn ə 'sɪl ən] *n.* a drug that was originally made from mold and is used to treat certain infections. (No plural form in this sense.) ♦ *The doctor prescribed some penicillin to fight my infection.* ♦ *Anne wore a bracelet warning of her allergy to penicillin.*

peninsula [pə 'nɪn sə lə] *n.* a piece of land surrounded by water on three sides. ♦ *The state of Michigan is composed of two peninsulas.* ♦ *The tourist traveled all over the Italian peninsula.*

peninsular [pə 'nɪn sə lɚ] *adj.* on a peninsula; concerning a peninsula. (Adv: *peninsularly.*) ♦ *The lighthouse was built on the peninsular extension of the coast.* ♦ *Maria left her cabin in the forest and moved to a peninsular village.*

penis ['pi nəs] *n.* the male organ of copulation and, in mammals, urination. (The Latin plural is *penes;* the English plural is *penises.*) ♦ *During circumcision, the foreskin is removed from the penis.* ♦ *Tom was surprised to learn that some fowl have penises.*

penitent ['pɛn ɪ tənt] *adj.* sorry for having done something wrong; showing that one is sorry for having done something wrong. (Adv: *penitently.*) ♦ *Penitent sinners pray for forgiveness.* ♦ *The penitent young man apologized to his mother for breaking her vase.*

penitentiary [pɛn ɪ 'tɛn ʃə ri] *n.* a prison. ♦ *The criminal was sentenced to the penitentiary for 20 years.* ♦ *The lawyer went to the penitentiary to speak to his client.*

penknife ['pɛn nɑɪf] *n.* a pocketknife; a small knife having blades that fold into the handle. (Pl: **penknives**. See also jackknife.) ♦ *Penknives can be used for sharpening pencils.* ♦ *The boy carried a penknife in his pocket for emergencies.*

penknives ['pɛn nɑɪvz] pl of penknife.

penlight ['pɛn lɑɪt] *n.* a small, thin flashlight, shaped like a pen. ♦ *The usher at the theater shined a penlight on my ticket.* ♦ *Bob aimed the penlight at the fuse box while I changed the fuse.*

penmanship ['pɛn mən ʃɪp] *n.* handwriting; the way someone writes or prints. (No plural form in this sense.) ♦ *The teacher told the students to practice their penmanship.* ♦ *My notes are hard to read because I have bad penmanship.*

pennant ['pɛn ənt] **1.** *n.* a narrow, three-sided flag. ♦ *Bill hung a school pennant in his dorm room.* ♦ *I bought a pennant with my favorite team's name on it.* **2.** *n.* the first-place prize in a sports league or division at the end of a season. ♦ *If our team wins this game, it will win the pennant.* ♦ *That baseball team is favored to win the pennant again this year.*

penniless ['pɛn i ləs] *adj.* broke; without a penny; having no money. (Adv: *pennilessly.*) ♦ *The penniless man* *begged for change downtown.* ♦ *Anne bought the penniless woman some food.*

Pennsylvania [pɛn sɪl 'ven jə] See Gazetteer.

penny ['pɛn i] *n.* a cent; 1/100 of a dollar in the U.S. and various other nations. ♦ *I got three pennies back when I gave the clerk one dollar for the item that cost 97 cents.* ♦ *I gave Bill 25 pennies in exchange for a quarter.*

pension ['pɛn ʃən] *n.* money that is paid to a former employee, from retirement until death, or some other period of time, to replace a salary. ♦ *Mary received her husband's pension after his death.* ♦ *The city raised taxes to maintain its employees' pensions.*

pensive ['pɛn sɪv] *adj.* deeply thoughtful and possibly sad. (Adv: *pensively.*) ♦ *The pensive teenager brooded about her boyfriend.* ♦ *A pensive poet sat quietly by the lake.*

pentagon ['pɛn tə gɑn] **1.** *n.* a geometric figure having five sides. ♦ *The sum of the interior angles of a pentagon equals 540 degrees.* ♦ *On the campus map, small pentagons indicated fraternity houses.* **2. the Pentagon** *n.* a five-sided building near Washington, D.C., where the U.S. Department of Defense is located. (No plural form in this sense. Treated as singular.) ♦ *The secretary of defense held a press conference at the Pentagon.* ♦ *The Pentagon is heavily guarded against terrorist attacks.* **3. the Pentagon** *n.* the U.S. Department of Defense and its personnel. (No plural form in this sense. Treated as singular.) ♦ *Congress increased the Pentagon's budget.* ♦ *The Pentagon issued a statement on the marine's death.*

penthouse ['pɛnt hɑʊs] *n., irreg.* a luxurious apartment on the top floor of a building. (Pl: [...hɑʊ zəz].) ♦ *The beautiful penthouse had an expansive view of the city.* ♦ *The rich lawyer rode the private elevator to her penthouse.*

pent-up ['pɛnt 'ʌp] *adj.* repressed; confined; kept enclosed; kept inside. ♦ *My psychiatrist encouraged me to release my pent-up emotions.* ♦ *Bob has a lot of pent-up anger.*

peony ['pi ə ni] **1.** *n.* a low, flowering bush having large red, pink, or white blossoms. ♦ *My wife planted peonies along the back of the house.* ♦ *The is only one peony left. The rest didn't survive the winter.* **2.** *n.* the blossom of ①. ♦ *Susan picked some peonies from her flower garden.* ♦ *David arranged the fragrant peonies in a vase.*

people ['pip əl] **1.** *n.* persons. (Used as a plural of person. Treated as plural.) ♦ *At the party, most of the people were dressed formally.* ♦ *Over 50,000 people attended the concert.* **2.** *n.* a specific group of ①; a race or ethnic group of ①. ♦ *Each student gave a report on the customs of an ancient people.* ♦ *Many different peoples lived within the old Soviet Union.* **3.** *n.* one's ancestors; one's family. (No plural form in this sense. Treated as plural.) ♦ *Mary's people came from Ireland in the 1800s.* ♦ *My father complained that my boyfriend's people weren't refined enough.*

pep ['pɛp] *n.* energy; vim; vigor. (No plural form in this sense.) ♦ *The cheerleaders jumped around with a lot of pep.* ♦ *The tired driver hoped the coffee would give him some pep.*

pepper ['pɛp ɚ] **1.** *n.* a green, yellow, or red vegetable that is mostly hollow and often very hot and spicy. ♦ *Red peppers can be roasted and served in many ways.* ♦ *Mary sliced up a green pepper and put the pieces in her salad.* **2.** *n.* the dried berry of various plants, usually ground, used to season food. (Usually black in the U.S. and white in Europe. No plural form in this sense.) ♦ *Mary sprinkled some pepper on her potato.* ♦ *The waiter ground some pepper onto my salad.* **3.** *tv.* to sprinkle ② on food as a seasoning. ♦ *Mary peppered her potato lightly.* ♦ *The cook peppered the fish while grilling it.* **4.** *tv.* [for many tiny things] to strike something lightly. ♦ *Stinging particles of sleet peppered my hands and face.* ♦ *Sand, blown by the wind, peppered the sides of the little cabin on the beach.*

peppermint ['pɛp ɚ mɪnt] **1.** *n.* an herb with a strong mint flavor, used to flavor foods, especially candy. (No plural form in this sense.) ♦ *John picked some peppermint from his herb garden.* ♦ *The gardener sucked on some peppermint while working.* **2.** *n.* a candy flavored with peppermint. ♦ *Tom doesn't care for peppermints.* ♦ *Max ate a peppermint to improve his breath.* **3.** *adj.* flavored with ①. ♦ *I prefer peppermint toothpaste.* ♦ *Susan offered me a stick of peppermint chewing gum.*

peppy ['pɛp i] *adj.* energetic; active; excited; vigorous. (Adv: *peppily.* Comp: *peppier;* sup: *peppiest.*) ♦ *The peppy cheerleaders did cartwheels when our team scored.* ♦ *The peppy young cat ran in circles, chasing its tail.*

pep talk ['pɛp tɔk] *n.* an inspiring talk; a speech given to make people feel energetic and enthusiastic. ♦ *The coach gave the losing team a pep talk during halftime.* ♦ *The head of the company gave the employees a pep talk before the annual raises were announced.*

per annum [pɚ 'æ nəm] *adv.* for each year; each year. (Latin for 'for every year.') ♦ *My hometown's population increased 5% per annum until last year.* ♦ *Taxes on our house are about $6,000 per annum.*

per capita [pɚ 'kæp ɪ tə] *adv.* for each person; each person. (Latin for 'for every head.') ♦ *The amount of energy used per capita has increased greatly.* ♦ *The federal income tax per capita was much higher in 1990 than in 1960.*

perceive [pɚ 'siv] *tv.* to be aware of someone or something with one's mind; to be aware of someone or something because of one's senses. ♦ *The eyes perceive color and the ears perceive sound.* ♦ *I perceived a slight cinnamon taste in the coffee.*

percent [pɚ 'sɛnt] *n.* a one-hundredth part. (No plural form in this sense. Usually expressed with a number ranging from 0 through 100. Also expressed as "%.") ♦ *Half of something can also be described as 50% of something.* ♦ *Thirty percent of the people surveyed had no opinion.*

percentage [pɚ 'sɛn tɪdʒ] *n.* a part that is less than the whole amount. (No plural form in this sense.) ♦ *The independent candidate received only a small percentage of the votes.* ♦ *The salesclerk earned a percentage of the price of the goods as a commission.*

perceptible [pɚ 'sɛp tə bəl] *adj.* able to be perceived; able to be seen, heard, smelled, tasted, touched, or felt. (Adv: *perceptibly.*) ♦ *Before we fixed the stove, there was always a perceptible odor of gas in the kitchen.* ♦ *The difference between those two very similar colors is barely perceptible.*

perception [pɚ 'sɛp ʃən] *n.* the ability to perceive; the ability to see, hear, taste, touch, or smell. (No plural form in this sense.) ♦ *The blind man's perception of sound was very precise.* ♦ *My depth perception is poor at night.*

perceptive [pɚ 'sɛp tɪv] *adj.* having good perception; able to perceive well with the mind or the senses. (Adv: *perceptively.*) ♦ *The perceptive detective discovered many clues.* ♦ *A perceptive scholar questioned the professor's theory.*

perch ['pɚtʃ] **1.** *n.* a branch or rod above the ground that a bird grasps with its feet when it is at rest. ♦ *The eagle's talons firmly grasped its perch.* ♦ *The bat hung upside down from its perch.* **2.** *n.* a place to sit that is high off the floor or ground; a high ledge. (Figurative on ①.) ♦ *From his perch, the lifeguard could see the whole beach.* ♦ *The queen waved at her subjects from her perch above the crowd.* **3.** *n., irreg.* any one of a number of edible freshwater fishes. (Pl: *perch.*) ♦ *I went fishing at the lake and caught several perch.* ♦ *David cleaned the perch and fried them for dinner.* **4.** *iv.* to sit atop something; to stand atop something, as does a bird. ♦ *A large bird perched on the roof.* ♦ *The cat perched on the top of the sofa.*

percolate ['pɚk ə let] **1.** *tv.* to make or brew coffee by causing hot water to pass through ground coffee beans. ♦ *Do you prefer to percolate your coffee or to pour hot water through coffee in a filter?* ♦ *My parents used to percolate coffee using an electric percolator.* **2.** *iv.* [for coffee] to brew as in ①. ♦ *I can hear the coffee percolating in the kitchen.* ♦ *We played cards while the coffee percolated.* **3. percolate through** *iv.* + *prep. phr.* [for a liquid] to trickle through something, such as loose soil or coffee grounds. ♦ *The hot water slowly percolated through the coffee grounds.* ♦ *The rainwater percolated through the loose soil.*

percolator ['pɚk ə let ɚ] *n.* a kind of coffeepot that percolates coffee. ♦ *My wedding gift to the newly married couple was a percolator.* ♦ *This red light means the percolator is turned on.*

percussion [pɚ 'kʌʃ ən] **1.** *n.* the impact of the hitting of one object against another. (No plural form in this sense.) ♦ *The percussion of my head against the windshield knocked me out.* ♦ *I felt the percussion of the rock striking my arm, and turned to see who threw it.* **2.** *n.* musical instruments that are struck, such as drums, bells, and xylophones, as a group in a band or orchestra. (No plural form in this sense.) ♦ *Percussion is to follow the brass as the marching band goes onto the football field.* ♦ *Mary played percussion for the city's symphony orchestra.*

percussionist [pɚ 'kʌʃ ə nəst] *n.* someone who plays instruments that are hit, such as drums, bells, and xylophones, especially in a band or orchestra. ♦ *The percussionists marched at the rear of the band.* ♦ *The percussionist was trained to play all kinds of drums.*

per diem [pɚ 'di əm] **1.** *adv.* for each day; daily. (Latin for 'for every day.') ♦ *I now earn $10 per diem more than I did last year.* ♦ *The consultant charged $200 per diem.* **2.** *adj.* daily; [allowed] for each day. ♦ *My company provides a per diem allowance for parking.* ♦ *The car rental company had various per diem rates.* **3.** *n.* something, especially money, that is given to someone to pay for daily expenses. (From ①.) ♦ *My boss handed me my per diem in cash before the conference.* ♦ *The businessman had spent his meager per diem by lunchtime.*

perennial [pə 'rɛn i əl] **1.** *adj.* [of a plant] living for two or more years. ♦ *Mary established an entire garden containing perennial flowers.* ♦ *Tom prefers perennial plants to those that last only a single year.* **2.** *adj.* constant; recurrent; happening over and over. (Figurative on ①. Adv: *perennially.*) ♦ *John is a perennial bore. He is always here and always dull.* ♦ *We have the perennial problem of leaks in the roof every spring.* **3.** *n.* a plant that lives for more than two years. ♦ *David planted some perennials alongside his driveway.* ♦ *Our winter is too harsh for most perennials.*

perfect 1. ['pɚ fɪkt] *adj.* being the best; completely correct; without flaws. (Adv: *perfectly.*) ♦ *The smart student got a perfect score on her test.* ♦ *I made sure my spelling was perfect before turning in my work.* **2.** ['pɚ fɪkt] *adj.* exactly suitable; very fitting; very appropriate. (Adv: *perfectly.*) ♦ *The young bride looked for the perfect wedding dress.* ♦ *A hot cup of coffee would be perfect with dessert.* **3.** ['pɚ fɪkt] *adj.* complete; total. (Adv: *perfectly.*) ♦ *A perfect stranger asked me for a dollar on the bus.* ♦ *After the party, my house was a perfect mess.* **4.** ['pɚ fɪkt] *n.* <a construction showing a completed action or condition; a form of the verb that shows that something was completed, is completed, or will be completed.> (In English, it consists of the past participle of the verb, preceded by a form of the auxiliary verb have ⑥. No plural form in this sense.) ♦ *"I had eaten" contains an example of the past perfect.* ♦ *"I have eaten" contains an example of the present perfect.* **5.** [pɚ 'fɛkt] *tv.* to make something perfect ①. ♦ *The chef perfected the meal by garnishing it.* ♦ *My boss perfected my design with a few small enhancements.*

perfection [pɚ 'fɛk ʃən] **1.** *n.* the condition of being perfect. (No plural form in this sense.) ♦ *I always hope for perfection in whatever I do.* ♦ *Perfection requires care and effort.* **2.** *n.* becoming perfect; making something perfect. (No plural form in this sense.) ♦ *She practiced the piano for many hours a day, working on the perfection of her technique.* ♦ *The perfection of the painter's skill is most evident in this painting.* **3. cook something to perfection** *idiom* to cook something perfectly. ♦ *John cooked my steak to perfection.* ♦ *The entire dinner was cooked to perfection!*

perforate ['pɚ fə ret] **1.** *tv.* to make a hole through something; to pierce something. ♦ *Anne accidentally perforated her papers with a pencil.* ♦ *Don't drive over that broken glass! It might perforate your tires.* **2.** *tv.* to make a row of holes in something so that it is easier to tear. ♦ *The machine failed to perforate the sheet of stamps, making it extremely valuable to stamp collectors.* ♦ *This machine perforates paper so you can tear it easily.*

perforated ['pɚ fə ret ɪd] **1.** *adj.* pierced; having a hole. ♦ *The surgeons repaired the survivor's perforated lung.* ♦ *The mechanic patched my perforated tire.* **2.** *adj.* having a row of holes so it is easier to tear. ♦ *The tickets were printed on perforated paper.* ♦ *I tore the paper off the note pad along the perforated edge.*

perforation [pɚ fə 're ʃən] **1.** *n.* a hole that is made through something; a piercing. ♦ *The perforation in John's lung almost killed him.* ♦ *The perforation in the tire allowed air to leak out.* **2.** *n.* a row of holes in a piece of paper, making it easier to tear. ♦ *I tore the bill along the perforation.* ♦ *Perforations allowed the tickets to be separated easily.*

perform [pɚ 'form] **1.** *tv.* to do something; to do an action. ♦ *Our maid performs many household tasks.* ♦ *The soldier performed his duties well during the war.* **2.** *tv.* to present a play, sing a song, play a piece of music, do a dance, etc. for a public audience. ♦ *Anne performed a song at the audition.* ♦ *Jimmy performed a dance for his class.* **3.** *iv.* to act, sing, dance, or play music, especially in front of people. ♦ *The students performed well at the concert.* ♦ *The famous singer performed for 2,000 people.* **4.** *iv.* to function; to do what is expected or has been assigned. ♦ *Our car performed as expected throughout the winter.* ♦ *The students performed well on the test.*

performance [pɚ 'for mәns] **1.** *n.* a presentation of a play, a piece of music, a song, a dance, etc. ♦ *I attended a performance at the theater last night.* ♦ *Each performance of the play lasted three hours.* **2.** *n.* the activity of presenting something; the execution of a task; accomplishing or performing something. (No plural form in this sense.) ♦ *Anne's performance at the sales meeting was impressive.* ♦ *The lawyer was praised for his performance in front of the jury.* **3.** *n.* the quality of performing or functioning; how well someone or something performs. (No plural form in this sense.) ♦ *My car's performance on ice is excellent.* ♦ *John's performance on the test was poor.*

performer [pɚ 'form ɚ] *n.* someone who performs; an actor, a singer, a musician, a dancer, or an entertainer. ♦ *The performer played the piano and sang.* ♦ *The audience applauded the performer after her act.*

perfume 1. ['pɚ fjum, pɚ 'fjum] *n.* a mixture of pleasant-smelling natural or artificial oils and alcohol that is put on people's skin. (No plural form in this sense.) ♦ *Anne wore perfume to the party.* ♦ *Susan sprayed some perfume on her neck.* **2. perfumes** [pɚ 'fjumz] *n.* kinds or types of ①. ♦ *They sell many perfumes at the department store.* ♦ *All the women at the party were wearing different perfumes.* **3.** [pɚ 'fjum] *tv.* to place a scented substance on someone; to add a scented substance to the air in a room. ♦ *Mary perfumed herself with an expensive scent.* ♦ *John perfumed the living room with a floral spray.*

perfunctory [pɚ 'fʌŋk tә ri] *adj.* done without interest or care. (Adv: *perfunctorily.*) ♦ *Whoever was supposed to clean this room did a very perfunctory job.* ♦ *Bill gave the letter from his lawyer a perfunctory glance and put it in a drawer.*

perhaps [pɚ 'hæps] *adv.* maybe; possibly; maybe yes, maybe no. ♦ *Perhaps I'll go to the party tonight, but I'm not sure now.* ♦ *Would you care for some coffee before dinner, perhaps?*

peril ['pɛr әl] **1.** *n.* great danger. (No plural form in this sense.) ♦ *The soldier's lives were in grave peril.* ♦ *The firefighters saved the family from peril.* **2.** *n.* something that causes danger; a great danger. ♦ *The senator said that drugs are a peril that children face every day.* ♦ *Hurricanes are among the perils of living on this island.*

perilous ['pɛr ә lәs] *adj.* dangerous; risky. (Adv: *perilously.*) ♦ *The climbers made a perilous journey up the mountain.* ♦ *The soldier went on a perilous mission behind enemy lines.*

perimeter [pә 'rɪm ɪ tɚ] *n.* the entire outside edge of something; the length of the outside edge of something. ♦ *Guards watched the perimeter of the prison yard.* ♦ *An electric fence ran around the perimeter of the ranch.*

period ['pɪr i әd] **1.** *n.* a punctuation mark "." used at the end of a sentence or at the end of an abbreviation. ♦ *Sentences that just make a simple statement end with a period.* ♦ Etc. *is an abbreviation that ends with a period.* **2.** *n.* a certain length of time, including certain times in history. ♦ *Mary waited for the bus for a period of twenty-five minutes.* ♦ *The 1920s were an interesting period in American history.* **3.** *n.* a section or part of certain games, such as basketball. ♦ *Our team took the lead in the third period.* ♦ *Halftime occurs between the second and third periods in basketball.* **4.** *n.* a subdivision the school day. ♦ *I have lunch during fourth period.* ♦ *The class in calculus is only offered during second period.* **5.** *n.* menstruation; a menstrual period. ♦ *Anne bought a box of tampons the day before her period started.* ♦ *Mary thought she was pregnant because she had missed a period.* **6.** *adj.* [of art, architecture, crafts, or literature] having to do with a certain time in history. ♦ *The designer created period costumes for the movie that was set in the 1920s.* ♦ *The old building was a period piece left over from the 1880s.*

periodic [pɪr i 'ɑd ɪk] **1.** *adj.* happening regularly; happening at regular intervals. (Adv: *periodically* [...ɪk li].) ♦ *The scientist measured the sound wave's periodic frequency.* ♦ *The astronomer lectured about the periodic return of the comet.* **2.** *adj.* happening occasionally; happening every so often. (Adv: *periodically* [...ɪk li].) ♦ *The old man looked forward to the periodic visits from his family.* ♦ *The worker took periodic breaks throughout the day.*

periodical [pɪr i 'ɑd ɪk әl] *n.* a magazine or journal that is published regularly, such as every week, every two weeks, every month, or quarterly. ♦ *Jane subscribes to two periodicals.* ♦ *A well-known periodical published some of my poetry.*

peripheral [pә 'rɪf ɚ әl] **1.** *adj.* at the distant border or edge of something; not in the center. (Adv: *peripherally.*) ♦ *The optometrist tested my peripheral vision.* ♦ *The city's transit system even reached several neighborhoods in peripheral parts of the county.* **2.** *adj.* not as important as other things; incidental. (Figurative on ①. Adv: *peripherally.*) ♦ *The committee was sidetracked by peripheral issues.* ♦ *The extensive report also addressed peripheral concerns.* **3.** *n.* a computer device that is added onto the main computer. ♦ *My printer is my only peripheral.* ♦ *John attached a new peripheral to his computer system.*

periphery [pә 'rɪf ә ri] *n.* the outer area or edge of something; an area near the border of something. (No plural form in this sense.) ♦ *Most of the offices and classrooms were in the center of the college campus, and the dormitories were on the periphery.* ♦ *Bill lives on the periphery of a big city, and he takes a bus downtown every day to work.*

perish ['pɛr ɪʃ] **1.** *iv.* to die. ♦ *Fourteen people perished in the hotel fire.* ♦ *The stray dog perished during the harsh winter.* **2.** *iv.* [for something] to go away or fade away. ♦ *Many native customs perished as a result of colonialism.* ♦ *Radio drama perished with the coming of television.*

perishable ['pɛr ɪʃ ә bәl] *adj.* quick to decay or spoil; likely to become rotten quickly. (Adv: *perishably.*) ♦ *Perishable food should be kept in the refrigerator.* ♦ *Those steaks are perishable, so put them in the freezer right away.*

peritoneum [pɛr i tә 'ni әm] *n.* the membrane that covers the inside of the abdomen and supports its contents. ♦ *The peritoneum is the lining of the abdominal cavity.* ♦ *The peritoneum helps to hold everything in the abdomen in place.*

peritonitis [pɛr ɪ tə 'nɑɪ tɪs] *n.* an infection of the peritoneum. (No plural form in this sense.) ♦ *Peritonitis can be quite serious and very painful.* ♦ *A ruptured appendix caused John's bout with peritonitis.*

perjury ['pɚ dʒə ri] *n.* lying in court after one has taken an oath promising not to lie. (No plural form in this sense.) ♦ *Perjury is a crime punishable by fine and imprisonment.* ♦ *Committing perjury in court can result in a prison sentence.*

perky ['pɚ ki] *adj.* lively; cheery and active. (Adv: *perkily.* Comp: *perkier;* sup: *perkiest.*) ♦ *Five perky cheerleaders cheered for the team.* ♦ *The photographer's perky assistant tried to make the children smile.*

perm ['pɛrm] **1.** *n.* a long-lasting hairdo; a **permanent.** ♦ *Jane went to the beauty salon for a perm.* ♦ *Bob's hair used to be straight until he got a perm.* **2.** *tv.* to give someone's hair ①. ♦ *The hairdresser permed and colored my hair.* ♦ *The stylist permed Mary's hair once a month.*

permanent ['pɚ mə nənt] **1.** *adj.* intended or designed to last forever or for a long time; not temporary. (Adv: *permanently.*) ♦ *Anne took a permanent position with the law firm.* ♦ *The fax machine seems to be a permanent fixture in our office.* **2.** *n.* a type of hair treatment where the hair is caused to be wavy or curly for a long time. ♦ *Jane went to the beauty salon for a permanent.* ♦ *Bob's hair used to be straight until he got a permanent.*

permeate ['pɚ mi et] **1.** *tv.* [for a gas, liquid, or odor] to spread or soak something throughout. ♦ *Nasty water from the flood permeated our carpeting.* ♦ *The cotton rags were permeated with gasoline.* **2.** *tv.* [for something abstract] to penetrate and mix with something. (Figurative on ①.) ♦ *Rebellious ideas permeated the song's lyrics.* ♦ *Annoying commercials permeate everything that is broadcast.*

permissible [pɚ 'mɪs ə bəl] *adj.* permitted; allowable. (Adv: *permissibly.*) ♦ *Smoking is permissible only in the smoking lounge.* ♦ *At the beach, swimming is permissible until sunset.*

permission [pɚ 'mɪ ʃən] *n.* authorization; consent. (No plural form in this sense.) ♦ *Jane asked her teacher's permission to leave class early.* ♦ *My father gave me permission to borrow his car.*

permissive [pɚ 'mɪs ɪv] *adj.* allowing too much freedom, especially concerning sexual behavior. (Adv: *permissively.*) ♦ *The minister condemned television's permissive messages.* ♦ *John's permissive parents don't mind if he smokes.*

permit 1. ['pɚ mɪt] *n.* an official document that allows someone to do something; an authorization. ♦ *John obtained a city permit before building his garage.* ♦ *Mary's permit allows her to carry a concealed weapon.* **2.** [pɚ 'mɪt] *tv.* to allow someone to do something; to let someone do something. ♦ *Jane permitted her children to stay up late on weekends.* ♦ *I permitted John to borrow my car.* **3. weather permitting** [...pɚ 'mɪt ɪŋ] *idiom* if the weather allows it. ♦ *Weather permitting, we will be there on time.* ♦ *The plane lands at midnight, weather permitting.*

pernicious [pɚ 'nɪʃ əs] *adj.* harmful or damaging; causing harm or damage. (Adv: *perniciously.*) ♦ *The pernicious gossip destroyed the actor's career.* ♦ *David's body was weakened by the pernicious disease.*

perpendicular [pɚ pən 'dɪk jə lɚ] *adj.* at a right angle to something; being at a 90-degree angle to a surface; upright. (Adv: *perpendicularly.*) ♦ *The road that runs north to south is perpendicular to the road that runs east to west.* ♦ *Any two adjacent sides of a square are perpendicular.*

perpetrate ['pɚp ə tret] **1.** *tv.* to commit a crime. ♦ *A well-known criminal perpetrated the fraud.* ♦ *The police want to know who perpetrated the crime.* **2.** *tv.* to do something badly; to perform or execute something badly. (Figurative on ①.) ♦ *These mistakes were perpetrated by an untrained worker.* ♦ *The actors who perpetrated this horrible performance are probably ashamed.*

perpetrator ['pɚp ə tret ɚ] **1.** *n.* someone who has committed a crime. ♦ *The police caught the perpetrator near the crime scene.* ♦ *The perpetrator of the murder escaped punishment.* **2.** *n.* someone who has done something very badly. (Figurative on ①.) ♦ *John is the perpetrator of this badly written report.* ♦ *The perpetrators of this horrible drama—the author, the actors, the director, and the stage crew—are probably ashamed.*

perpetual [pɚ 'pɛ tʃu əl] *adj.* lasting or continuing forever; eternal; never ending; continuous; permanent. (Adv: *perpetually.*) ♦ *A perpetual flame was lit in honor of the deceased leader.* ♦ *Everything seems to be in perpetual turmoil in my workplace.*

perpetually [pɚ 'pɛ tʃu ə li] *adv.* eternally; continuously; permanently; in a way that lasts or continues forever. ♦ *It seems as if my boss is perpetually criticizing me.* ♦ *The earth perpetually orbits the sun.*

perpetuate [pɚ 'pɛ tʃu et] *tv.* to cause someone or something to be remembered forever. ♦ *The memorial will perpetuate the memory of the soldiers who gave their lives.* ♦ *Storytellers have perpetuated ancient tales and legends since early times.*

perpetuity [pɚ pɪ 'tu ə ti] **in perpetuity** *phr.* for an indefinitely long period of time. ♦ *My trust fund generates income in perpetuity.* ♦ *The right for the road to cross my land was granted in perpetuity to the county.*

perplex [pɚ 'plɛks] *tv.* to puzzle someone; to confuse someone. ♦ *The difficult math problem perplexed the students.* ♦ *Mary's criticism of my good work perplexed me.*

perplexing [pɚ 'plɛks ɪŋ] *adj.* complicated; confusing; puzzling. (Adv: *perplexingly.*) ♦ *The perplexing problem baffled the researchers.* ♦ *I couldn't answer the perplexing riddle.*

persecute ['pɚ sə kjut] *tv.* to oppress or harass someone or some group of people, especially because of race, religion, or some other belief or status. ♦ *The stupid bully persecuted all the smart students.* ♦ *Millions of Jews were persecuted during World War II.*

persecution [pɚ sə 'kju ʃən] *n.* the persecuting of someone or some people; the oppression or harassment of people. (No plural form in this sense.) ♦ *The sociologist studied the causes for the frequent persecution of minority groups.* ♦ *The students' persecution of the disabled child was cruel.*

perseverance [pɚ sə 'vɪr əns] *n.* the continuous effort made to reach a goal; persistence. (No plural form in this sense.) ♦ *It required great effort and perseverance, but I fin-*

ished the marathon. ♦ *Through the mayor's perseverance, a new airport was built.*

persevere [pɚ sə 'vɪr] *iv.* to continue working to reach a goal, even though it is difficult; to struggle with a problem or difficulty. ♦ *The winter was very harsh, but the villagers persevered.* ♦ *Although Jane faced many obstacles, she persevered and got her degree.*

Persia ['pɚ ʒə] *n.* the former name of Iran. See Iran in the Gazetteer.

Persian ['pɚ ʒən] **1.** *adj.* of or about the people or culture of Persia or Iran. ♦ *Cyrus the Great established the Persian Empire in 549 B.C.* ♦ *People still pay a lot of money for an authentic Persian carpet.* **2.** *n.* the language spoken by the people of Iran. (No plural form in this sense.) ♦ *The Persian word for 'Persian' is* Farsi. ♦ *Persian is not related to Arabic.*

persist [pɚ 'sɪst] **1.** *iv.* to continue to do something; not to give up, even if it is difficult or if one faces opposition. ♦ *John won't give up. He persists in repeating his opinion.* ♦ *Keep persisting. They will agree eventually.* **2.** *iv.* to continue to exist. ♦ *It is claimed that cockroaches would persist in the world even after a nuclear war.* ♦ *My cough has persisted for two months.* **3. persist in doing something** *phr.* to continue doing something as in ①. ♦ *John persists in thinking that he's always right.* ♦ *Tom persists in demanding that I agree to his terms.* **4. persist with something** *phr.* to continue the state of something; to extend an action or state, as in ①. ♦ *Please do not persist with your demands that I agree to your terms.* ♦ *If you persist with this intrusion, I'm going to call the police.*

persistent [pɚ 'sɪs tənt] *adj.* not giving up; continuing; lasting; enduring. (Adv: *persistently.*) ♦ *I told the persistent salesman to leave me alone.* ♦ *The doctor gave me medicine for my persistent cough.*

person ['pɚ sən] **1.** *n.* a human being; a man, a woman, a boy, or a girl. (people is sometimes used as the plural.) ♦ *Not even one person showed up at my party!* ♦ *I asked the person standing next to me for the time.* **2.** *n.* <a grammar term, used to show the relationship of the speaker or writer to the receiver of the message.> (The first person refers to the speaker or writer, such as I, me, my, mine, we, us, our, and ours. The second person refers to the listener or reader, such as you, your, and yours. The third person refers to someone or something being spoken about, such as he, him, his, she, her, hers, it, its, they, them, their, and theirs.) ♦ Takes *is the third-person singular form of* take, *because it is used with third-person singular forms, such as* he. *For example:* He takes out the garbage. ♦ *In many languages, verbs are conjugated for person and number.* **3. in person** *phr.* [with someone] actually present in a place rather than appearing in a film, on a television screen, or through a radio broadcast. ♦ *All the famous movie stars were there in person.* ♦ *You must appear in the office in person to collect the money that is due to you.* **4. feel like a new person** *idiom* to feel refreshed and renewed, especially after getting well or getting dressed up. ♦ *I bought a new suit, and now I feel like a new person.* ♦ *Bob felt like a new person when he got out of the hospital.* **5. on one's person** *idiom* [of something] carried with one. ♦ *Always carry identification on your person.* ♦ *I'm sorry, I don't have any money on my person.*

personable ['pɚ sə nə bəl] *adj.* having pleasant behavior. (Adv: *personably.*) ♦ *Our firm hired a personable receptionist for the front desk.* ♦ *The thief was able to surprise his victims because he seemed so personable.*

personal ['pɚ sən əl] **1.** *adj.* of or about the private affairs of a particular person; belonging to or used primarily or exclusively by a particular person. (Adv: *personally.*) ♦ *I can't make any personal phone calls while at work.* ♦ *I bought a computer for my own personal use.* **2.** *adj.* done by a certain person, instead of by a representative of that person. (Adv: *personally.*) ♦ *I received a personal reply from the president of the company.* ♦ *The actress made a personal visit to a seriously ill fan of hers.* **3.** *adj.* relating to one's own self and how one looks or acts. (Adv: *personally.*) ♦ *Makeup can enhance one's personal appearance.* ♦ *The boisterous student didn't care about his personal demeanor.*

personality [pɚ sə 'næl ə ti] **1.** *n.* aspects of one's thinking and behavior that make one different from everyone else. ♦ *The brothers look similar, but they have quite different personalities.* ♦ *John is very quiet and shy, but Bill has a very outgoing personality and loves to meet people.* **2.** *n.* someone who is well known; a celebrity. ♦ *The charity sought the help of several television personalities to raise funds.* ♦ *I collect autographs of famous sports personalities.*

personalize ['pɚ sə nə lɑɪz] *tv.* to make something personal; to mark something with one's name or something about oneself. ♦ *Jane's stationery is personalized with her initials.* ♦ *Bob personalized his office by decorating it with his own artwork.*

personalized ['pɚ sə nə lɑɪzd] *adj.* marked with one's name or something about oneself. ♦ *My personalized luggage has my initials stamped on each piece.* ♦ *Jane's personalized coffee mug has her name on it.*

personally ['pɚ sə nə li] **1.** *adv.* as far as one is concerned; as for oneself; speaking for oneself. ♦ *Personally, I think you're wrong, but it's your decision.* ♦ *Mary personally didn't enjoy the party, but she was glad other people had a good time.* **2.** *adv.* by oneself, without other people's help; done by oneself. ♦ *I bought a painting personally signed by the artist.* ♦ *The governor demanded to speak with the mayor personally.* **3. take something personally** *idiom* to interpret a remark as if it were mean or critical about oneself. ♦ *Don't take it personally, but you really need a haircut.* ♦ *I want to tell you something, but please don't take it personally.*

personify [pɚ 'sɑn ɪ fɑɪ] **1.** *tv.* to regard animals or things as having human features. ♦ *The lonely girl personified her stuffed animals.* ♦ *The cartoonist personified the crow as a bandit wearing a black hat.* **2.** *tv.* to be the perfect example of something; to be the living example of something. ♦ *My grandmother personifies kindness and generosity.* ♦ *The dictator personified cruelty and evil.*

personnel [pɚ sə 'nɛl] **1.** *n.* the people who work for a company or organization. (No plural form in this sense.) ♦ *The company president sent a memo to all personnel.* ♦ *The parking lot is for company personnel only.* **2.** *n.* the department in a company that deals directly with the employees and is concerned with the hiring, training, and benefits of employees. (No plural form in this sense. Often capitalized; human resources (department) is more common.) ♦ *The new employees went to Personnel* *to fill out forms.* ♦ *The company president sent a memo to Personnel.*

perspective [pɚ 'spɛk tɪv] **1.** *n.* the appearance of depth or distance in a drawing or painting on a flat surface. (No plural form in this sense.) ♦ *Lisa is able to capture perspective very well in her paintings.* ♦ *Her ability to use perspective give the appearance of depth to her art.* **2. perspective on something** *phr.* a way of looking at a situation and determining what is important. ♦ *The jury did not have a good perspective on the crime since some of the evidence had to be ignored.* ♦ *Studying history gives one perspective on the past.*

perspiration [pɚ spə 're ʃən] *n.* sweat. (No plural form in this sense.) ♦ *The runner wiped the perspiration from his forehead.* ♦ *After working in the hot sun for an hour, the laborers were covered with perspiration.*

perspire [pɚ 'spɑɪr] *iv.* to sweat. ♦ *The ballet dancers perspired heavily under the hot stage lights.* ♦ *I was so nervous that I began to perspire.*

persuade [pɚ 'swed] *tv.* to use argument or discussion to convince someone to do or think something. ♦ *The salesman persuaded Mary to buy a new car.* ♦ *Anne persuaded her nephew to stay in school.*

persuasion [pɚ 'swe ʒən] **1.** *n.* an effort to persuade someone of something. (No plural form in this sense.) ♦ *Gentle persuasion is much better than using threats or force.* ♦ *No amount of persuasion could get Lisa to agree to sell her paintings to me.* **2. be of the persuasion that** *idiom* to hold a belief that something is true or is in existence. ♦ *Anne is of the persuasion that supports that candidate for mayor.* ♦ *The paranoid was of the persuasion that aliens lived among us.*

persuasive [pɚ 'swe sɪv] *adj.* serving to persuade; good at persuading. (Adv: *persuasively.*) ♦ *The persuasive saleswoman sold me a used car.* ♦ *The candidate's persuasive speech convinced me to vote for her.*

pertain [pɚ 'ten] **pertain to** *iv.* + *prep. phr.* to have to do with someone or something; to be relevant to someone or something. ♦ *Please leave. Our conversation doesn't pertain to you.* ♦ *Your comments don't pertain to the topic of conversation.*

pertinent ['pɚt n nənt] *adj.* relevant; related; important. (Adv: *pertinently.*) ♦ *My professor's criticisms about my paper were quite pertinent.* ♦ *The president addressed pertinent issues in his speech.*

perturb [pɚ 'tɚb] *tv.* to trouble and irritate someone; to agitate someone. ♦ *Drivers who go slow on the highway really perturb my father.* ♦ *Lisa was quite perturbed by Tom's strange behavior.*

Peru [pə 'ru] See Gazetteer.

peruse [pə 'ruz] *tv.* to read something carefully. ♦ *Mary perused the entire contract but understood little of it.* ♦ *Anne peruses her class notes every night.*

pervade [pɚ 'ved] *tv.* to spread throughout something; to spread throughout a place. ♦ *Fear pervaded the small town after the unexplained murder.* ♦ *A terrible stench of rotten food pervaded the kitchen.*

pervasive [pɚ 've sɪv] *adj.* spreading throughout; tending to pervade. (Adv: *pervasively.*) ♦ *A pervasive feeling of anger was evident throughout the jail.* ♦ *The pervasive rhythm of the drums brought the audience to its feet.*

perverse [pɚ 'vɚs] *adj.* stubborn; contrary; antagonistic. (Adv: *perversely.*) ♦ *John's so perverse—if I say it's day, he'll say it's night!* ♦ *The perverse child refused to eat the food his parents had prepared, even though it was his favorite.*

perversion [pɚ 'vɚ ʒən] *n.* something that has been changed to become abnormal or unnatural. ♦ *Sex crimes are considered by some to be perversions against nature.* ♦ *This movie is a perversion of the author's book.*

pervert 1. ['pɚ vɚt] *n.* someone who is perverted. ♦ *The police arrested the pervert for molesting a child.* ♦ *The angry parents chased the pervert away from the playground.* **2.** [pɚ 'vɚt] *tv.* to use something the wrong way; to use something in a way that was not intended. ♦ *The corrupt politician was accused of perverting the power of his office for his own gain.* ♦ *The lawyer perverted the judicial process by bribing the judge.*

perverted [pɚ 'vɚt ɪd] *adj.* [of persons or behavior] abnormal or unnatural, especially concerning sexual matters. (Adv: *pervertedly.*) ♦ *It is hard to determine exactly what perverted behavior is.* ♦ *Bill shocked everyone by saying that Bob was a perverted old man.*

pesky ['pɛs ki] *adj.* bothersome; annoying; troublesome. (Adv: *peskily.* Comp: *peskier;* sup: *peskiest.*) ♦ *A pesky fly buzzed around my sandwich.* ♦ *Anne asked her pesky brother to leave her alone.*

pessimism ['pɛs ə mɪz əm] *n.* the belief that everything is the worst it could be; the tendency to look at the bad side of everything; the opposite of optimism. (No plural form in this sense.) ♦ *Because of John's pessimism, he was rarely happy.* ♦ *Anne's pessimism makes all of her friends feel unhappy.*

pessimist ['pɛs ə məst] *n.* someone who assumes the worst; someone who exhibits pessimism. ♦ *The pessimist described every possible way that things could go wrong.* ♦ *The gloomy pessimist made the people around him miserable too.*

pessimistic [pɛs ə 'mɪs tɪk] *adj.* exhibiting pessimism. (Adv: *pessimistically* [...ɪk li].) ♦ *Thousands of pessimistic people said that we would lose the war.* ♦ *Pessimistic citizens don't expect politicians to keep promises.*

pest ['pɛst] **1.** *n.* someone or something that causes trouble; someone or something that is a nuisance. ♦ *My younger sister becomes a pest whenever my friends visit.* ♦ *Some pest on the bus kept bothering me for money.* **2.** *n.* any animal or insect that destroys crops, spreads disease, and intrudes into people's homes. ♦ *The farmer kept pests from ruining his crops by using insecticide.* ♦ *The city tried to kill the pests that carried the plague.*

pester ['pɛs tɚ] *tv.* to bother someone; to annoy someone. ♦ *The student pestered the professor with irrelevant questions.* ♦ *Some man I didn't know pestered me for money on the bus.*

pesticide ['pɛs tɪ sɑɪd] *n.* a chemical that kills **pests** ②. (No plural form in this sense.) ♦ *The farmer sprayed his crops with pesticide.* ♦ *You must wash the pesticide off the fruit before you eat it.*

pestilence ['pɛs tə ləns] *n.* a plague; an epidemic. (No plural form in this sense.) ♦ *They escaped the pestilence by fleeing to the mountains, away from the city.* ♦ *The terrible pestilence killed most of the people it infected.*

pestle ['pɛs təl] *n.* a sturdy rod or club-like tool used to crush substances in a bowl called a mortar. ♦ *The druggist used a mortar and pestle to grind the medicine into a powder.* ♦ *He pressed the pestle into the mortar and crushed the spices he was using for the evening meal.*

pet ['pɛt] **1.** *n.* an animal that is kept in one's home or yard as a companion. ♦ *My landlord won't let me have any pets.* ♦ *I have a few pets, including two dogs, a cat, and a rabbit.* **2.** *adj.* [of an animal] kept as ①. ♦ *I took my pet dog to the veterinarian's office.* ♦ *Anne's pet duck was always eating the houseplants.* **3.** *adj.* special; particular; favorite. ♦ *Bob puts a lot of work into his pet project.* ♦ *Lisa's pet theory is that there is life on Mars.* **4.** *tv.* to stroke or pat someone or some creature. ♦ *Anne petted her dog gently and scratched it between the ears.* ♦ *John petted his cat's soft fur.* **5. be the teacher's pet** *idiom* to be the teacher's favorite student. ♦ *Sally is the teacher's pet. She always gets special treatment.* ♦ *The other students don't like the teacher's pet.*

petal ['pɛt əl] *n.* one of the colored sections of the blossom of a flower. ♦ *As the flower died, its petals dried up.* ♦ *Mary picked the petals off the daisy, one by one.*

petite [pə 'tit] **1.** *adj.* [of a woman] small; [of a woman] short. (From French. Adv: *petitely.*) ♦ *Mary is quite petite and never finds airplane seats uncomfortable.* ♦ *The petite librarian stood on a chair to reach the top shelf.* **2.** *adj.* [of a clothing size or range of sizes] fitting women who are ①. ♦ *Petite sizes fit women who are shorter than average.* ♦ *This is a very nice skirt, but do you have it in a petite size?*

petition [pə 'tɪ ʃən] **1.** *n.* a document signed by many people who are demanding something from a someone. ♦ *I signed the petition to install a stop sign at the dangerous corner.* ♦ *The workers signed a petition demanding better working conditions.* **2.** *tv.* to request something formally of a government or of an authority, often through the use of ①. ♦ *The neighborhood petitioned the city for more parking.* ♦ *The students petitioned the university for a change in the grading policy.*

petrified ['pɛ trə fɑɪd] **1.** *adj.* changed into stone; made as hard as stone. ♦ *The museum displayed petrified fossils of dinosaurs.* ♦ *I bought a piece of petrified wood in Arizona.* **2.** *adj.* frightened; very scared. (Figurative on ①.) ♦ *The petrified woman gave the robber her purse.* ♦ *The deer stopped, petrified, in the middle of the road.*

petrify ['pɛ trə fɑɪ] **1.** *iv.* to change into stone; to become as hard as stone. ♦ *Over millions of years, the wood petrified.* ♦ *The bones of the dinosaur had petrified and become part of the rock millions of years ago.* **2.** *tv.* to cause someone or some creature to be frozen with fear. (Figurative on ①.) ♦ *I was petrified by the sound of the explosion.* ♦ *The thunderstorm petrified the children.*

petroleum [pə 'tro li əm] *n.* oil that is pumped from under the ground, used to make gasoline and other substances. (No plural form in this sense.) ♦ *The well produced thousands of barrels of petroleum each day.* ♦ *Petroleum is an extremely valuable fuel.*

petticoat ['pɛt i kot] *n.* a ruffled garment worn by women underneath a skirt or dress. ♦ *The dancer's petticoat was visible when she kicked her legs.* ♦ *Susan fled the burning farmhouse wearing only her petticoat.*

petty ['pɛt i] **1.** *adj.* not important; trivial. (Adv: *pettily.* Comp: *pettier;* sup: *pettiest.*) ♦ *The student bothered the professor with petty questions.* ♦ *The committee ignored petty matters and focused on major concerns.* **2.** *adj.* mean; unkind; narrow-minded; representing a desire to quibble. (Adv: *pettily.* Comp: *pettier;* sup: *pettiest.*) ♦ *The customer, who had lots of petty complaints, treated the clerk very rudely.* ♦ *The intolerant bully directed some petty remarks toward me.*

petulant ['pɛ tʃə lənt] *adj.* childish; impatient; irritable; bad-tempered. (Adv: *petulantly.*) ♦ *The petulant young boy stuck out his lower lip in defiance.* ♦ *Jane can be very petulant when she doesn't get her way.*

petunia [pə 'tun jə] *n.* an herb with bright flowers, cultivated as a popular garden plant. ♦ *There's a row of pink petunias growing in my front yard.* ♦ *John accidentally knocked over a pot of petunias.*

pew ['pju] *n.* a long bench with a back, used in churches. ♦ *I entered the church late and sat in the back pew.* ♦ *The church raised the money to purchase padding for its pews.*

phantom ['fæn təm] **1.** *n.* a ghost; a specter; an image or memory that is "seen" by the mind in a dream, or in a vision, but is not real. ♦ *The scary story was about a phantom that rode through town at midnight on a black horse.* ♦ *Phantoms of his long-forgotten friends raced through the dying man's mind.* **2.** *adj.* ghostlike; unreal; apparent, but not real. ♦ *According to the story, the phantom rider rode through town on a black horse at midnight.* ♦ *The beast is not real, of course. It's just a phantom.*

Pharaoh ['fɛr o] *n.* a king of ancient Egypt. ♦ *The pyramids are where great Pharaohs were buried.* ♦ *Thousands of years ago, the Israelites fled from the Pharaoh's rule.*

pharmaceutical [fɑr mə 'sut ɪk əl] **1.** *adj.* of or about drugs and medicines. (Adv: *pharmaceutically* [...ɪk li].) ♦ *The pharmaceutical company researched the new drug's effects.* ♦ *The researcher studied the pharmaceutical benefits of herbs.* **2. pharmaceuticals** *n.* drugs; medicines. (Treated as singular or plural.) ♦ *Legal drugs are called pharmaceuticals.* ♦ *You need a prescription to obtain many pharmaceuticals.*

pharmacist ['fɑr mə sɪst] *n.* someone who prepares and sells drugs or medicines that are prescribed by a doctor. ♦ *When my doctor gives me a prescription, I take it to a pharmacist to have it filled.* ♦ *There's always a pharmacist on duty at the drugstore near my house.*

pharmacology [fɑr mə 'kɑl ə dʒi] *n.* the science and study of drugs and medicines. (No plural form in this sense.) ♦ *The pharmacist has a degree in pharmacology.* ♦ *The chemist who specialized in pharmacology conducted research for a pharmaceutical company.*

pharmacy ['fɑr mə si] *n.* a place where drugs and medicines are prepared and sold; a drugstore. ♦ *I went to the pharmacy to have my prescription filled.* ♦ *Many pharmacies also stock vitamins and minerals.*

phase ['fez] **1.** *n.* a stage in the development of someone or something; a stage in a sequence of events. ♦ *The first phase of running for office is raising money.* ♦ *The doctor explained the different phases of the disease.* **2.** *n.* any of the stages of the appearance of the moon as seen from Earth. ♦ *The astrologer paid close attention to the moon's phases.* ♦ *A chart of the phases of the moon can be found in an almanac.*

pheasant ['fɛ zənt] **1.** *n., irreg.* a large, edible game bird with beautiful feathers and a long tail. (Pl: *pheasant* or *pheasants.*) ♦ *My uncle used to raise pheasants in a cage.* ♦ *What is the best time of year to hunt pheasant?* **2.** *n.* the meat of ①. (No plural form in this sense.) ♦ *The chef's specialty was roast pheasant.* ♦ *We enjoyed the casserole made of pheasant.*

phenomena [fɪ 'nɑm ə nə] pl of phenomenon.

phenomenal [fɪ 'nɑm ə nəl] *adj.* remarkable; interesting; hard to believe; extraordinary; unusual. (Adv: *phenomenally.*) ♦ *The phenomenal chess player was only 13 years old.* ♦ *Winning the lottery was a phenomenal event in my life.*

phenomenon [fɪ 'nɑm ə nɑn] *n., irreg.* a fact, circumstance, or event that can be observed, especially one that is unusual, remarkable, or interesting. (Pl: phenomena.) ♦ *Thunder and lightning are natural phenomena.* ♦ *The arrival of a ship from Mars was the greatest phenomenon human beings have ever witnessed.*

philanthropy [fɪ 'læn θrə pi] *n.* the love of humankind, especially as shown by helping other people by donating money and time to charities and organizations. (No plural form in this sense.) ♦ *If I had a lot of money to give away, I would be more interested in philanthropy.* ♦ *A committee of my club deals with philanthropy.*

philharmonic [fɪl (h)ɑr 'mɑn ɪk] *adj.* loving music; devoted to music. ♦ *The city's philharmonic orchestra performed a holiday concert.* ♦ *I attended a performance by the National Philharmonic Orchestra.*

Philippines ['fɪl ə pinz] See Gazetteer.

philosopher [fɪ 'lɑs ə fɚ] *n.* someone who practices, studies, or teaches philosophy. ♦ *The philosopher expounded his views on the meaning of life.* ♦ *The philosophers debated the truth of various sentences.*

philosophical [fɪl ə 'sɑf ɪk əl] **1.** *adj.* of, by, for, or about philosophy. (Adv: *philosophically* [...ɪk li].) ♦ *The nature of truth and goodness are matters of philosophical debate.* ♦ *I am studying a philosophical approach to language and its use.* **2.** *adj.* wise; full of knowledge and wisdom; calm; reasonable. (Adv: *philosophically* [...ɪk li].) ♦ *John, who rarely talked of philosophical things, chatted about death and dying after the funeral.* ♦ *I respected my professor's philosophical advice.*

philosophy [fɪ 'lɑs ə fi] **1.** *n.* the science and study of the meaning of truth, knowledge, reality, and existence. (No plural form in this sense.) ♦ *Most students of Western philosophy have studied Greek or Latin.* ♦ *A few of my friends decided to study philosophy.* **2.** *n.* the principles one uses to live one's life; the way one looks at life. (No plural form in this sense.) ♦ *Mary's personal philosophy is to treat people the way she would like to be treated.* ♦ *I use the golden rule as my philosophy of life.*

phlegm ['flɛm] *n.* mucus; the thick substance that comes from the throat and lungs when one is sick. (No plural form in this sense.) ♦ *John coughed up a little phlegm into his handkerchief.* ♦ *I wiped the phlegm from my nose.*

phlegmatic [flɛg 'mæt ɪk] *adj.* not easily excited; not caring; sluggish. (Adv: *phlegmatically* [...ɪk li].) ♦ *Bob seems phlegmatic, but if something really interests him, he gets excited.* ♦ *I am sometimes a little phlegmatic when I first get up in the morning.*

phobia ['fob i ə] *n.* an irrational fear; an unreasonable fear; a dread. (Also in combinations, such as claustrophobia, hydrophobia.) ♦ *Anne has a real phobia about elevators, so she always takes the stairs.* ♦ *Bill always stays at home because of his phobia for crowds.*

phone ['fon] **1.** *n.* a telephone. ♦ *I have a phone on my desk at work.* ♦ *John got into an accident while talking on his car phone.* **2.** *tv.* to call someone by telephone. ♦ *I phoned my mother to wish her a happy birthday.* ♦ *Bill phoned his boss to say that he was sick and couldn't come to work.* **3. (phone) call** See call ②.

phonetic [fə 'nɛt ɪk] **1.** *adj.* of or about the sounds of language and the way they are represented in writing or printing. (Adv: *phonetically* [...ɪk li].) ♦ [ə] *is the phonetic symbol for an unstressed central vowel called "schwa."* ♦ [bet] *is a phonetic transcription of "bait."* **2. phonetics** *n.* the science and study of the production and perception of speech sounds. (Treated as singular.) ♦ *My training in phonetics included transcribing conversations.* ♦ *Lisa studied phonetics in her first year of graduate school.* **3. phonetics** *n.* writing or printing done with phonetic ① symbols. (Usually treated as singular.) ♦ *I can't read phonetics. Please write it normally.* ♦ *I wrote an entire page of phonetics that reflected my own way of speaking.*

phonics ['fɑn ɪks] *n.* a way of teaching people how to read by interpreting standard spelling phonetically. (Treated as singular.) ♦ *Children who don't learn phonics are thought to memorize each word as a unit.* ♦ *To improve the students' poor reading skills, I suggested teaching them phonics.*

phonograph ['fon ə græf] *n.* a record player. ♦ *My phonograph's needle needs to be replaced.* ♦ *The record skipped when I bumped into the phonograph.*

phony ['fon i] **1.** *adj.* fake; not real; counterfeit; not genuine. (Informal. Adv: *phonily.* Comp: *phonier;* sup: *phoniest.*) ♦ *The phony diamond shattered because it was really glass.* ♦ *The phony doctor had no training at all.* **2.** *n.* a fake; a counterfeit; someone or something that is not genuine. (Informal.) ♦ *The police arrested the phony for impersonating a doctor.* ♦ *Thieves stole the valuable diamond and put a phony in its place.*

phosphorus ['fɑs fə rəs] *n.* a chemical element used in fertilizers, detergents, insecticides, and medicines. (No plural form in this sense.) ♦ *The atomic symbol for phosphorus is P.* ♦ *The atomic number of phosphorus is 15.*

photo ['fo to] *n.* a photograph; a snapshot; a picture taken by a camera. ♦ *The newspaper printed a photo of the crime scene.* ♦ *The tourist took some photos of the monument.*

photocopier ['fo to kɑp i ɚ] *n.* a copier; a machine that makes copies of documents. ♦ *Many photocopiers are able to make copies that are smaller or larger than the original document.* ♦ *New photocopiers can collate and staple sets of copies.*

photocopy ['fo to kɑp i] **1.** *n.* a copy of a document made by a photocopier. ♦ *I gave a photocopy of the report to my boss.* ♦ *Each employee received a photocopy of the schedule.* **2.** *tv.* to make ① on a photocopier. ♦ *I photocopied the report and gave the original to my boss.* ♦ *The secretary photocopied the holiday schedule for everyone.*

photogenic [fo to 'dʒɛn ɪk] *adj.* appearing especially good in photographs. (Adv: *photogenically* [...ɪk li].) ♦ *A photogenic model usually appears on the cover of my favorite magazine.* ♦ *Max isn't really ugly, but I've seen pictures of him, and he certainly is not photogenic.*

photograph ['fo tə græf] **1.** *n.* a picture made by a camera; a photo; a snapshot. ♦ *I want to take a photograph of the lake at sunset.* ♦ *I placed my vacation photographs in a large album.* **2.** *tv.* to take a picture of someone or something with a camera. ♦ *I photographed the monkeys at the zoo.* ♦ *The tourist photographed the historic monuments.*

photographer [fə 'tɑ grə fɚ] *n.* someone who takes pictures with a camera, especially for a living. ♦ *The photographer focused her camera on the child.* ♦ *The photographer checked the lighting before taking the picture.*

photographic [fo tə 'græf ɪk] *adj.* of, for, about, or involving photography. (Adv: *photographically* [...ɪk li].) ♦ *The museum exhibited many pieces of photographic art.* ♦ *Photographic film can be ruined if it is accidentally exposed to light.*

photography [fə 'tɑ grə fi] *n.* the science, study, art, or act of taking a picture with a camera. (No plural form in this sense.) ♦ *Photography is one of the newer forms of art.* ♦ *Anne studied photography to learn how to take better pictures.*

phr. See phrase ① and ②.

phrase ['frez] **1.** *n.* a group of words that functions as a part of speech within a sentence. (Abbreviated *phr.* here.) ♦ *The prepositional phrase "in the house" consists of a preposition ("in") and a nominal ("the house").* ♦ *In most declarative English sentences, the verb phrase follows the subject.* **2.** *n.* an expression usually including several words. (Abbreviated *phr.* here.) ♦ *What phrase did Mary use to describe her boss?* ♦ On vacation *is a common phrase.* **3.** *n.* a series of notes that is a part of a piece of music. ♦ *The conductor rehearsed the difficult phrase with the flute players.* ♦ *My piano teacher told me to play the first phrase again.* **4.** *tv.* to put communication into words. ♦ *Anne phrased her command in the form of a question.* ♦ *The speaker phrased his ideas in a confusing way, and the audience didn't understand what he meant.* **5.** *tv.* to perform music, grouping into a series the notes that belong to ③. ♦ *The conductor told the soloist that he had phrased the passage incorrectly.* ♦ *Please phrase the last line just as it was written.*

phrasing ['frez ɪŋ] **1.** *n.* the words that are chosen to express something; the way that something is expressed. (No plural form in this sense.) ♦ *I understood you even though your phrasing was confusing.* ♦ *The polite phrasing of Bob's request made it seem less offensive than it might have been.* **2.** *n.* the grouping together of a series of musical notes. (No plural form in this sense.) ♦ *The composer's phrasing in this section is difficult to follow.* ♦ *The singer's phrasing was punctuated with heavy breaths.*

physical ['fɪz ɪk əl] **1.** *adj.* of or about the body; bodily; of the body. (Adv: *physically* [...ɪk li].) ♦ *My doctor advised me to participate in physical activities.* ♦ *After the accident, I had a lot of physical symptoms as well as depression.* **2.** *adj.* of or about the laws of nature; of or about the study of physics. ♦ *Gravity is a physical force.* ♦ *The science students memorized physical laws.* **3.** *adj.* of or about real objects; of or about matter. (Adv: *physically* [...ɪk li].) ♦ *The physical world contrasts with the spiritual world.* ♦ *The ghost manifested itself as a physical presence.* **4. physical (examination)** *n.* an examination of someone's body and health by a doctor. ♦ *My grandma has a physical twice a year.* ♦ *The company doctor gave me a physical examination when I was hired.*

physical fitness ['fɪz ɪ kəl 'fɪt nəs] *n.* the state of a healthy body. (No plural form in this sense.) ♦ *Jane's physical fitness is due to a good exercise program.* ♦ *An important part of physical fitness is eating healthful foods.*

physical therapist ['fɪz ɪ kəl 'θɛr ə pəst] *n.* someone who practices or performs physical therapy. ♦ *After I sprained my ankle, I went to a physical therapist for months.* ♦ *The physical therapist massaged my legs and exercised the sore muscles.*

physical therapy ['fɪz ɪ kəl 'θɛr ə pi] *n.* the treatment of disease, injury, and deformity by using massage, heat, exercises, and other physical remedies. (No plural form in this sense.) ♦ *The injured athlete's doctor recommended physical therapy.* ♦ *My insurance doesn't pay for most forms of physical therapy.*

physician [fɪ 'zɪ ʃən] *n.* a medical doctor. ♦ *My physician prescribed some antibiotics for my illness.* ♦ *I asked my physician if I needed any X-rays.*

physicist ['fɪz ə sɪst] *n.* someone who studies or is an expert in physics. ♦ *The atom was first split by nuclear physicists.* ♦ *The physicist explained the law of gravity to the students.*

physics ['fɪz ɪks] *n.* the science and study of the properties of and relationships between matter and energy. (Treated as singular.) ♦ *Gravity demonstrates one of the laws of physics.* ♦ *Understanding physics is easier if you know calculus.*

physiology [fɪz i 'ɑl ə dʒi] *n.* the science and study of the functioning of the bodies and organs of living plants and animals. (No plural form in this sense.) ♦ *Anatomy and physiology deal with the structure and function of living organisms.* ♦ *The zoologist had studied physiology for many years.*

physique [fɪ 'zik] *n.* the shape and appearance of a human body, especially that of the male. ♦ *Jane admired the mechanic's muscular physique.* ♦ *Tom worked at the gym to improve his physique.*

pianist ['pi ə nəst, pi 'æn əst] *n.* someone who plays the piano. especially a professional piano player. ♦ *I hired a pianist to play at my party.* ♦ *John gave the pianist at the bar a tip.*

piano [pi 'æ no] *n.* a large musical instrument in which small, soft hammers connected to a keyboard strike tuned metal strings. (Pl in *-s*.) ♦ *Standard pianos have 88 keys.* ♦ *Bill taught himself how to play the piano.*

pick ['pɪk] **1.** *n.* a tool that is a heavy, pointed metal bar attached to a handle, used for breaking apart ice, rocks, and other objects. ♦ *Before ice fishing, I broke a hole in the ice with a pick.* ♦ *The mountain climber stuck a pick into the hard rock.* **2.** *n.* a choice; a selection. (No plural form in this sense.) ♦ *I've got chocolate, strawberry, and vanilla. Take your pick.* ♦ *If you had your pick, which of these shirts would you choose?* **3.** *tv.* to choose a particular person or thing. ♦ *The winner was picked randomly from a pool of contestants.* ♦ *Jane picked John as her part-*

ner for the card game. **4.** *tv.* to remove something from someplace, especially using one's fingers or a pointed tool. ♦ *I picked some lint off the carpet.* ♦ *Bill picked the piece of meat from between his teeth.* **5.** *tv.* to gather or harvest flowers, fruit, cotton, peas, beans, etc. ♦ *Bill picked some roses from the flower garden.* ♦ *The workers picked cotton in the hot sun.* **6. pick out** *tv. + adv.* to select or choose something, such as an item of clothing. ♦ *I picked out a new dress for the party.* ♦ *Max picked out some new shoes but didn't have enough money to pay for them.* **7. pick up** *tv. + adv.* to grasp and raise someone or something. ♦ *Please pick up that piece of paper you just dropped on the floor.* ♦ *Tom picked up the baby and took her into the living room.* **8. pick up** *tv. + adv.* to collect someone or something; to stop at a place and gather, obtain, or secure someone or something. ♦ *The letter carrier has just picked up the mail you left in the mailbox.* ♦ *I will stop by your house and pick you up at noon.* **9. pick at** *iv. + prep. phr.* to eat something a little bit at a time, without interest. ♦ *When Bill is sad, he just picks at his food.* ♦ *Jane usually has a hearty appetite, but she just picked at her dinner.* **10. pick a lock** *idiom* to open a lock without a key; to open a lock without using a key. ♦ *The robber picked the lock with a nail file.* ♦ *The thief picked the lock on the safe and stole the money.* **11. pick and choose** *idiom* to choose very carefully from a number of possibilities; to be selective. ♦ *You must take what you are given. You cannot pick and choose.* ♦ *Jane is so beautiful. She can pick and choose from a whole range of suitors.* **12. the pick of something** *idiom* the best of the group. ♦ *This playful puppy is the pick of the whole lot.* ♦ *These potatoes are the pick of the crop.*

picket ['pɪk ɪt] **1.** *n.* a pointed board, stick, or stake of wood. ♦ *The fence was made of white pickets.* ♦ *Tom stapled his poster to a picket so he could carry it in the protest.* **2.** *n.* someone—often a member of a labor union—who demonstrates or protests by marching or carrying signs attached to ①. ♦ *A group of pickets milled around the library, protesting a book they didn't like.* ♦ *The doors to the factory were blocked by pickets.* **3. picket fence** *n.* a fence made of ①, set upright and attached to a wooden frame. ♦ *There's a white picket fence around my yard.* ♦ *Picket fences can be seen all over the Midwest.* **4.** *iv.* to be part of demonstration or labor union strike. ♦ *The workers picketed demanding better working conditions.* ♦ *The union workers picketed against the wage reduction.* **5.** *tv.* to target someone or something as the object of a labor union strike or a demonstration. ♦ *The factory was picketed because of a contract dispute.* ♦ *When the workers picketed the store, the store lost money.*

pickle ['pɪk əl] **1.** *n.* a cucumber that has been preserved in salt water or vinegar. ♦ *Lisa bought some pickles at the deli.* ♦ *I put some sliced pickles on my hamburger.* **2.** *tv.* to preserve food, especially vegetables, in salt water or vinegar. ♦ *Anne pickled some cucumbers in vinegar.* ♦ *Sue's grandmother pickled the small onions she grew in her garden.*

pickpocket ['pɪk pɑk ɪt] *n.* someone who steals wallets from people's pockets or purses, especially in crowds. ♦ *The conductor warned the subway riders to beware of pickpockets.* ♦ *The pickpocket stole my wallet when he bumped into me.*

pickup truck ['pɪk əp trək] *n.* a truck having an enclosure for the driver and an open area in back for the load. ♦ *The farmer filled up his pickup truck with fertilizer.* ♦ *I moved my heavy desk to Anne's house in my pickup truck.*

picky ['pɪk i] *adj.* fussy; particular; choosy; hard to please; finding fault with the choices one is given. (Comp: *pickier;* sup: *pickiest.*) ♦ *The picky child refused to eat anything on her plate.* ♦ *The picky customer didn't like any of the shirts I showed him.*

picnic ['pɪk nɪk] **1.** *n.* a meal prepared to be eaten informally outdoors. ♦ *If it doesn't rain on Saturday, let's have a picnic in the park.* ♦ *I brought a blanket to sit on at the picnic.* **2.** *iv., irreg.* to go on a picnic; to have a meal outdoors, especially in the countryside. (Pt/pp: picnicked. Present participle is picnicking.) ♦ *On Saturday, many people picnicked in the park by the lake.* ♦ *My friends and I were picnicking when it started to rain.* **3.** *adj.* used for ①. ♦ *Anne packed food and plates into the picnic basket.* ♦ *All the picnic tables were being used, so we sat on the ground.*

picnicked ['pɪk nɪkt] pt/pp of picnic.

picnicking ['pɪk nɪk ɪŋ] present participle of picnic.

pictorial [pɪk 'tor i əl] **1.** *adj.* using or consisting of pictures. (Adv: *pictorially.*) ♦ *A pictorial exhibit in the museum showed how dinosaurs looked.* ♦ *The pictorial display showed pictures of Susie from ages 1 to 13.* **2.** *n.* a pictorial ① display. ♦ *The magazine produced a pictorial to document the history of the railroad.* ♦ *We only looked at the colorful pictorial and ignored the text.*

picture ['pɪk tʃɚ] **1.** *n.* a drawing, a painting, or a photograph; an image of someone or something. ♦ *The artist painted a picture of the countryside.* ♦ *Bill keeps a picture of his children in his wallet.* **2.** *n.* a movie; a motion picture. ♦ *Would you like to see a picture tonight?* ♦ *Which picture won the most awards last year?* **3.** *n.* the image on a television screen. ♦ *We bought a new antenna so we could get a clearer picture on our TV.* ♦ *Anne made the picture sharper by adjusting the tuner.* **4.** *tv.* to think of someone or something; to make a mental image of someone or something; to imagine something. ♦ *I just can't picture John acting so badly.* ♦ *Try to picture how Mary would act if she saw me now.* **5.** *tv.* to show someone or something in a picture. ♦ *The movie's opening scene pictured a cow eating grass.* ♦ *The death of the king was pictured in the painting.* **6. picture of something** *idiom* the perfect example of something; an exact image of something. ♦ *The young newlyweds were the picture of happiness.* ♦ *My doctor told me that I was the picture of good health.*

picturesque [pɪk tʃɚ 'ɛsk] *adj.* [of something] that is pretty enough to made a nice-looking picture. (Adv: *picturesquely.*) ♦ *The picturesque town was a popular tourist destination.* ♦ *I watched the picturesque sunset from the beach.*

pidgin ['pɪdʒ ən] **1.** *n.* a mixed language growing out of the need for communication between two peoples who speak different languages. ♦ *A pidgin is usually simpler than its component languages and has a smaller vocabulary.* ♦ *Traders in various parts of the world speak pidgins.* **2.** *adj.* of, by, for, or about ①. ♦ *Pidgin English is spoken in many parts of the world.* ♦ *A pidgin form of English is spoken in West Africa.*

pie ['pɑɪ] **1.** *n.* a kind of food that has a crust of pastry or something similar, and is filled with meat, fruit, or some sweet substance appropriate for dessert. (No plural form in this sense. The crust can be on the bottom or both bottom and top.) ♦ *Pie is good for dessert, especially with ice cream on it.* ♦ *Shall I make cake or pie for the banquet?* **2.** *n.* a single, complete, round unit of ①. ♦ *I baked three pies for dessert.* ♦ *The pie was cut into six triangular pieces.* **3. pie in the sky** *idiom* a future reward, especially one that is not likely to be granted. ♦ *You expect to get rich form this scheme, but that's just pie in the sky.* ♦ *His promises are just pie in the sky! He is a liar if I ever saw one.*

piece ['pis] **1.** *n.* a part of something; a part broken off of or removed from something; an object that is put together with other objects to make something. ♦ *Where is the other piece of the plate you broke?* ♦ *I've lost the last piece to this puzzle.* **2.** *n.* an example of something, especially of an art or craft, such as music. ♦ *The guide showed us an interesting piece by a famous artist.* ♦ *The pianist played a lovely piece and played it very well.* **3.** *n.* [in board games] an object that is placed on the board and, typically, moved to different places on the board according to the rules of the particular game. ♦ *Anne moved her piece around the board.* ♦ *The card said to move my piece back two spaces.* **4. piece together** *tv.* + *adv.* to join parts of something together. ♦ *Anne pieced the parts of the broken vase together.* ♦ *The plate was broken into so many parts that I could not piece it together.* **5. piece together** *tv.* + *adv.* to mentally connect facts in a way that allows a good understanding of an event or situation. ♦ *I was able to piece together the series of events that led to the argument.* ♦ *The detective pieced the solution to the crime together.*

piecemeal ['pis mil] **1.** *adv.* a little bit at a time; gradually. ♦ *Bob built a model plane piecemeal during his spare time.* ♦ *Anne read the long novel piecemeal during the summer.* **2.** *adj.* done a little bit at a time; done in pieces. ♦ *The artist painted a group of paintings in a piecemeal fashion, doing all the trees first, then all the fences, and so on.* ♦ *John's piecemeal approach to work annoyed his boss.*

piecrust ['paɪ krəst] **1.** *n.* pastry, in a layer or sheet, used to enclose a pie. (No plural form in this sense.) ♦ *Tom loves to bake and eat scraps of piecrust.* ♦ *Piecrust made of pastry is supposed to be light and flaky.* **2.** *n.* a piece of pastry found on the bottom and often the top of a pie. ♦ *Tom's piecrusts tend to be a bit soggy and hard.* ♦ *Anne made a piecrust for a cherry pie.*

pier ['pɪr] *n.* a dock; a structure like a bridge that extends into the water from the shore, supported by posts or columns. ♦ *The workers unloaded the ship's cargo onto the pier.* ♦ *The ship you want to board is at pier 4.*

pierce ['pɪrs] *tv.* to make a hole through someone or something; to cause something to go through something else; to penetrate something. ♦ *The bullet pierced the police officer's vest.* ♦ *I pierced the paper with my pencil.*

piercing ['pɪrs ɪŋ] **piercing scream** *idiom* a very loud and shrill scream. ♦ *Suddenly, there was a piercing scream from the next room.* ♦ *Bob heard Susan's piercing scream and ran to help her.*

pig ['pɪg] **1.** *n.* a farm animal with short legs and a curly tail, raised for food, especially bacon, ham, and pork. (Thought of as greedy and messy.) ♦ *The pigs ate from the trough in their sty.* ♦ *The pigs oinked loudly before they were slaughtered.* **2.** *n.* someone who eats a lot of food; a glutton. (Figurative on ①.) ♦ *The pig sitting next to me had four helpings of food.* ♦ *Don't be such a pig. Save some for me!* **3.** *n.* someone who is dirty or messy. (Figurative on ①.) ♦ *Clean up your room! You're such a pig!* ♦ *My roommates are pigs—they leave their dirty clothes and dishes everywhere.*

pigeon ['pɪdʒ ən] *n.* a bird, commonly found in cities, with short legs and a heavy body, whose head bobs as it walks. ♦ *The old man in the park threw breadcrumbs to the pigeons.* ♦ *As I walked up to the pigeons, they flew away.*

pigeonhole ['pɪdʒ ən hol] **1.** *n.* one of a set of boxes or compartments on a desk or shelf for holding papers. ♦ *Each teacher has a pigeonhole for mail in the school's main office.* ♦ *Bill kept his bills in their own pigeonhole on his desk.* **2.** *tv.* to rigidly classify something in one's mind as fitting a certain category. ♦ *Since first grade, Jimmy has been pigeonholed as a slow learner.* ♦ *The boss unfairly pigeonholed me as a troublemaker.*

piggyback ['pɪg i bæk] *adv.* [riding or being carried] on someone's back and shoulders. ♦ *John carried his son piggyback all around the zoo.* ♦ *Anne rode piggyback on her brother's shoulders.*

piglet ['pɪg lət] *n.* a young pig. ♦ *The piglet squealed loudly when I picked it up.* ♦ *The sow suckled her piglets.*

pigment ['pɪg mənt] **1.** *n.* a substance in a plant or animal that causes it to have a certain color. ♦ *People who have little pigment in their skin sunburn easily.* ♦ *Albinos have no pigment at all.* **2.** *n.* a colored substance that is mixed with a liquid to make paint or ink. ♦ *The artist used paint made with natural pigments.* ♦ *The dye contains green pigment.*

pigmentation [pɪg mən 'te ʃən] *n.* the natural coloring of a plant or animal. (No plural form in this sense.) ♦ *My pigmentation becomes darker after being in the sun.* ♦ *The plant's pigmentation was uneven, making a design in its leaves.*

pigpen ['pɪg pɛn] **1.** *n.* a sty; a place where pigs are kept. ♦ *The farmer fed the pigs in their pigpen.* ♦ *I got covered with mud when I fell into the pigpen.* **2.** *n.* a very messy or dirty place. (Figurative on ①.) ♦ *Your room is a pigpen. Clean it up.* ♦ *My house was a pigpen until I hired a maid.*

pigskin ['pɪg skɪn] **1.** *n.* leather made from the skin of a pig. (No plural form in this sense.) ♦ *The old book was bound with pigskin.* ♦ *The farmer wore a jacket made of pigskin.* **2.** *n.* a football, sometimes made of ①. (Informal.) ♦ *Let's go out to the park and throw the pigskin around.* ♦ *The receiver caught the pigskin and ran toward the goal.*

pigtail ['pɪg tel] *n.* a braid of hair, especially one hanging from the back of the head, or one of a pair, each hanging from one side of the head. ♦ *Susan separated her hair into two pigtails.* ♦ *Anne wore a ribbon in her pigtail.*

pike ['paɪk] **1.** *n., irreg.* a member of any of a number of species of large, slender freshwater fish. (Pl: *pike*.) ♦ *I caught a pike in the lake today.* ♦ *The cook broiled six small pike for dinner.* **2.** *n.* the meat of ①. (No plural form in this sense.) ♦ *I love broiled pike.* ♦ *We have enough pike for everyone to eat!*

pile ['paɪl] **1.** *n.* a heap of objects that lie on top of each other. ♦ *There's a pile of books on the corner of my desk.* ♦ *Bob sorted the magazines in to separate piles, one for each year.* **2.** *n.* a tall mound or heap of something, such as clothing, leaves, dirt. ♦ *I raked the fallen leaves into a large pile.* ♦ *There's a pile of dirty clothes in the laundry room.* **3.** *n.* a beam of wood or steel that is driven into the ground to support a building, bridge, or other structure. ♦ *Huge wooden piles support the fishing pier.* ♦ *One of the bridge's piles punctured a tunnel under the river.* **4.** *tv.* to place or form things or matter into a shape like ②. ♦ *Susie piled the sand into a pointed heap.* ♦ *Mary piled the files on top of her desk.* **5. pile up** *iv.* + *adv.* to accumulate. ♦ *Work was piling up while you were on vacation.* ♦ *All sorts of debris piled up in the alley.*

pileup ['paɪl əp] *n.* an accident involving several cars and trucks that collide into each other. ♦ *There's a six-car pileup at First Street and Western Avenue.* ♦ *The ambulance rushed to the scene of the pileup on the freeway.*

pilfer ['pɪl fɚ] *tv.* to steal a small amount of something; to steal things in small amounts. ♦ *The office worker who pilfered pens from the supply room was reprimanded.* ♦ *Jimmy pilfered a few cookies when his mother wasn't looking.*

pilgrim ['pɪl grɪm] **1.** *n.* someone who travels, especially to a holy place, as a religious act of devotion. ♦ *Many pilgrims travel to the holy city.* ♦ *The religious site attracted many devout pilgrims.* **2. Pilgrim** *n.* one of the settlers of Plymouth Colony in 1620. ♦ *The Pilgrims crossed the Atlantic Ocean in a ship called the* Mayflower. ♦ *Many Pilgrims did not survive the first winter in the new world.*

pilgrimage ['pɪl grə mɪdʒ] *n.* a journey, especially to a holy place as a religious act of devotion. ♦ *The devout monks made a pilgrimage to Jerusalem.* ♦ *Anne made a pilgrimage that took her across the world.*

piling ['paɪl ɪŋ] **1.** *n.* beams of wood or steel driven into the ground to support a building, bridge, or other structure. (No plural form in this sense.) ♦ *The old dock's piling crumbled during the earthquake.* ♦ *The weight of the bridge's piling crushed a tunnel underneath the river.* **2.** *n.* a beam of wood or steel as in ①. ♦ *The builders used wood pilings to support the dock.* ♦ *A huge machine drove steel pilings into the earth to form the base of the building.*

pill ['pɪl] **1.** *n.* a small, formed mass containing vitamins, medicine, or some other drug that is swallowed. ♦ *Mary takes a vitamin pill every morning at breakfast.* ♦ *My grandfather takes pills for his heart condition.* **2. the pill** *n.* ① taken by women to prevent conception. (No plural form in this sense. Treated as singular.) ♦ *Anne is on the pill because she doesn't want to get pregnant.* ♦ *Mary decided to have a baby, so she stopped taking the pill.*

pillar ['pɪl ɚ] **1.** *n.* a column; a strong upright structure used to support something or as decoration. ♦ *The pillars at the front of the museum are made of white marble.* ♦ *A banner was hung from a pillar in front of the building.* **2. pillar of strength; pillar of support** *idiom* someone or something that provides support as ① does. ♦ *My parents are my pillars of support.* ♦ *The minister looked to God as her pillar of strength.*

pillow ['pɪl o] *n.* a cloth bag filled with feathers or a similar soft material, typically used to support one's head while sleeping, or for decoration. ♦ *I bought three new pillows for my bed.* ♦ *My neck hurts because I slept without a pillow last night.*

pillowcase ['pɪl o kes] *n.* a fabric cover for a pillow. ♦ *The maid washed the pillowcases each week.* ♦ *I put the feather pillow inside the pillowcase.*

pilot ['paɪ lət] **1.** *n.* someone who flies a plane; someone who guides a boat along a channel. ♦ *The pilot flew the plane across the ocean.* ♦ *The pilot steered the boat through the shipping channel in the harbor.* **2.** *n.* the first episode of a television series that is shown as a test to see if people like it. ♦ *The star hoped his new pilot would be successful.* ♦ *The network aired the pilot immediately after a hit show.* **3.** *tv.* to fly an airplane; to guide a boat through a channel. ♦ *Captain Jones piloted the airplane through the storm.* ♦ *Dave piloted the ship away from the reef.* **4.** *adj.* preliminary; initial and serving as a test. ♦ *The funds for the pilot project came out of a special budget.* ♦ *The researchers refined the methods used in the pilot study.*

pimple ['pɪmp əl] *n.* a small, round infection on the skin. ♦ *Mary tried to cover up the pimple on her nose.* ♦ *Makeup gives me pimples.*

pin ['pɪn] **1.** *n.* a thin, stiff, pointed wire occurring in a variety of forms, such as with a flat top, a plastic end, a springy middle with a safety cover on the end, etc. (The simple ① is also called a *straight pin.*) ♦ *The tailor held the cloth sections together with pins.* ♦ *Mary accidentally pricked her finger on a pin.* **2.** *n.* a piece of jewelry that is attached to clothing with a variety of ①. ♦ *I attached the silver pin to my sweater.* ♦ *Mary wore an attractive pin on the lapel of her jacket.* **3.** *n.* one of the (usually) 10 wooden, club-like objects that are meant to be knocked down by a bowling ball in the sport of bowling. ♦ *Knocking down every pin on the first try is called a strike.* ♦ *In bowling, you score one point for each pin you knock over.* **4.** *tv.* to attach something to something else with some variety of ①. ♦ *The tailor pinned the pattern to the cloth.* ♦ *The secretary pinned an important message to the message board.* **5.** *tv.* to press someone or something against something. ♦ *The wrestler pinned his opponent to the mat.* ♦ *The police officer pinned the thief to the wall.* **6. pin in** *tv.* + *adv.* to block someone's or something's ability to move; to trap someone or something in a place. ♦ *I was pinned in by the crowd.* ♦ *The crowd pinned me in as I tried to get to the exit.* **7. pin someone down** *idiom* to force someone to make a decision or choice. ♦ *The doctor tried to pin Jane Smith down for her next appointment.* ♦ *I won't make up my mind for a week so don't try to pin me down now.* **8. pin something down** *idiom* to establish or identify something, such as date, time, source, cause, etc. ♦ *Mary and Bob pinned down a time for their date.* ♦ *The detective finally pinned down the identity of the killer.* **9. on pins and needles** *idiom* anxious; in suspense. ♦ *I've been on pins and needles all day, waiting for you to call with the news.* ♦ *We were on pins and needles until we heard that your plane had landed safely.* **10. pins and needles** *idiom* a tingling feeling in some part of one's body, especially the arms and legs. ♦ *I've got pins and needles in my legs.* ♦ *Mary gets pins and needles if she crosses her arms for long.*

pincer ['pɪn sɚz] **1.** *n.* one of the claws of lobsters and crabs. ♦ *The lobster snapped its pincers at the marine biologist.* ♦ *A crab's pincers are very sharp.* **2. pincers** *n.* a tool used to hold an object tightly. (Treated as singular or plural. Sometimes singular.) ♦ *Pincers are a pair of pivoting metal bars with jaws on one end and handles on the other.* ♦ *I pulled the nail from the wall with a pair of pincers.*

pinch ['pɪntʃ] **1.** *n.* an act of squeezing a fold of skin, usually causing pain. ♦ *Bill's pinch gave me a bruise.* ♦ *Susie returned Jimmy's insult with a pinch on the arm.* **2.** *n.* a small amount of something, such as a spice, that can be held between one's first finger and one's thumb. ♦ *The cook added a pinch of salt to the soup.* ♦ *This tomato sauce needs another pinch of oregano.* **3.** *tv.* to squeeze or hold something, such as a fold of flesh, between two surfaces. ♦ *Anne pinched me when I fell asleep in class.* ♦ *Mary got a bruise when Bob pinched her arm.* **4.** *tv.* to steal something. (Slang.) ♦ *Some thief pinched my leather coat at school.* ♦ *The shoplifter pinched a loaf of bread.* **5.** *tv.* to arrest someone. (Slang.) ♦ *The cops pinched the bank robbers before they could escape.* ♦ *The police pinched the thug in the alley behind the store.* **6. feel the pinch** *idiom* to experience hardship because of having too little money. ♦ *The Smiths used to go abroad every year, but now that he's retired, they're really feeling the pinch.* ♦ *You're bound to feel the pinch a bit when you're a student.* **7. in a pinch** *idiom* as a substitute. ♦ *A piece of clothing can be used as a bandage in a pinch.* ♦ *In a pinch, you can use folded paper to prop up the table leg so the table won't rock.* **8. in a pinch** *idiom* in an awkward situation where help is needed and alternatives do not exist. ♦ *I'm sort of in a pinch. Can you give me some help?* ♦ *If you are ever in a pinch, just ask me for help.*

pincushion ['pɪn kʊʃ ən] *n.* a small, padded cushion that pins and needles can be stuck into until they are needed. ♦ *The seamstress kept several sizes of needles in her pincushion.* ♦ *The tailor kept a pincushion next to the sewing machine.*

pine ['pɑɪn] **1.** *n.* a kind of tree that has long, thin, sharp needles for leaves. ♦ *Pines and spruce grow all over the world.* ♦ *The mountain cabin was surrounded by tall pines.* **2.** *n.* wood from ①. (No plural form in this sense.) ♦ *Our log cabin in the mountain is made of pine.* ♦ *The hunter carved a figure out of pine.* **3.** *adj.* made from ②; composed of ②. ♦ *The pine logs crackled in the fireplace.* ♦ *I stained the pine desk to protect the wood.* **4. pine for** *iv.* + *prep. phr.* to yearn for someone or something; to long for someone or something. ♦ *The soldier pined for his family back home.* ♦ *Bob pined for chocolate cake on his birthday.*

pineapple ['pɑɪn æp əl] **1.** *n.* a large, juicy tropical fruit that is yellow on the inside and has a very rough skin. ♦ *A rare frost killed most of the crop of pineapples.* ♦ *The cook used a sharp knife to slice through the pineapple.* **2.** *n.* the edible part of ①. (No plural form in this sense.) ♦ *A dish of fresh pineapple is as good as any dessert in the world.* ♦ *The cook added bits of pineapple to the cake batter.* **3.** *adj.* made from ②; containing or flavored with ②. ♦ *Anne had pineapple sherbet for dessert.* ♦ *Mary drank a glass of pineapple juice with her breakfast.*

Ping-Pong™ ['pɪŋ pɔŋ] *n.* a game in which two or four people on opposite ends of a table hit a small, light, hollow plastic ball back and forth over a low net using paddles. (Also called *table tennis.*) ♦ *It was raining, so we stayed indoors and played Ping-Pong.* ♦ *We played Ping-Pong at the recreation center.*

pink ['pɪŋk] **1.** *n.* the color of red mixed with white; a light, pale red. (No plural form in this sense.) ♦ *Most baby clothes are available in pink or light blue.* ♦ *For the Valentine's Day dance, the gym was decorated in pink and red.* **2.** *adj.* <the adj. use of ①.> (Comp: *pinker;* sup: *pinkest.*) ♦ *I picked some pink petunias from the flower garden.* ♦ *Mary is wearing a pink blouse today.* **3. in the pink (of condition)** *idiom* in very good health; in very good condition, physically or emotionally. ♦ *The garden is lovely. All the flowers are in the pink of condition.* ♦ *Jane looks quite healthy—in the pink, in fact.*

pinkeye ['pɪŋk ɑɪ] *n.* a contagious infection of the eye, in which the membrane that covers the eyeball and lines the inside of the eyelid becomes inflamed and sore. (No plural form in this sense.) ♦ *If you've got pinkeye, don't share your face towels with others.* ♦ *For my pinkeye, the doctor prescribed medicated eyedrops.*

pinkie ['pɪŋk i] *n.* the last, smallest finger of either hand; the little finger. (Informal.) ♦ *The man wore a large gold ring on his pinkie.* ♦ *I broke my pinkie when the window slammed shut on it.*

pinnacle ['pɪn ə kəl] *n.* the highest point of something. ♦ *Receiving the prestigious award became the pinnacle of the actor's career.* ♦ *The pinnacle of Bob's term as president was when he secured a large contribution to support the club.*

pinpoint ['pɪn pɔɪnt] **1.** *tv.* to identify a location exactly. ♦ *Radar can help pinpoint the location of an object within its range.* ♦ *The general pinpointed the site of the enemy fort on the map.* **2.** *tv.* to identify the cause of something exactly. (Figurative on ①.) ♦ *The doctors tried to pinpoint the cause of my illness.* ♦ *The expert mechanic finally pinpointed what was wrong with my car.* **3.** *adj.* extremely precise; exact. ♦ *Even in the dark, I was able to locate the small island in the lake with pinpoint accuracy.* ♦ *Surgery on a fetus requires pinpoint precision.*

pint ['pɑɪnt] **1.** *n.* a unit of liquid measure, equal to half a quart or ⅛ of a gallon or 16 fluid ounces. ♦ *Anne bought a pint of milk at the store.* ♦ *One quart equals two pints, and a pint equals two cups.* **2.** *n.* a unit of dry measure, equal to half a quart or 1/64 of a bushel. ♦ *John pickled a few pints of peppers.* ♦ *Mary bought a pint of fresh blueberries.* **3.** *adj.* [of a container] holding ① or ②. ♦ *Susan canned vegetables in pint jars.* ♦ *I sold the honey in plastic pint containers.*

pioneer [pɑɪ ə 'nɪr] **1.** *n.* someone who is one of the first of a particular group of people to settle a new area. (From the point of view of the particular group.) ♦ *In the 1800s, American pioneers moved across the West.* ♦ *Jimmy wants to be one of the first pioneers to live on the moon.* **2.** *n.* someone who is one of the first to investigate an area of science that has never been examined; someone who is one of the first people to do something, preparing the way for other people to do the same. ♦ *The early pioneers in science made many basic discoveries.* ♦ *My grandfather was an early pioneer in astronomy.* **3.** *tv.* to prepare the way for other people to do something; to help develop something for other people. ♦ *Cowboys helped pioneer the settlement of the West.* ♦ *Alexander Graham Bell pioneered the development of the telephone.*

pious ['pɑɪ əs] *adj.* very religious; expressing respect for God. (Adv: *piously.*) ♦ *Max is not a pious person, but he* *respects the beliefs of others.* ♦ *I am pious in church but very worldly outside of church.*

pipe ['paɪp] **1.** *n.* a hollow tube that is used to carry a fluid from one place to another. ♦ *Our kitchen flooded when a pipe burst.* ♦ *Oil was transported from the well through a very long pipe.* **2.** *n.* a tube connected to a small bowl, used to smoke tobacco. ♦ *Bob put some tobacco in the bowl of his pipe.* ♦ *Bill gave up smoking a pipe for the sake of his health.* **3. pipe from** *tv.* + *prep. phr.* to cause something to be carried through ①; to convey something through ①. ♦ *Oil was piped from the well to the refinery.* ♦ *We have to pipe our drinking water from our well to our house.* **4. pipe into** *tv.* + *prep. phr.* to send a sound or music into a room by wire. ♦ *Instrumental music was piped into the waiting room.* ♦ *The speech was piped into our classroom electronically.*

pipeline ['paɪp laɪn] **1.** *n.* a series of connected pipes for carrying water, gas, or other substances over a long distance. ♦ *An earthquake ruptured the oil pipeline.* ♦ *The workers repaired the gas pipeline after a leak was reported.* **2.** *n.* a source of information or gossip. (Figurative on ①.) ♦ *Anne's secretary is a good pipeline for information.* ♦ *After the aide was fired, the reporter lost his pipeline to the mayor's office.*

piping ['paɪp ɪŋ] **1.** *n.* a system of pipes that carry a fluid. (No plural form in this sense.) ♦ *The piping froze last night when it was so cold.* ♦ *I painted the overhead piping the same color as the ceiling.* **2. piping hot** *idiom* [of food] extremely hot. ♦ *On a cold day, I like to eat piping hot soup.* ♦ *Be careful! This coffee is piping hot!*

pique ['pik] **1. pique someone's curiosity; pique someone's interest** *idiom* to arouse interest; to arouse curiosity. ♦ *The advertisement piqued my curiosity about the product.* ♦ *The professor tried to pique the students' interest in French literature.* **2. in a pique** *idiom* having a feeling of resentment; feeling that one's pride has been hurt. ♦ *In a real pique, Anne insulted all of her friends.* ♦ *John's found himself in a pique over Bob's harsh criticism.*

piracy ['paɪ rə si] **1.** *n.* robbery done by pirates; robbery committed at sea. (No plural form in this sense.) ♦ *The crew of the ship lived by piracy, stealing valuable goods from other ships.* ♦ *The ship's cargo was lost to piracy.* **2.** *n.* duplicating and selling books, records, video, and software that are the property of someone else. (Figurative on ①. No plural form in this sense.) ♦ *The publishers were concerned about the increase in piracy.* ♦ *Copyright law protects authors' works from piracy.*

pirate ['paɪ rɪt] **1.** *n.* someone who robs ships at sea. ♦ *The pirates captured a fleet of ships carrying gold to Spain.* ♦ *The ship's cargo was stolen by pirates.* **2.** *tv.* to steal or capture something, especially while at sea. ♦ *A band of thieves pirated the entire fleet of ships.* ♦ *The rebels pirated the ship's cargo of gold and silver.* **3.** *tv.* to appropriate something; to use something when one does not have the right to use it. (Figurative on ②.) ♦ *My coworker pirated my computer software while I was at lunch.* ♦ *John pirated office supplies from his workplace.* **4.** *tv.* to duplicate and sell copies of books, records, videos, and software without the permission of the original publisher. (Figurative on ②.) ♦ *Someone pirated the software program that we paid $100,000 to develop.* ♦ *Some countries do not prosecute persons who pirate videos and records.*

pistol ['pɪs təl] *n.* a small gun that can be held and shot with one hand. ♦ *John was fined for carrying a pistol without a permit.* ♦ *The robber pointed the pistol at the clerk.*

piston ['pɪs tən] *n.* a solid cylinder that is moved up and down inside a tube by some force, such as that found in an engine. ♦ *The engine sputtered because some of its pistons weren't firing.* ♦ *Does your car's engine have six pistons or eight?*

pit ['pɪt] **1.** *n.* a large hole in the ground. ♦ *Jimmy fell into the abandoned gravel pit.* ♦ *My dog dug a shallow pit in the backyard.* **2.** *n.* a large, hard seed at the center of some kinds of fruit. ♦ *John threw the peach pit into the garbage.* ♦ *Anne spit the cherry pits into the sink.* **3. (orchestra) pit** *n.* the low area in a theater in front of the stage where the orchestra sits. ♦ *The ball fell out of the actor's hand and rolled into the pit.* ♦ *The musicians entered the pit from a room underneath the stage.* **4. pit against** *tv.* + *prep. phr.* to place someone or something in competition with someone or something else. ♦ *The champion was pitted against the young contender.* ♦ *I pitted my wits against the computer in a game of chess.* **5.** *tv.* to remove ② from fruit. ♦ *Max pitted the peach and then ate it.* ♦ *Are these chocolate-covered cherries pitted?*

pitch ['pɪtʃ] **1.** *tv.* to toss something to someone. ♦ *Pitch the ball to me and I will pitch it back.* ♦ *Lisa pitched a rock into the pond.* **2.** *tv.* [in baseball] to toss or throw a ball toward the batter. ♦ *Lisa pitched the ball, and Bob swung at it and missed.* ♦ *Don't pitch it so hard!* **3.** *tv.* to toss or throw someone or something. ♦ *The motion of the ship pitched the passenger against the wall.* ♦ *The farmer pitched the hay into the wagon with a pitchfork.* **4.** *iv.* [in baseball] to throw a baseball toward a batter; to be a pitcher. ♦ *John injured his wrist and could no longer pitch.* ♦ *My older brother pitches in the major leagues.* **5.** *iv.* [for a ship] to plunge up and down; [for the front of a ship] to rise and fall in rough water. ♦ *The ship pitched on the stormy sea.* ♦ *The heavy waves and wind caused the ship to pitch.* **6.** *n.* [in baseball] the movement of the ball from the pitcher toward the batter or the throw that propels the ball toward the batter. ♦ *The batter swung at the ball even though the pitch was wide.* ♦ *The catcher caught the fast pitch.* **7.** *n.* slope; the amount that something is slanted. (No plural form in this sense.) ♦ *The ball rolled down the driveway because of the driveway's steep pitch.* ♦ *It was hard to install shingles on the roof because of its pitch.* **8.** *n.* a speech that is used to persuade someone to do something or to promote something that is for sale. ♦ *Your sales pitch has impressed me. I'll buy two of these.* ♦ *John needs to work on his pitch, because he's not very persuasive.* **9.** *n.* the measure of highness or lowness of a sound. (No plural form in this sense.) ♦ *The singer's pitch is half a note too high.* ♦ *A note is flat if its pitch is too low.* **10.** *n.* the standard number of vibrations each second that makes a certain tone; the standard musical sound for a given note. ♦ *The pitch of A above middle C is 440 vibrations each second.* ♦ *Please sing exactly on this pitch, which is middle C.* **11.** *n.* a black substance made from tar, used to cover roofs. (No plural form in this sense.) ♦ *The workers covered the roof with pitch.* ♦ *On extremely hot days, pitch can become sticky.* **12. pitch a tent** *idiom* to erect a tent at a campsite. ♦ *The campers pitched their tent in a clearing in the woods.* ♦ *I pitched my tent next to a large oak tree.* **13. pitch black** *idiom* very black; as black as ⑪. ♦ *The hearse* *was pitch black.* ♦ *The bandit rode on a pitch black horse and wore black clothing.* **14. pitch camp** *idiom* to set up or arrange a campsite. ♦ *We pitched camp near the stream.* ♦ *Two campers went ahead of us to pitch camp while it was still light.* **15. pitch dark** *idiom* very dark; as dark as ⑪. ♦ *I couldn't see anything outside because it was pitch dark.* ♦ *The room was pitch dark, and I couldn't find the light switch!* **16. pitch in (and help)** *idiom* to get busy and help with something. ♦ *Pick up a paintbrush, and pitch in and help.* ♦ *Why don't some of you pitch in? We need all the help we can get.* **17. pitch someone a curve (ball)** *idiom* to surprise someone with an unexpected act or event. ♦ *You really pitched me a curve ball when you said I had done a poor job. I did my best.* ♦ *You asked Tom a hard question. You certainly pitched him a curve.*

pitcher ['pɪtʃ ɚ] **1.** *n.* the baseball player who pitches the baseball toward the other team's batters. ♦ *Do you think the pitcher can strike this batter out?* ♦ *The catcher threw the baseball back to the pitcher.* **2.** *n.* a tall container with a handle, used for serving liquids. ♦ *I poured iced tea from the pitcher for my guests.* ♦ *Bill carried water to the dinner table in a pitcher.* **3.** *n.* The contents of ②. ♦ *Do you think two pitchers of lemonade will be enough?* ♦ *I watered the plant with a pitcher of water.*

pitchfork ['pɪtʃ fork] *n.* a large tool shaped like a fork, used for moving hay, fodder, or other plant materials. ♦ *The farmer threw hay into the stable with a pitchfork.* ♦ *Jimmy hurt himself when he fell on the sharp prongs of the pitchfork.*

piteous ['pɪt i əs] *adj.* causing pity; worthy of pity. (Adv: *piteously.*) ♦ *The unhappy woman's piteous crying made Max rush to help her.* ♦ *The piteous look on Anne's face showed that she had heard the bad news.*

pitfall ['pɪt fɔl] *n.* a hidden or unexpected danger; a mistake that is easy to make. ♦ *Lisa was not aware of all the pitfalls she would encounter on her new job.* ♦ *You can avoid many of the common pitfalls people experience in buying a new house if you will hire a lawyer to help you.*

pithy ['pɪθ i] *adj.* full of meaning but using few words. (Adv: *pithily.* Comp: *pithier;* sup: *pithiest.*) ♦ *I enjoyed hearing the old man's pithy comments on the mayor and the police chief.* ♦ *Her speech was short and pithy.*

pitiful ['pɪt ə ful] **1.** *adj.* causing pity; worthy of pity; piteous. (Adv: *pitifully.*) ♦ *Many children orphaned during the war lived pitiful lives.* ♦ *The volunteer doctor helped the many pitiful people who suffered from serious diseases.* **2.** *adj.* worthless; worthy of contempt. (Adv: *pitifully.*) ♦ *The teacher gave the student's pitiful assignment a failing grade.* ♦ *You've made a pitiful attempt to wash these windows. There are streaks of dirt all over the glass!*

pitiless ['pɪt i ləs] *adj.* lacking pity; without pity; not showing mercy. (Adv: *pitilessly.*) ♦ *The pitiless thief beat the old man he was robbing.* ♦ *The pitiless miser gave no money to charity.*

pittance ['pɪt ns] *n.* a very small amount of something, especially money. (No plural form in this sense.) ♦ *The migrant workers received a pittance for their work.* ♦ *I refuse to work for a pittance. I want a good salary.*

pity ['pɪt i] **1.** *n.* a feeling of sorrow caused by seeing or learning about the suffering of other people; sympathy. (No plural form in this sense.) ♦ *Because of the pity she has for the poor, Anne became a social worker.* ♦ *The rich man was moved by pity and gave the charity a large donation.* **2.** *n.* a reason to feel regret; something to be sorry for. (No plural form in this sense.) ♦ *What a pity that you lost your job!* ♦ *It's such a pity that you can't go home for the holidays.* **3.** *tv.* to be sorry for someone or something; to feel ① for someone or something. ♦ *Anne pitied the victims of the war.* ♦ *I pitied the poor children of the cruel parents.* **4. take pity on someone** *idiom* to feel pity for someone. ♦ *I took pity on the hungry puppy and gave it some food.* ♦ *The owner of the house took pity on us and let us come in out of the rain.*

pivot ['pɪv ət] **1.** *n.* something that bears the weight of a person or thing that is turning, rocking, or rotating. ♦ *The kitchen shelf rested on a pivot that allowed it to turn in either direction.* ♦ *The seesaw rests on a pivot that allows it to rock up and down.* **2.** *iv.* [for someone or something] to turn, rock, or rotate on ①. ♦ *John pivoted to face the person behind him.* ♦ *This shelf pivots so that things in the back can be brought forward.*

pivotal ['pɪv ə təl] *adj.* very important; being a crucial turning point in a series of events. (Adv: *pivotally.*) ♦ *A British actor played the pivotal role of the detective.* ♦ *My parents' advice was pivotal in my decision to go to college.*

pizza ['pit sə] **1.** *n.* a food made of a baked disk of dough covered with spicy tomato sauce, cheese, and perhaps other foods. (No plural form in this sense. Number is expressed with *slice(s) of pizza.*) ♦ *I ordered pizza with pepperoni and mushrooms.* ♦ *Would you rather have pizza or hamburgers tonight?* **2.** *n.* a kind of round, flat pie made as in ①. ♦ *We ordered two pizzas for lunch.* ♦ *Half the pizza has onions, and the other half does not.*

pl See plural.

placard ['plæk ɚd] *n.* a poster; a large printed notice that is in a public place or carried about for people to see. ♦ *A placard on the wall stated that smoking wasn't allowed.* ♦ *Many activists carried placards at the protest march.*

placate ['ple ket] *tv.* to make someone or some creature less angry. ♦ *I placated the angry dog by throwing him some meat.* ♦ *John placated his landlord by paying half of the overdue rent.*

place ['ples] **1.** *n.* a position in space; a location; a certain area. ♦ *I led the police to the place where I'd seen the body.* ♦ *Anne put the clean dishes in their places.* **2. place setting** See setting ④. **3.** *n.* a house or apartment; a location where one lives. ♦ *Let's go back to my place after dinner.* ♦ *Would you like to visit my new place?* **4.** *n.* a position in relation to other positions in a numbered series. ♦ *The swimmer who won first place got a gold medal.* ♦ *I finished in last place because I had stumbled on the racetrack.* **5.** *tv.* to put something in a certain position; to put something on a certain surface. ♦ *I placed the milk in the refrigerator.* ♦ *Please place my drink on the table next to my salad.* **6.** *tv.* to remember when and where you have encountered someone or something in the past. ♦ *I'm sorry, I just can't place you.* ♦ *I know who you're talking about, but I can't place the face.* **7. feel out of place** *idiom* to feel that one does not belong in a ①. ♦ *I feel out of place at formal dances.* ♦ *Bob and Anne felt out of place at the picnic, so they went home.* **8. in place of someone or something** *idiom* instead of someone or something; as a substitute for someone or something. ♦ *I changed my mind. I want a red one in place of the blue one.*

♦ *John came to help in place of Max, who was sick.* **9. not one's place** *idiom* not one's role to do something. ♦ *It was not my place to criticize my boss.* ♦ *It was Bill's place to ask the questions, not yours.* **10. place an order** *idiom* to submit an order. ♦ *My secretary placed an order for a new computer.* ♦ *I placed my order only yesterday.* **11. take place** *idiom* to happen. ♦ *When will the party take place?* ♦ *The accident took place on the highway near the airport.*

placebo [plə 'si bo] *n.* a substance, usually in pill form, given to a person as medicine, but which actually contains no medicine. (Latin for 'I shall please'. Pl in *-s* or *-es*.) ♦ *Placebos are given to healthy patients who think they're sick to make them think they are being treated with medicine.* ♦ *Researchers use placebos to compare the effects of an actual drug in some people with the effects of the absence of the drug in other people.*

placement ['ples mənt] **1.** *n.* the placing of someone or something; putting someone or something somewhere. (No plural form in this sense.) ♦ *The placement of the grand piano in the corner required four strong movers.* ♦ *Bill helped with the placement of the decorations for the party.* **2.** *n.* the location where someone or something has been placed. (No plural form in this sense.) ♦ *The map shows the placement of each of the houses in the subdivision.* ♦ *The architect could not decide on the placement of the fountain in relation to the sidewalk.* **3.** *n.* the process of finding jobs for people; getting people hired in jobs. (No plural form in this sense.) ♦ *My college helps its graduates with placement.* ♦ *Placement is becoming an important service that more and more colleges offer.*

placenta [plə 'sɛn tə] *n.* the organ that connects a fetus to the inside of the uterus and passes nourishment from the mother to the fetus. (See also umbilical cord.) ♦ *The placenta is expelled from the womb after childbirth.* ♦ *After the birth, the placenta was examined by a pathologist.*

placid ['plæs ɪd] *adj.* calm; peaceful; hard to excite or arouse. (Adv: *placidly.*) ♦ *The raft floated on the placid lake.* ♦ *The baby looks so placid and content after she has been fed.*

plagiarism ['ple dʒə rɪz əm] *n.* copying something that is written by someone else and pretending that it is one's own work. (No plural form in this sense.) ♦ *The student was expelled from college for committing plagiarism.* ♦ *The famous author was accused of plagiarism by a book reviewer.*

plagiarize ['ple dʒə raɪz] **1.** *tv.* to copy something that someone else has written and pretend that it is one's own work. ♦ *The student was expelled for plagiarizing another student's term paper.* ♦ *Mary accused Bob of plagiarizing his article.* **2.** *iv.* to copy what other people write and pretend that it is one's own work. ♦ *Anne was too lazy to write a paper, so she plagiarized.* ♦ *The author plagiarized by not citing his sources.*

plague ['pleg] **1. the plague** *n.* an epidemic; a disease that kills people and is quickly spread. (No plural form in this sense. Treated as singular.) ♦ *The plague has killed millions through the centuries.* ♦ *The plague was transmitted by infected rats.* **2. plague with** *tv.* + *prep. phr.* to annoy someone with repeated questions, problems, etc. ♦ *The customer plagued the clerk with petty concerns.* ♦ *The bothersome student plagued the teacher with questions.*

plaid ['plæd] **1.** *n.* a design of stripes that cross each other at right angles. ♦ *Our kitchen wallpaper is a bright plaid.* ♦ *Mary's school uniform has a red plaid on the skirt.* **2.** *adj.* <the adj. use of ①.> ♦ *Our kitchen wallpaper has a plaid design.* ♦ *Anne wore a plaid skirt to the party.*

plain ['plen] **1.** *n.* a flat area of land; a prairie. ♦ *Before it was farmland, this county was a vast plain.* ♦ *Buffalo used to roam across the plains.* **2.** *adj.* obvious; easy to see or understand; evident. (Adv: *plainly.* Comp: *plainer;* sup: *plainest.*) ♦ *His distress was plain to see.* ♦ *It was plain to everyone at the office that Bill would soon be fired for his bad performance.* **3.** *adj.* simple; not complicated; not decorated; not adorned or encumbered. (Adv: *plainly.* Comp: *plainer;* sup: *plainest.*) ♦ *John wore a plain white shirt to work.* ♦ *Anne's presentation was rather plain, but it was easy to understand.* **4.** *adj.* not extremely good looking; average looking. (Adv: *plainly.* Comp: *plainer;* sup: *plainest.*) ♦ *I wear makeup because I think I have a plain face.* ♦ *My face is sort of plain, but I have a nice smile!* **5.** *adv.* simply, clearly; obviously. (Colloquial.) ♦ *Bob was plain foolish to go swimming during the thunderstorm.* ♦ *John didn't play basketball because he was just plain too short.* **6. plain English** *phr.* very direct and clear language; English that anyone can understand. ♦ *I told him what he was to do in plain English.* ♦ *That was too complicated. Please tell me again, this time in plain English.*

plaintiff ['plen tɪf] *n.* someone who sues someone else; someone who brings a lawsuit against someone else. ♦ *The plaintiff is suing the defendant for $100,000.* ♦ *The judge instructed the plaintiff to speak loudly so the jury could hear.*

plaintive ['plen tɪv] *adj.* [of sound] sad or expressing sadness. (Adv: *plaintively.*) ♦ *I heard the plaintive cry of a bird in the night, and it made me sad.* ♦ *The refugee's plaintive weeping was very depressing.*

plan ['plæn] **1.** *n.* the ideas for a future action or event; a detailed schedule for doing something. ♦ *The mayor announced his plans for reducing crime.* ♦ *Anne and John told me of their plans to get married.* **2. plans** *n.* a set of drawings of a house or building before it is built, used to help someone build the building. (Treated as plural.) ♦ *The client approved the designer's preliminary plans.* ♦ *An architect drafted the plans for the new office building.* **3.** *n.* a program or structure that provides a benefit to workers. ♦ *Our health plan pays for almost all our medical costs.* ♦ *The company has a retirement plan for all its workers.* **4.** *tv.* to make ① for an event. ♦ *Bob planned a party for his sister's birthday.* ♦ *Mary began planning her wedding a year in advance.* **5.** *iv.* to arrange [something] in advance. ♦ *My parents never plan very far in advance.* ♦ *Mary spent weeks planning for the party.* **6. plan to** *iv.* + *inf.* to intend to do something. ♦ *Do you plan to go to town today?* ♦ *Bill doesn't plan to go to college.*

plane ['plen] **1.** *n.* a flat surface. ♦ *Any three points define a plane.* ♦ *The intersection of two planes is a line.* **2.** *n.* an airplane. ♦ *What time will your plane land in Cleveland?* ♦ *Mary took a plane from New York to London.* **3.** *n.* a tool equipped with a blade that is scraped over wood to make it flat or smooth. ♦ *The carpenter ran the plane over the wooden surface.* ♦ *I used a plane to smooth the wooden railing.* **4.** *tv.* to make something flat or smooth by using ③. ♦ *The carpenter planed the railing before nailing it in place.*

♦ *When I planed the board, wood shavings fell to the ground.*

planet ['plæn ɪt] *n.* a huge sphere of matter that circles a single star in a permanent orbit. ♦ *Earth is the planet that we live on.* ♦ *Some planets are orbited by moons.*

planetarium [plæn ɪ 'tɛr i əm] *n.* a building containing a room with a dome-shaped ceiling onto which lights representing stars and planets are projected. ♦ *The class went to the planetarium to learn about constellations.* ♦ *The astronomer encouraged people to visit their local planetarium.*

planetary ['plæn ə tɛr i] **1.** *adj.* of or about a planet. ♦ *The astronomer studied the planetary radiation belt.* ♦ *Tiny rockets were sent to each planet in a study of planetary atmospheres.* **2.** *adj.* moving in an orbit around a central element. (Figurative on ①.) ♦ *The machine has a set of planetary gears that sometimes get out of alignment.* ♦ *This model shows the planetary motion of the moon.*

plank ['plæŋk] **1.** *n.* a board; a long, thin, narrow, flat piece of wood. ♦ *The theater's stage was made of wooden planks.* ♦ *Tom nailed some planks to a pair of logs to make a raft to float on the lake.* **2.** *n.* an issue or policy that a political party officially supports. (A plank ① in the party platform ③.) ♦ *The independent candidate disagreed with many of the planks in the platforms of both parties.* ♦ *Bob agreed with all the planks of his party's platform.*

plant ['plænt] **1.** *n.* a stationary living thing that takes its food from the soil or other substance that supports it. ♦ *Plants include trees, shrubs, flowers, grasses, cereals, and vines and usually have roots, stems, and leaves.* ♦ *Anne watered the plants in her yard.* **2.** *n.* a factory. ♦ *There was a small explosion at the plant today.* ♦ *My father worked at the car plant for 30 years.* **3.** *tv.* to put a seed or a small ① in the ground so that it will grow; to place [the seeds or young plant of] a crop into the soil. ♦ *The farmer planted carrot seeds each spring.* ♦ *The gardener planted roses in the flower garden.* **4. plant with** *tv. + prep. phr.* to cultivate and furnish an area of ground with seeds or small plants. ♦ *The farmer planted the field with corn.* ♦ *I planted the flower garden with roses.* **5.** *tv.* to place someone or something firmly in position. (Figurative on ③.) ♦ *The soldiers planted their feet solidly on the ground.* ♦ *Plant yourself in that doorway, and don't let anyone leave.* **6.** *tv.* to secretly place something somewhere. ♦ *Max planted a toy gun in his brother's luggage.* ♦ *A corrupt cop planted the evidence against me in my car.*

plantation [plæn 'te ʃən] *n.* a very large farm, especially in tropical or hot areas, where cotton, tobacco, rubber, coffee, or other tropical plants are grown. ♦ *In the 1800s, Mary's family owned a large cotton plantation.* ♦ *Many poorly paid workers toiled on the banana plantation.*

planter ['plæn tɚ] *n.* a container that holds plants. ♦ *The large plant outgrew its small planter.* ♦ *I put some petunia seeds in the outdoor planter.*

plaque ['plæk] **1.** *n.* a decorative panel with a message or a list of people's names printed on it. ♦ *Each employee is given a small plaque upon retirement.* ♦ *A bronze plaque listed the club members who died in the war.* **2.** *n.* a film of material on the teeth, in which bacteria live. (No plural form in this sense.) ♦ *Plaque can be removed by brushing one's teeth regularly.* ♦ *The dentist said my teeth were discolored due to plaque.*

plasma ['plæz mə] *n.* the liquid part of blood in which the red and white blood cells float. (No plural form in this sense.) ♦ *The patient needed more plasma during the difficult surgery.* ♦ *A technician removed some blood in order to study my plasma.*

plaster ['plæs tɚ] **1.** *n.* powdered gypsum; a mixture of lime, gypsum, water, and sand, which hardens when it dries. (No plural form in this sense.) ♦ *Plaster is put on walls, ceilings, and other surfaces.* ♦ *Plaster fell from the ceiling when something heavy crashed on the floor above.* **2.** *tv.* to apply ① to something. ♦ *The worker plastered the hole in the wall.* ♦ *The landlord plastered the ceiling and then painted it.* **3.** *tv.* to spread something thickly on a surface. (Informal. Figurative on ②.) ♦ *The cook plastered the tomato sauce onto the pizza.* ♦ *Make sure you plaster the glue onto the poster carefully.*

plasterboard ['plæs tɚ bord] *n.* a thin board made of plaster pressed between two layers of heavy paper, used for walls. (No plural form in this sense.) ♦ *The partition between the two offices was made of plasterboard.* ♦ *The angry man punched his fist through the plasterboard.*

plastered ['plæs tɚd] *adj.* covered with plaster. ♦ *I painted the plastered wall after the plaster was dry.* ♦ *The newly plastered ceiling was smooth and white.*

plastic ['plæs tɪk] **1.** *n.* an artificial material, made from resin or other materials, formed into different shapes. (No plural form in this sense.) ♦ *Things made from plastic won't rust.* ♦ *The lenses in my eyeglasses are made of plastic.* **2.** *adj.* made of ①. ♦ *At the picnic, Anne served juice in plastic glasses.* ♦ *The plastic spoon melted against the edge of the hot pan.* **3.** *adj.* [of something] easily molded or shaped. (Adv: *plastically* […ɪk li].) ♦ *The sculptor molded the plastic clay with her hands.* ♦ *Shape the wax figure while it is still warm and plastic.*

plate ['plet] **1.** *n.* an almost flat, round dish for holding food. ♦ *A plate's edge is slightly raised so that food does not roll off of it.* ♦ *Anne put some corn on my plate next to my potatoes.* **2.** *n.* a sheet of metal or glass. ♦ *The workers broke a plate of glass while installing new windows.* ♦ *The spy's car was reinforced with metal plates.* **3.** *n.* a sheet of metal or glass that is covered with a substance that is sensitive to light, used in photography to make pictures. ♦ *In the darkroom, I covered the photographic plate with a chemical solution.* ♦ *The scratch on the plate caused an imperfection in all the photos.* **4.** *n.* a denture; a fixture for the mouth that holds false teeth. ♦ *Grandpa's upper plate fell into his soup.* ♦ *Grandma took out her upper and lower plates when she went to bed.* **5.** *n.* a full-page picture in a book. ♦ *The art book included twelve four-color plates.* ♦ *A number of color plates depicted an ancient map of the world.* **6.** *n.* [in baseball] the base over which the batter stands when the ball is pitched; home plate. ♦ *The catch stands behind the plate.* ♦ *Susan stepped up to the plate and rested the bat on her shoulder.* **7. (license) plate** *n.* a rectangular panel, showing a car's license number, that is put on the rear and, in some states, the front of a car. ♦ *My plates have expired, and I have to get new ones.* ♦ *The new license plate is aluminum.* **8.** *tv.* to give one sort of metal a thin coating of a more valuable metal. ♦ *Our cutlery is plated with silver.* ♦ *The worker plated each piece of silverware with a new layer of silver.*

plateau [plæ 'to] **1.** *n.* a flat area of land that is raised up higher than the surrounding land. (From French.) ♦ *Most of northern Arizona is a huge plateau.* ♦ *The mountain climbers reached the first plateau by nightfall.* **2.** *iv.* [for a number or a measurement] to reach a higher level and then remain unchanged. ♦ *Her fever plateaued at 103 degrees and began to fall.* ♦ *Sales plateaued in the first quarter of the year.* **3. hit a plateau** *idiom* to reach a higher level of activity, sales, production, output, etc., and then stop and remain unchanged. ♦ *When my sales hit a plateau, my boss gave me a pep talk.* ♦ *When production hit a plateau, the company built a new factory.*

platform ['plæt form] **1.** *n.* a flat structure that is higher than the area around it, especially one that people can occupy standing or sitting. ♦ *The guest of honor tripped on the steps up to the platform.* ♦ *The guards prevented the fans from climbing onto the platform where the famous singer was performing.* **2.** *n.* the flat surface next to a railroad track where people get on and off trains. ♦ *The next train to Vienna leaves from platform 6.* ♦ *I set my luggage on the platform while I was waiting for the train.* **3.** *n.* a formal statement of the ideas and policies of a political party. ♦ *The Republicans and the Democrats have different platforms.* ♦ *Mary was upset with the philosophy of her party's platform.*

platinum ['plæt n əm] **1.** *n.* a valuable silvery, metallic chemical element used especially in jewelry, in parts for automobile exhaust systems, and to refine petroleum. (No plural form in this sense.) ♦ *The atomic symbol of platinum is Pt, and its atomic number is 78.* ♦ *The expensive ring was plated with platinum.* **2.** *adj.* made of ①. ♦ *John's platinum watch was very expensive.* ♦ *The jeweler repaired Mary's platinum necklace.*

platitude ['plæt ɪ tud] *n.* a true statement that is obvious, unoriginal, or uninteresting. ♦ *The reviewer attempted to say something good about the book but only gave a list of polite platitudes.* ♦ *My advisor's hollow platitudes weren't very helpful.*

Platonic [plə 'tɑn ɪk] **1.** *adj.* of or about the teachings of Plato, an ancient Greek philosopher. (Adv: *Platonically* [...ɪk li].) ♦ *The philosophy students discussed Platonic principles.* ♦ *The professor's argument involved Platonic reasoning.* **2. platonic** *adj.* of or about a relationship between two people that is not sexual; having affection for someone without sexual desire. (Adv: *platonically* [...ɪk li].) ♦ *Do you think men and women can have platonic relationships?* ♦ *Anne sees Bob a lot on the weekends, but they both say it's completely platonic.*

platoon [plə 'tun] *n.* a group of soldiers that is a part of a company. ♦ *The platoon was stationed four miles from the front lines.* ♦ *The platoon was ordered to attack the enemy at dawn.*

platter ['plæt ɚ] **1.** *n.* a large plate used for serving food. ♦ *I used a large platter to carry the roast to the table.* ♦ *The cook arranged the slices of baked ham on the platter.* **2.** *n.* the contents of ①. ♦ *I'm so hungry I could eat that whole platter of fried pork chops!* ♦ *Twenty platters of roast pork were served at the banquet.*

plausible ['plɔz ə bəl] *adj.* believable; seeming to be true or right. (Adv: *plausibly.*) ♦ *The jury believed the witness's plausible testimony.* ♦ *Susie's story about how she lost her books sounded plausible, but it wasn't actually true.*

play ['ple] **1.** *n.* fun; recreation; something that is done for fun or amusement. (No plural form in this sense.) ♦ *Bill watched his grandchildren at play.* ♦ *The children's play was interrupted by dinner.* **2.** *n.* one movement or action in a game or sport. ♦ *That last play was good, and it scored our team a point.* ♦ *The football team planned its next play in the huddle.* **3.** *n.* a piece of writing that is written as a series of lines that people say, for performance in a theater. ♦ *William Shakespeare wrote many plays.* ♦ *The director auditioned fifty actors for the cast of a new play.* **4.** *n.* a performance of ③. ♦ *The theater operator cancelled the play because of the bad weather.* ♦ *I have tickets to see a play tonight.* **5.** *iv.* [for a sound-making device] to operate or reproduce sounds that have been recorded previously. ♦ *I danced around the room while the record played.* ♦ *The radio played while I washed the dishes.* **6.** *iv.* to perform on the stage or in public; to perform. ♦ *Lisa was eager to play in front of a large audience.* ♦ *The actors played for the senior citizens' group.* **7.** *iv.* [for a performance] to be performed; [for a movie] to be shown. ♦ *The opening-night performance played to a full audience.* ♦ Hamlet *will play at that theater for two weeks, beginning tomorrow.* **8.** *iv.* to take one's turn in a game; to lay down a card in a card game. ♦ *After Mary played, I laid down all of my cards.* ♦ *John thought for a long time before he played.* **9.** *iv.* to perform [on a musical instrument as in ⑮]. ♦ *Bill has played in a band all his life.* ♦ *The violinist stopped playing when the music fell off the stand.* **10.** *iv.* to have fun; to amuse oneself; to be active in a sport or game. ♦ *The children played while the adults watched television.* ♦ *Jimmy and Susie got dirty when they played in the mud.* **11. play with** *iv.* + *prep. phr.* to play ⑩ [games] with someone or a group. ♦ *I love to play baseball. Can I play with your team?* ♦ *I am not good enough, and they won't let me play with them.* **12. play with** *iv.* + *prep. phr.* to toy with something; to fiddle with something. ♦ *Please don't play with that crystal vase.* ♦ *Stop playing with the television set. You'll break it.* **13.** *tv.* to perform a role in the theater or in a movie. ♦ *Bob plays tough guys in the movies.* ♦ *Anne played a leading role in the play.* **14.** *tv.* to take part in a certain game, sport, or activity; to participate in a certain game, sport, or activity. ♦ *Mary played softball in high school.* ♦ *John plays basketball every day after work.* **15.** *tv.* to make music with a musical instrument; to perform a particular piece of music on an instrument. ♦ *The pianist played a popular song on the piano.* ♦ *I can play "Home, Sweet Home" on the clarinet.* **16.** *tv.* to perform on a musical instrument. ♦ *Bill played the trumpet for the orchestra.* ♦ *Can you play the piano while I sing?* **17.** *tv.* [for an electronic device] to process tapes, records, or CDs in a way that produces the sounds or pictures that have been recorded. ♦ *David played tapes while he drove to work.* ♦ *Anne played the movie that she had rented.* **18.** *tv.* to cause an electronic device to produce sounds and pictures as in ⑰. ♦ *I want to play the new CD that I just bought.* ♦ *I can't play this record on my player!* **19.** *tv.* to cause an electronic device to reproduce a particular recording or video as in ⑰. ♦ *I bought a new recording of my favorite symphony, and I want to play it.* ♦ *Which movie are you playing now? I don't recognize it.* **20. at play** *phr.* [at this moment] involved in ①. ♦ *The children are at play, and I am doing household chores.* ♦ *Whether I am at work or at play, I try to be pleasant to people.* **21. foul play** *idiom* illegal or dishonest activity. ♦ *The police investi-*

gating the death suspect that foul play was involved. ♦ *Each student got an A on the test, and the teacher imagined it was the result of foul play.* **22. play both ends (against the middle)** *idiom* to scheme in a way that pits two sides against each other for one's own gain. ♦ *I told my brother that Mary doesn't like him. Then I told Mary that my brother doesn't like her. They broke up, so now I can have the car this weekend. I succeeded in playing both ends against the middle.* ♦ *If you try to play both ends, you're likely to get in trouble with both sides.* **23. play cat and mouse (with someone)** *idiom* to capture and release someone over and over; to pursue and then and withdraw over and over. ♦ *The police played cat and mouse with the suspect until they had sufficient evidence to make an arrest.* ♦ *Tom had been playing cat and mouse with Anne. Finally she got tired of it and broke up with him.* **24. play fast and loose (with someone or something)** *idiom* to act carelessly, thoughtlessly, and irresponsibly. ♦ *I'm tired of your playing fast and loose with me. Leave me alone.* ♦ *Bob got fired for playing fast and loose with the company's money.* **25. play ignorant** *idiom* to pretend to be ignorant [of something]. ♦ *I played ignorant even though I knew about the surprise party.* ♦ *John played ignorant when I asked him if he knew who had been on the telephone.* **26. play innocent** *idiom* to pretend to be innocent and not concerned. ♦ *There is no need to play innocent. I know you broke the lamp!* ♦ *John is playing innocent, and he knows more than he is telling us.* **27. play a (practical) joke on someone** See joke ⑧.

playboy ['ple bɔɪ] *n.* a man who loves to be entertained and have fun, especially with beautiful women. ♦ *When Anne found out that Bob was a playboy who really cared nothing for her, she refused to see him again.* ♦ *The playboy's wife demanded a divorce.*

player ['ple ɚ] **1.** *n.* someone who plays a game or sport. ♦ *My cousin is a player for the local baseball team.* ♦ *How many players are on each team?* **2.** *n.* someone who plays a particular musical instrument. ♦ *I was a trumpet player in my high-school's marching band.* ♦ *The conductor rehearsed the piece with the flute players.* **3.** *n.* an actor. ♦ *Mary was one of the best players in the stage show.* ♦ *The audience applauded the players after the show.* **4.** *n.* something that plays a recording. (Compare with recorder ③.) ♦ *Our record player needs a new needle.* ♦ *I listened to the cassette on my portable tape player.*

playful ['ple fʊl] **1.** *adj.* liking to play; full of fun. (Adv: *playfully.*) ♦ *The playful puppy licked my face.* ♦ *Playful children ran through the park, laughing and singing.* **2.** *adj.* funny; humorous; not serious. (Adv: *playfully.*) ♦ *My playful joke backfired and got me in trouble.* ♦ *Bob gave his friend a playful punch in the arm.*

playgoer ['ple go ɚ] *n.* someone who goes to theaters to see plays. ♦ *The playgoers applauded the cast at the end of the show.* ♦ *Our theater group surveyed playgoers for their opinions.*

playground ['ple graʊnd] **1.** *n.* an outdoor place for children to play. ♦ *Our school's playground has swings and a slide.* ♦ *Jimmy fell and hurt himself at the playground.* **2.** *adj.* <the adj. use of ①.> ♦ *The city purchased new playground equipment for the park.* ♦ *The playground supervisor blew his whistle at the fighting kids.*

playmate ['ple met] *n.* a child with whom another child plays. ♦ *Susie went to her playmate's house for lunch.* ♦ *Mary told her son's playmates that they had to leave at five o'clock.*

play-off ['ple ɔf] *n.* a sporting event, leading to a championship, that is played between the winning teams of two different divisions or leagues of teams. ♦ *My hometown football team made it to the play-offs this year.* ♦ *In baseball, the winners of the play-offs go to the World Series.*

playpen ['ple pɛn] *n.* an enclosure in which small children can play safely. ♦ *Mary put her son in his playpen while she cooked dinner.* ♦ *Susie was crying in her playpen, so her father gave her a hug.*

play school ['ple skul] *n.* a preschool; a school for children who are not old enough to go to kindergarten. ♦ *Jimmy went to play school on the days that his parents both worked.* ♦ *Anne picked up her children at play school at noon.*

plaything ['ple θɪŋ] *n.* a toy; something that is played with. ♦ *Jimmy must put his playthings away before he goes to bed.* ♦ *The puppy grabbed the plaything from Susie's hand.*

playwright ['ple rɑɪt] *n.* the author of a play; someone who writes plays. ♦ *William Shakespeare is a very famous English playwright.* ♦ *Many of that playwright's plays have been turned into movies.*

plea ['pli] **1.** *n.* a request; an appeal. ♦ *We asked for better law enforcement, but the legislature ignored our pleas.* ♦ *The group of citizens made a plea for lower tax rates.* **2.** *n.* a statement in court in which one declares one's guilt or innocence. ♦ *The defendant entered a plea of not guilty.* ♦ *A plea of guilty from a defendant means that he will spend time in prison.*

plead ['plid] **1. plead for** *iv., irreg.* + *prep. phr.* to beg for something; to ask for something. (Pt/pp: *pleaded* or pled.) ♦ *The beggar pleaded for some spare change.* ♦ *The condemned man pled for mercy.* **2.** *tv., irreg.* to declare in court that one is guilty or not guilty before the trial actually begins. ♦ *The defendant pled not guilty.* ♦ *Everyone expected the defendant to plead guilty.* **3.** *tv., irreg.* to claim something as an excuse. (Takes a clause.) ♦ *The teenager pled that his car had run out of gas as an excuse for being late.* ♦ *Mary pled that she did not have enough time to be as careful as she should.*

pleasant ['plɛz ənt] **1.** *adj.* [of something] enjoyable and pleasing. (Adv: *pleasantly.*) ♦ *I spent a pleasant weekend in the mountains.* ♦ *Jane played some pleasant music during dinner.* **2.** *adj.* [of someone] friendly and nice. (Adv: *pleasantly.*) ♦ *Thankfully, my roommate is a very pleasant person.* ♦ *The pleasant clerk helped me find what I was looking for.*

please ['pliz] **1.** *interj.* <a word used to make requests or commands more polite.> ♦ *Would you shut the door, please? It's cold in here.* ♦ *Could you please pass the salt?* **2.** *tv.* to cause someone to be happy or satisfied. ♦ *When we heard the loud applause, we knew the performance had pleased the audience.* ♦ *If your work pleases your boss, you may get a promotion.* **3. you please** *idiom* whatever pleases you; whoever please you. ♦ *Go to the kitchen and eat whatever you please.* ♦ *Do as you please. I'm not your boss.*

pleasing ['pliz ɪŋ] *adj.* pleasant; giving pleasure. (Adv: *pleasingly.*) ♦ *This is a very pleasing shade of blue.* ♦ *Because the meal was so pleasing, I left a large tip for the server.*

pleasurable ['plɛʒ ə rə bəl] *adj.* causing pleasure; enjoyable. (Adv: *pleasurably.*) ♦ *My vacation in Hawaii was very pleasurable, and cheap, too.* ♦ *The pleasurable massage helped the tense woman relax.*

pleasure ['plɛʒ ɚ] **1.** *n.* a feeling of happiness because of something that one likes; enjoyment; an enjoyable feeling or emotion. (No plural form in this sense.) ♦ *Some people devote themselves to seeking pleasure.* ♦ *The happily married couple brought pleasure to each other's life.* **2.** *n.* someone or something that causes enjoyment, happiness, or joy. ♦ *One of my favorite pleasures is smoking my old pipe.* ♦ *Bob thinks chocolate is one of life's small pleasures.*

pleat ['plit] *n.* a flat fold in a fabric, especially one fold in a series of folds, as found in skirts, draperies, and curtains. ♦ *The skirt's pleats were ironed, making nice, sharp creases.* ♦ *The small child hid among the pleats of the heavy draperies.*

plebiscite ['plɛb ə sɑɪt] *n.* a direct vote by all the voters of an area, state, or nation on an important issue. ♦ *The proposal was to be decided by plebiscite.* ♦ *The proposed law was defeated in the plebiscite.*

pled ['plɛd] a pt/pp of plead.

pledge ['plɛdʒ] **1.** *n.* a promise; a vow; a statement that one will do something. ♦ *The politician broke most of his campaign pledges.* ♦ *I made a pledge to stop smoking.* **2.** *n.* someone who is in the process of joining an organization, especially a fraternity or a sorority, but who is not yet a member. ♦ *Anne was a pledge at the most popular sorority on campus.* ♦ *The fraternity boys humiliated the pledges.* **3. pledge to** *iv.* + *inf.* to vow to do something. ♦ *The candidate pledged to cut taxes if elected.* ♦ *Bob pledged to stop smoking again.* **4.** *tv.* to promise something. ♦ *The workers pledged their support for the strike.* ♦ *We pledged $10 toward the total amount.*

plentiful ['plɛn tɪ fʊl] *adj.* abundant; having more than enough; ample. (Adv: *plentifully.*) ♦ *There was a plentiful supply of food at the party.* ♦ *When jobs are plentiful, the unemployment rate is low.*

plenty ['plɛn ti] **1.** *n.* abundance. (No plural form in this sense.) ♦ *We have plenty, so we donate a lot of money to charity.* ♦ *This year we had a good crop and experienced plenty as we never had before.* **2. plenty of something** *phr.* lots of something; an abundance of something; enough of something. ♦ *I have plenty of candy. Do you want some?* ♦ *This project is giving me plenty of trouble.* **3.** *adj.* enough; almost too much. (Not prenominal.) ♦ *Four slices of pizza will be plenty for me.* ♦ *I don't need any more soup. That's plenty.*

plethora ['plɛθ ə rə] *n.* a very large amount; an excessive amount. (No plural form in this sense.) ♦ *The picnic was ruined by a plethora of ants.* ♦ *The senator was bombarded by a plethora of questions.*

pleurisy ['plɚ ə si] *n.* an inflammation of the tissue that surrounds the lungs. (No plural form in this sense.) ♦ *If you've got pleurisy, each breath is painful.* ♦ *The doctor prescribed some antibiotics for my pleurisy.*

pliable ['plɑɪ ə bəl] **1.** *adj.* easily bent; flexible; not rigid. (Adv: *pliably.*) ♦ *The sheet of plastic becomes very pliable when it is warmed.* ♦ *I crumpled the pliable plastic into a little ball.* **2.** *adj.* [of someone] easily influenced and not stubborn. (Figurative on ①. Adv: *pliably.*) ♦ *Bob is much more pliable than his brother, Tom, who is very stubborn.* ♦ *Students should be exposed to new ideas when they are young and their minds are pliable.*

pliers ['plɑɪ ɚz] *n.* a tool with rough jaws, used to grasp objects. (Usually treated as plural. Number expressed with *pair(s) of pliers.*) ♦ *The carpenter kept two pairs of pliers in his toolbox.* ♦ *John looked in the garage for some pliers.*

plight ['plɑɪt] *n.* a difficult, serious, or bad situation. ♦ *I cried when I heard of the refugees' plight.* ♦ *Max sympathized with Bill, who was in a horrible plight.*

plod ['plɑd] **1.** *iv.* to progress slowly, with some difficulty. ♦ *He is so tired, he is just plodding.* ♦ *This hike is too difficult for her. She is plodding.* **2. plod along** *iv.* + *adv.* to walk or move along slowly but dependably. ♦ *Mary plodded along, even though she was tired.* ♦ *My baby brother plodded along behind me as I walked to the garden.* **3. plod through** *iv.* + *prep. phr.* to progress through something slowly. ♦ *Because I was sick, I only plodded through my work today.* ♦ *The students were all plodding through the tough algebra assignment.*

plodder ['plɑd ɚ] *n.* someone who makes progress overly slowly. ♦ *The plodder finished the project six months past the deadline.* ♦ *The teacher gave the plodders some extra help.*

plot ['plɑt] **1.** *n.* the story of a movie, book, opera, television show, play, etc. ♦ *Bob told me the whole plot of the movie he'd just seen.* ♦ *The TV show's plot was so predictable that I knew what would happen next.* **2.** *n.* a secret plan to do something wrong or illegal; a conspiracy. ♦ *The agents thwarted the terrorist's plot to kill the president.* ♦ *The rebels' plot to kidnap the prince was foiled.* **3.** *n.* a small garden or part of a garden; a small area of land. ♦ *Anne grew corn and carrots in her garden plot.* ♦ *My house sits on a half-acre plot of land.* **4.** *iv.* to plan in secret; to conspire. ♦ *Jealous of Bob's success, John plotted against him.* ♦ *The terrorists plotted late into the night.* **5.** *tv.* to plan in secret to do something. ♦ *The rebels plotted the overthrow of the government.* ♦ *The terrorists plotted the assassination of the ruler.* **6.** *tv.* to determine the position of something on a map, chart, or graph. ♦ *I plotted my journey to Toronto on the map.* ♦ *The driver plotted the easiest route to the village.* **7.** *tv.* to draw a graph, map, or chart. ♦ *David plotted a graph that showed how sales are increasing.* ♦ *The cartographer plotted a new map of South America.*

plotter ['plɑt ɚ] *n.* a machine that marks points, lines, or curves on a graph. ♦ *The plotter was capable of drawing in four different colors.* ♦ *The plotter graphed difficult equations accurately.*

plow ['plɑʊ] **1.** *n.* a farm tool made of a heavy metal blade used to break up and turn over soil. ♦ *Two mules pulled the plow over the field.* ♦ *The farmer used a tractor to pull the plow.* **2.** *n.* a large, curved blade in front of a vehicle that is used to move snow off a road or path. ♦ *The plow pushed the snow into the street.* ♦ *After clearing the road, John removed the plow from the front of his truck.* **3.** *n.* a vehicle equipped with ②. ♦ *The main road was not passable until the plow cleared the snow off of it.* ♦ *The plows cleared the main roads before rush hour.* **4.** *iv.* to use ①. ♦ *The farmer was plowing in the field when it began to rain.* ♦ *The workers plowed all day but couldn't finish by dark.* **5.** *tv.* to cut into land, making furrows for planting crops, with ①. ♦ *The farmer plowed the field before it rained.* ♦ *John plowed 90 acres today.* **6.** *tv.* to clear a road or path of snow with ②. ♦ *Anne plowed the snow from her driveway.* ♦ *The store owner plowed the snow from the sidewalk.* **7. plow through something** *idiom* to work through something with determination. (On ⑥.) ♦ *She plowed through the book to learn everything she could.* ♦ *Billy plowed through dinner and ran outside to play.*

ploy ['plɔɪ] *n.* a statement that is said or an action that is done in order to gain an advantage, especially if it is deceptive. ♦ *Her claim that she was lost was just a ploy to get into my house.* ♦ *The teacher ignored Bob's ploys to improve his grades.*

pluck ['plʌk] **1.** *tv.* to remove the feathers from a bird; to remove hairs from the body of a person or an animal. ♦ *Mary plucked the feathers off the chicken.* ♦ *John plucked the hair from his nose.* **2.** *tv.* to clean a bird of its feathers. ♦ *Mary plucked the chicken.* ♦ *Of course, the duck is dead when you pluck it.* **3.** *tv.* to pull something from some place. ♦ *The diver plucked the pearl from the oyster's shell.* ♦ *The father plucked the young child away from the dog.* **4.** *n.* courage; bravery. (No plural form in this sense.) ♦ *The queen praised the young knight's pluck.* ♦ *Because of the police officer's pluck, the robbery was thwarted.*

plug ['plʌg] **1.** *n.* a small device for closing a hole; a stopper. ♦ *The carpenter filled the hole with a small plug of wood.* ♦ *I put a plastic plug in the hole in the wall.* **2. (electric) plug** *n.* a device used to attach a lamp or appliance to an electrical outlet. ♦ *I pulled the toaster's plug from the socket before repairing it.* ♦ *John damaged the lamp's electrical plug when he stepped on it.* **3. (electric) plug** *n.* an electrical outlet or receptacle. (Informal.) ♦ *The electrician installed two new plugs in my bedroom.* ♦ *I moved my computer so that it would be closer to the electrical plug.* **4. (drain) plug** *n.* something used to cover or seal a hole or drain. ♦ *I pulled the plug from the drain so that the tub would empty.* ♦ *Dave pushed the drain plug in so he could fill the sink with water.* **5. (fire) plug** *n.* a fire hydrant. (Informal.) ♦ *The city repainted all of the plugs bright yellow.* ♦ *It's illegal to park in front of a fire plug.* **6.** *n.* a statement made while speaking on television or radio that encourages people to buy something or do something. ♦ *The guest on the talk show made a plug for her new book.* ♦ *The columnist made a plug for his favorite snack food.* **7. plug into** *tv.* + *prep. phr.* to attach an electrical appliance to an electrical outlet. ♦ *John plugged his stereo into an extension cord.* ♦ *Anne plugged the computer into the outlet.* **8. plug in** *tv.* + *adv.* to connect something to something else with an electrical plug. ♦ *Please plug your stereo in.* ♦ *Plug in this plug so the toaster will work.* **9. plug (up)** *tv.* (+ *adv.*) to cover or seal a hole or a drain with a plug. ♦ *Anne plugged the drain before she filled the tub with water.* ♦ *The carpenter plugged up the hole with a wooden peg.* **10.** *tv.* to mention a product and to encourage people to buy it. ♦ *The announcer plugged a new brand of dog food.* ♦ *The author plugged her new book on the talk show.* **11.** *iv.* to keep trying; to keep plodding. (Informal.) ♦ *My teacher encouraged me to keep plugging away at the assignment.* ♦ *David plugged along, trying to finish the job before 5 o'clock.*

plum ['plʌm] **1.** *n.* a fruit with a smooth skin and a soft, sweet, juicy pulp with a large pit. ♦ *A prune is a plum that has been dried.* ♦ *Anne bit into a ripe, juicy plum.* **2.** *n.* something that is good or desirable; something that is the best that is available. (Informal.) ♦ *The reporter was glad that her new assignment was a real plum.* ♦ *My boss gave me a plum of a task because I was a good worker.* **3.** *n.* a deep purple color. ♦ *My bathroom is decorated in plum and black.* ♦ *The actress wore plum to the awards ceremony.* **4.** *adj.* deep purple in color. ♦ *The fancy invitations were printed with plum ink.* ♦ *The actress wore a plum dress to the awards ceremony.*

plumage ['plum ɪdʒ] *n.* a bird's feathers. (No plural form in this sense.) ♦ *The plumage of the male peacock is very bright and colorful.* ♦ *The bird watcher distinguished many birds by their plumage.*

plumb ['plʌm] **1.** *n.* a small lead weight tied to the end of a string. ♦ *Eve lowered the plumb to the well's bottom to measure its depth.* ♦ *The plumb hung straight down, perpendicular to the earth's surface.* **2.** *tv.* to try to determine what something means; to try to understand something. ♦ *John plumbed the meaning of the confusing article.* ♦ *Anne plumbed her professor's words for meaning.* **3.** *adj.* vertical; straight up and down. ♦ *The carpenter used a level to make sure the wall was plumb.* ♦ *The carpenter marked a plumb line from the ceiling to the floor.* **4.** *adv.* vertically; straight up and down. ♦ *The string hung plumb from the top of the well.* ♦ *The farmer rested the hoe plumb against the wall.*

plumber ['plʌm ɚ] *n.* someone who is trained to install and repair sewer pipes, water pipes, and fixtures such as sinks, toilets, bathtubs, and drains. ♦ *The plumber fixed the leaky pipe under the sink.* ♦ *I hired a professional plumber to replace my old tub.*

plumbing ['plʌm ɪŋ] **1.** *n.* the work that a plumber does. (No plural form in this sense.) ♦ *The carpenter also did a little plumbing on the side.* ♦ *I fixed the leak because I'm pretty good at plumbing.* **2.** *n.* water and sewer pipes and fixtures. (No plural form in this sense.) ♦ *Our plumbing froze twice last winter.* ♦ *The rural family finally got indoor plumbing last year.*

plume ['plum] **1.** *n.* a feather, especially a bright, colorful one. ♦ *A few bright green plumes lay in the bottom of the parrot's cage.* ♦ *A bright red plume was attached to Anne's hat.* **2.** *n.* something that looks like a feather, especially a cloud of smoke or a jet of water. ♦ *Plumes of smoke billowed from the burning factory.* ♦ *A plume of water jetted up from the fountain.*

plummet ['plʌm ɪt] *iv.* to plunge; to drop quickly and suddenly. ♦ *The company's stock prices plummeted after it declared bankruptcy.* ♦ *The meteorite plummeted to earth.*

plump ['plʌmp] **1.** *adj.* chubby; somewhat fat; filled out. ♦ *The plump student decided to exercise more often.* ♦ *The plump turkey was juicy and delicious.* **2. plump down** *iv.* + *adv.* to fall with force; to drop with force. ♦ *Bob plumped down into his chair to watch TV.* ♦ *Anne plumped down onto her bed and fell asleep.* **3. plump down** *tv.* + *adv.* to drop something with force; to cause something to fall with force. ♦ *Sue plumped herself down onto the couch and watched TV.* ♦ *David plumped the heavy groceries down on the counter.*

plunder ['plʌn dɚ] **1.** *tv.* to rob someone or some place. ♦ *My apartment was plundered while I was on vacation.* ♦ *The pirates plundered the cargo ship at sea.* **2.** *n.* loot; things that are stolen. (No plural form in this sense.) ♦ *The thief sold his plunder at a pawn shop.* ♦ *The police found the plunder in the robber's car.* **3.** *n.* stealing; robbery. (No plural form in this sense.) ♦ *The enemy's plunder of the town was condemned by the citizens.* ♦ *The plunder of the royal necklace enraged the queen.*

plunge ['plʌndʒ] **1.** *n.* a dive; a jump into water. ♦ *The dog took a plunge into the cold lake.* ♦ *I took a plunge off the high diving board.* **2.** *iv.* to dive into a liquid. ♦ *The dog plunged into the cold lake.* ♦ *The swimmer plunged into the pool.* **3. plunge into** *iv.* + *prep. phr.* to enter hastily or suddenly into a situation. (Figurative on ②.) ♦ *John plunged into his decision without thinking about it.* ♦ *The country plunged into a depression.* **4. plunge into** *tv.* + *prep. phr.* to cause something to enter a liquid. ♦ *Bob plunged the dirty dishes into the dishwater.* ♦ *I plunged the clothes into the tub of water.* **5. plunge into** *tv.* + *prep. phr.* to cause someone or something to enter a situation. ♦ *My boss plunged my whole department into the middle of the crisis.* ♦ *The bad economy plunged the country into a depression.*

plunging ['plʌndʒ ɪŋ] *adj.* [of the neckline of a shirt or blouse] that is very low, especially one that shows part of a woman's breasts. (Adv: *plungingly.*) ♦ *The actress wore a dress with a plunging neckline.* ♦ *Anne's neckline was so plunging that she had to wear a shawl.*

plural ['plɚ əl] **1.** *n.* <the grammatical form of a part of speech that refers to more than one thing or person.> (No plural form in this sense. Abbreviated "pl" here.) ♦ *In English,* [z], [s], *or* [əz] *is added to regular nouns to form the plural.* ♦ *The plural of* child *is* children. **2.** *adj.* <the adj. use of ①.> ♦ *In English, plural nouns often end in* -s. ♦ *The plural form of English verbs is the same as the bare infinitive.*

pluralism ['plɚ əl ɪz əm] *n.* the quality of a society made of people with many different ethnic, cultural, religious, and physical characteristics. (No plural form in this sense.) ♦ *Pluralism is very evident in New York City.* ♦ *The bigot was afraid of changes caused by pluralism.*

plurality [plʊ 'ræl ə ti] **1.** *n.* the largest number of votes received by a candidate in an election. (No plural form in this sense. Compare with majority.) ♦ *That candidate received a plurality of the votes in the election.* ♦ *If the plurality of votes is over 50%, then it is also a majority.* **2.** *n.* the difference between the largest number of votes received by a candidate in an election and the number of votes received by the candidate who came in second place. (No plural form in this sense.) ♦ *The winner was elected to office with a plurality of 2,000 votes.* ♦ *The recount narrowed the winner's plurality to only 500 votes.* **3.** *n.* [of words] being plural. (No plural form in this sense.) ♦ *The plurality of English nouns is usually marked by* -s. ♦ *The plurality of words like* deer *and* sheep *depends on context.*

pluralize ['plɚ ə laɪz] *tv.* to express a word in its plural form; to make a word plural. ♦ *If you pluralize the word* cat, *you get* cats. ♦ *The editor pluralized the nouns standing for more than one thing.*

plus ['plʌs] **1.** *prep.* in addition to; added to. (Symbolized by "+".) ♦ *2 + 4 = 6 is to be read "Two plus four equals six."* ♦ *Any number plus zero equals that number.* **2.** *conj.* and also. ♦ *Let's eat now. I'm hungry. Plus, I have to leave in 20 minutes.* ♦ *I'd like to order eggs and bacon, plus some toast.* **3.** *adj.* above zero; [marking a number] greater than zero. (Symbolized as "+".) ♦ *Yesterday it was minus 5, but today it warmed up to plus 10.* ♦ *After the first round, Bob had scored −25, and Mary, +30.* **4.** *n.* an advantage; an extra. ♦ *A cellular phone is a plus in the business world.* ♦ *As a plus, the baker gave me an extra doughnut for free.*

plush ['plʌʃ] **1.** *n.* a fabric like velvet but softer with longer threads. (No plural form in this sense.) ♦ *The couch was covered with plush.* ♦ *The heavy stage curtains were made from a deep wool plush.* **2.** *adj.* <the adj. use of ①.> (Adv: *plushly.* Comp: *plusher;* sup: *plushest.*) ♦ *Susie rubbed the soft, plush stuffed animal against her cheek.* ♦ *I like to walk barefoot across the plush carpet.* **3.** *adj.* lavish; luxurious; expensive. (Adv: *plushly.* Comp: *plusher;* sup: *plushest.*) ♦ *The highly paid lawyer lived in a very plush apartment.* ♦ *The rich couple spent a plush two-week vacation in the Bahamas.*

plutonium [plu 'ton i əm] *n.* a radioactive chemical element used in nuclear reactors, spacecraft, and pacemakers. (No plural form in this sense.) ♦ *The atomic symbol of plutonium is Pu.* ♦ *Plutonium's atomic number is 94.*

ply ['plaɪ] **1.** *n.* a layer of thickness. (Hyphenated after a number.) ♦ *Two-ply tissue is softer than one-ply tissue.* ♦ *One-ply paper towels don't clean spills as well as two-ply kinds.* **2.** *tv.* to work doing one's job, especially at one's trade. ♦ *John plied his trade as a mechanic.* ♦ *Anne plies her skills as an independent bookkeeper.* **3. ply with** *tv.* + *prep. phr.* to provide someone with a lot of something, such as food or drink. ♦ *John plied his date with a lot of alcohol.* ♦ *The gracious host plied his guests with good food.*

plywood ['plaɪ wʊd] *n.* a wooden panel made of several thin sheets of wood that are glued together. (No plural form in this sense.) ♦ *Plywood is often sold in pieces that are eight feet long and four feet wide.* ♦ *The store owner put plywood in the frame in place of the broken window.*

P.M. ['pi 'ɛm] *abbr.* after noon. (Used to show that a time is between noon and midnight. From Latin *post meridiem,* meaning 'after midday.' Also **P.M.** and **p.m.**) ♦ *Ninety minutes after noon is 1:30 P.M.* ♦ *Jane's flight gets to the airport at 4:23 P.M.*

pneumatic [nu 'mæt ɪk] *adj.* operated by air pressure. (Adv: *pneumatically* [...ɪk li].) ♦ *The workers used a pneumatic drill to break up the asphalt.* ♦ *The bank teller put my deposit in the pneumatic tube, which sent it to the main bank.*

pneumonia [nə 'mon jə] *n.* an infection of the lungs involving fluid in the lungs. (No plural form in this sense.) ♦ *Elderly people are prone to pneumonia.* ♦ *John didn't take care of his cold, and it developed into pneumonia.*

poach ['potʃ] **1.** *tv.* to hunt for animals or fish illegally. ♦ *Many elephants are poached for their tusks.* ♦ *John poached a deer from his neighbor's property.* **2.** *tv.* to cook something (especially eggs and fish) in water or other liquid that is just above the boiling point. ♦ *The chef* *poached the eggs and fried the potatoes.* ♦ *After the fish were poached, the chef sprinkled pepper on them.* **3.** *iv.* to be cooked in water or other liquid that is just above the boiling point. ♦ *Dinner will be ready in 10 minutes. The fish is still poaching.* ♦ *The eggs poached for three minutes, and then I served them.*

poached ['potʃt] *adj.* cooked in water or other liquid that is just above the boiling point. ♦ *Mary ordered poached salmon for dinner.* ♦ *I sprinkled some pepper on my poached eggs.*

pocket ['pɑk ɪt] **1.** *n.* a small cloth bag that is sewn into clothing and is used to hold things, such as a wallet or keys. ♦ *My house keys fell through a hole in my pocket.* ♦ *The police searched my pockets for stolen property.* **2.** *n.* a small amount of something that is separated from other amounts of it; an isolated amount of something. ♦ *A small pocket of gold was found in the mine.* ♦ *This neighborhood is a pocket of wealth in an otherwise poor city.* **3.** *adj.* small enough to fit in ①; meant to be put in ①. ♦ *I gave my pocket change to the charity.* ♦ *I looked at my pocket watch to check the time.* **4.** *tv.* to put something in one's pocket ①. ♦ *I pocketed the change that the cashier gave me.* ♦ *Anne pocketed the pamphlet that the politician gave her.* **5.** *tv.* to steal something by putting it in one's pocket ①. ♦ *The thief pocketed the candy bar and walked out of the store.* ♦ *The clerk saw the teenager pocket a valuable watch.* **6. have someone in one's pocket** *idiom* to have control over someone. ♦ *Don't worry about the mayor. She'll cooperate. I've got her in my pocket.* ♦ *John will do just what I tell him. I've got him and his brother in my pocket.*

pocketbook ['pɑk ɪt bʊk] *n.* a woman's purse. ♦ *Anne forgot where she left her pocketbook.* ♦ *Mary put her change into her pocketbook.*

pocketful ['pɑk ɪt fʊl] *n.* the contents of a pocket. ♦ *I put a pocketful of coins on the table.* ♦ *The baker carried a pocketful of rye in her apron.*

pocketknife ['pɑk ɪt naɪf] *n., irreg.* a small knife whose blade folds into the handle and which is small enough to be carried in one's pocket. (Pl: pocketknives.) ♦ *I trimmed my fingernails with my pocketknife.* ♦ *The thief threatened the clerk with his pocketknife.*

pocketknives ['pɑk ɪt naɪvz] pl of pocketknife.

pockmark ['pɑk mɑrk] *n.* a small pit in the skin from acne, chickenpox, smallpox, or some other infection. ♦ *John has some pockmarks where he had picked his chickenpox.* ♦ *Sue covered her pockmarks with heavy makeup.*

pod ['pɑd] *n.* a long, soft, narrow shell that holds the seeds of certain plants, such as peas and beans. ♦ *The cook removed the peas from the pods.* ♦ *The large pod contained over ten peas.*

podiatrist [pə 'daɪ ə trəst] *n.* a doctor who is trained to treat feet. ♦ *I complained to my podiatrist about my bunions.* ♦ *The podiatrist removed my corns with laser surgery.*

podiatry [pə 'daɪ ə tri] *n.* the medical study and treatment of the feet. (No plural form in this sense.) ♦ *A foot doctor is a specialist in podiatry.* ♦ *The medical school offered several classes in podiatry.*

podium ['po di əm] *n.* a tall, narrow structure that a speaker, performer, or conductor stands behind. ♦ *The lecturer arranged her notes on the podium.* ♦ *The podium held the conductor's copy of the music.*

poem ['po əm] *n.* a piece of writing in a form that sometimes rhymes and often has a rhythm, usually expressing feelings, emotions, or imagination. ♦ *My English teacher read us a poem that she had written.* ♦ *Mary wrote a romantic poem to her best friend.*

poet ['po ɪt] *n.* someone who writes poetry. ♦ *The poet read his poetry aloud in the café.* ♦ *The literary journal rejected the young poet's work.*

poetic [po 'ɛt ɪk] **1.** *adj.* [of thoughts] expressed as a poem. (Adv: *poetically* [...ɪk li].) ♦ *Inside the card was a poetic expression of love.* ♦ *The poetic wedding invitation was printed on lavender paper.* **2.** *adj.* <the adj. form of poetry.> ♦ *The poet used poetic license in referring to her eyes as two bright suns.* ♦ *My writing teacher explained the different poetic structures.*

poetry ['po ə tri] **1.** *n.* a poem; a collection of poems. (No plural form in this sense.) ♦ *Jane read a collection of Japanese poetry.* ♦ *We studied Emily Dickinson's poetry in English class.* **2.** *n.* the art of writing poems. (No plural form in this sense.) ♦ *The popular author branched out into poetry.* ♦ *Not many people have made their livings from poetry.*

poignant ['poɪn jənt] *adj.* causing intense sadness, pity, or sympathy. (From French. Adv: *poignantly.*) ♦ *The dead man's best friend delivered a poignant eulogy.* ♦ *We watched a poignant film about refugees.*

poinsettia [poɪn 'sɛt i ə] *n.* a plant having stems of green leaves topped with specialized leaves of white, pink, or bright red. ♦ *Poinsettias are native to Central America.* ♦ *Poinsettias are very popular during the winter holiday season.*

point ['poɪnt] **1.** *n.* the sharp end of something. ♦ *I accidentally poked myself with the point of the needle.* ♦ *I broke the pencil point by writing too hard.* **2.** *n.* the main idea of something; the purpose of something. ♦ *I don't understand the point of this article.* ♦ *The lecturer reiterated the point of his speech.* **3.** *n.* one idea, argument, or statement in a series of ideas, arguments, or statements. ♦ *The first point I'd like to talk about is punctuality.* ♦ *The last point the report addressed was the budget.* **4.** *n.* a certain position in space or moment in time; a certain degree or position of something. ♦ *"At what point in time did you find the body?" the inspector asked.* ♦ *From this point on, I vow to stop drinking.* **5.** *n.* [in geometry] the place where two lines cross each other. ♦ *Any two points define a line.* ♦ *Any three points not in a line define a plane.* **6.** *n.* a dot; the decimal point. ♦ *3.14159 is read "Three point one four one five nine."* ♦ *Bob had a temperature of ninety-nine point four.* **7.** *n.* a feature, trait, or ability of someone or something. ♦ *John's best points are his friendliness and generosity.* ♦ *Anne's good points far outweigh her bad ones.* **8.** *n.* a unit of scoring in a game. ♦ *A football team scores six points for each touchdown.* ♦ *Anne beat David in cards by 200 points.* **9.** *n.* a helpful hint; a pointer. ♦ *The advice columnist printed some helpful household points.* ♦ *I asked the author for some points on getting published.* **10.** *n.* a unit for measuring how big a piece of type is in printing. ♦ *The author's name was set in 32-point type.* ♦ *Six-point type is almost too small to read comfortably.* **11.** *n.* a piece of land that sticks out into water. ♦ *There's a light-*

house at the end of the point. ♦ *The pier extended twenty yards into the lake from the point.* **12.** *tv.* to aim someone at someone or something; to direct someone to someone or something. ♦ *John pointed the tourists in the right direction.* ♦ *The receptionist pointed me toward the bathroom.* **13. point out** *tv.* + *adv.* to indicate something; to identify something and focus the discussion on it. ♦ *I would like to point out that you are twelve minutes late.* ♦ *The guide pointed out the house of a famous movie star as we passed by it.* **14.** *iv.* to indicate the location of someone or something by directing one's finger toward the location. ♦ *I asked John where Anne was, and he pointed toward the door.* ♦ *Mary pointed at the dog that had bitten her.* **15.** *iv.* to be facing in a certain direction. ♦ *The front of my car is pointing south.* ♦ *If you're pointing north, east is to your right.* **16. come to the point** *idiom* to get to the important part [of something]. ♦ *He has been talking a long time. I wish he would come to the point.* ♦ *We are talking about money, Bob! Get to the point.* **17. miss the point** *idiom* to fail to understand the ②, purpose, or intent. ♦ *I'm afraid you missed the point. Let me explain it again.* ♦ *You keep explaining, and I keep missing the point.* **18. point of view** *idiom* a way of thinking about something; [someone's] viewpoint; an attitude or expression of self-interest. ♦ *From my point of view, all this talk is a waste of time.* ♦ *I can understand her point of view. She has made some good observations about the problem.*

point-blank ['poɪnt 'blæŋk] **1.** *adv.* [of a gun fired] from a very close position. ♦ *The soldier fired at the enemy point-blank.* ♦ *The government agent shot the terrorist point-blank.* **2.** *adv.* straightforwardly; bluntly; directly. (Figurative on ①.) ♦ *John asked me point-blank how old I was.* ♦ *I told my boss point-blank that I wanted to quit.* **3.** *adj.* shot from a very close range; shot from a very close position. ♦ *The gunpowder burns indicated the shot was point-blank.* ♦ *The criminal was killed instantly by point-blank gunfire.* **4.** *adj.* very straightforward; blunt; directly. (Figurative on ③.) ♦ *My coworker ignored my point-blank request to stop smoking.* ♦ *The teacher issued a point-blank order to be quiet.*

pointed ['poɪn tɪd] **1.** *adj.* having a point; sharp; sharpened to a point. ♦ *My sweater got caught on the pointed picket fence.* ♦ *Jimmy jabbed the wood in the fire with a pointed stick.* **2.** *adj.* straightforward; directed in an obvious way. (Adv: *pointedly.*) ♦ *The mayor ignored the reporter's pointed questions.* ♦ *Bill's pointed criticism was rude and insulting.*

pointer ['poɪn tɚ] **1.** *n.* a helpful hint; a suggestion. ♦ *The columnist gave some pointers on applying for work.* ♦ *I asked John for some pointers on how to improve my golf score.* **2.** *n.* a long, thin stick used to point at a chalkboard, a map, a chart, or other things by someone who is speaking in front of people. ♦ *The general's pointer indicated the enemy's position on the map.* ♦ *The teacher referred to the equation with a pointer.* **3.** *n.* a kind of dog that is used in hunting. ♦ *The pointer indicated that there was a duck in the bushes.* ♦ *The pointer fetched the pheasant that John had shot.*

pointless ['poɪnt ləs] *adj.* having no purpose; having no reason; having no meaning; useless. (Adv: *pointlessly.*) ♦ *I stopped reading the article because it was pointless.* ♦ *I left the pointless movie after fifteen minutes.*

poise ['poɪz] **1.** *n.* the self-confident way one holds one's head or body; one's composure. (No plural form in this sense.) ♦ *Anne's poise indicated that she was feeling very powerful.* ♦ *Bob's lack of poise indicated that he was being threatened.* **2.** *tv.* [for one] to balance oneself in readiness; [for something] to balance itself in readiness. (Reflexive.) ♦ *The cat poised itself to jump.* ♦ *Anne poised herself to win the race.* **3. poised for something** *idiom* ready for something; in the right position and waiting for something. ♦ *The cat stared at the mouse, poised for action.* ♦ *The army was poised for battle.* **4. poised to do something** *idiom* ready to do something; in the right position to do something. ♦ *The cat is poised to jump on the mouse.* ♦ *The army is poised to attack at dawn.*

poison ['poɪ zən] **1.** *n.* a substance that can injure or kill a living creature, especially if eaten, drunk, breathed in, or absorbed through the skin. (No plural form in this sense.) ♦ *Bob and Sue kept poisons away from their child's reach.* ♦ *Mary baited the rat trap with poison.* **2.** *tv.* to kill someone or something with ①. ♦ *My landlord poisoned the rats in my attic.* ♦ *Anne was sent to jail for poisoning her husband.* **3.** *tv.* to put ① in something, especially food, in order to kill someone or something. ♦ *The cruel child poisoned the cat's food.* ♦ *The cook poisoned the rich man's breakfast.* **4.** *tv.* to have a harmful effect on someone or something; to corrupt someone or something. (Figurative on ③.) ♦ *The child's mind was poisoned by television.* ♦ *The government propaganda poisoned the citizens' minds.*

poisoning ['poɪ zən ɪŋ] *n.* a case of illness or death caused by poison. ♦ *Accidental poisonings can often be prevented.* ♦ *The coroner attributed the cause of death to poisoning.*

poisonous ['poɪ zən əs] *adj.* toxic; containing poison. (Adv: *poisonously.*) ♦ *John accidentally ate some poisonous mushrooms.* ♦ *The liquid flowing from the factory was poisonous.*

poke ['pok] **1.** *n.* a push with one's finger, fist, or elbow, or with a blunt object. ♦ *The man got my attention with a poke of his finger.* ♦ *Anne woke me up with a gentle poke.* **2.** *tv.* to push someone or something with one's finger, fist, or elbow, or with a blunt object. ♦ *Jimmy poked his brother in the ribs with his finger.* ♦ *Mary poked the logs in the fire.* **3.** *tv.* to move something through something by poking. ♦ *Anne poked her pencil through a piece of paper.* ♦ *John poked a pin through a piece of cork.* **4. poke a hole in something; poke a hole through something** *phr.* to make a hole by pushing something through something; to push something through a hole. ♦ *The carpenter poked a hole in the wall with a nail.* ♦ *The fisherman poked a hole through the ice with a pick.* **5. buy a pig in a poke** *idiom* to purchase or accept something without having seen or examined it. (This *poke* means 'bag' or 'sack.') ♦ *Buying a car without test-driving it is like buying a pig in a poke.* ♦ *He bought a pig in a poke when he ordered a diamond ring by mail.*

poker ['pok ɚ] **1.** *n.* a long, narrow metal rod that is used to move logs or coal in a fire. ♦ *Anne moved the burning logs around with a poker.* ♦ *I hung the poker in its stand next to the fireplace.* **2.** *n.* a card game where players win by having cards with the highest value. (No plural form in this sense.) ♦ *Bill won $100 playing poker last night.* ♦ *In poker, having four aces is very good.*

Poland ['po lənd] See Gazetteer.

polar ['po lɚ] *adj.* of or about the areas near the north or south pole. ♦ *The scientist studied the melting of the ice in the polar lands.* ♦ *The polar climate is very cold.*

polar bear ['po lɚ bɛr] *n.* a large white bear that lives on land surrounding the north pole. ♦ *The hunter killed the polar bear for its fur.* ♦ *The polar bear captured a seal and ate it.*

polarity [pə 'lɛr ə ti] *n.* alignment regarding some scale or standard, such as positive and negative electrical charges. (No plural form in this sense.) ♦ *The polarity of the electrical outlet was wrong, and I got a nasty shock.* ♦ *In electrical wiring, polarity is shown by the different colors of wire.*

pole ['pol] **1.** *n.* a long, thin, solid tube of wood, steel, plastic, or other material. ♦ *The soldiers ran their country's flag up the pole.* ♦ *My fishing pole jerked when I had caught a fish.* **2.** *n.* the place where the imaginary line on which a planet spins meets the surface of the planet, at the north and south ends of the planet. (See axis.) ♦ *The astronomer examined the white areas on the Martian poles.* ♦ *I wanted to place a flag at the north pole, but someone had already done it.* **3.** *n.* either side of a magnet; either end of a magnet; one of the two strongest points of a magnet that either attracts or repels metal objects. ♦ *The positive poles of the two magnets repelled each other.* ♦ *The positively charged object clung to the magnet's negative pole.* **4. be poles apart** *idiom* to be very different; to be far from coming to an agreement. ♦ *Mr. and Mrs. Jones don't get along well. They are poles apart.* ♦ *They'll never sign the contract because they are poles apart.*

police [pə 'lis] **1. the police** *n.* people who have the authority to maintain law and order by arresting people who break the law. (No plural form in this sense. Treated as singular. Number is expressed with *police officer(s).*) ♦ *My apartment had been robbed, so I called the police.* ♦ *The police raced to the scene of the crime.* **2.** *tv.* to patrol an area; to control, regulate, or protect an area. ♦ *Guards with dogs police the shopping mall.* ♦ *The security guard policed the building lobby.* **3.** *tv.* to regulate or control people, their behavior, or their actions. ♦ *The government policed reading materials through censorship.* ♦ *The students were policed by the authoritarian principal.*

policeman [pə 'lis mən] *n., irreg.* a police officer; a male member of a police force. (Pl: policemen or police officers.) ♦ *The policeman rushed to the scene of the crime.* ♦ *The witness told the policemen what she had seen.*

policemen [pə 'lis mən] pl of policeman.

police officer [pə 'lis ɔ fə sɚ] *n.* a member of a police department; a policeman; a policewoman. ♦ *A police officer helped me find the way to the train station.* ♦ *There is a police officer in the car behind us.*

policewoman [pə 'lis wʊm ən] *n., irreg.* a female police officer; a female member of a police force. (Pl: policewomen or police officers.) ♦ *The policewoman handcuffed the robbery suspect.* ♦ *The female customer was searched by a policewomen.*

policewomen [pə 'lis wɪm ən] pl of policewoman.

policy ['pɑl ə si] *n.* a plan of action used by management or government; a regulation. (No plural form in this sense.) ♦ *My company enforces a strict no-smoking policy.* ♦ *I can't issue a refund without a receipt. It's the store's policy.*

polio ['po li o] *n.* an infection of the nerves of the spine which causes its victims to become unable to move. (No plural form in this sense.) ♦ *A vaccine against polio was developed in the 1950s.* ♦ *Mary uses a wheelchair because she was paralyzed by polio.*

polish ['pɑl ɪʃ] **1.** *n.* a substance that is used to make something shiny or glossy. (No plural form in this sense.) ♦ *I put black polish on my shoes and rubbed them till they shined.* ♦ *The maid rubbed the silverware with a special polish.* **2.** *n.* a shiny or glossy condition of a surface. (No plural form in this sense.) ♦ *I waxed the floor to give it a brighter polish.* ♦ *The snow and dirt destroyed my shoes' fine polish.* **3.** *tv.* to make a surface shiny or glossy, especially by rubbing it. ♦ *The maid polished the silverware carefully.* ♦ *Please polish your shoes before you go to the wedding.* **4.** *tv.* to improve something; to make something better or perfect; to refine something. (Figurative on ③.) ♦ *Jane polished her speech by practicing it over and over.* ♦ *The author polished her manuscript before mailing it to the editor.*

polished ['pɑl ɪʃt] **1.** *adj.* shiny; glossy. ♦ *I saw my reflection in the polished marble of the lobby.* ♦ *I placed the polished silverware on the table.* **2.** *adj.* perfected; made better; improved; refined. ♦ *The polished presentation of Jane's speech was very professional.* ♦ *The editor though the polished manuscript was a big improvement over the first one.*

polite [pə 'lɑɪt] *adj.* courteous; having good behavior; having good manners; doing things in a helpful and kind way. (Adv: *politely.*) ♦ *Tom is a polite host and always makes us feel at home.* ♦ *That was polite of you to let me go first.*

politeness [pə 'lɑɪt nəs] *n.* courteousness; good behavior and good manners. (No plural form in this sense.) ♦ *The clerk's unexpected politeness put me in a good mood.* ♦ *Politeness prevented me from asking the actress her age.*

politic ['pɑl ə tɪk] **1. body politic** *n.* a population considered as a political force. (Pl: bodies politic.) ♦ *The body politic voted the mayor out of office.* ♦ *The body politic lost faith in the corrupt government.* **2. politics** *n.* the business or management of government; the study of the management of government. (Treated as singular or plural.) ♦ *Mary entered politics because she wanted to help people.* ♦ *Because of poor politics, the agency was overstaffed.* **3. politics** *n.* someone's beliefs about political issues. (Treated as singular or plural.) ♦ *Whenever I discuss politics with John, we begin to argue.* ♦ *My mother said to not mention politics during dinner.*

political [pə 'lɪ tɪ kəl] *adj.* of or about politics, politicians, or government. (Adv: *politically* [...ɪk li].) ♦ *In the primaries, my vote was limited to one political party.* ♦ *The government shutdown was a major political crisis.*

politician [pɑl ə 'tɪ ʃən] *n.* someone who has been elected or appointed to a government office; a person whose business is politics. ♦ *The career politician had been in public office for 50 years.* ♦ *The politician voted to cut taxes.*

polka ['pol kə] **1.** *n.* a fast German, Czech, or Polish dance for couples, and the kind of music that usually accompanies it. ♦ *David picked up his accordion and began playing a polka.* ♦ *After John and Mary did the polka, they* *were out of breath.* **2.** *iv.* to dance ①. (Pt: *polkaed.*) ♦ *After John and Mary polkaed, they were out of breath.* ♦ *My Czech grandmother taught me how to polka.*

poll ['pol] **1.** *n.* a survey that determines the popular opinion about an issue. ♦ *The latest poll indicated the mayor's popularity was improving.* ♦ *This poll of smokers indicates which brands they prefer.* **2. polls** *n.* the places where people vote. (Treated as plural.) ♦ *Because of the snowstorm, the polls stayed open an extra hour.* ♦ *The election results were announced an hour after the polls closed.* **3.** *tv.* to ask someone questions as part of a survey. ♦ *The researcher polled 1,000 people about their eating habits.* ♦ *The magazine polled college students about their political beliefs.*

pollen ['pɑl ən] *n.* a yellow powder made by flowers that is part of the process of causing flowers to make seeds. (No plural form in this sense.) ♦ *Pollen can cause hay fever if you're allergic to it.* ♦ *The bee transported pollen from flower to flower.*

polling booth ['pol ɪŋ buθ] *n.* the enclosure, desk, or stand in a polling place where a person votes. ♦ *The voter patiently waited for the next available polling booth.* ♦ *Anne closed the curtain to the polling booth while she voted.*

polling place ['pol ɪŋ ples] *n.* the place where people vote. ♦ *My precinct's polling place is the school in the next block.* ♦ *To protect the voters, the police patrolled the polling places.*

pollster ['pol stɚ] *n.* someone who conducts a poll; someone who asks people questions about issues to determine the general opinion of a group of people. ♦ *The pollster surveyed 1,000 people about their reading habits.* ♦ *I told the pollster I didn't have any time to answer questions.*

pollute [pə 'lut] **1.** *tv.* to cause something to become dirty or impure. ♦ *The factory polluted the river with waste.* ♦ *The city's air was polluted with car exhaust.* **2.** *iv.* to make something dirty or impure. ♦ *The government regulates businesses that pollute.* ♦ *Anne rides a bike because cars pollute.*

polluted [pə 'lut ɪd] *adj.* dirty or impure. (Adv: *pollutedly.*) ♦ *The factory was ordered to clean the polluted river.* ♦ *The polluted air made me gag.*

pollution [pə 'lu ʃən] **1.** *n.* something that makes air, water, or land dirty, impure, unclean, or unhealthy. (No plural form in this sense.) ♦ *There is a great deal of pollution in city air.* ♦ *The river next to the factory was clogged with pollution.* **2.** *n.* making air, water, or land dirty, impure, unclean, or unhealthy. (No plural form in this sense.) ♦ *The factory was fined for the pollution of the river.* ♦ *The car company worked to reduce pollution by cars.*

polyandry [pə li 'æn dri] *n.* the practice or state of having more than one husband at the same time. (No plural form in this sense.) ♦ *Polyandry is practiced among certain animals.* ♦ *A woman who practices polyandry is guilty of bigamy.*

polyester ['pɑl i ɛs tɚ] **1.** *n.* a synthetic substance used to make paint, plastic, thread, and many other products. (No plural form in this sense.) ♦ *Thread made from polyester is used to make durable fabrics.* ♦ *The factory produced polyester for commercial use.* **2.** *adj.* made from ①. ♦ *Most polyester clothing doesn't need to be ironed.* ♦ *The bright colors of paint all had a polyester base.*

polygamy [pə 'lɪg ə mi] *n.* the practice or state of being married to more than one spouse at the same time. (No plural form in this sense.) ♦ *Polygamy is acceptable in some religions.* ♦ *A man who practices polygamy is guilty of bigamy.*

polygyny [pə 'lɪdʒ ə ni] *n.* the practice or state of having more than one wife at the same time. (No plural form in this sense.) ♦ *Polygyny is practiced in some cultures.* ♦ *A man who practices polygyny is guilty of bigamy.*

polyp ['pɑl əp] **1.** *n.* a tumor that grows on a mucous membrane, such as in the colon, in the nose, or on the vocal cords. ♦ *The doctor removed some polyps from David's colon.* ♦ *The biopsy revealed that my polyps were not cancerous.* **2.** *n.* a simple sea creature that has a hollow tube for a body and tentacles that direct food into its mouth opening. ♦ *The deep sea diver took photos of the colorful polyps.* ♦ *The oil spill destroyed an entire species of polyp.*

polysyllabic [pɑl i sɪ 'læb ɪk] *adj.* [of a word] having two or more syllables. (Adv: *polysyllabically* [...ɪk li].) ♦ *Many polysyllabic English words have a Latin or Greek source.* ♦ Library *is an example of a polysyllabic word.*

pomp ['pɑmp] *n.* formal and dignified behavior; displays of splendor accompanying an important event. (No plural form in this sense.) ♦ *Graduation ceremonies are full of pomp.* ♦ *With great pomp, the famous professor was awarded a Nobel prize.*

pompous ['pɑmp əs] *adj.* arrogant; too solemn; too formal; overly dignified; stuffy; too showy. (Adv: *pompously.*) ♦ *The pompous explorer bragged about his achievements.* ♦ *The pompous judge never let anyone else talk.*

pond ['pɑnd] *n.* a small body of water; a body of water smaller than a lake. ♦ *Ponds are generally shallower than lakes.* ♦ *The swans swam across the pond gracefully.*

ponder ['pɑn dɚ] **1.** *iv.* to think carefully; to consider. ♦ *Anne pondered for a week before deciding to move to New York.* ♦ *The student pondered for a moment before writing her answer.* **2.** *tv.* to think about something carefully; to consider something. ♦ *I pondered the company's offer very carefully.* ♦ *John pondered the pros and cons of the situation.*

ponderous ['pɑn dɚ əs] *adj.* slow and awkward, especially because of being large or heavy. (Adv: *ponderously.*) ♦ *The ponderous elephant plodded toward the river.* ♦ *The man was so ponderous that he could hardly walk up the stairs.*

pontoon [pɑn 'tun] *n.* a floating structure that can support a floating bridge or serve as the floating base of a boat or raft. ♦ *I steered the pontoon by pushing a pole against the lake bottom.* ♦ *During the flood, the pontoons that supported the bridge were washed out to sea.*

pony ['pon i] *n.* a small horse. ♦ *Mary rode her pony around the ranch.* ♦ *John combed the pony's mane.*

ponytail ['pon i tel] *n.* a bunch of hair tied at the back of the head, larger than a pigtail. ♦ *John cut his ponytail before interviewing at the law firm.* ♦ *Anne tied her ponytail with a red ribbon.*

poodle ['pud əl] *n.* a kind of dog that is small and has very curly fur. ♦ *David cut his poodle's coat once a month.* ♦ *The poodle snapped at my ankles when I walked by it.*

pool ['pul] **1.** *n.* a puddle of water or other liquid. ♦ *The rain collected in pools of water on the sidewalk.* ♦ *The dead body was found in a pool of blood.* **2. (swimming) pool** *n.* a container that holds water for people to swim or play in. ♦ *Every child must be accompanied by a parent to swim in the pool.* ♦ *Jimmy filled the plastic pool with the garden hose.* **3.** *n.* a game played with a number of hard balls on a table covered with felt with raised sides and six pockets. ♦ *Most games of pool require balls to be knocked into certain holes in a certain order.* ♦ *Bill lost the game of pool when he knocked the eight ball into a pocket.* **4.** *n.* an amount of money that is gambled by several people on the outcome of a sporting event, lottery, or other kind of bet. ♦ *Our office's pool for tonight's football game is up to $500.* ♦ *Pools are illegal because the winners don't pay a tax.* **5.** *tv.* to put money or things together for common use. ♦ *If we pool our efforts, we can accomplish this task.* ♦ *My roommates and I pooled our money to buy a new television.*

poor ['por] **1.** *adj.* not rich; having very little money; not owning many things. (Comp: *poorer;* sup: *poorest.*) ♦ *The poor man was thankful for his good health.* ♦ *Although my family was poor, we were happy.* **2.** *adj.* below a certain level of quality; inferior in operation or function. (Adv: *poorly.* Comp: *poorer;* sup: *poorest.*) ♦ *The poor connection made it hard to hear the phone caller.* ♦ *My large car gets poor gas mileage.* **3.** *adj.* worthy of pity or sympathy. ♦ *Poor Susan is at home with chickenpox.* ♦ *Oh, you poor dear! You're soaking wet!* **4. the poor** *n.* people who are ①. (No plural form in this sense. Treated as plural.) ♦ *The poor are not often able to afford college.* ♦ *Who looks out for the welfare of the poor?*

pop ['pɑp] **1.** *n.* a quick, explosive noise. ♦ *There was a loud pop when I opened the champagne.* ♦ *The gun made a loud pop when it was fired.* **2.** *n.* father. (Informal. Also a term of address.) ♦ *What does your pop do for a living?* ♦ *Hey, Pop, can I borrow your car tonight?* **3. soda pop** See **soda** ①. **4.** *n.* popular music. (No plural form in this sense.) ♦ *The radio station played a mix of pop and jazz.* ♦ *The violinist preferred classical music to pop.* **5.** *adj.* popular; well liked; favored. ♦ *The radio station played pop music.* ♦ *The flamboyant actress was a pop star.* **6.** *iv.* to make a quick, explosive noise, especially when something explodes or bursts. ♦ *The balloon popped when I poked it with a pin.* ♦ *The football popped when the truck ran over it.* **7. pop by; pop in; pop over** *iv.* + *adv.* to visit somewhere; to stop by a place. ♦ *Do you mind if I pop over to watch television with you?* ♦ *My neighbor popped in unexpectedly.* **8.** *tv.* to cause something to make a quick, explosive noise; to cause something to explode or burst. ♦ *The children popped the balloons during the party.* ♦ *I popped the soap bubble with my finger.* **9.** *tv.* to hit something, especially a baseball, into the air. ♦ *The batter popped the ball into the air.* ♦ *John popped the baseball over the player's head.* **10. pop the question** *idiom* to ask someone to marry oneself. ♦ *I was surprised when he popped the question.* ♦ *I've been waiting for years for someone to pop the question.*

popcorn ['pɑp korn] **1.** *n.* kernels of various species of corn that explode into a soft, white, fluffy mass when heated. (No plural form in this sense. Number expressed with *kernel(s) of popcorn.*) ♦ *I covered the bottom of the frying pan with popcorn.* ♦ *David put the bag of popcorn in the microwave.* **2.** *n.* exploded and puffed up kernels of ① eaten as food. (No plural form in this sense.) ♦ *Sue ate popcorn while watching the movie.* ♦ *I poured melted butter on my popcorn.*

Pope ['pop] *n.* the spiritual leader of the Roman Catholic church. ♦ *Pope John spoke to a crowd of thousands of people.* ♦ *The majority of popes have been Italian.*

poplar ['pɑp lɚ] **1.** *n.* a kind of tall, thin tree that grows quickly. ♦ *At the end of the yard, there is a row of poplars.* ♦ *A robin built its nest in a poplar in my backyard.* **2.** *n.* wood from ①. (No plural form in this sense.) ♦ *My dresser is made from poplar.* ♦ *The carpenter bought some poplar from the lumberyard.* **3.** *adj.* made from ②. ♦ *Anne varnished her poplar bench to protect it.* ♦ *The picture was hung in a poplar frame.*

poppy ['pɑp i] *n.* a flowering herb with large red blossoms. ♦ *Poppy seeds, which are very small and black, are used in baking.* ♦ *The milky sap of the poppy is used to make opium.*

populace ['pɑp jə ləs] *n.* all the people who live in a country or an area. (No plural form in this sense. Compare with **populous.**) ♦ *The American populace elects a president every four years.* ♦ *The local populace is against the governor's proposal.*

popular ['pɑp jə lɚ] **1.** *adj.* liked by many people; favored by many people; well liked. (See **pop** ⑤. Adv: *popularly.*) ♦ *The radio station played popular music during the day.* ♦ *Vanilla and chocolate are popular ice-cream flavors.* **2.** *adj.* common to most people; shared by most people. (Adv: *popularly.*) ♦ *The pollster revealed popular opinions about many topics.* ♦ *The scientist refuted popular misconceptions about nuclear power.*

popularity [pɑp jə 'lɛr ə ti] *n.* a state of being popular. (No plural form in this sense.) ♦ *The president's popularity declined during the war.* ♦ *I was jealous of the football player's popularity in school.*

popularize ['pɑp jə lə rɑɪz] *tv.* to make someone or something popular and familiar. ♦ *Radio stations helped popularize rock and roll.* ♦ *Being a star in three movies popularized the young actor.*

populate ['pɑp jə let] *tv.* [for living creatures] to occupy an area. (Usually passive.) ♦ *Many species of birds populate this marsh.* ♦ *The United States is populated by numerous ethnic groups.*

population [pɑp jə 'le ʃən] **1.** *n.* the living creatures of one kind that live in a certain area. ♦ *The entire population of fish in the lake died due to pollution.* ♦ *A small population of farmers and merchants support the only store in town.* **2.** *n.* the number of people or creatures living in a certain place. (No plural form in this sense.) ♦ *My hometown has a population of about 10,000 people.* ♦ *What is the population of Adamsville?*

populous ['pɑp jə ləs] *adj.* having a large population. (Compare with **populace.** Adv: *populously.*) ♦ *Very populous cities have multiple area codes.* ♦ *California is the most populous state in the United States.*

porcelain ['por sə lɪn] **1.** *n.* a thin, strong ceramic material. (No plural form in this sense.) ♦ *Mary's coffee cup is made of fine porcelain.* ♦ *The sculptor fired the porcelain in the oven.* **2.** *n.* a set of dishes made from ①. (No plural form in this sense.) ♦ *John washed the porcelain in the sink.*

♦ *I used my best porcelain for the fancy dinner.* **3.** *adj.* made of ①. ♦ *I broke the porcelain plate when I dropped it.* ♦ *I showed Anne my porcelain doll collection.*

porch ['portʃ] *n.* a covered structure built in front of a house, usually at a doorway. ♦ *I sat on my porch, talking with my neighbors.* ♦ *The mail carrier left a package on my front porch.*

porcupine ['por kjə paɪn] *n.* a large rodent covered with sharp needles or spines that it uses to defend itself. ♦ *Anne removed the porcupine needles from her dog's skin.* ♦ *John made the mistake of trying to pick up the frightened porcupine.*

pore ['por] **1.** *n.* a tiny opening in the skin of plants and animals. ♦ *Sweat exits the human body through pores in the skin.* ♦ *I developed pimples because my pores were clogged with oil.* **2. pore over** *iv.* + *prep. phr.* to study something closely; to look over something thoroughly. ♦ *Bill pored over his notes the night before the exam.* ♦ *The architect pored over the designs carefully.*

pork ['pork] *n.* the meat of a pig, eaten as food. (No plural form in this sense.) ♦ *Jewish law prohibits the consumption of pork.* ♦ *We ate barbecued pork at the picnic.*

pornography [por 'nɑg rə fi] *n.* erotic pictures, movies, or books meant to cause someone to become sexually excited. (No plural form in this sense.) ♦ *The minister asked the store owner to stop selling pornography.* ♦ *Jane found some pornography hidden under her son's mattress.*

porous ['por əs] *adj.* having small openings through which gas or liquid can pass slowly. (Adv: *porously.*) ♦ *The porous sponge quickly soaked up the water.* ♦ *The helium escaped through the porous membrane.*

porpoise ['por pəs] *n.* a mammal that lives in the sea, swimming in groups, including the dolphin. ♦ *The porpoise was trapped in a tuna net.* ♦ *The crowd applauded when the porpoise performed tricks.*

port ['port] **1.** *n.* a city on an ocean, sea, or lake that has a harbor where ships can be loaded and unloaded. ♦ *New York City is an important port.* ♦ *John was born in Port Arthur, Texas.* **2.** *n.* a harbor. ♦ *When the ship pulled into the port, the passengers disembarked.* ♦ *The enemy bombed strategic ports during the war.* **3.** *n.* a very sweet wine, which is usually drunk after eating. (No plural form in this sense.) ♦ *After dinner, John ordered some port for the table.* ♦ *The waiter asked us if we'd like any port.* **4.** *adj.* on, at, or toward the left side of a ship or aircraft when one is facing the front of the ship or aircraft. ♦ *The iceberg tore a hole in the port side of the ship.* ♦ *The passengers boarded the ship from the port side.* **5. any port in a storm** *idiom* <a phrase indicating that when one is having trouble, one must accept any way out, whether one likes the solution or not.> ♦ *I don't want to live with my parents, but it's a case of any port in a storm. I can't find an apartment.* ♦ *He hates his job, but he can't get another. Any port in a storm, you know.*

portable ['port ə bəl] *adj.* able to be moved from place to place; able to be carried; not permanently placed in one position. (Adv: *portably.*) ♦ *John worked at his portable computer in the café.* ♦ *The musician carried the portable keyboard onto the stage.*

portal ['por təl] *n.* a doorway into a building, especially a large, beautiful, or impressive doorway. ♦ *The frame of the mansion's portal was made of granite.* ♦ *Thirty steps led to the museum's majestic portal.*

portentous [por 'tɛn təs] *adj.* threatening; warning; foreboding; indicating that something bad or evil will happen. (Adv: *portentously.*) ♦ *Portentous dark clouds loomed overhead.* ♦ *The portentous omen frightened the superstitious traveler.*

porter ['por tɚ] *n.* someone who carries luggage for other people, especially at a hotel, airport, or train station. ♦ *The porter took my luggage to my room.* ♦ *Mary tipped the porter for carrying her luggage.*

portfolio [port 'fol i o] **1.** *n.* a large, flat case used for carrying drawings or documents. (Pl in -s.) ♦ *The designer removed her drawings from her portfolio.* ♦ *The artist carried samples of his work in his portfolio.* **2.** *n.* a collection of drawings or documents that are samples of one's creative work. (Pl in -s.) ♦ *The interviewer took great interest in my portfolio.* ♦ *The designer included her résumé with her portfolio.* **3.** *n.* one's own set or mix of investments. (Pl in -s.) ♦ *John has a large stock portfolio.* ♦ *Lisa has a small investment portfolio, and she watches it very carefully.*

porthole ['port hol] *n.* a small, round opening on the side of the part of a ship that is above water, covered with a glass pane. ♦ *The portholes in the cruise ship do not open.* ♦ *Through the porthole, the passenger saw an iceberg.*

portion ['por ʃən] **1.** *n.* a part of something; a section. ♦ *Mary decorated her portion of the office.* ♦ *The grant paid for a portion of my tuition.* **2.** *n.* the amount of food given to someone at one time. ♦ *Would you like another portion of potatoes?* ♦ *The diner asked for a large portion of spaghetti.*

portly ['port li] *adj.* overweight; fat; stout. (Comp: *portlier;* sup: *portliest.*) ♦ *The portly man loved to eat rich, fatty foods.* ♦ *The doctor advised her portly patients to exercise.*

portrait ['por trɪt] *n.* a painting, especially of a person or a person's face. ♦ *A portrait of the mayor hung in city hall.* ♦ *Bill hung a portrait of his family in his living room.*

portray [por 'tre] **1.** *tv.* to make a picture, drawing, or painting of someone or something, or to describe someone or something in words. ♦ *The artist portrayed the battle in a colorful painting.* ♦ *This painting portrays the artist's idea of Hell.* **2.** *tv.* [for an actor] to represent someone or something in particular on the stage. ♦ *Peter Pan, the imaginary character, is often portrayed by a woman.* ♦ *My greatest challenge was having to portray Abraham Lincoln.*

Portugal ['por tʃə gəl] See Gazetteer.

Portuguese [por tʃə 'giz] **1.** *n., irreg.* a citizen or native of Portugal. (Pl: *Portuguese.*) ♦ *We met lots of Portuguese on the beach in Southern Portugal.* ♦ *A Portuguese and a Spaniard lectured about their countries.* **2. the Portuguese** *n.* the people of Portugal. (Treated as plural.) ♦ *The Portuguese are very polite and are happy to welcome visitors to Portugal.* ♦ *The Portuguese enjoy many beaches, especially in the south.* **3.** *n.* the language spoken in Portugal and Brazil. (No plural form in this sense.) ♦ *I have studied Portuguese in both Portugal and Brazil.* ♦ *Portuguese appears to be similar to Spanish.* **4.** *adj.* of or about Portugal, ①, ②, or ③. ♦ *Max is studying the Portuguese language in college.* ♦ *A famous Portuguese wine is called port.*

pose ['poz] **1.** *n.* a certain way that someone sits or stands, especially when one is getting one's picture taken or painted. ♦ *The photographer adjusted the model's pose.* ♦ *John's pose looks very unnatural in this picture.* **2.** *iv.* to sit or stand in a certain way when someone is taking or painting one's picture. ♦ *The model posed for the photographer.* ♦ *My friends posed for a picture.* **3.** *tv.* to place someone or something, as in ①. ♦ *The photographer posed the model in front of the car.* ♦ *I posed my friends in front of the fountain.* **4. pose as someone** *phr.* to pretend to be someone. ♦ *The impostor posed as the president of the company.* ♦ *My twin posed as me while I went on vacation.* **5. pose a question** *idiom* to ask a question; to imply the need for asking a question. ♦ *Genetic research poses many ethical questions.* ♦ *My interviewer posed a hypothetical question.* **6. strike a pose** *idiom* to position oneself in a certain posture. ♦ *Bob struck a pose in front of the mirror to see how much he had grown.* ♦ *Lisa walked into the room and struck a pose, hoping she would be noticed.*

posh ['pɑʃ] *adj.* very luxurious; elegant; full of style. (Adv: *poshly.* Comp: *posher;* sup: *poshest.*) ♦ *The lawyer's posh apartment was quite expensive.* ♦ *The floor of the posh hotel lobby was made of white marble.*

position [pə 'zɪ ʃən] **1.** *n.* the place where someone or something is or where someone or something belongs. ♦ *The librarian shelved the books in their proper positions.* ♦ *Your position is at the end of the line, not at the beginning.* **2.** *n.* the way that someone's body is placed, situated, or aligned. ♦ *Bob landed from his fall in an awkward position.* ♦ *John sat in a comfortable position with his legs crossed.* **3.** *n.* a point of view; an opinion; the way someone thinks about a certain subject or issue. ♦ *Mary explained her position on taxation.* ♦ *John disagreed with the mayor's position on crime.* **4.** *n.* a job. ♦ *After college, John took a position with his father's law firm.* ♦ *Mary was promoted to an important position at the bank.* **5.** *tv.* to put someone or something in a certain place. ♦ *John positioned the vase of flowers in the center of the table.* ♦ *Anne positioned herself in the doorway.*

positive ['pɑz ɪ tɪv] **1.** *adj.* meaning "yes." ♦ *Nodding one's head is a positive response.* ♦ *Raising one's thumb upward is a positive gesture for Americans.* **2.** *adj.* certain. (Adv: *positively.*) ♦ *I'm positive that I'm going to visit New York next month.* ♦ *Sue is positive that she left her coat here.* **3.** *adj.* in favor of something; accepting something. (Adv: *positively.*) ♦ *The critic gave a positive appraisal.* ♦ *The playwright hoped the audience's response would be positive.* **4.** *adj.* greater than zero; plus; above zero. (Adv: *positively.*) ♦ *Negative two times negative three is positive six. That is,* $-2 \times -3 = +6$. ♦ *The outside temperature is positive twelve.* **5.** *adj.* optimistic; having a happy or confident outlook. (Adv: *positively.*) ♦ *Mary's positive attitude makes everyone around her happy.* ♦ *The president was positive that the war would end soon.* **6.** *adj.* practical; helpful. (Adv: *positively.*) ♦ *My professor gave me some positive advice about my paper.* ♦ *The director gave the actor some positive criticism.* **7.** *adj.* [of some part of an electrical circuit] higher in electrical charge than other points in the same circuit, allowing electrical energy to flow to other parts of the circuit. (Adv: *positively.*) ♦ *I connected the wire to the positive terminal.* ♦ *There is a positive charge right at this point in the circuit.* **8.** *n.* the simple form of an adjective or adverb. ♦ *The positive of* better *and* best *is* good. ♦ *One way to form the comparative is to place* more *before the positive.* **9.** *n.* an image, especially a photograph, where dark and light are the same in the picture as they are in reality. ♦ *The developer made ten positives from the negative.* ♦ *The speck of dirt on the negatives showed up on the positives.* **10.** *n.* an advantage; a good quality; a benefit. ♦ *The report emphasized the positives of reform.* ♦ *I weighed the positives of moving against the negatives.* **11.** *n.* a quantity greater than zero. ♦ *The multiplication of two negatives results in a positive.* ♦ *Absolute value is expressed as a positive.*

possess [pə 'zɛs] **1.** *tv.* to have something; to own something. ♦ *John possesses five pairs of shoes.* ♦ *Anne possesses one dog and two cats.* **2.** *tv.* to influence someone or something completely; to be controlled by someone or something, especially by an evil spirit or the devil. ♦ *The evil spirit possessed the small child.* ♦ *The contestant in second place was possessed with jealousy.*

possession [pə 'zɛ ʃən] **1.** *n.* ownership. (No plural form in this sense.) ♦ *Possession of some firearms requires a license.* ♦ *Possession of certain drugs is a crime.* **2.** *n.* a belonging; something that belongs to someone; something that is owned by someone. ♦ *All of my possessions were destroyed by fire.* ♦ *John insured his possessions against theft.*

possessive [pə 'zɛs ɪv] **1.** *adj.* selfish; unwilling to share. (Adv: *possessively.*) ♦ *The possessive boy wouldn't share his crayons.* ♦ *John's possessive girlfriend won't let him speak to other women.* **2.** *adj.* [of a word] showing possession or belonging [to someone or something]. (Adv: *possessively.*) ♦ His, hers, *and* its *are possessive pronouns.* ♦ *Possessive nouns are usually written with apostrophes.* **3.** *n.* the form of a word that shows possession. ♦ *The possessive of* he *is* his. ♦ *The possessive of* woman *is written as* woman's.

possibility [pɑs ə 'bɪl ə ti] **1.** *n.* something that is possible. ♦ *Vacationing in Florida this year is a possibility.* ♦ *There are two possibilities, and neither one is good.* **2.** *n.* chance; likelihood. (No plural form in this sense.) ♦ *There is no possibility that it will rain tonight.* ♦ *What is the possibility of rain tomorrow?*

possible ['pɑs ə bəl] *adj.* able to be done; able to exist; able to happen; able to be true, but not necessarily true. (Adv: *possibly.*) ♦ *It's possible that I might want to go to the movies tonight.* ♦ *John's name was circulated as a possible candidate for governor.*

possum ['pɑs əm] *n.* the opossum, a furry animal with a tail like that of a rat. (Informal.) ♦ *The possum looked like a huge rat in the dim light.* ♦ *Possums are usually active at night.*

post ['post] **1.** *n.* an upright, thick length of wood, steel, or other material. ♦ *Mary's mailbox is attached to a post by the side of the road.* ♦ *The fence was made of wires attached to wooden posts.* **2.** *n.* the starting or finishing line in a race. ♦ *The race horses were led to the post.* ♦ *The first runner to cross the post wins the race.* **3.** *n.* a job; a position in a company or a government. ♦ *The company interviewed 20 people for one post.* ♦ *My uncle held the post of mayor for eight years.* **4.** *tv.* to place a written notice where people can see it. ♦ *The office manager posted a notice about the dress code.* ♦ *The city posted information* *about free vaccinations.* **5.** *tv.* to mail something; to send something by mail. ♦ *Mary posted a letter to her brother.* ♦ *John electronically posted a memo to all employees.*

postage ['pos tɪdʒ] **1.** *n.* the amount of stamps needed to send something through the mail; the cost of stamps. (No plural form in this sense.) ♦ *How much postage do I need to send this package overnight?* ♦ *The cost of postage is going up again.* **2.** *n.* the stamp or stamps that are placed on something that is mailed. (No plural form in this sense. Number is expressed with *postage stamp(s)*.) ♦ *Jane affixed the postage to the envelope.* ♦ *Most postage is canceled by machine.*

postal ['pos təl] *adj.* of or about mail or the post office. ♦ *The postal workers behind the counter at the post office are usually extremely polite.* ♦ *The postal system delivers tons of mail each day.*

postcard ['post kɑrd] *n.* a card that is thicker than paper, usually has a picture on one side of it, and is used to mail someone a short letter, especially when one is traveling. ♦ *I sent my friends postcards of Rome while vacationing in Italy.* ♦ *The artist sent postcards announcing the opening of his gallery.*

poster ['pos tɚ] *n.* a large sheet of thick paper carrying a message or a picture. ♦ *The demonstrators carried posters that listed their demands.* ♦ *John hung posters of his favorite bands in his bedroom.*

posterior [pɑ 'stɪr i ɚ] **1.** *n.* the back part of someone; the buttocks. (Euphemistic. Sometimes plural with the same meaning.) ♦ *The nurse gave me a shot in my posterior.* ♦ *Lisa fell on her posterior.* **2.** *adj.* back; rear; hind. (Adv: *posteriorly*.) ♦ *The posterior section of the plane was struck by a missile.* ♦ *The posterior door of the kitchen led to the alley.*

posterity [pɑ 'stɛr ə ti] *n.* the people of the future; the people who will live in the future. (No plural form in this sense.) ♦ *We are leaving all our debts to posterity.* ♦ *The author hoped her poems would survive for posterity.*

postgraduate [post 'græ dʒu ɪt] **1.** *n.* someone who studies in school after receiving one college degree. ♦ *Some academic journals are published by postgraduates.* ♦ *The postgraduate met with his committee to discuss his dissertation.* **2.** *adj.* <the adj. use of ①.> ♦ *Mary did her postgraduate work in history at Harvard.* ♦ *John was awarded a postgraduate degree in philosophy.*

posthaste ['post 'hest] *adv.* very quickly; with great speed. ♦ *The soldiers retreated from the battle posthaste.* ♦ *The ambulance sped to the hospital posthaste.*

posthumous ['pɑs tʃu məs] *adj.* happening after someone's death. (Adv: *posthumously*.) ♦ *The actor received a posthumous award.* ♦ *The policeman received posthumous recognition for his bravery.*

postman ['post mən] *n., irreg.* someone who brings the mail; a letter carrier; a man who delivers mail. (Pl: **postmen**.) ♦ *The postman rang my bell because I had to sign for a package.* ♦ *The postman usually comes here between noon and 1:00 P.M.*

postmark ['post mɑrk] **1.** *n.* the mark that is placed over a stamp on an envelope by the post office to cancel the stamp so that it cannot be used again and to show the date and place where the stamp was canceled. ♦ *The envelope bore a postmark from France.* ♦ *The postmark indicated the letter had been sent two weeks ago.* **2.** *tv.* to mark an envelope or stamp with ①. (Typically passive.) ♦ *This envelope was postmarked in England.* ♦ *Contest entries must be postmarked by December 1st.*

postmaster ['post mæ stɚ] *n.* someone who is in charge of a post office; the head of a post office. ♦ *The postmaster vowed to improve the speed of the mail.* ♦ *The chief of the U.S. Postal Service is the Postmaster General.*

postmen ['post mən] pl of **postman**.

postmortem [post 'mort əm] **1.** *adj.* done or happening after death. ♦ *A postmortem examination revealed that the victim had been strangled.* ♦ *Postmortem changes in the body include rigor mortis.* **2.** *n.* an autopsy; an examination of someone who is dead, especially to determine the reason of death. ♦ *The coroner performed a postmortem on the unidentified body.* ♦ *The postmortem revealed that the victim had been poisoned.*

post office ['post ɔf ɪs] *n.* a government building where mail is taken to, sorted, and sent to the proper addresses, and where other postal business can be taken care of. ♦ *I went to the post office to buy some stamps.* ♦ *Post offices are closed on federal holidays.*

postoperative ['post 'ɑ prə tɪv] *adj.* happening after surgery; happening after an operation. (Adv: *postoperatively*.) ♦ *The doctor ran some postoperative tests on me.* ♦ *The patient's postoperative condition was good.*

postpaid ['post 'ped] **1.** *adj.* having the postage paid in advance. ♦ *I mailed a postpaid package to my parents in Florida.* ♦ *The mail carrier left a postpaid parcel on my porch.* **2.** *adv.* with the postage already paid. ♦ *Please send your package postpaid.* ♦ *Bob sent the parcel postpaid so I wouldn't have to pay cash on delivery.*

postpone [post 'pon] *tv.* to delay something; to put something off; to schedule something for a later time than it was originally scheduled. ♦ *The meeting was postponed one day because my boss was sick.* ♦ *The nervous couple postponed their wedding until the next year.*

postscript ['post skrɪpt] *n.* a short message at the bottom of the letter, located below one's signature. (Abbreviated *P.S.*) ♦ *Bob quickly scrawled a postscript beneath his signature.* ♦ *In a postscript to his memo, my boss wished me a happy birthday.*

posture ['pɑs tʃɚ] **1.** *n.* the way that one sits, stands, or moves; the position of the body. (No plural form in this sense.) ♦ *With perfect posture, the model walked across the stage.* ♦ *Your posture is horrible! Sit up straight!* **2.** *iv.* to sit or stand in a certain way; to strike a pose. ♦ *The flamboyant actor postured on stage.* ♦ *The beautiful model postured in front of a mirror.*

postwar ['post 'wor] *adj.* after a war; happening after a war. (Compare with **prewar**.) ♦ *The postwar birth rate increased rapidly.* ♦ *The nation's postwar recession lasted three years.*

pot ['pɑt] **1.** *n.* a large, deep, round container, usually used to cook or hold food or liquid. ♦ *Anne sliced the potatoes and put them in a large pot.* ♦ *Bill washed the dirty pots after dinner.* **2.** *n.* a round container that holds soil and a flower or plant. ♦ *Mary planted some herbs in a pot.* ♦ *John moved the pot of flowers to a sunnier place.* **3.** *n.* the contents of ① or ②. ♦ *Mary made a pot of stew for dinner.* ♦ *John dumped a pot of water on the small fire.* **4.** *n.*

an amount of money that is collected together, especially money that is bet during a game while gambling. ♦ *When the pot had reached $20, Mary won it all.* ♦ *With each bet, each player added more money to the pot.* **5.** *tv.* to put a plant in soil in ②. ♦ *Anne potted the flowers in rich soil.* ♦ *John potted the small shrub and placed it on the window sill.*

potable ['pot ə bəl] *adj.* drinkable; not poisonous or unhealthy to drink. (Adv: *potably.*) ♦ *The soldiers carried potable water in their canteens.* ♦ *Gallons of potable water were delivered to the disaster site.*

potassium [pə 'tæs i əm] *n.* a soft, lightweight silvery element. (No plural form in this sense.) ♦ *Many kinds of fertilizers are rich in potassium.* ♦ *Potassium's atomic symbol is K, and its atomic number is 19.*

potato [pə 'tet o] **1.** *n.* an oval vegetable root. (Pl in -*es.*) ♦ *The gardener dug up potatoes from the ground.* ♦ *French fries are made from potatoes.* **2.** *n.* the plant that produces ①. (Pl in -*es.*) ♦ *The farmer planted potatoes in the spring.* ♦ *Jane went to the garden to water the potatoes.* **3.** *adj.* made of or with ①. ♦ *We had lots of potato salad at our picnic.* ♦ *My aunt used to make us potato pancakes when we visited her.* **4. potato chip** See chip ③.

potent ['pot nt] **1.** *adj.* powerful; having a strong effect. (Adv: *potently.*) ♦ *The potent drug knocked John unconscious.* ♦ *The potent stench made me gag.* **2.** *adj.* [of a male] virile and able to copulate. (Adv: *potently.*) ♦ *John longed to be potent again.* ♦ *Bill became potent after seeking help from his doctor.*

potentate ['pot n tet] *n.* a ruler; a monarch. ♦ *The potentate's empire stretched across three continents.* ♦ *The condemned prisoner begged the potentate for mercy.*

potential [pə 'tɛn ʃəl] **1.** *adj.* being a possibility; existing as a possibility; capable of becoming someone or something; capable of developing into someone or something. (Adv: *potentially.*) ♦ *The inventor determined potential markets for the new product.* ♦ *The clerk treated each customer as a potential purchaser.* **2.** *n.* a quality that makes it likely that someone or something will be a certain way or used in a certain way in the future. (No plural form in this sense.) ♦ *John had the potential to do well, but he was too lazy.* ♦ *The smart student showed potential for becoming a doctor.*

potholder ['pɑt hol dɚ] *n.* a pad of cloth used to hold hot things, such as containers of food. ♦ *Anne gripped the hot pan handle with a potholder.* ♦ *John set the pot of boiling soup onto the potholder.*

pothole ['pɑt hol] *n.* a large hole in the surface of a street. ♦ *I pleaded with the city to repair the large potholes on my street.* ♦ *I got into an accident when I hit a large pothole on 12th Street.*

potion ['po ʃən] *n.* a liquid mixture of different things, especially one that is a poison, a medicine, or thought to be magical. ♦ *The magical potion turned the handsome prince into a frog.* ♦ *The witch placed a drop of love potion on the king's lips.*

potluck ['pɑt lək] **1.** *n.* food that happens to be available; food that is given to people who show up uninvited because it is the only food that is ready to eat. (No plural form in this sense.) ♦ *I would love to come to dinner even if it's only potluck.* ♦ *My guest was upset that I could only offer potluck.* **2. potluck (dinner); potluck (supper)** *n.* a meal where different people bring different kinds of food, instead of one person cooking all the food for many people. ♦ *Mary brought a ham casserole to the potluck supper.* ♦ *All the guests collected their dishes after the potluck.*

potshot ['pɑt ʃɑt] **1.** *n.* a shot at game meant to be food. ♦ *The hunter's potshot missed the deer by several yards.* ♦ *The rabbit was scared away by the hunter's potshots.* **2. take a potshot at someone or something** *idiom* to criticize someone or something; to include a criticism of someone or something in a broader or more general criticism. ♦ *Daily, the media took potshots at the foolish politician.* ♦ *John is taking potshots at me in his condemnation of office workers.*

potted ['pɑt ɪd] *adj.* [of a plant] growing in a pot. ♦ *The hotel lobby was decorated with many potted palms.* ♦ *Bob killed the potted plant by watering it too much.*

potter ['pɑt ɚ] *n.* someone who makes pottery; someone who shapes clay into objects and then bakes the clay so that it hardens. ♦ *The potter sold several ashtrays at the crafts fair.* ♦ *The potter placed the wet clay in the oven.*

pottery ['pɑt ə ri] **1.** *n.* dishes, bowls, vases, and other objects that are made from baked clay. (No plural form in this sense.) ♦ *The artist sold her pottery at the county fair.* ♦ *After baking it, I painted the pottery with bright colors.* **2.** *n.* the art of making objects out of clay and baking them so that the clay hardens; ceramics. (No plural form in this sense.) ♦ *My art teacher taught pottery for an entire semester.* ♦ *John's hobbies include pottery and painting.*

pouch ['pɑʊtʃ] *n.* a small bag that is used to hold a small amount of something. ♦ *Bill pulled some tobacco from its pouch.* ♦ *Anne kept her change in a small canvas pouch.*

poultry ['pol tri] *n.* chickens, ducks, geese, and other birds that are used as meat or for providing eggs for humans to eat. (No plural form in this sense.) ♦ *Mary doesn't eat red meat, but she will eat fish and poultry.* ♦ *The farmer raised poultry for eggs and meat.*

pounce ['pɑʊns] *iv.* to jump suddenly onto, out of, or around someone or something. ♦ *The tiger pounced on the young deer.* ♦ *The children pounced out of the car and ran toward the lake.*

pound ['pɑʊnd] **1.** *n.* a unit of measure of weight, equal to 16 ounces or 0.454 kilogram. ♦ *Our baby weighed 7 pounds and 5 ounces at birth.* ♦ *I bought five pounds of flour at the grocery store.* **2.** *n.* the basic unit of money in the United Kingdom. (Symbolized as £.) ♦ *In 1993, one pound was worth about $1.50.* ♦ *I spent £10 on dinner at the British restaurant.* **3.** *n.* a place where stray animals are kept. ♦ *Stray animals are taken to the city pound.* ♦ *I adopted a cute puppy from the local dog pound.* **4.** *tv.* to hit someone or something very hard again and again; to beat something into a certain shape by hitting it very hard again and again. ♦ *The hurricane pounded the coastal city.* ♦ *The boxer pounded his opponent's face until it bled.* **5.** *iv.* [for the heart or blood pressure] to pulsate or beat very hard. ♦ *My heart pounded as my car slid off the road.* ♦ *The scary movie made my heart pound with fear.* **6. pound a beat** *idiom* to walk a route. ♦ *The cop pounded the same beat for years and years.* ♦ *Pounding a beat will wreck your feet.* **7. pound the pavement** *idiom* to walk through the streets looking for a job. ♦ *I spent two months* *pounding the pavement after the factory I worked for closed.* ♦ *Hey, Bob. You'd better get busy pounding those nails unless you want to be out pounding the pavement.*

pounding ['paʊn dɪŋ] *adj.* beating; throbbing. (Adv: *poundingly.*) ♦ *Do you have any aspirin? I have a pounding headache.* ♦ *The pounding music at the rock concert made my ears ache.*

pour ['por] **1.** *iv.* to flow from a place; to come out of a place quickly and continuously. ♦ *Rain just poured and poured all morning.* ♦ *Water poured out of the open faucet.* **2.** *tv.* to cause something to pour out of a place quickly and continuously. ♦ *David poured water onto the small fire.* ♦ *Anne poured juice into her glass from the pitcher.* **3. pouring rain** *idiom* very heavy rain. ♦ *The children's clothes were soaked after they played out in the pouring rain.* ♦ *I waited in the pouring rain for the next bus.*

pout ['paʊt] **1.** *n.* an expression on one's face when the bottom lip or both lips are pushed out. ♦ *Jimmy stuck out his bottom lip in a defiant pout.* ♦ *I told Susie to wipe the pout from her face and get dressed.* **2.** *iv.* to push out one's bottom lip or both lips when one is angry, upset, displeased, or showing that one is in a bad temper. ♦ *Jimmy pouted because his parents didn't buy him the toy he wanted.* ♦ *Susie pouted because she was told to be quiet.*

poverty ['pɑv ɚ ti] *n.* the lack of the necessities for life. (No plural form in this sense.) ♦ *The family had known only poverty for years.* ♦ *The mayor vowed to reduce poverty among the city's residents.*

powder ['paʊd ɚ] **1.** *n.* a substance that consists of tiny particles. (No plural form in this sense.) ♦ *After my shower, I sprinkled fragrant powder on my body.* ♦ *The scientist dissolved the chemical powder in water.* **2.** *tv.* to cover or dust something with ① or a powdered substance. ♦ *Mary powdered her baby's bottom after changing his diaper.* ♦ *The cook powdered the doughnuts with sugar.*

powdered ['paʊd ɚd] *adj.* made into a powder; in the form of powder; consisting of tiny particles. ♦ *The campers mixed a packet of powdered milk with water.* ♦ *The baker covered the doughnut with powdered sugar.*

power ['paʊ ɚ] **1.** *n.* the ability to do something; strength. (No plural form in this sense.) ♦ *The weightlifter has great muscle power.* ♦ *This detergent has the power to clean coffee stains.* **2.** *n.* the authority to do something; control. (No plural form in this sense.) ♦ *Our principal has the power to suspend unruly students.* ♦ *Congress has the power to pass new laws.* **3.** *n.* the number of times that a number is multiplied by itself. ♦ *The third power of 5 is 125, because 5 × 5 × 5 = 125.* ♦ *The second power of a number is also called its square.* **4.** *tv.* to supply energy to a machine or other consumer of energy. ♦ *Two batteries are needed to power this flashlight.* ♦ *Our heating system is powered by natural gas.* **5. the powers that be** *idiom* the people who are in authority. ♦ *The powers that be have decided to send back the immigrants.* ♦ *I have applied for a license, and the powers that be are considering my application.*

powerful ['paʊ ɚ fʊl] *adj.* having a lot of power, energy, or force; full of strength or influence. (Adv: *powerfully.*) ♦ *The driver revved the powerful engine at the intersection.* ♦ *The powerful senator urged the others to vote for the bill.*

powerfully ['paʊ ɚ fə li] *adv.* in a way that has a lot of energy, power, or force; in a way that is full of strength or influence. ♦ *The army tank drove powerfully through the woods, crushing trees as it went.* ♦ *We pushed against the door powerfully, but it would not move.*

powerhouse ['paʊ ɚ haʊs] **1.** *n., irreg.* a building that produces electric power. (Pl: [...haʊ zəz].) ♦ *There was a blackout when lightning struck the powerhouse.* ♦ *The utility company owned several powerhouses in the area.* **2.** *n., irreg.* someone or some people who are powerful, energetic, or forceful. (Figurative on ①.) ♦ *The football powerhouse won the championship six years in a row.* ♦ *Susan got the managerial job because she's an organizational powerhouse.*

powerless ['paʊ ɚ ləs] *adj.* having no power; lacking power, force, or energy; helpless; weak. (Adv: *powerlessly.*) ♦ *The powerless army surrendered.* ♦ *The severe illness left me completely powerless.*

powerlessness ['paʊ ɚ ləs nəs] *n.* a state of lacking authoritative power; helplessness. (No plural form in this sense.) ♦ *The army's powerlessness was evident from its complete defeat.* ♦ *The mayor's powerlessness against the governor angered him.*

pp See past participle.

practical ['præk tɪ kəl] **1.** *adj.* useful; able to be used; of or about actions and results, as opposed to ideas or theories. (Adv: *practically* [...ɪk li].) ♦ *The carpenter owned many practical tools for working with wood.* ♦ *Mary's practical approach solved the problem quickly.* **2.** *adj.* sensible; having common sense. (Adv: *practically* [...ɪk li].) ♦ *It isn't practical to have to go borrow the neighbor's lawn mower every time you need to mow the grass.* ♦ *My practical roommate sewed her name into all her clothes.*

practicality [præk tɪ 'kæl ə ti] *n.* the quality of being practical. (No plural form in this sense.) ♦ *The practicality of Jane's advice was very appealing.* ♦ *The supervisor rewarded workers for their practicality.*

practical joke ['præk tɪ kəl 'dʒok] *n.* a prank or trick that surprises, annoys, or embarrasses someone. ♦ *Bob did not like being the victim of Mary's practical joke.* ♦ *Max played a practical joke on his boss and nearly got fired.*

practically ['præk tɪk li] *adv.* almost; just about. ♦ *It's practically three o'clock. We're going to be late.* ♦ *I'm practically finished. Come back in two minutes.*

practice ['præk tɪs] **1.** *n.* an action that is done many times so that one will do it better and better; an action that is done many times so that one will become skilled at doing it. (No plural form in this sense.) ♦ *David has piano practice after school on Mondays.* ♦ *With practice, you'll be able to play the guitar as well as I do.* **2.** *n.* a custom; a tradition; the way something is usually done; a habit. ♦ *Shaking hands is one of our cultural practices.* ♦ *The anthropologist studied the rural village's local practices.* **3.** *n.* the business of a doctor or a lawyer. ♦ *The law firm advertised its practice on television.* ♦ *The plastic surgeon's practice was very successful.* **4.** *iv.* to rehearse. ♦ *I have a concert next week and I have to practice every day.* ♦ *The cast will practice for the play each night this week.* **5.** *tv.* to work at a skill over and over in order to be better at it. ♦ *Mary practices the piano every day after school.* ♦ *The actor practiced his monologue in front of a mirror.* **6.** *tv.* to do something; to make a habit of something. ♦ *Jane* *urged her children to practice telling the truth.* ♦ *Hypocrites do not practice what they preach.* **7.** *tv.* to work in medicine or law. ♦ *Mary practices law with a large firm downtown.* ♦ *Bob practices medicine at the county hospital.* **8.** *tv.* to follow and perform the tasks associated with a religion or profession. ♦ *Jane practices her religion only on the major holidays.* ♦ *My brother does not practice teaching any longer.* **9. in practice** *idiom* in real life; concerning actual events, as opposed to just talk or thinking. (No plural form in this sense.) ♦ *In practice, some of our policies are overlooked.* ♦ *In theory, my boss should do this job, but in practice, he doesn't.* **10. out of practice** *idiom* performing poorly due to a lack of ①. ♦ *I used to be able to play the piano extremely well, but now I'm out of practice.* ♦ *The baseball players lost the game because they were out of practice.*

practicing ['præk tə sɪŋ] *adj.* actively performing the tasks associated with a religion or profession. ♦ *Mary is a practicing Baptist.* ♦ *Bob is a practicing physician.*

practitioner [præk 'tɪʃ ən ɚ] *n.* someone who works at a certain profession, especially in medicine or law. ♦ *The legal practitioner agreed to take my case.* ♦ *A medical practitioner examined my sore throat.*

pragmatic [præg 'mæt ɪk] *adj.* practical; capable of dealing with the real world. (Adv: *pragmatically* [...ɪk li].) ♦ *The successful boss took a pragmatic approach to solving problems.* ♦ *The pragmatic social worker understood her clients' situations.*

pragmatism ['præg mə tɪz əm] *n.* the quality of being pragmatic or practical. (No plural form in this sense.) ♦ *Many politicians lack pragmatism because of lofty ideals.* ♦ *My unrealistic supervisor needs a good dose of pragmatism.*

pragmatist ['præg mə təst] *n.* someone who is pragmatic. ♦ *The pragmatist told me that my goals were unrealistic.* ♦ *I am a pragmatist, and I don't think your idea is practical.*

prairie ['prɛr i] *n.* a very large area of land that is covered with different kinds of grasses but which has no trees. ♦ *The farms of Illinois were once a vast prairie.* ♦ *The fox chased the rabbit through the tall grass of the prairie.*

praise ['prez] **1.** *n.* saying that someone or something is good; the use of words to express approval. (Sometimes plural with the same meaning.) ♦ *I appreciated my boss's praise of my work.* ♦ *My rude roommate offers many criticisms but rarely gives praise.* **2.** *tv.* to express approval of someone or something; to talk about the good things something does or how good someone or something is. ♦ *My boss praised my effort to finish the job on time.* ♦ *The parents praised their children's good behavior.* **3.** *tv.* to worship someone or God with words or songs. ♦ *Let us praise God, from whom all blessings flow.* ♦ *The congregation praised God in song.* **4. sing someone's praises; sing the praises of someone or something** *idiom* to praise ② someone highly and enthusiastically. ♦ *The boss is singing his new secretary's praises.* ♦ *The theater critics are singing the praises of the young actor.*

praiseworthy ['prez wɚ ði] *adj.* deserving praise; commendable. ♦ *The newspaper reported the firefighter's praiseworthy rescue.* ♦ *Your efforts to finish the project on time are praiseworthy.*

prance ['præns] **1.** *iv.* [for a horse or other animal] to move by raising its front legs and moving forward with its back legs. ♦ *The horse pranced across the field.* ♦ *The dog pranced when I held a toy over its head.* **2.** *iv.* to jump or bound about. ♦ *The children pranced across the playground.* ♦ *The dancers pranced on stage.*

prank ['præŋk] *n.* a harmless trick or joke that is played on someone. ♦ *The students laughed when Jimmy played a prank on the teacher.* ♦ *As a prank, Susie put sugar in the salt shaker.*

prankster ['præŋk stɚ] *n.* someone who plays a harmless trick or joke on someone. ♦ *The teacher sent the prankster to the principal's office.* ♦ *The prankster laughed when I found the fake worm in my soup.*

prate ['pret] *iv.* to talk a lot in a foolish way; to gossip. ♦ *The women prated about their husbands while playing cards.* ♦ *The men prated all afternoon while playing pool.*

prawn ['prɔn] *n.* a large shrimp. ♦ *I dipped the fried prawn in the spicy sauce.* ♦ *John bought a pound of prawns at the grocery store.*

pray ['pre] **1.** *iv.* to give thanks to God; to say a prayer to God; to ask God or someone for something. (Compare with **prey**.) ♦ *I prayed a lot when I was very sick.* ♦ *Jimmy prays every night before going to bed.* **2. pray for** *iv.* + *prep. phr.* to ask God for something. ♦ *I prayed for spring to come early this year.* ♦ *Bill prayed for good health and prosperity.* **3.** *tv.* to pray ① that something will happen the way one wants. (Takes a clause.) ♦ *The farmer prayed that it would rain.* ♦ *I prayed that Anne would have a safe trip.*

prayer ['pre ɚ] **1.** *n.* communication with a deity, especially God. ♦ *Prayer is practiced by millions of people daily.* ♦ *Ma felt that the power of prayer was enormous.* **2.** *n.* the words one uses when worshiping or praying to God. ♦ *John says his prayers every night before going to bed.* ♦ *Mary said a small prayer during the rough plane flight.*

preach ['pritʃ] **1.** *iv.* to give a sermon; to talk about something religious. ♦ *The minister preached about sin. He was against it.* ♦ *The preacher preached nearly an hour!* **2. preach at** *iv.* + *prep. phr.* to give advice to someone about something, especially when it is not wanted. ♦ *Jimmy resented being preached at for smoking.* ♦ *My teacher preached at me for being late.* **3.** *tv.* to deliver a sermon; to deliver a particular message through preaching as in ①. ♦ *The deacon preached that good people should help other people.* ♦ *My guru always preaches love and harmony.*

preacher ['pritʃ ɚ] *n.* someone who preaches; the leader of a church; a minister. ♦ *The preacher spoke about temptation today at church.* ♦ *Bill and Anne told their preacher that they wanted to get married.*

preamble ['pri æm bəl] *n.* the introduction to a speech or a text. (When capitalized, it refers to the introduction to the Constitution of the United States.) ♦ *We had to memorize the Preamble for our American history exam.* ♦ *The lengthy book's preamble was twenty pages long.*

prearrange [pri ə 'rendʒ] *tv.* to arrange something in advance; to schedule something in advance. ♦ *In some cultures, parents prearrange their children's marriages.* ♦ *My travel agent prearranged my rental car reservation.*

prearranged [pri ə 'rendʒd] *adj.* arranged in advance; scheduled in advance. ♦ *Anne warmed the prearranged* *meal in a microwave.* ♦ *The sociologist studied prearranged marriages in India.*

precancerous [pri 'kæn sə rəs] *adj.* of a medical condition where something may develop cancer but which is not yet cancerous. ♦ *The doctors removed the precancerous tumor from my neck.* ♦ *My doctor discovered a precancerous lump in my breast.*

precarious [prɪ 'kɛr i əs] *adj.* dangerous; not secure; not steady; likely to fall. (Adv: *precariously.*) ♦ *The vase was in a precarious position on the edge of the table.* ♦ *My trip down the icy mountain road was precarious.*

precaution [pri 'kɔ ʃən] *n.* an act that is done to prevent something bad from occurring. ♦ *Many diseases can be prevented if you take a few simple precautions.* ♦ *Despite all of my precautions, I still caught a bad cold.*

precede [prɪ 'sid] *tv.* to come before something else in time or space; to happen before something else; to be before something else. ♦ *World War II preceded the Korean War.* ♦ *In the alphabet,* A *precedes* B.

precedence ['prɛs ə dəns] **have precedence over someone or something; take precedence over someone or something** *idiom* have the right to come before someone or something else. ♦ *Ambulances have precedence over regular cars at intersections.* ♦ *My manager's concerns take precedence over mine.*

precedent ['prɛs ə dənt] *n.* something that can be used as an example in the future, especially a court ruling that can be used in the future in similar situations. ♦ *The precedent created by the trial resulted in similar lawsuits.* ♦ *Mary set a precedent by allowing Jimmy to stay up until 9:00* P.M.

preceding [prɪ 'sid ɪŋ] *adj.* coming before; happening before; being before something else. ♦ *The preceding summer had been a lot warmer than the current one.* ♦ *The preceding program was a paid political advertisement.*

precept ['pri sɛpt] *n.* a rule of behavior or morals. ♦ *In college, I studied precepts of Western religions.* ♦ *The precepts of the ancient religions have been recorded for thousands of years.*

precinct ['pri sɪŋkt] *n.* a district of a city; an administrative district of a city. ♦ *There is a polling place for each voting precinct.* ♦ *This map of the city shows the crime rate by police precinct.*

precious ['prɛʃ əs] **1.** *adj.* very valuable; worth a lot of money. (Adv: *preciously.*) ♦ *Mary kept her precious jewels in a safety-deposit box.* ♦ *The precious diamond was valued at over $100,000.* **2.** *adj.* very much loved; very dear to someone; cherished. (Figurative on ①. Adv: *preciously.*) ♦ *Good night, my precious child.* ♦ *I grabbed a few precious belongings and ran from the burning house.* **3.** *adj.* charming and cute. (Adv: *preciously.*) ♦ *Isn't that the most precious little poodle you've ever seen?* ♦ *Susie was a sweet and precious hostess at her birthday party.* **4.** *adv.* very [few]; very [little]. (In limited contexts.) ♦ *Precious few people showed up for the rally.* ♦ *There has been precious little rain this summer.*

precipice ['prɛs ə pɪs] *n.* a steep cliff; the side of a mountain or cliff, especially one that is almost straight up and down. ♦ *The car veered off the road and over the precipice.* ♦ *The mountain climbers inched up the precipice.*

precipitate [prɪ 'sɪp ɪ tet] **1.** *iv.* [for a vapor] to condense into a liquid. ♦ *It's supposed to precipitate today, so bring an umbrella.* ♦ *Water vapor precipitates in my refrigerator sometimes.* **2.** *tv.* to cause something to happen sooner than it would have on its own; to cause something to happen suddenly. (Figurative on ①.) ♦ *The senator precipitated a vote on the bill while its main opponent was gone.* ♦ *World War I was precipitated by a political assassination.* **3.** *n.* a solid substance that is removed from a liquid. ♦ *The chemist analyzed the precipitate for poison.* ♦ *The precipitate remained in the filter after the liquid drained.*

precipitation [prɪ sɪp ɪ 'te ʃən] **1.** *n.* the separation of a solid substance from a liquid. (No plural form in this sense.) ♦ *The precipitation of the substance was achieved by filtering it.* ♦ *After precipitation, the chemist analyzed the solid.* **2.** *n.* rain, snow, sleet, drizzle, or other moisture that is made by the atmosphere. (No plural form in this sense.) ♦ *Some form of precipitation was predicted for the weekend.* ♦ *If it gets cold, the precipitation will take the form of snow.* **3.** *n.* the hurried beginning of a bad situation. (No plural form in this sense.) ♦ *The expiration of the contract was the precipitation of the long strike.* ♦ *I do not know what caused the precipitation of the fighting.*

precipitous [prɪ 'sɪp ɪ təs] *adj.* steep; like the side of a cliff or mountain that is almost straight up and down. (Adv: *precipitously.*) ♦ *I drove carefully down the precipitous mountainside.* ♦ *The skier viewed the precipitous slope as a challenge.*

precise [prɪ 'sɑɪs] *adj.* exact; carefully and accurately detailed. (Adv: *precisely.*) ♦ *The witness gave a precise account of the murder.* ♦ *This ruler is precise to within a millimeter.*

precision [prɪ 'sɪ ʒən] *n.* exactness; the quality of being precise; doing something precisely. (No plural form in this sense.) ♦ *The experimenter's precision accounted for every variable.* ♦ *The missile's precision was accurate to within four feet.*

preclude [prɪ 'klud] *tv.* to make something impossible; to prevent something from happening. ♦ *My contract precluded a pay reduction.* ♦ *The lightning storm precluded swimming in the lake.*

precocious [prɪ 'ko ʃəs] *adj.* acting or behaving as though one were older or more mature than one is. (Adv: *precociously.*) ♦ *A precocious child flirted with me on the bus.* ♦ *The precocious six-year-old recited the names of all the states.*

preconceived ['pri kən sivd] *adj.* formed in advance; formed before there is evidence on which to base an opinion. ♦ *When his preconceived ideas didn't happen, Bob was disappointed.* ♦ *Your preconceived notion that I was quitting is wrong.*

precondition [pri kən 'dɪ ʃən] **1.** *n.* a prerequisite; a condition that must be met or fulfilled before something is done. ♦ *Understanding algebra is a precondition for learning calculus.* ♦ *The application listed all the preconditions for employment.* **2.** *tv.* to prepare someone or something for some activity or treatment. ♦ *The researcher preconditioned the subjects for the experiment.* ♦ *The soldiers were preconditioned for the uncomfortable weather.*

precursor [pri 'kɚ sɚ] *n.* someone or something that is an indication of someone or something that will follow.

♦ *Dark clouds are a precursor of rain.* ♦ *Thunder is a precursor of lightning.*

predator ['prɛd ə tɚ] *n.* a creature that preys on other creatures. ♦ *Cats are natural predators of birds.* ♦ *The most dangerous predators of many animals are human beings.*

predatory ['prɛd ə tor i] **1.** *adj.* living by killing and eating other animals. (Adv: *predatorily* [prɛd ə 'tor ə li].) ♦ *The predatory wolf killed the young lamb.* ♦ *The biologist studied the predatory habits of felines.* **2.** *adj.* making money by stealing and cheating; cruel and exploitative. (Figurative on ①. Adv: *predatorily* [prɛd ə 'tor ə li].) ♦ *The predatory thief preyed on innocent victims.* ♦ *A reporter exposed the lawyer's predatory practices.*

predecessor ['prɛd ə sɛs ɚ] *n.* someone who lived before someone else; someone who held a certain position before someone else. ♦ *Queen Elizabeth I is a predecessor of Queen Elizabeth II.* ♦ *The company president's immediate predecessor made most of the policies.*

predetermine [pri dɪ 'tɚ mɪn] *tv.* to determine something in advance; to determine something before it happens. ♦ *You cannot predetermine who the winner will be!* ♦ *The mayor tried to predetermine which company would get the valuable contract.*

predetermined [pri dɪ 'tɚ mɪnd] *adj.* decided in advance. ♦ *The rocket's predetermined path brought it near Mars.* ♦ *The predetermined winner feigned surprise when his raffle ticket was drawn.*

predicament [prɪ 'dɪk ə mənt] *n.* a difficult situation where one must make a difficult choice. ♦ *I asked my friend for advice about my awful predicament.* ♦ *I was in the predicament of competing against the best runner.*

predicate ['prɛd ə kət] **1.** *n.* the part of a sentence that expresses something about the subject of the sentence. ♦ *The predicate of "Snow is white" is "is white."* ♦ *Underline each predicate in your essay, and circle each subject.* **2.** *adj.* <the adj. use of ①.> ♦ *In "It is I," "I" is a predicate nominal.* ♦ *In "Snow is white," "white" is a predicate adjective.*

predicated ['prɛd ə ket ɪd] **predicated on** *adj.* + *prep. phr.* to base a statement or argument on some condition. ♦ *Future bonuses are predicated on good work.* ♦ *This formula is predicated on laws of physics.*

predict [prɪ 'dɪkt] *tv.* to say that something is going to happen before it happens; to prophesy that something will happen. ♦ *The psychic claimed to be able to predict the future.* ♦ *The weather forecaster predicted rain.*

prediction [prɪ 'dɪk ʃən] *n.* a statement made about something that is going to happen in the future; a prophecy. ♦ *The psychic's prediction of good luck pleased me.* ♦ *The weather forecaster's predictions were generally accurate.*

predictor [prɪ 'dɪk tɚ] *n.* someone or something that predicts that something will happen. ♦ *Interest rates are a good predictor of housing sales.* ♦ *Dark clouds are a dependable predictor of rain.*

predisposed [pri dɪ 'spozd] **1. predisposed to** *adj.* + *prep. phr.* likely to do something; likely to behave in a certain way. ♦ *I'm predisposed to going out to eat tonight.* ♦ *John is predisposed to anger when he's tired.* **2. predisposed to** *adj.* + *prep. phr.* susceptible; likely to suffer from a certain sickness. ♦ *People with AIDS are predisposed to pneumonia.* ♦ *People with allergies are predisposed to hay fever.*

predominance [prɪ 'dɑm ə nəns] *n.* the quality of being predominant, foremost, or primary. (No plural form in this sense.) ♦ *The predominance of hair salons in my neighborhood is surprising.* ♦ *My boss has predominance over me in making decisions.*

predominant [prɪ 'dɑm ə nənt] *adj.* primary; main; having a greater number or greater importance. (Adv: *predominantly.*) ♦ *The predominant reason for my wanting to go home is that I'm tired.* ♦ *The predominant crop in Idaho is potatoes.*

predominate [prɪ 'dɑm ə net] *iv.* to have more power, control, or importance than other things or people. ♦ *Green growing things predominate near the Amazon River.* ♦ *Young people predominate on the beaches in California.*

preeminent [pri 'ɛm ə nənt] *adj.* superior to other things or people; outstanding; very distinguished. (Adv: *preeminently.*) ♦ *The guest of honor is preeminent in her field.* ♦ *The preeminent author had received many awards.*

preen ['prin] **1.** *iv.* [for a bird] to clean and rearrange [its feathers]. ♦ *My parrot preens for hours at a time.* ♦ *Dozens of birds sat on the branch and preened.* **2.** *iv.* [for someone] to spend a lot of time arranging hair, makeup, clothing, etc. (Figurative on ①.) ♦ *Lisa was preening in the rearview mirror while she waited for the light to change.* ♦ *My roommate always preens in front of the mirror before he goes out on a date.* **3.** *tv.* [for a bird] to clean itself and its feathers as in ①. ♦ *The birds preened themselves for hours.* ♦ *My parrot preened its wings after each flight.*

prefab ['pri fæb] **1.** *n.* a house that was built in a factory and assembled on its foundation; a prefabricated house. ♦ *This neighborhood consists entirely of prefabs built in the 1960s.* ♦ *All the prefabs on my street look alike.* **2.** *adj.* <the adj. use of ①.> ♦ *The tornado destroyed the prefab houses.* ♦ *The large suburb consisted of prefab dwellings.*

prefabricated [pri 'fæb rə ket ɪd] *adj.* made in advance; having the parts of something made in a factory, taken to a location, and put together. ♦ *The tornado destroyed the neighborhood of prefabricated houses.* ♦ *The workers installed our prefabricated swimming pool.*

preface ['prɛf ɪs] **1.** *n.* an introduction to a speech or to something that is written. ♦ *The author wrote a new preface for the second edition of her book.* ♦ *The lecturer stated her main idea in the preface of his speech.* **2.** *tv.* to begin a speech or written piece with an introduction. ♦ *The lecturer prefaced her speech with a funny joke.* ♦ *The author prefaced the textbook with a list of acknowledgments.*

prefer [prɪ 'fɚ] **prefer (to); prefer (over)** *tv.* (+ *prep. phr.*) to like someone or something better than someone or something else. ♦ *I prefer summer to winter because I don't like snow.* ♦ *I prefer red over blue.*

preferable ['prɛf ə rə bəl] *adj.* more preferred; more desirable. (Adv: *preferably.*) ♦ *I find chocolate ice cream preferable to vanilla.* ♦ *Jane finds living in Florida preferable to here.*

preference ['prɛf ə rəns] **1.** *n.* special consideration that is given to certain people or things; favor. (No plural form in this sense.) ♦ *The king showed preference to his eldest son.* ♦ *The first people in line were given preference in seating.* **2.** *n.* someone or something that is preferred over someone or something else. ♦ *Strawberry ice cream is Jane's preference for dessert.* ♦ *Among wines, my preference is for white.*

preferential [prɛf ə 'rɛn ʃəl] *adj.* of or about getting or giving special treatment or consideration. (Adv: *preferentially.*) ♦ *Anne resented the preferential treatment shown toward David.* ♦ *The judge's preferential considerations were very biased.*

prefix ['pri fɪks] **1.** *n.* a letter or a group of letters at the beginning of a word that usually changes the meaning of the word. ♦ *Common English prefixes include* re-, in-, *and* un-. ♦ *Many Scottish surnames include the prefix* Mc *or* Mac. **2. prefix with** *tv.* + *prep. phr.* to use ① before a word. ♦ *If you prefix an adjective with* un-, *it usually means 'not.'* ♦ *Surnames that are prefixed with* O' *are usually Irish.*

pregnancy ['prɛg nən si] **1.** *n.* a state of being pregnant. (No plural form in this sense.) ♦ *Pregnancy in humans usually lasts for nine months.* ♦ *The doctor told Mary to rest in the last month of pregnancy.* **2.** *n.* an instance of being pregnant. ♦ *Mary's first two pregnancies were easier than her third.* ♦ *The cat is having her ninth pregnancy.*

pregnant ['prɛg nənt] *adj.* [of a woman or female creature] having conceived offspring. ♦ *The pregnant woman was carrying twins.* ♦ *The veterinarian said our dog was pregnant.*

prehensile [pri 'hɛn səl] *adj.* [of a living structure] designed or adapted to hold onto something. (Adv: *prehensilely.*) ♦ *The monkeys of South America have prehensile tails.* ♦ *Human beings have prehensile thumbs.*

prehistoric [pri hɪ 'stor ɪk] *adj.* happening before history was first recorded. (Adv: *prehistorically* [...ɪk li].) ♦ *The wheel is a prehistoric invention.* ♦ *In prehistoric times, dinosaurs walked the earth.*

prejudice ['prɛdʒ ə dɪs] **1.** *n.* opinion formed about someone or something before learning all the facts. (No plural form in this sense.) ♦ *Prejudice is often based on fear or ignorance.* ♦ *The hardworking immigrants faced irrational prejudice.* **2.** *n.* an instance of ①. ♦ *Bob has a prejudice against South Africans.* ♦ *The judge seemed to have a prejudice against the lawyer.* **3.** *tv.* to cause someone to have ①. ♦ *Being attacked in the city prejudiced Bob against visiting the city.* ♦ *The lawyer's rudeness prejudiced the jury against him.*

preliminary [prɪ 'lɪm ə nɛr i] **1.** *adj.* happening before something else; being an introduction to something that is more important or more difficult. (Adv: *preliminarily* [prɪ lɪm ə 'nɛr ə li].) ♦ *David made preliminary remarks at the start of the ceremony.* ♦ *Each applicant was required to take a preliminary examination.* **2.** *n.* an action or a preparation that is done before something that is more difficult or more important. ♦ *Algebra is a preliminary to calculus.* ♦ *Let's skip the preliminaries and get right to the point.* **3. preliminaries** *n.* an initial qualifying test that must be passed before someone is allowed to do something. (From preliminary ① *examination.* Treated as plural. Abbreviated *prelims.*) ♦ *Applicants must score above 80% on the preliminaries to be accepted.* ♦ *Forty skaters were eliminated in the preliminaries.*

prelude ['pre lud] **1.** *n.* an introduction, especially a short piece of music that comes before a longer work of music. ♦ *The composer wrote the symphony's prelude in the key of D.* ♦ *Having arrived at the concert hall late, we missed the prelude.* **2. prelude to something** *phr.* an act or event that comes before and signals another act or event. (Figurative on ①.) ♦ *Her rudeness to her boss was a prelude to her resignation.* ♦ *The invasion of Poland was a prelude to World War II.*

premarital [pri 'mɛr ɪ təl] *adj.* happening before marriage; of or about the time before one is married. (Adv: *premaritally.*) ♦ *Before marriage, premarital counseling is recommended.* ♦ *Premarital sex is an interesting moral issue.*

premature [pri mə 'tʃɚ] *adj.* early; before the expected time. (Adv: *prematurely.*) ♦ *The pregnant woman's accident triggered premature labor.* ♦ *Your present is premature. My birthday isn't until next week.*

premeditated [pri 'mɛd ɪ tet ɪd] *adj.* planned in advanced; thought out. (Adv: *premeditatedly.*) ♦ *The defendant is charged with premeditated murder.* ♦ *The police couldn't solve the premeditated crime.*

premier [prɪ 'mɪr] **1.** *adj.* first; initial. (Prenominal only.) ♦ *I bought the premier edition of the new magazine.* ♦ *The play's premier performance was a spectacular success.* **2.** *adj.* best; most notable. (Prenominal only.) ♦ *The premier software company hired the best programmers.* ♦ *The premier legal firm served very rich clients.* **3.** *n.* the prime minister of a country. ♦ *The premier met with the parliament about the new tax plan.* ♦ *The premier's assassination started a civil war.*

premiere [prɪ 'mɪr] **1.** *n.* the first performance or presentation of a play, film, symphony, etc. ♦ *Several critics attended the musical's premiere.* ♦ *The network advertised the season premieres heavily.* **2.** *iv.* [for a play, film, symphony, etc.] to be performed for the first time. ♦ *The musical premiered in Boston before playing on Broadway.* ♦ *The movie that I want to see premieres next Friday.*

premise ['prɛm ɪs] **1.** *n.* a statement that an argument or another statement is based on; a statement that is assumed to be true and on which another statement is based. ♦ *The illogical proof was based on a faulty premise.* ♦ *What is the premise for your argument?* **2.** *n.* a basic theme that is developed or built on. ♦ *The premise for my essay is that man is essentially good.* ♦ *The critic was disappointed by the film's basic premise.* **3. premises** *n.* a location; a piece of property, including the buildings that are built on it. (Treated as plural.) ♦ *The mortgage stated the legal description of the premises.* ♦ *The police wouldn't allow anyone to leave the premises.*

premium ['prim i əm] **1.** *n.* a regular payment to an insurance company for some kind of protection. ♦ *My insurance premiums are due on the first of each month.* ♦ *If your premium is late, you must pay a special fee.* **2.** *n.* an additional cost in addition to the regular cost. ♦ *The airplane passenger had to pay a premium for a seat by a window.* ♦ *I paid a premium for additional life insurance.* **3.** *n.* a small prize or reward that is given to someone to buy something or use a service. ♦ *The bank offered a toaster as a premium for opening an account.* ♦ *The cable company gave remote controls as a premium for starting service.* **4.** *adj.* of high quality; costing more; of greater value. ♦ *Premium gasoline provides more power than regular gasoline.* ♦ *Many amenities are available at premium hotels.* **5. at a premium** *phr.* at a high price; priced high because of something special. ♦ *Sally bought the shoes at a premium because they were of very high quality.* ♦ *This car model sells at a premium because so many people want to buy it.*

premonition [prɛm ə 'nɪ ʃən] *n.* a feeling that something is going to happen, especially that something bad is going to happen. ♦ *The elderly woman had a premonition that she would die.* ♦ *My premonition that the plane would crash made me feel uneasy.*

prenominal [pri 'nɑ mɪ nəl] *adj.* [of an adjective] occurring before the noun it modifies. (Adv: *prenominally.*) ♦ Late, *meaning 'dead,' can be used only as a prenominal adjective.* ♦ *Adjectives that are not prenominal cannot be used before the noun or nominal they modify.*

preoccupied [pri 'ɑk jə pɑɪd] *adj.* having all of one's time or attention taken up with someone or something. ♦ *The preoccupied driver crashed into a tree.* ♦ *Preoccupied with business, John stayed at the office late.*

prep. See preposition.

prepaid [pri 'ped] **1.** pt/pp of prepay. **2.** *adj.* paid in advance; paid beforehand. ♦ *Unless you have an account, prepaid postage is required.* ♦ *John picked up his prepaid tickets at the box office.* **3.** *adv.* with charges paid in advance. ♦ *She sent the package prepaid.* ♦ *It was shipped prepaid yesterday.*

preparation [prɛp ə 're ʃən] **1.** *n.* something that is done to prepare for something. (Sometimes plural with the same meaning.) ♦ *Anne's preparation for the party took all day.* ♦ *This recipe requires too much preparation.* **2.** *n.* something that is made by mixing things together, especially food or medicine. ♦ *The sick patient swallowed the bitter preparation.* ♦ *After adding the eggs, the cook put the preparation in the refrigerator for twenty minutes.*

preparatory [prɪ 'pɛr ə tor i] *adj.* preparing someone or something for something. ♦ *The gifted student went to a preparatory school.* ♦ *I took a preparatory class for the examination.*

prepare [prɪ 'pɛr] *tv.* to make something ready for someone or something; to make something ready for use. ♦ *The student prepared for the exam by studying all night.* ♦ *The maid prepared the beds for the hotel guests.*

prepared [prɪ 'pɛrd] *adj.* made ready ahead of time; made ready in advance. (Adv: *preparedly.* [prɪ 'pɛr əd li].) ♦ *I warmed the prepared food in the microwave oven.* ♦ *The president read a prepared speech.*

preparedness [prɪ 'pɛr ɪd nəs] *n.* a state of being prepared for something; readiness. (No plural form in this sense.) ♦ *Studying increased my preparedness for the examination.* ♦ *Exercise maintained the troops' preparedness to fight.*

prepay [pri 'pe] *tv., irreg.* to pay someone for something in advance; to pay someone for something before one receives it. (Pt/pp: prepaid.) ♦ *I prepaid the theater for my tickets with my credit card.* ♦ *Students prepaid the college for their tuition.*

preponderance [prɪ 'pɑn də rəns] *n.* a great amount of something. (No plural form in this sense.) ♦ *The preponderance of evidence led to the jury's guilty verdict.* ♦ *The preponderance of public sentiment is with the victim.*

preposition [prɛp ə 'zɪ ʃən] *n.* a word that is used to show the relationship of one word or phrase to another word or phrase. (Abbreviated *prep.* here. Prepositions take objects. For example: *aboard, about, across, after, against, along, alongside, among, around, astride, at, atop, before, behind, below, beneath, beside, between, beyond, but, by, concerning, despite, down, due to, during, except, except for, failing, for, from, in, in back of, inside, inside of, into, like, minus, near, of, off, on, onto, opposite, outside, outside of, over, past, pending, plus, round, save, since, through, throughout, till, times, to, toward(s), under, underneath, until, unto, up, upon, versus, vis-à-vis, with, within, without.*) ♦ In, on, under, *and* through *are all English prepositions.* ♦ *Pronouns following prepositions should be in the objective form: "John spoke to Jane and me."*

preposterous [prɪ 'pɑs trəs] *adj.* absurd; not making sense; outrageous; ridiculous. (Adv: *preposterously.*) ♦ *The police ignored the madman's preposterous confession.* ♦ *It would be preposterous to drive in this horrible blizzard.*

prerecorded [pri ri 'kord] *adj.* recorded ahead of time for use later. ♦ *This program was prerecorded in front of a live audience.* ♦ *When I watched the prerecorded baseball game, I already knew which team would win.*

prerequisite [prɪ 'rɛk wɪ zɪt] **1.** *n.* something that must be done before something else is done. ♦ *Passing the test is a prerequisite for graduating.* ♦ *Taking off your shoes is a prerequisite before entering my house.* **2.** *n.* a course that must be taken before one takes a more advanced course. ♦ *Algebra is a prerequisite for calculus.* ♦ *History 101 is a prerequisite for all other history courses.* **3.** *adj.* required before doing something else. ♦ *You must take the prerequisite classes before taking this one.* ♦ *Learning to type is prerequisite to using a computer.*

prerogative [prɪ 'rɑg ə tɪv] *n.* a right or privilege belonging to someone or something that has power or authority. ♦ *Ambulances have the prerogative to go through red lights.* ♦ *Dining in the executive dining room is a prerogative for club members.*

Presbyterian [prɛz bɪ 'tɪr i ən] **1.** *adj.* of or about the religion of the Presbyterian Church (U.S.A.) and its practitioners. ♦ *There are more than 12,000 Presbyterian churches in the U.S.* ♦ *Our wedding was performed by a Presbyterian minister.* **2.** *n.* a member of the Presbyterian church. ♦ *I married a Presbyterian.* ♦ *The Presbyterians donated clothing to charity.*

preschool ['pri skul] **1.** *n.* a school for small children before they are old enough to go to kindergarten. ♦ *When Susie was 4, she went to preschool in the mornings.* ♦ *Jimmy went to preschool because both of his parents worked.* **2.** *adj.* [of a child] not yet old enough to go to school; [concerning a child] not yet old enough to go to kindergarten. ♦ *The doctor vaccinated preschool children at the clinic.* ♦ *I bought some plastic preschool toys for my young nephew.*

prescribe [prɪ 'skrɑɪb] **1.** *tv.* [for a physician] to recommend or order that a certain medication be sold to and taken by a patient. ♦ *The doctor prescribed a mild tranquilizer.* ♦ *The doctor prescribed medicine for John's heart problem.* **2.** *tv.* [for a doctor] to advise a patient to do something to become or stay healthy. ♦ *The doctor prescribed daily walks for her overweight patients.* ♦ *My doctor prescribed exercise for my condition.* **3.** *tv.* to state something as a law; to establish something as a law. ♦ *The federal government prescribed the national speed limit.* ♦

Congress prescribed minimum sentences for certain offenses.

prescribed [prɪ 'skrɑɪbd] **1.** *adj.* of or about spoken or written instructions given by a doctor. ♦ *Mary took the prescribed dosage of medicine before each meal.* ♦ *John refrigerated his prescribed medicine.* **2.** *adj.* stated as law; established as a law. ♦ *What penalty is prescribed for murder.* ♦ *The prescribed penalty for certain crimes is life imprisonment.*

prescription [prɪ 'skrɪp ʃən] **1.** *n.* ordering or prescribing something, especially medicine or medical treatment. ♦ *My treatment required the prescription of a more powerful drug.* ♦ *I responded to my doctor's prescription of exercise with a laugh.* **2.** *n.* an order to do something or take medicine, especially a written order for medicine given to a patient by a doctor. ♦ *I handed my prescription to the pharmacist.* ♦ *My doctor gave me a prescription for penicillin.* **3.** *n.* the actual medicine that is ordered by ②. ♦ *I was told to take this prescription three times a day.* ♦ *I have to purchase a prescription at the drugstore.*

presence ['prɛz əns] **1.** *n.* the state of being present; being in the same place as someone or something else. (No plural form in this sense.) ♦ *The X-ray showed the presence of a tumor on my spine.* ♦ *The presence of dark clouds indicated that it would rain.* **2.** *n.* the power or influence one has in a group of people or in an institution. ♦ *The aging dean was a powerful presence in the university administration.* ♦ *John became an important presence in his law firm.* **3.** *n.* something that can be felt or sensed but not seen, such as a spirit. ♦ *Anne sensed her twin's presence even when they were miles apart.* ♦ *We can feel the presence of an evil spirit somewhere.* **4. have the presence of mind to do something** *idiom* to have the calmness and ability to act sensibly in an emergency or difficult situation. ♦ *Jane had the presence of mind to phone the police when the child disappeared.* ♦ *The child had the presence of mind to write down the car's license-plate number.*

present 1. ['prɛz ənt] *adj.* being in the same room or place as someone or something else; not absent; here. ♦ *All the students are present, so the teacher will begin class.* ♦ *Many of the actor's friends were present in the audience.* **2.** ['prɛz ənt] *adj.* now; at this time; happening now. (Adv: *presently.*) ♦ *The police cannot comment on that at the present time.* ♦ *The crime rate is one of the mayor's present concerns.* **3.** ['prɛz ənt] *adv.* here and not absent. ♦ *The teacher marked me present.* ♦ *The computer automatically reported the workers present.* **4.** ['prɛz ənt] *n.* now; this time; this moment in time. (No plural form in this sense.) ♦ *Cars look different in the present than they did in the 1920s.* ♦ *At present, five fire trucks are at the site of the accident.* **5.** ['prɛz ənt] *n.* a gift; something that is given to someone else. ♦ *My grandmother gave me a lovely present for my birthday.* ♦ *Anne sent a thank-you note for each present she had received.* **6.** present (tense) ['prɛz ənt…] *n.* a tense showing present time. (No plural form in this sense.) ♦ *The present of "John laughed" is "John laughs."* ♦ *The author rewrote her manuscript in the present.* **7.** [prɪ 'zɛnt] *tv.* to give something to someone, especially as part of a ceremony. ♦ *The groom presented the ring to his bride.* ♦ *The company presented a watch to each retired worker.* **8.** [prɪ 'zɛnt] *tv.* to make something available for the public to see; to bring something to someone's attention. ♦ *The movie studio presented a new film for the holiday season.* ♦ *The designer presented many ideas to the board of directors.* **9.** [prɪ 'zɛnt] *tv.* to introduce someone to someone else. ♦ *Mother, may I present my professor, Dr. Smith, to you?* ♦ *Jane presented her date to her parents.*

presentable [prɪ 'zɛn tə bəl] *adj.* suitable to be shown or seen. (Adv: *presentably.*) ♦ *Go change your clothes so you look more presentable!* ♦ *The report, although not perfect, was presentable.*

presentation [prɛz ən 'te ʃən] **1.** *n.* the way that something is shown to other people; the manner or style in which something is shown to other people. (No plural form in this sense.) ♦ *John's manner of presentation was calm and controlled.* ♦ *The skater's presentation received high marks from the judges.* **2.** *n.* the act of showing something to other people. ♦ *Mary's presentation at work went very smoothly.* ♦ *Although nervous, Anne enjoyed giving her presentation in class.* **3.** *n.* the ceremony of giving something to someone else. ♦ *Many celebrities attended the presentation of the awards.* ♦ *The presentation of the prizes will begin soon.*

present-day ['prɛz ənt 'de] *adj.* current; happening now; of or about the present time. ♦ *The magazine discussed present-day fashion trends.* ♦ *In English class, we read a lot of present-day literature.*

presenter [prɪ 'zɛn tɚ] *n.* someone who presents a gift or an award; someone who introduces someone; someone who presents a lecture. ♦ *The presenter announced the five nominees for "Best Picture."* ♦ *The audience applauded when the presenter finished her presentation.*

presently ['prɛz ənt li] **1.** *adv.* now; at this time. ♦ *Presently, John is the head cashier.* ♦ *Anne is busy presently. Can I take a message?* **2.** *adv.* soon. (Formal.) ♦ *I will do it presently.* ♦ *Flight 401 from Cleveland will be arriving presently.*

present participle ['prɛz ənt 'pɑr tə sɪp əl] *n.* <a form made by adding the suffix -ing to the bare verb.> (This form can function as a verb, noun, or adjective.) ♦ *"The cat is clawing the furniture to shreds" shows a present participle as a verb.* ♦ *"The laughing clowns failed to cheer her up" shows a present participle as an adjective.*

preservation [prɛ zɚ 've ʃən] *n.* the process of preserving something; keeping something safe or in good condition. (No plural form in this sense.) ♦ *The scientists lobbied for the preservation of endangered species.* ♦ *The prime minister supported the preservation of the rain forest.*

preservative [prɪ 'zɚ və tɪv] *n.* a substance that keeps something, such as food, from decaying. ♦ *The packaged doughnuts were full of artificial preservatives.* ♦ *Morticians use preservatives to keep bodies from decaying.*

preserve [prɪ 'zɚv] **1.** *tv.* to keep someone or something alive, healthy, safe, or in good condition. ♦ *Max eats only good things, hoping to preserve his health.* ♦ *I hope to preserve my peace of mind well into my old age.* **2.** *tv.* to do something or add something to something to keep it from spoiling or decaying. ♦ *The cook preserved the leftovers by freezing them.* ♦ *Tom preserved the frog in alcohol.* **3.** *n.* an area of land where plants and animals are protected. ♦ *Hunting is forbidden on game preserves.* ♦ *A staff of botanists helped to maintain the nature preserve.* **4. preserves** *n.* fruit cooked in sugar and sealed in a jar.

(Treated as plural.) ♦ *I spread some strawberry preserves on my toast.* ♦ *Grandma stores her preserves in the pantry.*

preside [prɪ 'zɑɪd] **1.** *iv.* to be in charge of a meeting or a business; to be in control. ♦ *When court is in session, the judge presides.* ♦ *As long as I preside, there will be order during meetings.* **2. preside over** *iv.* + *prep. phr.* to oversee something, such as a meeting. ♦ *The council president presided over the meeting.* ♦ *A judge presides over a courtroom.*

presidency ['prɛz ə dən si] *n.* the period of time when someone holds the office of president. ♦ *World War II was fought during Franklin Roosevelt's presidency.* ♦ *John's presidency at the company lasted for eight years.*

president ['prɛz ə dənt] **1.** *n.* the leader of the government of a republic, including the leader of the government of the United States of America. ♦ *The president answered questions during the press conference.* ♦ *President Reagan was in office from 1981 to 1989.* **2.** *n.* the leader or head officer of an organization, club, company, university, etc. ♦ *The president of the chess club arranged a tournament.* ♦ *The company president gave each employee an extra day off.* **3.** *n.* the office and position of power occupied by ① or ②. ♦ *Mary ran for class president.* ♦ *The talk-show host interviewed the candidates running for president.*

presidential [prɛz ə 'dɛn ʃəl] *adj.* of or about a president. (Adv: *presidentially.*) ♦ *Presidential elections are held on a Tuesday in November.* ♦ *The name of the presidential airplane is Air Force One.*

Presidents' Day ['prɛz ə dənts de] *n.* a U.S. holiday celebrated on the third Monday in February. ♦ *Presidents' Day marks the birthdays of the country's first president, George Washington, and the 16th president, Abraham Lincoln.* ♦ *Federal offices are closed on Presidents' Day.*

presiding [prɪ 'zɑɪd ɪŋ] *adj.* in charge; in control; running or controlling a meeting. ♦ *The presiding officer asked the treasurer to give a report.* ♦ *The presiding judge sentenced the criminal to jail.*

press ['prɛs] **1.** *n.* pressure; pushing. (No plural form in this sense.) ♦ *The press of the crowd moved me forward.* ♦ *I felt a gentle press on my shoulder, so I turned around.* **2. (printing) press** *n.* a machine used to print text and pictures on paper. ♦ *This printing press can produce thousands of copies each hour.* ♦ *Newspapers are printed on enormous, very fast printing presses.* **3.** *n.* a company that makes and sometimes sells or distributes books and other printed materials. ♦ *My manuscript is still at the press.* ♦ *This press has over 1,000 titles in stock.* **4. the press** *n.* newspapers and sometimes, radio and television; the mass media. (No plural form in this sense. Treated as a singular.) ♦ *Our publicity director faxed information to the press.* ♦ *The press is interested in events that people want to hear about.* **5.** *n.* the coverage of an action or event by newspapers and other media. (No plural form in this sense.) ♦ *The workers' protest got a lot of press.* ♦ *The publicity director tried to get more press for the new book.* **6.** *tv.* to push something against something else; to push something with force; to weigh down heavily on something. ♦ *In case of fire, press your hand against the alarm.* ♦ *John pressed the button to keep the elevator doors open.* **7.** *tv.* to move a hot iron over wrinkled clothing or fabric in order to make it smooth. ♦ *The launderer pressed each shirt after washing and drying it.* ♦ *I pressed the draperies because they were wrinkled.* **8.** *tv.* to ask for something again and again; to demand something. ♦ *I hate to press the issue, but could you give me an answer?* ♦ *John kept pressing his request for a raise.* **9.** *tv.* to lift a weight while weightlifting. ♦ *The athlete pressed 100 pounds.* ♦ *Jane pressed her own weight at the gym today.* **10. press for** *tv.* + *prep. phr.* to force someone to respond in some way. ♦ *Anne pressed her friend for an answer.* ♦ *John pressed his boss for a raise.* **11.** *iv.* to push against something else; to push with force; to weigh down heavily; to push forward. ♦ *Jane entered the elevator and pressed on the third-floor button.* ♦ *Bill pressed against the door to keep John from entering the room.*

pressing ['prɛs ɪŋ] *adj.* urgent; very important; very necessary. (Adv: *pressingly.*) ♦ *I interrupted my boss to report a pressing problem.* ♦ *I worked late to take care of a pressing issue.*

pressure ['prɛʃ ɚ] **1.** *n.* the effect of a force or a weight that is pushed against someone or something. (No plural form in this sense.) ♦ *The pressure from the flood water caused the dam to burst.* ♦ *If there's pressure against this button, an alarm will sound.* **2.** *n.* strong influence; strong persuasion. (Figurative on ①.) ♦ *The mayor put pressure on the council to pass his budget.* ♦ *Because of the lobbyist's pressure, the senator voted for the bill.* **3. under [some] pressure** *phr.* experiencing something that causes an amount of stress or anxiety. (Figurative on ①.) ♦ *I have a headache because I'm under a lot of pressure at work.* ♦ *The professor's children were under pressure to do well in school.* **4. pressure into** *tv.* + *prep. phr.* to succeed in persuading or forcing someone into doing something. ♦ *I pressured John into going to the movies with us.* ♦ *Anne pressured me into quitting smoking.*

prestige [prɛs 'tiʒ] *n.* good reputation and high distinction earned through success. (No plural form in this sense.) ♦ *Our mayor's prestige is known throughout the state.* ♦ *The influential researcher had a lot of prestige in her field.*

prestigious [prɛs 'tiʒ əs] *adj.* having great prestige. (Adv: *prestigiously.*) ♦ *A number of prestigious persons attended the wedding.* ♦ *The prestigious celebrity raised a lot of money for charity.*

presumably [prɪ 'zum ə bli] *adv.* as may be presumed; as may be supposed. ♦ *John presumably won't be coming, since he's sick.* ♦ *Presumably, the rally will be held indoors if it rains.*

presume ['prɪ zum] **1.** *tv.* to take something for granted; to suppose something; to assume something to be true. ♦ *Anne presumed the worst and was correct.* ♦ *Defendants are presumed innocent until proven guilty.* **2. presume to** *iv.* + *inf.* to dare to do something. ♦ *I would not presume to interfere in your business.* ♦ *John presumed to know what I was thinking.*

presumption [prɪ 'zʌm ʃən] **1.** *n.* boldness in supposing or assuming [arrogantly]. (No plural form in this sense.) ♦ *The presumption of innocence is part of every criminal trial.* ♦ *Your presumption in this matter is arrogant and unwelcome.* **2.** *n.* something that is taken for granted; a supposition; an assumption. ♦ *I'm operating under the presumption that the train will be late.* ♦ *Your presumption that John is guilty is unfounded.*

presumptuous [prɪ 'zʌm tʃu əs] *adj.* too bold; daring to do something that one should not do; tending to presume. (Adv: *presumptuously.*) ♦ *I told the presumptuous stranger to mind his own business.* ♦ *The bold student asked his teacher a presumptuous personal question.*

pretend [prɪ 'tɛnd] **1.** *iv.* to act [as if something were so]. ♦ *Jimmy couldn't fly, so he would pretend.* ♦ *I hate to pretend, so I will tell the truth.* **2.** *tv.* to make believe that something is so. (Takes a clause.) ♦ *The distraught man pretended he was happy.* ♦ *The children pretended that they lived in a castle.*

pretense ['pri tɛns] *n.* a false claim; a pretext. ♦ *I went to Anne's house on the pretense that I needed some sugar.* ♦ *The thief used the pretense that he was my nephew to get into my office.*

pretentious [prɪ 'tɛn ʃəs] *adj.* acting as though one were better or more important than one is; arrogant. (Adv: *pretentiously.*) ♦ *The pretentious woman talked for hours about herself.* ♦ *I asked the pretentious man to stop bragging about his accomplishments.*

pretext ['pri tɛkst] *n.* the reason that someone gives for doing something, which is different from the real reason. ♦ *John's claim of being sick was a pretext for skipping school.* ♦ *The thief entered the store on the pretext of buying shoes.*

pretty ['prɪt i] **1.** *adj.* attractive; pleasing; appealing. (Adv: *prettily.* Comp: *prettier;* sup: *prettiest.*) ♦ *There was a pretty bouquet of flowers in the vase.* ♦ *Mary wore a pretty blue dress to the dance.* **2.** *adv.* rather; quite; very. (Colloquial.) ♦ *I think I did pretty well on the examination.* ♦ *I think my interview went pretty smoothly.* **3. pretty much** *adv.* almost; just about. (Colloquial.) ♦ *Let's go. The concert is pretty much finished.* ♦ *I was pretty much done with my homework by midnight.*

pretzel ['prɛt səl] *n.* a salted, baked stick of bread, often twisted in the shape of a loose knot. ♦ *Pretzels are a snack that is very low in fat.* ♦ *I like pretzels better than potato chips.*

prevail [prɪ 'vel] **1.** *iv.* to exist in many places; to be widespread. ♦ *Sunny skies will prevail through the area all day.* ♦ *Despite crimes in the news, I believe that kindness prevails.* **2. prevail (over)** *iv.* (+ *prep. phr.*) to triumph [over someone or something]; to win [beating someone or something]. ♦ *The lawyer firmly believed that justice would prevail.* ♦ *Our triumphant army prevailed over the enemy.*

prevailing [prɪ 'vel ɪŋ] **1.** *adj.* most evident; most noticeable; predominant; widespread; common; general. (Adv: *prevailingly.*) ♦ *The market group researched prevailing trends among teenagers.* ♦ *The prevailing thought is that employers should pay for health care.* **2.** *adj.* of or about wind that usually blows over an area. (Adv: *prevailingly.*) ♦ *The prevailing winds brought cold and snow.* ♦ *The forecaster said the prevailing winds were out of the west.*

prevalent ['prɛv ə lənt] *adj.* evident; noticeable; predominant; widespread; common. (Adv: *prevalently.*) ♦ *It's a prevalent belief that smoking is harmful.* ♦ *The popular students established the prevalent fashion trends.*

prevaricate [prɪ 'vɛr ə ket] *iv.* to lie; to lie by answering a question vaguely, incompletely, or falsely. ♦ *The witness who prevaricated was charged with perjury.* ♦ *The thief prevaricated when questioned by the police.*

prevarication [prɪ vɛr ə 'ke ʃən] **1.** *n.* lying; not telling the truth. (No plural form in this sense.) ♦ *My lawyer exposed the defendant's constant prevarication.* ♦ *Prevarication can get you into a lot of trouble.* **2.** *n.* a lie. ♦ *A few small prevarications helped make Jane feel better about her failure to be promoted.* ♦ *Anne told a small prevarication to protect her friend's feelings.*

prevent [prɪ 'vɛnt] **prevent from** *tv.* + *prep. phr.* not to allow something to happen; not to allow someone to do something; to keep something from happening; to keep someone from doing something; to stop something before it begins. ♦ *The cement barrier prevented traffic from passing.* ♦ *John's parents prevented him from going to the party.*

preventable ['prɪ vɛnt ə bəl] *adj.* able to be prevented. (Adv: *preventably.*) ♦ *Mary's accident was preventable, but that doesn't help now.* ♦ *Many fires are preventable, but precautions must be taken.*

prevention [prɪ 'vɛn ʃən] *n.* preventing something. (No plural form in this sense.) ♦ *The firefighters went to the school to talk about fire prevention.* ♦ *The prevention of some diseases is possible with vaccinations.*

preventive [prɪ 'vɛn tɪv] *adj.* [of something] serving to prevent something from happening. ♦ *Mary took preventive measures to maintain her good health.* ♦ *Simple preventive steps will keep the equipment in good condition.*

preview ['pri vju] **1.** *n.* an opportunity to see something before it is available to the public. ♦ *Before the main feature, previews of other movies were shown.* ♦ *Most of the people who saw the preview of the new TV show liked it.* **2.** *iv.* [for something] to be shown as ①. ♦ *The movie previewed before a small party of the director's friends.* ♦ *The stage play previewed before a test audience.* **3.** *tv.* to watch or listen to something as ①. ♦ *I had the chance to preview the record before I bought it.* ♦ *The audience that previewed the new movie didn't like it.*

previous ['pri vi əs] **1.** *adj.* earlier; happening before something else; coming before. (Adv: *previously.*) ♦ *The previous owner of this house moved to Florida.* ♦ *For the previous ten hours, I had been sleeping.* **2. previous to** *adv.* + *prep. phr.* before something; prior to something. ♦ *Previous to our being here, there was a big argument.* ♦ *The president previous to George Bush was Ronald Reagan.*

previously ['pri vi əs li] *adv.* at an earlier time. ♦ *Previously, the law student had studied history.* ♦ *Previously, Texas was an independent republic.*

prewar ['pri 'wor] *adj.* before a war; of or about the time before a war. (Compare with **postwar**.) ♦ *The prewar treaties were broken during the war.* ♦ *The prewar boundaries were maintained after the war.*

prey ['pre] **1.** *n.* an animal that is hunted, killed, or eaten by another animal. (No plural form in this sense. Compare with **pray**.) ♦ *The eagle swooped down on its prey.* ♦ *The lion killed its prey by crushing its windpipe.* **2.** *n.* someone who is a victim of someone else. (No plural form in this sense. Figurative on ①.) ♦ *The thief chose foreign tourists as his prey.* ♦ *The criminal's prey sought compensation for their loss.* **3. prey on** *iv.* + *prep. phr.* to hunt and kill certain animals for food. ♦ *Wolves preyed on the shepherd's flock of sheep.* ♦ *The cat preys on birds and mice.* **4. prey on** *iv.* + *prep. phr.* to victimize someone. (Figurative on ③.) ♦ *The crook preyed on innocent citizens.* ♦

The corrupt stock broker preyed on the greed of his customers.

price ['prɑɪs] **1.** *n.* the amount of money that something costs; the amount of money that something will be sold for. ♦ *The price of this watch is $25.00.* ♦ *The price of gasoline rose two cents per gallon last week.* **2.** *tv.* to determine how much something will cost; to set the amount of money that something will cost. ♦ *This house is priced at $200,000.* ♦ *The salesman priced the used car below market value.* **3. have a price on one's head** *idiom* to be wanted by the authorities, who have offered a reward for one's capture. ♦ *We captured a thief who had a price on his head.* ♦ *The crook turned in his own brother, who had a price on his head.*

priceless ['prɑɪs ləs] **1.** *adj.* having a value that is too great to be determined; being worth so much that it doesn't have a price. (Adv: *pricelessly.*) ♦ *The priceless artwork was guarded 24 hours a day.* ♦ *The queen wore priceless jewels around her neck.* **2.** *adj.* amusing; charming; precious; delightful. (Figurative on ①. Adv: *pricelessly.*) ♦ *The old man told our class a priceless story about his youth.* ♦ *Jane's humorous observations were priceless!*

prick ['prɪk] **1.** *tv.* to make a small hole in someone or something with something sharp. ♦ *The tailor pricked his finger with a pin.* ♦ *The mosquito pricked my arm.* **2. pin prick** *n.* a tiny hole; a puncture. ♦ *The balloon was popped by a pin prick.* ♦ *John patched the pin prick in his leather couch.* **3.** *n.* a sudden, sharp pain or feeling, as if one were being pricked ①. ♦ *I felt a prick on my arm when the mosquito bit me.* ♦ *There was a slight prick of pain when the nurse gave me a shot.*

pride ['prɑɪd] **1.** *n.* the pleasure that one feels when one does something well; the feeling one has when one does something good. (No plural form in this sense.) ♦ *I have a feeling of pride when I an able to help someone.* ♦ *When my son won the championship, I was full of pride.* **2.** *n.* someone or something for which one has ①. (No plural form in this sense.) ♦ *Our new baby is our pride and joy.* ♦ *The Olympic skater was the pride of her hometown.* **3.** *n.* a good opinion of oneself; too high an opinion of oneself. (No plural form in this sense.) ♦ *The singer's excessive pride made her seem conceited.* ♦ *The mayor's pride made him blind to the problems in his city.* **4. pride oneself on something** *idiom* to feel one's pride about something one does or is. ♦ *The worker prided himself on his ability to do good work.* ♦ *The athlete prided herself on winning all the races she entered.* **5. take pride in something** *idiom* to do something with ①; to have ① for or about something. ♦ *The union workers took pride in their work.* ♦ *The artist took pride in her paintings.*

priest ['prist] *n.* someone who is trained to perform religious duties. (In the U.S., especially in the Roman Catholic, Orthodox Catholic, and Episcopal churches.) ♦ *During the full moon, the priest chanted a special prayer.* ♦ *Priests, ministers, and rabbis came to the convention of religious leaders.*

prim ['prɪm] *adj.* very proper; very formal; very exact; very precise; easily shocked by rude or rough behavior. (Adv: *primly.* Comp: *primmer;* sup: *primmest.*) ♦ *John's rude jokes offended the prim lady.* ♦ *Everything at the formal wedding was prim and proper.*

prima donna [prim ə 'dɑn ə] **1.** *n.* the leading female singer in an opera or in a musical group. (From Italian for 'first lady.') ♦ *The prima donna received a standing ovation after the opera.* ♦ *The director gave the prima donna a dozen roses on opening night.* **2.** *n.* someone who acts spoiled and demands to be catered to. (Figurative on ①.) ♦ *The prima donna treated the waiter very rudely.* ♦ *The prima donna demanded a private dressing room.*

primarily [prɑɪ 'mɛr ɪ li] *adv.* mainly; chiefly; for the most part; principally. ♦ *My classes are primarily within the department of history.* ♦ *Mary's duty was primarily to repair broken computers.*

primary ['prɑɪm ɚ i] **1.** *adj.* the most important; chief; main; principal. (Adv: *primarily* [prɑɪ 'mɛr ə li].) ♦ *The small island's primary source of revenue was tourism.* ♦ *My primary reason for running for mayor is to reduce crime.* **2.** *n.* an election that is held to determine who will represent a political party in the election for a political office. ♦ *The incumbent president won the primaries in every state.* ♦ *After winning the primary, Jane focused on the general election.* **3. primary color** *n.* one of the basic colors: red, blue, and yellow, because other colors can be made by mixing two or three of these together. ♦ *The painter mixed primary colors to create the others.* ♦ *The design was colored with primary colors only.* **4. primary school** *n.* a school having only the earliest grades. ♦ *My primary school is nearly a mile away.* ♦ *Students attend primary school before high school.*

primate ['prɑɪ met] *n.* a member of an advanced group of mammals, including humans, apes, and monkeys. ♦ *The archaeologist found the bones of a prehistoric primate.* ♦ *Humans are the most advanced of all the primates.*

prime ['prɑɪm] **1. prime (number)** *n.* a number that can only be evenly divided by itself and 1. ♦ *5 is a prime number, because it can only be divided evenly by 5 and 1.* ♦ *10 is not a prime, because it can be divided evenly by 10, 5, 2, and 1.* ♦ *Two is the only even-numbered prime.* **2.** *adj.* [of a state or condition] best or excellent. ♦ *The new car was in prime condition.* ♦ *The diners ate the prime roast beef.* **3.** *adj.* most important; chief; first in time, order, or importance. (Adv: *primely.*) ♦ *Location is the prime consideration for the new factory.* ♦ *The prime reason I'm moving to Florida is the weather.* **4.** *tv.* to add water or liquid to a pump to replace the air that is inside so that the pump is able to draw fluid. ♦ *You have to prime this pump before you can draw water from it.* ♦ *I poured a gallon of water into the pump to prime it.* **5.** *tv.* to make someone or something ready for something. (Figurative on ④.) ♦ *The announcer primed the audience for the next performer.* ♦ *We primed ourselves for the bad news at the hospital.* **6.** *tv.* to cover a surface with primer before painting it. ♦ *The carpenter primed the window frame twice.* ♦ *Mary primed the door with a paintbrush.* **7. in one's or its prime** *idiom* at one's or its peak or best time. ♦ *The program ended in its prime when we ran out of money.* ♦ *I could work long hours when I was in my prime.* **8. in the prime of life** *idiom* in the best and most productive period of one's life. ♦ *The good health of one's youth can carry over into the prime of life.* ♦ *He was struck down by a heart attack in the prime of life.* **9. prime mover** *idiom* the force that sets something going; someone or something that starts something off. ♦ *The assistant manager was the prime mover in getting the manager sacked.* ♦ *Dis-*

content with his job was the prime mover in John's deciding to emigrate.

prime minister ['prɑɪm 'mɪn ə stɚ] *n.* the head of government in countries that have a parliament. ♦ *The president invited the prime minister for dinner at the White House.* ♦ *The prime minister supports efforts to end pollution.*

primer 1. ['prɑɪm ɚ] *n.* a liquid that is spread over wood before one covers the wood with paint. (No plural form in this sense.) ♦ *Don't paint that door until the primer dries.* ♦ *The carpenter uses only high-quality primer to seal the wood.* **2.** ['prɪm ɚ] *n.* a book that is written to teach children how to read. ♦ *The children took their primers from their school desks.* ♦ *Susie said aloud the words that were written in her primer.*

primeval [prɑɪ 'mi vəl] *adj.* of or about the beginning and the earliest times of earth. (Adv: *primevally.*) ♦ *One-celled creatures swarmed in primeval ooze.* ♦ *In primeval times, there was one giant land mass on earth.*

primitive ['prɪm ə tɪv] **1.** *adj.* early in the development of something; early in the history of humankind. (Adv: *primitively.*) ♦ *The museum displayed the skeleton of a primitive ape.* ♦ *In its primitive stage, the plan was just a brief outline.* **2.** *adj.* very simple; not complicated. (Adv: *primitively.*) ♦ *The sociologist studied primitive cultures in the tropics.* ♦ *John's old computer is a primitive version of the latest model.*

primordial [prɑɪ 'mor di əl] *adj.* present from the earliest times; concerning the very beginning [of something]. (Adv: *primordially.*) ♦ *This insect arose from some sort of primordial life form.* ♦ *The earth was formed from a primordial mass of hot gases.*

primp ['prɪmp] *iv.* to preen; to dress and get ready for a social event very carefully. ♦ *John primped in front of the mirror before leaving the house.* ♦ *Anne primped for 30 minutes before going to the party.*

prince ['prɪns] **1.** *n.* the son or grandson of a king or a queen. ♦ *The handsome prince slew the dangerous dragon.* ♦ *Prince Charles is Queen Elizabeth II's eldest son.* **2.** *n.* the husband of a woman who inherits the throne and becomes queen. ♦ *Queen Victoria and Prince Albert were married in 1840.* ♦ *When the queen was crowned, she and her husband, the prince, moved to the castle.*

princely ['prɪns li] **1.** *adj.* like a prince; in the manner of a prince. ♦ *The princely gentleman was polite, charming, and well liked.* ♦ *The princely head of the company took us on a tour of the factory.* **2.** *adj.* elegant; refined; noble. (Figurative on ①.) ♦ *John's princely tastes are rather expensive.* ♦ *The princely feast featured very fine food.*

princess ['prɪns ɛs] **1.** *n.* the daughter or granddaughter of a king or queen. ♦ *Queen Elizabeth II's daughter is named Princess Anne.* ♦ *The knight rescued the princess from the enemy's castle.* **2.** *n.* the wife of a prince. ♦ *Sue dreamed of someday marrying a prince and becoming a princess.* ♦ *The princess was not allowed to retain her title after divorcing the prince.*

principal ['prɪns ə pəl] **1.** *n.* the head of an elementary, middle, or high school. (Compare with principle.) ♦ *The naughty student was sent to the principal's office.* ♦ *Ms. Jones spoke to Principal Davis about the truant student.* **2.** *n.* an amount of borrowed money on which the borrower must pay interest. ♦ *The bank added the late fees to my principal.* ♦ *Interest owed is a percentage of outstanding principal.* **3.** *n.* the most important or major person in a group. ♦ *The actors who played the principals in the play were paid more than the rest of the cast.* ♦ *The principals in the robbery were all sent to prison.* **4.** *adj.* main; chief; primary; most important. (Adv: *principally.*) ♦ *Security is the principal reason that Jane bought an alarm system.* ♦ *Anne is playing the principal female role in the play.*

principle ['prɪns ə pəl] **1.** *n.* obedience to ② and ③; honor. (No plural form in this sense. Compare with principal.) ♦ *Bill couldn't leave early. It was a matter of principle.* ♦ *Anne refused for the sake of principle.* **2.** *n.* a general or fundamental law or rule. ♦ *The final examination covered basic principles of physics.* ♦ *Formal proofs are based on the principles of logic.* **3.** *n.* a rule of behavior or conduct. ♦ *I live by the principles of my religion.* ♦ *The ambitious leader sacrificed her principles to gain power.*

print ['prɪnt] **1.** *tv.* to make letters of the alphabet by hand so that each letter is separate. ♦ *David learned to print his name when he was five.* ♦ *Please print your name on the dotted line.* **2.** *tv.* to put words or pictures on a blank piece of paper, one page at a time, using some kind of machine. ♦ *This printer prints twelve pages a minute.* ♦ *This picture was printed on a color copier.* **3.** *tv.* to publish a book, magazine, or newspaper using a printing press or a computer printer. ♦ *All of my books have been printed by the same publisher.* ♦ *The publisher printed 10,000 copies of the first edition.* **4.** *tv.* to publish something that is written in a book, newspaper, magazine, or other written material. ♦ *The magazine printed the whole story of the hostage crisis.* ♦ *The newspaper printed my comments out of context.* **5.** *tv.* to make a photograph from film. ♦ *Could you print some extra copies of that picture for me?* ♦ *Were these copies printed from the negative?* **6.** *tv.* to cause a computer to print ② something. ♦ *John printed the entire file.* ♦ *Jane printed the message that was on her computer screen.* **7.** *iv.* to make letters of the alphabet so that each letter is separate. ♦ *Mary learned to print in first grade.* ♦ *I asked Jane to print because I couldn't read her writing.* **8.** *iv.* to make books, magazines, newspapers, and other written material with a printing press. ♦ *The presses are printing now. It's too late to make any changes.* ♦ *The newspaper presses printed throughout the night.* **9.** *iv.* [for a computer printer] to print ② [something]. ♦ *The printer printed until it ran out of paper.* ♦ *This printer prints in many different colors.* **10.** *n.* letters or words that are printed ② with type ③. (No plural form in this sense.) ♦ *The print needs to be larger for me to see it well.* ♦ *The print was italic and was hard to read.* **11.** *n.* fabric that has a pattern on it. ♦ *I covered the sofa with a nice colorful print.* ♦ *Anne made a dress from a bright plaid print.* **12.** *n.* a copy of a movie. ♦ *The studio sent an advance print of the new movie to the critics.* ♦ *The projector destroyed a rare print when it burst into flames.* **13.** *n.* a photograph that is made from film; a photograph. ♦ *I have several prints of my dog in my photo album.* ♦ *The police showed me a print of the suspect.* **14.** *n.* a fingerprint. ♦ *The thief's prints were found on the doorknob.* ♦ *Whose prints are these on the gun?* **15. in print** *phr.* available in a book, magazine, newspaper, or other written material. ♦ *Ten thousands copies of the first edition remain in print.* ♦ *The publisher listed all of its books in print.* **16. out of print** *phr.*

no longer available in printed form. (In reference to books.) ♦ *I copied the article because it's out of print.* ♦ *This book is out of print, so I borrowed it from the library.* **17. small print; fine print** *idiom* an important part of a document that is not easily noticed, often because of the smallness of the printing. ♦ *You should have read the small print before signing the contract.* ♦ *You should always read the fine print of an insurance policy.*

printer ['prɪn tɚ] **1.** *n.* a business entity that prints books, magazines, and other materials. ♦ *The printer lost the last page of the author's manuscript.* ♦ *The printer shipped the books to its warehouse.* **2.** *n.* a machine that causes computer information to be put onto paper. (See also printing press at press.) ♦ *That laser printer prints five pages a minute.* ♦ *I sent the document to the printer.*

printing ['prɪn tɪŋ] **1.** *n.* letters or words that are printed by hand; letters that are put on paper so that the letters are separate, as opposed to handwriting. (No plural form in this sense.) ♦ *My printing is much neater than my handwriting.* ♦ *The printing on the poster was in a foreign language.* **2.** *n.* letters that are put on a page by a press or a computer. (No plural form in this sense.) ♦ *The printing on the first page is crooked.* ♦ *The printing in the second section is smeared.* **3.** *n.* all the copies of a book printed by machine at one time. ♦ *The popular book's first printing sold out in two weeks.* ♦ *Fifty thousand copies were made of the book's fourth printing.* **4. printing press** See press ②.

printout ['prɪnt ɑʊt] *n.* a copy of information from a computer, printed on paper. ♦ *The researcher read the experiment's results from the printout.* ♦ *I made a copy of the printout for everyone at the meeting.*

prior ['prɑɪ ɚ] **1.** *adj.* previous; earlier. ♦ *My prior attempts to finish the project failed.* ♦ *Anne's prior husband died five years ago.* **2. prior to** *adv.* + *prep. phr.* before. ♦ *Prior to lunch, I worked for four hours.* ♦ *Anne studied history prior to studying law.*

prioritize [prɑɪ 'or ə tɑɪz] *tv.* to arrange tasks into an order that puts the most important first. ♦ *If you would prioritize your tasks, you would be more efficient.* ♦ *Prioritize your assignments so that the most important ones get done first.*

priority [prɑɪ 'or ə ti] *n.* something that is more important than anything else; something that needs attention before everything else. ♦ *My boss said finishing the budget was my first priority.* ♦ *Going to the movies is not a priority this week.*

prism ['prɪz əm] *n.* a block of glass that has a flat, three-sided top and bottom, and edges that are straight up and down, and that projects the colors of the rainbow when light passes through it. ♦ *We made rainbows in science class by using a prism.* ♦ *Shafts of colored light beamed from the prism.*

prison ['prɪz ən] **1.** *n.* a building that criminals are kept in; a large jail. ♦ *The guilty criminal was sent to prison.* ♦ *The governor approved the construction of five new prisons.* **2.** *n.* a place where someone is not allowed to leave; a place where someone has no freedom. (Figurative on ①.) ♦ *The frail woman's apartment became her prison.* ♦ *The blind man lived in a prison of darkness.*

prisoner ['prɪz nɚ] **1.** *n.* someone who is kept in a prison. ♦ *The prisoner had been jailed for twenty years.* ♦ *The prisoner was led to his parole hearing.* **2.** *n.* someone or a creature that has been captured and is not free to go. (Figurative on ①.) ♦ *The garage door was closed, and the sleeping cat became a prisoner.* ♦ *The frail old couple were prisoners in their own home.*

prissy ['prɪs i] *adj.* fussy; too proper. (Adv: *prissily.* Comp: *prissier;* sup: *prissiest.*) ♦ *A prissy clerk gave me a disapproving look when I commented on the merchandise.* ♦ *The prissy waiter ignored my joke.*

pristine ['prɪs tin] *adj.* as fresh and clean as when it was new; spotless. (Adv: *pristinely.*) ♦ *This river is pristine before it flows through the city.* ♦ *I keep our house in pristine condition.*

privacy ['prɑɪv ə si] *n.* a state of being away from other people or away from the attention of the public. (No plural form in this sense.) ♦ *The accountant worked in the privacy of her own home.* ♦ *I demand that you respect my privacy.*

private ['prɑɪv ɪt] **1.** *adj.* not shared among everyone; meant only for a small number of people; not public. (Adv: *privately.*) ♦ *Only local residents were allowed access to the private beach.* ♦ *A locked gate blocked the private road.* **2.** *adj.* individual; concerning only one person. (Adv: *privately.*) ♦ *My private affairs are none of your business.* ♦ *The president refused to talk about his private life.* **3.** *adj.* secluded; isolated; quiet; away from other people. (Adv: *privately.*) ♦ *John and Mary went to a private area of the building to talk.* ♦ *I spent the winter in a private cabin in the woods.* **4.** *adj.* not owned, controlled, or managed by the government. (Adv: *privately.*) ♦ *John attends classes at a private university.* ♦ *The garbage in our town is collected by a private company.*

privilege ['prɪv (ə) lɪdʒ] **1.** *n.* special rights; special and exclusive status. (No plural form in this sense.) ♦ *The wealthy seem to have a great deal of privilege.* ♦ *Privilege and power are in the hands of only a few people.* **2.** *n.* a special right or favor that is given to someone or a certain group. ♦ *The use of this beach is a privilege for city residents.* ♦ *We had the privilege of meeting the reclusive celebrity.*

privileged ['prɪv (ə) lɪdʒd] **1.** *adj.* having a special right or favor. ♦ *Only a privileged few had access to the private beach.* ♦ *The privileged students were allowed to use the computers at school.* **2.** *adj.* [of a conversation or information] private and limited to the hearing or reading of the person it was intended for. ♦ *The attorney couldn't talk about the crook's privileged confession.* ♦ *The reporter refused to reveal privileged information.*

privy ['prɪv i] **1.** *n.* an outhouse; a building, separated from a house, where one can go to the bathroom. ♦ *The farmer put on his boots and walked out to the privy.* ♦ *When our power went out, we had to use the privy near the barn.* **2. privy to something** *idiom* uniquely knowledgeable about something. ♦ *The reporter became privy to the senator's evil plan.* ♦ *Why are you privy to this secret information?*

prize ['prɑɪz] **1.** *n.* an award that is given to a winner; an award that is given to someone who does well in a competition. ♦ *The fastest runner received first prize.* ♦ *The contestant in third place received a small prize.* **2.** *tv.* to consider something to be worth very much; to place a great value on something. ♦ *The actor prized his awards above all else.* ♦ *The large diamond was prized for its beauty.*

prized ['prɑɪzd] *adj.* considered to be worth very much; having a great value; greatly valued. ♦ *The prized diamond was stolen by a clever thief.* ♦ *The museum displayed the artist's prized works.*

prizewinner ['prɑɪz wɪn ɚ] *n.* someone who wins a prize. ♦ *The prizewinner won a trip to Florida.* ♦ *Prizewinners must pay taxes on their winnings.*

pro ['pro] **1.** *n.* an advantage; a reason for doing something. (The opposite of con ①. Pl in -s.) ♦ *There are several pros for lowering the interest rate.* ♦ *Anne listed the pros and cons of quitting her job.* **2.** *n.* someone who is in favor of something. (The opposite of con ②. Pl in -s.) ♦ *The pros outnumber the cons.* ♦ *In the final vote, the pros won.* **3.** *n.* professional. (Pl in -s.) ♦ *The charity auctioned a baseball signed by a sports pro.* ♦ *The pro baseball player demanded a higher salary.*

proactive ['pro æk tɪv] *adj.* likely to intervene; likely to act to prevent something from happening. (Compare with reactive. Adv: *proactively.*) ♦ *Vaccination programs are a proactive form of health care.* ♦ *The school board took a proactive stance against drug abuse.*

probability [prɑb ə 'bɪl ə ti] *n.* the likelihood or chance that something will happen. (No plural form in this sense.) ♦ *The probability of rain tonight is good.* ♦ *There is a remote probability that I may go to the party.*

probable ['prɑb ə bəl] *adj.* likely to happen; likely to be true. (Adv: *probably.*) ♦ *The coroner determined the probable cause of John's death.* ♦ *My father's probable response will be "no."*

probably ['prɑb ə bli] *adv.* in a way that is likely to happen or likely to be true. ♦ *It will probably rain tomorrow.* ♦ *Mary is probably at the bowling alley.*

probation [pro 'be ʃən] **1.** *n.* a state of existence where an offender remains out of jail and under observation as long as no further crimes are committed. (No plural form in this sense.) ♦ *During her period of probation, Anne reported to the police weekly.* ♦ *John managed to stay out of trouble during his probation.* **2.** *n.* a trial period. (Figurative on ①. No plural form in this sense.) ♦ *We had a period of probation as new members of the club.* ♦ *I had a year of probation in my new job before it became permanent.* **3. on probation** *phr.* serving a period of ①. ♦ *While Anne was on probation, she reported to the police regularly.* ♦ *John was on probation for a year.* **4. on probation** *phr.* serving a period of ②. ♦ *All new members are on probation for a year.* ♦ *I was on probation in my job for a full year before it became permanent.*

probationary [pro 'be ʃə nɛr i] *adj.* trial ④. ♦ *If you are unhappy with the product during the probationary period, we'll refund your money.* ♦ *The new member's first year in the fraternity was probationary.*

probe ['prob] **1.** *n.* a complete examination or investigation. ♦ *The investigator's probe didn't uncover any new clues.* ♦ *The senator demanded a probe of the president's affairs.* **2.** *n.* a thin rod with a rounded end that is used to examine the inside of a hole, wound, or cavity. ♦ *My dentist stuck the probe into my gums.* ♦ *The doctor examined my wound with a probe.* **3.** *n.* a rocket or satellite that is sent into space to relay information about space or other planets to scientists on earth. ♦ *The space probe drifted by the surface of Jupiter.* ♦ *The astronomers examined the data transmitted by the probe.* **4.** *tv.* to examine a hole, wound, or cavity with ②. ♦ *The dentist probed my teeth for cavities.* ♦ *The surgeon probed my wound for shrapnel.* **5.** *iv.* to examine; to search; to investigate. ♦ *The detective probed into the circumstances of the murder.* ♦ *The reporter probed into the president's affairs.*

probing ['prob ɪŋ] *adj.* searching; examining; investigating. (Adv: *probingly.*) ♦ *The doctor's probing hands found a lump on my neck.* ♦ *The inspector's probing questions made me uncomfortable.*

problem ['prɑb ləm] **1.** *n.* a question that must be answered; a difficulty. ♦ *I spoke to my counselor about my problems.* ♦ *There are too many problems to be solved in a single day!* **2.** *n.* a question put forward for solving, as in a school exercise or test. ♦ *The teacher assigned twenty algebra problems as homework.* ♦ *I was not able to solve the math problems before class.* **3.** *adj.* difficult to deal with; difficult to work with; causing difficulty. ♦ *The teacher sent the problem child to the principal's office.* ♦ *The dentist examined my problem tooth.*

problematic [prɑ blə 'mæt ɪk] *adj.* causing doubt; difficult to understand or deal with; hard to solve; causing problems. (Adv: *problematically* [...ɪk li].) ♦ *John needed to decide what to do about his problematic job.* ♦ *I avoided a problematic situation at work.*

problematical [prɑ blə 'mæt ɪk əl] *adj.* open to question; dependent on something. (Adv: *problematically* [...ɪk li].) ♦ *Whether I will be there on time is problematical.* ♦ *The time you suggest is somewhat problematical.*

procedure [prə 'si dʒɚ] *n.* the way that something is done; the way that a process is done; a method. ♦ *The manager explained company procedures to the new employees.* ♦ *Bill taught me the procedures for operating the machine.*

proceed [prə 'sid] **1.** *iv.* to continue to do something after stopping for a period of time; to do another activity after pausing or doing something else. ♦ *I stopped at the corner, looked both ways, and proceeded across the street.* ♦ *Bill went to the kitchen and proceeded to eat a piece of cheese.* **2. proceeds** *n.* money that is collected or received from someone or something. (Treated as plural.) ♦ *The proceeds from the auction were donated to charity.* ♦ *All proceeds from the telethon will support this station.*

proceeding [prə 'sid ɪŋ] **proceedings** *n.* a record of the speeches, lectures, testimony, questions, answers, and commentary that occurred in a conference or trial. (Treated as plural.) ♦ *The proceedings of the meeting were published as a book after the convention.* ♦ *The trial proceedings were available to both lawyers.*

process ['prɑ sɛs] **1.** *n.* a series of actions; a set of procedures used to do, make, achieve, prepare, or develop something. ♦ *The process of filming a movie is very expensive.* ♦ *This coffee maker brews coffee by a special process.* **2.** *tv.* to do a series of actions to something; to prepare, achieve, or develop something. ♦ *The computer processed all of the data in seconds.* ♦ *The clerk processed my request as soon as I placed my order.*

procession [prə 'sɛ ʃən] *n.* a moving line of people or things; a steady movement of people or things in a line.

♦ *Funeral processions have the right-of-way at intersections.* ♦ *There was a long procession of actors at the open auditions.*

processor ['prɑ sɛs ɚ] *n.* the part of a computer that performs the actual computing work. ♦ *Anne bought a computer with a more powerful processor.* ♦ *The processor was not powerful enough for the type of work John was doing.*

proclaim [prə 'klem] *tv.* to declare something officially; to make something public knowledge. ♦ *The soldier proclaimed his allegiance to his country.* ♦ *The senator proclaimed that he would seek reelection.*

proclamation [prɑk lə 'me ʃən] *n.* a statement that is proclaimed; something that is declared officially. ♦ *The mayor's proclamation was televised.* ♦ *I read the proclamation about the new national holiday.*

proclivity [prə 'klɪv ə ti] *n.* a tendency; an inclination. ♦ *Bill has a proclivity for listening to country music.* ♦ *John has a proclivity to cleanliness that Mary finds irritating.*

procrastinate [prə 'kræs tə net] **1.** *iv.* to delay. ♦ *Bob procrastinates because he never feels like working.* ♦ *If you hadn't procrastinated, you'd be done by now.* **2.** *tv.* to delay doing something until later. (Requires a clause with -ing.) ♦ *Sue procrastinated paying her bills, so she had to pay a late fee.* ♦ *I procrastinated returning the library book until it was overdue.*

procrastination [prə kræs tə 'ne ʃən] *n.* the practice of delaying doing something until later. (No plural form in this sense.) ♦ *Because of your procrastination, we missed the deadline.* ♦ *Sue's procrastination in paying her bills resulted in late fees.*

procreate ['pro kri et] *iv.* to produce offspring; to create life by reproducing. ♦ *Rabbits procreate very frequently.* ♦ *People tend to procreate at an older age than a few years ago.*

proctor ['prɑk tɚ] **1.** *n.* a school official who maintains discipline and is present during examinations. ♦ *The proctor handed me a newly sharpened pencil.* ♦ *Proctors do not tolerate cheating.* **2.** *iv.* to serve as ①. ♦ *When I took the placement exam, my counselor proctored.* ♦ *Because the principal was proctoring, no one dared to cheat.* **3.** *tv.* to monitor an examination as in ①. ♦ *One of the counselors proctored the placement examination.* ♦ *The departmental exam was proctored by a watchful secretary.*

procure [pro 'kjʊr] *tv.* to get something by work or effort. ♦ *My friend procured two concert tickets after waiting in line for hours.* ♦ *My boss procured upgraded computer equipment for our department.*

prod ['prɑd] **1.** *n.* a stick or rod that is used to push or poke someone or something. ♦ *The cowboy poked the steer with his cattle prod.* ♦ *John used his umbrella as a prod to push me forward.* **2.** *n.* a push; a poke; a nudge. ♦ *Anne's gentle prod moved me closer to the edge of the cliff.* ♦ *Mary's prod pushed me from the diving board.* **3.** *tv.* to push or poke someone or something with a stick or rod. ♦ *The cowboy prodded the cattle to make them move.* ♦ *The dentist prodded my gums with an instrument.* **4. prod to** *tv. + inf.* to urge someone to do something; to pressure someone to do something. (Figurative on ③.) ♦ *Bill prodded Susan to go dancing with him.* ♦ *The supervisor prodded the employees to work faster.*

prodigious [prə 'dɪ dʒəs] **1.** *adj.* large; enormous; vast. (Adv: *prodigiously.*) ♦ *I have a prodigious amount of work to do before I leave.* ♦ *The man with a prodigious appetite ate a pound of beef.* **2.** *adj.* amazing; wonderful; awesome. (Adv: *prodigiously.*) ♦ *The popular performer had a prodigious sense of comic timing.* ♦ *My five-year-old has a prodigious talent for playing the piano.*

prodigy ['prɑd ə dʒi] *n.* someone, especially a child, who has special abilities or talents. ♦ *The young prodigy spoke Latin and Greek before she was 5.* ♦ *The prodigy began college when he was only 9.*

produce 1. ['pro dus] *n.* food or food products that are farmed or grown; fruits and vegetables. (No plural form in this sense.) ♦ *Anne bought produce fresh from the farmers' market.* ♦ *Mary canned produce for use during the winter months.* **2.** [prə 'dus] *tv.* to grow something; to create something. ♦ *Kansas produces millions of bushels of wheat each year.* ♦ *Charles Dickens produced many well-known works of fiction.* **3.** [prə 'dus] *tv.* to cause something to be; to create a result. ♦ *Poverty produces much unhappiness.* ♦ *The tornado produced a lot of property damage.* **4.** [prə 'dus] *tv.* to make something from parts or materials. ♦ *This factory produces 400 engines a day.* ♦ *The terrorist produced a bomb from fertilizer.* **5.** [prə 'dus] *tv.* to coordinate and organize the details involved in making or presenting a movie, play, or other performance. ♦ *Our theater company produces five plays each season.* ♦ *The film studio produced a cartoon for the holiday season.* **6.** [prə 'dus] *iv.* to do what is expected or required, especially in terms of productivity. ♦ *These machines are producing at full speed.* ♦ *My boss fired the salespeople who couldn't produce.*

producer [prə 'dus ɚ] **1.** *n.* someone or something that produces something. ♦ *Kansas is a leading producer of wheat.* ♦ *Japan is an important producer of electronic equipment.* **2.** *n.* someone who coordinates and organizes the details involved in making or presenting a movie, television show, play, or other performance. ♦ *The producer determined each designer's budget.* ♦ *The director reported problems on the set to the producer.*

product ['prɑ dəkt] **1.** *n.* something that is produced; something that is made, created, or grown. ♦ *Many electronic products are made in East Asia.* ♦ *Paintings are the product of the artist's imagination.* **2.** *n.* someone or something that is the result of certain conditions; a result. ♦ *Mary's sorrow is the product of many years of sacrifice.* ♦ *Slippery roads are the product of snowy weather.* **3.** *n.* the number that is determined by multiplying two or more numbers together. ♦ *The product of 2 and 6 is 12.* ♦ *The product of any number and zero is zero.*

production [prə 'dʌk ʃən] **1.** *n.* producing something; making something. (No plural form in this sense.) ♦ *Oil production is very important to Saudi Arabia's economy.* ♦ *Many factories in Michigan are for car production.* **2.** *n.* the amount of or rate of ①. (No plural form in this sense.) ♦ *The factory's production had risen 10% over the previous year.* ♦ *The low production of the farm meant that the farm might fail.* **3.** *n.* a movie, television show, play, or other performance. ♦ *The award ceremony began with a lavish musical production.* ♦ *The famous actress had been in many productions.*

productive [prə 'dʌk tɪv] *adj.* producing good results. (Adv: *productively.*) ♦ *The owner gave the productive workers a raise.* ♦ *The productive factory was a boon to the local economy.*

productivity [pro dək 'tɪv ə ti] *n.* the rate that something is produced; the ability to produce products at a particular level of efficiency. (No plural form in this sense.) ♦ *The manager analyzed each employee's productivity.* ♦ *Productivity at this factory rose 10% last year.*

profane [pro 'fen] **1.** *tv.* to show disrespect or contempt for God or something sacred. ♦ *You have profaned the memory of your father by cursing him.* ♦ *Please don't profane things that are sacred to other people.* **2.** *adj.* showing disrespect or contempt for God or something sacred. (Adv: *profanely.*) ♦ *The network censored the performer's profane remarks.* ♦ *The protester's profane actions shocked the congregation.*

profanity [pro 'fæn ə ti] *n.* cursing; swearing. (No plural form in this sense.) ♦ *The angry customer's profanity shocked the cashier.* ♦ *Many viewers urged the network to forbid profanity on talk shows.*

profess [prə 'fɛs] **1.** *tv.* to declare something; to state something without shame. ♦ *John professed his love to Mary.* ♦ *The politician professed his loyalty to his party.* **2.** *tv.* to claim something; to believe something to be true. (Takes a clause.) ♦ *The crazy professor professed that the world was flat.* ♦ *Max professed that the end of the world was near.*

profession [prə 'fɛ ʃən] **1.** *n.* a job or career, especially one that requires education or training. ♦ *Please list your profession on line 2.* ♦ *Jane was satisfied with her chosen profession.* **2.** *n.* all of the people who work in a certain ①. ♦ *The medical profession regards smoking as harmful.* ♦ *The legal profession refused to support either candidate.* **3.** *n.* a declaration; a statement. ♦ *Mary's profession of love for her children was touching.* ♦ *The imprisoned man issued a profession of his innocence.*

professional [prə 'fɛʃ ə nəl] **1.** *adj.* <the adj. form of profession ①.> (Adv: *professionally.*) ♦ *The mayor belonged to several professional organizations.* ♦ *The injured man sought professional advice from his lawyer.* **2.** *adj.* showing the skill and standards of ③. (Adv: *professionally.*) ♦ *Mary did a professional job of landscaping our yard.* ♦ *Bob wanted the wiring in his house to be perfect, so he hired a professional electrician.* **3.** *n.* someone who works in a profession. ♦ *We hired a professional to design our house.* ♦ *Most health professionals agree that smoking is harmful.*

professor [prə 'fɛs ɚ] *n.* someone who holds a faculty position in a university or college. (Also a term of address.) ♦ *Anne is a full professor in the department of history.* ♦ *Professor Jones read my essay carefully.*

professorial [prɑ fə 'sor i əl] *adj.* in the manner of a professor; knowledgeable and refined. (Adv: *professorially.*) ♦ *The scholar's professorial manner was very dignified.* ♦ *Dr. Jones looked at me with his professorial gaze and frightened me.*

proficiency [prə 'fɪʃ ən si] *n.* the ability to do something properly and skillfully. (No plural form in this sense.) ♦ *Bill's proficiency at playing the piano is excellent.* ♦ *Jane's proficiency in German is as good as a native speaker's.*

proficient [prə 'fɪʃ ənt] *adj.* able to do something properly and skillfully; skillful. (Adv: *proficiently.*) ♦ *The proficient pianist played for the city orchestra.* ♦ *The linguist was proficient in five languages.*

profile ['pro fɑɪl] **1.** *n.* a side view of someone or something, especially of someone's face. ♦ *Bill preferred his right profile to his left.* ♦ *I saw John's profile through the window.* **2.** *n.* a short description of someone or something. ♦ *The program included a profile of each actor.* ♦ *Mary's profile stated that she spent four years in the Navy.* **3.** *tv.* to write about someone's life or achievements. ♦ *The documentary profiled the movies of the deceased actress.* ♦ *This book profiles the life of each president.*

profit ['prɑf ɪt] **1.** *n.* the amount of money made by a person or business after all expenses are paid. ♦ *Last year, our company made a modest profit.* ♦ *The four owners each had a share in the profits.* **2.** *tv.* to benefit someone or something. ♦ *Your help profited me a great deal.* ♦ *The opening of the new factory profited the local economy.* **3. profit from** *iv.* + *prep. phr.* to benefit from something. ♦ *The inspector profited from my information.* ♦ *The football team profited from playing in their hometown.*

profitable ['prɑf ɪt ə bəl] **1.** *adj.* providing a profit. (Adv: *profitably.*) ♦ *I sought a steady job at a profitable company.* ♦ *The profitable business pleased the investors.* **2.** *adj.* useful; worth doing; beneficial. (Adv: *profitably.*) ♦ *I hope that we will have a profitable meeting.* ♦ *The researcher spent a profitable day at the library.*

profiteer [prɑ fə 'tɪr] **1.** *n.* someone who makes money by charging a lot of money for things that are in short supply. ♦ *The profiteers charged $10 for a gallon of water when the supply was low.* ♦ *The profiteer sold items in short supply for very high prices.* **2.** *iv.* to make money by charging a lot of money for things that are in short supply. ♦ *Before the hurricane, the store profiteered by charging double for plywood.* ♦ *The merchant profiteered by selling tickets for triple their cost.*

profound [prə 'fɑʊnd] **1. profound depth(s)** *n.* a great distance, such as to the bottom of the sea or out into space. ♦ *The submarine descended to the profound depths of the sea.* ♦ *The rocket went into the profound depth of space.* **2.** *adj.* showing deep thought or understanding. (Figurative on ①. Adv: *profoundly.*) ♦ *It was hard to understand the philosopher's profound statements.* ♦ *I had nothing profound to say about the book, so I kept quiet.*

profuse [prə 'fjus] *adj.* abundant; in large amounts; plentiful. (Adv: *profusely.*) ♦ *The ancient ruins were covered with profuse plant growth.* ♦ *There was a profuse amount of ice on the airplane's wings.*

progenitor [pro 'dʒɛn ɪ tor] *n.* a direct ancestor of some creature. ♦ *One shares genetic material with one's progenitors.* ♦ *Humans and apes share a common progenitor.*

progeny ['prɑdʒ ə ni] *n.* the offspring of someone or some creature. (No plural form in this sense.) ♦ *Each of the senator's progeny became a politician.* ♦ *I took our cat's progeny to the animal pound.*

program ['pro græm] **1.** *n.* one episode of a broadcast show, such as on radio or television. ♦ *The radio program was to be continued the following week.* ♦ *None of the programs on television tonight look interesting to me.* **2.** *n.* a flyer or booklet provided to members of an audience, giving information about the performance. ♦ *The pro-*

gram listed the location of each scene of the play. ♦ *The program stated that there would be a 10-minute intermission.* **3.** *n.* a schedule of the parts of a performance. ♦ *The evening's program consisted of 12 acts.* ♦ *The ice skaters skillfully executed each part of their program.* **4.** *n.* a set of coded instructions given to a computer. ♦ *The program failed when I tried to run it.* ♦ *I installed the new program onto my computer.* **5. program to** *tv.* + *prep. phr.* to enter a set of instructions into a computer so that it will do a certain function. ♦ *My computer is programmed to perform difficult calculations.* ♦ *Mary programmed her computer to sound an alarm at noon.* **6.** *tv.* to train someone or something in a particular form of behavior. (Figurative on ⑤.) ♦ *I programmed my children so they do everything just as they should.* ♦ *Bob programmed his parrot to repeat whatever he says.*

programmer ['pro græm ɚ] *n.* someone who writes a computer program. ♦ *The programmer updated the old version of the operating system.* ♦ *The company hired programmers to write a new accounting program.*

progress 1. ['prɑ grɛs] *n.* the movement made toward a result or destination. (No plural form in this sense.) ♦ *The train's progress was quite slow because of the snow.* ♦ *The car's progress toward the intersection was slowed by traffic.* **2.** ['prɑ grɛs] *n.* the improvement that someone or something makes toward a qualitative goal. (No plural form in this sense.) ♦ *Our son didn't seem to be making much progress in school.* ♦ *My progress at work improved after I was properly trained.* **3.** [prə 'grɛs] *iv.* to move forward; to advance. ♦ *We progressed twenty yards before the traffic stopped again.* ♦ *The popular television show progressed in the rankings.* **4.** [prə 'grɛs] *iv.* to develop; to become better. ♦ *Teenagers progress toward adulthood.* ♦ *My experiment is progressing nicely.* **5. in progress** [... 'prɑ grɛs] *phr.* under way; happening; developing or moving right now. ♦ *Don't enter the studio. There's a show in progress.* ♦ *We now return you to the regularly scheduled show in progress.*

progression [prə 'grɛ ʃən] **1.** *n.* a sequence; a series. ♦ *The series 2, 4, 6, 8, 10 is a mathematical progression.* ♦ *The researcher analyzed each stage in the progression of the experiment.* **2.** *n.* movement towards a goal or ending point. (No plural form in this sense.) ♦ *The slow progression of the disease caused John to be depressed.* ♦ *I watched my brother's slow progression toward recovery.*

progressive [prə 'grɛs ɪv] **1.** *adj.* moving towards something. (Adv: *progressively.*) ♦ *Each progressive movement brought me closer to the edge of the cliff.* ♦ *At each progressive stage of the disease, I was given a different medicine.* **2.** *adj.* using new ideas, especially to improve or reform something. (Adv: *progressively.*) ♦ *The progressive school used many new teaching methods.* ♦ *The progressive political movement demanded free health care.* **3.** *adj.* [in grammar] of or about a word or words that show that an action is continuing or happening. ♦ *"I am singing" is in the present progressive form.* ♦ *Progressive forms in English are indicated by the suffix* -ing.

prohibit [pro 'hɪb ɪt] *tv.* to forbid something; to ban something. ♦ *The law prohibits the sale of most drugs.* ♦ *My parents prohibited me from watching many television shows.*

prohibition [pro ə 'bɪ ʃən] **1.** *n.* forbidding, banning, or not allowing something. (No plural form in this sense.) ♦ *Prohibition is a way to stop people from smoking, but it probably won't work.* ♦ *Prohibition and education have both been tried, but neither smoking or drinking can be stopped.* **2.** *n.* an instance of ①. ♦ *Many cities have a prohibition on smoking in public buildings.* ♦ *The mayor supported the prohibition of selling tobacco to minors.* **3. Prohibition** *n.* the period of time in American history when it was illegal to make, sell, or transport alcohol. (No plural form in this sense.) ♦ *Organized crime was a major problem during Prohibition.* ♦ *Prohibition was adopted in 1919 and repealed in 1933.*

prohibitive [pro 'hɪb ɪ tɪv] *adj.* preventing or prohibiting something. (Adv: *prohibitively.*) ♦ *The students flouted the principal's prohibitive rules.* ♦ *The school's prohibitive atmosphere stifled all creativity.*

project 1. ['prɑ dʒɛkt] *n.* an assignment or task that must be planned, researched, and executed. ♦ *I have to present plans for my project to the committee.* ♦ *Our project lost its funding due to budget cuts.* **2.** [prə 'dʒɛkt] *tv.* to cast a light onto something. ♦ *The projector projected a picture of a house on the screen.* ♦ *The flashlight projected a beam of light.* **3.** [prə 'dʒɛkt] *tv.* to make one's voice or words louder and carry further. ♦ *Please project your voice more.* ♦ *The speaker could not project his voice and I missed much of what he said.* **4.** [prə 'dʒɛkt] *tv.* to forecast or envision something; to estimate something. ♦ *The developer projected an annual growth rate of 10%.* ♦ *The report projected expenses for the next 10 years.* **5.** [prə 'dʒɛkt] *iv.* to be louder when speaking. ♦ *When you give your speech, make sure you project so we can hear you.* ♦ *You'll have to project more! I can't hear you in the back row.* **6.** [prə 'dʒɛkt] *iv.* to stick out; to extend from a surface. ♦ *The coat hooks projected from the wall.* ♦ *The broken arrow projected from the target.*

projected [prə 'dʒɛk tɪd] *adj.* planned; estimated. ♦ *This budget anticipates a projected tax increase of 5%.* ♦ *The president disagreed with the treasurer's projected figures.*

projectile [prə 'dʒɛk tɑɪl] *n.* something that is thrown or shot through the air or into space. ♦ *The bandit threw a large projectile into the sheriff's office.* ♦ *Rioters threw flaming projectiles at the building.*

projection [prə 'dʒɛk ʃən] **1.** *n.* something that sticks out or projects. ♦ *That metal projection from the building's facade is a flagpole.* ♦ *A sharp projection on the kitchen cabinet snagged my trousers.* **2.** *n.* a prediction; an estimate of a future state, often a financial state. ♦ *The financial projection was calculated by a computer program.* ♦ *The officers presented a number of projections of next year's profits.*

projector [prə 'dʒɛk tɚ] *n.* a machine that casts an image on a screen, wall, etc. (The image is recorded on film or digitally on tape.) ♦ *I threaded the film through the projector.* ♦ *The light bulb in the projector suddenly burned out.*

prolific [pro 'lɪf ɪk] *adj.* producing a lot of something, such as offspring, vegetation, works of art, etc. (Adv: *prolifically* [...ɪk li].) ♦ *The prolific author published over 80 novels.* ♦ *My prolific grandparents have 32 grandchildren.*

prologue AND **prolog** ['pro lɔg] *n.* the introduction to a book, play, poem, or other piece of writing. ♦ *The play's* *prologue was spoken by a chorus of six actors.* ♦ *The author's acknowledgments were listed in the textbook's prolog.*

prolong ['pro 'lɔŋ] *tv.* to cause something to last longer than it normally would; to lengthen the time it takes to do something. ♦ *The strong medications prolonged the sick man's life.* ♦ *The manager prolonged the interview in order to ask me more questions.*

prom ['pram] *n.* a formal high-school or college dance, especially one held at the end of the school year. ♦ *Anne wore a beautiful dress to her high-school prom.* ♦ *John and Mary attended their prom together.*

promenade [pram ə 'ned] **1.** *n.* a relaxing walk. ♦ *The young couple took a promenade along the beach.* ♦ *Our promenade through the park was very pleasurable.* **2.** *n.* a walkway where one can take a relaxing walk. ♦ *The couple walked down the promenade toward the lake.* ♦ *The beautiful promenade was lined with palm trees.* **3.** *iv.* to walk in a slow, relaxed way. ♦ *Anne and Bill promenaded along the beach.* ♦ *The pageant winner promenaded across the stage.*

prominence ['pram ə nəns] *n.* The condition of being prominent; fame. (No plural form in this sense.) ♦ *The president's prominence among leaders was deserved.* ♦ *The media gave prominence to the brave hero.*

prominent ['pram ə nənt] **1.** *adj.* famous; well known; renowned. (Adv: *prominently.*) ♦ *The prominent politician made an appeal to end the war.* ♦ *The reporter interviewed many prominent celebrities.* **2.** *adj.* noticeable; easy to see. (Adv: *prominently.*) ♦ *Huge bushes are the prominent feature of our yard.* ♦ *John has a very prominent nose.*

promiscuity [pra mɪ 'skju ə ti] **(sexual) promiscuity** *n.* the practice of having sex with many different people. (No plural form in this sense.) ♦ *Sexual promiscuity and unwanted pregnancies are modern social problems.* ♦ *Promiscuity makes one susceptible to sexually transmitted diseases.*

promiscuous [prə 'mɪs kju əs] *adj.* sexually casual and indiscriminate. (Adv: *promiscuously.*) ♦ *The promiscuous man spread herpes to his sex partners.* ♦ *Although she was promiscuous, she always used birth control.*

promise ['pram ɪs] **1.** *n.* an indication that someone will be successful or do good work. (No plural form in this sense.) ♦ *The new rookies have a lot of promise, don't you think?* ♦ *Your plans have promise, but I'll have to see the final results.* **2.** *n.* a pledge to do something. ♦ *I made a promise to go to the movies with my sister.* ♦ *John broke his promise to buy me a new watch.* **3.** *tv.* to pledge to do something; to vow to do something. (Takes a clause.) ♦ *I promised Mary that I would wash her car.* ♦ *I promised that I would be home by midnight.* **4.** *tv.* to cause someone to expect something. ♦ *The dark skies promise rain.* ♦ *I promise you a spanking if you don't behave.* **5. promise to** *iv.* + *inf.* to make a promise ② to do something. ♦ *I promise to leave at noon.* ♦ *You must come to my party. You promised to come!* **6. give something a lick and a promise** *idiom* to do something poorly—quickly and carelessly. ♦ *John! You didn't clean your room! You just gave it a lick and a promise.* ♦ *This time, Tom, comb your hair. It looks as if you just gave it a lick and a promise.*

promising ['pram ə sɪŋ] *adj.* suggesting good fortune in the future; indicating that something is likely to turn out well. (Adv: *promisingly.*) ♦ *The clear sky looks promising for a nice day at the park.* ♦ *A promising prognosis made the patient happy.*

promissory note ['pram ə sor i 'not] *n.* a document stating that the person who signs it will pay an amount of money to someone at some future time. ♦ *The bank lent me the money when I signed a promissory note.* ♦ *I signed a promissory note when the bank gave me a loan.*

promote [prə 'mot] **1.** *tv.* to work for the acceptance of someone or something through advertising and other public contacts. ♦ *The car company promoted its new models.* ♦ *The inventor promoted his products in trade journals.* **2.** *tv.* to raise someone to a new and higher level in employment or schooling. ♦ *The teacher promoted her entire class to fourth grade.* ♦ *The owner promoted Anne to the office of senior vice president.*

promotion [prə 'mo ʃən] **1.** *n.* the movement of someone to a higher level of employment or schooling. (No plural form in this sense.) ♦ *The owner's promotion of Anne to vice president was expected.* ♦ *Promotion is the way to get a better salary and a better-sounding job title.* **2.** *n.* a better job with higher pay. ♦ *My boss offered me a promotion today.* ♦ *Anne got her first promotion after six months on the job.* **3.** *n.* advertising and other activity intended to sell something. (No plural form in this sense.) ♦ *The promotion of the new product cost thousands of dollars.* ♦ *The advertisers managed the promotion of their clients' goods.*

prompt ['prampt] **1.** *adj.* punctual; on time. (Adv: *promptly.*) ♦ *Prompt patients make the dentist happy.* ♦ *We have to start on time, so please be prompt.* **2.** *tv.* to motivate or cause someone to do something. ♦ *John's criticism of Anne prompted me to defend her.* ♦ *The bad weather prompted me to dress warmly.* **3.** *tv.* to give someone a quiet reminder of what is to be said next. (Especially in stage performances.) ♦ *The stage manager prompted the actors during the rehearsal.* ♦ *Mary prompted her son to say "thank you."* **4.** *n.* a symbol on a computer screen that shows that the computer is ready to receive information. ♦ *At the prompt, there's a blinking cursor.* ♦ *Enter the appropriate command at the prompt.*

promulgate ['pram əl get] *tv.* to spread the news of something; to spread information. ♦ *The news of the layoffs was quickly promulgated throughout the factory.* ♦ *The reporter promulgated false information about the bus accident.*

pron. See pronoun.

prone ['pron] **1.** *adj.* lying flat with one's face toward the floor. ♦ *John was prone on the examining table.* ♦ *The paramedics rushed to the prone crash victim.* **2. prone to something** *idiom* likely to [do] something; apt to have something. ♦ *My boss is prone to fits of anger when my work isn't done.* ♦ *My sister is prone to sneezing because of her allergies.*

prong ['prɔŋ] *n.* one of the pointed ends of a fork; one of the branches of an antler. ♦ *The deer had antlers with many prongs.* ♦ *Someone bent the prongs of the fork.*

pronoun ['pro naʊn] *n.* a word that takes the place of a noun or nominal. (Abbreviated *pron.* here.) ♦ *In the sentence "I told Mary that she was next,"* she *is a pronoun that refers to* Mary. ♦ *After prepositions, pronouns should be in the objective case. For instance:* John gave the box to Anne and me.

pronounce [prə 'nɑʊns] **1.** *tv.* to speak the sound of a letter or a word; to make the sound of a letter or a word. ♦ *It was hard for the young child to pronounce long words.* ♦ *You don't pronounce the* gh *in* night. **2.** *tv.* to declare something about someone or something officially. ♦ *We were pronounced husband and wife.* ♦ *The judge pronounced the defendant guilty on all charges.*

pronounced [prə 'nɑʊnst] *adj.* evident; prominent; noticeable. ♦ *There's a pronounced bump on your head where you were hit.* ♦ *Bill's voice has a pronounced nasal quality.*

pronunciation [prə nən si 'e ʃən] *n.* the way a letter, group of letters, or word sounds when spoken; the way someone says things. (No plural form in this sense.) ♦ *The reporter's pronunciation was very clear.* ♦ *My pronunciation of French isn't very good.*

proof ['pruf] **1.** *n.* something that shows that something is definitely true. ♦ *The lawyer provided proof of the defendant's guilt.* ♦ *John's fingerprints were proof that he had held the gun.* **2.** *n.* a printed copy of something that is checked for mistakes before the final copy is printed; a preliminary version of a photograph. ♦ *The author examined the proofs carefully for mistakes.* ♦ *The photographer looked over the proofs and chose the best picture for the magazine cover.* **3.** *tv.* to proofread something. ♦ *The editor proofed the writer's work for errors.* ♦ *I proofed my roommate's term paper.*

proofread ['pruf rid] **1.** *tv., irreg.* to read something very carefully to look for mistakes. (Pt/pp: *proofread,* ['pruf rɛd].) ♦ *I proofread my paper before I gave it to my professor.* ♦ *The editor proofread my article before it was published.* **2.** *iv., irreg.* to read very carefully to look for mistakes. ♦ *The editor proofread carefully to avoid mistakes that would embarrass the author.* ♦ *Even though I always proofread, I sometimes miss a couple of mistakes.*

proofreader ['pruf rid ɚ] *n.* someone who reads text carefully to look for mistakes. ♦ *The proofreader circled the mistakes with red ink.* ♦ *The editor gave the manuscripts to the proofreaders for checking.*

prop ['prɑp] **1.** *n.* an object that is used in a play or in a movie by an actor. ♦ *Susan found the props needed for the play at a thrift store.* ♦ *The actor placed his prop on a shelf when he was finished with it.* **2.** *n.* a **propeller**. ♦ *The plane's prop broke in midair.* ♦ *Once, plane props were made of wood.* **3. prop up** *tv.* + *adv.* to support someone or something; to prevent someone or something from falling. ♦ *I propped up the books with a heavy brick.* ♦ *I had to prop up the injured woman until the doctor came.*

propaganda [prɑp ə 'gæn də] *n.* information that tries to influence or change how people think. (No plural form in this sense.) ♦ *The government broadcast propaganda to the enemy territory.* ♦ *This report is just propaganda designed to scare the public.*

propagandize [prɑp ə 'gæn dɑɪz] *tv.* to provide people with information designed to influence or change their thinking. ♦ *The government propagandized the citizens of the enemy nations with radio broadcasts.* ♦ *The government tried to propagandize its own people.*

propagate ['prɑp ə get] **1.** *iv.* to have offspring; to reproduce. ♦ *Our rabbits propagate continually.* ♦ *These flowers can propagate without help from people.* **2.** *tv.* to cause plants or other creatures to reproduce. ♦ *The farmer propagated different types of corn.* ♦ *We propagate fruits and vegetables for the market.* **3.** *tv.* to spread information or news. ♦ *The TV station propagated information about the bomb blast.* ♦ *Please don't propagate any gossip.*

propagation [prɑp ə 'ge ʃən] **1.** *n.* spreading something, such as news or information. (No plural form in this sense.) ♦ *A company newsletter was established for the propagation of information.* ♦ *The propagation of news is easy with the help of television.* **2.** *n.* the breeding and raising of plants or animals. (No plural form in this sense.) ♦ *The rancher oversaw the propagation of cattle.* ♦ *A botanist worked on the propagation of a new species of rose.*

propane ['pro pen] *n.* a colorless gas associated with oil and used as a fuel. (No plural form in this sense.) ♦ *A small tank of propane is used as fuel for the barbecue grill.* ♦ *There was an explosion when the train carrying propane derailed.*

propel [pro 'pɛl] *tv.* to cause someone or something to move ahead; to cause someone or something to move forward; to move something ahead. ♦ *The rocket was propelled into space from the launching pad.* ♦ *The football player propelled the ball forward with a good, hard kick.*

propellant [pro 'pɛl ənt] *n.* something, especially an explosion or chemical action, that causes **propulsion**; something that causes something to move forward. ♦ *An explosive propellant caused the rocket to launch.* ♦ *The propellant forced the hair spray out of the container.*

propeller [pro 'pɛl ɚ] *n.* a set of blades that rotate very fast in air or water, used to propel a boat or an airplane. ♦ *When you approach the plane, be careful of its rotating propellers.* ♦ *The boat's powerful propeller created large waves.*

propensity [pro 'pɛn sə ti] *n.* a tendency to do something; a tendency to behave a certain way. (No plural form in this sense.) ♦ *Anne has a propensity for eating when she's nervous.* ♦ *Bill's friends are aware of his propensity for gossiping.*

proper ['prɑp ɚ] **1.** *adj.* right; suitable; correct; appropriate. (Adv: *properly.*) ♦ *This printer won't work unless you've chosen the proper settings.* ♦ *The instructor showed me the proper way to hit the tennis ball.* **2.** *adj.* [in grammar] belonging to a person or place. ♦ Bill *is a proper noun, whereas* man *is a common noun.* ♦ *Almost all proper names are capitalized.* **3.** *adj.* <referring to a particular place itself, and not an area outside of that place.> (Not prenominal. Adv: *properly.*) ♦ *Mr. Jones does not live in Chicago proper, but in a suburb.* ♦ *Susan's office is in San Diego proper.*

properly ['prɑp ɚ li] **1.** *adv.* in the right way; suitably; appropriately; according to what is expected. ♦ *You should chew your food properly before swallowing.* ♦ *You must do your assignment properly in order to get a good grade.* **2.** *adv.* strictly. ♦ *What is commonly called an "orangutang" is properly known as an "orangutan."* ♦ *To be properly referred to as champagne, wine must come from the Champagne region of France.*

property ['prɑp ɚ ti] **1.** *n.* something that is owned. (No plural form in this sense.) ♦ *The police charged the thief with possession of stolen property.* ♦ *Please do not leave your property unattended in the airport.* **2.** *n.* an amount of land and any structures that have been built on it. (No plural form in this sense.) ♦ *My uncle owns some property* *next to the lake.* ♦ *The farmer sold some property to pay for his taxes.* **3.** *n.* a quality of something; a feature of something. ♦ *Sound quality is a very important property of a stereo system.* ♦ *Jealousy is one property that I don't like in people.*

prophecy ['prɑf ə si] **1.** *n.* the ability to foresee the future. (No plural form in this sense.) ♦ *The psychic claimed to have the gift of prophecy.* ♦ *Prophecy is not widely respected in our scientific age.* **2.** *n.* a prediction; a statement about what will happen in the future. ♦ *Jane's prophecy that I would win the lottery did not come true.* ♦ *The psychic's prophecy of danger frightened me.*

prophesy ['prɑf ə sɑɪ] *tv.* to predict what will happen in the future; to say that something is going to happen. ♦ *I prophesy that the president will be reelected.* ♦ *The psychic prophesied danger in my immediate future.*

prophet ['prɑf ɪt] **1.** *n.* someone who has the talent of being able to see into the future. ♦ *The prophet used his gift to warn others of danger.* ♦ *I asked the prophet for advice about my future.* **2.** *n.* [in some religions] a person chosen to speak for God. ♦ *The prophets often predicted doom, destruction, and exile.* ♦ *The false prophet was stoned to death.*

prophetic [prə 'fɛt ɪk] *adj.* telling or warning what will happen; predicting. (Adv: *prophetically* [...ɪk li].) ♦ *The prophetic message warned that we would die.* ♦ *Strangely, Bill's prophetic comments came true.*

prophylactic [pro fə 'læk tɪk] **1.** *adj.* preventing disease. (Adv: *prophylactically* [...ɪk li].) ♦ *The surgeon used the standard prophylactic measures to prevent infection.* ♦ *The operating room had to be made completely prophylactic before the surgery.* **2.** *n.* something that prevents disease or infection. ♦ *Some believe that taking lots of vitamin C is a good prophylactic to prevent a cold.* ♦ *A condom is a kind of prophylactic.*

propitiate [prə 'pɪ ʃi et] *tv.* to cause someone to stop being angry; to appease someone to avoid anger. ♦ *England tried to propitiate Germany before World War II.* ♦ *I propitiated the angry driver by offering to pay for damages.*

propitious [prə 'pɪ ʃəs] *adj.* favorable; being a good sign or omen. (Adv: *propitiously.*) ♦ *The propitious skies meant it would be a nice day at the beach.* ♦ *This is not a propitious time to buy stock in that company.*

proponent [prə 'pon ənt] *n.* someone who favors someone or something; a supporter. ♦ *The candidate's proponents applauded her speech.* ♦ *The proponents of the proposed law rallied in the street.*

proportion [prə 'por ʃən] **1.** *n.* the relationship between the sizes of different parts of someone or something. ♦ *The proportions of this figure are more realistic than that one.* ♦ *You have shown the wrong proportions in the drawing. The rear is larger than the front.* **2.** *tv.* to adjust the amount, degree, or size of something in comparison to something else. ♦ *The artist proportioned the dog's head to the rest of its body.* ♦ *The architect proportioned the doorway so that it was as wide as the lobby.* **3. in proportion; out of proportion** *phr.* showing the right or wrong ① relative to something else. (No plural form in this sense. See also ④.) ♦ *That man's large head is out of proportion to his small body.* ♦ *The cartoonist drew the dog in proportion to its surroundings.* **4. out of (all) proportion** *idiom* of exaggerated importance; of an unrealistic importance compared to something else. ♦ *This problem has grown out of all proportion.* ♦ *Yes, this thing is way out of proportion.*

proportional [prə 'por ʃə nəl] *adj.* having a suitable size, degree, or amount as compared with something else. (Essentially the same as **proportionate**. Adv: *proportionally.*) ♦ *In the cartoon, the cat's head was not proportional to its body.* ♦ *The number of representatives from each state is proportional to the state's population.*

proportionate [prə 'por ʃə nət] *adj.* having a suitable or expected size, degree, or amount as compared with something else. (Essentially the same as **proportional**. Adv: *proportionately.*) ♦ *The dog's head was proportionate to the rest of its body.* ♦ *The number of representatives from each state is proportionate to the state's population.*

proposal [prə 'poz əl] **1.** *n.* a suggestion; a plan. ♦ *My clients liked my design proposal.* ♦ *I disagreed with the president's proposal to raise taxes.* **2.** *n.* an offer of marriage made to someone. ♦ *Anne accepted Bill's proposal.* ♦ *Mary refused John's proposal, since she was in love with Bill.*

propose [prə 'poz] **1.** *tv.* to suggest something; to say something so that it is considered. ♦ *I would like to propose the following recommendations.* ♦ *John proposed that we eat pizza for dinner.* **2. propose (to)** *iv.* (+ *prep. phr.*) to ask someone to marry oneself. ♦ *Because John loved Mary, he proposed.* ♦ *Bill proposed to Susan in a very romantic way.* **3. propose a toast** *idiom* to make a toast before drinking. ♦ *I'd like to propose a toast in honor of your birthday.* ♦ *At the wedding reception, the bride's father proposed a toast.*

proposed [prə 'pozd] *adj.* suggested; planned. ♦ *The council approved the proposed budget.* ♦ *I agreed with the proposed changes to the plan.*

proposition [prɑp ə 'zɪ ʃən] **1.** *n.* a proposal; something that is being considered; a suggestion. ♦ *The council voted on the proposition to raise taxes.* ♦ *The minister fought against the proposition to build a casino.* **2.** *n.* a statement; a statement that is to be proved either true or false. ♦ *The logician proved the proposition by simple reasoning.* ♦ *The proposition "If a = b, then b = a" is true.*

proprietor [prə 'prɑɪ ɪ tɚ] *n.* an owner; someone who owns a business or establishment. ♦ *I spoke to the proprietor of the store about her merchandise.* ♦ *The proprietor apologized to me for the slow service.*

propriety [prə 'prɑɪ ə ti] *n.* the quality of being proper; appropriate behavior. (No plural form in this sense.) ♦ *Your rude friend is totally lacking in propriety.* ♦ *The reporters abandoned all propriety when questioning the grieving widow.*

propulsion [prə 'pʌl ʃən] *n.* a force that causes something to move forward. (No plural form in this sense.) ♦ *The plane was thrust forward by jet propulsion.* ♦ *The wind provided the propulsion necessary to move the sailboat.*

prorate [pro 'ret] *tv.* to divide something between things or people according to the percentage of the object that each thing or person used or will use. ♦ *The survivors prorated the rations among themselves.* ♦ *I prorated the long-distance phone calls among my roommates.*

proscribe [pro 'skrɑɪb] *tv.* to forbid something; to outlaw something; to ban something. ♦ *The city council pro-*

scribed smoking in public places. ♦ *The sale of liquor is proscribed in this town on Sundays.*

prose ['proz] *n.* the usual form of written language; writing that is not in verse. (No plural form in this sense.) ♦ *The professor's prose was very hard to understand.* ♦ *There were long sections of prose between the poems.*

prosecute ['prɑs ə kjut] *tv.* to seek to enforce a law against someone or some group in a court of law. ♦ *The store prosecuted John for shoplifting.* ♦ *Bob will be prosecuted for fraud.*

prosecution [prɑs ə 'kju ʃən] **1.** *n.* enforcement of the law against someone or an act in a court of law. (No plural form in this sense.) ♦ *Prosecution is a deterrent to crime.* ♦ *Anne's prosecution was brought about by the store she stole from.* **2.** *n.* the attorneys who work on the side of the state, and therefore the law, in court. ♦ *The witness for the prosecution saw the defendant commit the crime.* ♦ *The prosecution proved that the defendant was guilty.*

prosecutor ['prɑs ə kjut ɚ] *n.* an attorney who prosecutes someone in a court of law. ♦ *The prosecutor asked the defendant many questions.* ♦ *The judge asked the prosecutor to call the first witness.*

prospect ['prɑs pɛkt] **1.** *n.* something that is probable; something that is likely; a possibility; a likelihood. ♦ *My interview yielded a few interesting prospects for the future.* ♦ *There's a prospect that it might rain tomorrow.* **2.** *n.* the likelihood that something will be successful; the possibility that something will be successful. ♦ *My company's prospect for success is good.* ♦ *The team's prospect for winning the championship is excellent.* **3.** *n.* someone who will probably use a product or a service; someone who could become a customer. ♦ *Mary called a few sales prospects on the phone for appointments.* ♦ *The prospect left the store when no one offered to help her.* **4. prospect for** *iv.* + *prep. phr.* to search for minerals, oil, gold, silver, or precious stones in the earth. ♦ *The old miner still prospected for gold.* ♦ *I walked through the cave, prospecting for precious metals.*

prospective [prə 'spɛk tɪv] *adj.* probable; likely; expected to happen; expected to become something. (Adv: *prospectively.*) ♦ *The counselor showed the prospective students around the college.* ♦ *I handed a prospective employer my résumé.*

prospector ['prɑs pɛk tɚ] *n.* someone who searches for minerals, oil, gold, silver or precious stones in the earth. ♦ *The prospector looked for gold in the sands of the river.* ♦ *In the cave, I found a prospector looking for precious metals.*

prospectus [prə 'spɛk təs] *n.* a written statement that gives the official details about an event, school, or business. ♦ *The prospective client asked to see my company's prospectus.* ♦ *The school's prospectus presented a statement of its goals.*

prosper ['prɑs pɚ] *iv.* to become successful; to earn enough money so that one can live well; to thrive. ♦ *The banker prospered during the housing boom.* ♦ *The new toy store prospered at the mall.*

prosperity [prɑs 'pɛr ə ti] *n.* the condition of being prosperous; success; financial success. (No plural form in this sense.) ♦ *Because of the nation's prosperity, there was no need for taxes.* ♦ *The rich man credited his parents for his prosperity.*

prosperous ['prɑs pə rəs] *adj.* thriving; earning or having enough money so that one can live well. (Adv: *prosperously.*) ♦ *The prosperous lawyer lived in an expensive penthouse.* ♦ *The prosperous nation received its revenues from oil.*

prostate ['prɑs tet] **1. prostate (gland)** *n.* a gland in male humans located at the base of the bladder. ♦ *John's swollen prostate was very painful.* ♦ *The doctor examined Bob's prostate to see if it was enlarged.* **2.** *adj.* <the adj. use of ①.> ♦ *The doctor probed Bill's prostate gland.* ♦ *My uncle is suffering from prostate cancer.*

prostheses [prɑs 'θi siz] pl of prosthesis.

prosthesis [prɑs 'θi sɪs] *n., irreg.* an artificial body part. (Pl: prostheses.) ♦ *The doctor replaced the soldier's missing leg with a prosthesis.* ♦ *The amputee was fitted with a new prosthesis.*

prostitute ['prɑs tɪ tut] **1.** *n.* someone who makes money by having sex with people who pay for it. ♦ *The streets in the rough part of town were lined with prostitutes.* ♦ *A reporter caught the mayor in a hotel room with a prostitute.* **2.** *tv.* to make oneself available as ①. (Takes a reflexive object.) ♦ *She prostituted herself because she needed the money.* ♦ *The man prostituted himself to pay for his drug habit.* **3.** *tv.* to offer one's abilities or talents in a way that is not worthy of those abilities or talents. (Figurative on ②. Takes a reflexive object.) ♦ *The unknown artist prostituted himself by painting calendars.* ♦ *The once famous actress prostituted herself in cheap horror films.*

prostitution [prɑs tɪ 'tu ʃən] *n.* the business of a prostitute. (No plural form in this sense.) ♦ *Prostitution is legal in some counties in Nevada.* ♦ *The poor woman resorted to prostitution to support her drug habit.*

prostrate ['prɑs tret] **1.** *adj.* [lying] flat with one's face down. (Adv: *prostrately.*) ♦ *The king ordered the prostrate man to stand up.* ♦ *The police removed the prostrate protesters who had blocked the road.* **2.** *tv.* to lay oneself down flat on the ground. (Takes a reflexive object.) ♦ *The humble subject prostrated himself before the king.* ♦ *I prostrated myself from sheer exhaustion.*

protagonist [pro 'tæg ə nəst] *n.* the main character of a book, movie, television show, etc. ♦ *The protagonist of the story is portrayed by a famous actor.* ♦ *The protagonist of my book is an unemployed musician.*

protect [prə 'tɛkt] *tv.* to keep someone or something safe; to guard someone or something. ♦ *The bodyguard protected the president from harm.* ♦ *The glass panel protected the food and kept it clean.*

protection [prə 'tɛk ʃən] **1.** *n.* keeping someone or something safe; the quality offered by someone or something that protects. (No plural form in this sense.) ♦ *A bulletproof vest provides some protection from gunshot wounds.* ♦ *The bodyguard was responsible for the protection of the president.* **2.** *n.* something that protects someone or something; something that keeps something bad from happening to someone or something. ♦ *This alarm system is our protection against theft.* ♦ *Passwords are a protection against unauthorized usage or entry.*

protective [prə 'tɛk tɪv] *adj.* protecting; giving protection; defending; keeping someone or something safe. (Adv: *protectively.*) ♦ *The protective bear guarded her cubs.* ♦ *Anne's older brother was very protective of her.*

protector [prə 'tɛk tɚ] *n.* someone who protects someone or something; someone who defends or guards someone or something. ♦ *Anne resented her brother when he acted as her protector.* ♦ *Bill thanked his protector for saving his life.*

protégé ['pro tə ʒe] *n.* someone who is under the guidance of someone important, powerful, or knowledgeable. ♦ *The director's protégé studied all of his films closely.* ♦ *The pianist helped her protégé perfect her technique.*

protein ['pro tin] *n.* one of many kinds of chemical substances important to the cells of all living plants and animals. ♦ *The vegetarian ate beans to get protein.* ♦ *Meat, fish, and poultry are good sources of protein.*

protest 1. ['pro tɛst] *n.* a display of opposition or disapproval; a complaint. ♦ *The students held a protest to demand lower tuition rates.* ♦ *The workers' protest closed the factory for a week.* **2.** [prə 'tɛst] *tv.* to complain about something; to show disapproval of something. ♦ *The workers protested the reductions in their benefits.* ♦ *We protested the plans for a dump in our neighborhood.* **3.** [prə 'tɛst] *iv.* to complain about something. ♦ *Students protested by refusing to go to class.* ♦ *The workers protested about the reductions in their benefits.*

Protestant ['prɑt ə stənt] **1.** *adj.* of or about the Christian religions that separated from the Roman Catholic Church. ♦ *There are many different Protestant denominations.* ♦ *Protestant thinking has tended to be democratic on the organization of churches.* **2.** *n.* someone who is a member of a Protestant ① religion. ♦ *Protestants are in conflict with Catholics in Northern Ireland.* ♦ *The first Protestants disagreed with the notion of having a pope.*

protester AND **protestor** [pro 'tɛs tɚ] *n.* someone who protests something. ♦ *The protesters blocked traffic to the factory.* ♦ *The police arrested a dozen protestors at city hall.*

protocol ['pro tə kɔl] **1.** *n.* the system of etiquette, rules, and behavior in business, military, or social situations. (No plural form in this sense.) ♦ *The worker was reprimanded for not following proper protocol.* ♦ *Protocol demanded that the diplomat attend the king's funeral.* **2.** *n.* a class of patterns of communicating information in a computer system. ♦ *Computers using different protocols aren't compatible.* ♦ *My printer won't work because I have not used the proper protocols.*

proton ['pro tɑn] *n.* a particle in the center of an atom that carries a positive electrical charge. ♦ *The number of protons in an atom equals the atomic number of that element.* ♦ *The nucleus of a hydrogen atom has one proton.*

prototype ['pro tə tɑɪp] *n.* the original example of something from which later examples are developed. ♦ *The inventor constructed the prototype of the machine from scrap metal.* ♦ *The architect's novel design was the prototype on which more buildings were based.*

protractor [pro 'træk tɚ] *n.* an instrument used to measure and draw angles. ♦ *The designer used a protractor to draw a perfect right angle.* ♦ *The architect measured the angle with a protractor.*

protrude [pro 'trud] **1.** *iv.* to stick out. ♦ *A sharp nail protruded from the beam of wood.* ♦ *John's teeth protrude from his gums at an odd angle.* **2.** *tv.* to cause something to stick out. ♦ *A rude child protruded his tongue at me.* ♦ *John protruded his elbow as I walked by, nearly knocking me over.*

protrusion [pro 'tru ʒən] *n.* something that sticks out or protrudes. ♦ *Small protrusions on the outside of the large bottle made it easier to hold.* ♦ *John was bothered by a small protrusion of bone on his ankle.*

protuberance [pro 'tub ə rəns] *n.* a swelling, bulge, or bump that sticks out. ♦ *The doctor examined the protuberance on my neck.* ♦ *The new bud was a tiny protuberance on the twig.*

proud ['prɑʊd] **1.** *adj.* showing or feeling pride; having a good opinion about oneself and what one has accomplished. (Adv: *proudly.* Comp: *prouder;* sup: *proudest.*) ♦ *Jane was very proud of the hard work that she had done.* ♦ *The proud student showed her parents her good grades.* **2.** *adj.* causing someone to feel pride. (Adv: *proudly.* Comp: *prouder;* sup: *proudest.*) ♦ *The athlete's proudest moment was when he received the gold medal.* ♦ *Finishing college was a proud accomplishment for Mary.* **3.** *adj.* having too high an opinion about oneself; arrogant. (Adv: *proudly.* Comp: *prouder;* sup: *proudest.*) ♦ *The proud woman refused to speak to the servants in public.* ♦ *I laughed at the proud man when he finally failed.*

prove ['pruv] **1.** *tv., irreg.* to provide the proof of something; to be the proof of something. (Pp: *proved* or proven.) ♦ *The lawyer proved that his client was innocent.* ♦ *The experiment proved my hypothesis to be correct.* **2. prove to be something** *idiom* to be shown to be someone or something; to be found to be someone or something. (See ① for verb forms.) ♦ *Susan proved to be a good friend when she lent me some money.* ♦ *The food proved to be spoiled when I smelled it.*

proven ['pruv ən] a pp of prove.

proverb ['prɑ vɚb] *n.* a short saying that makes a wise comment. ♦ *We memorized some helpful proverbs in school.* ♦ *My grandmother dispenses advice by uttering proverbs.*

proverbial [prə 'vɚb i əl] *adj.* referred to in a well-known proverb; resembling a proverb; reminiscent of a proverb. (Adv: *proverbially.*) ♦ *My landlord is the proverbial wolf in sheep's clothing.* ♦ *As the proverbial expression goes, too many cooks spoil the broth.*

provide [prə 'vɑɪd] **1.** *tv.* to furnish someone or something with something. ♦ *The hotel clerk provided us with a comfortable room.* ♦ *The host provided the guests with party hats.* **2.** *tv.* to state or tell something. (Takes a clause.) ♦ *This paragraph provides that rent is due on the first of each month.* ♦ *This author's contract provided that he was to receive royalties.* **3. provide for** *iv.* + *prep. phr.* to allow something to be supplied or something to occur. ♦ *This agreement provides for the payment of rent by the first of the month.* ♦ *This mortgage provides for a repayment without penalty.* **4. provide for** *iv.* + *prep. phr.* to support people by earning enough money to supply them with food, clothing, and shelter. ♦ *John provided for a family of six.* ♦ *Anne provided for herself after she left her parents' home.* **5. provided that** *phr.* on the condition that. (Takes a clause.) ♦ *I will come, provided that I am invited.* ♦ *I will help you, provided that you pay me.*

providence ['prɑv ə dəns] **1. Providence** *n.* God. (No plural form in this sense.) ♦ *Providence has brought us all these blessings.* ♦ *It was Providence that steered us toward safety.* **2.** *n.* good fortune or the benevolence of ①. (No plural form in this sense.) ♦ *It was providence that* *kept everyone safe.* ♦ *Our good fortune is a result of divine providence.*

province ['prɑ vɪns] **1.** *n.* one of the main divisions of a country, such as Canada, similar to a state. ♦ *Toronto is in the province of Ontario.* ♦ *The Canadian rock band toured through all of the provinces.* **2.** *n.* an area of study, knowledge, or activity. ♦ *Biology was not in the historian's province of expertise.* ♦ *In the province of psychology, Dr. Smith is very respected.*

provincial [prə 'vɪn ʃəl] **1.** *adj.* of or about a province or provinces of a country. (Adv: *provincially.*) ♦ *John ran for an office in the provincial legislature.* ♦ *I crossed the provincial boundary between Quebec and Ontario.* **2.** *adj.* not sophisticated; rural; narrow-minded. (Usually derogatory. Adv: *provincially.*) ♦ *Mike is sort of provincial and does not accept new ideas.* ♦ *John's prejudice is an example of his provincial thinking.*

provision [prə 'vɪ ʒən] **1.** *n.* a condition; a statement that stipulates something; a stipulation. ♦ *This provision deals with your royalties after the third printing.* ♦ *I'll see a movie with you with the provision that you pay for it.* **2.** *n.* a preparation that is made beforehand; an arrangement that is made ahead of time. ♦ *My contract makes a provision for royalties.* ♦ *My lawyer closely examined the provisions in my will.* **3. provisions** *n.* food and supplies needed for everyday living. (Treated as plural.) ♦ *The hikers carried their provisions on their backs.* ♦ *My church sent provisions to the earthquake victims.*

provisional [prə 'vɪ ʒə nəl] *adj.* for the moment; for the time being; temporary; not permanent. (Adv: *provisionally.*) ♦ *Congress approved provisional aid for the earthquake victims.* ♦ *Enforcement of this law is provisional until the Supreme Court's final decision.*

provocation [prɑv ə 'ke ʃən] *n.* something that provokes anger, interest, or desire. ♦ *The enemy's provocation caused our nation to declare war.* ♦ *John's insult was the provocation that led Bob to hit him.*

provocative [prə 'vɑk ə tɪv] *adj.* causing anger, interest, or desire. (Adv: *provocatively.*) ♦ *The author's provocative book was also quite controversial.* ♦ *I listened to a provocative interview with an old veteran.*

provoke [prə 'vok] **1.** *tv.* to make someone angry; to irritate someone. ♦ *The bear provoked the bees by swatting at their hive.* ♦ *Anne provoked John by calling him inept.* **2.** *tv.* to cause an action to start or to happen. (Usually leading to negative results.) ♦ *The mayor's speech provoked an angry outburst of protest.* ♦ *Lisa's comments provoked a lot of criticism.*

provost ['pro vost] *n.* the head of certain colleges, schools, or churches. ♦ *The provost is in charge of the faculty of the university.* ♦ *The dean was just appointed to be provost.*

prowess ['prɑʊ ɪs] *n.* a powerful strength, skill, or ability. (No plural form in this sense.) ♦ *John's prowess enabled him to push the car from the mud.* ♦ *Anne's prowess in tennis is unmatched at my school.*

prowl ['prɑʊl] *iv.* to sneak around quietly, like an animal hunting for food or a thief looking for something to steal. ♦ *The dog prowled in the alley for scraps of food.* ♦ *The thief prowled in the dark room, looking for valuables.*

prowler ['prɑʊl ɚ] *n.* someone who prowls with the intention of doing something wrong; a thief; a burglar. ♦ *A prowler stole my brand-new computer.* ♦ *The police caught the prowler with a bag of stolen goods.*

proximity [prɑk 'sɪm ə ti] *n.* nearness; how close someone or something is to someone or something else. (No plural form in this sense.) ♦ *Mercury's surface is very hot during the day because of its proximity to the sun.* ♦ *Due to Bob's proximity to the microphone, his words were clearly recorded.*

proxy ['prɑk si] **1.** *n.* a substitute. ♦ *I'm acting as a proxy for the president while he's on vacation.* ♦ *Your proxy is supposed to vote the same way as you would.* **2.** *n.* the right to present someone else's vote at a meeting. ♦ *The council president gave his proxy to me while on vacation.* ♦ *The director controlled thousands of proxies at the annual board meeting.*

prude ['prud] *n.* someone who is easily offended or shocked; someone who is overly modest or proper. ♦ *The prude blushed when I told a slightly vulgar joke.* ♦ *Call me a prude, but I won't wear such a skimpy bathing suit!*

prudence ['prud ns] *n.* wisdom; care in thought and action; thoughtful judgment. (No plural form in this sense.) ♦ *Due to her prudence, Mary had made the correct choice.* ♦ *John's prudence kept him from criticizing his boss.*

prudent ['prud nt] *adj.* wise; thinking carefully before one does something. (Adv: *prudently.*) ♦ *It would be prudent to think carefully before you choose.* ♦ *The prudent worker did not tell his boss exactly how angry he was.*

prudish ['prud ɪʃ] *adj.* too easily shocked or offended; too modest. (Adv: *prudishly.*) ♦ *The prudish minister thought dancing was sinful.* ♦ *Because Jane is too prudish to wear a bathing suit, she doesn't swim at all.*

prune ['prun] **1.** *n.* a dried plum, eaten as food. ♦ *John cut up some prunes and sprinkled them on his cereal.* ♦ *As a snack between meals, Mary ate some prunes.* **2.** *iv.* to remove extra branches or leaves from a plant; to trim a tree, flower, bush, or shrub so that it has a nice, even shape. ♦ *The gardener wore heavy gloves while he pruned.* ♦ *After I mowed and raked, I spent an hour pruning.* **3.** *tv.* to make a plant look nice by removing extra branches or leaves. ♦ *The gardener pruned the hedges.* ♦ *The florist pruned the flower arrangement.* **4.** *tv.* to make something more useful or pleasant by removing things that are not needed or wanted. (Figurative on ③.) ♦ *The manager pruned the office staff to save money.* ♦ *The student pruned her long essay down to 500 words.*

pry ['prɑɪ] **1. pry open; pry up** *tv.* + *adv.* to open or raise something with a tool by using force; to force something open by using a tool. ♦ *The thief pried open the door with a crowbar.* ♦ *Anne pried the lid up with a screwdriver.* **2. pry into** *iv.* + *prep. phr.* to be too curious; to ask personal questions about things that should not concern oneself. ♦ *I resented my parents for prying into my personal life.* ♦ *My neighbor always pries into my financial affairs.*

P.S. See postscript.

psalm ['sɑm] *n.* a sacred song or hymn about God, especially one of the verses in the book of Psalms in the Bible. ♦ *The minister read Psalm 30.* ♦ *The book of Psalms is part of the Old Testament.*

pseudonym ['sud ə nɪm] *n.* a false name. ♦ *Jane used a pseudonym when she wrote romance novels.* ♦ *The criminal was known by many different pseudonyms.*

psyche ['sɑɪ ki] *n.* the mind, soul, or spirit of a person. (No plural form in this sense.) ♦ *After years of abuse, Mary's psyche was deeply scarred.* ♦ *The support Jane got from her friends was good for her psyche.*

psychiatric [sɑɪ ki 'æ trɪk] *adj.* <the adj. form of **psychiatry**.> (Adv: *psychiatrically* [...ɪk li].) ♦ *That doctor specializes in psychiatric medicine.* ♦ *The depressed woman decided to seek psychiatric treatment.*

psychiatrist [sɪ 'kɑɪ ə trəst] *n.* a doctor who treats people who have sicknesses of the mind. ♦ *The troubled man told his problems to his psychiatrist.* ♦ *My psychiatrist cured my depression through therapy and drugs.*

psychiatry [sɪ 'kɑɪ ə tri] *n.* the science of treating people who have sicknesses of the mind. (No plural form in this sense.) ♦ *People with degrees in psychiatry can prescribe medicine.* ♦ *David resorted to psychiatry to help cure his depression.*

psychic ['sɑɪ kɪk] **1.** *n.* someone who has or claims to have special powers of the mind to sense things that other people cannot sense. ♦ *The psychic helped the police find the missing person.* ♦ *The psychic warned me of impending danger.* **2.** *adj.* possessing or associated with the powers mentioned in ①. (Adv: *psychically* [...ɪk li].) ♦ *Mary used her psychic abilities to help find missing people.* ♦ *Moving objects with one's mind is a kind of psychic phenomenon.*

psychoanalysis [sɑɪ ko ə 'næl ɪ sɪs] *n.* the science and practice of examining people's minds in detail as a means of diagnosing and treating neuroses and other mental problems. (No plural form in this sense.) ♦ *I'm undergoing psychoanalysis to find the cause of my depression.* ♦ *The lecture on psychoanalysis explained the importance of dreams.*

psychoanalyst [sɑɪ ko 'æn ə ləst] *n.* someone who is trained in psychoanalysis. ♦ *My psychoanalyst listened as I talked about my childhood.* ♦ *The psychoanalyst helped the patient find the source of his compulsions.*

psychoanalyze [sɑɪ ko 'æn ə lɑɪz] *tv.* to examine someone's mind in detail, especially as a way of diagnosing and treating neuroses and other mental disorders. ♦ *We are looking for an analyst who psychoanalyzes children.* ♦ *Psychoanalysts psychoanalyze people, but psychiatrists usually do not.*

psychological [sɑɪ kə 'lɑdʒ ɪ kəl] **1.** *adj.* <the adj. form of **psychology** ①.> (Adv: *psychologically* [...ɪk li].) ♦ *David was paid to participate in a psychological study.* ♦ *Dr. Clark designed a psychological experiment.* **2.** *adj.* <the adj. form of **psychology** ②.> (Adv: *psychologically* [...ɪk li].) ♦ *Is there a psychological explanation for my depression?* ♦ *The crazed criminal had lot of psychological problems.*

psychologist [sɑɪ 'kɑl ə dʒəst] *n.* someone who is trained in psychology. ♦ *The psychologist wrote a book about the effects of brain lesions.* ♦ *Some psychologists study how people process language.*

psychology [sɑɪ 'kɑl ə dʒi] **1.** *n.* the study and science of the mind. (No plural form in this sense.) ♦ *The researcher incorporated psychology into his theory of language.* ♦ *Mental disorders are one facet of psychology.* **2.** *n.* the way a people behave; the way a person behaves. (No plural form in this sense.) ♦ *The bitter young man didn't understand the psychology of women.* ♦ *This book examines the psychology of serial killers.*

psychopath ['sɑɪ kə pæθ] *n.* someone who has a serious mental illness, causing criminal actions. ♦ *The psychopath was imprisoned in a private cell.* ♦ *The psychopath tortured his victims before killing them.*

psychopathic [sɑɪ kə 'pæθ ɪk] *adj.* <the adj. form of **psychopath**.> (Adv: *psychopathically* [...ɪk li].) ♦ *The psychopathic killer was sentenced to be executed.* ♦ *This explosion was the work of a psychopathic terrorist.*

psychoses [sɑɪ 'kos iz] pl of **psychosis**.

psychosis [sɑɪ 'kos ɪs] *n., irreg.* a serious mental illness that alters a person's sense of reality. (Pl: **psychoses**.) ♦ *John's psychoses were so severe that he never left his house.* ♦ *I took medication to treat my psychosis.*

psychosomatic [sɑɪ ko so 'mæt ɪk] *adj.* of or about an illness or a reaction in the body that is caused by the mind. (Adv: *psychosomatically* [...ɪk li].) ♦ *The doctor gave placebos to patients with psychosomatic illnesses.* ♦ *A psychologist thinks that Tom's back pain is psychosomatic.*

psychotherapy [sɑɪ ko 'θɛr ə pi] *n.* the treatment of mental disorders through psychology. (No plural form in this sense.) ♦ *After attempting suicide, the teenager underwent psychotherapy.* ♦ *I'm undergoing psychotherapy to determine why I'm so depressed.*

psychotic [sɑɪ 'kɑt ɪk] **1.** *adj.* suffering from a psychosis. (Adv: *psychotically* [...ɪk li].) ♦ *Max is acting a little psychotic, don't you think?* ♦ *The psychotic killer burned his victims.* **2.** *n.* a person who is ①. ♦ *A psychotic broke into the post office and set fire to the mail.* ♦ *Some of the prison inmates are psychotics.*

pt See **past tense** at **past** "②.

puberty ['pju bɚ ti] *n.* the period when the human body develops into sexual maturity. (No plural form in this sense.) ♦ *During puberty, boys' voices get lower.* ♦ *Sexual reproduction is not possible before puberty starts.*

pubic ['pju bɪk] *adj.* located in the area around the sex organs. ♦ *Pubic hair grows around the sexual organs.* ♦ *The baseball struck the batter in the pubic region.*

public ['pʌb lɪk] **1.** *adj.* available to everyone; available to people in general; not restricted; not private. (Adv: *publicly*.) ♦ *I went to a public school because I couldn't afford a private one.* ♦ *On hot days, I go to the public beach to swim.* **2.** *n.* people in general. (No plural form in this sense.) ♦ *The mayor hid his corrupt actions from the public.* ♦ *The once private files were made available to the public.* **3. one's public** *n.* a certain group of people, especially a group of fans. (No plural form in this sense.) ♦ *The actress thanked her public for their support when she was ill.* ♦ *The athlete angered his public by charging a fee for his autograph.* **4. in public** *phr.* in a place or way so that other people can see or know about something. ♦ *It's illegal to walk naked in public.* ♦ *John always tries to embarrass me whenever we're in public.* **5. wash one's dirty linen in public** *idiom* to discuss one's personal problems in public. ♦ *Bob is always telling us about his quarrels with his wife. I wish he wouldn't wash his dirty linen in* *public.* ♦ *Lisa will talk to anyone about her financial problems. Why does she wash her dirty linen in public?*

publication [pəb lə 'ke ʃən] **1.** *n.* making information in written form, such as in a book, magazine, or newspaper, available to the public. (No plural form in this sense.) ♦ *The publication of the blasphemous book endangered the author's life.* ♦ *You will receive payment upon the publication of your article.* **2.** *n.* any written document that is published. ♦ *This catalog lists our recent publications.* ♦ *My résumé includes a list of my academic publications.*

publicist ['pʌb lə sɪst] *n.* someone who is paid to make people aware of information about someone or something. ♦ *John's publicist denied the rumors about John.* ♦ *The singer's publicist sent me a press release about her new album.*

publicity [pəb 'lɪs ə ti] *n.* information that is brought to everyone's attention. (No plural form in this sense.) ♦ *Bad publicity hurt the mayor's chances for reelection.* ♦ *There was a lot of publicity surrounding the sensational trial.*

publicize ['pʌb lɪ saɪz] *tv.* to cause someone or something to be known by everyone; to inform everyone about someone or something. ♦ *The company publicized its fourth-quarter profits.* ♦ *The theater company publicized its new season of plays.*

publicly ['pʌb lɪk li] *adv.* [done] in public; [done] where people can see. ♦ *Tom insulted Bill publicly and made him very angry.* ♦ *You can think what you want about the company, as long as you don't say it publicly.*

public school ['pʌb lɪk 'skul] *n.* a school that is paid for by the government through taxes and that is available to all local children. ♦ *The real-estate agent said the area's public schools were great.* ♦ *Mary transferred from a public high school to a parochial one.*

publish ['pʌb lɪʃ] **1.** *tv.* to assemble, print, and sell books, magazines, newspapers, or other printed materials. ♦ *The university press published many academic journals.* ♦ *My professor's first book was published in 1970.* **2.** *tv.* to make something well known. ♦ *The company published the news of its record earnings.* ♦ *This newspaper publishes the scores of most sporting events.* **3.** *iv.* to assemble, print and sell books, magazines, newspapers, or other printed materials as a business. ♦ *Now that the book is finished, when will you be ready to publish?* ♦ *Our university's press doesn't publish during the summer.*

published ['pʌb lɪʃt] **1.** *adj.* assembled, printed, and made available for sale. ♦ *The professor kept a file of her published articles.* ♦ *Recently published books are placed on this shelf by the entrance.* **2.** *adj.* of someone whose written works have been published. ♦ *Lisa is a published author and lecturer.* ♦ *My friend is published but cannot make a living from her writing.*

publisher ['pʌb lɪʃ ɚ] *n.* someone or a company that assembles, prints, and makes written materials available for sale. ♦ *Bob's manuscript was rejected by five publishers.* ♦ *The publisher sends each author royalty checks twice a year.*

puck ['pʌk] *n.* a hard, thick disk used in hockey instead of a ball. ♦ *The hockey player knocked the puck across the ice.* ♦ *The goalie caught the puck with his mitt.*

pucker ['pʌk ɚ] **1.** *n.* a wrinkle, crease, or fold. ♦ *I ironed the puckers in the fabric.* ♦ *Mary smoothed out the pucker in her blouse.* **2.** *tv.* to cause something to be wrinkled; to collect something into folds. ♦ *The dryer puckered my delicate clothes.* ♦ *Anne puckered the fabric when she crumpled it into a ball.* **3. pucker (up)** *tv.* (+ *adv.*) to bring one's lips together for a kiss. ♦ *David puckered his lips before I kissed him.* ♦ *Mary puckered up her lips, waiting for me to kiss her.* **4.** *iv.* to move [one's lips] into a position for a kiss or when one has eaten something very bitter. ♦ *My lips puckered when I bit into the lime.* ♦ *The unsweetened lemonade made me pucker.*

pudding ['pʊd ɪŋ] **1.** *n.* a soft, sweet, creamy food, usually eaten as a dessert. (No plural form in this sense.) ♦ *I made some vanilla pudding for dessert.* ♦ *Jane put some strawberries on top of her pudding.* **2. puddings** *n.* kinds or types of ①. ♦ *I bought three different puddings at the store.* ♦ *Which puddings do you like?*

puddle ['pʌd l] *n.* a collection of water or other liquid on the ground or the surface of something. ♦ *Jimmy splashed mud when he jumped into the puddle.* ♦ *There's a puddle of water under the leaky pipe.*

puff ['pʌf] **1.** *n.* a short blast of air, smoke, steam, gas, etc. that is blown out from something. ♦ *With a puff of air, I blew the candle out.* ♦ *I felt a puff of cold wind on my neck.* **2.** *n.* a light pastry that is usually filled with a sweet, creamy filling. ♦ *The baker made a batch of delicious cream puffs.* ♦ *I ate a puff while sipping on a cup of coffee.* **3.** *tv.* to blow air, steam, smoke, etc. out a little bit at a time. ♦ *The iron puffed small amounts of steam.* ♦ *The exhaust pipe puffed dark clouds of smoke.* **4. puff on** *iv.* (+ *prep. phr.*) to breathe in smoke from a cigarette with small breaths; to smoke a cigarette. ♦ *The smokers puffed on their cigarettes.* ♦ *The executive puffed on a fat cigar.* **5.** *iv.* to pull smoke from a cigarette or a cigar with small breaths. ♦ *The smokers puffed at the building's front entrance because smoking was prohibited inside.* ♦ *The executive puffed and puffed and finished his cigar in a short time.* **6.** *iv.* to breathe when one is out of breath; to breathe with short, quick breaths. ♦ *The smoker puffed as she climbed the stairs.* ♦ *The overweight man puffed as he ran for the bus.* **7. puff out of** *iv.* + *adv.* + *prep. phr.* [for a vapor] to emerge from something as ①. ♦ *Steam puffed out of the open valve.* ♦ *Dark smoke puffed out of the exhaust pipe.*

puffy ['pʌf i] *adj.* swollen. (Adv: *puffily.* Comp: *puffier;* sup: *puffiest.*) ♦ *Bob wore sunglasses to cover his puffy eyes.* ♦ *When Anne had a cold, her nose was red and puffy.*

pugnacious [pəg 'ne ʃəs] *adj.* liking to fight; fond of fighting. (Adv: *pugnaciously.*) ♦ *The pugnacious student was sent to the principal's office.* ♦ *I was hit by the pugnacious bully after school.*

pull ['pʊl] **1. pull at** *iv.* + *prep. phr.* to tug at something. ♦ *The cat pulled at the string I dangled in front of it.* ♦ *The dog pulled at my slippers while I tried to rest.* **2.** *tv.* to move someone or something in some direction. ♦ *I pulled the door toward me.* ♦ *I pulled Anne away from the speeding car.* **3.** *tv.* to drag someone or something behind oneself; to move someone or something behind oneself while one is moving. ♦ *The tow truck pulled the illegally parked car to the pound.* ♦ *I pulled the children sitting in the wagon behind me.* **4.** *tv.* to stretch a limb or a muscle too far. ♦ *The athlete pulled a muscle while throwing a baseball.* ♦ *I* *pulled my leg because I didn't warm up before exercising.* **5.** *n.* a tug; an act of drawing something toward oneself. ♦ *I felt a sharp pull when my hair got caught in the door.* ♦ *Please help me give this rope another pull.* **6.** *n.* special influence. (No plural form in this sense. Informal.) ♦ *The charismatic politician had a lot of pull with the governor.* ♦ *John used his pull at city hall to get his street plowed.* **7. pull a gun (on someone); pull a knife (on someone)** *idiom* to bring out a gun or knife so that it is ready for use against someone. ♦ *I screamed when the mugger pulled a knife on me.* ♦ *The police shot the thief when he pulled a gun.*

pullback ['pʊl bæk] *n.* a return to one's earlier position; withdrawal of troops from an area. (No plural form in this sense.) ♦ *The general ordered the pullback of the front lines.* ♦ *The army's pullback was seen as a humiliating defeat.*

pulley ['pʊl i] *n.* a wheel with a grooved edge into which a rope, chain, or band fits. ♦ *A pulley can change the direction of the movement of a rope.* ♦ *There are pulleys attached to a car engine that allow belts to transfer power to various components.*

pullout ['pʊl ɑʊt] *n.* a withdrawal; the act of leaving a position that one was in. ♦ *The army's pullout from enemy territory was a humiliating defeat.* ♦ *The Baltic countries demanded a pullout of Russian troops.*

pullover ['pʊl ov ɚ] *n.* a sweater; a piece of clothing for the upper part of the body that is pulled over the head. ♦ *When I removed my pullover, it ruined my hairdo.* ♦ *I took off my pullover because I was becoming warm.*

pulmonary ['pʊl mə nɛr i] *adj.* of or about the lungs. (Adv: *pulmonarily* [pʊl mə 'nɛr ə li].) ♦ *The pulmonary inflammation made it painful to breathe.* ♦ *The smoker's pulmonary capacity is very small.*

pulp ['pʌlp] **1.** *n.* the soft part inside a fruit, vegetable, or plant. (No plural form in this sense.) ♦ *Mary strained the pulp from the orange juice.* ♦ *John removed the pulp from the inside of the pumpkin.* **2.** *n.* a paste-like liquid of crushed wood fiber used to make paper. (No plural form in this sense.) ♦ *The mill turned scrap wood into pulp for paper.* ♦ *Pigment was added to the pulp to make colored stationery.* **3.** *n.* any soft, partially solid, wet substance. (No plural form in this sense.) ♦ *The newspaper that landed in the puddle turned into pulp.* ♦ *The gray pulp next to your hamburger is overcooked rice.* **4.** *tv.* to make ②. ♦ *The paper mill pulped the wood chips in a large vat.* ♦ *We should pulp this paper so it can be recycled.*

pulpit ['pʊl pɪt] *n.* a raised platform that a preacher stands on when preaching. ♦ *The minister delivered a sermon from the pulpit.* ♦ *From his pulpit, the preacher talked about miracles.*

pulpy ['pʌl pi] *adj.* in the form of a wet mass. Comp: *pulpier;* sup: *pulpiest.*) ♦ *Before carving a pumpkin, you must remove the pulpy insides.* ♦ *The dog dragged a pulpy mass of wet newspaper from the puddle.*

pulsate ['pʌl set] *iv.* to throb; to expand and contract again and again in rhythm. ♦ *The distant star released energy as it pulsated.* ♦ *When I felt John's heart pulsate, I knew he was still alive.*

pulse ['pʌls] **1.** *n.* the rhythm of the flow of blood through one's body, caused by the beating of the heart. (No plural form in this sense.) ♦ *The patient's pulse was slowing, so the doctors acted quickly.* ♦ *His pulse is getting faster. He is getting better.* **2.** *n.* a rhythm with a regular beat; a movement of something with regular stops and starts. ♦ *The pulse of the music compelled me to dance.* ♦ *The other musicians followed the pulse of the drums.* **3.** *iv.* to beat regularly, like a heartbeat; to beat in rhythm. ♦ *The drums pulsed to the rhythm of the music.* ♦ *The ballroom pulsed with the beat of the dance music.* **4. take someone's pulse** *idiom* to measure the frequency of the beats of ①. ♦ *I can take my own pulse.* ♦ *The nurse took my pulse and said I was fine.*

pulverize ['pʌl və rɑɪz] *tv.* to make something into tiny bits, dust, or powder. ♦ *The tornado pulverized the small village.* ♦ *The sledgehammer pulverized the rock.*

pummel ['pʌm əl] **1.** *tv.* to beat someone or something with one's closed fists over and over. ♦ *The bully pummeled my nose until it bled.* ♦ *John pummeled the wall angrily with his fists.* **2. pummel against** *tv. + prep. phr.* to beat something against something. ♦ *The wind pummeled the branch against the side of the house.* ♦ *John pummeled his fists against the wall.*

pump ['pʌmp] **1.** *n.* a device that forces air, liquid, or gas through a tube or pipe. ♦ *Mary inflated her tire with a pump.* ♦ *John got a pitcher of water from the pump next to the house.* **2.** *tv.* to force air, liquid, or gas through a tube or pipe. ♦ *Oil has been pumped from the ground.* ♦ *John pumped gas into his car's gas tank.* **3.** *tv.* to move something up and down rapidly, like the handle of a pump. ♦ *I pumped the handle of the soap dispenser to get some more soap.* ♦ *When I met John, he pumped my hand with a vigorous handshake.*

pumpkin ['pʌmp kɪn] **1.** *n.* a large, round, heavy orange fruit that grows on a vine. ♦ *Many people carve pumpkins for Halloween.* ♦ *Seeds from pumpkins are very tasty when they're roasted.* **2.** *adj.* made with ①. ♦ *We have pumpkin pie at our Thanksgiving dinner.* ♦ *Pumpkin soup is good.*

pun ['pʌn] **1.** *n.* a play on words; the use of a word that has two different meanings in order to be funny. ♦ *The audience groaned when the speaker made a bad pun.* ♦ *This is an example of a pun: "What do you call a sad dog? A melan-collie." It is a pun because it is a play on the way that "collie"—a kind of dog—and part of "melancholy," meaning 'sad,' sound similar.* **2.** *iv.* to make ①. ♦ *Everyone groaned when the Bob punned.* ♦ *Mary punned when she said, "What kind of beans are they that you don't eat? Human beans!"*

punch ['pʌntʃ] **1.** *n.* a sweet drink made by mixing many different things to drink, but usually including some kind of fruit juice. (No plural form in this sense.) ♦ *The party guests ladled fruit punch into their glasses.* ♦ *We mixed some gin into a large bowl of punch.* **2.** *n.* a tool or machine that pierces holes through objects or that stamps or engraves designs on objects. ♦ *The oversized piece of metal jammed the punch.* ♦ *I made holes along the side of the paper with a paper punch.* **3.** *n.* a quick, forceful hit. ♦ *The punch to my face made my nose bleed.* ♦ *John's punch against the wall cracked the plaster.* **4.** *n.* forceful or effective power; strength. (Figurative on ③.) ♦ *Rewrite this story. It needs more punch.* ♦ *I gave the soup more punch by adding some spices.* **5.** *tv.* to hit someone or something forcefully with one's fist. ♦ *I angrily punched* *the wall with my fist.* ♦ *The boxer punched his opponent in his face.* **6. punch a hole in something** *idiom* to make a hole in something with ③. ♦ *John punched a hole in the wall with his fist.* ♦ *Mary punched a hole in the paper with her pencil.*

punchy ['pʌntʃ i] *adj.* having punch ④. (Comp: *punchier;* sup: *punchiest.*) ♦ *Your speech needs a punchy ending.* ♦ *This article isn't punchy enough. Rewrite it.*

punctual ['pʌŋk tʃu əl] *adj.* on time; prompt. (Adv: *punctually.*) ♦ *The punctual store owner expected his workers to arrive on time.* ♦ *Mary is punctual, so she is never late for an appointment.*

punctuality [pəŋk tʃu 'æl ə ti] *n.* the quality of doing something on time or being somewhere on time. (No plural form in this sense.) ♦ *The owner appreciated his workers' punctuality.* ♦ *The commuters depended on the punctuality of the train.*

punctuate ['pʌŋk tʃu et] **1.** *tv.* to use punctuation marks in something that one writes. ♦ *The student punctuated his essay properly.* ♦ *Questions are punctuated with question marks.* **2.** *tv.* to emphasize something; to stress something. ♦ *The speaker punctuated the main topic of her speech.* ♦ *The writer punctuated the topic sentence by underlining it.*

punctuation [pəŋk tʃu 'e ʃən] *n.* the use of punctuation marks to make writing easier to understand. (No plural form in this sense.) ♦ *The teacher circled mistakes in punctuation with a red pen.* ♦ *I made sure my essay had proper punctuation before I turned it in.*

punctuation mark [pəŋk tʃu 'e ʃən mɑrk] *n.* a symbol used to make writing easier to understand, such as the period (.), the comma (,), the colon (:), the question mark (?), the exclamation point (!), and the hyphen (-), among others. ♦ *The ransom note was written without punctuation marks.* ♦ *Punctuation marks usually aren't used in newspaper headlines.*

puncture ['pʌnk tʃɚ] **1.** *n.* a hole in the surface of something made by a sharp or pointed object. ♦ *The mechanic patched the puncture in the tire.* ♦ *A small puncture in the balloon caused it to deflate.* **2.** *tv.* to make a hole in the surface of something by using a sharp or pointed object. ♦ *The tacks thrown on the road punctured the car tires.* ♦ *Mary punctured the balloon with a pin.*

pundit ['pʌn dɪt] *n.* someone who is an expert in a certain subject; a critic or a commentator. ♦ *The political pundits criticized the president's speech.* ♦ *Thousands of pundits commented on the important football game.*

pungent ['pʌn dʒənt] *adj.* having a very strong, sharp taste or smell. (Adv: *pungently.*) ♦ *The strange spice emitted a pungent odor.* ♦ *The aged cheese had a pungent taste.*

punish ['pʌn ɪʃ] **1.** *tv.* to inflict a penalty on someone for doing something wrong. ♦ *The parents punished their child for lying.* ♦ *The criminal was punished for robbing the bank.* **2.** *tv.* to use something roughly. (Figurative on ①.) ♦ *The rough roads punished the car's new tires.* ♦ *Heavy waves punished the shore.*

punishment ['pʌn ɪʃ mənt] **1.** *n.* punishing; the practice of inflicting penalties for doing something wrong. (No plural form in this sense.) ♦ *Punishment is not always effective with children.* ♦ *The crafty thief escaped punishment.* **2.** *n.* rough treatment. (Figurative on ①. No plural form in this sense.) ♦ *The tires' tread eroded from the punishment of the rough roads.* ♦ *The army tank was built to withstand heavy punishment.* **3. glutton for punishment** *idiom* someone who seems to like doing or seeking out difficult, unpleasant, or badly paid tasks. ♦ *If you work for this firm, you'll have to be a glutton for punishment and work long hours for very little money.* ♦ *Jane must be a real glutton for punishment. She's typing Bill's manuscript free of charge.*

punitive ['pjun ə tɪv] *adj.* used as a punishment; acting as punishment. (Adv: *punitively.*) ♦ *Sue sought punitive damages from the firm that illegally fired her.* ♦ *The polluting factory had to pay an expensive punitive fine.*

punk ['pʌŋk] **1.** *n.* a young criminal; a young, anti-social person who gets into trouble a lot. ♦ *The police arrested the young punks for loitering.* ♦ *The punk shoplifted some food from the store.* **2.** *n.* a loud, harsh style of music first made popular in the late 1970s by rebellious youths. (No plural form in this sense.) ♦ *Many youths who listened to punk dyed their hair bright colors.* ♦ *The college radio station played punk after 10:00 P.M.* **3.** *n.* someone who listens to ②. ♦ *The punks slammed into each other as they danced.* ♦ *The punk wore eight silver earrings in each ear.* **4.** *adj.* <the adj. use of ②.> ♦ *The music at the punk concert was played very loudly.* ♦ *Punk songs are usually very short, fast, and loud.*

punt ['pʌnt] **1.** *tv.* to kick something, especially a football dropped from one's hands, before it hits the ground. ♦ *The kicker punted the football across the field.* ♦ *Mary punted her hat toward the couch.* **2.** *iv.* to kick as in ①. ♦ *He looked like he was going to punt, but resumed his run at the last instant.* ♦ *The kicker punted but missed the field goal.* **3.** *iv.* to delay; to evade an issue. (Figurative on ①.) ♦ *Lisa asked the senator a question, but he punted.* ♦ *The mayor punted on the tax increase until after the election.* **4.** *n.* the act of kicking a football as in ①. ♦ *The successful punt was worth a point.* ♦ *The punt was good, and the score became 7–0.* **5.** *n.* a shallow boat with a flat bottom that is moved by pushing a pole against the bottom of a river or lake. ♦ *I went across the lake on a punt.* ♦ *The fisherman placed the fish he'd caught in the punt.*

puny ['pju ni] *adj.* smaller and weaker than average. (Adv: *punily.* Comp: *punier;* sup: *puniest.*) ♦ *Mary ate the puny tomato in one bite.* ♦ *The puny child was teased by his classmates.*

pup ['pʌp] *n.* a young dog; a puppy; the young of certain animals, including the seal. ♦ *I trained the pup to bring me my slippers.* ♦ *The pups of the seal are adorable.* ♦ *The mother carried her pups to her den.*

pupil ['pju pəl] **1.** *n.* a student; someone who studies in school; someone who is taught by a teacher. ♦ *Mr. Brown has 32 pupils in his math class.* ♦ *This school was designed for 1,200 pupils.* **2.** *n.* the round, black opening in the middle of the colored part of the eye which allows light into the eye. ♦ *As lights dim, the pupil dilates.* ♦ *Pupils contract when light gets brighter.*

puppet ['pʌp ɪt] **1.** *n.* a movable doll that is used to perform a story. ♦ *John's hand controlled the mouth of the puppet.* ♦ *Mary pulled on the strings to make the puppet's arms move.* **2.** *n.* someone who is controlled by someone else. (Figurative on ①.) ♦ *The prime minister was merely a puppet of the army.* ♦ *The celebrity was a puppet of the media.*

3. *adj.* [of a government or official] controlled by something else. (Figurative on ①.) ♦ *The puppet state was governed by the powerful nation to its east.* ♦ *The military controlled the puppet government.*

puppeteer [pəp ə 'tɪr] *n.* someone who makes a puppet move in a performance. ♦ *The puppeteer spoke in a different voice for each puppet.* ♦ *The puppet appeared above a ledge that the puppeteer hid behind.*

puppy ['pʌp i] *n.* a young dog. ♦ *The veterinarian gave my puppy some shots.* ♦ *Our dog gave birth to six puppies.*

purchase ['pɚ tʃəs] **1.** *n.* the act of buying something. ♦ *My boss questioned my purchase of the new computer.* ♦ *Bill's purchase of a new car was done on impulse.* **2.** *n.* something that is bought. ♦ *Purchases cannot be returned without receipts.* ♦ *Mary paid for her purchase with a credit card.* **3.** *tv.* to buy something. ♦ *I purchased a new TV after my old one broke.* ♦ *Bob purchased groceries at the supermarket.*

purchaser ['pɚ tʃəs ɚ] *n.* a buyer; someone who buys something. ♦ *The purchaser paid for his goods with a check.* ♦ *The clerk returned some change to the purchaser.*

pure ['pjʊr] **1.** *adj.* completely made from only one thing; not mixed with anything. (Adv: *purely.* Comp: *purer;* sup: *purest.*) ♦ *Mary's necklace is made from pure gold.* ♦ *We drank pure water from the mountain spring.* **2.** *adj.* [of a color] clear and not cloudy. (Adv: *purely.* Comp: *purer;* sup: *purest.)* ♦ *Mary's eyes were pure green.* ♦ *The summer sky was pure blue.* **3.** *adj.* mere; absolute; nothing but. (Adv: *purely.* Comp: *purer;* sup: *purest.)* ♦ *Your accident was caused by pure foolishness.* ♦ *It was pure stupidity to throw rocks at that beehive.* **4.** *adj.* without sin; without evil. (Adv: *purely.* Comp: *purer;* sup: *purest.)* ♦ *The innocent young girl has a pure heart.* ♦ *The boy's intentions were completely pure.* **5.** *adj.* chaste; virginal; not having had sex. (Adv: *purely.* Comp: *purer;* sup: *purest.)* ♦ *Bob and Jane remained pure until their wedding night.* ♦ *A pure maiden was sacrificed to the gods.* **6.** *adj.* abstract; theoretical. (Adv: *purely.* Comp: *purer;* sup: *purest.)* ♦ *The logician appealed to pure reason in solving problems.* ♦ *The professor wrote theoretical articles about pure science.*

purée [pjʊ 're] **1.** *n.* food crushed into a paste. (No plural form in this sense.) ♦ *Mary fed the purée of vegetables to the baby.* ♦ *Bill added the apple purée to the sauce.* **2.** *tv.* to crush food to make ①. ♦ *John puréed the tomatoes and then let them cool.* ♦ *Jane puréed the peaches in the blender.*

purge ['pɚdʒ] **1.** *n.* the act of forcing unwanted people to leave a government, university, or other organization. ♦ *Hundreds of the ruler's opponents were killed in the purge.* ♦ *Twelve professors were fired as a result of the dean's purge.* **2.** *n.* the emptying of one's bowels, especially by using medicine or laxatives. ♦ *The purge of my bowels was caused by eating laxatives.* ♦ *I feel like I need a good purge.* **3.** *tv.* to empty one's bowels, especially by using medicine or laxatives. ♦ *I purged my bowels by taking a laxative.* ♦ *Bill had to purge his gut before his medical exam.* **4.** *tv.* to force a group of people who are not wanted someplace to leave. ♦ *The army purged the ethnic minority from the country.* ♦ *The mayor purged the city of its refugees.* **5.** *tv.* to make something clean by getting rid of what is dirty; to clean something out. ♦ *The plumber purged the dirty water from the tank.* ♦ *The cleaning crew purged the basin of its messy contents.* **6.** *tv.* to clear records or files by destroying everything that was in them. ♦ *The dictator purged the records of the previous government.* ♦ *The executive purged his files when he quit his job.*

purify ['pjʊr ə fɑɪ] *tv.* to make something pure or clean by removing something that is not pure. ♦ *The charcoal filter purified the water that passed through it.* ♦ *The air conditioner is supposed to purify the air in the entire house.*

purifying ['pjʊr ə fɑɪ ɪŋ] *adj.* making something pure or clean; causing something to become pure or clean. ♦ *I attached the purifying filter to the faucet.* ♦ *The purifying filter made the air suitable for breathing.*

Puritan ['pjʊr ə tən] **1.** *n.* one of the members of the Church of England in the 1500s and 1600s who wanted to simplify or purify the Church doctrines and worship practices. ♦ *Some Puritans fled England for America.* ♦ *The Puritans arrived at Plymouth Rock in 1620.* **2. puritan** *adj.* <the adj. use of ①.> ♦ *John was uncomfortable with puritan morals.* ♦ *The puritan citizens of the village disapproved of dancing.*

purity ['pjʊr ə ti] *n.* the quality of being pure. (No plural form in this sense.) ♦ *The scientist measured the purity of the polluted water.* ♦ *The jeweler guaranteed the purity of the gold in my ring.*

purloin [pɚ 'lɔɪn] *tv.* to steal something. (Formal.) ♦ *The butler purloined the incriminating letter from my desk.* ♦ *One of the guests has purloined a piece of my good silverware.*

purple ['pɚ pəl] **1.** *n.* the color made by mixing blue and red; the color of ripe grapes that are not green or red. (No plural form in this sense.) ♦ *This university's colors are purple and white.* ♦ *Anne's dress is a dark purple.* **2.** *adj.* of the color ①. ♦ *John's bruise began to turn purple.* ♦ *Grape-flavored drinks are often purple.*

purpose ['pɚ pəs] **1.** *n.* an intention; the reason that someone does something; a kind of goal. ♦ *The purpose of cutting my hair was that it was too long.* ♦ *My purpose for asking for a raise was that I needed the money.* **2. on purpose** *phr.* intentionally; in a way that is meant or intended; not an accident. ♦ *The bully stepped on my foot on purpose.* ♦ *Jealously, Jimmy destroyed Billy's sand castle on purpose.*

purr ['pɚ] **1.** *n.* the murmuring noise that a cat makes when it is satisfied. ♦ *The purr of the cat meant that it was content.* ♦ *I heard the cat's purr when I petted it.* **2.** *n.* the sound made by an engine that is running well. (Figurative on ①.) ♦ *As I started the car, I heard the familiar purr of the engine.* ♦ *The engine's purr was interrupted by a series of clanging sounds.* **3.** *iv.* to make a long, low sound as in ① or ②. ♦ *The cat purred when I petted it.* ♦ *The engine purred as I drove down the freeway.*

purse ['pɚs] **1.** *n.* a bag used, especially by women, to hold money and other personal items. ♦ *The tourist clutched her purse close to her while traveling.* ♦ *The thief grabbed Mary's purse as she walked through the mall.* **2.** *n.* an amount of money that is offered as a prize. ♦ *The horse's owner looked forward to winning the huge purse.* ♦ *The winner of the boxing match won a $25,000 purse.* **3. control the purse strings** *idiom* to be in charge of the money in a business or a household. ♦ *I control the purse strings at our house.* ♦ *Mr. Williams is the treasurer. He controls the purse strings.* **4. make a silk purse out of a sow's ear** *idiom* to create something of value out of something of no value. ♦ *Don't bother trying to fix up this old bicycle. You can't make a silk purse out of a sow's ear.* ♦ *My mother made a lovely jacket out of an old coat. She succeeded in making a silk purse out of a sow's ear.*

pursue [pɚ 'su] **1.** *tv.* to chase someone or something; to follow and attempt to catch someone or something. ♦ *The police pursued the thief down the alley.* ♦ *The dog pursued the cat across the yard.* **2.** *tv.* to continue to work toward something; to seek something. ♦ *Mary pursued a career in law.* ♦ *After retiring, Jane pursued her hobby of stamp collecting.* **3.** *tv.* to follow a plan of action. ♦ *The committee pursued a second plan after the first had failed.* ♦ *The football team pursued the plan that the coach had outlined.*

pursuit [pɚ 'sut] **1.** *n.* pursuing someone or something; chasing after someone or something. (No plural form in this sense.) ♦ *The pursuit of the missing child covered four states.* ♦ *In pursuit of happiness, Anne moved to California.* **2.** *n.* a hobby or job that fills one's time. ♦ *Bill's pursuit in sales began when he was 21.* ♦ *Bob's pursuit of coin collecting takes up all his spare time.*

purview ['pɚ vju] *n.* the scope or extent of an operation, activity, or understanding. ♦ *Calculus is beyond the purview of beginning algebra students.* ♦ *Your request doesn't fall into my purview. You must talk to my boss.*

pus ['pʊs] *n.* the liquid material found in an infection. (No plural form in this sense.) ♦ *The nurse drained the pus from my infection.* ♦ *I cleaned the pus from my sore with a cotton ball.*

push ['pʊʃ] **1. push ahead** *iv.* + *adv.* to move forward with force; to move by using pressure. ♦ *Bill pushed ahead until he was at the front of the crowd.* ♦ *Anne pushed ahead at her job until she ran the company.* **2. push through** *iv.* + *prep. phr.* to force one's way through a crowded place. ♦ *The thief pushed through the crowd in order to elude the police.* ♦ *The hiker pushed through the vines to get back to the path.* **3.** *iv.* to force movement in a certain direction. ♦ *The camper pushed against the sagging roof of the tent.* ♦ *The pilot pushed down on the red button and was ejected from the plane.* **4.** *tv.* to apply pressure to something, as if to move it. ♦ *The child pushed the cart into the wall.* ♦ *I pushed a button on the panel by the elevator door.* **5. push into** *tv.* + *prep. phr.* to urge someone to do something; to try to make someone do something; to encourage someone to do something. ♦ *Bill pushed his son into enlisting in the military.* ♦ *Mary pushed me into going to the movies with her.* **6.** *n.* a shove; a forceful movement that causes something to move. ♦ *I felt a push against my back, and I fell forward.* ♦ *The push of the panicking crowd propelled me toward the exit.* **7.** *tv.* to sell drugs; to sell something that is illegal or stolen. (Informal.) ♦ *The drug dealer was arrested for pushing marijuana.* ♦ *John was sent to jail for pushing stolen watches.*

pushbutton ['pʊʃ bət n] **1.** *n.* a disk or button that is pressed to activate a device. ♦ *On phones, the pushbutton marked with a 0 also stands for* operator. ♦ *The elevator's pushbuttons had a Braille plate next to them for the blind.* **2.** *adj.* operated by pushing buttons on a panel, such as a telephone. ♦ *To access the recorded information, you need a pushbutton phone.* ♦ *I activated the alarm system from the pushbutton panel.*

pushover ['pʊʃ ov ɚ] **1.** *n.* something that is very easy to do. ♦ *The smart student thought the math test was a pushover.* ♦ *That job was such a pushover that I finished it in 10 minutes.* **2.** *n.* someone who is easy to beat in a game; someone who is easily influenced to do or buy something. ♦ *The worst team in the league was a complete pushover.* ♦ *John's such a pushover. He'll do anything I tell him to.*

pushy ['pʊʃ i] *adj.* aggressive; insistent; too assertive. (Adv: *pushily.* Comp: *pushier;* sup: *pushiest.*) ♦ *The pushy salesclerk followed me around the store.* ♦ *When John became too pushy, I told him to relax.*

pussycat ['pʊs i kæt] **1.** *n.* a cat. ♦ *Mary fed her pussycat some warm milk.* ♦ *David's pussycat climbed onto my lap and fell asleep.* **2.** *n.* a timid person. (Figurative on ①.) ♦ *The pussycat was scared of her own shadow.* ♦ *Bob is quite a pussycat when it comes to driving in heavy traffic.*

pussyfoot ['pʊs i fʊt] **1.** *iv.* to move slowly, quietly, and carefully, so that one is not noticed. ♦ *The thief pussyfooted across the marble floor.* ♦ *The detective pussyfooted twenty yards behind the crook.* **2. pussyfoot around** *iv.* + *adv.* to avoid doing what needs to be done. ♦ *Stop pussyfooting around, and do your work!* ♦ *John pussyfooted around when he should have been working.*

put ['pʊt] **1.** *tv., irreg.* to place something in a certain position; to cause something to be in a certain place or position; to move something to a certain place or position. (Pt/pp: *put.*) ♦ *Mary put the book on the shelf.* ♦ *John put some food in his mouth.* **2.** *tv., irreg.* to express something; to say something in a certain way. ♦ *To say that I'm angry is putting it mildly!* ♦ *John didn't accept the job until the terms were put in writing.* **3. put someone on** *idiom* to tease or kid someone; to deceive someone playfully. ♦ *I don't believe you! You're just putting me on!* ♦ *He thought you were serious, but you were just putting him on.* **4. put someone off** *idiom* to avoid responding to someone; to delay a response to someone. ♦ *I keep asking her, but she just keeps putting me off.* ♦ *Don't put me off again. Answer me now!* **5. put something on** *idiom* to place clothing onto one's body; to get into a piece of clothing. ♦ *I put on a heavy coat to go outside in the cold.* ♦ *Please put this on and see if it fits.* **6. put something off** *idiom* to postpone something; to schedule something for a later time. ♦ *I have to put off our meeting until a later time.* ♦ *I put off a visit to the dentist as long as I could.* **7. put something to (good) use** *idiom* to apply a skill or ability; to use a skill or ability. ♦ *The lawyer put her training to good use for the charity.* ♦ *The pianist put his talents to use at the party.* **8. put upon someone** *idiom* to make use of someone to an unreasonable degree; to take advantage of someone for one's own benefit. ♦ *My mother was always put upon by her neighbors. She was too nice to refuse their requests for help.* ♦ *Jane feels put upon by her husband's parents. They're always coming to stay with her.* **9. put up with someone or something** *idiom* to tolerate or endure someone or something; to be able to stand someone or something. ♦ *I cannot put up with your constant whining any longer!* ♦ *We can put up with John's living here until he finds a place of his own.*

put-down ['pʊt daʊn] *n.* an insult; something that is insulting or humbling. ♦ *I left the party because I was angered by John's put-downs.* ♦ *Mary's criticism of my work was a real put-down.*

put-on ['pʊt ɔn] *n.* a trick; a hoax; something that is not meant to be taken seriously. ♦ *No, there aren't any aliens at city hall. That was just a put-on.* ♦ *A reporter exposed the students' claims as an elaborate put-on.*

putrid ['pju trɪd] *adj.* stinking and rotting; decaying. (Adv: *putridly.*) ♦ *Our dog dragged home a putrid carcass from the field behind our house.* ♦ *The vultures descended toward the putrid flesh.*

putter ['pʌt ɚ] **1. putter (around)** *iv.* (+ *adv.*) to move around doing small chores and bits of work. ♦ *After Bill retired, he puttered around all day.* ♦ *John puttered around in order to appear busy.* **2. putter around** *iv.* + *prep. phr.* to move around somewhere, doing little bits of works and chores. ♦ *John just putters around the office. He never gets anything done.* ♦ *I like to putter around the house on weekends.*

putty ['pʌt i] **1.** *n.* a soft, oily substance used to seal pipe connections, to seal the edges of glass in window frames, and to fill uneven surfaces. (No plural form in this sense.) ♦ *The plumber sealed the joint in the pipes with putty.* ♦ *The old putty around the panes of glass started to flake.* **2. be putty in someone's hands** *idiom* [for someone] to be easily influenced by someone else; excessively willing to do what someone else wishes. ♦ *Bob's wife is putty in his hands. She never thinks for herself.* ♦ *Jane is putty in her mother's hands. She always does exactly what her mother says.*

puzzle ['pʌz əl] **1.** *n.* a hard problem that needs to be solved; something that is hard to solve or understand. ♦ *Reducing crime was a real puzzle for the mayor.* ♦ *David found calculus to be a difficult puzzle.* **2.** See crossword puzzle, jigsaw puzzle. **3.** *tv.* to confuse someone. ♦ *Mary was puzzled by the difficult homework assignment.* ♦ *The bewildering array of wires puzzled the electrician.* **4. puzzle out** *tv.* + *adv.* to succeed in understanding something. ♦ *John puzzled out the complex logic problem.* ♦ *Mary puzzled out the translation of the poem from German.*

Pygmy ['pɪg mi] **1.** *n.* a member of a group of people in central Africa who are smaller than average. ♦ *The Belgian government colonized the lands where Pygmies lived.* ♦ *The missionary learned to speak the Pygmy's language.* **2. pygmy** *n.* someone or something that is much smaller than average. (Figurative on ①.) ♦ *Mary couldn't reach the top shelf because she's such a little pygmy.* ♦ *Our cat's a pygmy, and everyone thinks she's a kitten.* **3.** *adj.* very small. ♦ *I bought some pygmy tomatoes at the store.* ♦ *The pygmy dog snapped at my ankles.*

pyramid ['pɪr ə mɪd] **1.** *n.* a four-sided structure with triangular sides that meet at one point on top. ♦ *Jimmy set the base of the pyramid on top of a cube.* ♦ *Susie's pile of sand is shaped like a pyramid.* **2.** *n.* one of a group of large, Egyptian tombs—shaped like ①—in which Egyptian kings were buried. ♦ *The Great Pyramids are one of the seven wonders of the ancient world.* ♦ *The scientists found a mummy within the pyramid.*

pyrite ['paɪ raɪt] *n.* a kind of yellow mineral that looks like gold. (No plural form in this sense.) ♦ *Iron pyrite is called fool's gold.* ♦ *The chemist will determine if the powder is pyrite or gold.*

python ['paɪ θən] *n.* a large constrictor snake found in tropical areas of Asia, southeast India, Africa, and Australia. ♦ *The large python swallowed the rabbit whole.* ♦ *The python strangles its prey with its body.*

Q AND **q** ['kju] *n.* the seventeenth letter in the English alphabet. ♦ Q *is normally followed by the letter* U *in words.* ♦ *In the alphabet,* Q *comes after* P *and before* R.

quack ['kwæk] **1.** *iv.* to make the characteristic noise of a duck. ♦ *The ducks quacked as they swam in the pond.* ♦ *The duckling quacked and ran after its mother.* **2.** *n.* the noise that a duck makes. ♦ *I heard the quacks of ducks swimming in the pond.* ♦ *Jimmy, can you make a quack like a duck?* **3.** *n.* someone who claims to be a doctor but who is not trained to be a doctor. ♦ *The quack's remedy made the sick man feel even worse.* ♦ *I switched doctors because I thought my old one was a quack.*

quadrangle ['kwɑ dræŋ gəl] **1.** *n.* a geometric shape having four sides. ♦ *A rectangle is a quadrangle whose angles are all 90 degrees.* ♦ *Mary arranged four straws into the shape of a quadrangle.* **2.** *n.* an outdoor space, especially on a college campus, formed by being surrounded by a building or buildings on all four sides. ♦ *The history department is on the north side of the quadrangle.* ♦ *At noon, the quadrangle was full of students eating lunch.*

quadrant ['kwɑ drənt] *n.* one-quarter of a circle; a shape—like a piece of pie—equal to one-quarter of a circle. ♦ *My mother cut the pie into quadrants for the four of us.* ♦ *The garden is a large circle, and each quadrant is planted with a different kind of flower.*

quadruple [kwɑ 'dru pəl] **1.** *tv.* to do something four times as much; to make something four times as large; to multiply something by four. ♦ *If you quadruple five, you get twenty.* ♦ *In the last decade, the university has quadrupled the tuition rate.* **2.** *iv.* to become four times as large; to be four times greater; to be multiplied by four. ♦ *My insurance rates quadrupled after my second accident.* ♦ *My work load quadrupled when I got a promotion.* **3.** *adj.* of or about four of something. (Adv: *quadruply.*) ♦ *The food passed through the quadruple chambers of the cow's stomach.* ♦ *My uncle had quadruple bypass surgery.* **4.** *adj.* four times as much [as the regular amount]. (Adv: *quadruply.*) ♦ *The cook gave the hungry child a quadruple serving of potatoes.* ♦ *My insurance payments are quadruple what they were last year.*

quadruplet [kwɑ 'drup lɪt] *n.* one of four offspring born at the same time to the same mother. ♦ *The Smiths hired a nurse to help them care for their quadruplets.* ♦ *Anne was expecting twins, so she was surprised when she had quadruplets.*

quail ['kwel] **1.** *n., irreg.* a small bird that is often hunted for sport and eaten as food. (Pl: *quail* or *quails.*) ♦ *The dog frightened some quail from the deep grass.* ♦ *The hunter shot the quail as it flew overhead.* **2.** *n.* the meat of ①. (No plural form in this sense.) ♦ *The diner ordered quail at the fancy restaurant.* ♦ *The cook has a special recipe for preparing quail.*

quaint ['kwent] *adj.* strange in an interesting or funny way; charming in an old-fashioned way. (Adv: *quaintly.* Comp: *quainter;* sup: *quaintest.*) ♦ *The museum displayed quaint advertisements from the 1920s.* ♦ *My great-aunt told about the quaint clothes she wore as a child.*

quake ['kwek] **1.** *n.* an earthquake. ♦ *The quake broke all the dishes in my cabinets.* ♦ *The poorly made house crumbled during the quake.* **2.** *iv.* to shake; to tremble. ♦ *The earth was quaking and rolling during the earthquake.* ♦ *I was quaking from fear before the test.*

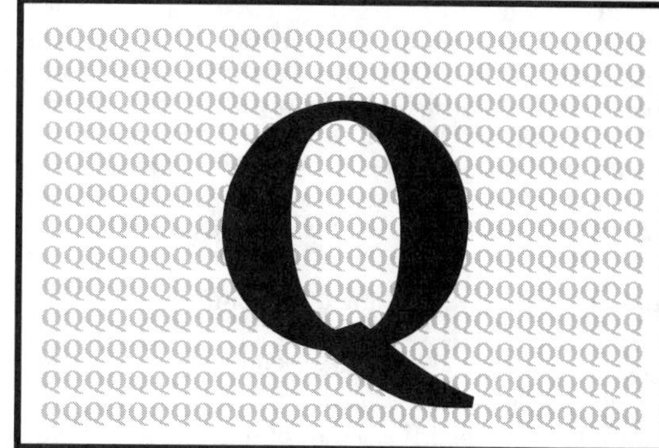

Quaker ['kwek ɚ] *n.* a member of a Christian denomination called the Society of Friends, whose followers oppose war and violence. ♦ *Quakers do not support wars or violence.* ♦ *There are many periods of silence during meetings of Quakers.*

qualification [kwɑl ə fɪ 'ke ʃən] **1.** *n.* the process of qualifying. (No plural form in this sense.) ♦ *Qualification for the job was achieved by way of an examination.* ♦ *The work is easy, but the process of qualification is difficult.* **2.** *n.* a quality or experience that makes someone an appropriate choice for something. ♦ *David has all the qualifications listed in the grant application.* ♦ *I described my qualifications for the job to the interviewer.* **3.** *n.* a statement of requirements for a job. ♦ *I am looking for a job with qualifications that match my skills.* ♦ *The qualifications for this job are very high.* **4.** *n.* a limitation; a restriction. ♦ *I support Anne as a candidate without qualification.* ♦ *The new law placed numerous qualifications on liquor licenses.*

qualified ['kwɑl ə fɑɪd] *adj.* having the qualities, experience, or skill that makes one acceptable for a job, position, award, or similar benefit. ♦ *The experienced lawyer was qualified for the assignment.* ♦ *The highly qualified student received a large scholarship.*

qualify ['kwɑl ə fɑɪ] **1. qualify (for)** *tv.* (+ *prep. phr.*) to cause someone meet the requirements for something, such as a job, responsibility, award, or acceptance into a school or organization. ♦ *Your excellent grades qualify you for a scholarship.* ♦ *Your years of experience qualify you for this job.* **2.** *tv.* to limit something; to restrict something; to narrow the meaning of something. ♦ *The mayor qualified his statement to clear up an ambiguity.* ♦ *I had to qualify my remarks to include all the facts.* **3. qualify for** *iv.* + *prep. phr.* to meet the requirements for something, such as a task or award as in ①. ♦ *Mary qualified for the early retirement program.* ♦ *Most of the flood victims qualified for low-interest loans.*

qualitative ['kwɑl ə te tɪv] **1.** *adj.* of or about quality; of or about something's level of excellence. (Adv: *qualitatively.*) ♦ *I expect some qualitative improvements in your grade next semester.* ♦ *The company promised qualitative excellence for its products.* **2.** *adj.* of or about qualities; of or about characteristics, especially as opposed to amounts. (Adv: *qualitatively.*) ♦ *The qualitative analysis of the powder showed that it was just starch.* ♦ *There are few qualitative differences in the two approaches.*

quality ['kwal ɪ ti] **1.** *n.* a characteristic; a distinguishing property of someone or something. ♦ *Bill's best quality is that he's so kind.* ♦ *Water has the important quality of conducting electricity.* **2.** *n.* a degree or level of excellence. (No plural form in this sense.) ♦ *Susan bought a luxury car of very high quality.* ♦ *I will not buy anything of low quality.* **3.** *adj.* of a good quality ②. ♦ *The customer demanded quality service.* ♦ *I insisted on buying a quality car.*

qualm ['kwam] *n.* a feeling of discomfort about someone or something. ♦ *Do you have any qualms about eating raw fish?* ♦ *Jane had a sudden qualm about going out on a blind date.*

quandary ['kwan dri] *n.* a state of uncertainty; a feeling that one is not sure of what one should do. ♦ *Bill asked his brother for advice on his quandary.* ♦ *After I lost my job, I found myself in a real quandary.*

quantitative ['kwan tə te tɪv] *adj.* of or about quantity or quantities. (Adv: *quantitatively.*) ♦ *A quantitative analysis showed that the cookie had 12 grams of fat.* ♦ *In addition to the differences in style, there's a quantitative difference in cost between the two plans.*

quantity ['kwan tə ti] *n.* an amount; a certain number of something that can be counted or measured. ♦ *I bought a large quantity of snacks for the party.* ♦ *The clerk who was taking inventory listed the quantities of all items in stock.*

quarantine ['kwar ən tin] **1.** *tv.* to isolate a living thing that has a disease or has been exposed to a disease. ♦ *Our dog was quarantined for a month when we moved to Asia.* ♦ *The travelers were quarantined until they passed a medical exam.* **2.** *n.* a period of isolation of living things that have an illness or have been exposed to an illness. (No plural form in this sense.) ♦ *During the quarantine, no one could leave the afflicted village.* ♦ *Our dog's quarantine lasted a month when we returned from abroad.*

quarrel ['kwar əl] **1.** *n.* an angry argument; an angry disagreement. ♦ *Don't yell at me. Why should we have a quarrel?* ♦ *The loud quarrel ended up in a brawl.* **2.** *iv.* to argue with someone angrily; for two or more people to argue angrily. ♦ *My brother and I quarreled over whose turn it was to wash dishes.* ♦ *The students in the ethics class quarreled about right and wrong.*

quarreling ['kwar (ə) lɪŋ] *adj.* arguing; angrily disagreeing. ♦ *The two quarreling men agreed to a duel.* ♦ *The quarreling neighbors yelled at each other across the fence.*

quarrelsome ['kwarl səm] *adj.* likely to cause an argument; fond of fighting or arguing. (Adv: *quarrelsomely.*) ♦ *My quarrelsome friend will argue about any subject.* ♦ *The quarrelsome couple decided to get a divorce.*

quarry ['kwar i] **1.** *n.* a place where marble, granite, and other kinds of stone are removed from the earth. ♦ *The sculptor went to the quarry to get a block of marble.* ♦ *The contractor bought a ton of gravel from the quarry.* **2.** *n.* the object of a hunt or search. ♦ *The dog retrieved its quarry from the bush.* ♦ *The hunter shot his quarry.* **3.** *tv.* to remove stone from ①. ♦ *This marble was quarried from a pit outside of town.* ♦ *They have been quarrying granite here for hundreds of years.*

quart ['kwort] **1.** *n.* a unit of measure of liquids, equal to one-fourth of a gallon, 32 ounces, or 0.95 liter. ♦ *I drank a quart of milk for breakfast.* ♦ *My car's engine needed two quarts of oil.* **2.** *adj.* [of something] holding ①. ♦ *Mike bought two quart containers of ice cream.* ♦ *We had 12 two-quart containers of milk left.*

quarter ['kwor tɚ] **1.** *n.* one-fourth of something; one of four equal parts; one of four parts. ♦ *Half of the apple is too much. Just give me a quarter.* ♦ *I cut the pizza into quarters.* **2.** *n.* a coin equal to 25 cents or one-fourth of a dollar. ♦ *I put two quarters in the pay phone before making my call.* ♦ *This vending machine only takes quarters.* **3.** *n.* fifteen minutes; one-fourth of an hour. (Limited to *quarter to; quarter till; quarter of; quarter after; quarter past.* No plural form in this sense.) ♦ *3:45 is a quarter to four, and also a quarter of four.* ♦ *2:15 is a quarter after two, and also a quarter past two.* **4.** *n.* three months; one-fourth of a year. ♦ *The corporation lost millions of dollars in the last quarter.* ♦ *The firm projected a large profit for the fourth quarter.* **5.** *n.* one of the four periods in football, basketball, and other games. ♦ *Our team won the game in the final minute of the fourth quarter.* ♦ *The basketball player was benched in the third quarter.* **6.** *n.* a neighborhood; a section of a town; a district. ♦ *Anne owns a hotel in the French Quarter of New Orleans.* ♦ *The mayor lived in a very fashionable quarter of town.* **7.** *n.* a period equal to one third of the school or academic year. ♦ *A semester is longer than an academic quarter.* ♦ *During third quarter, I took three math courses.* **8. quarters** *n.* the place where someone lives. (Treated a plural.) ♦ *I share my living quarters with two other roommates.* ♦ *My quarters were cramped while my house was being renovated.* **9.** *tv.* to divide something into four parts; to cut something into four parts; to split something into four parts. ♦ *I quartered the pizza before serving it.* ♦ *The inheritance was quartered and divided among my three siblings and me.* **10.** *tv.* to give someone, especially soldiers, a place to stay or live. ♦ *The soldiers were quartered in temporary barracks.* ♦ *During the war, the soldiers were quartered in farmhouses near the front.*

quarterback ['kwor tɚ bæk] *n.* a football player who gives the signals at the beginning of each play. ♦ *A player passed the football to the quarterback.* ♦ *In football, the quarterback directs the team's plays.*

quarterly ['kwor tɚ li] **1.** *adj.* happening or appearing four times a year; happening or appearing every three months. ♦ *The company issues a quarterly financial report.* ♦ *I prepared my office for the quarterly inspection.* **2.** *adv.* once every three months; four times each year. ♦ *I pay for my car insurance quarterly.* ♦ *The company paid stock dividends quarterly.* **3.** *n.* a magazine that has a new issue once every three months; an academic journal whose issues are three months apart. ♦ *Our school library subscribes to many academic quarterlies.* ♦ *My favorite magazine is a quarterly, so I only receive issues four times each year.*

quartet [kwor 'tɛt] **1.** *n.* a group of four things or people, especially a group of four singers or musicians. ♦ *A string quartet always includes two violins.* ♦ *The quartet sang a medley of folk songs.* **2.** *n.* a piece of music written for four instruments or four singers. ♦ *The composer wrote a quartet for strings.* ♦ *The leader of the choir chose four singers to perform the quartet.*

quartz ['kworts] *n.* a hard, and often crystalline, mineral commonly found as a constituent of rocks or as sand.

(No plural form in this sense.) ♦ *Quartz is one of the most common minerals on earth.* ♦ *Most of the sand in the desert is made of quartz.*

quash ['kwɑʃ] **1.** *tv.* to void something officially or legally; to cause something to be officially or legally not valid. ♦ *The lawyer asked the judge to quash the indictment.* ♦ *The legislation was quashed in the courts.* **2.** *tv.* to suppress something, such as a rebellion. ♦ *The king's army quashed the minor rebellion.* ♦ *We were not able to quash the uprising in time.*

quay ['ki] *n.* a wharf, usually made of stone, where people can load and unload cargo from ships. ♦ *The tidal wave destroyed the old stone quay.* ♦ *The sailor unloaded the cargo onto the quay.*

queasy ['kwiz i] *adj.* feeling sick, nauseated, or uneasy. (Adv: *queasily.* Comp: *queasier;* sup: *queasiest.*) ♦ *The rough waves made me queasy.* ♦ *The queasy passenger vomited.*

Quebec [kwə 'bɛk] See Gazetteer.

queen ['kwin] **1.** *n.* the female ruler of a country or the wife of a king. ♦ *Queen Elizabeth II became the queen of England in 1952.* ♦ *The country's currency was stamped with the queen's image.* **2.** *n.* the sole egg-laying female in a colony or hive of certain species of insects, such as bees, termites, or ants. ♦ *The queen of the colony is the only female that is allowed to breed.* ♦ *Every termite colony has a queen.* **3.** *n.* a playing card that has a picture of ① on it. ♦ *John had all four queens in his hand and won the poker game.* ♦ *Mary laid down the queen of spades.* **4.** *n.* a chess piece that can move any number of spaces in a straight line in any direction. ♦ *After I lost my queen, I knew I'd lose the game.* ♦ *I took my opponent's last rook with my queen.*

queen-size(d) ['kwin sɑɪz(d)] *adj.* [of bedding] larger than the standard bed for two people. ♦ *We are more comfortable on a queen-sized mattress.* ♦ *We can't get a queen-size bed through the bedroom door!*

queer ['kwɪr] **1.** *adj.* odd; strange; unusual; weird; peculiar. (Adv: *queerly.* Comp: *queerer;* sup: *queerest.*) ♦ *I had a queer feeling that something was wrong.* ♦ *The queer old man sat in the park and conversed with the pigeons.* **2.** *adj.* homosexual. (Usually rude and derogatory. Now used more openly by homosexuals in a nonderogatory manner. Adv: *queerly.*) ♦ *Max said he wouldn't be caught dead in a queer bar.* ♦ *The store owner refused to sell queer magazines.* **3.** *n.* a homosexual person. (Usually rude and derogatory slang.) ♦ *John really preferred being called gay to being called a queer.* ♦ *Bill told Max he was a queer simply to make him mad.*

quell ['kwɛl] *tv.* to calm or put an end to disorder or some other problem. ♦ *The police quelled the riot.* ♦ *The teacher quelled the loud disorder in the classroom.*

quench ['kwɛntʃ] **1.** *tv.* to put out a fire by using water. ♦ *The firefighters quenched the raging fire.* ♦ *Quick! Go get some water to quench the flames!* **2.** *tv.* to ease or eliminate one's thirst by drinking something. ♦ *A cold glass of lemonade would really quench my thirst.* ♦ *Jane quenched her thirst with a cup of juice.*

query ['kwɪr i] **1.** *n.* a question. ♦ *I have a query about your comments.* ♦ *I responded truthfully to the lawyer's query.* **2.** *tv.* to ask someone about something. ♦ *The lawyer queried the witness about the crime.* ♦ *The interviewer queried me about my past experience.* **3.** *tv.* to question the accuracy or advisability of something. ♦ *The researcher queried his hasty conclusions.* ♦ *The teacher queried Bill's ability to finish the project by noon.*

quest ['kwɛst] *n.* a search for someone or something. ♦ *The pirates were on a quest for the buried treasure.* ♦ *Bob's quest for a wife finally ended when he met Anne.*

question ['kwɛs tʃən] **1.** *n.* an inquiry; a speech utterance used to make an inquiry. ♦ *Would you please answer my question?* ♦ *"What time is it?" is a question.* **2.** *n.* a doubt; a concern; something that one is not sure about. (No plural form in this sense.) ♦ *There is some question as to whether you should go.* ♦ *Without question, you should do it.* **3.** *n.* a matter for consideration; a problem for solving. ♦ *The leaders discussed the question of ending the war.* ♦ *The manager addressed the question of overtime.* **4.** *tv.* to ask ① of someone. ♦ *The lawyer questioned the witness.* ♦ *I questioned my teacher about the homework assignment.* **5.** *tv.* to doubt something; to express one's doubts or concerns about something. ♦ *Do what I say, and don't question my motives.* ♦ *I questioned the appropriateness of red wallpaper for the bedroom.* **6. out of the question** *idiom* not possible; not permitted. ♦ *I'm sorry, but it's out of the question.* ♦ *You can't go to Florida this spring. We can't afford it. It's out of the question.*

questionable ['kwɛs tʃə nə bəl] **1.** *adj.* in doubt; inviting questions or scrutiny. (Adv: *questionably.*) ♦ *After I was fired, my future was questionable.* ♦ *Due to Bob's carelessness, the worth of the results of the experiment is questionable.* **2.** *adj.* possibly not honest or true. (Adv: *questionably.*) ♦ *The criminal had a questionable character.* ♦ *Some information in gossip columns is highly questionable.*

question mark ['kwɛs tʃən mɑrk] *n.* a punctuation mark "?" that is written at the end of a question. ♦ *You should put a question mark at the end of every question.* ♦ *Question marks are used after questions, while periods are used after declarative sentences.*

questionnaire [kwɛs tʃə 'ner] *n.* a printed set of questions. ♦ *The pollster gave me a questionnaire to fill out.* ♦ *I responded to a questionnaire about my political beliefs.*

queue ['kju] **1.** *n.* a line of people or things in a row waiting for something. ♦ *The tourists stood in a queue to tour the queen's palace.* ♦ *A queue of customers waited for the bank to open.* **2.** *n.* a series of telephone calls waiting to be answered or computer files waiting to be printed. ♦ *Your document is next in the printing queue.* ♦ *I deleted my document from the queue.* **3. queue up** *iv.* + *adv.* to line up; to form a line; to be in a line. ♦ *The tourists queued up in front of the palace.* ♦ *The cars in the funeral procession queued up at the church.*

quibble ['kwɪb əl] **1.** *iv.* to argue about, with, or over something that is not too important. ♦ *John quibbled with the waitress about the 25-cent charge for an extra plate.* ♦ *The student quibbled over his grade on an unimportant quiz.* **2.** *n.* a small disagreement over a minor point. ♦ *Bill had two or three quibbles he wanted to mention about Lisa's presentation.* ♦ *I have a small quibble about your last statement.*

quick ['kwɪk] **1.** *adj.* fast; rapid; swift. (Adv: *quickly.* Comp: *quicker;* sup: *quickest.*) ♦ *The express train is very quick.* ♦ *The quick fox managed to escape the hunters.*

2. *adj.* lasting only for a short period of time; having a short duration; beginning and ending in a short period of time. (Adv: *quickly.* Comp: *quicker;* sup: *quickest.*) ♦ *The teacher took a quick vacation between semesters.* ♦ *I took a quick look at the items on sale.* **3.** *adj.* able to understand or learn things in a short amount of time. (Adv: *quickly.* Comp: *quicker;* sup: *quickest.*) ♦ *John is very quick and doesn't require much help to learn new things.* ♦ *Lisa was quick, but not as bright as Jane.* **4.** *n.* the flesh under one's fingernails or toenails. (No plural form in this sense.) ♦ *Bill cut his nails to the quick.* ♦ *My crushed fingernail fell off, revealing the quick.* **5.** *adv.* quickly. (Colloquial. Comp: *quicker;* sup: *quickest.*) ♦ *Get here as quick as you can! It's an emergency.* ♦ *Come quick! I need help!*

quicken ['kwɪk ən] **1.** *iv.* to become faster; to move more quickly; to do something more quickly; to increase the speed of something. ♦ *My heartbeat quickened as I jumped out of the way of the oncoming car.* ♦ *The flow of water quickened as the hole in the pipe got larger.* **2.** *iv.* [for a fetus] to show movement in the uterus for the first time; to become alive. ♦ *Mary felt that the baby's life had begun when the fetus quickened.* ♦ *Anne had no idea of when her fetus actually quickened.* **3.** *tv.* to cause something to become faster; to cause something to move more quickly. ♦ *The supervisor quickened the movement of the assembly line.* ♦ *The jogger quickened his pace as he went down the hill.*

quickness ['kwɪk nəs] *n.* the quality of being quick. (No plural form in this sense.) ♦ *Because of the runner's quickness, she won first place.* ♦ *My friend's quickness in calling for help saved my life.*

quicksand ['kwɪk sænd] *n.* wet sand, often under water, into which living creatures can sink. (No plural form in this sense.) ♦ *The hunter pulled his friend from the quicksand with a rope.* ♦ *The dog became trapped in the quicksand.*

quiescent [kwi 'ɛs ənt] *adj.* inactive; not functioning. (Adv: *quiescently.*) ♦ *The patient's illness was quiescent for the moment.* ♦ *Bob's thinking became quiescent as he slept.*

quiet ['kwɑɪ ɪt] **1.** *adj.* not loud; making only a small amount of sound. (Adv: *quietly.* Comp: *quieter;* sup: *quietest.*) ♦ *The librarian asked me to be quiet.* ♦ *The quiet music was very soothing.* **2.** *adj.* [of a person] not assertive and not talkative. (Adv: *quietly.* Comp: *quieter;* sup: *quietest.*) ♦ *I advised the quiet student to be a little more aggressive.* ♦ *My quiet cousin left the party very early.* **3.** *adj.* not active; not moving; calm; still. (Adv: *quietly.* Comp: *quieter;* sup: *quietest.*) ♦ *Just before the tornado, all of nature was very quiet.* ♦ *The floating raft remained motionless on the quiet waters.* **4.** *adj.* peaceful; restful. (Adv: *quietly.* Comp: *quieter;* sup: *quietest.*) ♦ *I spent a quiet day at the beach.* ♦ *My grandparents like to spend a quiet evening at home.* **5. quiet down** *iv.* + *adv.* to become silent or less noisy. ♦ *The children quieted down when their teacher entered the room.* ♦ *The audience quieted down once the movie started.* **6.** *tv.* to cause someone or something to become ①. ♦ *Food quieted the barking dogs.* ♦ *I quieted the buzzing alarm clock by pressing the button on top.* **7.** *n.* silence. (No plural form in this sense.) ♦ *The quiet in the eye of a hurricane can be unnerving.* ♦ *After I moved to the city, I missed the quiet of the farm.*

quill ['kwɪl] *n.* a natural growth such as the spine of the porcupine or the main stem of the feather of a bird. ♦ *The porcupine has many sharp quills on its spiny back.* ♦ *Years ago, they made pens from quills.*

quilt ['kwɪlt] **1.** *n.* a bed covering made from a soft pad between two layers of decorative cloth, stitched together. ♦ *My aunts stitched a quilt for my baby.* ♦ *I made a quilt from leftover pieces of material.* **2.** *iv.* to work at making ①. ♦ *The women quilted together every Thursday afternoon.* ♦ *My mother taught me how to quilt.*

quintessential [kwɪn tə 'sɛn tʃəl] *adj.* most perfect; most representative of something; being the best example of something. (Adv: *quintessentially.*) ♦ *My boss is firm but fair. She's the quintessential supervisor.* ♦ *This chapel is the quintessential example of the architect's work.*

quintuple [kwɪn 'tʌp əl] **1.** *tv.* to multiply something by five. ♦ *If you quintuple six, you get thirty.* ♦ *Last year, my landlord quintupled my rent.* **2.** *iv.* to become five times greater. ♦ *My insurance rate quintupled when my teenage son began driving.* ♦ *My responsibilities quintupled when I got a promotion.* **3.** *adj.* five times greater than. (Adv: *quintuply.*) ♦ *My insurance payments are quintuple what they were last year.* ♦ *I examined the insect with a lens that had quintuple magnification.*

quintuplet [kwɪn 'tʌp lət] *n.* one of five offspring born at the same time to the same mother. ♦ *Our cat gave birth to quintuplets.* ♦ *The fertility medicine caused Jane to have quintuplets.*

quip ['kwɪp] **1.** *n.* a clever, witty, or sarcastic remark. ♦ *Lisa was insulted by Bob's sarcastic quip.* ♦ *The students sat in the café making witty quips.* **2.** *tv.* to say something in the manner of ①. ♦ *When I asked John which team he was rooting for, he quipped, "Whichever team is winning!"* ♦ *The conceited actress quipped that her rival was a better cook than an actress.*

quirk ['kwɚk] *n.* a strange habit; a strange characteristic. ♦ *After a while, I became used to my roommate's quirks.* ♦ *A quirk of this computer program is that the screen sometimes goes blank.*

quirky ['kwɚ ki] *adj.* strange, odd in an amusing way. (Adv: *quirkily.* Comp: *quirkier;* sup: *quirkiest.*) ♦ *The critic liked the quirky little film.* ♦ *My friends are quirky, but they're fun to be around.*

quit ['kwɪt] **1.** *tv., irreg.* to stop doing something. (Pt/pp: *quit.*) ♦ *Quit working! It's five o'clock.* ♦ *I hope it quits raining before we have to go outside.* **2.** *tv., irreg.* to leave a job; to resign a job. ♦ *Jane quit her job because she hated her boss.* ♦ *I won't quit this job until I find a new one.* **3.** *iv., irreg.* [for someone or something] to cease [doing something]. ♦ *I think it's time to quit today.* ♦ *The engine quit while I was driving down the freeway.* **4. call it quits** *idiom* to resign from something; to announce that one is stopping. ♦ *Okay! I've had enough! I'm calling it quits.* ♦ *Time to go home, John. Let's call it quits.*

quite ['kwɑɪt] **1.** *adv.* very; rather; completely. ♦ *I am quite full.* ♦ *Are you quite finished?* **2. quite a something** *phr.* definitely something; a good example of something. ♦ *The captain of the swim team is quite a swimmer.* ♦ *That's quite a bruise you have there.*

quitter ['kwɪt ɚ] *n.* someone who quits or gives up easily. ♦ *The coach told the team that quitters never win.* ♦

Don't be a quitter. If you've committed yourself to doing something, do it.

quiver ['kwɪv ɚ] *iv.* to shake; to tremble. ♦ *My hands quivered because I was so scared.* ♦ *The house quivered during the earthquake.*

quivering ['kwɪv ɚ ɪŋ] *adj.* shaking; trembling. (Adv: *quiveringly.*) ♦ *The quivering child began to cry.* ♦ *The quivering patient was rushed into the emergency room.*

quiz ['kwɪz] **1.** *n.* a small test; an informal test. (Pl: *quizzes.*) ♦ *Our teacher gave us a surprise quiz on yesterday's lecture.* ♦ *There's going to be a quiz tomorrow.* **2.** *tv.* to test someone on or about something; to ask someone questions about someone or something. ♦ *The teacher quizzed the students on the reading assignment.* ♦ *The police officer quizzed the witness about what she had seen.*

quorum ['kwor əm] *n.* the minimum number of members of an organization that must be present in order to hold a legitimate meeting. ♦ *The meeting was called to order as soon as there was a quorum.* ♦ *The eleven-member council voted to establish six as a quorum.*

quota ['kwot ə] *n.* a required amount of something; a required number of things or people. ♦ *The auto worker completed his quota of work by 3:00 P.M.* ♦ *The company vowed to maintain a certain quota of minority workers.*

quotation [kwo 'te ʃən] **1.** *n.* a statement that was said or written, used again by someone else; a statement that is quoted from someone or from someone's writing. ♦ *The critic's review of the novel included many quotations from the book itself.* ♦ *I consulted a book of famous quotations before writing my speech.* **2. quotation marks** *n.* <the marks “ ” and ‘ ’, which are *double quotation marks* and *single quotation marks*, respectively.> ♦ *That sentence is a quotation and should be in quotation marks.* ♦ *Put this word in single quotation marks like 'this.'*

quote ['kwot] **1.** *tv.* to use a quotation; to repeat part of something that someone else has said or written, at the same time telling who said or wrote it. ♦ *I like to quote Abraham Lincoln's clever remarks.* ♦ *The reporter quoted the mayor's speeches.* **2.** *tv.* to cite someone or a written source as the origin of a quotation. ♦ *John often quoted his father, who frequently said clever things.* ♦ *Don't quote the dictionary all the time! I know how to talk!* **3. quote from** *iv.* + *prep. phr.* to repeat [written or spoken language] from a named source. ♦ *Lisa often quotes from the writings of Thomas Jefferson.* ♦ *In his research, John always quotes from reliable sources.* **4.** *n.* a quotation; a statement that was said or written by someone else. ♦ *The newspaper printed a quote from the mayor.* ♦ *The speaker accidentally attributed a quote to the wrong person.* **5.** *n.* an estimate of the price of something. ♦ *Before remodeling our house, we asked several designers for quotes.* ♦ *I asked the mechanic for a quote before my car was serviced.* **6. quote a price** *idiom* to name or state the charge for doing or supplying something. ♦ *The mechanic quoted a price of $100 to repair my car.* ♦ *The carpenter quoted a price for fixing up the stairs.*

quotient ['kwo ʃənt] *n.* a number that is the result of one number being divided by another number. ♦ *The quotient of 50 divided by 10 is 5.* ♦ *8 is the quotient of 72 divided by 9.*

R

R AND **r** ['ɑr] *n.* the eighteenth letter of the alphabet. ♦ R *comes before* S *in the English alphabet.* ♦ *There is only one* r *in* sherbet.

rabbi ['ræb ɑɪ] *n.* the leader of a Jewish synagogue; a Jewish religious leader. (Also a term of address.) ♦ *Both a minister and a rabbi officiated at the mixed marriage.* ♦ *Tom spoke with Rabbi Simons at the temple about the service.*

rabbit ['ræb ət] **1.** *n.* a small animal with soft fur, long ears, and a fluffy tail. ♦ *A rabbit was nibbling lettuce in my garden.* ♦ *Sue fed carrots to her pet rabbit.* **2.** *n.* the skin and fur of ①. (No plural form in this sense.) ♦ *My gloves are lined with rabbit.* ♦ *Mary's coat is made of white rabbit.* **3.** *n.* the meat of ① used as food. (No plural form in this sense.) ♦ *The cook prepared rabbit for dinner.* ♦ *We roasted rabbit at the barbecue.* **4.** *adj.* <the adj. use of ①, ②, and ③.> ♦ *Mary wore a rabbit coat to the ski lodge.* ♦ *The hunter ate rabbit stew for dinner.*

rabble ['ræb əl] *n.* a crowd of loud people; a mob. (No plural form in this sense.) ♦ *The police tried to disperse the rabble in front of the park.* ♦ *The inflammatory newspaper article incited the rabble to riot.*

rabble-rouser ['ræb əl rɑʊz ɚ] *n.* someone who gets a crowd of people excited or aroused; an agitator. ♦ *The rabble-rouser screamed into a megaphone at the rally.* ♦ *The police arrested five rabble-rousers at the protest.*

rabid ['ræb ɪd] **1.** *adj.* having rabies; suffering from rabies. (Adv: *rabidly.*) ♦ *If you're bitten by a rabid animal, you need to see a doctor.* ♦ *The rabid dog foamed at the mouth.* **2.** *adj.* very angry; very mad. (Figurative on ①. Adv: *rabidly.*) ♦ *The school principal, rabid with anger, punished the insolent students.* ♦ *My parents were absolutely rabid when I got home two hours late last night.*

rabies ['re biz] *n.* hydrophobia. (A deadly disease that destroys the brain and causes convulsions and foaming at the mouth. Treated as singular.) ♦ *Our dog contracted rabies from an infected squirrel.* ♦ *I had to endure many painful shots because I'd been exposed to rabies.*

raccoon [ræ 'kun] **1.** *n.* an animal with a long bushy tail and black fur around the eyes, which makes it look like it is wearing a mask. ♦ *A raccoon pawed through the garbage can in the alley.* ♦ *The raccoon was chased up a tree by the barking dog.* **2.** *n.* the skin and fur of ①. (No plural form in this sense.) ♦ *My gloves are lined with raccoon.* ♦ *Anne bought a coat made of raccoon.* **3.** *adj.* made from ②. ♦ *Jimmy wore a raccoon hat outside.* ♦ *Mary's raccoon gloves kept her hands warm.*

race ['res] **1.** *n.* a contest that has to do with speed; a contest that has to do with how fast people, animals, or machines can move. ♦ *After running one mile in a race, the runner was tired.* ♦ *Many spectators gambled on the outcome of the horse race.* **2.** *n.* a political election, and the time of campaigning leading up to the election. ♦ *The reporter commented about the presidential race.* ♦ *Do you know who you're voting for in the mayoral race?* **3.** *n.* the physical differences between humans that have to do with dividing people into different groups, especially groups based on the color of skin. (No plural form in this sense.) ♦ *The city was torn apart by riots based on race.* ♦ *The company did not take race into account in hiring.* **4.** *n.* a division of humans based on certain characteristics, often the color of the skin. ♦ *Large nations are populated by citizens of many races.* ♦ *The leader wished people of all races could live together peacefully.* **5. human race** *n.* all humans as a group of people. (No plural form in this sense.) ♦ *The human race is spread across the planet Earth.* ♦ *As a member of the human race, the minister prayed for peace.* **6.** *n.* a certain kind of people, plant, animal, or other creature. ♦ *The farmers claimed a race of space aliens stole their cows.* ♦ *The biologist tried to create a race of plant life in the lab.* **7.** *iv.* to run rapidly, as if in a race; to move or operate very fast. ♦ *The runners raced toward the finish line.* ♦ *My thoughts were racing through my head as I tried to think of the answer.* **8.** *tv.* to cause someone or something to take part in ①. ♦ *The pilots raced their boats across the lake.* ♦ *The coach raced his best runners in the marathon.* **9.** *tv.* to cause an engine to run very rapidly. ♦ *The driver raced the car's engine at the intersection.* ♦ *Bob raced his motor every time he stopped the car.* **10.** *tv.* to compete against someone to reach a specific goal. ♦ *John raced Bill to the store.* ♦ *Mary raced Anne toward the finish line.* **11. rat race** *idiom* a fierce struggle for success, especially in one's career or business. ♦ *Bob is tired of the rat race. He's retired and lives in the country.* ♦ *Big business is a rat race, and many people who work in it die of the stress.*

racecar ['res kɑr] *n.* a car that participates in a race; a car that is built to move at very fast speeds. ♦ *The crew changed the racecar's tires in seconds.* ♦ *The racecar sped around the track very quickly.*

racehorse ['res hors] *n.* a horse that is bred for participating in races. ♦ *I bet $20 that my favorite racehorse would win.* ♦ *The racehorses were walked to the starting gate.*

racetrack ['res træk] *n.* the place, usually a large oval, where a race takes place, and the stadium or arena that contains it. ♦ *The racetrack was filled with spectators.* ♦ *The cars sped around the racetrack.*

racial ['reʃ əl] *adj.* of or about race ③. (Adv: *racially.*) ♦ *John was reprimanded for uttering racial slurs.* ♦ *Skin color, hair type, and eye shape are noticeable racial traits.*

racing ['res ɪŋ] *n.* the sport or business related to contests that involve speed. (No plural form in this sense.) ♦ *Insurance is expensive for people involved in automobile racing.* ♦ *My whole family enjoys racing with cars, horses, or dogs.*

racism ['res ɪz əm] *n.* prejudice, intolerance, hatred, or violence shown against someone of a particular race.

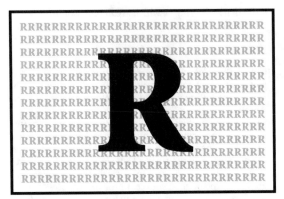

(No plural form in this sense.) ♦ *The journalist was disgusted by the candidate's racism.* ♦ *The protester accused the government of racism.*

racist ['res əst] **1.** *n.* someone who believes one race is better than another. ♦ *The racists threw stones at the immigrants in their neighborhood.* ♦ *The reporter exposed the candidate as a racist.* **2.** *adj.* exhibiting racism; showing prejudice, intolerance, or hatred against someone's race. ♦ *Some children's racist attitudes are instilled by their parents.* ♦ *The mayor was harshly criticized for using racist speech.*

rack ['ræk] **1.** *n.* a frame with shelves, rods, hooks, or pegs that is used to hang things from or put things on. ♦ *I have a rack in my closet for my shoes.* ♦ *Racks of clothing at the store were emptied during the sale.* **2.** *n.* the antlers of a deer, moose, elk, or similar animal. ♦ *The deer rubbed its rack against the tree trunk.* ♦ *The hunter hung the elk's rack on a wall in his den.* **3. be racked with pain** *idiom* suffering from severe pain. ♦ *My body was racked with pain, and I nearly passed out.* ♦ *My head was racked with pain.* **4. rack one's brain(s)** *idiom* to try very hard to think of something. ♦ *I racked my brains all afternoon but couldn't remember where I put the book.* ♦ *Don't waste any more time racking your brain. Go borrow the book from the library.*

racket ['ræk ɪt] **1.** AND **racquet** *n.* a device used to hit a ball or something similar back and forth, usually over a net. ♦ *The player was fined for throwing his racket to the ground in anger.* ♦ *Anne hit the tennis ball with her tennis racquet.* **2.** *n.* loud noise. (No plural form in this sense. Slang.) ♦ *What's all that racket in there? Keep it quiet!* ♦ *The pot made a loud racket when it fell to the floor.* **3.** *n.* a dishonest or illegal activity, such as fraud or extortion, done to make money. ♦ *David was arrested for his involvement in an illegal racket.* ♦ *The deli was a front for an illegal drug racket.*

racketeer [ræk ə 'tɪr] *n.* someone who makes money from a racket. ♦ *The police questioned the racketeer about the drug ring.* ♦ *The racketeers made a great deal of money from gambling.*

racquet ['ræk ət] See racket.

radar ['re dɑr] *n.* a device that uses radio waves to detect an object, usually a car or an aircraft, and to determine that object's location, distance, altitude, and speed. (An acronym for *radio detecting and ranging.* No plural form in this sense.) ♦ *With radar, the police can determine how fast someone is driving.* ♦ *The pilot's radar indicated there was another plane nearby.*

radial ['re di əl] **1.** *adj.* including radii in construction or design. (Adv: *radially.*) ♦ *Maple Avenue is a radial street going northwest out of the city.* ♦ *Anne bought four new radial tires for her car.* **2. radials** *n.* tires whose rubber layers have cords that radiate from the hub of the wheel instead of crossing each other. (Treated as plural.) ♦ *My car has steel-belted radials.* ♦ *The treads on my radials were wearing thin, so I replaced them.*

radiance ['re di əns] **1.** *n.* the radiation of brightness; a shine. (No plural form in this sense.) ♦ *The morning was brightened by the radiance of the sun.* ♦ *The radiance of the candle lit the room.* **2.** *n.* an aura of beauty, freshness, and glory. (Figurative on ①. No plural form in this sense.) ♦ *The photograph captured the bride's radiance at the wedding.* ♦ *Mary beamed with radiance as she held her newborn infant.*

radiant ['re di ənt] **1.** *adj.* bright; shining; giving off light. (Adv: *radiantly.*) ♦ *The earth is illuminated by the radiant sun.* ♦ *Dozens of radiant candle flames lit the room.* **2.** *adj.* looking very happy; glowing. (Figurative on ①. Adv: *radiantly.*) ♦ *The students were radiant after the graduation ceremony.* ♦ *Her radiant smile showed how happy she was.*

radiate ['re di et] **1.** *tv.* to cause something to spread out in all directions from a center point; to give off rays of something such as heat or light. ♦ *The lighted candle radiated heat and light.* ♦ *The hot stove radiated lots of heat.* **2. radiate from** *iv.* + *prep. phr.* [for rays] to come from something. ♦ *Sunlight radiated from the sun.* ♦ *Light radiated from the candle.* **3. radiate from** *iv.* + *prep. phr.* to extend outward from a central point. ♦ *Spokes radiated from the hub of the wheel.* ♦ *Thin wires radiated from the base of the antenna.*

radiation [re di 'e ʃən] **1.** *n.* the release of heat, light, or electromagnetic energy. (No plural form in this sense.) ♦ *The radiation of heat from the stove warmed the kitchen.* ♦ *Radiation of light from the sun reflects off the moon.* **2.** *n.* radioactive particles and energy used in medical treatment. (No plural form in this sense.) ♦ *The doctor used radiation to destroy the cancer cells.* ♦ *Many people were killed by the radiation from the bomb blast.*

radiator ['re di et ɚ] **1.** *n.* a device that sends out radiation, usually in the form of heat. ♦ *My apartment is heated by radiators.* ♦ *The cat slept on a mat in front of the warm radiator.* **2.** *n.* the part of an automobile that transfers engine heat to the surrounding air. ♦ *Hot steam escaped from the broken radiator.* ♦ *I burned my arm on the radiator when I tried to fix it.*

radical ['ræd ɪ kəl] **1.** *adj.* complete and thorough; extreme; drastic. (Adv: *radically* [...ɪk li].) ♦ *Our firm underwent radical changes to prevent bankruptcy.* ♦ *My editor said my article needed radical revisions.* **2.** *adj.* [of someone] favoring extreme change. (Adv: *radically* [...ɪk li].) ♦ *The radical activist protested in front of city hall.* ♦ *The radical professor's ideas were ignored.* **3.** *n.* someone who favors complete change; someone who favors extreme change. ♦ *The police stopped the radicals from overthrowing the government.* ♦ *The radicals demanded the release of the political prisoners.*

radicalism ['ræd ɪ kl ɪz əm] *n.* the belief in extreme, thorough, or drastic change. (No plural form in this sense.) ♦ *The politician's radicalism frightened the moderates.* ♦ *Urban unrest was fueled by the activist's radicalism.*

radii ['redi ɑɪ] a pl of radius.

radio ['re di o] **1.** *n.* the sending and receiving of sound through the air by using electromagnetic waves. (No plural form in this sense.) ♦ *The sound engineer was knowledgeable in the principles of radio.* ♦ *News of the war was broadcast solely by radio.* **2.** *n.* a device that is used to receive and decode electromagnetic waves into sound. (Pl in *-s.*) ♦ *I turned on the radio to listen to the news.* ♦ *I play the radio in my car when I'm stuck in traffic.* **3.** *n.* the business of broadcasting news, music, talk, and the sounds of an event by using electromagnetic waves. (No plural form in this sense.) ♦ *Some popular television soap operas were first broadcast on radio.* ♦ *The wealthy family's* *money was made in radio decades ago.* **4.** *adj.* <the adj. use of ①, ②, or ③.> ♦ *The mountains blocked radio waves coming from outside the valley.* ♦ *The radio announcer interrupted the music for a special bulletin.* **5.** *tv.* to send a message by ①. ♦ *The stranded campers radioed their plea for help.* ♦ *The police officer radioed a call for help to headquarters from the police car.* **6.** *tv.* to send [a message] to someone using radio receiver in a particular place. ♦ *Bob radioed headquarters that his car had run out of gas.* ♦ *Please radio the airport and ask if we can land.* **7.** *iv.* to use ② to send a message. ♦ *The stranded campers radioed for help.* ♦ *The policeman radioed in to headquarters.*

radioactive [red i o 'æk tɪv] *adj.* of or about an element or its compounds that spontaneously produce energy caused by changes in the nuclear structure of the atoms of the element. (Adv: *radioactively.*) ♦ *Uranium is a radioactive element.* ♦ *Exposure to radioactive materials can be fatal.*

radiology [red i 'ɑl ə dʒi] **1.** *n.* the science and study of X-rays or radioactive materials to treat and diagnose illness. (No plural form in this sense.) ♦ *The intern specialized in radiology.* ♦ *The doctor who took my X-rays is knowledgeable of radiology.* **2.** *n.* the department in a hospital or clinic where ① is used for diagnosis and treatment. (No plural form in this sense.) ♦ *Mary went to radiology to have her X-rays taken.* ♦ *The doctor sent the patient's files to radiology.*

radish ['ræd ɪʃ] *n.* a small, sharp-tasting, round root with a red or white skin and a white inside. ♦ *There were sliced carrots and radishes in my salad.* ♦ *The chef cut the radishes into decorative shapes.*

radium ['red i əm] *n.* a radioactive metallic element. (No plural form in this sense.) ♦ *As the atoms of radium break apart, it slowly turns into lead.* ♦ *The symbol for radium is Ra, its atomic weight is 226, and its number is 88.*

radius ['red i əs] **1.** *n., irreg.* the distance from the center of a circle to any point on the circle. (Pl: radii or radiuses.) ♦ *The radius of each wagon wheel is 3 feet.* ♦ *A circle's diameter is twice the length of its radius.* **2.** *n., irreg.* a line that goes from the center of a circle to any point on the circle. ♦ *A wheel's spokes are radii.* ♦ *The large hand on a clock is similar to a radius.*

radon ['re dɑn] *n.* a radioactive, gaseous chemical element. (No plural form in this sense.) ♦ *The atomic symbol of radon is Rn, and its atomic number is 86.* ♦ *Radon can seep from the earth and into people's homes.*

raffle ['ræf əl] **1.** *n.* a way of raising money where people buy tickets to win items or prizes that have been donated. (The winning ticket is chosen at random.) ♦ *The top prize for the raffle was a trip for two to Florida.* ♦ *The shopkeeper donated some goods for the school's raffle.* **2. raffle off** *tv. + adv.* to make an item available in ①. ♦ *The charity raffled off the signatures of famous people.* ♦ *Our school raffled off ten tickets to all the football games.*

raft ['ræft] **1.** *n.* boards or logs that are tied together and which float on water; a rubber boat that is filled with air that floats on water. ♦ *The wooden raft floated down the river.* ♦ *The passengers of the sinking ship climbed into rubber rafts.* **2.** *iv.* to travel across water on ①. ♦ *John rafted across the river.* ♦ *Mary rafted down the river for a couple of miles.*

rafter ['ræf tɚ] *n.* one of a series of parallel boards or beams that support a roof. ♦ *The workers nailed thick plywood to the rafters.* ♦ *The child's balloon soared up to the rafters.*

rag ['ræg] **1.** *n.* a piece of cloth, especially one that has no value or is used for cleaning. ♦ *The waiter wiped the table with a rag.* ♦ *The rags that I found in the trash were old torn shirts.* **2. from rags to riches** *idiom* from poverty to wealth; from modesty to elegance. ♦ *The princess used to be quite poor. She certainly moved from rags to riches.* ♦ *After I inherited the money, I went from rags to riches.* **3. in rags** *idiom* in worn-out and torn clothing. ♦ *Oh, look at my clothing. I can't go to the party in rags!* ♦ *I think the new casual fashions make you look as if you're in rags.*

rage ['redʒ] **1.** *n.* extreme, violent anger. ♦ *In his rage, Bill hit the wall with his fist.* ♦ *Susan's insults threw Jane into a wild rage.* **2.** *iv.* to show extreme, violent anger toward something. ♦ *The angry citizen raged against the new tax increase.* ♦ *The coach raged when the football team lost.*

ragged ['ræg əd] **1.** *adj.* torn; frayed; tattered. (Adv: *raggedly.*) ♦ *Susan convinced her son to throw away his ragged jacket.* ♦ *I wear comfortable, ragged clothes around the house.* **2. run someone ragged** *idiom* to keep someone or something very busy. ♦ *This busy season is running us all ragged at the store.* ♦ *What a busy day. I ran myself ragged.*

raging ['redʒ ɪŋ] *adj.* extremely violent; full of violent energy; furious. ♦ *Bill's raging temper frightens his friends.* ♦ *The raging fire destroyed many homes.*

ragweed ['ræg wid] *n.* a kind of weed that has pollen that causes hay fever. (No plural form in this sense.) ♦ *Ragweed grows wild in the field next to my house.* ♦ *My eyes were itchy and watery from ragweed.*

raid ['red] **1.** *n.* a surprise attack, especially by police or soldiers. ♦ *The police raid resulted in the arrests of five people.* ♦ *During the air raid, most of the village was destroyed.* **2.** *tv.* to enter someone's property or space and attack quickly, suddenly, and by surprise. ♦ *The police raided the drug dealer's apartment.* ♦ *The soldiers raided the enemy camp at dawn.*

rail ['rel] **1.** *n.* a thick strip of wood or metal, usually used to support or guide someone or something. ♦ *John gripped the rail for support as he walked down the stairs.* ♦ *There was a rail at the side of the road at the cliff's edge.* **2.** *n.* a metal rail ① on which a train travels. ♦ *I moved away from the rails when I heard a train approaching.* ♦ *At the horizon, parallel rails appear to come together.* **3. rail at someone (about something)** *idiom* to complain loudly or violently to someone about something. ♦ *Jane railed at the treasurer about not having received her check.* ♦ *I am not responsible for your problems. Don't rail at me!*

railing ['rel ɪŋ] *n.* a thick strip, rail, or tube of wood or metal that people can hold onto for support, usually found on a staircase or ramp. ♦ *David leaned on the railing for support as he walked down the stairs.* ♦ *Please hold the railing when using the stairs.*

railroad ['rel rod] **1.** *n.* two parallel metal rails on which a train travels. ♦ *I followed the railroad from the farm into the next village.* ♦ *Buses must stop before crossing railroads.* **2.** *n.* a network or system of train tracks, train stations, and trains. ♦ *I traveled from St. Louis to Chicago on a railroad.* ♦ *Most of America's system of railroads was built in* *the 19th century.* **3.** *n.* a business that operates trains. ♦ *The railroad bought acres of the farmers' lands to build new tracks.* ♦ *The conductor had worked for the same railroad for 40 years.* **4.** *tv.* to move something quickly and forcefully; to force someone to do something quickly. ♦ *The senator railroaded the bill through the legislature.* ♦ *The salesman tried to railroad me into buying a new car.* **5.** *adj.* <the adj. use of ② or ③.> ♦ *A railroad engine weighs many tons.* ♦ *We arrived at the railroad station exactly on time.*

railway ['rel we] **1.** *n.* a railroad; a railroad of a short length. ♦ *Mary rode on the local railway from Long Island to Manhattan.* ♦ *The city turned the abandoned railway into a bike path.* **2.** *adj.* <the adj. use of ①.> ♦ *The bus stopped at the railway crossing.* ♦ *The conductor announced the name of the next railway station.*

rain ['ren] **1.** *n.* water that falls down from the sky in drops. (No plural form in this sense.) ♦ *Three inches of rain fell last night.* ♦ *On the way home, I got soaked in the rain.* **2.** *n.* an instance of ①. ♦ *A cold rain fell on us as we walked.* ♦ *The rains came early this year.* **3.** *n.* the quick movement through the air of large amounts of anything. (Figurative on ①.) ♦ *The gangsters fired a rain of bullets at their enemy.* ♦ *The archers shot a rain of arrows toward the advancing army.* **4.** *iv.* [for drops of water] to fall from the sky. (The subject must be **it**.) ♦ *It is raining outside.* ♦ *It rained all through the night.* **5. rain down** *iv. + adv.* to fall from the sky like ①. (Figurative on ④.) ♦ *Bombs rained down from the warplanes.* ♦ *Bullets rained down on the gangsters.* **6.** *tv.* to cause something to fall from the sky like ①. ♦ *The storm rained hail on us as we ran for cover.* ♦ *The warplane rained bombs onto the village below.* **7. rain cats and dogs** *idiom* to rain ④ very hard. ♦ *It's raining cats and dogs. Look at it pour!* ♦ *I'm not going out in that storm. It's raining cats and dogs.* **8. rain or shine** *idiom* whether it **rains** ④ or the sun shines. ♦ *Don't worry. I'll be there rain or shine.* ♦ *We'll hold the picnic—rain or shine.*

rainbow ['ren bo] **1.** *n.* an arch of different colors of light that appears in the sky, caused by rays of sunlight passing through rain or mist. ♦ *The colors of the rainbow include red, orange, yellow, green, blue, and violet.* ♦ *After the storm, I saw a rainbow in the sky.* **2.** *adj.* consisting of the colors of the rainbow; from the group of colors of the rainbow. ♦ *The sherbet was available in rainbow colors.* ♦ *The nursery's wallpaper has a rainbow pattern of colors.*

raincoat ['ren kot] *n.* a waterproof coat that people wear when it rains to keep their clothes dry. ♦ *I wore my raincoat to work because it was raining this morning.* ♦ *The traffic guard's raincoat was bright orange.*

raindrop ['ren drɑp] *n.* one drop of rain. ♦ *I went inside when I felt the first raindrop.* ♦ *As the raindrops started to fall heavily, I became wetter.*

rainfall ['ren fɔl] **1.** *n.* the drops of rain that fall when it rains; a period of falling rain. (No plural form in this sense.) ♦ *Our crops needed last night's rainfall.* ♦ *The rainfall washed the dirt from the street.* **2.** *n.* the amount of rain that falls in a certain place over a certain length of time. (No plural form in this sense.) ♦ *Rainfall in desert areas is rare.* ♦ *We had two inches of rainfall last night.*

rain forest ['ren for əst] **1.** *n.* a forest that grows where there is a very high amount of rainfall. ♦ *Tropical rain forests always have many different kinds of trees and plants.* ♦ *The sloth is an animal that is found in American rain forests.* **2. rain-forest** *adj.* <the adj. use of ①.> ♦ *Many tropical rain-forest plants cannot be found anywhere else.* ♦ *Some rain-forest animals live high in the branches of trees.*

rainstorm ['ren storm] *n.* a storm that has a large amount of rain. ♦ *Some branches fell from the trees during the rainstorm.* ♦ *I got really wet when I was caught in the rainstorm.*

rainwater ['ren wɑt ɚ] *n.* water that falls as rain. (No plural form in this sense.) ♦ *Rainwater collected in the barrel behind the farmhouse.* ♦ *The rainwater soaked into the ground.*

rainy ['re ni] *adj.* having a lot of rain. (Adv: *rainily.* Comp: *rainier;* sup: *rainiest.*) ♦ *During the rainy season, it gets very hot and humid here.* ♦ *It was a rainy day, so I stayed indoors.*

raise ['rez] **1.** *tv.* to lift someone or something up; to move someone or something to a higher level; to move someone or something upward; to cause someone or something to rise. (Compare with **rise**.) ♦ *Mary raised her arms over her head.* ♦ *The soldier raised the flag to the top of the mast.* **2.** *tv.* to increase the amount of something; to increase the degree of something; to increase the force of something. ♦ *The heat of the oven raised the temperature in the kitchen.* ♦ *The pipe burst when the water pressure was raised.* **3.** *tv.* to cause plants to grow; to breed animals. ♦ *Mary raised rabbits, which she sold as pets and as meat.* ♦ *David raised rows of tulips alongside his house.* **4.** *tv.* to bring up a child; to rear a child. ♦ *John and Mary raised three daughters and one son.* ♦ *I was raised by my grandparents after my parents died.* **5.** *tv.* to collect or gather a certain amount of money. ♦ *The teacher raised enough money to buy a computer for the class.* ♦ *Mary raised $1,000 to help start her new business.* **6.** *tv.* to bring up a subject or issue; to mention something; to address a subject or an issue; to begin talking about something. ♦ *The student raised some issues not mentioned by the teacher.* ♦ *The reporter raised some questions that embarrassed the mayor.* **7.** *n.* an increase in one's salary; an increase in the amount of money one earns at a job. ♦ *Mary was happy to have received a raise of $2 per hour.* ♦ *John asked his boss for a raise.* **8. raise some eyebrows** *idiom* to shock or surprise people mildly (by doing or saying something). ♦ *What you just said may raise some eyebrows, but it shouldn't make anyone really angry.* ♦ *John's sudden marriage to Anne raised a few eyebrows.*

raisin ['rez ɪn] *n.* a dried grape, eaten as food. ♦ *I ate a box of raisins for lunch.* ♦ *Mary gave raisins to her children instead of candy.*

rake ['rek] **1.** *n.* a tool that has a long handle that is attached to a row of curved metal or plastic fingers, used to collect fallen leaves, loose grass, etc. ♦ *John collected the fallen leaves with a rake.* ♦ *David tripped over the rake he had left in the lawn.* **2.** *tv.* to collect something, especially leaves, hay, grass, or other objects on the ground. ♦ *Susie raked leaves for an hour when she got home from school.* ♦ *The farmer raked the hay into a large pile.* **3.** *tv.* to smooth or clean something by using ①. ♦ *The farmer raked the soil smooth.* ♦ *John raked his front yard after cut-*

ting the grass. **4.** *iv.* to use ①; to scrape with ①. ♦ *John raked after cutting the lawn.* ♦ *Mary raked until she got a blister on her hand.* **5. rake something up** *idiom* to uncover something unpleasant and remind people about it. ♦ *The young journalist raked up the old scandal about the president.* ♦ *The politician's opponents are trying to rake up some unpleasant details about his past.*

rally ['ræl i] **1.** *tv.* to bring people together for a certain reason or cause. ♦ *The candidate rallied a crowd of supporters.* ♦ *The professor rallied his students to support his cause.* **2.** *iv.* to come together for a certain reason or cause; to be brought together for a certain reason or cause. ♦ *The students rallied in support of their winning football team.* ♦ *Dozens of activists rallied against the death penalty.* **3.** *iv.* to improve or advance. ♦ *The stock market rallied throughout the afternoon.* ♦ *Finally, Bob's health rallied, and he left the hospital.* **4.** *n.* a large meeting, especially a large political meeting, held for a certain reason. ♦ *I heard a lot of speeches at the political rally.* ♦ *After winning the election, Anne addressed the large rally.* **5.** *n.* a quick increase in stock prices. ♦ *The afternoon rally was cut short when the market crashed at 3:00 P.M.* ♦ *The broker made a quick profit selling stock during the rally.* **6. rally (a)round someone or something** *idiom* to come together to support someone or something. ♦ *The family rallied around Bob when he lost his job.* ♦ *The former pupils rallied around their old school when it was in danger of being closed.*

ram ['ræm] **1.** *n.* a male sheep. ♦ *Mary sheared wool from the ram.* ♦ *The ram led the herd of sheep across the meadow.* **2.** *n.* a heavy pole, the end of which is thrust against something, possibly as part of a machine. ♦ *The soldiers used a huge ram to break down the door.* ♦ *The demolition crew used a ram to knock over the metal frame.* **3. ram into** *tv.* + *prep. phr.* to force something into something; to jam something into something. ♦ *David rammed his fist into the wall.* ♦ *Angrily, Jane rammed the book back into its place.* **4.** *tv.* to hit someone or something; to crash into someone or something. ♦ *A drunk driver rammed my car.* ♦ *David rammed the wall with his fist.* **5. ram into** *iv.* + *prep. phr.* to hit someone or something; to crash into someone or something. ♦ *The car rammed into a light post.* ♦ *David rammed into me because he wasn't watching where he was going.*

Ramadan ['rɑm ə dɑn] **1.** *n.* the ninth month of the Islamic year, commemorating the first revelation of the Koran to Muhammad. (No plural form in this sense.) ♦ *Muslims must fast every day in Ramadan.* ♦ *The old man made a pilgrimage to Mecca during Ramadan.* **2.** *n.* the daily fast from sunup to sundown, practiced by Muslims during ①. (No plural form in this sense.) ♦ *The obedient Muslim honored Ramadan for the whole month.* ♦ *Ramadan is rigidly observed in the world of Islam.*

ramble ['ræm bəl] **1.** *iv.* to talk or write about many different things with no connection between the different ideas; to talk or write in a way that is not organized. ♦ *The senile hospital patient rambled for hours about many things.* ♦ *Your writing rambles too much. Stick to your topic.* **2.** *iv.* to wander around in no particular direction; to go on a relaxing walk. ♦ *The hikers rambled through the forest.* ♦ *The students rambled around the lake.* **3.** *iv.* [for a pathway or road] to wander about, taking an indirect route. ♦ *The path rambled across the meadow.* ♦ *The river rambled across the plains.*

rambling ['ræm blɪŋ] **1.** *adj.* wandering; seeming to follow no particular direction or organization. (Adv: *ramblingly.*) ♦ *A rambling river twists through the canyon.* ♦ *The rambling road took us 10 miles out of our way.* **2.** *adj.* [of speech or writing] disorganized and disconnected. (Adv: *ramblingly.*) ♦ *The professor's rambling speech made no sense.* ♦ *The report's rambling structure makes it hard to understand.*

rambunctious [ræm 'bʌŋk ʃəs] *adj.* playing or behaving loudly and wildly; uncontrolled. (Adv: *rambunctiously.*) ♦ *The rambunctious children ran through the house, screaming.* ♦ *The rambunctious puppies rolled around in the dirt.*

ramp ['ræmp] **1.** *n.* a slanted path that is built or made to connect two surfaces with different heights. ♦ *Ramps make buildings accessible for people in wheelchairs.* ♦ *John wheeled the cartons of paper up the ramp behind the store.* **2.** *n.* a road that is an entrance or exit to an expressway or tollway. ♦ *The exit ramp was blocked by an accident.* ♦ *At the end of the ramp, I merged with traffic on the freeway.*

rampage ['ræm pedʒ] **1.** *n.* a period of wild, angry, or violent behavior. ♦ *I won't tolerate another of Jimmy's rampages!* ♦ *The boss's rampage frightened all the staff.* **2. rampage through** *iv.* + *prep. phr.* to move or behave in a wildly angry and violent way. ♦ *The terrorists rampaged through the airport, firing their guns.* ♦ *The worker rampaged through the manager's office when he was fired.* **3. go on a rampage** *idiom* to have ①. ♦ *The angry bull went on a rampage and broke the fence.* ♦ *My boss went on a rampage because the report wasn't finished.*

rampant ['ræm pənt] **1.** *adj.* growing, moving, or spreading out of control. (Adv: *rampantly.*) ♦ *Police were called in to help control the rampant violence in the school.* ♦ *The lawn of the abandoned house was choked with rampant weeds.* **2. run rampant** *idiom* to run, develop, or grow out of control. ♦ *The children ran rampant through the house.* ♦ *Weeds have run rampant around the abandoned house.*

ramshackle ['ræm ʃæk əl] *adj.* falling apart or likely to fall apart; not constructed very well. ♦ *The neighbors asked the city to demolish the ramshackle house.* ♦ *The heavy winds caused the ramshackle barn to collapse.*

ran ['ræn] pt of run.

ranch ['ræntʃ] *n.* a very large farm where cattle or other animals are raised. ♦ *Last summer, I worked on a cattle ranch in Wyoming.* ♦ *The cowboy rode his horse to the south part of the huge ranch.*

rancher ['ræntʃ ɚ] *n.* someone who works on a ranch; someone who owns a ranch. ♦ *The rancher's cattle grazed on government land.* ♦ *The poacher was arrested for trespassing on the rancher's property.*

rancid ['ræn sɪd] *adj.* spoiled; tasting or smelling sour or spoiled. (Adv: *rancidly.*) ♦ *Mary threw the rancid butter away.* ♦ *Rancid cheese smells very bad!*

rancor ['ræŋ kɚ] *n.* spite; ill will; a bitter feeling of hatred or anger. (No plural form in this sense.) ♦ *The old enemies had a great amount of rancor toward each other.* ♦ *Why do you show so much rancor toward your brother?*

rancorous ['ræŋ k ə rəs] *adj.* spiteful; bitter; malicious. (Adv: *rancorously.*) ♦ *The rancorous enemies refused to make peace.* ♦ *My rancorous neighbor spread terrible gossip about me.*

random ['ræn dəm] **1.** *adj.* by chance; haphazard. (Adv: *randomly.*) ♦ *The botanist studied random mutations in plants.* ♦ *The magician chose a random volunteer from the audience.* **2. at random** *phr.* by chance; haphazard. ♦ *The lottery numbers are chosen at random.* ♦ *As a prank, the children dialed phone numbers at random.*

rang ['ræŋ] a pt of ring.

range ['rendʒ] **1.** *n.* the area between two extremes; the choices, possibilities, or selections available. ♦ *The graduating students examined a range of possibilities.* ♦ *The talented singer had a range of three octaves.* **2.** *n.* the distance that something can operate or be used in, especially the distance that someone can see or hear, that a weapon can fire, or that something can travel without needing more fuel. (No plural form in this sense.) ♦ *When the enemy was within range, the soldiers fired their guns.* ♦ *My TV doesn't get Channel 10 because we're out of its range.* **3.** *n.* a field where cattle or other animals can range ⑦ to find food. (No plural form in this sense.) ♦ *The cattle were grazing in some part of the range.* ♦ *The cowboy felt at home on the range.* **4.** *n.* a stove with one or more ovens attached. ♦ *I cooked a dinner for 12 people on my new range.* ♦ *The cook cleans the range weekly.* **5. mountain range** *n.* a row or line of mountains. ♦ *The Rockies are a big mountain range in the western U.S.* ♦ *The map showed the world's major mountain ranges.* **6.** *iv.* to vary between two limits or extremes; to be located between an upper limit and a lower limit. ♦ *The ages of the students in my class range between 18 and 25.* ♦ *My musical tastes range from jazz to country.* **7.** *iv.* to wander or roam, especially in a certain area. ♦ *The buffalo ranged freely across the plains.* ♦ *Wild goats range in the hills.*

ranger ['rendʒ ɚ] *n.* someone who guards and patrols parks and forests. ♦ *The ranger prevented the small fire from spreading.* ♦ *The ranger warned us that there were bears in the area.*

rank ['ræŋk] **1.** *n.* one level in a series of levels; one level on a scale of authority, value, or importance. ♦ *Mary had worked her way up through the ranks to become the firm's president.* ♦ *The hierarchy of military titles are arranged by rank.* **2.** *n.* a row of things or people, especially soldiers. ♦ *The front ranks marched toward the enemy line.* ♦ *Three ranks of trumpeters marched in the parade.* **3.** *iv.* to occupy a certain position on a scale of authority, value, or importance; to be on a list in a certain position. ♦ *Honesty ranks high on my list of important qualities.* ♦ *The office of president ranks above the office of vice president.* **4.** *tv.* to place someone or something on a list in its proper order or place. ♦ *The news bureau ranked our football team first in the nation.* ♦ *The test ranked the students according to intelligence.* **5.** *adj.* smelling or tasting very bad or unpleasant. (Adv: *rankly.*) ♦ *I breathed a rank odor that made me feel ill.* ♦ *This milk tastes rank. How old is it?* **6.** *adj.* [of vegetation] growing thickly or coarsely. ♦ *The abandoned park was choked with rank vegetation.* ♦ *The field was covered with rank weeds.*

ransack ['ræn sæk] *tv.* to search a place completely, especially during a robbery. ♦ *My hotel apartment had been thoroughly ransacked.* ♦ *The spy ransacked Bob's office, looking for the secret file.*

ransom ['ræn səm] **1.** *n.* money demanded by kidnappers in exchange for releasing a hostage or someone who has been kidnapped. (No plural form in this sense.) ♦ *The wealthy parents paid the ransom that the kidnapper demanded.* ♦ *The kidnappers demanded a $100,000 ransom for the child's return.* **2.** *tv.* to pay money in order to release a hostage or someone who has been kidnapped. ♦ *The parents ransomed their child for $100,000.* ♦ *The firm ransomed the executive for a million dollars.* **3.** *tv.* [for a kidnapper] to offer to release someone who has been kidnapped upon payment of ①. ♦ *The terrorists ransomed the executive for $100,000.* ♦ *The police caught the criminal who had ransomed the young child.*

rant ['rænt] **rant (at someone) about someone or something** *idiom* to talk in a loud, violent way, about someone or something. ♦ *Anne ranted about the bad service she had received at the store.* ♦ *On the bus, someone was ranting at me about the end of the world.*

ranting ['ræn tɪŋ] *adj.* yelling; screaming; talking loudly and violently. (Adv: *rantingly.*) ♦ *The ranting crowd burned a large pile of books.* ♦ *The ranting man on the street corner was approached by the police.*

rap ['ræp] **1.** *n.* a quick, strong knock or hit. ♦ *My forceful rap dented the flimsy door.* ♦ *With a rap of the judge's gavel, court was in session.* **2.** *n.* a style of music where the words of the song are spoken in strong rhythm instead of sung. (No plural form in this sense.) ♦ *Do you prefer to listen to rock-and-roll, or to rap?* ♦ *John listened to rap over his headphones.* **3.** *n.* the sound made by a quick, strong knock or hit. ♦ *There was a sharp rap at my front door.* ♦ *The rap made by the judge's gavel caught everyone's attention.* **4. rap on** *iv.* + *prep. phr.* [for someone] to hit someone or something quickly and sharply, making a knocking sound. ♦ *Just rap lightly on the window to get her attention.* ♦ *I rapped on the door with my fist.* **5. rap at** *iv.* + *prep. phr.* to hit or knock on something quickly. ♦ *Someone was rapping at my door.* ♦ *The small branches rapped at my window during the storm.* **6. take the rap (for something)** *idiom* to receive the blame for something. (Informal.) ♦ *One criminal took the rap for the entire gang.* ♦ *David took the rap for his brother's crime.* **7. rap with someone** *idiom* to talk; to chat. (Informal.) ♦ *I rapped with the school counselor for half an hour.* ♦ *My neighbor rapped with me on my back porch all night.*

rape ['rep] **1.** *n.* the act and crime of forcing someone to have sex. ♦ *The sex offender was charged with rape.* ♦ *The instructor showed the women precautions to take against rape.* **2.** *n.* the abuse of something in a way that causes it to be ruined or spoiled. (Figurative on ①.) ♦ *The environmentalist decried the rape of the wilderness.* ♦ *He called the landfill a rape of the land.* **3.** *tv.* to force someone to have sex; to copulate forcibly with someone. ♦ *Mary identified the attacker who had attempted to rape her.* ♦ *The man who raped and killed five people was executed.*

rapid ['ræp ɪd] **1.** *adj.* quick; swift; moving fast; done quickly; happening quickly. (Adv: *rapidly.*) ♦ *My sister's rapid speech is hard to understand sometimes.* ♦ *The shoplifter made a rapid move toward the exit.* **2. rapids** *n.* the part of a river where the water moves very fast and is very active. (Treated as plural.) ♦ *My friends and I rafted down the rapids.* ♦ *Our rowboat was caught in the rapids, heading toward a waterfall.*

rapidity [rə 'pɪd ə ti] *n.* swiftness; quickness; speed. (No plural form in this sense.) ♦ *The rapidity of John's speech makes him difficult to understand.* ♦ *The rapidity with which the fire spread surprised me.*

rapist ['rep əst] *n.* someone who commits rape ①. ♦ *The judge sentenced the rapist to a long prison term.* ♦ *The strong woman confronted her rapist in the courtroom.*

rapport [rə 'por] *n.* a sympathetic understanding or relationship. (From French. No plural form in this sense.) ♦ *The popular professor had a good rapport with his students.* ♦ *The candidate had an amazing rapport with all kinds of people.*

rapt ['ræpt] *adj.* concentrated; alert. (Adv: *raptly.*) ♦ *The intense professor demanded the students' rapt attention.* ♦ *The woman's rapt gaze was directed at the movie screen.*

raptor ['ræp tɚ] *n.* any bird of prey such as the eagle, buzzard, hawk, or owl. ♦ *The raptor swooped down and picked up a mouse in its claws.* ♦ *The rabbit fled from the hungry raptor.*

rapture ['ræp tʃɚ] *n.* a feeling or expression of complete joy or delight. (No plural form in this sense.) ♦ *We felt great rapture when our son returned from the war safely.* ♦ *Anne's wedding day was filled with joyous rapture.*

rare ['rɛr] **1.** *adj.* not common; not often found, seen, or done. (Adv: *rarely.* Comp: *rarer;* sup: *rarest.*) ♦ *The rare species of bird was protected by law.* ♦ *John collects rare books.* **2.** *adj.* [of meat] cooked only a little. (Comp: *rarer;* sup: *rarest.*) ♦ *I ordered a rare steak.* ♦ *The inside of the rare hamburger was pink.* **3.** *adv.* cooked only a little. ♦ *The chef prepared the meat rare.* ♦ *I ordered my steak rare.*

rarin' to go See rear ⑧.

rascal ['ræs kəl] **1.** *n.* someone who is bad or not honest; a villain. ♦ *The sheriff dragged the rascal out of the bar.* ♦ *The rascal robbed the passengers in the covered wagon.* **2.** *n.* a playful or mischievous child. (Figurative on ①.) ♦ *That little rascal hid my slippers again!* ♦ *Which rascal left the bike in the driveway?*

rash ['ræʃ] **1.** *n.* an inflammation of the skin, making it red, itchy, and bumpy. ♦ *Some kinds of cloth give Jane a nasty rash.* ♦ *David put some salve on the rash on his chest.* **2.** *n.* an outbreak; many instances of something bad happening. (Figurative on ①.) ♦ *The police couldn't explain the recent rash of robberies.* ♦ *There was a rash of UFO sightings out west last year.* **3.** *adj.* hasty; not thinking about something carefully. (Adv: *rashly.* Comp: *rasher;* sup: *rashest.*) ♦ *John soon regretted his rash decision.* ♦ *It would be rash of you to quit your job today.*

rasp ['ræsp] **1.** *n.* a tool that is a strip of metal with a lot of raised bumps that is rubbed over an object to make it smooth. ♦ *The carpenter smoothed the piece of wood with a rasp.* ♦ *I smoothed the edge of the board with a rasp.* **2.** *tv.* to say something with a raspy voice. ♦ *The dying woman rasped her final words.* ♦ *The smoker rasped a request for a match.* **3.** *tv.* to smooth an object by using ①. ♦ *Jane rasped the wooden rail to make it smooth.* ♦ *The carpenter rasped the edge of the wood to remove the splinters.*

raspberry ['ræz bɛr i] **1.** *n.* a small, sweet, usually red or purple fruit that grows on a bush, and the bush itself. ♦ *Mary picked some raspberries from the bush in her garden.* ♦ *John put some raspberries on his cereal.* **2.** *n.* a noise made by sticking one's tongue out of one's mouth between the lips and blowing out. ♦ *When the team made an error, they heard a lot of raspberries.* ♦ *The student was punished for making raspberries in class.* **3.** *adj.* made or flavored with ①. ♦ *The raspberry flavor in this juice seems too strong.* ♦ *I made a raspberry tart for dessert.*

raspy ['ræs pi] *adj.* [of a voice] rough or hoarse. (Adv: *raspily.* Comp: *raspier;* sup: *raspiest.*) ♦ *The smoker spoke with a raspy voice.* ♦ *Anne's voice is very raspy because she's got a bad cold.*

rat ['ræt] **1.** *n.* a small rodent with a long tail. ♦ *Rats often feed on garbage and spread disease.* ♦ *I told my landlord that I'd seen rats in the kitchen.* **2.** *n.* someone who is mean, worthless, not honest, or not loyal. (Figurative on ①.) ♦ *John, that rat, informed the police about our plans.* ♦ *The mobsters had no tolerance for rats.* **3.** *iv.* to go to the police or authorities and tell them that someone is doing something wrong. ♦ *When the mobster ratted, he was granted immunity.* ♦ *Jimmy was unpopular, because he always ratted to the teacher.*

rate ['ret] **1.** *n.* an amount that is measured in relation to another amount, such as speed in relation to time. ♦ *The drivers all increased their rate of speed.* ♦ *At the rate we're going, we won't be finished until next week.* **2.** *n.* a price [for each unit of something]. ♦ *I asked the hotel clerk about their nightly rates.* ♦ *My health club's rates are cheaper than the rates at the one John goes to.* **3.** *tv.* to assign a value or rank to someone or something. ♦ *How would you rate this restaurant?* ♦ *The critic rated the movie highly.* **4.** *tv.* to deserve something; to be worthy of something. ♦ *The restaurant rated four stars.* ♦ *I think my letter rates a response, don't you?* **5. at any rate** *phr.* in any case; anyway. (Used before returning to a previous item of discussion.) ♦ *At any rate, what were we talking about?* ♦ *At any rate, I don't think you should quit your job.* **6. second-rate** *idiom* not of the best quality; inferior. ♦ *Bill's a second-rate tennis player compared with Bob.* ♦ *The government is building second-rate housing.*

rather ['ræð ɚ] **1. would rather** *phr.* would more willingly; would more readily. (Often *-'d rather.*) ♦ *I would rather have an apple than a pear. I don't like pears.* ♦ *I'd rather live in the north than the south, because I like snow.* **2.** *adv.* more exactly; more accurately; more truthfully. ♦ *This button is not red; rather, it is orange.* ♦ *No, I'm not sick; rather, I'm just tired.* **3.** *adv.* to an extent; to a degree; too; very; quite. ♦ *This shirt is rather red, don't you think?* ♦ *The music is rather loud, wouldn't you say?*

ratification [ræt ə fɪ 'ke ʃən] *n.* ratifying something; the legal act of indicating approval and acceptance of something, such as a law. ♦ *The ratification of the 21st Amendment took place in 1933.* ♦ *The ratification of the new law banned the sale of alcohol to minors.*

ratify ['ræt ə faɪ] *tv.* to approve something officially; to make something be valid officially. ♦ *The proposed rule has to be ratified by the members of the club.* ♦ *The city council ratified the mayor's proposed budget.*

rating ['ret ɪŋ] *n.* a level of popularity; the percentage of people that approve or disapprove of something; the records of a measurement of popularity or approval. (Often plural.) ♦ *The president was pleased to have approval ratings of 65%.* ♦ *Advertising costs are determined by a television show's ratings.*

ratio ['re ʃi o] *n.* the relationship between one amount as compared to another amount; a proportion. (Pl in *-s.*) ♦ *The ratio of boys to girls in the class was 2 to 1.* ♦ *The ratio of land to water on earth is roughly 1 to 3.*

ration ['ræ ʃən] **1.** *n.* an amount of something; an amount of something as prescribed by policy, rule, or law. ♦ *The citizens received food rations one week at a time.* ♦ *During the war, my family used our sugar ration slowly.* **2.** *tv.* to make a substance available to people only in certain small amounts. ♦ *During the war, the government rationed many kinds of food.* ♦ *During the oil crisis, gas was rationed.*

rational ['ræʃ ə nəl] **1.** *adj.* using the mind or the brain; sensible; reasonable; logical. (Adv: *rationally.*) ♦ *When I ask you a question, I expect a rational response.* ♦ *It isn't rational to walk barefoot in the snow.* **2.** *adj.* able to use sense or reason; aware. (Adv: *rationally.*) ♦ *I hardly seem rational when I wake up in the morning.* ♦ *After the accident, John was no longer rational.*

rationale [ræʃ ə 'næl] *n.* a reason; the reason for doing something; reasoning. (No plural form in this sense.) ♦ *The murderer's rationale was unclear to the detective.* ♦ *My professor disagreed with the rationale of my argument.*

rationalize ['ræʃ ə nə lɑɪz] **1.** *tv.* to explain one's reasons for doing something; to explain something. ♦ *The author rationalized her explanation of the theory.* ♦ *The criminal rationalized his theft as a means of survival.* **2.** *tv.* to improve a system so that it works in a logical or rational way. ♦ *The politician tried to rationalize the entire educational system.* ♦ *The scientist rationalized the theory so that it made sense.* **3.** *iv.* to justify why one did something; to make excuses. ♦ *John rationalized in his head why he had done what he did.* ♦ *You can rationalize all you want to, but you're still to blame.*

rattle ['ræt əl] **1.** *n.* a noise-making device, usually a toy for babies, consisting of a small container with bits of hard matter inside. ♦ *The baby dropped her rattle, and I picked it up.* ♦ *Sitting in his playpen, the toddler shook his rattle.* **2.** *n.* the noise made when a number of small things tap against something, such as with ①. ♦ *When Anne dropped a dozen marbles in the waste can, there was quite a rattle.* ♦ *During the earthquake, I heard the rattle of dishes.* **3.** *iv.* to make a quick set of short noises. ♦ *My car engine rattles when I'm waiting at intersections.* ♦ *The snake rattled as it approached its prey.* **4.** *tv.* to cause something to make a quick set of short noises. ♦ *The wind rattles the door if you don't shut it tightly.* ♦ *The musician rattled the tambourine.* **5.** *tv.* to make someone nervous, anxious, afraid, or upset; to affect someone's nerves. ♦ *The car accident rattled the driver's nerves.* ♦ *The large audience rattled Bob as he began to speak.*

rattlesnake ['ræt əl snek] *n.* a poisonous snake with hard rings of skin on its tail that make a rattling sound when it shakes its tail. ♦ *I jumped up from the ground when I heard a rattlesnake approach.* ♦ *The rattlesnake swallowed the rat.*

ratty ['ræt i] *adj.* shabby; unkempt; needing repair. (Adv: *rattily.* Comp: *rattier;* sup: *rattiest.*) ♦ *Robert finally threw out his ratty old tennis shoes.* ♦ *I wish my neighbors would paint their ratty house.*

raucous ['rɔk əs] *adj.* loud and hoarse. (Adv: *raucously.*) ♦ *The audience roared with raucous laughter when the performer fell.* ♦ *Someone with a raucous voice called me as I crossed the street.*

raunchy ['rɔn tʃi] *adj.* vulgar; obscene; smutty; risqué. (Adv: *raunchily.* Comp: *raunchier;* sup: *raunchiest.*) ♦ *Jimmy was punished for telling a raunchy joke in class.* ♦ *My parents turned off the TV because the show was raunchy.*

ravage ['ræv ɪdʒ] *tv.* to damage something badly; to destroy something; to ruin something. ♦ *The hurricane ravaged the Atlantic coast.* ♦ *The fire ravaged the office building.*

rave ['rev] **1. rave about** *iv.* + *prep. phr.* to praise or curse someone or something in a very excited or wild way; to praise someone or something. ♦ *I know you will rave about my new car when you see it.* ♦ *The critic raved about the movie in his review.* **2. rant and rave** *idiom* to shout angrily and wildly. ♦ *Bob rants and raves when anything displeases him.* ♦ *Father rants and raves if we arrive home late.*

raven ['rev ən] *n.* a large, black bird that makes a hoarse cry instead of singing. ♦ *A raven flew into my study through an open window.* ♦ *The cry of the ravens frightened the lost campers.*

ravenous ['ræv ə nəs] *adj.* very hungry. (Adv: *ravenously.*) ♦ *I'm ravenous. What's for dinner?* ♦ *The ravenous student ate a whole pizza.*

ravine [rə 'vin] *n.* a deep, narrow valley that is carved out by the movement of water in a river running through it. ♦ *The car rolled off the cliff and into a ravine.* ♦ *We rafted down the river running through the mountain ravine.*

raving ['rev ɪŋ] **1.** *adj.* talking wildly or in a very excited way. ♦ *Calm down. You sound like a raving maniac.* ♦ *The clerk told the raving customer to speak with the manager.* **2.** *n.* loud, excited, and wild talk. ♦ *What you are saying sounds like the ravings of a lunatic.* ♦ *I have heard enough of his raving. Let's leave.*

ravioli [ræv i 'o li] *n.* an amount of square pieces of pasta that are filled with cheese or meat, boiled, and eaten, usually with some kind of sauce. (From Italian. Treated as singular or plural.) ♦ *I ate cheese ravioli for dinner.* ♦ *John boiled some sausage ravioli for his guests.*

ravish ['ræv ɪʃ] **1.** *tv.* to rape someone. ♦ *The child molester ravished two young children.* ♦ *The explorers ravished the local population.* **2. ravished with delight** *idiom* to make someone very happy or delighted; to fill someone with happiness or delight. ♦ *Mary was ravished with delight by the dozen roses.* ♦ *My parents were ravished with delight when I graduated from college.*

ravishing ['ræv ɪʃ ɪŋ] *adj.* very delightful; very beautiful or attractive; causing great delight or happiness. (Adv: *ravishingly.*) ♦ *The ravishing princess married the handsome prince.* ♦ *Because of his ravishing good looks, David was very popular.*

raw ['rɔ] **1.** *adj.* not cooked; uncooked. (Comp: *rawer;* sup: *rawest.*) ♦ *My dog eats meat raw, but I only eat it cooked.* ♦ *The weightlifter added a raw egg to his milk.* **2.** *adj.* as found in nature; not treated or processed; in a natural condition. (Adv: *rawly.* Comp: *rawer;* sup: *rawest.*) ♦ *Coal is a raw material.* ♦ *Raw iron ore was dug from the mine.* **3.** *adj.* [of something that has been] rubbed until sore; having a layer of skin rubbed off. (Adv: *rawly.* Comp: *rawer;* sup: *rawest.*) ♦ *I soothed the baby's raw skin with powder.* ♦ *Your raw sunburn looks very painful.* **4.** *adj.* coarse and risqué. (Adv: *rawly.* Comp: *rawer;* sup: *rawest.*) ♦ *The raw joke offended me.* ♦ *The language in this movie is pretty raw.*

rawhide ['rɔ hɑɪd] **1.** *n.* the skin of cattle that has not been tanned; leather that has not been tanned. (No plural form in this sense.) ♦ *The rawhide was shipped to the tannery.* ♦ *The bandit's hands and feet were bound with rawhide.* **2.** *n.* a whip or rope made from strips of leather that have not been tanned. (No plural form in this sense.) ♦ *The cowboy cracked the rawhide against the cattle.* ♦ *The driver coiled up his rawhide and got up on the wagon.*

ray ['re] *n.* a beam of something that comes from a source, especially a line of light, heat, or radiation. ♦ *Rays of light streamed between the window blinds.* ♦ *The surgeon used a ray from a laser to destroy the tumor.*

rayon ['re ɑn] **1.** *n.* an artificial fiber made from cellulose. (No plural form in this sense.) ♦ *Rayon is easier to weave than some natural fibers.* ♦ *The scientist examined a strand of rayon under a microscope.* **2.** *n.* a fabric made from ①. ♦ *My league's bowling shirts are made from rayon.* ♦ *Can I put rayon in the dryer?* **3.** *adj.* made of ②. ♦ *Rayon clothing is difficult to tear.* ♦ *John's rayon shirt needs to be cleaned.*

raze ['rez] *tv.* to tear down a building completely; to demolish a building. ♦ *The city razed the abandoned building.* ♦ *The demolition crew razed the old factory.*

razor ['rez ɚ] **1.** *n.* a tool that holds a sharp blade that is used to shave whiskers or hair. ♦ *John bought new blades for his razor.* ♦ *Mary uses her razor in the shower.* **2.** *adj.* <the adj. use of ①.> ♦ *John covered his razor cut with medication.* ♦ *If your razor blade is dull, it won't shave you very well.*

razzle-dazzle ['ræz əl 'dæz əl] *n.* glitter; dazzle; a showy event. (No plural form in this sense.) ♦ *The razzle-dazzle of the circus amused the young children.* ♦ *The award ceremony was filled with razzle-dazzle.*

reach ['ritʃ] **1.** *tv.* to arrive at some place; to get to some place. ♦ *I left work at 5:00 and reached home at 5:45.* ♦ *The storm is supposed to reach Atlanta by noon.* **2.** *tv.* to get hold of someone by some means of communication; to contact someone. ♦ *I've been unable to reach Anne by telephone.* ♦ *I hope my letter reaches you before you move again.* **3.** *tv.* to stretch out to a certain place in space or time; to extend to a certain place in space or time. ♦ *Our property reaches the creek behind our house.* ♦ *The city limits reach the river to the west.* **4.** *tv.* to affect or influence someone; to make someone else understand something. ♦ *The refugee reached many people with her touching story.* ♦ *The counselor was unable to reach the troubled child.* **5.** *tv.* to total a certain amount. ♦ *The bill reached $400 by the time we were finished with dinner.* ♦ *The snowfall reached 24 inches before the night was over.* **6.** *iv.* to extend all the way. ♦ *I need a longer extension cord. This one doesn't reach.* ♦ *The storm reached from New York City to Boston.* **7. reach for** *iv.* + *prep. phr.* to move or stretch to touch or get something. ♦ *The child reached for the hot pan.* ♦ *I reached for the book on the top shelf.* **8. reach out** *iv.* + *adv.* to attempt to make contact with someone; to seek someone who can provide help. ♦ *The lonely student reached out to the guidance counselor.* ♦ *I reached out for help, but no one was there.* **9.** *n.* the distance that someone or something is able to stretch or extend; the range or capacity of someone or something. ♦ *John clung to the side of the cliff, a short reach from the rescuer.* ♦ *The tall man had a very long reach.*

react [ri 'ækt] **1.** *iv.* to show response [to something]; to make a response [to someone or something]. ♦ *I reacted to the gunfire by dropping to the ground.* ♦ *David reacted to my comments by leaving the room.* **2.** *iv.* [for a chemical] to do something when it touches another substance; [for two chemicals] to do something when they are brought together. ♦ *Salt dissolves when it reacts with water.* ♦ *Litmus changes color when it reacts to acids or alkalis.*

reaction [ri 'æk ʃən] **1.** *n.* a response to someone or something; an action that is done in response to someone or something; a feeling that is felt in response to someone or something. ♦ *John's reaction to Bob's insult was to leave the room.* ♦ *The experimenter monitored my reaction to the medicine.* **2.** *n.* the result of a chemical touching another substance; the result when two chemicals are brought together. ♦ *The explosion was caused by a chemical reaction.* ♦ *The chemist documented the changes caused by the reaction.*

reactionary [ri 'æk ʃə nɛr i] **1.** *n.* someone who is against liberal social or political change; someone who is very conservative. ♦ *The reactionary demanded a tax cut.* ♦ *Cutting welfare was popular among the reactionaries.* **2.** *adj.* <the adj. use of ①.> ♦ *The reactionary dean refused to listen to the students' demands.* ♦ *The reactionary pundit criticized the congressional action.*

reactivate [ri 'æk tɪ vet] *tv.* to activate something again; to make something usable again. ♦ *Mary reactivated the alarm when she left the office.* ♦ *The terrorist reactivated the bomb by remote control.*

reactive [ri 'æk tɪv] *adj.* likely to react. (Compare with proactive. Adv: *reactively.*) ♦ *Someone with a reactive personality waits for things to happen before trying to change them.* ♦ *We tried to hide the bad news from Bob because he is so reactive.*

reactor [ri 'æk tɚ] *n.* a complex device that makes atomic energy by splitting particles in the center of the atom. ♦ *The physicist worked at a nuclear reactor.* ♦ *All radiation was contained when the reactor melted down.*

read 1. ['rɛd] pt of read. **2.** ['rid] *tv., irreg.* to understand what is meant by written words; to get meaning from written words. (Pt/pp: read ① ['rɛd].) ♦ *Mary reads the newspaper every morning.* ♦ *I read the sign posted to the door.* **3.** ['rid] *tv., irreg.* to say written words out loud. ♦ *John read his poem to the patrons at the café.* ♦ *Anne read her speech in front of the class.* **4.** ['rid] *tv., irreg.* to interpret someone or something. ♦ *John doesn't know how to read his wife's actions.* ♦ *The psychic offered to read my palm.* **5.** ['rid] *iv., irreg.* to learn about something through written information. ♦ *I can't read right now because my eyes hurt.* ♦ *People who can't read are called illiterate.* **6. read about; read of** ['rid...] *iv., irreg.* + *prep. phr.* to learn about someone or something through reading. ♦ *The students read about the Revolutionary War in class.* ♦ *Jimmy liked to read about dinosaurs.* **7.** ['rid] *iv., irreg.* to say written words aloud. ♦ *"Could you please read more quietly?" the librarian asked.* ♦ *The teacher read to the class.* **8. read between the lines** ['rid...] *idiom* to infer something (from something else); to try to understand what is meant by something that is not written clearly or openly. ♦ *After listening to what she said, if you read between the lines, you can begin to see what she really means.* ♦ *Don't believe everything you hear. Learn to read between the lines.* **9. read someone like a book** ['rid...] *idiom* to understand someone very well. ♦ *I've got John figured out. I can read him like a book.* ♦ *Of course I understand you. I read you like a book.*

readable ['rid ə bəl] **1.** *adj.* able to be read; legible; written or printed neatly or clearly. (Adv: *readably.*) ♦ *The ransom note was barely readable.* ♦ *The poster was printed in a very readable font.* **2.** *adj.* easy to read; interesting or pleasant to read. (Adv: *readably.*) ♦ *The teacher assigned some readable articles.* ♦ *This popular book about discoveries in science is surprisingly readable—it's like a detective story!*

reader ['rid ɚ] **1.** *n.* someone who reads. ♦ *The reader found a mistake in the textbook.* ♦ *The library was filled with readers.* **2.** *n.* a book that is used for learning to read. ♦ *The young children took their readers to class.* ♦ *The teacher gave each student a new reader.*

readily ['rɛd ə li] **1.** *adv.* without difficulty or problems; easily. ♦ *The mechanic readily fixed my car's engine.* ♦ *The carpenter constructed a new door frame quite readily.* **2.** *adv.* willingly; eagerly. ♦ *The students helped their teacher readily.* ♦ *I readily let my best friend borrow my car.*

readiness ['rɛd i nəs] **1.** *n.* the state of being ready; the state of being prepared. (No plural form in this sense.) ♦ *The soldiers' readiness helped them win the war.* ♦ *The police officer's readiness to fight crime was noble.* **2.** *n.* eagerness; willingness; the condition of wanting to do something. (No plural form in this sense.) ♦ *My parents appreciated my readiness to help them.* ♦ *David thanked Anne for her readiness to drive him to the hospital.*

reading ['rid ɪŋ] **1.** *n.* something written that is meant to be read. ♦ *The first reading in this anthology is a piece of fiction.* ♦ *I have selected a reading from Shakespeare that I am sure you will recognize.* **2.** *n.* an interpretation; a meaning from something that is read; an opinion from something that is read. (No plural form in this sense.) ♦ *What is your reading of this situation?* ♦ *The doctor's reading of the patient's condition was crucial.* **3.** *n.* a measurement shown on a measuring device. ♦ *The gauge indicated a very high reading for poisonous fumes.* ♦ *The gas-company employee came to my house to check the meter reading.* **4.** *adj.* <the adj. use of ①.> ♦ *There was reading matter in the dentist's waiting room.* ♦ *Anne must wear reading glasses.*

readjust [ri ə 'dʒʌst] **1.** *tv.* to adjust something again; to put something back where it belongs. ♦ *Anne readjusted the volume control after I had changed it.* ♦ *The driver readjusted the car's rearview mirror after I bumped it.* **2. readjust to** *iv. + prep. phr.* to get used to someone or something again. ♦ *The miner's eyes readjusted to the bright daylight.* ♦ *I readjusted to school after summer vacation.*

readjustment [ri ə 'dʒʌst mənt] **1.** *n.* the process of getting used to something again. (No plural form in this sense.) ♦ *Jane's readjustment to the new school went quickly.* ♦ *My readjustment to winter takes quite some time.* **2.** *n.* the act of readjusting someone or something; a movement or change that is made when putting something back where it belongs. ♦ *The readjustment of my car engine gave me better gas mileage.* ♦ *The photographer's readjustment of the lens resulted in a clearer picture.*

readout ['rid ɑʊt] *n.* computer information that is displayed or printed out. ♦ *The analyst examined the readout.* ♦ *The readout indicated that the patient's tests were negative.*

ready ['rɛd i] **1.** *adj.* [of something] able to be used right now. (Comp: *readier;* sup: *readiest.*) ♦ *Dinner is ready to be eaten.* ♦ *The wall is ready for another coat of paint.* **2.** *tv.* to prepare something for use. ♦ *The teacher readied the class for the exam.* ♦ *The maid readied the hotel room for the next guest.* **3. ready to do something** *phr.* [of someone or some creature] prepared and willing. ♦ *Are you ready to leave for the airport?* ♦ *If you need me, I'm ready to help.*

ready-made ['rɛd i 'med] *adj.* already made; prepared; made ahead of time; ready to be used right now. ♦ *I bought a ready-made pie from the grocery store.* ♦ *Anne opened a bag of ready-made popcorn.*

ready-to-wear ['rɛd i tə 'wɛr] *adj.* [of clothes] already made and ready to be worn right now. ♦ *Bill buys custom-made suits because ready-to-wear clothing doesn't fit him well.* ♦ *We bought some ready-to-wear costumes for Halloween.*

real ['ril] **1.** *adj.* existing; actual; true. (Adv: *really.*) ♦ *What's the real value of your watch?* ♦ *David was unsure if what he was seeing was real.* **2.** *adj.* genuine; not fake; not phony; not counterfeit. (Adv: *really.*) ♦ *Anne's necklace was made of real diamonds.* ♦ *Is that painting real, or is it a copy?* **3.** *adv.* really; very; extremely. (Colloquial and widespread.) ♦ *My friends were real nice to me when I was sick.* ♦ *I don't want to go to the movies because I'm real tired.* **4. the real thing** *phr.* something that is genuine and not an imitation. ♦ *I don't want frozen yogurt, I want the real thing! Yes, ice cream!* ♦ *She hates plastic that looks like wood. She wants the real thing.*

real estate ['ril ə stet] **1.** *n.* land with all the buildings on it and all the minerals under it, which is bought and sold as a commodity. (No plural form in this sense.) ♦ *This real estate is valuable because it's on the lake.* ♦ *I bought a piece of real estate in the suburbs.* **2.** *n.* the business of dealing in ①. (No plural form in this sense.) ♦ *The rich retirees had made their money in real estate.* ♦ *I wish I had gotten into real estate before the housing boom.* **3. real-estate agent** *n.* someone who sells and arranges for the transfer of ①. ♦ *My real-estate agent took me to see a number of houses that are for sale.* ♦ *I rented an apartment with the help of a real-estate agent.* **4. real estate** *adj.* <the adj. use of ②.> (Hyphenated before nominals.) ♦ *I am involved in a real-estate deal with my brother.* ♦ *Anne went to the real-estate office to sign a contract.*

realism ['ri ə lɪz əm] *n.* the point of view concerned with reality in life and art. (No plural form in this sense.) ♦

The art museum had a special exhibit on realism. ♦ *The artist's best works were fine examples of realism.*

realistic [ri ə 'lɪs tɪk] **1.** *adj.* lifelike; appearing or seeming to be real. (Adv: *realistically* [...ɪk li].) ♦ *That portrait of me looks realistic.* ♦ *The artist drew a realistic sketch of herself.* **2.** *adj.* accepting life as it really is; practical. (Adv: *realistically* [...ɪk li].) ♦ *The realistic student knew he would never be famous.* ♦ *It's not realistic to expect me to do the work of two people.*

reality [ri 'æl ə ti] **1.** *n.* everything that is real; something that is real; that which exists. (No plural form in this sense.) ♦ *Bob's sense of reality seemed to be altered by his medication.* ♦ *It is time you quit dreaming and begin to face reality.* **2. in reality** *idiom* viewing things realistically; really. ♦ *Jane dreamed it was snowing, but in reality, it was very warm.* ♦ *John looks happy, but in reality, he is miserable.* **3. lose touch with reality** *idiom* to begin to think unrealistically; to become unrealistic. ♦ *I am so overworked that I am losing touch with reality.* ♦ *The psychotic criminal had lost touch with reality.* **4. the reality of the situation** *idiom* the truth or actuality of the situation; the way the situation really is. ♦ *The reality of the situation is that we must act right now.* ♦ *Let's face the reality of the situation and go out and get jobs so we can buy food.*

realization [ri əl ɪ 'ze ʃən] *n.* an understanding that something exists or has happened; a perception; an awareness. ♦ *The realization that my dog had died ruined my day.* ♦ *Jane came to the realization that Anne was right.*

realize ['ri ə lɑɪz] **1.** *tv.* to understand something; to be aware of something. ♦ *John realized that his father was correct.* ♦ *Anne realized the importance of the situation.* **2.** *tv.* to make something real; to cause something to exist. ♦ *The business realized a handsome profit last year.* ♦ *The thief's plans were slowly realized.*

really ['ri li] **1.** *adv.* actually; truly; in reality. ♦ *It's really raining outside. I'm not kidding.* ♦ *I'm serious. Jane is really an enemy spy.* **2.** *adv.* very; completely. ♦ *I brewed some really strong coffee this morning.* ♦ *I'm really tired. Can I call you back tomorrow?* **3. Really!** *interj.* "Indeed!" (Shows either interest or disgust.) ♦ *Really! I can't believe you are so rude!* ♦ *"I want you to give me $25." "Oh, really, do you?"*

realm ['rɛlm] **1.** *n.* an area that someone rules over; an area where a certain person is the most powerful. ♦ *The king was respected throughout his realm.* ♦ *The monarch ruled his realm justly.* **2.** *n.* domain; category. (Figurative on ①.) ♦ *Eye diseases fall into the realm of the ophthalmologist.* ♦ *The elderly professor was well known in the realm of biology.*

Realtor™ ['ri əl tɚ] *n.* A member of the National Association of Realtors who works in the business of selling real estate; a real-estate agent. ♦ *The Realtor showed the couple a nice house in an old neighborhood.* ♦ *I told the Realtor I wanted to buy a five-acre plot by the lake.*

ream ['rim] **1.** *n.* a unit of measurement—of sheets of paper—equal to 500 sheets. ♦ *The secretary put a ream of paper in the copier.* ♦ *The clerk loaded sixteen reams of paper into the supply cabinet.* **2. ream out** *tv.* + *adv.* to make a hole larger. ♦ *The plumber reamed the clogged pipe out.* ♦ *The carpenter reamed out the hole with a drill.*

reap ['rip] **1.** *tv.* to cut and gather crops from a field. ♦ *The migrant workers reaped the wheat in the field.* ♦ *The farmer reaped the fields with heavy machinery.* **2.** *tv.* to get something in return for doing something. (Figurative on ①.) ♦ *John reaped the rewards of his labor.* ♦ *A miserable person reaps misery.*

reaper ['ri pɚ] *n.* a person or machine that cuts and gathers crops from a field. ♦ *The reapers placed the newly mown wheat in large piles.* ♦ *The reaper ran out of fuel in the middle of the field.*

reappear [ri ə 'pɪr] **1.** *iv.* to appear again. ♦ *The sun reappeared from behind a cloud.* ♦ *The lost rubber ball reappeared behind the magician's ear.* **2.** *iv.* to occur again. ♦ *Jane's mysterious ailment reappeared after a month.* ♦ *The computer problem reappeared just when I thought I had fixed it.*

reapportion [ri ə 'por ʃən] *tv.* to apportion something again. ♦ *Congress reapportioned the legislative districts.* ♦ *The voting precincts were reapportioned after each census.*

rear ['rɪr] **1.** *n.* the buttocks; the backside; the part of the body one sits on. (Euphemistic.) ♦ *David hurt his rear when he fell on the ice.* ♦ *I spanked my son on the rear for misbehaving.* **2.** *adj.* in back; hind. ♦ *The clerk brought the delivery through the rear door.* ♦ *My dog hurt one of his rear legs when he fell off the porch.* **3.** *tv.* to raise offspring. ♦ *My parents reared four children.* ♦ *The bird reared the baby birds until they left the nest.* **4.** *iv.* to rise up, especially for a horse to stand on its back legs. ♦ *The horse reared, throwing the rider from its back.* ♦ *The horse reared in fright.* **5. at the rear of something** *phr.* located at the back part of something. ♦ *I keep my tools at the rear of my garage.* ♦ *There's a creek at the rear of my property.* **6. in the rear** *phr.* located in the space or area behind someone or something. ♦ *The waiter told me that the bathrooms were in the rear.* ♦ *All deliveries must be made in the rear.* **7. bring up the rear** *idiom* to move along behind everyone else; to be at the end of the line. ♦ *Here comes John, bringing up the rear.* ♦ *Hurry up, Tom! Why are you always bringing up the rear?* **8. rarin' to go** *idiom* extremely keen to act or do something. (*Raring* is an older form of *rearing*.) ♦ *Jane can't wait to start her job. She's rarin' to go.* ♦ *Mary is rarin' to go and can't wait for her university term to start.* **9. rear its ugly head** *idiom* [for something unpleasant] to appear or become obvious after lying hidden. ♦ *Jealousy reared its ugly head and destroyed their marriage.* ♦ *The question of money always rears its ugly head in matters of business.*

rearrange [ri ə 'rendʒ] *tv.* to arrange something again or in a different way, especially to place things or people in a different order or in different positions with respect to each other. ♦ *Mary rearranged the furniture after the new carpet was installed.* ♦ *If I rearrange my schedule of appointments, I may be able to meet you for lunch.*

rearrangement [ri ə 'rendʒ mənt] *n.* creating a new or different arrangement; changing the way that things or people are ordered or positioned with respect to each other. (No plural form in this sense.) ♦ *Rearrangement of the one-way streets improved traffic flow.* ♦ *Your rearrangement of the furniture has really made the room look bigger.*

rearview mirror ['rɪɚ vju 'mɪɚ ɚ] *n.* a mirror attached to the inside of a car's windshield, allowing the driver to see what is behind the car. ♦ *I adjusted my rearview mirror before I started the engine.* ♦ *In my rearview mirror, I saw a police car behind me.*

reason ['riz ən] **1.** *n.* the power or ability to think, understand, deduce, and form opinions and conclusions from facts and observations. (No plural form in this sense.) ♦ *Humans are the only creatures that have the power of reason.* ♦ *After the head injury, John lost all reason.* **2.** *n.* a cause; a motive; an explanation; a rationale. ♦ *The reason that I bought red roses is that Jane likes them.* ♦ *The reason for the seasons is the tilt of the earth.* **3.** *iv.* to think; to be able to think; to have the power or ability to think, understand, deduce, and form opinions and conclusions. ♦ *The jury reasoned carefully before delivering its verdict.* ♦ *The student reasoned thoughtfully before answering the question.* **4. reason with** *iv.* + *prep. phr.* to persuade someone by using ①; to argue with someone by using ①. ♦ *David is very stubborn. You just can't reason with him.* ♦ *John tried to reason with his parents, but they wouldn't let him go to the party.* **5.** *tv.* to have an opinion or conclusion based on ①. (Takes a clause.) ♦ *Brian reasoned that my plan would not work.* ♦ *The detective reasoned that David had been murdered for his money.*

reasonable ['riz ən ə bəl] **1.** *adj.* sensible; making sense; according to reason. (Adv: *reasonably.*) ♦ *The witness gave a reasonable account of the accident.* ♦ *Bill gave a reasonable excuse for his lateness.* **2.** *adj.* not expensive; having an appropriate cost. (Adv: *reasonably.*) ♦ *Anne bought her watch at a reasonable price.* ♦ *Although the neighborhood is expensive, this apartment is very reasonable.*

reasoning ['riz ən ɪŋ] **1.** *n.* the process or ability of forming opinions or conclusions from facts and observations. (No plural form in this sense.) ♦ *I don't agree with your reasoning.* ♦ *My English teacher showed me why my reasoning was faulty.* **2.** *adj.* <the adj. use of ①.> ♦ *Anne felt she had excellent reasoning ability.* ♦ *I had to put all my reasoning power to work on this problem.*

reassurance [ri ə 'ʃʊr əns] **1.** *n.* comfort and assurance that restores confidence and courage. (No plural form in this sense.) ♦ *I need reassurance that everything will be fine.* ♦ *Mary's comforting words provided the reassurance I needed.* **2.** *n.* an instance of ①. ♦ *John's reassurances were all I needed to complete the job.* ♦ *Mary's comforting words were quite a reassurance.*

reassure [ri ə 'ʃʊr] *tv.* to restore someone's courage or confidence. ♦ *The mayor reassured the citizens that she would not raise taxes.* ♦ *My boss reassured me that I would be getting a raise soon.*

rebate ['ri bet] **1.** *n.* money refunded from the purchase price of something. ♦ *If you buy a new car today, you'll get a $500 rebate!* ♦ *The company offered rebates as promotional gimmicks.* **2.** *tv.* to give a partial refund of a purchase price. ♦ *The company rebated $200 with each purchase of a new car.* ♦ *The company rebated the cost of new batteries.*

rebel 1. ['rɛb əl] *n.* someone who fights or resists power, authority, or government. ♦ *The rebels seized the capital city.* ♦ *The ruling general refused to bargain with the rebels.* **2. rebel against** [rɪ 'bɛl...] *iv.* + *prep. phr.* to fight against power, authority, or government; to disobey power, authority, or government. ♦ *The citizens rebelled against the corrupt government.* ♦ *The protesters rebelled against the police.* **3. rebel against** [rɪ 'bɛl...] *iv.* + *prep. phr.* to be against doing something; not to want to do something; to be opposed to doing something. (Figurative on ②.) ♦ *Jimmy rebelled against eating his vegetables.* ♦ *Jane rebelled against authority when she was a teenager.*

rebellion [rɪ 'bɛl jən] **1.** *n.* rebelling; the challenging of authority. (No plural form in this sense.) ♦ *Our child went through a stage of rebellion at age 13.* ♦ *Rebellion is part of becoming a teenager.* **2.** *n.* an organized and open resistance to power, authority, or government. ♦ *The leaders of the rebellion were all executed.* ♦ *The rebellion was infiltrated by government spies.*

rebellious [rɪ 'bɛl jəs] *adj.* resistant to power, authority, or government; not obedient. (Adv: *rebelliously.*) ♦ *The rebellious teenager disobeyed his parents frequently.* ♦ *The police arrested the rebellious protesters.*

rebirth [ri 'bɚθ] **1.** *n.* seeming to be being born again; a revival. (No plural form in this sense.) ♦ *After beginning to meditate, Jane experienced a feeling of rebirth.* ♦ *Belief in reincarnation is the belief in the rebirth of the soul.* **2.** *n.* the return of a belief, practice, or philosophy. (Figurative on ①.) ♦ *The aging senator hoped for a rebirth of conservatism.* ♦ *The politician urged for a rebirth of personal responsibility.*

reboot ['ri 'but] **1.** *tv.* to restart a computer. ♦ *I have to reboot this computer four or five times a day!* ♦ *Bob had to reboot the computer after he installed some new software.* **2.** *iv.* to restart [a computer]. ♦ *After I installed some new software, I had to reboot.* ♦ *Every time my computer crashes, I have to reboot.*

rebound 1. ['rɪ baʊnd] *n.* the return movement of something that bounced off something. ♦ *The tennis player hit the ball on the rebound.* ♦ *On the second rebound, the ball hit Bill on the head.* **2.** [rɪ 'baʊnd] *iv.* to bounce back after hitting something. ♦ *The tennis ball rebounded off the side of the wall.* ♦ *The rubber ball rebounded off the pavement.* **3.** [rɪ 'baʊnd] *iv.* to recover. (Figurative on ②.) ♦ *The firm rebounded from near bankruptcy.* ♦ *Anne rebounded from her last illness quickly.*

rebuff [ri 'bʌf] **1.** *n.* a snub; a blunt, harsh response to someone who is being friendly or to someone who is asking for help. ♦ *John's rebuff of my offer to help offended me.* ♦ *Mary's sharp rebuff took me by surprise.* **2.** *tv.* to respond bluntly or harshly to someone who is being friendly or asking for help. ♦ *Mary rebuffed John when he offered to help.* ♦ *David rebuffed his parents when they offered to lend him money.*

rebuild [rɪ 'bɪld] *tv., irreg.* to build something again. (Pt/pp: **rebuilt**.) ♦ *The citizens rebuilt the town after a tornado destroyed it.* ♦ *Dave rebuilt the sand castle after John knocked it over.*

rebuilt [rɪ 'bɪlt] pt/pp of **rebuild**.

rebuke [rɪ 'bjuk] **1.** *n.* scolding; disapproval; chiding. (No plural form in this sense.) ♦ *My efforts were met with rebuke and insults!* ♦ *I don't expect to make errors and escape without rebuke.* **2.** *n.* a scolding. ♦ *After frequent rebukes from the boss, I finally quit the job.* ♦ *David's rebukes became too much for Bill, and he finally lost his temper.* **3.** *tv.* to scold someone or some creature. ♦ *The* *manager rebuked the clerk for being rude to a customer.* ♦ *John rebuked the cat for scratching the furniture.*

rebut [rɪ 'bʌt] *tv.* to argue that something is false; to refute someone or something. ♦ *The liberal candidate rebutted the conservative's argument.* ♦ *The scientist rebutted the cigarette company's claims.*

rebuttal [rɪ 'bʌt əl] **1.** *n.* stating an argument against something; rebutting or refuting something. (No plural form in this sense.) ♦ *By way of rebuttal, I showed how each of her statements was false.* ♦ *In rebuttal, she proved them all wrong.* **2.** *n.* an argument that something is false; a statement intended to show that something is false. ♦ *Each candidate had five minutes for a rebuttal at the end of the debate.* ♦ *In my rebuttal, I pointed out the errors in the speaker's lecture.*

recall [rɪ 'kɔl] **1.** *tv.* to remember someone or something. ♦ *I can recall many happy events from my childhood.* ♦ *Do you recall the name of John's parents?* **2.** *tv.* to order someone to return. ♦ *The general recalled the troops from battle.* ♦ *The plumber was recalled to do the job right.* **3.** *tv.* [for a manufacturer] to request that a product be returned. ♦ *The company recalled the defective product.* ♦ *The car company recalled certain models for repair.* **4.** *n.* the ability to remember something. (No plural form in this sense.) ♦ *Amazingly, John has total recall of everything that he reads.* ♦ *Alcohol affects one's recall.* **5.** *n.* the act or process of asking that a product be returned to the seller or manufacturer. ♦ *The product recall cost the company millions of dollars.* ♦ *The consumers group demanded the recall of the faulty product.*

recant [ri 'kænt] *tv.* to cancel a statement or pledge that one has made. ♦ *The witness recanted her testimony and was charged with perjury.* ♦ *The prisoner recanted his confession.*

recap ['ri kæp] **1.** *tv.* to summarize something; to say briefly the important parts of what has been said; to recapitulate. ♦ *The speaker recapped the important points of her lecture.* ♦ *The main ideas of the book were recapped in the conclusion.* **2.** *n.* a summary; a brief statement about the important parts of what has been said. ♦ *As a recap, let me outline the five major points of my speech.* ♦ *The article concluded with a brief recap of the findings.*

recapitulate [ri kə 'pɪ tʃu let] **1.** *tv.* to summarize something; to state briefly the important parts of what has been said. ♦ *At the end of the lecture, the speaker recapitulated the main points.* ♦ *The experimental results were recapitulated in the article's last paragraph.* **2.** *iv.* to summarize; to state briefly the important parts of what has been said. ♦ *The speaker recapitulated at the end of her lecture.* ♦ *Let me recapitulate by reminding you of the experiment's results.*

recapitulation [ri kə pɪ tʃu 'le ʃən] *n.* a brief statement about the important parts of what has been said. ♦ *The article's conclusion was a succinct recapitulation.* ♦ *The speaker's recapitulation summarized the speech.*

recapture [ri 'kæp tʃɚ] **1.** *tv.* to capture someone or something again. ♦ *The prisoner was recaptured the day after he escaped.* ♦ *The antelope got away from the lion but was soon recaptured.* **2.** *n.* the capturing of someone or something again. (No plural form in this sense.) ♦ *Twenty soldiers were killed in the recapture of the capital.* ♦ *The recapture of the prisoner involved dozens of police.*

recede [rɪ 'sid] **1.** *iv.* to move backward in space or time. ♦ *The tide receded from the beach.* ♦ *The forest receded into the horizon as I drove away.* **2.** *iv.* [for the hairline] to move toward the top of the head, due to the loss of hair. (Figurative on ①.) ♦ *John bought a toupee when his hair began to recede.* ♦ *David's hair began to recede when he was a teenager.*

receipt [rɪ 'sit] **1.** *n.* a state of having been received. (No plural form in this sense.) ♦ *We await receipt of your check for the full amount.* ♦ *I expect receipt of the letter tomorrow.* **2.** *n.* a statement that proves that something has been received or paid for. ♦ *I showed the guard my receipt for my purchases.* ♦ *The clerk couldn't issue a refund because I lost my receipt.* **3. receipts** *n.* money that a business receives from customers; money that is collected by a business or at a performance. (Treated as plural.) ♦ *The manager took the receipts to the bank.* ♦ *The accountant examined the records of the store's receipts.* **4. in receipt of something** *idiom* in a state of having received something. (Formal.) ♦ *We are in receipt of your letter of request.* ♦ *When we are in receipt of your check for the full balance, we will mark your bill as paid.*

receive [rɪ 'siv] **1.** *tv.* to get something; to take something that is given. ♦ *I received a letter from my brother.* ♦ *John received an influenza shot from the nurse.* **2.** *tv.* to accept someone as a member of a group or organization; to welcome someone as a visitor. ♦ *The butler received the guests at the front door.* ♦ *The sorority received four new members in a secret ceremony.*

receiver [rɪ 'siv ɚ] **1.** *n.* someone or something that receives something. ♦ *The receiver of the package must sign for it.* ♦ *The receiver of the bad news called me to tell me.* **2.** *n.* the part of a telephone that one holds while one is talking. ♦ *I held the receiver close to my ear so I could hear the caller.* ♦ *After the call, Mary returned the receiver to the hook.* **3.** *n.* a radio or television set; something that receives broadcast signals. ♦ *The radio operator tuned the receiver to a clear channel.* ♦ *My neighbor's microwave oven affects my television receiver.* **4.** *n.* someone who is chosen to manage a property after it goes into bankruptcy. ♦ *The receiver sent the tenants' rent to the mortgage company.* ♦ *Mary's firm was appointed as the bankrupt office building's receiver.*

recent ['ri sənt] *adj.* happening only a short time ago; having existed for only a short time; not long ago. (Adv: *recently.*) ♦ *The most recent news was printed on page one of the newspaper.* ♦ *I told the manager about recent developments with the project.*

receptacle [rɪ 'sɛp tə kəl] **1.** *n.* a container designed to receive something. ♦ *John threw the old papers into the trash receptacle.* ♦ *I put my used paper towel into a receptacle by the door.* **2. (electric) receptacle** *n.* an electric outlet; a connection, usually in the wall, to which lamps and appliances can be attached. ♦ *Please plug the lamp into a receptacle.* ♦ *There is no electrical receptacle in the entire room!*

reception [rɪ 'sɛp ʃən] **1.** *n.* receiving or welcoming someone. (No plural form in this sense.) ♦ *The guests received a polite reception from the host.* ♦ *John's new in-laws gave him a cold reception.* **2.** *n.* the quality of broadcast signals that are received by a television set, a radio, or other receiver. (No plural form in this sense.) ♦ *The* *microwave oven affects the reception on my TV.* ♦ *The radio got better reception when I moved the antenna.* **3.** *n.* a party, gathering, or celebration where people are welcomed. ♦ *I met the groom's family at the wedding reception.* ♦ *Cheese and crackers were served at the reception after the conference.*

receptionist [rɪ 'sɛp ʃə nəst] *n.* someone who sits at the desk near the front door of an office, answers phone calls, and greets, helps, or directs clients or patients. ♦ *The dentist's receptionist scheduled my next appointment.* ♦ *I left a message for Anne with her receptionist.*

receptive [rɪ 'sɛp tɪv] **1.** *adj.* willing to listen to new ideas and suggestions; open to ideas and suggestions. (Adv: *receptively.*) ♦ *My boss is receptive to my input.* ♦ *Jane was receptive to changes in her work schedule.* **2.** *adj.* willing to receive the sexual attention of a mate. (Adv: *receptively.*) ♦ *The mare was receptive to the stallion.* ♦ *Anne was not receptive to John's interest.*

recess 1. ['ri sɛs] *n.* a period of time during the school day when the children are allowed to play, usually outside. (No plural form in this sense.) ♦ *The children played on the playground during recess.* ♦ *Recess ended when the school bell rang.* **2.** ['ri sɛs] *n.* a period of time during the work day where someone stops working for a few minutes and takes a break; a break. ♦ *David took a recess from work so he could smoke a cigarette.* ♦ *The judge declared a one-hour recess for lunch.* **3.** ['ri sɛs] *n.* a space cut or built into a wall; a space that is set back from a wall. ♦ *The painting was placed in a shallow recess next to the window.* ♦ *John put a vase of flowers in the recess in the front hallway.* **4.** [rɪ 'sɛs] *iv.* to take a break; to stop working for a short time. ♦ *The court recessed for lunch.* ♦ *The committee recessed while copies of the report were being made.*

recession [rɪ 'sɛ ʃən] **1.** *n.* backward movement or direction. (No plural form in this sense.) ♦ *The recession of the tide revealed some dead fish on the beach.* ♦ *The recession of the soldiers indicated an end to the siege.* **2.** *n.* a time when the economy is shrinking rather than growing. ♦ *Many auto workers were laid off during the last recession.* ♦ *The president's policies led the country into a recession.*

recessive [rɪ 'sɛs ɪv] *adj.* of or about a genetic trait that does not show up when there is a similar dominant trait present as well. (Adv: *recessively.*) ♦ *Blue eyes are recessive, and brown eyes are dominant.* ♦ *The botanist studied the recessive genes of the pea plant.*

recipe ['rɛs ə pi] **1.** *n.* a set of directions for making something to eat. ♦ *I used half the amount of salt that was listed in the recipe.* ♦ *There are a lot of delicious recipes in this cookbook.* **2.** *n.* a set of directions for preparing or causing anything. (Figurative on ①.) ♦ *Giving that job to someone lazy is a recipe for disaster.* ♦ *The couple outlined their recipe for a happy marriage.*

recipient [rɪ 'sɪp i ənt] *n.* someone who receives something. ♦ *The recipient of the lottery's grand prize quit her job.* ♦ *John is the grateful recipient of a heart that was transplanted into his body.*

reciprocal [rɪ 'sɪp rə kəl] *adj.* giving and receiving at the same time; giving as much as one gets; getting as much as one gives. (Adv: *reciprocally* [rɪ 'sɪ prə kli].) ♦ *The services that are provided should be reciprocal to the amount of taxes that are paid.* ♦ *John believed that all deeds were reciprocal, so if he did something nice for someone, someone would do something nice for him.*

reciprocate [rɪ 'sɪp rə ket] **1.** *tv.* to give something in return; to feel something in return; to do something in return. ♦ *I did an errand for Mary, and then she reciprocated the favor.* ♦ *I reciprocated John's kindness by buying him a gift.* **2.** *iv.* to return a favor. ♦ *I helped Anne, and then she reciprocated.* ♦ *I rubbed John's back, and then he reciprocated.*

reciprocity [rɛ sə 'prɑs ə ti] *n.* giving, feeling, or doing something in return. (No plural form in this sense.) ♦ *When John does favors, he expects reciprocity.* ♦ *This gift is in grateful reciprocity for the one you gave me.*

recital [rɪ 'sɑɪt əl] **1.** *n.* the telling of a story; a verbal account of something. (No plural form in this sense.) ♦ *The court reporter transcribed the witness's recital of facts.* ♦ *John's grandchildren never tired of the recital of his stories.* **2.** *n.* a concert or performance by students who play instruments, sing, or dance. ♦ *The parents attended the children's music recital.* ♦ *The young ballerinas were proud of their dance recital.* **3.** *n.* a concert or performance, often by a single performer playing an instrument, singing, or reading poetry. ♦ *The cellist performed in a recital at the Lincoln Center.* ♦ *The famous poet read her works at a private recital.*

recitation [rɛs ɪ 'te ʃən] **1.** *n.* something that is recited, usually from memory. (No plural form in this sense.) ♦ *The lazy boy had not memorized his weekly recitation.* ♦ *John was applauded for his recitation of original poetry.* **2.** *n.* the reciting of something, usually from memory, and usually poetry or Bible verses. ♦ *At school, each student did a recitation of a well-known speech.* ♦ *Anne performed a recitation of a famous poem.*

recite [rɪ 'sɑɪt] **1.** *tv.* to verbally deliver an answer in school; to tell in school what one has learned about a subject; to repeat something from memory. ♦ *Anne recited the poem perfectly.* ♦ *The class recited the multiplication tables.* **2.** *iv.* to state [something] aloud that has been memorized or learned. ♦ *The class recited in unison.* ♦ *The teacher asked a question, and the students recited.*

reckless ['rɛk ləs] *adj.* careless; not concerned with safety or danger. (Adv: *recklessly.*) ♦ *The reckless driver drove above the speed limit.* ♦ *It is reckless to go up so high on such a wobbly ladder.*

recklessness ['rɛk ləs nəs] *n.* being reckless; the deliberate taking of risks. (No plural form in this sense.) ♦ *The accident was caused by the driver's recklessness.* ♦ *The police were amazed at the criminal's recklessness.*

reckon ['rɛk ən] **1.** *tv.* to calculate something; to figure the amount of something; to determine the cost or the amount of something. ♦ *John reckoned the bill to be over $100.* ♦ *I reckon your share of the costs to be around $50.* **2.** *tv.* to think something; to suppose something. (Colloquial. Takes a clause.) ♦ *I reckon it's time to go home now.* ♦ *Mary reckoned that she would attend the party.*

reckoning ['rɛk ə nɪŋ] *n.* calculation; figuring out the amount of something. (No plural form in this sense.) ♦ *By my reckoning, everyone owes $10 for dinner.* ♦ *The reckoning of my taxes took my accountant a week.*

reclaim [rɪ 'klem] **1.** *tv.* to restore or return something to its original condition or to a usable condition; to make something able to be used. ♦ *The Netherlands has reclaimed large tracts of land from the sea.* ♦ *The workers reclaimed the old mansion from the squatters.* **2.** *tv.* to salvage something. ♦ *John reclaimed some of his belongings from the ashes of the fire.* ♦ *The librarian reclaimed a few of the books damaged by the flood.* **3.** *tv.* to demand or claim the return of something that has been given away or taken away. ♦ *I reclaimed the property stolen from my relatives during the war.* ♦ *Bob reclaimed his watch from the pawn shop.*

reclamation [rɛk lə 'me ʃən] **1.** *n.* a restoration; the return of something to its original condition; the restoration of something to a good condition. (No plural form in this sense.) ♦ *The environmentalists worked toward the reclamation of the prairie.* ♦ *The reclamation of the old mansion cost many thousands of dollars.* **2.** *n.* the salvaging of something. (No plural form in this sense.) ♦ *The reclamation of my possessions from the ashes was futile.* ♦ *Reclamation of the damaged books was time consuming.*

recline [rɪ 'klɑɪn] *iv.* to lie down; to lie back [on something]; to rest while lying down. ♦ *Mary reclined and put her feet up.* ♦ *When John reclined on the bed, he fell asleep instantly.*

recluse ['rɛk lus] *n.* someone isolated from the rest of the world; a hermit. ♦ *The recluse lived in a cabin deep in the woods.* ♦ *The recluse visited town once a month for supplies.*

recognition [rɛk ɪg 'nɪʃ ən] **1.** *n.* identifying someone or something as being the same person or thing that one has seen, heard, known, or experienced in the past. (No plural form in this sense.) ♦ *The witness's recognition of David led to his arrest.* ♦ *The fans' recognition of the actor caused him to leave the restaurant.* **2.** *n.* realization. (No plural form in this sense.) ♦ *Mary has no recognition of the kind of trouble she is in.* ♦ *Recognition that the house needed painting badly came when the neighbors complained.* **3.** *n.* the acknowledgment of the existence or legitimacy of someone or something. (No plural form in this sense.) ♦ *The secretary noted the chair's recognition of John.* ♦ *The country's recognition of Taiwan angered China.* **4.** *n.* acknowledgment of service or excellence. (No plural form in this sense.) ♦ *In recognition of 30 years of service, the company gave me a watch.* ♦ *As recognition of their bravery, the soldiers were given a medal.*

recognizable ['rɛk ɪg nɑɪz ə bəl] *adj.* in sufficient amount or degree to be noticed or identified. (Adv: *recognizably.*) ♦ *Bill is recognizable from the many movies he has appeared in.* ♦ *The mangled body found by the police was not recognizable.*

recognize ['rɛk ɪg nɑɪz] **1.** *tv.* to identify someone or something. ♦ *I recognized the man who tried to mug me.* ♦ *The baby recognized her mother's face.* **2.** *tv.* to acknowledge something as legitimate or in existence. ♦ *The United States recognizes each of the former Soviet republics.* ♦ *The university recognized the students' right to free speech.* **3.** *tv.* to give someone the right to speak, especially at a meeting. ♦ *The chairman recognized the treasurer, who gave the financial report.* ♦ *When Anne was recognized, she gave her report.* **4.** *tv.* to observe one's errors. ♦ *I recognize that I may have been wrong.* ♦ *My boss recognized his mistake.* **5. recognize something for what it is; recognize one for what one is** *idiom* to see and understand exactly what someone or something is or represents. ♦ *The disease represented a serious threat to all peoples, and Dr. Smith recognized it for what it was.* ♦ *I recognize you for what you are, you scoundrel!*

recoil 1. ['ri koɪl] *n.* the backward movement and force of a gun or weapon when it is fired. (No plural form in this sense.) ♦ *The recoil of the gun knocked it against my shoulder.* ♦ *The weapon's recoil knocked me backwards.* **2.** [rɪ 'koɪl] *iv.* to move backward forcefully; to spring backward. ♦ *The gun recoiled when I fired it.* ♦ *The rifle recoiled and knocked me against the wall.* **3.** [rɪ 'koɪl] *iv.* to step back in fear, disgust, or horror; to shrink back. (Figurative on ②.) ♦ *In fear, I recoiled from the robber with the knife.* ♦ *The dog recoiled from the snake.*

recollect [rɛk ə 'lɛkt] *tv.* to remember someone or something; to bring something back into one's mind; to recall something. ♦ *At the trial, the witness recollected the crime.* ♦ *Can you recollect when you were last in New York City?*

recollection [rɛk ə 'lɛk ʃən] *n.* a memory; something that is remembered. ♦ *Mary had many recollections of what it was like to be poor.* ♦ *My recollection of my childhood is very dim.*

recommend [rɛk ə 'mɛnd] **1.** *tv.* to suggest [making] a particular choice from a range of choices. ♦ *The server recommended the bean soup.* ♦ *The counselor recommended the easiest course of action.* **2.** *tv.* to suggest a particular course of action. ♦ *I recommend getting started to work earlier.* ♦ *The usher recommended that I stop smoking.*

recommendable [rɛk ə 'mɛn də bəl] *adj.* worthy of being recommended. (Adv: *recommendably.*) ♦ *The video store clerk mentioned movies she thought were recommendable.* ♦ *We ate dinner at a highly recommendable restaurant.*

recommendation [rɛk ə mɛn 'de ʃən] *n.* a suggestion of which selection someone should choose from a range of choices; someone or something that is recommended. ♦ *Do you have any recommendations for hotels that I might stay at?* ♦ *The critic's recommendation turned out to be a horrible movie.*

recompense ['rɛk əm pɛns] **1.** *tv.* to compensate someone for something. ♦ *There is no way I can recompense your kindness.* ♦ *The store where I fell recompensed the costs of my injury.* **2.** *tv.* to reward someone for doing something. ♦ *The company recompensed the hard worker with a bonus paycheck.* ♦ *The teacher recompensed the hard-working student with an A.* **3.** *n.* a payment given to someone as compensation, to make up for suffering or injury, or as a reward. (No plural form in this sense.) ♦ *The $20 bonus was an insufficient recompense for my hard work.* ♦ *The store was unable to pay the amount of recompense ordered by the judge.*

reconcile ['rɛk ən sɑɪl] **1.** *tv.* to make peace between people or groups of people by solving problems and ending disagreements. ♦ *A mediator reconciled the differences between the two sides.* ♦ *Anne reconciled her disagreement with Mary.* **2.** *tv.* to bring accounts into balance. ♦ *The treasurer reconciled the accounts.* ♦ *Mary reconciled her checking account.* **3. reconcile with** *iv.* + *prep. phr.* to make up with someone; to bring a disagreement with someone to an end. ♦ *Anne reconciled with Mary after 20 years of not speaking.* ♦ *Let's reconcile with each other and* *get on with our lives.* **4. reconcile oneself to something** *idiom* to grow to feel comfortable with an undesirable or challenging situation. ♦ *John reconciled himself to living alone.* ♦ *Anne reconciled herself to having to wear glasses.*

reconciliation [rɛk ən sɪl i 'e ʃən] **1.** *n.* making peace between people. (No plural form in this sense.) ♦ *I hoped for reconciliation, but John continued to fight and argue.* ♦ *Reconciliation may be the answer, but both people must be willing to try.* **2.** *n.* an act of ①. ♦ *After numerous reconciliations, we finally realized that we could not stay married.* ♦ *My reconciliation with my brother resulted in a tearful reunion.*

recondition [ri kən 'dɪ ʃən] *tv.* to restore something to its original condition; to return something to its original condition. ♦ *The mechanic reconditioned my car's engine.* ♦ *I managed to recondition my old bicycle so that it runs fine.*

reconnaissance [rɪ 'kɑn ə səns] **1.** *n.* the examination of an area in order to learn about it or get information about it, especially by the military. (No plural form in this sense. From French.) ♦ *The reconnaissance of the area was accomplished by satellite photos.* ♦ *The military reconnaissance was a secret mission.* **2.** *n.* the information gotten by means of ①. (No plural form in this sense.) ♦ *The soldiers studied the reconnaissance before being deployed.* ♦ *The reconnaissance indicated that many mines had been buried.* **3. reconnaissance mission** *n.* a journey or expedition for the purposes of ①. ♦ *The soldier was on a reconnaissance mission and wore a disguise.* ♦ *A plane crashed into the mountain while on a reconnaissance mission.*

reconsider [ri kən 'sɪd ɚ] **1.** *tv.* to consider something again; to think about something again. ♦ *Mary reconsidered the choice she had made yesterday.* ♦ *John reconsidered the things he had said to me in anger.* **2.** *iv.* to consider again; to think about again. ♦ *The company made a better offer, so I reconsidered.* ♦ *The actor reconsidered when I offered to rewrite his role.*

reconstitute [ri 'kɑn stɪ tut] *tv.* to return something to its earlier condition. ♦ *Add water to this powder to reconstitute the milk.* ♦ *I reconstituted the juice by adding water to the concentrate.*

reconstituted [ri 'kɑn stɪ tut ɪd] *adj.* made whole or normal again, as with condensed or dried food that has been made edible or drinkable. ♦ *The restaurant served reconstituted orange juice.* ♦ *The cook used reconstituted milk in the cake batter.*

reconstruct [ri kən 'strʌkt] **1.** *tv.* to construct something again; to build something again. ♦ *The company reconstructed its headquarters after the fire.* ♦ *Many cities in Europe were reconstructed after the war.* **2.** *tv.* to make a description of someone or something when one has only a part of the facts or information. ♦ *The witness reconstructed the crime based on what she had seen.* ♦ *The artist reconstructed an image of the assailant based on my input.*

reconstructed [ri kən 'strʌk tɪd] **1.** *adj.* rebuilt; built again; constructed again. ♦ *The reconstructed village lacked the charm it had before the war.* ♦ *The reconstructed barn was sturdier than the old one.* **2.** *adj.* [of an event] given a description based on only part of the facts or information. ♦ *The reconstructed scene of the crime was sketched on a chalkboard.* ♦ *The reconstructed picture of the terrorist was hung in post offices.*

reconstruction [ri kən 'strʌk ʃən] **1.** *n.* the process of reconstructing something; designing or building something again to match the original. (No plural form in this sense.) ♦ *The detective's reconstruction of the crime required lots of research.* ♦ *The reconstruction of the bombed town took years.* **2.** *n.* something that has been rebuilt; something that been reconstructed. ♦ *The artist drew a reconstruction of the criminal's face based on my input.* ♦ *This building is a reconstruction of an older building.* **3. Reconstruction** *n.* the period of American history from 1865 to 1877, when the Southern states were brought back into the Union after the War Between the States. (No plural form in this sense.) ♦ *During Reconstruction, slavery was abolished.* ♦ *Andrew Johnson and Ulysses S. Grant were presidents during Reconstruction.*

record 1. ['rɛk ɚd] *n.* a written account of facts or information about someone or something. ♦ *The government kept detailed records on the terrorists.* ♦ *My doctor examined my medical records.* **2.** ['rɛk ɚd] *n.* a flat plastic disk that has sound recorded on it, which is played on a machine that makes the recorded sounds able to be heard. ♦ *Records have been mostly replaced by compact discs.* ♦ *The record sounds bad because there are so many scratches on it.* **3.** ['rɛk ɚd] *n.* the most extreme example of something; the highest, lowest, fastest, slowest, longest, shortest, or any other extreme example of something. ♦ *In baseball, Hank Aaron broke Babe Ruth's record of home runs.* ♦ *John tried to break the world record for the long jump.* **4.** [rɪ 'kord] *tv.* to write down information about someone or something so that other people will be about to read the information. ♦ *The scribe recorded the details of the kingdom's treaties.* ♦ *Anne recorded her innermost thoughts in her diary.* **5.** [rɪ 'kord] *tv.* to store sound on audiotape or to store images on film or videotape; to put a sound or an image into a permanent form. ♦ *I recorded my sister's wedding on videocassette.* ♦ *The police officer recorded the senator's acceptance of the bribe on tape.* **6. for the record** [...'rɛk ɚd] *idiom* so there will be ① of a particular fact. ♦ *I'd like to say, for the record, that at no time have I ever accepted a bribe from anyone.* ♦ *For the record, I've never been able to get anything done around city hall without bribing someone.*

recorded [rɪ 'kor dɪd] **1.** *adj.* written down; having information about someone or something written down; known. ♦ *The historian studied recorded statements from the Middle Ages.* ♦ *Language began long before recorded history.* **2.** *adj.* stored on cassette, film, or videotape; stored in a permanent form. ♦ *The lawyer played a recorded conversation for the jury.* ♦ *The station broadcast a previously recorded television show.*

recorder [rɪ 'kor dɚ] **1.** *n.* someone who writes down and stores information. ♦ *The recorder wrote down everything that happened at the meeting.* ♦ *Someone called the recorder of deeds keeps track of property ownership.* **2.** *n.* a musical instrument, consisting of a hollow tube of wood that has holes down one side. ♦ *When you blow air through a recorder, you make different notes by covering different holes with your fingers.* ♦ *John played a folk tune on his recorder.* **3.** *n.* a machine that records sounds or images, and usually is able to play the sounds and images back. ♦ *I connected the videocassette recorder to my TV.* ♦ *Sue brought a battery-operated tape recorder to the interview.*

recording [rɪ 'kor dɪŋ] *n.* a record; music, speech, or other sound that has been recorded. ♦ *The old recording sounded very scratchy.* ♦ *The lawyer played a recording of the testimony for the jury.*

recount 1. ['ri kaʊnt] *n.* another counting; a second count; another count, especially in an election when the votes are counted for a second time because the first count is thought to be faulty. ♦ *The recount narrowed the margin between the two candidates.* ♦ *The election's outcome was reversed as a result of the recount.* **2.** [ri 'kaʊnt] *tv.* to tell a story; to tell about something that happened. ♦ *The witness recounted what she had seen.* ♦ *John recounted his day at work to me.* **3.** ['ri 'kaʊnt] *tv.* to count something again. ♦ *Each day, I recounted the classroom's ceiling tiles because I was bored.* ♦ *I recounted the playing cards to make sure there were 52.*

recoup [rɪ 'kup] *tv.* to make up for one's losses; to get at least as much money for something as the amount that was spent for it; to regain something, especially a loss. ♦ *The gambler was unable to recoup his losses.* ♦ *The investor could not recoup the money she had spent on the stock.*

recourse ['ri kors] **1.** *n.* access to a person or thing from which one can obtain help or protection. (No plural form in this sense.) ♦ *Each student has recourse to the school library for additional material.* ♦ *Very few people had recourse to the powerful senator.* **2. last recourse** *n.* a last chance or possibility. (No plural form in this sense.) ♦ *Finally, the dying patient took folk remedies as a last recourse.* ♦ *Alternative treatments were the patient's last recourse.*

recover [ri 'kʌv ɚ] **1.** *iv.* to get better after a sickness or injury; to return to health. ♦ *After a long bout with pneumonia, Anne finally recovered.* ♦ *John was slow to recover from the car accident.* **2.** *tv.* to get something back that went away or was lost, stolen, or taken away. ♦ *The police recovered the car that the thief had stolen from me.* ♦ *Our team recovered the ball after it had been lost to the other team.* **3.** *tv.* to reclaim something; to extract something useful from something that is not useful. ♦ *The prospector recovered small flecks of gold from sea water.* ♦ *This process can recover valuable minerals from salt water.*

recovery [ri 'kʌv ə ri] **1.** *n.* the process of getting something back that went away or was lost, stolen, or taken; receiving someone or something that went away or was lost, stolen, or taken. (No plural form in this sense.) ♦ *The recovery of the stolen jewels required two private detectives.* ♦ *I thanked the police for the recovery of my stolen car.* **2.** *n.* the return to someone or something's regular condition, especially the return of one's health after sickness or injury or the return of a good economy after a period of recession or depression. (No plural form in this sense.) ♦ *The doctor said that the crash victim had no chance of recovery.* ♦ *Many people found jobs after the state's economic recovery.*

recreation [rɛk ri 'e ʃən] *n.* amusement; play; activities that are done for pleasure, enjoyment, or fun. (No plural form in this sense.) ♦ *For recreation, I like to go hiking and camping.* ♦ *I went on vacation for rest and recreation.*

recreational [rɛk ri 'e ʃə nəl] *adj.* of or about recreation. (Adv: *recreationally.*) ♦ *The city park provided many recreational activities.* ♦ *The hotel's recreational facilities included a pool.*

recruit [rɪ 'krut] **1.** *tv.* to cause or persuade someone to become a new member of a group, an organization, or the military. ♦ *The senior recruited freshmen to join the fraternity.* ♦ *The sergeant recruited college graduates to join the army.* **2.** *n.* someone who has just joined a group or organization; someone who has just enlisted for the military. ♦ *The new recruits' heads were shaved.* ♦ *New recruits for a fraternity are called pledges.*

rectal ['rɛk təl] *adj.* of, for, or about the rectum. (Adv: *rectally.*) ♦ *The patient's temperature was taken with a rectal thermometer.* ♦ *The rectal exam showed that John's prostate was swollen.*

rectangle ['rɛk tæŋ gəl] *n.* a flat, four-sided figure with four right angles, whose opposite sides are parallel and the same length. ♦ *A square is a rectangle whose four sides are all equal.* ♦ *My garage is in the shape of a rectangle.*

rectangular [rɛk 'tæŋ gjə lɚ] *adj.* shaped like a rectangle. (Adv: *rectangularly.*) ♦ *John lives in a rectangular apartment.* ♦ *Anne arranged the data in a rectangular chart.*

rectify ['rɛk tə fɑɪ] *tv.* to make something right; to correct something. ♦ *The store rectified its error by giving me the product for free.* ♦ *I rectified the situation by offering to pay for the damage.*

rectum ['rɛk təm] *n.* the end of the lower intestine, which human waste passes through from the colon to the anus. ♦ *The nurse placed a thermometer in the patient's rectum.* ♦ *The man with hemorrhoids bled from the rectum.*

recuperate [rɪ 'kup ə ret] *iv.* to return to health after a sickness or an accident. ♦ *Anne recuperated from her illness in the hospital.* ♦ *It took John one year to recuperate from the accident.*

recur [rɪ 'kɚ] *iv.* to repeat; to happen again; to continue to happen. ♦ *The doctor asked Sue how often her pains recur.* ♦ *The same dream recurred night after night.*

recurrent [rɪ 'kɚ ənt] *adj.* happening over and over; happening again and again; repeating. (Adv: *recurrently.*) ♦ *I told my therapist about my recurrent dreams.* ♦ *The director used recurrent themes in all of his movies.*

recurring [rɪ 'kɚ ɪŋ] *adj.* happening over and over; happening again and again; repeating. (Adv: *recurringly.*) ♦ *I have a recurring nightmare that I'm being chased by wolves.* ♦ *The programmer tried to eliminate the recurring problem.*

recycle [ri 'sɑɪk əl] **1.** *tv.* to change glass, plastic, paper, or other material into a form that can be used again; to recover a resource. ♦ *They are able to recycle old glass into new glass.* ♦ *The plant recycled old newspapers into a fiber that can be used for insulation.* **2.** *tv.* to separate reusable trash from waste and make it available for collection with the assumption that it will be made into something useful. ♦ *My family recycles newspaper and glass bottles.* ♦ *You should recycle your grocery bags.* **3.** *iv.* to separate [reusable trash] as in ②. ♦ *Because I care about the environment, I recycle.* ♦ *Do you recycle?*

recycled [ri 'sɑɪk əld] *adj.* reused; made from a substance that has already been used. ♦ *This manual was printed on* *recycled paper.* ♦ *The shampoo bottle is made of recycled plastic.*

recycling [ri 'saɪk lɪŋ] *n.* the process of making waste material available for reuse. (No plural form in this sense.) ♦ *The city examined different methods of recycling.* ♦ *Recycling is encouraged at my office building.*

red ['rɛd] **1.** *n.* the color of blood and the traffic signal that means stop. (No plural form in this sense.) ♦ *The members of the marching band were dressed in red and white.* ♦ *John painted the walls of his room a dark red.* **2.** *adj.* <the adj. use of ①.> (Adv: *redly.* Comp: *redder;* sup: *reddest.*) ♦ *Mary placed the red rose in a vase.* ♦ *The dancer wore a pair of red shoes.* **3.** *adj.* [of hair] copper colored or rusty orange. (Comp: *redder;* sup: *reddest.*) ♦ *Lisa has lovely red hair.* ♦ *Red hair is actually more of a rusty orange color.* **4. in the red** *idiom* in debt. (See also in the black at black.) ♦ *My accounts are in the red at the end of every month.* ♦ *It's easy to get into the red if you don't pay close attention to the amount of money you spend.* **5. out of the red** *idiom* out of debt. ♦ *This year our firm is likely to get out of the red before fall.* ♦ *If we can cut down on expenses, we can get out of the red fairly soon.*

redbird ['rɛd bɚd] *n.* any of various birds having red feathers. ♦ *The cardinal is a redbird.* ♦ *A redbird flew across the yard and into a tree.*

red-blooded ['rɛd 'blʊd ɪd] *adj.* full of energy; full of strength; virile. ♦ *The red-blooded football player won the game.* ♦ *The red-blooded firefighter saved the family of six.*

red carpet ['rɛd 'kɑr pət] **roll out the red carpet (for someone)** *idiom* to put on a great show of honor and respect for a visitor. ♦ *The red carpet was put out for the foreign dignitary.* ♦ *The city rolled out the red carpet for the visiting queen.*

redden ['rɛd n] **1.** *iv.* to become red; to turn red. ♦ *My cheeks reddened in the wind.* ♦ *The apple's skin reddened as it ripened.* **2.** *tv.* to cause someone or something to become red; to cause someone or something to turn red. ♦ *The sunlight reddened the green tomatoes.* ♦ *The rash reddened my skin.*

reddish ['rɛd ɪʃ] *adj.* having some of the qualities of the color red. (Adv: *reddishly.*) ♦ *At sunset, reddish streaks of sunlight stretched over the lake.* ♦ *Mary's skin was reddish because of the cold.*

redeem [rɪ 'dim] **1.** *tv.* to get something back through the settlement of a debt. ♦ *I redeemed the watch that I had pawned at the pawn shop.* ♦ *Mary redeemed the car's title when she paid off the car loan.* **2.** *tv.* to convert something to cash, especially a coupon, token, lottery ticket, or other thing that is not money but which represents money. ♦ *The grocer redeemed the coupons that the customers used.* ♦ *I redeemed the lottery ticket for the $1,500 prize.* **3.** *tv.* to do something that restores someone's good opinion of oneself. (Takes a reflexive object.) ♦ *Mary redeemed herself by doing what she promised to do.* ♦ *If you want to redeem yourself, you can apologize to me.*

redeeming [rɪ 'dim ɪŋ] *adj.* making up for other faults or problems. ♦ *My apartment's one redeeming feature is that it is soundproof.* ♦ *The redeeming value of the car was that it got good gas mileage.*

redemption [rɪ 'dɛmp ʃən] **1.** *n.* the recovery of something through the settlement of a debt. (No plural form in this sense.) ♦ *The redemption of the watch I pawned cost $100.* ♦ *I had to pay off all my parking fines to effect the redemption of my car.* **2.** *n.* getting the monetary value of something. (No plural form in this sense.) ♦ *The grocer mailed the coupons to the manufacturer for redemption.* ♦ *The redemption of the lottery ticket required me to pay taxes on what I won.*

redeploy [ri dɪ 'plɔɪ] *tv.* to rearrange the placement of equipment, soldiers, employees, or other people. ♦ *The firm redeployed its work force to better suit its needs.* ♦ *The police were redeployed to an area of civil unrest.*

redevelop [ri dɪ 'vɛl əp] **1.** *tv.* to develop something again. ♦ *John redeveloped his old interest in piano playing.* ♦ *Bill redeveloped the ability to walk after the accident.* **2.** *tv.* to build in an area again; to construct buildings in an area again. ♦ *Investors redeveloped the abandoned factories into new housing.* ♦ *The city council voted to redevelop the public parks.*

redhead ['rɛd hɛd] *n.* someone who has red hair. ♦ *David prefers to date redheads.* ♦ *The redhead bought clothes that wouldn't clash with his hair.*

red-hot ['rɛd 'hɑt] **1.** *adj.* very hot; so hot as to be red. ♦ *In the furnace, the metal rods were red-hot.* ♦ *The worker cooled the red-hot steel in a vat of cold water.* **2.** *adj.* very spicy; causing a burning sensation in one's mouth. (Figurative on ①.) ♦ *This chili is red-hot, so don't burn your mouth.* ♦ *The Korean restaurant prepared many red-hot dishes.*

redid ['ri 'dɪd] pt of redo.

redirect [ri dɪ 'rɛkt] *tv.* to direct or send someone or something to a different place; to send someone or something in a different direction. ♦ *The reporter redirected her gaze to a different camera.* ♦ *The soldier redirected the missile toward the south.*

red-letter ['rɛd 'lɛt ɚ] *adj.* very happy or memorable, especially referring to a very happy or memorable event or day. ♦ *For most students, graduation is a red-letter event.* ♦ *For Anne, her wedding was a red-letter day she'd never forget.*

redness ['rɛd nəs] *n.* being red; the condition of having the color red. (No plural form in this sense.) ♦ *The redness of my eyes was caused by all the smoke in the meeting room.* ♦ *The redness of a tomato is an indication of its ripeness.*

redo [ri 'du] *tv., irreg.* to do something again; to do something over. (Pt: redid; pp: redone.) ♦ *My editor asked me to redo my article.* ♦ *After I had redone the assignment, I handed it to my teacher.*

redone ['ri 'dʌn] pp of redo.

redouble [ri 'dʌb əl] **1.** *tv.* to double the amount of something; to increase the amount of something. ♦ *The gambler redoubled the bet after he won.* ♦ *The firefighters redoubled their efforts as the fire spread.* **2.** *iv.* to double; to increase. ♦ *Problems redoubled when the bills came in for the wedding.* ♦ *My work redoubled when my boss went on vacation.*

redress 1. ['ri drɛs, ri 'drɛs] *n.* something that is done to make up for something; amends; compensation. (No plural form in this sense.) ♦ *The injured passenger sued the bus company for redress.* ♦ *The slandered celebrity demanded redress.* **2.** [rɪ 'drɛs] *tv.* to compensate for something; to do something to make up for something; to make amends. ♦ *The store redressed Anne's injury by paying for her medical costs.* ♦ *The newspaper was fined to redress the model they had slandered.*

Red Sea ['rɛd 'si] See Gazetteer.

reduce [rɪ 'dus] **1.** *tv.* to make something smaller or less important; to decrease something. ♦ *The politician promised to reduce taxes.* ♦ *John reduced the amount of unhealthy food that he ate.* **2.** *iv.* to lose [weight]. ♦ *Mary reduced after the winter holidays.* ♦ *My doctor ordered me to reduce.* **3. reduced to something** *idiom* brought into a certain condition or state. ♦ *The grieving family was reduced to tears.* ♦ *The poor man was reduced to begging for food.*

reduction [rɪ 'dʌk ʃən] **1.** *n.* making something smaller; reducing something. (No plural form in this sense.) ♦ *Congress's reduction of the budget was a lengthy process.* ♦ *I resented the reduction in my hours at work.* **2.** *n.* the amount by which something is made smaller. ♦ *This coupon is good for a ten-dollar reduction in price.* ♦ *The budget was subject to a 20% reduction.*

redundancy [rɪ 'dʌn dən si] **1.** *n.* the quality of being extra or in duplication [of something else]. (No plural form in this sense.) ♦ *Redundancy is both wasteful and inefficient.* ♦ *The redundancy of having two refrigerators is very costly.* **2.** *n.* something that is redundant, not necessary, or does the same thing as another part. ♦ *The editor deleted the redundancies in the article.* ♦ *To say "cease and desist" is a redundancy.*

redundant [rɪ 'dʌn dənt] *adj.* extra; not needed; doing the same thing as something else; superfluous. (Adv: *redundantly.*) ♦ *The editor deleted the redundant phrases from my article.* ♦ *These two words are redundant. Cross one out.*

redwood ['rɛd wʊd] **1.** *n.* a tall evergreen tree found in the western United States that lives to be very old. ♦ *The environmentalists sought to protect the redwoods from logging.* ♦ *The eagle soared among the redwoods.* **2.** *n.* the wood of ①. (No plural form in this sense.) ♦ *Redwood is very expensive.* ♦ *Redwood is resistant to insects and rot.* **3.** *adj.* <the adj. use of ②.> ♦ *Our house has redwood siding.* ♦ *The redwood fence will last forever!*

reed ['rid] **1.** *n.* a tall grass-like plant with hollow stems that grows in marshes and other wet places. ♦ *The hound retrieved the wounded duck from the reeds near the marsh.* ♦ *The developer chopped down the reeds before draining the pond.* **2.** *n.* a thin piece of wood in the mouthpiece of woodwind instruments like clarinets, saxophones, and oboes or a similar metal piece in harmonicas, accordions, and pipe organs. ♦ *The reed vibrates when the player blows air over it, making the sound of the instrument.* ♦ *The sax player moistened the reed before playing.* **3.** *adj.* <the adj. use of ②.> ♦ *Saxophones, clarinets, oboes, and bassoons are reed instruments.* ♦ *All of the reed pipes in the organ had to be tuned frequently.*

reef ['rif] *n.* a ridge of rocks, sand, or coral that extends from the bottom of a sea or ocean to or almost to the surface of the water. ♦ *Oil was spilled when the tanker's hull was torn on the reef.* ♦ *The undersea diver watched the fish swim along the coral reef.*

reek ['rik] **1.** *iv.* to smell very bad. ♦ *The meeting room reeked of stale cigar smoke.* ♦ *You should clean your refrigerator. It reeks.* **2.** *iv.* to be full of something disgusting or offensive. (Figurative on ①.) ♦ *The movie reeked of vulgarity.* ♦ *Bob's jokes reeked of rudeness and thoughtlessness.* **3.** *n.* a very bad odor. (No plural form in this sense.) ♦ *Mary detected a horrible reek coming from her garage can.* ♦ *The dead squirrel under our porch made an awful reek.*

reel ['ril] **1.** *n.* a round frame around which string, thread, yarn, fishing line, film, audiotape, videotape, or other long materials are wound. ♦ *The projectionist changed the film reels.* ♦ *I couldn't catch the fish because the reel had jammed.* **2.** *iv.* to twist or turn, as when struck a by powerful blow. ♦ *The car stuck the man, and he reeled to the curb.* ♦ *I reeled after I was hit in the face.* **3. reel in** *tv.* + *prep. phr.* to pull something inward, toward oneself by using ①. ♦ *I reeled the 10-pound fish in.* ♦ *Mary reeled in the large perch.*

reelect [ri ə 'lɛkt] *tv.* to elect someone again. ♦ *Ronald Reagan was reelected in 1984 to a second term.* ♦ *The voters reelected the mayor by a wide margin.*

reelection [ri ə 'lɛk ʃən] *n.* the election of someone to the same position for another term. ♦ *The senator's bid for reelection was unsuccessful.* ♦ *The mayor's reelection to city hall surprised no one.*

reentry [ri 'ɛn tri] *n.* entering a place again, especially describing a rocket or spaceship returning to the atmosphere of the earth. (No plural form in this sense.) ♦ *A rocket gets very hot upon reentry.* ♦ *Reentry is impossible without your ticket stub.*

reestablish [ri əs 'tæb lɪʃ] *tv.* to establish something again. ♦ *The speaker reestablished the points made before the interruption.* ♦ *Our school reestablished its annual bake sale after a two-year break.*

refer [rɪ 'fɚ] **1. refer to** *iv.* + *prep. phr.* to use something for help or information; to go to someone or something for help or information. ♦ *The secretary referred to the dictionary for the word's correct spelling.* ♦ *Anne referred to the computer manual for help.* **2. refer to** *iv.* + *prep. phr.* to have to do with something; to apply to something; to be related to something; to concern something. ♦ *My father's dying words referred to my brother, not me.* ♦ *The speaker referred to an experiment I had conducted last year.* **3. refer to** *tv.* + *prep. phr.* to direct someone to use something for help or information; to direct someone to go to someone or something for help or information. ♦ *The medical doctor referred me to a heart specialist.* ♦ *The guard referred the tourist to the museum's information desk.*

referee [rɛf ə 'ri] **1.** *n.* someone who judges the playing of sporting events; an umpire. ♦ *The referee declared that Robert had won the boxing match.* ♦ *The basketball referee blew his whistle.* **2.** *tv.* to judge the playing of a sporting event. ♦ *John refereed the boxing match.* ♦ *The game was refereed by a complete incompetent, in my opinion.* **3.** *iv.* to serve as ①. ♦ *I volunteered to referee for the high-school basketball games.* ♦ *My sister was a referee for the basketball team.*

reference ['rɛf rəns] **1.** *n.* words that refer to something else; something that has to do with something else; something that relates to something else. ♦ *John's comment was a reference to my eating habits.* ♦ *The movie made many references to current political events.* **2.** *n.* something that is used for help or information; someone or something that provides information about something. ♦ *I used the encyclopedia as a reference about the Civil War.* ♦ *The travel guide was a useful reference when I was in Europe.* **3.** *n.* a statement that someone writes about someone else for that other person's use when applying for something; a statement about someone or someone's character. ♦ *My former employer provided me with a glowing reference.* ♦ *The interviewer said that my references were full of praise.* **4.** *n.* someone who gives a statement about someone or someone's character. ♦ *Some of my references have since moved away or died.* ♦ *The applicant submitted a list of references.*

referenda [rɛf ə 'rɛn də] a pl of referendum.

referendum [rɛf ə 'rɛn dəm] *n.* a direct vote by the voters of an area about a specific issue; an issue to be determined directly by the voters. (Pl: *referendums* or referenda.) ♦ *The voters' referendum was voided by the Supreme Court.* ♦ *There's a referendum on the ballot to ban the sale of liquor here.*

referral [rɪ 'fɚ əl] **1.** *n.* mention. (No plural form in this sense.) ♦ *His constant referral to flying planes confused me.* ♦ *Referrals to death and dying always bother me.* **2.** *n.* a suggestion that a patient consult with another doctor or dentist. ♦ *I made an appointment with Dr. Jones based on Dr. Park's referral.* ♦ *I need a referral for a skin specialist.* **3.** *n.* a record of ②. ♦ *The patient lost the referral on the way to the doctor.* ♦ *I will need a copy of your referral before the doctor can see you.*

refill 1. [rɪ 'fɪl] *iv.* to fill again; to become full again. ♦ *After I drained it once, the sink refilled with water.* ♦ *The pond refilled naturally after the drought ended.* **2.** [rɪ 'fɪl] *tv.* to fill something again; to provide what is requested or needed. ♦ *The pharmacist refilled my prescription.* ♦ *The waiter refilled my cup with coffee.* **3.** ['ri fɪl] *n.* an amount of something that is used to refill a container. ♦ *The restaurant charges nothing for refills of coffee.* ♦ *Refills of pop are fifty cents apiece.* **4.** ['ri fɪl] *n.* an additional set of doses of medicine, as prescribed by a doctor. ♦ *I took the prescription to the pharmacy for a refill.* ♦ *The prescription allowed for four refills.*

refine [rɪ 'fɑɪn] **1.** *tv.* to make something purer; to remove impure substances from something. ♦ *The oil needed to be refined before it could be used.* ♦ *The factory refined sugar.* **2.** *tv.* to make something more detailed, rational, and effective. ♦ *The factory refined its hiring process.* ♦ *The author refined the manuscript.*

refined [rɪ 'fɑɪnd] **1.** *adj.* made purer; pure; having impure substances removed. ♦ *The recipe required refined sugar.* ♦ *Refined oil is used to make numerous products.* **2.** *adj.* elegant; cultured; cultivated; very proper. (Adv: *refinedly.*) ♦ *The very refined gentleman opened the door for me.* ♦ *The refined young lady curtsied before the queen.*

refinement [rɪ 'fɑɪn mənt] **1.** *n.* making someone or something refined. (No plural form in this sense.) ♦ *The young man's refinement was quite a challenge.* ♦ *The etiquette teacher's refinement of the wild students was amazing.* **2.** *n.* the appearance of being refined and cultivated. (No plural form in this sense.) ♦ *The hotel lobby's classical design was an example of elegant refinement.* ♦ *The gentleman's refinement was impressive.* **3.** *n.* an improvement; a better or more pure form of something. ♦ *The firm patented a refinement in its manufacturing process.* ♦ *The inventor made refinements to his design before patenting it.*

refinery [rɪ 'fɑɪn ə ri] *n.* a factory where substances, especially oil, sugar, or metal, are refined or purified. ♦ *Oil was piped to the refinery from the well.* ♦ *A new sugar refinery was built on the tropical island.*

refinish [ri 'fɪn ɪʃ] *tv.* to remove an old paint or varnish finish and apply a new one. ♦ *Jane refinished an antique desk that she had bought.* ♦ *John plans to refinish the woodwork around the windows.*

reflect [rɪ 'flɛkt] **1.** *tv.* to show an image in the manner of a mirror. ♦ *The mirror reflected my image.* ♦ *John's actions behind me were reflected in the mirror.* **2.** *tv.* to throw back heat, light, sound, or energy; to bounce back heat, light, sound, or energy. ♦ *The car's bumper reflected sunlight into my face.* ♦ *Acoustic panels reflected the music toward the audience.* **3.** *tv.* [for something] to show or reveal a personal characteristic of someone. ♦ *This book reflects the author's imagination.* ♦ *John's angry temper reflects his attitude.* **4. reflect on** *iv.* + *prep. phr.* to think deeply or carefully; to ponder; to examine one's thoughts. ♦ *Let me reflect on your idea for a while.* ♦ *My father reflected on my problem before giving me advice.* **5. reflect off** *iv.* + *prep. phr.* to be reflected ② away from something; [for light] to bounce off something. ♦ *The sunlight reflected off the water.* ♦ *The car lights reflected off the windows of the house.*

reflection [rɪ 'flɛk ʃən] **1.** *n.* a reflected glare; reflected light. ♦ *The sun's reflection off the windshield hurt my eyes.* ♦ *The shimmering reflection of the light off the snow was blinding.* **2.** *n.* something, especially an image, that is reflected. ♦ *I saw my reflection on the surface of the water.* ♦ *The reflection of my face in the mirror startled me.* **3.** *n.* something that is revealed about someone's character. (No plural form in this sense.) ♦ *Your tone of voice is a reflection of your attitude.* ♦ *His actions are a reflection of his anger and frustration.* **4.** *n.* deep thought; careful thought. (No plural form in this sense.) ♦ *The mayor was lost in reflection over the day's activities.* ♦ *Upon reflection of my action, I knew that I should apologize.*

reflector [rɪ 'flɛk tɚ] *n.* something that reflects light, especially when used in relation to vehicles. ♦ *The car's headlight lighted up the reflectors on my bike.* ♦ *Reflectors made the center of the road visible at night.*

reflex ['ri flɛks] **reflexes** *n.* movements of the body in response to an external stimulation. ♦ *The doctor tested my reflexes by tapping my knee with a mallet.* ♦ *My reflexes were okay, but my knee is bruised.*

reflexive [rɪ 'flɛks ɪv] **1. reflexive (pronoun)** *n.* <a form used as an object of a verb or preposition that is identical to the subject.> (Reflexive pronouns are myself, ourselves, yourself, yourselves, herself, himself, itself, themselves, oneself.) ♦ *I gave myself some medication for my headache.* ♦ *You must get yourself to work on time.* **2. reflexive (verb)** *n.* a verb or verb construction that uses ①. (Some verbs *must* have a reflexive object; others *can* have a reflexive object.) ♦ *"Please learn to behave yourself" contains a reflexive verb.* ♦ *"You need to compose yourself before answering the question" has a reflexive verb.*

reforest [ri 'for əst] *tv.* to cause an area that used to have trees to have trees again by planting them. ♦ *The rangers* *reforested the park after the fire.* ♦ *A government agency reforested the hillside.*

reform [ri 'form] **1.** *tv.* to change someone or something for the better; to make someone or something better; to improve someone or something. ♦ *The senator tried to reform the tax laws.* ♦ *Mary gave up trying to reform John.* **2.** *iv.* to improve; to become better; to change for the better. ♦ *The criminal reformed and became a productive member of society.* ♦ *The economy improved, and everyone stopped complaining.* **3.** *n.* a planned improvement; a change that eliminates past flaws or errors. ♦ *The government is in great need of reform.* ♦ *The reform lasted for only a few years. Then things became as bad as they ever were.*

reformation [rɛf ɚ 'me ʃən] **1.** *n.* the changing of something for the better. (No plural form in this sense.) ♦ *Reformation of the tax law failed in Congress.* ♦ *The citizens demanded reformation of the inept school system.* **2. Reformation** *n.* a period of European history in the 1500s when people tried to reform the Roman Catholic Church and started Protestant churches. (No plural form in this sense.) ♦ *Martin Luther was one of the leaders of the Reformation.* ♦ *During the Reformation, France and Italy remained mostly Catholic.*

reformatory [rɪ 'for mə tor i] *n.* a school or institution for children and teenagers who break the law but who are not sent to jail. ♦ *The shoplifter was sent to a reformatory.* ♦ *Maintaining discipline is of the utmost importance at a reformatory.*

reformer [ri 'for mɚ] *n.* someone who reforms and improves things or people. ♦ *Reformers are always trying to improve someone or something.* ♦ *The reformers brought about changes to the welfare system.*

refrain [rɪ 'fren] **1.** *n.* the part of a song that is sung after each verse; the chorus of a song. ♦ *The choir sang the song's refrain.* ♦ *At the end of the song, the refrain was repeated twice.* **2. refrain from** *iv.* + *prep. phr.* not to do something; to keep from doing something; to abstain from doing something. ♦ *Please refrain from smoking on the subway.* ♦ *The audience refrained from talking during the play.*

refresh [rɪ 'frɛʃ] **1.** *tv.* to make someone feel better or fresher. ♦ *Anne refreshed herself by splashing cold water on her face.* ♦ *The light meal refreshed the guests.* **2.** *tv.* to bring something into memory; to restore something to someone's memory. ♦ *Please refresh my memory on this point.* ♦ *Anne refreshed her knowledge of the material an hour before the test.*

refreshed [rɪ 'frɛʃt] *adj.* made to feel fresh again; made to feel better because of food, drink, sleep, or some activity. ♦ *The hot shower made me feel refreshed.* ♦ *After a good night's sleep, the refreshed travelers were ready to explore the city.*

refreshing [rɪ 'frɛʃ ɪŋ] *adj.* invigorating; reviving; new and stimulating. (Adv: *refreshingly.*) ♦ *After work, Jane took a long, refreshing shower.* ♦ *I had a refreshing conversation with my friends at work.*

refreshment [rɪ 'frɛʃ mənt] **1.** *n.* the process of making someone or something fresh; renewing someone or something. (No plural form in this sense.) ♦ *After a long, hot day, refreshment would be very welcome.* ♦ *Rest and refreshment will restore my energy.* **2.** *n.* **refreshments** food or drink that satisfies one's thirst or hunger. ♦ *Refreshments were served at the party.* ♦ *After the conference, I had some refreshments in the lobby.*

refrigerate [rɪ 'frɪdʒ ə ret] *tv.* to put something in a refrigerator; to keep something cold. ♦ *I refrigerated the leftovers after supper.* ♦ *John refrigerated the wine before serving it.*

refrigerator [rɪ 'frɪdʒ ə ret ɚ] *n.* an appliance into which food is placed to keep it cold. ♦ *I put the jar of pickles in the refrigerator.* ♦ *There's a special compartment in my refrigerator for eggs.*

refuel [ri 'fjul] **1.** *tv.* to put more fuel in something. ♦ *The plane was refueled shortly after it landed.* ♦ *Bob refueled the motorboat at the dock.* **2.** *iv.* to acquire more fuel; to get more fuel in the middle of a trip. ♦ *We refueled in the middle of Illinois.* ♦ *My flight to Australia refueled in Hawaii.*

refuge ['rɛf judʒ] *n.* shelter or protection from danger or trouble. ♦ *The soldiers took refuge in a cave.* ♦ *I took refuge from the storm inside a café.*

refugee [rɛf ju 'dʒi] *n.* one who flees one's homeland because of persecution, war, famine, or other reasons. ♦ *Thousands of refugees fled the warring country.* ♦ *The refugee wanted to emigrate to America.*

refund 1. ['ri fənd] *n.* the money that is given back when someone returns a product to a store. ♦ *John got a five-cent refund for returning his empty bottle.* ♦ *Mary took the gift to the store for a refund.* **2.** [rɪ 'fʌnd] *tv.* to give someone money back when a product is returned. ♦ *The store refunded $10 to Jane for the belt.* ♦ *The store refunded the money by check.*

refurbish [ri 'fɚ bɪʃ] *tv.* to fix something up; to polish something; to make something look bright or new; to restore something. ♦ *The young couple refurbished the old house.* ♦ *David refurbished his old car.*

refurbished [ri 'fɚ bɪʃt] *adj.* fixed up; polished; made to look bright or new again; restored. ♦ *I moved into a refurbished apartment.* ♦ *The collector locked the refurbished antique guns in a cabinet.*

refusal [rɪ 'fjuz əl] **1.** *n.* refusing something; saying no. (No plural form in this sense.) ♦ *When I asked for more, refusal was their only response.* ♦ *Refusal without any explanation simply made the protesters angry.* **2.** *n.* an act of ①. ♦ *My company's refusal to give me a raise angered me.* ♦ *Jimmy's refusal to do his chores resulted in a punishment.*

refuse 1. [rɪ 'fjuz] *tv.* not to accept something; to reject something. ♦ *The dog refused the bone I gave to it.* ♦ *The union refused the contract that management offered.* **2.** [rɪ 'fjuz] *tv.* to deny someone something; not to allow someone to have something. ♦ *I must refuse you your request.* ♦ *The company refused John his annual raise.* **3. refuse to** [rɪ 'fjuz...] *iv.* + *inf.* to decline to do something. ♦ *Anne refuses to get married before she is 25.* ♦ *The clerk refused to help the obnoxious customer.* **4.** [rɪ 'fjuz] *iv.* not to accept; to say no; to reject. ♦ *I asked David to help me, but he refused.* ♦ *John asked Anne to marry him, but she refused.* **5.** ['rɛf jus] *n.* garbage; trash; things that are thrown away. (No plural form in this sense.) ♦ *The busboy threw the refuse in the garbage.* ♦ *The sidewalks were littered with refuse.*

refute [rɪ 'fjut] *tv.* to disprove something; to prove that something is false or wrong. ♦ *The student boldly refuted the professor's claims.* ♦ *The newspaper refuted the results of the experiment.*

regain [rɪ 'gen] *tv.* to get something back; to recover something; to win something back. ♦ *John slowly regained his strength after the accident.* ♦ *Finally, Mary had regained her trust in me.*

regal ['ri gəl] **1.** *adj.* royal. (Adv: *regally.*) ♦ *The queen was crowned in a regal ceremony.* ♦ *The duke was invited to a regal dinner at the castle.* **2.** *adj.* refined; cultured. (Adv: *regally.*) ♦ *David wore a tuxedo to the regal banquet.* ♦ *There was a solemn, regal atmosphere at the dinner party.*

regale [rɪ 'gel] **regale with** *tv.* + *prep. phr.* to provide someone with amusement, entertainment, food, drink, stories, song, etc. ♦ *The entertainer regaled the audience with a funny routine.* ♦ *Tom regaled us with food and drink and then showed us his art collection.*

regard [rɪ 'gɑrd] **1.** *tv.* to think of someone or something in a certain way. ♦ *Mary regards her job as a way to pay her bills.* ♦ *John regards his neighbor as a thoughtless person.* **2.** *tv.* to respect someone. ♦ *The governor was well regarded throughout the state.* ♦ *The celebrity was regarded for her work with troubled young people.* **3.** *tv.* to notice someone or something. ♦ *The troops regarded the general attentively.* ♦ *The students barely regarded the teacher's presence.* **4.** *n.* respect; esteem. (No plural form in this sense.) ♦ *I have high regard for my boss.* ♦ *Mary's regard for her parents was immense.* **5.** *n.* thought; attention; consideration. (No plural form in this sense.) ♦ *David has shown an inadequate regard for details.* ♦ *The author gave much regard to his writing.* **6. with regard to someone or something** *idiom* concerning someone or something. ♦ *What shall we do with regard to planning dinner?* ♦ *With regard to Bill, I think he is working too hard.*

regardless [rɪ 'gɑrd ləs] **regardless of something** *phr.* without considering something; at any rate; whatever is done; whatever option is chosen. ♦ *Regardless of what you say, I'm still going to the club tonight.* ♦ *I still have to pay the bill, regardless of the facts.*

regenerate [rɪ 'dʒɛn ə ret] **1.** *tv.* to grow something again; to grow a part of the body again, especially after it has been removed or injured. ♦ *The starfish regenerated a new arm.* ♦ *The lobster regenerated the claw that had snapped off.* **2.** *iv.* [for a part of the body] to grow again. ♦ *The lizard's tail regenerated slowly.* ♦ *Both halves of the starfish regenerated.*

regent ['ri dʒənt] **1.** *n.* someone who rules an empire or kingdom when the reigning king or queen cannot rule. ♦ *Until the king turned 18, the empire was ruled by a regent.* ♦ *The prisoner appealed to the regent for clemency.* **2.** *n.* a member of certain boards of directors or governors, such as in a university. ♦ *The examination was administered by the board of regents.* ♦ *The regents were given the responsibility of raising $1,000,000.*

regime [rə 'ʒim] **1.** *n.* a group of people in control of a government; the government that is in power. ♦ *The cruel regime brutally repressed the people.* ♦ *The Nixon regime lasted from 1969 to 1974.* **2.** *n.* a regimen; the things that one does every day; a routine. ♦ *Anne follows the same regime daily, except for Sunday.* ♦ *An hour of exercise is part of Jane's daily regime.*

regimen ['rɛdʒ ə mən] *n.* a routine or one's habits that one does every day, especially to improve or keep one's health. ♦ *As part of his regimen, David ran a mile every day.* ♦ *Fatty foods were not in John's regimen.*

regiment 1. ['rɛdʒ ə mənt] *n.* a group of soldiers that function on land. ♦ *The soldier fought with the fifth regiment.* ♦ *The private's regiment was sent to the front lines.* **2.** ['rɛdʒ ə mənt] *n.* a large number of things or people. (Figurative on ①.) ♦ *A regiment of angry citizens marched into see the mayor.* ♦ *Our picnic was surrounded by a regiment of ants.* **3.** ['rɛdʒ ə mɛnt] *tv.* to treat someone strictly; to control someone. ♦ *The nutritionist regimented my diet.* ♦ *My personal trainer regimented my exercise program.*

region ['ri dʒən] **1.** *n.* an area of land that has a common social, cultural, economic, political, or natural feature; sometimes a political division of a country. ♦ *The nomads traveled throughout the desert region.* ♦ *Anne grew up in the Southern California region.* **2.** *n.* a part; an area that has a common feature throughout it. ♦ *Mary rubbed the muscles in the region of my back.* ♦ *There's a region of pain around my ankle joints.*

regional ['ridʒ ə nəl] *adj.* of or about a **region.** (Adv: *regionally.*) ♦ *The school's football team won the regional championship.* ♦ *I watched the regional weather forecast on the news.*

register ['rɛdʒ ɪ stɚ] **1.** *n.* a cash register; a machine in a store that cashiers use to keep track of money taken in or paid out. ♦ *The clerk gave me change from the register.* ♦ *The cashier couldn't open the register unless I made a purchase.* **2.** *n.* the book that a list or record of something is kept in. ♦ *The guests signed their name in the register.* ♦ *According to the register, John was in the office until 10:00.* **3. (heat) register** *n.* a small opening in a wall or floor that has a special cover that controls how much air or heat enters a room. ♦ *Anne moved the box off the register because it was blocking the heat.* ♦ *The room was getting rather warm, so I closed the heat register.* **4.** *n.* the range of a person's voice or of an instrument; the highest and lowest tone and all the tones in between that a human or an instrument can produce. ♦ *A female with a high singing register is called a soprano.* ♦ *A trombone's register is lower than a trumpet's.* **5.** *n.* a style of language that corresponds to social class or a range of formality. ♦ *The lawyer's documents were written in a very formal register.* ♦ *The linguist studied informal registers of speech.* **6.** *tv.* to write something down on a list or in a record; to record something; to sign up for something. ♦ *I registered my name in a raffle.* ♦ *John registered his car with the Department of Motor Vehicles.* **7.** *tv.* to show something such as a feeling or an attitude; to express something. ♦ *David registered dismay when he didn't get the promotion.* ♦ *John registered surprise when I remembered his birthday.* **8.** *tv.* [for a bride or her representative] to place or have placed the bride's name on a list at a certain store so that people who want to buy her a wedding gift can find out what is wanted. ♦ *At which department store did they register Mary?* ♦ *The matron of honor registered the bride at the fancy store.* **9.** *iv.* to put one's name and perhaps other information on an official list. ♦ *Dave registered for the draft many years ago.* ♦ *Mary registered to vote.*

registered ['rɛdʒ ɪ stɚd] *adj.* approved by the government; certified. ♦ *The registered nurse took my temperature.* ♦ *Only registered voters can participate in elections.*

registrar ['rɛdʒ ɪ strɑr] *n.* someone who keeps official records, especially at a school, college, or university. ♦ *When I moved, I gave the registrar my new address.* ♦ *I requested my transcripts from the registrar.*

registration [rɛdʒ ɪ 'stre ʃən] **1.** *n.* the process of registering; the condition of being registered. (No plural form in this sense.) ♦ *The registration of my car with the state required a fee.* ♦ *You need two pieces of identification for voter registration.* **2.** *n.* the time when people choose and reserve classes at a school, college, or university. (No plural form in this sense.) ♦ *Registration takes place the week before classes start.* ♦ *At registration, I got all of the classes I wanted.*

registry ['rɛdʒ ɪ stri] **1.** *n.* a book or place where records, lists, or registers are kept. ♦ *All of the baptisms were listed in the church registry.* ♦ *I have to go downtown to the registry to get a copy of my marriage license.* **2. (bridal) registry** *n.* a place where brides register their gift preferences. ♦ *I checked the registry to see if the bride needed a toaster.* ♦ *Mary was not listed in the store's bridal registry.*

regress [rɪ 'grɛs] *iv.* to go back to an earlier condition or stage of development. ♦ *When John is with his friends, he regresses into the behavior of a teenager.* ♦ *The dog was housebroken but seems to be regressing recently.*

regressive [rɪ 'grɛs ɪv] *adj.* going back to an earlier condition or stage of development. (Adv: *regressively.*) ♦ *The dog has a regressive tendency to forget it is housebroken.* ♦ *After a few regressive periods of severe pain, John began to recover from his surgery quickly.*

regret [rɪ 'grɛt] **1.** *n.* sorrow; the feeling of being sad or sorry about something. (No plural form in this sense.) ♦ *I felt deep regret for insulting David.* ♦ *Overcome with regret, he sat and sobbed.* **2.** *n.* something that one is sorry about; something that causes sorrow. ♦ *I have a few regrets, but there has been a lot of happiness in my life also.* ♦ *The dying man's only regret was that he'd never flown in a plane.* **3.** *tv.* to feel sad or sorry about doing something; to feel ① about doing something. ♦ *Anne regretted having told me John's secret.* ♦ *David regretted ruining his diet by eating all of the potato chips.*

regretful [rɪ 'grɛt fəl] *adj.* full of regret; feeling sad or sorry about something. (Adv: *regretfully.*) ♦ *I am regretful that you can't stay longer.* ♦ *The regretful student had failed to turn his homework in on time.*

regroup [rɪ 'grup] **1.** *iv.* to group together again; to form a group again; to get back together. ♦ *The famous band never regrouped after one of its members died.* ♦ *The football players regrouped for the huddle.* **2.** *tv.* to cause people or things to group together again; to cause people or things to form a group. ♦ *I regrouped the cards back into their piles after I examined them.* ♦ *We regrouped the vegetables into different portions that were more equal than the previous distribution.*

regular ['rɛg jə lɚ] **1.** *adj.* usual; normal; traditional; customary. (Adv: *regularly.*) ♦ *Shaking hands is a regular practice in this country.* ♦ *On a regular day, I work from 9 to 5.* **2.** *adj.* not large or small; medium; average. ♦ *I ordered a regular cola with my hamburger, not a large one.* ♦ *Do you have these shirts in regular sizes?* **3.** *adj.* not changing; even in size, shape, or speed; uniform. (Adv: *regularly.*) ♦ *The line I drew was not very regular because I was giggling.* ♦ *Each machine-made object was perfectly regular.* **4.** *adj.* following the usual pattern, especially concerning verb forms. (Adv: *regularly.*) ♦ To touch *is a regular verb in English.* ♦ *The word* tree *is regular, meaning that its plural ends in* -s. **5.** *n.* a customer who makes purchases at a place regularly. ♦ *Since I am a regular, I can get credit at the grocery store.* ♦ *The clerk knew all of the regulars' names.*

regularity [rɛg jə 'lɛr ə ti] *n.* the quality of being regular. (No plural form in this sense.) ♦ *David exercises with great regularity.* ♦ *Regularity in my studies and writing will make me a better scholar.*

regulate ['rɛg jə let] **1.** *tv.* to control someone or something by a rule or system; to limit someone or something by a rule or system. ♦ *The utility company was regulated by the state government.* ♦ *The city council regulates the money that the city spends.* **2.** *tv.* to fix or adjust something so that it will work at a certain level or standard. ♦ *The blinds regulate the amount of light coming into the room.* ♦ *The temperature of the greenhouse was regulated by computer.*

regulated ['rɛg jə let ɪd] *adj.* controlled or limited by a rule or system; controlled so that a certain level or standard is kept. ♦ *Air travel was a regulated industry until the 1980s.* ♦ *The regulated utility companies operate without competition.*

regulation [rɛg jə 'le ʃən] **1.** *n.* the control or order caused by rules, laws, principles, or systems. (No plural form in this sense.) ♦ *The police force maintained the regulation of traffic rules.* ♦ *The regulation of the airline industry was dismantled in the 1980s.* **2.** *n.* a rule; a law; an official principle that regulates someone or something. ♦ *The factory was fined for violating environmental regulations.* ♦ *The city's regulations forbid smoking inside public buildings.* **3.** *adj.* according to a rule, law, system, or standard; suitable according to a rule, law, system, or standard; standard. ♦ *All employees must wear regulation uniforms at work.* ♦ *The batter was fined for not using a regulation bat.*

regurgitate [rɪ 'gɚdʒ ə tet] **1.** *tv.* to bring up swallowed food from the stomach into the mouth; to vomit something. ♦ *The bird regurgitated the worm for the baby birds.* ♦ *John regurgitated his dinner after riding the roller coaster.* **2.** *iv.* to bring food from the stomach into the mouth; to vomit. (Often a euphemism for **vomit**.) ♦ *The horrible smell made me regurgitate.* ♦ *I nearly regurgitated when I saw the gory pictures.*

rehabilitate [ri hə 'bɪl ɪ tet] **1.** *tv.* to help someone whose body or mind is disabled or injured to return to a normal life. ♦ *The physical therapist rehabilitated David after his accident.* ♦ *The psychologist rehabilitated Anne without the use of drugs.* **2.** *tv.* to prepare a prisoner to have a normal life upon release. ♦ *The warden stated that some prisoners could not be rehabilitated.* ♦ *The social worker helped rehabilitate the hardened criminals.* **3.** *tv.* to renovate something; to restore something to its original condition. ♦ *The young couple bought an old house and rehabilitated it.* ♦ *David rehabilitated his car, and then he sold it.*

rehabilitated [ri hə 'bɪl ɪ tet ɪd] **1.** *adj.* trained or prepared to return to a normal life when one is disabled or has been injured or put in prison. ♦ *The rehabilitated veteran had learned to walk again.* ♦ *The rehabilitated felon became a productive member of society.* **2.** *adj.* renovated; restored. ♦ *Anne rented her rehabilitated basement apartment to students.* ♦ *Many rehabilitated antique cars were driven in the parade.*

rehabilitation [ri hə bɪl ɪ 'te ʃən] *n.* the process of restoring someone or something to its original, proper, or natural state. (No plural form in this sense.) ♦ *When rehabilitation of the criminal failed, he was returned to prison.* ♦ *The rehabilitation of the apartment required a lot of labor.*

rehash [ri 'hæʃ] **1.** *tv.* to discuss something that has already been discussed sufficiently. ♦ *Bill rehashed the gossip even though we'd all heard it.* ♦ *While debating, Anne rehashed the same arguments over and over.* **2.** *n.* a discussion of something that has been sufficiently discussed before; old ideas that have been put together in a new way without any improvement. ♦ *Her theory is just a rehash of Dr. Smith's theory.* ♦ *The rehash of Dave's arguments didn't cause me to change my mind.*

rehearsal [rɪ 'hɚs əl] **1.** *n.* a practice performance of a play, opera, concert, etc., devoted to perfecting the final performance. ♦ *The director expected the actors to be on time for rehearsals.* ♦ *We need a few more rehearsals before the play is ready to open.* **2. in rehearsal** *phr.* a stage of development in the production of a play, opera, or concert, involving many rehearsals ①. ♦ *The play is in rehearsal now and will open next month.* ♦ *While the opera was still in rehearsal, the star developed a hatred for the director.* **3.** *adj.* <the adj. use of ①.> ♦ *The shoddy production needed more rehearsal time.* ♦ *The actors wore rehearsal clothing until the costumes were made.*

rehearse [rɪ 'hɚs] **1.** *tv.* to practice a part in a play, concert, dance, or performance before performing it for the public. ♦ *The choir rehearsed the songs for weeks before the recital.* ♦ *The actor rehearsed his monologue before his audition.* **2.** *tv.* to order, direct, or lead performers in a rehearsal. ♦ *The director rehearsed the actors for six weeks.* ♦ *The conductor rehearsed the orchestra during the day.* **3.** *iv.* to practice [a role, musical instrument, play, piece of music, etc.]. ♦ *The choir rehearsed for weeks before the recital.* ♦ *The actors rehearsed for a month before the show was performed.*

reheat [ri 'hit] **1.** *tv.* to heat something again; to make something warm again. ♦ *I reheated the soup because it had gotten cold.* ♦ *The cook reheated the beans on the stove.* **2.** *iv.* [for something] to be made hot again. ♦ *The beans are reheating now and will be ready soon.* ♦ *When the leftover stew has reheated, I will serve it.*

reign ['ren] **1.** *iv.* to rule, especially as king, queen, emperor, or empress. ♦ *Queen Victoria reigned from 1837 to 1901.* ♦ *The monarch reigned during a time of peace.* **2.** *iv.* to be the current winner of a contest or holder of a title. ♦ *The winner of the beauty pageant reigns for a year.* ♦ *Tom reigned as the college chess champion for two years.* **3.** *iv.* to exist throughout a place; to be throughout a place. (Figurative on ①.) ♦ *Confusion reigned in the unorganized office.* ♦ *Peace reigned throughout the fortunate land.* **4.** *n.* the period of the rule of a king, queen, emperor, empress, as in ①; the winner of a contest or holder of a title, as in ②. ♦ *During the reign of King George III, the American colonies declared independence.* ♦ *Anne's reign as tennis champ ended when Mary defeated her.* **5.** *n.* domination by an abstract quality during a period of time. (Figurative on ④.) ♦ *Thousands of citizens were killed during the reign of terror.* ♦ *During the reign of confusion, the treasurer embezzled thousands of dollars.*

reigning ['ren ɪŋ] **1.** *adj.* ruling; in charge as a king, queen, emperor, or empress. ♦ *During World War I, the reigning British king was George V.* ♦ *The reigning monarch abdicated the throne to become a musician.* **2.** *adj.* being the current winner of a contest; being a champion. ♦ *The boxer unsuccessfully fought against the reigning champion.* ♦ *The reigning Miss America made many media appearances.*

reimburse [ri ɪm 'bɚs] **1.** *tv.* to pay someone back money. ♦ *I reimbursed John for the $25 I had borrowed.* ♦ *The treasurer reimbursed the officer for her travel expenses.* **2.** *tv.* to pay back money to someone. ♦ *When I was paid, I reimbursed $25 to John.* ♦ *The treasurer reimbursed the money I spent on the business trip.*

reimbursement [ri ɪm 'bɚs mənt] **1.** *n.* refunding money to someone; a repayment. (No plural form in this sense.) ♦ *For reimbursement, you'll have to fill out an expense report.* ♦ *I appreciated Bob's reimbursement of the money he owed me.* **2.** *n.* the money that is paid back, refunded, or reimbursed to someone. ♦ *I deposited the reimbursement in my bank account.* ♦ *The treasurer paid the reimbursement by check.*

rein ['ren] **1.** *n.* one of a pair of long straps attached to either side of the bridle of a horse, mule, donkey, etc. (Used to control the direction of movement of the animal.) ♦ *The jockey tightened the horse's reins.* ♦ *I pulled on the reins, and the horse stopped.* **2. keep a tight rein on someone or something; keep a close rein on someone or something** *idiom* to watch and control someone or something diligently. (On ①.) ♦ *The office manager kept a tight rein on the staff.* ♦ *Mary keeps a close rein on her children.*

reincarnation [ri ɪn kɑr 'ne ʃən] **1.** *n.* the return to life after death, in a new body, possibly of a different creature. (No plural form in this sense.) ♦ *If reincarnation exists, in what form would you like to return to Earth?* ♦ *The Buddhist monk believed in reincarnation.* **2.** *n.* an instance of ①. ♦ *One could go through a number of reincarnations, thousands, I guess.* ♦ *In my last reincarnation, I must have been a pig. I just love to eat!* **3.** *n.* a new version of something that has existed before in a different form. (Figurative on ②.) ♦ *Isn't your idea just a reincarnation of the idea you had last year?* ♦ *The architect presented a reincarnation of the plans that no one liked the last time he made a presentation.*

reindeer ['ren dɪr] *n., irreg.* a large deer with long antlers that lives in the Arctic areas of the world. (Pl: *reindeer.*) ♦ *Santa Claus's sleigh is said to be pulled by eight reindeer.* ♦ *In Finland, the reindeer is used for food.*

reinforce [ri ɪn 'fors] *tv.* to make something stronger, more durable, or longer lasting by adding something to it. ♦ *The carpenter reinforced the beam before putting any weight on it.* ♦ *The mayor reinforced the police department by hiring more cops.*

reinforced [ri ɪn 'forst] *adj.* made stronger or more durable by having added material to it; strengthened by having added material to it. ♦ *The reinforced beam could support many tons.* ♦ *The bridge was made of reinforced concrete.*

reinstate [ri ɪn 'stet] *tv.* to return someone or something to a former position or condition. ♦ *Anne was reinstated as chairwoman after a one-year sabbatical.* ♦ *The board reinstated the former president to office.*

reiterate [ri 'ɪt ə ret] *tv.* to say or do something again; to repeat an assertion. ♦ *The teacher reiterated the most important points of the lecture.* ♦ *Anne reiterated her claim that Tom was being unreasonable.*

reiterative [ri 'ɪt ə rə tɪv] *adj.* happening again and again; happening over and over; repeating. (Adv: *reiteratively.*) ♦ *The computer continued to run the reiterative program.* ♦ *The reiterative tapping on the ceiling was annoying me.*

reject 1. [rɪ 'dʒɛkt] *tv.* to refuse to take, accept, or use someone or something. ♦ *The union rejected the new contract.* ♦ *I rejected Bill's offer of help.* **2.** ['ri dʒɛkt] *n.* someone or something that has been refused as in ①. ♦ *The rejects were thrown in the garbage.* ♦ *The reject walked away from the schoolyard and cried.*

rejection [ri 'dʒɛk ʃən] *n.* the refusal of acceptance. (No plural form in this sense.) ♦ *The worker's rejection of the contract led to a strike.* ♦ *John was angered by his classmates' rejection of his ideas.*

rejoice [ri 'dʒoɪs] *iv.* to be very happy [about something]; to celebrate [something] joyfully. ♦ *The people rejoiced when the evil tyrant died.* ♦ *John and Mary rejoiced when she gave birth to a healthy child.*

rejoicing [ri 'dʒoɪs ɪŋ] *n.* great joy or happiness expressed by one or more people. (No plural form in this sense.) ♦ *After the war ended, there was much rejoicing.* ♦ *The students' rejoicing was interrupted by bad news.*

rejoin [ri 'dʒoɪn] **1.** *tv.* to join something again. ♦ *The confederate states rejoined the Union after the Civil War.* ♦ *I have to leave now, but I'll rejoin the group at noon.* **2.** *tv.* to join things together again. ♦ *I will have to rejoin the ends of the wire where it broke.* ♦ *Lisa will rejoin the table leg to the table with strong glue.* **3.** *iv.* [for things] to join again; [for things] to come back together again. ♦ *East and West Germany rejoined in 1990.* ♦ *Classes rejoined the week after winter break.*

rejuvenate [ri 'dʒuv ə net] *tv.* to cause someone to feel young again. ♦ *The relaxing massage rejuvenated the worn-out executive.* ♦ *Going to a circus always rejuvenates me.*

relapse 1. ['ri læps] *n.* a return to a bad condition after a period of improvement; a return to sickness after a period where one's health has improved. ♦ *Because of Anne's relapse, she had to return to the hospital.* ♦ *John was recovering nicely until his sudden relapse last week.* **2.** [rɪ 'læps] *iv.* to return to a bad condition after improvement, as in ①. ♦ *Bill recovered nicely after surgery, but then he relapsed.* ♦ *When Jane relapsed, she had to return to the hospital.*

relate [rɪ 'let] **1.** *tv.* to tell a story; to tell what was heard. ♦ *The witness related what she had heard.* ♦ *The reporter related the important news of the day.* **2. relate to** *tv.* to associate something with something else; to associate something and something else. ♦ *I relate your cold to your walk in the rain last week.* ♦ *Your works are related to those of Albert Einstein.* **3. relate to; relate with** *iv.* + *prep. phr.* to feel a bond of some type with someone because of shared experiences or a similar connection. ♦ *I can relate with Anne because I'm also adopted.* ♦ *Mary related to Jane because they had similar experiences.*

related [rɪ 'let ɪd] **1.** *adj.* connected. (Adv: *relatedly.*) ♦ *The professor lectured about many related ideas in class.* ♦ *In a related news story, the storm also closed many schools.* **2.** *adj.* part of the same family; in the same family. ♦ *Related children sometimes look alike.* ♦ *Related employees cannot work in the same department.* **3. related to** *adj.* + *prep. phr.* connected to someone as a relative. ♦ *Bill is related to Lisa. They are cousins.* ♦ *I am glad Anne is not related to me, because I don't like her.* **4. related to** *adj.* + *prep. phr.* associated with something. ♦ *Your cold is related to your walk in the rain last week.* ♦ *Is your theory related to the theory originated by Albert Einstein?*

relation [rɪ 'le ʃən] **1.** *n.* someone who is a member of one's family; a relative. ♦ *Anne visited her relations at Christmas.* ♦ *John is only a distant relation.* **2.** *n.* a connection between two or more things; relationship. ♦ *The report showed the relation between crime and poverty.* ♦ *The professor explained the relation between tides and the moon.*

relationship [rɪ 'le ʃən ʃɪp] **1.** *n.* a personal, romantic, business, or social connection between two people. ♦ *Jane's relationship with the mayor was merely social.* ♦ *Anne has been in a romantic relationship with John for four years.* **2.** *n.* a connection between two or more things. ♦ *The author showed the relationship of crime to poverty.* ♦ *The teacher explained the relationship between thunder and lightning.*

relative ['rɛl ə tɪv] **1.** *n.* someone who is a member of one's family. ♦ *I saw dozens of my relatives at my grandfather's funeral.* ♦ *The application required me to state the names of my nearest living relatives.* **2. relative clause** *n.* a subordinate clause; a clause that refers or is compared to someone or something. ♦ *Nonrestrictive relative clauses are usually set apart from main sentences by commas.* ♦ *The sentence "My left thumb, which I hit with a hammer yesterday, is bruised" contains a relative clause.* **3.** *adj.* compared to something else; having meaning only as compared with something else. (Adv: *relatively.*) ♦ *John's relative lack of ability makes him a poor choice.* ♦ *Mary's relative inexperience makes her an unlikely candidate.* **4. relative to** *adj.* + *prep. phr.* about; in connection with; concerning. ♦ *Relative to the matter we just discussed, I have nothing more to say.* ♦ *Relative to your concerns, I have spoken with the manager.* **5. relative to** *adj.* + *prep. phr.* corresponding to something; [of an amount] in proportion to something. ♦ *The occurrence of crime in a community is relative to the amount of poverty.* ♦ *The amount of postage needed is relative to the package's weight.*

relax [rɪ 'læks] **1.** *iv.* to become less tight, less stiff, less firm, less tense, or more loose. ♦ *As I became less tense, my grip on the steering wheel relaxed.* ♦ *When my hand relaxed, I dropped my pen.* **2.** *iv.* to become less worried, less busy with work, or less active; to rest, be calm, or slow down. ♦ *I need to relax more because I'm developing an ulcer.* ♦ *Bob took a sleeping pill to help him relax.* **3.** *tv.* to cause something to become less tight, less stiff, less firm, or less tense. ♦ *The physical therapist told me to relax my leg muscles.* ♦ *John relaxed his tight grip on the steering wheel.* **4.** *tv.* to cause something to become less strict, less harsh, or less severe. (Figurative on ③.) ♦ *The office manager relaxes the dress code on Fridays.* ♦ *Once the riots were over, law enforcement was relaxed.* **5.** *tv.* to cause someone to become less worried, less busy with work, or less active; to cause someone to rest, be calm, or slow down. ♦ *The magician relaxed the volunteer before hypnotizing her.* ♦ *The operator's soothing voice relaxed the panicking caller.*

relaxation [rɪ læk 'se ʃən] **1.** *n.* rest, especially after work or busy activity. (No plural form in this sense.) ♦ *The doctor advised the stressed man to seek relaxation.* ♦ *I spent my vacation in Bermuda in complete relaxation.* **2.** *n.* the lessening of tightness, stiffness, tenseness, or firmness; the loosening of something tight, stiff, tense, or firm. (No plural form in this sense.) ♦ *With the relaxation of my tight grip, my assailant broke free.* ♦ *A massage is good for the relaxation of one's muscles.* **3.** *n.* making something less severe; the easing of strict rules. (No plural form in this sense.) ♦ *On Fridays, John doesn't wear ties because of the relaxation of the dress code.* ♦ *The citizens appreciated the relaxation of martial law.*

relaxing [rɪ 'læk sɪŋ] *adj.* calming; soothing; restful; making one feel less tense, tight, stiff, or firm. (Adv: *relaxingly.*) ♦ *I spent a relaxing day at the beach.* ♦ *I took a long, relaxing shower.*

relay 1. [rɪ 'le] *tv.* to receive something and give it to someone else. ♦ *A government official relayed the bad news to the soldier's family.* ♦ *The reporter relayed the traffic information over the radio.* **2. relay (race)** ['ri le] *n.* a race in which a series of people run for individual segments of a great distance. ♦ *The first runner in a relay race passes a baton to the second, and so on.* ♦ *Each member of the relay passed the baton to the next runner.*

release [rɪ 'lis] **1.** *tv.* to let someone or something free; to let someone or something go; to let someone or something loose. ♦ *The prisoner was released from jail when his sentence was up.* ♦ *In the park John released his dog from its leash.* **2.** *tv.* to make a book, movie, information, or publication available to the public. ♦ *Four new movies were released last weekend.* ♦ *The singer's agent released her touring schedule to the media.* **3.** *n.* an act of letting someone or something go; an act of setting someone or something free. ♦ *The governor's release of the violent prisoner caused an uproar.* ♦ *The release of steam from the chimney looked like pollution.* **4.** *n.* a document that officially releases someone from control or responsibility. ♦ *Before the experiment, each participant had to sign a release.* ♦ *I signed a release shielding the doctor from a malpractice suit.* **5.** *n.* a document that frees someone from the control of an institution. ♦ *The government signed the convict's release.* ♦ *After the doctor signed my release, I left the hospital.* **6.** *n.* a book, movie, information, or publication that is made available to the public. ♦ *The press release stated that the film would open on Friday.* ♦ *The new release is playing at the movie theater downtown.*

relegate ['rɛl ə get] *tv.* to send someone to a job or position that is worse, less important, or less powerful. ♦ *The unskilled baseball player was relegated to the bench.* ♦ *The soldier was relegated to cleaning the latrine.*

relent [rɪ 'lɛnt] **1.** *iv.* to show pity; to be less mean or cruel; to be more merciful. ♦ *I relented and gave the beggar man a dollar.* ♦ *John relented and forgave me for yelling at him.* **2.** *iv.* to become less severe; to become more mild; to lose strength. ♦ *The harsh wind relented during the night.* ♦ *The floods finally relented, but only after extensive damage.*

relentless [rɪ 'lɛnt ləs] **1.** *adj.* without pity; severe; harsh; cruel; mean. (Adv: *relentlessly.*) ♦ *The relentless bully beat Jimmy up.* ♦ *The relentless landlord evicted the unemployed tenant.* **2.** *adj.* not stopping; endless. (Adv: *relentlessly.*) ♦ *The relentless winds battered the coast.* ♦ *The audience was relentless in its demands for another encore.*

relevance ['rɛl ə vəns] *n.* the quality of being relevant; the state of being related to something. (No plural form in this sense.) ♦ *Money is of great relevance to power.* ♦ *Because John's statement had no relevance, I ignored it.*

relevant ['rɛl ə vənt] *adj.* connected to something; of or about the subject being discussed; pertinent. (Adv: *relevantly.*) ♦ *The speaker asked if there were any relevant questions.* ♦ *The reporter provided relevant information about the blizzard.*

reliable [rɪ 'lɑɪ ə bəl] *adj.* able to be relied on; able to be trusted; loyal; dependable. (Adv: *reliably.*) ♦ *The subway is the most reliable way of getting to the airport during rush hour.* ♦ *If John were more reliable, I'd ask him to watch my dog.*

reliance [rɪ 'lɑɪ əns] **reliance on someone or something** *phr.* trust and dependence on someone or something. (No plural form in this sense.) ♦ *John's reliance on his family is holding him back.* ♦ *Reliance on sleeping pills is dangerous.*

reliant [rɪ 'lɑɪ ənt] **reliant on** *adj.* + *prep. phr.* dependent on. (See also **self-reliant**.) ♦ *When my car broke, I became reliant on my friends for transportation.* ♦ *The remote town was reliant on bottled water.*

relic ['rɛl ɪk] **1.** *n.* an important object from the distant past. ♦ *The anthropologist unearthed some Egyptian relics.* ♦ *The museum put the ancient relics on display.* **2.** *n.* a souvenir; something that brings back a memory. (Figurative on ①.) ♦ *The jersey was a relic of John's days on the football team.* ♦ *This injury is a relic of my time in the army.*

relief [rɪ 'lif] **1.** *n.* the feeling that is felt when pain, a burden, a strain, or a problem is eased. (No plural form in this sense.) ♦ *To my relief, my test results were negative.* ♦ *John felt relief when he dropped his heavy load.* **2.** *n.* something that eases pain, a burden, a strain, or a problem. (No plural form in this sense.) ♦ *I needed a relief from my stressful job.* ♦ *Hiring three extra workers was quite a relief at the office.* **3.** *n.* money, clothing, food, and other aid that is made available to help poor people or to help people who are victims of a disaster. (No plural form in this sense.) ♦ *Our church sent relief to the victims of the earthquake.* ♦ *The flooded city requested relief from the federal government.* **4.** *n.* replacement workers who start working to take the place of the workers who started earlier. (No plural form in this sense.) ♦ *After 12 hours at work, I was glad to see relief.* ♦ *The firefighters were replaced by relief after 16 hours.*

relieve [rɪ 'liv] **1.** *tv.* to ease or eliminate pain, anxiety, or strain. ♦ *The aspirin relieved my headache.* ♦ *I was relieved to hear the good news.* **2. relieve of** *tv.* + *prep.*

phr. to unburden someone or something by removing something. ♦ *Thank you for relieving me of the heavy load I was carrying.* ♦ *I relieved the suffering donkey of its burden.* **3. relieve of** *tv.* + *prep. phr.* to ease someone's state of being by removing fear or anxiety. ♦ *A kind explanation by the doctor relieved me of my fears.* ♦ *The presence of the security guard relieved me of my worries.* **4. relieve of** *tv.* + *prep. phr.* to make someone poorer by taking something away through robbery or costly expenditures. ♦ *The bill for the dinner relieved me of all my cash.* ♦ *The crook relieved me of my wallet and my watch.* **5.** *tv.* to begin working at a job as a replacement so that the person who was working can leave or take a break. ♦ *I was hired temporarily to relieve a woman who had just had a baby.* ♦ *The rookie was sent in to relieve the pitcher.* **6.** *tv.* to take the strain off one's bladder or bowels by urinating or defecating. (Euphemistic.) ♦ *I ran to the bathroom to relieve my bowels.* ♦ *The dog relieved itself on the rug.*

religion [rɪ 'lɪdʒ ən] **1.** *n.* belief in or worship of one or more gods or spirits. (No plural form in this sense.) ♦ *Religion and morals form a part of every culture.* ♦ *I am studying religion in school.* **2.** *n.* a belief in one or more gods or spirits. ♦ *The differences in religion led to an ethnic war.* ♦ *My mother said it was impolite to argue about religion during dinner.*

religious [rɪ 'lɪdʒ əs] **1.** *adj.* <the adj. form of religion.> (Adv: *religiously.*) ♦ *The two groups battled because of their religious differences.* ♦ *Mike loves to argue about religious matters.* **2.** *adj.* believing in or worshiping one or more gods or spirits. (Adv: *religiously.*) ♦ *Religious people are concerned about the morals of society.* ♦ *Although Anne is religious, she doesn't belong to a particular church.* **3. religious about doing something** *idiom* strict about something; conscientious about something. (On ②.) ♦ *Bob is religious about paying his bills on time.* ♦ *Max tries to be religious about being polite to everyone.* **4. (religious) order** See order ⑧.

religiously [ri 'lɪdʒ əs li] *adv.* strictly; conscientiously; exactly; carefully. ♦ *The maid cleaned the house religiously.* ♦ *The guard followed the rules religiously.*

relinquish [rɪ 'lɪŋ kwɪʃ] *tv.* to give something up; to let something go. ♦ *Max relinquished his ownership of a small piece of land needed by the city.* ♦ *The king relinquished the throne because of the scandal.*

relish ['rɛl ɪʃ] **1.** *tv.* to enjoy something very much. ♦ *My grandmother has always relished life.* ♦ *John relished his vacations.* **2.** *n.* a sweetened mixture of chopped pickled cucumbers or other pickled vegetables. (No plural form in this sense.) ♦ *John put some pickle relish on his hot dog.* ♦ *The meatloaf was served with corn relish.* **3. with relish** *idiom* with pleasure or enjoyment. ♦ *John ate his juicy hamburger with great relish.* ♦ *We sampled the excellent food with relish.*

relive [ri 'lɪv] *tv.* to experience something again in one's mind; to feel something again in one's mind. ♦ *The victim relived the horror of the accident over and over.* ♦ *The veteran relived the battle in which he had lost his legs.*

relocate [ri 'lo ket] **1.** *tv.* to move someone or something to a different place. ♦ *The company relocated its headquarters to Ohio.* ♦ *Mary was relocated to the suburban branch office.* **2. relocate to** *iv.* + *prep. phr.* to move to a different place; to move to a different house or to transfer to a different job site, especially in a different city. ♦ *The electronics company relocated to Japan.* ♦ *Bob relocated to Pittsburgh.*

reluctance [rɪ 'lʌk təns] **reluctance to do something** *phr.* a feeling of not wanting to do something; unwillingness to do something. ♦ *Mary showed great reluctance to go bowling with me.* ♦ *Because of John's reluctance to make friends, he was lonely.*

reluctant [rɪ 'lʌk tənt] **reluctant to do something** *phr.* unwilling to do something; not wanting to do something. ♦ *David was reluctant to admit his mistakes.* ♦ *The reluctant witness was ordered to appear in court.*

rely [rɪ 'lɑɪ] **rely (up)on** *iv.* + *prep. phr.* to depend on someone or something; to trust that someone will do something; to trust that something will happen. ♦ *I rely on my friends to tell me the truth.* ♦ *David relies on his car to get to work.*

remain [rɪ 'men] **1.** *iv.* to stay someplace; to continue to be in a certain place; to be left over after other parts or things are taken. ♦ *Very little remained of my house after the fire.* ♦ *Mary remained in the small town her whole life.* **2.** *iv.* to continue to be something; not to stop being something. ♦ *John remained sad throughout the winter.* ♦ *I remained unconvinced of John's argument.* **3. remains** *n.* things that are left behind. (Treated as plural.) ♦ *The mouse nibbled at the remains of a cheese sandwich.* ♦ *The archaeologist walked through the remains of the old city.* **4. remains** *n.* a corpse; a dead body. (Treated as plural.) ♦ *The soldier's remains were buried at the national cemetery.* ♦ *The family viewed the remains before the casket was closed.*

remainder [rɪ 'men dɚ] **1.** *n.* the part of something that is left over after part of it is taken. ♦ *Anne ate half of the pizza and left the remainder for me.* ♦ *Mary did most of the work, and Susan finished the remainder.* **2.** *n.* the number that is left over after a number is divided into another one. ♦ *3 divides into 14 four times, leaving a remainder of 2.* ♦ *Please write the remainder as a fraction.*

remaining [rɪ 'men ɪŋ] *adj.* yet to happen; yet to occur; not yet done or taken care of; not yet taken away; not yet happening; not yet occurring. ♦ *In his remaining years of life, John wants to travel.* ♦ *Susan addressed my only remaining doubts.*

remark [rɪ 'mɑrk] **1.** *n.* a comment; a statement; something that is said or written about something. ♦ *I agreed with Anne's remark about the president.* ♦ *Max's remarks about the meal were very kind.* **2.** *tv.* to say something; to comment about something; to state an opinion. (Takes a clause.) ♦ *Anne remarked that she was tired and wanted to leave.* ♦ *Jane remarked, "I like your haircut."*

remarkable [rɪ 'mɑrk ə bəl] *adj.* worth mentioning; worth talking about; noticeable; extraordinary; unusual. (Adv: *remarkably.*) ♦ *Anne talked about her remarkable trip to South America.* ♦ *John's stories of working in the circus are remarkable.*

remedial [rɪ 'mid i əl] **1.** *adj.* of or about a remedy. (Adv: *remedially.*) ♦ *The doctor suggested some kind of remedial exercises for my sore muscles.* ♦ *The sooner you receive remedial treatment for your injury, the sooner you will be well.* **2.** *adj.* [of teaching methods] designed for students who are slow to learn. (Adv: *remedially.*) ♦ *Don't make fun of* *the children in remedial education.* ♦ *The slow student was placed in a remedial math class.*

remedy ['rɛm ɪ di] **1.** *n.* a treatment; a cure; something that makes someone become healthy again. ♦ *There is no remedy for the common cold.* ♦ *The doctor's remedy was to rest and drink lots of liquid.* **2.** *n.* an improvement of bad conditions or the correction of a problem. (Figurative on ①.) ♦ *The manager's remedy of the difficult situation was brilliant.* ♦ *The unemployed workers expected a remedy from the government.* **3.** *tv.* to improve bad conditions; to correct a problem; to right something that is wrong or bad. ♦ *The situation was remedied by rearranging the schedule.* ♦ *The mayor's plan remedied the traffic problem.*

remember [rɪ 'mɛm bɚ] **1.** *tv.* to bring back the thought of someone or something into one's mind, memory, or imagination; to think about someone or something again. ♦ *Suddenly, Anne remembered a troubling incident from her childhood.* ♦ *Do you remember the time we went fishing with John?* **2.** *tv.* not to forget someone or something; to keep someone or something in one's mind. ♦ *I'll remember you forever.* ♦ *The soldier remembered the war throughout his life.* **3.** *iv.* to bring [someone or something] back into one's mind, memory, or imagination. ♦ *I just can't remember as well as I once could.* ♦ *What is that man's name? I can't remember.*

remind [rɪ 'mɑɪnd] *tv.* to tell someone about something again; to cause someone to remember someone or something. ♦ *May I remind you that smoking is not allowed?* ♦ *The librarian reminded the students to be quiet.*

reminder [rɪ 'mɑɪn dɚ] *n.* something that reminds someone about something. ♦ *The librarian put up signs as a reminder to be quiet.* ♦ *The secretary handed Anne a reminder about her 3:00 appointment.*

reminisce [rɛm ə 'nɪs] *iv.* to discuss memories with someone. ♦ *We sat by the fire and reminisced for hours.* ♦ *My friends and I reminisced about high school.*

reminiscence [rɛm ə 'nɪs əns] *n.* a memory; a recollection. ♦ *Max had some good reminiscences of college to share with Bill.* ♦ *The old friends shared happy reminiscences about their past.*

reminiscent [rɛm ə 'nɪs ənt] **reminiscent of someone or something** *phr.* reminding someone about someone or something; seeming like or suggesting someone or something. ♦ *This fragrance is reminiscent of fresh flowers.* ♦ *Jane's dress is reminiscent of the style worn in the 1920s.*

remiss [rɪ 'mɪs] *adj.* negligent; not paying attention to someone or something; neglecting someone or something; careless. (Not prenominal.) ♦ *The guard was remiss in his duty, so he was fired.* ♦ *I would be remiss if I did not offer to take your coat.*

remission [rɪ 'mɪ ʃən] **1. in remission** *phr.* at a time when a serious disease is not as bad or seems to be getting better. ♦ *While the disease was in remission, John got to leave the hospital.* ♦ *The doctor said my cancer was in remission.* **2.** *n.* remitting something; making a payment. (No plural form in this sense.) ♦ *The bank's remission of the money was done by wire.* ♦ *Upon remission of their last mortgage payment, the Smiths celebrated.*

remit [rɪ 'mɪt] **1.** *tv.* to send or deliver a payment. ♦ *Please remit payment in the envelope provided.* ♦ *Please remit your rent before the 1st of each month.* **2.** *iv.* to send or deliver [a payment]. ♦ *Please remit by check or money order only.* ♦ *Please remit before the 5th day of each month.*

remittance [rɪ 'mɪt ns] **1.** *n.* the sending or delivering of a payment. (No plural form in this sense.) ♦ *Remittance must be made by the date shown.* ♦ *Upon remittance of $100, your debt will thereby be paid.* **2.** *n.* a payment that is sent or delivered. ♦ *Please send your remittance in the envelope provided.* ♦ *Please include the lower portion of the bill with your remittance.*

remnant ['rɛm nənt] *n.* something that is left over, especially a piece of fabric that is left over after a large piece has been sold; a scrap. ♦ *We made a quilt from a pile of remnants.* ♦ *John used a small rug remnant as a mat for the front porch.*

remodel [ri 'mɑd l] *tv.* to decorate something in a new way; to construct something in a new way; to change a structure or room so it looks more modern. ♦ *We remodeled our old-fashioned kitchen.* ♦ *The young couple remodeled the house before they moved in.*

remorse [rɪ 'mors] *n.* sorrow or sadness that is felt when one does something wrong. (No plural form in this sense.) ♦ *The criminal showed no remorse at the trial.* ♦ *John's remorse for his criminal actions was sincere.*

remorseless [rɪ 'mors ləs] *adj.* without remorse; not feeling sorrow or sadness when one does something wrong. (Adv: *remorselessly.*) ♦ *The remorseless criminal smiled during the trial.* ♦ *The remorseless owner fired 20% of the work force.*

remote [rɪ 'mot] **1.** *adj.* far away in space or time; far off; not near; distant; isolated; secluded; not near other things or places. (Adv: *remotely.* Comp: *remoter;* sup: *remotest.*) ♦ *The doctor practiced medicine in a remote village in India.* ♦ *The astronomer studied remote stars through the telescope.* **2.** *adj.* slight; faint. (Figurative on ①. Adv: *remotely.* Comp: *remoter;* sup: *remotest.*) ♦ *There's a remote chance that I can see you on Friday.* ♦ *The chances of winning the lottery are very remote.* **3. remote (control)** *n.* a device that is held in the hand and used to operate a machine or appliance from a distance. ♦ *Anne took the remote because I kept changing the channel.* ♦ *Mary opened the garage door with her remote control.*

remotely [rɪ 'mot li] *adv.* barely; only slightly. ♦ *The lazy student was not even remotely prepared for class.* ♦ *I remotely recall hearing something about that problem.*

removal [rɪ 'muv əl] *n.* removing something; taking something away. (No plural form in this sense.) ♦ *Citizens demanded the removal of the ugly statue in front of city hall.* ♦ *My dentist suggested the removal of my wisdom teeth.*

remove [rɪ 'muv] **1.** *tv.* to take something away from a place; to eliminate something; to get rid of something. ♦ *The waiter removed our plates from the table.* ♦ *The plow removed the snow from the streets.* **2.** *tv.* to take off something, especially a piece of clothing. ♦ *Anne removed her sweater because it was so warm.* ♦ *John removed his clothes and put on a robe.*

removed [rɪ 'muvd] *adv.* a degree or a level of generations between two relatives. ♦ *My cousin's child is my first* *cousin once removed.* ♦ *My cousin's grandchild is my first cousin twice removed.*

remunerate [rɪ 'mjun ə ret] *tv.* to pay someone for work, time, or effort. ♦ *The firm remunerated me well for my work.* ♦ *The psychologist remunerated the people in the experiment.*

remuneration [rɪ mju nə 're ʃən] *n.* payment to someone for time or effort. (No plural form in this sense.) ♦ *My office wires my remuneration directly to my bank account.* ♦ *The official could not receive remuneration for her speech.*

renaissance ['rɛn ɪ sɑns] **1.** *n.* a cultural revival. (From French. No plural form in this sense.) ♦ *Cleveland's renaissance transformed its downtown.* ♦ *The old neighborhood enjoyed a renaissance as people began to repair their houses.* **2. Renaissance** *n.* the period of European history starting in the 1300s and lasting until the 1700s when art and education became highly valued. (No plural form in this sense.) ♦ *William Shakespeare was a famous playwright of the Renaissance.* ♦ *Perspective in art was developed during the Renaissance.* **3. Renaissance** *adj.* <the adj. use of ②.> ♦ *Shakespeare's works are part of Renaissance theater.* ♦ *The Italian town had several examples of Renaissance architecture.*

renal ['ri nəl] *adj.* of or about the kidneys. (Adv: *renally.*) ♦ *John suffered from renal cancer.* ♦ *I made an appointment with a renal specialist.*

render ['rɛn dɚ] **1.** *tv.* to cause someone or something to be in a certain condition; to cause someone or something to become a certain way. ♦ *The accident rendered John helpless.* ♦ *The surprise party rendered Jane speechless.* **2.** *tv.* to give an official verdict or opinion. ♦ *The Supreme Court rendered its opinion.* ♦ *The jury rendered its verdict.* **3.** *tv.* to sing something; to play a song. ♦ *Anne rendered a tune on the violin.* ♦ *Mary rendered a song in my honor.* **4.** *tv.* to melt down fat, purifying it by separating out the impurities. ♦ *The cook rendered the bacon fat.* ♦ *Mary rendered the fat out of the roast.* **5. render to** *tv.* + *prep. phr.* to give something or exchange something. ♦ *Bill rendered his last dollar to the tax collector.* ♦ *Anne rendered her final mortgage payment to the bank.*

rendering ['rɛn dɚ ɪŋ] **1.** *n.* a drawing that shows the design of a designer; a design. ♦ *The costume designer showed her renderings to the director.* ♦ *The rendering of the new headquarters was displayed in the lobby.* **2.** *n.* a performance. ♦ *The singer performed a delightful rendering of the song.* ♦ *John's rendering of the piece on the piano was flawless.* **3.** *n.* a translation of something written. ♦ *The teacher corrected John's rendering of the text from Italian.* ♦ *This text is a rendering of the original French version.*

rendezvous ['rɑn de vu] **1.** *n., irreg.* an arrangement to meet at a certain time and place. (Pl: *rendezvous.* From French.) ♦ *I met my lover at the park for a secret rendezvous.* ♦ *The spy scheduled a rendezvous with his client.* **2.** *n., irreg.* the place where two or more people arrange to meet. ♦ *The lovers' favorite rendezvous was a quiet little diner.* ♦ *The secret agent's rendezvous was bugged.* **3.** *iv.* to meet at a certain place and time. ♦ *The young lovers planned to rendezvous at midnight.* ♦ *The spy rendezvoused with the prime minister at the palace.*

rendition [rɛn 'dɪ ʃən] *n.* a performance of a piece of music, a drama or the reading of poetry. ♦ *Bill's rendition of the sonata was flawless.* ♦ *Anne's rendition of her poetry was touching.*

renegade ['rɛn ə ged] **1.** *n.* a traitor; someone who leaves an organization or a political party for a competing one or to be independent. ♦ *The renegade betrayed his political party.* ♦ *I was a renegade who preferred to do things my own way rather than obey someone else.* **2.** *adj.* disloyal; leaving one's religion or political party for another one. ♦ *The renegade senator from the South became a Republican.* ♦ *As a renegade novelist, John wrote a lot of highly original, but largely misunderstood books.*

renege [rɪ 'nɪg] **1. renege (on)** *iv.* (+ *prep. phr.*) not to keep a promise; to fail to do what was promised. ♦ *Once elected, many politicians renege on their promises.* ♦ *I know he promised, but he reneged.* **2.** *iv.* not to fulfill a promise. ♦ *He said he would join us, but he reneged and stayed home.* ♦ *Hey, you reneged! You told us you would, but you didn't do it.*

renew [rɪ 'nu] **1.** *tv.* to cause someone or something to become like new again; to restore someone or something. ♦ *The long, relaxing shower renewed the tired woman.* ♦ *The medicine renewed the sick man's strength.* **2.** *tv.* to cause something that has expired to become current again; to cause something to be valid for a longer period of time. ♦ *The baseball player renewed his contract for another two years.* ♦ *Mary renewed her driver's license.*

renounce [rɪ 'nɑʊns] *tv.* to give up something; to state formally that one is giving up something, especially a claim or a right. ♦ *The king renounced his claim on the neighboring kingdom's land.* ♦ *The philosopher renounced his faith in God.*

renovate ['rɛn ə vet] *tv.* to fix up something so that it is in good condition; to restore something to a good condition; to repair a structure. ♦ *The city renovated the ancient bridge.* ♦ *The landlord renovated the dilapidated building.*

renovated ['rɛn ə vet ɪd] *adj.* fixed up; restored to a good condition; repaired. ♦ *Mary lives in a renovated apartment in a nice neighborhood.* ♦ *The renovated lobby looked much more fashionable than before.*

renovation [rɛn ə 've ʃən] *n.* a restoration; something that has been renovated. ♦ *The tenants were pleased that the lobby had undergone renovation.* ♦ *As part of the renovation, marble floors were installed.*

renown [rɪ 'nɑʊn] *n.* fame; a state of being well known. (No plural form in this sense.) ♦ *Many celebrities of great renown were at the banquet.* ♦ *Our guest of honor was a politician of renown.*

renowned [rɪ 'nɑʊnd] *adj.* famous; well known. ♦ *The renowned baseball player charged a fee for his autograph.* ♦ *A renowned musician played at Orchestra Hall last night.*

rent ['rɛnt] **1.** *n.* the money paid for the use of something, especially for the use of a place to live. (No plural form in this sense.) ♦ *The student paid $300 each month for rent.* ♦ *I paid my landlady the rent on the second day of the month.* **2. rent (from)** *tv.* (+ *prep. phr.*) to get the right to use something (from someone) by paying ①. ♦ *I rented an apartment from my uncle.* ♦ *John rented a car so he could drive to Memphis.* **3. rent (out) (to)** *tv.* (+ *adv.*) (+ *prep. phr.*) to provide something that other people pay money to use. ♦ *The landlord rented out 24 apartments to college students.* ♦ *The hardware store rents out large* *floor sanders.* ♦ *I rent my garage to a neighbor.* **4.** *iv.* to live in an apartment that one does not own, but for which one pays ① to the owner. ♦ *I can't afford a house, so I rent.* ♦ *Mary moves a lot, so she prefers to rent.*

rental ['rɛn təl] **1.** *adj.* [of an apartment, office space, equipment, or other thing] rented or available to be rented. ♦ *My rental car cost $65 per day.* ♦ *Mary is looking for a small, inexpensive rental unit.* **2.** *n.* the amount of money that is paid as rent for something. (No plural form in this sense.) ♦ *The daily rental for the rowboat is $40 plus a deposit.* ♦ *John paid the car rental in cash.*

rented ['rɛn tɪd] *adj.* occupied or used for a fee, rather than owned. ♦ *I live in a small rented apartment.* ♦ *Insurance paid for the repairs when I wrecked the rented car.*

renunciation [rɪ nən si 'e ʃən] *n.* the process of renouncing someone or something. (No plural form in this sense.) ♦ *Max's renunciation of his faith surprised his mother.* ♦ *Renunciation of his country was difficult for the immigrant.*

reorganization [ri or gə nɪ 'ze ʃən] *n.* reorganizing something; organizing something in a different way, especially so that it works or operates better; the condition of having been reorganized. (No plural form in this sense.) ♦ *Under the company reorganization, 100 people lost their jobs.* ♦ *The new manager's reorganization of the office made it more efficient.*

reorganize [ri 'or gə naɪz] **1.** *tv.* to organize something in a different way, especially so that it works or operates better; to arrange something in a new or different way. ♦ *The new manager reorganized the office efficiently.* ♦ *David reorganized the messy papers on his desk.* **2.** *tv.* to reform a business, especially after it has gone bankrupt. ♦ *The investor profitably reorganized the failing company.* ♦ *The bankrupt firm was reorganized under a new owner.*

repaid [ri 'ped] pt/pp of repay.

repair [rɪ 'per] **1.** *tv.* to fix something; to mend something; to cause something to work again. ♦ *The mechanic repaired the car engine.* ♦ *The tailor repaired the tear in the shirt sleeve.* **2.** *n.* work that will fix or restore something. (Sometimes plural with the same meaning.) ♦ *My computer needs repair.* ♦ *Without repair and future maintenance, your furnace will not last another two years.* **3.** *n.* the act of mending something; the work that is done when mending something. ♦ *The jeweler's repair of my watch cost $75.* ♦ *The repair that the tailor made was almost unnoticeable.*

repairable [rɪ 'per ə bəl] *adj.* able to be repaired; able to be fixed. (Adv: *repairably.*) ♦ *Is this old TV repairable, or should I just throw it away?* ♦ *The mechanic said my car engine was not repairable.*

reparation [rɛp ə 're ʃən] **reparations** *n.* payment made to compensate for something. (Treated as plural.) ♦ *The refugees sought reparations from the warring nations.* ♦ *The injured worker sued the company for reparations.*

repast [rɪ 'pæst] *n.* a meal. (Formal.) ♦ *Thank you for a most enjoyable repast this evening.* ♦ *The guests were treated to a repast suitable for royalty.*

repatriate [ri 'pe tri et] *tv.* to send one back to one's country of origin. ♦ *The Mexican government repatriated the American criminal.* ♦ *The American government repatriated the illegal immigrants.*

repay [rɪ 'pe] *tv., irreg.* to pay someone back for something; to pay someone for an amount that is owed. (Pt/pp: repaid.) ♦ *I repaid John the money I owed him.* ♦ *Anne repaid all of her debts when she won the lottery.*

repayment [rɪ 'pe mənt] **1.** *n.* paying back something to someone. (No plural form in this sense.) ♦ *I asked John to speed up the repayment of my loan.* ♦ *My repayment was done in 6 monthly installments.* **2.** *n.* money that is paid back to someone; money that is returned to someone; something that is paid back to someone. ♦ *Mary gave me $40 as a partial repayment of the money she owes me.* ♦ *The plumber offered his labor as a repayment of his debt.*

repeal [rɪ 'pil] *tv.* to void a law; to cause a law to no longer be valid. ♦ *The 18th Amendment was repealed in 1933.* ♦ *The city council repealed the nonsmoking ordinance.*

repeat [rɪ 'pit] **1.** *tv.* to do or say something again. ♦ *The worker repeated the same task 240 times each hour.* ♦ *The singer repeated the chorus three times.* **2.** *tv.* to say something that someone else has just said, often for verification. ♦ *The students repeated the new word after the teacher said it.* ♦ *The clerk repeated my account number after hearing me say it.* **3.** *tv.* to say something that one has learned. ♦ *The students repeated the multiplication tables.* ♦ *Mary repeated the poem from memory.* **4.** *iv.* to do or say something again. ♦ *"Repeat after me," the language instructor said.* ♦ *Wash your hair thoroughly, rinse, and repeat.* **5.** *n.* something that is done again; an action that is done again. ♦ *Let's not have a repeat of last night, OK?* ♦ *The inattentive student's question was a repeat of my question.* **6.** *n.* a television program that has been on television before; a rerun. ♦ *I turned off the TV because nothing but repeats were on.* ♦ *We saw this repeat the first time it was on.*

repeated [rɪ 'pit ɪd] *adj.* previously done or said and being said or done again; done or said more than one time. (Adv: *repeatedly.*) ♦ *Her repeated asking of the same question irritated me.* ♦ *There was a repeated knocking at my door.*

repel [rɪ 'pɛl] **1.** *tv.* to keep someone or something away; to force someone or something away; to force someone or something back. ♦ *The soldiers repelled the enemy.* ♦ *Anne repelled her attacker by kicking him.* **2.** *tv.* to cause someone to be sickened or disgusted. (Figurative on ①.) ♦ *I was repelled by the smell coming from John's locker.* ♦ *Your bad attitude repels people.*

repellent [rɪ 'pɛl ənt] **1.** *n.* something that repels; something that keeps someone or something—especially insects—away. ♦ *I put on some insect repellent so that mosquitoes wouldn't bite me.* ♦ *I sprayed the room with a repellent to keep the cockroaches away.* **2.** *adj.* disgusting; sickening; not pleasing; repulsive. (Adv: *repellently.*) ♦ *The local theater refused to show the repellent movie.* ♦ *The comedian's jokes were lewd and repellent.*

repent [rɪ 'pɛnt] *iv.* to be sorry for one's wrongs and prepare to be better in the future. ♦ *The sinners repented and became good citizens.* ♦ *The criminal was not likely to repent and was not granted parole.*

repentance [rɪ 'pɛnt ns] *n.* regret; sorrow that is felt when one has done something wrong. (No plural form in this sense.) ♦ *As an act of repentance for my rudeness, I sent Jane flowers.* ♦ *Repentance is good for one's spirit and self-respect.*

repercussion [ri pɚ 'kʌ ʃən] *n.* a result that is indirectly caused by something. ♦ *One repercussion of the tax increase was that many senators were voted out of office.* ♦ *The soldier's loss of faith in humanity was a repercussion of the war.*

repertoire ['rɛp ɚ twɑr] See repertory.

repertory AND **repertoire** ['rɛp ɚ tor i, 'rɛp ɚ twɑr] **1.** *n.* a collection of songs, plays, monologues, or other performance pieces that a performer or a performance company is prepared to perform. ♦ *The actress had many comic monologues in her repertoire.* ♦ *The dance company's repertory was limited to ballet.* **2.** *n.* a collection of skills that someone has. (Figurative on ①.) ♦ *The crook's repertory included hundreds of small crimes.* ♦ *Lisa's repertoire of skills is extensive and varied.* **3.** *adj.* <the adj. use of ①.> ♦ *The repertory theater ran three different shows each weekend.* ♦ *I saw two different productions of the repertory dance company on the same day.*

repetition [rɛp ɪ 'tɪ ʃən] **1.** *n.* repeating something. (No plural form in this sense.) ♦ *Repetition can be boring.* ♦ *Repetition is a good way to learn a language.* **2.** *n.* something that is said or done again. ♦ *I do not want another repetition of what happened last night.* ♦ *The speaker's repetitions served to emphasize the important points.*

repetitive [rɪ 'pɛt ɪ tɪv] *adj.* repeated; said or done again and again. (Adv: *repetitively.*) ♦ *The repetitive barking of the dog was very annoying.* ♦ *The teacher tired of the students' repetitive questions.*

replace [rɪ 'ples] **1.** *tv.* to take the place of someone or something else. ♦ *This new phone replaces the old one I used to have.* ♦ *Nothing could replace my pet dog after he died.* **2.** *tv.* to exchange something for another thing that is more useful or newer. ♦ *Bill replaced the old carpet with a new one.* ♦ *Susan replaced the burnt-out light bulb.* **3.** *tv.* to return something to the place that it belongs; to put something back where it belongs. ♦ *Anne replaced the vase on the shelf after she dusted it.* ♦ *Mary replaced the hammer in the tool kit after she'd used it.*

replacement [rɪ 'ples mənt] **1.** *n.* replacing someone or something. (No plural form in this sense.) ♦ *The replacement of the broken part will cost $150.* ♦ *The replacement of the retiring worker would be a difficult task.* **2.** *n.* someone or something that takes the place of someone or something else. ♦ *David's temporary replacement was more efficient than he was.* ♦ *The replacement lasted longer than the original part.* **3.** *adj.* used to replace someone or something else. ♦ *The replacement secretary was more pleasant than the regular one.* ♦ *The replacement part cost $400.*

replay 1. ['ri ple] *n.* something that is played again; an event that is done over; a film clip that is played over, often in slow motion so one can see fast action better. ♦ *The instant replay was shown in slow motion.* ♦ *In the replay, you could see who won the race.* **2.** ['ri 'ple] *tv.* to play something again, especially a game or a piece of film. ♦ *The winning run was replayed on the evening news.* ♦ *Anne replayed the videotape of the party over and over.*

replenish [rɪ 'plɛn ɪʃ] *tv.* to fill something again; to supply something with more of what was taken from it. ♦ *The waitress replenished my glass with water.* ♦ *John replenished the pantry with boxes of food.*

replica ['rɛp lə kə] *n.* an exact copy of something, especially of a work of art; a reproduction. ♦ *This is not real. It's only a replica.* ♦ *I hung a replica of a famous painting above my fireplace.*

replicate ['rɛp lə ket] *tv.* to make a copy of something; to reproduce something. ♦ *The scientist replicated the important experiment.* ♦ *The counterfeiter could not replicate the currency accurately.*

reply [rɪ 'plɑɪ] **1.** *iv.* to answer. ♦ *Anne replied promptly when the lawyer asked her a question.* ♦ *I had no reply to the reporter's questions.* **2.** *tv.* to say or write something as an answer. (Takes a clause.) ♦ *When asked, Mary replied that she'd like cream with her coffee.* ♦ *John replied that he was feeling fine.* **3.** *n.* an answer; something that is said or written when answering a question. ♦ *John angrily shouted his reply to the rude clerk.* ♦ *Anne's reply was affirmative.*

report [rɪ 'port] **1.** *n.* an account that gives information about something. ♦ *The treasurer's report showed how much profit had been earned.* ♦ *Jimmy presented his report on dinosaurs to the class.* **2.** *n.* the noise made when a shot is fired. ♦ *The gun's report was muffled by a silencer.* ♦ *The rifle's report woke the neighbors.* **3.** *tv.* to describe news; to provide news. ♦ *A fire was reported to have started on 79th Street.* ♦ *The newscaster reported the latest events of the day.* **4. report to** *tv.* + *prep. phr.* to tell of someone or something to someone or something. ♦ *I reported the robbery to the police.* ♦ *Tom reported Bill to the supervisor.* **5. report to** *iv.* + *prep. phr.* to go to some place; to present oneself to someone at some place. ♦ *I have to report to headquarters immediately.* ♦ *Max reported to his boss when he came in late.*

reporter [rɪ 'por tɚ] **1.** *n.* someone who provides a newspaper, magazine, radio station, or television station with news; someone who reports news or information. ♦ *The reporter provided a traffic report every 10 minutes.* ♦ *The reporter finished the news article just before the deadline.* **2.** *n.* someone who writes down everything that is said in court. ♦ *The court reporter asked the witness to speak a little louder.* ♦ *The reporter repeated the lawyer's last question.*

repose [rɪ 'poz] **1.** *n.* sleep; quiet; rest; calm. (No plural form in this sense.) ♦ *My gentle repose was disturbed by the sound of arguing.* ♦ *For many, the final repose is in the graveyard.* **2.** *iv.* to rest; to sleep; to lie dead in a grave. ♦ *Midnight found John reposing peacefully in his bed.* ♦ *May the deceased repose in peace.*

repository [rɪ 'pɑz ɪ tor i] *n.* a place where something is kept. ♦ *At city hall, there's a repository of birth records.* ♦ *Grandma's pocket was a repository of candy.*

repossess [ri pə 'zɛs] *tv.* [for a company] to take back something purchased on credit when the purchaser fails to make payments on time. ♦ *The car company repossesses the cars of people who can't make payments.* ♦ *The furniture company repossessed my couch.*

repossessed [rɪ pə 'zɛst] *adj.* taken back from someone who is unable to make payments. ♦ *The dealership sold repossessed cars at a reduced price.* ♦ *The repossessed furniture was not suitable for resale.*

reprehensible [rɛp ri 'hɛn sɪ bəl] *adj.* worthy of blame or criticism; behaving very badly. (Adv: *reprehensibly.*) ♦ *The newspaper sharply criticized the mayor's reprehensi-*

ble behavior. ♦ *John was punished for his reprehensible actions.*

represent [rɛp rɪ 'zɛnt] **1.** *tv.* to stand for something; to portray someone or something; to express something. ♦ *This essay represents weeks of work.* ♦ *This painting represents the artist's emotions.* **2.** *tv.* to act on behalf of someone else; to speak for someone else. ♦ *The lawyer represented his client inside the courtroom.* ♦ *Someone who represented the company spoke at the press conference.*

representation [rɛp rɪ zɛn 'te ʃən] **1.** *n.* an action on behalf of someone or some organization; [someone's] presence that represents someone or some organization. (No plural form in this sense.) ♦ *The vice president served as representation of our company at the conference.* ♦ *The lawyer's representation of the client was costly.* **2.** *n.* something that represents someone or something; something that portrays or expresses something. ♦ *This painting is a representation of how the artist feels about violence.* ♦ *This gift of money is a representation of our concern for the elderly.*

representative [rɛp rɪ 'zɛn tə tɪv] **1.** *n.* someone who is chosen or elected to act, speak, or vote for other people, especially members elected to a legislature. ♦ *All of the representatives were present for the vote.* ♦ *I wrote a letter to my representative protesting the tax cut.* **2.** *adj.* typical of someone or something. (Adv: *representatively.*) ♦ *We need a representative example of the artist's work.* ♦ *This short poem is representative of the author's best works.*

repress [rɪ 'prɛs] *tv.* to hold back something, especially emotion or feeling. ♦ *Mary repressed her desire to laugh during the ceremony.* ♦ *John had repressed feelings of anger from his childhood.*

repression [rɪ 'prɛ ʃən] *n.* a mental condition caused by not allowing oneself to show one's emotions or feelings. (No plural form in this sense.) ♦ *David had a lot of repression that kept him from understanding himself.* ♦ *John's repression of his feelings led to his anger.*

reprieve [rɪ 'priv] **1.** *tv.* to delay someone's execution ② officially. ♦ *The condemned prisoner was reprieved at the last moment.* ♦ *The governor reprieved the prisoner from being executed.* **2.** *n.* an official order that delays someone's execution. ♦ *The protesters demanded a reprieve to the unjust execution.* ♦ *The governor granted a reprieve for the prisoner's execution.* **3.** *n.* a period of relief from something bad or unpleasant. (Figurative on ②.) ♦ *The rain was a reprieve from the horrible drought.* ♦ *The cool weather was a reprieve from the heat wave.*

reprimand ['rɛp rɪ mænd] **1.** *n.* censure; an official scolding; an official rebuke. ♦ *The police officer's reprimand included a $1,000 fine.* ♦ *The bully ignored the principal's reprimand.* **2.** *tv.* to scold someone for doing something; to censure someone; to rebuke someone. ♦ *Congress reprimanded the senator for accepting a bribe.* ♦ *The bad cop was reprimanded, but the protesters wanted him fired.*

reprint 1. [ri 'prɪnt] *tv.* to print something again, especially after all the copies of it have been sold. ♦ *The publishing company reprinted the popular book each year.* ♦ *So far, Jane's book has been reprinted six times.* **2.** ['ri prɪnt] *n.* a copy of a book or publication that has been reprinted ① from an earlier edition. ♦ *The book collector said this reprint isn't worth much.* ♦ *Only reprints were available of the rare 19th-century book.*

reprisal [rɪ 'praɪz əl] **1.** *n.* revenge. (No plural form in this sense.) ♦ *Reprisal against one's enemies is a form of retribution.* ♦ *In reprisal, the fired worker blackmailed his boss.* **2.** *n.* an act of ①. ♦ *The rebel's reprisal against the army was brutal and bloody.* ♦ *The president planned reprisals against his political enemies.*

reproach [rɪ 'protʃ] **1.** *n.* blame; censure. (No plural form in this sense.) ♦ *Reproach from a close friend can hurt your feelings.* ♦ *I earned reproach by my rude remark.* **2.** *tv.* to blame or censure someone. ♦ *The Senate reproached the senator for accepting bribes.* ♦ *The teacher reproached the students for cheating.* **3. above reproach** *idiom* not deserving of blame or criticism. ♦ *Some politicians behave as though they are above reproach.* ♦ *You must accept your punishment. You are not above reproach.*

reproduce [ri prə 'dus] **1.** *tv.* to make a copy of something. ♦ *I reproduced 100 copies of my résumé on the copier.* ♦ *The photo lab reproduced two copies of each print.* **2.** *tv.* to recreate something; to do something in the way it has already been done. ♦ *I could not reproduce the funny noise that Jane made.* ♦ *We were able to reproduce exactly the room where Lincoln died.* **3.** *iv.* to have offspring; to procreate. ♦ *Without the proper conditions, the fish will not reproduce.* ♦ *Our rabbits reproduced often, and soon we had 30 rabbits.*

reproduction [ri prə 'dʌk ʃən] **1.** *n.* the process of making a copy of something; duplicating something. (No plural form in this sense.) ♦ *The copier's reproduction of the image was flawless.* ♦ *Reproduction of the data was impossible, so the experiment must have been flawed.* **2.** *n.* creating offspring; reproducing. (No plural form in this sense.) ♦ *Reproduction is the way that living things replace themselves.* ♦ *The biology teacher explained the process of reproduction.* **3.** *n.* a copy of something, especially of a work of art or a book. ♦ *This is not an original, but a clever reproduction.* ♦ *A reproduction of an ornate temple filled the stage.*

reproductive [ri prə 'dʌk tɪv] *adj.* of or about reproduction. (Adv: *reproductively.*) ♦ *Anne's reproductive years ended when she was 45.* ♦ *The biology teacher lectured about the reproductive organs.*

reprove [rɪ 'pruv] *tv.* to scold someone; to criticize someone. ♦ *The teacher reproved the students for cheating.* ♦ *John reproved his child after the child had lied.*

reptile ['rɛp taɪl] *n.* a class of animals whose temperature is the same as the surrounding air, including dinosaurs, lizards, snakes, turtles, tortoises, alligators, and crocodiles. ♦ *The museum had dozens of fossils of ancient reptiles.* ♦ *Many kinds of reptiles live in the marsh behind my house.*

republic [rɪ 'pʌb lɪk] **1.** *n.* a nation where the people are governed by representatives that they elect. ♦ *The United States of America is a republic.* ♦ *The capital of the Czech Republic is Prague.* **2.** *n.* a system of government where the people elect representatives to represent them. ♦ *The U.S. gave aid to the struggling tropical republic.* ♦ *The cynical people had no faith in the republic.*

Republican [rɪ 'pʌb lɪ kən] **1. Republican Party** *n.* one of the two major political parties in the U.S. ♦ *The Republican Party generally opposes government control and reg-*

ulation. ♦ *The Republican Party is supportive of business and commerce.* **2.** *n.* a member of ①. ♦ *The southern Democrat became a Republican during his term.* ♦ *The young Republicans spoke on campus about term limits.* **3.** *adj.* <the adj. use of ①.> ♦ *The liberal disagreed with many planks of the Republican platform.* ♦ *The Republican philosophy is usually more socially and economically conservative than the Democratic Party.*

repudiate [rɪ 'pju di et] *tv.* to reject someone or something; to refuse to accept someone or something. ♦ *The scientist repudiated the results of the shoddy experiment.* ♦ *The court repudiated John's claim to the disputed territory.*

repugnant [rɪ 'pʌg nənt] *adj.* disgusting; offensive; very disagreeable. (Adv: *repugnantly.*) ♦ *The art exhibit was called repugnant and repellent.* ♦ *A repugnant odor was caused by rotten eggs.*

repulse [rɪ 'pʌls] **1.** *tv.* to drive back a force; to push back a force. ♦ *The army repulsed the rebels.* ♦ *Tom repulsed the attacker by punching him in the stomach.* **2.** *tv.* to cause someone to feel sick; to offend someone; to sicken someone; to disgust someone. (Often passive.) ♦ *John was repulsed by the disgusting movie.* ♦ *Television repulses many viewers.*

repulsive [rɪ 'pʌl sɪv] *adj.* causing disgust; offensive; sickening; causing someone to move or turn away from someone or something that is disgusting or offensive. (Adv: *repulsively.*) ♦ *Although the work of art was repulsive, it represented the artist's feelings.* ♦ *The repulsive food made me gag.*

reputable ['rɛp jə tə bəl] *adj.* respected; having a good reputation. (Adv: *reputably.*) ♦ *I trusted the reputable professor's analysis.* ♦ *This hotel is not expensive, but it is quite reputable.*

reputation [rep jə 'te ʃən] *n.* the opinion that people have about someone or something; what is said or thought about someone. ♦ *The candidate's reputation was spotless.* ♦ *A lurid newspaper story almost ruined the celebrity's good reputation.*

repute [rɪ 'pjut] *n.* a reputation, good unless otherwise stated. (No plural form in this sense.) ♦ *My friends took me to a restaurant of great repute.* ♦ *The Smiths are a family of good repute.*

reputed [rɪ 'pjut ɪd] **1.** *adj.* supposed; alleged. (Adv: *reputedly.*) ♦ *There was no evidence to convict the reputed thief.* ♦ *The popular candidate was also a reputed gang member.* **2. reputed to** *idiom* thought to do, be, or have someone or something. ♦ *My boss is reputed to have cancer.* ♦ *My neighbor was reputed to have been a spy during the war.*

request [rɪ 'kwɛst] **1.** *tv.* to ask for something politely. ♦ *Mary requested that she be allowed to leave the room.* ♦ *The office manager requested two new computers for the office.* **2.** *n.* the act of asking for something politely; a polite demand. ♦ *The manager's request for a new computer was denied.* ♦ *The student's request to leave the room was granted.*

require [rɪ 'kwaɪr] **1.** *tv.* to demand a particular qualification or skill. ♦ *This job requires a college degree.* ♦ *Calculus requires a knowledge of algebra.* **2.** *tv.* to demand that someone do something. ♦ *Everyone is required to wear a hard hat at the construction site.* ♦ *The icy roads require you to drive carefully.*

required [rɪ 'kwaɪrd] *adj.* needed; mandatory; ordered; necessary. ♦ *Anne submitted the form with the required signatures.* ♦ *The employee wore the required uniform.*

requirement [rɪ 'kwaɪr mənt] *n.* something that must be done; something that is mandatory; something that is necessary. ♦ *One of the school's requirements is that each student study math.* ♦ *The candidate met all of the requirements for the job.*

requisite ['rɛk wə zɪt] **1.** *n.* something that is needed or necessary for a certain purpose. ♦ *The chef collected all the requisites for the meal the day before she prepared it.* ♦ *Knowledge of computers is a requisite for this job.* **2.** *adj.* needed; necessary; required. (Adv: *requisitely.*) ♦ *Knowledge of algebra is requisite for a calculus course.* ♦ *The new employee completed the requisite training.*

requisition [rɛk wɪ 'zɪ ʃən] *n.* an official written request for goods or supplies. ♦ *The manager filled out a requisition for more office supplies.* ♦ *Anne's requisition for a new desk was sent to the supply office.*

rerun ['ri rən] *n.* a television program that is not new; a television program that has been on television before; a repeat. ♦ *The only shows on TV tonight were reruns, so I turned it off.* ♦ *The networks show mostly reruns during the summer.*

resale ['ri sel] **1.** *n.* the selling of something as a used or secondhand item. ♦ *The vintage store specialized in the resale of old clothes.* ♦ *The resale of some products is forbidden by law.* **2.** *adj.* of or about the selling of used items. ♦ *I bought the fancy old dress at a resale shop.* ♦ *The antique car's resale price was higher than its original cost.*

rescind [rɪ 'sɪnd] *tv.* to undo a law, an order, or an offer. ♦ *The city council rescinded the tax increase.* ♦ *The state rescinded many grants due to lack of funds.*

rescue ['rɛs kju] **1.** *tv.* to save someone or something that is in danger. ♦ *The firefighter rescued six people from the burning building.* ♦ *The Coast Guard rescued five people when their boat sank.* **2.** *n.* the act of saving someone or something from danger as performed by someone. ♦ *The firefighter's daring rescue of the child was extraordinary.* ♦ *My rescue of the cat in the tree was easy.* **3.** *n.* the act of saving someone or something from danger as performed on the person or thing. ♦ *The child's rescue by the fireman was extraordinary.* ♦ *The hostages' rescue ended in failure.*

research ['ri sɚtʃ] **1.** *n.* study and examination; the collection of information. (No plural form in this sense.) ♦ *The linguist's research required travel in India.* ♦ *The government grant paid for the biologist's research.* **2.** *tv.* to collect information about something in great detail. ♦ *The botanist researched the growth of herbs.* ♦ *The scientist researched the matter thoroughly.*

resemblance [rɪ 'zɛm bləns] *n.* the similarity between two things or people that look alike. ♦ *The resemblance between John and his son was obvious.* ♦ *David bears a striking resemblance to a famous actor.*

resemble [rɪ 'zɛm bəl] *tv.* to look like someone or something; to be like someone or something. ♦ *Mary resembles her mother in many ways.* ♦ *The fancy office building resembled a pyramid.*

resent [rɪ 'zɛnt] *tv.* to feel bitter at someone about something; to feel insulted by someone about something. ♦

Mary resented John's promotion because she deserved it. ♦ *Susan resented the work that her parents made her do.*

resentful [rɪ 'zɛnt fʊl] *adj.* full of anger or bitterness about someone or something; feeling that one has been insulted; showing anger or bitterness. (Adv: *resentfully.*) ♦ *The resentful child treated his parents rudely.* ♦ *A resentful worker damaged the office equipment.*

resentment [rɪ 'zɛnt mənt] **1.** *n.* a feeling that one has been insulted; a feeling of anger or bitterness toward someone or something. (No plural form in this sense.) ♦ *Bill's resentment of his inept coworkers was very strong.* ♦ *Do you have resentment for your parents?* **2.** *n.* a specific instance of ①. ♦ *I have a lot of resentments about my childhood.* ♦ *I have a resentment I would like to talk to you about.*

reservation [rɛ zɚ 've ʃən] **1.** *n.* a doubt about something; a concern; something that stops someone from accepting something. ♦ *I have reservations about going to unsafe neighborhoods at night.* ♦ *The manager had a reservation about giving the lazy worker a raise.* **2.** *n.* a previous claim on the use of something at a specific time, such as a seat in a theater, airplane, or concert; a room in a hotel; or a table at a restaurant. ♦ *I made reservations for a flight to London in May.* ♦ *The fancy restaurant did not accept reservations.* **3.** *n.* an area of land that is set aside for American Indians. ♦ *The anthropologist visited the reservation regularly.* ♦ *You need permission to enter some of the reservations.*

reserve [rɪ 'zɚv] **1.** *tv.* to schedule the use of something at a certain time; to record a claim for the future use of something at a certain time. ♦ *John and Bill reserved the tennis court for 3:00.* ♦ *Mary reserved four seats for the opera for next Friday.* **2.** *tv.* to save something for future use. ♦ *The surplus grain was reserved in a silo.* ♦ *John reserved the rest of the ham for a future meal.* **3.** *n.* something that is saved for future use. ♦ *The surplus was stored as a reserve for future use.* ♦ *A reserve of canned food is stored in the basement.* **4. reserves** *n.* troops or soldiers that are prepared to be called to war. (Treated as plural.) ♦ *The president sent the reserves to the war zone.* ♦ *During the war, the reserves were placed on alert.* **5.** *n.* land that is saved for a specific use or benefit. ♦ *Jane went hiking through the game reserve.* ♦ *The students went on a field trip to the nature reserve.*

reserved [rɪ 'zɚvd] **1.** *adj.* saved for a certain person or certain reason; scheduled to be used by someone at a certain time. ♦ *You need a ticket to sit in the reserved seats.* ♦ *This table is reserved for someone else.* **2.** *adj.* quiet; keeping to oneself; not talking about oneself. (Adv: *reservedly* [rɪ 'zɚv əd li].) ♦ *John is very reserved and doesn't like to go to parties.* ♦ *The reserved student ate in the cafeteria by herself.*

reservoir ['rɛ zɚ vwɑr] **1.** *n.* an artificial lake where water is stored for the use of people. ♦ *During the drought, the water level in the reservoir was low.* ♦ *Swimming is prohibited in the town reservoir.* **2.** *n.* a place where something, such as knowledge, is stored. (Figurative on ①.) ♦ *A library is a reservoir of knowledge.* ♦ *This encyclopedia is a reservoir of information.*

reshuffle [ri 'ʃʌf əl] *tv.* to shuffle something again; to change the position of things (especially playing cards) or people. ♦ *The dealer reshuffled the cards and handed them out.* ♦ *At the last minute, the host reshuffled the seating arrangement.*

reside [rɪ 'zɑɪd] *iv.* to live in a certain place. ♦ *The president resides in the White House.* ♦ *My boss resides in a very fancy apartment building.*

residence ['rɛz ɪ dəns] **1.** *n.* the period of time that someone lives in a certain place. (No plural form in this sense. Number is expressed with *period(s) of residence.*) ♦ *How long was your residence on the island?* ♦ *Jane's period of residence in New York City was short.* **2.** *n.* a house or an apartment; the place where someone lives. ♦ *Lisa's residence was not harmed by the fire next door.* ♦ *Bill and Mary live in a lovely brick residence on Maple Street.*

resident ['rɛz ɪ dənt] **1.** *n.* a person who lives in a certain house or apartment. ♦ *Five residents were injured in the apartment fire.* ♦ *The census counted each resident at each address.* **2.** *n.* a person who lives in a certain city, state, or country. ♦ *City workers must be residents of the city.* ♦ *The state college offered lower tuition to residents of the state.* **3.** *n.* a doctor who has finished serving as an intern and is getting specialized training. ♦ *The resident thoroughly examined the patient.* ♦ *The resident had worked for 24 hours without sleeping.* **4.** *adj.* living in or working at a certain place. ♦ *Our resident manager fixed the leak.* ♦ *The palace's resident poet wrote the queen a poem.*

residential [rɛz ɪ 'dɛn ʃəl] *adj.* of or about residences; of or about homes or apartments rather than offices, farms, or industry. (Adv: *residentially.*) ♦ *The quiet suburb was a residential community.* ♦ *Mary lived in a small house on a residential street.*

residual [rɪ 'zɪ dʒu əl] *adj.* left over; remaining; left behind; being a residue. (Adv: *residually.*) ♦ *The townspeople cleaned the residual debris left by the flood.* ♦ *The coroner found residual traces of gunpowder on the corpse.*

residue ['rɛz ɪ du] *n.* the part of something that remains after part of it has been taken; what is left over when something has been taken; a remainder. ♦ *After I washed the dishes, I rinsed the soapy residue away.* ♦ *The chemist filtered the liquid and examined the residue.*

resign [rɪ 'zɑɪn] **1.** *tv.* to quit a job officially; to give up a job; to leave a job. ♦ *Richard Nixon resigned the office of President in 1974.* ♦ *The office manager resigned her post amid scandal.* **2. resign to** *tv.* + *prep. phr.* to cause oneself to accept something without complaining; to cause oneself to yield to something. (Reflexive or passive.) ♦ *Mary resigned herself to finishing the book by midnight.* ♦ *David was resigned to losing ten pounds by summer.* **3. resign from** *iv.* + *prep. phr.* to quit; to give up a job; to leave a job. ♦ *I resigned from my job so I could spend more time with my family.* ♦ *The senator resigned from his post after his censure.*

resignation [rɛz ɪg 'ne ʃən] **1.** *n.* voluntarily leaving a job or an office. (No plural form in this sense.) ♦ *Resignation was the only way that the governor could save her reputation.* ♦ *Bill chose resignation rather than submit to the outrageous demands of the company president.* **2.** *n.* a formal statement or document made by someone who is leaving a job. ♦ *The company treasurer handed the owner his resignation.* ♦ *Jane gave her resignation to the chairman of the board.* **3.** *n.* the act of resigning from an office. ♦ *The pundits discussed the effects of the president's resigna-*

tion. ♦ *David's resignation left an opening on the board of directors.*

resilience [ri 'zɪl jəns] *n.* the state of being resilient; the ability to return to one's former condition or shape. (No plural form in this sense.) ♦ *Rubber has a great deal of resilience.* ♦ *The spring lost its resilience when it was wound too tightly.*

resilient [rɪ 'zɪl jənt] *adj.* able to return to one's former condition or shape. (Adv: *resiliently.*) ♦ *The resilient gymnast contorted her body into amazing positions.* ♦ *I stretched the resilient rubber band around the papers.*

resin ['rɛz ən] *n.* a naturally occurring, organic substance used in varnishes and plastics. (No plural form in this sense.) ♦ *When I touched the tree, the resin on its bark stuck to my hand.* ♦ *This varnish is made from natural resins.*

resinous ['rɛz ə nəs] *adj.* <the adj. form of resin.> (Adv: *resinously.*) ♦ *The resinous coating was very sticky.* ♦ *Resinous layers of varnish protect the wood from water.*

resist [rɪ 'zɪst] **1.** *tv.* to oppose something; to refuse to accept something. ♦ *Jimmy resisted his parents' help.* ♦ *The obstinate office manager resisted new technology.* **2.** *tv.* to keep from doing something; to prevent something from happening; to stop something from happening. (Takes a verb with *-ing.*) ♦ *The dieter couldn't resist eating chocolate.* ♦ *John resisted being sent to school every morning.* **3.** *tv.* to be undamaged by something; to be able to withstand something. ♦ *The rebels resisted the government soldiers' attack.* ♦ *The disease resisted all forms of treatment.*

resistance [rɪ 'zɪs təns] **1. resistance to** *n.* + *prep. phr.* resisting someone or something. (No plural form in this sense.) ♦ *Some metals show resistance to rusting.* ♦ *The old professor's resistance to new ideas was quite annoying.* **2. resistance to** *n.* + *prep. phr.* the ability to resist disease, poison, etc. (No plural form in this sense.) ♦ *A nutritious diet boosts one's resistance to infection.* ♦ *The insects developed a resistance to the insecticide.* **3.** *n.* the ability of a material to impede the flow of electricity. (No plural form in this sense.) ♦ *I doubled the voltage in the circuit to compensate for the resistance.* ♦ *What is the resistance of this electrical circuit?*

resistant [ri 'zɪs tənt] **resistant to** *adj.* + *prep. phr.* not affected by something; unreceptive to something; unfazed by something. ♦ *These pots are resistant to rust and stains.* ♦ *The old professor was resistant to new ideas.*

resole [ri 'sol] *tv.* to put a new sole on a shoe, boot, or other piece of footwear. ♦ *The cobbler resoled my boots.* ♦ *Anne's shoes were resoled at the shoe store.*

resolute ['rɛz ə lut] *adj.* determined; having one's mind made up. (Adv: *resolutely.*) ♦ *The resolute politician refused to be swayed by public opinion.* ♦ *Anne was resolute in her quest to prosecute her employer.*

resolution [rɛz ə 'lu ʃən] **1.** *n.* a formal statement, such as that voted on by a group of people. (See resolve ②.) ♦ *Congress issued a resolution honoring the war hero.* ♦ *The school board's resolution to fire two teachers was criticized.* **2.** *n.* a pledge or promise. ♦ *The governor had made a resolution to cut taxes.* ♦ *On New Year's Day, John made a resolution to lose ten pounds.* **3.** *n.* a solution to a problem. ♦ *The union and management sought a resolution of the contract dispute.* ♦ *The mediator crafted a resolution that pleased both parties.* **4.** *n.* the ability to do things in a determined way; the ability to focus on a purpose; determination. (No plural form in this sense.) ♦ *John does not have enough resolution to lose weight.* ♦ *Because of Anne's resolution, the office was made more efficient.*

resolve [rɪ 'zɑlv] **1. resolve to** *iv.* + *inf.* to decide to do something. ♦ *Susan resolved to take a course in English literature.* ♦ *David resolved to lose 10 pounds by the end of summer.* **2.** *tv.* [for a group of people] to vote to produce a statement making a request or statement. (Takes a clause.) ♦ *Be it resolved that funding of the budget is hereby approved.* ♦ *It was resolved that no smoking would be allowed in the building.* **3.** *tv.* to settle an issue; to solve a problem; to come to an agreeable solution; to explain something. ♦ *The budget issue was resolved before the meeting was adjourned.* ♦ *The mediator resolved the contract dispute.* **4.** *n.* determination; the ability to do things in a determined way. (No plural form in this sense.) ♦ *Anne's resolve to clean the neighborhood was appreciated.* ♦ *The school board was criticized for its lack of resolve.*

resonance ['rɛz ə nəns] **1.** *n.* the quality of being resonant and sounding rich and full. (No plural form in this sense.) ♦ *The opera singer's voice has very good resonance.* ♦ *The deep resonance of the cello evoked a somber feeling.* **2.** *n.* the property of a contained space, such as a room, that amplifies or enhances sounds or groups of sounds. (No plural form in this sense.) ♦ *The theater's resonance was such that every sound on stage was audible to the audience.* ♦ *Because of the room's resonance, whispered conversations were quite audible.*

resonant ['rɛz ə nənt] *adj.* echoing; making an echo; of or about sound that is vibrating. (Adv: *resonantly.*) ♦ *John's resonant laughter carried across the room.* ♦ *The clarinet's resonant tones were very soothing.*

resonator ['rɛz ə net ɚ] *n.* something that causes sound to continue or become louder; something that causes resonance. ♦ *The body of a violin serves as a resonator.* ♦ *The lower part of a harp is a kind of resonator.*

resort [rɪ 'zort] **1.** *n.* a place where people go for a vacation, consisting at least of a hotel. ♦ *For vacation, I went to the ski resort in Vermont.* ♦ *For their honeymoon, the couple went to a beach resort in Florida.* **2. resort to** *iv.* + *prep. phr.* to decide to do something as a useful alternative to something else. ♦ *David resorted to jogging as a way to lose weight.* ♦ *I resorted to walking after my bicycle was stolen.*

resound [rɪ 'zaʊnd] **1.** *iv.* [for a sound] to travel somewhere and seem to acquire volume. ♦ *My cry resounded throughout the valley.* ♦ *Mary's voice resounded across the empty room.* **2. resound with** *iv.* + *prep. phr.* to be filled with sound. ♦ *The valley resounded with the villagers' song.* ♦ *The kitchen resounded with noise when I dropped the dishes.*

resounding [rɪ 'zaʊn dɪŋ] **1.** *adj.* [of a space] echoing; causing sound to bounce back. (Adv: *resoundingly.*) ♦ *In the huge, resounding cathedral, sound echoes and bounces around.* ♦ *John's voice echoed in the resounding room.* **2.** *adj.* loud; able to be heard easily. (Adv: *resoundingly.*) ♦ *John's resounding voice carried across the river.* ♦ *The resounding explosion was heard for miles.* **3.** *adj.* very great; enormous. (Adv: *resoundingly.*) ♦ *Our company suffered a resounding loss last year.* ♦ *The dismal movie was a resounding failure.*

resource ['ri sors] *n.* someone or something that one can go to for help, information, support, or supplies. ♦ *An encyclopedia is an important resource for students.* ♦ *John's computer can access incredible resources of information.*

resourceful [ri 'sors fʊl] *adj.* able to think of different ways to solve a problem. (Adv: *resourcefully.*) ♦ *He is not resourceful enough to finish the difficult task.* ♦ *The resourceful cook substituted molasses for brown sugar.*

respect [rɪ 'spɛkt] **1.** *n.* the honor, admiration, or esteem that one feels for someone or something. (No plural form in this sense.) ♦ *The obedient child had great respect for his parents.* ♦ *Anne has the utmost respect for her college advisor.* **2.** *n.* the polite behavior one shows to someone whom one honors or admires. (No plural form in this sense.) ♦ *The official greeted the foreign diplomat with respect.* ♦ *The students showed their teacher the proper respect.* **3.** *tv.* to feel or show someone or something respect. ♦ *My boss respected the work I had done.* ♦ *The school respected the rights of each of the students.* **4. in some respects; in many respects** *phr.* with regard to some or many details. ♦ *In some respects, Anne's comments are similar to yours.* ♦ *The three proposals are quite different in many respects.* **5. with respect to someone or something** *idiom* of or about someone or something. ♦ *With respect to radiation, this power plant is very safe.* ♦ *This article examines experiments with respect to ethical issues.* **6. pay someone respect** *idiom* to honor someone; to have and show ① and ② for someone. ♦ *You really should pay your boss more respect.* ♦ *We have to pay our parents a lot of respect.*

respectable [rɪ 'spɛk tə bəl] **1.** *adj.* worthy of respect; deserving respect; honorable; admirable; decent. (Adv: *respectably.*) ♦ *Anne demanded that we eat at a respectable restaurant.* ♦ *The prosecuting attorney was a very respectable lawyer.* **2.** *adj.* good enough; adequate. (Informal. Adv: *respectably.*) ♦ *Mary washed her hands with a respectable amount of soap.* ♦ *There was a respectable amount of snowfall last night.*

respectful [rɪ 'spɛkt fʊl] *adj.* showing respect; honoring. (Adv: *respectfully.*) ♦ *The respectful soldier saluted his superiors.* ♦ *The respectful employees did not gossip about their boss.*

respective [rɪ 'spɛk tɪv] *adj.* separate; own; individual. (Relating each member in a group of people or things to someone or something specific. Adv: *respectively.*) ♦ *Ivan and Juan went to their respective countries during the summer; that is, Ivan went to Russia and Juan went to Spain.* ♦ *At the party, each woman danced with her respective husband.*

respectively [rɪ 'spɛk tɪv li] *adv.* individually; separately; in the order stated. (Used to link different things or people in one list with things or people on another list, with the first item in one series linking with the first item in the second series.) ♦ *Sue, Bob, and Dave lived in Rome, Paris, and Miami, respectively. That means that Sue lived in Rome, Bob lived in Paris, and Dave lived in Miami.* ♦ *I gave Mary and Jane a book and a magazine, respectively.*

respiration [rɛs pə 're ʃən] *n.* the process of breathing in and out. (No plural form in this sense.) ♦ *The thinning air hindered the climbers' respiration.* ♦ *The crash victim showed no signs of respiration.*

respirator ['rɛs pə ret ɚ] *n.* a device that fits over the mouth and nose and assists with breathing. ♦ *Respirators supply air or oxygen or filter the air.* ♦ *A respirator fills and empties the lungs alternately.*

respiratory ['rɛs pɚ ə tor i] *adj.* of or about respiration. ♦ *John's respiratory infection was caused by smoking.* ♦ *Asthma is one kind of respiratory ailment.*

respite ['rɛs pɪt] *n.* a short time of rest; a lull; a pause. (No plural form in this sense.) ♦ *During the respite in the war, thousands of citizens fled.* ♦ *The eye of the hurricane provided a brief respite from the storm.*

respond [rɪ 'spɑnd] **1. respond (to)** *iv.* (+ *prep. phr.*) to answer; to reply to someone or something. ♦ *The senator responded to the reporter's question.* ♦ *The judge asked the witness to respond to the question.* **2. respond (to)** *iv.* (+ *prep. phr.*) to react to something; to say or do something when something happens. ♦ *The dog responded to the shrill whistle by barking.* ♦ *David responded to the bad news by crying.* **3.** *tv.* to answer a question; to give an answer; to say something as a response. (Takes a clause.) ♦ *Mary responded that she wanted to have pizza for dinner.* ♦ *When the interviewer asked how old I was, I responded that I was 29.*

response [rɪ 'spɑns] **1.** *n.* an answer; a reply; something that is said or done to answer a question. ♦ *The judge asked the witness for his response.* ♦ *As a response to my question, Mary said she was angry at me.* **2.** *n.* a reaction; something that is done when something happens. ♦ *The senator's response to the allegations was one of denial.* ♦ *Max's lack of response to the invitation was predictable.*

responsibility [rɪ spɑn sə 'bɪl ə ti] **1.** *n.* the authority for something; the duty to take care of someone or something. (No plural form in this sense.) ♦ *Taking care of a younger sister is too much responsibility for a six-year-old child!* ♦ *The regional sales manager has responsibility for all of the company's sales in this part of the country.* **2.** *n.* liability for something going wrong; accountability; blame for causing something bad or, sometimes, credit for causing something good. (No plural form in this sense.) ♦ *Bill denied responsibility for the accident.* ♦ *After the doctor acknowledged her responsibility in the patient's death, the judge found her guilty of malpractice.* **3.** *n.* the quality of being responsible ②. (No plural form in this sense.) ♦ *The company owner looked for responsibility when hiring new employees.* ♦ *The teenager demonstrated his responsibility by taking care of the house while his parents were away.* **4.** *n.* someone or something that one is responsible for. ♦ *My children are my responsibility.* ♦ *Typing and filing are my responsibilities at work.*

responsible [rɪ 'spɑn sə bəl] **1. responsible for** *adj.* + *prep. phr.* having the authority or duty to take care of someone or something, and being liable for anything that goes wrong; accountable. ♦ *The treasurer is responsible for depositing the money.* ♦ *Susie is responsible for feeding the family dog.* **2.** *adj.* reliable; able to do something without being told what to do. (Adv: *responsibly.*) ♦ *The responsible student attended every class.* ♦ *The manager appreciated her responsible employees.* **3. responsible party** *idiom* the person or organization responsible ① or liable for something. ♦ *I intend to find the responsible party and get some answers to my questions.* ♦ *Mary sued the responsible party in the car crash.*

responsive [rɪ 'spɑn sɪv] **1.** *adj.* able to respond to a stimulus. (Adv: *responsively.*) ♦ *The patient was not responsive to the sound of my voice.* ♦ *Most plants are responsive to sunlight.* **2.** *adj.* responding quickly and eagerly to a suggestion or a question. (Adv: *responsively.*) ♦ *The teacher enjoyed the responsive students.* ♦ *The responsive employee did whatever the manager asked.*

rest ['rɛst] **1.** *n.* sleep. (No plural form in this sense.) ♦ *John's rest was interrupted by a loud crack of thunder.* ♦ *Rest was the most important thing on the tired driver's mind.* **2.** *n.* relaxation; a period of calm or quiet after work or activity. (No plural form in this sense.) ♦ *The doctor ordered me to a week of rest.* ♦ *After a long day at work, I needed some rest.* **3. at rest** *phr.* not moving; not active. ♦ *After the hectic day, the office was finally at rest at 8:00 P.M.* ♦ *Do not remove your seat belt until the plane is at rest.* **4.** *iv.* to relax after work or activity. ♦ *Bill rested on the couch after work.* ♦ *After playing tennis, Mary rested for an hour.* **5.** *iv.* to remain somewhere. ♦ *The huge dictionary rests on the bottom shelf.* ♦ *My computer rests on a large table by the door.* **6. rest against** *iv. + prep. phr.* to be supported by something; to lean against something. ♦ *The dictionary is on the shelf, resting against the encyclopedia.* ♦ *The rake rested against the side of the garage.* **7. rest on** *iv. + prep. phr.* to be based on someone or something. ♦ *The lawyer's case rested on weak evidence.* ♦ *The results of the experiment rested on faulty methodology.* **8.** *tv.* to cause someone or an animal to relax. ♦ *John rested the dogs after the hunt.* ♦ *The trainer rested the horses after the race.* **9.** *tv.* to support something; to lean something against something else. ♦ *John rested the rake against the garage door.* ♦ *The carpenter rested the board against the wall.* **10.** *pron.* the remainder; the things that are left over. (Singular form. Treated like a singular or plural.) ♦ *There are some flowers on the table. One is for Anne, but the rest are yours.* ♦ *I cooked rice for dinner. I ate some, but you can have the rest.* **11. rest in peace** *idiom* to lie dead peacefully for eternity. ♦ *We prayed that the deceased would rest in peace.* ♦ *The bodies of the soldiers will rest in peace.*

restate [ri 'stet] *tv.* to state something again; to state something in a different way. ♦ *The professor restated his idea in a less complex way.* ♦ *The senator restated her opposition to the legislation.*

restaurant ['rɛs tə rɑnt] *n.* a place where one buys and eats a meal, which is usually served at a table. ♦ *John and I ate dinner at an Italian restaurant.* ♦ *Mary works in a fancy restaurant as a waitress.*

restful ['rɛst fʊl] *adj.* causing one to feel rested; peaceful; calm; quiet. (Adv: *restfully.*) ♦ *The restful sound of flowing water helped me fall asleep.* ♦ *Jane sang a restful lullaby to the baby.*

restitution [rɛs tɪ 'tu ʃən] *n.* the return of something that was lost, taken, or stolen; the payment made to replace something that was lost, taken, or stolen. (No plural form in this sense.) ♦ *John sought restitution when David damaged his car.* ♦ *Restitution of the stolen painting pleased the museum director.*

restive ['rɛs tɪv] *adj.* unable to relax; always moving; fidgety; restless. (Adv: *restively.*) ♦ *The restive children ran around the house.* ♦ *The little boy was quite restive in church.*

restless ['rɛst ləs] **1.** *adj.* [of someone] fidgeting; not being still; not calm; not quiet; unable to relax; unable to be quiet. (Adv: *restlessly.*) ♦ *The restless man paced as he waited for the office to open.* ♦ *The doctor gave the restless patient a sedative.* **2.** *adj.* disturbed; not restful. ♦ *I spent a restless night trying to fall asleep.* ♦ *Max's restless sleep was not refreshing.*

restlessness ['rɛst ləs nəs] *n.* the inability to be calm, quiet, relaxed, or still; constant movement or fidgeting. (No plural form in this sense.) ♦ *I experience restlessness every night when I try to sleep.* ♦ *The children's restlessness annoyed the teacher.*

restoration [rɛs tə 're ʃən] **1.** *n.* the returning of something to its original or regular condition. (No plural form in this sense.) ♦ *The restoration of the oil painting was very time consuming.* ♦ *The restoration of the old mansion was quite expensive.* **2.** *n.* something that has been returned to its original or regular condition. ♦ *The restorations were more beautiful than the originals.* ♦ *We live in a large brick restoration of an older house.*

restorative [rɪ 'stor ə tɪv] *adj.* providing the power to restore; causing restoration. (Adv: *restoratively.*) ♦ *The restorative power of the medicine helped the sick man.* ♦ *The tired traveler needed a day of restorative sleep.*

restore [rɪ 'stor] *tv.* to return something to its original or regular condition; to put something back. ♦ *The designer restored the mansion to its original condition.* ♦ *The medicine restored Anne's health.*

restored [rɪ 'stord] *adj.* returned to an original or regular condition; returned. ♦ *The law firm moved into the restored office building.* ♦ *John was thankful for his restored health.*

restrain [rɪ 'stren] *tv.* to prevent someone or something from moving or doing something. ♦ *I restrained my urge to attack the bully.* ♦ *The doctors restrained the patient from hurting himself.*

restraint [rɪ 'strent] **1.** *n.* the quality of being restrained; the quality of not showing how one feels. (No plural form in this sense.) ♦ *John was rude to Anne, but she showed restraint by ignoring him.* ♦ *The diplomat's tactful restraint kept the crisis from escalating.* **2.** *n.* something that restrains someone or something; something that prevents someone or something from doing something or moving. ♦ *The prisoner escaped when he broke from his restraints.* ♦ *The patient with seizures was tied to the bed by restraints.*

restrict [rɪ 'strɪkt] *tv.* to limit someone or something's options; to keep someone or something within certain bounds. ♦ *The debaters were restricted to discussing certain topics.* ♦ *This bad legislation would restrict people's rights.*

restriction [rɪ 'strɪk ʃən] *n.* a limitation; a condition that limits action or movement; a rule against doing something; a regulation. ♦ *The airline placed restrictions on special travel offers.* ♦ *John obeyed Jewish dietary restrictions.*

restrictive [rɪ 'strɪk tɪv] *adj.* limiting; keeping someone or something within certain bounds; not allowing someone or something to do something. (Adv: *restrictively.* See a discussion of the *restrictive clause* at **which**. See also **nonrestrictive**.) ♦ *The restrictive government imposed a strict curfew.* ♦ *Mary took restrictive measures to keep Jimmy from eating too much.*

restroom ['rɛst rum] *n.* a room with a toilet, especially in a public building. ♦ *Excuse me, where is the nearest restroom?* ♦ *The janitor cleans the restroom four times each day.*

result [rɪ 'zʌlt] **1.** *n.* the outcome of an event; something that is caused by something else. ♦ *The researcher examined the results of the experiment.* ♦ *One of the results of the new policy was a lower inflation rate.* **2.** *n.* the answer to a math problem; a solution. ♦ *If you add 2 and 3, the result is 5.* ♦ *Please state your result in the form of a fraction.* **3. result from** *iv.* + *prep. phr.* to be an effect of something; to be caused by something. ♦ *Higher unemployment resulted from the disastrous policy.* ♦ *Mary's promotion resulted from her hard work.* **4. result in** *iv.* + *prep. phr.* to lead to a particular result. ♦ *John's interview resulted in his being offered the job.* ♦ *Mary's hard work resulted in a promotion.*

resulting [rɪ 'zʌl tɪŋ] *adj.* happening because of something else; being a result. ♦ *After her disastrous performance, Mary accepted the resulting dismissal.* ♦ *In the resulting panic during the fire, five people were trampled.*

résumé ['rɛz u me] *n.* a document that lists one's education, work history, and other important information. ♦ *The firm interviewed four clients with impressive résumés.* ♦ *Jane listed on her résumé that she spoke German fluently.*

resume [rɪ 'zum] **1.** *tv.* to do something again after having stopped for a time. ♦ *Mary resumed her search for her missing dog after a day of rest.* ♦ *The research was resumed after its funding was reinstated.* **2.** *iv.* to begin again after having stopped for a time. ♦ *My mail delivery resumed when I returned from vacation.* ♦ *The television show resumed after a commercial break.*

resumption [rɪ 'zʌmp ʃən] *n.* beginning to do something again after having stopped for a time. (No plural form in this sense.) ♦ *The mediator urged a resumption in contract talks.* ♦ *The resumption of the patient's vital signs pleased the surgeons.*

resurface [ri 'sɚ fɪs] **1.** *iv.* to come to the surface again. ♦ *The whale resurfaced and swam near the boat.* ♦ *I dove into the cold water and resurfaced very quickly.* **2.** *iv.* [for someone or something] to reappear or come out of concealment. (Figurative on ①.) ♦ *After years in hiding, the fugitive resurfaced in Seattle.* ♦ *My brother resurfaced after all of the chores were finished.* **3.** *tv.* to put a new surface on something. ♦ *Anne resurfaces the kitchen floor every other year.* ♦ *John resurfaced the porch with a new coat of varnish.*

resurgence [rɪ 'sɚ dʒəns] *n.* a return of power or energy; a rise in activity after destruction or loss. ♦ *The mayor was dismayed by the resurgence in violent crime.* ♦ *After years of decline, downtown businesses experienced a resurgence.*

resurgent [rɪ 'sɚ dʒənt] *adj.* having power or energy again; rising in activity after destruction or loss; becoming active again. (Adv: *resurgently.*) ♦ *The resurgent politician returned to office after a four-year absence.* ♦ *The media capitalized on a resurgent interest in the 1960s.*

resurrection [rɛz ə 'rɛk ʃən] **1.** *n.* the return to life of someone who has died; the bringing back to life of a dead person or creature. ♦ *The resurrection of all the creatures who have ever lived would make the earth a very crowded place.* ♦ *Do you believe in the resurrection of the dead?* **2.** *n.* the return to use of something that had been thought of as useless. (Figurative on ①.) ♦ *The resurrection of the old policies was met with antagonism.* ♦ *The resurrection of the run-down neighborhood surprised everyone.*

resuscitate *tv.* to cause someone who is unconscious to regain consciousness. ♦ *The lifeguard resuscitated the man who had almost drowned.* ♦ *Paramedics resuscitated the unconscious woman.*

retail ['ri tel] **1.** *adj.* [of a store] selling products to consumers directly. ♦ *Mary does all of her shopping at retail stores.* ♦ *What's the retail price of this television set?* **2. retail for** *iv.* + *prep. phr.* [for a product] to be available for purchase for a certain price in a retail ① store. ♦ *My new sofa retailed for $500.* ♦ *At John's store, everything retails for less!*

retailer ['ri tel ɚ] *n.* a shopkeeper; someone who sells products directly to consumers. ♦ *The retailer told me he had sold all of the toasters he had.* ♦ *The retailer bought her goods from a wholesaler.*

retain [rɪ 'ten] **1.** *tv.* to keep something; to continue to have something. ♦ *Mary retained all the information that she read.* ♦ *David retained his tax records for seven years.* **2.** *tv.* to hire a lawyer. ♦ *John retained a lawyer when he was sued.* ♦ *The defendant retained the best lawyer he could afford.*

retainer [rɪ 'ten ɚ] **1.** *n.* the payment that is given to someone, especially a lawyer, as a down payment on future services. ♦ *The lawyer requested a $2,500 retainer.* ♦ *After the initial interview, I gave the lawyer a $1,000 retainer.* **2.** *n.* a device worn in the mouth to hold the teeth in position. ♦ *After her braces were removed, Mary wore a retainer for a year.* ♦ *You shouldn't chew gum while you're wearing a retainer.*

retake 1. ['ri tek] *n.* the act of filming a part of a movie or television show again. ♦ *The director was satisfied with the third retake.* ♦ *The film crew spent the whole day doing retakes of the same scene.* **2.** [ri 'tek] *tv., irreg.* to take a picture again or to film a part of a movie or television show again. (Pt: retook; pp: retaken.) ♦ *The film crew had retaken the last scene seven times.* ♦ *The photographer retook the picture because my eyes were closed.*

retaken ['ri 'tek ən] pp of retake.

retaliate [rɪ 'tæl i et] *iv.* to get even with someone; to return a bad deed to someone who has done a bad deed to oneself. ♦ *When the mayor criticized the newspaper, it retaliated by endorsing his opponent.* ♦ *The slaves retaliated and attacked their masters.*

retaliation [rɪ tæl i 'e ʃən] *n.* returning a bad deed to someone who has done a bad deed to oneself. (No plural form in this sense.) ♦ *In retaliation against the tyrant, the citizens lynched him.* ♦ *He hit me, and for retaliation, I hit him.*

retaliatory [rɪ 'tæl i ə tor i] *adj.* of or about retaliation. (Adv: *retaliatorily* [rɪ tæl ə 'tor i ə li].) ♦ *The army's strike against the enemy was a retaliatory maneuver.* ♦ *In a retaliatory act, the discharged worker shot his employer.*

retard [rɪ 'tɑrd] *tv.* to cause someone or something to go slower. ♦ *The inflation rate was retarded by the government policies.* ♦ *The heavy winds retarded the plane's speed.*

retardant [rɪ 'tɑrd nt] *n.* something, especially a chemical, that slows the process of something, such as a fire.

♦ *Our draperies were sprayed with a chemical fire retardant.* ♦ *The steel was coated with a retardant that prevents rust.*

retarded [rɪ 'tɑr dɪd] *adj.* having low intelligence; not very developed in the mind. (Adv: *retardedly.*) ♦ *The retarded child was able to do only simple tasks.* ♦ *The mentally retarded man was polite and helpful.*

retch ['rɛtʃ] *iv.* to make the movements of vomiting without actually vomiting. ♦ *The horrible odor made me retch.* ♦ *Anne retched when she saw the disgusting pictures.*

retention [rɪ 'tɛn ʃən] **1.** *n.* retaining something; holding or keeping something. (No plural form in this sense.) ♦ *As an aid to memory retention, I copied my notes again after class.* ♦ *My retention of what I had read was hindered because I was tired.* **2.** *n.* the ability to remember things or people. (No plural form in this sense.) ♦ *The hyperactive child's reading retention was poor.* ♦ *My retention improves when the subject matter is interesting.*

retentive [rɪ 'tɛn tɪv] *adj.* able to remember; able to retain something well. (Adv: *retentively.*) ♦ *The retentive student did very well on the exam.* ♦ *Tom has a very retentive mind.*

reticent ['rɛt ə sənt] *adj.* not saying much; quiet; reserved; not saying what one feels or how one thinks. (Adv: *reticently.*) ♦ *I was reticent about correcting my manager's mistakes.* ♦ *David was reticent about asking Susan to the dance.*

retina ['rɛt n ə] *n.* the membrane on the inside of the back of the eyeball that sends the image of what the eye sees to the brain. ♦ *If your retinas ever become detached, you will be blind.* ♦ *Each retina has a unique pattern of blood vessels.*

retire [rɪ 'tɑɪr] **1.** *iv.* to stop working for a living and live on the money one has saved. ♦ *After working at the factory for 45 years, John retired.* ♦ *When Mary and Bob quit working, they retired and went to Florida.* **2. retire to** *iv. + prep. phr.* to quit work as in ① and move somewhere. ♦ *John retired to Arizona.* ♦ *When Mary and Bob quit working, they retired to Florida.* **3. retire to** *iv. + prep. phr.* to go to a different place; to go to a place away from other people. ♦ *After dinner, I retired to the living room to read.* ♦ *During the party, Mary retired to the bedroom to take a nap.* **4.** *iv.* to go to bed. ♦ *I normally retire for the night around 10:00.* ♦ *Jane retired earlier than normal because she was very tired.* **5.** *tv.* to cause someone to retire ①. ♦ *The team owner retired the star baseball player at 40.* ♦ *The university retired the senile professor.* **6.** *tv.* to cause something to no longer be used; to remove something from use. ♦ *Our neighbors retired their noisy old car last year.* ♦ *The Johnsons retired their broken toaster and bought a new one.* **7.** *tv.* to pay a debt. ♦ *My mortgage will be retired ten years from now.* ♦ *Mary retired her credit-card debt last month.*

retired [rɪ 'tɑɪrd] *adj.* having quit working altogether, usually to enjoy one's final years. ♦ *My retired grandparents live in Arizona.* ♦ *The retired senator received a very hefty pension.*

retirement [rɪ 'tɑɪr mənt] **1.** *n.* the period of time after one has retired. (No plural form in this sense.) ♦ *In her retirement, Mary began to garden as a hobby.* ♦ *John spent his retirement in Arizona.* **2.** *n.* an act of ①. ♦ *For John's retirement, his family threw him a big party.* ♦ *Anne celebrated her retirement by traveling to Europe.*

retiring [rɪ 'tɑɪr ɪŋ] *adj.* reserved; shy. (Adv: *retiringly.*) ♦ *Bill was always shy and retiring, and liked to eat alone.* ♦ *Lisa was a retiring child, but now she is very sociable.*

retook [ri 'tʊk] pt of retake.

retort [rɪ 'tort] **1.** *n.* a witty reply; an angry response. ♦ *Anne responded to the insult with a very clever retort.* ♦ *Bob's angry retort scared his employees.* **2.** *tv.* to make a response as in ①. ♦ *When I asked my boss for a raise, he retorted, "No!"* ♦ *When I asked if he was all right, the angry driver retorted that he was going to sue me.*

retouch [ri 'tʌtʃ] **1.** *tv.* to cause a photograph to look different, usually with paints or dyes. ♦ *Please retouch this photo so the subject looks more natural.* ♦ *The photographer retouched my photo to conceal my wrinkles.* **2.** *tv.* to make slight changes to a painting. ♦ *The artist retouched her painting before exhibiting it.* ♦ *Mary retouched my portrait so that I look younger.*

retrace [rɪ 'tres] *tv.* to go over something again; to travel or move over the same route again. ♦ *David retraced his path back to the cabin.* ♦ *Mary retraced her steps in order to find her lost keys.*

retract [rɪ 'trækt] **1.** *tv.* to cancel a statement, offer, or mistake. ♦ *The newspaper retracted the mistake.* ♦ *The company retracted its offer of a free ham, because it ran out of hams.* **2.** *tv.* to draw or pull something into something. ♦ *The turtle retracted its limbs into its shell.* ♦ *The lion retracts its claws when it plays with its cubs.* **3.** *iv.* [for something] to pull or draw back [into something]. ♦ *The turtle's limbs retract into its shell.* ♦ *The cat's claws retracted whenever it jumped up onto the furniture.*

retrain [ri 'tren] *tv.* to train someone again; to train someone to do something different. ♦ *The auto workers were retrained when the factory was modernized.* ♦ *The manager retrained the secretaries to use the new computer software.*

retread ['ri trɛd] *n.* a tire that has a new tread put on it. ♦ *The mechanic offered to sell me some retreads.* ♦ *My old tires were worn thin, so I bought some retreads.*

retreat [rɪ 'trit] **1.** *iv.* to go back, especially because one cannot fight or go forward. ♦ *The losing army retreated.* ♦ *The hikers retreated from the edge of the cliff.* **2.** *n.* the act of going back, especially during a battle, because one cannot fight or move forward. ♦ *The soldiers' retreat was a sign of defeat.* ♦ *The poorly trained troops made a hasty retreat from battle.* **3.** *n.* a quiet, isolated place; a place that one can go to for quiet, rest, or safety. ♦ *I spent a relaxing weekend at a remote mountain retreat.* ♦ *The old cathedral was a retreat for the poor and weary.*

retrench [rɪ 'trɛntʃ] *iv.* to reduce expenses; not to spend as much money. ♦ *If our company doesn't retrench, it will go bankrupt.* ♦ *The agency retrenched after the government cut its budget.*

retribution [rɛ trə 'bju ʃən] *n.* the reward or, more usually, punishment that is deserved. (No plural form in this sense.) ♦ *Tom believed that his many misfortunes were retribution for all the bad things he had done.* ♦ *A life in prison is just retribution for the suffering you have caused other people.*

retrieval [rɪ 'triv əl] *n.* getting, fetching, or bringing something. (No plural form in this sense.) ♦ *The old computer's retrieval of the data was very slow.* ♦ *The retrieval of the child from the well was very dangerous.*

retrieve [rɪ 'triv] **1.** *tv.* to get something and bring it to a place or to someone. ♦ *The dog retrieved the newspaper from the driveway.* ♦ *Jane retrieved the document from the computer's memory.* **2.** *tv.* to rescue someone or something; to save someone or something. ♦ *The police retrieved my stolen property.* ♦ *The cook retrieved the steak from the flames of the barbecue.*

retriever [rɪ 'triv ɚ] *n.* a dog that is trained to find animals that a hunter has killed and return those animals to the hunter. ♦ *The golden retriever carried the dead duck in its mouth.* ♦ *The retriever went into the bushes to find the pheasant I'd shot.*

retroactive [rɛ tro 'æk tɪv] *adj.* effective from a certain date in the past. (Adv: *retroactively.*) ♦ *Members of Congress approved retroactive raises in their salaries.* ♦ *The new tax increase was retroactive to last June.*

retrospect ['rɛ trə spɛkt] **in retrospect** *phr.* reconsidering the past with the knowledge one now has. ♦ *In retrospect, I would have gone to a better college.* ♦ *David realized, in retrospect, that he should have finished school.*

retrospective [rɛ trə 'spɛk tɪv] **1.** *adj.* looking at the past. (Adv: *retrospectively.*) ♦ *The book gave us a retrospective view of our grandparents' lives.* ♦ *Mary's retrospective study of piano tuning explained many current practices.* **2.** *n.* a display or presentation of something done in the past; a look back into the past. ♦ *The retrospective of Tom's works included things that should remain forgotten.* ♦ *The museum featured a retrospective of the artist's early works.*

return [rɪ 'tɚn] **1.** *iv.* to go back to a previous time, location, position, or condition. ♦ *I returned to my house at midnight.* ♦ *In October, we return to Standard Time.* **2.** *tv.* to give something back to the person it came from; to put something back in the place it came from. ♦ *Anne returned the earrings she had borrowed from her mother.* ♦ *I returned the book to the library.* **3.** *tv.* to cause someone or something to go back to a previous time, location, position, or condition. ♦ *Please return your book to the library.* ♦ *The pilot returned the plane to the gate.* **4.** *n.* the act of coming back as in ①. ♦ *The astronomers observed the return of the comet.* ♦ *On my return from Japan, my friends met me at the airport.* **5.** *n.* a report, especially an income-tax report. ♦ *You must file your tax return by April 15.* ♦ *The auditor examined my returns for the past seven years.* **6. return(s)** *n.* profit; the amount of money that is made. ♦ *The store's returns were deposited in its bank account.* ♦ *The manager noted that the weekend returns were low.* **7. returns** *n.* records or reports on the outcome of an election. (Treated as plural.) ♦ *Early returns indicated that the incumbent was losing.* ♦ *According to the final returns, Anne had beat her opponents.* **8. returns** *n.* items that are brought back to the place from which they were purchased. (Treated as plural.) ♦ *The day after Christmas, the cashiers dealt with numerous returns.* ♦ *No returns are accepted without a receipt.* **9.** *adj.* of, for, or about the part of a journey during which one returns ① to the starting point. ♦ *On the return trip, I took an express train.* ♦ *I kept my return ticket in my knapsack.* **10.** *adj.* repeated; for a second time; coming back to a place again. ♦ *The popular musical's return engagement was already sold out.* ♦ *The return performance of the play was not a success.* **11.** *adj.* enabling a return ① of something through the postal system. ♦ *The sender was charged for the return postage.* ♦ *A stamped and addressed return envelope was included with the inquiry.* **12. in return** *phr.* by way of giving something back; as a way of paying someone back for something; as part of an exchange. ♦ *I helped Tom yesterday, and he helped me in return today.* ♦ *I paid $20 and received four tickets in return.*

reunion [ri 'jun jən] *n.* a party or gathering of people who are coming together again, especially of people who have not seen each other in a long time. ♦ *Most of my high-school class attended the twentieth reunion.* ♦ *I saw dozens of relatives at the annual family reunion.*

reunite [ri ju 'nɑɪt] **1.** *tv.* to bring people or things together again; to unite people or things again. ♦ *Jane reunited her brother and sister who had been separated for many years.* ♦ *The police reunited the kidnapped children with their parents.* **2.** *iv.* to bring together again; to come together again; to unite again. ♦ *The former band members reunited for one last tour.* ♦ *Germany reunited in 1990.*

rev ['rɛv] **rev (up)** *tv.* (+ *adv.*) to run something, such as an engine, at a burst of full speed. ♦ *John revved his car's engine at the intersection.* ♦ *Mary pressed the gas pedal and revved up the motor.*

revamp [ri 'væmp] *tv.* to repair something; to improve something; to do something over so it is better. ♦ *The playwright revamped his script before opening night.* ♦ *The hotel lobby was revamped before the presidential convention.*

reveal [rɪ 'vil] **1.** *tv.* to allow or cause something to be seen. ♦ *The curtain was raised to reveal the singer.* ♦ *I lifted the lid to reveal the casserole to the guests.* **2.** *tv.* to make information known; to tell a piece of information. ♦ *The spy revealed secret information while being tortured.* ♦ *His testimony revealed that he was guilty of the crime.*

revealing [rɪ 'vil ɪŋ] **1.** *adj.* allowing or causing something to be seen; exposing something, especially skin. (Adv: *revealingly.*) ♦ *The models wore revealing bathing suits on the beach.* ♦ *Dave forbade his daughter to wear such a revealing dress.* **2.** *adj.* giving much information; allowing concealed information to be inferred. (Adv: *revealingly.*) ♦ *Under pressure, the defendant made some very revealing remarks.* ♦ *The revealing testimony was made known to the court.*

reveille ['rɛv ə li] *n.* the melody played on a bugle at the beginning of the day to wake up soldiers. (From French. No plural form in this sense.) ♦ *A soldier played reveille at 6:00 A.M.* ♦ *The troops were roused from sleep by the playing of reveille.*

revel ['rɛv əl] **1.** *iv.* to party; to be festive. ♦ *The college students reveled until 3:00 A.M.* ♦ *On New Year's Eve, thousands of tourists reveled in New Orleans.* **2. revel in** *iv.* + *prep. phr.* to take pleasure in something; to enjoy something very much. ♦ *The evil tyrant reveled in the people's misery.* ♦ *The celebrity reveled in his wealth and fame.*

revelation [rɛv ə 'le ʃən] **1.** *n.* revealing something; making something known. (No plural form in this sense.) ♦ *The professor's exciting lecture was more like revelation than explanation.* ♦ *Revelation of the new tax increase* *angered the voters.* **2.** *n.* something that is made known; a piece of information that is learned by someone. ♦ *The scientist's accidental discovery was quite a revelation.* ♦ *That Jane and Dave were getting married was a revelation to me.*

revenge [rɪ 'vɛndʒ] *n.* harm done, on behalf of oneself or another person, to someone in retaliation for something. (No plural form in this sense. See also **avenge**.) ♦ *The prince demanded revenge for his father's death.* ♦ *The gangster vowed revenge on those who killed his wife.*

revenue ['rɛv ə nu] **1.** *n.* income; money that is made from a business or an investment. ♦ *The company's owner reinvested the company's revenue in real estate.* ♦ *All companies must report their revenues to the government.* **2.** *n.* money that is collected by the government from taxes. ♦ *That program is funded by the revenue the government collects.* ♦ *Congress determines how tax revenues are spent.*

reverberate [rɪ 'vɚb ə ret] **1.** *iv.* [for sound] to echo again and again. ♦ *My loud shouting reverberated throughout the valley.* ♦ *The singer's shrill voice reverberated in the concert hall.* **2.** *iv.* [for a solid object] to vibrate or oscillate. ♦ *My bones reverberated from the loud bass beat coming from the speakers.* ♦ *The earth reverberated from the shock waves of the earthquake.*

revere [rɪ 'vɪr] *tv.* to have a deep respect for someone or something; to admire someone very much. ♦ *Respectful children revere their parents.* ♦ *The honest politician was revered by his constituents.*

reverence ['rɛv rəns] *n.* respect; admiration; awe. (No plural form in this sense.) ♦ *The pilgrims showed reverence by praying.* ♦ *I entered the sanctuary with great reverence.*

reverend ['rɛv rənd] **1. (the) Reverend** *n.* <the title used for a minister.> ♦ *We invited Reverend Jones to dinner after church.* ♦ *The butler announced the arrival of the Reverend Pratt.* **2. the reverend** *n.* a minister. (Informal. No plural form in this sense. Treated as singular.) ♦ *We invited the reverend to eat dinner at our house.* ♦ *The reverend spoke to the congregation about sin.*

reverie ['rɛv ə ri] *n.* a pleasant fantasy or daydream. ♦ *During the boring lecture, I was lost in a pleasant reverie.* ♦ *My reverie was interrupted when the teacher asked me a question.*

reversal [rɪ 'vɚ səl] *n.* a complete change to the opposite. ♦ *The Supreme Court's reversal of the lower court's decision was expected.* ♦ *In a reversal of roles, many children must one day care for their parents.*

reverse [rɪ 'vɚs] **1.** *tv.* to cause something to go or operate backwards. ♦ *Anne reversed the car and backed out of the parking space.* ♦ *Jane reversed the boat's motor so it ran the other way.* **2.** *tv.* to cause something to move the opposite way; to turn something the other way; to turn something upside down; to turn something inside out. ♦ *Mary reversed the piece of the puzzle so that it would fit.* ♦ *I reversed the socks that were inside out before washing them.* **3.** *iv.* to go or move backwards; to move in the opposite direction. ♦ *The videotape reversed automatically when it finished.* ♦ *As the storm approached, the direction of the wind reversed.* **4.** *n.* the opposite. (No plural form in this sense.) ♦ *I'm not mad at you. Quite the reverse, I'm pleased.* ♦ *The negative showed the image in reverse.* **5.** *n.* a setting of a vehicle's transmission that allows a vehicle to move backwards. ♦ *Anne put the car in reverse and backed out of the driveway.* ♦ *When I put the car in reverse, the engine makes a funny sound.* **6.** *n.* the back of something; the back side. ♦ *You must endorse the reverse of the check before cashing it.* ♦ *The bank teller stamped something on the reverse of the check I was cashing.*

revert [rɪ 'vɚt] **revert to** *iv.* + *prep. phr.* to change back into an original or earlier condition. ♦ *We were all disappointed when John reverted to cigarette smoking.* ♦ *In 1997, Hong Kong reverted to Chinese control.*

review [rɪ 'vju] **1.** *tv.* to examine something again. ♦ *My boss reviewed my request for more supplies.* ♦ *I reviewed my application once before submitting it.* **2.** *tv.* to study information again, especially before a test. ♦ *The student reviewed her notes before the test.* ♦ *Our teacher suggested that we review Chapter 6 tonight.* **3.** *tv.* to write or prepare ⑦ of a play, movie, book, dance, or other work of art. ♦ *A critic reviewed our play for an important newspaper.* ♦ *The popular movie was reviewed in many magazines.* **4.** *iv.* to study again. ♦ *Mary is reviewing for her test tomorrow.* ♦ *David reviewed for an hour in preparation for the quiz.* **5.** *n.* a formal examination or inspection. ♦ *During her review, the health inspector found many violations.* ♦ *In my review of the file, I found numerous errors.* **6.** *n.* the act of studying something again. ♦ *As a review, Anne read over her notes.* ♦ *During John's review, he read many things that he'd forgotten.* **7.** *n.* an essay that evaluates a book, play, movie, dance, or other work. ♦ *The review said the movie was bad. I thought it was great.* ♦ *Whoever wrote this review probably didn't even see the opera.*

reviewer [rɪ 'vju ɚ] *n.* a critic; someone who writes reviews. ♦ *The reviewer disliked the violent movie intensely.* ♦ *The usher led the reviewer to the best seat in the hall.*

revile [rɪ 'vɑɪl] *tv.* to swear at someone; to abuse someone with insults; to insult someone. ♦ *The captors reviled their hostages.* ♦ *The bully reviled the weakling on the playground.*

revise [rɪ 'vɑɪz] *tv.* to make something current or up-to-date; to change something to include new information. ♦ *The author revised her book for the second edition.* ♦ *The editor revised some facts in the article before publishing it.*

revised [rɪ 'vɑɪzd] *adj.* updated; made current; changed to include new information. ♦ *The revised edition of the textbook was completely updated.* ♦ *The revised dictionary contained many new slang words.*

revision [rɪ 'vɪ ʒən] **1.** *n.* a change made to a document or a manuscript. ♦ *The publisher asked the author to make a few simple revisions.* ♦ *The editor's revisions were necessary for accuracy.* **2.** *n.* a document that has been revised. ♦ *The journalist sent the revision to the editor.* ♦ *I have included all your suggestions in the revision.*

revitalize [rɪ 'vɑɪt ə lɑɪz] *tv.* to cause someone or something to have energy or power again. ♦ *The new businesses revitalized the downtown area.* ♦ *The nourishing meal revitalized the hungry man.*

revival [rɪ 'vɑɪv əl] **1.** *n.* reviving someone or something; the process of returning life or energy to someone or something. (No plural form in this sense.) ♦ *The new factory was responsible for the industrial town's revival.* ♦ *The ecologist encouraged the revival of endangered species.* **2.** *n.* a new production of play or a musical that has been done before; something that has been revived. ♦ *I* *attended a revival of an old Broadway musical.* ♦ *The playwright updated the script for the revival.*

revive [rɪ 'vɑɪv] **1.** *tv.* to cause someone to return to consciousness with a normal heartbeat and respiration. ♦ *The lifeguard revived the drowning man.* ♦ *The firefighter revived the victim pulled from the fire.* **2.** *tv.* to bring something back into use; to bring something back into style. ♦ *The designer revived clothing styles from the 1940s.* ♦ *The nostalgic movie revived interest in music from the 1960s.* **3.** *iv.* to return to consciousness, as in ①. ♦ *The drowning man revived in the ambulance.* ♦ *The woman who fainted revived a short time later.*

revoke [rɪ 'vok] *tv.* to cancel something, especially a law or a privilege; to repeal something. ♦ *I had to revoke my earlier statement of agreement.* ♦ *The company revoked the workers' contract.*

revolt [rɪ 'volt] **1.** *iv.* to fight against authority or the government. ♦ *The peasants revolted against the king.* ♦ *The army revolted against the ruling political party.* **2.** *tv.* to cause someone to feel sick with disgust; to offend someone strongly. ♦ *The violent movie revolted the audience.* ♦ *We were revolted by the pictures in the magazine.* **3.** *n.* a rebellion; a riot; an instance of revolting against authority. ♦ *The prime minister was assassinated during the revolt.* ♦ *Hundreds of innocent people died in the revolt.*

revolting [rɪ 'vol tɪŋ] *adj.* sickening; disgusting; very offensive. (Adv: *revoltingly.*) ♦ *The protesters burned the revolting magazines.* ♦ *My parents wouldn't let me see the revolting movie.*

revolution [rɛv ə 'lu ʃən] **1.** *n.* an act of seizing a government by force and replacing it with new rulers. ♦ *After the American Revolution, this country was independent.* ♦ *The government secretly aided revolutions in other countries.* **2.** *n.* a complete change. (Figurative on ①.) ♦ *Following a revolution in thinking, the liberal became a conservative.* ♦ *A revolution in hygiene helped prevent the further spread of disease.* **3.** *n.* the circular or rotating movement made by an object going around a fixed object. ♦ *The astronomer mapped the planet's revolution around the sun.* ♦ *The earth makes one revolution each day.*

revolutionary [rɛv ə 'lu ʃə nɛr i] **1.** *adj.* of or pertaining to a revolution ①. ♦ *George Washington was a general in the Revolutionary War.* ♦ *The revolutionary radical was imprisoned.* **2.** *adj.* of or pertaining to revolution ②. ♦ *A revolutionary improvement in the design made the product cheaper to produce.* ♦ *Computers caused a revolutionary change in the business world.* **3.** *n.* someone who fights to overthrow government or authority. ♦ *The revolutionaries were executed for treason.* ♦ *The government was toppled by young revolutionaries.*

Revolutionary War [rɛv ə 'lu ʃə nɛr ɪ 'wor] *n.* the American Revolution, which was a war between Britain and the American colonies, 1775–1783. ♦ *America won its independence from the English in the Revolutionary War.* ♦ *George Washington was a general in the Revolutionary War.*

revolve [rɪ 'vɑlv] **1. revolve around** *iv. + prep. phr.* to move in a circle or oval around a point; to orbit around something. ♦ *The planets rotate as they revolve around the sun.* ♦ *The moon revolves around the earth.* **2.** *iv.* [for someone or something] to rotate [around an axis]. ♦ *A wheel revolves as it moves along the ground.* ♦ *The revolving door was stuck and would not revolve.*

revolver [rɪ 'vɑl vɚ] *n.* a gun having spaces for bullets in a cylinder that revolves. ♦ *When a bullet is fired from a revolver, the cylinder revolves, putting a new bullet into place for firing.* ♦ *The robber held up the bank with a loaded revolver.*

revolving [rɪ 'vɑl vɪŋ] **1.** *adj.* moving in a circle or oval around something. ♦ *A revolving display let us see all sides of the beautiful vase.* ♦ *A revolving chamber holds the bullets in a revolver.* **2. revolving door** *n.* a doorway containing a set of four doors, each joined along one edge to the others, that rotates on an axis. ♦ *I entered the building through a revolving door.* ♦ *The revolving door moves faster than I can walk, so I have to find another way in and out.*

revulsion [rɪ 'vʌl ʃən] *n.* a strong, sickening feeling of disgust. (No plural form in this sense.) ♦ *A wave of revulsion swept over the audience watching the violent movie.* ♦ *I experienced severe revulsion when I saw the accident victim.*

reward [rɪ 'word] **1.** *n.* something, especially money, given to someone who returns something that is lost or gives information about a crime. ♦ *There's a $1,000 reward for clues leading to the murderer's arrest.* ♦ *Mary offered a reward to anyone who found her missing puppy.* **2.** *tv.* to give someone ①. ♦ *The good workers were rewarded with an extra day of vacation.* ♦ *Mary rewarded the woman who found her bracelet.*

rewarding [rɪ 'wor dɪŋ] *adj.* worthwhile; beneficial. (Adv: *rewardingly.*) ♦ *Our discussions have been most rewarding.* ♦ *My morning spent at the library was very rewarding.*

rewind [ri 'wɑɪnd] **1.** *tv.* to cause something, especially an audiotape, videotape, or film, to wind backward. (Pt/pp: rewound.) ♦ *After watching the movie, Mary rewound the videotape.* ♦ *The cassette player rewound the tape automatically.* **2.** *iv.* [for something that winds around an object, such as an audiotape, videotape, or film] to run backward. ♦ *The cassette tape rewound automatically when it finished.* ♦ *The film rewound around its reel.* **3.** *n.* a button or device that causes a movement as in ②. ♦ *When the movie ended, I pressed rewind on the remote control.* ♦ *Mary hit rewind in order to listen to the first song on the tape.*

rewire [ri 'wɑɪr] *tv.* to put new wires in something; to attach the wires of something again. ♦ *The electrician rewired the old apartment.* ♦ *We had to rewire the switch, since it had been installed wrong.*

reword [ri 'wɚd] *tv.* to use different words when saying something. ♦ *I reworded the phrase to clarify my meaning.* ♦ *The mayor's last sentence had been reworded to make it more inspiring.*

rewound [ri 'wɑʊnd] pt/pp of rewind.

rewrite 1. [ri 'rɑɪt] *tv., irreg.* to revise a something that has been written. (Pt: rewrote; pp: rewritten.) ♦ *The editor told the author to rewrite the last chapter.* ♦ *The scientist rewrote the conclusion to include the new data.* **2.** ['ri rɑɪt] *n.* a copy of writing that has been revised. ♦ *The author sent the latest rewrites to the publisher.* ♦ *Mary sent her rewrites to the editor for proofreading.*

rewritten ['ri 'rɪt n] **1.** pp of rewrite. **2.** *adj.* written in a different way; revised. ♦ *The rewritten article was more succinct than before.* ♦ *The rewritten textbook was clearer than the first edition.*

rewrote [rɪ 'rot] pt of rewrite.

rhapsodize ['ræp sə dɑɪz] **rhapsodize about** *iv.* + *prep. phr.* to talk or write about someone or something in a very excited or extravagant way. ♦ *The critic rhapsodized about the enjoyable play.* ♦ *The salesclerk rhapsodized about the new line of perfume.*

rhapsody ['ræp sə di] *n.* a piece of music that seems to be improvised instead of structured. ♦ *The composer wrote a rhapsody for a jazz quartet.* ♦ *Mary danced to Gershwin's "Rhapsody in Blue."*

rhetoric ['rɛt ə rɪk] **1.** *n.* the art of speaking or writing in a way that persuades or influences other people. (No plural form in this sense.) ♦ *The debater was highly skilled in the art of rhetoric.* ♦ *I studied rhetoric and logic in college because I wanted to become a politician.* **2.** *n.* the words that are used when trying to persuade or influence other people; the language used to persuade or influence other people. (No plural form in this sense.) ♦ *Sue's rhetoric didn't persuade me to go bowling with her.* ♦ *The politician's rhetoric convinced me to vote for him.*

rhetorical [rə 'tor ɪ kəl] *adj.* [of an instance of speech] used more for effect than essential communication. (Adv: *rhetorically* […ɪk li].) ♦ *I only asked a rhetorical question. I didn't really want an answer.* ♦ *Tom's remark was only a rhetorical one meant to get your attention.*

rheumatic fever [ru mæt ɪk 'fiv ɚ] *n.* a disease that causes inflammation in the joints and severe fever. (No plural form in this sense.) ♦ *Bill is confined to bed with rheumatic fever.* ♦ *When Mary had rheumatic fever, her joints were painfully swollen.*

rheumatism ['ru mə tɪz əm] *n.* a condition that causes painful swelling of the joints and muscles. (No plural form in this sense.) ♦ *Walking is painful for Jane because she's got rheumatism.* ♦ *Bill stopped going jogging when he developed rheumatism.*

rhinoceros [rɑɪ 'nɑs ə rəs] *n., irreg.* a large animal of Africa and South Asia that has one or two large horns on its nose. (Pl: *rhinoceros* or *rhinoceroses.*) ♦ *Jimmy was afraid of the rhinoceroses at the zoo.* ♦ *Is it illegal to hunt rhinoceros?*

Rhode Island [rod 'ɑɪ lənd] See Gazetteer.

rhodium ['rod i əm] *n.* a silverish, metallic chemical element used mainly in platinum alloys and to prevent corrosion. (No plural form in this sense.) ♦ *The atomic symbol of rhodium is Rh, and its atomic number is 45.* ♦ *Rhodium was discovered in 1803.*

rhododendron [ro də 'dɛn drən] *n.* a shrub that has pink, purple, or white flowers and is found in mountainous, arctic, and temperate zones. ♦ *The path to my front door is lined with rhododendrons.* ♦ *The florist added some rhododendrons to the bouquet.*

rhubarb ['ru bɑrb] **1.** *n.* a plant that has thick, sour stalks that can be boiled with sugar and eaten as food, especially in pies and other desserts. (No plural form in this sense.) ♦ *Mary went out to her garden and cut a few stalks of rhubarb.* ♦ *David made a pie from freshly cut rhubarb.* **2.** *adj.* made of ①. ♦ *Lisa loves hot rhubarb pie.* ♦ *I made a wonderful rhubarb cobbler for dessert.*

rhyme ['rɑɪm] **1.** *n.* a state existing where two or more words have phonetically similar or identical endings. (No plural form in this sense.) ♦ *Many poems have rhyme at the ends of each pair of lines.* ♦ *Rhyme is common in poetry and the lyrics of songs.* **2.** *n.* a word showing ① with another word. ♦ Time *is a rhyme for* lime. ♦ *The poet couldn't think of a rhyme for* silver. **3.** *n.* a short poem. ♦ *The teacher told nursery rhymes to the young children.* ♦ *The four-year-old had memorized a few rhymes.* **4.** *iv.* [for a word or phrase] to end with the same sound or sounds as another word or phrase; [for a poem] to include words or phrases ending with the same sound or sounds, especially at the ends of pairs of lines. ♦ Clown *and* frown *rhyme.* ♦ *I like your poem, even though it doesn't rhyme.* **5. rhyme with** *iv.* + *prep. phr.* [for a word] to match the same ending sound or sounds as another word. ♦ Clown *rhymes with* town. ♦ *What does* poplar *rhyme with?* **6. rhyme with** *tv.* + *prep. phr.* to choose a word that ends with the same sound or sounds as another word. ♦ *I wish poets would rhyme* June *with a word other than* moon. ♦ *The poet rhymed* king *with* ring.

rhythm ['rɪð əm] **1.** *n.* periodic beats that occur in a pattern, such as in music and rap ②. (No plural form in this sense.) ♦ *All music has rhythm.* ♦ *Rhythm is the basis for music and dance.* **2.** *n.* the repeating of a stressed beat or accent in each unit of speech, music, or movement. ♦ *The song's rhythm was carried by the heavy bass beat.* ♦ *The rhythm of the hypnotist's speech was very relaxing.*

rhythmic ['rɪð mɪk] *adj.* of or about rhythm. (Adv: *rhythmically* […ɪk li].) ♦ *We danced to the rhythmic drums.* ♦ *The rhythmic poem was easy to memorize.*

rib ['rɪb] **1.** *n.* one of the several pairs of bones that are attached to the backbone and curve around to the front of the chest. ♦ *One of the football player's ribs was cracked when he fell.* ♦ *I could see the starving child's ribs.* **2.** *n.* meat that contains a rib, eaten as food. ♦ *We ate barbecued ribs at the picnic.* ♦ *John ate ribs for dinner.* **3.** *tv.* to tease someone in a friendly way. (Informal.) ♦ *We ribbed John about his mistake.* ♦ *Mary ribbed Susan for getting lost.*

ribbon ['rɪb ən] **1.** *n.* a narrow band of fabric or material, often used as a decoration. ♦ *Mary tied ribbons in the horse's mane.* ♦ *David tied a ribbon around the wrapped gift.* **2.** *n.* a special kind of ①, coated with ink, used in a typewriter or computer printer; a special thin strip of plastic film used in an electric typewriter. ♦ *The typed letters weren't readable because the ribbon was so old.* ♦ *Mary installed a new ribbon in the electric typewriter.*

rice ['rɑɪs] **1.** *n.* a grass-like plant that produces edible seeds. (No plural form in this sense.) ♦ *The energetic farmers cultivated rice.* ♦ *This rice was harvested in China.* **2.** *n.* the edible grain of ①. (No plural form in this sense. Number is expressed with *grain(s) of rice.*) ♦ *I bought a bushel of rice at the market.* ♦ *Mary steamed some rice on the stove.*

rich ['rɪtʃ] **1.** *adj.* having a lot of money; wealthy; not poor. (Adv: *richly.* Comp: *richer;* sup: *richest.*) ♦ *A rich stockbroker donated $10,000 to charity last year.* ♦ *The rich lawyer lived in an expensive apartment.* **2.** *adj.* having a lot of cream, butter, or other fats. (Adv: *richly.* Comp: *richer;* sup: *richest.*) ♦ *The cream pie was so rich that I* *couldn't eat it all.* ♦ *Rich pastry is very fattening.* **3.** *adj.* [of soil] good for growing plants; fertile. (Adv: *richly.* Comp: *richer;* sup: *richest.*) ♦ *The rich soil yielded plentiful crops.* ♦ *The grass grew luxuriously in the rich earth.* **4.** *adj.* [of a color] vivid or deep. (Adv: *richly.* Comp: *richer;* sup: *richest.*) ♦ *The queen's robe was a rich purple.* ♦ *This shag carpeting is a rich crimson red.* **5.** *adj.* abundant; plentiful; causing or yielding abundance, benefit, or value. ♦ *A rich harvest meant there was plenty of grain for winter.* ♦ *We found a rich store of information in the library.* **6.** *adj.* elegant, beautiful, sumptuous, valuable. ♦ *The house was decorated with rich fabrics and fine furniture.* ♦ *A rich banquet of many meats and exotic fruits awaited the guests.* **7. riches** *n.* wealth; an abundant amount of anything good, especially money and property. (Treated as plural.) ♦ *All of the riches in the world couldn't get me to tell the secret.* ♦ *The wealthy man's riches were destroyed in the fire.* **8. the rich** *n.* people who are ①; the wealthy. (No plural form in this sense. Treated as plural.) ♦ *Congress sought to raise taxes on the rich.* ♦ *The rich contribute a great deal of money to charity.* **9. rich with something** *idiom* having a lot of something; not lacking; abundant. ♦ *The beautiful book was rich with color illustrations.* ♦ *The old town was rich with elegant Victorian houses.* **10. rich in something** *idiom* having valuable resources, characteristics, traditions, or history. ♦ *The entire region is rich in historical churches.* ♦ *Our soil is rich in important nutrients.* **11. strike it rich** *idiom* to acquire wealth suddenly. ♦ *If I could strike it rich, I wouldn't have to work anymore.* ♦ *Sally ordered a dozen oysters and found a huge pearl in one of them. She struck it rich!*

richly ['rɪtʃ li] **1.** *adj.* using large amounts; using valuable components. ♦ *The church was richly decorated for the big wedding.* ♦ *The prince dressed richly and very stylishly for the ball.* **2.** *adj.* fully; completely; absolutely. ♦ *The criminal's punishment was richly deserved.* ♦ *The person who found my wallet was richly rewarded.*

richness ['rɪtʃ nəs] *n.* the quality of being rich. (No plural form in this sense.) ♦ *Heavy cream gives the pastry its richness.* ♦ *The tycoon measured his richness in millions of dollars.*

rickety ['rɪk ə ti] *adj.* not well made; likely to break; likely to fall apart. (Comp: *ricketier;* sup: *ricketiest.*) ♦ *The wind destroyed the rickety shack.* ♦ *I was afraid to walk across the rickety bridge.*

rid ['rɪd] **1.** *tv., irreg.* to eliminate an area of something. (Pt/pp: rid.) ♦ *I rid my refrigerator of fattening foods before I started my diet.* ♦ *The exterminator rid the kitchen of cockroaches.* **2.** *tv., irreg.* to make oneself free of someone or something. (Takes a reflexive object.) ♦ *Mary rid herself of the annoying stranger.* ♦ *John rid himself of his coat and made himself comfortable.* **3. get rid of someone or something** *idiom* to make oneself free of someone or something. ♦ *I can't seem to get rid of my younger brother. He follows me everywhere.* ♦ *Lisa is trying to get rid of the mice in her house.*

ridden ['rɪd n] **1.** pp of ride. **2.** *adj.* burdened with something; full of something. (Only in combinations.) ♦ *The debt-ridden student declared bankruptcy.* ♦ *The flea-ridden cat needed a bath.*

riddle ['rɪd l] **1.** *n.* a puzzling question whose answer usually requires one to think in an unusual or ingenious way. ♦ *Anne asked me a riddle, but I couldn't think of the answer.* ♦ *The answers to many riddles are very bad puns.* **2.** *n.* someone or something that is difficult to understand; someone or something that is puzzling. (Figurative on ①.) ♦ *The detective solved the riddle of the stolen jewels.* ♦ *Why Mary changed her mind is a complete riddle to me.*

ride ['rɑɪd] **1.** *tv., irreg.* to sit on or in something that moves; to be a passenger in a vehicle that moves or travels. (Pt: rode; pp: ridden. With horse, donkey, burro, elephant, and other animals. With train, bicycle, roller coaster, carousel, elevator, trolley but not (transitively) in a vehicle such as a car, taxi, truck, Jeep.) ♦ *Mary rode a horse across the meadow.* ♦ *Dave rode an elevator to the second floor.* **2.** *tv., irreg.* to travel along on something. ♦ *A light feather gently rode the wind.* ♦ *The surfer rode the waves on a surfboard.* **3. ride in** *iv., irreg. + prep. phr.* to sit in and move along with [but not drive] certain vehicles that move. (With vehicles such as a car, taxi, truck, or Jeep.) ♦ *My dog rides in the car with me.* ♦ *We rode in a taxi to the airport.* **4.** *n.* a journey using a vehicle or an animal. ♦ *Mary went out for a ride in the country.* ♦ *I have always wanted to have a ride on a donkey.* **5.** *n.* a kind of entertainment in which people travel in some kind of conveyance to experience interesting sights and sounds, thrills, or enlightenment. ♦ *A roller coaster is a special kind of thrill ride.* ♦ *The amusement park has dozens and dozens of interesting rides.* **6. ride roughshod over someone or something** *idiom* to treat someone or something with disdain or scorn. ♦ *Tom seems to ride roughshod over his friends.* ♦ *You shouldn't have come into our town to ride roughshod over our laws and our traditions.*

rider ['rɑɪ dɚ] **1.** *n.* someone who rides on a vehicle or animal. ♦ *The horse threw the rider from its back.* ♦ *The rider fell off the motorcycle.* **2.** *n.* an extra note that is added to a legal document. ♦ *The author's royalties were set forth in a rider to her contract.* ♦ *The lease extension was added as a rider to the lease.*

ridge ['rɪdʒ] **1.** *n.* a long, narrow series of raised land, hills, or mountains. ♦ *From a ridge, an enemy scout spied on the soldiers in the valley.* ♦ *The sun set behind the rocky ridge.* **2.** *n.* a long, narrow, raised part of something. ♦ *The scar formed a ridge along David's arm.* ♦ *There were ridges in the lawn where moles had burrowed.* **3.** *n.* the line where two surfaces slanted upward meet, as with the top edge of a roof. ♦ *The bird landed on the roof's ridge.* ♦ *A squirrel sat on the ridge of the doghouse.*

ridicule ['rɪd ə kjul] **1.** *tv.* to make fun of someone or something; to mock someone or something. ♦ *The children ridiculed John because he wore old clothing.* ♦ *The bully ridiculed those who were smaller than he was.* **2.** *n.* laughter or mockery directed at someone or something, especially in a mean way. (No plural form in this sense.) ♦ *The bully's ridicule of Mary was horribly cruel.* ♦ *The crippled child ignored the ridicule she was subjected to.*

ridiculous [rɪ 'dɪk jə ləs] *adj.* deserving to be laughed at or mocked; deserving ridicule. (Adv: *ridiculously.*) ♦ *Your suggestions are too ridiculous to be taken seriously.* ♦ *John laughed at the ridiculous way in which Bill danced.*

rifle ['rɑɪ fʊl] **1.** *n.* a gun with a long barrel. ♦ *The farmer shot the wolf with a rifle.* ♦ *The hunter kept numerous rifles locked in a cabinet.* **2.** *tv.* to search an area thoroughly, stealing valuable things. ♦ *My bedroom was rifled, and* *all my jewelry was stolen.* ♦ *The spy rifled my apartment, looking for secret documents.* **3. rifle through** *iv. + prep. phr.* to search through an area, looking for something. ♦ *Someone rifled through my office, looking for valuables.* ♦ *The agent rifled through my luggage, looking for contraband.*

rift ['rɪft] **1.** *n.* a crack; a separation; a split in a surface or between two things. ♦ *During the earthquake, a huge rift opened in the earth.* ♦ *Some of the climber's supplies fell into a rift near the edge of the cliff.* **2.** *n.* a separation between people or groups of people. (Figurative on ①.) ♦ *The primary caused a rift among the party members.* ♦ *The rift between the union and management widened.*

rig ['rɪg] **1.** *n.* heavy machinery that is needed or built for a certain purpose. ♦ *The rig pumped thousands of gallons of oil daily.* ♦ *The lighting crew set up their rig on the movie studio lot.* **2.** *n.* a long, covered truck. ♦ *John drives a rig across the country each week.* ♦ *A rig full of oranges overturned on the freeway.* **3. rig up** *tv.* to put something together using whatever materials one has at the moment. ♦ *The castaway rigged up a transmitter with a battery and some wire.* ♦ *The terrorist rigged up a bomb using fertilizer.* **4.** *tv.* to provide a boat with masts and sails. ♦ *The sailors rigged the ship with masts and sails.* ♦ *The ship was rigged by the younger sailors.* **5.** *tv.* to arrange the results of a contest to make sure which contestant wins. ♦ *I knew which horse would win the race because the race was rigged.* ♦ *The gangster rigged the race and took part of the profits.*

rigging ['rɪg ɪŋ] *n.* lines (or ropes) used to support the masts and sails of a ship. (Sometimes plural.) ♦ *The heavy winds tore the rigging from the mast.* ♦ *The ship's rigging was meant to last for years.*

right ['rɑɪt] **1.** *adj.* the opposite of left; to the east when someone or something faces north. ♦ *David felt a pain in his right side.* ♦ *The utensils are kept in the right drawer.* **2.** *adj.* correct; true; not wrong; not false. (Adv: *rightly.*) ♦ *"What's the capital of France?" "Paris?" "That's right."* ♦ *Jimmy knew the right answer to the math problem.* **3.** *adj.* morally or ethically good; lawful; according to the law or social standards. (Adv: *rightly.*) ♦ *I did the right thing and took the wallet I found to the owner.* ♦ *The jury was right to have found the criminal guilty.* **4.** *adj.* proper; suitable; appropriate; being good for a situation. ♦ *A tuxedo is the right thing for a man to wear to a formal dinner.* ♦ *Do you know the right way to slice turkey?* **5.** *adv.* toward the right ① side. ♦ *Suddenly, the car in front of me veered right.* ♦ *At the intersection, turn right.* **6.** *adv.* correctly; not wrongly. ♦ *I know there is a problem, and we will make it right.* ♦ *Do your job right the first time, and you won't have to do it again.* **7.** *adv.* properly; suitably; appropriately; in a way that is good for a situation. ♦ *John tied his tie right.* ♦ *The coach taught Bill how to throw right.* **8.** *adv.* directly; straight. (Has nothing to do with movement to the right side.) ♦ *Mary went right into the apartment and turned on the light.* ♦ *Go right through the intersection and then turn left at the bank.* **9. right at** *phr.* exactly or precisely at a specific place or time. ♦ *Meet me at this corner right at 3:00 P.M.* ♦ *The restaurant is right at First and Main Streets.* **10.** *n.* the right ① side of someone or something. (No plural form in this sense.) ♦ *The car in front of me veered to the right.* ♦ *Mary placed her knife on the right, next to her plate.* **11.** *n.* correctness; righteousness; goodness. (No plural form in this sense.) ♦ *We were taught to love right and hate wrong.* ♦ *I can tell right from wrong.* **12. right(s)** *n.* something that is due a person according to civil or moral law. ♦ *There are ten amendments in the Bill of Rights.* ♦ *The factory was fined for violating the workers' rights.* **13. the Right** *n.* the right wing; radically conservative people. (No plural form in this sense. Treated as singular.) ♦ *The Right did not want the tax increase.* ♦ *The liberal representative was attacked by the Right.* **14.** *tv.* to cause something to be upright; to fix something that is leaning or has fallen so that it is standing up again. ♦ *Jane righted the vase that had tipped over.* ♦ *David righted the lamp after he knocked it over.* **15.** *tv.* to correct something. ♦ *Susan righted a wrong by apologizing to me.* ♦ *The restaurant owner righted the health violations after the inspector's visit.* **16. in the right** *idiom* on the moral or legal side of an issue; on the right ③ side of an issue. ♦ *I felt I was in the right, but the judge ruled against me.* ♦ *It's hard to argue with Jane. She always believes that she's in the right.*

right angle ['rɑɪt 'æŋ gəl] *n.* an angle whose sides join at 45-degrees. ♦ *A square contains four right angles.* ♦ *The letter L is a right angle.*

righteous ['rɑɪ tʃəs] *adj.* ethically or morally right. (Adv: *righteously.*) ♦ *We seek to be just and righteous at all times.* ♦ *The judge's righteous decision was hailed.*

righteousness ['rɑɪ tʃəs nəs] *n.* virtue; proper ethical or moral behavior. (No plural form in this sense.) ♦ *Righteousness and kindness are two good human qualities.* ♦ *One must seek righteousness and avoid being self-righteous.*

rightful ['rɑɪt fʊl] *adj.* legal; according to the law. (Adv: *rightfully.*) ♦ *The judge declared David to be his father's rightful heir.* ♦ *The stolen property was returned to its rightful owner.*

right-handed ['rɑɪt hæn dɪd] **1.** *adj.* able to use the right hand better than the left; using the right hand to write with. (Adv: *right-handedly.*) ♦ *Bill is right-handed, except when it comes to golfing.* ♦ *These scissors are designed for right-handed people.* **2.** *adj.* made to be used by the right hand. ♦ *Are those scissors right-handed or left-handed?* ♦ *Most of the desks in the classroom were right-handed.*

rightly ['rɑɪt li] **1.** *adv.* exactly; precisely; correctly. ♦ *My hypothesis rightly predicted the results.* ♦ *Anne rightly guessed the number I was thinking of.* **2.** *adv.* fairly; according to morals, ethics, or the law. ♦ *The criminal was rightly sentenced to jail.* ♦ *The jury rightly found the defendant to be guilty.*

right-of-way ['rɑɪt əv 'we] **1.** *n.* a strip of land that goes over someone else's property, especially for a path, sidewalk, or road that a public utility is placed under, on, or over. ♦ *The electric company compensated the farmer for the right-of-way through his farm.* ♦ *The city laid the sewer under the right-of-way in my front yard.* **2. have the right-of-way** *idiom* to possess the legal right to occupy a particular space on a public roadway. ♦ *I had a traffic accident yesterday, but it wasn't my fault. I had the right-of-way.* ♦ *Don't pull out onto a highway if you don't have the right-of-way.*

right wing ['rɑɪt wɪŋ] **1.** *n.* people holding a political philosophy that is conservative and traditional. (No plural form in this sense.) ♦ *The right wing wants a return* *to independence and self-reliance.* ♦ *Both the right wing and the left wing agree that the government has too much debt.* **2. right-wing** *adj.* <the adj. use of ①.> ♦ *Right-wing politicians dominate the Senate.* ♦ *Left-wing politicians and right-wing politicians both frighten me.*

rigid ['rɪdʒ ɪd] **1.** *adj.* stiff; not bending or hard to bend; not flexible. (Adv: *rigidly.*) ♦ *The rigid pencil snapped when I tried to bend it.* ♦ *My wet socks froze and became rigid.* **2.** *adj.* uncompromising. (Figurative on ①. Adv: *rigidly.*) ♦ *John has a very rigid attitude about the way he works.* ♦ *My rigid boss refused to break the company's rules.*

rigor ['rɪg ɚ] **1.** *n.* harshness; severity. ♦ *The southerner wasn't used to the rigor of winter in New York.* ♦ *The rigor of the job strained the laborer's muscles.* **2.** *n.* great carefulness. (No plural form in this sense.) ♦ *The editor proofread my article with the utmost rigor.* ♦ *With rigor, David translated the foreign document.*

rigor mortis ['rɪg ɚ 'mort ɪs] *n.* the stiffening of the muscles after death. (From Latin for 'the stiffness of death.' No plural form in this sense.) ♦ *Not only was the victim dead, but rigor mortis had already set in.* ♦ *The cadavers at the morgue had all undergone rigor mortis.*

rigorous ['rɪg ə rəs] **1.** *adj.* harsh; strict; severe; demanding. (Adv: *rigorously.*) ♦ *The soldiers' training was very rigorous.* ♦ *The team's final practice before the big game was rigorous.* **2.** *adj.* thorough; exact; according to strict scientific standards; scientifically accurate. (Adv: *rigorously.*) ♦ *The scientist conducted a very rigorous experiment.* ♦ *The rigorous accountant checked all his calculations twice.*

rim ['rɪm] **1.** *n.* the edge of something, especially of something that is circular. ♦ *The rim of the glass had a chip in it.* ♦ *Bill stuck a piece of gum on the rim of the wastebasket.* **2.** *n.* the part of a wheel that the tire is put around. ♦ *When I drove over the pothole, it bent the rim of my left front tire.* ♦ *Dave placed the bike tire around the rim and then inflated the tire.* **3.** *n.* a basketball hoop. ♦ *The basketball bounced off the rim.* ♦ *Mary shot the basketball through the rim for two points.*

rind ['raɪnd] *n.* the tough, outer skin of some fruits and vegetables; a peel; the hard, outer layer of cheese or bacon. ♦ *Anne removed the rind from the orange with a knife.* ♦ *I cut the rind from the cheese before serving it.*

ring ['rɪŋ] **1.** *n.* something made from a circle of material; a circular band. ♦ *The plumber placed a rubber ring in the pipe joint.* ♦ *A washer is a metal ring.* **2.** *n.* a piece of jewelry made from a circle of metal that is usually worn around fingers. (See also earring.) ♦ *Wedding rings are worn on the left hand.* ♦ *Mary wore her class ring on her right hand.* **3.** *n.* a circle. ♦ *The police stood in a ring around the suspect.* ♦ *I drew a ring around David's face in the photograph.* **4.** *n.* a group of things or people that are in a circle. ♦ *A ring of fans surrounded the celebrity.* ♦ *A ring of flowers encircled the tree.* **5.** *n.* an enclosed place where boxing and wrestling matches, circuses, and other forms of entertainment take place. ♦ *A boxing ring is actually square.* ♦ *There were three rings under the circus tent.* **6.** *n.* noise made by a bell or chime; noise that sounds like the noise of a bell or chime. (No plural form in this sense.) ♦ *This bell has a pleasant ring to it.* ♦ *The shrill ring of the alarm woke me up.* **7.** *n.* a feature; a characteristic; a quality. (No plural form in this sense.) ♦ *The politician's speech had a ring of sincerity to it.* ♦ *The suspect's alibi had a ring of truth.* **8.** *n.* a group of criminals, especially ones who work together as an illegal business. ♦ *The police uncovered the secret drug ring.* ♦ *The undercover ring was exposed by the reporter.* **9.** *tv., irreg.* to cause a bell or chime to ring. (Pt: rang; pp: rung.) ♦ *You should ring the alarm if there is a fire.* ♦ *I rang Jane's doorbell, but she didn't answer.* **10. ring up** *tv., irreg. + adv.* to call someone on the telephone. ♦ *Mary rang Susan up to tell her about her interview.* ♦ *Anne rang up David to ask him a question.* **11.** *tv.* to make a circle around someone or something; to form a circle around someone or something; to enclose someone or something in a circle. (Pt/pp: *ringed.*) ♦ *A line of police officers ringed the suspect and forced him to surrender.* ♦ *Moss ringed the tree trunk.* **12.** *iv., irreg.* to make a noise like a bell or chime; [for a bell or chime] to produce a noise. ♦ *The buzzer rang when Anne pushed the doorbell.* ♦ *The alarm is set to ring at 5:30 A.M.* **13.** *iv., irreg.* to sound; to have sound or a lot of sound. ♦ *Anne's voice rang out from her bedroom.* ♦ *The birds' song rang from the forest.* **14. ring for** *iv., irreg. + prep. phr.* to signal [someone or something] by ringing a bell. ♦ *Mary rang for the butler.* ♦ *The hospital patient rang for the nurse.* **15. give someone a ring** *idiom* to make a telephone call to someone. (Informal.) ♦ *Give me a ring when you get home.* ♦ *I gave Anne a ring just to say hello.* **16. have a familiar ring** *idiom* [for a story or an explanation] to sound familiar. ♦ *Your excuse has a familiar ring. Have you done this before?* ♦ *This term paper has a familiar ring. I think it has been copied.* **17. ring in the new year** *idiom* to celebrate the beginning of the new year at midnight on December 31. ♦ *We are planning a big party to ring in the new year.* ♦ *How did you ring in the new year?*

ringer ['rɪŋ ɚ] **1.** *n.* the part of a telephone, alarm, or other device that makes a ringing noise. ♦ *Mary turned the telephone ringer off when she went to bed.* ♦ *The ringer on my alarm clock broke, so I was late for work.* **2. (dead) ringer** *n.* someone who looks exactly like someone else. (Informal.) ♦ *Mary is a ringer for her mother.* ♦ *John is a dead ringer for my cousin Bill.*

ringleader ['rɪŋ lid ɚ] *n.* someone who is in charge of a group of people, typically outlaws, thieves, or rebels. ♦ *Bob was the ringleader of a bunch of thieves.* ♦ *The judge sentenced the ringleader of the criminals to life in prison.*

rink ['rɪŋk] *n.* a prepared surface—often indoors—on which one can skate and the building that houses it. ♦ *The roller-skating rink was swept twice a day.* ♦ *The hockey team arrived at the rink four hours before the game.*

rinse ['rɪns] **1. rinse (off)** *tv.* (+ *adv.*) to wash something with clean water without using soap. ♦ *After eating dinner, John rinsed the dirty plates.* ♦ *Mary rinsed her dirty shoes with the garden hose.* **2.** *n.* a washing with clean water, either for cleaning or to remove soap. ♦ *John added fabric softener to the washing machine during the first rinse.* ♦ *All of the dirt came out in the rinse.* **3.** *n.* a liquid that is put on hair to give color to the hair. ♦ *Anne colored Mary's hair with a rinse.* ♦ *John gave David a blond rinse at the salon.*

riot ['raɪ ət] **1.** *n.* a violent, uncontrolled disturbance by a crowd of angry people; a large, violent protest. ♦ *The protest became a riot when the cops started arresting people.* ♦ *Four guards were injured at the riot at the prison.* **2.** *n.* someone or something that is extremely funny. (Informal.) ♦ *You should read this book. It's a real riot!* ♦ *Thanks for inviting me to the party! It was a total riot!* **3.** *iv.* to participate in ①; to be part of ①. ♦ *When the prisoners rioted, forty were injured.* ♦ *Dozens of buildings were destroyed when the people rioted.* **4. read someone the riot act** *idiom* to give someone a severe scolding. ♦ *The manager read me the riot act for coming in late.* ♦ *The teacher read the students the riot act for their failure to do their assignments.*

riotous ['rɑɪ ə təs] *adj.* wild, violent, and disorderly; in a riot; unruly. (Adv: *riotously.*) ♦ *The riotous spectators threw bottles onto the field.* ♦ *The police sprayed water on the riotous crowd.*

rip ['rɪp] **1.** *n.* a tear; a gash; a ragged cut. ♦ *Anne had a rip in her coat.* ♦ *Mary taped the rip in the paper.* **2.** *tv.* to tear something apart; to tear something off; to cause something to come apart by pulling on it. ♦ *Mary ripped the cloth into strips.* ♦ *David ripped the wrapping from the present.* **3. rip off** *tv.* + *adv.* to steal from someone; to cheat someone. (Slang. See also rip-off.) ♦ *The thieves ripped the tourists off.* ♦ *The dishonest customer ripped off the cashier.* **4. rip off** *tv.* + *adv.* to steal something [from someone]. (Slang. See also rip-off.) ♦ *The thieves ripped off some television sets.* ♦ *The dishonest customer ripped off the silverware.* **5.** *iv.* to become torn; to be torn apart. ♦ *John's shirt ripped when it got caught on a nail.* ♦ *My newspaper ripped when David grabbed it from me.*

ripe ['rɑɪp] **1.** *adj.* ready to eaten or used; having developed enough so that it can be eaten or used; ready. (Adv: *ripely.* Comp: *riper;* sup: *ripest.*) ♦ *Anne peeled a ripe banana.* ♦ *John offered me a ripe peach.* **2. the time is ripe** *idiom* at exactly the right time. ♦ *I'll tell her the good news when the time is ripe.* ♦ *The time is right to ask the question again.*

ripen ['rɑɪ pən] *iv.* to become ripe. ♦ *Bananas ripen after they've been picked.* ♦ *I'll pick a bushel of apples when they have ripened.*

rip-off ['rɪp ɔf] *n.* something that is not worth the amount of money that one paid for it. (Slang. See also rip ③ and ④.) ♦ *You paid $100 for that watch? What a rip-off!* ♦ *My meal was a rip-off. I'll never eat there again.*

ripple ['rɪp əl] **1.** *n.* a small, gentle wave in water or fabric, caused by a light wind or by something falling onto the surface of water. ♦ *Each raindrop made a ripple when it hit the pond's surface.* ♦ *The lake was covered with small ripples.* **2.** *iv.* to develop into a series of ①. ♦ *The surface of the lake rippled in the wind.* ♦ *The flag rippled in the wind.* **3.** *iv.* to make a sound of gently running water; to flow like gently flowing water. ♦ *The creek rippled by behind our house.* ♦ *Water from the leak in the roof rippled down the wall.* **4.** *tv.* to cause something to have small waves. ♦ *The rain rippled the surface of the lake.* ♦ *A breeze rippled the flag gently.* **5. ripple of excitement** *idiom* a series of quiet but excited murmurs. ♦ *A ripple of excitement spread through the crowd.* ♦ *As the president came near, a ripple of excitement indicated that people could really see him.* **6. ripple of protest** *idiom* a few quiet remarks protesting something; a small amount of subdued protest. ♦ *There was only a ripple of protest about the new tax law.* ♦ *The rude comedian hardly drew a ripple of protest.*

rise ['rɑɪz] **1.** *iv., irreg.* to go upward; to move upward; to go to a higher level. (Pt: rose; pp: risen. Compare with raise.) ♦ *The elevator rose to the third floor.* ♦ *The helium balloon rose to the ceiling of the room.* **2.** *iv., irreg.* to wake up and get out of bed. ♦ *Jane rose at 7:00 A.M. and got ready for work.* ♦ *Bob rose when his alarm clock rang.* **3.** *iv., irreg.* [for the sun, moon, stars, and other objects in space] to appear to come up past the horizon. ♦ *The sun will rise tomorrow before 8:00 A.M.* ♦ *After the full moon rose, I could see across the field.* **4.** *iv., irreg.* to become stronger or more intense. ♦ *If your temperature is rising, you should take some medicine.* ♦ *As the tyrant rose to power, the people became more oppressed.* **5.** *iv., irreg.* [of dough] to become higher and lighter. ♦ *Once the dough rose, I flattened it into a pizza crust.* ♦ *After the dough rose, the baker kneaded it again.* **6. rise from** *iv., irreg.* to come from something. ♦ *Many rituals rise from mythical beliefs.* ♦ *The celebrity's rise from poverty is an interesting story.* **7. rise up (against)** *iv., irreg.* + *adv.* (+ *prep. phr.*) to revolt; to protest against authority. ♦ *The people rose up against the evil tyrant.* ♦ *The citizens rose up against the tax increase.* **8.** *n.* an upward movement; an increase; an ascent. ♦ *The reporter chronicled the politician's rise to power.* ♦ *The rise in crime worried the mayor.* **9.** *n.* a slope; a hill; land that slopes upward. ♦ *The sheep grazed along the gentle rise.* ♦ *The farmer's field was situated on a rise near the forest.* **10. get a rise out of someone** *idiom* to get a response, especially an angry response, from someone. ♦ *I ignored Anne, because she was trying to get a rise out of me.* ♦ *John's insults got a rise out of David.* **11. rise and shine** *idiom* to get out of bed and be lively and energetic. ♦ *Come on children! Rise and shine! We're going to the beach.* ♦ *Father always calls out "Rise and shine!" in the morning when we want to go on sleeping.*

risen ['rɪz ən] pp of rise.

rising ['rɑɪ zɪŋ] **1.** *adj.* going higher; moving higher; going to a higher level; increasing in amount, strength, or intensity. ♦ *The meteorologist predicted rising temperatures for the weekend.* ♦ *The rising tax rates angered the taxpayers.* **2.** *adj.* coming up above the horizon; moving above the horizon. ♦ *The rising sun glared into my eyes as I drove east.* ♦ *The dogs howled at the rising moon.*

risk ['rɪsk] **1.** *n.* a danger; a chance of harm or loss; a possibility of harm or loss; a hazard. ♦ *The traveler faced the risk of catching a disease.* ♦ *Mary explained the risks of driving without wearing a seat belt.* **2.** *tv.* to expose someone or something to loss, harm, or death. ♦ *The soldiers risked their lives on the battlefield.* ♦ *I can't risk any money on the purchase of stock.* **3. at risk** *idiom* in a situation where there is ①; at hazard; in danger. ♦ *I refuse to put my family's welfare at risk by quitting my job.* ♦ *Your whole future is at risk if you don't stop smoking.* **4. risk one's neck (to do something)** *idiom* to accept the risk of physical harm in order to accomplish something. ♦ *Look at that traffic! I refuse to risk my neck just to cross the street to buy a paper.* ♦ *I refuse to risk my neck at all.* **5. take a risk** *idiom* to enter a situation where there is ①; to expose oneself to ①. ♦ *I took a risk by standing too close to the edge of the cliff.* ♦ *I would never take a risk by buying stock on the stock market.*

risky ['rɪsk i] *adj.* dangerous; having a possibility of harm or loss; not safe; hazardous. (Adv: *riskily.* Comp: *riskier;*

sup: *riskiest.*) ♦ *Being an acrobat is a risky profession.* ♦ *Although it was risky, I drove on the icy roads.*

risqué [rɪ 'ske] *adj.* suggestive, especially of sex; referring to sex in an almost indecent way. (From French. Adv: *risquély.*) ♦ *I blushed when I heard the risqué joke.* ♦ *The risqué movie was banned in several cities.*

rite ['rɑɪt] *n.* a ceremony; a ritual; something, often a religious act, that is done in a certain way every time. ♦ *The priest performed the rite that was to purify the temple.* ♦ *An old man performed a rite that would keep us safe as we crossed the lake.*

ritual ['rɪtʃ ʊ əl] **1.** *n.* ceremony and rites. (No plural form in this sense.) ♦ *Too much ritual bores me.* ♦ *Ritual adds to the mystery of religion.* **2.** *n.* a ceremony; a complicated rite. ♦ *The old women performed a complicated ritual to make the bride live a long time.* ♦ *We witnessed an ancient ritual meant to drive evil spirits from the house.* **3.** *adj.* <the adj. use of ①.> (Adv: *ritually.*) ♦ *We became full members after we participated in a ritual exercise meant to frighten us.* ♦ *The secret meeting began with the ritual chant.*

rival ['rɑɪv əl] **1.** *n.* a person or team that one works or plays against; someone against whom one competes or plays. ♦ *The boxer vowed to beat any rival who challenged him.* ♦ *The tennis player shook hands with her rival after the game.* **2.** *adj.* <the adj. use of ①.> ♦ *The rival football team lost by 12 points.* ♦ *The rival armies attacked each other on the battlefield.* **3.** *tv.* to be as good as something else; to equal something else. ♦ *John's spaghetti sauce rivals David's.* ♦ *Anne's paintings rival the ones I see in art galleries.*

rivalry ['rɑɪ vəl ri] *n.* competition between two people or two groups of people. (No plural form in this sense.) ♦ *Bob and Anne encouraged sibling rivalry among their children.* ♦ *The rivalry between the two colleges was primarily friendly.*

river ['rɪv ɚ] *n.* a natural passage of fresh water that flows into a larger river or body of water. ♦ *The Mississippi River forms the border of many states.* ♦ *Anne crossed the river on a raft.*

riverbed ['rɪv ɚ bɛd] *n.* the bottom of a river; the ground that a river flows over. ♦ *During the drought, the riverbed was completely dry.* ♦ *The bottom of the boat scraped the riverbed.*

riverside ['rɪv ɚ sɑɪd] **1.** *n.* the land along either side of a river; the side of a river. (No plural form in this sense.) ♦ *On the riverside, a small shop sold bait and cold drinks.* ♦ *The developer built twelve houses along the riverside.* **2.** *adj.* beside a river; along the side of a river. ♦ *The riverside golf course was very beautiful.* ♦ *Riverside farms flooded during the spring.*

rivet ['rɪv ɪt] **1.** *n.* a metal bolt that is used to fasten things together. ♦ *There are rivets in the upper corners of the pockets of my jeans.* ♦ *The steel beams were held together by rivets.* **2.** *tv.* to fasten two or more things together with ①. ♦ *The steel worker riveted the beams together.* ♦ *The girders were riveted into place.* **3. rivet someone's attention** *idiom* to keep someone's attention fixed [on something]. ♦ *The movie riveted the audience's attention.* ♦ *Professor Jones's lecture riveted the students' attention.*

riveting ['rɪv ə tɪŋ] *adj.* keeping one's attention; very interesting. (Adv: *rivetingly.*) ♦ *The riveting documentary was very popular.* ♦ *I didn't go to sleep until I finished the riveting book.*

roach ['rotʃ] *n.* a cockroach. ♦ *David sprayed his kitchen with insecticide for roaches.* ♦ *Anne stepped on the roach and killed it.*

road ['rod] **1.** *n.* a path or way that people can drive cars and other vehicles on to get from one place to another. ♦ *The country roads are covered with ice and snow.* ♦ *My family has lived on Miller Road my whole life.* **2.** *n.* a path ② leading to a consequence. ♦ *Anne is following the road to ruin.* ♦ *Clean living is the road to a happy life.*

roadblock ['rod blɑk] *n.* something that is placed across a road to stop traffic or to prevent travel beyond that point. ♦ *The police set up a roadblock to trap the criminal.* ♦ *The workers set up a roadblock in front of the huge pit.*

roadside ['rod sɑɪd] **1.** *n.* the area alongside of a road. ♦ *Sue pulled over to the roadside to get something from the trunk.* ♦ *David rode his bicycle on the gravel roadside.* **2.** *adj.* beside a road. ♦ *John drove to a roadside rest stop.* ♦ *Mary ate lunch at the roadside park.*

roam ['rom] **1.** *tv.* to travel someplace with no definite destination in mind; to wander someplace. ♦ *The cows roamed the meadow as they grazed.* ♦ *The tourists roamed the streets, looking at the buildings.* **2.** *iv.* to travel around with no definite destination in mind; to wander. ♦ *Mary roamed throughout the south on her vacation.* ♦ *John roamed across Europe when he was 18.*

roar ['ror] **1.** *n.* a very loud, deep noise. ♦ *The lion's roar scared the hunter.* ♦ *The roars of laughter from the audience pleased the performers.* **2.** *iv.* to make ①. ♦ *The lion roared at the hunter.* ♦ *The engine roared when I turned the key.* **3.** *iv.* to laugh very hard and very long because someone or something is very funny. ♦ *The audience roared with laughter.* ♦ *Susan roared when I told her the funny joke.*

roast ['rost] **1.** *tv.* to cook something by using dry heat; to bake; to cook in an oven; to prepare something by using heat. (Most meats and vegetables are roasted. Bread and ham are baked. Potatoes are both roasted and baked.) ♦ *Bill roasted a squash for supper.* ♦ *Jane roasted the beef at 350 degrees.* **2.** *tv.* to cause something to become very hot. ♦ *The oven roasted the meat slowly.* ♦ *Mary roasted the turkey by placing it in the oven.* **3.** *iv.* to become cooked by using dry heat; to become cooked over fire. ♦ *The turkey roasted for five hours are 350 degrees.* ♦ *I could smell the potatoes as they roasted.* **4.** *n.* meat that is suitable for cooking in dry heat; meat that has been cooked with dry heat. ♦ *John removed the roast from the oven.* ♦ *Anne sliced the roast with a large knife.* **5.** *n.* an outdoor barbecue; an outdoor meal where food is cooked over an open fire. ♦ *We had a wiener roast at the picnic.* ♦ *Before we doused the campfire, we had a marshmallow roast.* **6.** *n.* a celebration where the guest of honor is insulted and ridiculed in a humorously. ♦ *At the roast, the host kept insulting the guest of honor.* ♦ *The network televised the celebrity roast.* **7.** *adj.* cooked with dry heat or over fire. ♦ *Mary ate roast beef with cheddar cheese.* ♦ *John served roast vegetables for dinner.*

roasted ['ros tɪd] *adj.* cooked or prepared with heat or over fire. ♦ *I put butter on the roasted ears of corn.* ♦ *I had wrapped the roasted potatoes in aluminum foil.*

roasting ['ros tɪŋ] *adj.* [of weather or air] very hot. ♦ *It's just roasting out there.* ♦ *Open a window, it's roasting in here.*

rob ['rɑb] **1.** *tv.* to steal something from someone; to take something from someone by force. ♦ *The thief robbed the tourists on a dark street.* ♦ *The thief robbed me of all my money.* **2.** *tv.* to deprive someone of something; to take something from someone. (Figurative on ①.) ♦ *The child laborers were robbed of their happy childhood.* ♦ *The lazy clerk robbed me of my patience.* **3. rob the cradle** *idiom* to marry or date someone who is much younger than oneself. ♦ *I hear that Bill is dating Anne. Isn't that sort of robbing the cradle? She's much younger than he is.* ♦ *Uncle Bill—who is nearly eighty—married a thirty-year-old woman. That is really robbing the cradle.*

robber ['rɑb ɚ] *n.* someone who robs people or places; a thief. ♦ *A robber had stolen my television set.* ♦ *The robber demanded all of my money.*

robbery ['rɑb (ə) ri] *n.* stealing something that belongs to someone else; theft. ♦ *I reported the robbery to the police.* ♦ *During the robbery, the thief held a gun to my head.*

robe ['rob] **1.** *n.* a long one-piece garment, especially worn to show one's rank or position. ♦ *A judge's robe is black.* ♦ *The king and queen wore fine, silk robes on the throne.* **2.** *n.* a bathrobe. ♦ *John wore a robe to the breakfast table.* ♦ *Anne put on a robe after her shower.*

robin ['rɑb ən] *n.* a songbird with orange feathers on its breast. ♦ *When I heard a robin outside my window, I knew spring had arrived.* ♦ *The cat tried to pounce on the robin.*

robot ['ro bɑt] *n.* a machine that does the work of a human and often moves like or looks like a human. ♦ *Some of the auto workers were replaced by robots.* ♦ *The robot was programmed to do some simple tasks.*

robust [ro 'bʌst] **1.** *adj.* [of someone] strong and sturdy. (Adv: *robustly.*) ♦ *Robust athletes eat a lot of fruits and vegetables.* ♦ *If you want to be healthy and robust, get lots of exercise.* **2.** *adj.* [of a flavor] strong and full. (Adv: *robustly.*) ♦ *Mary prefers a robust, red wine.* ♦ *Lisa's morning cup of coffee is robust and extra strong.*

rock ['rɑk] **1.** *n.* the mineral substances of which a planet is made. (No plural form in this sense.) ♦ *The miners blasted through rock, looking for precious ore.* ♦ *I built my house on solid rock.* **2.** *n.* a stone; a hard piece of earth; a piece of mineral. ♦ *The farmer removed rocks from the fields each year.* ♦ *I cut my foot when I stepped on a sharp rock.* **3.** *adj.* made of ①; consisting of ① or ②. ♦ *Anne put the rock sculpture on a pedestal.* ♦ *Grass won't grow here, so I built a rock garden.* **4.** *iv.* to move back and forth; to move from side to side; to sway. ♦ *The ship rocked on the waves.* ♦ *The wooden bridge rocked in the wind.* **5.** *tv.* to move something back and forth or from side to side. ♦ *Sit down or you'll rock the boat.* ♦ *The heavy waves rocked the raft.* **6.** *tv.* to shock or disturb someone greatly, especially because of bad news. (Figurative on ⑤.) ♦ *We were rocked by the news of our leader's death.* ♦ *The royal palace was rocked by scandal.* **7.** See rock-and-roll.

rock-and-roll AND **rock, rock 'n' roll** ['rɑk ən 'rol] **1.** *n.* a style of popular music, usually featuring drums and guitars. (No plural form in this sense.) ♦ *The most popular radio station in town plays nothing but rock.* ♦ *All of my friends like to listen to rock-and-roll.* **2.** *adj.* <the adj. use of ①.> ♦ *Lisa was in a rock-and-roll band when she was in college.* ♦ *Bob listens only to rock stations on the radio.*

rocker ['rɑk ɚ] See rocking chair.

rocket ['rɑk ət] **1.** *n.* a device used to travel in space or to carry missiles and bombs. ♦ *The rocket carried three astronauts toward the moon.* ♦ *An enemy rocket demolished the town's hospital.* **2.** *iv.* to travel somewhere very fast. ♦ *Cars rocketed by me as I stood on the side of the road.* ♦ *Our raft rocketed toward the waterfall through the rapids.* **3.** *iv.* to travel by ①. ♦ *The astronauts rocketed to the moon.* ♦ *The space shuttle rocketed into space.*

rocking chair AND **rocker** ['rɑk ɪŋ 'tʃɛr, 'rɑk ɚ] *n.* a chair whose legs are set into two curved pieces of wood so that it can rock back and forth. ♦ *John sat in his rocking chair as he watched television.* ♦ *Anne moved her rocker away from the edge of the carpet.*

rocky ['rɑk i] **1.** *adj.* having a lot of rocks; made of rocks. (Adv: *rockily.* Comp: *rockier;* sup: *rockiest.*) ♦ *Very little grows in rocky soil.* ♦ *The climbers inched up the rocky cliff.* **2.** *adj.* not smooth; difficult; uneven. (Figurative on ①. Adv: *rockily.* Comp: *rockier;* sup: *rockiest.*) ♦ *Many passengers became ill on the rocky flight.* ♦ *The rocky journey bounded us around.*

rod ['rɑd] *n.* a long, narrow cylinder of wood, metal, plastic, or other material. ♦ *The doctor put steel rods in the crash victim's hip.* ♦ *I hung the curtains from the rod over the window.*

rode ['rod] pt of ride.

rodent ['rod nt] *n.* a member of a group of mammals with large, strong, sharp front teeth. ♦ *Mice, rats, squirrels, and beavers are rodents.* ♦ *Dozens of rodents swarmed around the pile of garbage.*

rodeo ['ro di o] *n.* an event including contests involving roping cattle and riding horses. (Pl in *-s.*) ♦ *The cowboy rode a bronco at the rodeo.* ♦ *The veterinarian treated the horse that was injured at the rodeo.*

rogue ['rog] *n.* someone who is not honest. ♦ *Some rogue stole Anne's purse from the seat next to her.* ♦ *A rogue swindled the old couple's money from them.*

role ['rol] **1.** *n.* a part in a play or movie; the part that an actor plays in a play or movie. ♦ *Mary was cast in the role of Juliet.* ♦ *The director cast members of the ensemble in all of the roles.* **2.** *n.* the duty someone has in a group or organization. ♦ *In her role as chairwoman, Anne called the meeting to order.* ♦ *It is the secretary's role to take minutes of official meetings.*

roll ['rol] **1.** *n.* a small loaf of bread made for one person; a small, round piece of bread for one person. ♦ *The waiter brought our table a small basket of rolls.* ♦ *The salad was served with a warm roll.* **2.** *n.* a unit of something that has been formed into a tube. ♦ *The workers loaded three rolls of carpet onto the truck.* ♦ *I bought a roll of toilet paper at the store.* **3.** *n.* an ongoing movement of something from side to side or back and forth, such as the movement of a ship on rough water. ♦ *The roll of the ship made the passengers ill.* ♦ *The pilot controlled the roll of the plane as it turned.* **4.** *n.* the act of throwing dice. ♦ *It's my roll. Please give me the dice.* ♦ *If your roll is a 7 or an 11, you'll win the* *game.* **5. class roll** *n.* a list of the names of people, especially those who are enrolled in something. (See also ⑬.) ♦ *The class roll is too large for effective teaching.* ♦ *When the class roll is full, we will not enroll more students.* **6.** *iv.* to move forward by turning over and over; for a ball to move forward along a surface. ♦ *The ball rolled across the floor.* ♦ *The children became dirty when they rolled down the hill.* **7.** *iv.* to move on wheels. ♦ *The skaters rolled around the rink.* ♦ *The car rolled to a stop.* **8.** *iv.* to move back and forth or from side to side. ♦ *The ship rolled on the large waves.* ♦ *The raft rolled in the rough water.* **9.** *tv.* to move something forward by turning it over and over; to move a ball forward along a surface. ♦ *I rolled the tennis ball toward my dog.* ♦ *Bill rolled the barrel on its side.* **10.** *tv.* to move something on wheels; to cause something to move on wheels. ♦ *The attendant rolled the skates toward the customers.* ♦ *I rolled the stalled car past the intersection.* **11.** *tv.* to cause something to move back and forth or from side to side. ♦ *The heavy waves rolled the ship back and forth.* ♦ *The wind rolled the boat as it crossed the lake.* **12.** *tv.* to cause something to form the shape of a tube or cylinder. ♦ *This machine rolls the paper into tubes.* ♦ *The sculptor rolled the clay into a rod.* **13. call (the) roll; take (the) roll** *idiom* to call the names of people on the roll ⑤, expecting them to reply if they are present. ♦ *After I call the roll, please open your books to page 12.* ♦ *I will take roll, and then we will do arithmetic.* **14. heads will roll** *idiom* some people will get into trouble. ♦ *When the company's results become public, heads will roll.* ♦ *Heads will roll when the principal sees the damaged classroom.* **15. roll in** *idiom* to come in large numbers or amounts. ♦ *We didn't expect many people at the party, but they just kept rolling in.* ♦ *Money is simply rolling in for our charity.* **16. rolling in something** *idiom* having large amounts of something, usually money. ♦ *That family is rolling in money.* ♦ *Bob doesn't need to earn money. He's rolling in it.*

roller coaster ['rol ɚ kos tɚ] *n.* a ride ⑤ in an amusement park that consists of a string of cars or carriages that travels very fast over a track that follows a random course designed to thrill or terrify the rider. ♦ *I am always too frightened to ride a roller coaster.* ♦ *Modern roller coasters are fast, safe, and terrifying.*

roller skate ['rol ɚ sket] **1.** *n.* a shoe that is fitted with wheels underneath. ♦ *Roller skates are not permitted inside the store.* ♦ *I went to the lake on my roller skates.* **2. roller-skate** *iv.* to move on roller skates. ♦ *I roller-skated to the park.* ♦ *The children roller-skated around the rink.*

rolling ['rol ɪŋ] *adj.* having hills; [of land] high and low. (Adv: *rollingly.*) ♦ *The farmers planted crops on the rolling land.* ♦ *Susan jogged up and down the gently rolling hills.*

Roma ['ro mə] See Gypsy.

Roman ['ro mən] **1.** *n.* a citizen or native of Rome. ♦ *Susan spoke Italian to the Romans when she was on vacation.* ♦ *When I traveled through Italy, I fell in love with a Roman.* **2.** *adj.* of or about Rome. ♦ *The Roman taxi driver drove me to the museum.* ♦ *We ate pasta at the Roman restaurant.* **3.** *adj.* of or about an ancient empire centered in Rome from 27 B.C. to A.D. 395 when it was split in two. ♦ *Caesar was a Roman emperor.* ♦ *The English alphabet uses letters from the Roman alphabet.*

Roman Catholic ['ro mən 'kæθ (ə) lɪk] **1.** *n.* a follower of the Christian religion that is based in Roman and governed by the Pope. ♦ *Anne listens to the pope's teachings because she is a Roman Catholic.* ♦ *Roman Catholics aren't supposed to eat meat on Fridays during Lent.* **2.** *adj.* <the adj. use of ①.> ♦ *The Roman Catholic priest blessed the dying man.* ♦ *I play bingo at the local Roman Catholic church every week.*

romance [ro 'mæns] **1.** *n.* an interest in love and adventure. (No plural form in this sense.) ♦ *The busy executive had very little time for romance.* ♦ *Romance inspired me to buy my date a dozen roses.* **2.** *n.* a love story. ♦ *The delayed traveler bought a romance at the airport bookstore.* ♦ *This movie is a beautiful romance about two college students.* **3.** *n.* a love affair. ♦ *My lonely roommate longs for a romance with a lovely person.* ♦ *Sue told me about her brief romance during her trip to Europe.* **4. Romance** *n.* a group of languages that includes French, Italian, Spanish, Portuguese, and Romanian. ♦ *Romance includes languages spoken in the countries along the Mediterranean Sea.* ♦ *Romance is a group of languages spoken in Europe and South America.* **5.** *tv.* to woo someone; to treat someone in a romantic way; to show someone love. ♦ *Anne had romanced her lover for a month before they kissed.* ♦ *John romanced his neighbor with candy, flowers, and gifts.* **6. Romance** *adj.* <the adj. use of ④.> ♦ *Our university's Romance department specializes in Spanish literature.* ♦ *The linguist spoke French but understood all Romance languages.*

Romani AND **Roma** [ro 'mɑ ni, 'ro mə] See Gypsy.

Romania AND **Rumania** [ro 'men i ə] See Gazetteer.

Roman numeral ['rom ən 'num ə rəl] See numeral.

romantic [ro 'mæn tɪk] **1.** *adj.* full of love and adventure; of or about a love affair; of or about love. (Adv: *romantically* [...ɪk li].) ♦ *The romantic couple held hands as they watched the movie.* ♦ *My date surprised me with a very romantic kiss.* **2.** *adj.* causing romance; used to create a feeling of romance. (Adv: *romantically* [...ɪk li].) ♦ *The fireplace in the den is cozy and romantic.* ♦ *We went to a ski resort for a romantic winter vacation.* **3.** *n.* someone who is full of love and adventure. ♦ *John is a hopeless romantic and develops crushes too easily.* ♦ *Anne blushed when the romantic kissed her hand.*

Rome ['rom] See Rome at Italy in the Gazetteer.

romp ['rɑmp] **1.** *n.* rough but friendly play. ♦ *The puppy enjoyed its romp through the forest.* ♦ *The children became dirty from their romp in the sandbox.* **2.** *iv.* to play in a rough but friendly way; to run, jump, and be very active in play; to play wildly. ♦ *The silly children romped in the mud after the rainstorm.* ♦ *The puppies romped with each other in the park.*

roof ['ruf, 'rʊf] **1.** *n.* the outside covering of the top of a building, vehicle, or other enclosed object. ♦ *The workers covered the house's roof with shingles.* ♦ *Rain leaked through the hole in the roof.* **2.** *n.* the top part of the inside of something, such as the mouth or a cave. ♦ *The hot soup burned the roof of my mouth.* ♦ *Bats hung from the roof of the cave.* **3.** *tv.* to put ① over something; to build ①. ♦ *Eight men roofed the new barn in a day.* ♦ *The workers roofed the new condominiums in the scorching heat.* **4. go through the roof** *idiom* to go very high; to reach a very high degree (of something). ♦ *It's so hot! The temperature* *is going through the roof.* ♦ *Mr. Brown got so angry he almost went through the roof.*

roofer ['ruf ɚ, 'rʊf ɚ] *n.* someone who builds or fixes roofs as a job. ♦ *The roofer patched the hole in the roof.* ♦ *The roofer heated a batch of tar for the roof.*

roofing ['ruf ɪŋ, 'rʊf ɪŋ] *n.* the substance that roofs are covered with. (No plural form in this sense.) ♦ *Shingles are a common kind of roofing.* ♦ *The tornado blew the roofing from our house.*

roofless ['ruf ləs, 'rʊf ləs] *adj.* without a roof; not having a roof; open to the outdoor air. (Adv: *rooflessly.*) ♦ *The tornado caused many houses to become roofless.* ♦ *Mary sold merchandise from a roofless stall at the market.*

rookie ['rʊk i] *n.* a beginner; someone who is new to something; a newcomer. ♦ *The talented rookie was given a contract for a second year.* ♦ *The older players played a practical joke on the rookies.*

room ['rum] **1.** *n.* a part of a building that is separated from other parts of the building by a doorway. ♦ *My apartment has six rooms.* ♦ *Anne walked into the next room and shut the door.* **2.** *n.* space that is or could be taken up by someone or something. ♦ *Is there enough room for this couch in our living room?* ♦ *I moved my coat so there would be room for John to sit down.* **3. room with** *iv. + prep. phr.* to live with someone; to rent a room or an apartment with someone; to be someone's roommate. ♦ *Anne roomed with a different person each year in college.* ♦ *Bob roomed with his cousin when he first moved to Chicago.*

roomer ['rum ɚ] *n.* someone who lives in a rented apartment or room. ♦ *The landlady collected the roomers' rent each week.* ♦ *All of the roomers ate breakfast together on Saturday.*

roommate ['rum met] *n.* someone with whom one shares an apartment or room. ♦ *My roommate told me that my parents had called earlier.* ♦ *I helped my roommate wash the dishes.*

roomy ['rum i] *adj.* having plenty of room; having a lot of space; having a comfortable amount of space; not crowded; spacious. (Adv: *roomily.* Comp: *roomier;* sup: *roomiest.*) ♦ *The tall customer asked for an especially roomy car.* ♦ *The real-estate agent showed Susan the roomy apartment.*

roost ['rust] **1.** *n.* a place, such as a nest or branch, where birds rest or sleep. ♦ *The bird stood on the small roost in front of the birdhouse.* ♦ *Small birds use my clothesline as a roost.* **2.** *iv.* to occupy ① for rest or sleep. ♦ *A sparrow roosted on the small tree branch.* ♦ *The eagle wrapped its claws around the branch on which it roosted.* **3. rule the roost** *idiom* to be the boss or manager, especially at home. ♦ *Who rules the roost at your house?* ♦ *Our new office manager really rules the roost.*

rooster ['rust ɚ] *n.* an adult male chicken. ♦ *The rooster crows at sunrise.* ♦ *The rooster strutted around the barnyard.*

root 1. ['rut, rʊt] *n.* the part of a plant that is under the ground, taking nutrients from the soil and supporting the plant. ♦ *A root from the large tree cracked the sidewalk.* ♦ *Edible roots include carrots and turnips.* **2.** ['rut, rʊt] *n.* the part of something that is under a surface or that holds it in place in a surface. (Figurative on ①.) ♦ *The roots of your teeth are infected.* ♦ *This shampoo cleans down to the roots of your hair.* **3.** ['rut, rʊt] *n.* the origin of something; the source of something; something that causes something else. ♦ *The love of money is the root of all evil.* ♦ *I think that greed and anger are the roots of my problems.* **4.** ['rut, rʊt] *n.* the form of a word that other words are derived from. ♦ *The root of the word* interestingly *is* interest. ♦ *The progressive is formed by adding* -ing *to verb roots.* **5.** ['rut, rʊt] *n.* a number that is multiplied by itself a specific number of times to give another number. ♦ *5 is the square root of 25, because 5 × 5 = 25.* ♦ *4 is the cube root of 64, because 4 × 4 × 4 = 64.* **6.** ['rut, rʊt] *tv.* to cause a plant to grow roots. ♦ *The gardener rooted the plants in deep soil.* ♦ *You should root this plant in sandy soil.* **7.** ['rʊt] *iv.* to cheer for someone; to provide encouragement for someone or a team, especially for someone or a team in a contest or sporting event. ♦ *The fans rooted for their team.* ♦ *I was rooting for the challenger to upset the champion.* **8. root something out** ['rut...] *idiom* to get rid of something completely; to destroy something. ♦ *No government will ever root out crime completely.* ♦ *The headmaster wants to root troublemakers out at the local school.*

rooted ['rut ɪd] **rooted in something** *phr.* based on something; connected to a source or cause. ♦ *The civil war was rooted in old ethnic hatred.* ♦ *This fictional book was rooted in actual events.*

rope ['rop] **1.** *n.* a strong, thick cord made by twisting smaller cords together. (No plural form in this sense.) ♦ *Anne tied the mattress to the roof of her car with a heavy rope.* ♦ *The bank robber tied the tellers up with rope.* **2.** *tv.* to catch someone or something by using ① or lasso. ♦ *The cowboy roped a steer.* ♦ *In the movie, the sheriff roped the bandit and tied him up.* **3. at the end of one's rope** *idiom* at the limits of one's endurance. ♦ *I'm at the end of my rope! I just can't go on this way!* ♦ *These kids are driving me out of my mind. I'm at the end of my rope.* **4. know the ropes** *idiom* to know how to do something. ♦ *I can't do the job because I don't know the ropes.* ♦ *Ask Sally to do it. She knows the ropes.*

rose ['roz] **1.** pt of rise. **2.** *n.* a bright, sweet-smelling flower that grows on a thorny bush. ♦ *The florist arranged 12 roses in a vase.* ♦ *I sent some roses to my wife on our anniversary.* **3.** *n.* the bush that ② grows on. ♦ *The gardener planted roses next to the front porch.* ♦ *John tended to the roses growing alongside the fence.* **4.** *n.* a pink or reddish-pink color. (No plural form in this sense.) ♦ *The wind made my cheeks a bright rose.* ♦ *The carpet in the lobby is a dusty rose.* **5.** *adj.* pink; reddish-pink. ♦ *I bought some rose lipstick from the salesclerk.* ♦ *Mrs. Smith wrapped a rose shawl over her shoulders.*

rosebud ['roz bəd] *n.* the bud of a rose; a small rose blossom. ♦ *In the park, Anne bent over to smell the fragrant rosebuds.* ♦ *John pressed some rosebuds between the pages of the heavy book.*

rosebush ['roz bʊʃ] *n.* the thorny bush that roses grow on. ♦ *I pricked myself on a thorn when I trimmed the rosebush.* ♦ *The rosebushes by my house are very beautiful when they are in bloom.*

Rosh Hashanah ['rɑʃ hə 'ʃɑ nə] *n.* a holiday in the Jewish religion marking the Jewish New Year. ♦ *Rosh Hashanah occurs in the late summer or early fall.* ♦ *Rosh Hashanah is celebrated on the first day of the year.*

rosin ['rɑz ɪn] *n.* a hard substance that is made when turpentine is removed from pine sap, used to make ink, varnish, and wax and for rubbing on the bows of stringed instruments like the violin. (No plural form in this sense.) ♦ *The violinist kept some rosin in her case.* ♦ *It was difficult to remove the sticky rosin from my fingers.*

roster ['rɑst ɚ] *n.* a list of names or things, especially a list of people. ♦ *Only the people listed on the roster were allowed into the party.* ♦ *The supervisor assigned everyone on the roster a task.*

rostrum ['rɑs trəm] *n.* a raised platform that a speaker or conductor stands on, usually including a structure to hold papers and perhaps a glass of water. ♦ *The audience applauded as the speaker walked toward the rostrum.* ♦ *From the rostrum, the candidate pledged to cut taxes.*

rosy ['roz i] **1.** *adj.* pink; rose-colored. (Adv: *rosily.* Comp: *rosier;* sup: *rosiest.*) ♦ *The children's cheeks were rosy from the wind.* ♦ *The manicurist put some rosy polish on my nails.* **2.** *adj.* optimistic; hopeful. (Adv: *rosily.* Comp: *rosier;* sup: *rosiest.*) ♦ *The rosy economic outlook made the investors very happy.* ♦ *After surgery, the doctor said my prognosis was quite rosy.*

rot ['rɑt] **1.** *n.* decay; something that is rotten. (No plural form in this sense.) ♦ *The dentist removed my tooth because there was rot in it.* ♦ *I threw away the vegetable because of the rot.* **2.** *iv., irreg.* to decay; to decompose; [for plant or animal material] to lose its form because of bacteria. (Pt/pp: *rot.*) ♦ *The half-eaten apple rotted on the counter.* ♦ *A dead squirrel rotted by the side of the road.* **3.** *tv.* to cause something to decay. ♦ *The warm humid air helped rot the old fruit.* ♦ *Moisture and disease had rotted the old wooden bridge.*

rotary ['rot ə ri] **rotary dial** *n.* a telephone dial that turns in a circular movement around a fixed point. ♦ *The old farmhouse had a phone with a rotary dial.* ♦ *Because the phone had a rotary dial, I couldn't page Anne.*

rotate ['ro tet] **1.** *iv.* to move in a circle around a fixed point; to move around the center of something in a circle. ♦ *The earth rotates on its axis.* ♦ *The wheel rotated around its hub.* **2.** *iv.* to go in sequence; to occur in order or in sequence. ♦ *The duty of washing dishes rotated among my siblings and me.* ♦ *Before the serve, the members of the volleyball team rotated.* **3.** *tv.* to move something in a circle around a fixed point; to cause something to revolve; to move something around an axis. ♦ *Bill rotated the wheels of the bike to see if they needed lubrication.* ♦ *Jane rotated the basketball on her fingertip.* **4.** *tv.* to change things in a regular sequence. ♦ *The supervisor rotated the workers' shifts every month.* ♦ *Each year, the farmer rotated the crops that were grown.*

rotating ['ro tet ɪŋ] *adj.* moving in a circle around a fixed point; moving around an axis. ♦ *The rotating planet wobbled on its axis.* ♦ *The rotating wheel stopped when the brake was applied.*

rotation [ro 'te ʃən] **1.** *n.* the circular movement around a fixed point. (No plural form in this sense.) ♦ *Night and day are caused by the earth's rotation.* ♦ *Rotation can make you dizzy.* **2.** *n.* an instance of ①. ♦ *After two rotations, the wheel fell off.* ♦ *With each rotation of the bicycle wheel, I heard a click.* **3.** *n.* the alternation of people or things in a predetermined sequence. (No plural form in this sense.) ♦ *The supervisor practices the rotation of personnel in the three work shifts.* ♦ *The rotation of crops ensures that the soil won't be depleted of nutrients.*

rote ['rot] **by rote** *phr.* [of learning or memorizing] done as habit and without thinking. ♦ *I memorized the speech by rote. I don't know what it means.* ♦ *The student learns everything by rote and can't pass the test.*

rotisserie [ro 'tɪs ə ri] *n.* a rotating rod over a heat source, holding meat that cooks evenly as it turns. (From French.) ♦ *The chicken roasted evenly on the rotisserie.* ♦ *The pig cooked as it turned slowly on the rotisserie.*

rotted ['rɑt ɪd] *adj.* rotten; decayed. ♦ *The rotted wood crumbled when I picked it up.* ♦ *The vultures picked at the rotted carcass.*

rotten ['rɑt n] **1.** *adj.* decayed; spoiled; decomposed; putrid. (Adv: *rottenly.*) ♦ *The rotten fruit smelled horrible.* ♦ *Rotten eggs smell like sulfur.* **2.** *adj.* very bad; evil; nasty. (Adv: *rottenly.*) ♦ *My rotten boss makes me work on holidays.* ♦ *This TV show is really rotten.*

rotting ['rɑt ɪŋ] *adj.* decaying; decomposing; falling apart; deteriorating. ♦ *The rotting roof collapsed.* ♦ *The rotting flesh attracted vultures.*

rotund [ro 'tʌnd] *adj.* plump; having a round, somewhat fat body. (Adv: *rotundly.*) ♦ *The rotund man was asked to play Santa Claus at the mall.* ♦ *The doctor placed his rotund patients on diets.*

rouge ['ruʒ] *n.* a red powder or liquid that is put on the cheeks to give them color. (No plural form in this sense.) ♦ *The exotic dancers wore heavy rouge on their cheeks.* ♦ *Mary was wearing too much rouge, and she looked sunburned.*

rough ['rʌf] **1.** *adj.* not smooth; not even; having a surface that is uneven or bumpy. (Adv: *roughly.* Comp: *rougher;* sup: *roughest.*) ♦ *The rough road was difficult to drive on.* ♦ *The wound left a rough scar on my skin.* **2.** *adj.* forceful; using force; harsh; violent. (Adv: *roughly.* Comp: *rougher;* sup: *roughest.*) ♦ *This vase can't tolerate any rough treatment, so be careful.* ♦ *Our foster child had undergone a lot of rough abuse.* **3.** *adj.* coarse; not delicate; not refined. (Adv: *roughly.* Comp: *rougher;* sup: *roughest.*) ♦ *The poet captured the sailors' rough language.* ♦ *The musicians rented a cheap apartment in a rough part of town.* **4.** *adj.* hard; difficult; severe; not easy. (Comp: *rougher;* sup: *roughest.*) ♦ *We had a rough time finishing the difficult project.* ♦ *It was rough to drive in such a horrible snowstorm.* **5.** *adj.* not in final form; not finished; not exact; preliminary; not polished; rudimentary; not detailed; approximate. (Adv: *roughly.* Comp: *rougher;* sup: *roughest.*) ♦ *The architect made some rough designs for the client.* ♦ *My secretary made a rough outline of my schedule at the conference.* **6.** *n.* the part of a golf course where the grass is long. (No plural form in this sense.) ♦ *The golfer hit the ball into the rough.* ♦ *I couldn't find my ball in the rough.* **7. rough up** *tv. + adv.* to cause something to become rough. ♦ *I roughed up the surface of the floor before painting it.* ♦ *I accidentally roughed up the side of my new leather shoes.* **8. rough up** *tv. + adv.* to beat or assault someone. ♦ *The bank robbers roughed the tellers up during the robbery.* ♦ *The police officers roughed up the criminals in the alley.* **9. rough it** *idiom* to live without luxury; to live simply. ♦ *During the blackout, we roughed it without electricity.* ♦ *The campers roughed it in the remote cabin for a week.*

roughage ['rʌf ɪdʒ] *n.* coarse foods, such as celery; the coarse parts of food that provide dietary fiber. (No plural form in this sense.) ♦ *The nutritionist recommended I eat a lot of roughage.* ♦ *David eats roughage every day.*

roughhouse ['rʌf hɑʊs] **1.** *iv.* to play roughly; to play or behave in a rough way. ♦ *Don't roughhouse in the living room. You'll break something.* ♦ *The children roughhoused with the big dog.* **2.** *n., irreg.* someone who plays roughly or is a bully. (Pl: [...hɑʊ zəz].) ♦ *The roughhouse broke my arm when we played football.* ♦ *The small children gave the mean roughhouse their lunch money after he threatened them.*

roughness ['rʌf nəs] *n.* the quality of being rough. (No plural form in this sense.) ♦ *The roughness of the football players led to many injuries.* ♦ *The roughness of the path makes it difficult to drive on.*

roulette [ru 'lɛt] *n.* a gambling game where a wheel with numbered and colored slots is spun and people bet on which slot a ball will fall in. ♦ *In roulette, if the ball lands in a green slot, everyone loses.* ♦ *I played roulette at the casino until I'd lost all my money.*

round ['rɑʊnd] **1.** *adj.* shaped like a circle; circular; curved. (Adv: *roundly.* Comp: *rounder;* sup: *roundest.*) ♦ *My shirt has round buttons.* ♦ *The clock on the wall is round.* **2.** *adj.* shaped like a ball; spherical; curved. (Adv: *roundly.* Comp: *rounder;* sup: *roundest.*) ♦ *An orange is a round fruit.* ♦ *I pumped air into the basketball until it was round.* **3. round figures; round numbers** *n.* full; complete [with respect to numbers] to the nearest 1, 10, 100, 1,000, etc.). ♦ *How much will it cost—in round numbers?* ♦ *I used round figures when estimating my income tax.* **4. rounds** *n.* a circuit that ends where it begins, especially the path taken by a police officer or guard; a routine; a series of duties. ♦ *The guard read the newspaper between his rounds.* ♦ *The janitor made his rounds of the office building every evening.* **5.** *n.* a part of certain games or sports, especially boxing. ♦ *Anne won the last round of golf by four strokes.* ♦ *The boxer won the championship in five rounds.* **6.** *n.* the bullet or shell for a single shot from a gun. ♦ *The terrorist transported hundreds of rounds of ammunition.* ♦ *John shot two rounds before his gun jammed.* **7.** *n.* a burst of applause. ♦ *Let's give a big round of applause for our next performer.* ♦ *After the speech, there was a polite round of applause.* **8.** *n.* a song where people begin at different times so that the words and music of the different parts overlap. ♦ *The campers sang "Row, Row, Row Your Boat" as a round.* ♦ *When we sang the round, we were all singing different words at one time.* **9.** *n.* something—usually drinks—that is given to everyone in the group. ♦ *When I got a promotion, I bought everyone a round of drinks.* ♦ *If you pay for my beer, I'll buy the next round.* **10.** *prep.* around. (Informal. Round can be used informally for any of the preposition uses listed under around.) ♦ *Please put my coat round my shoulders.* ♦ *Run round the corner and buy me a paper.* **11.** *adv.* around. (Informal.) ♦ *The runner ran all the way round the lake.* ♦ *The detective looked round with a flashlight.* **12.** *tv.* to make something become round. ♦ *The sculptor rounded the clay in her hands.* ♦ *I rounded the cookie dough into small balls.* **13.** *tv.* to go around something. ♦ *The car rounded the corner.* ♦ *I rounded the last turn, looking for a parking space.* **14. round out** *tv. + adv.* to make something complete; to make something full. ♦ *David rounded out his diet with vitamin supplements.* ♦ *Anne rounded her workday out by exercising before dinner.* **15. round off to; round up to; round down to** *phr.* to express a number in the nearest whole amount or nearest group of 1, 10, 100, 1,000, 1/10, 1/100, 1/1,000, etc. ♦ *When doing taxes, Anne rounded her figures off to the nearest dollar.* ♦ *These census figures are rounded up to the nearest million.*

roundabout ['rɑʊnd ə bɑʊt] *adj.* indirect; not direct; not using the shortest path. ♦ *We walked to the lake in a very roundabout way.* ♦ *I accused the taxi driver of choosing a roundabout route.*

round-the-clock ['rɑʊnd ðə 'klɑk] **1.** *adj.* around-the-clock; 24 hours a day; all the time; never stopping; always happening, open, or available. ♦ *The hotel provided round-the-clock food service for its guests.* ♦ *Caring for an infant is a round-the-clock job.* **2.** *adv.* always; during the day and night; all the time. ♦ *This convenience store is open round-the-clock.* ♦ *The nuclear power plant was monitored round-the-clock.*

round trip ['rɑʊnd 'trɪp] **1.** *n.* a trip to a place and back to where one started. ♦ *John's round trip to New York was rather inexpensive.* ♦ *Anne makes one round trip between home and work each day.* **2.** *adv.* by way of a round-trip ③ journey. ♦ *Jane flew round trip to Rome for $500.* ♦ *Bill travels round trip to Cleveland every Wednesday. He spends the day there working and then comes back home.* **3. round-trip** *adj.* <the adj. use of ①.> ♦ *I bought a round-trip ticket to Tokyo for my vacation. Bill bought a one-way ticket, because he's moving there.* ♦ *Mary's round-trip commute is one hour each day.*

roundup ['rɑʊnd əp] **1.** *n.* the process of bringing cattle or other livestock together into a herd. ♦ *After the roundup, the cowboys ate dinner.* ♦ *They had a roundup to bring in all the cattle from the open pasture.* **2.** *n.* a gathering together of things or people. (Figurative on ①.) ♦ *All the campers were called together for a roundup before supper.* ♦ *The newscaster gave us a roundup of the day's events.*

roundworm ['rɑʊnd wɚm] *n.* any of many types of tiny worms that invade the intestines of humans and animals. ♦ *The veterinarian said that my dog had roundworms.* ♦ *Roundworms absorb many essential nutrients from the creatures they live in.*

rouse ['rɑʊz] **1.** *tv.* to wake someone up; to wake someone from sleep. ♦ *Mary roused her sister at 8:00 A.M.* ♦ *John's dog roused him when his house caught on fire.* **2.** *iv.* to waken; to wake from sleep; to become awake; to wake up. ♦ *Jane roused only with difficulty.* ♦ *David rouses late when he's on vacation.*

rousing ['rɑʊz ɪŋ] *adj.* exciting; vigorous; lively. (Adv: *rousingly.*) ♦ *The rousing cold shower woke me from my slumber.* ♦ *The choir marched as they sang the rousing chorus.*

rout ['rɑʊt] **1.** *n.* a complete defeat. ♦ *The unskilled team was facing a huge rout.* ♦ *The losing candidates got the routs they deserved.* **2.** *tv.* to defeat someone completely. ♦ *The challenger routed the champion by a very wide margin.* ♦ *Central High routed Southern 24–0 last night.*

route ['rut, 'rɑʊt] **1.** *n.* a road; a path; the way one travels; the way something is sent. ♦ *Do you know the route into town?* ♦ *This route will take you to the factory by way* *of the pond.* **2.** *tv.* to send something by a particular ①. ♦ *My flight to New York was routed through Atlanta.* ♦ *The travel agent routed me through Newark to Boston.*

routine [ru 'tin] **1.** *n.* a regular habit; something that is done regularly. (No plural form in this sense.) ♦ *The office worker did the same routine every weekday for 40 years.* ♦ *I took a vacation because I got tired of my daily routine.* **2.** *n.* a piece of entertainment; a skit; a sequence of actions in a performance. ♦ *The audience applauded my comedy routine.* ♦ *The skater's routine was perfect, and she won the gold medal.* **3.** *adj.* normal; habitual; usual; regular. (Adv: *routinely.*) ♦ *The workers did their routine tasks in silence.* ♦ *Anne took a routine coffee break at 2:30* P.M.

rove ['rov] **1.** *tv.* to roam over a place; to wander over a place. ♦ *The stray dog roved the city looking for food.* ♦ *The cow roved the meadow in search of good grass.* **2.** *iv.* to roam; to wander. ♦ *The traveler roved across the countryside.* ♦ *The orphan roved along the streets, begging for food.*

roving ['rov ɪŋ] *adj.* moving from place to place; wandering; roaming. (Adv: *rovingly.*) ♦ *The roving cattle grazed on government land.* ♦ *The roving reporter wrote about the dozens of places he'd visited.*

row 1. ['ro] *n.* a series of people or things in a line; a line of things or people. ♦ *The farmer planted many rows of corn.* ♦ *A row of people stood against the wall, waiting for the bank to open.* **2.** ['ro] *n.* a line of seats in a theater, church, auditorium, classroom, or other place. ♦ *John forgot his glasses, so he sat in the front row.* ♦ *The first six rows are reserved for important guests.* **3.** ['rɑʊ] *n.* a quarrel; an argument. ♦ *The neighbors' row woke me up at three o'clock this morning.* ♦ *The bus driver ignored the loud row at the back of the bus.* **4.** ['ro] *iv.* to move through water in a boat by using oars. ♦ *Mary rowed against the current.* ♦ *John rowed downstream.* **5.** ['ro] *tv.* to move a boat by using oars. ♦ *Susan and David took turns rowing the boat.* ♦ *Anne rowed the raft toward the bank.*

rowboat ['ro bot] *n.* a small boat that is moved by using oars. ♦ *The doctor reached the remote village by rowboat.* ♦ *During the flood, the police went through town in rowboats.*

rowdy ['rɑʊ di] *adj.* wild; disorderly; rough. (Adv: *rowdily.* Comp: *rowdier;* sup: *rowdiest.*) ♦ *The rowdy students made too much noise.* ♦ *The rowdy audience jeered the untalented opening act.*

royal ['rɔɪ əl] **1.** *adj.* belonging to kings and queens; of or about kings and queens. (Adv: *royally.*) ♦ *The royal juggler entertained the king and queen.* ♦ *The gallant knight was invited to the royal castle.* **2.** *adj.* elegant; fit for royalty. (Figurative on ①. Adv: *royally.*) ♦ *Mary and John prepared a royal feast for their guests.* ♦ *Mr. Brown treated his customer to a royal evening.*

royalty ['rɔɪ əl ti] **1.** *n.* the rank of king or queen; the power of a king or queen. (No plural form in this sense.) ♦ *The young prince was trained for royalty.* ♦ *The young children were in awe of the queen's royalty.* **2.** *n.* people who have attained ①. (No plural form in this sense.) ♦ *English royalty can be seen in public more now than in the past.* ♦ *This park is reserved for royalty.* **3.** *n.* money earned from the publication of a copyright holder's work. ♦ *Mary receives a small royalty each time one of her books is sold.* ♦ *John's contract doesn't provide for any royalties.*

rub ['rʌb] **1.** *tv.* to push or slide something with something else. ♦ *Anne rubbed the sticky spot on the table with a sponge.* ♦ *Sue rubbed the lottery ticket with the edge of a penny.* **2. rub against** *tv.* + *prep. phr.* to push or slide something against something else. ♦ *Please don't rub your hand against the wall.* ♦ *Sue rubbed the edge of a penny against the lottery ticket.* **3. rub against** *iv.* + *prep. phr.* to push or slide against something. ♦ *Please don't rub against the fresh paint.* ♦ *The damaged brake rubbed against the wheel.* **4.** *n.* the act of rubbing. ♦ *John gave his leather shoes a good rub before the party.* ♦ *I gave the silverware a thorough rub before my guests came over.*

rubber ['rʌb ɚ] **1.** *n.* a waterproof material that goes back to its original shape when stretched or compressed. (No plural form in this sense.) ♦ *Rubber is made from the sap of a tropical tree or by a chemical process.* ♦ *The soles of my shoes are made of rubber.* **2.** *adj.* made from ①. ♦ *Jane wore a rubber raincoat outside because it was raining.* ♦ *David's feet remained dry inside his rubber boots.*

rubber band [rəb ɚ 'bænd] *n.* a thin strip of rubber formed in a circle. ♦ *Bob put a rubber band around the stack of papers to hold them together.* ♦ *Lisa always keeps a rubber band around her wrist at work, in case she needs one.*

rubberneck(er) ['rʌb ɚ nɛk (ɚ)] *n.* a tourist; a sightseer; someone who stares at things foolishly. (Informal.) ♦ *The rubberneckers who gawked at the accident caused a traffic jam.* ♦ *A few rubbernecks were looking at the tall building as if it were leaning or growing or something.*

rubbish ['rʌb ɪʃ] *n.* trash; garbage; things that are thrown away. (No plural form in this sense.) ♦ *Mary emptied rubbish into the container behind her apartment.* ♦ *The janitor collected rubbish from the offices.*

rubble ['rʌb əl] *n.* broken stones, bricks, or other material. (No plural form in this sense.) ♦ *After the earthquake, the house was nothing but rubble.* ♦ *After the explosion, the building was reduced to rubble.*

rubdown ['rʌb dɑʊn] *n.* a massage; a rubbing of the muscles of the body. ♦ *John gave Jane a rubdown after she exercised.* ♦ *I'm under so much stress. I could really use a good rubdown.*

ruby ['rub i] **1.** *n.* a red gemstone. ♦ *The jeweler set a small ruby in my ring.* ♦ *The eyes of the statue of the goddess were made of rubies.* **2.** *adj.* <the adj. use of ①.> ♦ *Anne wore a ruby ring to the banquet.* ♦ *John's ruby earring sparkled in the light.*

ruckus ['rʌk əs] *n.* a noisy disturbance or argument; a fight; an uproar. (No plural form in this sense.) ♦ *I called the police when I heard a ruckus on the street.* ♦ *The referee's call caused quite a ruckus in the stands.*

rudder ['rʌd ɚ] *n.* a blade at the back of a ship or airplane that can be moved back and forth to control direction. ♦ *Mary turned the rudder sharply to avoid hitting the rock.* ♦ *John managed the sails while David steered the boat with the rudder.*

ruddy ['rʌd i] *adj.* reddish. (Adv: *ruddily.* Comp: *ruddier;* sup: *ruddiest.*) ♦ *Bill has a ruddy complexion and black hair.* ♦ *Anne's cheekbones are naturally ruddy, so she doesn't wear makeup.*

rude ['rud] **1.** *adj.* not polite; not well mannered; not courteous. (Adv: *rudely.* Comp: *ruder;* sup: *rudest.*) ♦ *The* *waiter ignored the diner's rude command.* ♦ *It was very rude of you to insult me in front of my friends.* **2.** *adj.* simple; not complex; primitive; coarse; rough; made without complex tools. (Adv: *rudely.* Comp: *ruder;* sup: *rudest.*) ♦ *Apes can use a few rude tools.* ♦ *Anne made a rude doghouse with some boards, a hammer, and nails.*

rudeness ['rud nəs] *n.* impoliteness; bad manners; bad behavior. (No plural form in this sense.) ♦ *Your rudeness is not excusable just because you were drunk.* ♦ *The student's rudeness shocked the teacher.*

rudiment ['rud ə mənt] **1.** *n.* something that is basic; something simple that is learned first. ♦ *You must learn the rudiments of algebra before calculus.* ♦ *I learned the rudiments of cooking in home economics.* **2.** *n.* something that is not completely developed; something that is only partially developed. ♦ *This software is merely the rudiment of a program in development.* ♦ *The architect explained the rudiments of the design plan to me.*

rudimentary [rud ə 'mɛn tri] **1.** *adj.* basic; simple; learned first. (Adv: *rudimentarily* [rud ə mɛn 'tɛr ə li].) ♦ *This manual provides a few rudimentary facts about computers.* ♦ *I took a rudimentary cooking class in high school.* **2.** *adj.* not completely developed; only partially developed. (Adv: *rudimentarily* [rud ə mɛn 'tɛr ə li].) ♦ *The two-year-old spoke a rudimentary form of English.* ♦ *This program is only rudimentary and is being developed for release next year.*

ruffle ['rʌf əl] **1.** *n.* a piece of cloth that is bunched in folds and is sewn onto a flat panel of cloth as a decoration. ♦ *The bottom hem of Mary's gown had a lot of ruffles.* ♦ *The shirt John wore with the tuxedo had light blue ruffles.* **2. ruffle its feathers** *phr.* [for a bird] to point its feathers outward. ♦ *The bird ruffled its feathers when it was annoyed.* ♦ *My parrot ruffles its feathers whenever it is ready to preen itself.* **3. ruffle someone's feathers** *idiom* to annoy or irritate someone. ♦ *I don't mean to ruffle your feathers, but you are late again.* ♦ *She is mad at me. I guess I ruffled her feathers.*

rug ['rʌg] **1.** *n.* a carpet; a thick piece of woven fabric that is used to cover a floor. ♦ *I replaced the rug in the bathroom with ceramic tile.* ♦ *John vacuumed the rug after he spilled popcorn.* **2. pull the rug out (from under someone)** *idiom* to make someone ineffective. ♦ *The treasurer pulled the rug out from under the mayor.* ♦ *Bob was doing well until Mary pulled the rug out from under him by telling everyone he had been arrested.*

rugby ['rʌg bi] *n.* a kind of British soccer game where the players are allowed to touch the ball. (No plural form in this sense.) ♦ *After the rugby game, the players were covered with mud.* ♦ *John got a bloody nose during the rough rugby match.*

rugged ['rʌg ɪd] **1.** *adj.* [of a trail] rough and jagged. (Adv: *ruggedly.*) ♦ *The hikers walked along the rugged path.* ♦ *We had to climb a rugged hill to get to the cabin.* **2.** *adj.* [of something] strong and durable; [of something] not easily broken. (Adv: *ruggedly.*) ♦ *These rugged tools are almost impossible to break.* ♦ *The soldier drove the rugged jeep across the field of rocks.* **3.** *adj.* [of someone] sturdy and strong. (Adv: *ruggedly.*) ♦ *The rugged football players played in the cold weather.* ♦ *The rugged campers lived in the woods for a month.*

ruin ['ru ɪn] **1.** *tv.* to destroy someone or something completely; to make something worthless. ♦ *The bomb ruined the ancient city.* ♦ *David ruined the cake by dropping it on the floor.* **2.** *n.* the remaining part of an old building. (Often plural.) ♦ *The tour guide led us through the old Roman ruins.* ♦ *The old house was a ruin and a firetrap.* **3.** *n.* a great amount of destruction. (No plural form in this sense.) ♦ *The powerful bomb caused widespread ruin.* ♦ *The massive ruin caused by the tornado will be costly to repair.* **4. in ruin** *phr.* a state of having been destroyed. ♦ *The enemy army left the cities they attacked in ruin.* ♦ *The crops laid in ruin after the flood.* **5. the ruin of someone or something** *idiom* the cause of destruction; a failure. ♦ *Your bad judgment will be the ruin of this company!* ♦ *The greedy politicians were the ruin of the old empire.*

ruined ['ru ɪnd] *adj.* destroyed; completely damaged; made worthless. ♦ *The ruined books were thrown into the trash.* ♦ *The townspeople slowly rebuilt the ruined city.*

rule ['rul] **1.** *n.* a statement that says what one is or is not allowed to do; a regulation. ♦ *There's a rule against smoking in this part of the restaurant.* ♦ *The coach explained the rules of the game.* **2.** *n.* government; the control of someone in authority. (No plural form in this sense.) ♦ *The citizens were repressed under military rule.* ♦ *Under the queen's rule, her word was law.* **3.** *tv.* to decide something officially. ♦ *The judge ruled on the lawyer's complaint.* ♦ *The Supreme Court ruled that the law was unconstitutional.* **4.** *tv.* to govern a country or its people. ♦ *The aged king had ruled his country for 43 years.* ♦ *A dictator ruled the Soviet Union during World War II.* **5.** *iv.* to govern; to have authority; to control. ♦ *The dictator ruled mercilessly over the Soviet Union.* ♦ *While the evil king ruled, many peasants starved.* **6. as a rule** *phr.* in general; usually. ♦ *As a rule, men should wear tuxedos at formal parties.* ♦ *As a rule, the bus usually picks me up at 7:30.* **7. hard-and-fast rule** *idiom* a strict rule ①. ♦ *It's a hard-and-fast rule that you must be home by midnight.* ♦ *You should have your project completed by the end of the month, but it's not a hard-and-fast rule.*

ruler ['rul ɚ] **1.** *n.* someone who rules; someone who governs. ♦ *The ruler demanded more taxes from the people.* ♦ *The peasants rebelled against the tyrannical ruler.* **2.** *n.* a straight strip of wood, plastic, metal, or other material that has marks on it that show measurement. ♦ *Mary used a ruler to measure the length of her kitchen table.* ♦ *Susan drew a straight line by tracing the edge of a ruler.*

ruling ['rul ɪŋ] **1.** *adj.* governing; controlling; being in authority; being in power. ♦ *The ruling party controlled the military.* ♦ *Only a few members of the ruling class influenced public policy.* **2.** *n.* an official decision, especially in a court of law. ♦ *The Supreme Court's ruling overturned the lower court's decision.* ♦ *The coach disputed the referee's ruling.*

rum ['rʌm] *n.* a liquor made from sugar or molasses. (No plural form in this sense.) ♦ *Rum tastes good with cola.* ♦ *This candy is flavored with rum.*

Rumania See Romania.

rumble ['rʌm bəl] **1.** *n.* a low vibrating sound, like the sound of thunder. ♦ *At the first rumble of thunder, the picnickers went home.* ♦ *I asked my mechanic to listen to the rumble under my car's hood.* **2.** *iv.* to make a low vibrating sound, like the sound of thunder. ♦ *The lightning* *flashed, and then the thunder rumbled.* ♦ *My car engine rumbles loudly when I accelerate.*

ruminant ['rum ə nənt] **1.** *n.* an animal that swallows food, brings it back from the stomach, and chews on it. ♦ *Cattle, deer, sheep, and goats are ruminants.* ♦ *The ruminant slowly chewed its cud.* **2.** *adj.* <the adj. use of ①.> ♦ *Cows are ruminant animals.* ♦ *The plains were covered with great herds of ruminant beasts.*

ruminate ['rum ɪ net] **1.** *iv.* to chew on a cud; to chew on food that has been brought back from the stomach. ♦ *The cows ruminated in the meadow.* ♦ *The sheep stood ruminating, waiting to be sheared.* **2.** *iv.* to think; to meditate; to ponder. (Figurative on ①.) ♦ *The owner ruminated about giving the workers a raise.* ♦ *I ruminated a while before answering the question.* **3.** *tv.* to chew food, as in ①. ♦ *The cows ruminated their cuds.* ♦ *The goat ruminated the grass it had just swallowed.*

rummage ['rʌm ɪdʒ] **1. rummage through** *iv.* + *prep. phr.* to search through something by moving things around in a disorderly way. ♦ *A thief had rummaged through my belongings, looking for valuables.* ♦ *David rummaged through the clean clothes, looking for socks.* **2. rummage sale** *n.* a sale of used clothing and other used items either to make a little money while getting rid of extra items in one's house, or to raise money for charity. ♦ *Susan bought an old toaster for $2 at a rummage sale.* ♦ *John sold a lot of old clothing at the neighborhood rummage sale.*

rumor ['rum ɚ] **1.** *n.* news about someone or something that may or may not be true; information that is passed from person to person about someone and that may or may not be true. ♦ *The rumors being spread about me are totally untrue.* ♦ *There's a rumor going around that you're moving to Florida.* **2.** *tv.* to spread information before it has been proved to be true. ♦ *The gossips are rumoring that our company is going to be sold.* ♦ *The tabloid rumored that a famous couple were going to divorce.*

rump ['rʌmp] **1.** *n.* the rear part of an animal; the buttocks. ♦ *The veterinarian gave the dog a shot in its rump.* ♦ *The father spanked the disobedient child on the rump.* **2.** *n.* meat from the rear part of an animal, used as food. (No plural form in this sense. Number expressed with *rump roast(s).*) ♦ *There's a sale on rump at the store.* ♦ *The butcher ground up some rump and sold me a pound of it.* **3. rump session** *idiom* a meeting held after a larger meeting. ♦ *A rump session continued after the meeting was adjourned.* ♦ *A lot of business was conducted in the rump session.*

rumpus ['rʌmp əs] *n.* a noisy argument; a commotion; an uproar. (No plural form in this sense.) ♦ *The police investigated the rumpus coming from the alley.* ♦ *My neighbors' early-morning rumpus woke me up.*

run ['rʌn] **1.** *iv., irreg.* to move quickly in such a way that both feet are off the ground during each stride. (Pt: ran; pp: *run.*) ♦ *The cat ran when the dog chased it.* ♦ *Susan ran toward the finish line.* **2.** *iv., irreg.* to work; to be working; to function; to be in operation. ♦ *My watch runs on batteries.* ♦ *The refrigerator isn't running because you haven't plugged it in.* **3.** *iv., irreg.* to extend to a certain length or distance; to reach a certain distance or time. ♦ *This railroad runs all the way to New York City.* ♦ *The production of this opera will run until May 31.* **4.** *iv., irreg.* to flow; [for liquids] to move. ♦ *The water ran over the edge of the sink.* ♦ *The waiter poured the coffee into my cup until it ran over.* **5.** *iv., irreg.* [for a liquid color] to spread, flow, or bleed. ♦ *The dye ran when I washed the shirt.* ♦ *The actors' makeup ran under the hot stage lights.* **6.** *iv., irreg.* to become unraveled; to unravel; to become snagged. ♦ *My nylons ran when I snagged them against a nail.* ♦ *Did your stockings run when the cat clawed you?* **7.** *iv., irreg.* to move quickly as a form of exercise or as a sport. ♦ *Susan runs for an hour every day.* ♦ *David runs on the high-school track team.* **8.** *iv., irreg.* [for one's nose] to drip fluid. ♦ *My nose is running. I need a handkerchief.* ♦ *Jimmy's nose is running, and he has a fever.* **9. run for** *iv., irreg.* + *prep. phr.* to be a candidate for an office in an election. ♦ *The young senator wants to run for president someday.* ♦ *Mary, John, and Susan are all running for class treasurer.* **10.** *tv., irreg.* to operate something; to cause something to work. ♦ *The workers ran the assembly line.* ♦ *Most cars are run on gasoline.* **11.** *tv., irreg.* to extend something to a certain length or distance; to cause something to reach a certain distance or time. ♦ *We will run this advertisement in the paper for three weeks.* ♦ *The railroad company runs an express train to downtown.* **12.** *tv., irreg.* to control, own, or manage a business. ♦ *My aunt runs an accounting service out of her home.* ♦ *My uncle ran a small newspaper stand on Elm Street.* **13.** *tv., irreg.* to publish something in a newspaper or magazine. ♦ *The newspaper ran an article about cancer research.* ♦ *The tabloid ran the scandalous gossip about the movie star.* **14.** *n.* an instance of running as in ①. ♦ *Anne goes out for a run every morning before going to work.* ♦ *After a short run, Max was winded.* **15.** *n.* a trip; a journey. ♦ *The executive made a quick run to Houston to sign a contract.* ♦ *I'm making a run to the store. Do you need anything?* **16.** *n.* a point scored in baseball when a player has run around the bases and has safely touched home plate. ♦ *At the bottom of ninth inning, our team still hadn't scored any runs.* ♦ *Jane got the first run of the softball game.* **17.** *n.* all the performances of a play, television show, or movie from opening to closing. ♦ *That musical has enjoyed a very long run on Broadway.* ♦ *The terrible movie's run lasted only one weekend.* **18.** *n.* a place where fabric has snagged or unraveled. ♦ *Your nylons have a run in them.* ♦ *I brushed against the bush, and my stockings got a run.* **19. run of something** *phr.* a continuous series of events. ♦ *The gambler had a run of bad luck at the roulette wheel.* ♦ *We had a run of very hot weather last July.* **20. dry run** *idiom* an attempt; a rehearsal. ♦ *We had better have a dry run for the official ceremony tomorrow.* ♦ *The children will need a dry run before their procession in the pageant.* **21. in the long run** *idiom* over a long period of time; ultimately. ♦ *We'd be better off in the long run buying one instead of renting one.* ♦ *In the long run, we'd be happier in the South.* **22. make a run for it** *idiom* to run fast to get away or get somewhere. ♦ *When the guard wasn't looking, the prisoner made a run for it.* ♦ *In the baseball game, the player on first base made a run for it, but he didn't make it to second base.* **23. out of the running** *idiom* no longer being considered; eliminated from a contest. ♦ *After the first part of the diving meet, three members of our team were out of the running.* ♦ *After the scandal was made public, I was no longer in the running. I pulled out of the election.* **24. run out of something** *idiom* to use up all of something and have no more. ♦ *We ran out of milk, so we will* *have to buy some more.* ♦ *I usually run out of money at the end of the month.* **25. run for it** *idiom* to try to escape by running. ♦ *The guard's not looking. Let's run for it!* ♦ *The convict tried to run for it, but the guard caught him.* **26. run for one's life** *idiom* to run away to save one's life. ♦ *The dam has burst! Run for your life!* ♦ *The captain told us all to run for our lives.* **27. run low (on something)** *idiom* to near the end of a supply of something. ♦ *We are running low on salt. It's time to buy more.* ♦ *The car is running low on gas.*

runaround ['rʌn ə raʊnd] *n.* confusion and frustration resulting from being sent to different people or places to take care of something. (No plural form in this sense.) ♦ *Mary got the runaround at city hall when she tried to file a complaint.* ♦ *The store gave David a runaround when he tried to get a refund.*

runaway ['rʌn ə we] **1.** *n.* someone, usually a child, who has run away from home. ♦ *We found a runaway sleeping under the bridge.* ♦ *The runaway had left home to live with his aunt.* **2.** *n.* a vehicle that is no longer under the control of it driver. ♦ *The huge truck is a runaway and will crash into the bridge.* ♦ *On the highway, at the bottom of the mountain is a special lane that runaways can use to slow down.* **3.** *adj.* <the adj. use of ①.> ♦ *The runaway children begged for money.* ♦ *The runaway teenager tried to get a job in the city.* **4.** *adj.* <the adj. use of ②.> ♦ *The runaway train crashed into the depot.* ♦ *The runaway car slid down the slope.*

run-down ['rʌn 'daʊn] **1.** *adj.* in poor health. ♦ *I am sort of run-down because I have been working too hard.* ♦ *I feel tired and run-down. I think I am going to get the flu.* **2.** *adj.* [of something] in bad condition owing to neglect. ♦ *The house on the corner is run-down and needs repairs.* ♦ *Who owns that run-down building?*

rung ['rʌŋ] **1.** a pp of ring. **2.** *n.* one of the poles forming a step of a ladder. ♦ *Bill fell from the ladder when one of the rungs broke.* ♦ *Mary stood on the top rung to change the light bulb.*

run-in ['rʌn ɪn] **have a run-in with someone** *idiom* to have an unpleasant and troublesome encounter with someone. ♦ *I had a run-in with Anne at the party, so I left early.* ♦ *David had a small run-in with the law last night.*

runner ['rʌn ɚ] **1.** *n.* someone who runs. ♦ *The runner sped around the track.* ♦ *I sat on a park bench and watched the runners go by.* **2.** *n.* a blade that moves over a surface, such as the blade of a skate or sled. ♦ *The skater sharpened her runners before the competition.* ♦ *The runners of the sled glided over the snow on the hill.* **3.** *n.* [in baseball] a player who is on the same team as the batter and who is at first, second, or third base. ♦ *The runner ran toward second base when the batter hit the ball.* ♦ *A runner who makes it to home plate safely scores a run.* **4.** *n.* a messenger; someone who delivers messages. ♦ *A runner from the hotel handed me an urgent message.* ♦ *I tipped the runner who had brought me an important message.*

runners-up ['rʌn ɚz əp] pl of runner-up.

runner-up ['rʌn ɚ əp] **1.** *n., irreg.* someone who comes in second place in a contest or competition. (Pl: runners-up.) ♦ *In the Olympics, the runner-up gets a silver medal.* ♦ *The runner-up nearly tied the winner.* **2.** *adj.* <the adj. use of ①.> ♦ *The runner-up prize is a $100 gift certificate.* ♦ *The coach of the runner-up team congratulated the winners.*

running ['rʌn ɪŋ] **1.** *n.* the activity of someone who runs for sport, health, or pleasure. (No plural form in this sense.) ♦ *Mary took up running when she was in high school.* ♦ *Bob has lost five pounds from running.* **2.** *adj.* <the adj. use of ①.> ♦ *Jane keeps her running shoes in her gym locker.* ♦ *The running coach told us to buy proper footwear.* **3.** *adj.* flowing; moving as a liquid. ♦ *Most modern houses have running water.* ♦ *The running river was blocked by a dam.* **4.** *adj.* [of talk] continuous. (Figurative on ③.) ♦ *Lisa's running narrative was a distraction from the movie.* ♦ *The reporter provided running commentary on the football game.* **5. days running; weeks running; months running; years running** *idiom* days in a series; months in a series; etc. (Follows a number.) ♦ *I had a bad cold for 5 days running.* ♦ *For two years running, I brought work home from the office every night.*

runny ['rʌn i] **1.** *adj.* [of eggs] not completely cooked and still somewhat liquid. (Adv: *runnily.* Comp: *runnier;* sup: *runniest.*) ♦ *Mary soaked up the runny eggs with toast.* ♦ *David doesn't like to eat runny yolks.* **2. runny nose** *n.* a person's nose that is dripping due to a cold, the flu, an allergy, etc. ♦ *Mary wiped her runny nose with a tissue.* ♦ *My cold has given me a terribly runny nose.*

run-of-the-mill [rən əv ðə 'mɪl] *adj.* average; ordinary; typical; normal; regular. ♦ *David lives in a quiet, run-of-the-mill suburb.* ♦ *Anne tolerated her run-of-the-mill job.*

runt ['rʌnt] **1.** *n.* the smallest animal in a litter. ♦ *The runt was not as well fed as the other offspring.* ♦ *When my cat had kittens, I gave my friend the runt of the litter.* **2.** *n.* one who is small for one's age. (Figurative on ①. Derogatory or jocular.) ♦ *The runt swung and hit the bully's chest.* ♦ *Jimmy was a runt until he went through puberty and grew ten inches.*

runway ['rʌn we] *n.* a landing strip for an airplane; a track that an airplane takes off from and lands on. ♦ *The crew removed the snow from the airport runways.* ♦ *The plane bounced a little when it made contact with the runway.*

rupture ['rʌp tʃɚ] **1.** *n.* a sudden break. ♦ *Water streamed from the rupture in the pipe.* ♦ *The engineers repaired the rupture in the dam.* **2.** *n.* the tearing of a body part, especially a tear that is a hernia. ♦ *The doctor felt the rupture in Jimmy's groin.* ♦ *Mary had to stop smoking following the rupture in her left lung.* **3.** *iv.* to break or burst suddenly. ♦ *There was a flash flood when the dam ruptured.* ♦ *Dave went to the hospital when his spleen ruptured.* **4.** *tv.* to break or burst something suddenly. ♦ *The bullet ruptured the victim's lung.* ♦ *The cold weather ruptured the water pipes.*

ruptured ['rʌp tʃɚd] **1.** *adj.* suddenly broken; burst. ♦ *The ruptured pipe released radioactive steam.* ♦ *A ruptured blood vessel endangered the patient's life.* **2.** *adj.* [of a location on the body] having a hernia. ♦ *The ruptured organ protruded through the wall of muscle.* ♦ *David's ruptured appendix caused him to become very ill.*

rural ['rɚ əl] *adj.* in the country; not like the city; not urban or suburban. (Adv: *rurally.*) ♦ *My grandparents raise cattle in a rural county in Nebraska.* ♦ *Tired of the big city, the writer moved to a quiet rural town.*

ruse ['ruz] *n.* a trick; a ploy; a deception. ♦ *Your kind acts were only a ruse to get money from me!* ♦ *The tourists lost $50 to the crook's ruse.*

rush ['rʌʃ] **1.** *n.* haste; hurry. (No plural form in this sense.) ♦ *In my rush, I had locked my keys inside my house.* ♦ *I was in a rush to get to work, but I was stuck in traffic.* **2.** *n.* a very sudden movement or flow. (No plural form in this sense.) ♦ *A rush of cold air entered the room when Anne opened the door.* ♦ *There was a rush for the exit when someone yelled, "Fire!"* **3. rush on something** *phr.* a large demand for something. ♦ *There was a rush on bottled water during the drought.* ♦ *During the hot summer, there was a rush on air conditioners.* **4.** *iv.* to move quickly; to hurry. ♦ *The cars rushed down the freeway.* ♦ *I rushed to answer the telephone when it rang.* **5.** *tv.* to cause someone or something to hurry or move quickly. ♦ *The workers rushed the important client's order to the warehouse.* ♦ *Don't rush me, I'm going as fast as I can.* **6.** *tv.* to run toward and crowd around or against someone or something. ♦ *The crowd rushed the gate as the usher approached it.* ♦ *The fan rushed the stage but was removed by security.* **7. in a mad rush** *idiom* in a great hurry. ♦ *I ran around all day today in a mad rush, looking for a present for Bill.* ♦ *Why are you always in a mad rush?*

rush hour ['rʌʃ ɑʊ ɚ] **1.** *n.* the time in the morning and the evening when streets, trains, and buses are crowded because people are going to or from work. ♦ *The freeway was backed up for miles during rush hour.* ♦ *If you have to come downtown during rush hour, take the train.* **2. rush-hour** *adj.* <the adj. use of ①.> ♦ *The large rush-hour crowd poured onto the expressway.* ♦ *We were stuck in rush-hour traffic for a long time.*

rushing ['rʌʃ ɪŋ] *adj.* moving quickly; hurrying. (Adv: *rushingly.*) ♦ *The rushing current swept the raft toward the sea.* ♦ *The rushing wind knocked my hat off my head.*

Russia ['rʌʃ ə] See Gazetteer.

Russian ['rʌʃ ən] **1.** *n.* a citizen or native of Russia. ♦ *We enjoyed visiting Moscow and meeting Russians.* ♦ *Tom and Bill attended a lecture given by a Russian visiting from Russia.* **2.** *n.* the language spoken in Russia by ①. (No plural form in this sense.) ♦ *Russian is a Slavic language.* ♦ *Russian uses the Cyrillic alphabet.* **3.** *adj.* of, for, or about Russia, ①, or ②. ♦ *Russian music is known all over the world.* ♦ *I am studying the Russian language in school.*

rust ['rʌst] **1.** *n.* a dark red or dark orange layer that forms on iron or steel when it is exposed to air or water; corrosion. (No plural form in this sense.) ♦ *The underside of my old car is covered with rust.* ♦ *The old metal garage door was coated with rust.* **2.** *iv.* to acquire a coating of ①. ♦ *The door hinges exposed to rain began to rust.* ♦ *John's bike rusted because he didn't take good care of it.* **3.** *tv.* to cause something to be covered with ①. ♦ *The salt poured on the snowy roads rusted my car.* ♦ *The rain rusted the nails holding the porch together.*

rustic ['rʌs tɪk] **1.** *adj.* of or about the countryside; rural; simple; suitable for the countryside. (Adv: *rustically* [...ɪk li].) ♦ *I spent a weekend at a rustic ski resort with my friends.* ♦ *David owned a rustic inn near the lake.* **2.** *n.* someone who lives in a rural area. (Slightly derogatory.) ♦ *The reporter polled the rustics in Iowa about the election.* ♦ *The rustics resented the city folk who moved to the area.*

rustle ['rʌs əl] **1.** *n.* a soft, crinkly sound, like the sound that leaves make when they are blown by the wind or the sound made when objects are rubbed together. (No plural form in this sense.) ♦ *I heard the rustle of leaves by my feet.* ♦ *I could hear the rustle of papers in the quiet library.* **2.** *iv.* [for objects] to make a soft, crinkly sound when rubbed together or blown by the wind. ♦ *The fallen leaves rustled as they blew by my feet.* ♦ *The pages of the old book rustled as Mary turned them.* **3.** *tv.* to cause objects to rustle ②. ♦ *Mary rustled the pages of the old book as she read it.* ♦ *The wind rustled the leaves in the tree.* **4.** *tv.* to steal cattle. ♦ *The rancher's cattle were rustled during the night.* ♦ *The thieves who rustled cattle were sent to jail.*

rustler ['rʌs lɚ] *n.* someone who steals cattle; a cattle thief. ♦ *The ranchers beat the rustler severely.* ♦ *The rural judge sentenced the rustler to a long prison term.*

rustproof ['rʌst pruf] **1.** *adj.* resistant to rust; not capable of rusting. ♦ *Make sure your car is rustproof, or it won't last long.* ♦ *Is this metal sink rustproof?* **2.** *tv.* to treat iron or steel with a chemical so that it will not rust. ♦ *The car company rustproofed each car in the factory.* ♦ *My car has not been rustproofed, and it is falling apart.*

rusty ['rʌst i] **1.** *adj.* covered with rust; rusted. (Adv: *rustily.* Comp: *rustier;* sup: *rustiest.*) ♦ *I got a tetanus shot because I stepped on a rusty nail.* ♦ *John junked his rusty old car.* **2.** *adj.* [of a skill or knowledge] deficient because it has been unused for so long a time. (Adv: *rustily.* Comp: *rustier;* sup: *rustiest.*) ♦ *I haven't played the piano in years, so I'm rusty.* ♦ *Although I was a little rusty, I solved the calculus problem.*

rut ['rʌt] **1.** *n.* a deep track that a wheel makes in soft ground; a groove. ♦ *The car became stuck in the muddy ruts of the path.* ♦ *The buggy wheels made deep ruts in the soft earth.* **2. (stuck) in a rut** *idiom* kept in an established way of living that never changes. ♦ *David felt like he was stuck in a rut, so he went back to school.* ♦ *Anne was tired of being in a rut, so she moved to Los Angeles.*

ruthless ['ruθ ləs] *adj.* without pity; without mercy; without compassion; cruel; evil. (Adv: *ruthlessly.*) ♦ *The ruthless tyrant caused the deaths of millions of people.* ♦ *The ruthless judge sentenced the innocent woman to jail.*

Rwanda [ru 'ɑn də] See Gazetteer.

rye ['rɑɪ] **1.** *n.* a tall grass that is farmed for its light brown grain. (No plural form in this sense.) ♦ *The farmer harvested the rye in September.* ♦ *The farmhouse was surrounded by acres of rye.* **2.** *n.* grain from ①. (No plural form in this sense. Number is expressed with *grain(s) of rye.*) ♦ *The mill grinds rye into flour.* ♦ *We've got rye stored in this silo.* **3.** *n.* a whiskey made from ②. ♦ *I ordered a shot of rye at the bar.* ♦ *Rye is not very popular in the U.S.* **4.** *adj.* made from ②. ♦ *We love sandwiches made with rye bread.* ♦ *Rye flour isn't as white as wheat flour.*

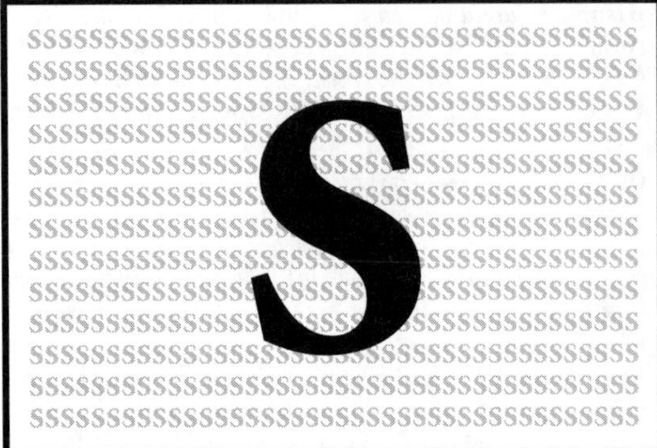

S AND **s** ['ɛs] **1.** *n.* the nineteenth letter of the alphabet. ♦ *S comes before* T *and after* R *in the English alphabet.* ♦ *The word* possesses *is spelled with five* S*'s.* **2. -'s** *suffix* See is, has. **3. -'s** *suffix* <a form attached to nouns that indicates possession.> ♦ *Where is Bob's hat?* ♦ *Mike's computer is broken.* **4. -s** *suffix* <a form, indicating the plural, that is attached to nouns ending in vowels and consonants other than *s, sh, ch, x, z.*> (Compare with -es.) ♦ *The* -s *in* hats *is a plural marker.* ♦ *Add* -s *to the word* bee *to make it plural.* **5. -s** *suffix* <a form added to present-tense verbs whose subjects are in the third-person singular and which do not end in *s, sh, ch, x, z.*> ♦ *The* -s *in* runs *goes with a third-person singular subject.* ♦ *"They runs" is a serious error in English because "they" is not third-person singular.*

Sabbath ['sæb əθ] **1.** *n.* the seventh day of the week, Saturday, a day of rest and worship in the Jewish religion and some Christian religions. (From Hebrew.) ♦ *Sabbath is observed from sundown on Friday to sundown on Saturday.* ♦ *David observed the strict laws against work on the Sabbath.* **2.** *n.* Sunday, as a day of rest and worship in most Christian religions. ♦ *Liquor stores are not open on the Sabbath in some states.* ♦ *Mary took her children to church on the Sabbath.*

sabbatical [sə 'bæt ɪ kəl] **1.** *n.* a professor's leave of absence from teaching for study or travel. (They were originally available every seventh year.) ♦ *The busy professor took a sabbatical for a much needed rest.* ♦ *Dr. Foster's sabbatical included doing research in Japan.* **2.** *adj.* <the adj. use of ①.> ♦ *Dr. Hubbard spent her sabbatical year in central Africa.* ♦ *Dr. Schwarz is on a sabbatical leave until next November.*

sabotage ['sæb ə tɑʒ] **1.** *n.* secret, intentional damage done to property or a project. (No plural form in this sense.) ♦ *The destruction of our computer files was an act of sabotage.* ♦ *The disgruntled employee committed sabotage against the firm.* **2.** *tv.* to damage something by ①; to harm something secretly. ♦ *The angry worker sabotaged the factory by stopping the assembly line.* ♦ *A secret agent sabotaged the government's plans.*

saccharine ['sæk (ə) rɪn] **1.** *adj.* very sweet; too sweet. (Adv: *saccharinely.*) ♦ *The punch tastes too saccharine.* ♦ *I couldn't stand the saccharine flavor of the candy.* **2.** *adj.* [of behavior] overly sentimental or overly sweet. (Figurative on ①. Adv: *saccharinely.*) ♦ *David's saccharine behavior is a sign of insincerity.* ♦ *When Jane becomes saccharine, she becomes slightly annoying.*

sack ['sæk] **1.** *n.* a bag or pouch made of paper, cloth, burlap, etc. (In some parts of the country, bag is more popular.) ♦ *The clerk put my groceries in a paper sack.* ♦ *The sack of potatoes is very heavy.* **2.** *n.* the contents of ①. ♦ *I need a lot of potatoes. At least two sacks.* ♦ *One sack was not enough.* **3.** *n.* a bed. (Slang.) ♦ *I'm really tired, so I'm going to stay in the sack.* ♦ *Bill spent too long in the sack this morning and was late for work.* **4.** *n.* dismissal from a job. (No plural form in this sense. Slang.) ♦ *John got the sack for stealing office supplies.* ♦ *She knew the sack was coming because of her poor language skills.* **5. sack (up)** *tv.* (+ *adv.*) to put something in ①. ♦ *The cashier sacked my groceries.* ♦ *It was busy at the store, so I sacked up my own purchases.* **6.** *tv.* to fire someone from a job. ♦ *John was sacked from his job for stealing office supplies.* ♦ *My manager sacked Mary today for embezzling.* **7. hit the sack** *idiom* to go to bed. (On ③.) ♦ *It's late. It's time to hit the sack.* ♦ *What time did you hit the sack last night?*

sacred ['se krɪd] *adj.* holy; blessed. (Adv: *sacredly.*) ♦ *The cemetery is a sacred burial place.* ♦ *The image of the Lord Buddha is sacred.*

sacrifice ['sæ krə fɑɪs] **1.** *n.* giving up something; not having something that is wanted or needed. (No plural form in this sense.) ♦ *We endured a lot of sacrifice to send you to college.* ♦ *Saving money for a new house required the financial sacrifice of not having things we wanted.* **2.** *n.* offering something to a deity or spirit. (No plural form in this sense.) ♦ *I gave up candy as a sacrifice during Lent.* ♦ *For a sacrifice, the worshipers offered food to their god.* **3.** *n.* something that is offered to a deity or spirit. ♦ *The goat was a sacrifice to the god.* ♦ *A sacrifice of food and milk was prepared for the gods.* **4.** *tv.* to take the life of a creature as in ②. ♦ *They sacrificed a goat to the god.* ♦ *We sacrificed two pigeons and a duck.* **5.** *tv.* to give up something of value [for someone else's benefit]. ♦ *The hero sacrificed his life so that mine would be saved.* ♦ *My parents sacrificed buying a second car so that I could go to college.*

sacrilege ['sæ krə lɪdʒ] *n.* disrespect for something sacred. (No plural form in this sense.) ♦ *Religious people condemned the antireligious film as a sacrilege.* ♦ *The desecration of the tombstones was a terrible sacrilege.*

sad ['sæd] **1.** *adj.* not happy; feeling sorrow. (Adv: *sadly.* Comp: *sadder;* sup: *saddest.*) ♦ *I tried to cheer John up because he seemed so sad.* ♦ *The sad children mourned at their mother's funeral.* **2.** *adj.* unfortunate; [of something] tainted by sadness because of sad events. (Adv: *sadly.* Comp: *sadder;* sup: *saddest.*) ♦ *It was a sad day when I lost my job.* ♦ *The accident that killed ten people was quite sad.*

sadden ['sæd n] **1.** *iv.* to become sad. ♦ *Mary saddened when she learned of her brother's death.* ♦ *John's mood saddened as the day of his departure got closer.* **2.** *tv.* to cause someone to become sad. ♦ *The horrible news of John's death saddened Bill.* ♦ *The plight of the refugees saddens me.*

saddle ['sæd l] **1.** *n.* a leather seat that fits on the back of a horse. ♦ *Anne put the saddle on the horse's back and rode away.* ♦ *When John fell off the horse, he got back in the saddle right away.* **2.** *n.* a bicycle or motorcycle seat. ♦ *The saddle was too high for Jimmy's feet to reach the pedals.* ♦ *Mary and I both sat on the saddle while she drove the motorcycle.* **3.** *tv.* to place ① on a horse or a similar animal. ♦ *It took an hour to saddle the horse for a 20-minute ride!* ♦ *Tell the servants to saddle the horses. We must leave at once.* **4. saddle someone with something** *idiom* to give someone something undesirable, annoying, or difficult to deal with. ♦ *Mary says she doesn't want to be saddled with a baby, but her husband would love one.* ♦ *Jane saddled Bob with the most boring job so that he would leave.*

saddlebag ['sæd l bæg] *n.* one of a pair of bags that hangs from either side of the back of a horse, bicycle, or motorcycle. ♦ *The mail was carried across the plains in saddlebags.* ♦ *John kept a small first-aid kit in a leather saddlebag.*

sadism ['sed ɪz əm] *n.* the desire to cause pain to someone else; satisfaction—especially sexual satisfaction—received by causing pain. (No plural form in this sense. Compare with masochism.) ♦ *John placed an advertisement seeking someone interested in sadism.* ♦ *Mary is shocked at the idea of sadism, especially harming other people.*

sadistic [sə 'dɪs tɪk] *adj.* receiving satisfaction by causing suffering. (Adv: *sadistically* [...ɪk li].) ♦ *The sadistic tyrant tortured the political prisoners.* ♦ *John's sadistic friend handcuffed him to the railing.*

sadly ['sæd li] *adv.* not happily; sorrowfully. ♦ *Sadly, Anne packed her possessions and left the only home she had ever known.* ♦ *Bill sat sadly at his father's funeral.*

sadness ['sæd nəs] *n.* unhappiness; sorrow. (No plural form in this sense.) ♦ *The mayor's death caused great sadness throughout the city.* ♦ *John felt sadness when his dog died.*

safari [sə 'fɑr i] *n.* a hunting or sightseeing trip, especially in eastern Africa. (From Swahili.) ♦ *The tourists saw many exotic animals on their safari.* ♦ *The reserve was stocked with lions for the photo safari.*

safe ['sef] **1.** *n.* a solid, sturdy, steel or iron box—with a strong lock—that money, jewelry, papers, or other valuable objects are kept in for protection. ♦ *Only the office manager knew how to get into the safe.* ♦ *The cashier deposited the $20 bills in the safe.* **2.** *adj.* not dangerous; not risky; not causing or creating danger. (Adv: *safely.* Comp: *safer;* sup: *safest.*) ♦ *I like to ride in John's car because he's a safe driver.* ♦ *Driving at such high speeds is not safe!* **3.** *adj.* protected; secure. (Adv: *safely.* Comp: *safer;* sup: *safest.*) ♦ *I have hidden the money in a safe location where no one will find it.* ♦ *Please put this gold ring in a safe place.* **4. safe (from)** *adj.* (+ *prep. phr.*) protected from someone or something. (Comp: *safer;* sup: *safest.*) ♦ *You will be safe from the dog if you don't go near it.* ♦ *This sunscreen makes you safe from ultraviolet rays.* **5. safe to** *adj.* + *inf.* suitable to do something with. (Comp: *safer;* sup: *safest.*) ♦ *The water is safe to drink here only after you boil it.* ♦ *The dilapidated bridge is not safe to walk on.* **6. to be safe** *phr.* to be cautious; to be careful; [to do something just] in case it is necessary; to be very well prepared. ♦ *Just to be safe, you should take some clean water with you.* ♦ *Other people like to drive over the speed limit, but I prefer to be safe.* **7. to be on the safe side** *idiom* to be safe ⑥; to be cautious; [to do something just] in case it is necessary; to be very well prepared. ♦ *To be on the safe side, carry some extra money in your shoe.* ♦ *I like to be on the safe side and stay in my hotel room at night.* **8. play it safe** *idiom* to be or act safe ⑥; to do something safely. ♦ *You should play it safe and take your umbrella.* ♦ *If you have a cold or the flu, play it safe and go to bed.* **9. safe and sound** *idiom* safe ③ and whole; safe ③ and healthy. ♦ *It was a rough trip, but we got there safe and sound.* ♦ *I'm glad to see you here safe and sound.*

safeguard ['sef gɑrd] **1.** *n.* something that protects someone or something from danger. ♦ *Bob wears a helmet as a safeguard against head injuries when he rides his motorcycle.* ♦ *The net is a safeguard for the tightrope walkers.* **2.** *tv.* to protect someone or something from danger; to keep someone or something safe. ♦ *The net safeguarded the acrobats from injury.* ♦ *Safety belts safeguard us from getting seriously injured in car accidents.*

safekeeping ['sef 'kip ɪŋ] **for safekeeping** *phr.* for the purpose of keeping someone or something safe. ♦ *I put my jewelry in the vault for safekeeping.* ♦ *I checked my fur coat at the entrance to the bar for safekeeping.*

safety ['sef ti] **1.** *n.* the state of being safe; freedom from harm or danger. (No plural form in this sense.) ♦ *I feared for the safety of the soldiers in the war.* ♦ *For your safety, please fasten your seat belts.* **2.** *adj.* <the adj. use of ①.> ♦ *You should wear a safety belt when you drive.* ♦ *This window is made of safety glass, so it won't shatter if it breaks.*

safety belt ['sef ti bɛlt] *n.* a seat belt; a set of straps that extend across one's lap and diagonally from the top of one's shoulder across the body to the opposite hip. ♦ *Our car has safety belts and air bags.* ♦ *Fasten your safety belt as soon as you get in the car.*

safe(ty)-deposit box ['sef (ti) də 'pɑz ət 'bɑks] *n.* a metal box for holding valuables that is locked in a large safe or vault. ♦ *I keep my important papers in my safe-deposit box.* ♦ *We rent a safety-deposit box at the bank.*

sag ['sæg] **1.** *iv.* to bend, hang, or curve downward. ♦ *The heavy tree branches sagged toward the ground.* ♦ *My mattress sags in the middle.* **2.** *iv.* to decrease in power, value, or strength. (Figurative on ①.) ♦ *Will the economy sag during the fourth quarter?* ♦ *The team's energy sagged toward the end of the game.*

saga ['sɑ gə] *n.* a long story about a person, family, or group of people that covers a long period of time. ♦ *In school, we read the saga of Eric the Red's adventures.* ♦ *The author wrote a five-volume saga about a powerful family.*

sage ['sedʒ] **1.** *n.* someone who is wise, especially someone who is old and has a lot of experience with life. ♦ *John spoke to a great sage about his problems.* ♦ *The sages were their tribe's spiritual leaders.* **2.** *n.* an herb used for flavoring stuffing and other foods. (No plural form in this sense.) ♦ *The cook added more sage to the stuffing.* ♦ *Jane grew sage in her herb garden.* **3. sage advice** *idiom* very good and wise advice. ♦ *My parents gave me some sage advice when I turned 18.* ♦ *I asked my uncle for some of his sage advice.*

said ['sɛd] pt/pp of say.

sail ['sel] **1.** *n.* a piece of cloth that is stretched on a mast of a ship to catch the energy of the wind. ♦ *The sails were torn by the heavy winds.* ♦ *The sailor raised the ship's sail before leaving the harbor.* **2.** *iv.* to travel by boat or ship on the water. ♦ *Mary sailed across the lake to visit her grandmother.* ♦ *The European emigrants sailed from Europe to America.* **3.** *iv.* [for a ship or boat] to travel on the water. ♦ *The ship sailed toward the remote island.* ♦ *The raft sailed down the river, carried by the current.* **4.** *iv.* to glide through the air the way a boat moves through water. ♦ *The jet sailed through the air high above the earth.* ♦ *The balloon sailed up to the clouds.* **5. sail through** *iv. + prep. phr.* to progress through something easily. ♦ *The smart student sailed right through the test.* ♦ *The job applicant sailed through the first interview.* **6.** *tv.* to steer a boat or ship on the water. ♦ *The captain sailed the ship through dangerous water.* ♦ *I sailed my boat across the bay.* **7.** *tv.* to cause something to glide through the air. ♦ *Jimmy sailed his kite high above the trees.* ♦ *Susie sailed her toy plane through the air.* **8. set sail (for somewhere)** *idiom* to begin a trip on a ship or boat. ♦ *The crew set sail at sunrise.* ♦ *After the sailors loaded the cargo, they set sail for Europe.*

sailboat ['sel bot] *n.* a boat that has at least one sail and that moves by the power of the wind. ♦ *The wind pushed the sailboat across the bay.* ♦ *We boarded my sailboat at the marina and sailed toward the lake.*

sailfish ['sel fɪʃ] *n., irreg.* a large fish having a sail-shaped fin on its back. (Pl: *sailfish.*) ♦ *When the sailfish leapt up, you could see its huge fin.* ♦ *The fishermen pulled the sailfish into the boat.*

sailor ['sel ɚ] **1.** *n.* someone who works on a boat or a ship. ♦ *The sailor swabbed the deck of the ship.* ♦ *The sailor notified the captain of a leak.* **2.** *n.* someone who is in the navy. ♦ *The sailors left the base for the evening and went into town.* ♦ *The sailors bravely fought the sea battle.*

saint ['sent] **1.** *n.* a dead person whom the Roman Catholic or Greek Orthodox Church has declared to have gone to heaven and who is therefore worthy of being honored. (Abbreviated *St.*) ♦ *The nun prayed to the saints for the health of her parents.* ♦ *St. Stephen was stoned to death.* **2.** *n.* someone who is very patient and kind. (Figurative on ①.) ♦ *These teachers are saints for dealing with such problem children.* ♦ *My boss is a saint for letting me leave work early again today.*

sake ['sek] **for someone or something's sake; for the sake of someone or something** *idiom* for the purpose or benefit of someone or something; to satisfy the demands of someone or something. ♦ *I made a meatless dinner for John's sake.* ♦ *The teacher repeated the assignment for the sake of the slower students.*

salad ['sæl əd] *n.* a dish of mixed vegetables, or other food mixed with vegetables, usually with a sauce called salad dressing. ♦ *Green salads contain mostly lettuce.* ♦ *I sprinkled some pieces of bacon over my spinach salad.*

salamander ['sæl ə mæn dɚ] *n.* a small, amphibious animal resembling a lizard. ♦ *The salamander stood still on the rock by the creek.* ♦ *I have a pet salamander that I keep in a glass tank.*

salami [sə 'lɑm i] **1.** *n.* a kind of spicy sausage. (No plural form in this sense. From Italian. Italian plural of *salame.* Number is expressed with *slice(s) of salami.*) ♦ *The butcher sliced the salami and wrapped it for me.* ♦ *I bought salami and potato salad at the store.* **2.** *n.* a whole roll or length of ①. ♦ *Three large salamis hung at the back of the butcher shop.* ♦ *For the party, we need a salami and six pounds of cheese.* **3.** *adj.* made with ①. ♦ *Anne eats a salami sandwich with mustard every day for lunch.* ♦ *John ordered a salami omelet.*

salary ['sæl (ə) ri] *n.* the amount of money that someone is paid for a period of working. ♦ *When my salary increased last year, so did my taxes.* ♦ *The terms of my salary were set forth in my contract.*

sale ['sel] **1.** *n.* the exchange of a product or service for money; an act of selling. ♦ *The cashier rang up my sale on the cash register.* ♦ *The sale of my car was easy because the buyer had cash.* **2. sales** *n.* the amount of products or services sold during a certain period of time. (Treated as plural. Singular is ①.) ♦ *This year's sales are 10% less than last year's.* ♦ *I reported the daily sales to the manager.* **3. sales** *n.* the occupation of selling things. (Treated as singular.) ♦ *I have been in sales for 20 years.* ♦ *Sales is a good way for a young person to start out in the company.* **4.** *n.* a special event where products or services are sold for less money than normal. ♦ *During the sale, everything at the store is reduced by 25%.* ♦ *I waited for a sale before I bought a new television set.* **5. for sale** *phr.* available to be sold. ♦ *Are the paintings on the wall for sale, or are they decorations?* ♦ *Susan told me that her vintage car was not for sale.* **6. on sale** *phr.* available for purchase at a reduced price. ♦ *These pots are on sale for $20.* ♦ *I bought these pants on sale for half price.*

salesclerk ['selz klɚk] *n.* someone who works in a store, helping customers and selling products. ♦ *The salesclerk showed me where the dressing room was.* ♦ *The salesclerk put my purchases in a shopping bag.*

salesman ['selz mən] *n., irreg.* someone who sells things for a living; a man who sells for a living. (Pl: salesmen.) ♦ *The salesman went from door to door selling encyclopedias.* ♦ *The used-car salesman sold me a good six-year-old car.*

salesmen ['selz mən] pl of salesman.

salespeople ['selz pi pəl] a pl of salesperson.

salesperson ['selz pɚ sən] *n.* someone who sells things for a living. (Pl: salespeople or *salespersons.*) ♦ *Each salesperson must wear a name tag at all times.* ♦ *The sales manager hired five new salespeople.*

sales tax ['selz tæks] *n.* a tax that is charged when products are sold. ♦ *A 5% sales tax means that a five-cent tax is charged for every dollar that an item costs.* ♦ *Everyone has to pay the same percentage of sales tax.*

saleswoman ['selz wʊ mən] *n., irreg.* a woman who sells things for a living. (Pl: saleswomen.) ♦ *Susan bought a new car from the knowledgeable saleswoman.* ♦ *Five saleswomen were hired to sell the new product.*

saleswomen ['selz wɪ mən] pl of saleswoman.

saliva [sə 'lɑɪ və] *n.* the liquid that is produced in the mouth, which helps people chew and digest food. (No plural form in this sense.) ♦ *Saliva dribbled from the baby's mouth.* ♦ *John spit some saliva onto the ground.*

sallow ['sæl o] *adj.* sickly pale; having yellowish skin; looking unhealthy. (Adv: *sallowly.*) ♦ *The teacher sent the student with the sallow face to the school nurse.* ♦ *After surgery, the patient's skin appeared sallow for a week.*

salmon ['sæm ən] **1.** *n., irreg.* a large food fish with soft, pale pink flesh. (Pl: *salmon.*) ♦ *You're only allowed to catch six salmon a day at this lake.* ♦ *A few salmon were caught by bears and eaten.* **2.** *n.* the meat of ①. (No plural form in this sense.) ♦ *Could I have some more salmon, please?* ♦ *I ate grilled salmon for dinner.*

salsa ['sɑl sə] **1.** *n.* a sauce made with tomatoes and spices that is eaten with food, especially Mexican food, to give it flavor. (From Spanish. No plural form in this sense.) ♦ *I asked the waiter for more salsa for my chips.* ♦ *David topped his omelet with some spicy salsa.* **2.** *n.* a style of sensuous, Latin American dance and music. (No plural form in this sense.) ♦ *The couple danced to salsa all night long.* ♦ *The band played salsa to make the atmosphere romantic.*

salt ['sɔlt] **1.** *n.* a white substance used to season or preserve food and to melt snow and ice; sodium chloride. (No plural form in this sense.) ♦ *Salt is found in a solid form in the earth and is found dissolved in sea water.* ♦ *Anne sprinkled a little salt on her vegetables.* **2.** *n.* a chemical substance made by combining an acid with a metal. (No plural form in this sense.) ♦ *This chemical salt is very corrosive.* ♦ *The shelves held bottles of acid and a jar of a bright blue salt.* **3.** *tv.* to season something by putting ① on it. ♦ *Jane salted her potatoes lightly.* ♦ *Don't salt the soup again!* **4.** *tv.* to cover something with ①. ♦ *Please salt the sidewalk so people won't slip and fall.* ♦ *The city workers salted the icy roads.* **5. salt of the earth** *idiom* the most worthy of people; a very good or worthy person. ♦ *Mrs. Jones is the salt of the earth. She is the first to help anyone in trouble.* ♦ *Bob's mother is the salt of the earth. She has five children of her own and cares for three others.* **6. worth one's salt** *idiom* worth one's salary. ♦ *Tom doesn't work very hard, and he's just barely worth his salt.* ♦ *I think he's more than worth his salt. He's a good worker.*

salted ['sɔl tɪd] *adj.* [of food] having salt added. ♦ *I avoid salted foods like pretzels.* ♦ *Tom loves to eat salted nuts.*

saltine [sɔl 'tin] *n.* a cracker that has salt on it. ♦ *As a snack, I ate some saltines with cheese.* ♦ *The soup was served with two saltines.*

salt water ['sɔlt 'wɑt ɚ] **1.** *n.* water with a high salt content as that found in the oceans. (No plural form in this sense.) ♦ *This fish can only live in salt water and will die in fresh water.* ♦ *Salt water is not suitable for drinking.* **2. saltwater** *adj.* [of water] having salt; found in the ocean or the sea. ♦ *I prefer saltwater fish over fish from fresh water.* ♦ *The biologist studied saltwater plants.*

salty ['sɔl ti] *adj.* tasting like salt; having salt. (Adv: *saltily.* Comp: *saltier;* sup: *saltiest.*) ♦ *These potato chips are too salty.* ♦ *The salty snacks made me thirsty.*

salutation [sæl jə 'te ʃən] *n.* something that is written to greet someone at the beginning of a letter. ♦ *The salutation belongs above the body of a letter.* ♦ *The letter's salutation contained a spelling error.*

salute [sə 'lut] **1.** *tv.* to show respect for someone by bringing the right hand to one's head. ♦ *The soldier saluted the general.* ♦ *Enlisted soldiers must salute their superiors.* **2.** *tv.* to show respect for someone or something by dipping a flag, firing a gun, or some other symbolic action. ♦ *The soldiers saluted the dead veteran by firing their guns.* ♦ *We saluted our deceased leader by dipping our flags as the hearse passed by.* **3.** *tv.* to greet someone with words, signs, or signals. (Formal.) ♦ *I saluted my guests from the window as they walked toward the door.* ♦ *Placards saluted the soldiers upon their return home.* **4.** *iv.* to show respect by making ⑤. ♦ *The soldier was reprimanded for failing to salute.* ♦ *When the privates saw their general, they saluted.* **5.** *n.* an act of saluting; a salutation. ♦ *The general returned the soldier's salute.* ♦ *A 21-gun salute was performed for the dead war hero.*

salvage ['sæl vɪdʒ] **1.** *tv.* to save something from destruction, damage, or ruin, especially to save a ship that has been wrecked or the cargo of a wrecked ship. ♦ *The divers salvaged chests of gold from the sunken ship.* ♦ *I was able to salvage some data from the ruined computer file.* **2.** *n.* something that has been saved from destruction or ruin. (No plural form in this sense.) ♦ *The salvage from the old ship was placed in the national museum.* ♦ *The salvage from the house that burned down was auctioned.*

salvation [sæl 've ʃən] **1.** *n.* saving something from being destroyed or ruined. (No plural form in this sense.) ♦ *The government agency depended on its salvation from the generosity of Congress.* ♦ *A bank loan was the old museum's salvation.* **2.** *n.* saving someone from the consequences of sin. (No plural form in this sense.) ♦ *The minister encouraged the salvation of the sinner's soul.* ♦ *The preacher praised the salvation of the converts.*

salve ['sæv] *n.* a soothing ointment put on wounds and sore places. (No plural form in this sense.) ♦ *Anne put some salve on my sunburned back.* ♦ *The doctor prescribed a salve for my rash.*

same ['sem] **1.** *adj.* not different; being the identical person or thing. ♦ *The evening star and the morning star are really the same thing: the planet Venus.* ♦ *Mary read the same book twice.* **2.** *adj.* being exactly like someone or something else; not different from someone or something else; alike. ♦ *Anne and Susan both have the same kind of car.* ♦ *David sent me the same birthday card as John did.* **3.** *pron.* <a form standing for something that has just been mentioned.> (No plural form in this sense. Typical of business correspondence.) ♦ *Please buy ten reams of paper and deliver same to my office.* ♦ *The defendant allegedly struck the plaintiff's car and then hit same with a baseball bat.* **4. the same as someone or something** *phr.* identical to someone or something. ♦ *Can you build me a birdhouse the same as yours?* ♦ *Have you noticed that Mary looks the same as her mother?*

sameness ['sem nəs] *n.* the quality of being the same; the degree of being very similar to someone or something. (No plural form in this sense.) ♦ *The sameness of the twins made it hard to tell them apart.* ♦ *John was bored with the sameness of each day at work.*

sample ['sæm pəl] **1.** *n.* a small portion of something that shows what the rest of it is like. ♦ *The clerk offered me a small sample of perfume.* ♦ *The drug company gave the doctors samples of many medicines.* **2.** *tv.* to take, try, or taste a small portion of something. ♦ *I sampled the cheese spread at the display table in the store.* ♦ *Mary sampled a piece of my apple pie.*

sanction ['sæŋk ʃən] **1.** *n.* approval by an authority to do something; permission. (No plural form in this sense.) ♦ *The reporter had an official sanction to meet with the mayor.* ♦ *Only with the dean's sanction could the professor go on a sabbatical.* **2.** *n.* a restriction placed against a country that has done something wrong. ♦ *The United Nations places sanctions on certain troubled countries.* ♦ *Many years after the war, the United States finally lifted the sanctions against Vietnam.* **3.** *tv.* to permit something; to allow something; to authorize something. ♦ *The government sanctioned the military research.* ♦ *The mayor refused to sanction the city council's actions.*

sanctity ['sæŋk tɪ ti] **1.** *n.* the quality of being holy or sacred. (No plural form in this sense.) ♦ *Mike felt that there was too much insincere sanctity among the church members.* ♦ *The tourist respected the sanctity of the mosque.* **2. odor of sanctity** *idiom* an atmosphere of excessive holiness or piety. ♦ *I hate their house. There's such an odor of sanctity with Bibles and holy pictures everywhere.* ♦ *People are nervous about Jane's odor of sanctity. She's always praying for people or doing good works and never has any fun.*

sanctuary ['sæŋk tʃu ɛr i] **1.** *n.* a state of safety or refuge traditionally provided by a house of worship. (No plural form in this sense.) ♦ *The exiled king sought sanctuary in the church.* ♦ *The pious woman found sanctuary in a convent.* **2.** *n.* a sacred or holy building; a holy place of worship. ♦ *This grotto is a sanctuary for the local monks.* ♦ *The developer was not allowed to build on the ruins of the sanctuary.* **3.** *n.* a place of safety or preservation, especially for birds and other wildlife. (Figurative on ②.) ♦ *You can see many exotic birds at the zoo's bird sanctuary.* ♦ *The county maintains a sanctuary for wild animals.*

sand ['sænd] **1.** *n.* very tiny particles of rock or seashells such as are found on beaches and in deserts. (No plural form in this sense. Number expressed with *grain(s) of sand*.) ♦ *I got sand in my shoes when I walked on the beach.* ♦ *There are millions of grains of sand on this small beach.* **2.** *tv.* to rub something with sandpaper to make it smooth; to smooth something with sandpaper. ♦ *The carpenter sanded the railing to remove the splinters.* ♦ *I sanded the floor before I coated it with varnish.* **3.** *tv.* to put or sprinkle ① on a surface, such as an icy street. ♦ *The city trucks sanded the icy roads.* ♦ *The store owner sanded the sidewalk in front of her store.* **4. bury one's head in the sand** *idiom* to ignore or hide from obvious signs of danger. ♦ *Stop burying your head in the sand. Look at the statistics on smoking and cancer.* ♦ *And stop burying your head in the sand. All of us will die somehow, whether we smoke or not.* **5. sands of time** *idiom* the accumulated tiny amounts of time; time represented by the sand ① in an hourglass. ♦ *The sands of time will make you grow old like everyone else.* ♦ *My only enemy is the sands of time.*

sandal ['sæn dəl] *n.* a light, open shoe consisting of a sole that is strapped to the foot. ♦ *John bought some sandals to wear to the beach.* ♦ *Jane's sandals slapped against the floor as she walked.*

sandbag ['sænd bæg] *n.* a bag that is filled with sand and used as a weight or in stacks to hold back water. ♦ *The townsfolk piled sandbags along the river to prevent flooding.* ♦ *The base of the temporary road sign is held in place by sandbags.*

sandblast ['sænd blæst] **1.** *tv.* to clean or cut a hard surface with a strong stream of air and sand. ♦ *The workers sandblasted the front of the building.* ♦ *John sandblasted the surface of the bricks.* **2.** *tv.* to remove something dirty from a surface using a strong stream of sand. ♦ *John sandblasted the soot from the surface of the bricks.* ♦ *Can you sandblast this mildew off?*

sandbox ['sænd bɑks] *n.* a low box that contains sand that young children can play in. ♦ *Tom played in the sandbox with his trucks and plastic shovel.* ♦ *Jimmy is dirty because he was playing in the sandbox.*

sandcastle ['sænd kæ səl] *n.* a mass of moist sand, shaped to look like a castle. ♦ *When the waves came in, they ruined my sandcastle.* ♦ *Mary made sandcastles on the beach during low tide.*

sander ['sæn dɚ] *n.* an electric tool that vibrates a piece of sandpaper for the purpose of smoothing and polishing. ♦ *With an electric sander, it's easy to get a smooth finish.* ♦ *Susan pushed the sander over the rough cabinet edges.*

sandlot ['sænd lɑt] **1.** *n.* an empty piece of land, usually in a city, on which baseball games are played. ♦ *All the neighborhood children are playing ball at the sandlot.* ♦ *The children cried when an office building was built on the old sandlot.* **2.** *adj.* <the adj. use of ①.> ♦ *The neighborhood children played sandlot baseball after school.* ♦ *When I was 8, I was a sandlot pitcher.*

sandpaper ['sænd pe pɚ] *n.* a paper lightly coated with sand particles, used to polish or smooth a surface. (No plural form in this sense.) ♦ *Mary sanded the wooden railing with sandpaper to remove the splinters.* ♦ *David attached a piece of sandpaper to the electric sander.*

sandstone ['sænd ston] **1.** *n.* a rock formed of sand and other mineral substances fused together under great pressure. (No plural form in this sense.) ♦ *The front of our fireplace is made of sandstone.* ♦ *Sandstone is usually red, tan, or brown.* **2.** *adj.* made of ①. ♦ *The sandstone front of the house is very attractive.* ♦ *Bob built a sandstone barbecue.*

sandstorm ['sænd storm] *n.* a strong wind that carries sand, especially a storm in a desert. ♦ *The nomads remained at the oasis during the sandstorm.* ♦ *The camel has developed special eyelids to protect it from sandstorms.*

sandwich ['sænd wɪtʃ] **1.** *n.* two pieces of bread with some kind of food in between. ♦ *Mary ate a peanut butter and jelly sandwich.* ♦ *John had a ham sandwich for lunch.* **2.** *tv.* to put someone or something tightly between or among other persons or objects. ♦ *Bob sandwiched his car between a red car and a blue truck.* ♦ *The librarian sandwiched the book into a tight space on the shelf.*

sandy ['sæn di] **1.** *adj.* covered with sand; having sand. (Comp: *sandier;* sup: *sandiest.*) ♦ *Bill washed his sandy feet when he returned from the beach.* ♦ *I cleaned the sandy picnic basket before putting it in the car.* **2.** *adj.* reddish-yellow or brownish-yellow in color; being the color of sand. (Comp: *sandier;* sup: *sandiest.*) ♦ *John has sandy blond hair.* ♦ *Mary's dog has sandy brown fur.*

sane ['sen] **1.** *adj.* having a healthy mind; not crazy. (Adv: *sanely.* Comp: *saner;* sup: *sanest.*) ♦ *The defendant was judged to be sane and competent to stand trial.* ♦ *Some patients at the mental hospital claimed they were sane.* **2.** *adj.* rational; sensible; having or showing common sense. (Adv: *sanely.* Comp: *saner;* sup: *sanest.*) ♦ *The professor presented sane arguments for nuclear disarmament.* ♦ *Do you have any sane reasons for not wearing your seat belt?*

sang ['sæŋ] pt of sing.

sanitarium [sæn ɪ 'tɛr i əm] *n.* a hospital where people who have a particular sickness, especially tuberculosis or mental diseases, stay while they are getting better. ♦ *Before a cure was found, tuberculosis sanitariums were commonplace.* ♦ *The mental patient was placed in the county sanitarium.*

sanitary ['sæn ɪ tɛr i] **1.** *adj.* very clean; not dangerous to one's health. (Adv: *sanitarily.*) ♦ *The doctor's office was extremely sanitary.* ♦ *The nurse applied some sanitary gauze to my wound.* **2.** *adj.* used for the disposal of waste that is harmful to health. ♦ *The storm sewer carries away rainwater and the sanitary sewer carries away household waste.* ♦ *The garbage was hauled to a sanitary landfill.*

sanitation [sæn ɪ 'te ʃən] *n.* the study and practice of preserving the health of the public, especially concerning the removal of waste. (No plural form in this sense.) ♦ *The city's Department of Sanitation oversees garbage removal.* ♦ *As sanitation improved, the incidence of disease dropped.*

sanity ['sæn ɪ ti] *n.* sound mental health. (No plural form in this sense.) ♦ *The defendant's sanity was questioned during the trial.* ♦ *Many soldiers lost their sanity during the war.*

sank ['sæŋk] pt of sink.

Sanskrit ['sæn skrɪt] *n.* an ancient Indo-European language; a classical language of India. (No plural form in this sense.) ♦ *Many ancient writings of India are written in Sanskrit.* ♦ *Latin, Greek, and Sanskrit all developed from a common language.*

Santa Claus ['sæn tə klɔz] *n.* the spirit of Christmas and the winter holiday season represented by a jolly old man in a red suit decorated with white fur. ♦ *Mother took the children to see Santa Claus at the department store.* ♦ *The legend says that Santa Claus comes down the chimney and brings toys to good little girls and boys.*

sap ['sæp] **1.** *n.* a fluid in a tree that carries important nutrients to all of its parts. (No plural form in this sense.) ♦ *The farmer made maple syrup by boiling sap from maple trees.* ♦ *The sap from the tree made my hands sticky when I touched it.* **2.** *tv.* to weaken or destroy someone or something; to take away someone or something's strength or energy. ♦ *The continuing war sapped the nation's economy.* ♦ *The losing streak sapped the football team's morale.*

sapling ['sæp lɪŋ] *n.* a young tree. ♦ *I planted a sapling in my yard.* ♦ *After the forest fire, saplings grew from the ashes.*

sapphire ['sæ fɑɪr] **1.** *n.* a hard mineral having a bluish color. (No plural form in this sense.) ♦ *David discovered a chunk of sapphire in the cave.* ♦ *Sapphire is very hard and transparent.* **2.** *n.* a bright blue gemstone made from ①. ♦ *Sapphires are very expensive jewels.* ♦ *The princess wore sapphires around her neck.* **3.** *adj.* made of ②. ♦ *What a lovely sapphire necklace!* ♦ *I would really like a pair of sapphire earrings.* **4.** *adj.* bright blue, like the color of ①. ♦ *The model's eyes were a beautiful sapphire blue.* ♦ *The sapphire water at the tropical beach was beautiful.*

sarcasm ['sɑr kæz əm] *n.* the use of words that have the opposite meaning from what is said; an ironic statement. (No plural form in this sense.) ♦ *Jane's voice was filled with sarcasm when she said her day went well.* ♦ *The critic enjoyed the playwright's witty sarcasm.*

sarcastic [sɑr 'kæs tɪk] *adj.* using sarcasm; ironic; mocking. (Adv: *sarcastically* [...ɪk li].) ♦ *I was being sarcastic when I said this movie was thrilling. It's really bad.* ♦ *John's sarcastic comments insulted David.*

sardine [sɑr 'din] *n.* a small, edible fish, usually sold in flat cans. ♦ *John ate sardines for dinner.* ♦ *You can eat a sardine's bones because they're so small.*

sardonic [sɑr 'dɑn ɪk] *adj.* mocking; cynical; sarcastic; grimly amusing. (Adv: *sardonically* [...ɪk li].) ♦ *Bill's sardonic sense of humor is often misunderstood.* ♦ *The reporter wrote a sardonic report on the progress of Congress.*

sash ['sæʃ] **1.** *n.* a long, wide strip of cloth, worn around the waist as a belt or over the shoulder as a decoration. ♦ *John's robe has a matching sash.* ♦ *The judge placed the sash over the winning contestant's shoulder.* **2.** *n.* the frame that holds glass in a window or door. ♦ *Be careful when you paint the sash so you don't drip paint on the glass of the window.* ♦ *We raised the sash and aired out the room.*

sat ['sæt] pt/pp of sit.

Satan ['set n] *n.* the devil. ♦ *Satan rules in hell.* ♦ *Satan and the devil are the same being.*

satanic [sə 'tæn ɪk] *adj.* <the adj. form of Satan.> (Adv: *satanically* [...ɪk li].) ♦ *The villain in the movie had a satanic laugh.* ♦ *The police found the meeting place of a satanic cult.*

satchel ['sætʃ əl] *n.* a small bag like a briefcase. ♦ *David entered the room with his satchel in his hand.* ♦ *The lawyer carried some legal briefs in his satchel.*

satellite ['sæt ə lɑɪt] **1.** *n.* a natural body of rock and minerals that orbits around a planet; a moon. ♦ *The moon is Earth's only satellite.* ♦ *Mars has two satellites, Phobos and Deimos.* **2.** *n.* a spacecraft that orbits a planet. ♦ *The old satellite burned up on reentry into the atmosphere.* ♦ *The television signal was broadcast live via satellite.* **3.** *adj.* dependent on something else that has more power. ♦ *The university operates a rural satellite college downstate.* ♦ *The TV station owns a smaller satellite station 200 miles away.*

satiate ['se ʃi et] *tv.* to satisfy someone fully; to satisfy a need fully. ♦ *The gourmet meal satiated my hunger.* ♦ *Some cold lemonade satiated my thirst.*

satin ['sæt n] **1.** *n.* a soft, silky, smooth cloth that is shiny on one side. (No plural form in this sense.) ♦ *The princess wore a gown of pink satin.* ♦ *Don't wash satin in a washing machine. Take it to the cleaners.* **2.** *adj.* made from ①. ♦ *The beds in the honeymoon suite have satin sheets.* ♦ *Anne's friends bought her a satin nightgown for her wedding night.*

satire ['sæ tɑɪr] **1.** *n.* a style of entertainment or communication in which sarcasm or irony is used to ridicule the faults of someone or something. (No plural form in this sense.) ♦ *The author used outrageous satire to make her point.* ♦ *Through satire, serious charges were made about the government.* **2.** *n.* a book, play, television show, editorial, etc., that uses ①. ♦ *This TV show is a satire of the ideal family.* ♦ *The political satire was censored by the government.*

satirical [sə 'tɪr ɪ kəl] *adj.* <the adj. form of satire.> (Adv: *satirically* [...ɪk li].) ♦ *The satirical article about the prime minister was censored.* ♦ *The lawyer laughed at the satirical movie about working in a law firm.*

satisfaction [sæt ɪs 'fæk ʃən] **1.** *n.* fulfillment; contentment. (No plural form in this sense.) ♦ *The salesclerk helped me achieve satisfaction with my purchase.* ♦ *The store strived for customer satisfaction.* **2.** *n.* something that satisfies; something that pleases someone; something that makes someone content. ♦ *Eating fine food is one of* *the satisfactions I get from being a food critic.* ♦ *Traveling abroad was a satisfaction John enjoyed once a year.*

satisfactorily [sæt ɪs 'fæk tə rə li] *adv.* in a satisfactory way. ♦ *The clerk satisfactorily took care of my problem.* ♦ *The mechanic satisfactorily repaired my car.*

satisfactory [sæt ɪs 'fæk tə ri] *adj.* adequate; meeting certain needs or requirements. (Adv: *satisfactorily.*) ♦ *The plumber did a satisfactory job of fixing my leaky sink.* ♦ *My children get satisfactory grades in school.*

satisfied ['sæt ɪs fɑɪd] *adj.* made content; happy with something. ♦ *The satisfied customer returned to the store again and again.* ♦ *I am completely satisfied with your explanation.*

satisfy ['sæt ɪs fɑɪ] **1.** *tv.* to make someone content; to please someone; to make someone happy with something. ♦ *The clerk satisfied me by helping me find what I wanted.* ♦ *The teacher was satisfied with the students' progress.* **2.** *tv.* to meet or fulfill certain needs or requirements. ♦ *I satisfied the foreign language requirement by learning French.* ♦ *Our current vendor satisfies our needs for supplies.*

satisfying ['sæt ɪs fɑɪ ɪŋ] *adj.* making someone content; pleasing; making someone happy; causing satisfaction. (Adv: *satisfyingly.*) ♦ *I spent a satisfying day at the beach relaxing.* ♦ *Dinner was very satisfying this evening.*

saturate ['sætʃ ə ret] **1.** *tv.* to soak something; to cause someone or something to become completely wet. ♦ *The heavy rains saturated the farmland.* ♦ *David saturated the white shirt in blue dye.* **2.** *tv.* to fill something with something; to cause something to become completely full. (Figurative on ①.) ♦ *She saturated her speech with allusions to death.* ♦ *The politician saturated the people's minds with promises.*

saturated ['sætʃ ə ret ɪd] *adj.* completely soaked; completely wet. ♦ *Water dripped from the saturated sponge.* ♦ *I came in from the rain and took off my saturated clothes.*

Saturday ['sæt ɚ de] **1.** *n.* the seventh day of the week, between Friday and Sunday. ♦ *This Saturday is the football game.* ♦ *Can you come to my party next Saturday?* **2.** *adv.* on the next ①. ♦ *Saturday I can sleep late if I want to.* ♦ *Please visit us Saturday.* **3. (on) Saturdays** *adv.* on each ①. ♦ *We always sleep late Saturdays.* ♦ *Often I have to work on Saturdays.*

Saturn ['sæt ɚn] **1.** *n.* [in Roman mythology] the god of the harvest. ♦ *The feast in honor of Saturn was held in the middle of the winter.* ♦ *If Saturn is pleased, the harvest will be good.* **2.** *n.* the sixth planet of the solar system, between Jupiter and Uranus. ♦ *Saturn is the second largest planet in our solar system.* ♦ *Saturn is famous for the rings of rocks that encircle it.*

sauce ['sɔs] *n.* a flavorful liquid that is put on food to add flavor to the food. (No plural form in this sense.) ♦ *I poured some tomato sauce on top of my spaghetti.* ♦ *Anne ate her potato with some cheese sauce.*

saucepan ['sɔs pæn] *n.* a round metal pan with a handle, used for cooking and boiling food. ♦ *I boiled some water for tea in a small saucepan.* ♦ *Jane heated some leftover stew in a saucepan on the stove.*

saucer ['sɔ sɚ] *n.* a small dish that cups are set on. ♦ *Anne spilled her coffee, but it landed on her saucer instead of on the tablecloth.* ♦ *Susan placed her cup on her saucer and carried them into the living room.*

Saudi Arabia [sɑu di ə 'reb i ə] See Gazetteer.

sauerkraut ['sɑʊ ɚ krɑʊt] *n.* shredded, pickled cabbage. (No plural form in this sense.) ♦ *We ordered bratwurst with sauerkraut at the German restaurant.* ♦ *John eats sausages with sauerkraut.*

sauna ['sɑʊ nɑ] *n.* a room with a small furnace that produces a lot of heat so that a person sitting it in sweats very much. ♦ *The health club had saunas in each locker room.* ♦ *After working out and before showering, Susan sat in the sauna.*

saunter ['sɔn tɚ] **1.** *iv.* to walk slowly or leisurely; to stroll. ♦ *The shoppers casually sauntered through the mall.* ♦ *The students sauntered toward school.* **2.** *n.* a slow, leisurely walk; a stroll. ♦ *We had a quiet saunter in the park.* ♦ *A sudden rainstorm interrupted my saunter through the woods.*

sausage ['sɔ sɪdʒ] **1.** *n.* a food made of chopped meat mixed with spices. (No plural form in this sense.) ♦ *David fried some sausage for dinner.* ♦ *Anne asked the butcher for some very spicy sausage.* **2.** *n.* ① stuffed into a thin tube of animal intestine or artificial material. ♦ *How many sausages did you have with breakfast?* ♦ *Please remember to buy a package of sausages.* **3.** *adj.* made with ①. ♦ *Would you like some sausage pizza, or would you prefer cheese?* ♦ *I prepared a sausage omelet for my supper.*

sauté [sɔ́ 'te] **1.** *tv.* to cook food quickly in a small amount of very hot oil or fat. (From French.) ♦ *The chef sautéed the onions before adding them to the salad.* ♦ *The cook is sautéing the green peppers for only 30 seconds.* **2.** *iv.* to be cooked quickly in a small amount of very hot oil or fat. (From French.) ♦ *The onions sautéed on the stove for 2 minutes.* ♦ *The mushrooms sautéed in a matter of moments.* **3.** *n.* a dish of food that has been cooked quickly in a small amount of very hot oil or fat. (No plural form in this sense. From French.) ♦ *The salad was topped with an onion sauté.* ♦ *The mushroom sauté smelled very delicious.*

savage ['sæv ɪdʒ] **1.** *adj.* wild; not tamed; not civilized; primitive. (Adv: *savagely.*) ♦ *The savage child had been raised by wolves in the forest.* ♦ *The explorer believed the indigenous people to be savage.* **2.** *adj.* fierce; ready to fight; violent; ferocious; vicious. (Adv: *savagely.*) ♦ *The savage lion slew its prey.* ♦ *The savage dog barked at the mail carrier.* **3.** *n.* someone who is wild, not tamed, and not civilized. ♦ *I assure you that I am not a savage! I am highly educated.* ♦ *The scientists studied the young savage who was raised by wolves.*

save ['sev] **1.** *tv.* to make someone or something safe from harm or danger; to rescue someone or something. ♦ *The firefighter saved the family from the burning house.* ♦ *The crew of another boat saved the passengers from the sinking boat.* **2.** *tv.* to keep a supply of something, especially money, for future use; to place something aside, especially money, for future use. ♦ *Mary saved enough money for a new car.* ♦ *Anne saved 25% of each paycheck for retirement.* **3.** *tv.* not to spend something; not to use something; to reserve something. ♦ *Don't eat all of the pizza. Save a slice for me.* ♦ *I saved gas by not making unnecessary trips.* **4.** *tv.* to cause something to be unnecessary; to prevent the need to do something. ♦ *Doing it* *now will save having to do it later.* ♦ *Buying the new model will save you time and money.* **5.** *prep.* but; except. (Old-fashioned.) ♦ *Everyone is here, save the Browns, who are always late.* ♦ *John has fulfilled his graduation requirements, save biology.* **6. save the day** *idiom* to produce a good result when a bad result was expected. ♦ *The team was expected to lose, but Sally made many points and saved the day.* ♦ *Your excellent speech saved the day.* **7. scrimp and save** *idiom* to be very thrifty; to live on very little money, often in order to save ② it for something. ♦ *We had to scrimp and save in order to send the children to college.* ♦ *The Smiths scrimp and save all year in order to go on a vacation.*

savings ['sev ɪŋz] **1.** *n.* money that is saved for future use; money that is set aside, especially in a bank account, for future use. (Treated as plural.) ♦ *John's surgery wiped out his life savings.* ♦ *My life savings are safely kept at the bank.* **2. savings account** *n.* a bank account that is intended for saving money over a long period of time. ♦ *I put half of each week's pay into my savings account.* ♦ *In 40 years, my savings account will be worth $1,000,000.*

savior ['sev jɚ] **1.** *n.* someone who saves someone or something; someone who rescues someone or something. ♦ *The army was the besieged town's savior.* ♦ *The Coast Guard was the savior of the passengers from the sinking ship.* **2. the Savior** *n.* Jesus Christ. (No plural form in this sense. Treated as singular.) ♦ *The congregation honored the Savior with singing.* ♦ *The minister raised his hands and praised the Savior.*

savor ['sev ɚ] *tv.* to enjoy the taste of food or drink, especially by eating or drinking it slowly. ♦ *Mary savored each sip of the fine wine.* ♦ *John savored a large bite of the rich dish.*

savory ['sev ə ri] **1.** *adj.* having a pleasant taste or smell; full of flavor. ♦ *The cook made a savory stew.* ♦ *This dish is far more savory than the plain food we are used to eating.* **2.** *adj.* salty or spicy; not sweet. ♦ *This soup has a very savory broth.* ♦ *Apple pie is sweet, but a meat pie is savory.*

savvy ['sæv i] **1.** *n.* a practical understanding; good common sense. (Informal. No plural form in this sense.) ♦ *The lost man's savvy about the streets kept him alive.* ♦ *The inspector's savvy helped him solve crimes.* **2.** *adj.* shrewd; having an understanding of how things are in the world. ♦ *The savvy mayor was popular with the city's working class.* ♦ *A savvy businessperson will usually be quite successful.* **3.** *tv.* to know something; to understand something; to comprehend something. ♦ *Our mayor just doesn't savvy urban problems.* ♦ *The student couldn't savvy complicated math problems.*

saw ['sɔ] **1.** pt of see. **2.** *n.* a cutting tool with a thin blade that is notched with tiny, sharp teeth. ♦ *The lumberjack cut down the tree with a saw.* ♦ *The carpenter replaced the blade of the saw with a sharper one.* **3. old saw** *n.* an old saying; a proverb; a maxim. ♦ *"Too many cooks spoil the broth" is an old saw.* ♦ *My grandfather has a clever old saw for every occasion.* **4.** *iv., irreg.* to cut with ②. (Pt: *sawed;* pp: *sawed* or sawn.) ♦ *The lumberjacks sawed until sunset.* ♦ *The carpenter sawed until the board had been cut.* **5.** *tv., irreg.* to cut something with ②. ♦ *The carpenter sawed the thick beam carefully.* ♦ *A huge blade sawed the lumber very quickly.*

sawdust ['sɔ dəst] *n.* tiny flakes of wood that are made when wood is sawed. (No plural form in this sense.) ♦ *After I sawed the wood, I swept up the sawdust on the floor.* ♦ *The floor of the carpenter's workshop was covered with sawdust.*

sawhorse ['sɔ hors] *n.* a support for holding the wood that is being cut with a saw. ♦ *The carpenter balanced the board on the sawhorse.* ♦ *I used a piece of plywood over two sawhorses as a table.*

sawmill ['sɔ mɪl] *n.* a building where logs are cut into boards and planks. ♦ *The trees were sent down the river to the sawmill.* ♦ *The sawmill sold planks to lumber companies.*

saxophone AND **sax** ['sæks ə fon, 'sæks] *n.* a musical instrument with a reed mouthpiece that the player blows air through, and on which different notes are made by pressing different keys. ♦ *The lower end of a saxophone curves upward, like the letter* J. ♦ *The singer performed with a musician playing a sax.*

say ['se] **1.** *tv., irreg.* to pronounce words; to speak words. (Pt/pp: said.) ♦ *The actor said each line in a raspy voice.* ♦ *Anne always says her words clearly and distinctly.* **2.** *tv., irreg.* to state something; to declare something; to express something in words. ♦ *Mary said, "We're leaving at ten o'clock."* ♦ *"This soup tastes delicious," said Jane.* **3. say that** *phr.* to assume something; to suppose that something were so. ♦ *Say that* x *is equal to a whole number greater than 10.* ♦ *Say that two trains leave two different cities at the same time.* **4.** *n.* an authoritative role [in making a decision]. (No plural form in this sense.) ♦ *I have no say in the matter.* ♦ *My boss has the final say in the department budget.*

saying ['se ɪŋ] *n.* a wise statement; a proverb; a well-known statement; an adage. ♦ *"A stitch in time saves nine" is an old saying.* ♦ *My grandmother had a saying about mean people like you!*

scab ['skæb] **1.** *n.* a crusty layer of dried blood that forms over a wound when it heals. ♦ *Don't pick your scab, or that cut will never heal.* ♦ *Susan covered her scab with a bandage.* **2.** *n.* a worker who works at a union job when the union workers are on strike. (Slang.) ♦ *The striking workers threw rocks at the scabs who went in the factory to work.* ♦ *The scabs were paid much less than the union workers had been.*

scaffold ['skæf əld] **1.** *n.* a temporary, elevated platform on which workers stand. ♦ *In many parts of the world, people make scaffolds from bamboo.* ♦ *The masons repairing the building's facade stood on a scaffold.* **2.** *n.* the platform where people stand during executions before they are hanged. ♦ *The condemned prisoner walked slowly to the scaffold.* ♦ *The hanged criminal dangled through an opening in the scaffold.*

scaffolding ['skæ fol dɪŋ] *n.* a complex construction of scaffolds, often very tall or very wide, covering the interior or exterior walls of a building. (No plural form in this sense.) ♦ *The building was almost concealed by the scaffolding.* ♦ *The scaffolding will remain in place until the building is completely painted.*

scald ['skɔld] *tv.* to expose someone or something to a boiling liquid or steam. ♦ *Hot steam from a broken pipe scalded the factory worker.* ♦ *I scalded my tongue on boiling tea.*

scalding ['skɔl dɪŋ] **1.** *adj.* [of a liquid] hot enough to boil. (Adv: *scaldingly.*) ♦ *Be careful. The coffee is scalding.* ♦ *John accidentally spilled some scalding water on his knee.* **2.** *adv.* extremely [hot]; boiling [hot]. ♦ *This coffee is scalding hot.* ♦ *The soup was served scalding hot.*

scale ['skel] **1.** *n.* a series of numbers at different levels, used for measuring something. ♦ *In America, temperature is measured on the Fahrenheit scale.* ♦ *In much of the world outside the U.S., temperature is measured on the Celsius scale.* **2.** *n.* the relation between a measurement on a map or design compared to the actual measurement it corresponds to. ♦ *This map's scale indicates an inch on the map is equal to 100 miles.* ♦ *The city map's scale was large enough so that each street could be shown.* **3.** *n.* a series of musical notes, from low notes to high notes or from high notes to low notes. ♦ *The musical scale in Western music is a mixture of whole steps and half steps.* ♦ *The opera singer warmed up her voice by practicing scales.* **4.** *n.* the size or extent of something, especially as compared to something else or an average. (No plural form in this sense.) ♦ *The earthquake caused misery on a very large scale.* ♦ *The war against drugs was fought on a wide scale.* **5.** *n.* a device that measures how much something weighs. (Singular or plural.) ♦ *The butcher weighed the sliced ham on a scale.* ♦ *At the gym, the dieters weighed themselves on the scales.* **6.** *n.* one of the small, thin pieces of hardened skin on the bodies of most fish and snakes. ♦ *John scraped the fish's scales off with a knife.* ♦ *Jane picked up the scales that the snake had shed.* **7.** *n.* a flake of something, especially dead skin. ♦ *There are scales of dandruff on John's shoulders.* ♦ *When Mary scratched her elbow, scales of dead skin flaked off.* **8.** *tv.* to climb something. ♦ *The climber scaled the mountain.* ♦ *Someone scaled the side of the office building.* **9.** *tv.* to remove ⑥ from a fish. ♦ *John scaled the perch with a knife.* ♦ *Mary scaled the fish we caught before frying them.* **10. scale something down** *idiom* to make something larger or smaller by a certain amount. ♦ *I scaled down the guest list because I couldn't invite so many people.* ♦ *Jane's salary was scaled down by 10% last year.* **11. tip the scales at something** *idiom* to weigh some amount. ♦ *Tom tips the scales at nearly 200 pounds.* ♦ *I'll be glad when I tip the scales at a few pounds less.*

scale model ['skel 'mɑd l] *n.* a model with each of its measurements proportional to the object being modeled. ♦ *The architect built a scale model of the new office building.* ♦ *The designer presented a scale model of the redecorated lobby.*

scallop ['skæl əp] **1.** *n.* an edible shellfish that lives in two fan-shaped shells that are hinged together. ♦ *There were a lot of scallops in my seafood chowder.* ♦ *John ordered fried scallops with a special sauce.* **2.** *n.* one of a series of half-circles or curves used as a decoration. ♦ *Fancy handwriting has a lot of loops and scallops.* ♦ *The grate over the window is decorated with ornate metal scallops.* **3.** *tv.* to cut something so that its edge consists of curves or half-circles. ♦ *The seamstress scalloped the neckline of the dress to make it more decorative.* ♦ *The carpenter scalloped the edge of the panel.*

scalp ['skælp] **1.** *n.* the skin and any hair growing on it on the top and back of the head. ♦ *Flakes of dead skin from the scalp are called dandruff.* ♦ *The bald man covered his scalp with a hat.* **2.** *tv.* to cut ① from a person's head. ♦ *The mercenary scalped the soldiers he killed.* ♦ *After the psychotic man killed his victims, he scalped them.* **3.** *tv.* to buy tickets for something and then sell them for a higher price to other people. (Informal.) ♦ *John makes his living scalping tickets for popular concerts.* ♦ *Mary scalped her ticket for twice what she'd paid for it.*

scalpel ['skæl pəl] *n.* a sharp knife that doctors use for cutting during surgery. ♦ *The nurse handed the doctor a scalpel during the operation.* ♦ *The scalpels were discarded after the operation.*

scalper ['skæl pɚ] *n.* someone who buys tickets for something and then sells them to other people at a higher price. ♦ *The police arrested the scalper in front of the football stadium.* ♦ *The ticket seller sold the scalper 50 tickets.*

scaly ['skel i] **1.** *adj.* having lots of scales; covered with scales. (Comp: *scalier;* sup: *scaliest.*) ♦ *The scaly snake felt dry to the touch.* ♦ *Most fish are quite scaly.* **2.** *adj.* flaky; having flakes. (Comp: *scalier;* sup: *scaliest.*) ♦ *I need some lotion because I've got scaly skin.* ♦ *David bought medicated shampoo for his scaly scalp.*

scamper ['skæm pɚ] *iv.* to run around in a playful way. ♦ *The puppies scampered in their kennel.* ♦ *The children scampered around the playground.*

scan ['skæn] **1.** *tv.* to examine something closely and carefully, as though one were searching for something. ♦ *The scout scanned the horizon for the enemy.* ♦ *The inspector scanned the room for clues.* **2.** *tv.* to look through something quickly and carelessly; to glance at something; to read through something quickly. ♦ *John scanned the reading assignment briefly before class.* ♦ *Mary only scanned the contract before signing it.* **3.** *tv.* to put a picture or a text into a computer file by placing the picture or book on a scanner. ♦ *John scanned a photo of himself and saved it in a file called "Me."* ♦ *Rather than type the article again, I scanned it into the computer.* **4.** *n.* an act of using a scanner. ♦ *The first scan was bad, so I had to do it again.* ♦ *Everything went fine, scan after scan.*

scandal ['skæn dəl] *n.* an event that causes disgrace; an instance of indecent or improper actions that become known by other people. ♦ *The sex scandal cost the senator his job.* ♦ *The embezzlement scandal caused the treasurer to be fired.*

scandalous ['skæn də ləs] *adj.* disgraceful; causing scandal. (Adv: *scandalously.*) ♦ *The tabloids printed scandalous news about the royal couple.* ♦ *David's behavior at the party last night was scandalous.*

Scandinavia [skæn də 'nev i ə] *n.* the countries of Denmark, Norway, and Sweden, and sometimes also Iceland and Finland. (No plural form in this sense.) ♦ *Parts of Scandinavia are north of the Arctic Circle.* ♦ *John goes to Scandinavia every winter to ski.*

Scandinavian [skæn də 'nev i ən] *adj.* of or about the people, land, and cultures of Denmark, Norway, and Sweden, and sometimes also Iceland and Finland. (Geographically, Iceland is not part of the group. Linguistically, Finland is not part of the group.) ♦ *The Scandinavian skiers did very well in the Olympics.* ♦ *The linguist studied each Scandinavian language.*

scanner ['skæn ɚ] *n.* a machine that converts a page of a book or a picture to an image that can be stored, viewed, or changed on a computer. ♦ *Anne bought a scanner so she could convert images to computer files.* ♦ *Bill placed his photograph on the scanner.*

scant ['skænt] *adj.* not enough of something. (Adv: *scantly.* Comp: *scanter;* sup: *scantest.*) ♦ *The youngest child received scant attention from his busy parents.* ♦ *The poor family lived on a very scant income.*

scanty ['skæn ti] *adj.* not sufficient; falling short of an amount that is needed. (Adv: *scantily.* Comp: *scantier;* sup: *scantiest.*) ♦ *That is a very scanty swimming suit!* ♦ *The editor made the scanty article twice as long.*

scapegoat ['skep got] **1.** *n.* someone who is blamed for the mistakes of others; someone who takes the blame for the mistakes of others. ♦ *The inept worker was a scapegoat for all of the company's problems.* ♦ *John portrayed himself as the scapegoat to protect his friend's job.* **2.** *tv.* to blame someone for the mistakes of others. ♦ *The manager scapegoated the staff for his own mistakes.* ♦ *Each political party scapegoated the other for all of Congress's problems.*

scar ['skɑr] **1.** *n.* a mark that is left on the surface of something, such as skin, that has been torn, cut, burned, or otherwise damaged. ♦ *John has a scar on his leg where he cut himself when he was a child.* ♦ *There's a scar on the table where I dragged a knife across it.* **2.** *tv.* to cause someone or something to have ①. ♦ *Chickenpox has scarred Dave's face badly.* ♦ *Jane scarred the marble floor by dragging a desk across it.*

scarce ['skɛrs] *adj.* rare; hard to find. (Adv: *scarcely.* Comp: *scarcer;* sup: *scarcest.*) ♦ *Fresh water was scarce during the drought.* ♦ *Scarce foods and other supplies were rationed during the war.*

scarcely ['skɛrs li] *adv.* hardly; barely; just almost. (Not used with other negative adverbs.) ♦ *Mary was scarcely 4 years old when she began to read.* ♦ *It was scarcely 7:00* A.M. *when the phone rang.* ♦ *There were scarcely any seats left when we arrived.*

scarcity ['skɛr sɪ ti] *n.* a lack; a very small supply. ♦ *There was a scarcity of fresh fruit during the war.* ♦ *There was no scarcity of water during the flood.*

scare ['skɛr] **1.** *tv.* to frighten someone; to cause someone to be afraid. ♦ *The thunder and lightning scared the small children.* ♦ *Please don't jump out and scare me like that!* **2.** *n.* a bad fright; an instance where one is afraid; a feeling of fear. ♦ *The angry dog gave the letter carrier a bad scare.* ♦ *I had a scare when the doctor said I might have cancer.*

scarecrow ['skɛr kro] *n.* a figure that looks human and is put in a field to scare away birds that will eat the crops. ♦ *The scarecrow was stuffed with straw.* ♦ *The farmer put a hat on top of the scarecrow.*

scared ['skɛrd] *adj.* frightened; filled with fear. ♦ *Badly scared, I walked faster toward my apartment.* ♦ *The airplane passenger was scared and clenched the armrests tightly.*

scarf ['skɑrf] *n., irreg.* a long strip of cloth that is wrapped around the neck or face to keep someone warm when it is cold. (Pl: **scarves.**) ♦ *Mary wrapped a scarf around her neck when she walked to the store.* ♦ *John covered his mouth and nose with his scarf while outside.*

scarlet ['skɑr lɪt] **1.** *n.* a bright red color. (No plural form in this sense.) ♦ *The artist painted the image of blood a deep scarlet.* ♦ *The scarlet in John's tie clashes with his orange shirt.* **2.** *adj.* bright red in color. ♦ *The cardinal has scarlet feathers.* ♦ *The performer wore scarlet lipstick onstage.*

scarves ['skɑrvz] pl of scarf.

scary ['skɛr i] *adj.* frightening; causing fear; filling one with fear; causing one to be afraid. (Adv: *scarily.* Comp: *scarier;* sup: *scariest.*) ♦ *The scary movie frightened the audience.* ♦ *Driving through the terrible blizzard was very scary.*

scathing ['skeð ɪŋ] *adj.* very cruel, severe, or critical. (Adv: *scathingly.*) ♦ *The scathing review caused the play to close sooner than planned.* ♦ *The professor's scathing comments hurt the student's feelings.*

scatter ['skæt ɚ] **1.** *tv.* to cause each person or thing in a group to move in a different direction. ♦ *The wind scattered the leaves on the ground.* ♦ *Dozens of books were scattered across my desk.* **2.** *tv.* to sprinkle something; to spread things over a wide area by throwing them. ♦ *The seeds had been scattered across the field.* ♦ *Mary scattered breadcrumbs on the ground for the pigeons.* **3.** *iv.* [for each person or thing in a group] to move in a different direction. ♦ *The papers on my desk scattered when the wind blew.* ♦ *The robbers scattered when the police arrived.*

scatterbrain ['skæt ɚ bren] *n.* someone who is incapable of serious thought; someone who is forgetful or thoughtless. ♦ *What scatterbrain forgot to lock the door?* ♦ *Don't depend on John to watch your pet when you're on vacation; he's a scatterbrain.*

scatterbrained ['skæt ɚ brend] *adj.* unable to think seriously; forgetful; thoughtless. ♦ *The scatterbrained secretary filed the letters incorrectly.* ♦ *My scatterbrained lawyer was an hour late for our appointment.*

scattered ['skæt ɚd] *adj.* sprinkled; spread over a wide area. (Adv: *scatteredly.*) ♦ *The scattered seeds sprouted into plants.* ♦ *The pigeons pecked at the scattered breadcrumbs.*

scavenger ['skæv ɪn dʒɚ] **1.** *n.* an animal that lives by eating anything it can find. ♦ *Vultures are scavengers that eat rotting carcasses.* ♦ *The campers' leftover food was soon eaten by scavengers.* **2.** *n.* someone who picks through trash, looking for useful things or things that can be sold. (Figurative on ①.) ♦ *The scavenger searched the garbage bin for scrap metal.* ♦ *I bought an old wooden desk from the neighborhood scavenger.* **3.** *n.* someone or a company that picks up and removes trash as a business. ♦ *I paid the scavenger $100 to take my trash away when I moved.* ♦ *The scavengers loaded my old refrigerator onto their truck.*

scenario [sɪ 'nɛr i o] **1.** *n.* a summary of the plot of a story, movie, or play. (Pl in *-s.*) ♦ *The scenario of* Romeo and Juliet *is similar to that of* West Side Story. ♦ *The teacher outlined the scenario of the play in class.* **2.** *n.* a possible outcome; a possible result of an event; a possible action. (Pl in *-s.*) ♦ *The report lists six possible scenarios if funds are not granted.* ♦ *The worst scenario would be if my credit card was stolen in a foreign country.*

scene ['sin] **1.** *n.* all that can be seen from one place. ♦ *The tourist surveyed the scene from the castle's window.* ♦ *The sun setting over the mountains was a beautiful scene.* **2.** *n.* the place where something happens; a setting. ♦ *The police rushed to the scene of the crime.* ♦ *This street corner is the scene of many fights.* **3.** *n.* a division of an act of a play; an incident in a movie or play. ♦ *I left the horrible play in the first scene of the first act.* ♦ *The opening scene of the movie was filmed on location.* **4.** *n.* a display of emotion or action, especially an angry or violent action. ♦ *Everyone stared at the customer who was making a terrible scene.* ♦ *If there is going to be a scene, I'm leaving.* **5.** *n.* a situation or a particular sphere of activity. (Informal.) ♦ *John was totally unfamiliar with the bowling scene.* ♦ *Since I'm new to this scene, could you explain a few things to me?*

scenery ['sin (ə) ri] **1.** *n.* the natural surroundings, trees, mountains, etc., of an area. (No plural form in this sense.) ♦ *The mountainous state was known for its beautiful scenery.* ♦ *The tourism department described the country's natural scenery.* **2.** *n.* the things that are built or bought and put on a stage to represent the place where the action of a play takes place. (No plural form in this sense.) ♦ *Four actors were injured when the scenery collapsed on the stage.* ♦ *Scenery can help establish the mood of a play.*

scenic ['sin ɪk] **1.** *adj.* <the adj. form of scenery ①.> (Adv: *scenically* [...ɪk li].) ♦ *The tourist marveled at the land's scenic beauty.* ♦ *The travelers stopped their car at the scenic overlook.* **2.** *adj.* <the adj. form of scenery ②.> (Adv: *scenically* [...ɪk li].) ♦ *The play's set was created by a professional scenic designer.* ♦ *The scenic artist painted the set realistically.*

scent ['sɛnt] **1.** *n.* a smell; an aroma; an odor; the way someone or something smells. ♦ *The scent of certain perfumes makes me sneeze.* ♦ *A chemical is added to natural gas to give it a scent.* **2.** *tv.* to sense the smell of someone or something. ♦ *The dogs scented the criminal's trail.* ♦ *I scented a cigarette smoker somewhere in the room.* **3.** *tv.* to cause an area to have a certain smell. ♦ *The room deodorizer scented the air with a pleasant smell.* ♦ *The cabin was scented with cedar.*

schedule ['skɛ dʒəl] **1.** *n.* a list showing the times that events are supposed to happen. ♦ *According to the schedule, the plane should have landed by now.* ♦ *My secretary showed me my schedule for the afternoon.* **2.** *n.* a form with blanks where information is written, especially a tax form. ♦ *My accountant remarked that I needed to complete Schedule A.* ♦ *Each schedule requires a different kind of detailed information.* **3.** *tv.* to put someone or something on a list or schedule for an event that happens at a particular time. ♦ *The dentist's first patient was scheduled for 9:30 A.M.* ♦ *They scheduled me for an early flight.* **4. behind schedule** *idiom* not done by the time listed on the schedule ①. ♦ *We have to hurry and finish soon because we are behind schedule.* ♦ *The project is behind schedule. Very late, in fact.* **5. ahead of schedule** *idiom* done before the time listed on the schedule ①. ♦ *I want to be able to finish the job ahead of schedule.* ♦ *We don't have to rush because we are ahead of schedule.*

scheduled ['skɛ dʒəld] *adj.* arranged; planned; placed on a schedule. ♦ *My scheduled appointment was canceled at the last minute.* ♦ *The scheduled flight to Cleveland will depart on time.*

schematic [ski 'mæt ɪk] **1.** *adj.* being in the form of a chart or graph; of or about a plan, chart, or diagram. (Adv: *schematically* [...ɪk li].) ♦ *The researcher's data was laid out in a schematic report.* ♦ *The architect showed the client some schematic drawings.* **2.** *n.* a chart, diagram, or plan. ♦ *Where are the schematics for the new radio circuit?* ♦ *I don't have the final drawings for the project, but there is one schematic in the conference room.*

scheme ['skim] **1.** *n.* a plan; a method for doing something; a way of doing something, possibly dishonestly. ♦ *The newspaper revealed the president's scheme to raise taxes.* ♦ *We discovered the crook's scheme for embezzling funds.* **2. color scheme** *n.* a set of selections of different colors that go well together. ♦ *The color scheme in my bathroom is pale blue and gray.* ♦ *I can't stand this color scheme!* **3.** *iv.* to plot; to make plans, especially dishonest ones. ♦ *The gambler schemed to recoup his losses.* ♦ *The criminal schemed and schemed, planning a bank robbery.*

scheming ['skim ɪŋ] *adj.* plotting or planning, especially in a dishonest way; crafty; sly. (Adv: *schemingly.*) ♦ *The scheming politician became very powerful.* ♦ *The scheming lawyer made a lot of money.*

schizophrenia [skɪt sə 'frɪn i ə] *n.* a mental illness that causes one to be unable to think or do things in a sane way and removes one from situations involving other people. (No plural form in this sense.) ♦ *The patient's schizophrenia could be controlled with medicine.* ♦ *Sometimes schizophrenia is triggered by a severe trauma.*

schizophrenic [skɪt sə 'frɛn ɪk] **1.** *adj.* <the adj. form of schizophrenia.> (Adv: *schizophrenically* [...ɪk li].) ♦ *The schizophrenic criminal received treatment in prison.* ♦ *A small percentage of drug addicts are also schizophrenic.* **2.** *n.* someone who has schizophrenia. ♦ *Many schizophrenics can function well as long as they take their medicine.* ♦ *The violent schizophrenic was committed to a mental institution.*

scholar ['skɑl ɚ] **1.** *n.* someone who studies a subject thoroughly. ♦ *My mother was a famous scholar in philosophy.* ♦ *The planetarium was operated by scholars and talented volunteers.* **2.** *n.* a student; a pupil. ♦ *In the library, many young scholars were studying for exams.* ♦ *The brilliant scholar learned Latin at the age of 12.* **3.** *n.* someone who has a scholarship. ♦ *The best scholars are housed on the dormitory's third floor.* ♦ *Each year, the scholars were required to apply again for their scholarships.*

scholarly ['skɑl ɚ li] **1.** *adj.* studious; concerning scholarship. ♦ *Her scholarly efforts earned her a fellowship at the university.* ♦ *The professor read dozens of scholarly journals.* **2.** *adj.* having a lot of knowledge about a certain subject. ♦ *Jane acts quite scholarly even though she has not gone to college.* ♦ *The old and scholarly professor lectured about physics.*

scholarship ['skɑl ɚ ʃɪp] **1.** *n.* knowledge that a person receives by studying; evidence of one's knowledge. (No plural form in this sense.) ♦ *Her scholarship in philosophy was quite weak.* ♦ *My four books are proof of my scholarship in economics.* **2.** *n.* money given by an organization to a student for tuition or other expenses related to studying. ♦ *Mary attended college on a sports scholarship.* ♦ *I applied for several scholarships to help pay for school.*

scholastic [skə 'læs tɪk] *adj.* of or about education or schools. (Adv: *scholastically* [...ɪk li].) ♦ *The students were known for their scholastic achievement.* ♦ *The educators debated about appropriate scholastic methods.*

school ['skul] **1.** *n.* a building for education and instruction. ♦ *The students have to be at school by 9:00 A.M.* ♦ *There are 800 students at the school where I teach.* **2.** *n.* all the people who work at and attend a school; all the people who study and teach at a school. ♦ *The whole school rooted for the football team.* ♦ *The principal spoke to the* *school about drug abuse.* **3.** *n.* a group of fish that swim together. ♦ *A school of fish swam toward the reef.* ♦ *We caught many fish from the school swimming under our boat.* **4.** *n.* the education system; school attendance. (No plural form in this sense.) ♦ *School is an important thing for young people.* ♦ *I am glad to be free from school.* **5. school in** *tv.* + *prep. phr.* to teach someone about something; to instruct someone about something; to train someone; to give someone an education. ♦ *My children are all schooled in the classics.* ♦ *The professor schooled her students in her own theoretical framework.* **6. school of thought** *idiom* a particular philosophy or way of thinking about something. ♦ *One school of thought holds that cats cause allergic reactions.* ♦ *I come from the school of thought that believes people should always be polite.* **7. from the old school** *idiom* holding attitudes or ideas that were popular and important in the past but are no longer considered relevant or in line with modern trends. ♦ *Grammar was not taught much in my son's school, but fortunately he had a teacher from the old school.* ♦ *Aunt Jane is from the old school. She never goes out without wearing a hat and gloves.*

schoolboy ['skul bɔɪ] *n.* a boy who attends school. ♦ *The schoolboys were required to wear dark blue ties.* ♦ *The teacher reprimanded the schoolboy for teasing Mary.*

schoolchild ['skul tʃaɪld] *n., irreg.* a child of elementary-school age; a child who attends school. (Pl: schoolchildren.) ♦ *Four schoolchildren were injured in the bus accident.* ♦ *The teacher told the schoolchild to stop running.*

schoolchildren ['skul tʃɪl drɪn] pl of schoolchild.

schoolgirl ['skul gɚl] *n.* a girl who attends school. ♦ *The nurse spoke to the schoolgirls about the onset of puberty.* ♦ *The schoolgirl answered the teacher's question.*

schooling ['skul ɪŋ] *n.* education, instruction, or training that is received at school. (No plural form in this sense.) ♦ *Where did you receive your schooling?* ♦ *The parents were not satisfied with their child's schooling.*

schoolroom ['skul rum] *n.* a room in a school building, especially one where students are taught. ♦ *The children decorated the schoolroom with their own art.* ♦ *Inside the schoolroom, there were 32 desks.*

schoolteacher ['skul titʃ ɚ] *n.* someone who teaches in a school. ♦ *The schoolteacher taught fractions to the students.* ♦ *Mary answered her schoolteacher's question.*

schoolwork ['skul wɚk] *n.* work that a student must do for a class; the assignments that a student must do. (See also homework. No plural form in this sense.) ♦ *Susie was not allowed to watch TV until she finished her schoolwork.* ♦ *Johnny left his schoolwork on the bus.*

schooner ['skun ɚ] *n.* a fast sailing ship that has at least two masts. ♦ *The schooner sailed from the harbor and into the bay.* ♦ *The wind carried the schooner across the ocean.*

schwa ['ʃwɑ] *n.* a vowel sound such as the *a* in *about* or the *o* in *bacon,* and represented in phonetics by [ə]. ♦ *In slurred speech, many vowels are pronounced as schwas.* ♦ *Schwas are usually found in the unstressed syllables of words.*

science ['saɪ əns] **1.** *n.* a system of knowledge obtained by testing and proving facts that describe the way something acts, functions, or exists. (No plural form in this sense.) ♦ *Science is the key to progress.* ♦ *The researcher's conclusions were well rooted in science.* **2.** *n.* one of the academic disciplines that results in a system of knowledge obtained by testing and proving facts that describe the way something acts, functions, or exists. ♦ *Biology is the science of living things.* ♦ *The science of sound is called acoustics.* **3.** *n.* a skill based on knowledge. (No plural form in this sense.) ♦ *Bob studied kitchen science in school.* ♦ *Getting the right kind of clothing for this cold weather is a real science!*

science fiction ['saɪ əns 'fɪk ʃən] *n.* literature that involves features of science, technology, or an imaginary future created by the author. (No plural form in this sense.) ♦ *In science fiction, many stories take place on other planets.* ♦ *Science fiction is a mixture of science and fantasy.*

scientific [saɪ ən 'tɪf ɪk] **1.** *adj.* using the laws or facts of a science. (Adv: *scientifically* [...ɪk li].) ♦ *I proved the theorem using scientific methods.* ♦ *The chemical was extracted by means of a scientific process.* **2.** *adj.* of or about science. (Adv: *scientifically* [...ɪk li].) ♦ *Our school purchased a lot of new scientific equipment.* ♦ *The library has a large number of scientific journals.*

scientist ['saɪ ən tɪst] *n.* someone who is skilled in a science; someone who works in a science. ♦ *The scientist exposed the laboratory mice to radiation.* ♦ *The scientist explained the theory of relativity to me.*

scissors ['sɪz ɚz] *n.* a set of two sharp blades that have handles on one end and are connected in the middle. (Treated as singular or plural. Number is expressed with *pair(s) of scissors.* Also a singular: **scissor**.) ♦ *You should carry scissors with the sharp end pointed downward.* ♦ *John cut the paper with scissors.*

scoff ['skɔf] *iv.* to ridicule (someone or something); to cast doubt on someone or something. ♦ *The scientist scoffed at the student's shoddy research.* ♦ *The atheist scoffed when John mentioned God.*

scold ['skold] **1.** *tv.* to speak angrily to someone who has done something wrong. ♦ *The teacher scolded Jimmy for running in the classroom.* ♦ *The boss scolded John for coming to work late.* **2.** *n.* someone who scolds as in ①. ♦ *My teacher is such a scold!* ♦ *Tom's mother is a terrible scold.*

scolding ['skold ɪŋ] *n.* speaking angrily to someone as punishment. ♦ *The principal gave Susie a scolding for swearing in class.* ♦ *Mary gave Johnny a scolding for knocking over her vase.*

scoop ['skup] **1.** *n.* a shovel-like utensil or tool. ♦ *The laundry detergent came with a small plastic scoop.* ♦ *John removed the dead leaves from the swimming pool with a scoop.* **2.** *n.* the contents of ①. ♦ *Mary added a scoop of sugar to the lemonade.* ♦ *David put a scoop of detergent in the washing machine.* **3.** *n.* an important piece of new information. (Informal.) ♦ *The star reporter gave us the scoop on the latest scandal.* ♦ *I finally got the scoop on the new tax laws.* **4.** *n.* the first and earliest report of a news event. ♦ *John's report of the robbery was a scoop for the local newspaper.* ♦ *Mary wanted to get a scoop for the television station she worked for.* **5.** *tv.* to beat someone by publishing or broadcasting a new piece of news first. ♦ *Channel 6 scooped Channel 2 on the mayor's tax increase.* ♦ *The reporter from the* Times *scooped the reporters from the other newspapers.* **6. scoop up** *tv.* + *adv.* to gather things together; to pick things up quickly or carelessly. ♦ *John* *scooped up his possessions and left the office.* ♦ *I quickly scooped up the papers I dropped on the sidewalk.*

scoot ['skut] *iv.* to move somewhere quickly. ♦ *David scooted to the bathroom because he felt sick.* ♦ *Mary scooted quickly to the comfortable chair before anyone else got it.*

scooter ['skut ɚ] **1.** *n.* a vehicle for children, made of two wheels, one in front of the other, having a platform in between, and a set of handlebars. ♦ *A scooter is moved by placing one foot on the platform and pushing against the ground with the other foot.* ♦ *The children rode around the park on their scooters.* **2.** *n.* a small motorcycle. ♦ *Mary drives a scooter from her apartment to school.* ♦ *The police officer patrolled the park on a scooter.*

scope ['skop] **1.** *n.* the range of something; the limit of something; the extent of something. (No plural form in this sense.) ♦ *Those questions aren't within the scope of my research.* ♦ *Calculus is beyond the scope of someone just learning algebra.* **2.** *n.* a small telescope on the barrel of a rifle or other weapon, used to aim the weapon. ♦ *The marksman looked through the scope and then fired the gun.* ♦ *If the scope is misaligned, you'll miss your target.*

scorch ['skortʃ] **1.** *tv.* to burn something so that burn marks are made but the object is not destroyed. ♦ *John scorched his shirt with an iron.* ♦ *Mary scorched her hair with a curling iron.* **2.** *iv.* to be burned as in ①. ♦ *The papers near the fire scorched but did not burn.* ♦ *My shirt will scorched if I set the iron on it.*

scorched ['skortʃt] **1.** *adj.* burned; having burn marks. ♦ *John threw away the scorched shirt.* ♦ *I ate the scorched potatoes anyway.* **2.** *adj.* very hot and dry. ♦ *The nomads crossed the scorched desert.* ♦ *The lawn is scorched and desperately needs rain.*

scorching ['skortʃ ɪŋ] *adj.* very hot and dry. (Adv: *scorchingly.*) ♦ *The pond dried up in the scorching heat.* ♦ *It was scorching outside, so I wore just a bathing suit.*

score ['skor] **1.** *n.* the number of points that a person or team has received in a game or contest; the number of points that a person has received on a test. ♦ *At the end of the baseball game, the score was 5–1.* ♦ *The best student only got a score of 89 on the difficult test.* **2.** *n.* a written piece of music for instruments or voices. ♦ *The violinist arranged the score on her music stand.* ♦ *The score was written for four voices.* **3.** *n.* a group of twenty things. ♦ *"Four score and seven years" means 87 years.* ♦ *Scores of people were injured in the accident.* **4.** *tv.* to earn one or more points in a game or contest. ♦ *When you score a touchdown in football, it's worth 6 points.* ♦ *Bill scored a point for the team when he touched home plate.* **5.** *tv.* to cut lines or grooves into a surface; to cut a surface with a series of lines. ♦ *The designer scored the cardboard before splitting it in half.* ♦ *Carefully score the pane of glass with a sharp tool and bend the glass to break it smoothly.* **6. score for** *tv.* + *prep. phr.* to write down the notes of a piece of music for instruments or voices. ♦ *The composer scored his composition for the orchestra in one year.* ♦ *This piece is scored for piano and violins.* **7.** *tv.* to earn a certain number of points on a test. ♦ *If you score a 90, you'll get an A.* ♦ *The best student scored a 100 on the final exam.* **8.** *iv.* to achieve [a level of performance in academic grades]. ♦ *None of the students in the class scored above an 80.* ♦ *Jane scored at the top of her class on the test.* **9.** *iv.* to earn [a point in a game or contest]. ♦ *Anne threw the basketball toward the hoop and scored.* ♦ *The contestant scores for each correct answer he gives.*

scoreboard ['skor bord] *n.* a display that shows the score of a game while the game is being played. ♦ *In addition to the score, the scoreboard showed the time.* ♦ *We could see the scoreboard clearly from our seats at the stadium.*

scorn ['skorn] **1.** *n.* contempt shown toward someone or something; derision; disdain. (No plural form in this sense.) ♦ *The disgruntled worker showed scorn towards his employer.* ♦ *The minister did not hide his scorn for sinners.* **2.** *n.* someone or something that is held in contempt; someone or something that is derided or disdained. ♦ *The player who lost the game was the scorn of the team.* ♦ *Traffic is the scorn of my workday.* **3.** *tv.* to show contempt toward someone or something; to look down on someone or something; to deride someone or something. ♦ *The hard workers scorned the lazy worker.* ♦ *The team scorned the player who lost the game.*

scornful ['skorn fʊl] *adj.* showing scorn; disdainful. (Adv: *scornfully.*) ♦ *The scornful worker damaged the office equipment.* ♦ *Scornful students shouted at the principal.*

scorpion ['skor pi ən] *n.* a large insect that has a long tail with a poisonous stinger on the end of it. ♦ *The camper stung by the scorpion was rushed to the hospital.* ♦ *Scorpions are often found in deserts.*

Scotch ['skɑtʃ] **1.** *adj.* of or about the people and culture of Scotland; Scottish. (Scottish is used more often than Scotch, especially when referring to people.) ♦ *David speaks English with a Scotch accent.* ♦ *We drank authentic Scotch whiskey in Glasgow.* **2. scotch** *n.* a kind of whiskey made in Scotland from barley. (No plural form in this sense.) ♦ *I drank a shot of scotch at the bar.* ♦ *We ordered some scotch to drink with our dinner.* **3. scotch** *n.* a drink or serving of ②. ♦ *David ordered scotches for his friends and a beer for himself.* ♦ *Would you like a scotch, or perhaps some pop?*

scot-free ['skɑt 'fri] *adv.* without burden; without punishment or harm. ♦ *Amazingly, the criminal walked away from the trial scot-free.* ♦ *The corrupt politician left office scot-free.*

Scotland ['skɑt lənd] See Gazetteer.

Scottish ['skɑt ɪʃ] *adj.* of or about the people, land, and culture of Scotland. (Scottish is used more often than Scotch, especially when referring to people.) ♦ *My family emigrated from the Scottish hills.* ♦ *Even though Bill left Scotland when he was a child, he still speaks with a Scottish accent.*

scoundrel ['skɑʊn drəl] *n.* a rascal; a villain; someone who is wicked or dishonest. ♦ *The scoundrel who stole my car was caught.* ♦ *The police arrested the scoundrel who tried to mug me.*

scour ['skɑʊ ɚ] **1.** *tv.* to clean something by rubbing with a lot of force. ♦ *I scoured the metal pans with steel wool.* ♦ *Dave scoured the carpet with rug cleaner.* **2.** *tv.* to search a place thoroughly while looking for someone or something. ♦ *The police scoured the area for the missing child.* ♦ *Bob scoured the park for his missing dog.*

scourge ['skordʒ] **1.** *n.* something, especially a whip, used to punish someone. ♦ *The master used a scourge to beat his slaves.* ♦ *The victim had wounds where he had been hit with a scourge.* **2.** *n.* someone or something that causes trouble or suffering. (Figurative on ①.) ♦ *Mary's rotten children are her scourge.* ♦ *My awful job is the scourge of my existence.* **3.** *tv.* to punish someone, especially with a whip. ♦ *The torturer scourged the prisoners with a whip.* ♦ *They scourged me and kicked me in prison.*

scout ['skaʊt] **1.** *n.* someone who is sent to get information about the terrain, an enemy, or a competitor. ♦ *The scout surveyed the valley from the ridge.* ♦ *The scout spied on the village during the night.* **2.** *tv.* to search a large area, looking for someone or something. ♦ *The inspector scouted the streets for the spy.* ♦ *The security guard scouted the whole city for the robber.* **3. scout around for someone or something** *idiom* to search here and there for someone or something. ♦ *Tom is scouting around for a date for Friday night.* ♦ *Please scout around for some ideas on what to cook for dinner.*

scowl ['skaʊl] **1.** *n.* a frown; an angry look. ♦ *From Anne's scowl, I knew that she was upset.* ♦ *Wipe that scowl off your face!* **2.** *iv.* to look angry; to frown. ♦ *When David scowls, he curls his lower lip.* ♦ *Mary scowled at the loud people sitting next to her.*

scowling ['skaʊl ɪŋ] *adj.* looking angry; frowning. (Adv: *scowlingly.*) ♦ *Mary sent her scowling daughter to her bedroom.* ♦ *The clerk tried to satisfy the scowling customer.*

scrabble ['skræb əl] **scrabble up** *iv.* + *prep. phr.* to climb or crawl up something quickly; to scramble, grasping with fingers or claws. ♦ *The squirrel scrabbled up the tree away from the dog.* ♦ *The soldiers scrabbled up the cliff.*

scramble ['skræm bəl] **1.** *tv.* to mix objects up; to move objects around; to put objects in a different order; to mix objects together. ♦ *The magician scrambled the cards that I had chosen with the rest of the deck.* ♦ *Someone scrambled the files in my drawer.* **2.** *tv.* to cook a mixture of egg whites and yolks. ♦ *Mary scrambled an egg for breakfast.* ♦ *John scrambled two eggs and served them with toast.* **3.** *tv.* to distort or change a radio or television signal, either to prevent people from receiving it or to prevent its reception without a special device to decode it. ♦ *The government scrambled the enemy's propaganda broadcasts.* ♦ *The cable channels that I don't pay for are scrambled.* **4. scramble for** *iv.* + *prep. phr.* to struggle for something; to struggle to reach something. ♦ *The six candidates all scrambled for the party's nomination.* ♦ *The women scrambled for the bouquet that the bride had thrown.* **5. scramble up** *iv.* + *prep. phr.* to climb up or crawl up something quickly. ♦ *The mountain goat scrambled up the hillside.* ♦ *Bob scrambled up the stairs to get to class on time.*

scrambled ['skræm bəld] **1.** *adj.* mixed up; put in a different order. ♦ *The magician put the scrambled deck of cards in the correct order.* ♦ *David rearranged the scrambled files.* **2.** *adj.* [of radio or television signals] distorted or changed, needing to be decoded. ♦ *The scrambled radio signal prevented the enemy's propaganda from being heard.* ♦ *The cable television channel broadcasts scrambled movies that you have to pay more money to see.* **3. scrambled eggs** *n.* eggs that have been cooked with the whites and the yolks mixed together. (Treated as plural.) ♦ *These scrambled eggs are too runny.* ♦ *John served some scrambled eggs with toast.*

scrap ['skræp] **1.** *n.* a small piece of something, especially a small piece of something that is left over from a larger piece, especially of food or cloth. ♦ *Jane fed scraps of meat to her dog.* ♦ *John threw all the scraps into the trash.* **2.** *n.* material, such as metal, that can be reused. (No plural form in this sense.) ♦ *John sold his old car for scrap.* ♦ *The old tin cans were sold as scrap.* **3.** *tv.* to throw something away that is no longer wanted, needed, or usable. ♦ *Mary scrapped her broken radio.* ♦ *The manager scrapped the failed project.*

scrapbook ['skræp bʊk] *n.* a book with blank pages that one fastens pictures, newspaper articles, small souvenirs, and other small objects to. ♦ *Mary kept pictures of her pets in her scrapbook.* ♦ *John taped the concert ticket stub in his scrapbook.*

scrape ['skrep] **1.** *tv.* to damage something by rubbing a sharp or rough object against it. ♦ *Bob scraped the wall with a knife, damaging the wallpaper.* ♦ *I scraped my car when I drove into the bushes.* **2.** *tv.* to remove something by scraping and rubbing. ♦ *Jane scraped crumbs off the counter.* ♦ *The janitor scraped the dried gum from the bottom of the chairs.* **3.** *iv.* to rub forcefully against something else. ♦ *The car scraped on the brick wall as it passed.* ♦ *The knife scraped against the wall.* **4. scrape by** *iv.* + *adv.* to have just enough; to survive. ♦ *I barely scraped by on minimum wage.* ♦ *The refugees scraped by on a day-to-day basis.* **5.** *n.* damage or injury to an object or skin caused by rubbing something sharp or rough against it. ♦ *I got a bad scrape on my knee when I fell onto the pavement.* ♦ *Bill was in an accident but only suffered a few minor scrapes.* **6.** *n.* the sound that is made when one object scrapes ③ against something else. ♦ *The scrape of fingernails against a chalkboard is horrendous.* ♦ *I heard the scrape of the car against the garage door.* **7. have a scrape (with someone or something)** *idiom* to have a small battle or encounter with someone or something. ♦ *I had a scrape with the county sheriff.* ♦ *John and Bill had a scrape, but they are friends again now.* **8. scrape something together; scrape something up** *idiom* to find and collect something; to locate and assemble a group of things. ♦ *Mary scraped a few dollars together for some new books.* ♦ *John barely scraped up enough money to pay his rent.*

scraper ['skrep ɚ] *n.* a tool that is used to scrape with, especially a tool with a sharp edge. ♦ *Mary used a scraper to remove the ice from her car's windshield.* ♦ *Jane removed paint from the window with a scraper.*

scratch ['skrætʃ] **1.** *tv.* to damage an object's surface by causing a sharp object to make a cut or tear in it; to make a cut or tear in the surface of something with a sharp object. ♦ *Mary scratched the marble floor when she dragged a chair across it.* ♦ *The cat scratched the piano leg with its claws.* **2.** *tv.* to remove something from the surface of something using a sharp object to cut or tear into it. ♦ *Bill scratched the paint off the window with his fingernail.* ♦ *Bob scratched the sticky price tag from the vase with the edge of a dime.* **3.** *tv.* to rub a location of the body that itches with one's fingers, fingernails, or a sharp object. ♦ *Dave scratched his arm because it itched.* ♦ *I scratched my shoulder.* **4.** *iv.* to rub [a part of the body that itches]. ♦ *Bob scratched because he felt itchy.* ♦ *Because the puppy was scratching, I gave it a bath.* **5.** *n.* a cut, tear, or mark made by scratching. ♦ *There are scratches on my arm where my cat clawed me.* ♦ *When you moved the desk, you put a scratch in the wall.* **6.** *n.* the sound of something scratching against something else. ♦ *I heard a scratch at the door,* *so I let the dog in.* ♦ *The scratch of branches against the window woke me up.* **7. make something from scratch** *idiom* to make something by starting with the basic ingredients. ♦ *We made the cake from scratch, using no prepared ingredients.* ♦ *I didn't have a ladder, so I made one from scratch.* **8. start from scratch** *idiom* to start from the beginning; to start from nothing. ♦ *Whenever I write a story, I start from scratch.* ♦ *I built every bit of my own house. I started from scratch and did everything with my own hands.*

scrawl ['skrɔl] **1.** *n.* bad handwriting; writing that is hard to read because it is messy. ♦ *The pharmacist couldn't read the doctor's scrawl on the prescription.* ♦ *Is this scrawl supposed to be your signature?* **2.** *tv.* to write something in a messy way; to write something using bad handwriting. ♦ *John scrawled his name at the bottom of the check.* ♦ *Because Mary scrawled the note so quickly, I couldn't read it.* **3.** *iv.* to write in a messy way; to write using bad handwriting. ♦ *Because the doctor scrawled, the pharmacist couldn't read the prescription.* ♦ *The teacher told the students to write neatly and not scrawl.*

scrawny ['skrɔn i] *adj.* skinny; not having much muscle. (Adv: *scrawnily.* Comp: *scrawnier;* sup: *scrawniest.*) ♦ *The scrawny child couldn't lift heavy objects.* ♦ *The scrawny woman studied karate so she could defend herself.*

scream ['skrim] **1.** *iv.* [for someone] to make a very loud noise, especially when hurt, afraid, excited, emotional, or surprised. ♦ *John screamed right before a truck hit our car.* ♦ *When the monster appeared on the screen, the audience screamed.* **2.** *iv.* to speak very loudly; to talk in a very loud voice. ♦ *I can hear you fine, you don't have to scream at me.* ♦ *This is a bad phone connection. You'll have to scream.* **3.** *tv.* to say something in a very loud voice. ♦ *Mary screamed her response because John doesn't hear well.* ♦ *David screamed, "Let's go home!" over the roar of the party.* **4.** *n.* a very loud noise, especially made by someone who is hurt, afraid, excited, emotional, or surprised. ♦ *John's scream from behind the curtain frightened me.* ♦ *Sue let out a scream of surprise when she opened the box.*

screaming ['skrim ɪŋ] **1.** *adj.* very loud; expressing oneself with screams. ♦ *The parents took their screaming children home early.* ♦ *The screaming speaker blamed everyone else for his problems.* **2.** *n.* the noise that is made when one screams. (No plural form in this sense.) ♦ *We heard the screaming of the tenants as they ran from their burning apartment building.* ♦ *My neighbor's screaming woke me up at 4:00 A.M.*

screech ['skritʃ] **1.** *n.* a shrill, high-pitched scream; a shrill, high-pitched noise made by a machine or when something rubs against something else. ♦ *The car came to a halt with a loud screech of its brakes.* ♦ *I couldn't hear music over the screech of the factory whistle.* **2.** *iv.* to make a shrill, high-pitched noise as in ①. ♦ *The car screeched to a halt at the intersection.* ♦ *The subway wheels screeched against the rails.* **3.** *tv.* to say something in a shrill, high-pitched voice. ♦ *John screeched "Yes!" when I asked if I was bothering him.* ♦ *Mary screeched her reply over the loud music.*

screeching ['skritʃ ɪŋ] *adj.* making a shrill, high-pitched noise. (Adv: *screechingly.*) ♦ *The screeching children gave the teacher a headache.* ♦ *After hearing the screeching brakes, I heard a loud crash.*

screen ['skrin] **1.** *n.* a mesh made of thin wires crossing each other. ♦ *The window screen lets air in and keeps flies out.* ♦ *John put screens on the windows in April.* **2.** *n.* a piece of cloth stretched over a frame, used to block, protect, or separate someone or something from someone or something else. ♦ *The spy hid behind a screen and heard everything.* ♦ *The actress changed costumes behind a screen backstage.* **3.** *n.* a large white surface that movies are projected onto. ♦ *The unruly audience threw popcorn at the movie screen.* ♦ *An image of a large red rose flashed onto the screen.* **4.** *n.* the glass part of a television set or computer monitor on which images are seen. ♦ *John wiped the dust from the television screen.* ♦ *Susan read the data on Mary's computer screen.* **5.** *tv.* to block, protect, or separate someone or something from someone or something. ♦ *The dark clouds screened the sun from my view.* ♦ *A partition screened the contestants from the audience.* **6.** *tv.* to determine if someone will be allowed to speak or meet with someone else. ♦ *A receptionist screened the executive's telephone calls.* ♦ *A butler screened the diplomat's visitors.* **7.** *tv.* to listen to a telephone caller leave a message on an answering machine instead of picking up the phone when it rings. ♦ *Jane bought an answering machine so she could screen her calls.* ♦ *David, if you're screening your calls, pick up the phone!* **8.** *tv.* to show a movie; to make a movie available to the public. ♦ *The new movie was screened at the auditorium last night.* ♦ *Hometown Theater will screen an award-winning drama tomorrow afternoon.*

screening ['skrin ɪŋ] **1.** *n.* the showing of a movie. ♦ *Dozens of celebrities attended the movie screening.* ♦ *Bill spoke to the director at the screening of her film.* **2.** *n.* a screen; the material used to make screens. (No plural form in this sense.) ♦ *The bullet tore a hole in the mesh screening.* ♦ *Fresh air can pass through screening.*

screenplay ['skrin ple] *n.* the script of a movie; the story of a movie written as a manuscript. ♦ *The studio asked the author to write two screenplays.* ♦ *The director adapted a famous novel into a screenplay.*

screw ['skru] **1.** *n.* a piece of metal, similar to a nail, having a spiral groove around its shaft. (A screw has a flat or rounded head that has a single groove or two crossed grooves.) ♦ *Mary tightened the screw with a screwdriver.* ♦ *The metal chair was held together with screws.* **2.** *tv.* to fasten something to something else with ①. ♦ *The carpenter screwed the boards to the wall.* ♦ *Mary screwed the hinges to the cabinet door.* **3.** *tv.* to twist ① into wood or metal with a screwdriver. ♦ *Tom screwed the screw into the wood.* ♦ *Screw one of these into each board.* **4.** *tv.* to turn the lid, cap, or top of a container to close it tightly. ♦ *John screwed the cap onto the tube of toothpaste.* ♦ *Mary screwed the lid on tightly.* **5. screw into** *tv.* + *prep. phr.* to twist or contort something into a shape. ♦ *Mary screwed her face into a grotesque grimace.* ♦ *The gymnast screwed his body into a knot.*

screwdriver ['skru draɪv ɚ] *n.* a very common tool used to tighten and loosen screws. ♦ *A regular screwdriver fits into a narrow groove.* ♦ *Jane kept a screwdriver in her tool kit.*

scribble ['skrɪb əl] **1.** *tv.* to draw or write something quickly or in a messy way, especially so that it is hard to recognize or read. ♦ *Write carefully and don't scribble your name.* ♦ *My professor scribbled a few comments in the mar-*

gins of my paper. **2.** *iv.* to draw or write quickly or in a messy way so that the result is hard to recognize or read. ♦ *The two-year-old child scribbled with a crayon.* ♦ *The artist scribbled on the canvas and called it art.* **3.** *n.* markings or words that are hard to recognize or read because they were drawn or written quickly or in a messy way. ♦ *John washed the child's scribble off the wall.* ♦ *How do you expect me to be able to read this scribble?*

scribe ['skrɑɪb] *n.* someone who made copies of documents by hand, especially in the days before books were printed. ♦ *The scribe wrote down the king's proclamation.* ♦ *Bibles were once copied one at a time by scribes.*

scrimmage ['skrɪm ɪdʒ] **1.** *n.* a football game played for practice. ♦ *The quarterback was injured during a scrimmage.* ♦ *The seniors played against the juniors in the scrimmage.* **2.** *iv.* to play a practice game of football. ♦ *The seniors scrimmaged against the juniors on the varsity team.* ♦ *As practice, the team scrimmaged the day before the big game.*

scrimp ['skrɪmp] *iv.* to attempt to preserve one's money by buying only what is needed and practicing thrift. ♦ *John scrimped and saved, but he still couldn't afford his rent.* ♦ *Mary scrimped until she had enough money to buy a car.*

script ['skrɪpt] **1.** *n.* a document containing the words of a play, movie, or speech. ♦ *The actors underlined their own lines in their scripts.* ♦ *The playwright refused to change a single word of his script.* **2.** *n.* a way of writing so that the letters of a word are joined together; handwriting. ♦ *Script is written by hand.* ♦ *The lawyer wrote with a neat, precise script.* **3.** *tv.* to write the words for a play, movie, or speech. ♦ *The playwright scripted the actors' words with great skill.* ♦ *A ghostwriter scripted the president's speech.*

scripture ['skrɪp tʃɚ] *n.* holy writings; one or more holy writings. ♦ *The minister quoted from New Testament scriptures.* ♦ *The Koran is the book of Islamic scripture.*

scroll ['skrol] **1.** *n.* a document that is rolled up. (It is unrolled to be read.) ♦ *The queen's proclamation was written on a scroll.* ♦ *The scribe wrote the information on a scroll.* **2.** *iv.* to move upward or downward through a computer file on a computer monitor. ♦ *Mary scrolled ahead in the document to read the end of it.* ♦ *John scrolled through the document, looking for mistakes.*

scrub ['skrʌb] **1.** *tv.* to clean or wash the surface of someone or something by rubbing. ♦ *Mary scrubbed her hands with soap.* ♦ *John scrubbed the carpet thoroughly.* **2.** *tv.* to remove something from something by rubbing. ♦ *Mary scrubbed the dirt from her hands.* ♦ *John scrubbed the stain from the carpet.* **3.** *tv.* to cancel something; to cause something not to happen. (Informal.) ♦ *We scrubbed the picnic because of the rain.* ♦ *The organizers scrubbed the conference due to lack of interest.* **4.** *iv.* to clean or wash [oneself] by rubbing, usually with a stiff brush, cloth, or sponge. ♦ *I scrubbed and scrubbed, but I couldn't remove the ink from my fingers.* ♦ *The doctors and nurses scrubbed before surgery.* **5.** *n.* an area of small trees and low bushes. (No plural form in this sense.) ♦ *Nothing will grow in this poor soil except scrub.* ♦ *I cleared the scrub from the soil, but grass wouldn't grow.*

scrumptious ['skrʌmp ʃəs] *adj.* very delicious; good to eat; tasty. (Adv: *scrumptiously.*) ♦ *This soup is scrumptious. Can I have some more?* ♦ *The children ate all of the scrumptious dessert.*

scruples ['skrup əlz] *n.* morals; a feeling that stops someone from doing something wrong. (Treated as plural.) ♦ *The lawyer had no scruples about defending rich guilty people.* ♦ *Because of my scruples, I was unable to keep the money I found.*

scrutinize ['skrut n ɑɪz] *tv.* to examine someone or something closely; to look at something very closely; to inspect someone or something. ♦ *My lawyer scrutinized my contract carefully.* ♦ *Jane scrutinized her lease before signing it.*

scrutiny ['skrut n i] **1.** *n.* a close examination; an inspection; looking at something closely. (No plural form in this sense.) ♦ *I gave the contract a lot of scrutiny, and it looks fine.* ♦ *This problem needs more scrutiny. I am sure it can be solved.* **2. under scrutiny** *idiom* being watched or examined closely. ♦ *Under close scrutiny, the jeweler found a flaw in the diamond.* ♦ *The suspect was kept under scrutiny throughout the investigation.*

scuba ['sku bə] **1. scuba (diving)** *n.* diving or exploration underwater with a portable breathing apparatus. (No plural form in this sense. An acronym for *self-contained underwater breathing apparatus.*) ♦ *Scuba requires special equipment and training.* ♦ *I wanted to learn scuba, but I don't swim well enough.* **2.** *iv.* to dive and explore underwater as in ①. ♦ *I took lessons so I could scuba in the nearby lake.* ♦ *I want to scuba, but I can't afford the equipment.* **3.** *adj.* <the adj. use of scuba.> ♦ *A good scuba tank is very expensive.* ♦ *I finally earned my scuba certification.*

scuba diver ['sku bə 'dɑɪv ɚ] *n.* someone who does scuba diving. ♦ *Some scuba divers appeared suddenly on the beach and frightened the swimmers.* ♦ *Scuba divers wear fins and use snorkels.*

scuba diving ['sku bə 'dɑɪv ɪŋ] See scuba.

scuff ['skʌf] **1.** *tv.* to make scratches in the surface of something clean and smooth; to make marks on the surface of something clean and smooth. ♦ *John scuffed the clean floor with his shoes.* ♦ *David scuffed the edges of my new book.* **2.** *tv.* to move one's feet as one walks without picking them up off the floor. ♦ *Tired, John scuffed his feet across the floor toward the couch.* ♦ *Mary scuffed her shoes across the marble floor.* **3.** *iv.* to walk somewhere without picking up one's feet; to slide one's feet along as one walks. ♦ *John built up static electricity as he scuffed across the rug.* ♦ *Tired, Mary scuffed along the carpet toward the bed.*

scuffed ['skʌft] *adj.* scratched or marked; having scratches or marks on a surface that was once clean or smooth. ♦ *I took the shoes back to the store because they were scuffed.* ♦ *I painted the scuffed and dented walls.*

scuffle ['skʌf əl] **1.** *iv.* to walk without picking up one's feet; to slide one's feet along as one walks. ♦ *The old man scuffled toward the door.* ♦ *Mary scuffled through the leaves as she walked through the park.* **2.** *tv.* to move one's feet as one walks without picking them up off the floor; to scuff or shuffle one's feet. ♦ *John scuffled his feet as he went toward the door.* ♦ *Don't scuffle your feet when you walk!* **3.** *n.* a walking movement that is made when one walks without picking up one's feet. ♦ *The hospital patient's scuffle was slow and weak.* ♦ *The children enjoyed* *a scuffle in the leaves.* **4.** *n.* a rough fight; a small battle. ♦ *There was a small scuffle over who was going to pay the bill.* ♦ *Three people were injured in a scuffle in the street.*

sculptor ['skʌlp tɚ] *n.* an artist who makes three-dimensional pieces of art out of clay, stone, metal, or other solid materials. ♦ *The sculptor shaped the clay into a bust of the president.* ♦ *The sculptor bent some metal rods into a work of art.*

sculpture ['skʌlp tʃɚ] **1.** *n.* the art of making three-dimensional pieces of art from clay, stone, metal, or another solid material. (No plural form in this sense.) ♦ *The art students all had to take a class in sculpture.* ♦ *Sculpture is the art of shaping solid materials.* **2.** *n.* a three-dimensional piece of art that is made out of clay, stone, metal, or another solid material. ♦ *With a pick, Mary made a sculpture from a block of ice.* ♦ *Don't touch any of the sculptures at the museum.* **3.** *tv.* to make a three-dimensional piece of art from clay, stone, metal, or another solid material. ♦ *The potter sculptured the clay into an ashtray.* ♦ *Bob sculptured the granite into a large round ball.*

scum ['skʌm] *n.* a layer of organic filth on the surface of something, especially water. (No plural form in this sense.) ♦ *After a week, the water in the bucket was covered with scum.* ♦ *The polluted river had a layer of green scum on its surface.*

scurry ['skɚ i] **1.** *iv.* to move quickly and busily; to hurry. ♦ *Mary scurried to class because she was late.* ♦ *John scurried around the office all morning.* **2.** *tv.* to cause someone to move quickly and busily. ♦ *Mary scurried her children out the door because they were late.* ♦ *Anne scurried the people into the meeting at 1:00 P.M.*

scuttle ['skʌt əl] *tv.* to cause a ship to sink by making holes in its bottom or sides; to sink a vessel by making holes in its bottom or sides. ♦ *A torpedo scuttled the large boat.* ♦ *The pirates scuttled the explorer's ship.*

scuttlebutt ['skʌt l bət] *n.* a rumor. (No plural form in this sense.) ♦ *What's the latest scuttlebutt about Bill?* ♦ *Have you heard the scuttlebutt about Mary's divorce?*

sea ['si] **1.** *n.* a large body of salt water that is smaller than an ocean. ♦ *The Mediterranean Sea is located south of Europe.* ♦ *The Baltic Sea separates Poland from Sweden.* **2.** *n.* one of the large bodies of salt water that cover almost three-fourths of the earth's surface; an ocean. ♦ *The ship set sail on the high seas.* ♦ *The old sailor had spent his life on the sea.* **3.** *n.* a large amount of things or people; an expanse; a large mass. (Figurative on ①.) ♦ *A sea of people moved toward the football stadium.* ♦ *The office manager's desk is invisible under a sea of paper.* **4. at sea** *phr.* on the sea ① or ②; away on a voyage on the ocean. ♦ *The ship is at sea now, and you can't disembark.* ♦ *I spent many happy days at sea on my cruise.* **5. at sea (about something)** *idiom* confused; lost and bewildered. ♦ *Mary is all at sea about getting married.* ♦ *When it comes to higher math, John is totally at sea.*

seacoast ['si kost] *n.* the land that borders a sea or an ocean; the coast of land along the sea. ♦ *We spent our vacation on the Mediterranean seacoast.* ♦ *The government protected the fragile seacoast from development.*

seafood ['si fud] *n.* animals from the sea, including fish, shellfish, octopus, and squid, that are eaten as food. (No plural form in this sense.) ♦ *The restaurants in the coastal town served a lot of seafood.* ♦ *Lobster is my favorite kind of seafood.*

seagull ['si gəl] *n.* a gull; a bird with long wings that lives near large bodies of water. ♦ *Hundreds of white seagulls flew above the beach.* ♦ *A seagull swooped down from the sky and caught a fish in its claws.*

seal ['sil] **1.** *n.* a large animal that has thick, bristly fur, lives in and near water, and has large flippers in place of arms and legs. ♦ *The circus seal was taught to clap its flippers together for the audience.* ♦ *Some seals can bark like a dog.* **2.** *n.* an official mark or design of a government, business, organization, or person, which is printed or stamped on objects for identification. ♦ *The flap of the envelope had the company's seal on it.* ♦ *The king placed his seal at the bottom of the proclamation.* **3.** *n.* a piece of wax, metal, or other material that has the mark or design of a government, business, organization, or person printed or stamped on it. ♦ *The scribe removed the wax seal from the scroll and unrolled it.* ♦ *Mary placed the company's seal on the confidential file.* **4.** *n.* something that causes an opening in an object to remain closed; something that prevents an opening from being opened without being detected. ♦ *When I twisted open the jar, I tore the plastic seal.* ♦ *Aspirin bottles have protective seals to prevent tampering.* **5.** *n.* a tight closure preventing an undetected opening. (No plural form in this sense.) ♦ *The seal was so tight that I couldn't open the container.* ♦ *The food inside the container spoiled because the seal was bad.* **6.** *n.* a type of paper stamp that functions as a ③. ♦ *I put a seal showing a picture of a dove on the back of my envelope.* ♦ *Mary uses decorative seals on her envelopes.* **7.** *n.* a mark or a sign that approves or confirms something. ♦ *The butcher sold only meat having the government's seal of approval.* ♦ *There was no government seal on the document.* **8.** *tv.* to close something tightly; to fasten something tightly, often with glue or pressure to create ⑤. ♦ *Please seal the soda bottle after you take what you want.* ♦ *I put the cucumbers in a quart jar and sealed the lid tightly.* **9.** *tv.* to fill cracks in an object with a substance so that air, water, or other things cannot pass through the cracks. ♦ *Dave sealed the space between the window and the frame with caulk.* ♦ *Mary sealed the cracks between the tiles with grout.* **10.** *tv.* to put or stamp ② or ③ onto a document. ♦ *The queen sealed the official document.* ♦ *The executive sealed the company's official letter.*

sealant ['si lənt] *n.* a substance that is put on the surface of an object to keep it from leaking; a substance used to seal something. (No plural form in this sense.) ♦ *The clerk sold me some sealant to protect my leather shoes.* ♦ *Mary painted her wooden patio with a waterproof sealant.*

sea level ['si lɛv əl] **1.** *n.* the altitude at the surface of the oceans, which is usually close to zero. ♦ *Sea level is exactly between low and high tide.* ♦ *The plane returned to sea level when it landed at an airport right by the ocean.* **2. at sea level** *phr.* located at ①. ♦ *It is easier to breathe at sea level than in the mountains.* ♦ *Boats on the ocean are at sea level, but those on rivers are not.*

sea lion ['si lɑɪ ən] *n.* a mammal with ears, related to the seal and found in the North Pacific Ocean and the waters of the Southern Hemisphere. ♦ *The city aquarium recently acquired a pair of sea lions.* ♦ *A sea lion died when it got stranded on the rocks.*

sealskin ['sil slɪn] **1.** *n.* the skin and fur of the seal. (No plural form in this sense.) ♦ *In the north, some people wear sealskin to keep warm.* ♦ *Sealskin is warm and soft.* **2.** *n.* a pelt of ①. ♦ *This coat is made of six sealskins.* ♦ *The merchant bought sealskins from the trapper.* **3.** *adj.* made from ①. ♦ *The fisherman wore a sealskin coat.* ♦ *The rich celebrity wore an expensive sealskin jacket.*

seam ['sim] **1.** *n.* the line of thread where two pieces of cloth have been sewn together. ♦ *The seam in my hem soon began to unravel.* ♦ *The seam in the seat of my pants split open!* **2.** *n.* the line where two edges of anything meet. ♦ *John caulked the seam between the window and the frame.* ♦ *A metal strip covered the seam between the carpet and the tile.* **3.** *tv.* to sew two pieces of cloth together; to make a ①. ♦ *The tailor seamed the hems of David's pant legs.* ♦ *I had to seam the skirt just a few minutes before the wedding.* **4. come apart at the seams** *idiom* to lose one's emotional self-control suddenly. ♦ *Bill was so upset that he almost came apart at the seams.* ♦ *I couldn't take any more. I just came apart at the seams.*

seaman ['si mən] *n., irreg.* a sailor or a member of the navy who is not an officer. (Pl: **seamen**.) ♦ *The seaman spotted the sinking ship.* ♦ *Dozens of seamen died in the naval battle.*

seamen ['si mən] pl of seaman.

seamstress ['sim strəs] *n.* a woman who earns her living by sewing; a woman who sews for a living. ♦ *The seamstress sewed the actors' torn costumes.* ♦ *The seamstress repaired the broken zipper in my jacket.*

séance ['se ɑns] *n.* a meeting in which a **medium** ⑥ tries to talk with the spirits of dead people. (From French.) ♦ *At the séance, the medium tried to contact the souls of the dead.* ♦ *Candles provided the only light during the séance.*

seaplane ['si plen] *n.* an airplane that can take off and land on water. ♦ *Food and supplies were brought to the tiny island by seaplane.* ♦ *The pilot landed the seaplane on the lagoon.*

seaport ['si port] *n.* a city on the coast of an ocean or sea that has a harbor where ships can dock. ♦ *Ships from around the globe were docked at the busy seaport.* ♦ *Anne lives in a quiet New England seaport.*

sear ['sɪr] **1.** *tv.* to burn the surface of someone or something with intense heat. ♦ *An intense laser beam seared the researcher's hand in the accident.* ♦ *The cook seared the chicken in the broiler.* **2.** *iv.* [for the surface of someone or something] to be burned in intense heat. ♦ *My skin seared in the hot summer sun.* ♦ *The meat seared over the campfire.*

search ['sɚtʃ] **1.** *iv.* to look carefully, trying to find someone or something. ♦ *The detective searched for hours, hoping to find a clue.* ♦ *David searched throughout the house for his lost keys.* **2.** *tv.* to examine someone or something closely to try to find something. ♦ *The police searched the scene of the crime for evidence.* ♦ *The townsfolk searched the woods for the missing child.* **3.** *n.* an attempt to find someone or something. ♦ *The inspector gave the crime scene a thorough search.* ♦ *John's search for his missing dog was fruitless.*

searchlight ['sɚtʃ lɑɪt] *n.* a very bright, strong beam of light that can be moved in any direction. ♦ *The searchlights swept back and forth over the prison grounds.* ♦ *The police cast their searchlights down the alley.*

seascape ['si skep] **1.** *n.* a view of the sea. ♦ *The seascape from my hotel window was breathtaking.* ♦ *Mary sat on the beach, admiring the seascape.* **2.** *n.* a picture or a painting of the sea. ♦ *Anne hung a seascape on her living-room wall.* ♦ *Standing on a cliff, the artist painted a brilliant seascape.*

seashell ['si ʃɛl] *n.* a shell of an animal that lives in the sea; a hard, protective covering made by an animal that lives in the sea, such as an oyster. ♦ *Anne walked along the beach, picking up pretty seashells.* ♦ *She sells seashells by the seashore.*

seashore ['si ʃor] *n.* the land that borders the sea; the shore that runs along a sea. ♦ *The seashore was coated with oil from a leaky ship.* ♦ *Anne rented a small cabin at the seashore for a relaxing week.*

seasick ['si sɪk] *adj.* being sick while on a boat or a ship because of the movement of the sea. ♦ *The seasick passenger went to the bathroom to vomit.* ♦ *Many passengers became seasick during the heavy storm.*

seasickness ['si sɪk nəs] *n.* the sickness that is caused by the movement of the sea while one is on a ship. (No plural form in this sense.) ♦ *Jane took a pill to prevent seasickness.* ♦ *Bill stayed in bed during the whole cruise because of seasickness.*

seaside ['si sɑɪd] **1.** *n.* the land that borders a sea; the seashore. (No plural form in this sense.) ♦ *The country protected its seaside from commercial development.* ♦ *The lifeguard sat at the seaside, watching the swimmers.* **2.** *adj.* on the seashore; at the side of the sea. ♦ *The seaside restaurant served fresh seafood.* ♦ *The seaside resort was a popular tourist destination.*

season ['siz ən] **1.** *n.* one of the four times of year: winter, spring, summer, and fall. ♦ *The seasons are caused by the tilt of the earth on its axis.* ♦ *Fall is my favorite season because the trees are so pretty.* **2.** *n.* a period of time marked by a certain kind of weather, an activity, or condition. ♦ *I went to the stadium every week during baseball season.* ♦ *The theater company presented four plays last season.* **3.** *tv.* to add spices to food to make it taste better or different. ♦ *The cook seasoned the stew with herbs and spices.* ♦ *I used oregano and basil to season the sauce.* **4.** *tv.* to cause someone to be experienced. ♦ *Tom had been seasoned in the business by 23 years of firsthand experience.* ♦ *Years at sea had seasoned John, and he was a fine captain.*

seasonable ['siz ən ə bəl] *adj.* [of weather] normal and typical for a certain time of year. (Adv: *seasonably.*) ♦ *In the Northern Hemisphere, hot weather is seasonable in the summer.* ♦ *Snow is seasonable for Minnesota in the winter.*

seasonably ['siz ən ə bli] *adv.* according to the season; having the normal kind of weather for a certain time of year. ♦ *After the cold snap, the May weather became seasonably warm again.* ♦ *Snow is seasonably appropriate for November in the north.*

seasonal ['siz ə nəl] *adj.* <the adj. form of **season** ②.> (Adv: *seasonally.*) ♦ *Football is a seasonal sport associated with autumn.* ♦ *One of the seasonal changes of spring is that the days become longer.*

seasoned ['siz ənd] **1.** *adj.* flavored with spices; having spices added; spicy; tasty; having seasoning. ♦ *The stew is seasoned quite nicely.* ♦ *John prefers bland food to seasoned dishes.* **2.** *adj.* matured; having a lot of experience.

♦ *The firm's decision to lay off its most seasoned employees was stupid.* ♦ *The seasoned lawyer was skilled at influencing juries.*

seasoning ['siz ə nɪŋ] *n.* a spice; a flavoring; an herb; something that is added to food to make it taste better or different. ♦ *This soup is bland. You should add some more seasoning.* ♦ *The seasoning in this salad is very tasty!*

season ticket ['siz ən 'tɪk ɪt] *n.* a ticket that allows one to do something for a certain period of time, such as see each production in a series of plays, attend each game of a sports team, or use certain facilities. ♦ *I saved 10% by buying season tickets instead of individual ones.* ♦ *People with season tickets often sit in the same seats throughout the season.*

seat ['sit] **1.** *n.* something that is used for sitting on; a place where someone can sit. ♦ *Each student found a seat at the start of class.* ♦ *I boarded the plane, and someone was sitting in my seat.* **2.** *n.* the part of a pair of pants that one sits on. ♦ *The dog tore the seat of the mail carrier's pants.* ♦ *The gum on the chair stuck to the seat of my pants.* **3.** *n.* the part of the body that one sits on; the behind; the buttocks. ♦ *Mary bruised her seat when she slipped on the ice.* ♦ *The bullet struck the robber in his seat.* **4.** *n.* a place where someone has the position of being a member, such as in Congress or on a stock exchange. ♦ *Mary bought the retiring banker's seat on the stock exchange.* ♦ *My neighbor holds a seat on the city council.* **5.** *tv.* to provide someone with ①; to lead someone to ①; to help someone sit down. ♦ *The usher seated the bride's parents in the front row.* ♦ *Bob help seat his mother and sat down next to her.* **6.** *tv.* to have a certain number of seats ①; to have room for a certain number of seated people. ♦ *This restaurant seats fifty.* ♦ *Anne's car comfortably seats five.* **7. show someone to a seat; show one to one's seat** *idiom* to lead or direct someone to a place to sit. ♦ *May I show you to your seat, sir?* ♦ *The ushers showed us to our seats politely and efficiently.*

seat belt ['sit bɛlt] *n.* a strap that buckles across one's lap, as in a car or an airplane. (See also safety belt.) ♦ *Anne told her passengers to fasten their seat belts.* ♦ *The flight attendant demonstrated how to fasten a seat belt.*

seated ['sit ɪd] *adj.* sitting down in or on something. ♦ *The seated audience listened attentively to the speaker.* ♦ *Seated passengers should wear their seat belts at all times.*

seating ['sit ɪŋ] **1.** *n.* a particular arrangement of seats. (No plural form in this sense.) ♦ *Anne arranged the seating at the dinner table.* ♦ *The seating at the party was indicated by name cards.* **2.** *n.* the number of seats that are available in a place. (No plural form in this sense.) ♦ *This restaurant has seating for fifty.* ♦ *The movie theater had seating for two hundred.* **3.** *n.* a specific mealtime for a number of people, as on a cruise ship. ♦ *We preferred the first seating but had to eat at the second seating.* ♦ *People in the early seating complained about the food.*

sea water ['si wɔt ɚ] *n.* salt water as found in the sea. ♦ *You cannot drink sea water.* ♦ *Whales live in sea water.*

seaweed ['si wid] *n.* a plant that grows in or at the edge of the sea. (No plural form in this sense.) ♦ *We couldn't see the bottom of the shallow part of the sea because there was too much seaweed.* ♦ *My oar became caught in the seaweed.*

seaworthy ['si wɚ ði] *adj.* [of a ship] in good enough condition for safe travel on water. ♦ *The inspector declared the boat to be seaworthy.* ♦ *The seaworthy ship sailed through the storm.*

secede [sɪ 'sid] **secede from** *iv.* + *prep. phr.* to leave an organization officially; to revoke one's own status as a member of an organization. ♦ *South Carolina seceded from the Union in 1861.* ♦ *Many citizens of Quebec want to secede from Canada.*

seclude [sɪ 'klud] *tv.* to keep someone away from other people; to keep something away from other things or places. ♦ *The police secluded the witness in a small cabin in the mountains.* ♦ *Mary secluded herself from her friends because she had to study.*

secluded [sɪ 'klud ɪd] *adj.* private; remote; set apart from other places; kept away from other places or people. (Adv: *secludedly.*) ♦ *My parents live in a secluded cabin in northern Michigan.* ♦ *I hid the money under a rock in a secluded spot.*

seclusion [sɪ 'klu ʒən] *n.* private and hidden; away from other people. (No plural form in this sense.) ♦ *The retired actress lived in seclusion in rural France.* ♦ *The remote village lay in total seclusion from the rest of the world.*

second ['sɛk ənd] **1.** *n.* a basic unit of the measurement of time; 1/60 of a minute; 1/3,600 of an hour. ♦ *One minute is equal to sixty seconds.* ♦ *The traffic light remained green for thirty seconds.* **2.** *n.* a moment; a very short period of time. ♦ *I'll be finished in a few seconds.* ♦ *Could I look at your newspaper for a second?* **3.** *n.* a unit of measurement of an angle equal to 1/60 of a minute or 1/3,600 of a degree. ♦ *The missile landed ten seconds north of its intended target.* ♦ *42 degrees, 10 minutes, and 6 seconds is written:* 42° 10′ 6″. **4.** *n.* someone or something that is second ⑥. ♦ *The second in line is my brother.* ♦ *I will choose the second from the right.* **5. seconds** *n.* an additional helping of food. (Treated as plural.) ♦ *Would anyone care for seconds?* ♦ *Can I have seconds on the green beans?* **6.** *adj.* coming, happening, or being after the first. (Adv: *secondly.*) ♦ *Texas is the second largest American state.* ♦ *The athlete in second place received a silver medal.* **7.** *adj.* an additional [thing or person]. ♦ *Mary went to another doctor for a second opinion.* ♦ *We bought a second car.* **8.** *adv.* in second position; in a position that is after the first position. ♦ *First, I will share my results; second, I will answer questions.* ♦ *I will discuss crime first and taxes second.*

secondarily [sɛk ən 'dɛr ɪ li] *adv.* in a way that is not the most important or that has less importance. ♦ *John moved to Miami to be near his parents, and secondarily because it is warmer than New York.* ♦ *The mediocre workers were considered for raises secondarily.*

secondary ['sɛk ən dɛr i] **1.** *adj.* second in importance; not primary; supplemental. (Adv: *secondarily.*) ♦ *After discussing the topic, we talked about some secondary issues.* ♦ *All of the mayor's concerns were secondary to fighting crime.* **2.** *adj.* [of the education of students] from the 6th to 12th or from the 9th to 12th grades, depending on the school district. ♦ *Mary is a principal at a large, urban secondary school.* ♦ *After graduating from a secondary school, Jane went to college.*

second class ['sɛk ənd 'klæs] **1.** *n.* a form of travel that is less comfortable and less costly than first class. ♦ *Our seats were in second class, but the tickets were much* *cheaper.* ♦ *Second class is a cheap way to travel.* **2.** *adv.* at a less comfortable level of service or accommodation. ♦ *I always travel second class on trains in Europe.* ♦ *The magazines were sent second class.* **3. second-class** *adj.* <the adj. use of ①.> ♦ *The traveler could only afford second-class seats on the train.* ♦ *The second-class tickets were cheap.* **4. second-class** *adj.* inferior; not as good; below a certain standard. ♦ *The company treated newly hired employees as second-class citizens.* ♦ *The accommodations in the second-class hotel were poor.*

secondhand ['sɛk ənd 'hænd] **1.** *adj.* [of goods] already used by someone else; not new. ♦ *Jimmy wore secondhand shirts from his older brothers.* ♦ *Mary bought a secondhand dress to wear to the banquet.* **2.** *adj.* [of stores] selling used products. ♦ *John buys his clothes cheaply at secondhand stores.* ♦ *I found an out-of-print atlas at a secondhand bookshop.* **3.** *adj.* not experienced directly but heard from another person. ♦ *Bill repeated the secondhand gossip to Mary.* ♦ *The newspaper would not print secondhand news reports.* **4.** *adv.* learned from someone else. ♦ *Susan became aware of the new policy secondhand by reading it in the newspaper.* ♦ *Anne heard the gossip secondhand from Bill.*

secondly ['sɛk ənd li] *adv.* second; in the second place. (Used before the second topic in a list of topics that are being discussed.) ♦ *Firstly, I want to discuss crime. Secondly, I want to discuss taxes.* ♦ *Anne spoke about France firstly and Germany secondly.*

second-rate ['sɛk ənd 'ret] *adj.* inferior; not as good; below a standard; not the best. ♦ *I complained about the second-rate service at the hotel.* ♦ *The student lived cheaply in a second-rate apartment.*

secrecy ['si krɪ si] *n.* the quality of being secret; concealment; keeping something a secret. (No plural form in this sense.) ♦ *The secrecy surrounding the lawyer's murder puzzled the reporter.* ♦ *The state's secrecy about the tax scandal angered the citizens.*

secret ['si krɪt] **1.** *n.* information known by a small number of people, especially people who have promised not to tell anyone else. ♦ *I'll tell you a secret, but you can't tell anyone.* ♦ *Mary kept Bob's secret to herself.* **2.** *n.* a mystery; something that cannot be explained. ♦ *The secrets of alien spacecraft intrigued the researcher.* ♦ *Only Tom understands the secret of getting his car to run.* **3.** *adj.* known only by a small number of people, especially when they have promised not to tell anyone else. (Adv: *secretly.*) ♦ *None of the audience knew the movie's secret ending.* ♦ *John used the secret information to blackmail the mayor.* **4.** *adj.* working at a job without others knowing what one does; doing something without others knowing what one is doing. (Adv: *secretly.*) ♦ *The secret agent couldn't tell me about her job.* ♦ *The terrorist was caught by the secret police.* **5. in secret** *phr.* secretly. ♦ *They planned in secret to blow up the bridge.* ♦ *I will tell her in secret so no one else will hear.* **6. open secret** *idiom* something that is supposed to be secret ③ but is known to a great many people. ♦ *Their engagement is an open secret. Only their friends are supposed to know, but in fact, the whole town knows.* ♦ *It's an open secret that Max is looking for a new job.*

secretary ['sɛk rɪ tɛr i] **1.** *n.* someone who is employed in an office to type letters, answer telephones, organize schedules and meetings, and do other clerical work. ♦ *Susan dictated a letter to her secretary.* ♦ *David's secretary opened his mail for him.* **2.** *n.* someone who keeps a written record of the things that are discussed at the official meetings of an organization. ♦ *The secretary passed out the minutes from the previous meeting.* ♦ *The secretary asked me to speak a little louder.* **3.** *n.* someone who is in charge of a department of the United States government. ♦ *The president's cabinet consists of the secretaries of federal departments.* ♦ *Henry Kissinger was the secretary of state from 1973 to 1977.* **4.** *n.* a writing desk with drawers and shelves. ♦ *I varnished the secretary when I bought it.* ♦ *John locked his papers inside the secretary.*

secrete [sɪ 'krit] **1.** *tv.* [for a part of a plant or an animal] to produce and release a fluid. (Pt: [sɪ 'kri tɪd].) ♦ *The eye secretes tears.* ♦ *The dog's infected wound secreted pus.* **2.** *tv.* to hide something; to put something in a place where others cannot see it or find it. (Pt: ['si krə tɪd].) ♦ *Mary secreted the money between the pages of a book.* ♦ *David secreted his house key under a brick by his house.*

secretion [sɪ 'kri ʃən] **1.** *n.* the production and release of fluid from living things. (No plural form in this sense.) ♦ *The secretion of the sap is quite slow.* ♦ *The liver produces a secretion of bile.* **2.** *n.* a fluid that is produced and released by a part of a plant or an animal, such as saliva or sap. ♦ *The researcher studied the secretions from the pig's glands.* ♦ *John collected the tree's secretion in a wooden bucket.*

secretive ['si krɪ tɪv] *adj.* tending to do things secretly; tending not to do things publicly or openly. (Adv: *secretively.*) ♦ *The secretive butler was uncooperative with the inspector.* ♦ *The secretive celebrity would not speak to reporters.*

secretly ['si krət li] *adv.* without being known or seen by others. ♦ *Anne was secretly stealing money from her employer.* ♦ *John secretly told the reporter sensitive political information.*

sect ['sɛkt] *n.* a group of people who have separated from an established religion because their religious beliefs are different. ♦ *After a dispute, half of the congregation formed its own sect.* ♦ *There are as many sects as there are beliefs.*

sectarian [sɛk 'tɛr i ən] *adj.* of or about sects. (Adv: *sectarianly.*) ♦ *Various sectarian leaders met to discuss their differences.* ♦ *The ministers sought to break down the sectarian divisions in the city's churches.*

section ['sɛk ʃən] **1.** *n.* a separate part of a larger group, place, or thing; a division. ♦ *The student read the introductory section of each chapter.* ♦ *I peeled an orange and ate each section of it one at a time.* **2.** *n.* a unit of measurement of land equal to one square mile or 640 acres. ♦ *Outside of New England, a township is usually a six-mile square of land, which is made up of 36 sections.* ♦ *The farmer owned half a section of land, or 320 acres.* **3.** *tv.* to divide something into ①. ♦ *The manager sectioned the work among the four workers.* ♦ *The old warehouse was sectioned into twelve condominiums.*

sector ['sɛk tɚ] *n.* a part of something, especially of society or the economy. ♦ *Economic growth in the nation's business sector improved last year.* ♦ *The agency tried to raise money from the private sector.*

secular ['sɛk jə lɚ] *adj.* not religious; separate from the church or religion. (Adv: *secularly.*) ♦ *Secular governments* *separate church from state.* ♦ *Advancement of a religion is not permitted in secular schools.*

secure [sɪ 'kjʊr] **1.** *adj.* safe from danger, harm, loss, injury, or theft. (Adv: *securely.*) ♦ *The jewels were secure in the hotel's vault.* ♦ *The tourists felt secure in the American embassy during the riot.* **2.** *tv.* to safely fasten or close something. ♦ *The passengers on the plane secured their seat belts.* ♦ *Jane secured her grip on her son's shoulder.* **3.** *tv.* to obtain something. ♦ *I secured the services of a good lawyer.* ♦ *Do you know where I can secure a good hotel room for the night?*

security [sɪ 'kjʊr ə ti] **1.** *n.* the state of being or feeling safe from danger, harm, loss, injury, or theft. (No plural form in this sense.) ♦ *There's security in traveling in pairs after dark.* ♦ *Anne liked the security of living in a small town.* **2.** *n.* an office or department concerned with protection of people and property. (No plural form in this sense.) ♦ *John lives in an apartment with 24-hour security in the lobby.* ♦ *Jane called security when the intruder entered the office.* **3.** *n.* property that is pledged to a bank or lender when money is borrowed. (If the money is not paid back, then the bank or lender will be given the property. No plural form in this sense.) ♦ *The security for a mortgage is usually a building or land.* ♦ *The bank retains ownership in your new car as security on the loan.* **4.** *n.* financial assets or debt agreements, such as stocks and bonds. ♦ *Jane's broker handled all her securities.* ♦ *Bill sold all his securities and retired.* **5. security against something** *phr.* something that keeps something safe; something that protects; a protection. ♦ *Insurance provides security against theft, loss, or damage.* ♦ *A good education is a security against unemployment.* **6.** *adj.* <the adj. use of ②.> ♦ *There is a security guard in the lobby of my apartment building.* ♦ *As a security measure, the workers showed their identification at the entrance.* **7. lull someone into a false sense of security** *idiom* to lead someone into believing that all is well before attacking or doing something bad. ♦ *We lulled the enemy into a false sense of security by pretending to retreat. Then we launched an attack.* ♦ *A strong economy lulled us into a false sense of security, and we were not prepared when the banks failed.*

sedan [sɪ 'dæn] *n.* a car with four doors, a front seat and a back seat, a fixed roof, and room for at least four people. (Compare with coupe.) ♦ *My friends and I rented a sedan when we drove to Texas.* ♦ *Anne loaded her sedan with her belongings when she moved.*

sedate [sɪ 'det] **1.** *adj.* quiet; calm; relaxed; not excited; not moved by excitement. (Adv: *sedately.*) ♦ *The sedate man quietly read his newspaper.* ♦ *After a long massage, I feel very sedate.* **2.** *tv.* to give someone or an animal a drug that causes relaxation. ♦ *The surgeons sedated me before the operation.* ♦ *The paramedics had to sedate the hysterical victim of the crash.*

sedation [sɪ 'de ʃən] **1.** *n.* the state caused by taking a sedative. (No plural form in this sense.) ♦ *Once the patient was under sedation, the surgeons began operating.* ♦ *With adequate sedation, the patient felt no pain.* **2.** *n.* giving a creature a drug that causes sleep or relaxation. (No plural form in this sense.) ♦ *The sedation of the large patient required an extra dose.* ♦ *Repeated sedation was required to calm the accident victim.*

sedative ['sɛd ə tɪv] **1.** *n.* a drug or medicine that causes one to sleep or relax. ♦ *The nurse gave the patients a sedative at bedtime.* ♦ *John takes sedatives when he can't fall asleep.* **2.** *adj.* <the adj. use of ①.> ♦ *Bill took a sedative tablet because he had insomnia.* ♦ *The soft music had a sedative effect on Anne.*

sedentary ['sɛd n tɛr i] **1.** *adj.* [of a creature] not very active and keeping still most of the time. (Adv: *sedentarily* [sɛd n 'tɛr ə li].) ♦ *Sedentary people often become overweight.* ♦ *Our old dog has become very sedentary.* **2.** *adj.* [of activity] not requiring a lot of movement. (Adv: *sedentarily* [sɛd n 'tɛr ə li].) ♦ *I exercise during lunch to compensate for my sedentary job.* ♦ *Driving a car is a sedentary activity.*

sediment ['sɛd ə mənt] *n.* pieces of solid matter that settle at the bottom of a liquid. (No plural form in this sense.) ♦ *The sediment in your orange juice is orange pulp.* ♦ *The chemist filtered the sediment from the liquid.*

sedition [sɪ 'dɪ ʃən] *n.* words or actions that cause or are intended to cause people to rebel against government or authority. (No plural form in this sense.) ♦ *The rebel was charged with sedition.* ♦ *During the war, people accused of sedition were imprisoned.*

seduce [sɪ 'dus] **1.** *tv.* to persuade someone to have sex; to talk someone into having sex. ♦ *The romantic executive seduced the young model with flowers.* ♦ *The innocent clerk was seduced by the scheming manager.* **2.** *tv.* to lure someone into doing something wrong by making it seem attractive. ♦ *Greed seduced the politician into accepting the bribe.* ♦ *The actor was seduced by fame and forgot about his old friends.*

seduction [sɪ 'dʌk ʃən] **1.** *n.* the process of seducing ① or ② someone. (No plural form in this sense.) ♦ *The seduction was interrupted by a knock at the door.* ♦ *The romantic young executive's seduction was a real challenge.* **2.** *n.* a temptation; a lure; an attraction; something that causes one to be seduced. (Figurative on ①.) ♦ *Greed was one of the seductions to which the politician succumbed.* ♦ *The seductions of fame and wealth lure many performers to Hollywood.*

seductive [sɪ 'dʌk tɪv] *adj.* tempting; alluring; enticing; having qualities that makes one able to seduce ① or ② someone. (Adv: *seductively.*) ♦ *My date's seductive glances beguiled me.* ♦ *Beware of the seductive power of greed.*

see ['si] **1.** *iv., irreg.* to perceive with the eyes. (Pt: saw; pp: seen.) ♦ *After the operation, I could see without my glasses.* ♦ *I know there's a stop sign ahead! I can see!* **2.** *tv., irreg.* to observe someone or something by the use of the eyes; to perceive someone or something with the eyes. ♦ *Mary saw the stain on the wall.* ♦ *Have you seen the new car that Jane has bought?* **3.** *tv., irreg.* to detect or understand something. (Takes a clause.) ♦ *John saw that the sun was setting.* ♦ *Mary saw that David was laughing.* **4.** *tv., irreg.* to understand something; to comprehend something. ♦ *I don't see the importance of your last statement.* ♦ *Clearly, you can see the reason for my concern.* **5.** *tv., irreg.* to learn something by reading or other direct observation. ♦ *In the newspaper, Mary saw how the economy was doing.* ♦ *In the last chapter, we see the hero fighting the bank robber.* **6.** *tv., irreg.* to visit someone; to stop by the place where someone lives. ♦ *I went into town last night and saw Mary.* ♦ *John went to the hospital to see his sick brother.*

7. *tv., irreg.* to meet with someone for an appointment. ♦ *You're supposed to see the dentist at 3:00 today.* ♦ *Anne saw a lawyer about her legal problems.* **8.** *tv., irreg.* to date someone; to have a romantic relationship with someone. ♦ *Mary has been seeing her boyfriend for over a year.* ♦ *David saw someone briefly last year, but he is still single.* **9. see someone as something** *idiom* to consider someone to be something; to deem someone or something as something. ♦ *The manager saw the skilled employee as a godsend.* ♦ *John saw the new salesman as a threat to his territory.* **10. see someone to someplace** *idiom* to escort someone to a place; to make sure that someone gets someplace safely; to accompany someone to a place. ♦ *I saw Mary to her door, and then got back in my car and left.* ♦ *Bill saw his cousin to the train station, and then they parted.* **11. see (to it) that something is done** *idiom* to make sure of something; to make certain of something; to be certain to do something. (Takes a clause.) ♦ *The manager saw to it that everyone began working on time.* ♦ *The mayor should see that the potholes are repaired.*

seed ['sid] **1.** *n.* a part of a plant that a new plant will grow from if it is fertilized, similar to a fertilized egg in animals. ♦ *The farmer planted seeds in the spring.* ♦ *Anne spit the apple seeds from her mouth.* **2.** *n.* the beginning of something; the source of something. (Figurative on ①.) ♦ *The seeds of my interest in science were sown by my biology teacher.* ♦ *Gossip is the seed of most of the problems at my office.* **3.** *tv.* to plant crops by scattering ① on land; to sow ①. ♦ *The rural farmer seeded the fields by hand.* ♦ *This tractor can seed dozens of acres a day.* **4. seed against** *tv. + prep. phr.* to arrange sporting matches, especially tennis, in a way that the best players don't play each other in the first round. ♦ *Last year's champion was seeded against a rookie.* ♦ *The novice tennis player was seeded against a powerhouse.* **5. go to seed** *idiom* to look badly maintained. ♦ *This neighborhood is going to seed because people don't take care of their homes.* ♦ *Uncle Tom seems to be going to seed in his old age.*

seedless ['sid ləs] *adj.* not having seeds; of or about fruit that is bred so that it doesn't have seeds. (Adv: *seedlessly.*) ♦ *Mary brought some seedless grapes to the party.* ♦ *John made juice from seedless oranges.*

seedling ['sid lɪŋ] *n.* a young plant or tree that is newly grown from a seed. ♦ *The seedlings were uprooted in the violent storm.* ♦ *Anne bought some seedlings and planted them in her yard.*

seedy ['si di] **1.** *adj.* having a lot of seeds. (Comp: *seedier;* sup: *seediest.*) ♦ *Watermelons are very seedy.* ♦ *I opened the seedy pumpkin and then roasted the seeds.* **2.** *adj.* rundown; shabby; dilapidated; going to seed. (Adv: *seedily.* Comp: *seedier;* sup: *seediest.*) ♦ *My rent is cheap, but I live in a seedy neighborhood.* ♦ *The police broke up a fight inside the seedy hotel.*

seek ['sik] **1.** *tv., irreg.* to try to find someone or something; to look for someone or something. (Pt/pp: sought.) ♦ *If you seek answers, be sure you know what you're asking for.* ♦ *If the symptoms persist, seek medical attention.* **2. seek to** *iv. + inf.* to try to do something; to attempt to do something; to endeavor to do something. ♦ *The president sought to end the war.* ♦ *The inspector sought to solve the crime.*

seem ['sim] *iv.* to appear; to appear to be; to give the impression of being. (Can be followed by (i) an adjective, (ii) an infinitive, (iii) *to be* plus an adjective, a noun phrase, or a pronoun in the nominative case [*I, you, he, she, it, we, they*], although in informal use the objective case is often used, or (iv) like or as though plus a clause. When seem follows it ②, it can also be followed by that plus a clause.) ♦ *"You seem to be very happy today," Mary remarked to Sue.* ♦ *"You seem very happy today," Mary remarked to Sue.* ♦ *"You seem as though you are very happy today," Mary remarked to Sue.* ♦ *"It seems as though you are very happy today," Mary remarked to Sue.* ♦ *The weather seems bad today.* ♦ *It seems to be rainy today.* ♦ *Even though Bob looks all right, he seems sick because he's so tired.* ♦ *Anne looked at the person walking toward her and thought, "I'm expecting Bill at 3:00, and it seems to be he, but I'm not sure."* ♦ *Anne looked at the person walking toward her and thought, "I'm expecting Bill at 3:00, and it seems to be him, but I'm not sure."*

seemingly ['sim ɪŋ li] *adv.* apparently; as far as one can tell. ♦ *Bob is seemingly interested in becoming a firefighter.* ♦ *Class is seemingly canceled, as the professor is not here.*

seen ['sin] pp of saw.

seep ['sip] *iv.* [for a liquid] to pass through something slowly; to leak. ♦ *Pollution seeped into the water supply.* ♦ *The muddy water seeped through the holes in my boots.*

seersucker ['sɪr sək ɚ] **1.** *n.* rayon, cotton, or linen that is woven so that the texture has alternate stripes of smooth fabric and wrinkled fabric. (No plural form in this sense.) ♦ *You shouldn't put delicate seersucker in the dryer.* ♦ *The designer's new clothing line featured seersucker.* **2.** *adj.* made of ①. ♦ *John wore a seersucker suit to the conference.* ♦ *I took my dirty seersucker clothing to the dry cleaners.*

seesaw ['si sɔ] **1.** *n.* a long, flat board whose middle rests on a raised object so the ends go up and down while one person sits on one end and another person sits on the other end. ♦ *Jimmy and Susie went up and down on the seesaw for hours.* ♦ *When I jumped off my end of the seesaw, Dave came crashing down.* **2.** *n.* something that moves up and down; something that moves back and forth; something that rises and falls. (Figurative on ①.) ♦ *During the financial crisis, the stock market moved like a seesaw.* ♦ *In the months before the election, the inflation rate rose and fell like a seesaw.* **3.** *iv.* [for two people] to ride ①. ♦ *Jimmy and Susie seesawed in the park until it got dark.* ♦ *The students seesawed for 24 hours to raise money for charity.* **4.** *iv.* to move up and down; to move back and forth. (Figurative on ③.) ♦ *The president's approval ratings seesawed in the polls.* ♦ *The car seesawed on the edge of the cliff and then dropped.*

seethe ['sið] **1.** *iv.* to boil and bubble; to bubble or foam as though boiling. ♦ *The soup seethed over the edge of the pot.* ♦ *The sea seethed around the rocks along the shore.* **2.** *iv.* to be very angry; to be very upset. (Figurative on ①.) ♦ *My boss seethed with rage when our computer system failed.* ♦ *The politician seethed about the unflattering article.*

seething ['sið ɪŋ] *adj.* very angry; very upset. (Adv: *seethingly.*) ♦ *The seething motorists stuck in traffic honked their car horns.* ♦ *John, seething with anger, thumped his fist on the table.*

segment ['sɛg mənt] **1.** *n.* a part of something; a part of something that can be easily separated. ♦ *John divided the line into one-inch segments.* ♦ *Jane gave her colleague a segment of her orange.* **2.** *tv.* to separate something into parts; to divide something into parts. ♦ *The manager segmented the task and gave part to me and part to Jane.* ♦ *The director segmented the long play into two acts.*

segregate ['sɛ grɪ get] **1.** *tv.* to separate someone or a group of people from other people; to isolate someone or a group of people. ♦ *The teacher segregated the students according to reading ability.* ♦ *The staff segregated the boys from the girls during gym class.* **2.** *tv.* to separate people of one race from people of another race. ♦ *In many cities, blacks were segregated from whites.* ♦ *Economic conditions segregated the blacks into their own neighborhoods.*

segregated ['sɛ grɪ get ɪd] *adj.* [of human races] separated by law or other forces. (Adv: *segregatedly.*) ♦ *The president called for an end to segregated society.* ♦ *Parents protested against segregated schools.*

segregation [sɛ grɪ 'ge ʃən] **1.** *n.* the state existing in a segregated society; the state of races being separated by law or other causes. (No plural form in this sense.) ♦ *Segregation is illegal, but many cities are still racially divided.* ♦ *Most people voted against the candidate who favored segregation.* **2.** *n.* the separation of someone or something from other things or people. (No plural form in this sense.) ♦ *The teacher advocated the segregation of smart students from the others.* ♦ *The jail enforced the segregation of dangerous criminals.*

seismic ['sɑɪz mɪk] *adj.* [of movement] associated with earthquakes. (Adv: *seismically* [...ɪk li].) ♦ *There's a lot of seismic activity in California.* ♦ *The Japanese are used to small seismic tremors.*

seismograph ['sɑɪz mə græf] *n.* a machine that measures and records the strength of an earthquake. ♦ *The seismograph's needle moved wildly when the earthquake hit.* ♦ *According to the seismograph, the earthquake was very, very small.*

seismologist [sɑɪz 'mɑl ə dʒəst] *n.* someone who is trained in the study of earthquakes. ♦ *The seismologist predicted a major earthquake would strike soon.* ♦ *After the quake, the seismologists said to expect additional jolts.*

seize ['siz] **1.** *tv.* to grab, take, and hold on to someone or something. ♦ *Mary seized a shovel and began to dig.* ♦ *The nurse seized the patient's arm as he fainted.* **2.** *tv.* to take control of something by force or by authority; to capture something by force or by authority. ♦ *The pirates seized the boat and killed the captain.* ♦ *The police seized the drug dealer's property.* **3.** *tv.* to take (figurative) possession or control of someone or some creature. (Figurative on ②.) ♦ *Fear seized the gigantic herd of buffalo.* ♦ *Panic seized John at the last minute before he was to jump.*

seizure ['si ʒɚ] **1.** *n.* seizing someone or something. ♦ *The police had a warrant for the seizure of the criminal's property.* ♦ *The army's seizure of the presidential palace was bloody.* **2.** *n.* a sudden attack of a sickness; a convulsion caused by a sudden attack of a sickness. ♦ *John shouldn't drive because sometimes he has epileptic seizures.* ♦ *Soon after being poisoned, Bill began to have seizures.*

seldom ['sɛl dəm] *adv.* almost never; rarely. ♦ *It seldom rains in the desert.* ♦ *The busy office manager seldom leaves work before 7:00 P.M.*

select [sə 'lɛkt] **1.** *tv.* to pick someone or something from a group of choices. ♦ *The diner selected an entrée from the menu.* ♦ *The faculty selected ten new students for the program.* **2.** *adj.* specifically chosen; exclusive; specially chosen. (Adv: *selectly.*) ♦ *A select few were invited to the mayor's party.* ♦ *I talk only to a select group of friends about my problems.*

selection [sə 'lɛk ʃən] **1.** *n.* a choice; someone or something that is chosen; someone or something that is selected. ♦ *Jane's selection was a chicken sandwich.* ♦ *The jukebox costs one dollar for three selections.* **2.** *n.* a group of things to choose from, especially in a store. (No plural form in this sense.) ♦ *The local hardware store has a large selection of tools.* ♦ *I shop at a grocery store that has only a small selection of fresh produce.*

selective [sə 'lɛk tɪv] *adj.* choosing carefully; making careful choices. (Adv: *selectively.*) ♦ *A selective buyer compares many brands.* ♦ *The selective customer examined the merchandise carefully.*

selenium [sə 'lɛn i əm] *n.* a chemical element used in photographic equipment, electronics, pigments, and xerography. (No plural form in this sense.) ♦ *The atomic symbol of selenium is Se, and its atomic number is 34.* ♦ *Selenium was discovered in 1817.*

self ['sɛlf] *n.* the inner being of a person. (Usually in compounds. See also **myself, yourself, herself, himself, itself, oneself, ourselves, yourselves, themselves.** No plural form in this sense.) ♦ *Tom was more concerned with self than with others.* ♦ *The boss likes employees who see the company as more important than self.*

self-addressed ['sɛlf ə 'drɛst] *adj.* addressed to oneself. ♦ *I included a self-addressed, stamped envelope with each invitation.* ♦ *I filled out the survey on the self-addressed business reply card.*

self-assertive [sɛlf ə 'sɚ tɪv] *adj.* asserting oneself aggressively or insistently. (Adv: *self-assertively.*) ♦ *The manager was too self-assertive and irritated the vice president.* ♦ *The counselor told the timid man to be more self-assertive and hold to his opinions.*

self-centered ['sɛlf 'sɛn tɚd] *adj.* selfish; inclined to think only of oneself instead of someone else. (Adv: *self-centeredly.*) ♦ *If you weren't so self-centered, you'd see that I'm unhappy, too.* ♦ *Dave is too self-centered to ask for my opinion.*

self-confidence [sɛlf 'kɑn fɪ dəns] *n.* the belief that one is able to do something; confidence in one's own ability. (No plural form in this sense.) ♦ *Anne's self-confidence has improved since she left home.* ♦ *Bill needs more self-confidence, or he'll never succeed.*

self-conscious [sɛlf 'kɑn ʃəs] *adj.* aware that one is being seen by other people, especially when one is shy or embarrassed around other people. (Adv: *self-consciously.*) ♦ *Bob is too self-conscious when he tries to talk in a group.* ♦ *The self-conscious lecturer began to stutter from nervousness.*

self-contained [sɛlf kən 'tend] *adj.* containing within itself everything that is necessary. ♦ *All of the parts needed for correct operation are self-contained.* ♦ *Our company's self-contained waste-disposal system doesn't harm the environment.*

self-control [sɛlf kən 'trol] *n.* the control of one's own actions or feelings. (No plural form in this sense.) ♦ *A dieter needs self-control to keep from eating between meals.* ♦ *Because Anne has self-control, she didn't respond to John's insults.*

self-defense [sɛlf dɪ 'fɛns] *n.* the defense of one's life by oneself; defending oneself. (No plural form in this sense.) ♦ *John killed the man in self-defense.* ♦ *Mary learned karate for self-defense.*

self-discipline ['sɛlf 'dɪs ə plɪn] *n.* the discipline one has to control one's feelings and actions. (No plural form in this sense.) ♦ *It took self-discipline for me to quit biting my fingernails.* ♦ *It takes self-discipline to accept criticism without becoming angry.*

self-educated [sɛlf 'ɛdʒ ə ket ɪd] *adj.* educated by studying and learning by oneself. ♦ *The self-educated woman established her own business.* ♦ *Many professionals in the 19th century were self-educated.*

self-employed [sɛlf ɛm 'plɔɪd] *adj.* working for one's own business; not working for other people. ♦ *Susan is self-employed because she dislikes having a boss.* ♦ *The self-employed accountant's office was in her home.*

self-esteem [sɛlf ə 'stim] *n.* the good opinion one has of oneself; the respect one shows for oneself. (No plural form in this sense.) ♦ *Anne has a high self-esteem, so she's not upset by criticism.* ♦ *People who allow others to order them around need more self-esteem.*

self-evident [sɛlf 'ɛv ɪ dənt] *adj.* obvious; easy to see; not needing proof. (Adv: *self-evidently.*) ♦ *It's self-evident that two plus two equals four.* ♦ *The importance of dressing warmly when it's cold is self-evident.*

self-explanatory [sɛlf ɛks 'plæn ə tor i] *adj.* not needing an explanation; obvious; evident. ♦ *What is self-explanatory for an expert may not be for a beginner.* ♦ *The author omitted self-explanatory words from the glossary.*

self-governing ['sɛlf 'gʌv ɚ nɪŋ] *adj.* governing itself; independent; autonomous; not governed by a foreign country. ♦ *Denmark granted Greenland self-governing status in 1979.* ♦ *In the 1960s, many African nations became self-governing.*

self-government [sɛlf 'gʌv ɚn mənt] *n.* the governing of a country by itself instead of by a foreign country; the government of a country by people from that country. (No plural form in this sense.) ♦ *Many Indians demand self-government from the national government.* ♦ *The Baltic Republics achieved self-government in the early 1990s.*

self-help ['sɛlf 'hɛlp] **1.** *n.* helping oneself without the help of others. (No plural form in this sense.) ♦ *Mary doesn't like therapists, so she relies on self-help.* ♦ *Bob's attempt at self-help failed, so he asked me for advice.* **2.** *adj.* [of books or techniques] showing people how to help themselves without the help of others. ♦ *Many bookstores have special sections for self-help books.* ♦ *Some self-help remedies do more harm than good.*

self-interest ['sɛlf 'ɪn trəst] *n.* interest only in one's personal advantage or gain. (No plural form in this sense.) ♦ *The greedy politician's votes were all based on self-interest.* ♦ *John is so absorbed in self-interest that he ignores his friends.*

selfish ['sɛl fɪʃ] *adj.* too concerned with oneself; too concerned with what one wants instead of what other people want; showing care for oneself more than for other people. (Adv: *selfishly.*) ♦ *The selfish girl wouldn't share her toys with the others.* ♦ *The rich but selfish lawyer wouldn't donate any money to charity.*

selfishness ['sɛl fɪʃ nəs] *n.* the state of being too concerned with oneself; greediness. (No plural form in this sense.) ♦ *Because of Bill's selfishness, no one wanted to be his friend.* ♦ *Selfishness and greed can be your downfall.*

self-made ['sɛlf 'med] **1.** *adj.* made by oneself; made without the help of other people. ♦ *All of Dave's self-made furniture is lovely.* ♦ *John's self-made computer actually works very well.* **2.** *adj.* having become successful without the help of other people. ♦ *The self-made businesswoman had faced many obstacles.* ♦ *The self-made man had not relied on family or friends for help.*

self-pity ['sɛlf 'pɪt i] *n.* pity for oneself, especially too much pity for oneself. (No plural form in this sense.) ♦ *It's depressing to be around Bob because he has so much self-pity.* ♦ *Sue's self-pity began to irritate her friends.*

self-possessed [sɛlf pə 'zɛst] *adj.* having strong control over one's own feelings and actions. ♦ *The self-possessed senator responded calmly to the accusations.* ♦ *Tom, a disciplined and self-possessed student, vowed to be the best.*

self-preservation [sɛlf prɛz ɚ 've ʃən] *n.* the instinct to keep oneself safe from danger, harm, or death; the instinct to survive. (No plural form in this sense.) ♦ *The skunk's foul odor is a tool of self-preservation.* ♦ *In the name of self-preservation, one of the survivors hid his food from the others.*

self-reliance [sɛlf rɪ 'lɑɪ əns] *n.* the quality of being self-reliant. (No plural form in this sense.) ♦ *The Smiths instilled a sense of self-reliance in their children.* ♦ *An employee with great self-reliance is what every boss would like.*

self-reliant [sɛlf rɪ 'lɑɪ ənt] *adj.* able to get along or do something without the help of others. (Adv: *self-reliantly.*) ♦ *Jane, a self-reliant worker, took care of the problem herself.* ♦ *The Smiths taught their children to be self-reliant at an early age.*

self-respect [sɛlf rɪ 'spɛkt] *n.* the respect and pride one has for oneself. (No plural form in this sense.) ♦ *Good grooming habits are a matter of self-respect.* ♦ *You must have self-respect if you expect others to respect you.*

self-respecting [sɛlf rɪ 'spɛk tɪŋ] *adj.* genuine and responsible. ♦ *What self-respecting person would do such a horrible thing?* ♦ *No self-respecting man would allow such things to be done to him!*

self-restraint [sɛlf rɪ 'strɑɪnt] *n.* the restraint that one shows; the control one has of one's emotions in difficult situations. (No plural form in this sense.) ♦ *The grieving family showed self-restraint at the funeral.* ♦ *Bill showed self-restraint by ignoring the names that the other kids called him.*

self-righteous [sɛlf 'rɑɪ tʃəs] *adj.* too proud or arrogant of one's righteousness, morality, or goodness. (Adv: *self-righteously.*) ♦ *Jane told the self-righteous old lady to mind her own business.* ♦ *When Bill became self-righteous, I pointed out his flaws to him.*

self-sacrifice [sɛlf 'sæ krɪ fɑɪs] *n.* giving up something one enjoys for the benefit of others; giving up one's desires for the sake of others. (No plural form in this sense.) ♦ *The soldiers and sailors were praised for their self-sacrifice.* ♦ *Spoiled children rarely appreciate their parents' self-sacrifice.*

self-satisfaction [sɛlf sæt ɪs 'fæk ʃən] *n.* the feeling of satisfaction that one has for oneself. (No plural form in this sense.) ♦ *Bob had a sense of self-satisfaction when things went as he predicted.* ♦ *Sue had great self-satisfaction in knowing that she had been right.*

self-satisfied [sɛlf 'sæt ɪs fɑɪd] *adj.* satisfied with oneself; happy with oneself; pleased with oneself; smug. ♦ *The cat that killed the mouse seemed to have a self-satisfied grin.* ♦ *"I knew I was right," Bill said with a self-satisfied laugh.*

self-service ['sɛlf 'sɚ vɪs] **1.** *n.* the system by which one must serve oneself in a store or a business. (No plural form in this sense.) ♦ *Self-service is much cheaper than having a clerk deal with every sale.* ♦ *Stores that offer self-service require fewer clerks.* **2.** AND **self-serve** ['sɛlf 'sɚv] *adj.* <the adj. use of ①.> ♦ *Jane filled her car's tank at the self-service gas station.* ♦ *The patrons filled their own plates at the self-serve buffet.*

self-sufficient ['sɛlf sə 'fɪʃ ənt] *adj.* able to support oneself without the help of other people; independent. (Adv: *self-sufficiently.*) ♦ *The self-sufficient farmer grew enough food to feed himself.* ♦ *The self-sufficient agency received no government grants.*

self-taught ['sɛlf 'tɔt] *adj.* taught by oneself; self-educated; taught by studying and learning by oneself. ♦ *John's ability to speak German is self-taught.* ♦ *The self-taught bakers opened their own business.*

sell ['sɛl] **1. sell for** *iv., irreg.* + *prep. phr.* to be offered for sale for an amount of money. (Pt/pp: **sold**.) ♦ *The rare book will sell for hundreds of dollars.* ♦ *This merchandise sells for more than it's worth.* **2.** *iv., irreg.* to be in demand by prospective buyers. ♦ *These chairs do not sell well.* ♦ *All the large sizes of clothing sell poorly.* **3. sell out** *iv., irreg.* + *adv.* [for all of something] to be **sold** as in ④. ♦ *The merchandise that was on sale sold out very quickly.* ♦ *I think these pictures are ugly, but they sell out every year.* **4.** *tv., irreg.* to transfer a product in exchange for money; to transfer a product to someone in exchange for money. ♦ *The clerk sold the vase to Anne.* ♦ *Have you sold your car yet?* **5.** *tv., irreg.* to make something available for purchase. ♦ *The baker sells bread and cakes.* ♦ *The artist sells paintings for $500 and sculptures for $750.* **6.** *tv., irreg.* to cause something to be more likely to be used or bought. ♦ *Often, good reporting doesn't sell news as well as sex and violence.* ♦ *The smell of fresh bread sells baked goods easily.* **7. sell like hot cakes** *idiom* [for something] to sell ② very well. ♦ *The delicious candy sold like hot cakes.* ♦ *The fancy new cars were selling like hot cakes.* **8. sell someone on something** *idiom* to convince someone to do something; to convince someone to accept an idea. ♦ *Mary sold me on ordering pizza for dinner.* ♦ *John sold Anne on switching long-distance phone companies.* **9. sell someone or something out** *idiom* to betray someone or something. ♦ *Max refused to sell his country out by revealing the secret information.* ♦ *Bob complained that Tom had sold him out when he testified against him.*

seller ['sɛl ɚ] **1.** *n.* someone who sells something for money. ♦ *The seller was asking $2,000 for the used car.* ♦ *The knowledgeable clerk was the top seller in the department.* **2.** *n.* a product that is selling in a specified way. ♦ *The auto manufacturer discontinued the car model that was a poor seller.* ♦ *This game is the top seller among children's toys.*

selling price ['sɛl ɪŋ prɑɪs] *n.* the price that a product is sold for. ♦ *The retailer reduced each item's selling price by 20%.* ♦ *The customer bargained with the seller over the selling price.*

sellout ['sɛl ɑʊt] *n.* a play, concert, sporting event, or other performance for which no tickets are available because they have all been sold. ♦ *The popular play was a sellout during its entire run.* ♦ *The boxing match became a sellout 10 minutes after tickets went on sale.*

semblance ['sɛm bləns] *n.* a resemblance to, or approximation of, something; a visible similarity with something. ♦ *I can't begin my speech until there's some semblance of order.* ♦ *The dilapidated house still had a semblance of dignity.*

semen ['si mən] *n.* the whitish fluid containing sperm that is made by the male sex organs. (No plural form in this sense.) ♦ *During a man's orgasm, he usually ejaculates semen.* ♦ *The cow was artificially inseminated with bull semen.*

semester [sɪ 'mɛs tɚ] *n.* half of a school year; a term; a 16-week to 18-week period of classes. ♦ *This college requires two semesters of calculus.* ♦ *Mary took five classes during the fall semester.*

semiannual [sɛm i 'æn ju əl] *adj.* happening twice a year; happening every half a year; happening every six months. (Adv: *semiannually.*) ♦ *The store held a semiannual sale in June and November.* ♦ *Each employee was given a semiannual review.*

semicircle ['sɛm ɪ sɚk əl] *n.* half of a circle; a shape like half of a circle. ♦ *The choir was arranged in a semicircle in front of the conductor.* ♦ *Anne cut each slice of lime in half, forming two semicircles from each slice.*

semicolon ['sɛm ɪ ko lən] *n.* a punctuation mark ";" that shows separation between two clauses, indicating more of a pause than a comma, but less of a pause than a period. (It is also used to separate items in a list, if any of the items use a comma, so that the reader is not confused.) ♦ *John replaced the comma between the sentences with a semicolon.* ♦ *The editor said using semicolons in the list would make it easier to read.*

semiconductor [sɛm i kən 'dʌk tɚ] *n.* a substance that allows electricity to pass through it, but not as well as some metals do. ♦ *Silicon is a common semiconductor.* ♦ *A semiconductor becomes more conductive to electricity as it becomes hotter.*

semiconscious [sɛm i 'kɑn ʃəs] *adj.* partially conscious; half-conscious. (Adv: *semiconsciously.*) ♦ *The lifeguard gave first aid to the semiconscious swimmer.* ♦ *The semiconscious crash victim moaned for help.*

semifinal [sɛm i 'fɑɪn əl] **1.** *n.* one of the two games in a contest whose winners will compete against each other in a final round for the championship. (Often plural.) ♦ *Only four teams will make it to the semifinals.* ♦ *Last year, we lost in the semifinals, but this year, we'll be champions!*

2. *adj.* <the adj. use of ①.> ♦ *Four tennis players competed in the semifinal competitions.* ♦ *Our high-school team made it to the semifinal rounds, then lost.*

semifinalist ['sɛm i 'fɑɪn ə ləst] *n.* one of the contestants competing in a semifinal. ♦ *Only two semifinalists would continue on to the finals.* ♦ *The judge congratulated each semifinalist for having done so well.*

semimonthly [sɛm i 'mʌnθ li] **1.** *adv.* twice a month; once every two weeks. ♦ *Some news magazines are published semimonthly.* ♦ *The treasurer provided a report to the manager semimonthly.* **2.** *adj.* happening twice a month; happening once every two weeks. ♦ *There are 24 issues of a semimonthly magazine each year.* ♦ *Every manager had to attend a semimonthly business meeting.*

seminar ['sɛm ə nɑr] **1.** *n.* one of the meetings of a type of course that meets regularly with a professor to discuss theories, studies, or research. ♦ *The biology professor conducted a seminar on primates.* ♦ *The students in the history seminar all presented original research.* **2.** *n.* a meeting where a speaker or panel of speakers talk, exchange information, or discuss ideas about a particular topic. ♦ *The sales manager attended a motivational seminar.* ♦ *Many lawyers attended a seminar on tort reform.*

seminary ['sɛm ə nɛr i] *n.* a school devoted to religious studies to prepare students for careers in religion. ♦ *Sally studies religious education at the seminary.* ♦ *Bill went to the seminary for three years to become a preacher.*

semiprecious [sɛm i 'prɛʃ əs] *adj.* of or about a jewel that is not as expensive as a precious jewel. ♦ *John could only afford to give Jane a semiprecious stone.* ♦ *The jeweler recommended some pretty semiprecious gems.*

semiskilled [sɛm i 'skɪld] *adj.* partly skilled. ♦ *John urged the semiskilled laborers to form a union.* ♦ *The semiskilled factory worker returned to college to get a degree.*

Semitic [sə 'mɪt ɪk] **1.** *n.* a group of languages that includes Arabic, Aramaic, and Hebrew. ♦ *David studied at the university to become a scholar in ancient Semitic.* ♦ *Semitic is a group of languages spoken in countries in the Middle East.* **2.** *adj.* <the adj. use of ①.> ♦ *The Middle East is the center of Semitic culture.* ♦ *Many Semitic peoples live on the Arabian peninsula.* **3.** *adj.* [of people and culture] Jewish. ♦ *John studies Semitic culture in the Jewish Studies Program at the university.* ♦ *The rabbi is very knowledgeable about Semitic history in the Middle East.*

senate ['sɛn ɪt] **1.** *n.* the smaller of the two groups of people who are elected to make the federal laws in the U.S. ♦ *The United States Senate has 100 senators, two from each state.* ♦ *One term in the United States Senate lasts six years.* **2.** *n.* the professors who are the governing body at some schools and universities. ♦ *The faculty senate voted to punish the students caught cheating.* ♦ *The administration asked the senate for input on the new curriculum.*

senator ['sɛn ə tɚ] *n.* someone who is a member of a senate. ♦ *President Lyndon Johnson had also been a senator from Texas.* ♦ *Senator Smith spoke at length about the proposed legislation.*

senatorial [sɛn ə 'tor i əl] *adj.* of or about a senator or senators. ♦ *The reporter covered the senatorial races throughout the country.* ♦ *The bill was subject to much senatorial debate.*

send ['sɛnd] **1.** *tv., irreg.* to cause someone or something to be transported or to go from one place to another. (Pt/pp: sent.) ♦ *Mary sent John a package in the mail.* ♦ *Susan sent her computer file to the printer.* **2. send for** *iv., irreg. + prep. phr.* to request that someone come. ♦ *The executive sent for the company treasurer.* ♦ *The doctor sent for an ambulance to take the injured man to the hospital.* **3. send someone off** *idiom* to participate in saying good-bye to someone who is leaving. ♦ *We had a party to send Tom off on his vacation.* ♦ *Bob's parents sent him off from the airport.* **4. send someone into something** *idiom* to cause someone to be in a certain state or condition. ♦ *The horrifying news sent our family into hysterics.* ♦ *The clerk's rude behavior sent the customer into a fit of anger.*

send-off ['sɛnd ɔf] *n.* a gathering in honor of someone who is beginning a trip or a new experience. ♦ *Mary gave Bob a lavish send-off when he left for graduate school.* ♦ *Anne was given a proper send-off before she began her journey.*

Senegal ['sɛn ə gɔl] See Gazetteer.

senile ['si nɑɪl] *adj.* becoming forgetful or mentally disoriented because of advancing age. (Adv: *senilely.*) ♦ *The senile woman could not remember her own name.* ♦ *As our father became senile, we hired a nurse to take care of him.*

senility [sə 'nɪl ə ti] *n.* a state of disorientation associated with old age. (No plural form in this sense.) ♦ *Owing to his senility, he could not handle his money matters.* ♦ *Keeping the mind and body active may prevent senility.*

senior ['sin jɚ] **1.** *adj.* [of people] older; [of employees] serving an employer longer than most other employees. ♦ *The senior professor was treated with respect and admiration.* ♦ *This new approach is difficult for the senior employees to understand.* **2.** *adj.* higher in rank or position. ♦ *A president is more senior than a vice president.* ♦ *The private spoke to a senior officer about the matter.* **3.** *adj.* of or for students in the fourth year of high school or college. ♦ *The shy boy didn't ask anyone to the senior prom.* ♦ *They handed out achievement awards at the senior banquet.* **4.** *adj.* for elderly people; serving elderly people. ♦ *The nurse gave a speech at the senior center.* ♦ *The elderly man demanded his senior discount.* **5.** *n.* an older person; a senior citizen. ♦ *This large retirement center is for seniors.* ♦ *When I am a senior, I hope to be able to afford medical care.* **6.** *n.* a student in the fourth year of high school (12th grade) or the fourth year of college. ♦ *Each senior had to write a thesis before graduating from college.* ♦ *The principal spoke to the seniors on graduation day.* **7. one's senior** *n.* someone who is older or who has a higher rank or position. ♦ *Tom is my senior in both age and rank.* ♦ *I will have to discuss this proposal with my seniors, who are more experienced in these matters.*

senior citizen ['sin jɚ 'sɪt ɪ zən] *n.* someone who is 65 years old or older. ♦ *The senior citizens were given a discount at the ticket office.* ♦ *Bob, a healthy and happy senior citizen, has no intention of retiring.*

seniority [sin 'jor ɪ ti] **1.** *n.* the quality of having been employed at one's place of work for a relatively longer period of time than someone else. (No plural form in this sense.) ♦ *The workers with the least seniority were laid off first.* ♦ *The employees' salaries were based on seniority.* **2.** *n.* the quality of being older than someone else. (No plural form in this sense.) ♦ *I respect my professors because of their seniority.* ♦ *Because of Dave's seniority, everyone called him Grandpa Dave.*

sensation [sɛn 'se ʃən] **1.** *n.* the ability to use the senses; the ability to see, hear, touch, taste, or smell. (No plural form in this sense.) ♦ *The sensation of taste is dulled by cigarettes.* ♦ *John lost all sensation after the horrible accident.* **2.** *n.* an awareness of someone or something because of sight, sound, touch, taste, or smell. ♦ *The very loud music caused painful sensations in my ear.* ♦ *The creamy dessert created a pleasant sensation on my tongue.* **3.** *n.* a vague feeling of awareness; a general feeling in the mind. (Figurative on ①.) ♦ *I had the eerie sensation that my best friend was in danger.* ♦ *Bill had a sensation that he was being followed.* **4.** *n.* someone or something that causes people to become very excited or interested. ♦ *The raunchy movie was quite a sensation in my hometown.* ♦ *The prominent politician was quite a sensation at the banquet.*

sensational [sɛn 'se ʃə nəl] **1.** *adj.* very exciting or interesting; fantastic. (Adv: *sensationally.*) ♦ *I told my friends about the sensational new film I'd seen.* ♦ *The singer gave a sensational performance yesterday.* **2.** *adj.* flamboyant or exaggerated; designed to excite and appeal to a mass audience. (Adv: *sensationally.*) ♦ *The tabloid's sensational coverage of the trial was criticized.* ♦ *The news presented mundane stories in a sensational manner.*

sense ['sɛns] **1.** *n.* each of the abilities allowing creatures to see, hear, touch, taste, or smell. ♦ *A blind person has no sense of sight.* ♦ *The thick smoke affected my senses of sight and smell.* **2.** *n.* a feeling or perception, especially one that cannot be described. (No plural form in this sense.) ♦ *John had a sense that he was being followed.* ♦ *Anne had a sense that something was wrong.* **3.** *n.* the ability to understand or appreciate something. (No plural form in this sense.) ♦ *Most musicians have a good sense of rhythm.* ♦ *The excellent comedian had a perfect sense of timing.* **4.** *n.* good judgment; the ability to make good decisions. (No plural form in this sense.) ♦ *Sometimes Bob does not use any sense when he is shopping.* ♦ *I put my faith in the sense of my elected officials.* **5.** *n.* the meaning or definition of something; meaning. ♦ *A dictionary defines the various senses of its entry words.* ♦ *The word* bank *has at least two completely different senses.* ♦ *Each sense in this dictionary has a number before it.* **6.** *n.* an impression; an understanding shared by a group of people. ♦ *The jury's initial sense was that the defendant was guilty.* ♦ *The class had a sense that the professor was unprepared.* **7.** *tv.* to be aware of something with the help of ①. ♦ *John sensed some cinnamon in the apple pie.* ♦ *Mary sensed the odor of gas in the air.* **8.** *tv.* to surmise something; to have a feeling about a situation. ♦ *Anne sensed the confusion in the meeting.* ♦ *John sensed that there was trouble between David and me.* **9. come to one's senses** *idiom* to become conscious; to start thinking clearly. ♦ *John, come to your senses. You're being quite stupid.* ♦ *In the morning I don't come to my senses until I have had two cups of coffee.* **10. horse sense** *idiom* common sense ④; practical thinking. ♦ *Bob is no scholar but he has a lot of horse sense.* ♦ *Horse sense tells me I should not be involved in that project.* **11. sixth sense** *idiom* a supposed power to know or feel things that are not perceptible by the five senses ① of sight, hearing, smell, taste, and touch. ♦ *My sixth sense told me to avoid going home by my usual route. Later I discovered there had been a fatal accident on it.* ♦ *Jane's sixth sense demanded that she not trust Tom, even though he seemed honest enough.*

senseless ['sɛns ləs] **1.** *adj.* without reason; having no purpose; stupid; foolish. (Adv: *senselessly.*) ♦ *There was no motive for the senseless murder.* ♦ *Your argument is based on senseless premises.* **2.** *adj.* unconscious. (Adv: *senselessly.*) ♦ *The paramedics tried to revive the senseless crash victim.* ♦ *The senseless patient lay in a coma for eight months.*

sensibility [sɛns ə 'bɪl ɪ ti] *n.* a delicate feeling or emotion, especially in someone who is easily offended. ♦ *Mary's vulgar language offended Sue's sensibilities.* ♦ *Bob took Dave's sensibilities into account when renting a movie.*

sensible ['sɛns ə bəl] **1.** *adj.* representing or showing common sense; wise. (Adv: *sensibly.*) ♦ *The sensible action would be to save as much money as possible.* ♦ *Jane is a sensible woman.* **2.** *adj.* practical instead of stylish. (Adv: *sensibly.*) ♦ *The nurse wore sensible shoes to work.* ♦ *The furniture is sensible instead of fancy.*

sensitive ['sɛns ə tɪv] **1.** *adj.* able to feel the effect of something, especially light, sound, smell, taste, or texture. (Adv: *sensitively.*) ♦ *My eyes are very sensitive to sunlight.* ♦ *Dogs are more sensitive to odors than people are.* **2.** *adj.* easily offended; [of someone] easily affected by something. (Figurative on ①. Adv: *sensitively.*) ♦ *Bob is too sensitive about what people think about him.* ♦ *This violent movie may upset sensitive viewers.* **3.** *adj.* easily able to detect a small change in something. ♦ *A sensitive seismograph can detect very minor earthquakes.* ♦ *Photographic film is very sensitive to light.* **4. sensitive to** *adj.* perceptive of something, such as someone else's feelings or preferences. ♦ *Mary is sensitive to other people's feelings.* ♦ *I wish you were more sensitive to my needs.*

sensitivity [sɛns ə 'tɪv ɪ ti] **1.** *n.* the ability to sense or detect something. (No plural form in this sense.) ♦ *The sensitivity of a dog's nose makes it a good animal for hunting.* ♦ *I wore sunglasses because of my eyes' sensitivity to bright light.* **2.** *n.* the tendency to detect or imagine even the smallest offense. (No plural form in this sense.) ♦ *Because of Bob's excessive sensitivity, he often feels insulted.* ♦ *Anne's sensitivity to vulgarity limits the books she can read.*

sensitize ['sɛns ə taɪz] *tv.* to cause someone or something to become sensitive. ♦ *An allergy has sensitized my eyes to pollution in the air.* ♦ *Being away from cigarette smoke has sensitized me to the slightest smell of it.*

sensor ['sɛns ɚ] *n.* a device that detects a change in something, such as temperature or air pressure. ♦ *The thief's movement triggered one of the alarm's sensors.* ♦ *The sensor indicated that the greenhouse's temperature was too low.*

sensory ['sɛns ə ri] *adj.* of the senses; of the ability to see, hear, taste, touch, or smell. ♦ *Some drugs inhibit sensory perception, while others enhance it.* ♦ *The prisoner who lived for months with no sensory stimulation went insane.*

sensual ['sɛn ʃu əl] *adj.* pleasurable to the body; concerning the pleasures of eating, drinking, sex, etc. (Adv: *sensually.*) ♦ *Sensual pleasures or thinking about them occupies much of Bob's time.* ♦ *He decided to enjoy all the sensual pleasures he could while he was young.*

sensuous [sɛn 'ʃu əs] *adj.* affecting the senses; perceived through the senses. (Adv: *sensuously.*) ♦ *The physical therapist gave me a very sensuous massage, using scented oils.* ♦ *Floating in the warm ocean water was a very sensuous experience.*

sent ['sɛnt] pt/pp of send.

sentence ['sɛnt ns] **1.** *n.* a group of words that forms an independent thought, usually including at least a subject and a verb. ♦ *"The cat is on the mat" is a sentence that is a statement.* ♦ *Jane's letter was only a few sentences long, but it said many important things.* **2.** *n.* the punishment given to a criminal by a judge in a court of law. ♦ *The judge gave the criminal the maximum sentence possible.* ♦ *The sentence of the killer was commuted.* **3.** *tv.* [for a judge] to assign a punishment to a criminal. ♦ *The judge sentenced the rapist to life in prison.* ♦ *The court sentenced the murderer one week after he was found guilty.*

sentencing ['sɛnt n sɪŋ] *n.* assigning a punishment to a criminal. (No plural form in this sense.) ♦ *The defendant was present in the courtroom for sentencing.* ♦ *The judge was criticized for such lenient sentencing.*

sentiment ['sɛn tə mənt] **1.** *n.* a tender feeling or emotion. (No plural form in this sense.) ♦ *We were shocked at John's lack of sentiment at the funeral.* ♦ *Bill's sentiment was expressed in a poem.* **2. sentiments** *n.* an expression of ①. (Treated as plural.) ♦ *I think preprinted sentiments in birthday cards are sometimes too emotional.* ♦ *I wrote my sentiments to the grieving family on a card.* **3.** *n.* a way of thinking about an issue; an attitude. (No plural form in this sense.) ♦ *We share the same sentiment about trying to help others.* ♦ *I understand your sentiment on this matter.*

sentimental [sɛn tə 'mɛn təl] *adj.* having tender feelings or emotions, often sad ones. (Adv: *sentimentally.*) ♦ *Mary felt sentimental about life each autumn.* ♦ *Everyone at the reunion had sentimental memories of high school.*

sentimentalism [sɛn tə 'mɛn tə lɪz əm] *n.* an exaggerated display of sentiment, filled with emotion and trivial sentiment. (No plural form in this sense.) ♦ *Since John hated Bill, his sentimentalism at Bill's funeral was insincere.* ♦ *Mary felt that there was too much sentimentalism in the poem I wrote.*

sentry ['sɛn tri] *n.* someone, usually a soldier, who guards a place; a soldier who stands guard. ♦ *The sentry allowed me to pass when I said the password.* ♦ *Two sentries guarded the building lobby during the night.*

separable ['sɛp ɚ ə bəl] *adj.* able to be separated; able to be divided. (Adv: *separably.*) ♦ *The parts of the stereo system were separable, so I put the speakers in the living room.* ♦ *The two parts of the idea are not separable.*

separate 1. ['sɛp rət] *adj.* not together; not joined; apart; single; individual. (Adv: *separately.*) ♦ *I've been to Europe on three separate occasions.* ♦ *Our garage is separate from our house.* **2.** ['sɛp ə ret] *tv.* to be between two or more things or people; to keep two or more things or people apart. ♦ *Only a thin wall separated the two apartments.* ♦ *A fence separated the sheep from the goats.* **3.** ['sɛp ə ret] *tv.* to cause two or more things or people to be apart. ♦ *Anne separated the orange and ate one section at a time.* ♦ *The teacher separated the children who were talking in class.* **4.** ['sɛp ə ret] *iv.* to break apart; to divide; to split. ♦ *Under the microscope, I saw one cell separate into two cells.* ♦ *Where the road separates, go left into town.* **5.** ['sɛp ə ret] *iv.* [for a husband and wife] to live apart for a period of time, often as a prelude to divorce. ♦ *John's parents were separated and he seldom saw his father any longer.* ♦ *Bob and Jane separated a year before their divorce.* **6. separate the men from the boys; separate the sheep from the goats** ['sɛp ə ret…] *idiom* to separate the competent from those who are less competent. (Not necessarily for males.) ♦ *This is the kind of task that separates the men from the boys.* ♦ *Working in a challenging place like this really separates the sheep from the goats.*

separated ['sɛp ə ret ɪd] *adj.* [of a married couple] no longer living together but not divorced. ♦ *The separated couple decided to file for divorce.* ♦ *Well, John is still married, but he's separated.*

separately ['sɛp rət li] *adv.* apart; not together; singly; individually. ♦ *John and Jane fly separately so they don't both die if either plane crashes.* ♦ *Oddly, each of my friends had come to the party separately.*

separation [sɛp ə 're ʃən] **1.** *n.* a state of having been separated. (No plural form in this sense.) ♦ *The separation of the children into reading groups was based on their ability.* ♦ *Dave's separation from his children made him sad.* **2.** *n.* a period of time when two people who are married no longer live together but have not yet divorced. ♦ *After a brief separation, the couple decided to remain married.* ♦ *After three trial separations, they were divorced.* **3.** *n.* the place where something divides, splits, or breaks apart. (No plural form in this sense.) ♦ *The separation in the broken bones was easily seen on the X-ray.* ♦ *At the separation of Route 6 and Route 10, stay on Route 10.*

September [sɛp 'tɛm bɚ] *n.* the ninth month of the year, coming after August and before October. ♦ *Our school began class in September, shortly after Labor Day.* ♦ *The first day of autumn occurs on or around September 22.*

septic tank ['sɛp tɪk tæŋk] *n.* a large underground tank for collecting household sewage, used when a municipal sewer is not available. ♦ *There was a bad odor when our septic tank cracked.* ♦ *Our house was so far from the city that we needed a septic tank.*

sequel ['si kwəl] **1.** *n.* a movie or book that is a continuation of an earlier movie or book, usually featuring some of the same characters or situations; a continuation. ♦ *There have been four sequels to that popular movie, all starring the same actor.* ♦ *The author wrote a sequel that was not as good as the original.* **2.** *n.* something that happens after something else, usually as a result. ♦ *As a sequel to his traffic accident, Bill lost his job for being late.* ♦ *The sequel to the story of my broken leg is that I broke the other one on the way home from the hospital.*

sequence ['si kwəns] **1.** *n.* the order in which a group of things or people are placed; the order in which a series of events happen. ♦ *The secretary placed the files in an alphabetical sequence.* ♦ *The class studied the sequence of events leading to World War II.* **2.** *tv.* to put things or people into ①. ♦ *The secretary sequenced the files in alphabetical order.* ♦ *The manager sequenced the buses five minutes apart.*

sequester [sɪ 'kwɛs tɚ] *tv.* to keep someone apart from other people, especially to isolate members of a jury during a trial. ♦ *The judge sequestered the jury in a hotel for weeks during the sensational trial.* ♦ *The actress sequestered herself from others while vacationing.*

sequin ['si kwɪn] *n.* a small, shiny, piece of plastic that is sewn onto clothing and cloth as a decoration. ♦ *The sequins on the dancers' costumes glittered onstage.* ♦ *Each sequin was attached to this dress by hand.*

Serbia ['sɚ bi ə] See Gazetteer.

serenade [sɛr ə 'ned] **1.** *n.* a song sung to someone; a love song. ♦ *John's serenade to his girlfriend was romantic, even though he sang off-key.* ♦ *At the restaurant, a quartet sang a serenade for the patrons.* **2.** *tv.* to sing a romantic song to someone; to play a romantic piece of music for someone. ♦ *David serenaded his date with a romantic love song.* ♦ *After Bill serenaded Jane, he proposed to her.*

serene [sə 'rin] *adj.* quiet; calm; peaceful; tranquil. (Adv: *serenely.*) ♦ *John spent a serene week resting in a remote cabin.* ♦ *Mary looked at the sun's reflection on the serene lake.*

serenity [sə 'rɛn ɪ ti] *n.* the quality of being serene. (No plural form in this sense.) ♦ *The village's peaceful serenity was shattered by gunfire.* ♦ *Bill meditates to achieve serenity.*

sergeant ['sɑr dʒənt] **1.** *n.* a noncommissioned officer in the air force, marines, or army, with a rank just above a corporal. ♦ *Sergeant Williams saluted his superior, who had just entered the room.* ♦ *The corporal felt honored to be promoted to sergeant.* **2.** *n.* a police officer with a rank just above the lowest rank. ♦ *The police captain sent Sergeant Wilson to the crime scene.* ♦ *The police officers had to pass an exam in order to become sergeants.*

serial ['sɪr i əl] **1.** *n.* a story that is presented in separate parts. ♦ *Daytime television serials are also known as soap operas.* ♦ *Each day, a new segment of the serial is broadcast.* **2. serial killer** *n.* a murderer who kills many people, one after the other. ♦ *A serial killer is loose in the city, terrifying everyone.* ♦ *The police finally caught the serial killer.* **3. serial murder; serial killing** *n.* murders that happen one after the other, presumably done by the same killer. ♦ *The detectives were puzzled by the serial murders.* ♦ *Serial killings had terrified the entire town.* **4.** *adj.* <the adj. use of ①.> (Adv: *serially.*) ♦ *A new serial drama starts next week on television.* ♦ *Lisa writes serial stories for daytime television.*

series ['sɪr iz] **1.** *n.* a group of similar things that happen or appear one after the other in a certain order; a group of similar things that are arranged in a row; a succession. (Treated as singular.) ♦ *The police investigated a series of arson attempts.* ♦ *The reporter asked the politician a series of questions.* **2.** *n.* an installment of a television entertainment program that is broadcast periodically, usually once per week. ♦ *An actor from a popular comedy series came to Mary's party.* ♦ *I really can't stand watching that series.*

serious ['sɪr i əs] **1.** *adj.* earnest; solemn; sincere. (Adv: *seriously.*) ♦ *The serious professor rarely smiled during class.* ♦ *Could you be serious for a minute and stop making jokes?* **2.** *adj.* important; severe; not trivial; not slight; not minor. (Adv: *seriously.*) ♦ *The crash victim's head wounds were very serious.* ♦ *John has a serious problem with his car. He may have to get a new one.*

seriousness ['sɪr i əs nəs] *n.* importance; gravity; a state of being serious ① or ②. (No plural form in this sense.) ♦ *The seriousness of Tom's frown makes people think that he has no fun.* ♦ *The seriousness of the situation frightened the children.*

sermon ['sɚ mən] **1.** *n.* a speech about religion or morals, especially one given by a clergyman or clergywoman. ♦ *Today's sermon was based on a story from the Bible.* ♦ *The minister's sermon on peace pleased everyone.* **2.** *n.* a long speech by someone who is giving advice or who is reprimanding someone else. (Figurative on ①.) ♦ *John expected a sermon from his parents for coming home late.* ♦ *My roommate gave me a sermon about being too messy.*

serpent ['sɚ pənt] *n.* a snake. (Literary.) ♦ *Serpents and alligators infest the swamp.* ♦ *The stone floor of the dungeon was covered with serpents.*

serpentine ['sɚ pən tin] *adj.* curved like a snake; shaped like the letter *S.* ♦ *The old city's serpentine streets are confusing.* ♦ *The chain was made up of serpentine links.*

serrated ['sɛr et ɪd] *adj.* having a notched edge, like the blade of a saw. ♦ *Dave cut the bread with a serrated knife.* ♦ *I placed a deeply serrated blade in the saw so I could cut the dense wood.*

serum ['sɪr əm] *n.* a liquid that is injected into the bloodstream to cure or prevent a disease. (Usually made from the blood of an animal that is immune to the disease. No plural form in this sense.) ♦ *The doctor brought needed serum to the remote village.* ♦ *The serum contains the antibodies the patient needs to fight the disease.*

servant ['sɚ vənt] *n.* someone who serves a person, the public, or God, especially someone who is paid to work for someone else in that person's house. ♦ *A trusted servant served dinner to the royal family.* ♦ *The palace has a staff of more than 40 servants.*

serve ['sɚv] **1.** *tv.* to provide someone with service. ♦ *The butler had served the same family for his entire life.* ♦ *Our old car has served us well for nearly ten years.* **2.** *tv.* to bring (previously ordered) food to someone, as in a restaurant. ♦ *The server served the salads first.* ♦ *The waitress served us our dinner.* **3.** *tv.* to provide a useful service or function. ♦ *The workers who no longer served a function were laid off.* ♦ *The human appendix no longer serves a useful purpose.* **4. serve (on)** *tv.* (+ *prep. phr.*) to present a subpoena [to someone]. ♦ *Who will serve these papers on Max?* ♦ *The law clerk served the subpoena while disguised as a waiter.* **5.** *tv.* to hit a ball first in order to start a play in tennis, Ping-Pong, and other similar sports. ♦ *Would you stop talking and serve the ball?* ♦ *Anne served the volleyball high above the net.* **6. serve with** *tv.* + *prep. phr.* to present someone with a subpoena. ♦ *Tom served Mary with the subpoena.* ♦ *The law clerk served Max with an order to be in court.* **7.** *iv.* to perform military service. ♦ *David served for twenty years in the air force.* ♦ *I spoke with a veteran who had served in the Vietnam War.* **8. serve as** *iv.* + *prep. phr.* to be used as; to fulfill a particular need. ♦ *Jimmy's hat had to serve as first base in the baseball game.* ♦ *The vice president will have to serve as president for the next two meetings.* **9.** *iv.* to begin a play in sports like tennis and Ping-Pong by hitting the ball toward the other player. ♦ *John served, but the ball hit the net.* ♦ *I threw the ball to Anne because it was her turn to serve.* **10.** *n.* the act of hitting a ball as in ⑨. ♦ *Bill's opening serve hit the net.* ♦ *Mary easily returned my serve back over the net.* **11. serve time** *idiom* to spend a certain amount of time in jail. ♦ *The criminal served ten years in jail.* ♦ *After the felon served his time, he was released from prison.* **12. serve as a guinea pig** *idiom* [for someone] to be experimented on; to allow some sort of test to be performed on one. ♦ *Try it on someone else! I don't want to serve as a guinea pig!* ♦ *Jane agreed to serve as a guinea pig. She'll be the one to try out the new flavor of ice cream.* **13. serve someone right** *idiom* [for an act or event] to punish someone fairly (for doing something). ♦ *John copied off my test paper. It would serve him right if he fails the test.* ♦ *It'd serve John right if he got arrested.*

server ['sɚ vɚ] **1.** *n.* a utensil used to serve certain foodstuffs. ♦ *Jane got a lovely silver pie server for her wedding anniversary.* ♦ *Tom put the jelly server in the sugar bowl by mistake.* **2.** *n.* someone who delivers subpoenas. ♦ *The server shoved the papers into my hand and left.* ♦ *The lawyer asked his secretary to act as server of the subpoenas.* **3.** *n.* a waitress; a waiter. ♦ *The server brought me the soup that I had ordered.* ♦ *I asked the server for more coffee.*

service ['sɚ vɪs] **1.** *n.* the work that someone does for the benefit of someone; work done by servants, clerks, food servers, taxi drivers, etc. (No plural form in this sense.) ♦ *I did not like the service in that restaurant.* ♦ *The clerk provided the service that I needed.* **2.** *n.* the repair of a machine or device; maintenance. (No plural form in this sense.) ♦ *I took my broken television to the repair shop for service.* ♦ *The service on my broken watch was costly.* **3. services** *n.* work that is done to help someone, especially the work done by a professional person. (Treated as plural.) ♦ *Our company needs the services of a good accountant.* ♦ *When I was sued, I sought the services of a lawyer.* **4.** *n.* the benefit provided by a company or organization that fulfills the needs of people and that usually does not manufacture products. (This includes *electric service, natural gas service, telephone service, water service, sewer service, message service, diaper service, lawn care service,* etc.) ♦ *We paid a diaper service to pick up our baby's dirty diapers and clean them.* ♦ *I left a message for Anne with her message service.* **5.** *n.* military service; serving [one's country] in a military organization. ♦ *John was in the service for four years.* ♦ *Anne was in the service during the Persian Gulf War.* **6.** *n.* a religious meeting or ceremony. ♦ *I went to the church service in honor of the dead mayor.* ♦ *The devout worshiper went to a service twice a week.* **7.** *n.* the set of dishes, glasses, silverware, etc., for a certain number of people. ♦ *Bob bought a fancy service for eight.* ♦ *Mary inherited her grandmother's fine porcelain service.* **8.** *n.* putting a ball into play in sports such as tennis and Ping-Pong. (No plural form in this sense.) ♦ *The service of the tennis ball hit the net.* ♦ *Before each service, the crowd became very quiet.* **9.** *tv.* to repair or adjust something mechanical or electronic. ♦ *Max serviced my broken washing machine.* ♦ *They are servicing my car in the shop.* **10. out of service** *idiom* inoperable; not currently operating. ♦ *Both elevators are out of service, so I had to use the stairs.* ♦ *The washroom is temporarily out of service.*

serviceable ['sɚ vɪs ə bəl] *adj.* useful; able to be used, especially for a long time; durable. (Adv: *serviceably.*) ♦ *My car may be old, but it's serviceable.* ♦ *I need to buy a sturdy, serviceable washing machine.*

serviceman ['sɚ vəs mæn] **1.** *n., irreg.* a man who is in the military. (Pl: servicemen.) ♦ *The gym near the military base is usually full of servicemen.* ♦ *Hundreds of servicemen died in the bloody battle.* **2.** *n., irreg.* someone, usually a male, who repairs machines or devices; someone who services machines or appliances. ♦ *The serviceman fixed my water heater in fifteen minutes.* ♦ *I called a serviceman to repair the refrigerator.*

servicemen ['sɚ vəs mɛn] pl of serviceman.

servicewoman ['sɚ vəs wʊm ən] **1.** *n., irreg.* a woman who is in the military. (Pl: servicewomen.) ♦ *The servicewoman showed her identification when entering the base.* ♦ *Six servicewomen were awarded medals in the military ceremony.* **2.** *n., irreg.* a woman who repairs machines, devices, or appliances. ♦ *The servicewoman rewired the airplane's control panel.* ♦ *A servicewoman charged $75 an hour to fix my furnace.*

servicewomen ['sɚ vəs wɪm ən] pl of servicewoman.

servile ['sɚv ɑɪl] *adj.* behaving like a slave; letting someone control oneself; submissive. (Adv: *servilely.*) ♦ *The cruel manager mistreated the servile employees.* ♦ *Tom refused to be a servile employee, so he contradicted his boss's statement.*

serving ['sɚ vɪŋ] *n.* a portion [of food]; the amount of food that is served at one time. ♦ *The cafeteria worker gave me a large serving of potatoes.* ♦ *This recipe provides eight servings.*

servitude ['sɚ vɪ tud] *n.* slavery; the condition of being forced to do what someone else wants. (No plural form in this sense.) ♦ *The children of slaves were also subject to a life of servitude.* ♦ *Many immigrants repaid their travel costs by a period of servitude.*

sesame ['sɛs ə mi] **1.** *n.* a tropical plant that is farmed for its small, oily seeds. (No plural form in this sense.) ♦ *Sesame is an herb.* ♦ *The farmer also raised sesame for cooking oil.* **2. sesame seeds** *n.* the seeds of ①. ♦ *The bread was topped with sesame seeds.* ♦ *Sesame seeds are sold in small bottles or jars.* **3. sesame oil** *n.* the oil pressed from toasted ②. (No plural form in this sense.) ♦ *Sesame oil is good in Chinese food.* ♦ *Bill used sesame oil in his casserole.*

session ['sɛ ʃən] **1.** *n.* a period of time during which a meeting is held or an activity is pursued. ♦ *Mary hasn't enrolled for the fall session of classes yet.* ♦ *We chose to attend the morning session of the seminar and skip the afternoon session.* **2. in session** *phr.* [of a court, congress, or other organization] operating or functioning. ♦ *Smoking is forbidden while the meeting is in session.* ♦ *The spectators must remain quiet while court is in session.*

set ['sɛt] **1.** *tv., irreg.* to put someone or something on a surface; to place someone or something somewhere. (Pt/pp: set.) ♦ *Anne set her glasses on the counter.* ♦ *Bill set a book on his desk.* **2.** *tv., irreg.* to move someone or something into a certain position. ♦ *Mary set the tilted vase upright.* ♦ *Dave set the bookshelf against the wall.* **3.** *tv., irreg.* to reposition and join the ends of a broken bone. ♦ *The doctor set Bill's broken arm.* ♦ *If your wrist is broken, the doctor will have to set it.* **4.** *tv., irreg.* to determine or establish a value, a standard, a time, an amount, etc. ♦ *We set the cost of the book at $27.95.* ♦ *Have you set a time for your appointment yet?* **5. set on** *tv., irreg. + prep. phr.* to order a dog to attack someone. ♦ *Mary set her dog on the mugger.* ♦ *John set his German shepherd on the robber.* **6.** *tv., irreg.* to adjust a machine so that it works correctly; to adjust something so that it will show the correct measurement. ♦ *The grocer set the scales to read "0" when empty.* ♦ *Mary set the thermostat on 68 degrees.* **7. set up** *tv.* + *adv.* to arrange the time and place of a meeting, appointment, interview, etc. ♦ *I called my dentist's office to set up an appointment.* ♦ *Can I set up a meeting with you early next week?* **8.** *iv., irreg.* to gel; to take a certain shape; to become shaped; to harden. ♦ *The glue set as it dried.* ♦ *I put the gelatin in the refrigerator to set.* **9.** *iv., irreg.* [for the sun] to drop below the horizon at night; to sink out of sight. ♦ *Tonight the sun will set at 5:39 P.M.* ♦ *As the sun set, the street lights came on.* **10.** *iv., irreg.* [for a color, stain, or dye] to become permanent. ♦ *The spilled red wine set into the white carpet.* ♦ *I needed to clean my shirt before the spilled coffee set.* **11.** *n.* a collection of related things; a group of things that are found or belong together. ♦ *{2, 4, 6, 8} is the set of even numbers between 1 and 9.* ♦ *Mary's blue salt and pepper shakers are a matched set.* **12. television set** See television ②. **13.** *n.* the scenery for a play, TV show, or movie. ♦ *The scenic designer built and painted the set.* ♦ *The news reporters took their places on the set.* **14.** *n.* the way the features of one's face are shaped or positioned. (No plural form in this sense.) ♦ *Bob's facial muscles have an evil set.* ♦ *John has a powerful set to his jaw.* **15.** *n.* a group of six or more tennis games. ♦ *The champion easily won the set in six games.* ♦ *The tennis player was exhausted after the grueling set.* **16.** *adj.* ready. (Not prenominal.) ♦ *Let me know when you're set to go.* ♦ *I'm all set. Let's leave.* **17.** *adj.* established; determined in advance; arranged. ♦ *We were provided with a set menu at the banquet.* ♦ *The guests arrived at the set time.* **18. not set foot somewhere** *idiom* not to go somewhere. ♦ *I wouldn't set foot in John's room. I'm very angry with him.* ♦ *He never set foot here.* **19. set a trap** *idiom* to adjust and prepare a trap to catch an animal. ♦ *Bill set a mousetrap and baited it with cheese.* ♦ *The old man set a trap to catch an annoying squirrel.* **20. set fire to something** *idiom* to light something on fire; to ignite something, often by accident. ♦ *The candle set fire to the curtains.* ♦ *I was afraid that the fire in the fireplace would set fire to the house.* **21. set someone or something free** *idiom* to release someone or something; to allow someone or something to leave, go away, depart, escape. ♦ *Jimmy went outside and set his balloon free.* ♦ *The army set the political prisoners free.* **22. set something to music** *idiom* to incorporate words into a piece of music; to write a piece of music to incorporate a set of words. ♦ *The musician set my lyrics to music.* ♦ *The rock band set the poem to music.* **23. set the table** *idiom* to arrange a table with plates and eating utensils in preparation for a meal. ♦ *Please help me get ready for dinner by setting the table.* ♦ *I set the table for six people, but only two dinner guests came.* **24. set type** *idiom* to arrange type ② for printing, now usually on a computer. ♦ *Have you finished setting the type for page one yet?* ♦ *John sets type for a living.*

setback ['sɛt bæk] **1.** *n.* something that causes something to change for the worse. ♦ *The candidate's death was a setback for the party.* ♦ *The loss of funds was a major setback to the agency.* **2.** *n.* the space between a building and the street, sidewalk, or property line. ♦ *The contractor was fined for building on the setback.* ♦ *The houses here all have a nine-foot setback from the street.*

settee [sɛ 'ti] *n.* a piece of furniture having a back and usually having arms, designed to seat two or more people; a kind of sofa. ♦ *I sat next to a stranger on a settee at the party.* ♦ *The tall man was unable to sleep on the settee.*

setter ['sɛt ɚ] *n.* a breed of dog that is trained to stand still and point its nose toward animals that are being hunted. ♦ *The setter indicated there were ducks in the marsh.* ♦ *The Irish setter retrieved the dead duck in its mouth.*

setting ['sɛt ɪŋ] **1.** *n.* the time and place where a story occurs. ♦ *The setting of this movie is New York City in the early 1960s.* ♦ *The dialogue in the first scene established the play's setting.* **2.** *n.* the frame or structure that holds a jewel or gem. ♦ *The diamond was held in a gold setting.* ♦ *Mary had her pearls put into a silver setting.* **3.** *n.* the surroundings or environment of something. ♦ *David didn't like the setting where the conference was held.* ♦ *Bill was accustomed to living in a more luxurious setting.* **4. (place) setting** *n.* the silverware, dishware, and glassware for one person. ♦ *Please get out four settings for dinner. I have guests.* ♦ *Mary received four place settings of her china as a birthday present.* **5.** *n.* a particular position of a calibrated control lever or knob; a particular amount of something as selected by a control device. ♦ *You should adjust the setting of your power saw. It is not cutting deeply enough.* ♦ *The volume setting of your stereo is too high! Please turn it down.*

settle ['sɛt əl] **1.** *tv.* to decide something, especially an argument or dispute; to resolve something. ♦ *Mary settled her argument with Bob by consulting an almanac.* ♦ *The union settled the strike when the contract was signed.* **2.** *tv.* to pay a bill or account. ♦ *We settled the bill at the end of the meal.* ♦ *I settled my account by paying everything I owed.* **3.** *tv.* to place oneself in a comfortable position; to place something in a comfortable position. (Takes a reflexive object.) ♦ *Bill settled himself into his easy chair.* ♦ *Anne settled herself into the hot, relaxing bathwater.* **4.** *tv.* to occupy land or a town and live there, often as a pioneer. ♦ *The pioneers settled the land alongside the great river.* ♦ *My ancestors settled this town in 1820.* **5. settle (down)** *tv.* (+ *adv.*) to cause someone or something to be calm, still, or less active. ♦ *I settled the children down by reading them a story.* ♦ *Some herbal tea will settle my nerves.* **6. settle in** *iv.* + *prep. phr.* to move to and reside somewhere. ♦ *My grandparents settled in the Cleveland area.* ♦ *My ancestors settled in this very town four generations ago.* **7. settle down** *iv.* + *adv.* to become calm, still, or less active. ♦ *If you children don't settle down, I'm taking you home!* ♦ *When tempers settled down, the meeting continued.* **8. settle (down)** *iv.* (+ *adv.*) to move into a comfortable position for resting or sleeping. ♦ *The dog settled down in front of the fireplace.* ♦ *Anne settled on the couch in front of the television.* **9.** *iv.* to sink, especially into the earth or to the bottom of something. ♦ *After the heavy rains, the house creaked as it settled.* ♦ *Undissolved sugar settled to the bottom of my glass of lemonade.* **10. settle (something) (out of court)** *idiom* to end a disagreement and reach an agreement without having to go through a court of justice. ♦ *The plaintiff and defendant decided to settle before the trial.* ♦ *Mary and Sue settled out of court before the trial.* **11. settle up with someone** *idiom* to pay someone what one owes; to pay one one's share of something. ♦ *I must settle up with Jim for the bike I bought for him.* ♦ *Bob paid the whole restaurant bill, and we all settled up with him later.*

settlement ['sɛt əl mənt] **1.** *n.* the establishing of towns or communities in new areas. (No plural form in this sense.) ♦ *The settlement of towns in the territory was mostly along the river.* ♦ *The government encouraged the settlement of the West.* **2.** *n.* a town established by people who move to an area where there was no town before. ♦ *The pioneers established settlements along the railway.* ♦ *The mayor of the pioneer settlement was also its founder.* **3.** *n.* an agreement that ends an argument, disagreement, or dispute. ♦ *Both parties must sign the settlement in order for it to go into effect.* ♦ *The union and management reached an acceptable settlement.*

settler ['sɛt lɚ] *n.* a pioneer; a colonist; someone who is one of the first people to live in an area that used to be undeveloped. ♦ *The frontier town was named for its first settler.* ♦ *The settlers crossed the plains in wagons and on horseback.*

setup ['sɛt əp] *n.* an arrangement; the way something is initially arranged or organized. ♦ *Mary thought the conference's setup was very unorganized.* ♦ *Every chess game has the same initial setup.*

seven ['sɛv ən] 7. See **four** for senses and examples.

seventeen ['sɛv ən 'tin] 17. See **four** for senses and examples.

seventeenth [sɛv ən 'tinθ] 17th. See **fourth** for senses and examples.

seventh ['sɛv ənθ] 7th. See **fourth** for senses and examples.

seventieth ['sɛv ən ti ɛθ] 70th. See **fourth** for senses and examples.

seventy ['sɛv ən ti] 70. See **forty** for senses and examples.

sever ['sɛv ɚ] **1.** *tv.* to cut through something; to cut something apart. ♦ *I severed the dead branches from the bushes and threw them away.* ♦ *Mary severed the string that bound the package.* **2.** *iv.* to break; to come apart; to separate. ♦ *When the wire severed, an alarm went off.* ♦ *Because it was rubbing against a sharp rock, the rope severed.* **3. sever ties with someone** *idiom* to end a relationship or agreement suddenly. ♦ *The company severed the embezzling employee's contract.* ♦ *John has severed all ties with his parents.*

several ['sɛv (ə) rəl] **1.** *adj.* some; a few, but not many. ♦ *Anne had several things to say about my presentation.* ♦ *It should be several degrees warmer tomorrow.* **2.** *n.* some people or things; a few people or things. (No plural form in this sense.) ♦ *Of the 15 people at the party, several had not been invited.* ♦ *John had many problems with the project and mentioned several to me.*

severance ['sɛv (ə) rəns] *n.* separating; ending of a relationship. (No plural form in this sense.) ♦ *The firm's severance of subsidiary companies saved a lot of money.* ♦ *Severance from my job when I retired was very difficult.*

severe [sə 'vɪr] **1.** *adj.* harsh; strict; not gentle. (Adv: *severely.* Comp: *severer;* sup: *severest.*) ♦ *The angry parents gave the naughty child a severe punishment.* ♦ *The judge gave the speeding driver a severe fine.* **2.** *adj.* strong; violent; causing harm; not mild. (Adv: *severely.* Comp: *severer;* sup: *severest.*) ♦ *The severe winds blew over large trees.* ♦ *The cold weather is so severe that you could easily get frostbite.* **3.** *adj.* plain; simple; not fancy; not decorated. (Adv: *severely.* Comp: *severer;* sup: *severest.*) ♦ *The teacher wore a very severe hairdo.* ♦ *The poor student could afford only a bleak and severe studio apartment.*

severed ['sɛv ɚd] *adj.* cut off; cut from; separated. ♦ *John threw the severed rope away.* ♦ *Mary tried to mend her severed ties to her family.*

severity [sɪ 'vɛr ɪ ti] *n.* the quality of being severe. (No plural form in this sense.) ♦ *The severity of the storm caused most people to stay inside.* ♦ *The severity of the crime disturbed the detective.*

sew ['so] **1.** *tv.* to attach two pieces of material together or to attach something to a piece of material by making stitches using a needle and thread. (Pt: **sewed**; pp: **sewed** or **sewn**.) ♦ *Bill sewed a patch over the hole in his trousers.* ♦ *The tailor has sewn the tear in my shirt.* **2.** *iv.* to attach with stitches using needle and thread. ♦ *As she sewed, Anne accidentally poked her finger with the needle.* ♦ *Bob learned how to sew in school.*

sewage ['su ɪdʒ] *n.* water and human waste that is carried away by sewers from homes and businesses. (No plural form in this sense.) ♦ *The city treated the sewage before releasing it into the river.* ♦ *Because of the storm, untreated sewage was washed into the bay.*

sewer 1. ['su ɚ] *n.* a pipe that carries waste away from homes and businesses. ♦ *There was an unpleasant smell when the sewers became clogged.* ♦ *When I dropped my keys, they fell through a grate and into the sewer.* **2.** ['so ɚ] *n.* someone who sews. ♦ *We helped make costumes for the play. I was a cutter and Tom was a sewer.* ♦ *We need a few sewers to help with the project.*

sewing ['so ɪŋ] **1.** *n.* the work that is done with needle and thread; the stitches made in material with needle and thread. (No plural form in this sense.) ♦ *In addition to laundry, these cleaners also do simple sewing.* ♦ *I ripped out the thread because Bob had done a bad job of sewing.* **2.** *n.* a piece of clothing or material that is being sewed. (No plural form in this sense.) ♦ *Mary put her sewing in her basket and went to bed.* ♦ *Where did I put the sewing I was working on?* **3.** *adj.* <the adj. use of ① or ②.> ♦ *The seamstress bought a new sewing machine with her profits.* ♦ *The tailor used only high-quality sewing needles.*

sewn ['son] a pp of sew.

sex ['sɛks] **1.** *n.* the topic of human sexual responses and sexual activity. (No plural form in this sense.) ♦ *Bob thought about sex often.* ♦ *Sex is a popular subject in movies, books, and all forms of entertainment.* **2.** *n.* sexual intercourse; copulation; sexual arousal leading to copulation; the urge to copulate; the subject of copulation. (No plural form in this sense.) ♦ *Bob thought often of sex.* ♦ *Sex is a powerful urge in all animals.* **3.** *n.* the state of being male or female. ♦ *The doctor announced the sex of the newborn infant.* ♦ *The children were assigned to groups according to sex.* **4. the sex act** *n.* an instance of sexual intercourse. ♦ *The anthropologist studied the sex acts of different cultures.* ♦ *Unable to perform the sex act, Bob became depressed.* **5.** *adj.* <the adj. use of ①.> ♦ *John and Mary visited a sex therapist.* ♦ *It was suggested that Dave buy a sex manual.*

sex appeal ['sɛks ə pil] *n.* attraction; a quality of a person that invites sexual interest. (No plural form in this sense.) ♦ *Advertisers use sex appeal to market products.* ♦ *The photographer captured the model's sex appeal on film.*

sexism ['sɛks ɪz əm] *n.* the belief that men are better than women; discrimination against women because they are women. (No plural form in this sense.) ♦ *Tom denied the charges of sexism placed against him.* ♦ *Mary claimed she wasn't promoted to the managerial position because of sexism.*

sexist ['sɛks əst] **1.** *n.* someone, usually a male, who practices sexism. ♦ *The female employees accused their boss of being a sexist.* ♦ *The female candidate claimed her opponent was a sexist.* **2.** *adj.* <the adj. use of ①.> (Adv: *sexistly.*) ♦ *Mary called Tom sexist because he held a door open for her.* ♦ *Anne accused her professor of making a sexist remark.*

sextet [sɛks 'tɛt] *n.* a group of six people, especially six musicians or six singers. ♦ *The sextet consisted of a piano, two violins, a viola, a cello, and a bass.* ♦ *The sextet sang an old German song at the concert.*

sexual ['sɛk ʃu əl] **1.** *adj.* of or about copulation or reproduction and the feelings and urges that are associated with that sphere of life. (Adv: *sexually.*) ♦ *The students studied the sexual life of the earthworm in biology.* ♦ *The sexual activity of many animals has been studied.* **2.** *adj.* requiring two creatures or organisms for reproduction; not asexual. ♦ *Unlike some plants, most animals practice sexual reproduction.* ♦ *Pollen is part of the sexual reproduction of plants.* **3. (sexual) intercourse** [sɛk ʃu ə 'ɪn tɚ kors] *n.* copulation; an act involving the genitals of two people for the purpose of creating pleasure or the production of offspring. (No plural form in this sense.) ♦ *Sexual intercourse represents a moral issue for many people.* ♦ *Anne used birth control every time she had intercourse.* **4. sexual promiscuity** See promiscuity.

sexuality [sɛk ʃu 'æl ɪ ti] *n.* human sexual matters and feelings; the involvement or interest a person has in sex. (No plural form in this sense.) ♦ *The artist had almost no interest in human sexuality.* ♦ *A group of parents condemned the rampant portrayal of sexuality in movies.*

sexually ['sɛks ju (ə) li] **1.** *adv.* in a sexual manner; in a way that concerns sex. ♦ *Anne believed that her date was sexually interested in her.* ♦ *The movie was claimed to be sexually stimulating.* **2. sexually promiscuous** See promiscuous.

sexy ['sɛk si] *adj.* of or about sex appeal; causing an interest in sex; sexually exciting. (Comp: *sexier;* sup: *sexiest.*) ♦ *Mary was wearing sexy lingerie under her dress.* ♦ *I was attracted to John's sexy smile.*

shabby ['ʃæb i] *adj.* having a messy appearance; looking run-down or worn out. (Adv: *shabbily.* Comp: *shabbier;* sup: *shabbiest.*) ♦ *The shabby old man asked me for a dollar.* ♦ *The shabby buildings made the neighborhood a bad place to live.*

shack ['ʃæk] *n.* a small house, hut, or shed that is quickly or poorly built; a shanty. ♦ *John kept his gardening equipment in a shack near the garden.* ♦ *The slum consisted of thousands of wooden shacks.*

shackle ['ʃæk əl] **1.** *n.* a set of metal bands that are locked around someone's wrists or ankles and that are attached to a chain fastened to something else. (Usually plural.) ♦ *The guard unlocked the prisoner's shackles.* ♦ *The prisoner's shackles were connected to the brick wall.* **2.** *n.* a restraint; something that prevents someone from being free. (Figurative on ①.) ♦ *Mary's debt from her student loans served as financial shackles.* ♦ *The shackle of guilt weighed heavily on the remorseful man.* **3.** *tv.* to restrain someone by using ①. ♦ *They shackled the prisoners to the wall.* ♦ *The cruel master shackled the slaves to their oars.*

shade ['ʃed] **1.** *n.* a place that is not directly exposed to sunlight because an object between that place and the sun blocks the sunlight. (No plural form in this sense.) ♦ *The shade under a tree is darker and cooler than direct sunlight.* ♦ *Mary sat in the shade in the park and read.* **2. (window) shade** *n.* a sheet of fabric designed to cover a window to keep the sun out and to prevent people from seeing in. ♦ *I pulled down the window shade so no one could see in.* ♦ *The shade keeps a lot of the sun's heat out.* **3.** *n.* a variety of a color; the paleness or deepness of a color; the lightness or darkness of a color. ♦ *Crimson, scarlet, and pink are all shades of red.* ♦ *The artist painted the sky a light shade of blue.* **4.** *n.* a slight amount of a quality; a nuance. ♦ *I detected a shade of irony in John's voice.* ♦ *There was a shade of panic in David's actions.* **5.** *tv.* to prevent light from reaching an area; to make something darker by blocking light. ♦ *Mary shaded her eyes with her hand.* ♦ *John's large hat shaded his face.* **6.** *tv.* to make something darker by painting or drawing on it with a darker color. ♦ *The artist shaded the outline with charcoal.* ♦ *The designer shaded the left side of the drawing of the house with a pencil.* **7. shades of someone or something** *idiom* reminders of someone or something; things reminiscent of someone or something. ♦ *When I met Jim's mother I thought, "shades of Aunt Mary."* ♦ *"Shades of high school," said Bob as the university lecturer rebuked him for being late.*

shading ['ʃed ɪŋ] *n.* the use of darker colors in paintings and drawings to make shadows. (No plural form in this sense.) ♦ *The artist's use of shading gave depth to the painting.* ♦ *Her expert shading made the picture look three-dimensional.*

shadow ['ʃæd o] **1.** *n.* the patch of shade created by someone or something blocking light. ♦ *Anne's house is in the shadow of a tall building.* ♦ *John moved his hand so that its shadow looked like a dog.* **2.** *n.* a slight suggestion; a trace. (No plural form in this sense.) ♦ *When our cat finally returned home and looked at us, there wasn't even a shadow of recognition.* ♦ *A shadow of uncertainty spread over the flawed project.* **3.** *n.* someone, especially a detective, who follows someone undetected. (Slang.) ♦ *Once the crook spotted his shadow, he got in a taxi and fled.* ♦ *The shadow followed the criminal to the scene of the crime.* **4.** *tv.* to follow someone secretly. ♦ *John hired a private detective to shadow his wife.* ♦ *A mysterious man was shadowing me all day, so I went to the police.* **5. shadow of oneself; shadow of itself** *idiom* someone or something that is not as strong, healthy, full, or lively as before. ♦ *The sick man was a shadow of his former self.* ♦ *The redecorated house was merely a shadow of its old self.* **6. without a shadow of a doubt; beyond the shadow of a doubt** *idiom* without the smallest amount of doubt. ♦ *I am certain that I am right, without a shadow of a doubt.* ♦ *I felt the man was guilty beyond the shadow of a doubt.*

shadowy ['ʃæd o i] *adj.* having many shadows or like a shadow; shady; dim. (Comp: *shadowier;* sup: *shadowiest.*) ♦ *Bill saw a shadowy figure near the bushes.* ♦ *Mary refused to walk down the shadowy alley.*

shady ['ʃe di] **1.** *adj.* in the shade; blocked from direct exposure to light; shaded. (Comp: *shadier;* sup: *shadiest.*) ♦ *We sat in a shady spot in the park and talked.* ♦ *It was much cooler in the shady area under the tree.* **2.** *adj.* not honest; scheming; dubious; not reputable. (Comp: *shadier;* sup: *shadiest.*) ♦ *The shady lawyer was not respected by his peers.* ♦ *The shady crooks left when they saw the police approach.*

shaft ['ʃæft] **1.** *n.* a rod or pole, such as that of a spear or an arrow. ♦ *The shaft of the arrow stuck out from the center of the target.* ♦ *The hunter held the spear by its shaft and threw it.* **2.** *n.* a pole that is used as a handle, including the handle of an axe, a golf club, and a sledgehammer. ♦ *The shaft of the axe broke when I slammed it against a rock.* ♦ *The worker gripped the sledgehammer's shaft and pounded on the wall.* **3.** *n.* a ray [of light]. ♦ *A shaft of light entered the room through the peephole.* ♦ *The laser emitted a shaft of red light.* **4.** *n.* a long, narrow passage, often vertical. ♦ *The miners were trapped in a remote shaft of the mine.* ♦ *An elevator travels up and down a shaft.*

shag ['ʃæg] **1.** *n.* carpeting that has thick, long, plush threads. (No plural form in this sense.) ♦ *The floors in the old apartment were covered with ugly orange shag.* ♦ *I replaced the shag in the living room with a carpet with shorter fibers.* **2.** *adj.* <the adj. use of ①.> ♦ *Mary installed shag carpet in her living room.* ♦ *John lost a contact lens in the shag rug.*

shaggy ['ʃæg i] *adj.* covered with long, thick, messy hair; [of hair] long, thick, and messy. (Adv: *shaggily.* Comp: *shaggier;* sup: *shaggiest.*) ♦ *The children loved their big, shaggy dog.* ♦ *Mr. Smith ordered John to cut his shaggy hair.*

shake ['ʃek] **1.** *iv., irreg.* [for something large] to move up and down, back and forth, or side to side many times very quickly. (Pt: shook; pp: shaken.) ♦ *The building shook during the earthquake.* ♦ *The walls shook when John jumped on the floor.* **2.** *iv., irreg.* [for someone] to tremble, waiver, or seem less secure. ♦ *John shook with fear when he saw the monster.* ♦ *Anne laughed until she shook when she heard the joke.* **3.** *iv., irreg.* to greet with a handshake; to agree on something by shaking someone's hand. ♦ *The arrogant man refused to shake when I held out my hand.* ♦ *John and Susan made an agreement and then shook on it.* **4.** *tv., irreg.* to cause someone or something to move up and down, back and forth, or side to side many times very quickly. ♦ *Mary shook the salt shaker over her vegetables.* ♦ *I shook the box to try to determine what was inside it.* **5. shake (up)** *tv., irreg.* (+ *adv.*) to upset someone; to bother someone; to disturb someone. ♦ *Seeing the accident shook Mary up.* ♦ *The awful news shook Bob up a lot.* **6.** *n.* an instance of shaking, as with ④. ♦ *The violent shake injured the young child.* ♦ *I gave the cloth a shake to get rid of the dust.* **7. (milk)shake** *n.* a drink made with chocolate, fruits, or other flavorings mixed with milk and ice cream. ♦ *I ordered a chocolate shake.* ♦ *Would you like a strawberry milkshake?* **8. shake hands; shake someone's hands** *idiom* to take someone's hand and move it up and down to greet someone or mark an agreement with someone. ♦ *David shook my hand when he greeted me.* ♦ *Anne and John shook hands before their business appointment.*

shakedown ['ʃek dɑʊn] **1.** *n.* an act of extortion; an illegal act of compelling people to give money to someone. ♦ *The small-business owners were forced to pay money in the shakedown.* ♦ *The aggressive charity telethon seemed like a shakedown.* **2.** *n.* a complete search; a thorough search. ♦ *In the shakedown of the victim's apartment, the inspector found a clue.* ♦ *During the shakedown of the suspect by the police, they found some drugs.*

shaken ['ʃek ən] **1.** pp of shake. **2.** *adj.* greatly upset; disturbed; bothered. (See also unshaken.) ♦ *The shaken victims of the crash refused to talk to reporters.* ♦ *The shaken widow cried at her husband's funeral.*

shaker ['ʃek ɚ] *n.* a small container that has a few tiny holes on one end from which salt, pepper, or other spices are sprinkled. ♦ *Can you pass the salt shaker?* ♦ *John added some ground pepper to the pepper shaker.*

Shakespearean [ʃek 'spɪr i ən] *adj.* of or about the plays and poetry of William Shakespeare. ♦ *Of all the Shakespearean tragedies, I like* Hamlet *the best.* ♦ *The students memorized Shakespearean sonnets for class.*

shake-up ['ʃek əp] *n.* a large change in the arrangement of an organization, including the movement, removal, or addition of people who have important jobs. ♦ *Five officers were fired during the board of director's shake-up.* ♦ *In the company shake-up, half of the employees were transferred.*

shaky ['ʃek i] **1.** *adj.* trembling; not steady. (Comp: *shakier;* sup: *shakiest.*) ♦ *Anne has shaky handwriting because she has arthritis.* ♦ *John's shaky voice was hard to understand.* **2.** *adj.* risky; not dependable; not reliable. (Comp: *shakier;* sup: *shakiest.*) ♦ *The bank declined to fund the shaky business deal.* ♦ *Although your references are shaky, we've decided to hire you.*

shall ['ʃæl] **1.** *aux.* <a form used with *I* and *we* to indicate something in the future.> (Formal. Followed by a bare verb. See will, should.) ♦ *I shall be at work by 9:00 A.M.* ♦ *We shall go to New York next Saturday.* **2.** *aux.* <a form used with *you, he, she, it, they,* and names of people or things to indicate obligation, command, or a promise.> (Formal. See will and should.) ♦ *You shall do your homework before you watch TV.* ♦ *The borrower shall make 36 monthly payments of $1,000 apiece.* **3.** *aux.* <a verb form used with *I* and *we* in questions that ask the hearer or reader to decide something concerning the speaker or writer.> (Formal. See will and should.) ♦ *Shall I go to the store now?* ♦ *Shall we be leaving for the market soon?*

shallow ['ʃæl o] **1.** *adj.* not deep; having only a small distance from the top of something to the bottom, especially used to describe water. (Adv: *shallowly.* Comp: *shallower;* sup: *shallowest.*) ♦ *The children waded in the shallow end of the pool.* ♦ *It is possible to drown even in shallow water.* **2.** *adj.* not having deep, important thoughts; superficial. (Figurative on ①. Adv: *shallowly.* Comp: *shallower;* sup: *shallowest.*) ♦ *Mary was bored by her date, who was very shallow.* ♦ *John yawned during the shallow lecture.*

sham ['ʃæm] **1.** *n.* a ruse; a trick; a hoax; a fraud. ♦ *I was shocked to learn that the charity was actually a sham.* ♦ *The tourist lost $100 in the sham.* **2.** *n.* a fake; a counterfeit; a phony; something that is not the real object that it is said to be; someone who pretends to be someone else. ♦ *The designer watch turned out to be a sham.* ♦ *The banker said my $50 bill was a sham.* **3.** *adj.* <the adj. use of ②.> ♦

Someone on the subway was selling sham designer watches. ♦ *The counterfeiter tried to pass a sham $20 bill.*

shambles ['ʃæm bəlz] **1.** *n.* something broken down or ruined. (Treated as singular or plural.) ♦ *Your room is a shambles. Clean it up now.* ♦ *After the scandal, the mayor's reputation was a shambles.* **2. in shambles** *phr.* in a messy state; destroyed. ♦ *After the earthquake, the town lay in shambles.* ♦ *The TV set was in shambles after John tried to fix it.*

shame ['ʃem] **1.** *n.* a bad feeling that someone has done something wrong or bad; a bad feeling of guilt. (No plural form in this sense.) ♦ *Have you no shame for all the bad things you've done?* ♦ *The shame I feel for what I have done will always haunt me.* **2.** *n.* an unfortunate situation. (No plural form in this sense.) ♦ *It's a shame that it rained during the picnic.* ♦ *You can't come to the gathering? What a shame!* **3.** *n.* disgrace; loss of good reputation; loss of honor. (No plural form in this sense.) ♦ *The shame of the scandal caused the mayor to resign.* ♦ *The accusations against John are a cause for great shame.* **4.** *tv.* to cause someone to feel ①. ♦ *Mary shamed her son in public.* ♦ *The critical article shamed the mayor's administration.* **5. put someone to shame** *idiom* to show someone up; to embarrass someone; to make someone ashamed. ♦ *Your excellent efforts put us all to shame.* ♦ *I put him to shame by telling everyone about his bad behavior.*

shameful ['ʃem fʊl] **1.** *adj.* causing shame, disgrace, or dishonor. (Adv: *shamefully.*) ♦ *John felt truly sorry for all of his shameful actions.* ♦ *The politician was criticized for his shameful speech.* **2.** *adj.* deserving shame; worthy of shame. (Adv: *shamefully.*) ♦ *I can't believe that you watched that shameful movie!* ♦ *The photographer took shameful photographs of the model.*

shameless ['ʃem ləs] *adj.* without shame, especially when one should feel shame; not modest. (Adv: *shamelessly.*) ♦ *The shameless model posed suggestively for the magazine.* ♦ *The shameless couple caressed each other on the bus.*

shampoo [ʃæm 'pu] **1.** *n.* a liquid soap used for washing hair. (No plural form in this sense.) ♦ *Mary squirted some shampoo into her hair.* ♦ *John rinsed the shampoo from his hair.* **2.** *n.* a washing of one's own or someone else's hair with ①. (Pl in *-s.*) ♦ *The stylist gave Anne a trim and then a shampoo.* ♦ *During her shampoo, Susan got some water in her ears.* **3.** *tv.* to wash someone's hair with ①. ♦ *Mary shampooed her hair while taking a shower.* ♦ *The hair stylist shampooed John's hair at the salon.* **4.** *iv.* to wash [hair] with ①. ♦ *Anne shampoos every morning.* ♦ *John shampooed in the shower at the gym.*

shamrock ['ʃæm rɑk] *n.* a small, green plant that has three or four heart-shaped leaves on its stem, usually associated with Ireland. ♦ *Shamrocks with four leaves are considered to be lucky.* ♦ *On St. Patrick's Day, we decorated the room with shamrocks.*

shanty ['ʃæn ti] *n.* a small house, hut, or shed that is quickly or poorly built; a shack. ♦ *The city's slums consisted of thousands of shanties.* ♦ *The violent windstorm destroyed the shanties in the neighborhood.*

shape ['ʃep] **1.** *n.* a form; a figure; a mass; an object. ♦ *The police officer saw a shape huddling behind the bushes.* ♦ *The shape in the road ahead of me was a dead raccoon.* **2.** *n.* condition; a state of being—good or bad. (No plural form in this sense.) ♦ *Although Anne was in an accident, she seems to be in good shape.* ♦ *The last time I saw my grandfather, he was in very bad shape.* **3.** *tv.* to cause something to have a certain form; to form something. ♦ *The sculptor shaped the clay into a vase.* ♦ *Anne shaped the branches to have a more graceful form.* **4.** *iv.* to be able to be put in a certain form in some manner. ♦ *This soft clay shapes easily.* ♦ *Plaster shapes well just as it is hardening.* **5. in shape** *phr.* [of someone] in good physical condition. ♦ *I exercise regularly to stay in shape.* ♦ *I am not in shape and I cannot run far without panting.* **6. shape up or ship out** *idiom* to either improve one's performance or behavior or to quit and leave. ♦ *Okay, Tom. That's the end. Shape up or ship out!* ♦ *John was late again, so I told him to shape up or ship out.* **7. take shape** *idiom* [for something, such as plans, writing, ideas, arguments, etc.] to begin to be organized and specific. ♦ *My plans are beginning to take shape.* ♦ *As my manuscript took shape, I started showing it to publishers.*

shapeless ['ʃep ləs] *adj.* without a shape; having no definite form. (Adv: *shapelessly.*) ♦ *The scientist looked at the shapeless amoeba under the microscope.* ♦ *The young child drew shapeless designs.*

shapely ['ʃep li] *adj.* having an attractive body; pretty; attractive, especially used to describe women. (Comp: *shapelier;* sup: *shapeliest.*) ♦ *The shapely actress insisted on wearing a swimsuit in the movie.* ♦ *A shapely dancer appeared onstage and the audience fell silent.*

share ['ʃɛr] **1.** *n.* one person's part of something that belongs to more than one person; a portion. ♦ *Jimmy, let Susie eat her pizza! You already had your share.* ♦ *I've certainly had my share of trouble for one evening!* **2.** *n.* a unit of stock; a unit into which the capital of a company or business is divided, and that is owned by a person or corporation. ♦ *Whoever owns 51% of the shares controls the firm.* ♦ *Anne sold some shares of stock so she could buy a computer.* **3.** *tv.* to use something together with another person or other people; to own something together with another person or other people. ♦ *John and David shared a two-bedroom apartment in college.* ♦ *Jimmy, share your toys with Susie.* **4.** *tv.* to divide something between two or among three or more people so that each person has a portion of it. ♦ *Bill, Anne, and Sue shared the cost of the meal.* ♦ *Anne and John shared the responsibility of walking the dog.* **5.** *iv.* to use together with another person or other people; to own together with another person or other people. ♦ *Jimmy, you mustn't be so selfish. Learn to share.* ♦ *Jane lived in a house that she shared with her best friend.*

shared ['ʃɛrd] *adj.* belonging to two or more people; divided among two or more people. ♦ *John and Mary have a shared interest in French literature.* ♦ *Susie and Jimmy have the shared responsibility of washing the dishes.*

shareholder ['ʃɛr hol dɚ] *n.* someone who owns a unit of a company's stock. ♦ *The shareholders demanded that the company president resign.* ♦ *Each shareholder received a dividend of $1.20 per share.*

shark ['ʃɑrk] *n.* a large, dangerous fish with a triangular fin on its back and long, sharp teeth. ♦ *The lifeguard saw a shark and ordered everyone to leave the water.* ♦ *A school of sharks circled our sailboat.*

sharp ['ʃɑrp] **1.** *adj.* having an edge that cuts things easily or having a point that pierces things easily; not dull. (Comp: *sharper;* sup: *sharpest.*) ♦ *Mary accidentally pierced her skin with a sharp tack.* ♦ *The sharp scissors cut the paper well.* **2.** *adj.* having a sudden change in direction; abrupt; turning at a narrow angle. (Adv: *sharply.* Comp: *sharper;* sup: *sharpest.*) ♦ *The taxi driver made a sharp left to avoid hitting a parked car.* ♦ *At the edge of the cliff, there's a sharp 600-foot drop.* **3.** *adj.* intelligent; smart; able to learn things quickly; aware. (Adv: *sharply.* Comp: *sharper;* sup: *sharpest.*) ♦ *The sharp student learned the foreign language quickly.* ♦ *A sharp manager runs our office efficiently.* **4.** *adj.* feeling like a sting, bite, cut, or prick; causing a stinging, biting, cutting, or pricking feeling. (Adv: *sharply.* Comp: *sharper;* sup: *sharpest.*) ♦ *I felt a sharp bee sting on my neck.* ♦ *Bill felt a sharp pain when the nurse gave him a shot.* **5.** *adj.* distinct; clear; easily seen or heard. (Adv: *sharply.* Comp: *sharper;* sup: *sharpest.*) ♦ *My television's reception is very sharp.* ♦ *The artist's lines were sharp and definite.* **6.** *adj.* [of speech or language] bitterly negative. (Adv: *sharply.* Comp: *sharper;* sup: *sharpest.*) ♦ *The critic's sharp criticism bothered the young director.* ♦ *Mary's sharp sarcasm ridiculed John's lack of intelligence.* **7.** *adj.* slightly higher in tone. (Comp: *sharper;* sup: *sharpest.*) ♦ *One sharp voice ruined the choir's overall harmony.* ♦ *The loud sharp note made the conductor cringe.* **8.** *adj.* excellent looking. (Adv: *sharply.* Comp: *sharper;* sup: *sharpest.*) ♦ *The vice president's clothes looked very sharp.* ♦ *John bought a sharp new sports car.* **9.** *n.* a tone that is half a step higher than the next lowest natural tone. ♦ *Please play a sharp there. It's F sharp, not F natural!* ♦ *There is not a single sharp in the whole piece of music.* **10.** *adv.* exactly at a stated time; on the dot. ♦ *The meeting will begin at three o'clock sharp.* ♦ *If you're not here at 4:20 sharp, I'm leaving.* **11.** *adv.* singing or playing music with tones that are slightly higher than they are supposed to be; out of tune. ♦ *One of the clarinets was playing very sharp.* ♦ *The flutist adjusted her instrument because she was playing sharp.*

sharpen ['ʃɑr pən] *tv.* to cause something to become sharp; to cause something to become sharper. ♦ *Anne sharpened her blunt pencil.* ♦ *Susan sharpened the knife on a whetstone.*

sharpener ['ʃɑr pən ɚ] **pencil sharpener** *n.* a machine that sharpens things, usually pencils. ♦ *Mary stuck a pencil in the automatic pencil sharpener.* ♦ *John cranked the pencil sharpener's handle.*

sharpshooter ['ʃɑrp ʃu tɚ] *n.* someone who can shoot things or people accurately; someone who is skilled at shooting. ♦ *The sharpshooter killed the terrorist without harming the hostages.* ♦ *The sharpshooter shot through the center of the target.*

shatter ['ʃæt ɚ] **1.** *iv.* to break into many tiny pieces. ♦ *The vase shattered when it fell off the table.* ♦ *The plate of glass shattered when John dropped it.* **2.** *tv.* to break something into many tiny pieces. ♦ *John shattered the vase when he threw it to the floor.* ♦ *The accident shattered John's collarbone.* **3.** *tv.* to destroy something. (Figurative on ②.) ♦ *The explosion shattered the peace of the rural farming village.* ♦ *The scandal shattered my confidence in the mayor.*

shattered ['ʃæt ɚd] *adj.* broken into many tiny pieces; smashed; destroyed. ♦ *The shattered vase could not be repaired.* ♦ *John swept up the shattered glass and threw it away.*

shattering ['ʃæt ɚ ɪŋ] *adj.* breaking [something] into tiny pieces; smashing [something]. (Adv: *shatteringly.*) ♦ *The shattering explosion destroyed the building.* ♦ *With one shattering blow, the old vase was ruined.*

shatterproof ['ʃæt ɚ pruf] *adj.* [of glass or plastic] unable to be shattered. ♦ *We have shatterproof glass in all the windows in our house.* ♦ *Jimmy uses a shatterproof drinking cup.*

shave ['ʃev] **1.** *tv., irreg.* to remove someone's or something's hair with a sharp blade; to cut off someone's or something's hair by moving a razor over the skin. (Often used reflexively. Pt: *shaved;* pp: *shaved* or **shaven**.) ♦ *Mary shaved her legs in the shower.* ♦ *John shaved his sideburns with a razor.* **2.** *tv.* to cut a thin slice from something. ♦ *Shave some more wood off this part so it will fit better.* ♦ *Anne shaved a slice of cheese from the big piece of cheese.* **3. shave off; shave from** *tv. + prep. phr.* to reduce the price of something; to discount something. (Figurative on ①.) ♦ *The retailer shaved 10% from the price of everything in stock.* ♦ *The store owner shaved fifty cents off laundry detergent.* **4.** *iv.* to move a razor over one's skin to remove hair. ♦ *Dave is quite hairy and has to shave twice a day.* ♦ *I hate to shave in cold water.* **5.** *n.* an instance of removing hair from the body by using a razor. ♦ *The barber gave John a very close shave.* ♦ *A blunt razor blade gives a poor shave.*

shaved ['ʃevd] **1.** *adj.* thinly cut; cut into thin pieces. ♦ *I bought a pound of shaved ham at the butcher shop.* ♦ *John arranged the shaved turkey meat on the platter.* **2.** *adj.* having had hair removed from the body. ♦ *The male swimmers all had shaved chests.* ♦ *Because he had a beard for years, Uncle Bob's shaved face looks funny!*

shaven ['ʃev ən] a pp of **shave**.

shaver ['ʃev ɚ] *n.* a razor; a device that holds a razor blade, used for shaving. ♦ *David plugged in his electric shaver.* ♦ *Anne replaced the blade in her shaver.*

shaving cream ['ʃev ɪŋ krim] *n.* a cream that is put on a part of the body before the hair on that part of the body is shaved off. (No plural form in this sense.) ♦ *John covered his face with shaving cream before shaving.* ♦ *Bob got some shaving cream on his robe.*

shawl ['ʃɔl] *n.* a piece of cloth, usually worn by women over the shoulders. ♦ *Grandma wrapped a shawl around her shoulders when it became cool.* ♦ *The warm shawl protected Jane's back from the chilly breeze.*

she ['ʃi] **1.** *pron.* <the third-person feminine singular pronoun.> (Used as the subject of a sentence or a clause.) ♦ *"Is Mary there?" I asked the woman who answered the telephone. "This is she," she replied.* ♦ *I took my cat to the veterinarian because she was sick.* **2.** *pron.* <the third-person feminine singular pronoun.> (Used to refer to certain objects, such as ships and cars.) ♦ *The boat was christened, and then she set sail.* ♦ *Ever since my car was wrecked, she just hasn't run quite right.* **3.** *n.* a female. ♦ *The shes outnumbered the hes in the room.* ♦ *Is your dog a she or a he?*

sheaf ['ʃif] *n., irreg.* a stack or bundle of things that are tied together. (Pl: **sheaves**.) ♦ *My boss put a sheaf of papers* *on my desk.* ♦ *The peasants threw sheaves of wheat onto the cart.*

shear ['ʃɪr] **1.** *tv., irreg.* to cut or remove something with ③ or scissors, especially wool from a sheep. (Pp: *sheared* or shorn.) ♦ *The farmer sheared the wool from the sheep.* ♦ *The barber sheared the soldier's hair.* **2.** *tv.* to trim a sheep totally, removing its wool. ♦ *The farmer sheared all his sheep.* ♦ *After the sheep were sheared, they looked naked.* **3. shears** *n.* large scissors; a heavy pair of scissors used for cutting thick materials. (Treated as plural. Number is usually expressed with *pair(s) of shears.*) ♦ *The seamstress cut through the thick cloth with shears.* ♦ *I used garden shears to trim the bushes.*

sheath ['ʃiθ] *n., irreg.* a covering for the blade of a knife or sword. (Pl: sheaths ['ʃɪðz].) ♦ *The knight pulled his sword from its sheath.* ♦ *The soldier's sheath was tied to his waist.*

sheaths ['ʃɪðz] pl of sheath.

sheaves ['ʃivz] pl of sheaf.

she'd ['ʃid] **1.** *cont.* "she had," where had is an auxiliary. ♦ *If Mary wants to see the play, she'd better buy tickets soon.* ♦ *She'd been sleeping for ten minutes when the phone rang.* **2.** *cont.* "she would." ♦ *Mary knew how to fire a gun, and she'd use it if she had to.* ♦ *Anne wondered if she'd arrive on time.*

shed ['ʃɛd] **1.** *n.* a small building, usually used for storage. ♦ *I keep my lawn mower in a shed in my backyard.* ♦ *Mary keeps her gardening supplies in a small shed.* **2.** *iv., irreg.* to release or lose hair, or skin in the case of a reptile. (Pt/pp: *shed.*) ♦ *When the cat sheds, I sneeze.* ♦ *My dog always sheds in the spring.* **3.** *tv., irreg.* [for an animal] to lose skin or hair. ♦ *The snake shed its skin.* ♦ *My dog shed its fur all over the furniture.* **4.** *tv., irreg.* to release a fluid, especially tears or blood. ♦ *The mourners shed many tears at the funeral.* ♦ *The wounded soldier shed a lot of blood.* **5.** *tv., irreg.* to rid oneself something burdensome or embarrassing. (Figurative on ②.) ♦ *John could not shed his bad reputation.* ♦ *He wanted to shed all his problems and get on with his life.* **6.** *tv., irreg.* to remove clothing. ♦ *Bob shed his sweatshirt in the hot sun.* ♦ *Mary shed her robe and stepped into the shower.*

shedding ['ʃɛd ɪŋ] *adj.* having hair, or skin in the case of reptiles, that is falling off. ♦ *John is allergic to shedding animals.* ♦ *My shedding pets left fur all around the house.*

sheep ['ʃip] **1.** *n., irreg.* an animal that grows wool on its body and is raised on farms for its wool and its meat. (Pl: *sheep.*) ♦ *The meat of the sheep is called mutton.* ♦ *Many sheep wandered about in the meadow.* **2.** *n.* someone who is a follower rather than a leader. (Figurative on ①.) ♦ *You need to be more aggressive and less of a sheep.* ♦ *The lackeys followed their boss around like sheep.* **3. black sheep of the family** *idiom* the worst member of the family; a member of the family who causes shame or embarrassment by being different in some way. ♦ *Mary is the black sheep of the family. She's always in trouble with the police.* ♦ *He keeps making a nuisance of himself. What do you expect from the black sheep of the family?*

sheepish ['ʃip ɪʃ] *adj.* weak; timid; easily scared; shy; easily embarrassed; bashful. (Adv: *sheepishly.*) ♦ *The sheepish student was afraid to ask the professor a question.* ♦ *The sheepish boy stayed at home instead of going to the dance.*

sheepskin ['ʃip skɪn] **1.** *n.* the skin of a sheep with wool on it, used as clothing or as a rug. (No plural form in this sense.) ♦ *Mary bundled up in sheepskin and went out into the cold.* ♦ *The tailor made a jacket from sheepskin.* **2.** *n.* the skin of sheep without wool on it, used as parchment or leather. (No plural form in this sense.) ♦ *The old book was bound with sheepskin.* ♦ *The scribe wrote the proclamation on sheepskin.* **3.** *n.* a diploma, especially a parchment one made from the skin of sheep. ♦ *Lisa hung her sheepskin on her office wall.* ♦ *It took five years, but John finally earned his sheepskin.* **4.** *adj.* made of ①. ♦ *Dave has a new sheepskin jacket.* ♦ *Mary's sheepskin slippers really keep her feet warm.*

sheer ['ʃɪr] **1.** *adj.* complete; utter. (Comp: *sheerer;* sup: *sheerest.*) ♦ *The customer's sheer rudeness shocked the clerk.* ♦ *Mary won the lottery by sheer luck.* **2.** *adj.* transparent; very thin; easy to see through. (Adv: *sheerly.* Comp: *sheerer;* sup: *sheerest.*) ♦ *Cotton fabrics can be quite sheer when wet.* ♦ *John peered through the sheer curtain.* **3.** *adj.* straight up and down; upright but not slanting or sloping. (Adv: *sheerly.* Comp: *sheerer;* sup: *sheerest.*) ♦ *The climbers slowly inched up the sheer slope.* ♦ *At the cliff's edge, there was a sheer drop of 400 feet.* **4.** *iv.* to turn to one side or another suddenly. ♦ *The taxi driver sheered to the left to avoid hitting the biker.* ♦ *The baseball sheered sharply to the right.*

sheet ['ʃit] **1.** *n.* a large, thin piece of fabric that is used in pairs on beds. (People sleep between sheets ①.) ♦ *The hotel maid changed our sheets each day.* ♦ *John tucked the edge of the bottom sheet under the mattress.* **2.** *n.* a thin, flat piece of something, such as paper, metal, glass, ice, etc., usually rectangular. ♦ *There is a lot of paper here. How many sheets do you need?* ♦ *The children skated on a thick sheet of ice.* **3.** *n.* a large mass or expanse of something such as fire or rain. ♦ *The heavy rain came down from the sky in sheets.* ♦ *Sheets of fire swallowed up the buildings.*

sheik ['ʃik] *n.* the leader of an Arab or Islamic town or mosque. ♦ *The rich sheik owned several oil wells along the coast.* ♦ *The sheik was highly regarded by the residents of the town.*

shelf ['ʃɛlf] *n.* a horizontal, flat piece of wood, metal, or something similar, that is put against or attached to a wall or is found in bookcases and other furniture. (Pl: shelves.) ♦ *Mary put the cans of soup on a shelf in the pantry.* ♦ *Susan took a heavy book from the top shelf of the bookcase.*

she'll ['ʃil] *cont.* "she will." ♦ *Mary just called to say she'll be here in thirty minutes.* ♦ *She'll be finished with the report tomorrow.*

shell ['ʃɛl] **1.** *n.* the hard covering on the outside of seeds, nuts, and eggs, and shellfish. ♦ *Anne removed the peanuts from their shells.* ♦ *John removed the oyster from its shell.* **2.** *n.* the exterior or public part of someone or something, as opposed to what is on the inside. (Figurative on ①.) ♦ *The shell of the building was covered with bricks.* ♦ *John has a tough shell, but he's really kindhearted inside.* **3.** *n.* a bullet. ♦ *The children picked up the empty shells on the street.* ♦ *The robber loaded shells into his gun.* **4.** *tv.* to free something from ① [by removing ①]. ♦ *Anne shelled the peanuts and ate them.* ♦ *The bird shelled the seeds with its beak.* **5.** *tv.* to attack people or a place with ③. ♦ *The* *enemy shelled the village in the valley from the mountains.* ♦ *The gang members shelled members of an opposing gang in the park.*

shellfish ['ʃɛl fɪʃ] **1.** *n., irreg.* an animal that lives in the water and has a shell, including clams, crabs, lobsters, oysters, and some other mollusks or crustaceans. (Pl: *shellfish.*) ♦ *Shrimp are a kind of shellfish.* ♦ *Some shellfish can crawl, but others have no legs.* **2.** *n.* the meat of ①. (No plural form in this sense.) ♦ *I put some shellfish in the chowder.* ♦ *The soup is full of delicious shellfish.*

shelter ['ʃɛl tɚ] **1.** *n.* something, especially a structure, that protects someone or something from the weather, danger, or harm. (No plural form in this sense.) ♦ *The picnickers sought shelter from the rainstorm.* ♦ *The soldiers took shelter in a trench.* **2.** *n.* a place where one can find ①. ♦ *There is a shelter at the picnic grounds where we can go if it rains.* ♦ *We stayed in the shelter all night, trying to keep warm.* **3.** *tv.* to protect someone or something from the weather, danger, or harm. ♦ *The tent sheltered the campers from the rain.* ♦ *The mother bird sheltered her chicks from the cold.*

sheltered ['ʃɛl tɚd] *adj.* [of an area] protected, especially from the weather. ♦ *The campers spent the night in a sheltered place under the ledge.* ♦ *The deer grazed in a sheltered area near the brook.*

shelve ['ʃɛlv] **1.** *tv.* to place something on a shelf. ♦ *The clerk in the grocery store shelved the produce.* ♦ *The librarian shelved the books that someone had been using.* **2.** *tv.* to postpone something until a later time. (Figurative on ①.) ♦ *The manager shelved the meeting until next week.* ♦ *The firm shelved its plans for the new product.*

shelves ['ʃɛlvz] pl of shelf.

shelving ['ʃɛl vɪŋ] *n.* shelves; a set of shelves. (No plural form in this sense.) ♦ *John lined his kitchen shelving with newspaper.* ♦ *Because the shelving in the basement was metal, it rusted.*

shenanigan [ʃə 'næn ə gən] *n.* mischief; something done while playing or goofing around. (Often plural.) ♦ *The babysitter tolerated the children's shenanigans.* ♦ *One more shenanigan like that and you are really in trouble.*

shepherd ['ʃɛp ɚd] **1.** *n.* someone who raises and protects sheep. ♦ *The shepherd sat in the meadow, watching the sheep.* ♦ *The shepherds gathered each night to keep warm by the fire.* **2.** *tv.* to guide someone in the way that a shepherd leads sheep. (Figurative on ①.) ♦ *Tom shepherded the young people into the bus.* ♦ *The tour guide shepherded the tourists through the castle.*

sherbet ['ʃɚ bət] *n.* a sweet, frozen dessert usually made of or flavored with fruit juice. (No plural form in this sense.) ♦ *Mary ate a dish of strawberry sherbet for dessert.* ♦ *John ate his sherbet too slowly and it melted.*

sheriff ['ʃɛr ɪf] *n.* the most important officer elected to enforce the law in a U.S. county. ♦ *The sheriff locked the villain in jail.* ♦ *The store owner told Sheriff Williams that his store had been robbed.*

sherry ['ʃɛr i] *n.* a strong wine made in Spain, often used as a flavoring in cooking. (No plural form in this sense.) ♦ *The chef added some sherry to the sauce.* ♦ *Each of the guests drank a glass of sherry.*

she's ['ʃiz] **1.** *cont.* "she is." ♦ *Last year, Susie was 6, and now she's 7.* ♦ *I don't know where Anne is, but she's supposed to be here soon.* **2.** *cont.* "she has," where **has** is an auxiliary. ♦ *Susie can't come out and play. She's got the measles.* ♦ *She's had more problems with her computer than I have had.*

shield ['ʃild] **1.** *n.* a cover for something (such as a part of a machine) that protects someone from being hurt. ♦ *If the protective shield is not in place, the machine will not operate.* ♦ *This shield protects your eyes from damage.* **2.** *n.* a large piece of metal or wood carried in front of the body to protect it during fighting. ♦ *The knight's sword struck the soldier's shield.* ♦ *The guard protected his body with his shield.* **3.** *tv.* to protect someone or something from someone or something; to keep someone or something safe from someone or something. ♦ *The heavy coat shielded me from the cold.* ♦ *Six bodyguards shield the president when he is in public.*

shift ['ʃɪft] **1.** *n.* a change in policy, position, opinion, or behavior. ♦ *The poll measured slight shifts of public opinion.* ♦ *The president's shift in foreign policy angered the senators.* **2.** *n.* a period during which a worker completes a day at work, such as day shift, night shift, afternoon shift. (In a workplace that operates more than 8 hours per day.) ♦ *Bob works the day shift, from 8 to 5.* ♦ *Jane's shift begins at 3:00 P.M. and ends at midnight.* **3.** *n.* a group of people who work during the same **shift** ②. ♦ *I'm friendly with most of the workers on my shift.* ♦ *The night crew replaces my shift at 5:00 P.M.* **4.** *tv.* to change the position of someone or something. ♦ *The driver shifted gears as the car went up the hill.* ♦ *The witness shifted his body nervously during his testimony.* **5.** *iv.* to alter behavior or opinion. ♦ *Voter opinion shifted dramatically after the election.* ♦ *Her attitude shifted from hostile to cooperative.*

shiftless ['ʃɪft ləs] *adj.* lazy; not resourceful. (Adv: *shiftlessly.*) ♦ *The shiftless worker was eventually fired.* ♦ *When the politician said that welfare recipients are shiftless, a group of hardworking poor people protested.*

shifty ['ʃɪf ti] *adj.* sneaky; dishonest; not trustworthy. (Adv: *shiftily.* Comp: *shiftier;* sup: *shiftiest.*) ♦ *The guard observed the shifty man hiding behind a tree.* ♦ *David is too shifty to be trusted with money.*

shimmer ['ʃɪm ɚ] **1.** *iv.* to shine with ripples of light; to shine with reflected light that quivers or trembles. ♦ *The pool shimmered in the moonlight.* ♦ *Jane's eyes shimmered as she stared into the fireplace.* **2.** *n.* a gleam or glow that ripples, quivers, or trembles. ♦ *The shimmer of moonlight on the lake was romantic.* ♦ *The shimmer of light reflected in the cat's eyes startled me.*

shin ['ʃɪn] *n.* the front of the leg between the knee and the ankle. ♦ *The young girl kicked the bully in the shins.* ♦ *John tripped over a fire hydrant and injured his shin.*

shinbone ['ʃɪn bon] *n.* the front bone of the leg between the knee and the ankle. ♦ *The scientific name for the shinbone is the tibia.* ♦ *David bruised his shinbone when he tripped and fell.*

shindig ['ʃɪn dɪg] *n.* a loud, exciting party. ♦ *The police halted the noisy shindig at 2:00 A.M.* ♦ *Anne brought two of her friends to the college shindig.*

shine ['ʃaɪn] **1.** *iv., irreg.* to be bright with light; to reflect light. (Pt/pp: *shined* or **shone**.) ♦ *John likes to work outside when the sun shines.* ♦ *A beam of light shined through the peephole.* **2.** *iv.* to do very well; to excel; to be outstanding. (Figurative on ①.) ♦ *The best student shined in* *every subject.* ♦ *David really shined when it was his turn to cook.* **3.** *tv.* to direct a beam or source of light in a certain direction. ♦ *The police shined a flashlight in my direction.* ♦ *John's lantern shined a beam of light down the path.* **4.** *tv.* to polish something; to cause something to become shiny. ♦ *John shined his shoes.* ♦ *The maid shined the mirror.* **5.** *n.* the brightness of a surface that has been polished. (No plural form in this sense.) ♦ *Tom got a great shine on the car by polishing it for hours.* ♦ *The polished marble floor had a nice shine.* **6.** *n.* an act of polishing. ♦ *John gave his shoes a good shine.* ♦ *The janitor gave the marble floor a wash and a shine.*

shingle ['ʃɪŋ gəl] **1.** *n.* a thin panel of wood or another material used to cover a roof in overlapping rows. ♦ *The heavy winds blew shingles from the roof.* ♦ *The roofer tacked each shingle into place.* **2. shingles** *n.* a severe, painful viral disease that inflames the ends of nerves, causing blisters to form on the skin. (Treated as singular or plural.) ♦ *John broke out in very painful shingles.* ♦ *The doctor told the patient not to scratch his shingles.*

shiny ['ʃɑɪn i] *adj.* bright; polished; reflecting a lot of light. (Adv: *shinily.* Comp: *shinier;* sup: *shiniest.*) ♦ *Johnny placed a shiny apple on his teacher's desk.* ♦ *The shiny marble floor was very slippery.*

ship ['ʃɪp] **1.** *n.* a large boat; a large vessel that travels on water and carries people and cargo. ♦ *A cruise ship sailed toward the tropical port.* ♦ *The immigrants traveled by ship from France to New York.* **2.** *tv.* to send something from one place to another by train, ①, or truck. ♦ *They shipped the produce to the market in a refrigerated truck.* ♦ *We shipped all of your order yesterday.*

shipbuilding ['ʃɪp bɪl dɪŋ] *n.* the design and construction of ships. (No plural form in this sense.) ♦ *Many of the island's residents were trained in shipbuilding.* ♦ *The sailor specialized in shipbuilding with the navy.*

shipment ['ʃɪp mənt] *n.* a load of goods and products ready to be shipped, being shipped, or just received. ♦ *The factory relied on timely shipments of parts from the warehouse.* ♦ *The grocery store received a shipment of fresh carrots.*

shipping ['ʃɪp ɪŋ] **1.** *n.* the activity or business of delivering products by ship, train, plane, or truck. (No plural form in this sense.) ♦ *John has worked in shipping for over ten years.* ♦ *The warehouse had a job opening for someone experienced in shipping.* **2.** *n.* the cost of transporting something. (No plural form in this sense.) ♦ *They charged me $30.00 for shipping!* ♦ *The purchaser paid the cost of shipping and handling.* **3.** *adj.* <the adj. use of ①.> ♦ *The shipping clerk loaded the crates onto the truck.* ♦ *The warehouse manager signed the shipping invoice.* **4.** *adj.* of and about ships and their movement and navigation. ♦ *The pilot guides the boat through the shipping channel.* ♦ *The shipping lanes near the port city are quite crowded.*

shipshape ['ʃɪp ʃep] *adj.* neat; tidy; clean; as orderly as a ship is meant to be. ♦ *You can't watch TV until your bedroom is shipshape.* ♦ *The guard determined that the tourists' papers were shipshape.*

shipwreck ['ʃɪp rɛk] **1.** *n.* the destruction of a ship caused by running into something. ♦ *The shipwreck was caused by extremely rough seas.* ♦ *Because of the shipwreck, the cargo sank to the bottom of the sea.* **2.** *n.* the remains of a ship that has undergone ①. ♦ *The scuba divers gathered around the shipwreck to watch the fish.* ♦ *The shipwreck at the entrance to the bay was a threat to navigation.* **3.** *tv.* to cause someone to be harmed or stranded owing to ①. ♦ *We feared the storm would shipwreck our crew and passengers.* ♦ *Who would have thought that the accident would shipwreck us on a desert island?*

shipwrecked ['ʃɪp rɛkt] *adj.* [of someone] involved in a shipwreck; stranded on an island or lost at sea after one's ship has been wrecked. ♦ *The shipwrecked sailors steered the life raft toward an island.* ♦ *The shipwrecked passengers were rescued from a desert island.*

shipyard ['ʃɪp jɑrd] *n.* a place where ships are built or repaired. ♦ *The navy submarine was built in a large shipyard.* ♦ *When the shipyard closed, unemployment in the port town soared.*

shirk ['ʃɚk] *tv.* to avoid doing something because one doesn't want to or because one is lazy; to avoid work or doing one's duty. ♦ *The guard shirked his duty and read the newspaper instead.* ♦ *Lisa shirked her responsibilities and left work early.*

shirt ['ʃɚt] **1.** *n.* a piece of clothing worn above the waist, worn either next to the skin or above an undershirt, and sometimes worn below a sweater, jacket, vest, or coat. ♦ *David buttoned his shirt.* ♦ *Anne wore an old shirt while she painted the ceiling.* **2. give someone the shirt off one's back** *idiom* to be very generous or solicitous to someone. ♦ *Tom really likes Bill. He'd give Bill the shirt off his back.* ♦ *John is so friendly that he'd give anyone the shirt off his back.*

shish kebab ['ʃɪʃ kə bɑb] *n.* pieces of meat and vegetables that are pierced on a thin rod and roasted. (From Turkish.) ♦ *We roasted the shish kebab over the campfire.* ♦ *The waiter brought us eight skewers of shish kebab.*

shiver ['ʃɪv ɚ] **1.** *iv.* to shake or tremble, especially because of cold, sickness, or fear. ♦ *Anne shivered terribly from the cold.* ♦ *John shivered in fear.* **2.** *n.* a shaking or trembling movement, especially because of cold, sickness, or fear. ♦ *A shiver of fear went through me when I entered the cold, dark castle.* ♦ *Mary walked out into the cold air and felt a shiver.*

shock ['ʃɑk] **1.** *n.* a sudden surprise, especially one that is violent or disturbing. ♦ *The accident was a terrible shock to the families of the victims.* ♦ *The shock of the gory sight made Bill ill.* **2.** *n.* a weakened condition of the body caused by a violent or disturbing event. (No plural form in this sense.) ♦ *The crash victim was suffering from shock when the police arrived.* ♦ *The people who barely escaped the fire were all in shock.* **3.** *n.* a strong, violent force, especially that caused by earthquakes or bombs. ♦ *The shock of the explosion shattered dozens of windows.* ♦ *The earthquake's first shock woke me.* **4.** *n.* the passing of electricity through someone's body. ♦ *I accidentally gave John a shock when I touched him lightly.* ♦ *Bob touched the electric fence and got quite a shock.* **5.** *n.* a large, thick, mass of hair. ♦ *The rock star had a long shock of blond hair.* ♦ *The eccentric poet had a shock of blue hair.* **6.** *tv.* to surprise someone, especially in a disturbing or violent way. ♦ *The news of Anne's accident shocked me.* ♦ *John's terrible lie shocked us all.* **7.** *tv.* to offend someone; to disgust someone. ♦ *The gory movie shocked the audience.* ♦ *The vulgar joke shocked Tom's parents.* **8.** *tv.* to give someone or some creature ④. ♦ *An electric fence shocks those who* *touch it.* ♦ *The loose wire shocked Mary when it touched her.* **9. get the shock of one's life** *idiom* to receive a serious (emotional) shock. ♦ *I opened the telegram and got the shock of my life.* ♦ *I had the shock of my life when I won $5,000.*

shocking ['ʃɑk ɪŋ] *adj.* surprising, especially in a disturbing or violent way; offensive; disgusting; causing disgust. (Adv: *shockingly.*) ♦ *The shocking movie made me physically ill.* ♦ *The shocking news made John speechless.*

shockproof ['ʃɑk pruf] *adj.* able to resist shock, especially electric shock. ♦ *The cable installer wore shockproof gloves.* ♦ *The electrician used shockproof tools.*

shod ['ʃɑd] a pt and a pp of **shoe**.

shoddy ['ʃɑd i] *adj.* done carelessly; poorly made or done. (Adv: *shoddily.* Comp: *shoddier;* sup: *shoddiest.*) ♦ *The shoddy house collapsed during the windstorm.* ♦ *The editor rejected the shoddy manuscript.*

shoe ['ʃu] **1.** *n.* an outer covering for one's foot, usually having a firm base, but less sturdy than a boot. ♦ *John bought a new pair of shoes for the party.* ♦ *Anne wears fancy shoes when she wears a dress.* **2.** *tv., irreg.* to put horseshoes on a horse. (Pt: *shoed* or **shod**; pp: *shoed* or **shod**.) ♦ *The blacksmith shod the horse.* ♦ *Do you know how to shoe a horse?* **3. fill someone's shoes** *idiom* to take the place of some other person and do that person's work satisfactorily. ♦ *I don't know how we'll be able to do without you. No one can fill your shoes.* ♦ *It'll be difficult to fill Jane's shoes. She did her job very well.*

shoebox ['ʃu bɑks] *n.* the box that a pair of shoes are sold in. ♦ *Bill kept all of his income-tax receipts in a shoebox.* ♦ *I found a shoebox full of old photos in my grandpa's attic.*

shoehorn ['ʃu horn] *n.* a small curved object that allows one to slip one's heel easily into a shoe without damaging the shoe. ♦ *I eased my foot into the shoe with a shoehorn.* ♦ *John squeezed the shoes onto his feet with a shoehorn.*

shoelace ['ʃu les] *n.* a fabric band or string that is put through the holes on top of a shoe or boot and tied. ♦ *Bill tripped on his untied shoelaces and fell.* ♦ *Anne tied her shoelaces into a bow.*

shoemaker ['ʃu mek ɚ] *n.* someone who makes or repairs shoes; a cobbler. ♦ *The shoemaker resoled my shoes.* ♦ *The executive's shoes were handcrafted by a shoemaker.*

shoeshine ['ʃu ʃɑɪn] *n.* the act of shining or polishing shoes. ♦ *Your scruffy shoes could use a good shoeshine.* ♦ *After the shoeshine, I could see my reflection in my shoes.*

shoestring ['ʃu strɪŋ] **1.** *n.* a shoelace, especially for shoes. ♦ *Anne tied her shoestrings quickly.* ♦ *John couldn't get the knot out of his shoestring.* **2. on a shoestring** *idiom* with a very small amount of money. ♦ *We lived on a shoestring for years before I got a good job.* ♦ *John traveled to Florida on a shoestring.*

shone ['ʃon] a pt/pp of **shine**.

shoo-in ['ʃu ɪn] *n.* someone or something that is almost certain to win. ♦ *The popular candidate was a shoo-in for the office.* ♦ *The former champion was a shoo-in to win against the rookie.*

shook ['ʃʊk] pt of **shake**.

shoot ['ʃut] **1.** *tv., irreg.* to fire a gun, missile, or similar weapon. (Pt/pp: **shot**.) ♦ *The robber shot his gun into the air.* ♦ *When the hunter shot his rifle, the bullet struck a bear.* **2.** *tv., irreg.* [for a weapon] to propel something. ♦ *The powerful gun shot the bullet through the wooden beam.* ♦ *The hunter used a strong bow to shoot the arrow to the target.* **3.** *tv., irreg.* to send something forward as though from a weapon; to thrust something forward. (Figurative on ②.) ♦ *The athlete shot the javelin across the stadium.* ♦ *The student shot a wad of paper toward the teacher.* **4.** *tv., irreg.* to strike someone or something with something, such as a bullet or an arrow, that has been propelled from a weapon. ♦ *The soldier shot the enemy.* ♦ *The police shot the criminal.* **5.** *tv., irreg.* to expose photographic film in a camera. ♦ *Anne shot four rolls of film in Europe.* ♦ *She shot all her film and had to buy some more.* **6.** *tv., irreg.* to make a photograph of someone or something on film or videotape; to record an image on videotape or motion picture film. ♦ *John shot a picture of his friends.* ♦ *The photographer shot a view of the students as they ran down the beach.* **7.** *iv., irreg.* to discharge [a weapon]. ♦ *The robber shot into the air.* ♦ *The police shot at the robber.* **8. shoot from** *iv., irreg.* + *prep. phr.* [for something] to be propelled from a gun, bow, or other weapon. ♦ *A stream of bullets shot from the automatic weapon.* ♦ *The arrow shot from the hunter's bow.* **9.** *iv., irreg.* to send [something] toward a goal in order to score points in a game or sport. ♦ *The hockey player shot and scored.* ♦ *The basketball player shot and scored two points.* **10.** *iv., irreg.* to move somewhere very quickly. ♦ *A sharp pain shot through John's body.* ♦ *The raft shot down the river.* **11.** *iv., irreg.* to discharge firearms as a hobby, as for target practice. ♦ *John shoots for fun on the weekend.* ♦ *You should always wear ear protection when you shoot.* **12.** *n.* a new bud or stem that sprouts from the ground or from an older part of a plant; a bit of new plant growth. ♦ *During the cold snap, the new shoots froze.* ♦ *Many shoots sprung up from the potato.* **13. shoot for something** *idiom* to try to do something; to attempt to do something; to aim toward a goal. ♦ *The industrious student shot for success.* ♦ *The worker shot for a $2 per hour raise.* **14. shoot from the hip** *idiom* to speak directly and frankly. ♦ *John has a tendency to shoot from the hip, but he generally speaks the truth.* ♦ *Don't pay any attention to John. He means no harm. It's just his nature to shoot from the hip.*

shooting ['ʃut ɪŋ] **1.** *n.* the sport and skill of hitting targets by firing a gun at them. (No plural form in this sense.) ♦ *Mary went to the range because she enjoys shooting.* ♦ *Bill is skilled at shooting and killed the deer on his first shot.* **2.** *n.* an act of murder, attempted murder, or assault using a gun. ♦ *The police were puzzled by the shooting at the university.* ♦ *Fortunately, no one was killed during the shooting.* **3.** *n.* a period of time in motion picture filming when the cameras are running, recording the action of the movie. (No plural form in this sense.) ♦ *The director demanded complete concentration during the shooting.* ♦ *The shooting of the film was done on location in Brazil.* **4. shooting pain** *n.* a pain that is sharp and moving. ♦ *Jane felt a shooting pain in her back.* ♦ *Bill took aspirin for the shooting pains in his legs.* **5.** *adj.* moving very rapidly or quickly. ♦ *The shooting rapids tossed the raft.* ♦ *The shooting star seemed to fall to earth.*

shop ['ʃɑp] **1.** *n.* a small store, especially where a single class of products is sold. ♦ *At the flower shop, Anne bought* *a dozen roses.* ♦ *Bob bought some cigars at the tobacco shop.* **2.** *n.* a place where things are built or repaired. ♦ *My car is in the shop being repaired.* ♦ *When my TV was in the shop, I read a lot.* **3.** *iv.* to go to a store to buy things. ♦ *John loves to shop.* ♦ *Mary shopped around the mall for clothes.* **4. shop at** *iv.* + *prep. phr.* to buy [something] at a particular place. ♦ *I shopped at every store in the mall.* ♦ *We don't shop at that store any longer.* **5.** *tv.* to visit a particular store, mall, or area in order to buy things. ♦ *Anne shopped every store inside the mall.* ♦ *John shopped the shops for bargains.* **6. talk shop** *idiom* to talk about business matters at a social event. ♦ *All right, everyone, we're not here to talk shop. Let's have a good time.* ♦ *Mary and Jane stood by the punch bowl, talking shop.* **7. window-shopping** *idiom* the habit or practice of looking at goods in shop windows or stores without actually buying anything. (No plural form in this sense.) ♦ *Mary and Jane do a lot of window-shopping in their lunch hour, looking for things to buy when they get paid.* ♦ *Jane said she was just window-shopping, but she bought a new coat.*

shopkeeper ['ʃɑp kip ɚ] *n.* someone who owns or manages a store. ♦ *The shopkeeper prosecuted the shoplifter.* ♦ *The shopkeeper fired the dishonest cashier.*

shoplift ['ʃɑp lɪft] **1.** *tv.* to steal merchandise from a shop or store. ♦ *If you shoplift anything here, you will be arrested!* ♦ *I saw a kid shoplift some candy.* **2.** *iv.* to steal [something] as in ①. ♦ *If you shoplift here, you will end up in jail.* ♦ *You had better not shoplift or do anything else wrong!*

shoplifter ['ʃɑp lɪft ɚ] *n.* someone who steals merchandise from a shop or store. ♦ *This store prosecutes shoplifters no matter how old they are.* ♦ *The shoplifter stole small items that he could fit in his pockets.*

shoplifting ['ʃɑp lɪft ɪŋ] *n.* the stealing of merchandise from a store. (No plural form in this sense.) ♦ *This store prosecutes shoplifting.* ♦ *A young thief was arrested for shoplifting.*

shopping ['ʃɑp ɪŋ] **1.** *n.* buying things; searching for the right thing to purchase. (No plural form in this sense.) ♦ *Anne is always in debt because her favorite activity is shopping.* ♦ *Grocery shopping is a chore for John.* **2. shopping bag** *n.* a bag or sack that is used to carry purchases. ♦ *When I bought a blanket, I was given a huge shopping bag to carry it in.* ♦ *I always take a shopping bag with me so I won't waste paper by getting another one.*

shopworn ['ʃɑp worn] *adj.* ruined or damaged from being on display in a store. ♦ *The shopworn items were sold at a reduced price.* ♦ *The shopkeeper gave the shopworn coat to one of the cashiers.*

shore ['ʃor] **1.** *n.* the land along the edge of a body of water. ♦ *The oil from the grounded tanker washed up onto the shore.* ♦ *The lifeguard stood on the shore, watching the swimmers.* **2. shore up** *tv.* + *adv.* to support something that is weak; to prop something up. ♦ *John shored up the sagging roof with a beam.* ♦ *The unprofitable agency was shored up with federal funds.*

shoreline ['ʃor laɪn] *n.* the land along the edge of a body of water, especially of an ocean, lake, or sea; the line where land meets water. ♦ *The house built too close to the shoreline slid into the sea.* ♦ *Florida has shoreline on both the Atlantic Ocean and the Gulf of Mexico.*

shorn ['ʃorn] pp of shear.

short ['ʃort] **1.** *adj.* not tall; less than average height from top to bottom. (Comp: *shorter;* sup: *shortest.*) ♦ *The short man jumped up to reach the book on the top shelf.* ♦ *Bill looks short because he stoops a little.* **2.** *adj.* not long; less than average length from side to side. (Comp: *shorter;* sup: *shortest.*) ♦ *The rope was too short to reach the drowning man.* ♦ *The short ruler wasn't long enough to measure the plank.* **3.** *adj.* not long in time; less than average duration; happening only for a small amount of time; brief. (Comp: *shorter;* sup: *shortest.*) ♦ *Could I borrow your newspaper for a short while?* ♦ *Mary took a short time to finish eating.* **4.** *adj.* not having enough of something; lacking enough of something. (Comp: *shorter;* sup: *shortest.*) ♦ *We're short of eggs, so I can't give you any.* ♦ *I'm short of sugar, so I'll go buy some more.* **5.** *adj.* curt; rude and impolite. (Not prenominal. Adv: *shortly.*) ♦ *I get upset when clerks are short with me.* ♦ *The ticket agent was rather short, so I angrily left the museum.* **6.** *adv.* suddenly; abruptly. ♦ *The movie was cut short because of technical difficulties.* ♦ *John stopped short before implicating himself in the crime.* **7.** *adv.* not close enough; not far enough; not enough. ♦ *Tom stopped short of losing his temper.* ♦ *The arrow fell short of the target.* **8.** *n.* See short-circuit ③. **9.** *n.* a movie that is not as long as a full-length movie, usually less than an hour. ♦ *The theater showed a series of entertaining shorts.* ♦ *The full-length movie was preceded by a dramatic short.* **10. shorts** *n.* a pair of pants whose legs do not reach the knees. (Treated as plural.) ♦ *On hot days, many people wear shorts outside.* ♦ *John made a pair of shorts by cutting off the legs of an old pair of jeans.* **11. shorts** *n.* underpants; boxers; briefs. (Treated as plural.) ♦ *David wore shorts to bed.* ♦ *John's zipper was open, and I could see his shorts.* **12. for short** *phr.* as an abbreviation. (See also ③.) ♦ *The Internal Revenue Service is known as the IRS for short.* ♦ *David goes by Dave for short.* **13. short for something** *phr.* <[of a form] being a shortened form of a word or phrase.> (See also ⑫.) ♦ Photo *is short for* photograph. ♦ Dave *is short for* David. **14. caught short** *idiom* to be without something you need, especially money. ♦ *I needed eggs for my cake, but I was caught short.* ♦ *Bob had to borrow money from John to pay for the meal. Bob is caught short quite often.* **15. run short (of something)** *idiom* to begin to run out of something. ♦ *We are running short of eggs.* ♦ *I always keep enough so I will never run short.* **16. sell someone or something short** *idiom* to underestimate someone or something; to fail to see the good qualities of someone or something. ♦ *This is a very good restaurant. Don't sell it short.* ♦ *When you say that John isn't interested in music, you're selling him short. Did you know he plays the violin quite well?*

shortage ['ʃor tɪdʒ] **1.** *n.* a lack; a state of not having enough of something. ♦ *When there was a gasoline shortage, gas was rationed.* ♦ *Due to a shortage of funds, the library closed.* **2.** *n.* the amount by which something is short; the amount of something that is needed in order to have enough. ♦ *Federal funds made up the shortage in the library's budget.* ♦ *Dave paid the shortage when I didn't have enough money for the bill.*

shortchange ['ʃort 'tʃendʒ] *tv.* to give less than is due someone; to give someone less change ③ than is due. ♦ *The dishonest cashier shortchanged the customer.* ♦ *The unfair contract shortchanged the workers.*

short-circuit ['ʃort 'sɚ kət] **1.** *tv.* to cause an electrical circuit to be completed before the electricity has flowed all the way though its intended circuit. ♦ *The electrical surge short-circuited the computer.* ♦ *The lightning short-circuited the electrical system.* **2.** *iv.* [for an electrical connection] to flow improperly, causing a problem that causes the flow of electricity to stop. ♦ *The lightning caused the electrical connection to short-circuit.* ♦ *The overloaded electrical outlet short-circuited.* **3. short (circuit)** *n.* a fault in an electrical circuit where the circuit is completed as in ①. ♦ *There must be a short circuit in the wiring because the fuse keeps blowing.* ♦ *John got a shock when he tried to repair the short.*

shortcoming ['ʃort kəm ɪŋ] *n.* a fault; a flaw; a defect. ♦ *Sue is an excellent employee, despite her shortcoming of talking too much.* ♦ *Bob compensates for his shortcomings by being very pleasant.*

shortcut ['ʃort kət] *n.* a path that is shorter, more direct, or quicker to travel than a different or more established route. ♦ *The shortcut to school saved the student five minutes.* ♦ *This path through the woods is a shortcut to the lake.*

shorten ['ʃort n] **1.** *iv.* to become shorter. ♦ *The days shortened as winter approached.* ♦ *The pencil shortened the more I sharpened it.* **2.** *tv.* to cause something to become shorter. ♦ *The principal shortened each class by five minutes.* ♦ *The new bridge shortened the route between the two cities.*

shortening ['ʃort nɪŋ] **1.** *n.* causing something to become shorter. (No plural form in this sense.) ♦ *Jane noticed the shortening of days as winter approached.* ♦ *The editor insisted on the shortening of the book.* **2.** *n.* butter or lard, used in frying and baking foods. (No plural form in this sense.) ♦ *The cook greased the frying pan with shortening.* ♦ *The rich pastries were fried in shortening.*

shortfall ['ʃort fɔl] *n.* the amount of money that is needed to reach a budgeted amount. ♦ *The president, who was responsible for the shortfall, was dismissed.* ♦ *The company treasurer hadn't anticipated a shortfall.*

shorthand ['ʃort hænd] *n.* a method of writing that uses special symbols that stand for a word or more than one sound so that one can write very rapidly while someone else is talking. (Compare with longhand. No plural form in this sense.) ♦ *The secretary wrote down in shorthand what the executive dictated.* ♦ *The receptionist typed a letter from Anne's shorthand.*

short-lived ['ʃort 'lɪvd] *adj.* not lasting very long. ♦ *The short-lived television series was canceled after four shows.* ♦ *The outbreak of gunfire ended the short-lived peace treaty.*

shortly ['ʃort li] *adv.* soon; in a few moments. ♦ *The movie will begin shortly.* ♦ *We're leaving the party shortly.*

shortsighted ['ʃort 'saɪt ɪd] **1.** *adj.* not able to see things clearly that are in the distance; nearsighted. (Adv: *shortsightedly.*) ♦ *The shortsighted man needed to wear glasses while driving.* ♦ *The shortsighted woman couldn't read the sign in the distance.* **2.** *adj.* acting without considering what will happen in the future. (Figurative on ①. Adv: *shortsightedly.*) ♦ *It was shortsighted of the firm to have fired half of its staff.* ♦ *The shortsighted manager never planned for the future.*

short-staffed ['ʃort 'stæft] *adj.* not having enough people to do a job properly; not having enough employees to run a business properly; needing more people in order to do a job properly. ♦ *Because our office is short-staffed, I have to work 12 hours a day.* ♦ *The company was short-staffed because ten employees quit.*

shortstop ['ʃort stɑp] *n.* a baseball player whose position is between second base and third base. ♦ *The shortstop caught the ball and threw it to first base.* ♦ *The ball flew past the pitcher and right into the glove of the shortstop.*

short-tempered ['ʃort 'tɛm pɚd] *adj.* easily made angry. (Adv: *short-temperedly.*) ♦ *The short-tempered boss screamed at everyone in the office.* ♦ *The owner asked the short-tempered customer to leave the store.*

short-term ['ʃort 'tɚm] *adj.* only for a short period of time; not permanent; temporary. ♦ *The accounting firm hired short-term workers during tax season.* ♦ *The medicine had some unpleasant short-term effects.*

shortwave ['ʃort 'wev] *adj.* transmitting or receiving radio waves that are sixty meters long or shorter. ♦ *The message was broadcast by shortwave radio.* ♦ *The shortwave radio operator broadcast constant propaganda.*

shot ['ʃɑt] **1.** pt/pp of shoot. **2.** *n.* the firing of a weapon; the shooting of a gun or other weapon; the explosion of an explosive. ♦ *When I heard the shot, I hid behind a brick wall.* ♦ *The robber fired the first shot and killed the cop.* **3.** *n.* someone who shoots in a particular way, such as good or bad. ♦ *Bob is a good shot. He always hits the target.* ♦ *You're a bad shot, Tom. You never hit it.* **4.** *n.* an injection of medicine, a vaccine, or a drug. ♦ *The doctor gave the baby a shot.* ♦ *Diabetics need shots of insulin to stay alive.* **5.** *n.* a ball or puck that is aimed and sent toward a goal in order to score a point. ♦ *The shot fell wide of the goal.* ♦ *The basketball player's shot went through the basket.* **6.** *n.* buckshot; small pellets of metal (especially lead) that are fired from a gun. ♦ *We found a lot of shot in the duck father brought home.* ♦ *The hunter fired his gun and sprayed shot at the ducks.* **7.** *n.* a photograph or a length of film or video. ♦ *John showed me some shots of his vacation in France.* ♦ *The last shot in the movie was a view from the bridge.* **8.** *n.* a small amount, usually an ounce, of hard liquor. ♦ *The bartender poured me a shot of whiskey.* ♦ *Jane added a shot of vodka to a glass of orange juice.* **9.** *adj.* completely used; no longer usable; no longer working. (Not prenominal.) ♦ *I threw out the toaster because it's shot.* ♦ *My engine is shot, so I had my car towed to the repair shop.* **10.** *adj.* tired; exhausted. (Not prenominal. Slang.) ♦ *After a long day at work, I was completely shot.* ♦ *After biking 80 miles, Jane was totally shot.* **11. give something a shot; take a shot at something** *idiom* to try something. ♦ *I have never dived before, but I will give it a shot.* ♦ *Tom decided to take a shot at writing a poem.*

shotgun ['ʃɑt gən] **1.** *n.* a gun that fires small metal pellets. ♦ *The farmer pointed a shotgun at the intruder.* ♦ *The hunter killed a rabbit with a shotgun.* **2. shotgun wedding** *idiom* a forced wedding. ♦ *Mary was six months pregnant when she married Bill. It was a real shotgun wedding.* ♦ *Bob would never have married Jane if she hadn't been pregnant. Jane's father forced the shotgun wedding.*

should ['ʃʊd] **1.** *aux.* ought ①. (Indicating obligation.) ♦ *You should stop swearing in front of your teachers.* ♦ *We should arrive at the airport in an hour, or else we'll miss our flight.* **2.** *aux.* ought ②. (Indicating that something is expected.) ♦ *We should arrive at the airport in an hour unless traffic becomes worse.* ♦ *It should be sunny tomorrow if the forecast is correct.*

shoulder ['ʃol dɚ] **1.** *n.* one of two parts of the body where an arm connects with the top of the chest below the neck. ♦ *Anne put her purse strap over her shoulder.* ♦ *The police officer grabbed the shoplifter's right shoulder.* **2.** *n.* the dirt or pavement along the side of a road. ♦ *Bill pulled over to the shoulder because he had a flat tire.* ♦ *The children rode their bicycles on the shoulder.* **3.** *tv.* to have responsibility for something; to take responsibility for something. ♦ *My boss shouldered the responsibility for my mistake.* ♦ *John shouldered the blame for David's problems.* **4. on someone's shoulders** *idiom* on someone's own self. ♦ *Why should all the responsibility fall on my shoulders?* ♦ *She carries a tremendous amount of responsibility on her shoulders.* **5. rub shoulders with someone** *idiom* to associate with someone; to work closely with someone. ♦ *I don't care to rub shoulders with someone who acts like that!* ♦ *I rub shoulders with John at work. We are good friends.* **6. shoulder-to-shoulder** *idiom* side-by-side; with a shared purpose. ♦ *The two armies fought shoulder-to-shoulder against the joint enemy.* ♦ *The strikers said they would stand shoulder-to-shoulder against management.*

shouldn't ['ʃʊd nt] *cont.* "should not." ♦ *You shouldn't have done that.* ♦ *I shouldn't be too late if I leave right now.*

should've ['ʃʊd əv] *cont.* "should have," where **have** is an auxiliary. ♦ *I should've ordered the salad instead of the soup.* ♦ *You should've solved the problem this way.*

shout ['ʃaʊt] **1.** *iv.* to speak, laugh, or make spoken noises loudly. ♦ *The children shouted on the playground.* ♦ *The speaker shouted because the microphone was broken.* **2.** *tv.* to speak something loudly; to say something by shouting. ♦ *Anne shouted her response from the other room.* ♦ *Dave shouted that he didn't care where we ate.* **3.** *n.* a loud utterance; a loud cry. ♦ *I heard the children's shouts from the other room.* ♦ *I called the police when I heard shouts for help.*

shouting ['ʃaʊt ɪŋ] **1.** *adj.* speaking, laughing, or making spoken noises loudly. ♦ *The shouting children gave me a headache.* ♦ *My guests could hear my shouting neighbors.* **2.** *n.* loud, forceful talking. (No plural form in this sense.) ♦ *I hear shouting somewhere down the street!* ♦ *Everyone could hear the shouting from next door.* **3. all over but the shouting** *idiom* decided and concluded; finished except for a celebration. ♦ *The last goal was made 12 seconds before the final whistle sounded. Tom said, "Well, it's all over but the shouting."* ♦ *When Tom finished his last final examination in college, he said, "It's all over but the shouting."*

shove ['ʃʌv] **1.** *iv.* to push forcefully. ♦ *I shoved against the door, but it wouldn't budge.* ♦ *I shoved and shoved, but it wouldn't move.* **2.** *tv.* to push someone or something forcefully in some direction. ♦ *I shoved Anne from the path of the oncoming car.* ♦ *Mary shoved the door open.* **3.** *n.* a forceful push. ♦ *I gave the door a shove, and it swung open.* ♦ *John gave Bill a shove, and he fell down.* **4. shove one's way somewhere** *idiom* to make a path through a crowd by pushing. ♦ *The impatient man shoved his way through the crowd.* ♦ *The reporter shoved her way to the front of the crowd.*

shovel ['ʃʌv əl] **1.** *n.* a tool—having a wide, flat blade attached to a handle—used to lift, move, or remove earth or other loose objects. ♦ *The cemetery workers dug the grave with shovels.* ♦ *Jimmy put sand into his pail with a plastic shovel.* **2.** *iv.* to work by using ①; to move, lift, or remove [something] by using a ①. ♦ *John shoveled until all the snow was removed from the sidewalk.* ♦ *Mary shoveled and shoveled, digging a huge hole.* **3.** *tv.* to move, lift, or remove something by using ①. ♦ *John shoveled sand into a bucket.* ♦ *Mary shoveled snow from the driveway.* **4.** *tv.* to clean something with ①. ♦ *Bill shoveled the driveway after it snowed.* ♦ *Anne shoveled the sidewalk and then salted it.*

show ['ʃo] **1.** *tv., irreg.* to cause someone to see something; to put something in someone's sight. (Pt: *showed;* pp: shown or *showed.*) ♦ *Jimmy showed me the cut on his finger.* ♦ *Anne showed her new book to me.* **2.** *tv., irreg.* to reveal something; to let something be known. ♦ *John's actions show that he's being sincere.* ♦ *Mary's test results show how hard she's been studying.* **3.** *tv., irreg.* to escort someone; to guide someone to a place. ♦ *The butler showed the guests to their room.* ♦ *The guide showed the tourists around the castle.* **4.** *tv., irreg.* to prove something; to make something clear. ♦ *This proof shows my hypothesis to be flawless.* ♦ *Ice on the pond shows that the temperature is below freezing.* **5.** *tv., irreg.* to display or deliver a kind of treatment to someone. ♦ *John showed his guests complete respect.* ♦ *We will show them the kind of treatment they deserve.* **6.** *tv., irreg.* to reveal a condition or illness. ♦ *John's skin is showing signs of dryness.* ♦ *Mary is showing the first symptoms of influenza.* **7.** *tv., irreg.* [for a movie theater] to present a movie. ♦ *The theater showed the new movie twice last night.* ♦ *The new cinema will show only the latest films.* **8.** *iv., irreg.* [for a condition] to appear or be visible; to be noticeable. ♦ *Anne's pregnancy is showing.* ♦ *Your slip is showing.* **9.** *iv., irreg.* [for a play or a film] to be shown ① or presented. ♦ *A classic play is showing at the theater tonight.* ♦ *My favorite movie is showing at the local cinema tomorrow.* **10.** *iv., irreg.* to finish in third place in a race. ♦ *The horse that I had bet on showed.* ♦ *The athlete who showed got a bronze medal.* **11.** *n.* a movie, television program, or theater performance. ♦ *Would you like to go see a show tonight?* ♦ *John left the boring show during intermission.* **12.** *n.* a grand spectacle; a noticeable display. ♦ *The poet made a great show of concern about the sick and elderly.* ♦ *The Smiths' huge house is a vulgar show of wealth.* **13.** *n.* an exhibition; something that is put on display for the public. ♦ *Mary went to the auto show at the convention hall.* ♦ *John's company was represented at the computer trade show.* **14.** *n.* an intentional display of something, such as raised hands, regard, praise, etc. ♦ *By a show of hands, who is available for the next meeting?* ♦ *The family made homeless by the fire appreciated the show of support from their community.* **15. make a great show of something** *idiom* to make something obvious; to do something in a showy fashion. (On ⑫.) ♦ *Anne made a great show of wiping up the drink that John spilled.* ♦ *Jane displayed her irritation at our late arrival by making a great show of serving the cold dinner.* **16. show off** *idiom* to do things in a way that is meant to attract attention. ♦ *Please stop showing off! You embarrass me.* ♦ *John is always showing off to his girlfriend.* **17. show something off** *idiom* to put someone or something on display. ♦ *Mary went to the party only to show off her new hairdo.* ♦ *Max likes to drive around and show his new car off.*

showcase [ˈʃo kes] **1.** *n.* a glass case that contains, protects, and displays objects of value—as in a museum—or trophies and awards—as in a school. ♦ *The football team's trophy was placed in the showcase.* ♦ *The museum kept the rare vase in a heavily guarded showcase.* **2.** *tv.* to exhibit, highlight, display, or feature someone or something. ♦ *The museum showcased rare vases from ancient China.* ♦ *The school showcased its brightest students in its newsletter.*

showdown [ˈʃo daʊn] *n.* the forceful settlement of an issue or argument. ♦ *The armed conflict ended in a bloody showdown.* ♦ *The showdown between the sheriff and the villain resulted in the villain's death.*

shower [ˈʃaʊ ɚ] **1.** *n.* a device that sprays water from a nozzle onto someone who is bathing. ♦ *Anne stood under the shower and washed her hair.* ♦ *David turned off the shower and dried himself with a towel.* **2.** *n.* the act of washing oneself under ①. ♦ *Mary needed a shower because she was hot and sweaty.* ♦ *After his shower, John put on clean clothes.* **3.** *n.* the place or compartment where one does ②. ♦ *Jane stepped into the shower and then turned on the water.* ♦ *John cleaned the mildew from the walls of the shower.* **4.** *n.* a brief fall of rain, snow, or other liquids in drops. ♦ *The shower lasted only a few minutes.* ♦ *The roads became slippery because of the snow shower.* **5.** *n.* a party for a woman who is about to get married or have a baby. ♦ *Mary threw a baby shower for her pregnant sister.* ♦ *Anne brought a gift to Susan's wedding shower.* **6.** *iv.* to rain; to fall like rain. ♦ *The rain showered down from the sky.* ♦ *It showered all day yesterday.* **7.** *iv.* to wash under ①. ♦ *Anne showered at the gym after exercising.* ♦ *John showers in the morning after he wakes up.* **8.** *tv.* to cause something to fall like rain. ♦ *People in buildings showered confetti on the parade route.* ♦ *The sunflower showered seeds on the ground.* **9. shower with** *tv.* + *prep. phr.* to give a lot of something to someone; to lavish someone with something. ♦ *Anne showered her grandchildren with gifts.* ♦ *The wealthy school showered the athletes with scholarships.* **10. send someone to the showers** *idiom* to send a player out of the game and off the field, court, etc. ♦ *John played so badly that the coach sent him to the showers after the third quarter.* ♦ *After the fistfight, the coaches sent both players to the showers.* **11. take a shower** See take ㉔.

showing [ˈʃo ɪŋ] **1.** *n.* a display or exhibit of something. ♦ *There's a showing of Picasso's paintings at the art museum.* ♦ *The sculptor had a showing of her works at her studio.* **2.** *n.* a display of one's success or lack of success. ♦ *The poor showing of the TV series disappointed the network.* ♦ *The politician made a good showing in the state primary.*

showmanship [ˈʃo mən ʃɪp] *n.* the skill or ability of presenting something in a showy or dramatic manner. (No plural form in this sense.) ♦ *The artistic director's showmanship ensured the play's success.* ♦ *The movie did poorly due to a lack of showmanship.*

shown [ˈʃon] a pp of show.

showroom [ˈʃo rum] *n.* a room where products that are available for purchase are displayed. ♦ *Mary walked around the showroom, looking at new cars.* ♦ *John bought the last bicycle in the showroom.*

showy [ˈʃo i] *adj.* very noticeable; flamboyant. (Adv: *showily.* Comp: *showier;* sup: *showiest.*) ♦ *The celebrities wore showy clothing to the award ceremony.* ♦ *I found the host's showy mannerisms to be pretentious.*

shrank [ˈʃræŋk] pt of shrink.

shrapnel [ˈʃræp nəl] *n.* tiny pieces of metal that are exploded from a shell or grenade. (No plural form in this sense.) ♦ *The surgeon removed shrapnel from the soldier's thigh.* ♦ *The bomb sent shrapnel flying in every direction.*

shred [ˈʃrɛd] **1.** *n.* a very small piece of something; a scrap of something; a fragment. ♦ *John tore the losing lottery ticket to shreds.* ♦ *The inspector found a shred of the missing child's clothing.* **2.** *tv.* to rip, cut, or grate something into ①. ♦ *The cook shredded the cheese into thin strips.* ♦ *David shredded the papers with his hands.*

shredded [ˈʃrɛd ɪd] *adj.* ripped, cut, or grated into shreds. ♦ *The secretary threw out the shredded papers.* ♦ *The pizza was topped with shredded cheese.*

shredder [ˈʃrɛd ɚ] *n.* a machine or tool that shreds objects. ♦ *A paper shredder cuts pieces of paper into tiny strips and is a good way to destroy documents.* ♦ *The cook rubbed the block of cheese against the shredder.*

shrew [ˈʃru] *n.* a small rodent, similar to a mouse, with a long nose. ♦ *There are shrews in the woods by the river.* ♦ *Mary killed the shrew in her kitchen with a broom.*

shrewd [ˈʃrud] *adj.* clever; astute; crafty; showing good judgment and common sense. (Adv: *shrewdly.* Comp: *shrewder;* sup: *shrewdest.*) ♦ *The shrewd business owner made large profits.* ♦ *The shrewd employee was soon promoted.*

shrewdness [ˈʃrud nəs] *n.* the quality of being shrewd. (No plural form in this sense.) ♦ *Because of her shrewdness, Sally earned a lot of money.* ♦ *Due to the lawyer's shrewdness, he won most of his cases.*

shriek [ˈʃrik] **1.** *n.* a loud, shrill, high-pitched scream or sound. ♦ *The woman let out a shriek when the window broke.* ♦ *When I heard the shriek of my car's brakes, I knew they had to be replaced.* **2.** *iv.* to scream with ①; to make ①. ♦ *The speeding car shrieked to a halt.* ♦ *John shrieked with pain when I accidentally dropped a bowling ball on his foot.*

shrill [ˈʃrɪl] *adj.* high-pitched and piercing; painfully loud or grating. (Adv: *shrilly.* Comp: *shriller;* sup: *shrillest.*) ♦ *The referee's shrill whistle hurt my ears.* ♦ *The teacher's shrill voice gave me a headache.*

shrimp [ˈʃrɪmp] **1.** *n., irreg.* a shellfish, about the size and shape of a finger, with a thin body, commonly eaten as food. (Pl: *shrimp* or *shrimps.*) ♦ *The waitress brought me a platter containing five jumbo shrimp.* ♦ *Do shrimp live at the bottom of the sea?* **2.** *n.* someone or something that is small. (Informal.) ♦ *Billy cried when the bigger kids called him a shrimp.* ♦ *The runt of the litter was quite a shrimp.* **3.** *adj.* <the adj. use of ①.> ♦ *I love shrimp casserole.* ♦ *Bill makes a wonderful shrimp dish that everyone likes.*

shrine [ˈʃraɪn] *n.* an altar, chapel, or other place of worship, especially one where there is a connection to a god, saint, or other revered being. ♦ *We stopped to photograph* *an ancient shrine along the road.* ♦ *The holy man built a shrine in the prophet's honor.*

shrink ['ʃrɪŋk] **1.** *iv., irreg.* to become smaller in size. (Pt: shrank; pp: shrunk or shrunken. Shrunk is usually used with auxiliary verbs, and shrunken is usually used as an adjective.) ♦ *My wool sweater shrank when I washed it.* ♦ *Because my shirt had shrunk, I gave it to my younger cousin.* **2. shrink from** *iv., irreg. + prep. phr.* to move away from something because of fear. ♦ *Mary shrank away from the snake in terror.* ♦ *John shrank from his attacker in fear.* **3.** *tv., irreg.* to cause someone or something to become smaller in size. ♦ *I shrank the raft by letting half of the air out of it.* ♦ *The president tried to shrink the size of the deficit.*

shrinkage ['ʃrɪŋ kɪdʒ] *n.* a reduction in size. (No plural form in this sense.) ♦ *Because of shrinkage, my sweater no longer fits.* ♦ *The shrinkage of our budget meant our salaries were much less.*

shrivel ['ʃrɪv əl] **1.** *iv.* to become wrinkly while drying up; to wither. ♦ *The crops shriveled in the drought.* ♦ *The old woman's skin had shriveled with age.* **2.** *tv.* to cause someone or something to wither. ♦ *The intense heat and lack of water shriveled the crops.* ♦ *Years of suntanning shriveled the sunbather's skin.*

shroud ['ʃrɑʊd] **1.** *n.* a cloth that is used to cover a dead body. ♦ *The undertaker covered the corpse with a shroud.* ♦ *The soldiers wrapped their dead friend in a shroud and buried him.* **2.** *n.* a covering; a layer of something that hides or conceals [something]. (Figurative on ①.) ♦ *The stones in the old garden wear a shroud of moss.* ♦ *The airport was closed under a shroud of fog.* **3.** *tv.* to cover something; to hide something by covering it. ♦ *Heavy fog shrouded the top of the tall building.* ♦ *A mass of smoke and pollution shrouds the city each morning.*

shrub ['ʃrʌb] *n.* a plant similar to a very small tree that has many stems coming from the ground; a bush. ♦ *The sidewalk in front of my house is lined with shrubs.* ♦ *John trimmed the shrubs with clippers.*

shrubbery ['ʃrʌb (ə) ri] *n.* a group of shrubs; shrubs in general. (No plural form in this sense.) ♦ *Some shrubbery grew next to the pond in the park.* ♦ *Mary trimmed the shrubbery into the shapes of animals.*

shrug ['ʃrʌg] **1.** *n.* the lifting of one's shoulders to indicate disinterest, doubt, or a lack of caring. ♦ *Bob responded to my question with a shrug of his shoulders.* ♦ *Anne's shrug indicated that she didn't care where we went.* **2.** *tv.* to lift one's shoulders as in ①. ♦ *When John yelled, Bill shrugged his shoulders and said, "Whatever."* ♦ *Mary shrugged her shoulders when I asked her what we should do.* **3.** *iv.* to gesture with ①. ♦ *I asked Anne what she wanted to eat, and she shrugged.* ♦ *Bill shrugged as he walked by the volunteer requesting money for charity.*

shrunk ['ʃrʌŋk] a pp of shrink.

shrunken ['ʃrʌŋ kən] a pp of shrink.

shuck ['ʃʌk] **1.** *tv.* to remove peas from a pod, corn from a husk, nuts from a shell, or an oyster from a shell. (See also hull and husk.) ♦ *The farmer shucked the peas for dinner.* ♦ *John shucked some peanuts and ate them.* **2.** *n.* a pod, husk, or shell, especially a corn husk. ♦ *Mary threw the shucks away.* ♦ *Dry out the shucks and use them to start a fire in the fireplace.*

shudder ['ʃʌd ɚ] **1.** *iv.* to tremble with fear, cold, or disgust. ♦ *John shuddered in fear when he saw the snake.* ♦ *Anne shuddered as she looked at the bloody photograph.* **2.** *n.* a brief, uncontrolled trembling of the body because of fear or disgust. ♦ *Bill felt a shudder when he saw the huge dog.* ♦ *Jane felt a shudder of disgust when she saw the sickening picture.*

shuffle ['ʃʌf əl] **1.** *iv.* to walk without picking up one's feet; to walk in a way that one's feet never leave the ground. (See also scuffle.) ♦ *The old man shuffled toward his mailbox.* ♦ *The tired woman shuffled across the carpet.* **2.** *iv.* to mix up [playing cards so that they are] in a different order. ♦ *Since John is the dealer, he will shuffle.* ♦ *The magician shuffled and then chose the card I had picked.* **3.** *tv.* to move one's feet without picking them up from the ground. ♦ *John shuffled his feet as he walked toward the kitchen.* ♦ *Anne shuffled her feet down the street.* **4.** *tv.* to mix up playing cards so that they are in a different order. ♦ *The dealer shuffled the cards and then dealt them.* ♦ *Please shuffle the cards before you deal them.* **5.** *n.* the dragging of one's feet along the ground; a walk where one's feet do not leave the ground. ♦ *I heard the shuffle of feet in the apartment above me.* ♦ *After Jimmy's shuffle through the leaves, I had to rake the yard again.* **6.** *n.* the act of mixing up playing cards so that they are in a different order. ♦ *Your shuffle was horrible. These are the same cards I just had.* ♦ *After each shuffle, the dealer dealt the cards clockwise.*

shuffleboard ['ʃʌf əl bord] *n.* a game played by pushing large disks on a narrow court with a long stick. ♦ *The travelers played shuffleboard on the cruise ship.* ♦ *I played shuffleboard at the park gymnasium.*

shun ['ʃʌn] *tv.* to avoid someone or something; to stay away from someone or something. ♦ *The arrogant students shunned the unpopular ones.* ♦ *John shuns businesses that don't employ union labor.*

shunt ['ʃʌnt] *tv.* to move or guide someone or something out of the way; to send someone to a place that is out of the way. ♦ *The rich parents' children had been shunted to boarding school.* ♦ *The engineer shunted the train onto an unused track.*

shut ['ʃʌt] **1.** *tv., irreg.* to close something, such as a door, window, or drawer. (Pt/pp: *shut.*) ♦ *Please shut the door. It's cold in here.* ♦ *Bill shut his desk drawer and left his office.* **2.** *tv., irreg.* to close something, such as an eye, mouth, or pocketknife. ♦ *Mary shut her eyes and relaxed for a few minutes.* ♦ *The students shut their mouths while the teacher spoke.* **3. shut (up)** *tv., irreg. + adv.* to confine someone or something; to keep someone or something in a place that has no exit. ♦ *The dog was shut in a kennel.* ♦ *The prisoners were shut in jail.* **4.** *iv., irreg.* to become closed. ♦ *The door shut when the wind blew.* ♦ *My eyes shut, and I fell asleep.* **5. shut up** to stop speaking. (Colloquial and rude when used as a command.) ♦ *Shut up and go home!* ♦ *I guess that I should shut up and listen.* **6.** *adj.* closed; moved into a closed position. (Not prenominal.) ♦ *Is the door shut?* ♦ *My eyes are shut.*

shutdown ['ʃʌt dɑʊn] *n.* the act of closing a factory or other place of industry for a period of time. ♦ *Because of the factory shutdown, 2,000 employees were jobless.* ♦ *The plant shutdown was caused by the employees' strike.*

shut-eye ['ʃʌt ɑɪ] *n.* sleep; a nap. (Informal. No plural form in this sense.) ♦ *I laid down on the sofa for a little shut-eye.* ♦ *The professor needed some shut-eye between classes.*

shut-in ['ʃʌt ɪn] *n.* someone who is not able or not allowed to go outside because of sickness. ♦ *The volunteers delivered food to shut-ins.* ♦ *A nurse took care of the shut-in 24 hours a day.*

shutout ['ʃʌt ɑʊt] *n.* a game in which one team has prevented another team from scoring any points. ♦ *Our school's championship game was a shutout.* ♦ *The game was a shutout because our pitcher struck out every batter.*

shutter ['ʃʌt ɚ] **1.** *n.* one of a pair of doors or panels that can be closed over the outside of a window. ♦ *To prepare for the hurricane, we closed the shutters.* ♦ *Sunlight filtered through the slots in the shutters.* **2.** *n.* a device in a camera that opens quickly and shuts in front of the lens in order to allow the proper amount of light when someone takes a picture. ♦ *I heard the shutter click when I took a picture.* ♦ *The speed of the shutter controls the amount of light the film is exposed to.*

shuttle ['ʃʌt əl] **1.** *n.* a bus or an airplane making regular trips back and forth between two places. ♦ *I took a shuttle from school to the train station.* ♦ *The pilot flew a shuttle from Chicago to Indianapolis.* **2. shuttle between** *iv.* + *prep. phr.* to travel back and forth between two places. ♦ *John shuttled between his offices in New York and Miami.* ♦ *Mary shuttled between work and school daily.* **3. shuttle someone or something from person to person; shuttle someone or something from place to place** *idiom* to move or pass someone or something from person to person; to move or pass someone or something from place to place. ♦ *My phone call was shuttled from person to person.* ♦ *Mary shuttled her children from home to school to practice.*

shy ['ʃɑɪ] **1.** *adj.* bashful; nervous around other people; not likely to talk around other people; timid; reserved. (Adv: *shyly.* Comp: *shyer;* sup: *shyest.*) ♦ *The shy teenager was afraid to talk to other students.* ♦ *The shy girl stood in the corner during the dance.* **2.** *adj.* not quite reaching a stated amount; almost having enough of something, but not quite. (Not prenominal. Comp: *shier;* sup: *shiest.*) ♦ *I realized I was five dollars shy of the amount I needed.* ♦ *The card player was one card shy of a flush.* **3. shy away from someone or something** *idiom* to avoid someone or something, especially because or as if one is ① or afraid. ♦ *The scared mail carrier shied away from the growling dog.* ♦ *John has shied away from snakes ever since he was bitten.*

shyness ['ʃɑɪ nəs] *n.* the quality of being shy; bashfulness; timidity. (No plural form in this sense.) ♦ *Because of John's shyness, he was afraid to speak to crowds.* ♦ *Mary tried to overcome her shyness by spending more time with people.*

sibilant ['sɪb ə lənt] **1.** *n.* each of the sounds [s, z, ʃ, ʒ]. ♦ *The word* success *begins and ends with sibilants.* ♦ *People who lisp have a hard time pronouncing sibilants.* **2.** *adj.* <the adj. use of ①.> (Adv: *sibilantly.*) ♦ *Bill's sibilant sounds made the loudspeaker hiss.* ♦ *John can't distinguish sibilant consonants over the telephone.*

sibling ['sɪb lɪŋ] *n.* a brother or sister. ♦ *How many siblings do you have?* ♦ *John fought with his siblings in the living room.*

sick ['sɪk] **1.** *adj.* not healthy; ill; having a disease. (Comp: *sicker;* sup: *sickest.*) ♦ *Mary stayed home from work because she was sick.* ♦ *The sick clerk sneezed all morning long.* **2.** *adj.* having an upset stomach and feeling like one has to vomit. (Comp: *sicker;* sup: *sickest.*) ♦ *Jane felt sick, so she ran to the bathroom.* ♦ *The smell of the rotten eggs made me sick.* **3. sick (and tired) of someone or something** *idiom* tired of someone or something, especially something that one must do again and again or someone or something that one must deal with repeatedly. ♦ *I am sick and tired of cleaning up after you.* ♦ *Mary was sick of being stuck in traffic.*

sicken ['sɪk ən] **1.** *tv.* to cause someone or some creature to become sick. ♦ *The smell of rotting flesh sickened the doctor.* ♦ *Anne was sickened by the maggots in the kitchen.* **2.** *tv.* to disgust someone. ♦ *These high taxes just sicken me.* ♦ *Your foul language sickens all of us.* **3.** *iv.* to become sick; to become ill. ♦ *As the workers sickened from the tainted food, they went home.* ♦ *The kittens sickened and died a short time after birth.* **4.** *iv.* to become disgusted [with something]. ♦ *We sickened of the high taxes and moved to another state.* ♦ *When John finally sickened of his messy room, he cleaned it up.*

sickening ['sɪk ə nɪŋ] *adj.* causing disgust; disgusting; nauseating. (Adv: *sickeningly.*) ♦ *John's parents punished him for telling a sickening joke during dinner.* ♦ *Anne left the sickening movie before it was over.*

sickle ['sɪk əl] *n.* a tool with a curved blade attached to a handle, used for cutting grass and grain. ♦ *The peasant cut the wheat with a sickle.* ♦ *The sickle's blade is very sharp.*

sickness ['sɪk nəs] *n.* the condition of being sick; illness; disease. ♦ *John was hospitalized for one week for his sickness.* ♦ *The doctor was unsure how to treat the mysterious sickness.*

sickroom ['sɪk rum] *n.* a room in which a sick person rests and recovers. ♦ *The nurse gave a pill to each patient in the sickroom.* ♦ *Anne visited her ill grandmother in her sickroom each day after school.*

side ['sɑɪd] **1.** *n.* one of the surfaces of a three-dimensional object, not including the top or the bottom; the vertical part of something; one of the edges of a two-dimensional object. ♦ *The side of the die that was facing up had one dot on it.* ♦ *The side of the box had the word "fragile" stamped on it.* **2.** *n.* any of the surfaces of a three-dimensional object; any of the edges of a two-dimensional object. ♦ *A cube has six sides; a square has four sides.* ♦ *A triangle has three sides.* **3.** *n.* either surface of something that is thin and flat. ♦ *Abraham Lincoln is on one side of the American penny.* ♦ *John put butter on one side of the toast.* **4.** *n.* a specified or particular surface of something. ♦ *The astronauts examined the dark side of the moon.* ♦ *The maid dusted the top side of the shelf.* **5.** *n.* the shore along either side of a river. ♦ *When the raft reached the other side, John pulled it ashore.* ♦ *Mary swam from one side of the river to the other.* **6.** *n.* a position or area that is to the right, left, or a certain direction from a central or reference point. ♦ *The heart is on the left side of your body.* ♦ *Mary sat on the right side of Susan.* **7.** *n.* the left or right part of a body. ♦ *The bullet lodged in the victim's* side. ♦ *David bruised his side when he fell down the stairs.* **8.** *n.* the position or opinion held by one group of people that opposes another group. ♦ *Which side of the issue do you support?* ♦ *The proponents of the two different sides held a debate.* **9.** *n.* a group of people that opposes another group, including sports teams, countries at war, or groups involved with political or social causes. ♦ *The other side defeated our team 12–3.* ♦ *The treasonous soldier defected to the other side.* **10.** *n.* a particular line of descendants in one's family. ♦ *My father's side came to America from Germany.* ♦ *Anne doesn't get along with her mother's side of the family.* **11.** *n.* a side dish; a separate dish or separate order of food. (Informal. Heard in restaurants.) ♦ *Max ordered a side of french fries with his meal.* ♦ *The broiled fish comes with a choice of two sides.* **12.** *adj.* [of a location] at, toward, or beside something. ♦ *David placed his coffee mug on a side table.* ♦ *Anne entered the house through the side door.* **13.** *adj.* not the most important; secondary; subordinate. ♦ *The mayor didn't have time to talk about side issues.* ♦ *One of the side effects of this medicine is a slight rash.* **14. side with** *iv.* + *prep. phr.* to agree with the opinions of someone or a group of people rather than the opinions of someone else or another group of people. ♦ *Jane sided with Bill on the issue.* ♦ *America sided with England during World Wars I and II.* **15.** *tv.* to put siding on a building. ♦ *The workers sided the old house with aluminum siding.* ♦ *They sided our house with gray siding.* **16. from side to side** *phr.* moving first to one side ⑥ and then to the other, repeatedly. ♦ *The pendulum of the clock swings from side to side.* ♦ *The singers swayed from side to side as they sang.*

sideburns ['sɑɪd bɚnz] *n.* hair grown long on the sides of the face, alongside the ears. (Treated as plural.) ♦ *David trimmed his sideburns before his job interview.* ♦ *Bill's sideburns extended all the way to his chin.*

side dish ['sɑɪd dɪʃ] *n.* food that is served in addition to the main meal, usually in a separate dish. (See also side ⑪.) ♦ *Mary served her guests a side dish of fresh asparagus along with rest of the meal.* ♦ *At the restaurant, I ordered two side dishes with my dinner.*

sidekick ['sɑɪd kɪk] *n.* a companion, especially one who is also a friend. ♦ *We rarely see Bill without his sidekick, John.* ♦ *In the movie, the cop's sidekick was a retired teacher.*

sideline ['sɑɪd lɑɪn] **1. sidelines** *n.* the line along the side of something, especially the line at the boundary of the playing area of a sport. (Treated as plural.) ♦ *The cheerleaders cheered the football team from the sidelines.* ♦ *The coach stood on the sidelines and watched the game.* **2.** *n.* an activity done in addition to one's primary interest or work. ♦ *John is a lawyer, but participates in community theater as a sideline.* ♦ *Anne is a banker, but as a sideline, she paints portraits.* **3.** *tv.* to prevent someone from participating in something; to prevent a player from participating in a sporting event. ♦ *The referee sidelined the player for using obscene language.* ♦ *The star football player was sidelined by a knee injury.*

sideshow ['sɑɪd ʃo] *n.* a minor show or event that is connected to a more important one. ♦ *The aide's allegations were a sideshow to the political crisis.* ♦ *Their argument was an unwelcome sideshow during the wedding celebration.*

sidesplitting ['sɑɪd splɪt ɪŋ] *adj.* very funny. (Adv: *sidesplittingly.*) ♦ *The critic gave the sidesplitting comedy an excellent review.* ♦ *The sidesplitting movie made me laugh so hard that I cried.*

sidestep ['sɑɪd stɛp] **1.** *tv.* to avoid injury or collision by stepping to the side. ♦ *The batter sidestepped the wild pitch.* ♦ *The woman sidestepped the bicycle that was veering toward her.* **2.** *tv.* to avoid or evade something. (Figurative on ①.) ♦ *The politician sidestepped the issue of tax evasion.* ♦ *The celebrity sidestepped the reporter's personal questions.*

side street ['sɑɪd strit] *n.* a residential street that is not a main street. ♦ *The cab driver escaped heavy traffic by driving on side streets.* ♦ *The quiet side street came to a dead end at the train tracks.*

sideswipe ['sɑɪd swɑɪp] *tv.* to hit something along its side; to hit something with one's side. ♦ *A player from the other team sideswiped the quarterback.* ♦ *The police officer sideswiped the man who stole Anne's purse.*

sidetrack ['sɑɪd træk] **1.** *tv.* to move a train from a main track to a minor one, alongside the major one. ♦ *An engineer sidetracked the idle train.* ♦ *The freight train was sidetracked at the depot.* **2.** *tv.* to distract someone from the main topic; to cause someone to digress. (Figurative on ①.) ♦ *Anne's comment sidetracked the speaker.* ♦ *Bill sidetracked his professor by asking an irrelevant question.* **3. get off on a sidetrack** *idiom* a digression; the discussion of a topic that is not the main topic. ♦ *Anne got off on a sidetrack and never returned to her topic.* ♦ *The ineffective committee got off on one sidetrack after another.*

sidewalk ['sɑɪd wɔk] *n.* a paved path, usually along the side of a street, for people to walk on. ♦ *Mary cleared the snow from the sidewalk in front of her house.* ♦ *Dave walked down the sidewalk along Main Street.*

sideways ['sɑɪd wez] **1.** *adj.* to or from a side. ♦ *I noticed the reporter's sideways glance from across the room.* ♦ *My sideways movement surprised the assailant.* **2.** *adv.* to, on, or from a side or both sides. ♦ *The silly children put the books in the bookcase sideways so that the covers faced outward.* ♦ *Anne looked sideways at the child walking past her.*

siding ['sɑɪd ɪŋ] *n.* strips of wood, aluminum, or vinyl attached to the outside of a building. (No plural form in this sense.) ♦ *The tornado blew the aluminum siding from our house.* ♦ *While renovating, we sided our house with vinyl siding.*

siege ['sidʒ] *n.* the surrounding of a city, fort, or place by people who are trying to capture it; an attack. ♦ *During the enemy's siege, no one could leave or enter the city.* ♦ *The siege of the soldier's camp ended in a violent battle.*

Sierra Leone [si 'ɛr ə li 'on] See Gazetteer.

siesta [si 'ɛs tə] *n.* a nap or rest period taken in the early afternoon during the hottest part of the day. (From Spanish.) ♦ *The workers took a siesta to escape the heat.* ♦ *Siestas are especially common in Spain and Latin America.*

sieve ['sɪv] *n.* a utensil, such as a strainer, used to separate solids from liquids or from powdered foods such as flour. ♦ *The cook removed the lumps from the flour with a sieve.* ♦ *The prospector used a sieve to lift pebbles from the river bed.*

sift ['sɪft] **1.** *tv.* to separate small pieces from larger pieces by using a sieve. ♦ *The cook sifted the flour to remove the lumps.* ♦ *Bob sifted the sugar because it had chunks in it.* **2. sift through** *iv.* + *prep. phr.* to flow through something. ♦ *Sand sifted slowly through the hourglass.* ♦ *Dust sifted through the cracks around the door.* **3. sift through** *iv. + prep. phr.* to look among a group of things closely. ♦ *The inspector sifted through the dead man's belongings.* ♦ *Jane sifted through the papers on her desk, looking for the important memo.*

sigh ['sɑɪ] **1.** *iv.* to breathe out slowly and noisily, especially to indicate that one is bored, relieved, sad, or tired. ♦ *Halfway through the long car trip, the driver sighed.* ♦ *After John's long tirade, Susan merely sighed.* **2.** *n.* the sound of sighing as in ①. ♦ *When my lost dog was found, I let out a sigh of relief.* ♦ *The speaker was unaware of the bored sighs coming from the audience.*

sight ['sɑɪt] **1.** *n.* the ability to see; the power to see; vision. (No plural form in this sense.) ♦ *The blind woman had lost her sight in a car accident.* ♦ *My sight is very good, so I don't need to wear glasses.* **2.** *n.* the distance that one can see; the range of vision. (No plural form in this sense.) ♦ *I didn't see the accident because it was out of my line of sight.* ♦ *Once the skyscrapers were in sight, I knew I was near the city.* **3.** *n.* something that is seen; something in one's range of vision; a view. ♦ *The sight from the scenic overlook was breathtaking.* ♦ *The sun setting over the lake was a beautiful sight.* **4.** *n.* something that is worth seeing. ♦ *When in Rome, we went to see all the tourist sights.* ♦ *John went to New York City to see the sights.* **5.** *n.* a device on a gun or other weapon that allows one to see exactly what one is aiming at. ♦ *The hunter looked through the sight and pulled the trigger.* ♦ *The marksman looked down the sights and shot.* **6.** *n.* something that looks funny or strange. (No plural form in this sense.) ♦ *John's weird clothing is quite a sight.* ♦ *The children laughed because the clowns were a funny sight.* **7.** *tv.* to see someone or something for the first time, especially when one is looking for that person or thing. ♦ *The sailor shouted to his mates when he sighted land.* ♦ *The new star was named for the astronomer who had sighted it.* **8. know someone by sight** *idiom* to know the name and recognize the face of someone. ♦ *I've never met the man, but I know him by sight.* ♦ *"Have you ever met Mary?" "No, but I know her by sight."* **9. raise one's sights** *idiom* to set higher goals for oneself. (On ⑤.) ♦ *When you're young, you tend to raise your sights too high.* ♦ *On the other hand, some people need to raise their sights.* **10. set one's sights on something** *idiom* to select something as one's goal. (On ⑤.) ♦ *I set my sights on a master's degree from the state university.* ♦ *Don't set your sights on something you cannot possibly do.* **11. in sight** *idiom* able to be seen. ♦ *I hear birds, but there are none in sight.* ♦ *The locusts ate everything in sight.*

sighted ['sɑɪt ɪd] *adj.* [of someone] able to see; [of someone] not blind. ♦ *The sighted woman helped her blind husband across the street.* ♦ *The blind students were guided by sighted friends.*

sighting ['sɑɪt ɪŋ] *n.* an event in which something is seen, especially something mysterious or supernatural. ♦ *Many sightings of UFOs were reported when the meteorite struck the earth.* ♦ *Even after his death, there were still many sightings of the famous entertainer.*

sightless ['sɑɪt ləs] *adj.* unable to see; without sight; blind. (Adv: *sightlessly.*) ♦ *The sightless woman relied on her guide dog.* ♦ *The sightless man knew how to read Braille.*

sightseeing ['sɑɪt si ɪŋ] *n.* visiting famous or interesting places, especially when one is on vacation. (No plural form in this sense.) ♦ *When Mary was in Japan, she did a lot of sightseeing.* ♦ *I'm going to go sightseeing on the first two days of my vacation.*

sign ['sɑɪn] **1.** *n.* a mark that represents something; a mark that indicates something. ♦ *The plus sign "+" is used to indicate addition.* ♦ *The dollar sign can be written with one or two vertical strokes.* **2.** *n.* something that indicates something else. ♦ *High blood pressure is a sign of many different health problems.* ♦ *Red spots can be a sign of measles.* **3.** *n.* an object that has information written on it. ♦ *Often, a sign is a flat piece of paper, wood, or metal that is attached to a post or wall.* ♦ *A sign on the freeway pointed to the exit to 55th Street.* **4.** *n.* a gesture used to communicate. ♦ *Mother made a sign for me to come to the door.* ♦ *Through the window, the clerk made a sign for me to come in.* **5.** *n.* one of the twelve divisions of the zodiac. ♦ *"What's your sign?" asked the man sitting next to me at the meeting.* ♦ *One of the signs looks like a scorpion.* **6.** *tv.* to write one's name on something. ♦ *John signed his name on the back of the check.* ♦ *Please sign your name on the line.* **7.** *tv.* to mark or validate something by writing one's name on it. ♦ *Mary signed the back of the check in order to endorse it.* ♦ *John signed his contract, thus making it official.* **8.** *tv.* to hire a new player to a sports team. ♦ *The team owner signed the best college football player.* ♦ *The hockey team signed four new players.* **9.** *tv.* to communicate something by using sign language. ♦ *The deaf man signed his request to his friend.* ♦ *Mary signed that she wanted to leave the party soon.* **10.** *tv.* [for a country or corporation] to agree to a document, treaty, or agreement by having an agreement signed ⑪ by one of its officers. ♦ *The warring nations signed the peace treaty.* ♦ *The large corporation signed the government contract.* **11.** *iv.* to write [one's name] on something. ♦ *The cashier handed me the receipt and a pen, and I signed.* ♦ *This car is yours as soon as you sign on the dotted line.* **12.** *iv.* to communicate in sign language. ♦ *Anne taught the deaf children how to sign.* ♦ *John signed with his deaf friends.* **13. signed, sealed, and delivered** *idiom* formally and officially signed ⑪; [for a formal document to be] executed. ♦ *Here is the deed to the property—signed, sealed, and delivered.* ♦ *I can't begin work on this project until I have the contract signed, sealed, and delivered.*

signal ['sɪg nəl] **1.** *n.* something that conveys a message by affecting one of the senses; a sound, light, movement, etc., that conveys a message. ♦ *When the traffic signal is red, you must stop.* ♦ *I waited for the customs agent's signal to proceed.* **2.** *n.* the waves sent by a radio or television transmitter. ♦ *I adjusted the antenna so that the signal would come in better.* ♦ *On clear days, we can get signals from stations 100 miles away.* **3.** *tv.* to indicate something. ♦ *The peace treaty signaled the end of the war.* ♦ *The test results signaled that John had cancer.* **4. signal (to) someone to do something** *idiom* [for someone] to give someone a command or instruction using ①. ♦ *The traffic cop signaled me to stop.* ♦ *Bill signaled the other driver to pull over to the side of the road.*

signatory ['sɪg nə tor i] *n.* someone who signs a document or agreement; a country whose representative signs an agreement or a treaty. ♦ *The signatories signed the peace* *treaty during a press conference.* ♦ *So far, the agreement has been signed by 25 signatories.*

signature ['sɪg nə tʃɚ] **1.** *n.* a person's name, handwritten by the person. ♦ *Jane wrote her signature on the bottom of the contract.* ♦ *The bank returned the check because it lacked a signature.* **2.** *n.* something distinctive that identifies someone or something. (Figurative on ①.) ♦ *A black bow tie was the politician's signature.* ♦ *The actress's high-pitched laugh was her signature.*

signed ['saɪnd] **1.** *adj.* having written one's signature on something. ♦ *The author sold signed copies of her book.* ♦ *The actor sent me a signed photograph of himself.* **2.** *adj.* using sign language; communicated in sign language. ♦ *I couldn't understand the deaf peoples' signed conversation.* ♦ *Anne interpreted the signed testimony of the deaf witness.*

significance [sɪg 'nɪf ə kəns] *n.* importance; meaning. (No plural form in this sense.) ♦ *The science professor explained the significance of gravity.* ♦ *The significance of my boss's promotion became clear at the meeting.*

significant [sɪg 'nɪf ə kənt] *adj.* important; meaningful. (Adv: *significantly.*) ♦ *The jury listened to the witness's significant testimony.* ♦ *Albert Einstein is a significant figure in the world of science.*

signify ['sɪg nə faɪ] *tv.* to mean something; to indicate something; to be a sign of something. ♦ *Dark clouds signify that it will rain soon.* ♦ *A written word signifies the concept associated with it.*

sign language ['saɪn læŋ gwɪdʒ] *n.* a visual form of communication where the hands assume specific positions that represent words or letters in the language. (No plural form in this sense.) ♦ *Many deaf people communicate with sign language.* ♦ *I learned sign language so I could converse with all of my friends.*

signpost ['saɪn post] *n.* a sign by the side of a road that gives information about where one is or how far a place is from where one is. ♦ *The signpost said that Washington was another 100 miles away.* ♦ *The signpost indicated that I was entering the village of Springfield.*

silence ['saɪ ləns] **1.** *n.* absolute quiet; the absence of all sound. (No plural form in this sense.) ♦ *The student needed complete silence in order to study.* ♦ *The silence in the library was appreciated by the readers.* **2.** *n.* the absence of comments about something. (No plural form in this sense.) ♦ *The lawyer maintained silence about his client's role in the crime.* ♦ *The government insisted on the newspaper's silence about the war.* **3.** *tv.* to cause someone to be quiet; to cause someone to stop talking or to stop making noise. ♦ *The usher silenced the people in the audience who were talking.* ♦ *The librarian silenced the loud students.* **4.** *tv.* to prevent someone or something from spreading information. ♦ *The government silenced the underground newspaper.* ♦ *The university silenced the unfavorable report.*

silent ['saɪ lənt] **1.** *adj.* quiet; not speaking or making noise; done without making noise. (Adv: *silently.*) ♦ *The silent students studied into the night.* ♦ *I didn't even realize Bob was here because he's so silent.* **2.** *adj.* not pronounced; not representing a sound. (Adv: *silently.*) ♦ *The* p *in* pneumonia *is silent.* ♦ *A silent* e *affects the pronunciation of an earlier vowel, as with the difference between* tap *and* tape.

silhouette [sɪl u 'ɛt] **1.** *n.* a side view image of someone or something in solid black against a contrasting background. ♦ *From the sidewalk, I could see the silhouette of an intruder on the window shade in my house.* ♦ *The artist painted a silhouette of the cathedral against the setting sun.* **2.** *tv.* to show the dark outline of something against a lighter background. ♦ *A bright light silhouetted a person's figure against the window shade.* ♦ *The moonlight silhouetted the ancient castle against the dark, night sky.*

silicon ['sil ə kɑn] *n.* a chemical element used in semiconductors. (No plural form in this sense.) ♦ *The atomic symbol of silicon is Si, and its atomic number is 14.* ♦ *Silicon is commonly found in nature as a component of rocks and sand.*

silk ['sɪlk] **1.** *n.* a smooth, fine thread that is created by a silkworm when making its cocoon. (No plural form in this sense.) ♦ *The silkworm produces silk to make its cocoon.* ♦ *Sally touched the soft silk of the cocoon.* **2.** *n.* cloth woven from ①. (No plural form in this sense.) ♦ *Silk is a delicate, expensive material.* ♦ *Mary bought some silk that was woven by hand.* **3.** *adj.* made of ②. ♦ *The silk shirt felt smooth against my skin.* ♦ *You should take this soiled silk blouse to the dry cleaners.*

silkworm ['sɪlk wɚm] *n.* a species of caterpillar that makes a cocoon of silk. ♦ *The silkworm is the larva of a Chinese moth.* ♦ *The silkworm is cultivated in China for its silk.*

silky ['sɪl ki] *adj.* like silk; soft and smooth; [of cloth] soft and shimmering. (Adv: *silkily.* Comp: *silkier;* sup: *silkiest.*) ♦ *Mary's shampooed hair felt silky.* ♦ *Anne wore a silky dress to the award ceremonies.*

sill ['sɪl] *n.* the bottom ledge of a window or door frame. ♦ *John placed his glasses on the window sill next to his bed.* ♦ *Bill tripped on the door sill as he entered the room.*

silly ['sɪl i] *adj.* foolish; not sensible. (Comp: *sillier;* sup: *silliest.*) ♦ *The silly children pretended that they were puppies.* ♦ *The professor ridiculed the silly hypothesis.*

silo ['saɪ lo] **1.** *n.* a tall, tube-shaped building used to store grain. (Pl in *-s.*) ♦ *The farmer stored the wheat in the silo next to the barn.* ♦ *Our silos are full of grain.* **2.** *n.* an underground structure where missiles are kept. (Pl in *-s.*) ♦ *The spy visited nuclear silos in eastern Montana.* ♦ *The missiles have been removed from the silos.*

silver ['sɪl vɚ] **1.** *n.* a bright, valuable metallic element, which in its pure form is soft and easily shaped. (No plural form in this sense.) ♦ *Silver is often mixed with other metals to make jewelry, eating utensils, coins, and other items.* ♦ *The atomic symbol of silver is Ag, and its atomic number is 47.* **2.** *n.* coins, as opposed to paper money. (From a time when major U.S. coins were made of ①. No plural form in this sense.) ♦ *I exchanged my dollar for silver so I could use the vending machine.* ♦ *John gave a handful of silver to the child who was collecting money for charity.* **3. silver (medal)** *n.* a medal given to someone who finishes a competition in second place. ♦ *The second-place competitor won the silver medal.* ♦ *An athlete from the United States won the silver, and another athlete won the gold.* **4.** *adj.* made of ①. ♦ *John collected old silver dollars.* ♦ *Anne wore silver earrings to the party.*

silver-plated ['sɪl vɚ plet ɪd] *adj.* coated with a thin layer of silver. ♦ *The jeweler sold me a silver-plated necklace.* ♦ *The collector examined the silver-plated coin.*

silverware ['sɪl vɚ wɛr] **1.** *n.* eating or serving utensils that are made from or plated with silver. (Often used in contrast to flatware. No plural form in this sense.) ♦ *The maid polished the silverware after washing it.* ♦ *After the party, Anne noticed that some of her silverware was missing.* **2.** *n.* flatware; knives, forks, and spoons made of steel, nickel, or metals other than silver. (No plural form in this sense.) ♦ *David put the silverware in the dishwasher.* ♦ *We took some old silverware to the picnic.*

silvery ['sɪl və ri] **1.** *adj.* looking like silver. ♦ *The chemist examined the silvery sediment.* ♦ *The cheap necklace was plated with a silvery metal.* **2.** *adj.* having a pleasing, gentle sound; having a nice melody. ♦ *The couple dreamed of happiness and danced to a silvery waltz.* ♦ *I fell asleep listening to gentle, silvery music.*

similar ['sɪm ə lɚ] *adj.* resembling something else, but not exactly the same. (Adv: *similarly.*) ♦ *Oranges and tangerines are similar.* ♦ *I bought a car that is similar to my last one, except for the color.*

similarity [sɪm ə 'lɛr ɪ ti] **1.** *n.* a way or an aspect in which someone or something is like or resembles someone or something else. ♦ *One similarity between me and my sister is that we are both tall.* ♦ *The researcher noticed the similarities between the two viruses.* **2.** *n.* resembling someone or something else; being like someone or something else. (No plural form in this sense.) ♦ *Mary's similarity to her mother is striking.* ♦ *The similarity between the author's first novel and his second one is intentional.*

simmer ['sɪm ɚ] **1.** *tv.* to boil something gently; to cook something at or just below its boiling point. ♦ *The cook simmered the stew for two hours.* ♦ *David simmered the sauce for five minutes before adding onions.* **2.** *iv.* to boil gently; to cook at or just below the boiling point. ♦ *The soup is simmering on the stove.* ♦ *As the water simmered, it slowly evaporated.* **3.** *iv.* to be angry without letting other people know that one is angry. (Figurative on ②.) ♦ *My boss simmered for days before telling us what was wrong.* ♦ *We later found out that Anne was actually simmering about her divorce, while we thought she was content.* **4.** *iv.* [for a situation] to be currently somewhat calm but progressing toward violence. (Figurative on ①.) ♦ *The ethnic unrest had simmered for months before the war.* ♦ *The voters' discontent simmered until it finally was made known at election time.*

simple ['sɪm pəl] **1.** *adj.* easy; not complicated; not complex. (Adv: *simply.* Comp: *simpler;* sup: *simplest.*) ♦ *The teacher taught simple math problems to the second graders.* ♦ *Unfortunately, there rarely are simple solutions to serious urban problems.* **2.** *adj.* plain; not complicated; not fancy. (Adv: *simply.* Comp: *simpler;* sup: *simplest.*) ♦ *Mary wore a simple dress to work.* ♦ *John and Mary had a small, simple wedding.*

simplicity [sɪm 'plɪs ɪ ti] *n.* ease; clearness; plainness. (No plural form in this sense.) ♦ *The simplicity of the teacher's explanation pleased me.* ♦ *I recommend this book for children because of its simplicity.*

simplify ['sɪm plə fɑɪ] *tv.* to make something more simple; to make something easier to do or understand; to make something more clear. ♦ *The teacher simplified the problem so I could understand it.* ♦ *The college simplified the complex requirements.*

simplistic [sɪm 'plɪs tɪk] *adj.* too simple; having been simplified too much. (Adv: *simplistically* [...ɪk li].) ♦ *The simplistic answer didn't explain all of the problems.* ♦ *The mayor's plan was too simplistic to do any good.*

simply ['sɪm pli] **1.** *adv.* easily; without difficulty. ♦ *The problem was solved quite simply.* ♦ *The remaining puzzle piece fit into place neatly and simply.* **2.** *adv.* merely; only. ♦ *Johnny was not dying of the plague. He simply had a case of chickenpox.* ♦ *All you have to do is simply tell me when you want to leave.* **3.** *adv.* absolutely; completely; very. ♦ *The critic was simply thrilled with the new movie.* ♦ *David is simply ecstatic about his upcoming vacation.*

simulate ['sɪm jə let] *tv.* to show the nature or effects of something, allowing the observer to learn about it without experiencing it. ♦ *The computer program simulated the effects of aging.* ♦ *The experiment simulated real weather conditions.*

simulation [sɪm jə 'le ʃən] **1.** *n.* a demonstration of the nature or effects of an event without really experiencing it. (No plural form in this sense.) ♦ *The documentary showed the simulation of a meteor striking the earth.* ♦ *The computer's simulation of the crime helped the inspectors solve it.* **2.** *n.* something that has been simulated. ♦ *The event shown in the news report was actually a simulation.* ♦ *The computer simulation showed what I would look like in 30 years.*

simultaneous [sɑɪ məl 'te ni əs] *adj.* happening or existing at the same time; concurrent. (Adv: *simultaneously.*) ♦ *There were five simultaneous explosions downtown caused by terrorists.* ♦ *The simultaneous responses from Anne and Mary show that they think alike.*

sin ['sɪn] **1.** *n.* evil; wickedness; a transgression. (No plural form in this sense.) ♦ *Sin will be the downfall of wicked people.* ♦ *Anne prayed to God to deliver her from the powers of sin.* **2.** *n.* the breaking of a religious or moral principle. ♦ *My sins are numerous, but I will behave properly in the future.* ♦ *One more little sin probably wouldn't do any harm.* **3.** *n.* any error or minor transgression. (Figurative on ②.) ♦ *Misspelling a word is not a serious sin, but try to avoid it.* ♦ *Her real sin was thinking she could outwit me.* **4.** *iv.* to break a religious or moral principle. ♦ *John sinned and then he prayed for forgiveness.* ♦ *Max sinned by stealing a car.*

since ['sɪns] **1.** *conj.* from a certain time in the past until now. ♦ *Mary has lived in Texas since she was born.* ♦ *John has been a lawyer ever since he graduated from law school.* **2.** *conj.* because. ♦ *Since Mary was tired, she left the party.* ♦ *Since two feet of snow fell yesterday, school has been canceled.* **3.** *prep.* from a certain time in the past until now. ♦ *Since yesterday, it has been raining.* ♦ *I have been awake since 6:00.* **4.** *adv.* from a certain time in the past until now. ♦ *John last saw Bill in high school and hasn't seen him since.* ♦ *Mary left town twenty years ago and hasn't been seen since.*

sincere [sɪn 'sɪr] *adj.* honest; real; genuine; true; not deceitful; without pretension. (Adv: *sincerely.* Comp: *sincerer;* sup: *sincerest.*) ♦ *Please accept my sincere gratitude for your help.* ♦ *I was being sincere when I told you how I felt.*

sincerely [sɪn 'sɪr li] **1.** *adv.* honestly; really; genuinely; truly; not deceitfully. ♦ *I sincerely wish the best for you in the future.* ♦ *We sincerely hope that you're mistaken about* *this.* **2.** *adv.* <a word used as a polite way to finish a letter, before one's signature.> ♦ *The letter was signed, "Sincerely, Anne."* ♦ *John's note was signed, "Sincerely, John."*

sincerity [sɪn 'sɛr ɪ ti] *n.* the quality of being sincere; honesty. (No plural form in this sense.) ♦ *Because of his sincerity, John could never lie to anyone.* ♦ *The jury believed the sincerity of the witness.*

sinew ['sɪn ju] *n.* a tendon; a strong cord that connects muscles to bones. ♦ *The weightlifter's muscles and sinews were well defined.* ♦ *The physical therapist placed an ice pack on my sore sinews.*

sinful ['sɪn fʊl] **1.** *adj.* full of sin; having committed a sin. (Adv: *sinfully.*) ♦ *I don't feel sinful, but I am sure I have committed a few bad deeds.* ♦ *The sinful man pledged that he would sin no more.* **2.** *adj.* wicked; bad; evil; leading people into sin. (Adv: *sinfully.*) ♦ *Miss Thompson was viewed as a sinful woman because of her different morals.* ♦ *The church members protested against the sinful movie.*

sing ['sɪŋ] **1.** *iv., irreg.* to make music with one's voice, uttering a melody with words. (Pt: sang; pp: sung.) ♦ *The children sang around the campfire.* ♦ *The performer will sing on the stage.* **2.** *tv., irreg.* to make music as in ①. ♦ *The choir sang the song beautifully.* ♦ *John sings the tenor part in the choir.*

Singapore ['sɪŋ ə por] See Gazetteer.

singe ['sɪndʒ] *tv.* to burn something slightly; to burn the edge or end of something. ♦ *Mary singed her hair when she bent over the stove.* ♦ *Bob singed his fingers when he lit a cigarette.*

singer ['sɪŋ ɚ] *n.* someone who sings something, especially as an occupation. ♦ *The singer performed a concert at the large auditorium.* ♦ *A famous singer sang the national anthem before the ballgame.*

single ['sɪŋ gəl] **1.** *adj.* one and only one; solitary. (Adv: *singly.*) ♦ *I placed a single slice of cheese on my hamburger.* ♦ *Tom has only a single dollar in his pocket.* **2.** *adj.* individual; meant for one thing or person. (Adv: *singly.*) ♦ *I rented a hotel room with a single bed.* ♦ *The instant soup was packaged in single portions.* **3.** *adj.* not married. (Adv: *singly.*) ♦ *The single lawyer was too busy to date.* ♦ *The single man was happy being a bachelor.* **4.** *adj.* having only one part; not double; not multiple. (Adv: *singly.*) ♦ *The encyclopedia came in a single, huge volume.* ♦ *My inexpensive bicycle only has a single gear.* **5.** *n.* something that is meant for one person. ♦ *The hotel patron asked the front-desk clerk for a single.* ♦ *The few remaining tickets for the performance were all singles, so my friend and I had to sit in different parts of the theater.* **6.** *n.* a $1 bill. ♦ *John paid for the $4 item with singles.* ♦ *Do you have five singles for a $5 bill?* **7.** *n.* [in baseball] a play where the batter reaches first base safely and stops there. ♦ *The batter got a single the first time he batted.* ♦ *Mary has gotten the most singles on her softball team.* **8.** *n.* someone who is not married. ♦ *The church sponsored a dance for the singles in the parish.* ♦ *Dozens of singles were seated around the bar.*

single-breasted ['sɪŋ gəl 'brɛs tɪd] *adj.* [of a coat, a jacket, or the jacket of a suit] overlapping a relatively small amount in the front and fastened with only one button or one row of buttons; not double-breasted. ♦ *The designer produced an inexpensive single-breasted jacket.* ♦ *David wore a single-breasted suit to the interview.*

single-handedly ['sɪŋ gəl 'hæn dɪd li] *adv.* without anyone else's help. ♦ *The hero stopped the robber single-handedly.* ♦ *The mayor was single-handedly responsible for firing the police chief.*

single-minded ['sɪŋ gəl 'maɪn dɪd] *adj.* having only one purpose. (Adv: *single-mindedly.*) ♦ *The single-minded politician focused on his new tax proposal.* ♦ *The suspect was questioned repeatedly by the single-minded detective.*

singsong ['sɪŋ sɔŋ] *adj.* with a repetitive or monotonous rising and falling rhythm. ♦ *The poet's singsong delivery detracted from the poem.* ♦ *The child recited the story in a singsong way.*

singular ['sɪŋ gjə lɚ] **1.** *adj.* referring to only one person or thing; the opposite of plural. ♦ Mouse *is the singular form of* mice. ♦ *Although* data *is a plural noun, many people use it as a singular noun.* **2.** *adj.* unusual; exceptional; remarkable. (Adv: *singularly.*) ♦ *Mary had a singular talent for painting realistic portraits.* ♦ *John developed a singular manner for dealing with angry people tactfully.* **3.** *n.* The form of a noun that refers to only one person or thing; the opposite of plural. ♦ Sheep *is a word that is the same in the singular as it is in the plural.* ♦ *The singular of* mice *is* mouse.

sinister ['sɪn ɪ stɚ] *adj.* suggesting evil or harm; threatening evil or harm. (Adv: *sinisterly.*) ♦ *The evil villain had a sinister laugh.* ♦ *The hero discovered the mad scientist's sinister plan.*

sink ['sɪŋk] **1.** *iv., irreg.* to go beneath a surface; to fall beneath a surface. (Pt: sank or sunk; pp: sunk or sunken.) ♦ *My shoes sank into the soft mud.* ♦ *The leaky boat sank beneath the surface of the water.* **2.** *iv., irreg.* to become smaller in number; to decrease. ♦ *The president's popularity rating sank below 30%.* ♦ *I turn up the heat when the temperature sinks to 65 degrees.* **3.** *iv., irreg.* [for someone] to collapse or fall to the ground because of weakness, fear, respect, etc. ♦ *The pleading woman sank to her knees before the king.* ♦ *The sick man clutched his heart and sank to the floor.* **4.** *tv., irreg.* to cause something to go lower and lower beneath the surface of water or some other liquid. ♦ *The torpedo sank the ship.* ♦ *The combined weight of all the children sank the raft.* **5. sink into** *tv., irreg. + prep. phr.* to force something into an object as far as it can go. ♦ *The carpenter sank the nail into the wall.* ♦ *The screw had been sunk too far into the beam, and I couldn't remove it.* **6.** *tv., irreg.* to dig a hole, shaft, or well into the earth. ♦ *The oil company plans to sink a new oil well in Texas.* ♦ *The farmer sank a hole and placed a fence post in it.* **7. sink into** *tv., irreg. + prep. phr.* to invest money or property. ♦ *John sank all of his income into real estate.* ♦ *Mary sank $100,000 into a mutual funds portfolio.* **8.** *n.* a permanent basin, especially in a kitchen or bathroom, for washing dishes, one's hands or face, etc. ♦ *John filled the sink before he shaved.* ♦ *David's dirty dishes piled up in his kitchen sink.* **9. sink or swim** *idiom* to fail or succeed. ♦ *After I've studied and learned all I can, I have to take the test and sink or swim.* ♦ *It's too late to help John now. It's sink or swim for him.*

sinking ['sɪŋ kɪŋ] *adj.* going further downward into a liquid; declining; diminishing. ♦ *The captain abandoned the sinking ship.* ♦ *The network canceled the television shows that had sinking ratings.*

sinner ['sɪn ɚ] *n.* someone who sins. ♦ *The sinner prayed to God for forgiveness.* ♦ *We are all sinners in one way or another.*

sinus ['sɑɪ nəs] **1.** *n.* one of a number of spaces inside the facial bones that are connected to the nasal passages. ♦ *Anne's not going to the party because her sinuses are clogged.* ♦ *When John gets headaches, his sinuses throb with pain.* **2.** *adj.* <the adj. use of ①.> ♦ *I have a terrible sinus headache.* ♦ *Anne is troubled with sinus congestion.*

sip ['sɪp] **1. sip at; sip on** *iv. + prep. phr.* to drink a little bit of something at a time. ♦ *Mary sipped on her tea while she read.* ♦ *Anne sipped at the coffee because it was hot.* **2.** *tv.* to drink something a little bit at a time. ♦ *David sipped some wine with dinner.* ♦ *The campers sipped hot chocolate around the campfire.* **3.** *n.* a small drink of something; a little taste of something liquid. ♦ *Could I have a sip of your juice?* ♦ *I could only swallow a sip of the bitter liquid.*

siphon AND **syphon** ['sɑɪ fən] **1.** *n.* a tube that has one end in a container of liquid and, through gravity, pulls the liquid down to another container placed at a lower level. ♦ *The crook placed a siphon in the gas tank of the parked car.* ♦ *John drained the water from the container with a siphon.* **2. siphon (off)** *tv.* (+ *adv.*) to remove liquid from a container by using ①. ♦ *The thief siphoned gasoline from the cars in the parking lot.* ♦ *The chemist siphoned off the oil at the top of the flask.*

sir ['sɚ] **1.** *n.* <a word used to address a man politely.> ♦ *How are you today, sir?* ♦ *Excuse me, sir, you dropped your hat.* **2. Sir** *n.* <the title of address for men who have been knighted.> (Used with the man's first name or first and last name, but never with just the last name.) ♦ *Sir Edward was a member of the British House of Lords.* ♦ *Sir Laurence Olivier was a famous actor.*

siren ['sɑɪ rən] *n.* a device that makes a loud noise of warning, such as that found on police cars, fire trucks, and ambulances. ♦ *When John heard the siren, he pulled his car over to the curb.* ♦ *The ambulance raced to the hospital with its siren blaring.*

sirloin ['sɚ lɔɪn] *n.* the meat cut from the upper part of the loin of cattle, considered to be the best cut of meat. (No plural form in this sense.) ♦ *The restaurant's choice sirloin was quite expensive.* ♦ *The tender sirloin that David cooked was delicious.*

sissy ['sɪs i] *n.* an effeminate boy; a boy who behaves like a girl. (Derogatory.) ♦ *The bully called Jimmy a sissy and then pushed him into the mud.* ♦ *Stop acting like a sissy, and face the guy who threatened you!*

sister ['sɪs tɚ] **1.** *n.* a female sibling; a daughter of one's mother or father. ♦ *I have two sisters, who are both younger than I am.* ♦ *Anne's sister let her borrow a nice pair of shoes.* **2.** *n.* a nun. (Also a term of address.) ♦ *Mary joined the convent because she wanted to become a sister.* ♦ *Sister Mary explained the concept of sin to the class.*

sisterhood ['sɪs tɚ hʊd] **1.** *n.* the relationship between two or more women who have a close friendship. (No plural form in this sense.) ♦ *Anne and Sue enjoyed a close sisterhood.* ♦ *The female soldiers developed a close bond of sisterhood.* **2.** *n.* a religious organization of women. ♦ *The novice joined the sisterhood when she was 21 years old.* ♦ *The sisterhood vowed to close the liquor store on their block.*

sister-in-law ['sɪs tɚ ɪn lɔ] *n., irreg.* the wife of one's brother or of one's brother-in-law; the sister of one's husband or one's wife. (Pl: sisters-in-law.) ♦ *Anne's husband and her sister-in-law inherited a fortune from their parents.* ♦ *My brother and sister-in-law visited me last night.*

sisters-in-law ['sɪs tɚz ɪn lɔ] pl of sister-in-law.

sit ['sɪt] **1.** *iv., irreg.* to be in a position where the upper part of the body is straight, and the buttocks are supported by a chair, a seat, the floor, or some other surface. (Pt/pp: sat.) ♦ *The patient sat on the hard chair for half an hour.* ♦ *John sat in the comfortable chair.* **2. sit (down)** *iv., irreg.* (+ *adv.*) to move or bend so that one sits ①. ♦ *Anne sat on the expensive couch.* ♦ *Please sit down, won't you?* **3.** *iv., irreg.* [for something] to be in a certain position; to be in a place. ♦ *Our television set sits in the living room.* ♦ *A large wastebasket sat next to John's desk.* **4.** *iv., irreg.* [for an animal] to be positioned with the back end resting on a surface. ♦ *John ordered the dog to sit.* ♦ *The cat sat on Anne's lap.* **5.** *tv., irreg.* to babysit someone. ♦ *I sat my sister's kids when she went to the doctor.* ♦ *My neighbor sat my daughter when I had to go to the dentist.* **6.** *tv., irreg.* to make someone sit ① in a location. ♦ *The nurse sat the frail patient on the bed.* ♦ *Tom's teacher sat him in the front row.* **7. sit around (somewhere)** *idiom* to sit somewhere and relax or do nothing; to sit idly somewhere. ♦ *Tom likes to sit around the house in shorts and a T-shirt on hot days.* ♦ *Too many people are just sitting around doing nothing at my office.* **8. sit at someone's feet** *idiom* to admire someone greatly; to be influenced by someone's teaching; to be taught by someone. ♦ *Bob sat at the feet of Picasso when he was studying in Europe.* ♦ *Tom would love to sit at the feet of his favorite musician.*

sitcom ['sɪt kɑm] *n.* a funny television program, as opposed to a serious or dramatic one. (From *sit*uation *com*edy.) ♦ *I prefer TV sitcoms to TV dramas.* ♦ *Most sitcoms are taped in front of a live audience.*

site ['sɑɪt] *n.* a location where something is, was, has happened, or will happen. ♦ *The site of the new shopping mall used to be a farm.* ♦ *The ambulance rushed to the accident site.*

sit-in ['sɪt ɪn] *n.* a protest or demonstration in which people take seats in an establishment and refuse to leave. ♦ *The protesters staged a sit-in at the lunch counter that wouldn't serve them.* ♦ *The police arrested those participating in the sit-in.*

sitting ['sɪt ɪŋ] **1.** *n.* the period of time that someone sits in a chair. ♦ *Jane read the interesting book in one sitting.* ♦ *It took more than two sittings to finish the work.* **2.** *n.* a time during which one poses to be photographed or painted. ♦ *My sitting with the portrait artist lasted four hours.* ♦ *The photographer scheduled me for a sitting at 1:00.*

situate ['sɪt ʃu et] *tv.* to place something; to have or make a place for something. ♦ *City hall is situated on Main Street.* ♦ *The king situated the castle at the top of the hill.*

situation [sɪt ʃu 'e ʃən] *n.* a condition; the circumstances of an event; the state of affairs. ♦ *The reporter commented on the tense situation with the hostages.* ♦ *I helped David when he was in a tough financial situation.*

six ['sɪks] **1.** 6. See four for senses and examples. **2. six of one and half a dozen of the other** *idiom* about the same one way or the other. ♦ *It doesn't matter to me which way you do it. It's six of one and half a dozen of the other.* ♦ *What difference does it make? They're both the same—six of one and half a dozen of the other.*

six-pack ['sɪks pæk] *n.* a package of six things, especially six cans of beer or soft drinks. ♦ *Anne brought a six-pack of soda to the party.* ♦ *John and Bob drank a six-pack last night.*

six-shooter ['sɪks ʃut ɚ] *n.* a gun that has six chambers; a gun that can shoot six bullets. ♦ *The sheriff pulled his six-shooter from his holster.* ♦ *The villain held the six-shooter against the victim's head.*

sixteen ['sɪks 'tin] 16. See four for senses and examples.

sixteenth ['sɪks 'tinθ] 16th. See fourth for senses and examples.

sixth ['sɪksθ] **1.** 6th. See fourth for senses and examples. **2. sixth sense** See sense ⑪.

sixtieth ['sɪks ti əθ] 60th. See fourth for senses and examples.

sixty ['sɪks ti] 60. See forty for senses and examples.

sizable ['sɑɪz ə bəl] *adj.* large; rather large; considerable. (Adv: *sizably.*) ♦ *The rich woman left a sizable part of her fortune to her daughter.* ♦ *I have a sizable amount of work to do before I leave the office.*

size ['sɑɪz] **1.** *n.* the degree to which someone or something is large or small. (No plural form in this sense.) ♦ *Considering David's small size, it's amazing that he's so strong.* ♦ *Because of the watermelon's large size, there was enough for everyone.* **2.** *n.* one measurement in a series of measurements, used to describe the size ① of a product one wants, such as an article of clothing, a portion of food or drink, certain hardware, etc. ♦ *The soft drinks were available in small, medium, and large sizes.* ♦ *Is this blue jacket available in a medium size?* **3.** *tv.* to make or construct something in a particular ②; to make or construct something to a particular measurement so that it will fit exactly. ♦ *The tailor sized Bob's suit so that it fit him exactly.* ♦ *The carpenter sized the board to cover the gap in the railing.* **4. -size(d)** <a suffix that permits a word to form an adjective describing the size of something.> (Either *size* or *sized* is used. Examples: *bean-size(d), bite-size(d), child-size(d), full-size(d), good-size(d), half-size(d), king-size(d), large-size(d), life-size(d), man-size(d), middle-size(d), oversize(d), queen-size(d), small-size(d), undersize(d).*)

sizzle ['sɪz əl] **1.** *n.* the hissing noise made when frying fat or frying food in fat. (No plural form in this sense.) ♦ *The first thing John heard in the morning was the sizzle of bacon frying.* ♦ *I heard a sizzle when I placed the butter in the hot pan.* **2.** *iv.* [for fat or cooking oil] to make a hissing noise when it is fried; to sound like fat when it fries. ♦ *The bacon sizzled in the frying pan.* ♦ *The steak sizzled in its own juices.*

sizzling ['sɪz lɪŋ] **1.** *adj.* frying; making the noise that fat does when it is heated. ♦ *The kitchen was filled with the smell of sizzling bacon.* ♦ *The cook removed the sizzling steak from the oven.* **2.** *adj.* very hot. ♦ *The sizzling weather made everyone sweat.* ♦ *I couldn't sit on the sizzling park bench for even a second.*

skate ['sket] **1.** *n.* an ice skate; a roller skate. ♦ *Mary put on her skates and rolled toward the rink.* ♦ *John tied his skates and entered the ice rink.* **2.** *iv.* to move (over a surface) while wearing ①. ♦ *Jane skated across the ice.* ♦ *The students skated around the roller rink.*

skateboard ['sket bord] **1.** *n.* a short board that is wide enough to stand on and has a pair of wheels in front and in back. ♦ *The police told the kids not to ride their skateboards in traffic.* ♦ *David fell off his skateboard and scraped his knee.* **2.** *iv.* to move (over a surface) using ①. ♦ *Bill skateboarded down the steep ramp.* ♦ *Mary skateboarded to the store.*

skater ['sket ɚ] *n.* someone who ice-skates or roller-skates. ♦ *A hockey player must be a good skater.* ♦ *The skaters moved clockwise around the roller rink.*

skating rink ['sket ɪŋ rɪŋk] *n.* a building or place where there is a large, smooth sheet of ice for ice skating, or where there is a large, smooth floor for roller skating. ♦ *The skating rink was kept below freezing.* ♦ *Organ music is played at the skating rink where we roller-skate.*

skein ['sken] *n.* a length of yarn wound into a shape that can be packaged and sold. ♦ *It took two skeins of wool yarn to make this scarf.* ♦ *Please buy three skeins of red yarn.*

skeleton ['skɛl ə tən] **1.** *n.* the bones of a person or an animal connected or assembled in their proper arrangement. ♦ *The police found a skeleton buried in the farmer's field.* ♦ *The science museum displayed several dinosaur skeletons.* **2.** *n.* a framework; an outline; the basic structure that supports something. (Figurative on ①.) ♦ *After the fire, only the building's skeleton remained.* ♦ *This outline is just the basic skeleton of the book I'm writing.*

skeptic ['skɛp tɪk] *n.* someone who doubts faith, claims, theories, or facts; someone who questions the truth of something, especially religion. ♦ *The skeptic questioned the existence of God.* ♦ *The skeptic dismissed the president's plan as unworkable.*

skeptical ['skɛp tɪ kəl] *adj.* doubting; questioning; finding something hard to believe. (Adv: *skeptically* [...ɪk li].) ♦ *The skeptical student refused to accept the theory of evolution.* ♦ *A skeptical jury doubted the witness's testimony.*

skepticism ['skɛp tə sɪz əm] *n.* doubt; disbelief; the condition of being skeptical; skeptical attitude or behavior. (No plural form in this sense.) ♦ *John's skepticism of evolution is based on his religious beliefs.* ♦ *The lawyer noted the jury's skepticism of the insincere witness.*

sketch ['skɛtʃ] **1.** *n.* a simple drawing; a rough drawing that is quickly made. ♦ *The artist drew a sketch of the city's skyline.* ♦ *John drew sketches of his teacher during class.* **2.** *n.* a brief description; an outline. ♦ *Mary included a sketch of her story along with the manuscript.* ♦ *An abstract provides a brief sketch of the contents of a document.* **3.** *n.* a short skit; a very short play that is usually funny. ♦ *The critic noted that each sketch went on too long.* ♦ *The comedy troupe did a hilarious sketch about the president's family.* **4.** *tv.* to draw someone or something roughly and quickly; to make a quick drawing. ♦ *The artist sketched the city's skyline.* ♦ *Mary sketched her mother, using a charcoal pencil.* **5. sketch (out)** *tv.* (+ *adv.*) to describe someone or something briefly; to outline something. ♦ *The witness sketched the events leading up to the crime.* ♦ *The lecturer sketched out her main points at the start of the talk.* **6.** *iv.* to draw roughly and quickly. ♦ *The artist sketched on his notepad.* ♦ *I always sketch while I am on a long telephone call.*

sketchy ['skɛtʃ i] *adj.* not complete; without details. (Adv: *sketchily.* Comp: *sketchier;* sup: *sketchiest.*) ♦ *The sleepy witness provided the police with sketchy details.* ♦ *The reporter only had sketchy information about the bomb blast.*

skewer ['skju ɚ] **1.** *n.* a long, thin rod used for holding pieces of meat, vegetables, or other foods while cooking them. ♦ *The camper put marshmallows on a skewer and then held them over the fire.* ♦ *The diner removed the cooked meat from the skewer with a fork.* **2.** *tv.* to pierce a piece of meat, vegetable, or other food with ①. ♦ *The camper skewered the hot dog and roasted it over the fire.* ♦ *The cook skewered the peppers and onions and grilled them.*

ski ['ski] **1.** *n.* one of two long, narrow, thin strips of wood, plastic, or metal attached to a boot and used to travel on the surface of snow. ♦ *John went down the mountain on skis.* ♦ *Mary took a pair of skis with her on vacation.* **2. (water) ski** *n.* one of two long, narrow, thin strips of wood or plastic worn while being towed across the surface of the water. ♦ *As he was being towed, both of Bob's skis came off.* ♦ *Fortunately, Bob's skis float, and he could recover them.* **3.** *iv.* to move on the surface of snow or water on ① or ②. ♦ *Anne skied down the slope.* ♦ *Susan skied across the snowy meadow.* **4. water-ski** *iv.* to move over the surface of the water on ②. ♦ *I am learning to water-ski.* ♦ *We water-skied on our vacation last summer.*

skid ['skɪd] **1.** *iv.* [for a wheel of a vehicle] to continue to move over a surface after the brakes have been applied. ♦ *The car skidded to a stop when I slammed on the brakes.* ♦ *The speeding truck skidded for one hundred yards before it stopped.* **2.** *iv.* to slip forward or sideways while moving. ♦ *The car skidded into the ditch.* ♦ *Mary skidded down the sidewalk on the ice.* **3.** *tv.* [for a driver] to cause a vehicle to move as in ②. ♦ *The driver skidded the car into a ditch.* ♦ *The trucker skidded his truck into the car beside him.* **4.** *n.* a forward or sideways slipping movement as with ① or ②. ♦ *The skid sent the car into the ditch.* ♦ *David couldn't control his skid because his tires had no tread.*

skid row ['skɪd 'ro] **1.** *n.* a run-down area where vagrants live in the streets. ♦ *After Dave lost his job, he ended up on skid row.* ♦ *The mayor vowed to clean up skid row.* **2. skid-row** *adj.* <the adj. use of ①.> ♦ *Bill's uncle was found living in a skid-row hotel.* ♦ *Max didn't want to end up as a skid-row bum.*

skier ['ski ɚ] **1.** *n.* someone who skis on water or snow. ♦ *The Olympic skier sped down the slope in under a minute.* ♦ *One of the skiers broke his leg.* **2. (water-)skier** *n.* someone who water-skis. ♦ *The water-skier was pulled by a motorboat.* ♦ *Water-skiers should wear life jackets.*

skiing ['ski ɪŋ] *n.* the sport or activity of moving over snow or water on skis. (No plural form in this sense. See also water-skiing.) ♦ *Anne went skiing in the mountains of Vermont.* ♦ *Skiing is very popular in our state.*

ski lift ['ski lɪft] *n.* an elevated cable with several seats, used to transport skiers up a mountain or slope. ♦ *You have to ride the ski lift to get to the top of the mountain.* ♦ *I looked down from the ski lift at the slope beneath me.*

skill ['skɪl] *n.* the ability to do something well, especially because of talent, experience, or practice. ♦ *Anne has a natural skill for playing the piano.* ♦ *David has many skills, but he is too lazy to use them.*

skilled ['skɪld] *adj.* having skill; experienced. ♦ *I commissioned the skilled artist to paint my portrait.* ♦ *The skilled workers organized a union.*

skillet ['skɪl ɪt] *n.* a shallow frying pan. ♦ *John fried some fish in a skillet.* ♦ *Mary held the hot skillet's handle with a potholder.*

skillful ['skɪl fʊl] *adj.* having skill; experienced; able to do something very well; adroit. (Adv: *skillfully.*) ♦ *The skillful tennis player won the championship.* ♦ *Lisa is skillful at repairing lamps.*

skim ['skɪm] **1.** *tv.* to remove something from the surface of a liquid. ♦ *The cook skimmed the fat from the top of the gravy.* ♦ *John skimmed the bugs from the surface of the swimming pool.* **2.** *tv.* to glide over the surface of something; to go over the surface of something quickly. ♦ *The plane skimmed the treetops before it crashed.* ♦ *The goose's feet just skimmed the surface of the lake as it landed.* **3.** *tv.* to scan reading material; to read something quickly. ♦ *The student skimmed the reading assignment before class.* ♦ *I skimmed the newspaper while eating breakfast.* **4. skim over** *iv.* + *prep. phr.* to glide over the surface of something, without touching it. ♦ *The plane skimmed over the treetops before it crashed.* ♦ *The airplane skimmed over the runway and took off again.* **5.** *adj.* [of milk] having the butterfat removed. ♦ *Skim milk has much less fat than whole milk.* ♦ *The dieter poured skim milk on top of some wheat bran.*

skimp ['skɪmp] **skimp (on)** *iv.* (+ *prep. phr.*) to provide or use too little of something. ♦ *The cook skimped on the shrimp in the chowder.* ♦ *The poor man skimped when it came to proper nutrition.*

skimpy ['skɪm pi] *adj.* not enough; needing more; not adequate. (Adv: *skimpily.* Comp: *skimpier;* sup: *skimpiest.*) ♦ *All the sunbathers wore skimpy swimsuits.* ♦ *Dave added irrelevant data to make his skimpy paper longer.*

skin ['skɪn] **1.** *n.* the outer covering of humans and most animals; the outer covering of (many) fruits and vegetables. (No plural form in this sense.) ♦ *My skin became sunburned when I spent all day outside.* ♦ *I peeled the brown skin from the potatoes.* **2.** *n.* the entire skin of a creature or of certain fruits or vegetables. ♦ *The cook peeled the skin from the potato.* ♦ *Mary removed the skin from the apple with a knife.* **3.** *tv.* to remove the skin from something. ♦ *The hunter skinned the deer.* ♦ *The cook skinned the chicken before grilling it.* **4. by the skin of one's teeth** *idiom* just barely; by an amount equal to the thickness of the (imaginary) skin on one's teeth. ♦ *I got through that class by the skin of my teeth.* ♦ *I got to the airport late and missed the plane by the skin of my teeth.* **5. get under someone's skin** *idiom* to bother or irritate someone. ♦ *I know he's bothersome, but don't let him get under your skin.* ♦ *This kind of problem gets under my skin.* **6. jump out of one's skin** *idiom* to react strongly to a shock or surprise. ♦ *Oh! You really scared me. I nearly jumped out of my skin.* ♦ *Bill was so startled he almost jumped out of his skin.*

skinflint ['skɪn flɪnt] *n.* someone who is stingy; a miser. ♦ *The skinflint refused to donate any money to charity.* ♦ *The skinflint ate only oatmeal and pasta to save money.*

skinny ['skɪn i] *adj.* very thin; without much fat. (Comp: *skinnier;* sup: *skinniest.*) ♦ *The skinny athlete could run very fast.* ♦ *The skinny model was very underweight.*

skintight ['skɪn 'tɑɪt] *adj.* fitting closely to the skin; as tight as one's skin is on one's body. ♦ *The model wore a pair of skintight jeans.* ♦ *These gloves are skintight. I need a larger size.*

skip ['skɪp] **1.** *iv.* to move so that one takes a step with one foot, hops on that foot, takes a step with the second foot, and then hops on the second foot, repeatedly. ♦ *The young children skipped through the park.* ♦ *The girls held hands as they skipped down the sidewalk.* **2. skip past; skip over** *iv.* + *prep. phr.* to pass over someone or something. ♦ *I skipped past the boring stories in the anthology.* ♦ *Just skip over the questions you cannot answer.* **3. skip about; skip around** *iv.* + *adv.* to move in a random order; to be random in doing things. ♦ *John skipped about when quizzing me on the vocabulary list.* ♦ *I skipped around when reading the collection of stories.* **4. skip off** *iv.* + *prep. phr.* to bounce off a surface. ♦ *The flat rock skipped off the surface of the pond.* ♦ *The bullet skipped off the bulletproof glass.* **5.** *tv.* to pass someone or something over; to omit something. ♦ *The intelligent child skipped second grade.* ♦ *Anne skipped lunch because she was very busy at work.* **6.** *tv.* to avoid a school class and go someplace else. ♦ *Jane skipped her history class and went to the mall instead.* ♦ *David skipped math because he didn't like the teacher.* **7.** *n.* a light step or jump. ♦ *Dave crossed the narrow creek with a skip.* ♦ *Mary walked with a skip in her step.* **8. skip rope** *phr.* to jump over an arc of rope that is passed beneath one's feet then over one's head, repeatedly. ♦ *The children skipped rope on the playground.* ♦ *The boxer skipped rope while training.*

skipper ['skɪp ɚ] *n.* the captain of a ship. (Also used as a form of address.) ♦ *The skipper piloted the ship around the reef.* ♦ *"We're near the harbor, Skipper," the first mate said.*

skirmish ['skɚ mɪʃ] *n.* a small battle or argument. ♦ *Five soldiers were killed in the bloody skirmish.* ♦ *The skirmish quickly turned into a fistfight.*

skirt ['skɚt] **1.** *n.* an item of women's clothing that wraps around the waist and hangs down, without separate compartments for each leg. ♦ *Anne's skirt extended to just above her knees.* ♦ *Mary had to lift the bottom of her long skirt as she walked up the stairs.* **2.** *tv.* to move along the edge of something; not to move through the center of something. ♦ *The police skirted the edge of the angry crowd.* ♦ *The hunting dogs skirted the marsh.* **3.** *tv.* to evade an issue, topic, or question; to fail to address an issue, topic, or question. ♦ *The politician skirted the accusations of fraud.* ♦ *My teacher's response skirted my question.*

skit ['skɪt] *n.* a short performance that is usually funny or that addresses a certain topic. ♦ *The popular TV show consisted of a series of funny skits.* ♦ *At the assembly, some students performed a skit about drug abuse.*

skittish ['skɪt ɪʃ] *adj.* easily scared. (Adv: *skittishly.*) ♦ *The skittish horse reared its legs.* ♦ *My skittish kitten ran into the other room when Anne came over.*

skull ['skʌl] *n.* the bone (or set of bones) of the head; the bone that protects the brain. ♦ *The driver's skull was cracked when his head hit the windshield in the crash.* ♦ *The anthropologist unearthed the skull of an ancient human.*

skunk ['skʌŋk] *n.* a small animal that has black fur with a white stripe down its back and a bushy tail, and that releases a very powerful bad smell when attacked or frightened. ♦ *Bill smelled horrible after he was sprayed by a skunk.* ♦ *The skunk sprayed the dog that was chasing it.*

sky ['skɑɪ] *n.* the space above the earth; the air above the earth. (Sometimes plural with the same meaning.) ♦ *Anne looked up at the nighttime sky and saw a lot of stars.* ♦ *The airplane flew high in the sky.*

skycap ['skɑɪ kæp] *n.* a porter at an airport. ♦ *The skycap took my luggage from my car to the ticket booth.* ♦ *John tipped the skycap for helping him with his luggage.*

skydive ['skɑɪ dɑɪv] **1.** *iv.* to jump from an airplane, fall through the air, and then open a parachute. (Pt/pp: *skydived.*) ♦ *Jane would not let her teenage son skydive.* ♦ *I'd like to skydive, but I'm too afraid.* **2.** *n.* the act of jumping from an airplane as in ①. ♦ *John went on his first skydive when he was 45 years old.* ♦ *The skydive was canceled because of high wind.*

skyjack ['skɑɪ dʒæk] *tv.* to hijack an airplane; to force a pilot to fly someplace other than where the plane is scheduled to go. (Compare with hijack.) ♦ *The terrorists skyjacked the jet and held the passengers hostage.* ♦ *The sharpshooters killed the men who skyjacked the plane.*

skylight ['skɑɪ lɑɪt] *n.* a window in the roof or ceiling of a building. ♦ *We installed a skylight in our living-room ceiling.* ♦ *Sunlight came through the skylight and lit the room naturally.*

skyline ['skɑɪ lɑɪn] *n.* the outline of buildings, mountains, or other scenery as viewed with the sky as a background. ♦ *The tourists looked at the city's skyline from the harbor.* ♦ *The mountainous skyline towered over the town in the valley.*

skyscraper ['skɑɪ skrep ɚ] *n.* a very tall building. ♦ *You can see for miles from the top of the skyscraper.* ♦ *The tops of the skyscrapers were concealed by low clouds.*

skywriting ['skɑɪ rɑɪt ɪŋ] *n.* writing words in the air with smoke that is released from an airplane. (No plural form in this sense.) ♦ *The skywriting above the stadium read, "Go, Tigers!"* ♦ *Skywriting is an expensive way to send a message.*

slab ['slæb] *n.* a thick slice of something; a thick, flat piece of something. ♦ *The butcher cut a thick slab of beef for me.* ♦ *I could not finish the huge slab of cake I was given.*

slack ['slæk] **1.** *adj.* loose; not tight; not taut. (Adv: *slackly.* Comp: *slacker;* sup: *slackest.*) ♦ *My fishing line was slack, so I knew the bait was sitting on the bottom of the lake.* ♦ *The firefighter unwound enough of the hose so that it was slack.* **2.** *adj.* not strict; relaxed. (Figurative on ①. Adv: *slackly.* Comp: *slacker;* sup: *slackest.*) ♦ *The workers took advantage of the slack rules.* ♦ *The teacher was very slack when it came to discipline.* **3.** *adj.* not active; not busy. (Adv: *slackly.* Comp: *slacker;* sup: *slackest.*) ♦ *Business was slack, so the owner closed the store early.* ♦ *John took his vacation while work was slack.* **4.** *n.* looseness; a part of something that is not pulled tight. ♦ *The climber took up the slack by coiling some of the rope.* ♦ *The electrician lessened the slack in the wire by tightening it.* **5. slacks** *n.* pants; trousers. (Treated as plural.) ♦ *The girls at the private school weren't allowed to wear slacks.* ♦ *David ironed his slacks before wearing them.* **6. slack off** *iv.* + *adv.* to be lazy; to work only when absolutely necessary. ♦ *While the guard slacked off, a thief entered the building.* ♦ *The worker slacked off by reading a newspaper on the job.*

slacken ['slæk ən] *iv.* to reduce, especially in speed or tightness; to become looser or slower. ♦ *The rope slackened as more of it became available.* ♦ *The increase in the crime rate slackened under the mayor's policies.*

slain ['slen] pp of slay.

slalom ['slɑ ləm] **1.** *iv.* to ski down a slope on a path full of twists and turns, especially as part of a race. ♦ *The professional skier slalomed down the hill.* ♦ *The Olympic athlete slalomed down the slope in record time.* **2.** *n.* a race as in ①. ♦ *The winner of the grand slalom was from Norway.* ♦ *Ten skiers participated in the local slalom.*

slam ['slæm] **1.** *tv.* to shut something forcefully and noisily. ♦ *David slammed the door because he was angry.* ♦ *Anne slammed the lid of the box shut.* **2. slam against** *tv.* + *prep. phr.* to propel someone or something against something very forcefully. ♦ *Anne slammed her fist against the table.* ♦ *The police officer slammed the criminal against the brick wall.* **3.** *tv.* to insult or criticize someone or something very strongly. (Informal.) ♦ *The critic slammed the boring play.* ♦ *The president's inept plan was slammed by the pundits.* **4.** *iv.* [for something] to shut very forcefully and noisily. ♦ *The door slammed shut.* ♦ *The lid slammed with a bang.* **5. slam into** *iv.* + *prep. phr.* to run into someone or something very forcefully; to collide with someone or something very forcefully. ♦ *The car slammed into a tree.* ♦ *The careless waiter slammed into me.* **6.** *n.* a loud and forceful closing or crash. ♦ *Susan shut the door with a slam.* ♦ *David closed the window with such a slam that the glass broke.*

slander ['slæn dɚ] **1.** *n.* a spoken lie that is meant to hurt someone's reputation; something false that is said in order to hurt someone's reputation. (No plural form in this sense. Compare with libel.) ♦ *John's slander damaged his manager's reputation.* ♦ *Mary ignored her enemy's slander against her.* **2.** *tv.* to damage someone's reputation by lying. ♦ *The newscaster slandered the politician by reporting gossip.* ♦ *The celebrity was slandered by malicious gossip.*

slanderous ['slæn dɚ əs] *adj.* understood or intended to be slander. (Adv: *slanderously.*) ♦ *The reporter's slanderous statements were too farfetched to be believed.* ♦ *The politician was sued for his slanderous tirade.*

slang ['slæŋ] **1.** *n.* words or expressions that are not expected in formal, educational, or business settings. (No plural form in this sense.) ♦ *The teenagers laughed at the adults who used slang incorrectly.* ♦ *The composition teacher did not approve of slang in formal papers.* **2.** *adj.* <the adj. use of ①.> ♦ *Please avoid using slang words in writing.* ♦ *The editor replaced the slang expression in the newspaper article.*

slant ['slænt] **1.** *n.* a slope; an angle. (No plural form in this sense.) ♦ *The roof was built at a slant so rain would run off it.* ♦ *The slant of the hill was very steep.* **2.** *n.* a way of looking at something; a way of thinking about something; a perspective. ♦ *Try getting a different slant on this for a minute.* ♦ *The reporter examined the subject from several slants.* **3.** *iv.* to slope; to angle; to move at an angle; to rise or fall while moving in a certain direction. ♦ *The roof slanted sharply so no water could collect on it.* ♦ *The cliffs slanted sharply up from the beach.* **4.** *tv.* to cause something to be angled; to cause something to move at an angle. ♦ *The contractor slanted the roof so that water would run off it.* ♦ *Mary slanted the antenna to improve the television reception.* **5.** *tv.* to express something in a way that favors one point of view. ♦ *The older politicians slanted the poll results to favor themselves rather than the other candidates.* ♦ *The newspaper slanted its news coverage of the president.*

slanted ['slæn tɪd] **1.** *adj.* sloped; angled. (Adv: *slantedly.*) ♦ *It was difficult for the workers to repair the slanted roof.* ♦ *John hit his head on the slanted ceiling.* **2.** *adj.* biased; favoring a certain point of view. (Adv: *slantedly.*) ♦ *The slanted newspaper did not provide objective information.* ♦ *Scientists dismissed the experiment's slanted results.*

slap ['slæp] **1.** *tv.* to hit someone or something with one's open hand; to hit someone or something with something flat. ♦ *Jane slapped David across the face for what he said.* ♦ *Bill slapped his brother's back as a greeting.* **2.** *tv.* to put something on a surface carelessly and with force. ♦ *My boss slapped some papers onto my desk.* ♦ *The workers just slapped the wallpaper onto the wall, and it didn't stick properly.* **3.** *n.* a hit with one's open hand or with something flat. ♦ *Mary gave her naughty son a slap with the paddle.* ♦ *I killed a fly with a slap of a folded newspaper.* **4.** *n.* the noise made when someone or something is hit with someone's open hand or with something flat. ♦ *John's palm hit the table with a loud slap.* ♦ *The slap of the thrown newspaper landing on the porch woke the dog.*

slapstick ['slæp stɪk] *n.* a style of comedy that is full of jokes, pranks, roughhousing, and physical action and abuse. (No plural form in this sense.) ♦ *The old comedian was known for slapstick when he was young.* ♦ *The critic thought the slapstick in the movie was too violent.*

slash ['slæʃ] **1.** *tv.* to cut something violently with a sharp object, using large, sweeping movements. ♦ *The vandal slashed the painting with a knife.* ♦ *The cat slashed the couch with its claws.* **2.** *tv.* to reduce numbers or amounts greatly. ♦ *The store owner slashed the prices of everything in stock.* ♦ *The president's policies slashed the unemployment rate.* **3. slash at** *iv.* + *prep. phr.* to cut at something as in ①. ♦ *The robber slashed at the clerk with a knife.* ♦ *The cat slashed at the mouse.* **4.** *n.* a violent movement as in ①. ♦ *The artist destroyed the canvas with wide slashes of a razor.* ♦ *The slash of a sharp knife ripped the bus seat open.* **5.** *n.* a cut made by a violent movement as in ①; a gash. ♦ *I covered the slash in the leather seat with a patch.* ♦ *The doctor stitched up the slash in the patient's skin.* **6.** *n.* the "/" symbol; the "\" symbol. ♦ *The "\" symbol is called a backslash as well as a slash.* ♦ *Mary placed a slash between her area code and her phone number.*

slat ['slæt] *n.* a thin, flat, narrow strip of wood, metal, or plastic. ♦ *My window blinds are made of plastic slats.* ♦ *This basket is made of wooden slats.*

slate ['slet] **1.** *n.* a rock that splits easily into flat, thin layers. (No plural form in this sense.) ♦ *The workers excavated slate from the quarry.* ♦ *Old chalkboards were made of slate.* **2.** *n.* a group of candidates of the same political party in an election. ♦ *Mary voted for the entire Democratic slate.* ♦ *Everyone on the Republican slate was over 50 years old.* **3.** *tv.* to appoint someone to do something; to schedule someone to do something. (Often passive.) ♦ *They slated Mary and Bill to run for class president.* ♦ *I slated my appointment with the dentist for next Tuesday.*

4. *adj.* made of ①. ♦ *My kitchen has a slate floor.* ♦ *Mary lives in a house with a slate roof.* **5. start (off) with a clean slate** *idiom* to start out again afresh; to ignore the past and start over again. ♦ *I plowed under all last year's flowers so I could start with a clean slate next spring.* ♦ *I got into some trouble at work, but I'm starting off with a clean slate.*

slaughter ['slɔt ɚ] **1.** *tv.* to kill and cut up an animal for food. ♦ *The workers slaughtered thousands of cows each day.* ♦ *The farmer slaughtered the pig by slitting its throat.* **2.** *tv.* to kill living creatures ruthlessly. ♦ *The government was accused of slaughtering innocent people.* ♦ *The fur trappers slaughtered hundreds of raccoons.* **3.** *n.* the act of killing many living creatures ruthlessly, as if killing for food. ♦ *The brutal soldiers walked away from the slaughter knowing they had done their job.* ♦ *The heartless slaughter of animals for food disgusted the vegetarian.*

slave ['slev] **1.** *n.* someone who is owned by someone else; someone who is the property of someone else. ♦ *Most southern plantation owners owned slaves before the Civil War.* ♦ *Slaves are forced to work against their will.* **2. be a slave to something** *idiom* someone who is under the control of something; someone who is controlled by something. (Figurative on ①.) ♦ *Mary is a slave to her job.* ♦ *Bill is a slave to his drug addiction.*

slavery ['slev ə ri] *n.* the ownership of slaves. (No plural form in this sense.) ♦ *In 1865, slavery was abolished in America.* ♦ *The brave woman fled slavery and helped others escape, too.*

Slavic ['slɑv ɪk] **1.** *n.* a group of languages that includes Polish, Czech, Slovak, Russian, Ukrainian, Byelorussian, Serbian, Croatian, Bosnian, Slovenian, and Bulgarian. (No plural form in this sense.) ♦ *Slavic includes the languages spoken in Russia and Eastern Europe.* ♦ *Slavic is best represented by Russian.* **2.** *adj.* of or about the people, languages, and cultures of central and eastern Europe, except for Hungary, Romania, Albania, and Greece. (Referring to Polish, Czech, Slovak, Russian, Ukrainian, Byelorussian, Serbian, Croatian, Bosnian, Slovenian, Bulgarian, and Macedonian people, languages, and cultures.) ♦ *The west Slavic languages include Czech, Polish, and Slovak.* ♦ *Mary studied Slavic culture in college, and she traveled to Moscow and Prague.*

slavish ['slev ɪʃ] *adj.* unoriginal; closely copied. (Adv: *slavishly.*) ♦ *Mary's house is a slavish copy of a famous design.* ♦ *The movie was slavish to the book on which it was based.*

slay ['sle] *tv., irreg.* to kill someone or some animal; to murder someone. (Pt: **slew**; pp: **slain.**) ♦ *The soldier slew the enemy guard.* ♦ *The bear was slain by the hunter.*

slaying ['sle ɪŋ] *n.* a murder; the killing of someone or some animal. ♦ *The police officer couldn't determine a motive for the slaying.* ♦ *The slaying of the rich executive remained unsolved for years.*

sleazy ['sliz i] *adj.* cheap; vulgar; sordid; of a bad reputation. (Adv: *sleazily.* Comp: *sleazier;* sup: *sleaziest.*) ♦ *There were cockroaches in the rooms at the sleazy motel.* ♦ *We don't spend much time in the sleazy part of town.*

sled ['slɛd] **1.** *n.* a flat, platform attached to long, thin runners that move easily over snow. ♦ *The children went down the snow-covered hill on a plastic sled.* ♦ *Larger sleds are pulled by dogs and used as transportation in polar regions where there is a lot of snow.* **2.** *iv.* to ride somewhere on ①; to play with ①; to travel by ①. ♦ *The children sledded down the hill.* ♦ *Pulled by dogs, the trapper sledded across the Arctic snow.*

sledgehammer ['slɛdʒ hæm ɚ] **1.** *n.* a large, durable hammer with a large, hard, heavy head, used to hammer or break something forcefully. ♦ *The workers broke the concrete with a sledgehammer.* ♦ *The vandal destroyed my car's windshield with a sledgehammer.* **2.** *adj.* powerful; forceful; pounding; driving; crushing. ♦ *The enemy's sledgehammer attack destroyed the village.* ♦ *The team's sledgehammer play resulted in a touchdown.*

sleek ['slik] **1.** *adj.* smooth and shiny. (Especially used to describe hair or fur of people or animals that is healthy or well cared for. Adv: *sleekly.* Comp: *sleeker*; sup: *sleekest.*) ♦ *The judges admired our dog's sleek coat of hair.* ♦ *The model's sleek hair shines in the sunlight.* **2.** *adj.* having neat, smooth lines; stylish. (Adv: *sleekly.* Comp: *sleeker*; sup: *sleekest.*) ♦ *The elegant car was very sleek.* ♦ *The client liked the architect's sleek design for the building.*

sleep ['slip] **1.** *n.* the period of rest when the mind is not conscious; the period of rest when the body is not awake. (No plural form in this sense.) ♦ *Mary's sleep was interrupted by a loud noise.* ♦ *Anne's sleep had been very restful.* **2.** *iv., irreg.* not to be awake; to rest the body and mind in an unconscious condition. (Pt/pp: **slept.**) ♦ *The infant slept almost 20 hours a day.* ♦ *Anne slept peacefully in her new bed.* **3.** *tv., irreg.* to provide space for a certain number of people to **sleep** ②; to have enough space for a certain number of people to **sleep** ②. ♦ *This double bed sleeps two comfortably.* ♦ *Jane's new tent sleeps four.* **4. not sleep a wink** *idiom* not to sleep ② at all; not to close one's eyes in ① even as long as it takes to blink. ♦ *I couldn't sleep a wink last night.* ♦ *Anne hasn't been able to sleep a wink for a week.* **5. put someone or something to sleep** *idiom* to make someone or something sleep ②; to make someone or something unconscious. ♦ *The anesthetic put the patient to sleep so the doctors could perform the operation.* ♦ *This movie is so boring it's putting me to sleep!* **6. put someone or something to sleep** *idiom* to kill someone or something. (Euphemistic.) ♦ *We had to put our dog to sleep.* ♦ *The robber said he'd put us to sleep forever if we didn't cooperate.* **7. sleep in** *idiom* to oversleep; to sleep ② late in the morning. ♦ *If you sleep in again, you'll get the sack.* ♦ *Get an alarm clock to stop you from sleeping in.* **8. sleep like a log** *idiom* to sleep ② very soundly. ♦ *Nothing can wake me up. I usually sleep like a log.* ♦ *Everyone in our family sleeps like a log, so no one heard the fire engines in the middle of the night.* **9. sleep on something** *idiom* to think about something overnight; to weigh a decision overnight. ♦ *I don't know whether I should agree to do it. Let me sleep on it.* ♦ *I slept on it, and I've decided to accept your offer.*

sleeper ['slip ɚ] **1.** *n.* a train car that has beds for passengers who want to sleep. ♦ *The newlyweds rented a private sleeper on the train.* ♦ *Bob couldn't afford a sleeper, so he slept in his seat.* **2.** *n.* an almost unknown event, candidate, proposal, etc., that becomes a large success. ♦ *The inexpensively produced film turned out to be a sleeper.* ♦ *The sleeper rocketed from obscurity to capture the party's nomination.*

sleepless ['slip ləs] *adj.* without sleep; unable to sleep. (Adv: *sleeplessly.*) ♦ *Jane spent a sleepless night tossing and turning in bed.* ♦ *Another period of sleeplessness started at 3:00, and I finally got to sleep when the sun came up.*

sleepwalk ['slip wɔk] *iv.* to walk while sleeping. ♦ *Mary sleepwalked every night at camp.* ♦ *Bill used to sleepwalk when he was young.*

sleepwalker ['slip wɔk ɚ] *n.* someone who walks around while sleeping. ♦ *The sleepwalker went to the kitchen and drank a glass of water.* ♦ *Mary is a sleepwalker, so she's always waking up in strange places.*

sleepy ['slip i] **1.** *adj.* tired; drowsy; needing to sleep. (Adv: *sleepily.* Comp: *sleepier;* sup: *sleepiest.*) ♦ *Mary put her sleepy children to bed.* ♦ *The sleepy driver almost caused an accident.* **2.** *adj.* not active; calm; reminding one of sleep. (Figurative on ①. Adv: *sleepily.* Comp: *sleepier;* sup: *sleepiest.*) ♦ *The sleepy river wound its way through the countryside.* ♦ *It had been a sleepy afternoon until tragedy struck.*

sleet ['slit] **1.** *n.* partly frozen rain; partly frozen rain mixed with snow or hail. (No plural form in this sense.) ♦ *The roads are very slippery from sleet.* ♦ *The sleet pelted against my face.* **2.** *iv.* [for ①] to fall from the sky. ♦ *It's sleeting, so drive very carefully.* ♦ *It sleeted last night, and everything is coated with ice.*

sleeve ['sliv] **1.** *n.* the part of an item of clothing that covers the arm. ♦ *The young child couldn't get his arm into his jacket sleeve.* ♦ *Be careful. You're dipping your sleeve into your food.* **2. laugh up one's sleeve** *idiom* to laugh secretly; to laugh quietly to oneself. ♦ *Jane looked very serious, but I knew she was laughing up her sleeve.* ♦ *I told Sally that her dress was darling, but I was laughing up my sleeve because her dress was too small.*

sleeveless ['sliv ləs] *adj.* without sleeves. (Adv: *sleevelessly.*) ♦ *Bill wore a sleeveless vest over his shirt.* ♦ *Anne likes to wear sleeveless dresses in the summer.*

sleigh ['sle] **1.** *n.* a large sled; a platform or carriage—usually pulled by horses or dogs—attached to long, metal runners for traveling over snow. ♦ *Santa's sleigh is pulled by eight reindeer.* ♦ *The visitors were taken to the castle by sleigh.* **2.** *iv.* to travel by ①; to ride on ①. ♦ *We sleighed over the tundra to the remote Arctic town.* ♦ *John sleighed across the frozen lake.*

slender ['slɛn dɚ] *adj.* slim; thin, in a pleasant or graceful way. (Adv: *slenderly.* Comp: *slenderer;* sup: *slenderest.*) ♦ *The photographer took pictures of the slender model.* ♦ *The slender ballet dancers glided across the stage.*

slept ['slɛpt] pt/pp of sleep.

sleuth ['sluθ] *n.* a detective; someone who solves crimes. ♦ *The brilliant sleuth solved the complex crime.* ♦ *The sleuth searched for clues at the scene of the murder.*

slew ['slu] **1.** pt of slay. **2.** *n.* a large amount of something. (Informal.) ♦ *Anne won a slew of money in the lottery.* ♦ *The reporters asked the politician a slew of questions.*

slice ['slɑɪs] **1.** *n.* a thin, flat piece that is cut from something. ♦ *Mary put a slice of ham on her sandwich.* ♦ *Each slice of cheese was individually wrapped.* **2.** *n.* a part; a portion; a share. ♦ *I ate a slice of pizza for dinner.* ♦ *Taxes take a large slice of my income.* **3.** *tv.* to cut a thin, flat piece from something; to cut something into thin, flat pieces. ♦ *The butcher sliced a pound of ham for me.* ♦ *John sliced the cheese with a knife.* **4. slice into** *tv.* + *prep. phr.* to divide something into parts or shares. ♦ *Anne sliced the pizza into eight pieces.* ♦ *Tom sliced the carrot into thin strips.*

slick ['slɪk] **1.** *adj.* wet, oily, or icy and slippery. (Adv: *slickly.* Comp: *slicker;* sup: *slickest.*) ♦ *David slipped on a slick patch of oil.* ♦ *The roads are slick with ice tonight.* **2.** *adj.* clever; sly; glib. (Informal. Adv: *slickly.* Comp: *slicker;* sup: *slickest.*) ♦ *Everyone laughed at John's slick response to Dave's insult.* ♦ *The slick criminal eluded the police.* **3.** *adj.* attractive or nicely designed, but without much content or meaning; superficial. (Adv: *slickly.* Comp: *slicker;* sup: *slickest.*) ♦ *Advertising is meant to be more slick than substantial.* ♦ *John's slick résumé listed very little job experience.*

slid ['slɪd] pt/pp of slide.

slide ['slɑɪd] **1.** *iv., irreg.* to move or glide along a smooth surface; to move down a surface; to move without resistance. (Pt/pp: slid.) ♦ *The kids slid down the slide on the playground.* ♦ *Cars slide easily on ice.* **2.** *iv., irreg.* to move backward or forward on a groove or track. ♦ *The folding closet doors slid along a track.* ♦ *The drapes do not slide well because the track needs cleaning.* **3.** *iv., irreg.* to move downward; to decline; to deteriorate. ♦ *This neighborhood slid after the local factories closed.* ♦ *The stock market slid after the bad economic news was released.* **4.** *tv., irreg.* to move someone or something or glide someone or something along a smooth surface; to cause someone or something to move or glide along a smooth surface. ♦ *The children slid pennies across the floor.* ♦ *Don't slide that heavy chair on the wooden floor!* **5.** *tv., irreg.* to move something backward or forward on a groove or track. ♦ *Jane slid the folding door shut.* ♦ *The factory worker slid the bar into position.* **6.** *tv., irreg.* to move something quietly, especially without anyone else noticing. ♦ *The robber cautiously slid the key into his pocket.* ♦ *The spy slid a message under the door.* **7.** *n.* a smooth piece of metal or plastic that slopes downward from the top of a ladder to the ground, usually found on playgrounds. ♦ *Bob landed in a puddle at the bottom of the slide.* ♦ *Susie giggled as she slid down the slide backwards.* **8.** *n.* a downward movement; a decline; a deterioration. (No plural form in this sense.) ♦ *The stock market's slide caused a recession.* ♦ *The neighborhood's slide into despair saddened the residents.* **9.** *n.* a movement along a smooth surface; a movement down a surface. (No plural form in this sense.) ♦ *The children each took a quick slide across the ice.* ♦ *The car's slide into the ditch caused a lot of damage.* **10.** *n.* a small, square frame with a picture on a piece of film in the center, the image of which can be projected onto a screen. ♦ *John showed us a lot of slides from his vacation.* ♦ *The architecture professor showed us slides of buildings.* **11.** *n.* a small, thin, rectangular piece of glass that small objects are placed on so that they can be examined under a microscope. ♦ *The lab technician placed a sample of blood on the slide.* ♦ *The scientist examined the slide under a microscope.* **12. let something slide** *idiom* to neglect something. ♦ *John let his lessons slide.* ♦ *Jane doesn't let her work slide.*

slight ['slɑɪt] **1.** *adj.* not very large; not very important. (Adv: *slightly.* Comp: *slighter;* sup: *slightest.*) ♦ *The pretty vase had a slight chip on its rim.* ♦ *The editor made only slight revisions to the author's manuscript.* **2.** *adj.* frail; delicate; not strong. (Adv: *slightly.* Comp: *slighter;* sup:

slightest.) ♦ *The slight lady had difficulty walking against the wind.* ♦ *John helped the slight old man walk up the stairs.* **3.** *tv.* to neglect mentioning someone or something; to insult a person by ignoring the person's presence or accomplishments. ♦ *The manager slighted his staff by not acknowledging their help.* ♦ *John intended to slight Dave by ignoring him.* **4.** *n.* the insult of treating someone as unimportant; the lack of attention paid to someone or something. ♦ *John's slight of Susan was very rude.* ♦ *What Mary thought was a slight turned out to be an oversight.*

slightly ['slɑɪt li] *adv.* a little; to a small degree. ♦ *I like pizza slightly more than I like spaghetti.* ♦ *It's slightly warmer out today than it was yesterday.*

slim ['slɪm] **1.** *adj.* very thin; slender. (Adv: *slimly.* Comp: *slimmer;* sup: *slimmest.*) ♦ *The slim model needed a belt to keep his pants around his waist.* ♦ *John read the slim book in half an hour.* **2.** *adj.* small in amount or quality; slight. (Adv: *slimly.* Comp: *slimmer;* sup: *slimmest.*) ♦ *There's a slim chance that I may take a vacation next week.* ♦ *The odds that the limping horse would win the race were slim.*

slime ['slɑɪm] *n.* a soft, sticky, unpleasant fluid; filth. (No plural form in this sense.) ♦ *I cleaned the slime out from underneath my refrigerator.* ♦ *The snail left a trail of slime as it moved.*

slimy ['slɑɪm i] *adj.* covered with slime; like slime; filthy. (Adv: *slimily.* Comp: *slimier;* sup: *slimiest.*) ♦ *David cleaned the slimy bathtub with bleach.* ♦ *The algae growing on the inside of the aquarium felt slimy.*

sling ['slɪŋ] **1.** *tv., irreg.* to throw something with force; to hurl something; to fling something. (Pt/pp: **slung.**) ♦ *The janitor slung the garbage into the garbage can.* ♦ *The pitcher slung the baseball toward the batter.* **2.** *tv., irreg.* to hang or suspend something from something or between two things. (Informal.) ♦ *Anne decided to sling the hammock between two trees.* ♦ *David slung the wire between the two poles.* **3.** *n.* a strip of cloth that is used to support an injured arm by being looped around the neck. ♦ *The nurse put John's fractured arm in a sling.* ♦ *Mary wore a sling while her broken arm healed.*

slingshot ['slɪŋ ʃɑt] *n.* a Y-shaped object with a rubber band that is stretched between the two posts of the Y, used to launch stones and other small objects. ♦ *Jimmy shot some pebbles into the air with his slingshot.* ♦ *Using her slingshot, Susie hit John in the head with a rock.*

slink ['slɪŋk] *iv., irreg.* to move quietly, as though one were embarrassed, ashamed, or guilty; to sneak. (Pt/pp: **slunk.**) ♦ *The embarrassed actor wanted to slink from the stage.* ♦ *The thief slunk out of the store unnoticed.*

slip ['slɪp] **1.** *iv.* to fall accidentally while moving or being moved; to slide from a place or position. ♦ *Mary slipped on the curb and twisted her ankle.* ♦ *The greasy knife slipped from my hand when I tried to cut the ham.* **2.** *iv.* to move or happen quietly, quickly, smoothly, easily, secretly, or without being noticed. ♦ *The thief slipped out of the police station.* ♦ *The spy slipped into the castle.* **3.** *iv.* to worsen; to lower; to diminish; to deteriorate; to decline. ♦ *The president's approval ratings slipped during the war.* ♦ *The stock market slipped when the bad economic news was released.* **4. slip to** *tv. + prep. phr.* to pass something to someone quietly, quickly, easily, secretly, or without being noticed. ♦ *Bill cautiously slipped a note to Mary during class.* ♦ *In the park, the soldier slipped the secret plans to the spy.* **5.** *n.* an accidental fall as in ①. ♦ *Mary blamed her slip on the wetness of the floor.* ♦ *John's slip resulted in a broken leg.* **6.** *n.* a mistake; an error; something that was done wrong. ♦ *Anne's slip at work caused her to be demoted.* ♦ *The accountant made a few slips when adding up the figures.* **7.** *n.* a thin, sleeveless article of women's clothing worn under dresses or skirts. ♦ *The edge of Mary's slip was visible below the hem of her skirt.* ♦ *Anne walked from the shower to her bedroom in her slip.* **8.** *n.* a place for a boat to dock between two piers. ♦ *The boat pulled into the slip and its passengers got out.* ♦ *The small cruise ship pulled into Southtown Slip.*

slipcover ['slɪp kəv ɚ] *n.* a cloth covering for the fabric that covers a piece of furniture or a cushion. ♦ *Cleaning slipcovers is easier than cleaning furniture.* ♦ *Mike spilled some wine and stained the slipcover.*

slipper ['slɪp ɚ] *n.* a lightweight foot covering that one wears indoors and that can be taken on and off easily; a lightweight shoe. ♦ *I took off my slippers and put on my shoes before going outside.* ♦ *David wears slippers around the house in the evening.*

slippery ['slɪp ə ri] **1.** *adj.* causing things or people to slip; hard for someone or something to stand or move on without falling. ♦ *The floor was slippery after I waxed it.* ♦ *Bill fell on the slippery ice.* **2.** *adj.* hard to catch or hold; likely to slip out of one's hands. ♦ *The slippery soap fell from my hands in the shower.* ♦ *The slippery fish squirmed out of Anne's hands.* **3.** *adj.* not to be trusted; not to be depended on. (Figurative on ②.) ♦ *The petty criminal was a slippery character.* ♦ *My landlord is slippery and dishonest.*

slipshod ['slɪp ʃɑd] *adj.* built or done poorly. ♦ *The slipshod shed collapsed in the storm.* ♦ *If your slipshod work doesn't improve, you'll be fired.*

slip-up ['slɪp əp] *n.* a mistake; an error; something that was done wrong. ♦ *The hotel clerk made a slip-up and gave me the wrong keys.* ♦ *The surgeon's slip-up almost killed the patient.*

slit ['slɪt] **1.** *n.* a straight, narrow cut or opening. ♦ *The surgeon made a slit in the patient's abdomen.* ♦ *My skirt has a slit on one side.* **2.** *tv., irreg.* to cut or tear something in a straight line so that there is a narrow opening. (Pt/pp: *slit.*) ♦ *The vandal slit the tire with a knife.* ♦ *The terrorist threatened to slit the hostage's throat.*

slither ['slɪð ɚ] *iv.* to slip or slide across something, especially on one's stomach; to move like a snake. ♦ *The snake slithered toward the rat.* ♦ *The children slithered across the floor to surprise their mom.*

sliver ['slɪv ɚ] **1.** *n.* a small, thin, sharp piece or stick of something. ♦ *Slivers of glass from the broken window littered the floor.* ♦ *I got a sliver of wood in my finger when I rubbed the rough board.* **2.** *iv.* to split or break into ①. ♦ *When the window broke, glass slivered all over the floor.* ♦ *The branch slivered when it broke.*

slob ['slɑb] *n.* someone who is very messy; someone who is rude and coarse. ♦ *The slob belched at the dinner table.* ♦ *My roommate is a slob who never washes his dirty dishes.*

slobber ['slɑb ɚ] **1.** *n.* spit; drool; saliva that runs from the mouth. (No plural form in this sense.) ♦ *Anne wiped the slobber from her baby's mouth.* ♦ *The puppy's slobber dripped to the floor.* **2.** *iv.* to drool; to have saliva running out of one's mouth. ♦ *The baby slobbered as I fed him.* ♦ *The dog slobbered all over me.*

slogan ['slo gən] *n.* a motto; a descriptive word or phrase used in advertising or politics. ♦ *Each candidate needs a clever slogan to attract the attention of the voters.* ♦ *The marketers developed a catchy slogan for the new product.*

slope ['slop] **1.** *n.* the slanted side of a mountain or hill. ♦ *The children sledded down the snowy slope.* ♦ *The tired worker walked up the steep slope.* **2.** *n.* the amount that a line or surface slopes ③. (No plural form in this sense.) ♦ *The slope of the roof caused the rain to roll off it.* ♦ *The ramp was built with a sharp slope.* **3.** *iv.* to lean, be set at, or be formed at an angle. ♦ *The roof sloped at a steep angle.* ♦ *The farmer's land sloped gently.* **4.** *tv.* to cause something to be at an angle; to cause something not to be level or straight up and down. ♦ *The builders sloped the roof so that rain wouldn't collect on it.* ♦ *The artist sloped his drawing board appropriately.*

sloping ['slop ɪŋ] *adj.* at an angle; not flat or straight up and down; sloped. (Adv: *slopingly.*) ♦ *The sloping driveway is dangerous in the winter.* ♦ *The worker fell off the sloping roof.*

sloppily ['slɑp ə li] *adv.* in a sloppy way. ♦ *Anne lived sloppily in a messy house.* ♦ *John was fired for doing his work sloppily.*

sloppy ['slɑp i] **1.** *adj.* muddy; slushy; very wet. (Adv: *sloppily.* Comp: *sloppier;* sup: *sloppiest.*) ♦ *It's very sloppy out, so wear your boots.* ♦ *My car got very dirty when I drove on the sloppy roads.* **2.** *adj.* messy; not tidy; careless. (Adv: *sloppily.* Comp: *sloppier;* sup: *sloppiest.*) ♦ *I couldn't read the doctor's sloppy handwriting.* ♦ *The sloppy employee made a lot of mistakes.*

slosh ['slɑʃ] **1.** *tv.* to splash mud, slush, water, or any liquid while moving. ♦ *Bill sloshed coffee from his cup while he gestured with his hand.* ♦ *The speeding car sloshed mud on the people waiting for the bus.* **2.** *iv.* [for mud, slush, water, etc.] to splash from a container or onto a surface. ♦ *Mud sloshed all over the car when I drove down the muddy road.* ♦ *Juice sloshed from the pitcher as I carried it to the table.*

slot ['slɑt] **1.** *n.* a narrow opening in an object or machine. ♦ *Anne placed a quarter into the slot of the vending machine.* ♦ *Mary placed her credit card in the slot on the gas pump.* **2.** *n.* a place on a list or schedule. ♦ *The dentist has a slot open at 3:00 next Monday.* ♦ *There aren't any slots available until next month.* **3.** *tv.* to place someone or something on a list or schedule. ♦ *The receptionist slotted the patient for next month.* ♦ *I've slotted a lunch date with you for the 10th of August.*

sloth ['slɔθ] **1.** *n.* a furry tropical animal that moves very slowly and hangs upside down from tree branches. ♦ *The shaggy sloth slept in its tree.* ♦ *The sloth slowly crept along the tree branch.* **2.** *n.* laziness; the desire to do nothing or to be lazy. (No plural form in this sense.) ♦ *Because of John's sloth, he won't look for a job.* ♦ *Because of your sloth, I always have to do the cleaning!*

slothful ['slɔθ fʊl] *adj.* lazy; idle; not liking work; unwilling to work. (Adv: *slothfully.*) ♦ *The slothful employee merely read the paper while at work.* ♦ *My slothful roommate sits and watches TV all day long.*

slouch ['slɑʊtʃ] **1.** *iv.* to sit, stand, or move with one's shoulders hunched; to sit or move without holding one's body erect. ♦ *The tall man slouched when he walked because he was self-conscious about his height.* ♦ *The instructor yelled at the dancers whenever they slouched.* **2.** *n.* someone who is lazy or awkward. ♦ *My roommate is a slouch and never helps clean the house.* ♦ *John can never keep a job for very long because he's a slouch.*

slough ['slʌf] **1. slough off** *tv.* + *adv.* to cast something aside, especially dead skin. ♦ *The snake sloughed its skin off.* ♦ *I sloughed the scab off my elbow with my fingernail.* **2. slough off** *iv.* + *adv.* to shirk something; to avoid one's responsibility. ♦ *Jane sloughed off when her boss went on vacation.* ♦ *John was reprimanded when he sloughed off on the job.*

Slovakia [slo 'vɑk i ɑ] See Gazetteer.

Slovenia [slo 'vin i ə] See Gazetteer.

slovenly ['slʌv ən li] *adj.* [of someone] dirty or messy in appearance. ♦ *John is simply a very slovenly person.* ♦ *Mary would never dress in such a slovenly fashion.*

slow ['slo] **1.** *adj.* not fast; not quick; taking a long time; taking more time than average; moving with less speed than average. (Adv: *slowly.* Comp: *slower;* sup: *slowest.*) ♦ *The slow turtle crossed the road.* ♦ *The old man's movements were very, very slow.* **2.** *adj.* behind schedule; happening later than the time something is supposed to happen. (Comp: *slower;* sup: *slowest.*) ♦ *My kitchen clock is five minutes slow.* ♦ *I'm late, so my watch must be slow.* **3.** *adj.* boring; dull; without much action or interest. (Comp: *slower;* sup: *slowest.*) ♦ *The audience yawned during the slow movie.* ♦ *This book is slow reading at first, but it becomes exciting later.* **4.** *adv.* at a slow ① pace. (Comp: *slower;* sup: *slowest.*) ♦ *This clock runs slow.* ♦ *Time moves slow when you are bored.* **5.** *iv.* to become ①; to become more ①; to move more ④. ♦ *People often slow as they become older.* ♦ *The driver slowed as she approached the intersection.* **6.** *tv.* to cause something to become ①; to cause something to move more ④. ♦ *Jane slowed the car as she approached the intersection.* ♦ *The president's policies slowed the inflation rate.* **7. slower and slower** *idiom* at a decreasing rate of speed; ① and then even more ①. ♦ *The car is going slower and slower and will stop soon.* ♦ *The dog's breathing got slower and slower as it went to sleep.*

slow motion ['slo 'mo ʃən] **1.** *n.* movement in a film or video image that appears slower than in real life. (No plural form in this sense.) ♦ *Slow motion made it possible to see the football play better.* ♦ *In slow motion, we were able to see the assassin dart from the crowd.* **2. slow-motion** *adj.* moving slower than normally; moving at a speed slower than what is normal; happening at a slower speed, especially on film or video. ♦ *The slow-motion footage showed the impact of the accident.* ♦ *The slow-motion sequence showed the gunman pull out his weapon.*

slug ['slʌg] **1.** *n.* a lump of metal, especially a bullet or a fake coin. ♦ *The sheriff's gun sent three slugs into the bandit.* ♦ *The teenager tried to use a slug in a vending machine.* **2.** *n.* a small, slimy creature, similar to a snail without a shell. ♦ *The slug left a slimy trail as it crawled across the pavement.* ♦ *The gardener removed all the slugs from the garden wall.* **3.** *n.* a hit or blow, especially with a closed fist. ♦ *The bully gave me a hard slug on the arm.* ♦ *John greeted his friend with a playful slug on the shoulder.* **4.** *tv.* to hit someone or something using one's closed fist. ♦ *The* *police officer slugged the thief in the alley.* ♦ *The angry man slugged the intrusive photographer.*

sluggish ['slʌg ɪʃ] *adj.* moving slowly or without energy; not very active. (Adv: *sluggishly.*) ♦ *The sluggish driver pulled into a rest stop for a nap.* ♦ *The snake was sluggish because of the cold weather.*

slum ['slʌm] *n.* a run-down neighborhood; a poor neighborhood where most of the people live in poverty. ♦ *The mayor vowed to rebuild the city's slums.* ♦ *The newspaper article focused on crime in the slums.*

slumber ['slʌm bɚ] **1.** *iv.* to sleep. (Literary.) ♦ *The young maiden slumbered after eating the magic apple.* ♦ *The prince killed the dragon as it slumbered in its cave.* **2.** *n.* sleep; deep rest. (Literary.) ♦ *The queen woke the king from his restful slumber.* ♦ *The princess's slumber was peaceful and long.*

slump ['slʌmp] **1.** *n.* a financial collapse; a sudden fall or decline; a recession or depression. ♦ *The new director helped the company out of its financial slump.* ♦ *The frivolous policies caused an economic slump.* **2.** *iv.* to sink; to slouch. ♦ *The tired worker slumped into a chair.* ♦ *People with bad posture slump as they walk.* **3.** *iv.* [for a value] to sink lower. (Figurative on ②.) ♦ *The price of gold slumped for the second day in a row.* ♦ *The stock market slumped because of the bad economic news.*

slung ['slʌŋ] pt/pp of sling.

slunk ['slʌŋk] pt/pp of slink.

slur ['slɚ] **1.** *tv.* to mumble something; to mispronounce something; to say something in a way that is not clear. ♦ *The drunken man slurred his words.* ♦ *The nervous lecturer slurred her speech.* **2.** *n.* an insult. ♦ *The mayor was criticized for making an ethnic slur.* ♦ *David apologized for his rude slur.*

slurp ['slɚp] **1.** *iv.* to drink noisily. ♦ *Mary slurped through a straw.* ♦ *John slurped rudely at the dinner table.* **2.** *tv.* to drink something noisily. ♦ *Mary slurped her soup.* ♦ *John always slurps his drinks.*

slush ['slʌʃ] *n.* a mixture of snow and water; snow that has started to melt. (No plural form in this sense.) ♦ *My foot got wet when I stepped in a puddle of slush.* ♦ *The snow, slush, and ice made driving difficult.*

slut ['slʌt] *n.* a woman who is willing to have sex with different people; a woman who has loose morals. (Derogatory and vulgar.) ♦ *David insulted Anne by calling her a slut.* ♦ *If you hang out with the bad crowd, people will think you're a slut.*

sly ['slɑɪ] *adj.* sneaky; clever; able to do things secretly; cunning. (Adv: *slyly.* Comp: *slyer;* sup: *slyest.*) ♦ *The sly salesman convinced me to buy the defective car.* ♦ *John would make a good spy because he's very sly.*

smack ['smæk] **1.** *tv.* to hit someone or something noisily with an open hand or flat object. ♦ *The angry man smacked the table with his hand.* ♦ *The teacher smacked the student's bottom with a paddle.* **2.** *tv.* to hit someone or something. ♦ *The door smacked me on the side of the head.* ♦ *Susan smacked the side of my car with her front bumper.* **3. smack into** *tv.* + *prep. phr.* to cause something to run into something, usually noisily. ♦ *Bob smacked his car into a tree.* ♦ *I was seriously injured after I smacked my bicycle into a car.* **4. smack into** *iv.* + *prep. phr.* to run into something noisily. ♦ *The car smacked into a tree.* ♦ *The guy on roller skates smacked into a wall.* **5.** *iv.* to be suggestive of something; to have a hint or trace of something. ♦ *Your behavior smacks of rudeness.* ♦ *This soup smacks of parsley.* **6.** *n.* a loud kiss. (Informal.) ♦ *Give me a smack before you leave.* ♦ *Susie gave her mother a smack on the cheek.* **7.** *n.* a loud hit, especially with an open hand or flat object, or when something runs into something else. ♦ *The car ran into the tree with a smack.* ♦ *Anne brought her hand down onto the table with a loud smack.* **8. smack(-dab)** *adv.* directly; squarely. ♦ *I ran smack into the closed door.* ♦ *Jane hit the target smack-dab in the center with an arrow.*

small ['smɔl] **1.** *adj.* not large; less than average size or weight. (Comp: *smaller;* sup: *smallest.*) ♦ *Can that small child eat such a big piece of cake?* ♦ *Jane has a problem trying to find shoes for her small feet.* **2.** *adj.* little; slight; not a lot; having less than an average amount of something. (Comp: *smaller;* sup: *smallest.*) ♦ *I gave a small amount of change to the beggar.* ♦ *I seem to have a small cold.* **3.** *n.* lowercase; not capital. ♦ *Several examples of small letters are* a, b, c, d, *and* e. ♦ *The penmanship teacher taught the children how to write both small and capital letters.* **4.** *adv.* into a small size. (Comp: *smaller;* sup: *smallest.*) ♦ *You are cutting the pieces of pie too small.* ♦ *Slice the pieces smaller or there won't be enough to go around.*

smallpox ['smɔl pɑks] *n.* a contagious viral disease which forms scabs on the skin that leave scars when they dry up and fall off. (No plural form in this sense.) ♦ *Smallpox has been virtually eradicated from the world.* ♦ *The elderly man had marks on his skin from smallpox.*

small talk ['smɔl tɔk] *n.* unimportant conversation; conversation about things that are not important. (No plural form in this sense.) ♦ *I engaged in small talk with the woman next to me in line.* ♦ *Weather is a common topic for small talk.*

smart ['smɑrt] **1.** *adj.* intelligent; not stupid; able to learn things quickly. (Comp: *smarter;* sup: *smartest.*) ♦ *The very smart child skipped fifth grade.* ♦ *Some of the smartest students received college scholarships.* **2.** *adj.* in style; fashionable. (Adv: *smartly.* Comp: *smarter;* sup: *smartest.*) ♦ *The celebrity wore a smart outfit to the awards ceremony.* ♦ *Mary wore smart accessories with her stylish clothes.* **3.** *iv.* to sting; to feel sharp pain; to cause sharp pain. ♦ *The bee sting smarted.* ♦ *When I stubbed my toe, it smarted.*

smart aleck ['smɑrt æl ɪk] **1.** *n.* someone who is rude or sarcastic in an obnoxious way; someone who is sassy. ♦ *The parents punished their teenager for being a smart aleck.* ♦ *Some smart aleck on the bus tried to start an argument with me.* **2. smart-aleck(y)** *adj.* behaving like ①. ♦ *Don't act so smart-alecky with me!* ♦ *That smart-aleck clerk refused to take my handful of pennies.*

smash ['smæʃ] **1.** *tv.* to break something into tiny pieces noisily or violently. ♦ *I accidentally smashed the window with a baseball.* ♦ *The vandal smashed the vase with a hammer.* **2. smash into** *tv.* + *prep. phr.* to crash something into something else; to cause something to collide with force or noise. ♦ *John smashed his car into a tree.* ♦ *David smashed his shopping cart into a stack of cans.* **3.** *iv.* to break into tiny pieces noisily or violently. ♦ *The glass smashed into tiny pieces when it fell from the table.* ♦ *The mirror smashed when I accidentally dropped it.* **4. smash into** *iv.* + *prep. phr.* to crash; to collide with force or noise. ♦ *My shopping cart smashed into a stack of cans.* ♦

The car rolled down my driveway and smashed into my garage. **5. smash (hit)** *n.* something that is very successful. ♦ *The popular play was a smash hit on Broadway.* ♦ *The gifted author wrote one smash after another.*

smash-up ['smæʃ əp] *n.* a wreck; a collision. ♦ *There was a six-car smash-up on the freeway tonight.* ♦ *Four people were injured in a smash-up on Maple Street today.*

smattering ['smæt ɚ ɪŋ] *n.* a small amount of something, especially of knowledge. (No plural form in this sense.) ♦ *Mary can understand a smattering of Russian.* ♦ *Anne knows a smattering of physics.*

smear ['smɪr] **1.** *tv.* to spread something on a surface, especially in a careless or messy fashion. ♦ *Susan smeared butter on her toast.* ♦ *The child smeared paint everywhere.* **2.** *tv.* to ruin someone's reputation; to make someone look bad; to say bad things about someone. ♦ *The gossip columnist smeared the celebrity's reputation.* ♦ *The politician was smeared by his opponent's accusations.* **3.** *n.* a stain; a mark made by wiping something on a surface. ♦ *Jane wiped a smear of jam from the kitchen counter.* ♦ *Go wash that smear of dirt from your face.*

smell ['smɛl] **1.** *n.* odor; something in the air, sensed with one's nose. ♦ *I lose my sense of smell when I have a cold.* ♦ *Smell and taste are closely related senses.* **2.** *n.* a scent; an odor; a particular variety of ①. ♦ *The smells of cooking dinner greeted me as I came in the door.* ♦ *There are bad smells in the basement.* **3.** *n.* the act of sensing ① or ②. ♦ *A quick smell told me that someone had been smoking.* ♦ *With one smell, I knew I didn't like John's cologne.* **4.** *tv.* to sense something with the nose; to sense an odor or scent; to sense something that has an odor or scent. ♦ *Mary smelled gas in her apartment.* ♦ *John smelled the roses on the table.* **5.** *tv.* to perceive something, especially danger or trouble. (Figurative on ④.) ♦ *Mary smelled trouble, so she quickly left the room.* ♦ *The spy smelled danger, so she hid behind a curtain.* **6.** *iv.* to have a certain quality of scent or odor. ♦ *These roses smell good.* ♦ *The rotten meat smelled bad.* **7.** *iv.* to stink; to have a bad smell. ♦ *A skunk's spray really smells!* ♦ *The sweaty jogger smelled.*

smelly ['smɛl i] *adj.* having a bad or strong odor. (Comp: *smellier;* sup: *smelliest.*) ♦ *Please wash your smelly shirt.* ♦ *Anne threw the smelly eggs into the trash.*

smidgen ['smɪdʒ ən] *n.* a tiny amount; a small portion. ♦ *Jimmy only ate a smidgen of his vegetables.* ♦ *There wasn't even a smidgen of sincerity in Bob's actions.*

smile ['smaɪl] **1.** *n.* a facial expression where the ends of the mouth are turned up, indicating happiness, amusement, or a good mood. ♦ *David has a nice smile in this photograph.* ♦ *John's smile let us know he was happy with our decision.* **2.** *iv.* to have ① on one's face; to look happy or pleased. ♦ *Mary smiled when I complimented her.* ♦ *John smiled in response to my funny joke.* **3.** *tv.* to express something by smiling, as in ②. ♦ *Mary smiled her agreement.* ♦ *John smiled his consent.* **4. crack a smile** *idiom* to smile ② a little, perhaps reluctantly. ♦ *She cracked a smile, so I knew she was kidding.* ♦ *The soldier cracked a smile at the wrong time and had to march for an hour as punishment.* **5. smile on someone or something** *idiom* to be favorable to someone or something. ♦ *Fate smiled on me and I got the job.* ♦ *Lady luck smiled on our venture and we made a profit.*

smiling ['smaɪl ɪŋ] *adj.* having a smile; happy; cheerful. (Adv: *smilingly.*) ♦ *The smiling cashier brightened the customer's day.* ♦ *A friendly photographer took a picture of the smiling children.*

smirk ['smɚk] **1.** *n.* a smug smile showing great self-satisfaction. ♦ *Bob had a smirk on his face because the plan failed just as he said it would.* ♦ *The overly proud man looked at me with a self-satisfied smirk.* **2.** *iv.* to smile in a way that shows one's self-satisfaction. ♦ *Bill smirked because he had been right and I had been wrong.* ♦ *Anne smirked because she was chosen and I wasn't.*

smithereens [smɪð ə 'rinz] **to smithereens** *adv.* [broken] into tiny, shattered pieces. ♦ *The vase had been smashed to smithereens.* ♦ *Bob accidentally stepped on the bowl and crushed it to smithereens.*

smock ['smɑk] *n.* a light covering that one wears over one's clothes to protect one's clothes from becoming dirty while working, especially as worn by a doctor, nurse, painter, etc. ♦ *The painter's clothes were protected by a smock.* ♦ *The members of the surgical team all wore green smocks during surgery.*

smog ['smɔg] *n.* smoke and fog that are trapped in the air; a mixture of fumes and smoke that are trapped like fog over a place. (A combination of *smoke* and *fog*. No plural form in this sense.) ♦ *People with asthma should stay indoors when there's a lot of smog.* ♦ *Smog is more common in industrial areas than in rural areas.*

smoke ['smok] **1.** *n.* a cloud of gas that can be seen in the air when something burns. (No plural form in this sense.) ♦ *Where there's smoke, there's fire.* ♦ *Smoke from the fireplace went up the chimney.* **2.** *n.* a cigarette. (Slang.) ♦ *Do you have an extra smoke I can have?* ♦ *John went to the bar to buy some smokes.* **3.** *n.* the act of inhaling ① of a cigarette. (Informal.) ♦ *The employees weren't allowed to have a smoke inside the building.* ♦ *The college students had a quick smoke between classes.* **4.** *iv.* to give off ①; to release ① into the air. ♦ *The house continued to smoke after the fire was extinguished.* ♦ *The overloaded electrical outlet began to smoke.* **5.** *iv.* to inhale and then exhale ① from burning tobacco. ♦ *The teachers smoked between classes.* ♦ *Once you begin to smoke, it's difficult to quit.* **6.** *tv.* to inhale ① of burning cigarettes, tobacco, etc., into the lungs. ♦ *You aren't allowed to smoke cigars here.* ♦ *John smoked a pipe in his office.* **7.** *tv.* to preserve food by exposing it to ① from wood. ♦ *We smoked the fish we had caught.* ♦ *Mary smoked the ham to give it a rich flavor.*

smoked ['smokt] *adj.* preserved by having been exposed to smoke. ♦ *The host served smoked cheese with crackers.* ♦ *Anne sliced the smoked ham.*

smoke screen ['smok skrin] *n.* something like a cloud of smoke that hides someone or something; something that hides one's intentions. ♦ *John's smile was a smoke screen for his evil intentions.* ♦ *Mary's laugh was a smoke screen for her anger at Bob.*

smokestack ['smok stæk] *n.* a tall chimney; a pipe that carries smoke from a building. ♦ *Smoke billowed from the factory's smokestacks.* ♦ *The chimney sweep cleaned the soot from the smokestack.*

smoking ['smok ɪŋ] **1.** *adj.* giving off smoke. ♦ *The smoking logs finally caught on fire.* ♦ *David unplugged the smoking toaster.* **2.** *adj.* designated as a place where one is allowed to smoke. ♦ *There was one small smoking section in the restaurant.* ♦ *David took a smoking flight to Europe.*

smoky ['smok i] **1.** *adj.* full of smoke; tasting or smelling like smoke. (Comp: *smokier;* sup: *smokiest.*) ♦ *The smoky room made Mary's eyes water.* ♦ *I began to cough in the smoky bar.* **2.** *adj.* giving off more smoke than normal or expected. (Adv: *smokily.* Comp: *smokier;* sup: *smokiest.*) ♦ *The firefighters wore masks when fighting the smoky fire.* ♦ *The campers sat far away from the smoky campfire.*

smolder ['smol dɚ] **1.** *iv.* [for wood or other fibers] to burn or give off smoke without having a flame. ♦ *The ashes from the fire smoldered for hours.* ♦ *When the toast began to smolder, I unplugged the toaster.* **2.** *iv.* [feelings that seem] to grow yet remain trapped and unexpressed. (Figurative on ①.) ♦ *David's crush on his teacher smoldered in his heart.* ♦ *Anne's anger toward her neighbor smoldered inside her.*

smoldering ['smol dɚ ɪŋ] **1.** *adj.* burning or giving off smoke without having a flame. (Adv: *smolderingly.*) ♦ *Anne dumped some sand on the smoldering ashes from the campfire.* ♦ *The firefighters put water on the smoldering house.* **2.** *adj.* [of a passionate feeling] that is **hot** ③ and sustained. (Figurative on ①. Adv: *smolderingly.*) ♦ *Anne's smoldering anger toward her neighbor gave her an ulcer.* ♦ *John's smoldering passion for Lisa occupied all of his thoughts.*

smooth ['smuð] **1.** *adj.* having an even surface; having a surface without bumps; not rough. (Adv: *smoothly.* Comp: *smoother;* sup: *smoothest.*) ♦ *After I sanded the wood, it was smooth.* ♦ *The baby's skin was soft and smooth.* **2.** *adj.* gentle; not rough; calm; not harsh. (Adv: *smoothly.* Comp: *smoother;* sup: *smoothest.*) ♦ *We had a smooth flight across the Atlantic.* ♦ *The train pulled into the station and came to a smooth stop.* **3.** *adj.* without lumps; having an even texture. (Adv: *smoothly.* Comp: *smoother;* sup: *smoothest.*) ♦ *Bill stirred the paint until it was smooth.* ♦ *I applied the smooth frosting to the cake with a plastic knife.* **4.** *tv.* to cause something to become smooth or smoother. ♦ *Anne smoothed the coarse wood with sandpaper.* ♦ *The mason smoothed the mortar with a trowel.* **5.** *adv.* to the point of being smooth. ♦ *Bob shaved his face smooth with a razor.* ♦ *Anne sanded the board smooth.*

smooth-talking ['smuð 'tɔk ɪŋ] *adj.* persuasive; suave. ♦ *The smooth-talking salesman convinced me to buy the car.* ♦ *Another smooth-talking politician won the election.*

smother ['smʌð ɚ] **1.** *iv.* to die because one cannot get enough oxygen, especially because something is covering one's mouth; to suffocate. ♦ *The victims had smothered from the smoke.* ♦ *The smallest kitten smothered under its mother.* **2.** *tv.* to kill a living creature by preventing it from breathing. ♦ *The murderer smothered his victims with a pillow.* ♦ *The farmer smothered the unwanted kittens with a rag.* **3.** *tv.* to cover something with a thick layer of something. ♦ *John smothered his sandwich with mustard.* ♦ *Anne smothered her dry skin with lotion.*

smudge ['smʌdʒ] **1.** *n.* a dirty mark or stain; a smear. ♦ *John cleaned the smudge of dirt from his shoe.* ♦ *The leaky pen left smudges of ink on the paper.* **2.** *tv.* to dirty something with a mark. ♦ *The wall near the light switch was smudged from dirty hands.* ♦ *I smudged my pants with the mustard that fell from my sandwich.*

smug ['smʌg] *adj.* overly pleased with oneself; too satisfied with oneself. (Adv: *smugly.* Comp: *smugger;* sup: *smuggest.*) ♦ *Bill was smug because he had been right and I had been wrong.* ♦ *The smug designer thought her designs were better than mine.*

smuggle ['smʌg əl] *tv.* to bring something into or take something out of a country illegally. ♦ *The criminals smuggled drugs into the country.* ♦ *The spy smuggled computer parts out of the country.*

smuggler ['smʌg lɚ] *n.* a criminal who brings something into or takes things from a country illegally. ♦ *The drug smuggler was sentenced to life in prison.* ♦ *The smugglers crossed the border on foot.*

smuggling ['smʌg lɪŋ] *n.* the illegal business of bringing something into or taking things out of a country. (No plural form in this sense.) ♦ *The drug dealer was also arrested for smuggling.* ♦ *Many products enter the country illegally by smuggling.*

smut ['smʌt] *n.* pornography; something that is morally offensive or obscene; offensive or obscene talk, pictures, movies, books, etc. (No plural form in this sense.) ♦ *The minister led a crusade against smut.* ♦ *The adult movie house showed smut.*

smutty ['smʌt i] *adj.* offensive; obscene. (Adv: *smuttily.* Comp: *smuttier;* sup: *smuttiest.*) ♦ *The smutty book was banned at my school.* ♦ *Bob's smutty jokes offended the other guests.*

snack ['snæk] **1.** *n.* food that is eaten between meals; a small amount of food. ♦ *I got hungry between breakfast and lunch, so I ate a small snack.* ♦ *John gained weight because he ate too many snacks.* **2.** *iv.* to eat a small amount of food between meals. ♦ *I try to eat only healthy foods when I snack.* ♦ *If you snack between meals, make sure you brush your teeth!* **3. snack on** *iv. + prep. phr.* to eat some of something as ①. ♦ *Mary snacked on some popcorn during the movie.* ♦ *Who has been snacking on the leftover cake?*

snag ['snæg] **1.** *n.* a thread that is pulled out of place from a fabric. ♦ *Mary had a snag in her nylons.* ♦ *John got a snag in his sweater when it caught on a hook.* **2.** *n.* an obstacle; something that gets in the way; a hindrance. ♦ *The project was delayed due to an unforeseeable snag.* ♦ *The upstart politician was a snag in the legislative process.* **3.** *tv.* to catch a piece of clothing or material by a thread. ♦ *A hook snagged Bob's sweater.* ♦ *The bush snagged Mary's nylons.* **4.** *tv.* to capture or catch someone or something. (Informal.) ♦ *The police snagged the criminal.* ♦ *The hunter snagged the bear.* **5. snag on** *iv. + prep. phr.* [for a piece of woven cloth or a thread] to become hooked or caught on something. ♦ *Susan's vest snagged on a hook.* ♦ *Anne's nylons snagged on the edge of her desk.* **6. hit a snag** *idiom* to run into a problem. ♦ *We've hit a snag with the building project.* ♦ *I stopped working on the job when I hit a snag.*

snail ['snel] *n.* a small, soft creature that has no limbs, has two small feelers, and carries a hard, spiral shell on its back. ♦ *The snail slowly inched across the leaf.* ♦ *The snail left a slimy trail as it moved.*

snake ['snek] **1.** *n.* a long, thin, scaly reptile that has no limbs. ♦ *Many snakes have huge mouths that stretch, enabling them to swallow their prey whole.* ♦ *The snake coiled around the rat and squeezed it.* **2.** *iv.* to move in twists and turns; to curve like a snake. ♦ *The path snaked through the forest.* ♦ *The river snaked toward the sea.* **3.** *tv.* to move something in twists and turns; to curve something like a snake. ♦ *Mary snaked the electrical cord around her furniture.* ♦ *Bill snaked his body through the narrow opening.*

snap ['snæp] **1.** *iv.* [for something] to make a sharp, popping sound, usually by breaking. ♦ *A branch snapped, frightening the deer.* ♦ *Something snapped in my foot, and I knew a bone was broken.* **2.** *iv.* [for something that is pulled tight or under pressure] to break suddenly. ♦ *The climber fell to his death when the rope snapped.* ♦ *My shoelace snapped when I pulled it too tightly.* **3. snap at** *iv. + prep. phr.* to speak to someone quickly, sharply, or angrily. ♦ *John snapped at the kids who kept asking him questions.* ♦ *Mary snapped at the reporters who hounded her.* **4.** *tv.* to break something that is pulled tight or under pressure. ♦ *The car accident snapped John's leg.* ♦ *The thief snapped the wire by stretching it.* **5.** *tv.* to take a picture with a camera. ♦ *John snapped a picture of his friends.* ♦ *Mary snapped a photo of the castle.* **6.** *tv.* to cause something to make a sharp, popping sound, as it breaks. ♦ *The branch snapped as Mary stepped on it.* ♦ *John's pencil snapped when he broke it.* **7.** *tv.* to close ⑪. ♦ *Anne snapped the snaps on her jeans.* ♦ *Bill snapped his jacket closed.* **8.** *n.* the noise made when someone or something snaps; a quick, sudden, popping sound. ♦ *When I heard the snap of the lock, I remembered I'd forgotten my keys.* ♦ *The snap of the lid closing caught my attention.* **9.** *n.* a sudden breaking of something; the breaking of something that is pulled tight or under pressure. ♦ *David felt the snap of a bone when he fell on ice.* ♦ *I felt a snap and my pants fell down.* **10. cold snap** *n.* a sudden period of very cold weather. ♦ *The buds on the trees froze during the cold snap.* ♦ *After the first cold snap, the lake was not quite frozen yet.* **11.** *n.* a metal or plastic fastener that closes firmly when pressed. ♦ *The top snap of John's shirt popped open.* ♦ *Mary fastened all of the snaps on her jacket.* **12.** *n.* something that is very easy to do; something that can be done without a problem. (Slang. No plural form in this sense.) ♦ *After studying all week, I found the test to be a snap.* ♦ *It was a snap for the champion to beat the rookie.* **13.** *adj.* sudden; without warning. ♦ *John's snap judgments are often wrong.* ♦ *The manager made a snap decision about the work schedule.*

snapdragon ['snæp dræg ən] *n.* a plant with long spikes of blossoms thought to resemble the snout of a dragon. ♦ *Snapdragons bloom in many colors.* ♦ *The florist added a few colorful snapdragons to the flower arrangement.*

snappy ['snæp i] *adj.* lively; exciting; in a hurry. (Adv: *snappily.* Comp: *snappier;* sup: *snappiest.*) ♦ *The audience applauded the snappy dance number.* ♦ *John told her to do it now and be snappy.*

snapshot ['snæp ʃɑt] *n.* a photograph; a picture taken with a camera. ♦ *John showed me snapshots of his vacation.* ♦ *Mary kept snapshots of her best friends in her wallet.*

snare ['snɛr] **1.** *tv.* to trap someone or something; to catch someone or something in a trap. ♦ *The hunter snared the fox.* ♦ *The police snared the crook.* **2.** *n.* a trap for catching animals. ♦ *The snare held the fox by its leg.* ♦ *The hunter checked the snare, but it was empty.*

snarl ['snɑrl] **1.** *iv.* to growl threateningly. ♦ *The angry dog snarled at the mail carrier.* ♦ *The surly clerk snarled at the pesky customer.* **2.** *iv.* to be tangled; to become tangled. ♦ *My long hair snarled after I washed it.* ♦ *My shoelaces had snarled into a knot.* **3.** *tv.* to tangle something. ♦ *The dog's hair was snarled with burrs.* ♦ *The accident snarled traffic for miles.* **4.** *n.* an angry growl. ♦ *The dog's snarl scared the mail carrier.* ♦ *The rude clerk's snarl offended the customer.* **5.** *n.* a clump of tangled hair. ♦ *Mary brushed out the snarl in her hair with a comb.* ♦ *Susan combed through the snarls in her dog's coat.*

snarling ['snɑr lɪŋ] *adj.* growling angrily. ♦ *The snarling dog barked at the mail carrier.* ♦ *The snarling manager criticized the staff.*

snatch ['snætʃ] *tv.* to grab someone or something suddenly; to steal something or kidnap someone. ♦ *The kidnapper snatched a four-year-old from the mall.* ♦ *The shoplifter snatched a watch that was on display.*

sneak ['snik] **1.** *iv., irreg.* to move quietly and secretly; to move without being noticed. (Pt/pp: *sneaked* or snuck.) ♦ *The thief sneaked around the house.* ♦ *The clerk snuck into the manager's office to read confidential files.* **2.** *tv., irreg.* to obtain or take something, such as a taste, a look, a peek, a touch, etc., quietly and secretly. ♦ *The boys sneaked a look at the raunchy magazine.* ♦ *Anne sneaked a taste of the cake's frosting when her mother wasn't looking.* **3.** *n.* someone who moves quietly about in secret. ♦ *Susan confronted the sneak who had been in her office.* ♦ *Bill trapped the sneak who had been going through his files.*

sneaker ['snik ɚ] *n.* one of a pair of gym shoes or tennis shoes; one of a pair of comfortable, casual canvas shoes with rubber soles. ♦ *Anne wore her sneakers to the gym.* ♦ *Bill played tennis in a pair of new sneakers.*

sneakily ['snik ə li] *adv.* without being noticed; quietly and secretly. ♦ *Sneakily, Mary took a look at the confidential file.* ♦ *John sneakily left work thirty minutes early.*

sneaky ['snik i] *adj.* doing something dishonest or wrong, quietly and secretly. (Adv: *sneakily.* Comp: *sneakier;* sup: *sneakiest.*) ♦ *The sneaky spy stole government secrets.* ♦ *It was sneaky of Bob to have looked at John's appointment book.*

sneer ['snɪr] **1.** *iv.* to show contempt with a facial gesture. ♦ *The rude celebrity sneered at the fan who asked for an autograph.* ♦ *The gourmet sneered at fast-food restaurants.* **2.** *n.* a look of contempt. ♦ *The arrogant socialite looked at me with a sneer of derision.* ♦ *The haughty man looked down on his neighbors with a sneer.*

sneeze ['sniz] **1.** *n.* a sudden and uncontrollable burst of air and mucus that is pushed out of the nose and mouth. ♦ *Mary's loud sneeze caught my attention.* ♦ *That was quite a sneeze! Do you need a tissue?* **2.** *iv.* to make ①. ♦ *John sneezed into a tissue.* ♦ *I sneeze frequently during allergy season.*

snicker ['snɪk ɚ] **1.** *iv.* to laugh; to laugh at someone; to laugh at someone disrespectfully. ♦ *Mary snickered at the slightly vulgar joke.* ♦ *Everyone was snickering because I fell down.* **2.** *n.* a laugh; a disrespectful laugh. ♦ *I responded to the joke with a snicker.* ♦ *With a snicker of ridicule, the popular students mocked John.*

sniff ['snɪf] **1.** *iv.* to breathe in through the nose in small, quick puffs that can be heard. ♦ *Mary sniffed a few times, and then she sneezed.* ♦ *David sniffed because his nose was running.* **2.** *iv.* to become aware of a smell by sniffing. ♦ *My dog sniffed at the base of the tree.* ♦ *I noticed the smell of gas when I sniffed.* **3.** *n.* a small, quick breath made through the nose, made especially when smelling something. ♦ *I caught a sniff of cinnamon and knew someone was baking.* ♦ *Mary tried just a sniff of the cologne.*

sniffle ['snɪf əl] **1.** *iv.* to sniff when one is sick or when one has been crying. ♦ *John sniffled during the sad movie.* ♦ *Anne sniffled and blew her nose into a tissue.* **2. the sniffles** *n.* a mild cold in the head. (Treated as plural.) ♦ *Susie stayed at home from school because she has the sniffles.* ♦ *I drink hot tea when I have the sniffles.*

snip ['snɪp] **1.** *tv.* to clip something; to cut something with scissors in short strokes; to cut something up into tiny pieces. ♦ *Mary snipped coupons from the newspaper.* ♦ *David snipped the contract into little pieces.* **2.** *n.* a short cutting movement; a short stroke made with scissors. ♦ *Anne cut the string with a snip of her scissors.* ♦ *The barber cut my hair in quick snips.* **3.** *n.* a small piece of something that has been cut with scissors. ♦ *Little snips of paper and string littered the tabletop.* ♦ *The detective found a little snip of cloth on the floor.*

sniper ['snɑɪp ɚ] *n.* a person with a gun who shoots at people from a hidden position. ♦ *The enemy sniper shot at the townsfolk from the mountainside.* ♦ *The sniper hid on the building's roof and shot at people on the street.*

snob ['snɑb] *n.* someone who is conceited; someone who is condescending. ♦ *The snob ridiculed the way the others were dressed.* ♦ *John is a snob who acts as though he is better than we are.*

snobbish ['snɑb ɪʃ] *adj.* arrogant; conceited; thinking that one is better than others. (Adv: *snobbishly.*) ♦ *My snobbish coworker thinks she is the most important employee in the company.* ♦ *The snobbish diner talked to the waiter as though he were stupid.*

snoop ['snup] **1.** *iv.* to sneak; to pry; to search through something without the owner's permission. ♦ *Mary snooped through Anne's desk for the confidential file.* ♦ *Bill snoops in kitchen cabinets when he visits people.* **2.** *n.* someone who sneaks; someone who pries; someone who searches through something without the owner's permission. ♦ *Anne accused Bob of being a snoop when she caught him in her office.* ♦ *The snoop looked through all of Mary's dresser drawers.*

snooping ['snup ɪŋ] *adj.* sneaking; prying; searching through something without the owner's permission. ♦ *The manager told the snooping employee to mind his own business.* ♦ *The snooping reporter went through the politician's wastebasket.*

snoot ['snut] *n.* the nose. (Informal.) ♦ *The children laughed at the clown's big snoot.* ♦ *The baseball hit Bill's snoot.*

snooty ['snut i] *adj.* arrogant and rude; haughty, with one's snoot in the air. (Adv: *snootily.* Comp: *snootier;* sup: *snootiest.*) ♦ *The snooty boy thought he was better than everyone else.* ♦ *The snooty cashier insulted the customer.*

snooze ['snuz] **1.** *iv.* to sleep; to nap. ♦ *The bored students snoozed during the lecture.* ♦ *Anne always snoozed for a few hours after work.* **2.** *n.* sleep; a nap. (Informal.) ♦ *Mary took a quick snooze between classes.* ♦ *John had a snooze before dinner.*

snore ['snor] **1.** *iv.* to breathe loudly while sleeping, especially to pass air through the nose so that it vibrates and makes a loud noise. ♦ *Mary couldn't sleep because her roommate snored.* ♦ *When John snored, I held his nose until he stopped.* **2.** *n.* the sound made by breathing loudly while sleeping. ♦ *Anne could hear her neighbor's snores through the thin walls.* ♦ *During the boring movie, I heard snores in the audience.*

snorkel ['snor kəl] **1.** *n.* a J-shaped tube that allows one to breathe while just under the surface of the water. ♦ *The snorkel's short end goes in one's mouth and the long end goes above the water's surface.* ♦ *I choked on some water when the end of the snorkel dipped underwater.* **2.** *iv.* to swim or float in the water while using ①. ♦ *The marine biologist examined the underwater reef while snorkeling.* ♦ *Anne snorkeled when she was at the Caribbean resort.*

snort ['snort] **1.** *iv.* to make a short, loud noise by blowing air through the nose. ♦ *The bull snorted before he charged.* ♦ *Anne snorted when the clerk told her the price of the watch.* **2.** *tv.* to inhale something, usually a drug, forcefully into the nose. (Informal.) ♦ *The drug addict snorted cocaine daily.* ♦ *Bob was caught snorting drugs in the alley.* **3.** *n.* the noise made by blowing through the nose. ♦ *Anne responded to Bill's rude comment with a sarcastic snort.* ♦ *The bull made a snort and ran toward the red cape.*

snot ['snɑt] **1.** *n.* nasal mucus. (Colloquial and unpleasant. No plural form in this sense.) ♦ *The dog's nose was covered with snot.* ♦ *John wiped his snot on his sleeve.* **2.** *n.* a rude and haughty person. (Colloquial and derogatory.) ♦ *That little snot refused to help me!* ♦ *John insulted the snot who laughed at him.*

snotty ['snɑt i] **1.** *adj.* covered with mucus. (Colloquial and unpleasant. Comp: *snottier;* sup: *snottiest.*) ♦ *David wiped his child's snotty nose.* ♦ *Anne cleaned her baby's snotty face.* **2.** *adj.* rude; nasty; conceited. (Colloquial. Adv: *snottily.* Comp: *snottier;* sup: *snottiest.*) ♦ *The snotty clerk refused to help me.* ♦ *The snotty student made fun of the other students' clothes.*

snout ['snɑʊt] *n.* a nose, especially the long nose of certain animals, like pigs and crocodiles. ♦ *The pig rooted in the mud with its snout.* ♦ *The crocodile's snout poked above the surface of the water.*

snow ['sno] **1.** *n.* water vapor that has frozen into small, white flakes that fall from the sky. (No plural form in this sense.) ♦ *Anne shoveled snow from the sidewalk in front of her house.* ♦ *The main roads were closed because there was so much snow.* **2.** *n.* the falling of ①. (No plural form in this sense.) ♦ *The snow stopped after six inches had fallen.* ♦ *The forecaster predicted snow for the entire weekend.* **3.** *n.* an instance of snowfall; a coating of snow on the ground. ♦ *We have had heavy snows every weekend this winter.* ♦ *After the snows were over, it was spring.* **4.** *n.* flecks of white light on a television screen when the reception is very bad or when no station is being broadcast. (Figurative on ①. No plural form in this sense.) ♦ *There was snow on every channel except channel 5.* ♦ *After the station signed off, the television screen filled with snow.* **5.** *iv.* [for ①] to fall from the sky. ♦ *It snowed last night.* ♦ *Because it snowed, driving was rather dangerous.*

snowball ['sno bɔl] **1.** *n.* a ball of snowflakes that have been pressed together. ♦ *The children threw snowballs at each other.* ♦ *Anne knocked the hat off my head with a snowball.* **2.** *iv.* to grow at a rapidly increasing rate. (Figurative on ①.) ♦ *If these problems aren't solved now, they'll snowball into something worse.* ♦ *The sales of the new product snowballed rapidly, making it very profitable.*

snowbank ['sno bæŋk] *n.* a big, long mound of snow. ♦ *My car slid into a snowbank next to the driveway.* ♦ *The wind swept the snow into large snowbanks.*

snow blower ['sno blo ɚ] *n.* a machine that clears snow from walks and pavements. ♦ *Bob's snow blower moved the snow from the sidewalk into the street.* ♦ *Mary cleared her driveway with a snow blower.*

snowbound ['sno bɑʊnd] *adj.* not able to travel because there is too much snow. ♦ *The snowbound tourists were stuck at the airport.* ♦ *The snowbound campers stayed in their tent for a week.*

snowdrift ['sno drɪft] *n.* a ridge of snow shaped by the wind that blows it along the ground. ♦ *It was hard for the young child to walk in the tall snowdrifts.* ♦ *The children hid among the large snowdrifts.*

snowfall ['sno fɔl] **1.** *n.* flakes of snow, falling or fallen from the sky. ♦ *The snowfall is expected to last until tomorrow.* ♦ *The most recent snowfall made the dangerous roads worse.* **2.** *n.* the amount of snow that falls; a coating of snow, fallen from the sky. ♦ *There was a six-inch snowfall last night.* ♦ *The two-inch snowfall made driving dangerous.*

snowflake ['sno flek] *n.* one individual piece of snow; a drop of water that freezes and falls from the sky as snow. ♦ *Susie opened her mouth to catch snowflakes on her tongue.* ♦ *No two snowflakes are identical in shape.*

snowman ['sno mæn] *n., irreg.* a mass of snow that has been shaped like a person. (Pl: snowmen.) ♦ *A snowman is usually a stack of three large balls of snow, with objects placed on the top one to represent eyes, a mouth, and other features, and two sticks placed in the middle one for arms.* ♦ *I made a snowman and my brother knocked it down.*

snowmen ['sno mɛn] pl of snowman.

snowmobile ['sno mo bil] **1.** *n.* a motor vehicle that moves on runners on a moving belt over the surface of snow. ♦ *John drove the snowmobile across the frozen, snow-covered lake.* ♦ *Anne traveled from her cabin into town on her snowmobile.* **2.** *iv.* to travel by ①. ♦ *Bill snowmobiled across the snowy meadow.* ♦ *After the blizzard, Jane snowmobiled to get into town.*

snowplow ['sno plɑʊ] *n.* a tractor or other vehicle with a large scoop or blade in front to clear snow from roads, driveways, and other surfaces. ♦ *The snowplows cleared the main roads first.* ♦ *The snow scooped by the snowplow covered my car.*

snowshoe ['sno ʃu] *n.* a light frame with leather straps stretched across it, which attaches to the bottom of shoes or boots so that one can walk on top of snow and not sink into it. ♦ *The trapper walked across the snow wearing snowshoes.* ♦ *David wore snowshoes in order to walk on the deep snow.*

snowstorm ['sno storm] *n.* a storm with lots of snow; a blizzard. ♦ *A terrible snowstorm closed the local airport.* ♦ *Mary couldn't get home because she was caught in a snowstorm.*

snow tire ['sno tɑɪr] *n.* a tire with heavy tread making it safer and easier to drive on snow and ice. ♦ *John puts snow tires on his car every November.* ♦ *The snow tires kept Anne's car from sliding into the ditch.*

snowy ['sno i] *adj.* covered with snow; having lots of snow. (Adv: *snowily.* Comp: *snowier;* sup: *snowiest.*) ♦ *The snowplow cleared the snowy streets.* ♦ *We climbed up the snowy mountain.*

snub ['snʌb] **1.** *tv.* to ignore someone; not to invite someone to an event. ♦ *Mary snubbed her brother by not inviting him to her wedding.* ♦ *The clerk snubbed me and spoke to someone else first.* **2.** *n.* an act of insulting someone or treating someone rudely. ♦ *Susan considered her manager's petty snub to be childish.* ♦ *David's snub of John caused John to feel angry.*

snuck ['snʌk] a pt/pp of sneak.

snuff ['snʌf] **1.** *n.* tobacco that is ground into powder and inhaled through the nose. ♦ *I prefer smoking cigarettes to inhaling snuff.* ♦ *The man inhaled some snuff, and then he sneezed.* **2. snuff out** *tv.* + *adv.* to extinguish a candle. ♦ *Please snuff out the candles before you go to bed.* ♦ *Jane snuffed out her birthday candles in one breath.*

snug ['snʌg] **1.** *adj.* warm; cozy; comfortable. (Adv: *snugly.* Comp: *snugger;* sup: *snuggest.*) ♦ *In front of the fireplace, I felt snug.* ♦ *The children were snug in their beds on the cold night.* **2.** *adj.* too tight; fitting too closely. (Adv: *snugly.* Comp: *snugger;* sup: *snuggest.*) ♦ *Anne didn't buy the shoes because they were too snug.* ♦ *Since I've gained weight, all of my clothes have become snug.*

snuggle ['snʌg əl] *iv.* to cuddle; to press against someone for warmth or to show affection. ♦ *The romantic couple snuggled in front of the fireplace.* ♦ *It was so cold that we snuggled in bed for warmth.*

so ['so] **1.** *adv.* to a certain degree; to such a degree. (Takes a clause.) ♦ *I am so tired that I think I will go to bed now.* ♦ *John was so hungry that he ate a whole pizza.* **2.** *adv.* very. ♦ *I am so tired!* ♦ *We are so relieved to hear that you're okay!* **3.** *adv.* in such a way; in that way; in this way. ♦ *This math problem is not too difficult if you solve it so.* ♦ *That won't work. You must do it so.* **4.** *adv.* also; too; as well. (Comes before an auxiliary verb, be, do, or have. In negative constructions, use neither or *not either.*) ♦ *Last year I visited Canada, and so did Mary.* ♦ *Mary is cold and so am I.* **5.** *conj.* in order that; with the result that. ♦ *Mary studied hard so she would pass the test.* ♦ *Dave went to the lake so he could go swimming.* **6.** *conj.* therefore; hence; consequently. ♦ *John is a human, and all humans are mortal, so John is mortal.* ♦ *Bill won the lottery, so he quit his job.* **7.** *interj.* <a mild exclamation of surprise or indignation.> ♦ *So! What do you have to say for yourself now?* ♦ *So! Do you think you can fool me?* **8.** *adj.* true. ♦ *Is that really so?* ♦ *Please tell me that it is not so!* **9. and so on** *idiom* continuing on in the same way [without saying all the details]; continuing to talk, saying more and more. ♦ *He told me about all his health problems, including his arthritis and so on.* ♦ *I need some help getting ready for dinner, setting the table, and so on.* **10. and so forth** *idiom* continuing talking in the same way; and so on as in ⑨. (Can be combined with *and so on.*) ♦ *She told me everything* *about her kids and so on and so forth.* ♦ *I heard about problems at work and so forth.*

soak ['sok] **1.** *iv.* to remain in [a container of] liquid for a period of time. ♦ *The dirty clothes soaked in the washing machine.* ♦ *John soaked in the tub.* **2.** *tv.* to cause something to become or remain completely wet; to saturate something with liquid. ♦ *Mary soaked the dirty dishes in the soapy water.* ♦ *The rain soaked my clothes.* **3.** *n.* a period of time spent in [a container of] liquid. ♦ *Anne had a nice long soak in the bathtub.* ♦ *These dirty clothes need a soak.*

so-and-so ['so ən so] *n.* <an expression for someone whose name is forgotten or someone at whom the speaker wishes to express displeasure.> (Pl in *-s.*) ♦ *I spoke to, uh, that so-and-so that John works with.* ♦ *Tell that old so-and-so that I want to see him right now!*

soap ['sop] **1.** *n.* a substance that helps clean objects being washed. (No plural form in this sense.) ♦ *Go wash your dirty hands with soap.* ♦ *Mary squirted some liquid soap into the dishwater.* **2. soap (opera)** *n.* a daily or weekly television drama that usually revolves around the lives and problems of people in a certain family, town, or place of work. ♦ *Anne has watched the same soap for twenty years.* ♦ *My friends and I watch our favorite soap every Monday evening.* **3.** *tv.* to clean someone or something with soap; to cover someone or something with soap while washing. ♦ *Anne soaped the car, and then she rinsed it.* ♦ *Bill soaped himself and then washed off the lather.*

soapsuds ['sop sədz] *n.* foam that is made from soap. (Treated as plural.) ♦ *Anne rinsed the soapsuds off herself.* ♦ *A layer of soapsuds floated on top of the dishwater.*

soapy ['sop i] *adj.* covered with soap. (Adv: *soapily.* Comp: *soapier;* sup: *soapiest.*) ♦ *The surgeons washed their hands with soapy water.* ♦ *John soaked the dirty dishes in soapy dishwater.*

soar ['sor] **1.** *iv.* to fly; to fly upwards; to glide. ♦ *The plane soared high in the sky.* ♦ *The kite soared over the trees.* **2.** *iv.* to increase suddenly and in a large amount; to go up suddenly and in a large amount. (Figurative on ①.) ♦ *The inflation rate soared during the war.* ♦ *The cost of gasoline soared during the oil crisis.*

soaring ['sor ɪŋ] **1.** *adj.* flying; flying high; flying high in the air; gliding. ♦ *The soaring kite became tangled in a tall tree.* ♦ *The soaring birds were flying south for the winter.* **2.** *adj.* increasing rapidly; increasing in large amounts; rising quickly. (Figurative on ①. Adv: *soaringly.*) ♦ *The soaring unemployment rate alarmed the president.* ♦ *The soaring cost of tuition angered the students.*

sob ['sɑb] **1.** *iv.* to cry while breathing short, quick breaths. ♦ *Mourners sobbed at the funeral.* ♦ *I sobbed during the sad movie.* **2.** *n.* a short, quick audible sound made while one is crying. ♦ *The mourners' loud sobs filled the church.* ♦ *I heard some sobs coming from Jimmy's bedroom.*

sober ['sob ɚ] **1.** *adj.* not drunk; not having been drinking alcohol. (Adv: *soberly.* Comp: *soberer;* sup: *soberest.*) ♦ *The drunk students looked for someone sober to drive them home.* ♦ *You should never drive a car if you are not sober.* **2.** *adj.* very serious; dignified. (Figurative on ①. Adv: *soberly.* Comp: *soberer;* sup: *soberest.*) ♦ *The sober and humorous presentation was dreadfully boring.* ♦ *A sober and frowning judge ordered the courtroom to be quiet.* **3. sober up** *iv.* + *adv.* to become ① after being drunk; to become ① all the time after being habitually drunk. ♦ *Tom left the party early to sober up.* ♦ *The alcoholic tried once again to sober up.* **4. sober up** *tv.* + *adv.* to cause someone to become ①. ♦ *Going to a doctor helped sober up the alcoholic.* ♦ *I tried to sober up my friend by making him drink coffee, but it didn't work.* **5. sober** *tv.* + *adv.* to cause someone to become serious. (Figurative on ④.) ♦ *The stern professor sobered the class with his announcement.* ♦ *The terrible news sobered us quickly.*

sobriety [sə 'brɑɪ ɪ ti] **1.** *n.* the quality of being sober. (No plural form in this sense.) ♦ *The blood test proved the driver's sobriety.* ♦ *The police doubted the sobriety of the driver.* **2.** *n.* the quality of remaining sober; the practice of never drinking alcohol. (No plural form in this sense.) ♦ *Recovering alcoholics intend to maintain their sobriety for the rest of their lives.* ♦ *The teacher preached sobriety to her students.* **3.** *n.* a sober ② bearing, look, or attitude. (No plural form in this sense.) ♦ *The look of sobriety on her face warned us of the trouble we were in.* ♦ *The judge's appearance of sternness and sobriety frightened the defendant.*

so-called ['so kɔld] *adj.* inappropriately named or called; wrongly named or called. ♦ *This so-called Picasso painting is really a forgery.* ♦ *My so-called doctor misdiagnosed my illness.*

soccer ['sɑk ɚ] *n.* a sport played by two teams of eleven people. (In Europe, soccer is called football. No plural form in this sense.) ♦ *In a game of soccer, each team tries to kick a ball across the other team's goal line, but players are not allowed to touch the ball with their hands or arms.* ♦ *John wanted to play soccer, but his school didn't have a team.*

sociable ['so ʃə bəl] *adj.* friendly; getting along well with other people, especially in social situations. (Adv: *sociably.*) ♦ *The sociable student invited his classmates to his party.* ♦ *Because Mary is sociable, she introduced herself to everyone at the party.*

social ['so ʃəl] **1.** *adj.* of or about friendship or companionship. (Adv: *socially.*) ♦ *My parents are at a social gathering tonight.* ♦ *John attended a social function last weekend.* **2.** *adj.* living together or forming groups in an organized way. (Adv: *socially.*) ♦ *Many insects are social creatures who live and work together.* ♦ *Since wolves travel in organized packs, they are considered to be social animals.*

socialism ['so ʃə lɪz əm] *n.* a belief and political system in which the production and distribution of all goods and services are owned and controlled by the government or by the workers themselves. (No plural form in this sense.) ♦ *Some Eastern European countries have moved from socialism to capitalism.* ♦ *The economist felt socialism wasn't practical because of human nature.*

socialist ['so ʃə ləst] **1.** *n.* someone who believes in socialism; someone who is a member of a political party that favors socialism. ♦ *Socialists tend to support government welfare programs.* ♦ *The socialist preached against the evils of capitalism.* **2.** *adj.* practicing socialism. ♦ *The Baltic countries were former Soviet Socialist Republics.* ♦ *Many socialist governments have immense bureaucracies.*

socialite ['so ʃə lɑɪt] *n.* someone who is wealthy and socially active, going to many parties. ♦ *The socialite went* *to many lavish parties each month.* ♦ *The elegant dance was attended by many socialites.*

socialize ['so ʃə lɑɪz] **1.** *iv.* to mingle with other people; to get to know other people; to be friendly with other people at a party or gathering. ♦ *John was too shy to socialize at the party.* ♦ *The teacher told the students not to socialize during class.* **2.** *tv.* to regulate something according to socialist principles. ♦ *The idealistic student wanted to socialize medicine.* ♦ *Some countries have socialized their hospital systems.*

socialized ['so ʃə lɑɪzd] *adj.* regulated according to socialist principles; owned or controlled by the government. ♦ *The people all favored socialized medicine.* ♦ *The economist wrote about the dangers of a socialized economy.*

social security ['so ʃəl sə 'kjɚ ɪ ti] **1.** *n.* a pension system operated by the government, making payments to people who have retired or to families of a worker who has died. (No plural form in this sense. Often capitalized.) ♦ *Generally, half of one's social security payments are paid by one's employer.* ♦ *After John turned 65, he received social security.* **2.** *adj.* <the adj. use of ①.> ♦ *Dave pays a large social security tax.* ♦ *Anne receives social security payments each month.*

social work ['so ʃəl wɚk] *n.* work done by people or the government in order to improve poor living conditions. (No plural form in this sense.) ♦ *Mary went into social work so she could help those less fortunate than she.* ♦ *Agencies involved in social work do not operate to make a profit.*

social worker ['so ʃəl wɚ kɚ] *n.* someone who is trained in social work; someone who is involved in social work. ♦ *The social worker took the child to her new foster home.* ♦ *The immense poverty in the community saddened the social worker.*

society [sə 'sɑɪ ə ti] **1.** *n.* all people; all humans. (No plural form in this sense.) ♦ *The president's policies were for the good of society.* ♦ *Society benefited greatly when smallpox was eradicated.* **2.** *n.* all people in a certain culture during a certain period of time. ♦ *I read about American society during the Revolutionary War.* ♦ *Anne studied the philosophy of Eastern societies.* **3.** *n.* an organization whose members have similar interests or goals; a club. ♦ *The smart students were inducted into the National Honor Society.* ♦ *The esteemed professor was a member of many academic societies.* **4.** *n.* the fashionable or upper-class people of a community; the community of people with good manners. (No plural form in this sense.) ♦ *Mary felt too many politicians were members of high society.* ♦ *That is not the proper way to behave in society.*

sociologist [so si 'ɑl ə dʒəst] *n.* someone who studies or practices sociology. ♦ *The sociologist studying politeness analyzed taped conversations.* ♦ *The sociologist tried to explain the increase in crime.*

sociology [so si 'ɑl ə dʒi] *n.* the study of the development, functioning, and organization of human society. (No plural form in this sense.) ♦ *John examined city life during his study of sociology.* ♦ *Mary majored in sociology and wrote about family structure.*

sock ['sɑk] **1.** *n.* a knitted or woven fabric covering for the foot, usually worn inside a shoe. ♦ *Mary put on her socks and then put on her shoes.* ♦ *The wool socks kept my feet warm.* **2.** *tv.* to hit someone or something hard. ♦ *The boxer socked his opponent in the face.* ♦ *A mugger socked me in the stomach and stole my wallet.*

socket ['sɑk ət] *n.* one of a number of types of opening that something round fits into. ♦ *The eyeball rests inside the eye socket.* ♦ *The blow knocked Bob's tooth right out of its socket.*

sod ['sɑd] *n.* turf; a piece of ground held together by the roots of grass. (No plural form in this sense.) ♦ *You should water your newly installed sod frequently.* ♦ *Workers replaced the dead grass with new sod.*

soda ['so də] **1. soda (pop)** *n.* a soft drink; a carbonated drink that has no alcohol. (No plural form in this sense.) ♦ *What kind of soda would you like to drink?* ♦ *Anne drank a diet soda with her meal.* **2. soda (water)** *n.* water that carbon dioxide has been added to so that it fizzes; carbonated water. ♦ *I like to mix soda with fruit juice for a soft drink.* ♦ *The soda fizzed when I added it to my drink.* **3. (ice-cream) soda** *n.* a confection made with ②, flavoring, and ice cream, served in a tall glass. ♦ *Bill had a chocolate soda with his hamburger.* ♦ *Anne made strawberry sodas for her guests.*

soda pop ['so də pɑp] See soda.

sodium ['so di əm] *n.* a soft, metallic element that is only found in nature as part of compounds, especially salt and soda. (No plural form in this sense.) ♦ *Table salt is a mixture of sodium (Na) and chlorine (Cl).* ♦ *The chemist had some pure sodium in the laboratory.*

sodium chloride [so di əm 'klor ɑɪd] *n.* common salt. (No plural form in this sense.) ♦ *The salty snack had a gram of sodium chloride per serving.* ♦ *The tomato juice had too much sodium chloride to be drinkable.*

sofa ['so fə] *n.* a davenport; a couch; a seat that is wide enough for more than one person. ♦ *Bill, Anne, and Sue sat on the living-room sofa and watched TV.* ♦ *I bought a matching sofa and chair for my living room.*

sofa bed ['so fə bɛd] *n.* a sofa whose seat can be pulled out to make a bed. ♦ *Mary's guests slept on the sofa bed in the living room.* ♦ *Each night, John would open his sofa bed and go to sleep.*

soft ['sɔft] **1.** *adj.* not hard; yielding to pressure; less hard than average. (Adv: *softly.* Comp: *softer;* sup: *softest.*) ♦ *Susan worked the soft clay with great skill.* ♦ *Anne's head sank into the soft pillow.* **2.** *adj.* delicate; smooth; calm; not rough; not coarse; not harsh; gently affecting the senses. (Adv: *softly.* Comp: *softer;* sup: *softest.*) ♦ *John put on some soft music while he studied.* ♦ *The soft light masked the model's facial wrinkles.* **3.** *adj.* not strong or strict; weak or lax. (Adv: *softly.* Comp: *softer;* sup: *softest.*) ♦ *The mayor was accused of being soft on crime.* ♦ *The students took advantage of their teacher's soft discipline.* **4.** *adj.* [of water] lacking certain minerals and able to make lather from soap easily. (Comp: *softer;* sup: *softest.*) ♦ *We don't need a water filter because we already have soft water.* ♦ *Soft water is usually better than hard water for washing clothes.* **5.** *adj.* [of a letter] pronounced as a fricative instead of a stop; pronounced like the *c* in *cent* or the *g* in *gin.* ♦ Genius *begins with a soft* g. ♦ *The* c *in the word* receive *is soft.*

softball ['sɔft bɔl] **1.** *n.* a game that is similar to baseball but uses a bigger, softer ball. (No plural form in this sense.) ♦ *Anne played softball in high school.* ♦ *My sister coaches a girls' softball team.* **2.** *n.* a ball that is like a baseball but is bigger and somewhat softer. ♦ *Susan caught the softball without a mitt.* ♦ *The pitcher threw the softball to the catcher.* **3.** *adj.* <the adj. use of ①.> ♦ *Lisa volunteered to be a softball coach for the new team.* ♦ *Tom joined a softball team to get some exercise.*

soft-boiled ['sɔft 'bɔɪld] **soft-boiled egg** *n.* an egg boiled slightly so that the yolk is still soft. ♦ *The soft-boiled egg had been cooked for less than three minutes.* ♦ *Anne peeled the soft-boiled egg and then ate it.*

soft drink ['sɔft drɪŋk] *n.* a carbonated drink without alcohol; pop; soda; soda pop. ♦ *I usually order a soft drink when I eat out.* ♦ *The parents served soft drinks at their child's party.*

soften ['sɔf ən] **1.** *iv.* to become more soft ①. ♦ *My jeans softened after I washed them.* ♦ *The clay softened as I added water.* **2.** *iv.* to become more gentle or less stern. ♦ *The tough administrator softened over the years.* ♦ *Her face softened as she saw the puppy.* **3.** *tv.* to make something softer. ♦ *The lotion softened my skin.* ♦ *Bill softened the music because it had been too loud.*

softhearted ['sɔft 'hɑrt əd] *adj.* gentle; kind; pitying someone or something easily. (Adv: *softheartedly.*) ♦ *The softhearted woman adopted the abandoned kitten.* ♦ *Some softhearted person fed our cat while we were away.*

softness ['sɔft nəs] *n.* the quality of being soft. (No plural form in this sense.) ♦ *The paper tissue's softness comforted my sore nose.* ♦ *The softness of the couch made it comfortable to sit on.*

soft-spoken [sɔft 'spok ən] *adj.* speaking softly, perhaps owing to shyness; speaking with a calm, quiet voice. ♦ *The soft-spoken lecturer could not be heard by those sitting in the back of the room.* ♦ *The professor encouraged the soft-spoken students to participate in class.*

software ['sɔft wɛr] *n.* one or more computer programs meant to be used or stored on a computer. (No plural form in this sense.) ♦ *Mary loaded some accounting software onto her computer.* ♦ *Susan updated the obsolete software on her computer.*

soggy ['sɔg i] *adj.* moist; wet; soaked. (Adv: *soggily.* Comp: *soggier;* sup: *soggiest.*) ♦ *The soggy cereal fell apart in the bowl.* ♦ *I removed the soggy clothes from the broken washing machine.*

soil ['sɔɪl] **1.** *n.* the ground; the top layer of dirt that plants grow in. (No plural form in this sense.) ♦ *The farmer planted the fertile soil with seed.* ♦ *The rainstorm washed a lot of soil into the river.* **2.** *tv.* to make something dirty. ♦ *You have soiled your new shirt, Jimmy!* ♦ *Anne soiled her shirt when she spilled coffee on it.* **3. soil one's diaper(s)** *idiom* [for a baby] to excrete waste into its diaper. (Euphemistic.) ♦ *The baby soiled his diapers.* ♦ *I detect that someone has soiled his diaper.*

soiled ['sɔɪld] *adj.* dirtied; made dirty. ♦ *I threw the baby's soiled diaper away.* ♦ *John put the soiled clothes into the washing machine.*

sojourn ['so dʒɚn] *n.* a short stay at some place. ♦ *Mary's sojourn in Los Angeles was quite pleasant.* ♦ *After a short sojourn in Dallas, I went back home.*

solace ['sɑ ləs] *n.* comfort or relief; something that comforts someone when one is upset, worried, or grieving. (No plural form in this sense.) ♦ *The student took solace in the fact that no one had done well on the test.* ♦ *David turned to food as solace from his anguish.*

solar ['so lɚ] *adj.* of or about the sun, the light of the sun, or the heat of the sun. ♦ *Anne's calculator is powered by solar energy.* ♦ *During a total solar eclipse, the sun is blocked by the moon.*

solar system ['so lɚ sɪs təm] *n.* a star and all of the planets, moons, asteroids, and comets that orbit around it. ♦ *There are nine planets in our solar system.* ♦ *Earth is the third planet from the sun in our solar system.*

sold ['sold] **1.** pt/pp of sell. **2. sold out** *phr.* [of a product] completely sold with no more items remaining; [of a store] having no more of a particular product. ♦ *The tickets were sold out so we couldn't go to the concert.* ♦ *I wanted new shoes like yours, but they were sold out.*

solder ['sɑd ɚ] **1.** *n.* a mixture of tin and lead that is melted and used to connect certain metals. (No plural form in this sense.) ♦ *I melted the solder with a torch.* ♦ *The two pipes were joined together with solder.* **2.** *tv.* to attach or connect things with ①. ♦ *Lisa soldered the two pipes together.* ♦ *Susan soldered the metal handle into place.*

soldier ['sol dʒɚ] *n.* someone who serves or fights in an army, especially one who is not an officer. ♦ *Hundreds of soldiers died in the bloody battle.* ♦ *The soldiers returning from the war were greeted with a parade.*

sole ['sol] **1.** *adj.* only; [the] only [one]. (Adv: *solely.*) ♦ *The reporter interviewed the plane wreck's sole survivor.* ♦ *The rich investor was the sole owner of the office building.* **2.** *n.* the bottom surface of the foot; the bottom part of a shoe, boot, or other piece of footwear. ♦ *As I walked on the beach, the hot sand burned the soles of my feet.* ♦ *The sole of my shoe needs to be replaced.* **3.** *n., irreg.* a flat-bodied, edible fish. (Pl: *sole.*) ♦ *Mary cleaned the sole before she baked it.* ♦ *Where do people fish for sole?* **4.** *n.* the edible flesh of ③. (No plural form in this sense.) ♦ *Susan ate some sole with rice.* ♦ *Sole is good with lemon and butter.* **5.** *tv.* to put a new bottom part on a shoe or boot. ♦ *I need to have these shoes soled.* ♦ *These boots were soled by a machine.*

solely ['sol li] *adv.* exclusively; for one person or group and no others. ♦ *The club facilities are to be used solely by club members.* ♦ *Bill was solely responsible for his mistakes.*

solemn ['sɑl əm] **1.** *adj.* [of someone] very serious. (Adv: *solemnly.*) ♦ *The solemn preacher rarely smiled.* ♦ *John gave his solemn promise that he'd meet me at five o'clock.* **2.** *adj.* very formal; associated with a religious or formal ceremony. (Adv: *solemnly.*) ♦ *The new members were initiated during a solemn rite.* ♦ *The judge had taken a solemn oath to uphold the Constitution.*

solemnity [sə 'lɛm nɪ ti] *n.* seriousness. (No plural form in this sense.) ♦ *The solemnity of the meeting seemed to make it take forever.* ♦ *Because of the professor's solemnity, I refrained from making jokes.*

solicit [sə 'lɪs ɪt] **1.** *tv.* to request something; to seek something. ♦ *Anne solicited help from her doctor.* ♦ *Bill solicited my opinion.* **2.** *tv.* to seek sexual activity in exchange for money. ♦ *Max solicited sex from the undercover police officer.* ♦ *The movie star was caught soliciting sexual favors from a model.* **3.** *iv.* to seek to sell something. ♦ *The law in this town does not allow anyone to solicit here.* ♦ *Bob was almost arrested for soliciting in an apartment building.* **4.** *iv.* to offer [one's body for sex] in exchange for money. ♦ *The model also secretly solicited to make extra money.* ♦ *The prostitute was arrested for soliciting.*

solicitor [sə 'lɪs ə tɚ] *n.* a peddler; someone who sells things, especially door to door. ♦ *Mary slammed the door in the solicitor's face.* ♦ *The sign on the door said "No solicitors."*

solicitous [sə 'lɪs ə təs] *adj.* anxious to please; concerned and eager. (Adv: *solicitously.*) ♦ *The waiter was solicitous and helpful.* ♦ *Mary was quite solicitous about Tom's injured foot.*

solid ['sɑl ɪd] **1.** *n.* something that is hard and does not allow its shape to be changed easily; something that is not a liquid and not a gas. ♦ *The geometry students determined the volume of solids like cubes and spheres.* ♦ *Solids don't change their shape to fit their containers.* **2. solids** *n.* food that is ① and not liquid. (Treated as plural.) ♦ *After a week of soup, I was eager to return to eating solids again.* ♦ *The hospital patient was unable to eat solids after surgery.* **3.** *adj.* not liquid or gas; having a shape that does not change on its own to fit its container. (Adv: *solidly.*) ♦ *Laser beams can bore holes through solid matter.* ♦ *Ice is the solid form of water.* **4.** *adj.* not hollow; having an inside that is full of something. (Adv: *solidly.*) ♦ *The solid block of cement was very heavy.* ♦ *The lead cube was completely solid.* **5.** *adj.* [of a period of time] continuous and not interrupted. (Adv: *solidly.* Before or after a noun.) ♦ *John studied for a solid hour.* ♦ *The movie lasted for three solid hours.* ♦ *The movie lasted for three hours solid.* **6.** *adj.* made of only one kind of thing; not mixed with anything else. (Adv: *solidly.*) ♦ *A flag of surrender is solid white.* ♦ *This ring is made of solid gold.* **7.** *adj.* sturdy; well made; dependable; reliable; strong; not likely to break, collapse, or fail. (Adv: *solidly.*) ♦ *My house has solid construction and is well maintained.* ♦ *The bridge was solid enough for heavy trucks to drive on.* **8.** *adj.* reliable. (Adv: *solidly.*) ♦ *The inspector had a few solid leads.* ♦ *John is my friend—solid and true.*

solidarity [sɑl ɪ 'dɛr ɪ ti] *n.* unity caused by having common interests or goals; agreement in interests or goals. (No plural form in this sense.) ♦ *Showing solidarity, the union rejected the factory's contract.* ♦ *Mary felt solidarity with other cancer survivors.*

solitaire ['sɑl ɪ tɛr] *n.* a card game for one person. (No plural form in this sense.) ♦ *Jane played solitaire while she waited for her date.* ♦ *Bill knows several different games of solitaire.*

solitary ['sɑl ɪ tɛr i] *adj.* alone; by oneself. (Adv: *solitarily* [sɑl ə 'tɛr ə li].) ♦ *The violent criminal was placed in solitary confinement.* ♦ *The solitary bachelor did not like Valentine's Day.*

solitude ['sɑl ɪ tud] **1.** *n.* aloneness; the state of being alone. (No plural form in this sense.) ♦ *The depressed student cried in solitude.* ♦ *After hard days at work, the teacher enjoyed the solitude of a hot bath.* **2.** *n.* loneliness. (No plural form in this sense.) ♦ *In his solitude, John became depressed.* ♦ *Mary combated her solitude by going to a movie.*

solo ['so lo] **1.** *n.* a musical piece performed by one person; a piece of music written primarily for one singer or one instrument. (Pl in *-s*.) ♦ *The composer wrote a solo for a violin.* ♦ *The soprano performed her solo excellently.* **2.** *adj.* done alone; done without help. ♦ *The pilot's first solo flight was successful.* ♦ *The spy undertook a dangerous solo mission.* **3.** *adv.* without help; alone. ♦ *Tom did the trip solo, with no one else to share the driving.* ♦ *Most of the people at the nightclub danced solo.* **4.** *iv.* to perform by oneself; to do something by oneself. ♦ *The dancer had to solo because her partner was ill.* ♦ *The pilot soloed for the first time after completing his training program.*

soloist ['so lo əst] *n.* a singer or musician who performs a solo; a singer or musician who performs music written for one person. ♦ *The soloist sang a beautiful ballad.* ♦ *The soloist who won first prize had played the piano flawlessly.*

soluble ['sɑl jə bəl] *adj.* able to dissolve; able to be dissolved. (Adv: *solubly.*) ♦ *Salt is soluble in water.* ♦ *Tom dissolved the soluble tablet in water.*

solution [sə 'lu ʃən] **1.** *n.* an answer to a problem or question; a way to fix a problem. ♦ *The solution to the math problem "What is 2 + 2?" is 4.* ♦ *Many social problems don't have easy solutions.* **2.** *n.* a liquid that has a solid or gas dissolved in it; a mixture of a liquid and a solid or gas that has been dissolved in it. ♦ *The doctor prepared a medicinal solution for me to drink.* ♦ *When the chemist added some powder, the solution turned cloudy.*

solve ['sɔlv] *tv.* to find the answer to a question or a problem. ♦ *The students had to solve 30 math problems in 60 minutes.* ♦ *The detective solved the terrible murder.*

solvent ['sɔlv ənt] **1.** *n.* a liquid that is able to dissolve something. ♦ *The powerful solvent dissolved the stains on the sidewalk.* ♦ *Water can serve as a solvent for salt.* **2.** *adj.* not in debt; having the money to pay one's debts. ♦ *Anne destroyed her credit cards in order to become solvent.* ♦ *Tom, always solvent and debt-free, pays cash for everything.*

Somalia [so 'mɑl i ə] See Gazetteer.

somber ['sɑm bɚ] *adj.* gloomy; very serious; dismal; depressing. (Adv: *somberly.* Comp: *somberer;* sup: *somberest.*) ♦ *The judge looked sober and somber as he sentenced the murderer to death.* ♦ *Mary left the somber party shortly after she arrived.*

some ['sʌm] **1.** *adj.* [of a person or creature] unnamed or unknown. ♦ *Some person has been reading my mail!* ♦ *Some dog has been walking through my flower garden.* **2.** *adj.* a few; more than one, but not too many. ♦ *David ate some cookies for lunch.* ♦ *Anne bought some books at the bookstore.* **3.** *adj.* [of something] excellent; exciting; severe; notable. (Informal.) ♦ *Anne threw some party last night, didn't she?* ♦ *I had some headache last night.* **4.** *adv.* about; approximately. ♦ *There were some 30 people at the party.* ♦ *The sculpture weighed some 500 pounds.* **5.** *n.* a number of people or things; a few people or things, but less than many. ♦ *I found that some left early because they had other things to do.* ♦ *Some were upset by the violent movie.*

somebody ['sʌm bɑd i] **1.** *pron.* some person; someone; a certain unnamed person. (Compare with anybody.) ♦ *Somebody sent me an anonymous letter.* ♦ *Somebody called an ambulance right after the accident.* **2.** *n.* a famous or important person. (Compare with anybody.) ♦ *I wish I were a somebody, not just an insignificant nobody.* ♦ *If you want to be somebody when you grow up, you should develop your talents now.*

someday ['sʌm de] *adv.* at some time in the future. ♦ *Someday I'd like to own a house.* ♦ *Anne thought she might travel to Japan someday.*

somehow ['sʌm haʊ] *adv.* in some way; in some manner; in a way that is not yet known. ♦ *Somehow, I'll get this report finished by noon.* ♦ *Somehow, we must find a way to reduce crime.*

someone ['sʌm wən] *pron.* somebody; some person; a person; a certain unnamed person. ♦ *There's someone on the phone who wants to talk to you.* ♦ *Someone had vandalized the office building.*

someplace ['sʌm ples] *adv.* somewhere; at, in, or to some place. (Informal. Somewhere is preferred by some people.) ♦ *John wanted to live someplace else.* ♦ *Do you want to go someplace for dinner?*

somersault ['sʌm ɚ sɔlt] *n.* a backward or forward roll of the body, started by placing one's head on the ground. ♦ *The gymnast did a double somersault in the middle of her routine.* ♦ *Bill knocked over a table when he did a somersault in the house.*

something ['sʌm θɪŋ] **1.** *pron.* some thing; a certain thing that is not known or named. (Compare with anything.) ♦ *Something is bothering Bob, but he won't tell us what it is.* ♦ *Anne told me something about the new worker, but I forgot what.* **2.** *n.* a thing that is more than nothing. (Compare with anything. No plural form in this sense.) ♦ *Getting a promotion is something, even if you didn't get a raise.* ♦ *I'm glad somebody finally did something about the crime problem.*

sometime ['sʌm tɑɪm] **1.** *adv.* at some point in time that is not known or specified. ♦ *I'd like to go out for dinner with you sometime.* ♦ *Could I make an appointment with you sometime soon?* **2. sometimes** *adv.* now and then; occasionally; from time to time. ♦ *Sometimes Mary likes to go shopping with her friends.* ♦ *Sometimes John just wants to be alone.*

somewhat ['sʌm ʍət] *adj.* rather; slightly; to some degree; kind of. ♦ *I was somewhat surprised that Bill wasn't home last night.* ♦ *Mary was somewhat upset that John had lied to her.*

somewhere ['sʌm ʍɛr] *adv.* at, in, or to some place. ♦ *John wanted to live somewhere quiet.* ♦ *Would you go away and stand somewhere else?*

son ['sʌn] *n.* someone's male child; the male child of a parent. (Also used as a term of address by an older person to any boy or young man.) ♦ *Son, go help your mother weed the garden.* ♦ *Mary has two sons and one daughter.*

sonar ['so nɑr] *n.* a device that reflects sound waves to determine the shape, position, and distance of something underwater. (No plural form in this sense. From **so**und **na**vigation **r**anging.) ♦ *The ship's sonar indicated there was a submarine directly beneath it.* ♦ *The captain tracked the torpedo by sonar.*

song ['sɔŋ] **1.** *n.* a story or words that are set to music; words that are sung. ♦ *The choir sang many songs at the concert.* ♦ *This song is a poem that has been set to music.* **2.** *n.* the art, practice, or action of singing. (No plural form in this sense.) ♦ *The morning was brightened by song, as the children practiced their singing.* ♦ *The choir lifted up their voices in song.* **3.** *n.* the musical noise that birds make. ♦ *The early-morning song of the robin woke me up.* ♦ *The bird watcher knew the different songs of different birds.* **4. swan song** *idiom* the last work or performance of a playwright, musician, actor, etc., before retirement. ♦ *The aging actor's portrayal of King Lear was his swan song.* ♦ *We didn't know that the singer's performance last night was her swan song.*

songbird ['sɔŋ bɚd] *n.* any common bird with a characteristic song. ♦ *The songbird's melodic chirp woke me up.* ♦ *Keeping a songbird in a cage should be illegal.*

sonic ['sɑn ɪk] *adj.* of or about sound or sound waves. (Adv: *sonically* [...ɪk li].) ♦ *The physicist measured the sonic energy created by the blast.* ♦ *The submarine emitted sonic waves that could be detected by sonar.*

sonic boom ['sɑn ɪk 'bum] *n.* a loud noise that an object makes when it goes faster than the speed of sound, about 760 miles per hour. ♦ *People living in the path of jet planes are used to hearing sonic booms.* ♦ *The jet's sonic boom was heard throughout my neighborhood.*

son-in-law ['sʌn ɪn lɔ] *n., irreg.* the husband of one's daughter. (Pl: sons-in-law.) ♦ *The bride's father shook his new son-in-law's hand.* ♦ *My son-in-law told me that my daughter went to New York on business.*

sonnet ['sɑn ət] *n.* a poem with 14 lines that has a certain pattern of rhythm and rhyme. ♦ *Each student had to memorize a sonnet for class.* ♦ *We had to outline the pattern of a sonnet on the English test.*

sons-in-law ['sʌnz ɪn lɔ] pl of son-in-law.

soon ['sun] **1.** *adv.* in a short period of time; before long; shortly. (Comp: *sooner;* sup: *soonest.*) ♦ *We should leave for the airport soon.* ♦ *Mary arrived at the party soon after John.* **2. so soon** *phr.* early; before the regular time; ahead of schedule. ♦ *I got there early because my bus arrived so soon.* ♦ *Because the meeting ended so soon, I had some extra time.* **3. as soon as** *phr.* at the moment that; at the time that; when. ♦ *I fell asleep as soon as I lay down.* ♦ *John ate dinner as soon as he came home.*

soot ['sʊt] *n.* a black powder that is made by burning something, such as coal or wood. (No plural form in this sense.) ♦ *Bill cleaned the soot from the fireplace.* ♦ *The buildings were covered with soot from the nearby factories.*

soothe ['suð] **1.** *tv.* to calm someone or something; to comfort someone or something; to ease pain or discomfort. ♦ *The medicine soothed my nerves.* ♦ *The cool lotion soothed my dry skin.* **2.** *iv.* to be a comfort; to be a relief. ♦ *This brand of ointment soothes better than the others.* ♦ *Kind words can soothe when someone is upset.*

soothing ['suð ɪŋ] *adj.* comforting; calming; relieving. (Adv: *soothingly.*) ♦ *The soothing music helped me fall asleep.* ♦ *The soothing lotion felt good on my dry skin.*

sophisticated [sə 'fɪs tə ket ɪd] **1.** *adj.* experienced; experienced in life; refined; cultured. (Adv: *sophisticatedly.*) ♦ *The opera's audience was rather sophisticated.* ♦ *The diplomat spoke in a sophisticated manner.* **2.** *adj.* not simple; complex; challenging. (Adv: *sophisticatedly.*) ♦ *Bill struggled with the sophisticated calculus problem.* ♦ *The sophisticated machinery is difficult to operate properly.*

sophomore ['sɔf (ə) mor] **1.** *n.* someone in the second year of high school or college. ♦ *The sophomore showed the freshman around the campus.* ♦ *Each sophomore was required to study algebra.* **2.** *adj.* of or about the second year of high school or college. ♦ *John studied in Brazil* *during his sophomore year.* ♦ *Mary was elected president of the sophomore class.*

sophomoric ['sɔf (ə) mor ɪk] *adj.* immature; crude; childish. (Adv: *sophomorically* [...ɪk li].) ♦ *Whoever plays another stupid, sophomoric trick will be punished!* ♦ *The mature audience members were insulted by the movie's sophomoric humor.*

soporific [sɑp ə 'rɪf ɪk] *adj.* causing sleep. (Adv: *soporifically* [...ɪk li].) ♦ *The soporific medicine made me drowsy.* ♦ *I yawned while the soporific lecture droned on.*

sopping ['sɑp ɪŋ] **sopping (wet)** *adj.* very wet. ♦ *I got caught in the rain, and now I'm sopping wet.* ♦ *Change out of those sopping clothes and put on some dry ones!*

soprano [sə 'præn o] **1.** *n.* someone, usually a woman, who sings in the highest vocal range. (Pl in *-s*.) ♦ *The sopranos sang the melody, and the altos sang only in the chorus.* ♦ *There are six sopranos in the choir.* **2. the soprano** *n.* the musical part written for ①; the notes usually sung by ①. (No plural form in this sense. Treated as singular.) ♦ *I am an alto, but I can sing the soprano if necessary.* ♦ *The soprano is really easy in this anthem.* **3.** *adj.* <the adj. use of ①.> ♦ *Mary sings the soprano part in the choir.* ♦ *The duet was written for soprano voices.*

sorcerer ['sors ə rɚ] *n.* a male magician who contacts evil spirits. ♦ *The wicked sorcerer cast an evil spell on the good king.* ♦ *The old man was accused of being a sorcerer.*

sorceress ['sor sə rəs] *n.* a female magician who contacts evil spirits. ♦ *The sorceress mixed a potion that would turn people into frogs.* ♦ *The evil sorceress, disguised as an old woman, tricked the queen.*

sorcery ['sor sə ri] *n.* magic practiced with the help of evil spirits. (No plural form in this sense.) ♦ *The church executed people it suspected of practicing sorcery.* ♦ *The large book of sorcery contained secret spells.*

sordid ['sor dɪd] *adj.* unpleasant; vile; degrading. (Adv: *sordidly*.) ♦ *The film's sordid plot offended most of the audience.* ♦ *The teenager told the judge the sordid story of how he became addicted to drugs and began living on the street.*

sore ['sor] **1.** *adj.* hurting; painful; aching. (Adv: *sorely*. Comp: *sorer;* sup: *sorest*.) ♦ *Mary rubbed her sore muscles.* ♦ *My feet were sore because I'd been walking all day.* **2.** *adj.* angry; irritable. (Informal. Comp: *sorer;* sup: *sorest*.) ♦ *Don't get sore at me. I only asked you a question.* ♦ *Mary was sore at John because he was an hour late.* **3.** *n.* a painful infection or injury on the skin. ♦ *The nurse cleaned and bandaged the soldier's infected sore.* ♦ *Blood oozed from the open sore.*

soreness ['sor nəs] *n.* the condition of being sore; pain. (No plural form in this sense.) ♦ *Susan took some aspirin for the soreness in her back.* ♦ *After the fall, I felt soreness throughout my body.*

sorority [sə 'ror ɪ ti] *n.* an organization of women, especially one for female students at a college or university. ♦ *Anne was accepted by the sorority she wanted to join.* ♦ *Ten sororities were affiliated with the women's college.*

sorrow ['sɑr o] **1.** *n.* sadness; grief. (No plural form in this sense.) ♦ *The grieving family's sorrow affected us all.* ♦ *Four touching poems expressed the poet's sorrow.* **2.** *n.* a cause of sadness, grief, or misfortune. ♦ *That her son was a criminal was one of Mary's greatest sorrows.* ♦ *My biggest sorrow in life was that I never finished school.* **3. sorrow over** *iv. + prep. phr.* to have regret about something; to feel sorry or grieve about something. ♦ *John sorrowed over the loss of his wife.* ♦ *The country sorrowed over the president's assassination.*

sorrowful ['sɑr ə fəl] **1.** *adj.* sorry; grieving. (Adv: *sorrowfully*.) ♦ *The sorrowful family wept at the funeral.* ♦ *We were sorrowful when we learned of your accident.* **2.** *adj.* causing sorrow; causing sadness. (Adv: *sorrowfully*.) ♦ *Everyone in the village attended the mayor's sorrowful funeral.* ♦ *I saw sorrowful images of famine in the newspaper.*

sorry ['sɑr i] **1.** *adj.* apologetic; expressing an apology. (Not prenominal. Comp: *sorrier;* sup: *sorriest*.) ♦ *John was sorry for stepping on my toes.* ♦ *Anne was sorry about being a few minutes late.* **2.** *adj.* sad; feeling pity; wishing that something had happened differently. (Not prenominal. Comp: *sorrier;* sup: *sorriest*.) ♦ *Mary's friends all told her how sorry they were that her husband had died.* ♦ *We were sorry to hear that the athlete had broken his leg.* **3.** *adj.* regretful; wishing that one had acted differently. (Not prenominal. Comp: *sorrier;* sup: *sorriest*.) ♦ *Bill is sorry now that he didn't finish high school.* ♦ *If you don't obey me, you'll be sorry!* **4.** *adj.* pitiable; worthy of pity; wretched; causing pity. (Only prenominal. Comp: *sorrier;* sup: *sorriest*.) ♦ *The child's sorry clothing was dirty and torn.* ♦ *I cannot accept your sorry excuse.* **5. (I'm) sorry.** *phr.* <an expression used to excuse oneself politely or apologize, especially when one has collided with someone, when one has offended someone, or to ask someone to repeat what has been said.> ♦ *"I'm sorry," I said to the woman I bumped into.* ♦ *I'm sorry, what did you say? I couldn't hear you.*

sort ['sort] **1.** *n.* a kind; a category; a group of similar persons, things, or qualities. ♦ *What sort of food would you like to eat tonight?* ♦ *John likes movies of the violent sort.* **2.** *tv.* to put things in a particular order; to arrange things by category; to separate things by category. ♦ *The students were sorted by height.* ♦ *The clerk sorted the invoices by their dates.* **3. sort of something** *idiom* somewhat; having a small amount of a characteristic; kind of. ♦ *I am sort of tired. Let's go home.* ♦ *Mary's eyes are sort of blue and sort of gray.* **4. in bad sorts** *idiom* in a bad mood. ♦ *Bill is in bad sorts today. He's very grouchy.* ♦ *I try to be extra nice to people when I'm in bad sorts.* **5. out of sorts** *idiom* not feeling well; grumpy and irritable. ♦ *I've been out of sorts for a day or two. I think I'm coming down with something.* ♦ *The baby is out of sorts. Maybe she's getting a tooth.*

so-so ['so 'so] **1.** *adj.* okay; adequate; moderate; not very good and not very bad. ♦ *Dinner was excellent, but the movie was only so-so.* ♦ *The teacher gave the so-so book report a C.* **2.** *adv.* okay; adequately; moderately; not very well and not very bad. ♦ *The potatoes are great, but the carrots taste only so-so.* ♦ *Our team only played so-so at the tournament.*

soufflé [su 'fle] *n.* a light, fluffy preparation of beaten eggs, flour, milk, and some other food cooked together. (From French.) ♦ *We ate a cheese soufflé for breakfast.* ♦ *Bill bought a special dish in which to make soufflés.*

sought ['sɔt] pt/pp of seek.

soul ['sol] **1.** *n.* the part of a human that is separate from the body (and that some religions believe never dies); the part of the body that controls emotion and intellect; the spirit. ♦ *The minister said that when we die, our souls go to heaven or hell.* ♦ *Anne believes that her deceased husband's soul is still with her.* **2.** *n.* a person; a human being. ♦ *I went to the meeting place, but there wasn't a soul in sight.* ♦ *The poor soul suffered in the cold weather.* **3.** *n.* the core or inspiration that gives something depth or meaning. (Figurative on ①.) ♦ *The book's soul was the author's extensive life experience.* ♦ *The soul of her singing was in her energy and passion.* **4. every living soul** *idiom* every person. ♦ *I expect every living soul to be there and be there on time.* ♦ *This is the kind of problem that affects every living soul.* **5. with all one's heart and soul** *idiom* very sincerely. ♦ *Oh, Bill, I love you with all my heart and soul, and I always will!* ♦ *She thanked us with all her heart and soul for the gift.*

soulful ['sol fəl] *adj.* passionate; emotional; full of feeling. (Adv: *soulfully.*) ♦ *The lovers danced to the soulful music of a saxophone.* ♦ *The soulful song made me cry.*

sound ['sɑʊnd] **1.** *n.* a property of vibrating air that can stimulate the ears and be heard. (No plural form in this sense.) ♦ *Sound cannot be heard in a vacuum.* ♦ *Sound travels at about 1,100 feet per second.* **2.** *n.* a noise; vibrations that stimulate the ears. ♦ *The car crash made a terrible sound.* ♦ *Loud sounds frighten me.* **3.** *n.* a narrow channel of water that connects two larger bodies of water; an inlet. ♦ *Long Island Sound is between Long Island and Connecticut.* ♦ *The sound froze during the harsh winter.* **4.** *tv.* to cause something to make a noise; to cause something to be heard. ♦ *The thief's movement sounded the alarm.* ♦ *The soldier sounded the bugle at 6:00 A.M.* **5.** *iv.* to make a characteristic noise. ♦ *I awoke when the alarm clock sounded.* ♦ *The church bells sound every hour.* **6.** *iv.* to be heard in a certain way. ♦ *Mary sounds hoarse because she has a cold.* ♦ *John's voice sounded funny after he inhaled some helium.* **7.** *adj.* [of sleep] deep. (Adv: *soundly.*) ♦ *I could not awaken her from her sound slumber.* ♦ *I need at least seven hours of sound sleep each night.* **8.** *adj.* healthy; not damaged or injured; in good condition. ♦ *The doctor said I was physically quite sound.* ♦ *Anne wrote her will while she was of sound mind and body.* **9.** *adj.* strong; sturdy; safe ⑨. (Adv: *soundly.* Comp: *sounder;* sup: *soundest.*) ♦ *The inspector stated that the bridge was sound and safe for travel.* ♦ *The sound building withstood the earthquake.* **10.** *adj.* sane; logical; reasonable; well reasoned; using good sense or judgment. (Adv: *soundly.* Comp: *sounder;* sup: *soundest.*) ♦ *You have sound reasons for being concerned. This place is not safe.* ♦ *Although your logic is sound, I still don't agree with you.* **11. sound as if _____; sound like _____** *idiom* to seem, from what has been said, as if something were so. (*Sound like* is colloquial.) ♦ *It sounds as if you had a good vacation.* ♦ *You sound like you are angry.* **12. sound like something** *idiom* to seem like something. ♦ *That sounds like a good idea.* ♦ *Your explanation sounds like an excuse!* **13. sound off** *idiom* to speak loudly and freely about something, especially when complaining. ♦ *The people at the bus stop were sounding off about the poor transportation services.* ♦ *Bob was sounding off about the government's economic policies.* **14. safe and sound** See safe.

soundly ['sɑʊnd li] **1.** *adv.* [of force used] severely. ♦ *Tom was soundly spanked and sent to bed.* ♦ *The opposing team beat us soundly.* **2.** *adv.* logically; reasonably; with good sense or judgment. ♦ *My counselor's advice was soundly based on experience.* ♦ *The philosopher presented his arguments soundly.* **3.** *adv.* [of sleep done] deeply. ♦ *John slept soundly when he was ill.* ♦ *I slept soundly even through the violent storm.*

soundproof ['sɑʊnd pruf] **1.** *adj.* not allowing sound to pass through. ♦ *The recording studio was soundproof.* ♦ *The game-show contestant was kept in a soundproof booth so she couldn't hear her opponent's answers.* **2.** *tv.* to make a place ①. ♦ *John soundproofed his bedroom so he could listen to loud music without disturbing anyone.* ♦ *Mary soundproofed her office so no one could eavesdrop.*

soundtrack ['sɑʊnd træk] **1.** *n.* the part of a film that contains the sound used in a movie. ♦ *The soundtrack contained all the sound effects used in the movie.* ♦ *The soundtrack must be synchronized with the video.* **2.** *n.* a recording of the music or the songs from a movie, sold separately from the movie. ♦ *The popular movie's soundtrack featured many famous bands.* ♦ *David played the movie's soundtrack on his stereo.*

soup ['sup] **1.** *n.* a liquid food that is made by boiling meat, fish, vegetables, or other foods. (No plural form in this sense.) ♦ *This soup is made from beans.* ♦ *I ate a bowl of hot soup with my lunch.* **2. soups** *n.* kinds or types of ①. ♦ *I bought my favorite soups at the store this week.* ♦ *We have a good choice of soups for our lunches.*

sour ['sɑʊ ɚ] **1.** *adj.* tasting like an acid; having a taste like lemons; not sweet, salty, or bitter. (Adv: *sourly.* Comp: *sourer;* sup: *sourest.*) ♦ *John added some sugar to the sour lemonade.* ♦ *I added some lime juice to my drink to make it sour.* **2.** *adj.* [of milk] spoiled. (Adv: *sourly.* Comp: *sourer;* sup: *sourest.*) ♦ *Anne poured the sour milk down the sink.* ♦ *Is there any way we can use this sour milk?* **3.** *adj.* unpleasant; disagreeable. (Adv: *sourly.* Comp: *sourer;* sup: *sourest.*) ♦ *I remained quiet because my boss was in a sour mood.* ♦ *The sour clerk was very rude to the customer.* **4.** *iv.* [for milk] to become ②. ♦ *The milk soured when I left it out of the refrigerator overnight.* ♦ *Let the milk sour before using it in the recipe.*

source ['sors] *n.* the origin of something; the place where something comes from. ♦ *The reporter refused to reveal her source of information.* ♦ *The river's source was an underground spring.*

south ['sɑʊθ] **1.** *n.* the direction to the right of someone or something facing east. (No plural form in this sense.) ♦ *Before winter came, the birds flew toward the south.* ♦ *The windows that face the south get a lot of sunlight.* **2.** *n.* the part of a region, country, or planet located toward ①, especially in the U.S. (No plural form in this sense.) ♦ *Florida, Georgia, South Carolina, North Carolina, Virginia, Kentucky, Tennessee, Alabama, Mississippi, Louisiana, and Arkansas are part of the American South.* ♦ *Mary has a small villa in the south of France.* **3. the South** *n.* the Confederacy. (No plural form in this sense. Treated as singular.) ♦ *The South separated from the rest of the country, leading to the Civil War.* ♦ *The South is now part of the nation again.* **4.** *adj.* to ①; toward ①; located in ②; facing ①. ♦ *Anne lived on the south side of town.* ♦ *Arizona is directly south of Utah.* **5.** *adj.* coming from ①, especially used to describe wind. ♦ *The south wind brought relief to the cold northern states.* ♦ *There were tornadoes where the warm south wind met the cool north* wind. **6.** *adv.* toward ①. ♦ *When you get to 10th Street, turn south away from the river.* ♦ *Jane drove south all the way to Florida.*

South Africa [sɑʊθ 'æf rɪ kə] See Gazetteer.

South America [sɑʊθ ə 'mɛr ɪ kə] See Gazetteer.

South Carolina ['sɑʊθ kɛr ə 'lɑɪ nə] See Gazetteer.

South Dakota ['sɑʊθ də 'ko tə] See Gazetteer.

southeast [sɑʊθ 'ist] **1.** *n.* the direction halfway between south and east. (No plural form in this sense.) ♦ *The pilot steered the ship toward the southeast.* ♦ *Mississippi is to the southeast of Arkansas.* **2.** *n.* an area in the southeastern part of a region or country. ♦ *Atlanta is the largest city in the American southeast.* ♦ *London lies in England's southeast.* **3.** *adj.* located in the ②; toward ①; facing ①. ♦ *Vietnam is a country in Southeast Asia.* ♦ *There's a freezer in the southeast corner of the basement.* **4.** *adj.* from ①, especially describing wind. ♦ *The southeast wind drove waves onto the South Carolina shores.* ♦ *The southeast breeze brought spray from the Atlantic Ocean.* **5.** *adv.* toward ①. ♦ *The plane flew southeast from Seattle to Salt Lake City.* ♦ *John drove southeast from Chicago to Indianapolis.*

southeastern [sɑʊθ 'is tɚn] *adj.* in the southeast; toward the southeast; facing the southeast. ♦ *Mary grew up in the southeastern states of Georgia and Florida.* ♦ *The morning sunlight streamed through the southeastern windows.*

southern ['sʌð ɚn] **1.** *adj.* in the south; toward the south; facing south. ♦ *The candidate campaigned heavily in the southern states.* ♦ *San Antonio is in the southern part of Texas.* **2.** *adj.* from the south ①, especially describing wind. ♦ *The southern wind was hot and dry.* ♦ *The spring day was warmed by southern winds.* **3.** *adj.* concerning the society and culture of the American South. ♦ *Southern hospitality is known all over the world.* ♦ *Mary's southern accent was obvious to the northerner.*

southerner ['sʌð ɚ nɚ] *n.* someone who lives in the south part of a country, especially someone from the southern United States. (Sometimes capitalized.) ♦ *The southerner and her friend from New York spoke with different accents.* ♦ *The southerner visited the north on occasion.*

Southern Hemisphere ['sʌð ɚn 'hɛm əs fir] *n.* the half of the earth that is south of the equator. ♦ *When it is winter in the Northern Hemisphere, it is summer in the Southern Hemisphere.* ♦ *All of New Zealand is in the Southern Hemisphere.*

southpaw ['sɑʊθ pɔ] *n.* a left-hander; someone who is left-handed. ♦ *The southpaw hit the baseball into right field.* ♦ *There are specially shaped scissors for southpaws.*

south pole ['sɑʊθ 'pol] **1.** *n.* the point in the Antarctic that is as far south as it is possible to go; the southern point on earth where the needle of a compass points straight down. ♦ *The south pole is at the southern end of earth's magnetic field.* ♦ *The south pole is exactly opposite the north pole.* **2. South Pole** *n.* the actual location of ①. ♦ *When you stand at the South Pole, all directions are south.* ♦ *Absolutely no one lives near the South Pole.*

southward ['sɑʊθ wɚd] *adv.* toward the south. ♦ *The birds flew southward for the winter.* ♦ *The Mississippi River flows southward toward the Gulf of Mexico.*

southwest [sɑʊθ 'wɛst] **1.** *n.* the direction halfway between south and west. (No plural form in this sense.) ♦ *From my compass, I determined I was walking toward the southwest.* ♦ *The pilot flew the plane toward the southwest.* **2. Southwest** *n.* the southwestern part of the United States. (No plural form in this sense.) ♦ *The American Southwest consists of Arizona, New Mexico, and west Texas.* ♦ *Susan attended school in the Southwest.* **3.** *adj.* located in ①; toward ①; facing ①. ♦ *I live in a suburb that is southwest of the city.* ♦ *Mary's office is in the southwest corner of the building.* **4.** *adj.* from ①, especially describing wind. ♦ *The southwest wind was blowing at 10 miles per hour.* ♦ *The southwest wind helped the eastbound flights.* **5.** *adv.* toward ①. ♦ *The trucker drove southwest from Nashville to Memphis.* ♦ *The pilot flew the plane southwest from Boston to New York City.*

southwestern [sɑʊθ 'wɛs tɚn] *adj.* in the southwest; toward the southwest; facing the southwest. ♦ *Anne lives in a southwestern suburb of Boston.* ♦ *Robert was born in a city in southwestern Germany.*

souvenir [su və 'nɪr] *n.* something that reminds one of someplace, someone, or one's travels; a keepsake. ♦ *The newlyweds bought a souvenir of their honeymoon in Florida.* ♦ *Many Germans kept a piece of the Berlin Wall as a souvenir.*

sovereign ['sɑv rɪn] **1.** *n.* a king or queen; a monarch; a ruler in a monarchy. ♦ *Queen Elizabeth became sovereign of the United Kingdom in 1952.* ♦ *The courier delivered a message to the sovereign of France.* **2.** *adj.* having the highest power. (Adv: *sovereignly.*) ♦ *The peasants paid taxes to their sovereign ruler.* ♦ *Long live our sovereign queen!* **3.** *adj.* independent; not controlled by another country; self-governing. (Adv: *sovereignly.*) ♦ *The United States declared itself a sovereign nation in 1776.* ♦ *The colony's struggle to become sovereign was crushed.*

sovereignty ['sɑv rɪn ti] **1.** *n.* independence; self-governance; the condition of being sovereign. (No plural form in this sense.) ♦ *Many African nations assumed sovereignty in the 1960s.* ♦ *Ukraine asserted its sovereignty in 1991.* **2.** *n.* a country that is independent; a country that is self-governing; a country that is not controlled by another country. ♦ *The tiny sovereignty's independence was threatened by its powerful neighbor.* ♦ *Now an independent sovereignty, the small country organized its own army.* **3.** *n.* supremacy; the quality of being supreme. (No plural form in this sense.) ♦ *The king killed anyone who questioned his sovereignty.* ♦ *The minister urged me to put my trust in the sovereignty of the Lord.*

Soviet ['sov i ɛt] **1.** *adj.* of or about the [former] Union of Soviet Socialist Republics. ♦ *The spy worked for the Soviet government.* ♦ *The Soviet leader met with the American president at the White House.* **2.** *n.* a citizen or native of the [former] Union of Soviet Socialist Republics. ♦ *The Soviets fought a bitter war in Afghanistan.* ♦ *Most Soviets were members of the Communist Party.*

Soviet Union ['sov i ɛt 'jun jən] *n.* the [former] Union of Soviet Socialist Republics (1917–1991). ♦ *Russia was the largest country in the Soviet Union.* ♦ *Mikhail Gorbachev was the last leader of the Soviet Union.*

sow 1. ['so] *tv., irreg.* to scatter seed on the ground; to plant crops by scattering seed on the ground. (Pp: **sown** or *sowed.*) ♦ *The farmer sowed the seeds for his crops in the* *spring.* ♦ *The wheat was sown in April.* **2.** ['so] *iv., irreg.* to plant [crops] by scattering seed on the ground. ♦ *The farmer sowed from morning to dusk.* ♦ *The gardener sowed in the springtime.* **3.** ['sɑʊ] *n.* a female pig. ♦ *The huge sow had a dozen tiny piglets.* ♦ *The farmer slaughtered the large sow.*

sown ['son] pp of sow.

soybean ['sɔɪ bin] *n.* a nutritious bean grown in Asia and North America, used to make flour and oil, and eaten as food. ♦ *The farmers harvested the soybeans late in the summer.* ♦ *This vegetarian burger is made mostly of soybeans.*

soy sauce ['sɔɪ sɔs] *n.* a salty brown sauce made from fermented soybeans. (No plural form in this sense.) ♦ *Anne added soy sauce to her rice.* ♦ *I asked the waiter at the Chinese restaurant for some soy sauce.*

spa ['spɑ] **1.** *n.* a spring that produces mineral water. ♦ *The small mountain village got its water from a natural spa.* ♦ *Water from this spa is bottled and sold by the liter.* **2.** *n.* a resort or health club, often built around a spring that produces mineral water. ♦ *I stayed at a German spa while on vacation.* ♦ *The elderly people go to the spa yearly for their health.* **3.** *n.* a large bathing tub, usually with water circulated throughout by a pump, sometimes heated. ♦ *After work, Susan relaxed in the spa at her health club.* ♦ *The mansion had its own bowling alley, swimming pool, and spa.*

space ['spes] **1.** *n.* the universe; the area that extends in every direction from the earth; every location in existence in the universe except the earth. (No plural form in this sense.) ♦ *No one knows how many stars there are in space.* ♦ *Some scientists believe that space is expanding.* **2.** *n.* outer space; every place past the air surrounding the earth. (No plural form in this sense.) ♦ *The rocket was shot into space.* ♦ *The astronaut viewed the earth from space.* **3.** *n.* a place or area that has length, width, or depth. (No plural form in this sense.) ♦ *There was a space of two feet between Bill and me.* ♦ *My apartment has 800 square feet of space.* **4.** *n.* a place where there is room for someone or something to be. (No plural form in this sense.) ♦ *There's no space in my apartment for that huge grand piano.* ♦ *John ran out of space on his bookshelf, so he piled the extra books on his floor.* **5.** *n.* a blank line or empty box on a piece of paper where something is to be written in. ♦ *Please write your answers in the spaces provided.* ♦ *Write your name in the first space.* **6.** *n.* a length of time; duration. ♦ *Within a space of one year, John visited the doctor six times.* ♦ *Jane's car was stolen in the space of five minutes.* **7.** *n.* an empty place between two words. ♦ *You should put a space between "high" and "school."* ♦ *Do I put a space or a hyphen between these two words?* **8.** *tv.* to place things with spaces between them. ♦ *The teacher spaced the students two feet apart.* ♦ *The lines of the poster were spaced four inches apart.*

spacecraft AND **spaceship** ['spes kræft, 'spes ʃɪp] *n.* a rocket or vehicle that travels in space. (Pl: *spacecraft, spaceships.*) ♦ *The United States and the Soviet Union launched many spacecraft in the 1960s.* ♦ *The astronauts landed the spaceship on the moon.*

space station ['spes ste ʃən] *n.* a laboratory built in space, especially one that orbits around Earth. ♦ *The astronauts worked in the space station orbiting Earth.* ♦ *Many science fiction novels take place on space stations near distant planets.*

spacesuit ['spes sut] *n.* an outfit that is worn by astronauts in outer space. ♦ *The spacesuit allows astronauts to breathe and to communicate with engineers on Earth.* ♦ *Spacesuits protect astronauts from the effects of radiation.*

spacing ['spes ɪŋ] *n.* the spaces between words or lines; the arrangement of spaces between words or lines. (No plural form in this sense.) ♦ *Mary increased the spacing between her words to make her paper more legible.* ♦ *This computer program changes the spacing between lines easily.*

spacious ['spe ʃəs] **1.** *adj.* roomy; having a lot of space; wide open. (Adv: *spaciously.*) ♦ *Mary moved from a cramped studio apartment to a spacious house.* ♦ *Bill's house was built on a spacious lot in the country.* **2.** *adj.* wide; vast; covering a wide area; extensive. (Adv: *spaciously.*) ♦ *This spacious ranch covers 20 square miles.* ♦ *The spacious forest is filled with wild animals.*

spade ['sped] **1.** *n.* a tool, similar to a small shovel, used for digging. ♦ *A spade is a handle with a blade attached at the end that can be pushed into the ground.* ♦ *Mary dug up the potatoes with a spade.* **2.** *n.* the black figure (♠) found on playing cards; one of the four suits found on playing cards. ♦ *In this game, spades rank lower than all of the other suits.* ♦ *John played the king of spades.* **3.** *iv.* to dig or work using a spade. ♦ *Anne spaded around her tomato plants.* ♦ *David spaded in the garden all afternoon.* **4.** *tv.* to dig something with a spade. ♦ *Anne spaded the dirt around her tomato plants.* ♦ *John spaded the weeds from around the strawberry bush.*

spaghetti [spə 'gɛt i] *n.* long, thin, (often dried) sticks made of a flour and water mixture, which are boiled and then eaten as food; long sticks of pasta. (No plural form in this sense.) ♦ *You must boil the spaghetti until it is limp.* ♦ *Anne spooned some tomato sauce over her spaghetti.*

Spain ['spen] See Gazetteer.

span ['spæn] **1.** *n.* the length of a bridge or arch between two supports. ♦ *The longest span of the bridge cracked during the earthquake.* ♦ *The span that made up the arch consisted of one piece of stone.* **2.** *n.* a period of time; a length of time. ♦ *Bill was sick for a two-month span last year.* ♦ *Mary received four anonymous letters over a two-week span.* **3.** *tv.* to stretch over a space or a period of time; to extend across a space or a period of time. ♦ *The bridge spanned the bay.* ♦ *My grandparents' marriage spanned fifty years.*

Spaniard ['spæn jɚd] *n.* a citizen or native of Spain. ♦ *We enjoyed visiting Spain and meeting Spaniards.* ♦ *Not all Spaniards speak the same kind of Spanish.*

spaniel ['spæn jəl] *n.* a breed of dog with long hair and long ears. ♦ *The spaniel yapped loudly when I walked by it.* ♦ *Mary took her spaniel to the veterinarian for shots.*

Spanish ['spæn ɪʃ] **1. the Spanish** *n.* the citizens and natives of Spain. (No plural form in this sense. Treated as plural. See also Spaniard.) ♦ *The Spanish are known for their bullfights.* ♦ *When we were in Spain, we found the Spanish very friendly.* **2.** *n.* the language spoken in Spain and many Central and South American countries. (No plural form in this sense.) ♦ *Spanish is a Romance language.* ♦ *Many Americans speak Spanish quite well.* **3.** *adj.* of or about Spain, ①, or ②. ♦ *I study the Spanish lan-*

guage in school. ♦ *The Spanish people are very interested in the New World.*

spank ['spæŋk] **1.** *tv.* to hit someone with one's open hand or some object, usually across the buttocks, as a form of punishment. ♦ *David spanked Jimmy for telling lies.* ♦ *The principal spanked the rowdy student with a paddle.* **2.** *n.* one slap with one's open hand or a flat object. ♦ *The naughty student was given two spanks with a paddle.* ♦ *Mary gave her daughter a spank for whining at the store.*

spanking ['spæŋ kɪŋ] *n.* a punishment inflicted by hitting someone with one's open hand or a flat object, usually across the buttocks. ♦ *The governor banned spanking in public schools.* ♦ *John threatened his naughty children with a spanking.*

spar ['spɑr] **1.** *iv.* to box; to practice fighting. ♦ *The boxer sparred with his coach before the match.* ♦ *The boys sparred on the playground for fun.* **2.** *n.* a post on ships for supporting ropes and sails. ♦ *Lighting struck the ship's tallest spar.* ♦ *The wind ripped the sail and wrapped it around the spar.*

spare ['spɛr] **1.** *adj.* surplus; extra; free; not needed. ♦ *I keep some spare lumber in the attic.* ♦ *The manufacturer donated spare glasses to charity.* **2.** *adj.* extra; saved in case of emergency; reserved for emergency use; kept for emergency use. ♦ *I keep a spare tire in the trunk of my car.* ♦ *Mary has a spare radio in her basement in case there is a tornado.* **3.** *n.* a fifth tire that is kept in a car in case a tire loses its air. ♦ *My spare is flat also.* ♦ *John changed the flat tire, replacing it with the spare.* **4.** *n.* something that is extra and not immediately needed. ♦ *My pen is broken. Do you have a spare I can use?* ♦ *I often forget to carry my office key, so I keep a spare in my purse.* **5.** *tv.* not to permit someone to undergo punishment or execution. ♦ *The benevolent king spared the prisoner's life.* ♦ *The governor spared the criminal from execution.* **6.** *tv.* to be able to give time, money, or energy. ♦ *Could you spare a dollar?* ♦ *If you can spare a minute, I need to speak with you.* **7. spare someone something** *idiom* to exempt someone from having to listen to or experience something. ♦ *I'll spare you the details and get to the point.* ♦ *Please, spare me the story and tell me what you want.* **8. have something to spare** *idiom* to have more than enough of something. ♦ *Ask John for some firewood. He has firewood to spare.* ♦ *Bob has pencils to spare. Just ask to borrow one.*

spare part ['spɛr 'pɑrt] *n.* an extra part used as a replacement or for repair; a part that is not needed to build something. ♦ *I found spare parts for my old car at the junkyard.* ♦ *The mechanic always kept important spare parts in stock.*

sparerib ['spɛr rɪb] *n.* a rib of pork that has most of the meat removed. ♦ *We ate barbecued spareribs at the picnic.* ♦ *The chef glazed the spareribs with a tasty sauce.*

spare time ['spɛr 'tɑɪm] *n.* free time; leisure time; time that is not spent at work or school. (No plural form in this sense.) ♦ *In my spare time, I like to ride my bicycle or read.* ♦ *Between work and school, Jane had very little spare time.*

sparingly ['spɛr ɪŋ li] *adv.* not wastefully; in very small amounts. ♦ *This detergent is concentrated, so use it sparingly.* ♦ *John used the expensive cologne sparingly.*

spark ['spɑrk] **1.** *n.* a flash of light made by electricity moving in the air between two points. ♦ *There was a spark between the plug and the receptacle.* ♦ *There were sparks of electricity flying everywhere after the wire was cut.* **2.** *n.* a small amount of something; an indication of something. (Figurative on ①.) ♦ *There was a spark of genius in the student's work.* ♦ *I helped the author put a spark of life into his boring story.* **3.** *iv.* to produce ①. ♦ *The lighter sparked but wouldn't stay lit.* ♦ *The flint sparked when I rubbed it against the cement.* **4.** *tv.* to cause something directly; to stimulate something. (Figurative on ③.) ♦ *The professor sparked the students' interest in reading.* ♦ *This movie has sparked my curiosity about World War II.*

sparkle ['spɑr kəl] **1.** *iv.* to shine as though producing sparks or small flashes; to glimmer. ♦ *The cat's eyes sparkled in the moonlight.* ♦ *The sequins on the dancer's dress sparkled under the lights.* **2.** *n.* shine; glitter; a bright flash of light. ♦ *This photograph captures the sparkle in your eye.* ♦ *The diamond had a beautiful sparkle to it.*

sparkling ['spɑr klɪŋ] **1.** *adj.* bright; flashing; giving off sparks. (Adv: *sparklingly.*) ♦ *The sparkling diamond on Anne's finger caught my eye.* ♦ *We gazed at the sparkling stars in the sky.* **2.** *adj.* lively; exciting. (Adv: *sparklingly.*) ♦ *Mary's sparkling wit is evident in her writing.* ♦ *John is always invited to parties because he has a sparkling personality.* **3.** *adj.* of champagne, water, or wine that contains bubbles of carbon dioxide. (Adv: *sparklingly.*) ♦ *John bought some sparkling water for use at home.* ♦ *Champagne is a sparkling drink that is made from the grapes in a certain area of France.*

sparrow ['spɛr o] *n.* a small, brown, common bird. ♦ *The sparrow flew away when it saw the cat approaching.* ♦ *A sparrow has built a nest in a tree outside my window.*

sparse ['spɑrs] *adj.* scattered; not having many people or things in a certain area; not dense; having a very small amount of people or things in an area. (Adv: *sparsely.* Comp: *sparser;* sup: *sparsest.*) ♦ *John always wears a hat because his hair is getting sparse.* ♦ *The population is very sparse in that remote, mountainous area.*

spasm ['spæz əm] **1.** *n.* a sudden, uncontrollable muscle contraction. ♦ *I stopped running because there was a spasm in my leg.* ♦ *John's back spasms forced him to lie down.* **2.** *n.* a sudden, uncontrollable display of emotion or activity. (Figurative on ①.) ♦ *During the panic, there was a spasm of selling at the stock exchange.* ♦ *The audience burst into a spasm of laughter at the joke.*

spastic ['spæs tɪk] *adj.* jerky; having spasms. (Adv: *spastically* [...ɪk li].) ♦ *My tic is caused by a spastic eye muscle.* ♦ *The woman made spastic movements while she was having an epileptic seizure.*

spat ['spæt] **1.** a pt/pp of spit. **2.** *n.* an argument; a quarrel; a disagreement. ♦ *John and Mary had a spat about washing the dishes.* ♦ *The childish spat turned into a real fight.*

spatial ['spe ʃəl] *adj.* of or about space or areas. (Adv: *spatially.*) ♦ *The artist had a good sense of spatial relations in perspective.* ♦ *The spatial arrangement of the furniture was pleasing to the eye.*

spatter ['spæt ɚ] **1.** *iv.* [for a liquid] to fall or splash against a surface in drops. ♦ *The victim's blood had spattered against the wall.* ♦ *Grease spattered from the frying pan.* **2.** *tv.* to scatter drops of a liquid against a surface.

♦ *The artist spattered paint against the canvas.* ♦ *Jimmy spattered mud on my pants when he jumped in the puddle.*

spatula ['spæ tʃu lə] *n.* a cooking tool that is a flat, square panel the size of the palm of the hand, attached to a long handle. ♦ *Tom used a spatula to turn the hamburgers.* ♦ *I have to use a plastic spatula because metal will scratch the special coating on my skillet.*

spawn ['spɔn] **1.** *n.* the eggs of fish, frogs, etc. (No plural form in this sense.) ♦ *The frog's spawn hatched into tadpoles.* ♦ *The spawn of sturgeon is called caviar.* **2.** *iv.* [for fish or frogs] to reproduce by laying hundreds of eggs; to reproduce. ♦ *The frogs spawned in the brook behind my house.* ♦ *Salmons spawn at the site where they themselves were spawned.* **3.** *tv.* [for fish or frogs] to lay hundreds of eggs. ♦ *The frogs spawned hundreds of eggs in the creek.* ♦ *The salmons spawned their eggs further up the river from here.* **4.** *tv.* to produce something; to produce a lot of something. (Figurative on ③.) ♦ *The excellent university spawned many Nobel prize winners.* ♦ *The research spawned further studies.*

speak ['spik] **1.** *tv., irreg.* to say something; to utter something; to express one's thoughts in words. (Pt: spoke; pp: spoken. Does not take a clause.) ♦ *Anne spoke her thoughts aloud.* ♦ *The shy student spoke his words softly.* **2.** *tv., irreg.* to use a language; to know how to talk in a language. ♦ *Mary speaks English, Spanish, and French.* ♦ *The immigrant learned to speak English by taking classes.* **3.** *iv., irreg.* to talk; to say words. ♦ *Mary began to speak when she was two years old.* ♦ *Please be quiet unless you are given permission to speak.* **4. speak to** *iv., irreg. + prep. phr.* to talk to someone or a group; to give a speech to someone. ♦ *The president spoke to the nation in a televised address.* ♦ *A famous scientist spoke to our biology class.* **5.** *iv., irreg.* to express something or communicate by some means other than talking. ♦ *Your actions speak louder than your words.* ♦ *The senator's silence spoke volumes.* **6. speak out on; speak out against** *iv., irreg. + adv. + prep. phr.* to express oneself boldly and negatively on a matter. (See outspoken.) ♦ *The protesters spoke out against the mayor's policies.* ♦ *The laborers spoke out on unfair hiring practices.* **7. speak the same language** *idiom* [for people] to have similar ideas, tastes, etc. ♦ *Jane and Bob get along very well. They really speak the same language about almost everything.* ♦ *Bob and his father didn't speak the same language when it came to politics.*

speaker ['spik ɚ] **1.** *n.* someone who speaks; someone who makes speeches; someone who speaks a particular language. ♦ *The speaker paused to drink a sip of water.* ♦ *My German class is taught by an authentic speaker of German.* **2. Speaker** *n.* the Speaker of the House; the presiding officer in the House of Representatives, the representative of the majority party who has the most seniority. ♦ *The Speaker stood next to the vice president and behind the president during the president's speech.* ♦ *The Speaker was present for every session of Congress.* **3.** *n.* a device that reproduces sound, as found in a stereo, television, computer, etc. ♦ *The stereo's left speaker is making a crackling noise.* ♦ *John balanced the sound between the two speakers.*

speaking ['spik ɪŋ] *n.* talking, especially the art and practice of making speeches. (No plural form in this sense.) ♦ *A politician should have training in public speaking.* ♦ *In debate class, the students learned the art of speaking.*

spear ['spɪr] **1.** *n.* a long stick or rod with a sharp, pointed end, used as a weapon. ♦ *The hunter threw a spear at the wild pig.* ♦ *The local fishermen caught fish in the river with spears.* **2.** *n.* a stalk, especially of asparagus or broccoli. ♦ *The spears of asparagus were covered in a light cheese sauce.* ♦ *David marinated the asparagus spears in soy sauce.* **3.** *tv.* to injure or pierce someone or something with ①. ♦ *The hunter speared the wild pig.* ♦ *The natives speared the fish in the shallow river.*

spearhead ['spɪr hɛd] **1.** *n.* the sharp, pointed end of a spear. ♦ *The hunter plunged the spearhead into the animal's neck.* ♦ *The spearhead had been sharpened against a rock.* **2.** *n.* the first part of an attack or an offense; the leader or the leading edge of an attack. (Figurative on ①.) ♦ *The rebel senator was the spearhead against the new tax increase.* ♦ *The huge rally was the spearhead against the mayor's new policy.* **3.** *tv.* to lead an attack; to take responsibility for an undertaking. ♦ *The president spearheaded the war against drugs.* ♦ *The police spearheaded the battle against crime.*

spearmint ['spɪr mɪnt] **1.** *n.* a mint herb that has a strong, fresh taste, used as a flavoring. (No plural form in this sense.) ♦ *This ice cream is flavored with real spearmint.* ♦ *I bought some gum that was flavored with spearmint.* **2.** *adj.* flavored with ①. ♦ *We each had a spearmint candy after dinner.* ♦ *I prefer a spearmint mouthwash to any other flavor.*

special ['spɛ ʃəl] **1.** *adj.* not ordinary; not regular; set apart from other things, especially for a particular purpose or reason; distinct. (Adv: *specially.*) ♦ *We use the good porcelain dishes only for special occasions.* ♦ *A child's birthday is a special day.* **2.** *n.* something that is set apart from other things, especially for a particular purpose or reason. ♦ *The regular TV program was replaced by a live special.* ♦ *I looked at the restaurant's menu to see what the special of the day was.* **3.** *n.* the offering of something for sale at a special ① price. ♦ *The drugstore has a special on toothpaste.* ♦ *I asked the butcher if there were any specials on meat today.*

specialist ['spɛ ʃə ləst] *n.* someone who is an expert at something; someone who is highly trained for something. ♦ *My doctor recommended that I see a throat specialist.* ♦ *A bomb specialist was called in to deactivate the suspicious device.*

specialize ['spɛ ʃə lɑɪz] *iv.* to focus one's study or training on a particular area within a larger field; to limit one's training to a particular area of study or research. ♦ *The medical student specialized in cancer research.* ♦ *The biology professor specialized in primates.*

specialty ['spɛ ʃəl ti] **1.** *n.* one's special area of business or study. ♦ *The doctor's specialty was infectious diseases.* ♦ *My literature professor's specialty is German literature.* **2.** *n.* a particular product or service for which someone or something is famous or well known. ♦ *Roast lamb is this restaurant's specialty.* ♦ *Making customers happy is our specialty!*

species ['spi ʃiz] *n.* a group of the same kind of plant or animal. (Two plants or animals are members of the same species if they are able to produce fertile offspring. Treated as singular or plural.) ♦ *The botanist classified plants according to their species.* ♦ *The scientist discovered a new species of insect.*

specific [spə 'sɪf ɪk] **1.** *adj.* particular; certain; definite; precise; exact. (Adv: *specifically* [...ɪk li].) ♦ *The witness gave specific facts and figures.* ♦ *David went to the store looking for a specific tie.* **2. specifics** *n.* the details and facts of a matter. (Treated as singular.) ♦ *The newspaper printed the specifics of the new tax law.* ♦ *I will not invest my money in your scheme until you give me the specifics.*

specifically [spɪ 'sɪf ɪk li] *adv.* particularly; certainly; definitely; precisely; exactly. ♦ *The crook was charged with a misdemeanor, specifically, breaking and entering.* ♦ *I specifically told you that I would be home at 6:00, and I am right on time.*

specification [spɛs ə fə 'ke ʃən] *n.* an exact requirement; a precise requirement; an exact direction; one aspect of a plan or a design. ♦ *The client gave the architect the specifications for the office building.* ♦ *The director told the designer the specifications for the set.*

specify ['spɛs ə fɑɪ] *tv.* to mention something in particular; to state something in detail; to mention something by name. ♦ *Specify the items you'd like by placing a check next to them.* ♦ *The contract specified the exact terms of my employment.*

specimen ['spɛs ə mən] **1.** *n.* an example from a group or species of something. ♦ *The florist showed me a fine specimen of a red rose.* ♦ *This tree is a good specimen of an oak tree.* **2.** *n.* a small amount of something, especially a fluid from the body. ♦ *The doctor asked me for a urine specimen.* ♦ *The lab technician examines hundreds of blood specimens each day.*

specious ['spi ʃəs] *adj.* seeming true, right, or reasonable, but actually not. (Adv: *speciously.*) ♦ *Mary proved that her colleague's specious theory was false.* ♦ *The experiment's specious results had, in fact, been miscalculated.*

speck ['spɛk] *n.* a small particle; a very small piece of something; a small spot. ♦ *I removed a speck of dust from my eye.* ♦ *There were a few specks of paint on the floor.*

speckled ['spɛk əld] *adj.* marked with small dots or flecks of color. ♦ *A speckled hen chased the duck.* ♦ *The speckled banana was very ripe.*

spectacle ['spɛk tə kəl] **1.** *n.* something to be viewed; something to be seen; a display; a scene. ♦ *The sunset over the ocean was a beautiful spectacle of nature.* ♦ *The arguing couple was quite a spectacle.* **2. spectacles** *n.* eyeglasses. (Old fashioned. Treated as plural.) ♦ *Grandma keeps her spectacles next to the bed when she sleeps.* ♦ *Grandpa can't see a thing without his spectacles.*

spectacular [spɛk 'tæk jə lɚ] *adj.* phenomenal; incredibly great or grand; awesome; attracting a lot of attention. (Adv: *spectacularly.*) ♦ *We saw a spectacular sunrise while we were camping.* ♦ *The spectacular pianist received five minutes of applause.*

spectator ['spɛk te tɚ] *n.* someone who watches something but does not take part in it. ♦ *The bleachers at the game were filled with spectators.* ♦ *I was merely a spectator to John and Mary's argument.*

specter ['spɛk tɚ] **1.** *n.* a ghost; a phantom. ♦ *The princess saw an eerie specter in the corridor.* ♦ *The psychic claimed to see the specter of my dead parents.* **2.** *n.* something that causes fear or dread. (Figurative on ①.) ♦ *John was haunted by the specter of his past sins.* ♦ *The specter of a lawsuit convinced me to settle out of court.*

spectrum ['spɛk trəm] **1.** *n.* the range of visible light, arranged in bands of colored light, formed when a beam of light is passed through a prism. ♦ *Raindrops or mist act as a prism through which the spectrum is seen as a rainbow.* ♦ *The computer monitor could display every color of the spectrum.* **2.** *n.* a range; a scope; a scale; a distribution. (Figurative on ①.) ♦ *At the trial, Anne felt the entire spectrum of emotion, from anger to joy.* ♦ *Mary's spectrum of scientific knowledge ranged from anatomy to zoology.*

speculate ['spɛk jə let] **1.** *iv.* to think about something, especially without knowing all the facts of the matter; to consider; to conjecture; to reflect on something. ♦ *The scientist speculated on the applications of the new medicine.* ♦ *The police would not speculate on a motive for the murder.* **2. speculate in** *iv.* + *prep. phr.* to invest in something without knowing whether it will bring profit; to invest in a risky business venture. ♦ *The banker speculated in mutual funds.* ♦ *The investor speculated in companies formed by young geniuses.* **3.** *tv.* to take or formulate a position on something by guessing or estimating. (Takes a clause.) ♦ *The expert speculated that the inflation rate would remain low.* ♦ *The president speculated that he would be reelected.*

speculation [spɛk jə 'le ʃən] **1.** *n.* conjecture; speculating; consideration of something, especially without knowing all of the facts. (No plural form in this sense.) ♦ *There was much speculation as to the outcome of the trial.* ♦ *Speculation is no substitute for facts.* **2.** *n.* an instance of ①. ♦ *The investigators provided only a few speculations about the cause of the accident.* ♦ *Your speculations ignore all the facts.* **3.** *n.* an investment in a risky business venture. ♦ *The investor's speculation was quite profitable.* ♦ *The banker lost thousands of dollars in risky speculations.*

speculative ['spɛk jə lə tɪv] **1.** *adj.* based on speculation; conjectured. (Adv: *speculatively.*) ♦ *The police inspectors were following a few speculative leads.* ♦ *A few speculative conclusions were drawn from the experiment's early results.* **2.** *adj.* [of investments] risky. (Adv: *speculatively.*) ♦ *John lost all of his savings in a speculative venture.* ♦ *Mary's speculative investments could make her either very rich or very poor.*

speculator ['spɛk jə le tɚ] *n.* someone who speculates, especially in investment. ♦ *The speculator suggested which stock I should buy.* ♦ *A speculator bought farmland near the highway junction.*

sped ['spɛd] pt/pp of speed.

speech ['spitʃ] **1.** *n.* the production of words by talking. (No plural form in this sense.) ♦ *In phonetics, one examines the components of speech.* ♦ *Dogs have no ability for creating speech.* **2.** *n.* a lecture; a formal talk to a group of listeners. ♦ *A famous athlete gave our class a speech about the dangers of drugs.* ♦ *The politician's speech was held in a large assembly hall.*

speechless ['spitʃ ləs] *adj.* unable to speak for a moment, especially because of surprise, shock, or other emotion. (Adv: *speechlessly.*) ♦ *The clerk's rudeness surprised me so much that I was speechless.* ♦ *When Anne won the lottery, she was speechless.*

speed ['spid] **1.** *iv., irreg.* to move fast; to go fast, especially to go faster than the legal limit. (Pt/pp: **sped.**) ♦ *Bill was speeding because he was late for work.* ♦ *The police gave tickets to the motorists who sped.* **2.** *tv., irreg.* to cause something to go or move fast; to cause something to go or move faster. ♦ *Mary sped her children out the door because they were late for school.* ♦ *Susan sped her car down the freeway because she was late for work.* **3.** *n.* the rate at which someone or something moves or does something during a period of time. ♦ *The car was traveling at a speed of 40 miles an hour.* ♦ *David's typing speed is sixty words per minute.* **4.** *n.* rapid movement; the quickness with which someone or something moves. (No plural form in this sense.) ♦ *The car was moving at great speed when it crashed.* ♦ *Susan needed a secretary who could type with speed and accuracy.*

speedboat ['spid bot] *n.* a small boat that has a powerful engine that can be driven at high speeds, especially for pleasure on lakes and rivers. ♦ *The man on water skis was being pulled by a powerful speedboat.* ♦ *The waves in the speedboat's wake were large.*

speedily ['spid ɪ li] *adv.* quickly; swiftly; rapidly; in a hurry. ♦ *Bill ran speedily toward the phone when it rang.* ♦ *John did his homework speedily so he could watch television.*

speeding ['spid ɪŋ] **1.** *n.* driving a car faster than the speed limit. (No plural form in this sense.) ♦ *John was stopped for speeding on the highway.* ♦ *The cop gave Mary a ticket for speeding.* **2.** *adj.* moving rapidly; traveling rapidly; moving at a high rate of speed. ♦ *The speeding bullets pounded into the target.* ♦ *The speeding car almost ran off the road.*

speed limit ['spid lɪm ɪt] *n.* the legal maximum speed that a vehicle is permitted to travel; the fastest speed that a driver can operate a vehicle under the law on a particular road. ♦ *The speed limit on this freeway is 65 miles per hour.* ♦ *Often, the speed limit is lower at night than during the day.*

speedometer [spɪ 'dɑm ɪ tɚ] *n.* a gauge on the control panel of a vehicle that indicates how fast the vehicle is moving. ♦ *According to the speedometer, I was 10 miles an hour above the speed limit.* ♦ *The speedometer showed the rate of speed in both miles and kilometers per hour.*

speedway ['spid we] *n.* a track for racing cars or other vehicles. ♦ *The racecars raced around the speedway.* ♦ *The accident at the speedway injured three drivers badly.*

speedy ['spid i] *adj.* rapid; swift; fast; above the speed limit; moving or passing quickly. (Adv: *speedily.* Comp: *speedier;* sup: *speediest.*) ♦ *A speedy express train zipped through the train crossings.* ♦ *The speedy messenger delivered the letter across town in 15 minutes.*

spell ['spɛl] **1.** *tv.* to say or write the letters of a word in the right order. (Pt/pp: *spelled,* or less frequently, spelt.) ♦ *The student spelled each word in his paper correctly.* ♦ *The teacher spelled the vocabulary words on the chalkboard.* **2.** *tv.* [for letters] to signify a word. ♦ W-o-r-d *spells* word. ♦ C-a-t *spells* cat. **3.** *tv.* to mean something. (Figurative on ②.) ♦ *Those dark clouds spell rain.* ♦ *Those mean dogs spell trouble.* **4.** *iv.* to know how to say or write the letters of many words; to be able to spell ① words. ♦ *You can use a dictionary to help you spell.* ♦ *The grammar school teacher taught children how to spell.* **5.** *n.* a set of words that are said because they are thought to have magical power; magic words. ♦ *The evil wizard put a spell on the handsome prince.* ♦ *The fairy's spell turned the pumpkin into a fancy carriage.* **6.** *n.* a period of time. ♦ *We had a long spell of hot weather last July.* ♦ *Uncle Bill stopped by our house for a spell.*

spellbinding ['spɛl bɑɪn dɪŋ] *adj.* enchanting; so interesting that one cannot leave or move; holding one's attention, especially as though one could not move because of a magic spell. (Adv: *spellbindingly.*) ♦ *The audience was absolutely quiet during the spellbinding movie.* ♦ *The spellbinding lecture seemed much shorter than it was.*

spellbound ['spɛl bɑʊnd] *adj.* fascinated; enchanted; having one's attention held as though one could not move because of a magic spell. ♦ *The spellbound students listened carefully to the teacher's story.* ♦ *The spellbound scientists gaped at Anne's new invention.*

spelt ['spɛlt] a pt/pp of spell.

spelunker [spɪ 'lʌŋ kɚ] *n.* someone who explores caves. ♦ *A group of bats flew by the spelunkers.* ♦ *The spelunkers were joined by a safety rope inside the cave.*

spend ['spɛnd] **1.** *tv., irreg.* to pay an amount of money for something that one buys. (Pt/pp: spent.) ♦ *Mary spent her entire paycheck on a new computer.* ♦ *Bill was willing to spend up to $100 for a new watch.* **2.** *tv., irreg.* to pass time; to use time or energy; to consume energy. ♦ *John spent four hours watching television last night.* ♦ *Mary spends a lot of time helping others with their work.*

spendthrift ['spɛnd θrɪft] *n.* someone who wastes money; someone who spends too much money. ♦ *The spendthrift owned a hundred pairs of shoes.* ♦ *The spendthrift's children were spoiled.*

spent ['spɛnt] **1.** pt/pp of spend. **2.** *adj.* used up; consumed; tired; exhausted. ♦ *After working for 12 hours, Mary felt completely spent.* ♦ *Mary bought more hair spray because her old can was spent.*

sperm ['spɚm] **1.** *n., irreg.* a male sex cell; a cell made by a male sex gland. (If it fertilizes a female sex cell—an egg or ovum—the two combine to form an embryo. Pl: *sperm* or *sperms.*) ♦ *Millions of sperm are released at one time.* ♦ *Many kinds of contraception prevent the sperms from reaching the egg.* **2.** *n.* a mass of the whitish fluid that contains ①; semen. (No plural form in this sense.) ♦ *The breeder bought frozen bull sperm from a ranch in Wyoming.* ♦ *The frozen sperm could still cause conception.*

spew ['spju] **1.** *iv.* to flow out with force. ♦ *Water spewed from the leaky pipe.* ♦ *Evil words spewed from his mouth.* **2.** *tv.* to force something out with power. ♦ *The bigot spewed hateful words.* ♦ *The baby spewed mashed vegetables all over the table.*

sphere ['sfir] **1.** *n.* a perfectly round object; a globe; a ball. ♦ *The sphere rolled across the floor.* ♦ *Each bead of the necklace was a sphere of colored glass.* **2.** *n.* the area or domain where someone or something has an influence or an effect; the place or environment in which someone or something exists or acts. ♦ *The politician's sphere of influence extended across the east coast.* ♦ *The researcher's work was well-known in scientific spheres.*

spherical ['sfɛr ɪ kəl] *adj.* shaped like a sphere. (Adv: *spherically* [...ɪk li].) ♦ *Spherical beads fell to the floor when Anne's necklace broke.* ♦ *The oranges were perfectly spherical and brilliantly colored.*

Sphinx ['sfɪŋks] **1.** *n.* a huge statue in Egypt of the head of a man attached to the body of a lion. ♦ *The nose of the*

Sphinx fell off a long time ago. ♦ *The tourists in Egypt wanted to visit the pyramids and the famous Sphinx.* **2.** *n.* a monster in Greek mythology that had the head of a woman, the wings of a bird, and the body of a lion. (She asked everyone who passed by her a riddle, and would kill the people who could not answer it.) ♦ *The man who solved the riddle angered the Sphinx.* ♦ *In mythology class, our teacher lectured about the Sphinx.*

spice ['spɑɪs] **1.** *n.* an herb or other vegetable seed or fiber that tastes or smells strong, used to give extra flavor to food. ♦ *The cook added some spices to the soup.* ♦ *Mary grew some spices in pots on her window sill.* **2.** *n.* something that adds excitement or flavor. (Figurative on ①. No plural form in this sense.) ♦ *Variety is the spice of life.* ♦ *The funny actor added some spice to the otherwise boring movie.* **3.** *tv.* to season or flavor food with ①. ♦ *I used oregano and basil to spice the sauce.* ♦ *The cook spiced the stew with curry powder.* **4. spice up** *tv.* + *adv.* to make something more exciting or interesting by adding something to it. (Figurative on ③.) ♦ *The lecturer spiced up her speech with funny jokes.* ♦ *The network spiced up the TV show by adding new characters.*

spiced ['spɑɪst] *adj.* seasoned; flavored; having had spice added. ♦ *The highly spiced soup was very flavorful.* ♦ *John gave each guest a slice of spiced ham.*

spicy ['spɑɪs i] **1.** *adj.* flavored with spices; seasoned with spices; having a sharp or pungent flavor. (Adv: *spicily.* Comp: *spicier;* sup: *spiciest.*) ♦ *The spicy food burned my mouth.* ♦ *Mary put some spicy salsa on her taco.* **2.** *adj.* risqué; somewhat vulgar. (Adv: *spicily.* Comp: *spicier;* sup: *spiciest.*) ♦ *Susan blushed when I told her the spicy joke.* ♦ *The spicy performance embarrassed the audience.*

spider ['spɑɪ dɚ] *n.* a small creature with eight legs whose body produces a silk thread that it uses to make a web, which is then used to trap insects, which it eats. ♦ *A spider had spun its web in the corner of the kitchen.* ♦ *Several mosquitoes were trapped in a spider's web.*

spiffy ['spɪf i] *adj.* very neat; well dressed; neat in appearance; well groomed. (Adv: *spiffily.* Comp: *spiffier;* sup: *spiffiest.*) ♦ *Bill looked spiffy at the dinner party.* ♦ *The real-estate agent showed a spiffy house to the young couple.*

spigot ['spɪg ət] *n.* a faucet that controls the flow of water into a sink; a valve that controls the flow of liquid from a pipe or a container. ♦ *Robert turned off the spigot when the sink was full of water.* ♦ *Don't drink directly from the spigot!*

spike ['spɑɪk] **1.** *n.* a large, thick, metal nail that comes to a sharp point. ♦ *Railroad ties are fixed in place with large spikes.* ♦ *The robber threatened to stab me with a sharp spike.* **2.** *n.* a cleat; a pointed metal or plastic object on the bottom of a shoe that gives the wearer extra traction. ♦ *The runner's spikes provided a great deal of traction.* ♦ *The spikes on the golfer's shoes clicked against the cement.* **3.** *n.* a sharp peak on a graph. ♦ *This spike shows the company's best week in sales.* ♦ *After the war, there was a sharp spike in the birthrate.* **4.** *tv.* to fasten something with ①. ♦ *The workers spiked the railroad ties together.* ♦ *John spiked the sign to the tree trunk.* **5.** *tv.* to add alcohol to a nonalcoholic drink. (Slang.) ♦ *The host spiked the punch with vodka.* ♦ *Everyone got drunk because someone had spiked the lemonade.*

spill ['spɪl] **1.** *tv.* to cause something, especially a liquid, to pour from a container by accident; to cause something, especially a liquid, to fall. ♦ *Anne spilled some coffee onto her shirt.* ♦ *John spilled a glass of milk during dinner.* **2.** *iv.* [for something, especially a liquid] to fall or be poured from a container by accident. ♦ *The milk spilled when I knocked the glass over.* ♦ *Oil spilled from the leaking pipe.* **3.** *n.* something, especially a liquid, that has fallen or poured from a container by accident. ♦ *Mary cleaned up the spill with a sponge.* ♦ *The coffee spill stained my shirt.* **4.** *n.* a fall from something. ♦ *John fell off his horse and took a nasty spill.* ♦ *The bicyclist was injured in a bad spill.*

spillway ['spɪl we] *n.* a channel that carries extra water away from a dam or a river. ♦ *Trespassing on the spillway is forbidden!* ♦ *The spillway emptied into a nearby stream.*

spin ['spɪn] **1.** *iv., irreg.* to turn around in circles quickly. (Pt/pp: spun. *Spinned* is often heard.) ♦ *The silly children became dizzy when they spun around repeatedly.* ♦ *The windmill spun when the wind blew.* **2.** *iv., irreg.* to rotate on an axis. ♦ *The earth spins around its axis once each day.* ♦ *The tire spun around its axle.* **3.** *iv., irreg.* [for one's surroundings] to seem to revolve. ♦ *Bill sat down when his head began to spin.* ♦ *The injured man thought the room was spinning.* **4.** *iv., irreg.* to pull and twist, making thread or yarn from wool, cotton, or other fibers. ♦ *Mary was spinning when her fingers started to feel cramped.* ♦ *She watched the children in the yard as she spun.* **5.** *tv., irreg.* to cause someone or something to turn around in circles quickly. ♦ *The player spun the basketball on his fingertip.* ♦ *The amusement park ride spun the riders faster and faster.* **6.** *tv., irreg.* to pull and twist fibers into thread or yarn. ♦ *John spun the wool into yarn.* ♦ *At the factory, cotton was spun into thread.* **7.** *tv., irreg.* [for a spider] to make a web. ♦ *The spider spun a web in the doorway.* ♦ *A tiny spider worked all night to spin that web!* **8.** *tv.* to create a tale, story, or lie. ♦ *The main suspect had spun lies to protect himself.* ♦ *Mary loved to spin tales for her children.* **9.** *n.* a short trip in or on a vehicle. ♦ *Would you like to take my new car for a spin?* ♦ *Bill took a spin on his new motorcycle.* **10.** *n.* the rotating motion of a ball or object when it is hit in a certain way. (No plural form in this sense.) ♦ *The spin of the pool ball sent it into the corner pocket.* ♦ *The baseball's spin caused it to curve away from the batter.* **11. put a spin on something** *idiom* to twist a report or story to one's advantage; to interpret an event to make it seem favorable or beneficial to oneself. ♦ *The mayor tried to put a positive spin on the damaging polls.* ♦ *The pundit's spin on the new legislation was highly critical.*

spinach ['spɪn ɪtʃ] **1.** *n.* a leafy, green vegetable. (No plural form in this sense.) ♦ *Spinach is very rich in iron and vitamin A.* ♦ *The dieter ate a plate of cooked spinach for lunch.* **2.** *adj.* made of or with ①. ♦ *Anne usually orders a spinach salad for lunch.* ♦ *I really don't care for spinach pizza.*

spinal ['spɑɪn əl] *adj.* of or about the spine. (Adv: *spinally.*) ♦ *Jane hoped that spinal surgery would relieve her back pain.* ♦ *Tom's spinal damage came from an accident.*

spinal cord ['spɑɪn əl kord] *n.* the bundle of nerves running through the spine. ♦ *The paraplegic's spinal cord had been severed in an accident.* ♦ *Bob's back pain was caused by pressure on his spinal cord.*

spindle [ˈspɪn dl] **1.** *n.* a rod or stick that rotates. ♦ *The machinist oiled the spindle so it would turn smoothly.* ♦ *Bob wound the yarn on a wooden spindle.* **2.** *tv.* to impale a piece of paper or a card onto a sharp spike. ♦ *The warning read, "Do not fold, spindle, or mutilate."* ♦ *The computer could not read punch cards that had been spindled.*

spine [ˈspɑɪn] **1.** *n.* the column of bones and the nerves within that are at the center of the back of humans and other animals. ♦ *Mary's legs were paralyzed when her spine was injured.* ♦ *The doctor examined each vertebra in John's spine.* **2.** *n.* any long, narrow, stiff thing that provides support, such as the side of a cover of a book where the pages are attached. (Figurative on ①.) ♦ *Angrily, Bill pulled the pages of the book from its spine.* ♦ *The spine of the book is held together with glue.* **3.** *n.* a stiff, pointed growth as found on certain plants and animals, providing protection against predators. (See **porcupine**.) ♦ *As I approached the porcupine, it raised its sharp spines.* ♦ *The hedgehog has spines on its back.*

spineless [ˈspɑɪn ləs] **1.** *adj.* without a spine; not having a spine; invertebrate. (Adv: *spinelessly.*) ♦ *The biologist examined spineless creatures in the laboratory.* ♦ *All insects are spineless.* **2.** *adj.* lacking courage; easily scared or frightened. (Figurative on ①. Adv: *spinelessly.*) ♦ *The spineless coward ran away from the fight.* ♦ *The spineless mayor was afraid to speak against the mob.*

spinning [ˈspɪn ɪŋ] *adj.* moving in circles rapidly; revolving. ♦ *The spinning top amused the child.* ♦ *The machine is filled with spinning gears and oily rods.*

spin-off [ˈspɪn ɔf] *n.* something that is derived from something else. ♦ *The popular sitcom spawned three spin-offs.* ♦ *Many innovations are spin-offs from military research.*

spinster [ˈspɪn stɚ] *n.* a woman—usually older—who has not married. (Now usually considered derogatory.) ♦ *The spinster paid a neighborhood boy to mow her lawn.* ♦ *The happy and contented single woman resented being called a spinster.*

spiny [ˈspɑɪ ni] **1.** *n.* having spines. ♦ *The hedgehog has a spiny coat.* ♦ *The porcupine is a very spiny creature.* **2.** *n.* having the shape of a spine. ♦ *Spiny leaves protected the small plant from creatures that might eat it.* ♦ *This fish has spiny fins that can stick you.*

spiral [ˈspɑɪ rəl] **1.** *n.* a curve that winds upward or downward around a center line while becoming wider or narrower; a coil. ♦ *Anne curled her hair into bouncy spirals.* ♦ *The caterer cut the radishes into decorative spirals.* **2.** *adj.* <the adj. use of ①.> ♦ *A spiral staircase takes up less space than a regular one.* ♦ *The tiny spiral spring in my watch snapped.* **3.** *iv.* to seem to follow the shape of ①. ♦ *A lovely climbing rose spiraled up the post.* ♦ *The staircase spiraled downward from the top floor.* **4.** *iv.* [for a measurement] to move upward or downward in a fast and uncontrolled manner. (Figurative on ③.) ♦ *The employment rate spiraled downward during the recession.* ♦ *Inflation spiraled upward at a frightening rate.*

spire [ˈspɑɪr] *n.* the top part of a steeple; the top part of a structure on top of a building that comes to a point. ♦ *The tower of city hall has a tall spire.* ♦ *The chapel's spire could be seen from three miles away.*

spirit [ˈspɪr ɪt] **1.** *n.* the part of a human that is separate from the body (and that some religions contend never dies); the part of the body that controls emotion and intellect; the soul. ♦ *Buddhists believe their spirits are reborn over and over.* ♦ *Christians believe their spirits will go to heaven or hell.* **2.** *n.* a supernatural being that does not have a body. ♦ *The castle was haunted by an evil spirit.* ♦ *Mysterious spirits seemed to haunt the old house.* **3.** *n.* the driving force of something; something that provides enthusiasm, energy, or force to something; zeal. (Figurative on ①. No plural form in this sense.) ♦ *The office manager was the spirit behind the new project.* ♦ *Mary exemplifies the true spirit of our team.* **4.** *n.* the meaning of something; the intent of something; the real meaning of something, instead of what is actually said or written. (No plural form in this sense.) ♦ *The court determined that the judge's ruling was within the spirit of the law.* ♦ *The students got into the spirit of the holiday season by decorating the classroom.* **5.** *n.* attitude; the character of a person or a group of people or an organization. (Singular or plural with the same meaning.) ♦ *Company spirits were low because of all the firings.* ♦ *School spirit was high because of the winning football team.* **6. spirits** *n.* a distilled alcoholic liquor. ♦ *People younger than 21 aren't allowed to buy spirits in most states.* ♦ *The owner was fined for selling spirits to minors.* **7. spirit away** *tv.* + *adv.* to carry someone or something away secretly or mysteriously. ♦ *The kidnappers spirited the young prince away.* ♦ *The treasure had been spirited away by the pirates.*

spirited [ˈspɪr ɪ tɪd] *adj.* excited; enthusiastic; vigorous; energetic; lively. (Adv: *spiritedly.*) ♦ *I listened to the politicians' spirited debate.* ♦ *The popular singer received a spirited response from the audience.*

spiritual [ˈspɪr ɪ tʃu əl] **1.** *adj.* of or about a relationship with the deity and other religious matters. (Adv: *spiritually.*) ♦ *Anne asked her minister for spiritual guidance.* ♦ *Jane thought it was rude to argue over her spiritual beliefs.* **2.** *n.* a folk religious song, especially one associated with early Protestant denominations in the U.S. ♦ *This spiritual about hope was written by a slave in 1856.* ♦ *The large choir sang spirituals during the service.*

spit [ˈspɪt] **1.** *iv., irreg.* to expel saliva from one's mouth; to push saliva out of one's mouth. (Pt/pp: **spit** or **spat**.) ♦ *Bill sometimes spits on the ground.* ♦ *The soldier spat at his enemy.* **2. spit up** *iv., irreg.* + *adv.* to throw up; to vomit. ♦ *The baby belched and then spit up.* ♦ *Oh, I feel like I'm going to spit up!* **3.** *tv., irreg.* to expel something from one's mouth; to push something out of one's mouth. ♦ *David spit his gum into a trash can.* ♦ *John quickly spit the sour milk onto the floor.* **4. spit up** *tv., irreg.* + *adv.* to throw up something; to vomit something. ♦ *The baby spit up all the milk it drank.* ♦ *I think I'm going to spit up my dinner!* **5.** *n.* saliva or mucus that comes from someone's mouth. (No plural form in this sense.) ♦ *Wipe the spit off your chin.* ♦ *Spit drooled from the baby's mouth.* **6.** *n.* a small area of land or beach that extends into a body of water. ♦ *Anne walked to the end of the spit and watched the sun set.* ♦ *We often fished about a hundred yards from the end of the sand spit.* **7.** *n.* a thin rod with a sharp end that food is pushed onto so that it can be roasted over a fire. ♦ *The pig on the spit roasted over the fire.* ♦ *We turned the spit over the fire to roast the meat evenly.*

spite [ˈspɑɪt] **1.** *n.* a desire to annoy someone else or get revenge; malice. (No plural form in this sense.) ♦ *John revealed a lot of spite in the way he talked to Bill.* ♦ *David's* *repeated acts of spite towards Anne frightened her.* **2. in spite of someone or something** *idiom* without regard to someone or something; even though another course had been prescribed; ignoring a warning. ♦ *In spite of her orders to stay, I left.* ♦ *In spite of the bad weather, I had fun on vacation.* **3. out of spite** *idiom* with the desire to harm someone or something. ♦ *Jane told some evil gossip about Bill out of spite.* ♦ *That was not an accident! You did it out of spite.*

spiteful ['spɑɪt fəl] *adj.* full of spite; wanting to annoy someone else or get revenge. (Adv: *spitefully.*) ♦ *The spiteful girl told lies about her teachers.* ♦ *Susie patiently tried to ignore the spiteful boy in class.*

splash ['splæʃ] **1.** *iv.* [for liquid] to scatter in many drops; [for liquid] to fall and spread in waves. ♦ *Water splashed from the sink as I washed the dishes.* ♦ *Gasoline splashed from my car's tank when I overfilled it.* **2.** *tv.* to cause a liquid to scatter in many drops or waves. ♦ *Jimmy splashed mud on me by jumping in the puddle.* ♦ *The speeding car splashed water on the people waiting for the bus.* **3. splash with** *tv.* + *prep. phr.* to cause someone or something to be covered with a liquid substance. ♦ *The car splashed me with mud.* ♦ *Bill splashed the wall with paint.* **4.** *n.* an instance of a liquid splashing, as in ①. ♦ *The waves sent splashes of water onto the beach.* ♦ *The truck drove through the mud and made a huge messy splash.* **5.** *n.* the sound of a splash ④. ♦ *The splash of the surf against the beach was quite loud.* ♦ *I heard the splashes of the children playing in the pool.* **6.** *n.* a mark or pool of liquid made by a splash ④; a puddle. ♦ *I cleaned up the splash of water on the floor.* ♦ *There were splashes of blood all over the ground at the crash site.*

splatter ['splæt ɚ] **1.** *iv.* to splash, especially in a careless, clumsy, or messy way. ♦ *When the pig was slaughtered, blood splattered everywhere.* ♦ *Mud had splattered all over Susan's clothes.* **2.** *tv.* to splash a liquid, especially in a careless, clumsy, or messy way. ♦ *Bill splattered water all over the floor while washing dishes.* ♦ *Dave splattered gas onto the car while filling his tank.*

spleen ['splin] **1.** *n.* an organ in the body, near the stomach, that filters the blood and destroys old, used blood cells. ♦ *The bullet hit John in the stomach and ruptured his spleen.* ♦ *The patient with a diseased spleen needed daily blood transfusions.* **2. vent one's spleen on someone or something** *idiom* to get rid of one's feelings of anger by attacking someone or something. ♦ *Bob vented his spleen on his wife by shouting at her.* ♦ *Tom vented his spleen on the car by kicking it.*

splendid ['splɛn dɪd] *adj.* excellent; very good; brilliant; wonderful; super; marvelous. (Adv: *splendidly.*) ♦ *Thank you for cooking a most splendid meal tonight!* ♦ *Our accommodations at the luxurious hotel were splendid.*

splendor ['splɛn dɚ] *n.* incredible beauty; glory; a magnificent display of wealth or beauty. (Sometimes plural with the same meaning.) ♦ *The tourists stood in awe of the Grand Canyon's splendor.* ♦ *The photographer took pictures of the bride in all her splendor.*

splice ['splɑɪs] **1.** *tv.* to fasten the ends of two pieces of something together by weaving, taping, or otherwise connecting them. ♦ *The electrician spliced the two wires together.* ♦ *The sailor spliced the lines together.* **2.** *n.* a joint or connection that has been made by weaving, taping, or otherwise connecting the ends of two pieces of something. ♦ *The electrician sealed the splice with electrical tape.* ♦ *The rope snapped because the splice was improperly tied.*

splint ['splɪnt] *n.* a flat object that is secured to a person's digit or limb in order to give support or keep a broken bone in place. ♦ *The doctor bandaged the splint to my broken finger.* ♦ *I couldn't wear a shoe over the splint on my broken toe.*

splinter ['splɪn tɚ] **1.** *n.* a sliver; a thin, sharp broken-off piece of wood, glass, or some other material. ♦ *I got a splinter in my finger from that rough piece of wood.* ♦ *Be careful! There are splinters of glass all over the floor.* **2.** *adj.* [of a group of people] separated from a larger group of people. ♦ *The splinter denomination held services in a member's garage.* ♦ *The splinter army fought against the king's soldiers.* **3.** *iv.* to separate from a larger object or group; to break into smaller pieces or groups. ♦ *The wood splintered into slivers after I hammered it.* ♦ *The rebel forces splintered into three armed factions.* **4.** *tv.* to break something into ①. ♦ *David splintered the firewood into kindling.* ♦ *One blow of the hammer splintered the brittle plastic.*

split ['splɪt] **1.** *tv., irreg.* to separate something into sections, layers, or groups; to divide something into sections, layers, or groups. (Pt/pp: *split.*) ♦ *The teacher split the class because it was too big.* ♦ *The dealer split the cards into two piles.* **2.** *tv., irreg.* to cut something lengthwise. ♦ *John split the orange with a knife.* ♦ *Mary split the log with an axe.* **3.** *tv., irreg.* to share something among members of a group; to divide something among members of a group. ♦ *The coworkers split the credit for the project.* ♦ *The students split the pizza among themselves.* **4.** *iv., irreg.* [for people or things] to separate into sections, layers, or groups. ♦ *The old tree split during the storm.* ♦ *Czechoslovakia split into two republics on January 1, 1993.* **5.** *iv., irreg.* to break or tear open, lengthwise. ♦ *The skin between my first two toes split painfully.* ♦ *The ground split in two during the earthquake.* **6. split (up)** *iv., irreg.* (+ *adv.*) [for a couple who are married or dating] to separate. ♦ *After 20 years of marriage, John and Anne split up.* ♦ *Since you and John have split, would you like to date me?* **7.** *n.* the cut or break made by splitting something, as in ②. ♦ *Mary put an iron wedge into the split in the log.* ♦ *I avoided walking near the split in the ice.* **8.** *n.* a separation within a group. ♦ *After the split, the two factions fought each other.* ♦ *The controversial minister's policies caused the split.* **9.** *adj.* separated; divided; cut from end to end. ♦ *Mary loaded the split firewood into the pickup truck.* ♦ *The electrician repaired the split wire.* **10. split the difference** *idiom* to divide the difference (with someone else). ♦ *You want to sell for $120, and I want to buy for $100. Let's split the difference and close the deal at $110.* ♦ *I don't want to split the difference. I want $120.*

splitting ['splɪt ɪŋ] **splitting headache** *n.* a very painful headache. ♦ *I took some aspirin for my splitting headache.* ♦ *I am suffering from a terrible splitting headache.*

splurge ['splɚdʒ] **1.** *tv.* to spend an amount of money on something extravagant. ♦ *Tom splurged $300 on a new chair.* ♦ *Mary is planning to splurge a fabulous sum on her computer.* **2.** *iv.* to spend a lot of money on something that is not necessary. ♦ *Mary splurged and bought herself a new sofa.* ♦ *Bill splurged and went on a vacation in*

Europe. **3. on a splurge** *phr.* an instance of extravagant spending. ♦ *Bob went on a splurge and bought a new car.* ♦ *Susan has been on another spending splurge! Look at that new furniture.*

spoil ['spɔɪl] **1.** *iv.* to become rotten; to rot; to decay. ♦ *The meat spoiled because someone didn't refrigerate it.* ♦ *When milk spoils, it smells very bad.* **2.** *tv.* to ruin something; to destroy something; to make something unusable. ♦ *Dave spoiled the book for me by telling me the ending.* ♦ *The warm temperatures helped spoil the meat before we could cook it.* **3.** *tv.* to pamper someone too well; to treat someone too leniently; to raise a child without discipline. ♦ *Mary spoiled her children with expensive toys.* ♦ *John's children are rude because he spoils them terribly.*

spoiled ['spɔɪld] **1.** *adj.* decayed; ruined; rotten; made unusable. ♦ *Mary threw the spoiled meat in the garbage.* ♦ *The spoiled eggs smelled terrible.* **2.** *adj.* pampered; not disciplined. ♦ *The spoiled children always got what they wanted.* ♦ *The spoiled kitten was fed real cream instead of milk.*

spoils ['spɔɪlz] *n.* loot; booty; plunder; things taken by an enemy during war. (Treated as plural.) ♦ *To the victor goes the spoils.* ♦ *The soldiers sold their spoils to collectors when they returned.*

spoilsport ['spɔɪl sport] *n.* someone who doesn't let other people have fun. ♦ *Some spoilsport called the police because our party was loud.* ♦ *The spoilsports sulked in the corner at the company party.*

spoke ['spok] **1.** pt of speak. **2.** *n.* one of the rods that are attached between the hub and the outer ring of a wheel. ♦ *The hubcaps covered the spokes of the car's wheels.* ♦ *Mary put reflectors in the spokes of her bike wheels.*

spoken ['spok ən] **1.** pp of speak. **2.** *adj.* oral; expressed by speaking; uttered; said. ♦ *The brilliant actor was a master of the spoken word.* ♦ *The teacher gave the naughty student a spoken warning.*

spokesman ['spoks mən] *n., irreg.* someone who officially speaks on behalf of other people. (Pl: spokesmen.) ♦ *Bill, as spokesman for his band, talked to the media after the concert.* ♦ *John was appointed spokesman for the mayor's office.*

spokesmen ['spoks mən] pl of spokesman.

spokesperson ['spoks pɚ sən] *n.* someone who officially speaks on behalf of other people. ♦ *The company spokesperson refused to comment on the accusations.* ♦ *The mayor's spokesperson prepared a statement for the press.*

spokeswoman ['spoks wʊm ən] *n., irreg.* a woman who officially speaks on behalf of other people. (Pl: spokeswomen.) ♦ *Mary is the spokeswoman at her company.* ♦ *The company spokeswoman had no comment on the lawsuit.*

spokeswomen ['spoks wɪm ən] pl of spokeswoman.

sponge ['spʌndʒ] **1.** *n.* any of a group of small animals that live in the water and attach themselves in large numbers to underwater objects, forming a rubbery, porous skeleton. ♦ *The deep-sea diver collected sponges from the underwater reef.* ♦ *While scuba diving, we observed sponges growing on the coral.* **2.** *n.* the soft skeleton of ① used for cleaning or absorbing of liquids, or an artificial substance having the same qualities. ♦ *Mary cleaned the spill with an absorbent sponge.* ♦ *John wrung out the sponge in the sink.* **3.** *n.* someone who lives on other people's money or kindness; someone who habitually takes advantage of other people's kindness. (Figurative on ②.) ♦ *Even though he is a sponge, I felt guilty about evicting my roommate.* ♦ *John's spoiled children are sponges who never do anything for him.* **4. sponge off** *tv.* + *adv.* to wipe a surface with a damp sponge ② in order to clean it. ♦ *Mary sponged off the counter with soapy water.* ♦ *Bill sponged the sticky table off after dinner.* **5. sponge off** *iv.* + *prep. phr.* to live by taking advantage of other people's kindness; to live on someone else's money. ♦ *Bill sponged off of his parents until he was 30 years old.* ♦ *I refuse to let my roommates sponge off me.*

spongy ['spʌn dʒi] **1.** *adj.* like a sponge; soft; wet; porous. (Adv: *spongily.* Comp: *spongier;* sup: *spongiest.*) ♦ *My shoes have spongy support cushions.* ♦ *My feet sank into the spongy earth.* **2.** *adj.* absorbent; able to take in liquid and have it squeezed back out. (Adv: *spongily.* Comp: *spongier;* sup: *spongiest.*) ♦ *I cleaned up the spill with the spongy rag.* ♦ *The spongy mop absorbed the water.*

sponsor ['spɑn sɚ] **1.** *n.* someone or an organization that supports and guides another person or organization. ♦ *Six companies sponsored the essay contest for high-school students.* ♦ *My baseball team is sponsored by our local hardware store.* **2.** *n.* someone who assumes responsibility for something. ♦ *The senator who sponsored the bill encouraged others to vote for it.* ♦ *The woman who sponsored the petition spoke before the city council.* **3.** *n.* a business that advertises during a radio or television program. ♦ *The sponsors of the offensive program were boycotted.* ♦ *Our program will continue after a message from our sponsors.* **4.** *tv.* to support someone or an organization, especially financially. ♦ *Anne asked me to sponsor her in the marathon for charity.* ♦ *The radio program was sponsored by local businesses.*

sponsorship ['spɑn sɚ ʃɪp] *n.* the state of being a sponsor; the responsibilities of being a sponsor. (No plural form in this sense.) ♦ *In exchange for its sponsorship, the company's name was printed on our uniforms.* ♦ *Our club sought the sponsorship of local shopkeepers.*

spontaneous [spɑn 'te ni əs] *adj.* not planned; happening naturally without outside influence or force. (Adv: *spontaneously.*) ♦ *Spontaneous combustion is what happens when something suddenly bursts into flames.* ♦ *There was spontaneous applause at the end of Mary's speech.*

spoof ['spuf] **1.** *n.* a parody; a satire; a funny but obvious imitation of something. ♦ *This play is a spoof of the government bureaucracy.* ♦ *Mary's paper is a spoof on intellectual prose.* **2.** *tv.* to parody someone or something; to imitate someone or something in a funny but obvious way. ♦ *That comedian spoofs the president very well in his act.* ♦ *It's easy to spoof the corny plots of soap operas.*

spook ['spuk] **1.** *n.* a ghost. ♦ *Susie dressed up as a spook for Halloween.* ♦ *Spooks wandered through the haunted house.* **2.** *tv.* to make someone or some creature wary and anxious. ♦ *John spooked me by jumping out from behind a tree.* ♦ *A snake spooked my horse and it threw me.*

spooky ['spuk i] *adj.* scary; eerie; creepy. (Adv: *spookily.* Comp: *spookier;* sup: *spookiest.*) ♦ *The campers heard a spooky noise in the forest.* ♦ *Mary had a spooky feeling that something bad was going to happen.*

spool ['spul] *n.* something that thread, film, wire, etc., can be wound around. ♦ *The seamstress put a spool of red thread on the sewing machine.* ♦ *The electrician took a spool of wire to the job site.*

spoon ['spun] **1.** *n.* a utensil that is made of a small, shallow oval bowl at the end of a handle, used for serving food, stirring drinks, and eating liquids. ♦ *John ate a bowl of cereal with a spoon.* ♦ *Mary stirred her coffee with a spoon.* **2.** *tv.* to move something to a place with a spoon. ♦ *Bill spooned the mashed potatoes onto his plate.* ♦ *The nurse spooned the soup into the patient's mouth.*

spoon-fed ['spun fɛd] **1.** pt/pp of spoon-feed. **2.** *adj.* pampered; coddled; given only exactly what is needed without encouraging independent thought. ♦ *The spoon-fed students wrote on the exam exactly what they were told in class.* ♦ *The spoon-fed graduates were unable to cope in the business world.*

spoon-feed ['spun fid] *tv., irreg.* to pamper someone; to coddle someone. (Pt/pp: spoon-fed.) ♦ *The teacher spoon-fed the students by giving them the questions that would be on the exam.* ♦ *The mother spoon-fed her adult children by doing their laundry and their shopping.*

spoonful ['spun fʊl] *n.* the contents of a spoon. ♦ *Mary ate a spoonful of dry cereal.* ♦ *John added two spoonfuls of sugar to his coffee.*

sporadic [spɔ 'ræd ɪk] *adj.* irregular; happening at various times or places; scattered. (Adv: *sporadically* [...ɪk li].) ♦ *We are having sporadic problems with our car.* ♦ *Sporadic rainfall is expected across the state tonight.*

spore ['spor] *n.* the reproductive cell of molds and funguses. ♦ *A mushroom's spores are on the underside of its cap.* ♦ *The disinfectant killed the mold spores growing in the bathroom.*

sport ['sport] **1.** *n.* competition and physical activity as found in games and some outdoor activities. (No plural form in this sense.) ♦ *I enjoy any kind of sport.* ♦ *There is a lot of sport in fishing.* **2.** *n.* a particular game involving physical activity and competition. ♦ *Baseball is Mary's favorite sport.* ♦ *John enjoys camping and most team sports.* **3.** *tv.* to wear a piece of clothing or accessory. ♦ *Tom always sports the latest fashions.* ♦ *Mary came to the party sporting a handmade leather jacket.*

sports car ['sports kɑr] *n.* a kind of expensive, stylish, small car, which usually can go very fast. ♦ *Only two people can fit comfortably into most sports cars.* ♦ *The driver of the sports car was given a ticket for speeding.*

sportscast ['sports kæst] *n.* a program of a sporting event on television or radio. ♦ *I couldn't afford tickets to the game, so I watched the sportscast on TV.* ♦ *We listened to a sportscast over the radio while we drove.*

sportsman ['sports mən] *n., irreg.* a man who participates in sporting events. (Pl: sportsmen.) ♦ *Bill is a general sportsman, liking hunting, fishing, and team sports.* ♦ *The coach was proud that his team consisted of well-trained sportsmen.*

sportsmanship ['sports mən ʃɪp] *n.* the behavior of someone who plays sports fairly and who wins and loses gracefully. (No plural form in this sense.) ♦ *It is good sportsmanship to shake hands with your opponent.* ♦ *The angry tennis player had enough sportsmanship to refrain from yelling.*

sportsmen ['sports mən] pl of sportsman.

sportswoman ['sports wʊm ən] *n., irreg.* a woman who participates in sporting events. (Pl: sportswomen.) ♦ *Mary is a general sportswoman, liking hunting, fishing, and team sports.* ♦ *The coach was proud that his team consisted of well-trained sportswomen.*

sportswomen ['sports wɪm ən] pl of sportswoman.

sporty ['spor ti] *adj.* stylish; fashionable. (Adv: *sportily.* Comp: *sportier;* sup: *sportiest.*) ♦ *Mary is wearing a sporty new jacket.* ♦ *Susan drives a sporty car.*

spot ['spɑt] **1.** *n.* a part (usually round) of a surface that is different from the rest of the surface in some way. ♦ *Bill's tie is blue with red spots.* ♦ *A leopard has dark spots on its fur.* **2.** *n.* a stain; a dirty mark; a blotch. ♦ *The wine left a spot on the rug when I spilled it.* ♦ *There were spots of blood on the murderer's hands.* **3.** *n.* a location; a place; a position. ♦ *My favorite vacation spot is in Hawaii.* ♦ *There's an open spot on the doctor's schedule for next Tuesday.* **4.** *tv.* to recognize someone or something; to see someone or something. ♦ *Mary spotted her brother in the crowd.* ♦ *I spotted the president walking down Pennsylvania Avenue today.* **5. hit the spot** *idiom* to be exactly right; to be refreshing. ♦ *This cool drink really hits the spot.* ♦ *That was a delicious meal, dear. It hit the spot.* **6. in a (tight) spot** *idiom* caught in a problem; in a difficult position. ♦ *Look, John, I'm in a tight spot. Can you lend me twenty dollars?* ♦ *I'm in a spot too. I need $300.* **7. on the spot** *idiom* in trouble; in a difficult situation. ♦ *There is a problem in the department I manage, and I'm really on the spot.* ♦ *My friend put me on the spot when he asked me to reveal a secret.* **8. rooted to the spot** *idiom* unable to move because of fear or surprise. ♦ *Jane stood rooted to the spot when she saw the ghostly figure.* ♦ *Mary stood rooted to the spot when the thief snatched her bag.*

spot-check ['spɑt tʃɛk] *tv.* to inspect something at random; to sample something at random. ♦ *An inspector spot-checked the material on the assembly line.* ♦ *The principal spot-checked the students' lockers for contraband.*

spotless ['spɑt ləs] *adj.* totally clean; without spots. (Adv: *spotlessly.*) ♦ *The cleaners made my stained shirt spotless once again.* ♦ *How do you keep your kitchen so spotless?*

spotlight ['spɑt lɑɪt] **1.** *n.* a spot or disk of strong, bright light. ♦ *The singer was lighted by a bright spotlight onstage.* ♦ *The taxi driver shined a spotlight on each house, looking for the right address.* **2.** *n.* a lamp that produces a circle of strong, bright light. ♦ *The guards turned the spotlight on the escaping thief.* ♦ *A technician operated the theater spotlight from a special booth.* **3.** *n.* something that is in the focus of public attention. (Figurative on ①.) ♦ *The mayor's tax plan was the spotlight of today's news.* ♦ *The spotlight is on the mayor's tax proposal today.* **4.** *tv.* to place someone or something in the focus of attention. ♦ *The news program spotlighted the rising crime rate.* ♦ *The tabloids spotlighted the private lives of famous celebrities.* **5. in the spotlight** *idiom* at the center of attention; being the thing or person receiving attention. ♦ *John really likes to be in the spotlight.* ♦ *Bill is shy and hates being in the spotlight.*

spotted ['spɑt ɪd] *adj.* having spots; covered with spots. ♦ *I saw a spotted leopard at the zoo.* ♦ *Jimmy's face is spotted with freckles.*

spouse ['spaʊs] *n.* a husband or a wife. ♦ *All employees and their spouses are invited to the company party.* ♦ *My spouse and I have been married for four years.*

spout ['spaʊt] **1.** *n.* the opening of something from which a liquid comes out. ♦ *The orange juice flowed from the spout of the pitcher.* ♦ *The gardener used a watering can with a long, narrow spout.* **2.** *tv.* to eject something, especially a liquid; to force a liquid out, especially through a narrow pipe or tube. ♦ *The shower nozzle spouted cold water on me.* ♦ *The beautiful fountain spouted streams of water.* **3.** *iv.* to flow into, out of, from, through, down, or onto someone or something. ♦ *Water spouted out from the broken pipe.* ♦ *Ketchup spouted from the bottle onto my shirt.*

sprain ['spren] **1.** *tv.* to twist a joint in the body in a way that causes injury or pain. ♦ *John sprained his ankle when he fell off the curb.* ♦ *Mary sprained her wrist while playing tennis.* **2.** *n.* the twisting of a joint in the body in a way that causes injury or pain; a joint that has been twisted in a way that causes injury or pain. ♦ *The nurse wrapped my sprain in a bandage.* ♦ *Susan put ice on her sprain.*

sprained ['sprend] *adj.* [of a joint] twisted in a way that causes injury or pain. ♦ *I walked on crutches when I had a sprained ankle.* ♦ *I couldn't write for three weeks when I had a sprained wrist.*

sprang ['spræŋ] pt of spring.

sprawl ['sprɔl] **1.** *iv.* to be spread out, especially in an unorganized or disorderly way. ♦ *The city's suburbs sprawled far into the countryside.* ♦ *The noisy students sprawled on the museum steps.* **2. sprawl (out)** *iv.* (+ *adv.*) to sit, stand, or lie so that one's limbs are stretched out, especially in an ungraceful way. ♦ *Susan sprawled out and took a nap.* ♦ *David sprawled on the chair in front of the television.* **3. sprawl (out)** *tv.* (+ *adv.*) to spread something or oneself out in an ungraceful, unorganized, or disorderly way. ♦ *Bill's sprawled his work all over his office.* ♦ *Mary sprawled herself out on the bed and took a nap.* **4.** *n.* something that is spread out, especially in an ungraceful, unorganized, or disorderly way. (No plural form in this sense.) ♦ *Suburban sprawl caused really bad traffic jams.* ♦ *Anne tried to organize the sprawl of papers in her office.*

sprawling ['sprɔl ɪŋ] *adj.* spread out, especially in an unorganized or disorderly way. (Adv: *sprawlingly.*) ♦ *The sprawling suburbs extended deep into what was once farmland.* ♦ *The sprawling student covered the length of the couch.*

spray ['spre] **1.** *tv.* to direct a stream of small drops of liquid onto a surface. ♦ *Mary sprayed paint on the wall.* ♦ *John sprayed insecticide on the plants.* **2.** *tv.* to coat a surface with a stream of small drops of liquid. ♦ *Mary sprayed the wall with paint.* ♦ *John sprayed the plants with insecticide.* **3.** *tv.* to direct a steady flow of bombs, bullets, or missiles onto an area. (Figurative on ①.) ♦ *The enemy sprayed missiles into the jungle.* ♦ *The gangster sprayed the bullets into the crowd.* **4.** *iv.* to be forced out in a spray ⑤. ♦ *The paint sprayed evenly on the wall.* ♦ *Steam sprayed from the kettle.* **5.** *n.* liquid that is pushed through the air in small drops, especially under pressure. ♦ *The spray from the vaporizer added moisture to the dry room.* ♦ *The spray of perfume made me sneeze.* **6.** *n.* one branch of leaves or flowers, used as a decoration. ♦ *The bouquet included a spray of lilac.* ♦ *David put a few sprays of flowers in the vase on the table.*

spread ['sprɛd] **1.** *iv., irreg.* to move outward; to become longer, wider, or broader; to extend to a larger extent or to the largest extent possible; to expand. (Pt/pp: *spread.*) ♦ *A terrible famine spread across the country.* ♦ *The wine stain spread across the tablecloth.* **2.** *iv., irreg.* to be passed on to many people. ♦ *Jane's cold spread to everyone in the office.* ♦ *The gossip spread quickly throughout the department.* **3.** *tv., irreg.* to distribute something to many people. ♦ *I spread the good news to everyone.* ♦ *John spread chickenpox to all of his classmates.* **4.** *tv., irreg.* to stretch something out; to cause something to become longer, wider, or broader. ♦ *Mary spread her arms wide.* ♦ *Mike spread the tablecloth on the table.* **5.** *tv., irreg.* to apply something onto something else by moving it around, making an even layer. ♦ *John spread some butter on his toast.* ♦ *They are spreading gravel on our street now.* **6. spread over** *tv., irreg.* + *prep. phr.* to distribute something over a period of time. ♦ *The company spreads our paychecks over twelve months.* ♦ *The teacher spread four tests over the course of the term.* **7.** *n.* the wide distribution [of something]. (No plural form in this sense.) ♦ *The scientists tried to stop the spread of the virus.* ♦ *The spread of gossip about Bill finally reached Bill himself.* **8.** *n.* the amount that something has been spread ④; the extent to which something has been spread ④. (No plural form in this sense.) ♦ *The spread of the drought went from coast to coast.* ♦ *The doctor assessed the spread of cancer in the patient's body.* **9.** *n.* a food, such as margarine or butter, that can be spread ⑤ on another food. ♦ *Mary put some cheese spread on the crackers.* ♦ *John put an artificial butter spread on his toast.* **10.** *n.* the difference between two amounts. ♦ *There was a 12-point spread between the two teams' final scores.* ♦ *There was a surprisingly large spread between the projected and actual election results.* **11.** *n.* a story or advertisement in a newspaper that takes up more than one column or more than one page. ♦ *Did you read the big spread about political fraud?* ♦ *The grocery store's advertising spread included many coupons.* **12.** *n.* a large display of food; many different foods set out for people to choose from. ♦ *There was a sumptuous spread on the buffet table.* ♦ *The generous hosts provided a lavish spread for their guests.* **13. spread oneself too thin** *idiom* to do so many things that you can do none of them well; to spread one's efforts or attention too widely. ♦ *It's a good idea to get involved in a lot of activities, but don't spread yourself too thin.* ♦ *I'm too busy these days. I'm afraid I've spread myself too thin.*

spreadsheet ['sprɛd ʃit] **1.** *n.* a computer program that calculates and manipulates rows and columns of numbers or data. ♦ *The accountant entered the monthly figures onto the spreadsheet.* ♦ *Anne programmed the spreadsheet to average the amounts in each column.* **2.** *n.* a printed display of ①. ♦ *May I see the spreadsheet for last year's financial statements?* ♦ *Susan included spreadsheets of data in her scientific report.*

spree ['spri] **1.** *n.* an episode of wild drinking, spending, or partying. ♦ *Bob remembered very little of the previous night's drunken spree.* ♦ *I spent $1,000 while on a shopping spree at the mall.* **2.** *n.* a period of activity and action. ♦ *The murderer went on a killing spree and killed three* *people.* ♦ *Our team went on a winning spree and won the championship.*

sprig ['sprɪg] *n.* a small stem or branch with its leaves or flowers still attached. ♦ *Anne pulled a sprig of blossoms from the cherry tree.* ♦ *Lisa made a wreath from a few sprigs of pine.*

sprightly ['sprɑɪt li] *adj.* active; lively; energetic. (Comp: *sprightlier;* sup: *sprightliest.*) ♦ *The sprightly dancers were sweating by the end of the song.* ♦ *Many sprightly children ran around the park, yelling and screaming.*

spring ['sprɪŋ] **1.** *n.* the season of the year between March 21 and June 21, between winter and summer. (No plural form in this sense.) ♦ *During spring in the Northern Hemisphere, it becomes warmer and leaves begin to grow on trees again.* ♦ *I'm planning to visit Europe in the spring.* **2.** *n.* a natural source of water from the ground; a place where water comes out of the earth. ♦ *The small town's water supply was a mineral spring.* ♦ *This bottled water comes from a spring in Wisconsin.* **3.** *n.* a metal coil; a metal object that is wound in the shape of a coil. ♦ *A spring returns to its original shape after being squeezed or pulled.* ♦ *When you wind a watch, you tighten a spring inside it.* **4.** *n.* the ability of something to return to its original shape after being bent, squeezed together, or pulled apart. (No plural form in this sense.) ♦ *Elastic objects have a great deal of spring.* ♦ *This diving board does not have enough spring.* **5.** *iv., irreg.* to jump; to leap. (Pt: sprang; pp: sprung.) ♦ *The dog sprang over the creek.* ♦ *Jimmy tried to spring 8 feet.* **6. spring up** *iv., irreg. + adv.* to grow suddenly; to sprout. (Figurative on ⑤.) ♦ *Weeds seem to be springing up everywhere in my garden.* ♦ *The flowers had sprung up from the ground within a week.* **7. spring over** *iv., irreg. + prep. phr.* to jump over something. ♦ *The dog sprang over the ditch.* ♦ *Susan tried to spring over the puddle.* **8.** *iv., irreg.* [for a spring ③] to fail and lose its elastic property. ♦ *The spring inside my watch has sprung, so it needs to be fixed.* ♦ *The springs inside my mattress had sprung, so I threw it away.* **9. spring on** *tv., irreg. + prep. phr.* to produce something in order to surprise someone; to say or do something that surprises someone. ♦ *Bill sprang the news on his boss that he was quitting.* ♦ *John sprang a $500 car repair bill on his parents.* **10.** *adj.* <the adj. use of ①.> ♦ *The department store had a big spring sale.* ♦ *Anne planned to take four classes during the spring term.*

springboard ['sprɪŋ bord] **1.** *n.* a diving board; a board that hangs over the edge of a pool and that people dive from. ♦ *The diver stood on the edge of the springboard above the pool.* ♦ *The swimmer jumped on the springboard and dived into the water.* **2.** *n.* something that is used as a means to move onto something else. (Figurative on ①.) ♦ *The company used its software as a springboard to enter the education market.* ♦ *The teacher thought marijuana was a springboard to more addictive drugs.*

spring-cleaning ['sprɪŋ 'klin ɪŋ] *n.* the thorough cleaning of a house or building in the spring. (No plural form in this sense.) ♦ *As part of spring-cleaning, John waxed the floors.* ♦ *Mary threw out ten bags of trash during spring-cleaning.*

spring fever ['sprɪŋ 'fi vɚ] *n.* a lazy feeling felt when the weather starts to become warmer. (No plural form in this sense.) ♦ *Toward the end of February, the students caught spring fever.* ♦ *John has spring fever and can't get his work done.*

springtime ['sprɪŋ tɑɪm] *n.* the period of time between March 21 and June 21; the season of spring. (No plural form in this sense.) ♦ *The birds returned from the south at the beginning of springtime.* ♦ *Anne planted her garden in the springtime.*

springy ['sprɪŋ i] *adj.* bouncy; elastic. (Adv: *springily.* Comp: *springier;* sup: *springiest.*) ♦ *The children bounced on the springy bed.* ♦ *Bill did a flip on the springy trampoline.*

sprinkle ['sprɪŋ kəl] **1.** *iv.* to fall in small drops or pieces; to scatter in small drops or pieces. ♦ *Snow sprinkled lightly on the ground.* ♦ *Rain is sprinkling against the window.* **2.** *iv.* to rain a little. (With *it* as a subject.) ♦ *It's sprinkling, so take your umbrella.* ♦ *Anne wore a raincoat because it was sprinkling when she left.* **3.** *tv.* to cause something to fall in small drops or pieces; to scatter something in small drops or pieces. ♦ *Bill sprinkled some cinnamon onto the cookies.* ♦ *Anne sprinkled some salt in her soup.* **4.** *tv.* to be scattered here and there; to be in a few locations here and there. (Usually passive.) ♦ *The company has sprinkled its offices all over town.* ♦ *A few oases were sprinkled across the desert.* **5.** *n.* a dust or powder that can be sprinkled as in ③. (No plural form in this sense.) ♦ *Anne put a sprinkle of sugar in her coffee.* ♦ *There was just a sprinkle of nutmeg in the cookies.* **6.** *n.* a small amount of rain. ♦ *I got caught in a light sprinkle, but I didn't get wet.* ♦ *The weather forecaster predicted a few sprinkles around noon.*

sprinkler ['sprɪŋk lɚ] *n.* a device that sprays water carried through a hose or pipe. ♦ *The gardener set the sprinkler next to the tomato plants.* ♦ *The fire activated the building's ceiling sprinklers, which sprayed water on the flames.*

sprint ['sprɪnt] **1.** *iv.* to run very fast over a short distance; to run a short distance very fast. ♦ *John sprinted for 100 yards.* ♦ *Anne sprinted faster than anyone else.* **2.** *n.* a very fast run over a short distance. ♦ *Bill got leg cramps during his sprint.* ♦ *The thief's sprint toward the door was stopped by a large dog.* **3.** *n.* a short race. ♦ *Anne won the 100-meter sprint.* ♦ *Eight athletes participated in the 50-meter sprint.*

sprout ['sprɑʊt] **1.** *iv.* [for a plant] to bud; [for a plant] to start growing leaves, flowers, or buds; [for a plant] to grow from a seed. ♦ *Buds sprouted from the tree branches in March.* ♦ *The plants sprouted from the ground a week after I planted seeds.* **2.** *tv.* to grow something [other than a plant]. ♦ *Bob has sprouted a mustache since I last saw him.* ♦ *The crab sprouted a new claw when an old one broke off.* **3.** *n.* new growth; a new bud, leaf, flower, or stem. ♦ *The new sprouts pushed through the surface of the soil.* ♦ *The sudden cold snap froze the young sprouts.* **4. sprouts** *n.* the first growth of the seeds of beans, alfalfa, etc., eaten as food. (Treated as plural.) ♦ *Mary put some bean sprouts on her salad.* ♦ *John ate some alfalfa sprouts with dinner.*

spruce ['sprus] **1.** *n.* a type of pine tree having short needles. ♦ *Many raccoons lived in the forest of spruce.* ♦ *I cut down a spruce that was blocking the view from my porch.* **2.** *n.* the wood of ①. (No plural form in this sense.) ♦ *Spruce is full of sap and burns very fast.* ♦ *Spruce is some-*

times used to make piano keys. **3. spruce up** *iv.* + *adv.* to make oneself or a place neat or clean. ♦ *Don't you think we should spruce up before our guests arrive?* ♦ *John went to the bathroom to spruce up before dinner.* **4. spruce up** *tv.* + *adv.* to tidy oneself or a place. ♦ *Mary spruced the house up before her parents visited.* ♦ *Anne spruced up her makeup before she left the office.*

sprung ['sprʌŋ] pp of spring.

spry ['spraɪ] *adj.* active; nimble; agile; able to move easily. (Especially used to describe older people. Adv: *spryly.* Comp: *spryer;* sup: *spryest.*) ♦ *The spry old man did his own shopping.* ♦ *The spry elderly women walked a mile every day through the park.*

spun ['spʌn] pt/pp of spin.

spunk ['spʌŋk] *n.* courage. (No plural form in this sense.) ♦ *The brave reporter with a lot of spunk covered the war.* ♦ *The soldiers survived living in tents and getting little to eat, because of their spunk and determination.*

spunky ['spʌŋ ki] *adj.* energetic; lively and alert. (Adv: *spunkily.* Comp: *spunkier;* sup: *spunkiest.*) ♦ *The spunky reporter kept asking questions until the mayor became angry.* ♦ *The spunky little boy kept running away from his mother.*

spur ['spɚ] **1.** *n.* a sharp object worn on the heel of a boot, used to prod a horse that one is riding to go faster. ♦ *The cowboy prodded the horse with the spurs on his boots.* ♦ *The spurs on Dave's boots sparkled in the sun.* **2.** *n.* a supplemental highway or railroad track that branches from the main one. ♦ *The driver took the spur around the town to avoid heavy traffic.* ♦ *The railroad ended service to towns on its secondary spurs.* **3. spur on** *tv.* + *adv.* to persuade, urge, or encourage someone. ♦ *The students spurred Jane on when she ran for class president.* ♦ *My parents spurred me on to study harder.* **4.** *tv.* to prod a horse with ①. ♦ *The cowboy spurred the horse to go faster.* ♦ *The rider spurred the horse gently.*

spurn ['spɚn] *tv.* to reject someone or something with contempt or disdain. ♦ *The politician spurned the support of anti-Semitic groups.* ♦ *Mary spurned her obnoxious coworker's attempts at flirting.*

spurt ['spɚt] **1.** *iv.* to burst from an opening; to gush; to flow out quickly. ♦ *Oil spurted from the leaky pipe.* ♦ *Water spurted from the broken faucet.* **2.** *tv.* to squirt something; to discharge something, making it flow fast. ♦ *The grounded tanker spurted oil into the bay.* ♦ *The gash on my arm spurted blood.* **3.** *n.* a burst of liquid or gas; a gush of liquid or gas. ♦ *The nurse stopped the spurt of blood by applying direct pressure.* ♦ *The water escaped from the leaky pipe in spurts.* **4.** *n.* a surge of activity or energy; a burst. (Figurative on ③.) ♦ *The graph showed each spurt of intense stock market activity.* ♦ *I was surprised by the spurt of anger from Bill.*

sputter ['spʌt ɚ] **1.** *iv.* to make small, quiet but explosive noises. ♦ *My car engine sputtered at the intersection.* ♦ *The fire in the fireplace sputtered as the pine burned.* **2.** *iv.* to speak in a confused or exasperated way. (Figurative on ①.) ♦ *The angry customer sputtered at the inept cashier.* ♦ *John fumed and sputtered when he was arrested for speeding.*

spy ['spaɪ] **1.** *n.* someone whose job is to secretly watch other people, organizations, or governments in order to learn information. ♦ *The Russian spy infiltrated the German government.* ♦ *The American spy obtained secret information about the foreign government.* **2. spy on** *iv.* + *prep. phr.* to watch other people, organizations, or governments in order to learn information. ♦ *The secretary spied on the prime minister's meetings.* ♦ *The government spied on the left-wing group.* **3.** *tv.* to see something; to discover something by sight; to see something for the first time. ♦ *I spied a red van following me home from work.* ♦ *The detective spied a piece of fabric on the floor near the corpse.*

squabble ['skwɑb əl] **1.** *n.* a small argument; a quarrel; a disagreement. ♦ *I got into a squabble with my parents about politics.* ♦ *I never resolved my squabble with Anne about philosophy.* **2.** *iv.* to argue about something; to disagree over something. ♦ *John squabbled with his neighbor about religion.* ♦ *Mary and John squabbled about money.*

squabbling ['skwɑb lɪŋ] **1.** *adj.* arguing; disagreeing; quarreling. ♦ *The teacher asked the squabbling students to be quiet.* ♦ *My squabbling neighbors kept me awake all night.* **2.** *n.* arguing; disagreeing; quarreling. (No plural form in this sense.) ♦ *The children's incessant squabbling is very annoying.* ♦ *The teacher asked us to postpone our squabbling until after class.*

squad ['skwɑd] *n.* a group of people who work together or who have been trained together for a job; a group of 11 soldiers and a leader who work together. ♦ *The squad of soldiers exercised every morning at sunrise.* ♦ *A police squad surrounded the robbers.*

squad car ['skwɑd kɑr] *n.* a patrol car; a police car used for patrolling a certain area that has a radio used to keep in contact with headquarters. ♦ *Five squad cars rushed toward the crime scene.* ♦ *The police put the suspect in the back of the squad car.*

squadron ['skwɑd rən] *n.* a large group of military ships, military aircraft, or soldiers and tanks that fight as a unit. ♦ *The squadron attacked the enemy during the night.* ♦ *The officer who commanded the victorious squadron was awarded a medal.*

squalid ['skwɑl ɪd] *adj.* very dirty, especially because of poverty; filthy; repulsive. (Adv: *squalidly.*) ♦ *The social worker removed the children from the squalid apartment.* ♦ *The mayor tried to revitalize the squalid neighborhood.*

squall ['skwɑl] *n.* a sudden burst of wind, often with rain or snow. ♦ *The sailboat headed toward shore as the squall approached.* ♦ *The violent squalls made driving along the coast dangerous.*

squalor ['skwɑl ɚ] *n.* dirt; filth, especially in reference to living conditions. (No plural form in this sense.) ♦ *The abandoned children had been living in squalor.* ♦ *The squalor of the slums saddened the social worker.*

squander ['skwɑn dɚ] *tv.* to waste something, including time or money; to spend something wastefully. ♦ *Anne squandered her time playing pool.* ♦ *Bill squandered his money on items he didn't really need.*

square ['skwɛr] **1.** *n.* a shape made with four straight sides that are the same length and four right angles. ♦ *A square with two-inch sides has an area of four square inches.* ♦ *The worker installed squares of tile on the floor.* **2.** *n.* a four-sided area in a city surrounded by streets or buildings. ♦ *The vendor sold peanuts and popcorn in the square.* ♦ *Mary took the subway from the town square to* *the suburbs.* **3.** *n.* an L-shaped or T-shaped tool, used for drawing and measuring right angles. ♦ *The architect kept his T-square near his drawing board.* ♦ *The carpenter drew a right angle on the board with a square.* **4.** *n.* a number that is the product of a number multiplied by itself. ♦ *64 is the square of 8 because 8 × 8 = 64.* ♦ *The area of a square is the square of the length of any one side.* **5. square meal** *n.* a meal that is complete and balanced. ♦ *Be sure to eat three square meals every day.* ♦ *The poor children's only square meals were at school.* **6.** *adj.* shaped like ①. (Adv: *squarely.*) ♦ *The youngster tried to place the square peg in a round hole.* ♦ *Mary's house was built on a square one-acre plot.* **7.** *adj.* forming a right angle; forming a 90-degree angle. (Adv: *squarely.*) ♦ *The carpenter made sure the window was plumb and square.* ♦ *The bookshelf was square with the side of the bookcase.* **8.** *adj.* [of an area] roughly equal in size and shape to a **square** ① that has sides of the specified length. (Follows the measurement of length.) ♦ *A room that is ten feet square has an area of 100 square feet because 10 × 10 is 100.* ♦ *The architect drew a shape that was two inches square.* **9.** *adj.* [of an area shaped like ①] having sides of a specified length. (A square inch is the area measured by a square that is one inch long and one inch wide. Adv: *squarely.*) ♦ *There are 640 acres in one square mile.* ♦ *A square mile is a measurement equal to the area of a square of land one mile long and one mile wide.* **10.** *adj.* having no debts; having settled all debts. ♦ *Ten years after graduation, Bill was finally square on his school loans.* ♦ *Are we square, or do I owe you more money?* **11.** *adj.* dull; boring; old-fashioned. (Slang. Adv: *squarely.*) ♦ *Mary voted for the square politician.* ♦ *John thought his parents were too square.* **12.** *tv.* to multiply a number by itself. ♦ *If you square 8, you get 64.* ♦ *If you square the length of one side of a square, you get its area.* **13. square (with)** *tv.* (+ *prep. phr.*) to settle a debt or balance with someone by paying the amount owed. ♦ *John squared his bill and left the restaurant.* ♦ *Mary squared her debt with the credit-card company.* **14.** *tv.* to make something ⑦. ♦ *The builders squared the wall with respect to the floor.* ♦ *The carpenter squared the shelf against the wall.* **15. square off (with)** *iv.* + *adv.* to take a position as if ready to fight; to prepare to oppose someone or something. ♦ *The two boxers squared off for a fight.* ♦ *The workers have squared off with management over the wage issue and are threatening to go on strike.* **16.** *adv.* directly or squarely ①, when making contact with someone or something. ♦ *John's punch landed square on Bill's nose.* ♦ *Mary's arrow hit the target square in the center.* **17. square up to someone or something** *idiom* to face someone or something bravely; to tackle someone or something. ♦ *You'll have to square up to the bully or he'll make your life miserable.* ♦ *It's time to square up to your financial problems. You can't just ignore them.* **18. square up with someone** *idiom* to pay someone what one owes; to pay one's share of something to someone. ♦ *I'll square up with you later if you pay the whole bill now.* ♦ *Bob said he would square up with Tom for his share of the gas.*

square dance ['skwɛr dæns] **1.** *n.* a U.S. folk dance performed by four pairs of dancers, who form a square and perform the dance steps that are called out by someone. ♦ *The rural townsfolk join in a square dance every Friday night.* ♦ *John called out the dance steps for the square dance last night.* **2. square-dance** *iv.* to participate in ①. ♦ *The students learned how to square-dance in gym class.* ♦ *The guests square-danced at the wedding.*

squarely ['skwɛr li] **1.** *adv.* directly; straight. ♦ *The drunken driver drove squarely into a tree.* ♦ *The bullet struck the target squarely in the center.* **2.** *adv.* honestly; straightforwardly. ♦ *The witness dealt squarely with the lawyer's questions.* ♦ *You must face this difficult problem squarely, or you will never resolve it.*

squash ['skwɑʃ] **1.** *n.* a fruit with a hard rind that grows from a vine on the ground, including the gourd and the pumpkin. (No plural form in this sense.) ♦ *Zucchini is a type of squash that grows in the summer.* ♦ *Squash is easy to grow in warm climates.* **2.** *n.* the flesh of ①. ♦ *Please pass me some more squash.* ♦ *We ate pork roast and squash for dinner.* **3.** *n.* an individual fruit of ①. ♦ *Please buy two squashes at the store today.* ♦ *Bill baked a squash for dinner.* **4.** *n.* a game played in an enclosed room with two or four people who hit a small rubber ball with a racket against one wall so that it strikes above a line painted on the wall. (No plural form in this sense.) ♦ *The lawyer played squash at the health club after work.* ♦ *Anne wore safety goggles while she played squash.* **5.** *tv.* to crush someone or something. ♦ *The strong man squashed the tin can in his fist.* ♦ *Mary squashed the trash further into the can with her foot.* **6.** *tv.* to belittle, embarrass, or overwhelm someone, causing silence or resignation. ♦ *Bill's rude remark absolutely squashed Tom, who will probably never come back to see us.* ♦ *The insulting teacher squashed the student's curiosity.* **7.** *iv.* to be crushed; to be pressed or squeezed into a tight space; to flatten. ♦ *The ripe tomato squashed when it fell to the floor.* ♦ *The pillow squashed as I sat on it.*

squat ['skwɑt] **1.** *iv.* to crouch; to rest, sitting with one's feet on the ground and one's legs bent under one's body. ♦ *The camper squatted next to the campfire.* ♦ *John squatted as he picked up the paper clips that he'd dropped.* **2.** *iv.* to take over and live in an empty building or on a piece of land without the owner's permission. ♦ *The poor family was squatting on land that belonged to the city.* ♦ *The runaway teenager had been squatting in a condemned apartment building.* **3.** *adj.* shorter or thicker than normal or expected. (Adv: *squatly.* Comp: *squatter;* sup: *squattest.*) ♦ *The squat football player couldn't run very fast.* ♦ *The vase seemed squat and ugly when I placed it on the table.* **4.** *n.* a crouching position. (No plural form in this sense.) ♦ *John crouched in a squat next to the campfire.* ♦ *The gymnast began her flip from a squat.*

squatter ['skwɑt ɚ] *n.* someone who lives in an empty building or on land without the permission of the owner. ♦ *The landlord drove the squatters from his building.* ♦ *A squatter set fire to the empty building while trying to warm himself.*

squawk ['skwɔk] **1.** *n.* a loud, harsh noise, especially one made by birds. ♦ *The parrot's squawk hurt my ears.* ♦ *If I hear one more squawk from you kids, you're all going to bed.* **2.** *iv.* to screech; to make a loud, harsh noise. ♦ *The bird squawked every morning at dawn.* ♦ *The horrible singer didn't sing, but rather squawked.*

squeak ['skwik] **1.** *n.* a short, high-pitched, quiet noise. ♦ *The door makes a squeak every time someone opens it.* ♦ *When I walk, my new shoes make squeaks.* **2.** *iv.* to make a short, high-pitched, quiet noise. ♦ *This door squeaks* *when it is opened or closed.* ♦ *The mouse squeaked when Susan accidentally stepped on it.* **3. squeak by; squeak through** *iv.* + *adv.* to barely be approved; to be approved by a very slim margin. ♦ *The mayor's budget barely squeaked by.* ♦ *The office manager's proposal barely squeaked through.*

squeal ['skwil] **1.** *n.* a loud, shrill noise or cry. ♦ *We heard horrible squeals when the wolf came near the pigs.* ♦ *The children made squeals of delight when I offered them cake.* **2.** *iv.* to make ①. ♦ *The pig squealed when it saw the food I was bringing it.* ♦ *When the baby squealed, I picked her up from her crib.*

squealing ['skwil ɪŋ] *adj.* making a loud, shrill noise or cry. ♦ *The farmer fed the squealing pigs.* ♦ *The squealing baby was hungry.*

squeamish ['skwim ɪʃ] *adj.* easily sickened; easily frightened. (Adv: *squeamishly.*) ♦ *This gory movie is not for squeamish audiences.* ♦ *The squeamish passengers became sick on their vacation cruise.*

squeeze ['skwiz] **1.** *tv.* to press something with force. ♦ *John squeezed the rubber ball with his hands.* ♦ *Anne squeezed the trigger of the gun with her finger.* **2.** *tv.* to force the liquid from something by pressing it; to extract something from something by using pressure or force. ♦ *Anne squeezed the oranges to make orange juice.* ♦ *John squeezed every drop of water from the wet rag.* **3. squeeze into** *tv.* + *prep. phr.* to fit someone or something into something by using force. ♦ *John squeezed his clothes into his suitcase.* ♦ *Anne squeezed herself into the crowded elevator.* **4. squeeze into** *iv.* + *prep. phr.* to fit by being pressed into a tight space. ♦ *The commuters squeezed into the crowded elevator.* ♦ *Mike squeezed into the tight pair of pants.* **5.** *n.* the act of pressing someone or something, as in ① or ②. ♦ *I gave the wet sponge a squeeze.* ♦ *John gave my hand a tight squeeze when we shook hands.*

squelch ['skwɛltʃ] *tv.* to suppress someone or something; to silence someone or something. ♦ *The tyrant squelched all opposition to the government.* ♦ *The army squelched the news about the war.*

squib ['skwɪb] *n.* a short note or essay, especially one used to fill space in a publication. ♦ *The journal editor wrote a humorous squib each month.* ♦ *The last page of the magazine always contains a political squib.*

squid ['skwɪd] **1.** *n., irreg.* a sea creature that has ten tentacles attached to its body and two triangular tail fins. (Pl: *squid* or *squids.*) ♦ *How many different types of squid are there?* ♦ *There was a picture of a giant squid on the cover of the nature magazine.* **2.** *n.* the flesh of ① used as food. (No plural form in this sense.) ♦ *Squid is often served at seafood restaurants.* ♦ *Susan loves fried squid.*

squiggle ['skwɪg əl] **1.** *n.* a line that is curved, wavy, or twisted. ♦ *The bored student drew squiggles in his notebook.* ♦ *Mary decorated the poster with colorful squiggles.* **2.** *tv.* to write something or draw something with curved, wavy, or twisted lines. ♦ *Tom quickly squiggled his signature on the check.* ♦ *The small children squiggled drawings on the wall with crayons.*

squint ['skwɪnt] **1.** *tv.* to close one's eyes almost all the way when looking at someone or something. ♦ *John squinted his eyes because the sun was so bright.* ♦ *I squinted my eyes so I could see enough to find my glasses.* **2.** *iv.* to have one's eyes almost closed because the light is so bright. ♦ *Driving west as the sun set, I had to squint.* ♦ *Facing the sun, Mary squinted as she watched the tennis game.*

squinting ['skwɪn tɪŋ] *adj.* having eyes almost completely closed. (Adv: *squintingly.*) ♦ *The squinting driver looked for her sunglasses.* ♦ *The teacher suggested that the squinting student might need glasses.*

squirm ['skwɚm] *iv.* to move around uncomfortably; to writhe. ♦ *The bored child squirmed in church.* ♦ *A dying squirrel squirmed on the road.*

squirming ['skwɚ mɪŋ] *adj.* moving around uncomfortably; writhing; twisting. ♦ *Mary told the squirming children to sit still.* ♦ *The nurse gave the squirming patient a sedative.*

squirrel ['skwɚ əl] **1.** *n.* a rodent that lives in trees and has a large, bushy tail. ♦ *The squirrel buried some acorns in the ground.* ♦ *The squirrels quickly ran up the tree.* **2. squirrel away** *tv.* + *adv.* to hide something; to store something in a hiding place. ♦ *My grandmother squirreled away money in her cookie jar.* ♦ *The militia members squirreled away ammunition in shelters.*

squirt ['skwɚt] **1.** *tv.* to force liquid through the air in a stream; to cause liquid to stream through the air. ♦ *Mary squirted water on the flowers with a hose.* ♦ *Susan squirted some hair spray onto her hair.* **2.** *tv.* to hit someone or something with a stream of liquid. ♦ *Mary squirted her brother with a stream of cold water.* ♦ *David squirted his dirty car with water from the hose.* **3.** *n.* a stream of liquid that is sent through the air. ♦ *Put a little squirt of oil on the squeaky hinges.* ♦ *Mary added a squirt of detergent to the dishwater.*

squish ['skwɪʃ] **1.** *tv.* to squeeze something; to crush something. ♦ *Jimmy squished the slice of bread into a small cube.* ♦ *Tom squished the banana flat.* **2.** *iv.* to walk in mud, making a wet, splashing noise; to splash through mud. ♦ *The children became dirty when they squished through the mud.* ♦ *Everyone squished across the soggy lawn.*

squishy ['skwɪʃ i] *adj.* soft and wet; making wet, splashing noises when squeezed. (Adv: *squishily.* Comp: *squishier;* sup: *squishiest.*) ♦ *John walked in the squishy mud.* ♦ *The squishy sponge held a quart of water.*

Sri Lanka [sri 'lɑŋ kə] See Gazetteer.

St. See saint, street.

stab ['stæb] **1.** *tv.* to thrust a pointed object into someone or something. ♦ *The robber stabbed the cashier with a knife.* ♦ *Mary stabbed the slab of ham and put it on her plate.* **2.** *n.* a thrust of a pointed object. ♦ *The stab to the victim's heart was fatal.* ♦ *The assailant made a stab at me, but he missed.* **3.** *n.* a sharp, painful feeling. ♦ *I felt a stab of pain in my stomach after overeating.* ♦ *Tom felt the stab of the knife as it slipped and cut his thumb.* **4. stab someone in the back** *idiom* to betray someone. ♦ *I thought we were friends! Why did you stab me in the back?* ♦ *You don't expect a person you trust to stab you in the back.* **5. have a stab at something; take a stab at something** *idiom* to try something; to make a try at doing something. ♦ *I would like to have a stab at operating the bulldozer.* ♦ *Why don't you take a stab at painting the fence?*

stabbing ['stæb ɪŋ] **1.** *n.* an incident in which someone is stabbed. ♦ *The reporter described the fatal stabbing of a prominent lawyer.* ♦ *The police investigated a pair of* *stabbings downtown.* **2.** *adj.* [of a pain] sharp. (Adv: *stabbingly.*) ♦ *Suddenly, I felt a stabbing pain in my leg.* ♦ *Tom felt a burning, stabbing sensation in his side.*

stability [stə 'bɪl ɪ ti] *n.* the quality of remaining stable. (No plural form in this sense.) ♦ *The stability of the government enabled its people to prosper.* ♦ *A new foster family brought stability to the young child's life.*

stabilize ['steb ə lɑɪz] **1.** *tv.* to make something steady; to fix something in place; to keep something from moving or fluctuating. ♦ *Congress's policies stabilized the employment rate.* ♦ *The soldiers stabilized the bridge before crossing it.* **2.** *iv.* to become steady; to be fixed in place. ♦ *The inflation rate stabilized after the war ended.* ♦ *The patient's heart rate stabilized after surgery.*

stable ['steb əl] **1.** *adj.* unlikely to fall or topple; steady; firm. (Adv: *stably.*) ♦ *The heavy bookcase was very stable.* ♦ *Don't lean on my desk! It's not stable.* **2.** *adj.* not likely to change; constant; permanent. (Adv: *stably.*) ♦ *The social worker placed the orphan with a stable family.* ♦ *Mary is looking for stable employment because she wants a steady income.* **3.** *n.* a building where horses are kept. ♦ *The horses fled the stable when it caught on fire.* ♦ *Anne locked the stable after grooming the horses.* **4.** *n.* a group of independent workers who are available to work for someone else. (Figurative on ③.) ♦ *The talk-show host's jokes were written by a stable of writers.* ♦ *The movie agent represented a stable of talent.*

staccato [stə 'kɑt o] **1.** *adj.* [of musical notes played] short, quick, and not connected. ♦ *The piano teacher told Bill to practice playing staccato notes.* ♦ *The dance song was punctuated by a crisp staccato drum beat.* **2.** *adj.* short, quick, and not connected, like music that is ①. (Figurative on ①.) ♦ *I couldn't understand the guide's rapid, staccato speech.* ♦ *The staccato beat of the rain against the window annoyed me.*

stack ['stæk] **1.** *n.* an orderly pile of something; a neat pile of something. ♦ *My boss set a stack of papers on my desk.* ♦ *The waiter served me a stack of blueberry pancakes.* **2.** *n.* a large number of something; a great amount of something. (Figurative on ①.) ♦ *I have a stack of problems that I must take care of.* ♦ *There is a whole stack of decisions facing me at work.* **3. the stacks** *n.* the part of a library where the books are kept on shelves. (Treated as plural.) ♦ *The book I needed wasn't in the stacks.* ♦ *The librarian had the new books taken to the stacks.* **4.** *tv.* to place things in a neat, orderly pile; to arrange things into a neat, orderly pile. ♦ *The boy stacked old newspapers in his wagon.* ♦ *My boss stacked a lot of work on my desk.*

stadium ['sted i əm] *n.* a playing field surrounded by rows of seats for spectators. ♦ *Over 40,000 people filled the stadium to watch the football game.* ♦ *When the home team won, the fans in the stadium cheered.*

staff ['stæf] **1.** *n.* the workers who operate and manage an organization. (No plural form in this sense.) ♦ *The library staff returns books to the shelves every day.* ♦ *The office staff meets every Monday to discuss the week's work.* **2.** *n.* a large, heavy stick used for support; a large cane. ♦ *The elderly man walked with the aid of a staff.* ♦ *The shepherd put his weight on his staff as he walked.* **3.** *tv.* to provide something with enough workers so that a job can be done properly. ♦ *The manager staffed the office with five new workers.* ♦ *We staffed the project with volunteers.* **4.** *tv.* [for workers] to provide services to do a task. ♦ *Volunteers staffed the phone lines at the charity's office.* ♦ *The charitable agency was staffed by trained counselors.*

stag ['stæg] **1.** *n.* a mature male deer. ♦ *The hunter kept the dead stag's antlers as a souvenir.* ♦ *We saw a stag and a doe in the woods.* **2.** *adj.* attended by men only; for men only. ♦ *I threw a stag party for the groom the night before his wedding.* ♦ *David joined a stag bowling league.* **3. go stag** *idiom* to attend something without an accompanying female when such accompaniment is expected. (Now also used for a female without a male.) ♦ *I went to the party stag because my wife was sick.* ♦ *Tom had to go stag because he couldn't find a date.*

stage ['stedʒ] **1.** *n.* a period of development; one part of a process. ♦ *In the first stage of our project, we must raise funds.* ♦ *Tadpoles are frogs in an early stage of development.* **2.** *n.* the floor, usually raised, in a theater where performers perform. ♦ *When the curtain was raised, the stage was empty.* ♦ *The performers walked onto the stage singing a song.* **3. the stage** *n.* theater; the business of producing and acting in live theater. (No plural form in this sense. Treated as singular.) ♦ *Mary moved to New York City to pursue a career on the stage.* ♦ *Susan was always fascinated by the stage.* **4.** *tv.* to produce a play at a theater; to put on a play. ♦ *Our theater company staged a new version of that play.* ♦ Romeo and Juliet *was staged by the high-school drama club.* **5.** *tv.* to plan and do something that attracts public attention. ♦ *The workers staged a strike over the factory's unfair labor practices.* ♦ *The protesters staged a riot in front of city hall.* **6. at this stage (of the game)** *idiom* at the current point in some event or situation; currently. ♦ *We'll have to wait and see. There isn't much we can do at this stage of the game.* ♦ *At this stage, we are better off not calling the doctor.*

stagecoach ['stedʒ kotʃ] *n.* a coach, used in the old West, pulled by horses. ♦ *Gunslingers robbed stagecoaches in the old West.* ♦ *My great-grandmother road a stagecoach from Ohio to Kansas.*

stagehand ['stedʒ hænd] *n.* a theater worker who helps move scenery during rehearsals and performances. ♦ *A stagehand lowered the curtain at the end of the play.* ♦ *The scenery was moved onstage by stagehands.*

stagger ['stæg ɚ] **1.** *iv.* to totter; to walk unsteadily from side to side, as though one were drunk, badly hurt, or very sick. ♦ *The drunk staggered through the bar.* ♦ *The injured soldier staggered toward shelter.* **2.** *tv.* to shock someone; to stun someone. ♦ *The sight of the burned building simply staggered the now homeless family.* ♦ *John was staggered by the horrifying news.* **3.** *tv.* to arrange different things so that they do not occur all at the same time. ♦ *The airline staggers its planes' arrival times so all the planes do not arrive at once.* ♦ *The doctor staggered his appointments throughout the week.*

staggering ['stæg ɚ ɪŋ] *adj.* unbelievable; incredible; shocking. (Adv: *staggeringly.*) ♦ *The plumber repaired our pipes for the staggering sum of $4,000.* ♦ *Mary faced a staggering amount of work when she returned from vacation.*

staging ['stedʒ ɪŋ] *n.* the production of a play; the way in which a play is staged. (No plural form in this sense.) ♦ *The theater's unique staging of the play received good reviews.* ♦ *The students applauded the drama club's staging of* Hamlet.

stagnant ['stæg nənt] **1.** *adj.* [of water or air] stale and not moving or circulating. (Adv: *stagnantly.*) ♦ *Do not drink water from a stagnant pond.* ♦ *The air in the room was quite stagnant, so I opened a window.* **2.** *adj.* never changing; not developing; stale. (Figurative on ①. Adv: *stagnantly.*) ♦ *The editor always rewrote the reporter's stagnant news articles.* ♦ *No one laughed at the comedian's stagnant routine.*

stagnate ['stæg net] **1.** *iv.* to become stagnant ①. ♦ *The pond stagnated when the natural spring beneath it ran dry.* ♦ *The air in the tiny room will stagnate if a window is not opened.* **2.** *iv.* to become stagnant ②. ♦ *Mary moved to New York because she was stagnating in her small hometown.* ♦ *I don't want to grow old and stagnate. I have to get out and be with people.*

staid ['sted] *adj.* quiet, serious, and dull. (Adv: *staidly.*) ♦ *Tom, a staid student, studied all weekend long.* ♦ *The staid gentleman at the library ignored my attempt at conversation.*

stain ['sten] **1.** *tv.* to discolor something; to make something dirty by changing its color. ♦ *A few drops of spilled coffee stained my shirt.* ♦ *Muddy water from the storm stained my shoes and socks.* **2.** *tv.* to coat a wooden surface with a liquid that gives it a color. ♦ *Mary stained the wooden deck to make it match the rest of the house.* ♦ *John stained the bookshelf to give it a darker hue.* **3.** *tv.* to color tissue or organisms so they can be observed or identified. ♦ *The scientist stained the bacteria so they could be identified.* ♦ *The technologist stained the cells purple.* **4.** *iv.* to cause discoloration; to have the ability to change the color of something permanently. ♦ *Coffee stains badly if you don't clean it up immediately.* ♦ *Mustard stains, especially on light-colored material.* **5.** *iv.* to accept and hold a stain ⑥. ♦ *Do you think this cloth will stain?* ♦ *My teeth stained because I drank too much coffee.* **6.** *n.* a mark, spot, or blemish; a discoloration. ♦ *Mary tried to scrub the stain from the rug.* ♦ *The cleaners removed the coffee stain from my tie.* **7.** *n.* a liquid that is used to give color to wood. (No plural form in this sense.) ♦ *Anne applied stain to the wooden make it match the house.* ♦ *John put a layer of stain on the bookshelf.*

stained ['stend] **1.** *adj.* marked; blemished; spotted; discolored. ♦ *Mary threw her stained blouse away.* ♦ *John covered the stained sofa with a blanket.* **2.** *adj.* [of wood] painted with a stain. ♦ *The stained wooden porch matched the color of the house.* ♦ *Our carefully stained table looked like an antique.*

stained glass ['stend glæs] *n.* colored glass that is arranged in tiny pieces in a metal framework to make a picture or design, especially used in windows in churches. (No plural form in this sense.) ♦ *We love to visit old churches and see the stained glass.* ♦ *The worker set the stained glass into the lead framing.*

stair ['ster] *n.* a step or series of steps that go from one level to another. (Usually plural.) ♦ *Mary held on to the railing as she walked down the stairs.* ♦ *To get to the second floor, you have to take the stairs.*

staircase ['ster kes] *n.* a set of stairs that allows one to go from one level to another; a stairway. ♦ *Jane ran up the staircase to the second floor.* ♦ *The mansion had an exquisite spiral staircase winding from the first floor to the second.*

stairway ['ster we] *n.* a set of stairs that allow one to go from one level to another; a staircase. ♦ *John held on to the railing as he walked down the stairway.* ♦ *The stairway was carpeted to prevent people from slipping.*

stake ['stek] **1.** *n.* a pointed piece of wood that is driven into the ground. ♦ *The camper pounded a stake into the ground to hold up the tent.* ♦ *I drove a stake in the ground to show where the tree should be planted.* **2. stakes** *n.* the amount of money bet in a game; the amount of risk involved in some activity. (Treated as plural.) ♦ *I matched my opponent's bet and raised the stakes another $100.* ♦ *John quit because the stakes were too high.* **3. burn someone at the stake** *idiom* to chastise or denounce someone severely, but without violence. ♦ *Stop yelling. I made a simple mistake, and you're burning me at the stake for it.* ♦ *Sally only spilled her milk. There is no need to shout. Don't burn her at the stake for it!* **4. pull up stakes** *idiom* to move to another place. ♦ *I've been here long enough. It's time to pull up stakes.* ♦ *I hate the thought of having to pull up stakes.*

stale ['stel] *adj.* no longer fresh, new, exciting, flavorful, or interesting. (Adv: *stalely.* Comp: *staler;* sup: *stalest.*) ♦ *The stale bread was dry and hard.* ♦ *The editor criticized the journalist's stale style.*

stalemate ['stel met] **1.** *n.* a situation in chess where neither player can win. ♦ *The players reached a stalemate, so a draw was declared.* ♦ *For the stalemate, each player received half a point.* **2.** *n.* a situation where no action can be taken; a standstill; a situation in which neither side of an issue can win. (Figurative on ①.) ♦ *A mediator was called in to help end the contract stalemate.* ♦ *The warring armies came to a stalemate and divided the country in half.*

stalk ['stɔk] **1.** *n.* the main stem of a plant, which is connected to the roots, and from which leaves grow. ♦ *David chopped up a stalk of celery.* ♦ *After the corn was picked, the farmer plowed the stalks into the ground.* **2.** *tv.* to pursue or approach an animal without being seen or heard. ♦ *The lion stalked its prey.* ♦ *The hunter stalked the deer through the forest.* **3.** *tv.* to follow or pursue someone menacingly or annoyingly. (Figurative on ②.) ♦ *The menacing man stalked his favorite actress.* ♦ *Mary placed a restraining order on the man who stalked her.*

stall ['stɔl] **1.** *n.* a small, enclosed space. ♦ *John cleaned the mildew from the shower stall.* ♦ *The janitor cleaned the bathroom stalls twice a day.* **2.** *n.* a space within a barn for one animal, especially a horse. ♦ *Mary led her horse back to its stall.* ♦ *Bill threw some fresh hay into the horse's stall.* **3.** *n.* a booth in a market, or in a building with an open wall in front, where products are sold. ♦ *At sunrise, the vendors set up their stalls in the town square.* ♦ *Anne sold handmade crafts at a stall at the fair.* **4.** *iv.* [for a vehicle] to stop because of engine trouble. ♦ *My car stalled at the intersection.* ♦ *There was an accident when the truck stalled on the freeway.* **5.** *iv.* [for an airplane] to point upward too sharply and go out of control. ♦ *The nose of the plane was too high and the plane stalled.* ♦ *When the plane started to stall, the pilot sped up the engine.* **6.** *iv.* to hesitate so that one has more time; to be evasive in order to gain time; to pause for time; to delay. ♦ *Stop stalling and tell me where you left your coat.* ♦ *John stalled for time while he tried to think of an excuse.* **7.** *tv.* to delay someone or something. ♦ *You stall the robber while I call the police!* ♦ *Something stalled the departure of the train.*

stallion ['stæl jən] *n.* an adult male horse capable of breeding. ♦ *Susan bred her mare with a strong black stallion.* ♦ *The stallion led his band of mares to the pond to drink.*

stalwart ['stɔl wɚt] **1.** *n.* someone who supports someone or something loyally and faithfully. ♦ *The former king's stalwarts were executed by the new regime.* ♦ *The stalwarts supported their party's entire slate.* **2.** *adj.* determined and loyal; steadfast. (Adv: *stalwartly.*) ♦ *The prince asked his stalwart aides for advice.* ♦ *The stalwart liberals would not vote for the conservative politician.*

stamina ['stæm ɪ nə] *n.* endurance; the ability of the body or mind to remain energetic. (No plural form in this sense.) ♦ *John lacks the stamina to run in a 24-mile marathon.* ♦ *It takes a lot of stamina to work and raise a family.*

stammer ['stæm ɚ] **1.** *n.* a speech condition where the speaker repeats the same sound many times while speaking. (No plural form in this sense.) ♦ *John's stammer became harder to understand when he was nervous.* ♦ *The speech therapist cured Anne of her stammer.* **2.** *iv.* to stutter; to repeat the same sound several times while speaking. ♦ *Susan stammered as she tried to explain why she was in my office.* ♦ *When David is scared, he begins to stammer.* **3.** *tv.* to say something while having ①. ♦ *"Wh-wh-what is that?" I stammered with surprise.* ♦ *When Mary is nervous, she stammers her words.*

stamp ['stæmp] **1.** *n.* a square of paper issued by the government that must be attached to certain documents to make them official or to indicate that a fee or tax has been paid, especially as used for postage. ♦ *I licked a stamp and affixed it to the envelope.* ♦ *In the small country, every purchase I made required a tax stamp on the receipt.* **2.** *n.* a tool that imprints a design (a picture or words) onto a surface. ♦ *The bottom of this stamp has a raised design, which is pressed in ink and then pressed onto a surface, causing the design to be printed.* ♦ *The banker had a stamp that said "APPROVED."* **3.** *n.* the design that is imprinted onto a surface by ②. ♦ *My teacher put a stamp of a smiling face on my homework.* ♦ *The stamp's fresh ink smeared when I rubbed against it.* **4.** *n.* a feature; a trait; a distinguishing mark. (Figurative on ③.) ♦ *Prejudice is the stamp of ignorance.* ♦ *This brand name is a stamp of excellence.* **5.** *tv.* to mark an object with ②, usually to make it official or to acknowledge that a fee has been paid or that requirements have been met. ♦ *The border guard stamped my passport when I entered the country.* ♦ *The city official stamped my building permit.* **6.** *tv.* to put a postage stamp ① on an envelope. ♦ *I stamped the envelopes and dropped them in the mailbox.* ♦ *The receptionist stamped the company's mail with a machine.* **7.** *tv.* to hit something or flatten something by bringing down one's foot with force. ♦ *David stamped the weeds down to make a path.* ♦ *Mary stamped the can flat with her boot.* **8.** *iv.* to walk heavily somewhere; to walk with heavy steps. ♦ *I could hear my upstairs neighbor stamp across his floor.* ♦ *Susan stamped loudly through the house in her heavy boots.*

stampede [stæm 'pid] **1.** *n.* a sudden rush of frightened horses or cattle. ♦ *The cowboys tried to stop the stampede of horses.* ♦ *The loud explosion caused the stampede of cattle.* **2.** *n.* a sudden rush of excited, angry, or impatient people. (Figurative on ①.) ♦ *There was a stampede toward the exit during the fire.* ♦ *Seven people were crushed in the stampede at the soccer stadium.* **3.** *iv.* to rush as part of a large crowd of people or creatures. ♦ *The fire caused the horses to stampede.* ♦ *The crowd stampeded toward the fire exit.* **4.** *tv.* to cause ① or ②. ♦ *The fire stampeded the crowd.* ♦ *The sound of thunder stampeded the cattle.*

stand ['stænd] **1.** *iv., irreg.* to be in a normal or typical upright position. (Pt/pp: **stood.**) ♦ *Mary stood by the door and waited for me.* ♦ *After the hurricane, very few trees or houses were still standing.* **2. stand (up)** *iv., irreg.* (+ *adv.*) to move to an upright position on one's feet. ♦ *Polite students stand up when their teacher enters the room.* ♦ *Mary stood and walked into the other room.* **3.** *iv., irreg.* to be a particular height when in an upright position on one's feet. ♦ *Jimmy stands 3 feet and 2 inches.* ♦ *Mary stands 5 feet 8 inches in her bare feet.* **4.** *iv., irreg.* to be in a particular location. ♦ *The coat rack stands behind the door.* ♦ *A police car stood right outside the bank.* **5.** *iv., irreg.* [for a law] to remain in force. ♦ *Because of the Supreme Court's ruling, the law still stood.* ♦ *The popular law stood for many years.* **6. stand for** *iv., irreg.* + *prep. phr.* to represent something; to symbolize something ♦ *The symbol "&" stands for "and."* ♦ *The word* o'clock *stands for "of the clock."* **7. stand for** *iv., irreg.* + *prep. phr.* to represent a quality that is either good or bad. ♦ *Our company stands for good products and good service.* ♦ *I personally stand for honesty and fairness for all people.* **8. stand for** *iv., irreg.* + *prep. phr.* to tolerate something; to endure something. ♦ *I will not stand for such insolence!* ♦ *Do you think the judge will stand for that kind of disruption in the courtroom?* **9.** *tv., irreg.* to move someone or something to an upright position. ♦ *The book fell on its side, so Bill stood it back on its end.* ♦ *The nurse stood the patient next to his bed.* **10.** *tv., irreg.* to withstand something; to endure something; to put up with something. ♦ *I can't stand much more of this!* ♦ *John can stand a lot of abuse.* **11.** *n.* the position one takes on an issue. ♦ *I disagree with your stand on gun control.* ♦ *The newspaper agreed with the president's stand on taxes.* **12. stands** *n.* the place where spectators sit during an event, consisting of rows of seats or benches; the grandstand. (Treated as plural.) ♦ *The fans cheered their team from the stands.* ♦ *The players looked up to the stands and saw the angry fans.* **13.** *n.* a booth at a market or on a street where products are sold. ♦ *I bought lunch at a stand on the corner.* ♦ *David sold handmade jewelry at a stand in the market square.* **14.** *n.* a base, frame, or piece of furniture that supports something. ♦ *The musician placed his music on the music stand.* ♦ *I put my umbrella in the umbrella stand as I entered.* **15.** *n.* a place where taxis line up while waiting for passengers. ♦ *I went to the first taxi at the stand and opened the door.* ♦ *There's room for only six taxis at this stand.* **16. (witness) stand** *n.* the place where someone gives testimony under oath in court. ♦ *The witness approached the stand after her name was called.* ♦ *You are under oath to tell the truth while you are on the stand.*

standard ['stæn dɚd] **1.** *n.* something against which something else is tested or measured; something that is the basis of comparison. ♦ *I used my own experience as a standard for comparison.* ♦ *The food critic used her grand-*

mother's cooking as the standard. **2.** *n.* something, especially gold or silver, that has a fixed value that backs the money system of a country. ♦ *The young country adopted the monetary standard of its powerful neighbor.* ♦ *The politician argued for a return to the gold standard.* **3.** *n.* a degree of quality or excellence. ♦ *This private school sets high standards for its students.* ♦ *The employees who didn't meet company standards were fired.* **4.** *adj.* ordinary; conforming to a certain degree or amount; normal. (Adv: *standardly.*) ♦ *The standard unit of metric measurement is the meter.* ♦ *Mary bought a new car with standard features because she couldn't afford extra gadgets.* **5.** *adj.* correct and acceptable according to the formal rules of a language. (Adv: *standardly.*) ♦ *In standard English, "ain't" is not considered acceptable.* ♦ *Lisa spoke the standard language at work and a nonstandard dialect at home.*

standardization [stæn dɚd ɪ 'ze ʃən] *n.* the process of creating a standard. (No plural form in this sense.) ♦ *The governor demanded a standardization of school curriculums throughout the state.* ♦ *The need for accurate train schedules led to the standardization of time zones.*

standardize ['stæn dɚ dɑɪz] *tv.* to cause something to conform to a standard. ♦ *Shoe sizes were standardized many years ago.* ♦ *The governor sought to standardize the curriculum of all the state's schools.*

standby ['stænd bɑɪ] **1.** *n.* an extra thing or person, nearby and ready. (Pl: *standbys.*) ♦ *This camera isn't working. Do you have a standby?* ♦ *If Tom does not come on time, Dave would make a good standby.* **2.** *n.* a person traveling on standby ④. (Pl: *standbys.*) ♦ *There were more standbys than there were seats on the plane!* ♦ *Three lucky standbys got on the flight.* **3.** *adv.* traveling where one is not able to reserve a seat and must travel as ②. ♦ *I hate to fly standby because I'm never sure if I'll get a seat.* ♦ *My cousin who works for an airline generally flies standby.* **4. on standby** *phr.* of waiting for one's turn, especially describing the status of travelers who wait near a train, plane, or bus, hoping that a seat will become available. ♦ *The passenger waited on standby for an available seat.* ♦ *The agent was able to seat all of the passengers on standby.*

stand-in ['stænd ɪn] *n.* someone who takes someone else's place temporarily. ♦ *The stand-in stood on the set while the lights were focused.* ♦ *Tom was a stand-in for the manager who was temporarily called away.*

standing ['stænd ɪŋ] **1.** *adj.* [of water] remaining at rest. ♦ *The standing water was muddy and still.* ♦ *Puddles of standing water made it hard to walk on the street.* **2.** *adj.* lasting; permanent; always in effect. ♦ *You have a standing invitation to stay at my house whenever you want.* ♦ *The guard has standing orders to question everyone who comes into the building.* **3.** *n.* one's position or rank, especially in society or in a business. (No plural form in this sense.) ♦ *The scandalous article ruined the banker's standing in town.* ♦ *The poor woman went to college to better her standing in life.*

stand-off ['stæn dɔf] *n.* a stalemate; a situation in which neither side of a dispute can win. ♦ *The stand-off between management and the union lasted for months.* ♦ *A stand-off between the two armies created peace temporarily.*

standoffish [stænd 'ɔf ɪʃ] *adj.* aloof; unfriendly; haughty. (Adv: *standoffishly.*) ♦ *The standoffish clerk wouldn't help me find what I wanted.* ♦ *David might seem standoffish, but he's really just shy.*

standpoint ['stænd pɔɪnt] *n.* one's point of view; the position from which opinions or policies are developed. ♦ *From the taxpayer's standpoint, taxes must be reduced.* ♦ *The witness described the accident from her standpoint.*

standstill ['stænd 'stɪl] *n.* a complete stop; a condition in which nothing is moving. (No plural form in this sense.) ♦ *Traffic came to a standstill because of an accident.* ♦ *Production was at a standstill during the factory strike.*

stank ['stæŋk] a pt of stink.

stanza ['stæn zə] *n.* a group of lines in a poem, designed to have a certain scheme of rhyme or rhythm. ♦ *One stanza of a poem is equivalent to one verse of a song.* ♦ *In this poem, the last word of each stanza rhymes.*

staple ['step əl] **1.** *n.* a small, thin, U-shaped piece of wire that fastens papers together, or that fastens things to a surface. ♦ *Mary pulled the staple from the document with her fingers.* ♦ *David loaded the stapler with staples.* **2.** *n.* the most basic foods. ♦ *Rice is a staple for many eastern Asians.* ♦ *We went to the store to buy staples for our camping trip.* **3.** *n.* the most basic element of something. (Figurative on ②.) ♦ *Automotive products are the staple of Michigan's economy.* ♦ *Mystery novels are the staple at the local bookstore.* **4.** *tv.* to fasten papers together or to attach something to something else with ①. ♦ *The clerk stapled my papers together.* ♦ *The manager stapled an important notice to the wall.*

stapler ['step lɚ] *n.* a machine that drives staples through paper or into objects. ♦ *John used an electric stapler to staple the thick stack of papers together.* ♦ *Every desk in the office has a stapler on it.*

star ['stɑr] **1.** *n.* a large object in space, such as the sun, that creates its own heat and light. ♦ *There are hundreds of stars in the sky.* ♦ *Alpha Centauri is the nearest star to Earth, besides our own sun.* **2.** *n.* a celebrity; a famous entertainer. ♦ *The movie featured six stars.* ♦ *The sports star demanded special treatment at the hotel.* **3.** *n.* a figure that has five points that radiate from a center point. ♦ *Mary drew a star on the paper.* ♦ *The American flag has white stars against a blue background.* **4.** *n.* ③ used as a mark of a degree of quality. (The more stars, the better something is.) ♦ *The excellent movie received four stars from many critics.* ♦ *The food critic gave the restaurant two stars because service was poor.* **5.** *tv.* [for a movie, play, or television show] to feature a particular performer. ♦ *Each week, the TV show stars different actors.* ♦ *Let's go see that movie that stars my favorite actress.* **6.** *iv.* [for a performer] to appear in a movie, play, or television show. ♦ *My talented friend once starred in a Broadway play.* ♦ *Mary hoped to star in a successful movie someday.* **7.** *adj.* most outstanding; most excellent; best. ♦ *The team's star player was injured during practice.* ♦ *The editor sent the paper's star reporter to cover the trial.* **8. get stars in one's eyes; have stars in one's eyes** *idiom* to be obsessed with movies and the theater. (On ②.) ♦ *Many young people get stars in their eyes at this age.* ♦ *Anne has stars in her eyes. She wants to go to Hollywood.* **9. see stars** *idiom* to see flashing lights after receiving a blow to the head. ♦ *I saw stars when I bumped my head on the attic ceiling.* ♦ *The little boy saw stars when he fell headfirst onto the concrete.*

starboard ['stɑr bɚd] **1.** *n.* the right side of a ship when one faces forward. (No plural form in this sense.) ♦ *I could see a bit of land from the starboard.* ♦ *Lisa quickly moved to the starboard to balance the small boat.* **2.** *adj.* on or at the right side of a ship. ♦ *The passenger requested a starboard cabin.* ♦ *A sailor fell from the starboard side during the storm.* **3.** *adv.* toward or in the direction of the right side of a ship when one faces forward. ♦ *If you look starboard, you can see a school of dolphins swimming.* ♦ *The cargo wasn't balanced, so the ship tilted starboard.*

starch ['stɑrtʃ] **1.** *n.* a white food substance that is part of potatoes, rice, and other grains. (No plural form in this sense.) ♦ *Starch is a kind of carbohydrate.* ♦ *Lisa eats a lot of foods that contain starch.* **2.** *n.* a substance used to stiffen cloth. (No plural form in this sense. ② is added while clothes are being washed or sprayed on afterward.) ♦ *There is too much starch in my shirts.* ♦ *It has been years since it was necessary to use starch when washing clothes.* **3.** *n.* food that contains ①. ♦ *Bill eats mostly starch on his diet.* ♦ *The nutritionist told me to eat fewer starches.* **4.** *tv.* to stiffen fabric or clothing by coating it with or soaking it in ②. ♦ *The launderer starched my shirts for free.* ♦ *Bill starched his shirt after ironing it.*

stardom ['stɑr dəm] *n.* fame; the state of being a famous performer or entertainer. (No plural form in this sense.) ♦ *The small role moved the actress into stardom.* ♦ *Mary dreamed of fame and stardom.*

stare ['stɛr] **1. stare (at)** *iv.* (+ *prep. phr.*) to look directly at someone or something with one's eyes wide open, as though in fear, shock, surprise, wonder, or stupidity. ♦ *The child stared curiously at the man on crutches.* ♦ *I just stared when Bill made a very rude comment.* **2.** *n.* a long, direct look at someone or something with one's eyes wide open. ♦ *On the bus, a stranger's stare made me very nervous.* ♦ *The flamboyant tourist ignored the stares of the local townspeople.*

starfish ['stɑr fɪʃ] *n., irreg.* a star-shaped sea animal with arm-like appendages. (Pl: *starfish.*) ♦ *A starfish's arm will grow back if it is cut off.* ♦ *The marine biologist studied the growth processes of starfish.*

stark ['stɑrk] **1.** *adj.* bare; desolate; empty. (Adv: *starkly.* Comp: *starker;* sup: *starkest.*) ♦ *Anne needs some furniture for her stark apartment.* ♦ *Susan surveyed the stark landscape of the tundra.* **2.** *adj.* complete; absolute. (Adv: *starkly.* (Typically with *terror, silence.* Comp: *starker;* sup: *starkest.*) ♦ *The mail carrier fled from the angry dog in stark terror.* ♦ *There was only a stark silence in the empty office building.* **3.** *adv.* completely; totally. (Typically with *naked, raving mad.*) ♦ *Jimmy ran stark naked through the living room.* ♦ *The person who murdered Mr. Smith was stark raving mad!*

starlight ['stɑr lɑɪt] *n.* light that comes from stars. (No plural form in this sense.) ♦ *On the clear summer night, the sky was aglow with starlight.* ♦ *The bright lights of the city prevented us from seeing starlight.*

starry ['stɑr i] *adj.* full of stars; bright with the light of many stars. (Adv: *starrily.* Comp: *starrier;* sup: *starriest.*) ♦ *The city resident was amazed at how starry the country skies were.* ♦ *I lay on the hill, gazing at the starry nighttime sky.*

starry-eyed ['stɑr i ɑɪd] *adj.* unrealistic; gullible; naive; idealistic. ♦ *The starry-eyed children waited in line to talk to Santa Claus.* ♦ *The director tricked the starry-eyed actor into working for almost no money.*

start ['stɑrt] **1.** *n.* the beginning point of something; the time or place where something begins. ♦ *January first is the start of the year.* ♦ *Susan always drinks coffee at the start of her day.* **2.** *n.* a shock that may jerk or jolt the body. ♦ *John gave me quite a start when he jumped out from behind the corner.* ♦ *The shocking news gave my heart a start.* **3.** *tv.* to begin a process; to begin doing something; to cause something to operate, work, or move. ♦ *We started the meeting by reading the minutes of the previous meeting.* ♦ *Susan started the lawn mower and mowed the lawn.* **4.** *tv.* to originate something. ♦ *My grandfather started the family business sixty years ago.* ♦ *The clothing designer started many fashion trends.* **5.** *iv.* to begin a movement; to begin a journey; to begin a process; to begin at the lower limit of something. ♦ *Bill started for class at 9:00 A.M.* ♦ *When should we start?* **6.** *iv.* to move or jerk suddenly, as though one were surprised or scared; to be startled. ♦ *John started when Bill jumped out from behind a corner.* ♦ *The horse started when a gunshot was fired.* **7. from start to finish** *idiom* entirely; throughout. ♦ *I disliked the whole business from start to finish.* ♦ *Mary caused problems from start to finish.* **8. get off to a flying start** *idiom* to have a very successful beginning to something. ♦ *The new business got off to a flying start with those export orders.* ♦ *We will need a large donation if the charity is to get off to a flying start.* **9. off to a running start** *idiom* with a good, fast beginning. ♦ *I got off to a running start in math this year.* ♦ *The new year got off to a running start with lots of excitement.*

starter ['stɑrt ɚ] **1.** *n.* someone or something that starts something. ♦ *Bill will be the starter for the race.* ♦ *My car won't run because its starter is broken.* **2.** *n.* a first course in a restaurant meal; an appetizer. ♦ *Lisa ordered a small salad for a starter.* ♦ *Anne skipped the starter and chose soup instead.*

startle ['stɑrt əl] *tv.* to cause someone to move or jump suddenly because of fear or surprise. ♦ *A loud gunshot startled me.* ♦ *The bad news startled John.*

startled ['stɑr təld] *adj.* surprised; suddenly surprised. (Adv: *startledly.*) ♦ *The startled horse galloped away.* ♦ *I tried to calm my startled friend.*

startling ['stɑr tl ɪŋ] *adj.* surprising or scary; causing someone to jump with fear or surprise. (Adv: *startlingly.*) ♦ *The startling explosion scared everyone in town.* ♦ *The startling news shocked the entire nation.*

starvation [stɑr 've ʃən] *n.* starving; suffering and possibly death caused by not having food. (No plural form in this sense.) ♦ *The abandoned child died of starvation.* ♦ *The tortured prisoners suffered from starvation.*

starve ['stɑrv] **1.** *iv.* to die because of a lack of food; to die because one does not or cannot eat. ♦ *The abandoned kittens starved to death.* ♦ *Thousands of people starved during the war.* **2.** *iv.* to be very hungry. ♦ *While the workers starved, the factory owner became rich.* ♦ *I'm starving. Let's go get some dinner.* **3.** *tv.* to cause someone or some creature to die of hunger. ♦ *The evil soldiers starved their prisoners.* ♦ *The abusive parents starved their child.*

starving ['stɑr vɪŋ] *adj.* extremely hungry; lacking enough food to survive. ♦ *The starving dog ate four bowls* *of dog food.* ♦ *Our church sent food to the starving victims of the famine.*

stash ['stæʃ] **1.** *tv.* to hide something somewhere secretly for future use. (Informal.) ♦ *John had stashed thousands of dollars in his house.* ♦ *Mary stashed some batteries in her tool box for emergencies.* **2.** *n.* something that is hidden; a hidden supply of something. (Informal.) ♦ *The police failed to find Bill's stash of gold.* ♦ *The old man's stash of money was destroyed in the fire.*

state ['stet] **1.** *n.* the condition that someone or something is in. ♦ *The happy children were in a state of excitement.* ♦ *The president spoke about the state of the economy.* **2.** *n.* the government of a country. (No plural form in this sense.) ♦ *The politician stressed the separation of church and state.* ♦ *The state censored the news about the war.* **3.** *n.* a division of government within a country or a republic. ♦ *A senator from the State of Ohio sponsored the bill.* ♦ *Both the U.S. and Mexico are divided into states.* **4.** *adj.* <the adj. use of ②.> ♦ *The spy was executed for selling state secrets to the enemy.* ♦ *During the state emergency, citizens' rights were suspended.* **5.** *adj.* <the adj. use of ③.> ♦ *You can get your driver's license renewed at any state office.* ♦ *The mayor decided to run for a seat in the state senate.* **6.** *adj.* [of a governmental event] involving formal ceremony. ♦ *Dozens of businesspeople were invited to a state dinner.* ♦ *Many politicians spoke during the state function.* **7.** *tv.* to express something; to say something. (Takes a clause.) ♦ *John stated that he was hungry.* ♦ *Mary stated that her client had no opinion on the rumor.*

stately ['stet li] *adj.* dignified; majestic; ceremonial; full of pomp. (Comp: *statelier;* sup: *stateliest.*) ♦ *Thousands of people attended the stately banquet.* ♦ *A Supreme Court justice presided over the stately inauguration.*

statement ['stet mənt] **1.** *n.* something that is said; something that is stated. ♦ *The lawyer issued a statement concerning the trial's outcome.* ♦ *The newspaper retracted its libelous statement.* **2.** *n.* a list showing the status of an account during a period of time. ♦ *My bank sends me a statement each month for my checking account.* ♦ *The accountant prepared the company's yearly financial statement.*

stateroom ['stet rum] *n.* a private cabin on a ship or train. ♦ *The newlyweds stayed in a fancy stateroom on their honeymoon.* ♦ *After dinner and dancing, Bob retired to his stateroom to sleep.*

statesman ['stets mən] *n., irreg.* someone who is a skilled political leader; a man who is a skilled political leader. (Pl: **statesmen**.) ♦ *The elder statesman drafted the intricate legislation.* ♦ *The president commended the statesman for his advice during the crisis.*

statesmen ['stets mən] pl of **statesman**.

stateswoman ['stets wʊm ən] *n., irreg.* a woman who is a skilled political leader. (Pl: **stateswomen**.) ♦ *The elder stateswoman drafted the intricate legislation.* ♦ *The president commended the stateswoman for her advice during the crisis.*

stateswomen ['stets wɪm ən] pl of **stateswoman**.

static ['stæt ɪk] **1.** *n.* interference with radio, television, or telephone reception; the buzzing noise made when a radio or television station is not tuned in properly. (No plural form in this sense.) ♦ *Could you tune the radio? We're getting a lot of static.* ♦ *I couldn't hear Bill on the phone because there was too much static.* **2.** *adj.* [of electricity] not confined to flowing in an electrical current. ♦ *A static charge causes clothes to cling together.* ♦ *Bill gave me a shock of static electricity when he touched me.* **3.** *adj.* not changing; stable; steady. (Adv: *statically* [...ɪk li].) ♦ *Interest rates are static at the moment, and the stock market is rising.* ♦ *Static air pressure indicates that the weather will not change soon.*

station ['ste ʃən] **1.** *n.* the building or platform where a train or bus stops to let people on and off. ♦ *The train pulled into Union Station.* ♦ *If you're going to the museum, get off at the next station.* **2.** *n.* a building where workers in a particular service work. ♦ *The post office built a new station in a suburb.* ♦ *The downtown electrical station was damaged in a fire.* **3.** *n.* the specific location where a worker is assigned to work. ♦ *During the emergency, I had to remain at my station and answer the telephone.* ♦ *My work station has a computer and a fax machine.* **4.** *n.* the building or offices from which a television or radio broadcast is transmitted. ♦ *The broadcast was interrupted when lightning struck the station.* ♦ *I called the station to complain about their news editorial.* **5.** *tv.* to place someone at a location for work; to assign someone to a location for work. ♦ *Hundreds of soldiers were stationed at a base in Germany.* ♦ *The firm stationed some of its employees downtown.*

stationary ['ste ʃə nɛr i] *adj.* remaining in place; not moving; standing still. (Compare with **stationery**.) ♦ *Because of an accident, traffic was stationary for an hour.* ♦ *I think your arm is broken. Try to keep it stationary until we get to the hospital.*

station break ['ste ʃən brek] *n.* a break between parts of a television or radio program so that the local station can be identified on the air. ♦ *The disc jockey paused for a station break.* ♦ *I went to the kitchen for some food during the station break.*

stationery ['ste ʃə nɛr i] *n.* writing paper; writing supplies, including paper, pen, ink, envelopes, etc. (No plural form in this sense. Compare with **stationary**.) ♦ *I bought some fancy stationery for my thank-you notes.* ♦ *Bob's stationery has his name printed on it in gold.*

station wagon ['ste ʃən wæg ən] *n.* a large car with a rear door and extra room in back for people or things. ♦ *The large family traveled in a station wagon.* ♦ *John loaded the groceries in the back of his station wagon.*

statistic [stə 'tɪs tɪk] **1.** *n.* a piece of data used in ②. ♦ *A gang member became the latest murder statistic last weekend.* ♦ *I don't want you to become another accident statistic.* **2. statistics** *n.* the science, study, and practice of grouping and analyzing data in order to show how it is important or significant. (Treated as singular.) ♦ *The mathematician specialized in statistics.* ♦ *The politician hired someone trained in statistics to interpret the polls.*

statistical [stə 'tɪs tɪk əl] *adj.* of or about statistics; determined by statistics. (Adv: *statistically* [...ɪk li].) ♦ *One subject's erratic results were a statistical anomaly for the experiment.* ♦ *The poll showed the two candidates to be in a statistical tie.*

statistician [stæt ɪ 'stɪ ʃən] *n.* someone who studies or works with statistics. ♦ *The company statistician produced all the sales reports.* ♦ *The unpopular politician ignored the statistician's predictions.*

statue ['stæ tʃu] *n.* a sculpture of someone or an animal, made of stone, clay, wood, plaster, etc. ♦ *I met Mary in the park by the statue of Abraham Lincoln.* ♦ *There's a statue of the company's founder in the main lobby.*

statuesque [stæ tʃu 'ɛsk] *adj.* [of a person] dignified or grand, like a statue. (Adv: *statuesquely.*) ♦ *Anne painted a picture of a statuesque general.* ♦ *The statuesque politician was reelected to Congress.*

statuette [stæ tʃu 'ɛt] *n.* a small statue. ♦ *At the awards banquet, each winner received a statuette.* ♦ *The captain of the first winning team placed its golden statuette in a trophy case.*

stature ['stæ tʃɚ] **1.** *n.* [someone's] height. (No plural form in this sense.) ♦ *The police asked the witness to estimate the thief's stature.* ♦ *Shoes with tall heels increased my stature by three inches.* **2.** *n.* reputation; how well someone or something is thought of. (No plural form in this sense.) ♦ *A scandal diminished John's stature in the community.* ♦ *The company's stature grew as it became more responsible to the community.*

status ['stæt əs] *n.* someone's position within society or business; rank. (No plural form in this sense.) ♦ *Mary's status as a brilliant lawyer helped her get many clients.* ♦ *The judge exploited his status to get preferential treatment.*

status quo ['stæt əs 'kwo] *n.* the way things are; the current state of affairs. (No plural form in this sense. Latin for 'the state in which.') ♦ *The new worker was warned against upsetting the status quo.* ♦ *The protesters intended to disrupt the status quo.*

status symbol ['stæt əs sɪm bəl] *n.* something that represents proof of one's social position or wealth. ♦ *The lawyer drove a luxury car as a status symbol.* ♦ *John can't swim. His expensive pool is merely a status symbol.*

statute ['stæ tʃut] *n.* a law. ♦ *The city council passed a statute prohibiting smoking in restaurants.* ♦ *The state supreme court voided one of the city's statutes.*

staunch ['stɔntʃ] *adj.* very loyal; dependable. (Adv: *staunchly.* Comp: *stauncher;* sup: *staunchest.*) ♦ *A staunch supporter of the mayor encouraged me to vote for him.* ♦ *The company owner paid his staunch advisers well.*

stay ['ste] **1.** *iv.* to remain in a place or position; to continue to be in a place or position. ♦ *The convict stayed in prison for the rest of his life.* ♦ *My keys stayed on the table until Anne moved them.* **2.** *iv.* to live someplace for a while, especially as a guest. ♦ *I stayed with my relatives in Europe last summer.* ♦ *Where are you staying while you are in town?* **3.** *iv.* to continue being in a certain condition; to remain in a certain condition. ♦ *John stayed unhappy for over a year after his parents' deaths.* ♦ *Mary stayed disappointed in me, and I couldn't regain her trust.* **4.** *n.* a visit; a period of time when one visits someplace or when one is a guest someplace; a period of time that one lives someplace. ♦ *Bill's short visit soon turned into a month-long stay.* ♦ *I very much enjoyed my stay at your house.* **5. stay (of execution)** *n.* a formal delay in an execution of a death sentence. (Pl: *stays...*) ♦ *The prisoner was executed when the governor wouldn't grant a stay.* ♦ *The prisoner's lawyer plead for a stay of execution.*

steadfast ['stɛd fæst] *adj.* loyal; dependable; faithful. (Adv: *steadfastly.*) ♦ *The manager rewarded the steadfast workers.* ♦ *The politician appreciated his steadfast supporters.*

steadily ['stɛd ɪ li] *adv.* in a steady way; without wavering; without faltering. ♦ *Lisa carried the large tray of plates steadily and confidently.* ♦ *It rained steadily for days.*

steady ['stɛd i] **1.** *adj.* not changing in condition, place, or position; firm. (Adv: *steadily.* Comp: *steadier;* sup: *steadiest.*) ♦ *The patient's medical condition remained steady.* ♦ *The driver kept a steady grip on the steering wheel.* **2.** *adj.* moving at an even, smooth pace; not moving in jerks and bursts. (Adv: *steadily.* Comp: *steadier;* sup: *steadiest.*) ♦ *There was a steady flow of water from the pipe.* ♦ *The generator provides a steady stream of electrical current.* **3.** *adj.* calm; not excited; not agitated. (Adv: *steadily.* Comp: *steadier;* sup: *steadiest.*) ♦ *She was steady even in the face of trouble.* ♦ *Despite the excitement, my nerves remained steady.* **4.** *tv.* to cause something to be stable and unwavering. ♦ *The medication steadied Dave's nerves after the accident.* ♦ *I put my weight on the table to steady it while Dave was writing.* **5.** *n.* a boyfriend or girlfriend that one regularly dates. ♦ *Mary went with her steady to the movies.* ♦ *John gave his steady a ring for Christmas.*

steak ['stek] *n.* a slab of a particular meat or fish, eaten as food. (A **steak** is beef unless stated otherwise.) ♦ *Lisa bought a large steak for dinner.* ♦ *I ate a salmon steak at the restaurant.*

steal ['stil] **1.** *tv., irreg.* to take something that does not belong to one without paying for it or without permission. (Pt: **stole;** pp: **stolen.**) ♦ *The shoplifter stole some shirts from the clothing store.* ♦ *My car was stolen last night from my driveway.* **2.** *tv., irreg.* [in baseball] to reach the next base before the pitcher throws the ball to the batter. ♦ *The runner stole second base during the pitch.* ♦ *Our team won the game when the player on third base stole home.* **3.** *iv., irreg.* to move somewhere secretly and quietly. ♦ *The cat stole across the garden, stalking a mouse.* ♦ *A thief stole through my apartment during the middle of the night.* **4. a steal** *n.* something that is sold for a very cheap price; a bargain; something that costs very little money. (Informal.) ♦ *This watch was a steal because I bought it on sale.* ♦ *This car was a steal because the owner wanted to get rid of it.* **5.** *n.* [in baseball] the act of reaching the next base before the pitcher throws the ball to the batter. ♦ *The runner reached third base by making a steal.* ♦ *The runner's steal to home plate won the game.*

stealthily ['stɛl θə li] *adv.* steadily and secretly; without being noticed. ♦ *The cat crawled stealthily toward the bird.* ♦ *The troops moved stealthily into enemy territory.*

steam ['stim] **1.** *n.* the gas that water is changed into when it is boiled. (No plural form in this sense.) ♦ *The tea kettle whistled as steam escaped through the spout.* ♦ *Our apartment is heated with steam.* **2.** *adj.* powered by ①; containing or using ①. ♦ *Our apartment is warmed by steam heat.* ♦ *A steam locomotive makes a distinctive noise.* **3.** *tv.* to cook something in ①. ♦ *Mary will steam some potatoes for dinner.* ♦ *Bill steamed some vegetables so that they remained crunchy.* **4.** *tv.* to subject someone or something to ① or very hot water vapor. ♦ *I steamed the wrinkles from the curtains.* ♦ *John steamed himself in the hot shower.* **5.** *iv.* to give off ①; to emit ①. ♦ *The overheated engine steamed fiercely.* ♦ *The kettle is steaming on the stove.* **6.** *iv.* [for food] to cook in ①. ♦ *The potatoes are steaming on the stove.* ♦ *The vegetables steamed for a minute, and then I turned off the heat.* **7. full steam ahead** *idiom* forward at the greatest speed possible; with as much energy and enthusiasm as possible. ♦ *It will have to be full steam ahead for everybody if the factory gets this order.* ♦ *It's going to be full steam ahead for me this week.* **8. under one's own steam** *idiom* by one's own power or effort. ♦ *I missed my ride to class, so I had to get there under my own steam.* ♦ *John will need some help with this project. He can't do it under his own steam.*

steamed ['stimd] *adj.* cooked in steam. ♦ *We ate steamed rice for dinner.* ♦ *I sprinkled some salt on the steamed vegetables.*

steamer ['stim ɚ] **1.** *n.* a ship that is powered by a steam engine. ♦ *Many immigrants traveled to America on steamers.* ♦ *The steamer sank when it crashed into an iceberg.* **2.** *n.* an enclosed pot or pan that uses steam to cook food. ♦ *Bill heated the fresh vegetables in a steamer.* ♦ *Susan removed the carrots from the steamer.*

steaming ['stim ɪŋ] **1. steaming (hot)** *adj.* very hot; sending off steam; boiling. ♦ *The waitress served me some hot, steaming coffee.* ♦ *The steaming soup smelled very good.* **2. steaming (mad)** *idiom* very angry; very mad; very upset. ♦ *The steaming coach yelled at the clumsy players.* ♦ *The principal was steaming mad when he found that his office had been vandalized.*

steamroller ['stim rol ɚ] *n.* a large vehicle with a wide, heavy roller that flattens materials used in the construction or repair of roads. (Once operated by a steam engine, now it is almost always diesel-powered.) ♦ *We saw two steamrollers at the construction site.* ♦ *The steamroller smoothed and compressed the hot asphalt.*

steamship ['stim ʃɪp] *n.* a ship that is powered by a steam engine. ♦ *My grandfather I took a steamship to Europe.* ♦ *The steamship traveled down the Pacific coastline.*

steamy ['stim i] *adj.* [of air] warm and full of moisture; hot and damp. (Adv: *steamily.* Comp: *steamier;* sup: *steamiest.*) ♦ *The steamy apartment was uncomfortable.* ♦ *When the weather is steamy, I turn on the air conditioning.*

steel ['stil] **1.** *n.* a very hard substance made of iron, carbon, and other metals, used in constructing tools, machines, and frameworks for buildings. (No plural form in this sense.) ♦ *The construction beams were made of solid steel.* ♦ *Untreated steel will rust in the rain.* **2.** *adj.* made of ①. ♦ *The building was supported by solid steel beams.* ♦ *The thick, steel vault door was impossible to penetrate.* **3.** *tv.* to make oneself, especially one's nerves, emotionally strong, as with ①. ♦ *The soldiers steeled their nerves and went into battle.* ♦ *Mary steeled herself and asked her boss for a raise.*

steel wool ['stil 'wʊl] *n.* a bundle of thin strands of steel used to scrub or polish surfaces. (No plural form in this sense.) ♦ *John scrubbed the dirty pot with steel wool.* ♦ *Anne cleaned the pans with steel wool that was impregnated with detergent.*

steep ['stip] **1.** *adj.* slanted at a sharp angle that is almost straight up and down. (Adv: *steeply.* Comp: *steeper;* sup: *steepest.*) ♦ *The children raced their sleds down the steep, snowy hill.* ♦ *The new year began with a steep rise in inflation.* **2.** *iv.* [for something, such as tea] to soak in hot liquid for a period of time. ♦ *Mary allowed her tea to steep before drinking it.* ♦ *The tea bag steeped for three minutes before the tea was ready.* **3.** *tv.* to soak something in liquid; to immerse something. ♦ *You must steep a tea bag in very, very hot water to release its flavor.* ♦ *You should have steeped the tea longer.*

steeple ['stip əl] *n.* a tower on the roof of a church, especially one that ends in a point. ♦ *During the storm, the steeple was struck by lightning.* ♦ *There is a tall steeple on the top of city hall.*

steeplechase ['stip əl tʃes] *n.* a horse race on an obstacle course; a horse race where the horses must jump over fences, water, hedges, etc. ♦ *A horse fell and broke its leg during the steeplechase.* ♦ *Lisa rode her favorite horse in the steeplechase.*

steer ['stɪr] **1.** *tv.* to cause something to go in a certain direction; to guide someone or something to go in a certain direction. ♦ *John steered the shopping cart toward the front of the store.* ♦ *The pilot steered the boat away from the shoals.* **2.** *tv.* to guide someone toward or away from a course of action. (Figurative on ①.) ♦ *The teacher steered the teenagers away from drug use.* ♦ *Max steered Lisa toward a sensible decision.* **3.** *iv.* to aim in a certain direction. ♦ *The truck driver steered away from the accident.* ♦ *The driver steered toward the expressway exit.* **4.** *n.* a castrated ox or bull, especially raised for its meat. ♦ *The rancher raised steers for gourmet steak restaurants.* ♦ *The steers were fed well before they were slaughtered.*

steering wheel ['stɪr ɪŋ wil] *n.* the wheel that a driver or pilot turns to control the direction of a vehicle. ♦ *Please keep both hands on the steering wheel while you drive.* ♦ *John suddenly turned the steering wheel to avoid an accident.*

stellar ['stɛl ɚ] **1.** *adj.* of, from, or about stars. ♦ *The very bright star is actually a stellar explosion.* ♦ *This instrument measures stellar light.* **2.** *adj.* superior; excellent; outstanding. ♦ *I recommend that you see the stellar movie I saw last night.* ♦ *The author won an award for her stellar novel.*

stem ['stɛm] **1.** *n.* the main part of a plant above the ground, which is connected to the roots below the ground, and from which leaves or flowers grow; a stalk. ♦ *The florist cut the rose stems diagonally.* ♦ *I grabbed the weeds by their stems and pulled them from the ground.* **2.** *n.* the part of a word that suffixes and prefixes are added to. ♦ *The stem of the word* uneatable *is* eat. ♦ *In English, gerunds are formed by adding the suffix* -ing *to verb stems.* **3. stem from** *iv.* + *prep. phr.* to develop from; to come from; to originate from. ♦ *The doctor said my lung cancer stemmed from smoking.* ♦ *John's selfish behavior stems from greed.* **4.** *tv.* to cause something to stop flowing; to stop the flow of something. ♦ *The dam stemmed the river's flow.* ♦ *Anne's response to her critics stemmed their accusations.*

stench ['stɛntʃ] *n.* a strong, unpleasant smell; a horrible odor. ♦ *The dead dog gave off a horrible stench.* ♦ *The stench of the rotten food made me gag.*

stencil ['stɛn səl] **1.** *n.* a piece of paper, plastic, wood, or metal in which letters or designs have been cut out. ♦ *The city worker used a stencil to make a No Parking sign.* ♦ *When Anne lifted the stencil, the marks on the paper were in the shape of the areas cut out of the stencil.* **2.** *tv.* to draw something using a piece of paper, plastic, wood, or metal with a design cut in it. ♦ *Bill stenciled the message by tracing the letters of the stencil.* ♦ *Jane stenciled the sign by spraying paint over the stencil.*

stenographer [stə 'nɑ grə fɚ] *n.* someone who uses shorthand to record what is said, and then prepares the document for other people to read in regular print. ♦ *The executive dictated a letter to the stenographer.* ♦ *The stenographer wrote 150 words per minute.*

step ['stɛp] **1.** *n.* the movement made by putting one foot in front of the other while walking. ♦ *The happy boy walked with a quick step.* ♦ *The soldier walked with uniform steps.* **2.** *n.* the distance traveled by a single ①. ♦ *The inspector took one step toward the dead body.* ♦ *Each step brought Mary closer to her destination.* **3.** *n.* a flat surface that one places one's foot on when going up or down stairs or a ladder. ♦ *The painter placed the can of paint on the ladder's top step.* ♦ *The wooden step creaked as I placed my foot on it.* **4.** *n.* an action in a series of actions in a particular order. ♦ *The first step in solving a problem is identifying the problem.* ♦ *In the last step of the experiment, we analyzed the results.* **5.** *iv.* to take a **step** ① in a certain direction. ♦ *John stepped toward the door and opened it.* ♦ *Anne stepped to the right so that Susan could pass her.* **6. step on** *iv.* + *prep. phr.* to put one's foot down on something. ♦ *Anne stepped on the car's brake pedal at the intersection.* ♦ *Bill stepped on the cockroach and killed it.* **7. watch one's step** *idiom* to act with care and caution so as not to make a mistake. ♦ *John had better watch his step with the new boss. He won't put up with his lateness.* ♦ *Mary was told by her adviser to watch her step and stop missing classes or she would be asked to leave college.*

step-by-step ['stɛp bɑɪ 'stɛp] *adj.* ordered; in order; meant to be performed in a certain order. ♦ *The manual gave step-by-step instructions for assembling the kit.* ♦ *John gave me step-by-step directions to his house.*

stepchild ['stɛp tʃɑɪld] *n., irreg.* a child of a person's husband or wife from a different marriage. (Pl: **stepchildren**.) ♦ *When John married Jane, he also got three new stepchildren.* ♦ *Bill treated his stepchildren as though they were his own.*

stepchildren ['stɛp tʃɪl drən] pl of **stepchild**.

stepfather ['stɛp fɑ ðɚ] *n.* the husband of one's mother, who is not one's father. ♦ *After Anne's father died, her mother married Bill, who became her stepfather.* ♦ *Mary calls her stepfather by his first name.*

stepladder ['stɛp læd ɚ] *n.* a small ladder that has flat, wide steps instead of rungs. ♦ *The librarian used a stepladder to reach books on the top shelf.* ♦ *Susan stood on a stepladder to change the light bulb in the ceiling light.*

stepmother ['stɛp mə ðɚ] *n.* the wife of one's father, who is not one's mother. ♦ *After John's mother died, his father married Anne, who became his stepmother.* ♦ *Bill invited both his mother and his stepmother to his wedding.*

stereo ['stɛr i o] **1.** *adj.* [of sound or electronic equipment making sound] coming from two or more speakers in a way that gives realistic effect. (See **stereophonic**.) ♦ *David listened to a stereo recording of the concert.* ♦ *Mary bought a new stereo television set.* **2.** *n.* an electronic device that produces sound coming from two or more sources, providing realistic sound reproduction. (Pl in *-s*.) ♦ *Tom's stereo was broken and he could only listen to one channel of music.* ♦ *Mary listened to her favorite record on the stereo.*

stereophonic [stɛr i o 'fɑn ɪk] *adj.* involving sound that comes from two or more speakers. (Each speaker receives a separate version of the original sound, for instance, one version for the left ear and one for the right. Adv: *stereophonically* [...ɪk li].) ♦ *The movie's soundtrack was recorded in stereophonic sound.* ♦ *Watching Bill's large, stereophonic TV is almost like being in a theater.*

stereotype ['stɛr i o tɑɪp] **1.** *n.* a feature or a trait that is thought of as typical of a certain group of things or people. ♦ *The teenager was angered by the stereotype of all young people as impolite.* ♦ *The lecturer alerted us to many stereotypes generated by the media.* **2.** *tv.* to consider someone to have features or traits that are thought of as typical of a certain group of people. ♦ *The blond actress feared being stereotyped as a silly woman.* ♦ *Tom was guilty of stereotyping Bill when he referred to him as "one of those carpenters."*

sterile ['stɛr ɪl] **1.** *adj.* free of germs or bacteria. ♦ *Surgery should be done in a sterile environment.* ♦ *The nurse put a sterile bandage on the patient's wound.* **2.** *adj.* barren; unable to produce offspring. ♦ *The sterile couple adopted two children.* ♦ *No crops could grow in the sterile soil.*

sterilize ['stɛr ɪ lɑɪz] **1.** *tv.* to rid something of germs or bacteria. ♦ *The surgical tools were sterilized after every operation.* ♦ *We sterilized the glass jars before filling them with homemade jam.* **2.** *tv.* to make someone or some creature unable to produce offspring. ♦ *We sterilized the cat to avoid having more kittens in the house.* ♦ *The veterinarian sterilizes several dogs and cats every day.*

sterling ['stɚ lɪŋ] **1.** *n.* silver that is at least 92.5% pure. (No plural form in this sense.) ♦ *Our silverware is really made of sterling.* ♦ *The jeweler said my ring was solid sterling.* **2.** *adj.* made of silver that is at least 92.5% pure. ♦ *Mary wore a sterling silver necklace to the party.* ♦ *David set the table with sterling silverware.* **3.** *adj.* dependable; having very good qualities; first-rate; excellent. ♦ *The company owner was thankful for his sterling staff.* ♦ *The worker was praised for doing a sterling job on the assignment.*

stern ['stɚn] **1.** *adj.* strict; rigid in discipline; not lenient. (Adv: *sternly*. Comp: *sterner*; sup: *sternest*.) ♦ *The stern principal suspended the troublemakers from school.* ♦ *The museum guard gave us a stern warning not to touch the paintings.* **2.** *n.* the rear part of a boat or ship. ♦ *The rudder is attached to the stern.* ♦ *Violent waves washed over the boat's stern.* **3. from stem to stern** *idiom* from one end to another. (On ②.) ♦ *Now, I have to clean the house from stem to stern.* ♦ *I polished my car carefully from stem to stern.*

sternly ['stɚn li] *adv.* strictly; not leniently. ♦ *The police officer sternly told us to leave the park.* ♦ *John's parents disciplined him sternly when he lied to them.*

sternum ['stɚn əm] *n.* the breastbone; the bone found in the front of the chest to which the ribs are connected. ♦ *The physician placed his stethoscope on my sternum.* ♦ *The driver bruised his sternum on the steering wheel during the accident.*

steroid ['stɛr ɔɪd] *n.* any of several chemical compounds important to the normal functioning of the human body. ♦ *Sex hormones are steroids.* ♦ *The football player took steroids in pill form to build up his muscles.*

stethoscope ['stɛθ ə skop] *n.* a medical instrument used to listen to a patient's heart and lungs at work. ♦ *One end* *of the stethoscope is placed on the skin near the heart, and the two tubes at the other end are placed in the examiner's ears.* ♦ *The doctor placed his stethoscope on my chest and asked me to breathe deeply.*

stew ['stu] **1.** *n.* a thick soup of meat and vegetables that are cooked slowly in water and their own juices. (No plural form in this sense.) ♦ *I ate beef stew for lunch.* ♦ *This stew is thick with potatoes and carrots.* **2.** *tv.* to cook something slowly in water and its own juices. ♦ *The cook stewed the ham hocks for a few hours.* ♦ *The vegetables were stewed before they were served.* **3.** *iv.* [for food] to cook slowly in water and juices. ♦ *The chicken stewed on the stove.* ♦ *The vegetables are stewing in the pot.* **4. stew about** *iv. + prep. phr.* to worry about something. ♦ *Mary stewed about her future.* ♦ *The workers stewed about their job security.*

steward ['stu ɚd] **1.** *n.* a male employee of a cruise ship whose job is to take care of passengers' needs. ♦ *The steward brought our breakfast to our cabin at sunrise.* ♦ *Has the steward cleaned our cabin yet?* **2.** *n.* a male employee of an airline whose job is to attend to passengers' needs; a male **flight attendant**. (The official name of the occupation is **flight attendant**.) ♦ *A steward brought us our meals soon after the plane took off.* ♦ *Among the flight attendants, there was only one steward.*

stewardess ['stu ɚ dəs] **1.** *n.* a female employee of a ship who takes care of passengers' needs. ♦ *The stewardess brought our breakfast to our cabin at sunrise.* ♦ *Has the stewardess cleaned our cabin yet?* **2.** *n.* a female employee of an airline whose job is to attend to passengers' needs; a female **flight attendant**. (The official name of the occupation is **flight attendant**.) ♦ *A stewardess brought us our meals soon after the plane took off.* ♦ *The flight attendants did not like being called stewardesses.*

stewed ['stud] *adj.* cooked slowly in water or in its own juices. ♦ *Mary served stewed prunes for dessert.* ♦ *Jane ordered stewed beef for dinner.*

stick ['stɪk] **1.** *n.* a small branch; a thin length of wood from a tree. ♦ *The bird built its nest with sticks.* ♦ *The children collected sticks and twigs for firewood.* **2.** *n.* a thin piece of wood used for a special purpose. ♦ *The camper hiked up the trail with a walking stick.* ♦ *Measure this board with a measuring stick.* **3.** *n.* a piece of something edible that is thin and flat, or shaped like ①. ♦ *John chewed a stick of gum.* ♦ *Bill bought some carrot sticks at the market.* **4.** *n.* the gear shift; the rod in a car that the driver uses to shift gears. (Informal.) ♦ *Anne put the stick in reverse and pulled out of the driveway.* ♦ *John moved the stick to second gear as he went up the hill.* **5.** *tv., irreg.* to attach something to something else with glue, tape, or something adhesive. (Pt/pp: **stuck**.) ♦ *Anne stuck a picture to the door of her office with tape.* ♦ *I spilled the glue that stuck the book's pages together.* **6. stick in(to)** *tv., irreg. + prep. phr.* to push the point of something into the surface of someone or something. ♦ *Don't stick the pin in the balloon.* ♦ *John stuck a knife into the watermelon.* **7. stick on** *tv., irreg. + prep. phr.* to fasten something to a surface by using a pin or something with a point. ♦ *Mary stuck an important message on the bulletin board.* ♦ *Susan stuck a sign on the tree.* **8.** *tv., irreg.* to put something in a position. (Informal.) ♦ *Stick the gallon of milk in the refrigerator.* ♦ *The librarian stuck the book on the shelf in its proper place.* **9. stick with** *tv., irreg. + prep. phr.* to make someone responsible for something when no one else wants to be responsible for it. (Informal.) ♦ *Anne stuck Mary with the bill for dinner.* ♦ *Dave stuck me with his work when he went on vacation.* **10.** *iv., irreg.* to remain attached or to something with glue, tape, or something adhesive. ♦ *The picture stuck securely to the wall.* ♦ *Some gum stuck to the bottom of my shoe.* **11.** *iv., irreg.* to remain; to stay. ♦ *The last guest stuck around at the party until midnight.* ♦ *Bill's high-school nickname stuck for life.*

sticker ['stɪk ɚ] *n.* a label with an adhesive side that sticks to things. ♦ *The butcher put price stickers on the hamburger packages.* ♦ *Susan put a sticker on her car window.*

stickler ['stɪk lɚ] *n.* someone who insists that everything be exact or precise. ♦ *My boss is a stickler for accuracy.* ♦ *I have to be prompt and neat at my house. My parents are sticklers.*

stickup ['stɪk əp] *n.* a robbery; a holdup. ♦ *Give me your wallet! This is a stickup!* ♦ *The thieves stole $10,000 in the bank stickup.*

sticky ['stɪk i] **1.** *adj.* adhesive. (Comp: *stickier;* sup: *stickiest.*) ♦ *I sealed the package with sticky tape.* ♦ *Some sticky glue has stuck to my fingers.* **2.** *adj.* hot and humid; causing one to sweat. (Comp: *stickier;* sup: *stickiest.*) ♦ *The workers sweat a lot in the sticky weather.* ♦ *During the sticky weather, I used an air conditioner.* **3.** *adj.* awkward. (Comp: *stickier;* sup: *stickiest.*) ♦ *Mary talked her way out of a sticky situation with the police.* ♦ *Bill had to make the sticky decision of whether to promote John or Anne.*

stiff ['stɪf] **1.** *adj.* rigid; not flexible; hard to bend. (Adv: *stiffly.* Comp: *stiffer;* sup: *stiffest.*) ♦ *The sturdy box was made of stiff cardboard.* ♦ *My neck was stiff from driving all day long.* **2.** *adj.* firm; almost solid; not fluid. (Adv: *stiffly.* Comp: *stiffer;* sup: *stiffest.*) ♦ *Beat the batter until it is stiff.* ♦ *As the wet cement became stiff, John wrote his initials in it.* **3.** *adj.* harsh; severe. (Informal. Comp: *stiffer;* sup: *stiffest.*) ♦ *The penalties for driving while drunk are very stiff here.* ♦ *The judge issued the dangerous criminal a stiff sentence.* **4.** *adj.* very formal; not relaxed. (Adv: *stiffly.* Comp: *stiffer;* sup: *stiffest.*) ♦ *The businessman was too stiff to enjoy the party.* ♦ *John is shy and seems stiff, but if you get to know him, he is a lot of fun.* **5.** *tv.* not to give someone a tip. (Slang.) ♦ *The diners stiffed the rude waiter.* ♦ *The rude students stiffed the accommodating waitress.*

stiffen ['stɪf ən] *iv.* to become stiff. ♦ *The human body stiffens shortly after death.* ♦ *Anne's muscles stiffened after she exercised for two hours.*

stifle ['staɪ fəl] **1.** *tv.* to suffocate someone; to cause someone to have a problem breathing. ♦ *The smoke stifled the people trapped in the burning building.* ♦ *A lack of oxygen stifled the miners.* **2.** *tv.* to suppress or withhold something. (Figurative on ①.) ♦ *Mary stifled the urge to laugh loudly during class.* ♦ *The editor stifled the controversial article.*

stifling ['staɪf lɪŋ] **1.** *adj.* suffocating; causing difficulty with breathing; smothering. (Adv: *stiflingly.*) ♦ *Stifling smoke rendered Bill unconscious.* ♦ *The stifling heat caused John to pass out.* **2.** *adj.* suppressing; preventing or hampering something. (Figurative on ①. Adv: *stiflingly.*) ♦ *Mary thought the strict rules at her parochial school were* *stifling.* ♦ *Advocates of free speech protested the stifling legislation.*

stigma ['stɪg mə] *n.* a mark of shame or disgrace. ♦ *The stigma of being divorced has lessened over the years.* ♦ *Bill had to live with the stigma of being fired from his job.*

stigmatize ['stɪg mə tɑɪz] *tv.* to mark someone or something as shameful or disgraceful. ♦ *The politicians stigmatized people who received welfare.* ♦ *The senator was stigmatized by his acceptance of bribes.*

still ['stɪl] **1.** *adj.* not moving; motionless; at rest. (Comp: *stiller;* sup: *stillest.*) ♦ *The raft floated on the still surface of the lake.* ♦ *The congregation could not remain still during the church service.* **2.** *adj.* quiet; not talking; not making noise. (Not prenominal.) ♦ *The children were still while the storyteller told a story.* ♦ *The teacher told the students to be still.* **3.** *adj.* of or about a single photograph, as opposed to a moving picture as in a movie or film. (Prenominal only.) ♦ *The artist specialized in still photography.* ♦ *The museum sponsored an exhibit of still photographs of fruit.* **4.** *n.* the quiet, calm, or restful part of something. (No plural form in this sense.) ♦ *In the still of the night, I could hear the crickets chirping.* ♦ *Mary rested on her porch during the still of the evening.* **5.** *n.* a device that distills alcohol; a place where alcohol is distilled. ♦ *Government agents destroyed many stills during Prohibition.* ♦ *John made gin in a homemade still.* **6.** *conj.* nevertheless. ♦ *Bob is shy, still it's strange that he'd leave without saying good-bye.* ♦ *I know you didn't intend to hurt Bill's feelings, still you should apologize to him.* **7.** *adv.* at a time past what was expected. ♦ *Are you still here?* ♦ *Tom was still not home at 3:00 A.M.* **8.** *adv.* up to a point in time. ♦ *It was still raining when I left the party.* ♦ *I was still tired when I woke up at noon.* **9.** *adv.* even ⑤; still more. (Comes after the adjective. Used with comparisons to make them stronger.) ♦ *Bill is tall, but Dave is taller still.* ♦ *Jane drives fast, but Mary drives faster still.*

stillborn ['stɪl born] **1.** *adj.* born dead; dead at birth. ♦ *Mary and Dave held a funeral for their stillborn infant.* ♦ *After having a stillborn child, Anne and John decided to try again.* **2.** *n.* a baby that is born dead. ♦ *The nurse wrapped the stillborn in a white blanket.* ♦ *Bill and Susan buried their stillborn in the family plot.*

stillness ['stɪl nəs] *n.* the absence of motion or noise; calm or silence. (No plural form in this sense.) ♦ *Because of the stillness of the air, the flag hung limply.* ♦ *Mary studied in the stillness of the library.*

stilt ['stɪlt] **1.** *n.* one of a pair of poles having a small support for the foot, used for walking elevated above the ground. (Usually plural.) ♦ *The clown walked around on stilts.* ♦ *Lisa was 8 feet tall when she walked on stilts.* **2.** *n.* poles that support a small building or house. ♦ *The people lived in the swamp in houses built on stilts.* ♦ *The house near the river is on stilts.*

stilted ['stɪl tɪd] *adj.* too dignified; too formal; formal in an unnatural way. (Adv: *stiltedly.*) ♦ *The foreigner spoke English in a stilted manner.* ♦ *The stilted ceremony made the guest of honor feel uncomfortable.*

stimulant ['stɪm jə lənt] *n.* something, especially a drug or chemical, that keeps someone awake or causes someone to be more active. ♦ *Caffeine, which is found in coffee and cola, is a common stimulant.* ♦ *John took a stimulant so he wouldn't fall asleep while driving.*

stimulate ['stɪm jə let] *tv.* to excite or arouse someone or something; to cause someone or something to be active or excited. ♦ *The lively conversation stimulated the people at the party.* ♦ *I stimulated the frog by touching it on the leg, and it jumped.*

stimulating ['stɪm jə let ɪŋ] *adj.* exciting; arousing; causing a reaction. ♦ *I had a stimulating conversation with my friends at the café.* ♦ *The stimulating shower refreshed me after a long day at work.*

stimuli ['stɪm jə lɑɪ] pl of stimulus.

stimulus ['stɪm jə ləs] *n.* something that causes a reaction; something that excites or arouses the body or the mind. (Pl: stimuli.) ♦ *Lisa's well-written book was a stimulus for Mary to write her own.* ♦ *The stimulus of bright light caused the subject to shield his eyes.*

sting ['stɪŋ] **1.** *tv., irreg.* to pierce the skin of someone or something with something sharp; [for an insect] to pierce the skin with a stinger and inject a poisonous chemical that causes a burning pain. (Pt/pp: stung.) ♦ *Bees stung the dog that was near their hive.* ♦ *A hornet stung the boy who swatted at it.* **2.** *tv., irreg.* to cause someone to feel a tingling or burning pain. ♦ *The injection stung my arm.* ♦ *The cigarette smoke stung my eyes.* **3.** *iv., irreg.* to be able to pierce skin as with ①. ♦ *Bees can only sting once.* ♦ *An angry wasp can sting again and again.* **4.** *iv., irreg.* to feel a tingling or burning pain. ♦ *The patient frowned because the injection stung.* ♦ *When the acid dripped on my arm, it stung badly.* **5.** *n.* the piercing of the skin as with ① and the pain that accompanies it. ♦ *Mary yelled when she felt the sting of the bee.* ♦ *The scorpion's sting is very poisonous.* **6.** *n.* a tingling or burning pain. ♦ *The sting of smoke made my eyes water.* ♦ *The nurse soothed the sting with some medicine.* **7.** *n.* an emotional impact; a sharp emotional stimulus. (No plural form in this sense. Figurative on ⑥.) ♦ *Our team felt the sting of defeat after we lost.* ♦ *The criminal wept with the sting of shame after the trial.*

stinger ['stɪŋ ɚ] *n.* the stinging organ of bees, scorpions, and other animals that sting. ♦ *A bee's stinger is ripped from its body when it stings someone.* ♦ *The stinger of a dead scorpion is still dangerous.*

stinginess ['stɪn dʒi nəs] *n.* an unwillingness to give or spend money. (No plural form in this sense.) ♦ *Nobody received a raise this year, due to the company owner's stinginess.* ♦ *The stinginess of the rich people baffled the charity officers.*

stinging ['stɪŋ ɪŋ] *adj.* causing a burning or tingling pain. (Adv: *stingingly.*) ♦ *The stinging smoke caused my eyes to water.* ♦ *When I stepped on some glass, I felt a stinging pain in my foot.*

stingray ['stɪŋ re] *n.* a flat, diamond-shaped fish with a powerful whip-like tail. ♦ *Stingrays can grow to be several feet wide.* ♦ *The tail of a stingray contains poison glands and a stinger.*

stingy ['stɪn dʒi] *adj.* unwilling to give or spend money; miserly. (Adv: *stingily.* Comp: *stingier;* sup: *stingiest.*) ♦ *The office manager repeatedly asked the stingy business owner for modern equipment.* ♦ *The stingy woman refused to donate any money to charity.*

stink ['stɪŋk] **1.** *n.* a terrible smell; a very bad smell. ♦ *An angry skunk emits a terrible stink.* ♦ *There's a horrible stink coming from the garbage can.* **2.** *iv., irreg.* to smell bad.

(Pt: stank or stunk; pp: stunk.) ♦ *Bill's bedroom stank, so his mother made him clean it.* ♦ *Those dirty clothes stink. Please wash them.* **3.** *iv., irreg.* to be terrible; to be very bad; to be awful; to be unpleasant. (Figurative on ②.) ♦ *The critic said the long, boring movie really stank.* ♦ *This book stinks and I refuse to read the rest of it.*

stinker ['stɪŋk ɚ] *n.* someone who is obnoxious, unpleasant, or annoying. (Informal.) ♦ *My brother, who is a little stinker, played a trick on me.* ♦ *What stinker ate the last piece of pizza?*

stint ['stɪnt] *n.* an amount of work; the time spent at a certain activity. ♦ *John had a four-year stint with the army.* ♦ *Before she became famous, Jane spent a long stint as a waitress.*

stipend ['stɑɪ pɛnd] *n.* a fixed payment of money, such as that paid as part of a scholarship or fellowship. ♦ *The university offered the best students a monthly stipend.* ♦ *Mary receives a stipend in addition to money to pay tuition.*

stipulate ['stɪp jə let] *tv.* to specify something as a condition of an agreement. ♦ *The workers' contract stipulated that they couldn't smoke on the job.* ♦ *The rental agreement stipulated that I was to return the car with a full tank of gas.*

stipulated ['stɪp jə let ɪd] *adj.* stated; agreed on; specified or demanded as a condition of an agreement. ♦ *I obeyed each of the stipulated requirements of the contract.* ♦ *I was paid the stipulated amount when I performed the required work.*

stipulation [stɪp jə 'le ʃən] *n.* a requirement; a demand; a condition of an agreement. ♦ *You can be my roommate with the stipulation that you don't smoke in the house.* ♦ *My parents paid my tuition on the stipulation that I kept a B average.*

stir ['stɚ] **1.** *tv.* to mix something with one's hand or with an object. ♦ *Anne stirred the sugar into the lemonade with a wooden spoon.* ♦ *Bill stirred the batter with a large spoon.* **2.** *tv.* to excite someone or an emotion; to cause someone to feel emotion or passion. ♦ *The band music stirred the crowd and made them feel patriotic.* ♦ *The speaker stirred us with an emotional presentation.* **3.** *iv.* to change position; to move about. ♦ *Mary stirred restlessly as she slept.* ♦ *The sleeping dog stirred in front of the fireplace.* **4.** *n.* the act of stirring something as in ①. ♦ *Mary gave her coffee a stir so that the sugar would dissolve.* ♦ *After a vigorous stir, my drink was completely mixed.* **5.** *n.* a commotion; an exciting event. ♦ *There was quite a stir when the governor came to our town.* ♦ *The scandal created a stir at the office.*

stirring ['stɚ ɪŋ] *adj.* exciting; causing someone to feel passion or emotion; rousing. (Adv: *stirringly.*) ♦ *The stirring movie made me cry.* ♦ *The band played a stirring march in the parade.*

stirrup ['stɚ əp] **1.** *n.* one of two metal loops that hang from the sides of a saddle to hold the feet of the rider. ♦ *Lisa got into the saddle and put her feet in the stirrups.* ♦ *John stepped into the left stirrup and hoisted himself onto the horse.* **2.** *n.* a tiny bone in the inner ear, shaped like ①. ♦ *The three tiny bones in the inner ear are called the hammer, anvil, and stirrup.* ♦ *The stirrup touches directly on the eardrum.*

stitch ['stɪtʃ] **1.** *n.* one movement of a threaded needle through an object while sewing. ♦ *John repaired the rip in his costume with quick stitches.* ♦ *Bill's gash required six stitches.* **2.** *n.* the thread that is seen after one movement of a threaded needle through an object while sewing. ♦ *The stitches in the dress's hem match the color of the dress.* ♦ *The doctor removed my stitches after my wound had healed.* **3.** *n.* a small amount of clothing. (No plural form in this sense. Usually in negative constructions.) ♦ *The child ran outdoors without a stitch of clothing.* ♦ *She sleeps without wearing a stitch.* **4.** *n.* a sharp pain. ♦ *After John ran a mile, he felt a stitch in his side.* ♦ *The stitch in Mary's neck made it hard for her to turn her head.* **5.** *tv.* to sew something; to sew things together. ♦ *The seamstress stitched the hem of the dress.* ♦ *The actors stitched their own costumes together.* **6.** *iv.* to sew. ♦ *The seamstress wore a thimble on her finger as she stitched.* ♦ *The tailor stitched for a living.* **7. keep someone in stitches** *idiom* to cause someone to laugh loud and hard, over and over. ♦ *The comedian kept us in stitches for nearly an hour.* ♦ *The teacher kept the class in stitches, but the students didn't learn anything.*

stock ['stɑk] **1.** *n.* a supply of something to be used or sold. (No plural form in this sense.) ♦ *Our stock of canned vegetables is getting low.* ♦ *The store's entire stock of winter clothes was on sale.* **2.** *n.* a heavy broth made from cooking meats, usually with vegetables for a long time, used to prepare sauce or soup. (No plural form in this sense.) ♦ *I made some soup from chicken stock.* ♦ *The cook added some spices to the beef stock.* **3.** *n.* the total assets of a company divided into equal shares that are usually bought and sold in a stock market. (No plural form in this sense.) ♦ *The owner of the company also owned 51% of its stock.* ♦ *Lisa sold her stock in the troubled company.* **4.** *n.* shares of ③ of a specific company. ♦ *Bob owns twelve different stocks.* ♦ *Lisa bought two stocks in the steel industry.* **5.** *n.* a group or type of people that someone is related to or descended from. (No plural form in this sense.) ♦ *David is descended from Slavic stock.* ♦ *Mary and Bill are from common stock.* **6.** *tv.* [for a store] to arrange to have ① of a product available for sale. ♦ *The grocery store always stocked fresh produce.* ♦ *This sporting goods store stocks team uniforms.* **7.** *tv.* to furnish land with animals; to furnish water with fish. ♦ *The farmer stocked his ponds with fish.* ♦ *One of the large lakes in the park was stocked with bass.* **8.** *adj.* [of a response that seems] trite, rehearsed, and not straightforward. ♦ *I don't want stock answers. I need all the details.* ♦ *The mayor's aide gave the reporter a stock response.* **9. in stock** *phr.* to have merchandise available and ready for sale. ♦ *Do you have extra-large sizes in stock?* ♦ *Of course, we have all sizes and colors in stock.*

stockade [stɑ 'ked] **1.** *n.* a wall of upright wooden posts driven into the ground for protection or defense. ♦ *The pioneers built a stockade around their settlement.* ♦ *The enemy army destroyed the stockade with its cannons.* **2.** *n.* a military jail; a building where people in the military are confined as a punishment. ♦ *The rowdy soldiers were put in the stockade overnight.* ♦ *The corporal suspected of treason was held in the stockade.*

stockbroker ['stɑk brok ɚ] *n.* someone who buys, sells, and trades stocks and bonds, often for a client. ♦ *I told my stockbroker to buy the stock of the Johnson Company.* ♦

My stockbroker told me how much value my stocks lost in the crash.

stock exchange ['stɑk ɛks tʃendʒ] *n.* the place where stocks and bonds are bought, sold, and traded. ♦ *My uncle works at the stock exchange downtown.* ♦ *The business of trading stocks is done at a stock exchange.*

stockholder ['stɑk hol dɚ] *n.* someone who owns at least one share of a company's stock. ♦ *The company stockholders can attend a meeting once a year at company headquarters.* ♦ *The firm issued a financial report to each of its stockholders.*

stocking ['stɑk ɪŋ] *n.* a knitted or woven sock. ♦ *Mary walked around her house in wool stockings.* ♦ *Anne wore nylon stockings to the party.*

stock market ['stɑk mɑr kət] **1.** *n.* the business of buying and selling of stocks in general. ♦ *The stock market crashed on October 29, 1929, and October 19, 1987.* ♦ *The retired teacher had made a fortune in the stock market.* **2.** *n.* some sort of measure of the general value of all the stocks at any one time. ♦ *The stock market is very high at this time.* ♦ *I hope the stock market will go down so I can afford to buy some shares.*

stockpile ['stɑk pɑɪl] **1.** *n.* a large amount of something that is stored for future use or in case of an emergency. ♦ *The militia kept a stockpile of arms in an underground bunker.* ♦ *During the winter, we keep a stockpile of canned goods in the pantry.* **2.** *tv.* to store a large amount of something for future use or in case of an emergency. ♦ *Mary stockpiled canned goods and batteries in her basement.* ♦ *David stockpiled ammunition in case of an attack.*

stocky ['stɑk i] *adj.* having a short, thick body; having a short, solid build. (Adv: *stockily.* Comp: *stockier;* sup: *stockiest.*) ♦ *Two stocky police officers broke the door down.* ♦ *Many football players are stocky.*

stockyard ['stɑk jɑrd] *n.* a place where cattle, pigs, and other livestock are kept before being sold or killed for food. ♦ *This stockyard contains only pigs.* ♦ *The cattle were transported to the stockyards by train.*

stodgy ['stɑdʒ i] *adj.* boring; old-fashioned; dull. (Adv: *stodgily.* Comp: *stodgier;* sup: *stodgiest.*) ♦ *Many students fell asleep during the stodgy lecture.* ♦ *Our stodgy old host bored us with trivial stories.*

stoic ['sto ɪk] *adj.* not showing pleasure or pain; not showing one's feelings; reserved. (Adv: *stoically* [...ɪk li].) ♦ *The stoic soldier didn't move while the doctor operated on him.* ♦ *The stoic refugee did not complain about his living conditions.*

stoke ['stok] *tv.* to maintain a fire; to try to make a smoldering fire burst into flame. ♦ *John stoked the fire in the fireplace with a poker.* ♦ *Mary stoked the campfire with a large stick.*

stole ['stol] **1.** pt of steal. **2.** *n.* a long strip of material or fur worn over a woman's shoulders. ♦ *Mary wore a warm, woolen stole during the winter.* ♦ *Anne asked the hotel clerk to put her mink stole in the safe.*

stolen ['stol ən] **1.** pp of steal. **2.** *adj.* taken without the owner's permission or knowledge. ♦ *Max discovered a warehouse full of stolen goods.* ♦ *The police returned the stolen bicycle to its rightful owner.*

stomach ['stʌm ək] **1.** *n.* the organ of the body in which food is digested. ♦ *A cow's stomach has four chambers.* ♦ *Spicy food upsets my stomach.* **2.** *n.* the front of the body below the chest and above the waist. ♦ *During the fight, Bill was punched in the stomach.* ♦ *Mary clasped her stomach because it hurt so much.* **3. not able to stomach someone or something; cannot stomach someone or something** *idiom* not to be able to put up with someone or something; not to be able to tolerate or endure someone or something. ♦ *Jane cannot stomach violent movies.* ♦ *The unpopular student could not stomach a lot of ridicule.* **4. turn someone's stomach** *idiom* to make someone (figuratively or literally) ill. ♦ *This milk is spoiled. The smell of it turns my stomach.* ♦ *The play was so bad that it turned my stomach.*

stomp ['stɑmp] **1.** *iv.* to walk with a very heavy step. (See also stamp.) ♦ *Bill stomped across the floor in his boots.* ♦ *Mary stomped through the garden, crushing flowers.* **2. stomp on** *tv.* + *prep. phr.* to bring one's foot down with force on top of something. ♦ *The surly child stomped her foot on the floor until she got her way.* ♦ *Anne stomped her heavy boot on the cockroach.* **3.** *tv.* to crush or press something down by bringing down one's foot with force. ♦ *David stomped the weeds down to make a path.* ♦ *Mary stomped the can flat with her boot.*

stone ['ston] **1.** *n.* the hard material of which rocks are made. (No plural form in this sense.) ♦ *The workers bored a tunnel through the mountain of stone.* ♦ *Bill's heavy paperweight is made of stone.* **2.** *n.* a rock; a chunk of ①. ♦ *The farmer removed a large stone from his field.* ♦ *Max threw a stone at Bob.* **3.** *n.* a jewel; a gem. ♦ *The jeweler appraised the stone in Mary's ring.* ♦ *A precious stone was stolen from the museum.* **4.** *n.* a small, hard object that forms in parts of the body, such as the kidney, that causes a lot of pain as it passes through the organ. ♦ *John screamed with pain as he passed a stone.* ♦ *The doctor informed Anne that she had kidney stones.* **5.** *adj.* made of ①. ♦ *The sculptor unveiled the stone statue of the president.* ♦ *Bill installed a stone patio in his backyard.* **6.** *tv.* to throw ② at someone or something, often as punishment or torment. ♦ *The rioters stoned the police.* ♦ *Two U.S. soldiers were stoned in Bosnia yesterday.* **7. a stone's throw away** *idiom* a short distance; a relatively short distance. ♦ *John saw Mary across the street, just a stone's throw away.* ♦ *Philadelphia is just a stone's throw away from New York City.*

stood ['stʊd] pt/pp of stand.

stooge ['studʒ] *n.* an inferior; a subordinate; someone who just takes orders. ♦ *One of the gang leader's stooges took the blame for the crime.* ♦ *The ignorant stooge carried out the mob leader's orders.*

stool ['stul] **1.** *n.* a tall seat that usually has no support for one's back or arms. ♦ *A dozen stools lined the bar.* ♦ *The professor sat on a stool in front of the class and lectured.* **2.** *n.* feces; waste matter that is expelled from the body. (No plural form in this sense.) ♦ *The doctor asked for a sample of my stool.* ♦ *I cleaned up my dog's stool from the sidewalk.* **3. fall between two stools** *idiom* to come somewhere between two possibilities and fail to meet the requirements of either. (On ①.) ♦ *The material is not suitable for an academic book or for a popular one. It falls between two stools.* ♦ *He tries to be both teacher and friend, but falls between two stools.*

stoop ['stup] **1.** *n.* a small porch at the door of a house. ♦ *Mary sat on her stoop and talked with her neighbors.* ♦ *The mail carrier left a package for me on the stoop.* **2.** *n.* a bent posture, as if carrying a heavy weight on the shoulders. ♦ *John's stoop is caused by a curved spine.* ♦ *The back brace helped correct Anne's stoop.* **3.** *iv.* to bend down; to bend forward; to hold one's head and shoulders downward in front of one's body. ♦ *John stooped and picked up a dime from the floor.* ♦ *Mary stooped so she wouldn't bump her head on the low ceiling.* **4. stoop to** *iv. + prep. phr.* to lower oneself to a lower level of behavior. (Figurative on ③.) ♦ *The queen refused to stoop to the peasant's level.* ♦ *David stooped to bribery to influence the senator's vote.*

stooped ['stupt] *adj.* having one's head and shoulders held downward in front of one's body; bent forward. ♦ *The very tall man walked with a stooped posture to avoid bumping his head on the low ceiling.* ♦ *The instructor made the stooped dancer stand up straight.*

stop ['stɑp] **1.** *tv.* to end movement, progress, an activity, or an existence. ♦ *Mary stopped the car by putting on the brakes.* ♦ *John stopped smoking because it was bad for his health.* **2.** *iv.* to move, progress, act, or function no longer; to cease. ♦ *The car stopped at the intersection.* ♦ *I hope it stops raining soon.* **3.** *iv.* to stay for a period of time. ♦ *Mary stopped by my house for half an hour.* ♦ *John stopped for a quick visit.* **4.** *n.* a short visit; a short stay. ♦ *John's stop by my house only lasted a few minutes.* ♦ *Mary hadn't planned her stop at the store.* **5.** *n.* a place where a bus, train, or other vehicle stops ② to let passengers get on and off the vehicle. ♦ *I waited at the bus stop for ten minutes in the rain.* ♦ *Someone announced each train stop as we approached it.* **6.** *n.* a consonant that is made by stopping the flow of the breath and suddenly releasing it. ♦ *In English, the stops are* [p, t, k, b, d, g]. ♦ *The word* wrap *ends with a stop.* **7. stop short of doing something** *idiom* to not go as far as doing something; to stop ② before one does something. ♦ *Fortunately Bob stopped short of hitting Tom.* ♦ *The boss criticized Jane's work, but stopped short of firing her.* **8. stop short of something** *idiom* not to go as far as something. ♦ *The bus stopped short of the end of the road.* ♦ *The speeding car stopped short of the child standing in the street.* **9. come to a stop** *idiom* [for someone or something] to stop ① moving or happening. ♦ *The bus finally came to a stop so I could get off.* ♦ *The loud noise finally came to a stop.* **10. put a stop to something** *idiom* to make something end; to stop ① something. (The same as put an end to something, at end ⑫.) ♦ *Why can't the police put a stop to crime?* ♦ *The mayor will put a stop to all this arguing.*

stopgap ['stɑp gæp] **1.** *n.* a temporary substitute or solution. ♦ *The law provided a one-month stopgap to fund the budget.* ♦ *The manager hired a temporary worker as a stopgap until a replacement was hired.* **2.** *adj.* <the adj. use of ①.> ♦ *Congress passed a stopgap bill to prevent a government shutdown.* ♦ *The ferry was a stopgap method of crossing the river until the bridge was rebuilt.*

stoplight ['stɑp lɑɪt] *n.* a traffic signal that has colored lights that indicate whether drivers should stop or go. ♦ *When the stoplight turned green, I crossed the intersection.* ♦ *The city installed a stoplight at the dangerous intersection.*

stopover ['stɑp ov ɚ] *n.* a place where one stops briefly during a journey, especially a stop at an airport between the city where one took off and the city that is the final destination. (See also layover.) ♦ *I flew from Boston to Chicago with a stopover in Cleveland.* ♦ *When Mary flew to Miami, she had a four-hour stopover in Atlanta.*

stoppage ['stɑp ɪdʒ] *n.* an organized strike; the organized stopping of work, such as during a labor dispute. ♦ *The factory was closed during the work stoppage.* ♦ *During the stoppage, the factory hired workers who did not belong to the union.*

stopper ['stɑp ɚ] *n.* a plug that is used to close the opening of a bottle or the drain in a sink or bathtub. ♦ *John put a rubber stopper in the wine bottle.* ♦ *Anne pulled the stopper from the drain when she finished bathing.*

stopwatch ['stɑp wɑtʃ] *n.* a watch that can be started or stopped at any moment, used to determine how long something lasts. ♦ *The judge clicked the stopwatch as the winner crossed the finish line.* ♦ *The coach timed the swimmers with a stopwatch.*

storage ['stor ɪdʒ] **1.** *n.* keeping or storing [things]. (No plural form in this sense.) ♦ *We use the basement and the attic for storage.* ♦ *Our large apartment had plenty of room for storage.* **2. in storage** *phr.* in a place where things are stored or kept. ♦ *Mary placed her winter clothes in storage during the summer.* ♦ *John's furniture is in storage while he is in the army.*

store ['stor] **1.** *n.* a shop where goods or products are sold. ♦ *Could you go to the store and buy some milk?* ♦ *At the store, there was a sale on towels.* **2.** *n.* a supply of something. ♦ *There's a large store of extra paper in the copy room.* ♦ *John built up a store of office supplies in his desk.* **3.** *tv.* to keep something someplace so that it can be used later. ♦ *John stored canned food in his bomb shelter.* ♦ *Mary stored bags of dog food in her garage.* **4. set great store by someone or something** *idiom* to have positive expectations for someone or something; to have high hopes for someone or something. ♦ *I set great store by my computer and its ability to help me in my work.* ♦ *Bill sets great store by his expensive tools.*

storefront ['stor frənt] *adj.* occupying a space originally designed for a retail store, where people enter directly from the sidewalk. ♦ *The storefront libraries served many of the older neighborhoods.* ♦ *The small storefront clinic was open two days a week.*

storehouse ['stor hɑʊs] *n., irreg.* a warehouse; a place where things are stored. (Pl: [...hɑʊ zəz].) ♦ *The company kept its business records in a nearby storehouse.* ♦ *A truck driver brought goods from the storehouse to the store.*

storekeeper ['stor kip ɚ] *n.* someone who owns or manages a store. ♦ *The storekeeper opened the store every morning at 7:00.* ♦ *The thief threatened to kill the storekeeper.*

storeroom ['stor rum] *n.* a room where things are stored. ♦ *The office manager kept the office supplies in the storeroom.* ♦ *The shop's excess stock is kept in a large storeroom.*

stork ['stork] *n.* a large bird with a long, sharp beak and a long neck. ♦ *The stork waded into the lake and caught a fish in its beak.* ♦ *There are many species of storks found around the world.*

storm ['storm] **1.** *n.* a period of severe weather with very strong winds, heavy rain or snow, or sometimes thunder and lightning. ♦ *The weather forecaster said to expect storms in the evening.* ♦ *Many trees were uprooted in the violent storm.* **2.** *n.* a violent attack or outburst. (Figurative on ①.) ♦ *The mayor's new policies set off a storm of criticism.* ♦ *The reporter's rude remarks caused a storm of protest.* **3.** *tv.* to attack something forcefully. ♦ *The government troops stormed the rebel hideout.* ♦ *The enemy army stormed the fort.* **4.** *iv.* [for the weather] to be severe, with strong winds, heavy rain or snow, or thunder and lightning. ♦ *It's supposed to storm all night long.* ♦ *Take your umbrella because it's going to storm today.* **5.** *iv.* to move to or from some place with great anger. (Figurative on ④.) ♦ *John stormed into my office, demanding an explanation.* ♦ *Customers stormed out of the restaurant because of the poor service.* **6. take someone or something by storm** *idiom* to attract a great deal of attention from someone or something. ♦ *Jane is madly in love with Tom. He took her by storm at the office party, and they've been together ever since.* ♦ *The singer took the world of opera by storm with her stunning performance.*

storm door ['storm dor] *n.* a second door, outside the regular door, that keeps cold, wind, snow, or rain from entering. ♦ *The storm door keeps the cold out and holds in the cooled air in the summer.* ♦ *Mary locked both the storm door and the inner door.*

storm window ['storm wɪn do] *n.* a second window placed outside a regular window, that keeps cold, wind, snow, or rain from entering a room or building. ♦ *Anne replaced the storm windows with screens in the spring.* ♦ *John put up the storm windows in October when it became cold.*

stormy ['stor mi] **1.** *adj.* of or about severe weather and storms. (Adv: *stormily.* Comp: *stormier;* sup: *stormiest.*) ♦ *The picnickers went home because of the stormy skies.* ♦ *The baseball game was canceled on account of stormy weather.* **2.** *adj.* full of conflict or turmoil. (Figurative on ①. Adv: *stormily.*) ♦ *John's stormy relationship with his wife ended in divorce.* ♦ *I abruptly left the stormy meeting.*

story ['stor i] **1.** *n.* an account of something that has happened. ♦ *The witness told his story to the jury.* ♦ *I read the story of President Roosevelt's life.* **2.** *n.* a tale; a fictional account of something, told or written for entertainment or amusement. ♦ *The teacher told the small children the story of "Cinderella."* ♦ *The author wrote fantastic adventure stories.* **3.** *n.* a lie. ♦ *Don't give me any stories; I want the truth.* ♦ *Bill told his boss a story about being stuck in traffic.* **4.** *n.* a news report; an article of news. ♦ *Our next story is about the terrible bombing overseas.* ♦ *The price of wheat is going up. For the story, here is our correspondent.* **5.** *n.* one level of a building; one layer from floor to ceiling in a building. (The floor on ground level is the first story.) ♦ *The main lobby is on the first story.* ♦ *My dentist's office is on the tenth story of this building.* **6. cock-and-bull story** *idiom* a silly, made-up ②; a ② that is a lie. ♦ *Don't give me that cock-and-bull story.* ♦ *I asked for an explanation, and all I got was your ridiculous cock-and-bull story!* **7. make a long story short** *idiom* to bring a ① to an end. ♦ *And—to make a long story short—I never got back the money that I lent him.* ♦ *To make a long story short, let me say that everything worked out fine.*

storybook ['stor i bʊk] **1.** *n.* a book that contains one or more fictional stories, usually for children. ♦ *The teacher read a storybook to the children.* ♦ *Mary draws colorful illustrations for storybooks.* **2.** *adj.* <the adj. use of ①.> ♦ *The famous actress lived in a storybook mansion.* ♦ *The prince and princess had a storybook romance.*

storyteller ['stor i tɛl ɚ] *n.* someone who tells stories as entertainment. ♦ *A storyteller entertained the children with fairy tales.* ♦ *The professional storyteller invented her own tales.*

storytelling ['stor ɪ tɛl ɪŋ] *n.* the art or skill of telling stories to people, either in writing or aloud. (No plural form in this sense.) ♦ *My hobby is storytelling for children in school.* ♦ *Storytelling is one of the oldest forms of art.*

stout ['staʊt] *adj.* wide; fat; overweight. (Adv: *stoutly.* Comp: *stouter;* sup: *stoutest.*) ♦ *A stout passenger took up two seats on the bus.* ♦ *The doctor put the stout patient on a diet.*

stove ['stov] *n.* an appliance that usually contains an oven and has burners on the top, used for cooking. ♦ *Dinner is cooking on the stove right now.* ♦ *Anne boiled some water on the stove for tea.*

stow ['sto] *tv.* to pack or store something, especially for travel. ♦ *Mary stowed her luggage in a large trunk.* ♦ *John stowed his knapsack under his seat.*

stowaway ['sto ə we] *n.* someone who hides on a ship, plane, or train in order to travel without paying for it. ♦ *A stowaway hid in the cargo section of the boat.* ♦ *The police will arrest the stowaway at the next train station.*

straddle ['stræd l̩] **1.** *tv.* to spread one's legs around something that one is sitting on or climbing. ♦ *David straddled the chair as he sat at the table.* ♦ *Jimmy straddled the tree trunk as he climbed the tree.* **2.** *tv.* to be on both sides of something; to support both sides of something. ♦ *The entire metropolitan area straddles parts of two states.* ♦ *The politician straddled both sides of the issue.*

straight ['stret] **1.** *adj.* not bent; not curved; direct; continuing in the same direction. (Adv: *straightly.* Comp: *straighter;* sup: *straightest.*) ♦ *Mary drew a straight line with a ruler.* ♦ *John walked in a straight line to prove he wasn't drunk.* **2.** *adj.* honest; sincere; telling the truth. (Adv: *straightly.* Comp: *straighter;* sup: *straightest.*) ♦ *The suspect gave the police officer a straight answer.* ♦ *Tell the truth! Be straight with me!* **3.** *adj.* without an interruption; continuous. (Before or after a noun.) ♦ *It rained for four straight hours.* ♦ *I slept for two days straight when I was ill.* **4.** *adj.* heterosexual; not homosexual or bisexual. (Comp: *straighter;* sup: *straightest.*) ♦ *John has some straight friends and some gay friends.* ♦ *Bill went with his straight friends to a straight bar.* **5.** *adj.* [of an alcoholic drink] not having water added. ♦ *John ordered a straight shot of whiskey.* ♦ *Mary drank a straight glass of vodka.* **6.** *adj.* sober; free from the influence of drugs. (Informal. Comp: *straighter;* sup: *straightest.*) ♦ *Mary will drive only when she is straight.* ♦ *The former addict was proud to say he'd been straight for three months.* **7.** *adv.* [going] directly [to a place without making a detour]. ♦ *David drove straight home after work.* ♦ *Mary went straight to bed when she got home.* **8.** *adv.* in a **straight** ① line; without turning. ♦ *Go straight through the intersection.* ♦ *John drove straight down Western Avenue from 47th Street to 35th Street.* **9.** *adv.* upright. ♦ *The dance instructor told everyone to stand straight.* ♦ *John sat straight in his chair.* **10. get something straight** *idiom* to understand something clearly. ♦ *Let me get this straight. I'm supposed to go there in the morning?* ♦ *The police officer made sure he had the witness's story straight.* **11. go straight** *idiom* to stop breaking the law and lead a lawful life instead. ♦ *The* *judge encouraged the thief to go straight.* ♦ *After Bob was arrested, he promised his mother he would go straight.*

straighten ['stret n] **1.** *tv.* to cause something to be straight. ♦ *Bill straightened his tie and entered the meeting room.* ♦ *Mary straightened her posture when she realized she was slouching.* **2. straighten out** *tv.* + *adv.* to solve a problem; to resolve a conflict. ♦ *I hope to be able to straighten this mess out soon.* ♦ *Can you straighten out this problem with my bill?* **3. straighten up** *tv.* + *adv.* to make something neat or orderly. ♦ *David straightened up the apartment before his guests arrived.* ♦ *The clerk straightened the disorganized files up.* **4. straighten (out)** *iv.* (+ *adv.*) to become straight ①. ♦ *The river straightens out just south of town.* ♦ *The curving road will straighten when you reach the border.* **5. straighten up** *iv.* + *adv.* [for someone] to begin to behave as desired or planned. ♦ *If you don't straighten up, you're going to get a spanking.* ♦ *The troublesome child straightened up as he matured.*

straight-faced ['stret 'fest] *adj.* without emotion; without showing one's emotion on one's face; appearing serious, especially when one thinks something is funny. ♦ *The straight-faced students played a practical joke on their teacher.* ♦ *The straight-faced witness calmly responded to the lawyer's questions.*

straightforward ['stret 'for wɚd] *adj.* direct; frank; not misleading. (Adv: *straightforwardly.*) ♦ *The student gave the teacher a straightforward answer.* ♦ *The reporter demanded a straightforward reply from the mayor.*

straightjacket ['stret dʒæk ət] See straitjacket.

straight-laced ['stret 'lest] See strait-laced.

strain ['stren] **1.** *tv.* to stretch or pull something, especially as much as possible or in a way that causes injury. ♦ *John strained his leg muscles while jogging.* ♦ *Mary strained her eyes while reading in the dim light.* **2.** *tv.* to separate liquid from something solid by pouring it through a strainer. ♦ *David strained the seeds from the orange juice.* ♦ *Jane strained the sediment from the chemical solution.* **3.** *tv.* to place something under a burden; to place tension on something. (Figurative on ①.) ♦ *You are straining my patience!* ♦ *Constant arguing strained the couple's marriage.* **4.** *iv.* to stretch tightly; to work hard and hold a heavy load. ♦ *The worker's muscles strained under the heavy load.* ♦ *The rope strained, but did not break, as I lifted the climber to safety.* **5.** *iv.* to use a lot of effort to do something. ♦ *The car engine strained as I drove up the hill.* ♦ *I strained to understand what my professor was talking about.* **6.** *n.* a burden or annoyance that causes someone distress. ♦ *Mary's disobedient children are a great strain on her.* ♦ *Insurance costs are a big strain on our budget.* **7.** *n.* an injury to a muscle caused by stretching it or pulling it too hard. ♦ *The strain in my neck was caused by a car accident.* ♦ *John got a strain because he didn't stretch his muscles before running.* **8.** *n.* a variety of plant, bacterium, or virus. ♦ *The scientist isolated a strain of the deadly virus.* ♦ *This strain of wheat is only grown in Kansas.* **9.** *n.* the melody of a song. (Formal.) ♦ *I heard the faint strains of an approaching marching band.* ♦ *We joined the chorus in the familiar strain.*

strained ['strend] **1.** *adj.* pulled, stretched, or overextended. ♦ *The dancer massaged her strained muscles after the performance.* ♦ *The company couldn't afford to give raises because of its strained budget.* **2.** *adj.* separated through a strainer. ♦ *Mary poured the strained juice into the glasses.* ♦ *The strained gravy was poured into a serving bowl.* **3.** *adj.* [of a response] requiring or showing much effort, politeness, or insincerity. ♦ *The inspector doubted John's strained response.* ♦ *Jane's strained "thank you" indicated that she was not really grateful.*

strainer ['stren ɚ] *n.* a container with holes in the bottom and sides that separates liquid from solid material. ♦ *I poured the cooked spaghetti from the pot into a strainer to drain the water from it.* ♦ *The strainer separated the seeds from the orange juice.*

strait ['stret] *n.* a narrow channel of water between two larger bodies of water. ♦ *The Strait of Mackinac separates Michigan's two peninsulas.* ♦ *The ferry took passengers across the narrow strait.*

straitjacket AND **straightjacket** ['stret dʒæk ɪt] *n.* a coat with long sleeves that can be tied so that one's arms are secured to one's sides. ♦ *A straitjacket prevents unstable people from moving violently or hurting themselves or others.* ♦ *The police sedated the insane man and put a straitjacket on him.*

strait-laced AND **straight-laced** ['stret 'lest] *adj.* prudish; too proper; having strict morals. ♦ *The strait-laced lady refused to go to the movies.* ♦ *The strait-laced teachers who were supervising the party kept the students from dancing close to each other.*

strand ['strænd] **1.** *n.* one thread of a rope; one wire of a cable; a thread; a fiber. ♦ *Anne removed the strands of hair from the hairbrush.* ♦ *The strands of the cut rope started to unravel.* **2.** *tv.* to cause someone or something to be stuck or held at a location. ♦ *Missing the last bus stranded John in the city.* ♦ *The blizzard stranded the passengers at the airport.*

stranded ['stræn dɪd] *adj.* left behind; abandoned; left someplace in a way that one is not able to leave. ♦ *The stranded shipwreck victims tried to radio for help.* ♦ *Hundreds of stranded passengers slept at the airport during the blizzard.*

strange ['strendʒ] **1.** *adj.* unusual; odd; peculiar; not normal or usual. (Adv: *strangely.* Comp: *stranger;* sup: *strangest.*) ♦ *The actions of the mentally unbalanced man were strange.* ♦ *Mary woke up when she heard a strange noise in the house.* **2.** *adj.* not familiar; not usually experienced. (Adv: *strangely.* Comp: *stranger;* sup: *strangest.*) ♦ *Warm weather in January seems quite strange to me.* ♦ *Susan is always willing to try strange foods.*

stranger ['strendʒ ɚ] **1.** *n.* someone who is not known to someone else; someone who is not familiar to someone else. ♦ *Mary told her children to stay away from strangers.* ♦ *A stranger at the bus stop asked me for a cigarette.* **2. stranger to something or someplace** *idiom* someone who is new to an area or place. ♦ *Although John was a stranger to big cities, he enjoyed visiting New York.* ♦ *You are a stranger to our town, and I hope you feel welcome.*

strangle ['stræŋ gəl] **1.** *tv.* to kill someone or some creature by crushing the throat to prevent breathing. ♦ *The killer strangled his victims with a telephone cord.* ♦ *One of the characters in the play is supposed to strangle the villain.* **2.** *iv.* to choke, possibly to death, because the throat is blocked. ♦ *I got tangled in the telephone cord and almost* *strangled.* ♦ *The puppy got its head caught in the fence and strangled.*

stranglehold ['stræŋ gəl hold] **1.** *n.* a tight hold around someone's neck. ♦ *David broke from the madman's stranglehold.* ♦ *The cop's stranglehold bruised the suspect's neck.* **2.** *n.* something that prevents the growth of something else; something that inhibits someone or something. (Figurative on ①.) ♦ *The heavy taxes were a stranglehold on economic development.* ♦ *The inflation rate put a stranglehold on new stock purchases.*

strangulation [stræŋ gju 'le ʃən] *n.* killing by squeezing the throat and cutting off the air. (No plural form in this sense.) ♦ *The coroner ruled that the victim had died of strangulation.* ♦ *A lion kills by strangulation when it clamps it teeth in its prey's throat.*

strap ['stræp] **1.** *n.* a strong, narrow strip of material used to secure something. ♦ *Anne picked up her book bag by its strap.* ♦ *The large crate was secured with thick plastic straps.* **2.** *tv.* to secure someone or something with a strong, narrow strip of leather or other material. ♦ *I had to strap my suitcase shut because it was so full.* ♦ *The assistant strapped the violent patient to the bed.*

strapping ['stræp ɪŋ] *adj.* tall, strong, and healthy; robust. ♦ *The beautiful princess married a strapping young prince.* ♦ *The farmer had five fine, strapping sons who worked in the fields.*

stratagem ['stræt ə dʒəm] *n.* a plan that is used to trick an enemy or opponent. ♦ *The spy informed the general of the opponent's stratagem.* ♦ *The candidate relied on ruthless stratagems to win the election.*

strategic [strə 'tidʒ ɪk] **1.** *adj.* of or about strategy; using strategy. (Adv: *strategically* [...ɪk li].) ♦ *The general devised a strategic plan to win the war.* ♦ *The strategic advisors suggested negotiating with the enemy.* **2.** *adj.* central, major, or crucial. (Adv: *strategically* [...ɪk li].) ♦ *Winning the strategic battle put us in a position to win the war.* ♦ *The soldiers gained control of the strategic port city.*

strategy ['stræt ə dʒi] *n.* the skill or science of planning something, especially planning military movements and making plans in the playing of games. (No plural form in this sense.) ♦ *Chess is a game of strategy.* ♦ *Because of our general's brilliant strategy, we won the war.*

straw ['strɔ] **1.** *n.* dried stalks left after the grain has been removed. (No plural form in this sense.) ♦ *The farmer bundled the straw into bales.* ♦ *David pitched clean straw into the horse's stable.* **2.** *n.* a plastic or paper tube used for drinking a liquid by sucking. ♦ *Susan sipped the juice from the glass through a straw.* ♦ *The patient with lockjaw drank soup through a straw.* **3.** *adj.* <the adj. use of ①.> ♦ *The farmer wore a straw hat in the field.* ♦ *Jane bought a straw purse at the market.*

strawberry ['strɔ bɛr i] **1.** *n.* a small, soft, red fruit that has tiny seeds embedded in its surface. ♦ *Anne served fresh strawberries for dessert.* ♦ *John put some sliced strawberries on his cereal.* **2.** *adj.* made with or flavored with ①. ♦ *I would like some strawberry ice cream.* ♦ *I put some whipped cream on my slice of strawberry pie.*

stray ['stre] **1.** *adj.* wandering. ♦ *The stray dog was taken to the city dog pound.* ♦ *Anne adopted the stray cat.* **2.** *adj.* occurring or arriving by chance. ♦ *The police officer was shot by a stray bullet.* ♦ *Stray radio signals interfered with my cellular telephone.* **3.** *iv.* to wander; to become lost; to leave the main path or topic. ♦ *My dog strays if she is not chained to a tree.* ♦ *The lecturer strayed from the subject.* **4.** *n.* an animal that is lost; an animal that wanders around and has no home. ♦ *The strays were taken to the animal shelter.* ♦ *Bill fed a stray he found in his backyard.*

streak ['strik] **1.** *n.* a long, thin line or stripe. ♦ *John's black hair has streaks of gray.* ♦ *A streak of lightning flashed across the sky.* **2.** *n.* a duration; a period of time during which something is constant; an unbroken period of something. ♦ *Our football team ended Central High's winning streak last night.* ♦ *David had an amazing streak of bad luck last month.* **3.** *tv.* to mark something with long, thin lines or stripes. ♦ *The hair stylist streaked my hair with blond dye.* ♦ *Rain streaked the dirty windows.* **4.** *iv.* to flow or race along in long, thin lines or stripes. ♦ *The lightning streaked across the sky.* ♦ *Tears streaked down the mourners' faces.* **5.** *iv.* to run or move somewhere very fast. ♦ *The bullet streaked past my head.* ♦ *The rocket streaked through space.*

stream ['strim] **1.** *n.* a small river. ♦ *Mary caught some fish in the stream near the cabin.* ♦ *Bill waded across the stream to the other bank.* **2.** *n.* a steady flow of something, especially something liquid. ♦ *A stream of water flowed toward the drain.* ♦ *From the cracked glass, a stream of juice ran to the edge of the table.* **3.** *n.* a flow of words, thoughts, ideas, etc. (Figurative on ②.) ♦ *A stream of happy thanks came from Bill's mouth.* ♦ *Tom's stream of thought was interrupted by a knock at the door.* **4.** *iv.* to flow somewhere steadily and in large amounts. ♦ *Tears streamed down my face during the sad movie.* ♦ *Blood streamed from the soldiers' wounds.*

streamer ['strim ɚ] *n.* a very long, thin strip of paper or ribbon used as a decoration during a ceremony, parade, or celebration. ♦ *Colorful streamers were hung from the ceiling at the birthday party.* ♦ *The people on the float threw streamers into the crowd.*

streamline ['strim lɑɪn] **1.** *tv.* to shape something so that it will move easily through air or water without a lot of resistance. ♦ *The designers streamlined the design of the car.* ♦ *They streamlined the ship for maximum energy efficiency.* **2.** *tv.* to change something in order to make it more efficient. (Figurative on ①.) ♦ *The clerk streamlined the company's procedures by eliminating several unnecessary steps.* ♦ *The state streamlined the process for renewing a driver's license.*

streamlined ['strim lɑɪnd] *adj.* having a shape that allows something to move easily through air or water without a lot of resistance. ♦ *The streamlined car got good gas mileage.* ♦ *The streamlined airplane broke the sound barrier.*

street ['strit] *n.* a road, usually one in a city or a town that has buildings or parks alongside it. (Abbreviated *St.*) ♦ *John lives on 42nd Street.* ♦ *Look both ways before you cross the street.*

streetlight ['strit lɑɪt] *n.* a light on a lamppost that lights a street when it is dark outside. ♦ *A streetlight was placed at every intersection.* ♦ *New streetlights were installed as a safety precaution.*

streetwise ['strit wɑɪz] *adj.* knowing how to survive in a large city. ♦ *Tom is streetwise and can take care of himself in the city.* ♦ *The streetwise tourist walked through the city unafraid.*

strength ['strɛŋkθ] **1.** *n.* the quality of being strong. (No plural form in this sense.) ♦ *The strength of the athlete impressed the Olympic judges.* ♦ *I have no strength in my left leg since the accident.* **2.** *n.* a virtue; a good feature of someone or something. ♦ *This car has a number of strengths and a number of weaknesses.* ♦ *Good and fast work is one of John's strengths.* **3. tower of strength** *idiom* a person who can always be depended on to provide support and encouragement, especially in times of trouble. ♦ *Mary was a tower of strength when Lisa was in the hospital. She looked after her whole family.* ♦ *Bob was a tower of strength while his father was unemployed.*

strengthen ['strɛŋk θən] **1.** *tv.* to make someone or something physically stronger. ♦ *John strengthened his muscles by exercising.* ♦ *Lisa felt that taking vitamins would strengthen her body.* **2.** *tv.* to make something more powerful and effective. ♦ *The legislature strengthened the law by revising it.* ♦ *If you would strengthen your complaint with facts, you would accomplish something.* **3.** *iv.* to become physically stronger. ♦ *The athlete's body strengthened as she exercised.* ♦ *The more I used my injured foot, the more it strengthened.* **4.** *iv.* to become more powerful and effective. ♦ *His resolve to win strengthened as he walked out onto the field.* ♦ *The economy strengthened because of the president's new policies.*

strenuous ['strɛn ju əs] *adj.* requiring hard work; requiring effort; requiring a lot of energy. (Adv: *strenuously.*) ♦ *After a strenuous day at work, Bill slept for 12 hours.* ♦ *The football players had a strenuous practice schedule.*

stress ['strɛs] **1.** *n.* the pressure caused by something that is heavy; strain. (No plural form in this sense.) ♦ *The stress caused by the heavy load strained John's back.* ♦ *Many heavy trucks put a lot of stress on the roadway.* **2.** *n.* the mental pressure caused by something that is difficult or demanding; mental tension. (No plural form in this sense. Figurative on ①.) ♦ *The stress of her job gave Mary headaches.* ♦ *Stress at work caused John to quit.* **3.** *n.* emphasis placed on a syllable when speaking by saying it louder or in a different tone. (No plural form in this sense.) ♦ Epitome *is pronounced with the stress on the second syllable.* ♦ *The teacher placed extra stress on the final syllable in the sentence.* **4.** *n.* a particular instance of ③; a particular syllable that should be given ③; a **stressed** syllable. ♦ *Sally marked each stress with an accent so she would know how to read the poem.* ♦ *There is only one stress in "White House" when it refers to the place where the president lives, but the phrase "white house" usually has two stresses.* **5.** *n.* emphasis or focus. (No plural form in this sense.) ♦ *Lisa placed a lot of stress on the need to be on time.* ♦ *The teacher put too much stress on dates and not enough on concepts.* **6.** *tv.* to place ③ on a syllable when speaking. ♦ *In the word* caravan, *the first syllable is stressed.* ♦ *Lisa stressed the wrong syllable, and we misunderstood her.* **7.** *tv.* to subject someone or something to ①. ♦ *The heavy weight of the piano stressed the wooden floor.* ♦ *Don't stress the glass panel in the door. It might break.* **8.** *tv.* to place emphasis or focus on something. ♦ *Lisa stressed the need to be on time.* ♦ *The history teacher stressed dates too much and didn't teach the children about the causes of events.*

stressed ['strɛst] *adj.* [of syllables] emphasized or given greater significance. ♦ *The stressed syllables were marked with an accent symbol.* ♦ *The stressed words in the article are printed in bold type.*

stressful ['strɛs fəl] *adj.* causing stress; causing tension; causing strain. (Adv: *stressfully.*) ♦ *The stressful situation caused David to quit his job.* ♦ *After a stressful day at work, Jane took a relaxing shower.*

stretch ['strɛtʃ] **1.** *tv.* to extend something. ♦ *Mary stretched the rubber band around the stack of papers.* ♦ *Anne stretched her arms wide and yawned.* **2. stretch (out)** *iv.* (+ *adv.*) to become wider; to become longer; to widen; to lengthen. ♦ *The sweater stretched out when I put it on a hanger.* ♦ *My pants stretched after I wore them a few days.* **3. stretch (out)** *iv.* (+ *adv.*) [for something] to spread out over time or space. ♦ *The trail stretched out all the way to the river.* ♦ *The lecture seemed to stretch to fill an hour and a half.* **4. stretch out** *iv.* + *adv.* to lie down on a bed and spread out to nap or sleep. ♦ *Mary stretched out on the bed and fell asleep.* ♦ *Dave stretched out and took a nap.* **5.** *iv.* to be elastic; to be able to be pulled without breaking. ♦ *The clay stretched as the sculptor pulled it.* ♦ *The rubber band stretched to double its own length.* **6.** *n.* a continuous area of land. ♦ *The farmer owned a 180-acre stretch of land along the river.* ♦ *The lifeguard protected a long stretch of beach.* **7.** *n.* a continuous period of time. ♦ *Each shift worked in eight-hour stretches.* ♦ *For a three-month stretch, Mary lived without a telephone.* **8. at a stretch** *idiom* continuously; without stopping. (On ⑦.) ♦ *We all had to do eight hours of duty at a stretch.* ♦ *The baby doesn't sleep for more than three hours at a stretch.*

stretcher ['strɛtʃ ɚ] *n.* a device like a light bed or cot, used to carry someone who is sick or dead. ♦ *The paramedics placed the crash victims on stretchers.* ♦ *The injured player was carried from the field on a stretcher.*

stricken ['strɪk ən] *adj.* affected by disaster, sickness, or something unpleasant. (From an older pp of **strike**.) ♦ *The murdered man's family was stricken with grief.* ♦ *The stricken woman sought treatment for her cancer.*

strict ['strɪkt] **1.** *adj.* [of rules or discipline] severe, harsh, or demanding. (Adv: *strictly.* Comp: *stricter;* sup: *strictest.*) ♦ *The strict principal punished the misbehaving students.* ♦ *The soldiers followed the strict military rules.* **2.** *adj.* absolute; exact. (Adv: *strictly.* Comp: *stricter;* sup: *strictest.*) ♦ *Mary told me the news in strict secrecy.* ♦ *The judge gave a strict interpretation of the law.*

strictly ['strɪkt li] **1.** *adv.* in a strict fashion. ♦ *The principal strictly maintained order in the school.* ♦ *The government strictly controlled interstate trade.* **2.** *adv.* absolutely; totally; completely. ♦ *Smoking in this building is strictly forbidden.* ♦ *The information in this file is strictly confidential.*

stridden ['strɪd n] pp of **stride**.

stride ['straɪd] **1.** *n.* the length of one's step while walking. ♦ *The tall man had a very long stride.* ♦ *An adult's stride is twice as long as a child's.* **2.** *n.* a long step made while walking. ♦ *Mary crossed the puddle in one stride.* ♦ *John needed only three long strides to cross the wet lawn.* **3.** *iv., irreg.* to walk by taking long steps. (Pt: **strode**; pp: **stridden**. The past participle is rarely used.) ♦ *Mary quickly strode toward her house because it was raining.* ♦ *The tall man strode across the park.* **4. take something in stride** *idiom* to accept something as natural or expected. ♦ *The argument surprised him, but he took it in stride.* ♦ *It was a very rude remark, but Mary took it in stride.*

strident ['straɪd nt] *adj.* harsh and shrill; grating; having a harsh voice. (Adv: *stridently.*) ♦ *The strident announcer gave me a headache.* ♦ *The politician's strident speech disturbed many voters.*

strife ['straɪf] *n.* feuding; fighting; a bitter struggle. (No plural form in this sense.) ♦ *The strife in her homeland caused the immigrant to flee.* ♦ *The controversial bill caused much strife in Congress.*

strike ['straɪk] **1.** *tv., irreg.* to hit someone or something; to hit something against something; to collide into something. (Pt/pp: struck.) ♦ *John struck Bill with his fist.* ♦ *The car struck a tree when it drove off the road.* **2.** *tv., irreg.* to attack someone or something. ♦ *The soldiers struck the enemy fort at dawn.* ♦ *The government forces struck the militia's compound.* **3.** *tv., irreg.* to light a match; to cause something to burn with fire. ♦ *Mary struck the match and lit her cigarette.* ♦ *John struck three matches before he could light the fire.* **4.** *tv., irreg.* to discover something underneath the ground by digging or drilling. ♦ *The miner struck gold.* ♦ *The workers struck oil.* **5. strike out** *tv., irreg. + adv.* [for a pitcher in baseball] to pitch so that the batter accumulates three strikes ⑬ and thus create an out ⑰. ♦ *When the batter was struck out, the game was over.* ♦ *John will probably strike the next batter out.* **6. strike out** *iv., irreg. + adv.* [for a batter in baseball] to accumulate three strikes ⑬ and thus create an out ⑰. ♦ *The batter struck out.* ♦ *One more strike and you will strike out!* **7. strike at** *iv., irreg. + prep. phr.* to hit at someone or something. ♦ *John struck at Bill with his fists.* ♦ *David struck at the ball with the bat.* **8.** *iv., irreg.* [for a group of workers] to refuse to work during the negotiation of a dispute. ♦ *The union workers struck without notice.* ♦ *The teachers voted to strike until they had a contract.* **9.** *iv., irreg.* to attack. ♦ *The soldiers struck at dawn.* ♦ *The mayor's policies struck at the heart of the crime problem.* **10.** *iv., irreg.* to make contact; to have a negative effect on someone or something. (See also stricken.) ♦ *Disaster struck in the form of a tornado.* ♦ *The terrible disease struck without warning.* **11.** *iv., irreg.* [for a clock] to chime to tell what time it is. ♦ *The clock struck at midnight.* ♦ *Shortly after the clock struck, I fell asleep.* **12.** *n.* the act of workers refusing to work during a labor dispute. ♦ *The bitter strike at the factory lasted for four months.* ♦ *The union settled the strike when the management offered a fair contract.* **13.** *n.* [in baseball] a penalty given to a batter who swings the bat and misses the ball, who hits the ball foul, or who does not swing the bat when the umpire thinks that the ball went by the batter in a way that the batter could have hit it. ♦ *A foul ball counts as a strike unless it would be the third strike.* ♦ *The batter swung at and missed the ball, and the umpire yelled "Strike!"* **14.** *n.* [in bowling] the act of knocking over all the pins at once. ♦ *A strike is worth 10 points, plus the number of pins knocked over in the next two attempts.* ♦ *The bowler needed a strike to win the game.* **15.** *n.* an attack, especially with bombs or bullets delivered by airplane. ♦ *The air strike destroyed the small town.* ♦ *Hundreds of civilians were killed in the surprise strike.* **16. have two strikes against one** *idiom* to have several things against one; to be in a position where success is unlikely. ♦ *Poor Bob had two strikes against him when he tried to explain where he was last night.* ♦ *I can't win. I have two strikes against me before I start.* **17. go (out) on strike** *idiom* [for a group of people] to quit working at their jobs until certain demands are met. ♦ *If we don't have a contract by noon tomorrow, we'll go out on strike.* ♦ *The entire work force went on strike at noon today.* **18. strike someone as something** *idiom* [for a thought or behavior] to affect someone a certain way. ♦ *John's rude behavior struck me as odd.* ♦ *Mary's attitude struck me as childish.*

striking ['straɪk ɪŋ] **1.** *adj.* very noticeable; getting attention. (Adv: *strikingly.*) ♦ *The celebrity wore a striking outfit to the award ceremony.* ♦ *The musician's green hair was striking.* **2.** *adj.* on strike; refusing to work during a dispute. ♦ *Management negotiated with the striking workers.* ♦ *The factory replaced the striking workers with nonunion employees.*

string ['strɪŋ] **1.** *n.* a thin rope or a thick thread, especially used for tying something, binding something, or suspending something in the air. (No plural form in this sense.) ♦ *The postal clerk tied my package with string.* ♦ *Where do you keep the string?* **2.** *n.* a length of ① or thread. ♦ *The mobile hung from the ceiling by a single string.* ♦ *I need a few strings to tie up my packages.* **3.** *n.* a wire or cord that is stretched tight and is used to produce sound in certain musical instruments. (See ⑤.) ♦ *Bob broke a string on his violin.* ♦ *Pianos have wire strings.* **4.** *n.* a cord used to form the tightly pulled net found in a tennis racket and similar sports equipment. ♦ *I broke a string in my tennis racket.* ♦ *The strings of the racket are made of nylon.* **5. strings** *n.* the orchestral instruments whose sounds are made by rubbing a bow across ③; the people who play the instruments having ③. (Treated as plural.) ♦ *The strings were too loud throughout the entire piece.* ♦ *This piece is written for strings.* **6.** *n.* a number of things or people in a row. ♦ *Our victory ended our opponent's string of wins.* ♦ *The manager interviewed a string of prospective employees.* **7.** *tv., irreg.* to put ③ or ④ on a guitar, violin, tennis racket, etc. (Pt/pp: strung.) ♦ *The musician strung his guitar before the show.* ♦ *The tennis racket was strung with thin plastic strings.* **8.** *tv., irreg.* to place something on a ②. ♦ *The children strung popcorn and placed it around the tree.* ♦ *The jewelry maker strung beads to make a necklace.* **9.** *tv., irreg.* to stretch ① or wire from one place to another. ♦ *The worker strung the cable from pole to pole.* ♦ *Sally strung paper streamers over the doorway as a decoration.*

stringent ['strɪn dʒənt] *adj.* strict; severe; demanding that laws be followed closely. (Adv: *stringently.*) ♦ *Our company has a stringent policy against smoking.* ♦ *The state passed stringent laws against drunk driving.*

stringy ['strɪŋ i] *adj.* thin like string; looking like string. (Comp: *stringier;* sup: *stringiest.*) ♦ *I told John to comb his stringy hair.* ♦ *Mary brushed her dog's stringy fur.*

strip ['strɪp] **1.** *n.* a long, flat piece of something. ♦ *The kitchen floor is made of narrow strips of wood.* ♦ *I used a strip of tape to stick the note to the wall.* **2.** *n.* a row of something. ♦ *The postal clerk sold me a strip of stamps.* ♦ *Most comic strips consist of a series of four panels.* **3.** *tv.* to undress someone; to remove someone's clothes; to remove something's covering. ♦ *Mary stripped her child and bathed him.* ♦ *Bob stripped himself for a shower.* **4.** *tv.* to make something empty or bare. ♦ *The car thieves* *stripped the car in minutes.* ♦ *The maid stripped the bed.* **5.** *iv.* to take off one's clothes; to undress. ♦ *The doctor told me to strip and put a sheet around myself.* ♦ *Max stripped and took a quick shower.*

stripe ['strɑɪp] **1.** *n.* a long band of color or texture; a wide line; a wide line of something that is different from what is around it. ♦ *A skunk has a white stripe down its back.* ♦ *The city worker painted yellow stripes down the middle of the road.* **2.** *tv.* to mark something with ①; to put ① on something. ♦ *The city worker striped the edge of the road with white paint.* ♦ *The artist striped the canvas with lines of red chalk.*

striped ['strɑɪpt] *adj.* having a stripe or stripes; marked with stripes. ♦ *The fur of a tiger is striped.* ♦ *The striped flag hung from the pole.*

strive ['strɑɪv] *iv., irreg.* to work very hard for something; to struggle against something. (Pt: strove or *strived;* pp: striven or strived.) ♦ *The poor family strived to pay the rent each month.* ♦ *The business owner strove for success.*

striven ['strɪv ən] a pp of strive.

strode ['strod] pt of stride.

stroke ['strok] **1.** *tv.* to caress someone or something lightly; to pet someone or something; to pass one's hand gently over something, especially a part of the body. ♦ *Mary stroked her pet dog between its ears.* ♦ *John stroked the back of Anne's head as he consoled her.* **2.** *n.* the gentle movement of one's hand across a body or a surface; a caress. ♦ *With a gentle stroke, I wiped away the baby's tears.* ♦ *I tried to calm the frightened puppy with soft strokes.* **3.** *n.* a single movement of the arms or a weapon as with swinging something, rowing a boat, or swimming. ♦ *The golfer's stroke sent the golf ball sailing.* ♦ *The swimmer practiced different kinds of swimming strokes.* **4.** *n.* a mark made by a pen or pencil when writing; a mark made by a paintbrush when painting. ♦ *The teacher printed with neat strokes.* ♦ *The artist painted wide strokes of color on the canvas.* **5.** *n.* the act of pressing a key of a typewriter or a computer keyboard. ♦ *Each stroke on the keyboard produced a character on the computer screen.* ♦ *He typed so fast that I could not count his strokes.* **6.** *n.* the sound made by a clock when it tells the time by chiming. ♦ *I expect you to be home by the stroke of midnight.* ♦ *At the stroke of five, the workers left the building.* **7.** *n.* a blocking of the flow of blood in the brain, which causes unconsciousness, paralysis, coma, or death. ♦ *My grandfather suffered a stroke and was taken to the hospital.* ♦ *Bill's stroke paralyzed the left side of his body.* **8.** *n.* an instance of luck. ♦ *Winning the lottery was a stroke of good luck!* ♦ *By a stroke of fortune, John found a good job.*

stroll ['strol] **1.** *n.* a pleasant walk. ♦ *Mary took a stroll toward the lake.* ♦ *The busy executive relaxed by taking a stroll during lunch.* **2.** *iv.* to go for a pleasant walk. ♦ *David strolled through the woods behind his house.* ♦ *Mary strolled for miles, enjoying the fresh air.*

stroller ['strol ɚ] *n.* a small chair on wheels that a baby or young child can lie or sit in. ♦ *Mary transported Jimmy around town in a stroller.* ♦ *When Bob goes shopping, he brings a stroller for his two-year-old.*

strong ['strɔŋ] **1.** *adj.* having strength in the mind or body; having power in the mind or the body; using strength. (Adv: *strongly.* Comp: *stronger;* sup: *strongest.*) ♦ *The strong weightlifter could lift 200 pounds.* ♦ *The strong firefighter carried John down the ladder.* **2.** *adj.* durable; able to last; able to withstand something; not easily broken; sturdy. (Adv: *strongly.* Comp: *stronger;* sup: *strongest.*) ♦ *The mechanic used a strong chain to lift the heavy engine.* ♦ *The strong pipes withstood intense water pressure.* **3.** *adj.* [of a taste, smell, or color] intense. (Adv: *strongly.* Comp: *stronger;* sup: *strongest.*) ♦ *Strong fishy smells came from the bay.* ♦ *A strong taste of ginger overpowered the soup.* **4.** *adj.* having a certain number [of people]. (Follows a specific number.) ♦ *The crowd at the rally was 200 strong.* ♦ *Our team of volunteers is 50 strong and still growing.*

stronghold ['strɔŋ hold] **1.** *n.* a fort; a fortress; a place that can be defended. ♦ *The country lost the war soon after its stronghold was destroyed.* ♦ *The enemy army surrounded our last remaining stronghold.* **2.** *n.* a place where something is widespread; a place where something is supported and defended. (Figurative on ①.) ♦ *Our college is a stronghold of academic freedom.* ♦ *Broadway is a stronghold of live theater.*

strontium ['strɑn ti əm] *n.* a silver-yellow metallic chemical element used in fireworks and flares. (No plural form in this sense.) ♦ *The atomic symbol of strontium is Sr.* ♦ *Strontium's atomic number is 38.*

strove ['strov] a pt of strive.

struck ['strʌk] pt/pp of strike.

structural ['strʌk tʃɚ əl] *adj.* of or about the structure of something, especially a building. (Adv: *structurally.*) ♦ *The earthquake caused much structural damage to the building.* ♦ *These beams serve as structural reinforcements to the ceiling.*

structurally ['strʌk tʃə rə li] *adv.* in the way that something is built or put together. ♦ *The inspector declared the bridge to be structurally sound.* ♦ *This building was structurally altered to withstand earthquakes.*

structure ['strʌk tʃɚ] **1.** *n.* the way that something is put together; the way that something is built; the way that something or some creature is arranged. (No plural form in this sense.) ♦ *The car's efficient structure increased its gas mileage.* ♦ *The building's structure resembled that of an old castle.* **2.** *n.* a building. ♦ *By law, no structures are to be built in the park.* ♦ *Many tall structures impeded my view of the horizon.* **3.** *n.* something that is made from different parts. ♦ *The manager explained the company's organizational structure.* ♦ *The biologist examined the complex structure of the cell.* **4.** *tv.* to arrange something so that it has a certain form; to form something in a certain way; to make something from different parts. ♦ *The teacher structured the children's school day.* ♦ *The writer structured the novel around a southern family.*

struggle ['strʌg əl] **1.** *iv.* to work hard for or against something; to fight for or against something, using a lot of effort or energy. ♦ *The poorly paid workers struggled to support their families.* ♦ *When he was injured, Max struggled for survival.* **2.** *n.* a hard fight for or against something; a difficult effort for or against something. ♦ *It was quite a struggle, but our team won the baseball game.* ♦ *Quitting smoking was the biggest struggle of John's life.*

struggling ['strʌg lɪŋ] *adj.* working hard for or against something; fighting for or against something, using a lot of effort or energy. ♦ *The struggling artist worked as a* *waiter to pay his rent.* ♦ *Four struggling climbers inched up the cliff.*

strum ['stʌm] **1.** *tv.* to play a stringed instrument by drawing the fingers or a small pick across the strings. ♦ *I sat under a tree and strummed my guitar.* ♦ *Mary sings while she strums her guitar.* **2.** *tv.* to play a melody on a stringed instrument, as in ①. ♦ *I strummed an old folk tune on the guitar.* ♦ *See if you can strum this piece with me.*

strung ['strʌŋ] pt/pp of string.

strut ['strʌt] **1.** *iv.* to walk somewhere arrogantly; to walk somewhere as though one were more important than one is. ♦ *The arrogant student strutted around campus.* ♦ *The celebrity strutted into the restaurant, demanding to be served.* **2.** *n.* a brace; a beam; a bar that supports a structure. ♦ *The roof collapsed when termites destroyed the struts in the attic.* ♦ *The steel struts that support the balcony are welded solidly into place.*

stub ['stʌb] **1.** *tv.* to hurt a toe by hitting it against something. ♦ *Anne stubbed her toe against the curb.* ♦ *John stubbed his toe on a log.* **2.** *n.* a short end of something that remains after the rest of it is taken or used. ♦ *The usher tore off the ticket and handed me my ticket stub.* ♦ *The stub of Max's cigarette is still smoldering.*

stubble ['stʌb əl] *n.* very short hair; hair that grows back shortly after one has shaved. (No plural form in this sense.) ♦ *Bob shaves in the morning, and by evening he has stubble.* ♦ *Mary shaved the stubble from her legs.*

stubborn ['stʌb ɚn] *adj.* obstinate; resistant to doing something that someone else wants; not yielding; not giving in; very determined. (Adv: *stubbornly.*) ♦ *The stubborn child refused to eat his vegetables.* ♦ *The stubborn student would not obey the teacher.*

stubbornly ['stʌb ɚn li] *adv.* in a stubborn way; obstinately; in a resistant way; very determinedly. ♦ *John stubbornly refused to help us.* ♦ *One juror stubbornly voted against the other eleven.*

stucco ['stʌk o] *n.* an external cement surface, usually on the sides of houses. (No plural form in this sense.) ♦ *Bill rubbed his hands over the rough stucco of the house.* ♦ *Mary painted the stucco after it dried.*

stuck ['stʌk] pt/pp of stick.

stuck-up ['stʌk 'əp] *adj.* conceited; thinking that one is better than one really is. ♦ *The stuck-up students ridiculed the unpopular ones.* ♦ *Jane seems so stuck-up since she got a new car.*

stud ['stʌd] **1.** *n.* a horse that is used for breeding; a stallion; any male animal that is used for breeding. ♦ *The horse breeder owned a stable of studs.* ♦ *Bob made money by renting his studs out to other breeders.* **2.** *n.* a nail, rivet, or tack with a large head, used as a decoration. ♦ *Max's leather belt was decorated with shiny silver studs.* ♦ *The desk drawers were decorated with gold studs.* **3.** *n.* an upright board that is part of the structure of a wall. ♦ *When you pound the nail into the wall, make sure you hit a stud.* ♦ *The studs in this wall are placed 16 inches apart.*

student ['stud nt] *n.* someone who studies or learns, especially at a school; a pupil. ♦ *There are twelve hundred students at my high school.* ♦ *The student asked the professor a question.*

studio ['stud i o] **1.** *n.* the room where an artist works. (Pl in -*s.*) ♦ *The artist's sculptures were placed around his studio.* ♦ *Jane invited me to her studio to look at her paintings.* **2. studio (apartment)** *n.* an apartment that consists of one room and a bathroom. ♦ *John lives in a studio downtown.* ♦ *There was no room for me to sleep at Anne's small studio apartment.* **3.** *n.* a building where movies are made or photography is done; a company that produces movies. (Pl in -*s.*) ♦ *The actors reported to the studio at six in the morning.* ♦ *The studio paid the famous director six million dollars.* **4.** *n.* the room from which a radio or television broadcast is made. (Pl in -*s.*) ♦ *John called the radio studio and talked with the disc jockey's guest.* ♦ *No one can enter the studio while the live TV show is on the air.*

studious ['stud i əs] *adj.* studying very much; in the manner of a serious student. (Adv: *studiously.*) ♦ *The studious student did very well on the test.* ♦ *Lisa was not studious and did horribly in school.*

study ['stʌd i] **1.** *tv.* to spend time learning information about something by reading, researching, observing, or experimenting. ♦ *Mary studies biology in college.* ♦ *The animal researcher studied advanced psychology.* **2.** *tv.* to examine something closely; to scrutinize something; to observe something closely. ♦ *Anne studied the spot on her desk and tried to figure out how to remove it.* ♦ *The detective studied some hairs found at the scene of the crime.* **3.** *iv.* to be a student; to read, research, observe, or experiment in order to learn about something. ♦ *Jane studies at the university.* ♦ *Bill works during the day and studies in the evening.* **4.** *n.* the work or effort involved in learning. (No plural form in this sense.) ♦ *A bachelor's degree usually involves four years of study.* ♦ *A program in medicine involves years of hard study.* **5.** *n.* an examination of something. ♦ *The researcher made a study of the development of language in children.* ♦ *Mary is deeply involved in her studies.* **6.** *n.* a room where someone studies ③. ♦ *Anne's study is lined with bookshelves.* ♦ *Bill closed the door to his study so he could concentrate.*

stuff ['stʌf] **1.** *n.* any substance that things are made of; the material that anything is made of. (No plural form in this sense.) ♦ *What kind of stuff is your artwork made from?* ♦ *The stuff inside John's walls began to rot.* **2.** *n.* things; unnamed objects; belongings; possessions. (No plural form in this sense.) ♦ *Mary lost all of her stuff in the fire.* ♦ *John bought a lot of stuff on sale at the store.* **3.** *tv.* to fill something with a substance; to pack something into a space or container until there is no room left. ♦ *The pillow was stuffed with synthetic fibers.* ♦ *I stuffed the bag with garbage and carried it out.* **4.** *tv.* to fill the inside of a dead animal with a material that preserves it and maintains its shape so that it can be displayed. ♦ *The taxidermist stuffed my pet dog after it died.* ♦ *The hunter stuffed his kill and then displayed it in his house.* **5. stuff the ballot box** *idiom* to fill a ballot box with more votes than the number of possible voters. ♦ *The politician was charged with stuffing the ballot box.* ♦ *The ballot box was stuffed with lots of votes for the crooked politician.*

stuffed ['stʌft] *adj.* [of a doll or a similar toy, often in the shape of an animal] filled with cotton or other fiber; [of a cooked food such as a whole fowl or fish] filled with seasoned, edible foodstuffs; [of a dead animal] filled with material to make it look lifelike. ♦ *The stuffed turkey* *looked beautiful on the table.* ♦ *The tall, scary stuffed bear at the museum is a real dead animal, unlike Susie's stuffed bear at home, which is cute and made of cloth.*

stuffing ['stʌf ɪŋ] *n.* various foods, especially breadcrumbs and spices, packed into a fowl before it is cooked. (No plural form in this sense.) ♦ *The cook filled the turkey with stuffing.* ♦ *I asked for another helping of the delicious stuffing.*

stuffy ['stʌf i] **1.** *adj.* having stale air; lacking air movement and fresh air. (Comp: *stuffier;* sup: *stuffiest.*) ♦ *The stuffy meeting room was filled with smoke.* ♦ *I opened the windows because my apartment was stuffy.* **2.** *adj.* prim; old-fashioned; very formal, proper, and strait-laced; easily offended. (Comp: *stuffier;* sup: *stuffiest.*) ♦ *Bob's stuffy neighbors were offended by his casual manner.* ♦ *The stuffy townspeople disapproved of the new teacher's innovative ideas.* **3.** *adj.* [of a nose that] does not allow air to pass easily. (Comp: *stuffier;* sup: *stuffiest.*) ♦ *This medicine should help clear your stuffy nose.* ♦ *I can't smell anything because my nose is stuffy.*

stumble ['stʌm bəl] **1.** *iv.* to trip; to fall over something; to almost fall while one is moving; to walk in a clumsy way. ♦ *Careful. Don't stumble and break a bone!* ♦ *John stumbled and fell down the hill.* **2.** *iv.* to speak in a clumsy way; to make mistakes while speaking; to trip on one's words. (Figurative on ①.) ♦ *The politician stumbled while making a speech.* ♦ *The nervous speaker stumbled over his words.*

stump ['stʌmp] **1.** *n.* the part of something that remains when the other part has been cut off, broken off, removed, or used. ♦ *The picnicker sat on a tree stump at the park.* ♦ *The nurse bandaged the amputee's stump.* **2.** *tv.* to puzzle someone; to baffle someone. ♦ *The difficult question stumped all of the students.* ♦ *The crime problem stumped even the mayor.* **3.** *tv.* [for a candidate] to direct an election campaign at a particular group or a particular location. ♦ *The politician stumped all of Iowa before the primaries.* ♦ *The candidate stumped the rally of union workers.* **4.** *iv.* [for a candidate] to campaign. ♦ *Lisa stumped day and night during the week before the election.* ♦ *She stumped in the city and in the country, talking to voters.*

stun ['stʌn] **1.** *tv.* to surprise someone completely; to astound someone; to amaze someone; to shock someone. ♦ *The president's assassination stunned the entire nation.* ♦ *The magician stunned the audience with amazing tricks.* **2.** *tv.* to render someone or something unconscious, by a blow or by electrical shock. ♦ *The boxer was stunned by repeated blows to the head.* ♦ *John was stunned when he touched the electrical fence.*

stung ['stʌŋ] pt/pp of sting.

stunk ['stʌŋk] a pt/pp of stink.

stunned ['stʌnd] **1.** *adj.* surprised; astounded; shocked; amazed. ♦ *The stunned employees cried when they learned they were laid off.* ♦ *The reporter interviewed the stunned survivor of the accident.* **2.** *adj.* knocked unconscious, especially by a blow on the head or with electricity. ♦ *The stunned man slowly regained consciousness.* ♦ *The stunned boxer lost the fight.*

stunning ['stʌn ɪŋ] **1.** *adj.* surprising; astounding; shocking; amazing. (Adv: *stunningly.*) ♦ *The company's stunning announcement surprised the employees.* ♦ *The stunning news that my dog died shocked me.* **2.** *adj.* very pretty; attractive; impressive. (Adv: *stunningly.*) ♦ *Mary wore a stunning gown to the ball.* ♦ *The stunning woman walked around the room, enjoying the attention.*

stunt ['stʌnt] **1.** *n.* a dangerous act that is filmed as part of a movie. ♦ *The athletic actor did his own stunts.* ♦ *The director filmed the dangerous stunt in one take.* **2.** *n.* a stupid action that is done to get attention. ♦ *The student pretended to be choking as a stunt to get attention.* ♦ *John's silly stunt almost got him killed.* **3.** *tv.* to prevent someone or something from reaching full growth. ♦ *Malnutrition stunts the growth of children around the world.* ♦ *The flowers were stunted by a lack of sunlight.*

stuntman ['stʌnt 'mæn] *n., irreg.* a man who does dangerous acts in a movie, especially one who does the action in place of the actor who is playing the character doing the dangerous action. (Pl: stuntmen.) ♦ *Stuntmen are trained how to fall without hurting themselves.* ♦ *The stuntman jumped from the exploding plane.*

stuntmen ['stʌnt mɛn] pl of stuntman.

stuntwoman ['stʌnt 'wʊm ən] *n., irreg.* a woman who does dangerous acts in a movie, especially one who does the action in place of the actor who is playing the character doing the dangerous action. (Pl: stuntwomen.) ♦ *The stuntwoman did all of the actress's dangerous scenes.* ♦ *The actress requested a stuntwoman for the life-threatening scene.*

stuntwomen ['stʌnt wɪm ən] pl of stuntwoman.

stupendous [stu 'pɛn dəs] *adj.* amazing; astounding; awesome; marvelous. (Adv: *stupendously.*) ♦ *The mayor has done a stupendous job of fighting crime.* ♦ *Bill told his grandchildren of his stupendous feats as a soldier.*

stupendously [stu 'pɛn dəs li] *adv.* amazingly; astoundingly; awesomely. ♦ *The popular singer's new record is selling stupendously well.* ♦ *This apple pie is stupendously delicious.*

stupid ['stu pɪd] **1.** *adj.* not intelligent; not smart. (Adv: *stupidly.* Comp: *stupider;* sup: *stupidest.*) ♦ *Bill felt stupid when he couldn't solve the math problem.* ♦ *The clerk is not stupid. He just made a simple mistake.* **2.** *adj.* silly; foolish. (Adv: *stupidly.* Comp: *stupider;* sup: *stupidest.*) ♦ *That is a stupid thing to say.* ♦ *What a stupid question! Of course, I do!* **3.** *adj.* [of something] annoying; [of something] causing anger or frustration. (Comp: *stupider;* sup: *stupidest.*) ♦ *I can't leave until I find my stupid coat.* ♦ *The stupid copy machine is broken again!*

stupidity [stu 'pɪd ɪ ti] **1.** *n.* a lack of intelligence. (No plural form in this sense.) ♦ *Due to John's unfortunate stupidity, he failed the test.* ♦ *The new teacher was disheartened by the stupidity of her students.* **2.** *n.* the condition of being stupid, incorrect, or inappropriate. (No plural form in this sense.) ♦ *I tried to explain the stupidity of the proposal to my boss.* ♦ *The stupidity of the television show amazed the critic.*

stupor ['stup ɚ] **in a stupor** *idiom* in a dazed condition; in a condition in which one cannot concentrate or think. ♦ *The drunk driver walked away from the car accident in a stupor.* ♦ *In the morning, Mary remains in a stupor until she drinks coffee.*

sturdy ['stɚ di] *adj.* strong; firm; not easily knocked over; not easily toppled. (Adv: *sturdily.* Comp: *sturdier;* sup:

sturdiest.) ♦ *The sturdy bridge withstood the shaking of the earthquake.* ♦ *Anne piled heavy weights on top of the sturdy table.*

stutter ['stʌt ɚ] **1.** *iv.* to have a problem with speech in which one repeats the first sound of a word or syllable several times when trying to speak. ♦ *Bill stutters when he has to give public speeches.* ♦ *Dave used to stutter when he was a child.* **2.** *tv.* to repeat the first sound of a word or syllable several times when trying to speak. ♦ *Anne stutters her words when she is nervous.* ♦ *Shocked, Mary stuttered her response to Bill's rude question.* **3.** *n.* a speech problem in which one stutters ①. (No plural form in this sense.) ♦ *The speech therapist helped Bill get rid of his stutter.* ♦ *Mary overcame her stutter and became a radio announcer.*

sty ['stɑɪ] **1.** *n.* a place where a pig lives on a farm. ♦ *The farmer kept ten pigs in a sty.* ♦ *The pigs wallowed in the mud in their sty.* **2.** *n.* a dirty, messy place; a messy room. (Figurative on ①.) ♦ *I want you to clean up this sty before you go to bed tonight.* ♦ *I don't like going to Bill's house because it's such a sty.* **3.** *n.* a swollen inflammation on the inside of the eyelid. ♦ *The eye doctor gave me medicated eye drops for my sty.* ♦ *The eye surgeon removed the dangerous sty from my eyelid.*

style ['stɑɪl] **1.** *n.* a way in which something is made, designed, done, said, or written. ♦ *The friends conversed in a very informal style.* ♦ *Dissertations should be written in a formal style.* **2.** *n.* a particular design or theme in clothing or products at a particular period of time. ♦ *The models wore the latest styles at the fashion show.* ♦ *The designer fashioned the actor's clothing in a 1920s style.* **3.** *n.* a fashionable way in which something is done, said, or written; the manner or nature of something that is done, said, or written. (No plural form in this sense.) ♦ *The poet wrote with elegant style.* ♦ *The socialite spoke in a highly cultivated style.* **4.** *n.* The manner in which someone behaves. (No plural form in this sense.) ♦ *I admired Jane's style in difficult situations.* ♦ *John's style of managing makes some workers uncomfortable.* **5.** *tv.* to design or form something in a certain way. ♦ *The writer styled his characters after his own family.* ♦ *The hairdresser styled the actor's hair before the show.* **6. cramp someone's style** *idiom* to limit someone in some way. ♦ *I hope this doesn't cramp your style, but could you please not hum while you work?* ♦ *To ask Bob to keep regular hours would really be cramping his style.* **7. out of style** *idiom* no longer stylish; not being suitable as a current style ②. (Hyphenated before nominals.) ♦ *Your clothes always look out of style!* ♦ *Tom has lots of out-of-style ideas.*

styling ['stɑɪl ɪŋ] **1.** *n.* the way something is styled. (No plural form in this sense.) ♦ *This luxury car has exquisite styling.* ♦ *The client liked the subtle styling of the room's decor.* **2.** *adj.* [of something] used to shape or arrange hair. ♦ *Mary curled her hair with a styling brush.* ♦ *David shaped his hair with styling gel.*

stylish ['stɑɪ lɪʃ] *adj.* fashionable; in style; current; up-to-date. (Adv: *stylishly.*) ♦ *The stylish teenager wore the latest designs.* ♦ *The popular students patronized the most stylish café.*

stylist ['stɑɪ ləst] **(hair) stylist** *n.* a hairdresser; someone who styles hair. ♦ *The hair stylist trimmed my hair and then dyed it.* ♦ *The stylist used hair spray to keep my hair in place.*

stymie ['stɑɪ mi] *tv.* to block, hinder, or impede someone or something. ♦ *Jane stymied my plans to run for office unopposed.* (Present participle: *stymieing.*) ♦ *The bodyguard stymied the assassin who sought to kill the prime minister.*

suave ['swɑv] *adj.* very polite; smooth; sophisticated. (Adv: *suavely.*) ♦ *The suave young man held the door open for his date.* ♦ *The suave entertainer graciously signed autographs for his fans.*

sub ['sʌb] See **submarine, substitute.**

subcommittee ['sʌb kə mɪt i] *n.* a group of people from a larger committee that is appointed to examine a particular issue or take on a special responsibility. ♦ *The council created a subcommittee to deal with traffic problems.* ♦ *The proposed bill was approved by the subcommittee before going to the full committee.*

subconscious [səb 'kɑn tʃəs] **1.** *n.* the part of one's mental processes of which one is not aware. (No plural form in this sense.) ♦ *Something in his subconscious kept him from expressing his feelings.* ♦ *Much of Mary's anxiety was linked to fears in her subconscious.* **2.** *adj.* <the adj. use of ①.> (Adv: *subconsciously.*) ♦ *The sleeping man's subconscious mind retained everything that was said around him.* ♦ *John finally faced his subconscious fear of snakes.*

subcontract ['sʌb 'kɑn trækt] **1.** *n.* a contract, to do some work, that is part of a larger contract. ♦ *The contractor kept track of each subcontract for the project.* ♦ *Max had a subcontract to install some marble tile in the lobby.* **2.** *tv.* [for a contractor] to assign part of the contractual responsibilities to another worker or company through ①. ♦ *The contractor subcontracted the electrical work to an electrician.* ♦ *The plumbing work was subcontracted, as was the painting.*

subdivide ['sʌb dɪ vɑɪd] *tv.* to divide something again into smaller parts, especially to divide a large tract of land into small lots for housing. ♦ *The developer subdivided the farm into half-acre plots.* ♦ *The landlord subdivided the second floor into two one-bedroom apartments.*

subdivision ['sʌb dɪ vɪ ʒən] **1.** *n.* a smaller part of a larger thing. ♦ *The manager assigned subdivisions of the project to individual workers.* ♦ *My office is a local subdivision of a national company.* **2.** *n.* a group of homes that are built on lots that were originally part of one tract of land. ♦ *All the kids in the subdivision waited for the school bus in one place.* ♦ *The large subdivision was filled with identical houses.*

subdue [səb 'du] **1.** *tv.* to bring someone or something under one's control; to overwhelm someone or something. ♦ *The army subdued the neighboring lands.* ♦ *The police subdued the excited suspect.* **2.** *tv.* to make someone or something less noticeable; to soften the strength or intensity of something. ♦ *Because the lighting was subdued, I couldn't see across the room.* ♦ *The artist subdued the bright colors in her painting.*

subject 1. ['sʌb dʒɪkt] *n.* a topic; something that is discussed, examined, or researched. ♦ *The subject of my paper is China.* ♦ *Lisa raised several subjects for discussion.* **2.** ['sʌb dʒɪkt] *n.* a course; something that is studied; a particular field of knowledge. ♦ *John is doing well in every subject except biology.* ♦ *Anne's favorite subject in college is French.* **3.** ['sʌb dʒɪkt] *n.* someone used in an experiment. ♦ *The researcher gave half of the subjects placebos.* ♦ *The scientist examined the subjects' reactions to bright light.* **4.** ['sʌb dʒɪkt] *n.* someone who is ruled by a government or a ruler. ♦ *The queen is supported by her subjects' tax money.* ♦ *The loyal subject would not speak against the government.* **5.** ['sʌb dʒɪkt] *n.* a person, object, or scene that is painted or photographed. ♦ *David is the subject of a new painting hanging in the lobby.* ♦ *Art students draw sketches of nude subjects.* **6.** ['sʌb dʒɪkt] *n.* the noun or noun phrase representing the doer of an action in active sentences, or that is the receiver of an action in passive sentences. ♦ *In the sentence "Mary gave Anne a present," "Mary" is the subject.* ♦ *The subject must agree with its verb.* **7. subject to** [səb 'dʒɛkt...] *tv.* + *prep. phr.* to make someone experience something. ♦ *The prisoner was subjected to torture.* ♦ *The master subjected the slave to harsh working conditions.* **8. subject to something** ['sʌb dʒɪkt...] *idiom* likely to have something, such as a physical disorder. ♦ *The sick man was subject to dizzy spells.* ♦ *I am subject to frequent headaches.* **9. subject to something** ['sʌb dʒɪkt...] *idiom* tentative, depending on something; vulnerable to something. ♦ *I have made all the necessary plans, subject to your approval, of course.* ♦ *My remarks are, of course, subject to your criticisms.* **10. change the subject** [...'sʌb dʒɪkt] *idiom* to begin talking about something different. (On ①.) ♦ *They changed the subject suddenly when the person whom they had been discussing entered the room.* ♦ *We'll change the subject if we are embarrassing you.*

subjective [səb 'dʒɛk tɪv] *adj.* of or about what someone thinks about something instead of the actual facts. (Adv: *subjectively.*) ♦ *The psychologist ignored his subjective thoughts regarding his research.* ♦ *Mary would not be a good juror because she is too subjective.*

sublease ['sʌb lis] **1.** *n.* a lease [for something] made by a renter rather than the owner. ♦ *Bill's lease allowed him to make a sublease with the approval of the owner.* ♦ *When the sublease expired, Lisa signed a regular lease with the landlord.* **2.** *tv.* to lease something [that one is renting] to someone else. ♦ *I subleased my apartment when I went to Europe for six months.* ♦ *The office manager subleased 400 square feet of space to a lawyer.*

sublet ['sʌb lɛt] **1.** *tv., irreg.* to sublease an apartment. (Pt/pp: sublet; present participle: *subletting.*) ♦ *Bill sublet his apartment while he went to Japan for three months.* ♦ *The professor sublet her apartment during the summer.* **2.** *n.* an apartment that is rented from someone who is renting it from someone else. ♦ *Mary lived in a cheap sublet for three months during the summer.* ♦ *My sublet was larger than the place I used to live.*

sublime [sə 'blɑɪm] *adj.* supreme; wonderful; grand; inspiring. (Adv: *sublimely.*) ♦ *Visiting the art museum was a sublime experience for Mary.* ♦ *David spent a sublime weekend resting in Florida.*

subliminal [səb 'lɪm ə nəl] *adj.* below the level of consciousness. (Adv: *subliminally.*) ♦ *Subliminal messages on the tape are supposed to help you lose weight.* ♦ *The advertisement contained subliminal suggestions to influence buyers.*

submarine AND **sub** ['sʌb mə rin, 'sʌb] **1.** *n.* a ship that can travel completely underwater, used especially in war and for research. ♦ *The submarine launched a torpedo at the cargo ship.* ♦ *The ship detected the submarine through the use of sonar.* **2.** *n.* a large sandwich; a sandwich made with two long pieces of bread. (Usually sub.) ♦ *Mary ate a ham sub for lunch.* ♦ *I ordered a salami sub that was one foot long.*

submerge [səb 'mɚdʒ] **1.** *tv.* to put something under the surface of a liquid; to immerse something in water. ♦ *Dave submerged the thermometer in alcohol to sterilize it.* ♦ *The coastal city was submerged by the flood.* **2.** *iv.* to go underwater; to go under the surface of liquid. ♦ *The submarine submerged and left the harbor.* ♦ *The scuba diver submerged and swam toward a coral reef.*

submerged [səb 'mɚdʒd] *adj.* underwater. ♦ *The divers discovered the submerged treasure.* ♦ *The police pulled the submerged truck from the river.*

submission [səb 'mɪ ʃən] **1.** *n.* something that is submitted for someone's consideration. ♦ *The editors rejected most of the submissions they received.* ♦ *The journal approved Anne's submission for publication.* **2.** *n.* surrender and submitting; the giving up of control or power of oneself. (No plural form in this sense.) ♦ *The master demanded total submission from his slaves.* ♦ *At college, one learns submission to authority, among other things.*

submissive [səb 'mɪs ɪv] *adj.* allowing someone else control or power; obedient; willing to let someone else have control over oneself. (Adv: *submissively.*) ♦ *The mean professor took advantage of submissive students.* ♦ *The submissive peasants remained steadfastly loyal to their king.*

submit [səb 'mɪt] **1. submit to** *tv.* + *prep. phr.* to give oneself over to the control of someone else. ♦ *The peasants submitted themselves to the queen's rule.* ♦ *The slaves could only submit themselves to their masters.* **2. submit to** *tv.* + *prep. phr.* to offer something to someone for consideration; to present something to someone for consideration. ♦ *Mary submitted an application to law school.* ♦ *David submitted his proposal to the company president.* **3. submit (to)** *iv.* + *prep. phr.* to yield to someone or something; to surrender to someone else's control. ♦ *I finally submitted to Mary's request after arguing with her for hours.* ♦ *Employees who refuse to submit to the authority of the boss are usually dismissed.*

subnormal [səb 'nor məl] *adj.* [of something] less than normal or below what is usual or average. (Adv: *subnormally.*) ♦ *The subnormal turnout of voters on election day was due to the bad weather.* ♦ *The forecaster said subnormal temperatures would last until Friday.*

subordinate [sə 'bor dn ət] **1.** *n.* someone who is lower in rank than someone else. ♦ *The manager issued all of her subordinates an important memo.* ♦ *The supervisor blamed one of his subordinates for the mistake.* **2. subordinate to** *adj.* + *prep. phr.* lower in rank; inferior. ♦ *The new recruit was subordinate to all of the officers.* ♦ *In chess, the pawns are subordinate to the other pieces.* **3.** *adj.* less important; secondary. (Adv: *subordinately.*) ♦ *The voter felt taxes were subordinate only to the crime problem.* ♦ *The lecturer discussed subordinate issues at the end of the talk.* **4.** *adj.* [of a clause that] cannot stand alone or is dependent [on the existence of some other clause]. (Adv: *sub-*

ordinately.) ♦ *In the sentence "If it rains, we'll stay home," "if it rains" is a subordinate clause.* ♦ *The verb in a German subordinate clause is placed at the end of the clause.*

subpoena [sə 'pi nə] **1.** *n.* an official written order that demands that a person appear in court. ♦ *The witness to the crime received a subpoena.* ♦ *The county official delivered a subpoena to me.* **2.** *tv.* to order someone to appear in court; to order something to be brought to court. ♦ *The primary witness was subpoenaed to appear in court.* ♦ *The court subpoenaed the defendant's medical records.*

subscribe [səb 'skrɑɪb] **1. subscribe to** *iv.* + *prep. phr.* to believe in a principle, theory, or viewpoint. ♦ *The student subscribed to the biblical story of creation.* ♦ *The revolutionary subscribed to communist ideas.* **2. subscribe to** *iv.* + *prep. phr.* to place a permanent order for and receive a series of issues of a magazine, newspaper, or newsletter. ♦ *The banker subscribes to a financial newsletter.* ♦ *John subscribes to many different computer magazines.*

subscriber [səb 'skrɑɪb ɚ] *n.* a customer who receives a newspaper, magazine, or newsletter on a regular basis; someone who receives information from a particular source on a regular basis. ♦ *Advertising rates are based on the number of subscribers a publication has.* ♦ *The sales representative received a bonus for each new subscriber.*

subscription [səb 'skrɪp ʃən] *n.* a standing order for a series of issues of a magazine or newspaper. ♦ *Mary has a yearly subscription to the local newspaper.* ♦ *Anne renewed her subscription to her favorite magazine.*

subsequent ['sʌb sə kwənt] *adj.* following; later; happening or coming afterward. (Adv: *subsequently.*) ♦ *The magazine informed its readers that subsequent issues would cost one dollar more.* ♦ *I hope the subsequent meetings are shorter than this first one has been.*

subservient [səb 'sɚ vi ənt] *adj.* always willing to do what someone demands; servile; submissive; very obedient. (Adv: *subserviently.*) ♦ *The subservient helper performed many errands for his boss.* ♦ *The high-school freshmen were subservient to the seniors.*

subside [səb 'sɑɪd] *iv.* to recede; to lessen; to become less strong or active. ♦ *The pain began to subside after I took medication.* ♦ *When the rain subsided, I went back outside.*

subsidence [səb 'sɪd əns] *n.* moving to a lower level; sinking. (No plural form in this sense.) ♦ *Upon the subsidence of the flood, the mayor inspected the damage.* ♦ *There is evidence of subsidence around the foundation of the building.*

subsidiary [səb 'sɪd i ɛr i] *n.* a company that is a small part of a larger company. ♦ *I work for a small subsidiary of a large corporation.* ♦ *The large conglomerate owned dozens of small subsidiaries.*

subsidize ['sʌb sɪ dɑɪz] *tv.* to pay part of the cost of something; to help a company or a person by paying part of its cost. ♦ *The federal government subsidized my college education because I couldn't afford to pay for it myself.* ♦ *The city subsidized the social-service agency's programs.*

subsidized ['sʌb sɪ dɑɪzd] *adj.* paid for by a subsidy, especially from a government, foundation, or corporation. ♦ *Max's family lived in subsidized housing.* ♦ *The subsidized program was discontinued after the government stopped funding it.*

subsidy ['sʌb sɪ di] *n.* [extra] money given to support someone or a group. ♦ *The needy students received a tuition subsidy.* ♦ *Poor families receive subsidies from the state.*

subsist [səb 'sɪst] *iv.* to remain alive on the least possible amount of food and other needs. ♦ *The poor farmer's family subsisted on potatoes.* ♦ *The homeless man could barely subsist.*

subsistence [səb 'sɪs təns] *n.* the absolute minimum amount of food and shelter that is required for one to live. (No plural form in this sense.) ♦ *The farmer's crops were his only subsistence.* ♦ *Millions of people depend on welfare for subsistence.*

subsoil ['sʌb sɔɪl] *n.* the layer of soil that lies below the surface of the earth. (No plural form in this sense.) ♦ *During spring, the subsoil thawed.* ♦ *The farmer plowed the fertilizer into the subsoil.*

substance ['sʌb stəns] **1.** *n.* the material that something is made of; matter. ♦ *I discovered that my furniture was stuffed with a flammable substance.* ♦ *The doctor flushed the poisonous substances from the child's stomach.* **2.** *n.* the essence; the important part of something. (No plural form in this sense.) ♦ *The teacher discussed the substance of the author's works.* ♦ *Lisa's report detailed the substance of her findings.*

substandard [səb 'stæn dɚd] *adj.* below a standard; not meeting required standards. (Adv: *substandardly.*) ♦ *The inspector condemned the substandard housing.* ♦ *John barely survived on his substandard income.*

substantial [səb 'stæn ʃəl] **1.** *adj.* sturdy; big and strong and not likely to break or collapse. (Adv: *substantially.*) ♦ *John placed the heavy objects on the substantial table.* ♦ *The substantial tree withstood the violent winds.* **2.** *adj.* ample; rather large; rather important. (Adv: *substantially.*) ♦ *Mary has a substantial amount of money in the bank.* ♦ *The TV news program received a substantial number of complaints about poor reporting.*

substantially [səb 'stæn ʃə li] *adv.* rather; quite; almost. (Used before an adjective.) ♦ *Substantially all of the victims were burned to death.* ♦ *John exercises substantially less in the winter than in the summer.*

substantiate [səb 'stæn ʃi et] *tv.* to prove something; to verify something; to show that something is true. ♦ *My experiment substantiated my claims.* ♦ *The researchers substantiated their figures with census data.*

substitute ['sʌb stɪ tut] **1. substitute for** *tv.* + *prep. phr.* to replace someone or something with someone or something else; to exchange someone for someone else. ♦ *John substituted margarine for butter in the recipe.* ♦ *The softball coach substituted Jane for the injured pitcher.* **2.** *iv.* to be put in someone else's or something else's place as a replacement. (Abbreviated **sub.**) ♦ *Mr. Wilson substituted for our regular teacher in my music class today.* ♦ *Bill's couch also substitutes as his bed.* **3.** *n.* a replacement; someone or something that is put in someone else's or something else's place. (Abbreviated **sub.**) ♦ *A substitute taught my English class because the teacher was sick.* ♦ *Susan stirred some sugar substitute in her coffee.*

substitution [səb stɪ 'tu ʃən] **1.** *n.* the replacement of someone or something with someone or something else. (No plural form in this sense.) ♦ *The substitution of but-*

ter with margarine in the recipe did not change the results. ♦ *The coach was criticized for the substitution of players he made late in the game.* **2.** *n.* someone or something that has been substituted as in ①. ♦ *We will not accept any substitutions.* ♦ *This is a very poor substitution for butter.*

subterfuge ['sʌb tɚ fjudʒ] *n.* lies or dishonesty used to hide something or evade something. (No plural form in this sense.) ♦ *The fraudulent treasurer was guilty of subterfuge.* ♦ *The boss remained unaware of the problem because of the employee's subterfuge.*

subterranean [səb tə 're ni ən] *adj.* underground. (Adv: *subterraneanly.*) ♦ *Subterranean steam tunnels carry heated water to the campus buildings.* ♦ *The prisoners were thrown into a subterranean dungeon.*

subtitle ['sʌb tɑɪt əl] **1.** *n.* a caption; words that appear with a picture or an image, including a translation of a film or television program into another language. ♦ *I rented a French film with subtitles.* ♦ *Hardly any of the television programs had English subtitles.* **2.** *n.* a secondary title of a book, film, or something similar. ♦ *A subtitle is generally separated from the title by a colon.* ♦ *The subtitle indicated that the book was based on a true story.* **3.** *tv.* to provide something with ①. ♦ *The French film was subtitled in English.* ♦ *A committee of translators subtitled the foreign film.* **4.** *tv.* to provide a book or article with ②. ♦ *The editor subtitled the journal article for clarification.* ♦ *The computer manual was subtitled "A guide for beginners."*

subtle ['sʌt əl] *adj.* barely noticeable; not noticeable right away; hard to detect, especially when something is delicate or clever. (Adv: *subtly.* Comp: *subtler;* sup: *subtlest.*) ♦ *Few people noticed Bill's subtle way of criticizing.* ♦ *I quietly laughed at Mary's subtle joke.*

subtlety ['sʌt l ti] **1.** *n.* delicacy; fine or subtle distinctions. (No plural form in this sense.) ♦ *It is the subtlety in the use of the spices in Chinese cooking that makes it such an art.* ♦ *Subtlety in the performance of music makes the difference between good music and great music.* **2.** *n.* a nuance; a slight suggestion or hint of something. ♦ *Only some of the audience members appreciated the subtlety of the speaker's humor.* ♦ *The food critic noticed the delicate subtlety of the herbs in the sauce.*

subtotal ['sʌb tot əl] **1.** *n.* an amount that is calculated, but is not the final amount, such as the total amount of one's purchase before tax is added. ♦ *The subtotal did not include the tax or tip.* ♦ *The clerk deducted 10% from my subtotal because the goods were on sale.* **2.** *tv.* to calculate ①. ♦ *The accountant subtotaled our expenses before taxes.* ♦ *After the bill was subtotaled, I added a 15% tip.*

subtract [səb 'trækt] **1.** *tv.* to take a part of something away; to take a quantity away from a quantity; to reduce something by a certain amount. (See also minus.) ♦ *Tom subtracted the smaller number from the larger number.* ♦ *Please remember to subtract the amount of the coupon.* **2.** *iv.* to lessen or reduce [something] as in ①. ♦ *I added when I should have subtracted!* ♦ *The first-grade teacher taught the students to subtract.*

subtraction [səb 'træk ʃən] **1.** *n.* the reduction of something by a certain amount; the reduction of a quantity by a quantity. (No plural form in this sense.) ♦ *The children learned how to perform subtraction in first grade.* ♦ *The subtraction of a number from a smaller number yields a negative number.* **2.** *n.* an amount that is subtracted. ♦ *After the subtractions of the cost of the items I returned, my bill was only $400.* ♦ *I made one small subtraction in my bank account to get it to balance.*

suburb ['sʌ bɚb] *adj.* a city, town, or village that is next to or near a large city. ♦ *Urban problems often stretch beyond city limits into the suburbs.* ♦ *Large cities are usually surrounded by many suburbs.*

suburban [sə 'bɚ bən] *adj.* of or about the suburbs. ♦ *John works at a large suburban shopping mall.* ♦ *Bill rode the train from a suburban station to the city.*

suburbanite [sə 'bɚ bə nɑɪt] *n.* someone who lives in a suburb. ♦ *The suburbanite commuted to the city every weekday.* ♦ *My friend, who is a suburbanite, lives about 15 miles from the city.*

suburbia [sə 'bɚ bi ə] *n.* the suburbs of a major city; suburbs in general. (No plural form in this sense.) ♦ *She prefers living in suburbia to living in a city.* ♦ *Many major urban problems have crept into suburbia.*

subversive [səb 'vɚ sɪv] **1.** *adj.* advocating the disruption or destruction of a government. (Adv: *subversively.*) ♦ *Over one hundred subversive rebels were imprisoned.* ♦ *The protesters spread subversive propaganda.* **2.** *n.* someone who wants to disrupt or overthrow a government. ♦ *The soldier shot the subversive.* ♦ *The government placed the subversives in jail.*

subway ['sʌb we] *n.* an underground electric train that provides transportation in large cities. ♦ *The New York City subway serves millions of passengers each year.* ♦ *Anne saves money by taking the subway to work instead of driving.*

succeed [sək 'sid] **1.** *iv.* to be successful; to reach a goal. ♦ *Anne tried and tried and finally succeeded.* ♦ *Bill succeeded in losing ten pounds.* **2.** *tv.* to follow someone or something into a job or office. ♦ *John Adams succeeded George Washington as president of the U.S.* ♦ *Susan succeeded Dave as the head of the department.*

success [sək 'sɛs] **1.** *n.* accomplishment; achievement. (No plural form in this sense.) ♦ *Success requires hard work.* ♦ *Most people would prefer success rather than failure.* **2.** *n.* a favorable outcome; a favorable result. ♦ *The project was a success.* ♦ *The producer was honored for his numerous successes in the movie industry.* **3.** *n.* someone or something that is successful, especially someone or something that has become famous, important, or rich. ♦ *The popular movie was a major Hollywood success.* ♦ *Through hard work, Susan became a success in her field.*

successful [sək 'sɛs fəl] *adj.* showing evidence of having accomplished something or having reached high status. (Adv: *successfully.*) ♦ *The successful banker had a very high salary.* ♦ *Mary has a successful career in finance.*

succession [sək 'sɛ ʃən] **1.** *n.* a series of things or people that follow one another. ♦ *The succession of presidents begins with George Washington.* ♦ *The company was hampered by a succession of problems.* **2.** *n.* the right by which someone is entitled to take a position after someone else. (No plural form in this sense.) ♦ *The heir apparent was denied succession to the throne.* ♦ *The succession of popes is determined by a secret ballot.*

successive [sək 'sɛs ɪv] *adj.* happening one after the other; following in order; consecutive. (Adv: *succes-*

sively.) ♦ *Six successive attempts finally brought success.* ♦ *The baseball player hit four successive home runs.*

successor [sək 'sɛs ɚ] *n.* someone who occupies a position after someone else; someone or something that follows someone or something else. ♦ *The office manager left detailed notes for his successor.* ♦ *George Bush's successor as president was Bill Clinton.*

succinct [sək 'sɪŋkt] *adj.* concise; expressed quickly and clearly. (Adv: *succinctly.*) ♦ *I easily understood my teacher's succinct remarks on my term paper.* ♦ *The winner of the award gave a succinct acceptance speech.*

succinctly [sək 'sɪŋkt li] *adv.* simply; briefly; concisely; in as few words as possible, yet still expressing what is necessary. ♦ *The customer succinctly stated his complaint.* ♦ *The professor explained the reading assignment succinctly.*

succor ['sʌk ɚ] *n.* something that provides help or assistance. (Formal. No plural form in this sense.) ♦ *Your kindness has been a great succor in my time of grief.* ♦ *The manual was the succor that I needed to complete the assembly.*

succulent ['sʌk jə lənt] *adj.* juicy and very good to eat. (Adv: *succulently.*) ♦ *Lisa enjoyed the succulent roast beef.* ♦ *Anne ate a ripe, succulent peach.*

succumb [sə 'kʌm] **1.** *iv.* to give in to someone or something; to yield to someone or something. ♦ *The politician succumbed to pressure and resigned.* ♦ *The manager succumbed and bought a new computer.* **2.** *iv.* to die. ♦ *Hundreds of soldiers succumbed on the battlefield.* ♦ *Many elderly people succumbed in the fire.*

such ['sʌtʃ] **1.** *adj.* so great; so much. ♦ *I've never had such fun in my life!* ♦ *There was such a noise from the explosion!* **2. as such** *phr.* the way something is; as someone or something is. ♦ *I cannot accept your manuscript as such. It needs revisions.* ♦ *You are new here, and as such, I will have to train you.* **3. such as** *phr.* for example. ♦ *Bill enjoys many kinds of fruit, such as apples, pears, and plums.* ♦ *Mary has many hobbies, such as swimming, bowling, and running.* **4. such as** *phr.* of a particular kind; of the sort that is. ♦ *Where can I get a haircut such as yours?* ♦ *I'd like to buy a vase such as the one in your display case.*

suck ['sʌk] **1.** *tv.* to pull liquid into one's mouth by putting one's lips around something and drawing in; to pull something into one's mouth with one's lips. ♦ *Bill sucked the poison from the snakebite.* ♦ *Anne sucked the soda through a straw.* **2.** *iv.* to be very unpleasant; to be disliked very much. (Rude slang.) ♦ *Anne thought the book sucked, so she didn't finish reading it.* ♦ *This party sucks. Let's leave.*

sucker ['sʌk ɚ] **1.** *n.* a piece of hard candy attached to a thin stick. ♦ *The photographer gave Jimmy a lemon-flavored sucker.* ♦ *Susie unwrapped the sucker and put it in her mouth.* **2.** *n.* someone who is easily deceived or cheated. (Slang.) ♦ *The crook cheated the sucker out of all of his money.* ♦ *I sold my defective car to a sucker from out of town.*

suckle ['sʌk əl] **1.** *iv.* [for a young mammal] to take milk at a breast or an udder. ♦ *The baby suckled quietly at Anne's breast.* ♦ *The piglets suckled while the sow snored.* **2.** *tv.* to feed a child milk from one's breast. ♦ *Anne suckled her infant.* ♦ *The sow suckled her piglets while she slept.*

suction ['sʌk ʃən] *n.* a difference in pressure that causes something to stick to something else or that causes something to flow into a vacuum; the force of a vacuum. (No plural form in this sense.) ♦ *A vacuum cleaner uses suction to pick up dirt.* ♦ *The toy stuck to the wall by suction.*

Sudan [su 'dæn] See Gazetteer.

sudden ['sʌd n] *adj.* unexpected; happening without warning. (Adv: *suddenly.*) ♦ *A sudden explosion destroyed the office building.* ♦ *I was unprepared for the sudden rainstorm and got all wet.*

suddenly ['sʌd n li] *adv.* unexpectedly; without warning. ♦ *Suddenly, the car slid off the road and into a ditch.* ♦ *The fire alarm suddenly rang, startling me.*

suds ['sʌdz] *n.* bubbles formed by soap mixing with water; lather; froth. (Treated as plural.) ♦ *John rinsed the soap suds from the dishes.* ♦ *The children played in the suds in the bathtub.*

sudsy ['sʌd zi] *adj.* bubbly; frothy; full of suds. (Comp: *sudsier;* sup: *sudsiest.*) ♦ *Anne washed the dishes in sudsy water.* ♦ *I rinsed off the sudsy car.*

sue ['su] **1.** *iv.* to start a lawsuit; to file a claim against someone or something in court. ♦ *The worker who had been fired sued for compensation.* ♦ *The woman who fell at the store sued to cover hospital costs.* **2.** *tv.* to bring a lawsuit against someone or something; to file a claim against someone or something in court. ♦ *The fired worker sued his company.* ♦ *John sued the driver who had caused the car accident.*

suede ['swed] **1.** *n.* a type of leather of which one side has been rubbed to give it a soft texture like velvet. (No plural form in this sense.) ♦ *The suede of my jacket feels very soft.* ♦ *Susan sprayed the suede with a protective waterproofing substance.* **2.** *adj.* made of ①. ♦ *Anne wore a new suede jacket to the party.* ♦ *John ruined his suede shoes by walking in mud.*

suffer ['sʌf ɚ] **1.** *tv.* to experience physical or emotional pain because of illness or emotional loss. ♦ *Susan suffered a great loss when her house burned down.* ♦ *Bill suffered a lot of pain before going to the doctor.* **2.** *iv.* to feel physical or emotional pain. ♦ *Mary is suffering from a toothache.* ♦ *John suffered over the death of his parents.* **3.** *iv.* to worsen; to decline in quality. ♦ *The economy suffered as more people lost their jobs.* ♦ *The city schools have suffered under the current administration.*

suffering ['sʌf ɚ ɪŋ] **1.** *adj.* feeling pain, trouble, or loss. ♦ *The suffering widower cried at the funeral.* ♦ *I donated clothing to the suffering victims of the war.* **2.** *n.* pain; the condition of being in pain. ♦ *Bill's suffering finally ended when they found the right medication for his illness.* ♦ *Aspirin eased the suffering caused by my headache.*

suffice [sə 'fɑɪs] *iv.* to be plenty; to be sufficient; to be enough. ♦ *No more, please. Two potatoes will suffice.* ♦ *You don't need a coat outside. A sweater will suffice.*

sufficient [sə 'fɪʃ ənt] *adj.* enough; adequate; meeting a need or requirement. (Adv: *sufficiently.*) ♦ *The troops were given sufficient provisions for a month.* ♦ *My office does not have sufficient desks for its employees.*

sufficiently [sə 'fɪʃ ənt li] *adv.* adequately; enough. ♦ *Retired federal politicians are sufficiently provided for.* ♦

Anne did sufficiently well in high school to be accepted to the college.

suffix ['sʌf ɪks] *n.* a form added to end of a word that changes or modifies the meaning or function of the word. ♦ *The most common plural suffix in English is spelled* -s. ♦ *The suffix* -ness *changes adjectives into nouns.*

suffocate ['sʌf ə ket] **1.** *tv.* to kill someone or a creature by preventing it from getting the oxygen that is needed. ♦ *The murderer suffocated his victim with a pillow.* ♦ *The thick smoke suffocated the victims of the fire.* **2.** *iv.* to die because one is unable to get the oxygen that is needed. ♦ *The dog suffocated in the hot car.* ♦ *Two people suffocated from the smoke in the building.*

suffocation [səf ə 'ke ʃən] *n.* death from a lack of oxygen. (No plural form in this sense.) ♦ *Many victims of fires actually die of suffocation.* ♦ *The coroner determined that the murder victim died from suffocation.*

suffrage ['sʌf rɪdʒ] *n.* the right to vote. (No plural form in this sense.) ♦ *In America, suffrage was granted to women in 1920.* ♦ *Suffrage for all citizens was not included in the U.S. Constitution when it was written.*

sugar ['ʃʊg ɚ] **1.** *n.* a sweet substance, usually in crystal form, that is made from certain plants and used to sweeten food and drinks. (No plural form in this sense.) ♦ *Mary added some sugar to her coffee.* ♦ *The donuts were covered with powdered sugar.* **2.** *n.* a sweet substance that is found naturally in many foods. (No plural form in this sense.) ♦ *The kind of sugar found in fruits is very easy to digest.* ♦ *Many fruits contain sugar.* **3.** *adj.* made with ①. ♦ *Anne bought some sugar cookies at the store.* ♦ *Bill ate two sugar donuts.*

sugarcoated ['ʃʊg ɚ kot əd] **1.** *adj.* covered or coated with sugar or a sweet coating. ♦ *The children's medicine was sugarcoated.* ♦ *Anne chewed on the sugarcoated vitamin.* **2.** *adj.* [of something unpleasant] made more agreeable in some way. (Figurative on ①.) ♦ *The company sugarcoated the decision to fire people by giving them a month's extra pay.* ♦ *John's criticism was sugarcoated with a few pleasant comments.*

sugary ['ʃʊg ə ri] *adj.* having a lot of sugar; made of sugar; sweet like sugar. ♦ *The children drank the sugary lemonade.* ♦ *Anne doesn't like sugary coffee.*

suggest [səg 'dʒɛst] **1.** *tv.* to propose something for consideration; to express something that one thinks should be considered; to offer something as an option. ♦ *Mary suggested that we order pizza for lunch.* ♦ *"I suggest ordering the meatloaf," said the waiter.* **2.** *tv.* to bring something to one's mind; to cause something to be thought of in a certain way; to cause something to be a reminder to someone. ♦ *The abstract painting suggested different things to different people.* ♦ *The rumbling in my stomach suggested that it was time for dinner.*

suggested [səg 'dʒɛs tɪd] *adj.* offered as an option. ♦ *The suggested retail price of this car is $12,000.* ♦ *The diner decided to order one of the suggested specials.*

suggestible [səg 'dʒɛs tə bəl] *adj.* [of someone] easily influenced by other things or people. (Adv: *suggestibly.*) ♦ *John is very suggestible and is likely to do anything you tell him to do.* ♦ *Members of the cult were highly suggestible, lonely people.*

suggestion [səg 'dʒɛs tʃən] **1.** *n.* a hint; a trace; something that reminds someone of someone or something. (No plural form in this sense.) ♦ *There's a slight suggestion of cinnamon in these cookies.* ♦ *I noticed a suggestion of anger in Susan's voice.* **2.** *n.* a proposal for consideration; an expression of something that one thinks should be considered; the offering of an option; the act of suggesting; something that is suggested. ♦ *The committee analyzed the three suggestions for the project.* ♦ *The diner ordered one of the waitress's suggestions.*

suggestive [səg 'dʒɛs tɪv] **1.** *adj.* seeming to suggest something sexual or indecent. (Adv: *suggestively.*) ♦ *Children were not allowed to watch the suggestive movie.* ♦ *Bob's act was too suggestive to be shown on television.* **2. suggestive of something** *phr.* reminiscent of something; seeming to suggest something. ♦ *Bill's homemade soup is suggestive of his mother's.* ♦ *The new movie was suggestive of an old one I had seen on TV.*

suicidal ['su ə saɪd l] **1.** *adj.* feeling the desire to kill oneself. (Adv: *suicidally.*) ♦ *The suicidal student called an emergency hotline.* ♦ *The lonely and depressed woman felt suicidal.* **2.** *adj.* [of an action] leading to one's death or destruction. (Adv: *suicidally.*) ♦ *The lonely man took a suicidal leap from the high bridge.* ♦ *Eating so much fat every day is suicidal.*

suicide ['su ə saɪd] **1.** *n.* killing oneself on purpose. (No plural form in this sense.) ♦ *The depressed man committed suicide by shooting himself.* ♦ *The terminally ill woman resorted to a painless suicide.* **2.** *n.* someone who has accomplished ①. ♦ *There were four potential suicides at my university last year.* ♦ *The coroner examined the suicide to determine the cause of death.*

suit ['sut] **1.** *n.* a set of formal clothes, consisting of a jacket, pants, and sometimes a vest, made from the same material. ♦ *David bought a tie to match his business suit.* ♦ *Each piece of my suit is brown.* **2.** *n.* a set of things, such as clothing or armor, that are worn together. ♦ *The gallant knight wore a metal suit of armor.* ♦ *Max put on his clown suit and entered the circus ring.* **3.** *n.* a lawsuit; a claim that is filed in court against someone or something. ♦ *Susan filed a suit against her neighbors because they built a deck on her property.* ♦ *The two parties decided to settle the suit out of court.* **4.** *n.* one of the four different sets of cards found in a deck of playing cards. ♦ *The four suits are diamonds, clubs, hearts, and spades.* ♦ *A poker hand of cards of the same suit is called a flush.* **5.** *tv.* to meet the requirements of someone or something. ♦ *Our present vendor suits all of our needs at this time.* ♦ *The new class suited Max perfectly.* **6.** *tv.* to look good with something; to look good on someone; to match someone. ♦ *Your outfit suits the color of your eyes.* ♦ *Do these pants suit me?* **7. in one's birthday suit** *idiom* naked; nude. ♦ *We used to go down to the river and swim in our birthday suits.* ♦ *You have to be in your birthday suit to bathe.*

suitable ['su tə bəl] *adj.* appropriate; fitting; right or proper for the circumstances. (Adv: *suitably.*) ♦ *Mary looked for a video that was suitable for young children.* ♦ *Employees must wear suitable business attire.*

suitcase ['sut kes] **1.** *n.* a piece of luggage used for carrying clothing and personal items while traveling. ♦ *Susan handed her suitcases to a porter at the airport.* ♦ *I packed my suitcase the evening before my trip.* **2. live out**

of a suitcase *idiom* to live briefly in a place, never unpacking one's luggage. ♦ *I hate living out of a suitcase. For my next vacation, I want to go to just one place and stay there the whole time.* ♦ *We were living out of suitcases in a motel while they repaired the damage the fire caused to our house.*

suite ['swit] **1.** *n.* two or more rooms that are connected, especially as found in a hotel or office building. ♦ *The family of six rented a two-room suite at the hotel.* ♦ *The receptionist sat in the main room of the office suite.* **2.** *n.* a set of furniture. ♦ *Bill won a living-room suite on a game show.* ♦ *Susan's dining-room suite is made of oak.* **3.** *n.* a piece of music made of two or more related movements in the same key or in related keys. ♦ *The pianist played the suite in D major during the party.* ♦ *Last winter, I attended a performance of* The Nutcracker Suite.

suitor ['sut ɚ] *n.* a man who courts a woman and hopes to marry her. ♦ *Mary's suitor gave her a diamond ring.* ♦ *Susan's suitor arrived early for their date.*

sulfur ['sʌl fɚ] *n.* a bright yellow chemical element that combines with many substances and has a very bad smell when it burns. (No plural form in this sense.) ♦ *The atomic symbol of sulfur is S, and its atomic number is 16.* ♦ *Sulfur is found in large quantities beneath the surface of the earth.*

sulfuric acid [səl fjɚ ɪk 'æs ɪd] *n.* a clear, corrosive liquid that is used in making explosives and fertilizers. (No plural form in this sense.) ♦ *Sulfuric acid eats into most surfaces it comes in contact with, including skin.* ♦ *The chemist corroded the metal with sulfuric acid.*

sulk ['sʌlk] *iv.* to look forlorn and sit without speaking because one is in a bad mood. ♦ *Susie sulked in the corner because she didn't get her way.* ♦ *My roommate sulked for days after we had an argument.*

sulking ['sʌl kɪŋ] *adj.* looking forlorn and sitting without speaking because one is in a bad mood. ♦ *The sulking child was sent to bed directly after supper.* ♦ *My sulking coworker refuses to talk to me.*

sullen ['sʌl ən] *adj.* being silent and looking angry and irritable because one is in a bad mood. (Adv: *sullenly.* Comp: *sullener;* sup: *sullenest.*) ♦ *The sullen child would not tell me what was wrong.* ♦ *The sullen waiter put the plates on our table and walked away.*

sultry ['sʌl tri] **1.** *adj.* [of or about weather] hot, sticky, and damp. (Adv: *sultrily.* Comp: *sultrier;* sup: *sultriest.*) ♦ *The workers sweated heavily in the sultry weather.* ♦ *We went swimming because the day was so sultry.* **2.** *adj.* sensual; showing passion or lust; sexually provocative; causing sexual attraction. (Adv: *sultrily.* Comp: *sultrier;* sup: *sultriest.*) ♦ *The sultry movie star danced suggestively.* ♦ *The performer sang a sultry ballad.*

sum ['sʌm] **1.** *n.* the total of two or more amounts. (No plural form in this sense.) ♦ *The sum of 2 and 3 is 5.* ♦ *Can you figure out the sum of these numbers?* **2.** *n.* an amount of money. ♦ *I paid my landlord the sum of $800.* ♦ *Jane donated the sum of $500 to the charity.*

summarize ['sʌm ə rɑɪz] *tv.* to express the main ideas of something. ♦ *The concluding paragraph summarized the main topics of the chapter.* ♦ *After Jane summarized her main points, she answered questions from the audience.*

summary ['sʌm ə ri] *n.* the main ideas of something; a short statement about the important points of a longer speech or text. ♦ *The textbook's first chapter was a summary of the whole text.* ♦ *The author submitted a summary along with the complete manuscript.*

summation [sə 'me ʃən] *n.* the final presentation of facts at a trial. ♦ *The jury listened attentively to the lawyers' summations.* ♦ *The lawyer made a strong plea for the defense in the summation.*

summer ['sʌm ɚ] **1.** *n.* one of the seasons of the year, after spring and before autumn. ♦ *In the Northern Hemisphere, summer lasts roughly from June 22 to September 22.* ♦ *Mary visited her grandparents during the summer.* **2.** *iv.* to live someplace during ①. ♦ *The Smiths summered on Long Island and wintered in Florida.* ♦ *The rich family summered in a luxurious cabin in Maine.* **3.** *adj.* <the adj. use of ①.> ♦ *Mary and Bill own a summer home in Europe.* ♦ *The student received extra help during summer school.*

summertime ['sʌm ɚ tɑɪm] *n.* summer; the season of summer. (No plural form in this sense.) ♦ *Jimmy mowed his neighbors' lawns in the summertime.* ♦ *During the cold winter, Anne looked forward to summertime.*

summit ['sʌm ət] **1.** *n.* the highest point of something, especially a mountain. ♦ *The climbers placed their country's flag at the mountain's summit.* ♦ *The highest summit in the world is the top of Mt. Everest.* **2.** *n.* a meeting involving very important people, especially leaders of governments. (Figurative on ①.) ♦ *A peace treaty was drafted at the political summit.* ♦ *The president met with his advisors at a secret summit.*

summon ['sʌm ən] **1.** *tv.* to order someone officially to do something. ♦ *The witness was summoned to testify in court.* ♦ *My boss summoned me to deliver an important package.* **2.** AND **summons** *tv.* to summon ① someone to court using ③. ♦ *The witness was summoned to testify in court.* ♦ *If you do not show up voluntarily, I will summons you.* **3. summons** *n.* an official order to appear in court. (Treated as singular.) ♦ *The county official handed me a summons.* ♦ *If I ignore the summons, I will face prosecution.*

sumptuous ['sʌmp tʃu əs] *adj.* lavish; very expensive; extravagant; very fine, but costing a lot of money. (Adv: *sumptuously.*) ♦ *The chef prepared sumptuous meals at the classy restaurant.* ♦ *The luxurious hotel offered sumptuous accommodations.*

sun ['sʌn] **1.** *n.* a star; a star that gives light and warmth to a planet; a star that is orbited by a planet. ♦ *The astronomer dreamed of traveling to distant suns.* ♦ *When the sun exploded, it engulfed the planets that orbited it.* **2. the sun** *n.* the star that gives light and warmth to Earth; the star that Earth orbits. (No plural form in this sense. Treated as singular.) ♦ *Nine planets, including Earth, orbit the sun.* ♦ *Earth is the third planet from the sun.* **3. the sun** *n.* sunlight; light and warmth that is radiated by ②. (No plural form in this sense. Treated as singular.) ♦ *I opened the curtains and let the sun in.* ♦ *Our kitten warmed itself in the sun.* **4.** *tv.* to expose oneself to ③; to bathe oneself in sunlight. (Takes a reflexive object.) ♦ *Dozens of people sunned themselves on the beach.* ♦ *If you sun yourself too much, you will develop wrinkles.* **5.** *iv.* to absorb the rays of ②; to sunbathe. ♦ *If you sun too much, you* *may get skin cancer.* ♦ *Dozens of people sunned on the beach.*

sunbathe ['sʌn beð] *iv.* to sit or lie down in the sunlight, especially in order to get a tan. ♦ *Jane protected her skin with sunblock while she sunbathed.* ♦ *If Bill sunbathes for too long, his skin turns bright red.*

sunbeam ['sʌn bim] *n.* a ray of sunlight; a beam of sunlight. ♦ *A sunbeam shone through the hole in the curtains.* ♦ *Early in the morning, I saw the first sunbeam peek over the horizon.*

sunblock See sunscreen.

sunburn ['sʌn bɚn] **1.** *n.* red, sore skin that has been exposed too long to sunlight. (No plural form in this sense.) ♦ *Bill rubbed some lotion on his sunburn.* ♦ *Jane prevented sunburn by wearing a good sunscreen.* **2.** *n.* an instance of ①. ♦ *I usually get two or three serious sunburns a year.* ♦ *Be careful with those sunburns. They may cause skin cancer.* **3.** *iv.* [for one's skin] to acquire ①. ♦ *John's arms sunburn because he wears short-sleeved shirts.* ♦ *Anne sunburns easily because her skin is fair.*

sundae ['sʌn de] *n.* a dessert made with ice cream and flavored toppings. ♦ *David ate a chocolate sundae after dinner.* ♦ *Jane made a caramel sundae with two scoops of vanilla ice cream.*

Sunday ['sʌn de] **1.** *n.* the first day of the week; the day between Saturday and Monday. ♦ *Sunday is the day I never work.* ♦ *John does his shopping and his laundry on Sunday.* **2.** *adv.* on the next ①. ♦ *Mary will sleep till noon Sunday.* ♦ *This store will be closed Sunday.* **3. (on) Sundays** *adv.* on each ①. ♦ *We always sleep till noon Sundays.* ♦ *We eat out Sundays.*

sundial ['sʌn dɑɪl] *n.* a device having a pointer that stands upright and indicates the time of day by casting a shadow on a flat dial. ♦ *On a sundial, the upright object's shadow falls on a number that corresponds to the time of day.* ♦ *The dark clouds blocked the sun, so the sundial was useless.*

sundown ['sʌn dɑʊn] *n.* the time of day when the sun sets in the west; sunset. ♦ *Bill tried to be home from work by sundown.* ♦ *Sundown is much later in the summer than in the winter.*

sundry ['sʌn dri] **1.** *adj.* various; several. (Adv: *sundrily.*) ♦ *The landlord charged me for sundry items of repair.* ♦ *The office assistant did sundry errands for the staff.* **2. sundries** *n.* various small items. (Treated as plural.) ♦ *Many airports have shops that sell sundries like magazines, candy, gum, souvenirs, etc.* ♦ *I went to the drugstore to buy aspirin and sundries.*

sunflower ['sʌn flɑʊ ɚ] *n.* a tall plant that has bright yellow petals that surround a large circular area of seeds. ♦ *The seeds of the sunflower are eaten as food and also made into cooking oil.* ♦ *Mary planted sunflowers in her garden.*

sung ['sʌŋ] pp of sing.

sunglasses ['sʌn glæs ɪz] *n.* glasses with dark lenses that are worn to block bright sunlight. (Treated as plural.) ♦ *The driver wore sunglasses to reduce glare from the sun.* ♦ *The celebrity hid her identity by wearing sunglasses and a wig.*

sunk ['sʌŋk] a pt/pp of sink.

sunken ['sʌŋ kən] **1.** *adj.* no longer floating; no longer above the surface of the water. ♦ *The divers examined the sunken ship.* ♦ *The sailors searched for sunken treasure.* **2.** *adj.* lower than the surface or usual level. ♦ *The sunken living room was connected to the foyer by three steps.* ♦ *The tired man's eyes appeared to be sunken.*

sunlamp ['sʌn læmp] *n.* a lamp that gives out light rays like the sun's. (Used for tanning the skin.) ♦ *I got my tan from lying under a sunlamp.* ♦ *Bob tans under a sunlamp because he's too busy to go to the beach.*

sunlight ['sʌn lɑɪt] *n.* the light that is given off by the sun. (No plural form in this sense.) ♦ *The plant grew toward the sunlight.* ♦ *Car windshields are often tinted to reduce the glare of sunlight.*

sunny ['sʌn i] **1.** *adj.* with bright sunshine. (Comp: *sunnier;* sup: *sunniest.*) ♦ *It was a nice, sunny day, so we decided to have a picnic.* ♦ *Mary grows a lot of plants in her sunny bedroom.* **2.** *adj.* cheerful; happy. (Figurative on ①. Adv: *sunnily.* Comp: *sunnier;* sup: *sunniest.*) ♦ *My best friend has a very sunny disposition.* ♦ *The sunny young clerk eagerly helped me find the clothes that I wanted.*

sunrise ['sʌn rɑɪz] *n.* the time of day when the sun is moving above the horizon in the east. ♦ *The rooster crowed at sunrise.* ♦ *Sunrise through the mist was beautiful.*

sunscreen AND **sunblock** ['sʌn skrin, 'sʌn blɑk] *n.* lotion or cream containing a chemical substance that helps prevent sun damage to the skin. (No plural form in this sense.) ♦ *Please rub some sunscreen on my back.* ♦ *To protect your skin from the sun, you should wear sunblock.*

sunset ['sʌn sɛt] *n.* the time of day when the sun moves below the horizon in the west. ♦ *This park closes at sunset.* ♦ *The tourists were in awe of the gorgeous sunset.*

sunshine ['sʌn ʃɑɪn] *n.* sunlight; light from the sun. (No plural form in this sense.) ♦ *The laborers sweated as they worked in the sunshine.* ♦ *I opened the curtains and let the sunshine into the room.*

sunstroke ['sʌn strok] *n.* an illness caused by remaining in sunlight for too long. (See also **heatstroke**. No plural form in this sense.) ♦ *The busy farmer passed out from sunstroke.* ♦ *John wore a hat with a large brim to help prevent sunstroke.*

suntan ['sʌn tæn] *n.* the state of human skin that has been darkened by being in sunlight. ♦ *Mary relaxed on the beach and got a suntan.* ♦ *Getting suntans dries out your skin and causes wrinkles.*

sunup ['sʌn əp] *n.* sunrise; the time that the sun rises. (No plural form in this sense.) ♦ *The farmer was up before sunup, milking the cows.* ♦ *Mary's busy day begins each morning at sunup.*

sup See superlative ①.

super ['sup ɚ] **1.** *adj.* excellent; wonderful; great; marvelous; fabulous. ♦ *We had a super time at your party; thanks for inviting us.* ♦ *Mary told me about the super movie she'd seen last night.* **2.** *adj.* extra large. ♦ *The super ice-cream sundae has five scoops of ice cream.* ♦ *After the first of year, there were super savings throughout the mall.* **3.** *adv.* very. (Informal. Usually hyphenated.) ♦ *I'd like a super-large soda, please.* ♦ *The baby wore super-small shoes.*

superb [sə 'pɚb] *adj.* very good; excellent; of the best quality. (Adv: *superbly.*) ♦ *This excellent restaurant serves superb steaks.* ♦ *The critic praised the superb movie highly.*

superficial [sup ɚ 'fɪʃ əl] **1.** *adj.* on the surface; not deep. (Adv: *superficially.*) ♦ *I didn't need stitches for my superficial wounds.* ♦ *Acne is a superficial skin problem.* **2.** *adj.* not profound; shallow ②. (Figurative on ①. Adv: *superficially.*) ♦ *Susan prefers deep thinkers to people who are superficial.* ♦ *The superficial report provided no solutions to the problem.*

superfluous [sə 'pɚ flu əs] *adj.* more than what is needed; excessive; unnecessary because the need has already been met. (Adv: *superfluously.*) ♦ *Because our foreign visitors were fluent in several languages, the translators we hired were superfluous.* ♦ *My editor deleted the superfluous information in my article.*

superhero ['su pɚ hɪr o] *n.* a fictional character who has extraordinary powers or strength. (Pl in *-s.*) ♦ *Most superheroes have one weakness which villains exploit.* ♦ *The villain's bullets bounced off the superhero's chest.*

superhuman [su pɚ 'hju mən] *adj.* having abilities or powers that are beyond those of humans. (Adv: *superhumanly.*) ♦ *To lift this car by yourself, I think you would need superhuman strength!* ♦ *The young boy fantasized about having the superhuman power of flight.*

superimpose [su pɚ ɪm 'poz] *tv.* to place one image in front of or on top of another, in a way that they can both be seen. ♦ *The director superimposed the end of one scene on the top of the next one.* ♦ *The photographer accidentally superimposed two images onto the film.*

superintendent [su pɚ ɪn 'tɛn dənt] **1.** *n.* someone who manages a school district or some other large enterprise, usually in government. ♦ *The superintendent interviewed the applicants for the teaching jobs.* ♦ *The superintendent of the sewer commission called the board meeting to order.* **2.** *n.* someone who maintains a building; a building manager. ♦ *The superintendent fixed my leaky faucet.* ♦ *I told the superintendent that the stairway light had burned out.*

superior [sə 'pɪr i ɚ] **1.** *n.* someone who has a higher rank or position in relationship to someone else. ♦ *The clerk promised to speak to his superiors about my problem.* ♦ *The soldier saluted his superior.* **2.** *adj.* very good; above average; better than something else. (Adv: *superiorly.*) ♦ *This meal is far superior to the one we ate last night.* ♦ *Mary spent the night in a superior room at the fancy hotel.*

superiority [sə pɪr i 'or ɪ ti] *n.* the condition of being superior to someone or something. (No plural form in this sense.) ♦ *Because of my boss's superiority in the area of customer service, he knew what to do in this situation.* ♦ *The superiority of the fine meal impressed everyone at the table.*

superlative [sə 'pɚl ə tɪv] **1.** *n.* the form of an adjective or adverb, usually created with *most* or *-est,* that indicates the highest degree of the comparison of that adjective or adverb. (Abbreviated "sup:" here.) ♦ *The superlative of "bad" is "worst."* ♦ *"Saddest" and "most sad" are both superlatives of "sad."* **2.** *adj.* best; having the highest quality. (Adv: *superlatively.*) ♦ *The expensive restaurant offered superlative gourmet food.* ♦ *Anne wore a diamond of superlative quality.*

supermarket ['su pɚ mɑr kɪt] *n.* a large store that stocks several kinds of each item, allowing customers a wide choice. ♦ *Bill bought enough groceries for a week at the supermarket.* ♦ *Anne handed her coupons to the cashier at the supermarket.*

supernatural [su pɚ 'nætʃ ə rəl] **1. the supernatural** *n.* the powers or forces that cannot be explained by science. (No plural form in this sense. Treated as singular.) ♦ *The superstitious man believed in the supernatural.* ♦ *Scientists scoff at reports of the supernatural.* **2.** *adj.* <the adj. use of ①.> (Adv: *supernaturally.*) ♦ *The psychic claimed her abilities were supernatural.* ♦ *The scientist disproved most supernatural claims.*

superpower ['su pɚ pɑʊ ɚ] *n.* one of the very powerful countries on the earth; a country that has a powerful military force. ♦ *During the 1950s, the United States and the Soviet Union were the undisputed superpowers.* ♦ *The superpower influenced the government of small neighboring countries.*

supersede [su pɚ 'sid] *tv.* to replace something similar that is out-of-date or no longer appropriate. ♦ *The new law superseded several old ones.* ♦ *A new list of problems supersedes the one I gave you last week.*

supersonic [su pɚ 'sɑn ɪk] *adj.* faster than the speed of sound. (Adv: *supersonically* [...ɪk li].) ♦ *When a supersonic jet exceeds the speed of sound, a sonic boom is heard.* ♦ *The executive took a supersonic flight from New York to London.*

superstition [su pɚ 'ʃtɪ ʃən] *n.* a belief that is based on tradition or legend instead of reason. ♦ *Fear of the number 13 is an old superstition.* ♦ *Breaking a mirror isn't bad luck; that's just a superstition.*

superstitious [su pɚ 'stɪʃ əs] *adj.* [of someone] believing in superstitions. (Adv: *superstitiously.*) ♦ *The superstitious actor refused to whistle backstage.* ♦ *The superstitious girl walked on the sidewalk without stepping on cracks.*

supervise ['su pɚ vɑɪz] *tv.* to direct a worker or a group of workers; to direct something; to oversee someone or something. ♦ *The office manager supervises a dozen clerks.* ♦ *The architect also supervised the construction workers.*

supervision [su pɚ 'vɪ ʒən] *n.* observation or watching over [someone or something]. (No plural form in this sense.) ♦ *Young children require constant supervision.* ♦ *Mature employees work diligently without supervision.*

supervisor ['su pɚ vɑɪz ɚ] *n.* someone who supervises other workers; a manager; an overseer. ♦ *Each assembly line at the factory had its own supervisor.* ♦ *The supervisor reprimanded the lazy worker.*

supervisory [su pɚ 'vɑɪz ə ri] *adj.* supervising; serving in the role of a supervisor. ♦ *My uncle has a supervisory position at an auto plant.* ♦ *Parents play an important supervisory role in their children's development.*

supine [su 'pɑɪn] *adj.* lying flat on one's back; lying face up. (Adv: *supinely.*) ♦ *Four surgeons operated on the supine patient.* ♦ *Hundreds of supine sunbathers cluttered the broad expanse of beach.*

supper ['sʌp ɚ] *n.* the meal eaten in the evening. ♦ *What would you like to eat for supper?* ♦ *Bill ordered pizza for his supper.*

suppertime ['sʌp ɚ tɑɪm] *n.* the time when supper is eaten. (No plural form in this sense.) ♦ *I'm always very hungry at suppertime.* ♦ *My mother called us to the dinner table at suppertime.*

supplant [sə 'plænt] *tv.* to take something's or someone's place. ♦ *The military plan of government supplanted the president's powers.* ♦ *Susan's plans supplanted my own plans.*

supple ['sʌp əl] *adj.* easily bent or moved; not rigid. (Adv: *supplely.*) ♦ *Supple gymnasts flipped around the parallel bars.* ♦ *John massaged my shoulder muscles until they were supple again.*

supplement 1. ['sʌp lə mənt] *n.* something that is added to something to make it better or bigger; an added part. ♦ *The evening newspaper included a few advertising supplements.* ♦ *As a supplement to my regular exercise program, I joined a softball team.* **2.** ['sʌp lə mənt] *n.* a vitamin; something that is eaten to improve one's diet. ♦ *Jane takes a daily supplement with extra iron.* ♦ *Bill ate a chewable supplement with breakfast.* **3.** ['sʌp lə mɛnt] *tv.* to supply something with something that is needed; to supply something with something in order to complete it. ♦ *Mary took a second job to supplement her income.* ♦ *Anne took an evening course to supplement her education.*

supplementary [səp lə 'mɛn t(ə)ri] *adj.* added; additional; providing something that is needed. ♦ *My teacher gave me supplementary help after school.* ♦ *John bought a car with supplementary income from a second job.*

supplier [sə 'plɑɪ ɚ] *n.* someone or a company that supplies goods or services. ♦ *My supplier delivers products directly to my store.* ♦ *The police arrested the drug addict's supplier.*

supply [sə 'plɑɪ] **1.** *tv.* to give someone something that is needed or wanted; to give something to someone who needs or wants it. ♦ *Each soldier was supplied with the necessary equipment.* ♦ *The high school supplies each student with textbooks.* **2.** *n.* an amount of something that is available. (Sometimes plural with the same meaning.) ♦ *Bill spent his weekly supply of money in one day.* ♦ *My coworkers and I quickly consumed our monthly supply of free coffee.* **3. in short supply** *idiom* scarce; not plentiful. ♦ *Fresh vegetables are in short supply in the winter.* ♦ *At this time of the year, fresh fruit is in short supply.*

support [sə 'port] **1.** *tv.* to provide someone with money, shelter, clothing, and food. ♦ *The Smiths supported their son until he turned 18.* ♦ *The college student was supported by her scholarship.* **2.** *tv.* to bear the weight of something; to keep something upright or in place so that it doesn't fall. ♦ *The sturdy bookcase supported the weight of 100 books.* ♦ *Three heavy wooden beams supported the ceiling.* **3.** *tv.* to give someone or something one's approval or favor; to show someone or something approval or favor. ♦ *John supported David's business proposal at the meeting.* ♦ *Bill's friends supported his decision to find a new job.* **4.** *n.* providing someone with money, shelter, food, and clothing. (No plural form in this sense.) ♦ *The Smith's support enabled their child to go to college.* ♦ *Mary provided support for her ailing mother.* **5.** *n.* the strength and structure needed to bear the weight of something. (No plural form in this sense.) ♦ *This beam provides enough support for the entire roof.* ♦ *These shoes provide the support my feet need when I run.* **6.** *n.* something that carries the weight of something; a beam; a prop. ♦ *When the earthquake cracked the supports, the building collapsed.* ♦ *The steel supports were firmly welded into place.* **7.** *n.* encouragement. (No plural form in this sense.) ♦ *Bill received support from his friends when he was ill.* ♦ *With Anne's support, Susan decided to look for a better job.*

supporter [sə 'port ɚ] *n.* someone who is loyal to someone or something. ♦ *The public television station thanked its supporters for their donations.* ♦ *The supporters of the proposed legislation urged everyone to vote for it.*

suppose [sə 'poz] *tv.* to consider or imagine that something is or will be true. (Takes a clause.) ♦ *Suppose that you get in an accident. Do you have insurance?* ♦ *I suppose you want me to leave, since everyone else has.*

supposed 1. [sə 'pozd, sə 'poz ɪd] *adj.* assumed; accepted as true, but not proved to be true. (Adv: *supposedly* [sə 'po zəd li].) ♦ *The lawyer questioned the supposed facts of the case.* ♦ *The supposed winner of the political race declared victory early.* **2.** [sə 'pozd] *adj.* probable; plausible; hypothetical. ♦ *In every supposed scenario, the chess player knew he'd lose.* ♦ *The new police recruits were asked what they would do in certain supposed situations.* **3. supposed to do something** [sə 'pozd...] *idiom* expected or intended to do something; obliged or allowed to do something. ♦ *You're supposed to say "excuse me" when you burp.* ♦ *Mom says you're supposed to come inside for dinner now.*

supposedly [sə 'poz ɪd li] *adv.* according to what is assumed to be true. ♦ *Supposedly, Anne is coming to the party after she's done with her work.* ♦ *Supposedly, the experiment was properly conducted.*

supposition [sə pə 'zɪ ʃən] *n.* a belief, especially one that has not been proved to be true; an assumption. ♦ *You are giving me only suppositions when I asked for facts!* ♦ *Lisa set out to prove her preliminary suppositions.*

suppress [sə 'prɛs] *tv.* to restrain something; to prevent something from happening; to prevent something from being seen, heard, or felt; to stop people from doing something. ♦ *The factory suppressed the unfavorable report about its working conditions.* ♦ *Bill suppressed his desire to yell at his boss.*

suppression [sə 'prɛ ʃən] *n.* not allowing something to be seen, heard, or felt. (No plural form in this sense.) ♦ *Dave realized that suppression of emotion is dangerous.* ♦ *The evil ruler insisted on the suppression of free speech.*

supremacy [sə 'prɛm ə si] *n.* being supreme; complete authority. (No plural form in this sense.) ♦ *Mary holds absolute supremacy in the world of golf.* ♦ *No one dared question the tyrant's supremacy.*

supreme [sə 'prim] **1.** *adj.* having total authority; having total power; having the highest rank; being the most important. (Adv: *supremely.*) ♦ *The supreme ruler ordered the execution of his enemies.* ♦ *The lawsuit was ruled on by the Supreme Court.* **2.** *adj.* of the highest degree of quality. (Adv: *supremely.*) ♦ *Lisa's playing of the concerto was simply supreme!* ♦ *The very rich couple lived in supreme luxury.*

surcharge ['sɚ tʃɑrdʒ] *n.* an amount of money that is added to the regular amount, especially as a tax or fee; an extra charge. ♦ *The city council imposed a surcharge on restaurant meals.* ♦ *A surcharge on our telephone bills pays for emergency services.*

sure ['ʃʊr] **1.** *adj.* certain; confident or knowing that something is the case. (Adv: *surely.* Comp: *surer;* sup: *surest.*) ♦ *Scientists are sure that the earth is not flat.* ♦ *Our* *team is a sure win in tonight's game.* **2.** *adv.* certainly. (Informal.) ♦ *It sure is hot outside!* ♦ *Your cat sure moves quickly!* **3.** *adv.* [in response to a yes-or-no question] yes. (Informal.) ♦ *"Would you like to go to the beach today?" "Sure!"* ♦ *"Will you help me move my furniture tomorrow?" "Sure."* **4.** *adv.* [in response to a negative assertion] on the contrary. ♦ *"Mars doesn't have any moons," said Tom. "Sure, it does! It has two," replied Mary.* ♦ *"I don't want any ice cream," screamed Jimmy. "Sure you do!" said Lisa, giving him a double serving.*

surefooted ['ʃʊr 'fʊt ɪd] *adj.* not clumsy; not likely to fall or trip. (Adv: *surefootedly.*) ♦ *A surefooted acrobat walked across the tightrope.* ♦ *The surefooted gymnast did a flip on the balance beam.*

surely ['ʃʊr li] *adv.* certainly; without doubt; definitely. ♦ *Surely you know you shouldn't eat cookies right before dinner!* ♦ *Mary will surely come here before going to the party.*

surf ['sɚf] **1.** *n.* waves of water hitting the beach. (No plural form in this sense.) ♦ *The violent surf pounded the beach during the storm.* ♦ *John's sand castle was washed away by the surf.* **2.** *iv.* to ride on a surfboard on a wave of water; to be carried along by a wave while standing or lying on top of a surfboard. ♦ *Teenagers surfed off the California beach all day long.* ♦ *The lifeguard wouldn't let us surf because the waves were too violent.*

surface ['sɚ fɪs] **1.** *n.* the outside of something; the outside layer of something. ♦ *Anne pricked the surface of the balloon with a pin.* ♦ *David dusted the surface of the shelf.* **2.** *n.* any one side or face of an object. ♦ *The title was written on the front surface of the book.* ♦ *The bottom surface of the glass left a wet ring on the table.* **3.** *n.* the top of a liquid. ♦ *These plants grow on the surface of the water.* ♦ *A fly floated on the surface of my soup.* **4. surface mail** *n.* mail sent on land by trucks or trains or on water by ships. (No plural form in this sense.) ♦ *I sent the package to Japan by surface mail.* ♦ *Surface mail is much slower than airmail.* **5.** *tv.* to seal a road with asphalt, pavement, or concrete. ♦ *The city workers surfaced the road with concrete.* ♦ *This parking lot was surfaced with asphalt last year.* **6.** *iv.* [for something underwater] to go up to or above the surface of the water. ♦ *The submarine surfaced when it entered the port.* ♦ *The fish surfaced to nibble at the fish food.* **7.** *iv.* to appear; to come to be known; to be discovered or found out. (Figurative on ⑥.) ♦ *The missing documents surfaced during the gangster's trial.* ♦ *The stolen paintings surfaced in a warehouse in Italy.* **8. scratch the surface** *idiom* to just begin to find out about something; to examine only the superficial aspects of something. ♦ *The investigation revealed some suspicious dealings. It is thought that the investigators have just scratched the surface.* ♦ *We don't know how bad the problem is. We've only scratched the surface.*

surfboard ['sɚf bord] **1.** *n.* a long narrow board on which someone lies or stands while being carried on top of a wave in the ocean. ♦ *Mary paddled the surfboard away from the beach toward the big waves.* ♦ *Dave rode his surfboard a quarter mile on the big wave.* **2.** *iv.* to ride ① on top of a wave in the ocean. ♦ *The teenagers drove to the beach to surfboard.* ♦ *John surfboarded on the large wave.*

surfeit ['sɚ fɪt] *n.* too large an amount of something, especially food; an excess of food and drink. (Formal. No plural form in this sense.) ♦ *A surfeit of food lay before the king.* ♦ *Because of the surfeit of goods, there was much waste.*

surfer ['sɚ fɚ] *n.* someone who rides on top of a wave while lying or standing on a surfboard. ♦ *The lifeguard ordered the surfers to come ashore because of sharks.* ♦ *A large wave knocked the inexperienced surfer into the water.*

surge ['sɚdʒ] **1.** *n.* a sudden, powerful burst of electricity. ♦ *An electrical surge damaged my computer.* ♦ *The power surge tripped the circuit breaker.* **2.** *n.* a strong forward movement. ♦ *When the dam broke, the huge surge of water crushed the town below.* ♦ *The surge of the crowd propelled me toward the fire exit.* **3.** *iv.* to push forward forcefully, like a wave of water. ♦ *The huge wave surged over the beach.* ♦ *When the electrical power surged, all of the fuses were blown.*

surgeon ['sɚ dʒən] *n.* a physician who performs surgery. ♦ *A well-trained surgeon removed John's appendix.* ♦ *The nurse handed a scalpel to the surgeon.*

surgery ['sɚ dʒə ri] **1.** *n.* the science and practice of curing sickness and treating injury by performing an **operation** ①. (No plural form in this sense.) ♦ *The interns were taught surgery in medical school.* ♦ *The doctors in the emergency room were trained in surgery.* **2.** *n.* the use of ① in treating illness and disease. (No plural form in this sense.) ♦ *Mary underwent surgery to remove a tumor on her neck.* ♦ *The use of sterile equipment during surgery prevents infection.* **3. in surgery** *phr.* involved in ②. ♦ *Dr. Smith is in surgery now.* ♦ *The patient is still in surgery.*

surgical ['sɚ dʒɪk əl] *adj.* of, for, or about surgery. (Adv: *surgically* [...ɪk li].) ♦ *With each surgical procedure, there is the danger of infection.* ♦ *Surgical tools should be sterilized after each patient.*

surly ['sɚ li] *adj.* angry and rude; having bad manners; impolite and mean. (Comp: *surlier;* sup: *surliest.*) ♦ *The surly clerk wouldn't help me find what I wanted.* ♦ *The diners gave the surly waiter a very small tip.*

surmise [sɚ 'mɑɪz] *tv.* to guess or figure that something is the case. (Takes a clause.) ♦ *I surmised that Mary had left because she didn't answer the door.* ♦ *The detective surmised that the murderer was left-handed.*

surmount [sɚ 'mɑʊnt] *tv.* to overcome a difficulty or obstacle. ♦ *Mary surmounted the problems caused by her handicap and finished college.* ♦ *I have surmounted the obstacles preventing me from getting a job.*

surname ['sɚ nem] *n.* the family name; [in the U.S.] the last name. ♦ *My brother and I have the same surname.* ♦ *Please print your surname first, and first name last.*

surpass [sɚ 'pæs] **1.** *tv.* to do better than someone or something; to be better than someone or something. ♦ *Mary surpassed all of her siblings in school.* ♦ *The excellent runner surpassed all previous records.* **2.** *tv.* to be larger or greater than something. ♦ *The national debt surpassed the level expected by the economists.* ♦ *When the inflation rate surpassed 5%, Congress took action.*

surplus ['sɚ pləs] **1.** *n.* an amount of something that is more than what is needed; an extra amount; an excess. ♦ *The clothing factory donated its surplus to charity.* ♦ *We have gotten a surplus of rain this season.* **2.** *adj.* <the adj. use of ①.> ♦ *The farmer's surplus grain was stored in silos.* ♦ *The government gave surplus cheese to needy families.*

surprise [sɚ 'prɑɪz] **1.** *n.* something that is not expected; something that happens without warning. ♦ *Winning the lottery was quite a surprise!* ♦ *The terrorist bombing was an unwelcome surprise.* **2.** *n.* the emotion that is caused by something unexpected happening. (No plural form in this sense.) ♦ *In his surprise, John dropped the package he was carrying.* ♦ *Mary screamed with surprise when we all shouted "Happy birthday!"* **3.** *tv.* to cause someone to feel ② by doing something or saying something unexpected. ♦ *My friends surprised me with a birthday party.* ♦ *The inexperienced politician surprised everyone by winning the election.* **4.** *tv.* to attack someone or something without warning. ♦ *The enemy army surprised the soldiers by attacking at dawn.* ♦ *The terrorists surprised the townsfolk with a late-night bombing.* **5.** *adj.* unexpected; without warning. ♦ *The surprise birthday party was the last thing Mary expected.* ♦ *The surprise attack killed dozens of innocent civilians.* **6. take someone by surprise** *idiom* to startle someone; to surprise ③ someone with something unexpected. ♦ *Oh! You took me by surprise because I didn't hear you come in.* ♦ *Bill took his mother by surprise by coming to the door and pretending to be a solicitor.*

surprising [sɚ 'prɑɪz ɪŋ] *adj.* causing surprise; unexpected. (Adv: *surprisingly.*) ♦ *The surprising news of the principal's arrest shocked the students.* ♦ *There was a surprising improvement in the economy last quarter.*

surrender [sə 'rɛn dɚ] **1.** *iv.* to give up, especially when one has lost a battle, argument, or fight; to yield to a force that one was fighting. ♦ *The army surrendered at noon.* ♦ *The soldiers surrendered because they were surrounded.* **2.** *tv.* to give someone or something up to someone; to yield someone or something to someone. ♦ *The criminals surrendered themselves to the police.* ♦ *The drunken driver surrendered his license.* **3.** *n.* surrendering as in ①; giving up. (No plural form in this sense.) ♦ *As part of their surrender, the soldiers laid down their weapons.* ♦ *The government demanded the terrorists' unconditional surrender.*

surreptitious [sə rɛp 'tɪʃ əs] *adj.* [of something] done in secret; [of something] not observed; clandestine. (Adv: *surreptitiously.*) ♦ *With a quick, surreptitious movement, the thief grabbed my purse and ran.* ♦ *I gave Anne a surreptitious nod of approval from across the room.*

surrogate ['sɚ ə gət] **1.** *adj.* substitute. ♦ *Tom is sort of a surrogate uncle who advises me when I am troubled.* ♦ *John served as a surrogate father for his niece when his brother died.* **2.** *n.* a substitute. ♦ *When our boss was on sick leave, John acted as his surrogate.* ♦ *The nun was a maternal surrogate to the orphaned children.* **3. surrogate mother** *n.* a woman who conceives and bears a child in place of another woman. ♦ *The couple hired a surrogate mother to bear a child for them.* ♦ *The surrogate mother decided that she wanted to keep the child after she gave birth to it.*

surround [sə 'rɑʊnd] *tv.* to enclose someone or something on all sides; to be on all sides of someone or something. ♦ *Bodyguards surrounded the president during the parade.* ♦ *Clear blue water surrounds the island.*

surrounding [sə 'rɑʊn dɪŋ] **1.** *adj.* nearby; neighboring; near; adjacent. ♦ *We searched the surrounding neighborhood for our missing dog.* ♦ *Mary wants to move to Chicago or one of its surrounding suburbs.* **2. surroundings** *n.* the immediate environment; that which surrounds someone or something. (Treated as plural.) ♦ *The man in a coma was unaware of his surroundings.* ♦ *The rich couple lived in luxurious surroundings.*

surtax ['sɚ tæks] *n.* an extra tax; a tax in addition to a regular tax. ♦ *The city imposed a 2% surtax on restaurant meals.* ♦ *The airline ticket surtax raised money for a new airport.*

surveillance [sɚ 've ləns] *n.* a close watch over someone, especially someone who is suspected of something or someone who requires protection. (No plural form in this sense.) ♦ *The suspect was placed under 24-hour surveillance.* ♦ *Police provided constant surveillance for the woman who had been threatened.*

survey 1. ['sɚ ve] *n.* a set of questions used to collect people's opinions, attitudes, and behavior. ♦ *Our survey of book purchases shows that people like picture books.* ♦ *The government agency conducted a survey about public health.* **2.** ['sɚ ve] *n.* a document containing ①. ♦ *John filled out a survey about his television viewing habits.* ♦ *Please complete this survey when you have time.* **3.** ['sɚ ve] *n.* an examination or study of the condition, contents, or details of something. ♦ *Tom did a survey of what was available in the shoe store and found many appealing styles of shoes.* ♦ *A quick survey of the kitchen revealed a lack of drinking glasses.* **4.** ['sɚ ve] *n.* a description or analysis of a subject of study. ♦ *This class is a general survey of English literature in the 19th century.* ♦ *Lisa's grant application included an in-depth survey of her work.* **5.** ['sɚ ve] *n.* the measurement of land so that accurate maps can be made or so that the legal description of property boundaries is exact. ♦ *The survey indicated my neighbor's fence was on my property.* ♦ *The Realtor checked the survey to see how far the property extended.* **6.** ['sɚ ve] *tv.* to collect people's opinions on an issue; to ask people for their opinions on an issue. ♦ *The pollster surveyed people about their political beliefs.* ♦ *The researcher surveyed students about their drug use.* **7.** [sɚ 've] *tv.* to examine or study the condition, contents, or details of something. ♦ *Tom surveys the contents of the kitchen cupboards weekly.* ♦ *The army general surveyed the losses on the battlefield.* **8.** [sɚ 've] *tv.* to measure part of the surface of the earth, or any celestial body exactly, so that accurate maps or legal descriptions of the land can be made. ♦ *When the Midwest was first surveyed, it was divided into 36-square-mile townships.* ♦ *Satellites are now used to survey the earth.*

surveyor [sɚ 've ɚ] *n.* someone who makes a survey ⑤. ♦ *The surveyor solved the boundary dispute between my neighbor and me.* ♦ *The surveyor determined the outline of the lake.*

survival [sɚ 'vɑɪ vəl] *n.* the process of remaining alive; surviving; remaining alive. (No plural form in this sense.) ♦ *Humans are dependent on oxygen and water for survival.* ♦ *Pollution in the river threatens the survival of thousands of fish.*

survive [sɚ 'vɑɪv] **1.** *iv.* to remain alive even after a threat to one's life; to live a very long life. ♦ *Relatively few people survive for 100 years.* ♦ *Those who survived rebuilt the city.* **2.** *tv.* to endure someone or something and remain alive or functional. ♦ *Mary survived the war.* ♦ *My car survived 15 years of hard service.* **3.** *tv.* to outlive someone; to live longer than someone. ♦ *Mary survived her husband by 5 years.* ♦ *David survived all of his siblings.*

surviving [sɚ 'vaɪv ɪŋ] **1.** *adj.* still alive after another person's death. ♦ *The surviving family members attended Bill's funeral.* ♦ *The reporter interviewed the surviving victims of the crash.* **2.** *adj.* still remaining after something else no longer remains. ♦ *The biologist examined the few surviving examples of the plant species.* ♦ *The linguist studied surviving Indian languages in Alaska.*

survivor [sɚ 'vaɪv ɚ] *n.* someone who remains alive; someone who did not die while others died. ♦ *There were only ten survivors of the terrible plane crash.* ♦ *The firefighters pulled two survivors from the burning house.*

susceptible [sə 'sɛp tə bəl] **1. susceptible to something** *phr.* likely to contract a sickness; likely to become sick. ♦ *People with AIDS are susceptible to pneumonia.* ♦ *Infants and the elderly are more susceptible to illness than other people.* **2. susceptible to something** *phr.* easily persuaded; easily influenced. ♦ *The students were susceptible to the allure of drugs.* ♦ *The young revolutionaries were susceptible to propaganda.*

suspect 1. ['sʌs pɛkt] *n.* someone who is thought to have committed a crime. ♦ *The police questioned five suspects in connection with the crime.* ♦ *The suspect was handcuffed and taken to the police station.* **2.** ['sʌs pɛkt] *adj.* suspicious; causing suspicion or doubt. (Adv: *suspectly.*) ♦ *John's reasons for leaving town were rather suspect.* ♦ *Jane's suspect testimony drew the attention of the lawyer.* **3.** [sə 'spɛkt] *tv.* to think or guess that someone is something or has done something. ♦ *The police suspected three people in connection with the crime.* ♦ *The mayor's aide was suspected of embezzling city funds.* **4.** [sə 'spɛkt] *tv.* to consider something to be likely. ♦ *Bob suspected that he was being followed.* ♦ *The general suspected John's disloyalty.*

suspected [sə 'spɛk tɪd] *adj.* considered to be likely. ♦ *The police questioned the suspected criminal.* ♦ *Poison was the suspected cause of death.*

suspend [sə 'spɛnd] **1.** *tv.* to hang something from something else; to cause something to hang down from something above it. ♦ *One bare light bulb was suspended from the ceiling.* ♦ *The executioner suspended a noose from a tree branch.* **2.** *tv.* to delay something; to stop something for a period of time. ♦ *The baseball game was suspended for an hour because of rain.* ♦ *The police suspended the investigation after three years.* **3.** *tv.* to prevent someone from working at a job, attending classes, etc., for a period of time, as a punishment. ♦ *The principal suspended the unruly students for two days.* ♦ *The boss suspended the drunken worker without pay for a week.* **4.** *tv.* to cause something to float in the air or in liquid. ♦ *A slight breeze suspended millions of dust particles in the air.* ♦ *The helium balloon was suspended in midair.*

suspended [sə 'spɛn dɪd] **1.** *adj.* hung; hung from something above. ♦ *A small potted plant—suspended from a tree branch—perfumed the air.* ♦ *Bill installed a suspended ceiling beneath the old one.* **2.** *adj.* delayed; temporarily stopped. ♦ *The suspended baseball game was finally canceled.* ♦ *The suspended students weren't allowed to go to football games.* **3.** *adj.* hanging in midair; floating in air or in a liquid. ♦ *The dancers seemed suspended in midair.* ♦ *The chemist measured the suspended particles in the heavy liquid.*

suspenders [sə 'spɛn dɚz] *n.* a pair of elastic bands or adjustable straps—to hold up trousers—connected to the front and back of the trousers at the waistline. (Treated as plural.) ♦ *Suspenders go up one's chest, over one's shoulders, down one's back, and are connected to the back of the waistline.* ♦ *John wore suspenders instead of a belt.*

suspense [sə 'spɛns] *n.* uncertainty; an anxious, scary, or uncertain feeling that is caused by not knowing what is going to happen next. (No plural form in this sense.) ♦ *There was a lot of suspense as to who would be promoted.* ♦ *The mysterious shooting left the audience in suspense until the final act of the play.*

suspension [sə 'spɛn ʃən] **1.** *n.* the suspending of something; holding something up. (No plural form in this sense.) ♦ *The equipment on the roof of the building is for the suspension of window cleaners on the face of the building.* ♦ *Workers are busy arranging for the suspension of strong cables to hold the decorations over the street.* **2.** *n.* a temporary stoppage; a delay. ♦ *There was a suspension of production during the workers' strike.* ♦ *The suspension of the baseball game was due to rain.* **3.** *n.* a punishment that prevents a person from participating in work, schooling, etc. ♦ *Workers found drinking on the job are subject to suspension.* ♦ *The principal gave Mary a one-day suspension for skipping class.*

suspicion [sə 'spɪ ʃən] **1.** *n.* an uneasy feeling in which one suspects something. (No plural form in this sense.) ♦ *Fear and suspicion cause bad feelings between people.* ♦ *Since her neighbor once stole her lawn furniture, Mary is always in a state of suspicion about him.* **2.** *n.* a feeling as in ① about someone or something. ♦ *The police inspector had suspicions that John was guilty.* ♦ *I have a suspicion it's going to rain soon.*

suspicious [sə 'spɪʃ əs] **1.** *adj.* suspecting something; suspecting that someone has bad intentions or has done something bad. (Adv: *suspiciously.*) ♦ *A suspicious detective questioned everyone about the crime.* ♦ *Aunt Jane was suspicious of everyone who came to her front door.* **2.** *adj.* causing suspicion. (Adv: *suspiciously.*) ♦ *Mary's suspicious movements caught the attention of the police.* ♦ *John's weak alibi seemed rather suspicious to the inspector.*

suspiciously [sə 'spɪʃ əs li] **1.** *adv.* in an untrusting way. ♦ *The detective looked around the room suspiciously.* ♦ *Aunt Jane looked at the letter carrier suspiciously whenever he walked by.* **2.** *adv.* in a way that causes distrust. ♦ *John's homework looks suspiciously just like Jane's.* ♦ *Someone was lurking suspiciously at the corner near Jane's house, so she called the police.*

sustain [sə 'sten] **1.** *tv.* to nourish and care for living plants and creatures. ♦ *Only bread and water sustained the prisoners.* ♦ *Mary sustained her plants with plenty of water and sunshine.* **2.** *tv.* to keep something moving, going, or working; to prolong something. ♦ *The arts agency was sustained by federal funds.* ♦ *Anne and Bill sustained their conversation for six hours.* **3.** *tv.* to suffer an injury; to have an injury. ♦ *Mary sustained a broken leg in the car crash.* ♦ *He sustained a concussion in the bus accident.*

sustained [sə 'stend] *adj.* continued without interruption; prolonged. (Adv: *sustainedly* [sə 'sten əd li].) ♦ *The* *sustained chatter at the café gave me a headache.* ♦ *The sustained high winds blew over many trees.*

sustenance ['sʌs tə nəns] *n.* food; nourishment. (No plural form in this sense.) ♦ *The homeless man scavenged through garbage for his meager sustenance.* ♦ *For sustenance, the vegetarian ate fruits, nuts, and vegetables.*

suture ['su tʃɚ] **1.** *n.* the line or joint where bones—especially the individual bones of the skull—fit tightly together. ♦ *The sutures of the skull look liked a number of winding lines.* ♦ *The blow to the skull created a fracture along a suture.* **2.** *n.* the surgical closure of a wound, possibly with ③. ♦ *The nurses bandaged the suture as soon as the surgeon finished.* ♦ *In three days, the suture was no longer visible.* **3.** *n.* a length of thread or a stitch used to sew up a wound. ♦ *The medic used dental floss as a suture during the emergency.* ♦ *The nurse handed each suture to the surgeon.* **4.** *tv.* to sew a wound closed. ♦ *A nurse sutured the soldier's gaping wound shut.* ♦ *The surgeon sutured the gash in my arm.*

swab ['swɑb] **1.** *n.* a piece of cotton or sometimes cloth, often attached to a small stick, used for cleaning something or applying medication. ♦ *The nurse put some disinfectant on a cotton swab and cleaned my wound.* ♦ *Anne cleaned her ears with a cotton swab.* **2.** *tv.* to clean something with ①. ♦ *Anne swabbed her ears to remove ear wax.* ♦ *The sailor swabbed the deck with a mop.*

swag ['swæg] *n.* a decorative band of cloth, fastened at each end and sagging in the middle. ♦ *The draperies in the hotel lobby were topped with graceful swags.* ♦ *The walls of the party room were covered with decorative swags of colored cloth.*

swagger ['swæg ɚ] **1.** *iv.* to walk very proudly or arrogantly. ♦ *The conceited speaker swaggered to the microphone.* ♦ *The arrogant couple swaggered to the front of the line.* **2.** *n.* an overly proud or arrogant walk. ♦ *With a boastful swagger, the winner went to the podium.* ♦ *I didn't let the tough guy's swagger intimidate me.*

Swahili [swɑ 'hi li] **1.** *n.* a language widely spoken in East Africa. (No plural form in this sense.) ♦ *Swahili has many Arabic words.* ♦ *You can study Swahili in many American universities.* **2.** *adj.* <the adj. use of ①.> ♦ *Swahili nouns have many different prefixes.* ♦ *The Swahili language is used by many Africans.*

swallow ['swɑl o] **1.** *tv.* to cause food or drink to go down one's throat and into the stomach. ♦ *John swallowed his food after chewing it thoroughly.* ♦ *Anne swallowed two vitamins with a glass of water.* **2.** *tv.* to believe something without question; to believe something that one is told, even if it is a lie; to accept something that one is told. (Figurative on ①. Informal.) ♦ *The citizens swallowed the mayor's lies.* ♦ *The jury swallowed the witness's testimony.* **3.** *iv.* to take [something] into the body by way of the throat. ♦ *Bill chewed his food carefully and then swallowed.* ♦ *When my throat was sore, it hurt to swallow.* **4.** *n.* the amount of something that is swallowed. ♦ *The man who nearly drowned took a deep swallow of air when he finally reached the beach.* ♦ *Could I have a swallow of your drink?* **5.** *n.* a kind of small songbird. ♦ *Some swallows have built a nest outside my bedroom window.* ♦ *Jane awoke at sunrise to the song of the swallows.*

swam ['swæm] pt of swim.

swamp ['swɑmp] **1.** *n.* an area of very wet, muddy ground, sometimes covered with water. ♦ *The trappers paddled their canoes through the swamp.* ♦ *An alligator swam through the swamp.* **2.** *adj.* associated with ①. ♦ *My oar was caught in swamp grass.* ♦ *Bill owns some swamp land in southern Louisiana.* **3.** *tv.* to flood something, especially a boat. ♦ *The large wave swamped our boat.* ♦ *The heavy rains swamped the port city.*

swampy ['swɑm pi] *adj.* like a swamp; of or about a swamp. (Adv: *swampily.* Comp: *swampier;* sup: *swampiest.*) ♦ *Alligators are found in swampy wetlands of the southeastern U.S.* ♦ *The heavy rains turned our backyard into a swampy mess.*

swan ['swɑn] *n.* a large, white, aquatic bird with a long, curving neck. ♦ *Several graceful swans swam on the surface of the pond.* ♦ *Many ducks, geese, and swans bred near the marsh.*

swap ['swɑp] **1. swap for** *tv.* + *prep. phr.* to exchange something for something else; to trade something for something else. ♦ *I swapped my old car for John's motorcycle.* ♦ *Bill swapped his desk for Mary's bookcase.* **2.** *iv.* to exchange; to trade. ♦ *I wanted John's car and he wanted my motorcycle, so we swapped.* ♦ *I offered to swap, but the merchant wanted cash.* **3.** *n.* an exchange; a trade. ♦ *John's old car for Mary's motorcycle is a fair swap.* ♦ *Jane felt she got the better deal in the swap.*

swarm ['swɔrm] **1.** *n.* a large number of people or animals, especially bees or other insects, that move together in a densely packed group. ♦ *A swarm of bees flew toward their hive.* ♦ *Swarms of people rushed toward the fire exit.* **2. swarm around** *iv.* + *prep. phr.* to gather around someone or something. ♦ *Thousands of bees swarmed around the hive.* ♦ *Dozens of reporters swarmed around the celebrity.*

swarthy ['swɑr ði] *adj.* [of a Caucasian] having a dark complexion. (Usually derogatory or unflattering. Comp: *swarthier;* sup: *swarthiest.*) ♦ *The swarthy sailor had spent many days in the sun.* ♦ *Max always looked swarthy in photographs.*

swat ['swɑt] **1.** *tv.* to hit someone or something hard. ♦ *Mary swatted the flies on the porch.* ♦ *Jane swatted my hand when I tried to eat her cookie.* **2.** *n.* a hard hit; a sharp blow. ♦ *Bill killed the fly with a well-aimed swat.* ♦ *John gave me a swat when I took some of his pizza.*

swatch ['swɑtʃ] *n.* a sample of cloth or material. ♦ *I took a swatch of my rug to the furniture store so I could buy a chair that matched.* ♦ *The designer attached swatches of material to her designs.*

swath ['swɑθ] **1.** *n.* the path that is cut by the movement of a blade. ♦ *The explorer cut a swath through the brush with his sword.* ♦ *John ran the razor across his cheek, leaving a swath of bare skin.* **2.** *n.* a path that is left by a tornado or some other destructive force. (Figurative on ①.) ♦ *The tornado cut a swath of destruction through town.* ♦ *The hurricane caused a 20-mile-wide swath of damage across Florida.*

sway ['swe] **1.** *iv.* to bend or swing back and forth; to bend to one side and then the other; to move back and forth. ♦ *The trees swayed in the wind.* ♦ *The ship swayed from side to side on the rough seas.* **2.** *tv.* to cause someone or something to bend or move back and forth; to bend or move someone or something back and forth. ♦

The heavy winds swayed the flagpole. ♦ *The violent sea swayed the ship from side to side.* **3.** *tv.* to change someone's opinion or judgment; to influence someone. (Figurative on ②.) ♦ *The persuasive politician swayed my opinion of the proposed law.* ♦ *The lobbyist swayed the senator who cast her vote against the bill.*

swear ['swɛr] **1.** *iv., irreg.* to curse; to say profane words; to blaspheme. (Pt: swore; pp: sworn.) ♦ *Jimmy was punished when he swore at the dinner table.* ♦ *The angry manager swore and yelled.* **2. swear to** *iv., irreg. + inf.* to vow to do something; to make a pledge to do something. ♦ *The police officer swore to uphold the law.* ♦ *The witness swore to tell the truth in court.* **3. swear in** *tv., irreg. + adv.* [for an officer of the court] to cause someone to swear to ② tell the truth or perform the duties required by law; to cause someone to take an oath. ♦ *After the defendant was sworn in, she took the witness stand.* ♦ *The Supreme Court justice swore the newly elected president in.*

sweat ['swɛt] **1.** *n.* the moisture that comes out of the body through pores in the skin. (No plural form in this sense.) ♦ *The construction worker wiped the sweat from his brow.* ♦ *After running 10 miles, Mary was covered with sweat.* **2.** *n.* hard work; labor; something that causes sweat. (No plural form in this sense.) ♦ *It took two years of real sweat to construct the bridge.* ♦ *A lot of sweat and planning went into this project.* **3.** *iv., irreg.* [for moisture] to come out of the body through pores in the skin. (Pt/pp: *sweat* or *sweated.*) ♦ *The tennis player sweated as she played.* ♦ *John sweat in the hot sun as he worked in his garden.* **4.** *iv.* to work very hard; to labor. ♦ *The construction workers sweated many hours at the job site.* ♦ *The architect sweated for days until the plans were finished.* **5. break out in a cold sweat** *idiom* to perspire from fever, fear, or anxiety; to begin to sweat profusely, suddenly. ♦ *I was so frightened I broke out in a cold sweat.* ♦ *The patient broke out in a cold sweat.*

sweater ['swɛt ɚ] *n.* a warm piece of clothing worn above the waist, usually woven or knitted from wool or cotton. ♦ *John always wears sweaters in the winter.* ♦ *Mary wore a sweater under her heavy coat because it was so cold.*

sweatpants ['swɛt pænts] *n.* warm pants, usually with a soft or fluffy inside layer. (Treated as plural.) ♦ *Tom pulled on his sweatpants and left for football practice.* ♦ *Mary has a sweatshirt to match her sweatpants.*

sweatshirt ['swɛt ʃɚt] *n.* a warm, long-sleeved shirt, usually with a soft or fluffy inside layer. ♦ *Jane bought a sweatshirt with her college emblem on it.* ♦ *The players wore matching sweatshirts while they practiced.*

sweatshop ['swɛt ʃɑp] *n.* a place where people work long hours for very little money. ♦ *The owners of the sweatshop were fined for violating labor laws.* ♦ *Dozens of immigrants worked at the sweatshop sewing garments.*

sweaty ['swɛt i] **1.** *adj.* covered with sweat. (Adv: *sweatily.* Comp: *sweatier;* sup: *sweatiest.*) ♦ *After gym class, the sweaty students showered.* ♦ *The sweaty runners drank lemonade at the end of the race.* **2.** *adj.* causing sweat, especially because of hot, muggy weather or hard work. (Comp: *sweatier;* sup: *sweatiest.*) ♦ *Construction work is a sweaty job.* ♦ *John uses an air conditioner in sweaty weather.*

Sweden ['swid n] See Gazetteer.

sweep ['swip] **1.** *tv., irreg.* to clean a floor by passing a broom over it; to clean a surface by moving a broom, brush, or one's hand over it to push the dirt away. (Pt: *sweeped* or swept; pp: swept.) ♦ *Mary swept the dirty floor with a broom.* ♦ *John swept the broken glass into a dustpan.* **2.** *tv., irreg.* to move something quickly, suddenly, or purposefully over an area. (Figurative on ①.) ♦ *The wind swept the snow everywhere!* ♦ *Bill swept his hand across the desk, knocking everything over.* **3.** *iv., irreg.* to clean as in ①. ♦ *The maid swept and then waxed.* ♦ *Bill swept after making a mess.* **4.** *iv., irreg.* to move quickly, suddenly, or purposefully over an area. (Figurative on ③.) ♦ *The plague swept across the country in a week.* ♦ *Gossip sweeps throughout the office almost instantly.* **5.** *n.* a smooth, flowing motion, especially in a curve; a swinging movement. ♦ *With a sweep of her hands, Mary accidentally hit me in the face.* ♦ *With each sweep of the searchlight, the guards could see the whole prison yard.* **6. sweep out of some place** *idiom* to move or leave in a flamboyant or theatrical way. ♦ *The insulted customer swept out of the store.* ♦ *The celebrity rose from his table and swept out of the restaurant.*

sweeping ['swip ɪŋ] *adj.* having a wide range; having a wide effect; general. (Adv: *sweepingly.*) ♦ *The sweeping effects of the legislation affected every taxpayer.* ♦ *The editor cautioned against making sweeping generalizations.*

sweepstakes ['swip steks] *n.* a contest or race where people win prizes at random or by gambling. (Treated as plural.) ♦ *Mary returned her entry form to the sweepstakes.* ♦ *John always plays the sweepstakes, but he's never won.*

sweet ['swit] **1.** *adj.* tasting like sugar; sugary. (Adv: *sweetly.* Comp: *sweeter;* sup: *sweetest.*) ♦ *This lemonade is too sweet. You put too much sugar in it.* ♦ *John likes to eat sweet chocolate.* **2.** *adj.* pleasant; pleasing; charming. (Adv: *sweetly.* Comp: *sweeter;* sup: *sweetest.*) ♦ *It was very sweet of you to help me.* ♦ *Mary helped the sweet old lady across the street.* **3. sweets** *n.* a candy; something that is sweet. (Treated as plural.) ♦ *You may not eat any sweets before dinner.* ♦ *I'm going to the candy store to buy some sweets.* **4. sweet tooth** *n.* a liking for candy, chocolate, or other sweet foods. (Always singular.) ♦ *Anne has a sweet tooth for chocolate.* ♦ *Bill's sweet tooth for desserts is ruining his diet.*

sweeten ['swit n] *tv.* to cause something to become sweet; to add sugar to something. ♦ *John sweetened the lemonade by adding more sugar.* ♦ *Mary sweetened her coffee before drinking it.*

sweetened ['swit nd] *adj.* having added sugar or other sweetener. ♦ *Mary bought some sweetened grapefruit juice.* ♦ *John ate some artificially sweetened cookies.*

sweetener ['swit n ɚ] *n.* sugar, or more often, a sweet-tasting substitute for sugar. (No plural form in this sense.) ♦ *Mary uses natural sweeteners like honey when she cooks.* ♦ *John added some artificial sweetener to his coffee.*

sweetheart ['swit hɑrt] *n.* a darling; someone that someone loves; a lover. (Also a term of address.) ♦ *Sweetheart, could you close the door for me?* ♦ *David gave his sweetheart a dozen roses.*

sweetness ['swit nəs] **1.** *n.* the quality of being sweet; the degree that something tastes sweet. (No plural form in this sense.) ♦ *The baker liked the natural sweetness of honey.* ♦ *Add sugar to the punch until you reach the desired* *sweetness.* **2.** *n.* kindness; pleasantness. (No plural form in this sense.) ♦ *The clerk's sweetness made the customer less angry.* ♦ *Mary's sweetness brightened my day.*

swell ['swɛl] **1.** *iv., irreg.* to grow larger; to grow fuller; to rise or grow past the regular amount. (Pt: *swelled;* pp: *swelled* or **swollen**.) ♦ *My ankle began to swell when I injured it.* ♦ *The river swelled over its banks and flooded the town.* **2.** *iv., irreg.* to increase in size, amount, or intensity. ♦ *The crime rate swelled during the economic recession.* ♦ *The music swelled majestically at the end of the symphony.* **3.** *tv., irreg.* to cause someone or something to grow larger or fuller; to increase something in size, amount, or intensity. ♦ *The recession swelled the ranks of the unemployed.* ♦ *A new assignment swelled the amount of work Susan had to do.* **4.** *n.* an increase in intensity, especially an increase in the loudness of sound. ♦ *The swell of the final notes of the symphony was quite dramatic.* ♦ *The swell of his opponent's popularity alarmed the president.* **5.** *n.* the rise and fall of waves. ♦ *The motion of the ship—meeting one swell after another—made some passengers sick.* ♦ *The captain increased the boat's speed because of the swells.*

swelter ['swɛl tɚ] *iv.* to suffer in very hot weather. ♦ *The construction workers sweltered in the heat.* ♦ *The ballplayers sweltered because it was such a hot day.*

sweltering ['swɛl tə rɪŋ] *adj.* very hot. (Adv: *swelteringly.*) ♦ *The traffic cop wiped his sweaty forehead in the sweltering heat.* ♦ *Mary bought an air conditioner because of the sweltering weather.*

swept ['swɛpt] pt/pp of **sweep**.

swerve ['swɚv] **1.** *iv.* to move suddenly to one side, especially when trying not to hit something or trying not to be hit by something. ♦ *The driver swerved to avoid hitting the stalled car.* ♦ *Anne aimed the golf ball toward the green, but it swerved to the left.* **2.** *tv.* to move something suddenly to one side, especially when one is trying not to hit something or trying not to be hit by something. ♦ *The driver swerved the car to avoid hitting the pedestrian.* ♦ *Bill swerved his shopping cart to avoid hitting a food display.*

swift ['swɪft] *adj.* rapid; quick; moving or passing fast. (Adv: *swiftly.* Comp: *swifter;* sup: *swiftest.*) ♦ *Bob's vengeance for the insult was swift and devastating.* ♦ *The swift current carried the raft downstream.*

swiftness ['swɪft nəs] *n.* the quality of being swift; rapidity; quickness. (No plural form in this sense.) ♦ *The swiftness of the current surprised the swimmers.* ♦ *The courier guaranteed the swiftness of his deliveries.*

swim ['swɪm] **1.** *iv., irreg.* [for someone] to travel through water by moving arms and legs; [for an animal] to travel through water by moving paws, legs, fins, tail, etc. (Pt: **swam**; pp: **swum**.) ♦ *Mary swam from the end of the dock to the shore.* ♦ *Bob watched the fish swim in his aquarium.* **2.** *iv., irreg.* [for something] to seem to spin or revolve owing to one's illness or disorientation. ♦ *I'm so tired that my head is swimming.* ♦ *The room swam in front of the sick patient's eyes.* **3.** *n.* an act of swimming. ♦ *Mary went for a quick swim in the lake before sundown.* ♦ *John took a refreshing swim after work.* **4. be swimming in something** *idiom* to be engulfed by an excess of something, as if it were a flood. ♦ *The war-torn city was swimming in blood.* ♦ *I am just swimming in paperwork.*

swimming ['swɪm ɪŋ] **1.** *n.* the sport or activity of traveling in water by moving one's arms and legs. (No plural form in this sense.) ♦ *Swimming is an excellent form of exercise.* ♦ *Students who are interested in swimming should report to the pool on Monday.* **2. swimming pool.** See pool.

swimsuit ['swɪm sut] *n.* a bathing suit; the clothing worn by someone who swims. ♦ *Mary always takes two or three swimsuits on her vacations.* ♦ *Bill got sand in his swimsuit when he lay on the beach.*

swindle ['swɪn dəl] **1.** *tv.* to defraud someone. ♦ *A clever thief swindled the tourist.* ♦ *The treasurer swindled the company by taking too much salary.* **2.** *n.* cheating; cheating people out of their money. ♦ *The newspaper reported the mayor's swindle of public money.* ♦ *No one discovered the company treasurer's elaborate swindle.*

swine ['swɑɪn] **1.** *n., irreg.* a hog or a pig. (Pl: *swine.*) ♦ *Bacon, ham, and pork are kinds of meat that come from swine.* ♦ *The farmer fattened the swine before slaughtering them.* **2.** *n., irreg.* someone who is disgusting, unpleasant, or contemptible. (Figurative on ①.) ♦ *The swine sitting behind me at the restaurant ruined my meal.* ♦ *That swine insulted my wife, then he insulted the hostess.*

swing ['swɪŋ] **1.** *tv., irreg.* to move something in a sweeping or curved pattern. (Pt/pp: **swung**.) ♦ *The cowboy swung the lasso over his head.* ♦ *Dave angrily swung the door open.* **2.** *tv., irreg.* to move something in a sweeping or circular movement. ♦ *Anne swung her tennis racket and hit the tennis ball.* ♦ *The clock swung the second hand to thirty minutes past the hour.* **3.** *iv., irreg.* to move in a sweeping or curved pattern. ♦ *The pendulum swung underneath the clock.* ♦ *The door swung open from the force of the wind.* **4.** *iv., irreg.* to move while hanging from a fixed point; to dangle. ♦ *A noose swung from a low branch of the tree.* ♦ *Mary's legs swung back and forth as she sat on the dock.* **5.** *iv., irreg.* to turn suddenly or quickly. ♦ *Suddenly, the car swung toward the ditch.* ♦ *Public opinion quickly swung against the lying politician.* **6.** *iv., irreg.* to play on a swing ⑨; to move one's body through the air on a swing ⑨. ♦ *Susan swung higher as Mary pushed her.* ♦ *The children swung on the swings at the park.* **7.** *n.* swinging; a swinging movement. ♦ *With each swing of the pendulum, another second passed.* ♦ *The swing of the door was accompanied by a horrible squeak.* **8.** *n.* a change; a fluctuation; a variation. ♦ *The mayor was alarmed by the swing in public opinion against her.* ♦ *The economist predicted a swing in the unemployment rate.* **9.** *n.* a seat that hangs on ropes or chains, which people, usually children, sit on and move back and forth. ♦ *The children played on the swings in the park.* ♦ *Bill sat on the porch swing and read his newspaper.* **10.** *n.* jazz music for dancing. (No plural form in this sense.) ♦ *We danced to swing at the jazz club all night long.* ♦ *The aerobics instructor played swing while we exercised.* **11. get into the swing of things** *idiom* to join into routines or activities. ♦ *Come on, Bill. Try to get into the swing of things.* ♦ *John just couldn't seem to get into the swing of things.* **12. in full swing** *idiom* in progress; operating or running without restraint. ♦ *We can't leave now! The party is in full swing.* ♦ *Just wait until our project gets into full swing.*

swinging ['swɪŋ ɪŋ] **1.** *adj.* moving back and forth in a sweeping curve. ♦ *The swinging pendulum in the clock caught my attention.* ♦ *The kitten tried to grab the swinging string above its head.* **2.** *adj.* moving in a sweeping or circular movement. ♦ *The swinging shutters kept banging against the wall.* ♦ *The suspect's violently swinging arms injured the police officer.* **3.** *adj.* turning suddenly or quickly. ♦ *The pollster measured the swinging directions of public opinion.* ♦ *The swinging stock prices frightened the inexperienced investors.*

swipe ['swɑɪp] **1.** *tv.* to steal something. (Informal.) ♦ *Someone swiped my leather jacket at the bar.* ♦ *The shoplifter swiped some socks from the clothing store.* **2.** *tv.* to move the magnetic strip of a plastic card through a slot that reads the information off the magnetic strip. ♦ *Mary swiped her subway pass through the turnstile when entering the station.* ♦ *The clerk swiped my credit card through the machine and handed it back to me.* **3. swipe at** *iv.* + *prep. phr.* to hit at someone or something; to strike at someone or something; to unsuccessfully attempt to hit someone or something. ♦ *The thief swiped at the homeowner with a lead pipe.* ♦ *Susan swiped at the fly with a folded newspaper.*

swirl ['swɚl] **1.** *iv.* to move in twists and turns; to move while twisting and turning. ♦ *Smoke swirled upward from the burning building.* ♦ *Couples swirled around the dance floor.* **2.** *n.* something moving in a swirling shape. ♦ *Swirls of smoke wafted from the fireplace.* ♦ *The ice skater's swirls on the ice were impressive.* **3.** *n.* something in a swirling shape. ♦ *The artist painted the canvas with swirls of color.* ♦ *Swirls of ribbons hung from the decorated table.*

swish ['swɪʃ] **1.** *iv.* to move rapidly and in a way that makes a rustling noise. ♦ *The wind swished through the tree branches.* ♦ *The water swished down the drain.* **2.** *tv.* to move something through the air in a way that makes a hissing or whistling noise. ♦ *Mary swished the basketball through the net.* ♦ *John swished his arm through the air, trying to hit a fly.* **3.** *n.* the sound made by swishing. ♦ *A swish of air escaped through the hole in the tire.* ♦ *With a loud swish, the wind blew the lamp over.*

Swiss ['swɪs] **1.** *n.* a citizen or native of Switzerland. (No plural form in this sense.) ♦ *My uncle married a Swiss when he was in Europe.* ♦ *We made good friends with some Swiss who spent the summer in our town.* **2.** *adj.* of or about Switzerland or ①. ♦ *We love to visit the Swiss countryside in the summer.* ♦ *Tom owns a very expensive Swiss watch.*

switch ['swɪtʃ] **1.** *n.* a lever that turns electricity on and off. ♦ *John flipped the switch and turned off the light.* ♦ *Jane turned the computer switch off.* **2.** *n.* a change from one thing to another. ♦ *The reporter spoke of the mayor's switch from Republican to Democrat.* ♦ *Our manager approved the switch in the brand of paper we use.* **3.** *n.* a thin, bendable stick that is cut from a tree. ♦ *The children were spanked with a switch when they were naughty.* ♦ *The farmer made a broom by tying many switches together.* **4. switch on; switch off** *tv.* + *adv.* to close or open an electric circuit; to turn something on or off. ♦ *Anne switched the television on.* ♦ *Bill switched the lights off.* **5.** *tv.* to change something; to swap or exchange things. ♦ *Bill and I switched seats so he could sit next to Mary.* ♦ *I switched pens when the one I was using ran out of ink.* **6. switch to** *iv.* + *prep. phr.* to change to something; to move from one to another. ♦ *The coffee drinker switched to a new brand of coffee.* ♦ *Anne switched to the Independent Party.*

switchboard ['swɪtʃ bord] *n.* a control panel that an operator uses to connect incoming telephone calls to the proper person. ♦ *No one could make phone calls while the switchboard was broken.* ♦ *The operator could listen to any call coming through the switchboard.*

switch-hitter ['swɪtʃ 'hɪt ɚ] *n.* [in baseball] a batter that can bat either left-handed or right-handed. ♦ *The switch-hitter hit the baseball into right field.* ♦ *The switch-hitter decided to bat left-handed against the pitcher.*

Switzerland ['swɪt sɚ lənd] See Gazetteer.

swivel ['swɪv əl] **1.** *n.* a device that allows something attached to it to spin easily. ♦ *My office chair is attached to a swivel that allows it to turn.* ♦ *The pulley has a swivel that keeps the ropes from becoming twisted.* **2. swivel around** *iv.* + *adv.* to rotate around something; to turn easily around something. ♦ *Mary swiveled around in her office chair to face me.* ♦ *I got wet when the sprinkler swiveled around.*

swollen ['swol ən] **1.** pp of swell. **2.** *adj.* puffed up; having gotten bigger; bulging. (Adv: *swollenly.*) ♦ *John put some ice on his swollen ankle.* ♦ *The swollen river caused the dam to burst.* **3.** *adj.* filled with pride. (Figurative on ①. Adv: *swollenly.*) ♦ *The winning player developed a swollen ego.* ♦ *John got a swollen sense of his worth from all the attention he got when he won.*

swoop ['swup] **1. swoop (down)** *iv.* (+ *adv.*) to move downward quickly through the air; to descend quickly from the sky. ♦ *The eagle swooped down from the sky and snatched a mouse.* ♦ *The plane swooped toward the ground when its engines died.* **2. swoop up** *tv.* + *adv.* to grab someone or something from above and pick it up. ♦ *Anne swooped up the $20 bill from the floor and put it in her pocket.* ♦ *The eagle swooped up the mouse with its talons.*

sword ['sord] **1.** *n.* a heavy metal weapon with a long, usually sharp blade attached to a handle. ♦ *Swords were often used to break a person's bones if the blade was not sharp enough for piercing.* ♦ *The knight lifted the heavy sword and slew the wild beast.* **2. cross swords (with someone)** *idiom* to enter into an argument with someone. ♦ *I don't want to cross swords with Tom.* ♦ *The last time we crossed swords, we had a terrible time.*

swordfish ['sord fɪʃ] **1.** *n., irreg.* a large fish whose upper jaw resembles a long sword. (Pl: *swordfish* or *swordfishes.*) ♦ *The marine biologist studied the breeding habits of the swordfish.* ♦ *Jimmy said the swordfish looked like it had a very long nose!* **2.** *n.* the flesh of ① used as food. (No plural form in this sense.) ♦ *Swordfish can be very tasty if it is not overcooked.* ♦ *Mary prepared grilled swordfish for dinner.*

swore ['swor] pt of swear.

sworn ['sworn] **1.** pp of swear. **2.** *adj.* having taken an oath; promised; vowed. ♦ *The deliberating jury asked to examine the sworn statements.* ♦ *The witness's sworn testimony helped to convict the defendant.*

swum ['swʌm] pp of swim.

swung ['swʌŋ] pt/pp of swing.

sycamore ['sɪk ə mor] *n.* a large variety of shade tree. ♦ *The road to the farmhouse was lined with sycamores.* ♦ *They cut down the old sycamore for lumber.*

syllabic [sɪ 'læb ɪk] *adj.* of or about syllables; consisting of syllables; constituting a syllable. (Adv: *syllabically* [...ɪk li].) ♦ *The linguist studied the syllabic structure of foreign languages.* ♦ [m], [n], *and* [l] *are common syllabic consonants; that is, they can form a syllable without being attached to a vowel sound.*

syllabification [sɪ læb ɪ fɪ 'ke ʃən] *n.* the way words are divided into syllables. (No plural form in this sense.) ♦ *Knowing the syllabification of a word makes it easier to pronounce.* ♦ *The syllabification of* radio *is* [re] [di] [o].

syllable ['sɪl ə bəl] *n.* an uninterrupted segment of speech consisting of a vowel possibly with adjacent consonants. ♦ *The words* cat, mat, red, *and* ant *are each a single syllable.* ♦ *The word* watermelon *has four syllables.*

syllabus ['sɪl ə bəs] *n.* a description or outline of the main points that will be addressed during a course of study. ♦ *The professor distributed a syllabus on the first day of class.* ♦ *According to the syllabus, there's an exam in the last week of class.*

symbol ['sɪm bəl] **1.** *n.* something that represents something else; something that is symbolic of something else. ♦ *The prophet regarded the full moon as a symbol of danger.* ♦ *Married people wear wedding rings as a symbol of their love and commitment.* **2.** *n.* a letter, number, or shape that represents a quantity, chemical element, mathematical operation, or other function. ♦ *The "+" sign is a symbol for addition.* ♦ *Au is the chemical symbol for gold.*

symbolic [sɪm 'bɑl ɪk] *adj.* used as a symbol; represented as a symbol; expressed as a symbol. (Adv: *symbolically* [...ɪk li].) ♦ *John gave Mary a ring as a symbolic gesture of his love.* ♦ *A dove is symbolic of peace.*

symbolize ['sɪm bə lɑɪz] *tv.* to represent something; to stand for something; to be a symbol of something. ♦ *The peace treaty symbolized the new trust between the former enemies.* ♦ *The dove is used to symbolize peace.*

symmetrical [sɪ 'mɛ trɪ kəl] *adj.* having the opposite sides of something being or looking exactly alike. (Adv: *symmetrically* [...ɪk li].) ♦ *John cut the pizza into two symmetrical halves.* ♦ *The painting of a vase of flowers and its mirror image was symmetrical.*

symmetry ['sɪm ə tri] *n.* the arrangement of the opposite sides of something so that they look exactly alike. (No plural form in this sense.) ♦ *The symmetry of the food placement on the buffet table meant that one could reach every kind of food from either side of the table.* ♦ *The symmetry of the building design was pleasing to the eye.*

sympathetic [sɪm pə 'θɛt ɪk] *adj.* having sympathy; kind and understanding. (Adv: *sympathetically* [...ɪk li].) ♦ *The depressed student spoke to a sympathetic counselor.* ♦ *A sympathetic man sent money to a charity.*

sympathize ['sɪm pə θɑɪz] *iv.* to feel sympathy for someone or something; to show sympathy for someone or something. ♦ *When Mary's parents died, Bill could sympathize, because his parents had died also.* ♦ *I sympathized with John when he lost his job.*

sympathizer ['sɪm pə θɑɪz ɚ] *n.* someone who agrees with a certain political philosophy. ♦ *The communist sympathizers were blacklisted in Hollywood.* ♦ *When the union went on strike, some sympathizers joined their picket.*

sympathy ['sɪm pə θi] *n.* supportive feelings for other people's problems and sorrows. (No plural form in this sense.) ♦ *Bill felt sympathy for the victims of the war.* ♦ *Anne expressed her sympathy for Jane's loss.*

symphonic [sɪm 'fɑn ɪk] *adj.* of or about a symphony. (Adv: *symphonically* [...ɪk li].) ♦ *Mary and I both love symphonic music.* ♦ *The orchestra played a short symphonic suite.*

symphony ['sɪm fə ni] **1.** *n.* a long piece of music written for an orchestra. ♦ *The orchestra performed Beethoven's Ninth Symphony.* ♦ *Mary listens to classical symphonies while she works.* **2. symphony (orchestra)** *n.* an orchestra that plays ①. ♦ *Tom goes to every concert given by the Cleveland Symphony.* ♦ *Mary plays violin for the local symphony orchestra.* **3.** *adj.* <the adj. use of ②.> (See also symphonic.) ♦ *Lisa has symphony tickets for tonight.* ♦ *The orchestra is performing in Symphony Hall.*

symposia [sɪm 'poz i ə] a pl of symposium.

symposium [sɪm 'poz i əm] *n., irreg.* a meeting where a specific topic is discussed. (Pl: *symposiums* or symposia.) ♦ *The social worker attended a symposium on urban problems.* ♦ *The movie critic spoke at many symposia on art films last year.*

symptom ['sɪmp təm] *n.* an indication that is evidence of the existence of something, especially of an illness. ♦ *A runny nose and coughing are symptoms of the common cold.* ♦ *High unemployment is a symptom of a troubled economy.*

synagogue AND **synagog** ['sɪn ə gɑg] *n.* a building for worship in the Jewish religion. (See also temple ②.) ♦ *The rabbi lived across the street from the synagogue.* ♦ *Religious training is available at our synagogue.*

synchronize ['sɪŋ krə nɑɪz] **1.** *tv.* to set two or more clocks, watches, or other timing devices so that they show the same time. ♦ *The spies synchronized their watches before leaving the meeting.* ♦ *Mary synchronized her watch to the clock at city hall.* **2.** *tv.* to cause two or more things to happen at the same time or at the same speed. ♦ *We synchronized our arrival so neither of us would be early.* ♦ *The actors synchronized their movements when practicing the fight for the play.*

synchronized ['sɪŋ krə nɑɪzd] *adj.* caused to happen at the same time or speed. ♦ *Synchronized traffic lights improved the flow of traffic.* ♦ *The synchronized swimmers moved in unison through the water.*

syndicate 1. ['sɪn də kət] *n.* people or businesses that are joined together for specific business reasons. ♦ *The office building was owned by a multinational syndicate.* ♦ *A powerful syndicate controlled the production of diamonds for the entire world.* **2.** ['sɪn də kət] *n.* an organization that sells news articles, comics, films, television shows, etc. ♦ *Lisa celebrated when her comic strip was accepted by a syndicate.* ♦ *The syndicate distributed the journalist's work to 154 newspapers.* **3.** ['sɪn də ket] *tv.* to publish an article, comic strip, other newspaper feature, television program, etc., by means of ②. ♦ *This comic strip is syndicated widely throughout the world.* ♦ *The producers syndicated the popular TV show after its fifth season.*

syndicated ['sɪn də ket ɪd] *adj.* published or distributed by a syndicate. (Adv: *syndicatedly.*) ♦ *The syndicated* *columnist's articles appeared in 154 newspapers.* ♦ *The syndicated television show could be seen five nights a week.*

syndication [sɪn də 'ke ʃən] *n.* publication or distribution through a syndicate. (No plural form in this sense.) ♦ *After its sixth season, the popular TV show was made available for syndication.* ♦ *Because of syndication, many people came to know the journalist's work.*

syndrome ['sɪn drom] *n.* a set of symptoms that are evidence of a certain sickness or condition. ♦ *The doctor noticed the symptoms of a serious mental syndrome in the patient.* ♦ *Often, a syndrome is named for the doctor who first detects it.*

synonym ['sɪ nə nɪm] *n.* a word that has the same or almost the same meaning as another word. ♦ Sofa, couch, *and* davenport *are synonyms.* ♦ *You should replace the overused words in your paper with synonyms.*

synonymous [sɪ 'nɑn ə məs] *adj.* having the same meaning as something else; meaning the same. (Adv: *synonymously.*) ♦ Carpet *and* rug *are often synonymous.* ♦ *Very few words are exactly synonymous.*

synopses [sɪ 'nɑp siz] pl of synopsis.

synopsis [sɪ 'nɑp sɪs] *n., irreg.* a summary of an event or story. (Pl: synopses.) ♦ *The reviewer provided a brief synopsis of the movie.* ♦ *The witness gave a synopsis of the events leading to the accident.*

syntax ['sɪn tæks] *n.* the arrangement of words in the proper order in sentences. (No plural form in this sense.) ♦ *It is a rule of English syntax that a preposition comes before its object.* ♦ *The improper syntax of the computer code caused the program to fail.*

syntheses ['sɪn θɪ siz] pl of synthesis.

synthesis ['sɪn θɪ sɪs] **1.** *n.* a combination of many parts to make a complete thing. (No plural form in this sense.) ♦ *This project is a synthesis of hard work and patience.* ♦ *The synthesis of the complicated compound required years of trying.* **2.** *n.* something created by synthesizing. (Pl: syntheses.) ♦ *This news report is the synthesis of many people's firsthand accounts.* ♦ *I need at least a week to make a synthesis of all the ideas I heard in the lecture!*

synthesize ['sɪn θə saɪz] **1.** *tv.* to make something by combining and organizing many parts. ♦ *John synthesized a computer from the parts of many broken computers.* ♦ *Mary synthesized her report from interviews with dozens of people.* **2.** *tv.* to make an artificial variety of something. ♦ *Finally, the technician succeeded in synthesizing rubber.* ♦ *The substance was rare in nature so it will have to be synthesized in the laboratory.*

synthetic [sɪn 'θɛt ɪk] *adj.* not found in nature; artificial. (Adv: *synthetically* [...ɪk li].) ♦ *Synthetic fabrics usually don't wrinkle as much as cotton.* ♦ *The chemist created a synthetic sweetener.*

syphon ['saɪ fən] See siphon.

syringe [sə 'rɪndʒ] *n.* a device from which liquids are pushed out or into which liquids are pulled, usually with a hypodermic needle attached. ♦ *The nurse removed blood from my arm with a needle and syringe.* ♦ *Dr. Smith needed a large syringe to hold the full dose of serum.*

syrup ['sɪr əp] *n.* a thick, sweet liquid eaten as food or used for the administration of medication through the mouth. (No plural form in this sense.) ♦ *Mary poured maple syrup over her pancakes.* ♦ *Anne drank some cough syrup to soothe her sore throat.*

system ['sɪs təm] **1.** *n.* a group of things that work together to form a network; a group of things arranged in a particular way that function as one thing. ♦ *Everyone at my office is linked to the same computer system.* ♦ *Consultants were hired to help improve the city's subway system.* **2.** *n.* a method of arrangement; a plan. ♦ *The workers developed an efficient system to get the job done.* ♦ *Can you explain the accounting system used in your firm?*

systematic [sɪs tə 'mæt ɪk] *adj.* organized and structured; based on a system or plan. (Adv: *systematically* [...ɪk li].) ♦ *Bill's systematic approach to problem-solving works with machines, but not people.* ♦ *The tyrant ordered the systematic destruction of his enemies.*

systematize ['sɪs tə mə taɪz] *tv.* to arrange something into a system. ♦ *The office manager systematized the assignment of work spaces.* ♦ *The city government systematized the building inspection process.*

systemic [sɪ 'stɛm ɪk] *adj.* affecting an entire living organism. (Adv: *systemically* [...ɪk li].) ♦ *The patient's violent seizures were a systemic disorder.* ♦ *The systemic poison paralyzed the man.*

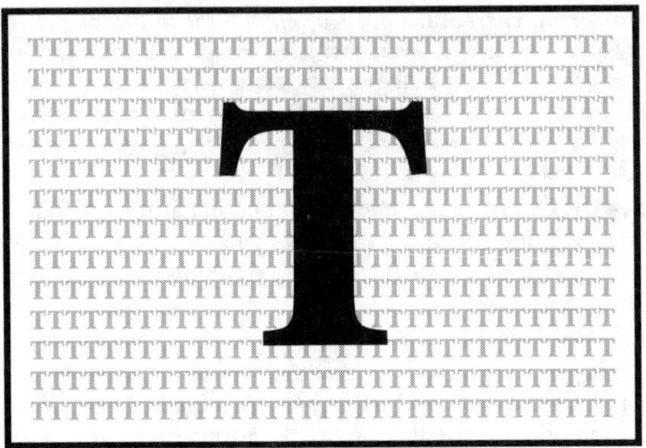

T AND **t** ['ti] **1.** *n.* the twentieth letter of the English alphabet. ♦ *The letter* T *comes after* S *and before* U. ♦ *There are two* Ts *in the word* letter. **2. 't** See not.

tab ['tæb] **1.** *n.* a small flap that sticks out from the edge of a sheet of paper, cardboard, or something similar. ♦ *The clerk wrote "Smith, John" on the tab of the folder containing Mr. Smith's medical records.* ♦ *The various sections of the cookbook were marked with colored tabs.* **2.** *n.* a bill that is presented to a customer for payment. ♦ *At the end of the meal, Mr. Smith asked for the tab.* ♦ *We ran up a large tab at the bar.* **3. pick up the tab** *idiom* to pay the bill. ♦ *Whenever we go out, my father picks up the tab.* ♦ *Order whatever you want. The company is picking up the tab.*

table ['teb əl] **1.** *n.* an item of furniture whose top is a raised, flat surface supported by legs. ♦ *Please place the book on that table.* ♦ *The table was laid with the best silver and china.* **2.** *n.* a chart of numbers, facts, or data presented in columns or rows. ♦ *This table shows the annual birth rate for the past 20 years.* ♦ *The researcher formatted her data into a table.* **3. table a motion** *idiom* to postpone the discussion of something during a meeting. ♦ *Mary suggested that they should table the motion.* ♦ *The motion for a new policy was tabled until the next meeting.*

tablecloth ['te bəl klɔθ] *n.* a piece of fabric that covers the top of a table and hangs over the side, for decoration or protection of the table's surface. ♦ *A lace tablecloth covers our kitchen table.* ♦ *Jane washed the tablecloth after the meal.*

table of contents ['teb əl əv 'kɑn tɛnts] See content ④.

tablespoon ['teb əl spun] **1.** *n.* a large spoon; a spoon that holds three times as much of something as a teaspoon. ♦ *We ate our soup with tablespoons.* ♦ *Jimmy couldn't fit the tablespoon into his mouth.* **2.** *n.* a tablespoonful. ♦ *The recipe calls for one tablespoon of sour cream.* ♦ *Three tablespoons of coffee beans make three cups of coffee.*

tablespoonful ['teb əl spun fʊl] *n.* the contents of a tablespoon. ♦ *I took a tablespoonful of cough syrup.* ♦ *There was only a tablespoonful of sugar left in the sugar bowl.*

tablet ['tæb lət] **1.** *n.* a pad of paper; blank sheets of paper that are bound together along the top or side. ♦ *The children each received a new tablet for drawing.* ♦ *The teacher instructed the students to take notes in their tablets.* **2.** *n.* a pill; a small, hard piece of medicine, drugs, vitamins, or minerals that a person swallows. ♦ *Aspirin comes in the form of a tablet or a capsule.* ♦ *The doctor gave Bill some tablets to take for his allergies.*

tabletop ['te bəl tɑp] *n.* the top, flat surface of a table. ♦ *We could see our reflection in the polished tabletop.* ♦ *A wet glass will leave a mark on a wooden tabletop.*

tableware ['te bəl wɛr] *n.* dishes, glasses, utensils, and related objects used while eating at a table. ♦ *Bob got out clean tableware each evening before dinner.* ♦ *Bill and Mary received a new set of tableware when they got married.*

tabloid ['tæb lɔɪd] **1.** *n.* a small newspaper with large, provocative headlines, a lot of pictures, and easy-to read news stories. ♦ *The tabloid published outrageous stories about celebrities.* ♦ *Mary does not read tabloids because she feels they are too sensational.* **2.** *adj.* <the adj. use of ①.> ♦ *Bill does not approve of tabloid journalism.* ♦ *The grocery store sells tabloid publications.*

taboo AND **tabu** [tə 'bu] **1.** *n.* something that is not socially acceptable; something that is not talked about because it is socially unacceptable. ♦ *Many cultures have some taboos concerning sex.* ♦ *The sociologist was criticized for violating a taboo.* **2.** *adj.* not approved; not acceptable socially; forbidden; not allowed. ♦ *Using vulgar language is taboo around my parents.* ♦ *Taboo topics from the 1930s are now discussed openly.*

tabulate ['tæb jə let] *tv.* to count something, such as votes. ♦ *All the votes were tabulated on election night.* ♦ *The computer tabulated the company's expenses automatically.*

tacit ['tæs ɪt] *adj.* understood, but not expressed in words. (Adv: *tacitly.*) ♦ *There was a tacit agreement among the group to leave before dark.* ♦ *I knew I had my parents' tacit approval for going to the party, but I had to ask to borrow the car.*

tack ['tæk] **1.** *n.* a small, thin nail with a large head. (See also thumbtack.) ♦ *Bob nailed down the carpet with tacks.* ♦ *David repaired the door frame with a few tacks.* **2.** *n.* a course of action that is different from an earlier one; an attempt to do something after earlier attempts have not worked. (Figurative on ③.) ♦ *After our first approach failed, we took another tack.* ♦ *A better tack than fighting would be to talk about the problem.* **3.** *n.* the direction that a ship travels as the result of the wind and the way that its sails are arranged. ♦ *The ship's tack took it straight toward the port.* ♦ *The boat changed tack because the wind shifted.* **4. tack to** *tv.* + *prep. phr.* to fasten something to a surface with ①. ♦ *Mary tacked her child's drawing to the wall.* ♦ *Dad tacked the top of the door frame to the sides.* **5.** *tv.* to sew something with a loose stitch. ♦ *The seamstress will tack the seams before she sews them tightly.* ♦ *I only tack the seams until someone buys the garment.* **6. tack on** *tv.* + *adv.* to add something to the end of something else. ♦ *Bill tacked an extra clause on to his will.* ♦ *Jane tacked another chapter on.* **7. get down to brass tacks** *idiom* to begin to talk about important things. ♦ *Let's get down to brass tacks. We've wasted too much time chatting.* ♦ *Don't you think that it's about time to get down to brass tacks?*

tackle ['tæk əl] **1.** *tv.* to run after, dive onto, and throw a person to the ground, especially in playing football. ♦ *The football player tackled the quarterback.* ♦ *The police officer tackled the mugger.* **2.** *n.* the act of tackling someone as in ①. ♦ *The football player was penalized for an illegal tackle.* ♦ *The tackle injured the quarterback.* **3.** *n.*

equipment used for fishing. (No plural form in this sense.) ♦ *Bill carried his tackle down to the fishing boat.* ♦ *Tom added the new lure to his tackle.* **4.** *tv.* to undertake a duty or a problem; to start working on something difficult. (Figurative on ①.) ♦ *After the plumber fixed the faucet, he tackled the drain.* ♦ *Susan tackled the problem and solved it easily.*

tacky ['tæk i] **1.** *adj.* sticky. (Especially said of something like wet paint that has not completely dried. Adv: *tackily.* Comp: *tackier;* sup: *tackiest.*) ♦ *The newly painted walls will be tacky for several hours.* ♦ *The counter was tacky and needed to be cleaned.* **2.** *adj.* shabby; cheap; not fashionable; not tasteful; lacking propriety or manners. (Adv: *tackily.* Comp: *tackier;* sup: *tackiest.*) ♦ *Belching in public is a tacky thing to do.* ♦ *Don't you think the tie John is wearing is really tacky?*

taco ['tɑ ko] *n.* a long, folded, soft or crispy circle of pastry filled with meat, cheese, tomatoes, lettuce, onions, and sour cream. (Pl in *-s.*) ♦ *We had vegetarian tacos for dinner.* ♦ *Mary ate two chicken tacos for lunch.*

tact ['tækt] *n.* the ability to deal with people without offending them; discretion. (No plural form in this sense.) ♦ *Asking someone not to smoke in your home requires tact.* ♦ *Mary lacks tact, so all of her requests seem rude.*

tactful ['tækt fʊl] *adj.* showing or having tact. (Adv: *tactfully.*) ♦ *In a tactful way, Mary asked her landlord to turn up her heat.* ♦ *If you want people to do as you say, try being more tactful.*

tactic ['tæk tɪk] *n.* a skillful way of doing something in order to reach a goal. (Often plural.) ♦ *Anne's tactic of confronting her boss directly was successful.* ♦ *The businessman's tactics were unscrupulous.*

tactical ['tæk tɪ kəl] *adj.* of or about tactics. (Adv: *tactically* [...ɪk li].) ♦ *The army's tactical maneuvers helped it win the war.* ♦ *The company's tactical leader laid off ten percent of the work force.*

tactician [tæk 'tɪʃ ən] *n.* someone who is skilled in tactics. ♦ *The tactician suggested that the army attack at dawn.* ♦ *The tactician doubled the company's profits.*

tactile ['tæk tɪl] *adj.* of or about the sense of touch. ♦ *Braille is a tactile system of reading.* ♦ *The paralyzed man had lost the tactile senses in his hands.*

tactless ['tækt ləs] *adj.* without tact; blunt. (Adv: *tactlessly.*) ♦ *Mary apologized for making a tactless comment about my husband.* ♦ *John is very tactless and will say whatever comes to his mind.*

tadpole ['tæd pol] *n.* a small, round water creature that has a long tail and develops into a frog or a toad. ♦ *The biology class watched the tadpoles develop into frogs.* ♦ *We could see several tadpoles swimming in the tank.*

taffy ['tæf i] *n.* a sticky, chewy, sweet candy, made by boiling brown sugar and butter or molasses and butter. ♦ *Each child chewed a piece of taffy.* ♦ *The taffy stuck to my teeth.*

tag ['tæg] **1.** *n.* a small label that has information about the object that it is attached to. ♦ *The tag on the shirt listed washing instructions.* ♦ *Jane took the tag off the gift before she wrapped it.* **2.** *n.* a game in which a player runs around trying to touch someone else—who then runs to touch another person. (No plural form in this sense.) ♦ *The children played tag in the backyard.* ♦ *Jimmy hated to play tag with the older, faster children.* **3.** *tv.* to put ① on something or some creature. ♦ *My mother tagged my clothes with my name.* ♦ *The scientist tagged the deer with a metal clip so the animal could be identified.* **4.** *tv.* to touch someone, especially in ②. ♦ *Jimmy tagged Mary and then she was "it."* ♦ *The slow runner couldn't tag any of the other players.* **5. tag along** *idiom* to go along with or follow someone, often when uninvited or unwanted. ♦ *Lisa always tags along when Tim and Sally go out on a date.* ♦ *I took my children to the zoo, and the neighbor's children tagged along.*

tail ['tel] **1.** *n.* the part of an animal that hangs off from its back, as an extension of the spine. ♦ *The cat ran in circles, chasing its tail.* ♦ *The dog happily wagged its tail as its master approached.* **2.** *n.* the rear part of something; the last part of something. (Figurative on ①.) ♦ *The smokers sat in the tail of the plane.* ♦ *The comet's tail stretched for thousands of miles.* **3.** *tv.* to follow someone closely. (Informal.) ♦ *The federal agent tailed the suspect.* ♦ *The police academy teaches how to discreetly tail someone.* **4. in two shakes of a lamb's tail** *idiom* in a very short time; very quickly. ♦ *Jane returned in two shakes of a lamb's tail.* ♦ *Mike was able to solve the problem in two shakes of a lamb's tail.* **5. tail wagging the dog** *idiom* [a situation in which] a small part [is] controlling the whole thing. ♦ *John was just hired yesterday, and today he's bossing everyone around. It's a case of the tail wagging the dog.* ♦ *Why is this small matter so important? Now the tail is wagging the dog!* **6. with one's tail between one's legs** *idiom* appearing frightened or cowardly, like a frightened or defeated dog; appearing threatened or humiliated. ♦ *John seems to lack courage. When people criticize him unjustly, he just goes away with his tail between his legs and doesn't tell them that they're wrong.* ♦ *The frightened dog ran away with its tail between its legs when the bigger dog growled.*

tailgate ['tel get] **1.** *n.* the panel at the back end of a vehicle, such as a truck, that folds down level. ♦ *The logs in the pickup truck were too long for the tailgate to close.* ♦ *I put the boxes in the back of the station wagon and shut the tailgate.* **2. tailgate party** *n.* a party or a barbecue where ① is used as a table. ♦ *There was plenty of beer at the tailgate party.* ♦ *Before the football game, we had a tailgate party in the parking lot.*

taillight ['tel lɑɪt] *n.* a light, usually red, at the back of a car or similar vehicle that is turned on at night so that people can see the vehicle. ♦ *One of the car's taillights was damaged in the collision.* ♦ *Bill watched the taillights of the car in front of him as he drove through the blizzard.*

tailor ['te lɚ] **1.** *n.* someone who makes or repairs clothes. ♦ *The tailor altered Mr. Smith's suit.* ♦ *The tailor put a new lining in my winter coat.* **2.** *tv.* to make or repair an item of clothing so that it fits a certain person. ♦ *The salesman suggested that the suit be tailored at the store.* ♦ *The tailor tailored the jacket to fit me.* **3. tailor to** *tv.* + *prep. phr.* to make or design a product or service so that it meets the needs of a specific person. (Figurative on ②.) ♦ *The payment plan was tailored to the couple's income.* ♦ *Tom tailored the computer program to his special needs.*

tailored ['te lɚd] **1.** *adj.* made by a tailor; made specifically for a person. ♦ *Mr. Jones wears expensive, tailored suits.* ♦ *My tailored coat fits me perfectly.* **2.** *adj.* cut and sewn with simple, straight lines without a lot of fancy decoration. ♦ *The businesswoman dressed in tailored suits.* ♦ *Mary wore a tailored outfit to the conference.*

tailpipe ['tel pɑɪp] *n.* the tube at the back of a car or other vehicle from which engine exhaust comes out. ♦ *Heavy smoke billowed from my tailpipe.* ♦ *The broken tailpipe clattered as it was dragged along the road.*

tailspin ['tel spɪn] **1.** *n.* the act of an airplane falling nose first, with the tail traveling in a circle. ♦ *The pilot was able to steer out of the tailspin.* ♦ *The pilot didn't know how to bring the plane out of the tailspin.* **2.** *n.* a chaotic decline in value. (Figurative on ①.) ♦ *The bankrupt company had gone into a financial tailspin.* ♦ *The stock's sudden tailspin could not be explained.* **3. go into a tailspin** *idiom* [for someone's life] to become chaotic and disorganized. ♦ *Although John was a great success, his life went into a tailspin. It took him a year to get straightened out.* ♦ *After her father died, Mary's life fell apart, and her world went into a tailspin.*

tailwind ['tel wɪnd] *n.* a wind that is moving in the same direction as an airplane and helping the airplane go faster. ♦ *The plane arrived early because it had a tailwind the whole way.* ♦ *The pilot flew the plane faster than normal because of the tailwinds.*

taint ['tent] **1.** *n.* a trace of something unpleasant or of contamination. ♦ *A rancid taint spoiled the taste of the meat.* ♦ *Anne's comments indicated a taint of jealousy.* **2.** *tv.* to spoil something; to change the character of someone or something for the worse. ♦ *The oil spill tainted the water of the bay.* ♦ *John's reputation was tainted by his corrupt friends.*

tainted ['ten təd] *adj.* spoiled; contaminated; corrupt. (Adv: *taintedly.*) ♦ *The tainted drug was removed from the pharmacy.* ♦ *Tainted meat killed several villagers.*

Taiwan [tɑɪ 'wɑn] See Gazetteer.

take ['tek] **1.** *tv., irreg.* to get or obtain something by one's own action. (Pt: **took**; pp: **taken**.) ♦ *Mary took a can of soup from the pantry.* ♦ *Bill took my coat instead of his own.* **2.** *tv., irreg.* to accept something that is offered. ♦ *Jane took the best offer for her used desk.* ♦ *The mayor took the man's hand and shook it heartily.* **3.** *tv., irreg.* to capture something; to win something. ♦ *The rebels took the palace and executed the king.* ♦ *The football team took first place in the conference.* **4.** *tv., irreg.* to ingest something, such as medicine. ♦ *The study recommended that pregnant women take extra vitamins.* ♦ *I don't take food supplements.* **5.** *tv., irreg.* to use something habitually; to require something habitually. ♦ *The car takes a bit of patience to start on a cold morning.* ♦ *Bill takes cream in his coffee.* **6.** *tv., irreg.* to transport someone or something somewhere. ♦ *I asked my brother to take me home.* ♦ *A taxi took me from the museum to the bank.* **7.** *tv., irreg.* to use a form of transportation. ♦ *I took a taxi home.* ♦ *We had to take a bus to the bank.* **8.** *tv., irreg.* to lead someone or something; to guide someone or something. ♦ *Mary had taken the children to the park.* ♦ *The guide took us on a hike in the forest.* **9.** *tv., irreg.* to record an image; to make a picture with a camera. ♦ *This camera takes great photos!* ♦ *Bill and Mary had their picture taken by a professional.* **10.** *tv., irreg.* to write a piece of information; to record a piece of information. ♦ *The students took notes during the lecture.* ♦ *When I'm out, Bill always takes my telephone messages.* **11.** *tv., irreg.* to have someone or something as a source; to quote someone or something; to copy something. ♦ *This quote is taken from the Bible.* ♦ *For my speech, I took a few lines from William Shakespeare.* **12.** *tv., irreg.* to interpret something in a certain way. ♦ *You could take that comment a number of ways.* ♦ *Mary took my statement out of context, and now she is mad.* **13.** *tv., irreg.* to measure something. ♦ *The nurse took Jimmy's temperature.* ♦ *The scientist took a reading from the barometer.* **14.** *tv., irreg.* to choose something among different options; to select something for oneself or as a course of action. ♦ *Hank hoped his son would take the right course of action.* ♦ *After several failures, the inventor took a new tack.* **15.** *tv., irreg.* to assume or accept the responsibility or blame for something. ♦ *Bill refused to take the blame for his boss's mistake.* ♦ *The child needed to learn to take responsibility for his actions.* **16.** *tv., irreg.* [in grammar] to use something in connection with something else. ♦ *All transitive verbs take a direct object.* ♦ *Some transitive verbs take a clause.* **17.** *tv., irreg.* to suffer something; to endure something; to accept something. ♦ *Jimmy took his punishment without crying.* ♦ *I couldn't take seeing the slaughter of the animals.* **18.** *tv., irreg.* to use up time; to consume time; to require that an amount of time be spent [doing something]. ♦ *This kind of work takes a lot of time.* ♦ *How long will this take?* **19.** *n.* the property or money stolen during a robbery. (Informal. No plural form in this sense.) ♦ *The police itemized the robber's take.* ♦ *The thieves tried to sell their take to a fence.* **20.** *n.* the amount of money that a business earns over a certain period of time. (Informal. No plural form in this sense.) ♦ *The company's take this year was over a million dollars.* ♦ *The manager deposited the day's take at the bank.* **21.** *n.* the amount of film that is recorded at one time for a movie. ♦ *The scene was shot in three takes.* ♦ *The director was unhappy with the first take of the commercial.* **22. take a course (in something)** *idiom* to enroll in a course and do the required work. ♦ *I decided to take a course in history.* ♦ *Bob drives into the city where he is taking a course.* **23. take it or leave it** *idiom* to accept something the way it is or forget it. ♦ *This is my last offer. Take it or leave it.* ♦ *It's not much, but it's the only food we have. You can take it or leave it.* **24. take a shower; take a bath** *idiom* to bathe. ♦ *I take a shower every morning.* ♦ *John takes a hot bath to relax.* **25. take over** *idiom* to begin doing something that someone else was doing. ♦ *When you get tired of washing dishes, I'll take over.* ♦ *You have been playing the drums long enough. Let me take over.* **26. take something over** *idiom* to assume control of something. ♦ *The large company took over a number of smaller ones.* ♦ *The dictator hoped to take over the world.* **27. take turns (doing something); take turns (at something); take turns (with something)** *idiom* [for two or more people] to alternate in doing something. ♦ *Bill and I take turns washing the dishes.* ♦ *Let's take turns with mowing the lawn.*

taken ['tek ən] pp of take.

takeoff ['tek ɔf] **1.** *n.* [an airplane's] leaving the ground and becoming airborne. ♦ *The plane's takeoff was rough.* ♦ *During the takeoff, the flight attendants were seated.* **2.** *n.* a parody; a humorous imitation of someone or something. ♦ *This movie is a takeoff on a famous play.* ♦ *The comedian's takeoff of the president was funny.*

takeout ['tek ɑʊt] **1.** *adj.* [of food] sold by a restaurant to someone who will eat it someplace else. ♦ *The children ate takeout food when their parents were away.* ♦ *Bill looked at the restaurant's takeout menu.* **2.** *n.* food to be eaten elsewhere as in ①. (No plural form in this sense.) ♦ *Let's order some kind of takeout for dinner.* ♦ *Is takeout available at the restaurant on the corner?*

takeover ['tek ov ɚ] *n.* taking control of a government or a company, especially in a hostile way. ♦ *The dictator planned a takeover of the neighboring country.* ♦ *The board of directors executed a takeover of a weaker company.*

talcum powder ['tæl kəm 'pɑʊ dɚ] *n.* a powder used for drying damp spots on the skin. (No plural form in this sense.) ♦ *Jane sprinkled some talcum powder on the baby's bottom.* ♦ *I rubbed some talcum powder on my body after my bath.*

tale ['tel] **1.** *n.* a story. ♦ *The storyteller told an interesting tale to the children.* ♦ *Mary told Jane her unhappy tale.* **2.** *n.* a lie. ♦ *Jimmy told his Grandpa a tale of how the window was broken.* ♦ *The girl's father admonished her not tell tales.* **3. tell tales out of school** *idiom* to tell secrets or spread rumors. ♦ *I wish that John would keep quiet. He's telling tales out of school again.* ♦ *If you tell tales out of school a lot, people will stop trusting you.*

talent ['tæl ənt] **1.** *n.* a special skill; a natural ability. ♦ *Bill's talent is with carpentry.* ♦ *Mary has quite a talent for music.* **2.** *n.* people who have a special skill or a natural ability, especially singers or actors; people employed or seeking employment in the entertainment industry. (No plural form in this sense.) ♦ *The director spent hours finding the talent for the commercial.* ♦ *Good talent is hard to find unless you go through an agent.*

talented ['tæl ənt ɪd] *adj.* having talent; skilled; able to do something naturally. (Adv: *talentedly.*) ♦ *The talented craftsman sold his work for a high price.* ♦ *Mary is a talented public speaker.*

talisman ['tæl ɪs mən] *n.* a charm; an object that is thought to protect its owner from evil. (Pl: *talismans.*) ♦ *I clutched my talisman when the old man looked threateningly at me.* ♦ *The witch wore a talisman to protect her from bad spirits.*

talk ['tɔk] **1.** *iv.* to communicate by speaking; to speak; to say words. ♦ *The two-year-old was just learning to talk.* ♦ *After I had jaw surgery, it was difficult for me to talk.* **2.** *iv.* to speak with someone; to converse with someone. ♦ *The old friends talked for hours.* ♦ *Would you like to talk about your problems?* **3.** *n.* the production of words; speech. (No plural form in this sense.) ♦ *There is a lot of talk coming from the conference room.* ♦ *I hear lots of talk but see no action.* **4.** *n.* a conversation; the act of speaking with someone. ♦ *I need to have a talk with you.* ♦ *Mary and I had a nice talk about politics.* **5.** *n.* a speech; a lecture. ♦ *Dr. Wu will give a talk on the politics of China.* ♦ *John fell asleep during the long talk.* **6. talks** *n.* negotiations. ♦ *The peace talks were held in a neutral nation.* ♦ *The contract talks were successful and the strike was ended.* **7.** *n.* gossip; rumors. (No plural form in this sense.) ♦ *The talk around town is that Mary has a new boyfriend.* ♦ *Hank never listens to the office talk.* **8. talk a blue streak** *idiom* to say a lot and talk very rapidly. ♦ *Billy didn't talk until he was six, and then he started talking a blue streak.* ♦ *I can't understand anything Bob says. He talks a blue streak, and I can't follow his thinking.* **9. talk of the town** *idiom* the subject of gossip; someone or something that everyone is talking about. ♦ *Jane's argument with Bob is the talk of the town.* ♦ *Mike's father is the talk of the town since the police arrested him.* **10. talk someone into doing something** *idiom* to persuade someone to do something; to convince someone to do something. ♦ *Mary talked Hank into going skiing with her.* ♦ *I never need to talk my friends into having a party.* **11. talk until one is blue in the face** *idiom* to talk until one is exhausted. ♦ *I talked until I was blue in the face, but I couldn't change her mind.* ♦ *She had to talk until she was blue in the face in order to convince him.* **12. the talk of somewhere** *idiom* someone or something who is the subject of a conversation somewhere, especially the town. ♦ *The handsome new teacher was the talk of the town.* ♦ *John's new car is the talk of the office.*

talkative ['tɔk ə tɪv] *adj.* liking to talk; fond of talking. (Adv: *talkatively.*) ♦ *Mary couldn't get away from the talkative woman at the party.* ♦ *The talkative toddler chatted to himself all day.*

talk show ['tɔk 'ʃo] **1.** *n.* a radio or television program devoted to discussion and opinion by different people. ♦ *I don't listen to talk shows because the people on them are so rude.* ♦ *Tom appeared on a talk show to discuss his new book.* **2. talk-show** *adj.* <the adj. use of ①.> ♦ *I listened to a talk-show program on the radio yesterday.* ♦ *The talk-show host tried to keep the discussion orderly.*

tall ['tɔl] **1.** *adj.* great in height; of a greater height than average; not short. (Comp: *taller;* sup: *tallest.*) ♦ *The tall trees seemed to touch the sky.* ♦ *Everyone in the Smith family is tall.* **2.** *adj.* extending a specified distance upward; at or reaching a specified distance above the ground. (Comp: *taller;* sup: *tallest.*) ♦ *Jimmy is three feet tall.* ♦ *This tree is twenty feet tall.*

tally ['tæl i] **1.** *n.* a score; a mark used to keep track of the number of something being counted; the number of points or votes someone has received. ♦ *The final tally indicated that the incumbent had won.* ♦ *According to the tally, I'm ahead by 25 points.* **2. tally (up)** *tv.* (+ *adv.*) to count the number of votes or points that someone has received. ♦ *The computer tallied the votes automatically.* ♦ *After the game was finished, I tallied up the score.* **3. tally (with)** *iv.* (+ *prep. phr.*) [for two amounts] to be equal; [for two stories] to be exactly the same or correspond closely. ♦ *The witness's testimony tallied with the defendant's.* ♦ *The accountant was glad that the two columns of figures tallied.*

Talmud ['tæl məd] *n.* the written record of Jewish law. ♦ *The Talmud includes a number of dietary restrictions.* ♦ *The laws in the Talmud were written down more than 1,500 years ago.*

tambourine [tæm bə 'rin] *n.* a musical instrument, made of a circular frame with a fabric stretched over it, like the head of a drum, and metal disks set in the side of the frame that make noise when shaken. ♦ *The children played tambourines in music class.* ♦ *Jane shook a tambourine as she danced.*

tame ['tem] **1.** *adj.* not in a natural wild state; domesticated; living with people; acting gentle rather than fierce. (Adv: *tamely.* Comp: *tamer;* sup: *tamest.*) ♦ *The tame deer came toward me to sniff my hands.* ♦ *The monkeys born at* *the zoo are tame.* **2.** *adj.* not shocking; not wild or unruly; not risky; not exciting; dull. (Figurative on ①. Adv: *tamely.* Comp: *tamer;* sup: *tamest.*) ♦ *Mary's parties are so tame that they are boring.* ♦ *Some old movies that used to be very shocking now seem quite tame.* **3.** *tv.* to train an animal to be ①. ♦ *The cowboy tamed the wild horse.* ♦ *Tigers are impossible to tame.*

tamper ['tæm pɚ] **tamper with** *iv.* + *prep. phr.* to alter something secretly, especially without permission; to fiddle around with something. ♦ *The secretary tampered with the prime minister's schedule.* ♦ *The terrorist tampered with the president's food.*

tampon ['tæm pɑn] *n.* a pad of cotton inserted to absorb body fluids, used especially during menstruation and in surgical procedures. ♦ *Tampons are available in the women's bathroom.* ♦ *Mary bought some tampons at the start of her period.*

tan ['tæn] **1.** *iv.* [especially of people with fair skin] to permit one's skin to darken by being outdoors in sunlight or by exposing oneself to artificial sunlight. ♦ *Jane has very fair skin and does not tan well.* ♦ *The teenagers tanned in the sun on the beach.* **2.** *tv.* to change the skin of an animal into leather by soaking it in a special chemical. ♦ *The worker tanned the cow's hide.* ♦ *The hunter tanned the animal skin before selling it.* **3.** *n.* darkened skin from exposure to sunlight as in ①. ♦ *Mary gets a tan every summer.* ♦ *The man's tan contrasted with his white shirt.* **4.** *n.* a light brown color. ♦ *The room was decorated in shades of tan.* ♦ *Tan is a light shade of brown.* **5.** *adj.* light brown in color. (Comp: *tanner;* sup: *tannest.*) ♦ *The man wore tan pants and a blue shirt.* ♦ *Mary rode the tan horse across the field.*

tandem ['tæn dəm] **1.** *adj.* [of two or more people or things] in sequence, one behind another. (Adv: *tandemly.*) ♦ *John and Bill exercised on the tandem rowing machine.* ♦ *Mary and Sue rode the tandem bicycle to town.* **2. in tandem** *phr.* in single file. ♦ *We marched to the door in tandem.* ♦ *They rode along in tandem.*

tangent ['tæn dʒənt] **1.** *n.* a line that touches a circle at only one point. ♦ *The geometry teacher drew a tangent to the circle on the chalkboard.* ♦ *The comet's path was a tangent to the planet's orbit.* **2. go off on a tangent** *idiom* to go off suddenly in another direction; suddenly to change one's line of thought, course of action, etc. ♦ *Please stick to one subject and don't go off on a tangent.* ♦ *If Mary would settle down and deal with one subject she would be all right, but she keeps going off on tangents.*

tangerine [tæn dʒə 'rin] **1.** *n.* a small, orange citrus fruit; a kind of orange whose peel is easy to remove. ♦ *Mary ate a tangerine for lunch.* ♦ *The fruit bowl is full of tangerines.* **2.** *adj.* deep orange in color. ♦ *Our apartment has tangerine carpeting.* ♦ *The dancer wore a tangerine costume.* **3.** *adj.* <the adj. use of ①.> ♦ *David served us some tangerine gelatin.* ♦ *I ate tangerine sherbet for dessert.*

tangible ['tæn dʒə bəl] **1.** *adj.* able to be touched or felt; real; material; physical. (Adv: *tangibly.*) ♦ *The rewards of volunteer work are not tangible.* ♦ *One tangible benefit of my new job is a company car.* **2.** *adj.* able to be measured; noticeable; not vague; specific. (Adv: *tangibly.*) ♦ *A tangible amount of rain fell during the night.* ♦ *There's a tangible level of lead in our drinking water.*

tangle ['tæŋ gəl] **1.** *n.* a twisted clump of hair, string, chain, rope, limbs, etc. ♦ *Susan's long hair was in tangles.* ♦ *The tangle in the necklace was hard to undo.* **2.** *n.* an argument; a disagreement. ♦ *I didn't want to get involved in the tangle between my brother and my sister.* ♦ *A little tangle between Bob and Bill became a fight.* **3.** *iv.* [for strands] to become twisted together. ♦ *The girl's hair tangled in the wind.* ♦ *The strings tangled together as I pulled on them.* **4. tangle with** *iv.* + *prep. phr.* to argue with someone; to disagree with someone; to have to deal with someone about a problem. ♦ *The cat tried to tangle with a raccoon and lost.* ♦ *Jane tangled with her boss about the marketing plan.* **5.** *tv.* to twist strands together; to snarl something. ♦ *The wind tangled the girl's hair.* ♦ *The washing machine tangled the pantyhose.*

tangy ['tæŋ i] *adj.* having a strong flavor; somewhat sour or spicy; pleasantly sharp in flavor. (Adv: *tangily.* Comp: *tangier;* sup: *tangiest.*) ♦ *The children snacked on tangy oranges.* ♦ *The special Chinese soup was really tangy.*

tank ['tæŋk] **1.** *n.* a container for storing air or liquid. ♦ *The scuba divers wore oxygen tanks on their backs.* ♦ *The gas tank in the car leaked slowly.* **2. (fish) tank** *n.* an aquarium; a container for holding fish or other creatures, usually with water. ♦ *Jimmy sat in front of the fish tank for hours.* ♦ *My tank contains a variety of aquatic plants.* **3.** *n.* a large armored vehicle, used by the military, that moves on heavy belts which are wrapped around a set of wheels. ♦ *Enemy tanks rolled into the town.* ♦ *The tank could travel over tough terrain.*

tanker ['tæŋ kɚ] *n.* a large ship or truck that has a special compartment for transporting fluids, such as milk, oil, liquid chemicals, etc. ♦ *The leaking tanker spread oil all over the seashore.* ♦ *A tanker transported milk from the farm to the dairy.*

tannery ['tæn ə ri] *n.* a factory where people tan animal skins. ♦ *The air around the tannery smelled terrible.* ♦ *Tom delivered skins and hides to the tannery.*

tantalize ['tæn tə lɑɪz] *tv.* to tease or torment someone or something. ♦ *Jimmy tantalized the dog by dangling a bone above its nose.* ♦ *We were tantalized by the sweet aroma coming from the bakery.*

tantalizing ['tæn tə lɑɪz ɪŋ] *adj.* elusive; causing desire but remaining out of one's reach; longed for but not accessible. (Adv: *tantalizingly.*) ♦ *Tantalizing smells wafted from Grandma's kitchen.* ♦ *The banquet table was a tantalizing sight to the hungry servant.*

tantamount ['tæn tə mɑʊnt] **tantamount to** *adj.* + *prep. phr.* as much as; having the same force as something else; having the same effect as something else. ♦ *The enemy's attack was tantamount to a declaration of war.* ♦ *John's volunteer work was tantamount to a full-time job.*

tantrum ['tæn trəm] **1.** *n.* a display of one's bad temper in hopes of getting what one wants. ♦ *The two-year-old had a tantrum because she wanted the toy.* ♦ *David's tantrum stunned everyone in the meeting.* **2. temper tantrum** See temper ③.

Tanzania [tænz ə 'ni ə] See Gazetteer.

tap ['tæp] **1.** *n.* a slight pressure or very light blow made by something. ♦ *I turned around when I felt a tap on my shoulder.* ♦ *I knew the roof was leaking when I felt the tap of water on my head.* **2.** *n.* a slight knocking noise; the sound of ①. ♦ *The mechanic heard a tap in the engine.* ♦ *The tap of the rain against the windows woke me up.* **3.** *n.* a device that controls the flow of a gas or a liquid from a pipe or a barrel; a faucet; a spigot. ♦ *The plumber fixed the dripping tap.* ♦ *Please turn the tap all the way off.* **4.** *n.* a device that allows someone to listen secretly to someone's phone calls. ♦ *The phone tap allowed us to record all of the mayor's conversations.* ♦ *The senator suspected that there was a tap on her phone.* **5.** *n.* a type of dancing where the dancer's shoes have metal **taps** ⑥ on the heels and toes that make a clicking noise when they touch the floor. (No plural form in this sense.) ♦ *The director looked for an actor who knew tap.* ♦ *The ballerina had also studied tap.* **6.** *n.* a steel plate that is attached to the bottom of a shoe used in **tap** ⑬ dancing, and that makes a clicking noise when it is struck against the floor. ♦ *The backstage was carpeted so the dancers' taps wouldn't click.* **7.** *tv.* to touch someone or something gently a number of times, especially with the tip of one's finger. ♦ *Mary gently tapped Grandpa to wake him for dinner.* ♦ *Anne impatiently tapped the table with her middle finger.* **8.** *tv.* to make noises by touching someone or something gently a number of times. ♦ *The rain tapped the windowpane.* ♦ *Hank tapped his pencil because he was nervous.* **9.** *tv.* to put ④ on someone's phone line so that one can listen secretly to that person's phone calls. ♦ *The spy tapped the prime minister's private phone.* ♦ *The corrupt candidate tapped his opponent's telephones.* **10.** *tv.* to cut something open so that liquid will flow out; to pierce something, such as a barrel, so that liquid will flow out. ♦ *The fraternity members tapped the beer keg and started the party.* ♦ *I tapped the tree to get sap for syrup.* **11.** *tv.* to use a supply of money. (Figurative on ⑩.) ♦ *Mary had to tap all of her resources to buy the house.* ♦ *I will have to tap my savings account to help pay for the car.* **12. tap on** *iv. + prep. phr.* to strike against something gently a number of times, especially with one's finger or with one's knuckles; to knock. ♦ *I gently tapped on the door to see if Anne was sleeping.* ♦ *The customer tapped on the counter to get the clerk's attention.* **13.** *adj.* <the adj. use of ⑤.> ♦ *The dancer put on her tap shoes for the next musical number.* ♦ *The musical featured a tap dance.*

tape ['tep] **1.** *n.* a narrow strip of something such as paper or plastic. (No plural form in this sense.) ♦ *Tom cut the strip of paper tape into labels.* ♦ *Bill used some red plastic tape to tie up the package.* **2.** *n.* a paper or plastic strip with one side that is sticky, used to stick something to something else. (No plural form in this sense.) ♦ *Mary needed scissors, tape, and wrapping paper to wrap the gift.* ♦ *The poster was stuck to the wall with tape.* **3.** *n.* a magnetic strip of plastic onto which sound or images can be recorded. ♦ *The jury listened to a tape of the defendant's confession.* ♦ *We watched a tape of Anne's birthday party.* **4.** *tv.* to stick something to something else with ②; to seal something with ②. ♦ *The movers taped the boxes shut.* ♦ *Bill taped the note to the refrigerator.* **5.** *tv.* to fix something that is torn by placing ② over the tear. ♦ *Susan taped the tear in the dollar bill.* ♦ *Jimmy taped his ripped art project back together.* **6.** *tv.* to record sound onto an audiotape; to record images onto a videotape. ♦ *Bill taped his sister's wedding on video.* ♦ *Mary taped her favorite radio program on a cassette.* **7.** *iv.* to make a sound or video recording; to record. ♦ *While the camera operator taped, the actors performed.* ♦ *Jane will start singing once you begin taping.* **8. red tape** *idiom* needless and annoying government forms and regulations. ♦ *Because of red tape, it took John weeks to get a visa.* ♦ *Red tape prevented Bob's wife from joining him abroad.*

tapestry ['tæp ə stri] *n.* a large cloth that has a design or decoration woven into it. ♦ *The tapestry had beautiful images of flowers in it.* ♦ *Tapestries were once used to cover the walls of drafty rooms.*

tapeworm ['tep wɚm] *n.* a long, flat worm that lives in a person's or an animal's intestines as a parasite. ♦ *The veterinarian said our dog had a tapeworm.* ♦ *The people in the remote village were afflicted with tapeworms.*

tapir ['te pɚ] *n.* an animal with hooves and a long snout, related to the horse and rhinoceros. ♦ *The tapir is found in tropical forests of the Americas and Southeast Asia.* ♦ *The tapir is a nocturnal animal.*

taproot ['tæp rut] **1.** *n.* the main root of a plant or tree. ♦ *Although Bill pulled the weed, its taproot remained in the ground.* ♦ *The taproot of the tree went deep into the ground.* **2.** *n.* the primary source of growth or development. (Figurative on ①.) ♦ *The research department was the taproot of the firm's development.* ♦ *The taproot of the lawyer's income was personal injury lawsuits.*

tar ['tɑr] **1.** *n.* a black substance made by distilling coal or wood, used to preserve or waterproof objects; asphalt. (No plural form in this sense.) ♦ *Tar is soft and sticky when hot, and it hardens as it cools.* ♦ *The building's roof was covered with tar.* **2.** *n.* a black substance made when tobacco is burned. (No plural form in this sense.) ♦ *The photo showed the effect of cigarette tar on human lungs.* ♦ *The smoker's teeth were stained with tar.* **3.** *tv.* to cover something with ①; to preserve or waterproof something with ①. ♦ *Bill tarred his driveway last week.* ♦ *The worker tarred the holes in the roof to prevent leakage.* **4. tarred with the same brush** *idiom* having the same faults or bad points as someone else. ♦ *Bob and his brother are tarred with the same brush. They're both crooks.* ♦ *The Smith children are tarred with the same brush. They're all lazy.*

tarantula [tə 'ræn tʃə lə] *n.* a large, hairy spider found in the southern and western United States and in tropical parts of the Americas. ♦ *There were some tarantulas in the crate of bananas.* ♦ *Some tarantulas have a poisonous bite.*

tardy ['tɑr di] **1.** *adj.* late; not prompt; not on time. (Adv: *tardily.* Comp: *tardier;* sup: *tardiest.*) ♦ *The tardy student tried to sneak into class.* ♦ *My boss lectured on the consequences of being tardy.* **2.** *n.* an instance of being ①. ♦ *If you have any more tardies, I will keep you after school.* ♦ *Each student was allowed two tardies each semester.*

target ['tɑr gət] **1.** *n.* someone or something that someone tries to hit or shoot when using a weapon. ♦ *The archer hit the center of the target.* ♦ *The shooting range has targets set up for practice.* **2.** *n.* someone who is ridiculed, blamed, or made fun of. (Figurative on ①.) ♦ *Jane was the target of ridicule when she ruined the project.* ♦ *Bill was the target of blame for causing the accident.* **3.** *n.* a goal that one would like to reach; an aim. (Figurative on ①.) ♦ *The charity has a target of a million dollars.* ♦ *Jane's target is to finish the project by Friday.* **4.** *tv.* to establish something as a goal. ♦ *Jane targeted Friday as the project's* *completion date.* ♦ *The charity targeted a million dollars as its goal.* **5.** *tv.* to focus on someone, something, or someplace; to give something, someone, or someplace the greatest amount of consideration. ♦ *The publishing company targets the school market with their books.* ♦ *The principal targeted five problems that needed to be solved.* **6. on target** *idiom* on schedule; exactly as predicted. ♦ *Your estimate of the cost was right on target.* ♦ *My prediction was not on target.* **7. sitting target** *idiom* someone or something in a position that is easily attacked. ♦ *The old man was a sitting target for the burglars. He lived alone and did not have a telephone.* ♦ *People recently hired will be sitting targets if the firm needs to reduce staff.*

tariff ['tɛr ɪf] **1.** *n.* a tax that a government charges on products entering or leaving a country. ♦ *The government imposed a tariff on all imported goods.* ♦ *The neighboring countries have tariffs on each other's goods.* **2.** *n.* the cost of a service, such as a utility. ♦ *The telephone company published its tariffs in the telephone book.* ♦ *The residents protested the increased tariff on electricity.*

Tarmac™ ['tɑr mæk] **1.** *n.* a paving material made of crushed rock and tar; black top. (No plural form in this sense.) ♦ *The airport runway was paved with Tarmac.* ♦ *The playground was covered with Tarmac.* **2. tarmac** *n.* an area paved with ①, especially at an airport. ♦ *The small plane approached the tarmac for a takeoff.* ♦ *Emergency vehicles sped toward the tarmac after the plane crashed.*

tarnish ['tɑr nɪʃ] **1.** *n.* a coating found especially on metals that makes them less shiny. ♦ *The antique silver bowl was covered with tarnish.* ♦ *Special chemicals were used to remove the tarnish from the brass.* **2.** *iv.* to acquire ①. ♦ *Silver and brass tarnish if not cleaned often.* ♦ *I wrapped the silver in cloth so it wouldn't tarnish.* **3.** *tv.* to dull the shiny metal surface of something. ♦ *Exposure to the open air tarnished the silver bowl.* ♦ *The elements tarnished the brass doorknob.* **4.** *tv.* to taint or spoil something. (Figurative on ③.) ♦ *The accident tarnished John's driving record.* ♦ *The ice skater tarnished her performance when she fell down.*

tarpaulin AND **tarp** ['tɑr pə lɪn, 'tɑrp] *n.* a heavy sheet of waterproof cloth, used to cover objects to protect them. ♦ *The campers made a tent from a tarp.* ♦ *The painter draped a tarpaulin over the furniture.*

tart ['tɑrt] **1.** *adj.* having a sharp, sour, or acidic taste. (Adv: *tartly.* Comp: *tarter;* sup: *tartest.*) ♦ *The tart cherries made an excellent pie.* ♦ *Mary grimaced as she bit a slice of the tart lemon.* **2.** *n.* a small pie, often made with fruit and usually having no top crust. ♦ *Tarts were served for dessert at the party.* ♦ *The baker filled the tarts with custard and fruit.*

tartan ['tɑrt n] *n.* a Scottish wool cloth made of colored stripes woven in a plaid pattern, especially the specific design belonging to a Scottish clan. ♦ *The dress was made of a beautiful tartan.* ♦ *Each clan is said to have a distinctive tartan.*

tartar ['tɑr tɚ] *n.* a hard substance that forms on teeth. (See also calculus. No plural form in this sense.) ♦ *The dentist removed the tartar from my teeth.* ♦ *This toothpaste supposedly reduces the accumulation of tartar.*

tartar sauce ['tɑr tɚ sɔs] *n.* a sauce made from mayonnaise and flavorings, eaten especially with seafood. ♦ *The fish sandwich is served with tartar sauce.* ♦ *Jane dipped the fried clam into the tartar sauce.*

task ['tæsk] *n.* a duty; an errand; a responsibility; a chore; an item of work that someone must do, especially a difficult one. ♦ *Mary checked each task off her list as she completed it.* ♦ *Mother gave Jimmy the task of vacuuming the house.*

task force ['tæsk fors] *n.* a group of people who are assigned a certain task, such as a military group that has a certain mission. ♦ *A task force was formed to design a strategy for the company.* ♦ *The report on poverty was submitted by the government task force.*

tassel ['tæs əl] **1.** *n.* a group of thin strings or cords, joined together at one end, used as a decoration, such as found on drapery. ♦ *John kept the tassel from his graduation cap as a souvenir.* ♦ *The curtains had long silken tassels.* **2.** *n.* the thin, silky strands at the top of a cornstalk. ♦ *Each corn stalk is topped with a tassel.* ♦ *The tassels in the cornfield blew in the wind.*

taste ['test] **1.** *n.* the ability to perceive sweetness, saltiness, bitterness, or sourness with one's tongue. (No plural form in this sense.) ♦ *Taste is one of the five senses.* ♦ *Mary's allergies affect her sense of taste.* **2.** *n.* a particular flavor as experienced through ①. ♦ *This candy has the distinctive taste of licorice.* ♦ *The boy tried to describe the taste of an orange.* **3.** *n.* a small sample of food or drink. ♦ *I took a taste of everything at the buffet table.* ♦ *Mary asked for a taste of Bill's hamburger.* **4.** *n.* the quality of one's choice or selection in beauty, fashion, or art; the ability to judge what is suitable or fitting. (No plural form in this sense.) ♦ *Mary's good taste is reflected in her clothes.* ♦ *Grandma's taste in furniture is impeccable.* **5.** *tv.* to perceive flavor with one's tongue. ♦ *Mary could taste the sugar in the cookies.* ♦ *John tasted the salt on the potato chips.* **6.** *tv.* to put something in one's mouth or on one's tongue so that one can know its flavor; to eat a very small amount of something so one can know its flavor. ♦ *Jimmy refused to even taste the vegetables.* ♦ *I tasted a small piece of pie before taking a whole slice.* **7.** *tv.* to experience something for a short while. ♦ *I tasted danger when I went skydiving.* ♦ *My family tasted the good life on the luxurious vacation.* **8.** *iv.* [for a food] to have a particular flavor. ♦ *This soup tastes too salty.* ♦ *A tangerine tastes a little like an orange.* **9. a taste of something** *idiom* an experience; an example. ♦ *Bill gave Sue a taste of her own rudeness.* ♦ *My friend used a parachute and got a taste of what it's like to be a bird.* **10. have a taste for something** *idiom* a desire for a particular food, drink, or experience. ♦ *The Smiths have a taste for adventure and take exotic vacations.* ♦ *When she was pregnant, Mary often had a taste for pickles.* **11. leave a bad taste in someone's mouth** *idiom* [for something] to leave a bad feeling or memory with someone. ♦ *The whole business about the missing money left a bad taste in his mouth.* ♦ *It was a very nice party, but something about it left a bad taste in my mouth.*

tasteful ['test fʊl] *adj.* aesthetically appealing; showing good taste ④. (Adv: *tastefully.*) ♦ *The elegant room was decorated in a tasteful way.* ♦ *I hope you can make a tasteful choice when deciding what to wear to the party.*

tasteless ['test ləs] **1.** *adj.* having no taste ②; having no flavor; bland. (Adv: *tastelessly.*) ♦ *Nobody liked the* *tasteless dinner.* ♦ *Mary added salt and pepper to the tasteless soup.* **2.** *adj.* showing poor taste ④; offensive; rude; vulgar. (Adv: *tastelessly.*) ♦ *Max always wears the most tasteless clothes!* ♦ *Mary regretted the tasteless comment the moment she said it.*

tasty ['test i] *adj.* full of flavor; delicious. (Adv: *tastily.* Comp: *tastier;* sup: *tastiest.*) ♦ *After eating one helping of the tasty stew, I asked for seconds.* ♦ *Anne's homemade cookies are always tasty.*

tatter ['tæt ɚ] **1.** *tv.* to tear a piece of cloth; to fray something. ♦ *The wind tattered the flag.* ♦ *The sharp edge of my desk tattered my skirt.* **2. in tatters** *phr.* in torn pieces of cloth. ♦ *The poor man's clothes hung in tatters.* ♦ *The flag was in tatters after the storm.*

tattered ['tæt ɚd] *adj.* frayed; torn, especially because something is old or used often. (Adv: *tatteredly.*) ♦ *The homeless man's tattered clothes were all he owned.* ♦ *Susan threw out the tattered towel.*

tattle ['tæt əl] **1.** *iv.* to tell someone about something bad that someone else has done, especially to get someone into trouble by telling people in authority what that person did. ♦ *Jimmy is always tattling.* ♦ *If you hit me again, I'll tattle to Mommy.* **2. tattle on** *iv.* + *prep. phr.* to report on someone; to report the bad things that someone has done. ♦ *Don't do that or I will tattle on you.* ♦ *Please don't tattle on me, Jimmy.*

tattletale ['tæt l tel] *n.* someone who tattles. ♦ *Jimmy's older sister told him not to be a tattletale.* ♦ *The tattletale ran to the teacher to tell what Mary had done.*

tattoo [tæ 'tu] **1.** *n.* a permanent design etched onto skin by pricking the skin with a needle and coloring it. (Pl in *-s.*) ♦ *The sailor had three tattoos on his chest.* ♦ *The biker had a tattoo of a snake on his shoulder.* **2.** *n.* a repeated knocking; a drumming. (Pl in *-s.*) ♦ *The tattoo of the rain against the window was annoying.* ♦ *The explorer heard the distant tattoo of tribal drums.* **3.** *tv.* to put ① on someone. ♦ *The artist tattooed Mary's back.* ♦ *John's thigh has been tattooed with a skull.* **4. tattoo on** *tv.* + *prep. phr.* to create ① on someone or something. ♦ *The artist tattooed a unicorn on my arm.* ♦ *A rose was tattooed on Anne's shoulder.*

taught ['tɔt] pt/pp of teach.

taunt ['tɔnt] **1.** *tv.* to tease someone; to make fun of someone; to goad someone; to ridicule someone; to provoke someone by saying something unkind. ♦ *The children cruelly taunted Jane by calling her names.* ♦ *Mary's brother taunted her mercilessly until she hit him.* **2.** *n.* an unkind remark that is made to tease or ridicule someone. ♦ *The cruel taunts from her classmates made the young girl cry.* ♦ *I was furious with John for directing taunts at me.*

taut ['tɔt] **1.** *adj.* pulled tight; having no slack; stretched. (Adv: *tautly.* Comp: *tauter;* sup: *tautest.*) ♦ *The sailor adjusted the sail until it was taut.* ♦ *We were afraid that the taut rope would break.* **2. pull something taut** *phr.* to make something become ① by stretching it. ♦ *The maid pulled the bedclothes taut.* ♦ *The electrician pulled the wire taut.*

tavern ['tæv ɚn] *n.* a bar; a place where alcohol is sold and drunk. ♦ *The townsfolk gather at the old tavern on Fridays.* ♦ *Mary and Sue went to the local tavern and ordered beer.*

tawdry ['tɔ dri] *adj.* cheap and gaudy; tacky; lacking quality. (Adv: *tawdrily.* Comp: *tawdrier;* sup: *tawdriest.*) ♦ *The actress was criticized for her tawdry clothes.* ♦ *The inexpensive motel room was quite tawdry.*

tax ['tæks] **1.** *n.* money charged by a government to pay for the cost of the government and its services. ♦ *The mayor proposed a higher tax on gasoline prices.* ♦ *The taxes you pay provide police and fire protection.* **2.** See sales tax. **3.** *tv.* to make someone pay ①; to levy ① on someone. ♦ *The border guards taxed the tourists.* ♦ *The government taxes its citizens at a flat rate.* **4.** *tv.* to charge ① on something; to burden something with ①. ♦ *The government taxed the citizens' incomes.* ♦ *The state taxes all money won at the casino.* **5.** *tv.* to burden someone or something; to place a strain on someone or something. (Figurative on ④.) ♦ *Insurance costs taxed the company's profits.* ♦ *The screaming children taxed the teacher's patience.*

taxable ['tæks ə bəl] *adj.* subject to a tax; eligible to be taxed. (Adv: *taxably.*) ♦ *The accountant determined my taxable income.* ♦ *I declared my taxable goods to the customs agent.*

taxation [tæk 'se ʃən] *n.* placing taxes on goods or transactions; collecting taxes. (No plural form in this sense.) ♦ *The colonists protested taxation without representation.* ♦ *The city resorted to taxation to pay for the stadium's construction.*

taxi ['tæk si] **1.** *n.* a taxicab. ♦ *Max took a taxi to the airport.* ♦ *Bill drives a taxi to make extra money.* **2.** *iv.* [for an airplane] to move on the ground. ♦ *The plane taxied to the runway before takeoff.* ♦ *After an hour's wait on the runway, the plane began to taxi.*

taxicab ['tæk si kæb] *n.* a car that, along with its driver, can be hired for short trips; a cab; a taxi. ♦ *Mary hailed a taxicab from her office building.* ♦ *The taxicab pulled over to the curb to pick up the passengers.*

taxidermist ['tæk sə dɚ məst] *n.* someone who practices taxidermy. ♦ *The hunter took his kill to the taxidermist to be stuffed.* ♦ *The taxidermist preserved the fish that Mary caught.*

taxidermy ['tæk sə dɚ mi] *n.* the craft of restoring the skins of dead animals to a realistic and lifelike state. (No plural form in this sense.) ♦ *The hunter was skilled in taxidermy and knew how to preserve the animals he killed.* ♦ *Workers trained in taxidermy posed the stuffed animals in the museum displays.*

taxing ['tæk sɪŋ] *adj.* burdened; strained. (Adv: *taxingly.*) ♦ *Mr. Jones had a taxing day at the office.* ♦ *Taking care of a sick relative is a taxing job.*

taxpayer ['tæks pe ɚ] *n.* someone who pays a tax. ♦ *The taxpayers demanded less spending by the government.* ♦ *Many taxpayers were fined for filing their tax returns late.*

tax return ['tæks rɪ tɚn] *n.* a form, filled out by a taxpayer, showing the amount of tax that is owed. ♦ *I sent my tax return and supporting documents to my accountant.* ♦ *Mary filed her tax return on time this year.*

T.B. See tuberculosis.

tea ['ti] **1.** *n.* a bush grown in Asia, whose leaves are dried and soaked in boiling water; the leaves of this bush. (No plural form in this sense.) ♦ *The region's economy was dependent on the production of tea.* ♦ *A local factory dried and processed tea.* **2.** *n.* a drink made from ①. ♦ *Many* *millions of people drink tea every day.* ♦ *Mary served tea and cookies to her guests.* **3.** *n.* a drink, like ②, made by soaking dried herbs or plants in boiling water. ♦ *The waitress brought me a glass of herbal tea.* ♦ *I drank some peppermint tea after dinner.* **4. not one's cup of tea** *idiom* not something one prefers. ♦ *Playing cards isn't her cup of tea.* ♦ *Sorry, that's not my cup of tea.*

teach ['titʃ] **1.** *tv., irreg.* to provide instruction in a particular subject. (Pt/pp: taught.) ♦ *The math teacher taught algebra in five classes each day.* ♦ *The Smiths taught swimming to their children.* **2.** *tv., irreg.* to instruct someone about something. ♦ *I hope Grandpa will teach me to play chess.* ♦ *My teacher taught me well.* **3.** *iv., irreg.* to work as a teacher. ♦ *After teaching for years, Jane was promoted to principal.* ♦ *It takes a lot of patience to teach.* **4. teach one's grandmother to suck eggs** *idiom* to try to tell or show someone more knowledgeable or experienced than oneself how to do something. ♦ *Don't suggest showing Mary how to knit. It will be teaching your grandmother to suck eggs. She's an expert.* ♦ *Don't teach your grandmother to suck eggs. Bob has been playing tennis for years.*

teacher ['titʃ ɚ] *n.* someone who teaches people something; someone who instructs people in some subject. ♦ *The teacher gave a lecture on modern literature.* ♦ *Mary asked her teacher for extra help.*

teaching ['titʃ ɪŋ] **1.** *n., irreg.* the job of a teacher; the practice or profession of supervising the education of someone. (No plural form in this sense.) ♦ *Teaching requires much patience.* ♦ *This college trains students who are interested in teaching.* **2. teachings** *n.* something that is taught; a philosophy. ♦ *The teachings of Buddha have endured for many years.* ♦ *Some of the major religions of the world share some of the same teachings.*

teacup ['ti kəp] *n.* a cup in which tea is served. ♦ *Mary's set of dishes includes teacups and saucers.* ♦ *Tea spilled from the teacup onto the saucer.*

teak ['tik] **1.** *n.* a large, tropical tree with dark, hard wood. (No plural form in this sense.) ♦ *The forest of teak was harvested for its lumber.* ♦ *Stately teaks lined the road to the banana plantation.* **2.** *n.* the wood from ①. ♦ *Our dining room table is made of teak.* ♦ *The lobby floors were laid with teak.* **3.** *adj.* made of ②. ♦ *John coated his teak desk with varnish.* ♦ *The expensive suite was decorated with teak paneling.*

teakettle ['ti kɛt əl] *n.* a kettle that is used for boiling water to make tea. ♦ *When the water is boiling, the teakettle will whistle.* ♦ *Mary put the copper teakettle on the stove.*

teal ['til] **1.** *n.* a dark, turquoise-blue color. (No plural form in this sense.) ♦ *The office was redecorated in ivory and teal.* ♦ *Teal is a popular color for clothing at the moment.* **2.** *adj.* dark turquoise-blue. ♦ *The teal dress looked stunning on Jane.* ♦ *The teal sea sparkled in the sun.*

team ['tim] **1.** *n.* a group of players who form one side in a game or sport. ♦ *A basketball team has many players, but only five play at once.* ♦ *The coach spoke to the team in the locker room before the game.* **2.** *n.* a group of people who work together. ♦ *Mary manages the team responsible for marketing.* ♦ *The construction team built the house in record time.* **3.** *n.* two or more animals that work together to pull a vehicle or farming equipment. ♦ *The farmer led his team to the field to begin plowing.* ♦ *A team of mules pulled the prospector's supplies.*

teammate ['tim met] *n.* a member of a team that one is a part of; another person on one's team. ♦ *One of my teammates was injured during the football game.* ♦ *The teammates supported each other in success and failure.*

teamwork ['tim wɚk] *n.* the action of working together as a team. (No plural form in this sense.) ♦ *With teamwork, we can finish this project tonight.* ♦ *Our side won the football game due to excellent teamwork.*

teapot ['ti pɑt] *n.* a container with a handle and a spout that is used to hold and pour tea. ♦ *David put several tea bags into the teapot.* ♦ *Mary poured each of us some tea from her new teapot.*

tear 1. ['tɪr] *n.* a drop of liquid that falls from one's eye when one cries. ♦ *Tears streamed down the lost child's face.* ♦ *Mary wiped the tears from her eyes during the sad movie.* **2.** ['tɛr] *n.* a rip; a place in a piece of cloth or paper that is ripped. ♦ *Bill noticed a small tear in his coat.* ♦ *Mary taped the tear in the page.* **3.** ['tɛr] *tv., irreg.* to make a hole or a rip in something, especially by pulling it; to pull something into pieces. (Pt: tore; pp: torn.) ♦ *Bill angrily tore the letter into tiny shreds.* ♦ *Mary took her skirt to the tailor because she had torn it.* **4. tear apart** ['tɛr…] *tv., irreg.* + *adv.* to cause people to disagree or split apart. ♦ *War tore the nation apart.* ♦ *The bitter divorce tore the family apart.* **5.** ['tɛr] *iv., irreg.* to be ripped apart. ♦ *The dress tore at the seams when I pulled on it.* ♦ *The paper tore when I grabbed it from David.* **6.** ['tɛr] *iv., irreg.* to move somewhere very quickly. ♦ *The rabid dog tore around the backyard.* ♦ *The sports car tore down the street and through the intersection.* **7.** ['tɪr] *iv., irreg.* to cry; to begin to cry; to have tears form in one's eyes. (Pt/pp: *teared.*) ♦ *The cold wind made my eyes tear.* ♦ *The toddler's eyes began to tear, and he let out a wail.* **8. torn between something and something else** *idiom* troubled by a choice or dilemma. ♦ *Jane was torn by the choice she faced.* ♦ *We were torn between telling our boss the bad news and keeping it a secret.*

teardrop ['tɪr drɑp] *n.* one tear; one drop of liquid that falls from one's eye. ♦ *Teardrops dripped down Mary's sad face.* ♦ *Mother brushed Jimmy's teardrops away.*

tearful ['tɪr fʊl] **1.** *adj.* [of or with eyes] full of tears; likely to cry; crying. (Adv: *tearfully.*) ♦ *The young couple said a tearful good-bye.* ♦ *The mourners at the funeral were tearful and sad.* **2.** *adj.* causing tears. (Adv: *tearfully.*) ♦ *The movie's tearful ending made me cry.* ♦ *The widow wept uncontrollably at the tearful memorial service.*

tease ['tiz] **1.** *tv.* to taunt someone; to make fun of someone. ♦ *Jimmy teased the dog with a bone, but didn't give it to him.* ♦ *Jane is always teasing Bill about his poor grades.* **2.** *tv.* to flirt with someone, especially with sexual hints. ♦ *Mary teased Bill for weeks and then started dating Tom.* ♦ *Sally teased John to get him interested, but then refused to go out with him.* **3.** *tv.* to separate strands of hair; to comb strands of hair apart. ♦ *The hairdresser teased the woman's hair.* ♦ *Mary teased her hair before going to the party.* **4.** *iv.* to taunt [someone or something]; to annoy on purpose. ♦ *Stop teasing!* ♦ *Bill didn't stop teasing until Mary cried.* **5.** *n.* someone who teases ②. ♦ *The tease winked at all the men at the party.* ♦ *My dance partner was a tease, so I left the party alone.*

teaser ['tiz ɚ] *n.* a puzzling problem; a question that is hard to solve. ♦ *The newspaper prints teasers one day and* *answers on the next day.* ♦ *The last algebra problem on the test was a real teaser.*

teaspoon ['ti spun] **1.** *n.* a small spoon, used especially for stirring tea or coffee; a spoon that holds ⅓ of a tablespoon. ♦ *Mary stirred her coffee with a teaspoon.* ♦ *The silver teaspoons are missing from the kitchen.* **2.** *n.* a teaspoonful. ♦ *There is a teaspoon of cinnamon in the gingerbread.* ♦ *The chef included a teaspoon of vinegar in the salad dressing.*

teaspoonful ['ti spun fʊl] *n.* the contents of a teaspoon. ♦ *No one could taste the teaspoonful of salt I put in the soup.* ♦ *Mary put a teaspoonful of sugar in her coffee.*

technical ['tɛk nɪ kəl] **1.** *adj.* of or about industrial or mechanical sciences. (Adv: *technically* [...ɪk li].) ♦ *John went to a two-year technical college to study engine repair.* ♦ *Anne studied engineering at the technical institute.* **2.** *adj.* of or about a particular subject; particular to a subject; belonging to the specialized knowledge of a subject. (Adv: *technically* [...ɪk li].) ♦ *Programming a computer is too technical for me.* ♦ *Repairing your television requires technical skills.* **3.** *adj.* using a strict, legal definition. (Adv: *technically* [...ɪk li].) ♦ *If you want to get technical about this, I will have to consult a lawyer.* ♦ *The technical terms of my work contract state that I get paid breaks.*

technicality [tɛk nɪ 'kæl ə ti] *n.* a detail, especially one that is expressed because of a strict, legal interpretation of a regulation. ♦ *The defendant was acquitted because of a legal technicality.* ♦ *Due to a technicality, the border guard refused my passport.*

technically ['tɛk nɪk li] according to rules or details; interpreting the rules strictly. ♦ *Technically, no one can enter the building after 5:00 P.M.* ♦ *Technically, that's not my job, but I'll help you anyway.*

technician [tɛk 'nɪ ʃən] **1.** *n.* someone who works in the field of industrial or mechanical sciences. ♦ *The technician checked the wiring beneath the dashboard.* ♦ *The technicians tested the elevator after it was installed.* **2.** *n.* someone who works in a laboratory, performing tests. ♦ *The technician tested the water for lead.* ♦ *The lab technician drew my blood.*

technique [tɛk 'nik] **1.** *n.* a special method of doing something. ♦ *The carpenter demonstrated the proper techniques for installing the window.* ♦ *John explained his technique for frying shrimp.* **2.** *n.* the skill involved in creating or performing art; the way that art is performed, displayed, or exhibited—showing the artist's skill. (No plural form in this sense.) ♦ *Bill plays tennis well, even though his technique is sloppy.* ♦ *The young violinist practiced her technique for hours every day.*

technological [tɛk nə 'lɑdʒ ɪ kəl] *adj.* of or about technology. (Adv: *technologically* [...ɪk li].) ♦ *Building a rocket requires many technological skills.* ♦ *Construction of this bridge is an amazing technological feat.*

technology [tɛk 'nɑl ə dʒi] **1.** *n.* the science and study of mechanical and industrial sciences. (No plural form in this sense.) ♦ *The engineers had all graduated from famous institutes of technology.* ♦ *John wants to attend a college that teaches technology.* **2.** *n.* the practical applications of mechanical and industrial sciences. ♦ *These frying pans were made to last, using the latest technology.* ♦ *The spaceship was built using very advanced technologies.*

tedious ['tid i əs] *adj.* boring; dull; not exciting; not stimulating. (Adv: *tediously.*) ♦ *John's job at the factory is very tedious.* ♦ *The tedious lecture went on endlessly.*

tedium ['tid i əm] *n., irreg.* the quality of being tedious; a lack of excitement. (No plural form in this sense.) ♦ *The tedium of the lecture made me fall asleep.* ♦ *Vacations relieve the tedium of work.*

teen ['tin] **1. teens** *n.* teenagers. ♦ *This magazine is written for teens.* ♦ *The teens congregated at the park after school.* **2. teens** *n.* the numbers 13–19 or 10–19. (When referring to age, it refers to the period of someone's life from the age of 13 through the age of 19.) ♦ *Tonight, the temperature will be in the teens, so dress warmly.* ♦ *Even though Anne was in her teens, she worked 40 hours a week.* **3.** *adj.* <the adj. use of ①.> ♦ *The rock star was a teen idol.* ♦ *Mary bought the teen magazine for her daughter.*

teenage ['tin edʒ] *adj.* of, for, or about teenagers; of the ages from 13 through 19. ♦ *Our church sponsors a teenage dance once a month.* ♦ *These advertisements are aimed at teenage shoppers.*

teenaged ['tin edʒd] *adj.* of the ages from 13 through 19. ♦ *The teenaged driver raced through the streets.* ♦ *The teenaged criminal was sent to jail.*

teenager ['tin edʒ ɚ] *n.* someone whose age is between 13 and 19. ♦ *Bill and Mary have two teenagers, aged 15 and 19.* ♦ *Those teenagers attend the local high school.*

teeny ['ti ni] *adj.* very small; tiny; very little. (Informal. Comp: *teenier;* sup: *teeniest.*) ♦ *The cat had three teeny kittens.* ♦ *I'd like a teeny bit of cake, please.*

teeter ['tit ɚ] *iv.* to sway back and forth; to move back and forth unsteadily. ♦ *The glass teetered on the edge of the counter before it fell.* ♦ *The hiker teetered on the edge of the path but didn't fall.*

teeth ['tiθ] pl of tooth.

teethe ['tið] *iv.* [for a child] to begin growing the first set of teeth. ♦ *The cranky toddler was teething.* ♦ *Our baby became irritable when he began to teethe.*

teetotaler ['ti 'tot l ɚ] *n.* someone who does not drink alcohol. ♦ *The teetotaler refused the wine I had offered him.* ♦ *Mary—a teetotaler—encouraged her friends to stop drinking booze.*

telecast ['tɛl ə kæst] **1.** *n.* a television show; the broadcasting of a television show. ♦ *The telecast of the opera was live.* ♦ *The news telecasts on all the channels were almost the same.* **2.** *tv., irreg.* to broadcast a television show. (Pt: *telecast.*) ♦ *The concert was telecast on last Wednesday.* ♦ *The network telecast the news from its studio in New York.*

telegram ['tɛl ə græm] *n.* a message sent by telegraph. ♦ *Grandma sent us a telegram announcing her arrival time.* ♦ *During the war, telegrams usually meant bad news.*

telegraph ['tɛl ə græf] **1.** *n.* a machine that sends messages in electrical code over electrical wires. ♦ *The widespread use of telephones replaced the telegraph.* ♦ *Telegraphs transmitted messages using a special code.* **2.** *tv.* to send a message by using ①. ♦ *I telegraphed a message to my brother, inviting him to the wedding.* ♦ *The reporter telegraphed the latest news to his office.* **3.** *tv.* to send [a message] to someone by ①. ♦ *He has no telephone, so I will telegraph him.* ♦ *We telegraphed all the winners, telling them of their good fortune.*

telepathy [tə 'lɛp ə θi] *n.* the ability to communicate by using one's mind. (No plural form in this sense.) ♦ *The psychic claimed to practice mental telepathy.* ♦ *The medium used telepathy to help the police find the missing body.*

telephone ['tɛl ə fon] **1.** *n.* a device that transmits sound by converting it into electrical signals; a phone. ♦ *Mary called Jane on the telephone to invite her for dinner.* ♦ *The telephone rang just as we were leaving the house.* **2. telephone call** *n.* a message or conversation using ①. (Also call, phone call.) ♦ *There was a telephone call for you earlier today.* ♦ *Is there somewhere here where I can make a telephone call?* **3.** *tv.* to call someone by using ①. ♦ *I'll telephone the store to see what time it closes.* ♦ *Please telephone me before you come over.* **4.** *tv.* to transmit a message [to someone] by using ①. ♦ *Please telephone me the good news when it happens.* ♦ *John telephoned that he would be late.* **5.** *iv.* to make a call with ①. ♦ *Telephone anytime you like.* ♦ *Someone always telephones when I'm taking a shower.*

telescope ['tɛl ə skop] **1.** *n.* a device that magnifies distant objects, especially objects that are in the sky, so that one can see them better. ♦ *The sailor scanned the horizon with the telescope.* ♦ *Through the telescope, I could see the mountains on the moon.* **2.** *iv.* to become shorter or longer by having one part slide over another. ♦ *The umbrella conveniently telescopes into a small tube.* ♦ *The three-foot walking cane telescoped into a foot-long rod.* **3.** *tv.* to make something shorter or longer by sliding one part of it over another. ♦ *The lecturer telescoped her pointer at the end of the lecture.* ♦ *I telescoped my fishing rod so it would fit in my trunk.*

telethon ['tɛl ə θɑn] *n.* a television show, usually lasting for several hours, that raises money for a charity. (Based on marathon.) ♦ *The telethon raised a million dollars for charity.* ♦ *During the telethon, regular programming was canceled.*

televise ['tɛl ə vɑɪz] *tv.* to broadcast something by television; to transmit a television broadcast signal; to show a program on television. ♦ *The network televised the president's speech.* ♦ *The football game will be televised after the news.*

television ['tel ə vɪ ʒən] **1.** *n.* the radio transmission of moving pictures with sound. (No plural form in this sense. Abbreviated *TV.*) ♦ *Thousands of programs have been broadcast by television.* ♦ *The science of television was developed in the 20th century.* **2. television (set)** *n.* an electronic device that receives ①. (Abbreviated *TV (set).*) ♦ *John watched the television in the kitchen as he made lunch.* ♦ *Jane turned off the television set because nothing good was on.* **3.** *n.* the business of producing programs for ①. (No plural form in this sense.) ♦ *The stage actor went into television in order to make more money.* ♦ *The playwright adapted his script for television.*

tell ['tɛl] **1.** *tv., irreg.* to express something in words. (Pt/pp: told.) ♦ *The student told a story about his vacation to the class.* ♦ *John told the truth.* **2.** *tv., irreg.* to inform someone [of something]. ♦ *I will tell you again.* ♦ *No one told me. I figured it out myself.* **3.** *tv.* to signal information [to someone]. ♦ *The clock told the time every hour.* ♦ *My watch tells the date and the time.* **4. tell about** *tv., irreg.* + *prep. phr.* to give someone information about someone or something. ♦ *Mary told Jane about the sale.* ♦ *Please tell me about what happened yesterday.* **5. tell to** *tv., irreg.* + *inf.* to order someone to do something. ♦ *Mother told Jimmy to go wash up.* ♦ *The army was told to attack.* **6.** *tv., irreg.* to know someone or something; to recognize someone or something. (Usually with can or able.) ♦ *I can't tell one brother from the other.* ♦ *John is always able to tell when I am unhappy.* **7.** *tv., irreg.* to reveal a secret. ♦ *You can confide in me; I'll never tell your secrets.* ♦ *Who told my secret?* **8.** *iv., irreg.* to reveal [a secret]. ♦ *I have a secret. Promise you won't tell.* ♦ *After you promised, I can't believe that you told!* **9.** *iv., irreg.* to tattle; to try to get someone in trouble by saying to someone in authority what that person did. ♦ *If you do it, I'll tell!* ♦ *I'm telling on you!* **10. a little bird told me** *idiom* something has been learned from a mysterious or secret source. ♦ *"All right," said Mary, "where did you get that information?" John replied, "A little bird told me."* ♦ *A little bird told me where I might find you.*

teller ['tɛl ɚ] *n.* someone who works at a bank, receiving and giving out money. ♦ *The teller processed my deposit of $50.* ♦ *The robber asked the teller for all the money in her drawer.*

telling ['tɛl ɪŋ] *adj.* having an effect; effective. (Adv: *tellingly.*) ♦ *John's telling remark indicates that he doesn't like me.* ♦ *The telling blow knocked David unconscious.*

temerity [tɪ 'mɛr ə ti] *n.* boldness; recklessness. (No plural form in this sense.) ♦ *Coming to a party without an invitation takes a lot of temerity.* ♦ *The employee's temerity got him fired.*

temper ['tɛm pɚ] **1.** *n.* mood; the condition of one's mind, especially in regard to anger. (No plural form in this sense.) ♦ *My boss was in a good temper all day today.* ♦ *One never knows what kind of temper Max is in.* **2.** *n.* an angry mood; the potential of being angry. (No plural form in this sense.) ♦ *Hank's temper was evident during the meeting.* ♦ *In a fit of temper, Jane threw the vase at the wall.* **3. temper tantrum** *n.* a burst of anger; an irrational or childish display of temper. ♦ *John's temper tantrum embarrassed us all.* ♦ *Jimmy had a temper tantrum because he was tired.* **4.** *tv.* to treat metal with heat to cause it to become harder or stronger. ♦ *The worker tempered the metal in a furnace.* ♦ *These pots and pans have all been tempered.* **5.** *tv.* to soften something; to mitigate something; to make something more moderate. ♦ *Mike's failings were tempered by his good intentions.* ♦ *Anne's harsh words were tempered with a kind smile.* **6. lose one's temper** *idiom* to become angry. ♦ *Please don't lose your temper. It's not good for you.* ♦ *I'm sorry that I lost my temper.*

temperament ['tɛm pɚ mənt] **1.** *n.* a person's mood; the way a person is or acts. ♦ *My grandmother has a fiery temperament.* ♦ *The nurse had a pleasant temperament.* **2.** *n.* the adjustment of musical pitches on a keyboard instrument by making slight changes in the pitch of the individual notes. ♦ *The amateur organ tuner ruined the temperament, and it had to be set again by a professional.* ♦ *The temperament of our piano was done by an experienced tuner.*

temperamental [tɛm pɚ 'mɛn təl] **1.** *adj.* easily angered or upset; moody; likely to change one's mood. (Adv: *temperamentally.*) ♦ *Mary tried not to be so temperamental around her parents.* ♦ *The temperamental customer* *screamed at the cashier.* **2.** *adj.* not dependable; likely to break or malfunction. (Figurative on ①. Adv: *temperamentally.*) ♦ *The dishwasher is temperamental and sometimes won't work.* ♦ *Since my car is temperamental, I've started taking the train to work.*

temperance ['tɛm pɚ əns] *n.* the practice of drinking no alcohol; abstinence. (No plural form in this sense.) ♦ *The nondrinkers urged temperance among the population.* ♦ *The movement for temperance resulted in making alcohol illegal.*

temperate ['tɛm pɚ ɪt] **1. temperate climate** *n.* a climate that is not hot and not cold; a moderate climate. ♦ *I want to retire to a place with a temperate climate.* ♦ *California has a temperate climate.* **2.** *adj.* controlled; moderate. (Adv: *temperately.*) ♦ *Your temperate response to the problem is most welcome.* ♦ *A temperate answer to a rude question is difficult to give.*

temperature ['tɛm pɚ ə tʃɚ] **1.** *n.* the degree of how cold or hot something is. ♦ *The temperature of the lake is too cold for swimming.* ♦ *What is the temperature outside?* **2.** *n.* the degree of the heat of one's blood, especially when it is above average; a fever. ♦ *John has a temperature. His fever is quite high.* ♦ *The sick child had a high temperature.*

tempered ['tɛm pɚd] *adj.* strengthened; hardened; treated so that a metal is strong and hard. ♦ *These tools are made from tempered steel.* ♦ *The factory produced all kinds of tempered metals.*

tempest ['tɛmp əst] **1.** *n.* a violent storm. ♦ *The boat was tossed about in the tempest.* ♦ *A late summer tempest racked the Florida coast.* **2. tempest in a teacup; tempest in a teapot** *idiom* an argument or disagreement over a very minor matter. ♦ *The entire issue of who was to present the report was just a tempest in a teapot.* ♦ *The argument at the office turned into a tempest in a teacup. No one really cared about the outcome.*

tempestuous [tɛm 'pɛs tʃu əs] *adj.* violent; wild. (Adv: *tempestuously.*) ♦ *The political rally became tempestuous.* ♦ *The tempestuous woman overturned the table.*

tempi ['tɛm pi] a pl of tempo.

template ['tɛm plɪt] *n.* a pattern that is cut out of cardboard, plastic, metal, or wood, and is used to cut the same shape from other material. ♦ *The children used a template to cut out paper snowflakes.* ♦ *I used a cardboard template so that all the figures would be identical.*

temple ['tɛm pəl] **1.** *n.* a building used for worship and ritual. ♦ *The tourist visited the temple of a goddess in Greece.* ♦ *The archaeologist unearthed the foundation of an ancient temple.* **2.** *n.* a synagogue. ♦ *Services are held at the temple on Friday night.* ♦ *We entered the temple early and took seats near the front.* **3.** *n.* the flat part on the side of the head between the eye and the ear and above the cheekbone. ♦ *Bill rubbed his temples to ease his headache.* ♦ *This cap is too tight on me. It hurts my temples.*

tempo [tɛm po] **1.** *n., irreg.* the relative frequency of the beats in musical rhythm. (The English plural is *tempos*, the Italian plural is tempi.) ♦ *This music should be played at a fast tempo.* ♦ *The famous orchestra conductor paid very close attention to the tempi of the music he conducted.* **2.** *n., irreg.* the pace of living or working. (Figurative on ①. Pl: *tempos.*) ♦ *We work at a very fast tempo in the sales department.* ♦ *The tempo of life at our house seems to decrease as we grow older.*

temporarily [tɛm pə 'rɛr ə li] *adv.* for the time being; for a little while; for a limited time. ♦ *The telephone lines were temporarily disconnected.* ♦ *I will have to take the bus temporarily until my car is fixed.*

temporary ['tɛm pə rɛr i] *adj.* for a limited time; not permanent. (Adv: *temporarily* [tɛm pə 'rɛr ə li].) ♦ *Bill's lapse of memory was only temporary.* ♦ *The temporary worker was soon replaced by a permanent employee.*

tempt ['tɛmpt] **1. tempt to** *tv.* + *inf.* to try to make someone do something bad or wrong. ♦ *I tried to tempt my coworker to leave work early.* ♦ *The children were tempted to disobey their parents.* **2.** *tv.* to arouse someone's desire. ♦ *The chocolate cake tempted me.* ♦ *The glamorous tease tempted Tom into strange thoughts.*

temptation [tɛmp 'te ʃən] **1.** *n.* someone or something that creates a desire; someone or something that tempts someone or something. (No plural form in this sense.) ♦ *Temptation can lead you into a lot of trouble.* ♦ *Bill had to struggle against the temptation to spend more money than he earned.* **2.** *n.* someone or something that tempts a person. ♦ *Chocolate is a big temptation for me.* ♦ *Bill has willpower and doesn't give in to the temptation to spend too much money.*

tempting ['tɛmp tɪŋ] *adj.* enticing; causing temptation. (Adv: *temptingly.*) ♦ *The restaurant had a tempting dessert tray.* ♦ *Bill made Mary a tempting offer for her car.*

ten ['tɛn] **1.** 10. See four for senses and examples. **2.** *n.* a $10 bill. ♦ *Mary handed Jane a ten.* ♦ *Bill's wallet was full of tens.*

tenable ['tɛn ə bəl] *adj.* able to be defended; defendable. (Adv: *tenably.*) ♦ *The thesis of the lawyer's argument was not the least bit tenable.* ♦ *The teenager's explanation was hardly tenable.*

tenacious [tə 'ne ʃəs] **1.** *adj.* [of a grasp] strong and tight. (Adv: *tenaciously.*) ♦ *Her tenacious grip on the railing kept her from falling.* ♦ *The monkey had a tenacious grasp on the tree.* **2.** *adj.* persistent; unyielding. (Adv: *tenaciously.*) ♦ *The tenacious applicant soon got the job.* ♦ *She was quite tenacious with her money. She would not part with a cent.*

tenacity [tə 'næs ə ti] *n.* persistence; stubbornness. (No plural form in this sense.) ♦ *Getting a job in a big company requires tenacity and talent.* ♦ *Because of Jane's tenacity, she was promoted to manager.*

tenant ['tɛn ənt] *n.* someone who rents a place to live from someone else; a company that rents a space in an office building. ♦ *This apartment building has fifty tenants.* ♦ *The tenants of the office building are mainly small firms.*

tend ['tɛnd] **1.** *tv.* to watch over someone or something; to protect someone or maintain someone. ♦ *The shepherds tended their flocks on the hillside.* ♦ *Jane loves to tend her garden.* **2. tend to** *iv.* + *prep. phr.* to mind someone or something; to take care of someone or something. ♦ *Bill tends to his own business and doesn't interfere with others.* ♦ *Mary must tend to her sick mother.* **3. tend to** *iv.* + *inf.* to be likely to do something; to be inclined to do something. ♦ *Mary tends to call her family on weekends.* ♦ *I tend to sleep late on Sundays.*

tendency ['tɛn dən si] *n.* an inclination to do something or toward something; a likelihood that someone or something will do something naturally. ♦ *My dog has a tendency to growl at strangers.* ♦ *John told me about his tendency to eat when he's depressed.*

tender ['tɛn dɚ] **1.** *adj.* soft; not tough; easy to chew. (Adv: *tenderly.*) ♦ *Marinating meat makes it tender.* ♦ *The tender roast beef was easy to slice.* **2.** *adj.* sore; sore when touched; painful. (Adv: *tenderly.*) ♦ *Bill's injured muscle was tender for several days.* ♦ *Mary flinched as the doctor touched the tender spot in her abdomen.* **3.** *adj.* kind; gentle; showing love or affection. (Adv: *tenderly.*) ♦ *The mother whispered tender words to her crying child.* ♦ *The young lovers were tender towards each other.* **4. (legal) tender** *n.* legal money; money that must be accepted as payment. ♦ *This store accepts all forms of tender except checks.* ♦ *I exchanged the huge check at the bank for a mountain of legal tender.* **5. tender age** *n.* a very young age. ♦ *The girl began to work at the tender age of 12.* ♦ *Bill was orphaned at the tender age of eight.* **6.** *tv.* to offer something formally or legally, such as to offer money in payment of a debt. ♦ *The borrower tendered each payment on time.* ♦ *I tendered my resignation in writing to the company president.*

tenderize ['tɛn də rɑɪz] *tv.* to make meat soft and easier to chew; to make meat tender. ♦ *The chef used a mallet to tenderize the meat.* ♦ *Marinade tenderizes meat.*

tenderness ['tɛn dɚ nəs] **1.** *n.* softness; the extent to which food can be easily chewed. (No plural form in this sense.) ♦ *A marinade would have improved the tenderness of this steak.* ♦ *Because of the steak's tenderness, I could cut it with my fork.* **2.** *n.* soreness; some slight pain. (No plural form in this sense.) ♦ *I went to the dentist because there was tenderness in my gums.* ♦ *My doctor said I'd feel tenderness around the stitches.* **3.** *n.* the state of being tender; kindness; gentleness; love and affection. (No plural form in this sense.) ♦ *The child showed the puppy much tenderness.* ♦ *Mary's heart was filled with tenderness for her elderly mother.*

tendon ['tɛn dən] *n.* a strong cord of body tissue that connects a muscle to a bone. ♦ *The skier tore a tendon in the fall.* ♦ *The football player pulled a tendon in his leg during the game.*

tenement ['tɛn ə mənt] *n.* a large building divided into smaller apartments that are rented to people, especially in poor neighborhoods of a city. ♦ *The overcrowded tenement was condemned by the city.* ♦ *The boy grew up in poverty in a tenement.*

tenet ['tɛn ət] *n.* a principle; a belief; an opinion. ♦ *The children were taught the tenets of their faith.* ♦ *Honesty is a tenet of good business.*

Tennessee [tɛn ə 'si] See Gazetteer.

tennis ['tɛn ɪs] *n.* a sport played by two people or two couples who hit a small ball with rackets from one side of the playing area, over a net, to the other side of the playing area. (No plural form in this sense.) ♦ *John learned to play tennis as soon as he could hold a racket.* ♦ *Bill and Sue play tennis every Saturday.*

tenor ['tɛn ɚ] **1.** *n.* a man having the higher of the two male singing voices. (See also bass.) ♦ *The director cast a tenor as the lead in the musical.* ♦ *A tenor sings higher notes than a bass.* **2. the tenor** *n.* the music written for ①; the musical part written for ①. (Treated as singular.) ♦ *I am a bass, but I can sing the tenor if necessary.* ♦ *The tenor is easy in this piece.* **3.** *n.* the mood or **tone** ② or ④ of an act of communication. ♦ *The tenor of the memo was demanding.* ♦ *The customer didn't like the tenor of the clerk's voice.* **4.** *adj.* <the adj. use of ①.> ♦ *The song's melody is in the tenor part.* ♦ *The tenor section sang louder than the sopranos.*

tense ['tɛns] **1.** *adj.* taut; not loose; not relaxed. (Adv: *tensely.* Comp: *tenser;* sup: *tensest.*) ♦ *The bath relaxed Mary's tense muscles.* ♦ *The strings on the violin became tense as I tuned it.* **2.** *adj.* nervous; not relaxed. (Adv: *tensely.* Comp: *tenser;* sup: *tensest.*) ♦ *Airplane travel makes me tense.* ♦ *The tense man paced up and down the halls.* **3. tense up** *iv.* + *adv.* to become tight; to tighten; to stiffen. ♦ *After the strenuous hike, Mary's muscles tensed up.* ♦ *John tensed up when his boss criticized him.* **4.** *tv.* to tighten something, such as a muscle; to stiffen something; to make something taut. ♦ *The ballet dancer tensed the muscle in her right leg.* ♦ *Bob tensed his jaw muscles and parachuted from the plane.* **5.** *n.* <a state of a verb that indicates the time that the action or state it expresses takes place.> ♦ *This sentence is written in the present tense.* ♦ *In English, verbs in the past tense often end in* -ed.

tension ['tɛn ʃən] **1.** *n.* the degree of tightness of something that is stretched. (No plural form in this sense.) ♦ *The pitch made by plucking a string depends on the string's tension.* ♦ *Because there was too much tension on the cable, it snapped.* **2.** *n.* an anxious or nervous feeling; hidden anxiety and anger. ♦ *Nervous tension gave Bill a headache.* ♦ *The extra work created a lot of tension at the office.*

tent ['tɛnt] *n.* a temporary, movable shelter made of fabric supported by poles and ropes. ♦ *The campers pitched their tent at the foot of the mountain.* ♦ *Bill purchased a waterproof tent for his camping trip.*

tentacle ['tɛn tə kəl] *n.* one of the flexible arms of an octopus or a squid. ♦ *The octopus has eight tentacles.* ♦ *A squid grasped the small creature in its tentacles.*

tentative ['tɛn tə tɪv] *adj.* not definite; not certain; provisional. (Adv: *tentatively.*) ♦ *Sue and Bill made a tentative date for Saturday night.* ♦ *The politician gave a tentative reply to the question.*

tenth ['tɛntθ] 10th. See **fourth** for senses and examples.

tenuous ['tɛn ju əs] **1.** *adj.* thin; not strong; not capable of supporting weight. (Adv: *tenuously.*) ♦ *The precious jewel hung only be a tenuous thread that appeared very fragile.* ♦ *The tiny cord tying the boat to the dock was tenuous and threatened to break at any moment.* **2.** *adj.* weak; without substance. (Figurative on ①. Adv: *tenuously.*) ♦ *The student's tenuous argument was quickly dismissed.* ♦ *The mayor's tenuous control over the city council is well known.*

tenure ['tɛn jɚ] **1.** *n.* the right to retain one's office or job permanently. (No plural form in this sense.) ♦ *The university granted the hardworking professor tenure.* ♦ *After six years of work, Jane earned tenure.* **2.** *n.* the length of time someone holds an office or a job. (No plural form in this sense.) ♦ *Mary's tenure as the club's president lasted eight years.* ♦ *John's tenure as chairman will end next year.*

tepee ['ti pi] *n.* a Native American dwelling, made by placing the ends of poles in a circle on the ground and fastening the tops of the poles together at one point, and then wrapping this frame with animal skins. ♦ *American Indians lived in tepees on the northern plains.* ♦ *Several tepees were erected near the stream.*

tepid ['tɛp ɪd] *adj.* slightly warm; lukewarm. (Adv: *tepidly.*) ♦ *The coffee that was hot fifteen minutes ago is now tepid.* ♦ *Houseplants should be watered with tepid water.*

term ['tɚm] **1.** *n.* the length of time that something lasts; a particular period of time. ♦ *The president's term of office is four years.* ♦ *The chairman served a two-year term.* **2.** *n.* a division of a school year; a quarter or semester. ♦ *Finals are given at the end of the term.* ♦ *Students take new classes each term.* **3.** *n.* an expression used in a particular field; a word. ♦ *The author listed the important terms in a glossary.* ♦ *I looked up the scientific term in the dictionary.* **4. terms** *n.* requirements; details; provisions. ♦ *My lawyer carefully read the terms of my contract.* ♦ *The editor objected to the terms of her employment.* **5. terms** *n.* charges; fee. ♦ *If I hire you, what are your terms?* ♦ *The lawyer's terms were too high, so I looked for another lawyer.* **6. in terms of something** *idiom* relating to something; with regard to something. ♦ *In terms of value to this company, how much do you think you are worth?* ♦ *Is this a good paint job on my car—in terms of the quality, not the color?* **7. on good terms (with someone)** *idiom* friendly with someone; able to interact well and be friends with someone. ♦ *Bill is on good terms with the people he works with.* ♦ *We are not on very good terms and don't speak to each other much.*

terminal ['tɚ mə nəl] **1.** *adj.* happening at the end of something; at the end; last. (Adv: *terminally.*) ♦ *John lost consciousness in the terminal stage of the disease.* ♦ *In the terminal session of the conference, the president concluded her remarks.* **2.** *adj.* resulting in death; causing death; not able to be cured. (Adv: *terminally.*) ♦ *Mary's grandmother suffered from a terminal illness for years.* ♦ *Cancer is not always terminal.* **3.** *n.* a building that passengers enter and leave from, especially at an airport, bus station, or train station. ♦ *The large international airport had several terminals.* ♦ *The taxi took the passenger directly to the terminal.* **4.** *n.* something that makes an electrical connection; the place where current enters or leaves a battery or a circuit. ♦ *I aligned the battery's negative terminal with the positive pole.* ♦ *John cleaned his car battery's terminals with a rag.* **5.** *n.* a computer device consisting of a keyboard and a screen that displays the messages sent to and from a computer. ♦ *The banker's terminal showed information about my account.* ♦ *I waited in the computer lab for the next available terminal.*

terminate ['tɚ mə net] **1.** *tv.* to end something; to cause something to no longer exist. ♦ *The author terminated his contract with the publisher.* ♦ *I terminated my relationship with my brother after he stole money from me.* **2.** *tv.* to fire someone from a job. ♦ *The personnel director terminated the lazy employee.* ♦ *John was terminated for repeated absences at work.* **3.** *iv.* to end; to come to an end; to no longer exist. ♦ *The workers' contract will terminate at midnight.* ♦ *John's insurance coverage terminated when he quit his job.*

termination [tɚ mə 'ne ʃən] **1.** *n.* ending; concluding; finishing; terminating; being terminated. (No plural form in this sense.) ♦ *The termination of the policy was cause for celebration.* ♦ *Did democracy arrive with the termination of communism?* **2.** *n.* an act of ①. ♦ *The company had three voluntary terminations this month.* ♦ *Several government programs were terminated this month, and citizens protested each termination.*

terminology [tɚ mə 'nɑ lə dʒi] *n.* the special words and phrases used in a particular science, profession, or other situation. (No plural form in this sense.) ♦ *The textbook contained a glossary of terminology used in the text.* ♦ *I did not understand the terminology of the computer manual.*

termite ['tɚ mɑɪt] *n.* an insect similar to an ant that eats a substance found in wood, causing great damage to wooden objects and structures. ♦ *Termites have eaten through the back door.* ♦ *The fallen tree was infested with termites.*

terrace ['tɛr əs] **1.** *n.* a flat area connected to or next to the side of a house or apartment; a balcony or patio. ♦ *We enjoyed the pleasant breeze on the terrace.* ♦ *The terrace was surrounded by a tiny hedge.* **2.** *n.* a flat area of land that has been cut into the side of a hill or mountain. ♦ *The mountain villagers farmed on narrow terraces.* ♦ *The state workers cut a terrace into the hill for the new freeway.* **3.** *tv.* to cut the side of a hill or mountain so that there are wide steps of flat areas of land, especially for farming. ♦ *The villagers terraced the hill for farmland.* ♦ *The roadway was terraced on the side of the mountain.*

terra cotta [tɛr ə 'kɑt ə] **1.** *n.* a reddish, baked clay, used especially for pottery and as decoration on the faces of buildings. (No plural form in this sense. It is sometimes glazed to give it different colors.) ♦ *The theater's facade was made of ornate slabs of terra cotta.* ♦ *The terra cotta began to crumble from the old apartment building.* **2. terra-cotta** *adj.* made of ①. ♦ *The garden was full of terra-cotta statues.* ♦ *I saved a piece of the theater's terra-cotta facade when it was demolished.*

terrain [tə 'ren] *n.* the physical features of an area of land. ♦ *The geographical map showed the terrain of the region.* ♦ *The mountainous terrain provided good hiking.*

terrapin ['tɛr ə pən] *n.* a turtle of North America found in fresh or brackish waters. ♦ *We could see a terrapin through the lake's clear water.* ♦ *The terrapin crawled out of the water and across the road.*

terrestrial [tə 'rɛs tri əl] **1.** *adj.* from the planet Earth; living on Earth; of Earth. (Adv: *terrestrially.*) ♦ *Monkeys were among the first terrestrial creatures to travel by rocket ship.* ♦ *The astronauts returned to their terrestrial home.* **2.** *adj.* living or growing on land, as opposed to living in the water, in the air, or in trees. (Adv: *terrestrially.*) ♦ *The eagle preys on small terrestrial creatures.* ♦ *Bats and whales are examples of mammals that aren't terrestrial.*

terrible ['tɛr ə bəl] *adj.* awful; horrible; extremely bad. (Adv: *terribly.*) ♦ *Bill related the tale of his terrible day.* ♦ *Mary had a terrible headache and spent the day in bed.*

terribly ['tɛr ə bli] **1.** *adv.* badly; horribly; awfully. ♦ *The orchestra performed terribly last night.* ♦ *This student writes terribly, so he is taking extra classes to learn to write better.* **2.** *adv.* very; extremely. ♦ *New furniture can be terribly expensive.* ♦ *Bill was terribly hurt by Mary's comment.*

terrier ['tɛr i ɚ] *n.* one of a group of breeds of small dogs, originally bred to be used in hunting. ♦ *Most Boston terriers have black and white fur.* ♦ *The terrier followed the trail of the fox.*

terrific ['tə 'rɪf ɪk] **1.** *adj.* great; wonderful; awesome; super; excellent. (Adv: *terrifically* [...ɪk li].) ♦ *We had a terrific time at the party.* ♦ *Bill is a terrific manager.* **2.** *adj.* extreme[ly bad]. (Adv: *terrifically* [...ɪk li].) ♦ *Losing his job was a terrific blow to Bill.* ♦ *Jane suffered a terrific loss in the stock market.*

terrifically [tə 'rɪf ɪk li] *adv.* wonderfully; awesomely; excellently. ♦ *We had a terrifically wonderful vacation in Mexico.* ♦ *I ate a terrifically delicious pie for dessert.*

terrified ['tɛr ɔɪ fɑɪd] *adj.* scared; frightened. ♦ *The terrified child hid under the bed.* ♦ *The terrified passengers panicked when the plane lost altitude.*

terrify ['tɛr ə fɑɪ] *tv.* to scare someone or something greatly. ♦ *The ghost story terrified the young children.* ♦ *Insects terrify Mary, so she never gardens.*

terrifying ['tɛr ə fɑɪ ɪŋ] *adj.* very scary; frightening; causing fear. (Adv: *terrifyingly.*) ♦ *The man related the terrifying experience to his friend.* ♦ *Nightmares are usually terrifying.*

territory ['tɛr ə tor i] **1.** *n.* an area of land. (No plural form in this sense.) ♦ *All the territory north of the river belongs to the Indians.* ♦ *Not many years ago, all this territory was still wilderness.* **2.** *n.* an area of land controlled by a specific government, especially a government that is far away. ♦ *The defeated nation lost control over two of its territories after the war.* ♦ *The island used to be a territory of that country, but now it is independent.* **3.** *n.* an area of land that is dominated by an animal or group of animals. ♦ *The bear guarded the territory around her cubs.* ♦ *The dog marked its territory with its scent.* **4.** *n.* an area of land that is covered by a salesperson; an area of land that a person is responsible for in some way. ♦ *Mary's territory includes the north part of downtown.* ♦ *The salesman did poorly because his territory was much too large.* **5. unfamiliar territory** *idiom* an area of knowledge unknown to the speaker. ♦ *We are in unfamiliar territory and I don't know the answer.* ♦ *Astronomy is unfamiliar territory, and I cannot answer any questions about the stars.*

terror ['tɛr ɚ] **1.** *n.* extreme fear. (No plural form in this sense.) ♦ *The movie inspired terror in its viewers.* ♦ *Jane awoke from her nightmare with a feeling of terror.* **2.** *n.* someone or something that causes extreme fear. ♦ *The tyrant was regarded as a menacing terror.* ♦ *The new vaccine brought the terror of the disease under control.* **3.** *n.* someone who is very annoying or obnoxious. (Figurative on ②.) ♦ *Mary has trouble finding a babysitter because her two-year-old is a terror.* ♦ *Jane's fiancé is a terror. No one likes him.*

terrorism ['tɛr ə rɪz əm] *n.* the use of violence and terror to achieve political goals. (No plural form in this sense.) ♦ *The country suffered many attacks of terrorism.* ♦ *The political group resorted to terrorism to advance its goals.*

terrorist ['tɛr ə rəst] *n.* someone who practices terrorism. ♦ *The terrorist claimed responsibility for the bombing.* ♦ *The police arrested three terrorists involved in the attack.*

terrorize ['tɛr ə rɑɪz] *tv.* to cause someone to feel extremely frightened. ♦ *The large dog terrorized the little girl.* ♦ *Bill terrorized Bob with a snake.*

terse ['tɚs] *adj.* concise; succinct; using few words. (Adv: *tersely.* Comp: *terser;* sup: *tersest.*) ♦ *The professor wrote a few terse comments on my research paper.* ♦ *The editorial was a terse indictment of the president's policies.*

test ['tɛst] **1.** *n.* a series of questions or activities that determine someone's knowledge or skill; a school examination. ♦ *Every Friday the students take a spelling test.* ♦ *The test had one very long question and thirty short questions.* **2.** *n.* an experiment; an action that is done to see how something works. ♦ *The inventor performed a test to see if the new device worked correctly.* ♦ *Climbing the mountain was a test of courage for Bill.* **3.** *tv.* to determine someone's knowledge or skill by evaluating answers to questions or performance of activities. ♦ *Miss Johnson tested her students frequently.* ♦ *Many colleges test students before accepting them.* **4.** *tv.* to subject something to ② in order to see how it works. ♦ *Climbing the mountain tested Bill's courage.* ♦ *Mary intended to test her boyfriend's loyalty.* **5. put someone or something to the test** *idiom* to see what someone or something can achieve. ♦ *I think I can jump that far, but no one has ever put me to the test.* ♦ *I'm going to put my car to the test right now, and see how fast it will go.*

testament ['tɛs tə mənt] **1.** *n.* a proof of something; a tribute to someone or something. ♦ *Mary's well-mannered children are a testament to her methods of discipline.* ♦ *Bill's success is a testament to his diligence.* **2. Old Testament; New Testament** *n.* either of the two divisions of the Christian Bible. ♦ *The story of the creation of the earth is in the Old Testament.* ♦ *The four gospels are found in the New Testament.* **3. last will and testament** *n.* a will; a set of instructions as to the disposition of the assets of a deceased person. ♦ *Mary's last will and testament was found in her safe-deposit box.* ♦ *The man amended his last will and testament a month before he died.*

testicle ['tɛs tɪ kəl] *n.* one of a pair of round sexual glands in males that produces sperm. ♦ *A cancerous tumor was found in one of Bill's testicles.* ♦ *The athlete wore special equipment to protect his testicles from injury.*

testify ['tɛs tə fɑɪ] **1.** *tv.* to say something under oath; to give evidence in court. (Takes a clause.) ♦ *Mary testified that she saw John commit the crime.* ♦ *The witness testified that the red car had struck the blue car.* **2. testify to** *iv.* + *prep. phr.* to give evidence that something is true or false. ♦ *I can testify to the value of this medicine.* ♦ *Tom testified to the helpfulness of the sermon.*

testimonial [tɛs tə 'mon i əl] **1.** *n.* a formal statement of someone's character; a recommendation. ♦ *The professor wrote a testimonial for the student looking for a job.* ♦ *David's testimonial for me was full of praise.* **2.** *adj.* <the adj. use of ①.> ♦ *The hero was honored at the testimonial dinner.* ♦ *The testimonial speech emphasized Mary's good works.*

testimony ['tɛs tə mo ni] *n.* the statements of a witness, especially in a court of law. (No plural form in this sense.) ♦ *John's testimony contradicted the defendant's testimony.* ♦ *The court recorder transcribed everyone's testimony.*

testosterone [tɛs 'tɑs tə ron] *n.* a male hormone produced by the testicles. (No plural form in this sense.) ♦ *Anne attributed John's aggression to too much testosterone.* ♦ *The body builder took small doses of testosterone to increase the size of his muscles.*

test tube ['tɛst tub] **1.** *n.* a glass tube with an open top and a rounded bottom that is used in chemistry and medicine. ♦ *The chemist heated the test tube over a burner.* ♦ *The nurse put a sample of my blood into a test tube.* **2. test-tube** *adj.* made in ①; made through the use of ①. ♦ *The test-tube baby had been implanted in her mother's womb as an embryo.* ♦ *The test-tube concoction exploded when I heated it.*

testy ['tɛs ti] *adj.* impatient; irritable; easily irritated. (Adv: *testily.* Comp: *testier;* sup: *testiest.*) ♦ *My testy roommate growled when I woke her up before noon.* ♦ *I avoided my testy boss all day long.*

tetanus ['tɛt nəs] *n.* a disease caused by a bacteria that enters the body through an infected wound, causing the muscles of the body to stiffen, and sometimes causing death. (No plural form in this sense.) ♦ *Tetanus is called lockjaw when it affects the lower jaw muscle.* ♦ *The nurse gave me a shot for tetanus when I stepped on the rusty nail.*

tether ['tɛð ɚ] **1.** *n.* a rope or something similar that is attached to an animal or a child to prevent straying or running away. ♦ *The young calf chewed on its tether.* ♦ *The dog broke from its tether and ran into the street.* **2.** *tv.* to attach ① to an animal or a child. ♦ *I tethered my dog before I went into the store.* ♦ *Mary tethered her young child to her wrist while she shopped.*

Texas ['tɛk səs] See Gazetteer.

text ['tɛkst] **1.** *n.* the main words in a book or article, as opposed to pictures, tables, graphs, appendixes, indexes, etc. (No plural form in this sense.) ♦ *The text appeared in large print.* ♦ *The author supplemented the text with graphs and charts.* **2.** *n.* the words of a speech in written form. ♦ *The newspaper printed the text of the president's speech.* ♦ *The lecturer read from a prepared text.* **3.** *n.* a textbook. ♦ *Mary bought her texts for the fall semester.* ♦ *The students had to read four texts for the biology course.*

textbook ['tɛkst bʊk] **1.** *n.* a book, designed for student use, that is used as a standard source of information about a specific subject. ♦ *I read the third chapter of the physics textbook last night.* ♦ *Mary studied her chemistry textbook the night before the test.* **2.** *adj.* the best possible example; quintessential. ♦ *The lawyer's first case was a textbook example of mail fraud.* ♦ *The accident was a textbook hit-and-run accident.*

textile ['tɛks tɑɪl] **1.** *n.* cloth; something that is made by weaving. ♦ *The tailor made a suit from the finest textiles.* ♦ *Anne purchased yards of textiles at the fabric store.* **2.** *adj.* <the adj. use of ①.> ♦ *The modern-art museum sponsored an exhibit of textile arts.* ♦ *There used to be many textile factories in New England.*

texture ['tɛks tʃɚ] **1.** *n.* the evenness, smoothness, or consistency of something. ♦ *Wood that has not been sanded has a rough texture.* ♦ *My oatmeal has a lumpy texture.* **2.** *n.* the appearance of having ①, such as with a design on paper or in art. ♦ *The background of the painting has an interesting texture.* ♦ *The computer screen has a texture that makes it hard to read the printing.*

Thailand ['tɑɪ lænd] See Gazetteer.

than ['ðæn] *conj.* as compared with someone or something; in comparison with someone or something. (Used before the second item of a comparison.) ♦ *Mary is younger than I am.* ♦ *Bill likes pizza more than chocolate.*

thank ['θæŋk] **1.** *tv.* to show someone gratitude by saying "thank you"; to express gratitude for something that has been given or done. ♦ *I thanked my hosts for their hospitality.* ♦ *John thanked the police officer for saving his life.* **2. thanks** *interj.* <a polite expression that is used by the recipient of an action, gift, or compliment, along with "yes" or "no" in response to a question, or to show gratitude.> (Less formal than Thank you ③.) ♦ *Thanks for helping me.* ♦ *"Would you like a sandwich?" "Yes, thanks. I'm hungry."* **3. Thank you.** *interj.* <a polite expression that is used by the recipient of an action, gift, or compliment, along with "yes" or "no" in response to a question, or to show gratitude.> ♦ *Thank you for helping me.* ♦ *"Would you like some coffee?" "Yes, thank you."* **4. thanks** *n.* gratitude; a feeling of appreciation toward someone. (Treated as plural.) ♦ *Bill expressed his thanks by buying me a small gift.* ♦ *We gave our thanks to God for the ample meal.* **5. thank-you** *n.* an expression of thanks. ♦ *I gave Mary a sincere thank-you for the gift.* ♦ *We sent out ten gifts, but have received only nine thank-yous.* **6. thank-you** *adj.* <the adj. use of ⑤.> ♦ *I wrote my host a thank-you note.* ♦ *A bouquet of flowers makes a good thank-you gift.* **7. vote of thanks** *idiom* a speech expressing appreciation and thanks to a speaker, lecturer, organizer, etc., and inviting the audience to applaud. ♦ *John gave a vote of thanks to Professor Jones for his talk.* ♦ *Mary was given a vote of thanks for organizing the dance.*

thankful ['θæŋk fʊl] *adj.* grateful; showing thanks; expressing thanks. (Adv: *thankfully.*) ♦ *The winning actor was thankful for the award.* ♦ *The thankful student appreciated the scholarship.*

thankfully ['θæŋk fə li] **1.** *adv.* gratefully; with thanks; with gratitude. ♦ *The young couple thankfully acknowledged my present.* ♦ *The actress thankfully accepted her award.* **2.** *adj.* [I am speaking] with gratitude. (Informal.) ♦ *Thankfully, we arrived in time for the celebration.* ♦ *Thankfully, it stopped raining before I left.*

thankless ['θæŋk ləs] **1.** *adj.* [of a deed] not rewarded with thanks. (Adv: *thanklessly.*) ♦ *Helping my grumpy roommate is a thankless task.* ♦ *Although my job is thankless, it pays my rent.* **2.** *adj.* [of a person] not showing gratitude. (Adv: *thanklessly.*) ♦ *The thankless diner did not leave the waiter a tip.* ♦ *My thankless guests made a mess of my house.*

Thanksgiving [θæŋks 'gɪv ɪŋ] *n.* a holiday celebrated in North America as an expression of thanks. ♦ *In Canada, Thanksgiving is celebrated on the second Monday of October.* ♦ *My family had dinner at my grandmother's house on Thanksgiving, which is on the fourth Thursday in November.*

that ['ðæt] **1.** *adj.* <a form referring to someone or something already mentioned or someone or something of which both the speaker and hearer are aware.> (Prenominal only. With plural nouns, use those.) ♦ *You know that guy I was telling you about? He quit his job today.* ♦ *The dog dug up that plant you planted last week.* **2.** *adj.* <the adj. use of ④; a form referring to someone or something further away or the furthest away from the speaker.> (Used in contrast with this. Prenominal only. With plural nouns, use those.) ♦ *That boy is taller than this one.* ♦ *This restaurant is too crowded. Let's go to that café over there.* **3.** *pron.* <a form standing for someone or something already referred to or someone or something of which

both the speaker and hearer are aware.> (Pl: those.) ♦ *So, that's what happened to me today.* ♦ *As the phone rang, John yelled, "Can someone get that?"* **4.** *pron.* <a form standing for someone or something that is further away or the furthest away from the speaker.> (Used in contrast with this. Pl: those.) ♦ *No, not this toy. Do you see the toy on the top shelf? That's what Jimmy wants.* ♦ *This is too small, but that is too big. Where is the right size?* **5.** *conj.* which. (Used to connect sentences, clauses, and phrases with noun phrases. Only used with restrictive clauses. Sometimes means 'when' or 'where' if it follows a noun phrase referring to a time or place.) ♦ *This is the toy that I bought for Jimmy.* ♦ *Do you remember the day that we bought this sled?* **6.** *conj.* who; whom. (Used to connect sentences, phrases, or clauses with noun phrases. Only used with restrictive clauses. Who or whom, as appropriate, is preferred by many people.) ♦ *I spoke to the man that knocked on the door.* ♦ *I apologized to the woman that I yelled at.* **7.** *conj.* <a form used to connect a verb with a sentence that is the object of the verb.> (This that can be omitted.) ♦ *I promise you that I will be there tomorrow.* ♦ *Jane already knows that Bill is giving her a ring.* **8. so...that** *conj.* and as a result; consequently. (This that can be omitted. Takes a clause.) ♦ *I'm so slow that I never seem to get anything done.* ♦ *David was so tired today that he fell asleep at work.* **9.** *adv.* so; to such a degree; to such an unwarranted degree. ♦ *I'm not that hungry, so I'll just have some soup.* ♦ *You can stop laughing now. John's joke wasn't that funny.*

that's ['ðæts] **1.** *cont.* "that is." ♦ *That's the hat I'd like to buy.* ♦ *Where is John? That's what I'd like to know.* **2.** *cont.* "that has," where has is an auxiliary. ♦ *That's got to be the most ridiculous thing I've ever heard!* ♦ *That's happened twice this week.*

thaw ['θɔ] **1.** *iv.* to melt; [for something frozen] to no longer be frozen; [for the weather] to be warm enough to melt ice or snow. ♦ *The frozen fish thawed when I placed it in the warm water.* ♦ *Last week it was so warm that the frozen pond thawed.* **2.** *iv.* to become less formal; to relax. (Figurative on ①.) ♦ *Jane thawed as she got to know more people at the party.* ♦ *The relations between the countries thawed after the war.* **3.** *tv.* to relax something; to cause something to become less formal, tense, or suspicious. (Figurative on ④.) ♦ *The end of the war thawed relations between the two former enemies.* ♦ *Fun games helped thaw the party where no one knew each other.* **4.** *tv.* to melt something; to cause something to no longer be frozen. ♦ *I thawed the frozen fish by placing it in warm water.* ♦ *We thawed the turkey by leaving it on the counter overnight.* **5.** *n.* a condition when the weather has become warm enough to melt ice or snow. ♦ *Our first thaw this winter came on March 3rd.* ♦ *The frozen pond melted during the thaw.* **6.** *n.* a relaxing of formality; making something less strict or formal. (Figurative on ⑤.) ♦ *A thaw in the relationship of the two countries allowed more dialogues to take place.* ♦ *The thaw in the contract negotiations helped to end the strike.*

the [ðə, ði] **1.** *article* a certain one; certain ones. (The definite article. Used before nouns or noun phrases to show that a definite thing, person, or group of things or people is being referred to. Pronounced ['ði] when emphasized or before vowels.) ♦ *I spoke to the man sitting next to me.* ♦ *I bought the candle with the long wick.* **2.** *article* the general category of ______. (Used before a noun that is used in a general sense.) ♦ *I saw a documentary about the life cycle of the mosquito.* ♦ *The moose lives, on the average, for 12 years.* **3.** *article* the special or specific one. (Used before some names and titles.) ♦ *The Gambia is a small country in western Africa.* ♦ *The mountain climber got lost in the Himalayas.* **4.** *article* the one and only. (Used to emphasize or stress a particular thing or person.) ♦ *Our new product is* the *solution to all of your cleaning problems!* ♦ *I don't want just any cup, I want* the *cup I bought today.* **5.** *adv.* to a certain degree, especially in comparison with something else. ♦ *The older I become, the happier I am.* ♦ *John invested his money foolishly, and now he's all the poorer for it.* **6.** *adv.* <a form used before *most* and *-est* constructions; used before adjectives and adverbs in their superlative forms.> ♦ *Today is the longest day of the year.* ♦ *Ten miles is the most I've ever walked in one day.* **7. by the** *phr.* each; per. (Used to show a unit of measure, but not a rate of a measure.) ♦ *Lettuce is sold by the head.* ♦ *Gas is sold by the gallon.*

theater AND **theatre** ['θi ə tɚ] **1.** *n.* a building where movies are shown or where plays are performed. (Very often the spelling *theatre* is used for buildings where plays are performed and in reference to live theater.) ♦ *John went to the theater to see the new movie.* ♦ *The actor auditioned for the play at the theater.* **2.** *n.* the business of producing plays for the stage; the study of drama, performance, and acting. (No plural form in this sense.) ♦ *Mary studied theater at a college in New York.* ♦ *Most people in theatre don't earn much money.* **3.** *n.* a place where something important happens, especially relating to war. ♦ *In the Pacific theater during World War II, the United States fought Japan.* ♦ *In the European theater, the United States fought Germany in both World Wars.*

theatergoer AND **theatregoer** ['θi ə tɚ go ɚ] *n.* someone who attends a theater; someone who goes to see a play or, especially, who goes to see plays frequently. ♦ *There are not enough theatergoers in this area to support a local theater.* ♦ *The acting company sent regular theatergoers a flier about its new play.*

theatrical [θi 'æ trɪ kəl] **1.** *adj.* of or about theater. (Adv: *theatrically* [...ɪk li].) ♦ *The producer arranged financing for a lavish theatrical production.* ♦ *This spotlight was designed for theatrical lighting.* **2.** *adj.* showy; exaggerated; not natural. (Adv: *theatrically* [...ɪk li].) ♦ *With a theatrical gesture, the magician pulled a rabbit from his hat.* ♦ *In a theatrical voice, the customer threatened to leave the store.*

theft ['θɛft] **1.** *n.* stealing; taking someone else's property without permission. (No plural form in this sense.) ♦ *Theft is just one kind of crime that frightens people.* ♦ *Theft is increasing in the major cities.* **2.** *n.* an instance of ①. ♦ *We reported a number of thefts of equipment to the police.* ♦ *We never found the thief responsible for the theft of my computer.*

their ['ðer] **1.** *pron.* <the possessive form of they>; belonging to people, animals, or things that have already been mentioned. (Used as a modifier before a noun.) ♦ *This is my coat. Those are their coats.* ♦ *Did you show the guests to their seats?* **2.** *pron.* <① standing for his ③>; belonging to a person who has already been mentioned. (Used to refer to a preceding noun or pronoun, the sexual reference of which is indeterminate, undetermined, or irrelevant. Adopted as a replacement for his

③ by those who see his ③ as referring to males only. Objected to by some as a needless violation of grammatical number when used for singular nouns.) ♦ *Everyone was told to take their seat.* ♦ *Each student took off their jacket.* **3. theirs** *pron.* <the possessive form of they>; belonging to people, animals, or things that have already been mentioned. (Do not use an apostrophe when writing theirs. Used in place of a noun.) ♦ *These coats are theirs.* ♦ *This cookie is mine. Theirs are on the counter.*

them ['ðɛm] **1.** *pron.* <the objective form of they.> (Used to refer to people, animals, and things, used after prepositions, and used as the object of verbs.) ♦ *Bob couldn't find his socks, so I helped him look for them.* ♦ *I washed the dishes, and then I dried them.* **2.** *pron.* <a form standing for him ②, referring to a person already mentioned.> (Used to refer to a noun or pronoun, the sexual reference of which is indeterminate, undetermined, or irrelevant. Adopted as a replacement for him ② by those who see him ② as referring to males only. Objected to by some as a needless violation of grammatical number when used for singular nouns.) ♦ *If a salesman comes while I am out, ask them to wait.* ♦ *If you do not know a person's name, you should ask them what it is.*

theme ['θim] **1.** *n.* a subject of a speech or a text; a topic. ♦ *The theme of the politician's speech was crime.* ♦ *The debate centered on the theme of eating less fat.* **2.** *n.* a melody that is used to identify a certain program, movie, character or emotion. ♦ *John hummed the theme from his favorite movie.* ♦ *The tragic victim's theme was written in a minor key.* **3.** *n.* the main melody of a piece of music. ♦ *I found myself humming the symphony's theme all day long.* ♦ *The triumphant theme recurred often throughout the musical piece.* **4.** *n.* a unifying idea; a motif; a concept that connects several parts of something. ♦ *This series of reports has a political theme.* ♦ *The restaurant was decorated around a southwestern theme.* **5.** *adj.* of or about a piece of music that is readily identified with someone or something. ♦ *When we heard the theme song of our favorite singer, we would gather around the radio.* ♦ *Every time the murderer's theme music was played in the movie, we knew someone was going to die.*

themselves [ðɛm 'sɛlvz] **1.** *pron.* <the reflexive form of they, used after a verb or a preposition when the subject of the sentence refers to the same people, animals, or things that the pronoun refers to.> ♦ *The barefoot children cut themselves on the pieces of glass.* ♦ *My brothers shave themselves every morning.* **2.** *pron.* <the reflexive form of they used after they or a plural noun phrase as an intensifier.> ♦ *The owners themselves signed the contract.* ♦ *They themselves cleaned up the park.* **3. by themselves** *phr.* with help from no one else. ♦ *Do you think they can do it by themselves?* ♦ *Mike and Max cannot lift the piano by themselves.* **4. by themselves** *phr.* with no one else present; alone. ♦ *They are sitting there by themselves. Let's sit with them.* ♦ *They enjoy spending the evening at home by themselves.*

then ['ðɛn] **1.** *adv.* at that time. ♦ *I don't remember President Kennedy. I wasn't alive then.* ♦ *In 1980, Anne, then only 12, learned to play the piano.* **2.** *adv.* next; following; after that. ♦ *I went to the store. Then, I went to the bank.* ♦ *Mary first told me the news, and then she told John.* **3.** *adv.* therefore; in that case; so. ♦ *If you are hurt, then you should go to the hospital.* ♦ *Since you like to draw, then you should make the poster.*

theologian [θi ə 'lo dʒən] *n.* someone who practices or studies theology; someone who works in theology. ♦ *The theologians argued about the nature of God.* ♦ *Theologians write books and teach at seminaries.*

theological [θi ə 'lɑdʒ ɪ kəl] *adj.* of or about theology. (Adv: *theologically* [...ɪk li].) ♦ *The young minister studied at a theological seminary.* ♦ *The atheist dismissed all theological teachings.*

theology [θi 'ɑl ə dʒi] *n.* the study and science of religion. (No plural form in this sense.) ♦ *John received a degree in theology at a divinity school.* ♦ *The expert in theology wrote a book comparing the world's major religions.*

theorem ['θɪr əm] *n.* a mathematical statement that can be proved to be true. ♦ *The mathematician proved the theorem using inductive reasoning.* ♦ *The geometry student proved five theorems.*

theoretical [θi ə 'rɛt ɪ kəl] **1.** *adj.* based on a theory; of or about a theory. (Adv: *theoretically* [...ɪk li].) ♦ *The evangelist condemned evolution as a theoretical heresy.* ♦ *The detective offered a theoretical explanation of the murder.* **2.** *adj.* existing only as a theory; not practical in real life. (Adv: *theoretically* [...ɪk li].) ♦ *I prefer functional explanations to theoretical ones.* ♦ *Theoretical methods are sometimes useless outside of the laboratory.*

theory ['θɪr (ə˞) i] **1.** *n.* the principles or abstract knowledge of a science or an art, as opposed to the actual practice of a science or an art; the principles on which a science or an art are based. (No plural form in this sense.) ♦ *Your skills are good, but your knowledge of theory is weak.* ♦ *The nuclear physicist studied atomic theory.* **2.** *n.* an explanation based on thought, observation, or reasoning from facts. ♦ *Charles Darwin developed the theory of evolution.* ♦ *Although it was just a theory, the detective thought he knew the murderer's identity.* **3. in theory** *phr.* according to a theory; theoretically. ♦ *In theory, if I take my medicine regularly, I will get well.* ♦ *How things work in theory doesn't always match with how things work in reality.*

therapeutic [θɛr ə 'pju tɪk] *adj.* of or about the treatment or the cure of a disease or illness; restoring one's health. (Adv: *therapeutically* [...ɪk li].) ♦ *Mary, who has arthritis, finds swimming to be very therapeutic.* ♦ *The nurse used various therapeutic techniques to exercise the patient's muscles.*

therapist ['θɛr ə pəst] **1.** *n.* someone who treats people by using certain kinds of therapy rather than medication, typically a speech therapist or a physical therapist. ♦ *My physical therapist massaged my pulled muscle.* ♦ *Bill went to a therapist to get help with a speech problem.* **2.** *n.* a psychiatrist; a psychologist, social worker, or similar professional who has been trained to help clients overcome psychological problems. ♦ *The depressed man told his therapist about his childhood.* ♦ *Mike is seeing a therapist about his anxiety.*

therapy ['θɛr ə pi] **1.** *n.* psychiatry; psychotherapy. ♦ *Mike spent two years in therapy because of depression.* ♦ *After the attack, I had a year of therapy to regain my confidence.* **2.** See physical therapy.

there ['ðer] **1.** *adv.* to or toward that place; at that place; in that place; in that respect; at that point in time; at that point during a process. (Compare with they're and their.) ♦ *I was hungry, so when I saw a restaurant, I decided to eat there.* ♦ *I knew what the third step of the experiment was, but when I got there, I forgot it.* **2.** *adv.* <a word used to focus someone's attention on a place, thing, or person, typically in the distance or moving away.> (Often the opposite of here.) ♦ *Look there, up in the sky!* ♦ *What's that large green thing there?* **3.** *adv.* <a form that begins a sentence or clause and is followed by a verb, which is then followed by the subject of the sentence.> (The verb is usually be—for example, *there is, there are*—but it can also be *go, come, stand, rest,* or another verb. In questions, the verb is placed before there.) ♦ *There are four cookies on the table.* ♦ *There was a lot of snow on the ground after the storm.* ♦ *In the doorway, there stood an old man with a long, gray beard.* ♦ *Is there a restaurant nearby?* **4.** *pron.* a particular place or location. ♦ *Turn right at Fifth Street. From there, walk toward the bank.* ♦ *Don't open that cabinet. I have a surprise in there.* **5. There, there; There, now** *phr.* <an expression used to comfort someone.> ♦ *There, there. You'll feel better after you take a nap.* ♦ *There, now. Everything will be all right.* **6. (way) over there** *phr.* in a place some distance away. ♦ *I see a house way over there in the field.* ♦ *My hat is over there on the table.*

thereabouts ['ðer ə bɑʊts] *adv.* near that place or time; near a number or amount; approximately. ♦ *I think John lives on 52nd Street or thereabouts.* ♦ *It was about 80 degrees today, or somewhere thereabouts.*

thereafter [ðer 'æf tɚ] *adv.* after that time; afterwards; subsequently. ♦ *Our favorite movie theater closed in 1972. Thereafter, we had to go to the one on Main Street.* ♦ *It rained until 8:30, and it snowed thereafter.*

thereby [ðer bɑɪ] *adv.* in such a way; in that way; by doing that; by those means. ♦ *Our team scored a touchdown, thereby winning the game.* ♦ *John called Mary an idiot, thereby insulting her.*

therefore ['ðer for] *adv.* for that reason; for those reasons; as a result; so; consequently. ♦ *I have two cookies, and you have three cookies. Therefore, we have five cookies.* ♦ *It's raining. Therefore, the picnic is canceled.*

there's ['ðerz] **1.** *cont.* "there has," where has is an auxiliary. ♦ *There's never been as much rain as today!* ♦ *There's got to be a better explanation.* **2.** *cont.* "there is." ♦ *There's more to this story than I've told you.* ♦ *There's a package for you at the post office.*

thermal ['θɚm əl] *adj.* of or about heat; producing or transmitting heat. (Adv: *thermally.*) ♦ *Most metals act as thermal conductors.* ♦ *It is very cold outside. You should wear your thermal underwear.*

thermometer [θɚ 'mɑm ə tɚ] *n.* a device that measures the temperature of someone or something. ♦ *The nurse put a thermometer in the patient's mouth.* ♦ *The thermometer indicated that it was too warm in the house.*

thermos ['θɚ məs] *n.* a container that has an empty space between its inner and outer walls, causing hot substances to remain hot or cold substances to remain cold. ♦ *I drank some hot soup from my thermos.* ♦ *Jimmy brought a thermos filled with juice to school for lunch.*

thermostat ['θɚm ə stæt] *n.* a device that maintains the temperature of a room or a machine. ♦ *Our thermostat is set at a comfortable 68 degrees.* ♦ *The machine's thermostat indicated it was overheating.*

thesaurus [θɪ 'sor əs] *n.* a reference book that arranges words according to their meanings, so that one can easily find synonyms or related words. ♦ *John referred to his thesaurus to find some synonyms for "nice."* ♦ *I couldn't think of the word I wanted to use, so I consulted a thesaurus.*

these ['ðiz] pl of this.

theses ['θi sis] pl of thesis.

thesis ['θi sɪs] **1.** *n., irreg.* the premise of an argument; a statement that will be proved and defended in an argument. (Pl: theses.) ♦ *My professor disagreed with the thesis of my article.* ♦ *Your thesis is sensible, but you don't defend it well.* **2.** *n., irreg.* a research paper written by someone in order to obtain a degree from a school, college, or university. ♦ *It took John three years to write his thesis.* ♦ *The topic of Susan's thesis concerns discourse.*

thespian ['θɛs pi ən] **1.** *n.* an actor or actress. ♦ *The director coached the young thespians.* ♦ *Mary moved to New York to become a professional thespian.* **2.** *adj.* dramatic; relating to drama or the theater. ♦ *The thespian club meets every Wednesday after school.* ♦ *My parents discouraged my thespian endeavors.*

they ['ðe] **1.** *pron.* <the third-person plural subject pronoun; the plural of he, she, or it.> ♦ *My neighbors are from France. They speak French fluently.* ♦ *It is they who need help most that should receive it first.* **2.** *pron.* <the third-person plural subject pronoun used as a singular.> (Used to refer to a preceding noun or pronoun, the sexual reference of which is indeterminate, undetermined, or irrelevant. Adopted as a replacement for he ② by those who see he ② as referring to males only. Objected to by some as a needless violation of grammatical number when used for singular nouns.) ♦ *Each student selected a poem that they wanted to read.* ♦ *Each one was told that they should be here at noon.* **3.** *pron.* <a form used to mean people in general; an unspecified number or group of people.> ♦ *It's going to be a very snowy winter, they say.* ♦ *They call this a city, but to me it's just a small town.*

they'd ['ðed] **1.** *cont.* "they would." ♦ *My friends would be healthier if they'd stop smoking.* ♦ *If they'd come on time, they could leave on time.* **2.** *cont.* "they had," where had is an auxiliary. ♦ *They'd gotten halfway home when they realized I was left behind.* ♦ *They'd better arrive soon if they're going to be on time.*

they'll ['ðel] *cont.* "they will." ♦ *They'll be here by 8:00.* ♦ *If John and Mary don't finish soon, they'll be in trouble.*

they're ['ðer] *cont.* "they are." (Compare with there, their.) ♦ *Dave and Bob are lucky because they're going on vacation tomorrow.* ♦ *They're trying to do the best they can.*

they've ['ðev] *cont.* "they have," where have is an auxiliary. ♦ *They've got to be here by noon, or they'll miss their flight.* ♦ *They've gone to the store, but they'll be back soon.*

thick ['θɪk] **1.** *adj.* not thin; having a greater than average distance between the two opposite sides; having a lot of space between the two opposite sides. (Adv: *thickly.* Comp: *thicker;* sup: *thickest.*) ♦ *The butcher gave me a thick slice of ham.* ♦ *Don't walk onto the ice unless you're sure that it's thick.* **2.** *adj.* measuring a certain distance between two opposite sides; having a certain depth or width. (Comp: *thicker.* No superlative.) ♦ *The ice on the pond is six inches thick.* ♦ *The strip of bacon was an eighth of an inch thick.* **3.** *adj.* dense; with very little space between things. (Adv: *thickly.* Comp: *thicker;* sup: *thickest.*) ♦ *The woods were thick with trees.* ♦ *It was difficult to move through the thick shrubbery.* **4.** *adj.* not pouring easily, like glue or molasses; being liquid but not flowing easily. (Adv: *thickly.* Comp: *thicker;* sup: *thickest.*) ♦ *I smeared the thick syrup over my pancakes.* ♦ *The cook spread the thick sauce over the pizza dough.* **5.** *adj.* [of air] not clear or full of humidity, smoke, or fog. (Comp: *thicker;* sup: *thickest.*) ♦ *The air was thick and humid.* ♦ *The early morning sky was thick with fog.* **6. thick accent** *n.* a unique way of speaking that shows where one is from. ♦ *My grandmother speaks English with a thick accent.* ♦ *The Germans laughed because I spoke with a thick American accent.* **7. through thick and thin** *idiom* through good times and bad times. ♦ *We've been together through thick and thin, and we won't desert each other now.* ♦ *Over the years, we went through thick and thin and enjoyed every minute of it.*

thicken ['θɪk ən] **1.** *tv.* to cause something to become thicker. ♦ *The cook thickened the gravy with flour.* ♦ *The artist used dry pigment to thicken the paint.* **2.** *iv.* [for a liquid] to become thicker. ♦ *The sauce thickened as it cooked.* ♦ *Blood thickens as it dries.*

thickness ['θɪk nəs] **1.** *n.* the quality of being thick ①. (No plural form in this sense.) ♦ *I had to cook the steak longer because of its thickness.* ♦ *John tested the thickness of the ice before walking on it.* **2.** *n.* the quality of being thick ④. (No plural form in this sense.) ♦ *The thickness of the sauce depends on the amount of water in it.* ♦ *The thickness of the mud made it hard to walk.* **3.** *n.* a layer of something, such as fabric. ♦ *The skirt is made with three thicknesses of the material.* ♦ *Fold the fabric over and over so that the pattern can be cut on as many thicknesses as possible.*

thick-skinned ['θɪk 'skɪnd] *adj.* not easily insulted; able to withstand criticism; not easily upset by criticism. ♦ *You wouldn't be so offended if you were more thick-skinned.* ♦ *The thick-skinned actor ignored the bad reviews of his performance.*

thief ['θif] *n.* someone who steals things. (Pl: thieves.) ♦ *The police caught the thief who stole my television set.* ♦ *My house was burglarized by professional thieves.*

thievery ['θiv ə ri] *n.* stealing things; theft. (No plural form in this sense.) ♦ *The criminals were punished for their thievery.* ♦ *The homeless man preferred to beg for money rather than resort to thievery.*

thieves ['θivz] pl of thief.

thigh ['θɑɪ] *n.* [in humans and many animals] the part of the leg between the hip and the knee. ♦ *Because I had been squatting for so long, the muscles in my thighs were sore.* ♦ *Mary wears shorts that go down to her knees because she likes her thighs to be covered.*

thighbone ['θɑɪ bon] *n.* the bone in the thigh. ♦ *John suffered a fractured thighbone in the motorcycle accident.* ♦ *The biologist pointed to the thighbone of the skeleton.*

thimble ['θɪm bəl] *n.* a small metal or plastic cap, which is worn over one's finger while sewing so the finger is not injured when pushing the needle through material. ♦ *The tailor tapped his thimble against the needle.* ♦ *The seamstress placed the thimble on her first finger.*

thin ['θɪn] **1.** *adj.* not thick; having less than the average distance between the two opposite sides; having very little space between the two opposite sides. (Adv: *thinly.* Comp: *thinner;* sup: *thinnest.*) ♦ *There's a thin layer of cheese on top of the pizza.* ♦ *Don't walk on the ice yet, because it's too thin to support you.* **2.** *adj.* not fat; slender; slim; not having much fat on one's body. (Adv: *thinly.* Comp: *thinner;* sup: *thinnest.*) ♦ *Mary went on a diet because she wanted to be thin.* ♦ *The thin student ate in moderation.* **3.** *adj.* not dense; spread out; scanty. (Adv: *thinly.* Comp: *thinner;* sup: *thinnest.*) ♦ *The grass is quite thin underneath the huge shade tree.* ♦ *John usually wears a hat because his hair is thin.* **4.** *adj.* not thick; watery; flowing easily. (Adv: *thinly.* Comp: *thinner;* sup: *thinnest.*) ♦ *The thin syrup poured out of the container quickly.* ♦ *The thin sauce soaked into the pizza crust.* **5. thin (out)** *tv.* (+ *adv.*) to make something thinner; to make a place less crowded. ♦ *The hair stylist thinned the actor's hair with scissors.* ♦ *The lecturer's boring speech thinned out the crowd.* **6.** *tv.* to make something more thin ④ or runny. ♦ *The chef thinned the sauce with water.* ♦ *You must thin this lumpy gravy.* **7. thin (out)** *iv.* (+ *adv.*) to become thinner; to become less crowded. ♦ *The crowd thinned as the boring speaker continued to talk.* ♦ *John's hair thinned out as he became older.*

thing ['θɪŋ] **1.** *n.* any object; an object whose name is not known; an object whose name is not important at that moment. ♦ *That thing in my car's engine is making a funny noise.* ♦ *Last night, I threw away some things from my refrigerator.* **2.** *n.* an event; an action; a deed; a statement; an idea; a perception. ♦ *What kind of horrible thing are you suggesting?* ♦ *I couldn't believe the offensive things coming from John's mouth.* **3.** *n.* a person or creature, especially as an object of pity. ♦ *You poor thing! Do you need some help?* ♦ *Look at that miserable thing tied up to the fence.* **4.** *n.* an obsession; a preoccupation. (Informal. No plural form in this sense.) ♦ *Anne's thing for silk dresses costs her a lot of money.* ♦ *David has a thing for expensive chocolate.* **5. things** *n.* possessions; what is owned by someone. ♦ *All of my things were destroyed in the fire.* ♦ *John insured his things against theft.* **6. seeing things** *idiom* to imagine one sees someone or something that is not there. ♦ *Lisa says that she saw a ghost, but she was just seeing things.* ♦ *I thought I was seeing things when Bill walked into the room. Someone had told me he was dead.*

think ['θɪŋk] **1.** *iv., irreg.* to use one's mind; to have thoughts or opinions; to form ideas in the mind. (Pt/pp: thought.) ♦ *Mary thinks carefully before making any decisions.* ♦ *John thought for a while before replying.* **2.** *iv., irreg.* to be able to use one's mind; to have the ability to use one's mind. ♦ *Are humans the only creatures who think?* ♦ *Dogs don't think, but instead rely on instinct.* **3. think about; think of** *iv., irreg.* + *prep. phr.* to have a thought or opinion about someone or something. ♦ *Mary thought about eating pizza for dinner.* ♦ *Jane thought of something at the last minute.* **4. think of** *iv., irreg.* to remember. (Used in negative constructions.) ♦ *I can't think of what I ate for breakfast.* ♦ *Mary couldn't think of where she had parked the car.* **5.** *tv., irreg.* to have a certain belief or opinion; to believe something. (Takes a clause.) ♦ *Anne thought that I had already left.* ♦ *Jimmy thinks the moon is closer than it really is.* **6. think better of something** *idiom* to reconsider something; to think again and decide not to do something. ♦ *Bob was going to escape, but he thought better of it.* ♦ *Jill had planned to resign but then* *thought better of it.* **7. think on one's feet** *idiom* to think while one is talking. ♦ *If you want to be a successful teacher, you must be able to think on your feet.* ♦ *I have to write out everything I'm going to say, because I can't think on my feet very well.*

thinker ['θɪŋk ɚ] *n.* someone who thinks, especially someone who thinks ponderously. ♦ *Mary, who spends a lot of time reading, is a real thinker.* ♦ *John's problem is that he's a thinker but never a doer.*

thinking ['θɪŋk ɪŋ] **1.** *adj.* able to think; forming thoughts, ideas, or opinions in one's mind; using one's mind. ♦ *Humans are thinking creatures.* ♦ *The scientist tried to invent a thinking computer.* **2.** *n.* the way that someone thinks; one's opinion. (No plural form in this sense.) ♦ *My thinking on this matter is that we should go to a movie tonight.* ♦ *The mayor's thinking was criticized in an editorial.* **3.** *n.* forming thoughts, ideas, or opinions with one's mind. (No plural form in this sense.) ♦ *Tom likes action and sports and not thinking.* ♦ *I do a lot of thinking when I'm alone.*

thinner ['θɪn ɚ] *n.* a liquid that is added to paint to dilute it or to make it easier to spread. ♦ *Turpentine is commonly used as a paint thinner.* ♦ *The fumes from the thinner made me dizzy.*

thinness ['θɪn nəs] **1.** *n.* the quality of being thin ①. (No plural form in this sense.) ♦ *The thinness of the ice means it's unsafe for walking.* ♦ *The book's thinness and small size made it look less valuable.* **2.** *n.* the quality of being thin ④. ♦ *The soup is too thin!* ♦ *Bob's gravy is always thin and watery.*

thin-skinned ['θɪn 'skɪnd] *adj.* easily hurt by criticism; easily upset by criticism; easily insulted. ♦ *The thin-skinned singer could not take criticism very well.* ♦ *My words weren't meant to be offensive. You're too thin-skinned.*

third ['θɚd] 3rd. See fourth for senses and examples.

thirdly ['θɚd li] *adv.* in the third place; as a third point of discussion. ♦ *I'd like to thank Anne. Secondly, I'd like to thank John. Thirdly, I'd like to thank my parents.* ♦ *Thirdly, as if two reasons aren't enough, you should stop smoking because it smells.*

third-rate ['θɚd 'ret] *adj.* inferior; not having very good quality; poor. ♦ *We found cockroaches in our third-rate hotel room.* ♦ *The bad movie featured third-rate actors.*

third world ['θɚd 'wɚld] **1.** *n.* the economically underdeveloped countries, primarily in the Southern Hemisphere, especially those not aligned with the United States or the former Soviet Union. ♦ *A measles epidemic ravaged the third world.* ♦ *The political prisoner from the third world fled to the United States.* **2. third-world** *adj.* <the adj. use of ①.> ♦ *The volunteer doctors served third-world nations.* ♦ *Third-world economies are usually not very robust.*

thirst ['θɚst] **1.** *n.* the feeling caused by having nothing to drink; the need to drink. (No plural form in this sense.) ♦ *I quenched my thirst with a tall glass of cold lemonade.* ♦ *The small sip of water didn't satisfy Mary's thirst.* **2. a thirst for something** *idiom* a craving or desire for something. ♦ *The tyrant had an intense thirst for power.* ♦ *The actor's thirst for fame caused him to become unscrupulous.*

thirsty ['θɚs ti] **1.** *adj.* needing to drink; having had nothing to drink; having thirst. (Adv: *thirstily.* Comp: *thirstier;* sup: *thirstiest.*) ♦ *I'm thirsty. Could I have a glass of water?* ♦ *The thirsty students drank a gallon of tea.* **2. thirsty for something** *idiom* craving or desiring something. ♦ *The students were thirsty for knowledge.* ♦ *That evil tyrant is thirsty for power.*

thirteen ['θɚt 'tin] 13. See four for senses and examples.

thirteenth ['θɚt 'tinθ] 13th. See fourth for senses and examples.

thirtieth ['θɚt i ɪθ] 30th. See fourth for senses and examples.

thirty ['θɚt i] 30. See forty for senses and examples.

this ['ðɪs] **1.** *adj.* <a form referring to a thing or person that has already been referred to or is obvious and present; a form referring to an object that one is pointing to or otherwise indicating.> (Prenominal only. Use these with plural nouns.) ♦ *This watch cost $100.* ♦ *This television program is really boring.* **2.** *adj.* <a form introducing a thing or person new to the conversation.> (Colloquial. Prenominal only. Use these with plural nouns.) ♦ *There was this woman on the bus today who had green hair!* ♦ *While I was driving today, suddenly there was this big pothole!* **3.** *adj.* <a form referring to the thing, person, or point in time that is closer or the closest to the speaker.> (Used in contrast with that. Prenominal only. Use these with plural nouns.) ♦ *You think your steak tastes bad? You should try this one.* ♦ *I don't like that painting over there. This one is much nicer.* **4.** *pron.* <a form standing for a thing or person that has already been mentioned or is obvious and present.> (Pl: these.) ♦ *This is exactly the kind of painting I wanted!* ♦ *"Could you buy me this?" Anne asked, pointing to a toy in a catalog.* **5.** *pron.* <a form standing for the thing, person, or point in time that is closer or the closest to the speaker.> (Used in contrast with that. Pl: these.) ♦ *I'll eat this, and you can eat that.* ♦ *If you don't like that sweater, try on this.* **6.** *adv.* to the indicated degree. ♦ *Please, take some of the ice cream back. I only want this much.* ♦ *"I saw a dog today that was this big!" Tom said, spreading his arms wide.*

thistle ['θɪs əl] *n.* any of several types of perennial plants with spiny leaves and large, usually purple, flowers. ♦ *There are thistles growing in my yard.* ♦ *Bob stepped on a thistle and got a small thorn in his foot.*

thorax ['θor æks] *n.* the chest; the technical name for the part of the body between the neck and the abdomen. ♦ *The biologist examined the dead bird's thorax.* ♦ *The patient's lung cancer had spread throughout his thorax.*

thorn ['θorn] **1.** *n.* a sharp, pointed growth on a plant. ♦ *Rose bushes have thorns along their stems.* ♦ *The florist accidentally poked her finger with a thorn.* **2. be a thorn in someone's side** *idiom* to be a constant bother or annoyance to someone. ♦ *This problem is a thorn in my side. I wish I had a solution to it.* ♦ *John was a thorn in my side for years before I finally got rid of him.*

thorny ['θorn i] **1.** *adj.* having thorns. (Adv: *thornily.* Comp: *thornier;* sup: *thorniest.*) ♦ *Bill cried out when he was pushed into a thorny bush.* ♦ *The gardener trimmed the thorny hedges with clippers.* **2.** *adj.* difficult; hard to solve. (Figurative on ①. Adv: *thornily.* Comp: *thornier;* sup: *thorniest.*) ♦ *David went to his boss with a thorny prob-*

lem. ♦ *The mayor tried to delicately handle the thorny situation.*

thorough ['θɚ o] *adj.* complete; doing something with great attention and in great detail. (Adv: *thoroughly.*) ♦ *You must be more thorough with your work. I found a lot of mistakes.* ♦ *The maid did such a thorough job of cleaning our kitchen that it looked new.*

thoroughbred ['θɚ o brɛd] **1.** *n.* an animal, usually a horse, all of whose ancestors are of the same breed or lineage. ♦ *The thoroughbreds raced around the track.* ♦ *The veterinarian examined my thoroughbred.* **2.** *adj.* <the adj. use of ①.> ♦ *Only thoroughbred horses were allowed to race at the track.* ♦ *I bought a thoroughbred stallion.*

thoroughfare ['θɚ o fer] *n.* a road, street, path, or passage that is open on both ends and leads to another similar route. ♦ *This alley is not to be used as a thoroughfare.* ♦ *An accident blocked the main thoroughfare, so I took an alternate street.*

thoroughly ['θɚ ə li] *adv.* completely; with great attention and great detail. ♦ *A surgeon's hands must be thoroughly clean.* ♦ *The editor proofread my article very thoroughly and found all the errors.*

those ['ðoz] pl of that.

though ['ðo] **1.** *conj.* in spite of something; in spite of the fact that; although. ♦ *Max doesn't do well in school, though he tries hard.* ♦ *Though it might rain, I want to go to the beach.* **2. as though** *conj.* as if. ♦ *John pretended to listen to my problems as though he really cared.* ♦ *This food tastes as though it were spoiled.* **3.** *adv.* however. ♦ *I could go to the store, though I could also go to the movies.* ♦ *You could get two slices of pizza, though that wouldn't be fair.*

thought ['θɔt] **1.** pt/pp of think. **2.** *n.* consideration; attention. (No plural form in this sense.) ♦ *After deep thought, I finally came to a decision.* ♦ *The mayor gave some thought to the citizens' request.* **3.** *n.* an idea; an opinion; something that one thinks. ♦ *My thought on the matter is that we should leave now.* ♦ *Mary shared her thoughts with her date.* **4. thoughts** *n.* one's conscious memory; one's conscious thinking. ♦ *My thoughts are always on you and your welfare.* ♦ *My sick friend is constantly in my thoughts.* **5. food for thought** *idiom* something to think about. ♦ *I don't like your idea very much, but it's food for thought.* ♦ *Your lecture was very good. It contained much food for thought.* **6. have second thoughts about someone or something** *idiom* to have doubts about someone or something. ♦ *I'm beginning to have second thoughts about Tom.* ♦ *We now have second thoughts about going to Canada.* **7. lose one's train of thought** *idiom* to forget what one was talking or thinking about. ♦ *Excuse me, I lost my train of thought. What was I talking about?* ♦ *You made Jane lose her train of thought.* **8. lost in thought** *idiom* busy thinking. ♦ *I'm sorry, I didn't hear what you said. I was lost in thought.* ♦ *Bill—lost in thought as always—went into the wrong room.* **9. on second thought** *idiom* having given something more thought; having reconsidered something. ♦ *On second thought, maybe you should sell your house and move into an apartment.* ♦ *On second thought, let's not go to a movie.*

thoughtful ['θɔt fʊl] **1.** *adj.* considerate; caring about someone's feelings; kind. (Adv: *thoughtfully.*) ♦ *The thoughtful students sent their sick teacher some flowers.* ♦ *The thoughtful woman helped the feeble old man up the stairs.* **2.** *adj.* [of something] showing thought and consideration. (Adv: *thoughtfully.*) ♦ *That was a very thoughtful thing to do.* ♦ *The thoughtful suggestion was the answer to our problem.*

thoughtfulness ['θɔt fʊl nəs] *n.* consideration; kindness; care for someone's feelings. (No plural form in this sense.) ♦ *John appreciated his friends' thoughtfulness toward him.* ♦ *I thanked my host for his thoughtfulness.*

thoughtless ['θɔt ləs] *adj.* doing something without thinking; not caring about someone's feelings. (Adv: *thoughtlessly.*) ♦ *The thoughtless woman trampled on the new grass.* ♦ *It was thoughtless of you to not invite Mary to lunch.*

thoughtlessly ['θɔt ləs li] *adv.* without considering someone's feelings; without thinking. ♦ *John thoughtlessly ignored Jane's repeated requests.* ♦ *The cook thoughtlessly served a pork roast to the vegetarians.*

thoughtlessness ['θɔt ləs nəs] *n.* the quality of being careless about someone's feelings or needs. (No plural form in this sense.) ♦ *Due to the waiter's thoughtlessness, I was served the wrong meal.* ♦ *The owner's thoughtlessness resulted in a decrease in business.*

thousand ['θɑʊ zənd] **1.** *n.* 1,000; the number between 999 and 1,001. (Additional numbers formed as with *two thousand, three thousand, four thousand,* etc.) ♦ *Ten times one hundred equals one thousand.* ♦ *Five hundred plus fifteen hundred equals two thousand.* **2.** *n.* a group of 1,000 things or people. ♦ *Thousands of people came to see the president speak.* ♦ *This theater seats a thousand.* **3.** *adj.* 1,000, consisting of 1,000 things; having 1,000 things. ♦ *A thousand soldiers were killed in the battle.* ♦ *This bridge is a thousand feet long.*

thousandth ['θɑʊ zəndθ] 1,000th. See fourth for senses and examples.

thrash ['θræʃ] **1.** *tv.* to move one's arms, legs, or body uncontrollably. ♦ *The epileptic thrashed his arms and legs during his seizure.* ♦ *Bob thrashed his arms, trying to get free from his attacker.* **2.** *tv.* to beat someone severely, especially as a punishment. ♦ *The police thrashed the child's murderer.* ♦ *The abusive father was arrested for thrashing his children.* **3.** *tv.* to separate grain from its stalk by beating it; to thresh grain. ♦ *The farmer thrashed the wheat after harvesting it.* ♦ *This rye was thrashed by a machine.* **4. thrash around; thrash about** *iv.* + *adv.* to move wildly or uncontrollably. ♦ *The poisoned rabbit thrashed around until it died.* ♦ *The drugged student thrashed about on the floor.* **5. thrash something out** *idiom* to discuss something thoroughly and solve any problems. ♦ *The committee took hours to thrash the whole matter out.* ♦ *John and Anne thrashed out the reasons for their constant disagreements.*

thread ['θrɛd] **1.** *n.* fine string, made of twisted strands of cotton, silk, or other fiber, that is used to sew pieces of cloth together or is woven to make cloth. (No plural form in this sense.) ♦ *Mary wanted to make a dress, so she bought some blue fabric and several spools of blue thread.* ♦ *The seamstress cut off the extra thread with a pair of scissors.* **2.** *n.* a very thin strand of something; a length of ①. ♦ *There are some threads hanging from your cuff.* ♦ *The spider's web was woven with silky threads.* **3.** *n.* a theme or idea that links parts of an argument or a story. (Figurative on ①.) ♦ *I was too tired to follow the thread of the* long movie. ♦ *The book's many threads were brought together in the last chapter.* **4. threads** *n.* the raised ridge that wraps around the length of a screw or a bolt. ♦ *The screw fell out because its threads were worn down.* ♦ *The nut turned around the threads of the bolt.* **5.** *tv.* to pass ① through something, usually a needle. ♦ *The tailor threaded the needle with red thread.* ♦ *The seamstress threaded her sewing-machine needle and began working.* **6.** *tv.* to place something on ① or on string, wire, etc. ♦ *The children threaded beads along the wire.* ♦ *As a decoration, I threaded popcorn onto the string.* **7. thread one's way through something** *idiom* to make a path for oneself through a crowded area; to make one's way through a crowded area. ♦ *The spy threaded his way through the crowd.* ♦ *The bicyclists threaded their way through the cars stopped in traffic.* **8. thread through something** *idiom* to travel through a crowded area; to travel through an area where there are many obstacles. ♦ *The spy threaded through the crowd at the palace.* ♦ *The joggers threaded through the shoppers on the sidewalks.*

threadbare ['θrɛd bɛr] *adj.* [of cloth] shabby or worn. ♦ *John replaced his threadbare jacket with a new one.* ♦ *The professor's jacket was almost threadbare.*

threat ['θrɛt] **1.** *n.* a warning; a statement or action that indicates that someone is going to hurt or punish someone in a certain way. ♦ *I hired a bodyguard because of John's threats to hurt me.* ♦ *The enemy made a threat to bomb the capital.* **2.** *n.* a sign of danger; a sign that something harmful or dangerous is going to happen. ♦ *The presence of nuclear weapons is a threat to peace.* ♦ *The workers considered robots to be a threat to their jobs.*

threaten ['θrɛt n] **1.** *tv.* to express a threat against someone. ♦ *Are you threatening me?* ♦ *Bill threatened his neighbor with a loaded gun.* **2.** *tv.* [for something] to pose a danger to someone or something. (Sometimes with an infinitive phrase.) ♦ *The tornado threatened the town before veering to the east.* ♦ *The wind threatened to blow the tree down.* **3.** *iv.* to be a threat; to be an indication of danger. ♦ *When danger threatened, the spy got a new disguise.* ♦ *When heavy rains threatened, we canceled our picnic.* **4. threaten to** *iv.* + *inf.* to make a threat to do something. ♦ *She threatened to leave if I did not stop singing.* ♦ *He is threatening to break every bone in my body!*

threatening ['θrɛt n ɪŋ] *adj.* indicating the possibility of harm or danger; expressing a threat. (Adv: *threateningly.*) ♦ *Because of the threatening weather, we canceled the picnic.* ♦ *Our air force dropped bombs on the threatening army.*

three ['θri] 3. See four for senses and examples.

three-dimensional ['θri dɪ 'mɛn ʃə nəl] **1.** *adj.* having three dimensions; having length, width, and depth. (Abbreviated *3-D.* Adv: *three-dimensionally.*) ♦ *The mathematician plotted the graph in three-dimensional space.* ♦ *I touched the three-dimensional sculpture.* **2.** *adj.* [of something flat, such as a picture on a printed page] seeming to have depth; seeming to have three dimensions. (Adv: *three-dimensionally.*) ♦ *The detailed painting seemed very three-dimensional.* ♦ *You need to wear special glasses with colored lenses to watch a 3-D movie.*

threefold ['θri fold] **1.** *adj.* triple. ♦ *The inflation rate is threefold what it was last year.* ♦ *My salary had a threefold increase over what it was before my promotion.* **2.** *adv.* three times as much. ♦ *Inflation rose threefold during the war.* ♦ *My strength increased threefold after I started to exercise.*

thresh ['θrɛʃ] **1.** *tv.* to separate the grain from its stalk by beating it; to thrash grain. ♦ *The farmer threshed the wheat by hand.* ♦ *This rye was threshed automatically by a machine.* **2.** *iv.* to work by threshing grain. ♦ *The farmer's family threshed for a week after the harvest.* ♦ *After the farmer threshed, the children gleaned a few more grains from the ground.*

threshold ['θrɛʃ hold] **1.** *n.* the piece of wood, metal, or stone across the bottom of a door frame; the entrance to a building, house, or room. ♦ *The wooden threshold has rotted and needs to be replaced.* ♦ *The marble threshold cracked during the very cold winter.* **2.** *n.* the beginning point of something. (Figurative on ①.) ♦ *The year 2001 is the threshold of a new millennium.* ♦ *The development of the computer marked the threshold of a new era of technology.*

threw ['θru] pt of throw.

thrift ['θrɪft] *n.* the careful use of money and things; the habit of not wasting money or things. (No plural form in this sense.) ♦ *Due to his thrift, John saved enough money to buy a car.* ♦ *Because of her thrift, Anne creates very little garbage.*

thriftiness ['θrɪf ti nəs] *n.* the quality of being thrifty. (No plural form in this sense.) ♦ *Through his thriftiness, John became very rich.* ♦ *Because of her thriftiness, Anne never spends money on herself.*

thrifty ['θrɪf ti] *adj.* saving money; using money and objects wisely; not wasting money or things; economical. (Adv: *thriftily.* Comp: *thriftier;* sup: *thriftiest.*) ♦ *The thrifty man lived in a barren apartment.* ♦ *My thrifty friend only buys grocery items that are on sale.*

thrill ['θrɪl] **1.** *n.* an exciting feeling of emotion, especially excitement, enjoyment, or fear. ♦ *Jane received quite a thrill when she met her favorite singer.* ♦ *Riding an old-fashioned train is a great thrill for me.* **2.** *tv.* to cause someone to feel excited with emotion, especially excitement, enjoyment, or fear. ♦ *Meeting her favorite singer thrilled Jane very much.* ♦ *The skydive thrilled me more than anything else I've ever done.*

thriller ['θrɪl ɚ] **1.** *n.* someone or something that causes excitement, enjoyment, or fear. ♦ *The amusement park was a real thriller for the young children.* ♦ *The scary movie was a thriller.* **2.** *n.* a detective or mystery story; a detective or mystery movie; a story or movie about the solving of a crime. ♦ *Anne's favorite books are thrillers.* ♦ *I have never been able to guess the ending of a mystery thriller.*

thrilling ['θrɪl ɪŋ] *adj.* causing excitement, enjoyment, or fear; exciting. (Adv: *thrillingly.*) ♦ *I just got back from a thrilling vacation in Hawaii.* ♦ *We had a lot of thrilling adventures while hiking.*

thrive ['θrɑɪv] **1.** *iv., irreg.* to grow and flourish; to develop in a very healthy way. (Pt: throve or *thrived;* pp: thriven or *thrived.*) ♦ *Most plants thrive in sunlight.* ♦ *My children thrived on my good cooking.* **2.** *iv., irreg.* to be successful; to become very rich. ♦ *The banker thrived in New York.* ♦ *The little café thrived because people loved the flavor of the coffee served there.*

thriven ['θrɪv ən] a pp of thrive.

thriving ['θraɪv ɪŋ] **1.** *adj.* growing; developing in a healthy way. (Adv: *thrivingly.*) ♦ *The thriving youngster quickly outgrew his clothes.* ♦ *My sunny apartment is filled with thriving plants.* **2.** *adj.* making a lot of money; profitable. (Adv: *thrivingly.*) ♦ *Anne's thriving café serves hundreds of people each day.* ♦ *The thriving banker saved a lot of money for retirement.*

throat ['θrot] **1.** *n.* the front of the neck. ♦ *I tied the warm scarf around my throat.* ♦ *The barber shaved John's beard from his throat to his temples.* **2.** *n.* the inside of the neck where food and air pass. ♦ *A small piece of food got stuck in my throat.* ♦ *I drank hot tea because my throat was sore.* **3. cut one's (own) throat** *idiom* to experience certain failure; to do damage to someone. ♦ *I wouldn't quit this job until I found a new one. To do otherwise would be cutting my own throat.* ♦ *Judges who take bribes are cutting their own throats.* **4. get a lump in one's throat** *idiom* to have the feeling of something in one's throat—as if one were going to cry. ♦ *Whenever they play the national anthem, I get a lump in my throat.* ♦ *I have a lump in my throat because I'm frightened.* **5. have a frog in one's throat** *idiom* to have a feeling of hoarseness. ♦ *I cannot speak more clearly. I have a frog in my throat.* ♦ *I had a frog in my throat, and the telephone receptionist couldn't understand me.* **6. have one's words stick in one's throat** *idiom* to be so overcome by emotion that one can hardly speak. ♦ *I sometimes have my words stick in my throat.* ♦ *John said that he never had his words stick in his throat.*

throb ['θrɑb] **1.** *iv.* to beat strongly and quickly, as with a heartbeat or some other rhythmic pulse. ♦ *My heart is throbbing because I have been running.* ♦ *Does your car's engine always throb like that, or is something wrong?* **2.** *iv.* to pulsate with a pain that occurs with each heartbeat. ♦ *Her infected finger throbbed painfully.* ♦ *When I have a headache, my head throbs with pain.* **3.** *n.* a pulsation; a strong pulse; one beat in a series of strong, quick beats. ♦ *The aspirin relieved the throb of pain in my head.* ♦ *With each throb of one's heart, blood is pumped through the body.*

throbbing ['θrɑb ɪŋ] **1.** *adj.* beating strongly and quickly. (Adv: *throbbingly.*) ♦ *I have a very painful, throbbing headache.* ♦ *We danced to the throbbing beat of the music.* **2.** *n.* strong beating. (No plural form in this sense.) ♦ *There is a painful throbbing in my head.* ♦ *The beat of the music was throbbing loudly and I wanted to dance.*

thrombosis [θrɑm 'bo sɪs] *n.* the formation of a blood clot in a blood vessel or in the heart. (No plural form in this sense.) ♦ *The patient had suffered a coronary thrombosis.* ♦ *The severe thrombosis cut the flow of blood to the patient's foot.*

throne ['θron] **1.** *n.* the chair that a king, queen, ruler, or other important person sits on. ♦ *The king's and queen's thrones were placed side by side.* ♦ *The royal throne was covered with jewels.* **2.** *n.* the position held by a king, queen, ruler, or other important person. ♦ *The present queen took the throne when her father died.* ♦ *King Edward VIII abdicated the British throne in 1936.*

throng ['θrɔŋ] **1.** *n.* a crowd; a large crowd of people. ♦ *A throng of fans came to hear the popular band perform.* ♦ *The president was surrounded by a throng of bodyguards.* **2.** *iv.* to form a crowd somewhere; to come together as a crowd. ♦ *Dozens of screaming fans thronged where the movie star was to appear.* ♦ *The bodyguards thronged around the president when shots rang out.* **3.** *tv.* [for many people] to fill an area as a crowd. ♦ *Thousands of fans thronged the arena to hear the band play.* ♦ *The fans thronged the street where the president would be speaking.*

throttle ['θrɑt əl] **1.** *n.* a valve that controls the amount of fuel that enters an engine. ♦ *John pulled the throttle before starting the engine.* ♦ *Turn off the throttle to stop the engine.* **2.** *tv.* to slow the speed of an engine by cutting back on the amount of fuel that goes into it. ♦ *John throttled the truck's engine as he approached the intersection.* ♦ *The pilot throttled the engine as the plane approached the runway.* **3.** *tv.* to choke someone violently; to strangle someone. ♦ *The mugger throttled his victim and then stole his wallet.* ♦ *John throttled his brother in anger.*

through ['θru] **1.** *prep.* from the outside of one end of something, into it, to the other end of it, and out of the other side of it. ♦ *A cold wind blew through my apartment.* ♦ *The jogger ran through the park.* **2.** *prep.* because of something; on account of something. ♦ *Through no fault of his own, John got into an accident.* ♦ *Anne got a promotion through her hard work.* **3.** *prep.* past something, without stopping. ♦ *The speeding driver drove through a red light.* ♦ *The powerful bullet tore through the victim.* **4.** *prep.* [proceeding] by a certain way; [following] along a certain route. ♦ *I traveled from Chicago to Boston through Cleveland.* ♦ *To speak with the manager, I had to go through her secretary.* **5.** *prep.* around; all over; throughout. ♦ *The poison spread through the victim's body.* ♦ *The fire swept through the forest.* **6.** *prep.* during the entire time from beginning to end; during the entire way from start to finish. ♦ *John slept through class.* ♦ *Bill worked through the night to finish the project.* **7.** *adv.* in one side and out the other. ♦ *Does this road go all the way through?* ♦ *While I rested in the park, a pack of kids ran through.* **8.** *adv.* from beginning to end; from start to finish. ♦ *The manager supervised the difficult project all the way through.* ♦ *I read my contract through carefully.* **9.** *adv.* in a way that is understood; in a way that allows communication. ♦ *Am I getting through to you?* ♦ *Operator, could you put this call through?* **10. through and through** *adv.* completely; totally. ♦ *I read the contract through and through.* ♦ *The maid cleaned the house through and through.* **11.** *adj.* [of a vehicle or vehicles] going all the way from one place to another directly or without stopping; [of a road, a route, or a ticket] allowing continuous or direct travel from one place to another. ♦ *I took a through train from New York to Washington, D.C.* ♦ *This lane is for through traffic only. If you want to turn, you must move your car into the other lane.* **12.** *adj.* finished; done. ♦ *When you're through in the kitchen, let me know.* ♦ *When Anne was through with the book, she let me borrow it.*

throughout [θru 'ɑʊt] *prep.* in every part of something; during every moment of something. ♦ *The cancer spread throughout John's body.* ♦ *Someone in the audience was talking throughout the movie.*

throughway AND **thruway** ['θru we] *n.* a traffic expressway. ♦ *Take the throughway to my house. It's much faster.* ♦ *The thruway was packed with traffic.*

throve [θrov] a pt of thrive.

throw ['θro] **1.** *tv., irreg.* to send something through the air; to hurl something; to cause something to move through the air. (Pt: **threw**; pp: **thrown**.) ♦ *The pitcher threw the baseball through the air.* ♦ *Please throw me those keys.* **2.** *tv., irreg.* to put someone or something someplace carelessly, forcefully, or in a hurry. ♦ *Mary angrily threw the groceries down on the counter.* ♦ *John threw himself onto the bed.* **3.** *tv., irreg.* [for an animal] to cause a rider to fall off. ♦ *The horse threw its rider from its back.* ♦ *The cowboy was thrown by the bucking bronco.* **4.** *tv., irreg.* to move a switch in order to start or stop the flow of electricity. ♦ *Anne threw the switch and turned off the light.* ♦ *The supervisor threw the switch to stop the assembly line.* **5.** *tv., irreg.* to cause someone to be in a certain condition, especially a confused one. ♦ *The hurricane threw the villagers into a panic.* ♦ *When Anne changed her mind, it really threw me.* **6. throw up** *tv. + adv.* to vomit something. ♦ *The dog threw up the entire rabbit it had eaten.* ♦ *Poor Jimmy threw up his dinner.* **7. throw up** *iv. + adv.* to vomit. ♦ *I feel terrible. I think I have to throw up.* ♦ *I just hate to throw up!* **8. throw a party (for someone)** *idiom* to have a party; to hold a party; to arrange a party. ♦ *Bill threw a party for his sister before she went away to college.* ♦ *Things seem sort of dull. Let's throw a party.* **9. throw one's voice** *idiom* to project one's voice so that it seems to be coming from some other place. ♦ *The ventriloquist threw his voice.* ♦ *Jane can throw her voice, so I thought she was standing behind me.*

throwaway ['θro ə we] **1.** *n.* something that can be discarded after it is used. ♦ *The flight attendant put the throwaways in the trash.* ♦ *Don't worry about washing the plastic spoons. They are just throwaways.* **2.** *adj.* <the adj. use of ①.> ♦ *Throwaway packaging materials create a lot of waste.* ♦ *We brought some throwaway plates to the picnic.*

throwback ['θro bæk] *n.* someone or some creature that has reverted to a more primitive form. ♦ *My roommate acts like a throwback to the apes.* ♦ *The genetic mutation seemed to be a throwback to an earlier form.*

thrown ['θron] pp of throw.

thrush ['θrʌʃ] *n.* a type of bird, brownish with a spotted belly, that is found throughout the world. ♦ *In the woods, Mary noticed a thrush sitting in its nest.* ♦ *A flock of thrushes rose up in front of me in the park.*

thrust ['θrʌst] **1.** *tv., irreg.* to push someone or something forward with force; to push someone or something in a certain direction with force. (Pt/pp: *thrust.*) ♦ *John thrust his body forward to open the stuck door.* ♦ *Anne thrust her dog through the door of the veterinarian's office.* **2.** *tv., irreg.* to drive a sharp object at or into someone or something. ♦ *The knight thrust his spear into the dragon.* ♦ *The soldier thrust his dagger at the enemy.* **3.** *iv., irreg.* to move forward with force; to lunge, especially with a sharp object. ♦ *The knight thrust forward towards the dragon.* ♦ *The robber thrust at me with a large knife.* **4.** *n.* a forceful movement in a certain direction; a lunge; a stab. ♦ *The student who was learning to fence practiced his forward thrust.* ♦ *With a powerful thrust of his body, the policeman broke open the door.* **5.** *n.* the force caused by propulsion that causes something, such as a plane or a rocket, to move. (No plural form in this sense.) ♦ *The rocket's thrust propelled it into space.* ♦ *The plane needed more thrust to reach cruising altitude.* **6.** *n.* a guiding force that provides momentum and direction. (No plural form in this sense.) ♦ *The thrust of David's argument was based on faulty premises.* ♦ *John's parents are the thrust behind his success.*

thruway ['θru we] See throughway.

thud ['θʌd] **1.** *n.* the dull sound of something heavy falling onto or hitting something firm but unbreakable. ♦ *The bowling ball fell to the floor with a heavy thud.* ♦ *I heard a thud as my car ran into the sandbags.* **2. thud on(to)** *iv. + prep. phr.* to fall onto someone or something with ①. ♦ *The bowling ball thudded onto the floor.* ♦ *The fainting clerk thudded onto the floor of the store.*

thug ['θʌg] *n.* a criminal; a crook; a robber. ♦ *The thug robbed the store with a gun.* ♦ *The thug ordered me to give him my wallet.*

thumb ['θʌm] **1.** *n.* the first and shortest finger on the hand, separate from the other four, having two knuckles instead of three. ♦ *The carpenter accidentally hit his thumb with a hammer.* ♦ *Anne used her thumb to tear into the peel of the orange.* **2.** *n.* the part of a glove or mitten that covers ①. ♦ *John removed a piece of lint from the thumb of his glove.* ♦ *The thumb of my mitten has a large hole in it.* **3. thumb through** *iv. + prep. phr.* to turn through the pages of a book quickly; to look through something quickly. ♦ *Mary thumbed through the newspaper, looking for the movie section.* ♦ *John thumbed through the magazine, only looking at the pictures.* **4. all thumbs** *idiom* very awkward and clumsy, especially with one's hands. ♦ *Poor Bob can't play the piano at all. He's all thumbs.* ♦ *Mary is all thumbs when it comes to gardening.* **5. have a green thumb** *idiom* to have the ability to grow plants well. ♦ *Just look at Mr. Simpson's garden. He has a green thumb.* ♦ *My mother has a green thumb when it comes to houseplants.* **6. rule of thumb** *idiom* a general principle developed through experiential rather than scientific means. ♦ *As a rule of thumb, I move my houseplants outside in May.* ♦ *Going by the rule of thumb, we stop for gas every 200 miles when we are traveling.* **7. thumb a ride** *idiom* to get a ride by hitchhiking. ♦ *I thumbed a ride to school.* ♦ *David had to thumb a ride because his bicycle was broken.* **8. twiddle one's thumbs** *idiom* to fill up time by playing with one's fingers. ♦ *What am I supposed to do while waiting for you? Sit here and twiddle my thumbs?* ♦ *Don't sit around twiddling your thumbs. Get busy!*

thumbnail ['θʌm nel] **1.** *n.* the nail on one's thumb. ♦ *I trimmed my thumbnails with a pair of clippers.* ♦ *I cracked my thumbnail when I accidentally hit it with a hammer.* **2.** *adj.* small; short; brief. (Prenominal only.) ♦ *The manager gave a thumbnail sketch of her plans.* ♦ *The student wrote a thumbnail description of his project.*

thumbtack ['θʌm tæk] **1.** *n.* a tack with a large, flat head that is pressed with one's thumb to drive the pointed part into a surface. ♦ *I pushed the extra thumbtacks into the board.* ♦ *John hung up the weekly schedule with a thumbtack.* **2.** *tv.* to attach something to a surface with ①. ♦ *Please thumbtack this notice to something that is visible to everyone.* ♦ *I thumbtacked the schedule to the bulletin board.*

thump ['θʌmp] **1.** *n.* a bump or hit. ♦ *Lisa felt a thump on her arm and turned to see who it was.* ♦ *The vacuum cleaner made a thump against the leg of the chair.* **2.** *n.* the sound made by hitting someone or something with something hard or against something hard. ♦ *The cart crashed into the wall with a loud thump.* ♦ *The pumpkin made a thump when I threw it to the ground.* **3.** *tv.* to hit someone or something with something hard; to hit someone or something against something hard. ♦ *I thumped the choking man's back with the palm of my hand.* ♦ *The old lady thumped the attacking dog with her cane.* **4.** *iv.* to hit hard, making ①; to pound [on something]. ♦ *The child thumped hard against the stairs as he fell.* ♦ *I thumped on the drum with the palms of my hands.*

thunder ['θʌn dɚ] **1.** *n.* the loud noise that follows lightning. (No plural form in this sense.) ♦ *The loud thunder scared the little children.* ♦ *Lightning and thunder accompanied the rain.* **2.** *n.* any loud noise or explosion that sounds like ①. ♦ *With a loud thunder, the building was demolished with explosives.* ♦ *There was a thunder of dissent when the jury announced the verdict.* **3.** *iv.* [for weather conditions] to make thunder. ♦ *During heavy rainstorms, it thunders quite loudly.* ♦ *It thundered for an hour, but our area didn't get any rain.* **4.** *iv.* to make a noise like ①; to walk or move making noise like ①. ♦ *The beast thundered toward its unsuspecting prey.* ♦ *John thundered down the hallway in his heavy boots.* **5. thunder at** *iv.* + *prep. phr.* to shout, especially angrily. ♦ *The angry man thundered at the clumsy waiter.* ♦ *Mary thundered at her boyfriend for being an hour late.* **6.** *tv.* to shout something, especially angrily. ♦ *Mary thundered curses at the reckless driver.* ♦ *The cruel boss thundered his orders to the workers.* **7. steal someone's thunder** *idiom* to lessen someone's force or authority. ♦ *What do you mean by coming in here and stealing my thunder? I'm in charge here!* ♦ *Someone stole my thunder by leaking my announcement to the press.*

thunderbolt ['θʌn dɚ bolt] *n.* one instance of thunder and lightning; a bolt of lightning followed by the sound of thunder. ♦ *The loud thunderbolt woke John from his nap.* ♦ *The terrible rainstorm was accompanied by thunderbolts.*

thunderclap ['θʌn dɚ klæp] *n.* a loud burst of thunder. ♦ *The sudden thunderclap made the nervous child jump.* ♦ *The flash of lightning was accompanied by a loud thunderclap.*

thundercloud ['θʌn dɚ klaʊd] *n.* a dark cloud that produces thunder and lightning. ♦ *Heavy rain poured from the thunderclouds in the sky.* ♦ *Dark thunderclouds hung over the park all day long.*

thundering ['θʌn dɚ ɪŋ] *adj.* loud like thunder; loud and explosive. (Adv: *thunderingly.*) ♦ *A thundering rainstorm lasted all night.* ♦ *The thundering explosion was heard for miles.*

thunderous ['θʌn dɚ əs] *adj.* loud like thunder; sounding like thunder. (Adv: *thunderously.*) ♦ *The singer's performance was met with thunderous applause.* ♦ *The villagers were wakened by a thunderous explosion.*

thundershower ['θʌn dɚ ʃaʊ ɚ] *n.* rain with thunder and lightning. ♦ *The picnic has been canceled because of thundershowers.* ♦ *The forecaster predicted thundershowers for the weekend.*

thunderstorm ['θʌn dɚ storm] *n.* a storm with thunder and lightning. ♦ *John was awakened by a loud thunderstorm.* ♦ *I don't like to drive during violent thunderstorms.*

Thursday ['θɚz de] **1.** *n.* the fifth day of the week, between Wednesday and Friday. ♦ *Thanksgiving always happens on a Thursday.* ♦ *I have an appointment with my doctor on Thursday.* **2.** *adv.* on the next ①. ♦ *What are you doing Thursday?* ♦ *I will leave Thursday for vacation.* **3. (on) Thursdays** *adv.* on each ①. ♦ *I do my laundry Thursdays.* ♦ *On Thursdays I have to go to town for physical therapy.*

thus ['ðʌs] *adv.* therefore; for this reason; for these reasons. ♦ *Mary worked very hard. Thus, she got a promotion.* ♦ *The defendant was found not guilty; thus he was freed.*

thwart ['θwɔrt] *tv.* to prevent someone from doing something; to prevent something from happening; to prevent someone from being successful. ♦ *The young hero thwarted the tyrant's evil plans.* ♦ *The police thwarted the criminal's escape.*

Tibet [tə 'bɛt] See Gazetteer.

tic ['tɪk] *n.* a small, uncontrolled movement of a muscle, especially in one's face; a twitch. ♦ *When I drink too much coffee, I get a tic in my left eye.* ♦ *John's stuttering is merely a nervous tic.*

tick ['tɪk] **1.** *n.* the short, quiet sound made by a watch or a clock. ♦ *The room was so quiet, I could hear the tick of my watch.* ♦ *The ticks of the large, old clock were annoying.* **2.** *n.* a small flat insect that attaches to the skin of animals and sucks their blood. ♦ *I removed the ticks from my dog's skin.* ♦ *While we were camping, our tent was invaded by ticks.* **3.** *n.* a mark that is made when counting something or checking something. ♦ *The teacher put a tick by the names of the absent students.* ♦ *There was a red tick by each spelling error in my essay.* **4. tick off** *tv.* + *adv.* to mark something with a check or other mark. ♦ *The clerk ticked off the items on the list.* ♦ *I ticked off the names of those on the list as they entered the room.* **5. tick off** *tv.* + *adv.* to make someone angry; to annoy someone. (Slang.) ♦ *She's lost her temper once today. Don't tick her off again.* ♦ *John really ticked me off when he insulted me.* **6.** *iv.* [for a timepiece] to make a short, quiet sound each second. ♦ *My watch ticked as each second passed.* ♦ *The package was ticking, so I was sure there was a timing device in it.* **7. tick away; tick by** *iv.* + *adv.* [for time or a unit of time] to pass. ♦ *The minutes quickly ticked by during Mary's interesting lecture.* ♦ *The hours ticked away slowly as I waited for John's plane to arrive.* **8. what makes something tick** *idiom* what causes something to run or function. ♦ *I don't know what makes it tick.* ♦ *I took apart the radio to find out what made it tick.* **9. what makes someone tick** *idiom* that which motivates someone; that which makes someone behave in a certain way. ♦ *William is sort of strange. I don't know what makes him tick.* ♦ *When you get to know people, you find out what makes them tick.*

ticket ['tɪk ɪt] **1.** *n.* a piece of paper that shows that its owner has paid for transportation or for entrance into a place that charges admission. ♦ *The travel agent handed me my ticket for my flight to Rome.* ♦ *An usher tore my ticket in half as I entered the theater.* **2.** *n.* a piece of paper that is given as a receipt when one leaves something at a repair shop, cleaners, or other business so that one can get it back. ♦ *You must present your ticket when claiming your car!* ♦ *My ticket from the cleaners listed all the clothes I'd brought in.* **3.** *n.* a piece of paper that is given to someone who has broken a traffic law or parking law, requiring that person to pay a fine or appear in court. ♦ *The cop* *gave me a ticket for speeding.* ♦ *When I returned to my car, there was a ticket on the windshield.* **4.** *tv.* to issue someone ③, requiring an appearance in court or a fine. ♦ *The cop ticketed me for speeding.* ♦ *My car was ticketed because it was parked illegally.* **5. vote a straight ticket** *idiom* to cast a ballot on which all the votes are for members of the same political party. ♦ *I'm not a member of any political party, so I never vote a straight ticket.* ♦ *I usually vote a straight ticket because I believe in the principles of one party and not in the other's.* **6. vote a split ticket** *idiom* to cast a ballot on which the votes are divided between two or more parties. ♦ *I always vote a split ticket since I detest both parties.* ♦ *Mary voted a split ticket for the first time in her life.*

ticking ['tɪk ɪŋ] *n.* the thick, coarse cloth that is used to cover mattresses and pillows. (No plural form in this sense.) ♦ *I covered the mattress with a sheet because the ticking was rough.* ♦ *The ticking on my pillow ripped, and feathers went everywhere.*

tickle ['tɪk əl] **1.** *tv.* to touch a person's body in a way that causes the person to laugh. ♦ *John tickled the baby gently.* ♦ *Mary tickled me until I was laughing hysterically.* **2.** *tv.* to amuse someone. (Figurative on ①.) ♦ *Mary was tickled by David's funny comments.* ♦ *Susan tickled me with her clever wit.* **3.** *tv.* to excite; to stimulate something, such as interest or curiosity. (Figurative on ②.) ♦ *The description of the movie tickled my interest.* ♦ *Does this new perfume tickle your fancy?* **4.** *iv.* to cause a feeling that causes someone to laugh. ♦ *This feather tickles. Get it out of my face.* ♦ *Stop touching me like that! It tickles.* **5.** *n.* an itchy feeling; a feeling that one needs to scratch or sneeze. ♦ *John felt a tickle in his nose just before he sneezed.* ♦ *I felt a tickle on my leg as the cat walked by it.*

ticklish ['tɪk lɪʃ] **1.** *adj.* sensitive to tickling; likely to laugh when tickled. (Adv: *ticklishly.*) ♦ *The ticklish baby giggled with laughter.* ♦ *My ticklish friend screamed as I touched his skin with a feather.* **2.** *adj.* difficult; hard to answer; delicate; requiring careful thought or action. (Figurative on ①. Adv: *ticklishly.*) ♦ *The mayor discussed the ticklish problem with his advisors.* ♦ *You must handle this ticklish situation with a lot of tact.*

tick-tock ['tɪk tɑk] *n.* the sound made by a watch or a clock each second. ♦ *"Tick-tock" went the clock as the seconds passed.* ♦ *It was so quiet, I could hear the tick-tock of the clock.*

tidal ['tɑɪd l] *adj.* of or about the tide; caused by tides; having tides. (Adv: *tidally.*) ♦ *The moon's gravity affects tidal patterns on Earth.* ♦ *The tidal basin filled with sea water twice a day.*

tidal wave ['tɑɪd l wev] **1.** *n.* a very large wave from an ocean, caused by an earthquake or hurricane. ♦ *The tidal wave crashed into the coastal town.* ♦ *The earthquake under the sea created a huge tidal wave.* **2.** *n.* an overwhelming or widespread movement in public opinion or public emotion. (Figurative on ①.) ♦ *There was a tidal wave of anger against the senator's comments.* ♦ *The president was elected with a tidal wave of support.*

tidbit ['tɪd bɪt] **1.** *n.* a small piece of food that tastes very good. ♦ *The host offered the guests some tidbits before dinner.* ♦ *For an appetizer, we ate some low-calorie tidbits.* **2.** *n.* a piece of trivia; a small, interesting piece of information. ♦ *Almanacs are filled with thousands of tidbits.* ♦ *The article was padded with interesting but irrelevant tidbits.*

tide ['tɑɪd] **1.** *n.* the rise and fall of the ocean, caused by the pull of the sun and the moon. ♦ *During high tide, most of this beach is covered with water.* ♦ *As the tide came in, it destroyed my sand castle.* **2. turn the tide** *idiom* to cause a reversal in the direction of events; to cause a reversal in public opinion. ♦ *It looked as if the team was going to lose, but near the end of the game, our star player turned the tide.* ♦ *At first, people were opposed to our plan. After a lot of discussion, we were able to turn the tide.*

tidings ['tɑɪd ɪŋz] *n.* news or information. (Older English. Treated as singular.) ♦ *News of the war's end was very good tidings, indeed.* ♦ *The soldier received the tidings of the birth of his son.*

tidy ['tɑɪ di] **1.** *adj.* very neat; orderly; not messy. (Adv: *tidily.* Comp: *tidier;* sup: *tidiest.*) ♦ *John's apartment is extremely tidy.* ♦ *My boss likes to have a tidy desk.* **2.** *adj.* liking to keep things clean, neat, and orderly. (Adv: *tidily.* Comp: *tidier;* sup: *tidiest.*) ♦ *My tidy roommate asked me to wash my dishes.* ♦ *The tidy secretary filed each document where it belonged.* **3.** *adj.* [of a sum of money] rather large. (Adv: *tidily.* Comp: *tidier;* sup: *tidiest.*) ♦ *John won the tidy sum of $100,000 in the lottery.* ♦ *We received a tidy amount of snow during the blizzard.* **4.** *tv.* to make something ①. ♦ *My boss tidies her desk at the end of each day.* ♦ *The maid had tidied the hotel room while I was out.*

tie ['tɑɪ] **1.** *tv.* to form string, rope, cord, or thread into a knot or bow, often as a way to connect it to something or to join two pieces or ends together. (The present participle is tying for all senses of the verb.) ♦ *Jimmy tied his shoelaces.* ♦ *Mary tied a ribbon in her hair.* **2.** *tv.* to join someone in occupying the same position in a list of the rank of a group of things; to have the same score as the opposite player or team. ♦ *Central High tied Northern High for first place.* ♦ *By the end of the inning, our team tied the opponent 4–4.* **3. tie (up)** *tv.* (+ *adv.*) to fasten something with string, rope, cord, or thread. ♦ *Mary tied her hair with a ribbon.* ♦ *The postal clerk tied the parcel up with string.* **4. tie down** *tv.* + *adv.* to restrain someone figuratively; to limit someone's freedom. ♦ *John's job and family tied him down.* ♦ *I don't want to tie you down. Leave if you must.* **5. tie to** *tv.* + *prep. phr.* to connect something to something; to link ④ something to something. ♦ *Studies have tied cancer to smoking.* ♦ *Her account of the accident ties the defendant to the car that did the damage.* **6.** *iv.* [for two teams] to have the same score; to occupy the same position as someone else in a list of the rank of a group of things. ♦ *The two teams tied at 7–7.* ♦ *Two runners tied for first place.* **7.** *n.* a string, rope, cord, or strand used for tying. ♦ *The parcel opened when its tie snapped.* ♦ *The tie around the package became tangled in knots.* **8.** *n.* a necktie; a strip of cloth that is looped around the neck and tied so there is a knot at the neck and the two ends hang down in front of one's shirt. ♦ *All male employees must wear ties to work.* ♦ *David spilled some coffee on his silk tie.* **9.** *n.* something that links, unites, or joins things or people together. ♦ *Love is the tie that binds John and Mary.* ♦ *John has family ties in New York City.* **10.** *n.* a long, heavy, wooden beam that train tracks are attached to. ♦ *The children hopped from one tie to another until they heard the train coming.* ♦ *The ties have to be inspected every few months.* **11.** *n.* a result of a game where both teams or players have the same score; a ranking where two or more people or things have the same rank. ♦ *The championship game ended in a tie.* ♦ *The baseball game was in a tie at the end of the ninth inning, so it went into extra innings.* **12. have one's hands tied** *idiom* to be prevented from doing something. ♦ *I can't help you. I was told not to, so I have my hands tied.* ♦ *John can help. He doesn't have his hands tied.* **13. tie the knot** *idiom* to get married. ♦ *Well, I hear that you and John are going to tie the knot.* ♦ *My parents tied the knot almost forty years ago.* **14. tied to one's mother's apron strings** *idiom* dominated by one's mother; dependent on one's mother. ♦ *Tom is still tied to his mother's apron strings.* ♦ *Isn't he a little old to be tied to his mother's apron strings?*

tier ['tɪr] **1.** *n.* one level in a series of levels, each higher than the one below and in front of it. ♦ *There were five tiers of seating at the arena.* ♦ *Each tier of the wedding cake was a different flavor.* **2.** *n.* a level or rank. (Figurative on ①.) ♦ *Mary was promoted to a higher job tier, so she had to work harder.* ♦ *That talented basketball player is in the top tier of professional athletes.*

tie-up ['tɑɪ əp] *n.* a traffic jam; a standstill in something that should be moving; a problem that causes something that should be moving or functioning to stop. ♦ *The accident caused a tie-up on the freeway.* ♦ *The assembly line stopped due to a tie-up at the end of the line.*

tiger ['tɑɪ gɚ] *n.* a large, fierce animal that is a member of the cat family and has orange or yellow fur with black stripes. ♦ *The poachers killed a rare tiger.* ♦ *The tiger stalked its prey.*

tight ['tɑɪt] **1.** *adj.* not loose; having no extra room on the sides or around the edges; fitting closely. (Adv: *tightly.* Comp: *tighter;* sup: *tightest.*) ♦ *These pants are too tight. I need a larger size.* ♦ *The tight shoes pinched Anne's feet.* **2.** *adj.* [of a schedule] having no extra time; having no appointments available. (Figurative on ①. Adv: *tightly.* Comp: *tighter;* sup: *tightest.*) ♦ *My time is very tight today. Can we meet next week?* ♦ *There is no room for lunch in my tight schedule.* **3.** *adj.* closely held; firmly fastened; fixed. (Adv: *tightly.* Comp: *tighter;* sup: *tightest.*) ♦ *Mary kept a tight grip on her child's hand at the mall.* ♦ *The contractor kept a tight rein on the workers.* **4.** *adj.* stretched; taut. (Adv: *tightly.* Comp: *tighter;* sup: *tightest.*) ♦ *The tight rope snapped under the pressure.* ♦ *My tight muscles were very sore.* **5.** *adj.* stingy; miserly; not likely to spend or give money. (Informal. Figurative on ③. Adv: *tightly.* Comp: *tighter;* sup: *tightest.*) ♦ *My boss is so tight that I haven't gotten a raise in two years.* ♦ *Because his landlord is so tight, John has almost no heat in the winter.* **6.** *adv.* tightly; in a tight ① way; firmly; closely. (Comp: *tighter;* sup: *tightest.*) ♦ *Anne held on tight to the railing.* ♦ *The crack in the pipe was sealed tight.* **7. tights** *n.* a garment that is worn below the waist and fits closely against one's body, generally worn by women and dancers; pantyhose; nylons. ♦ *Anne wore a pair of black tights under her skirt.* ♦ *The ballet dancers all wore white tights.* **8. sit tight** *idiom* to wait; to wait patiently. ♦ *Just relax and sit tight. I'll be right with you.* ♦ *We were waiting in line for the gates to open when someone came out and told us to sit tight because it wouldn't be much longer until we could go in.*

tighten ['tɑɪt n] **1.** *tv.* to make something tight; to make something tighter. ♦ *The plumber tightened the nut with a wrench.* ♦ *Mary tightened her grip on Jimmy's arm.* **2.** *iv.* to become tight; to become tighter. ♦ *The rope tightened as I pulled it.* ♦ *John's muscles tightened as he lifted the heavy crate.*

tight-fisted ['tɑɪt 'fɪs tɪd] *adj.* stingy; miserly; not likely to spend or give money. (Adv: *tight-fistedly.*) ♦ *My tight-fisted landlord turned off the heat in March.* ♦ *My tight-fisted boss won't give me a raise.*

tight-lipped ['tɑɪt lɪpt] *adj.* keeping a secret; not talking about something; saying nothing; keeping one's lips closely together. ♦ *The tight-lipped politician refused to talk to the reporter.* ♦ *David is being very tight-lipped about last night's incident.*

tightrope ['tɑɪt rop] **1.** *n.* a rope or cable that is stretched tight, high above the ground, and on which acrobats perform. ♦ *The acrobat fell from the tightrope onto the safety net.* ♦ *The clown rode a bicycle along the tightrope.* **2. walk a tightrope** *idiom* to be in a situation where one must be very cautious. ♦ *I've been walking a tightrope all day. I need to relax.* ♦ *Our business is about to fail. We've been walking a tightrope for three months.*

tightwad ['tɑɪt wɑd] *n.* someone who is tight with money; someone who is stingy; a miser. ♦ *The tightwad did not leave the waiter any tip.* ♦ *That tightwad refuses to give his workers bonuses.*

tile ['tɑɪl] **1.** *n.* baked clay or ceramic material formed into useful shapes for construction and decoration. (No plural form in this sense.) ♦ *The entire building was covered with tile.* ♦ *The floor was made of tile.* **2.** *n.* a thin, formed piece of ① used for covering floors, walls, roofs, and other surfaces in buildings and houses. ♦ *The swimming pool was lined with small ceramic tiles.* ♦ *The janitor polished the marble tiles in the lobby.* **3.** *n.* a square of soft material that absorbs sound and provides decoration, used in the construction of ceilings. ♦ *The ceiling was made of white tiles.* ♦ *John jumped up and touched the ceiling tiles.* **4.** *tv.* to cover a surface with ① or a similar substance. ♦ *The worker tiled the kitchen floor in one day.* ♦ *I tiled my bathroom walls with expensive white marble.* **5.** *iv.* to work by covering surfaces with ①. ♦ *John tiled while I brought him supplies.* ♦ *The contractor hired four workers who knew how to tile.*

till ['tɪl] **1.** *tv.* to plow land; to cultivate soil. ♦ *The farmer tilled the soil with a tractor.* ♦ *The field had been tilled before the seeds were planted.* **2.** *n.* the drawer in a cash register or counter where money is kept in a place of business. ♦ *The clerk opened the till to make change.* ♦ *There was no slot for a $2 bill in my till.* **3.** *prep.* until; up to a certain time; during a period of time up to a certain time. ♦ *We stayed at the bar till 5:00 A.M.* ♦ *Anne will be in Boston till Tuesday.* **4.** *conj.* until; up to a certain time. ♦ *Mary played with Susie till her mother called her home.* ♦ *We will be at the park till it gets dark.* **5.** *conj.* until; before. ♦ *Till John got his first job, he was supported by his parents.* ♦ *I never went to France till I learned French.* **6. have one's hand in the till** *idiom* to be stealing money from a company or an organization. (On ②.) ♦ *Mr. Jones had his hand in the till for years before he was caught.* ♦ *I think that the new clerk has her hand in the till. There is cash missing every morning.*

tiller ['tɪl ɚ] *n.* the handle attached to a rudder, used to steer a boat. ♦ *John pushed the tiller to the right to avoid the rock.* ♦ *My hands slipped from the tiller because it was wet.*

tilt ['tɪlt] **1.** *tv.* to turn something to its side; to slant something. ♦ *If you tilt your glass any more, it will fall over!* ♦ *The earthquake tilted the house to one side.* **2.** *iv.* to be turned to the side; to be tipped; to slant; to slope. ♦ *The old barn tilted to the left.* ♦ *The tree tilted toward the ground.* **3.** *n.* the condition of having been tilted; slope; slant; a tilting position. ♦ *The seasons are caused by the tilt of the earth on its axis.* ♦ *The tilt of the old building meant it was unsafe to live in.* **4. at full tilt** *idiom* at full speed; as fast as possible. ♦ *The driver sped down the road at full tilt.* ♦ *The runner raced at full tilt toward the finish line.*

timber ['tɪm bɚ] **1.** *n.* trees that are growing; a forest; woods. (No plural form in this sense.) ♦ *Much timber was destroyed in the forest fire.* ♦ *The farmer sold the timber growing behind the farm.* **2.** *n.* wood that is used to make or build things. (No plural form in this sense.) ♦ *The logging company harvested timber from the old forest.* ♦ *The carpenter bought some timber from the mill.* **3.** *n.* a thick length of wood. ♦ *The barn was built of sturdy timbers.* ♦ *The main beam is a very sturdy timber.*

timbre ['tɪm bɚ, 'tæm bɚ] *n.* the quality of a sound or a voice that distinguishes it from other kinds of sounds or voices. (No plural form in this sense.) ♦ *The opera singer's distinctive timbre gave the music a rich, full sound.* ♦ *The timbre of that singer's voice does not suit this kind of music.*

time ['tɑɪm] **1.** *n.* every moment that ever was, is now, and ever will be; a continuous passage of duration from the past, through now, and into the future. (No plural form in this sense.) ♦ *Time passes very slowly when you are bored.* ♦ *Humans cannot reverse the flow of time.* **2.** *n.* a period of ①; a period of ① between two events. (No plural form in this sense.) ♦ *Mary lived in Florida for a short time in the 1980s.* ♦ *For a long time, John had wanted to be an astronaut.* **3.** *n.* the measurement of the **time** ① that it takes to do something. (No plural form in this sense.) ♦ *Could I have five minutes of your time?* ♦ *How much time would it take to bake a cake?* **4.** *n.* an exact moment in the passage of ①; some moment in the passage of ①. ♦ *At what time do you usually eat breakfast?* ♦ *At what time is Mary's flight scheduled to arrive?* ♦ *"What time is it?" "The time is two o'clock."* **5.** *n.* the appropriate moment to do something. (No plural form in this sense.) ♦ *Let me know when it's time to leave the party.* ♦ *It's time to change our way of doing business.* **6.** *n.* a system of measuring ①. (No plural form in this sense.) ♦ *In the winter, New York City is on Eastern Standard Time.* ♦ *The news bureau used Greenwich Time in all its reports.* **7. times** *n.* periods of ① and the events that occurred during them. ♦ *We lived through some difficult times during the war.* ♦ *I had a lot of good times in college.* **8.** *n.* an occasion of doing something; an instance of something being done. ♦ *The first time I ate lobster, I didn't like it.* ♦ *"How many times have you seen this movie?" "I've seen it three times."* **9.** *n.* the rate of pay for a job, equal to the amount of money one makes for a regular period of time. (No plural form in this sense.) ♦ *After eight hours, I began earning time and a half.* ♦ *This company pays double time on holidays.* **10.** *adj.* <the adj. use of ①.> ♦ *The science-fiction writer wrote about time travel.* ♦ *The live broadcast was aired with a 7-second time delay.* **11.** *tv.* to measure the duration of something; to measure how long or how fast it takes someone to do something. ♦ *My boss timed how long it took me to do the project.* ♦ *The coach timed the runner in the race.* **12.** *tv.* to determine the best time for doing something, and do it then. ♦ *I timed my response to follow Anne's comments.* ♦ *The actor timed his entrance for the maximum comic effect.* **13.** *tv.* to set or arrange something so that it does something at a certain time ④. ♦ *The cook timed the eggs to finish cooking at the same time as the toast.* ♦ *Anne timed her arrival for 6:00 P.M.* **14. times** *prep.* multiplied by; multiplying ______ by. (Symbolized by "×.") ♦ *Four times four is eight.* ♦ *One times 1,000,000,000 is 1,000,000,000.* **15. on time** *phr.* before the deadline; by the stated time. ♦ *Please make sure that your essays are completed on time.* ♦ *My taxes were not done on time, so I had to pay a penalty.* **16. on time** *phr.* right at or just before the right time; soon enough [for something or to do something]. ♦ *I usually arrive right on time.* ♦ *Is the train on time, or will it be late?* **17. in time** *phr.* within the proper amount of time; before the deadline; before the time limit; within the allotted period of time. ♦ *I hope we get there in time to go swimming before dark.* ♦ *Am I in time for the cake and ice cream?* **18. ahead of one's time** *idiom* having ideas or attitudes that are too advanced to be acceptable to the society in which one is living. ♦ *People buy that artist's work now, but his paintings were laughed at when he was alive. He was ahead of his time.* ♦ *Mary's grandmother was ahead of her time in wanting to study medicine.* **19. from time to time** *idiom* irregularly; now and then; occasionally; sometimes; not predictably. ♦ *From time to time, I like to go fishing instead of going to work.* ♦ *Bob visits us at our house from time to time.* **20. have the time of one's life** *idiom* to have a very good time; to have the most exciting time or experience in one's life. ♦ *What a great party! I had the time of my life.* ♦ *We went to Florida last winter and had the time of our lives.* **21. in (less than) no time** *idiom* very quickly. ♦ *I'll be there in less than no time.* ♦ *Don't worry. This won't take long. It'll be over with in less than no time.* **22. in one's spare time** *idiom* in one's extra time; in the time not reserved for doing something else. ♦ *I write novels in my spare time.* ♦ *I'll try to paint the house in my spare time.* **23. in the nick of time** *idiom* just in time; at the last possible instant; just before it's too late. ♦ *The doctor arrived in the nick of time. The patient's life was saved.* ♦ *I reached the airport in the nick of time.* **24. kill time** *idiom* to waste time. ♦ *Stop killing time. Get to work!* ♦ *We went over to the record shop just to kill time.* **25. make up for lost time** *idiom* to do something quickly, especially to compensate for an earlier delay; to do something intensely or a lot, especially to compensate for not having done it earlier. ♦ *Because we took so long eating lunch, we have to drive faster to make up for lost time. Otherwise we won't arrive on time.* ♦ *At the age of sixty, Bill learned to play golf. Now he plays every day. He's making up for lost time.* **26. take one's time** *idiom* to go as slow as one wants or needs to; to use as much time as is required. ♦ *There is no hurry. Please take your time.* ♦ *Bill is very careful and takes his time so he won't make any mistakes.* **27. time flies** *idiom* time passes very quickly. ♦ *I didn't really think it was so late* *when the party ended. Doesn't time fly?* ♦ *Time simply flew when the old friends got together.* **28. time was (when)** *idiom* there was a time when; at a time in the past. ♦ *Time was when old people were taken care of at home.* ♦ *Time was when people didn't travel around so much.*

timeless ['taɪm ləs] *adj.* never beginning or ending; lasting forever; eternal. (Adv: *timelessly.*) ♦ *The human soul is thought to be timeless.* ♦ *Susan has a timeless beauty.*

timely ['taɪm li] *adj.* at the proper time; at the right time; at the appropriate time. ♦ *My counselor gave me some timely advice.* ♦ *John arrives at work in a timely manner.*

time off ['taɪm 'ɔf] *idiom* a period of time during which one does not have to work; free time. ♦ *The next time I have some time off, I want to go to Miami.* ♦ *I don't have any time off until next week.*

time-out ['taɪm 'aʊt] **1.** *n.* a period of time within a game when play is stopped. ♦ *The coach called a time-out to talk to his team about the next play.* ♦ *The injured player called for a time-out.* **2.** *n.* a period of time when one takes a break from something; a period of time when one stops doing something. (Figurative on ①.) ♦ *Jane told her arguing children to take a time-out and behave.* ♦ *Mary took a time-out during her busy day for a nap.* **3. time out** *iv.* [for a computer program] to cease working due to inactivity or lack of response. ♦ *My modem connection times out after 5 minutes.* ♦ *When I returned to my terminal, the program had already timed out.*

timepiece ['taɪm pis] *n.* a device, especially a clock or a watch, that keeps track of time. ♦ *My grandfather gave me his antique timepiece.* ♦ *The train conductor glanced at the timepiece in his hand.*

timer ['taɪm ɚ] *n.* someone or something that records time, especially a device that can be set to indicate when a certain amount of time has passed. ♦ *The cook set the timer for five minutes.* ♦ *Microwave ovens always come with timers.*

timetable ['taɪm te bəl] **1.** *n.* a schedule or chart that shows when a bus, train, plane, etc., arrives and departs. ♦ *According to the timetable, the train is ten minutes late.* ♦ *I consulted the timetable for the next departure.* **2.** *n.* a statement of when certain things are scheduled to happen. (Figurative on ①.) ♦ *We're on a timetable to finish construction by next spring.* ♦ *My boss pushed back the project's timetable by a week.*

time zone ['taɪm zon] *n.* an area of land running from pole to pole where the same standard time is used. ♦ *Earth is divided into 24 time zones, each about 15 degrees wide.* ♦ *New York City is in the Eastern time zone and is three hours ahead of Los Angeles, which is in the Pacific time zone.*

timid ['tɪm ɪd] *adj.* fearful; easily scared. (Adv: *timidly.* Comp: *timider;* sup: *timidest.*) ♦ *The timid student was afraid to talk to his teacher.* ♦ *The timid little mouse hid from the cat.*

timing ['taɪm ɪŋ] *n.* the control of the occurrence of events for the best effect possible. (No plural form in this sense.) ♦ *The timing of the comic's response was perfect.* ♦ *The press agent was in charge of the timing of the press conference.*

tin ['tɪn] **1.** *n.* a metal that is mixed with other metals to make bronze and is used as a coating for steel so that it doesn't rust. (No plural form in this sense.) ♦ *The atomic number of tin is 50, and its atomic symbol is Sn.* ♦ *The steel cans were coated with a layer of tin.* **2.** *n.* a can or a container made of ① or plated with ①, or a modern steel can containing no tin. (Usually limited to containers that hold cookies, crackers, and sardines.) ♦ *John stored the crackers in a tin.* ♦ *Mary bought a tin of sardines.* **3.** *adj.* made of or coated with ①. ♦ *John recycled the old tin cans.* ♦ *The soldier drank from a tin cup.*

tinderbox ['tɪn dɚ bɑks] **1.** *n.* a box that contains a dry substance that catches fire quickly, as well as a piece of flint and a piece of steel, which are used to make a spark to set the dry substance on fire. ♦ *Tinderboxes were in use in the 18th century.* ♦ *The hunter carried a tinderbox with him while hunting.* **2.** *n.* a situation that is likely to explode; someone or something that is explosive or excitable. (Figurative on ①.) ♦ *The nation was a tinderbox of ethnic hatred.* ♦ *John is a tinderbox of angry emotion.*

tinfoil ['tɪn foɪl] *n.* a very thin sheet of tin, as once used for wrapping food or tobacco. (Refers now to any thin metal foil, usually aluminum. No plural form in this sense.) ♦ *Aluminum foil and other products have almost totally replaced tinfoil.* ♦ *I wrapped tinfoil around the TV antenna to improve the reception.*

tinge ['tɪndʒ] **1.** *n.* a very small amount of something, such as color or an emotion. ♦ *There's a tinge of gray in my hair.* ♦ *I felt a tinge of guilt for eating Mary's cookie.* **2.** *tv.* to enhance something with a small amount of something. ♦ *The sun tinged the afternoon clouds with red.* ♦ *The routine news story was tinged with sensational details.*

tingle ['tɪŋ gəl] **1.** *n.* a light prickly or stinging feeling, as though one received a small shock or thrill. ♦ *I could feel only a tingle in my numb foot.* ♦ *The scary movie sent a tingle down my spine.* **2.** *iv.* to experience a light, prickly, or stinging feeling, as though one has received a small shock or thrill. ♦ *My body tingled on the amusement park ride.* ♦ *Lisa's foot tingled because she had been sitting on it.*

tinker ['tɪŋ kɚ] **tinker (with)** *iv.* (+ *prep. phr.*) to try to fix something; to meddle with something while trying to fix it. ♦ *Bob damaged the broken toaster even more when he tinkered with it.* ♦ *Anne tinkered with the antenna to improve the TV's reception.*

tinkle ['tɪŋ kəl] **1.** *n.* a short, quiet, high-pitched ring or clinking sound. ♦ *The small bell made a tinkle when I rang it.* ♦ *We heard the tinkle of glasses as Mother washed the dishes.* **2.** *iv.* to ring in a short, quiet, high-pitched way. ♦ *The tiny bells tinkled in the breeze.* ♦ *The charms on Mary's bracelet tinkle when she moves her arm.* **3.** *iv.* to urinate. (Juvenile.) ♦ *Jane told her mom that she had to tinkle.* ♦ *Billy laughed when the puppy tinkled on the rug.*

tinny ['tɪn i] **1.** *adj.* made of tin; seeming like tin. (Adv: *tinnily.* Comp: *tinnier;* sup: *tinniest.*) ♦ *The tinny bells did not have a clear ring.* ♦ *The tinny coating protected the metal core from rusting.* **2.** *adj.* having poor audio fidelity. (Adv: *tinnily.* Comp: *tinnier;* sup: *tinniest.*) ♦ *The inexpensive rental car had a tinny radio.* ♦ *The loud, tinny buzzer hurt my ears.*

tinsel ['tɪn səl] *n.* a very thin, shiny strip of a material, usually silver in color, used for decorating. ♦ *The caterer decorated the food cart with tinsel.* ♦ *The children hung tinsel around the doorway.*

tinsmith ['tɪn smɪθ] *n.* someone who makes things from sheets of metal. ♦ *The tinsmith pounded the metal sheet with a mallet.* ♦ *These metal cups were handmade by a tinsmith.*

tint ['tɪnt] **1.** *n.* a color; a weakened shade of a color. ♦ *Rose and pink are tints of red.* ♦ *Mary wanted to paint her bathroom walls in a lighter tint.* **2.** *tv.* to color something slightly; to give a small amount of color to something; to dye hair with ①. ♦ *The artist tinted the dab of yellow paint with some white.* ♦ *The hair stylist tinted my hair red.*

tinted ['tɪn tɪd] *adj.* slightly colored. ♦ *David wears tinted contact lenses.* ♦ *Mary's tinted hair is very attractive.*

tiny ['tɑɪ ni] *adj.* very small. (Adv: *tinily.* Comp: *tinier;* sup: *tiniest.*) ♦ *The tiny kitten licked its fur.* ♦ *A tiny insect walked across the floor.*

tip ['tɪp] **1.** *n.* the very end part of an object; the top of an object. ♦ *I scratched my ear with the tip of my finger.* ♦ *I tapped the tip of the pencil against the desk.* **2.** *n.* money that is given to someone for a service; a gratuity. ♦ *We gave the waiter a 15% tip.* ♦ *I gave my barber a large tip.* **3.** *n.* a hint; a suggestion; a piece of advice. ♦ *Can I give you a tip? Don't wear your sunglasses at night.* ♦ *The newscaster read a list of tips on safe driving.* **4.** *n.* a piece of secret information. ♦ *The police received an anonymous tip about the murder.* ♦ *John heard a tip about which horse would win the race.* **5.** *tv.* to lean something to the side; to cause something to slant. ♦ *John tipped the box of cereal onto its side.* ♦ *I tipped the barrel so the water would flow out.* **6. tip over** *tv.* + *adv.* to knock something over; to spill something; to overturn something. ♦ *The child tipped the vase over as he ran by.* ♦ *Tom tipped the container of cereal over.* **7.** *tv.* to give someone money for a service; to leave someone ②. ♦ *The satisfied diners tipped the server generously.* ♦ *I tipped the porter for carrying my luggage.* **8.** *tv.* to give a certain sum or percentage of money in gratitude for service. ♦ *At the restaurant, we tipped $5 on the bill of $30.* ♦ *I always tip at least 15%.* **9. tip off** *tv.* + *adv.* to advise someone of something that is about to happen. (Informal.) ♦ *The spy tipped off Mary that she was in danger.* ♦ *Go tip off your brother that Max is looking for him.* **10.** *iv.* to lean to the side; to slant. ♦ *The tree tipped in the wind.* ♦ *The rickety door tipped to one side.* **11. tip over** *iv.* + *adv.* to fall over; to spill; to overturn. ♦ *The top-heavy vase tipped over.* ♦ *The truck tipped over from the force of the collision.* **12.** *iv.* to give people money for their services on a regular basis. ♦ *The rich banker always tipped well.* ♦ *The newscaster always tips her hair stylist.*

tip-off ['tɪp ɔf] **1.** *n.* a piece of secret information. ♦ *The tip-off was phoned in anonymously.* ♦ *Mary got a tip-off that the horse race was fixed.* **2.** *n.* something that gives a secret away; something that exposes someone or something. ♦ *The fact that he didn't know basic facts of American history was the tip-off that John was a spy.* ♦ *Anne's accent is a tip-off that she's from Ireland.*

tiptoe ['tɪp to] **1.** *n.* the tips of the toes, referring to walking on the toes. ♦ *I walked about on tiptoe because my parents were sleeping.* ♦ *The ballerinas balanced on their tiptoes.* **2.** *iv.* to walk on the tips of one's toes; to walk very quietly or lightly. ♦ *I tiptoed when I got home so I wouldn't wake anyone up.* ♦ *The burglar tiptoed through the museum.* **3. on tiptoe** *idiom* [standing or walking] on the front part of the feet (the balls of the feet) with no weight put on the heels. ♦ *I had to stand on tiptoe in order to see over the fence.* ♦ *I came in late and walked on tiptoe so I wouldn't wake anybody up.*

tip-top ['tɪp 'tɑp] **1.** *n.* the highest point of something; the top of something. ♦ *The climbers placed their country's flag at the mountain's tip-top.* ♦ *I placed a cherry on the tip-top of the ice-cream sundae.* **2.** *adj.* [of a condition] excellent. (Informal.) ♦ *The doctor said I was in tip-top condition.* ♦ *John has a tip-top mind and is very bright.*

tirade ['tɑɪ red] *n.* a long, angry speech. ♦ *The politician's tirade offended many people.* ♦ *Bill expected a tirade from his parents because he was late.*

tire ['tɑɪr] **1.** *n.* a circular structure of rubber that surrounds a wheel and is filled with air. ♦ *One of my car's tires went flat when I was driving on the freeway.* ♦ *That rubber plant recycles old tires.* **2. tire of** *iv.* + *prep. phr.* to become impatient with someone or something. ♦ *John tired of his boss's constant complaining.* ♦ *I'm tired of your tardiness!* **3. tire (out)** *iv.* (+ *adv.*) to become weary or exhausted. ♦ *Jane quickly tired out during her long day at work.* ♦ *Bob tires easily because he has cancer.* **4. tire out** *tv.* + *adv.* to cause someone to become sleepy or weary. ♦ *The hard work tired Mary out.* ♦ *I was tired out by the hard work.* **5.** *tv.* to cause someone to become dissatisfied or impatient. ♦ *John tired Mary with the pictures from his vacation.* ♦ *The student's excuses tired the teacher and made him grouchy at times.*

tired ['tɑɪrd] **1.** *adj.* sleepy; wanting to sleep; exhausted. (Adv: *tiredly.*) ♦ *The tired traveler went to sleep early.* ♦ *Because I was so tired, I fell asleep at work.* **2.** *adj.* impatient with someone or something; annoyed with someone or something. (Adv: *tiredly.*) ♦ *I was tired of all the noise upstairs.* ♦ *The teacher became tired of explaining the same things over and over.*

tireless ['tɑɪr ləs] *adj.* never becoming tired; without tiring; not needing a lot of sleep. (Adv: *tirelessly.*) ♦ *The tireless doctor worked a 24-hour shift.* ♦ *The tireless firefighters labored until the fire was put out.*

tiresome ['tɑɪr səm] *adj.* boring; causing one to become tired. (Adv: *tiresomely.*) ♦ *My neighbor's tiresome stories made me yawn.* ♦ *We both fell asleep during the tiresome movie.*

tiring ['tɑɪr ɪŋ] *adj.* causing one to become tired, especially because it requires a lot of energy, patience, or attention; exhausting. (Adv: *tiringly.*) ♦ *After a tiring day at work, I went home and fell asleep.* ♦ *Mary spent a tiring afternoon preparing for the large party.*

tissue ['tɪʃ ju] **1.** *n.* a very soft piece of paper that is used to wipe the skin. ♦ *John wiped his runny nose with a tissue.* ♦ *Mary placed a box of tissues on her desk.* **2.** *n.* a part of a plant or an animal that is made of many cells having the same function; the group of cells in a plant or animal that form a particular organ. (No plural form in this sense.) ♦ *Layers of fatty tissue keep animals warm in the winter.* ♦ *The surgeon cut through the tissue surrounding the bone.*

titanic [tɑɪ 'tæn ɪk] *adj.* huge; very large; colossal. (Adv: *titanically* […ɪk li].) ♦ *Residents evacuated as the titanic storm approached.* ♦ *The politician tried to reduce the titanic deficit.*

titanium [tɑɪ 'ten i əm] *n.* a silver-gray metallic chemical element that resists corrosion and is used in aircraft, spacecraft, missiles, and ships. (No plural form in this sense.) ♦ *The atomic symbol of titanium is Ti, and its atomic number is 22.* ♦ *The government's defense department obtained titanium from a private mine.*

titillate ['tɪt ə let] *tv.* to excite someone, especially in a pleasant or sexual way; to arouse someone slightly. ♦ *Scantily dressed dancers sought to titillate the audience.* ♦ *Mary was titillated by David's suggestion.*

titillating ['tɪt ə let ɪŋ] *adj.* exciting, especially in a pleasant or sexual way; arousing. (Adv: *titillatingly.*) ♦ *I blushed while I watched the titillating movie.* ♦ *The librarian placed the titillating books in a separate section.*

title ['tɑɪt əl] **1.** *n.* the name of a book, movie, song, play, picture, or poem. ♦ East of Eden *is the title of a book by John Steinbeck.* ♦ *The title of the movie was changed twice during production.* **2.** *n.* a word, often abbreviated, that is placed before a person's name indicating rank, profession, or social position. ♦ *The honored guest addressed the queen by her formal title.* ♦ *Which title do you prefer, "Ms." or "Mrs."?* **3.** *n.* the official name of a job or position. ♦ *Mary's business card listed her title—Associate Director of Marketing—as well as her name.* ♦ *What will John's new title be after his promotion?* **4.** *n.* an official document showing that someone owns something. ♦ *After I paid my car loan, I got a copy of the title.* ♦ *Anne kept the title to her car in a safety-deposit box.* **5.** *n.* a championship. ♦ *The skilled boxer won the heavyweight boxing title.* ♦ *Tomorrow's game will decide the winner of the basketball title.* **6.** *tv.* to give something a title ①. (Often passive.) ♦ *What will you title your new song?* ♦ *The book was titled by the marketing department.*

titter ['tɪt ɚ] *iv.* to giggle quietly; to laugh in a nervous or restrained way. ♦ *The students tittered when Jimmy told a vulgar joke.* ♦ *John tittered when the speaker tripped and fell.*

titular ['tɪt jə lɚ] *adj.* signifying a title or an office, but having no power. (Adv: *titularly.*) ♦ *The retired officer was granted a titular post in the company.* ♦ *Some modern kings and queens hold titular offices.*

tizzy ['tɪz i] **in a tizzy** *idiom* an excited and confused condition; a fuss; a to-do. (Informal.) ♦ *John is in a tizzy because we're an hour late.* ♦ *Mary was in a tizzy when she couldn't find her keys.*

to [tu, tə] **1.** *prep.* in the direction of someone or something; toward someone or something; in the direction of a place, position, or condition; toward and reaching a destination. ♦ *Jane walked to the couch and sat down.* ♦ *We went to New York City last year for a vacation.* **2.** *prep.* as far as some time, place, thing, or person; until; through. (Often indicated with a hyphen or short dash, as in "1997–1999.") ♦ *This book is for children ages 6 to 8.* ♦ *Cut the potatoes into strips that are 4 to 6 inches long.* **3.** *prep.* <a form that marks the indirect object of a verb, showing the action of a verb toward someone or something.> ♦ *Mary gave the book to Susan.* ♦ *David sent a letter to his parents.* **4.** *prep.* for each; in each; included in each. ♦ *There are four quarters to a dollar.* ♦ *There are 5,280 feet to a mile.* **5.** *prep.* so as to touch someone or something; on someone or something; against someone or something. ♦ *Elizabeth taped the calendar to the refrigerator.* ♦ *I pushed the sofa to the wall to make more space in the room.* **6.** *prep.* in connection with something; along with something. ♦ *Jane and Sue danced to the beat of the music.* ♦ *This song is sung to the tune of the national anthem.* **7.** *prep.* before a certain time. ♦ *The train pulls into the station every day at ten minutes to three o'clock.* ♦ *There are only five minutes to halftime.* **8.** <the marker of the infinitive form of verbs.> (This use of to is often considered to be a preposition, but it has none of the qualities of a preposition. To is used alone when the verb is understood ②.) ♦ *I want to go home now.* ♦ *Bob must wash the dishes, even though he thinks he doesn't have to.* ♦ *You did it although I asked you not to!* **9.** *prep.* (Often indicated with a hyphen or short dash, as in "24–12.") as compared with something. ♦ *At halftime, the score was 24 to 12.* ♦ *The odds of my horse winning the race were 5 to 1.* **10. come to** *iv.* + *adv.* to become conscious. ♦ *Jane passed out when she fell, but after five minutes, she came to.* ♦ *The unconscious man came to when I threw cold water on his face.* **11. here's to someone or something** *idiom* <an expression used as a toast to someone or something to wish someone or something well.> ♦ *Here's to Jim and Mary! May they be very happy!* ♦ *Here's to your new job!*

toad ['tod] **1.** *n.* a small animal similar to a frog that lives mostly on land. ♦ *The toad hopped from the rock into leaves.* ♦ *Toads cannot leap as far as frogs.* **2.** *n.* someone who is disgusting. (Figurative on ①.) ♦ *Susan slapped the obnoxious toad who ridiculed her.* ♦ *I don't like sitting next to sloppy toads in the cafeteria.*

toadstool ['tod stul] *n.* a fungus, especially a poisonous mushroom. ♦ *The hunter became ill from eating a toadstool.* ♦ *The base of the tree was covered with moss and toadstools.*

toast ['tost] **1.** *n.* sliced bread that has been browned by heat. (No plural form in this sense. Number is expressed with *piece(s)* or *slice(s) of toast.*) ♦ *Anne spread some butter on her toast.* ♦ *John ate only a piece of toast for breakfast.* **2.** *n.* a pronouncement made as a prelude to everyone present taking a drink in approval or agreement. ♦ *I'd like to make a toast to my good friend Susan!* ♦ *My brother offered a toast in honor of my wedding.* **3.** *tv.* to brown a slice of bread by heating it; to brown something by heating it. ♦ *The toaster toasted the bread until it was golden.* ♦ *David toasted his bagel in the toaster.* **4.** *tv.* to warm something, especially marshmallows, over a fire. ♦ *The campers toasted marshmallows over the fire.* ♦ *Bob toasted his marshmallow until it burst into flame.* **5.** *tv.* to honor someone or something by taking a drink; to drink to the honor of someone or something. ♦ *I toasted my sister at her graduation party.* ♦ *We all toasted the birth of Anne's baby.* **6. propose a toast** See propose ③.

toaster ['tos tɚ] *n.* an electrical appliance that toasts bread. ♦ *The thick slice of bread became stuck in the toaster.* ♦ *I removed the hot toast from the toaster.*

toastmaster ['tost mæs tɚ] *n.* someone who introduces speakers or who proposes toasts at a formal dinner. ♦ *The toastmaster wished the newlyweds a happy life together.* ♦ *The toastmaster made a bad joke before each introduction.*

tobacco [tə 'bæk o] *n.* a plant whose leaves are dried to be smoked in cigars, cigarettes, or pipes or used as snuff. (No plural form in this sense.) ♦ *The workers harvested* *tobacco from the fields of the plantation.* ♦ *John rolled some tobacco in a paper and smoked it.*

toboggan [tə 'bɑg ən] **1.** *n.* a long sled without runners. ♦ *The kids slid down the hill on a toboggan.* ♦ *The toboggan overturned and threw Bob into a snowbank.* **2.** *iv.* to play on ①; to go down hills on ①. ♦ *The kids tobogganed down the steep hill.* ♦ *During the snowstorm, we tobogganed by the river.*

today [tə 'de] **1.** *n.* this day; the current day. ♦ *I'd like to make an appointment with Dr. Smith for today.* ♦ *Until today, I had never been on an airplane.* **2.** *n.* in this period of time. ♦ *The houses of today use much less energy than those of just a few years ago.* ♦ *John plans only for today. Tomorrow, he says, will take care of itself.* **3.** *adv.* nowadays; the current age or era. ♦ *Today, mail can be delivered electronically.* ♦ *Today, polio is no longer a serious threat.* **4.** *adv.* on this day. ♦ *We're going to go shopping today.* ♦ *Has the mail come today?*

toddler ['tɑd lɚ] *n.* a young child who is just learning to walk. ♦ *Mary stopped her toddler from walking up the staircase.* ♦ *The toddler pulled herself up into a standing position.*

to-do [tə 'du] *n.* a fuss; an excited, confused situation. (Pl in -*s*.) ♦ *There was quite a to-do surrounding the manager's announcement.* ♦ *The rude customer started a to-do with the cashier.*

toe ['to] **1.** *n.* one of the finger-like projections on the front of the foot; one of the digits on one's foot. ♦ *John stubbed his toe against the side of the couch.* ♦ *My toes were cramped in the narrow shoes.* **2.** *n.* the part of a shoe, boot, sock, or other piece of footwear that covers or encloses ①. ♦ *There was a pebble in the toe of my sock.* ♦ *The toes of my shoes need to be polished.* **3. on one's toes** *idiom* alert. ♦ *You have to be on your toes if you want to succeed.* ♦ *My boss keeps me on my toes.* **4. step on someone's toes** *idiom* to interfere with or offend someone. ♦ *When you're in public office, you have to avoid stepping on anyone's toes.* ♦ *Anne stepped on someone's toes during the last campaign and lost the election.*

toehold ['to hold] **1.** *n.* a small hole or bump suitable to support the foot of a mountain climber. ♦ *The climbers made toeholds in the cliff as they climbed up.* ♦ *The climber's toehold broke, and he fell five feet.* **2.** *n.* an entering point; access to something. (Figurative on ①.) ♦ *The secretarial job gave Mary a toehold in the industry.* ♦ *Bill's volunteer work on the campaign gave him a toehold in politics.*

toenail ['to nel] *n.* the thin, hard plate that covers the front part of the end of the toe. ♦ *Susan trimmed her toenails with a clipper.* ♦ *I cracked the toenail of my big toe when I bumped into the wall.*

together [tə 'gɛ ðɚ] **1.** *adv.* as one group of people or things. ♦ *John and David live together.* ♦ *Wales, England, and Scotland together are called Great Britain.* **2.** *adv.* at the same time; simultaneously. ♦ *Anne and Mary sang the song together.* ♦ *All of the bank's alarms rang together during the robbery.* **3. together with** *adv.* + *prep. phr.* and; as well as; in addition to. ♦ *David bought the cups together with the saucers.* ♦ *Anne and Mary came to the party together with John and Bill.* **4. put two and two together** *idiom* to figure something out from the information available. ♦ *Well, I put two and two together and came up with an idea of who did it.* ♦ *Don't worry. John won't figure it out. He can't put two and two together.*

togetherness [tə 'gɛ ðɚ nəs] *n.* a friendly feeling felt by a group of people who are joined or united. (No plural form in this sense.) ♦ *My friends and I enjoy our close togetherness.* ♦ *Anne missed the togetherness of her family when she moved away.*

toil ['tɔɪl] **1.** *n.* hard work; hard labor; work that requires a lot of physical energy or effort. (No plural form in this sense.) ♦ *The heavy toil made the workers sweat.* ♦ *All the toil made my hands blister.* **2.** *iv.* to work hard; to labor; to do work that requires a lot of physical energy or effort. ♦ *The workers toiled in the fields under the hot sun.* ♦ *The machinist toiled in the factory all day long.*

toilet ['tɔɪ lɪt] **1.** *n.* a bathroom; a room that has a ②; a restroom. ♦ *Could you tell me where the toilet is?* ♦ *The door to the toilet was locked, so I had to wait.* **2.** *n.* a porcelain bowl, connected to a drain and having a seat attached to it, into which one urinates or defecates. ♦ *Please flush the toilet after you use it.* ♦ *David woke up in the middle of the night needing to use the toilet.* **3. go to the toilet** *idiom* to use ② for defecation or urination. ♦ *Jimmy washed his hands after he went to the toilet.* ♦ *Excuse me, I have to go to the toilet.*

toilet paper ['tɔɪ lət pe pɚ] *n.* very thin, usually soft paper that is used to cleanse the affected areas of one's body after one has used the toilet. (No plural form in this sense.) ♦ *There is some more toilet paper in the cabinet if you need it.* ♦ *Mary buys the softest toilet paper that she can find.*

token ['tok ən] **1.** *n.* a sign of something; a reminder of something; visible proof of something; evidence of something. ♦ *Wear this ring as a token of our love.* ♦ *I keep a special penny in my pocket as a token of luck.* **2.** *n.* a small piece of metal, similar to a coin, that is used instead of money. ♦ *I handed the train conductor a token.* ♦ *The video game arcade sells six tokens for one dollar.* **3.** *adj.* only serving as a symbol of something; done for the sake of appearance. ♦ *John refused to join the club as a token black member.* ♦ *Mary deserved the job and had not been hired to be the token female.* **4. by the same token** *idiom* in the same way; reciprocally. ♦ *Tom must be good when he comes here, and, by the same token, I expect you to behave properly when you go to his house.* ♦ *The mayor votes for his friend's causes. By the same token, the friend votes for the mayor's causes.*

told ['told] pt/pp of tell.

tolerable ['tɑl ɚ ə bəl] *adj.* able to be tolerated; able to be endured; able to be withstood. (Adv: *tolerably.*) ♦ *The excessive heat in the sauna was barely tolerable.* ♦ *Although the diner's food wasn't very good, it was tolerable.*

tolerance ['tɑl ə rəns] **1.** *n.* the ability to endure pain, difficulty, or annoying behavior. (No plural form in this sense.) ♦ *The patient asked for a sedative as he had no tolerance for pain.* ♦ *The teacher has a lot of tolerance for bad behavior.* **2.** *n.* a resistance to the effects of a chemical, drug, or medicine built up after it has been taken for a long time. (No plural form in this sense.) ♦ *The species of insect built up a tolerance to the pesticide.* ♦ *I've developed a tolerance for caffeine, so I need to drink a lot of coffee to feel its effects.*

tolerant ['tɑl ə rənt] *adj.* willing to allow others to do something or to live the way they want to. (Adv: *tolerantly.*) ♦ *I think John's parents are too tolerant of his bad behavior.* ♦ *The prejudiced man was not at all tolerant.*

tolerate ['tɑl ə ret] *tv.* to put up with someone or something. ♦ *I could not tolerate my neighbor's loud stereo any longer.* ♦ *Mary barely tolerated her miserable living conditions.*

toll ['tol] **1.** *n.* a fee paid for the privilege of doing something, especially traveling on certain routes. ♦ *Drivers had to pay a toll to use the bridge.* ♦ *You have to pay a toll to drive on the turnpike.* **2.** *n.* the extra charge for certain nonlocal telephone calls. ♦ *I have to pay a toll just to call home from the office.* ♦ *Ask the operator if there is a toll for this call.* **3.** *iv.* [for a bell] to ring slowly and repeatedly. ♦ *The funeral bell tolled for the dead leader.* ♦ *The church bell tolls every morning at 6 A.M.* **4.** *tv.* to ring a bell slowly and repeatedly. ♦ *Bill tolled the church bell at the end of the funeral service.* ♦ *He tolled the bell by pulling on the rope.* **5. take a toll** *idiom* the damage or wear that is caused by using something or by hard living. ♦ *Years of sunbathing took a toll on Mary's skin.* ♦ *Drug abuse takes a heavy toll on the lives of people.*

tollgate ['tol get] *n.* the place on a tollway where a toll must be paid. ♦ *Traffic at the tollgate was backed up for half a mile.* ♦ *I handed forty-five cents to the worker at the tollgate.*

tollway ['tol we] *n.* a road or expressway on which one must pay a toll. ♦ *I took a different route because I had no money for the tollway.* ♦ *Tolls are used to maintain the condition of the tollways.*

tomato [tə 'me to] **1.** *n.* a roundish, soft, red fruit that grows on a vine and is eaten as food. (Pl in *-es.*) ♦ *Tomatoes are often thought of as vegetables, but they're really fruit.* ♦ *I sliced up a tomato for my salad.* **2.** *adj.* made or flavored with ①. ♦ *I covered the spaghetti with tomato sauce.* ♦ *Jane drank some tomato juice for breakfast.*

tomb ['tum] *n.* an enclosure where someone is buried, especially one that is above ground or in a mausoleum. ♦ *The tourists visited the tomb of a famous general.* ♦ *The pallbearers carried the coffin to the tomb.*

tomboy ['tɑm bɔɪ] *n.* a young girl who likes to act in a way usually associated with the way young boys act. ♦ *Susie is a tomboy and plays football better than Jimmy does.* ♦ *The tomboy refused to wear a dress to the wedding.*

tombstone ['tum ston] *n.* a gravestone; a grave marker; a large slab of stone at a grave that shows who is buried at that place and when that person was alive. ♦ *The vandals pushed over the tombstones in the cemetery.* ♦ *Mr. Wilson's tombstone indicated that he had been born in 1950.*

tomcat ['tɑm kæt] *n.* a male cat. ♦ *Our tomcat prowls in the alley behind our house.* ♦ *We didn't want a tomcat because they wander all about.*

tome ['tom] *n.* a large and important book. (Formal.) ♦ *The professor wrote a tome about her field of knowledge.* ♦ *These library shelves are lined with classical tomes.*

tomorrow [tə 'mɑr o] **1.** *n.* the day after today. (Usually singular.) ♦ *John postponed the meeting until tomorrow.* ♦ *You must finish this project by tomorrow.* **2.** *n.* the future. (No plural form in this sense.) ♦ *Nobody knows what tomorrow will bring.* ♦ *The science exhibit depicted the world of tomorrow.* **3.** *adv.* at some time during the day after today. ♦ *I will go to the store tomorrow.* ♦ *What time do you have to be at work tomorrow?*

ton ['tʌn] **1.** *n.* a unit of measure of weight equal to 2,000 pounds. (Also called a *short ton;* used in the United States and Canada.) ♦ *In England, a ton is 2,240 pounds. This is also called a "long ton."* ♦ *The ton of paper was loaded onto the large truck.* **2.** *n.* a large amount of something; a heavy amount of something. (An exaggeration. Often plural.) ♦ *I have a ton of work to do tomorrow.* ♦ *Tons of snow fell overnight.*

tone ['ton] **1.** *n.* a sound as it relates to its quality, intensity, or pitch. ♦ *The 12 different buttons of a phone each have a different tone.* ♦ *The fire alarm emitted a shrill, loud tone.* **2.** *n.* a quality of one's voice that reveals one's feelings or attitude. ♦ *I didn't appreciate the clerk's angry tone of voice.* ♦ *"Go away!" Jane said in an exasperated tone.* **3.** *n.* a shade of a color. ♦ *The depressing picture was painted in tones of blue and purple.* ♦ *The tone of the lobby's walls was very subdued.* **4.** *n.* a style, character, or mood of an event or circumstance. ♦ *The tone of the funeral was very somber.* ♦ *Our manager's cheerful demeanor set the tone for the meeting.* **5.** *n.* the firmness or definition of the body, especially the muscles. ♦ *The tone of the weightlifter's muscles was excellent.* ♦ *The advertiser wanted to hire a model with good body tone.* **6. tone up** *tv.* + *adv.* to firm or define one's muscles. ♦ *The weightlifter toned up his biceps.* ♦ *Jane toned her leg muscles up by running.*

tone-deaf ['ton 'dɛf] *adj.* unable to hear the difference between two different musical tones. ♦ *The tone-deaf student was unable to sing in the choir.* ♦ *Mary sings badly because she is tone-deaf.*

tongs ['tɔŋz] *n.* a tool or utensil that has two arms joined by a hinge or spring and is used for holding or moving something. (Treated as plural. Number is expressed with *pair(s) of tongs.*) ♦ *I removed a hot dog from the boiling water with a pair of tongs.* ♦ *John used tongs to serve the salad.*

tongue ['tʌŋ] **1.** *n.* the long, typically pink, movable organ in the mouth, used for tasting, managing food, and, in humans, speaking. ♦ *I burned my tongue when I sipped the hot soup.* ♦ *The kitten licked my hand with its tongue.* **2.** *n.* the ① of an animal, eaten as food. (No plural form in this sense.) ♦ *The cook served boiled tongue for dinner.* ♦ *These appetizers are made from beef tongue.* **3.** *n.* a language. ♦ *The cab driver spoke in a foreign tongue.* ♦ *The document was written in my native tongue.* **4.** *n.* the flap of material that is part of a shoe and fits under the laces. ♦ *When I put on my shoe quickly, the tongue was pushed all the way forward.* ♦ *Jane laid the tongue flat and laced the laces over it.* **5.** *n.* a flame; a pointed section of flame. ♦ *Tongues of fire licked at the logs in the fireplace.* ♦ *The yellow tongues of flame lighted the room.* **6. bite one's tongue** *idiom* to struggle not to say something that one really wants to say. ♦ *I had to bite my tongue to keep from telling her what I really thought.* ♦ *I sat through that whole conversation biting my tongue.* **7. cause (some) tongues to wag** *idiom* to cause people to gossip; to give people something to gossip about. ♦ *The way John was looking at Mary will surely cause some tongues to wag.* ♦ *The way Mary was dressed will also cause tongues to wag.* **8. hold one's tongue** *idiom* to refrain from speaking; to refrain from saying something unpleasant. ♦ *I felt like scolding her, but I held my tongue.* ♦ *Hold your tongue, John. You can't talk to me that way!* **9. keep a civil tongue (in one's head)** *idiom* to speak decently and politely. ♦ *Please, John. Don't talk like that. Keep a civil tongue in your head.* ♦ *John seems unable to keep a civil tongue.* **10. on the tip of one's tongue** *idiom* about to be said; almost remembered. ♦ *I have his name right on the tip of my tongue. I'll think of it in a second.* ♦ *John had the answer on the tip of his tongue, but Anne said it first.* **11. slip of the tongue** *idiom* an error in speaking in which a word is pronounced incorrectly, or in which the speaker says something unintentionally. ♦ *I didn't mean to tell her that. It was a slip of the tongue.* ♦ *I failed to understand the instructions because the speaker made a slip of the tongue at an important point.* **12. speak with a forked tongue** *idiom* to tell lies; to try to deceive someone. ♦ *Lisa's mother sounds very charming, but she speaks with a forked tongue.* ♦ *People tend to believe John because what he says seems plausible, but we know he speaks with a forked tongue.* **13. tongue-in-cheek** *idiom* insincere; joking. ♦ *The play seemed very serious at first, but then everyone saw that it was tongue-in-cheek, and they began laughing.* ♦ *Father spoke tongue-in-cheek of halving my allowance.*

tongue-lashing ['tʌŋ læʃ ɪŋ] *n.* a scolding; an angry lecture. ♦ *My parents gave me a tongue-lashing for being late.* ♦ *The principal gave the rowdy students a tongue-lashing.*

tongue-tied ['tʌŋ tɑɪd] *adj.* unable to speak properly, especially because of fear or nervousness. ♦ *The tongue-tied witness stuttered on the witness stand.* ♦ *I was so surprised by the party that I was tongue-tied.*

tonic ['tɑn ɪk] **1.** *n.* a remedy; something that is good for one's health; something that provides strength. ♦ *This tonic will cure what ails you.* ♦ *Jane made a tonic for her sick friend.* **2.** *n.* a kind of flavored soda water that is somewhat bitter. ♦ *Close the bottle of tonic tightly or it will lose its bubbles.* ♦ *Bill made a drink of gin and tonic for Bob.*

tonight [tə 'nɑɪt] **1.** *n.* this evening; this night. ♦ *Tonight is the night I planned to watch a movie.* ♦ *Do you have any plans for tonight?* **2.** *adv.* during this evening; at some time during this evening. ♦ *What are you wearing to the party tonight?* ♦ *I'd like to go out to a restaurant tonight.*

tonsil ['tɑn səl] *n.* one of two small organs in the very back of the mouth at the side of the throat. ♦ *When she was sick, Mary's tonsils were swollen.* ♦ *The surgeon removed the infected tonsils from the sick child.*

tonsillectomy [tɑn sə 'lɛk tə mi] *n.* a surgical operation in which the tonsils are removed. ♦ *That surgeon has performed dozens of tonsillectomies.* ♦ *David hasn't had a sore throat since his tonsillectomy.*

tonsillitis [tɑn sə 'lɑɪ tɪs] *n.* a medical condition in which the tonsils are infected, inflamed, or swollen. (No plural form in this sense.) ♦ *Bob stayed home from school because he had tonsillitis.* ♦ *Susie had tonsillitis five times before she had a tonsillectomy.*

too ['tu] **1.** *adv.* as well; also; in addition. ♦ *I'd like a hamburger, and I'd like french fries, too.* ♦ *I invited Bill to the party, and David, too.* **2.** *adv.* more than enough; more than is desired; beyond what is desired. ♦ *Oh, that's too much gravy!* ♦ *Your stereo is too loud.* **3.** *adv.* very; extremely. (An exaggeration.) ♦ *Thank you. You've been too kind.* ♦ *Thank you. You were just too helpful to bring me a glass of water.* **4.** *adv.* <a form used after **be, will, do, have, can, should, would,** and **could** to strengthen them in a response to a negative statement.> ♦ *"I won't eat my vegetables!" "You will too!"* ♦ *"I am not responsible for this problem." "You are too!"* **5. none too** *idiom* not very; not at all. ♦ *The towels in the bathroom were none too clean.* ♦ *It was none too warm in their house.*

took ['tʊk] pp of take.

tool ['tul] **1.** *n.* anything that helps someone work; an instrument that is used to help someone do work. ♦ *A carpenter's tools include drills, hammers, and screwdrivers.* ♦ *I brought some tools into the kitchen to fix the leaky faucet.* **2.** *n.* someone who is used by someone else, especially in an unfair way. (Figurative on ①.) ♦ *The workers were the tools of the greedy corporate owners.* ♦ *The citizens were tools of the corrupt government.* **3. tool around** *iv.* + *adv.* to cruise in a vehicle; to drive around in a vehicle. (Slang.) ♦ *John tooled around on the freeway in his new car.* ♦ *Mary tooled around the beaches in her jeep.*

toolbox ['tul bɑks] *n.* a container or cabinet in which one stores one's tools. ♦ *I put the hammer back in the toolbox when I was done with it.* ♦ *The carpenter locked up his toolbox at the end of the day.*

toolshed ['tul ʃɛd] *n.* a small building where gardening tools are stored. ♦ *We keep our toolshed locked, otherwise everything would be stolen.* ♦ *The Smiths stored their lawn mower in the toolshed.*

toot ['tut] **1.** *n.* a short blast of a horn or a whistle. ♦ *The train gave a loud toot when it pulled into the station.* ♦ *The toot of a car horn startled me.* **2.** *tv.* to cause a horn or whistle to make a short noise. ♦ *The engineer tooted the horn as the train approached the station.* ♦ *Bob tooted his horn, hoping Bill would hear him and come out.* **3.** *iv.* [for a whistle] to make a short noise. ♦ *The factory whistle tooted at noon.* ♦ *A car horn tooted and startled me.*

tooth ['tuθ] **1.** *n.* one of the hard, usually white, bony things in the mouth, used for biting and chewing while eating. (Pl: teeth.) ♦ *I brush my teeth twice a day.* ♦ *Susie wiggled her loose tooth with her fingers.* **2.** *n.* something shaped like a tooth, especially a small pointed object on a wheel that is part of a machine, the fingers of a rake, or the points along the length of a comb or saw. ♦ *The teeth of the saw blade ripped into John's finger.* ♦ *Mary prefers to use a comb that has wide spaces between the teeth.* **3. grit one's teeth** *idiom* to grind one's teeth together in anger or determination. ♦ *I was so mad, all I could do was stand there and grit my teeth.* ♦ *All through the race, Sally was gritting her teeth. She was really determined.* **4. have a sweet tooth** *idiom* to desire to eat sweet foods, especially candy and pastries. ♦ *I have a sweet tooth, and if I don't watch it, I'll really get fat.* ♦ *John eats candy all the time. He must have a sweet tooth.* **5. put some teeth into something** *idiom* to increase the power of something. ♦ *The mayor tried to put some teeth into the new law.* ♦ *The statement is too weak. Put some teeth into it.* **6. set someone's teeth on edge** *idiom* [for a person or a noise] to be irritating or get on one's nerves. ♦ *Please don't scrape your fingernails on the blackboard! It sets my teeth on edge!* ♦ *Here comes Bob. He's so annoying. He really sets my teeth on edge.* **7. set someone's teeth on edge** *idiom* [for a sour or bitter taste] to irritate one's mouth and make it feel funny. ♦ *Have you ever eaten a lemon? It'll set your teeth on edge.* ♦ *I can't stand food that sets my teeth on edge.* **8. sink one's teeth into something** *idiom* to get a chance to do, learn, or control something. ♦ *That appears to be a very challenging assignment. I can't wait to sink my teeth into it.* ♦ *Being the manager of this department is a big task. I'm very eager to sink my teeth into it.*

toothache ['tuθ ek] *n.* a pain in or around a tooth. ♦ *I told my dentist about my toothache.* ♦ *Very cold liquids sometimes give me toothaches.*

toothbrush ['tuθ brəʃ] *n.* a small brush that is used for cleaning the teeth. ♦ *I rinsed my toothbrush when I finished brushing my teeth.* ♦ *My dentist told me to brush my teeth with a toothbrush and toothpaste after every meal.*

toothpaste ['tuθ pest] *n.* a paste that is placed on a toothbrush and is used for cleaning the teeth. (No plural form in this sense.) ♦ *I brushed my teeth with a mint toothpaste.* ♦ *John removed the cap from the tube of toothpaste.*

toothpick ['tuθ pɪk] *n.* a small, thin piece of wood that is used to remove pieces of food from between one's teeth. ♦ *I removed the celery stuck between my teeth with a toothpick.* ♦ *There is a bowl of toothpicks on the counter at the diner.*

top ['tɑp] **1.** *n.* the highest part of something; the upper part of something; the peak of something; the upper surface of something. ♦ *The climbers climbed to the top of the mountain.* ♦ *Mary hid the candy on the top of the bookcase.* **2.** *n.* the highest position; the highest rank; the most successful position; the most important position. ♦ *The new employee hoped to eventually rise to the top.* ♦ *When I have a complaint, I go straight to the top.* **3.** *n.* a cover; a cap; a lid. ♦ *Please put the top back on the container when you're through.* ♦ *John drove his convertible with the top off.* **4.** *n.* a piece of clothing worn above the waist, especially on women. ♦ *Anne's bikini top was pale green.* ♦ *Mary bought a vest to go with her top.* **5.** *n.* the highest intensity; the highest degree of something. ♦ *The machine operated at the top of its capacity.* ♦ *Susan screamed at the top of her lungs.* **6. from the top** *phr.* from the beginning of something, such as a song or a script. ♦ *Okay, let's try it again from the top.* ♦ *Play it from the top one more time.* **7.** *adj.* on or at the highest part of something. ♦ *Anne placed the book on the top shelf.* ♦ *The top rung of the ladder is broken.* **8.** *adj.* first; best; most important. ♦ *David spoke to the top officer at the firm.* ♦ *Jane was the top performer at the competition.* **9.** *adj.* greatest; strongest; at the highest intensity. ♦ *Mary raced the car at its top speed.* ♦ *John played the stereo at its top volume.* **10.** *tv.* to place something on the highest part of something; to place something on something else. ♦ *I topped my slice of pie with ice cream.* ♦ *Mary topped the gift with a red bow.* **11.** *tv.* to be on ① of something; to be the ① of something. ♦ *A flag topped the mast.* ♦ *Our house is topped by a weather vane.* **12.** *tv.* to do or be better than someone or something; to be higher than someone or something. ♦ *Mary topped Susan on the biology exam.* ♦ *My firm topped our competitor in sales last year.* **13. from top to bottom** *idiom* from the highest point to the lowest point; throughout. ♦ *I have to clean the house from top to bottom today.* ♦ *We need to replace our elected officials from top to bottom.* **14. on top** *idiom* victorious over something; famous or notorious for something. ♦ *I have to study day and night to keep on top.* ♦ *Bill is on top in his field.* **15. over the top** *idiom* having achieved more than one's goal. ♦ *Our charity campaign went over the top by $3,000.* ♦ *We didn't go over the top. We didn't even get half of what we set out to collect.* **16. thin on top** *idiom* having sparse hair on the head. ♦ *James is wearing a hat because he's getting thin on top.* ♦ *Father got a little thin on top as he got older.*

topaz ['to pæz] **1.** *n.* a clear, usually yellow, mineral used to make jewelry. (No plural form in this sense.) ♦ *Topaz is relatively soft and can be damaged.* ♦ *The fine necklace was beaded with topaz.* **2.** *n.* a gemstone made from ①. ♦ *The jeweler set a beautiful topaz in the ring.* ♦ *The topaz fell out of its setting.* **3.** *adj.* made with ②. ♦ *The thief stole the topaz necklace.* ♦ *Mary wore a topaz ring.*

topcoat ['tɑp kot] *n.* an overcoat; a coat that is worn over a suit. ♦ *Since it was warm outside, John left his topcoat at home.* ♦ *Mr. Peters removed his topcoat when he entered the office.*

top-heavy ['tɑp hɛv i] *adj.* weighing more on top than on the bottom, and therefore likely to fall over; not balanced. (Adv: *top-heavily.*) ♦ *The top-heavy vase fell over and cracked.* ♦ *The coats laid over the back of the chair made it top-heavy.*

topic ['tɑp ɪk] *n.* the subject of something that is being written or talked about. ♦ *The topic of today's lecture is better nutrition.* ♦ *The essay's topic was stated in the opening paragraph.*

topical ['tɑp ɪ kəl] **1.** *adj.* of or about subjects that are currently being written or talked about; of current interest. (Adv: *topically* [...ɪk li].) ♦ *This newsletter discusses topical political issues.* ♦ *The radio station broadcast a topical debate on the election.* **2.** *adj.* to be applied to the surface of the body. (Adv: *topically* [...ɪk li].) ♦ *This medicine is for topical use only. Do not swallow it!* ♦ *I bought a soothing topical lotion for my rash.*

topless ['tɑp ləs] **1.** *adj.* [of a female] not wearing any clothing above the waist; showing one's bare breasts. ♦ *John went to a place where topless waitresses served lunch.* ♦ *The topless swimmers shocked some of the people at the beach.* **2.** *adj.* [of a garment] not covering one's body above the waist. (Adv: *toplessly.*) ♦ *The model posed in a topless bathing suit.* ♦ *In one scene, the actress wore a topless costume.* **3.** *adv.* without any clothing above one's waist. ♦ *Mary swam topless in her private pool.* ♦ *A photographer caught Mary topless by her own pool.*

top-level ['tɑp lɛv əl] *adj.* at the highest level of power; of the highest level of quality. ♦ *Even the firm's top-level executives didn't have any job security.* ♦ *The automobile manufacturer's top-level designs won many awards.*

topmost ['tɑp most] *adj.* highest. ♦ *I couldn't read the book on the topmost shelf.* ♦ *No climber has ever reached the topmost point of that mountain.*

top-notch ['tɑp 'nɑtʃ] *adj.* being the best; first-rate; excellent; outstanding. ♦ *Mary and I attended a top-notch play last night.* ♦ *I gave Susan a raise because she'd done a top-notch job on the project.*

topography [tə 'pɑ grə fi] **1.** *n.* the science of mapping the surface features of an area, especially showing in detail where there are lakes, rivers, streams, mountains, hills, valleys, etc., and what the various elevations are. (No plural form in this sense.) ♦ *The mountain range was surveyed by an expert in topography.* ♦ *The person who* *made these maps knows a lot about topography.* **2.** *n.* the features of an area of land or water. ♦ *The diver studied the topography of the reef before diving.* ♦ *The topography of Utah is very mountainous.*

topping ['tɑp ɪŋ] *n.* something that is put on top of something, especially something that is put on top of food. ♦ *I ordered a bowl of ice cream with caramel topping.* ♦ *The potato was served with an artificial cheese topping.*

topple ['tɑp əl] **1.** *iv.* to fall over; to fall down; to collapse. ♦ *The ladder toppled when I walked into it.* ♦ *All of our shelves toppled during the earthquake.* **2.** *tv.* to knock something over; to knock something down; to cause something to collapse. ♦ *Jimmy toppled a glass of milk at the dinner table.* ♦ *The earthquake toppled many expensive houses.*

top-secret ['tɑp 'si krɪt] *adj.* completely secret; very confidential. ♦ *The spy sold top-secret plans to a foreign government.* ♦ *I have some top-secret gossip. You must not tell anyone!*

topsoil ['tɑp sɔɪl] *n.* the top layer of soil; the highest layer of soil. ♦ *The farmer plowed the rich topsoil.* ♦ *A lot of the topsoil washed into the stream.*

topsy-turvy [tɑp si 'tɚ vi] *adj.* upside down; disordered; confused. (Adv: *topsy-turvily.*) ♦ *Things are topsy-turvy at the office when our secretary is on vacation.* ♦ *I knew my house had been robbed because everything was topsy-turvy.*

Torah ['tor ə] *n.* the holy scriptures of the Jewish religion. (The documents are the first five books of the Old Testament.) ♦ *Tom read from the Torah during the service in the temple.* ♦ *Our local synagogue has a very old Torah that was brought by the rabbi from Russia.*

torch ['tortʃ] **1.** *n.* a large stick or club whose upper end is on fire. ♦ *The villagers carried flaming torches through the dark forest.* ♦ *The castle's corridors were lit by large torches.* **2.** *n.* a machine that makes a very hot flame, used to cut or weld metal. ♦ *The welder held the torch against the pipe.* ♦ *The worker turned off the torch after welding the joint.* **3.** *tv.* to set something on fire; to destroy something with fire. ♦ *The arsonist torched an abandoned barn.* ♦ *The forest was torched by lightning.*

tore ['tor] pp of tear.

torment 1. ['tor mɛnt] *n.* a severe emotional or physical pain; agony. (No plural form in this sense.) ♦ *The driver of the car that caused the accident suffered great emotional torment.* ♦ *My arthritis is giving me constant torment.* **2.** ['tor mɛnt] *n.* someone or something that causes severe pain or agony. ♦ *Bill suffered the torment of a severe toothache.* ♦ *The villagers suffered under the torment of the evil ruler.* **3.** [tor 'mɛnt] *tv.* to cause someone severe pain or agony; to cause someone to suffer. ♦ *The bully tormented the clumsy young boy.* ♦ *The murderer was tormented by guilt.*

torn ['torn] **1.** pp of tear. **2.** *adj.* having a tear; ripped. ♦ *The tailor repaired my torn shirt.* ♦ *I taped the torn page back together.*

tornado [tor 'ne do] *n.* a violent wind that spins in circles very fast and can cause a great amount of damage. (Pl in *-s* or *-es.*) ♦ *The tornado destroyed half of the small village.* ♦ *There's a tornado coming! Get in the cellar!*

torpedo [tor 'pi do] **1.** *n.* an explosive device that is fired underwater from a submarine or ship toward another submarine or ship. (Pl in *-es.*) ♦ *The submarine launched a torpedo toward the ship.* ♦ *The ship exploded when the torpedo hit it.* **2.** *tv.* to attack something with ①; to explode something by firing ① at it. ♦ *The submarine torpedoed the enemy ship.* ♦ *The tanker was torpedoed by terrorists.*

torpid ['tor pɪd] *adj.* slow; sluggish; not active; lethargic. (Adv: *torpidly.*) ♦ *All of the workers were torpid because it was so hot.* ♦ *The torpid cat slept on the couch all day long.*

torrent ['tor ənt] **1.** *n.* a swift, dangerous current of water. ♦ *Dangerous torrents made the river a bad place to swim.* ♦ *The raft was carried toward the waterfall by the rough torrent.* **2.** *n.* a heavy rainstorm. ♦ *I got drenched in a sudden torrent.* ♦ *The rain was coming down in torrents.* **3.** *n.* a violent flowing of a fluid other than water. ♦ *A torrent of lava rushed down the side of the volcano.* ♦ *The speeding train spewed a torrent of smoke and exhaust.* **4.** *n.* a stream or flow of something. (Figurative on ③.) ♦ *A torrent of bees flew from the hive toward the bear.* ♦ *The horrible movie faced a torrent of criticism.*

torrid ['tor ɪd] *adj.* very hot. (Adv: *torridly.*) ♦ *This torrid weather makes me very thirsty.* ♦ *The explorer became lost in the torrid desert.*

torso ['tor so] *n.* the trunk of the body, without (or ignoring) the head, arms, and legs. (Pl in *-s.*) ♦ *The artist's model kept her torso draped with a sheet.* ♦ *The police found a mutilated torso in the river.*

torte ['tort] *n.* a rich, sweet, cake-like dessert, typically made with ground nuts or crumbs and layered with a creamy filling. ♦ *We ate a pecan torte for dessert.* ♦ *The cook baked a variety of cakes and tortes for the party.*

tortoise ['tor təs] *n.* a turtle, especially one that only lives on land. ♦ *The tortoise plodded slowly toward the pond.* ♦ *The tortoise withdrew into its shell to protect itself.*

tortuous ['tor tʃu əs] **1.** *adj.* full of twists, curves, and bends; winding. (Adv: *tortuously.*) ♦ *We drove slowly on the tortuous route through the mountains.* ♦ *Is there a simple, direct route, or must we take that tortuous path through the woods?* **2.** *adj.* complicated and indirect; convoluted. (Figurative on ①. Adv: *tortuously.*) ♦ *It was hard to follow the novel's tortuous plot.* ♦ *The lawyer's tortuous explanation confused the jury.*

torture ['tor tʃɚ] **1.** *n.* the act or method of inflicting pain in a cruel way. ♦ *Many martyrs have been killed by torture.* ♦ *The hostages underwent torture while they were held captive.* **2.** *tv.* to cause someone to suffer pain in a cruel way. ♦ *The cruel king tortured his political enemies.* ♦ *The sadistic killer tortured each victim.*

toss ['tɔs] **1.** *tv.* to throw something lightly or gently. ♦ *Jane tossed her keys in my direction, but I failed to catch them.* ♦ *Anne tossed the ball to John.* **2.** *tv.* to move something forcefully. ♦ *David tossed the empty boxes aside.* ♦ *Mary tossed the garbage into the trash can.* **3.** *tv.* to lift and throw something upward. ♦ *Anne tossed her long hair as she strutted down the walk.* ♦ *Our ship was tossed by the rough waves.* **4.** *tv.* to flip a coin into the air in order to decide a choice based on whether the head or reverse of the coin appears when it falls; to roll dice. ♦ *John and I tossed a coin to determine who would go first.* ♦ *Mary tossed the dice because it was her turn to play.* **5.** *iv.* to turn; to move restlessly. ♦ *The sick dog tossed on the ground.* ♦ *I tossed and turned in bed all night, unable to fall asleep.*

6. *iv.* to be thrown, especially by water; to be moved forcefully. ♦ *The passengers felt ill when the ship tossed.* ♦ *The boat tossed about in the heavy seas.* **7.** *n.* an instance of throwing something. ♦ *The football player dropped the easy toss.* ♦ *We decided the matter by the toss of a coin.* **8. toss a salad** *idiom* to mix the greens of a salad together with dressing. ♦ *The chef tossed the salad.* ♦ *I tossed the salad just before my guests arrived.*

tossed ['tɔst] **tossed salad** *n.* a salad made of a variety of greens that have been mixed together. ♦ *I ate a tossed salad before dinner.* ♦ *The cook poured some dressing over the tossed salad.*

tot ['tɑt] *n.* a small child. ♦ *The tots played on the slide.* ♦ *I babysat my neighbor's little tot last night.*

total ['tot əl] **1.** *n.* the whole amount; the sum; the number obtained by adding other numbers together. ♦ *The total of six and four is ten.* ♦ *Your total includes tax.* **2.** *adj.* whole; complete; entire. (Adv: *totally.*) ♦ *The total bill comes to $25.20.* ♦ *The total effects of the storm won't be known for a few days.* **3.** *tv.* to calculate ①. ♦ *The waiter totaled the bill.* ♦ *The students totaled the numbers in the left-hand column.* **4.** *tv.* to come to a certain amount; to reach a certain amount. ♦ *The bill totaled $60.* ♦ *My income taxes last year totaled $5,000.*

totalitarian [to tæl ə 'tɛr i ən] *adj.* of or about a government that is controlled by only one political party. ♦ *The totalitarian regime was ruled by a corrupt dictator.* ♦ *The citizens of the totalitarian society had very little freedom.*

totality [to 'tæl ə ti] *n.* wholeness; completeness. (No plural form in this sense.) ♦ *The totality of the bomb's destruction amazed the soldiers.* ♦ *Understood in their totality, John's remarks were encouraging.*

totally ['tot ə li] **1.** *adv.* completely; wholly; entirely. ♦ *At night, it becomes totally dark in my room.* ♦ *By the time we returned, the pizza was totally eaten.* **2.** *adv.* so; so very; incredibly. (Slang.) ♦ *That is totally cool!* ♦ *Mary bought a totally awesome new dress!*

tote ['tot] *tv.* to carry something. ♦ *The tourists toted their luggage to the airport.* ♦ *I had to tote my own golf clubs all day.*

totter ['tɑt ɚ] *iv.* to move or stand unsteadily; to shake while one moves or stands; to wobble. ♦ *The shelf tottered during the earthquake, but it didn't collapse.* ♦ *The drunken man tottered as he moved down the hall.*

touch ['tʌtʃ] **1.** *tv.* to place one's finger, hand, or some other body part on someone or something. ♦ *Bill touched the back of John's neck.* ♦ *I touched the button inside the elevator.* **2.** *tv.* to place one object against another; to place one object on another. ♦ *My hand touched the door just as you opened it.* ♦ *The blind man touched the edge of the sidewalk with his cane.* **3.** *tv.* to border something; to share a border with something. ♦ *Montana touches Canada to the north.* ♦ *Panama touches both the Atlantic and Pacific Oceans.* **4.** *tv.* to make contact with something; to have no space between two or more objects. ♦ *Make sure nothing plastic touches the heater.* ♦ *The tapestry just barely touches the wall.* **5.** *tv.* to affect someone, especially in a sad way. ♦ *The sad movie touched each member of the audience.* ♦ *The refugee's story touched me deeply.* **6.** *tv.* to compare with someone or something favorably. (Especially used in negative constructions.) ♦ *Your pizza doesn't touch mine in terms of flavor.* ♦ *John's work doesn't touch Bill's for efficiency.* **7.** *tv.* to handle something; to use something. (Especially in negative constructions.) ♦ *I would never touch someone else's toothbrush.* ♦ *Don't touch the exhibit.* **8.** *iv.* to make contact with someone or something; to have no space between two or more people or objects. ♦ *The wall and the tapestry touched.* ♦ *The two lovers touched when they met.* **9. touch on** *iv.* + *prep. phr.* to say something meaningful about something. ♦ *The lecturer touched on some of the audience's concerns.* ♦ *The article touched on the material we'd read in class.* **10.** *n.* an act of placing of one's finger or hand on someone or something. ♦ *Be careful! With just one touch, you can set off the alarm system.* ♦ *Jane repelled John's touch with a slap.* **11.** *n.* someone's handling or gentle pressure as sensed by the person being touched. (No plural form in this sense.) ♦ *John's touch sent shivers down my spine.* ♦ *The baby missed his mother's touch when she wasn't near him.* **12.** *n.* a detail that improves something or adds to something. ♦ *The artist added a few finishing touches to the painting.* ♦ *The vase of flowers on the dinner table was a nice touch.* **13.** *n.* a small amount of something; a little bit of something. (No plural form in this sense.) ♦ *Bob is tired because he has a touch of the flu.* ♦ *The cook put a touch of salt in the soup.* **14.** *n.* a special or unique skill or style; evidence of one's skill or style. ♦ *This movie certainly shows the director's touch.* ♦ *Even at her age, the veteran golfer had not lost her touch.* **15. keep in touch (with someone or something); remain in touch (with someone or something); stay in touch (with someone or something)** *idiom* to maintain communications with someone; to maintain up-to-date knowledge about someone or something. ♦ *After my neighbor moved, we still remained in touch.* ♦ *I want to stay in touch with my office over the weekend.* **16. lose touch (with someone or something)** *idiom* to break communication with someone or something. ♦ *The astronauts temporarily lost touch with Earth.* ♦ *I don't want to lose touch with my parents.* **17. touch someone for something** *idiom* to ask someone for a loan of money. (Slang.) ♦ *Mike's always trying to touch people for money.* ♦ *Bob touched John for ten dollars.*

touch-and-go ['tʌtʃ ən 'go] *adj.* risky; uncertain how something will end; not knowing the result. ♦ *The driver's chances for survival were touch-and-go after the accident.* ♦ *John's promotion was touch-and-go for a while. He was finally promoted, but only after several weeks of discussion among the managers.*

touchdown ['tʌtʃ dɑʊn] **1.** *n.* [in football] the act of placing the football behind the goal line of the other team, thus scoring six points. ♦ *Neither team scored a touchdown until the second quarter.* ♦ *We cheered when our team scored a touchdown.* **2.** *n.* the landing of a plane. ♦ *The air-traffic controllers monitor each touchdown.* ♦ *The plane's touchdown on the icy runway was dangerous.*

touching ['tʌtʃ ɪŋ] *adj.* moving; causing sympathy or sadness. (Adv: *touchingly.*) ♦ *The touching movie made me cry.* ♦ *The refugee's touching plight made me realize how lucky I was.*

touchy ['tʌtʃ i] *adj.* easily angered; easily upset; irritable; too sensitive. (Adv: *touchily.* Comp: *touchier;* sup: *touchiest.*) ♦ *My touchy boss yelled at everyone this morning.* ♦ *I can't even joke with my touchy brother.*

tough ['tʌf] **1.** *adj.* not tender; difficult to chew. (Comp: *tougher;* sup: *toughest.*) ♦ *This tough steak needs to be tenderized.* ♦ *The overcooked chicken was very tough.* **2.** *adj.* hard to do; difficult; not easy. (Comp: *tougher;* sup: *toughest.*) ♦ *It's tough to ride a bike against a strong wind.* ♦ *This math problem is very tough!* **3.** *adj.* strong and determined; not weak. (Adv: *toughly.* Comp: *tougher;* sup: *toughest.*) ♦ *Jane was tough enough to lift the whole box of books.* ♦ *The tough football player could lift 200 pounds over his head.* **4.** *adj.* stubborn; not likely to have a change of mind. (Adv: *toughly.* Comp: *tougher;* sup: *toughest.*) ♦ *The politician took a tough stance against drugs.* ♦ *The residents remained in tough opposition to the building project.* **5.** *adj.* rough; violent; dangerous. (Adv: *toughly.* Comp: *tougher;* sup: *toughest.*) ♦ *Don't get tough with me!* ♦ *The criminal grew up in a tough neighborhood.* **6.** *adj.* unfortunate; unlucky. (Comp: *tougher;* sup: *toughest.*) ♦ *Tough circumstances caused my uncle to lose all his money.* ♦ *The unfortunate woman had a very tough life.* **7.** *n.* a criminal; someone who is violent or dangerous. ♦ *The police officer arrested the tough for breaking and entering.* ♦ *The toughs in the jail cell all glared at each other.*

toughen ['tʌf ən] **1. toughen (up)** *iv.* (+ *adv.*) to become tough; to become tougher. ♦ *The roast will toughen if it is cooked too long.* ♦ *The tender young leaves will toughen up after a few days.* **2. toughen up** *iv.* + *adv.* to become stronger and more rugged. ♦ *After a week on the construction job, Bill began to toughen up.* ♦ *The football players practiced every day to toughen up.* **3. toughen** *tv.* to strengthen someone or something. ♦ *The college toughened the requirements for a degree.* ♦ *The politician toughened her stance against drugs.* **4. toughen up** *tv.* + *adv.* to make someone or some creature stronger and more rugged. ♦ *The hard work on the construction job toughened Bill up.* ♦ *Good food and exercise toughened up the football team.*

toupee [tu 'pe] *n.* a wig; a patch of artificial hair that covers a bald spot. (From French.) ♦ *The heavy wind blew John's toupee from his head.* ♦ *When Bill became bald, he bought a toupee.*

tour ['tʊ ɚ] **1.** *n.* a trip in which several places of interest are visited; a trip in which one visits an interesting place. ♦ *My biology class took a tour of the science museum.* ♦ *When I was in Rome, I went on a guided tour of the city.* **2.** *tv.* to travel through a place; to move through a place for entertainment. ♦ *Last year, John toured eastern Africa.* ♦ *Jane toured all the castles in Belgium.* **3.** *tv.* [for a performance and its performers] to visit or travel from place to place in order to be seen. ♦ *The popular play toured the country twice.* ♦ *The jazz band toured small college towns.* **4.** *iv.* to travel around, performing or exhibiting. ♦ *The band toured after the release of each of its CDs.* ♦ *Mary saw that art exhibit the last time it toured.*

touring ['tʊ ɚ ɪŋ] *adj.* concerned with presenting a play, playing a concert, or exhibiting works of art in several cities. ♦ *The touring company performed the musical in many major cities.* ♦ *The touring art exhibit came to our city's museum last year.*

tourism ['tʊɚ ɪz əm] **1.** *n.* travel; visiting interesting places, especially for a vacation. (No plural form in this sense.) ♦ *I love to travel. My hobby is tourism.* ♦ *The hurricane hurt tourism in several Caribbean islands.* **2.** *n.* the business of attracting and serving tourists. (No plural form in this sense.) ♦ *Tourism is an important part of many nations' economies.* ♦ *I work in tourism and get to visit new resorts for free.*

tourist ['tʊɚ əst] **1.** *n.* someone who travels for pleasure. ♦ *The tourist took a picture of the monument.* ♦ *A tourist asked me how to get to the lake.* **2.** *adj.* <the adj. use of ①.> ♦ *The rates at tourist hotels were rather expensive.* ♦ *Flights to Florida were heavily booked during tourist season.*

tournament ['tʊɚ nə mənt] *n.* a contest involving several people or teams who play several games in such a way that the winner of one game plays the winner of another game until there is only one champion remaining. ♦ *Mary won first prize in a chess tournament.* ♦ *Our school was selected to participate in the basketball tournament.*

tourniquet ['tɚ nə kət] *n.* a strip of cloth that is tied tightly around a part of the body, such as an arm or a leg, to stop the flow of blood. ♦ *At the accident site, I used a strip of my shirt as a tourniquet.* ♦ *The paramedic put a tourniquet above John's leg wound.*

tout ['tɑʊt] **1.** *tv.* to praise someone or something very much, especially in an extravagant way. ♦ *All the critics touted the new action movie.* ♦ *The political party touted its presidential candidate endlessly.* **2.** *tv.* to publicize or advertise something in an insistent or demanding way; to solicit business or support for someone or something in an insistent or demanding way. ♦ *The computer company touted its new product with heavy advertising.* ♦ *A clerk touted the new facial cream as a permanent end to wrinkles.*

tow ['to] **1.** *tv.* to pull something with a rope or chain. ♦ *The truck towed the illegally parked car away.* ♦ *The ship towed the barge of garbage.* **2.** *n.* an instance of pulling something with a rope or chain. ♦ *Could you please give me a tow?* ♦ *The stranded motorist had to pay $100 for a tow during the storm.* **3. in tow** *phr.* closely following; under someone's control. ♦ *The nanny walked into the park with three children in tow.* ♦ *The manager went to the meeting with her staff in tow.*

toward(s) ['tord(z)] **1.** *prep.* [facing] in a certain direction. ♦ *The ship sailed toward the port.* ♦ *I turned toward John when he called me.* **2.** *prep.* in relation to or about someone or something. ♦ *What are your feelings toward capital punishment?* ♦ *I have no ill will toward my neighbor.* **3.** *prep.* just before a certain time. ♦ *Toward dusk, I left work.* ♦ *Toward noon, we ate lunch.* **4.** *prep.* as a payment to someone or something. ♦ *I have $2,000 saved toward a new car.* ♦ *Your contribution will go toward building a new hospital.*

towel ['tɑʊ əl] **1.** *n.* a piece of cloth or paper that is used to take away moisture. ♦ *I stepped out of the shower and dried myself with a towel.* ♦ *John dried the dishes with a clean towel.* **2. towel off** *tv.* + *adv.* to dry someone with a towel. ♦ *Jane toweled the baby off after his bath.* ♦ *As soon as he toweled himself off, Tom got dressed.*

tower ['tɑʊ ɚ] **1.** *n.* a tall building or structure; a tall part of a building or structure. ♦ *The church bells are in the tower above the church.* ♦ *The treasure was kept in the highest tower of the castle.* **2. tower over; tower above** *iv.* + *prep. phr.* to be taller than someone or something else that is nearby. ♦ *The basketball player towered over the* *jockey.* ♦ *The mountains tower above the village in the valley.*

towering ['tau ɚ ɪŋ] *adj.* taller than everything else that is nearby; very high; very tall. (Adv: *toweringly.*) ♦ *Towering skyscrapers cast long shadows at dusk.* ♦ *The towering police officer helped the small children cross the street.*

town ['taʊn] **1.** *n.* an area where people live that is smaller than a city but larger than a village. ♦ *I grew up in a town of 5,000 people.* ♦ *Anne lives in a small town south of Philadelphia.* **2.** *n.* the part of a city where the businesses, stores, and markets are found. (No plural form in this sense.) ♦ *Mary went to town to buy some eggs.* ♦ *The new suburban shopping mall caused many stores in town to close.* **3.** *n.* a city. ♦ *What town were you born in?* ♦ *What's the largest town in Michigan?* **4.** *n.* all the people who live in a town ①. ♦ *The town voted to reelect the mayor.* ♦ *Most of the town worked for the local car factory.* **5.** *adj.* <the adj. use of ①.> ♦ *The mayor's office is in the town hall.* ♦ *The vendor sold hot dogs in the town square.* **6. go to town** *idiom* to work hard industriously. ♦ *Look at all those ants working. They are really going to town.* ♦ *Come on, you guys! Let's go to town. We have to finish this job before noon.* **7. out on the town** *idiom* celebrating at one or more places in a town. ♦ *I'm really tired. I was out on the town until dawn.* ♦ *We went out on the town to celebrate our wedding anniversary.*

town house ['taʊn haʊs] **1.** *n., irreg.* a house in the city; a house in town. (Pl: [...haʊ zəz].) ♦ *The rich couple owned both a town house and a country house.* ♦ *The Smiths sold their town house and moved to the suburbs.* **2.** *n., irreg.* a type of house, usually with two or three levels, that is attached on one or both sides to similar housing units. ♦ *I don't know who lives in the town houses next to me.* ♦ *I moved from an apartment to a town house when I graduated.*

townsfolk ['taʊnz fok] *n.* the population of a town; the people who live in a town. (No plural form in this sense.) ♦ *The townsfolk voted to reelect the mayor.* ♦ *The police officer knew most of the townsfolk by name.*

township ['taʊn ʃɪp] *n.* [in many areas of the United States] a division of a county, usually a square of land six miles long by six miles wide. ♦ *A township is often a unit of local government for people who do not live within the limits of a city or village.* ♦ *My grandparents own a farm in Clayton Township.*

townspeople ['taʊnz pip əl] *n.* the population of a town; the people who live in a town. (No plural form. Treated as plural.) ♦ *The mayor spoke to the townspeople about the recent robberies.* ♦ *Most of the townspeople work at the factory on Route 12.*

tow truck ['to trək] *n.* a truck that is equipped to tow cars that are parked illegally, that won't work, or that have been damaged in an accident. ♦ *When my car stalled on the freeway, I called a tow truck.* ♦ *The tow truck towed illegally parked cars out of the way.*

toxic ['tɑk sɪk] *adj.* poisonous. (Adv: *toxically* [...ɪk li].) ♦ *Toxic fumes seeped from the factory's chimneys.* ♦ *Some toxic waste was illegally buried in the landfill.*

toxicologist [tɑk sə 'kɑl ə dʒəst] *n.* someone who studies toxicology. ♦ *The toxicologist found that the cheese was tainted.* ♦ *The coroner consulted a toxicologist about the victim's death.*

toxicology [tɑk sə 'kɑl ə dʒi] *n.* the study and science of poisons, their effect on humans and animals, and the treatment of people who have been exposed to them. (No plural form in this sense.) ♦ *Management hired an expert in toxicology to study the factory's air.* ♦ *The coroner had studied toxicology in college.*

toxin ['tɑk sɪn] *n.* a poisonous chemical produced by a bacterium, plant, or animal. ♦ *The old factory released deadly toxins into the air.* ♦ *The toxin in the snake's venom killed the rat.*

toy ['tɔɪ] **1.** *n.* something that is made to amuse a child. ♦ *I gave Jimmy a toy for his birthday.* ♦ *Susie put her toys away when she was done playing with them.* **2.** *adj.* made to be played with. ♦ *The children's toy blocks were scattered on the floor.* ♦ *John tripped on his child's toy cars.* **3.** *adj.* of or about certain small breeds of dog. ♦ *Mary trims her toy poodle every month.* ♦ *David's toy terrier is tiny.*

trace ['tres] **1.** *n.* a very small amount of something. ♦ *The cook added a trace of salt to the soup.* ♦ *I smelled a trace of sulfur in the air.* **2.** *tv.* to draw or copy the outline of something by putting a thin piece of paper on top of it and then drawing over the lines one sees through the thin paper. ♦ *John traced a map of France from the atlas.* ♦ *Mary traced the picture of the cow and then colored it with crayons.* **3.** *tv.* to follow the path of something's growth, development, or history. ♦ *This book traces the development of the Soviet Union.* ♦ *These pictures trace the growth of my children.* **4.** *tv.* to seek the origin of something. ♦ *The reporter traced the history of corruption in city hall.* ♦ *The police detective traced the obscene phone call.*

trachea ['trek i ə] *n.* the passage in one's throat that conveys air from the mouth to the lungs. ♦ *The choking woman had a piece of food stuck in her trachea.* ♦ *An infection in John's trachea caused him to cough a lot.*

track ['træk] **1.** *n.* the marks made by a vehicle, person, or animal traveling from place to place. ♦ *The hunter followed the deer's tracks to a pond.* ♦ *John didn't wipe his shoes clean, so he left tracks on the rug.* **2.** *n.* a pair of parallel metal rails that trains travel on. ♦ *The freight train moved swiftly down the track.* ♦ *No train was coming, so John drove across the track.* **3.** *n.* a trail; a path; a rough road. ♦ *The track to the cabin was very muddy.* ♦ *Snow covered the only track to the remote village.* **4.** *n.* a circular pathway used for running or racing. ♦ *The track was built around the football field.* ♦ *Each lap around this track is a quarter of a mile.* **5.** *n.* a group of sports including running, jumping, and other tests of individual endurance and strength. (No plural form in this sense.) ♦ *My high school excels in track.* ♦ *Training for track, John ran 10 miles every day.* **6.** *tv.* to follow the trail of a person or other creature. ♦ *The hunter tracked the deer through the woods.* ♦ *The detective tracked the criminal across the country.* **7. drop in one's tracks** *idiom* to stop or collapse from exhaustion; to die suddenly. ♦ *If I keep working this way, I'll drop in my tracks.* ♦ *Uncle Bob was working in the garden and dropped in his tracks. We are all sorry that he's dead.* **8. get the inside track** *idiom* to get the advantage (over someone) because of special connections, special knowledge, or favoritism. ♦ *If I could get the inside track, I could win the contract.* ♦ *The boss likes me. Since I have the inside track, I'll probably be the new office manager.* **9. jump the track** *idiom* to change suddenly from one thing, thought, plan, or activity to another. ♦ *The entire project jumped the track, and we finally had to give up.* ♦ *John's mind jumped the track while he was in the play, and he forgot his lines.* **10. lose track (of someone or something)** *idiom* to lose contact with someone; to forget where something is. ♦ *I lost track of all my friends from high school.* ♦ *Tom has lost track of his glasses again.* **11. on the right track** *idiom* following the right set of assumptions. ♦ *Tom is on the right track and will solve the mystery soon.* ♦ *You are on the right track to find the answer.* **12. on the wrong track** *idiom* going the wrong way; following the wrong set of assumptions. ♦ *You'll never get the right answer. You're on the wrong track.* ♦ *They won't get it figured out because they are on the wrong track.* **13. the other side of the tracks** *idiom* the poorer part of a town, often near the railroad tracks. ♦ *Who cares if she's from the other side of the tracks?* ♦ *I came from a poor family—we lived on the other side of the tracks.*

tract ['trækt] **1.** *n.* a large piece of land; an area. ♦ *The farmer owned a 640-acre tract of land.* ♦ *The population of this census tract has doubled in 10 years.* **2.** *n.* a passageway within the body. ♦ *John was having problems with his digestive tract.* ♦ *The doctor removed some polyps from my intestinal tract.* **3.** *n.* a pamphlet, especially about a religious subject. ♦ *Some evangelists gave me a tract about their religion.* ♦ *The minister left some tracts on the bus seat for others to read.*

traction ['træk ʃən] *n.* the grip of a wheel or shoe on a surface that allows the wheel or shoe to apply energy to the surface in order to move ahead. (No plural form in this sense.) ♦ *Because the road was icy, my tires couldn't get any traction.* ♦ *The jogger's shoes have excellent traction.*

tractor ['træk tɚ] *n.* a motor vehicle with large, thick tires, used for pulling farm equipment in fields. ♦ *The farmer's tractors were kept in a large barn.* ♦ *The plow was pulled behind the tractor.*

trade ['tred] **1.** *n.* the business of buying and selling products; commerce. (No plural form in this sense.) ♦ *Trade declined during the recession.* ♦ *The nation practiced free trade with its neighboring countries.* **2.** *n.* a particular business. ♦ *The dentist plies his trade in a large office building.* ♦ *Anne made consulting into a lucrative trade.* **3.** *n.* a job that utilizes a skill. ♦ *The union consisted of people working in technical trades.* ♦ *The machinist's trade requires years of training.* **4.** *n.* the exchange of someone or something for someone or something else. ♦ *The team made a trade of its best pitcher for a player from another team.* ♦ *I regretted my trade of 4 rare stamps for 12 old maps.* **5.** *tv.* to exchange someone or something for someone or something else. ♦ *Jane traded her old van for a new car.* ♦ *The baseball team traded a new pitcher for an old catcher.* **6.** *iv.* to exchange; to swap. ♦ *Mary and Anne had what each other wanted, so they traded.* ♦ *I traded with Bill because I liked his lunch better than mine.*

trade-in ['tred ɪn] *n.* something, such as an old car, that is used as part of the payment for something new. ♦ *The car salesman offered $500 for any trade-in.* ♦ *When I bought a new TV, I asked if they took trade-ins.*

trademark ['tred mɑrk] **1.** *n.* a word, name, or symbol—used and owned by a manufacturer—that identifies a product. ♦ *A trademark can only be used by its owner.* ♦ *The symbol for a trademark is ™.* **2.** *n.* a mark or feature that is associated with a certain person or thing. (Figurative on ①.) ♦ *An unusual laugh is the actor's trademark.* ♦ *My teacher's trademark is her flamboyant clothing.* **3.** *tv.* [for a manufacturer] to protect ① by registering it with the government. ♦ *We trademarked the names of all of our products.* ♦ *You cannot trademark that symbol, because someone else already owns the rights to use it.*

trademarked ['tred mɑrkt] *adj.* bearing a trademark that is registered with the government. ♦ *The company protected its trademarked products in court.* ♦ *Trademarked names are denoted with the "™" symbol in the United States.*

trade name ['tred nem] *n.* the name by which a product is known. ♦ *Most companies trademark the trade names of their products.* ♦ Xerox™ *is the trade name of a particular brand of copiers.*

trader ['tred ɚ] *n.* a merchant; someone who buys and sells things as a business. ♦ *The merchant bought pelts directly from fur traders.* ♦ *The trader sold 10,000 shares of the troubled company.*

trade union ['tred jun jən] *n.* a worker's association that protects its members' interests and represents its members to management. ♦ *Management negotiated a new contract with the trade union.* ♦ *The trade union picketed the factory for higher wages.*

tradition [trə 'dɪ ʃən] **1.** *n.* the way that something has been done from generation to generation. (No plural form in this sense.) ♦ *My mother bakes pies following a family tradition.* ♦ *My family carefully follows religious tradition for Passover.* **2.** *n.* a custom, social practice, or belief. ♦ *It's a tradition in my family to eat Easter dinner at Grandma's.* ♦ *Our family's traditions have existed for decades.*

traditional [trə 'dɪʃ ə nəl] *adj.* relating to tradition. (Adv: *traditionally.*) ♦ *My grandma gave me her traditional recipes.* ♦ *Each week, the tribe performed traditional religious ceremonies.*

traditionally [trə 'dɪʃ ən (ə) li] *adv.* according to tradition. ♦ *Traditionally, my family goes to a restaurant for Thanksgiving.* ♦ *Our neighbors traditionally celebrate the end of summer with a barbecue.*

traffic ['træf ɪk] **1.** *n.* vehicles and their movement—or slowness of movement—on land, on water, or in the air. (No plural form in this sense.) ♦ *Air traffic came to a halt because of the blizzard.* ♦ *I'm late because I was caught in traffic.* **2.** *n.* the process of buying and selling. (No plural form in this sense.) ♦ *The agents tried to stop all drug traffic at the border.* ♦ *The agent monitored the traffic of goods into the country.* **3. traffic in** *iv., irreg.* + *prep. phr.* (Pt/pp: trafficked. The present participle is trafficking.) to be involved with buying and selling something, especially something illegal. ♦ *The crooks trafficked in stolen goods.* ♦ *The drug dealer trafficked in cocaine and heroin.*

traffic jam ['træf ɪk dʒæm] *n.* a situation in which vehicles on roads have stopped or slowed down because there are too many of them. ♦ *The terrible accident caused a large traffic jam.* ♦ *I was an hour late because I was stuck in a traffic jam.*

trafficked ['træf ɪkt] pt/pp of traffic ③.

traffic light ['træf ɪk lɑɪt] *n.* a signal, usually found at intersections, used to control traffic by a system of lights.

(Also light.) ♦ *At a traffic light, green means go, red means stop, and yellow means caution.* ♦ *The city installed a traffic light at the busy intersection.*

tragedy ['træ dʒə di] **1.** *n.* a serious play that has a sad ending. ♦ *In classical theater, tragedies are usually based on a personal flaw in the main character.* ♦ Hamlet *and* Othello *are two Shakespearean tragedies.* **2.** *n.* a disaster; a sad, unfortunate, or terrible event. ♦ *The train wreck was a tragedy that could have been avoided.* ♦ *It was a tragedy that we lost the game in the last minute.*

tragic ['træ dʒɪk] **1.** *adj.* of or about serious plays with sad endings. (Adv: *tragically* [...ɪk li].) ♦ *That playwright wrote many tragic plays.* ♦ Romeo and Juliet *is the tragic tale of two young lovers.* **2.** *adj.* disastrous; unfortunate. (Adv: *tragically* [...ɪk li].) ♦ *There was a tragic accident in front of my office today.* ♦ *The poor man's life came to a tragic end when he was hit by a bus.*

trail ['trel] **1.** *n.* the marks made by a vehicle, person, or animal as it travels from place to place; the scent left by a person or animal as it travels from place to place. (See also track.) ♦ *The hounds followed the fox's trail.* ♦ *John left a trail on the clean floor with his muddy shoes.* **2.** *n.* a path through an area that a car cannot travel over; a path for walking, biking, etc. ♦ *I biked on the trail to the pond.* ♦ *The trail to the cottage was covered with snow.* **3.** *tv.* to follow someone or an animal by its scent, footprints, or other clues that it leaves behind. ♦ *The dogs trailed the fox through the woods.* ♦ *The detective trailed the criminal across town.* **4.** *tv.* to leave something dirty on a surface by walking or dragging something across it. ♦ *Mary trailed mud on the carpet by walking on it with dirty shoes.* ♦ *The dying man trailed blood across the floor as he stumbled.* **5. trail behind** *iv.* + *prep. phr.* to follow behind someone or something. ♦ *The kite trailed behind Tom as he ran fast to try to get it in the air.* ♦ *Bob trailed behind his older sister in the mall.*

trailblazer ['trel blez ɚ] *n.* someone who travels someplace that no one has ever gone before; someone who discovers something that no one has ever known before; a pioneer. ♦ *Jonas Salk was a trailblazer in treating polio.* ♦ *Susan B. Anthony was a trailblazer in securing the vote for women.*

trailer ['tre lɚ] **1.** *n.* a vehicle that is pulled by another vehicle. ♦ *John hitched the trailer to the back of his pickup truck.* ♦ *Mary transported her furniture in a trailer.* **2.** *n.* a small, prefabricated house on wheels that is towed to a place and set on the ground; a mobile home. ♦ *My family owns a trailer near a lake in northern Michigan.* ♦ *The rural village consisted mostly of trailers.* **3.** *n.* an advertisement for a movie. ♦ *Before the movie, we saw trailers for six upcoming films.* ♦ *The movie's funniest lines were included in its trailer.*

trailer park ['tre lɚ pɑrk] *n.* a parcel of land where a number of trailers are set on the ground; a neighborhood consisting of trailers. ♦ *My grandparents live in a trailer park for retired people.* ♦ *After living in a trailer park for several years, the young couple had saved enough money to buy a small house.*

train ['tren] **1.** *n.* a line of railroad cars pulled by an engine. ♦ *The long train was made up of 60 cars.* ♦ *Susan took a train to St. Louis.* **2.** *n.* a group of things, animals, or people that are moving in a line. (Figurative on ①.) ♦ *The queen was followed by a train of attendants.* ♦ *A train of baby ducks waddled across the road.* **3.** *n.* a part of a very fancy dress that is carried by people or dragged on the ground behind oneself. ♦ *The train of Anne's bridal gown was 25 feet long.* ♦ *I tripped on the train of my sister's dress.* **4.** *tv.* to teach someone a skill; to give someone the knowledge needed to do a job. ♦ *The manager trained the new employees for the job.* ♦ *My father trained me in the proper way to use the lawn mower.* **5. train to** *tv.* + *inf.* to teach someone or some creature to do something or behave a certain way. ♦ *John trained the dog to roll over.* ♦ *Anne trained her children to be polite.* **6. train on** *tv.* + *prep. phr.* to aim something toward someone or something. ♦ *The marksman trained his sights on the target.* ♦ *Mary trained her eyes on the antique car coming up the road.* **7.** *iv.* to prepare [oneself] for a job, contest, or a performance. ♦ *The gymnast trained every day before school.* ♦ *The football team trains every day for two hours.* **8. train one's sights on something; have one's sights trained on something** *idiom* to have something as a goal; to direct something or oneself toward a goal. ♦ *You should train your sights on getting a promotion in the next year.* ♦ *Lisa has her sights trained on a new car.*

trainee [tre 'ni] *n.* someone who is being trained to do a job. ♦ *The trainees were given a copy of the company manual.* ♦ *The boss warned the trainees not to be late.*

traipse ['treps] *iv.* to walk about somewhere; to walk to a destination. ♦ *The children traipsed through the park on the sunny day.* ♦ *On Friday night, my friends and I traipsed around town.*

trait ['tret] *n.* a feature; a characteristic; a quality that is particular to someone or something. ♦ *Often, freckles are a trait of people with red hair.* ♦ *The color of one's eyes is a genetic trait.*

traitor ['tret ɚ] *n.* someone who betrays one's country or leader. ♦ *A traitor sold our country's secrets to the enemy during the war.* ♦ *The traitor will be executed at dawn.*

trajectory [trə 'dʒɛk tə ri] *n.* the path through space or through the air that something travels. ♦ *The ballistics expert determined the trajectory of the bullet.* ♦ *The missile's trajectory was too far to the right.*

tramp ['træmp] **1.** *n.* someone who lives by begging; a vagabond. ♦ *The tramp asked passersby for a dollar.* ♦ *Security guards evicted the tramp from the private office building.* **2.** *n.* the sound of someone marching. (No plural form in this sense.) ♦ *I was kept awake by the tramp of the invading army in the streets.* ♦ *The tramp of the soldier's boots alerted us to the danger.* **3.** *iv.* to walk heavily or steadily. ♦ *I asked my upstairs neighbor to stop tramping.* ♦ *The hikers tramped through the newly fallen snow.*

trample ['træm pəl] **1.** *tv.* to march over, across, or through, or to step on someone or something. ♦ *The neighbor's dog trampled my tulips.* ♦ *I was nearly trampled by the angry crowd.* **2. trample across; trample through** *iv.* + *prep. phr.* to step or walk heavily and roughly somewhere. ♦ *Please don't trample across my yard!* ♦ *Three dogs trampled through the playground, frightening the children.*

trampoline ['træm pə lin] *n.* an apparatus made of an elastic material tightly stretched from a frame, upon which someone bounces, especially as part of a gymnastic event. ♦ *Mary jumped up and down on the trampoline.* ♦ *Susan did a flip as she jumped from the trampoline.*

trance ['træns] *n.* a state where the mind is not conscious, as in hypnosis. ♦ *The magician put the volunteer into a deep trance.* ♦ *While in a trance, John revealed his inner secrets.*

tranquil ['træŋ kwɪl] *adj.* quiet; peaceful; calm. (Adv: *tranquilly.*) ♦ *A bird flew over the tranquil lake.* ♦ *I spent a tranquil day resting at home.*

tranquility [træŋ 'kwɪl ə ti] *n.* a quiet, peaceful, or calm condition. (No plural form in this sense.) ♦ *The tranquility of the woods appealed to the hiker.* ♦ *City people seek rest and tranquility in the country.*

tranquilizer ['træŋ kwə lɑɪ zɚ] *n.* a drug or medicine that relaxes someone or helps someone sleep. ♦ *David took a tranquilizer to help him sleep.* ♦ *The doctor prescribed tranquilizers for the anxious patient.*

transact [træn 'zækt] *tv.* to do a piece of business; to conduct business. ♦ *I transact business with my bank every day.* ♦ *The illegal deal was transacted in secret.*

transaction [træn 'zæk ʃən] **1.** *n.* a business deal; something that has been transacted. ♦ *My bank statement shows all of my transactions each month.* ♦ *The illegal transaction was filmed on videotape.* **2.** *n.* an act of doing business. ♦ *Our transaction was interrupted by an urgent matter.* ♦ *The business transaction was concluded with a handshake.*

transatlantic [trænz ət 'læn tɪk] *adj.* from one side of the Atlantic Ocean to the other; across the Atlantic Ocean. (Adv: *transatlantically* [...ɪk li].) ♦ *Transatlantic telephone calls can be expensive.* ♦ *The transatlantic flight went from New York to Paris.*

transcend [træn 'sɛnd] *tv.* to go beyond something; to go past a limit; to exceed something. ♦ *The gory movie transcended the boundaries of good taste.* ♦ *Passionate emotion transcends language.*

transcontinental [trænz kɑn tə 'nɛn təl] *adj.* across a continent; from one end of a continent to the other. (Adv: *transcontinentally.*) ♦ *The airline offers dozens of transcontinental flights.* ♦ *John took a transcontinental car trip from Boston to San Diego.*

transcribe [træn 'skrɑɪb] **1.** *tv.* to record something, such as sound, speech, or shorthand, in a permanent form. (Now usually refers to dictation notes and court reporting techniques.) ♦ *The reporter transcribed the notes she made during the interview she had taped.* ♦ *The court reporter transcribed the entire trial.* **2.** *tv.* to write down the phonetic symbols that correspond to something that is spoken. ♦ *The sociologist transcribed the story told by the old man.* ♦ *A trained linguist can transcribe almost any language.*

transcript ['træn skrɪpt] *n.* a written or printed copy, usually of something that was spoken. ♦ *The lawyer looked at the transcripts of the trial.* ♦ *You can order transcripts of many television talk shows.*

transcription [træn 'skrɪp ʃən] **1.** *n.* transcribing; writing something down in words. (No plural form in this sense.) ♦ *Transcription was difficult because the speaker had been mumbling.* ♦ *The court reporter's transcription took 24 hours to complete.* **2.** *n.* a copy; a transcript; something that has been transcribed. ♦ *The lawyer looked over the transcriptions of the trial.* ♦ *You can order the transcription of this radio program for $3.* **3.** *n.* a representation of speech, using phonetic symbols. ♦ *The linguist analyzed the transcription of the folktale.* ♦ *Anne was trained to read phonetic transcription.*

transfer ['træns fɚ] **1.** *n.* the movement of something from one place to another place. (No plural form in this sense.) ♦ *The transfer of the baby elephant was made carefully.* ♦ *Jane's transfer of funds was carried out electronically.* **2.** *n.* a ticket that allows someone to get off one vehicle, usually a bus, and get on another one without paying a second fare. ♦ *The transfer entitled John to a ride on a different bus route.* ♦ *I handed my transfer to the bus driver.* **3.** *n.* a movement of someone or something from one place to another. ♦ *The worker was angered by his transfer across the country.* ♦ *The bank manager must approve large transfers of funds.* **4.** *iv.* to move from one vehicle to another; to get off one vehicle and get on another one. ♦ *You have to transfer at Clark Street to the #22 bus.* ♦ *Mary transferred at the station to a different train.* **5.** *iv.* to move from one site to another site. ♦ *John transferred to the accounting department.* ♦ *The gifted student transferred away from the local school.* **6.** *tv.* to move something from one place to another place. ♦ *John transferred $100 from a savings account to a checking account.* ♦ *The broker transferred his investments out of the bond market.* **7.** *tv.* to cause someone to move from one job site to another job site. ♦ *The company transferred 200 employees to its Oregon plant.* ♦ *Mary was transferred from Chicago and had to sell her house.* **8. transfer to** *tv.* + *prep. phr.* to give the ownership of something to someone else. ♦ *I transferred the ownership of the car to Mary.* ♦ *Susan transferred her vacation home to her daughter.*

transferred ['træns fɚd] *adj.* moved from one's place of employment to a place of employment in another geographic location. ♦ *All the transferred workers were very disgruntled.* ♦ *The transferred manager wanted to return to New York.*

transfix [trænz 'fɪks] *tv.* to cause someone or something to be immobilized with interest or amazement. ♦ *The startled deer was transfixed by my car's headlights.* ♦ *The magician transfixed the entire audience.*

transform [træns 'form] **1.** *tv.* to change something's or someone's shape, form, nature, or appearance. ♦ *The sculptor transformed the clay into the form of a bird.* ♦ *Meditation transformed David from a grouch to a more likable person.* **2.** *iv.* to change shape, form, nature, or appearance. ♦ *The sand castle transformed into a heap of sand.* ♦ *John's personality transformed when he started meditating.*

transformation [træns for 'me ʃən] *n.* a change in shape, form, nature, or appearance. ♦ *John's transformation from a shy boy into an aggressive man surprised me.* ♦ *The rookie's transformation into a skilled player took many years.*

transfusion [træns 'fju ʒən] *n.* the process of transferring blood from one person to another. ♦ *The paramedics gave the crash victim a transfusion in the ambulance.* ♦ *Anne had three transfusions before she started getting better.*

transgress [trænz 'grɛs] *tv.* to exceed something; to pass a limit or a boundary. ♦ *The mayor transgressed the lim-*

its of his power when he fired the police chief. ♦ *This gory movie transgresses the limits of good taste.*

transgression [trænz 'grɛ ʃən] *n.* a breaking of a rule or law; the act of committing a crime; a sin. ♦ *Bob regretted his moral transgressions.* ♦ *Anne was imprisoned for her transgressions.*

transgressor [trænz 'grɛs ɚ] *n.* a sinner; someone who breaks a rule or a law. ♦ *Transgressors of the driving laws are numerous, and their number is growing.* ♦ *The transgressor was sent to jail.*

transient ['træn zi ənt] **1.** *adj.* lasting occasionally and only for a short period of time. (Adv: *transiently.*) ♦ *David's transient moods are quite unpredictable.* ♦ *The doctor warned me of the drug's transient side effects.* **2.** *n.* someone who stays someplace only for a short period of time. ♦ *The transient traveled across America by freight train.* ♦ *The farmer hired some transients to help with the harvest.*

transistor [træn 'zɪs tɚ] *n.* a small electrical device that controls the flow of current in electronic circuits. ♦ *The transistors were damaged by a surge of electrical power.* ♦ *When the transistor failed, the radio stopped working.*

transit ['træn zɪt] **1.** *n.* transportation; movement of people or goods. (No plural form in this sense.) ♦ *Subways are a form of urban mass transit.* ♦ *John's transit to safety was dangerous and courageous.* **2. in transit** *phr.* while in the process of being transported. ♦ *Dave is in transit from London to Chicago.* ♦ *The new stereo is now in transit from the manufacturer.*

transition [træn 'zɪ ʃən] *n.* a change; a change from one condition to another; a change from one thing to another. ♦ *Spring is a transition from winter into summer.* ♦ *Puberty is a transition from childhood into adolescence.*

transitive verb ['træn sə tɪv 'vɚb] *n.* a verb that is used with a direct object; a verb that requires a direct object. (Abbreviated *tv.* here.) ♦ *Transitive verbs take direct objects.* ♦ *Transitive sentences usually require at least two nominals.*

transitory ['træn sə tor i] *adj.* brief; lasting only for a short period of time; transient. (Adv: *transitorily.*) ♦ *Lisa was troubled by transitory headaches.* ♦ *In spite of some transitory anxiety, Bill is recovering nicely.*

translate ['træn slet] **1.** *tv.* to change something written or spoken from one language to another. ♦ *The poet translated her works from Italian to English.* ♦ *The guard translated the sign into English for me.* **2.** *iv.* to change [something written or spoken in one language] to another language. ♦ *I translated for John when he spoke to the German official.* ♦ *My friend translated while I gave my short speech.*

translation [trænz 'le ʃən] **1.** *n.* converting a message in one language into another language; converting a sequence of symbols in one code into another code. (No plural form in this sense.) ♦ *Translation of this language is impossible without a dictionary.* ♦ *We need someone who can supervise the translation of this document.* **2.** *n.* writing or speaking that is translated from another language. ♦ *I read a translation of the Spanish story in English.* ♦ *Hundreds of translations of the Bible have been prepared.*

translator ['træns le tɚ] *n.* someone who translates sentences of one language into another. ♦ *The translator told me what the diplomat wanted.* ♦ *I asked the translator to tell the guard that I was an American.*

transmission [trænz 'mɪ ʃən] **1.** *n.* sending electricity or electromagnetic waves. (No plural form in this sense.) ♦ *The transmission of the signal was hampered by the storm.* ♦ *The storm interfered with the transmission of electrical power.* **2.** *n.* transmitted electricity or radio waves. ♦ *A larger transmitter improved the daily radio transmissions.* ♦ *A storm ended the transmission.* **3.** *n.* the part of a motor vehicle that passes energy from the engine to one of the axles. ♦ *I asked the mechanic to check my car's transmission.* ♦ *My truck's transmission failed when I was on the freeway.*

transmit [trænz 'mɪt] *tv.* to send information by way of electricity or radio waves. ♦ *The clerk transmitted the message by telegraph.* ♦ *The radio station plans to transmit its broadcasts from a satellite.*

transmitter ['træns mɪt ɚ] *n.* a piece of electronic equipment that transmits electromagnetic waves, as for radio or television. ♦ *The TV station went off the air when its transmitter was damaged.* ♦ *The transmitter beamed its signal to a satellite.*

transom ['træn səm] *n.* a window that can be opened and closed, located between the top of a door and the ceiling. ♦ *Through my transom, I heard people talking in the hallway.* ♦ *I shut and locked the transom when I left the office.*

transparency [trænz 'pɛr ən si] **1.** *n.* the state of being transparent. (No plural form in this sense.) ♦ *The window's transparency was dimmed by dirt.* ♦ *Because of the transparency of Anne's deception, nobody believed her.* **2.** *n.* a clear sheet of film bearing an image, usually placed in a projector so the image is projected onto a surface; a slide ⑩. ♦ *The speaker's transparency was projected onto a large screen.* ♦ *Transparencies are good visual aids for speakers.*

transparent [trænz 'pɛr ənt] **1.** *adj.* clear and able to be seen through. (Adv: *transparently.*) ♦ *The sunset shined through the transparent glass.* ♦ *The lenses of my glasses are made of transparent plastic.* **2.** *adj.* obvious; evident; [of a deception] easy to figure out. (Figurative on ①. Adv: *transparently.*) ♦ *Lisa's transparent excuse fooled no one.* ♦ *My reasons for leaving town were transparent to my friends.*

transpire [træn 'spaɪr] *iv.* to happen; to occur over a period of time. ♦ *It was hard to figure out what had transpired in my absence.* ♦ *As the political scandal transpired, the taxpayers became angry.*

transplant 1. [trænz 'plænt] *tv.* to move a plant from one place and plant it in new soil. ♦ *Robert transplanted the begonia into a larger pot.* ♦ *Mary transplanted an elm tree into her backyard.* **2.** [trænz 'plænt] *tv.* to cause someone or something to move from one place (to another). ♦ *The employees were all transplanted from California.* ♦ *John transplanted his family from Ohio to Georgia.* **3.** [trænz 'plænt] *tv.* to move a part of someone's body to someone else's body. ♦ *The surgeons transplanted the crash victim's liver into a dying hospital patient.* ♦ *The doctors transplanted one of my kidneys into my brother.* **4.** ['træns plænt] *n.* a plant that has been moved from one place and planted in new soil. ♦ *I started all the new transplants in small pots.* ♦ *Make sure the transplants get plenty of water.* **5.** ['træns plænt] *n.* the surgical process of replacing a damaged limb or organ with a part from another body. ♦ *The heart transplant took over 9 hours.* ♦ *Her liver is diseased, and she will have to have a transplant.* **6.** ['træns plænt] *n.* someone who has moved to a place from another area. ♦ *The numerous California transplants annoyed the Utah native.* ♦ *My neighbor is a transplant from Washington.*

transport ['træns port] **1.** *n.* carrying things or people from one place to another. (No plural form in this sense.) ♦ *All the transport of goods between states is regulated.* ♦ *The transport of fresh produce requires refrigerated trucks.* **2.** *tv.* to carry someone or something from one place to another. ♦ *The criminal transported the stolen goods across the state line.* ♦ *The car parts were transported from the factory by train.* **3.** *tv.* to send someone to a remote place as punishment. ♦ *The exiled king was transported to a desert island.* ♦ *The sheriff transported the criminal to a remote jail.*

transportation [trænz pɚ 'te ʃən] **1.** *n.* the system of moving people and goods from one place to another. (No plural form in this sense.) ♦ *Subways and buses are forms of public transportation.* ♦ *My preferred mode of transportation is driving.* **2.** *n.* moving people or goods from one place to another. (No plural form in this sense.) ♦ *The transportation of certain drugs into the U.S. is illegal.* ♦ *The transportation of lettuce requires refrigeration.*

trap ['træp] **1.** *n.* a device used to catch animals or people. ♦ *The raccoon was caught in the hunter's trap.* ♦ *Mary baited the mouse trap with cheese.* **2.** *n.* a bend in a drain pipe in which water rests in order to prevent harmful gases from the sewer into a building. ♦ *The trap was clogged with hair.* ♦ *Mary's ring fell down the sink, but she found it in the trap.* **3.** *tv.* to catch someone or something in ①. ♦ *The hunter trapped the fox.* ♦ *Bob trapped the mouse in the garage and put it in the garbage.* **4.** *tv.* to prevent someone or something from escaping, leaving, or getting out. ♦ *The robbers were trapped inside the bank.* ♦ *A landslide trapped the hikers inside the cave.*

trapdoor ['træp 'dor] *n.* a door in a floor or a ceiling, especially one that can't be seen until it opens; a door that covers a hole in a floor or a ceiling. ♦ *The magician entered through a trapdoor in the stage floor.* ♦ *The terrorists escaped through a trapdoor in the ceiling.*

trapeze [træ 'piz] *n.* a bar suspended from two ropes far above the ground, used by acrobats. ♦ *When the acrobat fell from the trapeze, she landed in the safety net.* ♦ *A clown swung on the trapeze above the audience.*

trapper ['træp ɚ] *n.* someone who traps animals, skins them, and sells the pelts. ♦ *The trapper skinned the trapped animals.* ♦ *Some merchants from the east bought the pelts from the trapper.*

trappings ['træp ɪŋz] *n.* the dress, ornaments, or other outward signs characteristic of a status or condition. (Treated as plural.) ♦ *Jane was dressed with all of the trappings of a wealthy woman.* ♦ *The house seemed empty and cold without the usual trappings of the holidays.*

trash ['træʃ] **1.** *n.* things that are thrown away; rubbish; refuse. (No plural form in this sense.) ♦ *There was a pile of trash in the corner of the garage.* ♦ *John took the trash out to the bin in the alley.* **2.** *n.* someone or something that is worthless. (Derogatory. Figurative on ①. No plural form in this sense.) ♦ *I think everything John writes is trash.* ♦ *Why are you watching that trash? Isn't there anything better on TV?* **3.** *tv.* to destroy something; to wreck something. (Slang.) ♦ *An electrical surge trashed my computer.* ♦ *The thieves trashed my apartment.* **4.** *tv.* to throw something away; to discard something. (Slang.) ♦ *The students trashed the empty pizza boxes.* ♦ *Who trashed my old sweatshirt? I wanted to keep it.*

trash can ['træʃ kæn] *n.* a container that trash is thrown into; a wastebasket. ♦ *John threw the garbage in the trash can.* ♦ *Mary accidentally threw some important papers in the trash can.*

trauma ['trɔ mə] **1.** *n.* an emotional shock; an emotional response to an emotional shock. ♦ *The victims of the crash underwent serious trauma.* ♦ *The trauma caused by the explosion haunted John for years.* **2.** *n.* an injury; a wound; damage to the body. ♦ *The crash victim suffered severe medical trauma.* ♦ *The surgeon repaired the trauma near the victim's eye.*

traumatic [trɔ 'mæt ɪk] **1.** *adj.* disturbing to the mind. (Adv: *traumatically* [...ɪk li].) ♦ *The explosion was a traumatic experience for the survivors.* ♦ *She remembered the traumatic incident all through her life.* **2.** *adj.* medically serious or damaging to tissue. (Adv: *traumatically* [...ɪk li].) ♦ *The victim had a traumatic eye injury.* ♦ *He suffered a number of traumatic blows to the head.*

travel ['træv əl] **1.** *iv.* to visit [places other than where one lives]; to journey. ♦ *Jane traveled to Scotland to visit her grandmother.* ♦ *I have plans to travel to Asia next year.* **2.** *iv.* to move through space; to move across a distance. ♦ *Nothing travels faster than light.* ♦ *The comet traveled through space at a great speed.* **3.** *tv.* to move on a path or route as one travels ①. ♦ *Do you travel this road often?* ♦ *I traveled the main highway from Des Moines to Chicago.* **4.** *tv.* to move over a specific distance as one travels ①. ♦ *We traveled the entire way on interstate freeways.* ♦ *Tom traveled 10 miles, and then our car ran out of gas.* **5.** *n.* going to and visiting places other than where one lives. (No plural form in this sense.) ♦ *Mary spends thousands of dollars on travel each year.* ♦ *I couldn't afford any travel while I was a student.* **6.** *n.* the business of providing services to travelers. (No plural form in this sense.) ♦ *I spoke to an expert in travel about trips to Jerusalem.* ♦ *The economist noted that profits in travel were increasing.* **7. travels** *n.* [someone's] journeys or visits to other places, especially over a long period of time. ♦ *John talked about his travels through the Middle East.* ♦ *I had written to my parents about my travels that summer.* **8.** *adj.* <the adj. use of ⑤.> ♦ *The travel agent booked my flight for Rome.* ♦ *The travel guide listed the names of good hotels.*

traveler ['træv lɚ] *n.* someone who travels; someone who goes on trips or journeys. ♦ *The business traveler flew first-class.* ♦ *The hotel near the train station lodges many travelers.*

traveler's check ['træv lɚʒ 'tʃɛk] *n.* a special kind of bank check that can be cashed in most parts of the world without difficulty. ♦ *I took traveler's checks with me on my vacation.* ♦ *My traveler's checks were stolen, but I got replacements for them within one day.*

traveling ['træv (ə) lɪŋ] *adj.* going from place to place. ♦ *The traveling salesman sold encyclopedias.* ♦ *The traveling circus troupe set up in the park.*

travelogue AND **travelog** ['træv ə lɔg] *n.* a speech about travel in other countries or cities, usually along with slides or photographs. ♦ *The university sponsored travelogues on eastern Europe.* ♦ *The man giving the travelogue on Paris had never been there.*

traverse [trə 'vɚs] *tv.* to cross through something; to extend across a place. ♦ *The soldiers traversed the battlefield on foot.* ♦ *The river traverses several countries.*

travesty ['træv ɪs ti] **1.** *n.* a very bad and insulting copy, performance, or imitation of something that misrepresents the original work. ♦ *Her version of the story was simply a travesty.* ♦ *The terrible play was a travesty of Shakespeare's work.* **2. travesty of justice** *idiom* a miscarriage of justice; an act of the legal system that is an insult to the system of justice. ♦ *The jury's verdict was a travesty of justice.* ♦ *The lawyer complained that the judge's ruling was a travesty of justice.*

tray ['tre] *n.* a flat panel with a slightly raised rim, used to carry things, especially food. ♦ *The nurse put the food on a tray and carried it to the patient.* ♦ *The waitress carried drinks around the casino on a tray.*

treacherous ['trɛtʃ ə rəs] **1.** *adj.* dangerous; unstable. (Adv: *treacherously.*) ♦ *The treacherous current swept the raft toward the waterfall.* ♦ *The ice on the roads makes driving treacherous.* **2.** *adj.* not loyal; not trustworthy; not faithful. (Adv: *treacherously.*) ♦ *The treacherous official was hung for treason.* ♦ *The spy committed many treacherous crimes.*

treachery ['trɛtʃ ə ri] *n.* betrayal; a disloyal or unfaithful action. (No plural form in this sense.) ♦ *For the traitor's treachery, he was sent to prison for life.* ♦ *The king's penalty for treachery was torture and execution.*

tread ['trɛd] **1.** *n.* the raised pattern on a tire; the pattern on the bottom of shoes used for athletics. ♦ *The detective inspected the treads visible in the footprints around the murder victim.* ♦ *Because my tire treads are worn, my car slides on wet roads.* **2.** *n.* a step [in walking]; the way one walks. (No plural form in this sense.) ♦ *Mary has a light tread, so I didn't even hear her enter.* ♦ *Jane walked with such a heavy tread that the floor shook.* **3.** *n.* the sound made by walking or stepping. ♦ *I heard the tread of the postman on the porch.* ♦ *John listened to Anne's even tread as she walked away.* **4.** *n.* the top of a step; the part of a stair that one steps on. ♦ *Each stair tread must be big enough to hold someone's foot.* ♦ *David slipped on a cracked tread and fell down the stairs.* **5.** *iv., irreg.* to walk; to step. (Pt: trod; pp: trod or trodden. Less used than walk.) ♦ *Please tread very quietly. The baby is asleep.* ♦ *The criminals trod softly past the guard.* **6.** *tv., irreg.* to walk [on] a path; to travel a distance [by walking]. (Less used than walk.) ♦ *I trod the long distance to church with a sore foot.* ♦ *We wearily trod the path to town.*

treadmill ['trɛd mɪl] **1.** *n.* a device that is used to provide power by walking on the moving steps of a wheel or a continuous belt. ♦ *The horses on the treadmill powered the thresher's engine.* ♦ *The factory was powered by a giant treadmill operated by prisoners.* **2.** *n.* a piece of exercise equipment consisting of a wide belt ③ that moves continuously while one walks on it. ♦ *Mary walked on the treadmill for half an hour and then rested.* ♦ *All of the treadmills were being used, so I left the gym.*

treason ['tri zən] *n.* the betrayal of one's country; the betrayal of the leader of one's country. (No plural form in this sense.) ♦ *The traitor was charged with treason.* ♦ *The soldier accused of treason was severely punished.*

treasure ['trɛ ʒɚ] **1.** *n.* valuable objects, especially ones that are stored; someone or something that is highly valued. ♦ *The pirates found buried treasure on the desert island.* ♦ *The empress kept her treasures locked in a vault.* **2.** *tv.* to value someone or something highly. ♦ *Mary treasures her children more than anything else.* ♦ *Jane treasured her brand-new computer.*

treasurer ['trɛ ʒɚ ɚ] *n.* someone who is in charge of the money of an organization or unit of government. ♦ *The treasurer read the financial report at the meeting.* ♦ *The signature of the treasurer must appear on company checks.*

treasury ['trɛ ʒə ri] **1.** *n.* the money that is owned by an organization or unit of government. ♦ *The firm's treasury was spread among several banks.* ♦ *When the treasury ran out of money, the workers could not be paid.* **2.** *n.* the department of a government in charge of spending and saving public money. ♦ *The signature of the Secretary of the Treasury is on every bill.* ♦ *The U.S. Treasury tabulates how much money is in circulation.*

treat ['trit] **1.** *n.* a bit of tasty food, such as candy or ice cream. ♦ *We had ice cream as a treat.* ♦ *Mother gave us all treats because we were quiet.* **2.** *n.* something that is pleasing. ♦ *Lisa's visit was a real treat.* ♦ *It was a treat to go shopping with you.* **3. someone's treat** *n.* an act of paying for someone else's meal or entertainment. ♦ *Put your money away. Lunch is my treat.* ♦ *Where would you like to eat? It's my treat.* **4. treat to** *tv.* + *prep. phr.* to provide someone with food or entertainment. ♦ *Could I treat you to a movie?* ♦ *David treated me to lunch today.* **5.** *tv.* to handle or consider someone or something in a certain way. ♦ *David treats John very badly.* ♦ *Please stop treating me like a child!* **6.** *tv.* to try to cure something. ♦ *How do you treat a sore throat?* ♦ *Mary treated her cold by drinking hot tea.* **7. treat for** *tv.* + *prep. phr.* to provide someone with a treatment for a disease or disorder. ♦ *The doctor treated John for hepatitis.* ♦ *Bill treated Mary for shock.*

treatise ['trit ɪs] *n.* a formal book or article on a particular subject. ♦ *I read a colonial treatise on taxation without representation.* ♦ *Anne's treatise on the legal system was published last year.*

treatment ['trit mənt] **1.** *n.* the way someone or something is dealt with. (No plural form in this sense.) ♦ *The abusive parents' treatment of their children was deplorable.* ♦ *The captor's treatment of the hostages was relatively good.* **2.** *n.* the method by which someone tries to cure someone. ♦ *John's chemotherapy treatments made him very ill.* ♦ *Surgery is only one of the treatments for cancer.* **3.** *n.* a version of the portrayal of a story or script. ♦ *The film treatment is very faithful to the book.* ♦ *The director's treatment of the dead president was criticized.*

treaty ['trit i] *n.* a formal agreement between two or more nations. ♦ *The two nations signed a treaty to protect each other from attack.* ♦ *The country broke the treaty four days after signing it.*

treble ['trɛb əl] **1.** *tv.* to increase something by a factor of three; triple something. ♦ *The new law trebled the jail population within a year.* ♦ *The gambler trebled his bet.* **2.** *iv.* to triple; to increase by three times. ♦ *The inflation* *rate trebled last year.* ♦ *My rate of pay trebled when I received a promotion.* **3.** *n.* the high frequencies of an amplifier, radio, stereo, piano, or other musical instrument. ♦ *The treble sounded very tinny over the car radio.* ♦ *Please lower the amplifier's treble.* **4.** *adj.* <the adj. use of ③.> ♦ *The treble sounds of my radio are too intense.* ♦ *A pianist usually plays the treble notes with the right hand.*

tree ['tri] **1.** *n.* a tall plant whose stem and branches are made of wood, and that often has leaves growing from the branches. ♦ *A forest is filled with trees.* ♦ *We cut down the dead tree in our front yard.* **2.** *n.* a diagram that represents the relationship between different levels or hierarchies by expressing them as branches at different levels. ♦ *The linguist used a tree to show the structure of the sentence.* ♦ *John's family tree goes back to the 18th century.*

tree house ['tri hɑʊs] *n., irreg.* a platform or structure built in a tree for children to play in. (Pl: [...hɑʊ zəz].) ♦ *The children climbed up to their tree house.* ♦ *From their tree house, Mary and John threw snowballs down at me.*

treetop ['tri tɑp] *n.* the top of a tree. ♦ *A pretty bird sat in the treetop.* ♦ *The kite soared above the treetops.*

trek ['trɛk] **1.** *n.* a long journey, often on foot. ♦ *The astronomers' imaginary trek took them to distant planets.* ♦ *I went on a long trek across the state.* **2.** *iv.* to travel on a long journey, often on foot. ♦ *The hiker trekked through the forest for hours.* ♦ *John trekked across America.*

tremble ['trɛm bəl] **1.** *iv.* to shake, especially because of fear, excitement, sickness, or cold. ♦ *The poor girl trembled in the cold.* ♦ *When I heard the good news, I trembled with excitement.* **2.** *n.* a shaking movement. ♦ *Living near a fault, I felt the earth's tremble many times.* ♦ *With a momentary tremble, I turned to face my attacker.*

tremendous [trɪ 'mɛn dəs] **1.** *adj.* huge; enormous; very large; immense. (Adv: *tremendously.*) ♦ *The tornado caused a tremendous amount of damage.* ♦ *John is unable to repay his tremendous debts.* **2.** *adj.* wonderful; excellent; superb. (Adv: *tremendously.*) ♦ *The actor received an award for her tremendous performance.* ♦ *I always eat Thanksgiving dinner at John's house because he's a tremendous cook.*

tremendously [trɪ 'mɛn dəs li] *adv.* very; immensely. ♦ *I was tremendously happy when I won the lottery.* ♦ *The news reporter wanted to be tremendously famous.*

tremor ['trɛm ɚ] *n.* a shaking movement, especially one caused by an earthquake, fear, or disease. ♦ *The earth's tremors caused the building to crumble.* ♦ *The tremor in Lisa's hands was due to a nervous condition.*

trench ['trɛntʃ] *n.* a long ditch cut into the ground. ♦ *The soldiers slept in the wet, dark trench.* ♦ *The laborers laid sewer pipe in the trench.*

trend ['trɛnd] **1.** *n.* a tendency; the general direction in which something is heading. ♦ *The trend in the stock market is for higher and higher prices.* ♦ *The company followed the trend of marketing healthy products.* **2.** *n.* something that represents a fad or popular style. ♦ *The cheerleaders wore the latest trend in clothing at school.* ♦ *Thin ties were a fashion trend in the early 1980s.* **3.** *iv.* to tend to continue to move in a certain direction. ♦ *Lisa noticed that stock prices trended upward last year.* ♦ *Interest rates are trending downward.*

trendy ['trɛn di] *adj.* fashionable; in style; participating in a fad. (Adv: *trendily.* Comp: *trendier;* sup: *trendiest.*) ♦ *The popular students wore expensive, trendy clothing.* ♦ *The trendy teenagers ridiculed the unfashionable ones.*

trepidation [trɛp ɪ 'de ʃən] **1.** *n.* extreme fear; dread; anxiety. (No plural form in this sense.) ♦ *With much trepidation, John boarded a plane for the first time.* ♦ *Snakes always caused fear and trepidation in Mary.* **2.** *n.* a fear; an anxiety. ♦ *John had many trepidations about flying.* ♦ *With many trepidations, I opened the door and went into the dentist's office.*

trespass ['trɛs pæs] **1. trespass on** *iv.* + *prep. phr.* to go on someone's property without permission. ♦ *The hunter trespassed on the farmer's property.* ♦ *John shot at the burglar trespassing on his property.* **2. trespass against** *iv.* + *prep. phr.* to sin against someone or something; to do something against someone or something. ♦ *I forgave those who trespassed against me.* ♦ *The sinner trespassed against the laws of God.* **3.** *n.* going on someone's property without permission. (No plural form in this sense.) ♦ *The burglar was found guilty of trespass.* ♦ *The protester's trespass onto the military base was illegal.* **4. trespasses** *n.* sins; transgressions. ♦ *Forgive us our trespasses.* ♦ *We hoped for forgiveness of our trespasses.*

trestle ['trɛs əl] *n.* a braced structure that supports a road or railroad across a gap. ♦ *A trestle carried the tracks across the creek.* ♦ *The old wooden trestle collapsed into the river.*

trial ['trɑɪl] **1.** *n.* the examining of the evidence in a court of law by a judge or jury to settle a legal question, such as guilt or innocence. ♦ *The prosecution and the defense present their cases at a trial.* ♦ *The judge who presided over my trial was fair and impartial.* **2.** *n.* an experiment; a test to see if something works; a test to see if something is beneficial. ♦ *After dozens of trials, the drug was proven to be safe for humans.* ♦ *Susan explained the results of her experiment's first trial.* **3.** *n.* a difficult ordeal; an affliction. ♦ *John's alcoholism was a trial for his family.* ♦ *Jane's unruly children were a daily trial.* **4.** *adj.* experimental. ♦ *A dose of the trial drug was given to each volunteer.* ♦ *The trial results looked very promising to the researcher.* **5.** *adj.* <the adj. use of ①.> ♦ *The trial judge deliberated in his chambers.* ♦ *The court recorder transcribed the trial proceedings.* **6. on trial** *idiom* being tried in court. ♦ *My sister is on trial today, so I have to go to court.* ♦ *They placed the suspected thief on trial.*

triangle ['trɑɪ æŋ gəl] **1.** *n.* a figure that has three sides and three angles. ♦ *Each face of the pyramid was a triangle.* ♦ *A square divided along a diagonal creates two triangles.* **2.** *n.* a flat, three-sided object with three sides, used for drawing lines and angles. ♦ *The architect used a large triangle to draw a straight line.* ♦ *These angles were drawn with the aid of a triangle.* **3.** *n.* a metal musical instrument in the shape of ①, that is struck with a small rod to make a ringing noise. ♦ *The musician in the marching band carried a triangle.* ♦ *The conductor placed the triangle near the drummer.*

triangular [trɑɪ 'æŋ gjə lɚ] *adj.* shaped like a triangle. (Adv: *triangularly.*) ♦ *The bottom part of a clothes hanger usually has a triangular shape.* ♦ *The triangular park is bordered by three streets.*

tribe ['trɑɪb] *n.* a group of people—not usually industrialized—having the same customs, religion, language, and culture; a local division of a larger ethnic group, especially in North America. ♦ *The tribe held religious ceremonies next to a river.* ♦ *The warring tribes fought in the valley.*

tribulation [trɪb jə 'le ʃən] **1.** *n.* trouble or suffering. (No plural form in this sense.) ♦ *Tribulation seems to dominate my life lately.* ♦ *The unfortunate man faced much tribulation throughout life.* **2.** *n.* an instance of ①; a cause of ①. ♦ *Bill suffered many tribulations during the war.* ♦ *John's wayward son was his greatest tribulation.*

tribunal [trɑɪ 'bju nəl] *n.* a court of justice. ♦ *The tribunal found the defendant to be guilty.* ♦ *The lawyers pled their cases before the tribunal.*

tributary ['trɪb jə tɛr i] *n.* a branch of a river; a river that flows into a larger river. ♦ *The Ohio River is a tributary of the Mississippi River.* ♦ *The German factory flanked a tributary of the Rhine.*

tribute ['trɪb jut] *n.* a show of respect or honor. ♦ *The students wrote poems as a tribute to Martin Luther King, Jr.* ♦ *Lisa's acceptance speech was a tribute to her parents.*

trick ['trɪk] **1.** *n.* something that is done to deceive someone; a deception. ♦ *The swindler's trick cost the tourist $100.* ♦ *Jimmy played a funny trick on his parents.* **2.** *adj.* made to be used in ①; deceptive. ♦ *The magician's trick hat had a false bottom.* ♦ *Mary's trick cards are secretly marked on the back.* **3. play a trick on someone** *idiom* to do a trick ① that affects someone. ♦ *Somebody played a trick on me by hiding my shoes.* ♦ *The little boys planned to play a trick on their teacher by turning up the heat in the classroom.* **4. trick someone into doing something** *idiom* to fool, deceive, or cheat someone and in that way make the person do something. ♦ *The thief tricked John into giving him $10.* ♦ *Mary tricked her friends into paying for her dinner.* **5. use every trick in the book** *idiom* to use every method possible. ♦ *I used every trick in the book, but I still couldn't manage to get a ticket to the game Saturday.* ♦ *Bob tried to use every trick in the book, but he still failed.*

trickery ['trɪk ə ri] *n.* deception; the use of tricks to fool or cheat someone. (No plural form in this sense.) ♦ *Because of Mary's trickery, I didn't know that she was cheating.* ♦ *The thief obtained a lot of money through trickery.*

trickle ['trɪk əl] **1.** *n.* a very slow flow of something; the movement of a liquid one drop at a time. ♦ *A trickle of water dripped from the faucet.* ♦ *John wiped a trickle of blood from his nose.* **2.** *iv.* to flow very slowly; to move one drop at a time. ♦ *Water trickled from the broken pipe.* ♦ *Blood trickled from my nose.* **3.** *tv.* [for someone] to dribble a fluid onto something. ♦ *The baker trickled icing on the cake.* ♦ *The gardener trickled water into each pot.* **4.** *tv.* [for something] to leak or exude a fluid. ♦ *When Bill hit me, my nose trickled blood.* ♦ *The garden hose trickled water.*

tricky ['trɪk i] **1.** *adj.* difficult to do; puzzling; hard to deal with. (Adv: *trickily.* Comp: *trickier;* sup: *trickiest.*) ♦ *John struggled to solve the tricky algebra problem.* ♦ *Assembling appliances can be tricky without a manual.* **2.** *adj.* full of tricks; deceptive. (Adv: *trickily.* Comp: *trickier;* sup: *trickiest.*) ♦ *The rat ran through the tricky maze.* ♦ *I don't trust Jane because she is very tricky.*

tricycle ['trɑɪ sɪk əl] *n.* a small vehicle with three wheels, two in back and one in front, made for young children to ride on. ♦ *Susie rode her tricycle around the patio.* ♦ *Jimmy keeps his tricycle in the garage.*

triennial [trɑɪ 'ɛn i əl] **1.** *adj.* happening every three years; lasting for three years. (Adv: *triennially.*) ♦ *The town's triennial celebration is held in the town square.* ♦ *The mayor was in office for two triennial terms.* **2.** *n.* the third anniversary. ♦ *In honor of the school's triennial, we planted three trees.* ♦ *The young nation joyously celebrated its triennial of independence.*

trifle ['trɑɪ fəl] **1.** *n.* a small amount of something; a small amount of money. ♦ *I bought these cups for a trifle at the sale.* ♦ *Would you like some pizza? There's only a trifle left.* **2.** *n.* something that is very inexpensive; something that is not valuable. ♦ *Only a few trifles broke during the earthquake.* ♦ *The discount store sold inexpensive trifles.* **3. trifle with** *iv.* + *prep. phr.* to waste time with something. ♦ *Do you always have to trifle with my affairs?* ♦ *I trifled with the leaky pipe for hours before finally calling a plumber.* **4. trifle with** *iv.* + *prep. phr.* to toy with someone; to tease, annoy, or fiddle with someone. ♦ *If you trifle with the boss, you'll get in trouble.* ♦ *Don't trifle with me!*

trifocals ['trɑɪ fok əlz] *n.* a pair of eyeglasses whose lenses have three parts, one for distance, one for close viewing, and one for a medium distance. (Treated as plural.) ♦ *Grandma put on her trifocals so that she could read the letter.* ♦ *I can't wear contact lenses because I need trifocals.*

trigger ['trɪg ɚ] **1.** *n.* the small lever on a gun that is used to fire it. ♦ *You can't pull the trigger if the safety is locked.* ♦ *John pulled the trigger and shot the robber.* **2.** *n.* something that causes something else to happen. (Figurative on ①.) ♦ *The old song was a trigger to a repressed memory.* ♦ *John's movement was the trigger that set off the alarm.* **3.** *tv.* to cause something to happen; to cause something that starts a chain of events. ♦ *Even the slightest movement will trigger the alarm.* ♦ *The rise in interest rates was triggered by inflation.*

trigonometry [trɪg ə 'nɑm ə tri] *n.* the branch of mathematics that deals with the relationships between the sides and angles of triangles. (No plural form in this sense.) ♦ *The surveyor used trigonometry to determine the tree's height.* ♦ *We studied trigonometry in my geometry class.*

trill ['trɪl] **1.** *n.* a rapid alternation between two or three musical notes. ♦ *My piano teacher told me to practice my trills.* ♦ *The soprano finished the song with a trill.* **2.** *iv.* to alternate rapidly between two musical notes. ♦ *The soprano trilled as she practiced the song.* ♦ *The pianist trilled flawlessly.*

trillion ['trɪl jən] **1.** *n.* the number 1,000,000,000,000. (Additional numbers formed as with *two trillion, three trillion, four trillion,* etc.) ♦ *One trillion is a thousand billion.* ♦ *One million times one million is one trillion.* **2.** *n.* a group of 1,000,000,000,000 things or people. ♦ *Each year, the government spends over a trillion.* ♦ *"There must have been a trillion at the beach today," Bob exaggerated.* **3.** *adj.* consisting of 1,000,000,000,000 things. ♦ *The federal budget is over a trillion dollars annually.* ♦ *There must be a trillion water molecules in the ocean!*

trillionth ['trɪl jənθ] 1,000,000,000,000th. See fourth for senses and examples.

trilogy ['trɪl ə dʒi] *n.* a set of three books, plays, movies, etc., that share a common theme or characters and events. ♦ *The same actor starred in all three parts of the trilogy.* ♦ *The novelist wrote a trilogy of vampire stories.*

trim ['trɪm] **1.** *tv.* to make something neat by cutting; to cut something neatly. ♦ *The barber trimmed my hair.* ♦ *The gardener trimmed the hedges.* **2.** *tv.* to reduce something; to decrease something. ♦ *David trimmed 10 pounds from his body by exercising.* ♦ *The butcher trimmed the fat from the meat.* **3.** *tv.* to decorate something. ♦ *The children trimmed the Christmas tree with tinsel.* ♦ *Mary trimmed the old dress with a silk sash.* **4.** *adj.* [of someone] thin and of the proper weight. (Adv: *trimly.* Comp: *trimmer;* sup: *trimmest.*) ♦ *Through exercise, Mary has become trim and fit.* ♦ *Grandma is very trim for someone her age.* **5.** *n.* the act of cutting grass, hair, branches, fat from meat, etc. ♦ *The barber's trim cost $10.* ♦ *This hedge needs a good trim.* **6.** *n.* the woodwork around a door or window. ♦ *Mary painted the trim around the window blue.* ♦ *The trim around the door split when I pounded a nail into it.*

trimester ['traɪ mɛs tɚ] **1.** *n.* a division of a school year in institutions that divide the school year into three terms. ♦ *Each student must take three trimesters of biology.* ♦ *Last year, my college switched from semesters to trimesters.* **2.** *n.* a three-month period, such as ⅓ of a pregnancy. ♦ *Mary's pregnancy didn't begin to show until her third trimester.* ♦ *Anne saw her doctor three times each trimester.*

trimmings ['trɪm ɪŋz] **1.** *n.* the parts of something that were cut off when it was trimmed. (Treated as plural.) ♦ *David fed the meat trimmings to the dog.* ♦ *The gardener swept up the hedge trimmings with a rake.* **2.** *n.* extra items; accessories; especially vegetables, garnishes, and side dishes that are served with the main meal. (Treated as plural.) ♦ *This restaurant serves Sunday dinner with all the trimmings.* ♦ *Grandma made the ham, and everyone else brought the trimmings.*

Trinidad and Tobago ['trɪn ə dæd ænd tə 'be go] See Gazetteer.

trinket ['trɪŋ kɪt] *n.* a small, cheap piece of jewelry. ♦ *Mary wore a few cheap trinkets to the party.* ♦ *The crook tried to convince me that his trinkets were diamonds.*

trio ['tri o] **1.** *n.* a group of three, especially a group of three performers. (Pl in *-s.*) ♦ *The first act in the talent show was a trio of singers.* ♦ *Anne and her two best friends are an inseparable trio.* **2.** *n.* a piece of music written for three instruments or three voices. (Pl in *-s.*) ♦ *The composer wrote a trio for two violins and a viola.* ♦ *The musician wrote a trio for three tenors.*

trip ['trɪp] **1.** *n.* a journey between two places; a journey from one place to another. ♦ *Last year, I took a trip to India.* ♦ *Jane went on a business trip to Texas.* **2.** *iv.* to stumble; to fall over something; to hit one's foot against someone or something, causing a loss of balance. ♦ *Anne tripped on the stairs and fell down.* ♦ *There were toys all over the floor, causing Mary to trip.* **3.** *tv.* to cause someone to fall; to cause someone to stumble and lose balance. ♦ *Mary tripped Bob by sticking her leg out in front of him.* ♦ *The loose board tripped John when he walked past it.* **4.** *tv.* to release a lever or a switch, thus causing something to function. ♦ *The worker tripped the switch to start the assembly line.* ♦ *Mary tripped the lever to reset the fuse.*

triple ['trɪp əl] **1.** *adj.* 3 times as much; 3 times as many. (Adv: *triply.*) ♦ *My department's budget is triple that of Bill's department.* ♦ *The state's traffic fines are triple in construction zones.* **2.** *adj.* made of 3 parts; having 3 parts. ♦ *The triple sundae has three scoops of ice cream.* ♦ *Three outs are made during a triple play in baseball.* **3.** *n.* a number or amount that is 3 times greater than another amount. ♦ *12 is a triple of 4.* ♦ *The triple of 5 is 15.* **4.** *n.* [in baseball] a hit made by a batter who successfully reaches third base. ♦ *Two runners scored when the batter hit a triple.* ♦ *The player who just hit a triple is now on third base.* **5.** *iv.* to become 3 times as much; to become 3 times as many. ♦ *The inflation rate tripled last month from 0.1% to 0.3%.* ♦ *My work load tripled when Bob and Mary went on vacation.* **6.** *iv.* [in baseball] to hit the ball and successfully get to third base. ♦ *The batter tripled on his hit to right field.* ♦ *Although John tripled, another runner was put out.* **7. triple up** *iv.* + *adv.* [for three people] to join together to share something, such as a room. ♦ *Due to a lack of space, freshmen had to triple up in the dorm rooms.* ♦ *Anne, Susan, and Mary tripled up until another room was available.* **8.** *tv.* to multiply a number by 3; to cause something to have three times as much; to cause something to have three times as many. ♦ *If you triple four, you get 12.* ♦ *The merger tripled the amount of students in my school.*

triplet ['trɪp lət] **1.** *n.* one of three offspring born at the same time from the same mother. ♦ *Did you know that John is a triplet?* ♦ *Mary shared a room with her two triplets.* **2. triplets** *n.* a set of three children born at the same time to the same mother. ♦ *Anne was shocked to learn that she was pregnant with triplets.* ♦ *My grandma helped my parents when the triplets were born.*

triplicate ['trɪp lə kɪt] **1. in triplicate** *phr.* produced in three copies. ♦ *Mr. Smith asked me to type up his notes in triplicate.* ♦ *I completed each form in triplicate.* **2.** *adj.* [of a document] having three parts that are exactly alike. ♦ *Jane submitted triplicate copies of her insurance forms.* ♦ *The triplicate reports were a waste of paper.*

tripod ['traɪ pɑd] *n.* a support or stand that has three legs, especially one that supports a camera. ♦ *The photographer attached the camera to a tripod.* ♦ *The small movie screen was attached to a metal tripod.*

trite ['traɪt] *adj.* [of an expression] shallow and simple-minded. (Adv: *tritely.* Comp: *triter;* sup: *tritest.*) ♦ *The editor deleted the trite phrases from my article.* ♦ *The movie was filled with trite generalizations about teenagers.*

triumph ['traɪ əmf] **1.** *n.* celebration; the glory of victory. (No plural form in this sense.) ♦ *In the triumph, people hugged each other.* ♦ *In our moment of triumph, let's not forget those who made it all possible.* **2.** *n.* a victory; a great achievement; a great success. ♦ *Our team celebrated its triumph over our rival.* ♦ *The verdict was a triumph for the hardworking lawyers.* **3.** *iv.* to win; to be victorious; to be very successful. ♦ *Our team triumphed at the tournament.* ♦ *The lucky patient had triumphed over cancer.*

triumphant [traɪ 'ʌm fənt] *adj.* victorious; successful; joyful because of victory. (Adv: *triumphantly.*) ♦ *The tri-*

umphant soldiers returned from the battlefield. ♦ *Each triumphant winner thanked the voters.*

trivia ['trɪv i ə] *n.* trivial things; things that are insignificant; trivial facts. (No plural form in this sense.) ♦ *I'm trying to work. Please don't bother me with trivia.* ♦ *Trivia is something you should edit from important articles.*

trivial ['trɪv i əl] *adj.* not important; not significant. (Adv: *trivially.*) ♦ *Only a trivial amount of rain fell last night.* ♦ *I didn't bother Bob with my trivial concerns because he was busy.*

trod ['trɑd] pt and a pp of tread.

trodden ['trɑd n] a pp of tread.

trolley ['trɑ li] *n.* a streetcar that is operated by electricity and runs along a track. ♦ *The trolley stops in front of the hotel.* ♦ *Mary took a trolley from her apartment to work.*

trombone [trɑm 'bon] *n.* a brass musical instrument, played by blowing air into one end with tensed lips, while moving a long slide into different positions. ♦ *Trombones make lower notes than trumpets, but higher notes than tubas.* ♦ *Eight people played trombones in the marching band.*

troop ['trup] **1.** *n.* a group of people or animals, especially a group of soldiers. ♦ *The troop or soldiers marched all day.* ♦ *What troop are you in?* **2. troops** *n.* soldiers. (Treated as plural.) ♦ *The troops were sheltered in the trenches.* ♦ *The minister prayed for the troops on the battlefield.* **3.** *iv.* to walk or move as a group. ♦ *My friends and I trooped through the park.* ♦ *The soldiers trooped across the base.*

trooper ['trup ɚ] **(state) trooper.** *n.* a state police officer. ♦ *A trooper gave me a ticket for speeding.* ♦ *The state trooper rushed to the scene of the accident.*

trophy ['tro fi] **1.** *n.* something that is taken from a battle or a hunt as a symbol of one's success. ♦ *The mounted animal heads in the hunter's den were trophies of his kills.* ♦ *The soldiers kept trophies from the villages they ransacked.* **2.** *n.* a small statue or prize that is given to the winner of an event or competition. ♦ *The trophies of the school's teams were placed in a showcase.* ♦ *My bowling team won the league trophy last night.*

tropic ['trɑp ɪk] **1.** *n.* one of two imaginary circles around the earth, 23.45 degrees north and south of the equator. ♦ *The tropic of Cancer is in the Northern Hemisphere.* ♦ *New Zealand is south of the tropic of Capricorn.* **2. tropics** *n.* the area between the two tropics ①; the areas of the earth near the equator. (Treated as singular.) ♦ *The country of Indonesia is located in the tropics.* ♦ *Our cruise ship sailed to the tropics.* **3.** *adj.* tropical; hot and humid. ♦ *Many fruits grow best in tropic weather.* ♦ *I fainted in the tropic heat.*

tropical ['trɑp ɪ kəl] *adj.* of or about the tropics; of or about the weather conditions of the tropics; found in the tropics. (Adv: *tropically* [...ɪk li].) ♦ *Most bananas are grown on tropical plantations.* ♦ *The researcher explored the tropical jungle.*

trot ['trɑt] **1.** *n.* the gait of a horse between a walk and a gallop; the gait of a human between a walk and a run. ♦ *The galloping horse slowed to a trot.* ♦ *My short morning trots through the park are invigorating.* **2.** *iv.* to move faster than walking, but not as fast as running. ♦ *I trotted to the store to get some milk.* ♦ *The horse trotted all the way back to the barn.* **3.** *tv.* to cause a horse to ②. ♦ *The rider trotted the horse toward the barn.* ♦ *The jockey trotted the horse around the track.* **4. trot something out** *idiom* to mention something regularly or habitually, without giving it much thought. ♦ *When James disagreed with Mary, she simply trotted her same old political arguments out.* ♦ *Bob always trots out the same excuses for being late.*

trouble ['trʌb əl] **1.** *n.* worry; difficulty; anxiety. ♦ *Jane's marriage is giving her a lot of trouble.* ♦ *Dave's boss causes him too much trouble at work.* **2.** *n.* annoyance; bother. ♦ *Dave's injured back causes him a lot of trouble.* ♦ *John's unruly children are real trouble for him.* **3.** *n.* a sickness; an ailment. ♦ *The alcoholic developed liver trouble.* ♦ *John takes medicine for his heart trouble.* **4.** *n.* someone or something that causes worry, difficulty, anxiety, annoyance, bother, or problems. ♦ *John is trouble because he judges people too quickly.* ♦ *Those kids are trouble, and I refuse to babysit them.* **5.** *tv.* to worry someone; to cause someone difficulty or anxiety. ♦ *The problem of crime troubled the mayor.* ♦ *The new budget troubled the office manager.* **6.** *tv.* to bother or delay someone with an inquiry. ♦ *Could I trouble you for a moment of your time?* ♦ *The students troubled the teacher with trivial questions.* **7.** *tv.* to cause someone to feel pain. ♦ *John's back troubled him greatly.* ♦ *My sore feet trouble me a lot.* **8. in trouble** *phr.* in danger; at risk. ♦ *If you don't be quiet, you're going to be in trouble.* ♦ *The company was in trouble for months, and then went bankrupt.* **9. ask for trouble** *idiom* to do or say something that will cause trouble. ♦ *Stop talking to me that way, John. You're just asking for trouble.* ♦ *Anybody who threatens a police officer is just asking for trouble.* **10. teething troubles** *idiom* difficulties and problems experienced in the early stages of a project, activity, etc. ♦ *There have been a lot of teething troubles with the new computer system.* ♦ *We have finally gotten over the teething troubles connected with the new building complex.*

troubled ['trʌb əld] **1.** *adj.* worried; upset; anxious. (Adv: *troubledly.*) ♦ *The doctor comforted the patient's troubled family.* ♦ *The troubled parents called the police when their child didn't come home.* **2.** *adj.* having problems or difficulties. ♦ *The counselor spoke with the troubled students.* ♦ *The troubled company declared bankruptcy.*

troublemaker ['trʌb əl mek ɚ] *n.* someone who causes trouble; someone who causes problems. ♦ *The principal suspended the troublemaker for a week.* ♦ *The troublemaker set the abandoned barn on fire.*

troubleshooter ['trʌb əl ʃut ɚ] *n.* someone who tries to determine why something isn't working well. ♦ *Our company hired a troubleshooter to solve the morale problem.* ♦ *The troubleshooter found ten ways we could reduce costs.*

troublesome ['trʌb əl səm] *adj.* causing trouble; causing problems; annoying; bothersome. (Adv: *troublesomely.*) ♦ *I have a troublesome ache in my back.* ♦ *The teacher sent the troublesome students to the office.*

trough ['trɔf] **1.** *n.* the dip between two higher levels, as with a wave or on a wavy graph. ♦ *According to the chart, the economy is climbing out of a trough.* ♦ *The swimmer gasped for air in the trough between two waves.* **2.** *n.* a box or tank that contains food or water for animals. ♦ *The farmer put the pig's feed in their trough.* ♦ *The goats drank water from the trough.*

trounce ['trɑʊns] **1.** *tv.* to beat someone severely. ♦ *The bully trounced the small child every day.* ♦ *The army trounced the rebels within a week.* **2.** *tv.* to defeat someone, especially by a wide margin. ♦ *Our football team trounced Central High by 40 points.* ♦ *The baseball team trounced its opponent 15–2.*

troupe ['trup] *n.* a group of actors or performers; an ensemble. ♦ *The theater troupe performed* Romeo and Juliet. ♦ *The rich lawyer donated some money to the local dance troupe.*

trousers ['trɑʊ zɚz] *n.* an article of clothing worn below the waist, having a separate compartment for each leg and extending to the ankles. (Treated as plural. Number is expressed with *pair(s) of trousers.*) ♦ *The tailor repaired the rip in my trousers.* ♦ *John bought a new pair of trousers for his friend's wedding.*

trout ['trɑʊt] **1.** *n., irreg.* a freshwater fish commonly eaten as food. Pl: *trout.*) ♦ *Did you catch any trout during your fishing trip?* ♦ *The trout quickly swam downstream.* **2.** *n.* the flesh of ①, eaten as food. (No plural form in this sense.) ♦ *The trout I had at the restaurant was prepared perfectly.* ♦ *I would like some trout and boiled potatoes.*

trowel ['trɑʊ əl] **1.** *n.* a tool used to apply, manipulate, and smooth mortar or plaster. ♦ *The worker used a large trowel to spread the plaster.* ♦ *The mason scooped up some mortar with his trowel and placed it on the top level of bricks.* **2.** *n.* a tool used in gardening for digging small holes and planting individual plants. ♦ *The gardener always cleans his trowel after using it.* ♦ *When I plant small plants, I use a trowel rather than a shovel.*

truant ['tru ənt] **1.** *adj.* absent from school without permission. (Adv: *truantly.*) ♦ *Max was truant a number of times during the school year.* ♦ *The parents of the truant students were called by the principal.* **2.** *n.* someone who is absent from school without permission. ♦ *The truant was punished for skipping class.* ♦ *The principal found some truants at the fast-food restaurant.*

truce ['trus] *n.* an agreement to stop fighting. ♦ *The warring sides finally signed a truce after thousands had died.* ♦ *The rebels broke the truce by bombing the market square.*

truck ['trʌk] **1.** *n.* a large motor vehicle designed to carry objects or cargo rather than people. ♦ *Trucks must stay in the right lanes, except when passing.* ♦ *The worker loaded the car parts onto the truck.* **2.** *adj.* <the adj. use of ①.> ♦ *The truck parts were delivered to the warehouse on time.* ♦ *John works at a truck factory.* **3.** *tv.* to transport something by ①. ♦ *The parts were trucked from the factory to the warehouse.* ♦ *The farmer trucked the crops to the market.*

truck driver ['trʌk drɑɪv ɚ] *n.* someone who drives a truck for a living; someone who hauls cargo in a truck; a trucker. ♦ *The truck driver was carrying a load of fruit.* ♦ *The tired truck driver had been driving for 24 hours.*

trucker ['trʌk ɚ] *n.* someone who drives a truck for a living; someone who hauls cargo in a truck. ♦ *The police officer ticketed the trucker for speeding.* ♦ *The trucker slept during rush hour at a truck stop.*

trudge ['trʌdʒ] *iv.* to walk slowly and heavily, as though one were very tired; to plod. ♦ *The soldiers trudged through the thick mud.* ♦ *The children trudged toward class after recess.*

true ['tru] **1.** *adj.* being a fact; actual; real; not false. (Adv: *truly.* Comp: *truer;* sup: *truest.*) ♦ *Is it true that you are quitting your job?* ♦ *John's statement expressed a true proposition.* **2.** *adj.* sincere; genuine; not fake; not artificial. (Adv: *truly.* Comp: *truer;* sup: *truest.*) ♦ *John confessed his true feelings about his parents.* ♦ *David is a true friend of mine.* **3.** *adj.* properly fitted; at the proper angle. (Adv: *truly.* Comp: *truer;* sup: *truest.*) ♦ *If the sill is true to the frame, nail them together.* ♦ *The joint was not true and was finally knocked loose.* **4. come true** *idiom* to materialize as expected or hoped. ♦ *Jane's wishes had come true.* ♦ *Dave wondered if his dreams would ever come true.* **5. hold true** *idiom* [for something] to be ①; [for something] to remain ①. ♦ *Does this rule hold true all the time?* ♦ *Yes, it holds true no matter what.* **6. ring true** *idiom* to sound or seem true or likely. ♦ *The pupil's excuse for being late doesn't ring true.* ♦ *Do you think that Mary's explanation for her absence rang true?* **7. too good to be true** *idiom* almost unbelievable; so good as to be unbelievable. ♦ *The news was too good to be true.* ♦ *When I finally got a big raise, it was too good to be true.* **8. true to one's word** *idiom* keeping one's promise. ♦ *True to his word, Tom showed up at exactly eight o'clock.* ♦ *We'll soon know if Jane is true to her word. We'll see if she does what she promised.*

truism ['tru ɪz əm] *n.* a statement that is obviously true, so there is no need to say it. ♦ *The boring lecture was full of uninteresting truisms.* ♦ *"War is war" is a truism.*

truly ['tru li] *adv.* really; honestly; genuinely. ♦ *I truly apologize for my behavior.* ♦ *We truly hope you enjoy your stay in town.*

trump ['trʌmp] **trump up** *tv.* + *adv.* to make up false charges against someone; to invent or fabricate a story. ♦ *The crooked cop trumped up testimony against the mayor.* ♦ *All of the charges against me were trumped up by my boss.*

trumpet ['trʌmp ɪt] **1.** *n.* a brass musical instrument on which different notes are produced by blowing air into one end with tensed lips while pressing different combinations of three valves. ♦ *John played the trumpet with one hand.* ♦ *When I heard the trumpet blare, I knew the king had arrived.* **2.** *iv.* [for an elephant] to make a characteristic elephant noise. ♦ *The elephant trumpeted and frightened everyone.* ♦ *The huge elephant ran toward the keeper and trumpeted loudly.*

trunk ['trʌŋk] **1.** *n.* the main stem of a tree. ♦ *John carved his initials into the tree trunk.* ♦ *I sawed through the trunk of the dead tree.* **2.** *n.* the torso; the body of a human without its head, arms, or legs. ♦ *The police found the decaying trunk of a murder victim in the pond.* ♦ *The biology teacher showed a cross-section of a human trunk.* **3.** *n.* a large, sturdy box for transporting or storing clothes or other objects. ♦ *The passengers' trunks were loaded onto the steamer.* ♦ *I keep my sweaters in a large trunk during the summer.* **4.** *n.* the long, tube-shaped nose of an elephant. ♦ *The elephant sprayed water from its trunk into its mouth.* ♦ *The elephant picked up some hay with its trunk.* **5. trunks** *n.* a swimming suit for men. ♦ *John changed into his trunks and joined us in the pool.* ♦ *Bill's trunks slipped down when he dove into the water.*

truss ['trʌs] **1.** *n.* a framework of beams placed at angles that supports a bridge or roof. ♦ *As the truss burned, the roof began to collapse.* ♦ *The engineer designed the trusses* *that spanned the river.* **2. truss (up)** *tv.* (+ *adv.*) to tie someone or something up with rope. ♦ *The thieves trussed up the bank tellers with rope.* ♦ *The farmer trussed up the hog so he could take it to market.*

trust ['trʌst] **1.** *n.* a strong belief in the honesty or reliability of someone or something. (No plural form in this sense.) ♦ *The bank places its trust in no one.* ♦ *Trust is important in a good relationship.* **2.** *n.* a financial entity managed or controlled on behalf of someone else. ♦ *The executor managed the dead millionaire's trust.* ♦ *I receive $300 monthly from my grandparents' trust.* **3.** *tv.* to believe in the honesty and reliability of someone or something. ♦ *Mary trusted her instincts and refused to talk to the stranger.* ♦ *My parents trusted me to behave when they went out to dinner.* **4.** *tv.* to hope something. ♦ *I trust that you'll be coming to my party.* ♦ *I trust that you're merely joking about my dinner.* **5. trust in** *iv.* + *prep. phr.* to have confidence in someone or something. ♦ *The people trusted in God.* ♦ *The soldier trusted in the general's plans.* **6. in the trust of someone** *idiom* under a person's responsibility; in a person's care. (No plural form in this sense.) ♦ *The state placed the orphan in the trust of the foster parents.* ♦ *Our bonds are left in the trust of our broker.*

trusted ['trʌs tɪd] *adj.* [of someone] having one's full confidence. ♦ *I told the secret only to my trusted friends.* ♦ *One of the mayor's trusted allies leaked the news to the press.*

trustee [trə 'sti] *n.* someone, or one person of a group of people, who manages and controls the business affairs of an organization or person. ♦ *The Board of Trustees unanimously approved the budget.* ♦ *Some of the company's trustees were indicted for fraud.*

trusting ['trʌs tɪŋ] *adj.* confident in the honesty or reliability of someone or something. (Adv: *trustingly.*) ♦ *The thief took advantage of trusting people.* ♦ *The trusting students believed everything their teacher said.*

trustworthiness ['trʌst wɚ ði nəs] *n.* the quality of being trustworthy. (No plural form in this sense.) ♦ *Trustworthiness is essential for a good relationship.* ♦ *The judge doubted the defendant's trustworthiness.*

trustworthy ['trʌst wɚ ði] *adj.* deserving to be trusted; reliable. (Adv: *trustworthily.*) ♦ *Anne told her feelings to her trustworthy friend.* ♦ *My trustworthy old car has never broken down.*

trusty ['trʌs ti] *adj.* reliable; able to be depended on; trustworthy. (Adv: *trustily.* Comp: *trustier;* sup: *trustiest.*) ♦ *My trusty old car survived another harsh winter.* ♦ *My trusty dog defended me when I was threatened.*

truth ['truθ] **1.** *n.* the quality of being true or factual. (No plural form in this sense.) ♦ *In truth, I do not know who committed the crime.* ♦ *Philosophers discuss the truth of statements.* **2. moment of truth** *idiom* the point at which someone has to face the reality of a situation. ♦ *The moment of truth is here. Turn over your exam papers and begin.* ♦ *Now for the moment of truth when we find out whether we have got planning permission or not.*

truthful ['truθ fʊl] **1.** *adj.* [of a statement] able to be proven as true. (Adv: *truthfully.*) ♦ *I have never heard a truthful remark from Max!* ♦ *"Snow is white" is a truthful statement.* **2.** *adj.* regularly telling the truth; honest. (Adv: *truthfully.*) ♦ *The truthful man returned the extra change to the cashier.* ♦ *I was only being truthful when I told you your dress was ugly.*

try ['trɑɪ] **1.** *iv.* to attempt; to endeavor. ♦ *David tried and tried, but he eventually gave up.* ♦ *Although Anne tried very hard, she couldn't do it.* **2. try to** *iv.* + *inf.* to attempt to do something. ♦ *David tried to swim, but he kept sinking in the water.* ♦ *Anne tried to run, but her feet hurt.* **3. try out** *iv.* + *adv.* to audition for something. ♦ *Susan tried out for cheerleader yesterday.* ♦ *I plan to try out, but I probably won't get the part.* **4.** *tv.* to use something to see if one likes it; to test something to see if it works well. ♦ *Have you ever tried sweet potatoes?* ♦ *You should try my new bicycle!* **5.** *tv.* [for a judge or jury] to hear a [legal] case in a court of law. ♦ *The case against the accused will be tried tomorrow.* ♦ *They will try Anne's case next week.* **6.** *tv.* [for a judge or jury] to subject an accused person to undergo a trial in a court of law. ♦ *The man was tried for the murder of his boss.* ♦ *The jury that tried Anne had to spend a week in the courthouse.* **7.** *n.* an attempt; an endeavor; an effort to do something. ♦ *On the first try, David failed.* ♦ *Mary didn't pass the French test until her third try.* **8. try someone's patience** *idiom* to strain someone's patience; to bother someone. ♦ *My loud neighbors are trying my patience today.* ♦ *You really try my patience!*

trying ['trɑɪ ɪŋ] *adj.* burdensome; straining someone's patience; annoying; upsetting. (Adv: *tryingly.*) ♦ *Things at home have become trying since our grown son moved back in.* ♦ *Driving in heavy traffic can be a trying experience.*

tryout ['trɑɪ ɑʊt] **1** *n.* an audition; the process by which people are selected from a group of people. (Often plural.) ♦ *Tryouts for cheerleader are today in the gym.* ♦ *At the tryout, the actor forgot his monologue.*

tryst ['trɪst] *n.* a secret meeting between two people, especially two lovers. ♦ *Max set up a tryst with Susan.* ♦ *Mary planned a romantic tryst with her husband at a resort.*

tsar See czar.

T-shirt ['ti ʃɚt] *n.* a light, cotton shirt with short sleeves and no collar. ♦ *Anne wore a T-shirt to the game.* ♦ *I'm wearing a T-shirt under my sweater.*

tub ['tʌb] **1.** *n.* a large, round or oval container with a flat bottom. ♦ *The pioneers washed clothes in large metal tubs.* ♦ *The cook put the peeled potatoes in a large tub of water.* **2.** *n.* a bathtub. ♦ *Anne filled the tub with hot water and took a relaxing bath.* ♦ *The children played with plastic boats in the tub.*

tuba ['tub ə] *n.* a large brass instrument that makes very low notes. (Tubas are also sometimes made of lighter-weight material.) ♦ *The tuba was almost too heavy for me to carry in the parade.* ♦ *The composer wrote the bass line for the tuba.*

tube ['tub] **1.** *n.* a hollow pipe used for holding or conveying something. ♦ *A test tube is a glass tube with one open end.* ♦ *The painting was rolled up and placed in a cardboard tube.* **2.** *n.* a soft container that holds paste, such as toothpaste, icing, or medicine. ♦ *The baker bought a tube of blue frosting.* ♦ *There's a tube of toothpaste in the drawer.* **3. down the tube(s)** *idiom* ruined; wasted. ♦ *His political career went down the tubes after the scandal.* ♦ *The failing business is down the tube.*

tuberculosis [tə bɚ kjə 'lo sɪs] *n.* a serious infection in which a bacteria causes nodules to grow on body tissue, usually in the lungs. (Abbreviated *T.B.* No plural form in this sense.) ♦ *People with tuberculosis used to be placed in sanitariums.* ♦ *My grandmother died of tuberculosis just before a cure was found.*

tubing ['tub ɪŋ] *n.* a length of flexible tube made of a particular material. (No plural form in this sense.) ♦ *David needed some plastic tubing for his chemistry experiments.* ♦ *The plumber carried some metal tubing into the bathroom.*

tuck ['tʌk] **1. tuck into** *tv.* + *prep. phr.* to slip something flat and flexible into a space. ♦ *John tucked the bottom of his shirt into his pants.* ♦ *David tucked the money into his wallet.* **2.** *tv.* to sew a fold in an item of clothing to make it shorter or fit tighter. ♦ *The tailor tucked the waist of my trousers.* ♦ *The seamstress tucked the shoulders of my dress.* **3. tuck in** *iv.* + *adv.* to make something neater by slipping it into the place it belongs. ♦ *Please tuck your shirt in.* ♦ *There is a sock sticking out of your suitcase. Tuck it in.* **4.** *n.* a fold that is sewn shut to make an item of clothing shorter or fit tighter. ♦ *When David gained weight, he took the tucks out of his pants.* ♦ *When Mary lost weight, she put some tucks in her pants.*

Tuesday ['tuz de] **1.** *n.* the third day of the week, between Monday and Wednesday. ♦ *I have to go to the dentist next Tuesday.* ♦ *Election Day is generally a Tuesday.* **2.** *adv.* on the next ①. ♦ *We will go to town Tuesday.* ♦ *I get to sleep late Tuesday.* **3. (on) Tuesdays** *adv.* on each ①. ♦ *I work Tuesdays from 10:00 to 6:00.* ♦ *The store is closed Tuesdays.*

tuft ['tʌft] *n.* a soft bunch of something, especially hair, fur, or feathers. ♦ *Tufts of fur fell from the shedding dog.* ♦ *The angry man grabbed a tuft of my hair.*

tug ['tʌg] **1.** *n.* a hard pull; a yank. ♦ *Mary opened the door with a tug.* ♦ *I felt a tug on the back of my coat.* **2. tug at; tug on** *iv.* + *prep. phr.* to pull at someone or something with force. ♦ *The dog tugged on the leg of my pants.* ♦ *I tugged at the door but it was locked.* **3.** See **tugboat**.

tugboat AND **tug** ['tʌg bot] *n.* a small boat that pushes, pulls, or positions larger vessels, such as ships and barges. ♦ *The tugboat pushed the barge full of garbage through the harbor.* ♦ *Three tugboats nudged the gigantic cruise ship into its berth.*

tug-of-war ['tʌg əv 'wor] **1.** *n.* a game or contest where two groups of people pull a long rope, with one group on each end of the rope. ♦ *The object of a tug-of-war is to pull the other team past the line where the middle of the rope was at the start of the contest.* ♦ *Whoever loses this tug-of-war will be pulled into a large puddle of mud.* **2.** *n.* a difficult struggle, especially one that goes back and forth between the two sides. (Figurative on ①.) ♦ *The election was a fierce tug-of-war between the two candidates.* ♦ *There was a tug-of-war for control between the manager and the owner.*

tuition [tu 'ɪ ʃən] *n.* the money that a student must pay to attend classes at a school, college, or university. (No plural form in this sense.) ♦ *The university raised tuition by 4% last year.* ♦ *John took out a loan to pay his tuition.*

tulip ['tu ləp] *n.* a flower with a bright, colorful, cup-shaped bloom. ♦ *Holland is famous for its beautiful tulips.* ♦ *Anne planted a row of tulips in front of the porch.*

tumble ['tʌm bəl] **1.** *n.* a fall. ♦ *The football player was injured in his tumble.* ♦ *Mary took a tumble when she slipped on the ice.* **2.** *iv.* to fall over; to fall accidentally; to fall helplessly. ♦ *The toddler tumbled onto the floor.* ♦ *I tripped on my shoelace and tumbled into a bush.*

tumble-down ['tʌm bəl dɑʊn] *adj.* falling apart; dilapidated; run down. ♦ *The city condemned the tumble-down apartment building.* ♦ *Susan bought and renovated a tumble-down house in the city.*

tumbler ['tʌm blɚ] **1.** *n.* an acrobat; someone who performs gymnastic feats; a gymnast. ♦ *The tumbler did a perfect cartwheel.* ♦ *The tumbler did a flip on the balance beam.* **2.** *n.* a drinking glass that has a heavy, flat bottom and no handle. ♦ *I broke one of the tumblers this morning.* ♦ *I gave our empty tumblers to the waitress.* **3.** *n.* the contents of ②. ♦ *John swallowed a tumbler of whiskey.* ♦ *Mary ordered a tumbler of brandy.* **4.** *n.* the part of a lock that will not move until it is turned by the proper key. ♦ *The thief picked the lock until he heard the tumbler click.* ♦ *Max hammered the tumbler until it broke, and then opened the door.*

tummy ['tʌm i] *n.* the stomach or belly, the abdomen. (Informal; used especially with children.) ♦ *Mommy, my tummy hurts.* ♦ *Tom scratched the puppy's tummy.*

tumor ['tu mɚ] *n.* a group or cluster of diseased cells in a body that grow independently of the surrounding tissue or structure. ♦ *The doctors removed a tumor from my spine.* ♦ *The biopsy revealed that my tumor was not cancerous.*

tumult ['tu məlt] *n.* an uproar; a commotion. ♦ *When the mayor raised taxes, the citizens raised a loud tumult.* ♦ *The tumult at the party attracted the attention of the police.*

tumultuous [tu 'mʌl tʃu əs] *adj.* noisy; uncontrolled; violent; disturbing. (Adv: *tumultuously.*) ♦ *The police arrested 25 people at the tumultuous riot.* ♦ *Tumultuous waves crashed against the shore.*

tuna ['tu nə (fɪʃ)] **1.** *n., irreg.* a large ocean fish, commonly used for food. (Pl: *tuna* or *tunas.*) ♦ *The fishermen caught tons of tuna in their nets.* ♦ *The boat held two huge tunas.* **2. tuna (fish)** *n.* the flesh of ①, eaten as food. (No plural form in this sense.) ♦ *Anne bought three cans of tuna fish at the grocery store.* ♦ *Fresh tuna is very different from the inexpensive canned tuna that is used in sandwiches.* **3. tuna(-fish)** *adj.* made with or flavored with ②. ♦ *The cafeteria is serving tuna casserole today.* ♦ *John ate a tuna-fish sandwich for lunch.*

tune ['tun] **1.** *n.* a melody; a piece of music or a song. ♦ *What's the name of that tune?* ♦ *Mary whistled a happy tune.* **2. in tune; out of tune** *phr.* in or out of a state where musical notes are at their proper intervals so that none are flat or sharp. ♦ *Your piano is out of tune.* ♦ *The choir members all sang in tune.* **3.** *tv.* to adjust a musical instrument so that its tones are at the proper intervals from each other. ♦ *David tuned his guitar before the concert.* ♦ *Your piano needs to be tuned!* **4.** *tv.* to adjust something so that it works properly. ♦ *The mechanic tuned the car's engine.* ♦ *I tuned the television so that the picture was clearer.* **5. can't carry a tune** *idiom* unable to sing a simple melody; lacking musical ability. ♦ *I wish that Tom wouldn't try to sing. He can't carry a tune.* ♦ *Listen to poor old John. He really cannot carry a tune.* **6. dance to another tune** *idiom* to shift quickly to different behavior; to change one's behavior or attitude. ♦ *After being yelled at, Anne danced to another tune.* ♦ *A stern talking-to will make her dance to another tune.*

tune-up ['tun əp] *n.* the adjustment of an engine or a machine so that it works properly. ♦ *The car's tune-up cost $200.* ♦ *This old vacuum cleaner needs a good tune-up.*

tungsten ['tʌŋ stən] *n.* a metallic chemical element, ranging in color from silver-white to dark gray. (No plural form in this sense.) ♦ *Tungsten's atomic number is 74, and its atomic symbol is W.* ♦ *Tungsten is used for making lamps and lighting.*

Tunisia [tu 'ni ʒə] See Gazetteer.

tunnel ['tʌn əl] **1.** *n.* a passage that is underground, underwater, or through a mountain. ♦ *The workers bored a tunnel through the mountain for the freeway.* ♦ *A tunnel under the English Channel connects England with France.* **2.** *iv.* to make a passage that goes underground, underwater, or through a mountain. ♦ *The road construction crew tunneled through the mountain.* ♦ *The dog tunneled under the fence.*

turban ['tɚ bən] *n.* a long piece of cloth that is wrapped around one's head as a covering, worn especially by men in parts of southern Asia and the Middle East. ♦ *Do men in your country wear turbans?* ♦ *My friend from India showed me how to put on a turban.*

turbine ['tɚ bɪn] *n.* a large engine or motor that is powered by pressure from wind, water, or some other liquid or gas. ♦ *Dozens of turbines at the dam produced electricity.* ♦ *We get our electricity from wind-powered turbines.*

turbojet ['tɚ bo dʒɛt] *n.* a jet turbine whose powerful exhaust provides the thrust necessary to propel an aircraft. ♦ *The turbojets were inspected before each flight.* ♦ *A skilled mechanic repaired the complex turbojet.*

turbulence ['tɚ bjə ləns] *n.* the state of being turbulent, as with water, air, the stock market, emotions, or change. (No plural form in this sense.) ♦ *Turbulence in the stream made the water cloudy.* ♦ *The flight was bumpy because there was a lot of turbulence.*

turbulent ['tɚ bjə lənt] *adj.* violent; unruly; wild. (Adv: *turbulently.*) ♦ *The turbulent protest resulted in 50 arrests.* ♦ *Turbulent winds buffeted the airplane.*

turf ['tɚf] **1.** *n.* the surface of soil with plants or grass growing on it. (No plural form in this sense.) ♦ *The turf was eroded by a violent windstorm.* ♦ *The farmer enriched the turf with fertilizer.* **2.** *n.* the area that is controlled by a person or group of people. ♦ *The gangs marked their turf with graffiti.* ♦ *John accused me of making a sales call on his turf.*

turkey ['tɚ ki] **1.** *n.* a large North American bird that is often raised for its meat. ♦ *The farmer killed and cooked a turkey for Thanksgiving dinner.* ♦ *Some turkeys weigh over 40 pounds.* **2.** *n.* the meat of ① used as food. (No plural form in this sense.) ♦ *I eat turkey because it's cheaper than chicken.* ♦ *Turkey is my favorite food at Thanksgiving dinner.* **3.** *adj.* made with ②. ♦ *I made a turkey sandwich for lunch.* ♦ *We ate turkey casserole for dinner.*

Turkey ['tɚ ki] See Gazetteer.

turmoil ['tɚ mɔɪl] *n.* a condition of confusion or trouble; agitation. ♦ *The refugees had suffered from the turmoil of war.* ♦ *The turmoil of exams made the students very irritable.*

turn ['tɚn] **1.** *tv.* to move something around in a circle or an arc; to cause something to move in a circle or an arc. ♦ *Mary turned the crank to wind up the antique phonograph.* ♦ *I turned the bicycle's wheel to make sure it was securely attached.* **2.** *tv.* to aim a moving object or vehicle in a different direction. ♦ *John turned the car to the left.* ♦ *David turned his bicycle east at Maple Street.* **3.** *tv.* to change the position of something. ♦ *Mary turned the ugly painting so that it faced the wall.* ♦ *Please turn that switch to the "off" position.* **4.** *tv.* to reach a certain age. ♦ *When you turn 18, then you can vote.* ♦ *We had a party for Mary because she turned 21 last night.* **5. turn into** *tv.* + *prep. phr.* to change someone or something into a particular condition or state. ♦ *The witch turned the handsome prince into a frog.* ♦ *A sudden storm turned my happiness into sadness.* **6. turn into** *iv.* + *prep. phr.* to change to a particular condition or state. ♦ *The handsome prince turned into a frog to escape from the ugly princess.* ♦ *My happiness quickly turned into sadness.* **7. turn around** *iv.* + *prep. phr.* to move around in a circle; to move around an axis; to move around a center point. ♦ *The earth turns around its axis once every 24 hours.* ♦ *A wheel turns around an axle.* **8.** *iv.* to go in a different direction; to change direction. ♦ *Turn right at the next corner.* ♦ *The bus turned east at Maple Street.* **9.** *iv.* to change position by moving in a circle or an arc. ♦ *I turned to face the child who was following me.* ♦ *The taxi driver turned to ask me a question.* **10.** *iv.* to change, especially in form, state, color, or quality; to become some form, state, color, or quality. ♦ *The sky turned red just before the sun set.* ♦ *The water turned to ice in the freezer.* **11.** *n.* the movement of something that is going in a circle. ♦ *Night and day are caused by the turn of the earth around its axis.* ♦ *The wheel squeaked loudly with each turn.* **12.** *n.* a change in direction. ♦ *On that last turn, you should have gone right instead of left.* ♦ *There is a turn in this road up ahead.* **13.** *n.* a change in a situation; a change in circumstances. ♦ *The turn in the weather was a welcome relief.* ♦ *The reporter commented on the latest turn of events.* **14.** *n.* a chance to do something, especially when two or more people alternate an action in cycles. ♦ *Roll the dice. It's your turn.* ♦ *It's your turn to wash the dishes.* **15. in turn** *phr.* in the appropriate point in the series or order; when one's turn comes. ♦ *Someone has to wash the dishes after every meal. All of us will have to do it in turn.* ♦ *All three of them shared the task of carrying water in turn.* **16. do someone a good turn** *idiom* to do something that is helpful to someone. ♦ *My neighbor did me a good turn by lending me his car.* ♦ *The teacher did me a good turn when he told me to work harder.* **17. out of turn** *idiom* not at the proper time; not in the proper order. ♦ *We were permitted to be served out of turn, because we had to leave early.* ♦ *Bill tried to register out of turn and was sent to the back of the line.* **18. turn of the century** *idiom* the time when the year changes to one with two final zeros, such as from 1899 to 1900. ♦ *My family moved to America at the turn of the century.* ♦ *My uncle was born before the turn of the last century.* **19. turn on a dime** *idiom* to be able to turn ⑧ sharply in a very small space. ♦ *This car handles very well. It can turn on a dime.* ♦ *The speeding car turned on a dime and headed in the other direction.* **20. turn out (that)**

idiom to happen; to end up; to result. ♦ *After it was all over, it turned out that both of us were pleased with the bargain.* ♦ *Have you heard how the game turned out?* **21. turn someone's stomach** *idiom* to upset one's stomach. ♦ *The violent movie turned my stomach.* ♦ *The rich, creamy food turned John's stomach.*

turnabout ['tɚn ə bɑʊt] **1.** *n.* the act of turning so that one faces the opposite way. (No plural form in this sense.) ♦ *The car's sudden turnabout was caused by the ice on the road.* ♦ *Jane made a quick turnabout and glared at the man who was following her.* **2.** *n.* the act of changing one's mind so that one thinks the opposite of what one had been thinking. (Figurative on ①. No plural form in this sense.) ♦ *The manager made a complete turnabout and bought a new computer.* ♦ *Anne did a turnabout and decided to come with us after all.*

turnaround ['tɚn ə rɑʊnd] **1.** *n.* reversal; the act of changing direction. (No plural form in this sense.) ♦ *The turnaround of a boomerang has to do with its shape.* ♦ *The hijacker forced the turnaround of the jet.* **2.** *n.* the amount of time it takes to fill an order; the amount of time it takes to make something ready for the next task after the last task is finished. (No plural form in this sense.) ♦ *There's a one-week turnaround on each order placed.* ♦ *If I drop off the film tonight, what will the turnaround be?* **3.** *n.* a place for a vehicle to turn so that it goes in the opposite direction. ♦ *Don't back out into the street from the driveway; use the turnaround!* ♦ *The truck used the turnaround to back into the loading dock.*

turncoat ['tɚn kot] *n.* someone who changes beliefs or allegiances. ♦ *The turncoat switched from being a Republican to being a Democrat.* ♦ *Disillusioned with his company, Bob became a turncoat and went to work for a competitor.*

turning point ['tɚn ɪŋ pɔɪnt] *n.* the point in time when a decisive event takes place. ♦ *The Battle of Midway was a turning point in World War II.* ♦ *Going to college was an important turning point in my life.*

turnip ['tɚ nəp] *n.* a round yellow, white, or purplish-red root with a soft white inside, eaten as a vegetable. ♦ *Mother served roast beef and turnips for dinner.* ♦ *Anne made a salad from the leafy tops of the turnips.*

turnout ['tɚn ɑʊt] *n.* the number of people in a crowd; the number of people who have gathered together for something. ♦ *The organizers expected a turnout of 20,000 at the rally.* ♦ *In the last election, the turnout of voters was very low.*

turnover ['tɚn ov ɚ] **1.** *n.* the process of losing and gaining employees. ♦ *My department has a lot of turnover because the manager is inept.* ♦ *The company tried to keep its turnover to a minimum.* **2.** *n.* the amount of business that is done during a period of time. ♦ *The turnover at the restaurant was about 40 people an hour.* ♦ *The manager was pleased with the turnover this evening.* **3.** *n.* a kind of pastry consisting of a circle of dough folded in half and containing fruit and spices, then fried or baked. ♦ *Bob ordered a cherry turnover with his hamburger.* ♦ *Max made apple turnovers for dessert.*

turnpike ['tɚn pɑɪk] *n.* a road for which one must pay a toll to travel on it; a toll road. ♦ *Take the turnpike twenty miles out of town to Exit 5.* ♦ *John was ticketed for speeding on the Pennsylvania Turnpike.*

turnstile ['tɚn stɑɪl] *n.* a one-way gate or barrier placed at entrances or exits to control the flow of people. ♦ *The customers filed through the turnstile one at a time.* ♦ *This turnstile is equipped with a counter that counts the number of people passing through.*

turntable ['tɚn teb əl] *n.* a record player; the spinning surface that a record is played on. ♦ *Anne bought a used turntable to play some of her old records.* ♦ *After I bought a CD player, I sold my turntable.*

turpentine ['tɚ pən tɑɪn] *n.* a volatile oil obtained from pine trees. (No plural form in this sense.) ♦ *Jane thinned the paint with turpentine.* ♦ *The artist used turpentine to clean the paintbrushes.*

turquoise ['tɚ kɔɪz] **1.** *n.* a bluish-green stone, commonly used for jewelry. (No plural form in this sense.) ♦ *The singer's necklace was made of beads of turquoise.* ♦ *I found a huge chunk of turquoise in the mountains.* **2.** *n.* the color that is bluish green. (No plural form in this sense.) ♦ *Jane decorated the bathroom in turquoise.* ♦ *The artist used turquoise when painting the sea.* **3.** *adj.* bluish green in color. ♦ *The calm sea was a beautiful turquoise.* ♦ *Mary wore a turquoise dress to the party.*

turret ['tɚ ɪt] **1.** *n.* a small, round tower on the corner of a building or a castle. ♦ *The princess stood at the turret's window and waved.* ♦ *Our family's large castle has several turrets and one huge tower.* **2.** *n.* a dome-shaped structure on which guns are mounted, found on tanks, planes, and warships. ♦ *The tank's turret rotated toward the enemy and fired.* ♦ *The plane exploded when a missile hit one of its gun turrets.*

turtle ['tɚt əl] *n.* a reptile with a round body that is protected by a thick, hard, rounded shell. ♦ *A turtle can pull its head and legs into its shell for protection.* ♦ *Turtles walk very slowly.*

turtleneck ['tɚ təl nɛk] **1.** *n.* a sweater with a high collar that covers the lower part of the neck. ♦ *John wears a turtleneck to keep his neck warm.* ♦ *Anne knitted a woolen turtleneck for her grandchild.* **2.** *adj.* having a high collar that covers the lower part of the neck. ♦ *I wore a turtleneck sweater because it was cold outside.* ♦ *The actor looked funny in the tight turtleneck costume.*

tusk ['tʌsk] *n.* a very long, pointed tooth that projects from the face of some kinds of animals. ♦ *The hunters killed the walrus for its tusks.* ♦ *An elephant's tusks are made of ivory.*

tussle ['tʌs əl] **1.** *n.* a fight; a scuffle; a struggle. ♦ *The teacher stopped the tussle on the playground.* ♦ *There was a tussle for the football, but our team got it.* **2.** *iv.* to fight; to scuffle; to struggle; to wrestle. ♦ *The kids tussled in the dirt.* ♦ *The police tussled with the robber in the alley.*

tutelage ['tut ə lɪdʒ] *n.* instruction from a tutor or teacher; guidance from a guardian. (No plural form in this sense.) ♦ *I was indebted to my professor for her expert tutelage.* ♦ *Max's tutelage was much appreciated by his apprentice.*

tutor ['tut ɚ] **1.** *n.* someone who is employed as a private teacher; a teacher who gives private lessons. ♦ *Jimmy's tutor helped him learn his multiplication tables.* ♦ *Susie read aloud to her tutor.* **2.** *tv.* to teach someone privately. ♦ *John tutored the seven-year-old in math.* ♦ *Anne was tutored by professionals throughout high school.* **3.** *iv.*

to work as ①. ♦ *Bill tutored when he was in college.* ♦ *I decided to tutor to supplement my income.*

tutorial [tu 'tor i əl] *n.* a period of instruction by a tutor. ♦ *Today's tutorial is canceled because the tutor is sick.* ♦ *My tutorials were very rigorous because my tutor was demanding.*

tuxedo [tək 'si do] *n.* a man's outfit for very formal occasions, including a black jacket, a white shirt, a black bow tie, and pants. (Pl in *-s.*) ♦ *John rented a tuxedo to wear at his sister's wedding.* ♦ *David wore a tuxedo to the formal event.*

tv. See transitive verb.

TV ['ti 'vi] *n.* television. ♦ *You can't watch TV until you finish your homework.* ♦ *Is there anything good on TV tonight?*

twaddle ['twɑd əl] *n.* nonsense; foolishness. (No plural form in this sense.) ♦ *I don't want to hear any more of your twaddle.* ♦ *That's twaddle! Of course I'm not quitting my job.*

twang ['twæŋ] **1.** *n.* a nasal sound; the quality of one's voice when the sound is passed through one's nose. ♦ *When I was in Texas, it seemed like everyone had a twang.* ♦ *The customer's shrill twang annoyed the clerk.* **2.** *n.* a quick, vibrating sound, such as when one plucks a string. ♦ *I heard the twang of a banjo coming from John's room.* ♦ *There was a loud twang when David released the arrow from the bow.*

tweed ['twid] **1.** *n.* a rough wool fabric. ♦ *The professor's old jacket was made of tweed.* ♦ *Tweed feels rough against the skin.* **2.** *adj.* made of ①. ♦ *My tweed jacket keeps me warm.* ♦ *David wore a tweed suit to the banquet.*

tweezers ['twi zɚz] *n.* a small tool made of two strong, thin strips of metal joined at one end. (Treated as singular or plural. Number is usually expressed with *pair(s) of tweezers.*) ♦ *Tweezers are squeezed together to pick up small things or to pluck hair.* ♦ *Anne plucked the ticks from the dog's skin with tweezers.*

twelfth ['twɛlfθ] 12th. See fourth for senses and examples.

twelve ['twɛlv] 12. See four for senses and examples.

twentieth ['twɛn ti əθ] 20th. See fourth for senses and examples.

twenty ['twɛn ti] 20. See forty for senses and examples.

twice ['twɑɪs] **1.** *adv.* two times; on two occasions. ♦ *John has been to London twice.* ♦ *I told David twice to leave me alone.* **2.** *adv.* two times as much; double. ♦ *This shirt costs twice as much as that one.* ♦ *Tuition rates increased twice as much as I thought they would.* **3.** *adj.* two times as much. ♦ *Mary is twice as old as I am.* ♦ *This book is twice as long as it should be.*

twig ['twɪg] *n.* a small branch. ♦ *The heavy winds knocked a lot of twigs to the ground.* ♦ *The bird made its nest from grass and twigs.*

twilight ['twɑɪ lɑɪt] **1.** *n.* the time of day after the sun sets and before the sky is completely dark. (No plural form in this sense.) ♦ *At twilight, the streetlights went on.* ♦ *Anne didn't leave the office until twilight.* **2.** *n.* the dim light at ①. ♦ *In the twilight, I could see the outline of someone approaching me.* ♦ *I could not read in the fading twilight, so I turned on a lamp.*

twin ['twɪn] **1.** *n.* one of two children born at the same time from the same mother; one of two offspring born at the same time from the same mother. ♦ *David often dresses the same as his twin.* ♦ *Anne gave birth to a pair of twins.* **2.** *n.* one of two things that are part of a matched set. ♦ *I have one glove, but I misplaced its twin.* ♦ *That cup's twin was broken years ago when I dropped it.* **3.** *adj.* [of two offspring] born at the same time from the same mother. ♦ *Susan gave birth to twin girls.* ♦ *The lioness had twin cubs.* **4.** *adj.* forming a pair of two things that are similar or matching. ♦ *Mary bought Bill twin stereo speakers for his birthday.* ♦ *I chose twin lamps so I could put one on each side of the sofa.*

twine ['twɑɪn] *n.* strong string made of two or more strands that are twisted together. (No plural form in this sense.) ♦ *The postal clerk bound my package with sturdy twine.* ♦ *I tied the mattress to the roof of my car with heavy twine.*

twinge ['twɪndʒ] *n.* a sudden pain felt by the mind or the body. ♦ *I felt a twinge of guilt when I cheated on my diet.* ♦ *David felt a twinge of pain when he stepped on the tack.*

twinkle ['twɪŋ kəl] **1.** *iv.* to sparkle; to alternate between shining brightly and not so brightly; to flicker. ♦ *The stars twinkled in the night sky.* ♦ *The cat's eyes twinkle in the moonlight.* **2.** *n.* a light that alternates between shining brightly and dimly; a flicker. ♦ *The room was lit by the twinkle of a sole candle.* ♦ *There was a twinkle in John's eye as he laughed.* **3. in the twinkling of an eye** *idiom* very quickly. ♦ *In the twinkling of an eye, the deer had disappeared into the forest.* ♦ *I gave Bill ten dollars and, in the twinkling of an eye, he spent it.*

twirl ['twɚl] **1.** *n.* a spin; a whirl; a circular movement. ♦ *I gave the rope a twirl and tried to throw the loop over the post.* ♦ *The dancers' repeated twirls were very energetic.* **2.** *tv.* to spin something; to whirl something; to move something in circles. ♦ *The child twirled the top.* ♦ *I twirled the rope over my head like a cowboy.* **3.** *iv.* to spin; to whirl; to turn in circles. ♦ *While the propellers twirled round and round, I could only think of getting home.* ♦ *The gymnast twirled in the air.*

twist ['twɪst] **1.** *tv.* to turn something; to rotate something in an arc. ♦ *David twisted the key in the lock.* ♦ *Anne twisted the screw into place.* **2.** *tv.* to injure a body part by turning it sharply. ♦ *John twisted his ankle when he slipped on the ice.* ♦ *Susan twisted her back when she picked up the box.* **3.** *tv.* to bend and rotate part of something to change its shape. ♦ *Tom twisted the heavy cord into a knot.* ♦ *Years of hard work had twisted the tailor's hands.* **4.** *iv.* to curve; to bend; to change shape or direction; to rotate one part of a length while keeping another part in place. ♦ *The road twisted as it went up the mountain.* ♦ *The snake twisted and turned when I stepped on it.* **5.** *n.* a curve; a state resulting when one part of a length has been rotated while another part stays in one space. ♦ *The tree trunk had a twist in it.* ♦ *A twist in the hose kept the water from flowing.* **6.** *n.* the movement of twisting as in ①. ♦ *A quick twist of the wrist, and the door was opened.* ♦ *One twist and I had opened the jar of pickles.* **7.** *n.* a sudden change. (Figurative on ⑥.) ♦ *Due to a twist in fate, John was suddenly very lucky.* ♦ *Because of a twist in my schedule, I was late.* **8. twist someone's arm** *idiom* to force or persuade someone. ♦ *At first she refused, but after*

I twisted her arm a little, she agreed to help. ♦ *I didn't want to run for mayor, but everyone twisted my arm.*

twisted ['twɪs tɪd] **1.** *adj.* curved; bent; having a changed shape; contorted. (Adv: *twistedly.*) ♦ *Water couldn't pass through the twisted pipe.* ♦ *My twisted ankle was swollen and purple.* **2.** *adj.* evil; sadistic; cruel; mean. (Figurative on ①. Adv: *twistedly.*) ♦ *The twisted dictator tortured his enemies.* ♦ *The judge sent the twisted criminal to a mental hospital.*

twister ['twɪs tɚ] *n.* a tornado; a cyclone. ♦ *The twister destroyed a row of houses.* ♦ *I ran to the cellar when I saw the twister approaching.*

twisting ['twɪs tɪŋ] *adj.* turning; winding; contorting; bending; curving. (Adv: *twistingly.*) ♦ *I got lost in the subdivision's twisting streets.* ♦ *My hair got caught in the twisting vines.*

twitch ['twɪtʃ] **1.** *n.* a quick jerk of a muscle that one cannot control. ♦ *John's twitch is caused by a nervous tic.* ♦ *The twitch in my eye was starting to annoy me.* **2.** *iv.* [for a muscle] to jerk quickly and automatically. ♦ *When Anne's eyes twitch, it means she's tired.* ♦ *When I rubbed my dog's stomach, his body began to twitch.* **3.** *tv.* to jerk one's muscle quickly. ♦ *I twitched my leg muscles because my foot had fallen asleep.* ♦ *John twitched his arms when I tickled him.*

twitching ['twɪtʃ ɪŋ] *adj.* having a muscle that jerks quickly. (Adv: *twitchingly.*) ♦ *My twitching eye was very irritating.* ♦ *The twitching drug addict was taken to the hospital.*

twitter ['twɪt ɚ] **1.** *n.* the sounds made by chirping birds or people who talk quickly. ♦ *I heard a happy twitters from the room where John and Mary were.* ♦ *I was waked up by a loud twitter from outside my window.* **2.** *iv.* to chirp; to talk quickly. ♦ *The bird twittered in its nest.* ♦ *Anne twittered constantly during the party.*

two ['tu] **1.** 2. See four for senses and examples. **2. two of a kind** *idiom* people or things that are the same type or similar in character, attitude, etc. ♦ *Bob and Tom are two of a kind. They're both ambitious.* ♦ *The companies are two of a kind. They both pay their employees badly.* **3. two's company(, three's a crowd)** *idiom* two people want to be alone and a third person would be in the way. ♦ *Two's company. I'm sure Tom and Jill won't want his sister to go to the movies with them.* ♦ *John has been invited to join Jane and Tom on their picnic, but he says, "Two's company, three's a crowd."*

two-bit ['tu bɪt] *adj.* worth twenty-five cents; cheap; having very little value or importance. ♦ *I bought a two-bit newspaper from the vendor.* ♦ *I ignored David's two-bit advice.*

two-dimensional ['tu dɪ 'mɛn ʃə nəl] *adj.* having two dimensions; having length and width. (Adv: *two-dimensionally.*) ♦ *All the art in the museum is two-dimensional.* ♦ *The background of the painting was flat and two-dimensional, giving no sense of depth.*

two-door ['tu dor] *adj.* having two doors. (Used to described cars with two doors instead of four.) ♦ *To get into the back seat of a two-door vehicle, you have to fold down the front seat.* ♦ *I own a two-door car so my kids can't get out from the back seat when I'm driving.*

two-faced ['tu fest] **1.** *adj.* having two faces. ♦ *The rare two-faced coin was a collector's item.* ♦ *The two-faced doll had a smiling face on one side of its head and a crying face on the other.* **2.** *adj.* not sincere; hypocritical. (Figurative on ①. Adv: *two-facedly.*) ♦ *My two-faced friend gossips about me behind my back.* ♦ *My two-faced boss had only pretended to like my work.*

twofold ['tu fold] **1.** *adj.* double. ♦ *Last month, there was a twofold rise in inflation.* ♦ *The village had a twofold increase in population in only 10 years.* **2.** *adv.* twice; two times as much. ♦ *Prices rose twofold in one month.* ♦ *The landlord raised my rent twofold.*

two-seater ['tu 'sit ɚ] *n.* something, usually a car, seating only two people. ♦ *John just bought a sports car—a bright red two-seater.* ♦ *Anne and Bob's sofa is a two-seater.*

twosome ['tu səm] *n.* a group of two people; a couple. ♦ *The twosome decided to split a pizza.* ♦ *The twosome danced around the ballroom.*

two-timing ['tu taɪm ɪŋ] *adj.* dating two people at one time; not faithful ②. ♦ *Anne divorced her two-timing husband.* ♦ *David broke up with his two-timing girlfriend.*

two-way ['tu 'we] *adj.* allowing movement or travel in both directions. ♦ *At the next block, this street allows two-way traffic.* ♦ *Get over to the right! This street is two-way.*

tycoon [taɪ 'kun] *n.* a very important and wealthy person in business or industry. ♦ *The business tycoon donated a million dollars to the university.* ♦ *The workers installed marble floors in the tycoon's mansion.*

tyke ['taɪk] *n.* a young child. ♦ *The barber gave the tyke a lollipop after cutting his hair.* ♦ *The teacher watched all the little tykes playing on the playground.*

type ['taɪp] **1.** *n.* a kind, sort, or category; a group of related things or people. ♦ *What type of ice cream would you like?* ♦ *Mary wanted to buy the type of candles that her sister owned.* **2.** *n.* a block of wood or metal, with the raised shape of a letter or number on it, used in printing. (No plural form in this sense.) ♦ *The newspaper's type was still set by hand.* ♦ *Jane arranged the blocks of type for the headline.* **3.** *n.* a style of printing; a font. (No plural form in this sense.) ♦ *The report must be printed in 12-point type.* ♦ *The first word of the paragraph was set in bold type.* **4.** *tv.* to write something using a keyboard. ♦ *The ticket agent typed my name into a computer.* ♦ *Bill typed his paper on a typewriter because his computer was broken.* **5.** *iv.* to use a keyboard. ♦ *Good secretaries must know how to type well.* ♦ *I typed as fast as I could.*

typeface ['taɪp fes] *n.* a font; a style of type. ♦ *The script's stage directions were set in an italic typeface.* ♦ *Headlines appear in larger typefaces than the articles.*

typewriter ['taɪp raɪt ɚ] *n.* a machine for printing letters onto paper. ♦ *When one pushes a key of a typewriter, an arm with a raised letter swings against and strikes the paper through an inked ribbon.* ♦ *I found my old typewriter when my computer broke.*

typewritten ['taɪp rɪt n] *adj.* printed using a typewriter. (May also refer to computer printing.) ♦ *The teacher asked that the students' essays be typewritten.* ♦ *My typewritten note was very neat.*

typhoid ['taɪ foɪd] *n.* a serious, contagious disease that can cause death. (No plural form in this sense.) ♦ *The bacteria that cause typhoid are often spread by contaminated food and water.* ♦ *Symptoms of typhoid include severe fever and headaches.*

typical ['tɪp ɪ kəl] *adj.* average; usual; ordinary; regular; having the main qualities of a type of something. (Adv: *typically* [...ɪk li].) ♦ *My parents live in a typical suburb.* ♦ *In 1992, the life expectancy of a typical American woman was 72.*

typically ['tɪp ɪk li] *adv.* in a typical way; usually; ordinarily; regularly. ♦ *Typically, Anne and I go bowling on Fridays.* ♦ *Susan typically doesn't talk to strangers on the bus.*

typify ['tɪp ə fɑɪ] *tv.* to be the typical example of something; to exemplify something. ♦ *My brother typifies the average male.* ♦ *Parties at this college are typified by drinking and loud music.*

typist ['tɑɪp əst] *n.* someone who works at a typewriter as a job; someone who types on a typewriter or computer keyboard. ♦ *My firm hired a typist who can type sixty words a minute.* ♦ *The typist transcribed letters that were dictated into a tape recorder.*

typo ['tɑɪp o] *n.* an error made in printing or typing; a typographical error. (Pl in *-s*.) ♦ *Jane corrected the typo in her letter.* ♦ *The professor circled all of my typos with red ink.*

typographical [tɑɪp ə 'græf ɪ kəl] *adj.* of or about type ② or typewriting. (Adv: *typographically* [...ɪk li].) ♦ *Secretaries must have good typographical skills.* ♦ *John's report was full of typographical errors.*

tyrannical [tɪ 'ræn ɪ kəl] *adj.* like a tyrant; oppressive; cruel. (Adv: *tyrannically* [...ɪk li].) ♦ *The tyrannical ruler killed all of his opponents.* ♦ *The citizens despised the tyrannical police force.*

tyranny ['tɪr ə ni] *n.* cruel and unfair power; oppression. (No plural form in this sense.) ♦ *The evil king used tyranny to remain in control.* ♦ *The refugees fled to America to escape tyranny.*

tyrant ['tɑɪ rənt] *n.* a ruler who is cruel and unfair. ♦ *The tyrant's policies caused the deaths of thousands of peasants.* ♦ *The rebels who overthrew the tyrant were loved by the people.*

U

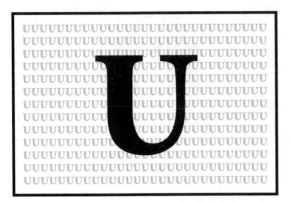

U AND **u** ['ju] *n.* the twenty-first letter of the English alphabet. ♦ *The letter* U *comes before* V *and after* T. ♦ *There is one* U *in* utopia.

ubiquitous [ju 'bɪ kwɪ təs] *adj.* in every place at the same time; being or happening everywhere at the same time. (Adv: *ubiquitously.*) ♦ *Telephones have become a ubiquitous feature of all homes and offices.* ♦ *The problem of crime is ubiquitous in large cities.*

udder ['ʌd ɚ] *n.* an organ shaped like a bag that hangs from the underside of female cows, goats, and other four-footed mammals, and that produces milk. ♦ *The cow's udder is quite full before milking time.* ♦ *The calf pushed at the cow's udder, wanting more milk.*

UFO ['ju 'ef 'o] *n.* something strange that flies in the air and cannot be identified, especially something that some people believe has come from outer space. (An acronym for *unidentified flying object.*) ♦ *The man claimed that he saw a UFO in the sky.* ♦ *The scientist debunked the theory about UFOs.*

Uganda [ju 'gæn də] See Gazetteer.

ugly ['ʌg li] **1.** *adj.* not pleasant to look at; not attractive. (Comp: *uglier;* sup: *ugliest.*) ♦ *Mary took the ugly painting off the wall.* ♦ *David sometimes felt he was very ugly.* **2.** *adj.* not pleasant; menacing. (Comp: *uglier;* sup: *ugliest.*) ♦ *Bill used some ugly words during the argument.* ♦ *The domestic squabble turned into an ugly fight.*

Ukraine [ju 'kren] See Gazetteer.

ulcer ['ʌl sɚ] *n.* a sore on a part of the body that may bleed and become infected. ♦ *The doctor noticed ulcers on the bedridden woman's skin.* ♦ *Spicy food irritates Bill's stomach ulcer.*

ulceration [əl sə 're ʃən] *n.* an ulcer on the surface of the body. ♦ *The nurse treated the patient's ulcerations with medicinal cream.* ♦ *Lying in one place caused the hospital patient's skin to develop ulcerations.*

ulterior [əl 'tɪr i ɚ] *adj.* further; beyond a certain limit; beyond what is seen and intentionally concealed (Adv: *ulteriorly.*) ♦ *Bill had ulterior motives when he offered to help Mary.* ♦ *The evil ruler's ulterior plan was to control the world.*

ultimate ['ʌl tə mɪt] **1.** *adj.* final and conclusive. (Adv: *ultimately.*) ♦ *As the pain reached the ultimate degree, Bill passed out.* ♦ *The ultimate decision in hiring is made by the company president.* **2. the ultimate** *n.* the best thing or person; the most superior thing or person. (Informal. No plural form in this sense. Treated as singular.) ♦ *This restaurant's cheese pizza is the ultimate in flavor!* ♦ *I love Tom because he's just the ultimate!*

ultimately ['ʌl tə mət li] *adv.* in the end; at the final reckoning of an issue. ♦ *Ultimately, the whole matter will be resolved.* ♦ *We will need a new car, ultimately.*

ultimatum [əl tə 'met əm] *n.* the final expression of conditions that must be met under the threat of punishment or retaliation. ♦ *Mary gave Bill an ultimatum—marry her or leave.* ♦ *Once the ultimatum was made, Mary had to follow through on it.*

ultra ['ʌl trə] *prefix* extreme; extra; going beyond the limit. (Occasionally hyphenated.) ♦ *Mr. Jones is ultra-conservative politically.* ♦ *The designer's clothes are ultra-chic.*

ultrasonic [əl trə 'sɑn ɪk] *adj.* of or about sound waves that are above the range that humans can hear. (Adv: *ultrasonically* [...ɪk li].) ♦ *Dogs can hear some ultrasonic tones.* ♦ *The intense ultrasonic waves caused the brick to crumble.*

ultrasound ['ʌl trə sɑʊnd] **1.** *n.* sound waves that are above the range that humans can hear, used to create images of things inside human bodies or other objects. (No plural form in this sense.) ♦ *Ultrasound can be used to find out what is going on inside the body.* ♦ *The gynecologist used ultrasound to observe the fetus inside Mary's uterus.* **2.** *n.* an image or picture of the inside of the body made by ①. ♦ *Ultrasounds indicated a tumor on the patient's spine.* ♦ *The doctor examined ultrasounds of his heart to see if it was working properly.*

ultraviolet [əl trə 'vɑɪ ə lɪt] *adj.* of or about light waves that are past purple in the spectrum of light. ♦ *This sunblock protects your skin from ultraviolet rays.* ♦ *The special paint on the wall glowed under ultraviolet light.*

umbilical cord [əm 'bɪl ɪ kəl kord] *n.* the tube that connects the placenta of a mother with the navel of an embryo or fetus in her womb. (From *umbilicus.*) ♦ *An unborn baby is nourished through the umbilical cord.* ♦ *The doctor cut the umbilical cord after the baby was born.*

umbrage ['ʌm brɪdʒ] **take umbrage at something** *idiom* to feel that one has been insulted by something. ♦ *The employee took umbrage at not getting a raise.* ♦ *Mary took umbrage at the suggestion that she was being unreasonable.*

umbrella [əm 'brɛl ə] *n.* a dome-shaped wire frame connected to a handle and covered with waterproof fabric. ♦ *I carried an umbrella to protect myself from the rain.* ♦ *The strong wind blew the umbrella from David's hands.*

umpire ['ʌm pɑɪr] **1.** *n.* a referee; someone who enforces the rules of certain sports; someone who judges the plays in certain sports. ♦ *The umpire called the ball foul.* ♦ *An umpire stood along the third baseline, watching the play.* **2.** *iv.* to act as ①. ♦ *Bill umpires for his son's little league.* ♦ *David umpires on the weekends.* **3.** *tv.* to referee a game; to judge the plays in certain sports. ♦ *I umpired the championship baseball game.* ♦ *Anne will umpire today's softball game.*

U.N. See United Nations.

un- [ən] **1.** *prefix* <a form that can be added freely to adjectives and words derived from them, giving them a negative meaning.> (Examples: *unable, unaccustomed, unattractive, unaware, unbent, unbreakable, uncalled-for, uncaring, unchanged, uncivilized, unconditional, uncon-*

ditionally, unconstant, uncooked, uncut, undeniable, undeveloped, undisciplined, unearthed, unease, unemployment, unequal, uninspired, unintentionally, unjust, unknowing, unknown, unlawfully, unlike, unlucky, unmentionable, unmoved, unnecessary, unnerving, unoriginal, unpaid, unpleasantly, unprecedented, unproven, unquestionable, unrealistic, unreasonable, unrestrained, unruly, unsavory, unsuccessful, unsure, unsweetened, unintelligible, untidy, untruthfulness, unusual, unwelcome, unwholesome, unworkable, unwritten, unzipped. **2.** *prefix* <a form used to show the reversing or undoing of an action, especially of the action of the verb.> (Examples: *unbend, unclog, uncover, undo, undress, unearth, unfasten, unfold, unlace, unload, unlock, unmask, unpack, unplug, unravel, unroll, unscrew, unseat, unstick, untie, unveil, unwind, unwrap, unzip.*)

unable [ən 'e bəl] **unable to** *adj.* + *inf.* not able to do something; not having the ability to do something. ♦ *David is unable to whistle.* ♦ *I regret that I was unable to attend the party.*

unacceptable [ən ɛk 'sɛp tə bəl] *adj.* not acceptable; completely wrong. (Adv: *unacceptably.*) ♦ *Mary thought Bill's politics were unacceptable.* ♦ *The shoddy workmanship of the furniture was unacceptable.*

unaccompanied [ən ə 'kʌm pə nid] **1.** *adj.* not accompanied; without anyone else; alone; [doing something] by oneself. ♦ *John went to the movie unaccompanied.* ♦ *No unaccompanied children are allowed on this train.* **2.** *adj.* without musical accompaniment. ♦ *The unaccompanied soloist sang a few songs.* ♦ *The choir performed one unaccompanied hymn and one hymn with the accompaniment of the church organ.*

unaccountable [ən ə 'kaʊn tə bəl] **1.** *adj.* not accountable for one's actions; not responsible. ♦ *The mentally ill woman was unaccountable for her actions.* ♦ *A baby is unaccountable for its behavior.* **2.** *adj.* puzzling; surprising; hard or impossible to explain. (Adv: *unaccountably.*) ♦ *For some unaccountable reason, I have not felt hungry all day.* ♦ *The unaccountable drop in stock prices surprised the investor.*

unaccustomed [ən ə 'kʌs təmd] **1.** *adj.* strange; different; unusual; weird. ♦ *The inspector investigated the unaccustomed noises.* ♦ *The stranger's unaccustomed behavior made me wary.* **2. unaccustomed to someone or something** *idiom* not used to someone or something. ♦ *The poor family was unaccustomed to going to fancy restaurants.* ♦ *Bill was unaccustomed to typing his own letters.*

unafraid [ən ə 'fred] *adj.* not afraid; brave; without fear. ♦ *The cancer patient was unafraid of facing his treatment.* ♦ *Jimmy is unafraid of the dark.*

un-American [ən ə 'mɛr ɪ kən] *adj.* not reflecting the politics, culture, or interests of the United States of America. ♦ *The patriot declared the war protester to be un-American.* ♦ *Some of the recent immigrants had very un-American political beliefs.*

unanimity [ju nə 'nɪm ə ti] *n.* a state of being unanimous; complete agreement. (No plural form in this sense.) ♦ *The contentious committee rarely experienced unanimity.* ♦ *The jury must have unanimity to convict the defendant.*

unanimous [ju 'næn ə məs] *adj.* in complete agreement; agreed to by everyone; without any dissent; with everyone saying "yes." (Adv: *unanimously.*) ♦ *The jury was unanimous about the defendant's guilt.* ♦ *My friends and I made a unanimous decision to order pizza.*

unannounced [ən ə 'naʊnst] *adj.* not announced; without being announced; without having told someone in advance. ♦ *The professor gave his students an unannounced quiz.* ♦ *Grandmother's arrival was unannounced and surprised us all.*

unanswered [ən 'æn sɚd] *adj.* not answered. ♦ *I wrote another letter to Bill, though my others were still unanswered.* ♦ *Mary had many unanswered prayers.*

unanticipated [ən æn 'tɪs ə pet ɪd] *adj.* not anticipated; not foreseen; not thought of beforehand. (Adv: *unanticipatedly.*) ♦ *Mary has no money because of unanticipated expenses.* ♦ *The pilot apologized for the unanticipated flight delay.*

unarmed [ən 'ɑrmd] *adj.* not armed; not carrying any weapons; without any weapons. ♦ *The police easily apprehended the unarmed thieves.* ♦ *The unarmed man could not defend himself against the attack.*

unashamed [ən ə 'ʃemd] *adj.* not ashamed; without shame. (Adv: *unashamedly.*) ♦ *The unashamed little boy sat and waited for his punishment.* ♦ *The couple made an unashamed declaration of their love.*

unassisted [ən ə 'sɪs tɪd] *adj.* without assistance; without help. (Adv: *unassistedly.*) ♦ *The woman in the wheelchair entered the building unassisted.* ♦ *Even an unassisted child can build this simple toy.*

unassuming [ən ə 'sum ɪŋ] *adj.* modest; sincere; not pretentious. (Adv: *unassumingly.*) ♦ *The unassuming man blended into the crowd.* ♦ *The Smiths, although rich, live in an unassuming house.*

unattached [ən ə 'tætʃt] **1.** *adj.* not attached; not connected. ♦ *The technician repaired the unattached cable.* ♦ *The lever became unattached because it had not been attached securely.* **2.** *adj.* single; not engaged or married. (Figurative on ①.) ♦ *Since Bill is unattached, let's introduce him to Mary.* ♦ *Mary had difficulty meeting unattached men.*

unattainable [ən ə 'ten ə bəl] *adj.* not attainable; not able to be attained. (Adv: *unattainably.*) ♦ *Sue's outlandish goals were unattainable.* ♦ *The untalented writer dreamed of unattainable fame.*

unattended [ən ə 'tɛn dɪd] *adj.* not attended; not watched or taken care of; left alone; without someone in charge. ♦ *The unattended baby began to choke.* ♦ *A thief stole all the money from the store's unattended cash register.*

unattractive [ən ə 'træk tɪv] *adj.* not attractive; plain; not pretty. (Adv: *unattractively.*) ♦ *I hid the unattractive painting in the closet.* ♦ *The unattractive man longed to be handsome.*

unauthorized [ən 'ɔθ ə rɑɪzd] *adj.* not authorized; without proper permission. (Adv: *unauthorizedly.*) ♦ *This book is an unauthorized account of the movie star's life.* ♦ *Bill was fired for taking an unauthorized vacation from work.*

unavailable [ən ə 'vel ə bəl] *adj.* not available. ♦ *The doctor was unavailable to see his patient.* ♦ *The restaurant was unavailable to cater the party.*

unavailing [ən ə 'vel ɪŋ] *adj.* useless; without success; to no avail. (Adv: *unavailingly.*) ♦ *Bob made several unavail-*

ing efforts to start a business. ♦ *Anne's attempts to sell her home were all unavailing.*

unaware [ən ə 'wɛr] *adj.* not aware; not conscious of someone or something; not knowing of someone or something. ♦ *The drunken man was unaware of his surroundings.* ♦ *Max is unaware of what is going on because he never listens to the news.*

unbaptized ['ʌn 'bæp tɑɪzd] *adj.* not baptized; never baptized. ♦ *The unbaptized atheist argued with the minister.* ♦ *The baby remained unbaptized until his first birthday.*

unbearable [ən 'bɛr ə bəl] *adj.* not bearable; not able to be endured. (Adv: *unbearably.*) ♦ *The patient complained of unbearable pain.* ♦ *Mary turned off the unbearable music.*

unbecoming [ən bɪ 'kʌm ɪŋ] *adj.* not becoming; not proper; not suitable; inappropriate. (Adv: *unbecomingly.*) ♦ *That behavior is unbecoming to a well-mannered student.* ♦ *The careless woman often wore unbecoming clothes to work.*

unbelievable [ən bə 'liv ə bəl] *adj.* not believable; incredible; surprising. (Adv: *unbelievably.*) ♦ *Grandpa tells unbelievable stories about his childhood.* ♦ *David spends an unbelievable amount of time watching television.*

unbend [ən 'bɛnd] **1.** *tv.* to cause something to become straight; to cause something not to be bent. (Pt/pp: unbent.) ♦ *This wire now has a 45-degree angle, but I can unbend it to make it straight.* ♦ *Anne unbent her arms and let them hang at her side.* **2.** *iv.* to unfold; to become less bent. ♦ *Anne unbent from a crouching position and stood erect.* ♦ *My fishing pole unbent after the fish I had caught freed itself.*

unbending [ən 'bɛn dɪŋ] *adj.* stubborn; not yielding. (Adv: *unbendingly.*) ♦ *The children endured the unbending rules of their strict parents.* ♦ *The woman was unbending in her religious convictions.*

unbent [ən 'bɛnt] pt/pp of unbend.

unbiased [ən 'bɑɪ əst] *adj.* not biased; fair; impartial; not favoring one side over another. (Adv: *unbiasedly.*) ♦ *The judge gave an unbiased decision in the case.* ♦ *The unbiased mediator helped solve the contract dispute.*

unborn [ən 'born] *adj.* not yet born. ♦ *The unborn child kicked in its mother's womb.* ♦ *The parents chose a name for their unborn son.*

unbreakable [ən 'brek ə bəl] *adj.* not able to be broken. (Adv: *unbreakably.*) ♦ *The company claimed to produce unbreakable baking dishes.* ♦ *The construction worker owned an unbreakable container for his lunch.*

unbroken [ən 'brok ən] *adj.* not broken; whole; complete; continuous; uninterrupted. (Adv: *unbrokenly.*) ♦ *Surprisingly, the ceramic dish remained unbroken after it fell off the shelf.* ♦ *The unbroken cycle of war doomed another generation to a hard life.*

unbutton [ən 'bʌt n] *tv.* to unfasten the buttons of something. ♦ *Mary unbuttoned her coat and took off her hat.* ♦ *Bill unbuttons his collar and loosens his tie every afternoon.*

unbuttoned [ən 'bʌt nd] *adj.* not having the buttons fastened; not buttoned. ♦ *David's unbuttoned collar made him look sloppy.* ♦ *Jimmy's mother would not let him go outside with an unbuttoned coat.*

uncalled-for [ən 'kɔld for] *adj.* not called for; improper; not deserved. ♦ *Jane scolded her children for their uncalled-for behavior.* ♦ *The uncalled-for comment hurt Bill's feelings.*

uncannily [ən 'kæn ɪ li] *adv.* weirdly; oddly. ♦ *Bill uncannily knew that I was lying.* ♦ *Uncannily, Mary telephones me whenever I think of her.*

uncanny [ən 'kæn i] *adj.* weird; odd; unusual. (Adv: *uncannily.* Comp: *uncannier;* sup: *uncanniest.*) ♦ *It's uncanny how Bob always knows when it's going to rain.* ♦ *Mary had an uncanny knack for guessing what I was thinking.*

uncaring [ən 'kɛr ɪŋ] *adj.* not caring; not concerned. (Adv: *uncaringly.*) ♦ *The rude nurse used an uncaring tone with her patients.* ♦ *John's uncaring actions toward Mary hurt her feelings.*

unceasing [ən 'sis ɪŋ] *adj.* not ceasing; never ending; continual; constant. (Adv: *unceasingly.*) ♦ *The manager's unceasing efforts to improve productivity were rewarded.* ♦ *The unceasing noise from the construction site was unbearable.*

uncensored [ən 'sɛn sɚd] *adj.* not censored. ♦ *The uncensored speech contained a lot of vulgar language.* ♦ *Children weren't allowed to view the uncensored movie.*

uncertain [ən 'sɚt n] **1.** *adj.* not certain; not sure. (Adv: *uncertainly.*) ♦ *Jimmy looked uncertain about diving into the pool.* ♦ *The uncertain doctor ordered some tests to confirm the diagnosis.* **2.** *adj.* not known for sure; not yet decided. ♦ *Mary will be visiting us at an uncertain time next summer.* ♦ *The exact date of our wedding is uncertain.* **3.** *adj.* changeable; not reliable. (Adv: *uncertainly.*) ♦ *The uncertain weather kept us guessing whether or not it would rain.* ♦ *Mary's uncertain temperament made her employees uncomfortable.*

uncertainty [ən 'sɚt n ti] **1.** *n.* the condition of being uncertain. (No plural form in this sense.) ♦ *With great uncertainty, the manager hired an inexperienced worker.* ♦ *The uncertainty of Bill's health kept him at home.* **2.** *n.* something that is uncertain. ♦ *The weather is always an uncertainty, especially when planning a picnic.* ♦ *The uncertainties of her job caused Mary to resign.*

unchangeable [ən 'tʃendʒ ə bəl] *adj.* not able to be changed. (Adv: *unchangeably.*) ♦ *The course of this illness is unchangeable.* ♦ *Once my boss makes a decision, it is unchangeable.*

unchanged [ən 'tʃendʒd] *adj.* not changed. ♦ *The unchanged bed linens angered the hotel guest.* ♦ *Jane found her college roommate unchanged after thirty years.*

unchanging [ən 'tʃen dʒɪŋ] *adj.* not changing; remaining the same. (Adv: *unchangingly.*) ♦ *The couple's devotion to each other is unchanging.* ♦ *John's unchanging dedication to his job delights his boss.*

unchecked [ən 'tʃɛkt] *adj.* not controlled or restrained. ♦ *Bill's unchecked comments got him into trouble.* ♦ *The unchecked illness soon became a global epidemic.*

uncivilized [ən 'sɪv ɪ lɑɪzd] *adj.* not civilized; wild; savage. (Often an exaggeration. Adv: *uncivilly.*) ♦ *Why must all of you act so uncivilized?* ♦ *Mary punished her children for their uncivilized behavior at the party.*

uncle ['ʌŋ kəl] *n.* the brother of one's father or mother; the husband of one's aunt. (Also a term of address.) ♦

Mary has a new uncle because her aunt just got married. ♦ *I asked my Uncle John what my mom was like when she was a girl.*

unclean [ən 'klin] **1.** *adj.* not clean; not pure. (Adv: *uncleanly.*) ♦ *Unclean food can make you sick.* ♦ *The ranger warned the campers not to drink the unclean water.* **2.** *adj.* immoral; dirty ②. (Adv: *uncleanly.*) ♦ *Bob felt guilty about having unclean thoughts.* ♦ *An unclean mind can lead to unclean deeds.*

unclear [ən 'klɪr] *adj.* not clear; not understood well. (Adv: *unclearly.*) ♦ *What happened the night of the crime remained unclear.* ♦ *John's confusing directions are unclear to me.*

uncomfortable [ən 'kʌmf tə bəl] **1.** *adj.* not comfortable; feeling uneasy. (Adv: *uncomfortably.*) ♦ *I always feel uncomfortable at funerals.* ♦ *John is uncomfortable speaking in front of a large group of people.* **2.** *adj.* causing discomfort; causing unease. (Adv: *uncomfortably.*) ♦ *The pilot apologized for the uncomfortable flight.* ♦ *Jane returned the uncomfortable furniture to the store.*

uncommon [ən 'kɑm ən] *adj.* not common; rare; unusual. (Adv: *uncommonly.*) ♦ *The botanist identified the uncommon plant.* ♦ *Changing careers is not uncommon nowadays.*

uncommonly [ən 'kɑm ən li] *adv.* very; to an unusual extent or degree. (Used as an intensifier.) ♦ *The movie was uncommonly stupid.* ♦ *These cookies taste uncommonly good.*

uncompromising [ən 'kɑm prə mɑɪz ɪŋ] *adj.* not compromising; not yielding; stubborn. (Adv: *uncompromisingly.*) ♦ *Our company has an uncompromising commitment to quality.* ♦ *Bill has uncompromising faith in his colleagues.*

unconcerned [ən kən 'sɚnd] *adj.* not concerned; apathetic; indifferent. (Adv: *unconcernedly.*) ♦ *The unconcerned salesperson did not offer to help us.* ♦ *Sadly, many of my friends are unconcerned about social issues.*

unconditional [ən kən 'dɪʃ ə nəl] *adj.* not conditional; without conditions; not restricted by conditions. (Adv: *unconditionally.*) ♦ *The parents offered their children their unconditional love.* ♦ *Bob gave Bill an unconditional personal loan.*

unconscious [ən 'kɑn ʃəs] **1.** *adj.* not conscious; having lost consciousness. (Adv: *unconsciously.*) ♦ *The unconscious accident victim was carried to an ambulance.* ♦ *The drunken man was unconscious on the park bench.* **2.** *adj.* not intentional; done without thinking. (Adv: *unconsciously.*) ♦ *Mary's comment about the surprise party was an unconscious slip.* ♦ *Susan made an unconscious glance in the direction of the door, indicating that she was expecting someone.* **3.** *n.* the part of one's mind of which one is not aware. (No plural form in this sense.) ♦ *The psychologist probed the woman's unconscious.* ♦ *The doctor used hypnosis to reveal the man's unconscious.*

unconsciousness [ən 'kɑn ʃəs nəs] *n.* a state of being unconscious. (No plural form in this sense.) ♦ *The accident victim's unconsciousness lasted for two days.* ♦ *The elderly man was brought to the hospital in a state of unconsciousness.*

unconstitutional [ən kɑn stɪ 'tu ʃə nəl] *adj.* not constitutional; not according to a constitution; against what is written in the U.S. Constitution. (Adv: *unconstitutionally.*) ♦ *The law was ruled unconstitutional and was repealed.* ♦ *Denying people their civil rights is unconstitutional.*

uncontrollable [ən kən 'trol ə bəl] *adj.* not able to be controlled; not controllable. (Adv: *uncontrollably.*) ♦ *The uncontrollable children were told to leave the theater.* ♦ *I had an uncontrollable urge to eat some more chocolate.*

unconventional [ən kən 'vɛn tʃə nəl] *adj.* not conventional; not regular; not ordinary; not traditional. (Adv: *unconventionally.*) ♦ *The musician wore an unconventional outfit to the awards ceremony.* ♦ *The professor with unconventional views was fired.*

uncooked [ən 'kʊkt] *adj.* not cooked; raw. ♦ *Susan likes to eat uncooked broccoli.* ♦ *The uncooked chicken made Bob ill.*

uncork [ən 'kork] *tv.* to open something by removing a cork from it; to remove a cork from something. ♦ *The waiter uncorked the bottle of wine.* ♦ *Mary uncorked the champagne shortly before midnight.*

uncouth [ən 'kuθ] *adj.* without good manners; rough; crude. (Adv: *uncouthly.*) ♦ *Belching at the table is uncouth behavior.* ♦ *The uncouth worker was never invited to company parties.*

uncover [ən 'kʌv ɚ] *tv.* to remove the cover from something; to expose someone or something by removing a cover. ♦ *The workers uncovered the baseball field by removing the tarp.* ♦ *Mary uncovered the pot of soup to let it cool before serving it.*

uncovered [ən 'kʌv ɚd] *adj.* not covered; not hidden; exposed. ♦ *The uncovered milk went sour very quickly.* ♦ *Mary's uncovered skin became sunburned.*

uncut [ən 'kʌt] **1.** *adj.* of or about a diamond or other gem that has not been shaped into a piece of jewelry. ♦ *The diamond buyer examined the uncut stones.* ♦ *Mary chose an uncut emerald from the jeweler's display.* **2.** *adj.* not shortened; not edited; not censored; of or about a film in its original condition. ♦ *The uncut version of the movie was ten minutes longer than the version shown on TV.* ♦ *The school board banned the uncut edition of the controversial book.*

undamaged [ən 'dæm ɪdʒd] *adj.* not damaged. ♦ *We salvaged a few undamaged goods from the house destroyed by fire.* ♦ *The fragile dishes remained undamaged when they were shipped.*

undaunted [ən 'dɔn tɪd] *adj.* not daunted; bold; brave; not afraid of or discouraged by danger. (Adv: *undauntedly.*) ♦ *The undaunted soldiers rebuilt their destroyed fort.* ♦ *Bob remained undaunted as he drove through the terrible storm.*

undecided [ən dɪ 'sɑɪd ɪd] **1.** *adj.* unsure of how one will decide; not having made a decision. (Adv: *undecidedly.*) ♦ *John is undecided whether to go to college or not.* ♦ *The undecided customer did not buy anything.* **2.** *adj.* [of a matter that has] not yet been determined. (Adv: *undecidedly.*) ♦ *By the end of the meeting, there were still some undecided issues.* ♦ *Bob left the undecided matters for his boss to answer.*

undefeated [ən dɪ 'fit ɪd] *adj.* not defeated; not having lost; always having won. (Adv: *undefeatedly.*) ♦ *The unde-*

feated team was confident of another victory. ♦ *The undefeated boxer easily overpowered his challenger.*

undefended [ən dɪ 'fɛn dɪd] *adj.* not defended; not protected; open to assault or attack. ♦ *The undefended fort soon fell to the invaders.* ♦ *The soldiers easily took control of the undefended town.*

undeniable [ən dɪ 'nɑɪ ə bəl] *adj.* not deniable; obvious. (Adv: *undeniably.*) ♦ *That fire can be destructive is undeniable.* ♦ *The testimony of the expert witness was undeniable.*

under ['ʌn dɚ] **1.** *prep.* in or at a place below someone or something; in or at a place beneath someone or something; to or into a place below someone or something; to or into a place beneath someone or something. ♦ *The couple snuggled under the covers.* ♦ *Bill reached under the desk to pick up his pen.* ♦ *A mouse just jumped off the chair and ran under the dresser.* **2.** *prep.* lower than someone or something; not as high as someone or something. ♦ *I hung my daughter's picture on the wall under the picture of my son.* ♦ *John placed the can of paint on the shelf under the window.* **3.** *prep.* less than something. ♦ *This couch cost under a hundred dollars.* ♦ *When it's under 32 degrees Fahrenheit, water freezes.* **4.** *prep.* affected by the control or influence of someone or something; ranked beneath someone or something. ♦ *Bill works under Mr. Jones.* ♦ *John is under a vice president who reports directly to the president.* **5.** *adv.* below; below the surface; beneath. ♦ *The undertow dragged the swimmer under.* ♦ *The ship started to sink, and then went under.* **6. under ____ circumstances; under ____ conditions** *phr.* depending on or influenced by something; because of something. ♦ *Under certain conditions, you can see across the lake.* ♦ *Under no circumstances are you to leave the house tonight.*

underage [ən dɚ 'edʒ] **1.** *adj.* not having reached a specific required age [for some activity or event]. ♦ *The underage students weren't allowed into the bar.* ♦ *John couldn't enlist in the army because he was underage.* **2.** *adj.* of or about the activities of minors. ♦ *The students were punished for underage drinking.* ♦ *No alcohol was served at the underage party.*

underarm ['ʌn dɚ ɑrm] **1.** *n.* the armpit. ♦ *The ape scratched its underarms.* ♦ *I sprayed my underarms with deodorant.* **2.** *adj.* <the adj. use of ①.> ♦ *I use an underarm deodorant that is a powder.* ♦ *Some women shave their underarm hair.*

underbrush ['ʌn dɚ brəʃ] *n.* small trees or plants that grow lower than the large trees in a forest. ♦ *The hikers walked on the path through the underbrush.* ♦ *My legs became scratched from the underbrush.*

undercharge [ən dɚ 'tʃɑrdʒ] *tv.* to charge someone less money than the proper price. ♦ *The plumber undercharges his friends.* ♦ *The cashier accidentally undercharged me for my purchase.*

underclassman [ən dɚ 'klæs mən] *n., irreg.* a freshman or sophomore. (Pl: underclassmen.) ♦ *The underclassmen looked up to the seniors.* ♦ *The upperclassmen refused to eat lunch with the underclassmen.*

underclassmen [ən dɚ 'klæs mən] pl of underclassman.

underclothes ['ʌn dɚ kloðz] *n.* underwear; underpants and undershirts; the clothing worn next to the skin, usually under other pieces of clothing. (Treated as plural.) ♦ *I put on fresh underclothes after taking a shower.* ♦ *Bill walked around the house in his underclothes.*

underclothing ['ʌn dɚ klo ðɪŋ] *n.* underwear; underclothes. (No plural form in this sense.) ♦ *I wore two layers of underclothing because it was so cold.* ♦ *Mary packed enough underclothing for the seven-day trip.*

undercoat ['ʌn dɚ kot] *n.* primer; the first coat of paint or varnish when more than one coat is applied. ♦ *The woodworker carefully put an undercoat on the bookcase.* ♦ *The painter let the undercoat dry before applying the next coat.*

undercover [ən dɚ 'kʌv ɚ] *adj.* done in secret; acting or working in secret. ♦ *The undercover cop helped break the drug ring.* ♦ *Spies usually work on undercover assignments.*

undercurrent ['ʌn dɚ kɚ ənt] *n.* a current of water underneath the surface of a body of water. ♦ *The strong undercurrent carried our raft out to sea.* ♦ *The swimmer tried to swim against the undercurrent and drowned.*

undercut ['ʌn dɚ kət] *tv., irreg.* to beat a competitor by selling the same good at a lower price. ♦ *The discount store undercut all of its competitors.* ♦ *When one airline undercut its major competitor, the others followed suit.*

underdeveloped [ən dɚ dɪ 'vɛl əpt] *adj.* not as developed as someone or something else; poorly developed, especially in comparison with other people or things. ♦ *The organs of the prematurely born infant were underdeveloped.* ♦ *The country suffered from an underdeveloped economy.*

underdog ['ʌn dɚ dɔg] *n.* someone who is expected to lose; someone who is considered to be inferior. ♦ *The odds that the underdog would win the race were 70–1.* ♦ *Although Anne was the underdog, she won the election.*

underdone [ən dɚ 'dʌn] *adj.* not cooked enough; somewhat raw. ♦ *The underdone hamburger was very pink.* ♦ *Bill became sick from eating underdone fish.*

underestimate [ən dɚ 'ɛs tə met] **1.** *tv.* to estimate the value of something at too low a value. ♦ *The business owner underestimated the value of his employees.* ♦ *The appraiser underestimated the worth of the rare gems.* **2.** *iv.* to estimate too low a value. ♦ *I tried to guess how many people were at the party, but I underestimated.* ♦ *Mary underestimated when she thought the watch would cost only $20.*

underfed [ən dɚ 'fɛd] **1.** pt/pp of underfeed. **2.** *adj.* not fed well enough; poorly fed; fed too little. ♦ *The underfed puppy begged for food.* ♦ *The underfed refugees looked very gaunt.*

underfeed ['ʌn dɚ 'fid] *tv., irreg.* to feed someone or some creature less than is required. (Pt/pp: underfed.) ♦ *Don't underfeed your new puppy.* ♦ *I underfed the tropical fish so the food wouldn't be wasted.*

underfoot [ən dɚ 'fʊt] **1.** *adv.* on the ground; under one's feet. ♦ *The leaves crunched underfoot as I walked through the park.* ♦ *I tripped over the toys that lay underfoot.* **2.** *adv.* bothersome and in someone's way. (Figurative on ①.) ♦ *The frisky puppy always runs underfoot.* ♦ *My children are well behaved and never underfoot.*

undergarment ['ʌn dɚ gɑr mənt] *n.* a piece of clothing that is worn under another layer of clothing, especially one that is next to one's skin; underwear. ♦ *The store sold* *luxurious undergarments and lingerie.* ♦ *The wool undergarments were itchy.*

undergo [ən dɚ 'go] *tv.* to experience something that is difficult. (Pt: underwent; pp: undergone.) ♦ *Bob must undergo surgery to remove a tumor.* ♦ *Mary told of the ordeal she underwent during the robbery.*

undergone [ən dɚ 'gɔn] pp of undergo.

undergraduate [ən dɚ 'græ dʒu ət] **1.** *n.* a college student who has not yet received a bachelor's degree. ♦ *The undergraduate signed up for new classes at the semester break.* ♦ *When Anne was an undergraduate, she declared chemistry as her major.* **2.** *adj.* <the adj. use of ①.> ♦ *Dave is attending undergraduate classes at night.* ♦ *Susan is an undergraduate advisor at the local college.*

underground ['ʌn dɚ graʊnd] **1.** *adj.* below the surface of the ground; in the earth. ♦ *The fox lived in an underground lair.* ♦ *The prisoner escaped from the jail through an underground tunnel.* **2.** *adj.* secret. (Figurative on ①.) ♦ *Underground rebels helped fight the corrupt leader.* ♦ *The politician did not know of the underground attempts to sabotage his campaign.* **3.** *adv.* below the surface of the ground; in the earth. ♦ *The groundhog burrows underground.* ♦ *The water pipes run underground through the city.* **4.** *adv.* in secret. (Figurative on ③.) ♦ *The political dissident was forced to live underground.* ♦ *The rebels went underground when their lives were threatened.*

undergrowth ['ʌn dɚ groθ] *n.* small trees or plants that grow under large trees in a forest. (No plural form in this sense.) ♦ *The farmer cleared the undergrowth from the small orchard.* ♦ *Hundreds of rabbits live in the undergrowth in this forest.*

underhanded ['ʌn dɚ 'hæn dɪd] *adj.* sneaky; dishonest; deceptive. (Adv: *underhandedly.*) ♦ *The corrupt politician used underhanded tactics to win the election.* ♦ *Jane made several underhanded attempts to get her coworker fired.*

underline ['ʌn dɚ laɪn] **1.** *tv.* to draw a line under a word to give the word emphasis; to emphasize a word by drawing a line under it. ♦ *The teacher underlined the incorrectly spelled words in my report.* ♦ *David underlined some words on the poster for emphasis.* **2.** *n.* a line that is drawn under a word to give the word emphasis. ♦ *The teacher drew an underline under the words spelled incorrectly.* ♦ *Mary erased the underline beneath the verb in the sentence.*

underlined ['ʌn dɚ laɪnd] *adj.* emphasized; stressed; [of words] having a line drawn beneath. ♦ *The underlined words are the ones the editor added in the new draft.* ♦ *The underlined words in the manuscript were printed in italics in the book.*

underling ['ʌn dɚ lɪŋ] *n.* someone who is inferior; someone who is subordinate; someone who does not have much power or rank. ♦ *The boss treated his underlings badly.* ♦ *The underling was finally promoted after two years of hard work.*

underlying [ən dɚ 'laɪ ɪŋ] *adj.* being the foundation of something; being the real reason for something. (Adv: *underlyingly.*) ♦ *The doctor could not determine the underlying cause of the disease.* ♦ *Lack of money was the underlying reason that I didn't go on vacation.*

undermine [ən dɚ 'maɪn] *tv.* to weaken something by wearing away support; to weaken someone or something gradually. ♦ *The project was undermined by lazy workers.* ♦ *The pesky journalist undermined the mayor's stature.*

underneath [ən dɚ 'niθ] **1.** *prep.* beneath someone or something; below someone or something; under someone or something. ♦ *The cold woman lay underneath three blankets.* ♦ *Bill stored empty boxes underneath the basement stairs.* **2.** *adv.* under someone or something that is on top; under someone or something. ♦ *On the sidewalk, I could hear the subway as it passed underneath.* ♦ *John jumped from the bridge to the river underneath.*

underpaid [ən dɚ 'ped] **1.** pt/pp of underpay. **2.** *adj.* not paid as well as one should be; not given enough money for one's work. ♦ *The underpaid worker requested a raise.* ♦ *The busy secretary felt underpaid and unappreciated.*

underpants ['ʌn dɚ pænts] *n.* an article of clothing worn next to the skin below the waist, usually under other clothing. (Treated as plural. Number is also expressed by *pair(s) of underpants.*) ♦ *I swam in my underpants because I'd forgotten to bring a bathing suit.* ♦ *Bob always wears underpants and an undershirt under his clothes.*

underpass ['ʌn dɚ pæs] *n.* a road or path that goes under another road, usually below the level of the surrounding land. ♦ *This low underpass floods when it rains a lot.* ♦ *The tall truck became stuck while driving through the underpass.*

underpay [ən dɚ 'pe] *tv., irreg.* not to pay someone or something enough money. (Pt/pp: underpaid.) ♦ *The exploitative company underpaid its workers.* ♦ *Mary underpaid her babysitter because she was short on cash.*

underpinning ['ʌn dɚ pɪn ɪŋ] **1.** *n.* the structures that support a building or a wall from beneath. (Often plural.) ♦ *Termites had destroyed the barn's wooden underpinnings.* ♦ *The office building's underpinnings withstood the earthquake.* **2.** *n.* something that provides support or a foundation. (Figurative on ①.) ♦ *Algebra is one of the underpinnings of calculus.* ♦ *The financial underpinning of the social agency was a federal grant.*

underprivileged [ən dɚ 'prɪv lɪdʒd] *adj.* not having the advantages that most people have, especially because of poverty. ♦ *The underprivileged family struggled to survive.* ♦ *The church helped provide scholarships to underprivileged students.*

underrate [ən dɚ 'ret] *tv.* to have too low an opinion of someone or something. ♦ *The picky critic had underrated the popular movie.* ♦ *Bill underrates his cooking, but I think it's delicious.*

underrated [ən dɚ 'ret ɪd] *adj.* better than generally thought. ♦ *The underrated writer struggled to have her manuscripts published.* ♦ *Few people saw the underrated movie, but it won a lot of awards.*

underscore ['ʌn dɚ skor] **1.** *tv.* to draw a line under a word to give the word emphasis. ♦ *The teacher underscored the verb of each sentence on the blackboard.* ♦ *Anne underscored the revised information in the new newsletter.* **2.** *tv.* to emphasize something. (Figurative on ①.) ♦ *The mayor underscored the need for more police officers.* ♦ *The job candidate underscored her previous experience in the field.* **3.** *n.* a line that is drawn under a word to give the word emphasis; an underline. ♦ *The lawyer placed an underscore under the important clauses in the contract.* ♦ *I* *drew an underscore under the change in the meeting time on the memo.*

underscored ['ʌn dɚ skord] *adj.* underlined. ♦ *The underscored passages are the ones you might want to delete.* ♦ *The lecturer emphasized the underscored words in the paper.*

undersell [ən dɚ 'sɛl] *tv., irreg.* to beat a competitor by selling the same goods at a lower price. (Pt/pp: undersold.) ♦ *Each store tried to undersell its competitors.* ♦ *The large grocery store undersold the local merchants by 10%.*

undershirt ['ʌn dɚ ʃɚt] *n.* a piece of clothing worn above the waist next to the skin, usually under other clothing. ♦ *John put on a clean undershirt and underpants after taking a shower.* ♦ *On warm days, I wear an undershirt with nothing over it.*

undershorts ['ʌn dɚ ʃorts] *n.* underpants; a piece of clothing worn below the waist next to the skin, usually under other clothing. (Treated as plural. Number is expressed with *pair(s) of undershorts.*) ♦ *The children jumped into the pool, wearing only their undershorts.* ♦ *Bill walks around the house in his undershorts in the evenings.*

underside ['ʌn dɚ saɪd] *n.* the surface of the bottom part of someone or something. (Usually singular.) ♦ *The underside of the snake is white.* ♦ *The underside of the car was covered with mud.*

undersold ['ʌn dɚ 'sold] pt/pp of undersell.

understand [ən dɚ 'stænd] **1.** *iv., irreg.* to know; to be aware of the meaning of something; to know about something; to be familiar with something. (Pt/pp: understood.) ♦ *After Susan explained the situation, I understood completely.* ♦ *I want to be left alone. Do you understand?* **2.** *tv., irreg.* to know something; to know the meaning of something. ♦ *Bill understood the directions that were given to him.* ♦ *I understand your concern about the situation.* **3.** *tv., irreg.* to assume something. ♦ *I'm sorry; I understood that you were leaving now.* ♦ *We understood that you would be on an earlier plane.*

understandable [ən dɚ 'stænd ə bəl] *adj.* able to be understood. (Adv: *understandably.*) ♦ *Your reasons for not coming to the party are understandable.* ♦ *It's understandable that Mary was promoted because she works so hard.*

understanding [ən dɚ 'stænd ɪŋ] **1.** *n.* the ability to understand. (No plural form in this sense.) ♦ *Mary has a profound understanding of biology.* ♦ *Alcoholism had affected the student's understanding.* **2.** *n.* an informal agreement. ♦ *The mediator helped the two sides to come to an understanding.* ♦ *The two former enemies reached an understanding and shook hands.* **3.** *adj.* able to understand; sympathetic. (Adv: *understandably.*) ♦ *My understanding teacher let me retake the exam I had failed.* ♦ *I appreciated my manager's understanding view of my personal problems.*

understatement ['ən dɚ stet mənt] *n.* a statement that expresses something too weakly. ♦ *To call that heavy rainstorm a drizzle is quite an understatement.* ♦ *That Mary helped with the project is an understatement. She did it all alone!*

understood [ən dɚ 'stʊd] **1.** pt/pp of understand. **2.** *adj.* of or about a language form that is not spoken or written, but is assumed to be part of an utterance. ♦ *In basic commands, there is an understood "you" before the verb.* ♦ *In "John wanted to go," "John" is the understood object of the verb "want"; that is, "John wanted for himself to go."*

understudy ['ʌn dɚ stəd i] **1.** a substitute actor who learns a part in a play in order to replace the real actor in case of illness. ♦ *The stage manager called the understudy when the star was injured.* ♦ *Signs in the lobby indicated that an understudy was playing the lead role.* **2.** *tv.* to learn a part in a play in order to serve as ①. ♦ *Mary understudied the role of Juliet in case the star became sick.* ♦ *Bill knows the part of Hamlet because he's understudied it before.*

undertake [ən dɚ 'tek] *tv., irreg.* to begin work on something; to begin an action; to start something. (Pt: undertook; pp: undertaken.) ♦ *Jane will undertake the project of renovating her house.* ♦ *The mechanic undertook rebuilding the engine.*

undertaken [ən dɚ 'tek ən] pp of undertake.

undertaker ['ʌn dɚ tek ɚ] *n.* someone who arranges funerals. ♦ *The undertaker spoke with the family about the service.* ♦ *The undertaker drove the hearse to the cemetery.*

undertaking ['ʌn dɚ tek ɪŋ] **1.** *n.* an important job that requires a lot of effort; a big effort needed to do something. ♦ *A dinner party for thirty people is a large undertaking.* ♦ *Managing my own business is an undertaking I have always wanted to pursue.* **2.** *n.* the business of arranging funerals. (No plural form in this sense.) ♦ *John taught his son everything he knew about undertaking.* ♦ *The funeral home director was trained in undertaking.*

under-the-table ['ʌn dɚ ðə 'te bəl] *adj.* secret; of or about something done secretly, especially something against the law. ♦ *The reporter discovered the senator's under-the-table bribe.* ♦ *Both parties profited from the lucrative under-the-table deal.*

undertook [ən dɚ 'tʊk] pt of undertake.

undertow ['ʌn dɚ to] *n.* a rapid current of water that runs away from the shore, opposite the direction of the tide. ♦ *The swimmer struggled against the undertow.* ♦ *The undertow pulled the shells and rocks back out to sea.*

underwater [ən dɚ 'wɑ tɚ] **1.** *adj.* under the surface of water. ♦ *The underwater photographs showed marine life on a reef.* ♦ *The diver explored the underwater cave.* **2.** *adj.* made for use under the water. ♦ *The diver wore an underwater watch.* ♦ *The underwater camera took magnificent photos of sea life.* **3.** *adv.* under the surface of water. ♦ *I swam underwater to the shore.* ♦ *The penguin dove underwater.*

underwear ['ʌn dɚ wɛr] *n.* underclothing; clothing worn next to the skin, usually under other clothing. (No plural form in this sense. Number is expressed with *pair(s) of underwear.*) ♦ *The traffic cop wore thermal underwear during the cold winter.* ♦ *The actors wore their own underwear under their costumes.*

underweight ['ʌn dɚ wet] *adj.* not weighing as much as one should; weighing too little. ♦ *The malnourished child was very underweight.* ♦ *The underweight wrestler was not allowed to wrestle in the match.*

underwent ['ʌn dɚ wɛnt] pt of undergo.

underworld ['ʌn dɚ wɚld] **1.** *n.* the world of crime; criminals and their society. ♦ *The undercover cop penetrated the underworld.* ♦ *The reporter wrote about the underworld of organized crime.* **2.** *n.* hell. (Sometimes capitalized.) ♦ *The minister said the sinner would burn in the Underworld.* ♦ *The sinner feared the flames of the eternal underworld.*

underwrite [ən dɚ 'rɑɪt] *tv., irreg.* to assume financial sponsorship of something. (Pt: **underwrote**; pp: **underwritten**.) ♦ *The new board of directors underwrote the firm's old debt.* ♦ *Bill's parents underwrote his student loans.*

underwriter ['ʌn dɚ rɑɪt ɚ] *n.* an insurer; someone who underwrites insurance policies or who determines whether someone or something is too risky to insure. ♦ *The underwriter inspected the huge factory before issuing insurance.* ♦ *The underwriter noted that my house was near an earthquake fault.*

underwritten [ən dɚ 'rɪt n] pp of **underwrite**.

underwrote [ən dɚ 'rot] pt of **underwrite**.

undeserved [ən dɪ 'zɚvd] *adj.* not deserved; not fitting the worth of something. (Adv: *undeservedly* [ən dɪ 'zɚv əd li].) ♦ *The lazy employee received an undeserved raise.* ♦ *The cast of the show felt the bad review was undeserved.*

undesirable [ən dɪ 'zɑɪr ə bəl] **1.** *adj.* not desirable; offensive; not wanted. (Adv: *undesirably.*) ♦ *Working at night is undesirable for many people.* ♦ *The undesirable refugees weren't admitted into the country.* **2.** *n.* someone who is not wanted. ♦ *At night, the undesirables roam the city streets.* ♦ *The cops chased the undesirables from the street corners.*

undetermined [ən dɪ 'tɚ mənd] *adj.* not counted, not decided, or not yet planned. ♦ *The president will arrive by way of an undetermined route.* ♦ *The number of guests Jane is inviting to her wedding is still undetermined.*

undeveloped [ən dɪ 'vɛl əpt] **1.** *adj.* not developed; not mature; not fully grown. ♦ *The ultrasound showed a picture of the undeveloped baby.* ♦ *Because my musical talent was undeveloped, I began taking classes.* **2.** *adj.* [of land] not having been exploited or used. ♦ *Colonists exploited the undeveloped countryside.* ♦ *A real-estate agent bought some undeveloped land near the freeway.*

undid [ən 'dɪd] pt of **undo**.

undignified [ən 'dɪg nə fɑɪd] *adj.* not dignified. ♦ *John's rude response to the reasonable question was undignified.* ♦ *The undignified man belched at the dinner table.*

undisturbed [ən də 'stɚbd] **1.** *adj.* not disturbed; left alone; calm; not bothered. ♦ *Amazingly, the fragile vase was undisturbed by the earthquake.* ♦ *The soldier was undisturbed by the violent movie.* **2.** *adj.* [of a place] in its natural or original condition. ♦ *Few parts of the earth are still undisturbed.* ♦ *The archaeologist discovered the undisturbed grave of an ancient king.* **3.** *adv.* not moved; not bothered. ♦ *The fragile vase lay undisturbed in the rubble.* ♦ *The dead soldier's body was left undisturbed by the enemy.*

undo [ən 'du] **1.** *tv., irreg.* to cancel the effects of something; to cause something to be as though something had never been done. (Pt: **undid**; pp: **undone**.) ♦ *I think you should try to undo the harm that you've done.* ♦ *This software allows you to undo changes that were accidentally made.* **2.** *tv., irreg.* to untie something; to unfasten something. ♦ *Jane undid the buttons on her coat.* ♦ *Bob couldn't undo his zipper because it was stuck.*

undoing [ən 'du ɪŋ] *n.* something that causes failure or ruin. (No plural form in this sense.) ♦ *Greed was the businessman's undoing.* ♦ *The rainstorm was the undoing of the outdoor wedding.*

undone [ən 'dʌn] pp of **undo**.

undoubtedly [ən 'dɑʊ tɪd li] *adv.* without doubt; certainly; obviously; surely. ♦ *Today was undoubtedly the hottest day of this summer.* ♦ *Most Americans undoubtedly know who the president is.*

undress [ən 'drɛs] **1.** *tv.* to remove someone's clothes. ♦ *The babysitter undressed the child and put her to bed.* ♦ *John undressed himself and took a shower.* **2.** *iv.* to take off one's own clothes. ♦ *Jane undressed and went to bed.* ♦ *Bill was caught in the rain, so he undressed when he got home.*

undue [ən 'du] *adj.* not deserved. (Adv: *unduly.*) ♦ *The newspaper gave the corrupt mayor undue respect.* ♦ *The employee flinched under the undue criticism.*

unduly [ən 'du li] *adv.* in an excessive way; excessively negative. ♦ *Tom got unduly excited over my error.* ♦ *Bill was unduly criticized for being late.*

undying [ən 'dɑɪ ɪŋ] *adj.* not dying; never dying; lasting forever. (Adv: *undyingly.*) ♦ *The bride and groom expressed their undying love to each other.* ♦ *I have undying gratitude for the firefighter who saved my life.*

unearned [ən 'ɚnd] **1.** *adj.* not earned; not deserved; not obtained by work or effort. ♦ *The embezzler was ordered to repay the unearned money.* ♦ *John, who copied the essay from an old magazine, received unearned praise for his fraudulent work.* **2.** *adj.* [in baseball] of or about a run that is scored because of an error. ♦ *When the player dropped the fly ball, an unearned run was scored.* ♦ *The other team was so bad that all of our runs were unearned.*

unearth [ən 'ɚθ] **1.** *tv.* to remove something from the ground; to dig something from the earth. ♦ *The archaeologist unearthed an ancient grave.* ♦ *The gardener unearthed some potatoes.* **2.** *tv.* to discover and reveal something; to disclose something; to expose something. (Figurative on ①.) ♦ *The spy's secret was unearthed by a federal agent.* ♦ *The newspaper reporter unearthed the lawyer's dark secret.*

unearthly [ən 'ɚθ li] *adj.* not from earth; alien; supernatural; not natural. ♦ *The yard was mysteriously bathed in an unearthly light.* ♦ *The injured dog gave an unearthly whine.*

uneasily [ən 'i zə li] *adv.* in a manner that is not at ease; uncomfortably. ♦ *Tom walked uneasily into the room full of strangers.* ♦ *Very worried, I tossed uneasily in bed.*

uneasiness [ən 'i zi nəs] *n.* the quality of being uneasy. (No plural form in this sense.) ♦ *The student felt an uneasiness about cheating.* ♦ *A feeling of uneasiness swept over the passengers on the rough flight.*

uneasy [ən 'i zi] **1.** *adj.* not comfortable; upset; anxious; worried. (Adv: *uneasily.*) ♦ *Being home alone makes me uneasy.* ♦ *The strange man on the bus made Bill uneasy.* **2.** *adj.* not certain; tentative; precarious; likely to collapse. (Adv: *uneasily.*) ♦ *The treaty resulted in an uneasy peace.* ♦ *The uneasy cease-fire was soon shattered by gunfire.*

uneducated [ən 'ɛdʒ ə ket ɪd] *adj.* not educated; not having attended school; not having been taught. ♦ *The uneducated man had difficulty finding a job.* ♦ *Jane taught the uneducated immigrants how to read.*

unemotional [ən ə 'mo ʃə nəl] *adj.* not emotional; not having emotion; not showing emotion. (Adv: *unemo-*

tionally.) ♦ *The touching movie did not affect the unemotional man.* ♦ *The doctor remained unemotional when his patient died.*

unemployed [ən ɛm 'plɔɪd] *adj.* not employed; not having a job; out of work. ♦ *The unemployed worker received benefits from the state.* ♦ *The unemployed student looked for a summer job.*

unemployment [ən ɛm 'plɔɪ mənt] *n.* the lack of a job or the lack of jobs in general. (No plural form in this sense.) ♦ *My family also suffered the strain of my unemployment.* ♦ *The governor promised to reduce unemployment in the state.*

unending [ən 'ɛn dɪŋ] *adj.* not ending; never ending; eternal; unceasing. (Adv: *unendingly.*) ♦ *The movie was incredibly boring and seemed unending.* ♦ *My coworker's unending chatter annoys me.*

unenthusiastic [ən ɪn θu zi 'æs tɪk] *adj.* not enthusiastic; not excited; without enthusiasm. (Adv: *unenthusiastically* [...ɪk li].) ♦ *The kids were unenthusiastic about another day at school.* ♦ *The unenthusiastic audience barely applauded the performers.*

unequal [ən 'i kwəl] *adj.* not equal in size, amount, degree, importance, or worth. (Adv: *unequally.*) ♦ *I resented that my salary was unequal to that of my colleague.* ♦ *The children complained that their portions of food were unequal.*

unerring [ən 'ɛr ɪŋ] *adj.* never wrong; making no mistakes; without error. (Adv: *unerringly.*) ♦ *I trusted my parents' unerring judgment.* ♦ *Jane completed her work with unerring accuracy.*

uneven [ən 'i vən] **1.** *adj.* [of a surface] not even; not smooth; rough; bumpy. (Adv: *unevenly.*) ♦ *Broken plaster gave the wall an uneven surface.* ♦ *The uneven road damaged the car's tires.* **2.** *adj.* [of a process or flow] not constant; varying; irregular. (Adv: *unevenly.*) ♦ *Bill's work is uneven, depending on how tired he is.* ♦ *The radio signal was uneven. It came in better on clear days.* **3.** *adj.* not equal; unequal. (Adv: *unevenly.*) ♦ *The cook had served the students uneven portions of food.* ♦ *The length of the boards is uneven and they must be made equal.*

uneventful [ən ɪ 'vɛnt fʊl] *adj.* not eventful; without anything important or interesting happening; tedious. (Adv: *uneventfully.*) ♦ *I left the uneventful football game at halftime.* ♦ *Bill had an uneventful day at the office and came home at the usual time.*

unexcused ['ʌn ɛk 'skuzd] *adj.* existing without excuse or explanation; without official pardon or excuse. ♦ *The teacher wouldn't allow any unexcused absences.* ♦ *Bill was forced to pay an unexcused late penalty on his water bill.*

unexpected [ən ɛk 'spɛk tɪd] *adj.* not expected; surprising; not known about beforehand. (Adv: *unexpectedly.*) ♦ *An unexpected event ruined the party.* ♦ *The unexpected news that Anne was moving surprised me.*

unexplained [ən ɛk 'splend] *adj.* not explained. ♦ *Mike said that unexplained events are due to chance.* ♦ *The professor told John to discuss his unexplained conclusions.*

unexplored [ən ɛk 'splord] *adj.* not explored; not examined. ♦ *The spaceship took pictures of unexplored planets.* ♦ *My boss told us to look closely at some unexplored options.*

unfailing [ən 'fel ɪŋ] *adj.* never failing; never tiring; continual; never ending. (Adv: *unfailingly.*) ♦ *The project was completed early due to Anne's unfailing efforts.* ♦ *Bob works sixteen hours a day with unfailing energy.*

unfair [ən 'fɛr] *adj.* not fair; unjust; not right; not equal. (Adv: *unfairly.*) ♦ *It's unfair that I have to work so hard!* ♦ *The loser challenged the unfair election.*

unfaithful [ən 'feθ fʊl] *adj.* not faithful to someone or something, especially to one's spouse; not loyal. (Adv: *unfaithfully.*) ♦ *Jane divorced her unfaithful husband.* ♦ *The king executed his unfaithful servants.*

unfamiliar [ən fə 'mɪl jɚ] *adj.* not familiar; not known; new to someone or something; not acquainted with someone or something. (Adv: *unfamiliarly.*) ♦ *The tourists were lost because they were unfamiliar with the area.* ♦ *Many Americans are unfamiliar with the metric system.*

unfashionable [ən 'fæʃ ə nə bəl] *adj.* not fashionable; not stylish. (Adv: *unfashionably.*) ♦ *The elderly man wore unfashionable clothing.* ♦ *The other children laughed at my unfashionable haircut.*

unfasten [ən 'fæ sən] **1.** *tv.* to open something by removing a fastener; to open something by loosening a fastener. ♦ *John stopped the car and unfastened his seat belt.* ♦ *Mary unfastened the buckles on her boots.* **2.** *iv.* to become loosened or opened. ♦ *My belt unfastened as I walked.* ♦ *A stage actor's clothing must unfasten easily for quick costume changes.*

unfavorable [ən 'fev ɚ ə bəl] *adj.* not favorable; adverse; harmful; not good; causing more harm than good. (Adv: *unfavorably.*) ♦ *The book sold badly after the unfavorable review was published.* ♦ *The candidate fired her advisors after the unfavorable poll results were released.*

unfazed [ən 'fezd] *adj.* not bothered or affected; not worried or upset. (Not prenominal.) ♦ *The unfazed professor continued his lecture as soon as the earthquake stopped.* ♦ *She acted unfazed when I told her, but I knew she was disturbed.*

unfeeling [ən 'fil ɪŋ] *adj.* not feeling; not kind; cruel; not having compassion; not showing compassion; without sympathy. (Adv: *unfeelingly.*) ♦ *The unfeeling man walked past the injured people on the street.* ♦ *The unfeeling critic yawned during the touching scene.*

unfinished [ən 'fɪn ɪʃt] **1.** *adj.* not complete; not done. ♦ *John has a great deal of unfinished work to do today.* ♦ *My deadline passed yesterday, and my manuscript is still unfinished.* **2.** *adj.* not polished; not smoothed. ♦ *I got a splinter from rubbing my fingers over the unfinished wood.* ♦ *The unfinished walls of the log cabin are quite rough.*

unfit [ən 'fɪt] *adj.* not fit; not appropriate; not qualified. ♦ *The insane defendant is unfit to stand trial.* ♦ *The children were removed from their unfit parents' care.*

unflagging [ən 'flæg ɪŋ] *adj.* not stopping; without weakening. (Adv: *unflaggingly.*) ♦ *With unflagging energy, Susan completed the project.* ♦ *The unflagging soldiers protected the fort from attack.*

unflinching [ən 'flɪntʃ ɪŋ] *adj.* not moving away from fear, pain, or danger. (Adv: *unflinchingly.*) ♦ *The doctor removed a bullet from the unflinching soldier's leg.* ♦ *The unflinching security guard chased the armed thief through the store.*

unfold [ən 'fold] **1.** *tv.* to spread something out; to open something that is folded. ♦ *I unfolded the new tablecloth and placed it on the table.* ♦ *Anne unfolded her napkin and* *set it on her lap.* **2.** *iv.* to develop; to become known; to be revealed. ♦ *The news story continued to unfold throughout the night.* ♦ *The movie bored me because the plot unfolded too slowly.*

unfolding [ən 'fol dɪŋ] *adj.* developing; becoming known; becoming revealed. (Adv: *unfoldingly.*) ♦ *The unfolding news story was broadcast live from the scene.* ♦ *As the unfolding plot became more clear, the story became more interesting.*

unforeseen [ən for 'sin] *adj.* not anticipated; not foreseen; not known beforehand. ♦ *Due to unforeseen circumstances, the meeting has been postponed.* ♦ *The computer program failed because of unforeseen difficulties.*

unforgettable [ən for 'gɛt ə bəl] *adj.* not forgettable; unable to be forgotten; always remembered. (Adv: *unforgettably.*) ♦ *David had an unforgettable time visiting his cousins in Mexico.* ♦ *My rough airplane flight through the storm was quite unforgettable.*

unforgivable [ən for 'gɪv ə bəl] *adj.* not forgivable; unpardonable. (Adv: *unforgivably.*) ♦ *The criminal's heinous crimes were unforgivable.* ♦ *The minister claimed that no sins were unforgivable.*

unfortunate [ən 'for tʃə nət] **1.** *adj.* not fortunate; not lucky. (Adv: *unfortunately.*) ♦ *The unfortunate victim died in the car crash.* ♦ *It's unfortunate that you have to leave so soon!* **2.** *adj.* not suitable; not appropriate; not proper. (Adv: *unfortunately.*) ♦ *Orange was an unfortunate choice for carpeting, I think.* ♦ *John made an unfortunate decision in hiring such a lazy worker.*

unfortunately [ən 'for tʃə nət li] *adv.* regrettably; sadly. ♦ *Unfortunately, the picnic has been postponed.* ♦ *Unfortunately, I didn't have as much fun as I thought I would.*

unfounded [ən 'faʊn dɪd] *adj.* without a basis; not based on facts. (Adv: *unfoundedly.*) ♦ *The journalist's accusations about the celebrity were unfounded.* ♦ *The professor rejected the student's unfounded conclusions.*

unfriendly [ən 'frɛnd li] *adj.* not friendly; hostile. (Comp: *unfriendlier;* sup: *unfriendliest.*) ♦ *We received poor service from the unfriendly waiter.* ♦ *The unfriendly clerk did not return my greeting.*

ungainly [ən 'gen li] *adj.* not graceful; awkward; clumsy. (Comp: *ungainlier;* sup: *ungainliest.*) ♦ *The ungainly teenager fell while climbing up the stairs.* ♦ *The ungainly puppy stumbled as it ran.*

ungodly [ən 'gɑd li] **1.** *adj.* not worshiping God. (Comp: *ungodlier;* sup: *ungodliest.*) ♦ *The ungodly ruler was assassinated by religious fanatics.* ♦ *The ungodly murderer begged for forgiveness.* **2.** *adj.* terrible; horrendous. (Comp: *ungodlier;* sup: *ungodliest.*) ♦ *It is so ungodly hot in here!* ♦ *Who is calling on the telephone at this ungodly hour?*

ungrateful [ən 'gret fʊl] *adj.* not grateful; not showing gratitude. (Adv: *ungratefully.*) ♦ *The ungrateful child threw my gift on the floor.* ♦ *The ungrateful worker refused the generous raise and demanded even more money.*

unguarded [ən 'gɑr dɪd] **1.** *adj.* not guarded; not protected; open to attack. ♦ *The enemy conquered the unguarded fort.* ♦ *The thief stole the unguarded jewelry.* **2.** *adj.* careless, especially in trying to keep secrets. (Adv: *unguardedly.*) ♦ *The agent foolishly spoke in a loud, unguarded voice.* ♦ *I overheard Mary's unguarded whisper.*

unhappily [ən 'hæp ə li] **1.** *adv.* sadly. ♦ *Mary listened unhappily to the bad news.* ♦ *The players on the losing team grumbled unhappily after the game.* **2.** *adv.* unfortunately [for someone]. ♦ *Unhappily, the party has been postponed for a month.* ♦ *Unhappily, the car wouldn't start.*

unhappiness [ən 'hæp i nəs] *n.* sadness; a lack of happiness. (No plural form in this sense.) ♦ *The clown tried to ease the child's unhappiness.* ♦ *Losing his job caused John much unhappiness.*

unhappy [ən 'hæp i] *adj.* sad; not happy; miserable. (Adv: *unhappily.* Comp: *unhappier;* sup: *unhappiest.*) ♦ *The unhappy child sat on the park bench and cried.* ♦ *The manager was very unhappy with Bill's poor work habits.*

unharmed [ən 'hɑrmd] **1.** *adj.* not harmed; not injured; not hurt. ♦ *The reporter interviewed the unharmed hostages.* ♦ *The unharmed soldier was thankful to be alive.* **2.** *adv.* suffering no harm. ♦ *The soldier returned unharmed.* ♦ *Few escaped from the plane crash unharmed.*

unhealthy [ən 'hɛl θi] **1.** *adj.* bad for one's health. (Adv: *unhealthily.* Comp: *unhealthier;* sup: *unhealthiest.*) ♦ *Smoking cigarettes is very unhealthy.* ♦ *John eats too many unhealthy foods.* **2.** *adj.* sick; having bad health. (Adv: *unhealthily.* Comp: *unhealthier;* sup: *unhealthiest.*) ♦ *The unhealthy student coughed loudly in class.* ♦ *The doctor tried to treat the unhealthy patient.*

unheard-of [ən 'hɚd əv] *adj.* not heard of; unknown; unprecedented. ♦ *Such vile behavior was unheard-of when I was young!* ♦ *This kind of computer was unheard-of in the 1970s.*

unhurt [ən 'hɚt] *adj.* not hurt; not injured. ♦ *The reporter interviewed some unhurt passengers from the wreck.* ♦ *The unhurt soldiers helped carry the injured ones away.*

unicorn ['ju nə korn] *n.* a mythical creature resembling a horse with a single horn on its brow. ♦ *In the fairy tale, the queen rode a unicorn to her castle.* ♦ *The unicorn's horn magically cured the sick knight.*

unidentified [ən ɑɪ 'dɛn tə fɑɪd] *adj.* not identified; unknown. ♦ *Bill filmed the unidentified flying object in the sky.* ♦ *The reporter's source was unidentified.*

unified ['ju nə fɑɪd] *adj.* brought together; made into one thing; united. ♦ *The unified colonies formed a new nation.* ♦ *The unified workers rejected the proposed contract.*

uniform ['ju nə form] **1.** *n.* the clothes that are worn by all the members of a certain group. ♦ *A nurse's uniform is typically white.* ♦ *Police officers often wear bulletproof vests under their uniforms.* **2.** *adj.* identical; alike; not varying; having no variation. (Adv: *uniformly.*) ♦ *I got lost in the subdivision because the houses were all uniform in appearance.* ♦ *Mornings, all the cars are moving at a uniform rate of speed.*

uniformity [ju nə 'form ə ti] *n.* the state of being uniform; sameness. (No plural form in this sense.) ♦ *I found the uniformity of the houses in the subdivision to be boring.* ♦ *The uniformity of the citizens' votes surprised the reporters.*

unify ['ju nə fɑɪ] **1.** *tv.* to unite something or a group; to bring many parts together to make one whole thing. ♦ *The charismatic leader unified the warring factions of his country.* ♦ *The religious leader unified many similar denominations.* **2.** *iv.* to become united; to be brought together to make one whole thing. ♦ *The colonies unified* *to form a sovereign nation.* ♦ *Dozens of rebels unified behind one leader.*

unilateral [ju nə 'læt ə rəl] *adj.* originating with only one group or thing. (Adv: *unilaterally.*) ♦ *The nation made a unilateral decision to disarm.* ♦ *The unilateral vote for sanctions was unanimous.*

unimaginative [ən ə 'mædʒ ə nə tɪv] *adj.* not imaginative; boring; bland. (Adv: *unimaginatively.*) ♦ *The unimaginative movie wasn't very exciting.* ♦ *The students yawned during the unimaginative lecture.*

unimportant [ən ɪm 'port nt] *adj.* not important; not significant; trivial. (Adv: *unimportantly.*) ♦ *My boss does not wish to be bothered with unimportant details.* ♦ *David spent a few dollars on some unimportant items at the store.*

uninformed [ən ɪn 'formd] *adj.* not informed; not having knowledge of something; unwise. ♦ *The uninformed citizen did not vote in the election.* ♦ *The owner's uninformed decision cost the company thousands of dollars.*

uninhabitable [ən ɪn 'hæb ɪ tə bəl] *adj.* [of a building or dwelling] not suitable for living in. (Adv: *uninhabitably.*) ♦ *The dilapidated building was completely uninhabitable.* ♦ *Over the years, the old house became uninhabitable.*

uninhabited [ən ɪn 'hæb ɪ tɪd] *adj.* not inhabited; not having a population. ♦ *The tiny, remote island was uninhabited by humans.* ♦ *The uninhabited building was demolished.*

uninjured [ən 'ɪn dʒɚd] *adj.* not injured; not hurt; not damaged; not harmed. ♦ *The uninjured passengers walked away from the crash.* ♦ *The soldier came out of the battle uninjured.*

uninsured [ən ɪn 'ʃʊrd] *adj.* not insured; not having insurance; without insurance. ♦ *The uninsured woman couldn't afford to see a doctor.* ♦ *The uninsured home owner lost everything in a terrible fire.*

unintelligible [ən ɪn 'tɛl ɪ dʒə bəl] *adj.* not intelligible; unable to be understood. (Adv: *unintelligibly.*) ♦ *The inspector tried to decipher the unintelligible note.* ♦ *The speaker's voice was unintelligible because he was so nervous.*

unintentional [ən ɪn 'tɛn ʃə nəl] *adj.* accidental. (Adv: *unintentionally.*) ♦ *The error was unintentional, I assure you.* ♦ *My revelation of Mary's secret was completely unintentional.*

uninterested [ən 'ɪn trɛs tɪd] *adj.* not interested; not showing an interest in someone or something; not concerned with someone or something. (See **disinterested**. Adv: *uninterestedly.*) ♦ *The uninterested students left the lecture soon after it started.* ♦ *The uninterested citizens didn't vote in the election.*

uninteresting [ən 'ɪn trɛs tɪŋ] *adj.* not interesting; not causing interest; boring. (Adv: *uninterestingly.*) ♦ *My uninteresting date didn't like to talk.* ♦ *Susan yawned during the uninteresting movie.*

uninterrupted [ən ɪn tə 'rʌp tɪd] *adj.* not interrupted; whole; complete; not having interruptions; continuous. (Adv: *uninterruptedly.*) ♦ *The cable channel featured uninterrupted movies.* ♦ *The senator's uninterrupted filibuster lasted for hours.*

union ['jun jən] **1.** *n.* joining two or more things together. (Usually singular.) ♦ *A judge presided over the union of the bride and groom.* ♦ *The union of the two companies resulted in a powerful corporation.* **2.** *n.* the bond between two or more things that are joined together. (No plural form in this sense.) ♦ *The union between the argumentative couple was fragile.* ♦ *The union among the related agencies began to weaken.* **3.** *n.* an organization whose members work together in support of a common interest; a trade union. ♦ *The workers in the textile union voted to strike.* ♦ *My mail is delivered by members of the American Postal Workers Union.* **4. the Union** *n.* the United States of America; especially the northern states during the Civil War. (No plural form in this sense. Treated as singular.) ♦ *Many southern states seceded from the Union before the Civil War.* ♦ *The Union finally won the war.* **5.** *adj.* <the adj. use of ③.> ♦ *Mary attends all the union meetings and will run for president of the union.* ♦ *The union workers approved the proposed contract.*

unionize ['jun jən ɑɪz] **1.** *tv.* to organize workers so that they form a labor union. ♦ *The labor leaders unionized the auto workers.* ♦ *The union helped to unionize laborers across the country.* **2.** *iv.* to form a labor union. ♦ *Many auto workers unionized in the 1930s.* ♦ *Management harassed the workers who wanted to unionize.*

unique [ju 'nik] **1.** *adj.* unlike anything else; having no equal; being the only one of its kind. (No comparative or superlative. Adv: *uniquely.*) ♦ *Everyone's fingerprints are unique.* ♦ *The letter was written in Anne's unique style.* **2.** *adj.* unusual; uncommon; remarkable. (In informal speech, in this sense, *more unique* and *most unique* are sometimes used. Adv: *uniquely.*) ♦ *The young author wrote a unique book about life in the city.* ♦ *The salesclerk showed me a most unique necklace.*

unisex ['jun i sɛks] *adj.* able to be used or worn by men or women; for men or women. ♦ *John and Mary waited in line for the unisex bathroom.* ♦ *Bill and Anne have the same unisex haircut.*

unison ['ju nə sən] **1. in unison** *phr.* [of musical notes, instruments, or voices] having the same pitch. ♦ *This part of the piece is performed in unison.* ♦ *The twins sang in unison.* **2. in unison** *phr.* acting as one; together and at the same time. ♦ *In unison, all of the workers voted "yes" for the new contract.* ♦ *John and his wife responded to my question in unison.*

unit ['ju nɪt] **1.** *n.* a single thing or person; one part of a group of things or people. ♦ *John owns only one unit of company stock.* ♦ *This school requires 180 units of coursework for graduation.* **2.** *n.* a group of things thought of as being one thing. ♦ *This hospital's surgical unit is regarded as the best in the state.* ♦ *Our company's sales unit is made up of fifty representatives and five district managers.* **3.** *n.* an amount of a standard measurement. ♦ *The meter is the standard metric unit for measuring distance or length.* ♦ *A pound is a standard unit for measuring weight.* **4.** *n.* an apartment within an apartment building. ♦ *The developer converted the old factory into 48 rental units.* ♦ *Mary rents a two-bedroom unit on the 12th floor of this building.*

Unitarian [ju nɪ 'tɛr i ən] **1.** *n.* someone who practices Unitarianism. ♦ *The Unitarian was actively involved in a local charity.* ♦ *Unitarians are generally liberal on social issues.* **2.** *adj.* of or about Unitarianism or ①. ♦ *Unitarians believe that God is one being.* ♦ *The Unitarian minister leads two services each Sunday.*

Unitarianism [ju nɪ 'tɛr i ən ɪs əm] *n.* a religion that asserts that God is one being. (No plural form in this sense.) ♦ *Anne left the Baptist church and converted to Unitarianism.* ♦ *Bill discussed the differences between Unitarianism and other religions.*

unite [ju 'nɑɪt] **1.** *tv.* to join two or more things together; to bring two or more things together. ♦ *Many Slavic groups had been united under the former Yugoslavia.* ♦ *The bride and groom were united in holy matrimony.* **2.** *iv.* to join together; to come together. ♦ *The two armies united to combat their common enemy.* ♦ *The two schools united to form one large one.*

united [ju 'nɑɪt ɪd] *adj.* brought together; joined together, especially because of a common purpose. (Adv: *unitedly.*) ♦ *The United Mine Workers of America was founded in 1890.* ♦ *The angry students presented a united front to the school administration.*

United Kingdom [ju 'nɑɪ tɪd 'kɪŋ dəm] See Gazetteer.

United Nations [ju 'nɑɪt ɪd 'ne ʃənz] **1.** *n.* an international organization formed in 1945 to promote world peace. (Abbreviated *UN* or *U.N.* Treated as singular.) ♦ *The United Nations is headquartered in New York City.* ♦ *The United Nations tries to mediate conflicts around the world.* **2.** *adj.* <the adj. use of ①.> ♦ *We planned to visit the U.N. headquarters in New York City.* ♦ *A small United Nations army tried to stop the fighting in Liberia.*

United States (of America) [ju 'nɑɪt əd 'stets (əv ə 'mɛr ɪ kə)] See Gazetteer.

unity ['ju nə ti] *n.* the condition of being together; the condition of being united. (No plural form in this sense.) ♦ *The mediator tried to bring unity to the divided groups.* ♦ *All the rebel groups sought unity with each other.*

universal [ju nə 'vɚ səl] **1.** *adj.* shared by every member of a group; of or about everyone; understood by everyone. (Adv: *universally.*) ♦ *Food and clothing are universal human needs.* ♦ *The desire to be wanted is universal.* **2.** *n.* a concept that is ①. ♦ *The linguist studied universals in language for many years.* ♦ *A universal similar to the golden rule exists in almost every religion.*

universe ['ju nə vɚs] *n.* everything that exists in space; all of space and everything that exists in it. ♦ *The astronomer mapped the different galaxies in the universe.* ♦ *Our solar system is just one very small part of the universe.*

university [ju nə 'vɚ sə ti] *n.* a school for higher education, usually consisting of one or more colleges for undergraduates and usually one or more schools for graduate students. ♦ *The undergraduate studies at the College of Arts and Sciences at the university.* ♦ *More than 8,000 students attend the local university.*

unjust [ən 'dʒʌst] *adj.* not just; not fair; not right. (Adv: *unjustly.*) ♦ *The protesters felt that the death penalty was unjust.* ♦ *The defendant appealed the unjust ruling.*

unjustly [ən 'dʒʌst li] *adv.* unfairly; in an unjust way. ♦ *The innocent defendant was unjustly sentenced to prison.* ♦ *Mary was unjustly fired for something she didn't do.*

unkempt [ən 'kɛmpt] *adj.* not clean or tidy; not properly groomed; messy; not cared for. (Used especially of one's hair or appearance. Adv: *unkemptly.*) ♦ *I discovered that the unkempt man at the train station was homeless.* ♦ *Please comb your unkempt hair.*

unkind [ən 'kɑɪnd] *adj.* not kind; mean; not compassionate. (Adv: *unkindly.* Comp: *unkinder;* sup: *unkindest.*) ♦ *Your insults were most unkind.* ♦ *Bill apologized for his unkind behavior.*

unknowing [ən 'no ɪŋ] *adj.* without knowing; without being aware; not having knowledge of something. (Prenominal only. Adv: *unknowingly.*) ♦ *Mary was the unknowing cause of the confusion at the bank.* ♦ *The taxi driver was an unknowing accomplice in the crime, because he drove the robbers away without realizing they had just robbed the store.*

unknown [ən 'non] **1.** *adj.* not known; not familiar. ♦ *I drove carefully down the unknown road.* ♦ *The actual number of stars in the universe is unknown.* **2.** *adj.* not famous; not recognized. ♦ *The article was written by an unknown author.* ♦ *The independent film featured unknown actors.* **3.** *n.* someone who is not known; something that is not known. ♦ *There are too many unknowns in this problem to make it easy to solve.* ♦ *The incumbent politician was beaten by an unknown.*

unlace [ən 'les] *tv.* to undo the laces of something; to loosen the laces of something. ♦ *Mary unlaced her shoes and slipped them off her feet.* ♦ *The actress unlaced her corset after the play.*

unlatched [ən 'lætʃt] *adj.* not latched; not locked. ♦ *The thief entered the house through an unlatched door.* ♦ *The dog escaped the yard through the unlatched gate.*

unlawful [ən 'lɔ fʊl] *adj.* not lawful; not legal; illegal; against the law. (Adv: *unlawfully.*) ♦ *Selling alcohol to minors is unlawful.* ♦ *Smoking in public buildings is unlawful in some cities.*

unleash [ən 'liʃ] **1.** *tv.* to let an animal off a leash. ♦ *Bob unleashed his dog so it could run around the park.* ♦ *When the puppy was unleashed, it ran toward the road.* **2.** *tv.* to set something free by removing a leash or as though removing a leash. (Figurative on ①.) ♦ *The violent winds unleashed their fury on the coastal town.* ♦ *David unleashed his anger by yelling at his dog.*

unless [ən 'lɛs] *conj.* except under the circumstances that.... (Takes a clause.) ♦ *Unless you pay me the money you owe me, I will sue you.* ♦ *I'm going to quit my job unless you give me a raise.*

unlettered [ən 'lɛt ɚd] *adj.* illiterate; not having learned to read or write; insufficiently educated. ♦ *The cowboy, though unlettered, managed to read the note.* ♦ *How can the government expect unlettered people to understand the tax forms?*

unlike [ən 'lɑɪk] **1.** *adj.* not like someone or something else; not similar; different. ♦ *Mary and her sister have unlike personalities.* ♦ *Our cars are unlike, but we have the same taste in clothes.* **2.** *prep.* not similar to someone or something; different from someone or something. ♦ *Bob's new car is quite unlike the one he used to own.* ♦ *Unlike her tall sisters, Sue is of average height.* **3.** *prep.* not characteristic or typical of someone or something. ♦ *It is unlike Jane to be so late. She is usually early.* ♦ *This wild behavior is quite unlike Bob. He's usually a very quiet person.*

unlikely [ən 'lɑɪk li] *adv.* improbable; not likely; likely to fail; not likely to succeed. ♦ *John is the most unlikely prospect for the job.* ♦ *Who is the candidate who is unlikely to lose?*

unlimited [ən 'lɪm ə tɪd] *adj.* not limited; without limits; not restricted. (Adv: *unlimitedly.*) ♦ *The film studio gave the gifted director an unlimited budget.* ♦ *I wished the newlyweds unlimited happiness.*

unlisted [ən 'lɪs tɪd] *adj.* not appearing on a list; [of a telephone number] not available to the public. ♦ *Mary requested an unlisted telephone number.* ♦ *How did you get my unlisted number?*

unlit [ən 'lɪt] **1.** *adj.* [of something that can burn] not yet set afire. (See lit.) ♦ *The camper only had one remaining unlit match.* ♦ *The fire is unlit, and I will start it just before the guests arrive.* **2.** *adj.* [of an electric lamp] not turned on. ♦ *The bulb remained unlit because the lamp was not plugged in.* ♦ *The office lighting remained unlit throughout the sunny day.*

unload [ən 'lod] **1.** *tv.* to remove a load from someone or something. ♦ *The workers unloaded the cargo from the ship.* ♦ *I unloaded the groceries from my car.* **2.** *tv.* to remove the ammunition from a gun. ♦ *Mary unloaded the ammunition from her gun before storing it.* ♦ *The police officer unloaded the remaining three bullets.* **3.** *tv.* to empty a gun of its ammunition. ♦ *The hunter unloaded his rifle when he was finished hunting.* ♦ *John unloaded his handgun and locked it in the safe.* **4.** *tv.* to remove the film from a camera. ♦ *I unloaded one roll of film and replaced it with a new one.* ♦ *The tourist unloaded the film from his camera.* **5.** *tv.* to empty a camera of its film. ♦ *The model waited while the photographer unloaded his camera.* ♦ *Don't expose the film to light when you unload your camera.*

unlock [ən 'lɑk] *tv.* to open a lock. ♦ *Mary unlocked the door and went into the room.* ♦ *Susan unlocked the safe and removed her valuables.*

unlocked [ən 'lɑkt] *adj.* not locked; not fastened with a lock. ♦ *The thief entered the building through an unlocked door.* ♦ *The radio was stolen from the unlocked car.*

unlucky [ən 'lʌk i] **1.** *adj.* not lucky; not having good luck; unfortunate. (Adv: *unluckily.* Comp: *unluckier;* sup: *unluckiest.*) ♦ *The unlucky man lost his job.* ♦ *The unlucky gambler lost $1,000.* **2.** *adj.* causing bad luck; causing misfortune. (Adv: *unluckily.* Comp: *unluckier;* sup: *unluckiest.*) ♦ *Many people think that 13 is an unlucky number.* ♦ *Some actors consider it unlucky to whistle backstage.*

unmarried [ən 'mɛr id] *adj.* not married; single. ♦ *The unmarried woman often went out on dates.* ♦ *Bill remained unmarried until he was nearly fifty.*

unmask [ən 'mæsk] **1.** *tv.* to remove a mask or other disguise from someone. ♦ *The police officer apprehended the bank robber and unmasked him.* ♦ *I didn't recognize my friend at the costume party until she unmasked herself.* **2.** *tv.* to reveal someone or something; to expose someone or something. (Figurative on ①.) ♦ *The inspector unmasked the killer, and we all learned who had committed the crime.* ♦ *At the meeting, the sales manager unmasked the plans for the new campaign.*

unmentionable [ən 'mɛn ʃə nə bəl] *adj.* not able to be mentioned; not mentionable, especially because it would not be polite to do so. (Adv: *unmentionably.*) ♦ *You should keep that unmentionable gossip to yourself.* ♦ *David just got a tattoo in an unmentionable place.*

unmistakable [ən mɪ 'stek ə bəl] *adj.* not able to be mistaken; able to be recognized easily. (Adv: *unmistakably.*) ♦ *The manager's role in the fraudulent scheme was unmistakable.* ♦ *The smell of smoke in the air is unmistakable.*

unmovable [ən 'muv ə bəl] **1.** *adj.* [of something] not subject to being moved. (Adv: *unmovably.*) ♦ *A tunnel was dug through the unmovable mountain.* ♦ *The large boulder was unmovable, so the farmer plowed around it.* **2.** *adj.* [of someone] firm and stubborn. (Figurative on ①. Adv: *unmovably.*) ♦ *Anne is unmovable once she's made up her mind.* ♦ *The unmovable professor refused to accept late homework.*

unmoved [ən 'muvd] **1.** *adj.* not sympathetic; not moved with emotion or pity. ♦ *The bitter critic remained unmoved by the tragic movie.* ♦ *The selfish miser was unmoved by the refugee's plight.* **2.** *adj.* not worried; not upset; not touched by emotion. ♦ *Anne was unmoved by the news of the plane crash.* ♦ *We are unmoved about the crime that we read about until someone we know is harmed.*

unnamed [ən 'nemd] **1.** *adj.* not having a name. ♦ *The streets in the new subdivision are still unnamed.* ♦ *An unnamed person sent a letter of complaint to the police.* **2.** *adj.* anonymous; not having a name that is known; not mentioned by name. ♦ *The reporter received information from an unnamed source.* ♦ *This beautiful poem was written by an unnamed poet.*

unnatural [ən 'nætʃ ə rəl] **1.** *adj.* strange; odd; unusual. (Adv: *unnaturally.*) ♦ *The meteor created an unnatural glow.* ♦ *Bob dyed his hair an unnatural shade of red.* **2.** *adj.* against the laws of nature or society; abnormal. (Adv: *unnaturally.*) ♦ *The criminal was accused of having unnatural lust.* ♦ *Cannibalism is considered unnatural among primates.*

unnecessary [ən 'nɛs ɪ sɛr i] *adj.* not necessary; not needed; not essential; extra; beyond what is needed. (Adv: *unnecessarily.*) ♦ *The hockey player was penalized for unnecessary roughness.* ♦ *Your rude insults were quite unnecessary.*

unnoticed [ən 'not əst] **1.** *adj.* not noticed; not seen; not having received attention; not observed. ♦ *An unnoticed thief left the room with John's wallet.* ♦ *The unnoticed traffic sign was moved to a location where it could easily be seen.* **2.** *adv.* not noticed; unobserved. ♦ *The fact that the computer had been stolen went unnoticed until someone needed it.* ♦ *The thief left the room unnoticed.*

unobserved [ən əb 'zɚvd] **1.** *adj.* not seen; not observed. ♦ *The unobserved missile destroyed its target.* ♦ *An unobserved thief seems to have stolen my purse from the counter.* **2.** *adv.* not seen. ♦ *I slipped into the room unobserved and removed my things.* ♦ *We left early, unobserved.*

unobtainable [ən əb 'ten ə bəl] *adj.* not able to be obtained; not obtainable. (Adv: *unobtainably.*) ♦ *Bill will never reach the unobtainable goals he has set for himself.* ♦ *Victory was unobtainable for the untalented athlete.*

unobtrusive [ən əb 'tru sɪv] *adj.* not obtrusive; inconspicuous; able to be present without being in the way. (Adv: *unobtrusively.*) ♦ *The shoplifter had been filmed by an unobtrusive security camera.* ♦ *The celebrity's unobtrusive secretary sat quietly during the interview.*

unoccupied [ən 'ɑk jə pɑɪd] *adj.* not occupied; empty; vacant. ♦ *Mary entered the unoccupied bathroom and* *locked the door.* ♦ *Susan showed a prospective tenant an unoccupied apartment.*

unofficial [ən ə 'fɪʃ əl] *adj.* not official; not officially confirmed or authorized. (Adv: *unofficially.*) ♦ *The TV network reported unofficial election returns.* ♦ *There was an unofficial report of a tornado in the next county.*

unopened [ən 'op ənd] *adj.* not opened; still closed or shut. ♦ *I handed my roommate her unopened mail.* ♦ *The unopened window was stuck.*

unorganized [ən 'or gə nɑɪzd] **1.** *adj.* not organized; lacking organization. ♦ *John couldn't find the memo in his unorganized files.* ♦ *The unorganized office really needed someone to organize it.* **2.** *adj.* not part of a labor union. ♦ *The unorganized workers were paid poorly.* ♦ *The unorganized employees decided to form a union.*

unpack [ən 'pæk] **1.** *tv.* to remove objects that have been packed; to remove objects that are in a box or suitcase. ♦ *Mary unpacked her luggage when she arrived at her hotel room.* ♦ *Anne unpacked the glasses from the crate.* **2.** *iv.* to remove objects that have been packed. ♦ *Upon returning from vacation, Anne unpacked and then took a nap.* ♦ *Bill unpacked as soon as he arrived at the hotel.*

unpaid [ən 'ped] **1.** *adj.* [of something] not paid [for]. ♦ *My bills have been unpaid for a month because I'm broke.* ♦ *I put the unpaid phone bill on my roommate's desk.* **2.** *adj.* [of someone] not having been paid wages due. ♦ *The unpaid office staff threatened to quit.* ♦ *The unpaid workers were angry with their boss.*

unparalleled [ən 'pɛr ə lɛld] *adj.* not paralleled; not equaled; without equal; superior. ♦ *Such a daring feat is unparalleled in history!* ♦ *The gourmet meal was unparalleled by any I had ever tasted.*

unpaved [ən 'pevd] *adj.* not paved. ♦ *When I drive on unpaved roads, my car gets dirty.* ♦ *The unpaved parking lot was muddy.*

unpleasant [ən 'plɛz ənt] *adj.* not pleasant; not pleasing; not nice; not enjoyable. (Adv: *unpleasantly.*) ♦ *There's an unpleasant odor coming from the refrigerator.* ♦ *My vacation was unpleasant because the weather was bad.*

unplug [ən 'plʌg] **1.** *tv.* to disconnect an appliance or machine by taking the plug out of its receptacle. ♦ *Jane unplugged the toaster when she finished using it.* ♦ *Susan unplugged her computer during the lightning storm.* **2.** *tv.* to remove the plug or stopper from a sink drain. ♦ *Unplug it so the water will flow out.* ♦ *I unplugged the sink and let the water drain from it.*

unplugged [ən 'plʌgd] *adj.* not plugged in; not connected to an electrical outlet. ♦ *The TV isn't working because it's unplugged.* ♦ *The unplugged computer still operated on batteries.*

unpopular [ən 'pɑp jə lɚ] *adj.* not popular; not preferred by many people. (Adv: *unpopularly.*) ♦ *The unpopular student was shunned by his classmates.* ♦ *The unpopular television show was soon canceled.*

unprecedented [ən 'prɛs ə dɛn tɪd] *adj.* not precedented; without precedent; not having happened before. (Adv: *unprecedentedly.*) ♦ *An unprecedented number of people voted in the important election.* ♦ *Such extremely cold weather is unprecedented in this century.*

unpredictable [ən prɪ 'dɪk tə bəl] *adj.* not able to be predicted; not predictable; uncertain; not able to tell how something will end. (Adv: *unpredictably.*) ♦ *Bill is so unpredictable that I never know what he's going to do.* ♦ *The exact path a tornado will take is unpredictable.*

unprepared [ən prɪ 'pɛrd] *adj.* [of someone] not prepared or ready. (Adv: *unpreparedly.*) ♦ *The unprepared student did poorly on the test.* ♦ *We are unprepared for such cold weather.*

unprincipled [ən 'prɪns ə pəld] *adj.* not having principles; without principles; not moral. ♦ *The unprincipled senator accepted the bribe.* ♦ *A few unprincipled youths tormented the dog.*

unprofessional [ən prə 'fɛʃ ə nəl] *adj.* not behaving in a professional way; contrary to the rules of a profession. (Adv: *unprofessionally.*) ♦ *The unprofessional lawyer was sued for malpractice.* ♦ *It is unprofessional to treat a customer rudely.*

unprofitable [ən 'prɑf ɪ tə bəl] *adj.* not making a profit; not profitable; losing money; not making money. (Adv: *unprofitably.*) ♦ *The owner sold his unprofitable business.* ♦ *The theater closed the unprofitable play three weeks early.*

unprotected [ən prə 'tɛk tɪd] **1.** *adj.* open to attack. ♦ *The unprotected fort was overtaken by the enemy.* ♦ *The soldiers easily took control of the unprotected island.* **2.** *adj.* not provided with a protective coating, covering, paint, shelter, etc. ♦ *Unprotected wood will warp.* ♦ *We were standing in an unprotected area, out in the rain.*

unpublished [ən 'pʌb lɪʃt] **1.** *adj.* not published; not appearing in print. ♦ *John kept his unpublished manuscript in his desk.* ♦ *Mary owns an unpublished cartoon drawn by her favorite cartoonist.* **2.** *adj.* not yet having any of one's writings appear in print; without any publications of one's own. ♦ *The unpublished professor was denied tenure.* ♦ *The unpublished author worked as a waiter to earn money.*

unpunished [ən 'pʌn ɪʃt] **1.** *adj.* not punished. ♦ *The unpunished criminal continued to commit more crimes.* ♦ *The unpunished troublemaker became more of a bully.* **2.** *adv.* without punishment. ♦ *The terrible crime went unpunished.* ♦ *The serial murderer died unpunished for his crimes.*

unqualified [ən 'kwɑl ə fɑɪd] **1.** *adj.* not qualified; not having the necessary skill or knowledge to do something. ♦ *We did not hire the unqualified applicants.* ♦ *The unqualified athletes were cut from the team.* **2.** *adj.* not restricted; not limited. (Adv: *unqualifiedly.*) ♦ *My professor gave an unqualified recommendation that I be hired.* ♦ *The skilled director's movie was an unqualified success.*

unquestionable [ən 'kwɛs tʃə nə bəl] *adj.* certain; sure. (Adv: *unquestionably.*) ♦ *My grandmother is a woman of unquestionable taste.* ♦ *I testified that David's morals were unquestionable.*

unravel [ən 'ræv əl] **1.** *tv.* to pull something apart by its threads; to separate the threads of something. ♦ *Anne unraveled the old sweater because she needed the yarn.* ♦ *Bill unraveled the wire and used the individual strands.* **2.** *tv.* to solve something; to figure something out. ♦ *The brilliant detective unraveled the complex crime.* ♦ *The student unraveled the solution to the difficult math problem.* **3.** *iv.* [for threads] to separate or be pulled apart. ♦ *My sweater began to unravel when it became caught on a hook.* ♦ *My knitted sock unraveled as my cat tugged on it.* **4.** *iv.* to become clear; to be solved. (Figurative on ③.) ♦ *The* *crime unraveled when a witness spoke to the inspector.* ♦ *The mystery began to unravel as the detective found more clues.* **5.** *iv.* [for the elements of a plan or scheme] to become uncoordinated and cause failure. (Figurative on ③.) ♦ *The conference schedule unraveled because the first speaker was late.* ♦ *The project unraveled as the volunteers quit working on it.*

unreal [ən 'ril] *adj.* not real; incredible; unbelievable. ♦ *The view from the top of the tower seemed unreal.* ♦ *Everything seemed unreal to Bill, as though he were dreaming.*

unrealistic [ən ri ə 'lɪs tɪk] **1.** *adj.* not seeming real; seeming fake; not realistic. (Adv: *unrealistically* [...ɪk li].) ♦ *The cheap movie's special effects were very unrealistic.* ♦ *Jane's unrealistic hair was actually a wig.* **2.** *adj.* not practical. (Adv: *unrealistically* [...ɪk li].) ♦ *Because John's goals are unrealistic, he never attains them.* ♦ *My boss expects me to finish an unrealistic amount of work before I leave today.*

unreasonable [ən 'ri zə nə bəl] **1.** *adj.* not reasonable; not sensible; irrational. (Adv: *unreasonably.*) ♦ *John was being unreasonable and refused to discuss the matter.* ♦ *The unreasonable clerk refused to accept my $20 bill.* **2.** *adj.* too much; excessive. (Adv: *unreasonably.*) ♦ *Jimmy wasn't allowed to watch movies with an unreasonable amount of violence.* ♦ *I waited an unreasonable amount of time for the delayed flight.*

unrelated [ən ri 'let ɪd] **1.** *adj.* not related; not of or about something else. (Adv: *unrelatedly.*) ♦ *The speaker refused to answer questions unrelated to the topic.* ♦ *Two banks were robbed today, but the events were unrelated.* **2.** *adj.* not related; not part of one's family. ♦ *Bob and John look like brothers, but they're actually unrelated.* ♦ *Anne and I were unrelated until our siblings married each other.*

unreliable [ən ri 'lɑɪ ə bəl] *adj.* not reliable; not able to be relied on; not dependable. (Adv: *unreliably.*) ♦ *The unreliable employee was not trusted with important tasks.* ♦ *The mayor complained about the city's unreliable mail service.*

unremitting [ən ri 'mɪt ɪŋ] *adj.* not stopping; continual; constant. (Adv: *unremittingly.*) ♦ *The unremitting rain ruined our picnic.* ♦ *The politician was subjected to unremitting criticism during the scandal.*

unrest [ən 'rɛst] **1.** *n.* an unsatisfied or dissatisfied feeling. (No plural form in this sense.) ♦ *The nervous man paced the hallway in a state of unrest.* ♦ *Susan suffered considerable unrest when I told her the disturbing news.* **2.** *n.* rebellion. (No plural form in this sense.) ♦ *The army put an end to the unrest.* ♦ *The leader's irresponsible rule caused unrest among the people.*

unroll [ən 'rol] **1.** *tv.* to spread something out that had been rolled up; to cause something no longer to be rolled. ♦ *The scribe unrolled the scroll and read the message aloud.* ♦ *The campers unrolled their sleeping bags in the tent.* **2.** *iv.* to spread out after having been rolled up; to become no longer rolled. ♦ *Susan's posters unrolled when she removed them from the tube.* ♦ *The ball of yarn unrolled as the kitten played with it.*

unruliness [ən 'rul i nəs] *n.* being unruly; bad behavior. (No plural form in this sense.) ♦ *The teacher would not tolerate unruliness in her classroom.* ♦ *The children were punished for their unruliness at the store.*

unruly [ən 'ru li] **1.** *adj.* badly behaved; not obedient; not paying attention to authority. ♦ *The clerk warned the unruly children to behave in the store.* ♦ *The unruly students were sent to the principal's office.* **2.** *adj.* [of hair] not orderly; hard to control. ♦ *I use hair spray to keep my unruly hair in place.* ♦ *John brushed his unruly hair out of his eyes.*

unsafe [ən 'sef] *adj.* not safe from danger; providing risk. (Adv: *unsafely.*) ♦ *I would never walk through that unsafe neighborhood at night.* ♦ *The unsafe driver drove into a ditch.*

unsatisfactory [ən sæt ɪs 'fæk tə ri] *adj.* not satisfactory; not good enough; not sufficient. (Adv: *unsatisfactorily.*) ♦ *I complained about the unsatisfactory service I had received.* ♦ *This food is unsatisfactory. Please return it to the kitchen.*

unscientific [ən sɑɪ ən 'tɪf ɪk] *adj.* not scientific; not using principles of science. (Adv: *unscientifically* [...ɪk li].) ♦ *The researchers ridiculed the unscientific theory.* ♦ *Your experiment was unscientific, so your conclusions are invalid.*

unscrew [ən 'skru] **1.** *tv.* to remove something, such as a screw or a lid, by turning it. ♦ *I unscrewed the burned-out light bulb and replaced it.* ♦ *Anne unscrewed the cap on the tube of toothpaste.* **2.** *iv.* [for a screw, lid, bolt, etc.] to rotate and become loose. ♦ *The loose bolt unscrewed because of the vibrations.* ♦ *The safety lid unscrews only if you push down on it.*

unscrupulous [ən 'skrup jə ləs] *adj.* not scrupulous; not worried about what is right and wrong. (Adv: *unscrupulously.*) ♦ *The unscrupulous lawyer goes to accident scenes to find prospective clients.* ♦ *The unscrupulous student cheated on the test.*

unseasonable [ən 'si zə nə bəl] *adj.* not typical of a season; not usually associated with a certain season. (Adv: *unseasonably.*) ♦ *We had some unseasonable snow last May.* ♦ *This warm weather is unseasonable for December.*

unseen [ən 'sin] *adj.* not seen; hidden; out of sight. ♦ *The unseen stagehands prepared the next set backstage.* ♦ *The puppets were manipulated by unseen people.*

unselfish [ən 'sɛl fɪʃ] *adj.* not selfish; generous. (Adv: *unselfishly.*) ♦ *The unselfish woman donated her time to a worthy charity.* ♦ *The unselfish man paid for his cousin's college tuition.*

unsettled [ən 'sɛt əld] **1.** *adj.* not populated; not having a population; empty of people. ♦ *The pioneers crossed the unsettled land.* ♦ *The rancher moved to an unsettled area of the state.* **2.** *adj.* disturbed; upset. ♦ *The children became unsettled by the loud thunder.* ♦ *Having guests in the house unsettled our cats.*

unshaken [ən 'ʃek ən] *adj.* not affected by misfortune, especially not emotionally upset or made to lose confidence. (See shaken ②. Adv: *unshakenly.*) ♦ *The wise investor remained unshaken after the stock-market crash.* ♦ *The strong villagers remained unshaken by tragedy.*

unshaven [ən 'ʃev ən] *adj.* not shaven; having hair or stubble. ♦ *Bill's unshaven face was rough to the touch.* ♦ *The unshaven applicant looked messy and unkempt.*

unsightly [ən 'sɑɪt li] *adj.* not pleasant to look at; disgusting in appearance. (Comp: *unsightlier;* sup: *unsightliest.*) ♦ *I couldn't clean the unsightly stain from the* *carpet.* ♦ *The doctor removed the unsightly mole from my nose.*

unskilled [ən 'skɪld] **1.** *adj.* not skilled; not trained. ♦ *The unskilled high-school graduate couldn't find a job.* ♦ *The unskilled apprentice slowly learned the trade.* **2.** *adj.* not requiring skill. ♦ *Unskilled work usually doesn't pay very well.* ♦ *The untrained worker looked for an unskilled job.*

unsold [ən 'sold] *adj.* not sold. ♦ *The haunted house remained unsold for years.* ♦ *The manager placed the unsold inventory on sale.*

unsolicited [ən sə 'lɪs ɪ tɪd] *adj.* not solicited; not asked for; given without having been asked for. (Adv: *unsolicitedly.*) ♦ *I ignored John's unsolicited advice.* ♦ *The charity was happy to receive the unsolicited donation.*

unsophisticated [ən sə 'fɪs tɪ ket ɪd] **1.** *adj.* not sophisticated; not complex; simple. (Adv: *unsophisticatedly.*) ♦ *Her approach to teaching math was unsophisticated and refreshingly simple.* ♦ *The client rejected the architect's unsophisticated designs.* **2.** *adj.* not sophisticated; not experienced; innocent; naive. (Adv: *unsophisticatedly.*) ♦ *The thief took advantage of the unsophisticated tourist.* ♦ *The unsophisticated student was frightened by the big city.*

unsound [ən 'saʊnd] **1.** *adj.* not providing support; not in good condition; likely to break. (Adv: *unsoundly.*) ♦ *Don't place more books on that shelf because it's unsound.* ♦ *The structurally unsound building was demolished.* **2.** *adj.* not valid; not based in fact. (Adv: *unsoundly.*) ♦ *The scientist's unsound theory was disproved.* ♦ *The researcher rejected the unsound data.*

unspeakable [ən 'spik ə bəl] *adj.* too horrible or disgusting to speak about; unable to be stated in words. (Adv: *unspeakably.*) ♦ *The jury was shocked by the unspeakable crime.* ♦ *The gory movie featured unspeakable acts of torture.*

unstable [ən 'ste bəl] **1.** *adj.* not stable; likely to fall apart; likely to break. (Adv: *unstably.*) ♦ *The unstable building was destroyed by the earthquake.* ♦ *The unstable shelf collapsed under the weight of the books.* **2.** *adj.* not secure; not having proper balance. (Adv: *unstably.*) ♦ *The table was unstable and wobbled whenever anyone touched it.* ♦ *The unstable chair fell over when I tried to sit down.* **3.** *adj.* not steady; likely to change. (Adv: *unstably.*) ♦ *The unstable radioactive element decayed rapidly.* ♦ *The unstable stock market made the investor very nervous.* **4.** *adj.* [of someone] distraught or insane. (Adv: *unstably.*) ♦ *Whoever committed this crime was very unstable!* ♦ *The unstable accountant stole thousands of dollars.*

unsteadily [ən 'stɛd ɪ li] *adv.* in an unsteady way. ♦ *I walked unsteadily on the icy sidewalk.* ♦ *The nervous witness gazed unsteadily at the accused person.*

unsteady [ən 'stɛd i] **1.** *adj.* shaky; not secure. (Adv: *unsteadily.*) ♦ *The unsteady ladder wobbled as I climbed up it.* ♦ *When I leaned on the unsteady desk, it collapsed.* **2.** *adj.* not dependable; likely to change. (Adv: *unsteadily.*) ♦ *The flow of water from the spring is unsteady, and sometimes there is not enough for our needs.* ♦ *The unsteady inflation rate worried the economists.*

unstoppable [ən 'stɑp ə bəl] *adj.* not able to be stopped; not able to be defeated. (Adv: *unstoppably.*) ♦ *The unstoppable baseball team won the World Series.* ♦ *A huge, unstoppable meteorite hurtled toward the earth.*

unstructured [ən 'strʌk tʃɚd] *adj.* not structured; not having a structure; not formally organized; having only a loose organization. (Adv: *unstructuredly.*) ♦ *Recess is usually unstructured play time for students.* ♦ *The unstructured office was highly inefficient.*

unstuck [ən 'stʌk] *adj.* no longer stuck. ♦ *The picture became unstuck and fell from its mounting.* ♦ *The stamp became unstuck and fell off the envelope.*

unsuccessful [ən sək 'sɛs fʊl] *adj.* not successful; without success. (Adv: *unsuccessfully.*) ♦ *The unsuccessful business owner filed for bankruptcy.* ♦ *After his unsuccessful campaign, David retired from politics.*

unsuitable [ən 'sut ə bəl] *adj.* not suitable; not appropriate; not proper. (Adv: *unsuitably.*) ♦ *This violent movie is unsuitable for younger children.* ♦ *The small hotel room was unsuitable for the foreign dignitary.*

unsure [ən 'ʃʊr] *adj.* not sure; not certain. (Adv: *unsurely.*) ♦ *I was unsure whether I'd locked my front door or not.* ♦ *The driver was unsure whether to turn right or left.*

unsuspecting [ən sə 'spɛk tɪŋ] *adj.* not suspecting; not suspicious; trusting; not aware that something is happening or about to happen. (Adv: *unsuspectingly.*) ♦ *The unsuspecting tourist fell prey to the crook.* ♦ *The unsuspecting man's wallet had been stolen on the train.*

unsympathetic [ən sɪm pə 'θɛt ɪk] *adj.* not having sympathy; without sympathy. (Adv: *unsympathetically* [...ɪk li].) ♦ *The unsympathetic woman walked by the beggar.* ♦ *The judge was unsympathetic to the criminal's excuses.*

untangle [ən 'tæŋ gəl] **1.** *tv.* to remove the tangles from something; to cause something that is tangled to be tangled no longer. ♦ *This conditioner will help untangle your hair.* ♦ *Anne untangled the string of Christmas lights.* **2.** *iv.* to become untangled; to become free of tangles. ♦ *My hair untangled when I applied the conditioner to it.* ♦ *The strings of Christmas lights untangled as I pulled them from the box.*

untapped [ən 'tæpt] *adj.* not made use of; yet unused. ♦ *The untapped natural resources in the wilderness were worth billions.* ♦ *My therapist helped me discover my untapped talents.*

unthankful [ən 'θæŋk fʊl] **1.** *adj.* not thankful; not grateful. (Adv: *unthankfully.*) ♦ *The child, angry and unthankful, threw my gift across the room.* ♦ *Bill was unthankful for our advice because he thought we were wrong.* **2.** *adj.* not appreciated; without thanks. (Adv: *unthankfully.*) ♦ *John had the unthankful task of washing the dishes.* ♦ *After working 35 years at an unthankful job, Anne was glad to retire.*

unthinkable [ən 'θɪŋk ə bəl] *adj.* not possible; out of the question. (Adv: *unthinkably.*) ♦ *In the 1800s, travel to the moon was unthinkable.* ♦ *Leaving before 5:00 is unthinkable at my office.*

untidy [ən 'tɑɪ di] *adj.* not tidy; not clean; messy. (Adv: *untidily.* Comp: *untidier;* sup: *untidiest.*) ♦ *I want you to clean your untidy room before dinner.* ♦ *John hired someone to clean his untidy apartment.*

untie [ən 'tɑɪ] **1.** *tv.* to loosen something that is tied; to undo something that is tied. (The present participle is untying.) ♦ *Mary untied her shoelaces and took her shoes off.* ♦ *Anne untied the string around the package.* **2.** *iv.* to become untied. (The present participle is untying.) ♦ *I tripped when my shoelaces untied.* ♦ *The knot untied because it was loose.*

until [ən 'tɪl] **1.** *prep.* up to a certain time; during a period of time up to a certain time. (See also till.) ♦ *The children sang songs until 4:00.* ♦ *These items will be on sale until next week.* **2.** *conj.* up to a certain time or at a time when a condition has been met. (Takes a clause.) ♦ *The children sang songs until it was time to go home.* ♦ *I had fun on my vacation until I became sick.* **3.** *conj.* before. (Used with a negative construction in the main clause.) ♦ *I didn't know happiness until I met you.* ♦ *John couldn't see well until he got glasses.*

untimely [ən 'taɪm li] **1.** *adj.* not timely; happening too soon; happening too early. ♦ *I mourned my young friend's untimely death.* ♦ *The actor's untimely entrance caused the audience to laugh.* **2.** *adj.* not suitable; not appropriate; at the wrong time. ♦ *Bill's untimely outburst made him look foolish.* ♦ *Because the company was losing money, Jane's request for a raise was untimely.*

unto ['ʌn tu] *prep.* to. (Literary.) ♦ *The worshipers offered their prayers unto the Lord.* ♦ *Splendid gifts were given unto the queen.*

untold [ən 'told] **1.** *adj.* not told; not expressed; not revealed. ♦ *The sealed envelope contained the untold truth.* ♦ *The reporter searched for the untold story about the scandal.* **2.** *adj.* countless; too great to be counted; innumerable. ♦ *The millionaire had made untold riches from selling oil.* ♦ *The pirates buried untold treasures on several islands.*

untouched [ən 'tʌtʃt] *adj.* not touched. ♦ *The remote wilderness remained untouched by human hands.* ♦ *The old manuscript must remain untouched, or it will crumble.*

untrained [ən 'trend] *adj.* not trained. ♦ *Mary took her untrained dog to obedience school.* ♦ *The untrained worker couldn't operate the machine.*

untranslatable [ən træns 'let ə bəl] *adj.* not able to be translated; not translatable. (Adv: *untranslatably.*) ♦ *A linguist studied the ancient, untranslatable text.* ♦ *The untranslatable message was written in a secret code.*

untrue [ən 'tru] **1.** *adj.* not true; false; not correct. (Adv: *untruly.*) ♦ *The newspaper retracted the untrue statements it had made.* ♦ *That Chicago is the capital of Illinois is untrue. Springfield is the capital.* **2. untrue (to)** *adj.* (+ *prep. phr.*) disloyal to someone or something; not faithful to someone or something. ♦ *Sally was untrue to John.* ♦ *Bill was untrue to the principles he once lived by.*

untruth [ən 'truθ] *n.* a lie; something that is not true. ♦ *The newspaper retracted the libelous untruths.* ♦ *If you utter untruths on the witness stand, you are guilty of perjury.*

unusable [ən 'juz ə bəl] *adj.* not able to be used; not usable. (Adv: *unusably.*) ♦ *My old car is unusable, so I am replacing it.* ♦ *When the storm knocked down the wires, the phones were unusable.*

unused [ən 'juzd] *adj.* not used; never having been used; new. ♦ *The party was so crowded that it was hard to find an unused glass.* ♦ *The dentist put on an unused pair of rubber gloves.*

unusual [ən 'ju ʒu əl] *adj.* not usual; strange; different; not ordinary. (Adv: *unusually.*) ♦ *John has an unusual lump on the back of his neck.* ♦ *My car engine made an unusual noise, so I took it to a mechanic.*

unveil [ən 'vel] **1.** *tv.* to expose someone or something by removing a veil or covering; to remove a veil from someone or something. ♦ *The groom unveiled the bride before he kissed her.* ♦ *Anne unveiled her painting at the opening of the art exhibit.* **2.** *tv.* to expose someone or something; to reveal someone or something; to uncover someone or something. (Figurative on ①.) ♦ *The reporter unveiled the truth about the rigged election.* ♦ *The sales manager unveiled the new advertising campaign.*

unwanted [ən 'wɑn tɪd] *adj.* not wanted. (Adv: *unwantedly.*) ♦ *The unwanted child lived with an aunt.* ♦ *I throw out the unwanted catalogs that I receive in the mail.*

unwarranted [ən 'wɑr ən tɪd] *adj.* not justified; without a good cause. (Adv: *unwarrantedly.*) ♦ *The patron's unwarranted complaints offended the waitress.* ♦ *The intrusion into the celebrity's private life was unwarranted.*

unwary [ən 'wɛr i] *adj.* not wary; not careful; careless. (Adv: *unwarily.* Comp: *unwarier;* sup: *unwariest.*) ♦ *The unwary tourist was robbed.* ♦ *The unwary driver caused an accident.*

unwashed [ən 'wæʃt] *adj.* not washed; dirty; soiled. ♦ *Several unwashed cars lined up at the entrance of the car wash.* ♦ *There's a pile of unwashed clothes on top of the clothes hamper.*

unwavering [ən 'wev ə rɪŋ] *adj.* firm; not yielding or changing. (Adv: *unwaveringly.*) ♦ *Lisa is unwavering in her refusal to give me a raise.* ♦ *The senator took an unwavering stand on the issue.*

unwed [ən 'wɛd] *adj.* not married. ♦ *The social worker met with the unwed mother once a week.* ♦ *The hotel clerk would not rent a room to the unwed couple.*

unwelcome [ən 'wɛl kəm] *adj.* not welcome; not wanted. (Adv: *unwelcomely.*) ♦ *The bad news was very unwelcome.* ♦ *I would not invite the unwelcome guest into my house.*

unwell [ən 'wɛl] *adj.* not well; sick; ill. ♦ *Susie is feeling unwell, so she can't go outside and play.* ♦ *After eating the undercooked meat, Anne felt unwell.*

unwholesome [ən 'hol səm] *adj.* not good for one's morals or one's health. (Adv: *unwholesomely.*) ♦ *My parents won't let me watch unwholesome TV programs.* ♦ *I stopped eating unwholesome foods and started eating better.*

unwieldy [ən 'wil di] *adj.* hard to move, especially because of size, shape, or weight. (Adv: *unwieldily.* Comp: *unwieldier;* sup: *unwieldiest.*) ♦ *Moving the unwieldy piano up the stairs was difficult.* ♦ *Anne tried to move the unwieldy crate through the doorway.*

unwilling [ən 'wɪl ɪŋ] *adj.* not willing; reluctant; not inclined to do something. (Adv: *unwillingly.*) ♦ *I am unwilling to change my mind because I know I am right.* ♦ *David could have done the job, but he was just unwilling.*

unwind [ən 'waɪnd] **1.** *tv., irreg.* to remove something that is wound around an object. (Pt/pp: unwound.) ♦ *I unwound the leash that the dog wrapped around the pole.* ♦ *The police unwound the rope that bound the hostage to the chair.* **2.** *iv., irreg.* to relax. ♦ *After a hard day at work, I unwound by taking a bath.* ♦ *Anne likes to unwind by riding her bike along the lake.* **3.** *iv., irreg.* [for something] to become unwrapped from an object that it is wound around. ♦ *When I untied the knot, the rope unwound from the post.* ♦ *The bandage unwound from my ankle by itself.*

unwise [ən 'waɪz] *adj.* not wise; foolish; silly. (Adv: *unwisely.*) ♦ *It is unwise to touch the electric fence.* ♦ *The unwise driver sped on the icy roads.*

unworldly [ən 'wɚld li] *adj.* not from Earth; supernatural; ghostly; belonging to another world. ♦ *Some psychics claim to receive unworldly messages.* ♦ *The strange object that fell from the sky looked unworldly.*

unworthy [ən 'wɚ ði] **1.** *adj.* not worthy; not deserving. (Adv: *unworthily.*) ♦ *Your remarks are unworthy of a rebuttal.* ♦ *The rich man omitted his unworthy children from his will.* **2. unworthy of** *adj.* + *prep. phr.* beneath a standard; not appropriate for someone or something; not fitting for someone or something. ♦ *The boring movie was unworthy of a second viewing.* ♦ *This poorly made product is unworthy of our company's name.*

unwound [ən 'waʊnd] pt/pp of unwind.

unwrap [ən 'ræp] *tv.* to expose something by removing its wrapper; to remove a wrapping from something. ♦ *Mary unwrapped her birthday presents during the party.* ♦ *John unwrapped a straw and placed it in his drink.*

unwrapped [ən 'ræpt] *adj.* having had its wrapper removed; not yet wrapped. ♦ *Mary placed the unwrapped straw in her drink.* ♦ *Anne hid the unwrapped gifts until she had time to wrap them.*

unwritten [ən 'rɪt n] **1.** *adj.* not written; not expressed in writing. ♦ *I asked Dave to tell Mary something, and he delivered my unwritten message.* ♦ *The unwritten stories were passed from generation to generation.* **2.** *adj.* understood or agreed on, but not expressed in writing. ♦ *Anne honored her unwritten agreement with the company.* ♦ *All the workers abide by certain unwritten rules.*

unzip [ən 'zɪp] **1.** *tv.* to open a zipper; to open something by opening its zipper. ♦ *Anne unzipped the tent and went inside.* ♦ *Bill unzipped his jacket because it was getting warm.* **2.** *iv.* [for a zipper] to become opened. ♦ *Bill was embarrassed because his pants zipper unzipped.* ♦ *My jacket unzipped when Jimmy pulled at it.*

up ['ʌp] **1.** *adv.* from a lower level toward a higher level. ♦ *The balloon rose up to the ceiling.* ♦ *The price of gas went up last week.* ♦ *Jane turned the radio's volume up.* **2.** *adv.* toward the north; northward; in the north. ♦ *When we drove up to Canada, we saw a lot of moose.* ♦ *My friends drove up from the south last week.* **3.** *adv.* into an upright position; in an upright position. ♦ *John awoke and sat up in bed.* ♦ *Mary stood up from her chair and looked out the window.* **4.** *adv.* completely; totally. (Used with verbs such as *use up, eat up, drink up, open up, wind up.*) ♦ *The campers used up their supplies before their return.* ♦ *The hungry man ate up everything on his plate.* **5.** *adv.* tightly; into a tight condition; firmly. ♦ *The drain was clogged up with old leaves.* ♦ *The garden hose is rolled up on its stand.* **6.** *adv.* together; into a condition in which things are together. ♦ *Mary added the bill up.* ♦ *The computer totaled up the figures in the column.* **7.** *adj.* over; finished. ♦ *Your time is up. Stop writing and submit your exam papers to the teacher.* ♦ *When the prisoner's term was up, he returned home.* **8. up to something** *idiom* doing something, especially something bad or scheming. ♦ *Max is up to no good, I see.* ♦ *The children are being quiet, so they must be up to something.* **9. up to doing something** *idiom* able to do something. ♦ *Do you feel up to going back to work today?* ♦ *She just isn't up to staying up all night.* **10. up for something** *idiom* enthusiastic about something. (Informal.) ♦ *Are you up for a hike through the woods?* ♦ *I'm really up for my job interview today.* **11.** *prep.* at a higher level or position; to a higher level or position. ♦ *The trees up the mountain are prettier than the ones in the valley.* ♦ *All of the bedrooms are up the stairs.*

up-and-coming ['ʌp ən 'kʌm ɪŋ] *adj.* about to succeed; becoming successful or famous; likely to become famous. ♦ *The journalist wrote about up-and-coming celebrities.* ♦ *The university offered to hire the up-and-coming scholar.*

upbeat ['ʌp bit] *adj.* optimistic; cheerful. ♦ *The upbeat movie made the audience smile.* ♦ *Mary was cheered by the upbeat news.*

upbringing ['ʌp brɪŋ ɪŋ] *n.* the way someone is raised as a child; the way someone is cared for as a child. (No plural form in this sense.) ♦ *David blames his personality problems on his bad upbringing.* ♦ *Anne is well disciplined because her upbringing was strict.*

upcoming ['ʌp kəm ɪŋ] *adj.* about to happen; coming soon; impending. ♦ *The club's newsletter lists upcoming events.* ♦ *Whom will you vote for in the upcoming election?*

update ['ʌp det] **1.** *n.* something that has new information, especially a news report that has more information about something. ♦ *The TV station will air an update of the story at 6:00.* ♦ *The latest weather update said a tornado was heading our way.* **2.** *tv.* to modernize something; to make something more modern; to make something up-to-date. ♦ *The designer updated the office building built in the 1960s.* ♦ *The office manager updated the office equipment.* **3.** *tv.* to provide the latest information; to inform someone of the latest news. ♦ *The network updated the sports scores every five minutes.* ♦ *Mary updated me about John's medical information.*

updated [əp 'det ɪd] *adj.* modernized. ♦ *The actors performed an updated version of* Romeo and Juliet. ♦ *The updated equipment was much easier to use.*

upgrade ['ʌp gred] **1.** *tv.* to promote someone or something; to bring someone or something to a higher position; to bring someone or something to a more important position; to raise someone or something's status. ♦ *The assistant vice president was upgraded to vice president.* ♦ *The ticket agent upgraded me from coach to first class.* **2.** *tv.* to replace something with something better. ♦ *The office manager upgraded the software on my computer.* ♦ *Anne upgraded her old TV by buying one with stereo sound.* **3.** *n.* something that has more features than the thing that it is replacing. ♦ *Anne installed the latest upgrade on her computer.* ♦ *The upgrade moved me from coach to first class.*

upheaval [əp 'hiv əl] *n.* unrest; turmoil; agitation; a violent social or political movement. ♦ *The historian studied the upheaval caused by the war.* ♦ *The prime minister called on the army to end the upheaval.*

upheld [əp 'hɛld] pt/pp of uphold.

uphill ['ʌp 'hɪl] **1.** *adj.* sloping upward; directed or moving up the side of a hill. ♦ *I walked on an uphill path toward the inn.* ♦ *Anne visited the village that was uphill from hers.* **2.** *adj.* difficult. (Figurative on ①.) ♦ *It was an uphill battle to convince Jimmy to eat his peas.* ♦ *The senator faced an uphill fight to get reelected.* **3.** *adv.* toward the top of a hill; upward. ♦ *The mountain goat ran uphill.* ♦ *I shifted gears as I started driving uphill.*

uphold [əp 'hold] **1.** *tv., irreg.* to confirm something, especially for a court to confirm or approve a lower court's ruling. (Pt/pp: **upheld.**) ♦ *The Supreme Court upheld the lower court's ruling.* ♦ *The district court's ruling was upheld by the state supreme court.* **2.** *tv., irreg.* to support something; to defend something against criticism. ♦ *Anne upheld her dignity in spite of Bob's libelous accusations.* ♦ *John couldn't uphold his innocence when he was caught stealing.*

upholster [ə 'pol stɚ] *tv.* to provide furniture with padding and coverings. ♦ *Mr. Smith upholstered the chairs with a stain-resistant fabric.* ♦ *The couch will be upholstered with leather.*

upholsterer [ə 'pol stɚ ɚ] *n.* someone who puts padding on furniture and covers it with material. ♦ *The upholsterer repaired the large tear in the chair's fabric.* ♦ *The upholsterer covered my old sofa with new fabric.*

upholstery [ə 'pol stɚ i] *n.* the padding used to stuff furniture and the material used to cover furniture. (No plural form in this sense.) ♦ *The upholstery of the old sofa was very worn.* ♦ *Anne put plastic over her chairs to protect the upholstery.*

upkeep ['ʌp kip] **1.** *n.* maintenance; the work required to maintain something. (No plural form in this sense.) ♦ *The janitor was responsible for the upkeep of the school.* ♦ *The upkeep of the large yard is very time consuming.* **2.** *n.* the cost of ①. (No plural form in this sense.) ♦ *Much of the store's operating budget went to upkeep.* ♦ *The upkeep of the old building rises each year.*

uplift [əp 'lɪft] *tv.* to raise someone's spirits; to cause someone to feel better spiritually. ♦ *The congregation was uplifted by the meaningful sermon.* ♦ *The choir's beautiful singing uplifted me.*

uplifting [ʌp 'lɪf tɪŋ] *adj.* inspirational; causing someone to feel spiritually refreshed. (Adv: *upliftingly.*) ♦ *Many were moved by the preacher's uplifting sermon.* ♦ *This novel about courageous deeds is very uplifting.*

upon [ə 'pɔn] **1.** *prep.* on. ♦ *Mary placed the groceries upon the table.* ♦ *The snow fell upon the ground.* **2.** *prep.* at the instance of; on the occasion of. ♦ *Upon seeing her friend, Mary ran to the window and waved.* ♦ *Upon returning home, I realized I had been robbed.*

upper ['ʌp ɚ] *adj.* the higher of two things; closer to the top of something than the bottom. ♦ *Grandpa's upper teeth are false.* ♦ *Mary placed the dangerous poison on an upper shelf.*

uppercase ['əp ɚ 'kes] *adj.* [of a letter or letters] capitalized; majuscule. (Compare with **lowercase.**) ♦ *The* T *that starts this sentence is uppercase.* ♦ *Use uppercase letters for the headline.*

upper class [əp ɚ 'klæs] *adj.* very rich; belonging to the upper class; of or about the people in a society who are rich. (Hyphenated when prenominal.) ♦ *The upper-class couple sent their children to expensive private schools.* ♦ *My upper-class friend dines only in the finest restaurants.*

upperclassman [əp ɚ 'klæs mən] *n., irreg.* a junior or senior in a high school or university. (Pl: **upperclassmen.**) ♦ *Only upperclassmen could play on the varsity sports team.* ♦ *The upperclassman tutored sophomores who needed help.*

upperclassmen [əp ɚ 'klæs mən] pl of **upperclassman.**

upper crust [əp ɚ 'krʌst] *idiom* the higher levels of society; the upper class. ♦ *Jane speaks like that because she pretends to be a wealthy upper-crust citizen, but her father was a miner.* ♦ *James is from the upper crust, but now he is penniless.*

uppermost ['ʌp ɚ most] *adj.* the highest; in the highest position; on the highest level. ♦ *The inexpensive tickets were for seats in the theater's uppermost row.* ♦ *Bill hid the file on the uppermost shelf.*

upright ['ʌp rɑɪt] **1.** *adj.* standing straight up; erect; perpendicular to a flat surface. ♦ *The bookends kept the upright books from falling over.* ♦ *I put flowers into the upright vase.* **2.** *adj.* [of someone] honest, moral, following the law. ♦ *The upright witness told the truth at the trial.* ♦ *The upright politician refused to accept the bribe.* **3.** *adv.* to an **upright** ① position. ♦ *If I sit upright, I am more comfortable.* ♦ *Please place the books upright.*

uprising ['ʌp rɑɪz ɪŋ] *n.* a rebellion; a revolution; a revolt; a riot. ♦ *The king's army stopped the violent uprising.* ♦ *The college dean was unable to control the student uprising.*

uproar ['ʌp ror] *n.* clamor; tumult; a loud, noisy, confused activity. ♦ *The scandalous news created an uproar in Hollywood.* ♦ *The crowd was in an uproar when gunshots were fired.*

uproarious [əp 'ror i əs] **1.** *adj.* noisy with laughter. (Adv: *uproariously.*) ♦ *The audience responded to the comedian with uproarious laughter.* ♦ *The uproarious audience laughed loudly in the movie theater.* **2.** *adj.* very funny; causing a lot of laughter. (Adv: *uproariously.*) ♦ *The critics enjoyed the uproarious comedy.* ♦ *The uproarious comedian entertained large audiences.*

uproot [əp 'rut] **1.** *tv.* to pull up a plant, including its roots. ♦ *The gardener uprooted the weeds.* ♦ *The carrots were uprooted during the harvest.* **2.** *tv.* to cause someone to move from where one lives. (Figurative on ①.) ♦ *The native tribe was uprooted and sent to a reservation.* ♦ *The refugees had been uprooted from their ancestral village.*

upset [əp 'sɛt] **1.** *adj.* worried about something; fretful. ♦ *Bill is upset because his wife is undergoing surgery today.* ♦ *Mary was upset because we were going to be late.* **2.** *adj.* [of someone's stomach] feeling bad or sick. ♦ *Anne lay down because she had an upset stomach.* ♦ *Bill's stomach gets upset when he eats spicy food.* **3.** *tv., irreg.* to knock something over; to tip something over; to overturn something. (Pt/pp: **upset.**) ♦ *The clumsy farmer upset the pail of milk.* ♦ *I upset my glass of milk when I gestured wildly.* **4.** *tv., irreg.* to defeat someone or something that was expected to win. ♦ *The rookie athlete upset the national champion.* ♦ *The last-place team upset the highest-ranked team.* **5.** *tv., irreg.* to disturb someone; to bother someone; to make someone worried. ♦ *Bill upset Mary with some bad news.* ♦ *I upset my parents when I didn't come home on time.* **6.** *tv., irreg.* to make someone's stomach sick. ♦ *Spicy foods upset my stomach.* ♦ *Coffee upsets Anne's stomach.* **7.** *n.* a surprise victory; the defeat of someone or something by someone or something that was not expected to win. ♦ *The rookie's upset surprised the former champion.* ♦ *The sports columnist was amazed by the last-place team's upset.*

upsetting [əp 'sɛt ɪŋ] *adj.* causing worry; bothersome. (Adv: *upsettingly.*) ♦ *The upsetting news made me cry.* ♦ *Anne's rude behavior is very upsetting to me.*

upshot ['ʌp ʃɑt] *n.* the final result; the outcome. (No plural form in this sense. Informal.) ♦ *The upshot of the story was that we ran out of gas and had to walk.* ♦ *The upshot of the trial was that the defendant was found guilty.*

upside ['ʌp sɑɪd] *n.* the positive side of something; the benefit of something. (Informal.) ♦ *The upside to being fired is that I'll have more free time.* ♦ *The upside of my move to Texas is that the weather will be warmer.*

upside down [əp sɑɪd 'dɑʊn] *adj.* having the top part at the bottom; having the wrong end or side up. (Hyphenated before a nominal.) ♦ *The museum curator righted the upside-down painting.* ♦ *The pen wouldn't write well because it had been upside down.*

upstairs [əp 'stɛrz] **1.** *adj.* located on an upper floor; located on a higher floor. ♦ *My guests stayed in the upstairs bedroom.* ♦ *Mary waved to me from an upstairs window.* **2.** *adv.* on or toward the next floor of a building; on or toward an upper floor of a building. ♦ *John walked upstairs to the second floor.* ♦ *I ran upstairs to find out why the baby was crying.* **3.** *n.* the top floor of a building; the upper floor of a building. (Treated as singular.) ♦ *I thoroughly cleaned the upstairs before my guests arrived.* ♦ *John heard a strange noise coming from upstairs.*

upstanding [əp 'stæn dɪŋ] *adj.* honorable; respectable. (Adv: *upstandingly.*) ♦ *The upstanding citizen had never been arrested.* ♦ *The principal awarded the upstanding student a scholarship.*

upstart ['ʌp stɑrt] **1.** *n.* a newcomer; someone who has become too important too soon, especially one who is arrogant. ♦ *The veteran gave the young upstart a stern lecture.* ♦ *That upstart treats the older staff members very rudely.* **2.** *adj.* <the adj. use of ①.> ♦ *John is an upstart politician who will probably not get reelected.* ♦ *Some upstart salesman tried to sell me a new car at full price!*

upstate ['ʌp 'stet] **1.** *adj.* in the northern part of a state. ♦ *My parents were married in upstate New York.* ♦ *The new student had transferred from one of the upstate counties.* **2.** *adv.* toward or at the part of a state that is further north than an important city. ♦ *We traveled upstate in the fall to see the leaves' changing colors.* ♦ *The reporter from New York City drove upstate to Albany.*

upstream ['ʌp 'strim] *adv.* against the current of a river. ♦ *The salmon swam upstream to spawn.* ♦ *John paddled the canoe upstream.*

upswing ['ʌp swɪŋ] *n.* an improvement. ♦ *The president was pleased that the economy was on an upswing.* ♦ *The upswing in employment was good news.*

uptight ['ʌp 'tɑɪt] *adj.* very tense; very repressed; irritable; unable to show how one really feels. (Informal. Adv: *uptightly.*) ♦ *David offered me a massage because I seemed so uptight.* ♦ *Susan considered the uptight professor to be a prude.*

up to date ['ʌp tə 'det] **1.** *adj.* current; based on the latest facts or information. (Hyphenated before nouns.) ♦ *Our library has up-to-date reference materials.* ♦ *The up-to-date map showed the latest changes in political boundaries.* **2.** *adj.* current; having the newest and best equipment or techniques. (Hyphenated before nouns.) ♦ *Mary's up-to-date computer runs twice as fast as mine.* ♦ *John's up-to-date TV has a 41-inch screen.* **3.** *adj.* current; in style; fashionable. (Hyphenated before nouns.) ♦ *The model wore very up-to-date fashions in public.* ♦ *David went to a trendy salon to get an up-to-date haircut.*

up to the minute ['ʌp tu ðə 'mɪn ɪt] *adj.* the most recent; the most up to date. (Hyphenated before nouns.) ♦ *The investor demanded up-to-the-minute stock quotes.* ♦ *The TV networks provided live, up-to-the-minute coverage of the earthquake.*

uptown ['ʌp tɑʊn] **1.** *adj.* concerning a part of town away from downtown or the better part of town. ♦ *Susan lives in a small uptown apartment.* ♦ *From Spring Street, take the uptown subway to 23rd Street.* **2.** *adv.* in or toward a better part of the city, away from the downtown part of the city. ♦ *Is this subway headed uptown?* ♦ *Mary walked uptown on Fifth Avenue.*

upturn ['ʌp tɚn] **1.** *n.* an improvement; an upward movement. ♦ *The economist predicted an upturn in the economy.* ♦ *The polls revealed an upturn in the president's popularity.* **2.** [əp 'tɚn] *tv.* to turn something up, over, or upside down. ♦ *The violent customer upturned the restaurant table.* ♦ *The garbage collector upturned the bin into the garbage truck.*

upward ['ʌp wɚd] **1. upward(s)** *adv.* to or toward a higher position; to or toward a higher level. ♦ *The inflation rate inched upward.* ♦ *The excellent worker rose upward in the company ranks.* **2. upward(s)** *adv.* to or toward the top part of something. ♦ *Anne looked upward toward the sky.* ♦ *The worker tiled the wall from the floor upward.* **3.** *adj.* moving upward ①; advancing. (Adv: *upwardly.*) ♦ *There is an upward trend to the inflation rate.* ♦ *American society is characterized by upward mobility, meaning that personal and financial advancement is a common goal.*

uranium [jə 'ren i əm] *n.* a metallic, radioactive chemical element used mainly as fuel for nuclear reactors. (No plural form in this sense.) ♦ *The atomic symbol for uranium is U, and its atomic number is 92.* ♦ *The terrorists smuggled uranium from Russia.*

urban ['ɚ bən] *adj.* of or about a city or cities in general; not suburban or rural. ♦ *The urban mayor requested more federal funds.* ♦ *The magazine had a special report about urban crime.*

urbane [ɚ 'ben] *adj.* refined; elegant; very polite. (Adv: *urbanely.*) ♦ *The urbane gentleman graciously accepted the honor bestowed upon him.* ♦ *A tall and urbane butler greeted the party guests at the door.*

urbanize ['ɚ bə nɑɪz] *tv.* to make an area urban. ♦ *The developer urbanized hundreds of acres of farmland.* ♦ *The influx of new businesses urbanized the small village.*

urbanized ['ɚ bə nɑɪzd] *adj.* like a city; adapted to a city; metropolitan. ♦ *The city's subways reach all of its urbanized neighborhoods.* ♦ *My urbanized friend is unaccustomed to rural life.*

urge ['ɚdʒ] **1.** *n.* a strong impulse, desire, or need. ♦ *Anne had a sudden urge to go for a walk.* ♦ *I repressed my urge to hit the rude cab driver.* **2. urge to** *tv.* + *inf.* to persuade someone to do something; to beg someone to do something. ♦ *Bill urged me to go to the movies with him.* ♦ *Anne urged Susan to seek psychiatric help.* **3.** *tv.* to force someone or something to go forward. ♦ *The jockey urged the horse forward by using a whip.* ♦ *The platoon leader urged the troops onward through the swamp.*

urgency ['ɚ dʒən si] *n.* the condition of being urgent; the need for immediate attention. (No plural form in this sense.) ♦ *There was a great urgency in John's voice as he yelled for help.* ♦ *Because of the urgency of the crisis, the networks provided a live broadcast of the events.*

urgent ['ɚ dʒənt] *adj.* very important; pressing; needing attention before anything else. (Adv: *urgently.*) ♦ *David sent an urgent message to his lawyer.* ♦ *It is urgent that you speak with me right now.*

urinal ['jʊr ə nəl] *n.* a container or receptacle for urine, usually made of porcelain, and usually for men. ♦ *Jimmy was too short to be able to use the urinal.* ♦ *David flushed the urinal after he used it.*

urinary ['jʊr ə nɛr i] *adj.* of or about urine or urination. ♦ *After leaving the bladder, urine travels through the urinary tract.* ♦ *The doctor treated me for a urinary disorder.*

urinate ['jʊr ə net] *iv.* to cause or allow urine to flow from the body. ♦ *The dog urinated on several trees in the park.* ♦ *David went into the bathroom so he could urinate.*

urination [jɚ rə 'ne ʃən] *n.* the production and elimination of urine from the body. (No plural form in this sense.) ♦ *Elimination includes defecation and urination.* ♦ *John had a problem with urination and made an appointment with the doctor.*

urine ['jʊr ɪn] *n.* a liquid waste product removed by the kidneys, passed through the bladder, and discharged from the body. (No plural form in this sense.) ♦ *The baby's diaper was soaked with urine.* ♦ *My doctor ran tests on the sample of urine I provided.*

urn ['ɚn] **1.** *n.* a large vase or pot, often used for plants or for ashes from a crematorium. ♦ *Mary placed the large plant into a decorative urn.* ♦ *We keep John's cremated remains in an urn next to the bookcase.* **2.** *n.* a large container for holding hot liquids, especially coffee. ♦ *The caterer brought a fresh urn of coffee to the buffet table.* ♦ *Don't touch the urn! It's filled with hot tea.*

urologist [jʊr 'ɑl ə dʒəst] *n.* a doctor who specializes in the medical care and treatment of the urinary tract. ♦ *The urologist asked me for a sample of my urine.* ♦ *I felt a burning sensation when I urinated, so I went to a urologist.*

urology [jʊr 'ɑl ə dʒi] *n.* the science and study of the medical care and treatment of the urinary tract. (No plural form in this sense.) ♦ *In medical school, Susan took a class in urology.* ♦ *I spoke with someone trained in urology about the pain I felt when urinating.*

Uruguay ['jʊr ə gwe] See Gazetteer.

U.S. See U.S.A.

us ['ʌs] *pron.* <the objective form of we, referring to a group of people including the speaker or writer.> ♦ *Would you please give us the ball?* ♦ *This matter is between Anne and us.*

U.S.A. AND **USA, U.S., US** ['ju 'ɛs ('e)] the abbreviation for United States (of America).

usable ['juz ə bəl] *adj.* able to be used; suitable for use; easy to use. (Adv: *usably.*) ♦ *This software is usable on most computers built after 1994.* ♦ *The batteries remained usable for about six months.*

usage ['ju sɪdʒ] **1.** *n.* the way something is used or operated. (No plural form in this sense.) ♦ *The manual describes the proper usage of the appliance.* ♦ *Incorrect usage of this tool will result in injury.* **2.** *n.* the way words in a language typically occur in speech. (No plural form in this sense.) ♦ *Most Americans aren't aware of the British usage of "shall."* ♦ *Anne uses a dictionary to find the correct usage of words she doesn't know.*

use 1. ['jus] *n.* consuming or operating something. (No plural form in this sense.) ♦ *John's drug use is troubling to me.* ♦ *The television set undergoes a lot of use in our house.* **2.** ['jus] *n.* the ability or authority to apply, consume, or operate something. (No plural form in this sense.) ♦ *The use of alcohol was restricted on campus.* ♦ *The use of cameras is forbidden inside the museum.* **3.** ['jus] *n.* the intended function of something; the purpose of something, especially the purpose of meeting people's needs. (No plural form in this sense.) ♦ *What use is there in studying when I know I'm going to fail?* ♦ *This elevator is for the use of employees only.* **4.** ['juz] *tv.* to employ someone or something for a certain purpose; to put something into service. ♦ *John used a vacuum cleaner to clean the carpet.* ♦ *The researcher used five students in the scientific experiment.* **5.** ['juz] *tv.* to consume a supply of something; to exhaust a supply of something. ♦ *We used a tank of gas when we drove to Grandma's house.* ♦ *John had used his weekly food ration in five days.* **6.** ['juz] *tv.* to treat someone badly or to one's own advantage. ♦ *David didn't really like Susan. He just used her for her money.* ♦ *Anne used her coworkers to get ahead in the business.* **7. use up** ['juz...] *tv.* + *adv.* to use ⑤ all of something; to consume all of something. ♦ *Who used up the mustard?* ♦ *Jimmy used all the milk up.* **8. make use of someone or something** [...'jus...] *idiom* to use ④ or utilize someone or something. ♦ *If you make use of all your talents and skills, you should succeed.* ♦ *The technician makes good use of a number of special tools.*

used 1. ['juzd] *adj.* already owned; not new; secondhand. ♦ *Mary bought a used car.* ♦ *David bought a used desk from an antique shop.* **2. used to do something** ['jus tə...] *idiom* to have done something [customarily] in the past. ♦ *We used to go swimming in the lake before it became polluted.* ♦ *I used to eat nuts, but then I became allergic to them.* **3. used to someone or something** ['jus tə...] *idiom* accustomed to someone or something; familiar and comfortable with someone or something. ♦ *I am used to eating better food than this.* ♦ *I am used to the doctor I have and I don't want to change.* **4. used to something; used to doing something** ['jus tə...] *idiom* accustomed to something; comfortable with something because it is familiar. ♦ *We are used to cooking our own food.* ♦ *I lived in Alaska so long that I am used to the cold.*

useful ['jus fʊl] *adj.* helpful; beneficial. (Adv: *usefully.*) ♦ *The student took many useful courses in college.* ♦ *Your advice has been very useful. Thank you.*

usefulness ['jus fʊl nəs] *n.* the utility or helpfulness of something. (No plural form in this sense.) ♦ *Susan praised her new screwdriver for its usefulness.* ♦ *The advertisement touted the usefulness of the new product.*

useless ['jus ləs] *adj.* not helpful; not beneficial; having no effect; having no purpose. (Adv: *uselessly.*) ♦ *It was useless trying to start the fire with wet matches.* ♦ *The manager fired the useless employees.*

user ['juz ɚ] *n.* someone who uses something. ♦ *This manual was written to aid new users of this appliance.* ♦ *The social worker convinced the drug user to seek help.*

user-friendly ['juz ɚ 'frɛnd li] *adj.* not complicated to use; designed for easy use. ♦ *The workers liked the user-friendly computer programs.* ♦ *The user-friendly videocassette recorder was easy to program.*

usher ['ʌʃ ɚ] **1.** *n.* someone who shows people to their seats in a church, auditorium, theater, or other place where people gather. ♦ *At the wedding, the usher escorted me to a pew.* ♦ *The usher tore my theater ticket in half and handed me the stub.* **2.** *tv.* to guide someone to a seat; to escort someone to a seat. ♦ *David ushered his mother to her seat.* ♦ *The groom's friends ushered the wedding guests down the aisle.* **3. usher in** *tv.* + *adv.* to bring something into existence; to introduce something new. (Figurative on ②.) ♦ *We ushered in the new year with a champagne toast.* ♦ *The company ushered in the new product line with expensive advertisements.*

usual ['ju ʒu wəl] **1.** *adj.* ordinary; typical; customary; common; regular. (Adv: *usually.*) ♦ *John ordered his usual scrambled eggs and bacon.* ♦ *An accident blocked my usual route to work.* **2. as usual** *phr.* as is the normal or typical situation. ♦ *John ordered eggs for breakfast as usual.* ♦ *He stood quietly as usual, waiting for the bus to come.*

usurp [ju 'sɚp] *tv.* to seize power or control by force. ♦ *The army usurped the prime minister's power.* ♦ *The owner's control was usurped by the Board of Directors.*

Utah ['ju tɔ] See Gazetteer.

utensil [ju 'tɛn səl] *n.* a tool that helps someone do something, especially a tool that helps someone cook or eat. ♦ *Bob rinsed the utensils before putting them in the dishwasher.* ♦ *Metal utensils will scratch the coating of these frying pans.*

uterus ['ju tə rəs] *n.* the womb; the organ in women and most other female mammals where the fetus is protected and supplied with nutrients until birth. ♦ *The uterus stretches as a fetus grows.* ♦ *The embryo attached itself to the wall of the uterus.*

utilitarian [ju tɪl ə 'tɛr i ən] *adj.* practical; more useful than attractive. ♦ *The utilitarian office was ugly, but had excellent equipment.* ♦ *John's truck isn't very stylish, but it's utilitarian.*

utility [ju 'tɪl ə ti] **1.** *n.* usefulness; the degree to which something is useful. (No plural form in this sense.) ♦ *The utility of the computer program made Anne more efficient.* ♦ *The utility of my college degree became apparent after graduation.* **2.** *n.* a service providing products such as electricity, water, gas, and waste removal to homes and businesses. ♦ *Electricity and water are two utilities.* ♦ *The cost of utilities is included in my monthly rent.* **3.** *n.* a company that provides a public service. ♦ *The gas, electric, and water companies are utilities.* ♦ *The utility announced that it will raise its rates this fall.* **4.** *adj.* having a basic function or service. ♦ *The designer cut the cardboard with a utility knife.* ♦ *The soldiers drove the utility vehicle across the field.*

utility room [ju 'tɪl ɪ ti rum] *n.* a room in a house where the water heater, washing machine, and related equipment are located. ♦ *David took his dirty clothes to the utility room.* ♦ *Our utility room flooded when our washing machine broke.*

utilization [jut ə lə 'ze ʃən] *n.* utilizing; using. (No plural form in this sense.) ♦ *The utilization of pesticides is discouraged.* ♦ *The utilization of nuclear weapons is to be avoided at all costs.*

utilize ['jut ə lɑɪz] *tv.* to use something practically; to make use of something; to employ something for a purpose. ♦ *Efficient workers utilize time wisely.* ♦ *John utilized the knife blade as a screwdriver.*

utmost ['ʌt most] *adj.* greatest possible; maximum. ♦ *Anne used her skills to the utmost level.* ♦ *I have the utmost respect for my parents.*

utopia [ju 'top i ə] *n.* an ideal geographical area having a perfect society, essentially imaginary. ♦ *My utopia would be a quiet Pacific island.* ♦ *Human nature led to the downfall of the carefully planned utopia.*

utter ['ʌt ɚ] **1.** *tv.* to say something; to express something aloud. ♦ *Susan uttered her explanation so softly we couldn't hear it.* ♦ *Not a word was uttered during the suspenseful movie.* **2.** *adj.* complete; total; absolute. (Adv: *utterly.*) ♦ *The rude customer acted like an utter fool at the store.* ♦ *The student held authority figures in utter contempt.*

utterance ['ʌt ə rəns] **1.** *n.* speaking; a stream of spoken words. (No plural form in this sense.) ♦ *John's utterance of the vulgar phrase shocked his parents.* ♦ *With the utterance of each word, my sore throat felt worse.* **2.** *n.* something that is said. ♦ *I asked Sue to repeat her utterance.* ♦ *Bill accentuated his utterances by snapping his fingers.*

utterly ['ʌt ɚ li] *adv.* completely; totally; absolutely. ♦ *The sunset behind the mountains was utterly beautiful.* ♦ *My vacation was utterly relaxing.*

U-turn ['ju tɚn] *n.* a reversal in direction. ♦ *I was driving the wrong way, so I made a U-turn.* ♦ *The decline in unemployment did a U-turn when the stock market crashed.*

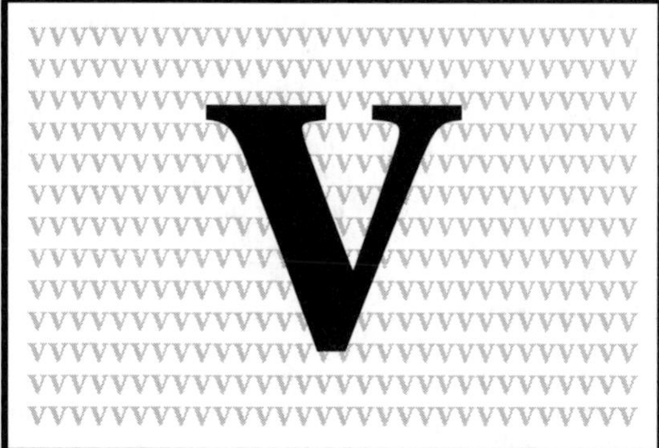

V AND **v** ['vi] *n.* the twenty-second letter of the English alphabet. ♦ V *comes after* U *and before* W *in the alphabet.* ♦ *There are two* Vs *in* valve.

vacancy ['ve kən si] **1.** *n.* a job or position that is not filled; an opening in employment; a job opening. ♦ *There is a vacancy in the accounting department because an employee quit.* ♦ *Bill's retirement left a vacancy in the production division.* **2.** *n.* an empty room or building that is available for rent. ♦ *Mary asked the hotel clerk if there were any vacancies.* ♦ *There are numerous vacancies in the city's older office buildings.* **3.** *n.* a facial expression showing a state of being **vacant** ②. (No plural form in this sense.) ♦ *Her eyes had a mysterious vacancy that led you to believe she was not awake or alive.* ♦ *Tom's stare had an eerie vacancy.*

vacant ['ve kənt] **1.** *adj.* not occupied; not being used; empty; not filled. ♦ *The real-estate developer purchased the vacant office building.* ♦ *Jane parked her car in the vacant lot.* **2.** *adj.* [a look on someone's face] blank, showing no thought or intelligent processes. (Figurative on ①. Adv: *vacantly.*) ♦ *I couldn't figure out Anne's mood from the vacant expression on her face.* ♦ *The stranger's vacant stare made me nervous.*

vacate ['ve ket] *tv.* to leave a place, which then becomes empty; to stop living, working, or using a place. ♦ *The landlord ordered the tenants to vacate the premises immediately.* ♦ *The tenants vacated the apartment before the end of the month.*

vacation [ve 'ke ʃən] **1.** *n.* a period of time when one does not have to work or go to school; a holiday. ♦ *I have a two-week vacation at the beginning of spring.* ♦ *School vacation is in the summer.* **2.** *n.* a trip during ① to a distant place for recreation. ♦ *Sue went to the Grand Canyon this year for her vacation.* ♦ *John showed us pictures from his vacation in Mexico.* **3.** *n.* vacating; leaving a place empty. (No plural form in this sense.) ♦ *The evicted tenants faced immediate vacation of the building.* ♦ *The landlord insisted upon vacation of his property.* **4. on vacation** *idiom* taking a trip; taking time off from work. ♦ *Where are you going on vacation this year?* ♦ *I'll be away on vacation for three weeks.* **5. take a vacation** *idiom* to go somewhere for ②; to stop work to have ①. ♦ *Sue took a vacation at the Grand Canyon last year.* ♦ *I need to take a vacation and relax.*

vacationing [ve 'ke ʃən ɪŋ] *adj.* taking a vacation; not at school or work. ♦ *The local residents easily recognized the vacationing tourists.* ♦ *The vacationing students crowded the beaches during spring break.*

vaccinate ['væk sə net] *tv.* to give someone a vaccine as a protection against disease. ♦ *The doctor vaccinated the children against measles.* ♦ *The pediatrician vaccinated Mary's infant.*

vaccination [væk sə 'ne ʃən] **1.** *n.* the use of a vaccine to protect people against disease. (No plural form in this sense.) ♦ *Vaccination is a good way to prevent measles.* ♦ *Children should be able to receive vaccination against diseases.* **2.** *n.* an instance of ①. ♦ *Jimmy's measles vaccination was almost painless.* ♦ *The doctor gave vaccinations by injection.*

vaccine [væk 'sin] *n.* a substance that is given to people in order to protect them from a certain disease. ♦ *A vaccine is usually a dead or weakened bacteria or virus that will cause the person to develop immunity to the disease that the bacteria or virus normally causes.* ♦ *The scientist was awarded a prize for a life-saving vaccine.*

vacillate ['væs ə let] *iv.* to be unable to make a decision; to go back and forth between different opinions. ♦ *Jane vacillated between wearing jeans or a dress to the party.* ♦ *Bob vacillated between making dinner or going to a restaurant.*

vacuum ['væk jum] **1.** *n.* a space that is completely empty and does not have any air in it. ♦ *Most of space is a huge vacuum.* ♦ *The vegetables were packed in a vacuum to ensure freshness.* **2. vacuum (cleaner)** *n.* a machine that cleans carpets or other materials by creating a partial ① that sucks up dirt. ♦ *My deluxe vacuum cleans and shampoos carpets.* ♦ *The vacuum is stored in the hallway closet.* **3.** *adj.* creating or causing ①. ♦ *The air was drained from the area with a vacuum pump.* ♦ *At the drive-in bank, I put the container holding my bank deposit in the vacuum tube.* **4.** *tv.* to clean a surface by sucking up dirt with ②. ♦ *John vacuumed the carpet in his bedroom.* ♦ *Anne vacuumed the hallway rugs.* **5.** *iv.* to clean by sucking up dirt with ②. ♦ *Jane vacuums on Saturdays.* ♦ *John vacuumed before his guests arrived.*

vagabond ['væg ə bɑnd] **1.** *n.* someone without a job who travels or wanders from place to place; a hobo. ♦ *The vagabond hitched a ride on the freight train.* ♦ *A few vagabonds set up camp just outside of town.* **2.** *adj.* <the adj. use of ①.> ♦ *The vagabond lifestyle can be adventurous but dangerous.* ♦ *The homeless man led a vagabond existence.*

vagina [və 'dʒaɪ nə] *n.* the channel in the body of a woman and some female animals that leads from the outside of the body to the uterus. ♦ *The gynecologist examined the pregnant woman's vagina.* ♦ *The birth canal runs from the uterus through the vagina.*

vagrant ['ve grənt] **1.** *n.* someone without a job who travels or wanders from place to place. ♦ *The vagrant will have no luck finding a job in this town.* ♦ *The police ordered the vagrants to leave the abandoned building.* **2.** *adj.* <the adj. use of ①.> (Adv: *vagrantly.*) ♦ *The vagrant man made a little money doing odd jobs.* ♦ *The police arrested the vagrant woman on suspicion of murder.*

vague ['veg] **1.** *adj.* not precise; not exact. (Adv: *vaguely.* Comp: *vaguer;* sup: *vaguest.*) ♦ *Tom evaded Jane's question by giving her a vague answer.* ♦ *The confusing movie had a rather vague ending.* **2.** *adj.* having no expression on one's face. (Figurative on ①. Adv: *vaguely.* Comp: *vaguer;* sup: *vaguest.*) ♦ *I couldn't tell what was bothering Anne from the vague look on her face.* ♦ *Bob's vague expression masked the stress I knew he was under.*

vain ['ven] **1.** *adj.* having too much pride about how one looks or about what one has done; conceited. (Adv: *vainly.* Comp: *vainer;* sup: *vainest.*) ♦ *You're so vain that you're always looking at your reflection in the mirror.* ♦ *The vain man spent a lot of money on the latest fashions.* **2. in vain** *adv.* futile; without having the result one wanted. ♦ *The firefighters worked in vain to control the fire.* ♦ *I tried in vain to convince my teacher to change my grade.*

valance ['væl ənts] *n.* a short, gathered curtain hung at the top of a window. ♦ *Jane hung the valance above the kitchen window.* ♦ *Dave took down the dusty valance so he could wash it.*

valentine ['væl ən tɑɪn] **1.** *n.* someone who is given a card or gift on St. Valentine's Day; a sweetheart. ♦ *I gave my valentine candy and flowers.* ♦ *Will you be my valentine?* **2.** *n.* a card or gift that is given on February 14, St. Valentine's Day. ♦ *Jimmy made a beautiful valentine for his mother.* ♦ *I received five valentines in the mail today.* **3. (St.) Valentine's Day** *n.* a minor holiday—occurring on February 14—celebrating love and friendship. ♦ *The candy manufacturers make a lot of money on St. Valentine's Day.* ♦ *She called her sweetheart on St. Valentine's Day.*

valet [væ 'le] **1.** *n.* a man who is another man's personal servant. ♦ *John has been Mr. Brown's valet for more than 20 years.* ♦ *David is Tom's loyal and trustworthy valet.* **2.** *n.* someone who parks cars for people who drive to a restaurant, theater, nightclub, or other business. ♦ *The valet parked patrons' cars near the theater.* ♦ *I gave my car keys to the valet in the restaurant parking lot.*

valiant ['væl jənt] *adj.* very brave; very courageous; heroic. (Adv: *valiantly.*) ♦ *The paramedics made a valiant effort to save the man's life.* ♦ *The valiant firefighter rescued the infant from the burning building.*

valiantly ['væl jənt li] *adv.* very bravely; very courageously. ♦ *The soldiers fought the battle valiantly.* ♦ *The troops valiantly stormed the castle.*

valid ['væl ɪd] **1.** *adj.* effective; legally usable or acceptable. (Adv: *validly.*) ♦ *This coupon is valid until the end of the month.* ♦ *Do you have a valid driver's license to operate this vehicle?* **2.** *adj.* true; factual; able to be defended or proved; based on facts. (Adv: *validly.*) ♦ *Your statement is valid, based on the evidence presented to this court.* ♦ *The data in your report seems to be valid to me.*

validate ['væl ɪ det] **1.** *tv.* to cause a document to become legally effective or acceptable; to declare that something is legally effective or acceptable. ♦ *The receptionist validated my parking ticket.* ♦ *The city clerk validated my building permit.* **2.** *tv.* to confirm something by proving that it is true; to show something to be factual or true. ♦ *This experiment has validated my hypothesis.* ♦ *Mary's testimony validated my alibi.*

validity [və 'lɪd ə ti] *n.* a state of being valid; authenticity. (No plural form in this sense.) ♦ *The doorman at the bar questioned the validity of my identification card.* ♦ *The validity of the blood test was disputed in court.*

valley ['væl i] *n.* a low area of land between two high areas of land; a low area of land that is drained by a large river and the smaller rivers that flow into the larger river. ♦ *The soldiers in the hills attacked the villages in the valley.* ♦ *Much of the Mississippi Valley was explored in the early 19th century.*

valor ['væl ɚ] *n.* bravery; courage. (No plural form in this sense.) ♦ *The soldier was decorated for his valor in battle.* ♦ *The terminally ill patient showed great valor in the last months of his life.*

valuable ['væl jə bəl] **1.** *adj.* worth a lot of money; having a great value. (Adv: *valuably.*) ♦ *Anne wore a valuable diamond ring to the party.* ♦ *A thief stole some valuable paintings from the museum.* **2.** *adj.* helpful; useful; important. (Adv: *valuably.*) ♦ *The firefighter taught the children valuable safety tips.* ♦ *Max learned a valuable lesson from his costly mistake at work.* **3. valuables** *n.* items that are ①. (No singular.) ♦ *You may store your valuables in the hotel safe.* ♦ *Susan insured her precious valuables.*

valuation [væl ju 'e ʃən] **1.** *n.* determining how much money something is worth. (No plural form in this sense.) ♦ *The jewelry valuation revealed my diamond to be a fake.* ♦ *The bank conducted a property valuation before offering me a mortgage.* **2.** *n.* the amount of money that something is determined to be worth. (No plural form in this sense.) ♦ *The bank determined the property's valuation at $10,000.* ♦ *This necklace has a $1,000 valuation.*

value ['væl ju] **1.** *n.* the amount of money that something is really worth. (No plural form in this sense.) ♦ *The jeweler determined the value of my ring.* ♦ *John's watch has a value of $75.* **2.** *n.* the actual worth compared to the amount of money one actually paid for it; a bargain. (Assumed to be a *good* value unless indicated otherwise. No plural form in this sense.) ♦ *These shoes were a real value because I bought them on sale.* ♦ *This appliance was a bad value because it broke soon after I bought it.* **3.** *n.* usefulness; benefit. (No plural form in this sense.) ♦ *Of what value is your expensive toy?* ♦ *The first-aid kit was of great value on our hiking trip.* **4.** *n.* an amount that is represented by a sign, symbol, or variable. ♦ *The math students determined the value of variables in equations.* ♦ *In the equation* x + 2 = y, *when* x *is 3,* y *has a value of 5.* **5.** *tv.* to believe that something is worth a certain amount of money. ♦ *This watch is valued at $100.* ♦ *The retailer valued the sofa at $450.* **6.** *tv.* to think someone or something is valuable; to regard someone or something as useful or worthy; to regard someone or something highly. ♦ *Mary values her medical skills.* ♦ *John valued the companionship of his trusty dog.* **7. take someone or something at face value** *idiom* to take someone or something by its outward appearance; to take someone or something as it first appears to be. ♦ *Don't just take her offer at face value. Think of the implications.* ♦ *Jane tends to take people at face value, so she is always getting hurt.*

valve ['vælv] *n.* a flap or other device in a tube that controls the amount of something that passes through the tube. ♦ *The automatic shut-off valve turned off the gas when the furnace flame blew out.* ♦ *The surgeons repaired one of John's heart valves.*

vampire ['væm pɑɪr] **1. vampire (bat)** *n.* any of several tiny bats found in Central and North America that drink the blood of other warm-blooded animals. ♦ *The vampire bat lighted on the sleeping dog's leg.* ♦ *Vampire bats sleep hanging upside down.* **2.** *n.* [in books and movies] a member of the living dead who sleeps in a coffin and leaves it only at night to suck the blood of people who are alive. ♦ *I love reading scary stories about vampires!* ♦ *The man killed the vampire by driving a wooden stake through its heart.*

van ['væn] *n.* a covered motor vehicle that has a large amount of space behind the driver's seat for carrying large objects or extra people. ♦ *Most vans have a large door that slides opens along the side of the vehicle as well as a pair of doors in the back.* ♦ *Bill borrowed my van to move some furniture.*

vanadium [və 'ned i əm] *n.* a silvery, metallic chemical element used in compounds in ceramics, glass, dyes, and the chemical industry. (No plural form in this sense.) ♦ *The atomic symbol of vanadium is V.* ♦ *Vanadium's atomic number is 23.*

vandal ['væn dəl] *n.* someone who damages other people's property or public property on purpose. ♦ *The vandals sprayed graffiti on the subway cars.* ♦ *The police caught the vandal who broke the school windows.*

vandalism ['væn də lɪz əm] *n.* the damaging of other people's property or public property on purpose. (No plural form in this sense.) ♦ *The judge ordered the juveniles to pay for their vandalism.* ♦ *The vandalism of the graveyard shocked the people in the town.*

vandalize ['væn də lɑɪz] *tv.* to damage other people's property or public property on purpose. ♦ *The juvenile delinquents vandalized the subway station.* ♦ *The youths who vandalized the school were caught and punished.*

vane ['ven] **1.** *n.* a part of a machine or structure that is a flat blade that is spun by wind, such as one of the blades of a windmill. ♦ *The windmill's vanes were a blur because it was so windy.* ♦ *Stand back from the windmill; its vanes are heavy and dangerous.* **2. weather vane** *n.* a metal object, including ①, that points in the direction that wind is blowing, so that one can determine the direction of the wind. ♦ *The weather vane indicated the wind was blowing from the west.* ♦ *The lightning bolt struck the weather vane on top of the barn.*

vanguard ['væn gɑrd] **1.** *n.* the group of soldiers positioned in front of the main part of the army. ♦ *The army slaughtered the enemy's vanguard.* ♦ *The vanguard of rebels surprised the unprepared soldiers.* **2.** *n.* the leaders of trends in fashion, style, politics, science, etc.; the position of the leaders of these trends. (Figurative on ①.) ♦ *Designers from Paris are often the vanguard of fashion.* ♦ *The professors in my department are in the vanguard of new theories.*

vanilla [və 'nɪl ə] **1.** *n.* a flavoring made from the bean of a certain tropical plant. (No plural form in this sense.) ♦ *I could see flecks of vanilla in the natural ice cream.* ♦ *I added a teaspoon of vanilla to the pancake batter.* **2.** *adj.* flavored with ①; tasting like ①. ♦ *I love chocolate syrup on vanilla ice cream.* ♦ *Anne ate a cup of vanilla yogurt for breakfast.*

vanish ['væn ɪʃ] **1.** *iv.* to disappear; to be seen no longer. ♦ *The spy vanished from his hotel room without a trace.* ♦ *The magician made the flowers vanish with a wave of his wand.* **2. vanish into thin air** *idiom* to disappear without leaving a trace. ♦ *My money gets spent so fast. It seems to vanish into thin air.* ♦ *When I came back, my car was gone. I had locked it, and it couldn't have vanished into thin air!*

vanishing ['væn ɪʃ ɪŋ] **1.** *adj.* disappearing; leaving someone's view. (Adv: *vanishingly.*) ♦ *The vanishing fog revealed the extent of the accident.* ♦ *The researcher of the supernatural chased the vanishing ghost.* **2.** *adj.* becoming extinct. ♦ *John is one of a vanishing breed of well-mannered gentlemen.* ♦ *The conservationist tried to protect vanishing species.*

vanity ['væn ə ti] **1.** *n.* the condition of being vain; the condition of having too much pride about how one looks or what one has done. (No plural form in this sense.) ♦ *Anne's vanity would not allow her to cut off her long hair.* ♦ *Because of Bill's vanity, we had to wait an hour while he primped in the bathroom.* **2.** *n.* a counter top and a sink on top of a cabinet with drawers, especially such a unit in bathrooms. ♦ *Jane designed the vanity to match the marble tile on the walls.* ♦ *I put extra towels in the bottom drawer of the vanity.*

vanquish ['væŋ kwɪʃ] *tv.* to defeat someone in a battle, sporting contest, argument, or other conflict. ♦ *Our army vanquished the enemy in a few months.* ♦ *Our football team vanquished the champions by a score of 21–0.*

vantage ['væn tɪdʒ] *n.* a condition or position that gives someone or something a special or unique way of looking at something. ♦ *The historian wrote about the Crusades from the vantage of the twentieth century.* ♦ *The journalist described the accident scene from his unique vantage.*

vapor ['ve pɚ] *n.* a liquid or solid in the form of a gas. ♦ *Steam, fog, and mist are water vapors.* ♦ *The cooking vapors were drawn out of the kitchen by a fan.*

vaporize ['ve pə rɑɪz] **1.** *tv.* to turn a liquid or solid into a gas; to cause a liquid or solid to become a gas. ♦ *The dry ice was vaporized on stage as a special effect.* ♦ *The wax figure was vaporized in the high heat.* **2.** *iv.* [for a liquid or solid] to become a gas. ♦ *Water vaporizes at 212 degrees Fahrenheit.* ♦ *The chemical liquids vaporized when they were combined.*

vaporizer ['ve pə rɑɪz ɚ] *n.* a machine that changes water into a vapor. ♦ *The air in my house was dry, so I bought a vaporizer.* ♦ *The Smiths put a vaporizer in their baby's nursery.*

variable ['vɛr i ə bəl] **1.** *adj.* able to be changed; flexible. (Adv: *variably.*) ♦ *The temperature of the water in the kitchen sink is variable.* ♦ *John worked variable hours, depending on when he was needed.* **2.** *adj.* likely to change; not staying the same. (Adv: *variably.*) ♦ *Spring weather in Chicago is highly variable.* ♦ *David's interest in sports is variable, depending on his mood.* **3.** *n.* something that changes, especially an amount that changes depending on other factors. ♦ *Anne plotted the graph of an equation with two variables.* ♦ *In an experiment, there should be as few variables as possible.*

variance ['vɛr i əns] **1.** *n.* a discrepancy or difference between two or more things. ♦ *A committee worked out the variances between the two bills.* ♦ *A mediator resolved the variances among the workers' opinions.* **2.** *n.* the amount that things are different. ♦ *The screw manufacturer allowed for a variance of up to half a millimeter.* ♦ *The variance in the calculations caused the rocket to crash.*

variant ['vɛr i ənt] **1.** *adj.* different; a particular difference as compared with something standard or the norm.

♦ *The researcher analyzed the variant data from his experiments.* ♦ *The variant spelling in England for* jail *is* gaol. **2.** *n.* a different form of something, especially a different way of spelling a word. ♦ Colour *is the British variant of* color. ♦ *David spoke a Canadian variant of French.*

variation [vɛr i 'e ʃən] **1.** *n.* (minor) differences. (No plural form in this sense.) ♦ *Variation among members of the same breed of dog is expected.* ♦ *Accepting variation in language is difficult for some people.* **2.** *n.* an instance of ①. ♦ *The color variations in a chameleon's skin depend on its environment.* ♦ *The constant variation of Bob's opinions is aggravating.*

varied ['vɛr ɪd] *adj.* having or representing a variety; diverse. (Adv: *variedly.*) ♦ *Mary has varied tastes in music. She like opera and rock.* ♦ *This restaurant offers a varied menu that should please anyone.*

variety [və 'rɑɪ ə ti] **1.** *n.* choice; diversity. (No plural form in this sense.) ♦ *Variety adds interest to living.* ♦ *I need more variety in my diet.* **2.** *n.* a wide selection of things to choose from; a large amount of different kinds of things; an assortment. ♦ *The electronics department had a wide variety of radios.* ♦ *There is quite a variety of food on the buffet table.*

various ['vɛr i əs] *adj.* different; several; several kinds of something; many kinds of something. (Adv: *variously.*) ♦ *The editor had various problems with the journalist's article.* ♦ *There are various ways of catching a cold.*

variously ['vɛr i əs li] *adv.* in different ways; differently. ♦ *My brother is variously referred to as Robert, Bob, and Bobby.* ♦ *The coastline was variously described by a number of early explorers.*

varnish ['vɑr nɪʃ] **1.** *n.* a clear liquid that is painted onto the surface of objects made from wood to protect the wood and give it a hard, shiny appearance. (No plural form in this sense.) ♦ *Please don't walk on the porch while the varnish is still wet.* ♦ *Anne cleaned the varnish from the brush with turpentine.* **2.** *tv.* to paint a surface with ①. ♦ *Mary will varnish the antique desk.* ♦ *The wooden porch was varnished to protect it from bad weather.*

varsity ['vɑr sə ti] *adj.* of or about the most experienced or skilled sports team in a school. ♦ *Most varsity sports are played by juniors and seniors.* ♦ *I went to the varsity basketball game with my friends.*

vary ['vɛr i] **1.** *iv.* to change; to be different; to appear or be used in different forms. ♦ *The position of the sun varies throughout the day.* ♦ *My work schedule varies depending on what time of year it is.* **2.** *tv.* to change something; to cause something to be different; to make something different. ♦ *John varied his appearance by shaving his beard every few months.* ♦ *Bill varied his writing style because he thought it was boring.*

vascular ['væs kjə lɚ] *adj.* concerning vessels that carry blood, sap, or other liquids. (Adv: *vascularly.*) ♦ *The botanist studied the vascular system of trees.* ♦ *His vascular system is slowed by narrow arteries.*

vase ['ves] *n.* a decorative container, often used for holding flowers. ♦ *Mary put the yellow roses in a crystal vase.* ♦ *John bought a porcelain vase at the antique shop.*

vast ['væst] *adj.* very large in size or amount; of an immense size or amount. (Adv: *vastly.* Comp: *vaster;* sup: *vastest.*) ♦ *The movie star got a vast amount of fan mail every week.* ♦ *The nomads wandered across the vast desert.*

vastly ['væst li] **1.** *adv.* in a way that is very large in size or amount; immensely. ♦ *Mary's singing ability improved vastly after she took lessons.* ♦ *The national debt increased vastly in the 1980s.* **2.** *adv.* very; extremely. ♦ *Even though Mary and Jane are twins, their personalities are vastly different.* ♦ *The critic thought the popular movie was vastly overrated.*

vat ['væt] *n.* a large container, used for storing liquid, especially liquor while it is being made. ♦ *The workers made wine by crushing grapes in a large vat.* ♦ *The factory carefully covered the vat of paint.*

vaudeville ['vɔd vɪl] **1.** *n.* a form of live theater, consisting of short, lively performances, including singing, dancing, comedy routines, magic acts, acrobatics, etc. (Based on French. No plural form in this sense.) ♦ *Vaudeville was very popular in the United States in the early 1900s.* ♦ *The movie studio's founder had gotten his start in vaudeville.* **2.** *adj.* <the adj. use of ①.> ♦ *Tom's grandfather was a vaudeville singer many years ago.* ♦ *The old vaudeville theater was torn down to make way for a new opera house.*

vault ['vɔlt] **1.** *n.* a secure, locked room where valuable things are kept and protected. ♦ *The bank keeps its money in a steel vault.* ♦ *The hotel clerk kept my valuables in the hotel's vault.* **2.** *n.* a ceiling made of several arches that support each other, as found in old churches. ♦ *During the war, the cathedral's majestic vault was bombed away.* ♦ *Religious art was painted on the church's main vault.* **3.** *n.* a leap; a jump made with the help of a pole or one's hands. ♦ *John cleared the puddle in a single vault.* ♦ *Jane's vault successfully took her over the beam.* **4.** *tv.* to jump a certain distance. ♦ *Tom knew he could not vault the width of the stream.* ♦ *The athlete vaulted fifteen feet.* **5. vault over** *iv. + prep. phr.* to jump over something. ♦ *The athlete vaulted over the raised beam.* ♦ *The horse vaulted over the fence.*

vaulted ['vɔlt ɪd] *adj.* arched; having several arches that support each other. ♦ *Religious art was painted on the church's vaulted ceilings.* ♦ *The lobby's vaulted ceiling was intricately tiled.*

've See have ⑥.

veal ['vil] *n.* the meat of a young cow used as food. (No plural form in this sense.) ♦ *The slaughter of young cows for veal disturbed the vegetarian.* ♦ *John ate breaded veal with mashed potatoes.*

veer ['vɪr] *iv.* to change from one position to another; to change the direction of movement, especially so that one does not collide with someone or something. ♦ *The driver veered to the left to avoid a large pothole.* ♦ *The conservative politician veered further right.*

vegetable ['vɛdʒ tə bəl] **1.** *n.* a plant that is eaten as food; a part of a plant that is eaten as food. ♦ *A carrot is an orange vegetable.* ♦ *You'd better eat all of the vegetables on your plate.* **2.** *adj.* made with or including ①. ♦ *I ordered some tasty vegetable soup at the restaurant.* ♦ *There's some vegetable stew cooking on the stove.*

vegetarian [vɛdʒ ɪ 'tɛr i ən] **1.** *n.* someone who practices vegetarianism; someone who does not eat the flesh of animals. ♦ *Vegetarians get their protein from rice and beans.* ♦ *Anne made special dishes for her guests who were* *vegetarians.* **2.** *adj.* [of food] made without the flesh of a once-living creature. ♦ *Anne ate a vegetarian pizza for lunch.* ♦ *I served my guests a vegetarian meal.* **3.** *adj.* practicing vegetarianism; serving or eating food other than animal tissue. ♦ *The vegetarian restaurant was popular with students.* ♦ *My vegetarian guests couldn't eat the hamburgers I'd made.*

vegetarianism [vɛdʒ ɪ 'tɛr i ə nɪz əm] *n.* the practice of not eating the flesh of once-living animals. (No plural form in this sense.) ♦ *Anne embraces vegetarianism because it's healthy.* ♦ *John practices vegetarianism because he's against killing animals.*

vegetate ['vɛdʒ ɪ tet] *iv.* to do nothing; to have a dull, boring life; to pursue no activities. ♦ *Bill vegetated on the couch all day in front of the TV.* ♦ *Jane vegetated at home while her car was being repaired.*

vegetation [vedʒ ɪ 'et ʃən] *n.* plant life; plants in general. (No plural form in this sense.) ♦ *Thick vegetation grows in tropical jungles.* ♦ *Vegetation was removed from the plot of land so a parking lot could be built.*

vehemence ['vi (h)ə məns] *n.* the strength of one's feelings or emotions; the passion of one's feelings or emotions. (No plural form in this sense.) ♦ *The vehemence of Anne's opinion persuaded me to agree with her.* ♦ *David expressed his vehemence by pounding his fist on the table.*

vehement ['vi (h)ə mənt] *adj.* [of expression] passionate, strong, or fierce. (Adv: *vehemently.*) ♦ *Many voters liked the politician's vehement expression of his ideas.* ♦ *The vehement lecturer gestured wildly as he spoke.*

vehicle ['vi hi əl] **1.** *n.* a machine that is used to carry people or things, especially on the ground on roads, including cars, buses, trucks, vans, motorcycles, bicycles, sleds, sleighs, and carriages. (But not trains or airplanes.) ♦ *Only certain motor vehicles are allowed on the expressways.* ♦ *Twenty vehicles were involved in the crash on the highway.* **2.** *n.* a means of carrying or delivering something. (Figurative on ①.) ♦ *Rats are often a vehicle for the spread of disease.* ♦ *The dramatic actress chose a comedy vehicle for her next project.*

vehicular [vɪ 'hi jə lɚ] *adj.* of or about vehicles. (Adv: *vehicularly.*) ♦ *The pedestrian was hindered by vehicular traffic.* ♦ *The automobile engineer studied vehicular accidents.*

veil ['vel] **1.** *n.* a piece of cloth used to hide something. ♦ *The widow wore a black veil to conceal her sorrow.* ♦ *At the exhibit, the new painting was covered with a veil.* **2.** *n.* something that covers something else. (Figurative on ①.) ♦ *A veil of fog clouded the airport.* ♦ *The mourners' faces were covered with a veil of sorrow.* **3.** *tv.* [for fog] to cover an area. ♦ *Thick fog veiled the airport.* ♦ *A blanket of fog veiled the entire neighborhood.*

veiled ['veld] **1.** *adj.* hidden; covered with a veil; covered by something like a veil. ♦ *The veiled portrait will be revealed at a special ceremony.* ♦ *The newly designed car was completely veiled at the introduction ceremony.* **2.** *adj.* not clearly stated; insinuated. (Figurative on ①.) ♦ *The criminal issued a veiled threat to the prosecuting attorney.* ♦ *David's sarcastic praise was really a thinly veiled insult.*

vein ['ven] **1.** *n.* a vessel that carries blood from parts of the body back to the heart. ♦ *The nurse found a prominent vein in my arm for the injection.* ♦ *His veins are clogged with fatty deposits.* **2.** *n.* a line that forms part of the framework of a leaf or the wing of an insect. ♦ *Mary examined the veins of a fly's wing under a microscope.* ♦ *John tore the leaf along one of its veins.* **3.** *n.* a layer of coal or a metal ore within a mass of rock. ♦ *The miner struck a rich vein of gold.* ♦ *The marble in the hotel lobby is white with colorful blue veins.* **4.** *n.* a mood; an attitude or style. ♦ *John spoke in a poetic vein, sounding pretty silly to most people.* ♦ *Bob, speaking in a jocular vein, invited everyone to my house for dinner.*

velocity [və 'lɑs ə ti] *n.* speed, especially the speed of an object moving in a specific direction. (No plural form in this sense.) ♦ *The police measured the velocity of cars with radar.* ♦ *At the current velocity, this plane will land in London in one hour.*

velour [və 'lʊr] **1.** *n.* a soft, plush fabric similar to velvet. (No plural form in this sense.) ♦ *Bill bought an old shirt made of velour at a thrift store.* ♦ *Can I put velour in the washing machine, or should it be dry-cleaned?* **2.** *adj.* made of ①. ♦ *John bought a warm velour shirt.* ♦ *Bill ran his hand along the soft velour fabric.*

velvet ['vɛl vɪt] **1.** *n.* a soft, plush fabric whose threads are short and close together and stick up on one side of the fabric. (No plural form in this sense.) ♦ *The smooth velvet felt nice against my skin.* ♦ *Few fabrics are as soft as velvet.* **2.** *adj.* made of ①. ♦ *Mary wore an elegant black velvet dress to the opera.* ♦ *I bought a fancy velvet vest to wear with my new skirt.*

vendetta [vɛn 'dɛt ə] *n.* a feud or bitterness against someone that lasts for a long time, especially in which someone seeks vengeance. (From Italian.) ♦ *David's vendetta against John lasted until his father's death was avenged.* ♦ *The counselor tried to resolve Bob's vendetta against Max.*

vending machine ['vɛn dɪŋ mə ʃin] *n.* a machine that gives a customer a product when the customer inserts the correct amount of money. ♦ *I put two quarters into the vending machine for a bag of potato chips.* ♦ *Jane got a carton of milk from the vending machine at school.*

vendor ['vɛn dɚ] *n.* a seller; someone who sells things. ♦ *That vendor sells cheap jewelry on the street corner.* ♦ *The retailer bought merchandise from three different vendors.*

veneer [və 'nɪr] **1.** *n.* a thin layer of wood or other decorative material that is glued on top of a surface. ♦ *The countertop's veneer was beginning to peel away.* ♦ *Unfortunately, the intricate veneer was covered with paint.* **2.** *n.* a pleasant appearance that covers up an unpleasant feeling. (Figurative on ①.) ♦ *Only Anne saw the turmoil behind Mary's happy veneer.* ♦ *John hid his anger behind a veneer of politeness.*

venerable ['vɛn ə rə bəl] *adj.* worthy of honor, esteem, or respect, especially because of age, experience, position, or importance. (Adv: *venerably.*) ♦ *The opera was performed in a venerable old building dating to the 1890s.* ♦ *It is my honor to introduce the venerable mayor of this fine city.*

venerate ['vɛn ə ret] *tv.* to honor someone with respect; to honor someone. ♦ *The devout Catholic venerated the saints.* ♦ *The art collector had always venerated Monet for the beautiful paintings he had done.*

veneration [vɛn ə 're ʃən] *n.* venerating; honor; esteem. (No plural form in this sense.) ♦ *Veneration of the aged* *is no longer practiced in western culture.* ♦ *A large feast was held in veneration of the queen.*

venereal [və 'nɪr i əl] *adj.* of or about sex, especially diseases that are transmitted sexually. (Adv: *venereally.*) ♦ *Bob was diagnosed with a serious venereal disease.* ♦ *Venereal ailments are now familiar to most medical doctors.*

Venezuela [vɛn ə 'zwe lə] See Gazetteer.

vengeance ['vɛn dʒəns] **1.** *n.* hurting someone or damaging someone's property as a form of revenge. (No plural form in this sense.) ♦ *Bob's urge to achieve vengeance after the fight was very strong.* ♦ *Most types of vengeance are illegal.* **2. with a vengeance** *idiom* with determination and eagerness. ♦ *The angry soldier attacked the enemy with a vengeance.* ♦ *Bill ate all his dinner and gobbled up his dessert with a vengeance.* **3. wreak vengeance (up)on someone or something** *idiom* to seek and get revenge on someone by harming someone or something. ♦ *The thief wreaked his vengeance on Mary by destroying her house.* ♦ *The general wanted to wreak vengeance on the opposing army for their recent successful attack.*

vengeful ['vɛndʒ fəl] **1.** *adj.* hurting someone or damaging someone's property in vengeance. (Adv: *vengefully.*) ♦ *The mobster was convicted of the vengeful murder of his rival.* ♦ *Mary prevented the vengeful destruction of her business by her rival.* **2.** *adj.* [of someone] eagerly seeking vengeance. (Adv: *vengefully.*) ♦ *The vengeful prince plotted the king's murder.* ♦ *The vengeful widow sued her husband's murderer.*

venison ['vɛn ɪ sən] **1.** *n.* the flesh of the deer eaten as food. (No plural form in this sense.) ♦ *The hunter ate some dried venison.* ♦ *The campers ate fresh venison for dinner.* **2.** *adj.* <the adj. use of ①.> ♦ *We had venison sausage for dinner.* ♦ *Most people eat venison as venison stew.*

venom ['vɛn əm] **1.** *n.* the poisonous liquid in the bite or sting of a snake, spider, scorpion, and other similar creatures. (No plural form in this sense.) ♦ *The snake's deadly venom killed the careless hiker.* ♦ *The paramedic drew the venom from the victim's snakebite.* **2.** *n.* extreme hatred; rancor. (Figurative on ①. No plural form in this sense.) ♦ *I can't understand your venom toward your boss.* ♦ *John's criticism of Jane was laced with venom.*

venomous ['vɛn ə məs] **1.** *adj.* full of venom; containing venom. (Adv: *venomously.*) ♦ *A venomous snake crawled across my toes, terrifying me.* ♦ *The venomous scorpion stung its prey.* **2.** *adj.* bitter and hateful; rancorous; full of extreme hatred. (Figurative on ①. Adv: *venomously.*) ♦ *Mary gave the leering stranger a venomous look.* ♦ *The politician's venomous speech disturbed many voters.*

venous ['vi nəs] *adj.* of or about veins or the circulation of blood in the veins. (Adv: *venously.*) ♦ *Venous blood is much darker than arterial blood.* ♦ *Max was afflicted with some sort of venous disorder.*

vent ['vɛnt] **1.** *n.* an opening to a duct through which air or other gases can move. ♦ *Cool air came through the ceiling vent in the office.* ♦ *The air vent was clogged with dust and dirt.* **2.** *tv.* to express one's feelings; to make one's feelings known. ♦ *Jane vented her anger in a destructive manner.* ♦ *John vented his frustration by kicking the tires on his car.*

ventilate ['vɛn tɪ let] *tv.* to bring fresh air into a room or an enclosed space; to expose something or someplace to fresh air. ♦ *This fan can ventilate 500 square feet of space.* ♦ *The teacher opened the windows to ventilate the stuffy classroom.*

ventilation [vɛn tɪ 'le ʃən] *n.* the movement of fresh air into or out of a place. (No plural form in this sense.) ♦ *The office building's poor ventilation impaired the worker's health.* ♦ *Make sure your baby's nursery has proper ventilation.*

ventilator ['vɛn tɪ le tɚ] **1.** *n.* a fan that moves air into or out of a room or enclosed space. ♦ *Bill turned on the ventilator because the room was stuffy.* ♦ *The ventilator was broken, so we all had to breathe stale air.* **2.** *n.* a device that supplies air or oxygen to someone who cannot breathe without help. ♦ *The man with emphysema was placed on a ventilator at the hospital.* ♦ *John, who had inhaled smoke during the fire, required a ventilator.*

ventriloquism [vɛn 'trɪl ə kwɪz əm] *n.* the skill and practice of speaking without moving one's lips or jaws so that the voice seems to come from someone or something else. (No plural form in this sense.) ♦ *Mary had studied ventriloquism and could make her doll seem to talk.* ♦ *To perform ventriloquism, one needs a mannequin of some sort.*

ventriloquist [vɛn 'trɪl ə kwəst] *n.* someone who practices ventriloquism. ♦ *The ventriloquist performed on stage with a wooden mannequin.* ♦ *The ventriloquist made it seem like the dummy was talking on its own.*

venture ['vɛn tʃɚ] **1.** *n.* a risky undertaking; especially an action taken in business where one risks one's money in order to gain more money. ♦ *The investor risked $1,000 in a business venture.* ♦ *John's venture into business wasn't very successful.* **2.** *tv.* to risk something; to expose something to danger; to place something in danger. ♦ *The lawyer ventured his reputation on the outcome of the trial.* ♦ *Mary ventured her paycheck on the bet.* **3.** *iv.* to go into a place that could be dangerous. ♦ *If I were you, I wouldn't venture near that dark cave alone.* ♦ *The young children ventured into the abandoned building.*

venturesome ['vɛn tʃɚ səm] **1.** *adj.* likely to take risks; daring. (Adv: *venturesomely.*) ♦ *The venturesome investor lost $100,000 in the stock-market crash.* ♦ *The venturesome hikers blazed their own trail.* **2.** *adj.* risky; hazardous; dangerous. (Adv: *venturesomely.*) ♦ *The venturesome investment promised a nice return if successful.* ♦ *No bank would finance the venturesome plans for the new office building.*

venue ['vɛn ju] **1.** *n.* the location of an event. ♦ *We had a discussion about the venue of the next meeting.* ♦ *This city will be the venue of the national convention.* **2.** *n.* the city or neighborhood where a trial is held and where the jurors are from. (Legal.) ♦ *The venue of the defendant's trial was moved out of state.* ♦ *The judge approved a change of venue for the trial.*

Venus ['vi nəs] **1.** *n.* the Roman goddess of love. ♦ *The Greek equivalent of Venus is called Aphrodite.* ♦ *Venus is the mother of Cupid and the wife of Vulcan.* **2.** *n.* the second planet in our solar system, found in an orbit between Mercury and Earth. (Named for ①.) ♦ *A space probe was sent toward Venus.* ♦ *Venus is shrouded by a thick layer of clouds.*

veracity [və 'ræs ə ti] *n.* truthfulness. (No plural form in this sense.) ♦ *The popular politician was criticized for his lack of veracity.* ♦ *The jury relied on the veracity of the witnesses.*

verb ['vɚb] *n.* a word that describes what someone or something is or does; a word that expresses being, action, or occurrence. ♦ *In the sentence "Mary touched the table," the verb is "touched."* ♦ *The past tense of many English verbs is formed by adding* -ed *or* -d.

verbal ['vɚb əl] **1.** *adj.* expressed in words; oral; spoken, not written. (Adv: *verbally.*) ♦ *The teacher issued a verbal warning to the unruly student.* ♦ *Anne gave a verbal committee report at the meeting.* **2.** *adj.* of or about a verb; formed from a verb. (Adv: *verbally.*) ♦ *The progressive verbal suffix is "-ing" in English.* ♦ *Past participles can be thought of as verbal adjectives.*

verbal auxiliary ['vɚb əl ɔg zɪl jə ri] See auxiliary verb.

verbalize ['vɚb ə lɑɪz] *tv.* to express something in words; to say something using words. ♦ *John verbalized his fears about snakes when we went to the zoo.* ♦ *Mary verbalized her thoughts when asked for her opinion.*

verbatim [vɚ 'bet əm] *adv.* word for word; in a way that repeats the exact words that someone else said or wrote. ♦ *The court reporter read back Mary's testimony verbatim.* ♦ *The article quoted the president's speech verbatim.*

verbose [vɚ 'bos] *adj.* using too many words; wordy. (Adv: *verbosely.*) ♦ *The editor rejected the verbose manuscript.* ♦ *Mary deleted many phrases in John's verbose report.*

verdant ['vɚd nt] *adj.* [of plant life] green; green with vegetation. (Adv: *verdantly.*) ♦ *The cows grazed in the verdant pasture.* ♦ *The hikers climbed up the verdant hillside.*

verdict ['vɚ dɪkt] **1.** *n.* the decision of a judge or a jury at the end of a trial. ♦ *The jury could not reach a verdict.* ♦ *The defendant appealed the guilty verdict.* **2.** *n.* a conclusion; a judgment; an opinion. ♦ *The critic's verdict was that the movie was worth seeing.* ♦ *David made me taste his soup and then awaited my verdict.*

verge ['vɚdʒ] **on the verge of (doing) something** *phr.* at the very beginning of doing something; just about to do something. ♦ *Bill was on the verge of leaving town when he found a job.* ♦ *Susan was on the verge of laughter, so she left the lecture hall.*

verifiable ['vɛr ɪ fɑɪ ə bəl] *adj.* able to be verified; able to be proved. (Adv: *verifiably.*) ♦ *My job references were easily verifiable.* ♦ *The scientific report contained verifiable data.*

verification [vɛr ɪ fɪ 'ke ʃən] *n.* evidence that proves something; proof. (No plural form in this sense.) ♦ *There is no independent verification that you are telling the truth.* ♦ *I handed my driver's license to the doorman as verification of my age.*

verify ['vɛr ɪ fɑɪ] *tv.* to provide evidence that something is true; to confirm that something is true. ♦ *Bill verified the identity of the corpse at the morgue.* ♦ *Your signature here will verify that you understand the terms of the agreement.*

vermilion [vɚ 'mɪl jən] **1.** *n.* a bright red color. (No plural form in this sense.) ♦ *The model's shirt was a brilliant vermilion.* ♦ *The bold design was printed in vermilion and gold.* **2.** *adj.* bright red in color. ♦ *The actress applied some vermilion lipstick.* ♦ *Anne bought a pair of vermilion shoes on sale.*

vermin ['vɚ mɪn] **1.** *n.* small destructive animals, including rats, fleas, and cockroaches. (No plural form in this sense. Treated as plural.) ♦ *The exterminator sprayed our house to rid it of vermin.* ♦ *The bins in the alley are infested with vermin.* **2.** *n.* someone who is vile, obnoxious, or unpleasant; vile and obnoxious people. (Figurative on ①. No plural form in this sense. Treated as plural.) ♦ *Anne moved away from the vermin sitting next to her in the movie theater.* ♦ *Some repugnant vermin were staring at me on the subway.*

Vermont [vɚ 'mɑnt] See Gazetteer.

vernacular [vɚ 'næk jə lɚ] **1.** *n.* the common spoken language of the people of a country or area. (No plural form in this sense.) ♦ *The politician spoke to the country folk in their vernacular.* ♦ *Formal writing should be done in the standard, not the vernacular.* **2.** *adj.* of or about the way language is commonly used by people, as opposed to the formal, literary style of language. (Adv: *vernacularly.*) ♦ *The popular play was written in a vernacular style.* ♦ *Please don't use vernacular expressions in your essay.*

versatile ['vɚ sə təl] **1.** *adj.* [of someone] able to do many different things; having many different skills. (Adv: *versatilely.*) ♦ *The versatile worker was assigned to many different jobs.* ♦ *Versatile actors can play many kinds of roles.* **2.** *adj.* [of something] able to be used in many different ways; adaptable. (Adv: *versatilely.*) ♦ *This versatile gadget slices, dices, peels, and chops.* ♦ *My versatile jackknife can also be used as a can opener.*

verse ['vɚs] **1.** *n.* poetry; language as it is used in poetry, as opposed to prose. (No plural form in this sense.) ♦ *Many of Shakespeare's plays are written in verse.* ♦ *The poet expressed her thoughts in verse.* **2.** *n.* a group of lines in a poem or song. ♦ *Mary knows all four verses to the national anthem.* ♦ *The choir sang the first two verses of the hymn.* **3.** *n.* a subdivision of a chapter of a book of the Bible. ♦ *The minister quoted the 16th verse of the 3rd chapter of the book of John.* ♦ *The shortest Bible verse is only two words long.*

version ['vɚ ʒən] **1.** *n.* one person's account or description of something that happens. ♦ *Bob gave his version of the accident in a statement to the police.* ♦ *Jane's version of the funny story was quite different from Tom's.* **2.** *n.* a form of something that is different from another form of it, such as being in a different language or medium. ♦ *I saw the movie version of that story before I read the book.* ♦ *The class read the English versions of famous Russian poems.*

versus ['vɚ səs] *prep.* in opposition with; in a contest with. (The abbreviation is either *vs.* or *v.* Used especially in law.) ♦ *The big game was the Badgers versus the Bulls.* ♦ *In the case of* Smith v. Jones, *the jury sided with Smith.*

vertebra ['vɚ tə brə] *n., irreg.* one of the bones of the spine; one of the bones of the backbone. (Pl: vertebrae or *vertebras.*) ♦ *The car accident shattered one of the driver's vertebrae.* ♦ *Anne bruised her lowest vertebra when she fell on the ice.*

vertebrae ['vɚ tə bre] a pl of vertebra.

vertebrate ['vɚ tə bret] **1.** *n.* an animal that has a spine; an animal that has a backbone. ♦ *Mammals, birds, reptiles, amphibians, and fish are classified as vertebrates.* ♦ *The archaeologist dug up the fossil of an ancient vertebrate.*

2. *adj.* <the adj. use of ①.> ♦ *Mary specializes in vertebrate biology.* ♦ *The scientist examined the vertebrate creature in detail.*

vertical ['vɝ tɪ kəl] *adj.* straight up and down; plumb. (Adv: *vertically* [...ɪk li].) ♦ *The vertical cliff was almost impossible to climb.* ♦ *The carpenter made sure the wall was vertical.*

vertigo ['vɝ tɪ go] *n.* a sick or dizzy feeling where one feels like everything is spinning around, especially when one looks down from a high place. (No plural form in this sense.) ♦ *If I looked down while crossing the bridge, I'd get vertigo.* ♦ *Looking out from the window of the 90th floor, David experienced vertigo.*

verve ['vɝv] *n.* enthusiasm; vigor; liveliness. (No plural form in this sense.) ♦ *The band played with verve and energy.* ♦ *Mary approached everything she did with a youthful verve.*

very ['vɛr i] **1.** *adv.* especially; quite; extremely; greatly; to a large degree. (Used to intensify an adjective or another adverb. *Very* is not used with the comparative forms, but is used with superlative forms, with *the,* as an intensifier.) ♦ *You did very well on the test. It's the very best you've ever done.* ♦ *Jane and Bill were very, very happy to win the lottery.* **2.** *adj.* same; actual; identical. ♦ *Mary bought the very dress that her twin sister had bought.* ♦ *This less expensive ring is the very one I saw in the jeweler's shop.* **3.** *adj.* mere; simple. ♦ *The very thought of eating liver makes me sick.* ♦ *The very idea of you telling me to mind my own business is insulting!* **4. the very thing** *idiom* the exact thing that is required. ♦ *The vacuum cleaner is the very thing for cleaning the stairs.* ♦ *I have the very thing to remove that stain.*

vessel ['vɛs əl] **1.** *n.* a large ship or boat. ♦ *The vessel contained exotic cargo from a distant port.* ♦ *The captain commanded the crew to board the vessel.* **2.** *n.* a container used to hold liquids. ♦ *The servant brought fresh water in some sort of a large vessel.* ♦ *Soup was served from a large, silver vessel.* **3. blood vessel** *n.* a tube that carries blood through the bodies of living things. ♦ *The clot blocked an important blood vessel.* ♦ *The drug constricted the patient's blood vessels.*

vest ['vɛst] **1.** *n.* a piece of clothing that has no sleeves and is worn above the waist on top of a shirt and usually under a suit coat or jacket. ♦ *The executive's vest matched his trousers.* ♦ *Susan wore a brightly colored vest over her blouse.* **2. vest with** *tv.* + *prep. phr.* to give someone or people the right or authority to do something. (Usually passive.) ♦ *Judges are vested by the state with the authority to perform marriages.* ♦ *The mayor was vested with the right to christen the ship.*

vested ['vɛs tɪd] **vested interest** *n.* a legally protected interest or ownership in something. ♦ *John has a vested interest in the outcome of the lawsuit.* ♦ *The judge asked if I had a vested interest in the real-estate project.*

vestibule ['vɛs tə bjul] *n.* a small room inside the entrance of a building; a lobby; a front hall. ♦ *I'll meet you in the hotel vestibule in an hour.* ♦ *The tenants' mailboxes are in the vestibule of the apartment building.*

vestige ['vɛs tɪdʒ] *n.* a trace; something that remains; a remainder. ♦ *A few artifacts were the only vestige of the once powerful city.* ♦ *The tyrant destroyed every vestige of the opposition.*

vet ['vɛt] **1.** *n.* a veteran. ♦ *David is a decorated vet from World War II.* ♦ *The local vets marched in a parade on Memorial Day.* **2.** *n.* a veterinarian. ♦ *The vet gave the cat his annual rabies shot.* ♦ *Our vet loves all types of animals.*

veteran ['vɛt (ə) rən] **1.** *n.* someone who has served in the military, especially during a war. (Abbreviated **vet.**) ♦ *Tom is a Persian Gulf War veteran, and his father was a Vietnam War veteran.* ♦ *The local veterans of foreign wars meet in this hall every Friday.* **2.** *n.* someone who has a lot of experience with something. (Figurative on ①.) ♦ *The retired principal is a veteran of the city's public school system.* ♦ *Veterans of the fire department hold a reunion once a year.* **3.** *adj.* experienced; having a lot of experience with something. ♦ *Susan is a veteran writer of mystery books.* ♦ *The veteran teacher would not tolerate misbehavior in his classroom.*

Veterans Day ['vɛt (ə) rənz de] *n.* a U.S. holiday celebrated on November 11, commemorating the end of World War I (1914–1918) and honoring all war veterans. ♦ *Every Veterans Day, there's a somber parade downtown.* ♦ *State and federal offices are closed on Veterans Day.*

veterinarian [vɛt (ə) rə 'nɛr i ən] *n.* a doctor of veterinary medicine; a doctor who treats animals. (Abbreviated **vet.**) ♦ *The rural veterinarian specialized in the health care of horses.* ♦ *Our veterinarian gives our dogs shots twice a year.*

veterinary ['vɛt ə rə nɛr i] *adj.* of or about the health of animals, including medical and surgical care. ♦ *Bill majored in veterinary science at the university.* ♦ *Susan was trained in veterinary medicine.*

veto ['vi to] **1.** *n.* an instance of using one's authority to stop legislation from becoming law. (Pl in *-es.*) ♦ *Thousands of voters were angered by the presidential veto.* ♦ *The Senate voted to override the veto.* **2.** *tv.* to stop legislation from becoming law; not to allow something to happen. ♦ *The president vetoed the budget proposed by Congress.* ♦ *If this proposed law isn't vetoed, the Supreme Court will find it unconstitutional anyway.*

vex ['vɛks] *tv.* to anger someone; to annoy someone; to trouble someone. ♦ *The difficult math problem vexed the student.* ♦ *The lazy workers vexed the supervisor.*

vexation [vɛk 'se ʃən] **1.** *n.* anger or irritation. (No plural form in this sense.) ♦ *In Mary's vexation, she angrily snapped her pencil in half.* ♦ *Bill's vexation is caused by his obnoxious roommates.* **2.** *n.* something that vexes; an annoyance; a bother; a trouble. ♦ *The worker's absence was a great vexation to the manager.* ♦ *Numerous vexations at the office gave David an ulcer.*

via ['vi ə, vɑɪ ə] *prep.* by way of someplace, someone, or some route. ♦ *Mary drove to Boston from Chicago via Cleveland.* ♦ *I heard the gossip via Bill.*

viable ['vɑɪ ə bəl] *adj.* able to succeed. (Adv: *viably.*) ♦ *The bank offered loans to viable businesses.* ♦ *Only two of the six plans were determined to be viable.*

viaduct ['vɑɪ ə dəkt] *n.* a bridge that carries a road or railroad over a valley or over another road. ♦ *The railroad company built viaducts over busy roads.* ♦ *The car slid from the viaduct and into the valley below.*

vial ['vɑɪl] *n.* a small bottle, usually used for holding medicine or perfume. ♦ *There are 100 tablets of aspirin in each* *vial.* ♦ *I bought a small vial of perfume at the department store.*

vibrant ['vaɪ brənt] *adj.* alive; exciting. (Adv: *vibrantly.*) ♦ *The artists lived in a vibrant neighborhood near downtown.* ♦ *The portrait was painted in bold, vibrant colors.*

vibrate ['vaɪ bret] **1.** *iv.* to move back and forth very quickly; to shake; to oscillate; to quiver. ♦ *The guitar string continued to vibrate after I plucked it.* ♦ *Mary felt the earth vibrate during the earthquake.* **2.** *tv.* to move something back and forth very quickly; to shake something; to cause something to oscillate or quiver. ♦ *My neighbor's loud music vibrated the wall between our apartments.* ♦ *What is vibrating the floor? Is it an earthquake?*

vibrating ['vaɪ bret ɪŋ] *adj.* moving back and forth very quickly; shaking; oscillating; quivering. (Adv: *vibratingly.*) ♦ *The vibrating bass beat from the stereo caused my walls to shake.* ♦ *The vibrating motion of the earthquake damaged my apartment.*

vibration [vaɪ 'bre ʃən] *n.* the motions of moving back and forth very quickly. ♦ *The vibrations of the earthquake shattered my crystal.* ♦ *The vibrations from a large truck set off my car alarm.*

vibrator ['vaɪ bre tɚ] *n.* something that vibrates, especially a device used to relax and soothe muscles. ♦ *Mary relaxed her sore muscles with a vibrator.* ♦ *The therapist massaged my neck with a vibrator.*

vicarious [vaɪ 'kɛr i əs] *adj.* experiencing something in one's mind that is being experienced by someone else; indirect; secondhand. (Adv: *vicariously.*) ♦ *I got a vicarious thrill from listening to Anne's adventurous stories.* ♦ *Looking at the explorer's photos provided me with a vicarious experience.*

vice ['vaɪs] *n.* a bad or immoral habit; wickedness. ♦ *Excessive drinking is an unhealthy and dangerous vice.* ♦ *David tried to quit the vice of smoking cigarettes.*

vice president ['vaɪs 'prɛz ə dənt] *n.* someone who is next in rank to a president. ♦ *The vice president held a press conference to discuss the economy.* ♦ *Anne has been promoted to senior vice president at the bank.*

vice versa ['vaɪs 'vɚ sə] *adv.* the other way around; in the opposite way. ♦ *Bill loves Jane and, vice versa, Jane loves Bill.* ♦ *Mary criticized David's work, and vice versa.*

vicinity [vɪ 'sɪn ə ti] *n.* a neighborhood; the location around someone or something; the surrounding area. ♦ *What stores are in the vicinity of 23rd Street and 7th Avenue?* ♦ *The storm hit the downtown area but passed over the outlying vicinities.*

vicious ['vɪʃ əs] **1.** *adj.* fierce; cruel; likely to cause pain; dangerous. (Adv: *viciously.*) ♦ *A vicious storm knocked down electrical wires.* ♦ *Keep that vicious dog away from me!* **2.** *adj.* malicious. (Adv: *viciously.*) ♦ *Susan's vicious remarks about my work upset me.* ♦ *Bob spread a vicious rumor about John at the office.*

viciously ['vɪʃ əs li] *adv.* in a vicious way. ♦ *The dog snarled at the stranger viciously.* ♦ *A cat hissed viciously at the dog.*

viciousness ['vɪʃ əs nəs] *n.* the quality of being vicious. (No plural form in this sense.) ♦ *The viciousness of the murder frightened the inspector.* ♦ *John's viciousness took David by surprise.*

victim ['vɪk təm] *n.* someone or an animal that dies, suffers, or loses something because of someone else's actions, a sickness, an accident, or a natural disaster. ♦ *The flood victims were given emergency funds.* ♦ *The new form of treatment gave hope to the cancer victims.*

victimize ['vɪk tə maɪz] *tv.* to cause someone to be a victim; to cause someone to suffer. ♦ *The police officers victimized the defenseless suspect.* ♦ *An unscrupulous shopkeeper victimized the illegal immigrants.*

victor ['vɪk tɚ] *n.* a winner; someone who wins a fight, game, contest, race, etc. ♦ *Susan was declared the victor of the chess tournament.* ♦ *Olympic victors are awarded medals.*

Victorian [vɪk 'tor i ən] **1.** *adj.* of or about things, styles, or people during the reign of the English Queen Victoria or showing the influence of this period. ♦ *John renovated a Victorian house in the inner-city neighborhood.* ♦ *The actors wore Victorian costumes on stage.* **2.** *adj.* prudish; [of attitudes] associated with reluctance to deal with sex in public. ♦ *My Victorian parents were very protective of me.* ♦ *The parents longed for a return to Victorian morals.*

victorious [vɪk 'tor i əs] **1.** *adj.* being a winner; having won a fight, game, contest, race, etc. (Adv: *victoriously.*) ♦ *The victorious team celebrated after the game.* ♦ *The victorious athlete was given a gold medal.* **2.** *adj.* causing victory; causing someone to be a winner. ♦ *The victorious touchdown was scored in the last minute of the game.* ♦ *The photographer took a picture of the victorious goal.*

victory ['vɪk tə ri] **1.** *n.* winning; achieving success over an adversary; the success of defeating an enemy or opponent. (No plural form in this sense.) ♦ *Victory is very satisfying.* ♦ *At the end of the long struggle, we would experience victory.* **2.** *n.* an instance of ①. ♦ *Our team needed a victory to continue on to the championship game.* ♦ *The citizens celebrated their army's victory overseas.* **3. landslide victory** *idiom* a victory ② by a large margin; a very substantial victory ②, particularly in an election. ♦ *The mayor won a landslide victory in the election.* ♦ *The younger man won a landslide victory in the presidential election.*

victuals ['vɪt lz] *n.* food. (Treated as plural.) ♦ *The cook prepared some tasty victuals for the hungry students.* ♦ *The campers heated some victuals on the campfire.*

video ['vɪd i o] **1.** *n.* moving visible images, such as what is recorded on videotape; the visible part of a television transmission; the display seen on a computer monitor. (No plural form in this sense.) ♦ *The video is poor, but the audio is good.* ♦ *Bill works with video in a television station.* **2.** *n.* a movie that is available on videotape; motion or action that is recorded on videotape. (Pl in *-s.*) ♦ *Bill rented some videos to watch after dinner.* ♦ *I watched a video of Mary's performance at the talent show.* **3.** *n.* a short film or taped version of a song. (Pl in *-s.*) ♦ *Dave watches music videos on cable television.* ♦ *The band recorded a video of their latest single.* **4. videocassette** *n.* a device that holds videotape, which is put into a video camera or videocassette recorder to record and play back images. ♦ *Bill crushed an important videocassette by accident.* ♦ *You should rewind videocassettes after watching them.* **5.** *adj.* <the adj. use of ①.> ♦ *I bought a video camera so I could record Anne's wedding.* ♦ *John rewound the videotape before returning it to the video rental store.*

videotape ['vɪd i o tep] **1.** *n.* a length of plastic tape that can be magnetized, by means of which images can be recorded and played back. (No plural form in this sense.) ♦ *All the videotape in the cassette was ruined by the heat.* ♦ *The film editor spliced two pieces of videotape together.* **2.** *n.* a reel or cassette of ①; a copy of a movie or a television show that is recorded on ①. ♦ *Bill watched a videotape of Mary's graduation party.* ♦ *Anne rented a videotape of her favorite movie after work.*

vie ['vaɪ] **vie for** *iv.* + *prep. phr.* to compete with someone; to compete for something; to compete with someone for something. (The present participle is *vying.*) ♦ *The two Olympic athletes vied for the gold medal.* ♦ *Mary vied with Susan for the open position in my department.*

Vietnam [vi ɛt 'nɑm] See Gazetteer.

view ['vju] **1.** *n.* the way something looks from a place; a scene. ♦ *The view from my hotel window was beautiful.* ♦ *From my office window, I have a view of the parking lot.* **2.** *n.* an opinion; the way someone thinks about something. ♦ *In my view, the mayor should do more to prevent crime.* ♦ *The article outlined the journalist's views on gun control.* **3.** *tv.* to examine someone or something; to look at someone or something closely. ♦ *John viewed the accident from his apartment window.* ♦ *Mary viewed a robin in its nest, feeding its young.* **4. view as** *tv.* + *prep. phr.* to consider someone or something in a certain way. ♦ *I viewed Mary as a good friend.* ♦ *John views his office as a dungeon.*

viewfinder ['vju fɑɪn dɚ] *n.* the device on a camera that one looks through in order to see what the camera will record or photograph. ♦ *The photographer focused the statue in the viewfinder and took its picture.* ♦ *I cleaned the viewfinder with a soft cloth so I could see through it clearly.*

viewpoint ['vju pɔɪnt] *n.* an opinion; the way someone thinks about something; a point of view. ♦ *Susan explained her viewpoints during the debate.* ♦ *Susan compared her viewpoint on gun control with mine.*

vigil ['vɪdʒ əl] *n.* the act of staying awake during the night in order to watch something, pray, take care of someone who is sick, or as a religious observance. ♦ *The guard remained awake throughout his vigil by drinking coffee.* ♦ *The family kept a vigil all night after the child was injured.*

vigilance ['vɪdʒ ə ləns] *n.* alertness; watching someone or something closely. (No plural form in this sense.) ♦ *Because of the police officer's vigilance, the crime was prevented.* ♦ *Due to the vigilance of the bank guard, the robber's plan was thwarted.*

vigilant ['vɪdʒ ə lənt] *adj.* on guard; watchful; watching over someone or something. (Adv: *vigilantly.*) ♦ *The vigilant guards protected the museum all day long.* ♦ *The president's vigilant bodyguard immediately noticed the man with a gun.*

vigilante [vɪdʒ ə 'læn ti] *n.* one who acts unofficially as judge and jury; one who takes the law into one's own hands. ♦ *The vigilante avenged his sister's murder by killing her murderer.* ♦ *Vigilantes patrolled the subways at night.*

vignette [vɪn 'jɛt] **1.** *n.* a short story, film, or production; a skit; a brief scene. (From French.) ♦ *This movie contains four short vignettes by the same director.* ♦ *The literary journal published Anne's vignette about learning to drive.* **2.** *n.* a small picture at the beginning or end of a book or chapter. ♦ *The vignettes in the old manuscript had been drawn by hand.* ♦ *The elaborate vignette contained the first letter of the chapter's first word.*

vigor ['vɪg ɚ] *n.* strength; eagerness and energy. (No plural form in this sense.) ♦ *The nutritious meal renewed the worker's vigor.* ♦ *The politician campaigned across the state with great vigor.*

vigorous ['vɪg ə rəs] *adj.* full of vigor; strong and active, especially in the mind or body; full of action; robust. (Adv: *vigorously.*) ♦ *The therapist gave the athlete a vigorous massage.* ♦ *Mary stretched her muscles before an hour of vigorous exercise.*

vile ['vaɪl] **1.** *adj.* very bad; very unpleasant; disgusting. (Adv: *vilely.* Comp: *viler;* sup: *vilest.*) ♦ *I spat the vile food out of my mouth.* ♦ *The vile stench of the rotting animal caused me to gag.* **2.** *adj.* evil; wicked; immoral. (Adv: *vilely.* Comp: *viler;* sup: *vilest.*) ♦ *The vile tyrant oppressed the citizens.* ♦ *The vile murderer tortured his victims.*

vilify ['vɪl ə fɑɪ] *tv.* to say vile things about someone or something. ♦ *The press vilified the corrupt politicians.* ♦ *The celebrity was vilified by the tabloid for his rudeness.*

villa ['vɪl ə] *n.* a house in the country, especially a vacation house; a fancy or elegant country house. ♦ *The rich couple owned a villa in the south of France.* ♦ *Each summer, Anne and Bob vacation at their country villa.*

village ['vɪl ɪdʒ] **1.** *n.* a small town; a group of houses and businesses in the country or suburbs. ♦ *I grew up in a small village of 500 people.* ♦ *The growing city annexed several small farm villages.* **2.** *n.* all the people who live in a particular village ①. ♦ *The village voted to construct a new fire station.* ♦ *The village objected to the way tax money was spent.* **3.** *adj.* <the adj. use of ①.> ♦ *I visited the mayor at the village hall.* ♦ *The park is located on village property.*

villager ['vɪl ɪdʒ ɚ] *n.* someone who lives in a village. ♦ *The villagers lived twenty miles from the nearest city.* ♦ *Many of the villagers go to the town pub on Friday night.*

villain ['vɪl ən] **1.** *n.* someone who is wicked or evil, especially someone who is the bad person in a story or movie. ♦ *The hero slew the villain in a sword fight at the end of the movie.* ♦ *The evil villain was very mean to everyone in the village.* **2. villain of the piece** *idiom* someone or something that is responsible for something bad or wrong. ♦ *I wonder who told the newspapers about the local scandal. I discovered that Jane was the villain of the piece.* ♦ *We couldn't think who had stolen the meat. The dog next door turned out to be the villain of the piece.*

vim ['vɪm] *n.* energy; vigor. (No plural form in this sense.) ♦ *The rookie played baseball with vim.* ♦ *The coffee gave me the vim I needed to remain awake.*

vindicate ['vɪn də ket] *tv.* to prove someone or something to be innocent. ♦ *Ten years after his execution, new evidence vindicated Bill of his alleged crimes.* ♦ *The surprising testimony vindicated the main suspect.*

vindication [vɪn də 'ke ʃən] *n.* the proving of innocence. (No plural form in this sense.) ♦ *The vindication of the executed prisoner was five years too late.* ♦ *John's vindication in the crime saved him from a ten-year prison sentence.*

vindictive [vɪn 'dɪk tɪv] *adj.* wanting to hurt someone who has hurt oneself; revengeful; holding a grudge. (Adv: *vindictively.*) ♦ *The vindictive employee spread lies* *about the manager who had reprimanded him.* ♦ *The vindictive clerk gave the rude customer incorrect information.*

vine ['vɑɪn] *n.* a plant that has long, thin stems that crawl along the ground or the sides of an object. ♦ *The workers removed vines of ivy from the side of the building.* ♦ *The farmer removed a large pumpkin from its vine.*

vinegar ['vɪn ɪ gɚ] *n.* a sour, acidic liquid, made by fermentation, used to flavor or preserve food. (No plural form in this sense.) ♦ *I put vinegar and oil on my salad.* ♦ *Mary sprinkled some vinegar on her french fries.*

vineyard ['vɪn jɚd] *n.* a place where grapes are grown. ♦ *The wine company owned its own vineyards.* ♦ *The sudden freeze destroyed the vineyard's entire grape crop.*

vintage ['vɪn tɪdʒ] **1.** *n.* the particular year in which a batch of wine was made. ♦ *The host served a very expensive vintage of wine.* ♦ *I arranged the bottles of wine in my cellar by their vintage.* **2.** *adj.* made in a very good year, especially wine made from a very good crop of grapes; outstanding in quality. ♦ *I tasted a sip of the vintage white wine.* ♦ *Mary served vintage wine at her dinner party.* **3.** *adj.* antique; of high quality from a period in the past. (Figurative on ②.) ♦ *Susan restores vintage cars from the 1930s.* ♦ *David collects vintage postcards from France.*

vinyl ['vɑɪ nəl] **1.** *n.* a common plastic. (No plural form in this sense.) ♦ *Since leather is expensive, Sue covered her chairs with vinyl.* ♦ *Our kitchen floor is covered with vinyl.* **2.** *adj.* made of ①. ♦ *My vinyl raincoat kept my clothes dry during the rainstorm.* ♦ *Mary bought a vinyl purse because it is easy to clean.*

viola [vi 'o lə] *n.* a stringed musical instrument that is similar to, but larger than, a violin. ♦ *David practices the viola hours at a time.* ♦ *Susan plays the viola in the local symphony orchestra.*

violate ['vɑɪ ə let] **1.** *tv.* to break a law, rule, or promise; not to observe a law or rule. ♦ *Anne received a ticket for violating a traffic law.* ♦ *Sadly, Bill has violated my trust by telling others my secret.* **2.** *tv.* to spoil something; to use something in a way it is not meant to be used. ♦ *The loud children violated my peace and quiet.* ♦ *The nosy reporter violated the celebrity's right to privacy.*

violation [vɑɪ ə 'le ʃən] *n.* the act of violating something, especially the breaking of a law or a rule. ♦ *The merchant sold beer to the minor in violation of the law.* ♦ *If you get one more traffic violation, your driver's license will be revoked.*

violence ['vɑɪ ə ləns] *n.* rough force; forceful actions that hurt or damage people or things. (No plural form in this sense. Number is expressed with *act(s) of violence.*) ♦ *Mary wouldn't let her children watch movies with lots of violence.* ♦ *The mayor was dismayed by all of the violence in the city.*

violent ['vɑɪ ə lənt] **1.** *adj.* using rough force that can hurt or damage people or things. (Adv: *violently.*) ♦ *The violent customer knocked over a table at the restaurant.* ♦ *The violent winds tore down many power lines.* **2.** *adj.* showing violence. (Adv: *violently.*) ♦ *I wouldn't let my children watch violent movies.* ♦ *In violent anger, Bill hit the wall with his fist.*

violet ['vɑɪ ə lɪt] **1.** *n.* a small plant that has dark purple flowers with a delicate smell. ♦ *Mary stopped to smell the violets growing in the park.* ♦ *David watered the pot of violets on his kitchen window sill.* **2.** *n.* the color purple or purplish-blue. ♦ *The bruise on my arm is a deep violet.* ♦ *The designer decorated my bathroom in violet and gray.* **3.** *adj.* purple or purplish-blue in color. ♦ *I picked the violet grapes from the vine.* ♦ *The spilled grape juice left a violet stain on the rug.*

violin [vɑɪ ə 'lɪn] *n.* a four-stringed musical instrument played with a bow. ♦ *The violin is smaller than and higher in pitch than the viola.* ♦ *There are six violins in our orchestra.*

violinist [vɑɪ ə 'lɪn əst] *n.* someone who plays a violin. ♦ *Four violinists auditioned for the open spot in the orchestra.* ♦ *The concert violinist practiced for eight hours every day.*

violist [vi 'o ləst] *n.* someone who plays a viola. ♦ *The violists sat behind the violinists in the orchestra pit.* ♦ *Dave intends to be a professional violist after he finishes school.*

viper ['vɑɪ pɚ] *n.* a poisonous snake, especially one with fangs. ♦ *The deadly viper sank its fangs into its prey.* ♦ *I clubbed the large viper to death before it could bite me.*

viral ['vɑɪ rəl] **1.** *adj.* of or about viruses. (Adv: *virally.*) ♦ *The researcher examined modes of viral transmission.* ♦ *The scientist discovered a new viral strain.* **2.** *adj.* caused by a virus. (Adv: *virally.*) ♦ *Bill is sick in bed with a viral infection.* ♦ *Many viral diseases cannot be cured.*

virgin ['vɚ dʒən] **1.** *n.* someone who has never had sexual intercourse. ♦ *The priest urged the students to remain virgins until marriage.* ♦ *The three teenagers vowed to remain virgins until they married.* **2.** *adj.* <the adj. use of ①.> ♦ *The virgin student asked the health teacher what sex was like.* ♦ *The nun taught us about the virgin martyrs.* **3.** *adj.* never touched by humans; unspoiled; spotless; pure; in the original condition. (Figurative on ②.) ♦ *The loggers could not cut the virgin forest in the national park.* ♦ *The explorer was the first to see the virgin wilderness.*

Virginia [vɚ 'dʒɪn jə] See Gazetteer.

virginity [vɚ 'dʒɪn ə ti] *n.* a state of never having had sexual intercourse. (No plural form in this sense.) ♦ *How old were you when you lost your virginity?* ♦ *The couple vowed to maintain their virginity until marriage.*

virile ['vɪr əl] *adj.* strong and masculine; able to procreate. (Adv: *virilely.*) ♦ *Tom looked strong and virile even after his heart transplant.* ♦ *The virile old man had fathered at least a dozen offspring.*

virologist [vɑɪ 'rɑl ə dʒəst] *n.* a scientist who studies viruses and viral diseases. ♦ *The virologist examined the virus under a microscope.* ♦ *A skilled virologist ran tests on the sick patient's blood.*

virology [vɑɪ 'rɑl ə dʒi] *n.* the science and study of viruses and diseases caused by viruses. (No plural form in this sense.) ♦ *The doctor who specialized in virology was consulted about the epidemic.* ♦ *The medical student studied virology at the university.*

virtual ['vɚ tʃu əl] **1.** *adj.* having an effect as though someone or something were the real thing or person. (Adv: *virtually.*) ♦ *The real-estate agent said the condo was located in a virtual paradise.* ♦ *The blizzard caused a virtual nightmare for the airport employees.* **2.** *adj.* of or about interaction in cyberspace; of or about interaction with other people through computers. (Adv: *virtually.*) ♦ *The virtual-reality program made it seem as though I* *were piloting a plane.* ♦ *A virtual business is one that exists in cyberspace.*

virtue ['vɚ tʃu] **1.** *n.* goodness, especially in behavior or morals. (No plural form in this sense.) ♦ *Virtue is a quality to which we should all aspire.* ♦ *What I lack in virtue, I make up for in good intentions.* **2.** *n.* a moral or admirable behavior or trait. ♦ *Faith, hope, and charity are all virtues.* ♦ *Mary looked for a potential husband with strong virtues.* **3.** *n.* an advantage. ♦ *My job isn't perfect, but it has many virtues.* ♦ *There are many virtues to owning your own house instead of renting.*

virtuoso [vɚ tʃu 'o so] *n.* a very skilled performer, especially a very skilled musician or singer. (From Italian. Pl in *-s*.) ♦ *The virtuoso sang before two thousand people at the concert hall.* ♦ *The piano virtuoso played the difficult sonata flawlessly.*

virtuous ['vɚ tʃu əs] *adj.* full of virtue; morally good; having or showing virtue. (Adv: *virtuously.*) ♦ *The virtuous boy returned to me the wallet I had lost.* ♦ *The teacher urged the students to be pure and virtuous.*

virulent ['vɪr jə lənt] **1.** *adj.* powerful and deadly; [of a serious disease capable of] spreading easily and quickly. (Adv: *virulently.*) ♦ *The virulent disease was spread by sneezing.* ♦ *Rats carried the virulent plague throughout the land.* **2.** *adj.* very hostile and hateful. (Figurative on ①. Adv: *virulently.*) ♦ *The journalist criticized the politician's virulent speech.* ♦ *The talk-show host spoke with a group of virulent bigots.*

virus ['vɑɪ rəs] *n.* a living thing so small it can only be seen under a microscope. (Viruses cause infections and diseases in humans, animals, and plants, including chickenpox, rabies, and the common cold.) ♦ *Viruses can reproduce only within the tissue of living animals or plants.* ♦ *The deadly virus was spread through casual contact.*

vis-à-vis ['vi zə 'vi] *prep.* relative to someone or something; in regard to someone or something. (From French.) ♦ *Vis-à-vis dinner, I'd like to go to a Mexican restaurant.* ♦ *The candidates explained their positions vis-à-vis the most important issue.*

visa ['vi zə] *n.* an official stamp, signature, or attachment put in a passport that allows its owner to enter a certain country. ♦ *The cost of the visa to enter a country depends on what country you are from.* ♦ *Mary went to the American embassy to renew her visa while abroad.*

visage ['vɪz ɪdʒ] *n.* the face; the appearance of the face. (Literary.) ♦ *The hero's visage was clouded with doubt.* ♦ *Mary's visage was shrouded by a veil.*

viscera ['vɪs ɚ ə] *n.* the internal organs of the body, especially the intestines. (The Latin plural of *viscus*, flesh.) ♦ *The buzzards ate the viscera of the dead deer.* ♦ *The mortician removed the viscera of the corpses before embalming them.*

visceral ['vɪs ɚ əl] **1.** *adj.* of or about or affecting the viscera. (Adv: *viscerally.*) ♦ *Bill had developed some sort of visceral infection.* ♦ *They suffered visceral lesions and bruises from the attack.* **2.** *adj.* of or about one's emotions or feelings, often a feeling centering in the viscera. (Adv: *viscerally.*) ♦ *I had a visceral reaction to the horrifying movie.* ♦ *Mary always follows her visceral instincts.*

viscosity [vɪ 'skɑs ə ti] *n.* the ability of a liquid to resist flowing. (No plural form in this sense.) ♦ *Molasses has a high viscosity.* ♦ *John reduced the viscosity of the ketchup by adding water.*

viscous ['vɪs kəs] *adj.* [of a liquid] thick and sticky, like syrup or glue. (Adv: *viscously.*) ♦ *The oil is too viscous to flow well in cold weather.* ♦ *My shoes stuck to the viscous tar as I walked across it.*

vise [vɑɪs] *n.* a machine made of metal jaws that can be pushed tightly together, used for clamping something tightly so that it doesn't move while someone works on it. ♦ *John clamped the rod in the vise while he sanded it.* ♦ *Anne tightened the two boards in the vise while she nailed them together.*

visibility [vɪz ə 'bɪl ə ti] **1.** *n.* the condition of being visible; the degree to which someone or something is noticed or causes someone or something to be seen. (No plural form in this sense.) ♦ *The hunters wore bright orange clothing to improve their visibility.* ♦ *Susan stained the object on the slide to improve its visibility under the microscope.* **2.** *n.* the degree to which the sky is clear; the distance that one can see because of weather conditions. (No plural form in this sense.) ♦ *The airport was closed because the visibility was only 300 feet.* ♦ *As the fog lifted, visibility improved.*

visible ['vɪz ə bəl] *adj.* able to be seen; not hidden. (Adv: *visibly.*) ♦ *Employees must wear their badges so they are visible.* ♦ *There were visible cracks in the old wall.*

vision ['vɪ ʒən] **1.** *n.* the ability to see; the power of sight. (No plural form in this sense.) ♦ *My vision is being destroyed by disease.* ♦ *Surgery restored the blind woman's vision.* **2.** *n.* something that is seen or experienced in a dream, in one's imagination, in one's memory, or in a supernatural occurrence. ♦ *Alone in the old house, Bill saw many ghostly visions.* ♦ *Anne was haunted in her dreams by visions of her past.* **3.** *n.* insight; the ability to understand what something means and how it will affect the future. (No plural form in this sense.) ♦ *Susan had the vision to sell her stock before the company went bankrupt.* ♦ *Because of the owner's vision, the company remained competitive.*

visionary ['vɪ ʒə nɛr i] **1.** *adj.* imaginary; existing only in the mind and therefore impractical or unreal. ♦ *John ridiculed Bill's visionary ideas as unrealistic.* ♦ *The owner's plans were too visionary to be practical.* **2.** *n.* someone who has great insight; someone who understands what something means and how it will affect the future. ♦ *John is the visionary who guided the company through the recession.* ♦ *The majority of citizens voted for the political visionary.*

visit ['vɪz ɪt] **1.** *tv.* to go to a person or a place for a period of time; to be with a person as a visitor; to be at a place as a visitor. ♦ *Mary visited Dave while he was in the hospital.* ♦ *John visited Europe for three weeks last summer.* **2.** *tv.* to examine or inspect something as part of one's job. ♦ *The company owner visited each branch once a month.* ♦ *The health inspector visited our restaurant for an inspection.* **3.** *iv.* to be someone's guest; to stay at someone's house or at a place as a guest or tourist. ♦ *We aren't living with my parents; we're just visiting.* ♦ *Some friends from Ohio are visiting this whole week.* **4.** *n.* the act of going to a place for a period of time in order to see someone or something, experience something, or talk with someone. ♦ *Would you like to come to my house for a visit next sum-*

mer? ♦ *John decided that his cousin in the hospital needed a visit.*

visitor ['vɪz ɪ tɚ] *n.* someone who visits someone or some place as a guest or tourist. ♦ *The hotel clerk recommended various restaurants to the visitors.* ♦ *Bill offered his visitors something to drink.*

visor ['vɑɪz ɚ] *n.* something that shields the eyes, especially from sunlight or glare. ♦ *Mary lowered her car's sun visor as she drove west.* ♦ *John wore a cap with a visor to protect his eyes from glare.*

vista ['vɪs tə] *n.* a view, especially a broad, sweeping view. ♦ *The vista of the river toward the waterfall was breathtaking.* ♦ *From his office window, John has a lovely vista of the lake.*

visual ['vɪ ʒu əl] **1.** *adj.* of or about vision. (Adv: *visually.*) ♦ *The colors of the visual spectrum range from red to violet.* ♦ *Special glasses corrected David's visual disorder.* **2.** *adj.* visible; designed to be seen; meant to be appreciated through sight. (Adv: *visually.*) ♦ *The artist's painting was a visual masterpiece.* ♦ *The movie had hundreds of special visual effects.*

visual aid ['vɪ ʒu əl 'ed] *n.* something involving vision, such as charts, pictures, movies, etc., that helps people remember or learn something. ♦ *The speaker used a colorful chart as a visual aid during her talk.* ♦ *Listeners retain more information if there are visual aids.*

visualization [vɪ ʒu əl ɪ 'ze ʃən] **1.** *n.* picturing something in one's mind. (No plural form in this sense.) ♦ *Visualization of the new building was hard without drawings.* ♦ *Visualization of what things should look like when they are completed is the architect's job.* **2.** *n.* an instance of ①. ♦ *I tried to describe my visualizations of what the new building should look like.* ♦ *The author's vivid description aided my visualization of the story's setting.*

visualize ['vɪ ʒu ə lɑɪz] *tv.* to imagine how someone or something appears. ♦ *I could visualize the action of the story because it was written so well.* ♦ *I closed my eyes and visualized walking through a field of wheat.*

vital ['vɑɪt əl] **1.** *adj.* very important; absolutely necessary; essential. (Adv: *vitally.*) ♦ *Secrecy is vital for national security.* ♦ *The soldiers protected the vital port from the enemy.* **2.** *adj.* of or about life; necessary for life. ♦ *The heart and brain are vital organs.* ♦ *The paramedic measured the injured man's vital signs.* **3.** *adj.* active; full of life. (Adv: *vitally.*) ♦ *The dancers performed in a vital, energetic way.* ♦ *John was quite a vital individual before his stroke.*

vitality [vɑɪ 'tæl ə ti] *n.* energy and enthusiasm; liveliness. (No plural form in this sense.) ♦ *The dancers performed on the stage with great vitality.* ♦ *John's vitality was drained by the end of the busy workday.*

vitalize ['vɑɪ tə lɑɪz] *tv.* to make someone or something active or energetic. ♦ *Coffee vitalized the sluggish man.* ♦ *A large donation of money vitalized our organization.*

vitamin ['vɑɪ tə mɪn] *n.* a chemical compound that is important for a person's health and cannot be made by the body. ♦ *Citrus fruit is rich in vitamin C.* ♦ *Mary swallowed a pill that contained essential vitamins and minerals.*

vivacious [vɑɪ 've ʃəs] *adj.* lively; full of life; active; robust. (Adv: *vivaciously.*) ♦ *The vivacious cheerleaders rallied the crowd at the football game.* ♦ *A charming and vivacious salesperson convinced me to buy a new car.*

vivid ['vɪv ɪd] **1.** *adj.* clear; distinct. (Adv: *vividly.*) ♦ *Mary remembered her vivid dream.* ♦ *John has vivid recollections of his childhood.* **2.** *adj.* strongly or brightly colored; deeply colored. (Adv: *vividly.*) ♦ *David's tie was a vivid green.* ♦ *As the sun set, the sky was streaked with vivid blues and pinks.*

vixen ['vɪk sən] *n.* a female fox. ♦ *The dog chased the vixen through the woods.* ♦ *The vixen protected her newborn offspring.*

V-neck ['vi nɛk] **1.** *adj.* having a collar that is shaped like a V. ♦ *Anne wore a beige V-neck sweater.* ♦ *Jane wore her blue V-neck jumper with a white blouse.* **2.** *n.* a shirt, sweater, dress, or other article of clothing whose collar is shaped like a V. ♦ *All the V-necks were on sale at the department store.* ♦ *John spilled some juice on his V-neck.*

vocabulary [vo 'kæb jə lɛr i] **1.** *n.* all of the words that someone knows. (No plural form in this sense.) ♦ *Mary studied the dictionary to improve her vocabulary.* ♦ *John's Russian vocabulary is limited to a few words and phrases.* **2.** *n.* the words used in a certain business, profession, or activity. (No plural form in this sense.) ♦ *The medical vocabulary confused the patient.* ♦ *The soldier quickly learned the military vocabulary.* **3.** *n.* a list of words with a brief meaning, like those found in foreign-language dictionaries; a glossary of words and their meanings. ♦ *The German textbook included an 800-word vocabulary.* ♦ *Every boldfaced word in the textbook was defined in the vocabulary at the end.* **4.** *n.* all the words of a language. (No plural form in this sense.) ♦ *Much of the English vocabulary consists of technical and scientific terms.* ♦ *An unabridged English dictionary presents the vocabulary of the language.*

vocal ['vo kəl] **1.** *adj.* of, with, or about the voice or the path along which the voice travels. (Adv: *vocally.*) ♦ *The choking man had a piece of food stuck in his vocal tract.* ♦ *The singer did some vocal exercises before performing.* **2.** *adj.* loud; making one's opinions known. (Adv: *vocally.*) ♦ *A few vocal politicians monopolized the debate.* ♦ *The more vocal citizens did not hesitate to complain about waste in government.*

vocal folds ['vok əl 'foldz] *n.* the part of human speech mechanism, located in the throat, that produces the sound of the voice. ♦ *When I have a sore throat, it affects my vocal folds, and I cannot speak well.* ♦ *The vocal folds are not used in the production of* [p], [t], *or* [k].

vocalist ['vo kə ləst] *n.* someone who sings; a singer. ♦ *The vocalist recorded a new album over the summer.* ♦ *My favorite singer won an award for Best Vocalist last year.*

vocalize ['vo kə lɑɪz] **1.** *iv.* to practice using the voice, as before a performance. ♦ *A very sore throat prevented him from vocalizing.* ♦ *John always had to vocalize for a while before a he gave a recital.* **2.** to make one's thoughts known by speaking; to speak one's thoughts; to say what one is thinking. ♦ *Mary vocalized her thoughts at the meeting.* ♦ *John vocalized his ideas in order to persuade us to agree with him.*

vocation [vo 'ke ʃən] *n.* an occupation; a trade; a profession; one's calling. ♦ *The guidance counselor helped the student choose a vocation.* ♦ *What vocation are you training for?*

vocational [vo 'ke ʃə nəl] *adj.* of or about working and occupations. (Adv: *vocationally.*) ♦ *Some high schools offer vocational programs.* ♦ *Bill learned to be an electrician at a vocational school.*

vociferous [vo 'sɪf ə rəs] *adj.* loud; noisy; expressing one's thoughts loudly. (Adv: *vociferously.*) ♦ *The police arrested the vociferous protester.* ♦ *The librarian asked the vociferous patrons to be quiet.*

vodka ['vɑd kə] *n.* a clear alcoholic liquor made from rye or other grains. (No plural form in this sense.) ♦ *Vodka is a very popular kind of alcohol in eastern Europe.* ♦ *The foreign dignitaries toasted each other with glasses of vodka.*

vogue ['vog] *n.* fashion; style. (No plural form in this sense.) ♦ *Fashion magazines will show you what is in vogue this season.* ♦ *Susan felt that the current vogue in clothing was ugly.*

voice ['vɔɪs] **1.** *n.* the sounds made by a person who is speaking or singing. ♦ *The operator had a nasal voice because she had a cold.* ♦ *I have never heard her voice over the telephone before.* **2.** *n.* the ability to make sounds by speaking or singing. ♦ *The show was canceled because the singer had lost her voice.* ♦ *Anne trained her voice to sing opera.* **3.** *n.* a medium or channel for representing someone's opinions. ♦ *I will serve as your voice in the planning meetings.* ♦ *The alderman was the neighborhood's voice on the city council.* **4.** *n.* <a grammar term that describes the relation of the subject of a sentence to the verb.> ♦ *I wrote this sentence in the active voice.* ♦ *This sentence was written in the passive voice.* **5.** *tv.* to express an opinion by speaking. ♦ *The local residents voiced their concerns about the landfill.* ♦ *Mary voiced a complaint about the rude clerk.* **6.** *tv.* [in phonetics] to give a certain quality to a sound by vibrating the vocal folds and making the sound of the voice. ♦ *John mistakenly voiced the consonant at the end of the word.* ♦ *In English, you must always voice nasal consonants.* **7. at the top of one's voice** *idiom* with a very loud ①; as loudly as is possible to speak or yell. ♦ *Bill called to Mary at the top of his voice.* ♦ *How can I work when you're all talking at the top of your voices?* **8. lower one's voice** *idiom* to speak more softly. ♦ *Please lower your voice, or you'll disturb the people who are working.* ♦ *He wouldn't lower his voice, so everyone heard what he said.*

voiced ['vɔɪst] *adj.* of or about sounds that are accompanied by a sounding of the voice. ♦ [b], [d], *and* [g] *are voiced consonants.* ♦ [z] *is the voiced counterpart of* [s].

voiceless ['vɔɪs ləs] **1.** *adj.* of or about sounds that are made when the vocal folds are not vibrating; made without vibrating the vocal folds. (Adv: *voicelessly.*) ♦ [p], [t], *and* [k] *are voiceless consonants.* ♦ *Whispers are voiceless sounds.* **2.** *adj.* mute; not having a voice; unable to speak. (Adv: *voicelessly.*) ♦ *The voiceless man communicated through sign language.* ♦ *The voiceless singer canceled the evening's performance.*

void ['vɔɪd] **1.** *adj.* not binding according to the law; having no legal authority; having no legal effect; no longer valid. ♦ *This commercial offer is void where prohibited.* ♦ *The judged ruled John's contract to be void.* **2. void of** *adj. + prep. phr.* empty [of someone or something]. ♦ *The arena was void of fans during the strike.* ♦ *The boring speech was void of interesting ideas.* **3.** *tv.* to cause a law to stop being a law; to invalidate something. ♦ *The Supreme Court voided the unconstitutional law.* ♦ *The marriage was voided by a judge.* **4.** *n.* emptiness; empty space. ♦ *Most of the universe is a large void.* ♦ *There was a void in John's life after his best friend died.*

volatile ['vɑl ə təl] **1.** *adj.* easily becoming a vapor or gas; changing easily into a vapor or gas. ♦ *The volatile chemical was stored at a temperature of –100 degrees Celsius.* ♦ *The volatile substance changed directly from solid to gas.* **2.** *adj.* likely to change suddenly. (Figurative on ①.) ♦ *I avoid Bill because his temper is so volatile.* ♦ *Mary's mood has been volatile because of trouble at home.*

volcanic [vɑl 'kæn ɪk] *adj.* of or about volcanoes. (Adv: *volcanically* [...ɪk li].) ♦ *Anne vacationed on a volcanic island in the Pacific Ocean.* ♦ *The volcanic mountain erupted after being dormant for centuries.*

volcano [vɑl 'ke no] *n.* a mountain with an opening at the top from which steam, gas, molten rock, and ash sometimes are ejected by pressure or force from inside the earth. (Pl in *-s* or *-es.*) ♦ *Mt. St. Helens is a volcano in Washington that erupted in 1980.* ♦ *The majority of the world's volcanoes encircle the Pacific Ocean.*

volition [vo 'lɪ ʃən] *n.* an exercise of one's will (No plural form in this sense.) ♦ *The criminal who had acted under his own volition was found guilty.* ♦ *Jane seemed to lack the volition to stand up for herself.*

volley ['vɑl i] **1.** *n.* many shots fired at the same time; many things that are sent through the air at the same time. ♦ *Our car was damaged by a volley of hail.* ♦ *The hunters shot a volley of arrows toward the deer.* **2.** *n.* [in tennis] the act of hitting a ball before it has touched the ground. ♦ *The tennis player returned her opponent's volley.* ♦ *The tennis player's volley struck the net.* **3.** *tv.* [in tennis] to hit the ball before it has touched the ground. ♦ *The tennis players volleyed the ball back and forth.* ♦ *Mary volleyed the tennis ball, and John returned it.*

volleyball ['vɑl i bɔl] **1.** *n.* a sport where two teams on opposite sides of a net try to hit a large, light ball back and forth over the net without letting the ball touch the ground. ♦ *The students erected a net and played volleyball at the beach.* ♦ *Anne played volleyball each year while in college.* **2.** *n.* the ball used to play ①. ♦ *Jane smacked the volleyball over the net.* ♦ *Bill hit the volleyball with his fist as he served it.*

volt ['volt] *n.* a unit of measurement of electrical force. ♦ *One watt of power is equal to one volt of electricity at the current of one ampere.* ♦ *Five thousand volts of electricity surged through the wire.*

voltage ['vol tɪdʒ] *n.* an amount of an electrical force, measured in volts. ♦ *Electrical power is determined by the product of voltage and current.* ♦ *The voltage in the electric fence was low enough to stun, not kill, anyone who touched it.*

volume ['vɑl jəm] **1.** *n.* a book, especially one book in a series of books. ♦ *The entries in the encyclopedia's second volume all began with* B. ♦ *One volume of the nature series was devoted to birds.* **2.** *n.* the loudness of sound. (No plural form in this sense.) ♦ *The music is too loud. Please turn down the volume.* ♦ *Adjust the volume so the walls don't shake!* **3.** *n.* an amount of something. ♦ *A large volume of oil washed up on shore from the spill.* ♦ *I have a considerable volume of work waiting for me at the office.* **4.** *n.* the expression of space in three dimensions, determined by multiplying an object's length, width, and depth. ♦ *The volume of a cube is determined by multiplying the length of one of its sides by itself twice. That is, the volume of a cube with a length of 3 inches is 3 × 3 × 3, or 27 cubic inches.* ♦ *The mathematician calculated the volume of the sphere.*

voluminous [və 'lu mə nəs] *adj.* bulky; large; to a large extent. (Adv: *voluminously.*) ♦ *The drapes, with their voluminous folds, cost hundreds of dollars to have dry-cleaned.* ♦ *The mayor faced the voluminous task of improving the schools.*

voluntarily [vɑl ən 'tɛr ə li] *adv.* by one's own choice; willingly; without being forced to do something. ♦ *John enlisted in the army voluntarily.* ♦ *David voluntarily offered to help me paint my house.*

voluntary ['vɑl ən tɛr ə i] **1.** *adj.* [done] by one's own choice. (Adv: *voluntarily* [vɑl ən tɛr ə li].) ♦ *Employees could make voluntary contributions to several charities.* ♦ *The charity relied solely on voluntary support.* **2.** *adj.* supported by volunteers or gifts. ♦ *Our voluntary agency provides nutritious meals to invalids.* ♦ *The association was run by a voluntary committee.*

volunteer [vɑl ən 'tɪr] **1.** *n.* someone who does work for free; someone who agrees to take on a job or task. ♦ *Mary is a volunteer at the local day-care center.* ♦ *Susan works as a volunteer on the mayor's reelection committee.* **2.** *tv.* to offer one's time, help, or energy at no cost; to give one's services for free. ♦ *Anne volunteered her services as a lawyer to the nonprofit agency.* ♦ *John volunteered his time to help organize the festival.* **3.** *tv.* to say something without being forced to talk; to say something by one's own choice. ♦ *John volunteered his comments when he felt they were appropriate.* ♦ *Mary volunteered some information about the computer program.* **4. volunteer to** *iv.* + *inf.* to help to do something at no cost. ♦ *David volunteered to help me move some furniture.* ♦ *The lawyer volunteered to represent the poor client for free.* **5.** *adj.* <the adj. use of ①.> ♦ *The volunteer group delivered food and blankets to the needy.* ♦ *The volunteer soldier served for four years.*

voluptuous [və 'lʌp tʃu əs] **1.** *adj.* luxurious; sensuous; causing a sensation of pleasure. (Adv: *voluptuously.*) ♦ *The car's imported leather interior was quite voluptuous.* ♦ *The decorations in the hotel lobby were voluptuous and looked quite expensive.* **2.** *adj.* having a sexually attractive female figure, especially with a sensuous figure. (Adv: *voluptuously.*) ♦ *The voluptuous actress modeled lingerie.* ♦ *The artist carved a voluptuous statue of the Roman goddess.*

vomit ['vɑm ɪt] **1.** *tv.* to throw food up after one has eaten it; to bring something up from the stomach. ♦ *The distraught man vomited the food he'd just eaten.* ♦ *The sick woman vomited the pizza she'd eaten for lunch.* **2.** *iv.* to throw [something] up from the stomach through the mouth. ♦ *The drunken student vomited into a trash can.* ♦ *The hospital patient vomited onto his pillow.* **3.** *n.* something that has been thrown up from the stomach through the mouth. (No plural form in this sense.) ♦ *The orderly cleaned up the patient's vomit.* ♦ *The dormitory bathroom smelled of vomit.*

voodoo ['vu du] *n.* a system of beliefs—practiced especially in the Caribbean—involving a mixture of established religion and magic. (No plural form in this sense.) ♦ *The tribal leader practiced voodoo to protect himself from evil spirits.* ♦ *The sorcerer used voodoo to curse his enemy.*

voracious [və 're ʃəs] *adj.* of or about a very strong appetite for something, especially food. (Adv: *voraciously.*) ♦ *The voracious student ate an entire pizza.* ♦ *Bill had a voracious appetite.*

vortex ['vor tɛks] *n.* a circular stream of water or wind that sucks everything in its path into its center; a whirlpool or whirlwind. ♦ *The abandoned raft was sucked into the swift vortex.* ♦ *Dirt and foliage swirled rapidly in the tornado's vortex.*

vote ['vot] **1.** *n.* a formal or legal expression of one's opinion on an issue, especially on political issues. ♦ *Jane cast her vote for the incumbent.* ♦ *Bill didn't want to give his vote to either candidate.* **2.** *n.* the right to vote ④. (No plural form in this sense.) ♦ *American women were granted the vote in 1920.* ♦ *The ethnic minority was denied the vote.* **3.** *n.* the votes ①, viewed collectively, of a large number of people who share a certain characteristic or background. (No plural form in this sense.) ♦ *The president received 75% of the Hispanic vote.* ♦ *The young candidate courted the youth vote.* **4.** *iv.* to express one's opinion on an issue by raising one's hand or marking one's choice on a ballot. ♦ *Only 25% of the eligible population voted in the election.* ♦ *Anne has voted since she turned 18.* **5. vote for; vote against** *iv.* + *prep. phr.* to act on a pending issue that is to be settled by voting for or against it. ♦ *Anne voted for the incumbent in the last election.* ♦ *The senator voted against the proposed legislation.*

voter ['vot ɚ] *n.* someone who has the right to vote in an election. ♦ *The candidate met with many voters before the election.* ♦ *The voters decided the presidential race by a slim margin.*

vouch ['vɑʊtʃ] **vouch for** *iv.* + *prep. phr.* to guarantee that something is true or accurate; to guarantee that someone is responsible. ♦ *The researcher vouched for the accuracy of the experiment.* ♦ *My former employer vouched for my good work record.*

voucher ['vɑʊ tʃɚ] *n.* a receipt; a document that proves that a monetary transaction has taken place. ♦ *I showed the delivery man the prepaid voucher the clerk had given me.* ♦ *John signed the credit-card voucher.*

vow ['vɑʊ] **1.** *n.* an oath; a solemn promise. ♦ *Tom and Mary took their wedding vows seriously.* ♦ *I made a vow to never reveal Jane's secret.* **2.** *tv.* to make ①; to promise something; to swear that one will do something. ♦ *Jimmy vowed that he would improve his grades next semester.* ♦ *Susan vowed to work hard until she paid off her debts.* ♦ *Bill vowed his loyalty to the cause.*

vowel ['vɑʊ əl] **1.** *n.* a speech sound that is made without closing any parts of the mouth while air passes through it. ♦ *The word* sweet *has only one sound that is a vowel, and it is* [i]. ♦ *The vowel* [e] *can be represented in writing by* ai, ay, *and* eigh. **2.** *n.* a letter of the alphabet that represents a speech sound that is not a consonant; [in English] the letters *a, e, i, o,* and *u.* ♦ *The word* sweet *contains two vowels.* ♦ *There are two vowels in the word* fought, *but only one vowel sound.* **3.** *adj.* <the adj. use of ①.> ♦ *The letter* e *stands for a vowel sound.* ♦ *We are studying vowel production in phonetics class.*

voyage ['vɔɪ ədʒ] **1.** *n.* a journey, especially one made over water, through the air, or in space; a journey made on a ship, airplane, or spacecraft. ♦ *The astronauts prepared for their voyage to the moon.* ♦ *We were excited about our upcoming voyage to Europe by ship.* **2. voyage to** *iv. + prep. phr.* to travel by ship, airplane, or spacecraft to a place; to travel on a long journey. ♦ *Our family voyaged to Australia by plane.* ♦ *The space shuttle crew voyaged to Mars on a discovery mission.* **3. maiden voyage** *idiom* the first voyage of a ship or boat. ♦ *The liner sank on its maiden voyage.* ♦ *Jim is taking his yacht on its maiden voyage.*

voyeur [vɔɪ 'jɚ] *n.* someone who becomes sexually excited by watching someone else in secret. ♦ *The police caught the voyeur looking into his neighbor's bedroom window.* ♦ *The voyeur watched as the woman changed her clothes.*

vulgar ['vʌl gɚ] **1.** *adj.* common; popular; for the common person; ordinary. (Adv: *vulgarly.*) ♦ *She doesn't take an interest in the concerns of the vulgar masses because she is too sophisticated.* ♦ *Tom spends his weekends with the typical vulgar college crowd.* **2.** *adj.* indecent; lewd. (Adv: *vulgarly.*) ♦ *She was criticized for telling vulgar jokes.* ♦ *Bill made a vulgar remark that offended everyone.*

vulgarity [vəl 'gɛr ə ti] **1.** *n.* a lack of good taste or good judgment. (No plural form in this sense.) ♦ *The comic's vulgarity offended most of the audience.* ♦ *The teacher tried to replace the students' vulgarity with good manners.* **2.** *n.* an obscene word or expression. ♦ *The disc jockey was fined for each vulgarity he used.* ♦ *The editor censored the vulgarities from the news report.*

vulnerable ['vʌl nə rə bəl] *adj.* unprotected; easily attacked or hurt; sensitive. (Adv: *vulnerably.*) ♦ *David felt very vulnerable after his manager criticized him.* ♦ *The inefficient company was vulnerable to the competition.*

vulture ['vʌl tʃɚ] *n.* a large bird that lives on the meat of dead animals. ♦ *Vultures circled over the dying animal.* ♦ *The vultures picked the meat from the rotting carcass.*

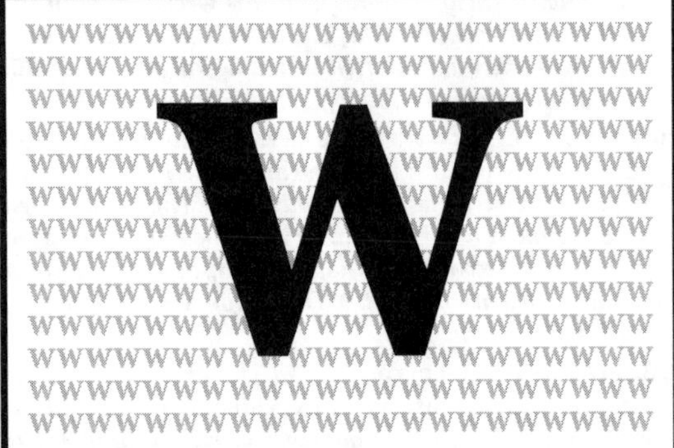

W AND **w** ['dʌb əl ju] *n.* the twenty-third letter of the English alphabet. ♦ W *comes after* V *and before* X. ♦ *There are two* Ws *in* wow.

wad ['wɑd] **1.** *n.* a thick, soft mass of something. ♦ *There are big wads of lint under the bed.* ♦ *Jimmy had a wad of gum in his mouth.* **2. wad up** *tv.* + *adv.* to form, shape, or roll something into ①. ♦ *Jane wadded up the paper and threw it away.* ♦ *David wadded up a wet rag and wiped the counter with it.*

waddle ['wɑd l] *iv.* to walk with slow, short steps while moving the body from side to side, as a duck walks. ♦ *The duck waddled toward the pond.* ♦ *The overweight man waddled across the street.*

wade ['wed] **1.** *iv.* to walk through shallow water or mud. ♦ *The horses waded across the stream.* ♦ *After the rainstorm we had to wade through the mud to get to the car.* **2.** *tv.* to cross a shallow body of water by walking through it. ♦ *The horses were carrying too much cargo to wade the creek.* ♦ *The children waded the length of the shallow pond.*

wafer ['we fɚ] *n.* a very thin biscuit, cracker, cookie, or piece of bread. ♦ *Sweet wafers were served with the ice cream.* ♦ *The delicate wafer broke as I put cheese on it.*

waffle ['wɑf əl] **1.** *n.* a thick round or square pancake with depressed squares that form a grid. ♦ *Jane poured lots of syrup on her waffles.* ♦ *My mother makes waffles for breakfast on Sundays.* **2.** *iv.* to change one's mind on an issue many times. ♦ *My manager waffled back and forth on whether to give me a raise.* ♦ *The president kept waffling about the important issues.*

waft ['wɑft] **1.** *iv.* to float on wind or water. ♦ *A feather slowly wafted toward the ground.* ♦ *The light raft wafted on the gentle waves.* **2.** *tv.* to carry or send something through the air or across the surface of the water. ♦ *The wind wafted the dry leaves over the garden wall.* ♦ *John wafted a ball across the park, and his dog chased it.*

wag ['wæg] **1.** *tv.* to move something up and down or from side to side many times. ♦ *Jane's dog wagged its tail happily when it saw her.* ♦ *Susan wagged her finger at her son as she scolded him.* **2.** *iv.* to move up and down or from side to side many times. ♦ *The dog's tail wagged very fast.* ♦ *The tree's branches wagged in the strong wind.*

wage ['wedʒ] **1.** *tv.* to begin and continue a war, battle, or struggle against someone or something. ♦ *The powerful country waged many wars.* ♦ *The residents waged a battle against the proposed landfill.* **2.** *n.* payment for work, especially if paid by the hour. (Often plural.) ♦ *Jane collects her wages once a week.* ♦ *Susan gets paid a good wage for her work.*

wager ['we dʒɚ] **1.** *n.* a bet. ♦ *The gamblers placed their wagers before the game started.* ♦ *John lost the wager that he had made on the horse race.* **2.** *tv.* to risk an amount of money on the outcome of an event. ♦ *John wagered $25 on the outcome of the race.* ♦ *I wagered $10 that my school's team would win the game.* **3.** *tv.* to bet that something will happen; to bet that something is or will be the case. (Takes a clause.) ♦ *Susan wagered that the train would be late.* ♦ *Bill wagered that I couldn't beat him in a game of tennis.*

wagon ['wæg ən] **1.** *n.* a strong four-wheeled vehicle with a flat bottom that is pulled by horses, mules, or oxen. ♦ *The pioneers crossed the plains in a covered wagon.* ♦ *The farmer hitched the horses to the wagon.* **2.** *n.* a small, light four-wheeled cart with a flat bottom that is pulled as a children's toy. ♦ *Susie gave her little brother a ride in his new red wagon.* ♦ *Jimmy filled his wagon with toys.* **3. fix someone's wagon** *idiom* to punish someone; to get even with someone; to plot against someone. ♦ *If you ever do that again, I'll fix your wagon!* ♦ *Tommy! You clean up your room this instant, or I'll fix your wagon!*

waif ['wef] *n.* a neglected child; a child who lives or works in the city streets. ♦ *The waif begged for food on the street corner.* ♦ *The sad waif was taken to the city orphanage.*

wail ['wel] **1.** *n.* a long, loud cry, especially one of pain or sadness. ♦ *After the earthquake, I heard the wails of the trapped victims.* ♦ *The mourners let out a loud wail of despair.* **2.** *iv.* to cry out with a long, loud sound because of pain or sadness. ♦ *The soldier wailed as he lay injured on the battlefield.* ♦ *The dead man's family wailed at his funeral.* **3.** *tv.* to utter something with a long, loud cry of pain or sadness. ♦ *The mourners wailed their anguish at the funeral.* ♦ *Jimmy wailed that his head hurt.*

wailing ['wel ɪŋ] *n.* intense, loud crying due to pain or sadness. (No plural form in this sense.) ♦ *The family's wailing continued throughout the funeral service.* ♦ *The wailing of the survivors helped the rescuers find them.*

waist ['west] **1.** *n.* the part of the body below the bottom of the ribs and above the hips. ♦ *John's belt fit tightly around his waist.* ♦ *Anne measured her waist before buying new pants.* **2.** *n.* the part of a piece of clothing that covers ①; the part of a piece of clothing that hangs from ①. ♦ *The tailor reduced the waist of my pants by two inches.* ♦ *A belt fits through loops sewn around the waist.*

waistline ['west lɑɪn] *n.* an imaginary line around the body at the smallest part of one's waist, usually where the top hem of a pair of pants or a skirt rests on the body. ♦ *The dieters measured their waistlines daily.* ♦ *The model had quite a small waistline.*

wait ['wet] **1.** *iv.* to stay in a place until someone or something else arrives or returns; to stay in a place until something happens. ♦ *I waited at the bus stop for the next bus.* ♦ *Anne waited in the doorway until it stopped raining.* **2. wait for; wait on** *iv.* + *prep. phr.* to anticipate the arrival of someone or something. ♦ *The diners waited for their meal for half an hour.* ♦ *Bill isn't ready, but we can't wait on him any longer. Let's go without him.* **3. wait on** *iv.* + *prep. phr.* to serve someone as a waiter or waitress or as a clerk behind a counter. ♦ *The waitress waited on five different tables full of diners at once.* ♦ *While the clerk* *was waiting on me, another customer rudely interrupted.* **4.** *n.* the period of time that one waits for someone or something; the act of waiting for someone or something. ♦ *There's a ten-minute wait until the next bus comes by.* ♦ *There was a short wait before the play while the theatergoers took their seats.* **5. can't wait (for something to happen)** *idiom* [to be very eager and] to be unable to endure the wait for something to happen. ♦ *I am so anxious for my birthday to come. I just can't wait.* ♦ *Tom can't wait for Mary to arrive.* **6. can't wait (to do something)** *idiom* [to be very eager and] unable to endure the wait until it is possible to do something. ♦ *I'm glad it's almost summertime—I just can't wait to go swimming!* ♦ *Jimmy can't wait to go to school tomorrow.* **7. wait on someone hand and foot** *idiom* to serve someone very well, attending to all personal needs. ♦ *I don't mind bringing you your coffee, but I don't intend to wait on you hand and foot.* ♦ *I don't want anyone to wait on me hand and foot. I can take care of myself.* **8. waiting in the wings** *idiom* ready or prepared to do something, especially to take over someone else's job or position. ♦ *Mr. Smith retires as manager next year, and Mr. Jones is just waiting in the wings.* ♦ *Jane was waiting in the wings, hoping that a member of the hockey team would drop out and she would get a place on the team.*

waiter ['we tɚ] *n.* a man who serves customers at a restaurant. ♦ *I asked my waiter for another cup of coffee.* ♦ *John did not leave the rude waiter a tip.*

waitress ['we trɪs] *n.* a woman who serves customers at a restaurant. ♦ *I asked my waitress what kind of soup was being served.* ♦ *The waitress asked us if we'd like to order dessert.*

waive ['wev] **1.** *tv.* to give up something, especially a right or a privilege. ♦ *The arrested man waived his right to make a phone call.* ♦ *Since John doesn't have a car, he waived his right to claim a parking space.* **2.** *tv.* to allow someone not to have to do something that is usually required; to excuse someone from fulfilling a requirement. ♦ *At college, my foreign-language requirement was waived because I had lived in Germany for five years.* ♦ *Tax payments are usually waived for charities.*

waiver ['wev ɚ] **1.** *n.* a form that indicates, when it is signed, that one is giving up a right or a privilege. ♦ *If you do not want to join the company's insurance plan, you must sign this waiver.* ♦ *The hikers each signed a waiver exempting the tour company from legal responsibility in case of injury.* **2.** *n.* permission from an authority that one is excused from having to do something. ♦ *Because of his medical condition, Bill was granted a waiver excusing him from gym class.* ♦ *Many charitable agencies have sales-tax waivers.*

wake ['wek] **1. wake (up)** *iv., irreg. (+ adv.)* to stop sleeping. (Pt: *waked* or **woke**; pp: *waked* or **woken**.) ♦ *I woke suddenly in the night when I heard a noise.* ♦ *Susan woke up at sunrise.* **2. wake (up)** *tv., irreg. (+ adv.)* to cause someone to stop sleeping. ♦ *I wake up Jane at 7:00 every day.* ♦ *Barking dogs woke me up at 3:00 A.M.* **3.** *n.* a gathering, shortly before a funeral, of friends and relatives of someone who has recently died. ♦ *I saw all of my cousins at my grandfather's wake.* ♦ *Mary said a prayer at her best friend's wake.* **4.** *n.* the path on the surface of a body of water caused by a boat or ship traveling through it. ♦ *The boat's wake sent waves toward the shore.* ♦ *The motorboat's rough wake overturned my rowboat.*

waken ['wek ən] **1.** *iv.* to wake from sleep; to stop sleeping. ♦ *Mary wakened shortly before dawn.* ♦ *John wakened to the sound of his neighbor's loud radio.* **2.** *tv.* to wake someone or something from sleep. ♦ *The sunlight wakened me early in the morning.* ♦ *Jane wakened Susan from her nap.*

waking ['wek ɪŋ] *adj.* being awake; while one is awake. ♦ *Bill spends every waking moment at work.* ♦ *Mary spent her waking hours doing errands.*

Wales ['welz] See Gazetteer.

walk ['wɔk] **1.** *iv.* to move on foot at a normal speed and in a way that each foot alternates being on the ground. ♦ *Anne walked to the bus stop.* ♦ *John walked down the hallway.* **2.** *iv.* [for a baseball batter] to go to first base after the pitcher has thrown four **balls** ③. ♦ *Susan walked her first time up at bat.* ♦ *Bill walked, so the player on first base moved to second base.* **3.** *tv.* to move in, on, or through a space as in ①. ♦ *Susan walked the trail along the lake.* ♦ *I walked the path that others had taken through the meadow.* **4.** *tv.* to exercise an animal, usually a dog, by taking it for ⑦. ♦ *Mary walks her dog twice a day.* ♦ *David walked his dog in the park.* **5.** *tv.* [for a baseball pitcher] to throw four **balls** ③ to a batter, which allows the batter to go to first base. ♦ *The skillful pitcher walked only one player during the game.* ♦ *The powerful batter was walked by the pitcher on purpose.* **6.** *tv.* to escort or accompany someone to a certain place. ♦ *The bodyguard walked Mary to her hotel room.* ♦ *The escort walks students home from the library at night.* **7.** *n.* an act of **walking** as in ①, especially as exercise or for pleasure; a journey on foot. ♦ *Susan took a long walk through the park after work.* ♦ *My dog enjoys his daily walks outside.* **8.** *n.* a path; a place where one can **walk** ①. ♦ *The walk to the pond was shaded by trees.* ♦ *Mary ran down the cobblestone walk near the hotel.* **9.** *n.* the placement of a [baseball] batter on first base after a pitcher has pitched four **balls** ③. ♦ *After four walks, the pitcher was replaced.* ♦ *The batter's walk moved the player on first base to second base.* **10. walk on eggs** *idiom* to be very cautious. ♦ *The manager is very hard to deal with. You really have to walk on eggs.* ♦ *I've been walking on eggs ever since I started working here.*

walker ['wɔk ɚ] **1.** *n.* a framework that supports someone who has difficulty walking. ♦ *David lifted the walker, moved it ahead, walked toward it, and repeated this until he reached his destination.* ♦ *My grandmother used a walker to get around after her hip surgery.* **2.** *n.* someone who walks, as opposed to a runner. ♦ *In the morning, there are many walkers exercising at the mall.* ♦ *Runners and walkers alike participated in the marathon for charity.*

walkout ['wɔk ɑʊt] *n.* a strike; the act of workers or others refusing to perform their duties until their demands are met. ♦ *The factory workers staged a walkout when their contract expired.* ♦ *The students held a walkout to protest the school's unfair policies.*

walkup ['wɔk əp] **1.** *n.* an apartment building that does not have an elevator. ♦ *Susan lives on the top floor of a five-story walkup.* ♦ *The older couple moved out of the four-story walkup and moved into a building with an elevator.* **2.** *n.* an apartment in a building that does not have an elevator, especially an apartment that is on the second floor or higher. ♦ *I hate carrying groceries to my walkup on the fourth floor.* ♦ *I was unable to move large furniture up to my walkup.* **3.** *adj.* <the adj. use of ① or ②.> ♦ *The landlady showed me the available walkup apartment.* ♦ *The city inspector condemned 20 unsafe walkup buildings.* **4.** *adj.* [of a counter, a window, or a similar location for service] arranged so that customers can walk directly up to someone who can help them. ♦ *I took my deposit slip to the bank's walkup window.* ♦ *The clerk at the walkup counter took my order.*

walkway ['wɔk we] *n.* a path or structure that people can walk on. ♦ *I placed my trash in the walkway between my building and the next one.* ♦ *The workers erected a walkway around the construction site.*

wall ['wɔl] **1.** *n.* the side of a room from the floor to the ceiling; the side of a building from the ground to the roof. ♦ *Anne tacked a calendar to the wall in her bedroom.* ♦ *John crashed his car through the wall of his garage.* **2.** *n.* a large, flat side of anything; anything that looks like ①. ♦ *The tidal wave slammed a large wall of water against the coast.* ♦ *The side of the house was covered with a wall of ivy.* **3.** *n.* a membrane that encloses a part of the body of a human, plant, or animal. ♦ *Mary looked at the cell walls of the onion under a microscope.* ♦ *Air passed through the cell wall by osmosis.* **4. wall in** *tv.* + *adv.* to build ① around something; to enclose something with ①. ♦ *The East Germans walled in West Berlin in the 1960s.* ♦ *I walled in the garden to prevent animals from eating the vegetables.* **5. wall up** *tv.* + *adv.* to close or seal something with ①. ♦ *Bill walled the old doorway up with bricks.* ♦ *Anne walled up the back portion of the large room with a wooden partition.* **6. go to the wall** *idiom* to fail or be defeated after being pushed to the extreme. ♦ *We really went to the wall on that deal.* ♦ *The company went to the wall because of that contract. Now it's broke.* **7. have one's back to the wall** *idiom* to be in a defensive position. ♦ *He'll have to give in. He has his back to the wall.* ♦ *How can I bargain when I've got my back to the wall?* **8. run into a stone wall** *idiom* to come to a barrier against further progress. ♦ *We've run into a stone wall in our investigation.* ♦ *Algebra was hard for Tom, but he really ran into a stone wall with geometry.* **9. Walls have ears.** *idiom* "We may be overheard." ♦ *Let's not discuss this matter here. Walls have ears, you know.* ♦ *Shhh. Walls have ears. Someone may be listening.*

wallboard ['wɔl bord] *n.* a thin panel made by pressing plaster between heavy paper, used to cover or create walls inside a building. (No plural form in this sense.) ♦ *The workers covered the wallboard with stucco.* ♦ *I screwed the wallboard into the studs.*

wallet ['wɑl ət] *n.* a small, flat case that is used for carrying money, identification, credit cards, etc. ♦ *I keep my driver's license in my wallet.* ♦ *Jane put the money in her wallet.*

wallow ['wɑl o] **1.** *iv.* to roll around in something, especially dirt, mud, or filth. ♦ *The young children wallowed in the mud and made their parents mad.* ♦ *Pigs love to wallow.* **2. wallow in** *iv.* + *prep. phr.* to take great pleasure in living in a certain way; to become deeply affected by one's emotions. (Figurative on ①.) ♦ *The guest in the fancy hotel wallowed in luxury.* ♦ *The miserable teenager wallowed in depression.*

wallpaper ['wɔl pe pɚ] **1.** *n.* paper, usually with a design on it, that is used to cover and decorate walls. (No plural form in this sense.) ♦ *Jane covered the ugly walls with bright wallpaper.* ♦ *David placed new wallpaper over the old, peeling layer.* **2.** *tv.* to cover a wall with ①. ♦ *Bob wallpapered his parents' kitchen for them.* ♦ *Anne wallpapered the living room with a bright print.* **3.** *iv.* to apply ① to a wall; to put up ①. ♦ *While Dave wallpapered, he became covered with paste.* ♦ *Mary decided to wallpaper instead of paint.*

wall-to-wall ['wɔl tə 'wɔl] **1.** *adj.* covering the entire floor, from one wall to the opposite wall. ♦ *Bob laid wall-to-wall carpeting in the living room.* ♦ *The wall-to-wall rug in the bathroom is damp.* **2. wall-to-wall with something** *idiom* having something in all places. (Figurative on ①.) ♦ *The hallway is wall-to-wall with Jimmy's toys.* ♦ *The beach was wall-to-wall with tourists.*

walnut ['wɔl nət] **1.** *n.* the hardwood tree that produces a delicious, edible nut. ♦ *There's a grove of walnuts behind the barn.* ♦ *A squirrel ran up the walnut in our front yard.* **2.** *n.* the nutmeat of ①; the nutmeat and shell of ①. ♦ *I added some chopped walnuts to the cookie dough.* ♦ *A squirrel sat under the tree, eating a walnut.* **3.** *n.* wood from ①. (No plural form in this sense.) ♦ *The carpenter made a desk from walnut.* ♦ *I coated the expensive walnut with a layer of varnish.* **4.** *adj.* made with or flavored with ②. ♦ *The walnut brownies taste delicious.* ♦ *Mary bought walnut ice cream.* **5.** *adj.* made from ③. ♦ *Jane protected the walnut table with a tablecloth.* ♦ *David polished the walnut bookshelves.*

walrus ['wɔl rəs] *n., irreg.* a large, thick-skinned animal that is similar to the seal and lives in the Arctic. (Pl: *walrus* or *walruses.*) ♦ *Walruses have very long tusks.* ♦ *The walrus dove into the sea to search for food.*

waltz ['wɔlts] **1.** *n.* a ballroom dance, with three beats to every measure of music, in which couples turn in a circle as they dance around the dance floor. ♦ *The couple danced a waltz around the ballroom.* ♦ *The dance instructors performed a waltz for the class.* **2.** *n.* music that has three beats to every measure and is written for ① or appropriate for ①. ♦ *Bill asked the band leader to play a waltz.* ♦ *The orchestra played a lively waltz.* **3.** *iv.* to dance ①. ♦ *Dozens of couples waltzed around the ballroom.* ♦ *I learned how to waltz when I took dance lessons.* **4. waltz in; waltz out** *iv.* + *adv.* to go in or out casually. ♦ *Our boss became angry when Anne waltzed in late for the third time this week.* ♦ *Instead of waiting for the meeting to end, John rudely waltzed out as soon as he got bored.*

wan ['wɑn] *adj.* [of a face or coloring] looking sick, pale, or tired. (Adv: *wanly.* Comp: *wanner;* sup: *wannest.*) ♦ *The doctor told Tom he looked wan.* ♦ *I offered my bus seat to the elderly passenger with a wan look on his face.*

wand ['wɑnd] **1.** *n.* a small, thin rod, such as the kind used by magicians during magic shows. ♦ *The magician tapped his magic wand against the hat, and a rabbit appeared.* ♦ *In the story, the fairy godmother waved her wand in the air.* **2.** *n.* the metal or plastic pipe that is attached to a vacuum-cleaner hose. ♦ *The vacuum cleaner had many different wands for hard-to-reach places.* ♦ *I used a long wand to clean along the edge of the walls.*

wander ['wɑn dɚ] **1.** *iv.* to travel in no specific direction without a specific destination in mind; to roam somewhere. ♦ *The nomads wandered across the desert from oasis to oasis.* ♦ *Anne wandered around the large park.* **2.** *tv.* to move over, through, or across an area in no specific direction or without a specific destination in mind. ♦ *Mary wandered the streets, looking for her dog.* ♦ *Bill wandered the countryside, working odd jobs.*

wanderlust ['wɑn dɚ ləst] *n.* the strong desire to travel. (No plural form in this sense.) ♦ *Bill quit his job to satisfy his wanderlust.* ♦ *Anne's wanderlust brought her to Florida.*

wane ['wen] **1.** *iv.* to become less important, less strong, less intense, or smaller. ♦ *The company's profits waned as competitors moved into its market.* ♦ *The politician's popularity waned as a result of the scandal.* **2.** *iv.* [for the moon] to gradually appear to be smaller after a full moon. (Compare with wax ④.) ♦ *The moon had visibly waned within a few days of the full moon.* ♦ *As the moon wanes, the nighttime sky is increasingly darker.*

want ['wɑnt] **1.** *tv.* to desire to have someone or something. ♦ *I want more potatoes, please.* ♦ *Jimmy wants a new toy.* **2. want to** *tv.* + *inf.* to desire to do something. ♦ *Anne wants to buy a new calendar.* ♦ *We want to go to Europe for a vacation.* **3.** *n.* a desire; a need; something that someone would like to have. ♦ *Jane's biggest want is a new car.* ♦ *Aunt Sally asked the children what their wants were.* **4.** *n.* a lack. (No plural form in this sense.) ♦ *A want of money led the youth to a life of crime.* ♦ *The beggar died for want of shelter and food.*

want ad ['wɑnt æd] *n.* an advertisement in a newspaper placed by someone who is looking for someone or something. ♦ *Jane placed a want ad for vintage automobiles.* ♦ *John looked through the want ads for job opportunities.*

wanted ['wɑn təd] *adj.* sought by the police or other law-enforcement agency. ♦ *The dangerous criminal was wanted in a dozen states.* ♦ *The federal agents tracked down the wanted suspect.*

wanton ['wɑnt n] *adj.* without a reason; without an excuse; for no reason; reckless; not restrained. (Adv: *wantonly.*) ♦ *The vandal was charged with wanton destruction.* ♦ *The wanton abuse of tax dollars by Congress angered the citizens.*

war ['wor] **1.** *n.* fighting or conflict between two or more nations, especially involving a military force of one country attacking another country. (No plural form in this sense.) ♦ *World War II ended in 1945.* ♦ *When John was 19, he joined the army and went to war.* **2.** *n.* a long fight or struggle against someone or something. ♦ *Congress struggled to win the war against drugs.* ♦ *Parents wanted to have a war on smut in the neighborhood.* **3.** *adj.* <the adj. use of ①.> ♦ *The war heroes marched in the veterans' parade.* ♦ *Max told us war stories of his experiences in the war.*

warbler ['worb lɚ] *n.* any of many species of small songbirds, known for their bright colors. ♦ *The bird watchers looked at the warblers through their binoculars.* ♦ *We heard the song of the warblers in the tree.*

ward ['word] **1.** *n.* someone, especially a child, who is under the protection of the state, the government, the court, or a guardian. ♦ *The abandoned child became a ward of the court.* ♦ *The foster parents eventually adopted their ward.* **2.** *n.* a political division of a city, especially one that is represented by someone in a city council. ♦ *I spoke to the alderman of my ward about trash collection.* ♦ *This city is divided into 50 wards.* **3.** *n.* a section of a hospital, usually containing the beds for patients having similar medical conditions. ♦ *I visited my sister in the maternity ward.* ♦ *The pediatrics ward is on the third floor of the hospital.* **4. ward off** *tv.* + *adv.* to deflect danger away from oneself. ♦ *Mary always wears a lucky charm to ward off evil spirits.* ♦ *Anne has an unlisted phone number to ward off unwanted callers.*

warden ['word n] **1.** *n.* someone who is in charge of a prison or jail. ♦ *The warden hired extra guards during the hot weather.* ♦ *The prison warden was unable to quell the riot.* **2. (game) warden** *n.* someone who enforces laws of or about hunting and fishing. ♦ *We had to show the game warden the ducks we shot.* ♦ *The warden asked to see our fishing permits.*

wardrobe ['word rob] **1.** *n.* a collection of clothes. ♦ *Mary's wardrobe contains many formal and casual outfits.* ♦ *Bill's wardrobe includes five different suits.* **2.** *n.* a piece of furniture that looks like a large box with a door, and is used to store clothing. ♦ *Anne folded her sweaters and placed them in the wardrobe.* ♦ *Bill keeps his ties inside the oak wardrobe.*

warehouse ['wɛr hɑʊs] **1.** *n., irreg.* a place where large amounts of goods are stored before they are sold or used. (Pl: [...hɑʊ zəz].) ♦ *A new shipment of paper should arrive from the warehouse soon.* ♦ *The manager took an inventory of the goods in the warehouse.* **2.** *tv.* to store something in ①. ♦ *The owner warehoused most of the stock because the store was small.* ♦ *The surplus inventory was warehoused in a large building.*

wares ['wɛrz] *n.* goods or products that are made or manufactured for sale. (Treated as plural.) ♦ *In her small jewelry shop, I asked Lisa to show me her wares.* ♦ *The sculptor's wares had been carved from mahogany.*

warfare ['wor fɛr] *n.* war, especially a particular method of fighting or killing. (No plural form in this sense.) ♦ *Atomic warfare could destroy the entire earth.* ♦ *Unleashing deadly viruses is a type of chemical warfare.*

warhead ['wor 'hɛd] *n.* the front end of a bomb or a missile that contains explosives. ♦ *Warheads rained down on the city from enemy planes.* ♦ *The bombs are equipped with nuclear warheads.*

warlike ['wor lɑɪk] *adj.* prepared for war; fond of war. ♦ *The United Nations condemned the army's warlike actions.* ♦ *The president viewed the warlike maneuvers as a threat.*

warlock ['wor lɑk] *n.* a wizard; a male witch; a sorcerer. ♦ *The warlock cast a magical spell on the princess.* ♦ *The king bought a potion from the warlock.*

warm ['worm] **1.** *adj.* somewhat hot; not too hot but not cold. (Adv: *warmly.* Comp: *warmer;* sup: *warmest.*) ♦ *The ice cream melted because it got warm.* ♦ *I like my coffee to be hot, not just warm.* **2.** *adj.* capable of retaining heat. (Adv: *warmly.* Comp: *warmer;* sup: *warmest.*) ♦ *Jane put on a pair of warm wool socks.* ♦ *John wears warm sweaters to work in winter.* **3.** *adj.* pleasant; friendly; indicating that one is pleasant or friendly. (Adv: *warmly.* Comp: *warmer;* sup: *warmest.*) ♦ *Tom gave Bill a warm handshake before the meeting.* ♦ *The guests received a warm reception at the banquet.* **4. warm (up)** *iv.* (+ *adv.*) to become ①. ♦ *The campers warmed up by the bonfire.* ♦ *The soup is warming on the stove.* **5. warm up** *iv.* + *adv.* to exercise and move the body about to prepare one's muscles for athletic activities. ♦ *I always warm up before I jog.* ♦ *If you don't warm up, you risk injuring yourself.* **6. warm to** *iv.* + *prep. phr.* to become agreeable to an idea. ♦ *Bill warmed to the idea of having pizza for dinner.* ♦ *Jane warmed to our plans of going to Florida.* **7. warm (up)** *tv.* (+ *adv.*) to cause someone or something to become ①. ♦ *Anne warmed her hands up by the fire.* ♦ *John warmed the soup on the stove.*

warm-blooded ['worm 'blʌd ɪd] *adj.* capable of maintaining a constant, warm body temperature. ♦ *The biologist studied warm-blooded mammals.* ♦ *Many large, warm-blooded creatures hibernate during the winter.*

warmer ['wor mɚ] *n.* something that makes heat to warm someone or something or to keep someone or something warm. ♦ *The cook kept the potatoes under a warmer.* ♦ *The coffee pot sat on a small warmer.*

warmhearted ['worm 'hɑrt ɪd] *adj.* kind; pleasant; friendly. (Adv: *warmheartedly.*) ♦ *The warmhearted hostess welcomed her guests.* ♦ *The small gift was a very warmhearted gesture.*

warmly ['worm li] *adv.* kindly; pleasantly; in a friendly way. ♦ *My mother warmly sends her regards to you.* ♦ *Susan thought warmly of her dear grandparents.*

warmonger ['wor mɑŋ gɚ] *n.* someone who is in favor of war or starting a war. ♦ *The warmongers in Congress urged the president to declare war.* ♦ *A few eager warmongers tried to influence the citizens.*

warmth ['wormθ] **1.** *n.* a small amount of heat. (No plural form in this sense.) ♦ *The warmth of the fire was a comfort to the cold campers.* ♦ *The warmth of the spring weather was a relief after the cold winter.* **2.** *n.* kindness; pleasantness; friendliness. (No plural form in this sense.) ♦ *The warmth of the doctor made the patient feel assured.* ♦ *Anne appreciated the warmth of her new neighbors.*

warn ['worn] **1.** *tv.* to alert someone to danger; to inform someone about something dangerous or risky. ♦ *The siren warned the residents of an approaching tornado.* ♦ *The spy warned the general of the enemy's plans.* **2.** *tv.* to tell someone not to do something, implying that punishment will follow repeated violations. ♦ *The museum guard warned us not to touch the paintings.* ♦ *The police officer warned me not to speed again.*

warning ['wor nɪŋ] *n.* a statement, sign, or indication of danger; something that warns. ♦ *The farmer posted a warning that read "No Trespassing!"* ♦ *My boss issued a verbal warning when I was late for work.*

warp ['worp] **1.** *tv.* to bend or twist something slightly and permanently out of shape. ♦ *The rain warped the boards that I'd left outside.* ♦ *The car's frame had been warped in the accident.* **2.** *tv.* to change someone or something for the worse; to corrupt someone. (Figurative on ①.) ♦ *John's unsavory friends warped his personality.* ♦ *Anne's mind became warped by excessive drug abuse.* **3.** *tv.* to change the meaning of something for the worse; to repeat what someone says and change the meaning to mean something bad. ♦ *The journalist warped the mayor's innocuous comments into an insult.* ♦ *The film director warped the author's simple story and made it too complicated.* **4.** *iv.* to become bent or twisted out of shape. ♦ *Wood warps if it is exposed to the elements.* ♦ *Over time, the shelf warped under the heavy weight of the books.* **5.** *n.* a bend, twist, or distortion of something. (No plural form in this sense.) ♦ *The warp of the board was so severe that it was no longer usable.* ♦ *The door won't close properly because of the warp of the door frame.*

warped ['worpt] **1.** *adj.* slightly twisted or bent out of shape. ♦ *John threw the warped boards into the fire.* ♦ *Anne pressed the warped door into its frame.* **2.** *adj.* characterized by distorted or corrupt thinking. (Figurative on ①.) ♦ *Max had a warped mind and had some terrible ideas.* ♦ *The warped thinking of the teenager worried his parents.*

warrant ['wor ənt] **1.** *n.* a written order that gives an authority the right to do something such as search someone, search a place, arrest someone, or carry out other legal orders. ♦ *The police officers arrived with a warrant for Bill's arrest.* ♦ *The judge signed a search warrant allowing the police to search Max's home.* **2.** *tv.* to justify something; to cause something to seem reasonable. ♦ *Your untrue comments warrant a lengthy reply.* ♦ *New evidence warranted a new trial.* **3. sign one's own death warrant** *idiom* to do something that ensures the failure of one's endeavors. (On ①.) ♦ *I wouldn't ever gamble a large sum of money. That would be signing my own death warrant.* ♦ *The killer signed his own death warrant when he walked into the police station and gave himself up.*

warranty ['wɑr ən ti] *n.* an official guarantee; a written promise from a manufacturer that something will function in the way that it is supposed to. ♦ *Anne's new computer came with a one-year warranty.* ♦ *John's new car has a limited warranty for parts and service.*

warring ['wor ɪŋ] *adj.* fighting; fighting a war; battling. ♦ *The warring factions agreed to a cease-fire.* ♦ *Both warring armies suffered heavy losses.*

warrior ['wor i jɚ] *n.* someone who is trained to fight; a soldier; a fighter. ♦ *The warrior rode into battle on his horse.* ♦ *The warriors fought on the battleground.*

warship ['wor ʃɪp] *n.* a ship equipped with weapons for making war. ♦ *The warship sank when it was struck by a torpedo.* ♦ *Two warships cruised into the enemy's harbor.*

wart ['wort] **1.** *n.* a hard, ugly bump that swells from the skin, especially on the face, neck, and hands. ♦ *Mary had a wart removed from her neck.* ♦ *A small wart developed on the end of John's nose.* **2. warts and all** *idiom* including all faults and disadvantages. ♦ *Jim has many faults, but Lisa loves him, warts and all.* ♦ *The place where we went on our holiday had some very run-down areas, but we liked it, warts and all.*

wartime ['wor tɑɪm] **1.** *n.* a period of time during war; a time of war. (No plural form in this sense.) ♦ *During wartime, our food was rationed.* ♦ *The citizens conserved energy during wartime.* **2.** *adj.* happening during war. ♦ *All wartime news reports were censored by the military.* ♦ *Wartime movies glorified the lives of soldiers.*

wary ['wɛr i] *adj.* aware; on guard against harm or danger; careful. (Adv: *warily.* Comp: *warier;* sup: *wariest.*) ♦ *The mail carrier was wary of dangerous dogs.* ♦ *The savvy tourist was wary of crooks.*

was ['wʌz, wɑz] *iv.* <a pt of be used with the first and third persons singular.> ♦ *The car was parked in the driveway all night.* ♦ *The house was red before they painted it white.*

wash ['wɑʃ] **1.** *tv.* to clean someone or something with water or some other liquid. ♦ *Anne washed her hands with soap and water.* ♦ *John always washes the dishes after dinner.* **2.** *tv.* to remove dirt through the use of water or some other liquid. ♦ *Wash the mud off your hands before you come to the table.* ♦ *The butcher washed the blood from the knife.* **3.** *tv.* [for water] to carry or move something. ♦ *The waves washed the log to the shore.* ♦ *The current washed the raft down the river.* **4.** *iv.* to clean [oneself or some part of oneself] with water or some other liquid. ♦ *Make sure you wash before dinner!* ♦ *Bob washed behind his ears.* **5.** *iv.* to be able to be washed without being damaged or losing color. ♦ *Do these dyed pants wash well?* ♦ *I took the dress to the cleaners because it doesn't wash.* **6.** *iv.* to be carried or moved by water. ♦ *The log washed ashore.* ♦ *The trash washed downstream.* **7.** *iv.* to be accepted. (Used in the negative.) ♦ *Your excuse won't wash with me!* ♦ *The suspect's alibi didn't wash in court.* **8.** *n.* laundry; clothes that need to be, are being, or have been washed; clothes that are washed together at one time. (No plural form in this sense.) ♦ *Anne carried the wash to the laundry room.* ♦ *Dave hung the wash out to dry on the clothesline.* **9.** *n.* an act or instance of washing or being washed as in ①, ②, or ④. ♦ *Your dirty clothes need a good wash.* ♦ *I gave my car a wash because I'd been driving on muddy roads.* **10. come out in the wash** *idiom* to work out all right. ♦ *Don't worry about that problem. It'll all come out in the wash.* ♦ *This trouble will go away. It'll come out in the wash.* **11. wash one's hands of someone or something** *idiom* to end one's association with someone or something. ♦ *I washed my hands of Tom. I wanted no more to do with him.* ♦ *That car was a real headache. I washed my hands of it long ago.*

washable ['wɑʃ ə bəl] *adj.* able to be washed without damage. ♦ *This shirt is washable, but don't put it in the dryer.* ♦ *I took the washable tablecloth to the Laundromat.*

wash-and-wear ['wɑʃ ən 'wɛr] *adj.* able to be worn after washing, without ironing. ♦ *I buy wash-and-wear clothes because I don't have time to iron.* ♦ *John hung the wash-and-wear shirt on a hanger after removing it from the dryer.*

washbowl ['wɑʃ bol] *n.* a bowl—as with a sink—that holds water with which one can wash one's face or hands. ♦ *Anne filled the washbowl with warm water and washed her face.* ♦ *Bill cleaned the washbowl after he finished shaving.*

washcloth ['wɑʃ klɔθ] *n.* a small cloth used for washing one's body, especially the face. ♦ *Mary cleaned her face with a wet washcloth.* ♦ *Who left the wet washcloth in the bathtub?*

washer ['wɑʃ ɚ] **1.** *n.* a washing machine; a machine that washes clothing. ♦ *Mary put the dirty clothes in the washer.* ♦ *Since I don't own a washer, I have to take my laundry to a Laundromat.* **2.** *n.* a small, flat circle of metal or rubber with a hole in the center that is put under the head of a bolt or screw or between a nut and a bolt to make a tighter seal. ♦ *You must put a washer on the bolt before you put the nut on.* ♦ *The metal washer protected the wood from being gouged by the screw.*

Washington ['wɑʃ ɪŋ tən] See Gazetteer.

Washington's Birthday [wɑʃ ɪŋ tənz 'bɚθ de] *n.* a U.S. holiday observing the birthday, on February 22, of George Washington, the country's first president. (See also **Presidents' Day**.) ♦ *Washington's Birthday is often observed in conjunction with Lincoln's Birthday on the third Monday in February.* ♦ *Our school is closed on Washington's Birthday.*

washout ['wɑʃ aʊt] *n.* a complete failure; a disaster. ♦ *John's ambitious plans were a complete washout.* ♦ *Mary's business was a washout, so she declared bankruptcy.*

washroom ['wɑʃ rum] *n.* a bathroom; a restroom; a room with a toilet. ♦ *Anne excused herself from the table to go to the washroom.* ♦ *When you're done in the washroom, turn out the light!*

wasn't ['wʌz ənt] *cont.* "was not." ♦ *Anne wasn't looking forward to going bowling with us.* ♦ *John wasn't at the party last night, was he?*

wasp ['wɑsp] *n.* a large stinging insect that is similar to a bee but is able to sting again and again. ♦ *The wasps stung the dog repeatedly.* ♦ *John angered the wasps by throwing rocks at their hive.*

waste ['west] **1.** *tv.* to use something foolishly or wrongly; to use too much of something. ♦ *John wasted his money on a pair of uncomfortable shoes.* ♦ *Anne wasted her time trying to convince John that she was right.* **2. waste (away)** *iv.* (+ *adv.*) to become weaker and weaker, often because of the lack of food. ♦ *The man in a coma was slowly wasting.* ♦ *Starving refugees wasted away at the border camp.* **3.** *n.* garbage; trash; something that is not used and is thrown away. (No plural form in this sense.) ♦ *Anne picked up the waste that littered the floor.* ♦ *The company illegally burned its waste.* **4.** *n.* a poor or foolish use of something; the failure to use all of the usable parts of something. (No plural form in this sense.) ♦ *Trying to convince John I was right was a waste of my time.* ♦ *This watch was a waste of money because it doesn't work.* **5.** *n.* material that is excreted from the body; urine and feces. (Sometimes plural with the same meaning.) ♦ *The filtration plant treated raw waste from the sewers.* ♦ *It's necessary to flush one's waste down the toilet.* **6. lay waste to something; lay something to waste** *idiom* to destroy something (literally or figuratively). ♦ *The kids came in and laid waste to my clean house.* ♦ *The invaders laid the village to waste.*

wastebasket ['west bæs kɪt] *n.* a container that is used to hold trash. ♦ *Anne's wastebasket is full of crumpled paper.* ♦ *The janitor emptied the wastebaskets in the office.*

wasteful ['west fʊl] *adj.* not saving; using something foolishly or wrongly; not conserving; using too much of something. (Adv: *wastefully.*) ♦ *The editorial criticized Congress's wasteful spending.* ♦ *It is wasteful to spend money on frivolous items.*

wasteland ['west lænd] *n.* an empty, barren, desolate, or unusable area of land. (Sometimes plural with the same meaning.) ♦ *The war had turned the town into a wasteland.* ♦ *No crops would grow on the rocky wasteland.*

wastepaper ['west pe pɚ] **1.** *n.* paper that is not needed and is thrown away or reused. (No plural form in this sense.) ♦ *Mary recycled wastepaper from the office.* ♦ *John threw the wastepaper in the trash.* **2. wastepaper basket** *n.* a container for receiving ①. ♦ *Please put this stuff in the wastepaper basket.* ♦ *You should empty the wastepaper basket into the large container outside.*

watch ['wɑtʃ] **1.** *tv.* to observe something as it happens; to pay someone or something attention; to look at someone or something to see what happens. ♦ *Susan watched the baseball game on television.* ♦ *David watched the parade from his apartment window.* **2.** *tv.* to guard someone or something; to protect someone or something. ♦ *Dozens of guards watch the paintings at the museum.* ♦ *Shepherds watched the flocks of sheep.* **3.** *iv.* to pay attention to someone or something; to look at someone or something carefully and attentively. ♦ *Mary played the piano while John watched.* ♦ *The audience watched closely as the magician performed the trick.* **4. watch over someone or something** *phr.* to monitor or guard someone or something ♦ *Please watch over my apartment while I am on vacation.* ♦ *I am looking for someone to watch over my grandmother during the day.* **5.** *n.* a device, typically worn on one's wrist, that keeps track of and displays the time. ♦ *I looked at my watch and realized I was late.* ♦ *What time does your watch say?*

watchband ['wɑtʃ bænd] *n.* the strap of a watch that keeps the watch on one's wrist. ♦ *The tight watchband left its imprint on my wrist.* ♦ *When my watchband snapped, the timepiece fell to the floor and broke.*

watchdog ['wɑtʃ dɔg] *n.* a dog that guards or protects someone or something. ♦ *The watchdog growled at the intruder.* ♦ *The robber always avoided houses with watchdogs.*

watchful ['wɑtʃ fʊl] *adj.* attentive; paying careful attention; paying close attention; vigilant. (Adv: *watchfully.*) ♦ *The celebrity was always under the bodyguard's watchful eye.* ♦ *The streets remained safe under the watchful care of the police.*

watchman ['wɑtʃ mən] *n., irreg.* someone, usually a male, who is hired to protect or guard something, especially during the night or when a building or place is empty. (Pl: watchmen.) ♦ *The night watchman was fired for sleeping on the job.* ♦ *The watchman called the police when he heard a suspicious noise.*

watchmen ['wɑtʃ mən] pl of watchman.

watchtower ['wɑtʃ taʊ ɚ] *n.* a tower from which guards are able to see over a wide area. ♦ *From the watchtower, the soldier saw the enemy advance.* ♦ *The troops tried to damage the stone watchtower with their cannons.*

water ['wɔt ɚ] **1.** *n.* the liquid that forms oceans, lakes, and rivers; the liquid that falls from the sky as rain and is drunk by humans and animals. (No plural form in this sense.) ♦ *Water boils at 100 degrees Celsius or 212 degrees Fahrenheit, and it freezes at 0 degrees Celsius or 32 degrees Fahrenheit.* ♦ *John swallowed some water when he was swimming.* **2.** *n.* the surface of a body of ①. (No plural form in this sense.) ♦ *I could see little fish swimming under the water.* ♦ *The calm water reflected my image.* **3. waters** *n.* vast amounts of ① as found in rivers, oceans, or large lakes. ♦ *The waters of the ocean were stirred into huge waves.* ♦ *The lake's waters provided swimming and boating.* **4.** *tv.* to provide a plant with ①; to put ① on the soil around a plant. ♦ *Mary watered the plants in her living room every day.* ♦ *John watered the tomato plants with a garden hose.* **5. water down** *tv.* + *adv.* to weaken the strength of a liquid by adding ① to it. ♦ *Someone has watered down the shampoo!* ♦ *Mary watered the lemonade down so that there would be enough for everyone.* **6.** *iv.* [for one's eyes] to fill with tears. ♦ *At the funeral, everyone's eyes were watering.* ♦ *My eyes watered because of the irritating fumes.* **7.** *iv.* [for one's mouth] to fill with saliva, especially when one is about to eat or is thinking eagerly about food. ♦ *My mouth watered when Anne described the lasagna she'd eaten.* ♦ *The children's mouths watered when they saw the delicious cake.* **8. hold water** *idiom* to be able to be proved; to be correct or true. ♦ *Bob's story doesn't hold water. It sounds too unlikely.* ♦ *The theory will not hold water, because the evidence is too weak.* **9. in deep water** *idiom* in a dangerous or vulnerable situation; in a serious situation, especially one that is too difficult or is beyond the level of one's abilities; in trouble. ♦ *John is having trouble with his taxes. He's in deep water.* ♦ *Bill is in deep water in algebra class. The class is too difficult for him, and he's almost failing.*

watercolor ['wɔt ɚ kəl ɚ] **1.** *n.* paint that has water as a base instead of oil. ♦ *The artist removed the watercolors from her hands with water and soap.* ♦ *Susan prefers to use watercolors over all other mediums.* **2.** *n.* a picture that is painted with ①. ♦ *David hung a cheery watercolor above his living-room sofa.* ♦ *Anne bought a watercolor from the art gallery.*

waterfall ['wɔt ɚ fɔl] *n.* a flow or cascade of water off the side of a mountain, rock, or dam. ♦ *We saw a beautiful waterfall in Hawaii.* ♦ *The daredevil went over the waterfall in a barrel.*

waterfowl ['wɔt ɚ faʊl] *n., irreg.* a bird that lives on or near the water. (Pl: *waterfowl* or *waterfowls.*) ♦ *Ducks, geese, and swans are types of waterfowl.* ♦ *The hunter shot several waterfowl by the marsh.*

waterfront ['wɔt ɚ frənt] **1.** *n.* the shore; the beach; land at the edge of a body of water. ♦ *We watched the sunset by the waterfront.* ♦ *The jogger ran along the waterfront for ten miles.* **2.** *n.* the part of a town alongside a body of water. ♦ *The industrial city's waterfront was badly polluted.* ♦ *We docked our boat at the waterfront.*

waterline ['wɔt ɚ lɑɪn] *n.* a real or imaginary line that marks how high the surface of a body of water reaches. ♦ *At the height of the flood, the waterline was higher than the dam.* ♦ *A layer of algae grew up to the waterline on the side of the pier.*

waterlogged ['wɔt ɚ lɔgd] *adj.* full of water; soaked through with water. ♦ *Mary wrung out her waterlogged boots.* ♦ *The waterlogged boat started to sink.*

watermark ['wɔt ɚ mɑrk] **1.** *n.* the mark on the side of an object in water that shows the height that the surface of the water has reached. ♦ *The flood left a watermark within an inch of the top of the dam.* ♦ *At low tide, the high tide's watermark was clearly visible.* **2.** *n.* a mark that is pressed onto paper when it is made. ♦ *If you hold a sheet of paper up to the light, you can see its watermark.* ♦ *The lawyer's stationery has a personalized watermark.*

watermelon ['wɔt ɚ mɛl ən] **1.** *n.* a large, round or oval fruit that grows on the ground on a vine and has a thick green rind and a juicy, pink inside containing a lot of black seeds. ♦ *Anne sliced the watermelon with a large knife.* ♦ *We all ate watermelon at the picnic.* **2.** *adj.* tasting like ①. ♦ *Mary ate watermelon candies.* ♦ *I chewed some watermelon gum.*

waterproof ['wɔt ɚ pruf] **1.** *adj.* not allowing water to pass through; able to keep water inside or outside; not leaking water. ♦ *Susan wore a waterproof raincoat during the rainstorm.* ♦ *John's waterproof boots keep his feet dry.* **2.** *tv.* to cause something to become waterproof ①. ♦ *Mary waterproofed her new leather shoes with a special spray.* ♦ *The wooden deck patio was waterproofed to protect it from the rain.*

water ski ['wɑt ɚ 'ski] **1.** *n.* a ski designed to be used on water instead of snow. ♦ *John took his water skis with him on vacation.* ♦ *You can water-ski on a single water ski, or on two.* **2. water-ski** *iv.* to use ① on the surface of the water. ♦ *I wanted to water-ski, but I could not find anyone to operate the boat to pull me along.* ♦ *I always wear a life vest when I water-ski.*

water-skiing ['wɑt ɚ ski ɪŋ] *n.* using water skis to water-ski. (See also skiing.) ♦ *Mike likes water-skiing, but it is an expensive sport.* ♦ *Lisa is an expert at water-skiing and has won some contests.*

watertight ['wɔt ɚ tɑɪt] **1.** *adj.* not allowing water to pass through; able to keep water inside or outside; not leaking water. ♦ *John caulked the windows to make them watertight.* ♦ *The watertight seal kept moisture from getting in the container.* **2.** *adj.* perfect; having no mistakes or loopholes. (Figurative on ①.) ♦ *No one could foil our watertight plan.* ♦ *The suspect was released because she had a watertight alibi.*

waterway ['wɔt ɚ we] *n.* a river, channel, canal, or body of water that ships can travel on. ♦ *The waterway was clogged with debris from the storm.* ♦ *The rescue team dredged the waterway to find the body of someone who had drowned.*

waterworks ['wɔt ɚ wɚks] *n.* the building and tanks wherein water is purified. (Treated as singular.) ♦ *The lake water was treated at the city's waterworks.* ♦ *Fluoride was added to the water supply at the waterworks.*

watery ['wɔt ɚ i] **1.** *adj.* wet; sodden; full of water; having too much water. ♦ *I sunk into the watery mud up to my ankles.* ♦ *The hunter avoided the watery quicksand.* **2.** *adj.* diluted; having had water added. ♦ *The watery soup tasted bland.* ♦ *The watery punch had very little flavor.*

watt ['wɑt] *n.* a measure of power expressing the amount of electrical power in a circuit where one ampere flows at the force of one volt. ♦ *One unit of horsepower is equal to 746 watts.* ♦ *Bright light bulbs use more watts of electrical energy than dim ones.*

wave ['wev] **1.** *n.* a moving ridge of water made by wind or the movement of something through water. ♦ *The waves crashed against the shore.* ♦ *The raft bobbed on the waves.* **2.** *n.* a ripple in the surface of something. ♦ *I used a sander to smooth the waves in the wood.* ♦ *The wind created small waves in the sand.* **3.** *n.* a movement of the hand as in ⑥. ♦ *I gave Anne a wave good-bye.* ♦ *The traffic cop's wave indicated that I should turn right.* **4.** *n.* an increase in crime, heat, or cold. ♦ *The police were baffled by the recent crime wave.* ♦ *The crops withered during the intense heat wave.* **5.** *tv.* to move something, especially one's hand, when greeting someone, trying to get someone's attention, or calling attention to oneself. ♦ *The surrendering army waved a white flag.* ♦ *Anne waved her hands wildly so that we would see her.* **6.** *iv.* to greet, to get someone's attention, or to call attention to oneself by moving one's hand. ♦ *John waved as I walked toward him.* ♦ *Mary was waving from her window.* **7.** *iv.* to move up and down or back and forth in the air. ♦ *The flag waved in the air.* ♦ *The kite waved as it hung from the tree.*

waver ['wev ɚ] **1.** *iv.* to flicker; to become stronger and weaker. ♦ *The candle wavered when the wind blew.* ♦ *The flame wavered and then went completely out.* **2.** *iv.* to move back and forth; to shake; to be unsteady. ♦ *The tall pole wavered in the heavy wind.* ♦ *The office building wavered during the earthquake.* **3.** *iv.* to be undecided between two or more options; to change one's opinion back and forth. (Figurative on ②.) ♦ *Mary wavered between going bowling and going to a movie.* ♦ *John wavered among the many choices on the menu.*

wavy ['wev i] *adj.* having waves; rippled; moving up and down or back and forth; rising and falling. (Adv: *wavily.* Comp: *wavier;* sup: *waviest.*) ♦ *These potato chips have wavy ridges.* ♦ *John's hair becomes wavy when it gets long.*

wax ['wæks] **1.** *n.* an oily or fatty substance that melts easily when it is warmed, but hardens when it is cool, used to make candles, floor polish, and other substances. (No plural form in this sense.) ♦ *The candle dripped wax as it burned.* ♦ *The floor shined with its new coat of wax.* **2.** *n.* an oily substance that is produced in the ears. (No plural form in this sense.) ♦ *Anne cleaned the wax from her ears with a cotton swab.* ♦ *John's slight deafness was caused by too much wax in his ears.* **3.** *tv.* to coat or polish a floor with wax. ♦ *David swept, mopped, and then waxed the floor.* ♦ *Anne just waxed the floor, so it's very slippery.* **4.** *tv.* [for the moon] to gradually appear to be brighter and fuller before a full moon. (Compare with wane.) ♦ *The moon waxed for days until it was again full.* ♦ *The psychic told me to leave town when the moon began to wax.*

waxed ['wækst] *adj.* coated or polished with wax. ♦ *John slipped on the waxed floor.* ♦ *The colorful, waxed tiles shined in the sunlight.*

waxy ['wæk si] **1.** *adj.* like wax. (Comp: *waxier;* sup: *waxiest.*) ♦ *Bill disliked the waxy chocolate.* ♦ *The soap left a waxy film on my skin.* **2.** *adj.* thick with wax; coated with wax. (Comp: *waxier;* sup: *waxiest.*) ♦ *The waxy floor was slippery.* ♦ *Mary cleaned her waxy ears.*

way ['we] **1.** *n.* a manner; the manner in which something is done; a method. ♦ *What way would you like your hamburger cooked?* ♦ *The teacher showed the students a new way to do division.* **2.** *n.* a habit; a custom; a regular manner in which something is done. ♦ *The sociologist studied the ways of the remote tribe.* ♦ *I am old-fashioned, and I adhered to the old way of doing it.* **3.** *n.* the route to a certain place. (No plural form in this sense.) ♦ *Do you know the way to the post office?* ♦ *The way to the stadium was blocked by an accident.* **4. one's way** *n.* one's desire; one's wish. ♦ *If I had my way, there would be no poverty.* ♦ *Jimmy cried until he got his way.* **5.** *adv.* far; far away in time or space. ♦ *The smart student was way ahead of the others.* ♦ *I'm way behind in my work.* **6. get something under way; have something under way** *idiom* to get something started. ♦ *The time has come to get this game under way.* ♦ *Now that the president has the meeting under way, I can relax.* **7. on the way (to something or some place); on one's way (to something or some place)** *idiom* moving toward a place; advancing toward a new status or condition. ♦ *Is he here yet or is he* *on the way?* ♦ *Mary is better now and on the way to recovery.*

waylaid ['we led] pt/pp of waylay.

waylay ['we le] *tv., irreg.* to attack someone from a hidden position. (Pt/pp: waylaid.) ♦ *The terrorists waylaid the secret police force.* ♦ *The robbers waylaid the unsuspecting tourists.*

wayside ['we sɑɪd] *adj.* along the way, road, or highway. ♦ *We finally found a wayside inn that had a vacancy.* ♦ *The motorist stopped at a wayside gas station.*

wayward ['we wɚd] *adj.* going the wrong way or any way except the right or expected one. (Adv: *waywardly.*) ♦ *The wayward teenager ran away from home.* ♦ *The driver could not control the wayward truck.*

we ['wi] **1.** *pron.* <the first-person plural subjective pronoun, referring to the speaker or writer—"I"—together with at least one other person.> (See also our, ours, us.) ♦ *Anne, do you think we should visit Susan today?* ♦ *I spoke for my friends when I said we were ready to order.* **2.** *pron.* <a special use of ① as a first-person singular subjective pronoun, meaning 'I, the speaker or writer.'> (Used by writers and sometimes by royalty.) ♦ *"We suggest a different analysis of the data," wrote the researcher.* ♦ *"We are not amused!" said the queen, speaking for herself.* **3.** *pron.* everyone; all humans. ♦ *We are all born, and we will all die.* ♦ *We must eat to live.*

weak ['wik] **1.** *adj.* lacking power or strength; not strong or powerful. (Adv: *weakly.* Comp: *weaker;* sup: *weakest.*) ♦ *The army toppled the weak government.* ♦ *The weak ballplayer collapsed on the field.* **2.** *adj.* lacking strong morals; lacking a moral character. (Adv: *weakly.* Comp: *weaker;* sup: *weakest.*) ♦ *Max is weak and can easily be pressured to do bad things.* ♦ *Bill was very weak against the temptation to cheat.* **3.** *adj.* having too much water; diluted. (Adv: *weakly.* Comp: *weaker;* sup: *weakest.*) ♦ *The weak punch wasn't very flavorful.* ♦ *This tea is far too weak for me. It hasn't steeped long enough.*

weaken ['wik ən] **1.** *iv.* to become weak. ♦ *The human body weakens as it gets older.* ♦ *The batteries in the flashlight had weakened over time.* **2.** *tv.* to cause someone or something to become weak. ♦ *Cancer weakened the patient's body.* ♦ *The army weakened the prime minister's power.*

weakling ['wik lɪŋ] *n.* someone who does not have much muscle and is not very strong. ♦ *The bully pushed the weakling around.* ♦ *The weakling was unable to lift the heavy package.*

weakness ['wik nəs] **1.** *n.* the condition of being weak, especially concerning the health of someone's mind or body. (No plural form in this sense.) ♦ *Mary's weakness was caused by pneumonia.* ♦ *Because of David's weakness, he dropped the heavy package.* **2.** *n.* a fault; a flaw; something that weakens someone or something. ♦ *The architect corrected the weaknesses in the building's design.* ♦ *One of the article's weaknesses was that it wasn't interesting.* **3. have a weakness for someone or something** *idiom* to be unable to resist someone or something; to be (figuratively) powerless against someone or something. ♦ *I have a weakness for chocolate.* ♦ *John has a weakness for Mary. I think he's in love.*

wealth ['wɛlθ] **1.** *n.* riches; a large amount of money or property. (No plural form in this sense.) ♦ *Anne inherited her parents' accumulated wealth.* ♦ *The rich investors donated part of their wealth to charity.* **2. wealth of something** *idiom* a large amount of something. (Figurative on ①.) ♦ *There's a wealth of information on parrots at the library.* ♦ *The junkyard had a wealth of used car parts.*

wealthy ['wɛl θi] **1.** *adj.* rich; having a large amount of money or property. (Adv: *wealthily.* Comp: *wealthier;* sup: *wealthiest.*) ♦ *The wealthy banker donated $100,000 to charity.* ♦ *Bill's wealthy parents paid for his college tuition.* **2. the wealthy** *n.* people who are ①. (No plural form in this sense. Treated as plural.) ♦ *The wealthy seek to protect their assets from taxation.* ♦ *The wealthy are able to afford the best of medical care.*

wean ['win] **1.** *tv.* to cause a child or young animal to begin to eat food other than milk from the mother. ♦ *Susan's children were all weaned before they were a year old.* ♦ *The farmer weaned the heifers as they got older.* **2. wean from** *tv. + prep. phr.* to cause someone to give up something gradually, especially a bad habit. (Figurative on ①.) ♦ *I was hard for me to wean myself from cigarettes.* ♦ *The nutritionist weaned John from red meat.*

weapon ['wɛp ən] *n.* any object or machine used to hurt someone, to kill someone, or to defend oneself during a fight or an attack. ♦ *The police searched for the weapon used to kill the victim.* ♦ *No weapons are permitted on the school grounds.*

weaponry ['wɛp ən ri] *n.* all weapons as a group. (No plural form in this sense.) ♦ *This legislation would ban many kinds of weaponry.* ♦ *The survivalist's shelter was stocked with a lot of weaponry.*

wear ['wɛr] **1.** *tv., irreg.* to have something on the body, including clothes, glasses, jewelry, perfume, makeup, and other accessories. (Pt: wore; pp: worn.) ♦ *John wears a uniform at work.* ♦ *Anne wore the necklace that I had given her.* **2.** *tv., irreg.* to have something on or related to the body postured in a particular way. ♦ *The actor wore his hair long for a movie role.* ♦ *The cashiers were all instructed to wear a smile.* **3.** *tv., irreg.* to damage something gradually because of continued use. ♦ *Many feet had worn the carpet to almost nothing.* ♦ *Over the centuries, the river wore the rocks down.* **4.** *iv., irreg.* to damage or worsen gradually. ♦ *My patience is wearing thin.* ♦ *The soil wore away with each rainstorm.* **5.** *n.* gradual damage that is caused because of continued use. (No plural form in this sense.) ♦ *John's favorite jeans show a lot of wear.* ♦ *Heavy wear on the car lessened its resale value.* **6.** *n.* clothing, especially a collection of clothing at a store available for sale. (No plural form in this sense.) ♦ *The pregnant woman shopped for maternity wear.* ♦ *The advertisement featured a new line of casual wear.* **7. none the worse for wear** *idiom* no worse because of use or effort. ♦ *I lent my car to John. When I got it back, it was none the worse for wear.* ♦ *I had a hard day today, but I'm none the worse for wear.* **8. wear and tear** *idiom* damage that is caused because of continued use. (No plural form in this sense.) ♦ *Children's clothing must withstand a lot of wear and tear.* ♦ *Due to five years of wear and tear, the dishwasher broke.*

wearable ['wɛr ə bəl] *adj.* able to be worn. (Adv: *wearably.*) ♦ *This shirt isn't wearable because it's too tight.* ♦ *My pants aren't wearable because the zipper is missing.*

wearily ['wɪr ə li] *adv.* in a tired way. ♦ *Bill wearily worked a double shift.* ♦ *Anne wearily finished her assignment at 3:00 in the morning.*

weariness ['wɪr i nəs] *n.* tiredness. (No plural form in this sense.) ♦ *The accident was caused by the driver's weariness.* ♦ *John's weariness was evident in the way he yawned.*

wearisome ['wɪr i səm] *adj.* causing tiredness, especially because of boredom; tiresome. (Adv: *wearisomely.*) ♦ *The wearisome speaker talked for three hours.* ♦ *I was bored by my friends' wearisome conversation.*

weary ['wɪr i] **1.** *adj.* tired; exhausted; fatigued. (Adv: *wearily.* Comp: *wearier;* sup: *weariest.*) ♦ *The weary workers walked slowly toward the train station after work.* ♦ *The weary driver fell asleep at the wheel and crashed into a tree.* **2. weary with** *tv.* + *prep. phr.* to cause someone to become tired, exhausted, or fatigued. ♦ *Bill wearied his friends with his boring stories.* ♦ *Mary wearied me with unimportant news.* **3.** *iv.* to become tired, exhausted, or fatigued. ♦ *The worker wearied as the day dragged on.* ♦ *The trucker wearied after driving for 18 hours.*

weasel ['wiz əl] *n.* a small, thin animal with a long body and short legs, related to the skunk. ♦ *Weasels eat birds' eggs and other small animals.* ♦ *The driver swerved to avoid the weasel crossing the road.*

weather ['wɛð ɚ] **1.** *n.* the condition of the outside air, including the temperature, the amount of moisture in the air, and the presence or absence of rain, snow, wind, clouds, and sunshine. (No plural form in this sense.) ♦ *The weather was very pleasant while I was on vacation.* ♦ *I use an air conditioner when the weather is hot.* **2.** *tv.* to withstand something (especially bad weather) without damage. ♦ *The boat weathered the storm.* ♦ *The plane easily weathered the rough journey.* **3.** *tv.* [for elements of weather] to damage something. ♦ *The rain weathered the wooden patio.* ♦ *The sun weathered the paint on the barn.* **4.** *iv.* to change because of exposure to ①. ♦ *When the porch weathered, the wood began to warp.* ♦ *Even well-built buildings weather over the course of time.* **5. under the weather** *idiom* sick. ♦ *I'm a bit under the weather today, so I can't go to the office.* ♦ *My head is aching, and I feel a little under the weather.*

weather-beaten ['wɛð ɚ bit n] *adj.* damaged or changed by wind, rain, snow, sun, or other aspects of weather. ♦ *The developer renovated the weather-beaten building.* ♦ *The weather-beaten shoreline was rapidly eroding.*

weather forecast ['wɛð ɚ for kæst] See forecast ②.

weatherproof ['wɛð ɚ pruf] **1.** *adj.* guarding against damage by or the intrusion of the weather. ♦ *The porch rotted because it was not weatherproof.* ♦ *Our windows are completely weatherproof.* **2.** *tv.* to make something weatherproof ①. ♦ *Anne weatherproofed the wooden deck with four coats of varnish.* ♦ *Bill weatherproofed his cabin so that he would be warm in the winter.*

weathervane ['wɛð ɚ ven] *n.* a wood or metal object that rotates to point in the direction that wind is blowing. ♦ *There's a weathervane on top of city hall.* ♦ *The weathervane indicated the wind was blowing from the west.*

weave ['wiv] **1.** *tv., irreg.* to make something by crossing threads or strips of material from side to side so that they go over and under threads or strips of material that are stretched up and down. (Pt: wove; pp: woven.) ♦ *Cloth is woven at this textile mill.* ♦ *I wove a wicker basket by hand.* **2.** *tv., irreg.* to cross threads or strips of material from side to side so that they go over and under threads or strips of material that are stretched up and down. ♦ *Anne wove her hair into a long braid.* ♦ *The machine wove wool thread into a bolt of material.* **3.** *tv., irreg.* to combine different things into a whole, as though one were crossing them back and forth. (Figurative on ②.) ♦ *The suspect wove many lies when trying to establish an alibi.* ♦ *Many cultures are woven together in large American cities.* **4.** *tv., irreg.* to make something by combining different things into a whole. (Figurative on ①.) ♦ *Grandpa wove many stories about his life as a boy.* ♦ *The suspect wove a web of lies when questioned by the police.* **5.** *iv., irreg.* to move so that one is always changing direction. (Pt: sometimes *weaved.*) ♦ *The drunk man weaved as he tried to walk.* ♦ *The police officer stopped the driver who kept weaving between lanes.* **6.** *n.* the way or pattern in which a material is woven. (No plural form in this sense.) ♦ *David bought a jacket with an unusual weave.* ♦ *Mary's sweater has a loose weave and snags easily.*

web ['wɛb] **1.** *n.* a net of thin, silky threads made by spiders in order to trap other insects for food. ♦ *The spider trapped small insects in its web.* ♦ *The corners of the room were covered with spider webs.* **2.** *n.* a network; a detailed arrangement of things that cross and connect each other. (Figurative on ①.) ♦ *The journalist had a wide web of information sources.* ♦ *The inspector unraveled the suspect's web of lies.* **3.** *n.* the piece of thin skin between the toes of ducks and other aquatic animals. ♦ *Beavers have webs between their toes.* ♦ *The webs of ducks' feet help them swim.* **4.** *n.* the World Wide Web; a branch of the computer Internet. (Often capitalized.) ♦ *There is something new on the web every day.* ♦ *Do you have any favorite locations on the Web?*

webbed ['wɛbd] *adj.* having skin between the toes, like those of ducks and other aquatic animals. ♦ *The duck's webbed feet help it swim.* ♦ *The beaver has webbed feet.*

we'd ['wid] **1.** *cont.* "we had," where had is an auxiliary. ♦ *We'd better go inside. It's starting to rain.* ♦ *If we'd had more time, we could have gone to the party.* **2.** *cont.* "we would." ♦ *We'd go to the party, but we weren't invited.* ♦ *We'd like to order our food now, please.*

wed ['wɛd] **1.** *tv., irreg.* to marry someone; to take someone as a husband or wife. (Pt/pp: *wedded* or *wed.*) ♦ *Anne wed Tom when she was 25.* ♦ *Mary wedded her high-school sweetheart.* **2.** *tv., irreg.* to cause two people to become married by performing a marriage ceremony. ♦ *The minister wedded the happy couple.* ♦ *A judge wed Jane and Bob.* **3.** *iv., irreg.* to become married. ♦ *John and Mary wedded in a small, quiet ceremony.* ♦ *After the couple wed, they honeymooned in Florida.* **4. wed(ded) to someone** *idiom* married to someone. ♦ *The couple will have been wed to each other for fifty years next June.* ♦ *Anne is wed to one of my cousins.* **5. wedded to something** *idiom* mentally attached to something; firmly committed to something. (Figurative on ④.) ♦ *The manager was wedded to the idea of getting new computers.* ♦ *The mayor was wedded to the new budget plan.*

wedding ['wɛd ɪŋ] **1.** *n.* the ceremony where two people become married to each other; a marriage ceremony. ♦ *The wedding was performed at a church.* ♦ *A rabbi presided over the couple's wedding.* **2.** *n.* a merger or formation of a close association. (Figurative on ①.) ♦ *A wedding of the two large firms would create a monopoly.* ♦ *Your theory is the wedding of two simple ideas.*

wedge ['wɛdʒ] **1.** *n.* a piece of wood, metal, or other material that is thick at one end and tapers to an edge at the other end. ♦ *A metal wedge can be used to split a log by placing the thin end on the end of the log and hitting the thick end with a hammer.* ♦ *Anne kept the door open by putting a rubber wedge under it.* **2.** *n.* any object shaped like ①. ♦ *I ate a wedge of chocolate cake.* ♦ *Tom placed a wedge of lime in my drink.* **3.** *n.* something that is used to separate things or people, like ①. (Figurative on ①.) ♦ *The court upheld the wedge between Church and State.* ♦ *John's drinking problem is a wedge between him and his friends.* **4.** *tv.* to stick someone or something in a tight space between two things or people, especially so that nothing or no one can move. ♦ *When Bill speaks, no one can wedge a word in edgewise.* ♦ *Susan wedged her car between two parked cars.*

wedlock ['wɛd lɑk] **1.** *n.* a state of marriage. (No plural form in this sense.) ♦ *Being united in wedlock was very important to the two young people.* ♦ *The minister united the two in holy wedlock.* **2. born out of wedlock** *idiom* born from parents who were not legally married. ♦ *The young infant had been born out of wedlock.* ♦ *A large proportion of births each year are of babies born out of wedlock.*

Wednesday ['wɛnz de] **1.** *n.* the fourth day of the week, between Tuesday and Thursday. ♦ *Next Wednesday, I will go to the bank.* ♦ *I have a dentist appointment next Wednesday.* **2.** *adv.* on the next ①. ♦ *Wednesday, I go to the dentist.* ♦ *We can sleep late Wednesday.* **3. (on) Wednesdays** *adv.* on each ①. ♦ *Tom cleans his room Wednesdays.* ♦ *I do my laundry Wednesdays.*

weed ['wid] **1.** *n.* a plant that grows in a place where it is not wanted. ♦ *The gardener removed the weeds from the tomato patch.* ♦ *The farmer killed the weeds with herbicide.* **2.** *tv.* to remove ① from an area of ground, such as a lawn or garden. ♦ *Anne weeded the garden with a hoe.* ♦ *John weeded the flower patch with a spade.* **3.** *tv.* to remove a specific kind of ①. ♦ *Bill weeded the dandelions from the tomato patch.* ♦ *Jane weeded the crab grass from the yard.* **4. weed out** *tv. + adv.* to eliminate someone or something that is not wanted. ♦ *The gifted students were weeded out from the regular program.* ♦ *The boss weeded out the bad workers.* **5.** *iv.* to clean or improve [a garden or lawn] by removing ①. ♦ *John went to the garden to weed.* ♦ *Mary weeds every week, but the weeds keep growing back.*

week ['wik] **1.** *n.* a period of seven days. ♦ *I was in the hospital for a week.* ♦ *Mary will go to Florida a week from Wednesday.* **2.** *n.* a period of seven days beginning on a Sunday and ending on a Saturday. ♦ *Anne promised to write the report sometime next week.* ♦ *John is going to visit during the third week of April.* **3.** *n.* the five or six days during which most workers work, especially Monday through Friday. ♦ *The store was open during the week and closed on the weekends.* ♦ *Jane spent the week analyzing last month's budget report.*

weekday ['wik de] **1.** *n.* Monday, Tuesday, Wednesday, Thursday, or Friday. ♦ *Every weekday, I awake at 7:00 A.M. and get ready for work.* ♦ *My dentist is only available on weekdays.* **2.** *adj.* happening on ①. ♦ *Anne took a weekday flight to New York City.* ♦ *Bill took a weekday vacation so that he could relax.* **3. (on) weekdays** *adv.* on every ①. ♦ *Jane works weekdays from 10:00 A.M. to 6:00 P.M.* ♦ *The bank is open on weekdays and closed on weekends.*

weekend ['wik ɛnd] **1.** *n.* the period of time from Friday evening to Sunday night. ♦ *What are you planning to do this weekend?* ♦ *We're going to have a party next weekend.* **2.** *adj.* happening at some time between Friday evening and Sunday night. ♦ *Mary took a weekend trip to Chicago and returned to work on Monday.* ♦ *The student works weekend shifts at the restaurant.* **3. (on) weekends** *adv.* on every ①. ♦ *Weekends, the drugstore is open all night long.* ♦ *The law office is closed on weekends.*

weekly ['wik li] **1.** *adj.* happening every week; happening once a week. ♦ *There's a weekly meeting in our office every Monday.* ♦ *Anne is at her parents' house for her weekly visit.* **2.** *adj.* payable every week. ♦ *Jane took her weekly pay to the bank.* ♦ *Bob spent his weekly allowance on a new book.* **3.** *adv.* every week; once a week. ♦ *Anne visits her parents weekly.* ♦ *The seminar class met weekly during the semester.* **4.** *n.* a magazine or newspaper that is issued once a week. ♦ *My favorite news weekly did a special feature on illegal drugs.* ♦ *Most of the news that was in the weekly had already appeared in my daily newspaper.*

weep ['wip] **1.** *iv., irreg.* to cry. (Pt/pp: **wept**.) ♦ *The mourners wept at the funeral.* ♦ *The audience wept during the sad movie.* **2.** *tv., irreg.* to shed tears; to cry and make tears. ♦ *All the neighbors wept tears of sorrow for the missing child.* ♦ *The hostages' families wept tears of joy upon their release.*

weeping ['wi pɪŋ] *adj.* crying; shedding tears. (Adv: *weepingly*.) ♦ *The teacher consoled the weeping children.* ♦ *The minister addressed the weeping mourners.*

weigh ['we] **1.** *tv.* to use a scale to determine the weight of someone or something. ♦ *The grocer weighed the fresh tomatoes.* ♦ *The doctor weighed the infant.* **2.** *tv.* to think carefully about and compare different options or alternatives when making a choice or decision. ♦ *Lisa weighed her options thoughtfully.* ♦ *The voter weighed the strengths and weaknesses of each candidate.* **3.** *iv.* to have a certain weight. ♦ *This chicken weighs four pounds.* ♦ *The wrestler weighed 135 pounds.* **4.** *iv.* to have a particular kind of influence on someone or something. ♦ *The trusted advisor's opinion weighed heavily with the mayor.* ♦ *Guilt weighed mightily on the sinner's conscience.*

weight ['wet] **1.** *n.* the degree of heaviness of someone or something or how heavy someone or something is, as measured according to a specific system. (No plural form in this sense.) ♦ *The weight of the load was too great for me to carry.* ♦ *Bill went on a diet to lose weight.* **2.** *n.* a heavy object, used for exercising. ♦ *Mary lifted forty-pound weights at the gym.* ♦ *John wore weights around his ankles while he jogged.* **3.** *n.* a heavy object, especially one that keeps something in place, holds something down, or balances something. ♦ *I placed a weight on the files on the desk in the windy room.* ♦ *The worker added a few weights to the pulleys.* **4.** *n.* a mental burden; something that occupies one's thoughts. (No plural form in this sense.) ♦ *The death of my friend was a heavy weight on my mind.* ♦ *The weight of my responsibility was very stressful.* **5.** *n.* importance; influence. (No plural form in this sense.) ♦ *The movie critic's review carried a lot of weight with audiences.* ♦ *The advisor used her weight to influence the mayor's decision.* **6. weight down** *tv.* + *adv.* to burden someone or something with something heavy. ♦ *The secretary was weighted down with too much work.* ♦ *Heavy clothing weighted down the drowning victim.* **7. carry weight (with someone)** *idiom* [for someone] to have influence with someone; [for something] to have significance for someone. ♦ *Everything Mary says carries weight with me.* ♦ *Don't pay any attention to John. What he says carries no weight around here.*

weightless ['wet ləs] *adj.* having no weight, especially when there is no gravity, as in space. (Adv: *weightlessly.*) ♦ *Three weightless astronauts floated around the spaceship.* ♦ *The weightless objects tumbled around the space capsule.*

weightlessness ['wet ləs nəs] *n.* a state of having no weight, especially because there is no gravity, as in space. (No plural form in this sense.) ♦ *The astronauts were trained in a machine that simulated weightlessness.* ♦ *Three astronauts floated around the rocket in a state of weightlessness.*

weightlifter ['wet lɪf tɚ] *n.* someone who lifts heavy weights, either as exercise or to compete with other people. ♦ *The weightlifter lifted 300 pounds over his head.* ♦ *Susan became a weightlifter to strengthen her muscles.*

weighty ['wet i] **1.** *adj.* heavy. (Comp: *weightier;* sup: *weightiest.*) ♦ *The weighty object sank to the bottom of the sea.* ♦ *Their weighty armor made it difficult for knights to move.* **2.** *adj.* important; serious. (Figurative on ①. Adv: *weightily.* Comp: *weightier;* sup: *weightiest.*) ♦ *The candidates discussed weighty issues during the debate.* ♦ *Lisa's weighty responsibilities were very stressful.*

weird ['wɪrd] *adj.* very strange; very odd; very unusual. (Adv: *weirdly.* Comp: *weirder;* sup: *weirdest.*) ♦ *Our dog barked at the weird glow in the sky.* ♦ *I called the police when I heard some weird noises in the alley.*

welcome ['wɛl kəm] **1.** *tv.* to greet someone in a friendly way. ♦ *The mayor welcomed the foreign diplomats at the airport.* ♦ *John welcomed his guests with open arms.* **2.** *tv.* to be happy to receive or experience something. (Figurative on ①.) ♦ *The office manager welcomed the new office policies.* ♦ *The teachers welcomed the adoption of a dress code.* **3.** *n.* the act of greeting or receiving someone or something with pleasure. ♦ *The tourists received a friendly welcome at the airport.* ♦ *The speaker received a hearty welcome of applause.* **4.** *adj.* accepted with pleasure; wanted. ♦ *A welcome breeze cooled the sweaty workers.* ♦ *I accepted the welcome promotion at work.* **5. welcome to do something** *idiom* free to do something; allowed to do something. ♦ *The audience is welcome to ask questions at the end of the speech.* ♦ *You are welcome to help yourself to anything in the kitchen.* **6. You are welcome.; You're welcome.** *phr.* a polite response to Thank you. ♦ *"Thank you for helping me." "You're welcome."* ♦ *"Thank you very much!" "You are welcome!"*

welcoming ['wɛl kəm ɪŋ] *adj.* inviting; causing one to feel welcome. (Adv: *welcomingly.*) ♦ *The adoptive parents gave their new child a welcoming hug.* ♦ *In a welcoming ceremony, the mayor gave the honored guest a key to the city.*

weld ['wɛld] **1.** *tv.* to join two pieces of metal together with high heat, sometimes using additional metal. ♦ *The metal worker welded the metal frame together.* ♦ *I'll need to weld these two pieces together.* **2.** *n.* the joint where two metals have been welded together. ♦ *After the weld cooled, it was very strong.* ♦ *The metal worker smoothed the weld with a file.*

welfare ['wɛl fɛr] **1.** *n.* a state of being healthy, comfortable, and having enough money to live satisfactorily. (No plural form in this sense.) ♦ *The parents looked out for their children's welfare.* ♦ *Going to college should improve your future welfare.* **2.** *n.* money provided by the government for poor people to live on. (No plural form in this sense.) ♦ *The poor family lived on welfare.* ♦ *The agency helped people find jobs and leave welfare.*

we'll ['wil] *cont.* "we will." ♦ *We'll be leaving in twenty minutes, so be ready.* ♦ *We'll be arriving at the restaurant around eight o'clock.*

well ['wɛl] **1.** *adv.* in a good way. (Comp: *better;* sup: *best.*) ♦ *Jane is a good singer. Jane sings well.* ♦ *Bob plays chess very well for someone who has just learned.* **2.** *adv.* enough; sufficiently; to a good degree. ♦ *This is not well done.* ♦ *Your plan is well thought out.* **3.** *adv.* completely; thoroughly; fully. ♦ *Anne likes her steak well cooked.* ♦ *Please wash your hands very well before cooking dinner.* **4.** *adv.* prosperously; showing prosperity. ♦ *The lawyer lived well in a fancy neighborhood.* ♦ *I ate very well when I was on vacation.* **5. well-** *adv.* <①–④ used in compounds.> (The examples are shown hyphenated. In actual use, the adjectival forms are usually hyphenated only when they are before a nominal and when there is no additional adverb such as very. Examples: *well-acquainted, well-adjusted, well-aimed, well-appointed, well-armed, well-balanced, well-behaved, well-being, well-bred, well-built, well-chosen, well-deserved, well-developed, well-disciplined, well-done, well-dressed, well-educated, well-established, well-fed, well-founded, well-groomed, well-grounded, well-heeled, well-informed, well-intentioned, well-known, well-liked, well-lit, well-loved, well-made, well-mannered, well-marbled, well-meaning, well-met, well-off, well-planned, well-qualified, well-read, well-reasoned, well-respected, well-rounded, well-run, well-spoken, well-tended, well-thought-of, well-to-do, well-trained, well-wisher, well-worn, well-written.*) **6. as well** *phr.* also; in addition. ♦ *Could I have some more potatoes as well?* ♦ *I'm feeling tired, and dizzy as well.* **7. as well as** *phr.* in addition to someone or something. ♦ *Mary and Jane are coming to the party, as well as Tom.* ♦ *I'm studying biology and chemistry, as well as history.* **8. as well as** *phr.* to the same high degree as someone or something; as much as. ♦ *Mary's parents treated me as well as they treated her.* ♦ *I did as well as you on the test.* **9.** *adj.* healthy; in good health. ♦ *I stayed home from work because I was not well.* ♦ *Anne asked me if I were feeling well.* **10. Well!** *interj.* <a word used to show surprise, dismay, agreement, or disagreement.> ♦ *Well! What do you think of that!* ♦ *Well! I've never been so insulted in all my life!* **11.** *n.* a deep hole that is dug in the ground to reach water, gas, or oil. ♦ *The oil shot up from the well.* ♦ *Bill lowered the bucket into the well.* **12.** *n.* a source. (Figurative on ⑪.) ♦ *The library is a well of information.* ♦ *My parents are a well of inspiration.* **13. well up** *iv.* + *adv.* [for a liquid] to rise from something. ♦ *Tears welled up in my eyes dur-*

ing the sad movie. ♦ *A flood of water welled up out of the sewer.*

well-adjusted [wɛl ə 'jʌs tɪd] *adj.* having a healthy mind; able to cope with life; not troubled by life. (Usually hyphenated only before a nominal.) ♦ *The well-adjusted children went on to have successful lives.* ♦ *The therapist helped the depressed student become well adjusted.*

well-appointed [wɛl ə 'pɔɪn tɪd] *adj.* [of something] having appropriate equipment or decorations. (Usually hyphenated only before a nominal.) ♦ *The well-appointed office contained a lot of computer equipment.* ♦ *Their living room was comfortable and well appointed.*

well-balanced ['wɛl 'bæl ənst] **1.** *adj.* having proper balance; properly balanced. (Usually hyphenated only before a nominal.) ♦ *Lisa carried the well-balanced tray to our table.* ♦ *John's load was not well balanced, and he nearly fell over.* **2.** *adj.* [of food] having a wide variety of nutrients. (Usually hyphenated only before a nominal.) ♦ *You should eat three well-balanced meals a day.* ♦ *I eat a well-balanced breakfast every morning.* **3.** *adj.* of a sound and balanced mental state. (Usually hyphenated.) ♦ *The prime suspect wasn't very well-balanced.* ♦ *The well-balanced manager was pleasant to work for.*

well-behaved ['wɛl bɪ 'hevd] *adj.* having proper behavior; properly behaved; obedient; not unruly. (Usually hyphenated only before a nominal.) ♦ *The teacher was pleased with the well-behaved students.* ♦ *The well-behaved audience applauded the performer.*

well-being ['wɛl 'bi ɪŋ] *n.* good health and prosperity; a state of having a comfortable life and good health. (No plural form in this sense.) ♦ *Parents are concerned for their children's well-being.* ♦ *The union protected the well-being of its members.*

well-bred ['wɛl 'brɛd] *adj.* raised in such a way that one has good manners; polite; courteous. (Usually hyphenated only before a nominal.) ♦ *The teacher was glad to have well-bred children in class.* ♦ *The well-bred man gave his seat on the bus to the elderly woman.*

well-built ['wɛl 'bɪlt] **1.** *adj.* properly built; solid; sturdy. (Usually hyphenated only before a nominal.) ♦ *The well-built fort withstood the enemy's attack.* ♦ *Only the well-built beach houses remained standing after the hurricane.* **2.** *adj.* muscular; having a good body shape. (Usually hyphenated only before a nominal.) ♦ *Well-built models posed for the clothing advertisement.* ♦ *A few well-built athletes trained at the gymnasium.*

well-chosen ['wɛl 'tʃo zən] *adj.* carefully picked; carefully selected; apt. (Usually hyphenated only before a nominal.) ♦ *Mary presented a well-chosen gift to the bride.* ♦ *Susan interviewed the well-chosen candidate for the newspaper.*

well-done ['wɛl 'dʌn] **1.** *adj.* properly or skillfully completed. (Usually hyphenated only before a nominal.) ♦ *The audience applauded the speaker's well-done presentation.* ♦ *Critics gave the well-done play an excellent review.* **2.** *adj.* thoroughly cooked; not rare. (Usually hyphenated.) ♦ *The inside of the well-done hamburger was not at all pink.* ♦ *The well-done pork was charred around the edges.*

well-dressed ['wɛl 'drɛst] *adj.* stylish; fashionable; wearing attractive or expensive clothing. (Usually hyphenated only before a nominal.) ♦ *Four or five well-dressed models showed off the new clothing.* ♦ *The well-dressed lawyer spent a lot of money on clothing.*

well-fed ['wɛl 'fɛd] *adj.* eating enough good food to be healthy; being served nutritious food. (Usually hyphenated only before a nominal.) ♦ *The well-fed orphans were taken care of by nuns.* ♦ *The well-fed prisoners didn't complain about the food.*

well-founded ['wɛl 'fɑʊn dɪd] *adj.* being a good reason or argument; factual; based on good reasons or fact. (Usually hyphenated only before a nominal.) ♦ *I can't disagree with your well-founded arguments.* ♦ *I have well-founded reasons for making my request.*

well-groomed ['wɛl 'grumd] *adj.* looking neat and clean; having a nice appearance. (Usually hyphenated only before a nominal.) ♦ *The well-groomed children smiled when their photo was taken.* ♦ *The judges examined the well-groomed horses.*

well-grounded ['wɛl 'grɑʊn dɪd] **1.** *adj.* factual; based on good reasons or fact. (Usually hyphenated only before a nominal.) ♦ *No one disputed the scientist's well-grounded conclusions.* ♦ *The speaker's arguments were well grounded, and she won the debate.* **2.** *adj.* having thorough education or experience in a certain subject. (Usually hyphenated only before a nominal.) ♦ *My teacher is well grounded in biological sciences.* ♦ *The mechanic was well grounded in foreign-car repair.*

well-heeled ['wɛl 'hild] *adj.* rich; prosperous; having a lot of money or property. ♦ *The well-heeled couple owned a second home in Paris.* ♦ *The poorer students were envious of their well-heeled classmates.*

well-informed ['wɛl ɪn 'formd] *adj.* having a lot of information about a certain subject or several subjects. (Usually hyphenated only before a nominal.) ♦ *The well-informed interviewer asked many insightful questions.* ♦ *The reporter got her news from a well-informed source.*

well-intentioned ['wɛl ɪn 'tɛn ʃənd] *adj.* having or showing good intentions, even if the results are not as good as expected. (Usually hyphenated only before a nominal.) ♦ *Although John was well intentioned, he shouldn't have gotten involved.* ♦ *Even well-intentioned actions can sometimes cause a lot of harm.*

well-known ['wɛl 'non] *adj.* known by many people; [of people who are] famous. (Usually hyphenated only before a nominal.) ♦ *The tourists saw a well-known musical in New York.* ♦ *The well-known actress disguised her identity when she appeared in public.*

well-liked ['wɛl 'lɑɪkt] *adj.* popular; liked by many people. (Usually hyphenated only before a nominal.) ♦ *The well-liked performer's show was sold out.* ♦ *The well-liked student won the office of class president.*

well-loved ['wɛl 'lʌvd] *adj.* popular; favorite; loved by many people. (Usually hyphenated only before a nominal.) ♦ *The reporter interviewed a well-loved author.* ♦ *The well-loved teacher's retirement party was rather sad.*

well-made ['wɛl 'med] *adj.* properly constructed; sturdy; made with skill. (Usually hyphenated only before a nominal.) ♦ *The well-made building withstood the earthquake.* ♦ *Even the most well-made plans sometimes go awry.*

well-mannered ['wɛl 'mæn ɚd] *adj.* having good manners; well behaved; polite; courteous; showing proper manners. (Usually hyphenated only before a nominal. Adv: *well-manneredly.*) ♦ *The well-mannered children rose when an adult entered the room.* ♦ *The well-mannered clerk was a pleasure to deal with.*

well-meaning ['wɛl 'min ɪŋ] *adj.* doing good things; having good intentions; well intentioned. (Usually hyphenated. Adv: *well-meaningly.*) ♦ *I know you're well-meaning, but you should mind your own business.* ♦ *Your proposal is well-meaning, but I'm afraid it's not feasible.*

well-off ['wɛl 'ɔf] *adj.* rich; wealthy; prosperous. ♦ *John doesn't work because his parents are quite well-off.* ♦ *Anne is so well-off that she owns three homes.*

well-read ['wɛl 'rɛd] *adj.* having learned many things from the books one has read; well educated. (Usually hyphenated only before a nominal.) ♦ *The well-read student did very well on the test.* ♦ *I had an interesting conversation with a well-read stranger.*

well-respected ['wɛl rɪ 'spɛk tɪd] *adj.* respected by many people; honored; admired. (Usually hyphenated only before a nominal.) ♦ *The well-respected mayor retired after 40 years in public service.* ♦ *The funeral of the well-respected citizen was well attended.*

well-rounded ['wɛl 'raʊn dɪd] *adj.* varied; balanced. (Usually hyphenated only before a nominal. Adv: *well-roundedly.*) ♦ *My advisor helped me plan a well-rounded education.* ♦ *The nutritionist urged me to eat a well-rounded diet.*

well-spoken ['wɛl 'spok ən] *adj.* able to use language effectively and politely when speaking; having good control of language when speaking; articulate. (Usually hyphenated only before a nominal.) ♦ *The well-spoken candidate did very well at the debate.* ♦ *The testimony of the well-spoken witness was impressive.*

well-thought-of ['wɛl 'θɔt əv] *adj.* respected; admired; honored; held in esteem; having a good reputation. (Hyphenated only before a nominal.) ♦ *The employees gave their well-thought-of manager a birthday gift.* ♦ *The president's policies are not well thought of around here.*

well-to-do ['wɛl tə 'du] *adj.* rich; prosperous; wealthy; having a lot of money. ♦ *My well-to-do grandparents live in luxury in Arizona.* ♦ *Because Dave's family is well-to-do, he'll never have to work.*

well-wisher ['wɛl wɪʃ ɚ] *n.* someone who wishes that someone will do well. ♦ *The well-wishers sent the opera star some flowers on opening night.* ♦ *Anne received cards from many well-wishers when she was ill.*

well-worn ['wɛl 'worn] **1.** *adj.* having been used a lot; showing damage because of use. (Usually hyphenated only before a nominal.) ♦ *The library replaced the well-worn dictionary.* ♦ *Our well-worn carpet is quite faded.* **2.** *adj.* [of words or phrases] used too often. (Usually hyphenated only before a nominal. Figurative on ①.) ♦ *The editor deleted the well-worn clichés from the manuscript.* ♦ *"Kick the bucket" is a well-worn euphemism meaning "to die."*

well-written ['wɛl 'rɪt n] *adj.* written in a clear, concise way; written in a way that is easy to understand and expresses what the writer wants to say. (Usually hyphenated only before a nominal.) ♦ *The well-written essay received the grade of A.* ♦ *The movie won several awards for its well-written screenplay.*

welt ['wɛlt] *n.* a ridge of reddened skin caused by being hit with a whip or belt. ♦ *There were welts on the horse's back where the whip had hit it.* ♦ *The doctor asked the boy about the welts on his arm.*

went ['wɛnt] pt of go.

wept ['wɛpt] pt/pp of weep.

we're ['wɪr] *cont.* "we are." ♦ *We're going to leave as soon as you're ready.* ♦ *When we're inside the store, I want you to behave.*

were ['wɚ] **1.** *iv.* <pt of be used with plural forms and you singular.> (Reduced to *'re* in contractions.) ♦ *The children were inside all day yesterday.* ♦ *You were very annoying last night.* **2.** *iv.* <the form of be used with all nouns and pronouns to indicate something that is contrary to fact.> ♦ *If I were you, I wouldn't drive to New York in this snowstorm.* ♦ *If you were I, what would you do?*

weren't ['wɚ ənt] *cont.* "were not." ♦ *We weren't in the park for more than five minutes when it started raining.* ♦ *You weren't at the party, were you?*

west ['wɛst] **1.** *n.* the direction to the left of someone or something facing north; the direction in which the sun sets. (No plural form in this sense.) ♦ *I saw dark clouds coming from the west.* ♦ *Mary lives to the west of Clark Street.* **2.** *n.* the western part of a region or country. (No plural form in this sense.) ♦ *El Paso is in the west of Texas.* ♦ *David vacationed in the west of France.* **3. West** *n.* the western part of the United States. (No plural form in this sense.) ♦ *Anne moved to the West after she graduated.* ♦ *The cowboy movie was set in the old wild West.* **4. West** *n.* Western Europe, North America, and South America, as contrasted with East Asia. (No plural form in this sense.) ♦ *Mary compared the philosophy of the West with that of the East.* ♦ *After years of living in Tokyo, Bill returned to the West.* **5. West** *n.* the part of Europe that was not communist or under the influence of the former Soviet Union. (No plural form in this sense.) ♦ *Many people were killed trying to escape to the West.* ♦ *Many formerly communist countries embraced the West after the Soviet Union fell.* **6.** *adj.* to ①; on the side that is toward ①; facing ①. ♦ *The fire damaged the west wing of the hospital.* ♦ *Bill painted the west side of his house green.* **7.** *adj.* from ①. (Especially used to describe wind.) ♦ *A cold west wind blew from the Rocky Mountains toward Omaha.* ♦ *The plane was flying against a strong west wind.* **8.** *adv.* towards ①; into the western part of something. ♦ *Anne drove west from Pittsburgh to Indianapolis.* ♦ *Turn west at the stop sign.*

westerly ['wɛs tɚ li] **1.** *adj.* toward the west; facing the west. ♦ *The westerly windows receive a lot of sunlight in the evening.* ♦ *The mayor campaigned in some of the westerly neighborhoods.* **2.** *adj.* from the west. (Especially used to describe wind.) ♦ *A cold westerly wind blew from the Rocky Mountains toward Omaha.* ♦ *The pilot flew westward against the strong westerly wind.* **3.** *adv.* toward the west. ♦ *The traveler slowly moved westerly across the continent.* ♦ *Anne walked westerly through the park.*

western ['wɛs tɚn] **1.** *adj.* in the west; toward the west; facing the west. ♦ *I watched the sunset through my apartment's western window.* ♦ *The candidate campaigned heavily in the western states.* **2.** *adj.* from the west, especially used to describe wind. ♦ *The western wind brought a lot of cold air.* ♦ *The plane flying from Chicago to New York* *was pushed along by western winds.* **3.** *n.* a movie, book, or television show about the development of the western ① United States during the 1800s. (Sometimes capitalized.) ♦ *Many Westerns inaccurately depict the plight of the Indians.* ♦ *Bill went to see a Western about a rancher trying to protect his cattle from outlaws.*

westerner ['wɛs tɚn ɚ] **1.** *n.* someone who lives in the western part of a country. ♦ *The westerner owns a 640-acre ranch in Nevada.* ♦ *Westerners in the U.S. seem to have a lot more space than folks in the East.* **2.** *n.* someone from the western non-Communist world. ♦ *The communist reviled westerners.* ♦ *The communist guard turned the westerner away at the border.*

Western Hemisphere ['wɛst ɚn 'hɛm əs fɪr] *n.* the half of the earth that includes North and South America. ♦ *The United States is in the Western Hemisphere.* ♦ *The Western Hemisphere includes what is called the "New World."*

West Virginia ['west vɚ 'dʒɪn jə] See Gazetteer.

westward ['wɛst wɚd] **1.** *adj.* toward the west; facing the west. (Adv: *westwardly.*) ♦ *The sunlight streamed through the westward windows around 6:00 P.M.* ♦ *The westward lanes of traffic were blocked by an accident.* **2.** *adv.* toward the west. ♦ *Mary drove westward toward California.* ♦ *The river ran westward toward the Pacific Ocean.*

wet ['wɛt] **1.** *adj.* not dry; covered with or soaked with liquid. (Adv: *wetly.* Comp: *wetter;* sup: *wettest.*) ♦ *I put the wet clothes in the dryer.* ♦ *I dried my wet hair with a towel.* **2.** *adj.* [of weather] rainy or humid. (Adv: *wetly.* Comp: *wetter;* sup: *wettest.*) ♦ *It's been a wet day, so I'm glad I brought my umbrella.* ♦ *My clothes are perpetually damp because of the wet weather.* **3.** *adj.* allowing liquor to be sold [legally]. ♦ *Wet states sell liquor every day except Sunday.* ♦ *The wet precinct contains most of the city's bars.* **4.** *tv.* to make someone or something ①; to cause someone or something to be ①. (Pt: usually *wetted.*) ♦ *The barber wetted my hair before cutting it.* ♦ *Anne wetted the flap and sealed the envelope.* **5.** *tv., irreg.* to urinate on oneself, on something, or in one's own clothes. (Pt: usually *wet.*) ♦ *The baby wet her diaper.* ♦ *The little boy wet his bed.* **6. wet behind the ears** *idiom* young and inexperienced. ♦ *John's too young to take on a job like this! He's still wet behind the ears!* ♦ *He may be wet behind the ears, but he's well trained and totally competent.*

wetness ['wɛt nəs] *n.* moisture; detectable liquid. (No plural form in this sense.) ♦ *The absorbent diapers keep wetness away from the baby's skin.* ♦ *The warm wetness of humid air is very uncomfortable.*

we've ['wiv] *cont.* "we have," where have is an auxiliary. ♦ *We've got to see each other more often!* ♦ *Do you think we've gotten lost?*

whack ['ʍæk] *tv.* to hit something with force. ♦ *The golfer whacked the golf ball with a club.* ♦ *I whacked the insect with a folded newspaper.*

whale ['ʍel] *n.* a very large mammal that lives in the ocean and breathes through an opening on top of its head. ♦ *Although whales live in the ocean, they are mammals.* ♦ *The fat of whales is called blubber.*

whaler ['ʍel ɚ] *n.* someone who hunts whales. ♦ *The whaler harpooned the large whale.* ♦ *The whalers were limited as to how many whales they could kill.*

wharf ['worf] *n., irreg.* a platform where ships can dock in order to load or unload people or cargo; a pier. (Pl: wharves.) ♦ *The cargo was taken from the ship and placed on the wharf.* ♦ *The part of town near the wharf is dangerous at night.*

wharves ['worvz] pl of wharf.

what ['ʍʌt] **1.** *interrog.* <a form used as the subject or object of a sentence or clause when asking questions to get more information about someone or something.> ♦ *What is the name of the person standing next to Aunt Mary?* ♦ *What did he say to you?* **2.** *interrog.* <a form used before nouns and nominals when asking questions to get more information about that noun or nominal.> ♦ *What gift did you bring to the wedding?* ♦ *What suit did John wear?* **3.** *pron.* that which; the thing that; the things that. ♦ *I understand what you're trying to do.* ♦ *Do what you want while I'm at the store.* **4.** *adv.* <an emphatic form.> ♦ *What a beautiful day!* ♦ *What a rude person!* **5.** *interj.* <a form showing great surprise.> ♦ *What? Are you telling me the truth?* ♦ *"Bill was fired today." "What? Are you kidding?"* **6. what for** *phr.* why?; for what reason? ♦ *"I want you to clean your room." "What for? It's clean enough."* ♦ *What did you do that for?* **7. what if** *phr.* what would be the result if something were true? ♦ *What if you had all the money you want?* ♦ *What if everyone thought you were great?*

whatever [ʍət 'ɛv ɚ] **1.** *pron.* anything that; everything that. ♦ *I'll listen to whatever you have to say.* ♦ *I'll eat whatever you decide to order.* **2.** *pron.* no matter what. ♦ *Whatever happens, I'll always be your friend.* ♦ *Whatever you tell me, I promise not to laugh.* **3.** *pron.* <an emphatic form of what, similar to *What possibly?* and used in questions.> ♦ *Whatever did you mean by that statement?* ♦ *Whatever did Bill do that made you so mad?* **4.** *adj.* any; no matter what. ♦ *Whatever shoes you want to get, I'll buy them for you.* ♦ *Whatever food you eat, eat it in moderation.* **5.** *interj.* <a form used to indicate resignation or lack of interest>; "Oh, well, it doesn't matter"; "Forget it!"; "I will not argue or discuss it anymore." (Informal.) ♦ *Please put the chair there. No there. I mean over there. Oh, whatever.* ♦ *So, you want me to do it this way? Oh, that's too hard. Whatever.*

what's ['ʍʌts] **1.** *cont.* "what is." ♦ *What's the answer to question five?* ♦ *What's going on in here?* **2.** *cont.* "what has," where has is an auxiliary. ♦ *What's been happening here since I left?* ♦ *What's Jimmy done today?*

whatsoever [ʍət so 'ɛv ɚ] **1.** *pron.* whatever. (Formal.) ♦ *I'll do whatsoever you ask me to do.* ♦ *Whatsoever could Anne have meant by that statement?* **2.** *adj.* any at all. (Used after nominals when *any* is before the nominal.) ♦ *"I can fix any clock whatsoever," the store owner said.* ♦ *You may buy any book whatsoever in the store.*

wheat ['ʍit] **1.** *n.* a kind of cereal plant grown for its seeds. (No plural form in this sense.) ♦ *The stalks of wheat in the field waved in the wind.* ♦ *The farmers harvested wheat towards the end of summer.* **2.** *n.* the seed of ①, ground to make flour. (No plural form in this sense. Number is expressed with *grain(s) of wheat.*) ♦ *I ground the wheat into meal.* ♦ *Wheat is carried to the mill in trucks or in barges on the river.* **3.** *adj.* made from ②. ♦ *Would you like wheat toast or rye toast?* ♦ *Anne ate some whole-wheat pancakes for breakfast.*

wheel ['ʍil] **1.** *n.* a sturdy circular object that turns around a central point and is connected to an axle. ♦ *Most cars have four wheels.* ♦ *Anne pumped some air into the front wheel of her bicycle.* **2.** *n.* something that is shaped like ① or works like ①. ♦ *Anne placed a wheel of cheese on the buffet table.* ♦ *The gamblers watched the roulette wheel spin.* **3.** *n.* the circular frame that a driver turns to control the direction of a car or truck; a steering wheel. ♦ *Susan turned the wheel sharply to avoid driving into the ditch.* ♦ *I got behind the wheel and started the engine.* **4. wheels** *n.* a car. (Slang.) ♦ *Anne bought a new set of wheels last week.* ♦ *I can't go to the concert because I don't have any wheels.* **5.** *tv.* to move or push something that has wheels ①. ♦ *John wheeled the grocery cart through the store.* ♦ *Anne wheeled her baby's stroller through the park.* **6.** *tv.* to carry someone or something in or on an object that has wheels ①. ♦ *Mary wheeled a load of newspapers in her wagon.* ♦ *Bill wheeled the baby around the park in a stroller.* **7. wheel around** *iv.* + *adv.* to turn around quickly. ♦ *Anne wheeled around to see who had been calling her name.* ♦ *Bill wheeled around when I tapped his back.* **8. put one's shoulder to the wheel** *idiom* to get busy. ♦ *You won't accomplish anything unless you put your shoulder to the wheel.* ♦ *I put my shoulder to the wheel and finished the job quickly.*

wheelbarrow ['ʍil bɛr o] *n.* an open container attached to a frame with one wheel in front. ♦ *A person uses a wheelbarrow by lifting the handles up and pushing it on its front wheel.* ♦ *The gardener picked weeds and threw them in the wheelbarrow.*

wheelchair ['ʍil tʃer] *n.* a chair that has wheels instead of legs, usually two large ones in back and two small ones in front, for people who are unable to walk. ♦ *A ramp was built next to the stairs for people in wheelchairs.* ♦ *John had to use a wheelchair after his legs were paralyzed in an accident.*

wheeze ['ʍiz] **1.** *iv.* to breathe with a heavy rasping or whistling sound, like a person who has trouble breathing. ♦ *Jane wheezed as she stumbled out of the burning building.* ♦ *When Bill contracted a lung disease, he began to wheeze.* **2.** *n.* a heavy rasping or whistling sound, like one made by someone who has trouble breathing. ♦ *The smoker's wheeze was so thick I couldn't understand him.* ♦ *The doctor listened to the patient's wheeze.*

when ['ʍɛn] **1.** *interrog.* at what time? ♦ *When does the next train leave the station?* ♦ *When was World War II fought?* **2.** *conj.* at the time that; at that certain time. ♦ *When the light turns green, you may proceed.* ♦ *Let's go see a movie when I'm finished with my homework.* **3.** *conj.* considering [the fact that]; as. ♦ *How do you expect to pass the test when you haven't studied?* ♦ *What am I supposed to think when you won't return my calls?*

whenever [ʍɛn 'ɛv ɚ] **1.** *conj.* at any time; at whatever time. ♦ *Wash the car whenever it's convenient for you.* ♦ *I'm ready to go whenever you are.* **2.** *conj.* every time; each time. ♦ *You are to clean your room whenever I tell you to.* ♦ *Whenever it rains, I stay indoors.* **3.** *adv.* when?; at what time? (Used for emphasis.) ♦ *Whenever will you get around to cleaning your room?* ♦ *Whenever will you stop smoking?*

where ['ʍɛr] **1.** *interrog.* in what place?; at what place?; in which location? ♦ *Where is your office located?* ♦ *Where is the post office?* **2.** *conj.* in that place; at that place; in that location. ♦ *Let's go to the restaurant where we ate last night.* ♦ *John led the police to the place where he'd seen the body.*

whereabouts ['ʍɛr ə bɑʊts] *n.* the place where someone or something is. (Treated as singular.) ♦ *The police did not know the whereabouts of the suspect.* ♦ *Her whereabouts is unknown.*

whereas [ʍɛr 'æz] **1.** *conj.* but; however; on the other hand; on the contrary. ♦ *Mary has never played the flute, whereas I have.* ♦ *Bill doesn't like large crowds, whereas John does.* **2.** *conj.* since; because. (Used to introduce legal documents.) ♦ *Whereas John Smith desires to purchase a house owned by Jane Brown, Jane Brown agrees to permit the house to be inspected by a qualified house inspector.* ♦ *Whereas my client has met the stated requirements, action is now called for.*

whereby [ʍɛr 'bɑɪ] *adv.* by which; according to which. (Formal.) ♦ *The gambler claimed to have found a system whereby he could win every bet.* ♦ *Show me the law whereby smoking is forbidden here.*

where's ['ʍɛrz] **1.** *cont.* "where has," where has is an auxiliary. ♦ *Where's he been?* ♦ *Where's the cat gone to?* **2.** *cont.* "where is." ♦ *Where's the dog?* ♦ *Where's the nearest bank?*

whereupon ['ʍɛr ə pɑn] *conj.* at which time; after which time; and then. ♦ *The thunder rumbled, whereupon the children screamed.* ♦ *The alarm sounded, whereupon everyone fled the building.*

wherever [ʍɛr 'ɛv ɚ] **1.** *adv.* to whatever place; at whatever place; in whatever place. ♦ *I'll go wherever you want.* ♦ *Let's go wherever this path will take us.* **2.** *adv.* where?; at what place? (Used for emphasis.) ♦ *Wherever are my glasses this time?* ♦ *Wherever have you been for the past hour?*

whet ['ʍɛt] **1.** *tv.* to sharpen something; to make something sharper. ♦ *Mary whetted the carving knife on the grindstone.* ♦ *John whetted the axe before chopping down the tree.* **2.** *tv.* to stimulate one's appetite. (Figurative on ①.) ♦ *The smell of roast lamb really whets my appetite.* ♦ *The juicy pie whetted our appetite.* **3.** *tv.* to stimulate one's interest or appetite for something. (Figurative on ②.) ♦ *The excerpt whetted my interest enough that I bought the book.* ♦ *The advertisement whetted Anne's appetite, so she went to see the movie.*

whether ['ʍɛð ɚ] **1.** *conj.* <a form used with indirect questions when more than one answer is possible>; if. ♦ *Do you know whether Jane is coming with us?* ♦ *I wonder whether Susan can help us with this problem.* **2. whether or not** *phr.* either if something is the case or if something is not the case; one way or the other. ♦ *I'll drive to New York tomorrow whether or not it rains.* ♦ *I'm going to the mall whether you come with me or not.*

whetstone ['ʍɛt ston] *n.* a stone used for sharpening knives, blades, and other tools. ♦ *Mary scraped the blade of the knife against the whetstone.* ♦ *John keeps a whetstone in the kitchen next to his set of knives.*

which ['ʍɪtʃ] **1.** *interrog.* <a form used in questions to ask about or distinguish among specific things or people>; what [one or ones]? (Used before a noun.) ♦ *Which television show do you want to watch tonight?* ♦ *Which students passed the test?* **2.** *interrog.* <a form used in questions to ask about or distinguish among specific things

or people>; what one or ones? (Treated as singular or plural.) ♦ *I have three kinds of cookies. Which would you prefer?* ♦ *Of all the books you've read, which were the most exciting?* **3.** *adj.* <a form used to distinguish among things or people already mentioned or known from the context>; what [one or ones]; the [one or ones]. (Prenominal only.) ♦ *I don't know which flavor of ice cream to choose.* ♦ *After looking at the three suspects, Bill told the police officers which person had robbed him.* **4.** *pron.* <a form used to distinguish among things or people already mentioned or known from the context>; what one or ones; the one or ones. (Treated as singular or plural.) ♦ *There are so many flavors of ice cream. I don't know which to choose.* ♦ *I have a lot of cousins, and it's hard to decide which to invite to my wedding.* **5.** *pron.* <a form used after a word, phrase, or clause and serving to introduce *incidental or descriptive* information about the word, phrase, or clause rather than information needed to identify it>; the one or ones that. (Treated as singular or plural. The phrase or clause that begins with which is set off by commas. This is called a *nonrestrictive clause.*) ♦ *There is only one car sitting in front of the house. I say: "The car, which is sitting in the driveway, belongs to my father." You already know which car I mean, but I am telling you more about it.* ♦ *I have been speaking about a wall, and it happens to face west. I say: "The wall, which faces west, has begun to crack." The direction that it faces is incidental information.* **6.** *pron.* <a word used after a word or phrase and serving to introduce *contrastive or distinctive* information about the word or phrase>; the one or ones that. (Treated as singular or plural. The phrase or clause that begins with which does not have commas around it because the phrase is needed to permit the hearer or reader to correctly identify the object or person referred to. This is called a *restrictive clause.* Some grammarians and editors do not accept this sense of which and require the use of that ⑤ instead.) ♦ *There are two cars in front of the house—one on the street and one in the driveway—so I say: "The car which is sitting in the driveway belongs to my father." You needed to know the location before you could identify the car I meant.* ♦ *There are two walls visible, and I am talking about only one of them. I say: "The wall which faces west has begun to crack." I have identified the relevant wall by saying where it faces.*

whichever [ʍɪtʃ ˈɛv ɚ] **1.** *pron.* anything that; anyone who. ♦ *I'll give this cookie to whichever of you wants it.* ♦ *I'd like either the pizza or the pasta, whichever is better.* **2.** *interrog.* <an emphatic form of which ②.> (Stilted.) ♦ *I have three good shirts. Whichever should I wear?* ♦ *There are so many options on the menu. Whichever should I pick?*

whiff [ˈʍɪf] *n.* a puff or short blast of air, especially one that has a certain smell. ♦ *I caught a whiff of Bill's cologne.* ♦ *One whiff of the skunk made me gag.*

while [ˈʍɑɪl] **1.** *conj.* during that time; during a certain time that; at the same time as that. ♦ *While Anne stayed at home, Mary went to work.* ♦ *While the teacher was talking, some students misbehaved.* **2.** *conj.* and, in contrast; although; on the other hand; and; whereas. ♦ *Bill's never gone skiing, while Jane has.* ♦ *I don't like tomatoes, while Mary loves them.* **3.** *n.* a length of time. (No plural form in this sense.) ♦ *I'll be out of the office for a while.* ♦ *We were stuck in the elevator for just a short while.*

whim [ˈʍɪm] *n.* a sudden wish to do something, especially an unreasonable wish. ♦ *On a whim, Mary decided to buy a new car.* ♦ *John's whim to take a vacation surprised me.*

whimper [ˈʍɪm pɚ] **1.** *n.* a small, quiet moan or cry, especially from someone or something that is afraid. ♦ *The small dog let out a whimper when I stepped on its tail.* ♦ *I could hear the baby's whimper from the next room.* **2.** *iv.* to moan quietly, as though one were afraid. ♦ *The coward whimpered in fear.* ♦ *The dog whimpered when I put him outside.* **3.** *tv.* to say something while whispering. ♦ *Bill whimpered his shameful admission of guilt.* ♦ *Mary whimpered an apology.*

whimpering [ˈʍɪm pɚ ɪŋ] *n.* small, quiet moans or cries, as though one were afraid; small moans made while cowering. (No plural form in this sense.) ♦ *The puppy's whimpering kept me awake.* ♦ *The baby's whimpering subsided when I sang a lullaby.*

whimsical [ˈʍɪm zɪ kəl] *adj.* fanciful; having unusually or strangely funny ideas. (Adv: *whimsically* […ɪk li].) ♦ *Mary read a whimsical fairy tale to the children.* ♦ *David's views are too whimsical to take seriously.*

whimsy [ˈʍɪm zi] **1.** *n.* strange humor or fantasy. (No plural form in this sense.) ♦ *The playwright's whimsy was evident in the odd play.* ♦ *The whimsy of the fairy tale amused the children.* **2.** *n.* an unusually or strangely funny idea; something that is unusually or strangely funny. ♦ *Bill's weird ideas were dismissed as mere whimsies.* ♦ *His plan for making money was a hopeless whimsy.*

whine [ˈʍɑɪn] **1.** *n.* a cry; a stifled cry. ♦ *When I heard the dog's whine, I knew he wanted to come inside.* ♦ *The baby's whines alerted the nurse to its fever.* **2.** *n.* a complaint, especially one made several times with a sad, annoying, childish voice. ♦ *The clerk ignored the customer's whines about lack of service.* ♦ *David's whine about wanting to leave started to annoy me.* **3.** *iv.* to complain in a sad, annoying, childish voice. ♦ *The children whined throughout the unpleasant trip.* ♦ *John whines whenever he doesn't get to do what he wants.* **4.** *tv.* to make a complaint in a sad, annoying, childish voice. ♦ *Lisa whined that her soup was too hot.* ♦ *Bill whined his displeasure.*

whining [ˈʍɑɪn ɪŋ] **1.** *adj.* using a sad, annoying, childish voice; complaining in an annoying way. (Adv: *whiningly.*) ♦ *The whining children gave the teacher a headache.* ♦ *The clerk ignored the whining customer.* **2.** *n.* constant complaining, as done by a weary child. (No plural form in this sense.) ♦ *The children's whining got on the teacher's nerves.* ♦ *If your whining doesn't stop, we're going home right now!*

whinny [ˈʍɪn i] **1.** *n.* the soft, gentle noise that horses make. ♦ *The horse let out a whinny when I groomed its hair.* ♦ *I heard the whinnies of the horses in the stable.* **2.** *iv.* to make ①. ♦ *The mare whinnied as I approached her foal.* ♦ *The horse whinnied when I let it out of its stable.*

whiny [ˈʍɑɪn i] *adj.* often whining; often complaining in an annoying way. (Comp: *whinier;* sup: *whiniest.*) ♦ *Mary told the whiny children to be quiet.* ♦ *The whiny diner kept complaining about the food.*

whip [ˈʍɪp] **1.** *n.* a long strip of leather, usually attached to a handle, used for hitting people or animals. ♦ *With a crack of his whip, John spurred the horse to move.* ♦ *The cowboy bought a long, slender whip at the leather shop.* **2.** *n.*

a member of a political party who organizes and manages members of the party serving in a legislative body. ♦ *The minority whip encouraged the senators to filibuster.* ♦ *The majority whip persuaded everyone in his party to vote for the measure.* **3.** *iv.* [for something] to move quickly and suddenly somewhere. ♦ *A bullet whipped by my head.* ♦ *The wind whipped down from the mountains.* **4.** *tv.* to hit or strike someone or an animal with ①. ♦ *Anne whipped her horse so that it would go faster.* ♦ *The criminals were whipped as a punishment.* **5.** *tv.* to beat eggs or cream until the mixture bubbles into a froth. ♦ *The cook whipped the eggs with a whisk.* ♦ *The cream had been whipped by hand.* **6.** *tv.* to beat an opponent in a contest or game by a wide margin. (Figurative on ④.) ♦ *I really whipped John at tennis.* ♦ *The home team whipped the visiting team by a score of 10–2.*

whiplash [ˈʍɪp læʃ] *n.* a neck injury caused by stopping suddenly in a moving vehicle so that the head moves forward and snaps back. (No plural form in this sense.) ♦ *Anne is wearing a neck brace because she's suffering from whiplash.* ♦ *The car crash gave John a severe case of whiplash.*

whipping [ˈʍɪp ɪŋ] *n.* punishment by beating someone with a whip, a paddle, or the hand. ♦ *Whipping will motivate mules, but it is not suitable for people.* ♦ *Mary and Bob don't believe in whipping as a method of discipline.*

whirl [ˈʍɚl] **1.** *tv.* to move something around quickly in a circle; to spin something quickly. ♦ *Anne whirled the top on the floor.* ♦ *The axle whirled the tire around it.* **2.** *iv.* to move around quickly in a circle; to spin quickly. ♦ *The clothes in the washing machine whirled around.* ♦ *The dancers whirled across the dance floor.* **3.** *n.* an act of spinning around quickly. ♦ *After two whirls of his sword, the knight stabbed the dragon.* ♦ *The whirl of the merry-go-round made me dizzy.* **4.** *n.* very busy movement or activity. (Figurative on ③.) ♦ *Things are in such a whirl that I haven't had time to relax.* ♦ *Anne was caught up in a whirl of schoolwork.* **5. give something a whirl** *idiom* to try or attempt something. ♦ *If at first you don't succeed, give it another whirl.* ♦ *John gave bowling a whirl last night.*

whirlpool [ˈʍɚl pul] **1.** *n.* a place in a body of water where the water flows quickly in a circle and pulls objects in the water into it. ♦ *The swimmer was caught in a whirlpool and drowned.* ♦ *The water draining from the bathtub formed a small whirlpool.* **2.** *n.* a large tub filled with water moving in a circular motion, used by people to relax in. ♦ *The penthouse apartment had a room with a whirlpool.* ♦ *Mary relaxed in the whirlpool at the health club after work.*

whirlwind [ˈʍɚl wɪnd] **1.** *n.* a current of air that moves very quickly in circles like a tornado. ♦ *We took shelter as the whirlwind approached from the west.* ♦ *A whirlwind knocked over most of the trees in our orchard.* **2.** *n.* a great deal of activity. (Figurative on ②.) ♦ *There was a whirlwind of preparation prior to the conference.* ♦ *The new students were caught up in a whirlwind of excitement.* **3.** *adj.* moving quickly and busily; being very active and always going from one place to another. (Figurative on ①.) ♦ *Mary embarked on a whirlwind tour when her book was published.* ♦ *John visited six countries in six days on his whirlwind trip.*

whisk [ˈʍɪsk] **1.** *n.* a wire tool for beating eggs, cream, batter, and other mixtures. ♦ *The cook beat the egg whites with a whisk.* ♦ *I washed the whisk and placed it with the other utensils.* **2.** *n.* a small brush or broom. ♦ *I swept the dust into the dustpan with a whisk.* ♦ *The barber used a whisk to brush the cut hair from my clothes.* **3.** *tv.* to beat eggs, cream, batter, and other mixtures into a froth. ♦ *You must whisk the eggs for two minutes.* ♦ *The cook whisked the batter until it was smooth.* **4. whisk away** *tv. + adv.* to brush dirt or crumbs from a surface. ♦ *David whisked the dirt away with a small broom.* ♦ *The barber whisked the loose hair away from my clothes.* **5. whisk away** *tv. + adv.* to move something away quickly; to remove something quickly. (Figurative on ④.) ♦ *The police whisked the suspect away.* ♦ *Mary whisked her children away from the reporters.*

whisker [ˈʍɪs kɚ] *n.* a hair that grows from near the mouth of a cat and certain other animals; a hair that is part of a beard. ♦ *I stroked my cat's whiskers.* ♦ *Bill trimmed his whiskers with a razor.*

whiskey [ˈʍɪs ki] **1.** *n.* a strong alcoholic drink made by fermenting corn, rye, or other grains. (No plural form in this sense.) ♦ *Anne added some whiskey to the punch.* ♦ *Bill kept a bottle of whiskey in the cupboard.* **2.** *n.* a glass of ①; a drink of ①. ♦ *Harry asked the bartender for two whiskeys.* ♦ *Anne asked for a whiskey with ice.*

whisper [ˈʍɪs pɚ] **1.** *tv.* to speak with the breath only, not using the full voice. ♦ *The witness whispered her response.* ♦ *Anne whispered that she had to leave the room.* **2.** *iv.* to speak as in ①. ♦ *I can't hear you when you whisper.* ♦ *You should whisper when you're in the library.* **3.** *n.* speaking done with the breath only, not using the voice. ♦ *The timid man barely spoke above a whisper.* ♦ *The librarian spoke in a whisper.*

whispering [ˈʍɪs pɚ ɪŋ] **1.** *n.* speech spoken in a whisper. (No plural form in this sense.) ♦ *I hear a lot of whispering in this classroom!* ♦ *Please stop your whispering.* **2.** *adj.* [of someone] speaking in a whisper. ♦ *The whispering librarian did not want to disturb the patrons.* ♦ *Too many whispering people spoiled the movie for us.* **3.** *adj.* rustling; making the sound of a whisper. (Figurative on ①. Adv: *whisperingly.*) ♦ *The whispering leaves rustled in the breeze.* ♦ *I closed my eyes and listened to the whispering wind.*

whistle [ˈʍɪs əl] **1.** *n.* a small metal or plastic instrument that makes a shrill, high-pitched sound when one blows air into it. ♦ *The child kept blowing on a plastic whistle.* ♦ *The football referees blew their whistles when a foul was made.* **2.** *n.* a shrill, high-pitched sound made by passing air through a small opening between one's lips or through ①. ♦ *The loud train whistle hurt my ears.* ♦ *The police officer's whistle alerted me to the danger.* **3.** *tv.* to make a shrill, high-pitched sound by passing air through ① or through one's lips. ♦ *Anne whistled a happy tune.* ♦ *The children whistled the simple song.* **4.** *iv.* to make a shrill, high-pitched sound by passing air through ① or through one's lips. ♦ *Bill whistled to get my attention.* ♦ *The train whistled as it approached the station.* **5. whistle at** *iv. + prep. phr.* to make a whistle ② of appreciation at a member of the opposite sex. ♦ *Jane whistled at John when he came into the room.* ♦ *The fireman whistled at the attractive woman who walked by the station.* **6.** *iv.* [for something] to move very quickly so that a shrill, high-pitched noise is made as it moves. ♦ *A bullet whistled by the criminal's ear.* ♦ *The express train whistled through the station without stopping.* **7. blow the whistle (on someone)** *idiom* to report someone's wrongdoing to someone (such as the police) who can stop the wrongdoing. ♦ *The citizens' group blew the whistle on the street gangs by calling the police.* ♦ *The gangs were getting very bad. It was definitely time to blow the whistle.*

white ['ʍɑɪt] **1.** *adj.* having the color of salt or milk. (Adv: *whitely.* Comp: *whiter;* sup: *whitest.*) ♦ *The artist began painting on the white canvas.* ♦ *The surrendering soldiers waved a white flag.* **2.** *adj.* pale. (Comp: *whiter;* sup: *whitest.*) ♦ *The frightened man turned white with fear.* ♦ *Mary's complexion is very white because she's ill.* **3.** *adj.* [of people, usually of European descent] having light-colored skin. (See Caucasian. Comp: *whiter;* sup: *whitest.*) ♦ *The assailant was described as a middle-aged white male.* ♦ *The white landlord happily rented to persons of any race.* **4.** *n.* the color of salt or milk. (No plural form in this sense.) ♦ *If you mix white with red, you get pink.* ♦ *I decorated the bathroom in white and light blue.* **5.** *n.* someone who has light-colored skin, usually persons of European descent. ♦ *The leader urged the whites and the blacks to live in peace.* ♦ *Five whites were arrested during the riot.* **6.** *n.* the clear part of an egg, which turns white when it is cooked. ♦ *The light cake was made with egg whites.* ♦ *The cook separated the white of the egg from the yolk.*

white-collar ['ʍɑɪt 'kɑl ɚ] *adj.* of or about an office job instead of a job involving manual labor. ♦ *Several white-collar executives were laid off due to cutbacks.* ♦ *The graduate wanted a white-collar position in management.*

white-hot ['ʍɑɪt 'hɑt] *adj.* extremely hot. ♦ *The steel worker removed the white-hot steel from the furnace.* ♦ *White-hot metal glowed in the huge furnace.*

White House ['ʍɑɪt hɑʊs] **1.** *n.* the building in which the President of the United States lives. (No plural form in this sense.) ♦ *The address of the White House is 1600 Pennsylvania Avenue in Washington, D.C.* ♦ *The White House is protected by special police.* **2.** *n.* the President of the United States and the administrative staff, considered as a center of authority. (No plural form in this sense.) ♦ *The White House expressed its condolences when the foreign leader died.* ♦ *The White House would not comment on the ongoing investigation.*

whiten ['ʍɑɪt n] **1.** *tv.* to cause something to become white; to make something white. ♦ *Lisa whitened her hair with bleach.* ♦ *The special toothpaste whitened my teeth.* **2.** *iv.* to turn pale. ♦ *The frightened guests whitened with fear.* ♦ *Tom's skin whitened while he was away from the sun in the hospital for three months.*

whiteness ['ʍɑɪt nəs] *n.* the degree to which someone or something is white. (No plural form in this sense.) ♦ *The whiteness of the snow was blinding in the daylight.* ♦ *Bleach brought out the whiteness of my old socks.*

whitewash ['ʍɑɪt wɑʃ] **1.** *n.* a substance made of lime and water used to paint things white. (No plural form in this sense.) ♦ *Lisa painted the garage walls with whitewash.* ♦ *Jane painted over the graffiti on her garage with whitewash.* **2.** *tv.* to cover a surface with ①. ♦ *Lisa whitewashed the dirty walls.* ♦ *David whitewashed the side of the building to cover up the graffiti.* **3.** *tv.* to say something or do something to hide a mistake; to cover up a wrongdoing. (Figurative on ②.) ♦ *An aide whitewashed the mayor's ridiculous comments.* ♦ *David whitewashed the accusations against him.*

whitish ['ʍɑɪt ɪʃ] *adj.* somewhat white. (Adv: *whitishly.*) ♦ *John's whitish socks were rather dirty.* ♦ *My whitish hair still has streaks of brown.*

whittle ['ʍɪt əl] **1.** *tv.* to cut pieces of wood away a little bit at a time with a knife; to shave off small strips from a piece of wood. ♦ *Susan whittled a stick with a knife to pass the time.* ♦ *David whittled a branch while he sat on the porch waiting for John.* **2.** *tv.* to sculpt an object from wood, cutting away small pieces. ♦ *John whittled a toy boat from a piece of wood.* ♦ *Jane used a small knife to whittle a peg of the proper size.*

whiz ['ʍɪz] **1.** *iv.* [for something] to move very quickly through the air while making a sound as it passes by someone or something. ♦ *The baseball whizzed by my head.* ♦ *A bullet whizzed by the police officer's shoulder.* **2. whiz through** *iv.* + *prep. phr.* to do something very fast, perhaps not too thoroughly. (Informal. Figurative on ①.) ♦ *The careless employee whizzed through his work.* ♦ *The student made a lot of mistakes when she whizzed through the test.* **3.** *n.* an expert; someone who is very skilled at something; someone who can do something quickly and reliably. (Figurative on ①.) ♦ *Bill is a whiz when it comes to fixing engines.* ♦ *I asked Mary for help because she's a whiz at biology.*

who ['hu] **1.** *interrog.* what or which person or people? (The possessive form is whose. The objective form is whom.) ♦ *Who wants to order some pizza?* ♦ *Who is the person sitting next to Jane?* **2.** *pron.* a person or people who have been mentioned. (Standard English requires whom instead of who as the object of a verb or preposition. Who can be used in restrictive and nonrestrictive clauses. See which.) ♦ *The man who is sitting next to my aunt is a lawyer.* ♦ *Do we know whom he saw?* ♦ *My father, who is a lawyer, gave me some good legal advice.*

whoa ['wo] *interj.* "Stop!"; "Slow down!" (Used especially to cause horses to stop moving.) ♦ *"Whoa!" the rider yelled as her horse approached town.* ♦ *"Whoa!" the driving instructor said. "You're going too fast!"*

who'd ['hud] **1.** *cont.* "who had," where had is an auxiliary. ♦ *John, who'd just returned from the beach, was covered with sand.* ♦ *Jane, who'd been working for twelve hours, was very tired.* **2.** *cont.* "who would." ♦ *Who'd have thought that David would lose the election?* ♦ *Who'd have believed that computers could do so much?*

whoever [hu 'ɛv ɚ] **1.** *pron.* anyone; any person who. ♦ *Whoever turns and runs away lives to fight another day.* ♦ *Whoever comes to the conference must pay a $10 fee.* **2.** *interrog.* Who? (An emphatic form of who.) ♦ *Whoever would do such a horrible thing?* ♦ *Whoever has heard of such a ridiculous idea?*

whole ['hol] **1.** *adj.* made of the entire amount; consisting of all parts; not divided; not separated; complete. (Adv: *wholly.*) ♦ *David ate the whole cake.* ♦ *Mary did the whole job herself.* **2.** *adj.* healthy or the feeling of good health, in the mind or body. ♦ *The medicine made John feel whole again.* ♦ *The therapist helped Anne become whole once more.* **3.** *adj.* not expressed as a fraction or a decimal. ♦ *3, 5, and 28,199 are examples of whole numbers.* ♦ *Please round your answer to the nearest whole number.*

4. *n.* something that is complete; something that has all of its parts; the entire amount. ♦ *This piece is just one part of the whole.* ♦ *If you look at the problem as a whole, the answer becomes clearer.*

wholehearted ['hol 'hɑrt ɪd] *adj.* sincere; enthusiastic; with all one's effort and desire. (Adv: *wholeheartedly.*) ♦ *The students had their teacher's wholehearted support.* ♦ *I appreciated Mary's wholehearted efforts to help me find a job.*

wholesale ['hol sel] **1.** *adj.* [of products] sold in large numbers to people who will sell the products one at a time to customers. ♦ *Wholesale prices are much cheaper than retail prices.* ♦ *The wholesale merchandise was sold in packages of 48.* **2.** *adj.* done on a large scale; in large amounts. (Figurative on ①.) ♦ *The war criminal was accused of wholesale slaughter.* ♦ *The wholesale destruction of the town devastated its residents.* **3.** *adv.* in large quantities at wholesale ① prices. ♦ *The store owner bought products wholesale and sold them at much higher prices.* ♦ *The merchant always bought goods wholesale.*

wholesaler ['hol sel ɚ] *n.* someone who buys products from a manufacturer and sells them to store owners. ♦ *I buy my clothing directly from a wholesaler.* ♦ *The wholesaler worked with dozens of merchants in town.*

wholesome ['hol səm] **1.** *adj.* causing good health; healthy to do or eat; good for one's health. (Adv: *wholesomely.*) ♦ *The school provides wholesome meals for the students.* ♦ *Anne drank a wholesome glass of orange juice.* **2.** *adj.* of or about good morals or good things in general. (Adv: *wholesomely.*) ♦ *The parents took their children to see a wholesome movie.* ♦ *The candidate's wholesome supporters each held a small flag.*

who'll ['hul] *cont.* "who will." ♦ *Who'll take my place after I retire?* ♦ *Do we know who'll be coming to fix the plumbing?*

wholly ['ho li] *adv.* completely; entirely; totally. ♦ *I was wholly satisfied with the service I received at the store.* ♦ *The manager was wholly disappointed with the lazy workers.*

whom ['hum] *pron.* <the objective form of who.> (Not common in informal English. Whom can be used in restrictive and nonrestrictive clauses. See which.) ♦ *To whom did you give the present?* ♦ *I gave it to Lisa, whom I saw yesterday.* ♦ *The man to whom I gave the present thanked me.*

whopper ['ʍɑp ɚ] **1.** *n.* something that is very large, often a fish. (Informal.) ♦ *Mary reeled the whopper into the boat.* ♦ *The hunter killed a whopper of a deer.* **2.** *n.* a very big lie. (Informal.) ♦ *Grandpa liked to tell whoppers about his life as a boy.* ♦ *Jimmy was punished for telling his parents a whopper.*

whore ['hor] *n.* a prostitute; someone who is paid money for sex. ♦ *The prostitute didn't like being called a whore.* ♦ *The police officer arrested the whore for prostitution.*

whorl ['ʍɚl] *n.* a loop or a curve of a spiral; the shape of a line that is a curve or a spiral, such as with a fingerprint. ♦ *One's fingerprints consist of curved lines and whorls.* ♦ *The artist traced the whorl of the seashell onto the canvas.*

who's ['huz] **1.** *cont.* "who has," where has is an auxiliary. ♦ *Who's got my hat?* ♦ *I wonder who's been sitting in my chair while I've been gone.* ♦ *John, who's lived in the city all his life, has never seen a cow.* **2.** *cont.* "who is." ♦ *Bill has a brother who's a famous actor.* ♦ *Who's standing next to Susan?* ♦ *Who's that girl in the red dress?*

whose ['huz] **1.** *pron.* <the possessive form of who and which>; of whom or of which. (Whose can be used in restrictive and nonrestrictive clauses. See which.) ♦ *The man whose house you passed is out of town.* ♦ *Some archaeologists found an ancient metal tool whose function is still unknown.* ♦ *John, whose mother owns a bakery, said he would bring us a box of cookies.* **2.** *interrog.* <a form used in questions to determine the identity of the person who owns, possesses, or is associated with something>; of or belonging to whom? ♦ *Whose jacket is this?* ♦ *Whose books are on the kitchen table?*

why 1. ['ʍɑɪ] *interrog.* for what reason? ♦ *Why would you do such a stupid thing?* ♦ *Why does it get cold in the winter?* **2.** ['ʍɑɪ] *pron.* the reason that; the reason for which. (Takes a clause.) ♦ *The teacher explained why there are clouds in the sky.* ♦ *Anne explained why she was upset with me.* **3.** ['wɑɪ] *interj.* <a form used to express surprise, dismay, disgust, or other emotion.> ♦ *Why, I've never been so insulted in all my life!* ♦ *Why, how could you say such a horrible thing!*

wick ['wɪk] *n.* the thread in a candle or oil lamp, one end of which sticks out and is lighted. ♦ *John lit the candle's wick with a match.* ♦ *Mary trimmed the wick of the oil lamp before lighting it.*

wicked ['wɪk əd] *adj.* evil; very bad; vile. (Adv: *wickedly.*) ♦ *All of the peasants hated the wicked king.* ♦ *The wicked owner treated the employees badly.*

wickedness ['wɪk əd nəs] *n.* the quality of being evil, very bad, or vile. (No plural form in this sense.) ♦ *The minister said the wickedness of evil people would condemn them to hell.* ♦ *The king was feared because of his wickedness.*

wicker ['wɪk ɚ] **1.** *n.* small branches and twigs woven into furniture. (No plural form in this sense.) ♦ *The delicate basket was made of wicker.* ♦ *Furniture made out of wicker is quite strong.* **2.** *adj.* made from ①. ♦ *Please don't sit on the delicate wicker chair.* ♦ *Mary placed the vase on the small wicker table.*

wide ['wɑɪd] **1.** *adj.* not narrow; broad. (Adv: *widely.* Comp: *wider;* sup: *widest.*) ♦ *The wide street contained three lanes of traffic in each direction.* ♦ *The wide truck could not fit into the narrow garage.* **2.** *adj.* being a certain or specified distance from side to side; measured from side to side. (Follows the measurement of width. Comp: *wider.*) ♦ *The room is 14 feet wide.* ♦ *The bookcase is three feet wide and six feet high.* **3.** *adj.* extensive; large in size, range, or scope. (Adv: *widely.* Comp: *wider;* sup: *widest.*) ♦ *The seminar covered a wide range of topics.* ♦ *Mary discussed a wide array of issues with her professor.* **4.** *adv.* as far as possible; to the greatest amount or extent. ♦ *The dentist asked me to open my mouth wide.* ♦ *Please open the door wide.*

wide-awake ['wɑɪd ə 'wek] *adj.* completely awake and alert; not sleepy. ♦ *The man with insomnia lay wide-awake in bed.* ♦ *After sleeping for ten hours, Susan was wide-awake.*

wide-eyed ['wɑɪd ɑɪd] *adj.* having one's eyes wide open, especially having to do with someone who is surprised or innocent. ♦ *The wide-eyed children looked at the candy* *in the display case.* ♦ *The thief took advantage of the wide-eyed tourists.*

widen ['waɪd n] **1.** *tv.* to make something wider; to cause something to become wider. ♦ *The workers widened the road so it would accommodate more traffic.* ♦ *John widened the hole where the bush was to be planted.* **2.** *iv.* to become wider. ♦ *The river widened as it approached the ocean.* ♦ *The gap between the winner and the loser widened as the votes were counted.*

widespread ['waɪd 'sprɛd] *adj.* spread over a large space; found in many places; experienced or felt by many people in many spaces. ♦ *There's a widespread rumor that you're quitting your job.* ♦ *The feeling of uncertainty was widespread during the war.*

widow ['wɪd o] *n.* a woman whose husband has died, and who has not married again. ♦ *The widow cried at her husband's funeral.* ♦ *The widow vowed never to marry again.*

widower ['wɪd o ɚ] *n.* a man whose wife has died, and who has not married again. ♦ *The widower cried at his wife's funeral.* ♦ *The widower vowed never to marry again.*

width ['wɪdθ] **1.** *n.* the distance of something from side to side; how wide something is from side to side. (No plural form in this sense.) ♦ *The width of this room is 12 feet.* ♦ *The width of your luggage cannot exceed six inches.* **2.** *n.* a piece of cloth that has a width ① of about 36 inches. ♦ *The tailor purchased a width of cloth four yards long.* ♦ *Anne made a tablecloth by sewing two widths of fabric together.*

wield ['wild] **1.** *tv.* to hold and use something, especially a weapon. ♦ *The warrior wielded a sharp spear.* ♦ *The athlete wielded the javelin and heaved it across the field.* **2.** *tv.* to have and use power, especially as though it were a weapon. (Figurative on ①.) ♦ *The manager wielded considerable power over his employees.* ♦ *The mayor wielded absolute control over the city council.*

wiener ['win ɚ] *n.* a frankfurter; a beef or pork sausage, often eaten on a long bun. ♦ *Anne boiled some wieners and ate them with mustard.* ♦ *The campers roasted some wieners over the fire.*

wife ['waɪf] *n., irreg.* the woman a man is married to. (Pl: wives.) ♦ *John married his wife when he was 28 and she was 26.* ♦ *Please inform your wife that she's invited to the party, too.*

wig ['wɪg] *n.* a head covering simulating one's own hair; a head covering made of real or artificial hair. ♦ *The actress wore a blond wig onstage.* ♦ *The cancer patient wore a wig after his hair fell out.*

wiggle ['wɪg əl] **1.** *iv.* to move back and forth in quick, little movements. ♦ *The children wiggled in their seats.* ♦ *The worm I used for bait wiggled as I put it on the hook.* **2.** *tv.* to cause something to move back and forth in quick, little movements. ♦ *Susan can wiggle her ears up and down.* ♦ *The rabbit wiggled its nose.*

wiggling ['wɪg (ə) lɪŋ] *adj.* moving from side to side in small, rapid movements. ♦ *The wiggling children were told to sit still.* ♦ *The puppy's wiggling tail indicated its excitement.*

wild ['waɪld] **1.** *adj.* growing or living in nature; not tame; not grown or kept by a human. (Comp: *wilder;* sup: *wildest.*) ♦ *Wild dogs howled in the night.* ♦ *A wild lion was captured and sent to a zoo.* **2.** *adj.* violent; strong; fierce; savage; not civilized. (Adv: *wildly.* Comp: *wilder;* sup: *wildest.*) ♦ *A wild storm uprooted several trees.* ♦ *The wild warriors brutally slew their enemies.* **3.** *adj.* not in control; out of control; uncontrolled; lacking control; disorderly; reckless. (Adv: *wildly.* Comp: *wilder;* sup: *wildest.*) ♦ *The wild guests destroyed the hotel room.* ♦ *Wild prisoners staged a riot.* **4. wild about someone or something** *idiom* very excited about someone or something. (Informal.) ♦ *I'm just wild about comedies.* ♦ *John is wild about antique cars.*

wildcat ['waɪld kæt] *n.* a cat of the lynx family. ♦ *Many wildcats live in mountainous regions.* ♦ *The wildcat chased and killed the mountain goat.*

wildebeest ['wɪld ə bist] *n., irreg.* a gnu. (Pl: *wildebeest* or *wildebeests.* From Dutch via Afrikaans.) ♦ *The poachers trapped a wildebeest on the African plains.* ♦ *The tourists on the safari saw a herd of wildebeest.*

wilderness ['wɪl dɚ nəs] *n.* a large area of land with no human residents. (No plural form in this sense.) ♦ *David dreamed of leaving society and living in the wilderness.* ♦ *Much of the natural wilderness is federally protected land.*

wildfire ['waɪld faɪr] **1.** *n.* an uncontrollable fire or flame. ♦ *Dozens of firefighters tried to extinguish the wildfire.* ♦ *The wildfire threatened to burn the houses close to the forest.* **2. spread like wildfire** *idiom* to spread rapidly and without control. ♦ *The epidemic is spreading like wildfire. Everyone is getting sick.* ♦ *John told a joke that was so funny that it spread like wildfire.*

wildflower ['waɪld flaʊ ɚ] *n.* a flower that is not cultivated by a person; a flower that grows in nature. ♦ *Wildflowers grew in the ditch alongside the road.* ♦ *The abandoned field was full of wildflowers.*

wild-goose chase ['waɪld 'gus tʃes] *n.* a foolish search; a useless search; a quest for something that cannot be obtained. ♦ *The inspector went on a wild-goose chase looking for a person who didn't exist.* ♦ *My search for my keys was a hopeless wild-goose chase.*

wildlife ['waɪld laɪf] *n.* wild animals as a group, especially as they live in their natural condition; wild plants and animals as a group. (No plural form in this sense.) ♦ *Environmentalists are committed to protecting wildlife.* ♦ *The coastal wildlife was threatened by an oil spill.*

will ['wɪl] **1.** *interrog.* <a form used with a verb to indicate politeness by turning a command into a question.> (See would ③.) ♦ *Will you shut the door, please?* ♦ *Will you please speak more quietly?* **2.** *aux.* <a form used with a verb to indicate the future tense.> (See also shall. Reduced to *'ll* in contractions.) ♦ *Mary will be in her office tomorrow morning.* ♦ *I will see you at the party next week.* **3.** *aux.* <a form used with a verb to command someone to do something.> ♦ *You will be quiet when I am talking.* ♦ *You will go to the store and get some milk!* **4.** *aux.* can; be able to. ♦ *A freezer will keep food from spoiling for a long time.* ♦ *This computer will organize your work for you.* **5.** *aux.* <a form used to express something that is always true or something that always happens.> ♦ *I will always be your friend.* ♦ *John will go on vacation twice a year.* **6.** *n.* the power one has in one's mind to do what one wants to do; the determination to do something; an intention to do something. (No plural form in this sense.) ♦ *Mary had the will to finish her degree in four years.* ♦ *The terminally ill patient lost the will to live.* **7.** *n.* a command or wish stated by someone. (No plural form in this sense.) ♦ *It was the king's will that the taxes were to be raised.* ♦ *The weak council always approved the will of the mayor.* **8.** *n.* a legal document that details how one's assets will be distributed after one's death. ♦ *According to Mary's will, her children will inherit her estate.* ♦ *Many greedy relatives contested the dead millionaire's will.* **9. will to** *tv.* + *prep. phr.* to give one's assets to someone or an organization when one dies. ♦ *Mary has willed her estate to her children.* ♦ *John willed his fortune to charity.* **10. will to** *tv.* + *inf.* to use the power of one's mind to do something; to intend something to happen by using the power of one's mind. ♦ *You cannot just will something to happen, you have to make it happen.* ♦ *The lone survivor had willed himself to survive after the crash.* **11. with a will** *idiom* with determination and enthusiasm. ♦ *The children worked with a will to finish the project on time.* ♦ *The workers set about manufacturing the new products with a will.*

willful ['wɪl fʊl] **1.** *adj.* intended; meant; done on purpose. (Adv: *willfully.*) ♦ *The lawyer argued the murder had not been willful.* ♦ *Mary's willful attempt to insult me drew much criticism.* **2.** *adj.* stubborn. (Adv: *willfully.*) ♦ *The willful child refused to eat his vegetables.* ♦ *Willful teenagers won't listen to their parents.*

willing ['wɪl ɪŋ] *adj.* eagerly ready to do something; happily prepared to do something or to be of service. (Adv: *willingly.*) ♦ *The employees were willing to work overtime.* ♦ *A willing helper gladly carried my heavy luggage.*

willingness ['wɪl ɪŋ nəs] *n.* a state of being eagerly ready to do something. (No plural form in this sense.) ♦ *Mary's willingness to help others is one of her best qualities.* ♦ *I appreciated John's willingness to lend me $100.*

willow ['wɪl o] **1.** *n.* a tree that has many long, thin, drooping branches with long, thin leaves. ♦ *The children played among the willows by the lake.* ♦ *I sat in the shade under the large willow.* **2.** *n.* wood from ①. (No plural form in this sense.) ♦ *The carpenter built a sturdy fence out of willow because it was plentiful.* ♦ *Willow is not strong enough for construction.* **3.** *adj.* made of or from ①. ♦ *The willow fence post grew into a tree!* ♦ *This basket is woven from willow branches.*

willpower ['wɪl paʊ ɚ] *n.* determination; the ability to control one's will. (No plural form in this sense.) ♦ *Anne had the willpower to quit smoking.* ♦ *I lacked the willpower to stay on my diet.*

wilt ['wɪlt] **1.** *iv.* to droop; to wither; [for the leaves or branches of a plant] to lose their strength. ♦ *The crops wilted during the drought.* ♦ *My flowers had wilted because I'd forgotten to water them.* **2.** *iv.* [for someone] to lose energy. (Figurative on ①.) ♦ *The construction workers wilted in the extreme heat.* ♦ *The horses wilted under the hot sun.* **3.** *tv.* to cause something to wilt ①. ♦ *The drought has severely wilted the crops.* ♦ *Tom wilted the lettuce for his special salad.*

wily ['waɪ li] *adj.* crafty; shrewd; sly; cunning. (Comp: *wilier;* sup: *wiliest.*) ♦ *The wily salesclerk convinced me to buy more than I had wanted.* ♦ *The wily coyote captured its prey.*

win ['wɪn] **1.** *tv., irreg.* to receive or achieve first place in a contest or competition. (Pt/pp: won.) ♦ *Our team won the football game.* ♦ *The fastest runner wins the gold medal.* **2.** *tv., irreg.* to achieve or earn something through hard work or effort. ♦ *I slowly won the respect of my manager.* ♦ *Women in America won the right to vote in 1920.* **3.** *iv., irreg.* to be in first place in a contest or competition; to be the best in a contest or competition. ♦ *Whoever wins will receive a trophy.* ♦ *I was surprised when the horse with the weak leg won.* **4.** *n.* a victory; a triumph. ♦ *Our team scored a win over the previous champions.* ♦ *The athlete needed a win to remain in the competition.* **5. win someone over** *idiom* to succeed in gaining the support and sympathy of someone. ♦ *Jane's parents disapproved of her engagement at first, but she won them over.* ♦ *I'm trying to win the boss over and get him to give us the day off.*

wince ['wɪns] **1.** *iv.* to flinch; to cringe. ♦ *Mary winced when a large bee flew around her head.* ♦ *David winced when the dentist touched his sore tooth.* **2.** *n.* a flinch; a small movement by one's body when one is scared or in pain. ♦ *From Bill's wince, I could tell that he was in severe pain.* ♦ *Mary's slight wince betrayed her fright.*

winch ['wɪntʃ] *n.* a powerful machine that can wind up a rope or a chain, managing to pull or lift something very heavy. ♦ *The mechanic lifted the motor from the car with a winch.* ♦ *The construction worker lifted the steal beams with a winch.*

wind 1. ['wɪnd] *n.* the movement of air; moving air. ♦ *A cold wind blew from the north.* ♦ *The wind blew the hat from my head.* **2.** ['wɪnd] *n.* a breath or the ability to breathe. ♦ *The football player lost his wind when he was tackled roughly.* ♦ *Toward the end of the marathon, the runner lost her wind.* **3.** ['wɪnd] *tv.* to cause someone to be out of breath; to cause someone to have a hard time breathing. ♦ *The rough tackle winded the football player.* ♦ *Running up the stairs winded Anne.* **4.** ['waɪnd] *tv., irreg.* to tighten the spring of a mechanical device. (Pt/pp: wound.) ♦ *Anne winds her watch every morning when she wakes up.* ♦ *Bill wound the music box, and it played a tune.* **5. wind around** ['waɪnd...] *tv., irreg.* + *prep. phr.* to wrap something around an object many times. ♦ *Please wind the rope around the pole and tie a knot.* ♦ *I wound the fishing line around the reel.* **6. wind around** ['waɪnd...] *iv., irreg.* + *prep. phr.* to wrap, turn, or twist around something many times. ♦ *The road wound around the mountain before it reached the top.* ♦ *The snake wound around its prey.* **7.** ['waɪnd] *iv., irreg.* to move in one direction and then another; to move in twists and turns. ♦ *The thief wound through the city streets to confuse the police.* ♦ *The path winds through the mountainous terrain.* **8. get wind of something; catch wind of something** [...wɪnd...] *idiom* to learn of something; to hear about something. (On ①.) ♦ *The police got wind of the illegal drug deal.* ♦ *John caught wind of the gossip being spread about him.* **9. in the wind** [...'wɪnd] *idiom* about to happen. (On ①.) ♦ *There are some major changes in the wind. Expect these changes to happen soon.* ♦ *There is something in the wind. We'll find out what it is soon.*

winded ['wɪn dɪd] *adj.* out of breath; gasping for breath; breathless. ♦ *The winded jogger collapsed.* ♦ *The winded football player was carried from the field on a stretcher.*

windfall ['wɪnd fɔl] *n.* a large sum of money or valuable goods, received as a surprise. ♦ *I received a windfall from the federal government.* ♦ *The surplus was a windfall that was divided up among the workers.*

winding ['waɪn dɪŋ] *adj.* twisting; turning; changing direction many times. (Adv: *windingly.*) ♦ *I drove along the winding mountain road.* ♦ *The winding route to the campground seemed much longer than the direct route.*

windmill ['wɪnd mɪl] **1.** *n.* a structure that uses metal or wooden blades to capture the power of the wind. ♦ *The irrigation pumps were powered by windmills.* ♦ *The windmills on the cliff provide power to the village.* **2. tilt at windmills** *idiom* to fight battles with imaginary enemies; to fight against unimportant enemies or issues. ♦ *Aren't you too smart to go around tilting at windmills?* ♦ *I'm not going to fight this issue. I've wasted too much of my life tilting at windmills.*

window ['wɪn do] **1.** *n.* an opening in a wall or door, usually covered with a sheet of glass, that allows light into a place. ♦ *When the morning sunlight streamed through the window, I awoke.* ♦ *Mary looked out the window to the street below.* **2.** *n.* the sheet of glass that covers an opening in a wall or door. ♦ *David washes the windows in his house once a week.* ♦ *A vandal broke my car window and stole my car radio.* **3.** *n.* an opening or opportunity to do something. (Figurative on ①.) ♦ *The shifting weather allowed the pilot a five-minute window of opportunity to land.* ♦ *We have a brief window between appointments when we can meet with the president.*

windowpane ['wɪn do pen] *n.* the sheet of glass that covers an opening in a wall or door. ♦ *I sealed the edges of the windowpane to the frame with caulk.* ♦ *The thief entered the house by breaking the windowpane in the front door.*

window shade ['wɪndo 'ʃed] See shade ②.

window sill ['wɪn do sɪl] *n.* the flat ledge adjacent to the place that a window sash touches when it is closed. ♦ *Mary placed a flowerpot on the window sill.* ♦ *The cat slept on the window sill.*

windpipe ['wɪnd paɪp] *n.* the tube in the body that air travels through between the mouth and the lungs; the trachea. ♦ *Bill choked when a piece of food was caught in his windpipe.* ♦ *Some water went down Mary's windpipe when she was swimming, and she started coughing.*

windshield ['wɪnd ʃild] *n.* the large, curved piece of glass in the front of a car above the dashboard. ♦ *The driver who didn't wear his seat belt crashed through the windshield in the accident.* ♦ *I cleared the snow and ice from my windshield.*

windstorm ['wɪnd storm] *n.* a storm with heavy winds. ♦ *The windstorm knocked over some trees in my yard.* ♦ *During the windstorm, we lost electrical power.*

windup ['waɪnd əp] **1.** *n.* a conclusion; a finish; an end. ♦ *The windup of the meeting was postponed to discuss an important issue.* ♦ *The movie's windup unfortunately left many questions unanswered.* **2.** *adj.* needing to be wound in order to operate. ♦ *Susie played with windup toys in her room.* ♦ *My windup watch stopped because I'd forgotten to wind it.*

windward ['wɪnd wɚd] **1.** *adv.* moving against the wind; moving toward the direction from which the wind is coming. ♦ *The boat sailed windward toward the islands.* ♦ *The plane flew windward, and progress was very slow.* **2.** *adj.* located or facing toward the direction from which the wind comes or is coming. ♦ *The hurricane approached the windward Caribbean Islands.* ♦ *I stood on the windward side of the boat and smelled the fresh air.*

windy ['wɪn di] *adj.* having a lot of wind; with a lot of wind. (Comp: *windier;* sup: *windiest.*) ♦ *It's difficult to have a picnic on a very windy day.* ♦ *I closed the window because it was too windy in the room.*

wine ['waɪn] **1.** *n.* an alcoholic drink made from fermented fruit juice, especially the juice of grapes. (No plural form in this sense. If the fruit or plant is not specified, it is almost always grape.) ♦ *Would you like some white wine or red wine with your meal?* ♦ *Our server poured wine in each glass.* **2. wines** *n.* different kinds or types of ①. ♦ *Tom prefers the wines of California.* ♦ *We only drink white wines.*

winery ['waɪn ə ri] *n.* a place where wine is made. ♦ *The tourists sampled different kinds of wine at the winery.* ♦ *The restaurant buys its wine directly from a winery.*

wing ['wɪŋ] **1.** *n.* one of the upper limbs of a bird, angel, or a flying mammal, used for flight. ♦ *The bird flapped its wings and flew away.* ♦ *The artist painted an angel with large, white, feathery wings.* **2.** *n.* an extension on the side of an insect's body, used for flight. ♦ *A fly's wings move very rapidly.* ♦ *Dragonflies have two pairs of wings.* **3.** *n.* a structure on an airplane that stands out from its body, which helps the airplane stay in the air during flight. ♦ *My seat on the airplane overlooked the left wing.* ♦ *There's an emergency exit over each wing of the plane.* **4.** *n.* a part of a building that is built out from the central or main part of the building. ♦ *Dr. Smith's office is in the west wing of the hospital.* ♦ *A new wing was added to the overcrowded school.* **5.** *iv.* [for birds or insects] to fly; [for humans] to travel by airplane. ♦ *The flock of birds winged south for the winter.* ♦ *While winging over Missouri, I could see the Missouri River.* **6.** *tv.* to shoot a bird in the wing without killing it. ♦ *The hunter winged the bird, and it fell to the earth.* ♦ *The injured duck had been winged by a hunter's bullet.* **7.** *tv.* to wound someone or some animal by grazing its skin with a bullet or other weapon. (Figurative on ⑥.) ♦ *The police winged the robber in the arm.* ♦ *The knight winged the enemy with a spear.* **8. clip someone's wings** *idiom* to restrain someone; to reduce or put an end to a teenager's privileges. ♦ *You had better learn to get home on time, or I will clip your wings.* ♦ *My mother clipped my wings. I can't go out tonight.* **9. take someone under one's wing(s)** *idiom* to care for a person's well-being or advancement. ♦ *John wasn't doing well in geometry until the teacher took him under her wing.* ♦ *I took the new workers under my wings, and they learned the job in no time.* **10. try one's wings (out)** *idiom* to try to do something one has recently become qualified to do. ♦ *I recently learned to snorkel, and I want to go to the seaside to try my wings.* ♦ *You've read about it enough. It's time to try your wings out.*

winged ['wɪŋd] *adj.* having wings; equipped with wings. ♦ *A fly is a winged insect.* ♦ *This fast plane is like a winged rocket.*

wingspan ['wɪŋ spæn] *n.* the distance between the tip of one wing to the tip of the other when both wings are opened as wide as possible. ♦ *An eagle's wingspan is much larger than a robin's wingspan.* ♦ *What is the wingspan of this jet?*

wink ['wɪŋk] **1.** *iv.* to shut and open one eye quickly, especially either as a signal or to show amusement or interest. ♦ *John winked at me to let me know that he had been joking.* ♦ *Mary ignored the stranger who winked at her in the bar.* **2.** *iv.* to blink; to shut and open the eyes quickly. ♦ *I winked rapidly to keep the blowing dust out of my eyes.* ♦ *Everyone in the dark room winked when I turned on the bright lights.* **3.** *n.* the act of shutting and opening one eye quickly, especially either as a signal or to show amusement or interest. ♦ *John's wink let me know he was aware of the practical joke.* ♦ *Lisa gave me a friendly wink when she got out of the car.* **4. take forty winks** *idiom* to take a nap; to go to sleep. ♦ *I think I'll go to bed and take forty winks. See you in the morning.* ♦ *Why don't you go take forty winks and call me in about an hour?*

winner ['wɪn ɚ] **1.** *n.* someone or something that wins. ♦ *A gold medal was placed around the winner's neck.* ♦ *The winner of the race received a prize.* **2.** *n.* someone or something that is the best. (Figurative on ①. Informal.) ♦ *Your delicious apple pie is a real winner!* ♦ *This car is a winner. I've never had any problems with it.*

winning ['wɪn ɪŋ] **1.** *adj.* of or about someone or something that wins. ♦ *The winning competitor will receive a blue ribbon.* ♦ *The winning time in the race was five seconds faster than the previous record.* **2.** *adj.* charming; attractive; intended to earn friends and friendship. (Adv: *winningly.*) ♦ *The model flashed a winning smile for the photographer.* ♦ *This winning outfit is made of pure silk.*

winter ['wɪn tɚ] **1.** *n.* one of the four seasons of the year, from about December 21 to March 21, between fall and spring. ♦ *In places north of the equator, winter is usually the coldest season.* ♦ *Many animals hibernate during the winter.* **2.** *adj.* Concerning or associated with ①. ♦ *In the winter months, I like to go skiing.* ♦ *David went to Florida for the winter holidays.* **3.** *iv.* to live in a certain place during ①. ♦ *The Smiths winter in Miami.* ♦ *My aunt and uncle winter in Arizona.*

winterize ['wɪn tə rɑɪz] **1.** *tv.* to prepare something for its use in the cold and snow. ♦ *John winterized the room by placing plastic over the windows.* ♦ *Susan winterized her car by checking the antifreeze.* **2.** *iv.* to prepare for the cold and snow. ♦ *At her small cabin in the woods, Mary winterizes every October.* ♦ *Dave winterized by adding insulation to his house.*

wintertime ['wɪn tɚ tɑɪm] *n.* the period of time during the winter season. (No plural form in this sense.) ♦ *In the wintertime, I often go to Vermont to ski.* ♦ *I like to vacation in a warm city during the wintertime.*

wintry ['wɪn tri] *adj.* like winter; cold and snowy. ♦ *The wintry wind froze my exposed skin.* ♦ *After the wintry storm, the roads were blocked with snow.*

wipe ['wɑɪp] **1.** *tv.* to rub the surface of someone or something with something in order to clean it. ♦ *Mary wiped the counter with a sponge.* ♦ *Bill wiped his hands with a towel.* **2.** *tv.* to remove something liquid from a surface, using something absorbent. ♦ *Anne wiped the mess from the counter with a sponge.* ♦ *David wiped the puddle on the floor with an absorbent mop.* **3. wipe off** *tv.* + *adv.* to clean something by wiping as in ②. ♦ *Please wipe off the table after you finish eating.* ♦ *Tom wiped off the hood of the car where rain had made some spots.* **4. wipe up** *tv.* + *adv.* to remove something by wiping as in ②. ♦ *Lisa wiped the spill up with a sponge.* ♦ *Mary wiped up the puddle of water with a rag.* **5.** *n.* the act of wiping as in ①. ♦ *This dirty table could use a good wipe.* ♦ *Give your nose a wipe.*

wire ['wɑɪr] **1.** *n.* a thin metal strand; a thread of metal, especially one used to transmit electricity. (No plural form in this sense.) ♦ *Wire is used to hold a bale of hay together.* ♦ *The electrician brought lots of wire to use in wiring the house.* **2.** *n.* a length or segment of ①. ♦ *The electrician replaced the broken wires near the outlet.* ♦ *Many colored wires were looped around the homemade bomb.* **3.** *n.* a message that is sent by telegram. ♦ *Wires of congratulations were sent to the actors after the successful performance.* ♦ *The wire informed me that my brother was coming to visit me.* **4.** *tv.* to send a telegram; to send a message or money by telegraph. ♦ *Could you wire me $100? It's an emergency.* ♦ *I wired a message of congratulations to Susan.* **5.** *tv.* to install ① in a building for electricity; to install or adjust any kind of ①. ♦ *A skilled electrician wired the new house.* ♦ *The alarm was wired to sound if anyone entered the room.* **6.** *tv.* to fasten or secure something with ①. ♦ *David wired the crate shut.* ♦ *The orthodontist wired my teeth to straighten them.* **7.** *tv.* to install hidden microphones in a place so that one can record what is said there. ♦ *The spy wired the diplomat's office.* ♦ *Don't discuss our secret plans on that phone. I think it's wired.* **8. down to the wire** *idiom* at the very last minute; up to the very last instant. ♦ *I have to turn this in tomorrow, and I'll be working down to the wire.* ♦ *When we get down to the wire, we'll know better what to do.* **9. under the wire** *idiom* just barely in time or on time. ♦ *I turned in my report just under the wire.* ♦ *Bill was the last person to get in the door. He got in under the wire.*

wireless ['wɑɪr ləs] *adj.* without wires; not having wires; [of something] functioning without wires. (Adv: *wirelessly.*) ♦ *Susan carried her wireless phone around the house as she talked.* ♦ *David bought a wireless mouse to use with his computer.*

wiretap ['wɑɪr tæp] **1.** *n.* a connection into a telephone line so that one can listen to or record telephone conversations. ♦ *A federal agent placed a wiretap on the suspect's phone.* ♦ *The spy installed a wiretap on the diplomat's personal phone.* **2.** *tv.* to make a connection into a telephone line so that one can listen to or record telephone conversations. ♦ *The agent wiretapped John's conversations and used them in court.* ♦ *The smugglers assumed that their phones were wiretapped.*

wiring ['wɑɪr ɪŋ] *n.* a network of wires that provides electricity to a building or a machine. (No plural form in this sense.) ♦ *The house fire had been caused by faulty wiring.* ♦ *The inspector examined the office building's wiring.*

wiry ['wɑɪr i] **1.** *adj.* like wire. (Comp: *wirier;* sup: *wiriest.*) ♦ *The wiry carpet fibers were rough to the touch.* ♦ *John's wiry hair is difficult to comb.* **2.** *adj.* very thin; very skinny. (Comp: *wirier;* sup: *wiriest.*) ♦ *The wiry teenager wanted to gain weight.* ♦ *The wiry woman slipped through the narrow entrance.*

Wisconsin [wɪs 'kɑn sən] See Gazetteer.

wisdom ['wɪz dəm] *n.* intelligence, especially intelligence that is a result of experience; the knowledge required to make good decisions; the quality of being wise. (No plural form in this sense.) ♦ *I appreciated my advisor's wisdom.* ♦ *Lisa is widely respected for her wisdom.*

wisdom teeth ['wɪz dəm tiθ] pl of wisdom tooth.

wisdom tooth ['wɪz dəm tuθ] *n., irreg.* the tooth that is the furthest back on either side of either jaw. (Pl: wisdom teeth.) ♦ *John still has all four of his wisdom teeth.* ♦ *The oral surgeon removed my impacted wisdom teeth.*

wise ['wɑɪz] **1.** *adj.* able to make good decisions; showing good judgment; intelligent. (Adv: *wisely.* Comp: *wiser;* sup: *wisest.*) ♦ *The wise judge was fair and impartial.* ♦ *Your decision to finish school is wise.* **2. none the wiser** *idiom* not knowing any more. ♦ *I was none the wiser about the project after the lecture. It was a complete waste of time.* ♦ *Anne tried to explain the situation tactfully to Bob, but in the end, he was none the wiser.*

wiseacre ['wɑɪz ek ɚ] *n.* a know-it-all; a person who seems to know everything. (Mildly derogatory.) ♦ *The teacher sent the wiseacre to the principal's office.* ♦ *Look, you wiseacre, why don't you fix the problem?*

wisecrack ['wɑɪz kræk] **1.** *n.* a sarcastic comment; a rude joke. ♦ *One more wisecrack from you, and you're going to the principal's office.* ♦ *The comedian's wisecracks in response to the heckling were very funny.* **2.** *tv.* to say or make ①; to make a sarcastic comment. ♦ *My young friend always wisecracks about my age.* ♦ *John wisecracked that the boring speech deserved a prize.*

wish ['wɪʃ] **1.** *n.* a desire for something; a longing for something; a yearning for something. ♦ *Mary has a wish to become a surgeon.* ♦ *My wish is to travel around the world.* **2.** *tv.* to express ①; to hope that something happens. (Takes a clause.) ♦ *I wish that it would stop snowing.* ♦ *Mary wished that she had more free time.* **3. wish for** *iv. + prep. phr.* to express a desire to have something or to make something happen. ♦ *The child wished for a new puppy.* ♦ *Susan wished for a better job.*

wishbone ['wɪʃ bon] *n.* a bone in the breast of chicken and other birds, which is shaped like a Y. ♦ *If two people each make a wish while pulling on the tips of the same wishbone until it breaks, the wish of the person getting the larger piece of the bone will come true.* ♦ *The cook removed the wishbone from the chicken.*

wishful ['wɪʃ fəl] **1.** *adj.* longing; appearing to be wishing for someone or something. (Adv: *wishfully.*) ♦ *Tom looked at the new red car with a wishful look in his eye.* ♦ *Bill had a wishful expression on his face when he asked Mary to marry him.* **2. wishful thinking** *idiom* believing that something is true or that something will happen just because one wishes that it were true or would happen. ♦ *Hoping for a car as a birthday present is just wishful thinking. Your parents can't afford it.* ♦ *Mary thinks that she is going to get a big raise, but that's wishful thinking. Her boss is so mean.*

wishy-washy ['wɪʃ i wɑʃ i] *adj.* weak; not strong; lacking substance; feeble; insipid. ♦ *The wishy-washy politician was very ineffective.* ♦ *The wishy-washy teacher never disciplined the students.*

wisp ['wɪsp] *n.* a small, thin amount of something; a small, thin portion of something. ♦ *Wisps of smoke started to rise from the campfire.* ♦ *Mary twirled the wisps of hair around her ears.*

wistful ['wɪst fʊl] *adj.* sad; showing sadness, yearning, or melancholy. (Adv: *wistfully.*) ♦ *The wistful child looked longingly at the expensive doll.* ♦ *The wistful prisoner knew that he would never be free.*

wit ['wɪt] **1.** *n.* the ability to understand ideas quickly and make intelligent, clever, and funny comments about them. (No plural form in this sense.) ♦ *The popular playwright had a wonderful wit.* ♦ *I like talking with Anne because of her bright wit.* **2.** *n.* someone who has the ability to understand ideas quickly and make intelligent, clever, and funny comments about them. ♦ *Mary is such a wit and is always making us laugh.* ♦ *The wit amused me with his funny observations.* **3. wits** *n.* cleverness; alertness and perceptiveness. (Treated as a plural.) ♦ *I get along in the world by my wits.* ♦ *If I'd had my wits about me, I would have challenged him.* **4. to wit** *phr.* namely; that is; that is to say. ♦ *The criminal was punished; to wit, he received a 20-year sentence.* ♦ *Many students, to wit Mary, Bill, Sue, and Anne, complained about their teacher.* **5. at one's wit's end** *idiom* at the limits of one's mental resources. ♦ *I'm at my wit's end with this problem. I cannot figure it out.* ♦ *Tom could do no more. He was at his wit's end.*

witch ['wɪtʃ] **1.** *n.* someone, usually a woman, who has or claims to have magical powers or who practices a pagan religion. ♦ *The witches stood in a circle and chanted.* ♦ *The witch handed the queen a magic potion.* **2.** *n.* a mean or ugly woman. (Derogatory.) ♦ *Bill called his boss a witch because he was intimidated by her.* ♦ *The old witch at the end of the street yells at her neighbors.*

witchcraft ['wɪtʃ kræft] *n.* magic; sorcery; the ability to use supernatural powers. (No plural form in this sense.) ♦ *I have a few books on witchcraft, but I am certainly not a witch.* ♦ *John wore a charm to protect him from the effects of witchcraft.*

with ['wɪθ] **1.** *prep.* among; including; in the company of someone or something; accompanied by someone or something. ♦ *Susan went to the party with Mary and Jane.* ♦ *I ate mashed potatoes with gravy.* **2.** *prep.* by means of someone or something; by using someone or something. ♦ *I swept the floor with a broom.* ♦ *The astronomer saw the huge star with a telescope.* **3.** *prep.* showing a quality or characteristic. ♦ *Bob always talked to people with ease.* ♦ *The soldier's eyes widened with fear.* **4. have to do with** *phr.* concerning someone or something; regarding someone or something. ♦ *My report has to do with the discovery of gold in California.* ♦ *This information has nothing to do with you.* **5.** *prep.* in the same direction as someone or something. ♦ *The fish swam with the current.* ♦ *Its easier to cut wood with the grain.* **6.** *prep.* in support of someone or something; on the side of someone or something. ♦ *I'm with Mary on this issue.* ♦ *Susan sided with me in the debate.* **7. not with it** *idiom* not able to think clearly; not able to understand things. ♦ *Lisa's mother is not really with it anymore. She's going senile.* ♦ *Tom's not with it yet. He's only just come round from the anesthetic.* **8. with it** *idiom* up-to-date; fashionable. ♦ *Bob thinks he's with it, but he's wearing clothes from the 1960s.* ♦ *Mary's mother embarrasses her by trying to be with it. She wears clothes that are too young for her.*

withdraw [wiθ 'drɔ] **1.** *tv., irreg.* to remove someone or something from someplace; to take someone or something away or back from someplace. (Pt: withdrew; pp:

withdrawn.) ♦ *John withdrew his suggestion when no one supported it.* ♦ *The general withdrew the army from the battleground.* **2.** *iv., irreg.* to move away from someplace; to step back; to step away; to leave; to go away. ♦ *The enemy withdrew as our army approached.* ♦ *The hostages withdrew in fear as the terrorist approached them.* **3.** *iv., irreg.* to no longer be a participant in a race; to drop out of a race. ♦ *The candidate caught cheating withdrew from the race.* ♦ *The injured athlete withdrew.*

withdrawal [wɪθ 'drɔ əl] **1.** *n.* taking something out or away from something. ♦ *Lisa's withdrawal from the race was a disappointment.* ♦ *There were a number of withdrawals at the last minute.* **2.** *n.* a sum of money removed from an account. ♦ *I made a withdrawal from my bank.* ♦ *I had four withdrawals and only one deposit last month.* **3.** *n.* stopping the use of an addictive substance. (No plural form in this sense.) ♦ *The alcoholic craved liquor while he went through withdrawal.* ♦ *Withdrawal from heroin is very difficult.*

withdrawn [wɪθ 'drɔn] **1.** pp of withdraw. **2.** *adj.* quiet, reserved, and unemotional; not likely to talk to others about one's feelings. ♦ *The withdrawn woman sat by herself in a corner of the cafeteria.* ♦ *Lisa seems very quiet and withdrawn sometimes.*

withdrew [wɪθ 'dru] pt of withdraw.

wither ['wɪð ɚ] **1.** *iv.* to shrivel; to droop; to wilt; [for a plant] to turn brown and dry out. ♦ *The crops withered during the drought.* ♦ *I forgot to water my plant and it withered.* **2.** *tv.* to cause a plant to shrivel, droop, or wilt; to cause a plant to turn brown and dry out. ♦ *The drought withered all of the farmers' crops.* ♦ *The hot sun has withered my flower garden.*

withheld [wɪθ 'hɛld] pt/pp of withhold.

withhold [wɪθ 'hold] *tv., irreg.* to hold or keep something back [from someone or something]. (Pt/pp: withheld.) ♦ *Twenty-five percent of my paycheck was withheld for taxes and social security.* ♦ *The audience members withheld their questions until the speech was over.*

within [wɪθ 'ɪn] **1.** *prep.* inside; in or into the inside part of someone or something. ♦ *The prisoners remained within the jail.* ♦ *News of the change had come from within the organization.* **2.** *prep.* not beyond a specific boundary; between certain limits. ♦ *Within three months, the dieter had lost 15 pounds.* ♦ *The bullet had come within three inches of striking me.* **3.** *adv.* into the inside of someone or something; inward. ♦ *The sign on the door read, "Interested applicants may inquire within."* ♦ *Don't look to others as the cause of your problems. Look within.*

without [wɪθ 'ɑʊt] **1.** *prep.* not including someone or something; lacking someone or something. ♦ *John completed the financial report without the help of his coworkers.* ♦ *I'd like to order some tacos without lettuce.* **2.** *prep.* by avoiding or not doing something; while avoiding or not doing something. (Takes the present participle of a verb.) ♦ *How long can you work without sleeping?* ♦ *I drove for 10 hours without stopping.* **3. go without; do without** *idiom* to manage while not having any; to not have any of something. ♦ *We were a poor family and usually went without.* ♦ *I didn't have enough money to buy a new coat so I did without.*

withstand [wɪθ 'stænd] *tv., irreg.* to resist someone or something; to oppose someone or something; to not yield to someone or something. (Pt/pp: withstood.) ♦ *The protected town withstood the onslaught of the enemy's army.* ♦ *The coastal town withstood the hurricane's force.*

withstood [wɪθ 'stʊd] pt/pp of withstand.

witness ['wɪt nəs] **1.** *n.* someone who sees something happen; someone who is in the same place where something happens; a spectator. ♦ *The police questioned the witness about the accident.* ♦ *In court, the witness described the murder in detail.* **2.** *n.* someone who sees the signing of a legal document. ♦ *The witnesses placed their signatures under mine.* ♦ *John and Anne served as witnesses to the signing of the contract.* **3.** *tv.* to see something happen; to be in the same place where something happens. ♦ *Mary witnessed the car crash from her bedroom window.* ♦ *I witnessed the eclipse of the moon last night.* **4.** *tv.* to sign a legal document as a way of swearing that one has watched another person, who is directly affected by the document, sign it, and thus that the other person's signature is real. ♦ *Two clerks witnessed the young couple's signatures on their marriage certificate.* ♦ *The notary public witnessed my signature.*

witness stand ['wit nəs stænd] See stand ⑯.

witticism ['wɪt ə sɪz əm] *n.* a witty remark. ♦ *The critic's witticisms were funnier than the play she reviewed.* ♦ *John's caustic witticisms were insulting but true.*

witty ['wɪt i] *adj.* full of wit; cleverly comical. (Adv: *wittily.* Comp: *wittier;* sup: *wittiest.*) ♦ *The two-act farce was filled with witty remarks.* ♦ *The friends' witty conversation was entertaining.*

wives ['wɑɪvz] pl of wife.

wizard ['wɪz ɚd] **1.** *n.* someone, usually a male, who has or claims to have magical powers. ♦ *The wizard mixed a magical potion in the large cauldron.* ♦ *The wizard chanted a magic spell.* **2.** *n.* an expert; someone who is very skilled at something. (Figurative on ①.) ♦ *Mary is a wizard at fixing radios.* ♦ *When it comes to calculus, Bill is a real wizard.*

wizardry ['wɪz ɚ dri] **1.** *n.* magic; the magical or supernatural skills of a wizard. (No plural form in this sense.) ♦ *The peasants accused the strange man of performing wizardry.* ♦ *The king blamed the famine on wizardry.* **2.** *n.* skill; cleverness. (No plural form in this sense. Figurative on ①.) ♦ *Her wizardry with a paintbrush turned the canvas into a work of art.* ♦ *Due to the mechanic's wizardry, my car was as good as new.*

wobble ['wɑb əl] **1.** *iv.* to shake or move unsteadily; to quiver; to rock back and forth unsteadily; to tremble. ♦ *After I bumped the vase, it wobbled and then fell over.* ♦ *The flimsy building wobbled during the earthquake.* **2.** *tv.* to shake or move something unsteadily; to cause something to quiver. ♦ *Anne wobbled a tree branch so that the apples would fall.* ♦ *The earthquake wobbled all of the glasses on the table.*

woe ['wo] **1.** *n.* sorrow; sad trouble; grief. (No plural form in this sense.) ♦ *Discomfort and woe make me grouchy.* ♦ *My sad friend told me her tale of woe.* **2.** *n.* unpleasant events or circumstances; something that causes ①. ♦ *Losing his job added to John's woes.* ♦

woebegone ['wo bi gɔn] *adj.* looking sad or miserable. ♦ *The woebegone child appeared to be lost.* ♦ *The college dean counseled the woebegone student.*

woeful ['wo fʊl] *adj.* full of woe; sad; sorrowful; miserable. (Adv: *woefully.*) ♦ *The woeful child sat on the curb and cried.* ♦ *The woeful mourners wept at the funeral.*

woke ['wok] pt/pp of wake.

woken ['wok ən] a pp of wake.

wolf ['wʊlf] **1.** *n., irreg.* a wild animal related to the dog that eats meat and travels in groups. (Pl: wolves.) ♦ *The wolves bayed at the moon.* ♦ *The wolf caught and killed one of the shepherd's sheep.* **2. wolf down** *tv.* + *adv.* to eat something quickly, taking large bites and swallowing in large gulps; to devour something. (Informal.) ♦ *The children wolfed the pizza down.* ♦ *Jane wolfed down a doughnut and left for work.* **3. cry wolf** *idiom* to cry or complain about something when nothing is really wrong. ♦ *Pay no attention. She's just crying wolf again.* ♦ *Don't cry wolf too often. No one will come.* **4. keep the wolf from the door** *idiom* to maintain oneself at a minimal level; to keep from starving, freezing, etc. ♦ *I don't make a lot of money, just enough to keep the wolf from the door.* ♦ *We have a small amount of money saved, hardly enough to keep the wolf from the door.* **5. throw someone to the wolves** *idiom* to sacrifice someone to something or some fate. ♦ *The press was demanding an explanation, so the mayor blamed the mess on John and threw him to the wolves.* ♦ *I wouldn't let them throw me to the wolves! I did nothing wrong, and I won't take the blame for their errors.*

wolverine ['wʊl vɚ in] *n.* a small bearlike mammal with dark brown fur, found in the mountains of North America, Europe, and Asia. ♦ *The wolverine is known for its viciousness.* ♦ *The wolverine tore into its prey with sharp claws.*

wolves ['wʊlvz] pl of wolf.

woman ['wʊm ən] **1.** *n., irreg.* an adult female person; an adult female human being. (Pl: women.) ♦ *I asked the woman sitting next to me what time it was.* ♦ *Sally Ride was the first American woman in space.* **2. young woman** *n.* a young adult female human; a female who is young, relative to the speaker. ♦ *Please invite the young woman to come in.* ♦ *Ask the young woman at the desk what office you should go to.* **3.** *adj.* <the adj. use of ①.> (In some contexts.) ♦ *Anne wanted to be called the first woman brain surgeon.* ♦ *A woman racecar driver won the race.*

womanly ['wʊ mən li] *adj.* like a woman; having features or qualities common to most women. ♦ *Mary's womanly intuition told her to distrust the stranger.* ♦ *Anne likes to be noticed for her accomplishments, not just for her womanly figure.*

womb ['wum] *n.* the uterus; the organ in women and some female animals where the fetus is protected and fed until birth. ♦ *Most female mammals have a womb.* ♦ *Jane's baby shifted in her womb.*

women ['wɪm ən] pl of woman.

won ['wʌn] pt/pp of win.

wonder ['wʌn dɚ] **1.** *n.* someone or something that is amazing, surprising, or like a miracle. ♦ *Of the Seven Wonders of the Ancient World, only the Great Pyramids of Egypt still stand.* ♦ *Mount Everest is one of the natural wonders of the world.* **2. wonder about** *iv.* + *prep. phr.* to wish to know about someone or something; to want to know about someone or something. ♦ *The curious student wondered about many things.* ♦ *Bill wondered about his future.* **3.** *tv.* to wish to know something; to want to know something. (Takes a clause.) ♦ *I wonder what Jane has been doing lately.* ♦ *Susan wondered what time it was.* **4.** *adj.* very good, helpful, or productive. ♦ *The wonder drug alleviated my pain.* ♦ *Certain wonder foods can help prevent cancer.* **5. nine days' wonder** *idiom* something that is of interest to people only for a short time. ♦ *Don't worry about the story about you in the newspaper. It'll be a nine days' wonder and then people will forget.* ♦ *The elopement of Bob and Anne was a nine days' wonder. Now people never mention it.*

wonderful ['wʌn dɚ fʊl] *adj.* very good; amazing; remarkable; marvelous. (Adv: *wonderfully.*) ♦ *We had a wonderful time on vacation.* ♦ *John was rewarded for the wonderful job he did.*

wonderland ['wʌn dɚ lænd] *n.* an area or place that is wonderful. ♦ *The snowy mountain village was a winter wonderland.* ♦ *The amusement park is a wonderland for children.*

won't ['wont] *cont.* "will not." ♦ *I won't be home until 8:00 tonight.* ♦ *If you don't eat your peas, you won't get any dessert.*

woo ['wu] **1.** *tv.* to court someone with the intention of marriage. ♦ *The amorous man wooed his beloved.* ♦ *David wooed Susan by writing romantic poetry for her.* **2.** *tv.* to attempt to attract someone or a group into some sort of interaction. ♦ *The Board of Directors wooed the executive to work for them.* ♦ *The salesclerk wooed customers with a lucrative sales pitch.*

wood ['wʊd] **1.** *n.* the substance of which trees are made. (No plural form in this sense.) ♦ *Susan placed some more wood in the fireplace.* ♦ *The sturdy beam was made of solid wood.* **2.** *n.* a kind or type of ①. ♦ *The tabletop was decorated with different woods.* ♦ *For the front of the cabinet, the carpenter chose a wood that would match the furniture in the room.* **3.** *n.* a small forest; an area where there are many trees. (Usually plural. The meaning is the same for the singular and the plural.) ♦ *I saw a deer run into the wood behind the field.* ♦ *Many foxes live in the woods.* **4.** *adj.* made of ①; wooden. ♦ *Mary varnished the wood deck so it wouldn't warp.* ♦ *The wood door split in two when the police battered it.* **5.** *adj.* <the adj. use of ①.> ♦ *Paper is made from wood pulp.* ♦ *The playground was covered with soft wood chips.* **6. knock on wood** *idiom* a phrase said to cancel out imaginary bad luck. ♦ *My stereo has never given me any trouble—knock on wood.* ♦ *We plan to be in Florida by tomorrow evening—knock on wood.* **7. out of the woods** *idiom* past a critical phase; out of the unknown. ♦ *When the patient got out of the woods, everyone relaxed.* ♦ *I can give you a better prediction for your future health when you are out of the woods.*

woodcarver ['wʊd kɑrv ɚ] *n.* someone who carves wood into objects; someone who makes woodcarvings. ♦ *The woodcarver whittled the wood into the shape of a bird.* ♦ *These wooden statues were made by a professional woodcarver.*

woodcarving ['wʊd kɑrv ɪŋ] **1.** *n.* the art and skill of making something by carving it from wood. (No plural form in this sense.) ♦ *Mary learned the craft of woodcarving to supplement her income.* ♦ *The students learned woodcarving in their art class.* **2.** *n.* something that has been carved from wood; a wood sculpture. ♦ *John placed* *the decorative woodcarving on the shelf.* ♦ *Susan sold mahogany woodcarvings at the county fair.*

woodchuck [ˈwʊd tʃək] *n.* a large, burrowing rodent with brown fur that lives in the United States and Canada; the groundhog. ♦ *A woodchuck burrowed into our lawn.* ♦ *The dog chased the woodchuck through the forest.*

wooded [ˈwʊd ɪd] *adj.* having a lot of trees; [of land] covered with trees. ♦ *A developer bought the wooded lot next to my house.* ♦ *The fire destroyed many heavily wooded acres of land.*

wooden [ˈwʊd n] **1.** *adj.* made of wood. ♦ *The wooden house burned quickly to the ground.* ♦ *The wooden staircase creaked as I walked up it.* **2.** *adj.* stiff; not easily moved; not moving easily; not flexible. (Figurative on ①. Adv: *woodenly.*) ♦ *John's wooden movement is caused by arthritis.* ♦ *The reviewer criticized the actor's wooden expressions.*

woodland [ˈwʊd lænd] *n.* an area of land that is covered with trees. (Sometimes plural with the same meaning.) ♦ *The federally protected woodland teemed with wildlife.* ♦ *The developer destroyed some woodlands to make a shopping mall.*

woodpecker [ˈwʊd pɛk ɚ] *n.* a bird that has a long, sharp beak for piercing holes in trees and a long tongue to catch insects inside the tree. ♦ *The woodpecker tapped at the dead tree trunk all day long.* ♦ *The woodpecker ate beetles living inside the tree trunk.*

woodpile [ˈwʊd paɪl] *n.* a pile of logs for burning as fuel. ♦ *Mary carried logs from the woodpile into the house.* ♦ *When our woodpile ran low, I cut down another tree.*

woodwind [ˈwʊd wɪnd] *n.* a group of musical instruments, many of which are made of wood or used to be made of wood, and many of which are played by blowing air across a reed. ♦ *Clarinets, oboes, and bassoons are woodwinds.* ♦ *Although a flute does not have a reed, it is a woodwind instrument.*

woodwork [ˈwʊd wɚk] *n.* something that is made of wood, especially the trimming on the inside of a house or building. (No plural form in this sense.) ♦ *Susan painted the woodwork around the windows blue.* ♦ *The ornate woodwork around the door frame was exquisite.*

woody [ˈwʊd i] **1.** *adj.* covered with woods; covered with trees. (Comp: *woodier;* sup: *woodiest.*) ♦ *We quickly became lost in the woody lot.* ♦ *The hikers walked up the woody hillside.* **2.** *adj.* [of a plant] containing wood. (Comp: *woodier;* sup: *woodiest.*) ♦ *The woody plant damaged the lawn mower's blades.* ♦ *I trimmed the woody shrub with electric clippers.*

woof [ˈwʊf] **1.** *n.* the sound made by a barking dog. ♦ *A periodic, loud woof from the neighbor's dog kept me awake all night.* ♦ *The dog let out a loud woof when it saw my cat.* **2.** *iv.* to utter or make the sound of a barking dog. ♦ *When I heard the dog woof, I suspected that someone was outside.* ♦ *The dog woofed excitedly when it saw the snake.*

wool [ˈwʊl] **1.** *n.* the soft, curly hair of sheep and goats. (No plural form in this sense.) ♦ *Anne sheared the wool from the sheep.* ♦ *John collected the sheep's wool and sold it at the market.* **2.** *n.* thread, yarn, or fabric, made from ①. (No plural form in this sense.) ♦ *Wool will shrink if you wash it in hot water.* ♦ *I knitted a sweater out of wool.* **3.** *adj.* made from ②. ♦ *I wore a wool sweater because it was so cold outside.* ♦ *The wool socks kept my feet warm and dry.* **4. pull the wool over someone's eyes** *idiom* to deceive someone. ♦ *You can't pull the wool over my eyes. I know what's going on.* ♦ *Don't try to pull the wool over her eyes. She's too smart.* **5. woolgathering** *idiom* daydreaming. ♦ *John never listens to the teacher. He's always woolgathering.* ♦ *I wish my new secretary would get on with the work and stop woolgathering.*

woolen [ˈwʊl ən] *adj.* made of wool. ♦ *I washed the dirty woolen sweater by hand.* ♦ *The woolen mittens keep my hands warm.*

woolly [ˈwʊl i] **1.** *adj.* made of wool. (Comp: *woollier;* sup: *woolliest.*) ♦ *The woolly sweater felt itchy.* ♦ *The woolly socks kept my feet warm.* **2.** *adj.* looking or feeling like wool; covered with wool or something that looks like wool. (Comp: *woollier;* sup: *woolliest.*) ♦ *The child touched Santa Claus's woolly beard.* ♦ *The large, woolly caterpillar crawled up the kitchen wall.*

woozy [ˈwu zi] *adj.* dizzy or confused, especially because one is sick or drunk. (Adv: *woozily.* Comp: *woozier;* sup: *wooziest.*) ♦ *Jane felt woozy after drinking too much vodka.* ♦ *The medicine made Bill feel woozy, so he took a nap.*

word [ˈwɚd] **1.** *n.* a speech sound or group of speech sounds that has a particular meaning; a written symbol or a group of written symbols that represent a speech sound or group of speech sounds that has a particular meaning. ♦ *The German word for 'three' is* drei. ♦ *I looked up the meaning of the unusual word in the dictionary.* **2. someone's word** *n.* someone's promise; someone's pledge. (No plural form in this sense.) ♦ *I give you my word that I will meet you at 8:00.* ♦ *The general kept his word that he would return.* **3. the word** *n.* an order; a command. (No plural form in this sense. Treated as singular.) ♦ *The soldiers attacked as soon as they got the word.* ♦ *When I give you the word, start the engine.* **4. the word** *n.* news; information. (No plural form in this sense. Treated as singular.) ♦ *The evening edition had the latest word on the day's news.* ♦ *What's the word about your test results?* **5.** *tv.* to express something by choosing words ① carefully. ♦ *Mary worded her request politely but firmly.* ♦ *Unfortunately, Bill worded his comments in an offensive way.* **6. have a word with someone** *idiom* to have a short chat with someone, usually a private chat. ♦ *Jane's boss asked if she could have a word with her.* ♦ *I had a word with Max about his work performance.* **7. break one's word** *idiom* not to do what one said one would do; not to keep one's promise. ♦ *Don't say you'll visit your grandmother if you can't go. She hates for people to break their word.* ♦ *If you break your word, she won't trust you again.* **8. by word of mouth** *idiom* by speaking rather than writing. ♦ *I learned about it by word of mouth.* ♦ *I need it in writing. I don't trust things I hear about by word of mouth.* **9. eat one's words** *idiom* to have to take back one's statements; to confess that one's predictions were wrong. ♦ *You shouldn't say that to me. I'll make you eat your words.* ♦ *John was wrong about the election and had to eat his words.* **10. go back on one's word** *idiom* to break a promise that one has made. ♦ *I hate to go back on my word, but I won't pay you $100 after all.* ♦ *Going back on your word makes you a liar.* **11. hang on someone's every word** *idiom* to listen carefully to everything someone says. ♦ *He gave a great lecture. We hung on his every word.* ♦ *Look at the way John hangs on Mary's every* *word. He must be in love with her.* **12. keep one's word** *idiom* to uphold one's promise; to keep one's promise. ♦ *I told her I'd be there to pick her up, and I intend to keep my word.* ♦ *Keeping one's word is necessary in the legal profession.* **13. put in a good word (for someone)** *idiom* to say something (to someone) in support of someone else. ♦ *I hope you get the job. I'll put in a good word for you.* ♦ *Yes, I want the job. If you see the boss, please put in a good word.* **14. put words into someone's mouth** *idiom* to speak for another person without permission. ♦ *Stop putting words into my mouth. I can speak for myself.* ♦ *The lawyer was scolded for putting words into the witness's mouth.* **15. take the words out of one's mouth** *idiom* [for someone else] to say what one was just about to say. ♦ *John said exactly what I was going to say. He took the words out of my mouth.* ♦ *I agree with you, and I wanted to say the same thing. You took the words right out of my mouth.*

wording ['wɚd ɪŋ] *n.* the way something is said or written; the choice and order of words that are used to express something. (No plural form in this sense.) ♦ *I understand what you said, but your wording could be more polite.* ♦ *The idiomatic wording was incorrectly translated.*

word processor ['wɚd prɑ sɛs ɚ] *n.* a type of computer program that aids in the production of written text, or the computer that runs such a program. ♦ *The author wrote her latest novel using a popular word processor.* ♦ *I prefer using a word processor to a typewriter when I write.*

wordy ['wɚd i] *adj.* having too many words; verbose; not concise. (Adv: *wordily.* Comp: *wordier;* sup: *wordiest.*) ♦ *The editor shortened the wordy document.* ♦ *The wordy speech was rather boring.*

wore ['wor] pt of wear.

work ['wɚk] **1.** *n.* an activity that requires effort. (No plural form in this sense.) ♦ *Digging ditches is difficult work.* ♦ *Hard work makes me sweat.* **2.** *n.* the effort required to do an activity. (No plural form in this sense.) ♦ *My staff had put a lot of work into the project.* ♦ *That job requires a lot of work!* **3.** *n.* something that is a result of effort or energy. ♦ *The artist's works are on display at the museum.* ♦ *Anne was proud of her handcrafted works of art.* **4.** *n.* a job; an occupation; a career; what one does for a living; what a person does to make money. (No plural form in this sense.) ♦ *What kind of work are you in?* ♦ *Her work is preparing other people's tax forms.* **5.** *n.* the place where one's job is located; the job site. (No plural form in this sense.) ♦ *I go to work every morning at 8:00.* ♦ *Yesterday, I left my car at work and took the train home.* **6.** *iv.* to be employed; to have a job; to labor; to earn money at a job. ♦ *Anne worked for thirty-five years before she retired.* ♦ *David works at a law firm downtown.* **7.** *iv.* to function properly; to operate properly. ♦ *The television is working again because I fixed it.* ♦ *Of course the radio works, but you have to plug it in first.* **8. work out** *iv.* + *adv.* to exercise; to lift weights and do exercises to build the body. (See also ⑳.) ♦ *I work out at least twice a week at the gym.* ♦ *Lisa doesn't have time to work out.* **9.** *tv.* to cause something to function as intended. ♦ *How do I work this machine?* ♦ *Bill doesn't know how to work his computer.* **10.** *tv.* to cause someone or something to move to a certain position while overcoming resistance or obstacles. ♦ *John worked his way through the crowd.* ♦ *The pin worked itself out from the hinge.* **11.** *tv.* to cover a certain territory while doing one's job. ♦ *The newspaper vendor worked the corner opposite city hall.* ♦ *The sales representative worked the whole state of Montana.* **12.** *tv.* to cause someone or something to operate or function; to cause someone or something to be active; to cause something to use energy. ♦ *My boss works me too hard.* ♦ *Dave really worked the car's engine when he drove up the hill.* **13.** *tv.* to plow or farm land. ♦ *The farmer works the land for eight months each year.* ♦ *I worked the soil with a plow.* **14. work up** *tv.* + *adv.* to excite or anger someone; to arouse someone's emotions. ♦ *Bill's offensive comments worked John up into a rage.* ♦ *Don't work yourself up over small details. It's not important.* **15. at work** *phr.* at the place where one does something to earn a living. ♦ *John's not here. He's at work.* ♦ *I will be at work tomorrow. Please call me there.* **16. at work** *phr.* involved in doing something. ♦ *John is not resting right now. He is at work.* ♦ *Whether at work or at play, I try to be pleasant to other people.* **17. all in a day's work** *idiom* part of what is expected; typical or normal. ♦ *I don't particularly like to cook, but it's all in a day's work.* ♦ *Putting up with rude customers isn't pleasant, but it's all in a day's work.* **18. work like a horse** *idiom* to work ⑥ very hard. ♦ *I've been working like a horse all day, and I'm tired.* ♦ *I'm too old to work like a horse. I'd prefer to relax more.* **19. work one's fingers to the bone** *idiom* to work ⑥ very hard. ♦ *I worked my fingers to the bone so you children could have everything you needed. Now look at the way you treat me!* ♦ *I spent the day working my fingers to the bone, and now I want to relax.* **20. work out (somehow)** *idiom* to result in a good conclusion; to finish positively. ♦ *Don't worry. I am sure that everything will work out all right.* ♦ *Things always work out.* **21. work something off** *idiom* to get rid of something by taking physical exercise. ♦ *Bob put on weight while on vacation and is trying to work it off by swimming regularly.* ♦ *Jane tried to work off her depression by playing a game of tennis.*

workable ['wɚk ə bəl] *adj.* able to be used; usable. (Adv: *workably.*) ♦ *The playwright's script wasn't perfect, but it was workable.* ♦ *After much kneading, the soft clay was workable.*

workaholic [wɚk ə 'hɔl ɪk] *n.* someone who is addicted to working all the time. ♦ *The workaholic stayed at the office overnight.* ♦ *I never see my roommate because she's a workaholic.*

workbench ['wɚk bɛntʃ] *n.* a table or surface that someone works at, which holds all the necessary tools and equipment. ♦ *The carpenter's tools were scattered across the workbench.* ♦ *Lisa sat at her workbench and drafted designs.*

workbook ['wɚk bʊk] *n.* a textbook for students, often including pages that assignments can be written on. ♦ *The teacher graded the students' workbooks every weekend.* ♦ *At the start of the school year, each student was given a workbook.*

workday ['wɚk de] **1.** *n.* a day on which people work. ♦ *For most Americans, workdays are Monday through Friday.* ♦ *Still, for many people Saturdays and Sundays are workdays, too.* **2.** *n.* the part of the day during which someone works. ♦ *Anne took a lunch break in the middle of her workday.* ♦ *Susan's workday was interrupted by numerous phone calls.*

worker ['wɚk ɚ] *n.* someone who works; someone who is employed. ♦ *This factory employs 4,000 workers.* ♦ *The workers were very unhappy with the new management.*

work force ['wɚk fors] *n.* the people who work, either at one place or in the entire country. (No plural form in this sense.) ♦ *The entire work force at our company is overworked and underpaid.* ♦ *I joined the work force when I was eighteen years old, and I have been in it ever since.*

workhorse ['wɚk hors] **1.** *n.* a horse that is used to do work. ♦ *The farmer hitched the workhorses to the plow.* ♦ *At the end of the day, Susan fed and groomed the workhorses.* **2.** *n.* someone or something that does a large amount of work. (Figurative on ①.) ♦ *Without a few real workhorses, this project would still be unfinished.* ♦ *The manager rewarded the workhorse with a year-end bonus.*

working ['wɚ kɪŋ] **1.** *adj.* functioning; operating; able to be used. ♦ *The inventor built a working model of the product.* ♦ *Anne has a working knowledge of French.* **2.** *adj.* [of someone] employed at a job for which one earns money; of or about employment. ♦ *The survey examined the leisure habits of working men and women.* ♦ *The working mother enrolled her child in day care.*

working class ['wɚk ɪŋ klæs] **1.** *n.* people who work at jobs usually requiring physical labor. ♦ *The working class is also known as blue-collar workers.* ♦ *The populist candidate was popular with the working class.* **2. working-class** *adj.* hardworking; appealing to or concerning ①. ♦ *The candidate stressed his working-class values.* ♦ *Apartments in a working-class neighborhood are usually reasonably priced.*

work load ['wɚk lod] *n.* one's assignment of work; the things that one must do as part of work. ♦ *My work load is too heavy, and I can't finish all my assignments.* ♦ *Bill asked for a lighter work load and was fired.*

workman ['wɚk mən] *n., irreg.* someone who works for a living; a man who works for a living, especially one who works with his hands or with machines. (Pl: workmen.) ♦ *The injured workman was taken to a hospital.* ♦ *All workmen are required to wear a hard hat at the construction site.*

workmanship ['wɚk mən ʃɪp] *n.* the quality of doing skilled work well; craftsmanship. (No plural form in this sense.) ♦ *Carpentry requires a high degree of workmanship.* ♦ *The laborers' workmanship was very professional.*

workmen ['wɚk mən] pl of workman.

workout ['wɚk aʊt] *n.* a period of physical exercise. ♦ *Anne goes to the health club for a workout each morning.* ♦ *After John's workout, he relaxed in the sauna.*

workplace ['wɚk ples] *n.* the place where people work. ♦ *The company tried to prevent accidents at the workplace.* ♦ *John's workplace is crowded with files.*

workshop ['wɚk ʃɑp] **1.** *n.* a room where things are made or repaired. ♦ *The carpenter made a table in his workshop.* ♦ *My car was towed to the mechanic's workshop.* **2.** *n.* a session where people study, discuss, or are taught a certain subject or craft. ♦ *Many students attended the workshop on interviewing techniques.* ♦ *The feuding couple attended a marriage workshop.*

work station ['wɚk ste ʃən] **1.** *n.* the space where one works and the equipment needed to do the job. ♦ *John requested a stapler for his work station.* ♦ *Susan completed the budget report at her work station.* **2.** *n.* a computer terminal and associated equipment. ♦ *Anne upgraded her work station's software.* ♦ *An hour's worth of work was lost when Bill's work station crashed.*

world ['wɚld] **1.** *n.* the planet Earth. ♦ *Our world is threatened by ecological disasters.* ♦ *The traveler had been to almost every country in the world.* **2.** *n.* the people who live on the planet Earth; the human race. ♦ *The entire world will feel the effects of this disease.* ♦ *The world awaited the passing of the comet.* **3.** *n.* a planet other than Earth, especially as the source of other life forms. ♦ *The astronomer searched for life forms from other worlds.* ♦ *The aliens from a distant world landed in the farmer's cornfield.* **4.** *n.* a certain part of ①. ♦ *The report focused on health care in the Third World.* ♦ *North and South America are sometimes referred to as the New World.* **5.** *n.* an area of human activity, thought, or interest. ♦ *Susan was fascinated by the world of biology.* ♦ *In the world of baseball, Babe Ruth is a familiar name.* **6. in a world of one's own** *idiom* aloof; detached; self-centered. ♦ *John lives in a world of his own. He has very few friends.* ♦ *Mary walks around in a world of her own, but she's very intelligent.* **7. not long for this world** *idiom* about to die. ♦ *Our dog is nearly twelve years old and not long for this world.* ♦ *I'm so tired. I think I'm not long for this world.* **8. on top of the world** *idiom* feeling wonderful; glorious; ecstatic. ♦ *Wow, I feel on top of the world.* ♦ *Since he got a new job, he's on top of the world.* **9. out of this world** *idiom* wonderful; extraordinary. ♦ *This pie is just out of this world.* ♦ *Look at you! How lovely you look—simply out of this world.* **10. set the world on fire** *idiom* to do exciting things that bring fame and glory. ♦ *I'm not very ambitious. I don't want to set the world on fire.* ♦ *You don't have to set the world on fire. Just do a good job.* **11. think the world of someone or something** *idiom* to be very fond of someone or something. ♦ *Mary thinks the world of her little sister.* ♦ *The old lady thinks the world of her cats.*

worldly ['wɚld li] *adj.* of or about people or society; not spiritual. (Comp: *worldlier;* sup: *worldliest.*) ♦ *The minister cautioned against pursuing worldly pleasures.* ♦ *The rebellious child's worldly views disturbed her parents.*

World War I ['wɚld 'wor 'wʌn] *n.* a major war fought between nations, mainly in Europe, 1914–1918. (Abbreviated *WW I.*) ♦ *My grandfather fought in World War I.* ♦ *Small airplanes were used in World War I.*

World War II ['wɚld 'wor 'tu] *n.* a major war fought between nations, in Europe and the Pacific area, 1939–1945. (Abbreviated *WW II.*) ♦ *During World War II, many things were rationed.* ♦ *Millions of human beings died in World War II.*

worldwide ['wɚld 'waɪd] **1.** *adj.* found or occurring throughout the world; involving everyone in the world. ♦ *The huge comet caused a worldwide panic.* ♦ *The local battle grew into a worldwide war.* **2.** *adv.* throughout the world; all over the world. ♦ *The flight attendant had traveled worldwide.* ♦ *The deadly virus spread worldwide.*

World Wide Web ['wɚld 'waɪd 'wɛb] *n.* an international network of data storage transfer and its visual display, designed to be accessed through a computer connection. (Abbreviated *WWW* and Web.) ♦ *Mary has her own site on the World Wide Web that describes her inter-*

ests. ♦ *I checked the World Wide Web for information on books.*

worm ['wɚm] **1.** *n.* any of numerous small, soft, tube-shaped animals having no legs or head, including some that crawl underground and others that live as parasites in animals or people. ♦ *When it rains, worms come out of the ground.* ♦ *Mary baited her fishing hook with a worm.* **2.** *n.* someone who is not worthy of being liked; someone who is lowly and despicable. (Figurative on ①. Derogatory.) ♦ *Susan finally kicked that worm out of her house.* ♦ *Some worm stole my leather jacket!* **3.** *tv.* to remove ① from an animal; to cause an animal to become free of ①. ♦ *The veterinarian wormed my cat.* ♦ *Our dog had to be wormed twice.* **4. open a can of worms** *idiom* to uncover a set of problems; to create unnecessary complications. ♦ *Now you are opening a whole new can of worms.* ♦ *How about cleaning up this mess before you open up a new can of worms?*

worn ['worn] **1.** pp of wear. **2.** *adj.* degraded or reduced in value or serviceability owing to wear. ♦ *The worn carpet had faded from exposure to sunlight.* ♦ *The worn stairs sagged in the middle.*

worn-out ['worn 'aʊt] **1.** *adj.* completely degraded or reduced in value or serviceability owing to wear. ♦ *Anne replaced the worn-out carpeting in her apartment.* ♦ *The mechanic replaced my car's worn-out motor.* **2.** *adj.* very tired; exhausted. ♦ *I'm worn-out. I need to go to bed.* ♦ *After a hard day at work, Mary was completely worn-out.*

worried ['wɚ id] **1.** *adj.* (Adv: *worriedly.*) upset; concerned; having worry. ♦ *Both worried parents remained awake until Jimmy came home.* ♦ *The worried pet owner took her sick dog to the veterinarian.* **2.** *adj.* showing worry. (Adv: *worriedly.*) ♦ *John's worried look indicated that something was wrong.* ♦ *With a worried glance, Mary watched the storm approach.*

worrisome ['wɚ i səm] *adj.* causing worry; causing someone to feel upset. (Adv: *worrisomely.*) ♦ *My assistant takes care of many worrisome problems every day.* ♦ *A few worrisome details threatened the success of the conference.*

worry ['wɚ i] **1.** *n.* a feeling of anxiety or nervousness. (No plural form in this sense.) ♦ *David developed an ulcer because of excessive worry.* ♦ *Worry kept Anne awake at night.* **2.** *n.* someone or something that causes ①. ♦ *Mary told her worries to her closest friend.* ♦ *Low approval ratings were a worry to the politician.* **3.** *tv.* to be anxious that...; to suspect, regrettably, that.... (Takes a clause.) ♦ *Anne worried that it would rain during the picnic.* ♦ *John worried that he wouldn't get to work on time.* **4.** *tv.* to cause someone to feel anxiety or nervousness. ♦ *The impending storm worried Susan.* ♦ *Max and his problems really worried Bill.*

worse ['wɚs] **1.** *adj.* more bad; less good; inferior. (The comparative form of bad.) ♦ *Each act at the talent show was worse than the previous one.* ♦ *John's sore throat is worse than it was yesterday.* **2.** *adv.* in a worse ① way. (The comparative form of *badly.*) ♦ *Unfortunately, my new car runs worse than my old one did.* ♦ *I scored worse on the test than everyone else did.*

worsen ['wɚs ən] **1.** *tv.* to make something worse. ♦ *Bill worsened the problem when he tried to fix the computer.* ♦ *The bad acting worsened an already tedious script.* **2.** *iv.* to become worse. ♦ *The boring picnic worsened when it began to rain.* ♦ *The horrible movie worsened with each passing minute.* **3.** *iv.* to become more sick. ♦ *Mary worsened during the night in the hospital.* ♦ *John's sore throat worsened throughout the week.*

worship ['wɚ ʃɪp] **1.** *tv.* to honor someone or something greatly; to adore someone or something. (Pt/pp: *worshiped.* Present participle: *worshiping.*) ♦ *The whole congregation worshiped the Lord.* ♦ *Anne worships her grandparents.* **2.** *iv.* to attend a church service. (Pt/pp: *worshiped.* Present participle: *worshiping.*) ♦ *Anne worships at the church down the street.* ♦ *Tom worships at the temple.* **3.** *n.* what is done at a church service. (No plural form in this sense.) ♦ *I tried to quiet my crying baby during worship.* ♦ *Worship requires peace and quiet.* **4.** *n.* extreme honor or adoration for someone or something that one holds dear. (Figurative on ③. No plural form in this sense.) ♦ *Bill is against the worship of professional athletes.* ♦ *Worship of the celebrities is the way of life for some people.*

worst ['wɚst] **1.** *adj.* most bad; least good; most inferior. (The superlative of bad.) ♦ *That was the worst movie I have ever seen!* ♦ *Our team has the worst record in the whole league.* **2. the worst** *adv.* in the worst ① way. (Functions as the superlative of badly.) ♦ *Of all of the children, Jimmy reads the best but he writes the worst.* ♦ *At the talent show, the off-key singer performed the worst.* **3. the worst** *n.* [among three or more] someone or something that is the most bad or least good. (Stands for singular or plural nominals.) ♦ *Anne voted against the worst of the three candidates.* ♦ *Of all the excuses I've ever heard, that is the worst.*

worth ['wɚθ] **1.** *n.* the value of something; the amount of money that something could sell for. (No plural form in this sense.) ♦ *What is the worth of your house?* ♦ *I calculated the worth of all my assets.* **2.** *n.* the importance of someone or something; usefulness. (No plural form in this sense.) ♦ *The efficient workers knew their true worth to the company.* ♦ *The firm paid me far less than my worth.* **3.** *n.* the amount of something that can be bought for a specific amount of money. (No plural form in this sense.) ♦ *Bill put $5 worth of gas in the tank.* ♦ *Could I have three dollars' worth of sliced ham?* **4.** *adj.* having a specific value; costing a specific amount of money. (Not prenominal.) ♦ *Do you think this umbrella is worth twenty dollars?* ♦ *This old car isn't worth the money I paid for it.* **5. make something worth someone's while** *idiom* to make something profitable enough for someone to do. ♦ *If you deliver this parcel for me, I'll make it worth your while.* ♦ *The boss said he'd make it worth our while if we worked late.* **6. worth someone's while** *idiom* worth one's time and trouble. ♦ *The job pays so badly it's not worth your while even going for an interview.* ♦ *It's not worth Mary's while going all that way just for a one-hour meeting.*

worthless ['wɚθ ləs] *adj.* having no value or importance; useless. (Adv: *worthlessly.*) ♦ *The worthless employees were fired.* ♦ *I threw away the worthless plastic jewelry.*

worthlessness ['wɚθ ləs nəs] *n.* a state of being worthless; uselessness. (No plural form in this sense.) ♦ *The philosopher pondered the worthlessness of war.* ♦ *The worthlessness of Mary's required classes amazed her.*

worthwhile ['wɚθ 'ʍaɪl] *adj.* deserving one's time, energy, or attention; worth doing. ♦ *Exercise is a worth-*

while activity. ♦ *It would be worthwhile to study for your next exam.*

worthy ['wɚ ði] *adj.* deserving one's time, energy, or attention; deserving; useful; having value or importance. (Adv: *worthily.* Comp: *worthier;* sup: *worthiest.*) ♦ *The diligent employee was worthy of a raise.* ♦ *I would praise him, but he is not worthy.* ♦ *The condemned criminal was not worthy of compassion.*

would ['wʊd] **1.** *aux.* <a form used as the past tense of will to express the future from a time in the past, especially in indirect quotes or in constructions where other past tense verbs are used.> (Contraction: *-'d.*) ♦ *Bob has said that he would like to go to the park tomorrow.* ♦ *Mary said she would have gone to the party if she had known about it.* **2.** *aux.* <a form used to express something that happened many times in the past.> (Contraction: *-'d.*) ♦ *We would visit Grandpa every Thursday except when it rained.* ♦ *I would play in the sandbox when I was young.* **3.** *aux.* <a form used instead of will to make commands more polite by turning them into questions.> (Contraction: *-'d.* See also will ①; using *would* is usually more polite than using *will.*) ♦ *Would you please close the door behind you?* ♦ *Would you mind being quiet while I'm talking?*

would-be ['wʊd bi] *adj.* meaning to be something; intending to be something; wishing to be something; wanting to be something. ♦ *The director auditioned several would-be actors.* ♦ *The publisher rejected the would-be author's first manuscript.*

wouldn't ['wʊd nt] *cont.* "would not." ♦ *I wouldn't do that if I were you.* ♦ *John wouldn't have gone to the party if he had known that I would be there, too.*

would've ['wʊd əv] *cont.* "would have," where have is an auxiliary. ♦ *We would've stayed on vacation longer if we could've afforded it.* ♦ *I would've phrased your request more politely.*

wound **1.** ['waʊnd] pt/pp of wind ④. **2.** ['wund] *n.* an injury where the skin is torn or punctured. ♦ *The paramedic bandaged the crash victim's wounds.* ♦ *The nurse cleaned the soldier's wounds.* **3.** ['wund] *n.* an injury to one's feelings. ♦ *The abusive insults created deep wounds.* ♦ *My therapist helped me heal my emotional wounds.* **4.** ['wund] *tv.* to injure someone; to cause someone to have ②. ♦ *The exploding grenade wounded several soldiers.* ♦ *Five people were wounded in the car accident.* **5. rub salt in a wound** [...'wund] *idiom* to deliberately make someone's unhappiness, shame, or misfortune worse. ♦ *Don't rub salt in the wound by telling me how enjoyable the party was.* ♦ *Bill is feeling miserable about losing his job, and Bob is rubbing salt in the wound by saying how good his replacement is.*

wounded ['wun dɪd] **1.** *adj.* injured; hurt and bleeding; having a wound. ♦ *The wounded soldiers were carried from the battlefield.* ♦ *The wounded accident victims were taken to the hospital.* **2. the wounded** *n.* injured, hurt, or bleeding people, as a group. (No plural form in this sense. Treated as plural.) ♦ *The wounded were removed from the field after the battle.* ♦ *Rescuers pulled the wounded from the rubble.*

wove ['wov] pt of weave.

woven ['wo vən] pp of weave.

Wow! ['waʊ] *interj.* "How exciting!" ♦ *Wow! That is great music.* ♦ *"Wow!" said Tom, when he saw that he had passed his calculus test.*

wrangle ['ræŋ gəl] **1.** *tv.* to herd and manage cattle on a ranch. ♦ *The cowboy had wrangled cattle in Wyoming for over ten years.* ♦ *Max didn't want to spend the rest of his life wrangling stupid animals.* **2.** *iv.* to argue; to quarrel. ♦ *Anne and Bill wrangled over where to go to dinner.* ♦ *Stop wrangling and get to work!*

wrap ['ræp] **1. wrap (up)** *tv.* (+ *adv.*) to enclose someone or something in a covering. ♦ *I wrapped Jimmy up in warm layers of clothing.* ♦ *Anne wrapped the present in colorful paper.* **2. wrap up** *tv.* + *adv.* to bring something to an end; to conclude something. ♦ *Anne wrapped up her lecture by taking questions from the audience.* ♦ *John wrapped up the financial report with some good news.* **3.** *n.* a shawl or a scarf; a coat or cape. ♦ *Mary hung her wrap on a coat hook.* ♦ *Susan covered her face with her wrap to protect it from the wind.* **4. keep something under wraps** *idiom* to keep something concealed (until some future time). ♦ *We kept the plan under wraps until after the election.* ♦ *The automobile company kept the new model under wraps until most of the old models had been sold.*

wrapper ['ræp ɚ] *n.* a piece of paper or cloth used to wrap an object. ♦ *Anne removed the wrapper from the stick of gum.* ♦ *Remove the frozen pizza's plastic wrapper before placing it in the oven.*

wrapping ['ræp ɪŋ] *n.* a piece of paper or other material used to wrap an object. ♦ *The gifts were wrapped with decorative wrapping.* ♦ *The clerk put the fish in a wrapping of newspaper.*

wrapping paper ['ræp ɪŋ pe pɚ] *n.* paper that is used to wrap objects, especially decorative paper used to wrap gifts. (No plural form in this sense.) ♦ *The gifts were wrapped with colorful wrapping paper.* ♦ *In January, the store held a sale on wrapping paper.*

wrap-up ['ræp əp] *n.* a conclusion; a summary. ♦ *During the wrap-up, the commentators discussed the game.* ♦ *As a wrap-up, the speaker took questions from the audience.*

wrath ['ræθ] *n.* severe anger, especially from someone with a lot of power. (No plural form in this sense.) ♦ *The young shoplifter faced his parents' wrath.* ♦ *The sinners feared the wrath of God.*

wreak ['rik] *tv.* to inflict damage or harm on someone or something. ♦ *The hurricane wreaked havoc on the coastal town.* ♦ *The gangster wreaked revenge on his brother's murderer.*

wreath ['riθ] *n., irreg.* an ornament of flowers and leaves arranged in a certain shape, especially a circle. (Pl is ['riθs] or ['riðz].) ♦ *Anne placed a wreath on her front door during the Christmas season.* ♦ *A mourner put a wreath of pine boughs on the casket.*

wreathe ['rið] *tv.* to encircle something; to make a circle around something. ♦ *The angel was wreathed with a halo.* ♦ *A circle of flowers wreathed the tree.*

wreck ['rɛk] **1.** *n.* a serious accident, especially where something is destroyed. ♦ *A wreck blocked traffic on the freeway for miles.* ♦ *The journalist reported live from the site of the wreck.* **2.** *n.* a ruined vehicle that remains after a serious accident. ♦ *The road crew cleared the wreck from the freeway.* ♦ *The police carefully pulled the injured man* *out of the wreck.* **3.** *n.* someone or something that is a mess. (Figurative on ②.) ♦ *Max was punished because his room was a wreck.* ♦ *I feel like a wreck because I drank too much last night.* **4.** *tv.* to destroy something. ♦ *Tom wrecked his brother's sand castle.* ♦ *The scandal wrecked the politician's chances of being elected.*

wreckage ['rɛk ɪdʒ] **1.** *n.* whatever remains after a serious accident or disaster. (No plural form in this sense.) ♦ *After the bomb went off, the police poked through the wreckage of the building.* ♦ *The inspectors examined the plane wreckage.* **2.** *n.* the remains of something that has been harmed or ruined. (No plural form in this sense. Figurative on ①.) ♦ *The scandal made a wreckage of my life.* ♦ *John carried the wreckage of previous relationships with him.*

wrecker ['rɛk ɚ] **1.** *n.* someone or something that tears something down or dismantles something, as in the course of performing a job. ♦ *The wreckers demolished the building in one day.* ♦ *Wreckers dismantled the ship to recover the steel.* **2.** *n.* a truck that removes wreckage after an accident. ♦ *The wrecker towed the twisted metal to the junkyard.* ♦ *Wreckers cleared the debris from the intersection.*

wren ['rɛn] *n.* a small songbird with a loud voice. ♦ *There's a nest of wrens outside my bedroom window.* ♦ *We heard the song of the nearby wrens.*

wrench ['rɛntʃ] **1.** *n.* a tool that turns nuts, bolts, pipes, and other objects that are rotated into or out of position. ♦ *The plumber used a wrench to unscrew the pipe.* ♦ *I tightened the wrench around the nut.* **2.** *n.* a strong twist. ♦ *My ankle got a painful wrench when I fell off the steps.* ♦ *With a powerful wrench, I removed the lid from the pickle jar.* **3.** *tv.* to twist or pull something forcefully. ♦ *The plumber wrenched the leaky pipe loose.* ♦ *Anne wrenched the stubborn lid from the jar.* **4.** *tv.* to injure a part of the body by twisting it or pulling it. ♦ *Anne wrenched her back when she picked up the heavy box.* ♦ *David wrenched his ankle when he fell off his skis.* **5. throw a monkey wrench in the works** *idiom* to cause problems for someone's plans. ♦ *I don't want to throw a monkey wrench in the works, but have you checked your plans with a lawyer?* ♦ *When John refused to help us, he really threw a monkey wrench in the works.*

wrest ['rɛst] *tv.* to pull or tear something away from someone by force; to take something from someone using great effort. ♦ *Bill had to wrest the remote control away from me.* ♦ *The police officer wrested the gun from the criminal.*

wrestle ['rɛs əl] **1.** *tv.* to force someone or something loose, down, away, etc., with force. ♦ *The police officer wrestled the burly criminal to the ground.* ♦ *Anne wrestled the knife from her assailant.* **2.** *iv.* to participate in the sport of wrestling. ♦ *John wrestled when he was in high school.* ♦ *My brother wrestled in the state championships.*

wrestling ['rɛs lɪŋ] *n.* a sport, usually done by males, where two competitors struggle to pin each other to the ground. (No plural form in this sense.) ♦ *Our school came in first place in its league for wrestling.* ♦ *David pursued wrestling in college.*

wretch ['rɛtʃ] **1.** *n.* someone who is poor and miserable. (Derogatory.) ♦ *I gave a quarter to the poor wretch on the street corner.* ♦ *An unfortunate wretch begged for money at the train station.* **2.** *n.* someone who is bad or despised. (Derogatory. Figurative on ①.) ♦ *I hated working for my wretch of a boss.* ♦ *The students often complained about the teacher who is just a wretch.*

wretched ['rɛtʃ əd] **1.** *adj.* poor; miserable; pitied. (Adv: *wretchedly.*) ♦ *I gave a dollar to the wretched beggar downtown.* ♦ *The impoverished family lived a wretched existence.* **2.** *adj.* despised; not liked. (Adv: *wretchedly.*) ♦ *Half of the audience left the wretched film before it was over.* ♦ *I couldn't eat the stew because it tasted wretched.*

wretchedness ['rɛtʃ əd nəs] **1.** *n.* a state of being wretched; misery; squalor; poverty. (No plural form in this sense.) ♦ *The wretchedness of his living conditions depressed Max.* ♦ *The wretchedness of the daily life of the beggar must have been agonizing.* **2.** *n.* the quality of being despised or hated. (No plural form in this sense.) ♦ *The wretchedness of my mean boss was known throughout the firm.* ♦ *The critic detailed the wretchedness of the horrible movie.*

wriggle ['rɪg əl] **1.** *iv.* to squirm; to move back and forth as though trying to escape. ♦ *The hostages wriggled free from their bonds.* ♦ *I wriggled into the tight pair of pants.* **2.** *tv.* to cause someone or something to twist; to cause someone or something to squirm; to cause someone or something to wiggle; to cause someone or something to move back and forth. ♦ *The doctor asked me to wriggle my injured finger.* ♦ *I had to wriggle the key in the lock in order to open the door.*

wring ['rɪŋ] **1.** *tv., irreg.* to squeeze or twist something very forcefully. (Pt/pp: wrung.) ♦ *The robber tried to wring the cashier's neck.* ♦ *I wrung my wet hat after I came inside from the rain.* **2. wring out** *tv., irreg. + prep. phr.* to squeeze and twist something to remove liquid. ♦ *Please wring out the wet rag when you finish with it.* ♦ *Susan wrung out the sponge.* **3. wring out of** *tv., irreg. + adv. + prep. phr.* to remove water from something by twisting and squeezing it very forcefully. ♦ *I wrung the water out of the sponge and wiped the counter.* ♦ *Mary wrung the water out of her wet socks in the sink.*

wringer ['rɪŋ ɚ] **1.** *n.* an old-fashioned washing machine that removes water from clothes by pressing them as the clothes are passed between two rollers. ♦ *I placed the wet clothes on the wringer.* ♦ *A button was torn from the shirt as it went through the wringer.* **2. put someone through the wringer** *idiom* to give someone difficulties. ♦ *They are really putting me through the wringer at school.* ♦ *The boss put Bob through the wringer over this contract.*

wrinkle ['rɪŋ kəl] **1.** *n.* a crease; a small fold or line, such as in clothing that has not been ironed or on the skin of an old person. ♦ *If you sunbathe, you're more likely to get wrinkles.* ♦ *I used an iron to remove the wrinkles from my cotton shirt.* **2.** *iv.* to become wrinkly; to get small lines in one's surface. ♦ *The cotton clothing wrinkled in the clothes dryer.* ♦ *John's face has wrinkled from excessive sunbathing.* **3.** *tv.* to cause someone's skin or the surface of something to have wrinkles ①; to cause creases, folds, or lines to form on the surface of someone or something. ♦ *Excessive exposure to the sun will wrinkle your skin.* ♦ *John wrinkled his pants by sleeping in them.*

wrinkled ['rɪŋ kəld] *adj.* having wrinkles; having creases, folds, or lines. ♦ *My grandfather's wrinkled skin felt dry and leathery.* ♦ *I ironed my wrinkled clothing.*

wrinkly ['rɪŋk li] *adj.* wrinkled; having wrinkles; having creases, folds, or lines. ♦ *You should iron your wrinkly pants.* ♦ *I put some moisturizer on my wrinkly skin.*

wrist ['rɪst] *n.* the part of the body where the hand joins the lower part of the arm. ♦ *David injured his wrist when he bent it backwards.* ♦ *I wear a bracelet around my wrist.*

wristwatch ['rɪst wɑtʃ] *n.* a watch that is worn on a band around the wrist. ♦ *Jane checked her wristwatch to see what time it was.* ♦ *My wristwatch has a leather band.*

write ['rɑɪt] **1.** *tv., irreg.* to make words or symbols on a surface with a pen, pencil, chalk, etc. (Pt: wrote; pp: written.) ♦ *The teacher wrote the letters on the chalkboard.* ♦ *Mary wrote a 4 on the check.* **2.** *tv., irreg.* to compose writing; to put thoughts or ideas into writing. ♦ *Anne had written a message on a note card and handed it to me.* ♦ *Susan wrote her term paper on a computer.* **3. write down** *tv. + adv.* to write information onto something, such as paper. ♦ *Please write this down so you don't forget it.* ♦ *I know I wrote her address down and put it in my desk.* **4.** *iv., irreg.* to mark on a surface with a pen, pencil, chalk, etc., as with ②. ♦ *Please write more carefully.* ♦ *The young children wrote on the walls with crayons.* **5.** *iv., irreg.* to work by writing ② books, articles, movies, plays, or other texts; to be an author; to be a writer. ♦ *David writes for a living.* ♦ *Jane writes now, but she used to be an editor.* **6.** *iv., irreg.* to write ② to someone in the form of a letter or note. ♦ *Anne wrote last week with news from abroad.* ♦ *Bill wrote to me asking if he could borrow $100.*

write-in ['rɑɪt ɪn] **1.** *n.* a candidate whose name is not already printed on a ballot, but whose name is written by the voter at the time of voting. ♦ *Anne announced that she was running as a write-in in the mayoral election.* ♦ *Four different write-ins captured less than 2% of the vote.* **2.** *adj.* <the adj. use of ①.> ♦ *I voted for a write-in candidate because I didn't like either major party's nominee.* ♦ *Write-in candidates received less than 1% of the vote.*

writer ['rɑɪt ɚ] *n.* an author who writes for a living; someone who has written something. ♦ *The publisher asked the writer to make a few revisions.* ♦ *Who is the writer of this report?*

writhe ['rɑɪð] *iv.* to twist and turn (as though) in pain. ♦ *The snake writhed as the truck rolled over it.* ♦ *Bill writhed in pain after he had been struck.*

writing ['rɑɪt ɪŋ] **1.** *n.* making words or letters with a pen, a pencil, chalk, and the like. (No plural form in this sense.) ♦ *John learned writing at a very young age.* ♦ *The writing of the complex contract took several weeks.* **2.** *n.* the style of making words whose letters are connected together, as opposed to printing. (No plural form in this sense.) ♦ *Please print, because it's easier to read than writing.* ♦ *After the children learned printing, they then learned writing.* **3.** *n.* something that is written; a book, poem, and the like. (Sometimes plural with the same meaning.) ♦ *I have an anthology of Emily Dickinson's writings.* ♦ *Susan bought a book of her favorite author's early writing.* **4.** *n.* penmanship; someone's own style of writing ②. (No plural form in this sense.) ♦ *The doctor's writing is difficult to read.* ♦ *The psychiatrist analyzed a sample of my writing.*

written ['rɪt n] **1.** pp of write. **2.** *adj.* placed in writing; printed or spelled out in writing. ♦ *Please provide written acknowledgment of your acceptance of our offer.* ♦ *Jane quit her job after receiving a written contract for a better one.*

wrong ['rɔŋ] **1.** *adj.* not correct; not true; mistaken; in error. (Adv: *wrongly.*) ♦ *Much of the data in the article was completely wrong.* ♦ *You're driving the wrong way down a one-way street!* **2.** *adj.* bad; evil; illegal; immoral; not lawful. (Adv: *wrongly.*) ♦ *It is wrong to kill others.* ♦ *Harming animals is wrong.* **3.** *adj.* not intended; not wanted; incorrect. (Adv: *wrongly.*) ♦ *Unfortunately, I had picked the wrong person for the job.* ♦ *I almost got on the wrong train this morning!* **4.** *adj.* out of order; not working properly; faulty. ♦ *Something's wrong with our television set.* ♦ *What is wrong with the elevator?* **5.** *adv.* in the wrong ③ way. ♦ *John did the project wrong, so he had to do it again.* ♦ *She sang the note wrong and it sounded very bad.* **6.** *n.* a bad, illegal, improper, or immoral action. ♦ *Bill tried to compensate for his past wrongs.* ♦ *This is a wrong that I cannot forgive you for.* **7.** *tv.* to treat someone badly or unfairly. ♦ *Anne was wronged when she was fired from her job.* ♦ *John wronged me when he spread malicious gossip about me.* **8. in the wrong** *idiom* on the wrong or illegal side of an issue; guilty or in error. ♦ *I felt she was in the wrong, but the judge ruled in her favor.* ♦ *It's hard to argue with Jane. She always believes that everyone else is in the wrong.*

wrongdoer ['rɔŋ du ɚ] *n.* someone who is bad or immoral; someone who does bad or immoral things. ♦ *The wrongdoer was sentenced to jail for two years.* ♦ *Most of the wrongdoers will never be caught by the police.*

wrongdoing ['rɔŋ du ɪŋ] *n.* a bad or immoral action or behavior. ♦ *The suspect said he was guilty of no wrongdoing.* ♦ *The owner suspected the fraudulent clerk of wrongdoing.*

wrote ['rot] pt of write.

wrung ['rʌŋ] pt/pp of wring.

WW I See World War I.

WW II See World War II.

WWW See World Wide Web.

Wyoming [wɑɪ 'o mɪŋ] See Gazetteer.

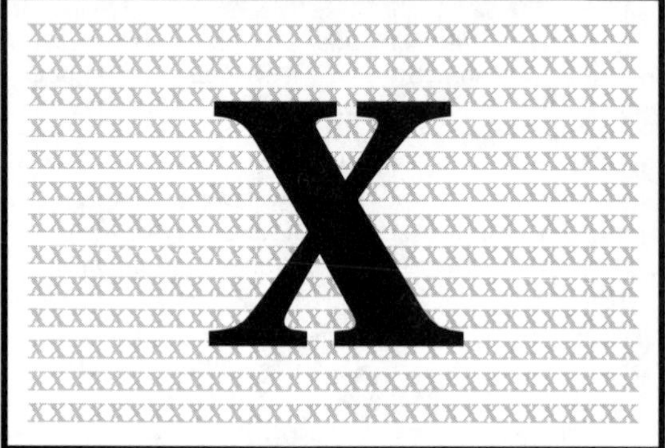

X AND **x** ['ɛks] *n.* the twenty-fourth letter of the English alphabet. ♦ *Few English words begin with* X. ♦ X *has the sound of a Z at the beginning of a word.*

xenon ['zi nɑn] *n.* a gaseous chemical element used in radiation-detection devices and electronic vacuum tubes. (No plural form in this sense.) ♦ *The atomic symbol of xenon is Xe, and its atomic number is 54.* ♦ *Since xenon is a noble gas, it doesn't combine easily with other elements.*

xerography [zɪr 'ɑ grə fi] *n.* the process used to make photocopies, which causes an image to be copied by using heat to fuse colored powder to a piece of paper. (No plural form in this sense.) ♦ *Before xerography's development, exact copies were expensive to make.* ♦ *Xerography has almost eliminated the need for carbon paper.*

Xerox™ ['zɪr ɑks] a copy of a document made on a copier manufactured by Xerox™. (A protected trade name for a type of xerography.) ♦ *Please make a Xerox of this for me.* ♦ *Mary handed a Xerox of the schedule to each employee.*

X-ray ['ɛks re] **1.** *n.* a ray of energy that can pass through opaque matter, such as the body. (Used especially to take pictures of the insides of people or objects.) ♦ *Prolonged exposure to X-rays is very dangerous.* ♦ *X-rays allow a doctor to examine possible bone fractures.* **2.** *n.* a picture of the inside of a person or an object, made by passing ① through the person or object onto photographic film. ♦ *The emergency-room doctor took an X-ray of Jane's foot.* ♦ *The X-ray revealed a hidden bomb in the suitcase.* **3.** *tv.* to take a picture of the inside of a person or an object as with ②. ♦ *The technician X-rayed Jane's foot.* ♦ *The airport guard X-rayed everyone's luggage.*

xylophone ['zɑɪ lə fon] *n.* a musical instrument made of a series of wooden bars of different sizes, each of which makes a different note when struck with a small hammer or mallet. ♦ *Mary plays the xylophone in the orchestra.* ♦ *The toddler banged the toy xylophone with a plastic mallet.*

Y AND **y** ['wɑɪ] *n.* the twenty-fifth letter in the English alphabet. ♦ Y *is the next to the last letter in the alphabet.* ♦ *There are two Ys in* yearly.

yacht ['jɑt] **1.** *n.* a large boat or ship used for pleasure or racing. (Powered by sails, engines, or both.) ♦ *I will never be wealthy enough to own a yacht.* ♦ *Mary's yacht pulled into the harbor.* **2.** *iv.* to travel somewhere on water in ①. ♦ *The Smiths yacht to their private island each spring.* ♦ *The rich couple yachted across the bay.*

yam ['jæm] **1.** *n.* a starchy vegetable similar to the potato, grown in tropical areas. ♦ *We ate roasted yams when we were in Africa.* ♦ *The tropical people's diet was mostly yams and rice.* **2.** *n.* a sweet potato. ♦ *We always have yams with our Thanksgiving dinner.* ♦ *I made a casserole with yams and marshmallows.*

yank ['jæŋk] **1.** *tv.* to pull someone or something quickly, with force. ♦ *Jane yanked the door open and left the room angrily.* ♦ *I yanked my hand away from the hot stove.* **2. yank (on)** *iv.* (+ *prep. phr.*) to pull or jerk on something, with force. ♦ *Susie yanked on the rope too hard and snapped it.* ♦ *I yanked on my dog's leash when he started to pull.* **3.** *n.* a forceful pull; a forceful tug. ♦ *I gave the stuck door a yank and it opened.* ♦ *Jimmy gave Susie's braids a yank.* **4.** *n.* **Yank** a Yankee ③, especially in Europe. (Sometimes lowercase.) ♦ *There are more Yanks in Europe on vacation than there are in Dallas each summer.* ♦ *The British soldier shared a train car with a couple of Yanks.*

Yankee ['jæŋ ki] **1.** *n.* a person from the northern part of the United States. (Used especially by southerners and often derogatory.) ♦ *After the Civil War, many Yankees went to the South to start businesses.* ♦ *Many southerners resented the Yankees after the Civil War.* **2.** *n.* a person from New England. ♦ *Those Yankees really know how to make good chowder.* ♦ *My great-grandfather was one of the first Yankees to settle in Pennsylvania.* **3.** *n.* a person from the United States of America. ♦ *The angry Mexicans protested against the Yankees' policies.* ♦ *The Englishman spoke with two Yankees at the pub.* **4.** *adj.* <the adj. use of ①, ②, or ③.> ♦ *It took a lot of Yankee ingenuity to figure out the puzzle.* ♦ *The British tourist spoke with two Yankee soldiers in Paris.*

yap ['jæp] *iv.* to make short, loud barks. ♦ *I couldn't sleep because the dog yapped all night long.* ♦ *The small terrier yapped at the burglar.*

yard ['jɑrd] **1.** *n.* a unit of measurement of length equal to 36 inches, 3 feet, or 91.44 centimeters. ♦ *The tailor bought three yards of fabric.* ♦ *The picnic table is about ten yards from the house.* **2.** *n.* the land that surrounds a house or other dwelling. ♦ *The dog is out in the yard.* ♦ *Our backyard is surrounded by a fence.* **3.** *n.* an enclosed area of land adjacent to a factory, used especially for storage or parking. ♦ *The company truck is parked out in the yard.* ♦ *That manufacturer stores crates of auto parts at its yard.*

yardstick ['jɑrd stɪk] **1.** *n.* a ruler that is 36 inches—that is, one yard—long. ♦ *Dave measured the couch with a yardstick before buying it.* ♦ *Mary used a yardstick to measure the room's perimeter.* **2.** *n.* something that other things are compared to; a standard. (Figurative on ①.) ♦ *I use my mother's cooking as a yardstick to judge all others.* ♦ *Don't use what you see on television as a yardstick to tell good from bad.*

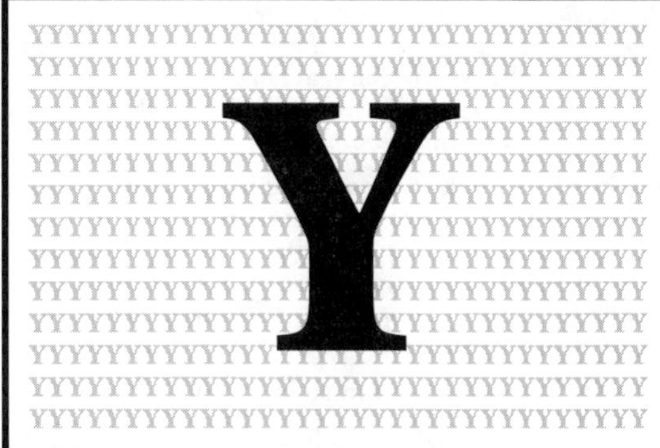

yard work ['jɑrd wɚk] *n.* work that is done on the land around a dwelling, such as mowing the grass, raking leaves, planting flowers, etc. (No plural form in this sense.) ♦ *My yard work is done by a boy in the neighborhood.* ♦ *On Saturday, Anne takes care of the yard work.*

yarn ['jɑrn] **1.** *n.* thick, soft thread that is used for knitting, crocheting, or weaving. (No plural form in this sense. Number is expressed with *ball(s)* or *skein(s) of yarn.*) ♦ *Mary knitted the sweater with cotton yarn.* ♦ *The kitten batted the ball of yarn with its paws.* **2.** *n.* a tale; a story that is not completely true. ♦ *Tell me another yarn about life in the old West.* ♦ *Max told Mary a yarn about his past.* **3. spin a yarn** *idiom* to tell a tale. ♦ *Grandpa spun an unbelievable yarn for us.* ♦ *My uncle is always spinning yarns about his childhood.*

yawn ['jɔn] **1.** *iv.* to stretch one's mouth open and breathe in and out slowly and deeply, especially when one is tired or bored. ♦ *The student yawned during the boring lecture.* ♦ *The sleepy woman yawned after dinner and took a nap.* **2.** *iv.* [for something like a hole] to have a very wide opening. (Figurative on ①.) ♦ *The deep ravine yawned in front of the hikers.* ♦ *A gaping pothole yawned in the middle of the road.* **3.** *n.* an act of opening one's mouth, as in ①. ♦ *Jane tried to stifle her yawns during the boring meeting.* ♦ *The cat opened its mouth with a big yawn.*

yawning ['jɔn ɪŋ] **1.** *adj.* having one's mouth open wide while breathing in and out slowly and deeply, such as when one is tired or bored. (Adv: *yawningly.*) ♦ *The professor stared at the yawning student.* ♦ *The yawning boy fidgeted during the church service.* **2.** *adj.* wide open; having a very wide opening. (Figurative on ①. Adv: *yawningly.*) ♦ *The tailor repaired the yawning hole in my trousers.* ♦ *The hikers entered the cave through its yawning entrance.*

yea ['je] *n.* a "yes" vote; an affirmative vote. ♦ *The motion passed with three "yeas" and two "nays."* ♦ *The manager added his "yea" to the votes for the proposal.*

year ['jɪr] **1.** *n.* 12 months; 365 or 366 days; the time it takes for Earth to revolve around the sun. ♦ *A year has passed since I've seen my parents.* ♦ *I threw last year's calendar away.* **2.** *n.* ① or part of ① spent doing a certain activity. ♦ *The school year lasts from September through May.* ♦ *The company's fiscal year ends in March.* **3.** *n.* a particular level of study in a school, college, or university. ♦ *Composition is a required course in freshman year.* ♦ *Bill is a first-year medical student.* **4. year after year** *phr.* for many years ①, one after another. ♦ *We go to the* *same place for our vacation year after year.* ♦ *I seem to earn the same salary year after year.* **5. year in, year out** *idiom* **year after year** ④; all year long. ♦ *I seem to have hay fever year in, year out. I never get over it.* ♦ *John wears the same old suit, year in, year out.*

yearbook ['jɪr bʊk] *n.* a book that has pictures of all the students who have attended a certain school, or at least all the students who are graduating from the school, during the year the book is published. ♦ *All of Jane's classmates signed her yearbook.* ♦ *A portrait of each student appears in the yearbook.*

yearling ['jɪr lɪŋ] *n.* an animal, especially a horse, in its second year. ♦ *The yearling was trained to be a racehorse.* ♦ *The farmer cleaned the yearling's stable.*

yearlong ['jɪr 'lɔŋ] *adj.* lasting for a year; lasting all year; happening all year. ♦ *Mary took a yearlong course at the local university.* ♦ *The designer had a yearlong contract with the company.*

yearly ['jɪr li] **1.** *adj.* once a year; each year; every year; annual. ♦ *The Smiths went to Florida for their yearly vacation.* ♦ *Jane makes a yearly visit to her mother in January.* **2.** *adv.* once a year; each year; every year; annually. ♦ *John sees his doctor yearly.* ♦ *The rich surgeon buys a new car yearly.*

yearn ['jɚn] **1. yearn for** *iv.* + prep. phr. to have a strong desire for someone or something. ♦ *I yearned for chocolate when I was dieting.* ♦ *The busy worker yearned for a vacation.* **2. yearn to** *iv.* + inf. to have a strong desire to do something. ♦ *Susan yearned to learn how to swim.* ♦ *David yearned to buy a new car.*

yearning ['jɚ nɪŋ] *n.* a strong desire; a longing; an intense feeling or emotion for someone or something. (No plural form in this sense.) ♦ *The busy worker had a yearning to go on a vacation.* ♦ *I always feel a yearning for spring during the winter.*

yeast ['jist] *n.* a very small plant that causes bread to rise and is also used to make alcoholic liquids. (No plural form in this sense.) ♦ *Yeast grows very quickly where there is sugar present.* ♦ *Yeast is an important ingredient of bread.*

yell ['jɛl] **1.** *tv.* to say something loudly; to scream something; to shout something. ♦ *Jane yelled the message to me from across the house.* ♦ *John yelled good-bye as he left.* **2.** *iv.* to speak loudly; to scream; to shout. ♦ *The kids yelled as they played in the yard.* ♦ *We try not to yell at our children.* **3.** *n.* a loud cry; a shout. ♦ *Mary thought she heard a yell from downstairs.* ♦ *Bill gave a yell to his friend across the street.*

yellow ['jɛl o] **1.** *n.* the color of a ripe lemon or the yolk of an egg. (No plural form in this sense.) ♦ *Yellow is the color of daffodils.* ♦ *The lemon trees made a dazzling display of yellow and green.* **2.** *adj.* being ① in color. (Comp: *yellower;* sup: *yellowest.*) ♦ *The daisy had a yellow center.* ♦ *John ate the yellow lemon cake.* **3.** *adj.* cowardly; timid; scared to do something. (Informal. Adv: *yellowly.* Comp: *yellower;* sup: *yellowest.*) ♦ *Bill was too yellow to stand up to the bully.* ♦ *The yellow soldiers ran from the enemy.*

yellowish ['jɛl o ɪʃ] *adj.* kind of yellow; somewhat yellow; partially yellow. (Adv: *yellowishly.*) ♦ *The old photographs have a yellowish cast to them.* ♦ *The newspaper was yellowish with age.*

yelp ['jɛlp] **1.** *n.* a short, high-pitched bark; a short, high-pitched shout of pain or emotion. ♦ *The puppy gave a yelp when I stepped on its tail.* ♦ *The child's yelp startled us.* **2.** *iv.* to make ①. ♦ *The puppy yelped in pain when its tail got closed in the door.* ♦ *Susie yelped as the doctor gave her a shot.*

yen ['jɛn] **1.** *n.* a strong desire; a yearning; a longing; a strong feeling of wanting something. (No plural form in this sense.) ♦ *Jane has a yen to go climbing in the Rockies.* ♦ *I have a yen for chocolate today.* **2.** *n., irreg.* the basic unit of money in Japan. (Also ¥. Pl: *yen.*) ♦ *There are more than 100 yen in a U.S. dollar.* ♦ *I exchanged my dollars for yen when I traveled to Tokyo.*

yeoman ['jo mən] *n., irreg.* a navy officer who does clerical work. (Pl: **yeomen.**) ♦ *A yeoman handed the captain an important message.* ♦ *The yeoman kept information about the sailors on a computer.*

yeomen ['jo mən] pl of **yeoman.**

yes ['jɛs] **1.** *n.* a statement of agreement or permission. ♦ *I need a yes or a no on this matter.* ♦ *The boss gave me a yes. We can do it.* **2.** *n.* a vote indicating agreement. ♦ *There were four yeses and two nos.* ♦ *Was your vote a yes?* **3.** *adv.* <a word showing agreement, acknowledgment, approval, consent, or willingness.> ♦ *Yes, I will.* ♦ *Yes, you should do it.* **4.** *adv.* <a word emphasizing a positive statement, especially when contradicting a negative one.> ♦ *"It's not raining outside." "Yes, it most certainly is."* ♦ *"I will not eat my peas." "Yes, you will."*

yesterday ['jɛs tɚ de] **1.** *n.* the day before today. ♦ *Yesterday was Friday, so that means today is Saturday.* ♦ *Yesterday was my birthday, so that's why I wasn't at work.* **2.** *adv.* on the day before today. ♦ *I am tired because I worked very hard yesterday.* ♦ *I sent the package yesterday. It should be there tomorrow.* **3. not born yesterday** *idiom* experienced; knowledgeable in the ways of the world. ♦ *I know what's going on. I wasn't born yesterday.* ♦ *Sally knows the score. She wasn't born yesterday.*

yet ['jɛt] **1.** *adv.* up to a certain point in time; by a certain point in time; as of a certain point in time. ♦ *Our guests have not arrived yet.* ♦ *I haven't made dinner yet. What would you like?* **2.** *adv.* eventually, in spite of barriers or impediments. ♦ *We'll make it to the beach yet.* ♦ *I will conquer this problem yet!* **3.** *adv.* still; even; even more. ♦ *The doorbell rang yet again.* ♦ *Grandpa told the same old story yet one more time.* **4.** *adv.* although; nevertheless. ♦ *The sadder yet wiser man learned from his mistakes.* ♦ *When the driver was pulled from the wreck, we saw that he was severely injured yet alive.* **5.** *conj.* but; however; nevertheless. ♦ *The soldier was small, yet he had a booming voice.* ♦ *I'm glad you got the promotion, yet I wish it had been me.*

Yiddish ['jɪd ɪʃ] *n.* a language belonging to the Germanic language family, with heavy Slavic and Hebrew components, originally spoken by the Jews of central and eastern Europe. (No plural form in this sense.) ♦ *My Jewish friend teaches Yiddish at the local college.* ♦ *Members of the rabbi's family often spoke Yiddish among themselves.*

yield ['jild] **1.** *iv.* to bend, break, or move out of the way because of someone or something that is stronger or more powerful. ♦ *Hard plastics will yield up to a point, but then they will snap.* ♦ *The streetlight yielded in the wind* *and fell over.* **2.** *iv.* to surrender to someone or something, especially someone or something that is stronger or more powerful; to submit to someone or something. ♦ *Mary yielded and gave her children more candy.* ♦ *The tiny country did not yield to the enemy's fierce domination.* **3.** *iv.* to allow other traffic or people to have the right of way; to allow another vehicle or person to move first. ♦ *The van yielded to the car at the stop sign.* ♦ *I failed to yield and smashed into an oncoming car.* **4.** *tv.* [for plants or animals] to supply or produce something such as food. ♦ *The damaged crops yielded very little.* ♦ *The vines yielded juicy grapes for wine.* **5. yield to** *tv.* + prep. phr. to surrender or give up something to someone. ♦ *The dying president yielded his power to the vice president.* ♦ *The villagers yielded their homes to the enemy soldiers.* **6.** *n.* the amount of something that is produced. ♦ *The field's high yield made the farmer rich.* ♦ *Last year's yield on my savings account was nominal.*

yodel ['jod l] **1.** *tv.* to sing a song that quickly changes back and forth between one's regular voice and a high-pitched voice. ♦ *The shepherd yodeled a happy song.* ♦ *Jane yodeled a greeting from across the valley.* **2.** *iv.* to sing as in ①. ♦ *The shepherd yodeled on the mountainside.* ♦ *The workers yodeled as they walked toward the valley.* **3.** *n.* an act of singing as in ①. (No plural form in this sense.) ♦ *The shepherd's yodel could be heard throughout the valley.* ♦ *We held a contest to see whose yodel was the best.*

yoga ['jo gə] *n.* a system of deep thought, mental exercise, and physical exercise, intended to give one a healthy mind and body. (No plural form in this sense.) ♦ *Yoga is often associated with Hindu philosophy.* ♦ *Mary uses yoga to relax after a busy day.*

yogurt ['jo gɚt] *n.* a thick, liquid dairy product made by adding certain bacteria to milk. (No plural form in this sense.) ♦ *Yogurt is often sold mixed with fruit.* ♦ *Anne ate a cup of yogurt for breakfast.*

yoke ['jok] **1.** *n.* a frame of wood that fits around the necks of animals so they can pull something heavy that is attached to it. (Compare with yolk.) ♦ *The wooden yoke hung in the barn.* ♦ *The oxen wore a yoke, which was attached to the plow.* **2.** *n.* two oxen that are connected with ①. ♦ *John plowed his field with a yoke of oxen.* ♦ *The farmer bought a yoke of oxen from his neighbor.* **3.** *tv.* to put ① on oxen. ♦ *The farmer yoked the team of oxen.* ♦ *Max yoked the mules and began to plow.* **4. a yoke around someone's neck** *idiom* something that oppresses people; a burden. (Figurative on ①.) ♦ *John's greedy children are a yoke around his neck.* ♦ *The Smiths have a huge mortgage that has become a yoke around their neck.*

yokel ['jok əl] *n.* someone who lives in the country; a rural person; someone who is not from the city or suburbs. (Derogatory.) ♦ *The yokels drove into town on Friday to buy supplies.* ♦ *The lost tourist asked a local yokel for directions.*

yolk ['jok] *n.* the yellow part inside an egg. (No plural form in this sense. Compare with yoke.) ♦ *I don't like to eat runny egg yolks.* ♦ *The chef separated the yolk from the egg white.*

Yom Kippur ['jom kɪ 'pur] *n.* a Jewish holiday of repentance on which fasting and prayer are practiced. (Also known as the Day of Atonement.) ♦ *The rabbi always fasted and prayed on Yom Kippur.* ♦ *Yom Kippur occurs in late September or early October.*

yonder ['jɑn dɚ] *adv.* over there. ♦ *My aunt lives yonder, past the bridge.* ♦ *Yonder in the distance lay the town.*

you ['ju] *pron.* <the second-person pronoun, singular and plural, nominative and objective.> (See also your, yours.) ♦ *You look very nice today.* ♦ *I gave you the letter yesterday.*

you'd ['jud] **1.** *cont.* "you would." ♦ *You said you'd do the grocery shopping.* ♦ *If you'd move over, I would sit down.* **2.** *cont.* "you had," where had is an auxiliary. ♦ *I called you, but you'd already gone out.* ♦ *If you'd bought the ingredients, I could have made a cake.*

you'll ['jul] *cont.* "you will." ♦ *You'll succeed if you try harder.* ♦ *You'll be finished with school before you know it!*

young ['jʌŋ] **1.** *adj.* in the early part of life; not old; having been alive for a short period of time as compared to an average age. (Comp: *younger;* sup: *youngest.*) ♦ *The young student was eager to experience the world.* ♦ *The young children believed in Santa Claus.* **2.** *adj.* new; in an early stage of development; recently formed or started. (Comp: *younger;* sup: *youngest.*) ♦ *The historian spoke of the time when the country was young.* ♦ *Our city was incorporated when the automobile was young.* **3.** *n.* the baby or babies of an animal or human; offspring. (No plural form in this sense. Treated as singular or plural.) ♦ *The bird fed worms to its young.* ♦ *Some wild animals abandon their young.*

youngster ['jʌŋ stɚ] *n.* a young person; a child. ♦ *The youngsters were seated at a separate table.* ♦ *All the youngsters gathered around Grandpa for a story.*

your ['jor] *pron.* <the possessive form of you, the second-person singular and plural pronoun>; belonging to the person(s) being spoken or written to. (Used as a modifier before a noun.) ♦ *This is your shirt. Please put it on.* ♦ *Please move your things so I can sit down.*

you're ['jʊɚ] *cont.* "you are." ♦ *You're late again.* ♦ *Please tell me when you're going to the store.*

yours ['jʊrz] *pron.* <the possessive form of you, the second-person singular and plural pronoun>; something belonging to the person(s) being spoken or written to. (Used in place of a noun.) ♦ *I have my sandwich. Where is yours?* ♦ *I already got my coat. I'll get yours for you.*

yourself ['jʊr 'sɛlf] **1.** *pron.* <the reflexive form of the singular of you.> ♦ *You can get your meal yourself.* ♦ *Be careful with those scissors! You'll cut yourself!* **2.** *pron.* <an emphatic form of you [singular].> ♦ *Can you yourself manage to lift this?* ♦ *You yourself must be there to accept the gift.* **3. by yourself** *phr.* with the help of no one else. ♦ *Can you really do this by yourself?* ♦ *Bill, can you lift this by yourself?* **4. by yourself** *phr.* with no one else present; alone. ♦ *Do you want to sit here by yourself, or can I sit here too?* ♦ *Don't sit at home by yourself. Come to the movie with me.*

yourselves ['jʊr 'sɛlvz] **1.** *pron.* <the reflexive form of the plural of you.> ♦ *I want you all to enjoy yourselves at the party tonight.* ♦ *I can't help all of you; you'll have to fend for yourselves.* **2.** *pron.* <an emphatic form of your [plural].> ♦ *You yourselves must decide what you will do with the rest of your time here.* ♦ *All of you listening to me* *here, you yourselves must make the decision, and it should be the right one.* **3. by yourselves** *phr.* with the help of no one else. ♦ *Can you do this by yourselves?* ♦ *Can all of you get to the meeting by yourselves?* **4. by yourselves** *phr.* with no one else present; alone. ♦ *Are you two going to sit here by yourselves all evening?* ♦ *Don't sit home by yourselves. Come to the party.*

yours truly ['jʊrz 'tru li] **1.** *phr.* <a conventional closing for a letter.> ♦ *Yours truly, John Jones.* ♦ *I always sign my letters "Yours truly, Anne Smith."* **2.** *phr.* I; me. (Sometimes informal.) ♦ *This short story was written by none other than yours truly.* ♦ *Yours truly fed your dog for you earlier today.*

youth ['juθ] **1.** *n.* the quality of being young. (No plural form in this sense.) ♦ *The older woman wished she still had her youth.* ♦ *The aging couple wanted their youth back.* **2.** *n.* the period of time when one is a child or teenager. (No plural form in this sense.) ♦ *In her youth, Anne tutored other students.* ♦ *Bill spent his youth in an orphanage.* **3.** *n.* children or teenagers, as a group. (No plural form in this sense.) ♦ *Tom worked with underprivileged youth in the city.* ♦ *The man expressed concern for the youth in his city.* **4.** *n.* someone who is young; a child or teenager. ♦ *The policeman apprehended the youth who stole the candy bar.* ♦ *The school choir consisted of 30 youths.*

youthful ['juθ fəl] *adj.* having the qualities of young people; looking or feeling young. (Adv: *youthfully.*) ♦ *My 50-year-old aunt wears youthful clothing.* ♦ *The elderly couple had a youthful outlook on life.*

you've ['juv] *cont.* "you have," where **have** is an auxiliary. ♦ *You've done an excellent job. Congratulations!* ♦ *Let me know when you've finished with the computer.*

Yuletide ['jul tɑɪd] **1.** *n.* the time around Christmas; Christmastime; the Christmas season. ♦ *The town was decorated for the Yuletide.* ♦ *Yuletide is meant to be a time of joy and peace.* **2.** *adj.* <the adj. use of ①.> ♦ *The town was decorated for the Yuletide season.* ♦ *The shoppers were filled with Yuletide cheer.*

yummy ['jʌm i] *adj.* having a good taste; delicious. (Adv: *yummily.* Comp: *yummier;* sup: *yummiest.*) ♦ *I had some yummy stew at the restaurant.* ♦ *Bill served us some yummy brownies.*

Z AND **z** ['zi] *n.* the twenty-sixth letter in the English alphabet. ♦ *There are two Zs in* zigzag. ♦ Z *is the last letter in the alphabet.*

Zaire [zɑ 'ɪr] See Gazetteer.

Zambia ['zæm bi ə] See Gazetteer.

zany ['zen i] *adj.* funny, foolish, and wild; crazy; comical. (Adv: *zanily.* Comp: *zanier;* sup: *zaniest.*) ♦ *The zany comedian made the audience laugh.* ♦ *The critic enjoyed the zany antics in the movie.*

zap ['zæp] *tv.* to attack, shock, or hit someone or something suddenly. (Informal.) ♦ *The bee zapped me when I wasn't looking.* ♦ *The electric fence zapped the dog.*

zeal ['zil] *n.* eagerness; a strong passion for a belief or cause; enthusiasm. (No plural form in this sense.) ♦ *The preacher pounded the lectern in his zeal.* ♦ *The choir sang with zeal.*

zealot ['zɛl ət] *n.* someone who has too much zeal for something; someone who is a fanatic about a belief or cause. ♦ *The animal-rights zealot sprayed Mary's fur coat with paint.* ♦ *The religious zealot handed out pamphlets on the street corner.*

zealous ['zɛl əs] *adj.* full of zeal; having a lot of enthusiasm; very eager. (Adv: *zealously.* ♦ *The zealous soldier hoped to be sent into battle.* ♦ *An overly zealous protester struck a police officer.*

zebra ['zi brə] *n., irreg.* a horse-like mammal that has a whitish hide with dark brown or black stripes and a short, thick mane. (Pl: *zebra* or *zebras.*) ♦ *The kids pointed at the zebra in the zoo.* ♦ *Zebras live on the plains of Africa.*

zenith ['zi nɪθ] **at the zenith of something** *idiom* at the highest point of something; at the pinnacle of something. ♦ *At the zenith of his career, the teacher died suddenly.* ♦ *The scientist was at the zenith of her career when she made her discovery.*

zephyr ['zɛf ɚ] *n.* a gentle wind; a breeze. ♦ *A zephyr rustled the tall grass by the shore.* ♦ *The zephyr brought the smell of the ocean to my doorstep.*

zero ['zɪr o] **1.** *n.* the number 0; 0. (Pl in *-s* or *-es.*) ♦ *Any number multiplied by zero is zero.* ♦ *Six plus zero is six.* **2.** *n.* nothing. (No plural form in this sense.) ♦ *The depressed man felt like his life was a big zero.* ♦ *I did absolutely zero at work today.* **3.** *adj.* not any. (Informal.) ♦ *I have zero energy tonight, so I don't want to go out.* ♦ *The critic thought the boring play had zero originality.* **4. zero in on something** *idiom* to aim or focus directly on something. ♦ *"Now," said Mr. Smith, "I would like to zero in on another important point."* ♦ *Mary is very good about zeroing in on the most important and helpful ideas.*

zest ['zɛst] **1.** *n.* enjoyment, especially for life; excitement. (No plural form in this sense.) ♦ *The hikers had a zest for adventure.* ♦ *The kids ran around the playground with zest.* **2.** *n.* a pleasant or sharp flavor. (No plural form in this sense.) ♦ *This soup has a delicious zest.* ♦ *The flavorful cookies had an incredible zest.* **3.** *n.* the outer peeling of a lemon or an orange, used for flavoring. (No plural form in this sense.) ♦ *The cooked fish was sprinkled with lemon zest.* ♦ *Sugar cookies sometimes have orange zest in them.*

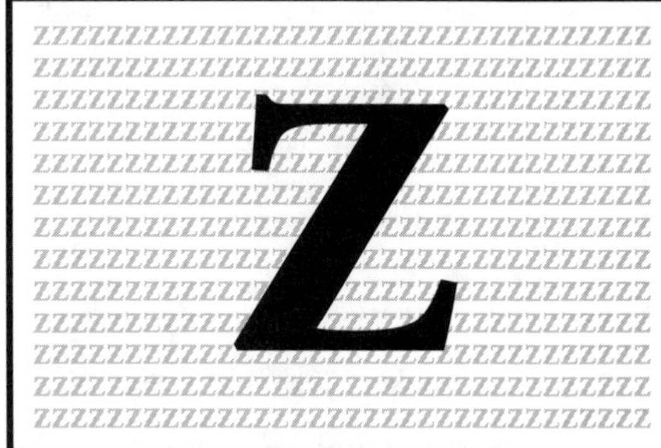

zestful ['zɛst fʊl] *adj.* full of zest; exciting; full of enjoyment. (Adv: *zestfully.*) ♦ *The zestful children played on the playground.* ♦ *The musical featured a troupe of zestful dancers.*

zigzag ['zɪg zæg] **1.** *n.* a series of short segments, each of which angle back sharply in the opposite direction of the segment before it. ♦ *The bored student drew dozens of zigzags on her notebook.* ♦ *Slow down! The road makes a dangerous zigzag ahead.* **2.** *adj.* in the shape of ①. ♦ *I followed the zigzag path through the woods.* ♦ *John has a small zigzag scar on his cheek.* **3.** *adv.* moving in a pattern like ①. ♦ *The drunk walked zigzag down the hallway.* ♦ *The rabbit ran zigzag through the forest.* **4.** *iv.* to move so that one goes straight, angles back sharply in the opposite direction, and repeats this process. (Pt/pp: *zigzagged.*) ♦ *The narrow path zigzagged up the cliff.* ♦ *The thief zigzagged through the city streets to elude the police.*

Zimbabwe [zɪm 'bɑb we] See Gazetteer.

zinc ['zɪŋk] *n.* a metal and an element, which is mixed with other metals to form alloys, some of which are used to cover steel so that it doesn't rust. (No plural form in this sense.) ♦ *Zinc is a metal that is used in making brass.* ♦ *Zinc's atomic number is 30, and its atomic symbol is Zn.*

zinnia ['zɪn i ə] *n.* a popular garden plant with coarse red, yellow, pink, or white flowers. ♦ *The vase held a bouquet of zinnias.* ♦ *The florist sold me an arrangement of pretty zinnias.*

Zionism ['zɑɪ ə nɪz əm] *n.* a political movement that sought to establish a Jewish homeland in what was once Palestine. (No plural form in this sense.) ♦ *The senators who supported Zionism voted to send financial aid.* ♦ *Zionism led to the creation of Israel after World War II.*

Zionist ['zɑɪ ə nəst] **1.** *n.* someone who supports Zionism. ♦ *The Zionist supported Jewish settlements in occupied territories.* ♦ *The radical Zionist tried to thwart the Middle East peace talks.* **2.** *adj.* <the adj. use of ①.> ♦ *Many Zionist settlers moved to the occupied West Bank.* ♦ *The Zionist rabbi raised money for the Jewish settlements.*

zip ['zɪp] **1.** *tv.* to open or close something, using a zipper. ♦ *Mary zipped Jimmy's coat.* ♦ *I zipped the pillowcase closed.* **2.** *iv.* to move somewhere very quickly. ♦ *The kitten zipped across the room.* ♦ *The car zipped in and out of traffic on the highway.* **3.** *n.* energy; vigor. (No plural form in this sense.) ♦ *The vitamins give Grandma some zip.* ♦ *Mary had lots of zip after her nap.*

zip code ['zɪp kod] *n.* one of the five-digit or nine-digit numbers that is part of the United States Postal Service's postal coding system. (An acronym for *Zoning Improvement Plan.* Often written *ZIP code.*) ♦ *You must include the ZIP code in the address.* ♦ *The postal worker sorted the mail by its zip code.*

zipper ['zɪp ɚ] **1.** *n.* a fastener made of two strips of tiny teeth that lock together when a sliding piece is moved over them. ♦ *The coat had a heavy-duty zipper.* ♦ *The zipper on Mike's pants jammed.* **2.** *tv.* to zip something; to open or close something using ①. ♦ *Mary zippered Jimmy's coat for him.* ♦ *Anne zippered her boots and went outside.*

zirconium [zɚ 'kon i əm] *n.* a grayish-white, metallic chemical element used to make nuclear reactors and ceramic glazes. (No plural form in this sense.) ♦ *The atomic symbol of zirconium is Zr, and its atomic number is 40.* ♦ *Zirconium is used to make inexpensive costume jewelry.*

zodiac ['zo di æk] *n.* an imaginary belt through space that includes the sun, moon, and some of the planets. (No plural form in this sense.) ♦ *The zodiac is divided into 12 sections or signs, each of which is named after a constellation of stars.* ♦ *The astrologer asked what sign of the zodiac I was born under.*

zombie ['zɑm bi] **1.** *n.* a dead person who is brought back to life, especially by voodoo. ♦ *The zombie arose from the grave and walked toward the village.* ♦ *The zombies in the horror movie were frightening.* **2.** *n.* someone who is very tired, lethargic, or seems to be lifeless. (Figurative on ①.) ♦ *Dave is a zombie today because he stayed up late last night.* ♦ *I'll be a zombie tomorrow if I don't get some sleep.*

zone ['zon] **1.** *n.* an area, especially one that is different in some way from nearby areas. ♦ *Ohio is in the Eastern time zone.* ♦ *The factory was built in an industrial zone.* **2.** *tv.* to divide a city into different areas limited only to specified uses. ♦ *The city council zoned the new neighborhood as residential.* ♦ *This neighborhood is not zoned for industry.*

zoo ['zu] *n.* a place or park where wild animals are kept so that they can be seen by people. ♦ *A baby gorilla was born at the local zoo.* ♦ *Jimmy's parents took him to the zoo to see the elephants.*

zookeeper ['zu kip ɚ] *n.* someone who takes care of animals at a zoo. ♦ *The zookeeper fed the baby gorilla.* ♦ *The city zoo employs dozens of zookeepers.*

zoological [zo ə 'lɑdʒ ɪ kəl] *adj.* of or about zoology. (Adv: *zoologically* [...ɪk li].) ♦ *The biologist joined the local zoological society.* ♦ *The scientist conducted a zoological study on local animals.*

zoologist [zo 'ɑl ə dʒəst] *n.* someone who studies or who is trained in zoology. ♦ *The zoo employs zoologists from all over the world.* ♦ *The zoologist studied the behavior of primates.*

zoology [zo 'ɑl ə dʒi] *n.* the science and study of animals and animal life. (No plural form in this sense.) ♦ *The biology student also took several courses in zoology.* ♦ *Zoology is the part of biology concerned with animals.*

zoom ['zum] **1.** *iv.* to move very quickly. ♦ *Mary zoomed into the room and zoomed out again.* ♦ *Dave zoomed over to the store for some bread.* **2.** *iv.* [for an aircraft or spacecraft] to move quickly. ♦ *The plane zoomed through the air.* ♦ *The rocket zoomed up into the clouds.*

zucchini [zu 'ki ni] *n.* a long, cylinder-shaped vegetable with a thin, dark green skin and a soft white inside, eaten as food. ♦ *Mary sliced up a zucchini for her salad.* ♦ *Susan grows zucchini in her vegetable garden.*

Idioms and Phrases Index

To find a particular idiom or phrase in this dictionary, consult the following index. Look up any major word in the phrase or idiom in the list of **boldface words** below. When you find the idiom or phrase you are seeking, look it up at the main entry that appears in *slanted type*. To find a particular phrasal verb, look at the main entry in the body of the dictionary for the verb in question.

Gazetteer

Listed below are cities, countries, continents, and bodies of water of the world. Pronunciation is given in brackets, and capitals are indicated by *Cap*. The circled number that follows the pronunciation leads you to the map that includes a place or body of water. The maps begin on page 1084.

Map ①: The United States of America
Map ②: Canada
Map ③: Mexico, Central America, and the Caribbean
Map ④: South America (and Antarctica)
Map ⑤: Africa
Map ⑥: Europe
Map ⑦: Asia, the Middle East, and Australia

Afghanistan [æf 'gæn ə stæn] ⑦ Cap: Kabul ['kɑ bul]
Africa ['æf rɪ kə] ⑤
Alabama [æ lə 'bæm ə] ① (A U.S. state.) Cap: Montgomery [mənt 'gʌm ɚ i]
Alaska [ə 'læs kə] ② (A U.S. state.) Cap: Juneau ['dʒu no]
Albania [æl 'be ni ə] ⑥ Cap: Tirane [tɪ 'rɑ nə]
Alberta [æl 'bɚ tə] ② (A province of Canada.) Cap: Edmonton ['ɛd mən tən]
Algeria [æl 'dʒɪr i ə] ⑤ Cap: Algiers [æl 'dʒɪɚz]
Angola [æŋ 'gol ə] ⑤ Cap: Luanda [lu 'ɑn də]
Antarctica [ænt 'ɑrk tɪ kə] ④
Arctic Ocean ['ɑrk tɪk...] ②
Argentina [ɑr dʒən 'ti nə] ④ Cap: Buenos Aires ['bwe nos 'ɛr iz]
Arizona [ɛr ɪ 'zon ə] ① (A U.S. state.) Cap: Phoenix ['fi nɪks]
Arkansas ['ɑr kən sɔ] ① (A U.S. state.) Cap: Little Rock ['lɪt əl rɑk]
Armenia [ɑr 'min i ə] ⑦ Cap: Yerevan [jɛ rə 'væn]
Asia ['e ʒə] ⑦
Atlantic Ocean [æt 'læn tɪk...] ① ⑥
Australia [ɔ 'strel jə] ⑦ Cap: Canberra ['kæn bɚ ə]
Austria ['ɔ stri ə] ⑥ Cap: Vienna [vi 'ɛn ə]
Bahamas [bə 'hɑ məz] ③ Cap: Nassau ['næ sɔ]
Bahrain [bɑ 'ren] Cap: (Al) Manamah [(ɑl) mə 'nɑ mə]
Baltic Sea ['bɔl tɪk...] ⑥
Bangladesh [bæŋ glə 'dɛʃ] ⑦ Cap: Dhaka, Dacca ['dɑk ə]
Barbados [bɑr 'be dos] ③ Cap: Bridgetown ['brɪdʒ taʊn]
Belarus [bɛl ə 'rus] ⑥ Cap: Minsk ['mɪnsk]
Belgium ['bɛl dʒəm] ⑥ Cap: Brussels ['brʌs əls]
Belize [bə 'liz] ③ Cap: Belmopan ['bɛl mo 'pɑn]
Benin [bɛ 'nɪn] ⑤ Cap: Porto Novo ['por to 'no vo]
Berlin See Germany.
Bermuda [bɚ 'mju də] Cap: Hamilton ['hæm əl tən]
Bhutan [bu 'tɑn] ⑦ Cap: Thimphu [tɪm 'pu]
Black Sea ['blæk...] ⑥
Bolivia [bo 'lɪv i ə] ④ Cap: La Paz [lɑ 'pɑz] (administrative); Sucre ['su kre] (official)
Bosnia and Herzegovina [bɑz ni ə...hɚt sə go 'vɪ nə] ⑥ Cap: Sarajevo [sɑr ə 'jev o]
Botswana [bɑt 'swɑn ə] ⑤ Cap: Gaborone [gæb ə 'ro ni]
Brazil [brə 'zɪl] ④ Cap: Brasilia [brə 'zɪl i ə]
Britain See Great Britain.
British Columbia [...kə 'lʌm bi ə] ② (A province of Canada.) Cap: Victoria [vɪk 'tor i ə]
Brunei [bru 'nɑɪ] ⑦ Cap: Bandar Seri Begawan ['bɑn dɑr 'sɛr i bɛ 'gɑ wɑn]
Bulgaria [bəl 'gɛr i ə] ⑥ Cap: Sofia [so 'fi ə]
Burkina Faso ['bɚ ki nə 'fɑ so] ⑤ Cap: Ouagadougou ['wɑ gɑ 'du gu]
Burma ['bɚ mə] See Myanmar.
Burundi [bʊ 'run di] ⑤ Cap: Bujumbura ['bʊ dʒum 'bɚ ə]
California [kæl ə 'forn jə] ① (A U.S. state.) Cap: Sacramento [sæ krə 'mɛn to]
Cambodia [kæm 'bod i ə] ⑦ Cap: Phnom Penh [nɑm 'pɛn]
Cameroon [kæm ə 'run] ⑤ Cap: Yaounde ['jaʊn de]
Canada ['kæn ə də] ② Cap: Ottawa ['ɑt ɑ wɑ]
Caribbean Sea [kɛr ə 'bi ən..., kə 'rɪb i ən...] ③
Caspian Sea ['kæs pi ən...] ⑦
Cayman Islands ['ke mən...] Cap: Georgetown ['dʒordʒ taʊn]
Central African Republic ⑤ Cap: Bangui ['bɑŋ gi]
Chad ['tʃæd] ⑤ Cap: N'Djamena [ən dʒɑ 'me nɑ]
Chicago [ʃə 'kɔ go] (A large city in Illinois.)
Chile ['tʃi le, 'tʃɪl i] ④ Cap: Santiago [sɑn ti 'ɑ go]
China ['tʃɑɪ nə] ⑦ Cap: Beijing [be 'dʒɪŋ]
Colombia [kə 'lʌm bi ə] ④ Cap: Bogota [bo gə 'tɑ]
Colorado [kɑ lə 'ræ do] ① (A U.S. state.) Cap: Denver ['dɛn vɚ]
Congo ['kɔn go] ⑤ Cap: Brazzaville ['bræz ə vɪl]
Connecticut [kə 'nɛt ɪ kət] ① (A U.S. state.) Cap: Hartford ['hɑrt fɚd]
Costa Rica [kɑs tə 'ri kə] ③ Cap: San Jose [sæn ho 'ze]
Côte d'Ivoire ['kot dɪ vwɑr] ⑤ Cap: Yamoussoukro [jɑ mu 'su kro] (administrative); Abidjan [ɑ bɪ 'dʒɑn] (commercial)
Croatia [kro 'e ʃə] ⑥ Cap: Zagreb ['zɑ grɛb]
Cuba ['kju bə] ③ Cap: Havana [hə 'væ nə]
Cyprus ['sɑɪ prəs] ⑦ Cap: Nicosia [nɪk ə 'si ə]
Czech Republic ['tʃɛk...] ⑥ Cap: Prague ['prɑg]
D.C. See District of Columbia.
Delaware ['dɛl ə wɛr] ① (A U.S. state.) Cap: Dover ['do vɚ]
Democratic Republic of the Congo [...'kɔŋ go] Cap: Kinshasa [kin 'ʃɑ sə]
Denmark ['dɛn mɑrk] ⑥ Cap: Copenhagen ['ko pən hɑ gən]
District of Columbia [...kə 'lʌm bi ə] (The capital of the United States of America. The District is comprised of the city of Washington. Abbreviated D.C.)
Dominican Republic [də 'mɪn ə kən...] ③ Cap: Santo Domingo ['sɑn to do 'mɪŋ go]
Ecuador ['ɛ kwə dor] ④ Cap: Quito ['ki to]

Egypt ['i dʒəpt] ⑤ Cap: Cairo ['kaɪ ro]
El Salvador [ɛl 'sæl və dor] ③ Cap: San Salvador [sæn 'sæl və dor]
England ['ɪŋ glənd] ⑥ Cap: London ['lʌn dən]
Equitorial Guinea [ɛk wɪ 'tor i əl 'gɪn i] ⑤ Cap: Malabo ['mɑ lə bo]
Eritrea [ɛ rə 'tri ə] ⑤ Cap: Asmara [ɑs 'mɑ rɑ]
Estonia [ɛs 'ton i ə] ⑥ Cap: Tallinn ['tɑ lɪn]
Ethiopia [i θi 'o pi ə] ⑤ Cap: Addis Ababa ['æd ɪs 'æ bə bə]
Eurasia [jɚ 'e ʒə] (Asia and Europe.)
Europe ['jɚ əp] ⑥
Finland ['fɪn lənd] ⑥ Cap: Helsinki ['hɛl sɪŋ ki]
Florida ['flor ə də] ① (A U.S. state.) Cap: Tallahassee [tæ lə 'hæs i]
France ['fræns] ⑥ Cap: Paris ['pɛ rɪs]
French Guiana ['frɛntʃ gi 'ɑ nə] ④ Cap: Cayenne [kɑi 'ɛn]
Gabon [gə 'bɑn] ⑤ Cap: Libreville ['lib rə vɪl]
Gambia, The [...'gæm bi ə] ⑤ Cap: Banjul [bɑn 'dʒul]
Georgia ['dʒor dʒə] ① (A U.S. state.) Cap: Atlanta [æt 'læn tə]
Georgia ['dʒor dʒə] ⑦ Cap: Tbilisi [tə bə 'li si]
Germany ['dʒɚ mə ni] ⑥ Cap: Berlin [bɚ 'lɪn]
Ghana ['gɑ nə] ⑤ Cap: Accra [ə 'krɑ]
Great Britain [...'brit n] ⑥ (The island that includes England, Wales, and Scotland.)
Greece ['gris] ⑥ Cap: Athens ['æ θəns]
Greenland See Kalaallit Nunaat.
Guatemala [gwɑt ə 'mɑl ə] ③ Cap: Guatemala City [gwɑt ə mɑ lə...]
Guinea ['gɪn i] ⑤ Cap: Conakry ['kon ə kri]
Guinea Bissau ['gɪn i 'bi so] ⑤ Cap: Bissau ['bi so]
Gulf of Mexico [...'mɛk sɪ ko] ① ③
Guyana [gɑɪ 'ɑ nə] ④ Cap: Georgetown ['dʒordz taʊn]
Haiti ['het i] ③ Cap: Port-au-Prince ['por to 'prɪns]
Hawaii [hə 'wɑɪ i] ① (A U.S. state.) Cap: Honolulu [hɑ nɑ 'lu lu]
Holland ['hɑl ənd] See Netherlands, The.
Honduras [hɑn 'dur əs] ③ Cap: Tegucigalpa [tə 'gus ɪ 'gɑl pə]
Hudson Bay ['hʌd sən 'be] ②
Hungary ['hʌŋ gə ri] ⑥ Cap: Budapest ['bud ə 'pɛst]
Iceland ['ɑɪs lənd] ⑥ Cap: Reykjavik ['re kjɑ vik]
Idaho ['ɑɪ də ho] ① (A U.S. state.) Cap: Boise ['boɪ zi]
Illinois [ɪl ə 'noɪ] ① (A U.S. state.) Cap: Springfield ['sprɪŋ fild]
India ['ɪn di ə] ⑦ Cap: New Delhi [nu 'dɛl i]
Indiana [ɪn di 'æ nə] ① (A U.S. state.) Cap: Indianapolis [ɪn di ə 'næp ə ləs]
Indian Ocean ['ɪn di ən...] ⑤ ⑦
Indonesia [ɪn do 'ni ʒə] ⑦ Cap: Jakarta [dʒə 'kɑr tə]
Iowa ['ɑɪ ə wə] ① (A U.S. state.) Cap: Des Moines [də 'moɪn]
Iran [ɪ 'ræn] ⑦ Cap: Tehran [tə 'rɑn]
Iraq [ɪ 'ræk] ⑦ Cap: Baghdad ['bæg 'dæd]
Ireland ['ɑɪr lənd] ⑥ Cap: Dublin ['dʌb lən]
Israel ['ɪz ri əl] ⑦ Cap: Jerusalem [dʒə 'ru sə ləm]; Tel Aviv ['tɛl ə 'viv]
Italy ['ɪt ə li] ⑥ Cap: Rome ['rom]
Ivory Coast ['ɑɪ vri 'kost] See Côte d'Ivoire.
Jamaica [dzə 'me kə] ③ Cap: Kingston ['kɪŋs tən]
Japan [dzə 'pæn] ⑦ Cap: Tokyo ['to ki o]
Jordan ['dʒor dn] ⑦ Cap: Amman ['ɑ mɑn]
Kalaallit Nunaat ['kɑ lɑ lit 'nu nɑt] ⑥ (Formerly Greenland.) Cap: Nuuk ['nuk]
Kansas ['kæn zəz] ① (A U.S. state.) Cap: Topeka [tə 'pi kə]
Kazakhstan [kɑ 'zɑk stæn] ⑦ Cap: Alma-Ata [ɑl mɑ 'ɑt ə]
Kentucky [kən 'tʌk i] ① (A U.S. state.) Cap: Frankfort ['fræŋk fɚt]
Kenya ['kɛn jə] ⑤ Cap: Nairobi [nɑɪ 'ro bi]
Kuwait [ku 'wet] ⑦ Cap: Kuwait City [ku 'wet...]
Kyrgyzstan ['kir gɪz stæn] ⑦ Cap: Bishkek ['bɪʃ kɛk]
Laos ['lɑ os] ⑦ Cap: Vientiane [vjɛn 'tjɑn]
Latvia ['læt vi ə] ⑥ Cap: Riga ['ri gə]
Lebanon ['lɛb ə nən] ⑦ Cap: Beirut [be 'rut]
Lesotho [lə 'so to] ⑤ Cap: Maseru ['mɑz ə 'ru]
Liberia [lɑɪ 'bɪr i ə] ⑤ Cap: Monrovia [mən 'ro vi ɑ]
Libya ['lɪb i ə] ⑤ Cap: Tripoli ['trɪp ə li]
Lithuania [lɪθ ʊ 'wen i ə] ⑥ Cap: Vilnius ['vɪl ni əs]
Los Angeles [lɑs 'æn dʒə ləs] ① (A large city in California.)
Louisiana [lu iz i 'æn ə] ① (A U.S. state.) Cap: Baton Rouge ['bæt n 'ruʒ]
Luxembourg ['lʌk səm bɚg] ⑥ Cap: Luxembourg ['lʌk səm bɚg]
Macedonia [mæ sə 'don i ə] ⑥ Cap: Skopje ['skɔp je]
Madagascar [mæd ə 'gæs kɚ] ⑤ Cap: Antananarivo [ɑn tə nɑ nə 'ri vo]
Maine ['men] ① (A U.S. state.) Cap: Augusta [ə 'gʌs tə]
Malawi [mə 'lɑ wi] ⑤ Cap: Lilongwe [lɪ 'lɔŋ we]
Malaysia [mə 'le ʒə] ⑦ Cap: Kuala Lumpur ['kwɑ lə 'lum 'pur]
Maldives ['mɑl dɑɪvz] Cap: Male ['mɑ le]
Mali ['mɑ li] ⑤ Cap: Bamako ['bɑm ə ko]
Malta ['mɑl tə] ⑥ Cap: Valletta [və 'lɛt ə]
Manitoba ['mæn ɪ 'tob ə] ② (A province of Canada.) Cap: Winnipeg ['wɪn ə pɛg]
Maryland ['mɛr ə lənd] ① (A U.S. state.) Cap: Baltimore ['bɑl tə mor]
Massachusetts [mæs ə 'tʃu sɪts] ① (A U.S. state.) Cap: Boston ['bɑs tən]
Mauritania [mor ə 'ten i ə] ⑤ Cap: Nouakchott [nwɑk 'ʃot]
Mauritius [mɑ 'rɪʃ əs] Cap: Port Louis [...'lu ɪs]
Mediterranean Sea ['mɛd ə tə ren i ən 'si] ⑥
Mexico ['mɛk sɪ ko] ③ Cap: Mexico City ['mɛk sɪ ko...]
Michigan ['mɪʃ ə gən] ① (A U.S. state.) Cap: Lansing ['læn sɪŋ]
Minnesota [mɪn ə 'sot ə] ① (A U.S. state.) Cap: St. Paul [sent 'pɔl]
Mississippi [mɪs ɪ 'sɪp i] ① (A U.S. state.) Cap: Jackson ['dʒæk sən]
Missouri [mə 'zɚ i] ① (A U.S. state.) Cap: Jefferson City ['dʒɛf ɚ sən...]
Moldova [mɑl 'do və] ⑥ Cap: Jassy ['jɑ si]
Monaco ['mɑn ə ko] Cap: Monaco ['mɑn ə ko]
Mongolia [mɑŋ 'go li ə] ⑦ Cap: Ulan Bator ['u lɑn 'bɑ tor]
Montana [mɑn 'tæn ə] ① (A U.S. state.) Cap: Helena ['hɛ lə nə]
Morocco [mə 'rɑk o] ⑤ Cap: Rabat [rɑ 'bɑt]
Mozambique [mo zəm 'bik] ⑤ Cap: Maputo [mɑ 'pu to]
Myanmar [mɪ 'jɑn mɑr] ⑦ (Formerly Burma.) Cap: Yangon [jæŋ 'gɔn]
Namibia [nə 'mɪb i ə] ⑤ Cap: Windhoek ['vɪnt huk]
Nebraska [nə 'bræs kə] ① (A U.S. state.) Cap: Lincoln ['lɪŋ kən]
Nepal [nɪ 'pɔl] ⑦ Cap: Kat(h)mandu [kæt mæn 'du]
Netherlands, The [ðə 'nɛ θɚ ləndz] ⑥ Cap: The Hague [ðə 'heg]; Amsterdam ['æm stɚ dæm]
Nevada [nə 'væd ə] ① (A U.S. state.) Cap: Carson City ['kɑr sən...]
New Brunswick [nu 'brʌnz wɪk] ② (A province of Canada.) Cap: Fredericton ['frɛd rɪk tən]
Newfoundland ['nuf ən lənd] ② (A province of Canada.) Cap: St. John's ['sent 'dʒɑns]
New Hampshire [nu 'hæmp ʃɚ] ① (A U.S. state.) Cap: Concord ['kɑn kɚd]
New Jersey [nu 'dʒɚ zi] ① (A U.S. state.) Cap: Trenton ['trɛnt n]
New Mexico [nu 'mɛk sɪ ko] ① (A U.S. state.) Cap: Santa Fe ['sæn tə 'fe]
New South Wales ['nu 'saʊθ 'wels] ⑦ (A state of Australia.) Cap: Sydney ['sɪd ni]
New York ['nu 'jork] ① (A U.S. state.) Cap: Albany ['ɑl bə ni]
New York (City) ['nu 'jork ('sɪt i)] (A large city in New York state.)
New Zealand [nu 'zi lənd] ⑦ Cap: Wellington ['wɛl ɪŋ tən]
Nicaragua [nɪk ə 'rɑg wə] ③ Cap: Managua [mə 'nɑg wə]
Niger ['nɑɪ dʒɚ] ⑤ Cap: Niamey [njɑ 'me]

Nigeria [nɑɪ 'dʒɪr i ə] ⑤ Cap: Abuja [ə 'bu dʒə]
North America [...ə 'mɛr ɪ kə]
North Carolina [...kɛr ə 'lɑɪ nə] ① (A U.S. state.) Cap: Raleigh ['rɑ li]
North Dakota ['norθ də 'ko tə] ① (A U.S. state.) Cap: Bismarck ['bɪz mɑrk]
Northern Ireland ['nor ðɚn 'ɑɪr lənd] ⑥ Cap: Belfast ['bɛl fæst]
Northern Territory ['nor ðɚn...] ⑦ (Territory of Australia.) Cap: Darwin ['dɑr wɪn]
North Korea [...ko 'ri ə] ⑦ Cap: Pyongyang ['pjuŋ 'jɑŋ]
North Sea ['norθ 'si] ⑥
Northwest Territories ['norθ 'wɛst...] ② (A territory of Canada.) Cap: Yellowknife ['jɛ lo nɑɪf]
Norway ['nor we] ⑥ Cap: Oslo ['ɑz lo]
Nova Scotia [no və 'sko ʃə] ② (A province of Canada.) Cap: Halifax ['hæ lɪ fæks]
Ohio [o 'hɑɪ o] ① (A U.S. state.) Cap: Columbus [kə 'lʌm bəs]
Oklahoma [ok lə 'hom ə] ① (A U.S. state.) Cap: Oklahoma City [ok lə 'hom ə...]
Oman [o 'mɑn] ⑦ Cap: Muscat ['mʌs kət]
Ontario [ɑn 'tɛr i o] ② (A province of Canada.) Cap: Toronto [tə 'rɑn to]
Oregon ['or ə gən] ① (A U.S. state.) Cap: Salem ['se ləm]
Pacific Ocean [pə 'sɪf ɪk...] ①
Pakistan ['pæk ə stæn] ⑦ Cap: Karachi [kə 'rætʃ i]
Panama ['pæn ə mɑ] ③ Cap: Panama City ['pæn ə mɑ...]
Papua New Guinea ['pɑp u ə nu 'gɪn ɪ] ⑦ Cap: Port Moresby [port 'morz bi]
Paraguay ['pɛr ə gwe] ④ Cap: Asuncion [ɑ 'sun sjɔn]
Pennsylvania [pɛn sɪl 'ven jə] ① (A U.S. state.) Cap: Harrisburg ['hɛr əs bɚg]
Persian Gulf ['pɚ ʒən...] ⑦
Peru [pə 'ru] ④ Cap: Lima ['li mə]
Philippines, The ['fɪl ɪ pinz] ⑦ Cap: Manila [mə 'nɪ lə]
Poland ['po lənd] ⑥ Cap: Warsaw ['wor sɔ]
Portugal ['por tʃə gəl] ⑥ Cap: Lisbon ['lɪz bən]
Prince Edward Island ['prɪns ɛd wɚd...] ② (A province of Canada.) Cap: Charlottetown ['ʃɑr lɪt tɑʊn]
Puerto Rico ['pwɛr tə 'ri ko] ③ Cap: San Juan [sɑn 'ʍɑn]
Qatar ['kɑ tɑr] ⑦ Cap: Doha ['do hɑ]
Quebec [kwə 'bɛk] ② (French: *Québec.* A province of Canada.) Cap: Quebec [kwə 'bɛk]
Queensland ['kwinz lənd] ⑦ (A state of Australia.) Cap: Brisbane ['bris ben]
Red Sea ['rɛd...] ⑤
Rhode Island ['rod...] ① (A U.S. state.) Cap: Providence ['prɑv ɪ dəns]
Romania [ro 'men i ə] ⑥ Cap: Bucharest ['buk ə rɛst]
Russia ['rʌʃ ə] ⑥ Cap: Moscow ['mɑs ko]
Rwanda [ru 'ɑn də] ⑤ Cap: Kigali [kɪ 'gɑ li]
Saskatchewan [sæs 'kætʃ ə wɑn] ② (A province of Canada.) Cap: Saskatoon ['sæs kə tun]
Saudi Arabia ['sɑu di ə 'reb i ə] ⑦ Cap: Riyadh [ri 'jɑd]
Scotland ['skɑt lənd] ⑥ Cap: Edinburgh ['ɛd ɪn bɚ ə]
Senegal ['sɛn ə gəl] ⑤ Cap: Dakar [dɑ 'kɑr]
Serbia ['sɚ bi ə] Cap: Belgrade ['bɛl gred]
Sierra Leone [si 'ɛr ə li 'on] ⑤ Cap: Freetown ['fri tɑʊn]
Singapore ['sɪŋ ə por] ⑦ Cap: Singapore ['sɪŋ ə por]
Slovakia [slo 'vɑk i ə] ⑥ Cap: Bratislava [brɑ tɪ 'slɑ və]
Slovenia [slo 'vin i ə] ⑥ Cap: Ljubljana [lu 'bli ɑ nɑ]
Somalia [so 'mɑl i ə] ⑤ Cap: Mogadishu [mo gɑ 'di ʃu]
South Africa ['sɑʊθ 'æf rɪ kə] ⑤ Cap: Cape Town (legislative) ['kep tɑʊn]; Pretoria (executive) [pri 'tor i ə]; Bloemfontein (judicial) ['blum fɑn ten]
South America ['sɑʊθ ə 'mɛr ɪ kə] ④
South Australia ['sɑʊθ ɑs 'tre li ə] ⑦ (A state of Australia.) Cap: Adelaide ['æ də led]
South Carolina ['sɑʊθ kɛr ə 'lɑɪ nə] ① (A U.S. state.) Cap: Columbia [kə 'lʌm bi ə]
South Dakota ['sɑʊθ də 'ko tə] ① (A U.S. state.) Cap: Pierre ['pir]
South Korea ['sɑʊθ kə 'ri ə] ⑦ Cap: Seoul ['sol]
Spain ['spen] ⑥ Cap: Madrid [mə 'drɪd]
Sri Lanka [sri 'lɑŋ kə] ⑦ Cap: Colombo [kə 'lʌm bo]
Sudan [su 'dæn] ⑤ Cap: Khartoum (executive) [kɑr 'tum]; Omdurman (legislative) [ɑm dur 'mɑn]
Surinam ['sɚ ɪ næm] ④ Cap: Paramaribo [pɛr ə 'mɑr ɪ bo]
Swaziland ['swɑ zɪ lænd] ⑤ Cap: Mbabane [bɑ 'bæn]
Sweden ['swid n] ⑥ Cap: Stockholm ['stɑk holm]
Switzerland ['swɪt sɚ lənd] ⑥ Cap: Bern (administrative) [bɚn]; Lausanne (judicial) [lo 'zæn]
Syria ['sɪr i ə] ⑦ Cap: Damascus [də 'mæs kəs]
Taiwan [tɑɪ 'wɑn] ⑦ Cap: Taipei [tɑɪ 'pe]
Tanzania [tænz ə 'ni ə] ⑤ Cap: Dar es Salaam [dɑr ɛs sə 'lɑm]
Tasmania [tæs 'me ni ə] ⑦ (An island state of Australia.) Cap: Hobart ['ho bɑrt]
Tennessee [tɛn ə 'si] ① (A U.S. state.) Cap: Nashville ['næʃ vɪl]
Texas ['tɛk səs] ① (A U.S. state.) Cap: Austin ['ɑs tɪn]
Thailand ['tɑɪ lænd] ⑦ Cap: Bangkok ['bæŋ kɑk]
The Gambia See Gambia, The.
The Netherlands See Netherlands, The.
The Philippines See Philippines, The.
Tibet [tə 'bɛt] Cap: Lhasa ['lɑ sə]
Togo ['to go] ⑤ Cap: Lome [lo 'me]
Trinidad and Tobago ['trɪn ə dæd ənd to 'be go] ④ Cap: Port-of-Spain [port əv 'spen]
Tunisia [tu 'ni ʒə] ⑤ Cap: Tunis ['tu nɪs]
Turkey ['tɚ ki] ⑦ Cap: Ankara ['æŋ kə rə]
Turkmenistan [tɚk mɛn ə 'stæn] ⑦ Cap: Ashkhabad [ɑʃ kə 'bɑd]
Uganda [ju 'gæn də] ⑤ Cap: Kampala [kəm 'pɑ lə]
Ukraine [ju 'kren] ⑥ Cap: Kiev [ki 'ɛv]
United Arab Emirates [...'ɛr əb 'ɛ mɚ əts] ⑦ Cap: Abu Dhabi ['ɑ bu 'dɑ bi]
United Kingdom [...'kɪŋ dəm] ⑥ Cap: London ['lʌn dən]
United States of America [...'stets əv ə 'mɛr ɪ kə] ① Cap: Washington, D.C. [District of Columbia] ['wɑʃ ɪŋ tən 'di 'si]
Uruguay ['jɚ ə gwe] ④ Cap: Montevideo [mɑn tə vɪ 'de o]
U.S. Virgin Islands ['ju 'ɛs 'vɪr dʒin...] ③ Cap: Charlotte Amalie ['ʃɑr lət ə 'mɑl jə]
Utah ['ju tɔ] ① (A U.S. state.) Cap: Salt Lake City ['sɑlt 'lek...]
Uzbekistan [uz 'bɛk ə stæn] ⑦ Cap: Tashkent ['tæʃ kɛnt]
Venezuela [vɛn ə 'zwe lə] ④ Cap: Caracas [kə 'rɑk əs]
Vermont [vɚ 'mɑnt] ① (A U.S. state.) Cap: Montpelier [mɑnt 'pil jɚ]
Victoria [vɪk 'tor i ə] ⑦ (A state of Australia.) Cap: Melbourne ['mɛl bɚn]
Vietnam [vi ɛt 'nɑm] ⑦ Cap: Hanoi [hə 'nɔɪ]
Virginia [vɚ 'dʒɪn jə] ① (A U.S. state.) Cap: Richmond ['rɪtʃ mənd]
Wales ['welz] ⑥ Cap: Cardiff ['kɑr dɪf]
Washington ['wɑʃ ɪŋ tən] ① (A U.S. state.) Cap: Olympia [ə 'lɪm pi ə]
Western Australia ['wɛs tɚn ɑs 'tre li ə] ⑦ (A state of Australia.) Cap: Perth ['pɚθ]
Western Sahara ['wɛs tɚn sə 'hɛr ə] ⑤
West Virginia ['wɛst vɚ 'dʒɪn jə] ① (A U.S. state.) Cap: Charleston ['tʃɑrls tən]
Wisconsin [wɪs 'kɑn sən] ① (A U.S. state.) Cap: Madison ['mæd ə sən]
Wyoming [wɑɪ 'o mɪŋ] ① (A U.S. state.) Cap: Cheyenne [ʃɑɪ 'æn]
Yemen ['jɛm ən] ⑦ Cap: Sanaa [sɑ 'nɑ]
Yugoslavia [ju go 'slɑv i ə] ⑥ Cap: Belgrade ['bɛl gred]
Yukon ['ju kɑn] ② (A territory of Canada.) Cap: Whitehorse ['ʍɑɪt hors]
Zaire [zɑ 'ɪr] ⑤ Cap: Kinshasa [kɪn 'ʃɑ sɑ]
Zambia ['zæm bi ə] ⑤ Cap: Lusaka [lu 'sɑ kə]
Zimbabwe [zɪm 'bɑb we] ⑤ Cap: Harare [hɑ 'rɑ re]

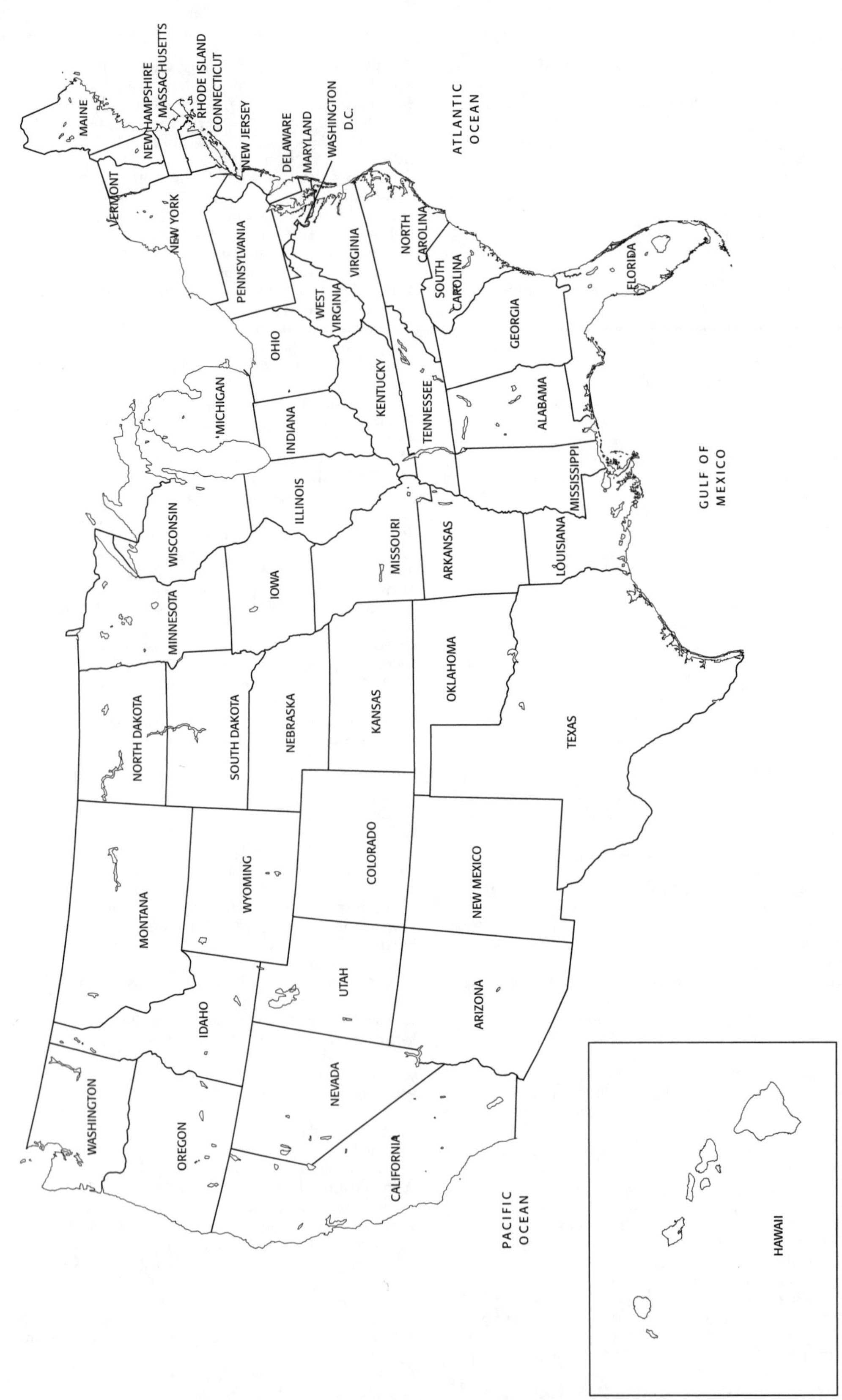

Map ①: The United States of America
(The state of Alaska appears on Map ②.)

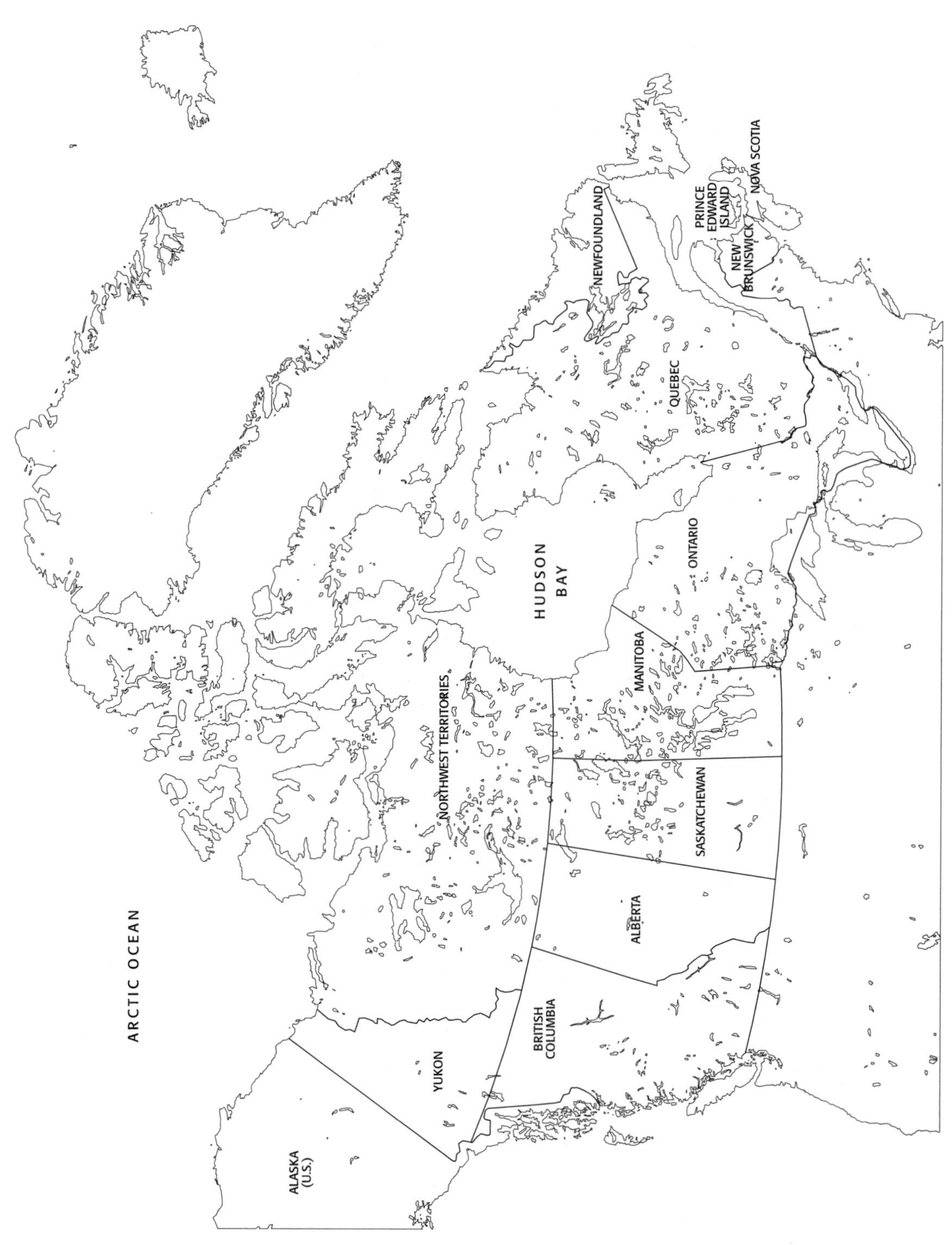
ARCTIC OCEAN
NEWFOUNDLAND
PRINCE
EDWARD
ISLAND
NOVA SCOTIA
NEW
BRUNSWICK
QUEBEC
HUDSON
BAY
ONTARIO
MANITOBA
NORTHWEST TERRITORIES
SASKATCHEWAN
ALBERTA
BRITISH
COLUMBIA
YUKON
ALASKA
(U.S.)

Map ②: Canada

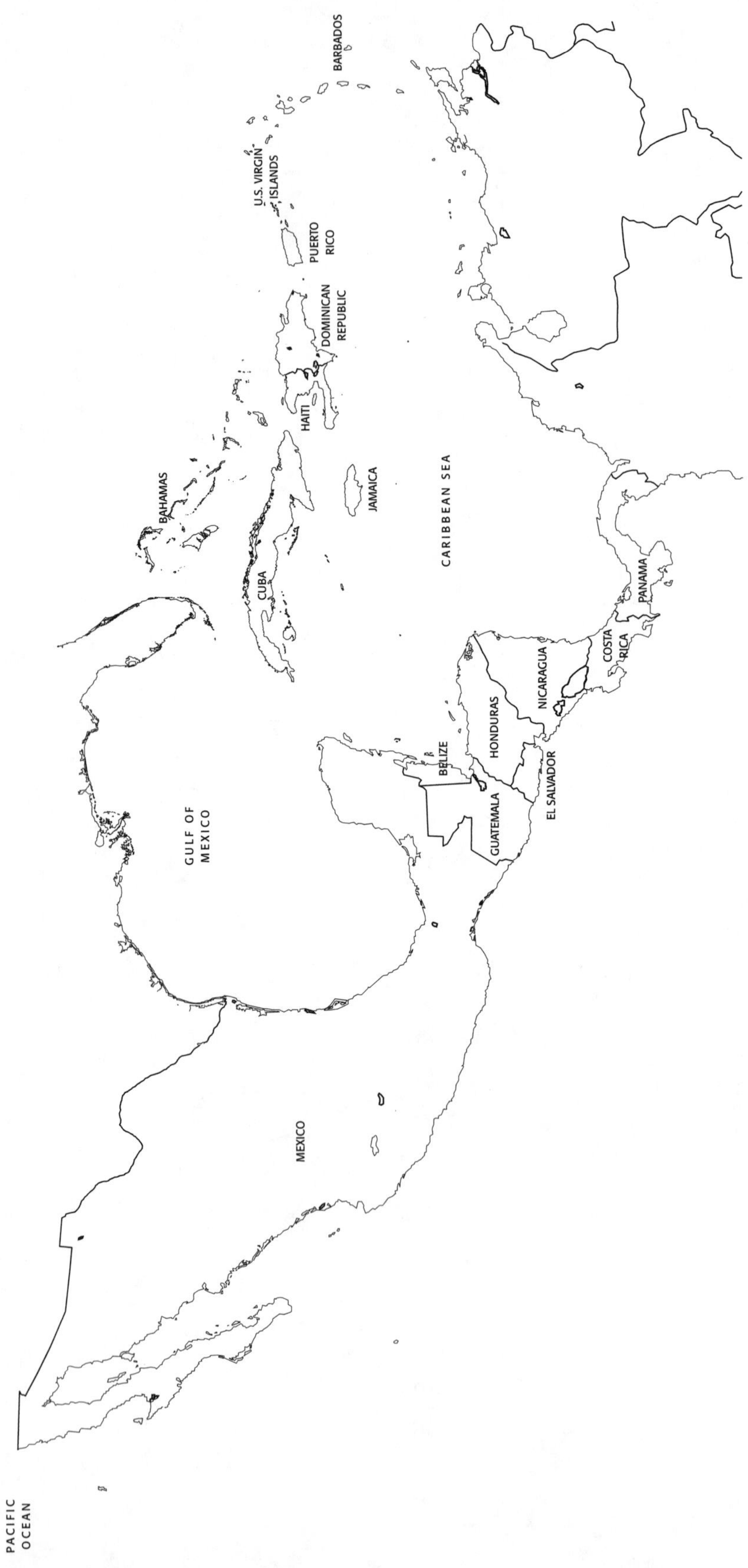

Map ③: Mexico, Central America, and the Caribbean

Map ④: South America (and Antarctica)

MEDITERRANEAN SEA
MOROCCO
ALGERIA
TUNISIA
LIBYA
EGYPT
WESTERN
SAHARA
MAURITANIA
MALI
NIGER
CHAD
SUDAN
RED SEA
ERITREA
SENEGAL
GAMBIA
GUINEA
BISSAU
GUINEA
SIERRA
LEONE
LIBERIA
BURKINA
FASO
CÔTE
D'IVOIRE
GHANA
TOGO
BENIN
NIGERIA
CENTRAL
AFRICAN
REPUBLIC
ETHIOPIA
SOMALIA
CAMEROON
EQUATORIAL GUINEA
GABON
CONGO
ZAIRE
RWANDA
UGANDA
KENYA
BURUNDI
TANZANIA
INDIAN OCEAN
ANGOLA
ZAMBIA
MALAWI
MOZAMBIQUE
NAMIBIA
ZIMBABWE
BOTSWANA
MADAGASCAR
SWAZILAND
LESOTHO
SOUTH AFRICA

Map ⑤: Africa

KALAALLIT NUNAAT (GREENLAND)
ICELAND
RUSSIA
FINLAND
SWEDEN
NORWAY
SCOTLAND
NORTHERN IRELAND
IRELAND
NORTH SEA
DENMARK
ESTONIA
LATVIA
BALTIC SEA
LITHUANIA
PRUSSIA
WALES
ENGLAND
NETHERLANDS
ATLANTIC OCEAN
BELARUS
POLAND
GERMANY
BELGIUM
UKRAINE
LUXEMBOURG
CZECH REPUBLIC
SLOVAKIA
MOLDOVA
SWITZERLAND
AUSTRIA
HUNGARY
FRANCE
ROMANIA
SLOVENIA
CROATIA
(GEORGIA)
PORTUGAL
BOSNIA- HERZEGOVINA
BLACK SEA
YUGOSLAVIA
ITALY
BULGARIA
SPAIN
MACEDONIA
(TURKEY)
ALBANIA
GREECE
MEDITERRANEAN SEA
(LEBANON)
(SYRIA)
MALTA
(CYPRUS)

Map ⑥: Europe

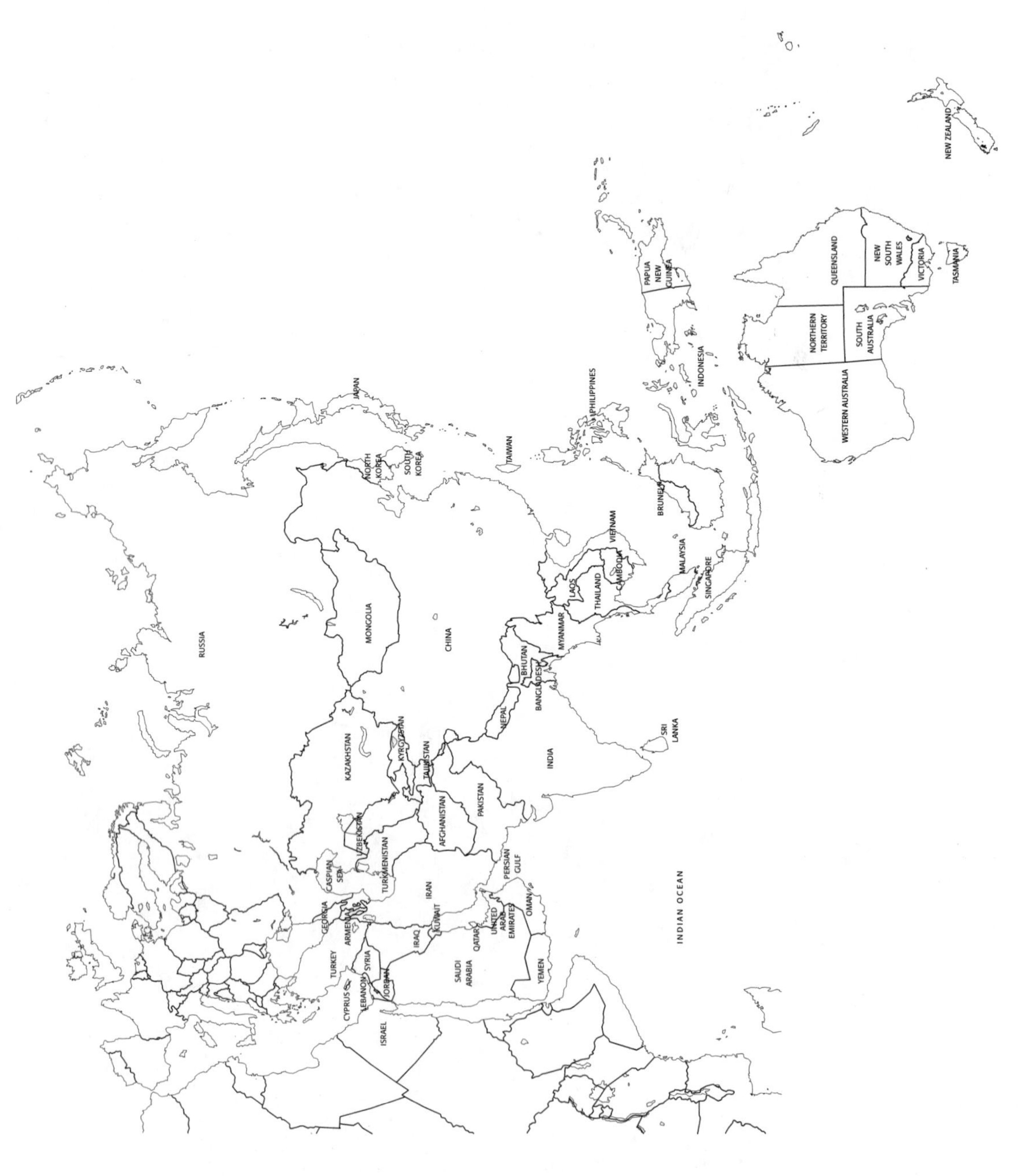

Map ⑦: Asia, the Middle East, and Australia